South-Western Federal Taxation

Internal Revenue Code of 1986 and Treasury Regulations

Annotated and Selected

2015 EDITION

James E. Smith

Ph.D., CPA

Prepared by

Mark P. Altieri

J.D., LL.M. (in Taxation), CPA/PFS

Australia • Brazil • Japan • Korea • Mexico • Singapore • Spain • United Kingdom • United States

South-Western Federal Taxation: Internal Revenue Code of 1986 and Treasury Regulations: Annotated and Selected, 2015 Edition
James E. Smith

Vice President, GM Science, Math & Quantitative Business: Balraj S. Kalsi

Product Director: Rob Dewey

Senior Product Manager: Sharon Oblinger

Associate Content Developer: Tristann Jones

Product Assistant: A.J. Smiley

Marketing Director: Natalie King

Senior Marketing Coordinator: Eileen Corcoran

Media Developer: Lysa Kosins

Senior Content Project Manager: Martha Conway

Manufacturing Planner: Doug Wilke

Production Service: MPS Limited

Senior Art Director: Michelle Kunkler

Cover Designer: Kim Torbeck/Imbue Design

Cover Image: Dennis Flaherty/Getty Images, Inc.

Intellectual Property:
Analyst: Christina Ciaramella
Project Manager: Anne Sheroff

Library of Congress Control Number: 2014939641

ISBN-13: 978-1-285-44149-8
ISBN-10: 1-285-44149-4

Student Edition ISBN-13: 978-1-285-44148-1
Student Edition ISBN-10: 1-285-44148-6

Cengage Learning
200 First Stamford Place, 4th Floor
Stamford, CT 06902
USA

Cengage Learning is a leading provider of customized learning solutions with office locations around the globe, including Singapore, the United Kingdom, Australia, Mexico, Brazil, and Japan. Locate your local office at: **www.cengage.com/global**

Cengage Learning products are represented in Canada by Nelson Education, Ltd.

To learn more about Cengage Learning Solutions, visit **www.cengage.com**

Purchase any of our products at your local college store or at our preferred online store **www.cengagebrain.com**

Printed in the United States of America
1 2 3 4 5 6 7 19 18 17 16 15 14

PREFACE

In the study of Federal tax law, the student should be exposed to the statute and the related regulations. This exposure can best be accomplished if the student has his or her complete copy of the Internal Revenue Code of 1986 and the Treasury Regulations for use inside and outside the classroom. However, cost (over $400) and size (over 5,000 pages in the code alone and 6 additional volumes of regulations) limit this option.

This book is designed to overcome the aforementioned limitations. In addition, the following features are included that make it superior, for educational purposes, to the complete code and regulations.

Annotations. The student is provided with insight into each major topical area of the code. Each such area is preceded by explanation, analysis, and cross-referencing in the form of an Editorial Summary. In order to continue to strengthen this distinguishing feature of the book, the annotations in the 2015 edition have been increased. To make it easy for the student to locate the Editorial Summary that relates to a particular topic, two features are included. First, a List of Editorial Summaries is on page xxix. Second, referencing is used in the text to indicate the page where the related Editorial Summary appears.

Selections. Expected frequency of use and the relationship among code sections were the principal criteria used in performing the selection process. Infrequently used and special purpose sections were either partially or completely omitted. The regulations were evaluated in terms of reflecting current law. A sanitizing process was applied that included the omission of out-of-date regulations, the reference to the specific legislation that produced the change, and the specification of the new tax result or the identification of the pertinent code section that contains the new result. Thus, potential student confusion resulting from disagreement between the language of the code and partially out-of-date regulations is reduced. In addition, footnote disclosure is used to replace code section numbers appearing in the regulations that have been modified by subsequent legislation with the current code section number.

Recent tax legislation. This edition includes changes in the tax law enacted in the Patient Protection and Affordable Care Act of 2010; Health Care and Education Reconciliation Act of 2010; Small Business Jobs Act of 2010; the Tax Relief Act of 2010, Temporary Payroll Tax Cut Continuation Act of 2011, Middle Class Tax Relief and Job Creation Act of 2012, and the American Taxpayer Relief Act of 2012. No 2013 legislation affected this edition. If other significant additional tax legislation is enacted in 2014 or early 2015, users will be provided with a supplement.

Future effective dates. Enacted tax legislation contains numerous provisions that will not take effect until a future effective date. For such a provision, the following treatment is provided:

- The provision that is effective for 2014 is presented.
- The provision that is effective in the future is presented with the effective date appearing in a footnote. This future effective date provision is preceded in

the text with the following warning: CAUTION: FUTURE EFFECTIVE DATE.

Comprehensive. Coverage is provided on the income, estate, and gift tax law and regulations.

Ease of usage. The annotations provide the student with an appreciation of the relationship among various code sections and assist the student in avoiding the tax trap of a wrong conclusion which frequently results if a code section is viewed in isolation. To aid the professor in making assignments, a list of included code sections and regulation sections is provided. A separate index, by code section, is provided for the income tax, the estate tax, the generation-skipping transfer tax, and the gift tax. Ease of entry in locating a topic is maximized by each topic having multiple entry words or phrases. The index is arranged with the additional objective of aiding the student in seeing relationships among code sections. Relevant temporary regulations are integrated into the same location as final regulations so the student does not have to turn to different parts of the book while using the regulations for a particular code section. Finally, a separate table of contents is provided for the code and for the regulations.

Flexibility of use. The book can be used as a supplement for any undergraduate or graduate tax course as well as by practicing tax professionals. However, the presence of the annotations makes it equally usable as the primary text in a course in which the professor uses a code and regulations approach in conducting the course. In the supplement format, if only the code is used by the professor, the annotated and abridged code portion of the book can be used.

Indexing. A procedure increasingly used by Congress is to index certain amounts in the code for the effect of inflation. Such indexing includes the individual income tax rates in Sec. 1, adoption expenses credit in Sec. 23, refundable component of child tax credit in Sec. 24, American opportunity and lifetime learning credits in Sec. 25A, earned income credit amounts in Sec. 32, standard deduction in Sec. 63(c), overall limitation on itemized deductions in Sec. 68, qualified transportation fringes exclusion in Sec. 132, educational savings bonds exclusion amounts in Sec. 135, adoption assistance programs exclusion in § 137, personal exemption and dependency deductions in Sec. 151 including the phase out, limited expensing of certain fixed assets in Sec. 179, long-term care premiums in Sec. 213(d)(10), AGI deduction limits for an IRA for an active participant under Sec. 217(g), medical savings account (MSA) limits in Sec. 220, deduction for interest on education loans in Sec. 221, health savings account (HSA) limits in Sec. 223, the limitation on the deduction for luxury automobiles in Sec. 280F, AGI limits in calculating Roth contributions under Sec. 408A(c)(3), the pension and profit-sharing amounts in Subchapter D of Chapter 1, foreign earned income exclusion limit under Sec. 911(b)(2), interest imputations under Sec. 1274A, the gift tax exclusion under Sec. 2503, and the long-term care insurance benefits exclusion under Sec. 7702B. These indexed amounts appear with the related code section and also in a table which begins on page xvi.

Depreciation and cost recovery tables. A popular feature is the inclusion of the depreciation and cost recovery tables in one location with descriptive headings that

aid the student and practitioner in selecting and applying the appropriate table. Such tables start on page xxii in the 2015 edition.

Glossary of Tax Terms. A feature that has been well received by adopters is the Glossary of Tax Terms. The Glossary is beneficial to the student and practitioner in reading, interpreting, and understanding the code and regulations. The Glossary is located before the Index.

Continued for 2015 Annual Edition for Students. Exclusive Access to RIA's Checkpoint® Student Edition Online Tax Research Database. This item provides *six months* of unlimited access to content from the online research database most widely used by tax professionals. As students use Checkpoint® in doing tax research, they are building research skills and familiarity with the database—valuable preparation for their professional future.

Since the book is revised annually, we encourage users to make recommendations that will increase the utility of the book to them and to their students. Every effort will be made to utilize such inputs as the basis for improvement. Several such recommendations are integrated into the current edition. James Smith's e-mail address is **james.smith@mason.wm.edu**. and Mark Altieri's is **maltieri@kent.edu**.

An expression of appreciation is appropriate for Cori Rich and Tristann Jones who provided much-needed editorial assistance.

JAMES E. SMITH
MARK ALTIERI

June, 2014

TABLE OF CONTENTS

*Omitted.

TABLE OF CONTENTS

*Omitted.

TABLE OF CONTENTS

*Omitted.

TABLE OF CONTENTS

*Omitted.

TABLE OF CONTENTS

*Omitted.

SUBTITLE B. ESTATE AND GIFT TAXES

SUBTITLE C. EMPLOYMENT TAXES

*Omitted.

SUBTITLE D. MISCELLANEOUS EXCISE TAXES

SUBTITLE E. ALCOHOL, TOBACCO, AND CERTAIN OTHER EXCISE TAXES

SUBTITLE F. PROCEDURE AND ADMINISTRATION

*Omitted.

TABLE OF CONTENTS

*Omitted.

TABLE OF CONTENTS

*Omitted.

SUBTITLE G. THE JOINT COMMITTEE ON TAXATION

SUBTITLE H. FINANCING OF PRESIDENTIAL ELECTION CAMPAIGNS

SUBTITLE I. TRUST FUND CODE

*Omitted.

TABLE OF INDEXED AMOUNTS

1. Tax rates in Sec. 1.

2014 Tax Rate Schedules for Individual Taxpayers

Single—Schedule X

If taxable income is: Over—	But not over—	The tax is:		of the amount over—
$0	$9,075	....	10%	$0
9,075	36,900	$907.50 +	15%	9,075
36,900	89,350	5,081.25 +	25%	36,900
89,350	186,350	18,193.75 +	28%	89,350
186,350	405,100	45,353.75 +	33%	186,350
405,100	406,750	117,541.25 +	35%	405,100
406,750	....	118,118.75 +	39.6%	406,750

Head of household—Schedule Z

If taxable income is: Over—	But not over—	The tax is:		of the amount over—
$0	$12,950	....	10%	$0
12,950	49,400	$1,295.00 +	15%	12,950
49,400	127,550	6,762.50 +	25%	49,400
127,550	206,600	26,300.00 +	28%	127,550
206,600	405,100	48,434.00 +	33%	206,600
405,100	432,200	113,939.00 +	35%	405,100
432,200	....	123,424.00 +	39.6%	432,200

Married filing jointly or Qualifying widow(er)—Schedule Y–1

If taxable income is: Over—	But not over—	The tax is:		of the amount over—
$0	$18,150	....	10%	$0
18,150	73,800	$1,815.00 +	15%	18,150
73,800	148,850	10,162.50 +	25%	73,800
148,850	226,850	28,925.00 +	28%	148,850
226,850	405,100	50,765.00 +	33%	226,850
405,100	457,600	109,587.50 +	35%	405,100
457,600	....	127,962.50 +	39.6%	457,600

Married filing separately—Schedule Y–2

If taxable income is: Over—	But not over—	The tax is:		of the amount over—
$0	$9,075	....	10%	$0
9,075	36,900	$907.50 +	15%	9,075
36,900	74,425	5,081.25 +	25%	36,900
74,425	113,425	14,462.50 +	28%	74,425
113,425	202,550	25,382.50 +	33%	113,425
202,550	228,800	54,793.75 +	35%	202,550
228,800	....	63,981.25 +	39.6%	228,800

2014 Tax Rate Schedule for Estates and Trusts

If taxable income is: Over—	But not over—	The tax is:		of the amount over—
$0	$2,500	....	15%	$0
2,500	5,800	$375.00 +	25%	2,500
5,800	8,900	1,200.00 +	28%	5,800
8,900	12,150	2,068.00 +	33%	8,900
12,150	____	3,140.50 +	39.6%	12,150

2013 Tax Rate Schedules for Individual Taxpayers

Single—Schedule X

If taxable income is: Over—	But not over—	The tax is:		of the amount over—
$0	$8,925	....	10%	$0
8,925	36,250	$892.50 +	15%	8,925
36,250	87,850	4,991.25 +	25%	36,250
87,850	183,250	17,891.25 +	28%	87,850
183,250	398,350	44,603.25 +	33%	183,250
398,350	400,000	115,586.25 +	35%	398,350
400,000	....	116,163.75 +	39.6%	400,000

Head of household—Schedule Z

If taxable income is: Over—	But not over—	The tax is:		of the amount over—
$0	$12,750	....	10%	$0
12,750	48,600	$1,275.00 +	15%	12,750
48,600	125,450	6,652.50 +	25%	48,600
125,450	203,150	25,865.00 +	28%	125,450
203,150	398,350	47,621.00 +	33%	203,150
398,350	425,000	112,037.00 +	35%	398,350
425,000	....	121,364.50 +	39.6%	425,000

Married filing jointly or Qualifying widow(er)—Schedule Y–1

If taxable income is: Over—	But not over—	The tax is:		of the amount over—
$0	$17,850	....	10%	$0
17,850	72,500	$1,785.00 +	15%	17,850
72,500	146,400	9,982.50 +	25%	72,500
146,400	223,050	28,457.50 +	28%	146,400
223,050	398,350	49,919.50 +	33%	223,050
398,350	450,000	107,768.50 +	35%	398,350
450,000	....	125,846.00 +	39.6%	450,000

Married filing separately—Schedule Y–2

If taxable income is: Over—	But not over—	The tax is:		of the amount over—
$0	$8,925	....	10%	$0
8,925	36,250	$892.50 +	15%	8,925
36,250	73,200	4,991.25 +	25%	36,250
73,200	111,525	14,228.75 +	28%	73,200
111,525	199,175	24,959.75 +	33%	111,525
199,175	225,000	53,884.25 +	35%	199,175
225,000	....	62,923.00 +	39.6%	225,000

2013 Tax Rate Schedule for Estates and Trusts

Taxable Income Over—	But not over—	The tax is:		of the amount over—
$0	$2,450	....	15%	$0
2,450	5,700	$367.50 +	25%	2,450
5,700	8,750	1,180.00 +	28%	5,700
8,750	11,950	2,034.00 +	33%	8,750
11,950	———	3,090.00 +	39.6%	11,950

2. Adoption expenses credit in Sec. 36C.

	Amount per Code	Indexed 2014 Amount	Indexed 2013 Amount
Maximum credit	$ 10,000	$ 13,190	$ 12,970
Phase-out begins	150,000	197,880	194,580
Phase-out range	40,000	40,000	40,000

3. Child tax credit in Sec. 24.

	Amount per Code	Indexed 2014 Amount	Indexed 2013 Amount
Phase-out of refundable component begins:	$10,000	$3,000	$3,000

4. Lifetime learning credits in Sec. 25A.

	Amount per Code	Indexed 2014 Amount	Indexed 2013 Amount
Phase-out begins			
Married filing jointly	$80,000	$108,000	$107,000
Other than married filing jointly	40,000	54,000	53,000
Phase-out range			
Married filing jointly	20,000	20,000	20,000
Other than married filing jointly	10,000	10,000	10,000

4A. American Opportunity credit in Sec. 25A (replaces Hope credit in taxable years 2009 through 2014).

Phase-out begins			
Married filing jointly	$160,000	$160,000	$160,000
Other than married filing jointly	80,000	80,000	80,000
Phase-out range			
Married filing jointly	20,000	20,000	20,000
Other than married filing jointly	10,000	10,000	10,000

5. Earned income credit amounts in Sec. 32.

	Amount per Code	Indexed 2014 Amount	Indexed 2013 Amount
Maximum amount eligible for credit:			
One child	$6,330	$ 9,720	$ 9,560
Two or more	8,890	13,650	13,430
Three or more*	8,890	13,650	13,430
No children	4,220	6,480	6,370
Credit percentage:			
One child	34.0%	34.0%	34.0%
Two or more	40.0%	40.0%	40.0%
Three or more*	45.0%	45.0%	45.0%
No children	7.65%	7.65%	7.65%
Phaseout of credit begins (married filing jointly):			
One child	$12,610	$23,260	$22,870
Two or more	12,610	23,260	22,870
Three or more*	12,610	23,260	22,870
No children	6,280	13,540	13,310
Phaseout of credit begins (other than married filing jointly):			
One child	$11,610	$17,830	$17,530
Two or more	11,610	17,830	17,530
Three or more*	11,610	17,830	17,530
No children	5,280	8,110	7,970

*For 2009–2017.

	Amount per Code	Indexed 2014 Amount	Indexed 2013 Amount
Phaseout of credit ends (married filing jointly):			
One child	$26,078	$43,941	$43,210
Two or more	29,495	49,186	48,378
Three or more*	29,495	52,427	51,567
No children	10,500	20,020	19,680
Phaseout of credit ends (other than married filing jointly):			
One child	$25,078	$38,511	$37,870
Two or more	28,495	43,756	43,087
Three or more*	28,495	46,997	46,227
No children	9,500	14,590	14,340
Phaseout percentage:			
One child	15.98%	15.98%	15.98%
Two or more	21.06%	21.06%	21.06%
Three or more*	21.06%	21.06%	21.06%
No children	7.65%	7.65%	7.65%
Excessive investment income limit	$2,200	$3,350	$3,300

6. Standard deduction in Sec. 63(c).

	Amount per Code	Indexed 2014 Amount	Indexed 2013 Amount
Category			
Single	$3,000	$6,200	$6,100
Head of household	4,400	9,100	8,950
Married filing jointly and surviving spouse	5,000	12,400	12,200
Married filing separately	2,500	6,200	6,100
Additional standard deduction for blind or aged	600	1,200	1,200
	or	or	or
	750	1,550	1,500
Dependent's amount to add to earned income	250	350	350

7. Overall limitation on itemized deductions under Sec. 68.

	Amount per Code	Indexed 2014 Amount	Indexed 2013 Amount
Married filing separately	$150,000	$152,525	150,000
Married filing jointly and surviving spouse	300,000	305,050	300,000
Single	250,000	254,200	250,000
Head of household	275,000	279,650	275,000

8. Qualified transportation fringe exclusion in Sec. 132.

	Amount per Code	Indexed 2014 Amount	Indexed 2013 Amount
Transportation in a commuter highway vehicle ?and transit pass	$100	$130	$125
Qualified parking	175	250	245

9. Education savings bonds exclusion in Sec. 135.

	Amount per Code	Indexed 2014 Amount	Indexed 2013 Amount
AGI ceiling			
Joint return	$60,000	$113,950	$112,050
Not a joint return	40,000	76,000	74,700
Phase-out range			
Joint return	$30,000	$30,000	$30,000
Not a joint return	15,000	15,000	15,000

10. Adoption assistance program exclusion in Sec. 137.

	Amount per Code	Indexed 2014 Amount	Indexed 2013 Amount
Maximum exclusion	$ 10,000	$ 13,190	$ 12,970
Phase-out begins	150,000	197,880	194,580
Phase-out range	40,000	40,000	40,000

*For 2009–2017.

11. Personal exemption and dependency deductions in Sec. 151.

Amount per Code	Indexed 2014 Amount	Indexed 2013 Amount
$2,000	$3,950	$3,900

12. Threshold amounts for phase-out of personal exemptions and dependency deductions under Sec. 151(d)(3).

	Amount per Code	Indexed 2014 Amount	Indexed 2013 Amount
Single	$250,000	254,200	250,000
Head of household	275,000	279,650	275,000
Married filing jointly and surviving spouse	300,000	305,050	300,000
Married filing separately	150,000	152,252	150,000

13. Limits on Sec. 179 expensing in Sec. 179(b).

	Amount per Code	Indexed 2014 Amount	Indexed 2013 Amount
Statutory ceiling on deduction	$ 500,000	$ 500,000*	$ 500,000
Limits on Sec. 179 assets placed in service	2,000,000	2,000,000	2,000,000

14. Eligible long-term care premiums under Sec. 213.

	Amount per Code	Indexed 2014 Amount	Indexed 2013 Amount
Age			
40 or less	$ 200	$ 370	$ 360
>40 but not more than 50	375	700	680
>50 but not more than 60	750	1,400	1,360
>60 but not more than 70	2,000	3,720	3,640
>70	2,500	4,660	4,550

15. IRA AGI deduction limits for active participants under Sec. 219(g).

	Amount per Code	Indexed 2014 Amount	Indexed 2013 Amount
Married filing jointly	$80,000	$96,000	$95,000
Other than married filing jointly	50,000	60,000	59,000
Spouse not an active participant	150,000	181,000	178,000

16. Archer MSAs under Sec. 220.

	Amount per Code	Indexed 2014 Amount	Indexed 2013 Amount
Definition of high-deductible plan: annual deductible range			
Individual	$1,500- 2,250	$2,200- 3,250	$2,150- 3,200
Family	3,000- 4,500	4,350 6,550	4,300- 6,450
Definition of high-deductible plan: out-of-pocket expenditures			
Individual	$3,000	$4,350	$4,300
Family	5,500	8,000	7,850

17. Deduction for interest on education loans under Sec. 221.

	Amount per Code	Indexed 2014 Amount	Indexed 2013 Amount
Phase-out begins			
Married filing jointly	$100,000	$130,000	$125,000
Other than married filing jointly	50,000	65,000	60,000
Phase-out range			
Married filing jointly	30,000	30,000	30,000
Other than married filing jointly	15,000	15,000	15,000

18. Health savings accounts (HSAs) under Sec. 223.

	Amount per Code	Indexed 2014 Amount	Indexed 2013 Amount
Monthly limitation			
Self-only coverage	$187.50	$275.00	$270.83
Family	375.00	545.83	537.50

*At the present time, this section has not been extended. There is pending legislation in the Senate, *The Tax Extenders Act of 2013 (S. 1859)*, that would extend Section 179(b) to 2014.

TABLE OF INDEXED AMOUNTS

	Amount per Code	Indexed 2014 Amount	Indexed 2013 Amount
Definition of high-deductible health plan: annual deductible (minimum)			
Self-only coverage	$1,000	$1,250	$1,250
Family	2,000	2,500	2,500
Definition of high-deductible health plan: out-of-pocket expenditures (maximum)			
Individual	$ 5,000	$ 6,350	$ 6,250
Family	10,000	12,700	12,500

19. Limitation on deduction for luxury automobiles in Sec. 208F.

Year	Amount per Code	Indexed 2014 Amount	Indexed 2013 Amount
1st	$2,560	$3,160 or $11,160	$3,160 or $11,160
2nd	4,100	5,100	5,100
3rd	2,450	3,050	3,050
Each succeeding year	1,475	1,875	1,875

20. AGI limits in calculating Roth contributions under Sec. 408A(c)(3).

	Amount per Code	Indexed 2014 Amount	Indexed 2013 Amount
Married filing jointly	$150,000	$181,000	$178,000
Single	95,000	114,000	112,000
Married filing separate returns	-0-	-0-	-0-
Phase-out range			
Married filing jointly	10,000	10,000	10,000
Single	15,000	15,000	15,000
Married filing separate returns	10,000	10,000	10,000

21. Statutory amounts for pension and profit-sharing plans.

Item	Amount per Code	Indexed 2014 Amount	Indexed 2013 Amount
Maximum annual benefits payable for a defined ?benefit plan	$ 90,000	$210,000	$205,000
Maximum annual contribution to a defined ?contribution plan	30,000	52,000	51,000
Definition of a highly compensated employee	80,000	115,000	115,000
Annual compensation ceiling	150,000	260,000	255,000
Section 401(k) plan ceiling	7,000	17,500	17,500
SEP compensation minimum	300	550	550
Tax credit ESOP distribution ceiling	100,000 or 500,000	210,000 or 1,050,000	205,000 or 1,035,000
SIMPLE plans	6,000	12,000	12,000

22. Foreign earned income exclusion limit under Sec. 911(b)(2).

	Amount per Code	Indexed 2014 Amount	Indexed 2013 Amount
Limit	$80,000	$99,200	$97,600

23. Interest imputations under Sec. 1274A.

	Amount per Code	Indexed 2014 Amount	Indexed 2013 Amount
Lower interest rate—principal amount ceiling on ?transactions to which applicable	$2,800,000	$5,557,200	$5,468,200
Election to use cash method—principal amount ?ceiling on transactions where election can be made	2,000,000	3,969,500	3,905,900

24. Per donee annual exclusion for the gift tax under Sec. 2503.

Amount per Code	Indexed 2014 Amount	Indexed 2013 Amount
$10,000	$14,000	$14,000

25. Long-term care insurance benefits under Sec. 7702B (per day).

Amount per Code	Indexed 2014 Amount	Indexed 2013 Amount
$175	$330	$320

DEPRECIATION AND COST RECOVERY TABLES

TABLE 1

MACRS Accelerated Depreciation for Personal Property
Assuming Half-Year Convention

For Property Placed in Service after December 31, 1986

Recovery Year	3-Year (200% DB)	5-Year (200% DB)	7-Year (200% DB)	10-Year (200% DB)	15-Year (150% DB)	20-Year (150% DB)
1	33.33	20.00	14.29	10.00	5.00	3.750
2	44.45	32.00	24.49	18.00	9.50	7.219
3	14.81*	19.20	17.49	14.40	8.55	6.677
4	7.41	11.52*	12.49	11.52	7.70	6.177
5		11.52	8.93*	9.22	6.93	5.713
6		5.76	8.92	7.37	6.23	5.285
7			8.93	6.55*	5.90*	4.888
8			4.46	6.55	5.90	4.522
9				6.56	5.91	4.462*
10				6.55	5.90	4.461
11				3.28	5.91	4.462
12					5.90	4.461
13					5.91	4.462
14					5.90	4.461
15					5.91	4.462
16					2.95	4.461
17						4.462
18						4.461
19						4.462
20						4.461
21						2.231

*Switchover to straight-line depreciation.

TABLE 2

MACRS Accelerated Depreciation for Personal Property Assuming Mid-Quarter Convention

For Property Placed in Service after December 31, 1986
(Partial Table*)

3-Year

Recovery Year	First Quarter	Second Quarter	Third Quarter	Fourth Quarter
1	58.33	41.67	25.00	8.33
2	27.78	38.89	50.00	61.11

5-Year

Recovery Year	First Quarter	Second Quarter	Third Quarter	Fourth Quarter
1	35.00	25.00	15.00	5.00
2	26.00	30.00	34.00	38.00

7-Year

Recovery Year	First Quarter	Second Quarter	Third Quarter	Fourth Quarter
1	25.00	17.85	10.71	3.57
2	21.43	23.47	25.51	27.55

* The figures in this table are taken from the official tables that appear in Rev.Proc. 87–57, 1987–2 C.B. 687. Because of their length, the complete tables are not presented.

TABLE 3
ACRS Cost Recovery Table for 19-Year Real Property

For Property Placed in Service after May 8, 1985, and before January 1, 1987
19-Year Real Property (19-Year 175% Declining Balance)
(Assuming Mid-Month Convention)

If the recovery year is:	And the month in the first recovery year the property is placed in service is:											
	1	2	3	4	5	6	7	8	9	10	11	12
	The applicable percentage is (use the column for the month in the first year the property is placed in service):											
1	8.8	8.1	7.3	6.5	5.8	5.0	4.2	3.5	2.7	1.9	1.1	0.4
2	8.4	8.5	8.5	8.6	8.7	8.8	8.8	8.9	9.0	9.0	9.1	9.2
3	7.6	7.7	7.7	7.8	7.9	7.9	8.0	8.1	8.1	8.2	8.3	8.3
4	6.9	7.0	7.0	7.1	7.1	7.2	7.3	7.3	7.4	7.4	7.5	7.6
5	6.3	6.3	6.4	6.4	6.5	6.5	6.6	6.6	6.7	6.8	6.8	6.9
6	5.7	5.7	5.8	5.9	5.9	5.9	6.0	6.0	6.1	6.1	6.2	6.2
7	5.2	5.2	5.3	5.3	5.3	5.4	5.4	5.5	5.5	5.6	5.6	5.6
8	4.7	4.7	4.8	4.8	4.8	4.9	4.9	5.0	5.0	5.1	5.1	5.1
9	4.2	4.3	4.3	4.4	4.4	4.5	4.5	4.5	4.5	4.6	4.6	4.7
10	4.2	4.2	4.2	4.2	4.2	4.2	4.2	4.2	4.2	4.2	4.2	4.2
11	4.2	4.2	4.2	4.2	4.2	4.2	4.2	4.2	4.2	4.2	4.2	4.2
12	4.2	4.2	4.2	4.2	4.2	4.2	4.2	4.2	4.2	4.2	4.2	4.2
13	4.2	4.2	4.2	4.2	4.2	4.2	4.2	4.2	4.2	4.2	4.2	4.2
14	4.2	4.2	4.2	4.2	4.2	4.2	4.2	4.2	4.2	4.2	4.2	4.2
15	4.2	4.2	4.2	4.2	4.2	4.2	4.2	4.2	4.2	4.2	4.2	4.2
16	4.2	4.2	4.2	4.2	4.2	4.2	4.2	4.2	4.2	4.2	4.2	4.2
17	4.2	4.2	4.2	4.2	4.2	4.2	4.2	4.2	4.2	4.2	4.2	4.2
18	4.2	4.2	4.2	4.2	4.2	4.2	4.2	4.2	4.2	4.2	4.2	4.2
19	4.2	4.2	4.2	4.2	4.2	4.2	4.2	4.2	4.2	4.2	4.2	4.2
20	0.2	0.5	0.9	1.2	1.6	1.9	2.3	2.6	3.0	3.3	3.7	4.0

TABLE 4

MACRS Straight-Line Depreciation for Real Property Assuming Mid-Month Convention*

For Property Placed in Service after December 31, 1986
27.5-Year Residential Real Property

The applicable percentage is (use the column for the month in the first year the property is placed in service):

Recovery Year(s)	1	2	3	4	5	6	7	8	9	10	11	12
1	3.485	3.182	2.879	2.576	2.273	1.970	1.667	1.364	1.061	0.758	0.455	0.152
2–18	3.636	3.636	3.636	3.636	3.636	3.636	3.636	3.636	3.636	3.636	3.636	3.636
19–27	3.637	3.637	3.637	3.637	3.637	3.637	3.637	3.637	3.637	3.637	3.637	3.637
28	1.970	2.273	2.576	2.879	3.182	3.485	3.636	3.636	3.636	3.636	3.636	3.636
29	0.000	0.000	0.000	0.000	0.000	0.000	0.152	0.455	0.758	1.061	1.364	1.667

For Property Placed in Service after December 31, 1986 and before May 13, 1993
31.5-Year Nonresidential Real Property

The applicable percentage is (use the column for the month in the first year the property is placed in service):

Recovery Year(s)	1	2	3	4	5	6	7	8	9	10	11	12
1	3.042	2.778	2.513	2.249	1.984	1.720	1.455	1.190	0.926	0.661	0.397	0.132
2–19	3.175	3.175	3.175	3.175	3.175	3.175	3.175	3.175	3.175	3.175	3.175	3.175
20–31	3.174	3.174	3.174	3.174	3.174	3.174	3.174	3.174	3.174	3.174	3.174	3.174
32	1.720	1.984	2.249	2.513	2.778	3.042	3.175	3.175	3.175	3.175	3.175	3.175
33	0.000	0.000	0.000	0.000	0.000	0.000	0.132	0.397	0.661	0.926	1.190	1.455

For Property Placed in Service after May 12, 1993
39-Year Nonresidential Real Property

Recovery Year(s)	1	2	3	4	5	6	7	8	9	10	11	12
1	2.461	2.247	2.033	1.819	1.605	1.391	1.177	0.963	0.749	0.535	0.321	0.107
2–39	2.564	2.564	2.564	2.564	2.564	2.564	2.564	2.564	2.564	2.564	2.564	2.564
40	0.107	0.321	0.535	0.749	0.963	1.177	1.391	1.605	1.819	2.033	2.247	2.461

* The official tables contain a separate row for each year. For ease of presentation, certain years are grouped in these three tables. In some instances, this will produce a difference of .001 for the last digit when compared with the official tables.

TABLE 5

ACRS Cost Recovery Table for 19-Year Real Property: Optional Straight-Line

For Property Placed in Service after May 8, 1985, and before January 1, 1987 19-Year Real Property for Which an Optional 19-Year Straight-Line Method Is Elected (Assuming Mid-Month Convention)

If the recovery year is:	And the month in the first recovery year the property is placed in service is:											
	1	2	3	4	5	6	7	8	9	10	11	12
	The applicable percentage is (use the column for the month in the first year the property is placed in service):											
1	5.0	4.6	4.2	3.7	3.3	2.9	2.4	2.0	1.5	1.1	0.7	0.2
2	5.3	5.3	5.3	5.3	5.3	5.3	5.3	5.3	5.3	5.3	5.3	5.3
3	5.3	5.3	5.3	5.3	5.3	5.3	5.3	5.3	5.3	5.3	5.3	5.3
4	5.3	5.3	5.3	5.3	5.3	5.3	5.3	5.3	5.3	5.3	5.3	5.3
5	5.3	5.3	5.3	5.3	5.3	5.3	5.3	5.3	5.3	5.3	5.3	5.3
6	5.3	5.3	5.3	5.3	5.3	5.3	5.3	5.3	5.3	5.3	5.3	5.3
7	5.3	5.3	5.3	5.3	5.3	5.3	5.3	5.3	5.3	5.3	5.3	5.3
8	5.3	5.3	5.3	5.3	5.3	5.3	5.3	5.3	5.3	5.3	5.3	5.3
9	5.3	5.3	5.3	5.3	5.3	5.3	5.3	5.3	5.3	5.3	5.3	5.3
10	5.3	5.3	5.3	5.3	5.3	5.3	5.3	5.3	5.3	5.3	5.3	5.3
11	5.3	5.3	5.3	5.3	5.3	5.3	5.3	5.3	5.3	5.3	5.3	5.3
12	5.3	5.3	5.3	5.3	5.3	5.3	5.3	5.3	5.3	5.3	5.3	5.3
13	5.3	5.3	5.3	5.3	5.3	5.3	5.3	5.3	5.3	5.3	5.3	5.3
14	5.2	5.2	5.2	5.2	5.2	5.2	5.2	5.2	5.2	5.2	5.2	5.2
15	5.2	5.2	5.2	5.2	5.2	5.2	5.2	5.2	5.2	5.2	5.2	5.2
16	5.2	5.2	5.2	5.2	5.2	5.2	5.2	5.2	5.2	5.2	5.2	5.2
17	5.2	5.2	5.2	5.2	5.2	5.2	5.2	5.2	5.2	5.2	5.2	5.2
18	5.2	5.2	5.2	5.2	5.2	5.2	5.2	5.2	5.2	5.2	5.2	5.2
19	5.2	5.2	5.2	5.2	5.2	5.2	5.2	5.2	5.2	5.2	5.2	5.2
20	0.2	0.6	1.0	1.5	1.9	2.3	2.8	3.2	3.7	4.1	4.5	5.0

TABLE 6
MACRS Straight-Line Depreciation for Personal Property Assuming Half-Year Convention*

For Property Placed in Service after December 31, 1986

MACRS Class	% First Recovery Year	Other Recovery Years: Years	Other Recovery Years: %	Last Recovery Year: Year	Last Recovery Year: %
3-Year	16.67	2–3	33.33	4	16.67
5-Year	10.00	2–5	20.00	6	10.00
7-Year	7.14	2–7	14.29	8	7.14
10-Year	5.00	2–10	10.00	11	5.00
15-Year	3.33	2–15	6.67	16	3.33
20-Year	2.50	2–20	5.00	21	2.50

* The official table contains a separate row for each year. For ease of presentation, certain years are grouped in this table. In some instances, this will produce a difference of .01 for the last digit when compared with the official table.

TABLE 7
Alternative Minimum Tax: 150% Declining-Balance Assuming Half-Year Convention

For Property Placed in Service after December 31, 1986 (Partial Table*)

Recovery Year	3-Year 150%	5-Year 150%	9.5-Year 150%	10-Year 150%
1	25.00	15.00	7.89	7.50
2	37.50	25.50	14.54	13.88
3	25.00**	17.85	12.25	11.79
4	12.50	16.66**	10.31	10.02
5		16.66	9.17**	8.74**
6		8.33	9.17	8.74
7			9.17	8.74
8			9.17	8.74
9			9.17	8.74
10			9.16	8.74
11				4.37

*The figures in this table are taken from the official table that appears in Rev.Proc. 87–57, 1987–2 C.B. 687. Because of its length, the complete table is not presented.

**Switchover to straight-line depreciation.

TABLE 8

ADS Straight-Line for Personal Property Assuming Half-Year Convention

For Property Placed in Service after December 31, 1986
(Partial Table*)

Recovery Year	5-Year Class	9.5-Year Class	12-Year Class
1	10.00	5.26	4.17
2	20.00	10.53	8.33
3	20.00	10.53	8.33
4	20.00	10.53	8.33
5	20.00	10.52	8.33
6	10.00	10.53	8.33
7		10.52	8.34
8		10.53	8.33
9		10.52	8.34
10		10.53	8.33
11			8.34
12			8.33
13			4.17

* The figures in this table are taken from the official table that appears in Rev.Proc. 87–57, 1987–2 C.B. 687. Because of its length, the complete table is not presented. The tables for the mid-quarter convention also appear in Rev.Proc. 87–57.

TABLE 9

ADS Straight-Line for Real Property Assuming Mid-Month Convention

For Property Placed in Service after December 31, 1986

Recovery Year	Month Placed in Service											
	1	2	3	4	5	6	7	8	9	10	11	12
1	2.396	2.188	1.979	1.771	1.563	1.354	1.146	0.938	0.729	0.521	0.313	0.104
2–40	2.500	2.500	2.500	2.500	2.500	2.500	2.500	2.500	2.500	2.500	2.500	2.500
41	0.104	0.312	0.521	0.729	0.937	1.146	1.354	1.562	1.771	1.979	2.187	2.396

LIST OF EDITORIAL SUMMARIES

LIST OF EDITORIAL SUMMARIES

LIST OF EDITORIAL SUMMARIES

LIST OF EDITORIAL SUMMARIES

LIST OF CODE SECTIONS AND REGULATION SECTIONS

CODE SECTIONS

1
2
3
5
11
12
15
21
22
23
24
25
25A
25B
26
27
29
30
31
32
33
34
35
36
36A
36C
37
38
39
41
42
44
45
45A
45B
45C
45D
45E
45F
45N
45R
46
47
48
49
50
51
52
53
55
56
57
58
59
59A
61
62
63
64
65
66
67
68
71
72
73
74
79
82
83
84
85
86
90
101
102
103
104
105
106
107
108
109
110
111
112
115
117
118
119
121
123
125
127
129
132
134
135
136
137
138
139
139A
151
152
153
161
162
163
164
165
166
167
168
169
170
171
172
173
174
175
178
179
180
183
190
194
195
196
197
199
211
212
213
215
217
219
220
221
222
223
241
243
246
246A
248
261
262
263
263A
264
265
266
267
268
269
269A
274
275
276
280A
280B
280C
280E
280F
280G
280H
291
301
302
303
304
305
306
307
311
312
316
317
318
331
332
334
336
337
338
346
351
354
355
356
357
358
361
362
368
381
382
383
384

CODE SECTIONS

385
401
402
402A
403
404
408
408A
409
409A
410
411
412
414
415
416
421
422
441
442
443
444
446
447
448
451
453
453A
453B
454
460
461
464
465
469
471
472
474
475
481
482
483
501
502
503
504
505
507
508
509
511
512
513
514
515
521
527
528
529
530
531
532
533
534
535
536
537
541
542
543
544
545
546
547
561
562
563
564
565
611
612
613
613A
616
631
641
642
643
644
645
651
652
661
662
663
664
665
666
667
671
672
673
674
675
676
677
678
681
682
691
692
701
702
703
704
705
706
707
708
709
721
722
723
724
731
732
733
734
735
736
737
741
742
743
751
752
753
754
755
761
771
772
773
774
775
776
777
901
904
905
911
1001
1011
1012
1013
1014
1015
1016
1017
1019
1022
1031
1032
1033
1035
1036
1038
1040
1041
1042
1043
1044
1045
1053
1059
1060
1091
1092
1201
1202
1211
1212
1221
1222
1223
1231
1233
1234
1234A
1234B
1235
1236
1237
1239
1241
1242
1243
1244
1245
1250
1252
1253
1254
1258
1259
1260
1271
1272
1273
1274
1274A
1275
1276
1277
1278
1281
1282
1283
1286
1287
1288
1301
1311
1312
1313
1314
1341
1361
1362
1363

CODE SECTIONS

1366
1367
1368
1371
1372
1373
1374
1375
1377
1378
1379
1401
1402
1403
1411
1501
1502
1503
1504
1551
1552
1561
1563
2001
2002
2010
2011
2012
2013
2014
2015
2016
2031
2032
2032A
2033
2034
2035
2036
2037
2038
2039
2040
2041
2042
2043
2044
2045
2046
2051
2053
2054
2055
2056
2056A
2058
2201
2501
2502
2503
2504
2505
2511
2512
2513
2514
2515
2516
2518
2519
2522
2523
2524
2601
2602
2603
2604
2611
2612
2613
2621
2622
2623
2624
2631
2632
2641
2642
2651
2652
2653
2654
2661
2662
2663
2664
2701
2702
2703
2704
4911
4912
4958
4971
4972
4973
4974
4975
4977
4979
4980C
4980D
4980E
4980G
4999
5881
6001
6011
6012
6013
6015
6018
6019
6031
6033
6037
6039D
6041
6041A
6053
6072
6075
6081
6104
6115
6151
6161
6163
6166
6211
6212
6213
6221
6222
6229
6231
6428
6429
6501
6502
6503
6511
6513
6601
6611
6621
6622
6631
6651
6654
6662
6662A
6663
6664
6665
6694
6695
6696
6701
6702
6703
7201
7202
7203
7204
7205
7206
7207
7216
7217
7441
7442
7443
7443A
7444
7445
7446
7451
7452
7453
7454
7463
7482
7483
7491
7508
7519
7701
7702B
7703
770
7[illegible]

REGULATION SECTION

1.1
1.2
1.25
1.61
1.62
1.63
1.67
1.71
1.72
1.73
1.74
1.79
1.82
1.83
1.101
1.104
1.105
1.106
1.107
1.109
1.118
1.119
1.121
1.127
1.132
1.151
1.152
1.162
1.163
1.164
1.165
1.166
1.170A
1.171
1.172
1.183
1.212
1.215
1.217
1.248
1.262
1.263A
1.265
1.267
1.269
1.274
1.280F
1.280H
1.301
1.302
1.305
1.306
1.307
1.312
1.316
1.318
1.331
1.332
1.334
1.351
1.354
1.355
1.356
1.357
1.358
1.361
1.362
1.368
1.441
1.442
1.443
1.446
1.448
1.461
1.469
1.471
1.472
1.482
1.483
1.532
1.533
1.534
1.535
1.536
1.537
1.541
1.542
1.543
1.544
1.545
1.547
1.561
1.562
1.563
1.564
1.565
1.611
1.612
1.613
1.631
1.641
1.642
1.643
1.651
1.652
1.661
1.662
1.665
1.666
1.671
1.672
1.674
1.675
1.676
1.677
1.678
1.691
1.701
1.702
1.703
1.704
1.705
1.706
1.707
1.708
1.709
1.721
1.722
1.723
1.731
1.732
1.733
1.734
1.735
1.736
1.737
1.741
1.742
1.743
1.751
1.752
1.753
1.754
1.755
1.761
1.1001
1.1011
1.1012
1.1013
1.1014
1.1015
1.1016
1.1017
1.1019
1.1031
1.1032
1.1033
1.1035
1.1036
1.1041
1.1042
1.1060
1.1091
1.1211
1.1212
1.1221
1.1222
1.1223
1.1231
1.1233
1.1234
1.1235
1.1236
1.1237
1.1239
1.1241
1.1244
1.1245
1.1250
1.1341
1.1375
1.1378
1.1502
1.1551
1.1561
1.1563
1.6001
1.6011
20.0
20.2011
20.2013
20.2015
20.2031
20.2032
20.2032A
20.2033
20.2034
20.2036
20.2037
20.2038
20.2039
20.2040
20.2041
20.2042
20.2043
20.2046
20.2053
20.2054
20.2055
20.2056
25.2501
25.2502
25.2503
25.2504
25.2511
25.2512
25.2513
25.2514
25.2516
25.2518
25.2522
25.2523
25.2524
301.7701

INTERNAL REVENUE CODE OF 1986

INTERNAL REVENUE TITLE

SUBTITLE A—INCOME TAXES

Chapter
1. Normal taxes and surtaxes.
2. Tax on self-employment income.*
3. Withholding of tax on nonresident aliens and foreign corporations.*
4. Rules applicable to recovery of excessive profits on government contracts.*
5. Tax on transfers to avoid income tax.*
6. Consolidated returns.

CHAPTER 1—NORMAL TAXES AND SURTAXES

Subchapter
A. Determination of tax liability.
B. Computation of taxable income.
C. Corporate distributions and adjustments.
D. Deferred compensation, etc.
E. Accounting periods and methods of accounting.
F. Exempt organizations.
G. Corporations used to avoid income tax on shareholders.
H. Banking institutions.*
I. Natural resources.
J. Estates, trusts, beneficiaries, and decedents.
K. Partners and partnerships.
L. Insurance companies.*
M. Regulated investment companies and real estate investment trusts.*
N. Tax based on income from sources within or without the United States.
O. Gain or loss on disposition of property.
P. Capital gains and losses.
Q. Readjustment of tax between years and special limitations.
[R. Repealed]
S. Tax treatment of S corporations and their shareholders.
T. Cooperatives and their patrons.*
U. General stock ownership corporations.*
V. Title 11 cases.*

SUBCHAPTER A—DETERMINATION OF TAX LIABILITY

Part
I. Tax on individuals.
II. Tax on corporations.
III. Changes in rates during a taxable year.
IV. Credits against tax.
[V. Repealed]
VI. Alternative minimum tax.
VII. Environmental tax.

Editorial Summary

Tax Rates

Subchapter A of Chapter 1 (Secs. 1–15)

Sections 1–15 provide the tax rates for the individual taxpayer and the corporate taxpayer. Rates are not provided for a partnership because the partnership is a conduit (i.e., a tax reporter rather than a taxpayer) [see Sec. 701].

For the individual taxpayer, two methods are provided for applying the tax rates to taxable income to calculate the tax liability. The first method is to use the tax rate schedule under which the taxpayer applies the statutory tax rates to taxable income [see Sec. 1]. The second method is to use the tax table [see Sec. 3]. In this case, the taxpayer locates the taxable income in the appropriate taxable income column in the table, and the tax liability is the related tax liability amount in the tax liability column. The tax table must be used unless the taxpayer is not eligible to use it. The tax rates are indexed for the effect of inflation [see Sec. 1(f)].

In calculating the tax liability under either the tax rate schedule approach or the tax table approach, the filing status of the taxpayer must be determined [see Secs. 1 and 2]. The available options include married individuals filing a joint return, surviving spouses, heads of households, single individuals, and married individuals filing separate returns.

In calculating the individual tax liability, the following must be considered:

1. The effective tax rate may be greater than the stated rate due to the phase-outs of personal exemptions [see Sec. 151(d)(3)]. The phase-out of personal exemptions expired at the end of 2009, but was reinstated by the American Taxpayer Relief Act of 2012 beginning in 2013.

2. The effective rate may be greater than the stated rate due to the phase-out of certain itemized deductions [see Sec. 68]. The phase-out of itemized deductions expired at the end of 2009, but was reinstated by the American Taxpayer Relief Act of 2012 beginning in 2013.

3. For a child under age 19 (under age 24 if a full-time student) with unearned income, the parents' rates may apply (i.e., the "kiddie" tax) [see Sec. 1(g)].

4. Maximum rates apply to certain capital gains and certain dividends. This alternative rate may produce a beneficial tax result [see Sec. 1(h)].

*Omitted.

5. The alternative minimum tax may apply rather than the regular income tax [see Sec. 55].

6. The filing status of the taxpayer affects the tax rates [see Secs. 1–2].

Section 1 also contains the income tax rates for estates and trusts.

Special tax rates (15% and 25% rather than 34%) apply for the small corporation. These beneficial rates are phased out as the taxable income of the corporation increases above $100,000 and are completely phased out once taxable income reaches $335,000. The Revenue Reconciliation Act of 1993 provided for an additional rate of 35% once taxable income exceeds $10 million. The beneficial rate on the first $10 million of 34% (rather than 35%) is phased out as the taxable income of the corporation increases above $15 million and is completely phased out once taxable income reaches $18,333,333 [see Sec. 11(b)].

Related items that may affect the corporate income tax liability include the following:

1. The alternative minimum tax [see Sec. 55].

2. The accumulated earnings tax [see Sec. 531].

3. The personal holding company tax [see Sec. 541].

4. The tax rate limitations imposed on corporations that are members of a controlled group [see Sec. 1561].

5. The ability to reduce the effective tax rate through the filing of a consolidated tax return [see Sec. 1501].

6. The alternative tax on certain capital gains if the regular corporate tax rates should be increased by Congress [see Sec. 1201(a)].

7. Certain corporations (personal service corporations) are ineligible for the beneficial rates [see Sec. 11(b)(2)].

As is the case with the partnership, certain corporations (i.e., S corporations) generally are not subject to taxation (see Sec. 1361). Instead, the tax liability is levied at the shareholder level (see Sec. 1366).

PART I—TAX ON INDIVIDUALS

§ 1. Tax imposed

(a) Married individuals filing joint returns and surviving spouses.*—There is hereby imposed on the taxable income of—

(1) every married individual (as defined in section 7703) who makes a single return jointly with his spouse under section 6013, and

(2) every surviving spouse (as defined in section 2(a)),

a tax determined in accordance with the following table:

If taxable income is:	The tax is:
Not over $36,900	15% of taxable income.
Over $36,900 but not over $89,150	$5,535, plus 28% of the excess over $36,900.
Over $89,150 but not over $140,000	$20,165, plus 31% of the excess over $89,150.
Over $140,000 but not over $250,000	$35,928.50, plus 36% of the excess over $140,000.
Over $250,000	$75,528.50, plus 39.6% of the excess over $250,000.

(b) Heads of households.*—There is hereby imposed on the taxable income of every head of a household (as defined in section 2(b)) a tax determined in accordance with the following table:

If taxable income is:	The tax is:
Not over $29,600	15% of taxable income.
Over $29,600 but not over $76,400	$4,440, plus 28% of the excess over $29,600.
Over $76,400 but not over $127,500	$17,544, plus 31% of the excess over $76,400.
Over $127,500 but not over $250,000	$33,385, plus 36% of the excess over $127,500.
Over $250,000	$77,485, plus 39.6% of the excess over $250,000.

(c) Unmarried individuals (other than surviving spouses and heads of households).*— There is hereby imposed on the taxable income of every individual (other than a surviving spouse as defined in section 2(a) or the head of a household as defined in section 2(b)) who is not a married individual (as defined in section 7703) a tax determined in accordance with the following table:

If taxable income is:	The tax is:
Not over $22,100	15% of taxable income.
Over $22,100 but not over $53,500	$3,315, plus 28% of the excess over $22,100.
Over $53,500 but not over $115,000	$12,107, plus 31% of the excess over $53,500.
Over $115,000 but not over $250,000	$31,172, plus 36% of the excess over $115,000.
Over $250,000	$79,772, plus 39.6% of the excess over $250,000.

*Editorial comment: See the indexed tax rates for 2014 after Sec. 1(i).

(d) Married individuals filing separate returns.*— There is hereby imposed on the taxable income of every married individual (as defined in section 7703) who does not make a single return jointly with his spouse under section 6013, a tax determined in accordance with the following table:

If taxable income is:	The tax is:
Not over $18,450	15% of taxable income.
Over $18,450 but not over $44,575	$2,767.50, plus 28% of the excess over $18,450.
Over $44,575 but not over $70,000	$10,082.50, plus 31% of the excess over $44,575.
Over $70,000 but not over $125,000	$17,964.25, plus 36% of the excess over $70,000.
Over $125,000	$37,764.25, plus 39.6% of the excess over $125,000.

(e) Estates and trusts.*—There is hereby imposed on the taxable income of—

(1) every estate, and

(2) every trust,

taxable under this subsection a tax determined in accordance with the following table:

If taxable income is:	The tax is:
Not over $1,500	15% of taxable income.
Over $1,500 but not over $3,500	$225, plus 28% of the excess over $1,500.
Over $3,500 but not over $5,500	$785, plus 31% of the excess over $3,500.
Over $5,500 but not over $7,500	$1,405, plus 36% of the excess over $5,500.
Over $7,500	$2,125, plus 39.6% of the excess over $7,500.

(f) Phaseout of marriage penalty in 15-percent bracket; adjustments in tax tables so that inflation will not result in tax increases.

(1) In general. Not later than December 15 of 1993, and each subsequent calendar year, the Secretary shall prescribe tables which shall apply in lieu of the tables contained in subsections (a), (b), (c), (d), and (e) with respect to taxable years beginning in the succeeding calendar year.

(2) Method of prescribing tables. The table which under paragraph (1) is to apply in lieu of the table contained in subsection (a), (b), (c), (d), or (e), as the case may be, with respect to taxable years beginning in any calendar year shall be prescribed—

(A) except as provided in paragraph (8), by increasing the minimum and maximum dollar amounts for each rate bracket for which a tax is imposed under such table by the cost-of-living adjustment for such calendar year.

(B) by not changing the rate applicable to any rate bracket as adjusted under subparagraph (A), and

(C) by adjusting the amounts setting forth the tax to the extent necessary to reflect the adjustments in the rate brackets.

(3) Cost-of-living adjustment. For purposes of paragraph (2), the cost-of-living adjustment for any calendar year is the percentage (if any) by which—

(A) the CPI for the preceding calendar year, exceeds

(B) the CPI for the calendar year 1992.

(4) CPI for any calendar year. For purposes of paragraph (3), the CPI for any calendar year is the average of the Consumer Price Index as of the close of the 12-month period ending on August 31 of such calendar year.

(5) Consumer price index. For purposes of paragraph (4), the term "Consumer Price Index" means the last Consumer Price Index for all-urban consumers published by the Department of Labor. For purposes of the preceding sentence, the revision of the Consumer Price Index which is most consistent with the Consumer Price Index for calendar year 1986 shall be used.

(6) Rounding.

(A) In general. If any increase determined under paragraph (2)(A), section 63(c)(4), section 68(b)(2) or section 151(d)(4) is not a multiple of $50, such increase shall be rounded to the next lowest multiple of $50.

(B) Table for married individuals filing separately. In the case of a married individual filing a separate return, subparagraph (A) (other than with respect to sections 63(c)(4) and

*Editorial comment: See the indexed tax rates for 2014 after Sec. 1(i).

151(d)(4)(A)) shall be applied by substituting "$25" for "$50" each place it appears.

(7) Special rule for certain brackets.

(A) Calendar year 1994. In prescribing the tables under paragraph (1) which apply with respect to taxable years beginning in calendar year 1994, the Secretary shall make no adjustment to the dollar amounts at which the 36 percent rate bracket begins or at which the 39.6 percent rate begins under any table contained in subsection (a), (b), (c), (d), or (e).

(B) Later calendar years. In prescribing tables under paragraph (1) which apply with respect to taxable years beginning in a calendar year after 1994, the cost-of-living adjustment used in making adjustments to the dollar amounts referred to in subparagraph (A) shall be determined under paragraph (3) by substituting "1993" for "1992."

(8) Elimination of marriage penalty in 15-percent bracket.—With respect to taxable years beginning after December 31, 2003, in prescribing the tables under paragraph (1)—

(A) the maximum taxable income in the 15-percent rate bracket in the table contained in subsection (a) (and the minimum taxable income in the next higher taxable income bracket in such table) shall be 200 percent of the maximum taxable income in the 15-percent rate bracket in the table contained in subsection (c) (after any other adjustment under this subsection), and

(B) the comparable taxable income amounts in the table contained in subsection (d) shall be ½ of the amounts determined under subparagraph (A).

(g) Certain unearned income of children taxed as if parent's income.—

(1) In general.—In the case of any child to whom this subsection applies, the tax imposed by this section shall be equal to the greater of—

(A) the tax imposed by this section without regard to this subsection, or

(B) the sum of—

(i) the tax which would be imposed by this section if the taxable income of such child for the taxable year were reduced by the net unearned income of such child, plus

(ii) such child's share of the allocable parental tax.

(2) Child to whom subsection applies.—This subsection shall apply to any child for any taxable year if—

(A) such child—

(i) has not attained age 18 before the close of the taxable year, or

(ii)(I) has attained age 18 before the close of the taxable year and meets the age requirements of section 152(c)(3) (determined without regard to subparagraph (B) thereof), and

(II) whose earned income (as defined in section 911(d)(2)) for such taxable year does not exceed one-half of the amount of the individual's support (within the meaning of section 152(c)(1)(D) after the application of section 152(f)(5) (without regard to subparagraph (A) thereof)) for such taxable year.

(B) either parent of such child is alive at the close of the taxable year, and

(C) such child does not file a joint return for the taxable year.

(3) Allocable parental tax.—For purposes of this subsection—

(A) In general.—The term "allocable parental tax" means the excess of—

(i) the tax which would be imposed by this section on the parent's taxable income if such income included the net unearned income of all children of the parent to whom this subsection applies, over

(ii) the tax imposed by this section on the parent without regard to this subsection.

For purposes of clause (i), net unearned income of all children of the parent shall not be taken into account in computing any exclusion, deduction, or credit of the parent.

(B) Child's share.—A child's share of any allocable parental tax of a parent shall be equal to an amount which bears the same ratio to the total allocable parental tax as the child's net unearned income bears to the aggregate net unearned income of all children of such parent to whom this subsection applies.

(C) Special rule where parent has different taxable year.—Except as provided in regulations, if the parent does not have the same taxable year as the child, the allocable parental tax shall be determined on the basis of the taxable year of the parent ending in the child's taxable year.

(4) Net unearned income.—For purposes of this subsection—

(A) In general.—The term "net unearned income" means the excess of—

(i) the portion of the adjusted gross income for the taxable year which is not attributable to earned income (as defined in section 911(d)(2)), over

(ii) the sum of—

(I) the amount in effect for the taxable year under section 63(c)(5)(A) (relating to limitation on standard deduction in the case of certain dependents), plus

(II) the greater of the amount described in subclause (I) or, if the child itemizes his deductions for the taxable year, the amount of the itemized deductions allowed by this chapter for the taxable year which are directly connected with the production of the portion of adjusted gross income referred to in clause (i).

(B) Limitation based on taxable income.—The amount of the net unearned income for any taxable year shall not exceed the individual's taxable income for such taxable year.

(C) Treatment of distributions from qualified disability trusts.—For purposes of this subsection, in the case of any child who is a beneficiary of a qualified disability trust (as defined in section 642(b)(2)(C)(ii)), any amount included in the income of such child under sections 652 and 662 during a taxable year shall be considered earned income of such child for such taxable year.

(5) Special rules for determining parent to whom subsection applies.—For purposes of this subsection, the parent whose taxable income shall be taken into account shall be—

(A) in the case of parents who are not married (within the meaning of section 7703), the custodial parent (within the meaning of section 152(e)) of the child, and

(B) in the case of married individuals filing separately, the individual with the greater taxable income.

(6) Providing of parent's TIN.—The parent of any child to whom this subsection applies for any taxable year shall provide the TIN of such parent to such child and such child shall include such TIN on the child's return of tax imposed by this section for such taxable year.

(7) Election to claim certain unearned income of child on parent's return.—

(A) In general.—If—

(i) any child to whom this subsection applies has gross income for the taxable year only from interest and dividends (including Alaska Permanent Fund dividends),

(ii) such gross income is more than the amount described in paragraph (4)(A)(ii)(I) and less than 10 times the amount so described,

(iii) no estimated tax payments for such year are made in the name and TIN of such child, and no amount has been deducted and withheld under section 3406, and

(iv) the parent of such child (as determined under paragraph (5)) elects the application of subparagraph (B),

such child shall be treated (other than for purposes of this paragraph) as having no gross income for such year and shall not be required to file a return under section 6012.

(B) Income included on parent's return.—In the case of a parent making the election under this paragraph—

(i) the gross income of each child to whom such election applies (to the extent the gross income of such child exceeds twice the amount described in paragraph (4)(A)(ii)(I)) shall be included in such parent's gross income for the taxable year,

(ii) the tax imposed by this section for such year with respect to such parent shall be the amount equal to the sum of—

(I) the amount determined under this section after the application of clause (i), plus

(II) for each such child, 10 percent of the lesser of the amount described in paragraph (4)(A)(ii)(I) or the excess of the gross income of such child over the amount so described, and

(iii) any interest which is an item of tax preference under section 57(a)(5) of the child shall be treated as an item of tax preference of such parent (and not of such child).

(C) Regulations.—The Secretary shall prescribe such regulations as may be necessary or appropriate to carry out the purposes of this paragraph.

(h) Maximum capital gains rate.—

(1) In general.—If a taxpayer has a net capital gain for any taxable year, the tax imposed by this section for such taxable year shall not exceed the sum of—

(A) a tax computed at the rates and in the same manner as if this subsection had not been enacted on the greater of—

(i) taxable income reduced by the net capital gain, or

(ii) the lesser of—

(I) the amount of taxable income taxed at a rate below 25 percent, or

(II) taxable income reduced by the adjusted net capital gain,

(B) 0 percent of so much of the adjusted net capital gain (or, if less, taxable income as does not exceed the excess (if any) of—

(i) the amount of taxable income which would (without regard to this paragraph) be taxed at a rate below 25 percent, over

(ii) the taxable income reduced by the adjusted net capital gain,

(C) 15 percent of the lesser of—

(i) so much of the adjusted net capital gain (or, if less, taxable income) as exceeds the amount on which a tax is determined under subparagraph (B), or

(ii) the excess of—

(I) the amount of taxable income which would (without regard to this paragraph) be taxed at a rate below 39.6 percent over,

(II) the sum of the amounts on which a tax is determined under subparagraphs (A) and (B),

(D) 20 percent of the adjusted net capital gain (or, if less, taxable income) in excess of the sum of the amounts on which tax is determined under subparagraphs (B) and (C),

(E) 25 percent of the excess (if any) of—

(i) the unrecaptured section 1250 gain (or, if less, the net capital gain (determined without regard to paragraph (11))), over

(ii) the excess (if any) of—

(I) the sum of the amount on which tax is determined under subparagraph (A) plus the net capital gain, over

(II) taxable income, and

(F) 28 percent of the amount of taxable income in excess of the sum of the amounts on which tax is determined under the preceding subparagraphs of this paragraph.

(2) Net capital gain taken into account as investment income.—For purposes of this subsection, the net capital gain for any taxable year shall be reduced (but not below zero) by the amount which the taxpayer takes into account as investment income under section 163(d)(4)(B)(iii).

(3) Adjusted net capital gain.—For purposes of this subsection, the term "adjusted net capital gain" means the sum of—

(A) net capital gain (determined without regard to paragraph (11)) reduced (but not below zero) by the sum of—

(i) unrecaptured section 1250 gain, and

(ii) 28-percent rate gain, plus

(B) qualified divided income (as defined in paragraph (11)).

(4) 28-percent rate gain.—For purposes of this subsection, the term "28-percent rate gain" means the excess (if any) of—

(A) the sum of—

(i) collectibles gain, and

(ii) section 1202 gain, over

(B) the sum of—

(i) collectibles loss,

(ii) the net short-term capital loss, and

(iii) the amount of long-term capital loss carried under section 1212(b)(1)(B) to the taxable year.

(5) Collectibles gain and loss.—For purposes of this subsection—

(A) In general.—The terms "collectibles gain" and "collectibles loss" mean gain or loss (respectively from the sale or exchange of a collectible (as defined in section 408(m) without regard to paragraph (3) thereof) which is a capital asset held for more than 1 year but only to the extent such gain is taken into account in computing gross income and such loss is taken into account in computing taxable income.

(B) Partnerships, etc.—For purposes of subparagraph (A), any gain from the sale of an interest in a partnership, S corporation, or trust which is attributable to unrealized appreciation in the value of collectibles shall be treated as gain from the sale or exchange of a collectible. Rules similar to the rules of section 751 shall apply for purposes of the preceding sentence.

(6) Unrecaptured section 1250 gain.—For purposes of this subsection—

(A) In general.—The term "unrecaptured section 1250 gain" means the excess (if any) of—

(i) the amount of long-term capital gain (not otherwise treated as ordinary income) which would be treated as ordinary income if section 1250(b)(1) included all depreciation and the applicable percentage under section 1250(a) were 100 percent, over

(ii) the excess (if any) of—

(I) the amount described in paragraph (4)(B), over

(II) the amount described in paragraph (4)(A).

(B) Limitation with respect to section 1231 property.—The amount described in subparagraph (A)(i) from sales, exchanges, and conversions described in section 1231(a)(3)(A) for any taxable year shall not exceed the net section 1231 gain (as defined in section 1231(c)(3)) for such year.

(7) Section 1202 gain.—For purposes of this subsection, the term "section 1202 gain" means the excess of—

(A) the gain which would be excluded from gross income under section 1202 but for the percentage limitation in section 1202(a), over

(B) the gain excluded from gross income under section 1202.

(8) Coordination with recapture of net ordinary losses under section 1231.—If any amount is treated as ordinary income under section 1231(c), such amount shall be allocated among the separate categories of net section 1231 gain (as defined in section 1231(c)(3)) in such manner as the Secretary may by forms or regulations prescribe.

(9) Regulations.—The Secretary may prescribe such regulations as are appropriate (including regulations requiring reporting) to apply this subsection in the case of sales and exchanges by pass-thru entities and of interests in such entities.

(10) Pass-thru entity defined.—For purposes of this subsection, the term "pass-thru entity" means—

(A) a regulated investment company,

(B) a real estate investment trust,

(C) an S corporation,

(D) a partnership,

(E) an estate or trust,

(F) a common trust fund, and

(G) a qualified electing fund (as defined in section 1295).

(11) Dividends taxed as net capital gain.—

(A) In general.—For purposes of this subsection, the term "net capital gain" means net capital gain (determined without regard to this paragraph) increased by qualified dividend income.

(B) Qualified dividend income.—For purposes of this paragraph—

(i) In general.—The term "qualified dividend income" means dividends received during the taxable year from—

(I) domestic corporations, and

(II) qualified foreign corporations.

(ii) Certain dividends excluded.—Such term shall not include—

(I) any dividend from a corporation which for the taxable year of the corporation in which the distribution is made, or the preceding taxable year, is a corporation exempt from tax under section 501 or 521,

(II) any amount allowed as a deduction under section 591 (relating to deduction for dividends paid by mutual savings banks, etc.), and

(III) any dividend described in section 404(k).

(iii) Coordination with section 246(c).—Such term shall not include any dividend on any share of stock—

(I) with respect to which the holding period requirements of section 246(c) are not met (determined by substituting in section 246(c) "60 days" for "45 days" each place it appears and by substituting "121-day period" for "91-day period"), or

(II) to the extent that the taxpayer is under an obligation (whether pursuant to a short sale or otherwise) to make related payments with respect to positions in substantially similar or related property.

(C) Qualified foreign corporations.—

(i) In general.—Except as otherwise provided in this paragraph, the term "qualified foreign corporation" means any foreign corporation if—

(I) such corporation is incorporated in a possession of the United States or

(II) such corporation is eligible for benefits of a comprehensive income tax treaty with the United States which the Secretary determines is satisfactory for purposes of this paragraph and which includes an exchange of information program.

(ii) Dividends on stock readily tradable on United States securities market.—A foreign corporation not otherwise treated as a qualified foreign corporation under clause (i) shall be so treated with respect to any dividend paid by such corporation if the stock with respect to which such dividend is paid is readily tradable on an established securities market in the United States.

(iii) Exclusion of dividends of certain foreign corporations.—Such term shall not include any foreign corporation which for the taxable year of the corporation in which the dividend was paid, or the preceding taxable year, is a passive foreign investment company (as defined in section 1297).

(iv) Coordination with foreign tax credit limitation.—Rules similar to the rules of section 904(b)(2)(B) shall apply with respect to the dividend rate differential under this paragraph.

(D) Special rules.—

(i) Amounts taken into account as investment income.—Qualified dividend income shall not include any amount which the taxpayer takes into account as investment income under section 163(d)(4)(B).

(ii) Extraordinary dividends.—If a taxpayer to whom this section applies receives, with respect to any share of stock, qualified dividend income from 1 or more dividends which are extraordinary dividends (within the meaning of section 1059(c)), any loss on the sale or exchange of such share shall, to the extent of such dividends, be treated as long-term capital loss.

(iii) Treatment of dividends from regulated investment companies and real estate investment trusts.—A dividend received from a regulated investment company or a real estate investment trust shall be subject to the limitations prescribed in sections 854 and 857.

(i) Rate reductions after 2000.—

(1) 10-percent rate bracket.—

(A) In general.—In the case of taxable years beginning after December 31, 2000—

(i) the rate of tax under subsections (a), (b), (c), and (d) on taxable income not over the initial bracket amount shall be 10 percent, and

(ii) the 15-percent rate of tax shall apply only to taxable income over the initial bracket amount but not over the maximum dollar amount for the 15-percent rate bracket.

(B) Initial bracket amount.—For purposes of this paragraph, the initial bracket amount is—

(i) $14,000 in the case of subsection (a).

(ii) $10,000 in the case of subsection (b), and

(iii) ½ the amount applicable under clause (i) (after adjustment, if any, under subparagraph (C)) in the case of subsections (c) and (d).

(C) Inflation adjustment.—In prescribing the tables under subsection (f) which apply with respect to taxable years beginning in calendar years after 2003—

(i) the cost-of-living adjustment shall be determined under subsection (f)(3) by substituting "2002" for "1992" in subparagraph (B) thereof, and

(ii) the adjustments under clause (i) shall not apply to the amount referred to in subparagraph (B)(iii).

If any amount after adjustment under the preceding sentence is not a multiple of $50, such amount shall be rounded to the next lowest multiple of $50.

* * *

(2) 25-, 28-, and 33-percent rate brackets.—The tables under subsections (a), (b), (c), (d), and (e) shall be applied—

(A) by substituting "25%" for "28%" each place it appears (before the application of subparagraph (B)),

(B) by substituting "28%" for "31%" each place it appears, and

(C) by substituting "33%" for "36%" each place it appears.

(3) Modifications to income tax brackets for high-income taxpayers.—

(A) **35 percent rate bracket.**— In the case of the taxable years beginning after December 31, 2012—

(i) the rate of tax under subsections (a), (b), (c), and (d) on a taxpayer's taxable income in the highest rate bracket shall be 35 percent to the extent such income does not exceed an amount equal to the excess of—

(I) the applicable threshold, over

(II) the dollar amount at which such bracket begins, and

(ii) the 39.6 percent rate of tax under such subsections shall apply only to the taxpayer's taxable income in such bracket in excess of the amount to which clause (i) applies.

(B) **Applicable threshold.**—For purposes of this paragraph, the term "applicable threshold" means—

(i) $450,000 in the case of subsection (a),

(ii) $425,000 in the case of subsection (b),

(iii) $400,000 in the case of subsection (c), and

(iv) ½ the amount applicable under clause (i) (after adjustment, if any, under subparagraph (C)) in the case of subsection (d)

(C) **Inflation adjustment.**—For purposes of this paragraph, with respect to taxable years beginning in calendar years after 2013, each of the dollar amounts under clauses (i), (ii), and (iii) of subparagraph (B) shall be adjusted in the same manner as under paragraph (1)(C)(i), except that subsection (f)(3)(B) shall be applied by substituting "2012" for "1992."

(4) **Adjustment of tables.**—The Secretary shall adjust the tables prescribed under subsection (f) to carry out this subsection.

Editorial Note

The indexed tax rates for 2014 are as follows:

2014 Tax Rate Schedules for Individual Taxpayers

Single—Schedule X

If taxable income is: Over—	But not over—	The tax is:		of the amount over—
$0	$9,075	....	10%	$0
9,075	36,900	$907.50 +	15%	9,075
36,900	89,350	5,081.25 +	25%	36,900
89,350	186,350	18,193.25 +	28%	89,350
186,350	405,100	45,353.75 +	33%	186,350
405,100	406,750	117,541.25 +	35%	405,100
406,750	....	118,118.75 +	39.6%	406,750

Head of household—Schedule Z

If taxable income is: Over—	But not over—	The tax is:		of the amount over—
$0	$12,950	....	10%	$0
12,950	49,400	$1,295.00 +	15%	12,950
49,400	127,550	6,762.50 +	25%	49,400
127,550	206,600	26,300.00 +	28%	127,550
206,600	405,100	48,434.00 +	33%	206,600
405,100	432,200	113,939.00 +	35%	405,100
432,200	....	123,424.00 +	39.6%	432,200

Married filing jointly or Qualifying widow(er)—Schedule Y–1

If taxable income is: Over—	But not over—	The tax is:		of the amount over—
$0	$18,150	....	10%	$0
18,150	73,800	$1,815.00 +	15%	18,150
73,800	148,850	10,162.50 +	25%	73,800
148,850	226,850	28,925.00 +	28%	148,850
226,850	405,100	50,765.00 +	33%	226,850
405,100	457,600	109,587.50 +	35%	405,100
457,600	....	127,962.50 +	39.6%	457,600

Married filing separately—Schedule Y–2

If taxable income is: Over—	But not over—	The tax is:		of the amount over—
$0	$9,075	....	10%	$0
9,075	36,900	$907.50 +	15%	9,075
36,900	74,425	5,081.25 +	25%	36,900
74,425	113,425	14,462.50 +	28%	74,425
113,425	202,550	25,382.50 +	33%	113,425
202,550	228,800	54,793.75 +	35%	202,550
228,800	....	63,981.25 +	39.6%	228,800

2014 Tax Rate Schedule for Estates and Trusts

If taxable income is: Over—	*But not over—*	**The tax is:**		*of the amount over—*
$0	$2,500	....	15%	$0
2,500	5,800	$375.00 +	25%	2,500
5,800	8,900	1,200.00 +	28%	5,800
8,900	12,150	2,068.00 +	33%	8,900
12,150	......	3,140.50 +	39.6%	12,150

§ 2. Definitions and special rules

(a) Definition of surviving spouse.—

(1) In general.—For purposes of section 1, the term "surviving spouse" means a taxpayer—

(A) whose spouse died during either of his two taxable years immediately preceding the taxable year, and

(B) who maintains as his home a household which constitutes for the taxable year the principal place of abode (as a member of such household) of a dependent (i) who (within the meaning of section 152, determined without regard to subsections (b)(1), (b)(2), and (d)(1)(B) thereof) is a son, stepson, daughter, or stepdaughter of the taxpayer, and (ii) with respect to whom the taxpayer is entitled to a deduction for the taxable year under section 151.

For purposes of this paragraph, an individual shall be considered as maintaining a household only if over half of the cost of maintaining the household during the taxable year is furnished by such individual.

(2) Limitations.—Notwithstanding paragraph (1), for purposes of section 1 a taxpayer shall not be considered to be a surviving spouse—

(A) if the taxpayer has remarried at any time before the close of the taxable year, or

(B) unless, for the taxpayer's taxable year during which his spouse died, a joint return could have been made under the provisions of section 6013 (without regard to subsection (a)(3) thereof).

* * *

(b) Definition of head of household.—

(1) In general.—For purposes of this subtitle, an individual shall be considered a head of a household if, and only if, such individual is not married at the close of his taxable year, is not a surviving spouse (as defined in subsection (a)), and either—

(A) maintains as his home a household which constitutes for more than one-half of such taxable year the principal place of abode, as a member of such household, of—

(i) a qualifying child of the individual (as defined in section 152(c), determined without regard to section 152(e)), but not if such child—

(I) is married at the close of the taxpayer's taxable year, and

(II) is not a dependent of such individual by reason of section 152(b)(2) or 152(b)(3), or both, or

(ii) any other person who is a dependent of the taxpayer, if the taxpayer is entitled to a deduction for the taxable year for such person under section 151, or

(B) maintains a household which constitutes for such taxable year the principal place of abode of the father or mother of the taxpayer, if the taxpayer is entitled to a deduction for the taxable year for such father or mother under section 151.

For purposes of this paragraph, an individual shall be considered as maintaining a household only if over half of the cost of maintaining the household during the taxable year is furnished by such individual.

(2) Determination of status.—For purposes of this subsection—

(A) an individual who is legally separated from his spouse under a decree of divorce or of separate maintenance shall not be considered as married;

(B) a taxpayer shall be considered as not married at the close of his taxable year if at any time during the taxable year his spouse is a nonresident alien; and

(C) a taxpayer shall be considered as married at the close of his taxable year if his spouse (other than a spouse described in subparagraph (B)) died during the taxable year.

(3) Limitations.—Notwithstanding paragraph (1), for purposes of this subtitle a taxpayer shall not be considered to be a head of a household—

(A) if at any time during the taxable year he is a nonresident alien; or

(B) by reason of an individual who would not be a dependent for the taxable year but for—

(i) subparagraph (H) of section 152(d)(2), or

(ii) paragraph (3) of section 152(d).

(c) Certain married individuals living apart.—For purposes of this part, an individual shall be treated as not married at the close of the taxable year if such individual is so treated under the provisions of section 7703(b).

(d) Nonresident aliens.—In the case of a nonresident alien individual, the taxes imposed by sections 1 and 55 shall apply only as provided by section 871 or 877.

(e) Cross reference.—

For definition of taxable income, see section 63.

§ 3. Tax tables for individuals

(a) Imposition of tax table tax.—

(1) In general.—In lieu of the tax imposed by section 1, there is hereby imposed for each taxable year on the taxable income of every individual—

(A) who does not itemize his deductions for the taxable year, and

(B) whose taxable income for such taxable year does not exceed the ceiling amount,

a tax determined under tables, applicable to such taxable year, which shall be prescribed by the Secretary and which shall be in such form as he determines appropriate. In the table so prescribed, the amounts of the tax shall be computed on the basis of the rates prescribed by section 1.

(2) Ceiling amount defined.— For purposes of paragraph (1), the term "ceiling amount" means, with respect to any taxpayer, the amount (not less than $20,000) determined by the Secretary for the tax rate category in which such taxpayer falls.

(3) Authority to prescribe tables for taxpayers who itemize deductions.—The Secretary may provide that this section shall apply also for any taxable year to individuals who itemize their deductions. Any tables prescribed under the preceding sentence shall be on the basis of taxable income.

(b) Section inapplicable to certain individuals.—This section shall not apply to—

(1) an individual making a return under section 443(a)(1) for a period of less than 12 months on account of a change in annual accounting period, and

(2) an estate or trust.

(c) Tax treated as imposed by section 1.—For purposes of this title, the tax imposed by this section shall be treated as tax imposed by section 1.

(d) Taxable income.—Whenever it is necessary to determine the taxable income of an individual to whom this section applies, the taxable income shall be determined under section 63.

(e) Cross reference.—

For computation of tax by Secretary, see section 6014.

* * *

§ 5. Cross references relating to tax on individuals

(a) Other rates of tax on individuals, etc.—

* * *

(4) For alternative minimum tax, see section 55.

(b) Special limitations on tax.—

(1) For limitation on tax in case of income of members of Armed Forces, astronauts, and victims of certain terrorist attacks on death, see section 692.

(2) For computation of tax where taxpayer restores substantial amount held under claim of right, see section 1341.

PART II—TAX ON CORPORATIONS

Editorial Summary

Corporate Tax Rates

Subchapter A of Chapter 1 (Sec. 11)

See the discussion under the Editorial Summary entitled Tax Rates which precedes Sec. 1.

The corporate tax rates are as follows:

Taxable Income	Tax Rate
Not over $50,000	15%
Over $50,000 but not over $75,000	25%
Over $75,000 but not over $100,000	34%
Over $100,000 but not over $335,000	39%*
Over $335,000 but not over $10,000,000	34%
Over $10,000,000 but not over $15,000,000	35%
Over $15,000,000 but not over $18,333,333	38%**
Over $18,333,333	35%

*Five percent of this rate represents a phase-out of the benefits of the lower tax rates on the first $75,000 of taxable income.

**Three percent of this rate represents a phase-out of the benefits of the lower tax rate (34% rather than 35%) on the first $10 million of taxable income.

§ 11. Tax imposed

(a) Corporations in general.—A tax is hereby imposed for each taxable year on the taxable income of every corporation.

(b) Amount of tax.—

(1) In general.—The amount of the tax imposed by subsection (a) shall be the sum of—

(A) 15 percent of so much of the taxable income as does not exceed $50,000,

(B) 25 percent of so much of the taxable income as exceeds $50,000 but does not exceed $75,000,

(C) 34 percent of so much of the taxable income as exceeds $75,000 but does not exceed $10,000,000, and

(D) 35 percent of so much of the taxable income as exceeds $10,000,000.

In the case of a corporation which has taxable income in excess of $100,000 for any taxable year, the amount of tax determined under the preceding sentence for such taxable year shall be increased by the lesser of (i) 5 percent of such excess, or (ii) $11,750. In the case of a corporation which has taxable income in excess of $15,000,000, the amount of the tax determined under the foregoing provisions of this paragraph shall be increased by an additional amount equal to the lesser of (i) 3 percent of such excess, or (ii) $100,000.

(2) Certain personal service corporations not eligible for graduated rates.—Notwithstanding paragraph (1), the amount of the tax imposed by subsection (a) on the tax able income of a qualified personal service corporation (as defined in section 448(d)(2)) shall be equal to 35 percent of the taxable income.

* * *

PART III—CHANGES IN RATES DURING A TAXABLE YEAR

Editorial Summary

Changes in Tax Rates

Subchapter A of Chapter 1 (Sec. 15)

See the discussion under the Editorial Summary entitled Tax Rates which precedes Sec. 1.

§ 15. Effect of changes

(a) General rule.—If any rate of tax imposed by this chapter changes, and if the taxable year includes the effective date of the change (unless that date is the first day of the taxable year), then—

(1) tentative taxes shall be computed by applying the rate for the period before the effective date of the change, and the rate for the period on and after such date, to the taxable income for the entire taxable year; and

(2) the tax for such taxable year shall be the sum of that proportion of each tentative tax which the number of days in each period bears to the number of days in the entire taxable year.

(b) Repeal of tax.—For purposes of subsection (a)—

(1) if a tax is repealed, the repeal shall be considered a change of rate; and

(2) the rate for the period after the repeal shall be zero.

(c) Effective date of change.—For purposes of subsections (a) and (b)—

(1) if the rate changes for taxable years "beginning after" or "ending after" a certain date, the following day shall be considered the effective date of the change; and

(2) if a rate changes for taxable years "beginning on or after" a certain date, that date shall be considered the effective date of the change.

(d) Section not to apply to inflation adjustments.—This section shall not apply to any change in rates under subsection (f) of section 1 (relating to adjustments in tax tables so that inflation will not result in tax increases).

(e) References to highest rate.—If the change referred to in subsection (a) involves a change in the highest rate of tax imposed by section 1 or 11(b), any reference in this chapter to such highest rate (other than in a provision imposing a tax by reference to such rate) shall be treated as a reference to the weighted average of the highest rates before and after the change determined on the basis of the respective portions of the taxable year before the date of the change and on or after the date of the change.

(f) Rate reductions enacted by Economic Growth and Tax Relief Reconciliation Act of 2001.—This section shall not apply to any change in rates under subsection (i) of section 1 (relating to rate reductions after 2000).

PART IV—CREDITS AGAINST TAX

Editorial Summary

Tax Credits

Subchapter A of Chapter 1 (Secs. 21–53)

From a cash flow perspective, a dollar of tax credit has the potential for producing a dollar of positive cash flow. This result occurs because a tax credit is a direct offset against the tax liability. To contrast, note that the tax benefit of an exclusion [see Secs. 101–139A] or a deduction [see Secs. 151–291] is dependent on the taxpayer's tax rates.

Tax credits can be beneficially classified in a variety of ways. Included are the following:

1. Business versus nonbusiness.
2. Refundable versus nonrefundable.
3. Eligible versus not eligible for carryback and/or carryover treatment.

Ideally, the taxpayer would prefer that a tax credit be refundable. A refundable credit produces a positive cash flow benefit to the taxpayer even though the taxpayer has no tax liability for the current tax year prior to the application of the tax credit (i.e., it is not necessary to have a tax liability to offset in order to be beneficial to the taxpayer in the current tax year). If the tax credit is not refundable, then the taxpayer would prefer that the credit be eligible for carryback and/or carryover treatment. In this way, the taxpayer has the potential for using the credit to offset tax liability in tax years other than the current tax year to the extent that the current tax liability is inadequate to absorb the credit. The utilization of a tax credit in a carryback year produces a tax refund, whereas utilization in a carryover year reduces the tax liability in a future tax year.

The following tax credits are refundable:

1. Credit for the tax withheld on wages (i.e., wage withholding) [see Sec. 31].
2. Earned income credit [see Sec. 32].
3. Credit for tax withheld at source on nonresident aliens and foreign corporations [see Sec. 33].
4. Credit for taxes paid associated with certain uses of gasoline and special fuels (i.e., nonhighway uses) [see Sec. 34].
5. Health insurance cost credit (see Sec. 35).
6. First-time homebuyer credit (see Sec. 36).*
7. Making work pay credit (see Sec. 36A).**
8. Credit for the overpayment of tax [see Sec. 37].

In addition, a portion of the child tax credit may be refundable [see Sec. 24] and a portion of the American Opportunity Tax Credit may be refundable [see Sec. 25A].

Generally, business credits qualify for carryback and/or carryover treatment whereas nonbusiness credits do not qualify (i.e., must be able to offset against tax liability in the current tax year or no tax benefit ever results). Qualifying for carryback and/or carryover treatment are the following tax credits:

1. Foreign tax credit [see Sec. 27].
2. Alcohol fuels credit [see Sec. 40].
3. Research activities credit [see Sec. 41].
4. Low-income housing credit [see Sec. 42].
5. Enhanced oil recovery credit [see Sec. 43].
6. Disabled access credit [see Sec. 44].

*Editorial comment: The First-Time Homebuyer credit expired on April 30, 2010.

**Editorial comment: The Making Work Pay credit expired at the end of 2010.

7. Renewable electricity production credit [see Sec. 45].

8. Investment tax credit (note that the regular ITC has been repealed for property placed in service after December 31, 1985) [see Sec. 46].

9. Indian employment credit [see Sec. 45A].

10. Employer Social Security credit [see Sec. 45B].

11. New markets tax credit [see Sec. 45D].

12. Work opportunity tax credit [see Sec. 51].

13. Minimum tax credit [see Sec. 53].

14. Home mortgage interest credit (see Sec. 25).

15. Adoption expenses credit (see Sec. 23 and 36C).

Not eligible for either carryback or carryover treatment are the following:

1. Household and dependent care credit [see Sec. 21].

2. Tax credit for the elderly and permanently disabled [see Sec. 22].

3. Child tax credit except to the extent indicated above [see Sec. 24].

4. Credit for clinical testing of certain drugs (i.e., orphan drug testing) [see Sec. 45C].

5. Credit for elective deferrals and IRA contributions by certain individuals [see Sec. 25B].

Another item of importance is the sequence in which tax credits are applied against tax liability. The sequence for the nonrefundable credits is as follows:

1. Household and dependent care credit, tax credit for the elderly and permanently disabled, adoption expenses credit, the child tax credit, the home mortgage interest credit, and the HOPE (American Opportunity Tax Credit for 2009 through 2017, extended by the American Taxpayer Relief Act of 2012) and lifetime learning credits (see Secs. 21, 22, 25, 25A, and 36C).

2. Foreign tax credit (see Sec. 27).

3. Credit for clinical testing of certain drugs (i.e., orphan drug testing) [see Sec. 45C].

4. Credit for producing fuel from a nonconventional source (see Sec. 29).

5. General business credit which is the summation of the investment tax credit, work opportunity tax credit, alcohol fuels credit, research activities credit, low-income housing credit, enhanced oil recovery credit, disabled access credit, renewable electricity production credit, Indian employment credit, new markets tax credit, credit for small employer pension plan startup costs, credit for employer-provided child care, and the employer Social Security credit (see Sec. 38).

Two other factors to consider with respect to tax credits are whether events can occur that can result in either partial or complete recapture of the credit (e.g., compare the absence of such a provision for the work opportunity tax credit with the presence of such a provision for the investment tax credit in Sec. 50) and whether any limitations exist on the ability to reduce the tax liability by the amount of the credit [e.g., see the limited offset rule for the general business credit contained in Sec. 38(c)].

Note that certain credits have termination dates. See Sec. 36(h) for the first-time homebuyer credit, Sec. 36A(e) for the making work pay credit, Sec. 41(h) for the research activities credit, Sec. 45A(f) for the Indian employment credit, Sec. 45N(e) for the mine rescue team training credit, and Sec. 51(c)(4) for the work opportunity tax credit.

SUBPART A—NONREFUNDABLE PERSONAL CREDITS

§ 21. Expenses for household and dependent care services necessary for gainful employment

(a) Allowance of credit.—

(1) In general.—In the case of an individual for which there are 1 or more qualifying individuals (as defined in subsection (b)(1)) with respect to such individual, there shall be allowed as a credit against the tax imposed by this chapter for the taxable year an amount equal to the applicable percentage of the employment-related expenses (as defined in subsection (b)(2)) paid by such individual during the taxable year.

(2) Applicable percentage defined.—For purposes of paragraph (1), the term "applicable percentage" means 35 percent reduced (but not below 20 percent) by 1 percentage point for each $2,000 (or fraction thereof) by which the taxpayer's adjusted gross income for the taxable year exceeds $15,000.

(b) Definitions of qualifying individual and employment-related expenses.—For purposes of this section—

(1) Qualifying individual.—The term "qualifying individual" means—

(A) a dependent of the taxpayer (as defined in section 152(a)(1)) who has not attained age 13,

(B) a dependent of the taxpayer (as defined in section 152, determined without regard to subsections (b)(1), (b)(2), and (d)(1)(B)) who is physically or mentally incapable of caring for himself or herself and who has the same principal place of abode as the taxpayer for more than one-half of such taxable year, or

(C) the spouse of the taxpayer, if the spouse is physically or mentally incapable of caring for himself or herself and who has the same principal place of abode as the taxpayer for more than one-half of such taxable year.

(2) Employment-related expenses.—

(A) In general.—The term "employment-related expenses" means amounts paid for the following expenses, but only if such expenses are incurred to enable the taxpayer to be gainfully employed for any period for which there are 1 or more qualifying individuals with respect to the taxpayer:

(i) expenses for household services, and

(ii) expenses for the care of a qualifying individual.

Such term shall not include any amount paid for services outside the taxpayer's household at a camp where the qualifying individual stays overnight.

(B) Exception.—Employment-related expenses described in subparagraph (A) which are incurred for services outside the taxpayer's household shall be taken into account only if incurred for the care of—

(i) a qualifying individual described in paragraph (1)(A), or

(ii) a qualifying individual (not described in paragraph (1)(A)) who regularly spends at least 8 hours each day in the taxpayer's household.

(C) Dependent care centers.—Employment-related expenses described in subparagraph (A) which are incurred for services provided outside the taxpayer's household by a dependent care center (as defined in subparagraph (D)) shall be taken into account only if—

(i) such center complies with all applicable laws and regulations of a State or unit of local government, and

(ii) the requirements of subparagraph (B) are met.

(D) Dependent care center defined.—For purposes of this paragraph, the term "dependent care center" means any facility which—

(i) provides care for more than six individuals (other than individuals who reside at the facility), and

(ii) receives a fee, payment, or grant for providing services for any of the individuals (regardless of whether such facility is operated for profit).

(c) Dollar limit on amount creditable.—The amount of the employment-related expenses incurred during any taxable year which may be taken into account under subsection (a) shall not exceed—

(1) $3,000 if there is 1 qualifying individual with respect to the taxpayer for such taxable year, or

(2) $6,000 if there are 2 or more qualifying individuals with respect to the taxpayer for such taxable year.

The amount determined under paragraph (1) or (2) (whichever is applicable) shall be reduced by the aggregate amount excludable from gross income under section 129 for the taxable year.

(d) Earned income limitation.—

(1) In general.—Except as otherwise provided in this subsection, the amount of the employment-related expenses incurred during any taxable year which may be taken into account under subsection (a) shall not exceed—

(A) in the case of an individual who is not married at the close of such year, such individual's earned income for such year, or

(B) in the case of an individual who is married at the close of such year, the lesser of such individual's earned income or the earned income of his spouse for such year.

(2) Special rule for spouse who is a student or incapable of caring for himself.—In the case of a spouse who is a student or a qualifying individual described in subsection (b)(1)(C), for purposes of paragraph (1), such spouse shall be deemed for each month during which such spouse is a full-time student at an educational institution, or is such a qualifying individual, to be gainfully employed and to have earned income of not less than—

(A) $250 if subsection (c)(1) applies for the taxable year, or

(B) $500 if subsection (c)(2) applies for the taxable year.

In the case of any husband and wife, this paragraph shall apply with respect to only one spouse for any one month.

(e) Special rules.—For purposes of this section—

(1) Place of abode.—An individual shall not be treated as having the same principal place of abode of the taxpayer if at any time during the taxable year of the taxpayer the relationship between the individual and the taxpayer is in violation of local law.

(2) Married couples must file joint return.—If the taxpayer is married at the close of the taxable year, the credit shall be allowed under subsection

(a) only if the taxpayer and his spouse file a joint return for the taxable year.

(3) Marital status.—An individual legally separated from his spouse under a decree of divorce or of separate maintenance shall not be considered as married.

(4) Certain married individuals living apart.—If—

(A) an individual who is married and who files a separate return—

(i) maintains as his home a household which constitutes for more than one-half of the taxable year the principal place of abode of a qualifying individual, and

(ii) furnishes over half of the cost of maintaining such household during the taxable year, and

(B) during the last 6 months of such taxable year such individual's spouse is not a member of such household, such individuals shall not be considered as married.

(5) Special dependency test in case of divorced parents, etc.—If—

(A) section 152(e) applies to any child with respect to any calendar year, and

(B) such child is under the age of 13 or is physically or mentally incapable of caring for himself,

in the case of any taxable year beginning in such calendar year, such child shall be treated as a qualifying individual described in subparagraph (A) or (B) of subsection (b)(1) (whichever is appropriate) with respect to the custodial parent (as defined in section 152(e)(4)(A)), and shall not be treated as a qualifying individual with respect to the noncustodial parent.

(6) Payments to related individuals.—No credit shall be allowed under subsection (a) for any amount paid by the taxpayer to an individual—

(A) with respect to whom, for the taxable year, a deduction under section 151(c) (relating to deduction for personal exemptions for dependents) is allowable either to the taxpayer or his spouse, or

(B) who is a child of the taxpayer (within the meaning of section 152(f)(1)) who has not attained the age of 19 at the close of the taxable year.

For purposes of this paragraph, the term "taxable year" means the taxable year of the taxpayer in which the service is performed.

(7) Student.—The term "student" means an individual who during each of 5 calendar months during the taxable year is a full-time student at an educational organization.

(8) Educational organization.—The term "educational organization" means an educational organization described in section 170(b)(1)(A)(ii).

(9) Identifying information required with respect to service provider.—No credit shall be allowed under subsection (a) for any amount paid to any person unless—

(A) the name, address, and taxpayer identification number of such person are included on the return claiming the credit, or

(B) if such person is an organization described in section 501(c)(3) and exempt from tax under section 501(a), the name and address of such person are included on the return claiming the credit.

In the case of a failure to provide the information required under the preceding sentence, the preceding sentence shall not apply if it is shown that the taxpayer exercised due diligence in attempting to provide the information so required.

(10) Identifying information required with respect to qualifying individuals.—No credit shall be allowed under this section with respect to any qualifying individual unless the TIN of such individual is included on the return claiming the credit.

(f) Regulations.—The Secretary shall prescribe such regulations as may be necessary to carry out the purposes of this section.

§ 22. Credit for the elderly and the permanently and totally disabled

(a) General rule.—In the case of a qualified individual, there shall be allowed as a credit against the tax imposed by this chapter for the taxable year an amount equal to 15 percent of such individual's section 22 amount for such taxable year.

(b) Qualified individual.—For purposes of this section, the term "qualified individual" means any individual—

(1) who has attained age 65 before the close of the taxable year, or

(2) who retired on disability before the close of the taxable year and who, when he retired, was permanently and totally disabled.

(c) Section 22 amount.—For purposes of subsection (a)—

(1) In general.—An individual's section 22 amount for the taxable year shall be the applicable initial amount determined under paragraph (2), reduced as provided in paragraph (3) and in subsection (d).

(2) Initial amount—

(A) In general.—Except as provided in subparagraph (B), the initial amount shall be—

(i) $5,000 in the case of a single individual, or a joint return where only one spouse is a qualified individual,

(ii) $7,500 in the case of a joint return where both spouses are qualified individuals, or

(iii) $3,750 in the case of a married individual filing a separate return.

(B) Limitation in case of individuals who have not attained age 65.—

(i) In general.—In the case of a qualified individual who has not attained age 65 before the close of the taxable year, except as provided in clause (ii), the initial amount shall not exceed the disability income for the taxable year.

(ii) Special rules in case of joint return. —In the case of a joint return where both spouses are qualified individuals and at least one spouse has not attained age 65 before the close of the taxable year—

(I) if both spouses have not attained age 65 before the close of the taxable year, the initial amount shall not exceed the sum of such spouses' disability income, or

(II) if one spouse has attained age 65 before the close of the taxable year, the initial amount shall not exceed the sum of $5,000 plus the disability income for the taxable year of the spouse who has not attained age 65 before the close of the taxable year.

(iii) Disability income.—For purposes of this subparagraph, the term "disability income" means the aggregate amount includible in the gross income of the individual for the taxable year under section 72 or 105(a) to the extent such amount constitutes wages (or payments in lieu of wages) for the period during which the individual is absent from work on account of permanent and total disability.

(3) Reduction.—

(A) In general.—The reduction under this paragraph is an amount equal to the sum of the amounts received by the individual (or, in the case of a joint return, by either spouse) as a pension or annuity or as a disability benefit—

(i) which is excluded from gross income and payable under—

(I) title II of the Social Security Act,

(II) the Railroad Retirement Act of 1974, or

(III) a law administered by the Veterans' Administration, or

(ii) which is excluded from gross income under any provision of law not contained in this title.

No reduction shall be made under clause (i)(III) for any amount described in section 104(a)(4).

(B) Treatment of certain workmen's compensation benefits.—For purposes of subparagraph (A), any amount treated as a social security benefit under section 86(d)(3) shall be treated as a disability benefit received under title II of the Social Security Act.

(d) Adjusted gross income limitation.—If the adjusted gross income of the taxpayer exceeds—

(1) $7,500 in the case of a single individual,

(2) $10,000 in the case of a joint return, or

(3) $5,000 in the case of a married individual filing a separate return,

the section 22 amount shall be reduced by one-half of the excess of the adjusted gross income over $7,500, $10,000, or $5,000, as the case may be.

(e) Definitions and special rules.—For purposes of this section—

(1) Married couple must file joint return.—Except in the case of a husband and wife who live apart at all times during the taxable year, if the taxpayer is married at the close of the taxable year, the credit provided by this section shall be allowed only if the taxpayer and his spouse file a joint return for the taxable year.

(2) Marital status.—Marital status shall be determined under section 7703.

(3) Permanent and total disability defined.—An individual is permanently and totally disabled if he is unable to engage in any substantial gainful activity by reason of any medically determinable physical or mental impairment which can be expected to result in death or which has lasted or can be expected to last for a continuous period of not less than 12 months. An individual shall not be considered to be permanently and totally disabled unless he furnishes proof of the existence thereof in such form and manner, and at such times, as the Secretary may require.

(f) Nonresident alien ineligible for credit.—No credit shall be allowed under this section to any nonresident alien.

§ 23. Adoption expenses*

(a) Allowance of credit.—

(1) In general.—In the case of an individual, there shall be allowed as a credit against the tax imposed by this chapter the amount of the qualified adoption expenses paid or incurred by the taxpayer.

(2) Year credit allowed.—The credit under paragraph (1) with respect to any expense shall be allowed—

(A) in the case of any expense paid or incurred before the taxable year in which such adoption becomes final, for the taxable year following the taxable year during which such expense is paid or incurred, and

(B) in the case of an expense paid or incurred during or after the taxable year in which such adoption becomes final, for the taxable year in which such expense is paid or incurred.

(3) $10,000 credit for adoption of child with special needs regardless of expenses.**—In the case of an adoption of a child with special needs which becomes final during a taxable year, the taxpayer shall be treated as having paid during such year qualified adoption expenses with respect to such adoption in an amount equal to the excess (if any) of $10,000** over the aggregate qualified adoption expenses actually paid or incurred by the taxpayer with respect to such adoption during such taxable year and all prior taxable years.

(b) Limitations.—

(1) Dollar limitation.—The aggregate amount of qualified adoption expenses which may be taken into account under subsection (a) for all taxable years with respect to the adoption of a child by the taxpayer shall not exceed $10,000.**

(2) Income limitation.—

(A) In general.—The amount allowable as a credit under subsection (a) for any taxable year (determined without regard to subsection (c)) shall be reduced (but not below zero) by an amount which bears the same ratio to the amount so allowable (determined without regard to this paragraph but with regard to paragraph (1)) as—

(i) the amount (if any) by which the taxpayer's adjusted gross income exceeds $150,000,*** bears to

(ii) $40,000.

(B) Determination of adjusted gross income.—For purposes of subparagraph (A), adjusted gross income shall be determined without regard to sections 911, 931, and 933.

(3) Denial of double benefit.—

(A) In general.—No credit shall be allowed under subsection (a) for any expense for which a deduction or credit is allowed under any other provision of this chapter.

(B) Grants.—No credit shall be allowed under subsection (a) for any expense to the extent that funds for such expense are received under any Federal, State, or local program.

(c) Carryforwards of unused credit.—

(1) In general.— If the credit allowable under subsection (a) for any taxable year exceeds the limitation imposed by section 26(a) for such taxable year reduced by the sum of the credits allowable under this subpart (other than this section and sections 25D and 1400C), such excess shall be carried to the succeeding taxable year and added to the credit allowable under subsection (a) for such taxable year.

(2) Limitation. — No credit may be carried forward under this subsection to any taxable year following the fifth taxable year in which the credit arose. For purposes of the preceding sentence, credits shall be treated as used on a first-in first-out basis.

*Editorial comment: For tax years beginning before January 1, 2012, the adoption expenses credit is designated §36C.

**Editorial comment: The indexed amount for 2013 is $12,970 and for 2014 is $13,190.

***Editorial comment: The indexed amount for 2013 is $194,580 and for 2014 is $197,880 (completely phased out at $237,880).

*(d) **Definitions.**—For purposes of this section—

(1) **Qualified adoption expenses.**—The term "qualified adoption expenses" means reasonable and necessary adoption fees, court costs, attorney fees, and other expenses—

(A) which are directly related to, and the principal purpose of which is for, the legal adoption of an eligible child by the taxpayer,

(B) which are not incurred in violation of State or Federal law or in carrying out any surrogate parenting agreement,

(C) which are not expenses in connection with the adoption by an individual of a child who is the child of such individual's spouse, and

(D) which are not reimbursed under an employer program or otherwise.

(2) **Eligible child.**—The term "eligible child" means any individual who—

(A) has not attained age 18, or

(B) is physically or mentally incapable of caring for himself.

(3) **Child with special needs.**—The term "child with special needs" means any child if—

(A) a State has determined that the child cannot or should not be returned to the home of his parents,

(B) such State has determined that there exists with respect to the child a specific factor or condition (such as his ethnic background, age, or membership in a minority or sibling group, or the presence of factors such as medical conditions or physical, mental, or emotional handicaps) because of which it is reasonable to conclude that such child cannot be placed with adoptive parents without providing adoption assistance, and

(C) such child is a citizen or resident of the United States (as defined in section 217(h)(3)).

(e) **Special rules for foreign adoptions.**—In the case of an adoption of a child who is not a citizen or resident of the United States (as defined in section 217(h)(3))—

(1) subsection (a) shall not apply to any qualified adoption expense with respect to such adoption unless such adoption becomes final, and

(2) any such expense which is paid or incurred before the taxable year in which such adoption becomes final shall be taken into account under this section as if such expense were paid or incurred during such year.

*Editorial comment: There is no subsection (c).

(f) **Filing requirements.**—

(1) **Married couples must file joint returns.**—Rules similar to the rules of paragraphs (2), (3), and (4) of section 21(e) shall apply for purposes of this section.

(2) **Taxpayer must include TIN.**—

(A) **In general.**—No credit shall be allowed under this section with respect to any eligible child unless the taxpayer includes (if known) the name, age, and TIN of such child on the return of tax for the taxable year.

(B) **Other methods.**—The Secretary may, in lieu of the information referred to in subparagraph (A), require other information meeting the purposes of subparagraph (A), including identification of an agent assisting with the adoption.

(g) **Basis adjustments.**—For purposes of this sub- title, if a credit is allowed under this section for any expenditure with respect to any property, the increase in the basis of such property which would (but for this subsection) result from such expenditure shall be reduced by the amount of the credit so allowed.

(h) **Adjustments for inflation.**—

(1) **Dollar limitations.**— In the case of a taxable year beginning after December 31, 2010, each of the dollar amounts in subsections (a)(3) and (b)(1) shall be increased by an amount equal to—

(A) such dollar amount, multiplied by

(B) the cost-of-living adjustment determined under section 1(f)(3) for the calendar year in which the taxable year begins, determined by substituting "calendar year 2009" for "calendar year 1992" in subparagraph (B) thereof.

If any amount as increased under the preceding sentence is not a multiple of $10, such amount shall be rounded to the nearest multiple of $10.

(2) **Income limitation.**—In the case of a taxable year beginning after December 31, 2002, the dollar amount in subsection (b)(2)(A)(i) shall be increased by an amount equal to—

(A) such dollar amount, multiplied by

(B) the cost-of-living adjustment determined under section 1(f)(3) for the calendar year in which the taxable year begins, determined by substituting "calendar year 2001" for "calendar year 1992" in subparagraph (B) thereof.

If any amount as increased under the preceding sentence is not a multiple of $10, such amount shall be rounded to the nearest multiple of $10.

(i) Regulations.—The Secretary shall prescribe such regulations as may be appropriate to carry out this section and section 137, including regulations which treat unmarried individuals who pay or incur qualified adoption expenses with respect to the same child as 1 taxpayer for purposes of applying the dollar amounts in subsections (a)(3) and (b)(1) of this section and in section 137(b)(1).

* * *

§ 24. Child tax credit

(a) Allowance of credit.—There shall be allowed as a credit against the tax imposed by this chapter for the taxable year with respect to each qualifying child of the taxpayer for which the taxpayer is allowed a deduction under section 151 an amount equal to $1,000.

(b) Limitations.—

(1) Limitations based on adjusted gross income.—The amount of the credit allowable under subsection (a) shall be reduced (but not below zero) by $50 for each $1,000 (or fraction thereof) by which the taxpayer's modified adjusted gross income exceeds the threshold amount. For purposes of the preceding sentence, the term "modified adjusted gross income" means adjusted gross income increased by any amount excluded from gross income under section 911, 931, or 933.

(2) Threshold amount.—For purposes of paragraph (1), the term "threshold amount" means—

(A) $110,000 in the case of a joint return,

(B) $75,000 in the case of an individual who is not married, and

(C) $55,000 in the case of a married individual filing a separate return.

For purposes of this paragraph, marital status shall be determined under section 7703.

(c) Qualifying child.—The term "qualifying child" means a qualifying child of the taxpayer (as defined in section 152(c)) who has not attained age 17.

(2) Exception for certain noncitizens.—The term "qualifying child" shall not include any individual who would not be a dependent if subparagraph (A) of section 152(b)(3) were applied without regard to all that follows "resident of the United States."

(d) Portion of credit refundable.—

(1) In general.—The aggregate credits allowed to a taxpayer under subpart C shall be increased by the lesser of—

(A) the credit which would be allowed under this section without regard to this subsection and the limitation under section 26(a), or

(B) the amount by which the aggregate amount of credits allowed by this subpart (determined without regard to this subsection) would increase if the limitation imposed by section 26(a) were increased by the greater of—

(i) 15 percent of so much of the taxpayer's earned income (within the meaning of section 32) which is taken into account in computing taxable income for the taxable year as exceeds $10,000,* or

(ii) in the case of a taxpayer with 3 or more qualifying children, the excess (if any) of—

(I) the taxpayer's social security taxes for the taxable year, over

(II) the credit allowed under section 32 for the taxable year.

The amount of the credit allowed under this subsection shall not be treated as a credit allowed under this subpart and shall reduce the amount of credit otherwise allowable under subsection (a) without regard to section 26(a) or subsection (b)(3), as the case may be. For purposes of sub-paragraph (B), any amount excluded from gross income by reason of section 112 shall be treated as earned income which is taken into account in computing taxable income for the taxable year.

(2) Social security taxes.—For purposes of paragraph (1)—

(A) In general.—The term "social security taxes" means, with respect to any taxpayer for any taxable year—

(i) the amount of the taxes imposed by sections 3101 and 3201(a) on amounts received by the taxpayer during the calendar year in which the taxable year begins,

(ii) 50 percent of the taxes imposed by section 1401 on the self-employment

*Editorial comment: The American Recovery and Reinvestment Tax Act of 2009 replaced the $10,000 indexed amount for 2009 through 2017 with $3,000. See § 24(d)(4).

income of the taxpayer for the taxable year, and

(iii) 50 percent of the taxes imposed by section 3211(a)(1) on amounts received by the taxpayer during the calendar year in which the taxable year begins.

(B) Coordination with special refund of social security taxes.—The term "social security taxes" shall not include any taxes to the extent the taxpayer is entitled to a special refund of such taxes under section 6413(c).

(C) Special rule.—Any amounts paid pursuant to an agreement under section 3121(l) (relating to agreements entered into by American employers with respect to foreign affiliates) which are equivalent to the taxes referred to in subparagraph (A)(i) shall be treated as taxes referred to in such subparagraph.

(3) Inflation adjustment.—In the case of any taxable year beginning in a calendar year after 2001, the $10,000 amount contained in paragraph (1)(B) shall be increased by an amount equal to—

(A) such dollar amount, multiplied by

(B) the cost-of-living adjustment determined under section 1(f)(3) for the calendar year in which the taxable year begins, determined by substituting "calendar year 2000" for "calendar year 1992" in subparagraph (B) thereof.

Any increase determined under the preceding sentence shall be rounded to the nearest multiple of $50.

(4) Special rule for certain years.—Notwithstanding paragraph (3), in the case of any taxable year beginning after 2008 and before 2018, the dollar amount in effect for such table year under paragraph (1)(B)(i) shall be $3,000.

(e) Identification requirement.—No credit shall be allowed under this section to a taxpayer with respect to a qualifying child unless the taxpayer includes the name and taxpayer identification number of such qualifying child on the return of tax for the taxable year.

(f) Taxable year must be full taxable year.—Except in the case of a taxable year closed by reason of the death of the taxpayer, no credit shall be allowable under this section in the case of a taxable year covering a period of less than 12 months.

§ 25. Interest on certain home mortgages

(a) Allowance of credit.—

(1) In general.—There shall be allowed as a credit against the tax imposed by this chapter for the taxable year an amount equal to the product of—

(A) the certificate credit rate, and

(B) the interest paid or accrued by the taxpayer during the taxable year on the remaining principal of the certified indebtedness amount.

(2) Limitation where credit rate exceeds 20 percent.—

(A) In general.—If the certificate credit rate exceeds 20 percent, the amount of the credit allowed to the taxpayer under paragraph (1) for any taxable year shall not exceed $2,000.

(B) Special rule where 2 or more persons hold interests in residence.—If 2 or more persons hold interests in any residence, the limitation of subparagraph (A) shall be allocated among such persons in proportion to their respective interests in the residence.

(b) Certificate credit rate; certified indebtedness amount.—For purposes of this section—

(1) Certificate credit rate.—The term "certificate credit rate" means the rate of the credit allowable by this section which is specified in the mortgage credit certificate.

(2) Certified indebtedness amount.—The term "certified indebtedness amount" means the amount of indebtedness which is—

(A) incurred by the taxpayer—

(i) to acquire the principal residence of the taxpayer,

(ii) as a qualified home improvement loan (as defined in section 143(k)(4)) with respect to such residence, or

(iii) as a qualified rehabilitation loan (as defined in section 143(k)(5)) with respect to such residence, and

(B) specified in the mortgage credit certificate.

(c) Mortgage credit certificate; qualified mortgage credit certificate program.—For purposes of this section—

(1) Mortgage credit certificate.—The term "mortgage credit certificate" means any certificate which—

(A) is issued under a qualified mortgage credit certificate program by the State or political subdivision having the authority to issue a qualified mortgage bond to provide financing on the principal residence of the taxpayer,

(B) is issued to the taxpayer in connection with the acquisition, qualified rehabilitation, or qualified home improvement of the taxpayer's principal residence,

(C) specifies—

(i) the certificate credit rate, and

(ii) the certified indebtedness amount, and

(D) is in such form as the Secretary may prescribe.

(2) Qualified mortgage credit certificate program.—

(A) In general.—The term "qualified mortgage credit certificate program" means any program—

(i) which is established by a State or political subdivision thereof for any calendar year for which it is authorized to issue qualified mortgage bonds,

(ii) under which the issuing authority elects (in such manner and form as the Secretary may prescribe) not to issue an amount of private activity bonds which it may otherwise issue during such calendar year under section 146,

(iii) under which the indebtedness certified by mortgage credit certificates meets the requirements of the following subsections of section 143 (as modified by subparagraph (B) of this paragraph):

(I) subsection (c) (relating to residence requirements),

(II) subsection (d) (relating to 3-year requirement),

(III) subsection (e) (relating to purchase price requirement),

(IV) subsection (f) (relating to income requirements),

(V) subsection (h) (relating to portion of loans required to be placed in targeted areas), and

(VI) paragraph (1) of subsection (i) (relating to other requirements),

(iv) under which no mortgage credit certificate may be issued with respect to any residence any of the financing of which is provided from the proceeds of a qualified mortgage bond or a qualified veterans' mortgage bond,

(v) except to the extent provided in regulations, which is not limited to indebtedness incurred from particular lenders,

(vi) except to the extent provided in regulations, which provides that a mortgage credit certificate is not transferrable, and

(vii) if the issuing authority allocates a block of mortgage credit certificates for use in connection with a particular development, which requires the developer to furnish to the issuing authority and the homebuyer a certificate that the price for the residence is no higher than it would be without the use of a mortgage credit certificate.

Under regulations, rules similar to the rules of subparagraphs (B) and (C) of section 143(a)(2) shall apply to the requirements of this subparagraph.

(B) Modifications of section 143.—Under regulations prescribed by the Secretary, in applying section 143 for purposes of subclauses (II), (IV), and (V) of subparagraph (A)(iii)—

(i) each qualified mortgage certificate credit program shall be treated as a separate issue,

(ii) the product determined by multiplying—

(I) the certified indebtedness amount of each mortgage credit certificate issued under such program, by

(II) the certificate credit rate specified in such certificate,

shall be treated as proceeds of such issue and the sum of such products shall be treated as the total proceeds of such issue, and

(iii) paragraph (1) of section 143(d) shall be applied by substituting "100 percent" for "95 percent or more."

Clause (iii) shall not apply if the issuing authority submits a plan to the Secretary for administering the 95-percent requirement of section 143(d)(1) and the Secretary is satisfied that such requirement will be met under such plan.

(d) Determination of certificate credit rate.—For purposes of this section—

(1) In general.—The certificate credit rate specified in any mortgage credit certificate shall not be less than 10 percent or more than 50 percent.

(2) Aggregate limit on certificate credit rates.—

(A) In general.—In the case of each qualified mortgage credit certificate program, the sum of the products determined by multiplying—

(i) the certified indebtedness amount of each mortgage credit certificate issued under such program, by

(ii) The certificate credit rate with respect to such certificate,

shall not exceed 25 percent of the nonissued bond amount.

(B) Nonissued bond amount.—For purposes of subparagraph (A), the term "nonissued bond amount" means, with respect to any qualified mortgage credit certificate program, the amount of qualified mortgage bonds which the issuing authority is otherwise authorized to issue and elects not to issue under subsection (c)(2)(A)(ii).

* * *

(e) Special rules and definitions.—For purposes of this section—

(1) Carryforward of unused credit.—

(A) In general.—If the credit allowable under subsection (a) for any taxable year exceeds the applicable tax limit for such taxable year, such excess shall be a carryover to each of the 3 succeeding taxable years and, subject to the limitations of subparagraph (B), shall be added to the credit allowable by subsection (a) for such succeeding taxable year.

(B) Limitation.—The amount of the unused credit which may be taken into account under subparagraph (A) for any taxable year shall not exceed the amount (if any) by which the applicable tax limit for such taxable year exceeds the sum of—

(i) the credit allowable under subsection (a) for such taxable year determined without regard to this paragraph, and

(ii) the amounts which, by reason of this paragraph, are carried to such taxable year and are attributable to taxable years before the unused credit year.

(C) Applicable tax limit.—For purposes of this paragraph, the term "applicable tax limit" means the limitation imposed by section 26(a) for the taxable year reduced by the sum of the credits allowable under this subpart (other than this section and sections 23, 25D, and 1400C).

(2) Indebtedness not treated as certified where certain requirements not in fact met.—Subsection (a) shall not apply to any indebtedness if all the requirements of subsections (c)(1), (d), (e), (f), and (i) of section 143 and clauses (iv), (v), and (vii) of subsection (c)(2)(A), were not in fact met with respect to such indebtedness. Except to the extent provided in regulations, the requirements described in the preceding sentence shall be treated as met if there is a certification, under penalty of perjury, that such requirements are met.

(3) Period for which certificate in effect.—

(A) In general.—Except as provided in subparagraph (B), a mortgage credit certificate shall be treated as in effect with respect to interest attributable to the period—

(i) beginning on the date such certificate is issued, and

(ii) ending on the earlier of the date on which—

(I) the certificate is revoked by the issuing authority, or

(II) the residence to which such certificate relates ceases to be the principal residence of the individual to whom the certificate relates.

(B) Certificate invalid unless indebtedness incurred within certain period.—A certificate shall not apply to any indebtedness which is incurred after the close of the second calendar year following the calendar year for which the issuing authority made the applicable election under subsection (c)(2)(A)(ii).

(C) Notice to Secretary when certificate revoked.—Any issuing authority which revokes any mortgage credit certificate shall notify the Secretary of such revocation at such time and in such manner as the Secretary shall prescribe by regulations.

* * *

(6) Interest paid or accrued to related persons.—No credit shall be allowed under subsection (a) for any interest paid or accrued to a person who is a related person to the taxpayer (within the meaning of section 144(a)(3)(A)).

(7) Principal residence.—The term "principal residence" has the same meaning as when used in section 121.

(8) Qualified rehabilitation and home improvement.—

(A) Qualified rehabilitation.—The term "qualified rehabilitation" has the meaning given such term by section 143(k)(5)(B).

(B) Qualified home improvement.—The term "qualified home improvement" means an alteration, repair, or improvement described in section 143(k)(4).

(9) Qualified mortgage bond.—The term "qualified mortgage bond" has the meaning given such term by section 143(a)(1).

(10) Manufactured housing.—For purposes of this section, the term "single family residence" includes any manufactured home which has a minimum of 400 square feet of living space and a minimum width in excess of 102 inches and which is of a kind customarily used at a fixed location. Nothing in the preceding sentence shall be construed as providing that such a home will be taken into account in making determinations under section 143.

* * *

(h) Regulations; contracts.—

(1) Regulations.—The Secretary shall prescribe such regulations as may be necessary to carry out the purposes of this section, including regulations which may require recipients of mortgage credit certificates to pay a reasonable processing fee to defray the expenses incurred in administering the program.

(2) Contracts.—The Secretary is authorized to enter into contracts with any person to provide services in connection with the administration of this section.

* * *

§ 25A. HOPE and lifetime learning credits

(a) Allowance of credit.—In the case of an individual, there shall be allowed as a credit against the tax imposed by this chapter for the taxable year the amount equal to the sum of—

(1) the Hope Scholarship Credit, plus,

(2) the Lifetime Learning Credit.

(b) Hope Scholarship Credit.*—

(1) Per student credit.—In the case of any eligible student for whom an election is in effect under this section for any taxable year, the Hope Scholarship Credit is an amount equal to the sum of—

(A) 100 percent of so much of the qualified tuition and related expenses paid by the taxpayer during the taxable year (for education furnished to the eligible student during any academic period beginning in such taxable year) as does not exceed $1,000,** plus

(B) 50 percent of such expenses so paid as exceeds $1,000** but does not exceed the applicable limit.

(2) Limitations applicable to Hope Scholarship Credit.—

(A) Credit allowed only for 2 taxable years.—An election to have this section apply with respect to any eligible student for purposes of the Hope Scholarship Credit under subsection (a)(1) may not be made for any taxable year if such an election (by the taxpayer or any other individual) is in effect with respect to such student for any 2 prior taxable years.

(B) Credit allowed for year only if individual is at least ½ time student for portion of year.—The Hope Scholarship Credit under subsection (a)(1) shall not be allowed for a taxable year with respect to the qualified tuition and related expenses of an individual unless such individual is an eligible student for at least one academic period which begins during such year.

(C) Credit allowed for first 2 years of postsecondary education.—The Hope Scholarship Credit under subsection (a)(1) shall not be allowed for a taxable year with respect to the qualified tuition and related expenses of an eligible student if the student has completed (before the beginning of such taxable year) the first 2 years of postsecondary education at an eligible educational institution.

(D) Denial of credit if student convicted of a felony drug offense.—The Hope Scholarship Credit under subsection (a)(1) shall not be allowed for qualified tuition and related expenses for the enrollment or attendance of a student for any academic period if such student has been convicted of a Federal or State felony offense consisting of

*Editorial comment: For 2009, 2010, 2011, 2012, 2013, and 2014 the Hope Scholarship Credit is renamed the American Opportunity Tax Credit and the amounts are increased to the amounts contained in section 25A(i).

**Editorial comment: The indexed amount for 2014 is $2,500.

the possession or distribution of a controlled substance before the end of the taxable year with or within which such period ends.

(3) Eligible student.—For purposes of this subsection, the term "eligible student" means, with respect to any academic period, a student who—

(A) meets the requirements of section 484(a)(1) of the Higher Education Act of 1965 (20 U.S.C. 1091(a)(1)), as in effect on the date of the enactment of this section, and

(B) is carrying at least ½ the normal full-time work load for the course of study the student is pursuing.

(4) Applicable limit.—For purposes of paragraph (1)(B), the applicable limit for any taxable year is an amount equal to 2 times the dollar amount in effect under paragraph (1)(A) for such taxable year.

(c) Lifetime Learning Credit.—

(1) Per taxpayer credit.—The Lifetime Learning Credit for any taxpayer for any taxable year is an amount equal to 20 percent of so much of the qualified tuition and related expenses paid by the taxpayer during the taxable year (for education furnished during any academic period beginning in such taxable year) as does not exceed $10,000 ($5,000 in the case of taxable years beginning before January 1, 2003).

(2) Special rules for determining expenses.—

(A) Coordination with Hope Scholarship.—The qualified tuition and related expenses with respect to an individual who is an eligible student for whom a Hope Scholarship Credit under subsection (a)(1) is allowed for the taxable year shall not be taken into account under this subsection.

(B) Expenses eligible for Lifetime Learning Credit.—For purposes of paragraph (1), qualified tuition and related expenses shall include expenses described in subsection (f)(1) with respect to any course of instruction at an eligible educational institution to acquire or improve job skills of the individual.

(d) Limitation based on modified adjusted gross income.—

(1) In general.—The amount which would (but for this subsection) be taken into account under subsection (a) for the taxable year shall be reduced (but not below zero) by the amount determined under paragraph (2).

(2) Amount of reduction.—The amount determined under this paragraph is the amount which bears the same ratio to the amount which would be so taken into account as—

(A) the excess of—

(i) the taxpayer's modified adjusted gross income for such taxable year, over

(ii) $40,000* ($80,000* in the case of a joint return), bears to

(B) $10,000 ($20,000 in the case of a joint return).

(3) Modified adjusted gross income.—The term "modified adjusted gross income" means the adjusted gross income of the taxpayer for the taxable year increased by any amount excluded from gross income under section 911, 931, or 933.

(e) Election not to have section apply.—A taxpayer may elect not to have this section apply with respect to the qualified tuition and related expenses of an individual for any taxable year.

(f) Definitions.—For purposes of this section—

(1) Qualified tuition and related expenses.—

(A) In general.—The term "qualified tuition and related expenses" means tuition and fees required for the enrollment or attendance of—

(i) the taxpayer,

(ii) the taxpayer's spouse, or

(iii) any dependent of the taxpayer with respect to whom the taxpayer is allowed a deduction under section 151, at an eligible educational institution for courses of instruction of such individual at such institution.

(B) Exception for education involving sports, etc.—Such term does not include expenses with respect to any course or other education involving sports, games, or hobbies, unless such course or other education is part of the individual's degree program.

(C) Exception for nonacademic fees.—Such term does not include student activity fees, athletic fees, insurance expenses, or other expenses unrelated to an individual's academic course of instruction.

*Editorial comment: The indexed amounts for 2013 for the Lifetime Learning Credit are $53,000 and $107,000 respectively and for 2014 are $54,000 and $108,000. For 2013 and 2014, the statutory amounts for the American Opportunity Tax Credit are not indexed and are $80,000 and $160,000 respectively. See section 25A(i)(4).

(2) Eligible educational institution.—The term "eligible educational institution" means an institution—

(A) which is described in section 481 of the Higher Education Act of 1965 (20 U.S.C. 1088), as in effect on the date of the enactment of this section, and

(B) which is eligible to participate in a program under title IV of such Act.

(g) Special rules.—

(1) Identification requirement.—No credit shall be allowed under subsection (a) to a taxpayer with respect to the qualified tuition and related expenses of an individual unless the taxpayer includes the name and taxpayer identification number of such individual on the return of tax for the taxable year.

(2) Adjustment for certain scholarships, etc.—The amount of qualified tuition and related expenses otherwise taken into account under subsection (a) with respect to an individual for an academic period shall be reduced (before the application of subsections (b), (c), and (d)) by the sum of any amounts paid for the benefit of such individual which are allocable to such period as—

(A) a qualified scholarship which is excludable from gross income under section 117,

(B) an educational assistance allowance under chapter 30, 31, 32, 34, or 35 or title 38, United States Code, or under chapter 1606 of title 10, United States Code, and

(C) a payment (other than a gift, bequest, devise, or inheritance within the meaning of section 102(a)) for such individual's educational expenses, or attributable to such individual's enrollment at an eligible educational institution, which is excludable from gross income under any law of the United States.

(3) Treatment of expenses paid by dependent.—If a deduction under section 151 with respect to an individual is allowed to another taxpayer for a taxable year beginning in the calendar year in which such individual's taxable year begins—

(A) no credit shall be allowed under subsection (a) to such individual for such individual's taxable year, and

(B) qualified tuition and related expenses paid by such individual during such individual's taxable year shall be related for purposes of this section as paid by such other taxpayer.

(4) Treatment of certain prepayments.—If qualified tuition and related expenses are paid by the taxpayer during a taxable year for an academic period which begins during the first 3 months following such taxable year, such academic period shall be treated for purposes of this section as beginning during such taxable year.

(5) Denial of double benefit.—No credit shall be allowed under this section for any expense for which a deduction is allowed under any other provision of this chapter.

(6) No credit for married individuals filing separate returns.—If the taxpayer is a married individual (within the meaning of section 7703), this section shall apply only if the taxpayer and the taxpayer's spouse file a joint return for the taxable year.

(7) Nonresident aliens.—If the taxpayer is a nonresident alien individual for any portion of the taxable year, this section shall apply only if such individual is treated as a resident alien of the United States for purposes of this chapter by reason of an election under subsection (g) or (h) of section 6013.

(h) Inflation adjustments.—

(1) Dollar limitation on amount of credit.—

(A) In general.—In the case of a taxable year beginning after 2001, each of the $1,000 amounts under subsection (b)(1) shall be increased by an amount equal to—

(i) such dollar amount, multiplied by

(ii) the cost-of-living adjustment determined under section 1(f)(3) for the calendar year in which the taxable year begins, determined by substituting "calendar year 2000" for "calendar year 1992" in subparagraph (B) thereof.

(B) Rounding.—If any amount as adjusted under subparagraph (A) is not a multiple of $100, such amount shall be rounded to the next lowest multiple of $100.

(2) Income limits.—

(A) In general.—In the case of a taxable year beginning after 2001, the $40,000 and $80,000 amounts in subsection (d)(2) shall each be increased by an amount equal to—

(i) such dollar amount, multiplied by

(ii) the cost-of-living adjustment determined under section 1(f)(3) for the calendar year in which the taxable year begins, determined by substituting "calendar year 2000" for "calendar year 1992" in subparagraph (B) thereof.

(B) Rounding.—If any amount as adjusted under subparagraph (A) is not a multiple of $1,000, such amount shall be rounded to the next lowest multiple of $1,000.

(i) American opportunity tax credit.*—In the case of any taxable year beginning after 2008 and before 2018—

(1) Increase in credit.—The Hope Scholarship Credit shall be an amount equal to the sum of—

(A) 100 percent of so much of the qualified tuition and related expenses paid by the taxpayer during the taxable year (for education furnished to the eligible student during any academic period beginning in such taxable year) as does not exceed $2,000, plus

(B) 25 percent of such expenses so paid as exceeds $2,000 but does not exceed $4,000.

(2) Credit allowed for first 4 years of post-secondary education.—Subparagraphs (A) and (C) of subsection (b)(2) shall be applied by substituting "4" for "2".

(3) Qualified tuition and related expenses to include required course materials.—Subsection (f)(1)(A) shall be applied by substituting "tuition, fees, and course materials" for "tuition and fees".

(4) Increase in AGI limits for Hope Scholarship Credit.—In lieu of applying subsection (d) with respect to the Hope Scholarship Credit, such credit (determined without regard to this paragraph) shall be reduced (but not below zero) by the amount which bears the same ratio to such credit (as so determined) as—

(A) the excess of—

(i) the taxpayer's modified adjusted gross income (as defined in subsection (d)(3)) for such taxable year, over

(ii) $80,000 ($160,000 in the case of a joint return), bears to

(B) $10,000 ($20,000 in the case of a joint return).

(5) Portion of credit made refundable.—40 percent of so much of the credit allowed under subsection (a) as is attributable to the Hope Scholarship Credit (determined after application of paragraph (4) and without regard to this paragraph and section 26(a)(2) or paragraph (5), as the case may be) shall be treated as a credit allowable under subpart C (and not allowed under subsection (a)). The preceding sentence shall not apply to any taxpayer for any taxable year if such taxpayer is a child to whom subsection (g) of section 1 applies for such taxable year.

(6) Coordination with midwestern disaster area benefits.—In the case of a taxpayer with respect to whom section 702(a)(1)(B) of the Heartland Disaster Tax Relief Act of 2008 applies for any taxable year, such taxpayer may elect to waive the application of this subsection to such taxpayer for such taxable year.

(j) Regulations.—The Secretary may prescribe such regulations as may be necessary or appropriate to carry out this section, including regulations providing for a recapture of the credit allowed under this section in cases where there is a refund in a subsequent taxable year of any amount which was taken into account in determining the amount of such credit.

§ 25B. Elective deferrals and IRA contributions by certain individuals

(a) Allowance of credit.—In the case of an eligible individual, there shall be allowed as a credit against the tax imposed by this subtitle for the taxable year an amount equal to the applicable percentage of so much of the qualified retirement savings contributions of the eligible individual for the taxable year as do not exceed $2,000.

(b) Applicable percentage.—For purposes of this section—

(1) Joint returns.—In the case of a joint return, the applicable percentage is—

(A) if the adjusted gross income of the taxpayer is not over $30,000, 50 percent,

(B) if the adjusted gross income of the taxpayer is over $30,000 but not over $32,500, 20 percent,

(C) if the adjusted gross income of the taxpayer is over $32,500 but not over $50,000, 10 percent, and

(D) if the adjusted gross income of the taxpayer is over $50,000, zero percent.

*Editorial comment: This provision applies to 2009, 2010, 2011, 2012, 2013, 2014, 2015, 2016, and 2017. See section 25A(i).

(2) Other returns.—In the case of—

(A) a head of household, the applicable percentage shall be determined under paragraph (1) except that such paragraph shall be applied by substituting for each dollar amount therein (as adjusted under paragraph (3)) a dollar amount equal to 75 percent of such dollar amount, and

(B) any taxpayer not described in paragraph (1) or subparagraph (A), the applicable percentage shall be determined under paragraph (1) except that such paragraph shall be applied by substituting for each dollar amount therein (as adjusted under paragraph (3)) a dollar amount equal to 50 percent of such dollar amount.

(3) Inflation adjustment.—In the case of any taxable year beginning in a calendar year after 2006, each of the dollar amount[s] in paragraph (1) shall be increased by an amount equal to—

(A) such dollar amount, multiplied by

(B) the cost-of-living adjustment determined under section 1(f)(3) for the calendar year in which the taxable year begins, determined by substituting "calendar year 2005" for "calendar year 1992" in subparagraph (B) thereof.

Any increase determined under the preceding sentence shall be rounded to the nearest multiple of $500.

(c) Eligible individual.—For purposes of this section—

(1) In general.—The term "eligible individual" means any individual if such individual has attained the age of 18 as of the close of the taxable year.

(2) Dependents and full-time students not eligible.—The term "eligible individual" shall not include—

(A) any individual with respect to whom a deduction under section 151 is allowed to another taxpayer for a taxable year beginning in the calendar year in which such individual's taxable year begins, and

(B) any individual who is a student (as defined in section 152(f)(2)).

(d) Qualified retirement savings contributions.—For purposes of this section—

(1) In general.—The term "qualified retirement savings contributions" means, with respect to any taxable year, the sum of—

(A) the amount of the qualified retirement contributions (as defined in section 219(e)) made by the eligible individual,

(B) the amount of—

(i) any elective deferrals (as defined in section 402(g)(3)) of such individual, and

(ii) any elective deferral of compensation by such individual under an eligible deferred compensation plan (as defined in section 457(b)) of an eligible employer described in section 457(e)(1)(A), and

(C) the amount of voluntary employee contributions by such individual to any qualified retirement plan (as defined in section 4974(c)).

(2) Reduction for certain distributions.—

(A) In general.—The qualified retirement savings contributions determined under paragraph (1) shall be reduced (but not below zero) by the aggregate distributions received by the individual during the testing period from any entity of a type to which contributions under paragraph (1) may be made. The preceding sentence shall not apply to the portion of any distribution which is not includible in gross income by reason of a trustee-to-trustee transfer or a rollover distribution.

(B) Testing period.—For purposes of subparagraph (A), the testing period, with respect to a taxable year, is the period which includes—

(i) such taxable year,

(ii) the 2 preceding taxable years, and

(iii) the period after such taxable year and before the due date (including extensions) for filing the return of tax for such taxable year.

(C) Excepted distributions.—There shall not be taken into account under subparagraph (A)—

(i) any distribution referred to in section 72(p), 401(k)(8), 401(m)(6), 402(g)(2), 404(k), or 408(d)(4), and

(ii) any distribution to which section 408A(d)(3) applies.

(D) Treatment of distributions received by spouse of individual.—For purposes of determining distributions received by an individual under subparagraph (A) for any taxable year, any distribution received by the spouse of such individual shall be treated as received by such individual if such individual and spouse file a joint return for such taxable year and for the taxable year during which the spouse receives the distribution.

(e) **Adjusted gross income.**—For purposes of this section, adjusted gross income shall be determined without regard to sections 911, 931, and 933.

(f) **Investment in the contract.**—Notwithstanding any other provision of law, a qualified retirement savings contribution shall not fail to be included in determining the investment in the contract for purposes of section 72 by reason of the credit under this section.

* * *

§ 26. Limitation based on tax liability; definition of tax liability

(a) **Limitation based on amount of tax.**—The aggregate amount of credits allowed by this subpart for the taxable year shall not exceed the sum of—

(1) the taxpayer's regular tax liability for the taxable year reduced by the foreign tax credit allowable under section 27(a), and

(2) the tax imposed by section 55(a) for the taxable year.

(b) **Regular tax liability.**—For purposes of this part—

(1) **In general.**—The term "regular tax liability" means the tax imposed by this chapter for the taxable year.

(2) **Exception for certain taxes.**—For purposes of paragraph (1), any tax imposed by any of the following provisions shall not be treated as tax imposed by this chapter:

(A) section 55 (relating to minimum tax),

(B) section 59A (relating to environmental tax),

(C) subsection (m)(5)(B), (q), (t), or (v) of section 72 (relating to additional taxes on certain distributions),

(D) section 143(m) (relating to recapture of proration of Federal subsidy from use of mortgage bonds and mortgage credit certificates,

(E) section 530(d)(4) (relating to additional tax on certain distributions from Coverdell education individual retirement accounts),

(F) section 531 (relating to accumulated earnings tax),

(G) section 541 (relating to personal holding company tax),

(H) section 1351(d)(1) (relating to recoveries of foreign expropriation losses),

(I) section 1374 (relating to tax on certain built-in gains of S corporations),

(J) section 1375 (relating to tax imposed when passive investment income of corporation having subchapter C earnings and profits exceeds 25 percent of gross receipts),

(K) subparagraph (A) of section 7518(g)(6) (relating to nonqualified withdrawals from capital construction funds taxed at highest marginal rate),

* * *

(O) sections 453(1)(3) and 453A(c) (relating to interest on certain deferred tax liabilities),

* * *

(Q) section 220(f)(4) (relating to additional tax on Archer MSA distributions not used for qualified medical expenses),

(R) section 138(c)(2) (relating to penalty for distributions from MedicareAdvantage MSA not used for qualified medical expenses if minimum balance not maintained),

(S) sections 106(e)(3)(A)(ii), 223(b)(8)(B)(i)(II), and 408(d)(9)(D)(i)(II) (relating to certain failures to maintain high deductible health plan coverage),

(T) section 170(o)(3)(B) (relating to recapture of certain deductions for fractional gifts),

(U) section 223(f)(4) (relating to additional tax on health savings account distributions not used for qualified medical expenses),

(V) subsections (a)(1)(B)(i) and (b)(4)(A) of section 409A (relating to interest and additional tax with respect to certain deferred compensation),

(W) section 36(f) (relating to recapture of homebuyer credit), and

(X) section 457A(c)(1)(B) (relating to determinability of amounts of compensation).

(c) **Tentative minimum tax.**—For purposes of this part, the term "tentative minimum tax" means the amount determined under section 55(b)(1).

SUBPART B—FOREIGN TAX CREDIT, ETC.

§ 27. Taxes of foreign countries and possessions of the United States; possession tax credit

(a) Foreign tax credit.—The amount of taxes imposed by foreign countries and possessions of the United States shall be allowed as a credit against the tax imposed by this chapter to the extent provided in section 901.

(b) Section 936 credit.—In the case of a domestic corporation, the amount provided by section 936 (relating to Puerto Rico and possession tax credit) shall be allowed as a credit against the tax imposed by this chapter.

§ 29. Credit for producing fuel from a nonconventional source

(a) Allowance of credit.—There shall be allowed as a credit against the tax imposed by this chapter for the taxable year an amount equal to—

(1) $3, multiplied by

(2) the barrel-of-oil equivalent of qualified fuels—

(A) sold by the taxpayer to an unrelated person during the taxable year, and

(B) the production of which is attributable to the taxpayer.

(b) Limitations and adjustments.—

(1) Phaseout of credit.—The amount of the credit allowable under subsection (a) shall be reduced by an amount which bears the same ratio to the amount of the credit (determined without regard to this paragraph) as—

(A) the amount by which the reference price for the calendar year in which the sale occurs exceeds $23.50, bears to

(B) $6.

(2) Credit and phaseout adjustment based on inflation.—The $3 amount in subsection (a) and the $23.50 and $6 amounts in paragraph (1) shall each be adjusted by multiplying such amount by the inflation adjustment factor for the calendar year in which the sale occurs. In the case of gas from a tight formation, the $3 amount in subsection (a) shall not be adjusted.

* * *

§ 30. Certain plug-in electric vehicles*

(a) Allowance of credit.—There shall be allowed as a credit against the tax imposed by this chapter for the taxable year an amount equal to 10 percent of the cost of any qualified plug-in electric vehicle placed in service by the taxpayer during the taxable year.

(b) Per vehicle dollar limitation.—The amount of the credit allowed under subsection (a) with respect to any vehicle shall not exceed $2,500.

(c) Application with other credits.—

(1) Business credit treated as part of general business credit.—So much of the credit which would be allowed under subsection (a) for any taxable year (determined without regard to this subsection) that is attributable to property of a character subject to an allowance for depreciation shall be treated as a credit listed in section 38(b) for such taxable year (and not allowed under subsection (a)).

(2) Personal credit.—For purposes of this title, the credit allowed under subsection (a) for any taxable year (determined after application of paragraph (1)) shall be treated as a credit allowable under subpart A for such taxable year.

(d) Qualified plug-in electric vehicle.—For purposes of this section—

(1) In general.—The term "qualified plug-in electric vehicle" means a specified vehicle—

(A) the original use of which commences with the taxpayer,

(B) which is acquired for use or lease by the taxpayer and not for resale,

(C) which is made by a manufacturer,

(D) which is manufactured primarily for use on public streets, roads, and highways,

(E) which has a gross vehicle weight rating of less than 14,000 pounds, and

(F) which is propelled to a significant extent by an electric motor which draws electricity from a battery which—

(i) has a capacity of not less than 4 kilowatt hours (2.5 kilowatt hours in the case of a vehicle with 2 or 3 wheels), and

(ii) is capable of being recharged from an external source of electricity.

(2) Specified vehicle.—The term "specified vehicle" means any vehicle which—

*Editorial comment: This credit does not apply to any property placed in service after December 31, 2011. See Sec. 30(f).

(A) is a low speed vehicle within the meaning of section 571.3 of title 49, Code of Federal Regulations (as in effect on the date of the enactment of the American Recovery and Reinvestment Tax Act of 2009), or

(B) has 2 or 3 wheels.

(3) **Manufacturer.**—The term "manufacturer" has the meaning given such term in regulations prescribed by the Administrator of the Environmental Protection Agency for purposes of the administration of title II of the Clean Air Act (42 U.S.C. 7521 et seq.).

(4) **Battery capacity.**—The term "capacity" means, with respect to any battery, the quantity of electricity which the battery is capable of storing, expressed in kilowatt hours, as measured from a 100 percent state of charge to a 0 percent state of charge.

(e) Special rules.—

(1) **Basis reduction.**—For purposes of this subtitle, the basis of any property for which a credit is allowable under subsection (a) shall be reduced by the amount of such credit so allowed.

(2) **No double benefit.**—The amount of any deduction or other credit allowable under this chapter for a new qualified plug-in electric drive motor vehicle shall be reduced by the amount of credit allowable under subsection (a) for such vehicle.

(3) **Property used by tax-exempt entity.**—In the case of a vehicle the use of which is described in paragraph (3) or (4) of section 50(b) and which is not subject to a lease, the person who sold such vehicle to the person or entity using such vehicle shall be treated as the taxpayer that placed such vehicle in service, but only if such person clearly discloses to such person or entity in a document the amount of any credit allowable under subsection (a) with respect to such vehicle (determined without regard to subsection (c)).

(4) **Property used outside United States not qualified.**—No credit shall be allowable under subsection (a) with respect to any property referred to in section 50(b)(1).

(5) **Recapture.**—The Secretary shall, by regulations, provide for recapturing the benefit of any credit allowable under subsection (a) with respect to any property which ceases to be property eligible for such credit.

(6) **Election not to take credit.**—No credit shall be allowed under subsection (a) for any vehicle if the taxpayer elects to not have this section apply to such vehicle.

(f) Termination.—This section shall not apply to any vehicle acquired after December 31, 2011.

* * *

SUBPART C—REFUNDABLE CREDITS

§ 31. Tax withheld on wages

(a) Wage withholding for income tax purposes.—

(1) **In general.**—The amount withheld as tax under chapter 24 shall be allowed to the recipient of the income as a credit against the tax imposed by this subtitle.

(2) **Year of credit.**—The amount so withheld during any calendar year shall be allowed as a credit for the taxable year beginning in such calendar year. If more than one taxable year begins in a calendar year, such amount shall be allowed as a credit for the last taxable year so beginning.

(b) Credit for special refunds of social security tax.—

(1) **In general.**—The Secretary may prescribe regulations providing for the crediting against the tax imposed by this subtitle of the amount determined by the taxpayer or the Secretary to be allowable under section 6413(c) as a special refund of tax imposed on wages. The amount allowed as a credit under such regulations shall, for purposes of this subtitle, be considered an amount withheld at source as tax under section 3402.

(2) **Year of credit.**—Any amount to which paragraph (1) applies shall be allowed as a credit for the taxable year beginning in the calendar year during which the wages were received. If more than one taxable year begins in the calendar year, such amount shall be allowed as a credit for the last taxable year so beginning.

(c) Special rule for backup withholding.—Any credit allowed by subsection (a) for any amount withheld under section 3406 shall be allowed for the taxable year of the recipient of the income in which the income is received.

§ 32. Earned income*

(a) Allowance of credit.—

(1) In general.—In the case of an eligible individual, there shall be allowed as a credit against the tax imposed by this subtitle for the taxable year an amount equal to the credit percentage of so much of the taxpayer's earned income for the taxable year as does not exceed the earned income amount.

(2) Limitation.—The amount of the credit allowable to a taxpayer under paragraph (1) for any taxable year shall not exceed the excess (if any) of—

(A) the credit percentage of the earned income amount, over

(B) the phaseout percentage of so much of the adjusted gross income (or, if greater, the earned income) of the taxpayer for the taxable year as exceeds the phaseout amount.

(b) Percentages and amounts.—For purposes of subsection (a)—

(1) Percentages.—The credit percentage and the phaseout percentage shall be determined as follows:

(A) In general.—In the case of taxable years beginning after 1995:

The credit

In the case of an eligible individual with:	The phaseout percentage is:	percentage is:
1 qualifying child	34	15.98
2 or more qualifying children	40	21.06
No qualifying children	7.65	7.65

(B) Transitional percentages for 1995.—In the case of taxable years beginning in 1995:

The credit

In the case of an eligible individual with:	The phaseout percentage is:	percentage is:
1 qualifying child	34	15.98
2 or more qualifying children	36	20.22
No qualifying children	7.65	7.65

(C) Transitional percentages for 1994.—In the case of a taxable year beginning in 1994:

In the case of an eligible individual with:	The credit percentage is:	The phaseout percentage is:
1 qualifying child	26.3	15.98
2 or more qualifying children	30	17.68
No qualifying children	7.65	7.65

(2) Amounts.—

(A) In general.—Subject to subparagraph (B), the earned income amount and the phaseout amount shall be determined as follows:

In the case of an eligible individual with:	The earned income amount is:	The phaseout amount is:
1 qualifying child	$6,330	$11,610
2 or more qualifying children	$8,890	$11,610
No qualifying children	$4,220	$ 5,280

(B) Joint returns.—In the case of a joint return filed by an eligible individual and such individual's spouse, the phaseout amount determined under subparagraph (A) shall be increased by—

(i) $1,000 in the case of taxable years beginning in 2002, 2003, and 2004.

(ii) $2,000 in the case of taxable years beginning in 2005, 2006, and 2007, and

(iii) $3,000 in the case of taxable years beginning after 2007.

(3) Special rules for certain years.—In the case of any taxable year beginning after 2008 and before 2018—

*Editorial comment: See the indexed amounts for the earned income credit after Sec. 32(k).

(A) Increased credit percentage for 3 or more qualifying children.—In the case of a taxpayer with 3 or more qualifying children, the credit percentage is 45 percent.

(B) Reduction of marriage penalty.—

(i) In general.—The dollar amount in effect under paragraph (2)(B) shall be $5,000.

(ii) Inflation adjustment.—In the case of any taxable year beginning in 2010, the $5,000 amount in clause (i) shall be increased by an amount equal to—

(I) such dollar amount, multiplied by

(II) the cost of living adjustment determined under section 1(f)(3) for the calendar year in which the taxable year begins determined by substituting "calendar year 2008" for "calendar year 1992" in subparagraph (B) thereof.

(iii) Rounding.—Subparagraph (A) of subsection (j)(2) shall apply after taking into account any increase under clause (ii).

(c) Definitions and special rules.—For purposes of this section—

(1) Eligible individual.—

(A) In general.—The term "eligible individual" means—

(i) any individual who has a qualifying child for the taxable year, or

(ii) any other individual who does not have a qualifying child for the taxable year, if—

(I) such individual's principal place of abode is in the United States for more than one-half of such taxable year,

(II) such individual (or, if the individual is married, either the individual or the individual's spouse) has attained age 25 but not attained age 65 before the close of the taxable year, and

(III) such individual is not a dependent for whom a deduction is allowable under section 151 to another taxpayer for any taxable year beginning in the same calendar year as such taxable year.

For purposes of the preceding sentence, marital status shall be determined under section 7703.

(B) Qualifying child ineligible.—If an individual is the qualifying child of a taxpayer for any taxable year of such taxpayer beginning in a calendar year, such individual shall not be treated as an eligible individual for any taxable year of such individual beginning in such calendar year.

(C) Exception for individual claiming benefits under section 911.—The term "eligible individual" does not include any individual who claims the benefits of section 911 (relating to citizens or residents living abroad) for the taxable year.

(D) Limitation on eligibility of nonresident aliens.—The term "eligible individual" shall not include any individual who is a nonresident alien individual for any portion of the taxable year unless such individual is treated for such taxable year as a resident of the United States for purposes of this chapter by reason of an election under subsection (g) or (h) of section 6013.

(E) Identification number requirement.—No credit shall be allowed under this section to an eligible individual who does not include on the return of tax for the taxable year—

(i) such individual's taxpayer identification number, and

(ii) if the individual is married (within the meaning of section 7703), the taxpayer identification number of such individual's spouse.

(F) Individuals who do not include TIN, etc., of any qualifying child.—No credit shall be allowed under this section to any eligible individual who has 1 or more qualifying children if no qualifying child of such individual is taken into account under subsection (b) by reason of paragraph (3)(D).

(2) Earned income.—

(A) The term "earned income" means—

(i) wages, salaries, tips, and other employee compensation, but only if such amounts are includible in gross income for the taxable year, plus

(ii) the amount of the taxpayer's net earnings from self-employment for the taxable year (within the meaning of section 1402(a)), but such net earnings shall be determined with regard to the deduction allowed to the taxpayer by section 164(f).

(B) For purposes of subparagraph (A)—

(i) the earned income of an individual shall be computed without regard to any community property laws,

(ii) no amount received as a pension or annuity shall be taken into account,

(iii) no amount to which section 871(a) applies (relating to income of nonresident alien individuals not connected with United States business) shall be taken into account,

(iv) no amount received for services provided by an individual while the individual is an inmate at a penal institution shall be taken into account,

(v) no amount described in subparagraph (A) received for service performed in work activities as defined in paragraph (4) or (7) of section 407(d) of the Social Security Act to which the taxpayer is assigned under any State program under part A of title IV of such Act shall be taken into account, but only to the extent such amount is subsidized under such State program, and

(vi) a taxpayer may elect to treat amounts excluded from gross income by reason of section 112 as earned income.

(3) Qualifying child.—

(A) In general.—The term "qualifying child" means a qualifying child of taxpayer (as defined in section 152(c), determined without regard to paragraph (1)(D) thereof and section 152(e)).

(B) Married individual.—The term "qualifying child" shall not include an individual who is married as of the close of the taxpayer's taxable year unless the taxpayer is entitled to a deduction under section 151 for such taxable year with respect to such individual (or would be so entitled but for section 152(e)).

(C) Place of abode.—For purposes of subparagraph (A), the requirements of section 152 (c)(1)(B) shall be met only if the principal place of abode is in the United States.

(D) Identification requirements.—

(i) In general.—A qualifying child shall not be taken into account under subsection (b) unless the taxpayer includes the name, age, and TIN of the qualifying child on the return of tax for the taxable year.

(ii) Other methods.—The Secretary may prescribe other methods for providing the information described in clause (i).

*Editorial comment: There is no subsection (g) or (h).

(4) Treatment of military personnel stationed outside the United States.—For purposes of paragraphs (1)(A)(ii)(I) and (3)(C), the principal place of abode of a member of the Armed Forces of the United States shall be treated as in the United States during any period during which such member is stationed outside the United States while serving on extended active duty with the Armed Forces of the United States. For purposes of the preceding sentence, the term "extended active duty" means any period of active duty pursuant to a call or order to such duty for a period in excess of 90 days or for an indefinite period.

(d) Married individuals.—In the case of an individual who is married (within the meaning of section 7703), this section shall apply only if a joint return is filed for the taxable year under section 6013.

(e) Taxable year must be full taxable year.—Except in the case of a taxable year closed by reason of the death of the taxpayer, no credit shall be allowable under this section in the case of a taxable year covering a period of less than 12 months.

(f) Amount of credit to be determined under tables.—

(1) In general.—The amount of the credit allowed by this section shall be determined under tables prescribed by the Secretary.

(2) Requirements for tables.—The tables prescribed under paragraph (1) shall reflect the provisions of subsections (a) and (b) and shall have income brackets of not greater than $50 each—

(A) for earned income between $0 and the amount of earned income at which the credit is phased out under subsection (b), and

(B) for adjusted gross income between the dollar amount at which the phase-out begins under subsection (b) and the amount of adjusted gross income at which the credit is phased out under subsection (b).

***(i) Denial of credit for individuals having excessive investment income.**—

(1) In general.—No credit shall be allowed under subsection (a) for the taxable year if the aggregate amount of disqualified income of the taxpayer for the taxable year exceeds $2,200.**

(2) Disqualified income.—For purposes of paragraph (1), the term "disqualified income" means—

**Editorial comment: The indexed amount for 2013 is $3,300 and for 2014 is $3,350.

(A) interest or dividends to the extent includible in gross income for the taxable year,

(B) interest received or accrued during the taxable year which is exempt from tax imposed by this chapter,

(C) the excess (if any) of—

(i) gross income from rents or royalties not derived in the ordinary course of a trade or business, over

(ii) the sum of—

(I) the deductions (other than interest) which are clearly and directly allocable to such gross income, plus

(II) interest deductions properly allocable to such gross income, and

(D) the capital gain net income (as defined in section 1222) of the taxpayer for such taxable year, and

(E) the excess (if any) of—

(i) the aggregate income from all passive activities for the taxable year (determined without regard to any amount included in earned income under subsection (c)(2) or described in a preceding subparagraph), over

(ii) the aggregate losses from all passive activities for the taxable year (as so determined).

For purposes of subparagraph (E), the term "passive activity" has the meaning given such term by section 469.

(j) Inflation adjustments.—

(1) In general.—In the case of any taxable year beginning after 1996, each of the dollar amounts contained in subsection (b)(2) and (i)(1) shall be increased by an amount equal to—

(A) such dollar amount, multiplied by

(B) the cost-of-living adjustment determined under section 1(f)(3), for the calendar year in which the taxable year begins, determined—

(i) in the case of amounts in subsections (b)(2)(A) and (i)(1), by substituting "calendar year 1995" for "calendar year 1992" in subparagraph (B) thereof, and

(ii) in the case of the $3,000 amount in subsection (b)(2)(B)(iii), by substituting "calendar year 2007" for "calendar year 1992" in subparagraph (B) of such section 1.

(2) Rounding.—

(A) In general.—If any dollar amount in subsection (b)(2)(A) (after being increased under subparagraph (B) thereof), after being increased under paragraph (1), is not a multiple of $10, such dollar amount shall be rounded to the nearest multiple of $10.

(B) Disqualified income threshold amount.—If the dollar amount in subsection (i)(1), after being increased under paragraph (1), is not a multiple of $50, such amount shall be rounded to the next lowest multiple of $50.

(k) Restrictions on taxpayers who improperly claimed credit in prior year.—

(1) Taxpayers making prior fraudulent or reckless claims.—

(A) In general.—No credit shall be allowed under this section for any taxable year in the disallowance period.

(B) Disallowance period.—For purposes of paragraph (1), the disallowance period is—

(i) the period of 10 taxable years after the most recent taxable year for which there was a final determination that the taxpayer's claim of credit under this section was due to fraud, and

(ii) the period of 2 taxable years after the most recent taxable year for which there was a final determination that the taxpayer's claim of credit under this section was due to reckless or intentional disregard to rules and regulations (but not due to fraud).

(2) Taxpayer's making improper prior claims.—In the case of a taxpayer who is denied credit under this section for any taxable year as a result of the deficiency procedures under Subchapter B of chapter 63, no credit shall be allowed under this section for any subsequent taxable year unless the taxpayer provides such information as the Secretary may require to demonstrate eligibility for such credit.

* * *

Editorial Note

The indexed amounts for 2014 and 2013 are:

	Amount per Code	Indexed 2014 Amount	Indexed 2013 Amount
Maximum amount eligible for credit:			
One child	$6,330	$9,720	$9,560
Two or more	8,890	13,650	13,430
Three or more	8,890	13,650	13,430
No children	4,220	6,480	6,370
Credit percentage:			
One child	34.0%	34.0%	34.0%
Two children	40.0%	40.0%	40.0%
Three or more	45.0%	45.0%	45.0%
No children	7.65%	7.65%	7.65%
Phaseout of credit begins (married filing jointly):			
One child	$11,610	$23,260	$22,870
Two or more	11,610	23,260	22,870
Three or more	11,610	23,260	22,870
No children	5,280	13,540	13,310
Phaseout of credit begins (other than married filing jointly):			
One child	$11,610	$17,830	$17,530
Two or more	11,610	17,830	17,530
Three or more	11,610	17,830	17,530
No children	5,280	8,110	7,970
Phaseout of credit ends (married filing jointly):			
One child	$25,078	$43,941	$43,210
Two or more	28,495	49,186	48,378
Three or more	28,495	52,427	51,567
No children	9,500	20,020	19,680
Phaseout of credit ends (other than married filing jointly):			
One child	$25,078	$38,511	$37,870
Two or more	28,495	43,756	43,087
Three or more	28,495	46,997	46,227
No children	9,500	14,590	14,340
Phaseout percentage:			
One child	15.98%	15.98%	15.98%
Two or more	21.06%	21.06%	21.06%
Three or more	21.06%	21.06%	21.06%
No children	7.65%	7.65%	7.65%
Maximum Credit (all taxpayers)			
One child		$3,305	$3,250
Two or more		5,460	5,372
Three or more		6,143	6,044
No children		496	487

§ 33. Tax withheld at source on nonresident aliens and foreign corporations

There shall be allowed as a credit against the tax imposed by this subtitle the amount of tax withheld at source under subchapter A of chapter 3 (relating to withholding of tax on nonresident aliens and on foreign corporations).

§ 34. Certain uses of gasoline and special fuels

(a) General rule.—There shall be allowed as a credit against the tax imposed by this subtitle for the taxable year an amount equal to the sum of the amounts payable to the taxpayer—

(1) under section 6420 (determined without regard to section 6420(g)),

(2) under section 6421 (determined without regard to section 6421(i)), and

(3) under section 6427 (determined without regard to section 6427(k)).

(b) Exception.—Credit shall not be allowed under subsection (a) for any amount payable under section 6421 or 6427, if a claim for such amount is timely filed and, under section 6421(i) or 6427(k), is payable under such section.

§ 35. Health insurance costs of eligible individuals

(a) In general.—In the case of an individual, there shall be allowed as a credit against the tax imposed by subtitle A an amount equal to 65 percent (80 percent in the case of eligible coverage months beginning before January 1, 2011) of the amount paid by the taxpayer for coverage of the taxpayer and qualifying family members under qualified health insurance for eligible coverage months beginning in the taxable year.

(b) Eligible coverage month.—For purposes of this section—

(1) In general.—The term "eligible coverage month" means any month if—

(A) as of the first day of such month, the taxpayer—

(i) is an eligible individual,

(ii) is covered by qualified health insurance, the premium for which is paid by the taxpayer,

(iii) does not have other specified coverage, and

(iv) is not imprisoned under Federal, State, or local authority, and

(B) such month begins more than 90 days after the date of the enactment of the Trade Act of 2002 [90 days after 8/6/2002].

(2) Joint returns.—In the case of a joint return, the requirements of paragraph (1)(A) shall be treated as met with respect to any month if at least 1 spouse satisfies such requirements.

(c) Eligible individual.—For purposes of this section—

(1) In general.—The term "eligible individual" means—

(A) an eligible TAA recipient,

(B) an eligible alternative TAA recipient, and

(C) an eligible PBGC pension recipient.

(2) Eligible TAA recipient.—

(A) In general.—Except as provided in subparagraph (B), the term "eligible TAA recipient" means, with respect to any month, any individual who is receiving for any day of such month a trade readjustment allowance under chapter 2 of title II of the Trade Act of 1974 or who would be eligible to receive such allowance if section 231 of such Act were applied without regard to subsection (a)(3)(B) of such section. An individual shall continue to be treated as an eligible TAA recipient during the first month that such individual would otherwise cease to be an eligible TAA recipient by reason of the preceding sentence.

(B) Special rule.—In the case of any eligible coverage month beginning after the date of the enactment of this paragraph and before February 13, 2011, the term "eligible TAA recipient" means, with respect to any month, any individual who—

(i) is receiving for any day of such month a trade readjustment allowance under chapter 2 of title II of the Trade Act of 1974,

(ii) would be eligible to receive such allowance except that such individual is in a break in training provided under a training program approved under section 236 of such Act that exceeds the period specified in section 233(e) of such Act, but is within the period for receiving such allowances provided under section 233(a) of such Act, or

(iii) is receiving unemployment compensation (as defined in section 85(b)) for any day of such month and who would be eligible to receive such allowance for such month if section 231 of such Act were applied without regard to subsections (a)(3)(B) and (a)(5) thereof.

An individual shall continue to be treated as an eligible TAA recipient during the first month that such individual would otherwise cease to be an eligible TAA recipient by reason of the preceding sentence.

(3) Eligible alternative TAA recipient.—The term "eligible alternative TAA recipient" means, with respect to any month, any individual who—

(A) is a worker described in section 246(a)(3)(B) of the Trade Act of 1974 who is participating in the program established under section 246(a)(1) of such Act, and

(B) is receiving a benefit for such month under section 246(a)(2) of such Act.

An individual shall continue to be treated as an eligible alternative TAA recipient during the first month that such individual would otherwise cease to be an eligible alternative TAA recipient by reason of the preceding sentence.

(4) Eligible PBGC pension recipient.—The term "eligible PBGC pension recipient" means, with respect to any month, any individual who—

(A) has attained age 55 as of the first day of such month, and

(B) is receiving a benefit for such month any portion of which is paid by the Pension Benefit Guaranty Corporation under title IV of the Employee Retirement Income Security Act of 1974.

(d) Qualifying family member.—For purposes of this section—

(1) In general.—The term "qualifying family member" means—

(A) the taxpayer's spouse, and

(B) any dependent of the taxpayer with respect to whom the taxpayer is entitled to a deduction under section 151(c).

Such term does not include any individual who has other specified coverage.

(2) Special dependency test in case of divorced parents, etc.—If section 152(e) applies to any child with respect to any calendar year, in the case of any taxable year beginning in such calendar year, such child shall be treated as described in paragraph (1)(B) with respect to the custodial parent (as defined in section 152(e)(4)(A)) and not with respect to the noncustodial parent.

(e) Qualified health insurance.—For purposes of this section—

(1) In general.—The term "qualified health insurance" means any of the following:

(A) Coverage under a COBRA continuation provision (as defined in section 9832(d)(1)).

(B) State-based continuation coverage provided by the State under a State law that requires such coverage.

(C) Coverage offered through a qualified State high risk pool (as defined in section 2744 (c)(2) of the Public Health Service Act).

(D) Coverage under a health insurance program offered for State employees.

(E) Coverage under a State-based health insurance program that is comparable to the health insurance program offered for State employees.

(F) Coverage through an arrangement entered into by a State and—

(i) a group health plan (including such a plan which is a multiemployer plan as defined in section 3(37) of the Employee Retirement Income Security Act of 1974),

(ii) an issuer of health insurance coverage,

(iii) an administrator, or

(iv) an employer.

(G) Coverage offered through a State arrangement with a private sector health care coverage purchasing pool.

(H) Coverage under a State-operated health plan that does not receive any Federal financial participation.

(I) Coverage under a group health plan that is available through the employment of the eligible individual's spouse.

(J) In the case of any eligible individual and such individual's qualifying family members, coverage under individual health insurance if the eligible individual was covered under individual health insurance during the entire 30-day period that ends on the date that such individual became separated from the employment which qualified such an individual for—

(i) in the case of an eligible TAA recipient, the allowance described in subsection (c)(2),

(ii) in the case of an eligible alternative TAA recipient, the benefit described in subsection (c)(3)(B), or

(iii) in the case of any eligible PBGC pension recipient, the benefit described in subsection (c)(4)(B).

For purposes of this subparagraph, the term "individual health insurance" means any insurance which constitutes medical care offered to individuals other than in connection with a group health plan and does not include Federal or State-based health insurance coverage.

(K) In the case of eligible coverage months beginning before February 13, 2011, coverage under an employee benefit plan funded by a voluntary employees' beneficiary association (as defined in section 501(c)(9)) established pursuant to an order of a bankruptcy court, or by agreement with an authorized representative, as provided in section 1114 of title 11, United States Code.

(2) Requirements for State-based coverage.—

(A) In general.—The term "qualified health insurance" does not include any coverage described in subparagraphs (B) through (H) of paragraph (1) unless the State involved has elected to have such coverage treated as qualified health insurance under this section and such coverage meets the following requirements:

(i) Guaranteed issue.—Each qualifying individual is guaranteed enrollment if the individual pays the premium for enrollment or provides a qualified health insurance costs credit eligibility certificate described in section 7527 and pays the remainder of such premium.

(ii) No imposition of pre-existing condition exclusion. No pre-existing condition limitations are imposed with respect to any qualifying individual.

(iii) Nondiscriminatory premium. The total premium (as determined without regard to any subsidies) with respect to a qualifying individual may not be greater than the total premium (as so determined) for a similarly situated individual who is not a qualifying individual.

(iv) Same benefits. Benefits under the coverage are the same as (or substantially similar to) the benefits provided to similarly situated individuals who are not qualifying individuals.

(B) Qualifying individual.—For purposes of this paragraph, the term "qualifying individual" means—

(i) an eligible individual for whom, as of the date on which the individual seeks to enroll in the coverage described in subparagraphs (B) through (H) of paragraph (1), the aggregate of the periods of creditable coverage (as defined in section 9801(c)) is 3 months or longer and who, with respect to any month, meets the requirements of clauses (iii) and (iv) of subsection (b)(1)(A); and

(ii) the qualifying family members of such eligible individual.

(3) Exception.—The term "qualified health insurance" shall not include—

(A) a flexible spending or similar arrangement, and

(B) any insurance if substantially all of its coverage is of expected benefits described in section 9832(c).

(f) Other specified coverage.—For purposes of this section, an individual has other specified coverage for any month if, as of the first day of such month—

(1) Subsidized coverage.—

(A) In general.—Such individual is covered under any insurance which constitutes medical care (except insurance substantially all of the coverage of which is of expected benefits described in section 9832(c)) under any health plan maintained by any employer (or former employer) of the taxpayer or the taxpayer's spouse and at least 50 percent of the cost of such coverage (determined under section 4980B) is paid or incurred by the employer.

(B) Eligible alternative TAA recipients.—In the case of an eligible alternative TAA recipient, such an individual is either—

(i) eligible for coverage under any qualified health insurance (other than insurance described in subparagraph (A), (B), or (F) of subsection (e)(1)) under which at least 50 percent of the cost of coverage (determined under section 4980B(f)(4)) is paid or incurred by an employer (or former employer) of the taxpayer or the taxpayer's spouse, or

(ii) covered under any such qualified health insurance under which any portion of the cost of coverage (as so determined) is paid or incurred by an employer (or former employer) of the taxpayer or the taxpayer's spouse.

(C) Treatment of cafeteria plans.—For purposes of subparagraphs (A) and (B), the cost of coverage shall be treated as paid or incurred by an employer to the extent the coverage is in lieu of a right to receive cash or other qualified benefits under a cafeteria plan (as defined in section 125(d)).

(2) Coverage under Medicare, Medicaid, or SCHIP.—Such individual—

(A) is entitled to benefits under part A of title XVIII of the Social Security Act or is enrolled under part B of such title, or

(B) is enrolled in the program under title XIX or XXI of such Act (other than under section 1928 of such Act).

(3) Certain other coverage.—Such individual—

(A) is enrolled in a health benefits plan under chapter 89 of title 5, United States Code, or

(B) is entitled to receive benefits under chapter 55 of title 10, United States Code.

(g) Special rules.—

(1) Coordination with advance payments of credit.—With respect to any taxable year, the amount which would (but for this subsection) be allowed as a credit to the taxpayer under subsection (a) shall be reduced (but not below zero) by the aggregate amount paid on behalf of such taxpayer under section 7527 for months beginning in such taxable year.

(2) Coordination with other deductions.—Amounts taken into account under subsection (a) shall not be taken into account in determining any deduction allowed under section 162(1) or 213.

(3) Medical and health savings accounts.—Amounts distributed from an Archer MSA (as defined in section 220(d)) or from a health savings account (as defined in section 223(d)) shall not be taken into account under subsection (a).

(4) Denial of credit to dependents.—No credit shall be allowed under this section to any individual with respect to whom a deduction under section 151 is allowable to another taxpayer for a taxable year beginning in the calendar year in which such individual's taxable year begins.

(5) Both spouses eligible individuals.—The spouse of the taxpayer shall not be treated as a qualifying family member for purposes of subsection (a), if—

(A) the taxpayer is married at the close of the taxable year,

(B) the taxpayer and the taxpayer's spouse are both eligible individuals during the taxable year, and

(C) the taxpayer files a separate return for the taxable year.

(6) Marital status; certain married individuals living apart.—Rules similar to the rules of paragraphs (3) and (4) of subsection 21(e) shall apply for purposes of this section.

(7) Insurance which covers other individuals.—For purposes of this section, rules similar to the rules of section 213(d)(6) shall apply with respect to any contract for qualified health insurance under which amounts are payable for coverage of an individual rather than the taxpayer and qualifying family members.

(8) Treatment of payments.—For purposes of this section—

(A) Payments by Secretary. Payments made by the Secretary on behalf of any individual under section 7527 (relating to advance payment of credit for health insurance costs of eligible individuals) shall be treated as having been made by the taxpayer on the first day of the month for which such payment was made.

(B) Payments made by taxpayer. Payments made by the taxpayer for eligible coverage months shall be treated as having been made by the taxpayer on the first day of the month for which such payment was made.

(9) Continued qualification of family members after certain events.—In the case of eligible coverage months beginning before February 13, 2011—

(A) Medicare eligibility.—In the case of any month which would be an eligible coverage month with respect to an eligible individual but for subsection (f)(2)(A), such month shall be treated as an eligible coverage month with respect to such eligible individual solely for purposes of determining the amount of the credit under this section with respect to any qualifying family members of such individual (and any advance payment of such credit under section 7527). This subparagraph shall only apply with respect to the first 24 months after such eligible individual is first entitled to the benefits described in subsection (f)(2)(A).

(B) Divorce.—In the case of the finalization of a divorce between an eligible individual and such individual's spouse, such spouse shall be treated as an eligible individual for purposes of this section and section 7527 for a period of 24 months beginning with the date of such finalization, except that the only qualifying family members who may be taken into account with respect to such spouse are those individuals who were qualifying family members immediately before such finalization.

(C) Death.—In the case of the death of an eligible individual—

(i) any spouse of such individual (determined at the time of such death) shall be treated as an eligible individual for purposes of this section and section 7527 for a period of 24 months beginning with the date of such death, except that the only qualifying family members who may be taken into account with respect to such spouse are those individuals who were qualifying family members immediately before such death, and

(ii) any individual who was a qualifying family member of the decedent immediately before such death (or, in the case of an individual to whom paragraph (4) applies, the taxpayer to whom the deduction under section 151 is allowable) shall be treated as an eligible individual for purposes of this section and section 7527 for a period of 24 months beginning with the date of such death, except that in determining the amount of such credit only such qualifying family member may be taken into account.

(10) Regulations.—The Secretary may prescribe such regulations and other guidance as may be necessary or appropriate to carry out this section, section 6050T, and section 7527.

§ 36. First-time homebuyer credit*

(a) Allowance of credit.—In the case of an individual who is a first-time homebuyer of a principal residence in the United States during a taxable year, there shall be allowed as a credit against the tax imposed by this subtitle for such taxable year an amount equal to 10 percent of the purchase price of the residence.

(b) Limitations.—

(1) Dollar limitation.—

(A) In general.—Except as otherwise provided in this paragraph, the credit allowed under subsection (a) shall not exceed $8,000.

(B) Married individuals filing separately.—In the case of a married individual filing a

*Editorial comment: This credit applies only to principal residences purchased on or after April 9, 2008 and before May 1, 2010. See Sec. 36(h).

separate return, subparagraph (A) shall be applied by substituting "$4,000" for "$8,000".

(C) Other individuals.—If two or more individuals who are not married purchase a principal residence, the amount of credit allowed under subsection (a) shall be allocated among such individuals in such manner as the Secretary may prescribe, except that the total amount of the credits allowed to all such individuals shall not exceed $8,000.

(D) Special rule for long-time residents of same principal residence.—In the case of a taxpayer to whom a credit under subsection (a) is allowed by reason of subsection (c)(6), subparagraphs (A), (B), and (C) shall be applied by substituting "$6,500" for "$8,000" and "$3,250" for "$4,000".

(2) Limitation based on modified adjusted gross income.—

(A) In general.—The amount allowable as a credit under subsection (a) (determined without regard to this paragraph) for the taxable year shall be reduced (but not below zero) by the amount which bears the same ratio to the amount which is so allowable as—

(i) the excess (if any) of—

(I) the taxpayer's modified adjusted gross income for such taxable year, over

(II) $125,000 ($225,000 in the case of a joint return), bears to

(ii) $20,000.

(B) Modified adjusted gross income.—For purposes of subparagraph (A), the term "modified adjusted gross income" means the adjusted gross income of the taxpayer for the taxable year increased by any amount excluded from gross income under section 911, 931, or 933.

(3) Limitation based on purchase price.—No credit shall be allowed under subsection (a) for the purchase of any residence if the purchase price of such residence exceeds $800,000.

(4) Age limitation.—No credit shall be allowed under subsection (a) with respect to the purchase of any residence unless the taxpayer has attained age 18 as of the date of such purchase. In the case of any taxpayer who is married (within the meaning of section 7703), the taxpayer shall be treated as meeting the age requirement of the preceding sentence if the taxpayer or the taxpayer's spouse meets such age requirement.

(c) Definitions.—For the purpose of this section—

(1) First-time homebuyer.—The term "first-time homebuyer" means any individual if such individual (and if married, such individual's spouse) had no present ownership interest in a principal residence during the 3-year period ending on the date of the purchase of the principal residence to which this section applies.

(2) Principal residence.—The term "principal residence" has the same meaning as when used in section 121.

(3) Purchase.—

(A) In general.—The term "purchase" means any acquisition, but only if—

(i) the property is not acquired from a person related to the person acquiring such property (or, if married, such individual's spouse), and

(ii) the basis of the property in the hands of the person acquiring such property is not determined—

(I) in whole or in part by reference to the adjusted basis of such property in the hands of the person from whom acquired, or

(II) under section 1014(a) (relating to property acquired from a decedent).

(B) Construction.—A residence which is constructed by the taxpayer shall be treated as purchased by the taxpayer on the date the taxpayer first occupies such residence.

(4) Purchase price.—The term "purchase price" means the adjusted basis of the principal residence on the date such residence is purchased.

(5) Related persons.—A person shall be treated as related to another person if the relationship between such persons would result in the disallowance of losses under section 267 or 707(b) (but, in applying section 267(b) and (c) for purposes of this section, paragraph (4) of section 267(c) shall be treated as providing that the family of an individual shall include only his spouse, ancestors, and lineal descendants).

(6) Exception for long-time residents of same principal residence.—In the case of an individual (and, if married, such individual's spouse) who has owned and used the same residence as such individual's principal residence for any 5-consecutive-year period during the 8-year period ending on the date of the purchase of a subsequent principal residence, such individual shall be treated as a first-time homebuyer for purposes of this section with respect to the purchase of such subsequent residence.

(d) Exceptions.—No credit under subsection (a) shall be allowed to any taxpayer for any taxable year with respect to the purchase of a residence if—

(1) the taxpayer is a nonresident alien,

(2) the taxpayer disposes of such residence (or such residence ceases to be the principal residence of the taxpayer (and, if married, the taxpayer's spouse)) before the close of such taxable year,

(3) a deduction under section 151 with respect to such taxpayer is allowable to another taxpayer for such taxable year, or

(4) the taxpayer fails to attach to the return of tax for such taxable year a properly executed copy of the settlement statement used to complete such purchase.

(e) Reporting.—If the Secretary requires information reporting under section 6045 by a person described in subsection (e)(2) thereof to verify the eligibility of taxpayers for the credit allowable by this section, the exception provided by section 6045 (e) shall not apply.

(f) Recapture of credit.—

(1) In general.—Except as otherwise provided in this subsection, if a credit under subsection (a) is allowed to a taxpayer, the tax imposed by this chapter shall be increased by 6 2/3 percent of the amount of such credit for each taxable year in the recapture period.

(2) Acceleration of recapture. — If a taxpayer disposes of the principal residence with respect to which a credit was allowed under subsection (a) (or such residence ceases to be the principal residence of the taxpayer (and, if married, the taxpayer's spouse)) before the end of the recapture period—

(A) the tax imposed by this chapter for the taxable year of such disposition or cessation shall be increased by the excess of the amount of the credit allowed over the amounts of tax imposed by paragraph (1) for preceding taxable years, and

(B) paragraph (1) shall not apply with respect to such credit for such taxable year or any subsequent taxable year.

(3) Limitation based on gain.—In the case of the sale of the principal residence to a person who is not related to the taxpayer, the increase in tax determined under paragraph (2) shall not exceed the amount of gain (if any) on such sale. Solely for the purposes of the preceding sentence, the adjusted basis of such residence shall be reduced by the amount of the credit allowed under subsection (a) to the extent not previously recaptured under paragraph (1).

(4) Exceptions.—

(A) Death of a taxpayer.—Paragraphs (1) and (2) shall not apply to any taxable year ending after the date of the taxpayer's death.

(B) Involuntary conversion.—Paragraph (2) shall not apply in the case of a residence which is compulsorily or involuntarily converted (within the meaning of section 1033(a) if the taxpayer acquires a new principal residence during the 2-year period beginning on the date of the disposition or cessation referred to in paragraph (2). Paragraph (2) shall apply to such new principal residence during the recapture period in the same manner as if such new principal residence were the converted residence.

(C) Transfers between spouses or incident to divorce.—In the case of a transfer of a residence to which section 1041(a) applies—

(i) paragraph (2) shall not apply to such transfer, and

(ii) in the case of taxable years ending after such transfer, paragraphs (1) and (2) shall apply to the transferee in the same manner as if such transferee were the transferor (and shall not apply to the transferor).

(D) Waiver of recapture for purchases in 2009 and 2010.—In the case of any credit allowed with respect to the purchase of a principal residence after December 31, 2008—

(i) paragraph (1) shall not apply, and

(ii) paragraph (2) shall not apply only if the disposition or cessation described in paragraph (2) with respect to such residence occurs during the 36-month period beginning on the date of the purchase of such residence by the taxpayer.

(E) Special rule for members of the armed forces, etc.—

(i) In general. In the case of the disposition of a principal residence by an individual (or a cessation referred to in paragraph (2)) after December 31, 2008, in connection with Government orders received by such individual, or such individual's spouse, for qualified official extended duty service—

(I) paragraph (2) and subsection (d)(2) shall not apply to such disposition (or cessation), and

(II) if such residence was acquired before January 1, 2009, paragraph (1) shall not apply to the taxable year in which such disposition (or cessation) occurs or any subsequent taxable year.

(ii) Qualified official extended duty service. For purposes of this section, the term "qualified official extended duty service" means service on qualified official extended duty as—

(I) a member of the uniformed services,

(II) a member of the Foreign Service of the United States, or

(III) an employee of the intelligence community.

(iii) Definitions. Any term used in this subparagraph which is also used in paragraph (9) of section 121(d) shall have the same meaning as when used in such paragraph.

(5) Joint returns.—In the case of a credit allowed under subsection (a) with respect to a joint return, half of such credit shall be treated as having been allowed to each individual filing such return for purposes of this subsection.

(6) Return requirement.—If the tax imposed by this chapter for the taxable year is increased under this subsection, the taxpayer shall, notwithstanding section 6012, be required to file a return with respect to the taxes imposed under this subtitle.

(7) Recapture period.—For purposes of this subsection, the term "recapture period" means the 15 taxable years beginning with the second taxable year following the taxable year in which the purchase of the principal residence for which a credit is allowed under subsection (a) was made.

(g) Election to treat purchase in prior year.—In the case of a purchase of a principal residence after December 31, 2008, a taxpayer may elect to treat such purchase as made on December 31 of the calendar year preceding such purchase for purposes of this section (other than subsections (b)(4), (c), (f)(4)(D), and (h)).

(h) Application of section.—

(1) In general.—This section shall only apply to a principal residence purchased by the taxpayer on or after April 9, 2008, and before May 1, 2010.

(2) Exception in case of binding contract.—In the case of any taxpayer who enters into a written binding contract before May 1, 2010, to close on the purchase of a principal residence before July 1, 2010, paragraph (1) shall be applied by substituting "July 1, 2010" for "May 1, 2010".

(3) Special rule for individuals on qualified official extended duty outside of the United States.—In the case of any individual who serves on qualified official extended duty service (as defined in section 121(d)(9)(C)(i)) outside of the United States for at least 90 days during the period beginning after December 31, 2008, and ending before May 1, 2010, and if married, such individual's spouse—

(A) paragraphs (1) and (2) shall each be applied by substituting "May 1, 2011" for "May 1, 2010", and

(B) paragraph (2) shall be applied by substituting "July 1, 2011" for "July 1, 2010".

§ 36A. Making work pay credit*

(a) Allowance of credit.—In the case of an eligible individual, there shall be allowed as a credit against the tax imposed by this subtitle for the taxable year an amount equal to the lesser of—

(1) 6.2 percent of earned income of the taxpayer, or

(2) $400 ($800 in the case of a joint return).

(b) Limitation based on modified adjusted gross income.—

(1) In general.—The amount allowable as a credit under subsection (a) (determined without regard to this paragraph and subsection (c)) for the taxable year shall be reduced (but not below zero) by 2 percent of so much of the taxpayer's modified adjusted gross income as exceeds $75,000 ($150,000 in the case of a joint return).

(2) Modified adjusted gross income.—For purposes of subparagraph (A), the term "modified adjusted gross income" means the adjusted gross income of the taxpayer for the taxable year increased by any amount excluded from gross income under section 911, 931, or 933.

(c) Reduction for certain other payments.—The credit allowed under subsection (a) for any taxable year shall be reduced by the amount of any

*Editorial comment: This credit shall not apply to taxable years beginning after December 31, 2010. See Sec. 36A(e).

payments received by the taxpayer during such taxable year under section 2201, or any credit allowed to the taxpayer under section 2202, of the American Recovery and Reinvestment Tax Act of 2009.

(d) Definitions and special rules.—For purposes of this section—

(1) Eligible individual.—

(A) In general.—The term "eligible individual" means any individual other than—

(i) any nonresident alien individual,

(ii) any individual with respect to whom a deduction under section 151 is allowable to another taxpayer for a taxable year beginning in the calendar year in which the individual's taxable year begins, and

(iii) an estate or trust.

(B) Identification number requirement.—Such term shall not include any individual who does not include on the return of tax for the taxable year—

(i) such individual's social security account number, and

(ii) in the case of a joint return, the social security account number of one of the taxpayers on such return.

For purposes of the preceding sentence, the social security account number shall not include a TIN issued by the Internal Revenue Service.

(2) Earned income.—The term "earned income" has the meaning given such term by section 32(c)(2), except that such term shall not include net earnings from self-employment which are not taken into account in computing taxable income. For purposes of the preceding sentence, any amount excluded from gross income by reason of section 112 shall be treated as earned income which is taken into account in computing taxable income for the taxable year.

(e) Termination.—This section shall not apply to taxable years beginning after December 31, 2010.

* * *

§ 36C. Adoption expenses*

* * *

§ 37. Overpayments of tax

For credit against the tax imposed by this subtitle for overpayments of tax, see section 6401.

SUBPART D—BUSINESS RELATED CREDITS

§ 38. General business credit

(a) Allowance of credit.—There shall be allowed as a credit against the tax imposed by this chapter for the taxable year an amount equal to the sum of—

(1) the business credit carryforwards carried to such taxable year,

(2) the amount of the current year business credit, plus

(3) the business credit carrybacks carried to such taxable year.

(b) Current year business credit.—For purposes of this subpart, the amount of the current year business credit is the sum of the following credits determined for the taxable year:

(1) the investment credit determined under section 46,

(2) work opportunity credit determined under section 51(a),

(3) the alcohol fuels credit determined under section 40(a),

(4) the research credit determined under section 41(a),

(5) the low-income housing credit determined under section 42(a),

(6) the enhanced oil recovery credit under section 43(a),

(7) in the case of an eligible small business (as defined in section 44(b)), the disabled access credit determined under section 44(a),

(8) the renewable electricity production credit under section 45(a),

(9) the empowerment zone employment credit determined under section 1396(a),

*Editorial comment: For tax years beginning after December 31, 2011, section 36C is redesignated as section 23.

(10) the Indian employment credit as determined under section 45A(a),

(11) the employer social security credit determined under section 45B(a), plus

(12) the orphan drug credit determined under section 45C(a),

(13) the new markets tax credit determined under section 45D(a).

(14) in the case of an eligible employer (as defined in section 45E(c)), the small employer pension plan startup cost credit determined under section 45E(a),

(15) the employer-provided child care credit determined under section 45F(a),

(16) the railroad track maintenance credit determined under section 45G(a),

(17) the biodiesel fuels credit determined under section 40A(a),

(18) the low sulfur diesel fuel production credit determined under section 45H(a),

(19) the marginal oil and gas well production credit determined under section 45I(a),

(20) the distilled spirits credit determined under section 5011(a),

(21) the advanced nuclear power facility productions credit determined under section 45J(a),

(22) the nonconventional source production credit determined under section 45K(a),

(23) the new energy efficient home credit determined under section 45L(a),

(24) the energy efficient appliance credit determined under section 45M(a),

(25) the portion of the alternative motor vehicle credit to which section 30B(g)(1) applies,

(26) the portion of the alternative fuel vehicle refueling property credit to which section 30C(d)(1) applies,

(27) the Hurricane Katrina housing credit determined under section 1400P(b),

(28) the Hurricane Katrina employee retention credit determined under section 1400R(a),

(29) the Hurricane Rita employee retention credit determined under section 1400R(b),

(30) the Hurricane Wilma employee retention credit determined under section 1400R(c),

(31) the mine rescue team training credit determined under Section 45N(a),

(32) in the case of an eligible agricultural business [as defined in section 45O(e)], the agricultural chemicals security credit determined under section 45O(a),

(33) the differential wage payment credit determined under section 45P(a),

(34) the carbon dioxide sequestration credit determined under section 45Q(a),

(35) the portion of the new qualified plug-in electric drive motor vehicle credit to which section 30D(c)(1) applies, plus

(36) the small employer health insurance credit determined under section 45R.

(c) Limitation based on amount of tax.—

(1) In general.—The credit allowed under subsection (a) for any taxable year shall not exceed the excess (if any) of the taxpayer's net income tax over the greater of—

(A) the tentative minimum tax for the taxable year, or

(B) 25 percent of so much of the taxpayer's net regular tax liability as exceeds $25,000.

For purposes of the preceding sentence, the term "net income tax" means the sum of the regular tax liability and the tax imposed by section 55, reduced by the credits allowable under subparts A and B of this part, and the term "net regular tax liability" means the regular tax liability reduced by the sum of the credits allowable under subparts A and B of this part.

(2) Empowerment zone employment credit may offset 25 percent of minimum tax.—

(A) In general.—In the case of the empowerment zone employment credit—

(i) this section and section 39 shall be applied separately with respect to such credit, and

(ii) for purposes of applying paragraph (1) to such credit—

(I) 75 percent of the tentative minimum tax shall be substituted for the tentative minimum tax under subparagraph (A) thereof, and

(II) the limitation under paragraph (1) (as modified by subclause (I)) shall be reduced by the credit allowed under subsection (a) for the taxable year (other than the empowerment zone employment credit, the New York Liberty Zone business employee credit, the eligible small business credits, and the specified credits).

(B) Empowerment zone employment credit.—For purposes of this paragraph, the term "empowerment zone employment credit" means the portion of the credit under subsection (a) which is attributable to the credit determined under section 1396 (relating to empowerment zone employment credit).

(3) Special rules for New York Liberty Zone business employee credit.—

(A) In general.—In the case of the New York Liberty Zone business employee credit—

(i) this section and section 39 shall be applied separately with respect to such credit, and

(ii) in applying paragraph (1) to such credit—

(I) the tentative minimum tax shall be treated as being zero, and

(II) the limitation under paragraph (1) (as modified by subclause (I)) shall be reduced by the credit allowed under subsection (a) for the taxable year (other than the New York Liberty Zone business employee credit, the eligible small business credits, and the specified credits).

(B) New York Liberty Zone business employee credit.—For purposes of this subsection, the term "New York Liberty Zone business employee credit" means the portion of work opportunity credit under section 51 determined under section 1400L(a).

(4) Special rules for specified credits.—

(A) In general.—In the case of specified credits—

(i) this section and section 39 shall be applied separately with respect to such credits, and

(ii) in applying paragraph (1) to such credits—

(I) the tentative minimum tax shall be treated as being zero, and

(II) the limitation under paragraph (1) (as modified by subclause (I)) shall be reduced by the credit allowed under subsection (a) for the taxable year (other than the eligible small business credits and the specified credits).

(B) Specified credits.—For purposes of this subsection, the term "specified credits" means—

(i) for taxable years beginning after December 31, 2004, the credit determined under section 40,

(ii) the credit determined under section 42 to the extent attributable to buildings placed in service after December 31, 2007,

(iii) the credit determined under section 45 to the extent that such credit is attributable to electricity or refined coal produced—

(I) at a facility which is originally placed in service after the date of the enactment of this paragraph, and

(II) during the 4-year period beginning on the date that such facility was originally placed in service,

(iv) the credit determined under section 45B,

(v) the credit determined under section 45G,

(vi) the credit determined under section 45R,

(vii) the credit determined under section 46 to the extent that such credit is attributable to the energy credit determined under section 48,

(viii) the credit determined under section 46 to the extent that such credit is attributable to the rehabilitation credit under section 47, but only with respect to qualified rehabilitation expenditures properly taken into account for periods after December 31, 2007, and

(ix) the credit determined under section 51.

* * *

(6) Special rules.—

(A) Married individuals.—In the case of a husband or wife who files a separate return, the amount specified under subparagraph (B) of paragraph (1) shall be $12,500 in lieu of $25,000. This subparagraph shall not apply if the spouse of the taxpayer has no business credit carryforward or carryback to, and has no current year business credit for, the taxable year of such spouse which ends within or with the taxpayer's taxable year.

(B) Controlled groups.—In the case of a controlled group, the $25,000 amount specified under subparagraph (B) of paragraph (1) shall be reduced for each component member of such group by apportioning $25,000 among the component members of such group in such manner as the Secretary shall by regulations prescribe. For purposes of the preceding sentence, the term "controlled group" has the meaning given to such term by section 1563(a).

(C) Limitations with respect to certain persons.—In the case of a person described in subparagraph (A) or (B) of section 46(e)(1) (as in effect on the day before the date of the enactment of the Revenue Reconciliation Act of 1990), the $25,000 amount specified under subparagraph (B) of paragraph (1) shall equal such person's ratable share (as determined under section 46(e)(2) (as so in effect)) of such amount.

(D) Estates and trusts.—In the case of an estate or trust, the $25,000 amount specified under subparagraph (B) of paragraph (1) shall be reduced to an amount which bears the same ratio to $25,000 as the portion of the income of the estate or trust which is not allocated to beneficiaries bears to the total income of the estate or trust.

(d) Ordering rules.—For purposes of any other provision of this title where it is necessary to ascertain the extent to which the credits determined under any section referred to in subsection (b) are used in a taxable year or as a carryback or carryforward—

(1) In general.—The order in which such credits are used shall be determined on the basis of the order in which they are listed in subsection (b) as of the close of the taxable year in which the credit is used.

(2) Components of investment credit.—The order in which the credits listed in section 46 are used shall be determined on the basis of the order in which such credits are listed in section 46 as of the close of the taxable year in which the credit is used.

(3) Credits no longer listed.—For purposes of this subsection—

(A) the credit allowable by section 40, as in effect on the day before the date of the enactment of the Tax Reform Act of 1984, (relating to expenses of work incentive programs) and the credit allowable by section 41(a), as in effect on the day before the date of the enactment of the Tax Reform Act of 1986, (relating to employee stock ownership credit) shall be treated as referred to in that order after the last paragraph of subsection (b), and

(B) the credit determined under section 46—

(i) to the extent attributable to the employee plan percentage (as defined in section 46(a)(2)(E) as in effect on the day before the date of the enactment of the Tax Reform Act of 1984) shall be treated as a credit listed under paragraph (1) of section 46, and

(ii) to the extent attributable to the regular percentage (as defined in section 46(b)(1) as in effect on the day before the date of the enactment of the Revenue Reconciliation Act of 1990) shall be treated as the first credit listed in section 46.

§ 39. Carryback and carryforward of unused credits

(a) In general.—

(1) 1-year carryback and 20-year carryforward.—If the sum of the business credit carry-forwards to the taxable year plus the amount of the current year business credit for the taxable year exceeds the amount of the limitation imposed by subsection (c) of section 38 for such taxable year (hereinafter in this section referred to as the "unused credit year"), such excess (to the extent attributable to the amount of the current year business credit) shall be—

(A) a business credit carryback to the taxable year preceding the unused credit year, and

(B) a business credit carryforward to each of the 20 taxable years following the unused credit year,

and, subject to the limitations imposed by subsections (b) and (c), shall be taken into account under the provisions of section 38(a) in the manner provided in section 38(a).

(2) Amount carried to each year.—

(A) Entire amount carried to first year.—The entire amount of the unused credit for an unused credit year shall be carried to the earliest of the 21 taxable years to which (by reason of paragraph (1)) such credit may be carried.

(B) Amount carried to other 20 years.—The amount of the unused credit for the unused credit year shall be carried to each of the other 20 taxable years to the extent that such unused credit may not be taken into account under section 38(a) for a prior taxable year because of the limitations of subsections (b) and (c).

(3) 5-year carryback for marginal oil and gas well production credit.—Notwithstanding subsection (d), in the case of the marginal oil and gas well production credit—

(A) this section shall be applied separately from the business credit (other than the marginal oil and gas well production credit or the eligible small business credits),

(B) paragraph (1) shall be applied by substituting "5 taxable years" for "the taxable year" in subparagraph (A) thereof, and

(C) paragraph (2) shall be applied—

(i) by substituting "25 taxable years" for "21 taxable years" in subparagraph (A) thereof, and

(ii) by substituting "24 taxable years" for "20 taxable years" in subparagraph (B) thereof.

(4) 5-year carryback for eligible small business credits.—

(A) In general.—Notwithstanding subsection (d), in the case of eligible small business credits determined in the first taxable year of the taxpayer beginning in 2010—

(i) paragraph (1) shall be applied by substituting "each of the 5 taxable years" for "the taxable year" in subparagraph (A) thereof, and

(ii) paragraph (2) shall be applied—

(I) by substituting "25 taxable years" for "21 taxable years" in subparagraph (A) thereof, and

(II) by substituting "24 taxable years" for "20 taxable years" in subparagraph (B) thereof.

(B) Eligible small business credits.—For purposes of this subsection, the term "eligible small business credits" has the meaning given such term by section 38(c)(5)(B).

(b) Limitation on carrybacks.—The amount of the unused credit which may be taken into account under section 38(a)(3) for any preceding taxable year shall not exceed the amount by which the limitation imposed by section 38(c) for such taxable year exceeds the sum of—

(1) the amounts determined under paragraphs (1) and (2) of section 38(a) for such taxable year, plus

(2) the amounts which (by reason of this section) are carried back to such taxable year and are attributable to taxable years preceding the unused credit year.

(c) Limitation on carryforwards.—The amount of the unused credit which may be taken into account under section 38(a)(1) for any succeeding taxable year shall not exceed the amount by which the limitation imposed by section 38(c) for such taxable year exceeds the sum of the amounts which, by reason of this section, are carried to such taxable year and are attributable to taxable years preceding the unused credit year.

(d) Transitional rule.—No portion of the unused business credit for any taxable year which is attributable to a credit specified in section 38(b) or any portion thereof may be carried back to any taxable year before the first taxable year for which such specified credit or such portion is allowable (without regard to subsection (a)).

* * *

§ 41. Credit for increasing research activities*

(a) General rule.—For purposes of section 38, the research credit determined under this section for the taxable year shall be an amount equal to the sum of—

(1) 20 percent of the excess (if any) of—

(A) the qualified research expenses for the taxable year, over

(B) the base amount, and

(2) 20 percent of the basic research payments determined under subsection (e)(1)(A), and

(3) 20 percent of the amounts paid or incurred by the taxpayer in carrying on any trade or business of the taxpayer during the taxable year (including as contributions) to an energy research consortium for energy research.

(b) Qualified research expenses.—For purposes of this section—

(1) Qualified research expenses.—The term "qualified research expenses" means the sum of the following amounts which are paid or incurred by the taxpayer during the taxable year in carrying on any trade or business of the taxpayer—

(A) in-house research expenses, and

(B) contract research expenses.

(2) In-house research expenses.—

(A) In general.—The term "in-house research expenses" means—

(i) any wages paid or incurred to an employee for qualified services performed by such employee,

*Editorial comment: This credit does not apply to any amount paid or incurred after June 30, 1995 and before July 1, 1996, or after December 31, 2013. At the present time, this section has not been extended. There is pending legislation in the Senate, *The Tax Extenders Act of 2013 (S. 1859)*, that would extend Section 41(h)(1) until after December 31, 2014.

(ii) any amount paid or incurred for supplies used in the conduct of qualified research, and

(iii) under regulations prescribed by the Secretary, any amount paid or incurred to another person for the right to use computers in the conduct of qualified research.

Clause (iii) shall not apply to any amount to the extent that the taxpayer (or any person with whom the taxpayer must aggregate expenditures under subsection (f)(1)) receives or accrues any amount from any other person for the right to use substantially identical personal property.

(B) Qualified services.—The term "qualified services" means services consisting of—

(i) engaging in qualified research, or

(ii) engaging in the direct supervision or direct support of research activities which constitute qualified research.

If substantially all of the services performed by an individual for the taxpayer during the taxable year consists of services meeting the requirements of clause (i) or (ii), the term "qualified services" means all of the services performed by such individual for the taxpayer during the taxable year.

(C) Supplies.—The term "supplies" means any tangible property other than—

(i) land or improvements to land, and

(ii) property of a character subject to the allowance for depreciation.

(D) Wages.—

(i) In general.—The term "wages" has the meaning given such term by section 3401(a).

(ii) Self-employed individuals and owner-employees.—In the case of an employee (within the meaning of section 401(c) (1)), the term "wages" includes the earned income (as defined in section 401(c) (2)) of such employee.

(iii) Exclusion for wages to which work opportunity credit applies.—The term "wages" shall not include any amount taken into account in determining the work opportunity credit under section 51(a).

(3) Contract research expenses.—

(A) In general.—The term "contract research expenses" means 65 percent of any amount paid or incurred by the taxpayer to any person (other than an employee of the taxpayer) for qualified research.

(B) Prepaid amounts.—If any contract research expenses paid or incurred during any taxable year are attributable to qualified research to be conducted after the close of such taxable year, such amount shall be treated as paid or incurred during the period during which the qualified research is conducted.

(C) Amounts paid to certain research consortia.—

(i) In general.—Subparagraph (A) shall be applied by substituting "75 percent" for "65 percent" with respect to amounts paid or incurred by the taxpayer to a qualified research consortium for qualified research on behalf of the taxpayer and 1 or more unrelated taxpayers. For purposes of the preceding sentence, all persons treated as a single employer under subsection (a) or (b) of section 52 shall be treated as related taxpayers.

(ii) Qualified research consortium.—The term "qualified research consortium" means any organization which—

(I) is described in section 501(c)(3) or 501(c)(6) and is exempt from tax under section 501(a),

(II) is organized and operated primarily to conduct scientific research, and

(III) is not a private foundation.

(D) Amounts paid to eligible small businesses, universities, and federal laboratories.—

(i) In general.—In the case of amounts paid by the taxpayer to—

(I) an eligible small business,

(II) an institution of higher education (as defined in section 3304(f)), or

(III) an organization which is a Federal laboratory,

for qualified research which is energy research, subparagraph (A) shall be applied by substituting "100 percent" for "65 percent".

(ii) Eligible small business.—For purposes of this subparagraph, the term "eligible small business" means a small business with respect to which the taxpayer does not own (within the meaning of section 318) 50 percent or more of—

(I) in the case of a corporation, the outstanding stock of the corporation (either by vote or value), and

(II) in the case of a small business which is not a corporation, the capital and profits interests of the small business.

(iii) Small business.—For purposes of this subparagraph—

(I) In general.—The term "small business" means, with respect to any calendar year, any person if the annual average number of employees employed by such person during either of the 2 preceding calendar years was 500 or fewer. For purposes of the preceding sentence, a preceding calendar year may be taken into account only if the person was in existence throughout the year.

(II) Startups, controlled groups, and predecessors.—Rules similar to the rules of subparagraphs (B) and (D) of section 220(c)(4) shall apply for purposes of this clause.

(iv) Federal laboratory.—For purposes of this subparagraph, the term "Federal laboratory" has the meaning given such term by section 4(6) of the Stevenson-Wydler Technology Innovation Act of 1980 (15 U.S.C. 3703(6)), as in effect on the date of the enactment of the Energy Tax Incentives Act of 2005.

(4) Trade or business requirement disregarded for in-house research expenses of certain startup ventures.—In the case of in-house research expenses, a taxpayer shall be treated as meeting the trade or business requirement of paragraph (1) if, at the time such in-house research expenses are paid or incurred, the principal purpose of the taxpayer in making such expenditures is to use the results of the research in the active conduct of a future trade or business—

(A) of the taxpayer, or

(B) of 1 or more other persons who with the taxpayer are treated as a single taxpayer under subsection (f)(1).

(c) Base amount.—For purposes of this section—

(1) In general.—The term "base amount" means the product of—

(A) the fixed-base percentage, and

(B) the average annual gross receipts of the taxpayer for the 4 taxable years preceding the taxable year for which the credit is being determined (hereinafter in this subsection referred to as the "credit year").

(2) Minimum base amount.—In no event shall the base amount be less than 50 percent of the qualified research expenses for the credit year.

(3) Fixed-base percentage.—

(A) In general.—Except as otherwise provided in this paragraph, the fixed-base percentage is the percentage which the aggregate qualified research expenses of the taxpayer for taxable years beginning after December 31, 1983, and before January 1, 1989, is of the aggregate gross receipts of the taxpayer for such taxable years.

(B) Start-up companies.—

(i) Taxpayers to which subparagraph applies.—The fixed-base percentage shall be determined under this subparagraph if—

(I) the first taxable year in which a taxpayer had both gross receipts and qualified research expenses begins after December 31, 1983, or

(II) there are fewer than 3 taxable years beginning after December 31, 1983, and before January 1, 1989, in which the taxpayer had both gross receipts and qualified research expenses.

(ii) Fixed-base percentage.—In a case to which this subparagraph applies, the fixed-base percentage is—

(I) 3 percent for each of the taxpayer's 1st 5 taxable years beginning after December 31, 1993, for which the taxpayer has qualified research expenses,

(II) in the case of the taxpayer's 6th such taxable year, $1/6$ of the percentage which the aggregate qualified research expenses of the taxpayer for the 4th and 5th such taxable years is of the aggregate gross receipts of the taxpayer for such years,

(III) in the case of the taxpayer's 7th such taxable year, $1/3$ of the percentage which the aggregate qualified research expenses of the taxpayer for the 5th and 6th such taxable years is of the aggregate gross receipts of the taxpayer for such years,

(IV) in the case of the taxpayer's 8th such taxable year, ½ of the percentage which the aggregate qualified research expenses of the taxpayer for the 5th, 6th, and 7th such taxable years is of the aggregate gross receipts of the taxpayer for such years,

(V) in the case of the taxpayer's 9th such taxable year, 2/3 of the percentage which the aggregate qualified research expenses of the taxpayer for the 5th, 6th, 7th, and 8th such taxable years is of the aggregate gross receipts of the taxpayer for such years,

(VI) in the case of the taxpayer's 10th such taxable year, 5/6 of the percentage which the aggregate qualified research expenses of the taxpayer for the 5th, 6th, 7th, 8th, and 9th such taxable years is of the aggregate gross receipts of the taxpayer for such years, and

(VII) for taxable years thereafter, the percentage which the aggregate qualified research expenses for any 5 taxable years selected by the taxpayer from among the 5th through the 10th such taxable years is of the aggregate gross receipts of the taxpayer for such selected years.

(iii) Treatment of de minimis amounts of gross receipts and qualified research expenses.—The Secretary may prescribe regulations providing that de minimis amounts of gross receipts and qualified research expenses shall be disregarded under clauses (i) and (ii).

(C) Maximum fixed-base percentage.—In no event shall the fixed-base percentage exceed 16 percent.

(D) Rounding.—The percentages determined under subparagraphs (A) and (B)(ii) shall be rounded to the nearest 1/100th of 1 percent.

(4) Election of alternative incremental credit.—

(A) In general.—At the election of the taxpayer, the credit determined under subsection (a)(1) shall be equal to the sum of—

(i) 3 percent of so much of the qualified research expenses for the taxable year as exceeds 1 percent of the average described in subsection (c)(1)(B) but does not exceed 1.5 percent of such average,

(ii) 4 percent of so much of such expenses as exceeds 1.5 percent of such average but does not exceed 2 percent of such average, and

(iii) 5 percent of so much of such expenses as exceeds 2 percent of such average.

(B) Election.—An election under this paragraph shall apply to the taxable year for which made and all succeeding taxable years unless revoked with the consent of the Secretary.

(5) Election of alternative simplified credit.—

(A) In general.—At the election of the taxpayer, the credit determined under subsection (a)(1) shall be equal to 14 percent (12 percent in the case of taxable years ending before January 1, 2009) of so much of the qualified research expenses for the taxable year as exceeds 50 percent of the average qualified research expenses for the 3 taxable years preceding the taxable year for which the credit is being determined.

(B) Special rule in case of no qualified research expenses in any of 3 preceding taxable years.—

(i) Taxpayers to which subparagraph applies.—The credit under this paragraph shall be determined under this subparagraph if the taxpayer has no qualified research expenses in any one of the 3 taxable years preceding the taxable year for which the credit is being determined.

(ii) Credit rate.—The credit determined under this subparagraph shall be equal to 6 percent of the qualified research expenses for the taxable year.

(C) Election.—An election under this paragraph shall apply to the taxable year for which made and all succeeding taxable years unless revoked with the consent of the Secretary. An election under this paragraph may not be made for any taxable year to which an election under paragraph (4) applies.

(6) Consistent treatment of expenses required.—

(A) In general.—Notwithstanding whether the period for filing a claim for credit or refund has expired for any taxable year taken into account in determining the fixed-base percentage, the qualified research expenses taken into account in computing such percentage shall be determined on a basis consistent with the determination of qualified research expenses for the credit year.

(B) Prevention of distortions.—The Secretary may prescribe regulations to prevent distortions in calculating a taxpayer's qualified research expenses or gross receipts caused by a change in accounting methods used by such taxpayer between the current year and a year taken into account in computing such taxpayer's fixed-base percentage.

(7) Gross receipts.—For purposes of this subsection, gross receipts for any taxable year shall be reduced by returns and allowances made during the taxable year. In the case of a foreign corporation, there shall be taken into account only gross receipts which are effectively connected with the conduct of a trade or business within the United States, the Commonwealth of Puerto Rico, or any possession of the United States.

(d) Qualified research defined.—For purposes of this section—

(1) In general.—The term "qualified research" means research—

(A) with respect to which expenditures may be treated as expenses under section 174,

(B) which is undertaken for the purpose of discovering information—

(i) which is technological in nature, and

(ii) the application of which is intended to be useful in the development of a new or improved business component of the taxpayer, and

(C) substantially all of the activities of which constitute elements of a process of experimentation for a purpose described in paragraph (3).

Such term does not include any activity described in paragraph (4).

(2) Tests to be applied separately to each business component.—For purposes of this subsection—

(A) In general.—Paragraph (1) shall be applied separately with respect to each business component of the taxpayer.

(B) Business component defined.—The term "business component" means any product, process, computer software, technique, formula, or invention which is to be—

(i) held for sale, lease, or license, or

(ii) used by the taxpayer in a trade or business of the taxpayer.

(C) Special rule for production processes.—Any plant process, machinery, or technique for commercial production of a business component shall be treated as a separate business component (and not as part of the business component being produced).

(3) Purposes for which research may qualify for credit.—For purposes of paragraph (1)(C)—

(A) In general.—Research shall be treated as conducted for a purpose described in this paragraph if it relates to—

(i) a new or improved function,

(ii) performance, or

(iii) reliability or quality.

(B) Certain purposes not qualified.—Research shall in no event be treated as conducted for a purpose described in this paragraph if it relates to style, taste, cosmetic, or seasonal design factors.

(4) Activities for which credit not allowed.—The term "qualified research" shall not include any of the following:

(A) Research after commercial production.—Any research conducted after the beginning of commercial production of the business component.

(B) Adaptation of existing business components.—Any research related to the adaptation of an existing business component to a particular customer's requirement or need.

(C) Duplication of existing business component.—Any research related to the reproduction of an existing business component (in whole or in part) from a physical examination of the business component itself or from plans, blueprints, detailed specifications, or publicly available information with respect to such business component.

(D) Surveys, studies, etc.—Any—

(i) efficiency survey,

(ii) activity relating to management function or technique,

(iii) market research, testing, or development (including advertising or promotions),

(iv) routine data collection, or

(v) routine or ordinary testing or inspection for quality control.

(E) Computer software.—Except to the extent provided in regulations, any research with respect to computer software which is developed by (or for the benefit of) the taxpayer primarily for internal use by the taxpayer, other than for use in—

(i) an activity which constitutes qualified research (determined with regard to this subparagraph), or

(ii) a production process with respect to which the requirements of paragraph (1) are met.

(F) Foreign research.—Any research conducted outside the United States, the Commonwealth of Puerto Rico, or any possession of the United States.

(G) Social sciences, etc.—Any research in the social sciences, arts, or humanities.

(H) Funded research.—Any research to the extent funded by any grant, contract, or otherwise by another person (or governmental entity).

(e) Credit allowable with respect to certain payments to qualified organizations for basic research.—For purposes of this section—

(1) In general.—In the case of any taxpayer who makes basic research payments for any taxable year—

(A) the amount of basic research payments taken into account under subsection (a)(2) shall be equal to the excess of—

(i) such basic research payments, over

(ii) the qualified organization base period amount, and

(B) that portion of such basic research payments which does not exceed the qualified organization base period amount shall be treated as contract research expenses for purposes of subsection (a)(1).

(2) Basic research payments defined.—For purposes of this subsection—

(A) In general.—The term "basic research payment" means, with respect to any taxable year, any amount paid in cash during such taxable year by a corporation to any qualified organization for basic research but only if—

(i) such payment is pursuant to a written agreement between such corporation and such qualified organization, and

(ii) such basic research is to be performed by such qualified organization.

(B) Exception to requirement that research be performed by the organization.—In the case of a qualified organization described in subparagraph (C) or (D) of paragraph (6), clause (ii) of subparagraph (A) shall not apply.

(3) Qualified organization base period amount.—For purposes of this subsection, the term "qualified organization base period amount" means an amount equal to the sum of—

(A) the minimum basic research amount, plus

(B) the maintenance-of-effort amount.

(4) Minimum basic research amount.—For purposes of this subsection—

(A) In general.—The term "minimum basic research amount" means an amount equal to the greater of—

(i) 1 percent of the average of the sum of amounts paid or incurred during the base period for—

(I) any in-house research expenses, and

(II) any contract research expenses, or

(ii) the amounts treated as contract research expenses during the base period by reason of this subsection (as in effect during the base period).

(B) Floor amount.—Except in the case of a taxpayer which was in existence during a taxable year (other than a short taxable year) in the base period, the minimum basic research amount for any base period shall not be less than 50 percent of the basic research payments for the taxable year for which a determination is being made under this subsection.

(5) Maintenance-of-effort amount.—For purposes of this subsection—

(A) In general.—The term "maintenance-of-effort amount" means, with respect to any taxable year, an amount equal to the excess (if any) of—

(i) an amount equal to—

(I) the average of the nondesignated university contributions paid by the taxpayer during the base period, multiplied by

(II) the cost-of-living adjustment for the calendar year in which such taxable year begins, over

(ii) the amount of nondesignated university contributions paid by the taxpayer during such taxable year.

(B) Nondesignated university contributions.—For purposes of this paragraph, the term "nondesignated university contribution" means any amount paid by a taxpayer to any qualified organization described in paragraph (6)(A)—

(i) for which a deduction was allowable under section 170, and

(ii) which was not taken into account—

(I) in computing the amount of the credit under this section (as in effect during the base period) during any taxable year in the base period, or

(II) as a basic research payment for purposes of this section.

(C) Cost-of-living adjustment defined.—

(i) In general.—The cost-of-living adjustment for any calendar year is the cost-of-living adjustment for such calendar year determined under section 1(f)(3), by substituting "calendar year 1987" for "calendar year 1992" in subparagraph (B) thereof.

(ii) Special rule where base period ends in a calendar year other than 1983 or 1984.—If the base period of any taxpayer does not end in 1983 or 1984, section 1(f)(3)(B) shall, for purposes of this paragraph, be applied by substituting the calendar year in which such base period ends for 1992. Such substitution shall be in lieu of the substitution under clause (i).

* * *

(7) Definitions and special rules.—For purposes of this subsection—

(A) Basic research.—The term "basic research" means any original investigation for the advancement of scientific knowledge not having a specific commercial objective, except that such term shall not include—

(i) basic research conducted outside of the United States, and

(ii) basic research in the social sciences, arts, or humanities.

(B) Base period.—The term "base period" means the 3-taxable-year period ending with the taxable year immediately preceding the 1st taxable year of the taxpayer beginning after December 31, 1983.

(C) Exclusion from incremental credit calculation.—For purposes of determining the amount of credit allowable under subsection (a)(1) for any taxable year, the amount of the basic research payments taken into account under subsection (a)(2)—

(i) shall not be treated as qualified research expenses under subsection (a)(1)(A), and

(ii) shall not be included in the computation of base amount under subsection (a)(1)(B).

(D) Trade or business qualification.—For purposes of applying subsection (b)(1) to this subsection, any basic research payments shall be treated as an amount paid in carrying on a trade or business of the taxpayer in the taxable year in which it is paid (without regard to the provisions of subsection (b)(3)(B)).

(E) Certain corporations not eligible.—The term "corporation" shall not include—

(i) an S corporation,

(ii) a personal holding company (as defined in section 542), or

(iii) a service organization (as defined in section 414(m)(3)).

(f) Special rules.—For purposes of this section—

(1) Aggregation of expenditures.—

(A) Controlled group of corporations.—In determining the amount of the credit under this section—

(i) all members of the same controlled group of corporations shall be treated as a single taxpayer, and

(ii) the credit (if any) allowable by this section to each such member shall be determined on a proportionate basis to its share of the aggregate of the qualified research expenses, basic research payments, and amounts paid or incurred to energy research consortiums, taken into account by such controlled group for purposes of this section.

(B) Common control.—Under regulations prescribed by the Secretary, in determining the amount of the credit under this section—

(i) all trades or businesses (whether or not incorporated) which are under common control shall be treated as a single taxpayer, and

(ii) the credit (if any) allowable by this section to each such person shall be determined on a proportionate basis to its share of the aggregate of the qualified research expenses, basic research payments, and amounts paid or incurred to energy research consortiums, taken into account by all such persons under common control for purposes of this section.

The regulations prescribed under this subparagraph shall be based on principles similar to the principles which apply in the case of subparagraph (A).

(2) Allocations.—

(A) Pass-thru in the case of estates and trusts.—Under regulations prescribed by the Secretary, rules similar to the rules of subsection (d) of section 52 shall apply.

(B) Allocation in the case of partnerships.—In the case of partnerships, the credit shall be allocated among partners under regulations prescribed by the Secretary.

* * *

(4) Short taxable years.—In the case of any short taxable year, qualified research expenses and gross receipts shall be annualized in such circumstances and under such methods as the Secretary may prescribe by regulation.

(5) Controlled group of corporations.—The term "controlled group of corporations" has the same meaning given to such term by section 1563 (a), except that—

(A) "more than 50 percent" shall be substituted for "at least 80 percent" each place it appears in section 1563(a)(1), and

(B) the determination shall be made without regard to subsections (a)(4) and (e)(3)(C) of section 1563.

(6) Energy research consortium.—

(A) In general.—The term "energy research consortium" means any organization—

(i) which is—

(I) described in section 501(c)(3) and is exempt from tax under section 501(a) and is organized and operated primarily to conduct energy research, or

(II) organized and operated primarily to conduct energy research in the public interest (within the meaning of section 501(c)(3)),

(ii) which is not a private foundation,

(iii) to which at least 5 unrelated persons paid or incurred during the calendar year in which the taxable year of the organization begins amounts (including as contributions) to such organization for energy research, and

(iv) to which no single person paid or incurred (including as contributions) during such calendar year an amount equal to more than 50 percent of the total amounts received by such organization during such calendar year for energy research.

(B) Treatment of persons.—All persons treated as a single employer under subsection (a) or (b) of section 52 shall be treated as related persons for purposes of subparagraph (A)(iii) and as a single person for purposes of subparagraph (A)(iv).

(C) Foreign research.—For purposes of subsection (a)(3), amounts paid or incurred for any energy research conducted outside the United States, the Commonwealth of Puerto Rico, or any possession of the United States shall not be taken into account.

(D) Denial of double benefit.—Any amount taken into account under subsection (a)(3) shall not be taken into account under paragraph (1) or (2) of subsection (a).

(E) Energy research.—The term "energy research" does not include any research which is not qualified research.

(g) Special rule for pass-thru of credit.—In the case of an individual who—

(1) owns an interest in an unincorporated trade or business,

(2) is a partner in a partnership,

(3) is a beneficiary of an estate or trust, or

(4) is a shareholder in an S corporation,

the amount determined under subsection (a) for any taxable year shall not exceed an amount (separately computed with respect to such person's interest in such trade or business or entity) equal to the amount of tax attributable to that portion of a person's taxable income which is allocable or apportionable to the person's interest in such trade or business or entity. If the amount determined under subsection (a) for any taxable year exceeds the limitation of the preceding sentence, such amount may be carried to other taxable years under the rules of section 39; except that the limitation of the preceding sentence shall be taken into account in lieu of the limitation of section 38(c) in applying section 39.

(h) Termination.—

(1) In general.—This section shall not apply to any amount paid or incurred—

(A) after June 30, 1995, and before July 1, 1996, or

(B) after December 31, 2013.*

(2) Termination of alternative incremental credit.—No election under subsection (c)(4) shall apply to taxable years beginning after December 31, 2008.

(3) Computation of taxable year in which credit terminates.—In the case of any taxable year with respect to which this section applies to a number of days which is less than the total number of days in such taxable year—

(A) the amount determined under subsection (c)(1)(B) with respect to such taxable year shall be the amount which bears the same ratio to such amount (determined without regard to this paragraph) as the number of days in such taxable year to which this section applies bears to the total number of days in such taxable year, and

(B) for purposes of subsection (c)(5), the average qualified research expenses for the preceding 3 taxable years shall be the amount which bears the same ratio to such average qualified research expenses (determined without regard to this paragraph) as the number of days in such taxable year to which this section applies bears to the total number of days in such taxable year.

§ 42. Low-income housing credit

(a) In general.—For purposes of section 38, the amount of the low-income housing credit determined under this section for any taxable year in the credit period shall be an amount equal to—

(1) the applicable percentage of

(2) the qualified basis of each qualified low-income building.

(b) Applicable percentage: 70 percent present value credit for certain new buildings; 30 percent present value credit for certain other buildings.—

(1) Determination of applicable percentage.—

(A) For purposes of this section, the term "applicable percentage" means, with respect to any building, the appropriate percentage prescribed by the Secretary for the earlier of—

(i) the month in which such building is placed in service, or

(ii) at the election of the taxpayer—

(I) the month in which the taxpayer and the housing credit agency enter into an agreement with respect to such building (which is binding on such agency, the taxpayer, and all successors in interest) as to the housing credit dollar amount to be allocated to such building, or

(II) in the case of any building to which subsection (h)(4)(B) applies, the month in which the tax-exempt obligations are issued.

A month may be elected under clause (ii) only if the election is made not later than the 5th day after the close of such month. Such an election, once made, shall be irrevocable.

(B) Method of prescribing percentages.—The percentages prescribed by the Secretary for any month shall be percentages which will yield over a 10-year period amounts of credit under subsection (a) which have a present value equal to—

(i) 70 percent of the qualified basis of a new building which is not federally subsidized for the table year, and

(ii) 30 percent of the qualified basis of a building not described in clause (i)

(C) Method of discounting.—The present value under subparagraph (B) shall be determined—

(i) as of the last day of the 1st year of the 10-year period referred to in subparagraph (B),

(ii) by using a discount rate equal to 72 percent of the average of the annual Federal mid-term rate and the annual Federal long-term rate applicable under section 1274(d)(1) to the month applicable under clause (i) or (ii) of subparagraph (A) and compounded annually, and

(iii) by assuming that the credit allowable under this section for any year is received on the last day of such year.

(2) Temporary minimum credit rate for non-federally subsidized new buildings.—In the case of any new building—

(A) which is placed in service by the taxpayer after the date of the enactment of this paragraph with respect to housing credit dollar amount allocations made before January 1, 2014,* and

*Editorial comment: At the present time, this section has not been extended. There is pending legislation in the Senate, *The Tax Extenders Act of 2013 (S.1859)*, that would extend Section 42(b)(2) until January 1, 2015.

(B) which is not federally subsidized for the taxable year, the applicable percentage shall not be less than 9 percent.

(3) Cross references.—

(A) For treatment of certain rehabilitation expenditures as separate new buildings, see subsection (e).

(B) For determination of applicable percentage for increases in qualified basis after the 1st year of the credit period, see subsection (f)(3).

(C) For authority of housing credit agency to limit applicable percentage and qualified basis which may be taken into account under this section with respect to any building, see subsection (h)(7).

(c) Qualified basis; qualified low-income building.—For purposes of this section—

(1) Qualified basis.—

(A) Determination.—The qualified basis of any qualified low-income building for any taxable year is an amount equal to—

(i) the applicable fraction (determined as of the close of such taxable year) of

(ii) the eligible basis of such building (determined under subsection (d)(5)).

(B) Applicable fraction.—For purposes of subparagraph (A), the term "applicable fraction" means the smaller of the unit fraction or the floor space fraction.

(C) Unit fraction.—For purposes of subparagraph (B), the term "unit fraction" means the fraction—

(i) the numerator of which is the number of low-income units in the building, and

(ii) the denominator of which is the number of residential rental units (whether or not occupied) in such building.

(D) Floor space fraction.—For purposes of subparagraph (B), the term "floor space fraction" means the fraction—

(i) the numerator of which is the total floor space of the low-income units in such building, and

(ii) the denominator of which is the total floor space of the residential rental units (whether or not occupied) in such building.

(E) Qualified basis to include portion of building used to provide supportive services for homeless.—In the case of a qualified low-income building described in subsection (i)(3) (B)(iii), the qualified basis of such building for any taxable year shall be increased by the lesser of—

(i) so much of the eligible basis of such building as is used throughout the year to provide supportive services designed to assist tenants in locating and retaining permanent housing, or

(ii) 20 percent of the qualified basis of such building (determined without regard to this subparagraph).

(2) Qualified low-income building.—The term "qualified low-income building" means any building—

(A) which is part of a qualified low-income housing project at all times during the period—

(i) beginning on the 1st day in the compliance period on which such building is part of such a project, and

(ii) ending on the last day of the compliance period with respect to such building, and

(B) to which the amendments made by section 201(a) of the Tax Reform Act of 1986 apply.

(d) Eligible basis.— For purposes of this section—

(1) New buildings.—The eligible basis of a new building is its adjusted basis as of the close of the 1st taxable year of the credit period.

(2) Existing buildings.—

(A) In general.—The eligible basis of an existing building is—

(i) in the case of a building which meets the requirements of subparagraph (B), its adjusted basis as of the close of the 1st taxable year of the credit period, and

(ii) zero in any other case.

(B) Requirements.—A building meets the requirements of this subparagraph if—

(i) the building is acquired by purchase (as defined in section 179(d)(2)),

(ii) there is a period of at least 10 years between the date of its acquisition by the taxpayer and the date the building was last placed in service,

(iii) the building was not previously placed in service by the taxpayer or by any person who was a related person with respect to the taxpayer as of the time previously placed in service, and

(iv) except as provided in subsection (f)(5), a credit is allowable under subsection (a) by reason of subsection (e) with respect to the building.

(C) Adjusted basis.—For purposes of subparagraph (A), the adjusted basis of any building shall not include so much of the basis of such building as is determined by reference to the basis of other property held at any time by the person acquiring the building.

(D) Special rules for subparagraph (B).—

(i) Special rule for certain transfers.—For purposes of determining under subparagraph (B)(ii) when a building was last placed in service, there shall not be taken into account any placement in service—

(I) in connection with the acquisition of the building in a transaction in which the basis of the building in the hands of the person acquiring it is determined in whole or in part by reference to the adjusted basis of such building in the hands of the person from whom acquired,

(II) by a person whose basis in such building is determined under section 1014(a) (relating to property acquired from a decedent),

(III) by any governmental unit or qualified non-profit organization (as defined in subsection (h)(5)) if the requirements of subparagraph (B)(ii) are met with respect to the placement in service by such unit or organization and all the income from such property is exempt from Federal income taxation,

(IV) by any person who acquired such building by foreclosure (or by instrument in lieu of foreclosure) of any purchase-money security interest held by such person if the requirements of subparagraph (B)(ii) are met with respect to the placement in service by such person and such building is resold within 12 months after the date such building is placed in service by such person after such foreclosure, or

(V) of a single-family residence by any individual who owned and used such residence for no other purpose than as his principal residence.

(ii) Related person.—For purposes of subparagraph (B) (iii), a person (hereinafter in this subclause referred to as the "related person") is related to any person if the related person bears a relationship to such person specified in section 267(b) or 707(b)(1), or the related person and such person are engaged in trades or businesses under common control (within the meaning of subsections (a) and (b) of section 52).

(3) Eligible basis reduced where disproportionate standards for units.—

(A) In general.—Except as provided in subparagraph (B), the eligible basis of any building shall be reduced by an amount equal to the portion of the adjusted basis of the building which is attributable to residential rental units in the building which are not low-income units and which are above the average quality standard of the low-income units in the building.

(B) Exception where taxpayer elects to exclude excess costs.—

(i) In general.—Subparagraph (A) shall not apply with respect to a residential rental unit in a building which is not a low-income unit if—

(I) the excess described in clause (ii) with respect to such unit is not greater than 15 percent of the cost described in clause (ii)(II), and

(II) the taxpayer elects to exclude from the eligible basis of such building the excess described in clause (ii) with respect to such unit.

(ii) Excess.—The excess described in this clause with respect to any unit is the excess of—

(I) the cost of such unit, over

(II) the amount which would be the cost of such unit if the average cost per square foot of low-income units in the building were substituted for the cost per square foot of such unit.

The Secretary may by regulation provide for the determination of the excess under this clause on a basis other than square foot costs.

(4) Special rules relating to determination of adjusted basis.—For purposes of this subsection—

(A) In general.—Except as provided in subparagraphs (B) and (C), the adjusted basis of any building shall be determined without regard to the adjusted basis of any property which is not residential rental property.

(B) Basis of property in common areas, etc., included.—The adjusted basis of any building shall be determined by taking into account the adjusted basis of property (of a character subject to the allowance for depreciation) used in common areas or provided as comparable amenities to all residential rental units in such building.

(C) Inclusion of basis of property used to provide services for certain nontenants.—

(i) In general.—The adjusted basis of any building located in a qualified census tract (as defined in paragraph (5)(C)) shall be determined by taking into account the adjusted basis of property (of a character subject to the allowance for depreciation and not otherwise taken into account) used throughout the taxable year in providing any community service facility.

(ii) Limitation.—The increase in the adjusted basis of any building which is taken into account by reason of clause (i) shall not exceed the sum of—

(I) 25 percent of so much of the eligible basis of the qualified low-income housing project of which it is a part as does not exceed $15,000,000, plus

(II) 10 percent of so much of the eligible basis of such project as is not taken into account under subclause (I).

For purposes of the preceding sentence, all community service facilities which are part of the same qualified low-income housing project shall be treated as one facility.

(iii) Community service facility.—For purposes of this subparagraph, the term "community service facility" means any facility designed to serve primarily individuals whose income is 60 percent or less of area median income (within the meaning of subsection (g)(1)(B)).

(D) No reduction for depreciation.—The adjusted basis of any building shall be determined without regard to paragraphs (2) and (3) of section 1016(a).

(5) Special rule for determining eligible basis.—

(A) Federal grants not taken into account in determining eligible basis.—The eligible basis of a building shall not include any costs financed with the proceeds of a federally funded grant.

(B) Increase in credit for buildings in high cost areas.—

(i) In general.—In the case of any building located in a qualified census tract or difficult development area which is designated for purposes of this subparagraph—

(I) in the case of a new building, the eligible basis of such building shall be 130 percent of such basis determined without regard to this subparagraph, and

(II) in the case of an existing building, the rehabilitation expenditures taken into account under subsection (e) shall be 130 percent of such expenditures determined without regard to this subparagraph.

(ii) Qualified census tract.—

(I) In general.—The term "qualified census tract" means any census tract which is designated by the Secretary of Housing and Urban Development and, for the most recent year for which census data are available on household income in such tract, either in which 50 percent or more of the households have an income which is less than 60 percent of the area median gross income for such year or which has a poverty rate of at least 25 percent. If the Secretary of Housing and Urban Development determines that sufficient data for any period are not available to apply this clause on the basis of census tracts, such Secretary shall apply this clause for such period on the basis of enumeration districts.

* * *

(7) Acquisition of building before end of prior compliance period.—

(A) In general.—Under regulations prescribed by the Secretary, in the case of a building described in subparagraph (B) (or interest therein) which is acquired by the taxpayer—

(i) paragraph (2)(B) shall not apply, but

(ii) the credit allowable by reason of subsection (a) to the taxpayer for any period after such acquisition shall be equal to the amount of credit which would have been allowable under subsection (a) for such period to the prior owner referred to in subparagraph (B) had such owner not disposed of the building.

(B) Description of building.—A building is described in this subparagraph if—

(i) a credit was allowed by reason of subsection (a) to any prior owner of such building, and

(ii) the taxpayer acquired such building before the end of the compliance period for such building with respect to such prior owner (determined without regard to any disposition by such prior owner).

(e) Rehabilitation expenditures treated as separate new building.—

(1) In general.—Rehabilitation expenditures paid or incurred by the taxpayer with respect to any building shall be treated for purposes of this section as a separate new building.

(2) Rehabilitation expenditures.—For purposes of paragraph (1)—

(A) In general.—The term "rehabilitation expenditures" means amounts chargeable to capital account and incurred for property (or additions or improvements to property) of a character subject to the allowance for depreciation in connection with the rehabilitation of a building.

(B) Cost of acquisition, etc., not included.—Such term does not include the cost of acquiring any building (or interest therein) or any amount not permitted to be taken into account under paragraph (3) or (4) of subsection (d).

(3) Minimum expenditures to qualify.—

(A) In general.—Paragraph (1) shall apply to rehabilitation expenditures with respect to any building only if—

(i) the expenditures are allocable to 1 or more low-income units or substantially benefit such units, and

(ii) the amount of such expenditures during any 24-month period meets the requirements of whichever of the following subclauses requires the greater amount of such expenditures:

(I) The requirement of this subclause is met if such amount is not less than 20 percent of the adjusted basis of the building (determined as of the 1st day of such period and without regard to paragraphs (2) and (3) of section 1016(a)).

(II) The requirement of this subclause is met if the qualified basis attributable to such amount, when divided by the number of low-income units in the building, is $6,000 or more.*

(B) Exception from 10 percent rehabilitation.—In the case of a building acquired by the taxpayer from a governmental unit, at the election of the taxpayer, subparagraph (A)(ii)(I) shall not apply and the credit under this section for such rehabilitation expenditures shall be determined using the percentage applicable under subsection (b)(2)(B)(ii).

(C) Date of determination.—The determination under subparagraph (A) shall be made as of the close of the 1st taxable year in the credit period with respect to such expenditures.

(D) Inflation adjustment.—In the case of any expenditures which are treated under paragraph (4) as placed in service during any calendar year after 2009, the $6,000 amount in subparagraph (A)(ii)(II) shall be increased by an amount equal to—

(i) such dollar amount, multiplied by

(ii) the cost-of-living adjustment determined under section 1(f)(3) for such calendar year by substituting "calendar year 2008" for "calendar year 1992" in subparagraph (B) thereof.

Any increase under the preceding sentence which is not a multiple of $100 shall be rounded to the nearest multiple of $100.

(4) Special rules.—For purposes of applying this section with respect to expenditures which are treated as a separate building by reason of this subsection—

*Editorial comment: For 2014, the indexed amount is $6,500.

(A) such expenditures shall be treated as placed in service at the close of the 24-month period referred to in paragraph (3)(A), and

(B) the applicable fraction under subsection (c)(1) shall be the applicable fraction for the building (without regard to paragraph (1)) with respect to which the expenditures were incurred.

Nothing in subsection (d)(2) shall prevent a credit from being allowed by reason of this subsection.

(5) No double counting.—Rehabilitation expenditures may, at the election of the taxpayer, be taken into account under this subsection or subsection (d)(2)(A)(i) but not under both such subsections.

(6) Regulations to apply subsection with respect to group of units in building.—The Secretary may prescribe regulations, consistent with the purposes of this subsection, treating a group of units with respect to which rehabilitation expenditures are incurred as a separate new building.

(f) Definition and special rules relating to credit period.—

(1) Credit period defined.—For purposes of this section, the term "credit period" means, with respect to any building, the period of 10 taxable years beginning with—

(A) the taxable year in which the building is placed in service, or

(B) at the election of the taxpayer, the succeeding taxable year,

but only if the building is a qualified low-income building as of the close of the 1st year of such period. The election under subparagraph (B), once made, shall be irrevocable.

(2) Special rule for 1st year of credit period.—

(A) In general.—The credit allowable under subsection (a) with respect to any building for the 1st taxable year of the credit period shall be determined by substituting for the applicable fraction under subsection (c)(1) the fraction—

(i) the numerator of which is the sum of the applicable fractions determined under subsection (c)(1) as of the close of each full month of such year during which such building was in service, and

(ii) the denominator of which is 12.

(B) Disallowed 1st year credit allowed in 11th year.—Any reduction by reason of subparagraph (A) in the credit allowable (without regard to subparagraph (A)) for the 1st taxable year of the credit period shall be allowable under subsection (a) for the 1st taxable year following the credit period.

(3) Determination of applicable percentage with respect to increases in qualified basis after 1st year of credit period.—

(A) In general.—In the case of any building which was a qualified low-income building as of the close of the 1st year of the credit period, if—

(i) as of the close of any taxable year in the compliance period (after the 1st year of the credit period) the qualified basis of such building exceeds

(ii) the qualified basis of such building as of the close of the 1st year of the credit period,

the applicable percentage which shall apply under subsection (a) for the taxable year to such excess shall be the percentage equal to $^2/_3$ of the applicable percentage which (after the application of subsection (h)) would but for this paragraph apply to such basis.

(B) 1st year computation applies.—A rule similar to the rule of paragraph (2)(A) shall apply to any increase in qualified basis to which subparagraph (A) applies for the 1st year of such increase.

(4) Dispositions of property.—If a building (or an interest therein) is disposed of during any year for which credit is allowable under subsection (a), such credit shall be allocated between the parties on the basis of the number of days during such year the building (or interest) was held by each. In any such case, proper adjustments shall be made in the application of subsection (j).

(5) Credit period for existing buildings not to begin before rehabilitation credit allowed.—

(A) In general.—The credit period for an existing building shall not begin before the 1st taxable year of the credit period for rehabilitation expenditures with respect to the building.

(B) Acquisition credit allowed for certain buildings not allowed a rehabilitation credit.—

(i) In general.—In the case of a building described in clause (ii)—

(I) subsection (d)(2)(B)(iv) shall not apply, and

(II) the credit period for such building shall not begin before the taxable year which would be the 1st taxable year of the credit period for rehabilitation expenditures with respect to the building under the modifications described in clause (ii)(II).

(ii) Building described.—A building is described in this clause if—

(I) a waiver is granted under subsection (d)(6)(C) with respect to the acquisition of the building, and

(II) a credit would be allowed for rehabilitation expenditures with respect to such building if subsection (e)(3)(A)(ii)(I) did not apply and if the dollar amount in effect under subsection (e)(3)(A)(ii)(II) were two-thirds of such amount.

(g) Qualified low-income housing project.—For purposes of this section—

(1) In general.—The term "qualified low-income housing project" means any project for residential rental property if the project meets the requirements of subparagraph (A) or (B) whichever is elected by the taxpayer:

(A) 20-50 test.—The project meets the requirements of this subparagraph if 20 percent or more of the residential units in such project are both rent-restricted and occupied by individuals whose income is 50 percent or less of area median gross income.

(B) 40-60 test.—The project meets the requirements of this subparagraph if 40 percent or more of the residential units in such project are both rent-restricted and occupied by individuals whose income is 60 percent or less of area median gross income.

Any election under this paragraph, once made, shall be irrevocable. For purposes of this paragraph, any property shall not be treated as failing to be residential rental property merely because part of the building in which such property is located is used for purposes other than residential rental purposes.

(2) Rent-restricted units.—

(A) In general.—For purposes of paragraph (1), a residential unit is rent-restricted if the gross rent with respect to such unit does not exceed 30 percent of the imputed income limitation applicable to such unit. For purposes of the preceding sentence, the amount of the income limitation under paragraph (1) applicable for any period shall not be less than such limitation applicable for the earliest period the building (which contains the unit) was included in the determination of whether the project is a qualified low-income housing project.

(B) Gross rent.—For purposes of subparagraph (A), gross rent—

(i) does not include any payment under section 8 of the United States Housing Act of 1937 or any comparable rental assistance program (with respect to such unit or occupants thereof),

(ii) includes any utility allowance determined by the Secretary after taking into account such determinations under section 8 of the United States Housing Act of 1937,

(iii) does not include any fee for a supportive service which is paid to the owner of the unit (on the basis of the low-income status of the tenant of the unit) by any governmental program of assistance (or by an organization described in section 501(c)(3) and exempt from tax under section 501(a)) if such program (or organization) provides assistance for rent and the amount of assistance provided for rent is not separable from the amount of assistance provided for supportive services, and

(iv) does not include any rental payment to the owner of the unit to the extent such owner pays an equivalent amount to the Farmers' Home Administration under section 515 of the Housing Act of 1949.

For purposes of clause (iii), the term "supportive service" means any service provided under a planned program of services designed to enable residents of a residential rental property to remain independent and avoid placement in a hospital, nursing home, or intermediate care facility for the mentally or physically handicapped. In the case of a single-room occupancy unit or building described in subsection (i)(3)(B)(iii), such term includes any service provided to assist tenants in locating and retaining permanent housing.

(C) Imputed income limitation applicable to unit.—For purposes of this paragraph, the imputed income limitation applicable to a unit is the income limitation which would apply under paragraph (1) to individuals occupying the unit if the number of individuals occupying the unit were as follows:

(i) In the case of a unit which does not have a separate bedroom, 1 individual.

(ii) In the case of a unit which has 1 or more bedrooms, 1.5 individuals for each separate bedroom.

In the case of a project with respect to which a credit is allowable by reason of this section and for which financing is provided by a bond described in section 142(a)(7), the imputed income limitation shall apply in lieu of the otherwise applicable income limitation for purposes of applying section 142(d)(4)(B)(ii).

(D) Treatment of units occupied by individuals whose incomes rise above limit.—

(i) In general.—Except as provided in clause (ii), notwithstanding an increase in the income of the occupants of a low-income unit above the income limitation applicable under paragraph (1), such unit shall continue to be treated as a low-income unit if the income of such occupants initially met such income limitation and such unit continues to be rent-restricted.

(ii) Next available unit must be rented to low-income tenant if income rises above 140 percent of income limit.—If the income of the occupants of the unit increases above 140 percent of the income limitation applicable under paragraph (1), clause (i) shall cease to apply to such unit if any residential rental unit in the building (of a size comparable to, or smaller than, such unit) is occupied by a new resident whose income exceeds such income limitation. In the case of a project described in section 142(d)(4)(B), the preceding sentence shall be applied by substituting "170 percent" for "140 percent" and by substituting "any low-income unit in the building is occupied by a new resident whose income exceeds 40 percent of area median gross income" for "any residential unit in the building (of a size comparable to, or smaller than, such unit) is occupied by a new resident whose income exceeds such income limitation."

(E) Units where federal rental assistance is reduced as tenant's income increases.—If the gross rent with respect to a residential unit exceeds the limitation under subparagraph (A) by reason of the fact that the income of the occupants thereof exceeds the income limitation applicable under paragraph (1), such unit shall, nevertheless, be treated as a rent-restricted unit for purposes of paragraph (1) if—

(i) a Federal rental assistance payment described in subparagraph (B)(i) is made with respect to such unit or its occupants, and

(ii) the sum of such payment and the gross rent with respect to such unit does not exceed the sum of the amount of such payment which would be made and the gross rent which would be payable with respect to such unit if—

(I) the income of the occupants thereof did not exceed the income limitation applicable under paragraph (1), and

(II) such units were rent-restricted within the meaning of subparagraph (A).

The preceding sentence shall apply to any unit only if the result described in clause (ii) is required by Federal statute as of the date of the enactment of this subparagraph and as of the date the Federal rental assistance payment is made.

(3) Date for meeting requirements.—

(A) In general.—Except as otherwise provided in this paragraph, a building shall be treated as a qualified low-income building only if the project (of which such building is a part) meets the requirements of paragraph (1) not later than the close of the 1st year of the credit period for such building.

(B) Buildings which rely on later buildings for qualification—

(i) In general.—In determining whether a building (hereinafter in this subparagraph referred to as the "prior building") is a qualified low-income building, the taxpayer may take into account 1 or more additional buildings placed in service during the 12-month period described in subparagraph (A) with respect to the prior building only if the taxpayer elects to apply clause (ii) with respect to each additional building taken into account.

(ii) Treatment of elected buildings.—In the case of a building which the taxpayer elects to take into account under clause (i), the period under subparagraph (A) for such building shall end at the close of the 12-month period applicable to the prior building.

(iii) Date prior building is treated as placed in service.—For purposes of determining the credit period and the compliance period for the prior building, the prior building shall be treated for purposes of this section as placed in service on the most recent date any additional building elected by the taxpayer (with respect to such prior building) was placed in service.

(C) Special rule.—A building—

(i) other than the 1st building placed in service as part of a project, and

(ii) other than a building which is placed in service during the 12-month period described in subparagraph (A) with respect to a prior building which becomes a qualified low-income building,

shall in no event be treated as a qualified low-income building unless the project is a qualified low-income housing project (without regard to such building) on the date such building is placed in service.

(D) Projects with more than 1 building must be identified.—For purposes of this section, a project shall be treated as consisting of only 1 building unless, before the close of the 1st calendar year in the project period (as defined in subsection (h)(1)(F)(ii)), each building which is (or will be) part of such project is identified in such form and manner as the Secretary may provide.

(4) Certain rules made applicable.—Paragraphs (2) (other than subparagraph (A) thereof), (3), (4), (5), (6), and (7) of section 142(d), and section 6652(j), shall apply for purposes of determining whether any project is a qualified low-income housing project and whether any unit is a low-income unit; except that, in applying such provisions for such purposes, the term "gross rent" shall have the meaning given such term by paragraph (2)(B) of this subsection.

(5) Election to treat building after compliance period as not part of a project.—For purposes of this section, the taxpayer may elect to treat any building as not part of a qualified low-income housing project for any period beginning after the compliance period for such building.

(6) Special rule where de minimis equity contribution.—Property shall not be treated as failing to be residential rental property for purposes of this section merely because the occupant of a residential unit in the project pays (on a voluntary basis) to the lessor a de minimis amount to be held toward the purchase by such occupant of a residential unit in such project if—

(A) all amounts so paid are refunded to the occupant on the cessation of his occupancy of a unit in the project, and

(B) the purchase of the unit is not permitted until after the close of the compliance period with respect to the building in which the unit is located.

Any amount paid to the lessor as described in the preceding sentence shall be included in gross rent under paragraph (2) for purposes of determining whether the unit is rent-restricted.

(7) Scattered site projects.—Buildings which would (but for their lack of proximity) be treated as a project for purposes of this section shall be so treated if all the dwelling units in each of the buildings are rent-restricted (within the meaning of paragraph (2)) residential rental units.

(8) Waiver of certain de minimis errors and recertifications.—On application by the taxpayer, the Secretary may waive—

(A) any recapture under subsection (j) in the case of any de minimis error in complying with paragraph (1), or

(B) any annual recertification of tenant income for purposes of this subsection, if the entire building is occupied by low-income tenants.

(9) Clarification of general public use requirement.—A project does not fail to meet the general public use requirement solely because of occupancy restrictions or preferences that favor tenants—

(A) with special needs,

(B) who are members of a specified group under a Federal program or State program or policy that supports housing for such a specified group, or

(C) who are involved in artistic or literary activities.

* * *

(i) Definitions and special rules.—For purposes of this section—

(1) Compliance period.—The term "compliance period" means, with respect to any building, the period of 15 taxable years beginning with the 1st taxable year of the credit period with respect thereto.

(2) Determination of whether building is federally subsidized.—

(A) In general.—Except as otherwise provided in this paragraph, for purposes of subsection (b)(l), a new building shall be treated as federally subsidized for any taxable year if, at any time during such taxable year or any prior taxable year, there is outstanding any obligation the interest on which is exempt from tax under section 103, the proceeds of which are or were used (directly or indirectly) with respect to such building or the operation thereof.

(B) Election to reduce eligible basis by proceeds of obligations.—A tax-exempt obligation shall not be taken into account under subparagraph (A) if the taxpayer elects to exclude from the eligible basis of the building for purposes of subsection (d) the proceeds of such obligation.

(C) Special rule for subsidized construction financing.—Subparagraph (A) shall not apply to any tax-exempt obligation used to provide construction financing for any building if—

(i) such obligation (when issued or made) identified the building for which the proceeds of such obligation would be used, and

(ii) such obligation is redeemed before such building is placed in service.

(3) Low-income unit.—

(A) In general.—The term "low-income unit" means any unit in a building if—

(i) such unit is rent-restricted (as defined in subsection (g)(2)), and

(ii) the individuals occupying such unit meet the income limitation applicable under subsection (g)(1) to the project of which such building is a part.

(B) Exceptions.—

(i) In general.—A unit shall not be treated as a low-income unit unless the unit is suitable for occupancy and used other than on a transient basis.

(ii) Suitability for occupancy.—For purposes of clause (i), the suitability of a unit for occupancy shall be determined under regulations prescribed by the Secretary taking into account local health, safety, and building codes.

(iii) Transitional housing for homeless.—For purposes of clause (i), a unit shall be considered to be used other than on a transient basis if the unit contains sleeping accommodations and kitchen and bathroom facilities and is located in a building—

(I) which is used exclusively to facilitate the transition of homeless individuals (within the meaning of section 103 of the Stewart B. McKinney Homeless Assistance Act (42 U.S.C. 11302), as in effect on the date of the enactment of this clause) to independent living within 24 months, and

(II) in which a governmental entity or qualified nonprofit organization (as defined in subsection (h)(5)) provides such individuals with temporary housing and supportive services designed to assist such individuals in locating and retaining permanent housing.

(iv) Single-room occupancy units.—For purposes of clause (i), a single-room occupancy unit shall not be treated as used on a transient basis merely because it is rented on a month-by-month basis.

(C) Special rule for buildings having 4 or fewer units.—In the case of any building which has 4 or fewer residential rental units, no unit in such building shall be treated as a low-income unit if the units in such building are owned by—

(i) any individual who occupies a residential unit in such building, or

(ii) any person who is related (as defined in subsection (d)(2)(D)(iii)) to such individual.

(D) Certain students not to disqualify unit.—A unit shall not fail to be treated as a low-income unit merely because it is occupied—

(i) by an individual who is—

(I) a student and receiving assistance under title IV of the Social Security Act,

(II) a student who was previously under the care and placement responsibility of the State agency responsible for administering a plan under part B or part E of title IV of the Social Security Act, or

(III) enrolled in a job training program receiving assistance under the Job Training Partnership Act or under other similar Federal, State, or local laws, or

(ii) entirely by full-time students if such students are—

(I) single parents and their children and such parents and children are not dependents (as defined in section 152, determined without regard to subsections (b)(1), (b)(2), and (d)(1)(B) thereof) of another individual, or

(II) married and file a joint return.

* * *

(4) New building.—The term "new building" means a building the original use of which begins with the taxpayer.

(5) Existing building.—The term "existing building" means any building which is not a new building.

* * *

(j) Recapture of credit.—

(1) In general.—If—

(A) as of the close of any taxable year in the compliance period, the amount of the qualified basis of any building with respect to the taxpayer is less than

(B) the amount of such basis as of the close of the preceding taxable year,

then the taxpayer's tax under this chapter for the taxable year shall be increased by the credit recapture amount.

(2) Credit recapture amount.—For purposes of paragraph (1), the credit recapture amount is an amount equal to the sum of—

(A) the aggregate decrease in the credits allowed to the taxpayer under section 38 for all prior taxable years which would have resulted if the accelerated portion of the credit allowable by reason of this section were not allowed for all prior taxable years with respect to the excess of the amount described in paragraph (1)(B) over the amount described in paragraph (1)(A), plus

(B) interest at the overpayment rate established under section 6621 on the amount determined under subparagraph (A) for each prior taxable year for the period beginning on the due date for filing the return for the prior taxable year involved.

No deduction shall be allowed under this chapter for interest described in subparagraph (B).

(3) Accelerated portion of credit.—For purposes of paragraph (2), the accelerated portion of the credit for the prior taxable years with respect to any amount of basis is the excess of—

(A) the aggregate credit allowed by reason of this section (without regard to this subsection) for such years with respect to such basis, over

(B) the aggregate credit which would be allowable by reason of this section for such years with respect to such basis if the aggregate credit which would (but for this subsection) have been allowable for the entire compliance period were allowable ratably over 15 years.

(4) Special rules.—

(A) Tax benefit rule.—The tax for the taxable year shall be increased under paragraph (1) only with respect to credits allowed by reason of this section which were used to reduce tax liability. In the case of credits not so used to reduce tax liability, the carryforwards and carrybacks under section 39 shall be appropriately adjusted.

(B) Only basis for which credit allowed taken into account.—Qualified basis shall be taken into account under paragraph (1)(B) only to the extent such basis was taken into account in determining the credit under subsection (a) for the preceding taxable year referred to in such paragraph.

(C) No recapture of additional credit allowable by reason of subsection (f)(3).—Paragraph (1) shall apply to a decrease in qualified basis only to the extent such decrease exceeds the amount of qualified basis with respect to which a credit was allowable for the taxable year referred to in paragraph (1)(B) by reason of subsection (f)(3).

(D) No credits against tax.—Any increase in tax under this subsection shall not be treated as a tax imposed by this chapter for purposes of determining the amount of any credit under this chapter.

(E) No recapture by reason of casualty loss.—The increase in tax under this subsection shall not apply to a reduction in qualified basis by reason of a casualty loss to the extent such loss is restored by reconstruction or replacement within a reasonable period established by the Secretary.

(F) No recapture where de minimis changes in floor space.—The Secretary may provide that the increase in tax under this subsection shall not apply with respect to any building if—

(i) such increase results from a de minimis change in the floor space fraction under subsection (c)(1), and

(ii) the building is a qualified low-income building after such change.

(5) Certain partnerships treated as the taxpayer.—

(A) In general.—For purposes of applying this subsection to a partnership to which this paragraph applies—

(i) such partnership shall be treated as the taxpayer to which the credit allowable under subsection (a) was allowed,

(ii) the amount of such credit allowed shall be treated as the amount which would have been allowed to the partnership were such credit allowable to such partnership,

(iii) paragraph (4)(A) shall not apply, and

(iv) the amount of the increase in tax under this subsection for any taxable year shall be allocated among the partners of such partnership in the same manner as such partnership's taxable income for such year is allocated among such partners.

(B) Partnerships to which paragraph applies.—This paragraph shall apply to any partnership which has 35 or more partners unless the partnership elects not to have this paragraph apply.

(C) Special rules.—

(i) Husband and wife treated as 1 partner.—For purposes of subparagraph (B)(i), a husband and wife (and their estates) shall be treated as 1 partner.

(ii) Election irrevocable.—Any election under subparagraph (B), once made, shall be irrevocable.

(6) No recapture on disposition of building which continues in qualified use.—

(A) In general.—The increase in tax under this subsection shall not apply solely by reason of the disposition of a building (or an interest therein) if it is reasonably expected that such building will continue to be operated as a qualified low-income building for the remaining compliance period with respect to such building.

(B) Statute of limitations.—If a building (or an interest therein) is disposed of during any taxable year and there is any reduction in the qualified basis of such building which results in an increase in tax under this subsection for such taxable or any subsequent taxable year, then—

(i) the statutory period for the assessment of any deficiency with respect to such increase in tax shall not expire before the expiration of 3 years from the date the Secretary is notified by the taxpayer (in such manner as the Secretary may prescribe) of such reduction in qualified basis, and

(ii) such deficiency may be assessed before the expiration of such 3-year period notwithstanding the provisions of any other law or rule of law which would otherwise prevent such assessment.

(k) Application of at-risk rules.—For purposes of this section—

(1) In general.—Except as otherwise provided in this subsection, rules similar to the rules of section 49(a)(1) (other than subparagraphs (D)(ii)

(II) and (D)(iv)(I) thereof), section 49(a)(2), and section 49(b)(1) shall apply in determining the qualified basis of any building in the same manner as such sections apply in determining the credit base of property.

* * *

(1) Certifications and other reports to secretary.—

(1) Certification with respect to 1st year of credit period.—Following the close of the 1st taxable year in the credit period with respect to any qualified low-income building, the taxpayer shall certify to the Secretary (at such time and in such form and in such manner as the Secretary prescribes)—

(A) the taxable year, and calendar year, in which such building was placed in service,

(B) the adjusted basis and eligible basis of such building as of the close of the 1st year of the credit period,

(C) the maximum applicable percentage and qualified basis permitted to be taken into account by the appropriate housing credit agency under subsection (h),

(D) the election made under subsection (g) with respect to the qualified low-income housing project of which such building is a part, and

(E) such other information as the Secretary may require.

In the case of a failure to make the certification required by the preceding sentence on the date prescribed therefor, unless it is shown that such failure is due to reasonable cause and not to willful neglect, no credit shall be allowable by reason of subsection (a) with respect to such building for any taxable year ending before such certification is made.

* * *

(n) Regulations.—The Secretary shall prescribe such regulations as may be necessary or appropriate to carry out the purposes of this section, including regulations—

(1) dealing with—

(A) projects which include more than 1 building or only a portion of a building,

(B) buildings which are placed in service in portions,

(2) providing for the application of this section to short taxable years,

(3) preventing the avoidance of the rules of this section, and

(4) providing the opportunity for housing credit agencies to correct administrative errors and omissions with respect to allocations and record keeping within a reasonable period after their discovery, taking into account the availability of regulations and other administrative guidance from the Secretary.

* * *

§ 44. Expenditures to provide access to disabled individuals

(a) General rule.—For purposes of section 38, in the case of an eligible small business, the amount of the disabled access credit determined under this section for any taxable year shall be an amount equal to 50 percent of so much of the eligible access expenditures for the taxable year as exceed $250 but do not exceed $10,250.

(b) Eligible small business.—For purposes of this section, the term "eligible small business" means any person if—

(1) either—

(A) the gross receipts of such person for the preceding taxable year did not exceed $1,000,000, or

(B) in the case of a person to which subparagraph (A) does not apply, such person employed not more than 30 full-time employees during the preceding taxable year, and

(2) such person elects the application of this section for the taxable year.

For purposes of paragraph (1)(B), an employee shall be considered full-time if such employee is employed at least 30 hours per week for 20 or more calendar weeks in the taxable year.

(c) Eligible access expenditures.—For purposes of this section—

(1) In general.—The term "eligible access expenditures" means amounts paid or incurred by an eligible small business for the purpose of enabling such eligible small business to comply with applicable requirements under the Americans With Disabilities Act of 1990 (as in effect on the date of the enactment of this section).

(2) Certain expenditures included.—The term "eligible access expenditures" includes amounts paid or incurred—

(A) for the purpose of removing architectural, communication, physical, or transportation barriers which prevent a business from being accessible to, or usable by, individuals with disabilities,

(B) to provide qualified interpreters or other effective methods of making aurally delivered materials available to individuals with hearing impairments,

(C) to provide qualified readers, taped texts, and other effective methods of making visually delivered materials available to individuals with visual impairments,

(D) to acquire or modify equipment or devices for individuals with disabilities, or

(E) to provide other similar services, modifications, materials, or equipment.

(3) Expenditures must be reasonable.—Amounts paid or incurred for the purposes described in paragraph (2) shall include only expenditures which are reasonable and shall not include expenditures which are unnecessary to accomplish such purposes.

(4) Expenses in connection with new construction are not eligible.—The term "eligible access expenditures" shall not include amounts described in paragraph (2)(A) which are paid or incurred in connection with any facility first placed in service after the date of the enactment of this section.

(5) Expenditures must meet standards.—The term "eligible access expenditures" shall not include any amount unless the taxpayer establishes, to the satisfaction of the Secretary, that the resulting removal of any barrier (or the provision of any services, modifications, materials, or equipment) meets the standards promulgated by the Secretary with the concurrence of the Architectural and Transportation Barriers Compliance Board and set forth in regulations prescribed by the Secretary.

(d) Definition of disability; special rules.—For purposes of this section—

(1) Disability.—The term "disability" has the same meaning as when used in the Americans With Disabilities Act of 1990 (as in effect on the date of the enactment of this section).

(2) Controlled groups.—

(A) In general.—All members of the same controlled group of corporations (within the meaning of section 52(a)) and all persons under common control (within the meaning of section 52(b)) shall be treated as 1 person for purposes of this section.

(B) Dollar limitation.—The Secretary shall apportion the dollar limitation under subsection (a) among the members of any group described in subparagraph (A) in such manner as the Secretary shall by regulations prescribe.

(3) Partnerships and S corporations.—In the case of a partnership, the limitation under subsection (a) shall apply with respect to the partnership and each partner. A similar rule shall apply in the case of an S corporation and its shareholders.

(4) Short years.—The Secretary shall prescribe such adjustments as may be appropriate for purposes of paragraph (1) of subsection (b) if the preceding taxable year is a taxable year of less than 12 months.

(5) Gross receipts.—Gross receipts for any taxable year shall be reduced by returns and allowances made during such year.

(6) Treatment of predecessors.—The reference to any person in paragraph (1) of subsection (b) shall be treated as including a reference to any predecessor.

(7) Denial of double benefit.—In the case of the amount of the credit determined under this section—

(A) no deduction or credit shall be allowed for such amount under any other provision of this chapter, and

(B) no increase in the adjusted basis of any property shall result from such amount.

(e) Regulations.—The Secretary shall prescribe regulations necessary to carry out the purposes of this section.

§ 45. Electricity produced from certain renewable resources, etc.

(a) General rule.—For purposes of section 38, the renewable electricity production credit for any taxable year is an amount equal to the product of—

(1) 1.5 cents, multiplied by

(2) the kilowatt hours of electricity—

(A) produced by the taxpayer—

(i) from qualified energy resources, and

(ii) at a qualified facility during the 10-year period beginning on the date the facility was originally placed in service, and

(B) sold by the taxpayer to an unrelated person during the taxable year.

(b) Limitations and adjustments.—

(1) Phaseout of credit.—The amount of the credit determined under subsection (a) shall be reduced by an amount which bears the same ratio to the amount of the credit (determined without regard to this paragraph) as—

(A) the amount by which the reference price for the calendar year in which the sale occurs exceeds 8 cents, bears to

(B) 3 cents.

(2) Credit and phaseout adjustment based on inflation.—The 1.5 cent amount in subsection (a), the 8 cent amount in paragraph (1), the $4.375 amount in subsection (e)(8)(A), the $3 amount in subsection (e)(8)(D)(ii)(I), and in subsection (e)(8)(B)(i) the reference price of fuel used as a feedstock (within the meaning of subsection (c)(7)(A) in 2002 shall each be adjusted by multiplying such amount by the inflation adjustment factor for the calendar year in which the sale occurs. If any amount as increased under the preceding sentence is not a multiple of 0.1 cent, such amount shall be rounded to the nearest multiple of 0.1 cent.

(3) Credit reduced for grants, tax-exempt bonds, subsidized energy financing, and other credits.—The amount of the credit determined under subsection (a) with respect to any project for any taxable year (determined after the application of paragraphs (1) and (2)) shall be reduced by the amount which is the product of the amount so determined for such year and the lesser of ½ or a fraction—

(A) the numerator of which is the sum, for the taxable year and all prior taxable years, of—

(i) grants provided by the United States, a State, or a political subdivision of a State for use in connection with the project,

(ii) proceeds of an issue of State or local government obligations used to provide financing for the project the interest on which is exempt from tax under section 103,

(iii) the aggregate amount of subsidized energy financing provided (directly or indirectly) under a Federal, State, or local program provided in connection with the project, and

(iv) the amount of any other credit allowable with respect to any property which is part of the project, and

(B) the denominator of which is the aggregate amount of additions to the capital account for the project for the taxable year and all prior taxable years.

The amounts under the preceding sentence for any taxable year shall be determined as of the close of the taxable year. This paragraph shall not apply with respect to any facility described in subsection (d)(2)(A)(ii).

(4) Credit rate and period for electricity produced and sold from certain facilities.—

(A) Credit rate.—In the case of electricity produced and sold in any calendar year after 2003 at any qualified facility described in paragraph (3), (5), (6), (7), (9), or (11) of subsection (d), the amount in effect under subsection (a)(1) for such calendar year (determined before the application of the last sentence of paragraph (2) of this subsection) shall be reduced by one-half.

(B) Credit period.—

(i) In general.—Except as provided in clause (ii) or clause (iii), in the case of any facility described in paragraph (3), (4), (5), (6), or (7) of subsection (d), the 5-year period beginning on the date the facility was originally placed in service shall be substituted for the 10-year period in subsection (a)(2)(A)(ii).

(ii) Certain open-loop biomass facilities.—In the case of any facility described in subsection (d)(3)(A)(ii) placed in service before the date of the enactment of this paragraph, the 5-year period beginning on January 1, 2005 shall be substituted for the 10-year period in subsection (a)(2)(A)(ii).

(iii) Termination.—Clause (i) shall not apply to any facility placed in service after the date of enactment of this clause.

(c) Resources— For purposes of this section:

(1) In general.—The term "qualified energy resources" means—

(A) wind,

(B) closed-loop biomass,

(C) open-loop biomass,

(D) geothermal energy,

(E) solar energy,

(F) small irrigation power,

(G) municipal solid waste,

(H) qualified hydropower production, and

(I) marine and hydrokinetic renewable energy.

(2) Closed-loop biomass.—The term "closed-loop biomass" means any organic material from a plant which is planted exclusively for purposes of being used at a qualified facility to produce electricity.

(3) Open-loop biomass.—

(A) In general.—The term "open-loop biomass" means—

(i) any agricultural livestock waste nutrients, or

(ii) any solid, nonhazardous, cellulosic waste material or any lignin material which is derived from—

(I) any of the following forest-related resources: mill and harvesting residues, precommercial thinnings, slash, and brush,

(II) solid wood waste materials, including waste pallets, crates, dunnage, manufacturing and construction wood wastes (other than pressure-treated, chemically-treated, or painted wood wastes), and landscape or right-of-way tree trimmings, but not including municipal solid waste, gas derived from the biodegradation of solid waste, or paper which is commonly recycled, or

(III) agriculture sources, including orchard tree crops, vineyard, grain, legumes, sugar, and other crop by-products or residues.

Such term shall not include closed-loop biomass or biomass burned in conjunction with fossil fuel (cofiring) beyond such fossil fuel required for startup and flame stabilization.

(B) Agricultural livestock waste nutrients.—

(i) In general.—The term "agricultural livestock waste nutrients" means agricultural livestock manure and litter, including wood shavings, straw, rice hulls, and other bedding material for the disposition of manure.

(ii) Agricultural livestock.—The term "agricultural livestock" includes bovine, swine, poultry, and sheep.

(4) Geothermal energy.—The term "geothermal energy" means energy derived from a geothermal deposit (within the meaning of section 613(e)(2)).

(5) Small irrigation power.—The term "small irrigation power" means power—

(A) generated without any dam or impoundment of water through an irrigation system canal or ditch, and

(B) the nameplate capacity rating of which is not less than 150 kilowatts but is less than 5 megawatts.

(6) Municipal solid waste.—The term "municipal solid waste" has the meaning given the term "solid waste" under section 2(27) of the Solid Waste Disposal Act (42 U.S.C. 6903), except that the term does not include paper which is commonly recycled and which has been segregated from other solid waste (as so defined).

(7) Refined coal.—

(A) In general.—The term "refined coal" means a fuel—

(i) which—

(I) is a liquid, gaseous, or solid fuel produced from coal (including lignite) or high carbon fish ash, including such fuel used as a feed stock,

(II) is sold by the taxpayer with the reasonable expectation that it will be used for purpose of producing steam, and

(III) is certified by the taxpayer as resulting (when used in the production of steam) in a qualified emission reduction.

(ii) which is steel industry fuel.

(B) Qualified emission reduction.—The term "qualified emission reduction" means a reduction of at least 20 percent of the emissions of nitrogen oxide and at least 40 percent of the emissions of either sulfur dioxide or mercury released when burning the refined coal (excluding any dilution caused by materials combined or added during the production process), as compared to the emissions released when burning the feedstock coal or comparable coal predominantly available in the marketplace as of January 1, 2003.

(C) Steel industry fuel.—

(i) In general.—The term "steel industry fuel" means a fuel which—

(I) is produced through a process of liquefying coal waste sludge and distributing it on coal, and

(II) is used as a feedstock for the manufacture of coke.

(ii) Coal waste sludge.—The term "coal waste sludge" means the tar decanter sludge and related byproducts of the coking process, including such materials that have been stored in ground, in tanks and in lagoons, that have been treated as hazardous wastes under applicable Federal environment rules absent liquefaction and processing with coal into a feedstock for the manufacture of coke.

(8) Qualified hydropower production.—

(A) In general.—The term "qualified hydropower production" means—

(i) in the case of any hydroelectric dam which was placed in service on or before the date of the enactment of this paragraph, the incremental hydropower production for the taxable year, and

(ii) in the case of any nonhydroelectric dam described in subparagraph (C), the hydropower production from the facility for the taxable year.

(B) Determination of incremental hydropower production.—

(i) In general.—For purposes of subparagraph (A), incremental hydropower production for any taxable year shall be equal to the percentage of average annual hydropower production at the facility attributable to the efficiency improvements or additions of capacity placed in service after the date of the enactment of this paragraph, determined by using the same water flow information used to determine an historic average annual hydropower production baseline for such facility. Such percentage and baseline shall be certified by the Federal Energy Regulatory Commission.

(ii) Operational changes disregarded.—For purposes of clause (i), the determination of incremental hydropower production shall not be based on any operational changes at such facility not directly associated with the efficiency improvements or additions of capacity.

(C) Nonhydroelectric dam.—For purposes of subparagraph (A), a facility is described in this subparagraph if—

(i) the hydroelectric project installed on the nonhydroelectric dam is licensed by the Federal Energy Regulatory Commission and meets all other applicable environmental, licensing, and regulatory requirements,

(ii) the nonhydroelectric dam was placed in service before the date of the enactment of this paragraph and operated for flood control, navigation, or water supply proposes and did not produce hydroelectric power on the date of the enactment of this paragraph, and

(iii) the hydroelectric project is operated so that the water surface elevation at any given location and time that would have occurred in the absence of the hydroelectric project is maintained, subject to any license retirements imposed under applicable law that change the water surface elevation for the purposes of improving environmental quality of the affected waterway.

The Secretary, in consultation with the Federal Energy Regulatory Commission, shall certify if a hydroelectric project licensed at a nonhydroelectric dam meets the criteria in clause (ii). Nothing in this section shall affect the standards under which the Federal Energy Regulatory Commission issues licenses for and regulates hydropower projects under part I of the Federal Power Act.

(9) Indian coal.—

(A) In general.—The term "Indian coal" means coal which is produced from coal reserves which, on June 14, 2005—

(i) were owned by an Indian tribe, or

(ii) were held in trust by the United States for the benefit of an Indian tribe or its members.

(B) Indian tribe.—For purposes of this paragraph, the term "Indian tribe" has the meaning given such term by section 7871(c)(3)(E)(ii).

(10) Marine and hydrokinetic renewable energy.—

(A) In general.—The term "marine and hydrokinetic renewable energy" means energy derived from—

(i) waves, tides, and currents in oceans, estuaries, and tidal areas,

(ii) free flowing water in rivers, lakes, and streams,

(iii) free flowing water in an irrigation system, canal, or other man-made channel, including projects that utilize non-mechanical structures to accelerate the flow of water for electric power production purposes, or

(iv) differentials in ocean temperature (ocean thermal energy conversion).

(B) Exceptions.—Such term shall not include any energy which is derived from any source which utilizes a dam, diversionary structure (except as provided in subparagraph (A)(iii)), or impoundment for electric power production purposes.

(d) Qualified facilities.*—For purposes of this section:

(1) Wind facility.—In the case of a facility using wind to produce electricity, the term "qualified facility" means any facility owned by the taxpayer which is originally placed in service after December 31, 1993, and the construction of which begins before January 1, 2014.* Such term shall not include any facility with respect to which any qualified small wind energy property expenditure (as defined in subsection (d)(4) of section 25D) is taken into account in determining the credit under such section.

(2) Closed-loop biomass facility.—

(A) In general.—In the case of a facility using closed-loop biomass to produce electricity, the term "qualified facility" means any facility—

(i) owned by the taxpayer which is originally placed in service after December 31, 1992, and the construction of which begins before January 1, 2014,* or

(ii) owned by the taxpayer which before January 1, 2014, is originally placed in service and modified to use closed-loop biomass to co-fire with coal, with other biomass, or with both, but only if the modification is approved under the Biomass Power for Rural Development Programs or is part of a pilot project of the Commodity Credit Corporation as described in 65 Fed. Reg. 63052.

For purposes of clause (ii), a facility shall be treated as modified before January 1, 2014,* if the construction of such modification begins before such date.

(B) Special rules.—In the case of a qualified facility described in subparagraph (A)(ii)—

(i) the 10-year period referred to in subsection (a) shall be treated as beginning no earlier than the date of the enactment of this clause, and

(ii) if the owner of such facility is not the producer of the electricity, the person eligible for the credit allowable under subsection (a) shall be the lessee or the operator of such facility.

(3) Open-loop biomass facilities.—

(A) In general.—In the case of a facility using open-loop biomass to produce electricity, the term "qualified facility" means any facility owned by the taxpayer which—

(i) in the case of a facility using agricultural livestock waste nutrients—

(I) is originally placed in service after the date of the enactment of this subclause and the construction of which begins before January 1, 2014,* and

(II) the nameplate capacity rating of which is not less than 150 kilowatts, and

(ii) in the case of any other facility, the construction of which begins before January 1, 2014.

(B) Expansion of facility.—Such term shall include a new unit placed in service after the date of the enactment of this subparagraph in connection with a facility described in subparagraph (A), but only to the extent of the increased amount of electricity produced at the facility by reason of such new unit.

(C) Credit eligibility.—In the case of any facility described in subparagraph (A), if the owner of such facility is not the producer of the electricity, the person eligible for the credit allowable under subsection (a) shall be the lessee or the operator of such facility.

(4) Geothermal or solar energy facility.—In the case of a facility using geothermal or solar energy to produce electricity, the term "qualified facility" means any facility owned by the taxpayer, which is originally placed in service after the date of the enactment of this paragraph and which—

*Editorial comment: At the present time, this section has not been extended. There is pending legislation in the Senate, *The Tax Extenders Act of 2013 (S.1859)*, that would extend Sections 45(d)(1), (d)(2)(A), (d)(3)(A), (d)(4)(B), (d)(6), (d)(7), (d)(9), and (d)(11)(B) until January 1, 2015.

(A) in the case of a facility using solar energy, is placed in service before January 1, 2006, or

(B) in the case of a facility using geothermal energy, the construction of which begins before January 1, 2014.*

Such term shall not include any property described in section 48(a)(3) the basis of which is taken into account by the taxpayer for purposes of determining the energy credit under section 48.

(5) Small irrigation power facility.—In the case of a facility using small irrigation power to produce electricity, the term "qualified facility" means any facility owned by the taxpayer which is originally placed in service after the date of the enactment of this paragraph and before October 3, 2008.

(6) Landfill gas facilities.—In the case of a facility producing electricity from gas derived from the biodegradation of municipal solid waste, the term "qualified facility" means any facility owned by the taxpayer which is originally placed in service after the date of the enactment of this paragraph and the construction of which begins before January 1, 2014.*

(7) Trash facilities.—In the case of a facility (other than a facility described in paragraph 6) which uses municipal solid waste to produce electricity, the term "qualified facility" means any facility owned by the taxpayer which is originally placed in service after the date of the enactment of this paragraph and the construction of which begins before January 1, 2014.* Such term shall include a new unit placed in service in connection with a facility placed in service on or before the date of the enactment of this paragraph, but only to the extent of the increased amount of electricity produced at the facility by reason of such new unit.

(8) Refined coal production facility—In the case of a facility that produces refined coal, the term "refined coal production facility" means—

(A) with respect to a facility producing steel industry fuel, any facility (or any modification to a facility) which is placed in service before January 1, 2010, and

(B) with respect to any other facility producing refined coal, and facility placed in service after the date of the enactment of the American Jobs Creation Act of 2004 and before January 1, 2012.

(9) Qualified hydropower facility.—

(A) In general.—In the case of a facility producing qualified hydroelectric production described in subsection (c)(8), the term "qualified facility" means—

(i) in the case of any facility producing incremental hydropower production, such facility but only to the extent of its incremental hydropower production attributable to efficiency improvements or additions to capacity described in subsection (c)(8)(B) placed in service after the date of the enactment of this paragraph and before January 1, 2014,* and

(ii) any other facility placed in service after the date of the enactment of this paragraph and the construction of which begins before January 1, 2014.*

(B) Credit period.—In the case of a qualified facility described in subparagraph (A), the 10-year period referred to in subsection (a) shall be treated as beginning on the date the efficiency improvements or additions to capacity are placed in service.

(C) Special rule.—For purposes of subparagraph (A)(i), an efficiency improvement or addition to capacity shall be treated as placed in service before January 1, 2014,* if the construction of such improvement or addition begins before such date.

(10) Indian coal production facility.—In the case of a facility that produces Indian coal, the term "Indian coal production facility" means a facility which is placed in service before January 1, 2009.

(11) Marine and hydrokinetic renewable energy facilities.—In the case of a facility producing electricity from marine and hydrokinetic renewable energy, the term "qualified facility" means any facility owned by the taxpayer—

(A) which has a nameplate capacity rating of at least 150 kilowatts, and

(B) which is originally placed in service on or after the date of the enactment of this paragraph and the construction of which begins before January 1, 2014.*

(e) Definitions and special rules.—For purposes of this section—

(1) Only production in the United States taken into account.—Sales shall be taken into account under this section only with respect to electricity the production of which is within—

(A) the United States (within the meaning of section 638(1)), or

(B) a possession of the United States (within the meaning of section 638(2)).

(2) Computation of inflation adjustment factor and reference price.—

(A) In general.—The Secretary shall, not later than April 1 of each calendar year, determine and publish in the Federal Register the inflation adjustment factor and the reference price for such calendar year in accordance with this paragraph.

(B) Inflation adjustment factor.—The term "inflation adjustment factor" means, with respect to a calendar year, a fraction the numerator of which is the GDP implicit price deflator for the preceding calendar year and the denominator of which is the GDP implicit price deflator for the calendar year 1992. The term "GDP implicit price deflator" means the most recent revision of the implicit price deflator for the gross domestic product as computed and published by the Department of Commerce before March 15 of the calendar year.

(C) Reference price.—The term "reference price" means, with respect to a calendar year, the Secretary's determination of the annual average contract price per kilowatt hour of electricity generated from the same qualified energy resource and sold in the previous year in the United States. For purposes of the preceding sentence, only contracts entered into after December 31, 1989, shall be taken into account.

(3) Production attributable to the taxpayer.— In the case of a facility in which more than 1 person has an ownership interest, except to the extent provided in regulations prescribed by the Secretary, production from the facility shall be allocated among such persons in proportion to their respective ownership interests in the gross sales from such facility.

(4) Related persons.—Persons shall be treated as related to each other if such persons would be treated as a single employer under the regulations prescribed under section 52(b). In the case of a corporation which is a member of an affiliated group of corporations filing a consolidated return, such corporation shall be treated as selling electricity to an unrelated person if such electricity is sold to such a person by another member of such group.

(5) Pass-thru in the case of estates and trusts.—Under regulations prescribed by the Secretary, rules similar to the rules of subsection (d) of section 52 shall apply.

***(7) Credit not to apply to electricity sold to utilities under certain contracts.—**

(A) In general.—The credit determined under subsection (a) shall not apply to electricity,

(i) produced at a qualified facility described in subsection (d)(1) which is placed in service by the taxpayer after June 30, 1999, and

(ii) sold to a utility pursuant to a contract originally entered into before January 1, 1987 (whether or not amended or restated after that date).

(B) Exception.—Subparagraph (A) shall not apply if—

(i) the prices for energy and capacity from such facility are established pursuant to an amendment to the contract referred to in subparagraph (A)(ii),

(ii) such amendment provides that the prices set forth in the contract which exceed avoided cost prices determined at the time of delivery shall apply only to annual quantities of electricity (prorated for partial years) which do not exceed the greater of—

(I) the average annual quantity of electricity sold to the utility under the contract during calendar years 1994, 1995, 1996, 1997, and 1998, or

(II) the estimate of the annual electricity production set forth in the contract, or, if there is no such estimate, the greatest annual quantity of electricity sold to the utility under the contract in any of the calendar years 1996, 1997, or 1998, and

(iii) such amendment provides that energy and capacity in excess of the limitation in clause (ii) may be—

(I) sold to the utility only at prices that do not exceed avoided cost prices determined at the time of delivery, or

(II) sold to a third party subject to a mutually agreed upon advance notice to the utility.

For purposes of this subparagraph, avoided cost prices shall be determined as provided for in 18 CFR 292.3049d)(1) or any successor regulation.

* * *

*Editorial comment: There is no subsection (e)(6).

§ 45A. Indian employment credit*

(a) Amount of credit.—For purposes of section 38, the amount of the Indian employment credit determined under this section with respect to any employer for any taxable year is an amount equal to 20 percent of the excess (if any) of—

(1) the sum of—

(A) the qualified wages paid or incurred during such taxable year, plus

(B) qualified employee health insurance costs paid or incurred during such taxable year, over

(2) the sum of the qualified wages and qualified employee health insurance costs (determined as if this section were in effect) which were paid or incurred by the employer (or any predecessor) during calendar year 1993.

(b) Qualified wages; qualified employee health insurance costs.—For purposes of this section—

(1) Qualified wages.—

(A) In general.—The term "qualified wages" means any wages paid or incurred by an employer for services performed by an employee while such employee is a qualified employee.

(B) Coordination with work opportunity credit.—The term "qualified wages" shall not include wages attributable to service rendered during the 1-year period beginning with the day the individual begins work for the employer if any portion of such wages is taken into account in determining the credit under section 51.

(2) Qualified employee health insurance costs.—

(A) In general.—The term "qualified employee health insurance costs" means any amount paid or incurred by an employer for health insurance to the extent such amount is attributable to coverage provided to any employee while such employee is a qualified employee.

(B) Exception for amounts paid under salary reduction arrangements.—No amount paid or incurred for health insurance pursuant to a salary reduction arrangement shall be taken into account under subparagraph (A).

(3) Limitation.—The aggregate amount of qualified wages and qualified employee health insurance costs taken into account with respect to any employee for any taxable year (and for the base period under subsection (a)(2)) shall not exceed $20,000.

(c) Qualified employee.—For purposes of this section—

(1) In general.—Except as otherwise provided in this subsection, the term "qualified employee" means, with respect to any period, any employee of an employer if—

(A) the employee is an enrolled member of an Indian tribe or the spouse of an enrolled member of an Indian tribe,

(B) substantially all of the services performed during such period by such employee for such employer are performed within an Indian reservation, and

(C) the principal place of abode of such employee while performing such services is on or near the reservation in which the services are performed.

(2) Individuals receiving wages in excess of $30,000 not eligible.—An employee shall not be treated as a qualified employee for any taxable year of the employer if the total amount of the wages paid or incurred by such employer to such employee during such taxable year (whether or not for services within an Indian reservation) exceeds the amount determined at an annual rate of $30,000.

(3) Inflation adjustment.—The Secretary shall adjust the $30,000 amount under paragraph (2) for years beginning after 1994 at the same time and in the same manner as under section 415(d), except that the base period taken into account for purposes of such adjustment shall be the calendar quarter beginning October 1, 1993.

(4) Employment must be trade or business employment.—An employee shall be treated as a qualified employee for any taxable year of the employer only if more than 50 percent of the wages paid or incurred by the employer to such employee during such taxable year are for services performed in a trade or business of the employer. Any determination as to whether the preceding sentence applies with respect to any employee for any taxable year shall be made without regard to subsection (e)(2).

*Editorial comment: At the present time, this section has not been extended. There is pending legislation in the Senate, *The Tax Extenders Act of 2013 (S.1859)*, that would extend Section 45A(f) until December 31, 2014.

(5) Certain employees not eligible.—The term "qualified employee" shall not include—

(A) any individual described in subparagraph (A), (B), or (C) of section 51(i)(1),

(B) any 5-percent owner (as defined in section 416(i)(1)(B)), and

(C) any individual if the services performed by such individual for the employer involve the conduct of class I, II, or III gaming as defined in section 4 of the Indian Gaming Regulatory Act (25 U.S.C. 2703), or are performed in a building housing such gaming activity.

(6) Indian tribe defined.—The term "Indian tribe" means any Indian tribe, band, nation, pueblo, or other organized group or community, including any Alaska Native village, or regional or village corporation, as defined in, or established pursuant to, the Alaska Native Claims Settlement Act (43 U.S.C. 1601 et seq.) which is recognized as eligible for the special programs and services provided by the United States to Indians because of their status as Indians.

(7) Indian reservation defined.—The term "Indian reservation" has the meaning given such term by section 168(j)(6).

(d) Early termination of employment by employer.—

(1) In general.—If the employment of any employee is terminated by the taxpayer before the day 1 year after the day on which such employee began work for the employer—

(A) no wages (or qualified employee health insurance costs) with respect to such employee shall be taken into account under subsection (a) for the taxable year in which such employment is terminated, and

(B) the tax under this chapter for the taxable year in which such employment is terminated shall be increased by the aggregate credits (if any) allowed under section 38(a) for prior taxable years by reason of wages (or qualified employee health insurance costs) taken into account with respect to such employee.

(2) Carrybacks and carryovers adjusted.—In the case of any termination of employment to which paragraph (1) applies, the carrybacks and carryovers under section 39 shall be properly adjusted.

(3) Subsection not to apply in certain cases.—

(A) In general.—Paragraph (1) shall not apply to—

(i) a termination of employment of an employee who voluntarily leaves the employment of the taxpayer,

(ii) a termination of employment of an individual who before the close of the period referred to in paragraph (1) becomes disabled to perform the services of such employment unless such disability is removed before the close of such period and the taxpayer fails to offer reemployment to such individual, or

(iii) a termination of employment of an individual if it is determined under the applicable State unemployment compensation law that the termination was due to the misconduct of such individual.

(B) Changes in form of business.—For purposes of paragraph (1), the employment relationship between the taxpayer and an employee shall not be treated as terminated—

(i) by a transaction to which section 381(a) applies if the employee continues to be employed by the acquiring corporation, or

(ii) by reason of a mere change in the form of conducting the trade or business of the taxpayer if the employee continues to be employed in such trade or business and the taxpayer retains a substantial interest in such trade or business.

(4) Special rule.—Any increase in tax under paragraph (1) shall not be treated as a tax imposed by this chapter for purposes of—

(A) determining the amount of any credit allowable under this chapter, and

(B) determining the amount of the tax imposed by section 55.

(e) Other definitions and special rules.—For purposes of this section—

(1) Wages.—The term "wages" has the same meaning given to such term in section 51.

(2) Controlled groups.—

(A) All employers treated as a single employer under section (a) or (b) of section 52 shall be treated as a single employer for purposes of this section.

(B) The credit (if any) determined under this section with respect to each such employer shall be its proportionate share of the wages and qualified employee health insurance costs giving rise to such credit.

(3) Certain other rules made applicable.—Rules similar to the rules of section 51(k) and subsections (c), (d), and (e) of section 52 shall apply.

(4) Coordination with nonrevenue laws.—Any reference in this section to a provision not contained in this title shall be treated for purposes of this section as a reference to such provision as in effect on the date of the enactment of this paragraph.

(5) Special rule for short taxable years.—For any taxable year having less than 12 months, the amount determined under subsection (a)(2) shall be multiplied by a fraction, the numerator of which is the number of days in the taxable year and the denominator of which is 365.

(f) Termination.—This section shall not apply to taxable years beginning after December 31, 2013.

§ 45B. Credit for portion of employer social security taxes paid with respect to employee cash tips

(a) General rule.—For purposes of section 38, the employer social security credit determined under this section for the taxable year is an amount equal to the excess employer social security tax paid or incurred by the taxpayer during the taxable year.

(b) Excess employer social security tax.—For purposes of this section—

(1) In general.—The term "excess employer social security tax" means any tax paid by an employer under section 3111 with respect to tips received by an employee during any month, to the extent such tips—

(A) are deemed to have been paid by the employer to the employee pursuant to section 3121(q) (without regard to whether such tips are reported under section 6053), and

(B) exceed the amount by which the wages (excluding tips) paid by the employer to the employee during such month are less than the total amount which would be payable (with respect to such employment) at the minimum wage rate applicable to such individual under section 6(a)(1) of the Fair Labor Standards Act of 1938 (as in effect on January 1, 2007, and determined without regard to section 3(m) of such Act).

(2) Only tips received for food or beverages taken into account.—In applying paragraph (1), there shall be taken into account only tips received from customers in connection with the providing, delivering, or serving of food or beverages for consumption if the tipping of employees delivering or serving food or beverages by customers is customary.

(c) Denial of double benefit.—No deduction shall be allowed under this chapter for any amount taken into account in determining the credit under this section.

(d) Election not to claim credit.—This section shall not apply to a taxpayer for any taxable year if such taxpayer elects to have this section not apply for such taxable year.

§ 45C. Clinical testing expenses for certain drugs for rare diseases or conditions*

(a) General rule.—For purposes of section 38, the credit determined under this section for the taxable year is an amount equal to 50 percent of the qualified clinical testing expenses for the taxable year.

(b) Qualified clinical testing expenses.—For purposes of this section—

(1) Qualified clinical testing expenses.—

(A) In general.—Except as otherwise provided in this paragraph, the term "qualified clinical testing expenses" means the amounts which are paid or incurred by the taxpayer during the taxable year which would be described in subsection (b) of section 41 if such subsection were applied with the modifications set forth in subparagraph (B).

(B) Modifications.—For purposes of subparagraph (A), subsection (b) of section 41 shall be applied—

(i) by substituting "clinical testing" for "qualified research" each place it appears in paragraphs (2) and (3) of such subsection, and

(ii) by substituting "100 percent" for "65 percent" in paragraph (3)(A) of such subsection.

(C) Exclusion for amounts funded by grants, etc.—The term "qualified clinical testing expenses" shall not include any amount to the extent such amount is funded by any grant, contract, or otherwise by another person (or any governmental entity).

(D) Special rule.—For purposes of this paragraph, section 41 shall be deemed to remain

*Editorial comment: At the present time, this section has not been extended. There is pending legislation in the Senate, *The Tax Extenders Act of 2013 (S. 1859)*, that would extend Section 45C until December 31, 2014.

in effect for periods after June 30, 1995, and before July 1, 1996, and periods after December 31, 2013.

(2) Clinical testing.—

(A) In general.—The term "clinical testing" means any human clinical testing—

(i) which is carried out under an exemption for a drug being tested for a rare disease or condition under section 505(i) of the Federal Food, Drug, and Cosmetic Act (or regulations issued under such section),

(ii) which occurs—

(I) after the date such drug is designated under section 526 of such Act, and

(II) before the date on which an application with respect to such drug is approved under section 505(b) or 507 of such Act or, if the drug is a biological product, before the date on which a license for such drug is issued under section 351 of the Public Health Service Act; and

(iii) which is conducted by or on behalf of the taxpayer to whom the designation under such section 526 applies.

(B) Testing must be related to use for rare disease or condition.—Human clinical testing shall be taken into account under subparagraph (A) only to the extent such testing is related to the use of a drug for the rare disease or condition for which it was designated under section 526 of the Federal Food, Drug, and Cosmetic Act.

(c) Coordination with credit for increased research expenditures.—

(1) In general.—Except as provided in paragraph (2), any qualified clinical testing expenses for a taxable year to which an election under this section applies shall not be taken into account for purposes of determining the credit allowable under section 41 for such taxable year.

(2) Expenses included in determining base period research expenses.—Any qualified clinical testing expenses for any taxable year which are qualified research expenses (within the meaning of section 41(b)) shall be taken into account in determining base period research expenses for purposes of applying section 41 to subsequent taxable years.

(d) Definition and special rules.—

(1) Rare disease or condition.—For purposes of this section, the term "rare disease or condition" means any disease or condition which—

(A) affects less than 200,000 persons in the United States, or

(B) affects more than 200,000 persons in the United States but for which there is no reasonable expectation that the cost of developing and making available in the United States a drug for such disease or condition will be recovered from sales in the United States of such drug.

Determination under the preceding sentence with respect to any drug shall be made on the basis of the facts and circumstances as of the date such drug is designated under section 526 of the Federal Food, Drug, and Cosmetic Act.

(2) Special limitations on foreign testing.—

(A) In general.—No credit shall be allowed under this section with respect to any clinical testing conducted outside the United States unless—

(i) such testing is conducted outside the United States because there is an insufficient testing population in the United States, and

(ii) such testing is conducted by a United States person or by any other person who is not related to the taxpayer to whom the designation under section 526 of the Federal Food, Drug, and Cosmetic Act applies.

(B) Special limitation for corporations to which section 936 applies.—No credit shall be allowed under this section with respect to any clinical testing conducted by a corporation to which an election under section 936 applies.

(3) Certain rules made applicable.—Rules similar to the rules of paragraphs (1) and (2) of section 41(f) shall apply for purposes of this section.

(4) Election.—This section shall apply to any taxpayer for any taxable year only if such taxpayer elects (at such time and in such manner as the Secretary may by regulations prescribe) to have this section apply for such taxable year.

§ 45D. New markets tax credit

(a) Allowance of credit.—

(1) In general.—For purposes of section 38, in the case of a taxpayer who holds a qualified equity investment on a credit allowance date of such investment which occurs during the taxable year, the new markets tax credit determined under this section for such taxable year is an amount equal to the applicable percentage of the amount paid to the qualified community development entity for such investment at its original issue.

(2) Applicable percentage.—For purposes of paragraph (1), the applicable percentage is—

(A) 5 percent with respect to the first 3 credit allowance dates, and

(B) 6 percent with respect to the remainder of the credit allowance dates.

(3) Credit allowance date.—For purposes of paragraph (1), the term "credit allowance date" means, with respect to any qualified equity investment—

(A) the date on which such investment is initially made, and

(B) each of the 6 anniversary dates of such date thereafter.

(b) Qualified equity investment.—For purposes of this section—

(1) In general.—The term "qualified equity investment" means any equity investment in a qualified community development entity if—

(A) such investment is acquired by the taxpayer at its original issue (directly or through an underwriter) solely in exchange for cash.

(B) substantially all of such cash is used by the qualified community development entity to make qualified low-income community investments, and

(C) such investment is designated for purposes of this section by the qualified community development entity.

Such term shall not include any equity investment issued by a qualified community development entity more than 5 years after the date that such entity receives an allocation under subsection (f). Any allocation not used within such 5-year period may be reallocated by the Secretary under subsection (f).

(2) Limitation.—The maximum amount of equity investments issued by a qualified community development entity which may be designated under paragraph (1)(C) by such entity shall not exceed the portion of the limitation amount allocated under subsection (f) to such entity.

(3) Safe harbor for determining use of cash.—The requirement of paragraph (1)(B) shall be treated as met if at least 85 percent of the aggregate gross assets of the qualified community development entity are invested in qualified low-income community investments.

(4) Treatment of subsequent purchasers.—The term "qualified equity investment" includes any equity investment which would (but for paragraph (1)(A)) be a qualified equity investment in the hands of the taxpayer if such investment was a qualified equity investment in the hands of a prior holder.

(5) Redemptions.—A rule similar to the rule of section 1202(c)(3) shall apply for purposes of this subsection.

(6) Equity investment.—The term "equity investment" means—

(A) any stock (other than nonqualified preferred stock as defined in section 351(g)(2)) in an entity which is a corporation, and

(B) any capital interest in an entity which is a partnership.

(c) Qualified community development entity.—For purposes of this section—

(1) In general.—The term "qualified community development entity" means any domestic corporation or partnership if—

(A) the primary mission of the entity is serving, or providing investment capital for, low-income communities or low-income persons,

(B) the entity maintains accountability to residents of low-income communities through their representation on any governing board of the entity or on any advisory board to the entity, and

(C) the entity is certified by the Secretary for purposes of this section as being a qualified community development entity.

(2) Special rules for certain organizations.—The requirements of paragraph (1) shall be treated as met by—

(A) any specialized small business investment company (as defined in section 1044(c)(3)), and

(B) any community development financial institution (as defined in section 103 of the Community Development Banking and Financial Institutions Act of 1994 (12 U.S.C. 4702)).

(d) Qualified low-income community investments.—For purposes of this section—

(1) In general.—The term "qualified low-income community investment" means—

(A) any capital or equity investment in, or loan to, any qualified active low-income community business,

(B) the purchase from another community development entity of any loan made by such entity which is a qualified low-income community investment,

(C) financial counseling and other services specified in regulations prescribed by the Secretary to businesses located in, and residents of, low-income communities, and

(D) any equity investment in, or loan to, any qualified community development entity.

(2) Qualified active low-income community business.—

(A) In general.—For purposes of paragraph (1), the term "qualified active low-income community business" means, with respect to any taxable year, any corporation (including a nonprofit corporation) or partnership if for such year—

(i) at least 50 percent of the total gross income of such entity is derived from the active conduct of a qualified business within any low-income community,

(ii) a substantial portion of the use of the tangible property of such entity (whether owned or leased) is within any low-income community,

(iii) a substantial portion of the services performed for such entity by its employees are performed in any low-income community,

(iv) less than 5 percent of the average of the aggregate unadjusted bases of the property of such entity is attributable to collectibles (as defined in section 408(m)(2)) other than collectibles that are held primarily for sale to customers in the ordinary course of such business, and

(v) less than 5 percent of the average of the aggregate unadjusted bases of the property of such entity is attributable to nonqualified financial property (as defined in section 1397C(e)).

(B) Proprietorship.—Such term shall include any business carried on by an individual as a proprietor if such business would meet the requirements of subparagraph (A) were it incorporated.

(C) Portions of business may be qualified active low-income community business.—The term "qualified active low-income community business" includes any trades or businesses which would qualify as a qualified active low-income community business if such trades or businesses were separately incorporated.

(3) Qualified business.—For purposes of this subsection, the term "qualified business" has the meaning given to such term by section 1397C(d); except that—

(A) In lieu of applying paragraph (2)(B) thereof, the rental to others of real property located in any low-income community shall be treated as a qualified business if there are substantial improvements located on such property, and

(B) paragraph (3) thereof shall not apply.

(e) Low-income community.—For purposes of this section—

(1) In general.—The term "low-income community" means any population census tract if—

(A) the poverty rate for such tract is at least 20 percent, or

(B) (i) in the case of a tract not located within a metropolitan area, the median family income for such tract does not exceed 80 percent of statewide median family income, or

(ii) in the case of a tract located within a metropolitan area, the median family income for such tract does not exceed 80 percent of the greater of statewide median family income or the metropolitan area median family income.

Subparagraph (B) shall be applied using possessionwide median family income in the case of census tracts located within a possession of the United States.

(2) Targeted populations.—The Secretary shall prescribe regulations under which 1 or more targeted populations (within the meaning of section 103(20) of the Riegle Community Development and Regulatory Improvement Act of 1994 (12 U.S.C. 4702(20))) may be treated as low-income communities. Such regulations shall include procedures for determining which entities are qualified active low-income community businesses with respect to such populations.

(3) Areas not within census tracts.—In the case of an area which is not tracted for population census tracts, the equivalent county divisions (as defined by the Bureau of the Census for purposes of defining poverty areas) shall be used for purposes of determining poverty rates and median family income.

(4) Tracts with low population.—A population census tract with a population of less than

2,000 shall be treated as a low-income community for purposes of this section if such tract—

(A) is within an empowerment zone the designation of which is in effect under section 1391, and

(B) is contiguous to 1 or more low-income communities (determined without regard to this paragraph).

(5) Modification of income requirement for census tracts within high migration rural counties.—

(A) In general.—In the case of a population census tract located within a high migration rural county, paragraph (1)(B)(i) shall be applied by substituting "85 percent" for "80 percent."

(B) High migration rural county.—For purposes of this paragraph, the term "high migration rural county" means any county which, during the 20-year period ending with the year in which the most recent census was conducted, has a net out-migration of inhabitants from the county of at least 10 percent of the population of the county at the beginning of such period.

(f) National limitation of amount of investments designated.*—

(1) In general.—There is a new markets tax credit limitation for each calendar year. Such limitation is—

(A) $1,000,000,000 for 2001,

(B) $1,500,000,000 for 2002 and 2003,

(C) $2,000,000,000 for 2004 and 2005,

(D) $3,500,000,000 for 2006 and 2007,

(E) $5,000,000,000 for 2008,

(F) $5,000,000,000 for 2009, and

(G) $3,500,000,000 for 2010, 2011, 2012, and 2013.*

(2) Allocation of limitation.—The limitation under paragraph (1) shall be allocated by the Secretary among qualified community development entities selected by the Secretary. In making allocations under the preceding sentence, the Secretary shall give priority to any entity—

(A) with a record of having successfully provided capital or technical assistance to disadvantaged businesses or communities, or

(B) which intends to satisfy the requirement under subsection (b)(1)(B) by making qualified low-income community investments in 1 or more businesses in which persons unrelated to such entity (within the meaning of section 267 (b) or 707(b)(1)) hold the majority equity interest.

(3) Carryover of unused limitation.—If the new markets tax credit limitation for any calendar year exceeds the aggregate amount allocated under paragraph (2) for such year, such limitation for the succeeding calendar year shall be increased by the amount of such excess. No amount may be carried under the preceding sentence to any calendar year after 2018.*

(g) Recapture of credit in certain cases.—

(1) In general.—If, at any time during the 7-year period beginning on the date of the original issue of a qualified equity investment in a qualified community development entity, there is a recapture event with respect to such investment, then the tax imposed by this chapter for the taxable year in which such event occurs shall be increased by the credit recapture amount.

(2) Credit recapture amount.—For purposes of paragraph (1), the credit recapture amount is an amount equal to the sum of—

(A) the aggregate decrease in the credits allowed to the taxpayer under section 38 for all prior taxable years which would have resulted if no credit had been determined under this section with respect to such investment, plus

(B) interest at the underpayment rate established under section 6621 on the amount determined under subparagraph (A) for each prior taxable year for the period beginning on the due date for filing the return for the prior taxable year involved.

No deduction shall be allowed under this chapter for interest described in subparagraph (B).

(3) Recapture event.—For purposes of paragraph (1), there is a recapture event with respect to an equity investment in a qualified community development entity if—

(A) such entity ceases to be a qualified community development entity,

*Editorial comment: At the present time, this section has not been extended. There is pending legislation in the Senate, *The Tax Extenders Act of 2013 (S. 1859)*, that would extend Section 45D(f)(1)(G) until 2014. This legislation would also extend Section 45(D)(f)(3) to 2019.

(B) the proceeds of the investment cease to be used as required of subsection (b)(1)(B), or

(C) such investment is redeemed by such entity.

(4) Special rules.—

(A) Tax benefit rule.—The tax for the taxable year shall be increased under paragraph (1) only with respect to credits allowed by reason of this section which were used to reduce tax liability. In the case of credits not so used to reduce tax liability, the carryforwards and carrybacks under section 39 shall be appropriately adjusted.

(B) No credits against tax.—Any increase in tax under this subsection shall not be treated as a tax imposed by this chapter for purposes of determining the amount of any credit under this chapter or for purposes of section 55.

(h) Basis reduction.—The basis of any qualified equity investment shall be reduced by the amount of any credit determined under this section with respect to such investment. This subsection shall not apply for purposes of sections 1202, 1400B, and 1400F.

(i) Regulations.—The Secretary shall prescribe such regulations—

(1) which limit the credit for investments which are directly or indirectly subsidized by other Federal tax benefits (including the credit under section 42 and the exclusion from gross income under section 103),

(2) which prevent the abuse of the purposes of this section,

(3) which provide rules for determining whether the requirement of subsection (b)(1)(B) is treated as met,

(4) which impose appropriate reporting requirements,

(5) which apply the provisions of this section to newly formed entities, and

(6) which ensure that non-metropolitan counties receive a proportional allocation of qualified equity investments.

§ 45E. Small employer pension plan startup costs

(a) General rule.—For purposes of section 38, in the case of an eligible employer, the small employer pension plan startup cost credit determined under this section for any taxable year is an amount equal to 50 percent of the qualified startup costs paid or incurred by the taxpayer during the taxable year.

(b) Dollar limitation.—The amount of the credit determined under this section for any taxable year shall not exceed—

(1) $500 for the first credit year and each of the 2 taxable years immediately following the first credit year, and

(2) zero for any other taxable year.

(c) Eligible employer.—For purposes of this section—

(1) In general.—The term "eligible employer" has the meaning given such term by section 408(p)(2)(C)(i).

(2) Requirement for new qualified employer plans.—Such term shall not include an employer if, during the 3-taxable year period immediately preceding the 1st taxable year for which the credit under this section is otherwise allowable for a qualified employer plan of the employer, the employer or any member of any controlled group including the employer (or any predecessor of either) established or maintained a qualified employer plan with respect to which contributions were made, or benefits were accrued, for substantially the same employees as are in the qualified employer plan.

(d) Other definitions.—For purposes of this section—

(1) Qualified startup costs.—

(A) In general.—The term "qualified startup costs" means any ordinary and necessary expenses of an eligible employer which are paid or incurred in connection with—

(i) the establishment or administration of an eligible employer plan, or

(ii) the retirement-related education of employees with respect to such plan.

(B) Plan must have at least 1 participant.—Such term shall not include any expense in connection with a plan that does not have at least 1 employee eligible to participate who is not a highly compensated employee.

(2) Eligible employer plan.—The term "eligible employer plan" means a qualified employer plan within the meaning of section 4972(d).

(3) First credit year.—The term "first credit year" means—

(A) the taxable year which includes the date that the eligible employer plan to which such costs relate becomes effective, or

(B) at the election of the eligible employer, the taxable year preceding the taxable year referred to in subparagraph (A).

(e) Special rules.—For purposes of this section—

(1) Aggregation rules.—All persons treated as a single employer under subsection (a) or (b) of section 52, or subsection (m) or (o) of section 414, shall be treated as one person. All eligible employer plans shall be treated as 1 eligible employer plan.

(2) Disallowance of deduction.—No deduction shall be allowed for that portion of the qualified startup costs paid or incurred for the taxable year which is equal to the credit determined under subsection (a).

(3) Election not to claim credit.—This section shall not apply to a taxpayer for any taxable year if such taxpayer elects to have this section not apply for such taxable year.

§ 45F. Employer-provided child care credit

(a) In general.—For purposes of section 38, the employer-provided child care credit determined under this section for the taxable year is an amount equal to the sum of—

(1) 25 percent of the qualified child care expenditures, and

(2) 10 percent of the qualified child care resource and referral expenditures, of the taxpayer for such taxable year.

(b) Dollar limitation.—The credit allowable under subsection (a) for any taxable year shall not exceed $150,000.

(c) Definitions.—For purposes of this section—

(1) Qualified child care expenditure.—

(A) In general.—The term "qualified child care expenditure" means any amount paid or incurred—

(i) to acquire, construct, rehabilitate, or expand property—

(I) which is to be used as part of a qualified child care facility of the taxpayer,

(II) with respect to which a deduction for depreciation (or amortization in lieu of depreciation) is allowable, and

(III) which does not constitute part of the principal residence (within the meaning of section 121) of the taxpayer or any employee of the taxpayer,

(ii) for the operating costs of a qualified child care facility of the taxpayer, including costs related to the training of employees, to scholarship programs, and to the providing of increased compensation to employees with higher levels of child care training, or

(iii) under a contract with a qualified child care facility to provide child care services to employees of the taxpayer.

(B) Fair market value.—The term "qualified child care expenditures" shall not include expenses in excess of the fair market value of such care.

(2) Qualified child care facility.—

(A) In general.—The term "qualified child care facility" means a facility—

(i) the principal use of which is to provide child care assistance, and

(ii) which meets the requirements of all applicable laws and regulations of the State or local government in which it is located, including the licensing of the facility as a child care facility.

Clause (i) shall not apply to a facility which is the principal residence (within the meaning of section 121) of the operator of the facility.

(B) Special rules with respect to a taxpayer.—A facility shall not be treated as a qualified child care facility with respect to a taxpayer unless—

(i) enrollment in the facility is open to employees of the taxpayer during the taxable year,

(ii) if the facility is the principal trade or business of the taxpayer, at least 30 percent of the enrollees of such facility are dependents of employees of the taxpayer, and

(iii) the use of such facility (or the eligibility to use such facility) does not discriminate in favor of employees of the taxpayer who are highly compensated employees (within the meaning of section 414(q)).

(3) Qualified child care resource and referral expenditure.—

(A) In general.—The term "qualified child care resource and referral expenditure" means any amount paid or incurred under a contract to provide child care resource and referral services to an employee of the taxpayer.

(B) Nondiscrimination.—The services shall not be treated as qualified unless the provision of such services (or the eligibility to use such services) does not discriminate in favor of employees of the taxpayer who are highly compensated employees (within the meaning of section 414(q)).

(d) Recapture of acquisition and construction credit.—

(1) In general.—If, as of the close of any taxable year, there is a recapture event with respect to any qualified child care facility of the taxpayer, then the tax of the taxpayer under this chapter for such taxable year shall be increased by an amount equal to the product of—

(A) the applicable recapture percentage, and

(B) the aggregate decrease in the credits allowed under section 38 for all prior taxable years which would have resulted if the qualified child care expenditures of the taxpayer described in subsection (c)(1)(A) with respect to such facility had been zero.

(2) Applicable recapture percentage.—

(A) In general.—For purposes of this subsection, the applicable recapture percentage shall be determined from the following table:

If the recapture event occurs in:	The applicable recapture percentage is:
Years 1–3	100
Year 4	85
Year 5	70
Year 6	55
Year 7	40
Year 8	25
Years 9 and 10	10
Years 11 and thereafter	0

(B) Years.—For purposes of subparagraph (A), year 1 shall begin on the first day of the taxable year in which the qualified child care facility is placed in service by the taxpayer.

(3) Recapture event defined.—For purposes of this subsection, the term "recapture event" means—

(A) Cessation of operation.—The cessation of the operation of the facility as a qualified child care facility.

(B) Change in ownership.—

(i) In general.—Except as provided in clause (ii), the disposition of a taxpayer's interest in a qualified child care facility with respect to which the credit described in subsection (a) was allowable.

(ii) Agreement to assume recapture liability.—Clause (i) shall not apply if the person acquiring such interest in the facility agrees in writing to assume the recapture liability of the person disposing of such interest in effect immediately before such disposition. In the event of such an assumption, the person acquiring the interest in the facility shall be treated as the taxpayer for purposes of assessing any recapture liability (computed as if there had been no change in ownership).

(4) Special rules.—

(A) Tax benefit rule.—The tax for the taxable year shall be increased under paragraph (1) only with respect to credits allowed by reason of this section which were used to reduce tax liability. In the case of credits not so used to reduce tax liability, the carryforwards and carrybacks under section 39 shall be appropriately adjusted.

(B) No credits against tax.—Any increase in tax under this subsection shall not be treated as a tax imposed by this chapter for purposes of determining the amount of any credit under this chapter or for purposes of section 55.

(C) No recapture by reason of casualty loss.—The increase in tax under this subsection shall not apply to a cessation of operation of the facility as a qualified child care facility by reason of a casualty loss to the extent such loss is restored by reconstruction or replacement within a reasonable period established by the Secretary.

(e) Special rules.—For purposes of this section—

(1) Aggregation rules.—All persons which are treated as a single employer under subsections (a) and (b) of section 52 shall be treated as a single taxpayer.

(2) Pass-thru in the case of estates and trusts.—Under regulations prescribed by the Secretary, rules similar to the rules of subsection (d) of section 52 shall apply.

(3) Allocation in the case of partnerships.—In the case of partnerships, the credit shall be allocated among partners under regulations prescribed by the Secretary.

(f) No double benefit.—

(1) Reduction in basis.—For purposes of this subtitle—

(A) In general.—If a credit is determined under this section with respect to any property by reason of expenditures described in subsection (c)(1)(A), the basis of such property shall be reduced by the amount of the credit so determined.

(B) Certain dispositions.—If, during any taxable year, there is a recapture amount determined with respect to any property the basis of which was reduced under subparagraph (A), the basis of such property (immediately before the event resulting in such recapture) shall be increased by an amount equal to such recapture amount. For purposes of the preceding sentence, the term "recapture amount" means any increase in tax (or adjustment in carrybacks or carryovers) determined under subsection (d).

(2) Other deductions and credits.—No deduction or credit shall be allowed under any other provision of this chapter with respect to the amount of the credit determined under this section.

* * *

§ 45N. Mine rescue team training credit*

(a) Amount of credit.—For purposes of section 38, the mine rescue team training credit determined under this section with respect to each qualified mine rescue team employee of an eligible employer for any taxable year is an amount equal to the lesser of—

(1) 20 percent of the amount paid or incurred by the taxpayer during the taxable year with respect to the training program costs of such qualified mine rescue team employee (including wages of such employee while attending such program), or

(2) $10,000.

(b) Qualified mine rescue team employee.—For purposes of this section, the term "qualified minerescue team employee" means with respect to any taxable year any full-time employee of the taxpayer who is—

(1) a miner eligible for more than 6 months of such taxable year to serve as a mine rescue team member as a result of completing, at a minimum, an initial 20-hour course of instruction as prescribed by the Mine Safety and Health Administration's Office of Educational Policy and Development, or

(2) a miner eligible for more than 6 months of such taxable year to serve as a mine rescue team member by virtue of receiving at least 40 hours of refresher training in such instruction.

(c) Eligible employer.—For purposes of this section, the term "eligible employer" means any taxpayer which employs individuals as miners in underground mines in the United States.

(d) Wages.—For purposes of this section, the term "wages" has the meaning given to such term by subsection (b) of section 3306 (determined without regard to any dollar limitation contained in such section).

(e) Termination.—This section shall not apply to taxable years beginning after December 31, 2013.*

* * *

§ 45R. Employee health insurance expenses of small employers

(a) General rule.—For purposes of section 38, in the case of an eligible small employer, the small employer health insurance credit determined under this section for any taxable year in the credit period is the amount determined under subsection (b).

(b) Health insurance credit amount.—Subject to subsection (c), the amount determined under this subsection with respect to any eligible small employer is equal to 50 percent (35 percent in the case of a tax-exempt eligible small employer) of the lesser of—

(1) the aggregate amount of nonelective contributions the employer made on behalf of its employees during the taxable year under the arrangement described in subsection (d)(4) for premiums for qualified health plans offered by the employer to its employees through an Exchange, or

(2) the aggregate amount of nonelective contributions which the employer would have made during the taxable year under the arrangement if each employee taken into account under paragraph (1) had enrolled in a qualified health plan which had a premium equal to the average premium (as determined by the Secretary of Health and Human Services) for the small group market in the rating area in which the employee enrolls for coverage.

(c) Phaseout of credit amount based on number of employees and average wages.—The amount of credit determined under subsection (b) without regard to this subsection shall be reduced (but not below zero) by the sum of the following amounts:

*Editorial comment: At the present time, this section has not been extended. There is pending legislation in the Senate, *The Tax Extenders Act of 2013 (S. 1859)*, that would extend Section 45N until December 31, 2014.

(1) Such amount multiplied by a fraction the numerator of which is the total number of full-time equivalent employees of the employer in excess of 10 and the denominator of which is 15.

(2) Such amount multiplied by a fraction the numerator of which is the average annual wages of the employer in excess of the dollar amount in effect under subsection (d)(3)(B) and the denominator of which is such dollar amount.

(d) Eligible small employer.—For purposes of this section—

(1) In general.—The term "eligible small employer" means, with respect to any taxable year, an employer—

(A) which has no more than 25 full-time equivalent employees for the taxable year,

(B) the average annual wages of which do not exceed an amount equal to twice the dollar amount in effect under paragraph (3)(B) for the taxable year, and

(C) which has in effect an arrangement described in paragraph (4).

(2) Full-time equivalent employees.—

(A) In general.—The term "full-time equivalent employees" means a number of employees equal to the number determined by dividing—

(i) the total number of hours of service for which wages were paid by the employer to employees during the taxable year, by

(ii) 2,080.

Such number shall be rounded to the next lowest whole number if not otherwise a whole number.

(B) Excess hours not counted.—If an employee works in excess of 2,080 hours of service during any taxable year, such excess shall not be taken into account under subparagraph (A).

(C) Hours of services.—The Secretary, in consultation with the Secretary of Labor, shall prescribe such regulations, rules, and guidance as may be necessary to determine the hours of service of an employee, including rules for the application of this paragraph to employees who are not compensated on an hourly basis.

(3) Average annual wages.—

(A) In general.—The average annual wages of an eligible small employer for any taxable year is the amount determined by dividing—

(i) the aggregate amount of wages which were paid by the employer to employees during the taxable year, by

(ii) the number of full-time equivalent employees of the employer determined under paragraph (2) for the taxable year.

Such amount shall be rounded to the next lowest multiple of $1,000 if not otherwise such a multiple.

(B) Dollar amount.*—For purposes of paragraph (1)(B) and subsection (c)(2)—

(i) 2010, 2011, 2012, and 2013.—The dollar amount in effect under this paragraph for taxable years beginning in 2010, 2011, 2012, or 2013 is $25,000.

(ii) Subsequent years.—In the case of a taxable year beginning in a calendar year after 2013, the dollar amount in effect under this paragraph shall be equal to $25,000, multiplied by the cost-of-living adjustment under section 1(f)(3) for the calendar year, determined by substituting "calendar year 2012" for "calendar year 1992" in subparagraph (B) thereof.

(4) Contribution agreement.—An arrangement is described in this paragraph if it requires an eligible small employer to make a nonelective contribution on behalf of each employee who enrolls in a qualified health plan offered to employees by the employer through an exchange in an amount equal to a uniform percentage (not less than 50 percent) of the premium cost of the qualified health plan.

(5) Seasonal worker hours and wages not counted.—For purposes of this subsection –

(A) In general.—The number of hours of services worked by, and wages paid to, a seasonal worker of an employer shall not be taken into account in determining the full-time equivalent employees and average

*Editorial comment: For 2014, the dollar amount in effect is $25,400.

annual wages of the employer unless the worker works for the employer on more than 120 days during the taxable year.

(B) Definition of a seasonal worker.—The term "seasonal worker" means a worker who performs labor or services on a seasonal basis as defined by the Secretary of Labor, including workers covered by section 500.20(s)(1) of title 29, Code of Federal Regulations section 500.20(s)(1) of title 29, Code of Federal Regulations and retail workers employed exclusively during holiday seasons.

(e) Other rules and definitions.—For purposes of this section—

(1) Employee.—

(A) Certain employees excluded.—The term "employee" shall not include—

(i) an employee within the meaning of section 401(c)(1),

(ii) any 2-percent shareholder (as defined in section 1372(b)) of an eligible small business which is an S corporation,

(iii) any 5-percent owner (as defined in section 416(i)(1)(B)(i)) of an eligible small business, or

(iv) any individual who bears any of the relationships described in subparagraphs (A) through (G) of section 152(d)(2) to, or is a dependent described in section 152(d)(2)(H) of, an individual described in clause (i), (ii), or (iii).

(B) Leased employees.—The term "employee" shall include a leased employee within the meaning of section 414(n).

(2) Credit period.—The term "credit period" means, with respect to any eligible small employer, the 2-consecutive-taxable year period beginning with the 1st taxable year in which the employer (or any predecessor) offers 1 or more qualified health plans to its employees through an Exchange.

(3) Nonelective contribution.—The term "nonelective contribution" means an employer contribution other than an employer contribution pursuant to a salary reduction agreement.

(4) Wages.—The term "wages" has the meaning given such term by section 3121(a) (determined without regard to any dollar limitation contained in such section).

(5) Aggregation and other rules made applicable.—

(A) Aggregation rules.—All employers treated as a single employer under subsection (b), (c), (m), or (o) of section 414 shall be treated as a single employer for purposes of this section.

(B) Other rules.—Rules similar to the rules of subsections (c), (d), and (e) of section 52 shall apply.

(f) Credit made available to tax-exempt eligible small employers.—

(1) In general.—In the case of a tax-exempt eligible small employer, there shall be treated as a credit allowable under subpart C (and not allowable under this subpart) the lesser of—

(A) the amount of the credit determined under this section with respect to such employer, or

(B) the amount of the payroll taxes of the employer during the calendar year in which the taxable year begins.

(2) Tax-exempt eligible small employer.—For purposes of this section, the term "tax-exempt eligible small employer" means an eligible small employer which is any organization described in section 501(c) which is exempt from taxation under section 501(a).

(3) Payroll taxes.—For purposes of this subsection—

(A) In general.—The term "payroll taxes" means—

(i) amounts required to be withheld from the employees of the tax-exempt eligible small employer under section 3401(a),

(ii) amounts required to be withheld from such employees under section 3101(b), and

(iii) amounts of taxes imposed on the tax-exempt eligible small employer under section 3111(b).

(B) Special rule.—A rule similar to the rule of section 24(d)(2)(C) shall apply for purposes of subparagraph (A).

(g) Application of section for calendar years 2010, 2011, 2012, and 2013.—In the case of any taxable year beginning in 2010, 2011, 2012, or 2013, the following modifications to this section shall apply in determining the amount of the credit under subsection (a):

(1) No credit period required.—The credit shall be determined without regard to whether the taxable year is in a credit period and for purposes of applying this section to taxable years beginning after 2013, no credit period shall be treated as beginning with a taxable year beginning before 2014.

(2) Amount of credit.—The amount of the credit determined under subsection (b) shall be determined—

(A) by substituting "35 percent (25 percent in the case of a tax-exempt eligible small employer)" for "50 percent (35 percent in the case of a tax-exempt eligible small employer)",

(B) by reference to an eligible small employer's nonelective contributions for premiums paid for health insurance coverage (within the meaning of section 9832(b)(1)) of an employee, and

(C) by substituting for the average premium determined under subsection (b)(2) the amount the Secretary of Health and Human Services determines is the average premium for the small group market in the State in which the employer is offering health insurance coverage (or for such area within the State as is specified by the Secretary).

(3) Contribution arrangement—An arrangement shall not fail to meet the requirements of subsection (d)(4) solely because it provides for the offering of insurance outside of an Exchange.

(h) Insurance definitions.—Any term used in this section which is also used in the Public Health Service Act of subtitle A of title I of the Patient Protection and Affordable Care Act shall have the meaning given such term by such Act or subtitle.

(i) Regulations.—The Secretary shall prescribe such regulations as may be necessary to carry out the provisions of this section, including regulations to prevent the avoidance of the 2-year limit on the credit period through the use of successor entities and the avoidance of the limitations under subsection (c) through the use of multiple entities.

* * *

SUBPART E—RULES FOR COMPUTING INVESTMENT CREDIT

§ 46. Amount of credit

For purposes of section 38, the amount of the investment credit determined under this section for any taxable year shall be the sum of—

(1) the rehabilitation credit,

(2) the energy credit,

(3) the qualifying advanced coal project credit,

(4) the qualifying gasification project credit,

(5) the qualifying advanced energy project credit, and

(6) the qualifying therapeutic discovery project credit.

§ 47. Rehabilitation credit

(a) General rule.—For purposes of section 46, the rehabilitation credit for any taxable year is the sum of—

(1) 10 percent of the qualified rehabilitation expenditures with respect to any qualified rehabilitated building other than a certified historic structure, and

(2) 20 percent of the qualified rehabilitation expenditures with respect to any certified historic structure.

(b) When expenditures taken into account.—

(1) In general.—Qualified rehabilitation expenditures with respect to any qualified rehabilitated building shall be taken into account for the taxable year in which such qualified rehabilitated building is placed in service.

(2) Coordination with subsection (d).—The amount which would (but for this paragraph) be taken into account under paragraph (1) with respect to any qualified rehabilitated building shall be reduced (but not below zero) by any amount of qualified rehabilitation expenditures taken into account under subsection (d) by the taxpayer or a predecessor of the taxpayer (or, in the case of a sale and leaseback described in section 50(a) (2)(C), by the lessee), to the extent any amount so taken into account has not been required to be recaptured under section 50(a).

(c) Definitions.—For purposes of this section—

(1) Qualified rehabilitated building.—

(A) In general.—The term "qualified rehabilitated building" means any building (and its structural components) if—

(i) such building has been substantially rehabilitated,

(ii) such building was placed in service before the beginning of the rehabilitation,

(iii) in the case of any building other than a certified historic structure, in the rehabilitation process—

(I) 50 percent or more of the existing external walls of such building are retained in place as external walls,

(II) 75 percent or more of the existing external walls of such building are retained in place as internal or external walls, and

(III) 75 percent or more of the existing internal structural framework of such building is retained in place, and

(iv) depreciation (or amortization in lieu of depreciation) is allowable with respect to such building.

(B) Building must be first placed in service before 1936.—In the case of a building other than a certified historic structure, a building shall not be a qualified rehabilitated building unless the building was first placed in service before 1936.

(C) Substantially rehabilitated defined.—

(i) In general.—For purposes of subparagraph (A)(i), a building shall be treated as having been substantially rehabilitated only if the qualified rehabilitation expenditures during the 24-month period selected by the taxpayer (at the time and in the manner prescribed by regulation) and ending with or within the taxable year exceed the greater of—

(I) the adjusted basis of such building (and its structural components), or

(II) $5,000.

The adjusted basis of the building (and its structural components) shall be determined as of the beginning of the 1st day of such 24-month period, or of the holding period of the building, whichever is later. For purposes of the preceding sentence, the determination of the beginning of the holding period shall be made without regard to any reconstruction by the taxpayer in connection with the rehabilitation.

(ii) Special rule for phased rehabilitation.—In the case of any rehabilitation which may reasonably be expected to be completed in phases set forth in architectural plans and specifications completed before the rehabilitation begins, clause (i) shall be applied by substituting "60-month period" for "24-month period".

(iii) Lessees.—The Secretary shall prescribe by regulation rules for applying this subparagraph to lessees.

(D) Reconstruction.—Rehabilitation includes reconstruction.

(2) Qualified rehabilitation expenditure defined.—

(A) In general.—The term "qualified rehabilitation expenditure" means any amount properly chargeable to capital account—

(i) for property for which depreciation is allowable under section 168 and which is—

(I) nonresidential real property,

(II) residential rental property,

(III) real property which has a class life of more than 12.5 years, or

(IV) an addition or improvement to property described in subclause (I), (II), or (III), and

(ii) in connection with the rehabilitation of a qualified rehabilitated building.

(B) Certain expenditures not included.—The term "qualified rehabilitation expenditure" does not include—

(i) Straight line depreciation must be used.—Any expenditure with respect to which the taxpayer does not use the straight line method over a recovery period determined under subsection (c) or (g) of section 168. The preceding sentence shall not apply to any expenditure to the extent the alternative depreciation system of section 168(g) applies to such expenditure by reason of subparagraph (B) or (C) of section 168(g)(1).

(ii) Cost of acquisition.—The cost of acquiring any building or interest therein.

(iii) Enlargements.—Any expenditure attributable to the enlargement of an existing building.

(iv) Certified historic structure, etc.—Any expenditure attributable to the rehabilitation of a certified historic structure or a building in a registered historic district, unless the rehabilitation is a certified rehabilitation (within the meaning of subparagraph (C)). The preceding sentence shall not apply to a building in a registered historic district if—

(I) such building was not a certified historic structure,

(II) the Secretary of the Interior certified to the Secretary that such building is not of historic significance to the district, and

(III) if the certification referred to in subclause (II) occurs after the beginning of the rehabilitation of such building, the taxpayer certifies to the Secretary that, at the beginning of such rehabilitation, he in good faith was not aware of the requirements of subclause (II).

(v) Tax-exempt use property.—

(I) In general.—Any expenditure in connection with the rehabilitation of a building which is allocable to the portion of such property which is (or may reasonably be expected to be) tax-exempt use property (within the meaning of section 168(h)), except that "50 percent" shall by substituted for "35 percent" in paragraph (1)(B)(iii) thereof.

(II) Clause not to apply for purposes of paragraph (1)(C).—This clause shall not apply for purposes of determining under paragraph (1)(C) whether a building has been substantially rehabilitated.

(vi) Expenditures of lessee.—Any expenditure of a lessee of a building if, on the date the rehabilitation is completed, the remaining term of the lease (determined without regard to any renewal periods) is less than the recovery period determined under section 168(c).

(C) Certified rehabilitation.—For purposes of subparagraph (B), the term "certified rehabilitation" means any rehabilitation of a certified historic structure which the Secretary of the Interior has certified to the Secretary as being consistent with the historic character of such property or the district in which such property is located.

(D) Nonresidential real property; residential rental property; class life.—For purposes of subparagraph (A), the terms "nonresidential real property," "residential rental property," and "class life" have the respective meanings given such terms by section 168.

(3) Certified historic structure defined.—

(A) In general.—The term "certified historic structure" means any building (and its structural components) which—

(i) is listed in the National Register, or

(ii) is located in a registered historic district and is certified by the Secretary of the Interior to the Secretary as being of historic significance to the district.

(B) Registered historic district.—The term "registered historic district" means—

(i) any district listed in the National Register, and

(ii) any district—

(I) which is designated under a statute of the appropriate State or local government, if such statute is certified by the Secretary of the Interior to the Secretary as containing criteria which will substantially achieve the purpose of preserving and rehabilitating buildings of historic significance to the district, and

(II) which is certified by the Secretary of the Interior to the Secretary as meeting substantially all of the requirements for the listing of districts in the National Register.

(d) Progress expenditures.—

(1) In general.—In the case of any building to which this subsection applies, except as provided in paragraph (3)—

(A) if such building is self-rehabilitated property, any qualified rehabilitation expenditure with respect to such building shall be taken into account for the taxable year for which such expenditure is properly chargeable to capital account with respect to such building, and

(B) if such building is not self-rehabilitated property, any qualified rehabilitation expenditure with respect to such building shall be taken into account for the taxable year in which paid.

(2) Property to which subsection applies.—

(A) In general.—This subsection shall apply to any building which is being rehabilitated by or for the taxpayer if—

(i) the normal rehabilitation period for such building is 2 years or more, and

(ii) it is reasonable to expect that such building will be a qualified rehabilitated building in the hands of the taxpayer when it is placed in service.

Clauses (i) and (ii) shall be applied on the basis of facts known as of the close of the taxable year of the taxpayer in which the rehabilitation begins (or, if later, at the close of the first taxable year to which an election under this subsection applies).

(B) Normal rehabilitation period.—For purposes of subparagraph (A), the term "normal rehabilitation period" means the period reasonably expected to be required for the rehabilitation of the building—

(i) beginning with the date on which physical work on the rehabilitation begins (or, if later, the first day of the first taxable year to which an election under this subsection applies), and

(ii) ending on the date on which it is expected that the property will be available for placing in service.

(3) Special rules for applying paragraph (1).—For purposes of paragraph (1)—

(A) Component parts, etc.—Property which is to be a component part of, or is otherwise to be included in, any building to which this subsection applies shall be taken into account—

(i) at a time not earlier than the time at which it becomes irrevocably devoted to use in the building, and

(ii) as if (at the time referred to in clause (i)) the taxpayer had expended an amount equal to that portion of the cost to the taxpayer of such component or other property which, for purposes of this subpart, is properly chargeable (during such taxable year) to capital account with respect to such building.

(B) Certain borrowing disregarded.—Any amount borrowed directly or indirectly by the taxpayer from the person rehabilitating the property for him shall not be treated as an amount expended for such rehabilitation.

(C) Limitation for buildings which are not self-rehabilitated.—

(i) In general.—In the case of a building which is not self-rehabilitated, the amount taken into account under paragraph (1)(B) for any taxable year shall not exceed the amount which represents the portion of the overall cost to the taxpayer of the rehabilitation which is properly attributable to the portion of the rehabilitation which is completed during such taxable year.

(ii) Carryover of certain amounts.—In the case of a building which is not a self-rehabilitated building, if for the taxable year—

(I) the amount which (but for clause (i)) would have been taken into account under paragraph (1)(B) exceeds the limitation of clause (i), then the amount of such excess shall be taken into account under paragraph (1)(B) for the succeeding taxable year, or

(II) the limitation of clause (i) exceeds the amount taken into account under paragraph (1)(B), then the amount of such excess shall increase the limitation of clause (i) for the succeeding taxable year.

(D) Determination of percentage of completion.—The determination under subparagraph (C)(i) of the portion of the overall cost to the taxpayer of the rehabilitation which is properly attributable to rehabilitation completed during any taxable year shall be made, under regulations prescribed by the Secretary, on the basis of engineering or architectural estimates or on the basis of cost accounting records. Unless the taxpayer establishes otherwise by clear and convincing evidence, the rehabilitation shall be deemed to be completed not more rapidly than ratably over the normal rehabilitation period.

(E) No progress expenditures for certain prior periods.—No qualified rehabilitation expenditures shall be taken into account under this subsection for any period before the first day of the first taxable year to which an election under this subsection applies.

(F) No progress expenditures for property for year it is placed in service, etc.—In the case of any building, no qualified rehabilitation expenditures shall be taken into account under this subsection for the earlier of—

(i) the taxable year in which the building is placed in service, or

(ii) the first taxable year for which recapture is required under section 50(a)(2) with respect to such property.

or for any taxable year thereafter.

(4) Self-rehabilitated building.—For purposes of this subsection, the term "self-rehabilitated building" means any building if it is reasonable to believe that more than half of the qualified rehabilitation expenditures for such building will be made directly by the taxpayer.

(5) Election.—This subsection shall apply to any taxpayer only if such taxpayer has made an election under this paragraph. Such an election shall apply to the taxable year for which made and all subsequent taxable years. Such an election, once made, may be revoked only with the consent of the Secretary.

§ 48. Energy credit

(a) Energy credit.—

(1) In general.—For purposes of section 46, except as provided in paragraphs (1)(B), (2)(B), (3)(B), and (4)(B) of subsection (c), the energy credit for any taxable year is the energy percentage of the basis of each energy property placed in service during such taxable year.

(2) Energy percentage.—

(A) In general.—The energy percentage is—

(i) 30 percent in the case of—

(I) qualified fuel cell property,

(II) energy property described in paragraph (3)(A)(i) but only with respect to periods ending before January 1, 2017,

(III) energy property described in paragraph (3)(A)(ii), and

(IV) qualified small wind energy property, and

(ii) in the case of any energy property to which clause (i) does not apply, 10 percent.

(B) Coordination with rehabilitation credit.—The energy percentage shall not apply to that portion of the basis of any property which is attributable to qualified rehabilitation expenditures.

(3) Energy property.—For purposes of this subpart, the term "energy property" means any property—

(A) which is—

(i) equipment which uses solar energy to generate electricity, to heat or cool (or provide hot water for use in) a structure, or to provide solar process heat, excepting property used to generate energy for the purposes of heating a swimming pool,

(ii) equipment which uses solar energy to illuminate the inside of a structure using fiber-optic distributed sunlight but only with respect to periods ending before January 1, 2009,

(iii) equipment used to produce, distribute, or use energy derived from a geothermal deposit (within the meaning of section 613(e)(2)), but only, in the case of electricity generated by geothermal power, up to (but not including) the electrical transmission stage,

(iv) qualified fuel cell property or qualified microturbine property,

(v) combined heat and power system property,

(vi) qualified small wind energy property, or

(vii) equipment which uses the ground or ground water as a thermal energy source to heat a structure or as a thermal energy sink to cool a structure, but only with respect to periods ending before January 1, 2017,

(B)(i) the construction, reconstruction, or erection of which is completed by the taxpayer, or

(ii) which is acquired by the taxpayer if the original use of such property commences with the taxpayer,

(C) with respect to which depreciation (or amortization in lieu of depreciation) is allowable, and

(D) which meets the performance and quality standards (if any) which—

(i) have been prescribed by the Secretary by regulations (after consultation with the Secretary of Energy), and

(ii) are in effect at the time of the acquisition of the property.

Such term shall not include any property which is part of a facility the production from which is allowed as a credit under section 45 for the taxable year or any prior taxable year.

(4) Special rule for property financed by subsidized energy financing or industrial development bonds.—

(A) Reduction of basis.—For purposes of applying the energy percentage to any property, if such property is financed in whole or in part by—

(i) subsidized energy financing, or

(ii) the proceeds of a private activity bond (within the meaning of section 141) the interest on which is exempt from tax under section 103,

the amount taken into account as the basis of such property shall not exceed the amount which (but for this subparagraph) would be so taken into account multiplied by the fraction determined under subparagraph (B).

(B) Determination of fraction.—For purposes of subparagraph (A), the fraction determined under this subparagraph is 1 reduced by a fraction—

(i) the numerator of which is that portion of the basis of the property which is allocable to such financing or proceeds, and

(ii) the denominator of which is the basis of the property.

(C) Subsidized energy financing.—For purpose of subparagraph (A), the term "subsidized energy financing" means financing provided under a Federal, State, or local program a principal purpose of which is to provide subsidized financing for projects designed to conserve or produce energy.

(D) Termination.—This paragraph shall not apply to periods after December 31, 2008, under rules similar to the rules of section 48(m) (as in effect on the day before the date of the enactment of the Revenue Reconciliation Act of 1990).

(5) Election to treat qualified facilities as energy property.—

(A) In general.—In the case of any qualified property which is part of a qualified investment credit facility—

(i) such property shall be treated as energy property for purposes of this section, and

(ii) the energy percentage with respect to such property shall be 30 percent.

(B) Denial of production credit.—No credit shall be allowed under section 45 for any taxable year with respect to any qualified investment credit facility.

(C) Qualified investment credit facility.—For purposes of this paragraph, the term "qualified investment credit facility" means any of the following facilities if no credit has been allowed under section 45 with respect to such facility and the taxpayer makes an irrevocable election to have this paragraph apply to such facility:

(i) Wind facilities.—Any qualified facility (within the meaning of section 45) described in paragraph (1) of section 45(d) if such facility is placed in service in 2009, 2010, 2011, or 2012.

(ii) Other facilities.—Any qualified facility (within the meaning of section 45) described in paragraph (2), (3), (4), (6), (7), (9), or (11) of section 45(d) if such facility is placed in service in 2009, 2010, 2011, 2012, or 2013.

(D) Qualified property.—For purposes of this paragraph, the term "qualified property" means property—

(i) which is—

(I) tangible personal property, or

(II) other tangible property (not including a building or its structural components), and

(ii) with respect to which depreciation (or amortization in lieu of depreciation) is allowable but only if such property is used as an integral part of the qualified investment credit facility.

(b) Certain progress expenditure rules made applicable.—Rules similar to the rules of subsections (c)(4) and (d) of section 46 (as in effect on the day before the date of the enactment of the Revenue Reconciliation Act of 1990) shall apply for purposes of subsection (a).

(c) Definitions.—For purposes of this subsection—

(1) Qualified fuel cell property.—

(A) In general.—The term "qualified fuel cell property" means a fuel cell power plant which—

(i) has a nameplate capacity of at least 0.5 kilowatt of electricity using an electrochemical process, and

(ii) has an electricity-only generation efficiency greater than 30 percent.

(B) Limitation.—In the case of qualified fuel cell property placed in service during the taxable year, the credit otherwise determined under subsection (a) for such year with respect to such property shall not exceed an amount equal to $1500 for each 0.5 kilowatt of capacity of such property.

(C) Fuel cell power plant.—The term "fuel cell power plant" means an integrated system comprised of a fuel cell stack assembly and associated balance of plant components which converts a fuel into electricity using electrochemical means.

(D) Termination.—The term "qualified fuel cell property" shall not include any property for any period after December 31, 2016.

(2) Qualified microturbine property.—

(A) In general.—The term "qualified microturbine property" means a stationary microturbine power plant which—

(i) has a nameplate capacity of less than 2,000 kilowatts, and

(ii) has an electricity-only generation efficiency of not less than 26 percent at International Standard Organization conditions.

(B) Limitation.—In the case of qualified microturbine property placed in service during the taxable year, the credit otherwise determined under subsection (a) for such year with respect to such property shall not exceed an amount equal $200 for each kilowatt of capacity of such property.

(C) Stationary microturbine power plant.—The term "stationary microturbine power plant" means an integrated system comprised of a gas turbine engine, a combustor, a recuperator or regenerator, a generator or alternator, and associated balance of plant components which converts a fuel into electricity and thermal energy. Such term also includes all secondary components located between the existing infrastructure for fuel delivery and the existing infrastructure for power distribution, including equipment and controls for meeting relevant power standards, such as voltage, frequency, and power factors.

(D) Termination.—The term "qualified microturbine property" shall not include any property for any period after December 31, 2016.

* * *

(4) Qualified small wind energy property.—

(A) In general.—The term "qualified small wind energy property" means property which uses a qualifying small wind turbine to generate electricity.

(B) Qualifying small wind turbine.—The term "qualifying small wind turbine" means a wind turbine which has a nameplate capacity of not more than 100 kilowatts.

(C) Termination.—The term "qualified small wind energy property" shall not include any property for any period after December 31, 2016.

(d) Coordination with Department of Treasury grants.—In the case of any property with respect to which the Secretary makes a grant under section 1603 of the American Recovery and Reinvestment Tax Act of 2009—

(1) Denial of production and investment credits.—No credit shall be determined under this section or section 45 with respect to such property for the taxable year in which such grant is made or any subsequent taxable year.

(2) Recapture of credits for progress expenditures made before grant.—If a credit was determined under this section with respect to such property for any taxable year ending before such grant is made—

(A) the tax imposed under subtitle A on the taxpayer for the taxable year in which such grant is made shall be increased by so much of such credit as was allowed under section 38,

(B) the general business carryforwards under section 39 shall be adjusted so as to recapture the portion of such credit which was not so allowed, and

(C) the amount of such grant shall be determined without regard to any reduction in the basis of such property by reason of such credit.

(3) Treatment of grants.—Any such grant shall—

(A) not be includible in the gross income of the taxpayer, but

(B) shall be taken into account in determining the basis of the property to which such grant relates, except that the basis of such property shall be reduced under section 50(c) in the same manner as a credit allowed under subsection (a).

* * *

§ 49. At-risk rules

(a) General rule.—

(1) Certain nonrecourse financing excluded from credit base.—

(A) Limitation.—The credit base of any property to which this paragraph applies shall be reduced by the nonqualified nonrecourse financing with respect to such credit base (as of the close of the taxable year in which placed in service).

(B) Property to which paragraph applies.—This paragraph applies to any property which—

(i) is placed in service during the taxable year by a taxpayer described in section 465 (a)(1), and

(ii) is used in connection with an activity with respect to which any loss is subject to limitation under section 465.

(C) Credit base defined.—For purposes of this paragraph, the term "credit base" means—

(i) the portion of the basis of any qualified rehabilitated building attributable to qualified rehabilitation expenditures,

(ii) the basis of any energy property,

(iii) the basis of any property which is part of a qualifying advanced coal project under section 48A,

(iv) the basis of any property which is part of a qualifying gasification project under section 48B,

(v) the basis of any property which is part of a qualifying advanced energy project under section 48C, and

(vi) the basis of any property to which paragraph (1) of section 48D(e) applies which is part of a qualifying therapeutic discovery project under section 48D.

(D) Nonqualified nonrecourse financing.—

(i) In general.—For purposes of this paragraph and paragraph (2), the term "nonqualified nonrecourse financing" means any nonrecourse financing which is not qualified commercial financing.

(ii) Qualified commercial financing.—For purposes of this paragraph, the term "qualified commercial financing" means any financing with respect to any property if—

(I) such property is acquired by the taxpayer from a person who is not a related person,

(II) the amount of the nonrecourse financing with respect to such property does not exceed 80 percent of the credit base of such property, and

(III) such financing is borrowed from a qualified person or represents a loan from any Federal, State, or local government or instrumentality thereof, or is guaranteed by any Federal, State, or local government.

Such term shall not include any convertible debt.

(iii) Nonrecourse financing.—For purposes of this subparagraph, the term "nonrecourse financing" includes—

(I) any amount with respect to which the taxpayer is protected against loss through guarantees, stop-loss agreements, or other similar arrangements, and

(II) except to the extent provided in regulations, any amount borrowed from a person who has an interest (other than as a creditor) in the activity in which the property is used or from a related person to a person (other than the taxpayer) having such an interest.

In the case of amounts borrowed by a corporation from a shareholder, subclause (II) shall not apply to an interest as a shareholder.

(iv) Qualified person.—For purposes of this paragraph, the term "qualified person" means any person which is actively and regularly engaged in the business of lending money and which is not—

(I) a related person with respect to the taxpayer,

(II) a person from which the taxpayer acquired the property (or a related person to such person), or

(III) a person who receives a fee with respect to the taxpayer's investment in the property (or a related person to such person).

(v) Related person.—For purposes of this subparagraph, the term "related person" has the meaning given such term by section 465(b)(3)

(C). Except as otherwise provided in regulations prescribed by the Secretary, the determination of whether a person is a related person shall be made as of the close of the taxable year in which the property is placed in service.

(E) Application to partnerships and S corporations.—For purposes of this paragraph and paragraph (2)—

(i) In general.—Except as otherwise provided in this subparagraph, in the case of any partnership or S corporation, the determination of whether a partner's or shareholder's allocable share of any financing is nonqualified nonrecourse financing shall be made at the partner or shareholder level.

(ii) Special rule for certain recourse financing of S corporation.—A shareholder of an S corporation shall be treated as liable for his allocable share of any financing provided by a qualified person to such corporation if—

(I) such financing is recourse financing (determined at the corporate level), and

(II) such financing is provided with respect to qualified business property of such corporation.

(iii) Qualified business property.—For purposes of clause (ii), the term "qualified business property" means any property if—

(I) such property is used by the corporation in the active conduct of a trade or business,

(II) during the entire 12-month period ending on the last day of the taxable year, such corporation had at least 3 full-time employees who were not owner-employees (as defined in section 465(c)(7) (E)(i)) and substantially all the services of whom were services directly related to such trade or business, and

(III) during the entire 12-month period ending on the last day of such taxable year, such corporation had at least 1 full-time employee substantially all the services of whom were in the active management of the trade or business.

(iv) Determination of allocable share.—The determination of any partner's or shareholder's allocable share of any financing shall be made in the same manner as the credit allowable by section 38 with respect to such property.

(F) Special rules for energy property.—Rules similar to the rules of subparagraph (F) of section 46(c)(8) (as in effect on the day before the date of the enactment of the Revenue Reconciliation Act of 1990) shall apply for purposes of this paragraph.

(2) Subsequent decreases in nonqualified nonrecourse financing with respect to the property.—

(A) In general.—If, at the close of a taxable year following the taxable year in which the property was placed in service, there is a net decrease in the amount of nonqualified nonrecourse financing with respect to such property, such net decrease shall be taken into account as an increase in the credit base for such property in accordance with subparagraph (C).

(B) Certain transactions not taken into account.—For purposes of this paragraph, nonqualified nonrecourse financing shall not be treated as decreased through the surrender or other use of property financed by nonqualified nonrecourse financing.

(C) Manner in which taken into account.—

(i) Credit determined by reference to taxable year property placed in service.—For purposes of determining the amount of credit allowable under section 38 and the amount of credit subject to the early disposition or cessation rules under section 50(a), any increase in a taxpayer's credit base for any property by reason of this paragraph shall be taken into account as if it were property placed in service by the taxpayer in the taxable year in which the property referred to in subparagraph (A) was first placed in service.

(ii) Credit allowed for year of decrease in nonqualified nonrecourse financing.—Any credit allowable under this subpart for any increase in qualified investment by reason of this paragraph shall be treated as earned during the taxable year of the decrease in the amount of nonqualified nonrecourse financing.

(b) Increases in nonqualified nonrecourse financing.—

(1) In general.—If, as of the close of the taxable year, there is a net increase with respect to the taxpayer in the amount of nonqualified nonrecourse financing (within the meaning of subsection (a)(1)) with respect to any property to which subsection (a)(1) applied, then the tax under this chapter for such taxable year shall be increased by an amount equal to the aggregate decrease in credits allowed under section 38 for all prior taxable years which would have resulted from reducing the credit base (as defined in subsection (a)(1)(C)) taken into account with respect to such property by the amount of such net increase. For purposes of determining the amount of credit subject to the early disposition or cessation rules of section 50(a), the net increase in the amount of the nonqualified nonrecourse financing with respect to the property shall be treated as reducing the property's credit base in the year in which the property was first placed in service.

(2) Transfers of debt more than 1 year after initial borrowing not treated as increasing nonqualified nonrecourse financing.—For purposes of paragraph (1), the amount of nonqualified nonrecourse financing (within the meaning of subsection (a)(1)(D)) with respect to the taxpayer shall not be treated as increased by reason of a transfer of (or agreement to transfer) any evidence of any indebtedness if such transfer occurs (or such agreement is entered into) more than 1 year after the date such indebtedness was incurred.

(3) Special rules for certain energy property.—Rules similar to the rules of section 47(d)(3) (as in effect on the day before the date of the enactment of the Revenue Reconciliation Act of 1990) shall apply for purposes of this subsection.

(4) Special rule.—Any increase in tax under paragraph (1) shall not be treated as tax imposed by this chapter for purposes of determining the amount of any credit allowable under this chapter.

§ 50. Other special rules

(a) Recapture in case of dispositions, etc.—Under regulations prescribed by the Secretary—

(1) Early disposition, etc.—

(A) General rule.—If, during any taxable year, investment credit property is disposed of, or otherwise ceases to be investment credit property with respect to the taxpayer, before the close of the recapture period, then the tax under this chapter for such taxable year shall be increased by the recapture percentage of the aggregate decrease in the credits allowed under section 38 for all prior taxable years which would have resulted solely from reducing to zero any credit determined under this subpart with respect to such property.

(B) Recapture percentage.—For purposes of subparagraph (A), the recapture percentage shall be determined in accordance with the following table:

If the property ceases to be investment credit property within—	The recapture percentage is:
(i) One full year after placed in service	100
(ii) One full year after the close of the period described in clause (i)	80
(iii) One full year after the close of the period described in clause (ii)	60
(iv) One full year after the close of the period described in clause (iii)	40
(v) One full year after the close of the period described in clause (iv)	20

(2) Property ceases to qualify for progress expenditures.—

(A) In general.—If during any taxable year any building to which section 47(d) applied ceases (by reason of sale or other disposition, cancellation or abandonment of contract, or otherwise) to be, with respect to the taxpayer, property which, when placed in service, will be a qualified rehabilitated building, then the tax under this chapter for such taxable year shall be increased by an amount equal to the aggregate decrease in the credits allowed under section 38 for all prior taxable years which would have resulted solely from reducing to zero the credit determined under this subpart with respect to such building.

(B) Certain excess credit recaptured.—Any amount which would have been applied as a reduction under paragraph (2) of section 47(b) but for the fact that reduction under such paragraph cannot reduce the amount taken into account under section 47(b)(1) below zero shall be treated as an amount required to be recaptured under subparagraph (A) for the taxable year during which the building is placed in service.

(C) Certain sales and leasebacks.—Under regulations prescribed by the Secretary, a sale by, and leaseback to, a taxpayer who, when the property is placed in service, will be a lessee to whom the rules referred to in subsection (d)(5) apply shall not be treated as a cessation described in subparagraph (A) to the extent that the amount which will be passed through to the lessee under such rules with respect to such property is not less than the qualified rehabilitation expenditures properly taken into account by the lessee under section 47(d) with respect to such property.

(D) Coordination with paragraph (1).—If, after property is placed in service, there is a disposition or other cessation described in paragraph (1), then paragraph (1) shall be applied as if any credit which was allowable by reason of section 47(d) and which has not been required to be recaptured before such disposition, cessation, or change in use were allowable for the taxable year the property was placed in service.

(E) Special rules.—Rules similar to the rules of this paragraph shall apply in cases where qualified progress expenditures were taken into account under the rules referred to in section 48(b).

(3) Carrybacks and carryovers adjusted.—In the case of any cessation described in paragraph (1) or (2), the carrybacks and carryovers under section 39 shall be adjusted by reason of such cessation.

(4) Subsection not to apply in certain cases.—Paragraphs (1) and (2) shall not apply to—

(A) a transfer by reason of death, or

(B) a transaction to which section 381(a) applies.

For purposes of this subsection, property shall not be treated as ceasing to be investment credit property with respect to the taxpayer by reason of a mere change in the form of conducting the trade or business so long as the property is retained in such trade or business as investment credit property and the taxpayer retains a substantial interest in such trade or business.

(5) Definitions and special rules.—

(A) Investment credit property.—For purposes of this subsection, the term "investment credit property" means any property eligible for a credit determined under this subpart.

(B) Transfer between spouses or incident to divorce.—In the case of any transfer described in subsection (a) of section 1041—

(i) the foregoing provisions of this subsection shall not apply, and

(ii) the same tax treatment under this subsection with respect to the transferred property shall apply to the transferee as would have applied to the transferor.

(C) Special rule.—Any increase in tax under paragraph (1) or (2) shall not be treated as tax imposed by this chapter for purposes of determining the amount of any credit allowable under this chapter.

(b) Certain property not eligible.—No credit shall be determined under this subpart with respect to—

(1) Property used outside United States.—

(A) In general.—Except as provided in subparagraph (B), no credit shall be determined under this subpart with respect to any property which is used predominantly outside the United States.

(B) Exceptions.—Subparagraph (A) shall not apply to any property described in section 168(g)(4).

(2) Property used for lodging.—No credit shall be determined under this subpart with respect to any property which is used predominantly to furnish lodging or in connection with the furnishing of lodging. The preceding sentence shall not apply to—

(A) nonlodging commercial facilities which are available to persons not using the lodging facilities on the same basis as they are available to persons using the lodging facilities.

(B) property used by a hotel or motel in connection with the trade or business of furnishing lodging where the predominant portion of the accommodations is used by transients;

(C) a certified historic structure to the extent of that portion of the basis which is attributable to qualified rehabilitation expenditures; and

(D) any energy property.

(3) Property used by certain tax-exempt organization.—No credit shall be determined under this subpart with respect to any property used by an organization (other than a cooperative described in section 521) which is exempt from the tax imposed by this chapter unless such property is used predominantly in an unrelated trade or business the income of which is subject to tax under section 511. If the property is debt-financed property (as defined in section 514(b)), the amount taken into account for purposes of determining the amount of the credit under this subpart with respect to such property shall be that percentage of the amount (which but for this paragraph would be so taken into account) which is the same percentage as is used under section 514(a), for the year the property is placed in service, in computing the amount of gross income to be taken into account during such taxable year with respect to such property. If any qualified rehabilitated building is used by the tax-exempt organization pursuant to a lease, this paragraph shall not apply for purposes of determining the amount of the rehabilitation credit.

(4) Property used by governmental units or foreign persons or entities.—

(A) In general.—No credit shall be determined under this subpart with respect to any property used—

(i) by the United States, any State or political subdivision thereof, any possession of the United States, or any agency or instrumentality of any of the foregoing, or

(ii) by any foreign person or entity (as defined in section 168(h)(2)(C)), but only with respect to property to which section 168 (h)(2)(A)(iii) applies (determined after the application of section 168(h)(2)(B)).

(B) Exception for short-term leases.—This paragraph and paragraph (3) shall not apply to any property by reason of use under a lease with a term of less than 6 months (determined under section 168(i)(3)).

(C) Exception for qualified rehabilitated buildings leased to governments, etc.—If any qualified rehabilitated building is leased to a governmental unit (or a foreign person or entity) this paragraph shall not apply for purposes of determining the rehabilitation credit with respect to such building.

(D) Special rules for partnerships, etc.—For purposes of this paragraph and paragraph (3), rules similar to the rules of paragraphs (5) and (6) of section 168(h) shall apply.

(E) Cross reference.—

For special rules for the application of this paragraph and paragraph (3), see section 168(h).

(c) Basis adjustment to investment credit property.—

(1) In general.—For purposes of this subtitle, if a credit is determined under this subpart with respect to any property, the basis of such property shall be reduced by the amount of the credit so determined.

(2) Certain dispositions.—If during any taxable year there is a recapture amount determined with respect to any property the basis of which was reduced under paragraph (1), the basis of such property (immediately before the event resulting in such recapture) shall be increased by an amount equal to such "recapture amount." For purposes of the preceding sentence, the term recapture amount means any increase in tax (or adjustment in carrybacks or carryovers) determined under subsection (a).

(3) Special rule.—In the case of any energy credit—

(A) only 50 percent of such credit shall be taken into account under paragraph (1), and

(B) only 50 percent of any recapture amount attributable to such credit shall be taken into account under paragraph (2).

(4) Recapture of reductions.—

(A) In general.—For purposes of sections 1245 and 1250, any reduction under this subsection shall be treated as a deduction allowed for depreciation.

(B) Special rule for section 1250.—For purposes of section 1250(b), the determination of what would have been the depreciation adjustments under the straight line method shall be made as if there had been no reduction under this section.

(5) Adjustment in basis of interest in partnership or S corporation.—The adjusted basis of—

(A) a partner's interest in a partnership, and

(B) stock in an S corporation,

shall be appropriately adjusted to take into account adjustments made under this subsection in the basis of property held by the partnership or S corporation (as the case may be).

* * *

SUBPART F—RULES FOR COMPUTING WORK OPPORTUNITY CREDIT

§ 51. Amount of credit*

(a) Determination of amount.—For purposes of section 38, the amount of the work opportunity credit determined under this section for the taxable year shall be equal to 40 percent of the qualified first-year wages for such year.

(b) Qualified wages defined.—For purposes of this subpart—

(1) In general.—The term "qualified wages" means the wages paid or incurred by the employer during the taxable year to individuals who are members of a targeted group.

(2) Qualified first-year wages.—The term "qualified first-year wages" means, with respect to any individual, qualified wages attributable to service rendered during the 1-year period beginning with the day the individual begins work for the employer.

(3) Limitation on wages per year taken into account.—The amount of the qualified first-year wages which may be taken into account with respect to any individual shall not exceed $6,000 per year ($12,000 per year in the case of any individual who is a qualified veteran by reason of subsection (d)(3)(A)(ii)).

(c) Wages defined.—For purposes of this subpart—

(1) In general.—Except as otherwise provided in this subsection and subsection (h)(2), the term "wages" has the meaning given to such term by subsection (b) of section 3306 (determined without regard to any dollar limitation contained in such section).

(2) On-the-job training and work supplementation payments.—

(A) Exclusion for employers receiving on-the-job training payments.—The term "wages" shall not include any amounts paid or incurred by an employer for any period to any individual for whom the employer receives federally funded payments for on-the-job training of such individual for such period.

(B) Reduction for work supplementation payments to employers.—The amount of wages which would (but for this subparagraph) be qualified wages under this section for an employer with respect to an individual for a taxable year shall be reduced by an amount equal to the amount of the payments made to such employer (however utilized by such employer) with respect to such individual for such taxable year under a program established under section 414 of the Social Security Act.

(3) Payments for services during labor disputes.—If—

(A) the principal place of employment of an individual with the employer is at a plant or facility, and

(B) there is a strike or lockout involving employees at such plant or facility, the term "wages" shall not include any amount paid or incurred by the employer to such individual for services which are the same as, or substantially similar to, those services performed by employees participating in, or affected by, the strike or lockout during the period of such strike or lockout.

(4) Termination.—The term "wages" shall not include any amount paid or incurred to an individual who begins work for the employer—

(A) after December 31, 1994, and before October 1, 1996, or

(B) after December 31, 2013.**

(5) Coordination with payroll tax forgiveness.— The term "wages" shall not include any amount paid or incurred to a qualified individual (as defined in section 3111(d)(3)) during the 1-year period beginning on the hiring date of such individual by a qualified employer (as defined in section 3111(d)) unless such qualified employer makes an election not to have section 3111(d) apply.

(d) Members of targeted groups.—For purposes of this subpart—

(1) In general.—An individual is a member of a targeted group if such individual is—

(A) a qualified IV-A recipient,

(B) a qualified veteran,

(C) a qualified ex-felon,

(D) a high-risk youth,

*Editorial comment: This credit does not apply to any amount of wages paid or incurred to an individual who began work for the employer after December 31, 1994 and before October 1, 1996, or after December 31, 2013.

**Editorial comment: At the present time, this section has not been extended. There is pending legislation in the Senate, *The Tax Extenders Act of 2013 (S. 1859)*, that would extend Section 51(c)(4) until December 31, 2014.

(E) a vocational rehabilitation referral,

(F) a qualified summer youth employee,

(G) a qualified food stamp recipient,

(H) a qualified SSI recipient, or

(I) a long-term family assistance recipient.

(2) Qualified IV-A recipient.—

(A) In general.—The term "qualified IV-A recipient" means any individual who is certified by the designated local agency as being a member of a family receiving assistance under a IV-A program any 9 months during the 18-month period ending on the hiring date.

(B) IV-A program.—For purposes of this paragraph, the term "IV-A program" means any program providing assistance under a State program funded under part A of title IV of the Social Security Act and any successor of such program.

(3) Qualified veteran.—

(A) In general.—The term "qualified veteran" means any veteran who is certified by the designated local agency as—

(i) being a member of a family receiving assistance under a food stamp program under the Food Stamp Act of 1977 for at least a 3-month period ending during the 12-month period ending on the hiring date, or

(ii) entitled to compensation for a service-connected disability, and—

(I) having a hiring date which is not more than 1 year after having been discharged or released from active duty in the Armed Forces of the United States, or

(II) having aggregate periods of unemployment during the 1-year period ending on the hiring date which equal or exceed 6 months.

(B) Veteran.—For purposes of subparagraph (A), the term "veteran" means any individual who is certified by the designated local agency as—

(i) (I) having served on active duty (other than active duty for training) in the Armed Forces of the United States for a period of more than 180 days, or

(II) having been discharged or released from active duty in the Armed Forces of the United States for a service-connected disability, and

(ii) not having any day during the 60-day period ending on the hiring date which was a day of extended active duty in the Armed Forces of the United States.

For purposes of clause (ii), the term "extended active duty" means a period of more than 90 days during which the individual was on active duty (other than active duty for training).

(C) Other definitions.—For purposes of subparagraph (A), the terms "compensation" and "service-connected" have the meanings given such terms under section 101 of title 38, United States Code.

(4) Qualified ex-felon.—The term "qualified ex-felon" means any individual who is certified by the designated local agency—

(A) as having been convicted of a felony under any statute of the United States or any State, and

(B) as having a hiring date which is not more than 1 year after the last date on which such individual was so convicted or was released from prison.

(5) Designated community residents.—

(A) In general.—The term "designated community resident" means any individual who is certified by the designated local agency—

(i) as having attained age 18 but not age 40 on the hiring date, and

(ii) as having his principal place of abode within an empowerment zone, enterprise community, renewal community, or rural renewal county.

(B) Individual must continue to reside in zone, community, or county.—In the case of a designated community resident, the term "qualified wages" shall not include wages paid or incurred for services performed while the individual's principal place of abode is outside an empowerment zone, enterprise community, renewal community, or rural renewal county.

(C) Rural renewal county.—For purposes of this paragraph, the term "rural renewal county" means any county which—

(i) is outside a metropolitan statistical area (defined as such by the Office of Management and Budget), and

(ii) during the 5-year periods 1990 through 1994 and 1995 through 1999 had a net population loss.

(6) Vocational rehabilitation referral.—The term "vocational rehabilitation referral" means any individual who is certified by the designated local agency as—

(A) having a physical or mental disability which, for such individual, constitutes or results in a substantial handicap to employment, and

(B) having been referred to the employer upon completion of (or while receiving) rehabilitative services pursuant to—

(i) an individualized written plan for employment under a State plan for vocational rehabilitation services approved under the Rehabilitation Act of 1973,

(ii) a program of vocational rehabilitation carried out under chapter 31 of title 38, United States Code, or

(iii) an individual work plan developed and implemented by an employment network pursuant to subsection (g) of section 1148 of the Social Security Act with respect to which the requirements of such subsection are met.

(7) Qualified summer youth employee.—

(A) In general.—The term "qualified summer youth employee" means any individual—

(i) who performs services for the employer between May 1 and September 15,

(ii) who is certified by the designated local agency as having attained age 16 but not 18 on the hiring date (or if later, on May 1 of the calendar year involved).

(iii) who has not been an employee of the employer during any period prior to the 90-day period described in subparagraph (B)(i), and

(iv) who is certified by the designated local agency as having his principal place of abode within an empowerment zone, enterprise community, or renewal community.

(B) Special rules for determining amount of credit.—For purposes of applying this subpart to wages paid or incurred to any qualified summer youth employee—

(i) subsection (b)(2) shall be applied by substituting "any 90-day period between May 1 and September 15" for "the 1-year period beginning with the day the individual begins work for the employer," and

(ii) subsection (b)(3) shall be applied by substituting "$3,000" for "$6,000."

The preceding sentence shall not apply to an individual who, with respect to the same employer, is certified as a member of another targeted group after such individual has been a qualified summer youth employee.

(C) Youth must continue to reside in zone or community.—Paragraph (5)(B) shall apply for purposes of subparagraph (A)(iv).

(8) Qualified food stamp recipient.—

(A) In general.—The term "qualified food stamp recipient" means any individual who is certified by the designated local agency—

(i) as having attained age 18 but not age 40 on the hiring date, and

(ii) as being a member of a family—

(I) receiving assistance under a food stamp program under the Food Stamp Act of 1977 for the 6-month period ending on the hiring date, or

(II) receiving such assistance for at least 3 months of the 5-month period ending on the hiring date, in the case of a member of a family who ceases to be eligible for such assistance under section 6(o) of the Food Stamp Act of 1977.

(B) Participation information.—Notwithstanding any other provision of law, the Secretary of the Treasury and the Secretary of Agriculture shall enter into an agreement to provide information to designated local agencies with respect to participation in the food stamp program.

(9) Qualified SSI recipient.—The term "qualified SSI recipient" means any individual who is certified by the designated local agency as receiving supplemental security income benefits under title XVI of the Social Security Act (including supplemental security income benefits of the type described in section 1616 of such Act or section 212 of Public Law 93-66) for any month ending within the 60-day period ending on the hiring date.

(10) Long-term family assistance recipient.—The term "long-term family assistance recipient" means any individual who is certified by the designated local agency—

(A) as being a member of a family receiving assistance under a IV-A program (as defined in paragraph (2)(B)) for at least the 18-month period ending on the hiring date,

(B)(i) as being a member of a family receiving such assistance for 18 months beginning after August 5, 1997, and

(ii) as having a hiring date which is not more than 2 years after the end of the earliest such 18-month period, or

(C)(i) as being a member of a family which ceased to be eligible for such assistance by reason of any limitation imposed by Federal or State law on the maximum period such assistance is payable to a family, and

(ii) as having a hiring date which is not more than 2 years after the date of such cessation.

(11) Hiring date.—The term "hiring date" means the day the individual is hired by the employer.

(12) Designated local agency.—The term "designated local agency" means a State employment security agency established in accordance with the Act of June 6, 1933, as amended (29 U.S.C. 49-49n).

(13) Special rules for certifications.—

(A) In general.—An individual shall not be treated as a member of a targeted group unless—

(i) on or before the day on which such individual begins work for the employer, the employer has received a certification from a designated local agency that such individual is a member of a targeted group, or

(ii) (I) on or before the day the individual is offered employment with the employer, a pre-screening notice is completed by the employer with respect to such individual, and

(II) not later than the 28th day after the individual begins work for the employer, the employer submits such notice, signed by the employer and the individual under penalties of perjury, to the designated local agency as part of a written request for such a certification from such agency.

For purposes of this paragraph, the term "prescreening notice" means a document (in such form as the Secretary shall prescribe) which contains information provided by the individual on the basis of which the employer believes that the individual is a member of a targeted group.

(B) Incorrect certifications.—If—

(i) an individual has been certified by a designated local agency as a member of a targeted group, and

(ii) such certification is incorrect because it was based on false information provided by such individual,

the certification shall be revoked and wages paid by the employer after the date on which notice of revocation is received by the employer shall not be treated as qualified wages.

(C) Explanation of denial of request.—If a designated local agency denies a request for certification of membership in a targeted group, such agency shall provide to the person making such request a written explanation of the reasons for such denial.

(14) Credit allowed for unemployed veterans and disconnected youth hired in 2009 or 2010.—

(A) In general.—Any unemployed veteran or disconnected youth who begins work for the employer during 2009 or 2010 shall be treated as a member of a targeted group for purposes of this subpart.

(B) Definitions.—For purposes of this paragraph—

(i) Unemployed veteran.—The term "unemployed veteran" means any veteran (as defined in paragraph (3)(B), determined without regard to clause (ii) thereof) who is certified by the designated local agency as—

(I) having been discharged or released from active duty in the Armed Forces at any time during the 5-year period ending on the hiring date, and

(II) being in receipt of unemployment compensation under State or Federal law for not less than 4 weeks during the 1-year period ending on the hiring date.

(ii) Disconnected youth.—The term "disconnected youth" means any individual who is certified by the designated local agency—

(I) as having attained age 16 but not age 25 on the hiring date,

(II) as not regularly attending any secondary, technical, or post-secondary school during the 6-month period preceding the hiring date,

(III) as not regularly employed during such 6-month period, and

(IV) as not readily employable by reason of lacking a sufficient number of basic skills.

(e) Credit for second-year wages for employment of long-term family assistance recipients.—

(1) In general.—With respect to the employment of a long-term family assistance recipient—

(A) the amount of the work opportunity credit determined under this section for the taxable year shall include 50 percent of the qualified second-year wages for such year, and

(B) in lieu of applying subsection (b)(3), the amount of the qualified first-year wages, and the amount of qualified second-year wages, which may be taken into account with respect to such a recipient shall not exceed $10,000 per year.

(2) Qualified second-year wages.—For purposes of this subsection, the term "qualified second-year wages" means qualified wages—

(A) which are paid to a long-term family assistance recipient, and

(B) which are attributable to service rendered during the 1-year period beginning on the day after the last day of the 1-year period with respect to such recipient determined under subsection (b)(2).

(3) Special rules for agricultural and railway labor.—If such recipient is an employee to whom subparagraph (A) or (B) of subsection (h)(1) applies, rules similar to the rules of such subparagraphs shall apply except that—

(A) such subparagraph (A) shall be applied by substituting "$10,000" for "$6,000", and

(B) such subparagraph (B) shall be applied by substituting "$833.33" for "$500".

(f) Remuneration must be for trade or business employment.—

(1) In general.—For purposes of this subpart, remuneration paid by an employer to an employee during any taxable year shall be taken into account only if more than one-half of the remuneration so paid is for services performed in a trade or business of the employer.

* * *

(i) Certain individuals ineligible.—

(1) Related individuals.—No wages shall be taken into account under subsection (a) with respect to an individual who—

(A) bears any of the relationships described in subparagraphs (A) through (G) of section 152(d)(2) to the taxpayer, or, if the taxpayer is a corporation, to an individual who owns, directly or indirectly, more than 50 percent in value of the outstanding stock of the corporation, or, if the taxpayer is an entity other than a corporation, to any individual who owns, directly or indirectly, more than 50 percent of the capital and profits interests in the entity (determined with the application of section 267(c)),

(B) if the taxpayer is an estate or trust, is a grantor, beneficiary, or fiduciary of the estate or trust, or is an individual who bears any of the relationships described in subparagraphs (A) through (G) of section 152(d)(2) to a grantor, beneficiary, or fiduciary of the estate or trust, or

(C) is a dependent (described in section 152 (d)(2)(H)) of the taxpayer, or, if the taxpayer is a corporation, of an individual described in subparagraph (A), or, if the taxpayer is an estate or trust, of a grantor, beneficiary, or fiduciary of the estate or trust.

(2) Nonqualifying rehires.—No wages shall be taken into account under subsection (a) with respect to any individual if, prior to the hiring date of such individual, such individual had been employed by the employer at any time.

(3) Individuals not meeting minimum employment period.—

(A) Reduction of credit for individuals performing fewer than 400 hours of service.—In the case of an individual who has performed at least 120 hours, but less than 400 hours, of service for the employer, subsection (a) shall be applied by substituting "25 percent" for "40 percent."

(B) Denial of credit for individuals performing fewer than 120 hours of service.—No wages shall be taken into account under subsection (a) with respect to any individual unless such individual has performed at least 120 hours of service for the employer.

* * *

(j) Election to have work opportunity credit not apply.—

(1) In general.—A taxpayer may elect to have this section not apply for any taxable year.

(2) Time for making election.—An election under paragraph (1) for any taxable year may be made (or revoked) at any time before the expiration of the 3-year period beginning on the last date prescribed by law for filing the return for such taxable year (determined without regard to extensions).

(3) Manner of making election.—An election under paragraph (1) (or revocation thereof) shall be made in such manner as the Secretary may by regulations prescribe.

* * *

§ 52. Special rules

(a) Controlled group of corporations.—For purposes of this subpart, all employees of all corporations which are members of the same controlled group of corporations shall be treated as employed by a single employer. In any such case, the credit (if any) determined under section 51(a) with respect to each such member shall be its proportionate share of the wages giving rise to such credit. For purposes of this subsection, the term "controlled group of corporations" has the meaning given to such term by section 1563(a), except that—

(1) "more than 50 percent" shall be substituted for "at least 80 percent" each place it appears in section 1563(a)(1), and

(2) the determination shall be made without regard to subsections (a)(4) and (e)(3)(C) of section 1563.

(b) Employees of partnerships, proprietorships, etc., which are under common control.—For purposes of this subpart, under regulations prescribed by the Secretary—

(1) all employees of trades or business (whether or not incorporated) which are under common control shall be treated as employed by a single employer, and

(2) the credit (if any) determined under section 51(a) with respect to each trade or business shall be its proportionate share of the wages giving rise to such credit.

The regulations prescribed under this subsection shall be based on principles similar to the principles which apply in the case of subsection (a).

(c) Tax-exempt organizations.—No credit shall be allowed under section 38 for any work opportunity credit determined under this subpart to any organization (other than a cooperative described in section 521) which is exempt from income tax under this chapter.

(d) Estates and trusts.—In the case of an estate or trust—

(1) the amount of the credit determined under this subpart for any taxable year shall be apportioned between the estate or trust and the beneficiaries on the basis of the income of the estate or trust allocable to each, and

(2) any beneficiary to whom any amount has been apportioned under paragraph (1) shall be allowed, subject to section 38(c), a credit under section 38(a) for such amount.

* * *

SUBPART G—CREDIT AGAINST REGULAR TAX FOR PRIOR YEAR MINIMUM TAX LIABILITY

§ 53. Credit for prior year minimum tax liability

(a) Allowance of credit.—There shall be allowed as a credit against the tax imposed by this chapter for any taxable year an amount equal to the minimum tax credit for such taxable year.

(b) Minimum tax credit.—For purposes of subsection (a), the minimum tax credit for any taxable year is the excess (if any) of—

(1) the adjusted net minimum tax imposed for all prior taxable years beginning after 1986, over

(2) the amount allowable as a credit under subsection (a) for such prior taxable years.

(c) Limitation.—The credit allowable under subsection (a) for any taxable year shall not exceed the excess (if any) of—

(1) the regular tax liability of the taxpayer for such taxable year reduced by the sum of the credits allowable under subparts A, B, D, E, and F of this part, over

(2) the tentative minimum tax for the taxable year.

(d) Definitions.—For purposes of this section—

(1) Net minimum tax.—

(A) In general.—The term "net minimum tax" means the tax imposed by section 55.

(B) Credit not allowed for exclusion preferences.—

(i) Adjusted net minimum tax.—The adjusted net minimum tax for any taxable year is—

(I) the amount of the net minimum tax for such taxable year, reduced by

(II) the amount which would be the net minimum tax for such taxable year if the only adjustments and items of tax pref erence taken into account were those specified in clause (ii).

(ii) Specified items.—The following are specified in this clause—

(I) the adjustments provided for in subsection (b)(1) of section 56, and

(II) the items of tax preference described in paragraphs (1), (5), and (7) of section 57(a).

(iii) Credit allowable for exclusion preferences of corporations.—In the case of a corporation—

(I) the preceding provisions of this subparagraph shall not apply, and

(II) the adjusted net minimum tax for any taxable year is the amount of the net minimum tax for such year.

In the case of taxable years beginning after 1989, the adjustments provided in section 56(g) shall be treated as specified in this clause to the extent attributable to items which are excluded from gross income for any taxable year for purposes of the regular tax, or are not deductible for any taxable year under the adjusted current earnings method of section 56(g).

(2) Tentative minimum tax.—The term "tentative minimum tax" has the meaning given to such term by section 55(b).

(e) Special rule for individuals with long-term unused credits.—

(1) In general.—If an individual has a long-term unused minimum tax credit for any taxable year beginning before January 1, 2013, the amount determined under subsection (c) for such taxable year shall not be less than the AMT refundable credit amount for such taxable year.

(2) AMT refundable credit amount.—For purposes of paragraph (1), the term "AMT refundable credit amount" means, with respect to any taxable year, the amount (not in excess of the long term unused minimum tax credit for such taxable year) equal to the greater of—

(A) 50 percent of the long-term unused minimum tax credit for such taxable year, or

(B) the amount (if any) of the AMT refundable credit amount determined under this paragraph for the taxpayer's preceding taxable year (determined without regard to subsection (f)(2)).

(3) Long-term unused minimum tax credit.—

(A) In general.—For purposes of this subsection, the term "long-term unused minimum tax credit" means, with respect to any taxable year, the portion of the minimum tax credit determined under subsection (b) attributable to the adjusted net minimum tax for taxable years before the 3rd taxable year immediately preceding such taxable year.

(B) First-in, first-out ordering rule.—For purposes of subparagraph (A), credits shall be treated as allowed under subsection (a) on a first-in, first-out basis.

(4) Credit refundable.—For purposes of this title (other than this section), the credit allowed by reason of this subsection shall be treated as if it were allowed under subpart C.

(f) Treatment of certain underpayments, interest, and penalties attributable to the treatment of incentive stock options.—

(1) Abatement.—Any underpayment of tax outstanding on the date of the enactment of this subsection which is attributable to the application of section 56(b)(3) for any taxable year ending before January 1, 2008 and any interest or penalty with respect to such underpayment which is outstanding on such date of enactment, is hereby abated. The amount determined under subsection (b)(1) shall not include any tax abated under the preceding sentence.

(2) Increase in credit for certain interest and penalties already paid.—The AMT refundable credit amount, and the minimum tax credit determined under subsection (b), for the taxpayer's first 2 taxable years beginning after December 31, 2007, shall each be increased by 50 percent of the aggregate amount of the interest and penalties which were paid by the taxpayer before the date of the enactment of this subsection and which would (but for such payment) have been abated under paragraph (1).

* * *

PART VI—ALTERNATIVE MINIMUM TAX

Editorial Summary

Alternative Minimum Tax

SubchapterA of Chapter1 (Secs. 55–59)

In order that the taxpayer not be able to avoid the Federal income tax liability completely, the minimum tax concept was introduced into the Code in 1969. To better achieve the objective, the statutory provisions have been amended on several occasions. The minimum tax, in its present form, is applicable to both the individual taxpayer (or estate or trust) and the corporate taxpayer. However, some differences exist in the calculation format.

The starting point for the calculation is taxable income. Certain adjustments are made to taxable income [see Secs. 56, 58]. This amount is increased by tax preferences [see Sec. 57] and is reduced by an exemption amount assuming that the exemption amount has not been phased out [see Sec. 55(d)]. The statutory rate of 20 percent for corporations or 26 and 28 percent for noncorporate taxpayers [see Sec. 55(b)] is applied to the above result to produce the tentative minimum tax.

In making the adjustment under Sec. 56, note in particular the adjustment which applies only to the corporation for business untaxed reported profits (i.e., the ACE adjustment) [see Sec. 56(c)(1)]. The adjustment is 75 percent of the excess (or the negative excess) of adjusted current earnings over alternative minimum taxable income (AMTI) [see Sec. 56(g)]. Note that under this calculation procedure the adjustment can be either positive or negative, but the total negative adjustments are limited to the amount of prior years positive adjustments. [see Secs. 56(g)(1) and (g)(2)].

The Code provides that the alternative minimum tax liability is the excess, if any, of the tentative minimum tax over the regular tax liability [see Sec. 55(a)]. Thus, this excess is the penalty tax that is imposed on the taxpayer. In effect, the taxpayer is required to pay the greater amount—the regular tax liability or the tax liability calculated in the preceding paragraph.

Tax credits impact differently on the calculation of the two tax liabilities. The regular tax liability, for purposes of the alternative minimum tax calculation, is normally defined in a special manner [see Sec. 55(c)]. The only credit that is permitted to be deducted is the foreign tax credit. The tentative minimum tax can also be reduced by the foreign tax credit, but it must be calculated in a special manner [see Sec. 59(a)]. The potential effect of this limitation on the use of credits in calculating both the regular tax liability and the tentative minimum tax liability is that substantial credits may be available, yet cannot be used to reduce the current taxable year tax liability.

For tax years after December 31, 2011, certain nonrefundable personal tax credits (e.g., child tax credit, adoption expenses credit, and credit for elective deferrals and IRA contributions) can offset both the regular income tax (less any foreign tax credit) and the AMT in full after all other nonrefundable personal tax credits have been utilized [see Sec. 26(a)(1) and (2)].

Timing differences in the reporting of income and the taking of deductions that produce an alternative minimum tax liability could result in the same item being taxed in the future as part of the regular tax liability calculation. To prevent this double taxation, the regular tax liability can be reduced by the minimum tax credit [see Sec. 53].

The calculation of the alternative minimum tax can be depicted as follows:

Regular taxable income before NOL deduction
± AMT adjustments
\+ Tax preferences
= Alternative minimum taxable income (AMTI) before AMT NOL deduction
− AMT NOL deduction
= Alternative minimum taxable income (AMTI)
− Exemption
= Alternative minimum tax base
x Rate (20 percent for corporation and 26 and 28 percent for individual)
= AMT before AMT foreign tax credit
− AMT foreign tax credit
= Tentative alternative minimum tax
− Regular tax liability before credits minus foreign tax credit
= Alternative minimum tax (AMT)
See Sec. 55(e) for the exemption from the AMT for small corporations.

For any tax year beginning in any calendar year after 2012, the exemption amounts are indexed for inflation.

§ 55. Alternative minimum tax imposed

(a) General rule.—There is hereby imposed (in addition to any other tax imposed by this subtitle) a tax equal to the excess (if any) of—

(1) the tentative minimum tax for the taxable year, over

(2) the regular tax for the taxable year.

(b) Tentative minimum tax.—For purposes of this part—

(1) Amount of tentative tax.—

(A) Noncorporate taxpayers.—

(i) In general.—In the case of a taxpayer other than a corporation, the tentative minimum tax for the taxable year is the sum of—

(I) 26 percent of so much of the taxable excess as does not exceed $175,000, plus

(II) 28 percent of so much of the taxable excess as exceeds $175,000.*

The amount determined under the preceding sentence shall be reduced by the alternative minimum tax foreign tax credit for the taxable year.

(ii) Taxable excess.—For purposes of this subsection, the term "taxable excess" means so much of the alternative minimum taxable income for the taxable year as exceeds the exemption amount.

(iii) Married individual filing separate return.—In the case of a married individual filing a separate return, clause (i) shall be applied by substituting 50 percent of the dollar amount otherwise applicable under subclause (I) and subclause (II) thereof. For purposes of the preceding sentence, marital status shall be determined under section 7703.

(B) Corporations.—In the case of a corporation, the tentative minimum tax for the taxable year is—

(i) 20 percent of so much of the alternative minimum taxable income for the taxable year as exceeds the exemption amount, reduced by

(ii) the alternative minimum tax foreign tax credit for the taxable year.

(2) Alternative minimum taxable income.—The term "alternative minimum taxable income" means the taxable income of the taxpayer for the taxable year—

(A) determined with the adjustments provided in section 56 and section 58, and

(B) increased by the amount of the items of tax preference described in section 57.

If a taxpayer is subject to the regular tax, such taxpayer shall be subject to the tax imposed by this section (and, if the regular tax is determined by reference to an amount other than taxable income, such amount shall be treated as the taxable income of such taxpayer for purposes of the preceding sentence).

(3) Maximum rate of tax on net capital gain of noncorporate taxpayers.—The amount determined under the first sentence of paragraph (1)(A)(i) shall not exceed the sum of—

(A) the amount determined under such first sentence computed at the rates and in the same manner as if this paragraph had not been enacted on the taxable excess reduced by the lesser of—

(i) the net capital gain, or

(ii) the sum of—

(I) the adjusted net capital gain, plus

(II) the unrecaptured section 1250 gain, plus

(B) 0 percent of so much of the adjusted net capital gain (or, if less, taxable excess) as does not exceed an amount equal to the excess described in section 1(h)(1)(B), plus

(C) 15 percent of the lesser of—

(i) so much of the adjusted net capital gain (or, if less, taxable excess) as exceeds the amount on which tax is determined under subparagraph (B), or

(ii) the excess described in section 1(h)(1)(C)(ii), plus

(D) 20 percent of the adjusted net capital gain (or, if less, taxable excess) in excess of the sum of the amounts on which tax is determined under subparagraphs (B) and (C), plus

(E) 25 percent of the amount of taxable excess in excess of the sum of the amounts on which tax is determined under the preceding subparagraphs of this paragraph.

Terms used in this paragraph which are also used in section 1(h) shall have the respective meanings given such terms by section 1(h) but computed with the adjustments under this part.

(4) Maximum rate of tax on qualified timber gain of corporations.—In the case of any taxable year to which section 1201(b) applies, the amount determined under clause (i) of subparagraph (B) shall not exceed the sum of—

(A) 20 percent of so much of the taxable excess (if any) as exceeds the qualified timber gain (or, if less, the net capital gain), plus

(B) 15 percent of the taxable excess in excess of the amount on which a tax is determined under subparagraph (A).

*Editorial comment: For all taxable years after January 1, 2014, the excess taxable income to which the 28% tax rate applies is $182,500.

treatment applicable for purposes of computing the regular tax):

(1) Depreciation.—

(A) In general.—

(i) Property other than certain personal property.—Except as provided in clause (ii), the depreciation deduction allowable under section 167 with respect to any tangible property placed in service after December 31, 1986, shall be determined under the alternative system of section 168(g). In the case of property placed in service after December 31, 1998, the preceding sentence shall not apply but clause (ii) shall continue to apply.

(ii) 150-percent declining balance method for certain property.—The method of depreciation used shall be—

(I) the 150-percent declining balance method,

(II) switching to the straight line method for the 1st taxable year for which using the straight line method with respect to the adjusted basis as of the beginning of the year will yield a higher allowance.

The preceding sentence shall not apply to any section 1250 property (as defined in section 1250 (c)) (and the straight line method shall be used for such section 1250 property) or to any other property if the depreciation deduction determined under section 168 with respect to such other property for purposes of the regular tax is determined by using the straight line method.

(B) Exception for certain property.—This paragraph shall not apply to property described in paragraph (1), (2), (3), or (4) of section 168 (f), or in section 168(e)(3)(C)(iv).

* * *

(2) Mining exploration and development costs.—

(A) In general.—With respect to each mine or other natural deposit (other than an oil, gas, or geothermal well) of the taxpayer, the amount allowable as a deduction under section 616(a) or 617(a) (determined without regard to section 291(b)) in computing the regular tax for costs paid or incurred after December 31, 1986, shall be capitalized and amortized ratably over the 10-year period beginning with the taxable year in which the expenditures were made.

(B) Loss allowed.—If a loss is sustained with respect to any property described in subparagraph (A), a deduction shall be allowed for the expenditures described in subparagraph (A) for the taxable year in which such loss is sustained in an amount equal to the lesser of—

(i) the amount allowable under section 165 (a) for the expenditures if they had remained capitalized, or

(ii) the amount of such expenditures which have not previously been amortized under subparagraph (A).

(3) Treatment of certain long-term contracts.—In the case of any long-term contract entered into by the taxpayer on or after March 1, 1986, the taxable income from such contract shall be determined under the percentage of completion method of accounting (as modified by section 460(b)). For purposes of the preceding sentence, in the case of a contract described in section 460(e)(1), the percentage of the contract completed shall be determined under section 460(b)(1) by using the simplified procedures for allocation of costs prescribed under section 460(b)(3). The first sentence of this paragraph shall not apply to any home construction contract (as defined in section 460(e)(6)).

(4) Alternative tax net operating loss deduction.—The alternative tax net operating loss deduction shall be allowed in lieu of the net operating loss deduction allowed under section 172.

(5) Pollution control facilities.—In the case of any certified pollution control facility placed in service after December 31, 1986, the deduction allowable under section 169 (without regard to section 291) shall be determined under the alternative system of section 168(g). In the case of such a facility placed in service after December 31, 1998, such deduction shall be determined under section 168 using the straight line method.

(6) Adjusted basis.—The adjusted basis of any property to which paragraph (1) or (5) applies (or with respect to which there are any expenditures to which paragraph (2) or subsection (b)(2) applies) shall be determined on the basis of the treatment prescribed in paragraph (1), (2), or (5), or subsection (b)(2), whichever applies.

* * *

(b) Adjustments applicable to individuals.—In determining the amount of the alternative minimum taxable income of any taxpayer (other than a corporation), the following treatment shall apply (in lieu of the treatment applicable for purposes of computing the regular tax):

(1) Limitation on deductions.—

(A) In general.—No deduction shall be allowed—

(i) for any miscellaneous itemized deduction (as defined in section 67(b)), or

(ii) for any taxes described in paragraph (1), (2), or (3) of section 164(a) or clause (ii) of section 164(b)(5)(A).

Clause (ii) shall not apply to any amount allowable in computing adjusted gross income.

(B) Medical expenses.—In determining the amount allowable as a deduction under section 213, subsection (a) of section 213 shall be applied without regard to subsection (f) of such subsection.

(C) Interest.—In determining the amount allowable as a deduction for interest, subsections (d) and (h) of section 163 shall apply, except that—

(i) in lieu of the exception under section 163(h)(2)(D), the term "personal interest" shall not include any qualified housing interest (as defined in subsection (e)),

(ii) sections 163(d)(6) and 163(h)(5) (relating to phase-ins) shall not apply,

(iii) interest on any specified private activity bond (and any amount treated as interest on a specified private activity bond under section 57(a)(5)(B)), and any deduction referred to in section 57(a)(5)(A), shall be treated as includible in gross income (or as deductible) for purposes of applying section 163(d),

(iv) in lieu of the exception under section 163(d)(3)(B)(i), the term "investment interest" shall not include any qualified housing interest (as defined in subsection (e)), and

(v) the adjustments of this section and sections 57 and 58 shall apply in determining net investment income under section 163(d).

(D) Treatment of certain recoveries.—No recovery of any tax to which subparagraph (A)(ii) applied shall be included in gross income for purposes of determining alternative minimum taxable income.

(E) Standard deduction and deduction for personal exemptions not allowed.—The standard deduction under section 63(c), the deduction for personal exemptions under section 151, and the deduction under section 642(b) shall not be allowed. The preceding sentence shall not apply to so much of the standard deduction as is determined under subparagraphs (D) and (E) of section 63(c)(1).

(F) Section 68 not applicable.—Section 68 shall not apply.

(2) Circulation and research and experimental expenditures.—

(A) In general.—The amount allowable as a deduction under section 173 or 174(a) in computing the regular tax for amounts paid or incurred after December 31, 1986, shall be capitalized and—

(i) in the case of circulation expenditures described in section 173, shall be amortized ratably over the 3-year period beginning with the taxable year in which the expenditures were made, or

(ii) in the case of research and experimental expenditures described in section 174(a), shall be amortized ratably over the 10-year period beginning with the taxable year in which the expenditures were made.

(B) Loss allowed.—If a loss is sustained with respect to any property described in subparagraph (A), a deduction shall be allowed for the expenditures described in subparagraph (A) for the taxable year in which such loss is sustained in an amount equal to the lesser of—

(i) the amount allowable under section 165(a) for the expenditures if they had remained capitalized, or

(ii) the amount of such expenditures which have not previously been amortized under subparagraph (A).

(C) Special rule for personal holding companies.—In the case of circulation expenditures described in section 173, the adjustments provided in this paragraph shall apply also to a personal holding company (as defined in section 542).

(D) Exception for certain research and experimental expenditures.—If the taxpayer materially participates (within the meaning of section 469(h)) in an activity, this paragraph shall not apply to any amount allowable as a deduction under section 174(a) for expenditures paid or incurred in connection with such activity.

(3) Treatment of incentive stock options.—Section 421 shall not apply to the transfer of stock acquired pursuant to the exercise of an incentive stock option (as defined in section 422). Section 422(c)(2) shall apply in any case where the disposition and the inclusion for purposes of this part are within the same taxable year and such section shall not apply in any other case. The adjusted basis of any stock so acquired shall be determined on the basis of the treatment prescribed by this paragraph.

(c) Adjustments applicable to corporations.—In determining the amount of the alternative minimum taxable income of a corporation, the following treatment shall apply:

(1) Adjustment for adjusted current earnings.—Alternative minimum taxable income shall be adjusted as provided in subsection (g).

* * *

(d) Alternative tax net operating loss deduction defined.—

(1) In general.—For purposes of subsection (a)(4), the term "alternative tax net operating loss deduction" means the net operating loss deduction allowable for the taxable year under section 172, except that—

(A) the amount of such deduction shall not exceed the sum of—

(i) the lesser of—

(I) the amount of such deduction attributable to net operating losses (other than the deduction described in clause (ii)(I)), or

(II) 90 percent of alternative minimum taxable income determined without regard to such deduction and the deduction under section 199, plus

(ii) the lesser of—

(I) the amount of such deduction attributable to an applicable net operating loss with respect to which an election is made under section 172(b)(1)(H), or

(II) alternative minimum taxable income determined without regard to such deduction and the deduction under section 199 reduced by the amount determined under clause (i), and

(B) in determining the amount of such deduction—

(i) the net operating loss (within the meaning of section 172(c)) for any loss year shall be adjusted as provided in paragraph (2), and

(ii) appropriate adjustments in the application of section 172(b)(2) shall be made to take into account the limitation of subparagraph (A).

(2) Adjustments to net operating loss computation.—

(A) Post-1986 loss years.—In the case of a loss year beginning after December 31, 1986, the net operating loss for such year under section 172(c) shall—

(i) be determined with the adjustments provided in this section and section 58, and

(ii) be reduced by the items of tax preference determined under section 57 for such year.

An item of tax preference shall be taken into account under clause (ii) only to the extent such item increased the amount of the net operating loss for the taxable year under section 172(c).

(B) Pre-1987 years.—In the case of loss years beginning before January 1, 1987, the amount of the net operating loss which may be carried over to taxable years beginning after December 31, 1986, for purposes of paragraph (2), shall be equal to the amount which may be carried from the loss year to the first taxable year of the taxpayer beginning after December 31, 1986.

(3) Net operating loss attributable to federally declared disasters.—In the case of a taxpayer which has a qualified disaster loss (as defined by section 172(b)(1)(J)) for the taxable year, paragraph (1) shall be applied by increasing the amount determined under subparagraph (A)(ii)(I) thereof by the sum of the carrybacks and carryovers of such loss.

(e) Qualified housing interest.—For purposes of this part—

(1) In general.—The term "qualified housing interest" means interest which is qualified residence interest (as defined in section 163(h)(3)) paid or accrued during the taxable year on indebtedness which is incurred in acquiring, constructing, or substantially improving any property which—

(A) is the principal residence (within the meaning of section 121) of the taxpayer at the time such interest accrues or is paid, or

(B) is a qualified dwelling which is a qualified residence (within the meaning of section 163(h)(4)).

Such term also includes interest on any indebtedness resulting from the refinancing of indebtedness meeting the requirements of the preceding sentence; but only to the extent that the amount of the indebtedness resulting from such refinancing does not exceed the amount of the refinanced indebtedness immediately before the refinancing.

(2) Qualified dwelling.—The term qualified dwelling" means any—

(A) house,

(B) apartment,

(C) condominium, or

(D) mobile home not used on a transient basis (within the meaning of section 7701(a) (19) (C)(v)),

including all structures or other property appurtenant thereto.

* * *

(g) Adjustments based on adjusted current earnings.—

(1) In general.—The alternative minimum taxable income of any corporation for any taxable year shall be increased by 75 percent of the excess (if any) of—

(A) the adjusted current earnings of the corporation, over

(B) the alternative minimum taxable income (determined without regard to this subsection and the alternative tax net operating loss deduction).

(2) Allowance of negative adjustments.—

(A) In general.—The alternative minimum taxable income for any corporation of any taxable year shall be reduced by 75 percent of the excess (if any) of—

(i) the amount referred to in subparagraph (B) of paragraph (1), over

(ii) the amount referred to in subparagraph (A) of paragraph (1).

(B) Limitation.—The reduction under subparagraph (A) for any taxable year shall not exceed the excess (if any) of—

(i) the aggregate increases in alternative minimum taxable income under paragraph (1) for prior taxable years, over

(ii) the aggregate reductions under subparagraph (A) of this paragraph for prior taxable years.

(3) Adjusted current earnings.—For purposes of this subsection, the term "adjusted current earnings" means the alternative minimum taxable income for the taxable year—

(A) determined with the adjustments provided in paragraph (4), and

(B) determined without regard to this subsection and the alternative tax net operating loss deduction.

(4) Adjustments.—In determining adjusted current earnings, the following adjustments shall apply:

(A) Depreciation.—

(i) Property placed in service after 1989.—The depreciation deduction with respect to any property placed in service in a taxable year beginning after 1989 shall be determined under the alternative system of section 168(g). The preceding sentence shall not apply to any property placed in service after December 31, 1993, and the depreciation deduction with respect to such property shall be determined under the rules of subsection (a)(1)(A).

(ii) Property to which new ACRS system applies.—In the case of any property to which the amendments made by section 201 of the Tax Reform Act of 1986 apply and which is placed in service in a taxable year beginning before 1990, the depreciation deduction shall be determined—

(I) by taking into account the adjusted basis of such property (as determined for purposes of computing alternative minimum taxable income) as of the close of the last taxable year beginning before January 1, 1990, and

(II) by using the straight-line method over the remainder of the recovery period applicable to such property under the alternative system of section 168(g).

(iii) Property to which original ACRS system applies.—In the case of any property to which section 168 (as in effect on the day before the date of the enactment of the Tax Reform Act of 1986 and without regard to subsection (d)(1)(A)(ii) thereof) applies and which is placed in service in a taxable year beginning before 1990, the depreciation deduction shall be determined—

(I) by taking into account the adjusted basis of such property (as determined for purposes of computing the regular tax) as of the close of the last taxable year beginning before January 1, 1990, and

(II) by using the straight line method over the remainder of the recovery period which would apply to such property under the alternative system of section 168(g).

(iv) Property placed in service before 1981.—In the case of any property not described in clause (i), (ii), or (iii), the amount allowable as depreciation or amortization with respect to such property shall be determined in the same manner as for purposes of computing taxable income.

(v) Special rule for certain property.—In the case of any property described in paragraph (1), (2), (3), or (4) of section 168 (f), the amount of depreciation allowable for purposes of the regular tax shall be treated as the amount allowable under the alternative system of section 168(g).

(B) Inclusion of items included for purposes of computing earnings and profits.—

(i) In general.—In the case of any amount which is excluded from gross income for purposes of computing alternative minimum taxable income but is taken into account in determining the amount of earnings and profits—

(I) such amount shall be included in income in the same manner as if such amount were includible in gross income for purposes of computing alternative minimum taxable income, and

(II) the amount of such income shall be reduced by any deduction which would have been allowable in computing alternative minimum taxable income if such amount were includible in gross income.

The preceding sentence shall not apply in the case of any amount excluded from gross income under section 108 (or the corresponding provisions of prior law) or under section 139A or 1357.

* * *

(iii) Tax exempt interest on certain housing bonds.—Clause (i) shall not apply in the case of any interest on a bond to which section 57(a)(5)(C)(iii) applies.

(iv) Tax exempt interest on bonds issued in 2009 and 2010.—

(I) In general.—Clause (i) shall not apply in the case of any interest on a bond issued after December 31, 2008, and before January 1, 2011.

(II) Treatment of refunding bonds.—For purposes of subclause (I), a refunding bond (whether a current or advance refunding) shall be treated as issued on the date of the issuance of the refunded bond (or in the case of a series of refundings, the original bond).

(III) Exception for certain refunding bonds.—Subclause (II) shall not apply to any refunding bond which is issued to refund any bond which was issued after December 31, 2003, and before January 1, 2009.

* * *

(C) Disallowance of items not deductible in computing earnings and profits.—

(i) In general.—A deduction shall not be allowed for any item if such item would not be deductible for any taxable year for purposes of computing earnings and profits.

* * *

(D) Certain other earnings and profits adjustments.—

(i) Intangible drilling costs.—The adjustments provided in section 312(n)(2)(A) shall apply in the case of amounts paid or incurred in taxable years beginning after December 31, 1989. In the case of a taxpayer other than an integrated oil company (as defined in section 291(b)(4)), in the case of any oil or gas well, this clause shall not apply in the case of amounts paid or incurred in taxable years beginning after December 31, 1992.

(ii) Certain amortization provisions not to apply.—Sections 173 and 248 shall not apply to expenditures paid or incurred in taxable years beginning after December 31, 1989.

(iii) LIFO inventory adjustments.—The adjustments provided in section 312(n)(4) shall apply, but only with respect to taxable years beginning after December 31, 1989.

(iv) Installment sales.—In the case of any installment sale in a taxable year beginning after December 31, 1989, adjusted current earnings shall be computed as if the corporation did not use the installment method.

The preceding sentence shall not apply to the applicable percentage (as determined under section 453A) of the gain from any installment sale with respect to which section 453A (a)(1) applies.

* * *

(F) Depletion.—

(i) In general.—The allowance for depletion with respect to any property placed in service in a taxable year beginning after December 31, 1989, shall be cost depletion determined under section 611.

(ii) Exception for independent oil and gas producers and royalty owners.—In the case of any taxable year beginning after December 31, 1992, clause (i) (and subparagraph (C)(i)) shall not apply to any deduction for depletion computed in accordance with section 613A(c).

* * *

(H) Adjusted basis.—The adjusted basis of any property with respect to which an adjustment under this paragraph applies shall be determined by applying the treatment prescribed in this paragraph.

***(J) Treatment of charitable contributions.**—Notwithstanding subparagraphs (B) and (C), no adjustment related to the earnings and profits effects of any charitable contribution shall be made in computing adjusted current earnings.

* * *

(6) Exception for certain corporations.—This subsection shall not apply to any S corporation.

* * *

§ 57. Items of tax preference

(a) General rule.—For purposes of this part, the items of tax preference determined under this section are—

(1) Depletion.—With respect to each property (as defined in section 614), the excess of the deduction for depletion allowable under section 611 for the taxable year over the adjusted basis of the property at the end of the taxable year (determined without regard to the depletion deduction for the taxable year). Effective with respect to taxable years beginning after December 31, 1992, this paragraph shall not apply to any deduction for depletion computed in accordance with section 613A(c).

(2) Intangible drilling costs.—

(A) In general.—With respect to all oil, gas, and geothermal properties of the taxpayer, the amount (if any) by which the amount of the excess intangible drilling costs arising in the taxable year is greater than 65 percent of the net income of the taxpayer from oil, gas, andgeothermal properties for the taxable year.

(B) Excess intangible drilling costs.—For purposes of subparagraph (A), the amount of the excess intangible drilling costs arising in the taxable year is the excess of—

(i) the intangible drilling and development costs paid or incurred in connection with oil, gas, and geothermal wells (other than costs incurred in drilling a nonproductive well) allowable under section 263(c) or 291(b) for the taxable year, over

(ii) the amount which would have been allowable for the taxable year if such costs had been capitalized and straight line recovery of intangibles (as defined in subsection (b)) had been used with respect to such costs.

(C) Net income from oil, gas, and geothermal properties.—For purposes of subparagraph (A), the amount of the net income of the taxpayer from oil, gas, and geothermal properties for the taxable year is the excess of—

(i) the aggregate amount of gross income (within the meaning of section 613(a)) from all oil, gas, and geothermal properties of the taxpayer received or accrued by the taxpayer during the taxable year, over

(ii) the amount of any deductions allocable to such properties reduced by the excess described in subparagraph (B) for such taxable year.

(D) Paragraph applied separately with respect to geothermal properties and oil and gas properties.—This paragraph shall be applied separately with respect to—

*Editorial comment: There is no subparagraph I.

(i) all oil and gas properties which are not described in clause (ii), and

(ii) all properties which are geothermal deposits (as defined in section 613(e)(2)).

(E) Exception for independent producers.—In the case of any oil or gas well—

(i) In general.—In the case of any taxable year beginning after December 31, 1992, this paragraph shall not apply to any taxpayer which is not an integrated oil company (as defined in section 291(b)(4)).

(ii) Limitation on benefit.—The reduction in alternative minimum taxable income by reason of clause (i) for any taxable year shall not exceed 40 percent (30 percent in case of taxable years beginning in 1993) of the alternative minimum taxable income for such year determined without regard to clause (i) and the alternative tax net operating loss deduction under section 56(a)(4).

*(5) **Tax-exempt interest.**—

(A) In general.—Interest on specified private activity bonds reduced by any deduction (not allowable in computing the regular tax) which would have been allowable if such interest were includible in gross income.

* * *

(vi) Exception for bonds issued in 2009 and 2010.—

(I) In general.—For purposes of clause (i), the term "private activity bond" shall not include any bond issued after December 31, 2008, and before January 1, 2011.

(II) Treatment of refunding bonds.—For purposes of subclause (I), a refunding bond (whether a current or advance refunding) shall be treated as issued on the date of the issuance of the refunded bond (or in the case of a series of refundings, the original bond).

(III) Exception for certain refunding bonds.—Subclause (II) shall not apply to any refunding bond which is issued to refund any bond which was issued after December 31, 2003, and before January 1, 2009.

(6) Accelerated depreciation or amortization on certain property placed in service before January 1, 1987.—The amounts which would be treated as items of tax preference with respect to the taxpayer under paragraphs (2), (3), (4), and (12) of this subsection (as in effect on the day before the date of the enactment of the Tax Reform Act of 1986). The preceding sentence shall not apply to any property to which section 56(a)(1) or (5) applies.

(7) **Exclusion for gains on sale of certain small business stock.—An amount equal to 7 percent of the amount excluded from gross income for the taxable year under section 1202.

(b) Straight line recovery of intangibles defined.—For purposes of paragraph (2) of subsection (a)—

(1) In general.—The term "straight line recovery of intangibles," when used with respect to intangible drilling and development costs for any well, means (except in the case of an election under paragraph (2)) ratable amortization of such costs over the 120-month period beginning with the month in which production from such well begins.

(2) Election.—If the taxpayer elects with respect to the intangible drilling and development costs for any well, the term "straight line recovery of intangibles" means any method which would be permitted for purposes of determining cost depletion with respect to such well and which is selected by the taxpayer for purposes of subsection (a)(2).

§ 58. Denial of certain losses

(a) Denial of farm loss.—

(1) In general.—For purposes of computing the amount of the alternative minimum taxable income for any taxable year of a taxpayer other than a corporation—

(A) Disallowance of farm loss.—No loss of the taxpayer for such taxable year from any tax shelter farm activity shall be allowed.

(B) Deduction in succeeding taxable year.—Any loss from a tax shelter farm activity disallowed under subparagraph (A) shall be treated as a deduction allocable to such activity in the 1st succeeding taxable year.

---

*Editorial comment: There is no paragraph (3) or paragraph (4).

**Editorial comment: The Jobs and Growth Tax Relief Reconciliation Act of 2003 decreased the exclusion percentage from 42 percent (28 percent if the holding period of the stock begins after December 31, 2000) to 7 percent. The reduced percentage applies only for dispositions on or after May 6, 2003.

(2) Tax shelter farm activity.—For purposes of this subsection, the term "tax shelter farm activity" means—

(A) any farming syndicate as defined in section 464(c), and

(B) any other activity consisting of farming which is a passive activity (within the meaning of section 469(c)).

(3) Application to personal service corporations.—For purposes of paragraph (1), a personal service corporation (within the meaning of section 469(j)(2)(C)) shall be treated as a taxpayer other than a corporation.

(4) Determination of loss.—In determining the amount of the loss from any tax shelter farm activity, the adjustments of sections 56 and 57 shall apply.

(b) Disallowance of passive activity loss.—In computing the alternative minimum taxable income of the taxpayer for any taxable year, section 469 shall apply, except that in applying section 469—

(1) the adjustments of sections 56 and 57 shall apply,

(2) the provisions of section 469(m) (relating to phase-in of disallowance) shall not apply, and

(3) in lieu of applying section 469(j)(7), the passive activity loss of a taxpayer shall be computed without regard to qualified housing interest (as defined in section 56(e)).

(c) Special rules.—For purposes of this section—

(1) Special rule for insolvent taxpayers.—

(A) In general.—The amount of losses to which subsection (a) or (b) applies shall be reduced by the amount (if any) by which the taxpayer is insolvent as of the close of the taxable year.

(B) Insolvent.—For purposes of this paragraph, the term "insolvent" means the excess of liabilities over the fair market value of assets.

(2) Loss allowed for year of disposition of farm shelter activity.—If the taxpayer disposes of his entire interest in any tax shelter farm activity during any taxable year, the amount of the loss attributable to such activity (determined after carryovers under subsection (a)(1)(B)) shall (to the extent otherwise allowable) be allowed for such taxable year in computing alternative minimum taxable income and not treated as a loss from a tax shelter farm activity.

§ 59. Other definitions and special rules

(a) Alternative minimum tax foreign tax credit.—For purposes of this part—

(1) In general.—The alternative minimum tax foreign tax credit for any taxable year shall be the credit which would be determined under section 27 (a) for such taxable year if—

(A) the pre-credit tentative minimum tax were the tax against which such credit was taken for purposes of section 904 for the taxable year and all prior taxable years beginning after December 31, 1986,

(B) section 904 were applied on the basis of alternative minimum taxable income instead of taxable income, and

* * *

(2) Pre-credit tentative minimum tax.—For purposes of this subsection, the term "pre-credit tentative minimum tax" means—

(A) in the case of a taxpayer other than a corporation, the amount determined under the first sentence of section 55(b)(1)(A)(i), or

(B) in the case of a corporation, the amount determined under section 55(b)(1)(B)(i).

* * *

(c) Treatment of estates and trusts.—In the case of any estate or trust, the alternative minimum taxable income of such estate or trust and any beneficiary thereof shall be determined by applying part I of subchapter J with the adjustments provided in this part.

* * *

(e) Optional 10-year writeoff of certain tax preferences.—

(1) In general.—For purposes of this title, any qualified expenditure to which an election under this paragraph applies shall be allowed as a deduction ratably over the 10-year period (3-year period in the case of circulation expenditures described in section 173) beginning with the taxable year in which such expenditure was made (or, in the case of a qualified expenditure described in paragraph (2)(C), over the 60-month period beginning with the month in which such expenditure was paid or incurred).

(2) Qualified expenditure.—For purposes of this subsection, the term "qualified expenditure" means any amount which, but for an election under this subsection, would have been allowable as a deduction (determined without regard to section 291) for the taxable year in which paid or incurred under—

(A) section 173 (relating to circulation expenditures),

(B) section 174(a) (relating to research and experimental expenditures),

(C) section 263(c) (relating to intangible drilling and development expenditures),

(D) section 616(a) (relating to development expenditures), or

(E) section 617(a) (relating to mining exploration expenditures).

(3) Other sections not applicable.—Except as provided in this subsection, no deduction shall be allowed under any other section for any qualified expenditure to which an election under this subsection applies.

(4) Election.—

(A) In general.—An election may be made under paragraph (1) with respect to any portion of any qualified expenditure.

(B) Revocable only with consent.—Any election under this subsection may be revoked only with the consent of the Secretary.

(C) Partners and shareholders of S corporations.—In the case of a partnership, any election under paragraph (1) shall be made separately by each partner with respect to the partner's allocable share of any qualified expenditure. A similar rule shall apply in the case of an S corporation and its shareholders.

(5) Dispositions.—

(A) Application of section 1254.—In the case of any disposition of property to which section 1254 applies (determined without regard to this section), any deduction under paragraph (1) with respect to amounts which are allocable to such property shall, for purposes of section 1254, be treated as a deduction allowable under section 263(c), 616(a), or 617(a), whichever is appropriate.

(B) Application of section 617(d).—In the case of any disposition of mining property to which section 617(d) applies (determined without regard to this subsection), any deduction under paragraph (1) with respect to amounts which are allocable to such property shall, for purposes of section 617(d), be treated as a deduction allowable under section 617(a).

(6) Amounts to which election apply not treated as tax preference.—Any portion of any qualified expenditure to which an election under paragraph (1) applies shall not be treated as an item of tax preference under section 57(a) and section 56 shall not apply to such expenditure.

(f) Coordination with section 291.—Except as otherwise provided in this part, section 291 (relating to cutback of corporate preferences) shall apply before the application of this part.

(g) Tax benefit rule.—The Secretary may prescribe regulations under which differently treated items shall be properly adjusted where the tax treatment giving rise to such items will not result in the reduction of the taxpayer's regular tax for the taxable year for which the item is taken into account or for any other taxable year.

(h) Coordination with certain limitations.—The limitations of sections 704(d), 465, and 1366 (d) (and such other provisions as may be specified in regulations) shall be applied for purposes of computing the alternative minimum taxable income of the taxpayer for the taxable year with the adjustments of sections 56, 57, and 58.

(i) Special rule for amounts treated as tax preference.—For purposes of this subtitle (other than this part), any amount shall not fail to be treated as wholly exempt from tax imposed by this subtitle solely by reason of being included in alternative minimum taxable income.

(j) Treatment of unearned income of minor children.—

(1) In general.—In the case of a child to whom section 1(g) applies, the exemption amount for purposes of section 55 shall not exceed the sum of—

(A) such child's earned income (as defined in section 911(d)(2)) for the taxable year, plus

(B) $5,000.*

(2) Inflation adjustment.—In the case of any taxable year beginning in a calendar year after 1998, the dollar amount in paragraph (1)(B) shall

*Editorial comment: The indexed amount for 2013 is $7,150 and for $2014 is $7,250.

be increased by an amount equal to the product of—

(A) such dollar amount, and

(B) the cost-of-living adjustment determined under section 1(f)(3) for the calendar year in which the taxable year begins, determined by substituting "1997" for "1992" in subparagraph (B) thereof.

If any increase determined under the preceding sentence is not a multiple of $50, such increase shall be rounded to the nearest multiple of $50.

* * *

SUBCHAPTER B—COMPUTATION OF TAXABLE INCOME

PART I—DEFINITION OF GROSS INCOME, ADJUSTED GROSS INCOME, TAXABLE INCOME, ETC.

Editorial Summary

Gross Income, Adjusted Gross Income, and Taxable Income

Subchapter B of Chapter 1 (Secs. 61–68)

In defining gross income, the Code takes a very broad perspective [see Sec. 61]. Note that the fifteen listed items are not intended to be all-inclusive. Rather, the listing serves two purposes. First, it specifies that these items definitely should be included in gross income. Second, the diversity of the items in the listing illustrates the breadth of the definition of gross income. A word of caution should accompany the phrase "except as otherwise provided in this subtitle." Other sections in the Code will provide specific rules for the determination of gross income associated with specific items or specific types of transactions (e.g., see Secs. 71–90, 101–139A). In such instances, the effect on gross income is to be determined under the specific rule in the particular section rather than under the general rule in Sec. 61.

Adjusted gross income [see Sec. 62] is a term that is peculiar to the tax model of the individual taxpayer.

	Income
–	Exclusions
=	Gross income
–	Deductions <u>for</u> adjusted gross income
=	Adjusted gross income
–	Deductions <u>from</u> adjusted gross income
	Itemized deductions or standard deduction
	Personal exemption and dependency deductions
=	Taxable income

The deductions for which the individual is eligible are classified into the two categories indicated in the tax model. In general, the "deductions for" are business-related deductions and the "deductions from" are deductions of a personal nature [see Sec. 62(a)(10) and Sec. 67 for examples of exceptions to this general rule]. It is beneficial for the deduction to be classified in the "deduction for" category for four reasons. First, certain deductions in the "deduction from" category, although permitted by the Code, will not result in reducing taxable income (i.e., itemized deductions will be wasted if the standard deduction is greater) [see Sec. 63(c)]. Second, certain of the deductions in the "deduction from" category have specific statutory floors that must be exceeded before the deduction is permitted [see Sec. 213(a)]. Third, certain deductions in the "deduction from" category are combined and then reduced by a general statutory floor (see Sec. 67). Fourth, as discussed below, part of the itemized deductions may be phased-out (see Sec. 68).

Rather than raising the individual tax rates above 31% (see Sec. 1) in the Revenue Reconciliation Act of 1990, Congress used an indirect approach to achieve the same revenue result. Section 68 provides for the phaseout of up to 80% of the covered itemized deductions of upper-income taxpayers [see Sec. 68(a)(2)]. Once adjusted gross income exceeds a statutory amount ($166,800 for 2009 and repealed for 2010) for all filing statuses except for married filing separately (which is $83,400 for 2009 and repealed for 2010), 3% of the excess amount is deducted from total itemized deductions. The covered itemized deductions are defined in Sec. 68(c). The statutory amounts are adjusted for the effect of inflation for taxable years beginning after 1991 [see Sec. 68(b)(2)]. This negative adjustment to itemized deductions is calculated after all other limits on itemized deductions [see Sec. 68(d)]. Note that when Congress raised the statutory rates above 31% in the Revenue Reconciliation Act of 1993, they retained the itemized deduction phaseout provision. In fact, Congress went a step further and repealed the "after December 31, 1995 termination date" which had been in Sec. 68(f). The Tax Relief Reconciliation Act of 2001 repeals the phaseout of itemized deductions. However, the phaseout was repealed using a phased approach. The repeal commenced in 2006 and was not completed until 2010 [see Sec. 68(f) and (g)]. The American Taxpayer Relief Act of 2012 reinstated the phaseout of itemized deductions beginning in 2013.

The amount of the standard deduction depends on the filing status of the taxpayer [see Secs. 1 and 63(c)(2)]. In calculating the standard deduction, note that special rules exist for the aged and blind [see Sec. 63(c)(3)] and for a taxpayer who is the dependent of another taxpayer [see Sec. 63(c)(5)]. Also, note that certain taxpayers are ineligible for the standard deduction [see Sec. 63(c)(6)]. See Sec. 63 (c)(1)(C) for the special standard deduction for the real property tax and Sec. 63(c)(1)(E) for the special standard deduction for the motor vehicle sales tax. These two

*Omitted.

provisions expired at the end of 2009 and were not extended in the 2010 or subsequent "extenders" tax legislation. The amount of the standard deduction is adjusted for the effect of inflation for taxable years beginning in calendar years after 1988 [see Sec. 63(c)(4)]. The Jobs and Growth Tax Relief Reconciliation Act of 2003 provides marriage penalty relief associated with the standard deduction.

"Local law" typically does not impact on the calculation of the federal income tax liability. However, generally it can with respect to "community income" (i.e., determination of whose income with respect to spouses) in the states which are community property states (i.e., Louisiana, Texas, New Mexico, Arizona, California, Washington, Idaho, Nevada, and Wisconsin). This effect will occur only if the spouses do not file a joint return (see Sec. 1). Section 66 is designed to eliminate certain inequities associated with the application of community property law (i.e., the so-called "innocent spouse" provision).

The tax model of the corporate taxpayer is as follows:

Income
– Exclusions
= Gross income
– Regular deductions
– Special deductions (see Secs. 241–250)
= Taxable income

The distinction between a special deduction and a regular deduction is presented later.

Income and deductions must be classified as ordinary or capital. Although the general definition appears in Secs. 64–65, one must refer to Subchapter P (Capital Gains and Losses) for the definition to be operationalized.

§ 61. Gross income defined

(a) General definition.—Except as otherwise provided in this subtitle, gross income means all income from whatever source derived, including (but not limited to) the following items:

(1) Compensation for services, including fees, commissions, fringe benefits, and similar items;

(2) Gross income derived from business;

(3) Gains derived from dealings in property;

(4) Interest;

(5) Rents;

(6) Royalties;

(7) Dividends;

(8) Alimony and separate maintenance payments;

(9) Annuities;

(10) Income from life insurance and endowment contracts;

(11) Pensions;

(12) Income from discharge of indebtedness;

(13) Distributive share of partnership gross income;

(14) Income in respect of a decedent; and

(15) Income from an interest in an estate or trust.

(b) Cross references.—

For items specifically included in gross income, see part II (sec. 71 and following). For items specifically excluded from gross income, see part III (sec. 101 and following).

§ 62. Adjusted gross income defined

(a) General rule.—For purposes of this subtitle, the term "adjusted gross income" means, in the case of an individual, gross income minus the following deductions:

(1) Trade and business deductions.—The deductions allowed by this chapter (other than by part VII of this subchapter) which are attributable to a trade or business carried on by the taxpayer, if such trade or business does not consist of the performance of services by the taxpayer as an employee.

(2) Certain trade and business deductions of employees.—

(A) Reimbursed expenses of employees.—The deductions allowed by part VI (section 161 and following) which consist of expenses paid or incurred by the taxpayer, in connection with the performance by him of services as an employee, under a reimbursement or other expense allowance arrangement with his employer. The fact that the reimbursement may be provided by a third party shall not be determinative of whether or not the preceding sentence applies.

(B) Certain expenses of performing artists.—The deductions allowed by section 162 which consist of expenses paid or incurred by a qualified performing artist in connection with the performances by him of services in the performing arts as an employee.

(C) Certain expenses of officials.—The deductions allowed by section 162 which consist of expenses paid or incurred with respect to services performed by an official as an employee of a State or a political subdivision thereof in a position compensated in whole or in part on a fee basis.

(D) Certain expenses of elementary and secondary school teachers.*—In the case of taxable years beginning during 2002, 2003, 2004, 2005, 2006, 2007, 2008, 2009, 2010, 2011, 2012, or 2013, the deductions allowed by section 162 which consist of expenses, not in excess of $250, paid or incurred by an eligible educator in connection with books, supplies (other than nonathletic supplies for courses of instruction in health or physical education), computer equipment (including related software and services) and other equipment, and supplementary materials used by the eligible educator in the classroom.

(E) Certain expenses of members of reserve components of the Armed Forces of the United States.—The deductions allowed by section 162 which consist of expenses, determined at a rate not in excess of the rates for travel expenses (including per diem in lieu of subsistence) authorized for employees of agencies under subchapter I of chapter 57 of title 5, United States Code, paid or incurred by the taxpayer in connection with the performance of services by such taxpayer as a member of a reserve component of the Armed Forces of the United States for any period during which such individual is more than 100 miles away from home in connection with such services.

(3) Losses from sale or exchange of property.—The deductions allowed by part VI (sec. 161 and following) as losses from the sale or exchange of property.

(4) Deductions attributable to rents and royalties.—The deductions allowed by part VI (sec. 161 and following), by section 212 (relating to expenses for production of income), and by section 611 (relating to depletion) which are attributable to property held for the production of rents or royalties.

(5) Certain deductions of life tenants and income beneficiaries of property.—In the case of a life tenant of property, or an income beneficiary of property held in trust, or an heir, legatee, or devisee of an estate, the deduction for depreciation allowed by section 167 and the deduction allowed by section 611.

(6) Pension, profit-sharing, and annuity plans of self-employed individuals.—In the case of an individual who is an employee within the meaning of section 401(c)(1), the deduction allowed by section 404.

(7) Retirement savings.—The deduction allowed by section 219 (relating to deduction of certain retirement savings).

****(9) Penalties forfeited because of premature withdrawal of funds from time savings accounts or deposits.**—The deductions allowed by section 165 for losses incurred in any transaction entered into for profit, though not connected with a trade or business to the extent that such losses include amounts forfeited to a bank, mutual savings bank, savings and loan association, building and loan association, cooperative bank or homestead association as a penalty for premature withdrawal of funds from a time savings account, certificate of deposit, or similar class of deposit.

(10) Alimony.—The deduction allowed by section 215.

(11) Reforestation expenses.—The deduction allowed by section 194.

* * *

(13) Jury duty pay remitted to employer.—Any deduction allowable under this chapter by reason of an individual remitting any portion of any jury pay to such individual's employer in exchange for payment by the employer of compensation for the period such individual was performing jury duty. For purposes of the preceding sentence, the term "jury pay" means any payment received by the individual for the discharge of jury duty.

(14) Deduction for clean-fuel vehicles and certain refueling property.—The deduction allowed by section 179A.

(15) Moving expenses.—The deduction allowed by section 217.

(16) Archer MSAs.—The deduction allowed by section 220.

(17) Interest on education loans.—The deduction allowed by section 221.

(18) Higher education expenses.—The deduction allowed by section 222.

*Editorial comment: This provision expired at the end of 2011. However, the American Taxpayer Relief Act of 2012 reinstated this provision through 2013. At the present time, this section has not been extended. There is pending legislation in the Senate, *The Tax Extenders Act of 2013 (S. 1859)*, that would extend Section 62(a)(2)(D) to 2014.

**Editorial comment: There is no paragraph (8).

(19) Health savings accounts.—The deduction allowed by section 223.

(20) Costs involving discrimination suits, etc.—Any deduction allowable under this chapter for attorney fees and court costs paid by, or on behalf of, the taxpayer in connection with any action involving a claim of unlawful discrimination (as defined in subsection (e)) or a claim of a violation of subchapter III of chapter 37 of title 31, United States Code or a claim made under section 1862(b)(3)(A) of the Social Security Act (42 U.S.C. 1395y(b)(3)(A)). The preceding sentence shall not apply to any deduction in excess of the amount includible in the taxpayer's gross income for the taxable year on account of a judgment or settlement (whether by suit or agreement and whether as lump sum or periodic payments) resulting from such claim.

(21) Attorney's fees relating to whistleblowers.—Any deduction allowable under this chapter for attorney fees and court costs paid by, or on behalf of, the taxpayer in connection with any award under section 7623(b) (relating to awards to whistleblowers). The preceding sentence shall not apply to any deduction in excess of the amount includible in the taxpayer's gross income for the taxable year on account of such award.

Nothing in this section shall permit the same item to be deducted more than once.

(b) Qualified performing artist.—

(1) In general.—For purposes of subsection (a)(2)(B), the term "qualified performing artist" means, with respect to any taxable year, any individual if—

(A) such individual performed services in the performing arts as an employee during the taxable year for at least 2 employers,

(B) the aggregate amount allowable as a deduction under section 162 in connection with the performance of such services exceeds 10 percent of such individual's gross income attributable to the performance of such services, and

(C) the adjusted gross income of such individual for the taxable year (determined without regard to subsection (a)(2)(B)) does not exceed $16,000.

(2) Nominal employer not taken into account.—An individual shall not be treated as performing services in the performing arts as an employee for any employer during any taxable year unless the amount received by such individual from such employer for the performance of such services during the taxable year equals or exceeds $200.

(3) Special rules for married couples.—

(A) In general.—Except in the case of a husband and wife who lived apart at all times during the taxable year, if the taxpayer is married at the close of the taxable year, subsection (a)(2)(B) shall apply only if the taxpayer and his spouse file a joint return for the taxable year.

(B) Application of paragraph (1).—In the case of a joint return—

(i) paragraph (1) (other than subparagraph (C) thereof) shall be applied separately with respect to each spouse, but

(ii) paragraph (1)(C) shall be applied with respect to their combined adjusted gross income.

(C) Determination of marital status.—For purposes of this subsection, marital status shall be determined under section 7703(a).

(D) Joint return.—For purposes of this subsection, the term "joint return" means the joint return of a husband and wife made under section 6013.

(c) Certain arrangements not treated as reimbursement arrangements.—For purposes of subsection (a)(2)(A), an arrangement shall in no event be treated as a reimbursement or other expense allowance arrangement if—

(1) such arrangement does not require the employee to substantiate the expenses covered by the arrangement to the person providing the reimbursement, or

(2) such arrangement provides the employee the right to retain any amount in excess of the substantiated expenses covered under the arrangement.

The substantiation requirements of the preceding sentence shall not apply to any expense to the extent that substantiation is not required under section 274(d) for such expense by reason of the regulations prescribed under the 2nd sentence thereof.

(d) Definition; special rules.—

(1) Eligible educator.—

(A) In general.—For purposes of subsection (a)(2)(D), the term "eligible educator" means, with respect to any taxable year, an individual who is a kindergarten through grade 12 teacher, instructor, counselor, principal, or aide in a school for at least 900 hours during a school year.

(B) School.—The term "school" means any school which provides elementary education or secondary education (kindergarten through grade 12), as determined under State law.

(2) Coordination with exclusions.—A deduction shall be allowed under subsection (a)(2)(D) for expenses only to the extent the amount of such expenses exceeds the amount excludable under section 135, 529(c)(1), or 530(d)(2) for the taxable year.

* * *

§ 63. Taxable income defined

(a) In general.—Except as provided in subsection (b), for purposes of this subtitle, the term "taxable income" means gross income minus the deductions allowed by this chapter (other than the standard deduction).

(b) Individuals who do not itemize their deductions.—In the case of an individual who does not elect to itemize his deductions for the taxable year, for purposes of this subtitle, the term "taxable income" means adjusted gross income, minus—

(1) the standard deduction, and

(2) the deduction for personal exemptions provided in section 151.

(c) Standard deduction.*—For purposes of this subtitle—

(1) In general.—Except as otherwise provided in this subsection, the term "standard deduction" means the sum of—

(A) the basic standard deduction,

(B) the additional standard deduction,

(C) in the case of any taxable year beginning in 2008 or 2009, the real property tax deduction,

(D) the disaster loss deduction, and

(E) the motor vehicle sales tax deduction.

(2) Basic standard deduction.—For purposes of paragraph (1), the basic standard deduction is—

(A) 200 percent of the dollar amount in effect under subparagraph (C) for the taxable year in the case of—

(i) a joint return, or

(ii) a surviving spouse (as defined in section 2(a)),

(B) $4,400 in the case of a head of household (as defined in section 2(b)), or

(C) $3,000 in any other case.

(3) Additional standard deduction for aged and blind.—For purposes of paragraph (1), the additional standard deduction is the sum of each additional amount to which the taxpayer is entitled under subsection (f).

(4) Adjustments for inflation.—In the case of any taxable year beginning in a calendar year after 1988, each dollar amount contained in paragraph (2)(B), (2)(C), or (5) or subsection (f) shall be increased by an amount equal to—

(A) such dollar amount, multiplied by

(B) the cost-of-living adjustment determined under section 1(f)(3) for the calendar year in which the taxable year begins, by substituting for "calendar year 1992" in subparagraph (B) thereof—

(i) "calendar year 1987" in the case of the dollar amounts contained in paragraph (2)(B), (2)(C), or (5)(A) or subsection (f), and

(ii) "calendar year 1997" in the case of the dollar amount contained in paragraph (5)(B).

(5) 'Limitation on basic standard deduction in the case of certain dependents.—In the case of an individual with respect to whom a deduction under section 151 is allowable to another taxpayer for a taxable year beginning in the calendar year in which the individual's taxable year begins, the basic standard deduction applicable to such individual for such individual's taxable year shall not exceed the greater of—

(A) $500, or

(B) the sum of $250 and such individual's earned income.

(6) Certain individuals, etc., not eligible for standard deduction.—In the case of—

(A) a married individual filing a separate return where either spouse itemizes deductions,

(B) a nonresident alien individual,

(C) an individual making a return under section 443(a)(1) for a period of less than 12 months on account of a change in his annual accounting period, or

(D) an estate or trust, common trust fund, or partnership,

the standard deduction shall be zero.

*Editorial comment: See the indexed standard deduction amounts for 2013 and 2014 after Sec. 63(g).Congress did not extend the real property tax standard deduction and the motor vehicle sales tax standard deduction when they expired at the end of 2009.

(7) Real property tax deduction.— For purposes of paragraph (1), the real property tax deduction is the lesser of—

(A) the amount allowable as a deduction under this chapter for State and local taxes described in section 164(a)(1), or

(B) $500 ($1,000 in the case of a joint return).

Any taxes taken into account under section 62(a) shall not be taken into account under this paragraph.

(8) Disaster loss deduction.—For the purposes of paragraph (1), the term "disaster loss deduction" means the net disaster loss (as defined in section 165(h)(3)(B)).

(9) Motor vehicle sales tax deduction.—For purposes of paragraph (1), the term "motor vehicle sales tax deduction" means the amount allowable as a deduction under section 164(a)(6). Such term shall not include any amount taken into account under section 62(a).

(d) Itemized deductions.—For purposes of this subtitle, the term "itemized deductions" means the deductions allowable under this chapter other than—

(1) the deductions allowable in arriving at adjusted gross income, and

(2) the deduction for personal exemptions provided by section 151.

(e) Election to itemize.—

(1) In general.—Unless an individual makes an election under this subsection for the taxable year, no itemized deduction shall be allowed for the taxable year. For purposes of this subtitle, the determination of whether a deduction is allowable under this chapter shall be made without regard to the preceding sentence.

(2) Time and manner of election.—Any election under this subsection shall be made on the taxpayer's return, and the Secretary shall prescribe the manner of signifying such election on the return.

(3) Change of election.—Under regulations prescribed by the Secretary, a change of election with respect to itemized deductions for any taxable year may be made after the filing of the return for such year. If the spouse of the taxpayer filed a separate return for any taxable year corresponding to the taxable year of the taxpayer, the change shall not be allowed unless, in accordance with such regulations—

(A) the spouse makes a change of election with respect to itemized deductions, for the taxable year covered in such separate return, consistent with the change of treatment sought by the taxpayer, and

(B) the taxpayer and his spouse consent in writing to the assessment (within such period as may be agreed on with the Secretary) of any deficiency, to the extent attributable to such change of election, even though at the time of the filing of such consent the assessment of such deficiency would otherwise be prevented by the operation of any law or rule of law.

This paragraph shall not apply if the tax liability of the taxpayer's spouse for the taxable year corresponding to the taxable year of the taxpayer has been compromised under section 7122.

(f) Aged or blind additional amounts.—

(1) Additional amounts for the aged.—The taxpayer shall be entitled to an additional amount of $600—

(A) for himself if he has attained age 65 before the close of his taxable year, and

(B) for the spouse of the taxpayer if the spouse has attained age 65 before the close of the taxable year and an additional exemption is allowable to the taxpayer for such spouse under section 151(b).

(2) Additional amount for blind.—The taxpayer shall be entitled to an additional amount of $600—

(A) for himself if he is blind at the close of the taxable year, and

(B) for the spouse of the taxpayer if the spouse is blind as of the close of the taxable year and an additional exemption is allowable to the taxpayer for such spouse under section 151(b).

For purposes of subparagraph (B), if the spouse dies during the taxable year the determination of whether such spouse is blind shall be made as of the time of such death.

(3) Higher amount for certain unmarried individuals.—In the case of an individual who is not married and is not a surviving spouse, paragraphs (1) and (2) shall be applied by substituting "$750" for "$600."

(4) Blindness defined.—For purposes of this subsection, an individual is blind only if his central visual acuity does not exceed 20/200 in the better eye with correcting lenses, or if his visual acuity is greater than 20/200 but is accompanied by a limitation in the fields of vision such that the widest diameter of the visual field subtends an angle no greater than 20 degrees.

(g) Marital status.—For purposes of this section, marital status shall be determined under section 7703.

Editorial Note

The indexed standard deduction amounts for 2014 and 2013 are as follows:

Category	2014 Amount	2013 Amount
Single	$6,200	$6,100
Head of household	9,100	8,950
Married filing jointly and surviving spouse	12,400	12,200
Married filing separately	6,200	6,100

The indexed additional standard deduction amounts for the blind and the aged for 2014 and 2013 are as follows:

Amount per Code	2014 Amount	2013 Amount
$600	$1,200	$1,200
750	1,550	1,500

The indexed limited standard deduction amounts for a taxpayer who is a dependent of another taxpayer for 2014 and 2013 are as follows:

Amount per Code	2014 Amount	2013 Amount
$500	$1,000	$1,000

The indexed amount that is added to earned income in calculating the limited standard deduction amount for a taxpayer who is a dependent of another taxpayer for 2014 and 2013 is as follows:

Amount per Code	2014 Amount	2013 Amount
$250	$350	$350

§ 64. Ordinary income defined

For purposes of this subtitle, the term "ordinary income" includes any gain from the sale or exchange of property which is neither a capital asset nor property described in section 1231(b). Any gain from the sale or exchange of property which is treated or considered, under other provisions of this subtitle, as "ordinary income" shall be treated as gain from the sale or exchange of property which is neither a capital asset nor property described in section 1231(b).

§ 65. Ordinary loss defined

For purposes of this subtitle, the term "ordinary loss" includes any loss from the sale or exchange of property which is not a capital asset. Any loss from the sale or exchange of property which is treated or considered, under other provisions of this subtitle, as "ordinary loss" shall be treated as loss from the sale or exchange of property which is not a capital asset.

§ 66. Treatment of community income

(a) Treatment of community income where spouses live apart.—If—

(1) 2 individuals are married to each other at any time during a calendar year;

(2) such individuals—

(A) live apart at all times during the calendar year, and

(B) do not file a joint return under section 6013 with each other for a taxable year beginning or ending in the calendar year;

(3) one or both of such individuals have earned income for the calendar year which is community income; and

(4) no portion of such earned income is transferred (directly or indirectly) between such individuals before the close of the calendar year,

then, for purposes of this title, any community income of such individuals for the calendar year shall be treated in accordance with the rules provided by section 879(a).

(b) Secretary may disregard community property laws where spouse not notified of community income.—The Secretary may disallow the benefits of any community property law to any taxpayer with respect to any income if such taxpayer acted as if solely entitled to such income and failed to notify the taxpayer's spouse before the due date (including extensions) for filing the return for the taxable year in which the income was derived of the nature and amount of such income.

(c) Spouse relieved of liability in certain other cases.—Under regulations prescribed by the Secretary, if—

(1) an individual does not file a joint return for any taxable year,

(2) such individual does not include in gross income for such taxable year an item of community income properly includible therein which, in accordance with the rules contained in section 879(a), would be treated as the income of the other spouse,

(3) the individual establishes that he or she did not know of, and had no reason to know of, such item of community income, and

(4) taking into account all facts and circumstances, it is inequitable to include such item of community income in such individual's gross income,

then, for purposes of this title, such item of community income shall be included in the gross income of the other spouse (and not in the gross income of the individual). Under procedures prescribed by the Secretary, if, taking into account all the facts and circumstances, it is inequitable to hold the individual liable for any unpaid tax or any deficiency (or any portion of either) attributable to any item for which relief is not available under the preceding sentence, the Secretary may relieve such individual of such liability.

* * *

§ 67. 2-percent floor on miscellaneous itemized deductions

(a) General rule.—In the case of an individual, the miscellaneous itemized deductions for any taxable year shall be allowed only to the extent that the aggregate of such deductions exceeds 2 percent of adjusted gross income.

(b) Miscellaneous itemized deductions.—For purposes of this section, the term "miscellaneous itemized deductions" means the itemized deductions other than—

(1) the deduction under section 163 (relating to interest),

(2) the deduction under section 164 (relating to taxes),

(3) the deduction under section 165(a) for casualty or theft losses described in paragraph (2) or (3) of section 165(c) or for losses described in section 165(d),

(4) the deductions under section 170 (relating to charitable, etc., contributions and gifts) and section 642(c) (relating to deduction for amounts paid or permanently set aside for a charitable purpose),

(5) the deduction under section 213 (relating to medical, dental, etc., expenses),

(6) any deduction allowable for impairment-related work expenses,

(7) the deduction under section 691(c) (relating to deduction for estate tax in case of income in respect of the decedent),

(8) any deduction allowable in connection with personal property used in a short sale,

(9) the deduction under section 1341 (relating to computation of tax where taxpayer restores substantial amount held under claim of right),

(10) the deduction under section 72(b)(3) (relating to deduction where annuity payments cease before investment recovered),

(11) the deduction under section 171 (relating to deduction for amortizable bond premium), and

(12) the deduction under section 216 (relating to deductions in connection with cooperative housing corporations).

(c) Disallowance of indirect deduction through pass-thru entity.—

(1) In general.—The Secretary shall prescribe regulations which prohibit the indirect deduction through pass-thru entities of amounts which are not allowable as a deduction if paid or incurred directly by an individual and which contain such reporting requirements as may be necessary to carry out the purposes of this subsection.

(2) Treatment of publicly offered regulated investment companies.—

(A) In general.—Paragraph (1) shall not apply with respect to any publicly offered regulated investment company.

(B) Publicly offered regulated investment companies.—For purposes of this subsection

(i) In general.—The term "publicly offered regulated investment company" means a regulated investment company the shares of which are—

(I) continuously offered pursuant to a public offering (within the meaning of section 4 of the Securities Act of 1933, as amended (14 U.S.C. 77a to 77aa)),

(II) regularly trade on an established securities market, or

(III) held by or for no fewer than 500 persons at all times during the taxable year.

(ii) Secretary may reduce 500 person requirement.—The Secretary may by regulation decrease the minimum shareholder requirement of clause (i)(III) in the case of regulated investment companies which experience a loss of shareholders through net redemptions of their shares.

(3) Treatment of certain other entities.—Paragraph (1) shall not apply—

(A) with respect to cooperatives and real estate investment trusts, and

(B) except as provided in regulations, with respect to estates and trusts.

* * *

(e) Determination of adjusted gross income in case of estates and trusts.—For purposes of this section, the adjusted gross income of an estate or trust shall be computed in the same manner as in the case of an individual, except that—

(1) the deductions for costs which are paid or incurred in connection with the administration of the estate or trust and which would not have been incurred if the property were not held in such trust or estate, and

(2) the deductions allowable under sections 642 (b), 651, and 661,

shall be treated as allowable in arriving at adjusted gross income.* * *

(f) Coordination with other limitation.—This section shall be applied before the application of the dollar limitation of the second sentence of section 162(a) (relating to trade or business expenses).

§ 68. Overall limitation on itemized deductions*

(a) General rule.—In the case of an individual whose adjusted gross income exceeds the applicable amount, the amount of the itemized deductions otherwise allowable for the taxable year shall be reduced by the lesser of—

(1) 3 percent of the excess of adjusted gross income over the applicable amount, or

(2) 80 percent of the amount of the itemized deductions otherwise allowable for such taxable year.

(b) Applicable amount.**—

(1) In general.—For purposes of this section, the term "applicable amount" means—

(A) $300,000** in the case of a joint return or a surviving spouse (as defined in section 2(a)),

(B) $275,000** in the case of a head of household (as defined in section 2(b)),

(C) $250,000** in the case of an individual who is not married and who is not a surviving spouse or head of household, and

(D) ½ the amount applicable under subparagraph (A) (after adjustment, if any, under paragraph (2)) in the case of a married individual filing a separate return.

For purposes of this paragraph, marital status shall be determined under section 7703.

(2) Inflation adjustments.—In the case of any taxable year beginning in calendar years after 2013, each of the dollar amounts under subparagraphs (A), (B), and (C) of paragraph (1) shall be increased by an amount equal to—

(A) such dollar amount, multiplied by

(B) the cost-of-living adjustment determined under section 1(f)(3) for the calendar year in which the taxable year begins, except that section 1(f)(3)(B) shall be applied by substituting "2012" for "1992".

If any amount after adjustment under the preceding sentence is not a multiple of $50, such amount shall be rounded to the next lowest multiple of $50.

(c) Exception for certain itemized deductions.—For purposes of this section, the term "itemized deductions does not include—

(1) the deduction under section 213 (relating to medical, etc. expenses),

(2) any deduction for investment interest (as defined in section 163(d)), and

(3) the deduction under section 165(a) for casualty or theft losses described in paragraph (2) or (3) of section 165(c) or for losses described in section 165(d).

(d) Coordination with other limitations.—This section shall be applied after the application of any other limitation on the allowance of any itemized deduction.

(e) Exception for estates and trusts.—This section shall not apply to any estate or trust.

*Editorial comment: The phaseout of itemized deductions terminated for taxable years beginning after December 31, 2009. However, the American Taxpayer Relief Act of 2012 reinstated the phaseout beginning in 2013.

**Editorial comment: For taxable years beginning after January 1, 2014, the indexed amounts in Section 68(b)(1) are $305,050, $279,650, and $254,200, respectively.

PART II—ITEMS SPECIFICALLY INCLUDED IN GROSS INCOME

Editorial Summary

Inclusions and Exclusions

Subchapter B of Chapter 1 (Secs. 71–139A)

These sections impact on the definition of gross income contained in Sec. 61. Absent these sections, the broad definition of gross income would result in these items being included in gross income. Part II (Inclusions: Secs. 71–90) provides specific rules for determining under what circumstances and in what amounts the covered items will be included in gross income. Part III (Exclusions: Secs. 101–139A) provides specific rules for detemining under what circumstances and in what amounts the covered items will be excluded from gross income.

The basic structural difference between classification as an inclusion versus classification as an exclusion is the form of the statutory language. For an inclusion, the format (i.e., general rule) is that the item is included in gross income unless otherwise specified. For the exclusion, the format is that the item is excluded from gross income unless otherwise provided.

Note that from a cash flow perspective, an inclusion, exclusion, or a deduction produces the same effect. That is, since the effect is before the tax rates are applied, a one dollar inclusion, exclusion, or deduction is worth less than one dollar. Contrast this treatment with a tax credit whereby a one dollar credit is worth one dollar (i.e., since the credit is applied directly against the tax liability rather than impacting on the calculation of taxable income).

Most of the inclusion/exclusion provisions that deal with employee benefits contain some type of antidiscrimination provision (e.g., Secs. 132(a)(1) and (a)(2)). Such provisions are intended to limit the ability of the employer to provide benefits to highly compensated employees that are not available to other employees. The Tax Reform Act of 1986 strengthened this antidiscrimination concept by enacting Sec. 89. However, Sec. 89, as the result of substantial negative reaction by the business community, was repealed in 1989 by Public Law 101–140. The repeal of this general antidiscrimination provision was accompanied by the reinstatement of the code section specific anti-discrimination rules which existed before the enactment of Sec. 89.

Editorial Summary

Alimony and Separate Maintenance Payments

Subchapter B of Chapter 1 (Sec. 71)

Pursuant to divorce or legal separation, state law generally requires a division of property. In addition, one spouse may incur the legal obligation to support the other spouse. The Code distinguishes between these two types of payments. Alimony and separate maintenance payments are includible in the gross income of the party receiving the payments [see Sec. 71(a)], and they are deductible from the gross income of the party making the payments [see Sec. 215(a)].

Child support payments are not alimony or separate maintenance payments. Their receipt is not taxable to the payee spouse or deductible by the payor spouse [see Sec. 71(c)].

Payments other than cash are considered a division of property which is not a taxable event to either party. It is often difficult to determine whether cash payments are a division of property or alimony and separate maintenance payments. In order to aid classification of these payments, in 1984 Congress developed certain rules. Cash payments made under post-1984 agreements and decrees are classified as alimony or separate maintenance payments only if the following are satisfied:

1. The agreement or decree does not specify that the payments are other than alimony or separate maintenance payments [see Sec. 71(b)(1)(B)].

2. The payor and the payee are not members of the same household at the time of such payments [see Sec. 71(b)(1)(C)].

3. There is no liability to make any payments for any period after the death of the payee [see Sec. 71(b)(1)(D)].

To further prevent a property division being disguised as alimony or separate maintenance payments through front-loaded payments, special rules apply to post-1984 agreements if payments in the first or second year exceed $15,000. The payor must include in gross income in the third post-separation year the excess alimony payments for the first post-separation year and the excess alimony payments for the second post-separation year [see Sec. 71(f)]. The excess alimony payments for the first post-separation year are the excess of the alimony or separate maintenance payments for that year over the sum of the average of (1) the payments made in the second post-separation year reduced by the excess payments in the second post-separation year and (2) the payments made during the third post-separation year, plus $15,000. The excess alimony payments for the second post-separation year are the excess of the payments for that year over the sum of the third post-separation year payments plus $15,000.

The following formula can be used to calculate the amount of the alimony recapture.

$$AR = Y1 + Y2$$
$$Y2 = P2 - (P3 + \$15{,}000)$$
$$Y1 = P1 - \left(\frac{P2 - Y2 + P3}{2} + \$15{,}000\right)$$

AR = Alimony recapture.
Y1 = Recapture associated with year #1 payments.
Y2 = Recapture associated with year #2 payments.
P1 = Payments in year 1.
P2 = Payments in year 2.
P3 = Payments in year 3.

Note that if the calculation of either Y1 or Y2 produces a negative amount, it is treated as zero.

A primary benefit of the approach taken by Sec. 71 in distinguishing between alimony or separate maintenance payments and property division payments is the objective nature of the provisions. Both the payor and the payee should be able to conduct negotiations associated with the divorce with a full awareness of the tax consequences.

A related section (Sec. 1041) provides that transfers of property between former spouses incident to the divorce are not taxable. Therefore, the transferee will have a carryover basis for the property received [see Sec. 1041(b)].

§ 71. Alimony and separate maintenance payments*

(a) General rule.—Gross income includes amounts received as alimony or separate maintenance payments.

(b) Alimony or separate maintenance payments defined.—For purposes of this section—

(1) In general.—The term "alimony or separate maintenance payment" means any payment in cash if—

(A) such payment is received by (or on behalf of) a spouse under a divorce or separation instrument,

(B) the divorce or separation instrument does not designate such payment as a payment which is not includible in gross income under this section and not allowable as a deduction under section 215,

(C) in the case of an individual legally separated from his spouse under a decree of divorce or of separate maintenance, the payee spouse and the payor spouse are not members of the same household at the time such payment is made, and

(D) there is no liability to make any such payment for any period after the death of the payee spouse and there is no liability to make any payment (in cash or property) as a substitute for such payments after the death of the payee spouse.

(2) Divorce or separation instrument.—The term "divorce or separation instrument" means—

(A) a decree of divorce or separate maintenance or a written instrument incident to such a decree,

(B) a written separation agreement, or

(C) a decree (not described in subparagraph (A)) requiring a spouse to make payments for the support or maintenance of the other spouse.

(c) Payments to support children.—

(1) In general.—Subsection (a) shall not apply to that part of any payment which the terms of the divorce or separation instrument fix (in terms of an amount of money or a part of the payment) as a sum which is payable for the support of children of the payor spouse.

(2) Treatment of certain reductions related to contingencies involving child.—For purposes of paragraph (1), if any amount specified in the instrument will be reduced—

(A) on the happening of a contingency specified in the instrument relating to a child (such as attaining a specified age, marrying, dying, leaving school, or a similar contingency), or

(B) at a time which can clearly be associated with a contingency of a kind specified in subparagraph (A),

an amount equal to the amount of such reduction will be treated as an amount fixed as payable for the support of children of the payor spouse.

(3) Special rule where payment is less than amount specified in instrument.—For purposes of this subsection, if any payment is less than the amount specified in the instrument, then so much of such payment as does not exceed the sum payable for support shall be considered a payment for such support.

(d) Spouse.—For purposes of this section, the term "spouse" includes a former spouse.

(e) Exception for joint returns.—This section and section 215 shall not apply if the spouses make a joint return with each other.

(f) Recomputation where excess front-loading of alimony payments.—

(1) In general.—If there are excess alimony payments—

(A) the payor spouse shall include the amount of such excess payments in gross income for the payor spouse's taxable year beginning in the 3rd post-separation year, and

(B) the payee spouse shall be allowed a deduction in computing adjusted gross income for the amount of such excess payments for the payee's taxable year beginning in the 3rd post-separation year.

(2) Excess alimony payments.—For purposes of this subsection, the term "excess alimony payments" mean the sum of—

(A) the excess payments for the 1st post-separation year, and

(B) the excess payments for the 2nd post-separation year.

*Editorial comment: See the related deduction provision in Sec. 215.

(3) Excess payments for 1st post-separation year.—For purposes of this subsection, the amount of the excess payments for the 1st post-separation year is the excess (if any) of—

(A) the amount of the alimony or separate maintenance payments paid by the payor spouse during the 1st post-separation year, over

(B) the sum of—

(i) the average of—

(I) the alimony or separate maintenance payments paid by the payor spouse during the 2nd post-separation year, reduced by the excess payments for the 2nd post-separation year, and

(II) the alimony or separate maintenance payments paid by the payor spouse during the 3rd post-separation year, plus

(ii) $15,000.

(4) Excess payments for 2nd post-separation year.—For purposes of this subsection, the amount of the excess payments for the 2nd post-separation year is the excess (if any) of—

(A) the amount of the alimony or separate maintenance payments paid by the payor spouse during the 2nd post-separation year, over

(B) the sum of—

(i) the amount of the alimony or separate maintenance payments paid by the payor spouse during the 3rd post-separation year, plus

(ii) $15,000.

(5) Exceptions.—

(A) Where payment ceases by reason of death or remarriage.—Paragraph (1) shall not apply if—

(i) either spouse dies before the close of the 3rd post-separation year, or the payee spouse remarries before the close of the 3rd post-separation year, and

(ii) the alimony or separate maintenance payments cease by reason of such death or remarriage.

(B) Support payments.—For purposes of this subsection, the term "alimony or separate maintenance payment" shall not include any payment received under a decree described in subsection (b)(2)(C).

(C) Fluctuating payments not within control of payor spouse.—For purposes of this subsection, the term "alimony or separate maintenance payment" shall not include any payment to the extent it is made pursuant to a continuing liability (over a period of not less than 3 years) to pay a fixed portion or portions of the income from a business or property or from compensation for employment or self-employment.

(6) Post-separation years.—For purposes of this subsection, the term "1st post-separation years means the 1st calendar year in which the payor spouse paid to the payee spouse alimony or separate maintenance payments to which this section applies. The 2nd and 3rd post-separation years shall be the 1st and 2nd succeeding calendar years, respectively.

(g) Cross references.—

(1) For deduction of alimony or separate maintenance payments, see section 215.

(2) For taxable status of income of an estate or trust in the case of divorce, etc., see section 682.

Editorial Summary

Annuities; Certain Proceeds of Endowment and Life Insurance Contracts

Subchapter B of Chapter 1 (Sec. 72)

Annuity contracts generally provide the purchaser (annuitant) with a right to receive a future stream of payments in return for a fixed payment. The issuer of the contract typically invests the fixed payment. The income earned is not taxable to the annuitant at this time because the annuitant has not constructively received the income.

Annuity payments can be either a nontaxable return of capital or includible in gross income. For amounts received prior to the annuity starting date, income is realized to the extent of the lesser of post-August 13, 1982 increases in cash value or amounts received [see Secs. 72(e)(2)(B) and (5)(B)]. Amounts received in excess of the increases in cash value are a return of capital to the extent of the initial investment. Amounts received in excess of the initial investment are included in gross income.

For annuity payments received on and after the annuity starting date, the annuitant can exclude from income the proportion of each payment that the investment in the contract bears to the expected return under the contract [see Sec. 72(b)]:

Investment/Expected return × Annuity payment = Exclusion amount

The expected return is the amount of each payment multiplied by the number of payments to be received. The number of payments can be fixed or determined over the life of the annuitant. In order to determine the expected return of an annuity to be paid over the life of the annuitant, the IRS has published life expectancy tables. The expected return is calculated by multiplying the amount of each payment by the life expectancy. The table for a single life annuity appears after Sec. 72(x).

Once the original investment is recovered, the remainder of the payments are taxable [see Sec. 72(b)(2)]. If the annuitant dies before his investment is recovered, the unrecovered investment is deductible on the final return of the annuitant [see Sec. 72(b)(3)].

Tax legislation enacted in 1996 provides for a simplified method for determining the tax consequences of annuity distributions from qualified employer retirement plans [see Sec. 72(d)]. Under this simplified method, a simplified life expectancy table [see Sec. 72(d)(1)(B)(iii)] provides the number of anticipated monthly payments rather than calculating the number using the more detailed life expectancy table normally used.

§ 72. Annuities; certain proceeds of endowment and life insurance contracts

(a) General rule for annuities.—

(1) Income inclusion.—Except as otherwise provided in this chapter, gross income includes any amount received as an annuity (whether for a period certain or during one or more lives) under an annuity, endowment, or life insurance contract.

(2) Partial annuitization.—If any amount is received as an annuity for a period of 10 years or more or during one or more lives under any portion of an annuity, endowment, or life insurance contract—

(A) such portion shall be treated as a separate contract for purposes of this section,

(B) for purposes of applying subsections (b), (c), and (e), the investment in the contract shall be allocated pro rata between each portion of the contract from which amounts are received as an annuity and the portion of the contract from which amounts are not received as an annuity, and

(C) a separate annuity starting date under subsection (c)(4) shall be determined with respect to each portion of the contract from which amounts are received as an annuity.

(b) Exclusion ratio.—

(1) In general.—Gross income does not include that part of any amount received as an annuity under an annuity, endowment, or life insurance contract which bears the same ratio to such amount as the investment in the contract (as of the annuity starting date) bears to the expected return under the contract (as of such date).

(2) Exclusion limited to investment.—The portion of any amount received as an annuity which is excluded from gross income under paragraph (1) shall not exceed the unrecovered investment in the contract immediately before the receipt of such amount.

(3) Deduction where annuity payments cease before entire investment recovered.—

(A) In general.—If—

(i) after the annuity starting date, payments as an annuity under the contract cease by reason of the death of an annuitant, and

(ii) as of the date of such cessation, there is unrecovered investment in the contract,

the amount of such unrecovered investment (in excess of any amount specified in subsection (e)(5) which was not included in gross income) shall be allowed as a deduction to the annuitant for his last taxable year.

(B) Payments to other persons.—In the case of any contract which provides for payments meeting the requirements of subparagraphs (B) and (C) of subsection (c)(2), the deduction under subparagraph (A) shall be allowed to the person entitled to such payments for the taxable year in which such payments are received.

(C) Net operating loss deductions provided.—For purposes of section 172, a deduction allowed under this paragraph shall be treated as if it were attributable to a trade or business of the taxpayer.

(4) Unrecovered investment.—For purposes of this subsection, the unrecovered investment in the contract as of any date is—

(A) the investment in the contract (determined without regard to subsection (c)(2)) as of the annuity starting date, reduced by

(B) the aggregate amount received under the contract on or after such annuity starting date and before the data as of which the determination is being made, to the extent such amount was excludable from gross income under this subtitle.

(c) Definitions.—

(1) Investment in the contract.—For purposes of subsection (b), the investment in the contract as of the annuity starting date is—

(A) the aggregate amount of premiums or other consideration paid for the contract, minus

(B) the aggregate amount received under the contract before such date, to the extent that such amount was excludable from gross income under this subtitle or prior income tax laws.

(2) Adjustment in investment where there is refund feature.—If—

(A) the expected return under the contract depends in whole or in part on the life expectancy of one or more individuals;

(B) the contract provides for payments to be made to a beneficiary (or to the estate of an annuitant) on or after the death of the annuitant or annuitants; and

(C) such payments are in the nature of a refund of the consideration paid,

then the value (computed without discount for interest) of such payments on the annuity starting date shall be subtracted from the amount determined under paragraph (1). Such value shall be computed in accordance with actuarial tables prescribed by the Secretary. For purposes of this paragraph and of subsection (e)(2)(A), the term "refund of the consideration paid" includes amounts payable after the death of an annuitant by reason of a provision in the contract for a life annuity with minimum period of payments certain, but (if part of the consideration was contributed by an employer) does not include that part of any payment to a beneficiary (or to the estate of the annuitant) which is not attributable to the consideration paid by the employee for the contract as determined under paragraph (1)(A).

(3) Expected return.—For purposes of subsection (b), the expected return under the contract shall be determined as follows:

(A) Life expectancy.*—If the expected return under the contract, for the period on and after the annuity starting date, depends in whole or in part on the life expectancy of one or more individuals, the expected return shall be computed with reference to actuarial tables prescribed by the Secretary.

(B) Installment payments.—If subparagraph (A) does not apply, the expected return is the aggregate of the amounts receivable under the contract as an annuity.

(4) Annuity starting date.—For purposes of this section, the annuity starting date in the case of any contract is the first day of the first period for which an amount is received as an annuity under the contract; except that if such date was before January 1, 1954, then the annuity starting date is January 1, 1954.

(d) Special rules for qualified employer retirement plans.—

(1) Simplified method of taxing annuity payments.—

(A) In general.—In the case of any amount received as an annuity under a qualified employer retirement plan—

(i) subsection (b) shall not apply, and

(ii) the investment in the contract shall be recovered as provided in this paragraph.

(B) Method of recovering investment in contract.—

(i) In general.—Gross income shall not include so much of any monthly annuity payment under a qualified employer retirement plan as does not exceed the amount obtained by dividing—

(I) the investment in the contract (as of the annuity starting date), by

(II) the number of anticipated payments determined under the table contained in clause (iii) (or, in the case of a contract to which subsection (c)(3)(B) applies, the number of monthly annuity payments under such contract).

(ii) Certain rules made applicable.—Rules similar to the rules of paragraphs (2) and (3) of subsection (b) shall apply for purposes of this paragraph.

(iii) Number of anticipated payments.—If the annuity is payable over the life of a single individual, the number of anticipated payments shall be determined as follows:

If the age of the annuitant on the annuity starting date is:	The number of anticipated payments is:
Not more than 55	360
More than 55 but not more than 60	310
More than 60 but not more than 65	260
More than 65 but not more than 70	210
More than 70	160

(iv) Number of anticipated payments where more than one life.—If the annuity is payable over the lives of more than 1

*Editorial comment: The table for a single life annuity appears after Sec. 72(x).

individual, the number of anticipated payments shall be determined as follows:

If the combined ages of annuitants are:	The number is:
Not more than 110	410
More than 110 but not more than 120	360
More than 120 but not more than 130	310
More than 130 but not more than 140	260
More than 140	210

(C) Adjustment for refund feature not applicable.—For purposes of this paragraph, investment in the contract shall be determined under subsection (c)(1) without regard to subsection (c)(2).

(D) Special rule where lump sum paid in connection with commencement of annuity payments.—If, in connection with the commencement of annuity payments under any qualified employer retirement plan, the taxpayer receives a lump-sum payment—

(i) such payment shall be taxable under subsection (e) as if received before the annuity starting date, and

(ii) the investment in the contract for purposes of this paragraph shall be determined as if such payment had been so received.

(E) Exception.—This paragraph shall not apply in any case where the primary annuitant has attained age 75 on the annuity starting date unless there are fewer than 5 years of guaranteed payments under the annuity.

(F) Adjustment where annuity payments not on monthly basis.—In any case where the annuity payments are not made on a monthly basis, appropriate adjustments in the application of this paragraph shall be made to take into account the period on the basis of which such payments are made.

(G) Qualified employer retirement plan.—For purposes of this paragraph, the term "qualified employer retirement plan" means any plan or contract described in paragraph (1), (2), or (3) of section 4974(c).

(2) Treatment of employee contributions under defined contribution plans.—For purposes of this section, employee contributions (and any income allocable thereto) under a defined contribution plan may be treated as a separate contract.

(e) Amounts not received as annuities.—

(1) Application of subsection.—

(A) In general.—This subsection shall apply to any amount which—

(i) is received under an annuity, endowment, or life insurance contract, and

(ii) is not received as an annuity,

if no provision of this subtitle (other than this subsection) applies with respect to such amount.

(B) Dividends.—For purposes of this section, any amount received which is in the nature of a dividend or similar distribution shall be treated as an amount not received as an annuity.

(2) General rule.—Any amount to which this subsection applies—

(A) if received on or after the annuity starting date, shall be included in gross income, or

(B) if received before the annuity starting date—

(i) shall be included in gross income to the extent allocable to income on the contract, and

(ii) shall not be included in gross income to the extent allocable to the investment in the contract.

(3) Allocation of amounts to income and investment.—For purposes of paragraph (2)(B)—

(A) Allocation to income.—Any amount to which this subsection applies shall be treated as allocable to income on the contract to the extent that such amount does not exceed the excess (if any) of—

(i) the cash value of the contract (determined without regard to any surrender charge) immediately before the amount is received, over

(ii) the investment in the contract at such time.

(B) Allocation to investment.—Any amount to which this subsection applies shall be treated as allocable to investment in the contract to the extent that such amount is not allocated to income under subparagraph (A).

(4) Special rules for application of paragraph (2)(B).—For purposes of paragraph (2)(B)—

(A) Loans treated as distributions.—If, during any taxable year, an individual—

(i) receives (directly or indirectly) any amount as a loan under any contract to which this subsection applies, or

(ii) assigns or pledges (or agrees to assign or pledge) any portion of the value of any such contract,

such amount or portion shall be treated as received under the contract as an amount not received as an annuity. The preceding sentence shall not apply for purposes of determining investment in the contract, except that the investment in the contract shall be increased by any amount included in gross income by reason of the amount treated as received under the preceding sentence.

(B) Treatment of policyholder dividends.—Any amount described in paragraph (1)(B) shall not be included in gross income under paragraph (2)(B)(i) to the extent such amount is retained by the insurer as a premium or other consideration paid for the contract.

(5) Retention of existing rules in certain cases.—

(A) In general.—In any case to which this paragraph applies—

(i) paragraphs (2)(B) and (4)(A) shall not apply, and

(ii) if paragraph (2)(A) does not apply,

the amount shall be included in gross income, but only to the extent it exceeds the investment in the contract.

(B) Existing contracts.—This paragraph shall apply to contracts entered into before August 14, 1982. Any amount allocable to investment in the contract after August 13, 1982, shall be treated as from a contract entered into after such date.

(C) Certain life insurance and endowment contracts.—Except as provided in paragraph (10) and except to the extent prescribed by the Secretary by regulations, this paragraph shall apply to any amount not received as an annuity which is received under a life insurance or endowment contract.

(D) Contracts under qualified plans.—Except as provided in paragraph (8), this paragraph shall apply to any amount received—

(i) from a trust described in section 401(a) which is exempt from tax under section 501(a),

(ii) from a contract—

(I) purchased by a trust described in clause (i),

(II) purchased as part of a plan described in section 403(a),

(III) described in section 403(b), or

(IV) provided for employees of a life insurance company under a plan described in section 818(a)(3), or

(iii) from an individual retirement account or an individual retirement annuity.

Any dividend described in section 404(k) which is received by a participant or beneficiary shall, for purposes of this subparagraph, be treated as paid under a separate contract to which clause (ii)(I) applies.

(E) Full refunds, surrenders, redemptions, and maturities.—This paragraph shall apply to—

(i) any amount received, whether in a single sum or otherwise, under a contract in full discharge of the obligation under the contract which is in the nature of a refund of the consideration paid for the contract, and

(ii) any amount received under a contract on its complete surrender, redemption, or maturity.

In the case of any amount to which the preceding sentence applies, the rule of paragraph (2)(A) shall not apply.

(6) Investment in the contract.—For purposes of this subsection, the investment in the contract as of any date is—

(A) the aggregate amount of premiums or other consideration paid for the contract before such date, minus

(B) the aggregate amount received under the contract before such date, to the extent that such amount was excludable from gross income under this subtitle or prior income tax laws.

* * *

(8) Extension of paragraph (2)(b) to qualified plans.—

(A) In general.—Notwithstanding any other provision of this subsection, in the case of any amount received before the annuity starting date from a trust or contract described in paragraph (5)(D), paragraph (2)(B) shall apply to such amounts.

(B) Allocation of amount received.—For purposes of paragraph (2)(B), the amount allocated to the investment in the contract shall be the portion of the amount described in subparagraph (A) which bears the same ratio to such amount as the investment in the contract bears to the account balance. The determination under the preceding sentence shall be made as of the time of the distribution or at such other time as the Secretary may prescribe.

(C) Treatment of forfeitable rights.—If an employee does not have a nonforfeitable right to any amount under any trust or contract to which subparagraph (A) applies, such amount shall not be treated as part of the account balance.

(D) Investment in the contract before 1987.—In the case of a plan which on May 5, 1986, permitted withdrawal of any employee contributions before separation from service, subparagraph (A) shall apply only to the extent that amounts received before the annuity starting date (when increased by amounts previously received under the contract after December 31, 1986) exceed the investment in the contract as of December 31, 1986.

(9) Extension of paragraph (2)(B) to qualified tuition programs and educational individual retirement accounts.—Notwithstanding any other provision of this subsection, paragraph (2)(B) shall apply to amounts received under a qualified tuition program (as defined in section 529(b)) or under an education individual retirement account (as defined in section 530(b)). The rule of paragraph (8)(B) shall apply for purposes of this paragraph.

* * *

(f) Special rules for computing employees' contributions.—In computing, for purposes of subsection (c)(1)(A), the aggregate amount of premiums or other consideration paid for the contract, and for purposes of subsection (e)(6), the aggregate premiums or other consideration paid, amounts contributed by the employer shall be included, but only to the extent that—

(1) such amounts were includible in the gross income of the employee under this subtitle or prior income tax laws; or

(2) if such amounts had been paid directly to the employee at the time they were contributed, they would not have been includible in the gross income of the employee under the law applicable at the time of such contribution.

Paragraph (2) shall not apply to amounts which were contributed by the employer after December 31, 1962, and which would not have been includible in the gross income of the employee by reason of the application of section 911 if such amounts had been paid directly to the employee at the time of contribution. The preceding sentence shall not apply to amounts which were contributed by the employer, as determined under regulations prescribed by the Secretary, to provide pension or annuity credits, to the extent such credits are attributable to services performed before January 1, 1963, and are provided pursuant to pension or annuity plan provisions in existence on March 12, 1962, and on that date applicable to such services or to the extent such credits are attributable to services performed as a foreign missionary (within the meaning of section 403(b)(2) (D)(iii)), as in effect before the enactment of the Economic Growth and Tax Relief Reconciliation Act of 2001).

(g) Rules for transferee where transfer was for value.—Where any contract (or any interest therein) is transferred (by assignment or otherwise) for a valuable consideration, to the extent that the contract (or interest therein) does not, in the hands of the transferee, have a basis which is determined by reference to the basis in the hands of the transferor, then—

(1) for purposes of this section, only the actual value of such consideration, plus the amount of the premiums and other consideration paid by the transferee after the transfer, shall be taken into account in computing the aggregate amount of the premiums or other consideration paid for the contract;

(2) for purposes of subsection (c)(1)(B), there shall be taken into account only the aggregate amount received under the contract by the transferee before the annuity starting date, to the extent that such amount was excludable from gross income under this subtitle or prior income tax laws; and

(3) the annuity starting date is January 1, 1954, or the first day of the first period for which the transferee received an amount under the contract as an annuity, whichever is the later.

For purposes of this subsection, the term "transferee" includes a beneficiary of, or the estate of, the transferee.

(h) Option to receive annuity in lieu of lump sum.—If—

(1) a contract provides for payment of a lump sum in full discharge of an obligation under the contract, subject to an option to receive an annuity in lieu of such lump sum;

(2) the option is exercised within 60 days after the day on which such lump sum first became payable; and

(3) part or all of such lump sum would (but for this subsection) be includible in gross income by reason of subsection (e)(1),

then, for purposes of this subtitle, no part of such lump sum shall be considered as includible in gross income at the time such lump sum first became payable.

* * *

(j) Interest.—Notwithstanding any other provision of this section, if any amount is held under an agreement to pay interest thereon, the interest payments shall be included in gross income.

* * *

(m) Special rules applicable to employee annuities and distributions under employee plans.—

* * *

(2) Computation of consideration paid by the employee.—In computing—

(A) the aggregate amount of premiums or other consideration paid for the contract for purposes of subsection (c)(1)(A) (and relating to the investment in the contract), and

(B) the aggregate premiums or other consideration paid for purposes of subsection (e)(6) (relating to certain amounts not received as an annuity),

any amount allowed as a deduction with respect to the contract under section 404 which was paid while the employee was an employee within the meaning of section 401(c)(1) shall be treated as consideration contributed by the employer, and there shall not be taken into account any portion of the premiums or other consideration for the contract paid while the employee was an owner-employee which is properly allocable (as determined under regulations prescribed by the Secretary) to the cost of life, accident, health, or other insurance.

* * *

(5) Penalties applicable to certain amounts received by 5-percent owners.—

(A) This paragraph applies to amounts which are received from a qualified trust described in section 401(a) or under a plan described in section 403(a) at any time by an individual who is, or has been, a 5-percent owner, or by a successor of such an individual, but only to the extent such amounts are determined, under regulations prescribed by the Secretary, to exceed the benefits provided for such individual under the plan formula.

(B) If a person receives an amount to which this paragraph applies, his tax under this chapter for the taxable year in which such amount is received shall be increased by an amount equal to 10 percent of the portion of the amount so received which is includible in his gross income for such taxable year.

(C) For purposes of this paragraph, the term "5-percent owner" means any individual who, at any time during the 5 plan years preceding the plan year ending in the taxable year in which the amount is received, is a 5-percent owner (as defined in section 416(i)(l)(B)).

(6) Owner-employee defined.—For purposes of this subsection, the term "owner-employee" has the meaning assigned to it by section 401(c)(3) and includes an individual for whose benefit an individual retirement account or annuity described in section 408(a) or (b) is maintained. For purposes of the preceding sentence, the term "owner-employee" shall include an employee within the meaning of section 401(c)(1).

* * *

(10) Determination of investment in the contract in the case of qualified domestic relations orders.—Under regulations prescribed by the Secretary, in the case of a distribution or payment made to an alternate payee who is the spouse or former spouse of the participant pursuant to a qualified domestic relations order (as defined in section 414(p)), the investment in the contract as of the date prescribed in such regulations shall be allocated on a pro rata basis between the present value of such distribution or payment and the present value of all other benefits payable with respect to the participant to which such order relates.

* * *

(o) Special rules for distributions from qualified plans to which employee made deductible contributions.—

(1) Treatment of contributions.—For purposes of this section and sections 402 and 403, notwithstanding section 414(h), any deductible employee contribution made to a qualified employer plan or government plan shall be treated as an amount contributed by the employer which is not includible in the gross income of the employee.

* * *

(3) Amounts constructively received.

(A) In general.—For purposes of this subsection, rules similar to the rules provided by subsection (p) (other than the exception contained in paragraph (2) thereof) shall apply.

(B) Purchase of life insurance.—To the extent any amount of accumulated deductible employee contributions of an employee are applied to the purchase of life insurance contracts, such amount shall be treated as distributed to the employee in the year so applied.

(4) Special rule for treatment of rollover amounts.—For purposes of sections 402(c), 403(a)(4), and 408(d)(3), the Secretary shall prescribe regulations providing for such allocations of amounts attributable to accumulated deductible employee contributions, and for such other rules, as may be necessary to insure that such accumulated deductible employee contributions do not become eligible for additional tax benefits (or freed from limitations) through the use of rollovers.

(5) Definitions and special rules.—For purposes of this subsection—

(A) Deductible employee contributions.—The term "deductible employee contributions" means any qualified voluntary employee contribution (as defined in section 219(e)(2)) made after December 31, 1981, in a taxable year beginning after such date and made for a taxable year beginning before January 1, 1987, and allowable as a deduction under section 219(a) for such taxable year.

(B) Accumulated deductible employee contributions.—The term "accumulated deductible employee contributions" means the deductible employee contributions—

(i) increased by the amount of income and gain allocable to such contributions, and

(ii) reduced by the sum of the amount of loss and expense allocable to such contributions and the amounts distributed with respect to the employee which are attributable to such contributions (or income or gain allocable to such contributions).

(C) Qualified employer plan.—The term "qualified employer plan" has the meaning given to such term by subsection (p)(3)(A)(i).

(D) Government plan.—The term "government plan" has the meaning given such term by subsection (p)(3)(B).

(6) Ordering rules.—Unless the plan specifies otherwise, any distribution from such plan shall not be treated as being made from the accumulated deductible employee contributions until all other amounts to the credit of the employee have been distributed.

(p) Loans treated as distributions.—For purposes of this section—

(1) Treatment as distributions.—

(A) Loans.—If during any taxable year a participant or beneficiary receives (directly or indirectly) any amount as a loan from a qualified employer plan, such amount shall be treated as having been received by such individual as a distribution under such plan.

(B) Assignments or pledges.—If during any taxable year a participant or beneficiary assigns (or agrees to assign) or pledges (or agrees to pledge) any portion of his interest in a qualified employer plan, such portion shall be treated as having been received by such individual as a loan from such plan.

(2) Exception for certain loans.—

(A) General rule.—Paragraph (1) shall not apply to any loan to the extent that such loan (when added to the outstanding balance of all other loans from such plan whether made on, before, or after August 13, 1982), does not exceed the lesser of—

(i) $50,000, reduced by the excess (if any) of—

(I) the highest outstanding balance of loans from the plan during the 1-year period ending on the day before the date on which such loan was made, over

(II) the outstanding balance of loans from the plan on the date on which such loan was made, or

(ii) the greater of (I) one-half of the present value of the nonforfeitable accrued benefit of the employee under the plan, or (II) $10,000.

For purposes of clause (ii), the present value of the nonforfeitable accrued benefit shall be determined without regard to any accumulated deductible employee contributions (as defined in subsection (o)(5)(B)).

(B) Requirement that loan be repayable within 5 years.—

(i) In general.—Subparagraph (A) shall not apply to any loan unless such loan, by its terms, is required to be repaid within 5 years.

(ii) Exception for home loans.—Clause (i) shall not apply to any loan used to acquire any dwelling unit which within a reasonable time is to be used (determined at the time the loan is made) as the principal residence of the participant.

(C) Requirement of level amortization.—Except as provided in regulations, this paragraph shall not apply to any loan unless substantially level amortization of such loan (with payments not less frequently than quarterly) is required over the term of the loan.

(D) Related employers and related plans.—For purposes of this paragraph—

(i) the rules of subsections (b), (c), and (m) of section 414 shall apply, and

(ii) all plans of an employer (determined after the application of such subsections) shall be treated as 1 plan.

(3) Denial of interest deductions in certain cases.—

(A) In general.—No deduction otherwise allowable under this chapter shall be allowed under this chapter for any interest paid or accrued on any loan to which paragraph (1) does not apply by reason of paragraph (2) during the period.

(B) Period to which subparagraph (A) applies.—For purposes of subparagraph (A), the period described in this subparagraph is the period—

(i) on or after the 1st day on which the individual to whom the loan is made is a key employee (as defined in section 416(i)), or

(ii) such loan is secured by amounts attributable to elective deferrals described in subparagraph (A) or (C) of section 402(g)(3).

(4) Qualified employer plan, etc.—For purposes of this subsection—

(A) Qualified employer plan.—

(i) In general.—The term "qualified employer plan" means—

(I) a plan described in section 401(a) which includes a trust exempt from tax under section 501(a),

(II) an annuity plan described in section 403(a), and

(III) a plan under which amounts are contributed by an individual's employer for an annuity contract described in section 403(b).

(ii) Special rule.—The term "qualified employer plan" shall include any plan which was (or was determined to be) a qualified employer plan or a government plan.

(B) Government plan.—The term "government plan" means any plan, whether or not qualified, established and maintained for its employees by the United States, by a State or political subdivision thereof, or by an agency or instrumentality of any of the foregoing.

(5) Special rules for loans, etc., from certain contracts.—For purposes of this subsection, any amount received as a loan under a contract purchased under a qualified employer plan (and any assignment or pledge with respect to such a contract) shall be treated as a loan under such employer plan.

(q) 10-percent penalty for premature distributions from annuity contracts.—

(1) Imposition of penalty.—If any taxpayer receives any amount under an annuity contract, the taxpayer's tax under this chapter for the taxable year in which such amount is received shall be increased by an amount equal to 10 percent of the portion of such amount which is includible in gross income.

(2) Subsection not to apply to certain distributions.—Paragraph (1) shall not apply to any distribution—

(A) made on or after the date on which the taxpayer attains age 59½,

(B) made on or after the death of the holder (or, when the holder is not an individual, the death of the primary annuitant (as defined in subsection (s)(6)(B))),

(C) attributable to the taxpayer's becoming disabled within the meaning of subsection (m)(7),

(D) which is a part of a series of substantially equal periodic payments (not less frequently than annually) made for the life (or life expectancy) of the taxpayer or the joint lives (or joint life expectancies) of such taxpayer and his designated beneficiary,

(E) from a plan, contract, account, trust, or annuity described in subsection (e)(5)(D),

(F) allocable to investment in the contract before August 14, 1982, or

(G) under a qualified funding asset (within the meaning of section 130(d), but without regard to whether there is a qualified assignment),

(H) to which subsection (t) applies (without regard to paragraph (2) thereof),

(I) under an immediate annuity contract (within the meaning of section 72(u)(4)), or

(J) which is purchased by an employer upon the termination of a plan described in section 401(a) or 403(a) and which is held by the employer until such time as the employee separates from service.

(3) Change in substantially equal payments.—If—

(A) paragraph (1) does not apply to a distribution by reason of paragraph (2)(D), and

(B) the series of payments under such paragraph are subsequently modified (other than by reason of death or disability)—

(i) before the close of the 5-year period beginning on the date of the first payment and after the taxpayer attains age 59½, or

(ii) before the taxpayer attains age 59½,

the taxpayer's tax for the 1st taxable year in which such modification occurs shall be increased by an amount, determined under regulations, equal to the tax which (but for paragraph (2)(D)) would have been imposed, plus interest for the deferral period (within the meaning of subsection (t)(4)(B)).

* * *

(s) Required distributions where holder dies before entire interest is distributed.—

(1) In general.—A contract shall not be treated as an annuity contract for purposes of this title unless it provides that—

(A) if the holder of such contract dies on or after the annuity starting date and before the entire interest in such contract has been distributed, the remaining portion of such interest will be distributed at least as rapidly as under the method of distributions being used as of the date of his death, and

(B) if the holder of such contract dies before the annuity starting date, the entire interest in such contract will be distributed within 5 years after the death of such holder.

(2) Exception for certain amounts payable over life of beneficiary.—If—

(A) any portion of the holder's interest is payable to (or for the benefit of) a designated beneficiary,

(B) such portion will be distributed (in accordance with regulations) over the life of such designated beneficiary (or over a period not extending beyond the life expectancy of such beneficiary), and

(C) such distributions begin not later than 1 year after the date of the holder's death or such later date as the Secretary may by regulations prescribe,

then for purposes of paragraph (1), the portion referred to in subparagraph (A) shall be treated as distributed on the day on which such distributions begin.

(3) Special rule where surviving spouse beneficiary.—If the designated beneficiary referred to in paragraph (2)(A) is the surviving spouse of the holder of the contract, paragraphs (1) and (2) shall be applied by treating such spouse as the holder of such contract.

(4) Designated beneficiary.—For purposes of this subsection, the term "designated beneficiary" means any individual designated a beneficiary by the holder of the contract.

(5) Exception for certain annuity contracts.—This subsection shall not apply to any annuity contract—

(A) which is provided—

(i) under a plan described in section 401(a) which includes a trust exempt from tax under section 501, or

(ii) under a plan described in section 403(a),

(B) which is described in section 403(b),

(C) which is an individual retirement annuity or provided under an individual retirement account or annuity, or

(D) which is a qualified funding asset (as defined in section 130(d), but without regard to whether there is a qualified assignment).

(6) Special rule where holder is corporation or other non-individual.—

(A) In general.—For purposes of this subsection, if the holder of the contract is not an individual, the primary annuitant shall be treated as the holder of the contract.

(7) Treatment of changes in primary annuitant where holder of contract is not an individual.—For purposes of this subsection, in the case of a holder of an annuity contract which is not an individual, if there is a change in the primary annuitant (as defined in paragraph (6)(B)), such change shall be treated as the death of the holder.

(t) 10-Percent additional tax on early distributions from qualified retirement plans.—

(1) Imposition of additional tax.—If any taxpayer receives any amount from a qualified retirement plan (as defined in section 4974(c)), the taxpayer's tax under this chapter for the taxable year in which such amount is received shall be increased by an amount equal to 10 percent of the portion of such amount which is includible in gross income.

(2) Subsection not to apply to certain distributions.—Except as provided in paragraphs (3) and (4), paragraph (1) shall not apply to any of the following distributions:

(A) In general.—Distributions which are—

(i) made on or after the date on which the employee attains age 59½,

(ii) made to a designated beneficiary (or to the estate of the employee) on or after the death of the employee,

(iii) attributable to the employee's being disabled within the meaning of subsection (m)(7),

(iv) part of a series of substantially equal periodic payments (not less frequently than annually) made for the life (or life expectancy) of the employee or the joint lives (or joint life expectancies) of such employee and his designated beneficiary,

(v) made to an employee after separation from service after attainment of age 55,

(vi) dividends paid with respect to stock of a corporation which are described in section 404(k), or

(vii) made on account of a levy under section 6331 on the qualified retirement plan.

(B) Medical expenses.—Distributions made to the employee (other than distributions described in subparagraph (A), (C), or (D)) to the extent such distributions do not exceed the amount allowable as a deduction under section 213 to the employee for amounts paid during the taxable year for medical care (determined without regard to whether the employee itemizes deductions for such taxable year).

(C) Payments to alternate payees pursuant to qualified domestic relations orders.—Any distribution to an alternate payee pursuant to a qualified domestic relations order (within the meaning of section 414(p)(1)).

(D) Distributions to unemployed individuals for health insurance premiums.—

(i) In general.—Distributions from an individual retirement plan to an individual after separation from employment—

(I) if such individual has received unemployment compensation for 12 consecutive weeks under any Federal or State unemployment compensation law by reason of such separation,

(II) if such distributions are made during any taxable year during which such unemployment compensation is paid or the succeeding taxable year, and

(III) to the extent such distributions do not exceed the amount paid during the taxable year for insurance described in section 213(d)(1)(D) with respect to the individual and the individual's spouse and dependents (as defined in section 152, determined without regard to subsections (b)(1), (b)(2), and (d)(1)(B) thereof).

(ii) Distributions after reemployment.—Clause (i) shall not apply to any distribution made after the individual has been employed for at least 60 days after the separation from employment to which clause (i) applies.

(iii) Self-employed individuals.—To the extent provided in regulations, a self-employed individual shall be treated as meeting the requirements of clause (i)(I) if, under Federal or State law, the individual would have received unemployment compensation but for the fact the individual was self-employed.

(E) Distributions from individual retirement plans for higher education expenses.—Distributions to an individual from an individual retirement plan to the extent such distributions do not exceed the qualified higher education expenses (as defined in paragraph (7)) of the taxpayer for the taxable year. Distributions shall not be taken into account under the preceding sentence if such distributions are described in subparagraph (A), (C), or (D) or to the extent paragraph (1) does not apply to such distributions by reason of subparagraph (B).

(F) Distributions from certain plans for first home purchases.—Distributions to an individual from an individual retirement plan which are qualified first-time homebuyer distributions (as defined in paragraph (8)). Distributions shall not be taken into account under the preceding sentence if such distributions are described in subparagraph (A), (C), (D), or (E) or to the extent paragraph (1) does not apply to such distributions by reason of subparagraph (B).

(G) Distributions from retirement plans to individuals called to active duty.—

(i) In general.—Any qualified reservist distribution.

(ii) Amount distributed may be repaid.—Any individual who receives a qualified reservist distribution may, at any time during the 2-year period beginning on the day after the end of the active duty period, make one or more contributions to an individual retirement plan of such individual in an aggregate amount not to exceed the amount of such distribution. The dollar limitations otherwise applicable to contributions to individual retirement plans shall not apply to any contribution made pursuant to the preceding sentence. No deduction shall be allowed for any contribution pursuant to this clause.

(iii) Qualified reservist distribution.—For purposes of this subparagraph, the term "qualified reservist distribution" means any distribution to an individual if—

(I) such distribution is from an individual retirement plan, or from amounts attributable to employer contributions made pursuant to elective deferrals described in subparagraph (A) or (C) of section 402(g)(3) or section 501(c)(18)(D)(iii),

(II) such individual was (by reason of being a member of a reserve component (as defined in section 101 of title 37, United States Code)) ordered or called to active duty for a period in excess of 179 days or for an indefinite period, and

(III) such distribution is made during the period beginning on the date of such order or call and ending at the close of the active duty period.

(iv) Application of subparagraph.—This subparagraph applies to individuals ordered or called to active duty after September 11, 2001. In no event shall the 2-year period referred to in clause (ii) end before the date which is 2 years after the date of the enactment of this subparagraph.

(3) Limitations.—

(A) Certain exceptions not to apply to individual retirement plans.—Subparagraphs (A)(v) and (C) of paragraph (2) shall not apply to distributions from an individual retirement plan.

(B) Periodic payments under qualified plans must begin after separation.—Paragraph (2)(A)(iv) shall not apply to any amount paid from a trust described in section 401(a) which is exempt from tax under section 501(a) or from a contract described in section 72(e)(5)(D)(ii) unless the series of payments begins after the employee separates from service.

(4) Change in substantially equal payments.—

(A) In general.—If—

(i) paragraph (1) does not apply to a distribution by reason of paragraph (2)(A)(iv), and

(ii) the series of payments under such paragraph are subsequently modified (other than by reason of death or disability)—

(I) before the close of the 5-year period beginning with the date of the first payment and after the employee attains age 59½, or

(II) before the employee attains age 59½, the taxpayer's tax for the 1st taxable year in which such modification occurs shall be increased by an amount, determined under regulations, equal to the tax which (but for paragraph (2)(A)(iv)) would have been imposed, plus interest for the deferral period.

(B) Deferral period.—For purposes of this paragraph, the term "deferral period" means the period beginning with the taxable year in which (without regard to paragraph (2)(A)(iv)) the distribution would have been includible in gross income and ending with the taxable year in which the modification described in subparagraph (A) occurs.

(5) Employee.—For purposes of this subsection, the term "employee" includes any participant, and in the case of an individual retirement plan, the individual for whose benefit such plan was established.

(6) Special rules for simple retirement accounts.—In the case of any amount received from a simple retirement account (within the meaning of section 408(p) during the 2-year period beginning on the date such individual first participated in any qualified salary reduction arrangement maintained by the individual's employer under section 408(p)(2), paragraph (1) shall be applied by substituting "25 percent" for "10 percent."

(7) Qualified higher education expenses.—For purposes of paragraph (2)(E)—

(A) In general.—The term "qualified higher education expenses" means qualified higher education expenses (as defined in section 529 (e)(3)) for education furnished to—

(i) the taxpayer,

(ii) the taxpayer's spouse, or

(iii) any child (as defined in section 152(f) (1)) or grandchild of the taxpayer or the taxpayer's spouse, at an eligible educational institution (as defined in section 529(e)(5)).

(B) Coordination with other benefits.—The amount of qualified higher education expenses for any taxable year shall be reduced as provided in section 25A(g)(2).

(8) Qualified first-time homebuyer distributions.—For purposes of paragraph (2)(F)—

(A) In general.—The term "qualified first-time homebuyer distribution" means any payment or distribution received by an individual to the extent such payment or distribution is used by the individual before the close of the 120th day after the day on which such payment or distribution is received to pay qualified acquisition costs with respect to a principal residence of a first-time homebuyer who is such individual, the spouse of such individual, or any child, grandchild, or ancestor of such individual or the individual's spouse.

(B) Lifetime dollar limitation.—The aggregate amount of payments or distributions received by an individual which may be treated as qualified first-time homebuyer distributions for any taxable year shall not exceed the excess (if any) of—

(i) $10,000, over

(ii) the aggregate amounts treated as qualified first-time homebuyer distributions with respect to such individual for all prior taxable years.

(C) Qualified acquisition costs.—For purposes of this paragraph, the term "qualified acquisition costs" means the costs of acquiring, constructing, or reconstructing a residence. Such term includes any usual or reasonable settlement, financing, or other closing costs.

(D) First-time homebuyer: Other definitions.—For purposes of this paragraph—

(i) First-time homebuyer.—The term "first-time homebuyer" means any individual if—

(I) such individual (and if married, such individual's spouse) had no present ownership interest in a principal residence during the 2-year period ending on the date of acquisition of the principal residence to which this paragraph applies, and

(II) subsection (h) or (k) of section 1034 (as in effect on the day before the date of the enactment of this paragraph) did not suspend the running of any period of time specified in section 1034 (as so in effect) with respect to such individual on the day before the date the distribution is applied pursuant to subparagraph (A).

(ii) Principal residence.—The term "principal residence" has the same meaning as when used in section 121.

(iii) Date of acquisition.—The term "date of acquisition" means the date—

(I) on which a binding contract to acquire the principal residence to which sub-paragraph (A) applies is entered into, or

(II) on which construction or reconstruction of such a principal residence is commenced.

(E) Special rule where delay in acquisition.—If any distribution from any individual retirement plan fails to meet the requirements of subparagraph (A) solely by reason of a delay or cancellation of the purchase or construction of the residence, the amount of the distribution may be contributed to an individual retirement plan as provided in section 408(d)(3)(A)(i) (determined by substituting "120th day" for "60th day" in such section), except that—

(i) section 408(d)(3)(B) shall not be applied to such contribution, and

(ii) such amount shall not be taken into account in determining whether section 408 (d)(3)(B) applies to any other amount.

(9) Special rule for rollovers to section 457 plans.—For purposes of this subsection, a distribution from an eligible deferred compensation plan (as defined in section 457(b)) of an eligible employer described in section 457(e)(1)(A) shall be treated as a distribution from a qualified retirement plan described in 4974(c)(1) to the extent that such distribution is attributable to an amount transferred to an eligible deferred compensation plan from a qualified retirement plan (as defined in section 4974(c)).

(10) Distributions to qualified public safety employees in governmental plans.—

(A) In general.—In the case of a distribution to a qualified public safety employee from a governmental plan (within the meaning of section 414(d)) which is a defined benefit plan, paragraph (2)(A)(v) shall be applied by substituting "age 50" for "age 55".

(B) Qualified public safety employee.—For purposes of this paragraph, the term "qualified public safety employee" means any employee of a State or political subdivision of a State who provides police protection, firefighting services, or emergency medical services for any area within the jurisdiction of such State or political subdivision.

(u) Treatment of annuity contracts not held by natural persons.—

(1) In general.—If any annuity contract is held by a person who is not a natural person—

(A) such contract shall not be treated as an annuity contract for purposes of this subtitle (other than subchapter L), and

(B) the income on the contract for any taxable year of the policyholder shall be treated as ordinary income received or accrued by the owner during such taxable year.

For purposes of this paragraph, holding by a trust or other entity as an agent for a natural person shall not be taken into account.

(2) Income on the contract.—

(A) In general.—For purposes of paragraph (1), the term "income on the contract" means, with respect to any taxable year of the policyholder, the excess of—

(i) the sum of the net surrender value of the contract as of the close of the taxable year plus all distributions under the contract received during the taxable year or any prior taxable year, reduced by

(ii) the sum of the amount of net premiums under the contract for the taxable year and prior taxable years and amounts includible in gross income for prior taxable years with respect to such contract under this subsection.

Where necessary to prevent the avoidance of this subsection, the Secretary may substitute "fair market value of the contract" for "net surrender value of the contract" each place it appears in the preceding sentence.

(B) Net premiums.—For purposes of this paragraph, the term "net premiums" means the amount of premiums paid under the contract reduced by any policyholder dividends.

(3) Exceptions.—This subsection shall not apply to any annuity contract which—

(A) is acquired by the estate of a decedent by reason of the death of the decedent,

(B) is held under a plan described in section 401(a) or 403(a), under a program described in section 403(b), or under an individual retirement plan,

(C) is a qualified funding asset (as defined in section 130(d), but without regard to whether there is a qualified assignment),

(D) is purchased by an employer upon the termination of a plan described in section 401(a) or 403(a) and which is held by the employer until all amounts under such contract are distributed to the employee for whom such contract was purchased or the employee's beneficiary, or

(E) is an immediate annuity.

(4) Immediate annuity.—For purposes of this subsection, the term "immediate annuity" means an annuity—

(A) which is purchased with a single premium or annuity consideration,

(B) the annuity starting date (as defined in subsection (c)(4)) of which commences no later than 1 year from the date of the purchase of the annuity, and

(C) which provides for a series of substantially equal periodic payments (to be made not less frequently than annually) during the annuity period.

(v) 10-percent additional tax for taxable distributions from modified endowment contracts.—

(1) Imposition of additional tax.—If any taxpayer receives any amount under a modified endowment contract (as defined in section 7702A), the taxpayer's tax under this chapter for the taxable year in which such amount is received shall be increased by an amount equal to 10 percent of the portion of such amount which is includible in gross income.

(2) Subsection not to apply to certain distributions.—Paragraph (1) shall not apply to any distribution—

(A) made on or after the date on which the taxpayer attains age 59½,

(B) which is attributable to the taxpayer's becoming disabled (within the meaning of subsection (m)(7)), or

(C) which is part of a series of substantially equal periodic payments (not less frequently than annually) made for the life (or life expectancy) of the taxpayer or the joint lives (or joint life expectancies) of such taxpayer and his beneficiary.

* * *

(x) Cross reference.—

For limitation on adjustments to basis of annuity contracts sold, see section 1021.

Editorial Note

Ordinary Life Annuities: One Life—Expected Return Multiples

Age	Multiple	Age	Multiple	Age	Multiple
5	76.6	29	53.1	53	30.4
6	75.6	30	52.2	54	29.5
7	74.7	31	51.2	55	28.6
8	73.7	32	50.2	56	27.7
9	72.7	33	49.3	57	26.8
10	71.7	34	48.3	58	25.9
11	70.7	35	47.3	59	25.0
12	69.7	36	46.4	60	24.2
13	68.8	37	45.4	61	23.3
14	67.8	38	44.4	62	22.5
15	66.8	39	43.5	63	21.6
16	65.8	40	42.5	64	20.8
17	64.8	41	41.5	65	20.0
18	63.9	42	40.6	66	19.2
19	62.9	43	39.6	67	18.4
20	61.9	44	38.7	68	17.6
21	60.9	45	37.7	69	16.8
22	59.9	46	36.8	70	16.0
23	59.0	47	35.9	71	15.3
24	58.0	48	34.9	72	14.6
25	57.0	49	34.0	73	13.9
26	56.0	50	33.1	74	13.2
27	55.1	51	32.2	75	12.5
28	54.1	52	31.3	76	11.9

Age	Multiple	Age	Multiple	Age	Multiple
77	11.2	90	5.0	103	2.1
78	10.6	91	4.7	104	1.9
79	10.0	92	4.4	105	1.8
80	9.5	93	4.1	106	1.6
81	8.9	94	3.9	107	1.4
82	8.4	95	3.7	108	1.3
83	7.9	96	3.4	109	1.1
84	7.4	97	3.2	110	1.0
85	6.9	98	3.0	111	.9
86	6.5	99	2.8	112	.8
87	6.1	100	2.7	113	.7
88	5.7	101	2.5	114	.6
89	5.3	102	2.3	115	.5

§ 73. Services of child

(a) Treatment of amounts received.—Amounts received in respect of the services of a child shall be included in his gross income and not in the gross income of the parent, even though such amounts are not received by the child.

(b) Treatment of expenditures.—All expenditures by the parent or the child attributable to amounts which are includible in the gross income of the child (and not of the parent) solely by reason of subsection (a) shall be treated as paid or incurred by the child.

(c) Parent defined.—For purposes of this section, the term "parent" includes an individual who is entitled to the services of a child by reason of having parental rights and duties in respect of the child.

(d) Cross reference.—For assessment of tax against parent in certain cases, see section 6201(c).

Editorial Summary

Prizes and Awards

Subchapter B of Chapter 1 (Sec. 74)

Under Sec. 74, the general rule is that gross income includes the fair market value of any prizes and awards (other than scholarships) received. An exception is made for prizes and awards received in recognition of religious, charitable, scientific, educational, artistic, literary, or civic achievement [see Sec. 74(b)]. This exclusion treatment is available only if (1) the recipient was selected without any action on his or her part to enter the contest or proceeding, (2) the recipient is not required to perform substantial future services to receive the prize or award, and (3) the prize or award is transferred by the payor to a qualified governmental unit or nonprofit organization. In effect, the exclusion permits the taxpayer to make a charitable contribution of the prize or award received and not have to be concerned with exceeding the AGI percentage limitations on the charitable contribution deduction under Sec. 170(b).

A second exception is made for certain employee achievement awards in the form of tangible personal property [see Sec. 74(c)]. An employee achievement award is not included in gross income if the award is made in recognition of length of service or safety achievement. The excluded amount cannot exceed $400 [$1,600 if the award is a qualified plan award as defined in Sec. 274(j)].

§ 74. Prizes and awards

(a) General rule.—Except as otherwise provided in this section or in section 117 (relating to qualified scholarships), gross income includes amounts received as prizes and awards.

(b) Exception for certain prizes and awards transferred to charities.—Gross income does not include amounts received as prizes and awards made primarily in recognition of religious, charitable, scientific, educational, artistic, literary, or civic achievement, but only if—

(1) the recipient was selected without any action on his part to enter the contest or proceeding;

(2) the recipient is not required to render substantial future services as a condition to receiving the prize or award; and

(3) the prize or award is transferred by the payor to a governmental unit or organization described in paragraph (1) or (2) of section 170(c) pursuant to a designation made by the recipient.

(c) Exception for certain employee achievement awards.—

(1) In general.—Gross income shall not include the value of an employee achievement award (as defined in section 274(j)) received by the taxpayer if the cost to the employer of the employee achievement award does not exceed the amount allowable as a deduction to the employer for the cost of the employee achievement award.

(2) Excess deduction award.—If the cost to the employer of the employee achievement award received by the taxpayer exceeds the amount allowable as a deduction to the employer, then gross income includes the greater of—

(A) an amount equal to the portion of the cost to the employer of the award that is not allowable as a deduction to the employer (but not in excess of the value of the award), or

(B) the amount by which the value of the award exceeds the amount allowable as a deduction to the employer.

The remaining portion of the value of such award shall not be included in the gross income of the recipient.

(3) Treatment of tax-exempt employers.—In the case of an employer exempt from taxation under this subtitle, any reference in this subsection to the amount allowable as a deduction to the employer shall be treated as a reference to the amount which would be allowable as a deduction to the employer if the employer were not exempt from taxation under this subtitle.

(4) Cross reference.—For provisions excluding certain de minimis fringes from gross income, see section 132(e).

* * *

Editorial Summary

Group-term Life Insurance Purchased for Employees

Subchapter B of Chapter 1 (Sec. 79)

Sec. 79 provides for an exclusion from gross income of premiums for the first $50,000 of group-term life insurance protection provided by an employer. This exclusion is available only to employees [see Sec. 79(a)]. The cost of coverage in excess of $50,000 is included in the employee's gross income using the uniform premium table in the regulations [see Reg.Sec. 1.79-3 for this table] to calculate such cost [see Secs. 79(a) and (c)].

The provision contains substantial nondiscrimination requirements [see Sec. 79(d)]. If discrimination does occur, key employees are required to include the greater of (1) the actual cost of the insurance or (2) the cost determined under the uniform premium table in their gross income [see Sec. 79 (d)(1)]. Other employees are still entitled to the exclusion.

§ 79. Group-term life insurance purchased for employees

(a) General rule.—There shall be included in the gross income of an employee for the taxable year an amount equal to the cost of group-term life insurance on his life provided for part or all of such year under a policy (or policies) carried directly or indirectly by his employer (or employers); but only to the extent that such cost exceeds the sum of—

(1) the cost of $50,000 of such insurance, and

(2) the amount (if any) paid by the employee toward the purchase of such insurance.

(b) Exceptions.—Subsection (a) shall not apply to—

(1) the cost of group-term life insurance on the life of an individual which is provided under a policy carried directly or indirectly by an employer after such individual has terminated his employment with such employer and is disabled (within the meaning of section 72(m)(7)),

(2) the cost of any portion of the group-term life insurance on the life of an employee provided during part or all of the taxable year of the employee under which—

(A) the employer is directly or indirectly the beneficiary, or

(B) a person described in section 170(c) is the sole beneficiary,

for the entire period during such taxable year for which the employee receives such insurance, and

(3) the cost of any group-term life insurance which is provided under a contract to which section 72(m)(3) applies.

(c) Determination of cost of insurance.—For purposes of this section and section 6052, the cost of group-term insurance on the life of an employee provided during any period shall be determined on the basis of uniform premiums (computed on the basis of 5-year age brackets) prescribed by regulations by the Secretary.

(d) Nondiscrimination requirements.—

(1) In general.—In the case of a discriminatory group-term life insurance plan—

(A) subsection (a)(1) shall not apply with respect to any key employee, and

(B) the cost of group-term life insurance on the life of any key employee shall be the greater of—

(i) such cost determined without regard to subsection (c), or

(ii) such cost determined with regard to subsection (c).

(2) Discriminatory group-term life insurance plan.—For purposes of this subsection, the term "discriminatory group-term life insurance plan" means any plan of an employer for providing group-term life insurance unless—

(A) the plan does not discriminate in favor of key employees as to eligibility to participate, and

(B) the type and amount of benefits available under the plan do not discriminate in favor of participants who are key employees.

(3) Nondiscriminatory eligibility classification.—

(A) In general.—A plan does not meet requirements of subparagraph (A) of paragraph (2) unless—

(i) such plan benefits 70 percent or more of all employees of the employer,

(ii) at least 85 percent of all employees who are participants under the plan are not key employees,

(iii) such plan benefits such employees as qualify under a classification set up by the employer and found by the Secretary not to be discriminatory in favor of key employees, or

(iv) in the case of a plan which is part of a cafeteria plan, the requirements of section 125 are met.

(B) Exclusion of certain employees.—For purposes of subparagraph (A), there may be excluded from consideration—

(i) employees who have not completed 3 years of service;

(ii) part-time or seasonal employees;

(iii) employees not included in the plan who are included in a unit of employees covered by an agreement between employee representatives and one or more employers which the Secretary finds to be a collective bargaining agreement, if the benefits provided under the plan were the subject of good faith bargaining between such employee representatives and such employer or employers; and

(iv) employees who are nonresident aliens and who receive no earned income (within the meaning of section 911(d)(2)) from the employer which constitutes income from sources within the United States (within the meaning of section 861(a)(3)).

(4) Nondiscriminatory benefits.—A plan does not meet the requirements of paragraph (2)(B) unless all benefits available to participants who are key employees are available to all other participants.

(5) Special rule.—A plan shall not fail to meet the requirements of paragraph (2)(B) merely because the amount of life insurance on behalf of the employees under the plan bears a uniform relationship to the total compensation or the basic or regular rate of compensation of such employees.

(6) Key employee defined.—For purposes of this subsection, the term "key employee" has the meaning given to such term by paragraph (1) of section 416(i). Such term also includes any former employee if such employee when he retired or separated from service was a key employee.

(7) Exemption for church plans.—

(A) In general.—This subsection shall not apply to a church plan maintained for church employees.

(B) Definitions.—For purposes of subparagraph (A), the terms "church plan" and "church employee" have the meaning given such terms by paragraphs (1) and (3)(B) of section 414(e), respectively, except that—

(i) section 414(e) shall be applied by substituting "section 501(c)(3)" for "section 501" each place it appears, and

(ii) the term "church employee" shall not include an employee of—

(I) an organization described in section 170(b)(1)(A)(ii) above the secondary school level (other than a school for religious training),

(II) an organization described in section 170(b)(1)(A)(iii), and

(III) an organization described in section 501(c)(3), the basis of the exemption for which is substantially similar to the basis for exemption of an organization described in subclause (II).

(8) Treatment of former employees.—To the extent provided in regulations, this subsection shall be applied separately with respect to former employees.

(e) Employee includes former employee.—For purposes of this section, the term "employee" includes a former employee.

* * *

§ 82. Reimbursement for expenses of moving*

Except as provided in section 132(a)(6), there shall be included in gross income (as compensation for services) any amount received or accrued,

*Editorial comment: See the related deduction provision in Sec. 217.

directly or indirectly, by an individual as a payment for or reimbursement of expenses of moving from one residence to another residence which is attributable to employment or self-employment.

Editorial Summary

Property Transferred in Connection With Performance of Services

Subchapter B of Chapter 1 (Sec. 83)

Section 83 provides for the taxation of property transferred in connection with the performance of services. Under Sec. 83(a), the excess of the fair market value of the property over the amount paid for the property is included in gross income in the year the property is transferred and becomes substantially vested. In order for the property to be substantially vested, it must be either transferable or not subject to a substantial risk of forfeiture. The rights of a person in property are transferable if the person can transfer any interest in the property to any person with the property rights not subject to substantial risk of forfeiture [see Sec. 83(c)(2)]. Substantial risk of forfeiture exists where the right to the enjoyment of the property is conditioned upon the future performance of substantial services by any individual [see Sec. 83(c)(1)].

Section 83(b) permits an election to be made to include in gross income for the taxable year in which the property is transferred the excess of the fair market value of the property over the amount paid for the property in the year of the transfer without regard to a substantial risk of forfeiture. A benefit of the election to the transferee is that any subsequent appreciation of the property between the transfer date and the date the property is not subject to a substantial risk of forfeiture qualifies for capital gain treatment. The potential disadvantage to the transferee is that a deduction will not be permitted to offset the income previously recognized if the property is forfeited [see Sec. 83(b)(1)].

The amount and timing of the deduction of the transferor is dependent on the amount and timing of the income recognition by the transferee [see Sec. 83(h)].

§ 83. Property transferred in connection with performance of services

(a) General rule.—If, in connection with the performance of services, property is transferred to any person other than the person for whom such services are performed, the excess of—

(1) the fair market value of such property (determined without regard to any restriction other than a restriction which by its terms will never lapse) at the first time the rights of the person having the beneficial interest in such property are transferable or are not subject to a substantial risk of forfeiture, whichever occurs earlier, over

(2) the amount (if any) paid for such property, shall be included in the gross income of the person who performed such services in the first taxable year in which the rights of the person having the beneficial interest in such property are transferable or are not subject to a substantial risk of forfeiture, whichever is applicable. The preceding sentence shall not apply if such person sells or otherwise disposes of such property in an arm's length transaction before his rights in such property become transferable or not subject to a substantial risk of forfeiture.

(b) Election to include in gross income in year of transfer.—

(1) In general.—Any person who performs services in connection with which property is transferred to any person may elect to include in his gross income, for the taxable year in which such property is transferred, the excess of—

(A) the fair market value of such property at the time of transfer (determined without regard to any restriction other than a restriction which by its terms will never lapse), over

(B) the amount (if any) paid for such property.

If such election is made, subsection (a) shall not apply with respect to the transfer of such property, and if such property is subsequently forfeited, no deduction shall be allowed in respect of such forfeiture.

(2) Election.—An election under paragraph (1) with respect to any transfer of property shall be made in such manner as the Secretary prescribes and shall be made not later than 30 days after the date of such transfer. Such election may not be revoked except with the consent of the Secretary.

(c) Special rules.—For purposes of this section—

(1) Substantial risk of forfeiture.—The rights of a person in property are subject to a substantial risk of forfeiture if such person's rights to full enjoyment of such property are conditioned upon the future performance of substantial services by any individual.

(2) Transferability of property.—The rights of a person in property are transferable only if the rights in such property of any transferee are not subject to a substantial risk of forfeiture.

* * *

(4) For purposes of determining an individual's basis in property in connection with the performance of services, rules similar to the rules of section 72(w) shall apply.

(d) Certain restrictions which will never lapse.—

(1) Valuation.—In the case of property subject to a restriction which by its terms will never lapse, and which allows the transferee to sell such property only at a price determined under a formula, the price so determined shall be deemed to be the fair market value of the property unless established to the contrary by the Secretary, and the burden of proof shall be on the Secretary with respect to such value.

(2) Cancellation.—If, in the case of property subject to a restriction which by its terms will never lapse, the restriction is canceled, then, unless the taxpayer establishes—

(A) that such cancellation was not compensatory, and

(B) that the person, if any, who would be allowed a deduction if the cancellation were treated as compensatory, will treat the transaction as not compensatory, as evidenced in such manner as the Secretary shall prescribe by regulations,

the excess of the fair market value of the property (computed without regard to the restrictions) at the time of cancellation over the sum of—

(C) the fair market value of such property (computed by taking the restriction into account) immediately before the cancellation, and

(D) the amount, if any, paid for the cancellation,

shall be treated as compensation for the taxable year in which such cancellation occurs.

(e) Applicability of section.—This section shall not apply to—

(1) a transaction to which section 421 applies,

(2) a transfer to or from a trust described in section 401(a) or a transfer under an annuity plan which meets the requirements of section 404(a)(2),

(3) the transfer of an option without a readily ascertainable fair market value,

(4) the transfer of property pursuant to the exercise of an option with a readily ascertainable fair market value at the date of grant, or

(5) group-term life insurance to which section 79 applies.

(f) Holding period.—In determining the period for which the taxpayer has held property to which subsection (a) applies, there shall be included only the period beginning at the first time his rights in such property are transferable or are not subject to a substantial risk of forfeiture, whichever occurs earlier.

(g) Certain exchanges.—If property to which subsection (a) applies is exchanged for property subject to restrictions and conditions substantially similar to those to which the property given in such exchange was subject, and if section 354, 355, 356, or 1036 (or so much of section 1031 as relates to section 1036) applied to such exchange, or if such exchange was pursuant to the exercise of a conversion privilege—

(1) such exchange shall be disregarded for purposes of subsection (a), and

(2) the property received shall be treated as property to which subsection (a) applies.

(h) Deduction by employer.—In the case of a transfer of property to which this section applies or a cancellation of a restriction described in subsection (d), there shall be allowed as a deduction under section 162, to the person for whom were performed the services in connection with which such property was transferred, an amount equal to the amount included under subsection (a), (b), or (d)(2) in the gross income of the person who performed such services. Such deduction shall be allowed for the taxable year of such person in which or with which ends the taxable year in which such amount is included in the gross income of the person who performed such services.

§ 84. Transfer of appreciated property to political organization

(a) General rule.—If—

(1) any person transfers property to a political organization, and

(2) the fair market value of such property exceeds its adjusted basis,

then for purposes of this chapter the transferor shall be treated as having sold such property to the political organization on the date of the transfer, and the transferor shall be treated as having realized an amount equal to the fair market value of such property on such date.

(b) Basis of property.—In the case of a transfer of property to a political organization to which subsection (a) applies, the basis of such property in the hands of the political organization shall be the same as it would be in the hands of the transferor, increased by the amount of gain recognized to the transferor by reason of such transfer.

(c) Political organization defined.—For purposes of this section, the term "political organization" has the meaning given to such term by section 527(e)(1).

§ 85. Unemployment compensation

(a) General rule.—In the case of an individual, gross income includes unemployment compensation.

(b) Unemployment compensation defined.—For purposes of this section, the term "unemployment compensation" means any amount received under a law of the United States or of a State which is in the nature of unemployment compensation.

(c) Special rule for 2009.*— In the case of any taxable year beginning in 2009, gross income shall not include so much of the unemployment compensation received by an individual as does not exceed $2,400.

Editorial Summary

Social Security Benefits

Subchapter B of Chapter 1 (Sec. 86)

Prior to 1984, Social Security benefits were excludable from gross income. Legislation in 1983 provided that the wherewithal to pay concept should apply in determining if Social Security benefits should be excluded. Applying this concept, Social Security benefits are included in gross income only if the summation of the taxpayer's modified adjusted gross income [see Sec. 86(b)(2)] and 50 percent of the Social Security benefits received exceed a base amount [see Sec. 86(c)(1)]. Even if there is such an excess, only one-half of it may be included in gross income (see the ceiling on the amount that will be included in the following paragraph). The logic for the 50 percent inclusion ceiling is that this represents the amount contributed by the employer (i.e., benefits received associated with amounts contributed by the employee should be excludable under the return of capital concept).

In the Revenue Reconciliation Act of 1993, the decision was made to expand the application of the wherewithal to pay concept even further by replacing the one-tier structure for taxing Social Security benefits with a two-tier structure. Applying this concept, Social Security benefits are included in gross income only if the summation of the taxpayer's modified adjusted gross income [see Sec. 86(b)(2)] and 50 percent of the Social Security benefits received exceed a base amount [see Sec. 86(c)(1)]. This calculation represents the first tier of taxation and the maximum amount included in gross income is 50 percent of the Social Security benefits received. Under the second tier, as much as 85 percent of the Social Security benefits received can be included if gross income depending on the extent to which the summation of the taxpayer's modified adjusted gross income and 50 percent of the Social Security benefits received exceed the adjusted base amount [see Sec. 86(c)(2)].

Note that tax-exempt income can affect the amount included in gross income [see Sec. 86(b)(2)(B)].

The formulas for the calculation of the Social Security benefits that must be included in gross income are as follows:

If modified adjusted gross income (MAGI) plus one-half of Social Security benefits exceeds the Sec. 86(c)(1) base amounts, but not the Sec. 86(c)(2) adjusted base amounts, the taxable amount of Social Security benefits is the lesser of the following:

—.50(Social Security benefits).
—.50[MAGI + .50(Social Security benefits) – Sec. 86(c)(1) base amount].

If MAGI plus one-half of Social Security benefits exceeds the Sec. 86(c)(2) adjusted base amounts, the taxable amount of Social Security benefits is the lesser of 1 or 2 below:

1. .85(Social Security benefits).
2. Sum of:
   a. .85[MAGI + .50(Social Security benefits) – Sec. 86(c)(2) adjusted base amount], and
   b. Lesser of:
      —Amount included through application of the first formula.
      —$4,500 ($6,000 for married filing jointly).

*Editorial comment: Congress has not extended the limited unemployment compensation exclusion in subsequent legislation.

§ 86. Social security and tier 1 railroad retirement benefits

(a) In general—

(1) In general—Except as provided in paragraph (2), gross income for the taxable year of any taxpayer described in subsection (b) (notwithstanding section 207 of the Social Security Act) includes social security benefits in an amount equal to the lesser of—

(A) one-half of the social security benefits received during the taxable year, or

(B) one-half of the excess described in subsection (b)(1).

(2) Additional amount—In the case of a taxpayer with respect to whom the amount determined under subsection (b)(1)(A) exceeds the adjusted base amount, the amount included in gross income under this section shall be equal to the lesser of—

(A) the sum of—

(i) 85 percent of such excess, plus

(ii) the lesser of the amount determined under paragraph (1) or an amount equal to one-half of the difference between the adjusted base amount and the base amount of the taxpayer, or

(B) 85 percent of the social security benefits received during the taxable year.

(b) Taxpayers to whom subsection (a) applies.—

(1) In general.—A taxpayer is described in this subsection if—

(A) the sum of—

(i) the modified adjusted gross income of the taxpayer for the taxable year, plus

(ii) one-half of the social security benefits received during the taxable year, exceeds

(B) the base amount.

(2) Modified adjusted gross income.—For purposes of this subsection, the term "modified adjusted gross income" means adjusted gross income—

(A) determined without regard to this section and sections 135, 137, 199, 221, 222, 911, 931, and 933, and

(B) increased by the amount of interest received or accrued by the taxpayer during the taxable year which is exempt from tax.

(c) Base amount and adjusted base amount.—For purposes of this section—

(1) Base amount. The term "base amount" means—

(A) except as otherwise provided in this subsection, $25,000,

(B) $32,000, in the case of a joint return, and

(C) zero, in the case of a taxpayer who—

(i) is married at the close of the taxable year (within the meaning of section 7703) but does not file a joint return for such year, and

(ii) does not live apart from his spouse at all times during the taxable year.

(2) Adjusted base amount.—The term "adjusted base amount" means—

(A) except as otherwise provided in this paragraph, $34,000,

(B) $44,000 in the case of a joint return, and

(C) zero in the case of a taxpayer described in paragraph (1)(C).

(d) Social security benefit.—

(1) In general.—For purposes of this section, the term "social security benefit" means any amount received by the taxpayer by reason of entitlement to—

(A) a monthly benefit under title II of the Social Security Act, or

(B) a tier 1 railroad retirement benefit.

(2) Adjustment for repayments during year.—

(A) In general.—For purposes of this section, the amount of social security benefits received during any taxable year shall be reduced by any repayment made by the taxpayer during the taxable year of a social security benefit previously received by the taxpayer (whether or not such benefit was received during the taxable year).

(B) Denial of deduction.—If (but for this sub-paragraph) any portion of the repayments referred to in subparagraph (A) would have been allowable as a deduction for the taxable year under section 165, such portion shall be allowable as a deduction only to the extent it exceeds the social security benefits received by the taxpayer during the taxable year (and not repaid during such taxable year).

* * *

(e) Limitation on amount included where taxpayer receives lump-sum payment.—

(1) Limitation.—If—

(A) any portion of a lump-sum payment of social security benefits received during the taxable year is attributable to prior taxable years, and

(B) the taxpayer makes an election under this subsection for the taxable year,

then the amount included in gross income under this section for the taxable year by reason of the receipt of such portion shall not exceed the sum of the increases in gross income under this chapter for prior taxable years which would result solely from taking into account such portion in the taxable years to which it is attributable.

(2) Special rules.—

(A) Year to which benefit attributable.—For purposes of this subsection, a social security benefit is attributable to a taxable year if the generally applicable payment date for such benefit occurred during such taxable year.

(B) Election.—An election under this subsection shall be made at such time and in such manner as the Secretary shall by regulations prescribe. Such election, once made, may be revoked only with the consent of the Secretary.

* * *

§ 90. Illegal federal irrigation subsidies

(a) General rule.—Gross income shall include an amount equal to any illegal Federal irrigation subsidy received by the taxpayer during the taxable year.

(b) Illegal Federal irrigation subsidy.—For purposes of this section—

(1) In general.—The term "illegal federal irrigation subsidy" means the excess (if any) of—

(A) the amount required to be paid for any Federal irrigation water delivered to the taxpayer during the taxpayer year, over

(B) the amount paid for such water.

(2) Federal irrigation water.—The term "Federal irrigation water" means any water made available for agricultural purposes from the operation of any reclamation or irrigation project referred to in paragraph (8) of section 202 of the Reclamation Reform Act of 1982.

(c) Denial of deduction.—No deduction shall be allowed under this subtitle by reason of any inclusion in gross income under subsection (a).

PART III—ITEMS SPECIFICALLY EXCLUDED FROM GROSS INCOME

Editorial Summary

Exclusions

Subchapter B of Chapter 1 (Secs. 101–139A)

See the discussion under the Editorial Summary entitled Inclusions and Exclusions which precedes Sec. 71.

Editorial Summary

Life Insurance Proceeds

Subchapter B of Chapter 1 (Sec. 101)

Section 101(a)(1) provides for the exclusion from gross income of life insurance proceeds. The exclusion applies regardless of whether the beneficiary is a family member or friend of the decedent or is an entity under a key person life insurance policy.

Section 101(a)(2) provides for an exception to the exclusion treatment. If the life insurance policy is transferred for valuable consideration, then return of capital treatment (i.e., cost plus additional premiums paid) applies rather than the exclusion treatment. Section 101(a)(2)(A) and §101(a)(2)(B) provide exception treatment to this return of capital provision.

Section 101(c) provides that if some or all of the excluded insurance proceeds are left with the insurance company to earn interest, such interest is included in the beneficiary's gross income. Under an installment payout arrangement for the insurance proceeds, part of each payment is a recovery of capital and part is interest income [Sec. 101(d)].

Section 101(g)(1) provides for exclusion treatment for insurance proceeds being paid before death (i.e., certain accelerated death benefits). However, for this provision to apply, the beneficiary must be either terminally ill [Sec. 101 (g)(1)(A)] or chronically ill [Sec. 101(g)(1)(B)].

See Sec. 264(a)(1) which disallows the deduction of the premiums paid by an employer under a key person life insurance policy.

§ 101. Certain death benefits

(a) Proceeds of life insurance contracts payable by reason of death.—

(1) General rule.—Except as otherwise provided in paragraph (2), subsection (d), subsection (f), and subsection (j), gross income does not include amounts received (whether in a single sum or otherwise) under a life insurance contract, if such amounts are paid by reason of the death of the insured.

(2) Transfer for valuable consideration.—In the case of a transfer for a valuable consideration, by assignment or otherwise, of a life insurance contract or any interest therein, the amount excluded from gross income by paragraph (1) shall not exceed an amount equal to the sum of the actual value of such consideration and the premiums and other amounts subsequently paid by the transferee. The preceding sentence shall not apply in the case of such a transfer—

(A) if such contract or interest therein has a basis for determining gain or loss in the hands of a transferee determined in whole or in part by reference to such basis of such contract or interest therein in the hands of the transferor, or

(B) if such transfer is to the insured, to a partner of the insured, to a partnership in which the insured is a partner, or to a corporation in which the insured is a shareholder or officer.

The term "other amounts" in the first sentence of this paragraph includes interest paid or accrued by the transferee on indebtedness with respect to such contract or any interest therein if such interest paid or accrued is not allowable as a deduction by reason of section 264(a)(4).

*(c) **Interest.**—If any amount excluded from gross income by subsection (a) is held under an agreement to pay interest thereon, the interest payments shall be included in gross income.

(d) Payment of life insurance proceeds at a date later than death.—

(1) General rule.—The amounts held by an insurer with respect to any beneficiary shall be prorated (in accordance with such regulations as may be prescribed by the Secretary) over the period or periods with respect to which such payments are to be made. There shall be excluded from the gross income of such beneficiary in the taxable year received any amount determined by such proration. Gross income includes, to the extent not excluded by the preceding sentence, amounts received under agreements to which this subsection applies.

(2) Amount held by an insurer.—An amount held by an insurer with respect to any beneficiary shall mean an amount to which subsection (a) applies which is—

(A) held by any insurer under an agreement provided for in the life insurance contract, whether as an option or otherwise, to pay such amount on a date or dates later than the death of the insured, and

(B) equal to the value of such agreement to such beneficiary

(i) as of the date of death of the insured (as if any option exercised under the life insurance contract were exercised at such time), and

(ii) as discounted on the basis of the interest rate used by the insurer in calculating payments under the agreement and mortality tables prescribed by the Secretary.

(3) Application of subsection.—This subsection shall not apply to any amount to which subsection (c) is applicable.

* * *

(f) Proceeds of flexible premium contracts issued before January 1, 1985 payable by reason of death.—

(1) In general.—Any amount paid by reason of the death of the insured under a flexible premium life insurance contract issued before January 1, 1985 shall be excluded from gross income only if—

(A) under such contract—

(i) the sum of the premiums paid under such contract does not at any time exceed the guideline premium limitation as of such time, and

(ii) any amount payable by reason of the death of the insured (determined without regard to any qualified additional benefit) is not at any time less than the applicable percentage of the cash value of such contract at such time, or

(B) by the terms of such contract, the cash value of such contract may not at any time exceed the net single premium with respect to the amount payable by reason of the death of the insured (determined without regard to any qualified additional benefit) at such time.

(2) Guideline premium limitation.—For purposes of this subsection—

(A) Guideline premium limitation.—The term "guideline premium limitation" means, as of any date, the greater of—

(i) the guideline single premium, or

(ii) the sum of the guideline level premiums to such date.

(B) Guideline single premium.—The term "guideline single premium" means the premium at issue with respect to future benefits under the contract (without regard to any qualified additional benefit), and with respect to any charges for qualified additional benefits, at the time of a determination under subparagraph (A) or (E) and which is based on—

(i) the mortality and other charges guaranteed under the contract, and

(ii) interest at the greater of an annual effective rate of 6 percent or the minimum rate or rates guaranteed upon issue of the contract.

(C) Guideline level premium.—The term "guideline level premium" means the level annual amount, payable over the longest period permitted under the contract (but ending not less than 20 years from date of issue or not later than age 95, if earlier), computed on the same basis as the guideline single premium, except that subparagraph (B)(ii) shall be applied by substituting "4 percent" for "6 percent."

*Editorial comment: There is no subsection (b).

(D) Computational rules.—In computing the guideline single premium or guideline level premium under subparagraph (B) or (C)—

(i) the excess of the amount payable by reason of the death of the insured (determined without regard to any qualified additional benefit) over the cash value of the contract shall be deemed to be not greater than such excess at the time the contract was issued,

(ii) the maturity date shall be the latest maturity date permitted under the contract, but not less than 20 years after the date of issue or (if earlier) age 95, and

(iii) the amount of any endowment benefit (or sum of endowment benefits) shall be deemed not to exceed the least amount payable by reason of the death of the insured (determined without regard to any qualified additional benefit) at any time under the contract.

(E) Adjustments.—The guideline single premium and guideline level premium shall be adjusted in the event of a change in the future benefits or any qualified additional benefit under the contract which was not reflected in any guideline single premiums or guideline level premium previously determined.

(g) Treatment of certain accelerated death benefits.—

(1) In general.—For purposes of this section, the following amounts shall be treated as an amount paid by reason of the death of an insured:

(A) Any amount received under a life insurance contract on the life of an insured who is a terminally ill individual.

(B) Any amount received under a life insurance contract on the life of an insured who is a chronically ill individual.

(2) Treatment of viatical settlements.—

(A) In general.—If any portion of the death benefit under a life insurance contract on the life of an insured described in paragraph (1) is sold or assigned to a viatical settlement provider, the amount paid for the sale or assignment of such portion shall be treated as an amount paid under the life insurance contract by reason of the death of such insured.

(B) Viatical settlement provider.—

(i) In general.—The term "viatical settlement provider" means any person regularly engaged in the trade or business of purchasing, or taking assignments of, life insurance contracts on the lives of insureds described in paragraph (1) if—

(I) such person is licensed for such purposes (with respect to insureds described in the same subparagraph of paragraph (1) as the insured) in the State in which the insured resides, or

(II) in the case of an insured who resides in a State not requiring the licensing of such persons for such purposes with respect to such insured, such person meets the requirements of clause (ii) or (iii), whichever applies to such insured.

(ii) Terminally ill insureds.—A person meets the requirements of this clause with respect to an insured who is a terminally ill individual if such person—

(I) meets the requirements of sections 8 and 9 of the Viatical Settlements Model Act of the National Association of Insurance Commissioners, and

(II) meets the requirements of the Model Regulations of the National Association of Insurance Commissioners (relating to standards for evaluation of reasonable payments) in determining amounts paid by such person in connection with such purchases or assignments.

(iii) Chronically ill insureds.—A person meets the requirements of this clause with respect to an insured who is a chronically ill individual if such person—

(I) meets requirements similar to the requirements referred to in clause (ii)(I), and

(II) meets the standards (if any) of the National Association of Insurance Commissioners for evaluating the reasonableness of amounts paid by such person in connection with such purchases or assignments with respect to chronically ill individuals.

(3) Special rules for chronically ill insureds.—In the case of an insured who is a chronically ill individual—

(A) In general.—Paragraphs (1) and (2) shall not apply to any payment received for any period unless—

(i) such payment is for costs incurred by the payee (not compensated for by insurance or otherwise) for qualified long-term care services provided for the insured for such period, and

(ii) the terms of the contract giving rise to such payment satisfy—

(I) the requirements of section 7702B(b)(1)(B), and

(II) the requirements (if any) applicable under subparagraph (B).

For purposes of the preceding sentence, the rule of section 7702B(b)(2)(B) shall apply.

(B) Other requirements.—The requirements applicable under this subparagraph are—

(i) those requirements of section 7702B(g) and section 4980C which the Secretary specifies as applying to such a purchase, assignment, or other arrangement,

(ii) standards adopted by the National Association of Insurance Commissioners which specifically apply to chronically ill individuals (and, if such standards are adopted, the analogous requirements specified under clause (i) shall cease to apply), and

(iii) standards adopted by the State in which the policyholder resides (and if such standards are adopted, the analogous requirements specified under clause (i) and (subject to section 4980C(f)) standards under clause (ii), shall cease to apply).

(C) Per diem payments.—A payment shall not fail to be described in subparagraph (A) by reason of being made on a per diem or other periodic basis without regard to the expenses incurred during the period to which the payment relates.

(D) Limitation on exclusion for periodic payments.—For limitation on amount of periodic payments which are treated as described in paragraph (1), see section 7702B(d).

(4) Definitions.—For purposes of this subsection—

(A) Terminally ill individual.—The term "terminally ill individual" means an individual who has been certified by a physician as having an illness or physical condition which can reasonably be expected to result in death in 24 months or less after the date of the certification.

(B) Chronically ill individual.—The term "chronically ill individual" has the meaning given such term by section 7702B(c)(2); except that such term shall not include a terminally ill individual.

(C) Qualified long-term care services.—The term "qualified long-term care services" has the meaning given such term by section 7702B(c).

(D) Physician.—The term "physician" has the meaning given to such term by section 1861(r)(1) of the Social Security Act (42 U.S.C. 1395x(r)(1)).

(5) Exception for business-related policies.—This subsection shall not apply in the case of any amount paid to any taxpayer other than the insured if such taxpayer has an insurable interest with respect to the life of the insured by reason of the insured being a director, officer, or employee of the taxpayer or by reason of the insured being financially interested in any trade or business carried on by the taxpayer.

(h) Survivor benefits attributable to service by a public safety officer who is killed in the line of duty.—

(1) In general.—Gross income shall not include any amount paid as a survivor annuity on account of the death of a public safety officer (as such term is defined in section 1204 of the Omnibus Crime Control and Safe Streets Act of 1968) killed in the line of duty—

(A) if such annuity is provided, under a governmental plan which meets the requirements of section 401(a), to the spouse (or a former spouse) of the public safety officer or to a child of such officer; and

(B) to the extent such annuity is attributable to such officer's service as a public safety officer.

(2) Exceptions.—Paragraph (1) shall not apply with respect to the death of any public safety officer if, as determined in accordance with the provisions of the Omnibus Crime Control and Safe Streets Act of 1968—

(A) the death was caused by the intentional misconduct of the officer or by such officer's intention to bring about such officer's death;

(B) the officer was voluntarily intoxicated (as defined in section 1204 of such Act) at the time of death;

(C) the officer was performing such officer's duties in a grossly negligent manner at the time of death; or

(D) the payment is to an individual whose actions were a substantial contributing factor to the death of the officer.

(i) Certain employee death benefits payable by reason of death of certain terrorist victims or astronauts.

(1) In general.—Gross income does not include amounts (whether in a single sum or otherwise) paid by an employer by reason of the death of an employee who is a specified terrorist victim (as defined in section 692(d)(4)).

(2) Limitation.—

(A) In general.—Subject to such rules as the Secretary may prescribe, paragraph (1) shall not apply to amounts which would have been payable after death if the individual had died other than as a specified terrorist victim (as so defined).

(B) Exception.—Subparagraph (A) shall not apply to incidental death benefits paid from a plan described in section 401(a) and exempt from tax under section 501(a).

(3) Treatment of self-employed individuals.—For purposes of paragraph (1), the term "employee" includes a self-employed individual (as defined in section 401(c)(1)).

(4) Relief with respect to astronauts.—The provisions of this subsection shall apply to any astronaut whose death occurs in the line of duty.

(j) Treatment of certain employer-owned life insurance contracts.—

(1) General rule.—In the case of an employer-owned life insurance contract, the amount excluded from gross income of an applicable policyholder by reason of paragraph (1) of subsection (a) shall not exceed an amount equal to the sum of the premiums and other amounts paid by the policyholder for the contract.

(2) Exceptions.—In the case of an employer-owned life insurance contract with respect to which the notice and consent requirements of paragraph (4) are met, paragraph (1) shall not apply to any of the following:

(A) Exceptions based on insured's status.—Any amount received by reason of the death of an insured who, with respect to an applicable policyholder—

(i) was an employee at any time during the 12-month period before the insured's death, or

(ii) is, at the time the contract is issued—

(I) a director,

(II) a highly compensated employee within the meaning of section 414(q) (without regard to paragraph (1)(B)(ii) thereof), or

(III) a highly compensated individual within the meaning of section 105(h)(5), except that "35 percent" shall be substituted for "25 percent" in subparagraph (C) thereof.

(B) Exception for amounts paid to insured's heirs.—Any amount received by reason of the death of an insured to the extent—

(i) the amount is paid to a member of the family (within the meaning of section 267(c)(4)) of the insured, any individual who is the designated beneficiary of the insured under the contract (other than the applicable policyholder), a trust established for the benefit of any such member of the family or designated beneficiary, or the estate of the insured, or

(ii) the amount is used to purchase an equity (or capital or profits) interest in the applicable policyholder from any person described in clause (i).

(3) Employer-owned life insurance contract.—

(A) In general.—For purposes of this subsection, the term "employer-owned life insurance contract" means a life insurance contract which—

(i) is owned by a person engaged in a trade or business and under which such person (or a related person described in subparagraph (B)(ii)) is directly or indirectly a beneficiary under the contract, and

(ii) covers the life of an insured who is an employee with respect to the trade or business of the applicable policyholder on the date the contract is issued.

For purposes of the preceding sentence, if coverage for each insured under a master contract is treated as a separate contract for purposes of sections 817(h), 7702, and 7702A, coverage for each such insured shall be treated as a separate contract.

(B) Applicable policyholder.—For purposes of this subsection—

(i) In general.—The term "applicable policyholder" means, with respect to any employerowned life insurance contract, the person described in subparagraph (A)(i) which owns the contract.

(ii) Related persons.—The term "applicable policyholder" includes any person which—

(I) bears a relationship to the person described in clause (i) which is specified in section 267(b) or 707(b)(1), or

(II) is engaged in trades or businesses with such person which are under common control (within the meaning of subsection (a) or (b) of section 52).

(4) Notice and consent requirements.—The notice and consent requirements of this paragraph are met if, before the issuance of the contract, the employee—

(A) is notified in writing that the applicable policyholder intends to insure the employee's life and the maximum face amount for which the employee could be insured at the time the contract was issued,

(B) provides written consent to being insured under the contract and that such coverage may continue after the insured terminates employment, and

(C) is informed in writing that an applicable policyholder will be a beneficiary of any proceeds payable upon the death of the employee.

(5) Definitions.—For purposes of this subsection—

(A) Employee.—The term "employee" includes an officer, director, and highly compensated employee (within the meaning of section 414(q)).

(B) Insured.—The term "insured" means, with respect to an employer-owned life insurance contract, an individual covered by the contract who is a United States citizen or resident. In the case of a contract covering the joint lives of 2 individuals, references to an insured include both of the individuals.

Editorial Summary

Gifts and Inheritances

Subchapter B of Chapter 1 (Sec. 102)

Property received by gift or by inheritance is excluded from gross income. While such transfers produce beneficial income tax treatment for the recipient, excise taxes in the form of the federal gift tax (see Chapter 12 of Subtitle) B and the federal estate tax (see Chapter 11 of Subtitle) B may be levied on the donor or the decedent's estate.

The exclusion provided for in Sec. 102 applies to property. Therefore, if only the income from the property is transferred, the income amount is included in the gross income of the transferor [see Sec. 102(b)].

Employee gifts are not eligible for exclusion treatment [see Sec. 102(c)] under Sec. 102.

§ 102. Gifts and inheritances

(a) General rule.—Gross income does not include the value of property acquired by gift, bequest, devise, or inheritance.

(b) Income.—Subsection (a) shall not exclude from gross income—

(1) the income from any property referred to in subsection (a); or

(2) where the gift, bequest, devise, or inheritance is of income from property, the amount of such income.

Where, under the terms of the gift, bequest, devise, or inheritance, the payment, crediting, or distribution thereof is to be made at intervals, then, to the extent that it is paid or credited or to be distributed out of income from property, it shall be treated for purposes of paragraph (2) as a gift, bequest, devise, or inheritance of income from property. Any amount included in the gross income of a beneficiary under subchapter J shall be treated for purposes of paragraph (2) as a gift, bequest, devise, or inheritance of income from property.

(c) Employee gifts.—

(1) In general.—Subsection (a) shall not exclude from gross income any amount transferred by or for an employer to, or for the benefit of, an employee.

(2) Cross references.—

For provisions excluding certain employee achievement awards from gross income, see section 74(c).

For provisions excluding certain de minimis fringes from gross income, see section 132(e).

§ 103. Interest on state and local bonds

(a) Exclusion.—Except as provided in subsection (b), gross income does not include interest on any State or local bond.

(b) Exceptions.—Subsection (a) shall not apply to—

(1) **Private activity bond which is not a qualified bond.**—Any private activity bond which is not a qualified bond (within the meaning of section 141).

(2) **Arbitrage bond.**—Any arbitrage bond (within the meaning of section 148).

(3) **Bond not in registered form, etc.**—Any bond unless such bond meets the applicable requirements of section 149.

(c) **Definitions.**—For purposes of this section and part IV—

(1) **State or local bond.**—The term "State or local bond" means an obligation of a State or political subdivision thereof.

(2) **State.**—The term "State" includes the District of Columbia and any possession of the United States.

* * *

§ 104. Compensation for injuries or sickness

(a) **In general.**—Except in the case of amounts attributable to (and not in excess of) deductions allowed under section 213 (relating to medical, etc., expenses) for any prior taxable year, gross income does not include—

(1) amounts received under workmen's compensation acts as compensation for personal injuries or sickness;

(2) the amount of any damages (other than punitive damages) received (whether by suit or agreement and whether as lump sums or as periodic payments) on account of personal physical injuries or physical sickness;

(3) amounts received through accident or health insurance (or through an arrangement having the effect of accident or health insurance) for personal injuries or sickness (other than amounts received by an employee, to the extent such amounts (A) are attributable to contributions by the employer which were not includible in the gross income of the employee, or (B) are paid by the employer);

(4) amounts received as a pension, annuity, or similar allowance for personal injuries or sickness resulting from active service in the armed forces of any country or in the Coast and Geodetic Survey or the Public Health Service, or as a disability annuity payable under the provisions of section 808 of the Foreign Service Act of 1980; and

(5) amounts received by an individual as disability income attributable to injuries incurred as a direct result of a terroristic or military action (as defined in section 692(c)(2)).

For purposes of paragraph (3), in the case of an individual who is, or has been, an employee within the meaning of section 401(c)(1) (relating to self-employed individuals), contributions made on behalf of such individual while he was such an employee to a trust described in section 401(a) which is exempt from tax under section 501(a), or under a plan described in section 403(a), shall, to the extent allowed as deductions under section 404, be treated as contributions by the employer which were not includible in the gross income of the employee. For purposes of paragraph (2), emotional distress shall not be treated as a physical injury or physical sickness. The preceding sentence shall not apply to an amount of damages not in excess of the amount paid for medical care (described in subparagraph (A) or (B) of section 213(d)(1)) attributable to emotional distress.

(b) **Termination of application of subsection (a)(4) in certain cases.**—

(1) **In general.**—Subsection (a)(4) shall not apply in the case of any individual who is not described in paragraph (2).

(2) **Individuals to whom subsection (a)(4) continues to apply.**—An individual is described in this paragraph if—

(A) on or before September 24, 1975, he was entitled to receive any amount described in subsection (a)(4),

(B) on September 24, 1975, he was a member of any organization (or reserve component thereof) referred to in subsection (a)(4) or under a binding written commitment to become such a member,

(C) he receives an amount described in subsection (a)(4) by reason of a combat-related injury, or

(D) on application therefor, he would be entitled to receive disability compensation from the Veterans' Administration.

(3) **Special rules for combat-related injuries.**—For purposes of this subsection, the term "combat-related injury" means personal injury or sickness—

(A) which is incurred—

(i) as a direct result of armed conflict,

(ii) while engaged in extra hazardous service, or

(iii) under conditions simulating war; or

(B) which is caused by an instrumentality of war.

In the case of an individual who is not described in subparagraph (A) or (B) of paragraph (2), except as provided in paragraph (4), the only amounts taken into account under subsection (a)(4) shall be the amounts which he receives by reason of a combat-related injury.

(4) Amount excluded to be not less than veterans' disability compensation.—In the case of any individual described in paragraph (2), the amounts excludable under subsection (a)(4) for any period with respect to any individual shall not be less than the maximum amount which such individual, on application therefor, would be entitled to receive as disability compensation from the Veterans' Administration.

(c) Application of prior law in certain cases.—The phrase "(other than punitive damages)" shall not apply to punitive damages awarded in a civil action—

(1) which is a wrongful death action, and

(2) with respect to which applicable State law (as in effect on September 13, 1995 and without regard to any modification after such date) provides, or has been construed to provide by a court of competent jurisdiction pursuant to a decision issued on or before September 13, 1995, that only punitive damages may be awarded in such an action.

This subsection shall cease to apply to any civil action filed on or after the first date on which the applicable State law ceases to provide (or is no longer construed to provide) the treatment described in paragraph (2).

(d) Cross references.—

(1) For exclusion from employee's gross income of employer contributions to accident and health plans, see section 106.

* * *

§ 105. Amounts received under accident and health plans

(a) Amounts attributable to employer contributions.—Except as otherwise provided in this section, amounts received by an employee through accident or health insurance for personal injuries or sickness shall be included in gross income to the extent such amounts (1) are attributable to contributions by the employer which were not includible in the gross income of the employee, or (2) are paid by the employer.

(b) Amounts expended for medical care.—Except in the case of amounts attributable to (and not in excess of) deductions allowed under section 213 (relating to medical, etc., expenses) for any prior taxable year, gross income does not include amounts referred to in subsection (a) if such amounts are paid, directly or indirectly, to the taxpayer to reimburse the taxpayer for expenses incurred by him for the medical care (as defined in section 213(d)) of the taxpayer, his spouse, his dependents (as defined in section 152, determined without regard to subsections (b)(1), (b)(2), and (d)(1)(B) thereof). Any child to whom section 152(e) applies shall be treated as a dependent of both parents for purposes of this subsection, and any child (as defined in section 152(f)(1)) of the taxpayer who as of the end of the taxable year has not attained age 27.

(c) Payments unrelated to absence from work.—Gross income does not include amounts referred to in subsection (a) to the extent such amounts—

(1) constitute payment for the permanent loss or loss of use of a member or function of the body, or the permanent disfigurement, of the taxpayer, his spouse, or a dependent (as defined in section 152, determined without regard to subsections (b)(1), (b)(2), and (d)(1)(B) thereof), and

(2) are computed with reference to the nature of the injury without regard to the period the employee is absent from work.

* * *

(e) Accident and health plans.—For purposes of this section and section 104—

(1) amounts received under an accident or health plan for employees, and

(2) amounts received from a sickness and disability fund for employees maintained under the law of a State or the District of Columbia,

shall be treated as amounts received through accident or health insurance.

(f) Rules for application of section 213.—For purposes of section 213(a) (relating to medical, dental, etc., expenses) amounts excluded from gross income under subsection (c) or (d) shall not be considered as compensation (by insurance or otherwise) for expenses paid for medical care.

(g) Self-employed individual not considered an employee.—For purposes of this section, the term "employee" does not include an individual who is an employee within the meaning of section 401(c)(1) (relating to self-employed individuals).

(h) Amount paid to highly compensated individuals under a discriminatory self-insured medical expense reimbursement plan.—

(1) In general.—In the case of amounts paid to a highly compensated individual under a self-insured medical reimbursement plan which does not satisfy the requirements of paragraph (2) for a plan year, subsection (b) shall not apply to such amounts to the extent they constitute an excess reimbursement of such highly compensated individual.

(2) Prohibition of discrimination.—A self-insured medical reimbursement plan satisfies the requirements of this paragraph only if—

(A) the plan does not discriminate in favor of highly compensated individuals as to eligibility to participate; and

(B) the benefits provided under the plan do not discriminate in favor of participants who are highly compensated individuals.

(3) Nondiscriminatory eligibility classifications.—

(A) In general.—A self-insured medical reimbursement plan does not satisfy the requirements of subparagraph (A) of paragraph (2) unless such plan benefits—

(i) 70 percent or more of all employees, or 80 percent or more of all the employees who are eligible to benefit under the plan if 70 percent or more of all employees are eligible to benefit under the plan; or

(ii) such employees as qualify under a classification set up by the employer and found by the Secretary not to be discriminatory in favor of highly compensated individuals.

(B) Exclusion of certain employees.—For purposes of subparagraph (A), there may be excluded from consideration—

(i) employees who have not completed 3 years of service;

(ii) employees who have not attained age 25;

(iii) part-time or seasonal employees;

(iv) employees not included in the plan who are included in a unit of employees covered by an agreement between employee representatives and one or more employers which the Secretary finds to be a collective bargaining agreement, if accident and health benefits were the subject of good faith bargaining between such employee representatives and employer or employers; and

(v) employees who are nonresident aliens and who receive no earned income (within the meaning of section 911(d)(2)) from the employer which constitutes income from sources within the United States (within the meaning of section 861(a)(3)).

(4) Nondiscriminatory benefits.—A self-insured medical reimbursement plan does not meet the requirements of subparagraph (B) of paragraph (2) unless all benefits provided for participants who are highly compensated individuals are provided for all other participants.

(5) Highly compensated individual defined.—For purposes of this subsection, the term "highly compensated individual" means an individual who is—

(A) one of the 5 highest paid officers,

(B) a shareholder who owns (with the application of section 318) more than 10 percent in value of the stock of the employer, or

(C) among the highest paid 25 percent of all employees (other than employees described in paragraph (3)(B) who are not participants).

(6) Self-insured medical reimbursement plan.—The term "self-insured medical reimbursement plan" means a plan of an employer to reimburse employees for expenses referred to in subsection (b) for which reimbursement is not provided under a policy of accident and health insurance.

(7) Excess reimbursement of highly compensated individual.—For purposes of this section, the excess reimbursement of a highly compensated individual which is attributable to a self-insured medical reimbursement plan is—

(A) in the case of a benefit available to highly compensated individuals but not to all other participants (or which otherwise fails to satisfy the requirements of paragraph (2)(B)), the amount reimbursed under the plan to the employee with respect to such benefit, and

(B) in the case of benefits (other than benefits described in subparagraph (A)) paid to a highly compensated individual by a plan which fails to satisfy the requirements of paragraph (2), the total amount reimbursed to the highly compensated individual for the plan year multiplied by a fraction—

(i) the numerator of which is the total amount reimbursed to all participants who are highly compensated individuals under the plan for the plan year, and

(ii) the denominator of which is the total amount reimbursed to all employees under the plan for such plan year.

In determining the fraction under subparagraph (B), there shall not be taken into account any reimbursement which is attributable to a benefit described in subparagraph (A).

(8) Certain controlled groups, etc.—All employees who are treated as employed by a single employer under subsection (b), (c), or (m) of section 414 shall be treated as employed by a single employer for purposes of this section.

(9) Regulations.—The Secretary shall prescribe such regulations as may be necessary to carry out the provisions of this section.

(10) Time of inclusion.—Any amount paid for a plan year that is included in income by reason of this subsection shall be treated as received or accrued in the taxable year of the participant in which the plan year ends.

* * *

§ 106. Contributions by employer to accident and health plans

(a) General rule.—Except as otherwise provided in this section, gross income of an employee does not include employer-provided coverage under an accident or health plan.

(b) Contributions to Archer MSAs.—

(1) In general.—In the case of an employee who is an eligible individual, amounts contributed by such employee's employer to any Archer MSA of such employee shall be treated as employer-provided coverage for medical expenses under an accident or health plan to the extent such amounts do not exceed the limitation under section 220(b)(1) (determined without regard to this subsection) which is applicable to such employee for such taxable year.

(2) No constructive receipt.—No amount shall be included in the gross income of any employee solely because the employee may choose between the contributions referred to in paragraph (1) and employer contributions to another health plan of the employer.

(3) Special rule for deduction of employer contributions.—Any employer contribution to an Archer MSA, if otherwise allowable as a deduction under this chapter, shall be allowed only for the taxable year in which paid.

(4) Employer MSA contributions required to be shown on return.—Every individual required to file a return under section 6012 for the taxable year shall include on such return the aggregate amount contributed by employers to the Archer MSAs of such individual or such individual's spouse for such taxable year.

(5) MSA contributions not part of COBRA coverage.—Paragraph (1) shall not apply for purposes of section 4980B.

(6) Definitions.—For purposes of this subsection, the terms "eligible individual" and "Archer MSA" have the respective meanings given to such terms by section 220.

(7) Cross reference.—**For penalty on failure by employer to make comparable contributions to the Archer MSAs of comparable employees, see section 4980E.**

(c) Inclusion of long-term care benefits provided through flexible spending arrangements.—

(1) In general.—Effective on and after January 1, 1997, gross income of an employee shall include employer-provided coverage for qualified long-term care services (as defined in section 7702B(c)) to the extent that such coverage is provided through a flexible spending or similar arrangement.

(2) Flexible spending arrangement.—For purposes of this subsection, a flexible spending arrangement is a benefit program which provides employees with coverage under which—

(A) specified incurred expenses may be reimbursed (subject to reimbursement maximums and other reasonable conditions), and

(B) the maximum amount of reimbursement which is reasonably available to a participant for such coverage is less than 500 percent of the value of such coverage,

In the case of an insured plan, the maximum amount reasonably available shall be determined on the basis of the underlying coverage.

(d) Contributions to health savings accounts.—

(1) In general.—In the case of an employee who is an eligible individual (as defined in section 223(c)(1)), amounts contributed by such employee's employer to any health savings account (as defined in section 223(d)) of such employee shall be treated as employer-provided coverage for medical expenses under an accident or health plan to the extent such amounts do not exceed the limitation under section 223(b) (determined without regard to this subsection) which is applicable to such employee for such taxable year.

(2) Special rules.—Rules similar to the rules of paragraphs (2), (3), (4), and (5) of subsection (b) shall apply for purposes of this subsection.

(3) Cross reference.—For penalty on failure by employer to make comparable contributions to the health savings accounts of comparable employees, see section 4980G.

(e) FSA and HRA terminations to fund HSAs.—

(1) In general.—A plan shall not fail to be treated as a health flexible spending arrangement or health reimbursement arrangement under this section or section 105 merely because such plan provides for a qualified HSA distribution.

(2) Qualified HSA distribution.—The term "qualified HSA distribution" means a distribution from a health flexible spending arrangement or health reimbursement arrangement to the extent that such distribution—

(A) does not exceed the lesser of the balance in such arrangement on September 21, 2006, or as of the date of such distribution, and,

(B) is contributed by the employer directly to the health savings account of the employee before January 1, 2012.

Such term shall not include more than 1 distribution with respect to any arrangement.

(3) Additional tax for failure to maintain high deductible health plan coverage.—(A) In general. If, at any time during the testing period, the employee is not an eligible individual, then the amount of the qualified HSA distribution—

(i) shall be includible in the gross income of the employee for the taxable year in which occurs the first month in the testing period for which such employee is not an eligible individual, and

(ii) the tax imposed by this chapter for such taxable year on the employee shall be increased by 10 percent of the amount which is so includible.

(B) Exception for disability or death. Clauses (i) and (ii) of subparagraph (A) shall not apply if the employee ceases to be an eligible individual by reason of the death of the employee or the employee becoming disabled (within the meaning of section 72(m)(7)).

(4) Definition and special rules.—For purposes of this subsection—

(A) Testing period. The term "testing period" means the period beginning with the month in which the qualified HSA distribution is contributed to the health savings account and ending on the last day of the 12th month following such month.

(B) Eligible individual. The term "eligible individual" has the meaning given such term by section 223(c)(1).

(C) Treatment as rollover contribution. A qualified HSA distribution shall be treated as a rollover contribution described in section 223(f)(5).

(5) Tax treatment relating to distributions.—For purposes of this title—

(A) In general. A qualified HSA distribution shall be treated as a payment described in subsection (d).

(B) Comparability excise tax.

(i) In general. Except as provided in clause (ii), section 4980G shall not apply to qualified HSA distributions.

(ii) Failure to offer too all employees. In the case of a qualified HSA distribution to any employee, the failure to offer such distribution to any eligible individual covered under a high deductible health plan of the employer shall (notwithstanding section 4980G(d)) be treated for purposes of section 4980G as a failure to meet the requirements of section 4980G(b).

(f) Reimbursements for medicine restricted to prescribed drugs and insulin.—For purposes of this section and section 105, reimbursement for expenses incurred for a medicine or a drug shall be treated as a reimbursement for medical expenses only if such medicine or drug is a prescribed drug (determined without regard to whether such drug is available without a prescription) or is insulin.

§ 107. Rental value of parsonages

In the case of a minister of the gospel, gross income does not include—

(1) the rental value of a home furnished to him as part of his compensation; or

(2) the rental allowance paid to him as part of his compensation, to the extent used by him to rent or provide a home and to the extent such allowance does not exceed the fair rental value of the home, including furnishings and appurtenances such as a garage, plus the cost of utilities.

§ 108. Income from discharge of indebtedness

(a) Exclusion from gross income.—

(1) In general.—Gross income does not include any amount which (but for this subsection) would be includible in gross income by reason of the discharge (in whole or in part) of indebtedness of the taxpayer if—

(A) the discharge occurs in a title 11 case,

(B) the discharge occurs when the taxpayer is insolvent,

(C) the indebtedness discharged is qualified farm indebtedness,

(D) in the case of a taxpayer other than a C corporation, the indebtedness discharged is qualified real property business indebtedness, or

(E) the indebtedness discharged is qualified principal residence indebtedness which is discharged before January 1, 2014.*

(2) Coordination of exclusions.—

(A) Title 11 exclusion takes precedence.—Subparagraphs (B), (C), (D), and (E) of paragraph (1) shall not apply to a discharge which occurs in a title 11 case.

(B) Insolvency exclusion takes precedence over qualified farm exclusion and qualified real property business exclusion.—Subparagraph (C) and (D) of paragraph (1) shall not apply to a discharge to the extent the taxpayer is insolvent.

(C) Principal residence exclusion takes precedence over insolvency exclusion unless elected otherwise.—Paragraph (1)(B) shall not apply to a discharge to which paragraph(1)(E) applies unless the taxpayer elects to apply paragraph(1)(B) in lieu of paragraph(1)(E).

(3) Insolvency exclusion limited to amount of insolvency.—In the case of a discharge to which paragraph (1)(B) applies, the amount excluded under paragraph (1)(B) shall not exceed the amount by which the taxpayer is insolvent.

(b) Reduction of tax attributes.—

(1) In general.—The amount excluded from gross income under subparagraph (A), (B), or (C) of subsection (a)(1) shall be applied to reduce the tax attributes of the taxpayer as provided in paragraph (2).

(2) Tax attributes affected; order of reduction.—Except as provided in paragraph (5), the reduction referred to in paragraph (1) shall be made in the following tax attributes in the following order:

(A) NOL.—Any net operating loss for the taxable year of the discharge, and any net operating loss carryover to such taxable year.

(B) General business credit.—Any carryover to or from the taxable year of a discharge of an amount for purposes for determining the amount allowable as a credit under section 38 (relating to general business credit).

(C) Minimum tax credit.—The amount of the minimum tax credit available under section 53(b) as of the beginning of the taxable year immediately following the taxable year of the discharge.

(D) Capital loss carryovers.—Any net capital loss for the taxable year of the discharge, and any capital loss carryover to such taxable year under section 1212.

(E) Basis reduction.—

(i) In general.—The basis of the property of the taxpayer.

(ii) Cross reference.—

For provisions for making the reduction described in clause (i), see section 1017.

(F) Passive activity loss and credit carryovers.—Any passive activity loss or credit carryover of the taxpayer under section 469(b) from the taxable year of the discharge.

(G) Foreign tax credit carryovers.—Any carryover to or from the taxable year of the discharge for purposes of determining the amount of the credit allowable under section 27.

(3) Amount of reduction.—

(A) In general.—Except as provided in subparagraph (B), the reductions described in paragraph (2) shall be one dollar for each dollar excluded by subsection (a).

*Editorial comment: At the present time, this section has not been extended. There is pending legislation in the Senate, *The Tax Extender's Act of 2013 (S. 1859)*, that would extend Section 108(a)(1)(E) until January 1, 2015.

(B) Credit carryover reduction.—The reductions described in subparagraphs (B), (C), and (G) shall be 33½ cents for each dollar excluded by subsection (a). The reduction described in subparagraph (F) in any passive activity credit carryover shall be 33½ cents for each dollar excluded by subsection (a).

(4) Ordering rules.—

(A) Reductions made after determination of tax for year.—The reductions described in paragraph (2) shall be made after the determination of the tax imposed by this chapter for the taxable year of the discharge.

(B) Reductions under subparagraph (A) or (D) of paragraph (2).—The reductions described in subparagraph (A) or (D) of paragraph (2) (as the case may be) shall be made first in the loss for the taxable year of the discharge and then in the carryovers to such taxable year in the order of the taxable years from which each such carryover arose.

(C) Reductions under subparagraphs (B) and (G) of paragraph (2).—The reductions described in subparagraphs (B) and (G) of paragraph (2) shall be made in the order in which carryovers are taken into account under this chapter for the taxable year of the discharge.

(5) Election to apply reduction first against depreciable property.—

(A) In general.—The taxpayer may elect to apply any portion of the reduction referred to in paragraph (1) to the reduction under section 1017 of the basis of the depreciable property of the taxpayer.

(B) Limitation.—The amount to which an election under subparagraph (A) applies shall not exceed the aggregate adjusted bases of the depreciable property held by the taxpayer as of the beginning of the taxable year following the taxable year in which the discharge occurs.

(C) Other tax attributes not reduced.—Paragraph (2) shall not apply to any amount to which an election under this paragraph applies.

(c) Treatment of discharge of qualified real property business indebtedness.—

(1) Basis reduction.—

(A) In general.—The amount excluded from gross income under subparagraph (D) of subsection (a)(1) shall be applied to reduce the basis of the depreciable real property of the taxpayer.

(B) Cross reference.—

For provisions making the reduction described in subparagraph (A), see section 1017.

(2) Limitations.—

(A) Indebtedness in excess of value.—The amount excluded under subparagraph (D) of subsection (a)(1) with respect to any qualified real property business indebtedness shall not exceed the excess (if any) of—

(i) the outstanding principal amount of such indebtedness (immediately before the discharge), over

(ii) the fair market value of the real property described in paragraph (3)(A) (as of such time), reduced by the outstanding principal amount of any other qualified real property business indebtedness secured by such property (as of such time).

(B) Overall limitation.—The amount excluded under subparagraph (D) of subsection (a)(l) shall not exceed the aggregate adjusted bases of depreciable real property (determined after any reductions under subsections (b) and (g)) held by the taxpayer immediately before the discharge (other than depreciable real property acquired in contemplation of such discharge).

(3) Qualified real property business indebtedness.—The term "qualified real property business indebtedness" means indebtedness which—

(A) was incurred or assumed by the taxpayer in connection with real property used in a trade or business and is secured by such real property,

(B) was incurred or assumed before January 1, 1993, or if incurred or assumed on or after such date, is qualified acquisition indebtedness, and

(C) with respect to which such taxpayer makes an election to have this paragraph apply.

Such term shall not include qualified farm indebtedness. Indebtedness under subparagraph (B) shall include indebtedness resulting from the refinancing of indebtedness under subparagraph (B) (or this sentence), but only to the extent it does not exceed the amount of the indebtedness being refinanced.

(4) Qualified acquisition indebtedness.—For purposes of paragraph (3)(B), the term "qualified acquisition indebtedness" means, with respect to any real property described in paragraph (3)(A), indebtedness incurred or assumed to acquire, construct, reconstruct, or substantially improve such property.

(5) Regulations.—The Secretary shall issue such regulations as are necessary to carry out this subsection, including regulations preventing the abuse of this subsection through cross-collateralization or other means.

(d) Meaning of terms; special rules relating to certain provisions.—

(1) Indebtedness of taxpayer.—For purposes of this section, the term "indebtedness of the taxpayer" means any indebtedness—

(A) for which the taxpayer is liable, or

(B) subject to which the taxpayer holds property.

(2) Title 11 case.—For purposes of this section, the term "title 11 case" means a case under title 11 of the United States Code (relating to bankruptcy), but only if the taxpayer is under the jurisdiction of the court in such case and the discharge of indebtedness is granted by the court or is pursuant to a plan approved by the court.

(3) Insolvent.—For purposes of this section, the term "insolvent" means the excess of liabilities over the fair market value of assets. With respect to any discharge, whether or not the taxpayer is insolvent, and the amount by which the taxpayer is insolvent, shall be determined on the basis of the taxpayer's assets and liabilities immediately before the discharge.

* * *

(5) Depreciable property.—The term "depreciable property" has the same meaning as when used in section 1017.

(6) Certain provisions to be applied at partner level.—In the case of a partnership, subsections (a), (b), (c), and (g) shall be applied at the partner level.

(7) Special rules for S corporation.—

(A) Certain provisions to be applied at corporate level.—In the case of an S corporation, subsections (a), (b), (c), and (g) shall be applied at the corporate level, including by not taking into account under section 1366(a) any amount excluded under subsection (a) of this section.

(B) Reduction in carryover of disallowed losses and deductions.—In the case of an S corporation, for purposes of subparagraph (A) of subsection (b)(2), any loss or deduction which is disallowed for the taxable year of the discharge under section 1366(d)(1) shall be treated as a net operating loss for such taxable year. The preceding sentence shall not apply to any discharge to the extent that subsection (a)(1)(D) applies to such discharge.

(C) Coordination with basis adjustments under section 1367(b)(2).—For purposes of subsection (e)(6), a shareholder's adjusted basis in indebtedness of an S corporation shall be determined without regard to any adjustments made under section 1367(b)(2).

(8) Reductions of tax attributes in title 11 cases of individuals to be made by estate.—In any case under chapter 7 or 11 of title 11 of the United States Code to which section 1398 applies, for purposes of paragraphs (1) and (5) of subsection (b) the estate (and not the individual) shall be treated as the taxpayer. The preceding sentence shall not apply for purposes of applying section 1017 to property transferred by the estate to the individual.

(9) Time for making election, etc.—

(A) Time.—An election under paragraph (5) of subsection (b) or under paragraph (3)(C) of subsection (c) shall be made on the taxpayer's return for the taxable year in which the discharge occurs or at such other time as may be permitted in regulations prescribed by the Secretary.

(B) Revocation only with consent.—An election referred to in subparagraph (A), once made, may be revoked only with the consent of the Secretary.

(C) Manner.—An election referred to in subparagraph (A) shall be made in such manner as the Secretary may by regulations prescribe.

(10) Cross reference.—

For provision that no reduction is to be made in the basis of exempt property of an individual debtor, see section 1017 (c)(1).

(e) General rules for discharge of indebtedness (including discharges not in title 11 cases or insolvency).—For purposes of this title—

(1) No other insolvency exception.—Except as otherwise provided in this section, there shall be no insolvency exception from the general rule that gross income includes income from the discharge of indebtedness.

(2) Income not realized to extent of lost deductions.—No income shall be realized from the discharge of indebtedness to the extent that payment of the liability would have given rise to a deduction.

(3) Adjustments for unamortized premium and discount.—The amount taken into account with respect to any discharge shall be properly adjusted for unamortized premium and unamortized discount with respect to the indebtedness discharged.

(4) Acquisition of indebtedness by person related to debtor.—

(A) Treated as acquisition by debtor.—For purposes of determining income of the debtor from discharge of indebtedness, to the extent provided in regulations prescribed by the Secretary, the acquisition of outstanding indebtedness by a person bearing a relationship to the debtor specified in section 267(b) or 707(b)(1) from a person who does not bear such a relationship to the debtor shall be treated as the acquisition of such indebtedness by the debtor. Such regulations shall provide for such adjustments in the treatment of any subsequent transactions involving the indebtedness as may be appropriate by reason of the application of the preceding sentence.

(B) Members of family.—For purposes of this paragraph, sections 267(b) and 707(b)(1) shall be applied as if section 267(c)(4) provided that the family of an individual consists of the individual's spouse, the individual's children, grandchildren, and parents, and any spouse of the individual's children or grandchildren.

(C) Entities under common control treated as related.—For purposes of this paragraph, two entities which are treated as a single employer under subsection (b) or (c) of section 414 shall be treated as bearing a relationship to each other which is described in section 267(b).

(5) Purchase-money debt reduction for solvent debtor treated as price reduction.—If—

(A) the debt of a purchaser of property to the seller of such property which arose out of the purchase of such property is reduced,

(B) such reduction does not occur—

(i) in a title 11 case, or

(ii) when the purchaser is insolvent, and

(C) but for this paragraph, such reduction would be treated as income to the purchaser from the discharge of indebtedness,

then such reduction shall be treated as a purchase price adjustment.

(6) Indebtedness contributed to capital.—Except as provided in regulations, for purposes of determining income of the debtor from discharge of indebtedness, if a debtor corporation acquires its indebtedness from a shareholder as a contribution to capital—

(A) section 118 shall not apply, but

(B) such corporation shall be treated as having satisfied the indebtedness with an amount of money equal to the shareholder's adjusted basis in the indebtedness.

(7) Recapture of gain on subsequent sale of stock.—

(A) In general.—If a creditor acquires stock of a debtor corporation in satisfaction of such corporation's indebtedness, for purposes of section 1245—

(i) such stock (and any other property the basis of which is determined in whole or in part by reference to the adjusted basis of such stock) shall be treated as section 1245 property,

(ii) the aggregate amount allowed to the creditor—

(I) as deductions under subsection (a) or (b) of section 166 (by reason of the worthlessness or partial worthlessness of the indebtedness), or

(II) as an ordinary loss on the exchange,

shall be treated as an amount allowed as a deduction for depreciation, and

(iii) an exchange of such stock qualifying under section 354(a), 355(a), or 356(a) shall be treated as an exchange to which section 1245(b)(3) applies.

The amount determined under clause (ii) shall be reduced by the amount (if any) included in the creditor's gross income on the exchange.

(B) Special rule for cash basis taxpayers.—In the case of any creditor who computes his taxable income under the cash receipts and disbursements method, proper adjustment shall be made in the amount taken into account under clause (ii) of subparagraph (A) for any amount which was not included in the creditor's gross income but which would have been included in such gross income if such indebtedness had been satisfied in full.

(C) Stock of parent corporation.—For purposes of this paragraph, stock of a corporation in control (within the meaning of section

368(c)) of the debtor corporation shall be treated as stock of the debtor corporation.

(D) Treatment of successor corporation.—For purposes of this paragraph, the term "debtor corporation" includes a successor corporation.

(E) Partnership rule.—Under regulations prescribed by the Secretary, rules similar to the rules of the foregoing subparagraphs of this paragraph shall apply with respect to the indebtedness of a partnership.

(8) Indebtedness satisfied by corporation's stock.—For purposes of determining income of a debtor from discharge of indebtedness, if a debtor corporation transfers stock to a creditor in satisfaction of its indebtedness, such corporation shall be treated as having satisfied the indebtedness with an amount of money equal to the fair market value of the stock.

* * *

(10) Indebtedness satisfied by issuance of debt instrument.—

(A) In general.—For purposes of determining income of a debtor from discharge of indebtedness, if a debtor issues a debt instrument in satisfaction of indebtedness, such debtor shall be treated as having satisfied the indebtedness with an amount of money equal to the issue price of such debt instrument.

(B) Issue price.—For purposes of subparagraph (A), the issue price of any debt instrument shall be determined under sections 1273 and 1274. For purposes of the preceding sentence, section 1273(b)(4) shall be applied by reducing the stated redemption price of any instrument by the portion of such stated redemption price which is treated as interest for purposes of this chapter.

(11) Indebtedness satisfied by issuance of debt instrument.—

(A) In general.—For purposes of determining income of a debtor from discharge of indebtedness, if a debtor issues a debt instrument in satisfaction of indebtedness, such debtor shall be treated as having satisfied the indebtedness with an amount of money equal to the issue price of such debt instrument.

(B) Issue price.—For purposes of subparagraph (A), the issue price of any debt instrument shall be determined under sections 1273 and 1274. For purposes of the preceding sentence, section 1273(b)(4) shall be applied by reducing the stated redemption price of any instrument by the portion of such stated redemption price which is treated as interest for purposes of this chapter.

(f) Student loans.—

(1) In general.—In the case of an individual, gross income does not include any amount which (but for this subsection) would be includible in gross income by reason of the discharge (in whole or in part) of any student loan if such discharge was pursuant to a provision of such loan under which all or part of the indebtedness of the individual would be discharged if the individual worked for a certain period of time in certain professions for any of a broad class of employers.

* * *

(g) Special rules for discharge of qualified farm indebtedness.—

(1) Discharge must be by qualified person.—

(A) In general.—Subparagraph (C) of subsection (a)(1) shall apply only if the discharge is by a qualified person.

(B) Qualified person.—For purposes of subparagraph (A), the term "qualified person" has the meaning given to such term by section 49(a)(1)(D)(iv); except that such term shall include any Federal, State, or local government or agency or instrumentality thereof.

(2) Qualified farm indebtedness.—For purposes of this section, indebtedness of a taxpayer shall be treated as qualified farm indebtedness if—

(A) such indebtedness was incurred directly in connection with the operation by the taxpayer of the trade or business of farming, and

(B) 50 percent or more of the aggregate gross receipts of the taxpayer for the 3 taxable years preceding the taxable year in which the discharge of such indebtedness occurs is attributable to the trade or business of farming.

(3) Amount excluded cannot exceed sum of tax attributes and business and investment assets.—

(A) In general.—The amount excluded under subparagraph (C) of subsection (a)(1) shall not exceed the sum of—

(i) the adjusted tax attributes of the taxpayer, and

(ii) the aggregate adjusted bases of qualified property held by the taxpayer as of the beginning of the taxable year following the taxable year in which the discharge occurs.

(B) Adjusted tax attributes.—For purposes of subparagraph (A), the term "adjusted tax attributes" means the sum of the tax attributes described in subparagraphs (A), (B), (C), (D), (F), and (G) of subsection (b)(2) determined by taking into account $3 for each $1 of the attributes described in subparagraphs (B), (C), and (G) of subsection (b)(2) and the attribute described in subparagraph (F) of subsection (b)(2) to the extent attributable to any passive activity credit carryover.

(C) Qualified property.—For purposes of this paragraph, the term "qualified property" means any property which is used or is held for use in a trade or business or for the production of income.

(D) Coordination with insolvency exclusion.—For purposes of this paragraph, the adjusted basis of any qualified property and the amount of the adjusted tax attributes shall be determined after any reduction under subsection (b) by reason of amounts excluded from gross income under subsection (a)(1)(B).

(h) Special rules relating to qualified principal residence indebtedness.—

(1) Basis reduction.—The amount excluded from gross income by reason of subsection (a)(1)(E) shall be applied to reduce (but not below zero) the basis of the principal residence of the taxpayer.

(2) Qualified principal residence indebtedness.—For purposes of this section, the term "qualified principal residence indebtedness" means acquisition indebtedness (within the meaning of section 163(h)(3)(B), applied by substituting "$2,000,000 ($1,000,000" for "$1,000,000 ($500,000" in clause (ii) thereof) with respect to the principal residence of taxpayer.

(3) Exception for certain discharges not related to taxpayer's financial conditions.—Subsection (a)(1)(E) shall not apply to the discharge of a loan if the discharge is on account of services performed for the lender or any other factor not directly related to a decline in the value of the residence or to the financial condition of the taxpayer.

(4) Ordering rules.—If any loan is discharged, in whole or in part, and only a portion of such loan is qualified principal residence indebtedness, subsection (a)(1)(E) shall apply only to so much of the amount discharged as exceeds the amount of the loan (as determined immediately before such discharge) which is not qualified principal residence indebtedness.

(5) Principal residences.—For purposes of this subsection, the term "principal residence" has the same meaning as when used in section 121.

(i) Deferral and ratable inclusion of income arising from business indebtedness discharged by the reacquisition of a debt instrument.—

(1) In general.—At the election of the taxpayer, income from the discharge of indebtedness in connection with the reacquisition after December 31, 2008, and before January 1, 2011, of an applicable debt instrument shall be includible in gross income ratably over the 5-taxable-year period beginning with—

(A) in the case of a reacquisition occurring in 2009, the fifth taxable year following the taxable year in which the reacquisition occurs, and

(B) in the case of a reacquisition occurring in 2010, the fourth taxable year following the taxable year in which the reacquisition occurs.

(2) Deferral of deduction for original issue discount in debt for debt exchanges.—

(A) In general.—If, as part of a reacquisition to which paragraph (1) applies, any debt instrument is issued for the applicable debt instrument being reacquired (or is treated as so issued under subsection (e)(4) and the regulations thereunder) and there is any original issue discount determined under subpart A of part V of subchapter P of this chapter with respect to the debt instrument so issued—

(i) except as provided in clause (ii), no deduction otherwise allowable under this chapter shall be allowed to the issuer of such debt instrument with respect to the portion of such original issue discount which—

(I) accrues before the 1st taxable year in the 5-taxable-year period in which income from the discharge of indebtedness attributable to the reacquisition of the debt instrument is includible under paragraph (1), and

(II) does not exceed the income from the discharge of indebtedness with respect to the debt instrument being reacquired, and

(ii) the aggregate amount of deductions disallowed under clause (i) shall be allowed as a deduction ratably over the 5-taxable-year period described in clause (i)(I).

If the amount of the original issue discount accruing before such 1st taxable year exceeds the income from the discharge of indebtedness with respect to the applicable debt instrument being reacquired, the deductions shall be disallowed in the order in which the original issue discount is accrued.

(B) Deemed debt for debt exchanges.—For purposes of subparagraph (A), if any debt instrument is issued by an issuer and the proceeds of such debt instrument are used directly or indirectly by the issuer to reacquire an applicable debt instrument of the issuer, the debt instrument so issued shall be treated as issued for the debt instrument being reacquired. If only a portion of the proceeds from a debt instrument are so used, the rules of subparagraph (A) shall apply to the portion of any original issue discount on the newly issued debt instrument which is equal to the portion of the proceeds from such instrument used to reacquire the outstanding instrument.

(3) Applicable debt instrument.—For purposes of this subsection—

(A) Applicable debt instrument.—The term "applicable debt instrument" means any debt instrument which was issued by—

(i) a C corporation, or

(ii) any other person in connection with the conduct of a trade or business by such person.

(B) Debt instrument.—The term "debt instrument" means a bond, debenture, note, certificate, or any other instrument or contractual arrangement constituting indebtedness (within the meaning of section 1275(a)(1)).

(4) Reacquisition.—For purposes of this subsection—

(A) In general.—The term "reacquisition" means, with respect to any applicable debt instrument, any acquisition of the debt instrument by

(i) the debtor which issued (or is otherwise the obligor under) the debt instrument, or

(ii) a related person to such debtor.

(B) Acquisition.—The term "acquisition" shall, with respect to any applicable debt instrument, include an acquisition of the debt instrument for cash, the exchange of the debt instrument for another debt instrument (including an exchange resulting from a modification of the debt instrument), the exchange of the debt instrument for corporate stock or a partnership interest, and the contribution of the debt instrument to capital. Such term shall also include the complete forgiveness of the indebtedness by the holder of the debt instrument.

(5) Other definitions and rules.—For purposes of this subsection—

(A) Related person.—The determination of whether a person is related to another person shall be made in the same manner as under subsection (e)(4).

(B) Election.—

(i) In general.—An election under this subsection with respect to any applicable debt instrument shall be made by including with the return of tax imposed by chapter 1 for the taxable year in which the reacquisition of the debt instrument occurs a statement which—

(I) clearly identifies such instrument, and

(II) includes the amount of income to which paragraph (1) applies and such other information as the Secretary may prescribe.

(ii) Election irrevocable.— Such election, once made, is irrevocable.

(iii) Pass through entities.—In the case of a partnership, S corporation, or other pass through entity, the election under this subsection shall be made by the partnership, the S corporation, or other entity involved.

(C) Coordination with other exclusions.—If a taxpayer elects to have this subsection apply to an applicable debt instrument, subparagraphs (A), (B), (C), and (D) of subsection (a)(1) shall not apply to the income from the discharge of such indebtedness for the taxable year of the election or any subsequent taxable year.

(D) Acceleration of deferred items.—

(i) In general.—In the case of the death of the taxpayer, the liquidation or sale of substantially all the assets of the taxpayer (including in a title 11 or similar case), the cessation of business by the taxpayer, or similar circumstances, any item of income or deduction which is deferred under this subsection (and has not previously been taken into account) shall be taken into account in the taxable year in which such event occurs (or in the case of a title 11 case, the day before the petition is filed).

(ii) Special rule for pass thru entities.—The rule of clause (i) shall also apply in the case of the sale or exchange or redemption of an interest in a partnership, S corporation, or other pass through entity by a partner, shareholder, or other person holding an ownership interest in such entity.

(6) Special rule for partnerships.—In the case of a partnership, any income or deduction deferred under this subsection shall be allocated to the partners in the partnership immediately before the discharge in the manner such amounts would have been included in the distributive shares of such partners under section 704 if such income were recognized at such time. Any decrease in a partner's share of partnership liabilities as a result of such discharge shall not be taken into account for purposes of section 752 at the time of the discharge to the extent it would cause the partner to recognize gain under section 731. Any decrease in partnership liabilities deferred under the preceding sentence shall be taken into account by such partner at the same time, and to the extent remaining in the same amount, as income deferred under this subsection is recognized.

(7) Secretarial authority.—The Secretary may prescribe such regulations, rules, or other guidance as may be necessary or appropriate for purposes of applying this subsection, including—

(A) extending the application of the rules of paragraph (5)(D) to other circumstances where appropriate,

(B) requiring reporting of the election (and such other information as the Secretary may require) on returns of tax for subsequent taxable years, and

(C) rules for the application of this subsection to partnerships, S corporations, and other pass-thru entities, including for the allocation of deferred deductions.

§ 109. Improvements by lessee on lessor's property

Gross income does not include income (other than rent) derived by a lessor of real property on the termination of a lease, representing the value of such property attributable to buildings erected or other improvements made by the lessee.

§ 110. Qualified lessee construction allowances for short-term leases

(a) In general.—Gross income of a lessee does not include any amount received in cash (or treated as a rent reduction) by a lessee from a lessor—

(1) under a short-term lease of retail space, and

(2) for the purpose of such lessee's constructing or improving qualified long-term real property for use in such lessee's trade or business at such retail space, but only to the extent that such amount does not exceed the amount expended by the lessee for such construction or improvement.

(b) Consistent treatment by lessor.—Qualified long-term real property constructed or improved in connection with any amount excluded from a lessee's income by reason of subsection (a) shall be treated as nonresidential real property of the lessor (including for purposes of section 168(i)(8)(B)).

(c) Definitions.—For purposes of this section—

(1) Qualified long-term real property.—The term "qualified long-term real property" means nonresidential real property which is part of, or otherwise present at, the retail space referred to in subsection (a) and which reverts to the lessor at the termination of the lease.

(2) Short-term lease.—The term "short-term lease" means a lease (or other agreement for occupancy or use) of retail space for 15 years or less (as determined under the rules of section 168 (i)(3)).

(3) Retail space.—The term "retail space" means real property leased, occupied, or otherwise used by a lessee in its trade or business of selling tangible personal property or services to the general public.

(d) Information required to be furnished to Secretary.—Under regulations, the lessee and lessor described in subsection (a) shall, at such times and in such manner as may be provided in such regulations, furnish to the Secretary—

(1) information concerning the amounts received (or treated as a rent reduction) and expended as described in subsection (a), and

(2) any other information which the Secretary deems necessary to carry out the provisions of this section.

§ 111. Recovery of tax benefit items

(a) Deductions.—Gross income does not include income attributable to the recovery during the taxable year of any amount deducted in any prior taxable year to the extent such amount did not reduce the amount of tax imposed by this chapter.

(b) Credits.—

(1) In general.—If—

(A) a credit was allowable with respect to any amount for any prior taxable year, and

(B) during the taxable year there is a downward price adjustment or similar adjustment,

the tax imposed by this chapter for the taxable year shall be increased by the amount of the credit attributable to the adjustment.

(2) Exception where credit did not reduce tax.—Paragraph (1) shall not apply to the extent that the credit allowable for the recovered amount did not reduce the amount of tax imposed by this chapter.

(3) Exception for investment tax credit and foreign tax credit.—This subsection shall not apply with respect to the credit determined under section 46 and the foreign tax credit.

(c) Treatment of carryovers.—For purposes of this section, an increase in a carryover which has not expired before the beginning of the taxable year in which the recovery or adjustment takes place shall be treated as reducing tax imposed by this chapter.

(d) Special rules for accumulated earnings tax and for personal holding company tax.—In applying subsection (a) for the purpose of determining the accumulated earnings tax under section 531 or the tax under section 541 (relating to personal holding companies)—

(1) any excluded amount under subsection (a) allowed for the purposes of this subtitle (other than section 531 or section 541) shall be allowed whether or not such amount resulted in a reduction of the tax under section 531 or the tax under section 541 for the prior taxable year; and

(2) where any excluded amount under subsection (a) was not allowable as a deduction for the prior taxable year for purposes of this subtitle other than of section 531 or section 541 but was allowable for the same taxable year under section 531 or section 541, then such excluded amount shall be allowable if it did not result in a reduction of the tax under section 531 or the tax under section 541.

§ 112. Certain combat zone compensation of members of the Armed Forces

(a) Enlisted personnel.—Gross income does not include compensation received for active service as a member below the grade of commissioned officer in the Armed Forces of the United States for any month during any part of which such member—

(1) served in a combat zone, or

(2) was hospitalized as a result of wounds, disease, or injury incurred while serving in a combat zone; but this paragraph shall not apply for any month beginning more than 2 years after the date of the termination of combatant activities in such zone.

With respect to service in the combat zone designated for purposes of the Vietnam conflict, paragraph (2) shall not apply to any month after January 1978.

(b) Commissioned officers.—Gross income does not include so much of the compensation as does not exceed the maximum enlisted amount received for active service as a commissioned officer in the Armed Forces of the United States for any month during any part of which such officer—

(1) served in a combat zone, or

(2) was hospitalized as a result of wounds, disease, or injury incurred while serving in a combat zone; but this paragraph shall not apply for any month beginning more than 2 years after the date of the termination of combatant activities in such zone.

With respect to service in the combat zone designated for purposes of the Vietnam conflict, paragraph (2) shall not apply to any month after January 1978.

(c) Definitions.—For purposes of this section—

(1) The term "commissioned officer" does not include a commissioned warrant officer.

(2) The term "combat zone" means any area which the President of the United States by Executive Order designates, for purposes of this section or corresponding provisions of prior income tax laws, as an area in which Armed Forces of the United States are or have (after June 24, 1950) engaged in combat.

(3) Service is performed in a combat zone only if performed on or after the date designated by the President by Executive Order as the date of the commencing of combatant activities in such zone, and on or before the date designated by the President by Executive Order as the date of the termination of combatant activities in such zone; except that June 25, 1950, shall be considered the date of the commencing of combatant activities in the combat zone designated in Executive order 10195.

(4) The term "compensation" does not include pensions and retirement pay.

(5) The term "maximum enlisted amount" means, for any month, the sum of—

(A) the highest rate of basic pay payable for such month to any enlisted member of the Armed Forces of the United States at the highest pay grade applicable to enlisted members, and

(B) in the case of an officer entitled to special pay under section 310 of title 37, United States Code, for such month, the amount of such special pay payable to such officer for such month.

(d) Prisoners of war, etc.—

(1) Members of the armed forces.—Gross income does not include compensation received for active service as a member of the Armed Forces of the United States for any month during any part of which such member is in a missing status (as defined in section 551(2) of title 37, United States Code) during the Vietnam conflict as a result of such conflict, other than a period with respect to which it is officially determined under section 552(c) of such title 37 that he is officially absent from his post of duty without authority.

(2) Civilian employees.—Gross income does not include compensation received for active service as an employee for any month during any part of which such employee is in a missing status during the Vietnam conflict as a result of such conflict. For purposes of this paragraph, the terms "active service," "employee," and "missing status" have the respective meanings given to such terms by section 5561 of title 5 of the United States Code.

(3) Period of conflict.—For purposes of this subsection, the Vietnam conflict began February 28, 1961, and ends on the date designated by the President by Executive order as the date of the termination of combatant activities in Vietnam. For purposes of this subsection, an individual is in a missing status as a result of the Vietnam conflict if immediately before such status began he was performing service in Vietnam or was performing service in Southeast Asia in direct support of military operations in Vietnam.

§ 115. Income of states, municipalities, etc.

Gross income does not include—

(1) income derived from any public utility or the exercise of any essential governmental function and accruing to a State or any political subdivision thereof, or the District of Columbia; or

(2) income accruing to the government of any possession of the United States, or any political subdivision thereof.

§ 117. Qualified scholarships

(a) General rule.—Gross income does not include any amount received as a qualified scholarship by an individual who is a candidate for a degree at an educational organization described in section 170(b) (1)(A)(ii).

(b) Qualified scholarship.—For purposes of this section—

(1) In general.—The term "qualified scholarship" means any amount received by an individual as a scholarship or fellowship grant to the extent the individual establishes that, in accordance with the conditions of the grant, such amount was used for qualified tuition and related expenses.

(2) Qualified tuition and related expenses.—For purposes of paragraph (1), the term "qualified tuition and related expenses" means—

(A) tuition and fees required for the enrollment or attendance of a student at an educational organization described in section 170(b) (l)(A)(ii), and

(B) fees, books, supplies, and equipment required for courses of instruction at such an educational organization.

(c) Limitation.—

(1) In general.—Except as provided in paragraph (2), subsections (a) and (d) shall not apply to that portion of any amount received which represents payment for teaching, research, or other services by the student required as a condition for receiving the qualified scholarship or qualified tuition reduction.

(2) Exceptions.—Paragraph (1) shall not apply to any amount received by an individual under—

(A) the National Health Service Corps Scholarship Program under section 338A(g)(1)(A) of the Public Health Service Act, or

(B) the Armed Forces Health Professions Scholarship and Financial Assistance program under subchapter I of chapter 105 of title 10, United States Code.

(d) Qualified tuition reduction.—

(1) In general.—Gross income shall not include any qualified tuition reduction.

(2) Qualified tuition reduction.—For purposes of this subsection, the term "qualified tuition reduction" means the amount of any reduction in tuition provided to an employee of an organization described in section 170(b)(1)(A)(ii) for the education (below the graduate level) at such organization (or another organization described in section 170(b)(1)(A)(ii)) of—

(A) such employee, or

(B) any person treated as an employee (or whose use is treated as an employee use) under the rules of section 132(h).

(3) Reduction must not discriminate in favor of highly compensated, etc.—Paragraph (1) shall apply with respect to any qualified tuition reduction provided with respect to any highly compensated employee only if such reduction is available on substantially the same terms to each member of a group of employees which is defined under a reasonable classification set up by the employer which does not discriminate in favor of highly compensated employees (within the meaning of section 414(q)).

* * *

(5) Special rules for teaching and research assistants.—In the case of the education of an individual who is a graduate student at an educational organization described in section 170(b) (l)(A)(ii) and who is engaged in teaching or research activities for such organization, paragraph (2) shall be applied as if it did not contain the phrase "(below the graduate level)."

§ 118. Contributions to the capital of a corporation

(a) General rule.—In the case of a corporation, gross income does not include any contribution to the capital of the taxpayer.

(b) Contributions in aid of construction, etc.—For purposes of subsection (a), except as provided in subsection (c), the term "contribution to the capital of the taxpayer" does not include any contribution in aid of construction or any other contribution as a customer or potential customer.

* * *

(e) Cross references.—

(1) For basis of property acquired by a corporation through a contribution to its capital, see section 362.

(2) For special rules in the case of contributions of indebtedness, see section 108(e)(6).

* * *

§ 119. Meals or lodging furnished for the convenience of the employer

(a) Meals and lodging furnished to employee, his spouse, and his dependents, pursuant to employment.—There shall be excluded from gross income of an employee the value of any meals or lodging furnished to him, his spouse, or any of his dependents by or on behalf of his employer for the convenience of the employer, but only if—

(1) in the case of meals, the meals are furnished on the business premises of the employer, or

(2) in the case of lodging, the employee is required to accept such lodging on the business premises of his employer as a condition of his employment.

(b) Special rules.—For purposes of subsection (a)—

(1) Provisions of employment contract or state statute not to be determinative.—In determining whether meals or lodging are furnished for the convenience of the employer, the provisions of an employment contract or of a State statute fixing terms of employment shall not be determinative of whether the meals or lodging are intended as compensation.

(2) Certain factors not taken into account with respect to meals.—In determining whether meals are furnished for the convenience of the employer, the fact that a charge is made for such meals, and the fact that the employee may accept or decline such meals, shall not be taken into account.

(3) Certain fixed charges for meals.—

(A) In general.—If—

(i) an employee is required to pay on a periodic basis a fixed charge for his meals, and

(ii) such meals are furnished by the employer for the convenience of the employer, there shall be excluded from the employee's gross income an amount equal to such fixed charge.

(B) Application of subparagraph (A).—Subparagraph (A) shall apply—

(i) whether the employee pays the fixed charge out of his stated compensation or out of his own funds, and

(ii) only if the employee is required to make the payment whether he accepts or declines the meals.

(4) Meals furnished to employees on business premises where meals of most employees are otherwise excludable.—All meals furnished on the business premises of an employer to such employer's employees shall be treated as furnished for the convenience of the employer if, without regard to this paragraph, more than half of the employees to whom such meals are furnished on such premises are furnished such meals for the convenience of the employer.

(c) Employees living in certain camps.—

(1) In general.—In the case of an individual who is furnished lodging in a camp located in a foreign country by or on behalf of his employer, such camp shall be considered to be part of the business premises of the employer.

(2) Camp.—For purposes of this section, a camp constitutes lodging which is—

(A) provided by or on behalf of the employer for the convenience of the employer because the place at which such individual renders services is in a remote area where satisfactory housing is not available on the open market,

(B) located, as near as practicable, in the vicinity of the place at which such individual renders services, and

(C) furnished in a common area (or enclave) which is not available to the public and which normally accommodates 10 or more employees.

(d) Lodging furnished by certain educational institutions to employees.—

(1) In general.—In the case of an employee of an educational institution, gross income shall not include the value of qualified campus lodging furnished to such employee during the taxable year.

(2) Exception in cases of inadequate rent.—Paragraph (1) shall not apply to the extent of the excess of—

(A) the lesser of—

(i) 5 percent of the appraised value of the qualified campus lodging, or

(ii) the average of the rentals paid by individuals (other than employees or students of the educational institution) during such calendar year for lodging provided by the educational institution which is comparable to the qualified campus lodging provided to the employee, over

(B) the rent paid by the employee for the qualified campus lodging during such calendar year.

The appraised value under subparagraph (A)(i) shall be determined as of the close of the calendar year in which the taxable year begins, or, in the case of a rental period not greater than 1 year, at any time during the calendar year in which such period begins.

(3) Qualified campus lodging.—For purposes of this subsection, the term "qualified campus lodging" means lodging to which subsection (a) does not apply and which is—

(A) located on, or in the proximity of, a campus of the educational institution, and

(B) furnished to the employee, his spouse, and any of his dependents by or on behalf of such institution for use as a residence.

(4) Educational institution, etc.—For purposes of this subsection—

(A) In general.—The term "educational institution" means—

(i) an institution described in section 170 (b)(1)(A)(ii) (or an entity organized under State law and composed of public institutions so described), or

(ii) an academic health center.

(B) Academic health center.—For purposes of subparagraph (A), the term "academic health center" means an entity—

(i) which is described in section 170(b) (1) (A)(iii),

(ii) which receives (during the calendar year in which the taxable year of the taxpayer begins) payments under subsection (d)(5)(B) or (h) of section 1886 of the Social Security Act (relating to graduate medical education), and

(iii) which has as one of its principal purposes or functions the providing and teaching of basic and clinical medical science and research with the entity's own faculty.

§ 121. Exclusion of gain from sale of principal residence

(a) Exclusion.—Gross income shall not include gain from the sale or exchange of property if, during the 5-year period ending on the date of the sale or exchange, such property has been owned and used by the taxpayer as the taxpayer's principal residence for periods aggregating 2 years or more.

(b) Limitations.—

(1) In general.—The amount of gain excluded from gross income under subsection (a) with respect to any sale or exchange shall not exceed $250,000.

(2) Special rules for joint returns.—In the case of a husband and wife who make a joint return for the taxable year of the sale or exchange of the property—

(A) $500,000 limitation for certain joint returns.—Paragraph (1) shall be applied by substituting "$500,000" for "$250,000" if—

(i) either spouse meets the ownership requirements of subsection (a) with respect to such property,

(ii) both spouses meet the use requirements of subsection (a) with respect to such property, and

(iii) neither spouse is ineligible for the benefits of subsection (a) with respect to such property by reason of paragraph (3).

(B) Other joint returns.—If such spouses do not meet the requirements of subparagraph (A), the limitation under paragraph (1) shall be the sum of the limitations under paragraph (1) to which each spouse would be entitled if such spouses had not been married. For purposes of the preceding sentence, each spouse shall be treated as owning the property during the period that either spouse owned the property.

(3) Application to only 1 sale or exchange every 2 years.—

(A) In general.—Subsection (a) shall not apply to any sale or exchange by the taxpayer if, during the 2-year period ending on the date of such sale or exchange, there was any other sale or exchange by the taxpayer to which subsection (a) applied.

(B) Pre-May 7, 1997, sales not taken into account.—Subparagraph(A) shall be applied without regard to any sale or exchange before May 7, 1997.

(4) Special rule for certain sales by surviving spouses.—In the case of a sale or exchange of property by an unmarried individual whose spouse is deceased on the date of such sale, paragraph (1) shall be applied by substituting "$500,000" for "$250,000" if such sale occurs not later than 2 years after the date of death of such spouse and the requirements of paragraph (2)(A) were met immediately before such date of death.

(5) Exclusion of gain allocated to nonqualified use.—

(A) In general.—Subsection (a) shall not apply to so much of the gain from the sale or exchange of property as is allocated to periods of nonqualified use.

(B) Gain allocated to periods of nonqualified use.—For purposes of subparagraph (A), gain shall be allocated to periods of nonqualified use based on the ratio which—

(i) the aggregate periods of nonqualified use during the period such property was owned by the taxpayer, bears to

(ii) the period such property was owned by the taxpayer.

(C) Period of nonqualified use.—For purposed of this paragraph—

(i) In general.—The term "period of nonqualified use" means any period (other than the portion of any period preceding January 1, 2009) during which the property is not used as the principal residence of the taxpayer or the taxpayer's spouse or former spouse.

(ii) Exceptions.—The term "period of nonqualified use" does not include—

(I) any portion of the 5-year period described in subsection (a) which is after the last date that such property is used as the principal residence of the taxpayer or the taxpayer's spouse,

(II) any period (not to exceed an aggregate period of 10 years) during which the taxpayer or the taxpayer's spouse is serving on qualified official extended duty (as defined subsection (d)(9)(C)) described in clause (i), (ii), or (iii) of subsection (d)(9)(A), and

(III) any other period of temporary absence (not to exceed an aggregate period of 2 years) due to change of employment, health conditions, or such other unforeseen circumstances as may be specified by the Secretary.

(D) Coordination with recognition of gain attributable to depreciation.— For purpose of this paragraph—

(i) subparagraph (A) shall be applied after the application of subsection (d)(6), and

(ii) subparagraph (B) shall be applied without regard to any gain to which subsection (d)(6) applies.

(c) Exclusion for taxpayers failing to meet certain requirements.—

(1) In general.—In the case of a sale or exchange to which this subsection applies, the ownership and use requirements of subsection (a) and subsection (b)(3) shall not apply; but the dollar limitation under paragraph (1) or (2) of subsection (b), whichever is applicable, shall be equal to—

(A) the amount which bears the same ratio to such limitation (determined without regard to this paragraph) as

(B)(i) the shorter of—

(I) the aggregate periods, during the 5-year period ending on the date of such sale or exchange, such property has been owned and used by the taxpayer as the taxpayer's principal residence, or

(II) the period after the date of the most recent prior sale or exchange by the taxpayer to which subsection (a) applied and before the date of such sale or exchange, bears to

(ii) 2 years.

(2) Sales and exchanges to which subsection applies.—This subsection shall apply to any sale or exchange if—

(A) subsection (a) would not (but for this subsection) apply to such sale or exchange by reason of—

(i) a failure to meet the ownership and use requirements of subsection (a), or

(ii) subsection (b)(3), and

(B) such sale or exchange is by reason of a change in place of employment, health, or, to the extent provided in regulations, unforeseen circumstances.

(d) Special rules.—

(1) Joint returns.—If a husband and wife make a joint return for the taxable year of the sale or exchange of the property, subsections (a) and (c) shall apply if either spouse meets the ownership and use requirements of subsection (a) with respect to such property.

(2) Property of deceased spouse.—For purposes of this section, in the case of an unmarried individual whose spouse is deceased on the date of the sale or exchange of property, the period such unmarried individual owned and used such property shall include the period such deceased spouse owned and used such property before death.

(3) Property by spouse or former spouse.—For purposes of this section—

(A) Property transferred to individual from spouse or former spouse.—In the case of an individual holding property transferred to such individual in a transaction described in section 1041(a), the period such individual owns such property shall include the period the transferor owned the property.

(B) Property used by former spouse pursuant to divorce decree, etc.—Solely for purposes of this section, an individual shall be treated as using property as such individual's principal residence during any period of ownership while such individual's spouse or former spouse is granted use of the property under a divorce or separation instrument (as defined in section 71(b)(2)).

(4) Tenant-stockholder in cooperative housing corporation.—For purposes of this section, if the taxpayer holds stock as a tenant-stockholder (as defined in section 216) in a cooperative housing corporation (as defined in such section), then—

(A) the holding requirements of subsection (a) shall be applied to the holding of such stock, and

(B) the use requirements of subsection (a) shall be applied to the house or apartment which the taxpayer was entitled to occupy as such stockholder.

(5) Involuntary conversions.—

(A) In general.—For purposes of this section, the destruction, theft, seizure, requisition, or condemnation of property shall be treated as the sale of such property.

(B) Application of section 1033.—In applying section 1033 (relating to involuntary conversions), the amount realized from the sale or exchange of property shall be treated as being the amount determined without regard to this section, reduced by the amount of gain not included in gross income pursuant to this section.

(C) Property acquired after involuntary conversion.—If the basis of the property sold or exchanged is determined (in whole or in part) under section 1033(b) (relating to basis of property acquired through involuntary conversion), then the holding and use by the taxpayer of the converted property shall be treated as holding and use by the taxpayer of the property sold or exchanged.

(6) Recognition of gain attributable to depreciation.—Subsection (a) shall not apply to so much of the gain from the sale of any property as does not exceed the portion of the depreciation adjustments (as defined in section 1250(b)(3)) attributable to periods after May 6, 1997, in respect of such property.

(7) Determination of use during periods of out-of-residence care.—In the case of a taxpayer who—

(A) becomes physically or mentally incapable of self-care, and

(B) owns property and uses such property as the taxpayer's principal residence during the 5-year period described in subsection (a) for periods aggregating at least 1 year, then the taxpayer shall be treated as using such property as the taxpayer's principal residence during any time during such 5-year period in which the taxpayer owns the property and resides in any facility (including a nursing home) licensed by a State or political subdivision to care for an individual in the taxpayer's condition.

(8) Sales of remainder interests.—For purposes of this section—

(A) In general.—At the election of the taxpayer, this section shall not fail to apply to the sale or exchange of an interest in a principal residence by reason of such interest being a remainder interest in such residence, but this section shall not apply to any other interest in such residence which is sold or exchanged separately.

(B) Exception for sales to related parties.—Subparagraph (A) shall not apply to any sale to, or exchange with, any person who bears a relationship to the taxpayer which is described in section 267(b) or 707(b).

(9) Uniformed services, foreign service, and intelligence community.—

(A) In general.—At the election of an individual with respect to a property, the running of the 5-year period described in subsections (a) and (c)(1)(B) and paragraph (7) of this subsection with respect to such property shall be suspended during any period that such individual or such individual's spouse is serving on qualified official extended duty—

(i) as a member of the uniformed services,

(ii) as a member of the Foreign Service of the United States, or

(iii) as an employee by the intelligence community.

(B) Maximum period of suspension.—The 5-year period described in subsection (a) shall not be extended more than 10 years by reason of subparagraph (A).

(C) Qualified official extended duty.—For purposes of this paragraph—

(i) In general.—The term "qualified official extended duty" means any extended duty while serving at a duty station which is at least 50 miles from such property or while residing under Government orders in Government quarters.

(ii) Uniformed services.—The term "uniformed services" has the meaning given such term by section 101(a)(5) of title 10, United States Code, as in effect on the date of the enactment of this paragraph.

(iii) Foreign Service of the United States.—The term "member of the Foreign Service of the United States" has the meaning given the term "member of the Service" by paragraph (1), (2), (3), (4), or (5) of section 103 of the Foreign Service Act of 1980, as in effect on the date of the enactment of this paragraph.

(iv) Employee of intelligence community.—The term "employee of the intelligence community" means an employee (as defined by section 2105 of title 5, United States Code) of—

(I) the Office of the Director of National Intelligence,

(II) the Central Intelligence Agency,

(III) the National Security Agency,

(IV) the Defense Intelligence Agency,

(V) the National Geospatial-Intelligence Agency,

(VI) the National Reconnaissance Office,

(VII) any other office within the Department of Defense for the collection of specialized national intelligence through reconnaissance programs,

(VIII) any of the intelligence elements of the Army, the Navy, the Air Force, the Marine Corps, the Federal Bureau of Investigation, the Department of Treasury, the Department of Energy, and the Coast Guard,

(IX) the Bureau of Intelligence and Research of the Department of State, or

(X) any of the elements of the Department of Homeland Security concerned with the analyses of foreign intelligence information.

(v) **Extended duty.**—The term "extended duty" means any period of active duty pursuant to a call or order to such duty for a period in excess of 90 days or for an indefinite period.

(D) Special rules relating to election.—

(i) Election limited to 1 property at a time.—An election under subparagraph (A) with respect to any property may not be made if such an election is in effect with respect to any other property.

(ii) Revocation of election.—An election under subparagraph (A) may be revoked at any time.

(10) Property acquired in like-kind exchange.—If a taxpayer acquires property in an exchange with respect to which gain is not recognized (in whole or in part) to the taxpayer under subsection (a) or (b) of section 1031, subsection (a) shall not apply to the sale or exchange of such property by such taxpayer (or by any person whose basis in such property is determined, in whole or in part, by reference to the basis in the hands of such taxpayer) during the 5-year period beginning with the date of such acquisition.

*__(11) Property acquired from a decedent.__—The exclusion under this section shall apply to property sold by—

(A) the estate of a decedent,

(B) any individual who acquired such property from the decedent (within the meaning of section 1022), and

(C) a trust which, immediately before the death of the decedent, was a qualified revocable trust (as defined in section 645(b)(1)) established by the decedent,

determined by taking into account the ownership and use by the decedent.

(12) Peace corps.—

(A) In general.—At the election of an individual with respect to a property, the running of the 5-year period described in subsections (a) and (c)(1)(B) and paragraph (7) of this subsection with respect to such property shall be suspended during any period that such individual or such individual's spouse is serving outside the United States—

(i) on qualified official extended duty (as defined in paragraph (9)(C)) as an employee of the Peace Corps, or

(ii) as an enrolled volunteer or volunteer leader under section 5 or 6 (as the case may be) of the Peace Corps Act (22 U.S.C. 2504, 2505).

(B) Applicable rules.—For purposes of subparagraph (A), rules similar to the rules of subparagraphs (B) and (D) shall apply.

(e) Denial of exclusion for expatriates.—This section shall not apply to any sale or exchange by an individual if the treatment provided by section 877 (a)(1) applies to such individual.

(f) Election to have section not apply.—This section shall not apply to any sale or exchange with respect to which the taxpayer elects not to have this section apply.

(g) Residences acquired in rollovers under section 1034.—For purposes of this section, in the case of property the acquisition of which by the taxpayer resulted under section 1034 (as in effect on the day before the date of the enactment of this section) in the nonrecognition of any part of the gain realized on the sale or exchange of another residence,

*Editorial comment: The Tax Relief Act of 2010 in effect retroactively repeals section 121(d)(11).

in determining the period for which the taxpayer has owned and used such property as the taxpayer's principal residence, there shall be included the aggregate periods for which such other residence (and each prior residence taken into account under section 1223(6) in determining the holding period of such property) had been so owned and used.

* * *

§ 123. Amounts received under insurance contracts for certain living expenses

(a) General rule.—In the case of an individual whose principal residence is damaged or destroyed by fire, storm, or other casualty, or who is denied access to his principal residence by governmental authorities because of the occurrence or threat of occurrence of such a casualty, gross income does not include amounts received by such individual under an insurance contract which are paid to compensate or reimburse such individual for living expenses incurred for himself and members of his household resulting from the loss of use or occupancy of such residence.

(b) Limitation.—Subsection (a) shall apply to amounts received by the taxpayer for living expenses incurred during any period only to the extent the amounts received do not exceed the amount by which—

(1) the actual living expenses incurred during such period for himself and members of his household resulting from the loss of use or occupancy of their residence, exceed

(2) the normal living expenses which would have been incurred for himself and members of his household during such period.

§ 125. Cafeteria plans

(a) General rule.—Except as provided in subsection (b), no amount shall be included in the gross income of a participant in a cafeteria plan solely because, under the plan, the participant may choose among the benefits of the plan.

(b) Exception for highly compensated participants and key employees.—

(1) Highly compensated participants.—In the case of a highly compensated participant, subsection (a) shall not apply to any benefit attributable to a plan year for which the plan discriminates in favor of—

(A) highly compensated individuals as to eligibility to participate, or

(B) highly compensated participants as to contributions and benefits.

(2) Key employees.—In the case of a key employee (within the meaning of section 416(i)(1)), subsection (a) shall not apply to any benefit attributable to a plan year for which the statutory non-taxable benefits provided to key employees exceed 25 percent of the aggregate of such benefits provided for all employees under the plan. For purposes of the preceding sentence, statutory non-taxable benefits shall be determined without regard to the second sentence of subsection (f).

(3) Year of inclusion.—For purposes of determining the taxable year of inclusion, any benefit described in paragraph (1) or (2) shall be treated as received or accrued in the taxable year of the participant or key employee in which the plan year ends.

(c) Discrimination as to benefits or contributions.—For purposes of subparagraph (B) of subsection (b)(1), a cafeteria plan does not discriminate where qualified benefits and total benefits (or employer contributions allocable to statutory non-taxable benefits and employer contributions for total benefits) do not discriminate in favor of highly compensated participants.

(d) Cafeteria plan defined.—For purposes of this section—

(1) In general.—The term "cafeteria plan" means a written plan under which—

(A) all participants are employees, and

(B) the participants may choose among 2 or more benefits consisting of cash and qualified benefits.

(2) Deferred compensation plans excluded.—

(A) In general.—The term "cafeteria plan" does not include any plan which provides for deferred compensation.

(B) Exception for cash and deferred arrangements.—Subparagraph (A) shall not apply to a profit-sharing or stock bonus plan or rural electric cooperative (within the meaning of section 401(k)(7)) which includes a qualified cash or deferred arrangement (as defined in section 401(k)(2)) to the extent of amounts which a covered employee may elect to have the employer pay as contributions to a trust under such plan on behalf of the employee.

(C) Exception for certain plans maintained by educational institutions.—Subparagraph (A) shall not apply to a plan maintained by an educational organization described in section 170(b)(1)(A)(ii) to the extent of amounts which a covered employee may elect to have the employer pay as contributions for post-retirement group life insurance if—

(i) all contributions for such insurance must be made before retirement, and

(ii) such life insurance does not have a cash surrender value at any time.

For purposes of section 79, any life insurance described in the preceding sentence shall be treated as group-term life insurance.

(D) Exception for health savings accounts.—Subparagraph (A) shall not apply to a plan to the extent of amounts which a covered employee may elect to have the employer pay as contributions to a health savings account established on behalf of the employee.

(e) Highly compensated participant and individual defined.—For purposes of this section—

(1) Highly compensated participant.—The term "highly compensated participant" means a participant who is—

(A) an officer,

(B) a shareholder owning more than 5 percent of the voting power or value of all classes of stock of the employer,

(C) highly compensated, or

(D) a spouse or dependent (within the meaning of section 152, determined without regard to subsections (b)(1), (b)(2), and (d)(1)(B) thereof) of an individual described in subparagraph (A), (B), or (C).

(2) Highly compensated individual.—The term "highly compensated individual" means an individual who is described in subparagraph (A), (B), (C), or (D) of paragraph (1).

Section 125(f) is amended by the Patient Protection and Affordable Care Act of 2010 effective for tax years beginning after 12/31/2013.

(f) Qualified benefits defined.—For purposes of this section, the term "qualified benefit" means any benefit which, with the application of subsection (a), is not includible in the gross income of the employee by reason of an express provision of this chapter (other than section 106(b), 117, 127, or 132). Such term includes any group term life insurance which is includible in gross income only because it exceeds the dollar limitation of section 79 and such term includes any other benefit permitted under regulations. Such term shall not include any product which is advertised, marketed, or offered as long-term care insurance.

(g) Special rules.—

(1) Collectively bargained plan not considered discriminatory.—For purposes of this section, a plan shall not be treated as discriminatory if the plan is maintained under an agreement which the Secretary finds to be a collective bargaining agreement between employee representatives and one or more employers.

(2) Health benefits.—For purposes of subparagraph (B) of subsection (b)(1), a cafeteria plan which provides health benefits shall not be treated as discriminatory if—

(A) contributions under the plan on behalf of each participant include an amount which—

(i) equals 100 percent of the cost of the health benefit coverage under the plan of the majority of the highly compensated participants similarly situated, or

(ii) equals or exceeds 75 percent of the cost of the health benefit coverage of the participant (similarly situated) having the highest cost health benefit coverage under the plan, and

(B) contributions or benefits under the plan in excess of those described in subparagraph (A) bear a uniform relationship to compensation.

(3) Certain participation eligibility rules not treated as discriminatory.—For purposes of subparagraph (A) of subsection (b)(1), a classification shall not be treated as discriminatory if the plan—

(A) benefits a group of employees described in section 410(b)(2)(A)(i), and

(B) meets the requirements of clauses (i) and (ii):

(i) No employee is required to complete more than 3 years of employment with the employer or employers maintaining the plan as a condition of participation in the plan, and the employment requirement for each employee is the same.

(ii) Any employee who has satisfied the employment requirement of clause (i) and who is otherwise entitled to participate in the plan commences participation no later than the first day of the first plan year beginning after the date the employment requirement was satisfied unless the employee was separated from service before the first day of that plan year.

(4) Certain controlled groups, etc.—All employees who are treated as employed by a single employer under subsection (b), (c), or (m) of section 414 shall be treated as employed by a single employer for purposes of this section.

(h) Special rule for unused benefits in health flexible spending arrangements of individuals called to active duty.—

(1) In general.—For purposes of this title, a plan or other arrangement shall not fail to be treated as a cafeteria plan or health flexible spending arrangement merely because such arrangement provides for qualified reservist distributions.

(2) Qualified reservist distribution.—For purposes of this subsection, the term "qualified reservist distribution" means, any distribution to an individual of all or a portion of the balance in the employee's account under such arrangement if—

(A) such individual was (by reason of being a member of a reserve component (as defined in section 101 of title 37, United States Code)) ordered or called to active duty for a period in excess of 179 days or for an indefinite period, and

(B) such distribution is made during the period beginning on the date of such order or call and ending on the last date that reimbursements could otherwise be made under such arrangement for the plan year which includes the date of such order or call.

(i) Limitation on health flexible spending arrangements.—

(1) In general.—For purposes of this section, if a benefit is provided under a cafeteria plan through employer contributions to a health flexible spending arrangement, such benefit shall not be treated as a qualified benefit unless the cafeteria plan provides that an employee may not elect for any taxable year to have salary reduction contributions in excess of $2,500 made to such arrangement.

(2) Adjustment for inflation.—In the case of any taxable year beginning after December 31, 2013, the dollar amount in paragraph (1) shall be increased by an amount equal to—

(A) such amount, multiplied by

(B) the cost-of-living adjustment determined under section 1(f)(3) for the calendar year in which such taxable year begins by substituting "calendar year 2012" for "calendar year 1992" in subparagraph (B) thereof.

If any increase determined under this paragraph is not a multiple of $50, such increase shall be rounded to the next lowest multiple of $50.

(j) Simple cafeteria plan for small businesses.—

(1) In general.—An eligible employer maintaining a simple cafeteria plan with respect to which the requirements of this subsection are met for any year shall be treated as meeting any applicable nondiscrimination requirement during such year.

(2) Simple cafeteria plan.—For purposes of this subsection, the term "simple cafeteria plan" means a cafeteria plan—

(A) which is established and maintained by an eligible employer, and

(B) with respect to which the contribution requirements of paragraph (3), and the eligibility and participation requirements of paragraph (4), are met.

(3) Contribution requirements.—

(A) In general.—The requirements of this paragraph are met if, under the plan the employer is required, without regard to whether a qualified employee makes any salary reduction contribution, to make a contribution to provide qualified benefits under the plan on behalf of each qualified employee in an amount equal to—

(i) a uniform percentage (not less than 2 percent) of the employee's compensation for the plan year, or

(ii) an amount which is not less than the lesser of

(I) 6 percent of the employee's compensation for the plan year, or

(II) twice the amount of the salary reduction contributions of each qualified employee.

(B) Matching contribution on behalf of highly compensated and key employees.—The requirements of subparagraph (A)(ii) shall not be treated as met if, under the plan, the rate of contributions with respect to any salary reduction contribution of a highly compensated or key employee at any rate of contribution is greater than that with respect to an employee who is not a highly compensated or key employee.

(C) Additional contributions.—Subject to subparagraph (B), nothing in this paragraph shall be treated as prohibiting an employer from making contributions to provide qualified benefits under the plan in addition to contributions required under subparagraph (A).

(D) Definitions.—For purposes of this paragraph—

(i) Salary reduction contribution.—The term "salary reduction contribution" means, with respect to a cafeteria plan, any amount which is contributed to the plan at the election of the employee and which is not includible in gross income by reason of this section.

(ii) Qualified employee.—The term "qualified employee" means, with respect to a cafeteria plan, any employee who is not a highly compensated or key employee and who is eligible to participate in the plan.

(iii) Highly compensated.—The term "highly compensated employee" has the meaning given such term by section 414(q).

(iv) Key employee.—The term "key employee" has the meaning given such term by section 416(i).

(4) Minimum eligibility and participation requirements.—

(A) In general.—The requirements of this paragraph shall be treated as met with respect to any year if, under the plan—

(i) all employees who had at least 1,000 hours of service for the preceding plan year are eligible to participate, and

(ii) each employee eligible to participate in the plan may, subject to terms and conditions applicable to all participants, elect any benefit available under the plan.

(B) Certain employees may be excluded.—For purposes of subparagraph (A)(i), an employer may elect to exclude under the plan employees—

(i) who have not attained the age of 21 before the close of a plan year,

(ii) who have less than 1 year of service with the employer as of any day during the plan year,

(iii) who are covered under an agreement which the Secretary of Labor finds to be a collective bargaining agreement if there is evidence that the benefits covered under the cafeteria plan were the subject of good faith bargaining between employee representatives and the employer, or

(iv) who are described in section 410(b)(3)(C) (relating to nonresident aliens working outside the United States). A plan may provide a shorter period of service or younger age for purposes of clause (i) or (ii).

(5) Eligible employer.—For purposes of this subsection—

(A) In general.—The term "eligible employer" means, with respect to any year, any employer if such employer employed an average of 100 of fewer employees on business days during either of the 2 preceding years. For purposes of this subparagraph, a year may only be taken into account if the employer was in existence throughout the year.

(B) Employer not in existence during the preceding year.—If an employer was not in existence throughout the preceding year, the determination under subparagraph (A) shall be based on the average number of employees that it is reasonably expected such employer will employ on business days in the current year.

(C) Growing employers retain treatment as small employer.—

(i) In general.—If—

(I) an employer was an eligible employer for any year (a "qualified year"), and

(II) such employer establishes a simple cafeteria plan for its employees for such year, then, notwithstanding the fact the employer fails to meet the requirements of subparagraph (A) for any subsequent year, such employer shall be treated as an eligible employer for such subsequent year with respect to employees (whether or not employees during a qualified year) of any trade or business which was covered by the plan during any qualified year.

(ii) Exception.—This subparagraph shall cease to apply if the employer employs an average of 200 or more employees on business days during any year preceding any such subsequent year.

(D) Special rules.—

(i) Predecessors.—Any reference in this paragraph to an employer shall include a reference to any predecessor of such employer.

(ii) Aggregation rules.—All persons treated as a single employer under subsection (a) or (b) of section 52, or subsection (n) or (o) of section 414, shall be treated as one person.

(6) Applicable nondiscrimination requirement.—For purposes of this subsection, the term "applicable nondiscrimation requirement" means any requirement under subsection (b) of this section, section 79(d), section 105(h), or paragraph (2), (3), (4), or (8) of section 129(d).

(7) Compensation.—The term "compensation" has the meaning given such term by section 414(s).

(k) Cross reference.—For reporting and recordkeeping requirements, see section 6039D.

(l) Regulations.—The Secretary shall prescribe such regulations as may be necessary to carry out the provisions of this section.

* * *

§ 127. Educational assistance programs

(a) Exclusion from gross income.—

(1) In general.—Gross income of an employee does not include amounts paid or expenses incurred by the employer for educational assistance to the employee if the assistance is furnished pursuant to a program which is described in subsection (b).

(2) $5,250 maximum exclusion.—If, but for this paragraph, this section would exclude from gross income more than $5,250 of educational assistance furnished to an individual during a calendar year, this section shall apply only to the first $5,250 of such assistance so furnished.

(b) Educational assistance program.—

(1) In general.—For purposes of this section an educational assistance program is a separate written plan of an employer for the exclusive benefit of his employees to provide such employees with educational assistance. The program must meet the requirements of paragraphs (2) through (6) of this subsection.

(2) Eligibility.—The program shall benefit employees who qualify under a classification set up by the employer and found by the Secretary not to be discriminatory in favor of employees who are highly compensated employees (within the meaning of section 414(q)) or their dependents. For purposes of this paragraph, there shall be excluded from consideration employees not included in the program who are included in a unit of employees covered by an agreement which the Secretary of Labor finds to be a collective bargaining agreement between employee representatives and one or more employers, if there is evidence that educational assistance benefits were the subject of good faith bargaining between such employee representatives and such employer or employers.

(3) Principal shareholders or owners.—Not more than 5 percent of the amounts paid or incurred by the employer for educational assistance during the year may be provided for the class of individuals who are shareholders or owners (or their spouses or dependents), each of whom (on any day of the year) owns more than 5 percent of the stock or of the capital or profits interest in the employer.

(4) Other benefits as an alternative.—A program must not provide eligible employees with a choice between educational assistance and other remuneration includible in gross income. For purposes of this section, the business practices of the employer (as well as the written program) will be taken into account.

(5) No funding required.—A program referred to in paragraph (1) is not required to be funded.

(6) Notification of employees.—Reasonable notification of the availability and terms of the program must be provided to eligible employees.

(c) Definitions; special rules.—For purposes of this section—

(1) Educational assistance.—The term "educational assistance" means—

(A) the payment, by an employer, of expenses incurred by or on behalf of an employee for education of the employee (including, but not limited to, tuition, fees, and similar payments, books, supplies, and equipment), and

(B) the provision, by an employer, of courses of instruction for such employee (including books, supplies, and equipment),

but does not include payment for, or the provision of, tools or supplies which may be retained by the employee after completion of a course of instruction, or meals, lodging, or transportation. The term "educational assistance" also does not include any payment for, or the provision of any benefits with respect to, any course or other education involving sports, games, or hobbies.

(2) Employee.—The term "employee" includes, for any year, an individual who is an employee within the meaning of section 401(c)(1) (relating to self-employed individuals).

(3) Employer.—An individual who owns the entire interest in an unincorporated trade or business shall be treated as his own employer. A partnership shall be treated as the employer of each partner who is an employee within the meaning of paragraph (2).

(4) Attribution rules.—

(A) Ownership of stock.—Ownership of stock in a corporation shall be determined in accordance with the rules provided under subsections (d) and (e) of section 1563 (without regard to section 1563(e)(3)(C)).

(B) Interest in unincorporated trade or business.—The interest of an employee in a trade or business which is not incorporated shall be determined in accordance with regulations prescribed by the Secretary, which shall be based on principles similar to the principles which apply in the case of subparagraph (A).

(5) Certain tests not applicable.—An educational assistance program shall not be held or considered to fail to meet any requirements of subsection (b) merely because—

(A) of utilization rates for the different types of educational assistance made available under the program; or

(B) successful completion, or attaining a particular course grade, is required for or considered in determining reimbursement under the program.

(6) Relationship to current law.—This section shall not be construed to affect the deduction or inclusion in income of amounts (not within the exclusion under this section) which are paid or incurred, or received as reimbursement, for educational expenses under section 117, 162 or 212.

(7) Disallowance of excluded amounts as credit or deduction.—No deduction or credit shall be allowed to the employee under any other section of this chapter for any amount excluded from income by reason of this section.

* * *

§ 129. Dependent care assistance programs

(a) Exclusion.—

(1) In general.—Gross income of an employee does not include amounts paid or incurred by the employer for dependent care assistance provided to such employee if the assistance is furnished pursuant to a program which is described in subsection (d).

(2) Limitation of exclusion.—

(A) In general.—The amount which may be excluded under paragraph (1) for dependent care assistance with respect to dependent care services provided during a taxable year shall not exceed $5,000 ($2,500 in the case of a separate return by a married individual).

(B) Year of inclusion.—The amount of any excess under subparagraph (A) shall be included in gross income in the taxable year in which the dependent care services were provided (even if payment of dependent care assistance for such services occurs in a subsequent taxable year).

(C) Marital status.—For purposes of this paragraph, marital status shall be determined under the rules of paragraphs (3) and (4) of section 21(e).

(b) Earned income limitation.—

(1) In general.—The amount excluded from the income of an employee under subsection (a) for any taxable year shall not exceed—

(A) in the case of an employee who is not married at the close of such taxable year, the earned income of such employee for such taxable year, or

(B) in the case of an employee who is married at the close of such taxable year, the lesser of—

(i) the earned income of such employee for such taxable year, or

(ii) the earned income of the spouse of such employee for such taxable year.

(2) Special rule for certain spouses.—For purposes of paragraph (1), the provisions of section 21(d)(2) shall apply in determining the earned income of a spouse who is a student or incapable of caring for himself.

(c) Payments to related individuals.—No amount paid or incurred during the taxable year of an employee by an employer in providing dependent care assistance to such employee shall be excluded under subsection (a) if such amount was paid or incurred to an individual—

(1) with respect to whom, for such taxable year, a deduction is allowable under section 151(c) (relating to personal exemptions for dependents) to such employee or the spouse of such employee, or

(2) who is a child of such employee (within the meaning of section 152(f)(1)) under the age of 19 at the close of such taxable year.

(d) Dependent care assistance program.—

(1) In general.—For purposes of this section a dependent care assistance program is a separate written plan of an employer for the exclusive benefit of his employees to provide such employees with dependent care assistance which meets the requirements of paragraphs (2) through (8) of this subsection. If any plan would qualify as a dependent care assistance program but for a failure to meet the requirements of this subsection, then, notwithstanding such failure, such plan shall be treated as a dependent care assistance program in the case of employees who are not highly compensated employees.

(2) Discrimination.—The contributions or benefits provided under the plan shall not discriminate in favor of employees who are highly compensated employees (within the meaning of section 414(q)), or their dependents.

(3) Eligibility.—The program shall benefit employees who qualify under a classification set up by the employer and found by the Secretary not to be discriminatory in favor of employees described in paragraph (2), or their dependents.

(4) Principal shareholders or owners.—Not more than 25 percent of the amounts paid or incurred by the employer for dependent care assistance during the year may be provided for the class of individuals who are shareholders or owners (or their spouses or dependents), each of whom (on any day of the year) owns more than 5 percent of the stock or of the capital or profits interest in the employer.

(5) No funding required.—A program referred to in paragraph (1) is not required to be funded.

(6) Notification of eligible employees.—Reasonable notification of the availability and terms of the program shall be provided to eligible employees.

(7) Statement of expenses.—The plan shall furnish to an employee, on or before January 31, a written statement showing the amounts paid or expenses incurred by the employer in providing dependent care assistance to such employee during the previous calendar year.

(8) Benefits.—

(A) In general.—A plan meets the requirements of this paragraph if the average benefits provided to employees who are not highly compensated employees under all plans of the employer is at least 55 percent of the average benefits provided to highly compensated employees under all plans of the employer.

(B) Salary reduction agreements.—For purposes of subparagraph (A), in the case of any benefits provided through a salary reduction agreement, a plan may disregard any employees whose compensation is less than $25,000. For purposes of this subparagraph, the term "compensation" has the meaning given such term by section 414(q)(4), except that, under rules prescribed by the Secretary, an employer may elect to determine compensation on any other basis which does not discriminate in favor of highly compensated employees.

(9) Excluded employees.—For purposes of paragraphs (3) and (8), there shall be excluded from consideration—

(A) subject to rules similar to the rules of section 410(b)(4), employees who have not attained the age of 21 and completed 1 year of service (as defined in section 410(a)(3)), and

(B) employees not included in a dependent care assistance program who are included in a unit of employees covered by an agreement which the Secretary finds to be a collective bargaining agreement between employee representatives and 1 or more employees, if there is evidence that dependent care benefits were the subject of good faith bargaining between such employee representatives and such employer or employers.

(e) Definitions and special rules.—For purposes of this section—

(1) Dependent care assistance.—The term "dependent care assistance" means the payment of, or provision of, those services which if paid for by the employee would be considered employment-related expenses under section 21(b)(2) (relating to expenses for household and dependent care services necessary for gainful employment).

(2) Earned income.—The term "earned income" shall have the meaning given such term in section 32(c)(2), but such term shall not include any amounts paid or incurred by an employer for dependent care assistance to an employee.

(3) Employee.—The term "employee" includes, for any year, an individual who is an employee within the meaning of section 401(c)(1) (relating to self-employed individuals).

(4) Employer.—An individual who owns the entire interest in an unincorporated trade or business shall be treated as his own employer. A partnership shall be treated as the employer of each partner who is an employee within the meaning of paragraph (3).

(5) Attribution rules.—

(A) Ownership of stock.—Ownership of stock in a corporation shall be determined in accordance with the rules provided under subsections (d) and (e) of section 1563 (without regard to section 1563(e)(3)(C)).

(B) Interest in unincorporated trade or business.—The interest of an employee in a trade or business which is not incorporated shall be determined in accordance with regulations prescribed by the Secretary, which shall be based on principles similar to the principles which apply in the case of subparagraph (A).

(6) Utilization test not applicable.—A dependent care assistance program shall not be held or considered to fail to meet any requirements of subsection (d) (other than paragraphs (4) and (8) thereof) merely because of utilization rates for the different types of assistance made available under the program.

(7) Disallowance of excluded amounts as credit or deduction.—No deduction or credit shall be allowed to the employee under any other section of this chapter for any amount excluded from the gross income of the employee by reason of this section.

(8) Treatment of onsite facilities.—In the case of an onsite facility maintained by an employer, except to the extent provided in regulations, the amount of dependent care assistance excluded with respect to any dependent shall be based on—

(A) utilization of the facility by a dependent of the employee, and

(B) the value of the services provided with respect to such dependent.

* * *

§ 132. Certain fringe benefits

(a) Exclusion from gross income.—Gross income shall not include any fringe benefit which qualifies as a—

(1) no-additional-cost service,

(2) qualified employee discount,

(3) working condition fringe,

(4) de minimis fringe,

(5) qualified transportation fringe,

(6) qualified moving expense reimbursement,

(7) qualified retirement planning services, or

(8) qualified military base realignment and closure fringe.

(b) No-additional-cost service defined.—For purposes of this section, the term "no-additional-cost service" means any service provided by an employer to an employee for use by such employee if—

(1) such service is offered for sale to customers in the ordinary course of the line of business of the employer in which the employee is performing services, and

(2) the employer incurs no substantial additional cost (including forgone revenue) in providing such service to the employee (determined without regard to any amount paid by the employee for such service).

(c) Qualified employee discount defined.—For purposes of this section—

(1) Qualified employee discount.—The term "qualified employee discount" means any employee discount with respect to qualified property or services to the extent such discount does not exceed—

(A) in the case of property, the gross profit percentage of the price at which the property is being offered by the employer to customers, or

(B) in the case of services, 20 percent of the price at which the services are being offered by the employer to customers.

(2) Gross profit percentage.—

(A) In general.—The term "gross profit percentage" means the percent which—

(i) the excess of the aggregate sales price of property sold by the employer to customers over the aggregate cost of such property to the employer, is of

(ii) the aggregate sale price of such property.

(B) Determination of gross profit percentage.—Gross profit percentage shall be determined on the basis of—

(i) all property offered to customers in the ordinary course of the line of business of the employer in which the employee is performing services (or a reasonable classification of property selected by the employer), and

(ii) the employer's experience during a representative period.

(3) Employee discount defined.—The term "employee discount" means the amount by which—

(A) the price at which the property or services are provided by the employer to an employee for use by such employee, is less than—

(B) the price at which such property or services are being offered by the employer to customers.

(4) Qualified property or services.—The term "qualified property or services" means any property (other than real property and other than personal property of a kind held for investment) or services which are offered for sale to customers in the ordinary course of the line of business of the employer in which the employee is performing services.

(d) Working condition fringe defined.—For purposes of this section, the term "working condition fringe" means any property or services provided to an employee of the employer to the extent that, if the employee paid for such property or services, such payment would be allowable as a deduction under section 162 or 167.

(e) De minimis fringe defined.—For purposes of this section—

(1) In general.—The term "de minimis fringe" means any property or service the value of which is (after taking into account the frequency with which similar fringes are provided by the employer to the employer's employees) so small as to make accounting for it unreasonable or administratively impracticable.

(2) Treatment of certain eating facilities.—The operation by an employer of any eating facility for employees shall be treated as a de minimis fringe if—

(A) such facility is located on or near the business premises of the employer, and

(B) revenue derived from such facility normally equals or exceeds the direct operating costs of such facility.

The preceding sentence shall apply with respect to any highly compensated employee only if access to the facility is available on substantially the same terms to each member of a group of employees which is defined under a reasonable classification set up by the employer which does not discriminate in favor of highly compensated employees. For purposes of subparagraph (B), an employee entitled under section 119 to exclude the value of a meal provided at such facility shall be treated as having paid an amount for such meal equal to the direct operating costs of the facility attributable to such meal.

(f) Qualified transportation fringe.—

(1) In general.—For purposes of this section, the term "qualified transportation fringe" means any of the following provided by an employer to an employee:

(A) Transportation in a commuter highway vehicle if such transportation is in connection with travel between the employee's residence and place of employment.

(B) Any transit pass.

(C) Qualified parking.

(D) Any qualified bicycle commuting reimbursement.

(2) Limitation on exclusion.—The amount of the fringe benefits which are provided by an employer to any employee and which may be excluded from gross income under subsection (a)(5) shall not exceed—

(A) $100* per month in the case of the aggregate of the benefits described in subparagraphs (A) and (B) of paragraph (1),

(B) $175** per month in the case of qualified parking, and

(C) the applicable annual limitation in the case of any qualified bicycle commuting reimbursement.

In the case of any month beginning on or after the date of enactment of this sentence and before January 1, 2014, subparagraph (A) shall be applied as if the dollar amount therein were the same as the dollar amount in effect for such month under subparagraph (B).***

(3) Cash reimbursements.—For purposes of this subsection, the term "qualified transportation fringe" includes a cash reimbursement by an employer to an employee for a benefit described

*Editorial comment: The indexed amount for 2013 is $125 and for 2014 is $130.

**Editorial comment: The indexed amount for 2013 is $245 and for 2014 is $250.

***Editorial comment: At the present time, this section has not been extended. There is pending legislation in the Senate, *The Tax Extenders Act of 2013 (S. 1859)*, that would extend Section 132(f)(2) until January 1, 2015.

in paragraph (1). The preceding sentence shall apply to a cash reimbursement for any transit pass only if a voucher or similar item which may be exchanged only for a transit pass is not readily available for direct distribution by the employer to the employee.

(4) No constructive receipt—No amount shall be included in the gross income of an employee solely because the employee may choose between any qualified transportation fringe (other than a qualified bicycle commuting reimbursement) and compensation which would otherwise be includible in gross income of such employee.

(5) Definitions.—For purposes of this subsection—

(A) Transit pass.—The term "transit pass" means any pass, token, farecard, voucher, or similar item entitling a person to transportation (or transportation at a reduced price) if such transportation is—

(i) on mass transit facilities (whether or not publicly owned), or

(ii) provided by any person in the business of transporting persons for compensation or hire if such transportation is provided in a vehicle meeting the requirements of subparagraph (B)(i).

(B) Commuter highway vehicle.—The term "commuter highway vehicle" means any highway vehicle—

(i) the seating capacity of which is at least 6 adults (not including the driver), and

(ii) at least 80 percent of the mileage use of which can reasonably be expected to be—

(I) for purposes of transporting employees in connection with travel between their residences and their place of employment, and

(II) on trips during which the number of employees transported for such purposes is at least ½ of the adult seating capacity of such vehicle (not including the driver).

(C) Qualified parking.—The term "qualified parking" means parking provided to an employee on or near the business premises of the employer or on or near a location from which the employee commutes to work by transportation described in subparagraph (A), in a commuter highway vehicle, or by carpool. Such term shall not include any parking on or near property used by the employee for residential purposes.

(D) Transportation provided by employer.—Transportation referred to in paragraph (1)(A) shall be considered to be provided by an employer if such transportation is furnished in a commuter highway vehicle operated by or for the employer.

(E) Employee.—For purposes of this subsection, the term "employee" does not include an individual who is an employee within the meaning of section 401(c)(1).

(F) Definitions related to bicycle commuting reimbursement.—

(i) Qualified bicycle commuting reimbursement.—The term "qualified bicycle commuting reimbursement" means, with respect to any calendar year, any employer reimbursement during the 15-month period beginning with the first day of such calendar year for reasonable expenses incurred by the employee during such calendar year for the purchase of a bicycle and bicycle improvements, repair, and storage, if such bicycle is regularly used for travel between the employee's residence and place of employment.

(ii) Applicable annual limitation.—The term "applicable annual limitation" means, with respect to any employee for any calendar year, the product of $20 multiplied by the number of qualified bicycle commuting months during such year.

(iii) Qualified bicycle commuting month.—The term "qualified bicycle commuting month" means, with respect to any employee, any month during which such employee—

(I) regularly uses the bicycle for a substantial portion of the travel between the employee's residence and place of employment, and

(II) does not receive any benefit described in subparagraph (A), (B), or (C) of paragraph (1).

(6) Inflation adjustment.—

(A) In general.—In the case of any taxable year beginning in a calendar year after 1999, the dollar amounts contained in subparagraphs (A)

and (B) of paragraph (2) shall be increased by an amount equal to—

(i) such dollar amount, multiplied by

(ii) the cost-of-living adjustment determined under section 1(f)(3) for the calendar year in which the taxable year begins, by substituting "calendar year 1998" for "calendar year 1992."

In the case of any taxable year beginning in a calendar year after 2002, clause (ii) shall be applied by substituting "calendar year 2001" for "calendar year 1998" for purposes of adjusting the dollar amount contained in paragraph (2)(A).

(B) Rounding.—If any increase determined under subparagraph (A) is not a multiple of $5, such increase shall be rounded to the next lowest multiple of $5.

(7) Coordination with other provisions.—For purposes of this section, the terms "working condition fringe" and "de minimis fringe" shall not include any qualified transportation fringe (determined without regard to paragraph (2)).

(g) Qualified moving expense reimbursement.—For purposes of this section, the term "qualified moving expense reimbursement" means any amount received (directly or indirectly) by an individual from an employer as a payment for (or a reimbursement of) expenses which would be deductible as moving expenses under section 217 if directly paid or incurred by the individual. Such term shall not include any payment for (or reimbursement of) an expense actually deducted by the individual in a prior taxable year.

(h) Certain individuals treated as employees for purposes of subsections (a)(1) and (2).—For purposes of paragraphs (1) and (2) of subsection (a),.
—

(1) Retired and disabled employees and surviving spouse of employee treated as employee.—With respect to a line of business of an employer, the term "employee" includes—

(A) any individual who was formerly employed by such employer in such line of business and who separated from service with such employer in such line of business by reason of retirement or disability, and

(B) any widow or widower of any individual who died while employed by such employer in such line of business or while an employee within the meaning of subparagraph (A).

(2) Spouse and dependent children.—

(A) In general.—Any use by the spouse or a dependent child of the employee shall be treated as use by the employee.

(B) Dependent child.—For purposes of subparagraph (A), the term "dependent child" means any child (as defined in section 152(f)(1) of the employee—

(i) who is a dependent of the employee, or

(ii) both of whose parents are deceased and who has not attained age 25.

For purposes of the preceding sentence, any child to whom section 152(e) applies shall be treated as the dependent of both parents.

(3) Special rule for parents in the case of air transportation.—Any use of air transportation by a parent of an employee (determined without regard to paragraph (1)(B)) shall be treated as use by the employee.

(i) Reciprocal agreements.—For purposes of paragraph (1) of subsection (a), any service provided by an employer to an employee of another employer shall be treated as provided by the employer of such employee if—

(1) such service is provided pursuant to a written agreement between such employers, and

(2) neither of such employers incurs any substantial additional costs (including foregone revenue) in providing such service or pursuant to such agreement.

(j) Special rules.—

(1) Exclusions under subsection (a)(1) and (2) apply to highly compensated employees only if no discrimination.—Paragraphs (1) and (2) of subsection (a) shall apply with respect to any fringe benefit described therein provided with respect to any highly compensated employee only if such fringe benefit is available on substantially the same terms to each member of a group of employees which is defined under a reasonable classification set up by the employer which does not discriminate in favor of highly compensated employees.

(2) Special rule for leased sections of department stores.—

(A) In general.—For purposes of paragraph (2) of subsection (a), in the case of a leased section of a department store—

(i) such section shall be treated as part of the line of business of the person operating the department store, and

(ii) employees in the leased section shall be treated as employees of the person operating the department store.

(B) Leased section of department store.—For purposes of subparagraph (A), a leased section of a department store is any part of a department store where over-the-counter sales of property are made under a lease or similar arrangement where it appears to the general public that individuals making such sales are employed by the person operating the department store.

(3) Auto salesmen.—

(A) In general.—For purposes of subsection (a)(3), qualified automobile demonstration use shall be treated as a working condition fringe.

(B) Qualified automobile demonstration use.—For purposes of subparagraph (A), the term "qualified automobile demonstration use" means any use of an automobile by a full-time automobile salesman in the sales area in which the automobile dealer's sales office is located if—

(i) such use is provided primarily to facilitate the salesman's performance of services for the employer, and

(ii) there are substantial restrictions on the personal use of such automobile by such salesman.

(4) On-premises gyms and other athletic facilities.—

(A) In general.—Gross income shall not include the value of any on-premises athletic facility provided by an employer to his employees.

(B) On-premises athletic facility.—For purposes of this paragraph, the term "on-premises athletic facility" means any gym or other athletic facility—

(i) which is located on the premises of the employer,

(ii) which is operated by the employer, and

(iii) substantially all the use of which is by employees of the employer, their spouses, and their dependent children (within the meaning of subsection (h)).

(5) Special rule for affiliates of airlines.—

(A) In general.—If—

(i) a qualified affiliate is a member of an affiliated group another member of which operates an airline, and

(ii) employees of the qualified affiliate who are directly engaged in providing airlinerelated services are entitled to no-additional-cost service with respect to air transportation provided by such other member,

then, for purposes of applying paragraph (1) of subsection (a) to such no-additional-cost service provided to such employees, such qualified affiliate shall be treated as engaged in the same line of business as such other member.

(B) Qualified affiliate.—For purposes of this paragraph, the term "qualified affiliate" means any corporation which is predominantly engaged in airline-related services.

(C) Airline-related services.—For purposes of this paragraph, the term "airline-related services" means any of the following services provided in connection with air transportation:

(i) Catering.

(ii) Baggage handling.

(iii) Ticketing and reservations.

(iv) Flight planning and weather analysis.

(v) Restaurants and gift shops located at an airport.

(vi) Such other similar services provided to the airline as the Secretary may prescribe.

(D) Affiliated group.—For purposes of this paragraph, the term "affiliated group" has the meaning given such term by section 1504(a).

(6) Highly compensated employee.—For purposes of this section, the term "highly compensated employee" has the meaning given such term by section 414(q).

(7) Air cargo.—For purposes of subsection (b), the transportation of cargo by air and the transportation of passengers by air shall be treated as the same service.

(8) Application of section to otherwise taxable educational or training benefits.—Amounts paid or expenses incurred by the employer for education or training provided to the employee which are not excludable from gross income under section 127 shall be excluded from gross income under this section if (and only if) such amounts or expenses are a working condition fringe.

(k) Customers not to include employees.—For purposes of this section (other than subsection (c)(2)), the term "customers" shall only include customers who are not employees.

(l) Section not to apply to fringe benefits expressly provided for elsewhere.—This section (other than subsection (e) and (g)) shall not apply to any fringe benefits of a type the tax treatment of which is expressly provided for in any other section of this chapter.

(m) Qualified retirement planning services.—

(1) In general.—For purposes of this section, the term "qualified retirement planning services" means any retirement planning advice or information provided to an employee and his spouse by an employer maintaining a qualified employer plan.

(2) Nondiscrimination rulc.—Subscction (a)(7) shall apply in the case of highly compensated employees only if such services are available on substantially the same terms to each member of the group of employees normally provided education and information regarding the employer's qualified employer plan.

(3) Qualified employer plan.—For purposes of this subsection, the term "qualified employer plan" means a plan, contract, pension, or account described in section 219(g)(5).

(n) Qualified military base realignment and closure fringe.—

(1) In general.—The term "qualified military base realignment and closure fringe" means 1 or more payments under the authority of section 1013 of the Demonstration Cities and Metropolitan Development Act of 1966 (42 U.S.C. 3374) (as in effect on the date of the enactment of the American Recovery and Reinvestment Tax Act of 2009).

(2) Limitation.—With respect to any property, such term shall not include any payment referred to in paragraph (1) to the extent that the sum of all of such payments related to such property exceeds the maximum amount described in subsection (c) of such section (as in effect on such date).

(o) Regulations.—The Secretary shall prescribe such regulations as may be necessary or appropriate to carry out the purposes of this section.

§ 134. Certain military benefits

(a) General rule.—Gross income shall not include any qualified military benefit.

(b) Qualified military benefit.—For purposes of this section—

(1) In general.—The term "qualified military benefit" means any allowance or in-kind benefit (other than personal use of a vehicle) which—

(A) is received by any member or former member of the uniformed services of the United States or any dependent of such member by reason of such member's status or service as a member of such uniformed services, and

(B) was excludable from gross income on September 9, 1986, under any provision of law, regulation, or administrative practice which was in effect on such date (other than a provision of this title).

(2) No other benefit to be excludable except as provided by this title.—Notwithstanding any other provision of law, no benefit shall be treated as a qualified military benefit unless such benefit—

(A) is a benefit described in paragraph (1), or

(B) is excludable from gross income under this title without regard to any provision of law which is not contained in this title and which is not contained in a revenue Act.

(3) Limitations on modifications.—

(A) In general.—Except as provided in subparagraphs (B) and (C) and paragraph (4), no modification or adjustment of any qualified military benefit after September 9, 1986, shall be taken into account.

(B) Exception for certain adjustments to cash benefits.—Subparagraph (A) shall not apply to any adjustment to any qualified military benefit payable in cash which—

(i) is pursuant to a provision of law or regulation (as in effect on September 9, 1986), and

(ii) is determined by reference to any fluctuation in cost, price, currency, or other similar index.

(C) Exception for death gratuity adjustments made by law.—Subparagraph (A) shall not apply to any adjustment to the amount of death gratuity payable under chapter 75 of title 10, United States Code, which is pursuant to a provision of law enacted after September 9, 1986.

(4) Clarification of certain benefits.—For purposes of paragraph (1), such term includes any dependent care assistance program (as in effect on the date of the enactment of this paragraph) for any individual described in paragraph (1)(A).

(5) Travel benefits under operation hero miles.—The term "qualified military benefit" includes a travel benefit provided under section 2613 of title 10, United States Code (as in effect on the date of enactment of this paragraph).

(6) Certain State payments.—The term "qualified military benefit" includes any bonus payment by a State or political subdivision thereof to any member or former member of the uniformed services of the United States or any dependent of such member only by reason of such member's service in a combat zone (as defined in section 112(c)(2), determined without regard to the parenthetical).

§ 135. Income from United States savings bonds used to pay higher education tuition and fees

(a) General rule.—In the case of an individual who pays qualified higher education expenses during the taxable year, no amount shall be includible in gross income by reason of the redemption during such year of any qualified United States savings bond.

(b) Limitations.—

(1) Limitation where redemption proceeds exceed higher education expenses.—

(A) In general.—If—

(i) the aggregate proceeds of qualified United States savings bonds redeemed by the taxpayer during the taxable year exceed

(ii) the qualified higher education expenses paid by the taxpayer during such taxable year,

the amount excludable from gross income under subsection (a) shall not exceed the applicable fraction of the amount excludable from gross income under subsection (a) without regard to this subsection.

(B) Applicable fraction.—For purposes of subparagraph (A), the term "applicable fraction" means the fraction the numerator of which is the amount described in subparagraph (A)(ii) and the denominator of which is the amount described in subparagraph (A)(i).

(2) Limitation based on modified adjusted gross income.—

(A) In general.—If the modified adjusted gross income of the taxpayer for the taxable year exceeds $40,000 ($60,000 in the case of a joint return),* the amount which would (but for this paragraph) be excludable from gross income under subsection (a) shall be reduced (but not below zero) by the amount which bears the same ratio to the amount which would be so excludable as such excess bears to $15,000 ($30,000 in the case of a joint return).

(B) Inflation adjustment.*—In the case of any taxable year beginning in a calendar year after 1990, the $40,000 and $60,000 amounts contained in subparagraph (A) shall be increased by an amount equal to—

(i) such dollar amount, multiplied by

(ii) the cost-of-living adjustment under section 1(f)(3) for the calendar year in which the taxable year begins, determined by substituting "calendar year 1989" for "calendar year 1992" in subparagraph (B) thereof.

(C) Rounding.—If any amount as adjusted under subparagraph (B) is not a multiple of $50, such amount shall be rounded to the nearest multiple of $50 (or if such amount is a multiple of $25, such amount shall be rounded to the next highest multiple of $50).

(c) Definitions.—For purposes of this section—

(1) Qualified United States savings bond.—The term "qualified United States savings bond" means any United States savings bond issued—

(A) after December 31, 1989,

(B) to an individual who has attained age 24 before the date of issuance, and

(C) at discount under section 3105 of title 31, United States Code.

(2) Qualified higher education expenses.—

(A) In general.—The term "qualified higher education expenses" means tuition and fees required for the enrollment or attendance of—

(i) the taxpayer,

(ii) the taxpayer's spouse, or

(iii) any dependent of the taxpayer with respect to whom the taxpayer is allowed a deduction under section 151,

at an eligible educational institution.

(B) Exception for education involving sports, etc.—Such term shall not include expenses with respect to any course or other

*Editorial comment: The indexed amounts for 2013 are $74,700 and $112,050 and for 2014 are $76,000 and $113,950. The exclusion is completely phased out for a modified adjusted gross income of $143,950 for joint returns or $91,000 for all other returns.

education involving sports, games, or hobbies other than as part of a degree program.

(C) Contributions to qualified tuition program and education individual retirement accounts.—Such term shall include any contribution to a qualified tuition program (as defined in section 529) on behalf of a designated beneficiary (as defined in such section), or to an education individual retirement account (as defined in section 530) on behalf of an account beneficiary, who is an individual described in subparagraph (A); but there shall be no increase in the investment in the contract for purposes of applying section 529(c)(3)(A) by reason of any portion of such contribution which is not includible in gross income of this subparagraph.

(3) Eligible educational institution.—The term "eligible educational institution" has the meaning given such term by section 529(e)(5).

(4) Modified adjusted gross income.—The term "modified adjusted gross income" means the adjusted gross income of the taxpayer for the taxable year determined—

(A) without regard to this section and sections 137, 199, 221, 222, 911, 931, and 933, and

(B) after the application of sections 86, 469, and 219.

(d) Special rules.—

(1) Adjustment for certain scholarships and veterans benefits.—The amount of qualified higher education expenses otherwise taken into account under subsection (a) with respect to the education of an individual shall be reduced (before the application of subsection (b)) by the sum of the amounts received with respect to such individual for the taxable year as—

(A) a qualified scholarship which under section 117 is not includible in gross income,

(B) an educational assistance allowance under chapter 30, 31, 32, 34, or 35 of title 38, United States Code,

(C) a payment (other than a gift, bequest, devise, or inheritance within the meaning of section 102(a)) for educational expenses, or attributable to attendance at an eligible educational institution, which is exempt from income taxation by any law of the United States, or

(D) a payment, waiver, or reimbursement of qualified higher education expenses under a qualified tuition program (within the meaning of section 529(b)).

(2) Coordination with other higher education benefits.—The amount of the qualified higher education expenses otherwise taken into account under subsection (a) with respect to the education of an individual shall be reduced (before the application of subsection (b)) by—

(A) the amount of such expenses which are taken into account in determining the credit allowed to the taxpayer or any other person under section 25A with respect to such expenses, and

(B) the amount of such expenses which are taken into account in determining the exclusions under sections 529(c)(3)(B) and 530(d)(2).

(3) No exclusion for married individuals filing separate returns.—If the taxpayer is a married individual (within the meaning of section 7703), this section shall apply only if the taxpayer and his spouse file a joint return for the taxable year.

(4) Regulations.—The Secretary may prescribe such regulations as may be necessary or appropriate to carry out this section, including regulations requiring record keeping and information reporting.

§ 136. Energy conservation subsidies provided by public utilities

(a) Exclusion.—Gross income shall not include the value of any subsidy provided (directly or indirectly) by a public utility to a customer for the purchase or installation of any energy conservation measure.

(b) Denial of double benefit.—Notwithstanding any other provision of this subtitle, no deduction or credit shall be allowed for, or by reason of, any expenditure to the extent of the amount excluded under subsection (a) for any subsidy which was provided with respect to such expenditure. The adjusted basis of any property shall be reduced by the amount excluded under subsection (a) which was provided with respect to such property.

(c) Energy conservation measure.—

(1) In general.—For purposes of this section, the term "energy conservation measure" means any installation or modification primarily designed to reduce consumption of electricity or natural gas or to improve the management of energy demand with respect to a dwelling unit.

(2) Other definitions and special rules.—For purposes of this subsection—

(A) Dwelling unit.—The term "dwelling unit" has the meaning given such term by section 280A(f)(1).

(B) Public utility.—The term "public utility" means a person engaged in the sale of electricity or natural gas to residential, commercial, or industrial customers for use by such customers. For purposes of the preceding sentence, the term "person" includes the Federal Government, a State or local government or any political subdivision thereof, or any instrumentality of any of the foregoing.

(d) Exception.—This section shall not apply to any payment to or from a qualified cogeneration facility or qualifying small power production facility pursuant to section 210 of the Public Utility Regulatory Policy Act of 1978.

§ 137. Adoption assistance programs

(a) Exclusion.—

(1) In general.—Gross income of an employee does not include amounts paid or expenses incurred by the employer for qualified adoption expenses in connection with the adoption of a child by an employee if such amounts are furnished pursuant to an adoption assistance program.

(2) $10,000* exclusion for adoption of child with special needs regardless of expenses.—In the case of an adoption of a child with special needs which becomes final during a taxable year, the qualified adoption expenses with respect to such adoption for such year shall be increased by an amount equal to the excess (if any) of $10,000* over the actual aggregate qualified adoption expenses with respect to such adoption during such taxable year and all prior taxable years.

(b) Limitations.—

(1) Dollar limitation.—The aggregate of the amounts paid or expenses incurred which may be taken into account under subsection (a)(1) for all taxable years with respect to the adoption of a child by the taxpayer shall not exceed $10,000.*

(2) Income limitation.—The amount excludable from gross income under subsection (a) for any taxable year shall be reduced (but not below zero) by an amount which bears the same ratio to the amount so excludable (determined without regard to this paragraph but with regard to paragraph (1)) as—

(A) the amount (if any) by which the taxpayer's adjusted gross income exceeds $150,000,** bears to

(B) $40,000.

(3) Determination of adjusted gross income.—For purposes of paragraph (2), adjusted gross income shall be determined—

(A) without regard to this section and sections 199, 221, 222, 911, 931, and 933, and

(B) after the application of sections 86, 135, 219, and 469.

(c) Adoption assistance program.—For purposes of this section, an adoption assistance program is a separate written plan of an employer for the exclusive benefit of such employer's employees—

(1) under which the employer provides such employees with adoption assistance, and

(2) which meets requirements similar to the requirements of paragraphs (2), (3), (5), and (6) of section 127(b).

An adoption reimbursement program operated under section 1052 of title 10, United States Code (relating to armed forces) or section 514 or title 14, United States Code (relating to members of the Coast Guard) shall be treated as an adoption assistance program for purposes of this section.

(d) Qualified adoption expenses.—For purposes of this section, the term "qualified adoption expenses" has the meaning given such term by section 23(d)*** (determined without regard to reimbursements under this section).

(e) Certain rules to apply.—Rules similar to the rules of subsections (e), (f), and (g) of section 23**** shall apply for purposes of this section.

*Editorial comment: The indexed amount for 2014 is $13,190 ($12,970 in 2013).

**Editorial comment: The indexed amount for 2014 is $197,880 ($194,580 in 2013). The amount excludable from an employee's gross income is completely phased out for taxpayers with a modified adjusted gross income of $237,880.

***Editorial comment: For tax years beginning after December 31, 2012, the Tax Relief Act of 2010 replaced "section 36C(d)" with "section 23(d)."

****Editorial comment: For tax years beginning after December 31, 2012, the Tax Relief Act of 2010 replaced "section 36C" with "section 23."

(f) Adjustments for inflation.—

(1) Dollar limitations.—In the case of a taxable year beginning after December 31, 2002, each of the dollar amounts in subsections (a)(2) and (b)(1) shall be increased by an amount equal to—

(A) such dollar amount, multiplied by

(B) the cost-of-living adjustment determined under section 1(f)(3) for the calendar year in which the taxable year begins, determined by substituting "calendar year 2001" for "calendar year 1992" in subparagraph (B) thereof.

If any amount as increased under the preceding sentence is not a multiple of $10, such amount shall be rounded to the nearest multiple of $10.

(2) Income limitation.—In the case of a taxable year beginning after December 31, 2002, the dollar amount in subsection (b)(2)(A) shall be increased by an amount equal to—

(A) such dollar amount, multiplied by

(B) the cost-of-living adjustment determined under section 1(f)(3) for the calendar year in which the taxable year begins, determined by substituting "calendar year 2001" for "calendar year 1992" in subparagraph thereof.

If any amount as increased under the preceding sentence is not a multiple of $10, such amount shall be rounded to the nearest multiple of $10.

§ 138. MedicareAdvantage MSA

(a) Exclusion.—Gross income shall not include any payment to the MedicareAdvantage MSA of an individual by the Secretary of Health and Human Services under part C of title XVIII of the Social Security Act.

(b) MedicareAdvantage MSA.—For purposes of this section, the term "MedicareAdvantage MSA" means an Archer MSA (as defined in section 220(d))—

(1) which is designated as a MedicareAdvantage MSA,

(2) with respect to which no contribution may be made other than—

(A) a contribution made by the Secretary of Health and Human Services pursuant to part C of title XVIII of the Social Security Act, or

(B) a trustee-to-trustee transfer described in subsection (c)(4),

(3) the governing instrument of which provides that trustee-to-trustee transfers described in subsection (c)(4) may be made to and from such account, and

(4) which is established in connection with an MSA plan described in section 1859(b)(3) of the Social Security Act.

(c) Special rules for distributions.—

(1) Distributions for qualified medical expenses.—In applying section 220 to a MedicareAdvantage MSA—

(A) qualified medical expenses shall not include amounts paid for medical care for any individual other than the account holder, and

(B) section 220(d)(2)(C) shall not apply.

(2) Penalty for distributions from MedicareAdvantage MSA not used for qualified medical expenses if minimum balance not maintained.—

(A) In general.—The tax imposed by this chapter for any taxable year in which there is a payment or distribution from a MedicareAdvantage MSA which is not used exclusively to pay the qualified medical expenses of the account holder shall be increased by 50 percent of the excess (if any) of—

(i) the amount of such payment or distribution, over

(ii) the excess (if any) of—

(I) the fair market value of the assets in such MSA as of the close of the calendar year preceding the calendar year in which the taxable year begins, over

(II) an amount equal to 60 percent of the deductible under the MedicareAdvantage MSA plan covering the account holder as of January 1 of the calendar year in which the taxable year begins.

Section 220(f)(4) shall not apply to any payment or distribution from a MedicareAdvantage MSA.

(B) Exceptions.—Subparagraph (A) shall not apply if the payment or distribution is made on or after the date the account holder—

(i) becomes disabled within the meaning of section 72(m)(7), or

(ii) dies.

(C) Special rules.—For purposes of subparagraph A—

(i) all MedicareAdvantage MSAs of the account holder shall be treated as 1 account,

(ii) all payments and distributions not used exclusively to pay the qualified medical expenses of the account holder during any taxable year shall be treated as 1 distribution, and

(iii) any distribution of property shall be taken into account at its fair market value on the date of the distribution.

(3) Withdrawal of erroneous contributions.—Section 220(f)(2) and paragraph (2) of this subsection shall not apply to any payment or distribution from a MedicareAdvantage MSA to the Secretary of Health and Human Services of an erroneous contribution to such MSA and of the net income attributable to such contribution.

(4) Trustee-to-trustee transfers.—Section 220 (f)(2) and paragraph (2) of this subsection shall not apply to any trustee-to-trustee transfer from a MedicareAdvantage MSA of an account holder to another MedicareAdvantage MSA of such account holder.

(d) Special rules for treatment of account after death of account holder.—In applying section 220 (f)(8)(A) to an account which was a Medicare-Advantage MSA of a decedent, the rules of section 220(f) shall apply in lieu of the rules of subsection (c) of this section with respect to the spouse as the account holder of such MedicareAdvantage MSA.

(e) Reports.—In the case of a MedicareAdvantage MSA, the report under section 220(h)—

(1) shall include the fair market value of the assets in such MedicareAdvantage MSA as of the close of each calendar year, and

(2) shall be furnished to the account holder—

(A) not later than January 31 of the calendar year following the calendar year to which such reports relate, and

(B) in such manner as the Secretary prescribes in such regulations.

(f) Coordination with limitation on number of taxpayers having Archer MSAs.—Subsection (i) of section 220 shall not apply to an individual with respect to a MedicareAdvantage MSA, and Medicare-Advantage MSA's shall not be taken into account in determining whether the numerical limitations under section 220(j) are exceeded.

§ 139. Disaster relief payments

(a) General rule.—Gross income shall not include any amount received by an individual as a qualified disaster relief payment.

(b) Qualified disaster relief payment defined.—For purposes of this section, the term "qualified disaster relief payment" means any amount paid to or for the benefit of an individual—

(1) to reimburse or pay reasonable and necessary personal, family, living, or funeral expenses incurred as a result of a qualified disaster,

(2) to reimburse or pay reasonable and necessary expenses incurred for the repair or rehabilitation of a personal residence or repair or replacement of its contents to the extent that the need for such repair, rehabilitation, or replacement is attributable to a qualified disaster,

(3) by a person engaged in the furnishing or sale of transportation as a common carrier by reason of the death or personal physical injuries incurred as a result of a qualified disaster, or

(4) if such amount is paid by a Federal, State, or local government, or agency or instrumentality thereof, in connection with a qualified disaster in order to promote the general welfare,

but only to the extent any expense compensated by such payment is not otherwise compensated for by insurance or otherwise.

(c) Qualified disaster defined.—For purposes of this section, the term "qualified disaster" means—

(1) a disaster which results from a terroristic or military action (as defined in section 692(c)(2)),

(2) Federally declared disaster (as defined by section 165(h)(3)(C)(i)),

(3) a disaster which results from an accident involving a common carrier, or from any other event, which is determined by the Secretary to be of a catastrophic nature, or

(4) with respect to amounts described in subsection (b)(4), a disaster which is determined by an applicable Federal, State, or local authority (as determined by the Secretary) to warrant assistance from the Federal, State, or local government or agency or instrumentality thereof.

(d) Coordination with employment taxes.—For purposes of chapter 22 and subtitle C, a qualified disaster relief payment shall not be treated as net earnings from self-employment, wages, or compensation subject to tax.

(e) No relief for certain individuals.—Subsections (a) and (f) shall not apply with respect to any individual identified by the Attorney General to have been a participant or conspirator in a terroristic action (as so defined), or a representative of such individual.

(f) Exclusion of certain additional payments.—Gross income shall not include any amount received as payment under section 406 of the Air Transportation Safety and System Stabilization Act.

(g) Qualified disaster mitigation payments.—

(1) In general.—Gross income shall not include any amount received as a qualified disaster mitigation payment.

(2) Qualified disaster mitigation payment defined.—For purposes of this section, the term "qualified disaster mitigation payment" means any amount which is paid pursuant to the Robert T. Stafford Disaster Relief and Emergency Assistance Act (as in effect on the date of the enactment of this subsection) or the National Flood Insurance Act (as in effect on such date) to or for the benefit of the owner of any property for hazard mitigation with respect to such property. Such term shall not include any amount received for the sale or disposition of any property.

(3) No increase in basis.—Notwithstanding any other provision of this subtitle, no increase in the basis or adjusted basis of any property shall result from any amount excluded under this subsection with respect to such property.

(h) Denial of double benefit.—Notwithstanding any other provision of this subtitle, no deduction or credit shall be allowed (to the person for whose benefit a qualified disaster relief payment or qualified disaster mitigation payment is made) for, or by reason of, any expenditure to the extent of the amount excluded under this section with respect to such expenditure.

§ 139A. Federal subsidies for prescription drug plans

Gross income shall not include any special subsidy payment received under section 1860D–22 of the Social Security Act.

* * *

PART IV—TAX EXEMPTION REQUIREMENTS FOR STATE AND LOCAL BONDS*

PART V—DEDUCTIONS FOR PERSONAL EXEMPTIONS

Editorial Summary

Personal Exemptions and Dependency Deductions

Subchapter B of Chapter 1 (Secs. 151–153)

The Code refers to this entire category as the personal exemption deduction [see Sec. 151(a)]. However, for clarity of presentation, it is preferable to dichotomize the category as follows:

1. Personal exemption deductions [see Sec. 151(b)].
2. Dependency deductions [see Secs. 151(c) and 152].

The value of these deductions to the taxpayer is the same (i.e., $3,950 in 2014 and $3,900 for 2013) [see Sec. 151(d)]. Note that for taxable years beginning after 1989, the amount is adjusted annually for the effect of inflation [see Sec. 151(d)(4)(A)]. Also note that it is not possible for a taxpayer to be claimed as a dependent on another taxpayer's return and to be claimed as a personal exemption on the taxpayer's own return (e.g., the taxpayer who is a child is a dependent on the parents' return). In this case, the personal exemption deduction is disallowed to the taxpayer [see Sec. 151(d)(2)].

The personal exemption deduction is provided merely for existing during the taxable year. The only other taxpayer for whom a personal exemption may be claimed is the taxpayer's spouse. To qualify for this additional personal exemption, certain rules must be satisfied [see Sec. 151(b)].

A dependency deduction may be claimed only if certain statutory requirements are satisfied. The two options are the potential dependent is (1) a qualifying child (see Sec. 152(a)(1)) or (2) a qualifying relative (see Sec. 152(a)(2)). A qualifying child must meet the following requirements (see Sec. 152(c), Sec. 152(b)(2), and Sec. 152(b)(3)): relationship, abode, age, not be self-supporting, absence of a joint return by the dependent, and citizenship or resident status. A qualifying relative must meet the following requirements (see Sec. 152(d), Sec. 152(b)(2), and Sec. 152(b)(3)): support, relationship, dependent's gross income, absence of a joint return by the dependent, and citizenship or resident status). A taxpayer's spouse can never qualify as his or her dependent. Special rules exist in the case of a child who is under age 19 or a student [see Sec. 152(c)(3)], children of divorced parents [see Sec. 152(e)], and multiple support agreements [see Sec. 152(d)(3)].

The Tax Reform Act of 1986 provided for the phaseout of the personal exemption and dependency deductions for

*Omitted

upper-income taxpayers. Although the procedure and the statutory location [i.e., moved from Sec. 1(g) to Sec. 151(d)(3)] is modified by the Revenue Reconciliation Act of 1990, the concept of phasing-out the personal exemption and dependency deductions of upper-income taxpayers remained through 2009. This had the effect of increasing the individual taxpayer's effective tax rate above the statutory 28, 33, or 35 percent for 2009. This phaseout commenced once the threshold amount (i.e:, ranges from $75,000 to $150,000 depending on filing status) was exceeded [see Sec. 151(d)(3)(C)]. For taxable years beginning after 1991, the threshold amounts are adjusted annually for the effect of inflation [see Sec. 151(d)(4)(B)]. Under the sunset legislation concept, the phaseout provision was scheduled to expire for taxable years beginning after December 31, 1996. However, this termination date was repealed by the Revenue Reconciliation Act of 1993 [see Sec. 151 (d)(3)(E) prior to repeal by RRA of 1993].

TRRA of 2001 repealed the personal exemption and dependency deduction phaseout provision. However, a phased approach was used for the repeal. That is, the repeal takes place over a 5-year period which began in tax year 2006 and is not completed until tax years beginning after December 31, 2009. The American Taxpayer Relief Act of 2012 reinstated the phaseout of the personal exemption and dependency deduction beginning in 2013.

Other Code sections will use the term "dependent." Generally, the term will have the meaning assigned above (i.e., must satisfy one of the two options). In some instances, however, not all of the statutory tests will need to be satisfied (e.g., see Sec. 213(a) for the modified definition of dependent for medical expense deduction purposes).

§ 151. Allowance of deductions for personal exemptions

(a) Allowance of deductions.—In the case of an individual, the exemptions provided by this section shall be allowed as deductions in computing taxable income.

(b) Taxpayer and spouse.—An exemption of the exemption amount for the taxpayer; and an additional exemption of the exemption amount for the spouse of the taxpayer if a joint return is not made by the taxpayer and his spouse, and if the spouse, for the calendar year in which the taxable year of the taxpayer begins, has no gross income and is not the dependent of another taxpayer.

(c) Additional exemption for dependents.—An exemption of the exemption amount for each individual who is a dependent (as defined in section 152) of the taxpayer for the taxable year.

*Editorial comment: The indexed amount for 2014 is $3,950 and for 2013 is $3,900.

(d) Exemption amount.*—For purposes of this section—

(1) In general.—Except as otherwise provided in this subsection, the term "exemption amount" means $2,000.*

(2) Exemption amount disallowed in case of certain dependents.—In the case of an individual with respect to whom a deduction under this section is allowable to another taxpayer for a taxable year beginning in the calendar year in which the individual's taxable year begins, the exemption amount applicable to such individual for such individual's taxable year shall be zero.

(3) Phaseout.—

(A) In general.—In the case of any taxpayer whose adjusted gross income for the taxable year exceeds the applicable amount in effect under section 68(b), the exemption amount shall be reduced by the applicable percentage.

(B) Applicable percentage.—For purposes of subparagraph (A), the term "applicable percentage" means 2 percentage points for each $2,500 (or fraction thereof) by which the taxpayer's adjusted gross income for the taxable year exceeds the applicable amount in effect under section 68(b). In the case of a married individual filing a separate return, the preceding sentence shall be applied by substituting "$1,250" for "$2,500." In no event shall the applicable percentage exceed 100 percent.

(C) Coordination with other provisions.—The provisions of this paragraph shall not apply for purposes of determining whether a deduction under this section with respect to any individual is allowable to another taxpayer for any taxable year.

(4) Inflation adjustments.**—In the case of any taxable year beginning in a calendar year after 1989, the dollar amount contained in paragraph (1) shall be increased by an amount equal to—

(A) such dollar amount, multiplied by

(B) the cost-of-living adjustment determined under section 1(f)(3) for the calendar year in which the taxable year begins, by substituting "calendar year 1988" for "calendar year 1992" in subparagraph (B) therof.

**Editorial comment: See the indexed phaseouts after Section 151(e).

(e) Identifying information required.—No exemption shall be allowed under this section with respect to an individual unless the TIN of such individual is included on the return claiming the exemption.

Editorial Note

For taxable years beginning in 2014, the personal exemption phases out for taxpayers with the following AGI amounts:

Filing Status	AGI-Beginning of Phaseout	AGI-Completed Phaseout
Married Individuals Filing Joint Returns and Surviving Spouses	$305,050	$427,550
Heads of Household	279,650	402,150
Unmarried Individuals (other than Surviving Spouses and Heads of Households)	254,200	376,700
Married Individuals Filing Separate Returns	152,525	213,775

§ 152. Dependent defined

(a) In general.—For purposes of this subtitle, the term "dependent" means—

(1) a qualifying child, or

(2) a qualifying relative.

(b) Exceptions.—For purposes of this section—

(1) Dependents ineligible.—If an individual is a dependent of a taxpayer for any taxable year of such taxpayer beginning in a calendar year, such individual shall be treated as having no dependents for any taxable year of such individual beginning in such calendar year.

(2) Married dependents.—An individual shall not be treated as a dependent of a taxpayer under subsection (a) if such individual has made a joint return with the individual's spouse under section 6013 for the taxable year beginning in the calendar year in which the taxable year of the taxpayer begins.

(3) Citizens or nationals of other countries.—

(A) In general.—The term "dependent" does not include an individual who is not a citizen or national of the United States unless such individual is a resident of the United States or a country contiguous to the United States.

(B) Exception for adopted child.—Subparagraph (A) shall not exclude any child of a taxpayer (within the meaning of subsection (f)(1)(B)) from the definition of "dependent" if—

(i) for the taxable year of the taxpayer, the child has the same principal place of abode as the taxpayer and is a member of the taxpayer's household, and

(ii) the taxpayer is a citizen or national of the United States.

(c) Qualifying child.—For purposes of this section—

(1) In general.—The term "qualifying child" means, with respect to any taxpayer for any taxable year, an individual—

(A) who bears a relationship to the taxpayer described in paragraph (2),

(B) who has the same principal place of abode as the taxpayer for more than one-half of such taxable year,

(C) who meets the age requirements of paragraph (3),

(D) who has not provided over one-half of such individual's own support for the calendar year in which the taxable year of the taxpayer begins, and

(E) who has not filed a joint return (other than only for a claim of refund) with the individual's spouse under section 6013 for the taxable year beginning in the calendar year in which the taxable year of the taxpayer begins.

(2) Relationship.—For purposes of paragraph (1)(A), an individual bears a relationship to the taxpayer described in this paragraph if such individual is—

(A) a child of the taxpayer or a descendant of such a child, or

(B) a brother, sister, stepbrother, or stepsister of the taxpayer or a descendant of any such relative.

(3) Age requirements.—

(A) In general.—For purposes of paragraph (1)(C), an individual meets the requirements of this paragraph if such individual is younger than the taxpayer claiming such individual as a qualifying child and—

(i) has not attained the age of 19 as of the close of the calendar year in which the taxable year of the taxpayer begins, or

(ii) is a student who has not attained the age of 24 as of the close of such calendar year.

(B) Special rule for disabled.—In the case of an individual who is permanently and totally disabled (as defined in section 22(e)(3)) at any time during such calendar year, the requirements of subparagraph (A) shall be treated as met with respect to such individual.

(4) Special rule relating to 2 or more who can claim the same qualifying child.—

(A) In general.—Except as provided in subparagraph (B) and (C), if (but for this paragraph) an individual may be claimed as a qualifying child by 2 or more taxpayers for a taxable year beginning in the same calendar year, such individual shall be treated as the qualifying child of the taxpayer who is—

(i) a parent of the individual, or

(ii) if clause (i) does not apply, the taxpayer with the highest adjusted gross income for such taxable year.

(B) More than 1 parent claiming qualifying child.—If the parents claiming any qualifying child do not file a joint return together, such child shall be treated as the qualifying child of—

(i) the parent with whom the child resided for the longest period of time during the taxable year, or

(ii) if the child resides with both parents for the same amount of time during such taxable year, the parent with the highest adjusted gross income.

(C) No parent claiming qualifying child.—If the parents of an individual may claim such individual as a qualifying child but no parent so claims the individual, such individual may be claimed as the qualifying child of another taxpayer but only if the adjusted gross income of such taxpayer is higher than the highest adjusted gross income of any parent of the individual.

(d) Qualifying relative.—For purposes of this section—

(1) In general.—The term "qualifying relative" means, with respect to any taxpayer for any taxable year, an individual—

(A) who bears a relationship to the taxpayer describe in paragraph (2),

(B) whose gross income for the calendar year in which such taxable year begins is less than the exemption amount (as defined in section 151(d)),

(C) with respect to whom the taxpayer provides over one-half of the individual's support for the calendar year in which such taxable year begins, and

(D) who is not a qualifying child of such taxpayer or of any other taxpayer for any taxable year beginning in the calendar year in which such taxable year begins.

(2) Relationship.—For purposes of paragraph (1)(A), an individual bears a relationship to the taxpayer described in this paragraph if the individual is any of the following with respect to the taxpayer.

(A) A child or a descendant of a child.

(B) A brother, sister, stepbrother, or stepsister.

(C) The father or mother, or an ancestor of either.

(D) A stepfather or stepmother.

(E) A son or daughter of a brother or sister of the taxpayer.

(F) A brother or sister of the father or mother of the taxpayer.

(G) A son-in-law, daughter-in-law, father-in-law, mother-in-law, brother-in-law, or sister-in-law.

(H) An individual (other than an individual who at any time during the taxable year was the spouse, determined without regard to section 7703, of the taxpayer) who, for the taxable year of the taxpayer, has the same principal place of abode as the taxpayer and is a member of the taxpayer's household.

(3) Special rule relating to multiple support agreements.—For purposes of paragraph (1)(C), over one-half of the support of an individual for a calendar year shall be treated as received from the taxpayer if—

(A) no one person contributed over one-half of such support,

(B) over one-half of such support was received from 2 or more persons each of whom, but for the fact that any such person alone did not contribute over one-half of such support, would have been entitled to claim such individual as a dependent for a taxable year beginning in such calendar year,

(C) the taxpayer contributed over 10 percent of such support, and

(D) each person described in subparagraph (B) (other than the taxpayer) who contributed over 10 percent of such support files a written declaration (in such manner and form as the Secretary may by regulations prescribe) that such person will not claim such individual as a dependent for any taxable year beginning in such calendar year.

(4) Special rule relating to income of handicapped dependents.—

(A) In general.—For purposes of paragraph (1)(B), the gross income of an individual who is permanently and totally disabled (as defined in section 22(e)(3)) at any time during the taxable year shall not include income attributable to services performed by the individual at a sheltered workshop if—

(i) the availability of medical care at such workshop is the principal reason for the individual's presence there, and

(ii) the income arises solely from activities at such workshop which are incident to such medical care.

(B) Sheltered workshop defined.—For purposes of subparagraph (A), the term "sheltered workshop" means a school—

(i) which provides special instruction or training designed to alleviate the disability of the individual, and

(ii) which is operated by an organization described in section 501(c)(3) and exempt from tax under section 501(a), or by a State, a possession of the United States, any political subdivision of any of the foregoing, the United States, or the District of Columbia.

(5) Special rules for support.—For purposes of this subsection—

(A) payments to a spouse which are includible in the gross income of such spouse under section 71 or 682 shall not be treated as a payment by the payor spouse for the support of any dependent, and

(B) in the case of the remarriage of a parent, support of a child received from the parent's spouse shall be treated as received from the parent.

(e) Special rule for divorced parents, etc.—

(1) In general.—Notwithstanding subsection (c)(1)(B), (c)(4), or (d)(1)(C), if—

(A) a child receives over one-half of the child's support during the calendar year from the child's parents—

(i) who are divorced or legally separated under a decree of divorce or separate maintenance,

(ii) who are separated under a written separation agreement, or

(iii) who live apart at all times during the last 6 months of the calendar year, and

(B) such child is in the custody of 1 or both of the child's parents for more than one-half of the calendar year,

such child shall be treated as being the qualifying child or qualifying relative of the noncustodial parent for a calendar year if the requirements described in paragraph (2) or (3) are met.

(2) Exception where custodial parent releases claim to exemption for the year.—For purposes of paragraph (1), the requirements described in this paragraph are met with respect to any calendar year if—

(A) the custodial parent signs a written declaration (in such manner and form as the Secretary may by regulations prescribe) that such custodial parent will not claim such child as a dependent for any taxable year beginning in such calendar year, and

(B) the noncustodial parent attaches such written declaration to the noncustodial parent's return for the taxable year beginning during such calendar year.

(3) Exception for certain pre-1985 instruments.—

(A) In general.—For purposes of paragraph (1), the requirements described in this paragraph are met with respect to any calendar year if—

(i) a qualified pre-1985 instrument between the parents applicable to the taxable year beginning in such calendar year provides that the noncustodial parent shall be entitled to any deduction allowable under section 151 for such child, and

(ii) the noncustodial parent provides at least $600 for the support of such child during such calendar year.

For purposes of this subparagraph, amounts expended for the support of a child or children shall be treated as received from the noncustodial parent to the extent that such parent provided amounts for such support.

(B) Qualified pre-1985 instrument.—For purposes of this paragraph, the term "qualified pre-1985 instrument" means any decree of divorce or separate maintenance or written agreement—

(i) which is executed before January 1, 1985,

(ii) which on such date contains the provision described in subparagraph (A)(i), and

(iii) which is not modified on or after such date in a modification which expressly provides that this paragraph shall not apply to such decree or agreement.

(4) Custodial parent and noncustodial parent.—For purposes of this subsection—

(A) Custodial parent.—The term "custodial parent" means the parent having custody for the greater portion of the calendar year.

(B) Noncustodial parent.—The term "noncustodial parent" means the parent who is not the custodial parent.

(5) Exception for multiple-support agreements.—This subsection shall not apply in any case where over one-half of the support of the child is treated as having been received from a taxpayer under the provision of subsection (d)(3).

(6) Special rule for support received from new spouse of parent.—For purposes of this subsection, in the case of the remarriage of a parent, support of a child received from the parent's spouse shall be treated as received from the parent.

(f) Other definitions and rules.—For purposes of this section—

(1) Child defined.—

(A) In general.—The term "child" means an individual who is—

(i) a son, daughter, stepson, or stepdaughter of the taxpayer, or

(ii) an eligible foster child of the taxpayer.

(B) Adopted child.—In determining whether any of the relationships specified in subparagraph (A)(i) or paragraph (4) exists, a legally adopted individual of the taxpayer, or an individual who is lawfully placed with the taxpayer for legal adoption by the taxpayer, shall be treated as a child of such individual by blood.

(C) Eligible foster child.—For purposes of subparagraph (A)(ii), the term "eligible foster child" means an individual who is placed with the taxpayer by an authorized placement agency or by judgment, decree, or other order of any court of competent jurisdiction.

(2) Student defined.—The term "student' means an individual who during each of 5 calendar months during the calendar year in which the taxable year of the taxpayer begins—

(A) is a full-time student at an educational organization described in section 170(b) (1)(A)(ii), or

(B) is pursuing a full-time course of institutional on-farm training under the supervision of an accredited agent of an educational organization described in section 170(b)(1)(A)(ii) or of a State or political subdivision of a State.

(3) Determination of household status.—An individual shall not be treated as a member of the taxpayer's household if at any time during the taxable year of the taxpayer the relationship between such individual and the taxpayer is in violation of local law.

(4) Brother and sister.—The terms "brother" and "sister" include a brother or sister by the half blood.

(5) Special support test in case of students.—For purposes of subsections (c)(1)(D) and (d)(1)(C), in the case of an individual who is—

(A) a child of the taxpayer, and

(B) a student,

amounts received as scholarships for study at an educational organization described in section 170 (b)(1)(A)(ii) shall not be taken into account.

(6) Treatment of missing children.—

(A) In general.—Solely for the purposes referred to in subparagraph (B), a child of the taxpayer—

(i) who is presumed by law enforcement authorities to have been kidnapped by someone who is not a member of the family of such child or the taxpayer, and

(ii) who had, for the taxable year in which the kidnapping occurred, the same principal place of abode as the taxpayer for more than one-half of the portion of such year before the date of the kidnapping,

shall be treated as meeting the requirement of subsection (c)(1)(B) with respect to a taxpayer for all taxable years ending during the period that the child is kidnapped.

(B) Purposes.—Subparagraph (A) shall apply solely for purposes of determining—

(i) the deduction under section 151(c),

(ii) the credit under section 24 (relating to child tax credit),

(iii) whether an individual is a surviving spouse or a head of a household (as such terms are defined in section 2), and

(iv) the earned income credit under section 32.

(C) Comparable treatment of certain qualifying relatives.—For purposes of this section, a child of the taxpayer—

(i) who is presumed by law enforcement authorities to have been kidnapped by someone who is not a member of the family of such child or the taxpayer, and

(ii) who was (without regard to this paragraph) a qualifying relative of the taxpayer for the portion of the taxable year before the date of the kidnapping,

shall be treated as a qualifying relative of the taxpayer for all taxable years ending during the period that the child is kidnapped.

(D) Termination of treatment.—Subparagraphs (A) and (C) shall cease to apply as of the first taxable year of the taxpayer beginning after the calendar year in which there is a determination that the child is dead (or, if earlier, in which the child would have attained age 18).

(7) Cross references.—For provision treating child as dependent of both parents for purposes of certain provisions, see sections 105(b), 132(h)(2)(B), and 213(d)(5).

§ 153. Cross references

* * *

(3) For determination of marital status, see section 7703.

Editorial Summary

Deductions

Subchapter B of Chapter 1 (Secs. 161–291)

Deductions are classified in the Code into the following major areas:

1. Itemized deductions for individuals and corporations (Part VI).
2. Additional itemized deductions for individuals (Part VII).
3. Special deductions for corporations (Part VIII).
4. Items not deductible (Part IX).
5. Other.

All deductions are statutory in nature [see Sec. 63(a)]. That is, a particular item of expense cannot be deducted unless authorization for doing so exists in the Code. One must be careful to correlate deduction Code sections with deduction disallowance Code sections. Otherwise, deductions may be taken which are, in fact, denied by a disallowance Code section.

The use of the term "itemized" in category 1 and category 2 above can lead to confusion. Tax terminology normally associates the term with the itemized deduction subcategory which is part of the "deduction from" category on the return of the individual taxpayer. While the term generally is used this way with respect to category 2, that is not the intent with respect to category 1. This will be further clarified in the discussion of category 1.

It is useful at this stage in the presentation of deductions to categorize more precisely the deductions for the individual taxpayer into the "deduction for" category and the "deduction from" category [see Sec. 62].

Type	For	From
Trade or business expense	X	
Production of income expense	1	X
Deductible personal expenses	2	X

X = normal classification.

1 = This is an exception classification. It will apply only if the expense is associated with royalty property or rental property or is a penalty for a premature withdrawal from a time savings account.

2 = This is an exception classification. It will apply only if the expense is a reimbursed employee expense, a contribution to retirement savings, an alimony payment, or a qualified moving expense.

The statutory language of the Code refers to the deduction Code sections being applicable to the individual taxpayer and/or the corporate taxpayer. No mention is made of the partnership. In effect, many of these Code sections are applicable to the partnership. However, the partnership is merely a tax reporter rather than being a taxpayer. The tax liability is levied at the partner level. Thus, the partnership is a conduit [see Secs. 701, 702, 703].

For presentation purposes, the Code sections relating to deductions are arranged into the following categories:

1. Trade or business deduction.
2. Production of income deduction.
3. Deductible personal expenses.
4. Disallowance of deductions.

Note that some Code sections appear in more than one category.

Code Sec.	T or B	P of I	DPE	D of D
161	X	X	X	X
162	X			X
163	X	X	X	X
164	X	X	X	X
165	X	X	X	X
166	X	X	X	
167	X	X		
168	X	X		
169	X			
170	X	X	X	X
171	X	X		
172	X			
173	X			
174	X			
175	X			
176	X			
178	X	X		
179	X	X		
180	X			

Code Sec.	T or B	P of I	DPE	D of D
183		X		X
184	X	X		
186	X			
188	X			
190	X			
192	X			
193	X			
194	X	X		
194A	X			
195	X			
196	X			
197	X	X		
199	X			
211		X	X	
212		X		
213			X	X
215			X	
216			X	X
217	X		X	
219	X	X	X	X
220	X	X	X	
221			X	
222			X	
223	X	X	X	
241	X			
243	X			
244	X			
245	X			
246				X
246A				X
247	X			
248	X			
249				X
250	X			
261-280H				X

Trade or business deduction. The ability to deduct expenses associated with a trade or business is permitted under Sec. 162. However, Sec. 162 is not intended to provide all-inclusive justification for deducting the expenses of a trade or business. Rather, Sec. 162 provides the general authority. Particular types of expenses are deductible in accordance with the provisions contained in other Code sections. Depreciation and cost recovery, for example, are deductible under Secs. 167 and 168 respectively, and bad debts are deductible under Sec. 166.

Key terms that affect the ability to deduct trade or business expenses are ordinary, necessary, reasonable, lavish or extravagant, and away from home. Through various administrative and judicial interpretations, special meanings have developed for each of these terms. In addition, in certain circumstances, the statute specifically defines through a dollar amount or percentage the amount that can be deducted rather than relying on the interpretation of the aforementioned terms. Utilizing this approach are the following:

1. Statutory ceiling amount for members of Congress for living expenses while away from home [see Sec. 162(a)].

2. Maximum deduction for state legislator's living expenses while away from home [see Sec. 162(h)].

3. Percentage limitation on self-employed individuals' health insurance costs prior to 2003 [see Sec. 162(1)].

4. Limit on executive compensation deduction [see Sec. 162(m)].

5. Statutory ceiling amounts on acquisition indebtedness and home equity indebtedness [see Sec. 163(h)(3)].

6. Materiality amounts and percentage for personal casualty and theft losses [see Sec. 165(h)].

7. Percentage limitations on charitable contributions [see Sec. 170(b)].

8. Standard mileage rate for charitable contributions [see Sec. 170(i)].

9. Maximum deduction for limited expensing of certain fixed assets (see Sec. 179).

10. Percentage of adjusted gross income requirement for medical expenses [see Sec. 213(a)].

11. Statutory ceiling amount of lodging while away from home for medical purposes [see Sec. 213(d)(2)].

12. Statutory ceiling amounts on Individual Retirement Accounts [see Secs. 219(b) and (c)].

13. Percentage limitations on the deduction allowed for Archer MSAs [see Sec. 220(b)(2)] and dollar limits on what is a high deductible health plan [see Sec. 220(c)(2)].

14. Dollar limitation on the deduction for interest on education loans [see Sec. 221(b)(2)].

15. Dollar limitation on the deduction allowed for health savings accounts [see Sec. 223(b)(2)] and dollar limits on what is a high deductible plan [see Sec. 223(c)(2)].

16. Percentage limitations on dividends received deduction [see Sec. 243(a)].

17. Statutory ceiling amount for conventions on cruise ships [see Sec. 274(h)(2)].

18. Statutory ceiling amounts for employee achievement awards [see Sec. 274(j)(2)].

19. Percentage limitation on meal and entertainment expenses [see Sec. 274(n)].

20. Statutory ceiling amounts on depreciation deduction for luxury automobiles [see Sec. 280F(a)(1)].

21. Limitation on golden parachute payments [see Sec. 280G(b)].

What is considered a trade or business by the taxpayer may not satisfy the statutory intent [refer to the hobby loss provision under Sec. 183]. If the activity is a hobby rather than a trade or business, the deductions are limited to the gross income produced by the activity.

Production of income deduction. Like Sec. 162 for trade or business expenses, Sec. 212 provides the general authority for deducting the expenses associated with activities which constitute the production of income (e.g., investment) rather than being a trade or business. Likewise, Sec. 212 is not allinclusive; that is, other Code sections provide the authority for deducting particular types of production of income expenses.

Note that the deductions under Sec. 212 also are referred to as "nonbusiness" expenses. This term is sometimes used because the term "production of income" is not broad enough to cover certain items which are deductible under Sec. 212.

That is, in addition to providing the statutory authority for "production of income" expenses, Sec. 212 also provides the statutory authority for deducting expenses associated with the determination, collection, or refund of any tax [see Sec. 212(3)].

Deductible personal expenses. Section 262 provides that personal, living, and family expenses are not deductible unless specifically provided in the Code. Such statutory authority exists in the following Code sections.

163	Interest
164	Taxes
165	Losses
166	Bad Debts
170	Charitable Contributions
183	Hobby Loss
213	Medical and Dental Expenses
215	Alimony
217	Moving Expenses
219	Retirement Savings
220	Medical Savings Accounts (Archer MSAs)
221	Interest on Education Loans
222	Qualified tuition and related expenses
223	Health Savings Account

The deduction authority, provided in each of the Code sections, is limited.

Disallowance of deductions. Deductions are denied for a variety of reasons that can be classified as follows:

1. Personal expenses [see Sec. 262].
2. Capital expenditures [see Secs. 263, 263A, 280B].
3. Expenses associated with generating tax-exempt income [see Sec. 265].
4. Expenses that are contrary to public policy [see Secs. 162, 280E, 280G, 280H].
5. Expenses associated with activities that are classified as hobbies rather than as trades or businesses [see Sec. 183].
6. Certain transactions between related parties [see Secs. 267, 280H, 707(b)(1)].
7. Certain tax avoidance transactions [see Secs. 269, 269A].
8. Certain meal or entertainment expenses associated with a trade or business or the production of income [see Sec. 274].
9. Expenses associated with certain business uses of taxpayer's home or vacation home [see Sec. 280A].
10. Others [see Secs. 162, 280F].

Even though a deduction Code section may appear to provide authority for a deduction, the deduction may either be limited or prohibited by one of the deduction disallowance provisions.

In dealing with the deduction disallowance provisions, distinction needs to be made between those provisions which produce a permanent disallowance and those which provide for only a temporary disallowance. For example, an expenditure for a building to be used in the taxpayer's trade or business is appropriately classified as a capital expenditure under Sec. 263. However, Sec. 168 permits the cost of the building to be deducted through the application of the cost recovery process. Contrast this with the permanent nature of the deduction disallowance under Sec. 162(c) for certain illegal payments.

Employee business expenses. The treatment of employee business expenses deserves special attention. In general, Sec. 162 provides the statutory authority for the deduction of such expenses. Illustrative of the types of items appropriately included in this category for an employee are the following:

1. Travel expenses while away from home.
2. Transportation expenses (i.e., as contrasted with non-deductible commuting expenses).
3. Education expenses.
4. Professional dues and subscriptions.
5. Union dues.
6. Entertainment expenses (but see Sec. 274).
7. Office in the home expenses (but see Sec. 280A).
8. Participation in professional meetings and conferences.
9. Special required clothing not adaptable for regular wear.

For the individual taxpayer, these expenses must be classified as "deductions for" adjusted gross income or "deductions from" adjusted gross income (see the Editorial Summary associated with Sec. 62). Since the "deduction for" category generally includes business-related deductions whereas the "deduction from" category generally includes personal-type deductions, it would appear logical that deductible employee business expenses be included in the "deduction for" category. Prior to the Tax Reform Act of 1986, some of the items in this category were so included (e.g., travel expenses and transportation expenses). However, the extant classification includes all deductible employee business expenses in the "deduction from" category unless such expenses are reimbursed. Section 62(a)(2)(A) specifically provides that deductible employee business expenses which are reimbursed by the employer are to be classified in the "deduction for" category. Note, also the special rule for performing artists in Sec. 62(a)(2)(B) which provides for "deduction for" treatment in limited circumstances. Also note the deduction *for* AGI treatment for (1) certain expenses of officials who are employees of state or local governments [Sec. 62(a)(2)(C)], (2) certain expenses of elementary and secondary school teachers [Sec. 62(a)(2)(D)], and (3) certain expenses of reserve employees of the U.S. military [Sec. 62(a)(2)(E)].

Classification of employee business expenses in the "deduction for" category has three potential advantages. First, if the taxpayer uses the standard deduction rather than itemizing deductions [see Sec. 63(c) and (d)], the potential deduction for employee business expenses is not wasted. Second, even if the taxpayer itemizes deductions, employee business expenses classified in the "deduction from" category are subject to the 2 percent floor rule of Sec. 67 and may be subject to the 3 percent phaseout rule of Sec. 68 (through 2009). Third, employee business expenses are included in the covered itemized deductions which prior to 2010 were subject to phaseout [see Sec. 68(c)] (through 2009). Note that the American Taxpayer

Relief Act of 2012 reinstated the phaseout of itemized deductions beginning in 2013.

The moving expenses of an employee also can be classified as an employee business expense. However, the statutory authority for the deduction is under Sec. 217 rather than under Sec. 162. Prior to the Revenue Reconciliation Act of 1993 (RRA of 1993), moving expenses were classified in the "deduction from" category, but were not subject to the 2 percent floor of Sec. 67. RRA of 1993 reclassified moving expenses as a "deduction for" adjusted gross income [see Sec. 62(a)(15)].

PART VI—ITEMIZED DEDUCTIONS FOR INDIVIDUALS AND CORPORATIONS

§ 161. Allowance of deductions

In computing taxable income under section 63, there shall be allowed as deductions the items specified in this part, subject to the exceptions provided in part IX (sec. 261 and following, relating to items not deductible).

§ 162. Trade or business expenses

(a) In general.—There shall be allowed as a deduction all the ordinary and necessary expenses paid or incurred during the taxable year in carrying on any trade or business, including—

(1) a reasonable allowance for salaries or other compensation for personal services actually rendered;

(2) traveling expenses (including amounts expended for meals and lodging other than amounts which are lavish or extravagant under the circumstances) while away from home in the pursuit of a trade or business; and

(3) rentals or other payments required to be made as a condition to the continued use or possession, for purposes of the trade or business, of property to which the taxpayer has not taken or is not taking title or in which he has no equity.

For purposes of the preceding sentence, the place of residence of a Member of Congress (including any Delegate and Resident Commissioner) within the State, congressional district, or possession which he represents in Congress shall be considered his home, but amounts expended by such Members within each taxable year for living expenses shall not be deductible for income tax purposes in excess of $3,000. For purposes of paragraph (2), the taxpayer shall not be treated as being temporarily away from home during any period of employment if such period exceeds 1 year. The preceding sentence shall not apply to any Federal employee during any period for which such employee is certified by the Attorney General (or the designee thereof) as traveling on behalf of the United States in temporary duty status to investigate or prosecute, or provide support services for the investigation or prosecution of, a Federal crime.

(b) Charitable contributions and gifts excepted.—No deduction shall be allowed under subsection (a) for any contribution or gift which would be allowable as a deduction under section 170 were it not for the percentage limitations, the dollar limitations, or the requirements as to the time of payment, set forth in such section.

(c) Illegal bribes, kickbacks, and other payments.—

(1) Illegal payments to government officials or employees.—No deduction shall be allowed under subsection (a) for any payment made, directly or indirectly, to an official or employee of any government, or of any agency or instrumentality of any government, if the payment constitutes an illegal bribe or kickback or, if the payment is to an official or employee of a foreign government, the payment is unlawful under the Foreign Corrupt Practices Act of 1977. The burden of proof in respect of the issue, for the purposes of this paragraph, as to whether a payment constitutes an illegal bribe or kickback (or is unlawful under the Foreign Corrupt Practices Act of 1977) shall be upon the Secretary to the same extent as he bears the burden of proof under section 7454 (concerning the burden of proof when the issue relates to fraud).

(2) Other illegal payments.—No deduction shall be allowed under subsection (a) for any payment (other than a payment described in paragraph (1)) made, directly or indirectly, to any person, if the payment constitutes an illegal bribe, illegal kickback, or other illegal payment under any law of the United States, or under any law of a State (but only if such State law is generally enforced), which subjects the payor to a criminal penalty or the loss of license or privilege to engage in a trade or business. For purposes of this paragraph, a kickback includes a payment in consideration of the referral of a client, patient, or customer. The burden of proof in respect of the issue, for purposes of this paragraph, as to whether a payment constitutes an illegal bribe, illegal kickback, or other illegal payment shall be upon the Secretary to the same extent as he bears the burden of proof under section 7454 (concerning the burden of proof when the issue relates to fraud).

(3) Kickbacks, rebates, and bribes under medicare and medicaid.—No deduction shall be allowed under subsection (a) for any kickback, rebate, or bribe made by any provider of services, supplier, physician, or other person who furnishes items or services for which payment is or may be made under the Social Security Act, or in whole or in part out of Federal funds under a State plan approved under such Act, if such kickback, rebate, or bribe is made in connection with the furnishing of such items or services or the making or receipt of such payments. For purposes of this paragraph, a kickback includes a payment in consideration of the referral of a client, patient, or customer.

* * *

(e) Denial of deduction for certain lobbying and political expenditures.—

(1) In general.—No deduction shall be allowed under subsection (a) for any amount paid or incurred in connection with—

(A) influencing legislation,

(B) participation in, or intervention in, any political campaign on behalf of (or in opposition to) any candidate for public office,

(C) any attempt to influence the general public, or segments thereof, with respect to elections, legislative matters, or referendums, or

(D) any direct communication with a covered executive branch official in an attempt to influence the official actions or positions of such official.

(2) Exception for local legislation.—In the case of any legislation of any local council or similar governing body—

(A) paragraph (1)(A) shall not apply, and

(B) the deduction allowed by subsection (a) shall include all ordinary and necessary expenses (including, but not limited to, traveling expenses described in subsection (a)(2) and the cost of preparing testimony) paid or incurred during the taxable year in carrying on any trade or business—

(i) in direct connection with appearances before, submission of statements to, or sending communications to the committees, or individual members, of such council or body with respect to legislation or proposed legislation of direct interest to the taxpayer, or

(ii) in direct connection with communication of information between the taxpayer and an organization of which the taxpayer is a member with respect to any such legislation or proposed legislation which is of direct interest to the taxpayer and to such organization,

and that portion of the dues so paid or incurred with respect to any organization of which the taxpayer is a member which is attributable to the expenses of the activities described in clauses (i) and (ii) carried on by such organization.

(3) Application to dues of tax-exempt organizations.—No deduction shall be allowed under subsection (a) for the portion of dues or other similar amounts paid by the taxpayer to an organization which is exempt from tax under this subtitle which the organization notifies the taxpayer under section 6033(e)(1)(A)(ii) is allocable to expenditures to which paragraph (1) applies.

(4) Influencing legislation.—For purposes of this subsection—

(A) In general.—The term "influencing legislation" means any attempt to influence any legislation through communication with any member or employee of a legislative body, or with any government official or employee who may participate in the formulation of legislation.

(B) Legislation.—The term "legislation" has the meaning given such term by section 4911(e)(2).

(5) Other special rules.—

(A) Exception for certain taxpayers.—In the case of any taxpayer engaged in the trade or business of conducting activities described in paragraph (1), paragraph (1) shall not apply to expenditures of the taxpayer in conducting such activities directly on behalf of another person (but shall apply to payments by such other person to the taxpayer for conducting such activities).

(B) De minimis exception.—

(i) In general.—Paragraph (1) shall not apply to any in-house expenditures for any taxable year if such expenditures do not exceed $2,000. In determining whether a taxpayer exceeds the $2,000 limit under this clause, there shall not be taken into account overhead costs otherwise allocable to activities described in paragraphs (1)(A) and (D).

(ii) In-house expenditures.—For purposes of clause (i), the term "in-house expenditures" means expenditures described in paragraphs (1)(A) and (D) other than—

(I) payments by the taxpayer to a person engaged in the trade or business of conducting activities described in paragraph (1) for the conduct of such activities on behalf of the taxpayer, or

(II) dues or other similar amounts paid or incurred by the taxpayer which are allocable to activities described in paragraph (1).

(C) Expenses incurred in connection with lobbying and political activities.—Any amount paid or incurred for research for, or preparation, planning, or coordination of, any activity described in paragraph (1) shall be treated as paid or incurred in connection with such activity.

(6) Covered executive branch official.—For purposes of this subsection, the term "covered executive branch official" means—

(A) the President,

(B) the Vice President,

(C) any officer or employee of the White House Office of the Executive Office of the President, and the 2 most senior level officers of each of the other agencies in such Executive Office, and

(D) **(i)** any individual serving in a position in level I of the Executive Schedule under section 5312 of title 5, United States Code, (ii) any other individual designated by the President as having Cabinet level status, and (iii) any immediate deputy of an individual described in clause (i) or (ii).

(7) Special rule for Indian tribal governments.—For purposes of this subsection, an Indian tribal government shall be treated in the same manner as a local council or similar governing body.

(8) Cross reference.—

For reporting requirements and alternative taxes related to this subsection, see section 6033(e).

(f) Fines and penalties.—No deduction shall be allowed under subsection (a) for any fine or similar penalty paid to a government for the violation of any law.

(g) Treble damage payments under the antitrust laws.—If in a criminal proceeding a taxpayer is convicted of a violation of the antitrust laws, or his plea of guilty or nolo contendere to an indictment or information charging such a violation is entered or accepted in such a proceeding, no deduction shall be allowed under subsection (a) for two-thirds of any amount paid or incurred—

(1) on any judgment for damages entered against the taxpayer under section 4 of the Act entitled "An Act to supplement existing laws against unlawful restraints and monopolies, and for other purposes," approved October 15, 1914 (commonly known as the Clayton Act), on account of such violation or any related violation of the antitrust laws which occurred prior to the date of the final judgment of such conviction, or

(2) in settlement of any action brought under such section 4 on account of such violation or related violation.

The preceding sentence shall not apply with respect to any conviction or plea before January 1, 1970, or to any conviction or plea on or after such date in a new trial following an appeal of a conviction before such date.

(h) State legislators' travel expenses away from home.—

(1) In general.—For purposes of subsection (a), in the case of any individual who is a State legislator at any time during the taxable year and who makes an election under this subsection for the taxable year—

(A) the place of residence of such individual within the legislative district which he represented shall be considered his home,

(B) he shall be deemed to have expended for living expenses (in connection with his trade or business as a legislator) an amount equal to the sum of the amounts determined by multiplying each legislative day of such individual during the taxable year by the greater of—

(i) the amount generally allowable with respect to such day to employees of the State of which he is a legislator for per diem while away from home, to the extent such amount does not exceed 110 percent of the amount described in clause (ii) with respect to such day, or

(ii) the amount generally allowable with respect to such day to employees of the executive branch of the Federal Government for per diem while away from home but serving in the United States, and

(C) he shall be deemed to be away from home in the pursuit of a trade or business on each legislative day.

(2) Legislative days.—For purposes of paragraph (1), a legislative day during any taxable year for any individual shall be any day during such year on which—

(A) the legislature was in session (including any day in which the legislature was not in session for a period of 4 consecutive days or less), or

(B) the legislature was not in session but the physical presence of the individual was formally recorded at a meeting of a committee of such legislature.

(3) Election.—An election under this subsection for any taxable year shall be made at such time and in such manner as the Secretary shall by regulations prescribe.

(4) Section not to apply to legislators who reside near capitol.—For taxable years beginning after December 31, 1980, this subsection shall not apply to any legislator whose place of residence within the legislative district which he represents is 50 or fewer miles from the capitol building of the State.

* * *

(k) Stock reacquisition expenses.—

(1) In general.—Except as provided in paragraph (2), no deduction otherwise allowable shall be allowed under this chapter for any amount paid or incurred by a corporation in connection with the reacquisition of its stock or of the stock of any related person (as defined in section 465(b)(3)(C)).

(2) Exceptions.—Paragraph (1) shall not apply to—

(A) Certain specific deductions.—Any—

(i) deduction allowable under section 163 (relating to interest),

(ii) deduction for amounts which are properly allocable to indebtedness and amortized over the term of such indebtedness, or

(iii) deduction for dividends paid (within the meaning of section 561).

* * *

(l) Special rules for health insurance costs of self-employed individuals.

(1) Allowance of deduction.—In the case of a taxpayer who is an employee within the meaning of section 401(c)(1), there shall be allowed as a deduction under this section an amount equal to the amount paid during the taxable year for insurance which constitutes medical care for—

(A) the taxpayer,

(B) the taxpayer's spouse,

(C) the taxpayer's dependents, and

(D) any child (as defined in section 152(f)(1)) of the taxpayer who as of the end of the taxable year has not attained age 27.

(2) Limitations.—

(A) Dollar amount.—No deduction shall be allowed under paragraph (1) to the extent that the amount of such deduction exceeds the taxpayer's earned income (within the meaning of section 401(c)) derived by the taxpayer from the trade or business with respect to which the plan providing the medical care coverage is established.

(B) Other coverage.—Paragraph (1) shall not apply to any taxpayer for any calendar month for which the taxpayer is eligible to participate in any subsidized health plan maintained by any employer of the taxpayer or of the spouse of, or any dependent, or individual described in subparagraph (D) of paragraph (1) with respect to the taxpayer. The preceding sentence shall be applied separately with respect to—

(i) plans which include coverage for qualified long-term care services (as defined in section 7702B(c)) or are qualified long-term care insurance contracts (as defined in section 7702B(b)), and

(ii) plans which do not include such coverage and are not such contracts.

(C) Long-term care premiums.—In the case of a qualified long-term care insurance contract (as defined in section 7702B(b)), only eligible long-term care premiums (as defined in section 213(d)(10)) shall be taken into account under paragraph (1).

(3) Coordination with medical deduction.—Any amount paid by a taxpayer for insurance to which paragraph (1) applies shall not be taken into account in computing the amount allowable to the taxpayer as a deduction under section 213(a).

(4) Deduction not allowed for self-employment tax purposes.—The deduction allowable by reason of this subsection shall not be taken into account in determining an individual's net earnings from self-employment (within the meaning of section 1402(a)) for purposes of chapter 2 for taxable years beginning before January 1, 2010, or after December 31, 2010.

(5) Treatment of certain S corporation shareholders.—This subsection shall apply in the case of any individual treated as a partner under section 1372(a), except that—

(A) for purposes of this subsection such individual's wages (as defined in section 3121) from the S corporation shall be treated as such individual's earned income (within the meaning of section 401(c)(1)), and

(B) there shall be such adjustments in the application of this subsection as the Secretary may by regulations prescribe.

(m) Certain excessive employee remuneration.—

(1) In general.—In the case of any publicly held corporation, no deduction shall be allowed under this chapter for applicable employee remuneration with respect to any covered employee to the extent that the amount of such remuneration for the taxable year with respect to such employee exceeds $1,000,000.

(2) Publicly held corporation.—For purposes of this subsection, the term "publicly held corporation" means any corporation issuing any class of common equity securities required to be registered under section 12 of the Securities Exchange Act of 1934.

(3) Covered employee.—For purposes of this subsection, the term "covered employee" means any employee of the taxpayer if—

(A) as of the close of the taxable year, such employee is the chief executive officer of the taxpayer or is an individual acting in such a capacity, or

(B) the total compensation of such employee for the taxable year is required to be reported to shareholders under the Securities Exchange Act of 1934 by reason of such employee being among the 4 highest compensated officers for the taxable year (other than the chief executive officer).

(4) Applicable employee remuneration.—For purposes of this subsection—

(A) In general.—Except as otherwise provided in this paragraph, the term "applicable employee remuneration" means, with respect to any covered employee for any taxable year, the aggregate amount allowable as a deduction under this chapter for such taxable year (determined without regard to this subsection) for remuneration for services performed by such employee (whether or not during the taxable year).

(B) Exception for remuneration payable on commission basis.—The term "applicable employee remuneration" shall not include any remuneration payable on a commission basis solely on account of income generated directly by the individual performance of the individual to whom such remuneration is payable.

(C) Other performance-based compensation.—The term "applicable employee remuneration" shall not include any remuneration payable solely on account of the attainment of one or more performance goals, but only if—

(i) the performance goals are determined by a compensation committee of the board of directors of the taxpayer which is comprised solely of 2 or more outside directors,

(ii) the material terms under which the remuneration is to be paid, including the performance goals, are disclosed to shareholders and approved by a majority of the vote in a separate shareholder vote before the payment of such remuneration, and

(iii) before any payment of such remuneration, the compensation committee referred to in clause (i) certifies that the performance goals and any other material terms were in fact satisfied.

(D) Exception for existing binding contracts.—The term "applicable employee remuneration" shall not include any remuneration payable under a written binding contract which was in effect on February 17, 1993, and which was not modified thereafter in any material respect before such remuneration is paid.

(E) Remuneration.—For purposes of this paragraph, the term "remuneration" includes any remuneration (including benefits) in any medium other than cash, but shall not include—

(i) any payment referred to in so much of section 3121(a)(5) as precedes subparagraph (E) thereof, and

(ii) any benefit provided to or on behalf of an employee if at the time such benefit is provided it is reasonable to believe that the employee will be able to exclude such benefit from gross income under this chapter.

For purposes of clause (i), section 3121(a)(5) shall be applied without regard to section 3121(v)(1).

(F) Coordination with disallowed golden parachute payments.—The dollar limitation contained in paragraph (1) shall be reduced (but not below zero) by the amount (if any) which would have been included in the applicable employee remuneration of the covered employee for the taxable year but for being disallowed under section 280G.

(G) Coordination with excise tax on specified stock compensation.—The dollar limitation contained in paragraph (1) with respect to any covered employee shall be reduced (but not below zero) by the amount of any payment (with respect to such employee) of the tax imposed by section 4985 directly or indirectly by the expatriated corporation (as defined in such section) or by any member of the expanded affiliated group (as defined in such section) which includes such corporation.

(5) Special rule for application to employers participating in the troubled assets relief program.—

(A) In general.—In the case of an applicable employer, no deduction shall be allowed under this chapter—

(i) in the case of executive remuneration for any applicable taxable year which is attributable to services performed by a covered executive during such applicable taxable year, to the extent that the amount of such remuneration exceeds $500,000, or

(ii) in the case of deferred deduction executive remuneration for any taxable year for services performed during any applicable taxable year by a covered executive, to the extent that the amount of such remuneration exceeds $500,000 reduced (but not below zero) by the sum of—

(I) the executive remuneration for such applicable taxable year, plus

(II) the portion of the deferred deduction executive remuneration for such services which was taken into account under this clause in a preceding taxable year.

(B) Applicable employer.—For purposes of this paragraph —

(i) In general.—Except as provided in clause (ii), the term "applicable employer" means any employer from whom 1 or more troubled assets are acquired under a program established by the Secretary under section 101(a) of the Emergency Economic Stabilization Act of 2008 if the aggregate amount of the assets so acquired for all taxable years exceeds $300,000,000.

(ii) Disregard of certain assets sold through direct purchase.—If the only sales of troubled assets by an employer under the program described in clause (i) are through 1 or more direct purchases (within the meaning of section 113(c) of the Emergency Economic Stabilization Act of 2008), such assets shall not be taken into account under clause (i) in determining whether the employer is an applicable employer for purposes of this paragraph.

(iii) Aggregation rules.—Two or more persons who are treated as a single employer under subsection (b) or (c) of section 414 shall be treated as a single employer, except that in applying section 1563(a) for purposes of either such subsection, paragraphs (2) and (3) thereof shall be disregarded.

(C) Applicable taxable year.—For purposes of this paragraph, the term "applicable taxable year" means, with respect to any employer—

(i) the first taxable year of the employer—

(I) which includes any portion of the period during which the authorities under section 101(a) of the Emergency Economic Stabilization Act of 2008 are in effect (determined under section 120 thereof), and

(II) in which the aggregate amount of troubled assets acquired from the employer during the taxable year pursuant to such authorities (other than assets to which subparagraph (B)(ii) applies), when added to the aggregate amount so acquired for all preceding taxable years, exceeds $300,000,000, and

(ii) any subsequent taxable year which includes any portion of such period.

(D) Covered executive.—For purposes of this paragraph—

(i) In general.—The term "covered executive" means, with respect to any applicable taxable year, any employee—

(I) who, at any time during the portion of the taxable year during which the authorities under section 101(a) of the Emergency Economic Stabilization Act of 2008 are in effect (determined under section 120 thereof), is the chief executive officer of the applicable employer or the chief financial officer of the applicable employer, or an individual acting in either such capacity, or

(II) who is described in clause (ii).

(ii) Highest compensated employees.—An employee is described in this clause if the employee is 1 of the 3 highest compensated officers of the applicable employer for the taxable year (other than an individual described in clause (i)(I)), determined—

(I) on the basis of the shareholder disclosure rules for compensation under the Securities Exchange Act of 1934 (without regard to whether those rules apply to the employer), and

(II) by only taking into account employees employed during the portion of the taxable year described in clause (i)(I).

(iii) Employee remains covered executive.—If an employee is a covered executive with respect to an applicable employer for any applicable taxable year, such employee shall be treated as a covered executive with respect to such employer for all subsequent applicable taxable years and for all subsequent taxable years in which deferred deduction executive remuneration with respect to services performed in all such applicable taxable years would (but for this paragraph) be deductible.

(E) Executive remuneration.—For purposes of this paragraph, the term "executive remuneration" means the applicable employee remuneration of the covered executive, as determined under paragraph (4) without regard to subparagraphs (B), (C), and (D) thereof. Such term shall not include any deferred deduction executive remuneration with respect to services performed in a prior applicable taxable year.

(F) Deferred deduction executive remuneration.—For purposes of this paragraph, the term "deferred deduction executive remuneration" means remuneration which would be executive remuneration for services performed in an applicable taxable year but for the fact that the deduction under this chapter (determined without regard to this paragraph) for such remuneration is allowable in a subsequent taxable year.

(G) Coordination.—Rules similar to the rules of subparagraphs (F) and (G) of paragraph (4) shall apply for purposes of this paragraph.

(H) Regulatory authority.—The Secretary may prescribe such guidance, rules, or regulations as are necessary to carry out the purposes of this paragraph and the Emergency Economic Stabilization Act of 2008, including the extent to which this paragraph applies in the case of any acquisition, merger, or reorganization of an applicable employer.

* * *

(n) Special rule for certain group health plans.—

(1) In general.—No deduction shall be allowed under this chapter to an employer for any amount paid or incurred in connection with a group health plan if the plan does not reimburse for inpatient hospital care services provided in the State of New York—

(A) except as provided in subparagraphs (B) and (C), at the same rate as licensed commercial insurers are required to reimburse hospitals for such services when such reimbursement is not through such a plan,

(B) in the case of any reimbursement through a health maintenance organization, at the same rate as health maintenance organizations are required to reimburse hospitals for such services for individuals not covered by such a plan (determined without regard to any government-supported individuals exempt from such rate), or

(C) in the case of any reimbursement through any corporation organized under Article 43 of the New York State Insurance Law, at the same rate as any such corporation is required to reimburse hospitals for such services for individuals not covered by such a plan.

(2) State law exception.—Paragraph (1) shall not apply to any group health plan which is not required under the laws of the State of New York (determined without regard to this subsection or other provisions of Federal law) to reimburse at the rates provided in paragraph (1).

(3) Group health plan.—For purposes of this subsection, the term "group health plan" means a plan of, or contributed to by, an employer or employee organization (including a self-insured plan) to provide health care (directly or otherwise) to any employee, any former employee, the employer, or any other individual associated or formerly associated with the employer in a business relationship, or any member of their family.

(o) Treatment of certain reimbursed expenses of rural mail carriers.—

(1) General rule.—In the case of any employee of the United States Postal Service who performs services involving the collection and delivery of mail on a rural route and who receives qualified reimbursements for the expenses incurred by such employee for the use of a vehicle in performing such services—

(A) the amount allowable as a deduction under this chapter for the use of a vehicle in performing such services shall be equal to the amount of such qualified reimbursements; and

(B) such qualified reimbursements shall be treated as paid under a reimbursement or other expense allowance arrangement for purposes of section 62(a)(2)(A) (and section 62(c) shall not apply to such qualified reimbursements).

(2) Special rule where expenses exceed reimbursements.—Notwithstanding paragraph (1)(A), if the expenses incurred by an employee for the use of a vehicle in performing services described in paragraph (1) exceed the qualified reimbursements for such expenses, such excess shall be taken into account in computing the miscellaneous itemized deductions of the employee under section 67.

(3) Definition of qualified reimbursements.—For purposes of this subsection, the term "qualified reimbursements" means the amounts paid by the United States Postal Service to employees as an equipment maintenance allowance under the 1991 collective bargaining agreement between the United States Postal Service and the National Rural Letter Carriers' Association. Amounts paid as an equipment maintenance allowance by such Postal Service under later collective bargaining agreements that supersede the 1991 agreement shall be considered qualified reimbursements if such amounts do not exceed the amounts that would have been paid under the 1991 agreement, adjusted for changes in the Consumer Price Index (as defined in section 1(f)(5)) since 1991.

(p) Treatment of expenses of members of reserve component of Armed Forces of the United States.—For purposes of subsection (a)(2), in the case of an individual who performs services as a member of a reserve component of the Armed Forces of the United States at any time during the taxable year, such individual shall be deemed to be away from home in the pursuit of a trade or business for any period during which such individual is away from home in connection with such service.

(q) Cross references.—

(1) For special rule relating to expenses in connection with subdividing real property for sale, see section 1237.

(2) For special rule relating to the treatment of payments by a transferee of a franchise, trademark, or trade name, see section 1253.

(3) For special rules relating to—

(A) funded welfare benefit plans, see section 419, and

(B) deferred compensation and other deferred benefits, see section 404.

* * *

Editorial Summary

Interest

Subchapter B of Chapter 1 (Sec. 163)

The Tax Reform Act of 1986 not only increased the complexity of the interest deduction under Sec. 163 but also placed additional limitations on the interest deduction. Particular attention must be given to the limitations on the interest deduction and the time period during which the ability to deduct certain types of interest is being phased out. Interest is classified into the following categories:

1. Trade or business interest.
2. Investment interest.
3. Consumer interest.
4. Qualified residence interest.
5. Passive activity interest.

The disallowance provision impacts on investment interest, consumer interest, and passive activity interest. Therefore, if investment interest can be classified instead as trade or business interest or passive activity interest can be classified as non-passive activity interest, the disallowance provision can be avoided. Likewise, if consumer interest can be classified instead as qualified residence interest, the disallowance provision can be avoided. Note that the Revenue Act of 1987 modified the statutory provisions for qualified residence interest [see Sec. 163(h)(3)].

Differentiation must be made between interest that is disallowed and interest that merely cannot be deducted in the current taxable year (i.e., is eligible for carryover to future taxable years). For example, investment interest has both a phaseout (i.e., disallowance) provision [see Sec. 163(d)(6)] and a carryover provision [see Sec. 163(d)(2)].

In dealing with the interest deduction, consideration must be given to both the actual interest paid or accrued and to imputed interest (i.e., interest on deferred payment contracts and on below-market loans). See Secs. 163(b), 483, 1272, 1274, 1274A, and 7872.

See Sec. 221 for the special provision on interest on student loans.

§ 163. Interest

(a) General rule.—There shall be allowed as a deduction all interest paid or accrued within the taxable year on indebtedness.

(b) Installment purchases where interest charge is not separately stated.—

(1) General rule.—If personal property or educational services are purchased under a contract—

(A) which provides that payment of part or all of the purchase price is to be made in installments, and

(B) in which carrying charges are separately stated but the interest charge cannot be ascertained,

then the payments made during the taxable year under the contract shall be treated for purposes of this section as if they included interest equal to 6 percent of the average unpaid balance under the contract during the taxable year. For purposes of the preceding sentence, the average unpaid balance is the sum of the unpaid balance outstanding on the first day of each month beginning during the taxable year, divided by 12. For purposes of this paragraph, the term "educational services" means any service (including lodging) which is purchased from an educational organization described in section 170(b)(1)(A)(ii) and which is provided for a student of such organization.

(2) Limitation.—In the case of any contract to which paragraph (1) applies, the amount treated as interest for any taxable year shall not exceed the aggregate carrying charges which are properly attributable to such taxable year.

(c) Redeemable ground rents.—For purposes of this subtitle, any annual or periodic rental under a redeemable ground rent (excluding amounts in redemption thereof) shall be treated as interest on an indebtedness secured by a mortgage.

(d) Limitation on investment interest.—

(1) In general.—In the case of a taxpayer other than a corporation, the amount allowed as a deduction under this chapter for investment interest for any taxable year shall not exceed the net investment income of the taxpayer for the taxable year.

(2) Carryforward of disallowed interest.—The amount not allowed as a deduction for any taxable year by reason of paragraph (1) shall be treated as investment interest paid or accrued by the taxpayer in the succeeding taxable year.

(3) Investment interest.—For purposes of this subsection—

(A) In general.—The term "investment interest" means any interest allowable as a deduction under this chapter (determined without regard to paragraph (1)) which is paid or accrued on indebtedness properly allocable to property held for investment.

(B) Exceptions.—The term "investment interest" shall not include—

(i) any qualified residence interest (as defined in subsection (h)(3)), or

(ii) any interest which is taken into account under section 469 in computing income or loss from a passive activity of the taxpayer.

(C) Personal property used in short sale.—For purposes of this paragraph, the term "interest" includes any amount allowable as a deduction in connection with personal property used in a short sale.

(4) Net investment income.—For purposes of this subsection—

(A) In general.—The term "net investment income" means the excess of—

(i) investment income, over

(ii) investment expenses.

(B) Investment income.—The term "investment income" means the sum of—

(i) gross income from property held for investment (other than any gain taken into account under clause (ii)(I)),

(ii) the excess (if any) of—

(I) the net gain attributable to the disposition of property held for investment, over

(II) the net capital gain determined by only taking into account gains and losses from dispositions of property held for investment, plus

(iii) so much of the net capital gain referred to in clause (ii)(II) (or, if lesser, the net gain referred to in clause (ii)(I)) as the taxpayer elects to take into account under this clause.

Such term shall include qualified dividend income (as defined in section 1(h)(11)(b)) only to the extent the taxpayer elects to treat such income as investment income for purposes of this subsection.

(C) Investment expenses.—The term "investment expenses" means the deductions allowed under this chapter (other than for interest) which are directly connected with the production of investment income.

(D) Income and expenses from passive activities.—Investment income and investment expenses shall not include any income or expenses taken into account under section 469 in computing income or loss from a passive activity.

(E) Reduction in investment income during phase-in of passive loss rules.—Investment income of the taxpayer for any taxable year shall be reduced by the amount of the passive activity loss to which section 469(a) does not apply for such taxable year by reason of section 469(m). The preceding sentence shall not apply to any portion of such passive activity loss which is attributable to a rental real estate activity with respect to which the taxpayer actively participates (within the meaning of section 469(i)(6)) during such taxable year.

(5) Property held for investment.—For purposes of this subsection—

(A) In general.—The term "property held for investment" shall include—

(i) any property which produces income of a type described in section 469(e)(1), and

(ii) any interest held by a taxpayer in an activity involving the conduct of a trade or business—

(I) which is not a passive activity, and

(II) with respect to which the taxpayer does not materially participate.

(B) Investment expenses.—In the case of property described in subparagraph (A)(i), expenses shall be allocated to such property in the same manner as under section 469.

(C) Terms.—For purposes of this paragraph, the terms "activity," "passive activity,, and "materially participate" have the meanings given such terms by section 469.

(6) Phase-in of disallowance.—In the case of any taxable year beginning in calendar years 1987 through 1990—

(A) In general.—The amount of interest paid or accrued during any such taxable year which is disallowed under this subsection shall not exceed the sum of—

(i) the amount which would be disallowed under this subsection if—

(I) paragraph (1) were applied by substituting "the sum of the ceiling amount and the net investment income" for "the net investment income," and

(II) paragraphs (4)(E) and (5)(A)(ii) did not apply, and

(ii) the applicable percentage of the excess of—

(I) the amount which (without regard to this paragraph) is not allowable as a deduction under this subsection for the taxable year, over

(II) the amount described in clause (i).

The preceding sentence shall not apply to any interest treated as paid or accrued during the taxable year under paragraph (2).

(B) Applicable percentage.—For purposes of this paragraph, the applicable percentage shall be determined in accordance with the following table:

In the case of taxable years beginning in:	The applicable percentage is:
1987	35
1988	60
1989	80
1990	90

(C) Ceiling amount.—For purposes of this paragraph, the term "ceiling amount" means—

(i) $10,000 in the case of a taxpayer not described in clause (ii) or (iii),

(ii) $5,000 in the case of a married individual filing a separate return, and

(iii) zero in the case of a trust.

(e) Original issue discount.—

(1) In general.—In the case of any debt instrument issued after July 1, 1982, the portion of the original issue discount with respect to such debt instrument which is allowable as a deduction to the issuer for any taxable year shall be equal to the aggregate daily portions of the original issue discount for days during such taxable year.

(2) Definitions and special rules.—For purposes of this subsection—

(A) Debt instrument.—The term "debt instrument" has the meaning given such term by section 1275(a)(1).

(B) Daily portions.—The daily portion of the original issue discount for any day shall be determined under section 1272(a) (without regard to paragraph (7) thereof and without regard to section 1273(a)(3)).

(C) Short-term obligations.—In the case of an obligor of a short-term obligation (as defined in section 1283(a)(l)(A)) who uses the cash receipts and disbursements method of accounting, the original issue discount (and any other interest payable) on such obligation shall be deductible only when paid.

*   *   *

(f) Denial of deduction for interest on certain obligations not in registered form.—

(1) In general.—Nothing in subsection (a) or in any other provision of law shall be construed to provide a deduction for interest on any registration-required obligation unless such obligation is in registered form.

(2) Registration-required obligation.—For purposes of this section—

(A) In general.—The term "registration-required obligation" means any obligation (including any obligation issued by a governmental entity) other than an obligation which—

(i) is issued by a natural person,

(ii) is not of a type offered to the public, on

(iii) has a maturity (at issue) of not more than 1 year.

(B) Authority to include other obligations.—Clauses (ii) and (iii) of subparagraph (A) shall not apply to any obligation if—

(i) such obligation is of a type which the Secretary has determined by regulations to be used frequently in avoiding Federal taxes, and

(ii) such obligation is issued after the date on which the regulations referred to in clause (i) take effect.

(3) Book entries permitted, etc.—For purposes of this subsection, rules similar to the rules of section 149(a)(3) shall apply, except that a dematerialized book entry system or other book entry system specified by the Secretary shall be treated as a book entry system described in such section.

*   *   *

(g) Reduction of deduction where section 25 credit taken.—The amount of the deduction under this section for interest paid or accrued during any taxable year on indebtedness with respect to which a mortgage credit certificate has been issued under section 25 shall be reduced by the amount of the credit allowable with respect to such interest under section 25 (determined without regard to section 26).

(h) Disallowance of deduction for personal interest.—

(1) In general.—In the case of a taxpayer other than a corporation, no deduction shall be allowed under this chapter for personal interest paid or accrued during the taxable year.

(2) Personal interest.—For purposes of this subsection, the term "personal interest" means any interest allowable as a deduction under this chapter other than—

(A) interest paid or accrued on indebtedness properly allocable to a trade or business (other than the trade or business of performing services as an employee),

(B) any investment interest (within the meaning of subsection (d)),

(C) any interest which is taken into account under section 469 in computing income or loss from a passive activity of the taxpayer,

(D) any qualified residence interest (within the meaning of paragraph (3)),

(E) any interest payable under section 6601 on any unpaid portion of the tax imposed by section 2001 for the period during which an extension of time for payment of such tax is in effect under section 6163, and

(F) any interest allowable as a deduction under section 221 (relating to interest on educational loans).

(3) Qualified residence interest.—For purposes of this subsection—

(A) In general.—The term "qualified residence interest" means any interest which is paid or accrued during the taxable year on—

(i) acquisition indebtedness with respect to any qualified residence of the taxpayer, or

(ii) home equity indebtedness with respect to any qualified residence of the taxpayer.

For purposes of the preceding sentence, the determination of whether any property is a qualified residence of the taxpayer shall be made as of the time the interest is accrued.

(B) Acquisition indebtedness.—

(i) In general.—The term "acquisition indebtedness" means any indebtedness which—

(I) is incurred in acquiring, constructing, or substantially improving any qualified residence of the taxpayer, and

(II) is secured by such residence.

Such term also includes any indebtedness secured by such residence resulting from the refinancing of indebtedness meeting the requirements of the preceding sentence (or this sentence); but only to the extent the amount of the indebtedness resulting from such refinancing does not exceed the amount of the refinanced indebtedness.

(ii) $1,000,000 limitation.—The aggregate amount treated as acquisition indebtedness for any period shall not exceed $1,000,000 ($500,000 in the case of a married individual filing a separate return).

(C) Home equity indebtedness.—

(i) In general.—The term "home equity indebtedness" means any indebtedness (other than acquisition indebtedness) secured by a qualified residence to the extent the aggregate amount of such indebtedness does not exceed—

(I) the fair market value of such qualified residence, reduced by

(II) the amount of acquisition indebtedness with respect to such residence.

(ii) Limitation.—The aggregate amount treated as home equity indebtedness for any period shall not exceed $100,000 ($50,000 in the case of a separate return by a married individual).

(D) Treatment of indebtedness incurred on or before October 13, 1987.—

(i) In general.—In the case of any pre-October 13, 1987, indebtedness—

(I) such indebtedness shall be treated as acquisition indebtedness, and

(II) the limitation of subparagraph (B)(ii) shall not apply.

(ii) Reduction in $1,000,000 limitation.—The limitation of subparagraph (B)(ii) shall be reduced (but not below zero) by the aggregate amount of outstanding pre-October 13, 1987, indebtedness.

(iii) Pre-October 13, 1987, indebtedness.—The term "pre-October 13, 1987, indebtedness" means—

(I) any indebtedness which was incurred on or before October 13, 1987, and which was secured by a qualified residence on October 13, 1987, and at all times thereafter before the interest is paid or accrued, or

(II) any indebtedness which is secured by the qualified residence and was incurred after October 13, 1987, to refinance indebtedness described in subclause (I) (or refinanced indebtedness meeting the requirements of this subclause) to the extent (immediately after the refinancing) the principal amount of the indebtedness resulting from the refinancing does not exceed the principal amount of the refinanced indebtedness (immediately before the refinancing).

(iv) Limitation on period of refinancing.—Subclause (II) of clause (iii) shall not apply to any indebtedness after—

(I) the expiration of the term of the indebtedness described in clause (iii)(I), or

(II) if the principal of the indebtedness described in clause (iii)(I) is not amortized over its term, the expiration of the term of the 1st refinancing of such indebtedness (or if earlier, the date which is 30 years after the date of such 1st refinancing).

(E) Mortgage insurance premiums treated as interest.—

(i) In general.—Premiums paid or accrued for qualified mortgage insurance by a taxpayer during the taxable year in connection with acquisition indebtedness with respect to a qualified residence of the taxpayer shall be treated for purposes of this section as interest which is qualified residence interest.

(ii) Phaseout.—The amount otherwise treated as interest under clause (i) shall be reduced (but not below zero) by 10 percent of such amount for each $1,000 ($500 in the case of a married individual filing a separate return) (or fraction thereof) that the taxpayer's adjusted gross income for the taxable year exceeds $100,000 ($50,000 in the case of a married individual filing a separate return).

(iii) Limitation.—Clause (i) shall not apply with respect to any mortgage insurance contracts issued before January 1, 2007.

(iv) Termination.*—Clause (i) shall not apply to amounts—

(I) paid or accrued after December 31, 2013, or

(II) properly allocable to any period after such date.

(4) Other definitions and special rules.—

(A) Qualified residence.—For purposes of this subsection—

(i) In general.—The term "qualified residence" means—

(I) the principal residence (within the meaning of section 121) of the taxpayer, and

(II) 1 other residence of the taxpayer which is selected by the taxpayer for the taxable year and which is used by the taxpayer as a residence (within the meaning of section 280A(d)(1)).

(ii) Married individuals filing separate returns.—If a married couple does not file a joint return for the taxable year—

(I) such couple shall be treated as 1 taxpayer for purposes of clause (i), and

(II) each individual shall be entitled to take into account 1 residence unless both individuals consent in writing to 1 individual taking into account the principal residence and 1 other residence.

(iii) Residence not rented.—For purposes of clause (i)(II), notwithstanding section 280A(d)(l), if the taxpayer does not rent a dwelling unit at any time during a taxable year, such unit may be treated as a residence for such taxable year.

(B) Special rule for cooperative housing corporations.—Any indebtedness secured by stock held by the taxpayer as a tenant-stockholder (as defined in section 216) in a cooperative housing corporation (as so defined) shall be treated as secured by the house or apartment which the taxpayer is entitled to occupy as such a tenant-stockholder. If stock described in the preceding sentence may not be used to secure indebtedness, indebtedness shall be treated as so secured if the taxpayer establishes to the satisfaction of the Secretary that such indebtedness was incurred to acquire such stock.

(C) Unenforceable security interests. Indebtedness shall not fail to be treated as secured by any property solely because, under any applicable State or local homestead or other debtor protection law in effect on August 16, 1986, the security interest is ineffective or the enforceability of the security interest is restricted.

(D) Special rules for estates and trusts.—For purposes of determining whether any interest paid or accrued by an estate or trust is qualified residence interest, any residence held by such estate or trust shall be treated as a qualified residence of such estate or trust if such estate or trust establishes that such residence is a qualified residence of a beneficiary who has a present interest in such estate or trust or an interest in the residuary of such estate or trust.

(E) Qualified mortgage insurance.—The term "qualified mortgage insurance" means—

(i) mortgage insurance provided by the Department of Veterans Affairs, the Federal Housing Administration, or the Rural Housing Service, and

(ii) private mortgage insurance (as defined by section 2 of the Homeowners Protection Act

*Editorial comment: At the present time, this section has not been extended. There is pending legislation in the Senate, *The Tax Extender's Act of 2013 (S. 1859)*, that would extend Section 163(h)(3)(E)(iv)(I) until December 31, 2014.

of 1998 (12 U.S.C. 4901), as in effect on the date of the enactment of this subparagraph).

(F) Special rules for prepaid qualified mortgage insurance.—Any amount paid by the taxpayer for qualified mortgage insurance that is properly allocable to any mortgage the payment of which extends to periods that are after the close of the taxable year in which such amount is paid shall be chargeable to capital account and shall be treated as paid in such periods to which so allocated. No deduction shall be allowed for the unamortized balance of such account if such mortgage is satisfied before the end of its term. The preceding sentences shall not apply to amounts paid for qualified mortgage insurance provided by the Veterans Administration or the Rural Housing Administration.

(5) Phase-in of limitation.—In the case of any taxable year beginning in calendar years 1987 through 1990, the amount of interest with respect to which a deduction is disallowed under this subsection shall be equal to the applicable percentage (within the meaning of subsection (d)(6)(B)) of the amount which (but for this paragraph) would have been so disallowed.

* * *

(j) Limitation of deduction for interest on certain indebtedness.—

(1) Limitation.—

(A) In general.—If this subsection applies to any corporation for any taxable year, no deduction shall be allowed under this chapter for disqualified interest paid or accrued by such corporation during such taxable year. The amount disallowed under the preceding sentence shall not exceed the corporation's excess interest expense for the taxable year.

(B) Disallowed amount carried to succeeding taxable year.—Any amount disallowed under subparagraph (A) for any taxable year shall be treated as disqualified interest paid or accrued in the succeeding taxable year (and clause (ii) of paragraph (2)(A) shall not apply for purposes of applying this section to the amount so treated).

(2) Corporations to which subsection applies.—

(A) In general.—This subsection shall apply to any corporation for any taxable year if—

(i) such corporation has excess interest expense for such taxable year, and

(ii) the ratio of debt to equity of such corporation as of the close of such taxable year (and on any other day during the taxable year as the Secretary may by regulations prescribe) exceeds 1.5 to 1.

(B) Excess interest expense.—

(i) In general.—For purposes of this subsection, the term "excess interest expense" means the excess (if any) of—

(I) the corporation's net interest expense, over

(II) the sum of 50 percent of the adjusted taxable income of the corporation plus any excess limitation carryforward under clause (ii).

(ii) Excess limitation carryforward.—If a corporation has an excess limitation for any taxable year, the amount of such excess limitation shall be an excess limitation carryforward to the 1st succeeding taxable year and to the 2nd and 3rd succeeding taxable years to the extent not previously taken into account under this clause. The amount of such a carryforward taken into account for any such succeeding taxable year shall not exceed the excess interest expense for such succeeding taxable year (determined without regard to the carryforward from the taxable year of such excess limitation).

(iii) Excess limitation.—For purposes of clause (ii), the term "excess limitation" means the excess (if any) of—

(I) 50 percent of the adjusted taxable income of the corporation, over

(II) the corporation's net interest expense.

(C) Ratio of debt to equity.—For purposes of this paragraph, the term "ratio of debt to equity" means the ratio which the total indebtedness of the corporation bears to the sum of its money and all other assets reduced (but not below zero) by such total indebtedness. For purposes of the preceding sentence.—

(i) the amount taken into account with respect to any asset shall be the adjusted basis thereof for purposes of determining gain.

(ii) the amount taken into account with respect to any indebtedness with original issue discount shall be its issue price plus the portion of the original issue discount previously accrued as determined under the rules of section 1272 (determined without regard to subsection (a)(7) or (b)(4) thereof), and

(iii) there shall be such other adjustments as the Secretary may by regulations prescribe.

(3) Disqualified interest.—For purposes of this subsection, the term "disqualified interest" means—

(A) any interest paid or accrued by the taxpayer (directly or indirectly) to a related person if no tax is imposed by this subtitle with respect to such interest,

(B) any interest paid or accrued by the taxpayer with respect to any indebtedness to a person who is not a related person if—

(i) there is a disqualified guarantee of such indebtedness, and

(ii) no gross basis tax is imposed by this subtitle with respect to such interest, and

* * *

(4) Related person.—For purposes of this subsection—

(A) In general.—Except as provided in subparagraph (B), the term "related person" means any person who is related (within the meaning of section 267(b) or 707(b)(1)) to the taxpayer.

(B) Special rule for certain partnerships.—

(i) In general.—Any interest paid or accrued to a partnership which (without regard to this subparagraph) is a related person shall not be treated as paid or accrued to a related person if less than 10 percent of the profits and capital interests in such partnership are held by persons with respect to whom no tax is imposed by this subtitle on such interest. The preceding sentence shall not apply to any interest allocable to any partner in such partnership who is a related person to the taxpayer.

(ii) Special rule where treaty reduction.—If any treaty between the United States and any foreign country reduces the rate of tax imposed by this subtitle on a partner's share of any interest paid or accrued to a partnership, such partner's interests in such partnership shall, for purposes of clause (i), be treated as held in part by a tax-exempt person and in part by a taxable person under rules similar to the rules of paragraph (5)(B).

(5) Special rules for determining whether interest is subject to tax.—

(A) Treatment of pass-thru entities.—In the case of any interest paid or accrued to a partnership, the determination of whether any tax is imposed by this subtitle on such interest shall be made at the partner level. Rules similar to the rules of the preceding sentence shall apply in the case of any pass-thru entity other than a partnership and in the case of tiered partnerships and other entities.

(B) Interest treated as tax-exempt to extent of treaty reduction.—If any treaty between the United States and any foreign country reduces the rate of tax imposed by this subtitle on any interest paid or accrued by the taxpayer, such interest shall be treated as interest on which no tax is imposed by this subtitle to the extent of the same proportion of such interest as—

(i) the rate of tax imposed without regard to such treaty, reduced by the rate of tax imposed under the treaty, bears to

(ii) the rate of tax imposed without regard to the treaty.

(6) Other definitions and special rules.—For purposes of this subsection—

(A) Adjusted taxable income.—The term "adjusted taxable income" means the taxable income of the taxpayer—

(i) computed without regard to—

(I) any deduction allowable under this chapter for the net interest expense,

(II) the amount of any net operating loss deduction under section 172,

(III) any deduction allowable under section 199, and

(IV) any deduction allowable for depreciation, amortization, or depletion, and

(ii) computed with such other adjustments as the Secretary may by regulations prescribe.

(B) Net interest expense.—The term "net interest expense" means the excess (if any) of—

(i) the interest paid or accrued by the taxpayer during the taxable year, over

(ii) the amount of interest includible in the gross income of such taxpayer for such taxable year.

The Secretary may by regulations provide for adjustments in determining the amount of net interest expense.

(C) Treatment of affiliated group.—All members of the same affiliated group (within the meaning of section 1504(a)) shall be treated as 1 taxpayer.

(D) Disqualified guarantee.—

(i) In general.—Except as provided in clause (ii), the term "disqualified guarantee" means any guarantee by a related person which is—

(I) an organization exempt from taxation under this subtitle, or

(II) a foreign person.

(ii) Exceptions.—The term "disqualified guarantee" shall not include a guarantee—

(I) in any circumstances identified by the Secretary by regulation, where the interest on the indebtedness would have been subject to a net basis tax if the interest had been paid to the guarantor, or

(II) if the taxpayer owns a controlling interest in the guarantor.

For purposes of subclause (II), except as provided in regulations, the term "a controlling interest" means direct or indirect ownership of at least 80 percent of the total voting power and value of all classes of stock of a corporation, or 80 percent of the profit and capital interests in any other entity. For purposes of the preceding sentence, the rules of paragraphs (1) and (5) of section 267(c) shall apply; except that such rules shall also apply to interest in entities other than corporations.

(iii) Guarantee.—Except as provided in regulations, the term "guarantee" includes any arrangement under which a person (directly or indirectly through an entity or otherwise) assures, on a conditional or unconditional basis, the payment of another person's obligation under any indebtedness.

(E) Gross basis and net basis taxation.—

(i) Gross basis tax.—The term "gross basis tax" means any tax imposed by this subtitle which is determined by reference to the gross amount of any item of income without any reduction for any deduction allowed by this subtitle.

(ii) Net basis tax.—The term "net basis tax" means any tax imposed by this subtitle which is not a gross basis tax.

(7) Coordination with passive loss rules, etc.—This subsection shall be applied before sections 465 and 469.

(8) Treatment of corporate partners.—Except to the extent provided by regulations, in applying this subsection to a corporation which owns (directly or indirectly) an interest in a partnership—

(A) such corporation's distributive share of interest income paid or accrued to such partnership shall be treated as interest income paid or accrued to such corporation,

(B) such corporation's distributive share of interest paid or accrued by such partnership shall be treated as interest paid or accrued by such corporation, and

(C) such corporation's share of the liabilities of such partnership shall be treated as liabilities of such corporation.

(9) Regulations.—The Secretary shall prescribe such regulations as may be appropriate to carry out the purposes of this subsection, including—

(A) such regulations as may be appropriate to prevent the avoidance of the purposes of this subsection,

(B) regulations providing such adjustments in the case of corporations which are members of an affiliated group as may be appropriate to carry out the purposes of this subsection,

(C) regulations for the coordination of this subsection with section 884, and

(D) regulations providing for the reallocation of shares of partnership indebtedness, or distributive shares of the partnership's interest income or interest expense.

(k) Section 6166 interest.—No deduction shall be allowed under this section for any interest payable under section 6601 on any unpaid portion of the tax imposed by section 2001 for the period during which an extension of time for payment of such tax is in effect under section 6166.

(l) Disallowance of deduction of certain debt instruments of corporations.—

(1) In general.—No deduction shall be allowed under this chapter for any interest paid or accrued on a disqualified debt instrument.

(2) Disqualified debt instrument.—For purposes of this subsection, the term "qualified debt instrument" means any indebtedness of a corporation which is payable in equity of the issuer or a related party or equity held by the issuer (or any related party) in any other person.

(3) Special rules for amounts payable in equity.—For purposes of paragraph (2), indebtedness shall be treated as payable in equity of the issuer or any other person only if—

(A) a substantial amount of the principal or interest is required to be paid or converted, or at the option of the issuer or a related party is payable in, or convertible into, such equity,

(B) a substantial amount of the principal or interest is required to be determined, or at the option of the issuer or a related party is determined, by reference to the value of such equity, or

(C) the indebtedness is part of an arrangement which is reasonably expected to result in a transaction described in subparagraph (A) or (B).

For purposes of this paragraph, principal or interest shall be treated as required to be so paid, converted, or determined if it may be required at the option of the holder or a related party and there is a substantial certainty the option will be exercised.

(4) Capitalization allowed with respect to equity of persons other than issuer and related parties.—If the disqualified debt instrument of a corporation is payable in equity held by the issuer (or any related party) in any other person (other than a related party), the basis of such equity shall be increased by the amount not allowed as a deduction by reason of paragraph (1) with respect to the instrument.

(5) Exception for certain instruments issued by dealers in securities.—For purposes of this subsection, the term "disqualified debt instrument" does not include indebtedness issued by a dealer in securities (or a related party) which is payable in, or by reference to, equity (other than equity of the issuer or a related party) held by such dealer in its capacity as a dealer in securities. For purposes of this paragraph, the term "dealer in securities" has the meaning given such term by section 475.

(6) Related party.—For purposes of this subsection, a person is a related party with respect to another person if such person bears a relationship to such other person described in section 267(b) or 707(b).

(7) Regulations.—The Secretary shall prescribe such regulations as may be necessary or appropriate to carry out the purposes of this subsection, including regulations preventing avoidance of this subsection through the use of an issuer other than a corporation.

(m) Interest on unpaid taxes attributable to nondisclosed reportable transactions.—No deduction shall be allowed under this chapter for any interest paid or accrued under section 6601 on any underpayment of tax which is attributable to the portion of any reportable transaction understatement (as defined in section 6662A(b)) with respect to which the requirement of section 6664(d)(2)(A) is not met.

(n) Cross references.—

(1) For disallowance of certain amounts paid in connection with insurance, endowment, or annuity contracts, see section 264.

(2) For disallowance of deduction for interest relating to tax-exempt income, see section 265(a)(2).

(3) For disallowance of deduction for carrying charges chargeable to capital account, see section 266.

(4) For disallowance of interest with respect to transactions between related taxpayers, see section 267.

(5) For treatment of redeemable ground rents and real property held subject to liabilities under redeemable ground rents, see section 1055.

Editorial Summary

Taxes

Subchapter B of Chapter 1 (Sec. 164)

Section 164 deals with three major issues. These are as follows:

1. Is the item a tax?
2. May the tax be deducted?
3. By whom is the tax deductible?

Section 164(b) defines personal property taxes, state or local taxes, foreign taxes, GST taxes, and sales taxes. Note that the real property tax is not included in this definition section. The apparent reason is that the real property tax is adequately defined under local law.

Section 164(a) provides that, except as otherwise limited in the section, the following types of taxes are deductible.

1. State, local, and foreign real property taxes.
2. State and local personal property taxes.
3. State, local, and foreign income, war profits, and excess profits taxes.
4. GST tax on income distributions.
5. Qualified motor vehicle taxes.*

*Editorial comment: The deduction for the qualified motor vehicle tax does not apply to purchases after December 31, 2009 (See §164(b)(6)(G)).

Note that Sec. 164 did not provide the authority for either the federal income tax or the sales tax to be deducted as a tax. However, the American Jobs Creation Act of 2004 provides for 2004 and 2005 a choice between deducting as a tax the state and local sales taxes rather than state and local income taxes. The Tax Relief and Health Care Act of 2006 extended this sales tax option through 2007. Subsequent legislation extended the provision through 2013. Congress is likely to extend this deduction to 2014. Federal income taxes continue to be nondeductible as a tax.

A deductible tax generally is deducted by the taxpayer on whom it is imposed. However, a special provision provides for the mandatory statutory apportionment between the buyer and the seller of real property taxes [see Sec. 164(d)]. Note that depending on whether such taxes are prorated in the sales contract, this mandatory allocation may affect the calculation of the seller's amount realized and the buyer's adjusted basis. In addition, another special provision permits a corporation to deduct certain taxes the corporation pays which are imposed on a shareholder [see Sec. 164(e)].

The deduction for the qualified motor vehicle tax does not apply to purchases after December 31, 2009.

§ 164. Taxes

(a) General rule.—Except as otherwise provided in this section, the following taxes shall be allowed as a deduction for the taxable year within which paid or accrued:

(1) State and local, and foreign, real property taxes.

(2) State and local personal property taxes.

(3) State and local, and foreign, income, war profits, and excess profits taxes.

(4) The GST tax imposed on income distributions.

(5) The environmental tax imposed by section 59A.

(6) Qualified motor vehicle taxes.

In addition, there shall be allowed as a deduction State and local, and foreign, taxes not described in the preceding sentence which are paid or accrued within the taxable year in carrying on a trade or business or an activity described in section 212 (relating to expenses for production of income).

Notwithstanding the preceding sentence, any tax (not described in the first sentence of this subsection) which is paid or accrued by the taxpayer in connection with an acquisition or disposition of property shall be treated as part of the cost of the acquired property or, in the case of a disposition, as a reduction in the amount realized on the disposition.

(b) Definitions and special rules.—For purposes of this section—

(1) Personal property taxes.—The term "personal property tax" means an ad valorem tax which is imposed on an annual basis in respect of personal property.

(2) State or local taxes.—A State or local tax includes only a tax imposed by a State, a possession of the United States, or a political subdivision of any of the foregoing, or by the District of Columbia.

(3) Foreign taxes.—A foreign tax includes only a tax imposed by the authority of a foreign country.

(4) Special rules for GST tax.—

(A) In general.—The GST tax imposed on income distributions is—

(i) the tax imposed by section 2601, and

(ii) any State tax described in section 2604,

but only to the extent such tax is imposed on a transfer which is included in the gross income of the distributee and to which section 666 does not apply.

(B) Special rule for tax paid before due date.—Any tax referred to in subparagraph(A) imposed with respect to a transfer occurring during the taxable year of the distributee (or, in the case of a taxable termination, the trust) which is paid not later than the time prescribed by law (including extensions) for filing the return with respect to such transfer shall be treated as having been paid on the last day of the taxable year in which the transfer was made.

*(5) **General sales taxes.**—For purposes of subsection (a)—

(A) Election to deduct state and local sales taxes in lieu of state and local income taxes.—At the election of the taxpayer for the taxable year, subsection (a) shall be applied—

(i) without regard to the reference to State and local income taxes, and

(ii) as if State and local general sales taxes were referred to in a paragraph thereof.

*Editorial comment: This provision applied only for taxable years beginning after December 31, 2003 and before January 1, 2006. The Tax Relief and Health Care Act of 2006 extended this sales tax option to taxable years ending before January 1, 2008. Subsequent legislation extended the provision through 2013. At the present time, this section has not been extended further. There is pending legislation in the Senate, the *Tax Extenders Act of 2013 (S. 1859)*, that would extend Section 164(b)(5) until January 1, 2015.

(B) Definition of general sales tax.—The term "general sales tax" means a tax imposed at one rate with respect to the sale at retail of a broad range of classes of items.

(C) Special rules for food, etc.—In the case of items of food, clothing, medical supplies, and motor vehicles—

(i) the fact that the tax does not apply with respect to some or all of such items shall not be taken into account in determining whether the tax applies with respect to a broad range of classes of items, and

(ii) the fact that the rate of tax applicable with respect to some or all of such items is lower than the general rate of tax shall not be taken into account in determining whether the tax is imposed at one rate.

(D) Items taxed at different rates.—Except in the case of a lower rate of tax applicable with respect to an item described in subparagraph (C), no deduction shall be allowed under this paragraph for any general sales tax imposed with respect to an item at a rate other than the general rate of tax.

(E) Compensating use taxes.—A compensating use tax with respect to an item shall be treated as a general sales tax. For purposes of the preceding sentence, the term "compensating use tax" means, with respect to any item, a tax which—

(i) is imposed on the use, storage, or consumption of such item, and

(ii) is complementary to a general sales tax, but only if a deduction is allowable under this paragraph with respect to items sold at retail in the taxing jurisdiction which are similar to such item.

(F) Special rule for motor vehicles.—In the case of motor vehicles, if the rate of tax exceeds the general rate, such excess shall be disregarded and the general rate shall be treated as the rate of tax.

(G) Separately stated general sales taxes.—If the amount of any general sales tax is separately stated, then, to the extent that the amount so stated is paid by the consumer (other than in connection with the consumer's trade or business) to the seller, such amount shall be treated as a tax imposed on, and paid by, such consumer.

(H) Amount of deduction may be determined under tables.—

(i) In general.—At the election of the taxpayer for the taxable year, the amount of the deduction allowed under this paragraph for such year shall be—

(I) the amount determined under this paragraph (without regard to this subparagraph) with respect to motor vehicles, boats, and other items specified by the Secretary, and

(II) the amount determined under tables prescribed by the Secretary with respect to items to which subclause (I) does not apply.

(ii) Requirements for tables.—The tables prescribed under clause (i)—

(I) shall reflect the provisions of this paragraph,

(II) shall be based on the average consumption by taxpayers on a State-by-State basis (as determined by the Secretary) of items to which clause (i)(I) does not apply, taking into account filing status, number of dependents, adjusted gross income, and rates of State and local general sales taxation, and

(III) need only be determined with respect to adjusted gross incomes up to the applicable amount (as determined under section 68(b)).

(I) Application of paragraph.—This paragraph shall apply to taxable years beginning after December 31, 2003, and before January 1, 2014.

(6) Qualified motor vehicle taxes.—*

(A) In general.—For purposes of this section, the term "qualified motor vehicle taxes" means any State or local sales or excise tax imposed on the purchase of a qualified motor vehicle.

(B) Limitation based on vehicle price.—The amount of any State or local sales or excise tax imposed on the purchase of a qualified motor vehicle taken into account under subparagraph (A) shall not exceed the portion of such tax attributable to so much of the purchase price as does not exceed $49,500.

*Editorial comment: The qualified motor vehicle sales tax deduction does not apply to purchases after December 31, 2009. This provision was not extended by the extender's legislation enacted in late 2010 or in subsequent legislation.

(C) Income limitation.—The amount otherwise taken into account under subparagraph (A) (after the application of subparagraph (B)) for any taxable year shall be reduced (but not below zero) by the amount which bears the same ratio to the amount which is so treated as—

(i) the excess (if any) of—

(I) the taxpayer's modified adjusted gross income for such taxable year, over

(II) $125,000 ($250,000 in the case of a joint return), bears to

(ii) $10,000.

For purposes of the preceding sentence, the term "modified adjusted gross income" means the adjusted gross income of the taxpayer for the taxable year (determined without regard to sections 911, 931, and 933).

(D) Qualified motor vehicle.—For purposes of this paragraph—

(i) In general.—The term "qualified motor vehicle" means—

(I) a passenger automobile or light truck which is treated as a motor vehicle for purposes of title II of the Clean Air Act, the gross vehicle weight rating of which is not more than 8,500 pounds, and the original use of which commences with the taxpayer,

(II) a motorcycle the gross vehicle weight rating of which is not more than 8,500 pounds and the original use of which commences with the taxpayer, and

(III) a motor home the original use of which commences with the taxpayer.

(ii) Other terms.—The terms "motorcycle" and "motor home" have the meanings given such terms under section 571.3 of title 49, Code of Federal Regulations (as in effect on the date of the enactment of this paragraph).

(E) Qualified motor vehicle taxes not included in cost of acquired property.—The last sentence of subsection (a) shall not apply to any qualified motor vehicle taxes.

(F) Coordination with general sales tax.—This paragraph shall not apply in the case of a taxpayer who makes an election under paragraph (5) for the taxable year.

(G) Termination.—This paragraph shall not apply to purchases after December 31, 2009.

(c) Deduction denied in case of certain taxes.—No deduction shall be allowed for the following taxes:

(1) Taxes assessed against local benefits of a kind tending to increase the value of the property assessed; but this paragraph shall not prevent the deduction of so much of such taxes as is properly allocable to maintenance or interest charges.

(2) Taxes on real property, to the extent that subsection (d) requires such taxes to be treated as imposed on another taxpayer.

(d) Apportionment of taxes on real property between seller and purchaser.—

(1) General rule.—For purposes of subsection (a), if real property is sold during any real property tax year, then—

(A) so much of the real property tax as is properly allocable to that part of such year which ends on the day before the date of the sale shall be treated as a tax imposed on the seller, and

(B) so much of such tax as is properly allocable to that part of such year which begins on the date of the sale shall be treated as a tax imposed on the purchaser.

(2) Special rules.—

(A) In the case of any sale of real property, if—

(i) a taxpayer may not, by reason of his method of accounting, deduct any amount for taxes unless paid, and

(ii) the other party to the sale is (under the law imposing the real property tax) liable for the real property tax for the real property tax year,

then for purposes of subsection (a) the taxpayer shall be treated as having paid, on the date of the sale, so much of such tax as, under paragraph (1) of this subsection, is treated as imposed on the taxpayer. For purposes of the preceding sentence, if neither party is liable for the tax, then the party holding the property at the time the tax becomes a lien on the property shall be considered liable for the real property tax for the real property tax year.

(B) In the case of any sale of real property, if the taxpayer's taxable income for the taxable year during which the sale occurs is computed under an accrual method of accounting, and if no election under section 461(c) (relating to the accrual of real property taxes) applies, then, for purposes of subsection (a), that portion of such tax which—

(i) is treated, under paragraph (1) of this subsection, as imposed on the taxpayer, and

(ii) may not, by reason of the taxpayer's method of accounting, be deducted by the taxpayer for any taxable year,

shall be treated as having accrued on the date of the sale.

(e) Taxes of shareholder paid by corporation.—Where a corporation pays a tax imposed on a shareholder on his interest as a shareholder, and where the shareholder does not reimburse the corporation, then—

(1) the deduction allowed by subsection (a) shall be allowed to the corporation; and

(2) no deduction shall be allowed the shareholder for such tax.

(f) Deduction for one-half of self-employment taxes.—

(1) In general.—In the case of an individual, in addition to the taxes described in subsection (a), there shall be allowed as a deduction for the taxable year an amount equal to one-half of the taxes imposed by section 1401 (other than the taxes imposed by section 1401(b)(2)) for such taxable year.

(2) Deduction treated as attributable to trade or business.—For purposes of this chapter, the deduction allowed by paragraph (1) shall be treated as attributable to a trade or business carried on by the taxpayer which does not consist of the performance of services by the taxpayer as an employee.

(g) Cross references.—

(1) For provisions disallowing any deduction for certain taxes, see section 275.

* * *

Editorial Summary

Losses

Subchapter B of Chapter 1 (Sec. 165)

Section 165 provides the authority to deduct losses. The general statutory treatment is that all losses are deductible. However, numerous exceptions to this general rule are provided. Included are the following:

1. Losses on personal use assets of the individual taxpayer [see Sec. 165(c)].
2. Losses on capital assets (see Sec. 1211).
3. Hobby losses (see Sec. 183).
4. Office in the home losses (see Sec. 280A).
5. Wagering losses [see Sec. 165(d)].
6. Vacation home losses (see Sec. 280A).
7. Losses for which the taxpayer is not at risk (see Sec. 465).
8. Passive activity losses (see Sec. 469).

A special rule is provided for casualty and theft losses of the individual taxpayer for personal use assets [see Sec. 165(h)]. For trade or business property or income-producing property, the regular loss deduction rules apply. That is, if the property is completely destroyed, the maximum deduction (i.e., no proceeds are received from insurance or otherwise) is the adjusted basis of the asset. If the property is only partially destroyed, the maximum deduction is the lesser of the value decline (i.e., fair market value before the casualty or theft versus the fair market value after) or the adjusted basis of the asset.

The aforementioned special provision for the individual taxpayer associated with personal use assets initially limits the maximum deduction to the lesser of the value decline or the adjusted basis of the asset (i.e., regardless of whether the asset is completely destroyed or only partially destroyed). This amount must then be reduced by a materiality amount of $100 ($500 in 2009) per casualty or theft event. Finally, the resultant total amount of casualties or thefts must be reduced by a floor provision of 10 percent of adjusted gross income. Note that the $100 ($500 in 2009) reduction is per *event* and the 10 percent reduction is per *taxable year.* Also, note that the provision enabling a loss deduction for personal use casualties and thefts does not apply to the third form of an involuntary conversion (i.e., condemnations) [see Sec. 1033(a)].

The amount of any potential loss deduction must be reduced to the extent "compensated for by insurance or otherwise". The judicial interpretation of "compensated for" appears to be moving in the direction of the taxpayer being disallowed a loss deduction to the extent that it is covered by insurance. In addition, the Code now provides that personal-use property casualty and theft losses that are covered by insurance are not deductible unless the taxpayer files a timely insurance claim [see Sec. 165(h)(4)(E)].

Losses from bad debts are not covered by Sec. 165. Instead, they are subject to Sec. 166. Note, however, that Sec. 165, rather than Sec. 166, does apply to worthless securities [see Secs. 165(g) and 166(e)].

§ 165. Losses

(a) General rule.—There shall be allowed as a deduction any loss sustained during the taxable year and not compensated for by insurance or otherwise.

(b) Amount of deduction.—For purposes of subsection (a), the basis for determining the amount of the deduction for any loss shall be the adjusted basis provided in section 1011 for determining the loss from the sale or other disposition of property.

(c) Limitation on losses of individuals.—In the case of an individual, the deduction under subsection (a) shall be limited to—

(1) losses incurred in a trade or business;

(2) losses incurred in any transaction entered into for profit, though not connected with a trade or business; and

(3) except as provided in subsection (h), losses of property not connected with a trade or business or a transaction entered into for profit, if such losses arise from fire, storm, shipwreck, or other casualty, or from theft.

(d) Wagering losses.—Losses from wagering transactions shall be allowed only to the extent of the gains from such transactions.

(e) Theft losses.—For purposes of subsection (a), any loss arising from theft shall be treated as sustained during the taxable year in which the taxpayer discovers such loss.

(f) Capital losses.—Losses from sales or exchanges of capital assets shall be allowed only to the extent allowed in sections 1211 and 1212.

(g) Worthless securities.—

(1) General rule.—If any security which is a capital asset becomes worthless during the taxable year, the loss resulting therefrom shall, for purposes of this subtitle, be treated as a loss from the sale or exchange, on the last day of the taxable year, of a capital asset.

(2) Security defined.—For purposes of this subsection, the term "security" means—

(A) a share of stock in a corporation;

(B) a right to subscribe for, or to receive, a share of stock in a corporation; or

(C) a bond, debenture, note, or certificate, or other evidence of indebtedness, issued by a corporation or by a government or political subdivision thereof, with interest coupons or in registered form.

(3) Securities in affiliated corporation.—For purposes of paragraph (1), any security in a corporation affiliated with a taxpayer which is a domestic corporation shall not be treated as a capital asset. For purposes of the preceding sentence, a corporation shall be treated as affiliated with the taxpayer only if—

(A) the taxpayer owns directly stock in such corporation meeting the requirements of section 1504(a)(2), and

(B) more than 90 percent of the aggregate of its gross receipts for all taxable years has been from sources other than royalties, rents (except rents derived from rental of properties to employees of the corporation in the ordinary course of its operating business), dividends, interest (except interest received on deferred purchase price of operating assets sold), annuities, and gains from sales or exchanges of stocks and securities.

In computing gross receipts for purposes of the preceding sentence, gross receipts from sales or exchanges of stocks and securities shall be taken into account only to the extent of gains therefrom.

(h) Treatment of casualty gains and losses.—

(1) $100 limitation per casualty.*—Any loss of an individual described in subsection (c)(3) shall be allowed only to the extent that the amount of the loss to such individual arising from each casualty, or from each theft, exceeds $500 ($100 for taxable years beginning after December 31, 2009).

(2) Net casualty loss allowed only to the extent it exceeds 10 percent of adjusted gross income.—

(A) In general.—If the personal casualty losses for any taxable year exceed the personal casualty gains for such taxable year, such losses shall be allowed for the taxable year only to the extent of the sum of—

(i) the amount of the personal casualty gains for the taxable year, plus

(ii) so much of such excess as exceeds 10 percent of the adjusted gross income of the individual.

(B) Special rule where personal casualty gains exceed personal casualty losses.—If the personal casualty gains for any taxable year exceed the personal casualty losses for such taxable year—

(i) all such gains shall be treated as gains from sales or exchanges of capital assets, and

(ii) all such losses shall be treated as losses from sales or exchanges of capital assets.

(3) Special rule for losses in federally declared disasters.—

(A) In general.—If an individual has a net disaster loss for any taxable year, the amount

*Editorial comment: Congress did not extend the $500 materiality amount in the extender's legislation enacted in late 2010 or in subsequent legislation.

determined under paragraph (2)(A)(ii) shall be the sum of—

(i) such net disaster loss, and

(ii) so much of the excess referred to in the matter preceding clause (i) of paragraph (2)(A) (reduced by the amount in clause (i) of this subparagraph) as exceeds 10 percent of the adjusted gross income of the individual.

(B) Net disaster loss.—For purposes of subparagraph (A), the term "net disaster loss: means the excess of—

(i) the personal casualty losses—

(I) attributable to a federally declared disaster occurring before January 1, 2010, and

(II) occurring in a disaster area, over

(ii) personal casualty gains.

(C) Federally declared disaster.—For purposes of this paragraph—

(i) Federally declared disaster.—The term "federally declared disaster" means any disaster subsequently determined by the President of the United States to warrant assistance by the Federal Government under the Robert T. Stafford Disaster Relief and Emergency Assistance Act.

(ii) Disaster area.—The term "disaster area" means the area so determined to warrant such assistance.

(4) Definitions of personal casualty gain and personal casualty loss.—For purposes of this subsection—

(A) Personal casualty gain.—The term "personal casualty gain" means the recognized gain from any involuntary conversion of property which is described in subsection (c)(3) arising from fire, storm, shipwreck, or other casualty, or from theft.

(B) Personal casualty loss.—The term "personal casualty loss" means any loss described in subsection (c)(3). For purposes of paragraph (2) and (3), the amount of any personal casualty loss shall be determined after the application of paragraph (1).

(5) Special rules.—

(A) Personal casualty losses allowable in computing adjusted gross income to the extent of personal casualty gains.—In any case to which paragraph (2)(A) applies, the deduction for personal casualty losses for any taxable year shall be treated as a deduction allowable in computing adjusted gross income to the extent such losses do not exceed the personal casualty gains for the taxable year.

(B) Joint returns.—For purposes of this subsection, a husband and wife making a joint return for the taxable year shall be treated as 1 individual.

(C) Determination of adjusted gross income in case of estates and trusts.—For purposes of paragraph (2), the adjusted gross income of an estate or trust shall be computed in the same manner as in the case of an individual, except that the deductions for costs paid or incurred in connection with the administration of the estate or trust shall be treated as allowable in arriving at adjusted gross income.

(D) Coordination with estate tax.—No loss described in subsection (c)(3) shall be allowed if, at the time of filing the return, such loss has been claimed for estate tax purposes in the estate tax return.

(E) Claim required to be filed in certain cases.—Any loss of an individual described in subsection (c)(3) to the extent covered by insurance shall be taken into account under this section only if the individual files a timely insurance claim with respect to such loss.

(i) Disaster losses.—

(1) Election to take deduction for preceding year.—Notwithstanding the provisions of subsection (a), any loss occurring in a disaster area (as defined by clause (ii) of subsection (h)(3)(C)) and attributable to a federally declared disaster (as defined by clause (i) of such subsection) may, at the election of the taxpayer, be taken into account for the taxable year immediately preceding the taxable year in which the disaster occurred.

(2) Year of loss.— If an election is made under this subsection, the casualty resulting in the loss shall be treated for purposes of this title as having occurred in the taxable year for which the deduction is claimed.

(3) Amount of loss.—The amount of the loss taken into account in the preceding taxable year by reason of paragraph (1) shall not exceed the un-compensated amount determined on the basis of the facts existing at the date the taxpayer claims the loss.

(4) Use of disaster loan appraisals to establish amount of loss.—Nothing in this title shall be construed to prohibit the Secretary from prescribing regulations or other guidance under which an appraisal for the purpose of obtaining a loan of Federal funds or a loan guarantee from the Federal Government as a result of a federally declared disaster (as defined by section (h)(3)(C)(i)) may be used to establish the amount of any loss described in paragraph (1) or (2).

* * *

(k) Treatment as disaster loss where taxpayer ordered to demolish or relocate residence in disaster area because of disaster.—In the case of a taxpayer whose residence is located in an area which has been determined by the President of the United States to warrant assistance by the Federal Government under the Robert T. Stafford Disaster Relief and Emergency Assistance Act, if—

(1) not later than the 120th day after the date of such determination, the taxpayer is ordered, by the government of the State or any political subdivision thereof in which such residence is located, to demolish or relocate such residence, and

(2) the residence has been rendered unsafe for use as a residence by reason of the disaster,

any loss attributable to such disaster shall be treated as a loss which arises from a casualty and which is described in subsection (i).

(l) Treatment of certain losses in insolvent financial institutions.—

(1) In general.—If—

(A) as of the close of the taxable year, it can reasonably be estimated that there is a loss on a qualified individual's deposit in a qualified financial institution, and

(B) such loss is on account of the bankruptcy or insolvency of such institution,

then the taxpayer may elect to treat the amount so estimated as a loss described in subsection (c)(3) incurred during the taxable year.

(2) Qualified individual defined.—For purposes of this subsection, the term "qualified individual" means any individual, except an individual—

(A) who owns at least 1 percent in value of the outstanding stock of the qualified financial institution,

(B) who is an officer of the qualified financial institution,

(C) who is a sibling (whether by the whole or half blood), spouse, aunt, uncle, nephew, niece, ancestor, or lineal descendant of an individual described in subparagraph (A) or (B), or

(D) who otherwise is a related person (as defined in section 267(b)) with respect to an individual described in subparagraph (A) or (B).

(3) Qualified financial institution.—For purposes of this subsection, the term "qualified financial institution" means—

(A) any bank (as defined in section 581),

(B) any institution described in section 591,

(C) any credit union the deposits or accounts in which are insured under Federal or State law or are protected or guaranteed under State law, or

(D) any similar institution chartered and supervised under Federal or State law.

(4) Deposit.—For purposes of this subsection, the term "deposit" means any deposit, withdrawable account, or withdrawable or repurchasable share.

(5) Election to treat as ordinary loss.—

(A) In general.—In lieu of any election under paragraph (1), the taxpayer may elect to treat the amount referred to in paragraph (1) for the taxable year as an ordinary loss described in subsection (c)(2) incurred during the taxable year.

(B) Limitations.—

(i) Deposit may not be federally insured.—No election may be made under subparagraph (A) with respect to any loss on a deposit in a qualified financial institution if part or all of such deposit is insured under Federal law.

(ii) Dollar limitation.—With respect to each financial institution, the aggregate amount of losses attributable to deposits in such financial institution to which an election under subparagraph (A) may be made by the taxpayer for any taxable year shall not exceed $20,000 ($10,000 in the case of a separate return by a married individual). The limitation of the preceding sentence shall be reduced by the amount of any insurance proceeds under any State law which can reasonably be expected to be received with respect to losses on deposits in such institution.

(6) Election.—Any election by the taxpayer under this subsection for any taxable year—

(A) shall apply to all losses for such taxable year of the taxpayer on deposits in the institution with respect to which such election was made, and

(B) may be revoked only with the consent of the Secretary.

(7) Coordination with section 166.—Section 166 shall not apply to any loss to which an election under this subsection applies.

* * *

Editorial Summary

Bad Debts

Subchapter B of Chapter 1 (Sec. 166)

Although bad debts represent a type of loss, they are subject to the provisions contained in Sec. 166 rather than the general rules of Sec. 165. Prior to the Tax Reform Act of 1986, the financial reporting treatment of bad debts and the tax treatment were similar. That is, the taxpayer had the choice of using either the reserve method (i.e., allowance for bad debts) or the direct charge-off method. However, the Tax Reform Act of 1986 repealed the reserve method except for certain financial institutions.

The other primary factor that remains in Sec. 166 relates to whether the bad debt is a business bad debt or a nonbusiness bad debt. The differences in treatment are as follows:

Type of bad debt	Tax result
Business	1. Can deduct based on either partial worthlessness or complete worthlessness.
	2. Classified as an ordinary deduction.
Nonbusiness	1. Can deduct only based on complete worthlessness.
	2. Classified as a short-term capital loss.

The nonbusiness label can apply only to noncorporate taxpayers.

Section 165 applies to worthless securities rather than Sec. 166 [see Secs. 165(g) and 166(e)].

§ 166. Bad debts

(a) General rule.—

(1) Wholly worthless debts.—There shall be allowed as a deduction any debt which becomes worthless within the taxable year.

(2) Partially worthless debts.—When satisfied that a debt is recoverable only in part, the Secretary may allow such debt, in an amount not in excess of the part charged off within the taxable year, as a deduction.

(b) Amount of deduction.—For purposes of subsection (a), the basis for determining the amount of the deduction for any bad debt shall be the adjusted basis provided in section 1011 for determining the loss from the sale or other disposition of property.

* * *

(d) Nonbusiness debts.—

(1) General rule.—In the case of a taxpayer other than a corporation—

(A) subsection (a) shall not apply to any nonbusiness debt; and

(B) where any nonbusiness debt becomes worthless within the taxable year, the loss resulting therefrom shall be considered a loss from the sale or exchange, during the taxable year, of a capital asset held for not more than 1 year.

(2) Nonbusiness debt defined.—For purposes of paragraph (1), the term "nonbusiness debt" means a debt other than—

(A) a debt created or acquired (as the case may be) in connection with a trade or business of the taxpayer; or

(B) a debt the loss from the worthlessness of which is incurred in the taxpayer's trade or business.

(e) Worthless securities.—This section shall not apply to a debt which is evidenced by a security as defined in section 165(g)(2)(C).

* * *

Editorial Summary

Depreciation and Cost Recovery*

Subchapter B of Chapter 1 (Secs. 167 and 168)

Sections 167 and 168 should be viewed as companion provisions for writing off depreciable tangible personalty and realty. Section 168 was enacted as part of the Economic Recovery Tax Act (ERTA) of 1981 for the purposes of economic stimulus and simplification. Modifications to Sec. 168 were made by the Tax Equity and Fiscal Responsibility Act of 1982 and the Deficit Reduction Act of 1984. Section 168 was completely revised by the Tax Reform Act of 1986. The result of these changes is that, depending on when an asset was placed in service, one of three depreciation/cost

*See the depreciation and cost recovery tables on page xxii.

recovery systems may be applicable. The principal dates of significance are as follows:

1. Property placed in service prior to 1981. For this category, depreciation is calculated using the traditional approach under Sec. 167.

2. Property placed in service after 1980 and prior to 1987 (ACRS). For this category, depreciation (i.e., cost recovery) generally is calculated under the original version of Sec. 168 as amended by the 1982 Act and the 1984 Act.

3. Property placed in service after 1986 (MACRS). For this category, depreciation (i.e., cost recovery) generally is calculated under the revised version of Sec. 168.

The enactment of ERTA in 1981 was intended to simplify depreciation calculations by replacing, in general, the depreciation concept with the cost recovery concept. Perceived complexities and related taxpayer/IRS conflicts associated with depreciation under Sec. 167 were as follows:

1. Determination of estimated useful life. Conflicts between the taxpayer and the IRS previously had been reduced through the promulgation of the guideline class system and later the asset depreciation range system.

2. Determination of salvage value. This potential problem previously had been reduced through the enactment of Sec. 167(f)(1) [prior to repeal by the Revenue Reconciliation Act of 1990] which enabled salvage value for certain personal property to be ignored up to 10 percent of the asset basis.

3. Depreciation method. While various methods could be used, as specified in Sec. 167(b) [prior to repeal by the Revenue Reconciliation Act of 1990], the prior enactment of Sec. 167(j) [prior to repeal by the Revenue Reconciliation Act of 1990] limited the taxpayer's choice for certain property.

The enactment of the Sec. 168 Accelerated Cost Recovery System (ACRS) in 1981 responded to the aforementioned complexities and conflicts by substituting the concept of cost recovery for the concept of depreciation. Since the objective of a cost recovery system is to enable the taxpayer to deduct the entire cost of an asset, salvage value became irrelevant. The estimated useful life issue was resolved by classifying all personalty into four categories (i.e., 3, 5, 10, and 15 years) and all realty into one category (i.e., 15 years). The cost recovery method issue was addressed by specifying the taxpayer must use either the statutory percentage method (i.e., the taxpayer merely selects the appropriate percentage from a table) or the optional straight-line method (i.e., with a choice of 3 statutorily provided recovery periods).

Even with the simplification provided by ERTA, a short-run complexity was created which, in certain limited cases, will be a long-run complexity. One depreciation system was replaced by two systems (i.e., the depreciation system under Sec. 167 and the cost recovery system under Sec. 168). That is, the Sec. 168 cost recovery system applied only to property placed in service after 1980. In addition, the Sec. 167 depreciation system, rather than the Sec. 168 cost recovery system, will continue to apply to certain assets placed in service after 1980 (e.g., assets whose life is not based on years; assets subject to the anti-churning rules, etc.) [see Sec. 168(f)].

Unfortunately, substantial additional complexity has been created during the intervening years by the following:

1. Increase in the recovery period for realty from 15 years to 18 years, followed by a subsequent increase to 19 years.

2. Reduction in the basis of certain personalty by 50 percent or 100 percent of the calculated investment tax credit.

3. Replacement of the whole-month convention for realty with the mid-month convention.

4. Replacement of the original ACRS with a completely revised, and more complex, MACRS by the Tax Reform Act of 1986. [Note: Only revised ACRS (MACRS) is included in this book].

5. Increase in the recovery period for nonresidential realty from 31.5 years to 39 years by the Revenue Reconciliation Act of 1993.

Therefore, the taxpayer must now contend with one depreciation system under Sec. 167 and two cost recovery systems under Sec. 168.

In applying the Secs. 167 and 168 Code provisions, consideration should be given to the limited expensing [(i.e., statutory ceiling amount of $100,000 (indexed amount for 2007 is $125,000); $25,000 for tax years beginning after 2010)] available under Sec. 179. The Economic Stimulus Act of 2008 increased the amount eligible for limited expensing to $250,000 for 2008. The American Recovery and Reinvestment Tax Act of 2009 extended the $250,000 amount to 2009. The Hiring Incentives to Restore Employment (HIRE) Act of 2010 extended the $250,000 amount to 2010, but the Tax Relief Act of 2010 increased the $250,000 to $500,000 for both 2010 and 2011. For 2012, the statutory amount is $500,000 and the indexed amount is $500,000. The American Taxpayer Relief Act of 2012 retained the amount at $500,000. Likewise, for luxury automobiles and other listed property, consideration must be given to the limitations imposed by Sec. 280F.

In considering the tax effects of depreciation and cost recovery, consideration must be given to the depreciation recapture provisions (see Secs. 291, 1245, and 1250). Depreciation also affects the Sec. 121 exclusion on the sale of a principal residence [see Sec. 121(d)(6)].

The Job Creation and Worker Assistance Act of 2002 provided for an additional first-year depreciation deduction of 30% for selected property acquired by the taxpayer after September 10, 2001 and before September 11, 2004, and placed in service before 2005 [see Sec. 168(k)]. The Jobs and Growth Tax Relief Reconciliation Act of 2003 increased the 30% to 50% and extended the eligible acquisition period to "before January 1, 2005" [see Sec. 168(k)(4)]. The 50% applied to property that was acquired by the taxpayer after May 5, 2003 and whose original use commenced with the taxpayer after May 5, 2003. Note that a taxpayer who is eligible for 50% bonus depreciation could (1) elect to use 30% bonus depreciation instead or (2) elect to forego bonus depreciation. The Economic Stimulus Act of 2008 reinstated 50 percent additional first-year depreciation for 2008. The American Recovery and Reinvestment Tax Act of 2009 extended 50 percent additional first-year depreciation to 2009. The Small Business Jobs Act of 2010 extended 50 percent additional first-year depreciation to 2010. The Tax Relief Act of 2010 increased the percentage to 100 percent for 2011. For 2012, the percentage is reduced to 50 percent. The American Taxpayer Relief Act of 2012 retained the percentage at 50 percent.

§ 167. Depreciation

(a) General rule.—There shall be allowed as a depreciation deduction a reasonable allowance for the exhaustion, wear and tear (including a reasonable allowance for obsolescence)—

(1) of property used in the trade or business, or

(2) of property held for the production of income.

(b) Cross reference.—

For determination of depreciation deduction in case of property to which section 168 applies, see section 168.

(c) Basis for depreciation.—

(1) In general.—The basis on which exhaustion, wear and tear, and obsolescence are to be allowed in respect of any property shall be the adjusted basis provided in section 1011, for the purpose of determining the gain on the sale or other disposition of such property.

(2) Special rule for property subject to lease.—If any property is acquired subject to a lease—

(A) no portion of the adjusted basis shall be allocated to the leasehold interest, and

(B) the entire adjusted basis shall be taken into account in determining the depreciation deduction (if any) with respect to the property subject to the lease.

(d) Life tenants and beneficiaries of trusts and estates.—In the case of property held by one person for life with remainder to another person, the deduction shall be computed as if the life tenant were the absolute owner of the property and shall be allowed to the life tenant. In the case of property held in trust, the allowable deduction shall be apportioned between the income beneficiaries and the trustee in accordance with the pertinent provisions of the instrument creating the trust, or, in the absence of such provisions, on the basis of the trust income allocable to each. In the case of an estate, the allowable deduction shall be apportioned between the estate and the heirs, legatees, and devisees on the basis of the income of the estate allocable to each.

(e) Certain term interests not depreciable.—

(1) In general.—No depreciation deduction shall be allowed under this section (and no depreciation or amortization deduction shall be allowed under any other provision of this subtitle) to the taxpayer for any term interest in property for any period during which the remainder interest in such property is held (directly or indirectly) by a related person.

(2) Coordination with other provisions.—

(A) Section 273.—This subsection shall not apply to any term interest to which section 273 applies.

(B) Section 305(e).—This subsection shall not apply to the holder of the dividend rights which were separated from any stripped preferred stock to which section 305(e)(1) applies.

(3) Basis adjustments.—If, but for this subsection, a depreciation or amortization deduction would be allowable to the taxpayer with respect to any term interest in property—

(A) the taxpayer's basis in such property shall be reduced by any depreciation or amortization deductions disallowed under this subsection, and

(B) the basis of the remainder interest in such property shall be increased by the amount of such disallowed deductions (properly adjusted for any depreciation deductions allowable under subsection (d) to the taxpayer).

(4) Special rules.—

(A) Denial of increase in basis of remainderman.—No increase in the basis of the remainder interest shall be made under paragraph (3)(B) for any disallowed deductions attributable to periods during which the term interest was held—

(i) by an organization exempt from tax under this subtitle, or

(ii) by a nonresident alien individual or foreign corporation but only if income from the term interest is not effectively connected with the conduct of a trade or business in the United States.

(B) Coordination with subsection (d).—If, but for this subsection, a depreciation or amortization deduction would be allowable to any person with respect to any term interest in property, the principles of subsection (d) shall apply to such person with respect to such term interest.

(5) Definitions.—For purposes of this subsection—

(A) Term interest in property.—The term "term interest in property" has the meaning given such term by section 1001(e)(2).

(B) Related person.—The term "related person" means any person bearing a relationship to the taxpayer described in subsection (b) or (e) of section 267.

(6) Regulations.—The Secretary shall prescribe such regulations as may be necessary to carry out the purposes of this subsection, including regulations preventing avoidance of this subsection through cross-ownership arrangements or otherwise.

(f) Treatment of certain property excluded from section 197.—

(1) Computer software.—

(A) In general.—If a depreciation deduction is allowable under subsection (a) with respect to any computer software, such deduction shall be computed by using the straight line method and a useful life of 36 months.

(B) Computer software.—For purposes of this section, the term "computer software" has the meaning given to such term by section 197 (e)(3)(B); except that such term shall not include any such software which is an amortizable section 197 intangible.

(C) Tax-exempt use property subject to lease.—In the case of computer software which would be tax-exempt use property as defined in subsection (h) of section 168 if such section applied to computer software, the useful life under subparagraph (A) shall not be less than 125 percent of the lease term (within the meaning of section 168(i)(3)).

(2) Certain interests or rights acquired separately.—If a depreciation deduction is allowable under subsection (a) with respect to any property described in subparagraph (B), (C), or (D) of section 197(e)(4), such deduction shall be computed in accordance with regulations prescribed by the Secretary. If such property would be tax-exempt use property as defined in subsection (h) of section 168 if such section applied to such property, the useful life under such regulations shall not be less than 125 percent of the lease term (within the meaning of subsection 168(i)(3)).

(3) Mortgage servicing rights.—If a depreciation deduction is allowable under subsection (a) with respect to any right described in section 197(e)(6), such deduction shall be computed by using the straight line method and a useful life of 108 months.

(g) Depreciation under income forecast method.—

(1) In general.—If the depreciation deduction allowable under this section to any taxpayer with respect to any property is determined under the income forecast method or any similar method—

(A) the income from the property to be taken into account in determining the depreciation deduction under such method shall be equal to the amount of income earned in connection with the property before the close of the 10th taxable year following the taxable year in which the property was placed in service.

(B) the adjusted basis of the property shall only include amounts with respect to which the requirements of section 461(h) are satisfied,

(C) the depreciation deduction under such method for the 10th taxable year beginning after the taxable year in which the property was placed in service shall be equal to the adjusted basis of such property as of the beginning of such 10th taxable year, and

(D) such taxpayer shall pay (or be entitled to receive) interest computed under the look-back method of paragraph (2) for any recomputation year.

(2) Look-back method.—The interest computed under the look-back method of this paragraph for any recomputation year shall be determined by—

(A) first determining the depreciation deductions under this section with respect to such property which would have been allowable for prior taxable years if the determination of the amounts so allowable had been made on the basis of the sum of the following (instead of the estimated income from such property)—

(i) the actual income earned in connection with such property for periods before the close of the recomputation year, and

(ii) an estimate of the future income to be earned in connection with such property for periods after the recomputation year and before the close of the 10th taxable year following the taxable year in which the property was placed in service,

(B) second, determining (solely for purposes of computing such interest) the overpayment or underpayment of tax for each such prior taxable year which would result solely from the application of subparagraph (A), and

(C) then using the adjusted overpayment rate (as defined in section 460(b)(7)), compounded daily, on the overpayment or underpayment determined under subparagraph (B).

For purposes of the preceding sentence, any cost incurred after the property is placed in service (which is not treated as a separate property under paragraph (5)) shall be taken into account by discounting (using the Federal mid-term rate determined under section 1274(d) as of the time such cost is incurred) such cost to its value as of the date the property is placed in service. The taxpayer may elect with respect to any property to have the preceding sentence not apply to such property.

(3) Exception from look-back method.—Paragraph (1)(D) shall not apply with respect to any property which had a cost basis of $100,000 or less.

(4) Recomputation year.—For purposes of this subsection, except as provided in regulations, the term "recomputation year" means, with respect to any property, the 3d and the 10th taxable years beginning after the taxable year in which the property was placed in service, unless the actual income earned in connection with the property for the period before the close of such 3d or 10th taxable year is within 10 percent of the income earned in connection with the property for such period which was taken into account under paragraph (1)(A).

(5) Special rules.—

(A) Certain costs treated as separate property.—For purposes of this subsection, the following costs shall be treated as separate properties:

(i) Any costs incurred with respect to any property after the 10th taxable year beginning after the taxable year in which the property was placed in service.

(ii) Any costs incurred after the property is placed in service and before the close of such 10th taxable year if such costs are significant and give rise to a significant increase in the income from the property which was not included in the estimated income from the property.

(B) Syndication income from television series.—In the case of property which is 1 or more episodes in a television series, income from syndicating such series shall not be required to be taken into account under this subsection before the earlier of—

(i) the 4th taxable year beginning after the date the first episode in such series is placed in service, or

(ii) the earliest taxable year in which the taxpayer has an arrangement relating to the future syndication of such series.

(C) Special rules for financial exploitation of characters, etc.—For purposes of this subsection, in the case of television and motion picture films, the income from the property shall include income from the exploitation of characters, designs, scripts, scores, and other incidental income associated with such films, but only to the extent that such income is earned in connection with the ultimate use of such items by, or the ultimate sale of merchandise to, persons who are not related persons (within the meaning of section 267(b)) to the taxpayer.

(D) Collection of interest.—For purposes of subtitle F (other than sections 6654 and 6655), any interest required to be paid by the taxpayer under paragraph (1) for any recomputation year shall be treated as an increase in the tax imposed by this chapter for such year.

(E) Treatment of distribution costs.—For purposes of this subsection, the income with respect to any property shall be the taxpayer's gross income from such property.

(F) Determinations.—For purposes of paragraph (2), determinations of the amount of income earned in connection with any property shall be made in the same manner as for purposes of applying the income forecast method; except that any income from the disposition of such property shall be taken into account.

(G) Treatment of pass-thru entities.—Rules similar to the rules of section 460(b)(4) shall apply for purposes of this subsection.

(6) Limitation on property for which income forecast method may be used.—The depreciation deduction allowable under this section may be determined under the income forecast method or any similar method only with respect to—

(A) property described in paragraph (3) or (4) of section 168(f),

(B) copyrights,

(C) books,

(D) patents, and

(E) other property specified in regulations.

Such methods may not be used with any amortizable section 197 intangible (as defined in section 197(c)).

(7) Treatment of participations and residuals.—

(A) In general.—For purposes of determining the depreciation deduction allowable with respect to a property under this subsection, the taxpayer may include participations and residuals with respect to such property in the adjusted basis of such property for the taxable year in which the property is placed in service, but only to the extent that such participations and residuals relate to income estimated (for purposes of this subsection) to be earned in connection with the property before the close of the 10th taxable year referred to in paragraph (1)(A).

(B) Participations and residuals.—For purposes of this paragraph, the term "participations and residuals" means, with respect to any property, costs the amount of which by contract varies with the amount of income earned in connection with such property.

(C) Special rules relating to recomputation years.—If the adjusted basis of any property is determined under this paragraph, paragraph (4) shall be applied by substituting "for each taxable year in such period" for "for such period."

(D) Other special rules.—

(i) Participations and residuals.—Notwithstanding subparagraph (A), the taxpayer may exclude participations and residuals from the adjusted basis of such property and deduct such participations and residuals in the taxable year that such participations and residuals are paid.

(ii) Coordination with other rules.—Deductions computed in accordance with this paragraph shall be allowable notwithstanding paragraph (1)(B), section 263, 263A, 404, 419, or 461(h).

(E) Authority to make adjustments.—The Secretary shall prescribe appropriate adjustments to the basis of property and to the lookback method for the additional amounts allowable as a deduction solely by reason of this paragraph.

(8) Special rules for certain musical works and copyrights.—

(A) In general.—If an election is in effect under this paragraph for any taxable year, then, notwithstanding paragraph (1), any expense which—

(i) is paid or incurred by the taxpayer in creating or acquiring any applicable musical property placed in service during the taxable year, and

(ii) is otherwise properly chargeable to capital account,

shall be amortized ratably over the 5-year period beginning with the month in which the property was placed in service. The preceding sentence shall not apply to any expense which, without regard to this paragraph, would not be allowable as a deduction.

(B) Exclusive method.—Except as provided in this paragraph, no depreciation or amortization deduction shall be allowed with respect to any expense to which subparagraph (A) applies.

(C) Applicable musical property.—For purposes of this paragraph—

(i) In general.—The term "applicable musical property" means any musical composition (including any accompanying words), or any copyright with respect to a musical composition, which is property to which this subsection applies without regard to this paragraph.

(ii) Exceptions.—Such term shall not include any property—

(I) with respect to which expenses are treated as qualified creative expenses to which section 263A(h) applies,

(II) to which a simplified procedure established under section 263A(i)(2) applies, or

(III) which is an amortizable section 197 intangible (as defined in section 197(c)).

(D) Election.—An election under this paragraph shall be made at such time and in such form as the Secretary may prescribe and shall apply to all applicable musical property placed in service during the taxable year for which the election applies.

(E) Termination.—An election may not be made under this paragraph for any taxable year beginning after December 31, 2010.

(h) Amortization of geological and geophysical expenditures.—

(1) **In general.**—Any geological and geophysical expenses paid or incurred in connection with the exploration for, or development of, oil or gas within the United States (as defined in section 638) shall be allowed as a deduction ratably over the 24-month period beginning on the date that such expense was paid or incurred.

(2) **Half-year convention.**—For purposes of paragraph (1), any payment paid or incurred during the taxable year shall be treated as paid or incurred on the mid-point of such taxable year.

(3) **Exclusive method.**—Except as provided in this subsection, no depreciation or amortization deduction shall be allowed with respect to such payments.

(4) **Treatment upon abandonment.**—If any property with respect to which geological and geophysical expenses are paid or incurred is retired or abandoned during the 24-month period described in paragraph (1), no deduction shall be allowed on account of such retirement or abandonment and the amortization deduction under this subsection shall continue with respect to such payment.

* * *

(i) **Cross references.**—

(1) For additional rule applicable to depreciation of improvements in the case of mines, oil and gas wells, other natural deposits, and timber, see section 611.

(2) For amortization of goodwill and certain other intangibles, see section 197.

* * *

Editorial Summary
Cost Recovery
Subchapter B of Chapter 1 (Sec. 168)

See the discussion under the Editorial Summary entitled Depreciation and Cost Recovery which precedes Sec. 167.

§ 168. Accelerated cost recovery system

(a) **General rule.**—Except as otherwise provided in this section, the depreciation deduction provided by section 167(a) for any tangible property shall be determined by using—

(1) the applicable depreciation method,

(2) the applicable recovery period, and

(3) the applicable convention.

(b) **Applicable depreciation method.**—For purposes of this section—

(1) **In general.**—Except as provided in paragraphs (2) and (3), the applicable depreciation method is—

(A) the 200 percent declining balance method,

(B) switching to the straight line method for the 1st taxable year for which using the straight line method with respect to the adjusted basis as of the beginning of such year will yield a larger allowance.

(2) **150 percent declining balance method in certain cases.**—Paragraph (1) shall be applied by substituting "150 percent" for "200 percent" in the case of—

(A) any 15-year or 20-year property not referred to in paragraph (3),

(B) any property used in a farming business (within the meaning of section 263A(e)(4)),

(C) any property (other than property described in paragraph (3)) which is a qualified smart electric meter or qualified smart electric grid system, or

(D) any property (other than property described in paragraph (3)) with respect to which the taxpayer elects under paragraph (5) to have the provisions of this paragraph apply.

(3) **Property to which straight line method applies.**—The applicable depreciation method shall be the straight line method in the case of the following property:

(A) Nonresidential real property.

(B) Residential rental property.

(C) Any railroad grading or tunnel bore.

(D) Property with respect to which the taxpayer elects under paragraph (5) to have the provisions of this paragraph apply.

(E) Property described in subsection (e)(3)(D)(ii).

(F) Water utility property described in subsection (e)(5).

(G) Qualified leasehold improvement property described in subsection (e)(6).

(H) Qualified restaurant property described in subsection (e)(7).

(I) Qualified retail improvement property described in subsection (e)(8).

(4) Salvage value treated as zero.—Salvage value shall be treated as zero.

(5) Election.—An election under paragraph 2 (C) or (3)(D) may be made with respect to 1 or more classes of property for any taxable year and once made with respect to any class shall apply to all property in such class placed in service during such taxable year. Such an election, once made, shall be irrevocable.

(c) Applicable recovery period.—For purposes of this section, the applicable recovery period shall be determined in accordance with the following table:

In the case of:	The applicable recovery period is:
3-year property	3 years
5-year property	5 years
7-year property	7 years
10-year property	10 years
15-year property	15 years
20-year property	20 years
Water utility property	25 years
Residential rental property	27.5 years
Nonresidential real property	39 years*
Any railroad grading or tunnel bore	50 years

(d) Applicable convention.—For purposes of this section—

(1) In general.—Except as otherwise provided in this subsection, the applicable convention is the half-year convention.

(2) Real property.—In the case of—

(A) nonresidential real property,

(B) residential rental property, and

(C) any railroad grading or tunnel bore,

the applicable convention is the mid-month convention.

(3) Special rule where substantial property placed in service during last 3 months of taxable year.—

(A) In general.—Except as provided in regulations, if during any taxable year—

(i) the aggregate bases of property to which this section applies placed in service during the last 3 months of the taxable year, exceed

(ii) 40 percent of the aggregate bases of property to which this section applies placed in service during such taxable year,

the applicable convention for all property to which this section applies placed in service during such taxable year shall be the mid-quarter convention.

(B) Certain real property not taken into account.—For purposes of subparagraph (A), there shall not be taken into account—

(i) any nonresidential real property, residential rental property, and railroad grading or tunnel bore, and

(ii) any other property placed in service and disposed of during the same taxable year.

(4) Definitions.—

(A) Half-year convention.—The half-year convention is a convention which treats all property placed in service during any taxable year (or disposed of during any taxable year) as placed in service (or disposed of) on the midpoint of such taxable year.

(B) Mid-month convention.—The mid-month convention is a convention which treats all property placed in service during any month (or disposed of during any month) as placed in service (or disposed of) on the mid-point of such month.

(C) Mid-quarter convention.—The mid-quarter convention is a convention which treats all property placed in service during any quarter of a taxable year (or disposed of during any quarter of a taxable year) as placed in service (or disposed of) on the mid-point of such quarter.

(e) Classification of property.—For purposes of this section—

(1) In general.—Except as otherwise provided in this subsection, property shall be classified under the following table:

Property shall be treated as:	If such property has a class life (in years) of:
3-year property	4 or less
5-year property	More than 4 but less than 10
7-year property	10 or more but less than 16
10-year property	16 or more but less than 20
15-year property	20 or more but less than 25
20-year property	25 or more.

(2) Residential rental or nonresidential real property.—

(A) Residential rental property.—

(i) Residential rental property.—The term "residential rental property" means any building or structure if 80 percent or more of the gross rental income from such

*Editorial comment: Prior to the effect of the Revenue Reconciliation Act of 1993 (qualifying property placed in service on or after May 13, 1993), the recovery period for nonresidential real property was 31.5 years.

building or structure for the taxable year is rental income from dwelling units.

(ii) Definitions.—For purposes of clause (i)—

(I) the term "dwelling unit" means a house or apartment used to provide living accommodations in a building or structure, but does not include a unit in a hotel, motel, or other establishment more than one-half of the units in which are used on a transient basis, and

(II) if any portion of the building or structure is occupied by the taxpayer, the gross rental income from such building or structure shall include the rental value of the portion so occupied.

(B) Nonresidential real property.—The term "nonresidential real property" means section 1250 property which is not—

(i) residential rental property, or

(ii) property with a class life of less than 27.5 years.

(3) Classification of certain property.—

(A) 3-year property.—The term "3-year property" includes—

(i) any race horse—

(I) which is placed in service before January 1, 2014,* and

(II) which is placed in service after December 31, 2013,* and which is more than 2 years old at the time such horse is placed in service by such purchaser.

(ii) any horse other than a race horse which is more than 12 years old at the time it is placed in service, and

(iii) any qualified rent-to-own property.

(B) 5-year property.—The term "5-year property" includes—

(i) any automobile or light general purpose truck,

(ii) any semi-conductor manufacturing equipment,

(iii) any computer-based telephone central office switching equipment,

(iv) any qualified technological equipment,

(v) any section 1245 property used in connection with research and experimentation,

(vi) any property which—

(I) is described in subparagraph (A) of section 48(a)(3) (or would be so described if "solar or wind energy" were substituted for "solar energy" in clause (i) thereof and the last sentence of such section did not apply to such subparagraph),

(II) is described in paragraph (15) of section 48(1) (as in effect on the day before the date of the enactment of the Revenue Reconciliation Act of 1990) and is a qualifying small power production facility within the meaning of section 3(17)(C) of the Federal Power Act (16 U.S.C. 796(17)(C)), as in effect on September 1, 1986, or

(III) is described in section 48(1)(3) (A)(ix) (as in effect on the day before the date of the enactment of the Revenue Reconciliation Act of 1990), and

(vii) any machinery or equipment (other than any grain bin, cotton ginning asset, fence, or other land improvement) which is used in a farming business (as defined in section 263A(e)(4)), the original use of which commences with the taxpayer after December 31, 2008, and which is placed in service before January 1, 2010.

Nothing in any provision of law shall be construed to treat property as not being described in clause (vi)(I) (or the corresponding provision or prior law) by reason of being public utility property (within the meaning of section 48(a)(3)).

(C) 7-year property.—The term "7-year property" includes—

(i) any railroad track,

(ii) any motorsports entertainment complex,

(iii) any Alaska natural gas pipeline,

(iv) any natural gas gathering line the original use of which commences with the taxpayer after April 11, 2005, and

(v) any property which—

(I) does not have a class life, and

(II) is not otherwise classified under paragraph (2) or this paragraph.

---

*Editorial comment: At the present time, this section has not been extended. There is pending legislation in the Senate, *The Tax Extenders Act of 2013 (S. 1859)*, that would extend Section 168(e)(3)(A)(i)(I) until January 1, 2015 and 168(e)(3)(A)(i)(II) until December 31, 2014.

(D) 10-year property.—The term "10-year property" includes

(i) any single purpose agricultural or horticultural structure (within the meaning of subsection (i)(13)),

(ii) any tree or vine bearing fruit or nuts,

(iii) any qualified smart electric meter, and

(iv) any qualified smart electric grid system.

(E) 15-year property.*—The term "15-year property" includes—

(i) any municipal wastewater treatment plant,

(ii) any telephone distribution plant and comparable equipment used for 2-way exchange of voice and data communications,

(iii) any section 1250 property which is a retail motor fuels outlet (whether or not food or other convenience items are sold at the outlet),

(iv) any qualified leasehold improvement property placed in service before January 1, 2014,*

(v) any qualified restaurant property placed in service before January 1, 2014,*

(vi) initial clearing and grading land improvements with respect to gas utility property,

(vii) any section 1245 property (as defined in section 1245(a)(3)) used in the transmission at 69 or more kilovolts of electricity for sale and the original use of which commences with the taxpayer after April 11, 2005,

(viii) any natural gas distribution line the original use of which commences with the taxpayer after April 11, 2005, and which is placed in service before January 1, 2011, and

(ix) any qualified retail improvement property placed in service after December 31, 2008, and before January 1, 2014.*

(F) 20-year property.—The term "20-year property" means initial clearing and grading land improvements with respect to any electric utility transmission and distribution plants.

(4) Railroad grading or tunnel bore.—The term "railroad grading or tunnel bore" means all improvements resulting from excavations (including tunneling), construction of embankments, clearings, diversions of roads and streams, sodding of slopes, and from similar work necessary to provide, construct, reconstruct, alter, protect, improve, replace, or restore a roadbed or right-of-way for railroad track.

(5) Water utility property.—The term "water utility property" means property—

(A) which is an integral part of the gathering, treatment, or commercial distribution of water, and which, without regard to this paragraph, would be 20-year property, and

(B) any municipal sewer.

(6) Qualified leasehold improvement property.—The term "qualified leasehold improvement property" has the meaning given such term in section 168(k)(3) except that the following special rules shall apply:

(A) Improvements made by lessor.—In the case of an improvement made by the person who was the lessor of such improvement when such improvement was placed in service, such improvement shall be qualified leasehold improvement property (if at all) only so long as such improvement is held by such person.

(B) Exception for changes in form of business.—Property shall not cease to be qualified leasehold improvement property under subparagraph (A) by reason of—

(i) death,

(ii) a transaction to which section 381(a) applies,

(iii) a mere change in the form of conducting the trade or business so long as the property is retained in such trade or business as qualified leasehold improvement property and the taxpayer retains a substantial interest in such trade or business,

(iv) the acquisition of such property in an exchange described in section 1031, 1033, or 1038 to the extent that the basis of such property includes an amount representing the adjusted basis of other property owned by the taxpayer or a related person, or

(v) the acquisition of such property by the taxpayer in a transaction described in section 332, 251, 361, 721, or 731 (or the acquisition of such property by the taxpayer from the transferee or acquiring corporation in a transaction described in such section), to

*Editorial comment: At the present time this section has not been extended. There is pending legislation in the Senate, *The Tax Extenders Act of 2013 (S. 1859)*, that would extend Sections 168(e)(3)(E)(iv), (v), and (ix) until January 1, 2015.

the extent that the basis of the property in the hands of the taxpayer is determined by reference to its basis in the hands of the transferor or distributor.

(7) Qualified restaurant property.—

(A) In general.—The term "qualified restaurant property" means any section 1250 property which is—

(i) a building, or

(ii) an improvement to a building,

if more than 50 percent of the building's square footage is devoted to preparation of, and seating for on-premises consumption of, prepared meals.

(B) Exclusion from bonus depreciation.—Property described in this paragraph shall not be considered qualified property for purposes of subsection (k).

(8) Qualified retail improvement property.—

(A) In general.—The term "qualified retail improvement property" means any improvement to an interior portion of a building which is nonresidential real property if—

(i) such portion is open to the general public and is used in the retail trade or business of selling tangible personal property to the general public, and

(ii) such improvement is placed in service more than 3 years after the date the building was first placed in service.

(B) Improvements made by owner.—In the case of an improvement made by the owner of such improvement, such improvement shall be qualified retail improvement property (if at all) only so long as such improvement is held by such owner. Rules similar to the rules under paragraph (6)(B) shall apply for purposes of the preceding sentence.

(C) Certain improvements not included.—Such term shall not include any improvement for which the expenditure is attributable to—

(i) the enlargement of the building,

(ii) any elevator or escalator,

(iii) any structural component benefiting a common area, or

(iv) the internal structural framework of the building.

(D) Exclusion from bonus depreciation.—Property described in this paragraph shall not be considered qualified property for purposes of subsection (k).

(f) Property to which section does not apply.—This section shall not apply to—

(1) Certain methods of depreciation.—Any property if—

(A) the taxpayer elects to exclude such property from the application of this section, and

(B) for the 1st taxable year for which a depreciation deduction would be allowable with respect to such property in the hands of the taxpayer, the property is properly depreciated under the unit-of-production method or any method of depreciation not expressed in a term of years (other than the retirement replacement-betterment method or similar method).

* * *

(3) Films and video tape.—Any motion picture film or video tape.

(4) Sound recordings.—Any works which result from the fixation of a series of musical, spoken, or other sounds, regardless of the nature of the material (such as discs, tapes, or other phonorecordings) in which such sounds are embodied.

(5) Certain property placed in service in churning transactions.—

(A) In general.—Property—

(i) described in paragraph (4) of section 168(e) (as in effect before the amendments made by the Tax Reform Act of 1986), or

(ii) which would be described in such paragraph if such paragraph were applied by substituting "1987" for "1981" and "1986" for "1980" each place such terms appear.

(B) Subparagraph (A)(ii) not to apply.—Clause (ii) of subparagraph (A) shall not apply to—

(i) any residential rental property or nonresidential real property,

(ii) any property if, for the 1st taxable year in which such property is placed in service—

(I) the amount allowable as a deduction under this section (as in effect before the date of the enactment of this paragraph) with respect to such property is greater than

(II) the amount allowable as a deduction under this section (as in effect on or after such date and using the half-year convention) for such taxable year, or

(iii) any property to which this section (as amended by the Tax Reform Act of 1986) applied in the hands of the transferor.

(C) Special rule. In the case of any property to which this section would apply but for this paragraph, the depreciation deduction under section 167 shall be determined under the provisions of this section as in effect before the amendments made by section 201 of the Tax Reform Act of 1986.

(g) Alternative depreciation system for certain property.—

(1) In general.—In the case of—

(A) any tangible property which during the taxable year is used predominantly outside the United States,

(B) any tax-exempt use property,

(C) any tax-exempt bond financed property,

(D) any imported property covered by an Executive order under paragraph (6), and

(E) any property to which an election under paragraph (7) applies,

the depreciation deduction provided by section 167 (a) shall be determined under the alternative depreciation system.

(2) Alternative depreciation system.—For purposes of paragraph (1), the alternative depreciation system is depreciation determined by using—

(A) the straight line method (without regard to salvage value),

(B) the applicable convention determined under subsection (d), and

(C) a recovery period determined under the following table:

In the case of:	The recovery period shall be:
(i) Property not described in clause (ii) or (iii)	The class life
(ii) Personal property with no class life	12 years
(iii) Nonresidential real and residential rental property	40 years
(iv) Any railroad grading or tunnel bore or water utility property	50 years

(3) Special rules for determining class life.—

(A) Tax-exempt use property subject to lease.—In the case of any tax-exempt use property subject to a lease, the recovery period used for purposes of paragraph (2) shall (notwithstanding any other subparagraph of this paragraph) in no event be less than 125 percent of the lease term.

(B) Special rule for certain property assigned to classes.—For purposes of paragraph (2), in the case of property described in any of the following subparagraphs of subsection (e)(3), the class life shall be determined as follows:

If property is described in subparagraph:	The class life is:
(A)(iii)	4
(B)(ii)	5
(B)(iii)	9.5
(C)(i)	10
(C)(iii)	22
(C)(iv)	14
(D)(i)	15
(D)(ii)	20
(E)(i)	24
(E)(ii)	24
(E)(iii)	20
(E)(iv)	39
(E)(v)	39
(E)(vi)	20
(E)(vii)	30
(E)(viii)	35
(F)	25

(C) Qualified technological equipment.—In the case of any qualified technological equipment, the recovery period used for purposes of paragraph (2) shall be 5 years.

(D) Automobiles, etc.—In the case of any automobile or light general purpose truck, the recovery period used for purposes of paragraph (2) shall be 5 years.

(E) Certain real property.—In the case of any section 1245 property which is real property with no class life, the recovery period used for purposes of paragraph (2) shall be 40 years.

(4) Exception for certain property used outside United States.—Subparagraph (A) of paragraph (1) shall not apply to—

(A) any aircraft which is registered by the Administrator of the Federal Aviation Agency and which is operated to and from the United States or is operated under contract with the United States;

(B) rolling stock which is used within and without the United States and which is—

(i) of a domestic railroad corporation providing transportation subject to subchapter I of chapter 105 of title 49, or

(ii) of a United States person (other than a corporation described in clause (i)) but only if the rolling stock is not leased to one or more foreign persons for periods aggregating more than 12 months in any 24-month period;

(C) any vessel documented under the laws of the United States which is operated in the foreign or domestic commerce of the United States;

(D) any motor vehicle of a United States person (as defined in section 7701(a)(30)) which is operated to and from the United States;

(E) any container of a United States person which is used in the transportation of property to and from the United States;

(F) any property (other than a vessel or an aircraft) of a United States person which is used for the purpose of exploring for, developing, removing, or transporting resources from the outer continental shelf (within the meaning of section 2 of the Outer Continental Shelf Lands Act, as amended and supplemented; (43 U.S.C. 1331));

(G) any property which is owned by a domestic corporation (other than a corporation which has an election in effect under section 936) or by a United States citizen (other than a citizen entitled to the benefits of section 931 or 933) and which is used predominantly in a possession of the United States by such a corporation or such a citizen, or by a corporation created or organized in, or under the law of, a possession of the United States;

(H) any communications satellite (as defined in section 103(3) of the Communications Satellite Act of 1962, 47 U.S.C. 702(3)), or any interest therein, of a United States person;

(I) any cable, or any interest therein, of a domestic corporation engaged in furnishing telephone service to which section 168(i) (10)(C) applies (or of a wholly owned domestic subsidiary of such a corporation), if such cable is part of a submarine cable system which constitutes part of a communication link exclusively between the United States and one or more foreign countries;

(J) any property (other than a vessel or an aircraft) of a United States person which is used in international or territorial waters within the northern portion of the Western Hemisphere for the purpose of exploring for, developing, removing, or transporting resources from ocean waters or deposits under such waters;

(K) any property described in section 48(l)(3)(A)(ix) (as in effect on the day before the date of the enactment of the Revenue Reconciliation Act of 1990) which is owned by a United States person and which is used in international or territorial waters to generate energy for use in the United States; and

(L) any satellite (not described in subparagraph (H)) or other spacecraft (or any interest therein) held by a United States person if such satellite or other spacecraft was launched from within the United States.

For purposes of subparagraph (J), the term "northern portion of the Western Hemisphere" means the area lying west of the 30th meridian west of Greenwich, east of the international dateline, and north of the Equator, but not including any foreign country which is a country of South America.

(5) Tax-exempt bond financed property.—For purposes of this subsection—

(A) In general.—Except as otherwise provided in this paragraph, the term "tax-exempt bond financed property" means any property to the extent such property is financed (directly or indirectly) by an obligation the interest on which is exempt from tax under section 103(a).

(B) Allocation of bond proceeds.—For purposes of subparagraph (A), the proceeds of any obligation shall be treated as used to finance property acquired in connection with the issuance of such obligation in the order in which such property is placed in service.

(C) Qualified residential rental projects.—The term "tax-exempt bond financed property" shall not include any qualified residential rental project (within the meaning of section 142(a)(7)).

(6) Imported property.—

(A) Countries maintaining trade restrictions or engaging in discriminatory acts.—If the President determines that a foreign country—

(i) maintains nontariff trade restrictions, including variable import fees, which substantially burden United States commerce in a manner inconsistent with provisions of trade agreements, or

(ii) engages in discriminatory or other acts (including tolerance of international cartels) or policies unjustifiably restricting United States commerce, the President may by Executive order provide for the application of paragraph (1)(D) to any article or class of articles manufactured or produced in such foreign country for such period as may be provided by such Executive order. Any period specified in the preceding sentence shall not apply to any property ordered before (or the construction, reconstruction, or erection of which began before) the date of the Executive order unless the President determines an earlier date to be in the public interest and specifies such date in the Executive order.

(B) Imported property.—For purposes of this subsection, the term "imported property" means any property if—

(i) such property was completed outside the United States, or

(ii) less than 50 percent of the basis of such property is attributable to value added within the United States.

For purposes of this subparagraph, the term "United States" includes the Commonwealth of Puerto Rico and the possessions of the United States.

(7) Election to use alternative depreciation system.—

(A) In general.—If the taxpayer makes an election under this paragraph with respect to any class of property for any taxable year, the alternative depreciation system under this subsection shall apply to all property in such class placed in service during such taxable year. Notwithstanding the preceding sentence, in the case of nonresidential real property or residential rental property, such election may be made separately with respect to each property.

(B) Election irrevocable.—An election under subparagraph (A), once made, shall be irrevocable.

* * *

(i) Definitions and special rules.—For purposes of this section—

(1) Class life.—Except as provided in this section, the term "class life" means the class life (if any) which would be applicable with respect to any property as of January 1, 1986, under subsection (m) of section 167 (determined without regard to paragraph (4) and as if the taxpayer had made an election under such subsection). The Secretary, through an office established in the Treasury, shall monitor and analyze actual experience with respect to all depreciable assets. The reference in this paragraph to subsection (m) of section 167 shall be treated as a reference to such subsection as in effect on the day before the date of the enactment of the Revenue Reconciliation Act of 1990.

* * *

(4) General asset accounts.—Under regulations, a taxpayer may maintain 1 or more general asset accounts for any property to which this section applies. Except as provided in regulations, all proceeds realized on any disposition of property in a general asset account shall be included in income as ordinary income.

(5) Changes in use.—The Secretary shall, by regulations, provide for the method of determining the deduction allowable under section 167(a) with respect to any tangible property for any taxable year (and the succeeding taxable years) during which such property changes status under this section but continues to be held by the same person.

(6) Treatments of additions or improvements to property.—In the case of any addition to (or improvement of) any property—

(A) any deduction under subsection (a) for such addition or improvement shall be computed in the same manner as the deduction for such property would be computed if such property had been placed in service at the same time as such addition or improvement, and

(B) the applicable recovery period for such addition or improvement shall begin on the later of—

(i) the date on which such addition (or improvement) is placed in service, or

(ii) the date on which the property with respect to which such addition (or improvement) was made is placed in service.

(7) Treatment of certain transferees.—

(A) In general.—In the case of any property transferred in a transaction described in subparagraph (B), the transferee shall be treated as the transferor for purposes of computing the depreciation deduction determined under this section with respect to so much of the basis in the hands of the transferee as does not exceed the adjusted basis in the hands of the transferor. In any case where this section as in effect before the amendments made by section 201 of the Tax Reform Act of 1986 applied to the property in the hands of the transferor, the reference in the preceding sentence to this section shall be treated as a reference to this section as so in effect.

(B) Transactions covered.—The transactions described in this subparagraph are—

(i) any transaction described in section 332, 351, 361, 721, or 731, and

(ii) any transaction between members of the same affiliated group during any taxable year for which a consolidated return is made by such group.

Subparagraph (A) shall not apply in the case of a termination of a partnership under section 708(b)(1)(B).

(C) Property reacquired by the taxpayer.—Under regulations, property which is disposed of and then reacquired by the taxpayer shall be treated for purposes of computing the deduction allowable under subsection (a) as if such property had not been disposed of.

(8) Treatment of leasehold improvements.—

(A) In general.—In the case of any building erected (or improvements made) on leased property, if such building or improvement is property to which this section applies, the depreciation deduction shall be determined under the provisions of this section.

(B) Treatment of lessor improvements which are abandoned at termination of lease.—An improvement—

(i) which is made by the lessor of leased property for the lessee of such property, and

(ii) which is irrevocably disposed of or abandoned by the lessor at the termination of the lease by such lessee,

shall be treated for purposes of determining gain or loss under this title as disposed of by the lessor when so disposed of or abandoned.

(C) Cross reference.—

For treatment of qualified long-term real property constructed or improved in connection with cash or rent reduction from lessor to lessee, see section 110(b).

* * *

(12) Section 1245 and Section 1250 property.—The terms "section 1245 property" and "section 1250 property" have the meanings given them by sections 1245(a)(3) and 1250(c), respectively.

(13) Single purpose agricultural or horticultural structure.—

(A) In general.—The term "single purpose agricultural or horticultural structure" means—

(i) a single purpose livestock structure, and

(ii) a single purpose horticultural structure.

(B) Definitions.—For purposes of this paragraph—

(i) Single purpose livestock structure.—The term "single purpose livestock structure" means any enclosure or structure specifically designed, constructed, and used—

(I) for housing, raising, and feeding a particular type of livestock and their produce, and

(II) for housing the equipment (including any replacements) necessary for the housing, raising, and feeding referred to in subclause (I).

(ii) Single purpose horticultural structure.—The term "single purpose horticultural structure" means—

(I) a greenhouse specifically designed, constructed, and used for the commercial production of plants, and

(II) a structure specifically designed, constructed, and used for the commercial production of mushrooms.

(iii) Structures which include work space.—An enclosure or structure which provides work space shall be treated as a single purpose agricultural or horticultural structure only if such work space is solely for—

(I) the stocking, caring for, or collecting of livestock or plants (as the case may be) or their produce,

(II) the maintenance of the enclosure or structure, and

(III) the maintenance or replacement of the equipment or stock enclosed or housed therein.

(iv) Livestock.—The term "livestock" includes poultry.

(14) Qualified rent-to-own property.—

(A) In general.—The term "qualified rent-to-own property" means property held by a rent-to-own dealer for purposes of being subject to a rent-to-own contract.

(B) Rent-to-own dealer.—The term "rent-to-own dealer" means a person that, in the ordinary course of business, regularly enters into rent-to-own contracts with customers for the use of consumer property, if a substantial portion of those contracts terminate and the property is returned to such person before the receipt of all payments required to transfer ownership of the property from such person to the customer.

(C) Consumer property.—The term "consumer property" means tangible personal property of a type generally used within the home for personal use.

(D) Rent-to-own contract.—The term "rent-to-own contract" means any lease for the use of consumer property between a rent-to-own dealer and a customer who is an individual which—

(i) is titled "Rent-to-Own Agreement" or "Lease Agreement with Ownership Option," or uses other similar language,

(ii) provides for level (or decreasing where no payment is less than 40 percent of the largest payment), regular periodic payments (for a payment period which is a week or month),

(iii) provides that legal title to such property remains with the rent-to-own dealer until the customer makes all the payments described in clause (ii) or early purchase payments required under the contract to acquire legal title to the item of property,

(iv) provides a beginning date and a maximum period of time for which the contract may be in effect that does not exceed 156 weeks or 36 months from such beginning date (including renewals or options to extend),

(v) provides for payments within the 156-week or 36-month period that, in the aggregate, generally exceed the normal retail price of the consumer property plus interest,

(vi) provides for payments under the contract that, in the aggregate, do not exceed $10,000 per item of consumer property,

(vii) provides that the customer does not have any legal obligation to make all the payments referred to in clause (ii) set forth under the contract, and that at the end of each payment period the customer may either continue to use the consumer properly by making the payment for the next payment period or return such property to the rent-to-own dealer in good working order, in which case the customer does not incur any further obligations under the contract and is not entitled to a return of any payments previously made under the contract, and

(viii) provides that the customer has no right to sell, sublease, mortgage, pawn, pledge, encumber, or otherwise dispose of the consumer property until all payments stated in the contract have been made.

(15) Motorsports entertainment complex.—

(A) In general.—The term "motorsports entertainment complex" means a racing track facility which—

(i) is permanently situated on land, and

(ii) during the 36-month period following the first day of the month in which the asset is placed in service, hosts 1 or more racing events for automobiles (of any type), trucks, or motorcycles which are open to the public for the price of admission.

(B) Ancillary and support facilities.—Such term shall include, if owned by the taxpayer who owns the complex and provided for the benefit of patrons of the complex—

(i) ancillary facilities and land improvements in support of the complex's activities (including parking lots, sidewalks, waterways, bridges, fences, and landscaping),

(ii) support facilities (including food and beverage retailing, souvenir vending, and other nonlodging accommodations), and

(iii) appurtenances associated with such facilities and related attractions and amusements (including ticket booths, race track surfaces, suites and hospitality facilities, grandstands and viewing structures, props, walls, facilities that support the delivery of entertainment services, other special purpose structures, facades, shop interiors, and buildings).

(C) Exception.—Such term shall not include any transportation equipment, administrative services assets, warehouses, administrative buildings, hotels, or motels.

(D) Termination.*—Such term shall not apply to any property placed in service after December 31, 2013.

(16) Alaska natural gas pipeline.—The term "Alaska natural gas pipeline" means the natural gas pipeline system located in the State of Alaska which—

(A) has a capacity of more than 500,000,000,000 BTU of natural gas per day, and

(B) is—

(i) placed in service after December 31, 2013, or

(ii) treated as placed in service on January 1, 2014, if the taxpayer who places such system in service before January 1, 2014, elects such treatment.

*Editorial comment: At the present time, this section has not been extended. There is pending legislation in the Senate, *The Tax Extenders Act of 2013 (S. 1859)*, that would extend Section 168(i)(15) until December 31, 2014.

Such term includes the pipe, trunk lines, related equipment, and appurtenances used to carry natural gas, but does not include any gas processing plant.

(17) Natural gas gathering line.—The term "natural gas gathering line" means—

(A) the pipe, equipment, and appurtenances determined to be a gathering line by the Federal Energy Regulatory Commission, and

(B) the pipe, equipment, and appurtenances used to deliver natural gas from the wellhead or a common-point to the point at which such gas first reaches—

(i) a gas processing plant,

(ii) an interconnection with a transmission pipeline for which a certificate as an interstate transmission pipeline has been issued by the Federal Energy Regulatory Commission,

(iii) an interconnection with an intrastate transmission pipeline, or

(iv) a direct interconnection with a local distribution company, a gas storage facility, or an industrial consumer.

(18) Qualified smart electric meters.—

(A) In general.—The term "qualified smart electric meter" means any smart electric meter which—

(i) is placed in service by a taxpayer who is a supplier of electric energy or a provider of electric energy services, and

(ii) does not have a class life (determined without regard to subsection (e)) of less than 10 years.

(B) Smart electric meter.—For purposes of subparagraph (A), the term "smart electric meter" means any time based meter and related communication equipment which is capable of being used by the taxpayer as part of a system that—

(i) measures and records electricity usage data on a time-differentiated basis in at least 24 separate time segments per day,

(ii) provides for the exchange of information between supplier or provider and the customer's electric meter in support of time-based rates or other forms of demand response,

(iii) provides data to such supplier or provider so that the supplier or provider can provide energy usage information to customers electronically, and

(iv) provides net metering.

(19) Qualified smart electric grid systems.—

(A) In general.—The term "qualified smart electric grid system" means any smart grid property which—

(i) is used as part of a system for electric distribution grid communications, monitoring and management placed in service by a taxpayer who is a supplier of electric energy or a provider of electric energy services, and

(ii) does not have a class life (determined without regard to subsection (e)) of less than 10 years.

(B) Smart grid property.—For purposes of subparagraph (A), the term "smart grid property" means electronics and related equipment that is capable of—

(i) sensing, collecting, and monitoring data of or from all portions of a utility's electric distribution grid,

(ii) providing real-time, two-way communications to monitor or manage such grid, and

(iii) providing real time analysis of and event prediction based upon collected data that can be used to improve electric distribution system reliability, quality, and performance.

(j) Property on Indian reservations.—*

(1) In general.—For purposes of subsection (a), the applicable recovery period for qualified Indian reservation property shall be determined in accordance with the table contained in paragraph (2) in lieu of the table contained in subsection (c).

(2) Applicable recovery period for Indian reservation property.—For purposes of paragraph (1)—

In the case of:	The applicable recovery period is:
3-year property	2 years
5-year property	3 years
7-year property	4 years
10-year property	6 years
15-year property	9 years
20-year property	12 years
Nonresidential real property	22 years

(3) Deduction allowed in computing minimum tax.—For purposes of determining alternative minimum taxable income under section 55, the deduction under subsection (a) for property to which paragraph (1) applies shall be determined under this section without regard to any adjustment under section 56.

*Editorial comment: This subsection does not apply for property placed in service after December 31, 2013 [see Sec. 168(j)(8)].

(4) Qualified Indian reservation property defined.—For purposes of this subsection—

(A) In general.—The term "qualified Indian reservation property" means property which is property described in the table in paragraph (2) and which is—

(i) used by the taxpayer predominantly in the active conduct of a trade or business within an Indian reservation,

(ii) not used or located outside the Indian reservation on a regular basis,

(iii) not acquired (directly or indirectly) by the taxpayer from a person who is related to the taxpayer (within the meaning of section 465(b)(3)(C)), and

(iv) not property (or any portion thereof) placed in service for purposes of conducting or housing class I, II, or III gaming (as defined in section 4 of the Indian Regulatory Act (25 U.S.C. 2703)).

(B) Exception for alternative depreciation property.—The term "qualified Indian reservation property" does not include any property to which the alternative depreciation system under subsection (g) applies, determined—

(i) without regard to subsection (g)(7) (relating to election to use alternative depreciation system), and

(ii) after the application of section 280F(b) (relating to listed property with limited business use).

(C) Special rule for reservation infrastructure investment.—

(i) In general.—Subparagraph (A)(ii) shall not apply to qualified infrastructure property located outside of the Indian reservation if the purpose of such property is to connect with qualified infrastructure property located within the Indian reservation.

(ii) Qualified infrastructure property.—For purposes of this subparagraph, the term "qualified infrastructure property" means qualified Indian reservation property (determined without regard to subparagraph (A)(ii)) which—

(I) benefits the tribal infrastructure,

(II) is available to the general public, and

(III) is placed in service in connection with the taxpayer's active conduct of a trade or business within an Indian reservation.

Such term includes, but is not limited to, roads, power lines, water systems, railroad spurs, and communications facilities.

(5) Real estate rentals.—For purposes of this subsection, the rental to others of real property located within an Indian reservation shall be treated as the active conduct of a trade or business within an Indian reservation.

(6) Indian reservation defined.—For purposes of this subsection, the term "Indian reservation" means a reservation, as defined in—

(A) section 3(d) of the Indian Financing Act of 1974 (25 U.S.C. 1452(d)), or

(B) section 4(10) of the Indian Child Welfare Act of 1978 (25 U.S.C. 1903(10)).

* * *

(7) Coordination with nonrevenue laws.—Any reference in this subsection to a provision not contained in this title shall be treated for purposes of this subsection as a reference to such provision as in effect on the date of the enactment of this paragraph.

(8) Termination.*—This subsection shall not apply to property placed in service after December 31, 2013.

****(k) Special allowance for certain property acquired after December 31, 2007, and before January 1, 2014.*****—

---

*Editorial comment: At the present time, this section has not been extended. There is pending legislation in the Senate, *The Tax Extenders Act of 2013 (S.1859)*, that would extend Section 168(j)(8) until December 31, 2014.

**Editorial comment: The additional 30% (or 50%) deduction did not apply to property acquired after December 31, 2004. The property generally must have been placed in service before January 1, 2005. However, the Economic Stimulus Act of 2008 reinstated 50 percent additional first-year depreciation for 2008. The American Recovery and Reinvestment Tax Act of 2009 extended 50 percent additional first-year depreciation to 2009. The Small Business Jobs Act of 2010 extended 50 percent additional first-year depreciation to 2010. The Tax Relief Act of 2010 increased the percentage to 100 percent for 2011. For 2012, the percentage is reduced to 50 percent. The American Taxpayer Relief Act of 2012 retained the percentage at 50 percent.

***Editorial comment: At the present time, this section has not been extended. There is pending legislation in the Senate, *The Tax Extenders Act of 2013 (S.1859)*, that would extend the Section 168(k) heading until January 1, 2015, 168(k)(2)(A)(iii)(II) until January 1, 2015, and 168(k)(2)(A)(iv) until January 1, 2015 and 2016.

(1) Additional allowance.—In the case of any qualified property—

(A) the depreciation deduction provided by section 167(a) for the taxable year in which such property is placed in service shall include an allowance equal to 50 percent of the adjusted basis of the qualified property, and

(B) the adjusted basis of the qualified property shall be reduced by the amount of such deduction before computing the amount otherwise allowable as a depreciation deduction under this chapter for such taxable year and any subsequent taxable year.

(2) Qualified property.—For purposes of this subsection—

(A) In general.—The term "qualified property" means property—

(i) (I) to which this section applies which has a recovery period for 20 years or less,

(II) which is computer software (as defined in section 167(f)(1)(B)) for which a deduction is allowable under section 167 (a) without regard to this subsection,

(III) which is water utility property, or

(IV) which is qualified leasehold improvement property,

(ii) the original use of which commences with the taxpayer after December 31, 2007,

(iii) which is—

(I) acquired by the taxpayer after December 31, 2007, and before January 1, 2014, but only if no written binding contract for the acquisition was in effect before January 1, 2008, or

(II) acquired by the taxpayer pursuant to a written binding contract which was entered into after December 31, 2007, and before January 1, 2014,* and

(iv) which is placed in service by the taxpayer before January 1, 2014,* or, in the case of property described in subparagraph (B) or (C), before January 1, 2015.*

(B) Certain property having longer production periods treated as qualified property.—

(i) In general.—The term "qualified property" includes any property if such property—

(I) meets the requirements of clauses (i), (ii), (iii) and (iv) of subparagraph (A),

(II) has a recovery period of at least 10 years or is transportation property,

(III) is subject to section 263A, and

(IV) meets the requirements of clause (iii) of section 263(A)(f)(1)(B) (determined as if such clauses also apply to property which has a long useful life (within the meaning of section 263A(f))).

(ii) Only pre-January 1, 2014, basis eligible for additional allowance.—In the case of property which is qualified property solely by reason of clause (i), paragraph (1) shall apply only to the extent of the adjusted basis thereof attributable to manufacture, construction, or production before January 1, 2014.

(iii) Transportation property.—For purposes of this subparagraph, the term "transportation property" means tangible personal property used in the trade or business of transporting persons or property.

(iv) Application of subparagraph.—This subparagraph shall not apply to any property which is described in subparagraph (C).

(C) Certain aircraft.—The term "qualified property" includes property—

(i) which meets the requirements of clauses (ii), (iii) and (iv) of subparagraph (A),

(ii) which is an aircraft which is not a transportation property (as defined in subparagraph (B)(iii) other than for agricultural or firefighting purposes,

(iii) which is purchased and on which such purchaser, at the time of the contract for purchase, has made a nonrefundable deposit of the lesser of—

(I) 10 percent of the cost, or

(II) $100,000, and

(iv) which has—

(I) an estimated production period exceeding 4 months, and

(II) a cost exceeding $200,000.

(D) Exceptions.—

(i) Alternative depreciation property.—The term "qualified property" shall not include any property to which the alternative depreciation system under subsection (g) applies, determined—

(I) without regard to paragraph (7) of subsection (g) (relating to election to have system apply), and

(II) after application of section 280(F)(b) (relating to listed property with limited business use).

(ii) Qualified New York Liberty Zone leasehold improvement property.—The term "qualified property" shall not include any qualified New York Liberty Zone leasehold improvement property (as defined in section 1400L(c)(2)).

(iii) Election out.—If a taxpayer makes an election under this clause with respect to any class of property for any taxable year, this subsection shall not apply to all property in such class placed in service during such taxable year.

(E) Special rules.—

(i) Self-constructed property.—In the case of a taxpayer manufacturing, constructing, or producing property for the taxpayer's own use, the requirements of clause (iii) of subparagraph (A) shall be treated as met if the taxpayer begins manufacturing, constructing, or producing the property after December 31, 2007, and before January 1, 2014.

(ii) Sale-leasebacks.—For purposes of clause (iii) and subparagraph (A)(ii), if property is—

(I) originally placed in service after December 31, 2007, by a person, and

(II) sold and leased back by such person within 3 months after the date such property was originally place in service,

such property shall be treated as originally placed in service not earlier than the date on which such property is used under the leaseback referred to in subclause (II).

(iii) Syndication.—For purposes of subparagraph (A)(ii), if—

(I) property is originally placed in service after December 31, 2007, by the lessor of such property,

(II) such property is sold by such lessor or any subsequent purchaser within 3 months after the date such property was originally placed in service (or, in the case of multiple units of property subject to the same lease, within 3 months after the date the final unit is placed in service, so long as the period between the time the first unit is placed in service and the time the last unit is placed in service does not exceed 12 months), and

(III) the user of such property after the last sale during such 3-month period remains the same as when such property was originally placed in service,

such property shall be treated as originally placed in service not earlier than the date of such last sale.

(iv) Limitations related to users and related parties.—The term "qualified property" shall not include any property if—

(I) the user of such property (as of the date on which such property is originally placed in service) or a person which is related (within the meaning of section 267(b) or 707(b)) to such user or to the taxpayer had a written binding contract in effect for the acquisition of such property at any time on or before December 31, 2007, or

(II) in the case of property manufactured, constructed, or produced for such user's or person's own use, the manufacture, construction, or production of such property began at any time on or before December 31, 2007.

(F) Coordination with section 280F.—For purposes of section 280F—

(i) Automobiles.—In the case of a passenger automobile (as defined in section 280F(d)(5)) which is qualified property, the Secretary shall increase the limitation under section 280F(a)(1)(A)(i) by $8,000.

(ii) Listed property.—The deduction allowable under paragraph (1) shall be taken into account in computing any recapture amount under section 280F(b)(2).

(G) Deduction allowed in computing minimum tax.—For purposes of determining alternative minimum taxable income under section 55, the deduction under subsection (a) for qualified property shall be determined under this section without regard to any adjustment under section 56.

(3) Qualified leasehold improvement property.—For purposes of this subsection—

(A) In general.—The term "qualified leasehold improvement property" means any improvement to an interior portion of a building which is nonresidential real property if—

(i) such improvement is made under or pursuant to a lease (as defined in subsection (h)(7))—

(I) by the lessee (or any sublessee) of such portion, or

(II) by the lessor of such portion,

(ii) such portion is to be occupied exclusively by the lessee (or any sublessee) of such portion, and

(iii) such improvement is placed in service more than 3 years after the date the building was first placed in service.

(B) Certain improvements not included.—Such term shall not include any improvement for which the expenditure is attributable to—

(i) the enlargement of the building,

(ii) any elevator or escalator,

(iii) any structural component benefiting a common area, and

(iv) the internal structural framework of the building.

(C) Definitions and special rules.—For purposes of this paragraph—

(i) Commitment to lease treated as lease.—A commitment to enter into a lease shall be treated as a lease, and the parties to such commitment shall be treated as lessor and lessee, respectively.

(ii) Related persons.—A lease between related persons shall not be considered a lease. For purposes of the preceding sentence, the term "related persons" means—

(I) members of an affiliated group (as defined in section 1504), and

(II) persons having a relationship described in subsection (b) of section 267; except that, for purposes of this clause, the phrase "80 percent or more" shall be substituted for the phrase "more than 50 percent" each place it appears in such subsection.

(4) Election to accelerate the AMT and research credits in lieu of bonus depreciation.—

(A) In general.—If a corporation elects to have this paragraph apply for the first taxable year of the taxpayer ending after March 31, 2008, in the case of such taxable year and each subsequent taxable year—

(i) paragraph (1) shall not apply to any eligible qualified property placed in service by the taxpayer,

(ii) the applicable depreciation method used under this section with respect to such property shall be the straight line method, and

(iii) each of the limitations described in subparagraph (B) for any such taxable year shall be increased by the bonus depreciation amount which is—

(I) determined for such taxable year under subparagraph (C), and

(II) allocated to such limitation under subparagraph (E).

(B) Limitations to be increased.—The limitations described in this subparagraph are—

(i) the limitation imposed by section 38(c), and

(ii) the limitation imposed by section 53(c).

(C) Bonus depreciation amount.—For purposes of this paragraph—

(i) In general.—The bonus depreciation amount for any taxable year is an amount equal to 20 percent of the excess (if any) of—

(I) the aggregate amount of depreciation which would be allowed under this section for eligible qualified property placed in service by the taxpayer during such taxable year if paragraph (1) applied to all such property, over

(II) the aggregate amount of depreciation which would be allowed under this section for eligible qualified property placed in service by the taxpayer during such taxable year if paragraph (1) did not apply to any such property.

The aggregate amounts determined under subclauses (I) and (II) shall be determined without regard to any election made under subsection (b)(2)(C), (b)(3)(D), or (g)(7) and without regard to subparagraph (A)(ii).

(ii) Maximum amount.—The bonus depreciation amount for any taxable year shall not exceed the maximum increase amount under clause (iii), reduced (but not below zero) by the sum of the bonus depreciation amounts for all preceding taxable years.

(iii) Maximum increase amount.—For purposes of clause (ii), the term "maximum increase amount" means, with respect to any corporation, the lesser of—

(I) $30,000,000, or

(II) 6 percent of the sum of the business credit increase amount, and the AMT credit increase amount, determined with respect to such corporation under subparagraph (E).

(iv) Aggregation rule.—All corporations which are treated as a single employer under section 52(a) shall be treated—

(I) as 1 taxpayer for purposes of this paragraph, and

(II) as having elected the application of this paragraph if any such corporation so elects.

(D) Eligible qualified property.—For purposes of this paragraph, the term "eligible qualified property" means qualified property under paragraph (2), except that in applying paragraph (2) for purposes of this paragraph—

(i) "March 31, 2008" shall be substituted for "December 31, 2007" each place it appears in subparagraph (A) and clauses (i) and (ii) of subparagraph (E) thereof,

(ii) "April 1, 2008" shall be substituted for "January 1, 2008" in subparagraph (A)(iii)(I) thereof,

(iii) only adjusted basis attributable to manufacture, construction, or production—

(I) after March 31, 2008, and before January 1, 2010, and

(II) after December 31, 2010, and before January 1, 2014,*

shall be taken into account under subparagraph (B)(ii) thereof.

(E) Allocation of bonus depreciation amounts.—

(i) In general.—Subject to clauses (ii) and (iii), the taxpayer shall, at such time and in such manner as the Secretary may prescribe, specify the portion (if any) of the bonus depreciation amount for the taxable year which is to be allocated to each of the limitations described in subparagraph (B) for such taxable year.

(ii) Limitation on allocations.—The portion of the bonus depreciation amount which may be allocated under clause (i) to the limitations described in subparagraph (B) for any taxable year shall not exceed—

(I) in the case of the limitation described in subparagraph (B)(i), the excess of the business credit increase amount over the bonus depreciation amount allocated to such limitation for all preceding taxable years, and

(II) in the case of the limitation described in subparagraph (B)(ii), the excess of the AMT credit increase amount over the bonus depreciation amount allocated to such limitation for all preceding taxable years.

(iii) Business credit increase amount.—For purposes of this paragraph, the term "business credit increase amount" means the amount equal to the portion of the credit allowable under section 38 (determined without regard to subsection (c) thereof) for the first taxable year ending after March 31, 2008, which is allocable to business credit carryforwards to such taxable year which are—

(I) from taxable years beginning before January 1, 2006, and

(II) properly allocable (determined under the rules of section 38(d)) to the research credit determined under section 41(a).

(iv) AMT credit increase amount.—For purposes of this paragraph, the term "AMT credit increase amount" means the amount equal to the portion of the minimum tax credit under section 53(b) for the first taxable year ending after March 31, 2008, determined by taking into account only the adjusted minimum tax for taxable years beginning before January 1, 2006. For purposes of the preceding sentence, credits shall be treated as allowed on a first-in, first-out basis.

(F) Credit refundable.—For purposes of section 6401(b), the aggregate increase in the credits allowable under part IV of subchapter A for any taxable year resulting from the application of this paragraph shall be treated as allowed under subpart C of such part (and not any other subpart).

(G) Other rules.—

(i) Election.—Any election under this paragraph (including any allocation under

*Editorial comment: At the present time, this section has not been extended. There is pending legislation in the Senate, *The Tax Extenders Act of 2013 (S. 1859)* that would extend Section 168(k)(4)(D)(iii)(II) until January 1, 2015.

subparagraph (E)) may be revoked only with the consent of the Secretary.

(ii) Partnerships with electing partners.—In the case of a corporation making an election under subparagraph (A) and which is a partner in a partnership, for purposes of determining such corporation's distributive share of partnership items under section 702—

(I) paragraph (1) shall not apply to any eligible qualified property, and

(II) the applicable depreciation method used under this section with respect to such property shall be the straight line method.

(iii) Special rule for passenger aircraft.—In the case of any passenger aircraft, the written binding contract limitation under paragraph (2)(A)(iii)(I) shall not apply for purposes of subparagraphs (C)(i)(I) and (D).

(H) Special rules for extension property.—

(i) Taxpayers previously electing acceleration.—In the case of a taxpayer who made the election under subparagraph (A) for its first taxable year ending after March 31, 2008—

(I) the taxpayer may elect not to have this paragraph apply to extension property, but

(II) if the taxpayer does not make the election under subclause (I), in applying this paragraph to the taxpayer a separate bonus depreciation amount, maximum amount, and maximum increase amount shall be computed and applied to eligible qualified property which is extension property and to eligible qualified property which is not extension property.

(ii) Taxpayers not previously electing acceleration.—In the case of a taxpayer who did not make the election under subparagraph (A) for its first taxable year ending after March 31, 2008—

(I) the taxpayer may elect to have this paragraph apply to its first taxable year ending after December 31, 2008, and each subsequent taxable year, and

(II) if the taxpayer makes the election under subclause (I), this paragraph shall only apply to eligible qualified property which is extension property.

(iii) Extension property.—For purposes of this subparagraph, the term "extension property" means property which is eligible qualified property solely by reason of the extension of the application of the special allowance under paragraph (1) pursuant to the amendments made by section 1201(a) of the American Recovery and Reinvestment Tax Act of 2009 (and the application of such extension to this paragraph pursuant to the amendment made by section 1201(b)(1) of such Act).

(I) Special rules for round 2 extension property.—

(i) In general.—In the case of round 2 extension property, this paragraph shall be applied without regard to—

(I) the limitation described in subparagraph (B)(i) thereof, and

(II) the business credit increase amount under subparagraph (E)(iii) thereof.

(ii) Taxpayers previously electing acceleration.—In the case of a taxpayer who made the election under subparagraph (A) for its first taxable year ending after March 31, 2008, or a taxpayer who made the election under subparagraph (H)(ii) for its first taxable year ending after December 31, 2008—

(I) the taxpayer may elect not to have this paragraph apply to round 2 extension property, but

(II) if the taxpayer does not make the election under subclause (I), in applying this paragraph to the taxpayer the bonus depreciation amount, maximum amount, and maximum increase amount shall be computed and applied to eligible qualified property which is round 2 extension property.

The amounts described in subclause (II) shall be computed separately from any amounts computed with respect to eligible qualified property which is not round 2 extension property.

(iii) Taxpayers not previously electing acceleration.—In the case of a taxpayer who neither made the election under subparagraph (A) for its first taxable year ending after March 31, 2008, nor made the election under subparagraph (H)(ii) for its first taxable year ending after December 31, 2008—

(I) the taxpayer may elect to have this paragraph apply to its first taxable year ending after December 31, 2010, and each subsequent taxable year, and

(II) if the taxpayer makes the election under subclause (I), this paragraph shall only apply to eligible qualified property which is round 2 extension property.

(iv) Round 2 extension property.—For purposes of this subparagraph, the term "round 2 extension property" means property which is eligible qualified property solely by reason of the extension of the application of the special allowance under paragraph (1) pursuant to the amendments made by section 401(a) of the Tax Relief, Unemployment Insurance Reauthorization, and Job Creation Act of 2010 (and the application of such extension to this paragraph pursuant to the amendment made by section 401(c)(1) of such Act).

(5) Special rule for property acquired during certain pre-2012 periods.—In the case of qualified property acquired by the taxpayer (under rules similar to the rules of clauses (ii) and (iii) of paragraph (2)(A)) after September 8, 2010, and before January 1, 2012, and which is placed in service by the taxpayer before January 1, 2012 (January 1, 2013, in the case of property described in subparagraph (2)(B) or (2)(C)), paragraph (1)(A) shall be applied by substituting "100 percent" for "50 percent".

* * *

(n) Special allowance for qualified disaster assistance property.—

(1) In general.—In the case of any qualified disaster assistance property—

(A) the depreciation deduction provided by section 167(a) for the taxable year in which such property is placed in service shall include an allowance equal to 50 percent of the adjusted basis of the qualified disaster assistance property, and

(B) the adjusted basis of the qualified disaster assistance property shall be reduced by the amount of such deduction before computing the amount otherwise allowable as a depreciation deduction under this chapter for such taxable year and any subsequent taxable year.

(2) Qualified disaster assistance property.—For purposes of this subsection—

(A) In general.—The term "qualified disaster assistance property" means any property—

(i)

(I) which is described in subsection (k)(2)(A)(i), or

(II) which is nonresidential real property or residential rental property,

(ii) substantially all of the use of which is—

(I) in a disaster area with respect to a federally declared disaster occurring before January 1, 2010, and

(II) in the active conduct of a trade or business by the taxpayer in such disaster area,

(iii) which—

(I) rehabilitates property damaged, or replaces property destroyed or condemned, as a result of such federally declared disaster, except that, for purposes of this clause, property shall be treated as replacing property destroyed or condemned if, as part of an integrated plan, such property replaces property which is included in a continuous area which includes real property destroyed or condemned, and

(II) is similar in nature to, and located in the same county as, the property being rehabilitated or replaced,

(iv) the original use of which in such disaster area commences with an eligible taxpayer on or after the applicable disaster date,

(v) which is acquired by such eligible taxpayer by purchase (as defined in section 179(d)) on or after the applicable disaster date, but only if no written binding contract for the acquisition was in effect before such date, and

(vi) which is placed in service by such eligible taxpayer on or before the date which is the last day of the third calendar year following the applicable disaster date (the fourth calendar year in the case of nonresidential real property and residential rental property).

(B) Exceptions.—

(i) Other bonus depreciation property.—The term "qualified disaster assistance property" shall not include—

(I) any property to which subsection (k) (determined without regard to paragraph (4)), (l), or (m) applies,

(II) any property to which section 1400N(d) applies, and

(III) any property described in section 1400N(p)(3).

(ii) Alternative depreciation property.—The term "qualified disaster assistance property" shall not include any property to which the alternative depreciation system under subsection (g) applies, determined without regard to paragraph (7) of subsection (g) (relating to election to have system apply).

(iii) Tax-exempt bond financed property.—Such term shall not include any property any portion of which is financed with the proceeds of any obligation the interest on which is exempt from tax under section 103.

(iv) Qualified revitalization buildings.—Such term shall not include any qualified revitalization building with respect to which the taxpayer has elected the application of paragraph (1) or (2) of section 1400I(a).

(v) Election out.—If a taxpayer makes an election under this clause with respect to any class of property for any taxable year, this subsection shall not apply to all property in such class placed in service during such taxable year.

* * *

§ 169. Amortization of pollution control facilities

(a) Allowance of deduction.—Every person, at his election, shall be entitled to a deduction with respect to the amortization of the amortizable basis of any certified pollution control facility (as defined in subsection (d)), based on a period of 60 months. Such amortization deduction shall be an amount, with respect to each month of such period within the taxable year, equal to the amortizable basis of the pollution control facility at the end of such month divided by the number of months (including the month for which the deduction is computed) remaining in the period. Such amortizable basis at the end of the month shall be computed without regard to the amortization deduction for such month. The amortization deduction provided by this section with respect to any month shall be in lieu of the depreciation deduction with respect to such pollution control facility for such month provided by section 167. The 60-month period shall begin, as to any pollution control facility, at the election of the taxpayer, with the month following the month in which such facility was completed or acquired, or with the succeeding taxable year.

(b) Election of amortization.—The election of the taxpayer to take the amortization deduction and to begin the 60-month period with the month following the month in which the facility is completed or acquired, or with the taxable year succeeding the taxable year in which such facility is completed or acquired, shall be made by filing with the Secretary, in such manner, in such form, and within such time, as the Secretary may by regulations prescribe, a statement of such election.

(c) Termination of amortization deduction.—A taxpayer which has elected under subsection (b) to take the amortization deduction provided in subsection (a) may, at any time after making such election, discontinue the amortization deduction with respect to the remainder of the amortization period, such discontinuance to begin as of the beginning of any month specified by the taxpayer in a notice in writing filed with the Secretary before the beginning of such month. The depreciation deduction provided under section 167 shall be allowed, beginning with the first month as to which the amortization deduction does not apply, and the taxpayer shall not be entitled to any further amortization deduction under this section with respect to such pollution control facility.

* * *

(f) Amortizable basis.—

(1) Defined.—For purposes of this section, the term "amortizable basis" means that portion of the adjusted basis (for determining gain) of a certified pollution control facility which may be amortized under this section.

(2) Special rules.—

(A) If a certified pollution control facility has a useful life (determined as of the first day of the first month for which a deduction is allowable under this section) in excess of 15 years, the amortizable basis of such facility shall be equal to an amount which bears the same ratio to the portion of the adjusted basis of such facility, which would be eligible for amortization but for the application of this subparagraph, as 15 bears to the number of years of useful life of such facility.

(B) The amortizable basis of a certified pollution control facility with respect to which an election under this section is in effect shall not be increased, for purposes of this section, for additions or improvements after the amortization period has begun.

(g) Depreciation deduction.—The depreciation deduction provided by section 167 shall, despite the provisions of subsection (a), be allowed with respect to the portion of the adjusted basis which is not the amortizable basis.

* * *

(i) Life tenant and remainderman.—In the case of property held by one person for life with remainder to another person, the deduction under this section shall be computed as if the life tenant were the absolute owner of the property and shall be allowable to the life tenant.

(j) Cross reference.—

For special rule with respect to certain gain derived from the disposition of property the adjusted basis of which is determined with regard to this section, see section 1245.

Editorial Summary

Charitable Contributions

Subchapter B of Chapter1 (Sec. 170)

The following differences exist with respect to the charitable contribution deduction for the corporate and noncorporate taxpayer.

1. Ability for an accrual-basis taxpayer to deduct a charitable contribution prior to payment [see Sec. 170(a)(1) and (a)(2)].
2. Ceiling percentage limitation on the charitable contribution deduction [see Sec. 170(b)(1) and (b)(2)].
3. Ability to deduct contribution of inventory in excess of the basis of the inventory [see Sec. 170(e)(3)].

In determining the charitable contribution deduction for the current taxable year, the taxpayer must ascertain each of the following:

1. The allowable *value* of the contributed property
2. The amount of the *deduction* for the current taxable year.
3. The amount of the *carryover*, if any.

The general rule is that the allowable value is the fair market value of the contributed property. However, in two circumstances, the fair market value must be reduced by a negative adjustment [see Sec. 170(e)(1)]. First, assuming that the taxpayer had sold the property rather than contributing it, a negative adjustment is made for the amount of the gain which *would not* have been long-term capital gain [i.e., either ordinary income or short-term capital gain under Sec. 1222(1)].

Value = FMV – 100% (not LTCG)

Second, assuming that the taxpayer had sold the property rather than contributing it, a negative adjustment is made for the gain which *would* have been long-term capital gain [see Sec. 1222(3)] if any of the following conditions are satisfied:

1. The donee is a private nonoperating foundation.
2. The property is tangible, personal property and the use by the donee is unrelated to the purpose for which the donee is tax-exempt under Sec. 501.
3. The property is certain intangible property (i.e., patent, certain copyrights, trademarks, trade name, trade secret, know-how, and certain software).

In this case, the formula is as follows:

Value = FMV – 100% (LTCG)

The amount of the charitable contribution deduction for the current taxable year is dependent on the following:

1. Whether the taxpayer is a corporate or noncorporate taxpayer.
2. Whether the form of the contribution is cash or property.
3. Whether or not the donee is a private nonoperating foundation.
4. Whether or not the property is long-term capital gain property for which no negative adjustment was made in the "value" calculation.

The first and third factors affect both corporate and noncorporate taxpayers whereas the other factors affect only the noncorporate taxpayer.

The corporate taxpayer can deduct up to 10 percent of taxable income as adjusted [see Sec. 170(b)(2) for the definition of taxable income as adjusted]. Any excess amount is eligible for a 5-year carryover [see Sec. 170(d)(2)].

The general rule for the individual taxpayer provides that the deduction is limited to 50 percent of adjusted gross income [see Sec. 170(b)(1)(A)]. However, in particular circumstances, the deduction is limited to either 30 percent [see Sec. 170(b)(1)(B)] or 20 percent [see Sec. 170(b)(1)(D)] of adjusted gross income. Note that in one circumstance the taxpayer is permitted to elect to increase the 30 percent limit to 50 percent in exchange for voluntarily making the negative adjustment provided for under Sec. 170(e)(1)(B) in the "value" calculation [see Sec. 170(b)(1)(C)]. In no circumstance may the charitable contribution deduction exceed 50 percent of adjusted gross income. Excess contributions qualify for a 5-year carryover [see Sec. 170(d)(1)].

Only contributions of *property* qualify for deduction. That is, the contribution of *services* cannot be deducted as a charitable contribution. However, out-of-pocket expenses incurred associated with the contribution of services can be deducted.

See the disclosure requirements imposed on charitable organizations in Sec. 6115 for quid pro quo contributions.

§ 170. Charitable, etc., contributions and gifts

(a) Allowance of deduction.—

(1) General rule.—There shall be allowed as a deduction any charitable contribution (as defined in subsection (c)) payment of which is made within the taxable year. A charitable contribution shall be allowable as a deduction only if verified under regulations prescribed by the Secretary.

(2) Corporations on accrual basis.—In the case of a corporation reporting its taxable income on the accrual basis, if—

(A) the board of directors authorizes a charitable contribution during any taxable year, and

(B) payment of such contribution is made after the close of such taxable year and on or before the 15th day of the third month following the close of such taxable year,

then the taxpayer may elect to treat such contribution as paid during such taxable year. The election may be made only at the time of the filing of the return for such taxable year, and shall be signified in such manner as the Secretary shall by regulations prescribe.

(3) Future interests in tangible personal property.—For purposes of this section, payment of a charitable contribution which consists of a future interest in tangible personal property shall be treated as made only when all intervening interests in, and rights to the actual possession or enjoyment of, the property have expired or are held by persons other than the taxpayer or those standing in a relationship to the taxpayer described in section 267(b) or 707(b). For purposes of the preceding sentence, a fixture which is intended to be severed from the real property shall be treated as tangible personal property.

(b) Percentage limitations.—

(1) Individuals.—In the case of an individual, the deduction provided in subsection (a) shall be limited as provided in the succeeding subparagraphs.

(A) General rule.—Any charitable contribution to—

(i) a church or a convention or association of churches,

(ii) an educational organization which normally maintains a regular faculty and curriculum and normally has a regularly enrolled body of pupils or students in attendance at the place where its educational activities are regularly carried on,

(iii) an organization the principal purpose or functions of which are the providing of medical or hospital care or medical education or medical research, if the organization is a hospital, or if the organization is a medical research organization directly engaged in the continuous active conduct of medical research in conjunction with a hospital, and during the calendar year in which the contribution is made such organization is committed to spend such contributions for such research before January 1 of the fifth calendar year which begins after the date such contribution is made,

(iv) an organization which normally receives a substantial part of its support (exclusive of income received in the exercise or performance by such organization of its charitable, educational, or other purpose or function constituting the basis for its exemption under section 501(a)) from the United States or any State or political subdivision thereof or from direct or indirect contributions from the general public, and which is organized and operated exclusively to receive, hold, invest, and administer property and to make expenditures to or for the benefit of a college or university which is an organization referred to in clause (ii) of this subparagraph and which is an agency or instrumentality of a State or political subdivision thereof, or which is owned or operated by a State or political subdivision thereof or by an agency or instrumentality of one or more States or political subdivisions,

(v) a governmental unit referred to in subsection (c) (1),

(vi) an organization referred to in subsection (c) (2) which normally receives a substantial part of its support (exclusive of income received in the exercise or performance by such organization of its charitable, educational, or other purpose or function constituting the basis for its exemption under section 501(a)) from a governmental unit referred to in subsection (c) (1) or from direct or indirect contributions from the general public,

(vii) a private foundation described in subparagraph (F), or

(viii) an organization described in section 509(a) (2) or (3),

shall be allowed to the extent that the aggregate of such contributions does not exceed 50 percent of the taxpayer's contribution base for the taxable year.

(B) Other contributions.—Any charitable contribution other than a charitable contribution to which subparagraph (A) applies shall be allowed to the extent that the aggregate of such contributions does not exceed the lesser of—

(i) 30 percent of the taxpayer's contribution base for the taxable year, or

(ii) the excess of 50 percent of the taxpayer's contribution base for the taxable year over the amount of charitable contributions allowable under subparagraph (A) (determined without regard to subparagraph (C)).

If the aggregate of such contributions exceeds the limitation of the preceding sentence, such excess shall be treated (in a manner consistent with the rules of subsection (d)(1)) as a charitable contribution (to which subparagraph (A) does not apply) in each of the 5 succeeding taxable years in order of time.

(C) Special limitation with respect to contributions described in subparagraph (A) of certain capital gain property.—

(i) In the case of charitable contributions described in subparagraph (A) of capital gain property to which subsection (e)(1)(B) does not apply, the total amount of contributions of such property which may be taken into account under subsection (a) for any taxable year shall not exceed 30 percent of the taxpayer's contribution base for such year. For purposes of this subsection, contributions of capital gain property to which this subparagraph applies shall be taken into account after all other charitable contributions (other than charitable contributions to which subparagraph (D) applies).

(ii) If charitable contributions described in subparagraph (A) of capital gain property to which clause (i) applies exceeds 30 percent of the taxpayer's contribution base for any taxable year, such excess shall be treated, in a manner consistent with the rules of subsection (d)(1), as a charitable contribution of capital gain property to which clause (i) applies in each of the 5 succeeding taxable years in order of time.

(iii) At the election of the taxpayer (made at such time and in such manner as the Secretary prescribes by regulations), subsection (e)(1) shall apply to all contributions of capital gain property (to which subsection (e)(1)(B) does not otherwise apply) made by the taxpayer during the taxable year. If such an election is made, clauses (i) and (ii) shall not apply to contributions of capital gain property made during the taxable year, and, in applying subsection (d)(1) for such taxable year with respect to contributions of capital gain property made in any prior contribution year for which an election was not made under this clause, such contributions shall be reduced as if subsection (e)(1) had applied to such contributions in the year in which made.

(iv) For purposes of this paragraph, the term "capital gain property" means, with respect to any contribution, any capital asset the sale of which at its fair market value at the time of the contribution would have resulted in gain which would have been long-term capital gain. For purposes of the preceding sentence, any property which is property used in the trade or business (as defined in section 1231(b)) shall be treated as a capital asset.

(D) Special limitation with respect to contributions of capital gain property to organizations not described in subparagraph (A).—

(i) In general.—In the case of charitable contributions (other than charitable contributions to which subparagraph (A) applies) of capital gain property, the total amount of such contributions of such property taken into account under subsection (a) for any taxable year shall not exceed the lesser of—

(I) 20 percent of the taxpayer's contribution base for the taxable year, or

(II) the excess of 30 percent of the taxpayer's contribution base for the taxable year over the amount of the contributions of capital gain property to which subparagraph (C) applies.

For purposes of this subsection, contributions of capital gain property to which this subparagraph applies shall be taken into account after all other charitable contributions.

(ii) Carryover.—If the aggregate amount of contributions described in clause (i) exceeds the limitation of clause (i), such excess shall be treated (in a manner consistent with the rules of subsection (d)(l)) as a charitable contribution of capital gain property to which clause (i) applies in each of the 5 succeeding taxable years in order of time.

(E) Contributions of qualified conservation contributions.—*

(i) In general.—Any qualified conservation contribution (as defined in subsection (h)(1)) shall be allowed to the extent the

*Editorial comment: At the present time, this section has not been extended. There is pending legislation in the Senate, *The Tax Extenders Act of 2013 (S. 1859)*, that would extend Section 170(b)(1)(E)(vi) until December 31, 2014.

aggregate of such contributions does not exceed the excess of 50 percent of the taxpayer's contribution base over the amount of all other charitable contributions allowable under this paragraph.

(ii) Carryover.—If the aggregate amount of contributions described in clause (i) exceeds the limitation of clause (i), such excess shall be treated (in a manner consistent with the rules of subsection (d)(1)) as a charitable contribution to which clause (i) applies in each of the 15 succeeding years in order of time.

(iii) Coordination with other subparagraphs.—For purposes of applying this subsection and subsection (d)(1), contributions described in clause (i) shall not be treated as described in subparagraph (A), (B), (C), or (D) and such subparagraphs shall apply without regard to such contributions.

(iv) Special rule for contribution of property used in agriculture or livestock production.—

(I) In general.—If the individual is a qualified farmer or rancher for the taxable year for which the contribution is made, clause (i) shall be applied by substituting "100 percent" for "50 percent".

(II) Exception.—Subclause (I) shall not apply to any contribution of property made after the date of the enactment of this subparagraph which is used in agriculture or livestock production (or available for such production) unless such contribution is subject to a restriction that such property remain available for such production. This subparagraph shall be applied separately with respect to property to which subclause (I) does not apply by reason of the preceding sentence prior to its application to property to which subclause (I) does apply.

(v) Definition.—For purposes of clause (iv), the term "qualified farmer or rancher" means a taxpayer whose gross income from the trade or business of farming (within the meaning of section 2032A(e)(5)) is greater than 50 percent of the taxpayer's gross income for the taxable year.

(vi) Termination.—This subparagraph shall not apply to any contribution made in taxable years beginning after December 31, 2013.

* * *

(G) Contribution base defined.—For purposes of this section, the term "contribution base" means adjusted gross income (computed without regard to any net operating loss carryback to the taxable year under section 172).

(2) Corporations.—In the case of a corporation—

(A) In general.—The total deductions under subsection (a) for any taxable year (other than for contributions to which subparagraph (B) applies) shall not exceed 10 percent of the taxpayer's taxable income.

(B) Qualified conservation contributions by certain corporate farmers and ranchers.—*

(i) In general.—Any qualified conservation contribution (as defined in subsection (h)(1))—

(I) which is made by a corporation which, for the taxable year during which the contribution is made, is a qualified farmer or rancher (as defined in paragraph (1)(E)(v)) and the stock of which is not readily tradable on an established securities market at any time during such year, and

(II) which, in the case of contributions made after the date of the enactment of this subparagraph, is a contribution of property which is used in agriculture or livestock production (or available for such production) and which is subject to a restriction that such property remain available for such production,

shall be allowed to the extent the aggregate of such contributions does not exceed the excess of the taxpayer's taxable income over the amount of charitable contributions allowable under subparagraph (A).

(ii) Carryover.—If the aggregate amount of contributions described in clause (i) exceeds the limitation of clause (i), such excess shall be treated (in a manner

*Editorial comment: At the present time, this section has not been extended. There is pending legislation in the Senate, *The Tax Extenders Act of 2013 (S. 1859)*, that would extend Section 170(b)(2)(B)(iii) until December 31, 2014.

consistent with the rules of subsection (d)(2)) as a charitable contribution to which clause (i) applies in each of the 15 succeeding years in order of time.

(iii) Termination.—This subparagraph shall not apply to any contribution made in taxable years beginning after December 31, 2013.

(C) Taxable income.—For purposes of this paragraph, taxable income shall be computed without regard to—

(i) this section,

(ii) part VIII (except section 248),

(iii) any net operating loss carryback to the taxable year under section 172,

(iv) section 199, and

(v) any capital loss carryback to the taxable year under section 1212(a)(1).

(c) Charitable contribution defined.—For purposes of this section, the term "charitable contribution" means a contribution or gift to or for the use of—

(1) A State, a possession of the United States, or any political subdivision of any of the foregoing, or the United States or the District of Columbia, but only if the contribution or gift is made for exclusively public purposes.

(2) A corporation, trust, or community chest, fund, or foundation—

(A) created or organized in the United States or in any possession thereof, or under the law of the United States, any State, the District of Columbia, or any possession of the United States;

(B) organized and operated exclusively for religious, charitable, scientific, literary, or educational purposes, or to foster national or international amateur sports competition (but only if no part of its activities involve the provision of athletic facilities or equipment), or for the prevention of cruelty to children or animals;

(C) no part of the net earnings of which inures to the benefit of any private shareholder or individual; and

(D) which is not disqualified for tax exemption under section 501(c)(3) by reason of attempting to influence legislation, and which does not participate in, or intervene in (including the publishing or distributing of statements), any political campaign on behalf of (or in opposition to) any candidate for public office.

A contribution or gift by a corporation to a trust, chest, fund, or foundation shall be deductible by reason of this paragraph only if it is to be used within the United States or any of its possessions exclusively for purposes specified in subparagraph (B). Rules similar to the rules of section 501(j) shall apply for purposes of this paragraph.

(3) A post or organization of war veterans, or an auxiliary unit or society of, or trust or foundation for, any such post or organization—

(A) organized in the United States or any of its possessions, and

(B) no part of the net earnings of which inures to the benefit of any private shareholder or individual.

(4) In the case of a contribution or gift by an individual, a domestic fraternal society, order, or association, operating under the lodge system, but only if such contribution or gift is to be used exclusively for religious, charitable, scientific, literary, or educational purposes, or for the prevention of cruelty to children or animals.

(5) A cemetery company owned and operated exclusively for the benefit of its members, or any corporation chartered solely for burial purposes as a cemetery corporation and not permitted by its charter to engage in any business not necessarily incident to that purpose, if such company or corporation is not operated for profit and no part of the net earnings of such company or corporation inures to the benefit of any private shareholder or individual.

For purposes of this section, the term "charitable contribution" also means an amount treated under subsection (g) as paid for the use of an organization described in paragraph (2), (3), or (4).

(d) Carryovers of excess contributions.—

(1) Individuals.—

(A) In general.—In the case of an individual, if the amount of charitable contributions described in subsection (b)(1)(A) payment of which is made within a taxable year (hereinafter in this paragraph referred to as the "contribution year") exceeds 50 percent of the taxpayer's contribution base for such year, such excess shall be treated as a charitable contribution described in subsection (b)(l)(A) paid in each of the 5 succeeding taxable years in order of time, but, with respect to any such succeeding taxable year, only to the extent of the lesser of the two following amounts:

(i) the amount by which 50 percent of the taxpayer's contribution base for such succeeding taxable year exceeds the sum of the charitable contributions described in subsection (b)(1)(A) payment of which is made by the taxpayer within such succeeding taxable year (determined without regard to this subparagraph) and the charitable contributions described in subsection (b)(l)(A) payment of which was made in taxable years before the contribution year which are treated under this subparagraph as having been paid in such succeeding taxable year; or

(ii) in the case of the first succeeding taxable year, the amount of such excess, and in the case of the second, third, fourth, or fifth succeeding taxable year, the portion of such excess not treated under this subparagraph as a charitable contribution described in subsection (b)(1)(A) paid in any taxable year intervening between the contribution year and such succeeding taxable year.

(B) Special rule for net operating loss carryovers.—In applying subparagraph (A), the excess determined under subparagraph (A) for the contribution year shall be reduced to the extent that such excess reduces taxable income (as computed for purposes of the second sentence of section 172(b) (2)) and increases the net operating loss deduction for a taxable year succeeding the contribution year.

(2) Corporations.—

(A) In general.—Any contribution made by a corporation in a taxable year (hereinafter in this paragraph referred to as the "contribution year") in excess of the amount deductible for such year under subsection (b)(2) (A) shall be deductible for each of the 5 succeeding taxable years in order of time, but only to the extent of the lesser of the two following amounts: (i) the excess of the maximum amount deductible for such succeeding taxable year under subsection (b) (2) over the sum of the contributions made in such year plus the aggregate of the excess contributions which were made in taxable years before the contribution year and which are deductible under this subparagraph for such succeeding taxable year; or (ii) in the case of the first succeeding taxable year, the amount of such excess contribution, and in the case of the second, third, fourth, or fifth succeeding taxable year, the portion of such excess contribution not deductible under this subparagraph for any taxable year intervening between the contribution year and such succeeding taxable year.

(B) Special rule for net operating loss carryovers.—For purposes of subparagraph (A), the excess of—

(i) the contributions made by a corporation in a taxable year to which this section applies, over

(ii) the amount deductible in such year under the limitation in subsection (b)(2) (A),

shall be reduced to the extent that such excess reduces taxable income (as computed for purposes of the second sentence of section 172 (b)(2)) and increases a net operating loss carryover under section 172 to a succeeding taxable year.

(e) Certain contributions of ordinary income and capital gain property.—

(1) General rule.—The amount of any charitable contribution of property otherwise taken into account under this section shall be reduced by the sum of—

(A) the amount of gain which would not have been long-term capital gain (determined without regard to section 1221(b)(3)) if the property contributed had been sold by the taxpayer at its fair market value (determined at the time of such contribution), and

(B) in the case of a charitable contribution—

(i) of tangible personal property,—

(I) if the use by the donee is unrelated to the purpose or function constituting the basis for its exemption under section 501 (or, in the case of a governmental unit, to any purpose or function described in subsection (c)), or

(II) which is applicable property (as defined in paragraph (7)(C), but without regard to clause (ii) thereof)) which is sold, exchanged, or otherwise disposed of by the donee before the last day of the taxable year in which the contribution was made and with respect to which the donee has not made a certification in accordance with paragraph (7)(D),

(ii) to or for the use of a private foundation (as defined in section 509(a)), other than a private foundation described in subsection (b)(1)(F), or

(iii) of any patent, copyright (other than a copyright described in section 1221(a)(3) or 1231(b)(1)(C)), trademark, trade name, trade secret, know-how, software (other than software described in section 197(e)(3)(A)(i)), or similar property, or applications or registrations of such property, or

(iv) of any taxidermy property which is contributed by the person who prepared, stuffed, or mounted the property or by any person who paid or incurred the cost of such preparation, stuffing, or mounting,

the amount of gain which would have been long-term capital gain if the property contributed had been sold by the taxpayer at its fair market value (determined at the time of such contribution).

For purposes of applying this paragraph (other than in the case of gain to which section 617(d)(1), 1245(a), 1250(a), 1252(a), or 1254(a) applies), property which is property used in the trade or business (as defined in section 1231(b)) shall be treated as a capital asset. For purposes of applying this paragraph in the case of a charitable contribution of stock in an S corporation, rules similar to the rules of section 751 shall apply in determining whether gain on such stock would have been long-term capital gain if such stock were sold by the taxpayer.

(2) Allocation of basis.—For purposes of paragraph (1), in the case of a charitable contribution of less than the taxpayer's entire interest in the property contributed, the taxpayer's adjusted basis in such property shall be allocated between the interest contributed and any interest not contributed in accordance with regulations prescribed by the Secretary.

(3) Special rule for certain contributions of inventory and other property.—

(A) Qualified contributions.—For purposes of this paragraph, a qualified contribution shall mean a charitable contribution of property described in paragraph (1) or (2) of section 1221, by a corporation (other than a corporation which is an S corporation) to an organization which is described in section 501(c) (3) and is exempt under section 501(a) (other than a private foundation, as defined in section 509(a), which is not an operating foundation, as defined in section 4942(j) (3)), but only if—

(i) the use of the property by the donee is related to the purpose or function constituting the basis for its exemption under section 501 and the property is to be used by the donee solely for the care of the ill, the needy, or infants;

(ii) the property is not transferred by the donee in exchange for money, other property, or services;

(iii) the taxpayer receives from the donee a written statement representing that its use and disposition of the property will be in accordance with the provisions of clauses (i) and (ii); and

(iv) in the case where the property is subject to regulation under the Federal Food, Drug, and Cosmetic Act, as amended, such property must fully satisfy the applicable requirements of such Act and regulations promulgated thereunder on the date of transfer and for one hundred and eighty days prior thereto.

(B) Amount of reduction.—The reduction under paragraph (1) (A) for any qualified contribution (as defined in subparagraph (A)) shall be no greater than the sum of—

(i) one-half of the amount computed under paragraph (1)(A) (computed without regard to this paragraph), and

(ii) the amount (if any) by which the charitable contribution deduction under this section for any qualified contribution (computed by taking into account the amount determined in clause (i), but without regard to this clause) exceeds twice the basis of such property.

(C) Special rule for contributions of food inventory.—

(i) General rule.—In the case of a charitable contribution of food from any trade or business of the taxpayer, this paragraph shall be applied—

(I) without regard to whether the contribution is made by a C corporation, and

(II) only to food that is apparently wholesome food.

(ii) Limitation.—In the case of a taxpayer other than a C corporation, the aggregate amount of such contributions for any taxable year which may be taken into account under this section shall not exceed 10 percent of the taxpayer's aggregate net income for such taxable year from all trades or businesses from which such contributions were made for such year, computed without regard to this section.

(iii) Apparently wholesome food.—For purposes of this subparagraph, the term "apparently wholesome food" has the meaning given to such term by section 22(b)(2) of the Bill Emerson Good Samaritan Food Donation Act (42 U.S.C. 1791(b)(2)), as in effect on the date of the enactment of this subparagraph.

(iv) Termination.—This subparagraph shall not apply to contributions made after December 31, 2013.*

(D) Special rule for contributions of book inventory to public schools.

(i) Contributions of book inventory.—In determining whether a qualified book contribution is a qualified contribution, subparagraph (A) shall be applied without regard to whether the donee is an organization described in the matter preceding clause (i) of subparagraph (A).

(ii) Qualified book contribution.—For purpose of this paragraph, the term "qualified book contribution" means a charitable contribution of books to a public school which is an educational organization described in subsection (b)(l)(A)(ii) and which provides elementary education or secondary education (kindergarten through grade 12).

(iii) Certification by donee.—Subparagraph (A) shall not apply to any contribution unless (in addition to the certifications required by subparagraph (A) (as modified by this subparagraph)), the donee certifies in writing that—

(I) the books are suitable, in terms of currency, content, and quantity, for use in the donee's educational programs, and

(II) the donee will use the books in its educational programs.

(iv) Termination.—This subparagraph shall not apply to contributions made after December 31, 2011.**

(E) This paragraph shall not apply to so much of the amount of the gain described in paragraph (1)(A) which would be long-term capital gain but for the application of sections 617, 1245, 1250, or 1252.

(4) Special rule for contributions of scientific property used for research.—

(A) Limit on reduction.—In the case of a qualified research contribution, the reduction under paragraph (1)(A) shall be no greater than the amount determined under paragraph (3)(B).

(B) Qualified research contributions.—For purposes of this paragraph, the term "qualified research contribution" means a charitable contribution by a corporation of tangible personal property described in paragraph (1) of section 1221, but only if—

(i) the contribution is to an organization described in subparagraph (A) or subparagraph (B) of section 41(e)(6),

(ii) the property is constructed or assembled by the taxpayer,

(iii) the contribution is made not later than 2 years after the date the construction or assembly of the property is substantially completed,

(iv) the original use of the property is by the donee,

(v) the property is scientific equipment or apparatus substantially all of the use of which by the donee is for research or experimentation (within the meaning of section 174), or for research training, in the United States in physical or biological sciences,

(vi) the property is not transferred by the donee in exchange for money, other property, or services, and

(vii) the taxpayer receives from the donee a written statement representing that its use and disposition of the property will be in accordance with the provisions of clauses (v) and (vi).

(C) Construction of property by taxpayer.—For purposes of this paragraph, property shall be treated as constructed by the taxpayer only if the cost of the parts used in the

*Editorial comment: At the present time, this section has not been extended. There is pending legislation in the Senate, *The Tax Extenders Act of 2013 (S. 1859)*, that would extend Section 170(e)(3)(C)(iv) until December 2014.

**Editorial comment: Congress did not extend this provision in extender legislation.

construction of such property (other than parts manufactured by the taxpayer or a related person) do not exceed 50 percent of the taxpayer's basis in such property.

(D) Corporation.—For purposes of this paragraph, the term "corporation" shall not include—

(i) an S corporation,

(ii) a personal holding company (as defined in section 542), and

(iii) a service organization (as defined in section 414(m)(3)).

(5) Special rule for contributions of stock for which market quotations are readily available.—

(A) In general.—Subparagraph (B)(ii) of paragraph (1) shall not apply to any contribution of qualified appreciated stock.

(B) Qualified appreciated stock.—Except as provided in subparagraph (C), for purposes of this paragraph, the term "qualified appreciated stock" means any stock of a corporation—

(i) for which (as of the date of the contribution) market quotations are readily available on an established securities market, and

(ii) which is capital gain property (as defined in subsection (b)(1)(C)(iv)).

(C) Donor may not contribute more than 10 percent of stock of corporation.—

(i) In general.—In the case of any donor, the term "qualified appreciated stock" shall not include any stock of a corporation contributed by the donor in a contribution to which paragraph (1)(B)(ii) applies (determined without regard to this paragraph) to the extent that the amount of the stock so contributed (when increased by the aggregate amount of all prior such contributions by the donor of stock in such corporation) exceeds 10 percent (in value) of all of the outstanding stock of such corporation.

(ii) Special rule.—For purposes of clause (i), an individual shall be treated as making all contributions made by any member of his family (as defined in section 267(c)(4)).

(6) Special rule for contributions of computer technology and equipment for educational purposes.—

(A) Limit on reduction.—In the case of a qualified computer contribution, the reduction under paragraph (1)(A) shall be no greater than the amount determined under paragraph (3)(B).

(B) Qualified computer contribution.—For purposes of this paragraph, the term "qualified computer contribution" means a charitable contribution by a corporation of any computer technology or equipment, but only if—

(i) the contribution is to—

(I) an educational organization described in subsection (b)(1)(A)(ii),

(II) an entity described in section 501(c)(3) and exempt from tax under section 501(a) (other than an entity described in subclause (I)) that is organized primarily for purposes of supporting elementary and secondary education, or

(III) a public library (within the meaning of section 213(2)(A) of the Library Services and Technology Act (20 U.S.C. 9122(2)(A)), as in effect on the date of the enactment of the Community Renewal Tax Relief Act of 2000), established and maintained by an entity described in subsection (c)(1).

(ii) the contribution is made not later than 3 years after the date the taxpayer acquired the property (or in the case of property constructed or assembled by the taxpayer, the date the construction or assembling of the property is substantially completed),

(iii) the original use of the property is by the donor or the donee,

(iv) substantially all of the use of the property by the donee is for use within the United States for educational purposes that are related to the purpose or function of the donee,

(v) the property is not transferred by the donee in exchange for money, other property, or services, except for shipping, installation and transfer costs,

(vi) the property will fit productively into the donee's education plan,

(vii) the donee's use and disposition of the property will be in accordance with the provisions of clauses (iv) and (v), and

(viii) the property meets such standards, if any, as the Secretary may prescribe by regulation to assure that the property meets minimum functionality and suitability standards for educational purposes.

(C) Contribution to private foundation.—A contribution by a corporation of any computer technology or equipment to a private foundation (as defined in section 509) shall be treated as a qualified computer contribution for purposes of this paragraph if—

(i) the contribution to the private foundation satisfies the requirements of clauses (ii) and (v) of subparagraph (B), and

(ii) within 30 days after such contribution, the private foundation—

(I) contributes the property to an entity described in clause (i) of subparagraph (B) that satisfies the requirements of clauses (iv) through (vii) of subparagraph (B), and

(II) notifies the donor of such contribution.

(D) Donations of property reacquired by manufacturer.—In the case of property which is reacquired by the person who constructed or assembled the property—

(i) subparagraph (B)(ii) shall be applied to a contribution of such property by such person by taking into account the date that the original construction or assembly of the property was substantially completed, and

(ii) subparagraph (B)(iii) shall not apply to such contribution.

(E) Special rule relating to construction of property.—For the purposes of this paragraph, the rules of paragraph (4)(C) shall apply.

(F) Definitions.—For the purposes of this paragraph—

(i) Computer technology or equipment.—The term "computer technology or equipment" means computer software (as defined by section 197(e)(3)(B)), computer or peripheral equipment (as defined by section 168(i)(2)(B)), and fiber optic cable related to computer use.

(ii) Corporation.—The term "corporation" has the meaning given to such term by paragraph (4)(D).

(G) Termination.—This paragraph shall not apply to any contribution made during any taxable year beginning after December 31, 2011.

* * *

(f) Disallowance of deduction in certain cases and special rules.—

* * *

(6) Deductions for out-of-pocket expenditures.—No deduction shall be allowed under this section for an out-of-pocket expenditure made by any person on behalf of an organization described in subsection (c) (other than an organization described in section 501(h)(5) (relating to churches, etc.)) if the expenditure is made for the purpose of influencing legislation (within the meaning of section 501 (c)(3)).

* * *

(8) Substantiation requirement for certain contributions.—

(A) General rule.—No deduction shall be allowed under subsection (a) for any contribution of $250 or more unless the taxpayer substantiates the contribution by a contemporaneous written acknowledgment of the contribution by the donee organization that meets the requirements of subparagraph (B).

(B) Content of acknowledgement.—An acknowledgement meets the requirements of this subparagraph if it includes the following information:

(i) The amount of cash and a description (but not value) of any property other than cash contributed.

(ii) Whether the donee organization provided any goods or services in consideration, in whole or in part, for any property described in clause (i).

(iii) A description and good faith estimate of the value of any goods or services referred to in clause (ii) or, if such goods or services consist solely of intangible religious benefits, a statement to that effect.

For purposes of this subparagraph, the term "intangible religious benefit" means any intangible religious benefit which is provided by an organization organized exclusively for religious purposes and which generally is not sold in a commercial transaction outside the donative context.

(C) Contemporaneous.—For purposes of subparagraph (A), an acknowledgment shall be considered to be contemporaneous if the taxpayer obtains the acknowledgment on or before the earlier of—

(i) the date on which the taxpayer files a return for the taxable year in which the contribution was made, or

(ii) the due date (including extensions) for filing such return.

(D) Substantiation not required for contributions reported by the donee organization.—Subparagraph (A) shall not apply to a contribution if the donee organization files a return, on such form and in accordance with such regulations as the Secretary may prescribe, which includes the information described in subparagraph (B) with respect to the contribution.

(E) Regulations.—The Secretary shall prescribe such regulations as may be necessary or appropriate to carry out the purposes of this paragraph, including regulations that may provide that some or all of the requirements of this paragraph do not apply in appropriate cases.

(9) Denial of deduction where contribution for lobbying activities.—No deduction shall be allowed under this section for a contribution to an organization which conducts activities to which section 162(e)(1) applies on matters of direct financial interest to the donor's trade or business, if a principal purpose of the contribution was to avoid Federal income tax by securing a deduction for such activities under this section which would be disallowed by reason of section 162(e) if the donor had conducted such activities directly. No deduction shall be allowed under section 162(a) for any amount for which a deduction is disallowed under the preceding sentence.

* * *

(11) Qualified appraisal and other documentation for certain contributions.—

(A) In general.—

(i) Denial of deduction.—In the case of an individual, partnership, or corporation, no deduction shall be allowed under subsection (a) for any contribution of property for which a deduction of more than $500 is claimed unless such person meets the requirements of subparagraphs (B), (C), and (D), as the case may be, with respect to such contribution.

(ii) Exceptions.—

(I) Readily valued property.—Subparagraphs (C) and (D) shall not apply to cash, property described in subsection (e)(1)(B)(iii) or section 1221(a)(1), publicly traded securities (as defined in section 6050L(a)(2)(B)), and any qualified vehicle described in paragraph (12)(A)(ii) for which an acknowledgement under paragraph (12)(B)(iii) is provided.

(II) Reasonable cause.—Clause (i) shall not apply if it is shown that the failure to meet such requirements is due to reasonable cause and not to willful neglect.

(B) Property description for contributions of more than $500.—In the case of contributions of property for which a deduction of more than $500 is claimed, the requirements of this subparagraph are met if the individual, partnership or corporation includes with the return for the taxable year in which the contribution is made a description of such property and such other information as the Secretary may require. The requirements of this subparagraph shall not apply to a C corporation which is not a personal service corporation or a closely held C corporation.

(C) Qualified appraisal for contributions of more than $5,000.—In the case of contributions of property for which a deduction of more than $5,000 is claimed, the requirements of this subparagraph are met if the individual, partnership, or corporation obtains a qualified appraisal of such property and attaches to the return for the taxable year in which such contribution is made such information regarding such property and such appraisal as the Secretary may require.

(D) Substantiation for contributions of more than $500,000.—In the case of contributions of property for which a deduction of more than $500,000 is claimed, the requirements of this subparagraph are met if the individual, partnership, or corporation attaches to the return for the taxable year a qualified appraisal of such property.

(E) Qualified appraisal and appraises.—For purposes of this paragraph—

(i) Qualified appraisal.— the term "qualified appraisal" means, with respect to any property, an appraisal of such property which—

(I) is treated for purposes of this paragraph as a qualified appraisal under regulations or other guidance prescribed by the Secretary, and

(II) is conducted by a qualified appraiser in accordance with generally accepted appraisal standards and any regulations or other guidance prescribed under subclause (I).

(ii) Qualified appraisal.—Except as provided in clause (iii), the term "qualified appraisal" means an individual who—

(I) has earned anappraisal designation fromar ecognized professional appraiser organization or has otherwise met minimume ducation and experience requirements set forth in regulation sprescribed by the Secretary,

(II) regularly performs appraisals for which the individual receives compensation, and

(III) meets such other requirements as may be prescribed by the Secretary in regulations or other guidance.

(iii) Specific appraisals.—An individual shall not be treated as a qualified appraiser with respect to any specific appraisal unless—

(I) the individual demonstrates verifiable education and experience invaluing the type of property subject to the appraisal, and

(II) the individual has not been prohibited from practicing before the Internal Revenue Service by the Secretary under section 330(c) of title 31, United States Code, at any time during the 3-year period ending on the date of the appraisal.

(F) Aggregation of similar items of property.—For purposes of determining thresholds under this paragraph, property and all similar items of property donated to 1 or more donees shall be treated as 1 property.

(G) Special rule for pass-thru entities.—In the case of a partnership or S corporation, this paragraph shall be applied at the entity level, except that the deduction shall be denied at the partner or shareholder level.

(H) Regulations.—The Secretary may prescribe such regulations as may be necessary or appropriate to carry out the purposes of this paragraph, including regulations that may provide that some or all of the requirements of this paragraph do not apply in appropriate cases.

(12) Contributions of used motor vehicles, boats, and airplanes.—

(A) In general.—In the case of a contribution of a qualified vehicle the claimed value of which exceeds $500—

(i) paragraph (8) shall not apply and no deduction shall be allowed under subsection (a) for such contribution unless the taxpayer substantiates the contribution by a contemporaneous written acknowledgement of the contribution by the donee organization that meets the requirements of subparagraph (B) and includes the acknowledgement with the taxpayer's return of tax which includes the deduction, and

(ii) if the organization sells the vehicle without any significant intervening use or material improvement of such vehicle by the organization, the amount of the deduction allowed under subsection (a) shall not exceed the gross proceeds received from such sale.

(B) Content of acknowledgement.—An acknowledgement meets the requirements of this subparagraph if it includes the following information:

(i) The name and taxpayer identification number of the donor.

(ii) The vehicle identification number or similar number.

(iii) In the case of a qualified vehicle to which subparagraph (A)(ii) applies—

(I) a certification that the vehicle was sold in an arm's length transaction between unrelated parties,

(II) the gross proceeds from the sale, and

(III) a statement that the deductible amount may not exceed the amount of such gross proceeds.

(iv) In the case of a qualified vehicle to which subparagraph (A)(ii) does not apply—

(I) a certification of the intended use or material improvement of the vehicle and the intended duration of such use, and

(II) a certification that the vehicle would not be transferred in exchange for money, other property, or services before completion of such use or improvement.

(v) Whether the donee organization provided any goods or services in consideration, in whole or inpart, for the qualified vehicle.

(vi) A description and good faith estimate of the value of any goods or services referred to in clause (v) or, if such goods or services consist solely of intangible religious benefits (as defined in paragraph (8)(B)), a statement to that effect.

(C) Contemporaneous.—For purposes of subparagraph (A), an acknowledgement shall be considered to be contemporaneous if the donee organization provides it within 30 days of—

(i) the sale of the qualified vehicle, or

(ii) in the case of an acknowledgement including a certification described in subparagraph (B)(iv), the contribution of the qualified vehicle.

(D) Information to Secretary.—A donee organization required to provide an acknowledgement under this paragraph shall provide to the Secretary the information contained in the acknowledgement. Such information shall be provided at such time and in such manner as the Secretary may prescribe.

(E) Qualified vehicle.—For purposes of this paragraph, the term "qualified vehicle" means any—

(i) motor vehicle manufactured primarily for use on public streets, roads, and highways,

(ii) boat, or

(iii) airplane.

Such term shall not include any property which is described in section 1221(a)(1).

(F) Regulations or other guidance.—The Secretary shall prescribe such regulations or other guidance as may be necessary to carry out the purposes of this paragraph. The Secretary may prescribe regulations or other guidance which exempts sales by the donee organization which are in direct furtherance of such organization's charitable purpose from the requirements of subparagraphs (A)(ii) and (B)(iv)(II).

* * *

(16) Contributions of clothing and household items.—

(A) In general.—In the case of an individual, partnership, or corporation, no deduction shall be allowed under subsection (a) for any contribution of clothing or a household item unless such clothing or household item is in good used condition or better.

(B) Items of minimal value.—Notwithstanding subparagraph (A), the Secretary may by regulation deny a deduction under subsection (a) for any contribution of clothing or a household item which has minimal monetary value.

(C) Exception for certain property.—Subparagraphs (A) and (B) shall not apply to any contribution of a single item of clothing or a household item for which a deduction of more than $500 is claimed if the taxpayer includes with the taxpayer's return a qualified appraisal with respect to the property.

(D) Household items.—For purposes of this paragraph—

(i) In general.—The term "household items" includes furniture, furnishings, electronics, appliances, linens, and other similar items.

(ii) Excluded items.—Such term does not include—

(I) food,

(II) paintings, antiques, and other objects of art,

(III) jewelry and gems, and

(IV) collections.

(E) Special rule for pass-thru entities.—In the case of a partnership or S corporation, this paragraph shall be applied at the entity level, except that the deduction shall be denied at the partner or shareholder level.

(17) Recordkeeping.—No deduction shall be allowed under subsection (a) for any contribution of a cash, check, or other monetary gift unless the donor maintains as a record of such contribution a bank record or a written communication from the donee showing the name of the donee organization, the date of the contribution, and the amount of the contribution.

(18) Contributions to donor advised funds.—A deduction otherwise allowed under subsection (a) for any contribution to a donor advised fund (as defined in section 4966(d)2)) shall only be allowed if—

(A) the sponsoring organization (as defined in section 4966(d)(1)) with respect to such donor advised fund is not—

(i) described in paragraph (3), (4), or (5) of subsection (c), or

(ii) a type III supporting organization (as defined in section 4943(f)(5)(A)) which is not a functionally integrated type III supporting organization (as defined in section 4943 (f)(5)(B)), and

(B) the taxpayer obtains a contemporaneous written acknowledgment (determined under rules similar to the rules of paragraph (8)(C)) from the sponsoring organization (as so defined) of such donor advised fund that such organization has exclusive legal control over the assets contributed

(g) Amounts paid to maintain certain students as members of taxpayer's household.—

(1) In general.—Subject to the limitations provided by paragraph (2), amounts paid by the taxpayer to maintain an individual (other than a dependent, as defined in section 152 (determined without regard to subsections (b)(1), (b)(2), and (d) (1)(B) thereof), or a relative of the taxpayer) as a member of his household during the period that such individual is—

(A) a member of the taxpayer's household under a written agreement between the taxpayer and an organization described in paragraph (2), (3), or (4) of subsection (c) to implement a program of the organization to provide educational opportunities for pupils or students in private homes, and

(B) a full-time pupil or student in the twelfth or any lower grade at an educational organization described in section 170(b)(1)(A)(ii) located in the United States,

shall be treated as amounts paid for the use of the organization.

(2) Limitations.—

(A) Amount.—Paragraph (1) shall apply to amounts paid within the taxable year only to the extent that such amounts do not exceed $50 multiplied by the number of full calendar months during the taxable year which fall within the period described in paragraph (1). For purposes of the preceding sentence, if 15 or more days of a calendar month fall within such period such month shall be considered as a full calendar month.

(B) Compensation or reimbursement.—Paragraph (1) shall not apply to any amount paid by the taxpayer within the taxable year if the taxpayer receives any money or other property as compensation or reimbursement for maintaining the individual in his household during the period described in paragraph (1).

(3) Relative defined.—For purposes of paragraph (1), the term "relative of the taxpayer" means an individual who, with respect to the taxpayer, bears any of the relationships described in subparagraphs (A) through (G) of section 152(d)(2).

(4) No other amount allowed as deduction.—No deduction shall be allowed under subsection (a) for any amount paid by a taxpayer to maintain an individual as a member of his household under a program described in paragraph (1) (A) except as provided in this subsection.

* * *

(i) Standard mileage rate for use of passenger automobile.—For purposes of computing the deduction under this section for use of a passenger automobile the standard mileage rate shall be 14 cents per mile.

(j) Denial of deduction for certain travel expenses.—No deduction shall be allowed under this section for traveling expenses (including amounts expended for meals and lodging) while away from home, whether paid directly or by reimbursement, unless there is no significant element of personal pleasure, recreation, or vacation in such travel.

* * *

(l) Treatment of certain amounts paid to or for the benefit of institutions of higher education.—

(1) In general.—For purposes of this section, 80 percent of any amount described in paragraph (2) shall be treated as a charitable contribution.

(2) Amount described. For purposes of paragraph (1), an amount is described in this paragraph if—

(A) the amount is paid by the taxpayer to or for the benefit of an educational organization—

(i) which is described in subsection (b)(1) (A)(ii), and

(ii) which is an institution of higher education (as defined in section 3304(f)), and

(B) such amount would be allowable as a deduction under this section but for the fact that the taxpayer receives (directly or indirectly) as a result of paying such amount the right to purchase tickets for seating at an athletic event in an athletic stadium of such institution.

If any portion of a payment is for the purchase of such tickets, such portion and the remaining portion (if any) of such payment shall be treated as separate amounts for purposes of this subsection.

(m) Certain donee income from intellectual property treated as an additional charitable contribution.—

(1) Treatment as additional contribution.—In the case of a taxpayer who makes a qualified intellectual property contribution, the deduction allowed under subsection (a) for each taxable year of the taxpayer ending on or after the date of such contribution shall be increased (subject to the limitations under subsection (b)) by the applicable percentage of qualified donee income with respect to such contribution which is properly allocable to such year under this subsection.

(2) Reduction in additional deductions to extent of initial deduction.—With respect to any qualified intellectual property contribution, the deduction allowed under subsection (a) shall be increased under paragraph (1) only to the extent that the aggregate amount of such increases with respect to such contribution exceed the amount allowed as a deduction under subsection (a) with respect to such contribution determined without regard to this subsection.

(3) Qualified donee income.—For purposes of this subsection, the term "qualified donee income" means any net income received by or accrued to the donee which is properly allocable to the qualified intellectual property.

(4) Allocation of qualified donee income to taxable years of donor.—For purposes of this subsection, qualified donee income shall be treated as properly allocable to a taxable year of the donor if such income is received by or accrued to the donee for the taxable year of the donee which ends within or with such taxable year of the donor.

(5) 10-year limitation.—Income shall not be treated as properly allocable to qualified intellectual property for purposes of this subsection if such income is received by or accrued to the donee after the 10-year period beginning on the date of the contribution of such property.

(6) Benefit limited to life of intellectual property.—Income shall not be treated as properly allocable to qualified intellectual property for purposes of this subsection if such income is received by or accrued to the donee after the expiration of the legal life of such property.

(7) Applicable percentage.—For purposes of this subsection, the term "applicable percentage" means the percentage determined under the following table which corresponds to a taxable year of the donor ending on or after the date of the qualified intellectual property contribution:

Taxable Year of Donor Ending on or After Date of Contribution	Applicable Percentage:
1st	100
2nd	100
3rd	90
4th	80
5th	70
6th	60
7th	50
8th	40
9th	30
10th	20
11th	10
12th	10

(8) Qualified intellectual property contribution.—For purposes of this subsection, the term "qualified intellectual property contribution" means any charitable contribution of qualified intellectual property—

(A) the amount of which taken into account under this section is reduced by reason of subsection (e)(1), and

(B) with respect to which the donor informs the donee at the time of such contribution that the donor intends to treat such contribution as a qualified intellectual property contribution for purposes of this subsection and section 6050L.

(9) Qualified intellectual property.—For purposes of this subsection, the term "qualified intellectual property" means property described in subsection (e)(1)(B)(iii) (other than property contributed to or for the use of an organization described in subsection (e)(1)(B)(ii)).

(10) Other special rules.—

(A) Application of limitations on charitable contributions.—Any increase under this subsection of the deduction provided under subsection (a) shall be treated for purposes of subsection (b) as a deduction which is attributable to a charitable contribution to the donee to which such increase relates.

(B) Net income determined by donee.—The net income taken into account under paragraph (3) shall not exceed the amount of such income reported under section 6050L(b)(l).

(C) Deduction limited to 12 taxable years.—Except as may be provided under subparagraph (D)(i), this subsection shall not apply with respect to any qualified intellectual property contribution for any taxable year of the donor after the 12th taxable year of the donor which ends on or after the date of such contribution.

(D) Regulations.—The Secretary may issue regulations or other guidance to carry out the purposes of this subsection, including regulations or guidance—

(i) modifying the application of this subsection in the case of a donor or donee with a short taxable year, and

(ii) providing for the determination of an amount to be treated as net income of the donee which is properly allocable to qualified intellectual property in the case of a donee who uses such property to further a purpose or function constituting the basis of the donee's exemption under section 501 (or, in the case of a governmental unit, any purpose described in section 170(c)) and does not possess a right to receive any payment from a third party with respect to such property.

* * *

§ 171. Amortizable bond premium

(a) General rule.—In the case of any bond, as defined in subsection (d), the following rules shall apply to the amortizable bond premium (determined under subsection (b)) on the bond:

(1) Taxable bonds.—In the case of a bond (other than a bond the interest on which is excludable from gross income), the amount of the amortizable bond premium for the taxable year shall be allowed as a deduction.

(2) Tax-exempt bonds.—In the case of any bond the interest on which is excludable from gross income, no deduction shall be allowed for the amortizable bond premium for the taxable year.

(3) Cross reference.—

For adjustment to basis on account of amortizable bond premium, see section 1016(a)(5).

(b) Amortizable bond premium.—

(1) Amount of bond premium.—For purposes of paragraph (2), the amount of bond premium, in the case of the holder of any bond, shall be determined—

(A) with reference to the amount of the basis (for determining loss on sale or exchange) of such bond,

(B) (i) with reference to the amount payable on maturity or on earlier call date, in the case of any bond other than a bond to which clause (ii) applies, or

(ii) with reference to the amount payable on maturity (or if it results in a smaller amortizable bond premium attributable to the period to earlier call date, with reference to the amount payable on earlier call date), in the case of any bond described in subsection (a)(1) which is acquired after December 31, 1957, and

(C) with adjustments proper to reflect unamortized bond premium, with respect to the bond, for the period before the date as of which subsection (a) becomes applicable with respect to the taxpayer with respect to such bond.

In no case shall the amount of bond premium on a convertible bond include any amount attributable to the conversion features of the bond.

(2) Amount amortizable.—The amortizable bond premium of the taxable year shall be the amount of the bond premium attributable to such year. In the case of a bond to which paragraph (1)(B)(ii) applies and which has a call date, the amount of bond premium attributable to the taxable year in which the bond is called shall include an amount equal to the excess of the amount of the adjusted basis (for determining loss on sale or exchange) of such bond as of the beginning of the taxable year over the amount received on redemption of the bond or (if greater) the amount payable on maturity.

(3) Method of determination.—

(A) In general.—Except as provided in regulations prescribed by the Secretary, the determinations required under paragraphs (1) and (2) shall be made on the basis of the taxpayer's yield to maturity determined by—

(i) using the taxpayer's basis (for purposes of determining loss on sale or exchange) of the obligation, and

(ii) compounding at the close of each accrual period (as defined in section 1272(a)(5)).

(B) Special rule where earlier call date is used.—For purposes of subparagraph (A), if the amount payable on an earlier call date is used under paragraph (1)(B)(ii) in determining the amortizable bond premium attributable to the period before the earlier call date, such bond shall be treated as maturing on such date for the amount so payable and then reissued on such date for the amount so payable.

(4) Treatment of certain bonds acquired in exchange for other property.—

(A) In general.—If—

(i) a bond is acquired by any person in exchange for other property, and

(ii) the basis of such bond is determined (in whole or in part) by reference to the basis of such other property,

for purposes of applying this subsection to such bond while held by such person, the basis of such bond shall not exceed its fair market value immediately after the exchange. A similar rule shall apply in the case of such bond while held by any other person whose basis is determined (in whole or in part) by reference to the basis in the hands of the person referred to in clause (i).

(B) Special rule where bond exchanged in reorganization.—Subparagraph (A) shall not apply to an exchange by the taxpayer of a bond for another bond if such exchange is a part of a reorganization (as defined in section 368). If any portion of the basis of the taxpayer in a bond transferred in such an exchange is not taken into account in determining bond premium by reason of this paragraph, such portion shall not be taken into account in determining the amount of bond premium on any bond received in the exchange.

(c) Election as to taxable bonds.—

(1) Eligibility to elect; bonds with respect to which election permitted.—In the case of bonds the interest on which is not excludible from gross income, this section shall apply only if the taxpayer has so elected.

(2) Manner and effect of election.—The election authorized under this subsection shall be made in accordance with such regulations as the Secretary shall prescribe. If such election is made with respect to any bond (described in paragraph (1)) of the taxpayer, it shall also apply to all such bonds held by the taxpayer at the beginning of the first taxable year to which the election applies and to all such bonds thereafter acquired by him and shall be binding for all subsequent taxable years with respect to all such bonds of the taxpayer, unless, on application by the taxpayer, the Secretary permits him, subject to such conditions as the Secretary deems necessary, to revoke such election. In the case of bonds held by a common trust fund, as defined in section 584(a), the election authorized under this subsection shall be exercisable with respect to such bonds only by the common trust fund. In case of bonds held by an estate or trust, the election authorized under this subsection shall be exercisable with respect to such bonds only by the fiduciary.

(d) Bond defined.—For purposes of this section, the term "bond" means any bond, debenture, note, or certificate or other evidence of indebtedness, but does not include any such obligation which constitutes stock in trade of the taxpayer or any such obligation of a kind which would properly be included in the inventory of the taxpayer if on hand at the close of the taxable year, or any such obligation held by the taxpayer primarily for sale to customers in the ordinary course of his trade or business.

(e) Treatment as offset to interest payments.—Except as provided in regulations, in the case of any taxable bond—

(1) the amount of any bond premium shall be allocated among the interest payments on the bond under rules similar to the rules of subsection (b)(3), and

(2) in lieu of any deduction under subsection (a), the amount of any premium so allocated to any interest payment shall be applied against (and operate to reduce) the amount of such interest payment.

* * *

Editorial Summary

Net Operating Loss

Subchapter B of Chapter 1 (Sec. 172)

If allowable deductions exceed gross income, it may be possible to utilize the resultant loss in a different taxable year or years. The purpose of the net operating loss provision is to provide relief to the taxpayer whose taxable income is positive in some years and negative in others. Otherwise, taxes would be levied in the positive years and no tax benefit would result for the taxpayer in the negative years. The beneficial treatment is accomplished by Sec. 172 through the carryback and/or carryforward of the net operating loss (i.e., produces a tax refund associated with the carryback years and a reduced tax liability associated with the carryover years) [see Sec. 172(b)].

Several calculations must be made, associated with the net operating loss. First, the amount of the net operating loss must be calculated. Second, if the net operating loss is carried back, the amount of the claim for refund for the carryback period must be determined. Third, if all of the net operating loss is not absorbed in a single taxable year, the remaining amount of the net operating loss available for use in other taxable years must be calculated.

The net operating loss is not identical to the amount of the negative taxable income. Rather, certain adjustments must be made to convert negative taxable income to a net operating loss [see Sec. 172(d)].

Caution needs to be exercised with respect to the adjustments depending on the starting point. If the starting point is merely the excess of the available deductions over gross income, certain amounts will have been deducted that are not deductible in the regular calculation of taxable income (e.g., for the individual taxpayer, net capital losses in excess of $3,000 may have been deducted). Therefore, the adjustments will be in accord with the statutory provisions contained in Sec. 172(d) [e.g., see Sec. 172(d)(2) for excess capital losses]. However, if the starting point is taxable income (i.e., with all relevant limitations already being applied), then certain adjustments will not be required in part or in full (e.g., no net capital loss in excess of $3,000 will have been deducted).

Note that substantially more adjustments must be made for the individual taxpayer than for the corporate taxpayer. This results because the corporate taxpayer has not deducted such items in calculating taxable income (e.g., net capital loss, personal exemption and dependency deductions, nonbusiness deductions).

The starting point for the claim for refund for a particular taxable year is the taxable income of the carryback year. Such taxable income is reduced by the amount of the net operating loss in calculating revised taxable income for that taxable year. Since the net operating loss will reduce the amount of the adjusted gross income, both the amount of the medical expense deduction and the charitable contribution deduction could be affected (i.e., increase the medical expenses deduction and decrease the charitable contribution deduction) as a result of the percentage of adjusted gross income calculations required by Secs. 170(b) and 213(a). However, for this purpose, the amount of the charitable contribution deduction is to be the amount included on the original return.

If the net operating loss is carried to more than a single tax year, another set of adjustments referred to as intervening year adjustments must be made [see Sec. 172(b)(2)]. The general effect of intervening year adjustments is to reduce the amount of the net operating loss remaining for carryover to another taxable year. The relationship can be depicted as follows:

Original net operating loss
− Taxable income of year to which NOL was carried
± Intervening year adjustments (i.e., generally negative)
= NOL remaining for carryover to another taxable year

Therefore, the greater the number of taxable years to which the net operating loss is carried, (i.e., potentially 2 carryback years and 20 carryforward years for a total of 22 years) the more of the net operating loss that is consumed (i.e., wasted) by the intervening year adjustments. The Job Creation and Worker Assistance Act of 2002 temporarily increased the NOL carryback period from 2 years to 5 years [see Sec. 172 (b)(1)(H)]. The Gulf Opportunity Zone Act of 2005 temporarily increases the NOL carryback period from 2 years to 5 years in limited circumstances [see Sec. 172(b)(1)(I)]. The American Recovery and Reinvestment Tax Act of 2009 permits an eligible small business to extend the carryback period from 2 years up to 5 years associated with a 2008 NOL. The Worker, Homeownership, and Business Assistance Act of 2009 provides for a five-year carryback associated with 2008 and 2009 net operating losses (subject to limitations).

In recognition of the potential negative effects of intervening year adjustments and other items (e.g., NOL produces no benefit because credits had already eliminated the tax liability of the carryback years; low tax rates in carryback years), the taxpayer may elect to forgo the two-year carryback period and instead carry the NOL forward (i.e., 20-year carryforward period) [see Sec. 172(b)(3)]. The only potential disadvantage of the election is that it is irrevocable with respect to the NOL for which it was made.

Section 172 interacts with the calculation of the dividends received deduction for corporate taxpayers under Sec. 243. The "taxable income as adjusted" limitation on the amount of the dividends received deduction is not applicable if deducting the full amount of the dividends received reduction produces or increases the amount of net operating loss [see Sec. 246(b)].

From a conceptual perspective, the net operating loss may be thought of as the summation of the net business loss plus the personal casualty and theft losses.

§ 172. Net operating loss deduction

(a) Deduction allowed.—There shall be allowed as a deduction for the taxable year an amount equal to the aggregate of (1) the net operating loss carryovers to such year, plus (2) the net operating loss carrybacks to such year. For purposes of this subtitle, the term "net operating loss deduction" means the deduction allowed by this subsection.

(b) Net operating loss carrybacks and carryovers.—

(1) Years to which loss may be carried.—

(A) General rule.—Except as otherwise provided in this paragraph, a net operating loss for any taxable year—

(i) shall be a net operating loss carryback to each of the 2 taxable years preceding the taxable year of such loss, and

(ii) shall be a net operating loss carryover to each of the 20 taxable years following the taxable year of the loss.

* * *

(C) Specified liability losses.—In the case of a taxpayer which has a specified liability loss (as defined in subsection (f)) for a taxable year, such specified liability loss shall be a net operating loss carryback to each of the 10 taxable years preceding the taxable year of such loss.

* * *

(F) Retention of 3-year carryback in certain cases.—

(i) In general.—Subparagraph (A)(i) shall be applied by substituting "3 taxable years" for "2 taxable years" with respect to the portion of the net operating loss for the taxable year which is an eligible loss with respect to the taxpayer.

(ii) Eligible loss.—For purposes of clause (i), the term "eligible loss" means—

(I) in the case of an individual, loss of property arising from fire, storm, shipwreck, or other casualty, or from theft,

(II) in the case of a taxpayer which is a small business, net operating losses attributable to federally declared disasters (as defined by subsection (h)(3)(C)(i)), and

(III) in the case of a taxpayer engaged in the trade or business of farming (as defined in section 263A(e)(4)), net operating losses attributable to such federally declared disasters.

Such term shall not include any farming loss (as defined in subsection (i)) or qualified disaster loss (as defined in subsection (j)).

(iii) Small business.—For purposes of this subparagraph, the term "small business" means a corporation or partnership which meets the gross receipts test of section 448(c) for the taxable year in which the loss arose (or, in the case of a sole proprietorship, which would meet such test if such proprietorship were a corporation).

(iv) Coordination with paragraph (2). For purposes of applying paragraph (2), an eligible loss for any taxable year shall be treated in a manner similar in which a specified liability loss is treated.

(G) Farming losses.—In the case of a taxpayer which has a farming loss (as defined in subsection (i)) for a taxable year, such farming loss shall be a net operating loss carryback to each of the 5 taxable years preceding the taxable year of such loss.

(H) Carrybacks for 2008 or 2009 net operating losses.—

(i) In general.—In the case of an applicable net operating loss with respect to which the taxpayer has elected the application of this subparagraph—

(I) subparagraph (A)(i) shall be applied by substituting any whole number elected by the taxpayer which is more than 2 and less than 6 for "2",

(II) subparagraph (E)(ii) shall be applied by substituting the whole number which is one less than the whole number substituted under subclause (I) for "2", and

(III) subparagraph (F) shall not apply.

(ii) Applicable net operating loss.—For purposes of this subparagraph, the term "applicable net operating loss" means the taxpayer's net operating loss for a taxable year ending after December 31, 2007, and beginning before January 1, 2010.

(iii) Election.—

(I) In general.—Any election under this subparagraph may be made only with respect to 1 taxable year.

(II) Procedure.—Any election under this subparagraph shall be made in such manner as may be prescribed by the Secretary, and shall be made by the due date (including extension of time) for filing the return for the taxpayer's last taxable year beginning in 2009. Any such election, once made, shall be irrevocable.

(iv) Limitation on amount of loss carryback to 5th preceding taxable year.—

(I) In general.—The amount of any net operating loss which may be carried back to the 5th taxable year preceding the taxable year of such loss under clause (i) shall not exceed 50 percent of the taxpayer's taxable income (computed without regard to the net operating loss for the loss year or any taxable year thereafter) for such preceding taxable year.

(II) Carrybacks and carryovers to other taxable years.—Appropriate adjustments in the application of the second sentence of paragraph (2) shall be made to take into account the limitation of subclause (I).

(III) Exception for 2008 elections by small businesses.—Subclause (I) shall not apply to any loss of an eligible small business with respect to any election made under this subparagraph as in effect on the day before the date of the enactment of the Worker, Homeownership, and Business Assistance Act of 2009.

(v) Special rules for small business.—

(I) In general.—In the case of an eligible small business which made or makes an election under this subparagraph as in effect on the day before the date of the enactment of the Worker, Homeownership, and Business Assistance Act of 2009., clause (iii)(I) shall be applied by substituting "2 taxable years" for "1 taxable year".

(II) Eligible small business.—For purposes of this subparagraph, the term "eligible small business" has the meaning given such term by subparagraph (F)(iii), except that in applying such subparagraph, section 448(c) shall be applied by substituting "$15,000,000" for "$5,000,000" each place it appears.

(I) Transmission property and pollution control investment.—

(i) In general.—At the election of the taxpayer in any taxable year ending after December 31, 2005, and before January 1, 2009, in the case of a net operating loss in a taxable year ending after December 31, 2002, and before January 1, 2006, there shall be a net operating loss carryback to each of the 5 years preceding the taxable year of such loss to the extent that such loss does not exceed 20 percent of the sum of electric transmission property capital expenditures and pollution control facility capital expenditures of the taxpayer for the taxable year preceding the taxable year in which such election is made.

(ii) Limitations.—For purpose of this subsection—

(I) not more than one election may be made under clause (i) with respect to any net operating loss for a taxable year, and

(II) an election may not be made under clause (i) for more than 1 taxable year beginning in any calendar year.

(III) Coordination with ordering rule.—For purposes of applying subsection (b)(2), the portion of any loss which is carried back 5 years by reason of clause (i) shall be treated in a manner similar to the manner in which a specified liability loss is treated.

(iv) Special rules relating to credit or refund.—In the case of the portion of the loss which is carried back 5 years by reasons of clause (i)—

(I) an application under section 6411(a) with respect to such portion shall not fail to be treated as timely filed if filed within 24 months after the due date specified under such section, and

(II) references in sections 6501(h), 6511(d)(2)(A), and 6611(f)(1) to the taxable year in which such net operating loss arises or results in a net operating loss carryback shall be treated as references to the taxable year for which such election is made.

(v) Definitions.—For purposes of this subparagraph—

(I) Electric transmission property capital expenditures.—The term "electric transmission property capital expenditures" means any expenditure, chargeable to capital account, made by the taxpayer which is attributable to electric transmission property used by the taxpayer in the transmission at 69 or more kilovolts of electricity for sale. Such term shall not include any expenditure which may be refunded or the purpose of which may be modified at the option of the taxpayer so as to cease to be treated as an expenditure within the meaning of such term.

(II) Pollution control facility capital expenditure.—The term "pollution control facility capital expenditures" means any expenditure, chargeable to capital account, made by an electric utility company (as defined in section 2(3) of the Public Utility Holding Company Act (15 U.S.C. 79b(3)), as in effect on the day before the date of the enactment of the Energy Tax Incentives Act of 2005) which is attributable to a facility which will qualify as a certified pollution control facility as determined under section 169 (d)(1) by striking "before January 1, 1976," and by substituting "an identifiable" for "a new identifiable". Such term shall not include any expenditure which may be refunded or the purpose of which may be modified at the option of the taxpayer so as to cease to be treated as an expenditure within the meaning of such term.

(J) Certain losses attributable to federally declared disasters.—In the case of a taxpayer who has a qualified disaster loss (as defined in subsection (j)), such loss shall be a net operating loss carryback to each of the 5 taxable years preceding the taxable year of such loss.

(2) Amount of carrybacks and carryovers.—The entire amount of the net operating loss for any taxable year (hereinafter in this section referred to as the "loss year") shall be carried to the earliest of the taxable years to which (by reason of paragraph (1)) such loss may be carried. The portion of such loss which shall be carried to each of the other taxable years shall be the excess, if any, of the amount of such loss over the sum of the taxable income for each of the prior taxable years to which such loss may be carried. For purposes of the preceding sentence, the taxable income for any such prior taxable year shall be computed—

(A) with the modifications specified in subsection (d) other than paragraphs (1), (4), and (5) thereof, and

(B) by determining the amount of the net operating loss deduction without regard to the net operating loss for the loss year or for any taxable year thereafter,

and the taxable income so computed shall not be considered to be less than zero.

(3) Election to waive carryback.—Any taxpayer entitled to a carryback period under paragraph (1) may elect to relinquish the entire carryback period with respect to a net operating loss for any taxable year. Such election shall be made in such manner as may be prescribed by the Secretary, and shall be made by the due date (including extensions of time) for filing the taxpayer's return for the taxable year of the net operating loss for which the election is to be in effect. Such election, once made for any taxable year, shall be irrevocable for such taxable year.

(c) Net operating loss defined.—For purposes of this section, the term "net operating loss" means the excess of the deductions allowed by this chapter over the gross income. Such excess shall be computed with the modifications specified in subsection (d).

(d) Modifications.—The modifications referred to in this section are as follows:

(1) Net operating loss deduction.—No net operating loss deduction shall be allowed.

(2) Capital gains and losses of taxpayers other than corporations.—In the case of a taxpayer other than a corporation—

(A) the amount deductible on account of losses from sales or exchanges of capital assets shall not exceed the amount includible on account of gains from sales or exchanges of capital assets; and

(B) the exclusion provided by section 1202 shall not be allowed.

(3) Deduction for personal exemptions.—No deduction shall be allowed under section 151 (relating to personal exemptions). No deduction in lieu of any such deduction shall be allowed.

(4) Nonbusiness deductions of taxpayers other than corporations.—In the case of a taxpayer other than a corporation, the deductions allowable by this chapter which are not attributable to a tax-payer's trade or business shall be allowed only to the extent of the amount of the gross income not derived from such trade or business. For purposes of the preceding sentence—

(A) any gain or loss from the sale or other disposition of—

(i) property, used in the trade or business, of a character which is subject to the allowance for depreciation provided in section 167, or

(ii) real property used in the trade or business,

shall be treated as attributable to the trade or business;

(B) the modifications specified in paragraphs (1), (2), and (3) shall be taken into account;

(C) any deduction for casualty or theft losses allowable under paragraph (2) or (3) of section 165(c) shall be treated as attributable to the trade or business, and

(D) any deduction allowed under section 404 to the extent attributable to contributions which are made on behalf of an individual who is an employee within the meaning of section 401(c) (1) shall not be treated as attributable to the trade or business of such individual.

(5) Computation of deduction for dividends received, etc.—The deductions allowed by sections 243 (relating to dividends received by corporations), * * * shall be computed without regard to section 246(b) (relating to limitation on aggregate amount of deductions); * * *

(7) Manufacturing deduction.—The deduction under section 199 shall not be allowed.

(e) Law applicable to computations.—In determining the amount of any net operating loss carryback or carryover to any taxable year, the necessary computations involving any other taxable year shall be made under the law applicable to such other taxable year.

(f) Rules relating to specified liability loss.—For purposes of this section—

(1) In general.—The term "specified liability loss" means the sum of the following amounts to the extent taken into account in computing the net operating loss for the taxable year:

(A) Any amount allowable as a deduction under section 162 or 165 which is attributable to—

(i) product liability, or

(ii) expenses incurred in the investigation or settlement of, or opposition to, claims against the taxpayer on account of product liability.

(B) (i) Any amount allowable as a deduction under this chapter (other than section 468(a) (1) or 468A(a)) which is in satisfaction of a liability under a Federal or State law requiring—

(I) the reclamation of land,

(II) the decommissioning of a nuclear power plant (or any unit thereof),

(III) the dismantlement of a drilling platform,

(IV) the remediation of environmental contamination, or

(V) a payment under any workers compensation act (within the meaning of section 461(h)(2)(C)(i)).

(ii) A liability shall be taken into account under this subparagraph only if—

(I) the act (or failure to act) giving rise to such liability occurs at least 3 years before the beginning of the taxable year, and

(II) the taxpayer used an accrual method of accounting throughout the period or periods during which such act (or failure to act) occurred.

(2) Limitation.—The amount of the specified liability loss for any taxable year shall not exceed the amount of the net operating loss for such taxable year.

(3) Special rule for nuclear powerplants.—Except as provided in regulations prescribed by the Secretary, that portion of a specified liability loss which is attributable to amounts incurred in the decommissioning of a nuclear powerplant (or any unit thereof) may, for purposes of subsection (b)(1) (C), be carried back to each of the taxable years during the period—

(A) beginning with the taxable year in which such plant (or unit thereof) was placed in service, and

(B) ending with the taxable year preceding the loss year.

(4) Product liability.—The term "product liability" means—

(A) liability of the taxpayer for damages on account of physical injury or emotional harm to individuals, or damage to or loss of the use of property, on account of any defect in any product which is manufactured, leased, or sold by the taxpayer, but only if

(B) such injury, harm, or damage arises after the taxpayer has completed or terminated operations with respect to, and has relinquished possession of, such product.

(5) Coordination with subsection (b)(2).—For purposes of applying subsection (b)(2), a specified liability loss for any taxable year shall be treated as a separate net operating loss for such taxable year to be taken into account after the remaining portion of the net operating loss for such taxable year.

(6) Election.—Any taxpayer entitled to a 10-year carryback under subsection (b)(1)(C) from any loss year may elect to have the carryback period with respect to such loss year determined without regard to subsection (b)(1)(C). Such election shall be made in such manner as may be prescribed by the Secretary and shall be made by the due date (including extensions of time) for filing the taxpayer's return for the taxable year of the net operating loss. Such election, once made for any taxable year, shall be irrevocable for that taxable year.

* * *

(i) Rules relating to farming losses.—For purposes of this section—

(1) In general.—The term "farming loss" means the lesser of—

(A) the amount which would be the net operating loss for the taxable year if only income and deductions attributable to farming businesses (as defined in section 263A(e)(4)) are taken into account, or

(B) the amount of the net operating loss for such taxable year.

Such term shall not include any qualified disaster area loss (as defined in subsection (j)).

(2) Coordination with subsection (b)(2).—For purposes of applying subsection (b)(2), a farming loss for any taxable year shall be treated in a manner similar to the manner in which a specified liability loss is treated.

(3) Election.—Any taxpayer entitled to a 5-year carryback under subsection (b)(1)(G) from any loss year may elect to have the carryback period with respect to such loss year determined without regard to subsection (b)(1)(G). Such election shall be made in such manner as may be prescribed by the Secretary and shall be made by the due date (including extensions of time) for filing the taxpayer's return for the taxable year of the net operating loss. Such election, once made for any taxable year, shall be irrevocable for such taxable year.

(j) Rules relating to qualified disaster losses.—For purposes of this section—

(1) In general.—The term "qualified disaster loss" means the lesser of—

(A) the sum of—

(i) the losses allowable under section 165 for the taxable year—

(I) attributable to a federally declared disaster (as defined in section 165(h)(3)(C)(i)) occurring before January 1, 2010, and

(II) occurring in a disaster area (as defined in section 165(h)(3)(C)(ii)), and

(ii) the deduction for the taxable year for qualified disaster expenses which is allowable under section 198A(a) or which would be so allowable if not otherwise treated as an expense, or

(B) the net operating loss for such taxable year.

(2) Coordination with subsection (b)(2).—For purposes of applying subsection (b)(2), a qualified disaster loss for any taxable year shall be treated in a manner similar to the manner in which a specified liability loss is treated.

(3) Election.—Any taxpayer entitled to a 5-year carryback under subsection (b)(1)(J) from any loss year may elect to have the carryback period with respect to such loss year determined without regard to subsection (b)(1)(J). Such election shall be made in such manner as may be prescribed by the Secretary and shall be made by the due date (including extensions of time) for filing the taxpayer's return for the taxable year of the net operating loss. Such election, once made for any taxable year, shall be irrevocable for such taxable year.

(4) Exclusion.—The term "qualified disaster loss" shall not include any loss with respect to any property described in section 1400N(p)(3).

(k) Cross references.—

(1) For treatment of net operating loss carryovers in certain corporate acquisitions, see section 381.

(2) For special limitation on net operating loss carryovers in case of a corporate change of ownership, see section 382.

§ 173. Circulation expenditures

(a) General rule.—

Notwithstanding section 263, all expenditures (other than expenditures for the purchase of land or depreciable property or for the acquisition of circulation through the purchase of any part of the business of another publisher of a newspaper, magazine, or other periodical) to establish, maintain, or increase the circulation of a newspaper, magazine, or other periodical shall be allowed as a deduction;

except that the deduction shall not be allowed with respect to the portion of such expenditures as, under regulations prescribed by the Secretary, is chargeable to capital account if the taxpayer elects, in accordance with such regulations, to treat such portion as so chargeable. Such election, if made, must be for the total amount of such portion of the expenditures which is so chargeable to capital account, and shall be binding for all subsequent taxable years unless, upon application by the taxpayer, the Secretary permits a revocation of such election subject to such conditions as he deems necessary.

(b) Cross reference.—

For election of 3-year amortization of expenditures allowable as a deduction under subsection (a), see section 59(e).

§ 174. Research and experimental expenditures

(a) Treatment as expenses.—

(1) In general.—A taxpayer may treat research or experimental expenditures which are paid or incurred by him during the taxable year in connection with his trade or business as expenses which are not chargeable to capital account. The expenditures so treated shall be allowed as a deduction.

(2) When method may be adopted.—

(A) Without consent.—A taxpayer may, without the consent of the Secretary, adopt the method provided in this subsection for his first taxable year—

(i) which begins after December 31, 1953, and ends after August 16, 1954, and

(ii) for which expenditures described in paragraph (1) are paid or incurred.

(B) With consent.—A taxpayer may, with the consent of the Secretary, adopt at any time the method provided in this subsection.

(3) Scope.—The method adopted under this subsection shall apply to all expenditures described in paragraph (1). The method adopted shall be adhered to in computing taxable income for the taxable year and for all subsequent taxable years unless, with the approval of the Secretary, a change to a different method is authorized with respect to part or all of such expenditures.

(b) Amortization of certain research and experimental expenditures.—

(1) In general.—At the election of the taxpayer, made in accordance with regulations prescribed by the Secretary, research or experimental expenditures which are—

(A) paid or incurred by the taxpayer in connection with his trade or business,

(B) not treated as expenses under subsection (a), and

(C) chargeable to capital account but not chargeable to property of a character which is subject to the allowance under section 167 (relating to allowance for depreciation, etc.) or section 611 (relating to allowance for depletion),

may be treated as deferred expenses. In computing taxable income, such deferred expenses shall be allowed as a deduction ratably over such period of not less than 60 months as may be selected by the taxpayer (beginning with the month in which the taxpayer first realizes benefits from such expenditures). Such deferred expenses are expenditures properly chargeable to capital account for purposes of section 1016(a) (1) (relating to adjustments to basis of property).

(2) Time for and scope of election.—The election provided by paragraph (1) may be made for any taxable year beginning after December 31, 1953, but only if made not later than the time prescribed by law for filing the return for such taxable year (including extensions thereof). The method so elected, and the period selected by the taxpayer, shall be adhered to in computing taxable income for the taxable year for which the election is made and for all subsequent taxable years unless, with the approval of the Secretary, a change to a different method (or to a different period) is authorized with respect to part or all of such expenditures. The election shall not apply to any expenditure paid or incurred during any taxable year before the taxable year for which the taxpayer makes the election.

(c) Land and other property.—This section shall not apply to any expenditure for the acquisition or improvement of land, or for the acquisition or improvement of property to be used in connection with the research or experimentation and of a character which is subject to the allowance under section 167 (relating to allowance for depreciation, etc.) or section 611 (relating to allowance for depletion); but for purposes of this section allowances under section 167, and allowances under section 611, shall be considered as expenditures.

(d) Exploration expenditures.—This section shall not apply to any expenditure paid or incurred for the purpose of ascertaining the existence, location, extent, or quality of any deposit of ore or other mineral (including oil and gas).

(e) Only reasonable research expenditures eligible.—This section shall apply to a research or experimental expenditure only to the extent that the amount thereof is reasonable under the circumstances.

(f) Cross references.—

(1) For adjustments to basis of property for amounts allowed as deductions as deferred expenses under subsection (b), see section 1016(a)(14).

(2) For election of 10-year amortization of expenditures allowable as a deduction under subsection (a), see section 59(e).

§ 175. Soil and water conservation expenditures; endangered species recovery expenditures

(a) In general.—A taxpayer engaged in the business of farming may treat expenditures which are paid or incurred by him during the taxable year for the purpose of soil or water conservation in respect of land used in farming, or for the prevention of erosion of land used in farming, or for endangered species recovery, as expenses which are not chargeable to capital account. The expenditures so treated shall be allowed as a deduction.

(b) Limitation.—The amount deductible under subsection (a) for any taxable year shall not exceed 25 percent of the gross income derived from farming during the taxable year. If for any taxable year the total of the expenditures treated as expenses which are not chargeable to capital account exceeds 25 percent of the gross income derived from farming during the taxable year, such excess shall be deductible for succeeding taxable years in order of time; but the amount deductible under this section for any one such succeeding taxable year (including the expenditures actually paid or incurred during the taxable year) shall not exceed 25 percent of the gross income derived from farming during the taxable year.

*   *   *

§ 178. Amortization of cost of acquiring a lease

(a) General rule.—In determining the amount of the deduction allowable to a lessee for exhaustion, wear or tear, obsolescence, or amortization in respect of any cost of acquiring the lease, the term of the lease shall be treated as including all renewal options (and any other period for which the parties reasonably expect the lease to be renewed) if less than 75 percent of such cost is attributable to the period of the term of the lease remaining on the date of its acquisition.

(b) Certain periods excluded.—For purposes of subsection (a), in determining the period of the term of the lease remaining on the date of acquisition, there shall not be taken into account any period for which the lease may subsequently be renewed, extended, or continued pursuant to an option exercisable by the lessee.

Editorial Summary

Limited Expensing

Subchapter B of Chapter 1 (Sec. 179)

Expenditures that benefit more than the current taxable year generally must be capitalized (e.g., see Secs. 263 and 263A). To the extent the resultant asset has a limited life (i.e., either in fact or per the statute), the basis of the asset is written off (i.e., depreciated, depleted, or amortized) over the benefit period.

To a limited extent, Sec. 179 permits the expensing of a capital expenditure for certain depreciable business property [see Sec. 179(d)(1)]. In effect, Sec. 179 permits the expensing of certain fixed assets used in a trade or business based on the concepts of materiality and simplicity.

The expensing provided under Sec. 179 is subject to the following limitations:

1. The annual amount of the deduction cannot exceed the amount specified in Sec. 179(b)(1) (the indexed amount for 2008 and 2009 is $250,000). Note the limitations on married taxpayers filing separately in Sec. 179(b)(4), on controlled groups of corporations in Sec. 179(d)(6), and on partnerships and S corporations in Sec. 179(d)(8). For 2010, the statutory amount remains at $250,000. In light of the economic downturn, Congress increased this amount for 2010 from $134,000 to $250,000 (i.e., the 2009 amount) in the Hiring Incentives to Restore Employment (HIRE) Act. The Small Business Jobs Act of 2010 increased the $250,000 to $500,000 for 2010 and 2011. For 2012, the statutory amount is $500,000 and the indexed amount is $500,000.
2. Phaseout of the amount available for limited expensing begins once qualifying expenditures for the taxable year exceed $800,000 for 2008 and 2009. For 2010, the amount was going to be reduced to $530,000. However, in light of the economic downturn, Congress increased this amount for 2010 to $800,000 (i.e., the 2009 amount) in the Hiring Incentives to Restore Employment (HIRE) Act. The Small

Business Jobs Act of 2010 increased the $800,000 to $2 million for 2010 and 2011. For 2012 and 2013, the statutory amount is $500,000 and $2 million respectively as a result of the American Taxpayer Relief Act of 2012.

3. The available Sec. 179 deduction, after reduction in items 1 and 2 above, may not exceed the income derived by the taxpayer from the conduct of any trade or business [see Sec. 179(b)(3)(A)]. Note, however, that any reduction required under this provision is not wasted, but is eligible for carryover [see Sec. 179(b)(3)(B)].

The Job Creation and Worker Assistance Act of 2002 provided for an additional first-year depreciation deduction of 30% for selected property acquired by the taxpayer after September 10, 2001 and before September 11, 2004, and placed in service before 2008 [see Sec. 168(k)]. The Jobs and Growth Tax Relief Reconciliation Act of 2003 increased the 30% to 50% and extended the eligible acquisition period to "before January 1, 2005" [see Sec. 168(k)(4)]. The 50% applied to property that was acquired by the taxpayer after May 5, 2003 and whose original use commenced with the taxpayer after May 5, 2003. The Economic Stimulus Act of 2008 reinstated additional first-year depreciation for 2008. The American Recovery and Reinvestment Tax Act of 2009 extended 50 percent additional first-year depreciation to 2009. The Small Business Jobs Act of 2010 extended 50 percent additional first-year depreciation to 2010. The Tax Relief Act of 2010 increased the percentage to 100 percent for 2011. For 2012, the percentage is reduced to 50 percent.

Under the American Taxpayer Relief Act of 2012, the percentage remains at 50 percent for 2013.

§ 179. Election to expense certain depreciable business assets

(a) Treatment as expenses.—A taxpayer may elect to treat the cost of any section 179 property as an expense which is not chargeable to capital account. Any cost so treated shall be allowed as a deduction for the taxable year in which the section 179 property is placed in service.

(b) Limitations.—

(1) Dollar limitation.—The aggregate cost which may be taken into account under subsection (a) for any taxable year shall not exceed—

(A) $250,000 in the case of taxable years beginning after 2007 and before 2010,

(B) $500,000 in the case of taxable years beginning in 2010, 2011, 2012, or 2013,* and

(C) $25,000 in the case of taxable years beginning after 2013.*

(2) Reduction in limitation.—The limitation under paragraph (1) for any taxable year shall be reduced (but not below zero) by the amount by which the cost of section 179 property placed in service during such taxable year exceeds—

(A) $800,000 in the case of taxable years beginning after 2007 and before 2010,

(B) $2,000,000 in the case of taxable years beginning in 2010, 2011, 2012, or 2013,* and

(C) $200,000 in the case of taxable years beginning after 2013.*

(3) Limitation based on income from trade or business.—

(A) In general.—The amount allowed as a deduction under subsection (a) for any taxable year (determined after the application of paragraphs (1) and (2)) shall not exceed the aggregate amount of taxable income of the taxpayer for such taxable year which is derived from the active conduct by the taxpayer of any trade or business during such taxable year.

(B) Carryover of disallowed deduction.—The amount allowable as a deduction under subsection (a) for any taxable year shall be increased by the lesser of—

(i) the aggregate amount disallowed under subparagraph (A) for all prior taxable years (to the extent not previously allowed as a deduction by reason of this subparagraph), or

(ii) the excess (if any) of—

(I) the limitation of paragraphs (1) and (2) (or if lesser, the aggregate amount of taxable income referred to in subparagraph (A)), over

(II) the amount allowable as a deduction under subsection (a) for such taxable year without regard to this subparagraph.

(C) Computation of taxable income.—For purposes of this paragraph, taxable income derived from the conduct of a trade or business shall be computed without regard to the deduction allowable under this section.

(4) Married individuals filing separately.—In the case of a husband and wife filing separate returns for the taxable year—

(A) such individuals shall be treated as 1 taxpayer for purposes of paragraphs (1) and (2), and

(B) unless such individuals elect otherwise, 50 percent of the cost which may be taken into account under subsection (a) for such taxable

*Editorial comment: At the present time, this section has not been extended. There is pending legislation in the Senate, *The Tax Extenders Act of 2013 (S. 1859)*, that would extend Sections 179(b)(1) and 179(b)(2) to 2014.

year (before application of paragraph (3)) shall be allocated to each such individual.

(A) In general.—In the case of any taxable year beginning in a calendar year after 2007 and before 2011, the $125,000 and $500,000 amounts in paragraphs (1) and (2) shall each be increased by an amount equal to—

(i) such dollar amount, multiplied by

(ii) the cost-of-living adjustment determined under section 1(f)(3) for the calendar year in which the taxable year begins, by substituting "calendar year 2006" for "calendar year 1992" in subparagraph (B) thereof.

(B) Rounding.—

(i) Dollar limitation.—If the amount in paragraph (1) as increased under subparagraph (A) is not a multiple of $1,000, such amount shall be rounded to the nearest multiple of $1,000.

(ii) Phaseout amount.—If the amount in paragraph (2) as increased under subparagraph (A) is not a multiple of $10,000, such amount shall be rounded to the nearest multiple of $10,000.

(5) Limitation on cost taken into account for certain passenger vehicles.—

(A) In general.—The cost of any sport utility vehicle for any taxable year which may be taken into account under this section shall not exceed $25,000.

(B) Sport utility vehicle.—For purposes of subparagraph (A)—

(i) In general.—The term "sport utility vehicle" means any 4-wheeled vehicle—

(I) which is primarily designed or which can be used to carry passengers over public streets, roads, or highways (except any vehicle operated exclusively on a rail or rails),

(II) which is not subject to section 280F, and

(III) which is rated at not more than 14,000 pounds gross vehicle weight.

(ii) Certain vehicles excluded.—Such term does not include any vehicle which—

(I) is designed to have a seating capacity of more than 9 persons behind the driver's seat,

(II) is equipped with a cargo area of at least 6 feet in interior length which is an open area or is designed for use as an open area but is enclosed by a cap and is not readily accessible directly from the passenger compartment, or

(III) has an integral enclosure, fully enclosing the driver compartment and load carrying device, does not have seating rearward of the driver's seat, and has no body section protruding more than 30 inches ahead of the leading edge of the windshield.

(c) Election.—

(1) In general.—An election under this section for any taxable year shall—

(A) specify the items of section 179 property to which the election applies and the portion of the cost of each of such items which is to be taken into account under subsection (a), and

(B) be made on the taxpayer's return of the tax imposed by this chapter for the taxable year.

Such election shall be made in such manner as the Secretary may by regulations prescribe.

(2) Election irrevocable.—Any election made under this section, and any specification contained in any such election, may not be revoked except with the consent of the Secretary. Any such election or specification with respect to any taxable year beginning after 2002 and before 2014 may be revoked by the taxpayer with respect to any property, and such revocation, once made, shall be irrevocable.*

(d) Definitions and special rules.—

(1) Section 179 property.—For purposes of this section, the term "section 179 property" means property—

(A) which is—

(i) tangible property (to which section 168 applies), or

(ii) computer software (as defined in section 197(e)(3)(B)) which is described in section 197(e)(3)(A)(i), to which section 167 applies, and which is placed in service in a taxable year beginning after 2002 and before 2014,*

*Editorial comment: At the present time, this section has not been extended. There is pending legislation in the Senate, *The Tax Extenders Act of 2013 (S. 1859)*, that would extend Sections 179(c)(2) and 179(d)(1)(A)(ii) until 2015.

(B) which is section 1245 property (as defined in section 1245(a)(3)), and

(C) which is acquired by purchase for use in the active conduct of a trade or business.

Such term shall not include any property described in section 50(b) and shall not include air conditioning or heating units.

(2) Purchase defined.—For purposes of paragraph (1), the term "purchase" means any acquisition of property, but only if—

(A) the property is not acquired from a person whose relationship to the person acquiring it would result in the disallowance of losses under section 267 or 707(b) (but, in applying section 267(b) and (c) for purposes of this section, paragraph (4) of section 267(c) shall be treated as providing that fthe family of an individual shall include only his spouse, ancestors, and lineal descendants),

(B) the property is not acquired by one component member of a controlled group from another component member of the same controlled group, and

(C) the basis of the property in the hands of the person acquiring it is not determined—

(i) in whole or in part by reference to the adjusted basis of such property in the hands of the person from whom acquired, or

(ii) under section 1014(a) (relating to property acquired from a decedent).

(3) Cost.—For purposes of this section, the cost of property does not include so much of the basis of such property as is determined by reference to the basis of other property held at any time by the person acquiring such property.

(4) Section not to apply to estates and trusts.—This section shall not apply to estates and trusts.

(5) Section not to apply to certain noncorporate lessors.—This section shall not apply to any section 179 property which is purchased by a person who is not a corporation and with respect to which such person is the lessor unless—

(A) the property subject to the lease has been manufactured or produced by the lessor, or

(B) the term of the lease (taking into account options to renew) is less than 50 percent of the class life of the property (as defined in section 168 (i)(1)), and for the period consisting of the first 12 months after the date on which the property is transferred to the lessee the sum of the deductions with respect to such property which are allowable to the lessor solely by reason of section 162 (other than rents and reimbursed amounts with respect to such property) exceeds 15 percent of the rental income produced by such property.

(6) Dollar limitation of controlled group.—For purposes of subsection (b) of this section—

(A) all component members of a controlled group shall be treated as one taxpayer, and

(B) the Secretary shall apportion the dollar limitation contained in subsection (b)(1) among the component members of such controlled group in such manner as he shall by regulations prescribe.

(7) Controlled group defined.—For purposes of paragraphs (2) and (6), the term "controlled group" has the meaning assigned to it by section 1563(a), except that, for such purposes, the phrase "more than 50 percent" shall be substituted for the phrase "at least 80 percent" each place it appears in section 1563(a)(1).

(8) Treatment of partnerships and S corporations.—In the case of a partnership, the limitations of subsection (b) shall apply with respect to the partnership and with respect to each partner. A similar rule shall apply in the case of an S corporation and its shareholders.

(9) Coordination with section 38.—No credit shall be allowed under section 38 with respect to any amount for which a deduction is allowed under subsection (a).

(10) Recapture in certain cases.—The Secretary shall, by regulations, provide for recapturing the benefit under any deduction allowable under subsection (a) with respect to any property which is not used predominantly in a trade or business at any time.

(e) Special rules for qualified disaster assistance property.—

(1) In general.—For purposes of this section—

(A) the dollar amount in effect under subsection (b)(1) for the taxable year shall be increased by the lesser of—

(i) $100,000, or

(ii) the cost of qualified section 179 disaster assistance property placed in service during the taxable year, and

(B) the dollar amount in effect under subsection (b)(2) for the taxable year shall be increased by the lesser of—

(i) $600,000, or

(ii) the cost of qualified section 179 disaster assistance property placed in service during the taxable year.

(2) Qualified section 179 disaster assistance property.—For purposes of this subsection, the term "qualified section 179 disaster assistance property" means section 179 property (as defined in subsection (d)) which is qualified disaster assistance property (as defined in section 168(n)(2)).

(3) Coordination with empowerment zones and renewal communities.—For purposes of sections 1397A and 1400J, qualified section 179 disaster assistance property shall not be treated as qualified zone property or qualified renewal property, unless the taxpayer elects not to take such qualified section 179 disaster assistance property into account for purposes of this subsection.

(4) Recapture.—For purposes of this subsection, rules similar to the rules under subsection (d)(10) shall apply with respect to any qualified section 179 disaster assistance property which ceases to be qualified section 179 disaster assistance property.

(f) Special rules for qualified real property.—

(1) In general.—If a taxpayer elects the application of this subsection for any taxable year beginning in 2010, 2011, 2012, or 2013,* the term "section 179 property" shall include any qualified real property which is—

(A) of a character subject to an allowance for depreciation,

(B) acquired by purchase for use in the active conduct of a trade or business, and

(C) not described in the last sentence of subsection (d)(1).

(2) Qualified real property.—For purposes of this subsection, the term "qualified real property means—

(A) qualified leasehold improvement property described in section 168(e)(6),

(B) qualified restaurant property described in section 168(e)(7) (without regard to the dates specified in subparagraph (A)(i) thereof), and

(C) qualified retail improvement property described in section 168(e)(8) (without regard to subparagraph (E) thereof).

(3) Limitation.—For purposes of applying the limitation under subsection (b)(1)(B), not more than $250,000 of the aggregate cost which is taken into account under subsection (a) for any taxable year may be attributable to qualified real property.

(4) Carryover limitation.—

(A) In general.—Notwithstanding subsection (b)(3)(B), no amount attributable to qualified real property may be carried over to a taxable year beginning after 2013.*

(B) Treatment of disallowed amounts.—Except as provided in subparagraph (C), to the extent that any amount is not allowed to be carried over to a taxable year beginning after 2013* by reason of subparagraph (A), this title shall be applied as if no election under this section had been made with respect to such amount.

(C) Amounts carried over from 2010, 2011, and 2012.*—If subparagraph (B) applies to any amount (or portion of an amount) which is carried over from a taxable year other than the taxpayer's last taxable year beginning in 2013,* such amount (or portion of an amount) shall be treated for purposes of this subtitle as attributable to property placed in service on the first day of the taxpayer's last taxable year beginning in 2013.* For the last taxable year beginning in 2013,* the amount determined under subsection (b)(3)(A) for such taxable year shall be determined without regard to this paragraph.

(D) Allocation of amounts.—For purposes of applying this paragraph and subsection (b)(3)(B) to any taxable year, the amount which is disallowed under subsection (b)(3)(A) for such taxable year which is attributed to qualified real property shall be the amount which bears the same ratio to the total amount so disallowed as—

(i) the aggregate amount attributable to qualified real property placed in service during such taxable year, increased by the portion of any amount carried over to such taxable year from a prior taxable year which is attributable to such property, bears to

(ii) the total amount of section 179 property placed in service during such taxable year, increased by the aggregate amount

*Editorial comment: At the present time, this section has not been extended. There is pending legislation in the Senate, *The Tax Extenders Act of 2013 (S. 1859)*, that would extend Sections 179(f)(1) and 179(f)(4)(C) until 2014 and the 179(f)(4)(C) heading to 2013.

carried over to such taxable year from any prior taxable year.

For purposes of the preceding sentence, only section 179 property with respect to which an election was made under subsection (c)(1) (determined without regard to subparagraph (B) of this paragraph) shall be taken into account.

* * *

§ 180. Expenditures by farmers for fertilizer, etc.

(a) In general.—A taxpayer engaged in the business of farming may elect to treat as expenses which are not chargeable to capital account expenditures (otherwise chargeable to capital account) which are paid or incurred by him during the taxable year for the purchase or acquisition of fertilizer, lime, ground limestone, marl, or other materials to enrich, neutralize, or condition land used in farming, or for the application of such materials to such land. The expenditures so treated shall be allowed as a deduction.

(b) Land used in farming.—For purposes of subsection (a), the term "land used in farming" means land used (before or simultaneously with the expenditures described in subsection (a)) by the taxpayer or his tenant for the production of crops, fruits, or other agricultural products or for the sustenance of livestock.

(c) Election.—The election under subsection (a) for any taxable year shall be made within the time prescribed by law (including extensions thereof) for filing the return for such taxable year. Such election shall be made in such manner as the Secretary may by regulations prescribe. Such election may not be revoked except with the consent of the Secretary.

* * *

Editorial Summary

Hobby Loss Limitation

Subchapter Bof Chapter 1 (Sec. 183)

Sections 162 and 212 permit deductions for expenses incurred in a trade or business or for the production of income. In general, personal expenses are not deductible. Thus, if a taxpayer engages in an activity, it is beneficial for the activity to be classified as a trade or business or as a production of income activity. Whether the conduct of an activity is the conduct of a trade or business or an income-producing activity is a factual determination and is subject to substantial taxpayer and IRS conflict.

Section 183 addresses two major issues. First, it provides that if an activity is ascertained to be neither a Sec. 162 trade or business nor a Sec. 212 income-producing activity (i.e., is a hobby), then, in general, no deductions are permitted [see Sec. 183(a)]. However, the following exceptions are provided [see Sec. 183(b)].

1. Deductions are permitted for *deductions otherwise allowable* (i.e., deductions which are permitted under various Code sections for personal expenses such as mortgage interest and property taxes).

2. Deductions are permitted for the amount that would be deductible if the hobby were either a Sec. 162 trade or business or a Sec. 212 income-producing activity, subject to the limitation that such amount is permitted only to the extent of the gross income from the activity.

The second issue addressed by Sec. 183 is intended to reduce taxpayer and IRS conflict over the factual determination of whether the activity is a hobby, or instead is a Sec. 162 trade or business or Sec. 212 income-producing activity. This is accomplished through the application of the *presumption* concept [see Sec. 183(d)]. This concept provides the taxpayer with a statutory time period (i.e., either 5 or 7 years) during which he or she can demonstrate that the conduct of the activity is not a hobby.

The model for an activity which is appropriately treated as a hobby is as follows:

Gross income from activity
– Deductions otherwise allowable (item 1 above)
= Ceiling on remaining deductions
– Deductions allowable if the activity were not a hobby (item 2 above), *limited* to the aforementioned ceiling
= Balance of zero

Thus, deductions are permitted to exceed gross income only for item 1 deductions. If this should occur, then none of the item 2 amounts are deductible. Also note that the item 2 amounts are subject to the 2% floor on miscellaneous itemized deductions in Sec. 67.

§ 183. Activities not engaged in for profit

(a) General rule.—In the case of an activity engaged in by an individual or an S corporation, if such activity is not engaged in for profit, no deduction attributable to such activity shall be allowed under this chapter except as provided in this section.

(b) Deductions allowable.—In the case of an activity not engaged in for profit to which subsection (a) applies, there shall be allowed—

(1) the deductions which would be allowable under this chapter for the taxable year without regard to whether or not such activity is engaged in for profit, and

(2) a deduction equal to the amount of the deductions which would be allowable under this chapter for the taxable year only if such activity were engaged in for profit, but only to the extent that the gross income derived from such activity for the taxable year exceeds the deductions allowable by reason of paragraph (1).

(c) Activity not engaged in for profit defined.—For purposes of this section, the term "activity not engaged in for profit" means any activity other than one with respect to which deductions are allowable for the taxable year under section 162 or under paragraph (1) or (2) of section 212.

(d) Presumption.—If the gross income derived from an activity for 3 or more of the taxable years in the period of 5 consecutive taxable years which ends with the taxable year exceeds the deductions attributable to such activity (determined without regard to whether or not such activity is engaged in for profit), then, unless the Secretary establishes to the contrary, such activity shall be presumed for purposes of this chapter for such taxable year to be an activity engaged in for profit. In the case of an activity which consists in major part of the breeding, training, showing, or racing of horses, the preceding sentence shall be applied by substituting "2" for "3" and "7" for "5".

(e) Special rule.—

(1) In general.—A determination as to whether the presumption provided by subsection (d) applies with respect to any activity shall, if the taxpayer so elects, not be made before the close of the fourth taxable year (sixth taxable year, in the case of an activity described in the last sentence of such subsection) following the taxable year in which the taxpayer first engages in the activity. For purposes of the preceding sentence, a taxpayer shall be treated as not having engaged in an activity during any taxable year beginning before January 1, 1970.

(2) Initial period.—If the taxpayer makes an election under paragraph (1), the presumption provided by subsection (d) shall apply to each taxable year in the 5-taxable year (or 7-taxable year) period beginning with the taxable year in which the taxpayer first engages in the activity, if the gross income derived from the activity for 3 (or 2 if applicable) or more of the taxable years in such period exceeds the deductions attributable to the activity (determined without regard to whether or not the activity is engaged in for profit).

(3) Election.—An election under paragraph (1) shall be made at such time and manner, and subject to such terms and conditions, as the Secretary may prescribe.

(4) Time for assessing deficiency attributable to activity.—If a taxpayer makes an election under paragraph (1) with respect to an activity, the statutory period for the assessment of any deficiency attributable to such activity shall not expire before the expiration of 2 years after the date prescribed by law (determined without extensions) for filing the return of tax under chapter 1 for the last taxable year in the period of 5 taxable years (or 7 taxable years) to which the election relates. Such deficiency may be assessed notwithstanding the provisions of any law or rule of law which would otherwise prevent such an assessment.

* * *

§ 190. Expenditures to remove architectural and transportation barriers to the handicapped and elderly

(a) Treatment as expenses.—

(1) In general.—A taxpayer may elect to treat qualified architectural and transportation barrier removal expenses which are paid or incurred by him during the taxable year as expenses which are not chargeable to capital account. The expenditures so treated shall be allowed as a deduction.

(2) Election.—An election under paragraph (1) shall be made at such time and in such manner as the Secretary prescribes by regulations.

(b) Definitions.—For purposes of this section—

(1) Architectural and transportation barrier removal expenses.—The term "architectural and transportation barrier removal expenses" means an expenditure for the purpose of making any facility or public transportation vehicle owned or leased by the taxpayer for use in connection with his trade or business more accessible to, and usable by, handicapped and elderly individuals.

(2) Qualified architectural and transportation barrier removal expense.—The term "qualified architectural and transportation barrier removal expense" means, with respect to any such facility or public transportation vehicle, an architectural or transportation barrier removal expense with respect to which the taxpayer establishes, to the satisfaction of the Secretary, that the resulting removal of any such barrier meets the standards promulgated by the Secretary with the concurrence of the Architectural and Transportation Barriers Compliance Board and set forth in regulations prescribed by the Secretary.

(3) Handicapped individual.—The term "handicapped individual" means any individual who has a physical or mental disability (including, but not limited to, blindness or deafness) which for such individual constitutes or results in a functional limitation to employment, or who has any physical or mental impairment (including, but not limited to, a sight or hearing impairment) which substantially limits one or more major life activities of such individual.

(c) Limitation.—The deduction allowed by subsection (a) for any taxable year shall not exceed $15,000.

* * *

§ 194. Treatment of reforestation expenditures

(a) Allowance of deduction.—In the case of any qualified timber property with respect to which the taxpayer has made (in accordance with regulations prescribed by the Secretary) an election under this subsection, the taxpayer shall be entitled to a deduction with respect to the amortization of the amortizable basis of qualified timber property based on a period of 84 months. Such amortization deduction shall be an amount, with respect to each month of such period within the taxable year, equal to the amortizable basis at the end of such month divided by the number of months (including the month for which the deduction is computed) remaining in the period. Such amortizable basis at the end of the month shall be computed without regard to the amortization deduction for such month. The 84-month period shall begin on the first day of the first month of the second half of the taxable year in which the amortizable basis is acquired.

(b) Treatment as expenses.—

(1) Election to treat certain reforestation expenditures as expenses.—

(A) In general.—In the case of any qualified timber property with respect to which the taxpayer has made (in accordance with regulations prescribed by the Secretary) an election under this subsection, the taxpayer shall treat reforestation expenditures which are paid or incurred during the taxable year with respect to such property as an expense which is not chargeable to capital account. The reforestation expenditures so treated shall be allowed as a deduction.

(B) Dollar limitation.—The aggregate amount of reforestation expenditures which may be taken into account under subparagraph (A) with respect to each qualified timber property for any taxable year shall not exceed—

(i) except as provided in clause (ii) or (iii), $10,000,

(ii) in the case of a separate return by a married individual (as defined in section 7703), $5,000, and

(iii) in the case of a trust, zero.

(2) Allocation of dollar limit.—

(A) Controlled group.—For purposes of applying the dollar limitation under paragraph (1)—

(i) all component members of a controlled group shall be treated as one taxpayer, and

(ii) the Secretary shall, under regulations prescribed by him, apportion such dollar limitation among the component members of such controlled group.

For purposes of the preceding sentence, the term "controlled group" has the meaning assigned to it by section 1563(a), except that the phrase "more than 50 percent" shall be substituted for the phrase "at least 80 percent" each place it appears in section 1563(a)(1).

(B) Partnerships and S corporations.—In the case of a partnership, the dollar limitation contained in paragraph (1)(B) shall apply with respect to the partnership and with respect to each partner. A similar rule shall apply in the case of an S corporation and its shareholders.

(c) Definitions and special rule.—For purposes of this section—

(1) Qualified timber property.—The term "qualified timber property" means a woodlot or other site located in the United States which will contain trees in significant commercial quantities and which is held by the taxpayer for the planting, cultivating, caring for, and cutting of trees for sale or use in the commercial production of timber products.

(2) Amortizable basis.—The term "amortizable basis" means that portion of the basis of the qualified timber property attributable to reforestation expenditures which have not been taken into account under subsection (b).

(3) Reforestation expenditures.—

(A) In general.—The term "reforestation expenditures" means direct costs incurred in connection with forestation or reforestation by planting or artificial or natural seeding, including costs—

(i) for the preparation of the site:

(ii) of seeds or seedlings; and

(iii) for labor and tools, including depreciation of equipment such as tractors, trucks, tree planters, and similar machines used in planting or seeding.

(B) Cost-sharing programs.—Reforestation expenditures shall not include any expenditures for which the taxpayer has been reimbursed under any governmental reforestation cost-sharing program unless the amounts reimbursed have been included in the gross income of the taxpayer.

(4) Treatment of trusts and estates.—The aggregate amount of reforestation expenditures incurred by any trust or estate shall be apportioned between the income beneficiaries and the fiduciary under regulations prescribed by the Secretary. Any amount so apportioned to a beneficiary shall be taken into account as expenditures incurred by such beneficiary in applying this section to such beneficiary.

(5) Application with other deductions.—No deduction shall be allowed under any other provision of this chapter with respect to any expenditure with respect to which a deduction is allowed or allowable under this section to the taxpayer.

(d) Life tenant and remainderman.—In the case of property held by one person for life with remainder to another person, the deduction under this section shall be computed as if the life tenant were the absolute owner of the property and shall be allowed to the life tenant.

* * *

Editorial Summary

Investigation Expenses versus Start-up Expenses

Subchapter B of Chapter 1 (Sec. 195)

Investigation expenses associated with an ongoing trade or business provide a greater tax benefit than those incurred associated with a business in which the taxpayer is not already involved. In the former situation, the deduction of the investigation expenses incurred is deductible under Sec. 162. In the latter situation, the only deduction opportunity is under Sec. 195.

If the taxpayer is already in a business that is the same as, or similar to the one being investigated, beneficial tax treatment results. If the taxpayer acquires the business being investigated, a full deduction is allowed for the investigation expenses incurred. Likewise, if the taxpayer does not acquire the business being investigated, a full deduction still is allowed for the investigation expenses incurred. The investigation expenses qualify for deduction treatment under Sec. 162(a).

Start-up expenses produce different tax consequences. If the taxpayer does not acquire the business under consideration, no deduction is permitted for the related expenses incurred. Conversely, if the taxpayer does acquire the business under consideration, the related expenses incurred must be capitalized. An election can be made to deduct up to $5,000 of the start-up costs in the year in which business is begun [Sec. 195(b)]. The full $5,000 deduction is available only to small businesses as defined in Sec. 195(b)(1)(A) with the balance of the start-up expenses being amortized over a 180-month period beginning in the month the business begins. [Sec. 195(b)(1)(B)].

The Small Business Jobs Act of 2010 increases the $5,000 and $50,000 amounts to $10,000 and $60,000 respectively for 2010 (note the increase is only for 2010).

The reason for the difference in the tax treatment of investigation expenses and start-up costs is that Sec. 162, because a business already exists, provides the statutory authority for investigation expenses [excluding those that only satisfy the definition of start-up expenses under Sec. 195(c)(1)] whereas Sec. 195 provides the statutory authority for start-up expenses.

§ 195. Start-up expenditures

(a) Capitalization of expenditures.—Except as otherwise provided in this section, no deduction shall be allowed for start-up expenditures.

(b) Election to deduct.—

(1) Allowance of deduction.—If a taxpayer elects the application of this subsection with respect to any start-up expenditures—

(A) the taxpayer shall be allowed a deduction for the taxable year in which the active trade or business begins in an amount equal to the lesser of—

(i) the amount of start-up expenditures with respect to the active trade or business, or

(ii) $5,000, reduced (but not below zero) by the amount by which such start-up expenditures exceed $50,000, and

(B) the remainder of such start-up expenditures shall be allowed as a deduction ratably over the 180-month period beginning with the month in which the active trade or business begins.

(2) Dispositions before close of amortization period.—In any case in which a trade or business is completely disposed of by the taxpayer before the end of the period to which paragraph (1) applies, any deferred expenses attributable to such trade or business which were not allowed as a deduction by reason of this section may be deducted to the extent allowable under section 165.

(3) Special rule for taxable years beginning in 2010.—In the case of a taxable year beginning in 2010, paragraph (1)(A)(ii) shall be applied—

(A) by substituting "$10,000" for "$5,000", and

(B) by substituting "$60,000" for "$50,000".

(c) **Definitions.**—For purposes of this section—

(1) **Start-up expenditures.**—The term "start-up expenditure" means any amount—

(A) paid or incurred in connection with—

(i) investigating the creation or acquisition of an active trade or business, or

(ii) creating an active trade or business, or

(iii) any activity engaged in for profit and for the production of income before the date on which the active trade or business begins, in anticipation of such activity becoming an active trade or business, and

(B) which, if paid or incurred in connection with the operation of an existing active trade or business (in the same field as the trade or business referred to in subparagraph (A)), would be allowable as a deduction for the taxable year in which paid or incurred.

The term "start-up expenditure" does not include any amount with respect to which a deduction is allowable under section 163(a), 164, or 174.

(2) **Beginning of trade or business.**—

(A) **In general.**—Except as provided in subparagraph (B), the determination of when an active trade or business begins shall be made in accordance with such regulations as the Secretary may prescribe.

(B) **Acquired trade or business.**—An acquired active trade or business shall be treated as beginning when the taxpayer acquires it.

(d) **Election.**—

(1) **Time for making election.**—An election under subsection (b) shall be made not later than the time prescribed by law for filing the return for the taxable year in which the trade or business begins (including extensions thereof).

(2) **Scope of election.**—The period selected under subsection (b) shall be adhered to in computing taxable income for the taxable year for which the election is made and all subsequent taxable years.

§ 196. Deduction for certain unused business credits

(a) **Allowance of deduction.**—If any portion of the qualified business credits determined for any taxable year has not, after the application of section 38(c), been allowed to the taxpayer as a credit under section 38 for any taxable year, an amount equal to the credit not so allowed shall be allowed to the taxpayer as a deduction for the first taxable year following the last taxable year for which such credit could, under section 39, have been allowed as credit.

(b) **Taxpayer's dying or ceasing to exist.**—If a taxpayer dies or ceases to exist before the first taxable year following the last taxable year for which the qualified business credits could, under section 39, have been allowed as a credit, the amount described in subsection (a) (or the proper portion thereof) shall, under regulations prescribed by the Secretary, be allowed to the taxpayer as a deduction for the taxable year in which such death or cessation occurs.

(c) **Qualified business credits.**—For purposes of this section, the term "qualified business credits" means—

(1) the investment credit determined under section 46 (but only to the extent attributable to property the basis of which is reduced by section 50(c)),

(2) the work opportunity credit determined under section 51(a),

(3) the alcohol fuels credit determined under section 40(a),

(4) the research credit determined under section 41(a) (other than such credit determined under section 280C(c)(3)) for taxable years beginning after December 31, 1988,

(5) the enhanced oil recovery credit determined under section 43(a),

(6) the empowerment zone employment credit determined under section 1396(a),

(7) the Indian employment credit determined under section 45A(a),

(8) the employer social security credit determined under section 45B(a),

(9) the new markets tax credit determined under section 45D(a),

(10) the small employer pension startup cost credit determined under section 45E(a),

(11) the biodiesel fuel credit determined under section 40A(a),

(12) the low sulfur diesel fuel production credit determined under section 45H(a),

(13) the new energy efficient home credit determined under section 45L(a), and

(14) the small employer health insurance credit determined under section 45R(a).

(d) Special rule for investment tax credit and research credit.—Subsection (a) shall be applied by substituting "an amount equal to 50 percent of" for "an amount equal to" in the case of—

(1) the investment credit determined under section 46 (other than the rehabilitation credit), and

(2) the research credit determined under section 41(a) for a taxable year beginning before January 1, 1990.

Editorial Summary

Amortization of Intangibles

Subchapter B of Chapter 1 (Sec. 197)

Prior to the effect of the Revenue Reconciliation Act of 1993 (RRA of 1993), intangibles with a definite limited life (e.g., patents, franchises, and covenants not to compete) were eligible for amortization whereas intangibles with an indefinite limited life (e.g., goodwill) could not be amortized. The amortization period was the identified life (e.g., a 5-year covenant was amortized over a 5-year period). Thus, in acquiring a business, the purchaser preferred that excess amounts not paid for identifiable assets be associated with a covenant rather than with goodwill. Such an allocation possessed both legal and tax benefits.

RRA of 1993 resulted in the classification of most intangibles as Sec. 197 intangibles [see Sec. 197(d)]. Section 197 intangibles are amortized over a statutory 15-year period [see Sec. 197(a)] regardless of the actual life of the asset (e. g., a 5-year covenant must be amortized over the statutory 15-year period). Thus, the aforementioned purchaser of a business would have no tax benefit in allocating the excess purchase price to a covenant rather than goodwill since both would be amortized over 15 years.

Certain self-created assets [see Sec. 197(c)(2)] are not Sec. 197 intangibles. In addition, certain assets are specifically excluded from being Sec. 197 intangibles [see Sec. 197 (e)]. See Sec. 167(f) for the related depreciation provision for certain property excluded from Sec. 197 treatment.

§ 197. Amortization of goodwill and certain other intangibles

(a) General rule.—A taxpayer shall be entitled to an amortization deduction with respect to any amortizable section 197 intangible. The amount of such deduction shall be determined by amortizing the adjusted basis (for purposes of determining gain) of such intangible ratably over the 15-year period beginning with the month in which such intangible was acquired.

(b) No other depreciation or amortization deduction allowable.—Except as provided in subsection (a), no depreciation or amortization deduction shall be allowable with respect to any amortizable section 197 intangible.

(c) Amortizable section 197 intangible.—For purposes of this section—

(1) In general.—Except as otherwise provided in this section, the term "amortizable section 197 intangible" means any section 197 intangible—

(A) which is acquired by the taxpayer after the date of the enactment of this section, and

(B) which is held in connection with the conduct of a trade or business or an activity described in section 212.

(2) Exclusion of self-created intangibles, etc.—The term "amortizable section 197 intangible" shall not include any section 197 intangible—

(A) which is not described in subparagraph (D), (E), or (F) of subsection (d)(1), and

(B) which is created by the taxpayer.

This paragraph shall not apply if the intangible is created in connection with a transaction (or series of related transactions) involving the acquisition of assets constituting a trade or business or substantial portion thereof.

(3) Anti-churning rules.—

For exclusion of intangibles acquired in certain transactions, see subsection (f)(9).

(d) Section 197 intangible.—For purposes of this section—

(1) In general.—Except as otherwise provided in this section, the term "section 197 intangible" means—

(A) goodwill,

(B) going concern value,

(C) any of the following intangible items:

(i) workforce in place including its composition and terms and conditions (contractual or otherwise) of its employment,

(ii) business books and records, operating systems, or any other information base (including lists or other information with respect to current or prospective customers),

(iii) any patent, copyright, formula, process, design, pattern, know how, format, or other similar item,

(iv) any customer-based intangible,

(v) any supplier-based intangible, and

(vi) any other similar item

(D) any license, permit, or other right granted by a governmental unit or an agency or instrumentality thereof,

(E) any covenant not to compete (or other arrangement to the extent such arrangement has substantially the same effect as a covenant not to compete) entered into in connection with an acquisition (directly or indirectly) of an interest in a trade or business or substantial portion thereof, and

(F) any franchise, trademark, or trade name.

(2) Customer-based intangible.—

(A) In general.—The term "customer-based intangible" means—

(i) composition of market,

(ii) market share, and

(iii) any other value resulting from future provision of goods or services pursuant to relationships (contractual or otherwise) in the ordinary course of business with customers.

(B) Special rule for financial institutions.—In the case of a financial institution, the term "customer-based intangible" includes deposit base and similar items.

(3) Supplier-based intangible.—The term "supplier-based intangible" means any value resulting from future acquisitions of goods or services pursuant to relationships (contractual or otherwise) in the ordinary course of business with suppliers of goods or services to be used or sold by the taxpayer.

(e) Exceptions.—For purposes of this section, the term "section 197 intangible" shall not include any of the following:

(1) Financial interests.—Any interest—

(A) in a corporation, partnership, trust, or estate, or

(B) under an existing futures contract, foreign currency contract, notional principal contract, or other similar financial contract.

(2) Land.—Any interest in land.

(3) Computer software.—

(A) In general.—Any—

(i) computer software which is readily available for purchase by the general public, is subject to a nonexclusive license, and has not been substantially modified, and

(ii) other computer software which is not acquired in a transaction (or series of related transactions) involving the acquisition of assets constituting a trade or business or substantial portion thereof.

(B) Computer software defined.—For purposes of subparagraph (A), the term "computer software" means any program designed to cause a computer to perform a desired function. Such term shall not include any data base or similar item unless the data base or item is in the public domain and is incidental to the operation of otherwise qualifying computer software.

(4) Certain interests or rights acquired separately.—Any of the following not acquired in a transaction (or series of related transactions) involving the acquisition of assets constituting a trade business or substantial portion thereof:

(A) Any interest in a film, sound recording, video tape, book, or similar property.

(B) Any right to receive tangible property or services under a contract or granted by a governmental unit or agency or instrumentality thereof.

(C) Any interest in a patent or copyright.

(D) To the extent provided in regulations, any right under a contract (or granted by a governmental unit or an agency or instrumentality thereof) if such right—

(i) has a fixed duration of less than 15 years, or

(ii) is fixed as to amount and, without regard to this section, would be recoverable under a method similar to the unit-of-production method.

(5) Interests under leases and debt instruments.—Any interest under—

(A) an existing lease of tangible property, or

(B) except as provided in subsection (d)(2)(B), any existing indebtedness.

(6) Mortgage servicing.—Any right to service indebtedness which is secured by residential real property unless such right is acquired in a transaction (or series of related transactions) involving the acquisition of assets (other than rights described in this paragraph) constituting a trade or business or substantial portion thereof.

(7) Certain transaction costs.—Any fees for professional services, and any transaction costs, incurred by parties to a transaction with respect to which any portion of the gain or loss is not recognized under part III of subchapter C.

(f) Special rules.—

(1) Treatment of certain dispositions, etc.—

(A) In general.—If there is a disposition of any amortizable section 197 intangible acquired in a transaction or series of related transactions (or any such intangible becomes worthless) and one or more other amortizable section 197 intangibles acquired in such transaction or series of related transactions are retained—

(i) no loss shall be recognized by reason of such disposition (or such worthlessness), and

(ii) appropriate adjustments to the adjusted bases of such retained intangibles shall be made for any loss not recognized under clause (i).

(B) Special rule for covenants not to compete.—In the case of any section 197 intangible which is a covenant not to compete (or other arrangement) described in subsection (d)(1)(E), in no event shall such covenant or other arrangement be treated as disposed of (or becoming worthless) before the disposition of the entire interest described in such subsection in connection with which such covenant (or other arrangement) was entered into.

(C) Special rule.—All persons treated as a single taxpayer under section 41(f)(1) shall be so treated for purposes of this paragraph.

(2) Treatment of certain transfers.—

(A) In general.—In the case of any section 197 intangible transferred in a transaction described in subparagraph (B), the transferee shall be treated as the transferor for purposes of applying this section with respect to so much of the adjusted basis in the hands of the transferee as does not exceed the adjusted basis in the hands of the transferor.

(B) Transactions covered.—The transactions described in this subparagraph are—

(i) any transaction described in section 332, 351, 361, 721, 731, 1031, or 1033, and

(ii) any transaction between members of the same affiliated group during any taxable year for which a consolidated return is made by such group.

(3) Treatment of amounts paid pursuant to covenants not to compete, etc.—Any amount paid or incurred pursuant to a covenant or arrangement referred to in subsection (d)(1)(E) shall be treated as an amount chargeable to capital account.

(4) Treatment of franchises, etc.—

(A) Franchise.—The term "franchise" has the meaning given to such term by section 1253(b)(1).

(B) Treatment of renewals.—Any renewal of a franchise, trademark, or trade name (or of a license, a permit, or other right referred to in subsection (d)(1)(D)) shall be treated as an acquisition. The preceding sentence shall only apply with respect to costs incurred in connection with such renewal.

(C) Certain amounts not taken into account.—Any amount to which section 1253(d)(1) applies shall not be taken into account under this section.

(5) Treatment of certain reinsurance transactions.—In the case of any amortizable section 197 intangible resulting from an assumption reinsurance transaction, the amount taken into account as the adjusted basis of such intangible under this section shall be the excess of—

(A) the amount paid or incurred by the acquirer under the assumption reinsurance transaction, over

(B) the amount required to be capitalized under section 848 in connection with such transaction.

Subsection (b) shall not apply to any amount required to be capitalized under section 848.

(6) Treatment of certain subleases.—For purposes of this section, a sublease shall be treated in the same manner as a lease of the underlying property involved.

(7) Treatment as depreciable.—For purposes of this chapter, any amortizable section 197 intangible shall be treated as property which is of a character subject to the allowance for depreciation provided in section 167.

(8) Treatment of certain increments in value.—This section shall not apply to any increment in value if, without regard to this section, such increment is properly taken into account in determining the cost of property which is not a section 197 intangible.

(9) Anti-churning rules.—For purposes of this section—

(A) In general.—The term "amortizable section 197 intangible" shall not include any section 197 intangible which is described in subparagraph (A) or (B) of subsection (d)(1) (or for which depreciation or amortization would not have been allowable but for this section) and which is acquired by the taxpayer after the date of the enactment of this section, if—

(i) the intangible was held or used at any time on or after July 25, 1991, and on or before such date of enactment by the taxpayer or a related person,

(ii) the intangible was acquired from a person who held such intangible at any time on or after July 25, 1991, and on or before such date of enactment, and, as part of the transaction, the user of such intangible does not change, or

(iii) the taxpayer grants the right to use such intangible to a person (or a person related to such person) who held or used such intangible at any time on or after July 25, 1991, and on or before such date of enactment.

For purposes of this subparagraph, the determination of whether the user of property changes as part of a transaction shall be determined in accordance with regulations prescribed by the Secretary. For purposes of this subparagraph, deductions allowable under section 1253(d) shall be treated as deductions allowable for amortization.

(B) Exception where gain recognized.—If—

(i) subparagraph (A) would not apply to an intangible acquired by the taxpayer but for the last sentence of subparagraph (C)(i), and

(ii) the person from whom the taxpayer acquired the intangible elects, notwithstanding any other provision of this title—

(I) to recognize gain on the disposition of the intangible, and

(II) to pay a tax on such gain which, when added to any other income tax on such gain under this title, equals such gain multiplied by the highest rate of income tax applicable to such person under this title,

then subparagraph (A) shall apply to the intangible only to the extent that the taxpayer's adjusted basis in the intangible exceeds the gain recognized under clause (ii)(I).

(C) Related person defined.—For purposes of this paragraph—

(i) Related person.—A person (hereinafter in this paragraph referred to as the "related person") is related to any person if—

(I) the related person bears a relationship to such person specified in section 267(b) or section 707(b)(1), or

(II) the related person and such person are engaged in trades or businesses under common control (within the meaning of subparagraphs (A) and (B) of section 41(f)(1)).

For purposes of subclause (I), in applying section 267(b) or 707(b)(1), "20 percent" shall be substituted for "50 percent."

(ii) Time for making determination.—A person shall be treated as related to another person if such relationship exists immediately before or immediately after the acquisition of the intangible involved.

(D) Acquisitions by reason of death.—Subparagraph (A) shall not apply to the acquisition of any property by the taxpayer if the basis of the property in the hands of the taxpayer is determined under section 1014(a).

(E) Special rule for partnerships.—With respect to any increase in the basis of partnership property under section 732, 734, or 743, determinations under this paragraph shall be made at the partner level and each partner shall be treated as having owned and used such partner's proportionate share of the partnership assets.

(F) Anti-abuse rules.—The term "amortizable section 197 intangible" does not include any section 197 intangible acquired in a transaction, one of the principal purposes of which is to avoid the requirement of subsection (c)(1) that the intangible be acquired after the date of the enactment of this section or to avoid the provisions of subparagraph (A).

(10) Tax-exempt use property subject to lease.—In the case of any section 197 intangible which would be tax-exempt use property as defined in subsection (h) of section 168 if such section applied to such intangible, the amortization period under this section shall not be less than 125 percent of the lease term (within the meaning of section 168(i)(3)).

(g) Regulations.—The Secretary shall prescribe such regulations as may be appropriate to carry out the purposes of this section, including such regulations as may be appropriate to prevent avoidance of the purposes of this section through related persons or otherwise.

* * *

Editorial Summary

Domestic Production Activities Deduction (DPAD)

Subchapter B of Chapter 1 (Sec. 199)

Section 199 was enacted as the result of a trade dispute with our trading partners. An export incentive, the extraterritorial regime (ETI), was found to be an illegal export subsidiary by the World Trade Organization (WTO). So it was necessary for this provision to be repealed by Congress. In doing so in 2004, rather than immediately repealing the ETI, Congress did so using a phaseout approach.

Given major consideration to replace the ETI in terms of the economic effect of its repeal was a decrease in the corporate income tax rate. Proposals ranged from one to one and one-half percentage points. Rather than adopting this approach, Congress decided to follow the stealth approach by enacting Sec. 199 (i.e., with the impact on the less visible tax base rather than on the more visible tax rates).

In enacting the Domestic Production Activities Deduction, Congress took a novel approach. Section 199 provides for deduction treatment. However, the calculation of DPAD is dependent on an income measure [Sec. 199(a)]. In addition, Congress recognized the negative direct economic effect on domestic jobs of the outsourcing of jobs to foreign countries. Therefore, the calculated amount of DPAD is limited by the amount of domestic production W-2 wages [Sec. 199(b)].

The statutory rate to be used in calculating DPAD is 9% [Sec. 199(a)(1)]. However, Congress used a phase-in approach with the 9% rate not being effective until 2010 [Sec. 199(a)(2)].

§ 199. Income attributable to domestic production activities.

(a) Allowance of deduction.—

(1) In general.—There shall be allowed as a deduction an amount equal to 9 percent of the lesser of—

(A) the qualified production activities income of the taxpayer for the taxable year, or

(B) taxable income (determined without regard to this section) for the taxable year.

(2) Phasein.—In the case of any taxable year beginning after 2004 and before 2010, paragraph (1) shall be applied by substituting for the percentage contained therein the transition percentage determined under the following table:

For taxable years beginning in:	The transition percentage is:
2005 or 2006	3
2007, 2008, or 2009	6

(b) Deduction limited to wages paid.—

(1) In general.—The amount of the deduction allowable under subsection (a) for any taxable year shall not exceed 50 percent of the W-2 wages of the taxpayer for the taxable year.

(2) W-2 Wages.— For purposes of this section—

(A) In general.—The term "W-2 wages" means, with respect to any person for any taxable year of such person, the sum of the amounts described in paragraphs (3) and (8) of section 6051(a) paid by such person with respect to employment of employees by such person during the calendar year ending during such taxable year.

(B) Limitation to wages attributable to domestic production.—Such term shall not include any amount which is not properly allocable to domestic production gross receipts for purposes of subsection (c)(1).

(C) Return requirement.—Such term shall not include any amount which is not properly included in a return filed with the Social Security Administration on or before the 60th day after the due date (including extensions) for such return.

(D) Special rule for qualified film.—In the case of a qualified film, such term shall include compensation for services performed in the United States by actors, production personnel, directors, and producers.

(3) Acquisitions and dispositions.—The Secretary shall provide for the application of this subsection in cases where the taxpayer acquires, or disposes of, the major portion of a trade or business or the major portion of a separate unit of a trade or business during the taxable year.

(c) Qualified production activities income.—For purposes of this section—

(1) In general.—The term "qualified production activities income" for any taxable year means an amount equal to the excess (if any) of—

(A) the taxpayer's domestic production gross receipts for such taxable year, over

(B) the sum of—

(i) the cost of goods sold that are allocable to such receipts, and

(ii) other expenses, losses, or deductions (other than the deduction allowed under this section), which are properly allocable to such receipts.

(2) Allocation method.—The Secretary shall prescribe rules for the proper allocation of items described in paragraph (1) for purposes of determining qualified production activities income. Such rules shall provide for the proper allocation of items whether or not such items are directly allocable to domestic production gross receipts.

(3) Special rules for determining costs.—

(A) In general.—For purposes of determining costs under clause (i) of paragraph (1)(B), any item or service brought into the United States shall be treated as acquired by purchase, and its cost shall be treated as not less than its value immediately after it entered the United States. A similar rule shall apply in determining the adjusted basis of leased or rented property where the lease or rental gives rise to domestic production gross receipts.

(B) Exports for further manufacture.—In the case of any property described in subparagraph (A) that had been exported by the taxpayer for further manufacture, the increase in cost or adjusted basis under subparagraph (A) shall not exceed the difference between the value of the property when exported and the value of the property when brought back into the United States after the further manufacture.

(4) Domestic production gross receipts.—

(A) In general.—The term "domestic production gross receipts" means the gross receipts of the taxpayer which are derived from—

(i) any lease, rental, license, sale, exchange, or other disposition of—

(I) qualifying production property which was manufactured, produced, grown, or extracted by the taxpayer in whole or in significant part within the United States,

(II) any qualified film produced by the taxpayer, or

(III) electricity, natural gas, or potable water produced by the taxpayer in the United States,

(ii) in the case of a taxpayer engaged in the active conduct of a construction trade or business, construction of real property performed in the United States by the taxpayer in the ordinary course of such trade or business, or

(iii) in the case of a taxpayer engaged in the active conduct of an engineering or architectural services trade or business, engineering or architectural services performed in the United States by the taxpayer in the ordinary course of such trade or business with respect to the construction of real property in the United States.

(B) Exceptions.—Such term shall not include gross receipts of the taxpayer which are derived from—

(i) the sale of food and beverages prepared by the taxpayer at a retail establishment,

(ii) the transmission or distribution of electricity, natural gas, or potable water, or

(iii) the lease, rental, license, sale, exchange, or other disposition of land.

(C) Special rule for certain government contracts.—Gross receipts derived from the manufacture or production of any property described in subparagraph (A)(i)(I) shall be treated as meeting the requirement of subparagraph (A)(i) if—

(i) such property is manufactured or produced by the taxpayer pursuant to a contract with the Federal Government, and

(ii) the Federal Acquisition Regulation requires that title or risk of loss with respect to such property be transferred to the Federal Government before the manufacture or production of such property is complete.

(D) Partnerships owned by expanded affiliated groups.—For purposes of this paragraph, if all of the interests in the capital and profits of a partnership are owned by members of a single expanded affiliated group at all times during the taxable year of such partnership, the partnership and all members of such group shall be treated as a single taxpayer during such period.

(5) Qualifying production property.—The term "qualifying production property" means—

(A) tangible personal property,

(B) any computer software, and

(C) any property described in section 168(f)(4).

(6) Qualified film.—The term "qualified film" means any property described in section 168(f)(3) if not less than 50 percent of the total compensation relating to the production of such property is compensation for services performed in the United States by actors, production personnel, directors, and producers. Such term does not include property with respect to which records are required to be maintained under section 2257 of title 18, United States Code. A qualified film shall include any copyrights, trademarks, or other intangibles with respect to such film. The methods and means of distributing a qualified film shall not affect the availability of the deduction under this section.

(7) Related persons.—

(A) In general.—The term "domestic production gross receipts" shall not include any gross receipts of the taxpayer derived from property leased, licensed, or rented by the taxpayer for use by any related person.

(B) Related person.—For purposes of subparagraph (A), a person shall be treated as related to another person if such persons are treated as a single employer under subsection (a) or (b) of section 52 or subsection (m) or (o) of section 414, except that determinations under subsections (a) and (b) of section 52 shall be made without regard to section 1563(b).

(d) Definitions and special rules.—

(1) Application of section to pass-thru entities.—

(A) Partnerships and S corporations.—In the case of a partnership or S corporation—

(i) this section shall be applied at the partner or shareholder level,

(ii) each partner or shareholder shall take into account such person's allocable share of each item described in subparagraph (A) or (B) of subsection (c)(1) (determined without regard to whether the items described in such subparagraph (A) exceed the items described in such subparagraph (B)),

(iii) each partner or shareholder shall be treated for purposes of subsection (b) as having W-2 wages for the taxable year in an amount equal to such person's allocable share of the W-2 wages of the partnership or S corporation for the taxable year (as determined under regulations prescribed by the Secretary), and

(iv) in the case of each partner of a partnership, or shareholder of an S corporation, who owns (directly or indirectly) at least 20 percent of the capital interest in such partnership or of the stock of such S corporation—

(I) such partner or shareholder shall be treated as having engaged directly in any film produced by such partnership or S corporation, and

(II) such partnership or S corporation shall be treated as having engaged directly in any film produced by such partner or shareholder.

(B) Trusts and estates.—In the case of a trust or estate—

(i) the items referred to in subparagraph (A)(ii) (as determined therein) and the W-2 wages of the trust or estate for the taxable year, shall be apportioned between the beneficiaries and the fiduciary (and among the beneficiaries) under regulations prescribed by the Secretary, and

(ii) for purposes of paragraph (2), adjusted gross income of the trust or estate shall be determined as provided in section 67(e) with the adjustments described in such paragraph.

(C) Regulations.—The Secretary may prescribe rules requiring or restricting the allocation of items and wages under this paragraph and may prescribe such reporting requirements as the Secretary determines appropriate

(2) Application to individuals.—In the case of an individual, subsection (a)(1)(B) shall be applied by substituting "adjusted gross income" for "taxable income." For purposes of the preceding sentence, adjusted gross income shall be determined—

(A) after application of sections 86, 135, 137, 219, 221, 222, and 469, and

(B) without regard to this section.

(3) Agricultural and horticultural cooperatives.—

(A) Deduction allowed to patrons.—Any person who receives a qualified payment from a specified agricultural or horticultural cooperative shall be allowed for the taxable year in which such payment is received a deduction under subsection (a) equal to the portion of the deduction allowed under subsection (a) to such cooperative which is—

(i) allowed with respect to the portion of the qualified production activities income to which such payment is attributable, and

(ii) identified by such cooperative in a written notice mailed to such person during the payment period described in section 1382(d).

(B) Cooperative denied deduction for portion of qualified payments.—The taxable income of a specified agricultural or horticultural cooperative shall not be reduced under section 1382 by reason of that portion of any qualified payment as does not exceed the deduction allowable under subparagraph (A) with respect to such payment.

(C) Taxable income of cooperatives determined without regard to certain deductions. — For purposes of this section, the taxable income of a specified agricultural or horticultural cooperative shall be computed without regard to any deduction allowable under subsection (b) or (c) of section 1382 (relating to patronage dividends, per-unit retain allocations, and nonpatronage distributions).

(D) Special rule for marketing cooperatives.—For purposes of this section, a specified agricultural or horticultural cooperative described in subparagraph (F)(ii) shall be treated as having manufactured, produced, grown, or extracted in whole or significant part any qualifying production property marketed by the organization which its patrons have so manufactured, produced, grown, or extracted.

(E) Qualified payment.—For purposes of this paragraph, the term "qualified payment" means, with respect to any person, any amount which—

(i) is described in paragraph (1) or (3) of section 1385(a),

(ii) is received by such person from a specified agricultural or horticultural cooperative, and

(iii) is attributable to qualified production activities income with respect to which a deduction is allowed to such cooperative under subsection (a).

(F) Specified agricultural or horticultural cooperative.—For purposes of this paragraph, the term "specified agricultural or horticultural cooperative" means an organization to which part I of subchapter T applies which is engaged—

(i) in the manufacturing, production, growth, or extraction in whole or significant part of any agricultural or horticultural product, or

(ii) in the marketing of agricultural or horticultural products.

(4) Special rule for affiliated groups.—

(A) In general.—All members of an expanded affiliated group shall be treated as a single corporation for purposes of this section.

(B) Expanded affiliated group.—For purposes of this section, the term "expanded affiliated group" means an affiliated group as defined in section 1504(a), determined—

(i) by substituting "more than 50 percent" for "at least 80 percent" each place it appears, and

(ii) without regard to paragraphs (2) and (4) of section 1504(b).

(C) Allocation of deduction.—Except as provided in regulations, the deduction under subsection (a) shall be allocated among the members of the expanded affiliated group in proportion to each member's respective amount (if any) of qualified production activities income.

(5) Trade or business requirement.—This section shall be applied by only taking into account items which are attributable to the actual conduct of a trade or business.

(6) Coordination with minimum tax.—For purposes of determining alternative minimum taxable income under section 55—

(A) qualified production activities income shall be determined without regard to any adjustments under sections 56 through 59, and

(B) in the case of a corporation, subsection (a)(1)(B) shall be applied by substituting "alternative minimum taxable income" for "taxable income."

(7) Unrelated business taxable income.—For purposes of determining the tax imposed by section 511, subsection (a)(1)(B) shall be applied by substituting "unrelated business taxable income" for "taxable income."

(8) Treatment of activities in Puerto Rico.—

(A) In general.—In the case of any taxpayer with gross receipts for any taxable year from sources within the Commonwealth of Puerto Rico, if all of such receipts are taxable under section 1 or 11 for such taxable year, then for purposes of determining the domestic production gross receipts of such taxpayer for such taxable year under subsection (c)(4), the term United States shall include the Commonwealth of Puerto Rico.

(B) Special rule for applying wage limitation.—In the case of any taxpayer described in subparagraph (A), for purposes of applying the limitation under subsection (b) for any taxable year, the determination of W-2 wages of such taxpayer shall be made without regard to any exclusion under section 3401(a)(8) for remuneration paid for services performed in Puerto Rico.

(C) Termination.—This paragraph shall apply only with respect to the first 8 taxable years of the taxpayer beginning after December 31, 2005, and before January 1, 2014.*

(9) Special rule for taxpayers with oil related qualified production activities income.—

(A) In general.—If a taxpayer has oil related qualified production activities income for any taxable year beginning after 2009, the amount otherwise allowable as a deduction under subsection (a) shall be reduced by 3 percent of the least of—

(i) the oil related qualified production activities income of the taxpayer for the taxable year,

(ii) the qualified production activities income of the taxpayer for the taxable year, or

(iii) taxable income (determined without regard to this section).

(B) Oil related qualified production activities income.—For purposes of this paragraph, the term "oil related qualified production activities income" means for any taxable year the qualified production activities income which is attributable to the production, refining, processing, transportation, or distribution of oil, gas, or any primary product thereof during such taxable year.

(C) Primary product.—For purposes of this paragraph, the term "primary product" has the same meaning as when used in section 927(a)(2)(C), as in effect before its repeal.

(10) Regulations.—The Secretary shall prescribe such regulations as are necessary to carry out the purposes of this section, including regulations which prevent more than 1 taxpayer from being allowed a deduction under this section with respect to any activity described in subsection (c)(4)(A)(i).

PART VII—ADDITIONAL ITEMIZED DEDUCTIONS FOR INDIVIDUALS

Editorial Summary

Itemized Deductions for Individuals

Subchapter B of Chapter 1 (Secs. 211–222)

Individual taxpayers are eligible for the deductions contained in Part VII (i.e., Secs. 211–222) and also for the deductions contained in Part VI (i.e., Secs. 161–199). The reason for the separate classification is that Part VII deductions apply only to the individual taxpayer whereas Part VI deductions apply to both the individual taxpayer and the corporate taxpayer.

See also the discussion under the Editorial Summary entitled Deductions which precedes Sec. 161.

§ 211. Allowance of deductions

In computing taxable income under section 63, there shall be allowed as deductions the items specified in this part, subject to the exceptions provided in part IX (section 261 and following, relating to items not deductible).

§ 212. Expenses for production of income

In the case of an individual, there shall be allowed as a deduction all the ordinary and necessary expenses paid or incurred during the taxable year—

(1) for the production or collection of income;

(2) for the management, conservation, or maintenance of property held for the production of income; or

(3) in connection with the determination, collection, or refund of any tax.

§ 213. Medical, dental, etc., expenses

(a) Allowance of deduction.—There shall be allowed as a deduction the expenses paid during the taxable year, not compensated for by insurance or otherwise, for medical care of the taxpayer, his spouse, or a dependent (as defined in section 152,

*Editorial comment: At the present time, this section has not been extended. There is pending legislation in the Senate, *The Tax Extenders Act of 2013 (S. 1859)*, that would extend Section 199(D)(8)(c) until January 1, 2015.

determined without regard to subsections (b)(1), (b)(2), and (d)(1)(B) thereof), to the extent that such expenses exceed 10 percent of adjusted gross income.

(b) Limitation with respect to medicine and drugs.—An amount paid during the taxable year for medicine or a drug shall be taken into account under subsection (a) only if such medicine or drug is a prescribed drug or is insulin.

(c) Special rule for decedents.—

(1) Treatment of expenses paid after death.—For purposes of subsection (a), expenses for the medical care of the taxpayer which are paid out of his estate during the 1-year period beginning with the day after the date of his death shall be treated as paid by the taxpayer at the time incurred.

(2) Limitation.—Paragraph (1) shall not apply if the amount paid is allowable under section 2053 as a deduction in computing the taxable estate of the decedent, but this paragraph shall not apply if (within the time and in the manner and form prescribed by the Secretary) there is filed—

(A) a statement that such amount has not been allowed as a deduction under section 2053, and

(B) a waiver of the right to have such amount allowed at any time as a deduction under section 2053.

(d) Definitions.—For purposes of this section—

(1) The term "medical care" means amounts paid—

(A) for the diagnosis, cure, mitigation, treatment, or prevention of disease, or for the purpose of affecting any structure or function of the body,

(B) for transportation primarily for and essential to medical care referred to in subparagraph (A),

(C) for qualified long-term care services (as defined in section 7702B(c)), or

(D) for insurance (including amounts paid as premiums under part B of title XVIII of the Social Security Act, relating to supplementary medical insurance for the aged) covering medical care referred to in subparagraphs (A) and (B) or for any qualified long-term care insurance contract (as defined in section 7702(B)(b)).

In the case of a qualified long-term care insurance contract (as defined in section 7702B(b)), only eligible long-term care premiums (as defined in paragraph (10)) shall be taken into account under subparagraph (D).

(2) Amounts paid for certain lodging away from home treated as paid for medical care.—Amounts paid for lodging (not lavish or extravagant under the circumstances) while away from home primarily for and essential to medical care referred to in paragraph (1)(A) shall be treated as amounts paid for medical care if—

(A) the medical care referred to in paragraph (1)(A) is provided by a physician in a licensed hospital (or in a medical care facility which is related to, or the equivalent of, a licensed hospital), and

(B) there is no significant element of personal pleasure, recreation, or vacation in the travel away from home.

The amount taken into account under the preceding sentence shall not exceed $50 for each night for each individual.

(3) Prescribed drug.—The term "prescribed drug" means a drug or biological which requires a prescription of a physician for its use by an individual.

(4) Physician.—The term "physician" has the meaning given to such term by section 1861(r) of the Social Security Act (42 U.S.C. 1395x(r)).

(5) Special rule in the case of child of divorced parents, etc.—Any child to whom section 152(e) applies shall be treated as a dependent of both parents for purposes of this section.

(6) In the case of an insurance contract under which amounts are payable for other than medical care referred to in subparagraphs (A), (B), and (C) of paragraph (1)—

(A) no amount shall be treated as paid for insurance to which paragraph (1) (D) applies unless the charge for such insurance is either separately stated in the contract, or furnished to the policyholder by the insurance company in a separate statement,

(B) the amount taken into account as the amount paid for such insurance shall not exceed such charge, and

(C) no amount shall be treated as paid for such insurance if the amount specified in the contract (or furnished to the policyholder by the insurance company in a separate statement) as the charge for such insurance is unreasonably large in relation to the total charges under the contract.

(7) Subject to the limitations of paragraph (6), premiums paid during the taxable year by a taxpayer before he attains the age of 65 for insurance covering medical care (within the meaning of sub paragraphs (A), (B), and (C) of paragraph (1)) for the taxpayer, his spouse, or a dependent after the taxpayer attains the age of 65 shall be treated as expenses paid during the taxable year for insurance which constitutes medical care if premiums for such insurance are payable (on a level payment basis) under the contract for a period of 10 years or more or until the year in which the taxpayer attains the age of 65 (but in no case for a period of less than 5 years).

(8) The determination of whether an individual is married at any time during the taxable year shall be made in accordance with the provisions of section 6013(d) (relating to determination of status as husband and wife).

(9) Cosmetic surgery.—

(A) In general.—The term "medical care" does not include cosmetic surgery or other similar procedures, unless the surgery or procedure is necessary to ameliorate a deformity arising from, or directly related to, a congenital abnormality, a personal injury resulting from an accident or trauma, or disfiguring disease.

(B) Cosmetic surgery defined.—For purposes of this paragraph, the term "cosmetic surgery" means any procedure which is directed at improving the patient's appearance and does not meaningfully promote the proper function of the body or prevent or treat illness or disease.

(10) Eligible long-term care premiums.—

(A) In general.—For purposes of this section, the term "eligible long-term care premiums" means the amount paid during a taxable year for any qualified long-term care insurance contract (as defined in section 7702B(b)) covering an individual, to the extent such amount does not exceed the limitation determined under the following table:

In the case of an individual with an attained age before the close of the taxable year of:	The limitation is:*
40 or less	$200
More than 40 but not more than 50	375
More than 50 but not more than 60	750
More than 60 but not more than 70	2,000
More than 70	2,500

(B) Indexing.—

(i) In general.—In the case of any taxable year beginning in a calendar year after 1997, each dollar amount contained in subparagraph (A) shall be increased by the medical care cost adjustment of such amount for such calendar year. If any increase determined under the preceding sentence is not a multiple of $10, such increase shall be rounded to the nearest multiple of $10.

(ii) Medical care cost adjustment.—For purposes of clause (i), the medical care cost adjustment for any calendar year is the percentage (if any) by which—

(I) the medical care component of the Consumer Price Index (as defined in section 1(f)(5)) August of the preceding calendar year, exceeds

(II) such component for August of 1996. The Secretary shall, in consultation with the Secretary of Health and Human Services, prescribe an adjustment which the Secretary determines is more appropriate for purposes of this paragraph than the adjustment described in the preceding sentence, and the adjustment so prescribed shall apply in lieu of the adjustment described in the preceding sentence.

(11) Certain payments to relatives treated as not paid for medical care.—An amount paid for a qualified long-term care service (as defined in section 7702B(c)) provided to an individual shall be treated as not paid for medical care if such service is provided—

(A) by the spouse of the individual or by a relative (directly or through a partnership, corporation, or other entity) unless the service is provided by a licensed professional with respect to such service, or

(B) by a corporation or partnership which is related (within the meaning of section 267(b) or 707 (b)) to the individual.

*Editorial comment: The indexed amounts for 2014 and 2013 are as follows:

Amount per Code	2014	2013
$ 200	$ 370	$ 360
375	700	680
750	1,400	1,360
2,000	3,720	3,640
2,500	4,660	4,550

For purposes of this paragraph, the term "relative" means an individual bearing a relationship to the individual which is described in any of subparagraphs (A) through (G) of section 152(d)(2). This paragraph shall not apply for purposes of section 105(b) with respect to reimbursements through insurance.

(e) Exclusion of amounts allowed for care of certain dependents.—Any expense allowed as a credit under section 21 shall not be treated as an expense paid for medical care.

(f) Special rule for 2013, 2014, 2015, and 2016.—In the case of any taxable year beginning after December 31, 2012, and ending before January 1, 2017, subsection (a) shall be applied with respect to a taxpayer by substituting "7.5 percent" for "10 percent" if such taxpayer or such taxpayer's spouse has attained age 65 before the close of such taxable year.

§ 215. Alimony, etc., payments*

(a) General rule.—In the case of an individual, there shall be allowed as a deduction an amount equal to the alimony or separate maintenance payments paid during such individual's taxable year.

(b) Alimony or separate maintenance payments defined.—For purposes of this section, the term "alimony or separate maintenance payment" means any alimony or separate maintenance payment (as defined in section 71(b)) which is includible in the gross income of the recipient under section 71.

(c) Requirement of identification number.—The Secretary may prescribe regulations under which—

(1) any individual receiving alimony or separate maintenance payments is required to furnish such individual's taxpayer identification number to the individual making such payments, and

(2) the individual making such payments is required to include such taxpayer identification number on such individual's return for the taxable year in which such payments are made.

(d) Coordination with section 682.—No deduction shall be allowed under this section with respect to any payment if, by reason of section 682 (relating to income of alimony trusts), the amount thereof is not includible in such individual's gross income.

* * *

*Editorial comment: See the related exclusion provision in Sec. 71.

Editorial Summary

Moving Expenses

Subchapter B of Chapter 1 (Sec. 217)

Moving expenses may be deductible. To qualify for deduction treatment, the moving expenses must qualify as direct moving expense [see Sec. 217(b)(1)]. Prior to the effect of the Revenue Reconciliation Act of 1993 (RRA of 1993), certain indirect moving expenses, within statutory limits of $1,500 or $3,000, were deductible [see Sec. 217(b)(1)(C), (D), and (E) prior to repeal by RRA of 1993]. Not only did RRA of 1993 repeal the deduction for indirect moving expenses, it also repealed the deduction for meals en route associated with the move [see Sec. 217(b)(1)(B)].

To be eligible for the moving expense deduction, the taxpayer must satisfy both a distance requirement and a length of employment requirement [see Sec. 217(c)]. Note that RRA of 1993 increased the distance requirement from 35 miles to 50 miles [see Sec. 217(c)(1)].

For an employee, prior to the effect of RRA of 1993, moving expenses were deductible "from" adjusted gross income unless they were reimbursed by the employer. If reimbursed, the moving expenses were deductible "for" adjusted gross income [see Sec. 62(a)(2)(A)]. Unreimbursed moving expenses of an employee were not subject to the 2-percent floor on miscellaneous itemized deductions [see Sec. 67(b)(6) prior to repeal by RRA of 1993].

RRA of 1993 reclassified moving expenses as a "deduction for" adjusted gross income [see Sec. 62(a)(15)]. If the moving expenses of an employee are paid or reimbursed by the employer and the moving expenses are qualified moving expenses, they are excluded from the employee's gross income (see Sec. 82). In this case, the employee receives no moving expense deduction.

§ 217. Moving expenses**

(a) Deduction allowed.—There shall be allowed as a deduction moving expenses paid or incurred during the taxable year in connection with the commencement of work by the taxpayer as an employee or as a self-employed individual at a new principal place of work.

(b) Definition of moving expenses.—

(1) In general.—For purposes of this section, the term "moving expenses" means only the reasonable expenses—

(A) of moving household goods and personal effects from the former residence to the new residence, and

(B) of traveling (including lodging) from the former residence to the new place of residence.

Such term shall not include any expenses for meals.

**Editorial comment: See the related exclusion provision in Sec. 82.

(2) Individuals other than taxpayer.—In the case of any individual other than the taxpayer, expenses referred to in paragraph (1) shall be taken into account only if such individual has both the former residence and the new residence as his principal place of abode and is a member of the taxpayer's household.

(c) Conditions for allowance.—No deduction shall be allowed under this section unless—

(1) the taxpayer's new principal place of work—

(A) is at least 50 miles farther from his former residence than was his former principal place of work, or

(B) if he had no former principal place of work, is at least 50 miles from his former residence, and

(2) either—

(A) during the 12-month period immediately following his arrival in the general location of his new principal place of work, the taxpayer is a full-time employee, in such general location, during at least 39 weeks, or

(B) during the 24-month period immediately following his arrival in the general location of his new principal place of work, the taxpayer is a full-time employee or performs services as a self-employed individual on a full-time basis, in such general location, during at least 78 weeks, of which not less than 39 weeks are during the 12-month period referred to in subparagraph (A).

For purposes of paragraph (1), the distance between two points shall be the shortest of the more commonly traveled routes between such two points.

(d) Rules for application of subsection (c)(2).—

(1) The condition of subsection (c)(2) shall not apply if the taxpayer is unable to satisfy such condition by reason of—

(A) death or disability, or

(B) involuntary separation (other than for willful misconduct) from the service of, or transfer for the benefit of, an employer after obtaining full-time employment in which the taxpayer could reasonably have been expected to satisfy such condition.

(2) If a taxpayer has not satisfied the condition of subsection (c)(2) before the time prescribed by law (including extensions thereof) for filing the return for the taxable year during which he paid or incurred moving expenses which would otherwise be deductible under this section, but may still satisfy such condition, then such expenses may (at the election of the taxpayer) be deducted for such taxable year notwithstanding subsection (c)(2).

(3) If—

(A) for any taxable year moving expenses have been deducted in accordance with the rule provided in paragraph (2), and

(B) the condition of subsection (c)(2) cannot be satisfied at the close of a subsequent taxable year,

then an amount equal to the expenses which were so deducted shall be included in gross income for the first such subsequent taxable year.

*__(f) Self-employed individual.__—For purposes of this section, the term "self-employed individual" means an individual who performs personal services—

(1) as the owner of the entire interest in an unincorporated trade or business, or

(2) as a partner in a partnership carrying on a trade or business.

(g) Rules for members of the Armed Forces of the United States.—In the case of a member of the Armed Forces of the United States on active duty who moves pursuant to a military order and incident to a permanent change of station—

(1) the limitations under subsection (c) shall not apply;

(2) any moving and storage expenses which are furnished in kind (or for which reimbursement or an allowance is provided, but only to the extent of the expenses paid or incurred) to such member, his spouse, or his dependents, shall not be includible in gross income, and no reporting with respect to such expenses shall be required by the Secretary of Defense or the Secretary of Transportation, as the case may be; and

(3) if moving and storage expenses are furnished in kind (or if reimbursement or an allowance for such expenses is provided) to such member's spouse and his dependents with regard to moving to a location other than the one to which such member moves (or from a location other than the one from which such member moves), this section shall apply with respect to the moving expenses of his spouse and dependents—

(A) as if his spouse commenced work as an employee at a new principal place of work at such location;

*Editorial comment: There is no subsection (e).

(B) without regard to the limitations under subsection (c).

(h) Special rules for foreign moves.—

(1) Allowance of certain storage fees.—In the case of a foreign move, for purposes of this section, the moving expenses described in subsection (b)(1)(A) include the reasonable expenses—

(A) of moving household goods and personal effects to and from storage, and

(B) of storing such goods and effects for part or all of the period during which the new place of work continues to be the taxpayer's principal place of work.

(2) Foreign move.—For purposes of this subsection, the term "foreign move" means the commencement of work by the taxpayer at a new principal place of work located outside the United States.

(3) United States defined.—For purposes of this subsection and subsection (i), the term "United States" includes the possessions of the United States.

(i) Allowance of deductions in case of retirees or decedents who were working abroad.—

(1) In general.—In the case of any qualified retiree moving expenses or qualified survivor moving expenses—

(A) this section (other than subsection (h)) shall be applied with respect to such expenses as if they were incurred in connection with the commencement of work by the taxpayer as an employee at a new principal place of work located within the United States, and

(B) the limitations of subsection (c)(2) shall not apply.

(2) Qualified retiree moving expenses.—For purposes of paragraph (1), the term "qualified retiree moving expenses" means any moving expenses—

(A) which are incurred by an individual whose former principal place of work and former residence were outside the United States, and

(B) which are incurred for a move to a new residence in the United States in connection with the bona fide retirement of the individual.

(3) Qualified survivor moving expenses.—For purposes of paragraph (1), the term "qualified survivor moving expenses" means moving expenses—

(A) which are paid or incurred by the spouse or any dependent of any decedent who (as of the time of his death) had a principal place of work outside the United States, and

(B) which are incurred for a move which begins within 6 months after the death of such decedent and which is to a residence in the United States from a former residence outside the United States which (as of the time of the decedent's death) was the residence of such decedent and the individual paying or incurring the expense.

(j) Regulations.—The Secretary shall prescribe such regulations as may be necessary to carry out the purposes of this section.

§ 219. Retirement savings

Editorial Summary

Traditional IRAs*

Subchapter B of Chapter 1 (Sec. 219)

Individual taxpayers who have earned income are provided with the opportunity to make a limited contribution to their retirement savings and receive beneficial tax results. The ceiling on the amount of the annual contribution is the lower of $5,500 in 2014 (unchanged since 2013) or the individual's earned income (i.e., compensation) [Sec. 219(b)]. For married individuals who are eligible to make a contribution for the spouse, the combined dollar ceiling for the taxpayer and spouse is $11,000 in 2014 [Sec. 219(c)]. See the catch-up provision in Sec. 219(b)(5)(b) which permits an additional $1,000 to be contributed in 2006 and thereafter for taxpayers age 50 or over.

The contribution may be deductible. If the contribution is deductible, it is a deduction *for* AGI [Sec. 62(a)(7)]. The amount of the deduction for an active participant in certain pension plans is limited based on the wherewithal to pay concept [Sec. 219(g)]. If the taxpayer's AGI exceeds the applicable dollar amount, the amount otherwise deductible is phased out over a $10,000 range ($20,000 for married filing jointly) [Sec. 219(g)(2) and (3)]. Thus, for married filing jointly, the phaseout is complete at $116,000 in 2014; for married filing separately, the phaseout is complete at $10,000 in 2014; and for other filing statuses, the phaseout is complete at $70,000 in 2014.

To the extent not eligible to make deductible contributions because of Sec. 219(g), nondeductible contributions can be made [Sec. 408(o)]. The earnings of both deductible contributions and nondeductible contributions are tax-deferred [Sec. 408(e)]. The basis for a deductible contribution is zero whereas the basis for a nondeductible contribution is the amount of the contribution. An election can be made to

*Editorial comment: See the discussion of Roth IRAs in Sec. 408A.

treat deductible contributions as nondeductible contributions [Sec. 219(f)(7) and Sec. 408(o)].

An IRA can be established by the taxpayer up to the return due date (not including extensions). Likewise, contributions can be made up to the return due date (not including extensions) [Sec. 219(f)(3)].

Contributions cannot be made if the individual has reached age 70 and one-half before the close of the tax year [Sec. 219 (d)(1)]. Excess contributions [Sec. 219(f)(6)] are subject to a 6 percent penalty tax under Sec. 4973.

Distributions are not eligible for lump-sum distribution treatment (i.e. special 10-year averaging and limited capital gain treatment). An early distribution is subject to a 10 percent penalty tax [Sec. 72(t)]. Certain contributions and distributions qualify for rollover treatment and are not presently subject to tax [Sec. 408(d)(3)].

(a) Allowance of deduction.—In the case of an individual, there shall be allowed as a deduction an amount equal to the qualified retirement contributions of the individual for the taxable year.

(b) Maximum amount of deduction.—

(1) In general.—The amount allowable as a deduction under subsection (a) to any individual for any taxable year shall not exceed the lesser of—

(A) the deductible amount, or

(B) an amount equal to the compensation includible in the individual's gross income for such taxable year.

(2) Special rule for employer contributions under simplified employee pensions.—This section shall not apply with respect to an employer contribution to a simplified employee pension.

(3) Plans under section 501(c)(18).—Notwithstanding paragraph (1), the amount allowable as a deduction under subsection (a) with respect to any contributions on behalf of an employee to a plan described in section 501(c)(18) shall not exceed the lesser of—

(A) $7,000, or

(B) an amount equal to 25 percent of the compensation (as defined in section 415(c)(3)) includible in the individual's gross income for such taxable year.

(4) Special rule for simple retirement accounts.—This section should not apply with respect to any amount contributed to a simple retirement account established under section 408(p).

(5) Deductible amount.—For purposes of paragraph (1)(A)—

(A) In general.—The deductible amount shall be determined in accordance with the following table:

For taxable years beginning in	The deductible amount is:
2002 through 2004	$3,000
2005 through 2007	$4,000
2008 and thereafter	$5,000

(B) Catch-up contributions for individuals 50 or older.—

(i) In general.—In the case of an individual who has attained the age of 50 before the close of the taxable year, the deductible amount for such taxable year shall be increased by the applicable amount.

(ii) Applicable amount.—For purposes of clause (i), the applicable amount shall be the amount determined in accordance with the following table:

For taxable years beginning in	The applicable amount is:
2002 through 2005	$500
2006 and thereafter	$1,000

(C) Catchup contributions for certain individuals.—

(i) In general.—In the case of an applicable individual who elects to make a qualified retirement contribution in addition to the deductible amount determined under subparagraph (A)—

(I) the deductible amount for any taxable year shall be increased by an amount equal to 3 times the applicable amount determined under subparagraph (B) for such taxable year, and

(II) subparagraph (B) shall not apply.

(ii) Applicable individual.—For purposes of this subparagraph, the term "applicable individual" means, with respect to any taxable year, any individual who was a qualified participant in a qualified cash or deferred arrangement (as defined in section 401(k)) of an employer described in clause (iii) under which the employer matched at least 50 percent of the employee's contributions to such arrangement with stock of such employer.

(iii) Employer described.—An employer is described in this clause if, in any taxable year preceding the taxable year described in clause (ii)—

(I) such employer (or any controlling corporation of such employer) was a debtor in a case under title 11 of the United States Code, or similar Federal or State law, and

(II) such employer (or any other person) was subject to an indictment or conviction resulting from business transactions related to such case.

(iv) Qualified participant.—For purposes of clause (ii), the term "qualified participant" means any applicable individual who was a participant in the cash or deferred arrangement described in such clause on the date that is 6 months before the filing of the case described in clause (iii).

(v) Termination.—This subparagraph shall not apply to taxable years beginning after December 31, 2009.

(D) Cost-of-living adjustment.—

(i) In general.—In the case of any taxable year beginning in a calendar year after 2008, the $5,000 amount under subparagraph (A) shall be increased by an amount equal to—

(I) such dollar amount, multiplied by

(II) the cost-of-living adjustment determined under section 1(f)(3) for the calendar year in which the taxable year begins, determined by substituting "calendar year 2007" for "calendar year 1992" in subparagraph (b) thereof.

(ii) Rounding rules.—If any amount after adjustment under clause (i) is not a multiple of $500, such amount shall be rounded to the next lower multiple of $500.

(c) Special rules for certain married individuals.—

(1) In general.—In the case of an individual to whom this paragraph applies for the taxable year, the limitation of paragraph (1) of subsection (b) shall be equal to the lesser of—

(A) the dollar amount in effect under subsection (b)(l)(A) for the taxable year, or

(B) the sum of—

(i) the compensation includible in such individual's gross income for the taxable year, plus

(ii) the compensation includible in the gross income of such individual's spouse for the taxable year reduced by—

(I) the amount allowed as a deduction under subsection (a) to such spouse for such taxable year,

(II) the amount of any designated nondeductible contribution (as defined in section 408(o)) on behalf of such spouse for such taxable year, and

(III) the amount of any contribution on behalf of such spouse to a Roth IRA under section 408A for such taxable year.

(2) Individuals to whom paragraph (1) applies.—Paragraph (1) shall apply to any individual if—

(A) such individual files a joint return for the taxable year, and

(B) the sum of—

(i) the compensation includible in such individual's gross income for the taxable year, plus

(ii) the compensation includible in the gross income of such individual's spouse for the taxable year reduced by—

(I) the amount allowed as a deduction under subsection (a) to such spouse for such taxable year, and

(II) the amount of any contribution on behalf of such spouse to a Roth IRA under section 408A for such taxable year.

(d) Other limitations and restrictions.—

(1) Beneficiary must be under age 70½.—No deduction shall be allowed under this section with respect to any qualified retirement contribution for the benefit of an individual if such individual has attained age 70½ before the close of such individual's taxable year for which the contribution was made.

(2) Recontributed amounts.—No deduction shall be allowed under this section with respect to a rollover contribution described in section 402(c), 403(a)(4), 403(b)(8), 408(d)(3), or 457(e)(16).

(3) Amounts contributed under endowment contract.—In the case of an endowment contract described in section 408(b), no deduction shall be allowed under this section for that portion of the amounts paid under the contract for the taxable year which is properly allocable, under regulations prescribed by the Secretary, to the cost of life insurance.

(4) Denial of deduction for amount contributed to inherited annuities or accounts.—No deduction shall be allowed under this section with respect to any amount paid to an inherited individual retirement account or individual retirement annuity (within the meaning of section 408 (d)(3)(C)(ii)).

(e) Qualified retirement contribution.—For purposes of this section, the term "qualified retirement contribution" means—

(1) any amount paid in cash for the taxable year by or on behalf of an individual to an individual retirement plan for such individual's benefit, and

(2) any amount contributed on behalf of any individual to a plan described in section 501(c)(18).

(f) Other definitions and special rules.—

(1) Compensation.—For purposes of this section, the term "compensation" includes earned income (as defined in section 401(c)(2)). The term "compensation" does not include any amount received as a pension or annuity and does not include any amount received as deferred compensation. The term "compensation" shall include any amount includible in the individual's gross income under section 71 with respect to a divorce or separation instrument described in subparagraph (A) of section 71(b)(2). For purposes of this paragraph, section 401(c)(2) shall be applied as if the term trade or business for purposes of section 1402 included service described in subsection (c)(6). The term compensation includes any differential wage payment (as defined in section 3401(h)(2)).

(2) Married individuals.—The maximum deduction under subsection (b) shall be computed separately for each individual, and this section shall be applied without regard to any community property laws.

(3) Time when contributions deemed made.—For purposes of this section, a taxpayer shall be deemed to have made a contribution to an individual retirement plan on the last day of the preceding taxable year if the contribution is made on account of such taxable year and is made not later than the time prescribed by law for filing the return for such taxable year (not including extensions thereof).

(4) Reports.—The Secretary shall prescribe regulations which prescribe the time and the manner in which reports to the Secretary and plan participants shall be made by the plan administrator of a qualified employer or government plan receiving qualified voluntary employee contributions.

(5) Employer payments.—For purposes of this title, any amount paid by an employer to an individual retirement plan shall be treated as payment of compensation to the employee (other than a self-employed individual who is an employee within the meaning of section 401(c) (1)) includible in his gross income in the taxable year for which the amount was contributed, whether or not a deduction for such payment is allowable under this section to the employee.

(6) Excess contributions treated as contribution made during subsequent year for which there is an unused limitation.—

(A) In general.—If for the taxable year the maximum amount allowable as a deduction under this section for contributions to an individual retirement plan exceeds the amount contributed, then the taxpayer shall be treated as having made an additional contribution for the taxable year in an amount equal to the lesser of—

(i) the amount of such excess, or

(ii) the amount of the excess contributions for such taxable year (determined under section 4973(b)(2) without regard to subparagraph (C) thereof).

(B) Amount contributed.—For purposes of this paragraph, the amount contributed—

(i) shall be determined without regard to this paragraph, and

(ii) shall not include any rollover contribution.

(C) Special rule where excess deduction was allowed for closed year.—Proper reduction shall be made in the amount allowable as a deduction by reason of this paragraph for any amount allowed as a deduction under this section for a prior taxable year for which the period for assessing deficiency has expired if the amount so allowed exceeds the amount which should have been allowed for such prior taxable year.

(7) Election not to deduct contributions.—

For election not to deduct contributions to individual retirement plans, see section 408(o)(2) (B)(ii).

(g) Limitation on deduction for active participants in certain pension plans.—

(1) In general.—If (for any part of any plan year ending with or within a taxable year) an individual or the individual's spouse is an active participant, each of the dollar limitations contained in subsections (b)(1)(A) and (c)(1)(A) for such taxable year shall be reduced (but not below zero) by the amount determined under paragraph (2).

(2) Amount of reduction.—

(A) In general.—The amount determined under this paragraph with respect to any dollar limitation shall be the amount which bears the same ratio to such limitation as—

(i) the excess of—

(I) the taxpayer's adjusted gross income for such taxable year, over

(II) the applicable dollar amount, bears to

(ii) $10,000 ($20,000 in the case of a joint return for a taxable year beginning after December 31, 2006).

(B) No reduction below $200 until complete phaseout.—No dollar limitation shall be reduced below $200 under paragraph (1) unless (without regard to this subparagraph) such limitation is reduced to zero.

(C) Rounding.—Any amount determined under this paragraph which is not a multiple of $10 shall be rounded to the next lowest $10.

(3) Adjusted gross income; applicable dollar amount.—For purposes of this subsection—

(A) Adjusted gross income.—Adjusted gross income of any taxpayer shall be determined—

(i) after application of sections 86 and 469, and

(ii) without regard to sections 135, 137, 199, 221, 222, and 911 or the deduction allowable under this section.

(B) Applicable dollar amount.—The term "applicable dollar amount" means the following:

(i) In the case of a taxpayer filing a joint return:

For taxable years beginning in:	The applicable dollar amount is:
1998	$50,000
1999	$51,000
2000	$52,000
2001	$53,000
2002	$54,000
2003	$60,000
2004	$65,000
2005	$70,000
2006	$75,000
2007 and thereafter	$80,000*

(ii) in the case of any other taxpayer (other than a married individual filing a separate return)

For taxable years beginning in:	The applicable dollar amount is:
1998	$30,000
1999	$31,000
2000	$32,000
2001	$33,000
200	$34,000
2003	$40,000
2004	$45,000
2005 and thereafter	$50,000**

(iii) in the case of a married individual filing a separate return, zero.

(4) Special rule for married individuals filing separately and living apart.—A husband and wife who—

(A) file separate returns for any taxable year, and

(B) live apart at all times during such taxable year, shall not be treated as married individuals for purposes of this subsection.

(5) Active participant.—For purposes of this subsection, the term "active participant" means, with respect to any plan year, an individual—

(A) who is an active participant in—

(i) a plan described in section 401(a) which includes a trust exempt from tax under section 501(a),

(ii) an annuity plan described in section 403(a),

(iii) a plan established for its employees by the United States, by a State or political subdivision thereof, or by an agency or instrumentality of any of the foregoing,

(iv) an annuity contract described in section 403(b),

*Editorial comment: The indexed amount for 2013 is $95,000 and for 2014 is $96,000.

**Editorial comment: The indexed amount for 2013 is $59,000 and for 2014 is $60,000.

(v) a simplified employee pension (within the meaning of section 408(k)), or

(vi) any simple retirement account (within the meaning of section 408(p)).

(B) who makes deductible contributions to a trust described in section 501(c)(18).

The determination of whether an individual is an active participant shall be made without regard to whether or not such individual's rights under a plan, trust, or contract are nonforfeitable. An eligible deferred compensation plan (within the meaning of section 457(b)) shall not be treated as a plan described in subparagraph (A)(iii).

(6) Certain individuals not treated as active participants.—For purposes of this subsection, any individual described in any of the following subparagraphs shall not be treated as an active participant for any taxable year solely because of any participation so described:

(A) Members of reserve components.—Participation in a plan described in subparagraph (A)(iii) of paragraph (5) by reason of service as a member of a reserve component of the Armed Forces (as defined in section 10101 of title 10), unless such individual has served in excess of 90 days on active duty (other than active duty for training) during the year.

(B) Volunteer firefighters.—A volunteer firefighter—

(i) who is a participant in a plan described in subparagraph (A)(iii) of paragraph (5) based on his activity as a volunteer firefighter, and

(ii) whose accrued benefit as of the beginning of the taxable year is not more than an annual benefit of $1,800 (when expressed as a single life annuity commencing at age 65).

(7) Special rule for spouses who are not active participants.—If this subsection applies to an individual for any taxable year solely because their spouse is an active participant, then, in applying this subsection to the individual (but not their spouse)—

(A) the applicable dollar amount under paragraph (3)(B)(i) shall be $150,000,* and

(B) the amount applicable under paragraph (2)(A)(ii) shall be $10,000.

(8) Inflation adjustment.—In the case of any taxable year beginning in a calendar year after 2006, the dollar amount in the last row of the table contained in paragraph (3)(B)(i), the dollar amount in the last row of the table contained in paragraph (3)(B)(ii), and the dollar amount contained in paragraph (7)(A), shall each be increased by an amount equal to—

(A) such dollar amount, multiplied by

(B) the cost-of-living adjustment determined under section 1(f)(3) for the calendar year in which the taxable year begins, determined by substituting "calendar year 2005" for "calendar year 1992" in subparagraph (B) thereof.

Any increase determined under the preceding sentence shall be rounded to the nearest multiple of $1,000.

* * *

§ 220. Archer MSAs

(a) Deduction allowed.—In the case of an individual who is an eligible individual for any month during the taxable year, there shall be allowed as a deduction for the taxable year an amount equal to the aggregate amount paid in cash during such taxable year by such individual to an Archer MSA of such individual.

(b) Limitations.—

(1) In general.—The amount allowable as a deduction under subsection (a) to an individual for the taxable year shall not exceed the sum of the monthly limitations for months during such taxable year that the individual is an eligible individual.

(2) Monthly limitation.—The monthly limitation for any month is the amount equal to 1/12 of—

(A) in the case of an individual who has self-only coverage under the high deductible health plan as of the first day of such month, 65 percent of the annual deductible under such coverage, and

(B) in the case of an individual who has family coverage under the high deductible health plan as of the first day of such month, 75 percent of the annual deductible under such coverage.

(3) Special rule for married individuals.—In the case of individuals who are married to each other, if either spouse has family coverage—

(A) both spouses shall be treated as having only such family coverage (and if such spouses

*Editorial comment: The indexed amount for 2013 is $178,000 and for 2014 is $181,000.

each have family coverage under different plans, as having the family coverage with the lowest annual deductible), and

(B) the limitation under paragraph (1) (after the application of subparagraph (A) of this paragraph) shall be divided equally between them unless they agree on a different division.

(4) Deduction not to exceed compensation.—

(A) Employees.—The deduction allowed under subsection (a) for contributions as an eligible individual described in subclause (I) of subsection (c)(1)(A)(iii) shall not exceed such individual's wages, salaries, tips, and other employee compensation which are attributable to such individual's employment by the employer referred to in such subclause.

(B) Self-employed individuals.—The deduction allowed under subsection (a) for contributions as an eligible individual described in subclause (II) of subsection (c)(1)(A)(iii) shall not exceed such individual's earned income (as defined in section 401(c)(1)) derived by the taxpayer from the trade or business with respect to which the high deductible health plan is established.

(C) Community property laws not to apply.—The limitations under this paragraph shall be determined without regard to community property laws.

(5) Coordination with exclusion for employer contributions.—No deduction shall be allowed under this section for any amount paid for any taxable year to an Archer MSA of an individual if—

(A) any amount is contributed to any Archer MSA of such individual for such year which is excludable from gross income under section 106(b), or

(B) if such individual's spouse is covered under the high deductible health plan covering such individual, any amount is contributed for such year to any Archer MSA of such spouse which is so excludable.

(6) Denial of deduction to dependents.—No deduction shall be allowed under this section to any individual with respect to whom a deduction under section 151 is allowable to another taxpayer for a taxable year beginning in the calendar year in which such individual's taxable year begins.

(c) Definitions.—For purposes of this section—

(1) Eligible individual.—

(A) In general.—The term "eligible individual" means, with respect to any month, any individual if—

(i) such individual is covered under a high deductible health plan as of the 1st day of such month,

(ii) such individual is not, while covered under a high deductible health plan, covered under any health plan—

(I) which is not a high deductible health plan, and

(II) which provides coverage for any benefit which is covered under the high deductible health plan, and

(iii) **(I)** the high deductible health plan covering such individual is established and maintained by the employer of such individual or of the spouse of such individual and such employer is a small employer, or

(II) such individual is an employee (within the meaning of section 401(c)(1)) or the spouse of such an employee and the high deductible health plan covering such individual is not established or maintained by any employer of such individual or spouse.

(B) Certain coverage disregarded.—Subparagraph (A)(ii) shall be applied without regard to—

(i) coverage for any benefit provided by permitted insurance, and

(ii) coverage (whether through insurance or otherwise) for accidents, disability, dental care, vision care, or long-term care.

(C) Continued eligibility of employee and spouse establishing Archer MSAs.—If, while an employer is a small employer—

(i) any amount is contributed to an Archer MSA of an individual who is an employee of such employer or the spouse of such an employee, and

(ii) such amount is excludable from gross income under section 106(b) or allowable as a deduction under this section,

such individual shall not cease to meet the requirement of subparagraph (A)(iii)(I) by reason of such employer ceasing to be a small employer so long as such employee continues to be an employee of such employer.

(D) Limitations on eligibility.—For limitations on number of taxpayers who are eligible to have Archer MSAs, see subsection (i).

(2) High deductible health plan.*—

(A) In general.—The term "high deductible health plan" means a health plan—

(i) in the case of self-only coverage, which has an annual deductible which is not less than $1,500 and not more than $2,250,

(ii) in the case of family coverage, which has an annual deductible which is not less than $3,000 and not more than $4,500, and

(iii) the annual out-of-pocket expenses required to be paid under the plan (other than for premiums) for covered benefits does not exceed—

(I) $3,000 for self-only coverage, and

(II) $5,500 for family coverage.

(B) Special rules.—

(i) Exclusion of certain plans.—Such term does not include a health plan if substantially all of its coverage is coverage described in paragraph (1)(B).

(ii) Safe harbor for absence of preventive care deductible.—A plan shall not fail to be treated as a high deductible health plan by reason of failing to have a deductible for preventive care if the absence of a deductible for such care is required by State law.

(3) Permitted insurance.—The term "permitted insurance" means—

(A) insurance if substantially all of the coverage provided under such insurance relates to—

(i) liabilities incurred under workers' compensation laws,

(ii) tort liabilities,

(iii) liabilities relating to ownership or use of property, or

(iv) such other similar liabilities as the Secretary may specify by regulations,

(B) insurance for a specified disease or illness, and

(C) insurance paying a fixed amount per day (or other period) of hospitalization.

(4) Small employer.—

(A) In general.—The term "small employer" means, with respect to any calendar year, any employer if such employer employed an average of 50 or fewer employees on business days during either of the 2 preceding calendar years. For purposes of the preceding sentence, a preceding calendar year may be taken into account only if the employer was in existence throughout such year.

(B) Employer not in existence in preceding year.—In the case of an employer which was not in existence throughout the 1st preceding calendar year, the determination under subparagraph (A) shall be based on the average number of employees that it is reasonably expected such employer will employ on business days in the current calendar year.

(C) Certain growing employers retain treatment as small employer.—The term "small employer" includes, with respect to any calendar year, any employer if—

(i) such employer met the requirement of subparagraph (A) (determined without regard to subparagraph (B)) for any preceding calendar year after 1996,

(ii) any amount was contributed to the Archer MSA of any employee of such employer with respect to coverage of such employee under a high deductible health plan of such employer during such preceding calendar year and such amount was excludable from gross income under section 106(b) or allowable as a deduction under this section, and

(iii) such employer employed an average of 200 or fewer employees on business days during each preceding calendar year after 1996.

(D) Special rules.—

(i) Controlled groups.—For purposes of this paragraph, all persons treated as a single employer under subsection (b), (c), (m), or (o) of section 414 shall be treated as 1 employer.

(ii) Predecessors.—Any reference in this paragraph to an employer shall include a

*Editorial comment: The indexed annual deductible range in 2014 for self-only coverage is $2,200 to $3,250 and for family coverage is $4,350 to $6,550. The indexed maximum for out-of-pocket expenditures in 2014 for self-only coverage is $4,350 and for family coverage is $8,000.

reference to any predecessor of such employer.

(5) Family coverage.—The term "family coverage" means any coverage other than self-only coverage.

(d) Archer MSA.—For purposes of this section—

(1) Archer MSA.—The term "Archer MSA" means a trust created or organized in the United States as a medical savings account exclusively for the purpose of paying the qualified medical expenses of the account holder, but only if the written governing instrument creating the trust meets the following requirements:

(A) Except in the case of a rollover contribution described in subsection (f)(5), no contribution will be accepted—

(i) unless it is in cash, or

(ii) to the extent such contribution, when added to previous contributions to the trust for the calendar year, exceeds 75 percent of the highest annual limit deductible permitted under subsection (c)(2)(A)(ii) for such calendar year.

(B) The trustee is a bank (as defined in section 408(n)), an insurance company (as defined in section 816), or another person who demonstrates to the satisfaction of the Secretary that the manner in which such person will administer the trust will be consistent with the requirements of this section.

(C) No part of the trust assets will be invested in life insurance contracts.

(D) The assets of the trust will not be commingled with other property except in a common trust fund or common investment fund.

(E) The interest of an individual in the balance in his account is nonforfeitable.

(2) Qualified medical expenses.—

(A) In general.—The term "qualified medical expenses" means, with respect to an account holder, amounts paid by such holder for medical care (as defined in section 213(d)) for such individual, the spouse of such individual, and any dependent (as defined in section 152, determined without regard to subsections (b)(1), (b)(2), and (d)(1)(B) thereof) of such individual, but only to the extent such amounts are not compensated for by insurance or otherwise. Such term shall include an amount paid for medicine or a drug only if such medicine or drug is a prescribed drug (determined without regard to whether such drug is available without a prescription) or is insulin.

(B) Health insurance may not be purchased from account.—

(i) In general.—Subparagraph (A) shall not apply to any payment for insurance,

(ii) Exceptions.—Clause (i) shall not apply to any expense for coverage under—

(I) a health plan during any period of continuation coverage required under any Federal law,

(II) a qualified long-term care insurance contract (as defined in section 7702B(b)), or

(III) a health plan during a period in which the individual is receiving unemployment compensation under any Federal or State law.

(C) Medical expenses of individuals who are not eligible individuals.—Subparagraph (A) shall apply to an amount paid by an account holder for medical care of an individual who is not described in clauses (i) and (ii) of subsection (c)(1)(A) for the month in which the expense for such care is incurred only if no amount is contributed (other than a rollover contribution) to any Archer MSA of such account holder for the taxable year which includes such month. This subparagraph shall not apply to any expense for coverage described in subclause (I) or (III) of subparagraph (B)(ii).

(3) Account holder.—The term "account holder" means the individual on whose behalf the Archer MSA was established.

(4) Certain rules to apply.—Rules similar to the following rules shall apply for purposes of this section:

(A) Section 219(d)(2) (relating to no deduction for rollovers).

(B) Section 219(f)(3) (relating to time when contributions deemed made).

(C) Except as provided in section 106(b), section 219(f)(5) (relating to employer payments).

(D) Section 408(g) (relating to community property laws).

(E) Section 408(h) (relating to custodial accounts).

(e) Tax treatment of accounts.—

(1) In general.—An Archer MSA is exempt from taxation under this subtitle unless such account has ceased to be an Archer MSA. Notwithstanding the preceding sentence, any such account is subject to the taxes imposed by section 511 (relating to imposition of tax on unrelated business income of charitable, etc. organizations).

(2) Account terminations.—Rules similar to the rules of paragraphs (2) and (4) of section 408 (e) shall apply to Archer MSAs, and any amount treated as distributed under such rules shall be treated as not used to pay qualified medical expenses.

(f) Tax treatment of distributions.—

(1) Amounts used for qualified medical expenses.—Any amount paid or distributed out of an Archer MSA which is not used exclusively to pay the qualified medical expenses of any account holder shall not be includible in gross income.

(2) Inclusion of amounts not used for qualified medical expenses.—Any amount paid or distributed out of an Archer MSA which is not used exclusively to pay the qualified medical expenses of the account holder shall be included in the gross income of such holder.

(3) Excess contributions returned before date of return.—

(A) In general.—If any excess contribution is contributed for a taxable year to any Archer MSA of an individual, paragraph (2) shall not apply to distributions from the Archer MSAs of such individual (to the extent such distributions do not exceed the aggregate excess contributions to all such accounts of such individual for such year) if—

(i) such distribution is received by the individual on or before the last day prescribed by law (including extensions of time) for filing such individual's return for such taxable year, and

(ii) such distribution is accompanied by the amount of net income attributable to such excess contribution.

Any net income described in clause (ii) shall be included in the gross income of the individual for the taxable year in which it is received.

(B) Excess contribution.—For purposes of subparagraph (A), the term "excess contribution" means any contribution (other than a rollover contribution) which is neither excludable from gross income under section 106(b) nor deductible under this section.

(4) Additional tax on distributions not used for qualified medical expenses.—

(A) In general.—The tax imposed by this chapter on the account holder for any taxable year in which there is a payment or distribution from an Archer MSA of such holder which is includible in gross income under paragraph (2) shall be increased by 20 percent of the amount which is so includible.

(B) Exception for disability or death.—Subparagraph (A) shall not apply if the payment or distribution is made after the account holder becomes disabled within the meaning of section 72(m)(7) or dies.

(C) Exception for distributions after Medicare eligibility.—Subparagraph (A) shall not apply to any payment or distribution after the date on which the account holder attains the age specified in section 1811 of the Social Security Act.

(5) Rollover contribution.—An amount is described in this paragraph as a rollover contribution if it meets the requirements of subparagraphs (A) and (B).

(A) In general.—Paragraph (2) shall not apply to any amount paid or distributed from an Archer MSA to the account holder to the extent the amount received is paid into an Archer MSA or a health savings account (as defined in section 223(d)) for the benefit of such holder not later than the 60th day after the day on which the holder receives the payment or distribution.

(B) Limitation.—This paragraph shall not apply to any amount described in subparagraph (A) received by an individual from an Archer MSA if, at any time during the 1-year period ending on the day of such receipt, such individual received any other amount described in subparagraph (A) from an Archer MSA which was not includible in the individual's gross income because of the application of this paragraph.

(6) Coordination with medical expense deduction.—For purposes of determining the amount of the deduction under section 213, any payment or distribution out of an Archer MSA for qualified medical expenses shall not be treated as an expense paid for medical care.

(7) Transfer of account incident to divorce.—The transfer of an individual's interest in an Archer MSA to an individual's spouse or former spouse under a divorce or separation instrument described in subparagraph (A) of section 71(b)(2) shall not be considered a taxable transfer made by such individual notwithstanding any other provision of this subtitle, and such interest shall, after such transfer, be treated as an Archer MSA with respect to which such spouse is the account holder.

(8) Treatment after death of account holder.—

(A) Treatment if designated beneficiary is spouse.—If the account holder's surviving spouse acquires such holder's interest in an Archer MSA by reason of being the designated beneficiary of such account at the death of the account holder, such an Archer MSA shall be treated as if the spouse were the account holder.

(B) Other cases.—

(i) In general.—If, by reason of the death of the account holder, any person acquires the account holder's interest in an Archer MSA in a case to which subparagraph (A) does not apply—

(I) such account shall cease to be an Archer MSA as of the date of death, and

(II) an amount equal to the fair market value of the assets in such account on such date shall be includible, if such person is not the estate of such holder, in such person's gross income for the taxable year which includes such date, or if such person is the estate of such holder, in such holder's gross income for the last taxable year of such holder.

(ii) Special rules.—

(I) Reduction of inclusion for pre-death expenses.—The amount includible in gross income under clause (i) by any person (other than the estate) shall be reduced by the amount of qualified medical expenses which were incurred by the decedent before the date of the decedent's death and paid by such person within 1 year after such date.

(II) Deduction for estate taxes.—An appropriate deduction shall be allowed under section 691(c) to any person (other than the decedent or the decedent's spouse) with respect to amounts included in gross income under clause (i) by such person.

(g) Cost-of-living adjustment.—In the case of any taxable year beginning in a calendar year after 1998, each dollar amount in subsection (c)(2) shall be increased by an amount equal to—

(1) such dollar amount, multiplied by

(2) the cost-of-living adjustment determined under section 1(f)(3) for the calendar year in which such taxable year begins by substituting "calendar year 1997" for "calendar year 1992" in subparagraph (B) thereof.

If any increase under the preceding sentence is not a multiple of $50, such increase shall be rounded to the nearest multiple of $50.

(h) Reports.—The Secretary may require the trustee of an Archer MSA to make such reports regarding such account to the Secretary and to the account holder with respect to contributions, distributions, and such other matters as the Secretary determines appropriate. The reports required by this subsection shall be filed at such time and in such manner and furnished to individuals at such time and in such matter as may be required by the Secretary.

(i) Limitation of number of taxpayers having Archer MSAs.—

(1) In general.—Except as provided in paragraph (5), no individual shall be treated as an eligible individual for any taxable year beginning after the cut-off year unless—

(A) such individual was an active MSA participant for any taxable year ending on or before the close of the cut-off year, or

(B) Such individual first became an active MSA participant for a taxable year ending after the cut-off year by reason of coverage under a high deductible health plan of an MSA-participating employer.

(2) Cut-off year.—For purposes of paragraph (1), the term "cut-off year" means the earlier of—

(A) calendar year 2007, or

(B) the first calendar year before 2007 for which the Secretary determines under subsection (j) that the numerical limitation for such year has been exceeded.

(3) Active MSA participant.—For purposes of this subsection—

(A) In general.—The term "active MSA participant" means, with respect to any taxable year, any individual who is the account holder of any Archer MSA into which any contribution was made which was excludable from gross income under section 106(b), or allowable as a deduction under this section, for such taxable year.

(B) Special rule for cut-off years before 2007.—In the case of a cut-off year before 2007—

(i) an individual shall not be treated as an eligible individual for any month of such year or an active MSA participant under paragraph (1)(A) unless such individual is, on or before the cut-off date, covered under a high deductible health plan, and

(ii) an employer shall not be treated as an MSA-participating employer unless the employer, on or before the cut-off date, offered coverage under a high deductible health plan to any employee.

(C) Cut-off date.—For purposes of subparagraph (B)—

(i) In general.—Except as otherwise provided in this subparagraph, the cut-off date is October 1 of the cut-off year.

(ii) Employees with enrollment periods after October 1.—In the case of an individual described in subclause (I) of subsection (c)(1)(A)(iii), if the regularly scheduled enrollment period for health plans of the individual's employer occurs during the last 3 months of the cut-off year, the cut-off date is December 31 of the cut-off year.

(iii) Self-employed individuals.—In the case of an individual described in subclause (II) of subsection (c)(1)(A)(iii), the cut-off date is November 1 of the cut-off year.

(iv) Special rules for 1997.—If 1997 is a cut-off year by reason of subsection (j)(1)(A) —

(I) each of the cut-off dates under clauses (i) and (iii) shall be 1 month earlier than the date determined without regard to this clause, and

(II) clause (ii) shall be applied by substituting "4 months" for "3 months."

(4) MSA-participating employer.—For purposes of this subsection, the term "MSA-participating employer" means any small employer if—

(A) such employer made any contribution to the Archer MSA of any employee during the cut-off year or any preceding calendar year which was excludable from gross income under section 106(b), or

(B) at least 20 percent of the employees of such employer who are eligible individuals for any month of the cut-off year by reason of coverage under a high deductible health plan of such employer each made a contribution of at least $100 to their Archer MSAs for any taxable year ending with or within the cut-off year which was allowable as a deduction under this section.

(5) Additional eligibility after cut-off year.—If the Secretary determines under subsection (j)(2)(A) that the numerical limit for the calendar year following a cut-off year described in paragraph (2)(B) has not been exceeded—

(A) this subsection shall not apply to any otherwise eligible individual who is covered under a high deductible health plan during the first 6 months of the second calendar year following the cut-off year (and such individual shall be treated as an active MSA participant for purposes of this subsection if a contribution is made to any Archer MSA with respect to such coverage), and

(B) any employer who offers coverage under a high deductible health plan to any employee during such 6-month period shall be treated as an MSA-participating employer for purposes of this subsection if the requirements of paragraph (4) are met with respect to such coverage.

For purposes of this paragraph, subsection (j)(2)(A) shall be applied for 1998 by substituting "750,000" for "600,000."

(j) Determination of whether numerical limits are exceeded.—

(1) Determination of whether limit exceeded for 1997.—The numerical limitation for 1997 is exceeded if, based on the reports required under paragraph (4), the number of Archer MSAs established as of—

(A) April 30, 1997, exceeds 375,000, or

(B) June 30, 1997, exceeds 525,000.

(2) Determination of whether limit exceeded for 1998, 1999, 2001, 2002, 2004, 2005, or 2006.—

(A) In general.—The numerical limitation for 1998, 1999, 2001, 2002, 2004, 2005, or 2006. is exceeded if the sum of—

(i) the number of MSA returns filed on or before April 15 of such calendar year for taxable years ending with or within the preceding calendar year, plus

(ii) the Secretary's estimate (determined on the basis of the returns described in clause (i)) of the number of MSA returns for such taxable years which will be filed after such date, exceeds 750,000 (600,000 in the case of 1998). For purposes of the preceding sentence, the term "MSA return" means any return on which any exclusion is claimed under section 106(b) or any deduction is claimed under this section.

(B) Alternative computation of limitation.— The numerical limitation for 1998, 1999, 2001, 2002, 2004, 2005, or 2006. is also exceeded if the sum of—

(i) 90 percent of the sum determined under subparagraph (A) for such calendar year, plus

(ii) the product of 2.5 and the number of Archer MSAs established during the portion of such year preceding July 1 (based on the reports required under paragraph (4)) for taxable years beginning in such year, exceeds 750,000.

(C) No limitation for 2000 or 2003.—The numerical limitation shall not apply for 2000 or 2003.

(3) Previously uninsured individuals not included in determination.—

(A) In general.—The determination of whether any calendar year is a cut-off year shall be made by not counting the Archer MSA of any previously uninsured individual.

(B) Previously uninsured individual.—For purposes of this subsection, the term "previously uninsured individual" means, with respect to any Archer MSA, any individual who had no health plan coverage (other than coverage referred to in subsection (c)(1)(B)) at any time during the 6-month period before the date such individual's coverage under the high deductible health plan commences.

(4) Reporting by MSA trustees.—

(A) In general.—Not later than August 1 of 1997, 1998, 1999, 2001, 2002, 2004, 2005, or 2006, each person who is the trustee of an Archer MSA established before July 1 of such calendar year shall make a report to the Secretary (in such form and manner as the Secretary shall specify) which specifies—

(i) the number of Archer MSAs established before such July 1 (for taxable years beginning in such calendar year) of which such person is the trustee,

(ii) the name and TIN of the account holder of each such account, and

(iii) the number of such accounts which are accounts of previously uninsured individuals.

(B) Additional report for 1997.—Not later than June 1, 1997, each person who is the trustee of an Archer MSA established before May 1, 1997, shall make an additional report described in subparagraph (A) but only with respect to accounts established before May 1, 1997.

(C) Penalty for failure to file report.—The penalty provided in section 6693(a) shall apply to any report required by this paragraph, except that—

(i) such section shall be applied by substituting "$25" for "$50," and

(ii) the maximum penalty imposed on any trustee shall not exceed $5,000.

(D) Aggregation of accounts.—To the extent practicable, in determining the number of medical savings accounts on the basis of the reports under this paragraph, all Archer MSAs of an individual shall be treated as 1 account and all accounts of individuals who are married to each other shall be treated as 1 account.

(5) Date of making determinations.—Any determination under this subsection that a calendar year is a cut-off year shall be made by the Secretary and shall be published not later than October 1 of such year.

§ 221. Interest on education loans

(a) Allowance of deduction.—In the case of an individual, there shall be allowed as a deduction for the taxable year an amount equal to the interest paid by the taxpayer during the taxable year on any qualified education loan.

(b) Maximum deduction.—

(1) In general.—Except as provided in paragraph (2), the deduction allowed by subsection (a) for the taxable year shall not exceed the amount determined in accordance with the following table:

In the case of taxable years beginning in:	The dollar amount is:
1998	$1,000
1999	$1,500
2000	$2,000
2001 or thereafter	$2,500

(2) Limitation based on modified adjusted gross income.—

(A) In general.—The amount which would (but not for this paragraph) be allowable as a deduction under this section shall be reduced (but not below zero) by the amount determined under subparagraph (B).

(B) Amount of reduction*.—The amount determined under this subparagraph is the amount which bears the same ratio to the amount which would be so taken into account as—

(i) the excess of—

(I) the taxpayer's modified adjusted gross income for such taxable year, over

(II) $50,000 ($100,000 in the case of a joint return), bears to

(ii) $15,000 ($30,000 in the case of a joint return).

(C) Modified adjusted gross income.—The term "modified adjusted gross income" means adjusted gross income determined—

(i) without regard to this section and sections 199, 222, 911, 931, and 933, and

(ii) after application of sections 86, 135, 137, 219, and 469.

(c) Dependents not eligible for deduction.—No deduction shall be allowed by this section to an individual for the taxable year if a deduction under section 151 with respect to such individual is allowed to another taxpayer for the taxable year beginning in the calendar year in which such individual's taxable year begins.

(d) Definitions.—For purposes of this section—

(1) Qualified education loan.—The term "qualified education loan" means any indebtedness incurred by the taxpayer solely to pay qualified higher education expenses—

(A) which are incurred on behalf of the taxpayer, the taxpayer's spouse, or any dependent of the taxpayer as of the time the indebtedness was incurred,

(B) which are paid or incurred within a reasonable period of time before or after the indebtedness is incurred, and

(C) which are attributable to education furnished during a period which the recipient was an eligible student.

Such term includes indebtedness used to refinance indebtedness which qualifies as a qualified education loan. The term "qualified education loan" shall not include any indebtedness owed to a person who is related (within the meaning of section 267(b) or 707(b) (1)) to the taxpayer or to any person by reason of a loan under any qualified employer plan (as defined in section 72(p)(4)) or under any contract referred to in section 72(p)(5).

(2) Qualified higher education expenses.—The term "qualified higher education expenses" means the cost of attendance (as defined in section 472 of the Higher Education Act of 1965, 20 U.S.C. 108711, as in effect on the day before the date of the enactment of the Taxpayer Relief Act of 1997) at an eligible educational institution, reduced by the sum of—

(A) the amount excluded from gross income under section 127, 135, 529, or 530 by reason of such expenses, and

(B) the amount of any scholarship, allowance, or payment described in section 25A(g)(2).

For purposes of the preceding sentence, the term "eligible educational institution" has the same meaning given such term by section 25(A)(f)(2), except that such term shall also include an institution conducting an internship or residency program leading to a degree or certificate awarded by an institution of higher education, a hospital, or a health care facility which offers postgraduate training.

(3) Eligible student.—The term "eligible student" has the meaning given such term by section 25A(b)(3).

(4) Dependent.—The term "dependent" has the meaning given such term by section 152

*Editorial comment: Although subject to indexing for tax years beginning after 2003, the amounts remained unchanged through 2006. The indexed amount is $55,000 for 2007 for the $50,000, and the indexed amount for the $100,000 is $110,000. For 2008, the indexed amounts are $55,000 and $115,000 respectively. For 2009, 2010 and 2011, the indexed amounts are $60,000 and $120,000 respectively. For 2012 and 2013, the indexed amounts are $60,000 and $125,000 respectively. The 2014 indexed amounts are $65,000 and $130,000. The deduction is completely phased out for taxpayers with a modified adjusted gross income of $80,000 ($160,000 for joint filers).

(determined without regard to subsections (b)(1), (b)(2), and (d)(1)(B) thereof).

(e) Special rules.—

(1) Denial of double benefit.—No deduction shall be allowed under this section for any amount for which a deduction is allowable under any other provision of this chapter.

(2) Married couples must file joint return.—If the taxpayer is married at the close of the taxable year, the deduction shall be allowed under subsection (a) only if the taxpayer and the taxpayer's spouse file a joint return for the taxable year.

(3) Marital status.—Marital status shall be determined in accordance with section 7703.

(f) Inflation adjustments.—

(1) In general.—In the case of a taxable year beginning after 2002, the $50,000 and $100,000 amounts in subsection (b)(2) shall each be increased by an amount equal to—

(A) such dollar amount, multiplied by

(B) the cost-of-living adjustment determined under section 1(f)(3) for the calendar year in which the taxable year begins, determined by substituting "calendar year 2001" for "calendar year 1992" in subparagraph (B) thereof.

(2) Rounding.—If any amount as adjusted under paragraph (1) is not a multiple of $5,000, such amount shall be rounded to the next lowest multiple of $5,000.

§ 222. Qualified tuition and related expenses*

(a) Allowance of deduction.—In the case of an individual, there shall be allowed as a deduction an amount equal to the qualified tuition and related expenses paid by the taxpayer during the taxable year.

(b) Dollar limitations.—

(1) In general.—The amount allowed as a deduction under subsection (a) with respect to the taxpayer for any taxable year shall not exceed the applicable dollar limit.

(2) Applicable dollar limit.—

(A) 2002 and 2003.—In the case of a taxable year beginning in 2002 or 2003, the applicable dollar limit shall be equal to—

(i) in the case of a taxpayer whose adjusted gross income for the taxable year does not exceed $65,000 ($130,000 in the case of a joint return), $3,000, and—

(ii) in the case of any other taxpayer, zero.

(B) After 2003.—In the case of a taxable year beginning in after 2003, the applicable dollar amount shall be equal to—

(i) in the case of a taxpayer whose adjusted gross income for the taxable year does not exceed $65,000 ($130,000 in the case of a joint return), $4,000,

(ii) in the case of a taxpayer not described in clause (i) whose adjusted gross income for the taxable year does not exceed $80,000 ($160,000 in the case of a joint return), $2,000, and

(iii) in the case of any other taxpayer, zero.

(C) Adjusted gross income.—For purposes of this paragraph, adjusted gross income shall be determined—

(i) without regard to this section and sections 199, 911, 931, and 933, and

(ii) after application of sections 86, 135, 137, 219, 221, and 469.

(c) No double benefit.—

(1) In general.—No deduction shall be allowed under subsection (a) for any expense for which a deduction is allowed to the taxpayer under any other provision of this chapter.

(2) Coordination with other education incentives.—

(A) Denial of deduction if credit elected.—No deduction shall be allowed under subsection (a) for a taxable year with respect to the qualified tuition and related expenses with respect to an individual if the taxpayer or any other person elects to have section 25A apply with respect to such individual for such year.

(B) Coordination with exclusions.—The total amount of qualified tuition and related expenses shall be reduced by the amount of such expenses taken into account in determining any amount excluded under section 135, 529(c)(1), or 530(d)(2). For purposes of the preceding sentence, the amount taken into account in

*Editorial comment: At the present time, this section has not been extended. There is pending legislation in the Senate, *The Tax Extenders Act of 2013 (S. 1859)*, that would extend Section 222(e) until December 31, 2014.

determining the amount excluded under section 529(c)(1) shall not include that portion of the distribution which represents a return of any contributions to the plan.

(3) Dependents.—No deduction shall be allowed under subsection (a) to any individual with respect to whom a deduction under section 151 is allowable to another taxpayer for a taxable year beginning in the calendar year in which such individual's taxable year begins.

(d) Definitions and special rules.—For purposes of this section—

(1) Qualified tuition and related expenses.—The term "qualified tuition and related expenses" has the meaning given such term by section 25A (f). Such expenses shall be reduced in the same manner as under section 25A(g)(2).

(2) Identification requirement.—No deduction shall be allowed under subsection (a) to a taxpayer with respect to the qualified tuition and related expenses of an individual unless the taxpayer includes the name and taxpayer identification number of the individual on the return of tax for the taxable year.

(3) Limitation of taxable year of deduction.—

(A) In general.—A deduction shall be allowed under subsection (a) for qualified tuition and related expenses for any taxable year only to the extent such expenses are in connection with enrollment at an institution of higher education during the taxable year.

(B) Certain prepayments allowed.—Subparagraph (A) shall not apply to qualified tuition and related expenses paid during a taxable year if such expenses are in connection with an academic term beginning during such taxable year or during the first 3 months of the next taxable year.

(4) No deduction for married individuals filing separate returns.—If the taxpayer is a married individual (within the meaning of section 7703), this section shall apply only if the taxpayer and the taxpayer's spouse file a joint return for the taxable year.

(5) Nonresident aliens.—If the taxpayer is a nonresident alien individual for any portion of the taxable year, this section shall apply only if such individual is treated as a resident alien of the United States for purposes of this chapter by reason of an election under subsection (g) or (h) of section 6013.

(6) Regulations.—The Secretary may prescribe such regulations as may be necessary or appropriate to carry out this section, including regulations requiring recordkeeping and information reporting.

(e) Termination.—This section shall not apply to taxable years beginning after December 31, 2013.

§ 223. Health savings accounts

(a) Deduction allowed.—In the case of an individual who is an eligible individual for any month during the taxable year, there shall be allowed as a deduction for the taxable year an amount equal to the aggregate amount paid in cash during such taxable year by or on behalf of such individual to a health savings account of such individual.

(b) Limitations.—

(1) In general.—The amount allowable as a deduction under subsection (a) to an individual for the taxable year shall not exceed the sum of the monthly limitations for months during such taxable year that the individual is an eligible individual.

(2) Monthly limitation.—The monthly limitation for any month is 1/12 of—

(A) in the case of an eligible individual who has self-only coverage under a high deductible health plan as of the first day of such month, $2,250.*

(B) in the case of an eligible individual who has family coverage under a high deductible health plan as of the first day of such month, $4,500.*

(3) Additional contributions for individuals 55 or older.—

(A) In general.—In the case of an individual who has attained age 55 before the close of the taxable year, the applicable limitation under subparagraphs (A) and (B) of paragraph (2) shall be increased by the additional contribution amount.

(B) Additional contribution amount.—For purposes of this section, the additional contribution amount is the amount determined in accordance with the following table:

*Editorial comment: The indexed amounts for 2014 are $3,300 ($3,250 in 2013) and $6,550 ($6,450 in 2013) respectively.

For taxable years beginning in:	The additional contribution amount is:
2004	$500
2005	$600
2006	$700
2007	$800
2008	$900
2009 and thereafter	$1,000.

(4) Coordination with other contributions.—The limitation which would (but for this paragraph) apply under this subsection to an individual for any taxable year shall be reduced (but not below zero) by the sum of—

(A) the aggregate amount paid for such taxable year to Archer MSAs of such individual,

(B) the aggregate amount contributed to health savings accounts of such individual which is excludable from the taxpayer's gross income for such taxable year under section 106 (d) (and such amount shall not be allowed as a deduction under subsection (a)), and

(C) the aggregate amount contributed to health savings accounts of such individual for such taxable year under section 408(d)(9) (and such amount shall not be allowed as a deduction under subsection (a)).

Subparagraph (A) shall not apply with respect to any individual to whom paragraph (5) applies.

(5) Special rule for married individuals.—In the case of individuals who are married to each other, if either spouse has family coverage—

(A) both spouses shall be treated as having only such family coverage (and if such spouses each have family coverage under different plans, as having the family coverage with the lowest annual deductible), and

(B) the limitation under paragraph (1) (after the application of subparagraph (A) and without regard to any additional contribution amount under paragraph (3))—

(i) shall be reduced by the aggregate amount paid to Archer MSAs of such spouses for the taxable year, and

(ii) after such reduction, shall be divided equally between them unless they agree on a different division.

(6) Denial of deduction to dependents.—No deduction shall be allowed under this section to any individual with respect to whom a deduction under section 151 is allowable to another taxpayer for a taxable year beginning in the calendar year in which such individual's taxable year begins.

(7) Medicare eligible individuals.—The limitation under this subsection for any month with respect to an individual shall be zero for the first month such individual is entitled to benefits under title XVIII of the Social Security Act and for each month thereafter.

(8) Increase in limit for individuals becoming eligible individuals after the beginning of the year.—

(A) In general.—For purposes of computing the limitation under paragraph (1) for any taxable year, an individual who is an eligible individual during the last month of such taxable year shall be treated—

(i) as having been an eligible individual during each of the months in such taxable year, and

(ii) as having been enrolled, during each of the months such individual is treated as an eligible individual solely by reason of clause (i), in the same high deductible health plan in which the individual was enrolled for the last month of such taxable year.

(B) Failure to maintain high deductible health plan coverage.—

(i) In general.—If, at any time during the testing period, the individual is not an eligible individual, then—

(I) gross income of the individual for the taxable year in which occurs the first month in the testing period for which such individual is not an eligible individual is increased by the aggregate amount of all contributions to the health savings account of the individual which could not have been made but for subparagraph (A), and

(II) the tax imposed by this chapter for any taxable year on the individual shall be increased by 10 percent of the amount of such increase.

(ii) Exception for disability or death.—Subclauses (I) and (II) of clause (i) shall not apply if the individual ceased to be an eligible individual by reason of the death of the individual or the individual becoming disabled (within the meaning of section 72 (m)(7)).

(iii) Testing period.—The term "testing period" means the period beginning with the last month of the taxable year referred to in subparagraph (A) and ending on the last day of the 12th month following such month.

(c) Definitions and special rules.—For purposes of this section—

(1) Eligible individual.—

(A) In general.—The term "eligible individual" means, with respect to any month, any individual if—

(i) such individual is covered under a high deductible health plan as of the 1st day of such month, and

(ii) such individual is not, while covered under a high deductible health plan, covered under any health plan—

(I) which is not a high deductible health plan, and

(II) which provides coverage for any benefit which is covered under the high deductible health plan.

(B) Certain coverage disregarded.—Subparagraph (A)(ii) shall be applied without regard to—

(i) coverage for any benefit provided by permitted insurance,

(ii) coverage (whether through insurance or otherwise) for accidents, disability, dental care, vision care, or long-term care, and

(iii) for taxable years beginning after December 31, 2006, coverage under a health flexible spending arrangement during any period immediately following the end of a plan year of such arrangement during which unused benefits or contributions remaining at the end of such plan year may be paid or reimbursed to plan participants for qualified benefit expenses incurred during such period if—

(I) the balance in such arrangement at the end of such plan year is zero, or

(II) the individual is making a qualified HSA distribution (as defined in section 106(e)) in an amount equal to the remaining balance in such arrangement as of the end of such plan year, in accordance with rules prescribed by the Secretary.

(2) High deductible health plan.—

(A) In general.—The term "high deductible health plan" means a health plan—

(i) which has an annual deductible which is not less than—

(I) $1,000* for self-only coverage, and

(II) twice* the dollar amount in subclause (I) for family coverage, and

(ii) the sum of the annual deductible and the other annual out-of-pocket expenses required to be paid under the plan (other than for premiums) for covered benefits does not exceed—

(I) $5,000** for self-only coverage, and

(II) twice** the dollar amount in subclause (I) for family coverage.

(B) Exclusion of certain plans.—Such term does not include a health plan if substantially all of its coverage is coverage described in paragraph (1)(B).

(C) Safe harbor for absence of preventive care deductible.—A plan shall not fail to be treated as a high deductible health plan by reason of failing to have a deductible for preventive care (within the meaning of section 1871 of the Social Security Act, except as otherwise provided by the Secretary).

(D) Special rules for network plans.—In the case of a plan using a network of providers—

(i) Annual out-of-pocket limitation.—Such plan shall not fail to be treated as a high deductible health plan by reason of having an out-of-pocket limitation for services provided outside of such network which exceeds the applicable limitation under subparagraph (A)(ii).

(ii) Annual deductible.—Such plan's annual deductible for services provided outside of such network shall not be taken into account for purposes of subsection (b)(2).

---

*Editorial comment: The indexed amounts for 2014 are $1,250 and $2,500 respectively.

**Editorial comment: The indexed amounts for 2014 are $6,350 and $12,700 respectively.

(3) **Permitted insurance.**—The term "permitted insurance" means—

(A) insurance if substantially all of the coverage provided under such insurance relates to—

(i) liabilities incurred under workers' compensation laws,

(ii) tort liabilities,

(iii) liabilities relating to ownership or use of property, or

(iv) such other similar liabilities as the Secretary may specify by regulations,

(B) insurance for a specified disease or illness, and

(C) insurance paying a fixed amount per day (or other period) of hospitalization.

(4) **Family coverage.**—The term "family coverage" means any coverage other than self-only coverage.

(5) **Archer MSA.**—The term "Archer MSA" has the meaning given such term in section 220(d).

(d) **Health savings account.**—For purposes of this section—

(1) **In general.**—The term "health savings account" means a trust created or organized in the United States as a health savings account exclusively for the purpose of paying the qualified medical expenses of the account beneficiary, but only if the written governing instrument creating the trust meets the following requirements:

(A) Except in the case of a rollover contribution described in subsection (f)(5) or section 220(f)(5), no contribution will be accepted.—

(i) unless it is in cash, or

(ii) to the extent such contribution, when added to previous contributions to the trust for the calendar year, exceeds the sum of—

(I) the dollar amount in effect under subsection (b)(2)(B), and

(II) the dollar amount in effect under subsection (b)(3)(B).

(B) The trustee is a bank (as defined in section 408(n)), an insurance company (as defined in section 816), or another person who demonstrates to the satisfaction of the Secretary that the manner in which such person will administer the trust will be consistent with the requirements of this section.

(C) No part of the trust assets will be invested in life insurance contracts.

(D) The assets of the trust will not be commingled with other property except in a common trust fund or common investment fund.

(E) The interest of an individual in the balance in his account is nonforfeitable.

(2) **Qualified medical expenses.**—

(A) **In general.**—The term "qualified medical expenses" means, with respect to an account beneficiary, amounts paid by such beneficiary for medical care (as defined in section 213(d) for such individual, the spouse of such individual, and any dependent (as defined in section 152, determined without regard to subsections (b)(1), (b)(2), and (d)(1)(B) thereof) of such individual, but only to the extent such amounts are not compensated for by insurance or otherwise. Such term shall include an amount paid for medicine or a drug only if such medicine or drug is a prescribed drug (determined without regard to whether such drug is available without a prescription) or is insulin.

(B) **Health insurance may not be purchased from account.**—Subparagraph (A) shall not apply to any payment for insurance.

(C) **Exceptions.**—Subparagraph (B) shall not apply to any expense for coverage under—

(i) a health plan during any period of continuation coverage required under any Federal law,

(ii) a qualified long-term care insurance contract (as defined in section 7702B(b)),

(iii) a health plan during a period in which the individual is receiving unemployment compensation under any Federal or State law, or

(iv) in the case of an account beneficiary who has attained the age specified in section 1811 of the Social Security Act, any health insurance other than a Medicare supplemental policy (as defined in section 1882 of the Social Security Act).

(3) **Account beneficiary.**—The term "account beneficiary" means the individual on whose behalf the health savings account was established.

(4) **Certain rules to apply.**—Rules similar to the following rules shall apply for purposes of this section:

(A) Section 219(d)(2) (relating to no deduction for rollovers).

(B) Section 219(f)(3) (relating to time when contributions deemed made).

(C) Except as provided in section 106(d), section 219(f)(5) (relating to employer payments).

(D) Section 408(g) (relating to community property laws).

(E) Section 408(h) (relating to custodial accounts).

(e) Tax treatment of accounts.—

(1) In general.—A health savings account is exempt from taxation under this subtitle unless such account has ceased to be a health savings account. Notwithstanding the preceding sentence, any such account is subject to the taxes imposed by section 511 (relating to imposition of tax on unrelated business income of charitable, etc. organizations).

(2) Account terminations.—Rules similar to the rules of paragraphs (2) and (4) of section 408(e) shall apply to health savings accounts, and any amount treated as distributed under such rules shall be treated as not used to pay qualified medical expenses.

(f) Tax treatment of distributions.—

(1) Amounts used for qualified medical expenses.—Any amount paid or distributed out of a health savings account which is used exclusively to pay qualified medical expenses of any account beneficiary shall not be includible in gross income.

(2) Inclusions of amounts not used for qualified medical expenses.—Any amount paid or distributed out of a health savings account which is not used exclusively to pay the qualified medical expenses of the account beneficiary shall be included in the gross income of such beneficiary.

(3) Excess contributions returned before due date of return.—

(A) In general.—If any excess contribution is contributed for a taxable year to any health savings account of an individual, paragraph (2) shall not apply to distributions from the health savings accounts of such individual (to the extent such distributions do not exceed the aggregate excess contributions to all such accounts of such individual for such year) if—

(i) such distribution is received by the individual on or before the last day prescribed by law (including extensions of time) for filing such individual's return for such taxable year, and

(ii) such distribution is accompanied by the amount of net income attributable to such excess contribution.

Any net income described in clause (ii) shall be included in the gross income of the individual for the taxable year in which it is received.

(B) Excess contribution.—For purposes of subparagraph (A), the terms "excess contribution" means any contribution (other than a rollover contribution described in paragraph (5) or section 220(f)(5)) which is neither excludable from gross income under section 106(d) nor deductible under this section.

(4) Additional tax on distributions not used for qualified medical expenses.—

(A) In general.—The tax imposed by this chapter on the account beneficiary for any taxable year in which there is a payment or distribution from a health savings account of such beneficiary which is includible in gross income under paragraph (2) shall be increased by 20 percent of the amount which is so includible.

(B) Exception for disability or death.—Subparagraph (A) shall not apply if the payment or distribution is made after the account beneficiary becomes disabled within the meaning of section 72(m)(7) or dies.

(C) Exception for distributions after Medicare eligibility.—Subparagraph (A) shall not apply to any payment or distribution after the date on which the account beneficiary attains the age specified in section 1811 of the Social Security Act.

(5) Rollover contribution.—An amount is described in this paragraph as a rollover contribution if it meets the requirements of subparagraphs (A) and (B).

(A) In general.—Paragraph (2) shall not apply to any amount paid or distributed from a health savings account to the account beneficiary to the extent the amount received is paid into a health savings account for the benefit of such beneficiary not later than the 60th day after the day on which the beneficiary receives the payment or distribution.

(B) Limitation.—This paragraph shall not apply to any amount described in subparagraph (A) received by an individual from a health savings account if, at any time during the 1-year period ending on the day of such receipt, such individual received any other amount described in subparagraph (A) from a health savings account which was not includible in the individual's gross income because of the application of this paragraph.

(6) Coordination with medical expense deduction.—For purposes of determining the amount of the deduction under section 213, any payment or distribution out of a health savings account for qualified medical expenses shall not be treated as an expense paid for medical care.

(7) Transfer of account incident to divorce.—The transfer of an individual's interest in a health savings account to an individual's spouse or former spouse under a divorce or separation instrument described in subparagraph (A) of section 71(b)(2) shall not be considered a taxable transfer made by such individual notwithstanding any other provision of this subtitle, and such interest shall, after such transfer, be treated as a health savings account with respect to which such spouse is the account beneficiary.

(8) Treatment after death of account beneficiary.—

(A) Treatment if designated beneficiary is spouse.—If the account beneficiary's surviving spouse acquires such beneficiary's interest in a health savings account by reason of being the designated beneficiary of such account at the death of the account beneficiary, such health savings account shall be treated as if the spouse were the account beneficiary.

(B) Other cases.—

(i) In general.—If, by reason of the death of the account beneficiary, any person acquires the account beneficiary's interest in a health savings account in a case to which subparagraph (A) does not apply—

(I) such account shall cease to be a health savings account as of the date of death, and

(II) an amount equal to the fair market value of the assets in such account on such date shall be includible if such person is not the estate of such beneficiary, in such person's gross income for the taxable year which includes such date, or if such person is the estate of such beneficiary, in such beneficiary's gross income for the last taxable year of such beneficiary.

(ii) Special rules.—

(I) Reduction of inclusion for predeath expenses.—The amount includible in gross income under clause (i) by any person (other than the estate) shall be reduced by the amount of qualified medical expenses which were incurred by the decedent before the date of the decedent's death and paid by such person within 1 year after such date.

(II) Deduction for estate taxes.—An appropriate deduction shall be allowed under section 691(c) to any person (other than the decedent or the decedent's spouse) with respect to amounts included in gross income under clause (i) by such person.

(g) Cost-of-living adjustment.—

(1) In general.—Each dollar amount in subsections (b)(2) and (c)(2)(A) shall be increased by an amount equal to—

(A) such dollar amount, multiplied by

(B) the cost-of-living adjustment determined under section 1(f)(3) for the calendar year in which such taxable year begins determined by substituting for "calendar year 1992" in subparagraph (B) thereof—

(i) except as provided in clause (ii), "calendar year 1997," and

(ii) in the case of each dollar amount in subsection (c)(2)(A), "calendar year 2003."

In the case of adjustments made for any taxable year beginning after 2007, section (1)(f)(4) shall be applied for purposes of this paragraph by substituting "March 31" for "August 31," and the Secretary shall publish the adjustment amounts under subsections (b)(2) and (c)(2)(A) for taxable years beginning in any calendar year no later than June 1 of the preceding calendar year.

(2) Rounding.—If any increase under paragraph (1) is not a multiple of $50, such increase shall be rounded to the nearest multiple of $50.

(h) Reports.—The Secretary may require—

(1) the trustee of a health savings account to make such reports regarding such account to the Secretary and to the account beneficiary with respect to contributions, distributions, the return of excess contributions, and such other matters as the Secretary determines appropriate, and

(2) any person who provides an individual with a high deductible health plan to make such reports to the Secretary and to the account beneficiary with respect to such plan as the Secretary determines appropriate.

The reports required by this subsection shall be filed at such time and in such matter and furnished to such individuals at such time and in such manner as may be required by the Secretary.

* * *

PART VIII—SPECIAL DEDUCTIONS FOR CORPORATIONS

Editorial Summary

Special Deductions for Corporations

Subchapter B of Chapter 1 (Secs. 241–248)

Corporations are eligible for the deductions contained in Part VIII (i.e., Secs. 241–248) and also for the deductions contained in Part VI (i.e., Secs. 161–199). The reason for the separate classification is that Part VIII deductions apply only to the corporate taxpayer whereas Part VI deductions apply to both the individual taxpayer and the corporate taxpayer.

The two special deductions most likely to apply to the typical corporation are the dividends received deduction (see Sec. 243) and the deduction for organization expenses (see Sec. 248).

The justification for the dividends received deduction is to avoid, or at least limit the occurrence of, triple taxation. Corporations are subject to taxation on their taxable income [see Sec. 11(a)]. If a corporation distributes part or all of its earnings to its shareholders (i.e., a dividend), no deduction is available to the corporation associated with the distribution. At the shareholder level, the dividends received are required to be included in gross income [see Sec. 61(7)]. Thus, double taxation has occurred. If the shareholder were a corporation and such corporate shareholder distributed its earnings to its shareholders, triple taxation would result.

The calculation of the dividends received deduction consists of these three steps [see Secs. 243(a) and 246(b)]:

1. Multiply the dividends received during the taxable year by a statutory percentage (discussed below).

2. Multiply "taxable income as adjusted" (discussed below) by the statutory percentage used in Step 1.

3. The dividends received deduction generally is the lower of the amounts calculated in Steps 1 and 2. However, if deducting the amount calculated in Step 1 either creates or increases a net operating loss (see Sec. 172), then the dividends received deduction is the amount calculated in Step 1.

The Revenue Act of 1987 modified the statutory percentage to be used. Prior to the Act, the general statutory percentage was 80 percent. However, in the case of a corporation which receives dividends from a corporation that is a member of the same affiliated group [see Sec. 243(b)(2)], the statutory percentage can be increased from 80 percent to 100 percent. The Revenue Act dichotomized the general statutory percentage as follows:

1. If the percentage of stock ownership by the corporate shareholder is less than 20 percent, the statutory percentage is 70 percent.

2. If the percentage of stock ownership by the corporate shareholder is at least 20 percent but less than 80 percent, the statutory percentage is 80 percent. Note that if the percentage of stock ownership is at least 80 percent and if affiliated group status is present, the statutory percentage is increased to 100 percent.

"Taxable income as adjusted" is defined in Sec. 246(b)(1). In general, it consists of taxable income before giving consideration to the dividends received deduction, the net operating loss deduction, and any capital loss carryback.

The organizational expenditures [see Sec. 248(b)] incurred by a corporation must be capitalized. Since such expenditures benefit the corporation over its entire life, it would appear that organizational expenditures could not be deducted (i.e., expensed and amortized) because of the indefinite life of the corporation. However, Sec. 248(a) enables the corporation to elect limited expensing with the amortization of the balance of these expenditures over a minimum 180-month period. Absent a timely election [see Sec. 248(c)], the capitalized amount cannot be deducted until the end of the life of the corporation.

§ 241. Allowance of special deductions

In addition to the deductions provided in part VI (sec. 161 and following), there shall be allowed as deductions in computing taxable income the items specified in this part.

§ 243. Dividends received by corporations

(a) General rule.—In the case of a corporation, there shall be allowed as a deduction an amount equal to the following percentages of the amount received as dividends from a domestic corporation which is subject to taxation under this chapter:

(1) 70 percent, in the case of dividends other than dividends described in paragraph (2) or (3);

(2) 100 percent, in the case of dividends received by a small business investment company operating under the Small Business Investment Act of 1958 (15 U.S.C. 661 and following); and

(3) 100 percent, in the case of qualifying dividends (as defined in subsection (b)(1)).

(b) Qualifying dividends.—

(1) In general.—For purposes of this section, the term "qualifying dividend" means any dividend received by a corporation—

(A) if at the close of the day on which such dividend is received, such corporation is a member of the same affiliated group as the corporation distributing such dividend, and

(B) if—

(i) such dividend is distributed out of the earnings and profits of a taxable year of the distributing corporation which ends after

December 31, 1963, for which an election under section 1562 was not in effect, and on each day of which the distributing corporation and the corporation receiving the dividend were members of such affiliated group, or

(ii) such dividend is paid by a corporation with respect to which an election under section 936 is in effect for the taxable year in which such dividend is paid.

(2) Affiliated group.—For purposes of this subsection:

(A) In general.—The term "affiliated group" has the meaning given such term by section 1504(a), except that for such purposes sections 1504(b)(2), 1504(b)(4), and 1504(c) shall not apply.

(B) Group must be consistent in foreign tax treatment.—The requirements of paragraph (1)(A) shall not be treated as being met with respect to any dividend received by a corporation if, for any taxable year which includes the day on which such dividend is received—

(i) 1 or more members of the affiliated group referred to in paragraph (1)(A) choose to any extent to take the benefits of section 901, and

(ii) 1 or more other members of such group claim to any extent a deduction for taxes otherwise creditable under section 901.

* * *

(3) Special rule for groups which include life insurance companies.—

(A) In general.—In the case an affiliated group which includes 1 or more insurance companies under section 801, no dividend by any member of such group shall be treated as a qualifying dividend unless an election under this paragraph is in effect for the taxable year in which the dividend is received. The preceding sentence shall not apply in the case of a dividend described in paragraph (1)(B)(ii).

(B) Effect of election.—If an election under this paragraph is in effect with respect to any affiliated group—

(i) part II of subchapter B of chapter 6 (relating to certain controlled corporations) shall be applied with respect to the members of such group without regard to sections 1563(a)(4) and 1563(b)(2)(D), and

(ii) for purposes of this subsection, a distribution by any member of such group which is subject to tax under section 801 shall not be treated as a qualifying dividend if such distribution is out of earnings and profits for a taxable year for which an election under this paragraph is not effective and for which such distributing corporation was not a component member of a controlled group of corporations within the meaning of section 1563 solely by reason of section 1563(b)(2)(D).

(C) Election.—An election under this paragraph shall be made by the common parent of the affiliated group and at such time and in such manner as the Secretary shall by regulations prescribe. Any such election shall be binding on all members of such group and may be revoked only with the consent of the Secretary.

(c) Retention of 80-percent dividends received deduction for dividends from 20-percent owned corporations.—

(1) In general.—In the case of any dividend received from a 20-percent owned corporation—

(A) subsection (a)(1) of this section, and

(B) subsections (a)(3) and (b)(2) of section 244,

shall be applied by substituting "80 percent" for "70 percent."

(2) 20-percent owned corporation.—For purposes of this section, the term "20-percent owned corporation" means any corporation if 20 percent or more of the stock of such corporation (by vote and value) is owned by the taxpayer. For purposes of the preceding sentence, stock described in section 1504(a)(4) shall not be taken into account.

* * *

§ 246. Rules applying to deductions for dividends received

(a) Deduction not allowed for dividends from certain corporations.—

(1) In general.—The deductions allowed by sections 243, 244, and 245 shall not apply to any dividend from a corporation which, for the taxable year of the corporation in which the distribution is made, or for the next preceding taxable year of the corporation, is a corporation exempt from tax under section 501 (relating to certain charitable, etc., organizations) or section 521 (relating to farmers' cooperative associations).

* * *

(b) Limitation on aggregate amount of deductions.—

(1) General rule.—Except as provided in paragraph (2), the aggregate amount of the deductions allowed by sections 243(a)(1), 244(a), and 245 shall not exceed the percentage determined under paragraph (3) of the taxable income computed without regard to the deductions allowed by sections 172, 192, 243(a)(l), 244(a), subsection (a) or (b) of section 245, and 247, without regard to any adjustment under section 1059, and without regard to any capital loss carryback to the taxable year under section 1212(a)(l).

(2) Effect of net operating loss.—Paragraph (1) shall not apply for any taxable year for which there is a net operating loss (as determined under section 172).

(3) Special rules.—The provisions of paragraph (1) shall be applied—

(A) first separately with respect to dividends from 20-percent owned corporations (as defined in section 243(c)(2)) and the percentage determined under this paragraph shall be 80 percent, and

(B) then separately with respect to dividends not from 20-percent owned corporations and the percentage determined under this paragraph shall be 70 percent and the taxable income shall be reduced by the aggregate amount of dividends from 20-percent owned corporations (as so defined).

(c) Exclusion of certain dividends.—

(1) In general.—No deduction shall be allowed under section 243, 244, or 245, in respect of any dividend on any share of stock—

(A) which is held by the taxpayer for 45 days or less during the 91-day period beginning on the date which is 45 days before the date on which such share becomes ex-dividend with respect to such dividend, or

(B) to the extent that the taxpayer is under an obligation (whether pursuant to a short sale or otherwise) to make related payments with respect to positions in substantially similar or related property.

(2) 90-day rule in the case of certain preference dividends.—In the case of stock having preference in dividends, if the taxpayer receives dividends with respect to such stock which are attributable to a period or periods aggregating in excess of 366 days, paragraph (1)(A) shall be applied—

(A) by substituting "90 days" for "45 days" each place it appears, and

(B) by substituting "181-day period" for "91-day period."

(3) Determination of holding periods.—For purposes of this subsection, in determining the period for which the taxpayer has held any share of stock—

(A) the day of disposition, but not the day of acquisition, shall be taken into account, and

(B) paragraph (3) of section 1223 shall not apply.

(4) Holding period reduced for periods where risk of loss diminished.—The holding periods determined for purposes of this subsection shall be appropriately reduced (in the manner provided in regulations prescribed by the Secretary) for any period (during such periods) in which—

(A) the taxpayer has an option to sell, is under a contractual obligation to sell, or has made (and not closed) a short sale of, substantially identical stock or securities,

(B) the taxpayer is the grantor of an option to buy substantially identical stock or securities, or

(C) under regulations prescribed by the Secretary, a taxpayer has diminished his risk of loss by holding 1 or more other positions with respect to substantially similar or related property.

The preceding sentence shall not apply in the case of any qualified covered call (as defined in section 1092(c)(4) but without regard to the requirement that gain or loss with respect to the option not be ordinary income or loss), other than a qualified covered call option to which section 1092(f) applies.

* * *

§ 246A. Dividends received deduction reduced where portfolio stock is debt financed

(a) General rule.—In the case of any dividend on debt-financed portfolio stock, there shall be substituted for the percentage which (but for this subsection) would be used in determining the amount of the deduction allowable under section 243, 244, or 245(a) a percentage equal to the product of—

(1) 70 percent (80 percent in the case of any dividend from a 20-percent owned corporation as defined in section 243(c)(2)), and

(2) 100 percent minus the average indebtedness percentage.

(b) Section not to apply to dividends for which 100 percent dividends received deduction allowable.—Subsection (a) shall not apply to—

(1) qualifying dividends (as defined in section 243(b) without regard to section 243(d)(4)), and

(2) dividends received by a small business investment company operating under the Small Business Investment Act of 1958.

(c) Debt financed portfolio stock.—For purposes of this section—

(1) In general.—The term "debt financed portfolio stock" means any portfolio stock if at some time during the base period there is portfolio indebtedness with respect to such stock.

(2) Portfolio stock.—The term "portfolio stock" means any stock of a corporation unless—

(A) as of the beginning of the ex-dividend date, the taxpayer owns stock of such corporation—

(i) possessing at least 50 percent of the total voting power of the stock of such corporation, and

(ii) having a value equal to at least 50 percent of the total value of the stock of such corporation, or

(B) as of the beginning of the ex-dividend date—

(i) the taxpayer owns stock of such corporation which would meet the requirements of subparagraph (A) if "20 percent" were substituted for "50 percent" each place it appears in such subparagraph, and

(ii) stock meeting the requirements of subparagraph (A) is owned by 5 or fewer corporate shareholders.

* * *

(d) Average indebtedness percentage.—For purposes of this section—

(1) In general.—Except as provided in paragraph (2), the term "average indebtedness percentage" means the percentage obtained by dividing—

(A) the average amount (determined under regulations prescribed by the Secretary) of the portfolio indebtedness with respect to the stock during the base period, by

(B) the average amount (determined under regulations prescribed by the Secretary) of the adjusted basis of the stock during the base period.

(2) Special rule where stock not held throughout base period.—In the case of any stock which was not held by the taxpayer throughout the base period, paragraph (1) shall be applied as if the base period consisted only of that portion of the base period during which the stock was held by the taxpayer.

(3) Portfolio indebtedness.—

(A) In general.—The term "portfolio indebtedness" means any indebtedness directly attributable to investment in the portfolio stock.

(B) Certain amounts received from short sale treated as indebtedness.—For purposes of subparagraph (A), any amount received from a short sale shall be treated as indebtedness for the period beginning on the day on which such amount is received and ending on the day the short sale is closed.

(4) Base period.—The term "base period" means, with respect to any dividend, the shorter of—

(A) the period beginning on the ex-dividend date for the most recent previous dividend on the stock and ending on the day before the ex-dividend date for the dividend involved, or

(B) the 1-year period ending on the day before the ex-dividend date for the dividend involved.

(e) Reduction in dividends received deduction not to exceed allocable interest.—Under regulations prescribed by the Secretary, any reduction under this section in the amount allowable as a deduction under section 243, 244, or 245 with respect to any dividend shall not exceed the amount of any interest deduction (including any deductible short sale expense) allocable to such dividend.

(f) Regulations.—The regulations prescribed for purposes of this section under section 7701(f) shall include regulations providing for the disallowance of interest deductions or other appropriate treatment (in lieu of reducing the dividend received deduction) where the obligor of the indebtedness is a person other than the person receiving the dividend.

* * *

§ 248. Organizational expenditures

(a) Election to deduct.—If a corporation elects the application of this subsection (in accordance with regulations prescribed by the Secretary) with respect to any organizational expenditures—

(1) the corporation shall be allowed a deduction for the taxable year in which the corporation begins business in an amount equal to the lesser of—

(A) the amount of organizational expenditures with respect to the taxpayer, or

(B) $5,000, reduced (but not below zero) by the amount by which such organizational expenditures exceed $50,000, and

(2) the remainder of such organizational expenditures shall be allowed as a deduction ratably over the 180-month period beginning with the month in which the corporation begins business.

(b) Organizational expenditures defined.—The term "organizational expenditures" means any expenditure which—

(1) is incident to the creation of the corporation;

(2) is chargeable to capital account; and

(3) is of a character which, if expended incident to the creation of a corporation having a limited life, would be amortizable over such life.

(c) Time for and scope of election.—The election provided by subsection (a) may be made for any taxable year beginning after December 31, 1953, but only if made not later than the time prescribed by law for filing the return for such taxable year (including extensions thereof). The period so elected shall be adhered to in computing the taxable income of the corporation for the taxable year for which the election is made and all subsequent taxable years. The election shall apply only with respect to expenditures paid or incurred on or after August 16, 1954.

* * *

PART IX—ITEMS NOT DEDUCTIBLE

Editorial Summary

Disallowance of Deductions

Subchapter B of Chapter 1 (Secs. 261–291)

See the discussion under the Editorial Summary entitled Deductions which precedes Sec. 161.

§ 261. General rule for disallowance of deductions

In computing taxable income, no deduction shall in any case be allowed in respect of the items specified in this part.

§ 262. Personal, living, and family expenses

(a) General rule.—Except as otherwise expressly provided in this chapter, no deduction shall be allowed for personal, living, or family expenses.

(b) Treatment of certain phone expenses.—For purposes of subsection (a), in the case of an individual, any charge (including taxes thereon) for basic local telephone service with respect to the 1st telephone line provided to any residence of the taxpayer shall be treated as a personal expense.

§ 263. Capital expenditures

(a) General rule.—No deduction shall be allowed for—

(1) Any amount paid out for new buildings or for permanent improvements or betterments made to increase the value of any property or estate. This paragraph shall not apply to—

(A) expenditures for the development of mines or deposits deductible under section 616,

(B) research and experimental expenditures deductible under section 174,

(C) soil and water conservation expenditures deductible under section 175,

(D) expenditures by farmers for fertilizer, etc., deductible under section 180,

(E) expenditures for removal of architectural and transportation barriers to the handicapped and elderly which the taxpayer elects to deduct under section 190,

(F) expenditures for tertiary injectants with respect to which a deduction is allowed under section 193,

(G) expenditures for which a deduction is allowed under section 179,

(H) expenditures for which a deduction is allowed under section 179A,

(I) expenditures for which a deduction is allowed under section 179B,

(J) expenditures for which a deduction is allowed under section 179C,

(K) expenditures for which a deduction is allowed under section 179D, or

(L) expenditures for which a deduction is allowed under section 179E.

(2) Any amount expended in restoring property or in making good the exhaustion thereof for which an allowance is or has been made.

*__(c) Intangible drilling and development costs in the case of oil and gas wells and geothermal wells.__—Notwithstanding subsection (a), and except as provided in subsection (i), regulations shall be prescribed by the Secretary under this subtitle corresponding to the regulations which granted the option to deduct as expenses intangible drilling and development costs in the case of oil and gas wells and which were recognized and approved by the Congress in House Concurrent Resolution 50, Seventy-ninth Congress. Such regulations shall also grant the option to deduct as expenses intangible drilling and development costs in the case of wells drilled for any geothermal deposit (as defined in section 613(e)(2)) to the same extent and in the same manner as such expenses are deductible in the case of oil and gas wells. This subsection shall not apply with respect to any costs to which any deduction is allowed under section 59(e) or 291.

* * *

(g) Certain interest and carrying costs in the case of straddles.—

(1) General rule.—No deduction shall be allowed for interest and carrying charges properly allocable to personal property which is part of a straddle (as defined in section 1092(c)). Any amount not allowed as a deduction by reason of the preceding sentence shall be chargeable to the capital account with respect to the personal property to which such amount relates.

(2) Interest and carrying charges defined.—For purposes of paragraph (1), the term "interest and carrying charges" means the excess of—

(A) the sum of—

(i) interest on indebtedness incurred or continued to purchase or carry the personal property, and

(ii) all other amounts (including charges to insure, store, or transport the personal property) paid or incurred to carry the personal property, over

(B) the sum of—

(i) the amount of interest (including original issue discount) includible in gross income for the taxable year with respect to the property described in subparagraph (A),

(ii) any amount treated as ordinary income under section 1271(a)(3)(A), 1276, 1278, or 1281(a) with respect to such property for the taxable year,

(iii) the excess of any dividends includible in gross income with respect to such property for the taxable year over the amount of any deduction allowable with respect to such dividends under section 243, 244, or 245, and

(iv) any amount which is a payment with respect to a security loan (within the meaning of section 512(a)(5)) includible in gross income with respect to such property for the taxable year.

For purposes of subparagraph (A), the term "interest" includes any amount paid or incurred in connection with personal property used in a short sale.

(3) Exception for hedging transactions.—This subsection shall not apply in the case of any hedging transaction (as defined in section 1256(e)).

(4) Application with other provisions.—

(A) Subsection (c).—In the case of any short sale, this subsection shall be applied after subsection (h).

(B) Section 1277 or 1282.—In the case of any obligation to which section 1277 or 1282 applies, this subsection shall be applied after section 1277 or 1282.

* * *

§ 263A. Capitalization and inclusion in inventory costs of certain expenses

(a) Nondeductibility of certain direct and indirect costs.—

(1) In general.—In the case of any property to which this section applies, any costs described in paragraph (2)—

(A) in the case of property which is inventory in the hands of the taxpayer, shall be included in inventory costs, and

*Editorial comment: There is no subsection (b).

(B) in the case of any other property, shall be capitalized.

(2) **Allocable costs.**—The costs described in this paragraph with respect to any property are—

(A) the direct costs of such property, and

(B) such property's proper share of those indirect costs (including taxes) part or all of which are allocable to such property.

Any cost which (but for this subsection) could not be taken into account in computing taxable income for any taxable year shall not be treated as a cost described in this paragraph.

(b) **Property to which section applies.**—Except as otherwise provided in this section, this section shall apply to—

(1) **Property produced by taxpayer.**—Real or tangible personal property produced by the taxpayer.

(2) **Property acquired for resale.**—

(A) **In general.**—Real or personal property described in section 1221(1) which is acquired by the taxpayer for resale.

(B) **Exception for taxpayer with gross receipts of $10,000,000 or less.**—Subparagraph (A) shall not apply to any personal property acquired during any taxable year by the taxpayer for resale if the average annual gross receipts of the taxpayer (or any predecessor) for the 3-taxable year period ending with the taxable year preceding such taxable year do not exceed $10,000,000.

(C) **Aggregation rules, etc.**—For purposes of subparagraph (B), rules similar to the rules of paragraphs (2) and (3) of section 448(c) shall apply.

For purposes of paragraph (1), the term "tangible personal property" shall include a film, sound recording, video tape, book, or similar property.

(c) **General exceptions.**—

(1) **Personal use property.**—This section shall not apply to any property produced by the taxpayer for use by the taxpayer other than in a trade or business or an activity conducted for profit.

(2) **Research and experimental expenditures.**—This section shall not apply to any amount allowable as a deduction under section 174.

(3) **Certain development and other costs of oil and gas wells or other mineral property.**—This section shall not apply to any cost allowable as a deduction under section 167(h), 179(b), 263(c), 263(i), 291(b)(2), 616, or 617.

(4) **Coordination with long-term contract rules.**—This section shall not apply to any property produced by the taxpayer pursuant to a long-term contract.

(5) **Timber and certain ornamental trees.**—This section shall not apply to—

(A) trees raised, harvested, or grown by the taxpayer other than trees described in clause (ii) of subsection (e)(4)(B) (after application of the last sentence thereof), and

(B) any real property underlying such trees.

(6) **Coordination with section 59(e).**—Paragraphs (2) and (3) shall apply to any amount allowable as a deduction under section 59(e) for qualified expenditures described in subparagraphs (B), (C), (D), and (E) of paragraph (2) thereof.

(d) **Exception for farming businesses.**—

(1) **Section not to apply to certain property.**—

(A) **In general.**—This section shall not apply to any of the following which is produced by the taxpayer in a farming business:

(i) Any animal.

(ii) Any plant which has a preproductive period of 2 years or less.

(B) **Exception for taxpayers required to use accrual method.**—Subparagraph (A) shall not apply to any corporation, partnership, or tax shelter required to use an accrual method of accounting under section 447 or 448(a)(3).

(2) **Treatment of certain plants lost by reason of casualty.**—

(A) **In general.**—If plants bearing an edible crop for human consumption were lost or damaged (while in the hands of the taxpayer) by reason of freezing temperatures, disease, drought, pests, or casualty, this section shall not apply to any costs of the taxpayer of replanting plants bearing the same type of crop (whether on the same parcel of land on which such lost or damaged plants were located or any other parcel of land of the same acreage in the United States).

(B) **Special rule for person with minority interest who materially participates.**—Subparagraph (A) shall apply to amounts paid or incurred by a person (other than the taxpayer described in subparagraph (A)) if—

(i) the taxpayer described in subparagraph (A) has an equity interest of more than 50 percent in the plants described in subparagraph (A) during the taxable year in which such amounts were paid or incurred, and

(ii) such other person holds any part of the remaining equity interest and materially participates in the planting, maintenance, cultivation, or development of the plants described in subparagraph (A) at all times during the taxable year in which such amounts were paid or incurred.

The determination of whether an individual materially participates in any activity shall be made in a manner similar to the manner in which such determination is made under section 2032A(e)(6).

(3) Election to have this section not apply.—

(A) In general.—If a taxpayer makes an election under this paragraph, this section shall not apply to any plant produced in any farming business carried on by such taxpayer.

(B) Certain persons not eligible.—No election may be made under this paragraph by a corporation, partnership, or tax shelter, if such corporation, partnership, or tax shelter is required to use an accrual method of accounting under section 447 or 448(a)(3).

(C) Special rule for citrus and almond growers.—An election under this paragraph shall not apply with respect to any item which is attributable to the planting, cultivation, maintenance, or development of any citrus or almond grove (or part thereof) and which is incurred before the close of the 4th taxable year beginning with the taxable year in which the trees were planted. For purposes of the preceding sentence, the portion of a citrus or almond grove planted in 1 taxable year shall be treated separately from the portion of such grove planted in another taxable year.

(D) Election.—Unless the Secretary otherwise consents, an election under this paragraph may be made only for the taxpayer's 1st taxable year which begins after December 31, 1986, and during which the taxpayer engages in a farming business. Any such election, once made, may be revoked only with the consent of the Secretary.

(e) Definitions and special rules for purposes of subsection (d).—

(1) Recapture of expensed amounts on disposition.—

(A) In general.—In the case of any plant with respect to which amounts would have been capitalized under subsection (a) but for an election under subsection (d)(3)—

(i) such plant (if not otherwise section 1245 property) shall be treated as section 1245 property, and

(ii) for purposes of section 1245, the recapture amount shall be treated as a deduction allowed for depreciation with respect to such property.

(B) Recapture amount.—For purposes of subparagraph (A), the term "recapture amount" means any amount allowable as a deduction to the taxpayer which, but for an election under subsection (d)(3), would have been capitalized with respect to the plant.

(2) Effects of election on depreciation.—

(A) In general.—If the taxpayer (or any related person) makes an election under subsection (d)(3), the provisions of section 168(g)(2) (relating to alternative depreciation) shall apply to all property of the taxpayer used predominantly in the farming business and placed in service in any taxable year during which any such election is in effect.

(B) Related person.—For purposes of subparagraph (A), the term "related person" means—

(i) the taxpayer and members of the taxpayer's family,

(ii) any corporation (including an S corporation) if 50 percent or more (in value) of the stock of such corporation is owned (directly or through the application of section 318) by the taxpayer or members of the taxpayer's family,

(iii) a corporation and any other corporation which is a member of the same controlled group described in section 1563(a)(1), and

(iv) any partnership if 50 percent or more (in value) of the interests in such partnership is owned directly or indirectly by the taxpayer or members of the taxpayer's family.

(C) Members of family.—For purposes of this paragraph, the term "family" means the taxpayer, the spouse of the taxpayer, and any of their children who have not attained age 18 before the close of the taxable year.

(3) Preproductive period.—

(A) In general.—For purposes of this section, the term "preproductive period" means—

(i) in the case of a plant which will have more than 1 crop or yield, the period before the 1st marketable crop or yield from such plant, or

(ii) in the case of any other plant, the period before such plant is reasonably expected to be disposed of.

For purposes of this subparagraph, use by the taxpayer in a farming business of any supply produced in such business shall be treated as a disposition.

(B) Rule for determining period.—In the case of a plant grown in commercial quantities in the United States, the preproductive period for such plant if grown in the United States shall be based on the nationwide weighted average preproductive period for such plant.

(4) Farming business.—For purposes of this section—

(A) In general.—The term "farming business" means the trade or business of farming.

(B) Certain trades and businesses included.—The term "farming business" shall include the trade or business of—

(i) operating a nursery or sod farm, or

(ii) the raising or harvesting of trees bearing fruit, nuts, or other crops, or ornamental trees.

For purposes of clause (ii), an evergreen tree which is more than 6 years old at the time severed from the roots shall not be treated as an ornamental tree.

(5) Certain inventory valuation methods permitted.—The Secretary shall by regulations permit the taxpayer to use reasonable inventory valuation methods to compute the amount required to be capitalized under subsection (a) in the case of any plant.

(f) Special rules for allocation of interest to property produced by the taxpayer.—

(1) Interest capitalized only in certain cases.—Subsection (a) shall only apply to interest costs which are—

(A) paid or incurred during the production period, and

(B) allocable to property which is described in subsection (B)(l) and which has—

(i) a long useful life,

(ii) an estimated production period exceeding 2 years, or

(iii) an estimated production period exceeding 1 year and a cost exceeding $1,000,000.

(2) Allocation rules.—

(A) In general.—In determining the amount of interest required to be capitalized under subsection (a) with respect to any property—

(i) interest on any indebtedness directly attributable to production expenditures with respect to such property shall be assigned to such property, and

(ii) interest on any other indebtedness shall be assigned to such property to the extent that the taxpayer's interest costs could have been reduced if production expenditures (not attributable to indebtedness described in clause (i)) had not been incurred.

(B) Exception for qualified residence interest.—Subparagraph (A) shall not apply to any qualified residence interest (within the meaning of section 163(h)).

(C) Special rule for flow-through entities.—Except as provided in regulations, in the case of any flow-through entity, this paragraph shall be applied first at the entity level and then at the beneficiary level.

(3) Interest relating to property used to produce property.—This subsection shall apply to any interest on indebtedness allocable (as determined under paragraph (2)) to property used to produce property to which this subsection applies to the extent such interest is allocable (as so determined) to the produced property.

(4) Definitions.—For purposes of this subsection—

(A) Long useful life.—Property has a long useful life if such property is—

(i) real property, or

(ii) property with a class life of 20 years or more (as determined under section 168).

(B) Production period.—The term "production period" means, when used with respect to any property, the period—

(i) beginning on the date on which production of the property begins, and

(ii) ending on the date on which the property is ready to be placed in service or is ready to be held for sale.

(C) Production expenditures.—The term "production expenditures" means the costs (whether or not incurred during the production period) required to be capitalized under subsection (a) with respect to the property.

(g) Production.—For purposes of this section—

(1) In general.—The term "produce" includes construct, build, install, manufacture, develop, or improve.

(2) Treatment of property produced under contract for the taxpayer.—The taxpayer shall be treated as producing any property produced for the taxpayer under a contract with the taxpayer; except that only costs paid or incurred by the taxpayer (whether under such contract or otherwise) shall be taken into account in applying subsection (a) to the taxpayer.

(h) Exemption for freelance authors, photographers, and artists.—

(1) In general.—Nothing in this section shall require the capitalization of any qualified creative expense.

(2) Qualified creative expense.—For purposes of this subsection, the term "qualified creative expense" means any expense—

(A) which is paid or incurred by an individual in the trade or business of such individual (other than as an employee) of being a writer, photographer, or artist, and

(B) which, without regard to this section, would be allowable as a deduction for the taxable year.

Such term does not include any expense related to printing, photographic plates, motion picture films, video tapes, or similar items.

(3) Definitions.—For purposes of this subsection—

(A) Writer.—The term "writer" means any individual if the personal efforts of such individual create (or may reasonably be expected to create) a literary manuscript, musical composition (including any accompanying words), or dance score.

(B) Photographer.— The term "photographer" means any individual if the personal efforts of such individual create (or may reasonably be expected to create) a photograph or photographic negative or transparency.

(C) Artist.—

(i) In general.—The term "artist" means any individual if the personal efforts of such individual create (or may reasonably be expected to create) a picture, painting, sculpture, statute, etching, drawing, cartoon, graphic design, or original print edition.

(ii) Criteria.—In determining whether any expense is paid or incurred in the trade or business of being an artist, the following criteria shall be taken into account:

(I) The originality and uniqueness of the item created (or to be created).

(II) The predominance of aesthetic value over utilitarian value of the item created (or to be created).

(D) Treatment of certain corporations.—

(i) In general.—If—

(I) substantially all of the stock of a corporation is owned by a qualified employee-owner and members of his family (as defined in section 267(c)(4)), and

(II) the principal activity of such corporation is performance of personal services directly related to the activities of the qualified employee-owner and such services are substantially performed by the qualified employee-owner,

this subsection shall apply to any expense of such corporation which directly relates to the activities of such employee-owner in the same manner as if such expense were incurred by such employee-owner.

(ii) Qualified employee-owner.—For purposes of this subparagraph, the term "qualified employee-owner" means any individual who is an employee-owner of the corporation (as defined in section 269A(b)(2)) and who is a writer, photographer, or artist.

(i) Regulations.—The Secretary shall prescribe such regulations as may be necessary or appropriate to carry out the purposes of this section, including—

(1) regulations to prevent the use of related parties, pass-thru entities, or intermediaries to avoid the application of this section, and

(2) regulations providing for simplified procedures for the application of this section in the case of property described in subsection (b)(2).

§ 264. Certain amounts paid in connection with insurance contracts

(a) General rule.—No deduction shall be allowed for—

(1) Premiums on any life insurance policy, or endowment or annuity contract, if the taxpayer is directly or indirectly a beneficiary under the policy or contract.

(2) Any amount paid or accrued on indebtedness incurred or continued to purchase or carry a single premium life insurance, endowment, or annuity contract.

(3) Except as provided in subsection (d), any amount paid or accrued on indebtedness incurred or continued to purchase or carry a life insurance, endowment, or annuity contract (other than a single premium contract or a contract treated as a single premium contract) pursuant to a plan of purchase which contemplates the systematic direct or indirect borrowing of part or all of the increases in the cash value of such contract (either from the insurer or otherwise).

(4) Except as provided in subsection (e), any interest paid or accrued on any indebtedness with respect to 1 or more life insurance policies owned by the taxpayer covering the life of any individual, or any endowment or annuity contracts owned by the taxpayer covering any individual.

Paragraph (2) shall apply in respect of annuity contracts only as to contracts purchased after March 1, 1954. Paragraph (3) shall apply only in respect of contracts purchased after August 6, 1963.

Paragraph (4) shall apply with respect to contracts purchased after June 20, 1986.

* * *

§ 265. Expenses and interest relating to taxexempt income

(a) General rule.—No deduction shall be allowed for—

(1) Expenses.—Any amount otherwise allowable as a deduction which is allocable to one or more classes of income other than interest (whether or not any amount of income of that class or classes is received or accrued) wholly exempt from the taxes imposed by this subtitle, or any amount otherwise allowable under section 212 (relating to expenses for production of income) which is allocable to interest (whether or not any amount of such interest is received or accrued) wholly exempt from the taxes imposed by this subtitle.

(2) Interest.—Interest on indebtedness incurred or continued to purchase or carry obligations the interest on which is wholly exempt from the taxes imposed by this subtitle.

* * *

(6) Section not to apply with respect to parsonage and military housing allowances.—No deduction shall be denied under this section for interest on a mortgage on, or real property taxes on, the home of the taxpayer by reason of the receipt of an amount as—

(A) a military housing allowance, or

(B) a parsonage allowance excludable from gross income under section 107.

* * *

§ 266. Carrying charges

No deduction shall be allowed for amounts paid or accrued for such taxes and carrying charges as, under regulations prescribed by the Secretary, are chargeable to capital account with respect to property, if the taxpayer elects, in accordance with such regulations, to treat such taxes or charges as so chargeable.

§ 267. Losses, expenses, and interest with respect to transactions between related taxpayers

(a) In general.—

(1) Deduction for losses disallowed.—No deduction shall be allowed in respect of any loss from the sale or exchange of property, directly or indirectly, between persons specified in any of the paragraphs of subsection (b). The preceding sentence shall not apply to any loss of the distributing corporation (or the distributee) in the case of a distribution in complete liquidation.

(2) Matching of deduction and payee income item in the case of expenses and interest.—If—

(A) by reason of the method of accounting of the person to whom the payment is to be made, the amount thereof is not (unless paid) includible in the gross income of such person, and

(B) at the close of the taxable year of the taxpayer for which (but for this paragraph) the amount would be deductible under this chapter, both the taxpayer and the person to whom the payment is to be made are persons specified in any of the paragraphs of subsection (b),

then any deduction allowable under this chapter in respect of such amount shall be allowable as of the day as of which such amount is includible in the gross income of the person to whom the payment is made (or, if later, as of the day on which it would be so allowable but for this paragraph).

(3) Payments to foreign persons.—

(A) In general.—The Secretary shall by regulations apply the matching principle of paragraph (2) in cases in which the person to whom the payment is to be made is not a United States person.

* * *

(b) Relationships.—The persons referred to in subsection (a) are:

(1) Members of a family, as defined in subsection (c)(4);

(2) An individual and a corporation more than 50 percent in value of the outstanding stock of which is owned, directly or indirectly, by or for such individual;

(3) Two corporations which are members of the same controlled group (as defined in subsection (f));

(4) A grantor and a fiduciary of any trust;

(5) A fiduciary of a trust and a fiduciary of another trust, if the same person is a grantor of both trusts;

(6) A fiduciary of a trust and a beneficiary of such trust;

(7) A fiduciary of a trust and a beneficiary of another trust, if the same person is a grantor of both trusts;

(8) A fiduciary of a trust and a corporation more than 50 percent in value of the outstanding stock of which is owned, directly or indirectly, by or for the trust or by or for a person who is a grantor of the trust;

(9) A person and an organization to which section 501 (relating to certain educational and charitable organizations which are exempt from tax) applies and which is controlled directly or indirectly by such person or (if such person is an individual) by members of the family of such individual;

(10) A corporation and a partnership if the same persons own—

(A) more than 50 percent in value of the outstanding stock of the corporation, and

(B) more than 50 percent of the capital interest, or the profits interest, in the partnership;

(11) An S corporation and another S corporation if the same persons own more than 50 percent in value of the outstanding stock of each corporation;

(12) An S corporation and a C corporation, if the same persons own more than 50 percent in value of the outstanding stock of each corporation; or

(13) Except in the case of a sale or exchange in satisfaction of a pecuniary bequest, an executor of an estate and a beneficiary of such estate.

(c) Constructive ownership of stock.—For purposes of determining, in applying subsection (b), the ownership of stock—

(1) Stock owned, directly or indirectly, by or for a corporation, partnership, estate, or trust shall be considered as being owned proportionately by or for its shareholders, partners, or beneficiaries;

(2) An individual shall be considered as owning the stock owned, directly or indirectly, by or for his family;

(3) An individual owning (otherwise than by the application of paragraph (2)) any stock in a corporation shall be considered as owning the stock owned, directly or indirectly, by or for his partner;

(4) The family of an individual shall include only his brothers and sisters (whether by the whole or half blood), spouse, ancestors, and lineal descendants; and

(5) Stock constructively owned by a person by reason of the application of paragraph (1) shall, for the purpose of applying paragraph (1), (2), or (3), be treated as actually owned by such person, but stock constructively owned by an individual by reason of the application of paragraph (2) or (3) shall not be treated as owned by him for the purpose of again applying either of such paragraphs in order to make another the constructive owner of such stock.

(d) Amount of gain where loss previously disallowed.—If—

(1) in the case of a sale or exchange of property to the taxpayer a loss sustained by the transferor is not allowable to the transferor as a deduction by reason of subsection (a)(1); *** and

(2) after December 31, 1953, the taxpayer sells or otherwise disposes of such property (or of other property the basis of which in his hands is determined directly or indirectly by reference to such property) at a gain,

then such gain shall be recognized only to the extent that it exceeds so much of such loss as is properly allocable to the property sold or otherwise disposed of by the taxpayer. This subsection applies with respect to taxable years ending after December 31, 1953. This subsection shall not apply if the loss sustained by the transferor is not allowable to the transferor as a deduction by reason of section 1091 (relating to wash sales).***

(e) Special rules for pass-thru entities.—

(1) In general.—In the case of any amount paid or incurred by, to, or on behalf of, a pass-thru entity, for purposes of applying subsection (a)(2)—

(A) such entity,

(B) in the case of—

(i) a partnership, any person who owns (directly or indirectly) any capital interest or profits interest of such partnership, or

(ii) an S corporation, any person who owns (directly or indirectly) any of the stock of such corporation,

(C) any person who owns (directly or indirectly) any capital interest or profits interest of a partnership in which such entity owns (directly or indirectly) any capital interest or profits interest, and

(D) any person related (within the meaning of subsection (b) of this section or section 707(b)(1)) to a person described in subparagraph (B) or (C),

shall be treated as persons specified in a paragraph of subsection (b). Subparagraph (C) shall apply to a transaction only if such transaction is related either to the operations of the partnership described in such subparagraph or to an interest in such partnership.

(2) Pass-thru entity.—For purposes of this section, the term "pass-thru entity" means—

(A) a partnership, and

(B) an S corporation.

(3) Constructive ownership in the case of partnerships.—For purposes of determining ownership of a capital interest or profits interest of a partnership, the principles of subsection (c) shall apply, except that—

(A) paragraph (3) of subsection (c) shall not apply, and

(B) interests owned (directly or indirectly) by or for a C corporation shall be considered as owned by or for any shareholder only if such shareholder owns (directly or indirectly) 5 percent or more in value of the stock of such corporation.

(4) Subsection (a)(2) not to apply to certain guaranteed payments of partnerships.—In the case of any amount paid or incurred by a partnership, subsection (a)(2) shall not apply to the extent that section 707(c) applies to such amount.

(5) Exception for certain expenses and interest of partnerships owning low-income housing.—

(A) In general.—This subsection shall not apply with respect to qualified expenses and interest paid or incurred by a partnership owning low-income housing to—

(i) any qualified 5-percent or less partner of such partnership, or

(ii) any person related (within the meaning of subsection (b) of this section or section 707(b)(1)) to any qualified 5-percent or less partner of such partnership.

(B) Qualified 5-percent or less partner.—For purposes of this paragraph, the term "qualified 5-percent or less partner" means any partner who has (directly or indirectly) an interest of 5 percent or less in the aggregate capital and profits interests of the partnership but only if—

(i) such partner owned the low-income housing at all times during the 2-year period ending on the date such housing was transferred to the partnership, or

(ii) such partnership acquired the low-income housing pursuant to a purchase, assignment, or other transfer from the Department of Housing and Urban Development or any State or local housing authority.

For purposes of the preceding sentence, a partner shall be treated as holding any interest in the partnership which is held (directly or indirectly) by any person related (within the meaning of subsection (b) of this section or section 707(b)(1)) to such partner.

(C) Qualified expenses and interest.—For purpose of this paragraph, the term "qualified expenses and interest" means any expense or interest incurred by the partnership with respect to low-income housing held by the partnership but—

(i) only if the amount of such expense or interest (as the case may be) is unconditionally required to be paid by the partnership not later than 10 years after the date such amount was incurred, and

(ii) in the case of such interest, only if such interest is incurred at an annual rate not in excess of 12 percent.

(D) Low-income housing.—For purposes of this paragraph, the term "low-income housing" means—

(i) any interest in property described in clause (i), (ii), (iii), or (iv) of section 1250 (a)(1)(B), and

(ii) any interest in a partnership owning such property.

(6) Cross reference.—

For additional rules relating to partnerships, see section 707(b).

(f) Controlled group defined; special rules applicable to controlled groups.—

(1) Controlled group defined.—For purposes of this section, the term "controlled group" has the meaning given to such term by section 1563(a), except that—

(A) "more than 50 percent" shall be substituted for "at least 80 percent" each place it appears in section 1563(a), and

(B) the determination shall be made without regard to subsections (a)(4) and (e)(3)(C) of section 1563.

(2) Deferral (rather than denial) of loss from sale or exchange between members.—In the case of any loss from the sale or exchange of property which is between members of the same controlled group and to which subsection (a)(1) applies (determined without regard to this paragraph but with regard to paragraph (3))—

(A) subsections (a)(1) and (d) shall not apply to such loss, but

(B) such loss shall be deferred until the property is transferred outside such controlled group and there would be recognition of loss under consolidated return principles or until such other time as may be prescribed in regulations.

(3) Loss deferral rules not to apply in certain cases.—

* * *

(B) Certain sales of inventory.—Except to the extent provided in regulations prescribed by the Secretary, subsection (a)(1) shall not apply to the sale or exchange of property between members of the same controlled group (or persons described in subsection (b)(10)) if—

(i) such property in the hands of the transferor is property described in section 1221(1),

(ii) such sale or exchange is in the ordinary course of the transferor's trade or business,

(iii) such property in the hands of the transferee is property described in section 1221(1), and

(iv) the transferee or the transferor is a foreign corporation.

* * *

(g) Coordination with section 1041.—Subsection (a)(1) shall not apply to any transfer described in section 1041(a) (relating to transfers of property between spouses or incident to divorce).

§ 268. Sale of land with unharvested crop

Where an unharvested crop sold by the taxpayer is considered under the provisions of section 1231 as "property used in the trade or business," in computing taxable income no deduction (whether or not for the taxable year of the sale and whether for expenses, depreciation, or otherwise) attributable to the production of such crop shall be allowed.

§ 269. Acquisitions made to evade or avoid income tax

(a) In general.—If—

(1) any person or persons acquire, or acquired on or after October 8, 1940, directly or indirectly, control of a corporation, or

(2) any corporation acquires, or acquired on or after October 8, 1940, directly or indirectly, property of another corporation, not controlled, directly or indirectly, immediately before such acquisition, by such acquiring corporation or its stockholders, the basis of which property, in the hands of the acquiring corporation, is determined by reference to the basis in the hands of the transferor corporation,

and the principal purpose for which such acquisition was made is evasion or avoidance of Federal income tax by securing the benefit of a deduction, credit, or other allowance which such person or corporation would not otherwise enjoy, then the Secretary may disallow such deduction, credit, or other allowance. For purposes of paragraphs (1) and (2), control means the ownership of stock possessing at least 50 percent of the total combined voting power of all classes of stock entitled to vote or at least 50 percent of the total value of shares of all classes of stock of the corporation.

(b) Certain liquidations after qualified stock purchases.—

(1) In general.—If—

(A) there is a qualified stock purchase by a corporation of another corporation,

(B) an election is not made under section 338 with respect to such purchase,

(C) the acquired corporation is liquidated pursuant to a plan of liquidation adopted not more than 2 years after the acquisition date, and

(D) the principal purpose for such liquidation is the evasion or avoidance of Federal income tax by securing the benefit of a deduction, credit, or other allowance which the acquiring corporation would not otherwise enjoy,

then the Secretary may disallow such deduction, credit, or other allowance.

(2) Meaning of terms.—For purposes of paragraph (1), the terms "qualified stock purchase" and "acquisition date" have the same respective meanings as when used in section 338.

(c) Power of Secretary to allow deduction, etc., in part.—In any case to which subsection (a) or (b) applies the Secretary is authorized—

(1) to allow as a deduction, credit, or allowance any part of any amount disallowed by such subsection, if he determines that such allowance will not result in the evasion or avoidance of Federal income tax for which the acquisition was made; or

(2) to distribute, apportion, or allocate gross income, and distribute, apportion, or allocate the deductions, credits, or allowances the benefit of which was sought to be secured, between or among the corporations, or properties, or parts thereof, involved, and to allow such deductions, credits, or allowances so distributed, apportioned, or allocated, but to give effect to such allowance only to such extent as he determines will not result in the evasion or avoidance of Federal income tax for which the acquisition was made; or

(3) to exercise his powers in part under paragraph (1) and in part under paragraph (2).

§ 269A. Personal service corporations formed or availed of to avoid or evade income tax

(a) General rule.—If—

(1) substantially all of the services of a personal service corporation are performed for (or on behalf of) 1 other corporation, partnership, or other entity, and

(2) the principal purpose for forming, or availing of, such personal service corporation is the avoidance or evasion of Federal income tax by reducing the income of, or securing the benefit of any expense, deduction, credit, exclusion, or other allowance for, any employee-owner which would not otherwise be available,

then the Secretary may allocate all income, deductions, credits, exclusions, and other allowances between such personal service corporation and its employee-owners, if such allocation is necessary to prevent avoidance or evasion of Federal income tax or clearly to reflect the income of the personal service corporation or any of its employee-owners.

(b) Definitions.—For purposes of this section—

(1) Personal service corporation.— The term "personal service corporation" means a corporation the principal activity of which is the performance of personal services and such services are substantially performed by employee-owners.

(2) Employee-owner.—The term "employee-owner" means any employee who owns, on any day during the taxable year, more than 10 percent of the outstanding stock of the personal service corporation. For purposes of the preceding sentence, section 318 shall apply, except that "5 percent" shall be substituted for "50 percent" in section 318(a)(2)(C).

(3) Related persons.—All related persons (within the meaning of section 144(a)(3)) shall be treated as 1 entity.

* * *

§ 274. Disallowance of certain entertainment, etc., expenses

(a) Entertainment, amusement, or recreation.—

(1) In general.—No deduction otherwise allowable under this chapter shall be allowed for any item—

(A) Activity.—With respect to an activity which is of a type generally considered to constitute entertainment, amusement, or recreation, unless the taxpayer establishes that the item was directly related to, or, in the case of an item directly preceding or following a substantial and bona fide business discussion (including business meetings at a convention or otherwise), that such item was associated with, the active conduct of the taxpayer's trade or business, or

(B) Facility.—With respect to a facility used in connection with an activity referred to in subparagraph (A).

In the case of an item described in subparagraph (A), the deduction shall in no event exceed the portion of such item which meets the requirements of subparagraph (A).

(2) Special rules.—For purposes of applying paragraph (1)—

(A) Dues or fees to any social, athletic, or sporting club or organization shall be treated as items with respect to facilities.

(B) An activity described in section 212 shall be treated as a trade or business.

(C) In the case of a club, paragraph (1)(B) shall apply unless the taxpayer establishes that the facility was used primarily for the furtherance of the taxpayer's trade or business and that the item was directly related to the active conduct of such trade or business.

(3) Denial of deduction for club dues.—Notwithstanding the preceding provisions of this subsection, no deduction shall be allowed under this chapter for amounts paid or incurred for membership in any club organized for business, pleasure, recreation, or other social purpose.

(b) Gifts.—

(1) Limitation.—No deduction shall be allowed under section 162 or section 212 for any expense for gifts made directly or indirectly to any individual to the extent that such expense, when added to prior expenses of the taxpayer for gifts made to such individual during the same taxable year, exceeds $25. For purposes of this section, the term "gift" means any item excludable from gross income of the recipient under section 102 which is not excludable from his gross income under any other provision of this chapter, but such term does not include—

(A) an item having a cost to the taxpayer not in excess of $4.00 on which the name of the taxpayer is clearly and permanently imprinted and which is one of a number of identical items distributed generally by the taxpayer, or

(B) a sign, display rack, or other promotional material to be used on the business premises of the recipient.

(2) Special rules.—

(A) In the case of a gift by a partnership, the limitation contained in paragraph (1) shall apply to the partnership as well as to each member thereof.

(B) For purposes of paragraph (1), a husband and wife shall be treated as one taxpayer.

(c) Certain foreign travel.—

(1) In general.—In the case of any individual who travels outside the United States away from home in pursuit of a trade or business or in pursuit of an activity described in section 212, no deduction shall be allowed under section 162 or section 212 for that portion of the expenses of such travel otherwise allowable under such section which, under regulations prescribed by the Secretary, is not allocable to such trade or business or to such activity.

(2) Exception.—Paragraph (1) shall not apply to the expenses of any travel outside the United States away from home if—

(A) such travel does not exceed one week, or

(B) the portion of the time of travel outside the United States away from home which is not attributable to the pursuit of the taxpayer's trade or business or an activity described in section 212 is less than 25 percent of the total time on such travel.

(3) Domestic travel excluded.—For purposes of this subsection, travel outside the United States does not include any travel from one point in the United States to another point in the United States.

(d) Substantiation required.—No deduction or credit shall be allowed—

(1) under section 162 or 212 for any traveling expense (including meals and lodging while away from home),

(2) for any item with respect to an activity which is of a type generally considered to constitute entertainment, amusement, or recreation, or with respect to a facility used in connection with such an activity,

(3) for any expense for gifts, or

(4) with respect to any listed property (as defined in section 280F(d)(4)),

unless the taxpayer substantiates by adequate records or by sufficient evidence corroborating the taxpayer's own statement (A) the amount of such expense or other item, (B) the time and place of the travel, entertainment, amusement, recreation, or use of the facility or property, or the date and description of the gift, (C) the business purpose of the expense or other item, and (D) the business relationship to the taxpayer of persons entertained, using the facility or property, or receiving the gift. The Secretary may by regulations provide that some or all of the requirements of the preceding sentence shall not apply in the case of an expense which does not exceed an amount prescribed pursuant to such regulations. This subsection shall not apply to any qualified nonpersonal use vehicle (as defined in subsection (i)).

(e) Specific exceptions to application of subsection (a).—Subsection (a) shall not apply to—

(1) Food and beverages for employees.—Expenses for food and beverages (and facilities used in connection therewith) furnished on the business premises of the taxpayer primarily for his employees.

(2) Expenses treated as compensation.—

(A) In general.—Except as provided in subparagraph (B), expenses for goods, services, and facilities, to the extent that the expenses are treated by the taxpayer, with respect to the recipient of the entertainment, amusement, or recreation, as compensation to an employee on the taxpayer's return of tax under this chapter and as wages to such employee for purposes of chapter 24 (relating to withholding of income tax at source on wages).

(B) Specified individuals.—

(i) In general.—In the case of a recipient who is a specified individual, subparagraph (A) and paragraph (9) shall each be applied by substituting "to the extent that the expenses do not exceed the amount of the expenses which" for "to the extent that the expenses."

(ii) Specified individual.—For purposes of clause (i), the term "specified individual" means any individual who—

(I) is subject to the requirements of section 16(a) of the Securities Exchange Act of 1934 with respect to the taxpayer or a related party of the taxpayer, or

(II) would be subject to such requirements if the taxpayer (or such related party) were an issuer of equity securities referred to in such section.

For purposes of this clause, a person is a related party with respect to another person if such person bears a relationship to such other person described in section 267(b) or 707(b).

(3) Reimbursed expenses.—Expenses paid or incurred by the taxpayer, in connection with the performance by him of services for another person (whether or not such other person is his employer), under a reimbursement or other expense allowance arrangement with such other person, but this paragraph shall apply—

(A) where the services are performed for an employer, only if the employer has not treated such expenses in the manner provided in paragraph (2), or

(B) where the services are performed for a person other than an employer, only if the taxpayer accounts (to the extent provided by subsection (d)) to such person.

(4) Recreational, etc., expenses for employees.—Expenses for recreational, social, or similar activities (including facilities therefor) primarily for the benefit of employees (other than employees who are highly compensated employees (within the meaning of section 414(q)). For purposes of this paragraph, an individual owning less than a 10-percent interest in the tax-payer's trade or business shall not be considered a shareholder or other owner, and for such purposes an individual shall be treated as owning any interest owned by a member of his family (within the meaning of section 267(c)(4)). This paragraph shall not apply for purposes of subsection (a)(3).

(5) Employee, stockholder, etc., business meetings.—Expenses incurred by a taxpayer which are directly related to business meetings of his employees, stockholders, agents, or directors.

(6) Meetings of business leagues, etc.—Expenses directly related and necessary to attendance at a business meeting or convention of any organization described in section 501(c)(6) (relating to business leagues, chambers of commerce, real estate boards, and boards of trade) and exempt from taxation under section 501(a).

(7) Items available to public.—Expenses for goods, services, and facilities made available by the taxpayer to the general public.

(8) Entertainment sold to customers.—Expenses for goods or services (including the use of facilities) which are sold by the taxpayer in a bona fide transaction for an adequate and full consideration in money or money's worth.

(9) Expenses includible in income of persons who are not employees.—Expenses paid or incurred by the taxpayer for goods, services, and facilities to the extent that the expenses are includible in the gross income of a recipient of the entertainment, amusement, or recreation who is not an employee of the taxpayer as compensation for services rendered or as a prize or award under section 74. The preceding sentence shall not apply to any amount paid or incurred by the taxpayer if such amount is required to be included (or would be so required except that the amount is less than $600) in any information return filed by such taxpayer under part III of subchapter A of chapter 61 and is not so included.

For purposes of this subsection, any item referred to in subsection (a) shall be treated as an expense.

(f) Interest, taxes, casualty losses, etc.—This section shall not apply to any deduction allowable to the taxpayer without regard to its connection with his trade or business (or with his income-producing activity). In the case of a taxpayer which is not an individual, the preceding sentence shall be applied as if it were an individual.

(g) Treatment of entertainment, etc., type facility.—For purposes of this chapter, if deductions are disallowed under subsection (a) with respect to any portion of a facility, such portion shall be treated as an asset which is used for personal, living, and family purposes (and not as an asset used in the trade or business).

(h) Attendance at conventions, etc.—

(1) In general.—In the case of any individual who attends a convention, seminar, or similar meeting which is held outside the North American area, no deduction shall be allowed under section 162 for expenses allocable to such meeting unless the taxpayer establishes that the meeting is directly related to the active conduct of his trade or business and that, after taking into account in the manner provided by regulations prescribed by the Secretary—

(A) the purpose of such meeting and the activities taking place at such meeting,

(B) the purposes and activities of the sponsoring organizations or groups,

(C) the residences of the active members of the sponsoring organization and the places at which other meetings of the sponsoring organization or groups have been held or will be held, and

(D) such other relevant factors as the taxpayer may present,

it is as reasonable for the meeting to be held outside the North American area as within the North American area.

(2) Conventions on cruise ships.—In the case of any individual who attends a convention, seminar, or other meeting which is held on any cruise ship, no deduction shall be allowed under section 162 for expenses allocable to such meeting, unless the taxpayer meets the requirements of paragraph (5) and establishes that the meeting is directly related to the active conduct of his trade or business and that—

(A) the cruise ship is a vessel registered in the United States; and

(B) all ports of call of such cruise ship are located in the United States or in possessions of the United States.

With respect to cruises beginning in any calendar year, not more than $2,000 of the expenses attributable to an individual attending one or more meetings may be taken into account under section 162 by reason of the preceding sentence.

(3) Definitions.—For purposes of this subsection—

(A) North American area.—The term "North American area" means the United States, its possessions, and the Trust Territory of the Pacific Islands, and Canada and Mexico.

(B) Cruise ship.—The term "cruise ship" means any vessel sailing within or without the territorial waters of the United States.

(4) Subsection to apply to employer as well as to traveler.—

(A) Except as provided in subparagraph (B), this subsection shall apply to deductions otherwise allowable under section 162 to any person, whether or not such person is the individual attending the convention, seminar, or similar meeting.

(B) This subsection shall not deny a deduction to any person other than the individual attending the convention, seminar, or similar meeting with respect to any amount paid by such person to or on behalf of such individual if includible in the gross income of such individual. The preceding sentence shall not apply if the amount is required to be included in any information return filed by such person under part III of subchapter A of chapter 61 and is not so included.

(5) Reporting requirements.—No deduction shall be allowed under section 162 for expenses allocable to attendance at a convention, seminar, or similar meeting on any cruise ship unless the taxpayer claiming the deduction attaches to the return of tax on which the deduction is claimed—

(A) a written statement signed by the individual attending the meeting which includes—

(i) information with respect to the total days of the trip, excluding the days of transportation to and from the cruise ship port, and the number of hours of each day of the trip which such individual devoted to scheduled business activities,

(ii) a program of the scheduled business activities of the meeting, and

(iii) such other information as may be required in regulations prescribed by the Secretary; and

(B) a written statement signed by an officer of the organization or group sponsoring the meeting which includes—

(i) a schedule of the business activities of each day of the meeting,

(ii) the number of hours which the individual attending the meeting attended such scheduled business activities, and

(iii) such other information as may be required in regulations prescribed by the Secretary.

* * *

(7) Seminars, etc. for section 212 purposes.—No deduction shall be allowed under section 212 for expenses allocable to a convention, seminar, or similar meeting.

(i) Qualified nonpersonal use vehicle.—For purposes of subsection (d), the term "qualified nonpersonal use vehicle" means any vehicle which, by reason of its nature, is not likely to be used more than a de minimis amount for personal purposes.

(j) Employee achievement awards.—

(1) General rule.—No deduction shall be allowed under section 162 or section 212 for the cost of an employee achievement award except to the extent that such cost does not exceed the deduction limitations of paragraph (2).

(2) Deduction limitations.—The deduction for the cost of an employee achievement award made by an employer to an employee—

(A) which is not a qualified plan award, when added to the cost to the employer for all other employee achievement awards made to such employee during the taxable year which are not qualified plan awards, shall not exceed $400, and

(B) which is a qualified plan award, when added to the cost to the employer for all other employee achievement awards made to such employee during the taxable year (including employee achievement awards which are not qualified plan awards), shall not exceed $1,600.

(3) Definitions.—For purposes of this subsection—

(A) Employee achievement award.—The term "employee achievement award" means an item of tangible personal property which is—

(i) transferred by an employer to an employee for length of service achievement or safety achievement,

(ii) awarded as part of a meaningful presentation, and

(iii) awarded under conditions and circumstances that do not create a significant likelihood of the payment of disguised compensation.

(B) Qualified plan award.—

(i) In general.—The term "qualified plan award" means an employee achievement award awarded as part of an established written plan or program of the taxpayer which does not discriminate in favor of highly compensated employees (within the meaning of section 414(q)) as to eligibility or benefits.

(ii) Limitation.—An employee achievement award shall not be treated as a qualified plan award for any taxable year if the average cost of all employee achievement awards which are provided by the employer during the year, and which would be qualified plan awards but for this subparagraph, exceeds $400. For purposes of the preceding sentence, average cost shall be determined by including the entire cost of qualified plan awards, without taking into account employee achievement awards of nominal value.

(4) Special rules.—For purposes of this subsection—

(A) Partnerships.—In the case of an employee achievement award made by a partnership, the deduction limitations contained in paragraph (2) shall apply to the partnership as well as to each member thereof.

(B) Length of service awards.—An item shall not be treated as having been provided for length of service achievement if the item is received during the recipient's 1st 5 years of employment or if the recipient received a length of service achievement award (other than an award excludable under section 132(e)(1)) during that year or any of the prior 4 years.

(C) Safety achievement awards.—An item provided by an employer to an employee shall not be treated as having been provided for safety achievement if—

(i) during the taxable year, employee achievement awards (other than awards excludable under section 132(e)(1)) for safety achievement have previously been awarded by the employer to more than 10 percent of the employees of the employer (excluding employees described in clause (ii)), or

(ii) such item is awarded to a manager, administrator, clerical employee, or other professional employee.

(k) Business meals.—

(1) In general.—No deduction shall be allowed under this chapter for the expense of any food or beverages unless—

(A) such expense is not lavish or extravagant under the circumstances, and

(B) the taxpayer (or an employee of the taxpayer) is present at the furnishing of such food or beverages.

(2) Exceptions.—Paragraph (1) shall not apply to—

(A) any expense described in paragraph (2), (3), (4), (7), (8), or (9) of subsection (e), and

(B) any other expense to the extent provided in regulations.

(l) Additional limitations on entertainment tickets.—

(1) Entertainment tickets.—

(A) In general.—In determining the amount allowable as a deduction under this chapter for any ticket for any activity or facility described in subsection (d)(2), the amount taken into account shall not exceed the face value of such ticket.

(B) Exception for certain charitable sports events.—Subparagraph (A) shall not apply to any ticket for any sports event—

(i) which is organized for the primary purpose of benefiting an organization which is described in section 501(c)(3) and exempt from tax under section 501(a),

(ii) all of the net proceeds of which are contributed to such organization, and

(iii) which utilizes volunteers for substantially all of the work performed in carrying out such event.

(2) Skyboxes, etc.—In the case of a skybox or other private luxury box leased for more than 1 event, the amount allowable as a deduction under this chapter with respect to such events shall not exceed the sum of the face value of non-luxury box seat tickets for the seats in such box covered by the lease. For purposes of the preceding sentence, 2 or more related leases shall be treated as 1 lease.

(m) Additional limitations on travel expenses.—

(1) Luxury water transportation.—

(A) In general.—No deduction shall be allowed under this chapter for expenses incurred for transportation by water to the extent such expenses exceed twice the aggregate per diem amounts for days of such transportation. For purposes of the preceding sentence, the term "per diem amounts" means the highest amount generally allowable with respect to a day to employees of the executive branch of the Federal Government for per diem while away from home but serving in the United States.

(B) Exceptions.—Subparagraph (A) shall not apply to—

(i) any expense allocable to a convention, seminar, or other meeting which is held on any cruise ship, and

(ii) any expense described in paragraph (2), (3), (4), (7), (8), or (9) of subsection (e).

(2) Travel as form of education.—No deduction shall be allowed under this chapter for expenses for travel as a form of education.

(3) Travel expenses of spouse, dependent, or others.—No deduction shall be allowed under this chapter (other than section 217) for travel expenses paid or incurred with respect to a spouse, dependent, or other individual accompanying the taxpayer (or an officer or employee of the taxpayer) on business travel, unless—

(A) the spouse, dependent, or other individual is an employee of the taxpayer,

(B) the travel of the spouse, dependent, or other individual is for a bona fide business purpose, and

(C) such expenses would otherwise be deductible by the spouse, dependent, or other individual.

(n) Only 50 percent of meal and entertainment expenses allowed as deduction.—

(1) In general.—The amount allowable as a deduction under this chapter for—

(A) any expense for food or beverages, and

(B) any item with respect to an activity which is of a type generally considered to constitute entertainment, amusement, or recreation, or with respect to a facility used in connection with such activity,

shall not exceed 50 percent of the amount of such expense or item which would (but for this paragraph) be allowable as a deduction under this chapter.

(2) Exceptions.—Paragraph (1) shall not apply to any expense if—

(A) such expense is described in paragraph (2), (3), (4), (7), (8), or (9) of subsection (e),

(B) in the case of an expense for food or beverages, such expense is excludable from the gross income of the recipient under section 132 by reason of subsection (e) thereof (relating to de minimis fringes),

(C) such expense is covered by a package involving a ticket described in subsection (l)(1)(B),

(D) in the case of an employer who pays or reimburses moving expenses of an employee, such expenses are includible in the income of the employee under section 82, or

(E) such expense is for food or beverages—

(i) required by any Federal law to be provided to crew members of a commercial vessel,

(ii) provided to crew members of a commercial vessel—

(I) which is operating on the Great Lakes, the Saint Lawrence Seaway, or any inland waterway of the United States, and

(II) which is of a kind which would be required by Federal law to provide food and beverages to crew members if it were operated at sea,

(iii) provided on an oil or gas platform or drilling rig if the platform or rig is located offshore, or

(iv) provided on an oil or gas platform or drilling rig, or at a support camp which is in proximity and integral to such platform or rig, if the platform or rig is located in the United States north of 54 degrees north latitude.

In the case of the employee, the exception of subparagraph (A) shall not apply to expenses described in subparagraph (D). Clauses (i) and (ii) of subparagraph (E) shall not apply to vessels primarily engaged in providing luxury water transportation (determined under the principles of subsection (m)).

(3) Special rule for individuals subject to federal hours of service.—

(A) In general.—In the case of any expenses for food or beverages consumed while away from home (within the meaning of section 162(a)(2)) by an individual during, or incident to, the period of duty subject to the hours of service limitations of the Department of Transportation, paragraph (1) shall be applied by substituting "the applicable percentage" for "50 percent."

(B) Applicable percentage.—For purposes of this paragraph, the term "applicable percentage" means the percentage determined under the following table:

For taxable years beginning in calendar year:	The applicable percentage is:
1998 or 1999	55
2000 or 2001	60
2002 or 2003	65
2004 or 2005	70
2006 or 2007	75
2008 or thereafter	80

(o) Regulatory authority.—The Secretary shall prescribe such regulations as he may deem necessary to carry out the purposes of this section, including regulations prescribing whether subsection (a) or subsection (b) applies in cases where both such subsections would otherwise apply.

§ 275. Certain taxes

(a) General rule.—No deduction shall be allowed for the following taxes:

(1) Federal income taxes, including—

(A) the tax imposed by section 3101 (relating to the tax on employees under the Federal Insurance Contributions Act);

(B) the taxes imposed by sections 3201 and 3211 (relating to the taxes on railroad employees and railroad employee representatives); and

(C) the tax withheld at source on wages under section 3402.

(2) Federal war profits and excess profits taxes.

(3) Estate, inheritance, legacy, succession, and gift taxes.

(4) Income, war profits, and excess profits taxes imposed by the authority of any foreign country or possession of the United States if the taxpayer chooses to take to any extent the benefits of section 901.

(5) Taxes on real property, to the extent that section 164(d) requires such taxes to be treated as imposed on another taxpayer.

(6) Taxes imposed by chapters 41, 42, 43, 44, 46, and 54.

Paragraph (1) shall not apply to any taxes to the extent such taxes are allowable as a deduction under section 164(f). Paragraph (1) shall not apply to the tax imposed by section 59A.

(b) Cross reference.—

For disallowance of certain other taxes, see section 164(c).

§ 276. Certain indirect contributions to political parties

(a) Disallowance of deduction.—No deduction otherwise allowable under this chapter shall be allowed for any amount paid or incurred for—

(1) advertising in a convention program of a political party, or in any other publication if any part of the proceeds of such publication directly or indirectly inures (or is intended to inure) to or for the use of a political party or a political candidate,

(2) admission to any dinner or program, if any part of the proceeds of such dinner or program directly or indirectly inures (or is intended to inure) to or for the use of a political party or a political candidate, or

(3) admission to an inaugural ball, inaugural gala, inaugural parade, or inaugural concert, or to any similar event which is identified with a political party or a political candidate.

* * *

§ 280A. Disallowance of certain expenses in connection with business use of home, rental of vacation homes, etc.

Editorial Summary

Home Office and Vacation Home

Subchapter B of Chapter 1 (Sec. 280A)

Section 280A results in the disallowance of deductions associated with (1) home office expenses and (2) vacation homes. Combining these two disallowance provisions into a single code section makes it more complex than if a separate code section were provided for each.

Home Office. Expenses for a home office can be deducted only if the home office is a qualified home office under any of the following options [Sec. 280A(c)(1)]:

1. Principal place of business.
2. Place of business which is used by patients, clients, or customers in meeting with the taxpayer in the normal course of his or her trade or business.
3. A separate unattached structure which is used in connection with the taxpayer's trade or business.

For each of the options, there is an additional requirement of exclusive use on a regular basis. If the home office is not a qualified home office, then the only expenses that can be deducted are those that otherwise are deductible as personal expenses on Schedule A (e.g., property taxes, mortgage interest, and personal casualties) [Sec. 280A(b)].

If the home office is a qualified home office then business-type expenses (e.g., maintenance, repairs, utilities, insurance, depreciation) for the home office can be deducted. However, the total expenses allocable to the home office that can be deducted are limited to the gross income derived from such use [Sec. 280A(c)(5)]. In making this calculation, the sequence of the deduction of expenses to be offset against gross income is as follows:

1. Other non-home office expenses associated with the business (e.g., secretary's salary).
2. Schedule A expenses allocated to the home office.
3. Business-type expenses allocated to the home office which do not offset basis (e.g., maintenance, utilities, insurance).
4. Business-type expenses which do affect basis (e.g., depreciation).

Any deduction not permitted in the current tax year because of the gross income limit is carried over to the following tax year.

Vacation home. Expenses for a vacation home are disallowed [Sec. 280A(a)]. However, two exceptions are provided. First, expenses that otherwise are deductible as personal expenses on Schedule A (e.g., property taxes, mortgage interest, and personal casualties) are permitted. Second, if there is limited personal use, then the business-type expenses (e.g., maintenance, utilities, insurance, and depreciation) can be deducted subject to limitation.

A vacation home can be classified into the following categories for determining whether business-type expenses can be deducted.

1. Only rental use.
2. Only personal use.
3. Combined rental use and personal use.

If there is *only rental use* of the vacation home, then it is treated as rental property and is not subject to the limits on deducting expenses contained in Sec. 280A [Sec. 280A(c) (3)].

If there is *only personal use* of the vacation home, then only the personal expenses that are deductible on Schedule A (e.g., property taxes, mortgage interest, and personal casualties) are permitted.

If there is *combined rental use and personal use*, then one must ascertain if there has been excessive personal use. If there has not been excessive personal use, then the vacation home is treated the same as "only rental use" property except the expenses must be allocated to rental use and personal use. Excessive personal use is defined in Sec. 280A(d)(1) as personal use in excess of the greater of the following:

1. 14 days.
2. 10% of rental days.

If there is excessive personal use, then the allocable business-type expenses that can be deducted are limited to the gross rental income reduced by the allocable deductible personal expenses. The sequence of the deductions of business-type expenses is (1) business-type expenses allocable to rental use which do not affect basis (e.g., rental agent's commission, maintenance, utilities, insurance) and (2) business-type expenses allocable to rental use which do affect basis (e.g., depreciation). Any deduction not permitted in the current year because of the gross income limit is carried over to the following year [Sec. 280A(c)(5)].

There is a materiality provision associated with vacation homes. If the rental use is less than 15 days, then the rental income can be excluded from gross income [Sec. 280A(g)].

(a) General rule.—Except as otherwise provided in this section, in the case of a taxpayer who is an individual or an S corporation, no deduction otherwise allowable under this chapter shall be allowed with respect to the use of a dwelling unit which is used by the taxpayer during the taxable year as a residence.

(b) Exception for interest, taxes, casualty losses, etc.—Subsection (a) shall not apply to any deduction allowable to the taxpayer without regard to its connection with his trade or business (or with his income-producing activity).

(c) Exceptions for certain business or rental use; limitation on deductions for such use.—

(1) Certain business use.—Subsection (a) shall not apply to any item to the extent such item is allocable to a portion of the dwelling unit which is exclusively used on a regular basis—

(A) as the principal place of business for any trade or business of the taxpayer.

(B) as a place of business which is used by patients, clients, or customers in meeting or dealing with the taxpayer in the normal course of his trade or business, or

(C) in the case of a separate structure which is not attached to the dwelling unit, in connection with the taxpayer's trade or business.

In the case of an employee, the preceding sentence shall apply only if the exclusive use referred to in the preceding sentence is for the convenience of his employer. For purposes of subparagraph (A), the term "principal place of business" includes a place of business which is used by the taxpayer for the administrative or management activities of any trade or business of the taxpayer if there is no other fixed location of such trade or business where the taxpayer conducts substantial administrative or management activities of such trade or business.

(2) Certain storage use.—Subsection (a) shall not apply to any item to the extent such item is allocable to space within the dwelling unit which is used on a regular basis as a storage unit for the inventory or product samples of the taxpayer held for use in the taxpayer's trade or business of selling products at retail or wholesale, but only if the dwelling unit is the sole fixed location of such trade or business.

(3) Rental use.—Subsection (a) shall not apply to any item which is attributable to the rental of the dwelling unit or portion thereof (determined after the application of subsection (e)).

(4) Use in providing day care services.—

(A) In general.—Subsection (a) shall not apply to any item to the extent that such item is allocable to the use of any portion of the dwelling unit on a regular basis in the taxpayer's trade or business of providing day care for children, for individuals who have attained age 65, or for individuals who are physically or mentally incapable of caring for themselves.

(B) Licensing, etc., requirement.—Subparagraph (A) shall apply to items accruing for a period only if the owner or operator of the trade or business referred to in subparagraph (A)—

(i) has applied for (and such application has not been rejected),

(ii) has been granted (and such granting has not been revoked), or

(iii) is exempt from having,

a license, certification, registration, or approval as a day care center or as a family or group day care home under the provisions of any applicable State law. This subparagraph shall apply only to items accruing in periods beginning on or after the first day of the first month which begins more than 90 days after the date of the enactment of the Tax Reduction and Simplification Act of 1977.

(C) Allocation formula.—If a portion of the taxpayer's dwelling unit used for the purposes described in subparagraph (A) is not used exclusively for those purposes, the amount of the expenses attributable to that portion shall not exceed an amount which bears the same ratio to the total amount of the items allocable to such portion as the number of hours the portion is used for such purposes bears to the number of hours the portion is available for use.

(5) Limitation on deductions.—In the case of a use described in paragraph (1), (2), or (4), and in the case of a use described in paragraph (3) where the dwelling unit is used by the taxpayer during the taxable year as a residence, the deductions allowed under this chapter for the taxable year by reason of being attributed to such use shall not exceed the excess of—

(A) the gross income derived from such use for the taxable year, over

(B) the sum of—

(i) the deductions allocable to such use which are allowable under this chapter for the taxable year whether or not such unit (or portion thereof) was so used, and

(ii) the deductions allocable to the trade or business or rental activity in which such use occurs (but which are not allocable to such use) for such taxable year.

Any amount not allowable as a deduction under this chapter by reason of the preceding sentence shall be taken into account as a deduction (allocable to such use) under this chapter for the succeeding taxable year. Any amount taken into account for any taxable year under the preceding sentence shall be subject to the limitation of the 1st sentence of this paragraph whether or not the dwelling unit is used as a residence during such taxable year.

(6) Treatment of rental to employer.—Paragraphs (1) and (3) shall not apply to any item which is attributable to the rental of the dwelling unit (or any portion thereof) by the taxpayer to his employer during any period in which the taxpayer uses the dwelling unit (or portion) in performing services as an employee of the employer.

(d) Use as residence.—

(1) In general.—For purposes of this section, a taxpayer uses a dwelling unit during the taxable year as a residence if he uses such unit (or portion thereof) for personal purposes for a number of days which exceeds the greater of—

(A) 14 days, or

(B) 10 percent of the number of days during such year for which such unit is rented at a fair rental.

For purposes of subparagraph (B), a unit shall not be treated as rented at a fair rental for any day for which it is used for personal purposes.

(2) Personal use of unit.—For purposes of this section, the taxpayer shall be deemed to have used a dwelling unit for personal purposes for a day if, for any part of such day, the unit is used—

(A) for personal purposes by the taxpayer or any other person who has an interest in such unit, or by any member of the family (as defined in section 267(c)(4)) of the taxpayer or such other person;

(B) by any individual who uses the unit under an arrangement which enables the taxpayer to use some other dwelling unit (whether or not a rental is charged for the use of such other unit); or

(C) by any individual (other than an employee with respect to whose use section 119 applies), unless for such day the dwelling unit is rented for a rental which, under the facts and circumstances, is fair rental.

The Secretary shall prescribe regulations with respect to the circumstances under which use of the unit for repairs and annual maintenance will not constitute personal use under this paragraph, except that if the taxpayer is engaged in repair and maintenance on a substantially full time basis for any day, such authority shall not allow the Secretary to treat a dwelling unit as being used for personal use by the taxpayer on such day merely because other individuals who are on the premises on such day are not so engaged.

(3) Rental to family member, etc., for use as principal residence.—

(A) In general.—A taxpayer shall not be treated as using a dwelling unit for personal purposes by reason of a rental arrangement for any period if for such period such dwelling unit is rented, at a fair rental, to any person for use as such person's principal residence.

(B) Special rules for rental to person having interest in unit.—

(i) Rental must be pursuant to shared equity financing agreement.—Subparagraph (A) shall apply to a rental to a person who has an interest in the dwelling unit only if such rental is pursuant to a shared equity financing agreement.

(ii) Determination of fair rental.—In the case of a rental pursuant to a shared equity financing agreement, fair rental shall be determined as of the time the agreement is entered into and by taking into account the occupant's qualified ownership interest.

(C) Shared equity financing agreement.—For purposes of this paragraph, the term "shared equity financing agreement" means an agreement under which—

(i) 2 or more persons acquire qualified ownership interests in a dwelling unit, and

(ii) the person (or persons) holding 1 or more of such interests—

(I) is entitled to occupy the dwelling unit for use as a principal residence, and

(II) is required to pay rent to 1 or more other persons holding qualified ownership interests in the dwelling unit.

(D) Qualified ownership interest.—For purposes of this paragraph, the term "qualified ownership interest" means an undivided interest for more than 50 years in the entire dwelling unit and appurtenant land being acquired in the transaction to which the shared equity financing agreement relates.

(4) Rental of principal residence.—

(A) In general.—For purposes of applying subsection (c)(5) to deductions allocable to a qualified rental period, a taxpayer shall not be considered to have used a dwelling unit for personal purposes for any day during the taxable year which occurs before or after a qualified rental period described in subparagraph (B)(i), or before a qualified rental period described in subparagraph (B)(ii), if with respect to such day such unit constitutes the principal residence (within the meaning of section 121) of the taxpayer.

(B) Qualified rental period.—For purposes of subparagraph (A), the term "qualified rental period" means a consecutive period of—

(i) 12 or more months which begins or ends in such taxable year, or

(ii) less than 12 months which begins in such taxable year and at the end of which such dwelling unit is sold or exchanged, and

for which such unit is rented, or is held for rental, at a fair rental.

(e) Expenses attributable to rental.—

(1) In general.—In any case where a taxpayer who is an individual or an S corporation uses a dwelling unit for personal purposes on any day during the taxable year (whether or not he is treated under this section as using such unit as a residence), the amount deductible under this chapter with respect to expenses attributable to the rental of the unit (or portion thereof) for the taxable year shall not exceed an amount which bears the same relationship to such expenses as the number of days during each year that the unit (or portion thereof) is rented at a fair rental bears to the total number of days during such year that the unit (or portion thereof) is used.

(2) Exception for deductions otherwise allowable.—This subsection shall not apply with respect to deductions which would be allowable under this chapter for the taxable year whether or not such unit (or portion thereof) was rented.

(f) Definitions and special rules.—

(1) Dwelling unit defined.—For purposes of this section—

(A) In general.—The term "dwelling unit" includes a house, apartment, condominium, mobile home, boat, or similar property, and all structures or other property appurtenant to such dwelling unit.

(B) Exception.—The term "dwelling unit" does not include that portion of a unit which is used exclusively as a hotel, motel, inn, or similar establishment.

(2) Personal use by shareholders of S corporation.—In the case of an S corporation, subparagraphs (A) and (B) of subsection (d)(2) shall be applied by substituting "any shareholder of the S corporation" for "the taxpayer" each place it appears.

(3) Coordination with section 183.—If subsection (a) applies with respect to any dwelling unit (or portion thereof) for the taxable year—

(A) section 183 (relating to activities not engaged in for profit) shall not apply to such unit (or portion thereof) for such year, but

(B) such year shall be taken into account as a taxable year for purposes of applying subsection (d) of section 183 (relating to 5-year presumption).

(4) Coordination with section 162(a)(2).—Nothing in this section shall be construed to disallow any deduction allowable under section 162(a)(2) (or any deduction which meets the tests of section 162(a)(2) but is allowable under another provision of this title) by reason of the taxpayer's being away from home in the pursuit of a trade or business (other than the trade or business of renting dwelling units).

(g) Special rule for certain rental use.— Notwithstanding any other provision of this section or section 183, if a dwelling unit is used during the taxable year by the taxpayer as a residence and such dwelling unit is actually rented for less than 15 days during the taxable year, then—

(1) no deduction otherwise allowable under this chapter because of the rental use of such dwelling unit shall be allowed, and

(2) the income derived from such use for the taxable year shall not be included in the gross income of such taxpayer under section 61.

§ 280B. Demolition of structures

In the case of the demolition of any structure—

(1) no deduction otherwise allowable under this chapter shall be allowed to the owner or lessee of such structure for—

(A) any amount expended for such demolition, or

(B) any loss sustained on account of such demolition; and

(2) amounts described in paragraph (1) shall be treated as properly chargeable to capital account with respect to the land on which the demolished structure was located.

§ 280C. Certain expenses for which credits are allowable

(a) Rule for employment credits.—No deduction shall be allowed for that portion of the wages or salaries paid or incurred for the taxable year which is equal to the sum of the credits determined for the taxable year under sections 45A, 51(a), 1396(a), 1400P(b), and 1400R. In the case of a corporation which is a member of a controlled group of corpo-rations (within the meaning of section 52(a)) or a trade or business which is treated as being under common control with other trades or businesses (within the meaning of section 52(b)), this subsection shall be applied under rules prescribed by the Secretary similar to the rules applicable under subsections (a) and (b) of section 52.

(b) Credit for qualified clinical testing expenses for certain drugs.—

(1) In general.—No deduction shall be allowed for that portion of the qualified clinical testing expenses (as defined in section 45C(b)) otherwise allowable as a deduction for the taxable year which is equal to the amount of the credit allowable for the taxable year under section 45C (determined without regard to section 38(c)).

(2) Similar rule where taxpayer capitalizes rather than deducts expenses.—If—

(A) the amount of the credit allowable for the taxable year under section 45C (determined without regard to section 38(c)), exceeds

(B) the amount allowable as a deduction for the taxable year for qualified clinical testing expenses (determined without regard to paragraph (1)),

the amount chargeable to capital account for the taxable year for such expenses shall be reduced by the amount of such excess.

(c) Credit for increasing research activities.—

(1) In general.—No deduction shall be allowed for that portion of the qualified research expenses (as defined in section 41(b)) or basic research expenses (as defined in section 41(e)(2) otherwise allowable as a deduction for the taxable year which is equal to the amount of the credit determined for such taxable year under section 41(a).

(2) Similar rule where taxpayer capitalizes rather than deducts expenses.—If—

(A) the amount of the credit determined for the taxable year under section 41(a)(1), exceeds

(B) the amount allowable as a deduction for such taxable year for qualified research expenses or basic research expenses (determined without regard to paragraph (1)),

the amount chargeable to capital account for the taxable year for such expenses shall be reduced by the amount of such excess.

(3) Election of reduced credit.—

(A) In general.—In the case of any taxable year for which an election is made under this paragraph—

(i) paragraphs (1) and (2) shall not apply, and

(ii) the amount of the credit under section 41(a) shall be the amount determined under subparagraph (B).

(B) Amount of reduced credit.—The amount of credit determined under this subparagraph for any taxable year shall be the amount equal to the excess of—

(i) the amount of credit determined under section 41(a) without regard to this paragraph, over

(ii) the product of—

(I) the amount described in clause (i), and

(II) the maximum rate of tax under section 11(b)(1).

(C) Election.—An election under this paragraph for any taxable year shall be made not later than the time for filing the return of tax for such year (including extensions), shall be made on such return, and shall be made in such manner as the Secretary may prescribe. Such an election, once made, shall be irrevocable.

(4) Controlled groups.—Paragraph (3) of subsection (b) shall apply for purposes of this subsection.

* * *

CAUTION: FUTURE EFFECTIVE DATE

Section 280C(g) is amended by the Patient Protection and Affordable Care Act of 2010 effective for taxable years ending after 12/31/2013.

(g) Qualifying therapeutic discovery project credit.—

(1) In general.—No deduction shall be allowed for that portion of the qualified investment (as defined in section 48D(b)) otherwise allowable as a deduction for the taxable year which—

(A) would be qualified research expenses (as defined in section 41(b)), basic research expenses (as defined in section 41(e)(2)), or qualified clinical testing expenses (as defined in section 45C(b)) if the credit under section 41 or section 45C were allowed with respect to such expenses for such taxable year, and

(B) is equal to the amount of the credit determined for such taxable year under section 48D(a), reduced by—

(i) the amount disallowed as a deduction by reason of section 48D(e)(2)(B), and

(ii) the amount of any basis reduction under section 48D(e)(1).

(2) Similar rule where taxpayer capitalizes rather than deducts expenses.—In the case of expenses described in paragraph (1)(A) taken into account in determining the credit under section 48D for the taxable year, if—

(A) the amount of the portion of the credit determined under such section with respect to such expenses, exceeds

(B) the amount allowable as a deduction for such taxable year for such expenses (determined without regard to paragraph (1)), the amount chargeable to capital account for the taxable year for such expenses shall be reduced by the amount of such excess.

(3) Controlled groups.—Paragraph (3) of subsection (b) shall apply for purposes of this subsection.

(h) Credit for employee health insurance expenses of small employers.—No deduction shall be allowed for that portion of the premiums for qualified health plans (as defined in section 1301(a) of the Patient Protection and Affordable Care Act), or for health insurance coverage in the case of taxable years beginning in 2010, 2011, 2012, or 2013, paid by an employer which is equal to the amount of the credit determined under section 45R(a) with respect to the premiums.

§ 280E. Expenditures in connection with the illegal sale of drugs

No deduction or credit shall be allowed for any amount paid or incurred during the taxable year in carrying on any trade or business if such trade or business (or the activities which comprise such trade or business) consists of trafficking in controlled substances (within the meaning of schedule I and II of the Controlled Substances Act) which is prohibited by Federal law or the law of any State in which such trade or business is conducted.

§ 280F. Limitation on depreciation for luxury automobiles; limitation where certain property used for personal purposes

Editorial Summary

Limitations on Listed Property and Luxury Automobiles

Subchapter B of Chapter 1 (Sec. 280F)

Section 280F contains two sets of limitations. The first limitation applies to all listed property as defined in Sec. 280F (d)(4). Under this limitation, if the business use of the listed property is not greater than 50%, only the straight-line method of cost recovery can be used [Sec. 280F(b)(1)]. In addition, if accelerated cost recovery has been used in the past and the percentage of business use for the current tax year fails the greater than 50% test, the excess depreciation (i.e., amount calculated under the accelerated method over the amount calculated under the straight-line method) must be recaptured as ordinary income [Sec. 280F(b)(2)]. In calculating the business use percentage, only Sec. 162 trade or business use is counted. That is, Sec. 212 production of income use is not counted in this calculation [Sec. 280F(d)(6)].

The second limitation applies only to luxury automobiles as defined in Sec. 280F(d)(5). Note that for this purpose, "luxury" has a rather low threshold. The amount of the cost recovery deduction (which includes the amount elected under Sec. 179 limited expensing) is limited to statutory dollar amounts [Sec. 280F(a)]. These dollar amounts are indexed annually. The indexed amounts for property placed in service in 2013 and 2014 are as follows:

Year of Use	Amount per Code	2013 Amount	2014 Amount
1st	$2,560	$3,160*	$3,160*
2nd	4,100	5,100	5,100
3rd	2,450	3,050	3,050
4th & succeeding	1,475	1,875	1,875

*Increased by $8,000 in 2012 and 2013 if eligible for additional first-year depreciation under §168(k).

(a) Limitation on amount of depreciation for luxury automobiles.—

(1) Depreciation.—

(A) Limitation.*—The amount of the depreciation deduction for any taxable year for any passenger automobile shall not exceed—

*Editorial comment: See the indexed amounts for 2013 and 2014 after Sec. 280F(e).

(i) $2,560 for the 1st taxable year in the recovery period,

(ii) $4,100 for the 2nd taxable year in the recovery period,

(iii) $2,450 for the 3rd taxable year in the recovery period, and

(iv) $1,475 for each succeeding taxable year in the recovery period.

(B) Disallowed deductions allowed for years after recovery period.—

(i) In general.—Except as provided in clause (ii), the unrecovered basis of any passenger automobile shall be treated as an expense for the 1st taxable year after the recovery period. Any excess of the unrecovered basis over the limitation of clause (ii) shall be treated as an expense in the succeeding taxable year.

(ii) $1,475 limitation.—The amount treated as an expense under clause (i) for any taxable year shall not exceed $1,475.

(iii) Property must be depreciable.—No amount shall be allowable as a deduction by reason of this subparagraph with respect to any property for any taxable year unless a depreciation deduction would be allowable with respect to such property for such taxable year.

(iv) Amount treated as depreciation deduction.—For purposes of this subtitle, any amount allowable as a deduction by reason of this subparagraph shall be treated as a depreciation deduction allowable under section 168.

(C) Special rule for certain clean-fuel passenger automobiles.—

(i) Modified automobiles.—In the case of a passenger automobile which is propelled by a fuel which is not a clean-burning fuel and to which is installed qualified clean-fuel vehicle property (as defined in section 179(c) (1)(A)) for purposes of permitting such vehicle to be propelled by a clean-burning fuel (as defined in section 179A(e)(1)), subparagraph (A) shall not apply to the cost of the installed qualified clean-burning vehicle property.

(ii) Purpose built passenger vehicles.—In the case of a purpose built passenger vehicle (as defined in section 4001(a)(2)(C)(ii)), each of the annual limitations specified in subparagraphs (A) and (B) shall be tripled.

(iii) Application of subparagraph.—This subparagraph shall apply to property placed in service after August 5, 1997, and before January 1, 2007.

(2) Coordination with reductions in amount allowable by reason of personal use, etc.—This subsection shall be applied before—

(A) the application of subsection (b), and

(B) the application of any other reduction in the amount of any depreciation deduction allowable under section 168 by reason of any use not qualifying the property for such credit or depreciation deduction.

(b) Limitation where business use of listed property not greater than 50 percent.—

(1) Depreciation.—If any listed property is not predominantly used in a qualified business use for any taxable year, the deduction allowed under section 168 with respect to such property for such taxable year and any subsequent taxable year shall be determined under section 168(g) (relating to alternative depreciation system).

(2) Recapture.—

(A) Where business use percentage does not exceed 50 percent.—If—

(i) property is predominantly used in a qualified business use in a taxable year in which it is placed in service, and

(ii) such property is not predominantly used in a qualified business use for any subsequent taxable year,

then any excess depreciation shall be included in gross income for the taxable year referred to in clause (ii), and the depreciation deduction for the taxable year referred to in clause (ii) and any subsequent taxable years shall be determined under section 168(g) (relating to alternative depreciation system).

(B) Excess depreciation.—For purposes of subparagraph (A), the term "excess depreciation" means the excess (if any) of—

(i) the amount of the depreciation deductions allowable with respect to the property for taxable years before the 1st taxable year in which the property was not predominantly used in a qualified business use, over

(ii) the amount which would have been so allowable if the property had not been predominantly used in a qualified business use for the taxable year in which it was placed in service.

(3) Property predominantly used in qualified business use.—For purposes of this subsection, property shall be treated as predominantly used in a qualified business use for any taxable year if the business use percentage for such taxable year exceeds 50 percent.

(c) Treatment of leases.—

(1) Lessor's deductions not affected.—This section shall not apply to any listed property leased or held for leasing by any person regularly engaged in the business of leasing such property.

(2) Lessee's deductions reduced.—For purposes of determining the amount allowable as a deduction under this chapter for rentals or other payments under a lease for a period of 30 days or more of listed property, only the allowable percentage of such payments shall be taken into account.

(3) Allowable percentage.—For purposes of paragraph (2), the allowable percentage shall be determined under tables prescribed by the Secretary. Such tables shall be prescribed so that the reduction in the deduction under paragraph (2) is substantially equivalent to the applicable restrictions contained in subsections (a) and (b).

(4) Lease term.—In determining the term of any lease for purposes of paragraph (2), the rules of section 168(i)(3)(A) shall apply.

(5) Lessee recapture.—Under regulations prescribed by the Secretary, rules similar to the rules of subsection (b)(3) shall apply to any lessee to which paragraph (2) applies.

(d) Definitions and special rules.—For purposes of this section—

(1) Coordination with section 179.—Any deduction allowable under section 179 with respect to any listed property shall be subject to the limitations of subsections (a) and (b), and the limitation of paragraph (3) of this subsection, in the same manner as if it were a depreciation deduction allowable under section 168.

(2) Subsequent depreciation deductions reduced for deductions allocable to personal use.—Solely for purposes of determining the amount of the depreciation deduction for subsequent taxable years, if less than 100 percent of the use of any listed property during any taxable year is use in a trade or business (including the holding for the production of income), all of the use of such property during such taxable year shall be treated as use so described.

(3) Deductions of employee.—

(A) In general.—Any employee use of listed property shall not be treated as use in a trade or business for purposes of determining the amount of any depreciation deduction allowable to the employee (or the amount of any deduction allowable to the employee for rentals or other payments under a lease of listed property) unless such use is for the convenience of the employer and required as a condition of employment.

(B) Employee use.—For purposes of subparagraph (A), the term "employee use" means any use in connection with the performance of services as an employee.

(4) Listed property.—

(A) In general.—Except as provided in subparagraph (B), the term "listed property" means—

(i) any passenger automobile,

(ii) any other property used as a means of transportation,

(iii) any property of a type generally used for purposes of entertainment, recreation, or amusement,

(iv) any computer or peripheral equipment (as defined in section 168(i)(2)(B)), and

(v) any other property of a type specified by the Secretary by regulations.

(B) Exception for certain computers.—The term "listed property" shall not include any computer or peripheral equipment (as so defined) used exclusively at a regular business establishment and owned or leased by the person operating such establishment. For purposes of the preceding sentence, any portion of a dwelling unit shall be treated as a regular business establishment if (and only if) the requirements of section 280A(c)(1) are met with respect to such portion.

(C) Exception for property used in business of transporting persons or property.—Except to the extent provided in regulations, clause (ii) of subparagraph (A) shall not apply to any property substantially all of the use of which is in a trade or business of providing to unrelated persons services consisting of the transportation of persons or property for compensation or hire.

(5) Passenger automobile.—

(A) In general.—Except as provided in subparagraph (B), the term "passenger automobile" means any 4-wheeled vehicle—

(i) which is manufactured primarily for use on public streets, roads, and highways, and

(ii) which is rated at 6,000 pounds unloaded gross vehicle weight or less.

In the case of a truck or van, clause (ii) shall be applied by substituting "gross vehicle weight" for "unloaded gross vehicle weight."

(B) Exception for certain vehicles.—The term "passenger automobile" shall not include—

(i) any ambulance, hearse, or combination ambulance-hearse used by the taxpayer directly in a trade or business,

(ii) any vehicle used by the taxpayer directly in the trade or business of transporting persons or property for compensation or hire, and

(iii) under regulations, any truck or van.

(6) Business use percentage.—

(A) In general.—The term "business use percentage" means the percentage of the use of any listed property during any taxable year which is a qualified business use.

(B) Qualified business use.—Except as provided in subparagraph (C), the term "qualified business use" means any use in a trade or business of the taxpayer.

(C) Exception for certain use by 5-percent owners and related persons.—

(i) In general.—The term "qualified business use" shall not include—

(I) leasing property to any 5-percent owner or related person,

(II) use of property provided as compensation for the performance of services by a 5-percent owner or related person, or

(III) use of property provided as compensation for the performance of services by any person not described in subclause (II) unless an amount is included in the gross income of such person with respect to such use, and, where required, there was withholding under chapter 24.

(ii) Special rule for aircraft.—Clause (i) shall not apply with respect to any aircraft if at least 25 percent of the total use of the aircraft during the taxable year consists of qualified business use not described in clause (i).

(D) Definitions.—For purposes of this paragraph—

(i) 5-percent owner.—The term "5-percent owner" means any person who is a 5-percent owner with respect to the taxpayer (as defined in section 416(i)(1)(B)(i)).

(ii) Related person.—The term "related person" means any person related to the taxpayer (within the meaning of section 267(b)).

(7) Automobile price inflation adjustment.—

(A) In general.—In the case of any passenger automobile placed in service after 1988, subsection (a) shall be applied by increasing each dollar amount contained in such subsection by the automobile price inflation adjustment for the calendar year in which such automobile is placed in service. Any increase under the preceding sentence shall be rounded to the nearest multiple of $100 (or if the increase is a multiple of $50, such increase shall be increased to the next higher multiple of $100).

(B) Automobile price inflation adjustment.—For purposes of this paragraph—

(i) In general.—The automobile price inflation adjustment for any calendar year is the percentage (if any) by which—

(I) the CPI automobile component for October of the preceding calendar year, exceeds

(II) the CPI automobile component for October of 1987.

(ii) CPI automobile component.—The term "CPI automobile component" means the automobile component of the Consumer Price Index for All Urban Consumers published by the Department of Labor.

(8) Unrecovered basis.—For purposes of subsection (a)(2), the term "unrecovered basis" means the adjusted basis of the passenger automobile determined after the application of subsection (a) and as if all use during the recovery period were use in a trade or business (including the holding of property for the production of income).

(9) All taxpayers holding interests in passenger automobile treated as 1 taxpayer.—All taxpayers holding interests in any passenger automobile shall be treated as 1 taxpayer for purposes of applying subsection (a) to such automobile, and the limitations of subsection (a) shall be allocated among such taxpayers in proportion to their interests in such automobile.

(10) Special rule for property acquired in nonrecognition transactions.—For purposes of subsection (a)(2), any property acquired in a nonrecognition transaction shall be treated as a single property originally placed in service in the taxable year in which it was placed in service after being so acquired.

(e) Regulations.—The Secretary shall prescribe such regulations as may be necessary or appropriate to carry out the purposes of this section, including regulations with respect to items properly included in, or excluded from, the adjusted basis of any listed property.

Editorial Note

The indexed amounts for luxury automobiles for 2013 and 2014 are as follows:

Amount per Code	2013 Amount	2014 Amount
$1,475	$1,875	$1,875
2,450	3,050	3,050
2,560	3,160*	3,160*
4,100	5,100	5,100

*Increased by $8,000 in 2013 and 2014 if eligible for additional first-year depreciation under §168(k).

§ 280G. Golden parachute payments

(a) General rule.—No deduction shall be allowed under this chapter for any excess parachute payment.

(b) Excess parachute payment.—For purposes of this section—

(1) In general.—The term "excess parachute payment" means an amount equal to the excess of any parachute payment over the portion of the base amount allocated to such payment.

(2) Parachute payment defined.—

(A) In general.—The term "parachute payment" means any payment in the nature of compensation to (or for the benefit of) a disqualified individual if—

(i) such payment is contingent on a change—

(I) in the ownership or effective control of the corporation, or

(II) in the ownership of a substantial portion of the assets of the corporation, and

(ii) the aggregate present value of the payments in the nature of compensation to (or for the benefit of) such individual which are contingent on such change equals or exceeds an amount equal to 3 times the base amount.

For purposes of clause (ii), payments not treated as parachute payments under paragraph (4)(A), (5), or (6) shall not be taken into account.

(B) Agreements.—The term "parachute payment" shall also include any payment in the nature of compensation to (or for the benefit of) a disqualified individual if such payment is made pursuant to an agreement which violates any generally enforced securities laws or regulations. In any proceeding involving the issue of whether any payment made to a disqualified individual is a parachute payment on account of a violation of any generally enforced securities laws or regulations, the burden of proof with respect to establishing the occurrence of a violation of such a law or regulation shall be upon the Secretary.

(C) Treatment of certain agreements entered into within 1 year before change of ownership.—For purposes of subparagraph (A)(i), any payment pursuant to—

(i) an agreement entered into within 1 year before the change described in subparagraph (A)(i), or

(ii) an amendment made within such 1-year period of a previous agreement,

shall be presumed to be contingent on such change unless the contrary is establish by clear and convincing evidence.

(3) Base amount.—

(A) In general.—The term "base amount" means the individual's annualized includible compensation for the base period.

(B) Allocation.—The portion of the base amount allocated to any parachute payment shall be an amount which bears the same ratio to the base amount as—

(i) the present value of such payment, bears to

(ii) the aggregate present value of all such payments.

(4) Treatment of amounts which taxpayer establishes as reasonable compensation.—In the case of any payment described in paragraph (2)(A)—

(A) the amount treated as a parachute payment shall not include the portion of such payment which the taxpayer establishes by clear and convincing evidence is reasonable compensation for personal services to be rendered on or after the date of the change described in paragraph (2)(A)(i), and

(B) the amount treated as an excess parachute payment shall be reduced by the portion of such payment which the taxpayer establishes by clear and convincing evidence is reasonable compensation for personal services actually rendered before the date of the change described in paragraph (2)(A)(i).

For purposes of subparagraph (B), reasonable compensation for services actually rendered before the date of the change described in paragraph (2)(A)(i) shall be first offset against the base amount.

(5) Exemption for small business corporations, etc.—

(A) In general.—Notwithstanding paragraph (2), the term "parachute payment" does not include—

(i) any payment to a disqualified individual with respect to a corporation which (immediately before the change described in paragraph (2)(A)(i)) was a small business corporation (as defined in section 1361(b) but without regard to paragraph (1)(C) thereof), and

(ii) any payment to a disqualified individual with respect to a corporation (other than a corporation described in clause (i)) if—

(I) immediately before the change described in paragraph (2)(A)(i), no stock in such corporation was readily tradeable on an established securities market or otherwise, and

(II) the shareholder approval requirements of subparagraph (B) are met with respect to such payment.

The Secretary may, by regulations, prescribe that the requirements of subclause (I) of clause (ii) are not met where a substantial portion of the assets of any entity consists (directly or indirectly) of stock in such corporation and interests in such other entity are readily tradeable on an established securities market, or otherwise. Stock described in section 1504(a)(4) shall not be taken into account under clause (ii)(I) if the payment does not adversely affect the shareholder's redemption and liquidation rights.

(B) Shareholder approval requirements.—The shareholder approval requirements of this subparagraph are met with respect to any payment if—

(i) such payment was approved by a vote of the persons who owned, immediately before the change described in paragraph (2)(A)(i), more than 75 percent of the voting power of all outstanding stock of the corporation, and

(ii) there was adequate disclosure to shareholders of all material facts concerning all payments which (but for this paragraph) would be parachute payments with respect to a disqualified individual.

The regulations prescribed under subsection (e) shall include regulations providing for the application of this subparagraph in the case of shareholders which are not individuals (including the treatment of nonvoting interests in an entity which is a shareholder) and where an entity holds a de minimis amount of stock in the corporation.

(6) Exemption for payments under qualified plans.—Notwithstanding paragraph (2), the term "parachute payment" shall not include any payment to or from—

(A) a plan described in section 401(a) which includes a trust exempt from tax under section 501(a),

(B) an annuity plan described in section 403(a),

(C) a simplified employee pension (as defined in section 408(k)), or

(D) a simple retirement account described in section 408(p).

(c) Disqualified individuals.—For purposes of this section, the term "disqualified individual" means any individual who is—

(1) an employee, independent contractor, or other person specified in regulations by the

Secretary who performs personal services for any corporation, and

(2) is an officer, shareholder, or highly-compensated individual.

For purposes of this section, a personal service corporation (or similar entity) shall be treated as an individual. For purposes of paragraph (2), the term "highly-compensated individual" only includes an individual who is (or would be if the individual were an employee) a member of the group consisting of the highest paid 1 percent of the employees of the corporation or, if less, the highest paid 250 employees of the corporation.

(d) Other definitions and special rules.—For purposes of this section—

(1) Annualized includible compensation for base period.—The term "annualized includible compensation for the base period" means the average annual compensation which—

(A) was payable by the corporation with respect to which the change in ownership or control described in paragraph (2)(A) of subsection (b) occurs, and

(B) was includible in the gross income of the disqualified individual for taxable years in the base period.

(2) Base period.—The term "base period" means the period consisting of the most recent 5 taxable years ending before the date on which the change in ownership or control described in paragraph (2)(A) of subsection (b) occurs (or such portion of such period during which the disqualified individual performed personal services for the corporation).

(3) Property transfers.—Any transfer of property—

(A) shall be treated as a payment, and

(B) shall be taken into account as its fair market value.

(4) Present value.—Present value shall be determined by using a discount rate equal to 120 percent of the applicable Federal rate (determined under section 1274(d)), compounded semiannually.

(5) Treatment of affiliated groups.—Except as otherwise provided in regulations, all members of the same affiliated group (as defined in section 1504, determined without regard to section 1504 (b)) shall be treated as 1 corporation for purposes of this section. Any person who is an officer of any member of such group shall be treated as an officer of such 1 corporation.

(e) Special rule for application to employers participating in the troubled assets relief program.—

(1) In general.—In the case of the severance from employment of a covered executive of an applicable employer during the period during which the authorities under section 101(a) of the Emergency Economic Stabilization Act of 2008 are in effect (determined under section 120 of such Act), this section shall be applied to payments to such executive with the following modifications:

(A) Any reference to a disqualified individual (other than in subsection (c)) shall be treated as a reference to a covered executive.

(B) Any reference to a change described in subsection (b)(2)(A)(i) shall be treated as a reference to an applicable severance from employment of a covered executive, and any reference to a payment contingent on such a change shall be treated as a reference to any payment made during an applicable taxable year of the employer on account of such applicable severance from employment.

(C) Any reference to a corporation shall be treated as a reference to an applicable employer.

(D) The provisions of subsections (b)(2)(C), (b)(4), (b)(5), and (d)(5) shall not apply.

(2) Definitions and special rules.—For purposes of this subsection:

(A) Definitions.—Any term used in this subsection which is also used in section 162 (m)(5) shall have the meaning given such term by such section.

(B) Applicable severance from employment.—The term "applicable severance from employment" means any severance from employment of a covered executive—

(i) by reason of an involuntary termination of the executive by the employer, or

(ii) in connection with any bankruptcy, liquidation, or receivership of the employer.

(C) Coordination and other rules.—

(i) In general.—If a payment which is treated as a parachute payment by reason of this subsection is also a parachute payment determined without regard to this subsection, this subsection shall not apply to such payment.

(ii) Regulatory authority.—The Secretary may prescribe such guidance, rules, or regulations as are necessary—

(I) to carry out the purposes of this subsection and the Emergency Economic Stabilization Act of 2008, including the extent to which this subsection applies in the case of any acquisition, merger, or reorganization of an applicable employer,

(II) to apply this section and section 4999 in cases where one or more payments with respect to any individual are treated as parachute payments by reason of this subsection, and other payments with respect to such individual are treated as parachute payments under this section without regard to this subsection, and

(III) to prevent the avoidance of the application of this section through the mischaracterization of a severance from employment as other than an applicable severance from employment.

(f) Regulations.—The Secretary shall prescribe such regulations as may be necessary or appropriate to carry out the purposes of this section (including regulations for the application of this section in the case of related corporations and in the case of personal service corporations).

§ 280H. Limitation on certain amounts paid to employee-owners by personal service corporations electing alternative taxable years

(a) General rule.—If—

(1) an election by a personal service corporation under section 444 is in effect for a taxable year, and

(2) such corporation does not meet the minimum distribution requirements of subsection (c) for such taxable year,

then the deduction otherwise allowed under this chapter for applicable amounts paid or incurred by such corporation to employee-owners shall not exceed the maximum deductible amount. The preceding sentence shall not apply for purposes of subchapter G (relating to personal holding companies).

(b) Carryover of nondeductible amounts.—If any amount is not allowed as a deduction for a taxable year under subsection (a), such amount shall be treated as paid or incurred in the succeeding taxable year.

(c) Minimum distribution requirement.—For purposes of this section—

(1) In general.—A personal service corporation meets the minimum distribution requirements of this subsection if the applicable amounts paid or incurred during the deferral period of the taxable year (determined without regard to subsection (b)) equal or exceed the lesser of—

(A) the product of—

(i) the applicable amounts paid during the preceding taxable year, divided by the number of months in such taxable year, multiplied by

(ii) the number of months in the deferral period of the preceding taxable year, or

(B) The applicable percentage of the adjusted taxable income for the deferral period of the taxable year.

(2) Applicable percentage.—The term "applicable percentage" means the percentage (not in excess of 95 percent) determined by dividing—

(A) the applicable amounts paid or incurred during the 3 taxable years immediately preceding the taxable year, by

(B) the adjusted taxable income of such corporation for such 3 taxable years.

(d) Maximum deductible amount.—For purposes of this section, the term "maximum deductible amount" means the sum of—

(1) the applicable amounts paid during the deferral period, plus

(2) an amount equal to the product of—

(A) the amount determined under paragraph (1), divided by the number of months in the deferral period, multiplied by

(B) the number of months in the nondeferral period.

(e) Disallowance of net operating loss carrybacks.—No net operating loss carryback shall be allowed to (or from) any taxable year of a personal service corporation to which an election under section 444 applies.

(f) Other definitions and special rules.—For purposes of this section—

(1) Applicable amount.—The term "applicable amount" means any amount paid to an employee-owner which is includible in the gross income of such employee, other than—

(A) any gain from the sale or exchange of property between the owner-employee and the corporation, or

(B) any dividend paid by the corporation.

(2) Employee-Owner.—The term "employee-owner" has the meaning given such term by section 269A(b)(2) (as modified by section 441(i)(2)).

(3) Nondeferral and deferral periods.—

(A) Deferral period.—The term "deferral period" has the meaning given to such term by section 444(b)(4).

(B) Nondeferral period.—The term "nondeferral period" means the portion of the taxable year of the personal service corporation which occurs after the portion of such year constituting the deferral period.

(4) Adjusted taxable income.—The term "adjusted taxable income" means taxable income determined without regard to—

(A) any amount paid to an employee-owner which is includible in the gross income of such employee-owner, and

(B) any net operating loss carryover to the extent such carryover is attributable to amounts described in subparagraph (A).

(5) Personal service corporation.—The term "personal service corporation" has the meaning given to such term by section 441(i)(2).

PART X—TERMINAL RAILROAD CORPORATIONS AND THEIR SHAREHOLDERS*

PART XI—SPECIAL RULES RELATING TO CORPORATE PREFERENCE ITEMS

Editorial Summary

Section 291 Depreciation Recapture

Subchapter B of Chapter 1 (Sec. 291)

For both the individual and the corporate taxpayer, Sec. 1231 property is subject to depreciation recapture under Sec. 1245 and Sec. 1250. The amount recaptured is classified as ordinary income rather than as Sec. 1231 gain which can qualify for long-term capital gain treatment. Section 1245 property is principally personalty and Sec. 1250 property is principally realty.

Section 291 depreciation recapture applies only to the corporate taxpayer and only to Sec. 1250 property [see Sec. 291 (a)]. It is calculated as 20 percent of the excess of what depreciation recapture would have been under Sec. 1245 over what depreciation recapture actually is under Sec. 1250. Like depreciation recapture under Sec. 1245 and Sec. 1250, Sec. 291 recapture is classified as ordinary income.

§ 291. Special rules relating to corporate preference items

(a) Reduction in certain preference items, etc.—For purposes of this subtitle, in the case of a corporation—

(1) Section 1250 capital gain treatment.—In the case of section 1250 property which is disposed of during the taxable year, 20 percent of the excess (if any) of—

(A) the amount which would be treated as ordinary income if such property was section 1245 property, over

(B) the amount treated as ordinary income under section 1250 (determined without regard to this paragraph),

shall be treated as gain which is ordinary income under section 1250 and shall be recognized notwithstanding any other provision of this title. Under regulations prescribed by the Secretary, the provisions of this paragraph shall not apply to the disposition of any property to the extent section 1250(a) does not apply to such disposition by reason of section 1250(d).

(2) Reduction in percentage depletion.—In the case of iron ore and coal (including lignite), the amount allowable as a deduction under section 613 with respect to any property (as defined in section 614) shall be reduced by 20 percent of the amount of the excess (if any) of—

(A) the amount of the deduction allowable under section 613 for the taxable year (determined without regard to this paragraph), over

*Omitted.

(B) the adjusted basis of the property at the close of the taxable year (determined without regard to the depletion deduction for the taxable year).

* * *

(5) Amortization of pollution control facilities.—If an election is made under section 169 with respect to any certified pollution control facility, the amortizable basis of such facility for purposes of such section shall be reduced by 20 percent.

(b) Special rules for treatment of intangible drilling costs and mineral exploration and development costs.—For purposes of this subtitle, in the case of a corporation—

(1) In general.—The amount allowable as a deduction for any taxable year (determined without regard to this section)—

(A) under section 263(c) in the case of an integrated oil company, or

(B) under section 616(a) or 617(a), shall be reduced by 30 percent.

(2) Amortization of amounts not allowable as deductions under paragraph (1).—The amount not allowable as a deduction under section 263(c), 616(a), or 617(a) (as the case may be) for any taxable year by reason of paragraph (1) shall be allowable as a deduction ratably over the 60-month period beginning with the month in which the costs are paid or incurred.

(3) Dispositions.—For purposes of section 1254, any deduction under paragraph (2) shall be treated as a deduction allowable under section 263 (c), 616(a), or 617(a) (whichever is appropriate).

(4) Integrated oil company defined.—For purposes of this subsection, the term "integrated oil company" means, with respect to any taxable year, any producer (within the meaning of section 4996(a)(1)) of crude oil other than an independent producer (within the meaning of section 4992(b)).

(5) Coordination with cost depletion.—The portion of the adjusted basis of any property which is attributable to amounts to which paragraph (1) applied shall not be taken into account for purposes of determining depletion under section 611.

(c) Special rules relating to pollution control facilities.—For purposes of this subtitle—

(1) Accelerated cost recovery deduction.—Section 168 shall apply with respect to that portion of the basis of any property not taken into account under section 169 by reason of subsection (a)(4).

(2) 1250 recapture.—Subsection (a)(1) shall not apply to any section 1250 property which is part of a certified pollution control facility (within the meaning of section 169(d)(1)) with respect to which an election under section 169 was made.

* * *

(e) Definitions.—For purposes of this section—

* * *

(2) Section 1245 and 1250 property.—The terms "section 1245 property" and "section 1250 property" have the meanings given such terms by sections 1245(a)(3) and 1250(c), respectively.

SUBCHAPTER C—CORPORATE DISTRIBUTIONS AND ADJUSTMENTS

Editorial Summary

Corporate Distributions: General

Subchapter C of Chapter 1

Corporate distributions impact on two parties (i.e., the corporation and the shareholder); therefore, the tax consequences to each party must be considered.

From the viewpoint of the recipient shareholder, distributions can produce the following results:

1. Dividend income. Dividends are taxed as ordinary income.

2. Return of capital. The amount of the distribution reduces the shareholder's stock basis (tax-free). Distributions in excess of basis receive capital gain treatment.

3. Tax-free. The distribution is not a taxable transaction.

Forms in which corporate distributions can be structured are as follows:

Form	Result
1. Dividend.	1. Ordinary income.
2. Stock redemption.	2. Return of capital.
3. Partial liquidation.	3. Return of capital.
4. Complete liquidation.	4. Return of capital.
5. Reorganization.	5. Tax-free.

Corporate distributions generally reduce the net assets of the corporation, and in certain instances, may produce recognition at the corporate level. In addition, the earnings and profits of the corporation may be reduced. Finally, the corporation's basis for its remaining assets may be affected.

PART I—DISTRIBUTIONS BY CORPORATIONS

Editorial Summary

Corporate Distributions: Dividend or Stock Redemption

Subchapter C of Chapter 1 (Secs. 301–318)

Effect on shareholder. If the distribution is a dividend, the shareholder has ordinary income [see Secs. 301(c), 316]. The form of the distribution can be in cash or property. The dividend may be one that is declared by the board of directors of the corporation or one that constructively produces dividend treatment to the shareholder even though no formal declaration occurs (e.g., use of corporate property, bargain purchase). The Jobs and Growth Tax Relief Reconciliation Act of 2003 permits certain dividends to be taxed at beneficial capital gains rates [see Sec. 301(f)(4)].

Differences exist with respect to dividends received by an individual shareholder versus those received by a corporate shareholder. A corporate shareholder is eligible for the dividends received deduction [see Sec. 243], whereas no such opportunity is available to the individual shareholder. This can affect the decision of the shareholder to invest in income stock rather than in growth stock. However, in the case of property dividends, different rules no longer exist (i.e., as the result of the change made by the Technical and Miscellaneous Revenue Act of 1988) for determining the amount of the dividend [see Secs. 301(b), 317(a)].

If the distribution is a stock redemption, the shareholder receives return of capital treatment [see Secs. 301(c), 317 (b)]. Differences again no longer exist between the individual and corporate shareholder for determining the amount of the stock redemption if the shareholder receives property from the corporation [see Sec. 301(b)]. Be aware that the number of shares redeemed is not necessarily determinative of the portion of shareholder basis that is used in the return of capital calculation.

The general stock redemption rules appear in Sec. 302. Five types of stock redemptions are provided for in Sec. 302:

1. Redemption not essentially equivalent to a dividend.
2. Substantially disproportionate redemption.
3. Termination of a shareholder's interest.
4. Partial liquidation.
5. Redemptions by certain regulated investment companies.

A basic difference exists between the partial liquidation and the three other types of stock redemptions. For the partial liquidation, the testing to determine if the statutory requirements are satisfied is done at the corporate level rather than at the shareholder level. This produces the results that all of the shareholders qualify for stock redemption treatment, rather than some shareholders qualifying and other shareholders not qualifying. (Note that Sec. 302(b)(4)(A) provides that corporate shareholders are not eligible for type 4 treatment.)

*Omitted.

In determining stock ownership under Sec. 302, both direct and indirect ownership must be considered [see the constructive ownership rules in Sec. 318]. Note that the constructive ownership rules are different than those for related party transactions under Sec. 267. Also note that under certain conditions the constructive ownership rules do not apply to the third type (i.e., termination of shareholder's interest) of stock redemption [see Sec. 302(c)(2)].

Section 301(d) contains the basis rules for property received as a dividend or as a stock redemption. Differences again no longer exist with respect to the calculation methodology for the individual and corporate shareholder.

Two special purpose types of stock redemptions are covered in Secs. 303 and 304.

Effect on corporation. The general rule under Sec. 311 provides that a distribution by the corporation with respect to its stock is not a taxable event. However, two major exceptions exist that are frequently applicable [see Sec. 311(b)].

The earnings and profits of a corporation are both influenced by and influence corporate distributions. For dividend treatment to occur at the shareholder level, earnings and profits must be adequate to cover the amount of the distribution [see Sec. 316(a)]. Note that in evaluating this adequacy of earnings and profits, one first looks to the *current* earnings and profits account [see Sec. 316(a)]. Only if this account is inadequate does one look to the *accumulated* earnings and profits account. Because of this sequence, there could be a negative balance in the accumulated earnings and profits account and yet dividend treatment could result due to earnings for the current taxable year. Both dividends and stock redemptions reduce the earnings and profits of the corporation [see Sec. 312(a)]. Earnings and profits can be negative as the result of corporate losses, but distributions cannot reduce earnings and profits below zero.

The earnings and profits of the corporation are a derivative of the accounting concept of retained earnings. The adjustments contained in Sec. 312, however, produce numerous reasons for the amount of retained earnings and earnings and profits not being equal.

SUBPART A—EFFECTS ON RECIPIENTS

§ 301. Distributions of property

(a) In general.—Except as otherwise provided in this chapter, a distribution of property (as defined in section 317(a)) made by a corporation to a shareholder with respect to its stock shall be treated in the manner provided in subsection (c).

(b) Amount distributed.—

(1) General rule.—For purposes of this section, the amount of any distribution shall be the amount of money received, plus the fair market value of the other property received.

(2) Reduction for liabilities.—The amount of any distribution determined under paragraph (1) shall be reduced (but not below zero) by—

(A) the amount of any liability of the corporation assumed by the shareholder in connection with the distribution, and

(B) the amount of any liability to which the property received by the shareholder is subject immediately before, and immediately after, the distribution.

(3) Determination of fair market value.—For purposes of this section, fair market value shall be determined as of the date of the distribution.

(c) Amount taxable.—In the case of a distribution to which subsection (a) applies—

(1) Amount constituting dividend.—That portion of the distribution which is a dividend (as defined in section 316) shall be included in gross income.

(2) Amount applied against basis.—That portion of the distribution which is not a dividend shall be applied against and reduce the adjusted basis of the stock.

(3) Amount in excess of basis.—

(A) In general.—Except as provided in subparagraph (B), that portion of the distribution which is not a dividend, to the extent that it exceeds the adjusted basis of the stock, shall be treated as gain from the sale or exchange of property.

(B) Distributions out of increase in value accrued before March 1, 1913.—That portion of the distribution which is not a dividend, to the extent that it exceeds the adjusted basis of the stock and to the extent that it is out of increase in value accrued before March 1, 1913, shall be exempt from tax.

(d) Basis.—The basis of property received in a distribution to which subsection (a) applies shall be the fair market value of such property.

(e) Special rule for certain distributions received by 20 percent corporate shareholder.—

(1) In general.—Except to the extent otherwise provided in regulations, solely for purposes of determining the taxable income of any 20 percent corporate shareholder (and its adjusted basis in the stock of the distributing corporation), section 312 shall be applied with respect to the distributing corporation as if it did not contain subsections (k) and (n) thereof.

(2) 20 percent corporate shareholder.—For purposes of this subsection, the term "20 percent corporate shareholder" means, with respect to any distribution, any corporation which owns (directly or through the application of section 318)—

(A) stock in the corporation making the distribution possessing at least 20 percent of the total combined voting power of all classes of stock entitled to vote, or

(B) at least 20 percent of the total value of all stock of the distributing corporation (except nonvoting stock which is limited and preferred as to dividends),

but only if, but for this subsection, the distributee corporation would be entitled to a deduction under section 243, 244, or 245 with respect to such distribution.

(3) Application of section 312(n)(7) not affected.—The reference in paragraph (1) to subsection (n) of section 312 shall be treated as not including a reference to paragraph (7) of such subsection.

(4) Regulations.—The Secretary shall prescribe such regulations as may be necessary or appropriate to carry out the purposes of this subsection.

(f) Special rules.—

(1) For distributions in redemption of stock, see section 302.

(2) For distributions in complete liquidation, see part II (sec. 331 and following).

(3) For distributions in corporate organizations and reorganizations, see part III (sec. 351 and following).

(4) For taxation of dividends received by individuals at capital gain rates, see section 1(h)(11).

§ 302. Distributions in redemption of stock

(a) General rule.—If a corporation redeems its stock (within the meaning of section 317(b)), and if paragraph (1), (2), (3), (4), or (5) of subsection (b) applies, such redemption shall be treated as a distribution in part or full payment in exchange for the stock.

(b) Redemptions treated as exchanges.—

(1) Redemptions not equivalent to dividends.—Subsection (a) shall apply if the redemption is not essentially equivalent to a dividend.

(2) Substantially disproportionate redemption of stock.—

(A) In general.—Subsection (a) shall apply if the distribution is substantially disproportionate with respect to the shareholder.

(B) Limitation.—This paragraph shall not apply unless immediately after the redemption the shareholder owns less than 50 percent of the total combined voting power of all classes of stock entitled to vote.

(C) Definitions.—For purposes of this paragraph, the distribution is substantially disproportionate if—

(i) the ratio which the voting stock of the corporation owned by the shareholder immediately after the redemption bears to all of the voting stock of the corporation at such time,

is less than 80 percent of—

(ii) the ratio which the voting stock of the corporation owned by the shareholder immediately before the redemption bears to all of the voting stock of the corporation at such time.

For purposes of this paragraph, no distribution shall be treated as substantially disproportionate unless the shareholder's ownership of the common stock of the corporation (whether voting or nonvoting) after and before redemption also meets the 80 percent requirement of the preceding sentence. For purposes of the preceding sentence, if there is more than one class of common stock, the determinations shall be made by reference to fair market value.

(D) Series of redemptions.—This paragraph shall not apply to any redemption made pursuant to a plan the purpose or effect of which is a series of redemptions resulting in a distribution which (in the aggregate) is not substantially disproportionate with respect to the shareholder.

(3) Termination of shareholder's interest.—Subsection (a) shall apply if the redemption is in complete redemption of all of the stock of the corporation owned by the shareholder.

(4) Redemption from noncorporate shareholder in partial liquidation.—Subsection (a) shall apply to a distribution if such distribution is —

(A) in redemption of stock held by a shareholder who is not a corporation, and

(B) in partial liquidation of the distributing corporation.

(5) Redemptions by certain regulated investment companies.—Except to the extent provided in regulations prescribed by the Secretary, subsection (a) shall apply to any distribution in redemption of stock of a publicly offered regulated investment company (within the meaning of section 67(c)(2)(B)) if—

(A) such redemption is upon the demand of the stockholder, and

(B) such company issues only stock which is redeemable upon the demand of the stockholder.

(6) Application of paragraphs.—In determining whether a redemption meets the requirements of paragraph (1), the fact that such redemption fails to meet the requirements of paragraph (2), (3), or (4) shall not be taken into account. If a redemption meets the requirements of paragraph (3) and also the requirements of paragraph (1), (2), or (4), then so much of subsection (c)(2) as would (but for this sentence) apply in respect of the acquisition of an interest in the corporation within the 10-year period beginning on the date of the distribution shall not apply.

(c) Constructive ownership of stock.—

(1) In general.—Except as provided in paragraph (2) of this subsection, section 318(a) shall apply in determining the ownership of stock for purposes of this section.

(2) For determining termination of interest.—

(A) In the case of a distribution described in subsection (b)(3), section 318(a)(1) shall not apply if—

(i) immediately after the distribution the distributee has no interest in the corporation (including an interest as officer, director, or employee), other than an interest as a creditor,

(ii) the distributee does not acquire any such interest (other than stock acquired by bequest or inheritance) within 10 years from the date of such distribution, and

(iii) the distributee, at such time and in such manner as the Secretary by regulations prescribes, files an agreement to notify the Secretary of any acquisition described in clause (ii) and to retain such records as may be necessary for the application of this paragraph.

If the distributee acquires such an interest in the corporation (other than by bequest or inheritance) within 10 years from the date of the distribution, then the periods of limitation provided in sections 6501 and 6502 on the making of an assessment and the collection by levy or a proceeding in court shall, with respect to any deficiency (including interest and additions to the tax) resulting from such acquisition, include one year immediately following the date on which the distributee (in accordance with regulations prescribed by the Secretary) notifies the Secretary of such acquisition; and such assessment and collection may be made notwithstanding any provision of law or rule of law which otherwise would prevent such assessment and collection.

(B) Subparagraph (A) of this paragraph shall not apply if—

(i) any portion of the stock redeemed was acquired, directly or indirectly, within the 10-year period ending on the date of the distribution by the distributee from a person the ownership of whose stock would (at the time of distribution) be attributable to the distributee under section 318(a), or

(ii) any person owns (at the time of the distribution) stock the ownership of which is attributable to the distributee under section 318(a) and such person acquired any stock in the corporation, directly or indirectly, from the distributee within the 10-year period ending on the date of the distribution, unless such stock so acquired from the distributee is redeemed in the same transaction.

The preceding sentence shall not apply if the acquisition (or, in the case of clause (ii), the disposition) by the distributee did not have as one of its principal purposes the avoidance of Federal income tax.

(C) Special rule for waivers by entities.—

(i) Ingeneral.—Subparagraph (A) shall not apply to a distribution to any entity unless—

(I) such entity and each related person meet the requirements of clauses (i), (ii), and (iii) of subparagraph (A), and

(II) each related person agrees to be jointly and severally liable for any deficiency (including interest and additions to tax) resulting from an acquisition described in clause (ii) of subparagraph (A).

In any case to which the preceding sentence applies, the second sentence of subparagraph (A) and subparagraph (B)(ii) shall be applied by substituting "distributee or any related person" for "distributee" each place it appears.

(ii) Definitions.—For purposes of this subparagraph—

(I) the term "entity" means a partnership, estate, trust, or corporation; and

(II) the term "related person" means any person to whom ownership of stock in the corporation is (at the time of the distribution) attributable under section 318(a)(1) if such stock is further attributable to the entity under section 318(a)(3).

(d) Redemptions treated as distributions of property.—Except as otherwise provided in this subchapter, if a corporation redeems its stock (within the meaning of section 317(b)), and if subsection (a) of this section does not apply, such redemption shall be treated as a distribution of property to which section 301 applies.

(e) Partial liquidation defined.—

(1) In general.—For purposes of subsection (b)(4), a distribution shall be treated as in partial liquidation of a corporation if—

(A) the distribution is not essentially equivalent to a dividend (determined at the corporate level rather than at the shareholder level), and

(B) the distribution is pursuant to a plan and occurs within the taxable year in which the plan is adopted or within the succeeding taxable year.

(2) Termination of business.—The distributions which meet the requirements of paragraph (1)(A) shall include (but shall not be limited to) a distribution which meets the requirements of subparagraphs (A) and (B) of this paragraph:

(A) The distribution is attributable to the distributing corporation's ceasing to conduct, or consists of the assets of, a qualified trade or business.

(B) Immediately after the distribution, the distributing corporation is actively engaged in the conduct of a qualified trade or business.

(3) Qualified trade or business.—For purposes of paragraph (2), the term "qualified trade or business" means any trade or business which—

(A) was actively conducted throughout the 5-year period ending on the date of the redemption, and

(B) was not acquired by the corporation within such period in a transaction in which gain or loss was recognized in whole or in part.

(4) Redemption may be pro rata.—Whether or not a redemption meets the requirements of subparagraphs (A) and (B) of paragraph (2) shall be determined without regard to whether or not the redemption is pro rata with respect to all of the shareholders of the corporation.

(5) Treatment of certain pass-thru entities.—For purposes of determining under subsection (b)(4) whether any stock is held by a shareholder who is not a corporation, any stock held by a partnership, estate, or trust shall be treated as if it were actually held proportionately by its partners or beneficiaries.

(f) Cross references.—

For special rules relating to redemption—

(1) Death Taxes.—Of stock to pay death taxes, see section 303.

(2) Section 306 Stock.—Of section 306 stock, see section 306.

(3) Liquidations.—Of stock in complete liquidation, see section 331.

§ 303. Distributions in redemption of stock to pay death taxes

(a) In general.—A distribution of property to a shareholder by a corporation in redemption of part or all of the stock of such corporation which (for Federal estate tax purposes) is included in determining the gross estate of a decedent, to the extent that the amount of such distribution does not exceed the sum of—

(1) the estate, inheritance, legacy, and succession taxes (including any interest collected as a part of such taxes) imposed because of such decedent's death, and

(2) the amount of funeral and administration expenses allowable as deductions to the estate under section 2053 (or under section 2106 in the case of the estate of a decedent nonresident, not a citizen of the United States),

shall be treated as a distribution in full payment in exchange for the stock so redeemed.

(b) Limitations on application of subsection (a).—

(1) Period for distribution.—Subsection (a) shall apply only to amounts distributed after the death of the decedent and—

(A) within the period of limitations provided in section 6501(a) for the assessment of the Federal estate tax (determined without the application of any provision other than section 6501(a)), or within 90 days after the expiration of such period,

(B) if a petition for redetermination of a deficiency in such estate tax has been filed with the Tax Court within the time prescribed in section 6213, at any time before the expiration of 60 days after the decision of the Tax Court becomes final, or

(C) if an election has been made under section 6166 and if the time prescribed by this subparagraph expires at a later date than the time prescribed by subparagraph (B) of this paragraph, within the time determined under section 6166 for the payment of the installments.

(2) Relationship of stock to decedent's estate. —

(A) In general.—Subsection (a) shall apply to a distribution by a corporation only if the value (for Federal estate tax purposes) of all of the stock of such corporation which is included in determining the value of the decedent's gross estate exceeds 35 percent of the excess of—

(i) the value of the gross estate of such decedent, over

(ii) the sum of the amounts allowable as a deduction under section 2053 or 2054.

(B) Special rule for stock in 2 or more corporations.—For purposes of subparagraph (A), stock of 2 or more corporations, with respect to each of which there is included in determining the value of the decedent's gross estate 20 percent or more in value of the outstanding stock, shall be treated as the stock of a single corporation. For purposes of the 20-percent requirement of the preceding sentence, stock which, at the decedent's death, represents the surviving spouse's interest in property held by the decedent and the surviving spouse as community property or as joint tenants, tenants by the entirety, or tenants in common shall be treated as having been included in determining the value of the decedent's gross estate.

(3) Relationship of shareholder to estate tax. —Subsection (a) shall apply to a distribution by a corporation only to the extent that the interest of the shareholder is reduced directly (or through a binding obligation to contribute) by any payment of an amount described in paragraph (1) or (2) of subsection (a).

(4) Additional requirements for distributions made more than 4 years after decedent's death.—In the case of amounts distributed more than 4 years after the date of the decedent's death, subsection (a) shall apply to a distribution by a corporation only to the extent of the lesser of—

(A) the aggregate of the amounts referred to in paragraph (1) or (2) of subsection (a) which remained unpaid immediately before the distribution, or

(B) the aggregate of the amounts referred to in paragraph (1) or (2) of subsection (a) which are paid during the 1-year period beginning on the date of such distribution.

(c) Stock with substituted basis.—If—

(1) a shareholder owns stock of a corporation (referred to in this subsection as "new stock") the basis of which is determined by reference to the basis of stock of a corporation (referred to in this subsection as "old stock"),

(2) the old stock was included (for Federal estate tax purposes) in determining the gross estate of a decedent, and

(3) subsection (a) would apply to a distribution of property to such shareholder in redemption of the old stock,

then, subject to the limitations specified in subsection (b), subsection (a) shall apply in respect of a distribution in redemption of the new stock.

(d) Special rules for generation-skipping transfers.—Where stock in a corporation is the subject of a generation-skipping transfer (within the meaning of section 2611 (a)) occurring at the same time as and as a result of the death of an individual—

(1) the stock shall be deemed to be included in the gross estate of such individual;

(2) taxes of the kind referred to in subsection (a)(1) which are imposed because of the generation-skipping transfer shall be treated as imposed because of such individual's death (and for this purpose the tax imposed by section 2601 shall be treated as an estate tax);

(3) the period of distribution shall be measured from the date of the generation-skipping transfer; and

(4) the relationship of stock to the decedent's estate shall be measured with reference solely to the amount of the generation-skipping transfer.

§ 304. Redemption through use of related corporations

(a) Treatment of certain stock purchases.—

(1) Acquisition by related corporation (other than subsidiary).—For purposes of sections 302 and 303, if—

(A) one or more persons are in control of each of two corporations, and

(B) in return for property, one of the corporations acquires stock in the other corporation from the person (or persons) so in control,

then (unless paragraph (2) applies) such property shall be treated as a distribution in redemption of the stock of the corporation acquiring such stock. To the extent that such distribution is treated as a distribution to which section 301 applies, the transferor and the acquiring corporation shall be treated in the same manner as if the transferor had transferred the stock so acquired to the acquiring corporation in exchange for stock of the acquiring corporation in a transaction to which section 351(a) applies, and then the acquiring corporation had redeemed the stock it was treated as issuing in such transaction.

(2) Acquisition by subsidiary.—For purposes of sections 302 and 303, if—

(A) in return for property, one corporation acquires from a shareholder of another corporation stock in such other corporation, and

(B) the issuing corporation controls the acquiring corporation,

then such property shall be treated as a distribution in redemption of the stock of the issuing corporation.

(b) Special rules for application of subsection (a).—

(1) Rule for determinations under section 302(b).—In the case of any acquisition of stock to which subsection (a) of this section applies, determinations as to whether the acquisition is, by reason of section 302(b), to be treated as a distribution in part or full payment in exchange for the stock shall be made by reference to the stock of the issuing corporation. In applying section 318(a) (relating to constructive ownership of stock) with respect to section 302(b) for purposes of this paragraph, sections 318(a)(2)(C) and 318(a)(3)(C) shall be applied without regard to the 50 percent limitation contained therein.

(2) Amount constituting dividend.—In the case of any acquisition of stock to which subsection (a) applies, the determination of the amount which is a dividend (and the source thereof) shall be made as if the property were distributed—

(A) by the acquiring corporation to the extent of its earnings and profits, and

(B) then by the issuing corporation to the extent of its earnings and profits.

(3) Coordination with section 351.—

(A) Property treated as received in redemption.—Except as otherwise provided in this paragraph, subsection (a) (and not section 351 and not so much of sections 357 and 358 as relates to section 351) shall apply to any property received in a distribution described in subsection (a).

(B) Certain assumptions of liability, etc.—

(i) In general.—In the case of an acquisition described in section 351, subsection (a) shall not apply to any liability—

(I) assumed by the acquiring corporation, or

(II) to which the stock is subject,

if such liability was incurred by the transferor to acquire the stock. For purposes of the preceding sentence, the term "stock" means stock referred to in paragraph (1)(B) or (2)(A) of subsection (a).

(ii) Extension of obligations, etc.—For purposes of clause (i), an extension, renewal, or refinancing of a liability which meets the requirements of clause (i) shall be treated as meeting such requirements.

(iii) Clause (i) does not apply to stock acquired from related person except where complete termination.—Clause (i) shall apply only to stock acquired by the transferor from a person—

(I) none of whose stock is attributable to the transferor under section 318(a) (other than paragraph (4) thereof), or

(II) who satisfies rules similar to the rules of section 302(c)(2) with respect to both the acquiring and the issuing corporations (determined as if such person were a distributee of each such corporation).

* * *

(4) Treatment of certain intragroup transactions.—

(A) In general.—In the case of any transfer described in subsection (a) of stock from 1 member of an affiliated group to another member of such group, proper adjustments shall be made to—

(i) the adjusted basis of any intragroup stock, and

(ii) the earnings and profits of any member of such group,

to the extent necessary to carry out the purposes of this section.

(B) Definitions.—For purposes of this paragraph—

(i) Affiliated group.—The term "affiliated group" has the meaning given such term by section 1504(a).

(ii) Intragroup stock.—The term "intragroup stock" means any stock which—

(I) is in a corporation which is a member of an affiliated group, and

(II) is held by another member of such group.

* * *

(c) Control.—

(1) In general.—For purposes of this section, control means the ownership of stock possessing at least 50 percent of the total combined voting power of all classes of stock entitled to vote, or at least 50 percent of the total value of shares of all classes of stock. If a person (or persons) is in control (within the meaning of the preceding sentence) of a corporation which in turn owns at least 50 percent of the total combined voting power of all stock entitled to vote of another corporation, or owns at least 50 percent of the total value of the shares of all classes of stock of another corporation, then such person (or persons) shall be treated as in control of such other corporation.

(2) Stock acquired in the transaction.—For purposes of subsection (a)(1)—

(A) General rule.—Where 1 or more persons in control of the issuing corporation transfer stock of such corporation in exchange for stock of the acquiring corporation, the stock of the acquiring corporation received shall be taken into account in determining whether such person or persons are in control of the acquiring corporation.

(B) Definition of control group.—Where 2 or more persons in control of the issuing corporation transfer stock of such corporation to the acquiring corporation and, after the transfer, the transferors are in control of the acquiring corporation, the person or persons in control of each corporation shall include each of the persons who so transfer stock.

(3) Constructive ownership.—

(A) In general.—Section 318(a) (relating to constructive ownership of stock) shall apply for purposes of determining control under this section.

(B) Modification of 50-percent limitations in section 318.—For purposes of subparagraph (A)—

(i) paragraph (2)(C) of section 318(a) shall be applied by substituting "5 percent" for "50 percent", and

(ii) paragraph (3)(C) of section 318(a) shall be applied—

(I) by substituting "5 percent" for "50 percent", and

(II) in any case where such paragraph would not apply but for subclause (I), by considering a corporation as owning the stock (other than stock in such corporation) owned by or for any shareholder of such corporation in that proportion which the value of the stock which such shareholder owned in such corporation bears to the value of all stock in such corporation.

§ 305. Distributions of stock and stock rights

(a) General rule.—Except as otherwise provided in this section, gross income does not include the amount of any distribution of the stock of a corporation made by such corporation to its shareholders with respect to its stock.

(b) Exceptions.—Subsection (a) shall not apply to a distribution by a corporation of its stock, and the distribution shall be treated as a distribution of property to which section 301 applies—

(1) Distributions in lieu of money.—If the distribution is, at the election of any of the shareholders (whether exercised before or after the declaration thereof), payable either—

(A) in its stock, or

(B) in property.

(2) Disproportionate distributions.—If the distribution (or a series of distributions of which such distribution is one) has the result of—

(A) the receipt of property by some shareholders, and

(B) an increase in the proportionate interests of other shareholders in the assets or earnings and profits of the corporation.

(3) Distributions of common and preferred stock.—If the distribution (or a series of distributions of which such distribution is one) has the result of—

(A) the receipt of preferred stock by some common shareholders, and

(B) the receipt of common stock by other common shareholders.

(4) Distributions on preferred stock.—If the distribution is with respect to preferred stock, other than an increase in the conversion ratio of convertible preferred stock made solely to take account of a stock dividend or stock split with respect to the stock into which such convertible stock is convertible.

(5) Distributions of convertible preferred stock.—If the distribution is of convertible preferred stock, unless it is established to the satisfaction of the Secretary that such distribution will not have the result described in paragraph (2).

(c) Certain transactions treated as distributions.—For purposes of this section and section 301, the Secretary shall prescribe regulations under which a change in conversion ratio, a change in redemption price, a difference between redemption price and issue price, a redemption which is treated as a distribution to which section 301 applies, or any transaction (including a recapitalization) having a similar effect on the interest of any shareholder shall be treated as a distribution with respect to any shareholder whose proportionate interest in the earnings and profits or assets of the corporation is increased by such change, difference, redemption, or similar transaction. Regulations prescribed under the preceding sentence shall provide that—

(1) where the issuer of stock is required to redeem the stock at a specified time or the holder of stock has the option to require the issuer to redeem the stock, a redemption premium resulting from such requirement or option shall be treated as reasonable only if the amount of such premium does not exceed the amount determined under the principles of section 1273(a)(3),

(2) a redemption premium shall not fail to be treated as a distribution (or series of distributions) merely because the stock is callable, and

(3) in any case in which a redemption premium is treated as a distribution (or series of distributions), such premium shall be taken into account under principles similar to the principles of section 1272(a).

(d) Definitions.—

(1) Rights to acquire stock.—For purposes of this section, the term "stock" includes rights to acquire such stock.

(2) Shareholders.—For purposes of subsections (b) and (c), the term "shareholder" includes a holder of rights or of convertible securities.

(e) Treatment of purchaser of stripped preferred stock.—

(1) In general.—If any person purchases after April 30, 1993, any stripped preferred stock, then such person, while holding such stock, shall include in gross income amounts equal to the amounts which would have been so includible if such stripped preferred stock were a bond issued on the purchase date and having original issue discount equal to the excess, if any, of—

(A) the redemption price for such stock, over

(B) the price at which such person purchased such stock.

The preceding sentence shall also apply in the case of any person whose basis in such stock is determined by reference to the basis in the hands of such purchaser.

(2) Basis adjustments.—Appropriate adjustments to basis shall be made for amounts includible in gross income under paragraph (1).

(3) Tax treatment of person stripping stock.—If any person strips the rights to 1 or more dividends from any stock described in paragraph (5)(B) and after April 30, 1993, disposes of such dividend rights, for purposes of paragraph (1), such person shall be treated as having purchased the stripped preferred stock on the date of such disposition for a purchase price equal to such person's adjusted basis in such stripped preferred stock.

(4) Amounts treated as ordinary income.—Any amount included in gross income under paragraph (1) shall be treated as ordinary income.

(5) Stripped preferred stock.—For purposes of this subsection—

(A) In general.—The term "stripped preferred stock" means any stock described in subparagraph (B) if there has been a separation in ownership between such stock and any dividend on such stock which has not become payable.

(B) Description of stock.—Stock is described in this subsection if such stock—

(i) is limited and preferred as to dividends and does not participate in corporate growth to any significant extent, and

(ii) has a fixed redemption price.

(6) Purchase.—For purposes of this subsection, the term "purchase" means—

(A) any acquisition of stock, where

(B) the basis of such stock is not determined in whole or in part by the reference to the adjusted basis of such stock in the hands of the person from whom acquired.

* * *

(f) Cross references.—

For special rules—

(1) Relating to the receipt of stock and stock rights in corporate organizations and reorganizations, see part III (sec. 351 and following).

(2) In the case of a distribution which results in a gift, see section 2501 and following.

(3) In the case of a distribution which has the effect of the payment of compensation, see section 61(a)(1).

§ 306. Dispositions of certain stock

(a) General rule.—If a shareholder sells or otherwise disposes of section 306 stock (as defined in subsection (c))—

(1) Dispositions other than redemptions.—If such disposition is not a redemption (within the meaning of section 317(b))—

(A) The amount realized shall be treated as ordinary income. This subparagraph shall not apply to the extent that—

(i) the amount realized, exceeds

(ii) such stock's ratable share of the amount which would have been a dividend at the time of distribution if (in lieu of section 306 stock) the corporation had distributed money in an amount equal to the fair market value of the stock at the time of distribution.

(B) Any excess of the amount realized over the sum of—

(i) the amount treated under subparagraph (A) as ordinary income, plus

(ii) the adjusted basis of the stock,

shall be treated as gain from the sale of such stock.

(C) No loss shall be recognized.

(D) Treatment as dividend.—For purposes of section 1(h)(11) and such other provisions as the Secretary may specify, any amount treated as ordinary income under this paragraph shall be treated as a dividend received from the corporation.

(2) Redemption.—If the disposition is a redemption, the amount realized shall be treated as a distribution of property to which section 301 applies.

(b) Exceptions.—Subsection (a) shall not apply—

(1) Termination of shareholder's interest, etc.—

(A) Not in redemption.—If the disposition—

(i) is not a redemption;

(ii) is not, directly or indirectly, to a person the ownership of whose stock would (under section 318 (a)) be attributable to the shareholder; and

(iii) terminates the entire stock interest of the shareholder in the corporation (and for purposes of this clause, section 318(a) shall apply).

(B) In redemption.—If the disposition is a redemption and paragraph (3) or (4) of section 302(b) applies.

(2) Liquidations.—If the section 306 stock is redeemed in a distribution in complete liquidation to which part II (sec. 331 and following) applies.

(3) Where gain or loss is not recognized.—To the extent that, under any provision of this subtitle, gain or loss to the shareholder is not recognized with respect to the disposition of the section 306 stock.

(4) Transactions not in avoidance.—If it is established to the satisfaction of the Secretary—

(A) that the distribution, and the disposition or redemption, or

(B) in the case of a prior or simultaneous disposition (or redemption) of the stock with respect to which the section 306 stock disposed of (or redeemed) was issued, that the disposition (or redemption) of the section 306 stock,

was not in pursuance of a plan having as one of its principal purposes the avoidance of Federal income tax.

(c) Section 306 stock defined.—

(1) In general.—For purposes of this subchapter, the term "section 306 stock" means stock which meets the requirements of subparagraph (A), (B), or (C) of this paragraph.

(A) Distributed to seller.—Stock (other than common stock issued with respect to common stock) which was distributed to the shareholder selling or otherwise disposing of such stock if, by reason of section 305(a), any part of such distribution was not includible in the gross income of the shareholder.

(B) Received in a corporate reorganization or separation.—Stock which is not common stock and—

(i) which was received, by the shareholder selling or otherwise disposing of such stock, in pursuance of a plan of reorganization (within the meaning of section 368(a)), or in a distribution or exchange to which section 355 (or so much of section 356 as relates to section 355) applied, and

(ii) with respect to the receipt of which gain or loss to the shareholder was to any extent not recognized by reason of part III, but only to the extent that either the effect of the transaction was substantially the same as the receipt of a stock dividend, or the stock was received in exchange for section 306 stock.

For purposes of this section, a receipt of stock to which the foregoing provisions of this subparagraph apply shall be treated as a distribution of stock.

(C) Stock having transferred or substituted basis.—Except as otherwise provided in subparagraph (B), stock the basis of which (in the hands of the shareholder selling or otherwise disposing of such stock) is determined by reference to the basis (in the hands of such shareholder or any other person) of section 306 stock.

(2) Exception where no earnings and profits.—For purposes of this section, the term "section 306 stock" does not include any stock no part of the distribution of which would have been a dividend at the time of the distribution if money had been distributed in lieu of the stock.

(3) Certain stock acquired in section 351 exchange.—The term "section 306 stock" also includes any stock which is not common stock acquired in an exchange to which section 351 applied if receipt of money (in lieu of the stock) would have been treated as a dividend to any extent. Rules similar to the rules of section 304(b)(2) shall apply—

(A) for purposes of the preceding sentence, and

(B) for purposes of determining the application of this section to any subsequent disposition of stock which is section 306 stock by reason of an exchange described in the preceding sentence.

(4) Application of attribution rules for certain purposes.—For purposes of paragraphs (1)(B)(ii) and (3), section 318(a) shall apply. For purposes of applying the preceding sentence to paragraph (3), the rules of section 304(c)(3)(B) shall apply.

(d) Stock rights.—For purposes of this section—

(1) stock rights shall be treated as stock, and

(2) stock acquired through the exercise of stock rights shall be treated as stock distributed at the time of the distribution of the stock rights, to the extent of the fair market value of such rights at the time of the distribution.

(e) Convertible stock.—For purposes of subsection (c)—

(1) if section 306 stock was issued with respect to common stock and later such section 306 stock is exchanged for common stock in the same corporation (whether or not such exchange is pursuant to a conversion privilege contained in the section 306 stock), then (except as provided in paragraph (2)) the common stock so received shall not be treated as section 306 stock; and

(2) common stock with respect to which there is a privilege of converting into stock other than common stock (or into property), whether or not the conversion privilege is contained in such stock, shall not be treated as common stock.

(f) Source of gain.—The amount treated under subsection (a)(1)(A) as ordinary income shall, for purposes of part I of subchapter N (sec. 861 and following, relating to determination of sources of income), be treated as derived from the same source as would have been the source if money had been received from the corporation as a dividend at the time of the distribution of such stock. If under the preceding sentence such amount is determined to be derived from sources within the United States, such amount shall be considered to be fixed or determinable annual or periodical gains, profits, and income within the meaning of section 871(a) or section 881 (a), as the case may be.

(g) Change in terms and conditions of stock.—If a substantial change is made in the terms and conditions of any stock, then, for purposes of this section—

(1) the fair market value of such stock shall be the fair market value at the time of the distribution or at the time of such change, whichever such value is higher;

(2) such stock's ratable share of the amount which would have been a dividend if money had been distributed in lieu of stock shall be determined as of the time of distribution or as of the time of such change, whichever such ratable share is higher; and

(3) subsection (c)(2) shall not apply unless the stock meets the requirements of such subsection both at the time of such distribution and at the time of such change.

§ 307. Basis of stock and stock rights acquired in distributions

(a) General rule.—If a shareholder in a corporation receives its stock or rights to acquire its stock (referred to in this subsection as "new stock") in a distribution to which section 305(a) applies, then the basis of such new stock and of the stock with respect to which it is distributed (referred to in this section as "old stock"), respectively, shall, in the shareholder's hands, be determined by allocating between the old stock and the new stock the adjusted basis of the old stock. Such allocation shall be made under regulations prescribed by the Secretary.

(b) Exception for certain stock rights.—

(1) In general.—If—

(A) a corporation distributes rights to acquire its stock to a shareholder in a distribution to which section 305(a) applies, and

(B) the fair market value of such rights at the time of the distribution is less than 15 percent of the fair market value of the old stock at such time,

then subsection (a) shall not apply and the basis of such rights shall be zero, unless the taxpayer elects under paragraph (2) of this subsection to determine the basis of the old stock and of the stock rights under the method of allocation provided in subsection (a).

(2) Election.—The election referred to in paragraph (1) shall be made in the return filed within the time prescribed by law (including extensions thereof) for the taxable year in which such rights were received. Such election shall be made in such manner as the Secretary may by regulations prescribe, and shall be irrevocable when made.

* * *

SUBPART B—EFFECTS ON CORPORATION

Editorial Summary

Corporate Distributions: Effect on Corporation

Subchapter C of Chapter 1 (Secs. 311 and 312)

See the discussion under the Editorial Summary entitled Corporate Distributions: Dividend or Stock Redemption which precedes Sec. 301.

§ 311. Taxability of corporation on distribution

(a) General rule.—Except as provided in subsection (b), no gain or loss shall be recognized to a corporation on the distribution (not in complete liquidation), with respect to its stock of—

(1) its stock (or rights to acquire its stock), or

(2) property.

(b) Distributions of appreciated property.—

(1) In general.—If—

(A) a corporation distributes property (other than an obligation of such corporation) to a shareholder in a distribution to which subpart A applies, and

(B) the fair market value of such property exceeds its adjusted basis (in the hands of the distributing corporation),

then gain shall be recognized to the distributing corporation as if such property were sold to the distributee at its fair market value.

(2) Treatment of liabilities.—Rules similar to the rules of section 336(b) shall apply for purposes of this subsection.

(3) Special rule for certain distributions of partnership or trust interests.—If the property distributed consists of an interest in a partnership or trust, the Secretary may by regulations provide that the amount of the gain recognized under paragraph (1) shall be computed without regard to any loss attributable to property contributed to the partnership or trust for the principal purpose of recognizing such loss on the distribution.

§ 312. Effect on earnings and profits

(a) General rule.—Except as otherwise provided in this section, on the distribution of property by a corporation with respect to its stock, the earnings and profits of the corporation (to the extent thereof) shall be decreased by the sum of—

(1) the amount of money,

(2) the principal amount of the obligations of such corporation (or, in the case of obligations having original issue discount, the aggregate issue price of such obligations), and

(3) the adjusted basis of the other property, so distributed.

(b) Distributions of appreciated property.—On the distribution by a corporation, with respect to its stock, of any property (other than an obligation of such corporation) the fair market value of which exceeds the adjusted basis thereof—

(1) the earnings and profits of the corporation shall be increased by the amount of such excess, and

(2) subsection (a)(3) shall be applied by substituting "fair market value" for "adjusted basis."

For purposes of this subsection and subsection (a), the adjusted basis of any property is its adjusted basis as determined for purposes of computing earnings and profits.

(c) Adjustments for liabilities.—In making the adjustments to the earnings and profits of a corporation under subsection (a) or (b), proper adjustment shall be made for—

(1) the amount of any liability to which the property distributed is subject,

(2) the amount of any liability of the corporation assumed by a shareholder in connection with the distribution, and

(3) any gain recognized to the corporation on the distribution.

(d) Certain distributions of stock and securities.—

(1) In general.—The distribution to a distributee by or on behalf of a corporation of its stock or securities, of stock or securities in another corporation, or of property, in a distribution to which this title applies, shall not be considered a distribution of the earnings and profits of any corporation—

(A) if no gain to such distributee from the receipt of such stock or securities, or property, was recognized under this title, or

(B) if the distribution was not subject to tax in the hands of such distributee by reason of section 305(a).

(2) Prior distributions.—In the case of a distribution of stock or securities, or property, to which section 115(h) of the Internal Revenue Code of 1939 (or the corresponding provision of prior law) applied, the effect on earnings and profits of such distribution shall be determined under such section 115(h), or the corresponding provision of prior law, as the case may be.

(3) Stock or securities.—For purposes of this subsection, the term "stock or securities" includes rights to acquire stock or securities.

***(f) Effect on earnings and profits of gain or loss and of receipt of tax-free distributions.—**

*Editorial comment: There is no subsection (e).

(1) **Effect on earnings and profits of gain or loss.**—The gain or loss realized from the sale or other disposition (after February 28, 1913) of property by a corporation—

(A) for the purpose of the computation of the earnings and profits of the corporation, shall (except as provided in subparagraph (B)) be determined by using as the adjusted basis the adjusted basis (under the law applicable to the year in which the sale or other disposition was made) for determining gain, except that no regard shall be had to the value of the property as of March 1, 1913; but

(B) for purposes of the computation of the earnings and profits of the corporation for any period beginning after February 28, 1913, shall be determined by using as the adjusted basis the adjusted basis (under the law applicable to the year in which the sale or other disposition was made) for determining gain.

Gain or loss so realized shall increase or decrease the earnings and profits to, but not beyond, the extent to which such a realized gain or loss was recognized in computing taxable income under the law applicable to the year in which such sale or disposition was made. Where, in determining the adjusted basis used in computing such realized gain or loss, the adjustment to the basis differs from the adjustment proper for the purpose of determining earnings and profits, then the latter adjustment shall be used in determining the increase or decrease above provided. For purposes of this subsection, a loss with respect to which a deduction is disallowed under section 1091 (relating to wash sales of stock or securities), or the corresponding provision of prior law, shall not be deemed to be recognized.

(2) **Effect on earnings and profits of receipt of tax-free distributions.**—Where a corporation receives (after February 28, 1913) a distribution from a second corporation which (under the law applicable to the year in which the distribution was made) was not a taxable dividend to the shareholders of the second corporation, the amount of such distribution shall not increase the earnings and profits of the first corporation in the following cases:

(A) no such increase shall be made in respect of the part of such distribution which (under such law) is directly applied in reduction of the basis of the stock in respect of which the distribution was made; and

(B) no such increase shall be made if (under such law) the distribution causes the basis of the stock in respect of which the distribution was made to be allocated between such stock and the property received (or such basis would, but for section 307(b), be so allocated).

(g) Earnings and profits—Increase in value accrued before March 1, 1913.—

(1) If any increase or decrease in the earnings and profits for any period beginning after February 28, 1913, with respect to any matter would be different had the adjusted basis of the property involved been determined without regard to its March 1, 1913, value, then, except as provided in paragraph (2), an increase (properly reflecting such difference) shall be made in that part of the earnings and profits consisting of increase in value of property accrued before March 1, 1913.

(2) If the application of subsection (f) to a sale or other disposition after February 28, 1913, results in a loss which is to be applied in decrease of earnings and profits for any period beginning after February 28, 1913, then, notwithstanding subsection (f) and in lieu of the rule provided in paragraph (1) of this subsection, the amount of such loss so to be applied shall be reduced by the amount, if any, by which the adjusted basis of the property used in determining the loss exceeds the adjusted basis computed without regard to the value of the property on March 1, 1913, and if such amount so applied in reduction of the decrease exceeds such loss, the excess over such loss shall increase that part of the earnings and profits consisting of increase in value of property accrued before March 1, 1913.

(h) Allocation in certain corporate separations and reorganizations.—

(1) **Section 355.**—In the case of a distribution or exchange to which section 355 (or so much of section 356 as relates to section 355) applies, proper allocation with respect to the earnings and profits of the distributing corporation and the controlled corporation (or corporations) shall be made under regulations prescribed by the Secretary.

(2) **Section 368(a)(1)(C) or (D).**—In the case of a reorganization described in subparagraph (C) or (D) of section 368(a)(1), proper allocation with respect to the earnings and profits of the acquired corporation shall, under regulations prescribed by the Secretary, be made between the acquiring

corporation and the acquired corporation (or any corporation which had control of the acquired corporation before the reorganization).

(i) Distribution of proceeds of loan insured by the United States.—If a corporation distributes property with respect to its stock and if, at the time of distribution—

(1) there is outstanding a loan to such corporation which was made, guaranteed, or insured by the United States (or by any agency or instrumentality thereof), and

(2) the amount of such loan so outstanding exceeds the adjusted basis of the property constituting security for such loan,

then the earnings and profits of the corporation shall be increased by the amount of such excess, and (immediately after the distribution) shall be decreased by the amount of such excess. For purposes of paragraph (2), the adjusted basis of the property at the time of distribution shall be determined without regard to any adjustment under section 1016(a)(2) (relating to adjustment for depreciation, etc.). For purposes of this subsection, a commitment to make, guarantee, or insure a loan shall be treated as the making, guaranteeing, or insuring of a loan.

***(k) Effect of depreciation on earnings and profits.**—

(1) General rule.—For purposes of computing the earnings and profits of a corporation for any taxable year beginning after June 30, 1972, the allowance for depreciation (and amortization, if any) shall be deemed to be the amount which would be allowable for such year if the straight line method of depreciation had been used for each taxable year beginning after June 30, 1972.

(2) Exception.—If for any taxable year a method of depreciation was used by the taxpayer which the Secretary has determined results in a reasonable allowance under section 167(a) and which is the unit-of-production method or other method not expressed in a term of years, then the adjustment to earnings and profits for depreciation for such year shall be determined under the method so used (in lieu of the straight line method).

(3) Exception for tangible property.—

(A) In general.—Except as provided in subparagraph (B), in the case of tangible property to which section 168 applies, the adjustment to earnings and profits for depreciation for any taxable year shall be determined under the alternative depreciation system (within the meaning of section 168(g)(2)).

(B) Treatment of amounts deductible under section 179, 179A, 179B, 179C, 179D, or 179E.—For purposes of computing the earnings and profits of a corporation, any amount deductible under section 179, 179A, 179B, 179C, 179D, or 179E shall be allowed as a deduction ratably over the period of 5 taxable years (beginning with the taxable year for which such amount is deductible under section 179, 179A, 179B, 179C, 179D, or 179E, as the case may be).

* * *

(5) Basis adjustment not taken into account.—In computing the earnings and profits of a corporation for any taxable year, the allowance for depreciation (and amortization, if any) shall be computed without regard to any basis adjustment under section 50(c).

(l) Discharge of indebtedness income.—

(1) Does not increase earnings and profits if applied to reduce basis.—The earnings and profits of a corporation shall not include income from the discharge of indebtedness to the extent of the amount applied to reduce basis under section 1017.

(2) Reduction of deficit in earnings and profits in certain cases.—If—

(A) the interest of any shareholder of a corporation is terminated or extinguished in a title 11 or similar case (within the meaning of section 368(a)(3)(A)), and

(B) there is a deficit in the earnings and profits of the corporation,

then such deficit shall be reduced by an amount equal to the paid-in capital which is allocable to the interest of the shareholder which is so terminated or extinguished.

* * *

(n) Adjustments to earnings and profits to more accurately reflect economic gain and loss.—For purposes of computing the earnings and profits of a corporation, the following adjustments shall be made:

*Editorial comment: There is no subsection (j).

(1) Construction period carrying charges.—

(A) In general.—In the case of any amount paid or incurred for construction period carrying charges—

(i) no deduction shall be allowed with respect to such amount, and

(ii) the basis of the property with respect to which such charges are allocable shall be increased by such amount.

(B) Construction period carrying charges defined.—For purposes of this paragraph, the term "construction period carrying charges" means all—

(i) interest paid or accrued on indebtedness incurred or continued to acquire, construct, or carry property,

(ii) property taxes, and

(iii) similar carrying charges,

to the extent such interest, taxes, or charges are attributable to the construction period for such property and would be allowable as a deduction in determining taxable income under this chapter for the taxable year in which paid or incurred.

(C) Construction period.—The term "construction period" has the meaning given the term production period under section 263A(f)(4)(B).

(2) Intangible drilling costs and mineral exploration and development costs.—

(A) Intangible drilling costs.—Any amount allowable as a deduction under section 263(c) in determining taxable income (other than costs incurred in connection with a nonproductive well)—

(i) shall be capitalized, and

(ii) shall be allowed as a deduction ratably over the 60-month period beginning with the month in which such amount was paid or incurred.

(B) Mineral exploration and development costs.—Any amount allowable as a deduction under section 616(a) or 617 in determining taxable income—

(i) shall be capitalized, and

(ii) shall be allowed as a deduction ratably over the 120-month period beginning with the later of—

(I) the month in which production from the deposit begins, or

(II) the month in which such amount was paid or incurred.

(3) Certain amortization provisions not to apply.—Sections 173 and 248 shall not apply.

(4) LIFO inventory adjustments.—

(A) In general.—Earnings and profits shall be increased or decreased by the amount of any increase or decrease in the LIFO recapture amount as of the close of each taxable year; except that any decrease below the LIFO recapture amount as of the close of the taxable year preceding the 1st taxable year to which this paragraph applies to the taxpayer shall be taken into account only to the extent provided in regulations prescribed by the Secretary.

(B) LIFO recapture amount.—For purposes of this paragraph, the term "LIFO recapture amount" means the amount (if any) by which—

(i) the inventory amount of the inventory assets under the first-in, first-out method authorized by section 471, exceeds

(ii) the inventory amount of such assets under the LIFO method.

(C) Definitions.—For purposes of this paragraph—

(i) LIFO method.—The term "LIFO method" means the method authorized by section 472 (relating to last-in, first-out inventories).

(ii) Inventory assets.—The term "inventory assets" means stock in trade of the corporation, or other property of a kind which would properly be included in the inventory of the corporation if on hand at the close of the taxable year.

(iii) Inventory amount.—The inventory amount of assets under the first-in, first-out method authorized by section 471 shall be determined—

(I) if the corporation uses the retail method of valuing inventories under section 472, by using such method, or

(II) if subclause (I) does not apply, by using cost or market, whichever is lower.

(5) Installment sales.—In the case of any installment sale, earnings and profits shall be computed as if the corporation did not use the installment method.

(6) Completed contract method of accounting.—In the case of a taxpayer who uses the completed contract method of accounting, earnings and profits shall be computed as if such taxpayer used the percentage of completion method of accounting.

(7) Redemptions.—If a corporation distributes amounts in a redemption to which section 302(a) or 303 applies, the part of such distribution which is properly chargeable to earnings and profits shall be an amount which is not in excess of the ratable share of the earnings and profits of such corporation accumulated after February 28, 1913, attributable to the stock so redeemed.

* * *

(o) Definition of original issue discount and issue price for purposes of subsection (a)(2).—For purposes of subsection (a)(2), the terms "original issue discount" and "issue price" have the same respective meanings as when used in subpart A of part V of subchapter P of this chapter.

SUBPART C—DEFINITIONS; CONSTRUCTIVE OWNERSHIP OF STOCK

Editorial Summary

Corporate Distributions: Definitions

Subchapter C of Chapter 1 (Secs. 316–318)

See the discussion under the Editorial Summary entitled Corporate Distributions: Dividend or Stock Redemption, which precedes Sec. 301.

§ 316. Dividend defined

(a) General rule.—For purposes of this subtitle, the term "dividend" means any distribution of property made by a corporation to its shareholders—

(1) out of its earnings and profits accumulated after February 28, 1913, or

(2) out of its earnings and profits of the taxable year (computed as of the close of the taxable year without diminution by reason of any distributions made during the taxable year), without regard to the amount of the earnings and profits at the time the distribution was made.

Except as otherwise provided in this subtitle, every distribution is made out of earnings and profits to the extent thereof, and from the most recently accumulated earnings and profits. To the extent that any distribution is, under any provision of this subchapter, treated as a distribution of property to which section 301 applies, such distribution shall be treated as a distribution of property for purposes of this subsection.

(b) Special rules.—

(1) Certain insurance company dividends.—The definition in subsection (a) shall not apply to the term "dividend" as used in Subchapter L in any case where the reference is to dividends of insurance companies paid to policyholders as such.

(2) Distributions by personal holding companies.—

(A) In the case of a corporation which—

(i) under the law applicable to the taxable year in which the distribution is made, is a personal holding company (as defined in section 542), or

(ii) for the taxable year in respect of which the distribution is made under section 563(b) (relating to dividends paid after the close of the taxable year), or section 547 (relating to deficiency dividends), or the corresponding provisions of prior law, is a personal holding company under the law applicable to such taxable year,

the term "dividend" also means any distribution of property (whether or not a dividend as defined in subsection (a)) made by the corporation to its shareholders, to the extent of its undistributed personal holding company income (determined under section 545 without regard to distributions under this paragraph) for such year.

(B) For purposes of subparagraph (A), the term "distribution of property" includes a distribution in complete liquidation occurring within 24 months after the adoption of a plan of liquidation, but—

(i) only to the extent of the amounts distributed to distributees other than corporate shareholders, and

(ii) only to the extent that the corporation designates such amounts as a dividend distribution and duly notifies such distributees of such designation, under regulations prescribed by the Secretary, but

(iii) not in excess of the sum of such distributes' allocable share of the undistributed personal holding company income for such year, computed without regard to this subparagraph or section 562(b).

* * *

§ 317. Other definitions

(a) Property.—For purposes of this part, the term "property" means money, securities, and any other property; except that such term does not include stock in the corporation making the distribution (or rights to acquire such stock).

(b) Redemption of stock.—For purposes of this part, stock shall be treated as redeemed by a corporation if the corporation acquires its stock from a shareholder in exchange for property, whether or not the stock so acquired is cancelled, retired, or held as treasury stock.

§ 318. Constructive ownership of stock

(a) General rule.—For purposes of those provisions of this subchapter to which the rules contained in this section are expressly made applicable—

(1) Members of family.—

(A) In general.—An individual shall be considered as owning the stock owned, directly or indirectly, by or for—

(i) his spouse (other than a spouse who is legally separated from the individual under a decree of divorce or separate maintenance), and

(ii) his children, grandchildren, and parents.

(B) Effect of adoption.—For purposes of subparagraph (A)(ii), a legally adopted child of an individual shall be treated as a child of such individual by blood.

(2) Attribution from partnerships, estates, trusts, and corporations.—

(A) From partnerships and estates.—Stock owned, directly or indirectly, by or for a partnership or estate shall be considered as owned proportionately by its partners or beneficiaries.

(B) From trusts.—

(i) Stock owned, directly or indirectly, by or for a trust (other than an employees' trust described in section 401(a) which is exempt from tax under section 501(a)) shall be considered as owned by its beneficiaries in proportion to the actuarial interest of such beneficiaries in such trust.

(ii) Stock owned, directly or indirectly, by or for any portion of a trust of which a person is considered the owner under subpart E of part I of subchapter J (relating to grantors and others treated as substantial owners) shall be considered as owned by such person.

(C) From corporations.—If 50 percent or more in value of the stock in a corporation is owned, directly or indirectly, by or for any person, such person shall be considered as owning the stock owned, directly or indirectly, by or for such corporation, in that proportion which the value of the stock which such person so owns bears to the value of all the stock in such corporation.

(3) Attribution to partnerships, estates, trusts, and corporations.—

(A) To partnerships and estates.—Stock owned, directly or indirectly, by or for a partner or a beneficiary of an estate shall be considered as owned by the partnership or estate.

(B) To trusts.—

(i) Stock owned, directly or indirectly, by or for a beneficiary of a trust (other than an employees' trust described in section 401(a) which is exempt from tax under section 501 (a)) shall be considered as owned by the trust, unless such beneficiary's interest in the trust is a remote contingent interest. For purposes of this clause, a contingent interest of a beneficiary in a trust shall be considered remote if, under the maximum exercise of discretion by the trustee in favor of such beneficiary, the value of such interest, computed actuarially, is 5 percent or less of the value of the trust property.

(ii) Stock owned, directly or indirectly, by or for a person who is considered the owner of any portion of a trust under subpart E of part I of subchapter J (relating to grantors and others treated as substantial owners) shall be considered as owned by the trust.

(C) To corporations.—If 50 percent or more in value of the stock in a corporation is owned, directly or indirectly, by or for any person, such corporation shall be considered as owning the stock owned, directly or indirectly, by or for such person.

(4) Options.—If any person has an option to acquire stock, such stock shall be considered as owned by such person. For purposes of this paragraph, an option to acquire such an option, and each one of a series of such options, shall be considered as an option to acquire such stock.

(5) Operating rules.—

(A) In general.—Except as provided in subparagraphs (B) and (C), stock constructively owned by a person by reason of the application of paragraph (1), (2), (3), or (4), shall, for purposes of applying paragraphs (1), (2), (3), and (4), be considered as actually owned by such person.

(B) Members of family.—Stock constructively owned by an individual by reason of the application of paragraph (1) shall not be considered as owned by him for purposes of again applying paragraph (1) in order to make another the constructive owner of such stock.

(C) Partnerships, estates, trusts, and corporations.—Stock constructively owned by a partnership, estate, trust, or corporation by reason of the application of paragraph (3) shall not be considered as owned by it for purposes of applying paragraph (2) in order to make another the constructive owner of such stock.

(D) Option rule in lieu of family rule.—For purposes of this paragraph, if stock may be considered as owned by an individual under paragraph (1) or (4), it shall be considered as owned by him under paragraph (4).

(E) S corporation treated as partnership.—For purposes of this subsection—

(i) an S corporation shall be treated as a partnership, and

(ii) any shareholder of the S corporation shall be treated as a partner of such partnership.

The preceding sentence shall not apply for purposes of determining whether stock in the S corporation is constructively owned by any person.

(b) Cross references.—

For provisions to which the rules contained in subsection (a) apply, see—

(1) section 302 (relating to redemption of stock);

(2) section 304 (relating to redemption by related corporations);

(3) section 306(b)(1)(A) (relating to disposition of section 306 stock);

(4) section 338(h)(3) (defining purchase);

(5) section 382(l)(3) (relating to special limitations on net operating loss carryovers);

* * *

PART II—CORPORATE LIQUIDATIONS

Subpart

A. Effects on recipients.
B. Effects on corporation.
C. Collapsible corporations [Repealed].
D. Definition and special rule.

Editorial Summary

Corporate Liquidations: General*

Subchapter C of Chapter 1

A complete liquidation [see Sec. 346(a)] of a corporation results in the dissolution of the entity in corporate form. The corporation pays the creditors and distributes the remaining assets to the shareholders. The shareholders surrender their stock to the corporation.

The liquidation of the corporation usually takes one of three forms. First, the assets can be distributed to the shareholders (i.e., either *pro rata* or not *pro rata*). Second, the corporation can sell the assets and distribute the cash to the shareholders. Third, a combination of the two aforementioned forms can occur; that is, some of the assets are sold by the corporation and the remaining property and cash are distributed to the shareholders.

From a tax perspective, four issues need to be resolved. First, does the asset sale (if any) at the corporate level produce any

*Editorial Note: If the coverage is on current law only, the pre-TRA of 1986 material can be ignored since the transition period has expired. This material is included in the book for several reasons. First, in the opinion of the editor, the present corporate liquidation provisions can be understood better within the historical framework of pre-TRA law. Second, tax literature frequently refers to the corporate liquidation provisions prior to the repeal of *General Utilities* (i.e., pre-TRA 1986 law). Third, the instructor may want to include case law under the pre-TRA of 1986 law in the coverage of corporate liquidations.

recognition of gain or loss at the corporate level? Second, does the shareholders' surrendering of stock and related receipt of assets from the corporation result in the recognition of gain or loss? Third, what is the shareholders' basis for the assets received? Fourth, if gain or loss is recognized at the corporate level or at the shareholder level, is it classified as ordinary income (loss) or is it classified as capital gain (loss)?

In dealing with any corporate liquidation, consideration must be given to both the effect on the corporation and the effect on the shareholders. Sections 331 through 334 cover the effect on the shareholders (i.e., recognition of gain or loss and basis for assets received) and Secs. 336 through 338 cover the effect on the corporation (i.e., recognition of gain or loss and a stock purchase treated as an asset purchase). Thus, in dealing with a corporate liquidation, one must deal with a minimum of three code sections (i.e., recognition of gain or loss at the corporate level, recognition of gain or loss at the shareholder level, and basis for assets received at the shareholder level).

In general, the classification of recognized gain or loss is determined under the provisions of Subchapter P (Capital Gains and Losses).

If the entity is going to continue to be operated in corporate form (i.e., one ownership group is selling and another ownership group is buying), there is usually a conflict in the form of the transaction with respect to the buyer and the seller. The normal position of the seller is to want to sell stock rather than the corporate assets (i.e., in order to avoid double taxation and to qualify for capital gain treatment). The normal position of the buyer is to want to purchase the corporate assets (assuming they have appreciated) rather than the stock (i.e., in order to be able to assign fair market value as the basis for the corporate assets rather than to use a carryover basis). Prior to the effective date of the Tax Reform Act (TRA) of 1986, the corporate liquidation provisions could be used to neutralize (although normally not completely) the differences in the tax consequences to the buyer and the seller depending on whether the form of the transaction was a sale of stock versus a sale of assets. See the coverage in the subsequent Editorial Summary entitled Corporate Liquidations: Effect on Corporation. Unfortunately, the TRA of 1986 has severely limited this neutralization function of the corporate liquidation provisions.

The corporation liquidation provisions were further complicated by the transitional approach taken by the TRA of 1986 with respect to corporate liquidations. Under these transitional rules, the transactions associated with the corporate liquidation could be taxed under any of the following:

1. Pre-TRA of 1986 provisions.
2. Post-TRA of 1986 provisions.
3. Partially under Pre-TRA of 1986 provisions and partially under Post-TRA of 1986 provisions.

The general effective date for the Tax Reform Act of 1986 with respect to corporate liquidations was for liquidating sales and distributions after July 31, 1986. However, two sets of transitional rules were provided. The first set applied to any corporation. However, for this set to apply, the liquidation must have been completed before January 1, 1988. The other set applied to so-called "small, closely-held corporations." In this case, the liquidation had to be completed before January 1, 1989. For this transition rule to apply, both of the following conditions had to be satisfied:

1. The fair market value of the stock of the corporation was less than \$5 million on the date of the adoption of the plan of complete liquidation (or on January 1, 1986 if the fair market value at that date is greater).

2. More than 50 percent in value of the stock of the corporation was held by 10 or fewer qualified persons (i.e., individual, estate, trust).

Even though the first requirement was not satisfied, partial transitional relief was available if the fair market value of the stock was less than \$10 million. In this circumstance, the following formula was applied to determine the phaseout percentage (i.e., the percentage that did not qualify for transitional relief).

$$\frac{\text{FMV of stock} - \$5 \text{ million}}{\$5 \text{ million}}$$

Thus, for example, if the fair market value of the stock was \$7 million, the phase-out percentage was 40 and the percentage qualifying for transitional relief was 60 (100 – 40). Likewise, if the fair market value was \$10 million or greater, the phase-out percentage was 100 and the percentage qualifying for transitional relief was 0 (100 – 100).

While the expiration of this transition period has resulted in less beneficial tax treatment for corporate liquidations, it should be obvious that such expiration has produced the beneficial result of simplification.

SUBPART A—EFFECTS ON RECIPIENTS

Editorial Summary

Corporation Liquidations: Effect on Shareholders

Subchapter C of Chapter 1 (Secs. 331–334)

Pre-TRA of 1986 (Code sections not reproduced). Pre-TRA of 1986 provisions no longer are applicable as the result of the expiration of the transitional period provided for in the TRA of 1986. However, awareness of the tax consequences under these repealed provisions provides a historical perspective that helps the student to better understand the post-TRA of 1986 provisions and the resultant tax consequences. In addition, the student may be dealing with a tax year for which pre-TRA of 1986 provisions are applicable (i.e., in terms of case law). Section 331 (Gain or Loss to Shareholders in Corporate Liquidations) provided that, from the shareholder's perspective, the liquidation was treated as being equivalent to a stock sale (i.e., return of capital treatment). Therefore, the shareholder calculated his or her recognized gain or loss by comparing the fair market value of the assets received with the adjusted basis for his or her stock. Section 331 was a mandatory provision. That is, if neither Sec. 332 nor Sec. 333 (i.e., must be elected) applied, then the recognized gain or loss to the shareholder on the liquidation was calculated under Sec. 331.

Section 332 (Complete Liquidation of Subsidiaries) provided an exception to the aforementioned taxable treatment under Sec. 331. As the title indicated, for Sec. 332 to be available, the qualifying shareholder must be a corporation. That is, a parent and subsidiary relationship must exist (i.e., 80 percent control requirement). Thus, if Section 332 was applicable, no gain or loss was recognized at the qualifying shareholder (i.e., parent corporation) level.

Section 333 (Election as to Recognition of Gain in Certain Liquidations) provided the shareholder with the opportunity to elect to limit the amount of gain recognition. A corporation which controlled another corporation (i.e., at least 50 percent) could not qualify for Sec. 333 treatment. Section 333 required that all of the assets of the corporation be distributed to the shareholders within one calendar month (i.e., a so-called "one-month liquidation"). Under a qualifying election, the gain recognized at the shareholder level was limited to the greater of the following:

1. Ratable share of earnings and profits.

2. Assets distributed to shareholder which consisted of money, stock, or securities.

A qualifying corporate shareholder would classify the recognized gain as a capital gain. A noncorporate shareholder would classify the amount recognized in item 1 above as ordinary income (i.e., dividend income) and the amount recognized in item 2 above in *excess* of the item 1 amount, if any, as capital gain.

Sections 331 through 333 dealt with the issue of recognition of gain or loss at the shareholder level associated with a corporate liquidation. Section 334 (Basis of Property Received in Liquidations) dealt with the related issue of the basis of the property received by the shareholder from the corporation.

The general determination of basis was dependent on whether the distribution transaction at the shareholder level was treated as a taxable event or as a nontaxable event. If treated as a taxable event (e.g., Sec. 331), the basis of the assets received was the fair market value at the date of the distribution. Conversely, if treated as a nontaxable event (e.g., Sec. 332), the basis of the assets received was a carryover basis. Finally, if the transaction was treated as partially taxable and partially nontaxable at the shareholder level (e.g., Sec. 333), then the basis was a combination of a carryover basis and a fair market value basis (i.e., in between the two amounts).

Post-TRA of 1986. The statutory language of Sec. 331 was not affected by the Tax Reform Act of 1986. Therefore, the return of capital approach contained in Sec. 331 remains in effect. The shareholder calculates his or her recognized gain or loss by comparing the fair market value of the assets received with the adjusted basis of his or her stock.

While several minor changes were made in the statutory language of Sec. 332 by the Tax Reform Act of 1986, the changes do not result in the modification of the previous discussion of the Sec. 332 tax consequences. Thus, the opportunity still exists for a parent corporation to liquidate a subsidiary and not have any gain or loss recognized at the parent corporation (i.e., shareholder) level.

Section 333 was repealed by the Tax Reform Act of 1986.

The statutory language of Sec. 334 was not modified by the Tax Reform Act of 1986 except to delete the provisions which related to Sec. 333. That is, if the liquidation is treated as a taxable event at the shareholder level (i.e., the general rule under Sec. 331), the basis of the assets received by the shareholder is the fair market value on the date of the distribution. Conversely, if the liquidation is treated as a nontaxable event at the shareholder level (i.e., the exception under Sec. 332), the basis of the assets received is a carryover basis from the corporation. However, changes were made in Sec. 334(b) by the Technical and Miscellaneous Revenue Act of 1988 such that this Code section now provides for an exception to the carryover basis rule for property received in a Sec. 332 liquidation of a subsidiary. That is, if gain or loss is recognized by the liquidating corporation with respect to property, then the basis of the property is increased by the amount of the recognized gain and is decreased by the amount of the recognized loss (i.e., the basis is equal to the fair market value of the property).

§ 331. Gain or loss to shareholders in corporate liquidations

(a) Distributions in complete liquidation treated as exchanges.—Amounts received by a shareholder in a distribution in complete liquidation of a corporation shall be treated as in full payment in exchange for the stock.

(b) Nonapplication of section 301.—Section 301 (relating to effects on shareholder of distributions of property) shall not apply to any distribution of property (other than a distribution referred to in paragraph (2) (B) of section 316(b)) in complete liquidation.

(c) Cross reference.—

For general rule for determination of the amount of gain or loss recognized, see section 1001.

§ 332. Complete liquidations of subsidiaries

(a) General rule.—No gain or loss shall be recognized on the receipt by a corporation of property distributed in complete liquidation of another corporation.

(b) Liquidations to which section applies.—For purposes of this section, a distribution shall be considered to be in complete liquidation only if—

(1) the corporation receiving such property was, on the date of the adoption of the plan of liquidation, and has continued to be at all times until the receipt of the property, the owner of stock (in such other corporation) meeting the requirements of section 1504(a)(2); and either:

(2) the distribution is by such other corporation in complete cancellation or redemption of all its stock, and the transfer of all the property occurs within the taxable year; in such case the adoption by the shareholders of the resolution under which is authorized the distribution of all the assets of such corporation in complete cancellation or redemption of all its stock shall be considered an adoption of a plan of liquidation, even though no time for the completion of the transfer of the property is specified in such resolution; or

(3) such distribution is one of a series of distributions by such other corporation in complete cancellation or redemption of all its stock in accordance with a plan of liquidation under which the transfer of all the property under the liquidation is to be completed within 3 years from the close of the taxable year during which is made the first of the series of distributions under the plan, except that if such transfer is not completed within such period, or if the taxpayer does not continue qualified under paragraph (1) until the completion of such transfer, no distribution under the plan shall be considered a distribution in complete liquidation.

If such transfer of all the property does not occur within the taxable year, the Secretary may require of the taxpayer such bond, or waiver of the statute of limitations on assessment and collection, or both, as he may deem necessary to insure, if the transfer of the property is not completed within such 3-year period, or if the taxpayer does not continue qualified under paragraph (1) until the completion of such transfer, the assessment and collection of all income taxes then imposed by law for such taxable year or subsequent taxable years, to the extent attributable to property so received. A distribution otherwise constituting a distribution in complete liquidation within the meaning of this subsection shall not be considered as not constituting such a distribution merely because it does not constitute a distribution or liquidation within the meaning of the corporate law under which the distribution is made; and for purposes of this subsection a transfer of property of such other corporation to the taxpayer shall not be considered as not constituting a distribution (or one of a series of distributions) in complete cancellation or redemption of all the stock of such other corporation, merely because the carrying out of the plan involves (A) the transfer under the plan to the taxpayer by such other corporation of property, not attributable to shares owned by the taxpayer, on an exchange described in section 361, and (B) the complete cancellation or redemption under the plan, as a result of exchanges described in section 354, of the shares not owned by the taxpayer.

(c) Deductible liquidating distributions of regulated investment companies and real estate investment trusts.—If a corporation receives a distribution from a regulated investment company or a real estate investment trust which is considered under subsection (b) as being in complete liquidation of such company or trust, then, notwithstanding any other provision of this chapter, such corporation shall recognize and treat as a divided from such company or trust an amount equal to the deduction for dividends paid allowable to such company or trust by reason of such distribution.

* * *

§ 334. Basis of property received in liquidations

(a) General rule.—If property is received in a distribution in complete liquidation, and if gain or loss is recognized on receipt of such property, then the basis of the property in the hands of the distributee shall be the fair market value of such property at the time of the distribution.

(b) Liquidation of subsidiary.—

(1) In general.—If property is received by a corporate distributee in a distribution in a complete liquidation to which section 332 applies (or in a transfer described in section 337(b)(1)), the basis of such property in the hands of such distributee shall be the same as it would be in the hands of the transferor; except that, in the hands of such distributee—

(A) the basis of such property shall be the fair market value of the property at the time of the distribution in any case in which gain or loss is recognized by the liquidating corporation with respect to such property, and

(B) the basis of any property described in section 362(e)(1)(B) shall be the fair market value of the property at the time of the distribution in any case in which such distributee's aggregate adjusted basis of such property would (but for this subparagraph) exceed the fair market value of such property immediately after such liquidation.

(2) Corporate distributee.—For purposes of this subsection, the term "corporate distributee" means only the corporation which meets the stock ownership requirements specified in section 332(b).

SUBPART B—EFFECTS ON CORPORATION

Editorial Summary

Corporate Liquidations: Effect on Corporation

Subchapter C of Chapter 1 (Sec. 336–338)

Pre-TRA of 1986 (Code sections not reproduced). Pre-TRA of 1986 provisions no longer are applicable as the result of the expiration of the transitional period provided for in the TRA of 1986. However, awareness of the tax consequences under these repealed provisions provides a historical perspective that helps the student to better understand the post-TRA of 1986 provisions and the resultant tax consequences. In addition, the student may be dealing with a tax year for which the pre-TRA of 1986 provisions are applicable (i.e., in terms of case law). Section 336 (Distributions of Property in Liquidation) provided the liquidating corporation with the potential for no recognition of gain or loss (i.e., and thus the opportunity for the corporate liquidation not to be subject to double taxation) on the distribution of the corporate assets to the shareholders. While the general rule of Sec. 336 provided for no recognition, exceptions were contained in the Code section and others had developed as the result of judicial decisions. Included were the following:

1. Certain installment receivables (excess of fair market value over adjusted basis).
2. Lifo inventory (excess of Fifo over Lifo).
3. Depreciation recapture under Secs. 1245, 1250, and 291.
4. Tax benefit rule (to the extent the corporation has previously taken a deduction which produced a tax benefit).
5. Anticipatory assignment of income.
6. Investment tax credit recapture.
7. Treat actual sale of assets by the shareholders as deemed sale of assets by the corporation under the *Court Holding Company doctrine.*

Section 337 (Gain or Loss on Sales or Exchanges in Connection with Certain Liquidations) originally was enacted in response to the deemed sale approach problem for Sec. 336-type liquidations created by *Court Holding Company.* Under Sec. 337, no gain or loss was recognized at the corporate level on the sale of the assets by the corporation in complete liquidation. To qualify for such nonrecognition, the corporation was required to distribute all of its assets, less those retained to meet claims, within a 12-month period beginning on the date on which the corporation adopted a plan of complete liquidation (i.e., a so-called "12-month liquidation"). As was the case for Sec. 336, the general rule of nonrecognition under Sec. 337 was subject to certain statutory and judicial exceptions including the following:

1. Inventory unless a bulk sale to one person.
2. Installment obligations with respect to a non-bulk sale of inventory.
3. Installment notes acquired before the adoption of the plan of complete liquidation.
4. Lifo inventory (excess of Fifo over Lifo) for a bulk sale.
5. Depreciation recapture under Secs. 1245, 1250, and 291.
6. Tax benefit rule (to the extent the corporation has previously taken a deduction which produced a tax benefit).
7. Anticipatory assignment of income.
8. Investment tax credit recapture.

Quite often the form of the corporate liquidation was a combination sale/distribution (i.e., sale of most corporate assets by the corporation with the remaining non-cash assets and the cash being distributed to the shareholders). In such a circumstance, both Sec. 336 and Sec. 337 were applicable.

In the Editorial Summary entitled Corporate Liquidations: General, mention was made of the potential conflict between the buyer and the seller with respect to a sale of stock versus a sale of assets. The following example can be used to show how the corporate liquidation provisions could be used to neutralize, at least partially, the conflict.

Example: Corporation L has assets with a basis of $50,000 and a fair market value of $150,000. All the stock of the corporation is owned by Ms. S. Her basis for the stock is $50,000 and the fair market value is $150,000. Assume that none of the exceptions that produce recognition associated with a Sec. 337 liquidation are applicable.

If Ms. S sells her stock for $150,000, the tax consequences to her are as follows:

Amount realized	$150,000
– Basis for stock	50,000
= Recognized gain	$100,000

No recognition occurs at the corporate level because the corporation is not involved in the transaction. The tax disadvantage in this case is to the purchaser, Mr. P. While his basis for the stock is the fair market value of $150,000, Corporation L's basis for its assets remains at $50,000 because it was not involved in the transaction.

If Mr. P had been able to purchase the assets of Corporation L for $150,000 rather than Ms. S's stock, his basis for the assets would have been the amount paid of $150,000. Then, Mr. P could have contributed the assets to a corporation, Corporation M, under Sec. 351. Corporation M's basis for the corporate assets would have been a carryover basis of $150,000.

Absent the corporate liquidation provisions, a conflict does exist with respect to the transaction for Ms. S and Mr. P. Ms. S wants to sell the stock in order to avoid the double taxation that would result if the corporation sold the assets to Mr. P (i.e., gain to the corporation on the sale of the assets and gain to Ms. S on the distribution of the available cash by the corporation). Mr. P wants to purchase the assets in order to step the basis up to $150,000.

With the corporate liquidation provisions, the conflict could be eliminated. Corporation L could adopt a plan of complete liquidation under Sec. 337 and then sell the assets to Mr. P.

The tax consequences at the corporate level under Sec. 337 would be as follows:

Amount realized	$150,000
– Basis for assets	50,000
= Realized gain	$100,000
= Recognized gain	$ 0

Corporation L could then distribute the available cash of $150,000 to Ms. S in redemption of her stock. The tax consequences to Ms. S under Sec. 331 would be as follows:

Amount realized	$150,000
– Basis for stock	50,000
= Recognized gain	$100,000

Mr. P could contribute the assets to Corporation M under Sec. 351. Corporation M's basis for its assets would be $150,000. Thus, double taxation was avoided and the basis for the assets was stepped-up to fair market value. This is the same tax result to Ms. S as if she had sold her stock.

Another point illustrated in the example is that when determining the tax consequences of a corporate liquidation, both Subpart A (Effects on Recipients) and Subpart B (Effects on Corporation) must be consulted. Since the form of the transaction in the example was an asset sale by the corporation, Sec. 337 governed the effect on the corporation and Sec. 331 governed the effect on the shareholder. In addition, Sec. 334 governed the basis of the assets received. If the form of the transaction had been a distribution of corporate assets to the shareholder, then the section governing the effect for the corporation would have been Sec. 336 and Secs. 331 and 334 would once again have determined the tax consequences at the shareholder level.

Section 338 (Certain Stock Purchases Treated As Asset Acquisitions) provided the opportunity for the acquisition of corporate stock to be treated as if the corporate assets had been acquired instead. In effect, this section enabled the elimination, at least partially, of the conflict mentioned in the previous example: if the purchaser must buy the corporate stock when he would prefer to buy the corporate assets in order to step-up the basis of the assets to the fair market value.

In order to qualify for this deemed purchase of corporate assets, the purchasing shareholder must be a corporation. In addition, the purchasing corporation must have acquired control (i.e., 80 percent) of the acquired corporation during a 12-month acquisition period.

The statutory language of Sec. 338 assumed that the following steps occurred in association with the purchase of the stock of acquired corporation.

1. Acquired corporation is treated as having sold all of its assets for the fair market value. Section 337 applies to this deemed sale transaction (i.e., no recognition at the corporate level except for the aforementioned exceptions).

2. Acquired corporation is treated as a new corporation which purchased all of the corporate assets for the fair market value.

3. Assuming the acquiring corporation had acquired 100 percent of the stock of acquired corporation in qualifying purchase transactions during the 12-month acquisition period, the basis of the assets is the fair market value. However, if less than 100 percent was so purchased, then more complex rules are applied to determine the basis for the corporate assets.

In general, Sec. 338 was an elective provision. However, in order to negate certain tax avoidance opportunities, the consistency requirement of Sec. 338 provided for a deemed Sec. 338 election in certain circumstances.

Section 338 could also be used in conjunction with a Sec. 332 liquidation of a subsidiary. By doing so, the basis of the assets received from the liquidating subsidiary could be stepped-up under Sec. 338 rather than having a carryover basis under Sec. 334.

Post-TRA of 1986. Both Secs. 336 and 337 were repealed by the Tax Reform Act of 1986. The intent of the legislation was to repeal the doctrine initially established in *General Utilities* (i.e., the distribution of appreciated property by a corporation to its shareholders is not a taxable event). From a Code section perspective, the impact was on Secs. 311, 336, and 337. Therefore, the general statutory intent with respect to corporate liquidations now is that the sale or distribution of property is subject to recognition at the corporate level.

As was the case prior to the Tax Reform Act of 1986, post-TRA of 1986 Sec. 336 deals with the topic of distributions of property to the shareholders in complete liquidation of the corporation. However, the general rule contained in Sec. 336 is that realized gains or losses associated with the distributions are recognized at the corporate level [see Sec. 336(a)]. However, in drafting the legislation, Congress was aware that taxpayers may attempt to use the loss recognition provision to produce deductions that otherwise would not be permitted. Therefore, Sec. 336 contains two rules which either disallow or limit the recognition of loss in particular circumstances.

Section 336(d)(1) is the loss disallowance provision. It is applicable only if the distribution is to a Sec. 267-related party and then only if the distribution is not *pro rata* or the distributed property is disqualified property [see Sec. 336(d)(1)(B)]. Thus, to avoid this loss disallowance rule on distributions to related parties, the distribution must be *pro rata* and must not consist of disqualified property.

Section 336(d)(2) limits the amount of realized loss that can be recognized. The amount of the realized loss on the disposition of property subject to the Sec. 336(d)(2) limit is reduced by the amount of the built-in loss (i.e., excess of the basis of the property over the fair market value at the time of the contribution of the property to the corporation). Note that disposition is defined to include a sale, exchange, or distribution of the property. For Sec. 336(d)(2) to apply, both of the following conditions must be satisfied:

1. The property is acquired by the corporation either in a Sec. 351 transaction or as a contribution to capital. Note that if the loss were fully recognized by the shareholder at the time of contribution of the property to the corporation, it would not be carryover basis property and there would be no built-in loss.

2. A principal purpose of the acquisition of the property by the liquidating corporation was to recognize loss on such property associated with the liquidation of the corporation.

There is overlap with respect to the property described in Sec. 336(d)(1) and Sec. 336(d)(2). Also, note that a safe harbor is provided only with respect to Sec. 336(d)(1) in terms of the required time period between the date of the contribution of the property to the corporation and the date of the distribution [see Sec. 336(d)(1)(B)]. In fact, Sec. 336(d)(2)(B)(ii) goes in the opposite direction of a safe harbor by presuming a tax avoidance motive if the time period between the contribution and the date of the adoption of the plan of complete liquidation is not greater than two years.

Section 336 also contains an exception rule associated with Sec. 332 liquidations of subsidiaries [see Sec. 336(d)] and an exception rule associated with liquidations which are part of a reorganization [see Sec. 336(c)].

Section 337 now deals with a completely different topic when compared with Sec. 337 prior to the Tax Reform Act of 1986. It now covers the tax consequences to the subsidiary corporation associated with a Sec. 332 liquidation of a subsidiary. The general rule of Sec. 337 provides that no gain or loss will be recognized at the subsidiary corporation level.

In order that the S corporation rules (see Sec. 1363) not be used to avoid taxation at the corporate level (i.e., the corporation elects S corporation status under Sec. 1362 prior to liquidation), the Tax Reform Act of 1986 amended Sec. 1374 to provide that "built-in gains" are subject to taxation at the corporate level (see Sec. 1374 and the Editorial Summary entitled Taxation at the Corporate Level, which precedes Sec. 1371).

At the surface level, Sec. 338 basically remains intact as a result of the Tax Reform Act of 1986. The only changes appear to be of a minor technical nature and do not modify the basic statutory intent or framework of Sec. 338. For example, prior to amendment, the definition of control with respect to a qualified stock purchase was contained in Sec. 338(d)(3). The amended statutory language of Sec. 338(d)(3) defines control by reference to the definition contained in Sec. 1504(a)(2). However, the relationship between Sec. 338 and other corporate liquidation provisions has resulted in a substantial change with respect to the tax consequences of a Sec. 338 election. Note the following difference in the general rule of Sec. 338 for pre-TRA of 1986 and for post-TRA of 1986:

Pre-TRA of 1986. For purposes of this subtitle, if a purchasing corporation makes an election under this section (or is treated under subsection (e) as having made such an election), then, in the case of any qualified stock purchase, the target corporation—

1. shall be treated as having sold all of its assets at the close of the acquisition date at fair market value in a single transaction *to which Section 337 applies*, and

2. shall be treated as a new corporation which purchased all of the assets referred to in paragraph (1) as of the beginning of the day after the acquisition date.

Post-TRA of 1986. For purposes of this subtitle, if a purchasing corporation makes an election under this section (or is treated under subsection (e) as having made such an election), then, in the case of any qualified stock purchase, the target corporation—

1. shall be treated as having sold all of its assets at the close of the acquisition date at fair market value in a single transaction, and

2. shall be treated as a new corporation which purchased all of the assets referred to in paragraph (1) as of the beginning of the day after the acquisition date.

The change in the general rule is italicized (i.e., deletion of "to which section 337 applies"). Recall that the TRA of 1986 repealed the nonrecognition provision of Sec. 337. Therefore, while Sec. 338 can still be used to step-up the basis of the assets deemed purchased to the basis (i.e., purchase price) of the stock actually purchased, there is a negative factor involved. That is, because the pre-TRA of 1986 Sec. 337 nonrecognition provision has been repealed, the Sec. 338 election will trigger recognition at the target corporation level.

§ 336. Gain or loss recognized on property distributed in complete liquidation

(a) General rule.—Except as otherwise provided in this section or section 337, gain or loss shall be recognized to a liquidating corporation on the distribution of property in complete liquidation as if such property were sold to the distributee at its fair market value.

(b) Treatment of liabilities.—If any property distributed in the liquidation is subject to a liability or the shareholder assumes a liability of the liquidating corporation in connection with the distribution, for purposes of subsection (a) and section 337, the fair market value of such property shall be treated as not less than the amount of such liability.

(c) Exception for liquidations which are part of a reorganization.—

For provision providing that this subpart does not apply to distributions in pursuance of a plan of reorganization, see section 361(c)(4).

(d) Limitations on recognition of loss.—

(1) No loss recognized in certain distributions to related persons.—

(A) In general.—No loss shall be recognized to a liquidating corporation on the distribution of any property to a related person (within the meaning of section 267) if—

(i) such distribution is not pro rata, or

(ii) such property is disqualified property.

(B) Disqualified property.—For purposes of subparagraph (A), the term "disqualified property" means any property which is acquired by the liquidating corporation in a transaction to which section 351 applied, or as a contribution to capital, during the 5-year period ending on the date of the distribution. Such term includes any property if the adjusted basis of such property is determined (in whole or in part) by reference to the adjusted basis of property described in the preceding sentence.

(2) Special rule for certain property acquired in certain carryover basis transactions.—

(A) In general.—For purposes of determining the amount of loss recognized by any liquidating corporation on any sale, exchange, or distribution of property described in subparagraph (B), the adjusted basis of such property shall be reduced (but not below zero) by the excess (if any) of—

(i) the adjusted basis of such property immediately after its acquisition by such corporation, over

(ii) the fair market value of such property as of such time.

(B) Description of property.—

(i) In general.—For purposes of subparagraph (A), property is described in this subparagraph if—

(I) such property is acquired by the liquidating corporation in a transaction to which section 351 applied or as a contribution to capital, and

(II) the acquisition of such property by the liquidating corporation was part of a plan a principal purpose of which was to recognize loss by the liquidating corporation with respect to such property in connection with the liquidation.

Other property shall be treated as so described if the adjusted basis of such other property is determined (in whole or in part) by reference to the adjusted basis of property described in the preceding sentence.

(ii) Certain acquisitions treated as part of plan.—For purposes of clause (i), any property described in clause (i)(I) acquired by the liquidated corporation after the date 2 years before the date of the adoption of the plan of complete liquidation shall, except as provided in regulations, be treated as acquired as part of a plan described in clause (i)(II).

(C) Recapture in lieu of disallowance.—The Secretary may prescribe regulations under which, in lieu of disallowing a loss under subparagraph (A) for a prior taxable year, the gross income of the liquidating corporation for the taxable year in which the plan of complete liquidation is adopted shall be increased by the amount of the disallowed loss.

(3) Special rule in case of liquidation to which section 332 applies.—In the case of any liquidation to which section 332 applies, no loss shall be recognized to the liquidating corporation on any distribution in such liquidation. The preceding sentence shall apply to any distribution to the 80-percent distributee only if subsection (a) or (b)(1) of section 337 applies to such distribution.

(e) Certain stock sales and distributions may be treated as asset transfers.—Under regulations prescribed by the Secretary, if—

(1) a corporation owns stock in another corporation meeting the requirements of section 1504(a)(2), and

(2) such corporation sells, exchanges, or distributes all of such stock,

an election may be made to treat such sale, exchange, or distribution as a disposition of all of the assets of such other corporation, and no gain or loss shall be recognized on the sale, exchange, or distribution of such stock.

§ 337. Nonrecognition for property distributed to parent in complete liquidation of subsidiary

(a) In general.—No gain or loss shall be recognized to the liquidating corporation on the distribution to the 80-percent distributee of any property in a complete liquidation to which section 332 applies.

(b) Treatment of indebtedness of subsidiary, etc.—

(1) Indebtedness of subsidiary to parent.—If—

(A) a corporation is liquidated in a liquidation to which section 332 applies, and

(B) on the date of the adoption of the plan of liquidation, such corporation was indebted to the 80-percent distributee,

for purposes of this section and section 336, any transfer of property to the 80-percent distributee in satisfaction of such indebtedness shall be treated as a distribution to such distributee in such liquidation.

(2) Treatment of tax-exempt distributee.—

(A) In general.—Except as provided in subparagraph (B), paragraph (1) and subsection (a) shall not apply where the 80-percent distributee is an organization (other than a cooperative described in section 521) which is exempt from the tax imposed by this chapter.

(B) Exception where property will be used in unrelated business.—

(i) In general.—Subparagraph (A) shall not apply to any distribution of property to an organization described in section 511 (a)(2) if, immediately after such distribution, such organization uses such property in an activity the income from which is subject to tax under section 511(a).

(ii) Later disposition or change in use.—If any property to which clause (i) applied is disposed of by the organization acquiring such property, notwithstanding any other provision of law, any gain (not in excess of the amount not recognized by reason of clause (i) shall be included in such organization's unrelated business taxable income. For purposes of the preceding sentence, if such property ceases to be used in an activity referred to in clause (i), such organization shall be treated as having disposed of such property on the date of such cessation.

(c) 80-percent distributee.—For purposes of this section, the term "80-percent distributee" means only the corporation which meets the 80-percent stock ownership requirements specified in section 332(b). For purposes of this section, the determination of whether any corporation is an 80-percent distributee shall be made without regard to any consolidated return regulation.

(d) Regulations.—The Secretary shall prescribe such regulations as may be necessary or appropriate to carry out the purposes of the amendments made by subtitle D of title VI of the Tax Reform Act of 1986, including—

(1) regulations to ensure that such purposes may not be circumvented through the use of any provision of law or regulations (including the consolidated return regulations and part III of this subchapter) or through the use of a regulated investment company, real estate investment trust, or tax-exempt entity, and

(2) regulations providing for appropriate coordination of the provisions of this section with the provisions of this title relating to taxation of foreign corporations and their shareholders.

§ 338. Certain stock purchases treated as asset acquisitions

(a) General rule.—For purposes of this subtitle, if a purchasing corporation makes an election under this section (or is treated under subsection (e) as having made such an election), then, in the case of any qualified stock purchase, the target corporation—

(1) shall be treated as having sold all of its assets at the close of the acquisition date at fair market value in a single transaction, and

(2) shall be treated as a new corporation which purchased all of the assets referred to in paragraph (1) as of the beginning of the day after the acquisition date.

(b) Basis of assets after deemed purchase.—

(1) In general.—For purposes of subsection (a), the assets of the target corporation shall be treated as purchased for an amount equal to the sum of—

(A) the grossed-up basis of the purchasing corporation's recently purchased stock, and

(B) the basis of the purchasing corporation's nonrecently purchased stock.

(2) Adjustment for liabilities and other relevant items.—The amount described in paragraph (1) shall be adjusted under regulations prescribed by the Secretary for liabilities of the target corporation and other relevant items.

(3) Election to step-up the basis of certain target stock.—

(A) In general.—Under regulations prescribed by the Secretary, the basis of the purchasing corporation's nonrecently purchased stock shall be the basis amount determined under subparagraph (B) of this paragraph if the purchasing corporation makes an election to recognize gain as if such stock were sold on the acquisition date for an amount equal to the basis amount determined under subparagraph (B).

(B) Determination of basis amount.—For purposes of subparagraph (A), the basis amount determined under this subparagraph shall be an amount equal to the grossed-up basis determined under subparagraph (A) of paragraph (1) multiplied by a fraction—

(i) the numerator of which is the percentage of stock (by value) in the target corporation attributable to the purchasing corporation's nonrecently purchased stock, and

(ii) the denominator of which is 100 percent minus the percentage referred to in clause (i).

(4) Grossed-up basis.—For purposes of paragraph (1), the grossed-up basis shall be an amount equal to the basis of the corporation's recently purchased stock, multiplied by a fraction—

(A) the numerator of which is 100 percent, minus the percentage of stock (by value) in the target corporation attributable to the purchasing corporation's nonrecently purchased stock, and

(B) the denominator of which is the percentage of stock (by value) in the target corporation attributable to the purchasing corporation's recently purchased stock.

(5) Allocation among assets.—The amount determined under paragraphs (1) and (2) shall be allocated among the assets of the target corporation under regulations prescribed by the Secretary.

(6) Definitions of recently purchased stock and nonrecently purchased stock.—For purposes of this subsection—

(A) Recently purchased stock.—The term "recently purchased stock" means any stock in the target corporation which is held by the purchasing corporation on the acquisition date and which was purchased by such corporation during the 12-month acquisition period.

(B) Nonrecently purchased stock.—The term "nonrecently purchased stock" means any stock in the target corporation which is held by the purchasing corporation on the acquisition date and which is not recently purchased stock.

***(d) Purchasing corporation; target corporation; qualified stock purchase.**—For purposes of this section—

(1) Purchasing corporation.—The term "purchasing corporation" means any corporation which makes a qualified stock purchase of stock of another corporation.

(2) Target corporation.—The term "target corporation" means any corporation the stock of which is acquired by another corporation in a qualified stock purchase.

(3) Qualified stock purchase.—The term "qualified stock purchase" means any transaction or series of transactions in which stock (meeting the requirements of section 1504(a)(2)) of 1 corporation is acquired by another corporation by purchase during the 12-month acquisition period.

(e) Deemed election where purchasing corporation acquires asset of target corporation.—

(1) In general.—A purchasing corporation shall be treated as having made an election under this section with respect to any target corporation if, at any time during the consistency period, it acquires any asset of the target corporation (or a target affiliate).

(2) Exceptions.—Paragraph (1) shall not apply with respect to any acquisition by the purchasing corporation if—

(A) such acquisition is pursuant to a sale by the target corporation (or the target affiliate) in the ordinary course of its trade or business,

(B) the basis of the property acquired is determined (wholly) by reference to the adjusted basis of such property in the hands of the person from whom acquired,

(C) such acquisition was before September 1, 1982, or

(D) such acquisition is described in regulations prescribed by the Secretary and meets such conditions as such regulations may provide.

(3) Anti-avoidance rule.—Whenever necessary to carry out the purpose of this subsection and subsection (f), the Secretary may treat stock acquisitions which are pursuant to a plan and which meet the requirements of section 1504(a)(2) as qualified stock purchases.

(f) Consistency required for all stock acquisitions from same affiliated group.—If a purchasing corporation makes qualified stock purchases with respect to the target corporation and 1 or more target affiliates during any consistency period, then (except as otherwise provided in subsection (e))—

(1) any election under this section with respect to the first such purchase shall apply to each other such purchase, and

(2) no election may be made under this section with respect to the second or subsequent such purchase if such an election was not made with respect to the first such purchase.

(g) Election.—

(1) When made.—Except as otherwise provided in regulations, an election under this section

*Editorial comment: There is no subsection (c).

shall be made not later than the 15th day of the 9th month beginning after the month in which the acquisition date occurs.

(2) Manner.—An election by the purchasing corporation under this section shall be made in such manner as the Secretary shall by regulations prescribe.

(3) Election irrevocable.—An election by a purchasing corporation under this section, once made, shall be irrevocable.

(h) Definitions and special rules.—For purposes of this section—

(1) 12-month acquisition period.—The term "12-month acquisition period" means the 12-month period beginning with the date of the first acquisition by purchase of stock included in a qualified stock purchase (or, if any of such stock was acquired in an acquisition which is a purchase by reason of subparagraph (C) of paragraph (3), the date on which the acquiring corporation is first considered under section 318(a) (other than paragraph (4) thereof) as owning stock owned by the corporation from which such acquisition was made).

(2) Acquisition date.—The term "acquisition date" means, with respect to any corporation, the first day on which there is a qualified stock purchase with respect to the stock of such corporation.

(3) Purchase.—

(A) In general.—The term "purchase" means any acquisition of stock, but only if—

(i) the basis of the stock in the hands of the purchasing corporation is not determined (I) in whole or in part by reference to the adjusted basis of such stock in the hands of the person from whom acquired, or (II) under section 1014(a) (relating to property acquired from a decedent),

(ii) the stock is not acquired in an exchange to which section 351, 354, 355, or 356 applies and is not acquired in any other transaction described in regulations in which the transferor does not recognize the entire amount of the gain or loss realized on the transaction, and

(iii) the stock is not acquired from a person the ownership of whose stock would, under section 318(a) (other than paragraph (4) thereof), be attributed to the person acquiring such stock.

(B) Deemed purchase under subsection (a).—The term "purchase" includes any deemed purchase under subsection (a)(2). The acquisition date for a corporation which is deemed purchased under subsection (a)(2) shall be determined under regulations prescribed by the Secretary.

(C) Certain stock acquisitions from related corporations.—

(i) In general.— Clause (iii) of subparagraph (A) shall not apply to an acquisition of stock from a related corporation if at least 50 percent in value of the stock of such related corporation was acquired by purchase (within the meaning of subparagraphs (A) and (B)).

(ii) Certain distributions.—Clause (i) of subparagraph (A) shall not apply to an acquisition of stock described in clause (i) of this subparagraph if the corporation acquiring such stock—

(I) made a qualified stock purchase of stock of the related corporation, and

(II) made an election under this section (or is treated under subsection (e) as having made such an election) with respect to such qualified stock purchase.

(iii) Related corporation defined.—For purposes of this subparagraph, a corporation is a related corporation if stock owned by such corporation is treated (under section 318(a) other than paragraph (4) thereof) as owned by the corporation acquiring the stock.

(4) Consistency period.—

(A) In general.—Except as provided in subparagraph (B), the term "consistency period" means the period consisting of—

(i) the 1-year period before the beginning of the 12-month acquisition period for the target corporation,

(ii) such acquisition period (up to and including the acquisition date), and

(iii) the 1-year period beginning on the day after the acquisition date.

(B) Extension where there is plan.—The period referred to in subparagraph (A) shall also include any period during which the Secretary determines that there was in effect a plan to make a qualified stock purchase plus 1 or more other qualified stock purchases (or asset acquisitions described in subsection (e)) with respect to the target corporation or any target affiliate.

(5) Affiliated group.—The term "affiliated group" has the meaning given to such term by section 1504(a) (determined without regard to the exceptions contained in section 1504(b)).

(6) Target affiliate.—

(A) In general.—A corporation shall be treated as a target affiliate of the target corporation if each of such corporations was, at any time during so much of the consistency period as ends on the acquisition date of the target corporation, a member of an affiliated group which had the same common parent.

* * *

*__(8) Acquisitions by affiliated group treated as made by 1 corporation.__—Except as provided in regulations prescribed by the Secretary, stock and asset acquisitions made by members of the same affiliated group shall be treated as made by 1 corporation.

(9) Target not treated as member of affiliated group.—Except as otherwise provided in paragraph (10) or in regulations prescribed under this paragraph, the target corporation shall not be treated as a member of an affiliated group with respect to the sale described in subsection (a)(1).

(10) Elective recognition of gain or loss by target corporation, together with nonrecognition of gain or loss on stock sold by selling consolidated group.—

(A) In general.—Under regulations prescribed by the Secretary, an election may be made under which if—

(i) the target corporation was, before the transaction, a member of the selling consolidated group, and

(ii) the target corporation recognizes gain or loss with respect to the transaction as if it sold all of its assets in a single transaction,

then the target corporation shall be treated as a member of the selling consolidated group with respect to such sale, and (to the extent provided in regulations) no gain or loss will be recognized on stock sold or exchanged in the transaction by members of the selling consolidated group.

(B) Selling consolidated group.—For purposes of subparagraph (A), the term "selling consolidated group" means any group of corporations which (for the taxable period which includes the transaction)—

(i) includes the target corporation, and

(ii) files a consolidated return.

To the extent provided in regulations, such term also includes any affiliated group of corporations which includes the target corporation (whether or not such group files a consolidated return).

(C) Information required to be furnished to the Secretary.—Under regulations, where an election is made under subparagraph (A), the purchasing corporation and the common parent of the selling consolidated group shall, at such times and in such manner as may be provided in regulations, furnish to the Secretary the following information:

(i) The amount allocated under subsection (b)(5) to goodwill or going concern value.

(ii) Any modification of the amount described in clause (i).

(iii) Any other information as the Secretary deems necessary to carry out the provisions of this paragraph.

(11) Elective formula for determining fair market value.—For purposes of subsection (a)(1), fair market value may be determined on the basis of a formula provided in regulations prescribed by the Secretary which takes into account liabilities and other relevant items.

**__(13) Tax on deemed sale not taken into account for estimated tax purposes.__—For purposes of section 6655, tax attributable to the sale described in subsection (a)(1) shall not be taken into account. The preceding sentence shall not apply with respect to a qualified stock purchase for which an election is made under paragraph (10).

***__(15) Combined deemed sale return.__—Under regulations prescribed by the Secretary, a combined deemed sale return may be filed by all

*Editorial comment: There is no paragraph (7).

**Editorial comment: There is no paragraph (12).

***Editorial comment: There is no paragraph (14).

target corporations acquired by a purchasing corporation on the same acquisition date if such target corporations were members of the same selling consolidated group (as defined in subparagraph (B) of paragraph (10)).

* * *

(i) Regulations.—The Secretary shall prescribe such regulations as may be necessary or appropriate to carry out the purposes of this section, including—

(1) regulations to ensure that the purpose of this section to require consistency of treatment of stock and asset sales and purchases may not be circumvented through the use of any provision of law or regulations (including the consolidated return regulations) and

(2) regulations providing for the coordination of the provisions of this section with the provision of this title relating to foreign corporations and their shareholders.

SUBPART C—COLLAPSIBLE CORPORATIONS [REPEALED]

SUBPART D—DEFINITION AND SPECIAL RULE

Editorial Summary

Corporate Liquidations: Definition

Subchapter C of Chapter 1 (Sec. 346)

See the discussion under the Editorial Summary entitled Corporate Liquidations: General, which follows Sec. 318.

§ 346. Definition and special rule

(a) Complete liquidation.— For purposes of this subchapter, a distribution shall be treated as in complete liquidation of a corporation if the distribution is one of a series of distributions in redemption of all of the stock of the corporation pursuant to a plan.

(b) Transactions which might reach same result as partial liquidations.—The Secretary shall prescribe such regulations as may be necessary to ensure that the purposes of subsections (a) and (b) of section 222 of the Tax Equity and Fiscal Responsibility Act of 1982 (which repeal the special tax treatment for partial liquidations) may not be circumvented through the use of section 355, 351, or any other provision of law or regulations (including the consolidated return regulations).

PART III—CORPORATE ORGANIZATIONS AND REORGANIZATIONS

SubPart

A. Corporate organizations.
B. Effects on shareholders and security holders.
C. Effects on corporation.
D. Special rule; definitions.

Editorial Summary

Transfers to a Controlled Corporation

Subchapter C of Chapter 1 (Secs. 351-362)

Effect on shareholder. For tax purposes, the corporation is considered an entity separate and apart from the owners of the corporation. Thus, transactions between the shareholders and the corporation generally are treated as taxable. Therefore, if property is transferred to the corporation in exchange for its stock, gain or loss is recognized to the shareholder based on the difference between the basis and the fair market of the property. This tax treatment is an application of entity theory.

Section 351 provides an exception to the taxable treatment by substituting aggregate or proprietary theory (i.e., the owner and the corporation are treated as one and the same) for entity theory. Since the realized gain or loss is not recognized, the basis of the stock to the shareholders is a carryover basis (i.e., same as the basis of the property transferred to the corporation) under Sec. 358, and the basis of the property to the corporation is a carryover basis under Sec. 362. For Sec. 351 to produce nonrecognition treatment, the shareholders who are transferring property to the corporation must be in control of the corporation immediately after the transfer [see Sec. 368(c)]. Section 351 applies only with respect to stock issued for property and not to stock issued for services [see Sec. 351(d)].

The general rule of Sec. 351 provides for the mandatory nonrecognition of realized gain or loss. However, if boot is received, the receipt of boot will trigger the recognition of realized gain to the extent of the lesser of (1) the boot received, or (2) the realized gain [see Sec. 351(b)]. The receipt of boot does not trigger the recognition of realized loss. Since Sec. 351 is mandatory, if the taxpayer wants to avoid Sec. 351 nonrecognition (i.e., in order to either recognize realized loss or realized gain), then the transaction must be structured so that the requirements of Sec. 351 are not satisfied. A benefit of recognizing gain at the shareholder level is the ability to step-up the basis of the contributed property at the corporation level [see Sec. 362(b)].

Section 357, associated with the corporation's assumption of shareholder liabilities, produces gain recognition to the shareholder in certain circumstances. The general rule of Sec. 357 provides that if in a Sec. 351 contribution the corporation assumes shareholder liabilities or acquires shareholder property subject to a liability, the liability is not considered to be boot. However, two exceptions exist. First, Sec. 357(c) provides that if such liabilities exceed the basis of all the property transferred by a shareholder, the excess (i.e., liabilities in excess of basis) is treated as a boot. Second, Sec. 357(b) provides that all of such liabilities, rather than just the excess, is treated as boot if a tax avoidance motive exists (i.e., the principal purpose) with the liability transfer. It is important to distinguish between liabilities for which the corporation can take a deduction and those for which no such deduction is permitted [see Sec. 357(c)] and also to ascertain if the principal purpose was tax avoidance [see Sec. 357(b)].

Effect on corporation. The receipt by a corporation of property in exchange for its stock is not a taxable transaction (see Sec. 1032). As indicated above, if no recognition occurs under Sec. 351 for the shareholder, the basis of the property contributed by the shareholder to the corporation is a carryover basis [see Sec. 362]. If, however, gain is recognized at the shareholder level, then the adjusted basis of the property to the corporation is increased by the amount of gain recognized by the shareholder.

SUBPART A—CORPORATE ORGANIZATIONS

§ 351. Transfer to corporation controlled by transferor

(a) General rule.—No gain or loss shall be recognized if property is transferred to a corporation by one or more persons solely in exchange for stock in such corporation and immediately after the exchange such person or persons are in control (as defined in section 368(c)) of the corporation.

(b) Receipt of property.—If subsection (a) would apply to an exchange but for the fact that there is received, in addition to the stock permitted to be received under subsection (a), other property or money, then—

(1) gain (if any) to such recipient shall be recognized, but not in excess of—

(A) the amount of money received, plus

(B) the fair market value of such other property received; and

(2) no loss to such recipient shall be recognized.

(c) Special rules where distribution to shareholders.—

(1) In general.—In determining control for purposes of this section, the fact that any corporate transferor distributes part or all of the stock in the corporation which it receives in the exchange to its shareholders shall not be taken into account.

(2) Special rule for section 355.—If the requirements of section 355 (or so much of section 356 as relates to section 355) are met with respect to a distribution described in paragraph (1), then, solely for purposes of determining the tax treatment of the transfers of property to the controlled corporation by the distributing corporation, the fact that the shareholders of the distributing corporation dispose of part or all of the distributed stock, or the fact that the corporation whose stock was distributed issues additional stock, shall not be taken into account in determining control for purposes of this section.

(d) Services, certain indebtedness, and accrued interest not treated as property.—For purposes of this section, stock issued for—

(1) services,

(2) indebtedness of the transferee corporation which is not evidenced by a security, or

(3) interest on indebtedness of the transferee corporation which accrued on or after the beginning of the transferor's holding period for the debt,

shall not be considered as issued in return for property.

(e) Exceptions.—This section shall not apply to—

(1) Transfer of property to an investment company.—A transfer of property to an investment company. For purposes of the preceding sentence, the determination of whether a company is an investment company shall be made—

(A) by taking into account all stock and securities held by the company, and

(B) by treating as stock and securities—

(i) money,

(ii) stocks and other equity interests in a corporation, evidences of indebtedness, options, forward or futures contracts, notional principal contracts and derivatives,

(iii) any foreign currency,

(iv) any interest in a real estate investment trust, a common trust fund, a regulated investment company, a publicly-traded partnership (as defined in section 7704(b)) or any other equity interest (other than in a corporation) which pursuant to its terms or any other arrangement is readily convertible into, or exchangeable for, any asset described in any preceding clause, this clause or clause (v) or (viii),

(v) except to the extent provided in regulations prescribed by the Secretary, any interest in a precious metal, unless such metal is used or held in the active conduct of a trade or business after the contribution,

(vi) except as otherwise provided in regulations prescribed by the Secretary, interests in any entity if substantially all of the assets of such entity consist (directly or indirectly) of any assets described in any preceding clause or clause (viii),

(vii) to the extent provided in regulations prescribed by the Secretary, any interest in any entity not described in clause (vi), but only to the extent of the value of such interest that is attributable to assets listed in clauses (i) through (v) or clause (viii), or

(viii) any other asset specified in regulations prescribed by the Secretary.

The Secretary may prescribe regulations that, under appropriate circumstances, treat any asset described in clauses (i) through (v) as not so listed.

* * *

(f) Treatment of controlled corporation.—If—

(1) property is transferred to a corporation (hereinafter in this subsection referred to as the "controlled corporation") in an exchange with respect to which gain or loss is not recognized (in whole or in part) to the transferor under this section, and

(2) such exchange is not in pursuance of a plan of reorganization,

section 311 shall apply to any transfer in such exchange by the controlled corporation in the same manner as if such transfer were a distribution to which subpart A of part I applies.

(g) Nonqualified preferred stock not treated as stock.—

(1) In general.—In the case of a person who transfers property to a corporation and receives nonqualified preferred stock—

(A) subsection (a) shall not apply to such transferor, and

(B) if (and only if) the transferor receives stock other than nonqualified preferred stock—

(i) subsection (b) shall apply to such transferor, and

(ii) such nonqualified preferred stock shall be treated as other property for purposes of applying subsection (b).

(2) Nonqualified preferred stock.—For purposes of paragraph (1)—

(A) In general.—The term "nonqualified preferred stock" means preferred stock if—

(i) the holder of such stock has the right to require the issuer or a related person to redeem or purchase the stock,

(ii) the issuer or a related person is required to redeem or purchase the stock,

(iii) the issuer or a related person has the right to redeem or purchase the stock and, as of the issue date, it is more likely than not that such right will be exercised, or

(iv) the dividend rate on such stock varies in whole or in part (directly or indirectly) with reference to interest rates, commodity prices, or other similar indices.

(B) Limitations.—Clauses (i), (ii), and (iii) of subparagraph (A) shall apply only if the right or obligation referred to therein may be exercised within the 20-year period beginning on the issue date of such stock and such right or obligation is not subject to a contingency which, as of the issue date, makes remote the likelihood of the redemption or purchase.

(C) Exceptions for certain rights or obligations.—

(i) In general.—A right or obligation shall not be treated as described in clause (i), (ii), or (iii) of subparagraph (A) if—

(I) it may be exercised only upon death, disability, or mental incompetency of the holder, or

(II) in the case of a right or obligation to redeem or purchase stock transferred in connection with the performance of services for the issuer or a related person (and which represents reasonable compensation), it may be exercised only upon the holder's separation from service from the issuer or a related person.

(ii) Exception.—Clause (i)(I) shall not apply if the stock relinquished in the exchange, or the stock acquired in the exchange is in—

(I) a corporation if any class of stock in such corporation or a related party is readily tradable on an established securities market or otherwise, or

(II) any other corporation if such exchange is part of a transaction or series of transactions in which such corporation is to become a corporation described in subclause (I).

(3) Definitions.—For purposes of this subsection—

(A) Preferred stock.—The term "preferred stock" means stock which is limited and preferred as to dividends and does not participate in corporate growth to any significant extent. Stock shall not be treated as participating in corporate growth to any significant extent unless there is a real and meaningful likelihood of the shareholder actually participating in the earnings and growth of the corporation. If there is not a real and meaningful likelihood that dividends beyond any limitation or preference will actually be paid, the possibility of such payments will be disregarded in determining whether stock is limited and preferred as to dividends.

(B) Related person.—A person shall be treated as related to another person if they bear a relationship to such other person described in section 267(b) or 707(b).

(4) Regulations.—The Secretary may prescribe such regulations as may be necessary or appropriate to carry out the purposes of this subsection and sections 354(a)(2)(C), 355(a)(3)(D), and 356(e). The Secretary may also prescribe regulations, consistent with the treatment under this subsection and such sections, for the treatment of nonqualified preferred stock under other provisions of this title.

(h) Cross references.—

(1) For special rule where another party to the exchange assumes a liability, see section 357.

(2) For the basis of stock or property received in an exchange to which this section applies, see sections 358 and 362.

(3) For special rule in the case of an exchange described in this section but which results in a gift, see section 2501 and following.

(4) For special rule in the case of an exchange described in this section but which has the effect of the payment of compensation by the corporation or by a transferor, see section 61(a)(1).

(5) For coordination of this section with section 304, see section 304(b)(3).

SUBPART B—EFFECTS ON SHAREHOLDERS AND SECURITY HOLDERS

Editorial Summary

Transfers to Controlled Corporations and Corporate Reorganizations: Effect on Shareholders

Subchapter C of Chapter 1 (Secs. 354–358)

See the discussion under the Editorial Summary entitled Transfers to a Controlled Corporation, which precedes Sec. 351, and the Editorial Summary entitled Corporate Reorganizations, which precedes Sec. 368.

§ 354. Exchanges of stock and securities in certain reorganizations

(a) General rule.—

(1) In general.—No gain or loss shall be recognized if stock or securities in a corporation a party to a reorganization are, in pursuance of the plan of reorganization, exchanged solely for stock or securities in such corporation or in another corporation a party to the reorganization.

(2) Limitations.—

(A) Excess principal amount.—Paragraph (1) shall not apply if—

(i) the principal amount of any such securities received exceeds the principal amount of any such securities surrendered, or

(ii) any such securities are received and no such securities are surrendered.

(B) Property attributable to accrued interest.—Neither paragraph (1) nor so much of section 356 as relates to paragraph (1) shall apply to the extent that any stock (including nonqualified preferred stock, as defined in section 351(g)(2)), securities, or other property received is attributable to interest which has accrued on securities on or after the beginning of the holder's holding period.

(C) Nonqualified preferred stock.—

(i) In general.—Nonqualified preferred stock (as defined in section 351(g)(2)) received in exchange for stock other than nonqualified preferred stock (as so defined) shall not be treated as stock or securities.

(ii) Recapitalization of family-owned corporations.—

(I) In general.—Clause (i) shall not apply in the case of a recapitalization under section 368(a)(1)(E) of a family-owned corporation.

(II) Family-owned corporation.—For purposes of this clause, except as provided in regulations, the term "family-owned corporation" means any corporation which is described in clause (i) of section 447(d)(2)(C) throughout the 8-year period beginning on the date which is 5 years before the date of the recapitalization. For purposes of the preceding sentence, stock shall not be treated as owned by a family member during any period described in section 355(d)(6)(B).

(III) Extension of statute of limitations.—The statutory period for the assessment of any deficiency attributable to a corporation failing to be a family-owned corporation shall not expire before the expiration of 3 years after the date the Secretary is notified by the corporation (in such manner as the Secretary may prescribe) of such failure, and such deficiency may be assessed before the expiration of such 3-year period notwithstanding the provisions of any other law or rule of law which would otherwise prevent such assessment.

(3) Cross references.—

(A) For treatment of the exchange if any property is received which is not permitted to be received under this subsection (including nonqualified preferred stock and an excess principal amount of securities received over securities surrendered, but not including property to which paragraph (2)(B) applies), see section 356.

(B) For treatment of accrued interest in the case of an exchange described in paragraph (2)(B), see section 61.

(b) Exception.—

(1) In general.—Subsection (a) shall not apply to an exchange in pursuance of a plan of reorganization within the meaning of subparagraph (D) or (G) of section 368(a)(1), unless—

(A) the corporation to which the assets are transferred acquires substantially all of the assets of the transferor of such assets; and

(B) the stock, securities, and other properties received by such transferor, as well as the other properties of such transferor, are distributed in pursuance of the plan of reorganization.

(2) Cross reference.—

For special rules for certain exchanges in pursuance of plans of reorganization within the meaning of subparagraph (D) or (G) of section 368(a)(1), see section 355.

* * *

§ 355. Distribution of stock and securities of a controlled corporation

(a) Effect on distributees.—

(1) General rule.—If—

(A) a corporation (referred to in this section as the "distributing corporation")—

(i) distributes to a shareholder, with respect to its stock, or

(ii) distributes to a security holder, in exchange for its securities,

solely stock or securities of a corporation (referred to in this section as "controlled corporation") which it controls immediately before the distribution,

(B) the transaction was not used principally as a device for the distribution of the earnings and profits of the distributing corporation or the controlled corporation or both (but the mere fact that subsequent to the distribution stock or securities in one or more of such corporations are sold or exchanged by all or some of the distributees (other than pursuant to an arrangement negotiated or agreed upon prior to such distribution) shall not be construed to mean that the transaction was used principally as such a device),

(C) the requirements of subsection (b) (relating to active businesses) are satisfied, and

(D) as part of the distribution, the distributing corporation distributes—

(i) all of the stock and securities in the controlled corporation held by it immediately before the distribution, or

(ii) an amount of stock in the controlled corporation constituting control within the meaning of section 368(c), and it is established to the satisfaction of the Secretary that the retention by the distributing corporation of stock (or stock and securities) in the controlled corporation was not in pursuance of a plan having as one of its principal purposes the avoidance of Federal income tax,

then no gain or loss shall be recognized to (and no amount shall be includible in the income of) such shareholder or security holder on the receipt of such stock or securities.

(2) Non pro rata distributions, etc.—Paragraph (1) shall be applied without regard to the following:

(A) whether or not the distribution is pro rata with respect to all of the shareholders of the distributing corporation,

(B) whether or not the shareholder surrenders stock in the distributing corporation, and

(C) whether or not the distribution is in pursuance of a plan of reorganization (within the meaning of section 368(a)(1)(D)).

(3) Limitations.—

(A) Excess principal amount.—Paragraph (1) shall not apply if—

(i) the principal amount of the securities in the controlled corporation which are received exceeds the principal amount of the securities which are surrendered in connection with such distribution, or

(ii) securities in the controlled corporation are received and no securities are surrendered in connection with such distribution.

(B) Stock acquired in taxable transactions within 5 years treated as boot.—For purposes of this section (other than paragraph (1)(D) of this subsection) and so much of section 356 as relates to this section, stock of a controlled corporation acquired by the distributing corporation by reason of any transaction—

(i) which occurs within 5 years of the distribution of such stock, and

(ii) in which gain or loss was recognized in whole or in part,

shall not be treated as stock of such controlled corporation, but as other property.

(C) Property attributable to accrued interest.—Neither paragraph (1) nor so much of section 356 as relates to paragraph (1) shall apply to the extent that any stock (including nonqualified preferred stock, as defined in section 351(g)(2)), securities, or other property received is attributable to interest which has accrued on securities on or after the beginning of the holder's holding period.

(D) Nonqualified preferred stock.—Nonqualified preferred stock (as defined in section 351(g)(2)) received in a distribution with respect to stock other than nonqualified preferred stock (as so defined) shall not be treated as stock or securities.

(4) Cross references.—

(A) For treatment of the exchange if any property is received which is not permitted to be received under this subsection (including nonqualified preferred stock and an excess principal amount of securities received over securities surrendered, but not including property to which paragraph (3)(C) applies), see section 356.

(B) For treatment of accrued interest in the case of an exchange described in paragraph (3)(C), see section 61.

(b) Requirements as to active business.—

(1) In general.—Subsection (a) shall apply only if either—

(A) the distributing corporation, and the controlled corporation (or, if stock of more than one controlled corporation is distributed, each of such corporations), is engaged immediately after the distribution in the active conduct of a trade or business, or

(B) immediately before the distribution, the distributing corporation had no assets other than stock or securities in the controlled corporations and each of the controlled corporations is engaged immediately after the distribution in the active conduct of a trade or business.

(2) Definition.—For purposes of paragraph (1), a corporation shall be treated as engaged in the active conduct of a trade or business if and only if—

(A) it is engaged in the active conduct of a trade or business,

(B) such trade or business has been actively conducted throughout the 5-year period ending on the date of the distribution,

(C) such trade or business was not acquired within the period described in subparagraph (B) in a transaction in which gain or loss was recognized in whole or in part, and

(D) control of a corporation which (at the time of acquisition of control) was conducting such trade or business—

(i) was not acquired by any distributee corporation directly (or through 1 or more corporations, whether through the distributing corporation or otherwise) within the period described in subparagraph (B) and was not acquired by the distributing corporation directly (or through 1 or more corporations) within such period, or

(ii) was so acquired by any such corporation within such period, but, in each case in which such control was so acquired, only by reason of transactions in which gain or loss was not recognized in whole or in part, or only by reason of such transactions combined with acquisitions before the beginning of such period.

For purposes of subparagraph (D), all distributee corporations which are members of the same affiliated group (as defined in section 1504(a) without regard to section 1504(b) shall be treated as 1 distributee corporation.

* * *

(c) Taxability of corporation on distribution.—

(1) In general.—Except as provided in paragraph (2), no gain or loss shall be recognized to a corporation on any distribution to which this section (or so much of section 356 as relates to this section) applies and which is not in pursuance of a plan of reorganization.

(2) Distribution of appreciated property.—

(A) In general.—If—

(i) in a distribution referred to in paragraph (1), the corporation distributes property other than qualified property, and

(ii) the fair market value of such property exceeds its adjusted basis (in the hands of the distributing corporation),

then gain shall be recognized to the distributing corporation as if such property were sold to the distributee at its fair market value.

(B) Qualified property.—For purposes of subparagraph (A), the term "qualified property" means any stock or securities in the controlled corporation.

(C) Treatment of liabilities.—If any property distributed in the distribution referred to in paragraph (1) is subject to a liability or the shareholder assumes a liability of the distributing corporation in connection with the distribution, then, for purposes of subparagraph (A), the fair market value of such property shall be treated as not less than the amount of such liability.

(3) Coordination with sections 311 and 336 (a).—Sections 311 and 336(a) shall not apply to any distribution referred to in paragraph (1).

(d) Recognition of gain on certain distributions of stock or securities in controlled corporation.—

(1) In general.—In the case of a disqualified distribution, any stock or securities in the controlled corporation shall not be treated as qualified property for purposes of subsection (c)(2) of this section or section 361(c)(2).

(2) Disqualified distribution.—For purposes of this subsection, the term "disqualified distribution" means any distribution to which this section (or so much of section 356 as relates to this section) applies if, immediately after the distribution—

(A) any person holds disqualified stock in the distributing corporation which constitutes a 50-percent or greater interest in such corporation, or

(B) any person holds disqualified stock in the controlled corporation (or, if stock of more than 1 controlled corporation is distributed, in any controlled corporation) which constitutes a 50-percent or greater interest in such corporation.

(3) Disqualified stock.—For purposes of this subsection, the term "disqualified stock" means—

(A) any stock in the distributing corporation acquired by purchase after October 9, 1990, and during the 5-year period ending on the date of the distribution, and

(B) any stock in any controlled corporation—

(i) acquired by purchase after October 9, 1990, and during the 5-year period ending on the date of the distribution, or

(ii) received in the distribution to the extent attributable to distributions on—

(I) stock described in subparagraph (A), or

(II) any securities in the distributing corporation acquired by purchase after October 9, 1990, and during the 5-year period ending on the date of the distribution.

(4) 50-percent or greater interest.—For purposes of this subsection, the term "50-percent or greater interest" means stock possessing at least 50 percent of the total combined voting power of all classes of stock entitled to vote or at least 50 percent of the total value of shares of all classes of stock.

(5) Purchase.—For purposes of this subsection—

(A) In general.—Except as otherwise provided in this paragraph, the term "purchase" means any acquisition but only if—

(i) the basis of the property acquired in the hands of the acquirer is not determined (I) in whole or in part by reference to the adjusted basis of such property in the hands of the person from whom acquired, or (II) under section 1014(a), and

(ii) the property is not acquired in an exchange to which section 351, 354, 355, or 356 applies.

(B) Certain section 351 exchanges treated as purchases.—The term "purchase" includes any acquisition of property in an exchange to which section 351 applies to the extent such property is acquired in exchange for—

(i) any cash or cash item,

(ii) any marketable stock or security, or

(iii) any debt of the transferor.

(C) Carryover basis transactions.—If—

(i) any person acquires property from another person who acquired such property by purchase (as determined under this paragraph with regard to this subparagraph), and

(ii) the adjusted basis of such property in the hands of such acquirer is determined in whole or in part by reference to the adjusted basis of such property in the hands of such other person,

such acquirer shall be treated as having acquired such property by purchase on the date it was so acquired by such other person.

(6) Special rule where substantial diminution of risk.—

(A) In general.—If this paragraph applies to any stock or securities for any period, the running of any 5-year period set forth in subparagraph (A) or (B) of paragraph (3) (whichever applies) shall be suspended during such period.

(B) Property to which suspension applies.—This paragraph applies to any stock or securities for any period during which the holder's risk of loss with respect to such stock or securities, or with respect to any portion of the activities of the corporation, is (directly or indirectly) substantially diminished by—

(i) an option,

(ii) a short sale,

(iii) any special class of stock, or

(iv) any other device or transaction.

(7) Aggregation rules.—

(A) In general.—For purposes of this subsection, a person and all persons related to such person (within the meaning of section 267(b) of section 707(b)(1)) shall be treated as one person.

(B) Persons acting pursuant to plans or arrangements.—If two or more persons act pursuant to a plan or arrangement with respect to acquisitions of stock or securities in the distributing corporation or controlled corporation, such persons shall be treated as one person for purposes of this subsection.

(8) Attribution from entities.—

(A) In general.—Paragraph (2) of section 318(a) shall apply in determining whether a person holds stock or securities in any corporation (determined by substituting "10 percent" for "50 percent" in subparagraph (C) of such paragraph (2) and by treating any reference to stock as including a reference to securities).

(B) Deemed purchase rule.—If—

(i) any person acquires by purchase an interest in any entity, and

(ii) such person is treated under subparagraph (A) as holding any stock or securities by reason of holding such interest,

such stock or securities shall be treated as acquired by purchase by such person on the later of the date of the purchase of the interest in such entity or the date such stock or securities are acquired by purchase by such entity.

(9) Regulations.—The Secretary shall prescribe such regulations as may be necessary to carry out the purposes of this subsection, including—

(A) regulations to prevent the avoidance of the purposes of this subsection through the use of related persons, intermediaries, pass-thru entities, options, or other arrangements, and

(B) regulations modifying the definition of the term "purchase."

(e) Recognition of gain on certain distributions of stock or securities in connection with acquisitions.—

(1) General rule.—If there is a distribution to which this subsection applies, any stock or securities in the controlled corporation shall not be treated as qualified property for purposes of subsection (c)(2) of this section or section 361(c)(2).

(2) Distributions to which subsection applies.—

(A) In general.—This subsection shall apply to any distribution—

(i) to which this section (or so much of section 356 as relates to this section) applies, and

(ii) which is part of a plan (or series of related transactions) pursuant to which 1 or more persons acquire directly or indirectly stock representing a 50-percent or greater interest in the distributing corporation or any controlled corporation.

(B) Plan presumed to exist in certain cases.—If 1 or more persons acquire directly or indirectly stock representing a 50-percent or greater interest in the distributing corporation or any controlled corporation during the 4-year period beginning on the date which is 2 years before the date of the distribution, such acquisition shall be treated as pursuant to a plan described in subparagraph (A)(ii) unless it is established that the distribution and the acquisition are not pursuant to a plan or series of related transactions.

(C) Certain plans disregarded.—A plan (or series of related transactions) shall not be treated as described in subparagraph (A)(ii) if, immediately after the completion of such plan or transactions, the distributing corporation and all controlled corporations are members of a single affiliated group (as defined in section 1504 without regard to subsection (b) thereof).

(D) Coordination with subsection (d).—This subsection shall not apply to any distribution to which subsection (d) applies.

(3) Special rules relating to acquisitions.—

(A) Certain acquisitions not taken into account.—Except as provided in regulations, the following acquisitions shall not be taken into account in applying paragraph (2)(A)(ii):

(i) The acquisition of stock in any controlled corporation by the distributing corporation.

(ii) The acquisition by a person of stock in any controlled corporation by reason of holding stock or securities in the distributing corporation.

(iii) The acquisition by a person of stock in any successor corporation of the distributing corporation or any controlled corporation by reason of holding stock or securities in such distributing or controlled corporation.

(iv) The acquisition of stock in the distributing corporation or any controlled corporation to the extent that the percentage of stock owned directly or indirectly in such corporation by each person owning stock in such corporation immediately before the acquisition does not decrease.

This subparagraph shall not apply to any acquisition if the stock held before the acquisition was acquired pursuant to a plan (or series of related transactions) described in paragraph (2)(A)(ii).

(B) Asset acquisitions.—Except as provided in regulations, for purposes of this subsection, if the assets of the distributing corporation or any controlled corporation are acquired by a successor corporation in a transaction described in subparagraph (A), (C), or (D) of section 368(a)(1) or any other transaction specified in regulations by the Secretary, the shareholders (immediately before the acquisition) of the corporation acquiring such assets shall be treated as acquiring stock in the corporation from which the assets were acquired.

(4) Definition and special rules.—For purposes of this subsection—

(A) 50-percent or greater interest.—The term "50-percent or greater interest" has the meaning given such term by subsection (d)(4).

(B) Distributions in title 11 or similar case.—Paragraph (1) shall not apply to any distribution made in a title 11 or similar case (as defined in section 368(a)(3)).

(C) Aggregation and attribution rules.—

(i) Aggregation.—The rules of paragraph (7)(A) of subsection (d) shall apply.

(ii) Attribution.—Section 318(a)(2) shall apply in determining whether a person holds stock or securities in any corporation. Except as provided in regulations, section 318(a) (2) (C) shall be applied without regard to the phrase "50 percent or more in value" for purposes of the preceding sentence.

(D) Successors and predecessors.—For purposes of this subsection, any reference to a controlled corporation or a distributing corporation shall include a reference to any predecessor or successor of such corporation.

(E) Statute of limitations.—If there is a distribution to which paragraph (1) applies—

(i) the statutory period for the assessment of any deficiency attributable to any part of the gain recognized under this subsection by reason of such distribution shall not expire before the expiration of 3 years from the date the Secretary is notified by the taxpayer (in such manner as the Secretary may by regulations prescribe) that such distribution occurred, and

(ii) such deficiency may be assessed before the expiration of such 3-year period notwithstanding the provisions of any other law or rule of law which would otherwise prevent such assessment.

(5) Regulations.—The Secretary shall prescribe such regulations as may be necessary to carry out the purposes of this subsection, including regulations—

(A) providing for the application of this subsection where there is more than 1 controlled corporation,

(B) treating 2 or more distributions as 1 distribution where necessary to prevent the avoidance of such purposes, and

(C) providing for the application of rules similar to the rules of subsection (d)(6) where appropriate for purposes of paragraph (2)(B).

(f) Section not to apply to certain intragroup distributions.—Except as provided in regulations, this section (or so much of section 356 as relates to this section) shall not apply to the distribution of stock from 1 member of an affiliated group (as defined in section 1504(a)) to another member of such group if such distribution is part of a plan (or series of related transactions) described in subsection (e)(2)(A)(ii) (determined after the application of subsection (e)).

* * *

§ 356. Receipt of additional consideration

(a) Gain on exchanges.—

(1) Recognition of gain.—If—

(A) section 354 or 355 would apply to an exchange but for the fact that

(B) the property received in the exchange consists not only of property permitted by section 354 or 355 to be received without the recognition of gain but also of other property or money,

then the gain, if any, to the recipient shall be recognized, but in an amount not in excess of the sum of such money and the fair market value of such other property.

(2) Treatment as dividend.—If an exchange is described in paragraph (1) but has the effect of the distribution of a dividend (determined with the application of section 318(a)), then there shall be treated as a dividend to each distributee such an amount of the gain recognized under paragraph (1) as is not in excess of his ratable share of the undistributed earnings and profits of the corporation accumulated after February 28, 1913. The remainder, if any, of the gain recognized under paragraph (1) shall be treated as gain from the exchange of property.

(b) Additional consideration received in certain distributions.—If—

(1) section 355 would apply to a distribution but for the fact that

(2) the property received in the distribution consists not only of property permitted by section 355 to be received without the recognition of gain, but also of other property or money,

then an amount equal to the sum of such money and the fair market value of such other property shall be treated as a distribution of property to which section 301 applies.

(c) Loss.—If—

(1) section 354 would apply to an exchange, or section 355 would apply to an exchange or distribution, but for the fact that

(2) the property received in the exchange or distribution consists not only of property permitted by section 354 or 355 to be received without the recognition of gain or loss, but also of other property or money,

then no loss from the exchange or distribution shall be recognized.

(d) Securities as other property.—For purposes of this section—

(1) In general.—Except as provided in paragraph (2), the term "other property" includes securities.

(2) Exceptions.—

(A) Securities with respect to which nonrecognition of gain would be permitted.—The term "other property" does not include securities to the extent that, under section 354 or 355, such securities would be permitted to be received without the recognition of gain.

(B) Greater principal amount in section 354 exchange.—If—

(i) in an exchange described in section 354 (other than subsection (c) thereof), securities of a corporation a party to the reorganization are surrendered and securities of any corporation a party to the reorganization are received, and

(ii) the principal amount of such securities received exceeds the principal amount of such securities surrendered,

then, with respect to such securities received, the term "other property" means only the fair market value of such excess. For purposes of this subparagraph and subparagraph (C), if no securities are surrendered, the excess shall be the entire principal amount of the securities received.

(C) Greater principal amount in section 355 transaction.—If, in an exchange or distribution described in section 355, the principal amount of the securities in the controlled corporation which are received exceeds the principal amount of the securities in the distributing corporation which are surrendered, then, with respect to such securities received, the term "other property" means only the fair market value of such excess.

(e) Nonqualified preferred stock treated as other property.—For purposes of this section—

(1) In general.—Except as provided in paragraph (2), the term "other property" includes nonqualified preferred stock (as defined in section 351 (g)(2)).

(2) Exception.—The term "other property" does not include nonqualified preferred stock (as so defined) to the extent that, under section 354 or 355, such preferred stock would be permitted to be received without the recognition of gain.

(f) Exchanges for section 306 stock.—Notwithstanding any other provision of this section, to the extent that any of the other property (or money) is received in exchange for section 306 stock, an amount equal to the fair market value of such other property (or the amount of such money) shall be treated as a distribution of property to which section 301 applies.

(g) Transactions involving gift or compensation.—

For special rules for a transaction described in section 354, 355, or this section, but which—

(1) results in a gift, see section 2501 and following, or

(2) has the effect of the payment of compensation, see section 61(a)(1).

§ 357. Assumption of liability

(a) General rule.—Except as provided in subsections (b) and (c), if—

(1) the taxpayer receives property which would be permitted to be received under section 351 or 361 without the recognition of gain if it were the sole consideration, and

(2) as part of the consideration, another party to the exchange assumes a liability of the taxpayer, or acquires from the taxpayer property subject to a liability,

then such assumption or acquisition shall not be treated as money or other property, and shall not prevent the exchange from being within the provisions of section 351 or 361 as the case may be.

(b) Tax avoidance purpose.—

(1) In general.—If, taking into consideration the nature of the liability and the circumstances in the light of which the arrangement for the assumption or acquisition was made, it appears that the principal purpose of the taxpayer with respect to the assumption or acquisition described in subsection (a)—

(A) was a purpose to avoid Federal income tax on the exchange, or

(B) if not such purpose, was not a bona fide business purpose,

then such assumption or acquisition (in the total amount of the liability assumed or acquired pursuant to such exchange) shall, for purposes of section 351 or 361 (as the case may be), be considered as money received by the taxpayer on the exchange.

(2) Burden of proof.—In any suit or proceeding where the burden is on the taxpayer to prove such assumption or acquisition is not to be treated as money received by the taxpayer, such burden shall not be considered as sustained unless the taxpayer sustains such burden by the clear preponderance of the evidence.

(c) Liabilities in excess of basis.—

(1) In general.—In the case of an exchange—

(A) to which section 351 applies, or

(B) to which section 361 applies by reason of a plan of reorganization within the meaning of section 368(a)(1)(D) with respect to which stock or securities of the corporation to which the assets are transferred are distributed in a transaction which qualifies under section 355,

if the sum of the amount of the liabilities assumed, plus the amount of the liabilities to which the property is subject, exceeds the total of the adjusted basis of the property transferred pursuant to such exchange, then such excess shall be considered as a gain from the sale or exchange of a capital asset or of property which is not a capital asset, as the case may be.

(2) Exceptions.—Paragraph (1) shall not apply to any exchange—

(A) to which subsection (b)(1) of this section applies, or

(B) which is pursuant to a plan of reorganization within the meaning of section 368(a)(1)(G) where no former shareholder of the transferor corporation receives any consideration for his stock.

(3) Certain liabilities excluded.—

(A) In general.—If a taxpayer transfers, in an exchange to which section 351 applies, a liability the payment of which either—

(i) would give rise to a deduction, or

(ii) would be described in section 736(a),

then, for purposes of paragraph (1), the amount of such liability shall be excluded in determining the amount of liabilities assumed or to which the property transferred is subject.

(B) Exception.—Subparagraph (A) shall not apply to any liability to the extent that the incurrence of the liability resulted in the creation of, or an increase in, the basis of any property.

(d) Determination of amount of liability assumed.—

(1) In general.—For purposes of this section, 358(d), section 358(h), section 361(b)(3), section 362(d), section 368(a)(1)(C), and section 368(a)(2)(B), except as provided in regulations—

(A) a recourse liability (or portion thereof) shall be treated as having been assumed if, as determined on the basis of all facts and circumstances, the transferee has agreed to, and is expected to, satisfy such liability (or portion), whether or not the transferor has been relieved of such liability; and

(B) except to the extent provided in paragraph (2), a nonrecourse liability shall be treated as having been assumed by the transferee of any asset subject to such liability.

(2) Exception for nonrecourse liability.—The amount of the nonrecourse liability treated as described in paragraph (1)(B) shall be reduced by the lesser of—

(A) the amount of such liability which an owner of other assets not transferred to the transferee and also subject to such liability has agreed with the transferee to, and is expected to, satisfy, or

(B) the fair market value of such other assets (determined without regard to section 7701(g)).

(3) Regulations.—The Secretary shall prescribe such regulations as may be necessary to carry out the purposes of this subsection and section 362(d). The Secretary may also prescribe regulations which provide that the manner in which a liability is treated as assumed under this subsection is applied, where appropriate, elsewhere in this title.

§ 358. Basis to distributees

(a) General rule.—In the case of an exchange to which section 351, 354, 355, 356, or 361 applies—

(1) Nonrecognition property.—The basis of the property permitted to be received under such section without the recognition of gain or loss shall be the same as that of the property exchanged—

(A) decreased by—

(i) the fair market value of any other

property (except money) received by the taxpayer,

(ii) the amount of any money received by the taxpayer, and

(iii) the amount of loss to the taxpayer which was recognized on such exchange, and

(B) increased by—

(i) the amount which was treated as a dividend, and

(ii) the amount of gain to the taxpayer which was recognized on such exchange (not including any portion of such gain which was treated as a dividend).

(2) Other property.—The basis of any other property (except money) received by the taxpayer shall be its fair market value.

(b) Allocation of basis.—

(1) In general.—Under regulations prescribed by the Secretary, the basis determined under subsection (a)(1) shall be allocated among the properties permitted to be received without the recognition of gain or loss.

(2) Special rule for section 355.—In the case of an exchange to which section 355 (or so much of section 356 as relates to section 355) applies, then in making the allocation under paragraph (1) of this subsection, there shall be taken into account not only the property so permitted to be received without the recognition of gain or loss, but also the stock or securities (if any) of the distributing corporation which are retained, and the allocation of basis shall be made among all such properties.

(c) Section 355 transactions which are not exchanges.—For purposes of this section, a distribution to which section 355 (or so much of section 356 as relates to section 355) applies shall be treated as an exchange, and for such purposes the stock and securities of the distributing corporation which are retained shall be treated as surrendered, and received back, in the exchange.

(d) Assumption of liability.—

(1) In general.—Where, as part of the consideration to the taxpayer, another party to the exchange assumed a liability of the taxpayer or acquired from the taxpayer property subject to a liability, such assumption or acquisition (in the amount of the liability) shall, for purposes of this section, be treated as money received by the taxpayer on the exchange.

(2) Exception.—Paragraph (1) shall not apply to the amount of any liability excluded under section 357(c)(3).

(e) Exception.—This section shall not apply to property acquired by a corporation by the exchange of its stock or securities (or the stock or securities of a corporation which is in control of the acquiring corporation) as consideration in whole or in part for the transfer of the property to it.

(f) Definition of nonrecognition property in case of section 361 exchange.—For purposes of this section, the property permitted to be received under section 361 without the recognition of gain or loss shall be treated as consisting only of stock or securities in another corporation a party to the reorganization.

(g) Adjustments in intragroup transactions involving section 355.—In the case of a distribution to which section 355 (or so much of section 356 as relates to section 355) applies and which involves the distribution of stock from 1 member of an affiliated group (as defined in section 1504(a) without regard to subsection (b) thereof) to another member of such group, the Secretary may, notwithstanding any other provision of this section, provide adjustments to the adjusted basis of any stock which—

(1) is in a corporation which is a member of such group, and

(2) is held by another member of such group, to appropriately reflect the proper treatment of such distribution.

(h) Special rules for assumption of liabilities to which subsection (d) does not apply.—

(1) In general.—If, after application of the other provisions of this section to an exchange or series of exchanges, the basis of property to which subsection (a)(1) applies exceeds the fair market value of such property, then such basis shall be reduced (but not below such fair market value) by the amount (determined as of the date of the exchange) of any liability—

(A) which is assumed by another person as part of the exchange, and

(B) with respect to which subsection (d)(1) does not apply to the assumption.

(2) Exceptions—Except as provided by the

Secretary, paragraph (1) shall not apply to any liability if—

(A) the trade or business with which the liability is associated is transferred to the person assuming the liability as part of the exchange, or

(B) substantially all of the assets with which the liability is associated are transferred to the person assuming the liability as part of the exchange.

(3) Liability.—For purposes of this subsection, the term "liability" shall include any fixed or contingent obligation to make payment, without regard to whether the obligation is otherwise taken into account for purposes of this title.

SUBPART C—EFFECTS ON CORPORATION

Editorial Summary

Transfers to Controlled Corporations and Corporate Reorganizations: Effect on Corporation

Subchapter C of Chapter 1 (Secs. 361 and 362)

See the discussion under the Editorial Summary entitled Transfers to a Controlled Corporation, which precedes Sec. 351, and the Editorial Summary entitled Corporate Reorganizations, which precedes Sec. 368.

§ 361. Nonrecognition of gain or loss to corporations; treatment of distributions

(a) General rule.—No gain or loss shall be recognized to a corporation if such corporation is a party to a reorganization and exchanges property, in pursuance of the plan of reorganization, solely for stock or securities in another corporation a party to the reorganization.

(b) Exchanges not solely in kind.—

(1) Gain.—If subsection (a) would apply to an exchange but for the fact that the property received in exchange consists not only of stock or securities permitted by subsection (a) to be received without the recognition of gain, but also of other property or money, then—

(A) Property distributed.—If the corporation receiving such other property or money distributes it in pursuance of the plan of reorganization, no gain to the corporation shall be recognized from the exchange, but

(B) Property not distributed.—If the corporation receiving such other property or money does not distribute it in pursuance of the plan of reorganization, the gain, if any, to the corporation shall be recognized.

The amount of gain recognized under subparagraph (B) shall not exceed the sum of the money and the fair market value of the other property so received which is not so distributed.

(2) Loss.—If subsection (a) would apply to an exchange but for the fact that the property received in exchange consists not only of property permitted by subsection (a) to be received without the recognition of gain or loss, but also of other property or money, then no loss from the exchange shall be recognized.

(3) Treatment of transfers to creditors.—For purposes of paragraph (1), any transfer of the other property or money received in the exchange by the corporation to its creditors in connection with the reorganization shall be treated as a distribution in pursuance of the plan of reorganization. The Secretary may prescribe such regulations as may be necessary to prevent avoidance of tax through abuse of the preceding sentence or subsection (c)(3). In the case of a reorganization described in section 368(a)(1)(D) with respect to which stock or securities of the corporation to which the assets are transferred are distributed in a transaction which qualifies under section 355, this paragraph shall apply only to the extent that the sum of the money and the fair market value of other property transferred to such creditors does not exceed the adjusted bases of such assets transferred (reduced by the amount of the liabilities assumed (within the meaning of section 357(c))).

(c) Treatment of distributions.—

(1) In general.—Except as provided in paragraph (2), no gain or loss shall be recognized to a corporation, a party to a reorganization on the distribution to its shareholders of property in pursuance of the plan of reorganization.

(2) Distributions of appreciated property.—

(A) In general.—If—

(i) in a distribution referred to in paragraph (1), the corporation distributes property other than qualified property, and

(ii) the fair market value of such property exceeds its adjusted basis (in the hands of the distributing corporation),

then gain shall be recognized to the distributing corporation as if such property were sold to the distributee at its fair market value.

(B) Qualified property.—For purposes of this subsection, the term "qualified property" means—

(i) any stock in (or right to acquire stock in) the distributing corporation or obligation of the distributing corporation, or

(ii) any stock in (or right to acquire stock in) another corporation which is a party to the reorganization or obligation of another corporation, which is such a party if such stock (or right) or obligation is received by the distributing corporation in the exchange.

(C) Treatment of liabilities.—If any property distributed in the distribution referred to in paragraph (1) is subject to a liability or the shareholder assumes a liability of the distributing corporation in connection with the distribution, then, for purposes of subparagraph (A), the fair market value of such property shall be treated as not less than the amount of such liability.

(3) Treatment of certain transfers to creditors.—For purposes of this subsection, any transfer of qualified property by the corporation to its creditors in connection with the reorganization shall be treated as a distribution to its shareholders pursuant to the plan of reorganization.

(4) Coordination with other provisions.—Section 311 and subpart B of part II of this subchapter shall not apply to any distribution referred to in paragraph (1).

(5) Cross reference.—For provision providing for recognition of gain in certain distributions, see section 355(d).

§ 362. Basis to corporations

(a) Property acquired by issuance of stock or as paid-in surplus.—If property was acquired on or after June 22, 1954, by a corporation—

(1) in connection with a transaction to which section 351 (relating to transfer of property to corporation controlled by transferor) applies, or

(2) as paid-in surplus or as a contribution to capital,

then the basis shall be the same as it would be in the hands of the transferor, increased in the amount of gain recognized to the transferor on such transfer.

(b) Transfers to corporations.—If property was acquired by a corporation in connection with a reorganization to which this part applies, then the basis shall be the same as it would be in the hands of the transferor, increased in the amount of gain recognized to the transferor on such transfer. This subsection shall not apply if the property acquired consists of stock or securities in a corporation a party to the reorganization, unless acquired by the exchange of stock or securities of the transferee (or of a corporation which is in control of the transferee) as the consideration in whole or in part for the transfer.

(c) Special rule for certain contributions to capital.—

(1) Property other than money.—Notwithstanding subsection (a)(2), if property other than money—

(A) is acquired by a corporation, on or after June 22, 1954, as a contribution to capital, and

(B) is not contributed by a shareholder as such,

then the basis of such property shall be zero.

(2) Money.—Notwithstanding subsection (a)(2), if money—

(A) is received by a corporation, on or after June 22, 1954, as a contribution to capital, and

(B) is not contributed by a shareholder as such,

then the basis of any property acquired with such money during the 12-month period beginning on the day the contribution is received shall be reduced by the amount of such contribution. The excess (if any) of the amount of such contribution over the amount of the reduction under the preceding sentence shall be applied to the reduction (as of the last day of the period specified in the preceding sentence) of the basis of any other property held by the taxpayer. The particular properties to which the reductions required by this paragraph shall be allocated shall be determined under regulations prescribed by the Secretary.

(d) Limitation on basis increase attributable to assumption of liability.

(1) In general.—In no event shall the basis of any property be increased under subsection (a) or (b) above the fair market value of such property (determined without regard to section 7701(g)) by reason of any gain recognized to the transferor as a result of the assumption of a liability.

(2) Treatment of gain not subject to tax.—Except as provided in regulations, if—

(A) gain is recognized to the transferor as a result of an assumption of a nonrecourse liability by a transferee which is also secured by assets not transferred to such transferee; and

(B) no person is subject to tax under this title on such gain,

then, for purposes of determining basis under subsections (a) and (b), the amount of gain recognized by the transferor as a result of the assumption of the liability shall be determined as if the liability assumed by the transferee equaled such transferee's ratable portion of such liability determined on the basis of the relative fair market values (determined without regard to section 7701 (g)) of all of the assets subject to such liability.

(e) Limitations on built-in losses.—

(1) Limitation on importation of built-in losses.—

(A) In general.—If in any transaction described in subsection (a) or (b) there would (but for this subsection) be an importation of a net built-in loss, the basis of each property described in subparagraph (B) which is acquired in such transaction shall (notwithstanding subsections (a) and (b)) be its fair market value immediately after such transaction.

(B) Property described.—For purposes of subparagraph (A), property is described in this subparagraph if—

(i) gain or loss with respect to such property is not subject to tax under this subtitle in the hands of the transferor immediately before the transfer, and

(ii) gain or loss with respect to such property is subject to such tax in the hands of the transferee immediately after such transfer.

In any case in which the transferor is a partnership, the preceding sentence shall be applied by treating each partner in such partnership as holding such partner's proportionate share of the property of each partnership.

(C) Importation of net built-in loss.—For purposes of subparagraph (A), there is an importation of a net built-in loss in a transaction if the transferee's aggregate adjusted bases of property described in subparagraph (B) which is transferred in such transaction would (but for this paragraph) exceed the fair market value of such property immediately after such transaction.

(2) Limitation on transfer of built-in losses in section 351 transactions.—

(A) In general.—If—

(i) property is transferred by a transferor in any transaction which is described in subsection (a) and which is not described in paragraph (1) of this subsection, and

(ii) the transferee's aggregated adjusted bases of such property so transferred would (but for this paragraph) exceed the fair market value of such property immediately after such transaction,

then, notwithstanding subsection (a), the transferee's aggregate adjusted bases of the property so transferred shall not exceed the fair market value of such property immediately after such transaction.

(B) Allocation of basis reduction.—The aggregate reduction in basis by reason of subparagraph (A) shall be allocated among the property so transferred in proportion to their respective built-in losses immediately before the transaction.

(C) Election to apply limitation to transferor's stock basis.—

(i) In general.—If the transferor and transferee of a transaction described in subparagraph (A) both elect the application of this subparagraph—

(I) subparagraph (A) shall not apply, and

(II) the transferor's basis in the stock received for property to which subparagraph (A) does not apply by reason of the election shall not exceed its fair market value immediately after the transfer.

(ii) Election.—An election under clause (i) shall be made at such time and in such form and manner as the Secretary may prescribe, and, once made, shall be irrevocable.

SUBPART D—SPECIAL RULE; DEFINITIONS

Editorial Summary

Corporate Reorganizations

Subchapter C of Chapter 1 (Secs. 354–367, 368)

Corporate reorganizations generally can be classified as acquisitive reorganizations and as divisive reorganizations. The types of acquisitive reorganizations are as follows:

1. Statutory merger or consolidation (type A).
2. Stock for stock acquisition (type B).
3. Stock for asset acquisition (type C).

The types of divisive reorganizations (type D) are as follows:

1. One-step.
2. Two-step.

An acquisitive reorganization produces nontaxable treatment for the parties to the reorganization (i.e., acquired corporation, acquiring corporation, and shareholders) and a carryover basis to the shareholders and the corporations [see Secs. 354(a), 361 (a)].

The basis for the classification of a divisive reorganization as a one-step or a two-step divisive reorganization is whether the corporate division encompasses both Secs. 355 and 368 or only Sec. 355.

A one-step divisive reorganization is a corporate division which is in compliance with the provisions of Sec. 355. The transaction involved is the distribution of the stock of the subsidiary corporation or corporations. The transaction can take one of several forms. First, there can be a *spin-off* in which one corporation distributes the stock of a subsidiary corporation. In this form, no stock is turned in by the recipient shareholders. Second, there can be a *split-off* in which one corporation distributes the stock of a subsidiary in return for some, but not all, of its own stock. Third, there can be a *split-up* in which one corporation distributes the stock of two or more subsidiaries in complete liquidation. In this form, the recipient shareholders turn in all the stock of the transferor corporation.

Absent qualification as a one-step divisive reorganization, the distribution in each of the three forms has the following appearance.

Form	*Appearance*
Spin-off	Dividend
Split-off	Stock redemption
Split-up	Complete liquidation

The tax consequences must be evaluated for the three parties directly or indirectly involved in the one-step divisive reorganization (i.e., distributee, distributing corporation, and the controlled corporation). Section 355(a)(1) contains the general rule that such shareholders and security holders shall recognize no gain or loss on the distribution. Section 356(a)(1) contains the exception rule that if boot is received in an exchange transaction (i.e., split-off or split-up), gain is recongnized to the extent of the lower of the boot received or the realized gain. Section 356(b) contains the exception rule that if boot is received in a distribution transaction (i.e., spin-off), gain is recognized to the extent of the boot received. Loss is not recognized in an exchange or distribution transaction regardless of whether or not boot is received [see Sec. 356(c)]. The distributing corporation recognizes no gain or loss as a result of distributing the stock and securities of the controlled corporation, and there is no recognition effect on the controlled corporation.

A two-step divisive reorganization is a corporate reorganization which is in compliance with both the provisions of Sec. 368 (a)(1)(D) and Sec. 355. The first step consists of a qualifying asset transfer under Sec. 368(a)(1)(D) and the second step consists of the stock and securities transfer under Sec. 355 (i.e., the only step in a one-step divisive reorganization).

For the two-step divisive reorganization, the tax consequences of the first step are those of the transferor corporation and the transferee corporation. Section 361(a), which contains the rule for the transferor corporation, provides for no recognition of gain or loss on the transfer of assets if the corporation is a party to a reorganization and the exchange is pursuant to a plan of reorganization. Section 1032 provides that there is no recognition of gain or loss on the receipt of money or other property in exchange for stock.

Acquisitive reorganizations generally take one of the three forms mentioned above. While they do produce the same tax results (i.e., nonrecognition and a carryover basis) in the case of full qualification, structurally they are different and do provide different opportunities and limitations with respect to the form of the transaction.

The Type A acquisitive reorganization under Sec. 368(a)(1)(A) is referred to as a statutory merger or consolidation. The form can be depicted as follows:

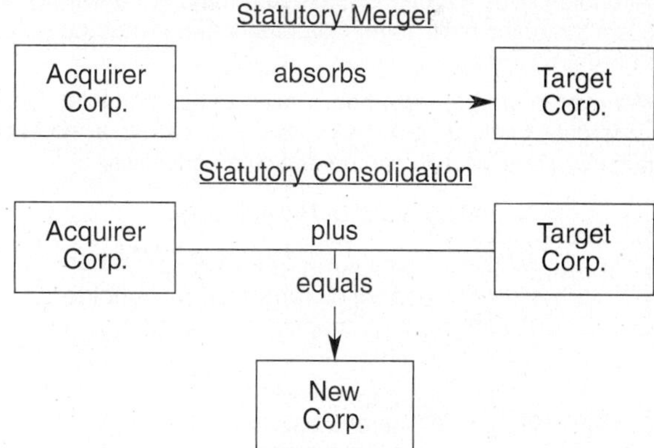

By operation of law, Target Corporation ceases to exist in the case of a statutory merger and both Acquirer and Target Corporations cease to exist in the case of a statutory consolidation. Acquirer Corporation is the survivor for the statutory merger and New Corporation is the survivor for the statutory consolidation.

The term "statutory" connotes that the merger or consolidation must comply with the requirements of the state law under which it is being consummated. Obviously, these requirements vary somewhat from state to state. Failure to meet the state law requirements results in the merger or consolidation not being a qualified Type A reorganization.

The Type A reorganization under state law provides Acquirer Corporation with substantial flexibility with respect to the form of the consideration to be used in acquiring Target Corporation (i.e., not limited only to voting stock). One must be cautious, however, that enough voting stock is received by Target shareholders so that the requisite *continuity of interest* is maintained. Thus, assuming that this continuity of interest is maintained, considerable boot can be used as consideration.

A major disadvantage of the Type A reorganization is the assumption by Acquirer Corporation of Target Corporation's liabilities. The potential burden such assumption can produce can be limited through the use of the triangular form of the Type A reorganization which can be depicted as follows:

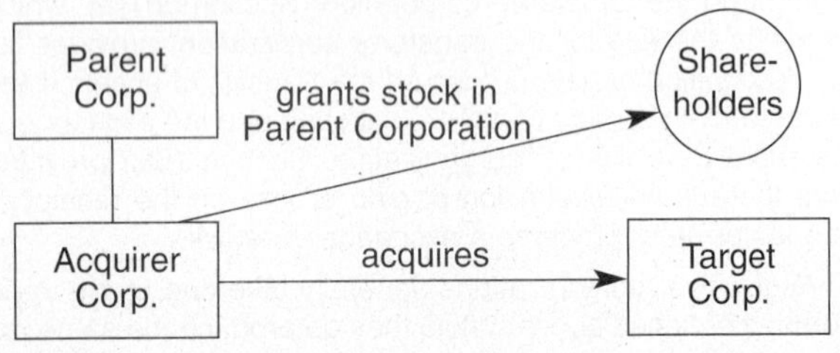

In this case, since the subsidiary is Acquirer Corporation, the assumed liabilities of Target Corporation become those of the subsidiary and Parent Corporation is effectively shielded. The use of the stock of Parent Corporation potentially achieves two objectives. First, the potential loss of control of the subsidiary (i.e., Acquirer Corporation) is avoided. Second, the shareholders of Target Corporation may be unwilling to accept the stock of Acquirer Corporation (i.e., want the stock of Parent Corporation).

An even more sophisticated version of the triangular Type A reorganization is permitted which is called a reverse triangular. This version can be depicted as follows:

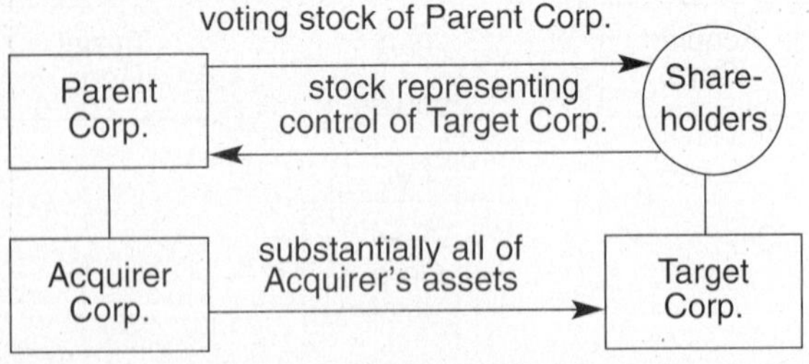

This version achieves the same purposes as the triangular reorganization with the additional benefit of the Target Corporation being the survivor rather than the original subsidiary (i.e., Acquirer Corporation). Quite often the original subsidiary is a newly-created corporation. Thus, permitting the Target Corporation to become the subsidiary of Parent Corporation enables retention of the identity of Target Corporation.

The authority for the triangular Type A reorganization appears in Sec. 368(a)(2)(D) [i.e., the authority to use the stock of Acquirer Corporation's parent]. Likewise, the authority for a reverse triangular Type A reorganization appears in Sec. 368(a)(2)(E). However, this authority is meaningless if state law will not permit such usage.

A Type B acquisitive reorganization is referred to as a stock-for-stock reorganization and can be depicted as follows:

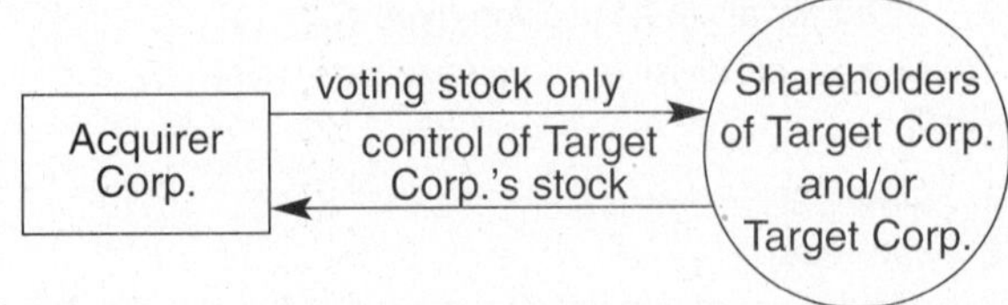

A major disadvantage of the Type A reorganization is the state law requirement that the reorganization must be approved by the board of directors and shareholders of both Acquirer Corporation and Target Corporation. This can be partially offset through the use of the triangular Type A reorganization (i.e., the shareholder of Acquirer Corporation is Parent Corporation). However, even in this circumstance, formal approval at the Target Corporation level still is required.

The Type B reorganization eliminates the necessity for shareholder approval at the Acquirer Corporation level (unless an adequate amount of unissued stock is not available). Equally beneficial, formal board and shareholder approval is not required at the Target Corporation level because the stock can be acquired from individual shareholders. Note that it is permissible to obtain Target Corporation stock both from Target Corporation shareholders and from Target Corporation itself (i.e., unissued stock).

The major disadvantage of the Type B form of reorganization is the rigidity regarding the form of the consideration Acquirer Corporation is permitted to use. Only voting stock can be used. The use of nonvoting stock or other boot to acquire the requisite 80 percent control will result in the failure to qualify as a Type B reorganization. Other related disadvantages are the usual problems associated with a minority interest if less than 100 percent of the stock of Target Corporation is acquired.

Section 368(a)(2)(C) permits the use of the triangular Type B reorganization which can be depicted as follows:

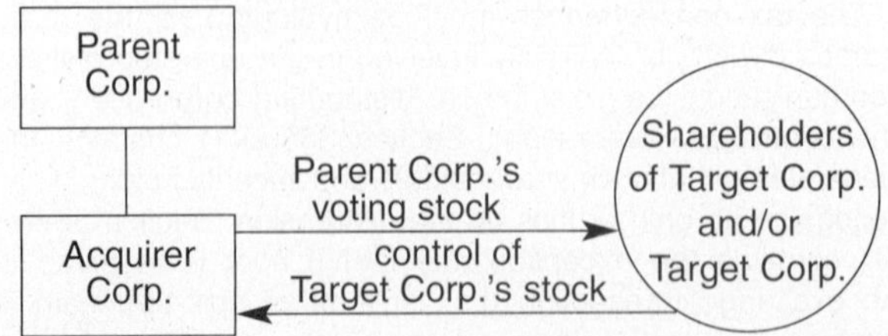

A Type C acquisitive reorganization is referred to as a stock-for-asset reorganization and can be depicted as follows:

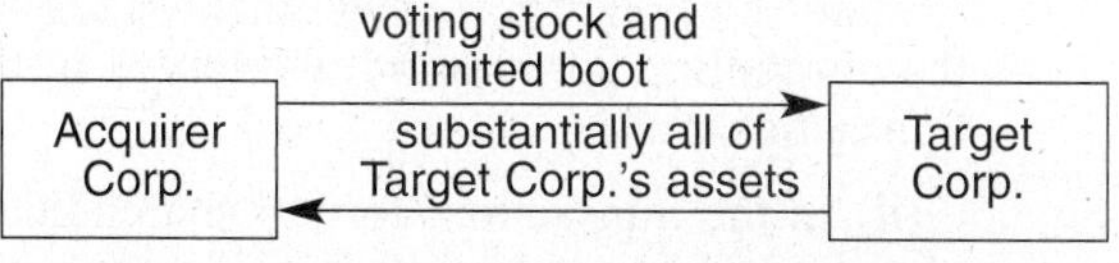

The Type C reorganization is more flexible with respect to the consideration used in that only 80 percent of the fair market value of the acquired assets need be acquired with voting stock. Note, however, that the choice of consideration used is less flexible than that for a Type A reorganization.

Another advantage of the Type C reorganization is the ability to specify the liabilities, if any, for which Acquirer is responsible. Thus, normally no problem with contingent or undisclosed liabilities is present.

All of the assets of Target Corporation do not have to be acquired. However, the assets acquired must be adequate to satisfy the "substantially all" provision.

Section 368(a)(2)(C) permits the use of the triangular Type C reorganization which can be depicted as follows:

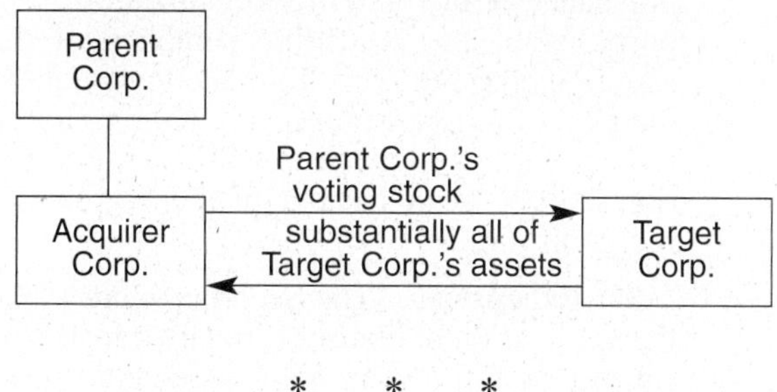

* * *

§ 368. Definitions relating to corporate reorganizations

(a) Reorganization.—

(1) In general.—For purposes of parts I and II and this part, the term "reorganization" means—

(A) a statutory merger or consolidation;

(B) the acquisition by one corporation, in exchange solely for all or a part of its voting stock (or in exchange solely for all or a part of the voting stock of a corporation which is in control of the acquiring corporation), of stock of another corporation if, immediately after the acquisition, the acquiring corporation has control of such other corporation (whether or not such acquiring corporation had control immediately before the acquisition);

(C) the acquisition by one corporation, in exchange solely for all or a part of its voting stock (or in exchange solely for all or a part of the voting stock of a corporation which is in control of the acquiring corporation), of substantially all of the properties of another corporation, but in determining whether the exchange is solely for stock the assumption by the acquiring corporation of a liability of the other, or the fact that property acquired is subject to a liability, shall be disregarded;

(D) a transfer by a corporation of all or a part of its assets to another corporation if immediately after the transfer the transferor, or one or more of its shareholders (including persons who were shareholders immediately before the transfer), or any combination thereof, is in control of the corporation to which the assets are transferred; but only if, in pursuance of the plan, stock or securities of the corporation to which the assets are transferred are distributed in a transaction which qualifies under section 354, 355, or 356;

(E) a recapitalization;

(F) a mere change in identity, form, or place of organization of one corporation, however effected; or

(G) a transfer by a corporation of all or part of its assets to another corporation in a title 11 or similar case; but only if, in pursuance of the plan, stock or securities of the corporation to which the assets are transferred are distributed in a transaction which qualifies under section 354, 355, or 356.

(2) Special rules relating to paragraph (1).—

(A) Reorganizations described in both paragraph (1)(C) and paragraph (1)(D).—If a transaction is described in both paragraph (1)(C) and paragraph (1)(D), then, for purposes of this subchapter (other than for purposes of subparagraph (C)), such transaction shall be treated as described only in paragraph (1)(D).

(B) Additional consideration in certain paragraph (1)(C) cases.—If—

(i) one corporation acquires substantially all of the properties of another corporation,

(ii) the acquisition would qualify under paragraph (1)(C) but for the fact that the acquiring corporation exchanges money or other property in addition to voting stock, and

(iii) the acquiring corporation acquires, solely for voting stock described in paragraph (1)(C), property of the other corporation having a fair market value which is at least 80 percent of the fair market value of all of the property of the other corporation,

then such acquisition shall (subject to subparagraph (A) of this paragraph) be treated as qualifying under paragraph (1)(C). Solely for the purpose of determining whether clause (iii) of the preceding sentence applies, the amount of any liability assumed by the acquiring corporation, and the amount of any liability to which any property acquired by the acquiring corporation is subject, shall be treated as money paid for the property.

(C) Transfers of assets or stock to subsidiaries in certain paragraph (1)(A), (1)(B), (1)(C), and (1)(G) cases.—A transaction otherwise qualifying under paragraph (1)(A), (1)(B), or (1)(C) shall not be disqualified by reason of the fact that part or all of the assets or stock which were acquired in the transaction are transferred to a corporation controlled by the corporation acquiring such assets or stock. A similar rule shall apply to a transaction otherwise qualifying under paragraph (1)(G) where the requirements of subparagraphs (A) and (B) of section 354(b)(1) are met with respect to the acquisition of the assets.

(D) Use of stock of controlling corporation in paragraph (1)(A) and (1)(G) cases.—The acquisition by one corporation, in exchange for stock of a corporation (referred to in this subparagraph as "controlling corporation") which is in control of the acquiring corporation, of substantially all of the properties of another corporation shall not disqualify a transaction under paragraph (1)(A) or (1)(G) if—

(i) no stock of the acquiring corporation is used in the transaction, and

(ii) in the case of a transaction under paragraph (1)(A), such transaction would have qualified under paragraph (1)(A) had the merger been into the controlling corporation.

(E) Statutory merger using voting stock of corporation controlling merged corporation.—A transaction otherwise qualifying under paragraph (1)(A) shall not be disqualified by reason of the fact that stock of a corporation (referred to in this subparagraph as the "controlling corporation") which before the merger was in control of the merged corporation is used in the transaction, if—

(i) after the transaction, the corporation surviving the merger holds substantially all of its properties and of the properties of the merged corporation (other than stock of the controlling corporation distributed in the transaction); and

(ii) in the transaction, former shareholders of the surviving corporation exchanged, for an amount of voting stock of the controlling corporation, an amount of stock in the surviving corporation which constitutes control of such corporation.

* * *

(G) Distribution requirement for paragraph (1)(C).—

(i) In general.—A transaction shall fail to meet the requirements of paragraph (1)(C) unless the acquired corporation distributes the stock, securities, and other properties it receives, as well as its other properties, in pursuance of the plan of reorganization. "For purposes of the preceding sentence, if the acquired corporation is liquidated pursuant to the plan of reorganization, any distribution to its creditors in connection with such liquidation shall be treated as pursuant to the plan of reorganization."

(ii) Exception.—The Secretary may waive the application of clause (i) to any transaction subject to any conditions the Secretary may prescribe.

(H) Special rule for determining whether certain transactions are qualified under paragraph (1)(D).—For purposes of determining whether a transaction qualifies under paragraph (1)(D)—

(i) in the case of a transaction with respect to which the requirements of subparagraphs (A) and (B) of section 354(b)(1) are met, the term "control" has the meaning given such term by section 304(c), and

(ii) in the case of a transaction with respect to which the requirements of section 355 (or so much of section 356 as relates to section 355) are met, the fact that the shareholders of the distributing corporation dispose of part or all of the distributed stock shall not be taken into account.

* * *

(b) Party to a reorganization.—For purposes of this part, the term "a party to a reorganization" includes—

(1) a corporation resulting from a reorganization, and

(2) both corporations, in the case of a reorganization resulting from the acquisition by one corporation of stock or properties of another.

In the case of a reorganization qualifying under paragraph (1)(B) or (1)(C) of subsection (a), if the stock exchanged for the stock or properties is stock of a corporation which is in control of the acquiring corporation, the term "a party to a reorganization" includes the corporation so controlling the acquiring corporation. In the case of a reorganization qualifying under paragraph (1)(A), (1)(B), (1)(C), or (1)(G) of subsection (a) by reason of paragraph (2)(C) of subsection (a), the term "a party to a reorganization" includes the corporation controlling the corporation to which the acquired assets or stock are transferred. In the case of a reorganization qualifying under paragraph (1)(A) or (1)(G) of subsection (a) by reason of paragraph (2)(D) of that subsection, the term "a party to a reorganization" includes the controlling corporation referred to in such paragraph (2)(D). In the case of a reorganization qualifying under subsection (a)(1)(A) by reason of subsection (a)(2)(E), the term "party to a reorganization" includes the controlling corporation referred to in subsection (a)(2)(E).

(c) Control defined.—For purposes of part I (other than section 304), part II, this part, and part V, the term "control" means the ownership of stock possessing at least 80 percent of the total combined voting power of all classes of stock entitled to vote and at least 80 percent of the total number of shares of all other classes of stock of the corporation.

PART IV—INSOLVENCY REORGANIZATIONS*

PART V—CARRYOVERS

Editorial Summary

Corporate Carryovers

Subchapter C of Chapter 1 (Secs. 381–384)

Frequent legislative changes by Congress has kept the provisions and the related planning opportunities associated with corporate carryovers for successor corporations in a state of fluctuation. The most recent substantive changes were made by the Tax Reform Act of 1986 and the Revenue Act of 1987.

Section 381 contains the general rules covering the carryover of corporate attributes associated with certain liquidations and reorganizations. Note that Sec. 381 does not deal with all corporate attributes [see Sec. 381(c)] or with all liquidations and reorganizations [see Sec. 381 (a)].

Section 382 deals with the narrower topic of the carryover of a net operating loss and whether the requisite continuity of interest is present. Absent the requisite continuity of interest, the acquiring corporation will not be able to fully use the net operating loss of the acquired corporation. The Tax Reform Act of 1986 completely revamped the rules for NOL carryovers. In addition to covering NOL carryovers, new Sec. 382 also deals with certain built-in losses.

Section 382 deals with two continuity factors. These are the continuity of business enterprise and the continuity of interest. The former of these factors has the potential for creating the greater damage to the taxpayer. Generally, if the continuity of the business enterprise (i.e., the "new corporation" must continue the business enterprise of the "old corporation") requirement is not satisfied, then none of the net operating loss carryforward can be used [see Sec. 382(c)]. Continuing the business enterprise entails the continuation of the loss corporation's historical business or the use of a significant portion of the loss corporation's assets in a business. The continuity of business enterprise requirement must be satisfied for a two-year period following an owner shift or equity structure shift (as discussed below).

In dealing with the continuity of interest factor, Sec. 382 provides two types of ownership changes that must be evaluated. These are as follows:

1. Owners shift [see Sec. 382(g)(1) and (2)].
2. Equity structure shift [see Sec. 382(g)(1) and (3)].

If either type of ownership change occurs, the ability to use the NOL carryforward is limited. The general thrust of Sec. 382 is that the NOL carryover of a corporation will be fully allowed only if there has been no ownership change. If there has been an ownership change, then the NOL carryover that can be used in the current taxable year to offset taxable income is limited to the following [see Sec. 382(b)]:

Value of corporation's stock on the date of ownerships change × Prescribed interest rate

A key to deciding whether an ownership change has occurred is the testing period (i.e., the period of time over which owner

*Omitted.

shifts or equity structure shifts are summed in making the cumulative calculation). Generally, the testing period is a three-year period [see Sec. 382(i)].

§ 381. Carryovers in certain corporate acquisitions

(a) General rule.—In the case of the acquisition of assets of a corporation by another corporation—

(1) in a distribution to such other corporation to which section 332 (relating to liquidations of subsidiaries) applies; or

(2) in a transfer to which section 361 (relating to nonrecognition of gain or loss to corporations) applies, but only if the transfer is in connection with a reorganization described in subparagraph (A), (C), (D), (F), or (G) of section 368(a)(1),

the acquiring corporation shall succeed to and take into account, as of the close of the day of distribution or transfer, the items described in subsection (c) of the distributor or transferor corporation, subject to the conditions and limitations specified in subsections (b) and (c). For purposes of the preceding sentence, a reorganization shall be treated as meeting the requirements of subparagraph (D) or (G) of section 368(a)(1) only if the requirements of subparagraphs (A) and (B) of section 354(b)(1) are met.

(b) Operating rules.—Except in the case of an acquisition in connection with a reorganization described in subparagraph (F) of section 368(a)(1)—

(1) The taxable year of the distributor or transferor corporation shall end on the date of distribution or transfer.

(2) For purposes of this section, the date of distribution or transfer shall be the day on which the distribution or transfer is completed; except that, under regulations prescribed by the Secretary, the date when substantially all of the property has been distributed or transferred may be used if the distributor or transferor corporation ceases all operations, other than liquidating activities, after such date.

(3) The corporation acquiring property in a distribution or transfer described in subsection (a) shall not be entitled to carry back a net operating loss or a net capital loss for a taxable year ending after the date of distribution or transfer to a taxable year of the distributor or transferor corporation.

(c) Items of the distributor or transferor corporation.—The items referred to in subsection (a) are:

(1) Net operating loss carryovers.—The net operating loss carryovers determined under section 172, subject to the following conditions and limitations:

(A) The taxable year of the acquiring corporation to which the net operating loss carryovers of the distributor or transferor corporation are first carried shall be the first taxable year ending after the date of distribution or transfer.

(B) In determining the net operating loss deduction, the portion of such deduction attributable to the net operating loss carryovers of the distributor or transferor corporation to the first taxable year of the acquiring corporation ending after the date of distribution or transfer shall be limited to an amount which bears the same ratio to the taxable income (determined without regard to a net operating loss deduction) of the acquiring corporation in such taxable year as the number of days in the taxable year after the date of distribution or transfer bears to the total number of days in the taxable year.

(C) For the purpose of determining the amount of the net operating loss carryovers under section 172(b)(2), a net operating loss for a taxable year (hereinafter in this subparagraph referred to as the "loss year") of a distributor or transferor corporation which ends on or before the end of a loss year of the acquiring corporation shall be considered to be a net operating loss for a year prior to such loss year of the acquiring corporation. For the same purpose, the taxable income for a "prior taxable year" (as the term is used in section 172(b)(2)) shall be computed as provided in such section; except that, if the date of distribution or transfer is on a day other than the last day of a taxable year of the acquiring corporation—

(i) such taxable year shall (for the purpose of this subparagraph only) be considered to be 2 taxable years (hereinafter in this subparagraph referred to as the "pre-acquisition part year" and the "post-acquisition part year");

(ii) the pre-acquisition part year shall begin on the same day as such taxable year begins and shall end on the date of distribution or transfer;

(iii) the post-acquisition part year shall

begin on the day following the date of distribution or transfer and shall end on the same day as the end of such taxable year;

(iv) the taxable income for such taxable year (computed with the modifications specified in section 172(b)(2)(A) but without a net operating loss deduction) shall be divided between the pre-acquisition part year and the post-acquisition part year in proportion to the number of days in each;

(v) the net operating loss deduction for the pre-acquisition part year shall be determined as provided in section 172(b)(2)(B), but without regard to a net operating loss year of the distributor or transferor corporation; and

(vi) the net operating loss deduction for the post-acquisition part year shall be determined as provided in section 172(b)(2)(B).

(2) Earnings and profits.—In the case of a distribution or transfer described in subsection (a)—

(A) the earnings and profits or deficit in earnings and profits, as the case may be, of the distributor or transferor corporation shall, subject to subparagraph (B), be deemed to have been received or incurred by the acquiring corporation as of the close of the date of the distribution or transfer; and

(B) a deficit in earnings and profits of the distributor, transferor, or acquiring corporation shall be used only to offset earnings and profits accumulated after the date of transfer. For this purpose, the earnings and profits for the taxable year of the acquiring corporation in which the distribution or transfer occurs shall be deemed to have been accumulated after such distribution or transfer in an amount which bears the same ratio to the undistributed earnings and profits of the acquiring corporation for such taxable year (computed without regard to any earnings and profits received from the distributor or transferor corporation, as described in subparagraph (A) of this paragraph) as the number of days in the taxable year after the date of distribution or transfer bears to the total number of days in the taxable year.

(3) Capital loss carryover.—The capital loss carryover determined under section 1212, subject to the following conditions and limitations:

(A) The taxable year of the acquiring corporation to which the capital loss carryover of the distributor or transferor corporation is first carried shall be the first taxable year ending after the date of distribution or transfer.

(B) The capital loss carryover shall be a short-term capital loss in the taxable year determined under subparagraph (A) but shall be limited to an amount which bears the same ratio to the capital gain net income (determined without regard to a short-term capital loss attributable to capital loss carryover), if any, of the acquiring corporation in such taxable year as the number of days in the taxable year after the date of distribution or transfer bears to the total number of days in the taxable year.

(C) For purposes of determining the amount of such capital loss carryover to taxable years following the taxable year determined under subparagraph (A), the capital gain net income in the taxable year determined under subparagraph (A) shall be considered to be an amount equal to the amount determined under subparagraph (B).

(4) Method of accounting.—The acquiring corporation shall use the method of accounting used by the distributor or transferor corporation on the date of distribution or transfer unless different methods were used by several distributor or transferor corporations or by a distributor or transferor corporation and the acquiring corporation. If different methods were used, the acquiring corporation shall use the method or combination of methods of computing taxable income adopted pursuant to regulations prescribed by the Secretary.

(5) Inventories.—In any case in which inventories are received by the acquiring corporation, such inventories shall be taken by such corporation (in determining its income) on the same basis on which such inventories were taken by the distributor or transferor corporation, unless different methods were used by several distributor or transferor corporations or by a distributor or transferor corporation and the acquiring corporation. If different methods were used, the acquiring corporation shall use the method or combination of methods of taking inventory adopted pursuant to regulations prescribed by the Secretary.

(6) Method of computing depreciation allowance.—The acquiring corporation shall be treated as the distributor or transferor corporation for purposes of computing the depreciation allowance under sections 167 and 168 on property acquired in a distribution or transfer with respect to so much of the basis in the hands of the acquiring corporation as does not exceed the adjusted basis in the hands of the distributor or transferor corporation.

*(8) **Installment method.**—If the acquiring corporation acquires installment obligations (the income from which the distributor or transferor corporation reports on the installment basis under section 453) the acquiring corporation shall, for purposes of section 453, be treated as if it were the distributor or transferor corporation.

(9) Amortization of bond discount or premium.—If the acquiring corporation assumes liability for bonds of the distributor or transferor corporation issued at a discount or premium, the acquiring corporation shall be treated as the distributor or transferor corporation after the date of distribution or transfer for purposes of determining the amount of amortization allowable or includible with respect to such discount or premium.

(10) Treatment of certain mining development and exploration expenses of distributor or transferor corporation.—The acquiring corporation shall be entitled to deduct, as if it were the distributor or transferor corporation, expenses deferred under section 616 (relating to certain development expenditures) if the distributor or transferor corporation has so elected.

(11) Contributions to pension plans, employees' annuity plans, and stock bonus and profit-sharing plans.—The acquiring corporation shall be considered to be the distributor or transferor corporation after the date of distribution or transfer for the purpose of determining the amounts deductible under section 404 with respect to pension plans, employees' annuity plans, and stock bonus and profit-sharing plans.

(12) Recovery of tax benefit items.—If the acquiring corporation is entitled to the recovery of any amounts previously deducted by (or allowable as credits to) the distributor or transferor corporation, the acquiring corporation shall succeed to the treatment under section 111 which would apply to such amounts in the hands of the distributor or transferor corporation.

(13) Involuntary conversions under section 1033.—The acquiring corporation shall be treated as the distributor or transferor corporation after the date of distribution or transfer for purposes of applying section 1033.

(14) Dividend carryover to personal holding company.—The dividend carryover (described in section 564) to taxable years ending after the date of distribution or transfer.

(16) Certain obligations of distributor or transferor corporation.—If the acquiring corporation—

(A) assumes an obligation of the distributor or transferor corporation which, after the date of the distribution or transfer, gives rise to a liability, and

(B) such liability, if paid or accrued by the distributor or transferor corporation, would have been deductible in computing its taxable income,

the acquiring corporation shall be entitled to deduct such items when paid or accrued, as the case may be, as if such corporation were the distributor or transferor corporation. A corporation which would have been an acquiring corporation under this section if the date of distribution or transfer had occurred on or after the effective date of the provisions of this subchapter applicable to a liquidation or reorganization, as the case may be, shall be entitled, even though the date of distribution or transfer occurred before such effective date, to apply this paragraph with respect to amounts paid or accrued in taxable years beginning after December 31, 1953, on account of such obligations of the distributor or transferor corporation. This paragraph shall not apply if such obligations are reflected in the amount of stock, securities, or property transferred by the acquiring corporation to the transferor corporation for the property of the transferor corporation.

(17) Deficiency dividend of personal holding company.—If the acquiring corporation pays a deficiency dividend (as defined in section 547(d)) with respect to the distributor or transferor corporation, such distributor or transferor corporation shall, with respect to such payments, be entitled to the deficiency dividend deduction provided in section 547.

(18) Percentage depletion on extraction of ores or minerals from the waste or residue of prior mining.—The acquiring corporation shall be considered to be the distributor or transferor corporation for the purpose of determining the

*Editorial comment: There is no paragraph (7).

**Editorial comment: There is no paragraph 15.

applicability of section 613(c)(3) (relating to extraction of ores or minerals from the ground).

(19) Charitable contributions in excess of prior years' limitations.—Contributions made in the taxable year ending on the date of distribution or transfer and the 4 prior taxable years by the distributor or transferor corporation in excess of the amount deductible under section 170(b) (2) for such taxable years shall be deductible by the acquiring corporation for its taxable years which begin after the date of distribution or transfer, subject to the limitations imposed in section 170(b)(2). In applying the preceding sentence, each taxable year of the distributor or transferor corporation beginning on or before the date of distribution or transfer shall be treated as a prior taxable year with reference to the acquiring corporation's taxable years beginning after such date.

* * *

(24) Credit under section 38.—The acquiring corporation shall take into account (to the extent proper to carry out the purposes of this section and section 38, and under such regulations as may be prescribed by the Secretary) the items required to be taken into account for purposes of section 38 in respect of the distributor or transferor corporation.

(25) Credit under section 53.—The acquiring corporation shall take into account (to the extent proper to carry out the purposes of this section and section 53, and under such regulations as may be prescribed by the Secretary) the items required to be taken into account for purposes of section 53 in respect of the distributor or transferor corporation.

(26) Enterprise zone provisions.—The acquiring corporation shall take into account (to the extent proper to carry out the purposes of this section and subchapter U, and under such regulations as may be prescribed by the Secretary) the items required to be taken into account for purposes of subchapter U in respect of the distributor or transferor corporation.

* * *

§ 382. Limitation on net operating loss carryforwards and certain built-in losses following ownership change

(a) General rule.—The amount of the taxable income of any new loss corporation for any post-change year which may be offset by pre-change losses shall not exceed the section 382 limitation for such year.

(b) Section 382 limitation.—For purposes of this section—

(1) In general.—Except as otherwise provided in this section, the section 382 limitation for any post-change year is an amount equal to—

(A) the value of the old loss corporation, multiplied by

(B) the long-term tax-exempt rate.

(2) Carryforward of unused limitation.—If the section 382 limitation for any post-change year exceeds the taxable income of the new loss corporation for such year which was offset by pre-change losses, the section 382 limitation for the next post-change year shall be increased by the amount of such excess.

(3) Special rule for post-change year which includes change date.—In the case of any post-change year which includes the change date—

(A) Limitation does not apply to taxable income before change.—Subsection (a) shall not apply to the portion of the taxable income for such year which is allocable to the period in such year on or before the change date. Except as provided in subsection (h)(5) and in regulations, taxable income shall be allocated ratably to each day in the year.

(B) Limitation for period after change.—For purposes of applying the limitation of subsection (a) to the remainder of the taxable income for such year, the section 382 limitation shall be an amount which bears the same ratio to such limitation (determined without regard to this paragraph) as—

(i) the number of days in such year after the change date, bears to

(ii) the total number of days in such year.

(c) Carryforwards disallowed if continuity of business requirements not met.—

(1) In general.—Except as provided in paragraph (2), if the new loss corporation does not continue the business enterprise of the old loss corporation at all times during the 2-year period beginning on the change date, the section 382 limitation for any post-change year shall be zero.

(2) Exception for certain gains.—The section 382 limitation for any post-change year shall not be less than the sum of—

(A) any increase in such limitation under—

(i) subsection (h)(1)(A) for recognized built-in gains for such year, and

(ii) subsection (h)(1)(C) for gain recognized by reason of an election under section 338, plus

(B) any increase in such limitation under subsection (b)(2) for amounts described in subparagraph (A) which are carried forward to such year.

(d) Pre-change loss and post-change year.—For purposes of this section—

(1) Pre-change loss.—The term "pre-change loss" means—

(A) any net operating loss carryforward of the old loss corporation to the taxable year ending with the ownership change or in which the change date occurs, and

(B) the net operating loss of the old loss corporation for the taxable year in which the ownership change occurs to the extent such loss is allocable to the period in such year on or before the change date.

Except as provided in subsection (h)(5) and in regulations, the net operating loss shall, for purposes of subparagraph (B), be allocated ratably to each day in the year.

(2) Post-change year.—The term "post-change year" means any taxable year ending after the change date.

(e) Value of old loss corporation.—For purposes of this section—

(1) In general.—Except as otherwise provided in this subsection, the value of the old loss corporation is the value of the stock of such corporation (including any stock described in section 1504(a)(4)) immediately before the ownership change.

(2) Special rule in the case of redemption or other corporate contraction.—If a redemption or other corporate contraction occurs in connection with an ownership change, the value under paragraph (1) shall be determined after taking such redemption or other corporate contraction into account.

* * *

(f) Long-term tax-exempt rate.—For purposes of this section—

(1) In general.—The long-term tax-exempt rate shall be the highest of the adjusted Federal long-term rates in effect for any month in the 3-calendar-month period ending with the calendar month in which the change date occurs.

(2) Adjusted federal long-term rate.—For purposes of paragraph (1), the term "adjusted Federal long-term rate" means the Federal long-term rate determined under section 1274(d), except that—

(A) paragraphs (2) and (3) thereof shall not apply, and

(B) such rate shall be properly adjusted for differences between rates on long-term taxable and tax-exempt obligations.

(g) Ownership change.—For purposes of this section—

(1) In general.—There is an ownership change if, immediately after any owner shift involving a 5-percent shareholder or any equity structure shift—

(A) the percentage of the stock of the loss corporation owned by 1 or more 5-percent shareholders has increased by more than 50 percentage points, over

(B) the lowest percentage of stock of the loss corporation (or any predecessor corporation) owned by such shareholders at any time during the testing period.

(2) Owner shift involving 5-percent shareholder.—There is an owner shift involving a 5-percent shareholder if—

(A) there is any change in the respective ownership of stock of a corporation, and

(B) such change affects the percentage of stock of such corporation owned by any person who is a 5-percent shareholder before or after such change.

(3) Equity structure shift defined.—

(A) In general.—The term "equity structure shift" means any reorganization (within the meaning of section 368). Such term shall not include—

(i) any reorganization described in subparagraph (D) or (G) of section 368(a)(1) unless the requirements of section 354(b)(1) are met, and

(ii) any reorganization described in subparagraph (F) of section 368(a)(1).

(B) Taxable reorganization-type transactions, etc.—To the extent provided in regulations, the term "equity structure shift" includes taxable reorganization-type transactions, public offerings, and similar transactions.

(4) Special rules for application of subsection.—

(A) Treatment of less than 5-percent shareholders.—Except as provided in subparagraphs (B)(i) and (C), in determining whether an ownership change has occurred, all stock owned by shareholders of a corporation who are not 5-percent shareholders of such corporation shall be treated as stock owned by 1 5-percent shareholder of such corporation.

(B) Coordination with equity structure shifts.—For purposes of determining whether an equity structure shift (or subsequent transaction) is an ownership change—

(i) Less than 5-percent shareholders.—Subparagraph (A) shall be applied separately with respect to each group of shareholders (immediately before such equity structure shift) of each corporation which was a party to the reorganization involved in such equity structure shift.

(ii) Acquisitions of stock.—Unless a different proportion is established, acquisitions of stock after such equity structure shift shall be treated as being made proportionately from all shareholders immediately before such acquisition.

(C) Coordination with other owner shifts.—Except as provided in regulations, rules similar to the rules of subparagraph (B) shall apply in determining whether there has been an owner shift involving a 5-percent shareholder and whether such shift (or subsequent transaction) results in an ownership change.

(i) shall be treated as having acquired such stock on the 1st day of his 1st succeeding taxable year, and

(ii) shall not be treated as having owned such stock during any prior period.

For purposes of the preceding sentence, the term "50-percent shareholder" means any person owning 50 percent or more of the stock of the corporation at any time during the 3-year period ending on the last day of the taxable year with respect to which the stock was so treated.

(D) Treatment of worthless stock.—If any stock held by a 50-percent shareholder is treated by such shareholder as becoming worthless during any taxable year of such shareholder and such stock is held by such shareholder as of the close of such taxable year, for purposes of determining whether an ownership change occurs after the close of such taxable year, such shareholder—

(i) shall be treated as having acquired such stock on the 1st day of his 1st succeeding taxable year, and

(ii) shall not be treated as having owned such stock during any prior period.

For purposes of the preceding sentence, the term "50-percent shareholder" means any person owning 50 percent or more of the stock of the corporation at any time during the 3-year period ending on the last day of the taxable year with respect to which the stock was so treated.

(h) Special rules for built-in gains and losses and section 338 gains.—For purposes of this section—

(1) In general.—

(A) Net unrealized built-in gain.—

(i) In general.—If the old loss corporation has a net unrealized built-in gain, the section 382 limitation for any recognition period taxable year shall be increased by the recognized built-in gains for such taxable year.

(ii) Limitation.—The increase under clause (i) for any recognition period taxable year shall not exceed—

(I) the net unrealized built-in gain, reduced by

(II) recognized built-in gains for prior years ending in the recognition period.

(B) Net unrealized built-in loss.—

(i) In general.—If the old loss corporation has a net unrealized built-in loss, the recognized built-in loss for any recognition period taxable year shall be subject to limitation under this section in the same manner as if such loss were a pre-change loss.

(ii) Limitation.—Clause (i) shall apply to recognized built-in losses for any recognition period taxable year only to the extent such losses do not exceed—

(I) the net unrealized built-in loss, reduced by

(II) recognized built-in losses for prior taxable years ending in the recognition period.

(C) **Special rules for certain section 338 gains.**—If an election under section 338 is made in connection with an ownership change and the net unrealized built-in gain is zero by reason of paragraph (3)(B), then, with respect to such change, the section 382 limitation for the post-change year in which gain is recognized by reason of such election shall be increased by the lesser of—

(i) the recognized built-in gains by reason of such election, or

(ii) the net unrealized built-in gain (determined without regard to paragraph (3)(B)).

(2) **Recognized built-in gain and loss.**—

(A) **Recognized built-in gain.**—The term "recognized built-in gain" means any gain recognized during the recognition period on the disposition of any asset to the extent the new loss corporation establishes that—

(i) such asset was held by the old loss corporation immediately before the change date, and

(ii) such gain does not exceed the excess of —

(I) the fair market value of such asset on the change date, over

(II) the adjusted basis of such asset on such date.

(B) **Recognized built-in loss.**—The term "recognized built-in loss" means any loss recognized during the recognition period on the disposition of any asset except to the extent the new loss corporation establishes that—

(i) such asset was not held by the old loss corporation immediately before the change date, or

(ii) such loss exceeds the excess of—

(I) the adjusted basis of such asset on the change date, over

(II) the fair market value of such asset on such date.

Such term includes any amount allowable as depreciation, amortization, or depletion for any period within the recognition period except to the extent the new loss corporation establishes that the amount so allowable is not attributable to the excess described in clause (ii).

(3) **Net unrealized built-in gain and loss defined.**—

(A) **Net unrealized built-in gain and loss.**—

(i) **In general.**—The terms "net unrealized built-in gain" and "net unrealized built-in loss" mean, with respect to any old loss corporation, the amount by which—

(I) the fair market value of the assets of such corporation immediately before an ownership change is more or less, respectively, than

(II) the aggregate adjusted basis of such assets at such time.

(ii) **Special rule for redemptions or other corporate contractions.**—If a redemption or other corporate contraction occurs in connection with an ownership change, to the extent provided in regulations, determinations under clause (i) shall be made after taking such redemption or other corporate contraction into account.

(B) **Threshold requirement.**—

(i) **In general.**—If the amount of the net unrealized built-in gain or net unrealized built-in loss (determined without regard to this subparagraph) of any old loss corporation is not greater than the lesser of—

(I) 15 percent of the amount determined for purposes of subparagraph (A)(i)(I), or

(II) $10,000,000,

the net unrealized built-in gain or net unrealized built-in loss shall be zero.

(ii) **Cash and cash items not taken into account.**—In computing any net unrealized built-in gain or net unrealized built-in loss under clause (i), except as provided in regulations, there shall not be taken into account—

(I) any cash or cash item, or

(II) any marketable security which has a value which does not substantially differ from adjusted basis.

(4) **Disallowed loss allowed as a carryforward.**—If a deduction for any portion of a recognized built-in loss is disallowed for any post-change year, such portion—

(A) shall be carried forward to subsequent

taxable years under rules similar to the rules for the carrying forward of net operating losses (or to the extent the amount so disallowed is attributable to capital losses, under rules similar to the rules for the carrying forward of net capital losses), but

(B) shall be subject to limitation under this section in the same manner as a pre-change loss.

(5) Special rules for post-change year which includes change date.—For purposes of subsection (b)(3)—

(A) in applying subparagraph (A) thereof, taxable income shall be computed without regard to recognized built-in gains to the extent such gains increased the section 382 limitation for the year (or recognized built-in losses to the extent such losses are treated as pre-change losses), and gain described in paragraph (1)(C), for the year, and

(B) in applying subparagraph (B) thereof, the section 382 limitation shall be computed without regard to recognized built-in gains, and gain described in paragraph (1)(C), for the year.

(6) Treatment of certain built-in items—

(A) Income items.—Any item of income which is properly taken into account during the recognition period but which is attributable to periods before the change date shall be treated as a recognized built-in gain for the taxable year in which it is properly taken into account.

(B) Deduction items.—Any amount which is allowable as a deduction during the recognition period (determined without regard to any carryover) but which is attributable to periods before the change date shall be treated as a recognized built-in loss for the taxable year for which it is allowable as a deduction.

(C) Adjustments.—The amount of the net unrealized built-in gain or loss shall be properly adjusted for amounts which would be treated as recognized built-in gains or losses under this paragraph if such amounts were properly taken into account (or allowable as a deduction) during the recognition period.

(7) Recognition period, etc.—

(A) Recognition period.—The term "recognition period" means, with respect to any ownership change, the 5-year period beginning on the change date.

(B) Recognition period taxable year.—The term "recognition period taxable year" means any taxable year any portion of which is in the recognition period.

(8) Determination of fair market value in certain cases.—If 80 percent or more in value of the stock of a corporation is acquired in 1 transaction (or in a series of related transactions during any 12-month period), for purposes of determining the net unrealized built-in loss, the fair market value of the assets of such corporation shall not exceed the grossed up amount paid for such stock properly adjusted for indebtedness of the corporation and other relevant items.

(9) Tax-free exchanges or transfers.—The Secretary shall prescribe such regulations as may be necessary to carry out the purposes of this subsection where property held on the change date was acquired (or is subsequently transferred) in a transaction where gain or loss is not recognized (in whole or in part).

(i) Testing period.—For purposes of this section—

(1) 3-year period.—Except as otherwise provided in this section, the testing period is the 3-year period ending on the day of any owner shift involving a 5-percent shareholder or equity structure shift.

(2) Shorter period where there has been recent ownership change.—If there has been an ownership change under this section, the testing period for determining whether a 2nd ownership change has occurred shall not begin before the 1st day following the change date for such earlier ownership change.

(3) Shorter period where all losses arise after 3-year period begins.—The testing period shall not begin before the earlier of the 1st day of the 1st taxable year from which there is a carryforward of a loss or of an excess credit to the 1st post-change year or in the taxable year in which the transaction being tested occurs. Except as provided in regulations, this paragraph shall not apply to any loss corporation which has a net unrealized built-in loss (determined after application of subsection (h)(3)(B)).

(j) Change date.—For purposes of this section, the change date is—

(1) in the case where the last component of an ownership change is an owner shift involving a

5-percent shareholder, the date on which such shift occurs, and

(2) in the case where the last component of an ownership change is an equity structure shift, the date of the reorganization.

(k) Definitions and special rules.—For purposes of this section—

(1) Loss corporation.—The term "loss corporation" means a corporation entitled to use a net operating loss carryover or having a net operating loss for the taxable year in which the ownership change occurs. Except to the extent provided in regulations, such term includes any corporation with a net unrealized built-in loss.

(2) Old loss corporation.—The term "old loss corporation" means any corporation—

(A) with respect to which there is an ownership change, and

(B) which (before the ownership change) was a loss corporation.

(3) New loss corporation.—The term "new loss corporation" means a corporation which (after an ownership change) is a loss corporation. Nothing in this section shall be treated as implying that the same corporation may not be both the old loss corporation and the new loss corporation.

(4) Taxable income.—Taxable income shall be computed with the modifications set forth in section 172(d).

(5) Value.—The term "value" means fair market value.

(6) Rules relating to stock.—

(A) Preferred stock.—Except as provided in regulations and subsection (e), the term "stock" means stock other than stock described in section 1504(a)(4).

(B) Treatment of certain rights, etc.—The Secretary shall prescribe such regulations as may be necessary—

(i) to treat warrants, options, contracts to acquire stock, convertible debt interests, and other similar interests as stock, and

(ii) to treat stock as not stock.

(C) Determinations on basis of value.—Determinations of the percentage of stock of any corporation held by any person shall be made on the basis of value.

(7) 5-percent shareholder.—The term "5-percent shareholder" means any person holding 5-percent or more of the stock of the corporation at any time during the testing period.

(l) Certain additional operating rules.—For purposes of this section—

(1) Certain capital contributions not taken into account.—

(A) In general.—Any capital contribution received by an old loss corporation as part of a plan a principal purpose of which is to avoid or increase any limitation under this section shall not be taken into account for purposes of this section.

(B) Certain contributions treated as part of plan.—For purposes of subparagraph (A), any capital contribution made during the 2-year period ending on the change date shall, except as provided in regulations, be treated as part of a plan described in subparagraph (A).

(2) Ordering rules for application of section.—

(A) Coordination with section 172(b) carryover rules.—In the case of any pre-change loss for any taxable year (hereinafter in this subparagraph referred to as the "loss year") subject to limitation under this section, for purposes of determining under the 2nd sentence of section 172(b)(2) the amount of such loss which may be carried to any taxable year, taxable income for any taxable year shall be treated as not greater than—

(i) the section 382 limitation for such taxable year, reduced by

(ii) the unused pre-change losses for taxable years preceding the loss year.

Similar rules shall apply in the case of any credit or loss subject to limitation under section 383.

(B) Ordering rule for losses carried from same taxable year.—In any case in which—

(i) a pre-change loss of a loss corporation for any taxable year is subject to a section 382 limitation, and

(ii) a net operating loss of such corporation from such taxable year is not subject to such limitation,

taxable income shall be treated as having been offset first by the loss subject to such limitation.

(3) Operating rules relating to ownership of stock.—

(A) Constructive ownership.—Section 318 (relating to constructive ownership of stock) shall apply in determining ownership of stock, except that—

(i) paragraphs (1) and (5)(B) of section 318(a) shall not apply and an individual and all members of his family described in paragraph (1) of section 318(a) shall be treated as 1 individual for purposes of applying this section,

(ii) paragraph (2) of section 318(a) shall be applied—

(I) without regard to the 50-percent limitation contained in subparagraph (C) thereof, and

(II) except as provided in regulations, by treating stock attributed thereunder as no longer being held by the entity from which attributed,

(iii) paragraph (3) of section 318(a) shall be applied only to the extent provided in regulations, and

(iv) except to the extent provided in regulations, an option to acquire stock shall be treated as exercised if such exercise results in an ownership change, and

(v) in attributing stock from an entity under paragraph (2) of section 318(a), there shall not be taken into account—

(I) in the case of attribution from a corporation, stock which is not treated as stock for purposes of this section, or

(II) in the case of attribution from another entity, an interest in such entity similar to stock described in subclause (I).

A rule similar to the rule of clause (iv) shall apply in the case of any contingent purchase, warrant, convertible debt, put, stock subject to a risk of forfeiture, contract to acquire stock, or similar interests.

(B) Stock acquired by reason of death, gift, divorce, separation, etc.—If—

(i) the basis of any stock in the hands of any person is determined—

(I) under section 1014 (relating to property acquired from a decedent),

(II) section 1014 (relating to property acquired by a gift or transfer in trust), or

(III) section 1041(b)(2) (relating to transfers of property between spouses or incident to divorce).

(ii) stock is received by any person in satisfaction of a right to receive a pecuniary bequest, or

(iii) stock is acquired by a person pursuant to any divorce or separation instrument (within the meaning of section 71(b)(2)),

such person shall be treated as owning such stock during the period such stock was owned by the person from whom it was acquired.

(C) Certain changes in percentage ownership which are attributable to fluctuations in value not taken into account.—Except as provided in regulations, any change in proportionate ownership which is attributable solely to fluctuations in the relative fair market values of different classes of stock shall not be taken into account.

(4) Reduction in value where substantial non-business assets.—

(A) In general.—If, immediately after an ownership change, the new loss corporation has substantial nonbusiness assets, the value of the old loss corporation shall be reduced by the excess (if any) of—

(i) the fair market value of the nonbusiness assets of the old loss corporation, over

(ii) the nonbusiness asset share of indebtedness for which such corporation is liable.

(B) Corporation having substantial non-business assets.—For purposes of subparagraph (A)—

(i) In general.—The old loss corporation shall be treated as having substantial non-business assets if at least $\frac{1}{3}$ of the value of the total assets of such corporation consists of nonbusiness assets.

(ii) Exception for certain investment entities.—A regulated investment company to which part I of subchapter M applies, a real estate investment trust to which part II of subchapter M applies, or a REMIC to which part IV of subchapter M applies shall not be treated as a new loss corporation having substantial nonbusiness assets.

(C) Nonbusiness assets.—For purposes of this paragraph, the term "nonbusiness assets" means assets held for investment.

(D) Nonbusiness asset share.—For purposes of this paragraph, the nonbusiness asset share of the indebtedness of the corporation is an amount which bears the same ratio to such indebtedness as—

(i) the fair market value of the nonbusiness assets of the corporation, bears to

(ii) the fair market value of all assets of such corporation.

(E) Treatment of subsidiaries.—For purposes of this paragraph, stock and securities in any subsidiary corporation shall be disregarded and the parent corporation shall be deemed to own its ratable share of the subsidiary's assets. For purposes of the preceding sentence, a corporation shall be treated as a subsidiary if the parent owns 50 percent or more of the combined voting power of all classes of stock entitled to vote, and 50 percent or more of the total value of shares of all classes of stock.

* * *

(7) Coordination with alternative minimum tax.—The Secretary shall by regulation provide for the application of this section to the alternative tax net operating loss deduction under section 56 (d).

(8) Predecessor and successor entities.—Except as provided in regulations, any entity and any predecessor or successor entities of such entity shall be treated as 1 entity.

(m) Regulations.—The Secretary shall prescribe such regulations as may be necessary or appropriate to carry out the purposes of this section and section 383, including (but not limited to) regulations—

(1) providing for the application of this section and section 383 where an ownership change with respect to the old loss corporation is followed by an ownership change with respect to the new loss corporation, and

(2) providing for the application of this section and section 383 in the case of a short taxable year,

(3) providing for such adjustments to the application of this section and section 383 as is necessary to prevent the avoidance of the purposes of this section and section 383, including the avoidance of such purposes through the use of related persons, pass-thru entities, or other intermediaries,

(4) providing for the application of subsection (g)(4) where there is only 1 corporation involved, and

(5) providing, in the case of any group of corporations described in section 1563(a) (determined by substituting "50 percent" for "80 percent" each place it appears and determined without regard to paragraph (4) thereof), appropriate adjustments to value, built-in gain or loss, and other items so that items are not omitted or taken into account more than once.

(n) Special rule for certain ownership changes.—

(1) In general.—The limitation contained in subsection (a) shall not apply in the case of an ownership change which is pursuant to a restructuring plan of a taxpayer which—

(A) is required under a loan agreement or a commitment for a line of credit entered into with the Department of the Treasury under the Emergency Economic Stabilization Act of 2008, and

(B) is intended to result in a rationalization of the costs, capitalization, and capacity with respect to the manufacturing workforce of, and suppliers to, the taxpayer and its subsidiaries.

(2) Subsequent acquisitions.—Paragraph (1) shall not apply in the case of any subsequent ownership change unless such ownership change is described in such paragraph.

(3) Limitation based on control in corporation.—

(A) In general.—Paragraph (1) shall not apply in the case of any ownership change if, immediately after such ownership change, any person (other than a voluntary employees' beneficiary association under section 501(c)(9)) owns stock of the old loss corporation possessing 50 percent or more of the total combined voting power of all classes of stock entitled to vote, or of the total value of the stock of such corporation.

(B) Treatment of related persons.—

(i) In general.—Related persons shall be treated as a single person for purposes of this paragraph.

(ii) Related persons.—For purposes of clause (i), a person shall be treated as related to another person if—

(I) such person bears a relationship to such other person described in section 267 (b) or 707(b), or

(II) such persons are members of a group of persons acting in concert.

§ 383. Special limitations on certain excess credits, etc.

(a) Excess credits.—

(1) In general.—Under regulations, if an ownership change occurs with respect to a corporation, the amount of any excess credit for any taxable year which may be used in any post-change year shall be limited to an amount determined on the basis of the tax liability which is attributable to so much of the taxable income as does not exceed the section 382 limitation for such post-change year to the extent available after the application of section 382 and subsections (b) and (c) of this section.

(2) Excess credit.—For purposes of paragraph (1), the term "excess credit" means—

(A) any unused general business credit of the corporation under section 39, and

(B) any unused minimum tax credit of the corporation under section 53.

(b) Limitation on net capital loss.—If an ownership change occurs with respect to a corporation, the amount of any net capital loss under section 1212 for any taxable year before the 1st post-change year which may be used in any post-change year shall be limited under regulations which shall be based on the principles applicable under section 382. Such regulations shall provide that any such net capital loss used in a post-change year shall reduce the section 382 limitation which is applied to pre-change losses under section 382 for such year.

(c) Foreign tax credits.—If an ownership change occurs with respect to a corporation, the amount of any excess foreign taxes under section 904(c) for any taxable year before the 1st post-change taxable year shall be limited under regulations which shall be consistent with purposes of this section and section 382.

(d) Proration rules for year which includes change.—For purposes of this section, rules similar to the rules of subsections (b)(3) and (d)(l)(B) of section 382 shall apply.

(e) Definitions.—Terms used in this section shall have the same respective meanings as when used in section 382, except that appropriate adjustments shall be made to take into account that the limitations of this section apply to credits and net capital losses.

§ 384. Limitation on use of preacquisition losses to offset built-in gains

(a) General rule.—If—

(1) (A) a corporation acquires directly (or through 1 or more other corporations) control of another corporation, or

(B) the assets of a corporation are acquired by another corporation in a reorganization described in subparagraph (A), (C), or (D) of section 368(a)(1), and

(2) either of such corporations is a gain corporation,

income for any recognition period taxable year (to the extent attributable to recognized built-in gains) shall not be offset by any preacquisition loss (other than a preacquisition loss of the gain corporation).

(b) Exception where corporations under common control.—

(1) In general.—Subsection (a) shall not apply to the preacquisition loss of any corporation if such corporation and the gain corporation were members of the same controlled group at all times during the 5-year period ending on the acquisition date.

(2) Controlled group.—For purposes of this subsection, the term "controlled group" means a controlled group of corporations (as defined in section 1563(a)); except that—

(A) "more than 50 percent" shall be substituted for "at least 80 percent" each place it appears,

(B) the ownership requirements of section 1563(a) must be met both with respect to voting power and value, and

(C) the determination shall be made without regard to subsection (a)(4) of section 1563.

(3) Shorter period where corporations not in existence for 5 years.—If either of the corporations referred to in paragraph (1) was not in existence throughout the 5-year period referred to in paragraph (1), the period during which such corporation was in existence (or if both, the shorter of such periods) shall be substituted for such 5-year period.

(c) Definitions.—For purposes of this section—

(1) **Recognized built-in gain.**—

(A) **In general.**—The term "recognized built- in gain" means any gain recognized during the recognition period on the disposition of any asset except to the extent the gain corporation (or, in any case described in subsection (a)(1)(b), the acquiring corporation) establishes that—

(i) such asset was not held by the gain corporation on the acquisition date, or

(ii) such gain exceeds the excess (if any) of—

(I) the fair market value of such asset on the acquisition date, over

(II) the adjusted basis of such asset on such date.

(B) **Treatment of certain income items.**—Any item of income which is properly taken into account for any recognition period taxable year but which is attributable to periods before the acquisition date shall be treated as a recognized built-in gain for the taxable year in which it is properly taken into account and shall be taken into account in determining the amount of the net unrealized built-in gain.

(C) **Limitation.**—The amount of the recognized built-in gains for any recognition period taxable year shall not exceed—

(i) the net unrealized built-in gain, reduced by

(ii) the recognized built-in gains for prior years ending in the recognition period which (but for this section) would have been offset by preacquisition losses.

(2) **Acquisition date.**—The term "acquisition date" means

(A) in any case described in subsection (a)(1)(A), the date on which the acquisition of control occurs, or

(B) in any case described in subsection (a)(1)(B), the date of the transfer in the reorganization.

(3) **Preacquisition loss.**—

(A) **In general.**—The term "preacquisition loss" means—

(i) any net operating loss carryforward to the taxable year in which the acquisition date occurs, and

(ii) any net operating loss for the taxable year in which the acquisition date occurs to the extent such loss is allocable to the period in such year on or before the acquisition date.

Except as provided in regulations, the net operating loss shall, for purposes of clause (ii), be allocated ratably to each day in the year.

(B) **Treatment of recognized built-in loss.**—In the case of a corporation with a net unrealized built-in loss, the term "preacquisition loss" includes any recognized built-in loss.

(4) **Gain corporation.**—The term "gain corporation" means any corporation with a net unrealized built-in gain.

(5) **Control.**— The term "control" means ownership of stock in a corporation which meets the requirements of section 1504(a)(2).

(6) **Treatment of members of same group.**—Except as provided in regulations and except for purposes of subsection (b), all corporations which are members of the same affiliated group immediately before the acquisition date shall be treated as 1 corporation. To the extent provided in regulations, section 1504 shall be applied without regard to subsection (b) thereof for purposes of the preceding sentence.

(7) **Treatment of predecessors and successors.**—Any reference in this section to a corporation shall include a reference to any predecessor or successor thereof.

(8) **Other definitions.**—Except as provided in regulations, the terms "net unrealized built-in gain," "net unrealized built-in loss," "recognized built-in loss," "recognition period," and "recognition period taxable year," have the same respective meanings as when used in section 382(h), except that the acquisition date shall be taken into account in lieu of the change date.

(d) **Limitation also to apply to excess credits or net capital losses.**—Rules similar to the rules of subsection (a) shall also apply in the case of any excess credit (as defined in section 383(a)(2)) or net capital loss.

(e) **Ordering rules for net operating losses, etc.**—

(1) **Carryover rules.**—If any preacquisition loss may not offset a recognized built-in gain by reason of this section, such gain shall not be taken into account in determining under section 172(b)(2) the amount of such loss which may be carried

to other taxable years. A similar rule shall apply in the case of any excess credit or net capital loss limited by reason of subsection (d).

(2) Ordering rule for losses carried from same taxable year.—In any case in which—

(A) a preacquisition loss for any taxable year is subject to limitation under subsection (a), and

(B) a net operating loss from such taxable year is not subject to such limitation,

taxable income shall be treated as having been offset 1st by the loss subject to such limitation.

(f) Regulations.—The Secretary shall prescribe such regulations as may be necessary to carry out the purposes of this section, including regulations to ensure that the purposes of this section may not be circumvented through—

(1) the use of any provision of law or regulations (including subchapter K of this chapter), or

(2) contributions of property to a corporation.

PART VI—TREATMENT OF CERTAIN CORPORATE INTERESTS AS STOCK OR INDEBTEDNESS

Editorial Summary

Debt Versus Equity

Subchapter C of Chapter 1 (Sec. 385)

Corporate assets can be financed through the use of equity and through the use of debt. From the shareholders' perspective, a benefit of using debt provided by others is the ability to apply the concept of leverage and thereby earn a greater return on the invested capital.

However, rather than having the debt financing (all or some part thereof) provided by others, the shareholder may choose to provide the debt financing. This is achieved by the shareholder investing a certain amount in the corporation and loaning a certain amount to the corporation. Tax benefits of such an approach include the following:

1. Interest payments made on the debt are deductible to the corporation whereas dividend payments are not.

2. The shareholder can withdraw the debt financing (i.e., the loans are repaid) tax-free whereas withdrawing invested capital as a return of capital is difficult to achieve.

In recognition of such tax opportunities associated with shareholder debt, the IRS may conclude that the corporation is "thinly capitalized" (i.e., too much shareholder debt an too little shareholder equity). Thus, the IRS may reclassify debt as equity. If this occurs, the aforementioned tax benefits disappear with respect to the debt that is reclassified as equity.

Substantial taxpayer and IRS conflict resulted with respect to this issue. Therefore, as part of the Tax Reform Act of 1969, Sec. 385 was enacted to provide a statutory basis for distinguishing between such debt and equity [see Sec. 385 (b)]. The major shortcoming of Sec. 385 is that, while it does list five factors that may be used in distinguishing debt from equity, it leaves to the issuance of interpretive regulations the actual application of these factors and other factors in so distinguishing. An attempt was made to issue such regulations in the early 1980s (i.e., in proposed form). However, these regulations were quickly withdrawn. Thus, at this point in time, no such regulations have been promulgated.

§ 385. Treatment of certain interests in corporations as stock or indebtedness

(a) Authority to prescribe regulations.*—The Secretary is authorized to prescribe such regulations as may be necessary or appropriate to determine whether an interest in a corporation is to be treated for purposes of this title as stock or indebtedness (or as in part stock and in part indebtedness).

(b) Factors.—The regulations prescribed under this section shall set forth factors which are to be taken into account in determining with respect to a particular factual situation whether a debtor-creditor relationship exists or a corporation-shareholder relationship exists. The factors so set forth in the regulations may include among other factors:

(1) whether there is a written unconditional promise to pay on demand or on a specified date a sum certain in money in return for an adequate consideration in money or money's worth, and to pay a fixed rate of interest,

(2) whether there is subordination to or preference over any indebtedness of the corporation,

(3) the ratio of debt to equity of the corporation,

(4) whether there is convertibility into the stock of the corporation, and

*Editorial Note: Regulations not to be applied retroactively.—Any regulations issued pursuant to the authority granted by the above amendment (treating an interest as part stock and part indebtedness) shall only apply with respect to instruments issued after the date on which the Secretary of the Treasury or his delegate provides public guidance as to the characterization of such instruments whether by regulation, ruling, or otherwise.

(5) the relationship between holdings of stock in the corporation and holdings of the interest in question.

(c) Effect of classification by issuer.—

(1) In general.—The characterization (as of the time of issuance) by the issuer as to whether an interest in a corporation is stock or indebtedness shall be binding on such issuer and on all holders of such interest (but shall not be binding on the Secretary).

(2) Notification of inconsistent treatment.—Except as provided in regulations, paragraph (1) shall not apply to any holder of an interest if such holder on his return discloses that he is treating such interest in a manner inconsistent with the characterization referred to in paragraph (1).

(3) Regulations.—The Secretary is authorized to require such information as the Secretary determines to be necessary to carry out the provisions of this subsection.

SUBCHAPTER D—DEFERRED COMPENSATION, ETC.

Editorial Summary

Deferred Compensation
Subchapter D of Chapter 1 (Secs. 401–425)

The payment of compensation produces a deduction for the employer. The payment likewise results in income to the employee. Subchapter D provides the opportunity for the employee to have a "wealth increase," yet to have no current period taxable income. This is achieved by structuring the compensation in the form of deferred compensation rather than in the form of current period compensation. Included in the deferred compensation area are the following:

1. Pension and profit-sharing plans.
2. Stock bonus plans.
3. Individual retirement accounts.
4. Simplified employee pension plans.
5. Keogh plans.
6. Employee stock ownership plans.
7. Stock options.

The tax consequences of deferred compensation potentially impact on three taxpayers: the employer, the trust, and the employee. The ideal tax consequences are as follows: the employer takes a current period deduction for the deferred compensation, the trust is tax-exempt, and the employee defers the reporting of the deferred compensation until some subsequent taxable year or years. Note that the only way this tax treatment could be improved would be for the employee to permanently exclude the deferred compensation from gross income. While such exclusion treatment is available for certain types of fringe benefits [see Sec. 79 group-term life insurance; Sec. 82 moving expenses; Secs. 104-106 accident and health plans; Sec. 107 rental value of parsonages; Sec. 112 combat zone compensation for members of the armed forces; Sec. 119 meals and lodging furnished for the convenience of the employer; Sec. 127 educational assistance programs; Sec. 129 dependent care assistance programs; Sec. 132 certain fringe benefits; Sec. 134 certain military benefits, and Sec. 137 adoption expenses], deferral treatment is the best employee tax treatment provided for deferred compensation. The following listing includes the potential tax consequences for the employer and the employee for deferred compensation.

Employer	Employee
Deduction now	Deferral
Deduction now	Include in gross income now
Employer	Employee
Deduction in the future when the employee includes in gross income	Include in gross income in the future
Deduction now	Include in gross income now and qualify for a deduction now

A number of statutory requirements must be satisfied in order to receive the ideal tax consequences for the three parties. Included are the following:

1. Nondiscrimination requirements (Sec. 401).
2. Minimum participation and coverage requirements (Sec. 410).
3. Minimum vesting standards (Sec. 411).
4. Minimum funding standards (Sec. 412).
5. Limitations on employer deductions (Sec. 404).
6. Limitations on contributions (Sec. 415).
7. Limitations on benefits (Sec. 415).
8. Distribution requirements (Secs. 401, 403).

Benefits are usually distributed to the employee in the form of an annuity [see Secs. 402(a), 72] or as a lump-sum distribution [see Sec. 402(e)].

PART I—PENSION, PROFIT–SHARING, STOCK BONUS PLANS, ETC.

SUBPART A—GENERAL RULE

§ 401. Qualified pension, profit-sharing, and stock bonus plans

(a) Requirements for qualification.—A trust created or organized in the United States and forming part of a stock bonus, pension, or profit-sharing plan of an employer for the exclusive benefit of his employees or their beneficiaries shall constitute a qualified trust under this section—

(1) if contributions are made to the trust by such employer, or employees, or both, or by another employer who is entitled to deduct his contributions under section 404(a)(3)(B) (relating to deduction for contributions to profit-sharing and stock bonus plans), or by a charitable remainder trust pursuant to a qualified gratuitous transfer (as defined in section 664(g)(1)), for the purpose of distributing to such employees or their beneficiaries the corpus and income of the fund accumulated by the trust in accordance with such plan;

(2) if under the trust instrument it is impossible, at any time prior to the satisfaction of all liabilities with respect to employees and their beneficiaries under the trust, for any part of the corpus or income to be (within the taxable year or thereafter) used for, or diverted to, purposes other than for the exclusive benefit of his employees or their beneficiaries (but this paragraph shall not be construed, in the case of a multiemployer plan, to prohibit the return of a contribution within 6 months after the plan administrator determines that the contribution was made by a mistake of fact or law (other than a mistake relating to whether the plan is described in section 401(a) or the trust which is part of such plan is exempt from taxation under section 501(a), or the return of any withdrawal liability payment determined to be an overpayment within 6 months of such determination);

(3) if the plan of which such trust is a part satisfies the requirements of section 410 (relating to minimum participation standards); and

(4) if the contributions or benefits provided under the plan do not discriminate in favor of highly compensated employees (within the meaning of section 414(q)). For purposes of this paragraph, there shall be excluded from consideration employees described in section 410(b)(3)(A) and (C).

(5) Special rules relating to nondiscrimination requirements.—

(A) Salaried or clerical employees.—A classification shall not be considered discriminatory within the meaning of paragraph (4) or section 410(b)(2)(A)(i) merely because it is limited to salaried or clerical employees.

(B) Contributions and benefits may bear uniform relationship to compensation.—A plan shall not be considered discriminatory within the meaning of paragraph (4) merely because the contributions or benefits of, or on behalf of, the employees under the plan bear a uniform relationship to the compensation (within the meaning of section 414(a)) of such employees.

(C) Certain disparity permitted.—A plan shall not be considered discriminatory within the meaning of paragraph (4) merely because the contributions or benefits of, or on behalf of, the employees under the plan favor highly compensated employees (as defined in section 414(q)) in the manner permitted under subsection (1).

(D) Integrated defined benefit plan.—

(i) In general.—A defined benefit plan shall not be considered discriminatory within the meaning of paragraph (4) merely because the plan provides that the employer-derived accrued retirement benefit for any participant under the plan may not exceed the excess (if any) of—

(I) the participant's final pay with the employer, over

(II) the employer-derived retirement benefit created under Federal law attributable to service by the participant with the employer.

For purposes of this clause, the employer-derived retirement benefit created under Federal law shall be treated as accruing ratably over 35 years.

(ii) Final pay.—For purposes of this subparagraph, the participant's final pay is the compensation (as defined in section 414(q)

*Omitted

(4)) paid to the participant by the employer for any year—

(I) which ends during the 5-year period ending with the year in which the participant separated from service for the employer, and

(II) for which the participant's total compensation from the employer was highest.

(E) 2 or more plans treated as single plan.—For purposes of determining whether 2 or more plans of an employer satisfy the requirements of paragraph (4) when considered as a single plan—

(i) Contributions.—If the amount of contributions on behalf of the employees allowed as a deduction under section 404 for the taxable year with respect to such plans, taken together, bears a uniform relationship to the compensation (within the meaning of section 414(s)) of such employees, the plans shall not be considered discriminatory merely because the rights of employees to, or derived from, the employer contributions under the separate plans do not become nonforfeitable at the same rate.

(ii) Benefits.—If the employees' rights to benefits under the separate plans do not become nonforfeitable at the same rate, but the levels of benefits provided by the separate plans satisfy the requirements of regulations prescribed by the Secretary to take account of the differences in such rates, the plans shall not be considered discriminatory merely because of the difference in such rates.

(F) Social security retirement age.—For purposes of testing for discrimination under paragraph (4)—

(i) the social security retirement age (as defined in section 415(b)(8)) shall be treated as a uniform retirement age, and

(ii) subsidized early retirement benefits and joint and survivor annuities shall not be treated as being unavailable to employees on the same terms merely because such benefits or annuities are based in whole or in part on an employee's social security retirement age (as so defined).

(G) Governmental plans.—Paragraphs (3) and (4) shall not apply to a governmental plan (within the meaning of section 414(d)).

(6) A plan shall be considered as meeting the requirements of paragraph (3) during the whole of any taxable year of the plan if on one day in each quarter it satisfied such requirements.

(7) A trust shall not constitute a qualified trust under this section unless the plan of which such trust is a part satisfies the requirements of section 411 (relating to minimum vesting standards).

(8) A trust forming part of a defined benefit plan shall not constitute a qualified trust under this section unless the plan provides that forfeitures must not be applied to increase the benefits any employee would otherwise receive under the plan.

(9) Required distributions.—

(A) In general.—A trust shall not constitute a qualified trust under this subsection unless the plan provides that the entire interest of each employee—

(i) will be distributed to such employee not later than the required beginning date, or

(ii) will be distributed, beginning not later than the required beginning date, in accordance with regulations, over the life of such employee or over the lives of such employee and a designated beneficiary (or over a period not extending beyond the life expectancy of such employee or the life expectancy of such employee and a designated beneficiary).

(B) Required distribution where employee dies before entire interest is distributed.—

(i) Where distributions have begun under subparagraph (A)(ii).—A trust shall not constitute a qualified trust under this section unless the plan provides that if—

(I) the distribution of the employee's interest has begun in accordance with subparagraph (A)(ii), and

(II) the employee dies before his entire interest has been distributed to him,

the remaining portion of such interest will be distributed at least as rapidly as under the method of distributions being used under subparagraph (A)(ii) as of the date of his death.

(ii) 5-year rule for other cases.—A trust shall not constitute a qualified trust under this section unless the plan provides that, if an employee dies before the distribution of the employee's interest has begun in accordance with subparagraph (A)(ii), the entire interest of the employee will be distributed within 5 years after the death of such employee.

(iii) Exception to 5-year rule for certain amounts payable over life of beneficiary.—If—

(I) any portion of the employee's interest is payable to (or for the benefit of) a designated beneficiary,

(II) such portion will be distributed (in accordance with regulations) over the life of such designated beneficiary (or over a period not extending beyond the life expectancy of such beneficiary), and

(III) such distributions begin not later than year after the date of the employee's death or such later date as the Secretary may by regulations prescribe,

for purposes of clause (ii), the portion referred to in subclause (I) shall be treated as distributed on the date on which such distributions begin.

(iv) Special rule for surviving spouse of employee.—If the designated beneficiary referred to in clause (iii)(I) is the surviving spouse of the employee—

(I) the date on which the distributions are required to begin under clause (iii)(III) shall not be earlier than the date on which the employee would have attained age 70½, and

(II) if the surviving spouse dies before the distributions to such spouse begin, this subparagraph shall be applied as if the surviving spouse were the employee.

(C) Required beginning date.—For purposes of this paragraph—

(i) In general.—The term "required beginning date" means April 1 of the calendar year following the later of—

(I) the calendar year in which the employee attains age 70½, or

(II) the calendar year in which the employee retires.

(ii) Exception.—Subclause (II) of clause (i) shall not apply—

(I) except as provided in section 409(d), in the case of an employee who is a 5-percent owner (as defined in section 416) with respect to the plan year ending in the calendar year in which the employee attains age 70½, or

(II) for purposes of section 408(a)(6) or (b)(3).

(iii) Actuarial adjustment.—In the case of an employee to whom clause (i)(II) applies who retires in a calendar year after the calendar year in which the employee attains age 70½, the employee's accrued benefit shall be actuarially increased to take into account the period after age 70½ in which the employee was not receiving any benefits under the plan.

(iv) Exception for governmental and church plans.—Clauses (ii) and (iii) shall not apply in the case of a governmental plan or church plan. For purposes of this clause, the term "church plan" means a plan maintained by a church for church employees, and the term "church" means any church (as defined in section 3121(w)(3)(A)) or qualified church-controlled organization (as defined in section 3121(w)(3)(B)).

(D) Life expectancy.—For purposes of this paragraph, the life expectancy of an employee and the employee's spouse (other than in the case of a life annuity) may be redetermined but not more frequently than annually.

(E) Designated beneficiary.—For purposes of this paragraph, the term "designated beneficiary" means any individual designated as a beneficiary by the employee.

(F) Treatment of payments to children.—Under regulations prescribed by the Secretary, for purposes of this paragraph, any amount paid to a child shall be treated as if it had been paid to the surviving spouse if such amount will become payable to the surviving spouse upon such child reaching majority (or other designated event permitted under regulations).

(G) Treatment of incidental death benefit distributions.—For purposes of this title, any distribution required under the incidental death benefit requirements of this subsection shall be treated as a distribution required under this paragraph.

(H) Temporary waiver of minimum required distribution.—

(i) In general.—The requirements of this paragraph shall not apply for the calendar year 2009 to—

(I) a defined contribution plan which is described in this subsection or in section 403(a) or 403(b),

(II) a defined contribution plan which is an eligible deferred compensation plan described in section 457(b) but only if such plan is maintained by an employer described in section 457(e)(1)(A), or

(III) an individual retirement plan.

(ii) Special rules regarding waiver period.—For purposes of this paragraph—

(I) the required beginning date with respect to any individual shall be determined without regard to this subparagraph for purposes of applying this paragraph for calendar years after 2009, and

(II) if clause (ii) of subparagraph (B) applies, the 5-year period described in such clause shall be determined without regard to calendar year 2009.

(10) Other requirements.—

(A) Plans benefiting owner-employees.—In the case of any plan which provides contributions or benefits for employees some or all of whom are owner-employees (as defined in subsection (c)(3)), a trust forming part of such plan shall constitute a qualified trust under this section only if the requirements of subsection (d) are also met.

(B) Top-heavy plans.—

(i) In general.—In the case of any top-heavy plan, a trust forming part of such plan shall constitute a qualified trust under this section only if the requirements of section 416 are met.

(ii) Plans which may become top-heavy.—Except to the extent provided in regulations, a trust forming part of a plan (whether or not a top-heavy plan) shall constitute a qualified trust under this section only if such plan contains provisions—

(I) which will take effect if such plan becomes a top-heavy plan, and

(II) which meet the requirements of section 416.

(iii) Exemption for governmental plans.—This subparagraph shall not apply to any governmental plan.

(11) Requirement of joint and survivor annuity and preretirement survivor annuity.—

(A) In general.—In the case of any plan to which this paragraph applies, except as provided in section 417, a trust forming part of such plan shall not constitute a qualified trust under this section unless—

(i) in the case of a vested participant who does not die before the annuity starting date, the accrued benefit payable to such participant is provided in the form of a qualified joint and survivor annuity, and

(ii) in the case of a vested participant who dies before the annuity starting date and who has a surviving spouse, a qualified preretirement survivor annuity is provided to the surviving spouse of such participant.

(B) Plans to which paragraph applies.—This paragraph shall apply to—

(i) any defined benefit plan,

(ii) any defined contribution plan which is subject to the funding standards of section 412, and

(iii) any participant under any other defined contribution plan unless—

(I) such plan provides that the participant's nonforfeitable accrued benefit (reduced by any security interest held by the plan by reason of a loan outstanding to such participant) is payable in full, on the death of the participant, to the participant's surviving spouse (or, if there is no surviving spouse or the surviving spouse consents in the manner required under section 417(a)(2), to a designated beneficiary),

(II) such participant does not elect a payment of benefits in the form of a life annuity, and

(III) with respect to such participant, such plan is not a direct or indirect transferee (in a transfer after December 31, 1984) of a plan which is described in clause (i) or (ii) or to which this clause applied with respect to the participant.

Clause (iii)(III) shall apply only with respect to the transferred assets (and income therefrom) if the plan separately accounts for such assets and any income therefrom.

(C) Exception for certain ESOP benefits.—

(i) In general.—In the case of—

(I) a tax credit employee stock ownership plan (as defined in section 409(a)), or

(II) an employee stock ownership plan (as defined in section 4975(e)(7)),

subparagraph (A) shall not apply to that portion of the employee's accrued benefit to which the requirements of section 409(h) apply.

(ii) Nonforfeitable benefit must be paid in full, etc.—In the case of any participant, clause (i) shall apply only if the requirements of subclauses (I), (II), and (III) of subparagraph (B)(iii) are met with respect to such participant.

(D) Special rule where participant and spouse married less than 1 year.—A plan shall not be treated as failing to meet the requirements of subparagraphs (B)(iii) or (C) merely because the plan provides that benefits will not be payable to the surviving spouse of the participant unless the participant and such spouse had been married throughout the 1-year period ending on the earlier of the participant's annuity starting date or the date of the participant's death.

(E) Exception for plans described in section 404(c).—This paragraph shall not apply to a plan which the Secretary has determined is a plan described in section 404(c) (or a continuation thereof) in which participation is substantially limited to individuals who, before January 1, 1976, ceased employment covered by the plan.

(F) Cross reference.—For—

(i) provisions under which participants may elect to waive the requirements of this paragraph, and

(ii) other definitions and special rules for purposes of this paragraph,

see section 417.

(12) A trust shall not constitute a qualified trust under this section unless the plan of which such trust is a part provides that in the case of any merger or consolidation with, or transfer of assets or liabilities to, any other plan after September 2, 1974, each participant in the plan would (if the plan then terminated) receive a benefit immediately after the merger, consolidation, or transfer which is equal to or greater than the benefit he would have been entitled to receive immediately before the merger, consolidation, or transfer (if the plan had then terminated). The preceding sentence does not apply to any multiemployer plan with respect to any transaction to the extent that participants either before or after the transaction are covered under a multi-employer plan to which title IV of the Employee Retirement Income Security Act of 1974 applies.

(13) Assignment and alienation.—

(A) In general.—A trust shall not constitute a qualified trust under this section unless the plan of which such trust is a part provides that benefits provided under the plan may not be assigned or alienated. For purposes of the preceding sentence, there shall not be taken into account any voluntary and revocable assignment of not to exceed 10 percent of any benefit payment made by any participant who is receiving benefits under the plan unless the assignment or alienation is made for purposes of defraying plan administration costs. For purposes of this paragraph a loan made to a participant or beneficiary shall not be treated as an assignment or alienation if such loan is secured by the participant's accrued nonforfeitable benefit and is exempt from the tax imposed by section 4975 (relating to tax on prohibited transactions) by reason of section 4975(d)(1). This paragraph shall take effect on January 1, 1976, and shall not apply to assignments which were irrevocable on September 2, 1974.

(B) Special rules for domestic relations orders.—Subparagraph (A) shall apply to the creation, assignment, or recognition of a right to any benefit payable with respect to a participant pursuant to a domestic relations order, except that subparagraph (A) shall not apply if the order is determined to be a qualified domestic relations order.

(C) Special rule for certain judgments and settlements.—Subparagraph (A) shall not apply to any offset of a participant's benefits provided under a plan against an amount that the participant is ordered or required to pay to the plan if—

(i) the order or requirement to pay arises—

(I) under a judgment of conviction for a crime involving such plan,

(II) under a civil judgment (including a consent order or decree) entered by a court in an action brought in connection with a violation (or alleged violation) of part 4 of subtitle B of title I of the Employee Retirement Income Security Act of 1974, or

(III) pursuant to a settlement agreement between the Secretary of Labor and the participant, or a settlement agreement between the Pension Benefit Guaranty Corporation and the participant, in connection with a violation (or alleged violation) of part 4 of such subtitle by a fiduciary or any other person,

(ii) the judgment, order, decree, or settlement agreement expressly provides for the offset of all or part of the amount ordered or required to be paid to the plan against the participant's benefits provided under the plan, and

(iii) in a case in which the survivor annuity requirements of section 401(a)(11) apply with respect to distributions from the plan to the participant, if the participant has a spouse at the time at which the offset is to be made—

(I) either such spouse has consented in writing to such offset and such consent is witnessed by a notary public or representative of the plan (or it is established to the satisfaction of a plan representative that such consent may not be obtained by reason of circumstances described in section 417(a)(2)(B)), or an election to waive the right of the spouse to either a qualified joint and survivor annuity or a qualified preretirement survivor annuity is in effect in accordance with the requirements of section 417(a),

(II) such spouse is ordered or required in such judgment, order, decree, or settlement to apply an amount to the plan in connection with a violation of part 4 of such subtitle, or

(III) in such judgment, order, decree, or settlement, such spouse retains the right to receive the survivor annuity under a qualified joint and survivor annuity provided pursuant to section 401(a)(11)(A)(i) and under a qualified preretirement survivor annuity provided pursuant to section 401(a)(11)(A)(ii), determined in accordance with subparagraph (D).

A plan shall not be treated as failing to meet the requirements of this subsection, subsection (k), section 403(b), or section 409(d) solely by reason of an offset described in this subparagraph.

(D) Survivor annuity.—

(i) In general.—The survivor annuity described in subparagraph (C)(iii)(III) shall be determined as if—

(I) the participant terminated employment on the date of the offset,

(II) there was no offset,

(III) the plan permitted commencement of benefits only on or after normal retirement age,

(IV) the plan provided only the minimum-required qualified joint and survivor annuity, and

(V) the amount of the qualified preretirement survivor annuity under the plan is equal to the amount of the survivor annuity payable under the minimum-required qualified joint and survivor annuity.

(ii) Definition.—For purposes of this subparagraph, the term "minimum-required qualified joint and survivor annuity" means the qualified joint and survivor annuity which is the actuarial equivalent of the participant's accrued benefit (within the meaning of section 411(a)(7)) and under which the survivor annuity is 50 percent of the amount of the annuity which is payable during the joint lives of the participant and the spouse.

(14) A trust shall not constitute a qualified trust under this section unless the plan of which such trust is a part provides that, unless the participant otherwise elects, the payment of benefits under the plan to the participant will begin not later than the 60th day after the latest of the close of the plan year in which—

(A) the date on which the participant attains the earlier of age 65 or the normal retirement age specified under the plan,

(B) occurs the 10th anniversary of the year in which the participant commenced participation in the plan, or

(C) the participant terminates his service with the employer.

In the case of a plan which provides for the payment of an early retirement benefit, a trust forming a part of such plan shall not constitute a qualified trust under this section unless a participant who satisfied the service requirements for such early retirement benefit, but separated from the service (with any nonforfeitable right to an accrued benefit) before satisfying the age requirement for such early retirement benefit, is entitled upon satisfaction of such age requirement to receive a benefit not less than the benefit to which he would be entitled at the normal retirement age, actuarially, reduced under regulations prescribed by the Secretary.

(15) A trust shall not constitute a qualified trust under this section unless under the plan of which such trust is a part—

(A) in the case of a participant or beneficiary who is receiving benefits under such plan, or

(B) in the case of a participant who is separated from the service and who has nonforfeitable rights to benefits,

such benefits are not decreased by reason of any increase in the benefit levels payable under title II of the Social Security Act or any increase in the wage base under such title II, if such increase takes place after September 2, 1974, or (if later) the earlier of the date of first receipt of such benefits or the date of such separation, as the case may be.

(16) A trust shall not constitute a qualified trust under this section if the plan of which such trust is a part provides for benefits or contributions which exceed the limitations of section 415.

(17) Compensation limit.—

(A) In general.—A trust shall not constitute a qualified trust under this section unless, under the plan of which such trust is a part, the annual compensation of each employee taken into account under the plan for any year does not exceed $200,000.*

(B) Cost-of-living adjustment—The Secretary shall adjust annually the $200,000* amount in subparagraph (A) for increases in the cost-of-living at the same time and in the same manner as adjustments under section 415(d); except that the base period shall be the calendar quarter beginning July 1, 2001, and any increase which is not a multiple of $5,000 shall be rounded to the next lowest multiple of $5,000.

****(19)** A trust shall not constitute a qualified trust under this section if under the plan of which such trust is a part any part of a participant's accrued benefit derived from employer contributions (whether or not otherwise nonforfeitable), is forfeitable solely because of withdrawal by such participant of any amount attributable to the benefit derived from contributions made by such participant. The preceding sentence shall not apply to the accrued benefit of any participant unless, at the time of such withdrawal, such participant has a nonforfeitable right to at least 50 percent of such accrued benefit (as determined under section 411). The first sentence of this paragraph shall not apply to the extent that an accrued benefit is permitted to be forfeited in accordance with section 411(a)(3)(D)(iii) (relating to proportional forfeitures of benefits accrued before September 2, 1974, in the event of withdrawal of certain mandatory contributions).

(20) A trust forming part of a pension plan shall not be treated as failing to constitute a qualified trust under this section merely because the pension plan of which such trust is a part makes 1 or more distributions within 1 taxable year to a distributee on account of a termination of the plan of which the trust is a part, or in the case of a profit-sharing or stock bonus plan, a complete discontinuance of contributions under such plan. This paragraph shall not apply to a defined benefit plan unless the employer maintaining such plan files a notice with the Pension Benefit Guaranty Corporation (at the time and in the manner prescribed by the Pension Benefit Guaranty Corporation) notifying the Corporation of such payment or distribution and the Corporation has approved such payment or distribution or, within 90 days after the date on which such notice was filed, has failed to disapprove such

*Editorial comment: The $200,000 amount is subject to indexing. For 2013 the indexed amount is $255,000, and for 2014 is $260,000.

**Editorial comment: There is no paragraph (18).

payment or distribution. For purposes of this paragraph, rules similar to the rules of section 402(a)(6)(B) (as in effect before its repeal by section 521 of the Unemployment Compensation Amendments of 1992) shall apply.

***(22)** If a defined contribution plan (other than a profit-sharing plan)—

(A) is established by an employer whose stock is not readily tradable on an established market, and

(B) after acquiring securities of the employer, more than 10 percent of the total assets of the plan are securities of the employer, any trust forming part of such plan shall not constitute a qualified trust under this section unless the plan meets the requirements of subsection (e) of section 409. The requirements of subsection (e) of section 409 shall not apply to any employees of an employer who are participants in any defined contribution plan established and maintained by such employer if the stock of such employer is not readily tradable on an established market and the trade or business of such employer consists of publishing on a regular basis a newspaper for general circulation. For purposes of the preceding sentence, subsections (b), (c), (m), and (o) of section 414 shall not apply except for determining whether stock of the employer is not readily tradable on an established market.

(23) A stock bonus plan shall not be treated as meeting the requirements of this section unless such plan meets the requirements of subsections (h) and (o) of section 409, except that in applying section 409(h) for purposes of this paragraph, the term "employer securities" shall include any securities of the employer held by the plan.

(24) Any group trust which otherwise meets the requirements of this section shall not be treated as not meeting such requirements on account of the participation or inclusion in such trust of the moneys of any plan or governmental unit described in section 818(a)(6).

(25) Requirement that actuarial assumptions be specified.—A defined benefit plan shall not be treated as providing definitely determinable benefits unless, whenever the amount of any benefit is to be determined on the basis of actuarial assumptions, such assumptions are specified in the plan in a way which precludes employer discretion.

(26) Additional participation requirements.—

(A) In general.—In the case of a trust which is part of a defined benefit plan, such trust shall not constitute a qualified trust under this subsection unless on each day of the plan year such trust benefits the lesser of—

(i) 50 employees of the employer, or

(ii) the greater of—

(I) 40 percent of all employees of the employer, or

(II) 2 employees (or if there is only 1 employee, such employee).

(B) Treatment of excludable employees.—

(i) In general.—A plan may exclude from consideration under this paragraph employees described in paragraphs (3) and (4)(A) of section 410(b).

(ii) Separate application for certain excludable employees.—If employees described in section 410(b)(4)(B) are covered under a plan which meets the requirements of subparagraph (A) separately with respect to such employees, such employees may be excluded from consideration in determining whether any plan of the employer meets such requirements if—

(I) the benefits for such employees are provided under the same plan as benefits for other employees,

(II) the benefits provided to such employees are not greater than comparable benefits provided to other employees under the plan, and

(III) no highly compensated employee (within the meaning of section 414(q)) is included in the group of such employees for more than 1 year.

(C) Special rule for collective bargaining units.—Except to the extent provided in regulations, a plan covering only employees described in section 410(b)(3)(A) may exclude from consideration any employees who are not included in the unit or units in which the covered employees are included.

*Editorial comment: There is no paragraph (21).

(D) Paragraph not to apply to multiemployer plans.—Except to the extent provided in regulations, this paragraph shall not apply to employees in a multiemployer plan (within the meaning of section 414(f)) who are covered by collective bargaining agreements.

(E) Special rule for certain dispositions or acquisitions.—Rules similar to the rules of section 410(b)(6)(C) shall apply for purposes of this paragraph.

(F) Separate lines of business.—At the election of the employer and with the consent of the Secretary, this paragraph may be applied separately with respect to each separate line of business of the employer. For purposes of this paragraph, the term "separate line of business" has the meaning given such term by section 414 (r) (without regard to paragraph (2)(a) or (7) thereof).

(G) Exception for state and local governmental plans.—This paragraph shall not apply to a governmental plan (within the meaning of section 414(d)) maintained by a State or local government or political subdivision thereof (or agency or instrumentality thereof).

(H) Regulations.—The Secretary may by regulation provide that any separate benefit structure, any separate trust, or any other separate arrangement is to be treated as a separate plan for purposes of applying this paragraph.

(27) Determination as to profit-sharing plans.—

(A) Contributions need not be based on profits.—The determination of whether the plan under which any contributions are made is a profit-sharing plan shall be made without regard to current or accumulated profits of the employer and without regard to whether the employer is a tax-exempt organization.

(B) Plan must designate type.—In the case of a plan which is intended to be a money purchase pension plan or a profit-sharing plan, a trust forming part of such plan shall not constitute a qualified trust under this subsection unless the plan designates such intent at such time and in such manner as the Secretary may prescribe.

(28) Additional requirements relating to employee stock ownership plans.—

(A) In general.—In the case of a trust which is part of an employee stock ownership plan (within the meaning of section 4975(e)(7)) or a plan which meets the requirements of section 409(a), such trust shall not constitute a qualified trust under this section unless such plan meets the requirements of subparagraphs (B) and (C).

(B) Diversification of investments.—

(i) In general.—A plan meets the requirements of this subparagraph if each qualified participant in the plan may elect within 90 days after the close of each plan year in the qualified election period to direct the plan as to the investment of at least 25 percent of the participant's account in the plan (to the extent such portion exceeds the amount to which a prior election under this subparagraph applies). In the case of the election year in which the participant can make his last election, the preceding sentence shall be applied by substituting "50 percent" for "25 percent."

(ii) Method of meeting requirements.—A plan shall be treated as meeting the requirements of clause (i) if—

(I) the portion of the participant's account covered by the election under clause (i) is distributed within 90 days after the period during which the election may be made, or

(II) the plan offers at least 3 investment options (not inconsistent with regulations prescribed by the Secretary) to each participant making an election under clause (i) and within 90 days after the period during which the election may be made, the plan invests the portion of the participant's account covered by the election in accordance with such election.

(iii) Qualified participant.—For purposes of this subparagraph, the term "qualified participant" means any employee who has completed at least 10 years of participation under the plan and has attained age 55.

(iv) Qualified election period.—For purposes of this subparagraph, the term "qualified election period" means the 6-plan-year period beginning with the later of—

(I) the 1st plan year in which the individual first became a qualified participant, or

(II) the 1st plan year beginning after December 31, 1986.

For purposes of the preceding sentence, an employer may elect to treat an individual first becoming a qualified participant in the 1st plan year beginning in 1987 as having become a participant in the 1st plan year beginning in 1988.

(C) Use of independent appraiser.—A plan meets the requirements of this subparagraph if all valuations of employer securities which are not readily tradable on an established securities market with respect to activities carried on by the plan are by an independent appraiser. For purposes of the preceding sentence, the term "independent appraiser" means any appraiser meeting requirements similar to the requirements of the regulations prescribed under section 170(a)(1).

(v) Exception.—This subparagraph shall not apply to an applicable defined contribution plan (as defined in paragraph (35)(E)).

(29) Benefit limitations on plans in at-risk status.—In the case of a defined benefit plan (other than a multiemployer plan) to which the requirements of section 412 apply, the trust of which the plan is a part shall not constitute a qualified trust under this subsection unless the plan meets the requirements of section 436.

(30) Limitations on elective deferrals.—In the case of a trust which is part of a plan under which elective deferrals (within the meaning of section 402 (g)(3)) may be made with respect to any individual during a calendar year, such trust shall not constitute a qualified trust under this subsection unless the plan provides that the amount of such deferrals under such plan and all other plans, contracts, or arrangements of an employer maintaining such plan may not exceed the amount of the limitation in effect under section 402(g)(1)(A) for taxable years beginning in such calendar year.

(31) Direct transfer of eligible rollover distributions.—

(A) In general.—A trust shall not constitute a qualified trust under this section unless the plan of which such trust is a part provides that if the distributee of any eligible rollover distribution—

(i) elects to have such distribution paid directly to an eligible retirement plan, and

(ii) specifies the eligible retirement plan to which such distribution is to be paid (in such form and at such time as the plan administrator may prescribe),

such distribution shall be made in the form of a direct trustee-to-trustee transfer to the eligible retirement plan so specified.

(B) Certain mandatory distributions.—

(i) In general.—In case of a trust which is part of an eligible plan, such trust shall not constitute a qualified trust under this section unless the plan of which such trust is a part provides that if—

(I) a distribution described in clause (ii) in excess of $1,000 is made, and

(II) the distributee does not make an election under subparagraph (A) and does not elect to receive the distribution directly.

the plan administrator shall make such transfer to an individual retirement plan of a designated trustee or issuer and shall notify the distributee in writing (either separately or as part of the notice under section 402(f)) that the distribution may be transferred to another individual retirement plan.

(ii) Eligible plan.—For purposes of clause (i), the term "eligible plan" makes a plan which provides that any nonforfeitable accrued benefit for which the present value (as determined under section 411(a)(11)) does not exceed $5,000 shall be immediately distributed to the participant.

(C) Limitation.—Subparagraphs (A) and (B) shall apply only to the extent that the eligible rollover distribution would be includible in gross income if not transferred as provided in subparagraph (A) (determined without regard to sections 402(c), 403(a)(4), 403(b)(8), and 457(e)(16)). The preceding sentence shall not apply to such distribution if the plan to which such distribution is transferred—

(i) is a qualified trust which is part of a plan which is a defined contribution plan and agrees to separately account for amounts so transferred, including separately accounting for the portion of such distribution which is includible in gross income and the portion of such distribution which is not so includible, or

(ii) is an eligible retirement plan described in clause (i) or (ii) or section 402(c)(8)(B).

(D) Eligible rollover distribution.—For purposes of this paragraph, the term "eligible rollover distribution" has the meaning given such term by section 402(f)(2)(A).

(E) Eligible retirement plan.—For purposes of this paragraph, the term "eligible retirement plan" has the meaning given such term by section 402(c)(8)(B), except that a qualified trust shall be considered an eligible retirement plan only if it is a defined contribution plan, the terms of which permit the acceptance of rollover distributions.

(32) Treatment of failure to make certain payments if plan has liquidity shortfall.—

(A) In general.—A trust forming part of a pension plan to which section 430(j)(4) applies shall not be treated as failing to constitute a qualified trust under this section merely because such plan ceases to make any payment described in subparagraph (B) during any period that such plan has a liquidity shortfall (as defined in section 430(j)(4)).

(B) Payments described.—A payment is described in this subparagraph if such payment is—

(i) any payment, in excess of the monthly amount paid under a single life annuity (plus any social security supplements described in the last sentence of section 411(a)(9)), to a participant or beneficiary whose annuity starting date (as defined in section 417(f)(2)) occurs during the period referred to in subparagraph (A),

(ii) any payment for the purchase of an irrevocable commitment from an insurer to pay benefits, and

(iii) any other payment specified by the Secretary by regulations.

(C) Period of shortfall.—For purposes of this paragraph, a plan has a liquidity shortfall during the period that there is an underpayment of an installment under section 430(j)(3) by reason of section 430(j)(4)(A) thereof.

(33) Prohibition on benefit increases while sponsor is in bankruptcy.—

(A) In general.—A trust which is part of a plan to which this paragraph applies shall not constitute a qualified trust under this section if an amendment to such plan is adopted while the employer is a debtor in a case under title 11, United States Code, or similar Federal or State law, if such amend-ment increases liabilities of the plan by reason of—

(i) any increase in benefits,

(ii) any change in the accrual of benefits, or

(iii) any change in the rate at which benefits become nonforfeitable under the plan,

with respect to employees of the debtor, and such amendment is effective prior to the effective date of such employer's plan of reorganization.

(B) Exceptions.—This paragraph shall not apply to any plan amendment if—

(i) the plan, were such amendment to take effect, would have a funding target attainment percentage (as defined in section 430(d)(2)) of 100 percent or more.

(ii) the Secretary determines that such amendment is reasonable and provides for only de minimis increases in the liabilities of the plan with respect to employees of the debtor,

(iii) such amendment only repeals an amendment described in subsection 412(d)(2), or

(iv) such amendment is required as a condition of qualification under this part.

(C) Plans to which this paragraph applies.—This paragraph shall apply only to plans (other than multiemployer plans) covered under section 4021 of the Employee Retirement Income Security Act of 1974.

(D) Employer.—For purposes of this paragraph, the term "employer" means the employer referred to in section 412(c)(11) (without regard to subparagraph (B) thereof).

(34) Benefits of missing participants on plan termination.—In the case of a plan covered by title IV of the Employee Retirement Income Security Act of 1974, a trust forming part of such plan shall not be treated as failing to constitute a qualified trust under this section merely because the pension plan of which such trust is a part, upon its termination, transfers benefits of missing participants to the Pension Benefit Guaranty Corporation in accordance with section 4050 of such Act.

(35) Diversification requirements for certain defined contribution plans.—

(A) In general.—A trust which is part of an applicable defined contribution plan shall not be treated as a qualified trust unless the plan meets the diversification requirements of subparagraphs (B), (C), and (D).

(B) Employee contributions and elective deferrals invested in employer securities.—In the case of the portion of an applicable individual's account attributable to employee contributions and elective deferrals which is invested in employer securities, a plan meets the requirements of this subparagraph if the applicable individual may elect to direct the plan to divest any such securities and to reinvest an equivalent amount in other investment options meeting the requirements of subparagraph (D).

(C) Employer contributions invested in employer securities.—In the case of the portion of the account attributable to employer contributions other than elective deferrals which is invested in employer securities, a plan meets the requirements of this subparagraph if each applicable individual who—

(i) is a participant who has completed at least 3 years of service, or

(ii) is a beneficiary of a participant described in clause (i) or of a deceased participant, may elect to direct the plan to divest any such securities and to reinvest an equivalent amount in other investment options meeting the requirements of subparagraph (D).

(D) Investment options.—

(i) In general.—The requirements of this subparagraph are met if the plan offers not less than 3 investment options, other than employer securities, to which an applicable individual may direct the proceeds from the divestment of employer securities pursuant to this paragraph, each of which is diversified and has materially different risk and return characteristics.

(ii) Treatment of certain restrictions and conditions.—

(I) Time for making investment choices.—A plan shall not be treated as failing to meet the requirements of this subparagraph merely because the plan limits the time for divestment and reinvestment to periodic, reasonable opportunities occurring no less frequently than quarterly.

(II) Certain restrictions and conditions not allowed.—Except as provided in regulations, a plan shall not meet the requirements of this subparagraph if the plan imposes restrictions or conditions with respect to the investment of employer securities which are not imposed on the investment of other assets of the plan. This subclause shall not apply to any restrictions or conditions imposed by reason of the application of securities laws.

(E) Applicable defined contribution plan.—For purposes of this paragraph—

(i) In general.—The term "applicable defined contribution plan" means any defined contribution plan which holds any publicly traded employer securities.

(ii) Exception for certain ESOPs.—Such term does not include an employee stock ownership plan if—

(I) there are no contributions to such plan (or earnings thereunder) which are held within such plan and are subject to subsection (k) or (m), and

(II) such plan is a separate plan for purposes of section 414(l) with respect to any other defined benefit plan or defined contribution plan maintained by the same employer or employers.

(iii) Exception for one-participant plans.—Such term does not include a one-participant retirement plan.

(iv) One-participant retirement plan.—For purposes of clause (iii), the term "one-participant retirement plan" means a retirement plan that—

(I) covered only one individual (or the individual and the individual's spouse) and the individual (or the individual and the individual's spouse) owned 100 percent of the plan sponsor (whether or not incorporated), or

(II) covered only one or more partners (or partners and their spouses) in the plan sponsor.

(F) Certain plans treated as holding publicly traded employer securities.—

(i) In general.—Except as provided in regulations or in clause (ii), a plan holding employer securities which are not publicly traded employer securities shall be treated as holding publicly traded employer securities if any employer corporation, or any member of a controlled group of corporations which includes such employer corporation, has issued a class of stock which is a publicly traded employer security.

(ii) Exception for certain controlled groups with publicly traded securities.—Clause (i) shall not apply to a plan if—

(I) no employer corporation, or parent corporation of an employer corporation, has issued any publicly traded employer security, and

(II) no employer corporation, or parent corporation of an employer corporation, has issued any special class of stock which grants particular rights to, or bears particular risks for, the holder or issuer with respect to any corporation described in clause (i) which has issued any publicly traded employer security.

(iii) Definitions.—For purposes of this subparagraph, the term—

(I) "controlled group of corporations" has the meaning given such term by section 1563 (a), except that "50 percent" shall be substituted for "80 percent" each place it appears,

(II) "employer corporation" means a corporation which is an employer maintaining the plan, and

(III) "parent corporation" has the meaning given such term by section 424(e).

(G) Other definitions.—For purposes of this paragraph—

(i) Applicable individual.—The term "applicable individual" means—

(I) any participant in the plan, and

(II) any beneficiary who has an account under the plan with respect to which the beneficiary is entitled to exercise the rights of a participant.

(ii) Elective deferral.—The term "elective deferral" means an employer contribution described in section 402(g)(3)(A).

(iii) Employer security.—The term "employer security" has the meaning given such term by section 407(d)(1) of the Employee Retirement Income Security Act of 1974.

(iv) Employee stock ownership plan.—The term "employee stock ownership plan" has the meaning given such term by section 4975(e)(7).

(v) Publicly traded employer securities.—The term "publicly traded employer securities" means employer securities which are readily tradable on an established securities market.

(vi) Year of service.—The term "year of service" has the meaning given such term by section 411(a)(5).

(H) Transition rule for securities attributable to employer contributions.—

(i) Rules phased in over 3 years.—

(I) In general.—In the case of the portion of an account to which subparagraph (C) applies and which consists of employer securities acquired in a plan year beginning before January 1, 2007, subparagraph (C) shall only apply to the applicable percentage of such securities. This subparagraph shall be applied separately with respect to each class of securities.

(II) Exception for certain participants aged 55 or over.—Subclause (I) shall not apply to an applicable individual who is a participant who has attained age 55 and completed at least 3 years of service before the first plan year beginning after December 31, 2005.

(ii) Applicable percentage.—For purposes of clause (i), the applicable percentage shall be determined as follows:

Plan year to which subparagraph (C) applies:	The applicable percentage is:
1st	33
2d	66
3d and following	100.

(36) Distributions during working retirement.—A trust forming part of a pension plan shall not be treated as failing to constitute a qualified trust under this section solely because the plan provides that a distribution may be made from such trust to an employee who has attained age 62 and who is not separated from employment at the time of such distribution.

(37) Death benefits under USERRA-qualified active military service.—A trust shall not constitute a qualified trust unless the plan provides that, in the case of a participant who dies while performing qualified military service (as defined in section 414 (u)), the survivors of the participant are entitled to any additional benefits (other than benefit accruals relating to the period of qualified military service) provided under the plan had the participant resumed and then terminated employment on account of death.

Paragraphs (11), (12), (13), (14), (15), (19), and (20) shall apply only in the case of a plan to which section 411 (relating to minimum vesting standards) applies without regard to subsection (e)(2) of such section.

(b) Certain retroactive changes in plan.—A stock bonus, pension, profit-sharing, or annuity plan shall be considered as satisfying the requirements of subsection (a) for the period beginning with the date on which it was put into effect, or for the period beginning with the earlier of the date on which there was adopted or put into effect any amendment which caused the plan to fail to satisfy such requirements, and ending with the time prescribed by law for filing the return of the employer for his taxable year in which such plan or amendment was adopted (including extensions thereof) or such later time as the Secretary may designate, if all provisions of the plan which are necessary to satisfy such requirements are in effect by the end of such period and have been made effective for all purposes for the whole of such period.

(c) Definitions and rules relating to self-employed individuals and owner-employees.—For purposes of this section—

(1) Self-employed individual treated as employee.—

(A) In general.—The term "employee" includes, for any taxable year, an individual who is a self-employed individual for such taxable year.

(B) Self-employed individual.—The term "self-employed individual" means, with respect to any taxable year, an individual who has earned income (as defined in paragraph (2)) for such taxable year. To the extent provided in regulations prescribed by the Secretary, such term also includes, for any taxable year—

(i) an individual who would be a self-employed individual within the meaning of the preceding sentence but for the fact that the trade or business carried on by such individual did not have net profits for the taxable year, and

(ii) an individual who has been a self-employed individual within the meaning of the preceding sentence for any prior taxable year.

(2) Earned income.—

(A) In general.—The term "earned income" means the net earnings from self-employment (as defined in section 1402(a)), but such net earnings shall be determined—

(i) only with respect to a trade or business in which personal services of the taxpayer are a material income-producing factor,

(ii) without regard to paragraphs (4) and (5) of section 1402(c),

(iii) in the case of any individual who is treated as an employee under sections 3121(d)(3)(A), (C), or (D), without regard to paragraph (2) of section 1402(c),

(iv) without regard to items which are not included in gross income for purposes of this chapter, and the deductions properly allocable to or chargeable against such items,

(v) with regard to the deductions allowed by section 404 to the taxpayer, and

(vi) with regard to the deduction allowed to the taxpayer by section 164(f).

For purposes of this subparagraph, section 1402, as in effect for a taxable year ending on December 31, 1962, shall be treated as having been in effect for all taxable years ending before such date. For purposes of this part only (other than sections 419 and 419A), this subparagraph shall be applied as if the term "trade or business" for purposes of section 1402 included service described in section 1402(c)(6).

*__(C) Income from disposition of certain property.__—For purposes of this section, the term "earned income" includes gains (other than any gain which is treated under any provision of this chapter as gain from the sale or exchange of a capital asset) and net earnings derived from the sale or other disposition of, the transfer of any interest in, or the licensing of the use of property (other than good will) by an individual whose personal efforts created such property.

(3) Owner-employee.—The term "owner-employee" means an employee who—

(A) owns the entire interest in an unincorporated trade or business, or

*Editorial comment: There is no paragraph (B).

(B) in the case of a partnership, is a partner who owns more than 10 percent of either the capital interest or the profits interest in such partnership.

To the extent provided in regulations prescribed by the Secretary, such term also means an individual who has been an owner-employee within the meaning of the preceding sentence.

(4) Employer.—An individual who owns the entire interest in an unincorporated trade or business shall be treated as his own employer. A partnership shall be treated as the employer of each partner who is an employee within the meaning of paragraph (1).

(5) Contributions on behalf of owner-employees.—The term "contribution on behalf of an owner-employee" includes, except as the context otherwise requires, a contribution under a plan—

(A) by the employer for an owner-employee, and

(B) by an owner-employee as an employee.

(6) Special rule for certain fishermen.—For purposes of this subsection, the term "self-employed individual" includes an individual described in section 3121(b)(20) (relating to certain fishermen).

(d) Contribution limit on owner-employees.—A trust forming part of a pension or profit-sharing plan which provides contributions or benefits for employees some or all of whom are owner-employees shall constitute a qualified trust under this section only if, in addition to meeting the requirements of subsection (a), the plan provides that contributions on behalf of any owner-employee may be made only with respect to the earned income of such owner-employee which is derived from the trade or business with respect to which such plan is established.

***(f) Certain custodial accounts and contracts.**—For purposes of this title, a custodial account, an annuity contract, or a contract (other than a life, health or accident, property, casualty, or liability insurance contract) issued by an insurance company qualified to do business in a State shall be treated as a qualified trust under this section if—

(1) the custodial account or contract would, except for the fact that it is not a trust, constitute a qualified trust under this section, and

(2) in the case of a custodial account the assets thereof are held by a bank (as defined in section 408(n)) or another person who demonstrates, to the satisfaction of the Secretary, that the manner in which he will hold the assets will be consistent with the requirements of this section.

For purposes of this title, in the case of a custodial account or contract treated as a qualified trust under this section by reason of this subsection, the person holding the assets of such account or holding such contract shall be treated as the trustee thereof.

(g) Annuity defined.—For purposes of this section and sections 402, 403, and 404, the term "annuity" includes a face-amount certificate, as defined in section 2(a)(15) of the Investment Company Act of 1940 (15 U.S.C., sec. 80a-2); but does not include any contract or certificate issued after December 31, 1962, which is transferable, if any person other than the trustee of a trust described in section 401(a) which is exempt from tax under section 501(a) is the owner of such contract or certificate.

(h) Medical, etc., benefits for retired employees and their spouses and dependents.—Under regulations prescribed by the Secretary, and subject to the provisions of section 420, a pension or annuity plan may provide for the payment of benefits for sickness, accident, hospitalization, and medical expenses of retired employees, their spouses and their dependents, but only if—

(1) such benefits are subordinate to the retirement benefits provided by the plan,

(2) a separate account is established and maintained for such benefits,

(3) the employer's contributions to such separate account are reasonable and ascertainable,

(4) it is impossible, at any time prior to the satisfaction of all liabilities under the plan to provide such benefits, for any part of the corpus or income of such separate account to be (within the taxable year or thereafter) used for, or diverted to, any purpose other than the providing of such benefits,

*Editorial comment: There is no subsection (e).

(5) notwithstanding the provisions of subsection (a)(2), upon the satisfaction of all liabilities under the plan to provide such benefits, any amount remaining in such separate account must, under the terms of the plan, be returned to the employer, and

(6) in the case of an employee who is a key employee, a separate account is established and maintained for such benefits payable to such employee (and his spouse and dependents) and such benefits (to the extent attributable to plan years beginning after March 31, 1984, for which the employee is a key employee) are only payable to such employee (and his spouse and dependents) from such separate account.

For purposes of paragraph (6), the term "key employee" means any employee, who at any time during the plan year or any preceding plan year during which contributions were made on behalf of such employee, is or was a key employee as defined in section 416(i). In no event shall the requirements of paragraph (1) be treated as met if the aggregate actual contributions for medical benefits, when added to actual contributions for life insurance protection under the plan, exceed 25 percent of the total actual contributions to the plan (other than contributions to fund past service credits) after the date on which the account is established. For purposes of this subsection, the term "dependent" shall include any individual who is a child (as defined in section 152(f)(1)) of a retired employee who at the end of the calendar year has not attained age 27.

(i) Certain union-negotiated pension plans.—In the case of a trust forming part of a pension plan which has been determined by the Secretary to constitute a qualified trust under subsection (a) and to be exempt from taxation under section 501(a) for a period beginning after contributions were first made to or for such trust, if it is shown to the satisfaction of the Secretary that—

(1) such trust was created pursuant to a collective bargaining agreement between employee representatives and one or more employers,

(2) any disbursements of contributions, made to or for such trust before the time as of which the Secretary determined that the trust constituted a qualified trust, substantially complied with the terms of the trust, and the plan of which the trust is a part, as subsequently qualified, and

(3) before the time as of which the Secretary determined that the trust constitutes a qualified trust, the contributions to or for such trust were not used in a manner which would jeopardize the interests of its beneficiaries,

then such trust shall be considered as having constituted a qualified trust under subsection (a) and as having been exempt from taxation under section 501(a) for the period beginning on the date on which contributions were first made to or for such trust and ending on the date such trust first constituted (without regard to this subsection) a qualified trust under subsection (a).

***(k) Cash or deferred arrangements.**—

(1) General rule.—A profit-sharing or stock bonus plan, a pre-ERISA money purchase plan, or a rural cooperative plan shall not be considered as not satisfying the requirements of subsection (a) merely because the plan includes a qualified cash or deferred arrangement.

(2) Qualified cash or deferred arrangement.—A qualified cash or deferred arrangement is any arrangement which is part of a profit-sharing or stock bonus plan, a pre-ERISA money purchase plan, or a rural cooperative plan which meets the requirements of subsection (a)—

(A) under which a covered employee may elect to have the employer make payments as contributions to a trust under the plan on behalf of the employee, or to the employee directly in cash;

(B) under which amounts held by the trust which are attributable to employer contributions made pursuant to the employee's election,—

(i) may not be distributable to participants or other beneficiaries earlier than—

(I) severance from employment, death, or disability,

(II) an event described in paragraph (10),

(III) in the case of a profit-sharing or stock bonus plan, the attainment of age 59½, or

(IV) in the case of contributions to a profit-sharing or stock bonus plan to which section 402(e)(3) applies, upon hardship of the employee, or

*Editorial comment: There is no subsection (j).

(V) in the case of a qualified reservist distribution (as defined in section 72(t)(2)(G)(iii)), the date on which a period referred to in subclause (III) of such section begins, and

(ii) will not be distributable merely by reason of the completion of a stated period of participation or the lapse of a fixed number of years; and

(C) which provides that an employee's right to his accrued benefit derived from employer contributions made to the trust pursuant to his election is nonforfeitable, and

(D) which does not require, as a condition of participation in the arrangement, that an employee complete a period of service with the employer (or employers) maintaining the plan extending beyond the period permitted under section 410(a)(1) (determined without regard to subparagraph (B)(i) thereof).

(3) Application of participation and discrimination standards.—

(A) A cash or deferred arrangement shall not be treated as a qualified cash or deferred arrangement unless—

(i) those employees eligible to benefit under the arrangement satisfy the provisions of section 410(b)(1), and

(ii) the actual deferral percentage for eligible highly compensated employees (as defined in paragraph (5)) for the plan year bears a relationship to the actual deferral percentage for all other eligible employees for the preceding plan year which meets either of the following tests:

(I) The actual deferral percentage for the group of eligible highly compensated employees is not more than the actual deferral percentage of all other eligible employees multiplied by 1.25.

(II) The excess of the actual deferral percentage for the group of eligible highly compensated employees over that of all other eligible employees is not more than 2 percentage points, and the actual deferral percentage for the group of eligible highly compensated employees is not more than the actual deferral percentage of all other eligible employees multiplied by 2.

If 2 or more plans which include cash or deferred arrangements are considered as 1 plan for purposes of section 401(a)(4) or 410(b), the cash or deferred arrangements included in such plans shall be treated as 1 arrangement for purposes of this subparagraph.

If any employee is a participant under 2 or more cash or deferred arrangements of the employer, for purposes of determining the deferral percentage with respect to such employee, all such cash or deferred arrangements shall be treated as 1 cash or deferred arrangement. An arrangement may apply clause (ii) by using the plan year rather than the preceding plan year if the employer so elects, except that if such an election is made, it may not be changed except as provided by the Secretary.

(B) For purposes of subparagraph (A), the actual deferral percentage for a specified group of employees for a plan year shall be the average of the ratios (calculated separately for each employee in such group) of—

(i) the amount of employer contributions actually paid over to the trust on behalf of each such employee for such plan year, to

(ii) the employee's compensation for such plan year.

(C) A cash or deferred arrangement shall be treated as meeting the requirements of subsection (a)(4) with respect to contributions if the requirements of subparagraph (A)(ii) are met.

(D) For purposes of subparagraph (B), the employer contributions on behalf of any employee—

(i) shall include any employer contributions made pursuant to the employee's election under paragraph (2), and

(ii) under such rules as the Secretary may prescribe, may, at the election of the employer, include—

(I) matching contributions (as defined in 401(m)(4)(A)) which meet the requirements of paragraph (2)(B) and (C), and

(II) qualified nonelective contributions (within the meaning of section 401(m)(4)(C)).

(E) For purposes of this paragraph, in the case of the first plan year of any plan (other than a successor plan), the amount taken into account as the actual deferral percentage of nonhighly compensated employees for the preceding plan year shall be—

(i) 3 percent, or

(ii) if the employer makes an election under this subclause, the actual deferral percentage of nonhighly compensated employees determined for such first plan year.

(F) Special rule for early participation.—If an employer elects to apply section 410(b)(4)(B) in determining whether a cash or deferred arrangement meets the requirements of subparagraph (A)(i), the employer may, in determining whether the arrangement meets the requirements of subparagraph (A)(ii), exclude from consideration all eligible employees (other than highly compensated employees) who have not met the minimum age and service requirements of section 410(a)(1)(A).

(G) Governmental plan.— A governmental plan (within the meaning of section 414(d)) shall be treated as meeting the requirements of this paragraph.

(4) Other requirements.—

(A) Benefits (other than matching contributions) must not be contingent on election to defer.—A cash or deferred arrangement of any employer shall not be treated as a qualified cash or deferred arrangement if any other benefit is conditioned (directly or indirectly) on the employee electing to have the employer make or not make contributions under the arrangement in lieu of receiving cash. The preceding sentence shall not apply to any matching contribution (as defined in section 401(m)) made by reason of such an election.

(B) Eligibility of state and local governments and tax-exempt organizations.—

(i) Tax-exempts eligible.—Except as provided in clause (ii), any organization exempt from tax under this subtitle may include a qualified cash or deferred arrangement as part of a plan maintained by it.

(ii) Governments ineligible.—A cash or deferred arrangement shall not be treated as a qualified cash or deferred arrangement if it is part of a plan maintained by a State or local government or political subdivision thereof, or any agency or instrumentality thereof. This clause shall not apply to a rural cooperative plan or to a plan of an employer described in clause (iii).

(iii) Treatment of Indian tribal governments.—An employer which is an Indian tribal government (as defined in section 7701(a)(40)), a subdivision of an Indian tribal government (determined in accordance with section 7871(d)), an agency or instrumentality of an Indian tribal government or subdivision thereof, or a corporation chartered under Federal, State, or tribal law which is owned in whole or in part by any of the foregoing may include a qualified cash or deferred arrangement as part of a plan maintained by the employer.

(C) Coordination with other plans.—Except as provided in section 401(m), any employer contribution made pursuant to an employee's election under a qualified cash or deferred arrangement shall not be taken into account for purposes of determining whether any other plan meets the requirements of section 401(a) or 410(b). This subparagraph shall not apply for purposes of determining whether a plan meets the average benefit requirement of section 410(b)(2)(A)(ii).

(5) Highly compensated employee.—For purposes of this subsection, the term "highly compensated employee" has the meaning given such term by section 414(q).

(6) Pre-ERISA money purchase plan.—For purposes of this subsection, the term "pre-ERISA money purchase plan" means a pension plan—

(A) which is a defined contribution plan (as defined in section 414(i)),

(B) which was in existence on June 27, 1974, and which, on such date, included a salary reduction arrangement, and

(C) under which neither the employee contributions nor the employer contributions may exceed the levels provided for by the contribution formula in effect under the plan on such date.

(7) Rural cooperative plan.—For purposes of this subsection—

(A) In general.—The term "rural electric cooperative plan" means any pension plan—

(i) which is a defined contribution plan (as defined in section 414(i)), and

(ii) which is established and maintained by a rural electric cooperative.

(B) Rural cooperative defined.—For purposes of subparagraph (A), the term "rural cooperative" means—

(i) any organization which—

(I) is engaged primarily in providing electric service on a mutual or cooperative basis, or

(II) is engaged primarily in providing electric service to the public in its area of service and which is exempt from tax under this subtitle or which is a State or local government (or an agency or instrumentality thereof), other than a municipality (or an agency or instrumentality thereof),

(ii) any organization described in paragraph (4) or (6) of section 501(c) and at least 80 percent of the members of which are organizations described in clause (i),

(iii) a cooperative telephone company described in section 501(c)(12),

(iv) any organization which—

(I) is a mutual irrigation or ditch company described in section 501(c)(12) (without regard to the 85 percent requirement thereof), or

(II) is a district organized under the laws of a State as a municipal corporation for the purpose of irrigation, water conservation, or drainage, and

(v) an organization which is a national association of organizations described in clause (i), (ii), (iii), or (iv).

(C) Special rule for certain distributions.—A rural cooperative plan which includes a qualified cash or deferred arrangement shall not be treated as violating the requirements of section 401(a) or of paragraph (2) merely by reason of a hardship distribution or a distribution to a participant after attainment of age 59½. For purposes of this section, the term "hardship distribution" means a distribution described in paragraph (2)(B)(i)(IV) (without regard to the limitation of its application to profit-sharing or stock bonus plans).

(8) Arrangement not disqualified if excess contributions distributed.—

(A) In general.—A cash or deferred arrangement shall not be treated as failing to meet the requirements of clause (ii) of paragraph (3)(A) for any plan year if, before the close of the following plan year—

(i) the amount of the excess contributions for such plan year (and any income allocable to such contributions through the end of such year) is distributed, or

(ii) to the extent provided in regulations, the employee elects to treat the amount of the excess contributions as an amount distributed to the employee and then contributed by the employee to the plan.

Any distribution of excess contributions (and income) may be made without regard to any other provision of law.

(B) Excess contributions.—For purposes of subparagraph (A), the term "excess contributions" means, with respect to any plan year, the excess of—

(i) the aggregate amount of employer contributions actually paid over to the trust on behalf of highly compensated employees for such plan year, over

(ii) the maximum amount of such contributions permitted under the limitations of clause (ii) of paragraph (3)(A) (determined by reducing contributions made on behalf of highly compensated employees in order of the actual deferral percentages beginning with the highest of such percentages).

(C) Method of distributing excess contributions.—Any distribution of the excess contributions for any plan year shall be made to highly compensated employees on the basis of the amount of contributions by, or on behalf of, each of such employees.

(D) Additional tax under section 72(t) not to apply.—No tax shall be imposed under section 72(t) on any amount required to be distributed under this paragraph.

(E) Treatment of matching contributions forfeited by reason of excess deferral or contribution or permissible withdrawal.—For purposes of paragraph (2)(C), a matching contribution (within the meaning of subsection (m)) shall not be treated as forfeitable merely because such contribution is forfeitable if the contribution to which the matching contribution relates is treated as an excess contribution under subparagraph (B), an excess deferral under section 402(g)(2)(A), a permissible withdrawal under section 414(w), or an excess aggregate contribution under section 401(m)(6)(B).

(F) Cross reference.—

For excise tax on certain excess contributions, see section 4979.

(9) Compensation.—For purposes of this subsection, the term "compensation" has the meaning given such term by section 414(s).

(10) Distributions upon termination of plan.—

(A) In general.—An event described in this subparagraph is the termination of the plan without establishment or maintenance of another defined contribution plan (other than an employee stock ownership plan as defined in section 4975(e)(7)).

(B) Distributions must be lump-sum distributions.—

(i) In general.—A termination shall not be treated as described in subparagraph (A) with respect to any employee unless the employee receives a lump sum distribution by reason of the termination.

(ii) Lump-sum distribution.—For purposes of this subparagraph, the term "lump-sum distribution" has the meaning given such term by section 402(e)(4)(D) (without regard to subclauses (I), (II), (III), and (IV) of clause (i) thereof.) Such term includes a distribution of an annuity contract from—

(I) a trust which forms a part of a plan described in section 401(a) and which is exempt from tax under section 501(a), or

(II) an annuity plan described in section 403(a).

(11) Adoption of simple plan to meet nondiscrimination tests.—

(A) In general.—A cash or deferred arrangement maintained by an eligible employer shall be treated as meeting the requirements of paragraph (3)(A)(ii) if such arrangement meets—

(i) the contribution requirements of subparagraph (B),

(ii) the exclusive plan requirements of subparagraph (C), and

(iii) the vesting requirements of section 408(p)(3).

(B) Contribution requirements.—

(i) In general.—The requirements of this subparagraph are met if, under the arrangement—

(I) an employee may elect to have the employer make elective contributions for the year on behalf of the employee to a trust under the plan in an amount which is expressed as a percentage of compensation of the employee but which in no event exceeds the amount in effect under section 408(p)(2)(A)(ii),

(II) the employer is required to make a matching contribution to the trust for the year in an amount equal to so much of the amount the employee elects under subclause (I) as does not exceed 3 percent of compensation for the year, and

(III) no other contributions may be made other than contributions described in subclause (I) or (II).

(ii) Employer may elect 2-percent nonelective contribution.—An employer shall be treated as meeting the requirements of clause (i)(II) for any year if, in lieu of the contributions described in such clause, the employer elects (pursuant to the terms of the arrangement) to make nonelective contributions of 2 percent of compensation for each employee who is eligible to participate in the arrangement and who has at least $5,000 of compensation from the employer for the year. If an employer makes an election under this subparagraph for any year, the employer shall notify employees of such election within a reasonable period of time before the 60th day before the beginning of such year.

(iii) Administrative requirements.—

(I) In general.—Rules similar to the rules of subparagraphs (B) and (C) of section 408(p)(5) shall apply for purposes of this subparagraph.

(II) Notice of election period.—The requirements of this subparagraph shall not be treated as met with respect to any year unless the employer notifies each employee eligible to participate, within a reasonable period of time before the 60th day before the beginning of such year (and, for the first year the employee is so eligible, the 60th day before the first day such employee is so eligible), of the rules similar to the rules of section 408(p)(5)(C) which apply by reason of subclause (I).

(C) Exclusive plan requirement.—The requirements of this subparagraph are met for any year to which this paragraph applies if no contributions were made, or benefits were accrued, for services during such year under any qualified plan of the employer on behalf of any employee eligible to participate in the cash or deferred arrangement, other than contributions described in subparagraph (B).

(D) Definitions and special rule.—

(i) Definitions.—For purposes of this paragraph, any term used in this paragraph which is also used in section 408(p) shall have the meaning given such term by such section.

(ii) Coordination with top-heavy rules.—A plan meeting the requirements of this paragraph for any year shall not be treated as a top-heavy plan under section 416 for such year if such plan allows only contributions required under this paragraph.

(12) Alternative methods of meeting nondiscrimination requirements.—

(A) In general.—A cash or deferred arrangement shall be treated as meeting the requirements of paragraph (3)(A)(ii) if such arrangement—

(i) meets the contribution requirements of subparagraph (B) or (C), and

(ii) meets the notice requirements of subparagraph (D).

(B) Matching contributions.—

(i) In general.—The requirements of this subparagraph are met if, under the arrangement, the employer makes matching contributions on behalf of each employee who is not a highly compensated employee in an amount equal to—

(I) 100 percent of the elective contributions of the employee to the extent such elective contributions do not exceed 3 percent of the employee's compensation, and

(II) 50 percent of the elective contributions of the employee to the extent that such elective contributions exceed 3 percent but do not exceed 5 percent of the employee's compensation.

(ii) Rate for highly compensated employees.—The requirements of this subparagraph are not met if, under the arrangement, the rate of matching contribution with respect to any elective contribution of a highly compensated employee at any rate of elective contribution is greater than that with respect to an employee who is not a highly compensated employee.

(iii) Alternative plan designs.—If the rate of any matching contribution with respect to any rate of elective contribution is not equal to the percentage required under clause (i), an arrangement shall not be treated as failing to meet the requirements of clause (i) if—

(I) the rate of an employer's matching contribution does not increase as an employee's rate of elective contributions increases, and

(II) the aggregate amount of matching contributions at such rate of elective contribution is at least equal to the aggregate amount of matching contributions which would be made if matching contributions were made on the basis of the percentages described in clause (i).

(C) Nonelective contributions.—The requirements of this subparagraph are met if, under the arrangement, the employer is required, without regard to whether the employee makes an elective contribution or employee contribution, to make a contribution to a defined contribution plan on behalf of each employee who is not a highly compensated employee and who is eligible to participate in the arrangement in an amount equal to at least 3 percent of the employee's compensation.

(D) Notice requirement.—An arrangement meets the requirements of this paragraph if, under the arrangement, each employee eligible to participate is, within a reasonable period before any year, given written notice of the employee's rights and obligations under the arrangement which—

(i) is sufficiently accurate and comprehensive to appraise the employer of such rights and obligations, and

(ii) is written in a manner calculated to be understood by the average employee eligible to participate.

(E) Other requirements.—

(i) Withdrawal and vesting restrictions.—An arrangement shall not be treated as meeting the requirements of subparagraph (B) or (C) or this paragraph unless the requirements of subparagraphs (B) and (C) of paragraph (2) are met with respect to all employer contributions (including matching contributions) taken into account in determining whether the requirements of subparagraphs (B) and (C) of this paragraph are met.

(ii) Social security and similar contributions taken into account.—An arrangement shall not be treated as meeting the requirements of subparagraph (B) or (C) unless such requirements are met without regard to subsection (1), and for purposes of subsection (1), employer contributions under subparagraph (B) or (C) shall not be taken into account.

(F) Other plans.—An arrangement shall be treated as meeting the requirements under subparagraph (A)(i) if any other plan maintained by the employer meets such requirements with respect to employees eligible under the arrangement.

(13) Alternative method for automatic contribution arrangements to meet nondiscrimination requirements.—

(A) In general.—A qualified automatic contribution arrangement shall be treated as meeting the requirements of paragraph (3)(A)(ii).

(B) Qualified automatic contribution arrangement.—For purposes of this paragraph, the term "qualified automatic contribution arrangement" means any cash or deferred arrangement which meets the requirements of subparagraphs (C) through (E).

(C) Automatic deferral.—

(i) In general.—The requirements of this subparagraph are met if, under the arrangement, each employee eligible to participate in the arrangement is treated as having elected to have the employer make elective contributions in an amount equal to a qualified percentage of compensation.

(ii) Election out.—The election treated as having been made under clause (i) shall cease to apply with respect to any employee if such employee makes an affirmative election—

(I) to not have such contributions made, or

(II) to make elective contributions at a level specified in such affirmative election.

(iii) Qualified percentage.—For purposes of this subparagraph, the term "qualified percentage" means, with respect to any employee, any percentage determined under the arrangement if such percentage is applied uniformly, does not exceed 10 percent, and is at least—

(I) 3 percent during the period ending on the last day of the first plan year which begins after the date on which the first elective contribution described in clause (i) is made with respect to such employee,

(II) 4 percent during the first plan year following the plan year described in subclause (I),

(III) 5 percent during the second plan year following the plan year described in subclause (I), and

(IV) 6 percent during any subsequent plan year.

(iv) Automatic deferral for current employees not required.—Clause (i) may be applied without taking into account any employee who—

(I) was eligible to participate in an arrangement (or a predecessor arrangement) immediately before the date on which such arrangement becomes a qualified automatic contribution arrangement (determined after application of this clause), and

(II) had an election in effect on such date either to participate in the arrangement or to not participate in the arrangement.

(D) Matching or nonelective contributions.—

(i) In general.—The requirements of this subparagraph are met if, under the arrangement, the employer—

(I) makes matching contributions on behalf of each employee who is not a highly compensated employee in an amount equal to the sum of 100 percent of the elective contributions of the employee to the extent that such contributions do not exceed 1 percent of compensation plus 50 percent of so much of such contributions as exceeds 1 percent but does not exceed 6 percent of compensation, or

(II) is required, without regard to whether the employee makes an elective contribution or employee contribution, to make a contribution to a defined contribution plan on behalf of each employee who is not a highly compensated employee and who is eligible to participate in the arrangement in an amount equal to at least 3 percent of the employee's compensation.

(ii) Application of rules for matching contributions.—The rules of clauses (ii) and (iii) of paragraph (12)(B) shall apply for purposes of clause (i)(I).

(iii) Withdrawal and vesting restrictions.—An arrangement shall not be treated as meeting the requirements of clause (i) unless, with respect to employer contributions (including matching contributions) taken into account in determining whether the requirements of clause (i) are met-

(I) any employee who has completed at least 2 years of service (within the meaning of section 411(a)) has a nonforfeitable right to 100 percent of the employee's accrued benefit derived from such employer contributions, and

(II) the requirements of subparagraph (B) of paragraph (2) are met with respect to all such employer contributions.

(iv) Application of certain other rules.—The rules of subparagraphs (E)(ii) and (F) of paragraph (12) shall apply for purposes of subclauses (I) and (II) of clause (i).

(E) Notice requirements.—

(i) In general.—The requirements of this subparagraph are met if, within a reasonable period before each plan year, each employee eligible to participate in the arrangement for such year receives written notice of the employee's rights and obligations under the arrangement which—

(I) is sufficiently accurate and comprehensive to apprise the employee of such rights and obligations, and

(II) is written in a manner calculated to be understood by the average employee to whom the arrangement applies.

(ii) Timing and content requirements.—A notice shall not be treated as meeting the requirements of clause (i) with respect to an employee unless—

(I) the notice explains the employee's right under the arrangement to elect not to have elective contributions made

on the employee's behalf (or to elect to have such contributions made at a different percentage),

(II) in case of an arrangement under which the employee may elect among 2 or more investment options, the notice explains how contributions made under the arrangement will be invested in the absence of any investment election by the employee, and

(III) the employee has a reasonable period of time after receipt of the notice described in subclause (I) and (II) and before the first elective contribution is made to make either such election.

(l) Permitted disparity in plan contributions or benefits.—

(1) In general.—The requirements of this subsection are met with respect to a plan if—

(A) in the case of a defined contribution plan, the requirements of paragraph (2) are met, and

(B) in the case of a defined benefit plan, the requirements of paragraph (3) are met.

(2) Defined contribution plan.—

(A) In general.—A defined contribution plan meets the requirements of this paragraph if the excess contribution percentage does not exceed the base contribution percentage by more than the lesser of—

(i) the base contribution percentage, or

(ii) the greater of—

(I) 5.7 percentage points, or

(II) the percentage equal to the portion of the rate of tax under section 3111 (a) (in effect as of the beginning of the year) which is attributable to old-age insurance.

(B) Contribution percentages.—For purposes of this paragraph—

(i) Excess contribution percentage.—The term "excess contribution percentage" means the percentage of compensation which is contributed by the employer under the plan with respect to that portion of each participant's compensation in excess of the integration level.

(ii) Base contribution percentage.—The term "base contribution percentage" means the percentage of compensation contributed by the employer under the plan with respect to that portion of each participant's compensation not in excess of the integration level.

(3) Defined benefit plan.—A defined benefit plan meets the requirements of this paragraph if—

(A) Excess plans.—

(i) In general.—In the case of a plan other than an offset plan—

(I) the excess benefit percentage does not exceed the base benefit percentage by more than the maximum excess allowance,

(II) any optional form of benefit, preretirement benefit, actuarial factor, or other benefit or feature provided with respect to compensation in excess of the integration level is provided with respect to compensation not in excess of such level, and

(III) benefits are based on average annual compensation.

(ii) Benefit percentages.—For purposes of this subparagraph, the excess and base benefit percentages shall be computed in the same manner as the excess and base contribution percentages under paragraph (2)(B), except that such determination shall be made on the basis of benefits attributable to employer contributions rather than contributions.

(B) Offset plans.—In the case of an offset plan, the plan provides that—

(i) a participant's accrued benefit attributable to employer contributions (within the meaning of section 411(c) (1)) may not be reduced (by reason of the offset) by more than the maximum offset allowance, and

(ii) benefits are based on average annual compensation.

(4) Definitions relating to paragraph (3).—For purposes of paragraph (3)—

(A) Maximum excess allowance.—The maximum excess allowance is equal to—

(i) in the case of benefits attributable to any year of service with the employer taken into account under the plan, $\frac{3}{4}$ of a percentage point, and

(ii) in the case of total benefits, $\frac{3}{4}$ of a percentage point, multiplied by the participant's years of service (not in excess of 35) with the employer taken into account under the plan.

In no event shall the maximum excess allowance exceed the base benefit percentage.

(B) Maximum offset allowance.—The maximum offset allowance is equal to—

(i) in the case of benefits attributable to any year of service with the employer taken into account under the plan, $\frac{3}{4}$ percent of the participant's final average compensation, and

(ii) in the case of total benefits, $\frac{3}{4}$ percent of the participant's final average compensation, multiplied by the participant's years of service (not in excess of 35) with the employer taken into account under the plan.

In no event shall the maximum offset allowance exceed 50 percent of the benefit which would have accrued without regard to the offset reduction.

(C) Reductions.—

(i) In general.—The Secretary shall prescribe regulations requiring the reduction of the 3/4 percentage factor under subparagraph (A) or (B)—

(I) in the case of a plan other than an offset plan which has an integration level in excess of covered compensation, or

(II) with respect to any participant in an offset plan who has final average compensation in excess of covered compensation.

(ii) Basis of reductions.—Any reductions under clause (i) shall be based on the percentages of compensation replaced by the employer-derived portions of primary insurance amounts under the Social Security Act for participants with compensation in excess of covered compensation.

(D) Offset plan.—The term "offset plan" means any plan with respect to which the benefit attributable to employer contributions for each participant is reduced by an amount specified in the plan.

(5) Other definitions and special rules.—For purposes of this subsection—

(A) Integration level.—

(i) In general.—The term "integration level" means the amount of compensation specified under the plan (by dollar amount or formula) at or below which the rate at which contributions or benefits are provided (expressed as a percentage) is less than such rate above such amount.

(ii) Limitation.—The integration level for any year may not exceed the contribution and benefit base in effect under section 230 of the Social Security Act for such year.

(iii) Level to apply to all participants.— A plan's integration level shall apply with respect to all participants in the plan.

(iv) Multiple integration levels.—Under rules prescribed by the Secretary, a defined benefit plan may specify multiple integration levels.

(B) Compensation.—The term "compensation" has the meaning given such term by section 414(s).

(C) Average annual compensation.—The term "average annual compensation" means the participant's highest average annual compensation for—

(i) any period of at least 3 consecutive years, or

(ii) if shorter, the participant's full period of service.

(D) Final average compensation.—

(i) In general.—The term "final average compensation" means the participant's average annual compensation for—

(I) the 3-consecutive year period ending with the current year, or

(II) if shorter, the participant's full period of service.

(ii) Limitation.—A participant's final average compensation shall be determined by not taking into account in any year compensation in excess of the contribution and benefit base in effect under section 230 of the Social Security Act for such year.

(E) Covered compensation.—

(i) In general.—The term "covered compensation" means, with respect to an employee, the average of the contribution and benefit bases in effect under section 230 of the Social Security Act for each year in the 35-year period ending with the year in which the employee attains the social security retirement age.

(ii) Computation for any year.—For purposes of clause (i), the determination for any year preceding the year in which the employee attains the social security retirement age shall be made by assuming that there is no increase in the bases described in clause (i) after the determination year and before the employee attains the social security retirement age.

(iii) Social security retirement age.—For purposes of this subparagraph, the term "social security retirement age" has the meaning given such term by section 415(b)(8).

(F) Regulations.—The Secretary shall prescribe such regulations as are necessary or appropriate to carry out the purposes of this subsection, including—

(i) in the case of a defined benefit plan which provides for unreduced benefits commencing before the social security retirement age (as defined in section 415(b)(8)), rules providing for the reduction of the maximum excess allowance and the maximum offset allowance, and

(ii) in the case of an employee covered by 2 or more plans of the employer which fail to meet the requirements of subsection (a)(4) (without regard to this subsection,) rules preventing the multiple use of the disparity permitted under this subsection with respect to any employee.

For purposes of clause (i), unreduced benefits shall not include benefits for disability (within the meaning of section 223(d) of the Social Security Act).

(6) Special rule for plan maintained by railroads.—In determining whether a plan which includes employees of a railroad employer who are entitled to benefits under the Railroad Retirement Act of 1974 meets the requirements of this subsection, rules similar to the rules set forth in this subsection shall apply. Such rules shall take into account the employer-derived portion of the employees' tier 2 railroad retirement benefits and any supplemental annuity under the Railroad Retirement Act of 1974.

(m) Nondiscrimination test for matching contributions and employee contributions.—

(1) In general.—A defined contribution plan shall be treated as meeting the requirements of subsection (a)(4) with respect to the amount of any matching contribution or employee contribution for any plan year only if the contribution percentage requirement of paragraph (2) of this subsection is met for such plan year.

(2) Requirements.—

(A) Contribution percentage requirement.—A plan meets the contribution percentage requirement of this paragraph for any plan year only if the contribution percentage for eligible highly compensated employees for such plan year does not exceed the greater of—

(i) 125 percent of such percentage for all other eligible employees, or

(ii) the lesser of 200 percent of such percentage for all other eligible employees, or such percentage for all other eligible employees for the preceding plan year plus 2 percentage points.

This subparagraph may be applied by using the plan year rather than the preceding plan year if the employer so elects, except that if such an election is made, it may not be changed except as provided by the Secretary.

(B) Multiple plans treated as a single plan.—If two or more plans of an employer to which matching contributions, employee contributions, or elective deferrals are made are treated as one plan for purposes of section 410(b), such plans shall be treated as one plan for purposes of this subsection. If a highly compensated employee participates in two or more plans of an employer to which contributions are made to which this subsection applies, all such contributions shall be aggregated for purposes of this subsection.

(3) Contribution percentage.—For purposes of paragraph (2), the contribution percentage for a specified group of employees for a plan year shall be the average of the ratios (calculated separately for each employee in such group) of—

(A) the sum of the matching contributions and employee contributions paid under the plan on behalf of each such employee for such plan year, to

(B) the employee's compensation (within the meaning of section 414(s)) for such plan year.

Under regulations, an employer may elect to take into account (in computing the contribution percentage) elective deferrals and qualified non-elective contributions under the plan or any other plan of the employer. If matching contributions are taken into account for purposes of subsection (k)(3)(A)(ii) for any plan year, such contributions shall not be taken into account under subparagraph (A) for such year. Rules similar to the rules of subsection (k)(3)(E) shall apply for purposes of this subsection.

(4) Definitions.—For purposes of this subsection—

(A) Matching contribution.—The term "matching contribution" means—

(i) any employer contribution made to a defined contribution plan on behalf of an employee on account of an employee contribution made by such employee, and

(ii) any employer contribution made to a defined contribution plan on behalf of an employee on account of an employee's elective deferral.

(B) Elective deferral.—The term "elective deferral" means any employer contribution described in section 402(g)(3).

(C) Qualified nonelective contributions.— The term "qualified nonelective contribution" means any employer contribution (other than a matching contribution) with respect to which—

(i) the employee may not elect to have the contribution paid to the employee in cash instead of being contributed to the plan, and

(ii) the requirements of subparagraphs (B) and (C) of subsection (k)(2) are met.

(5) Employees taken into consideration.—

(A) In general.—Any employee who is eligible to make an employee contribution (or, if the employer takes elective contributions into account, elective contributions) or to receive a matching contribution under the plan being tested under paragraph (1) shall be considered an eligible employee for purposes of this subsection.

(B) Certain nonparticipants.—If an employee contribution is required as a condition of participation in the plan, any employee who would be a participant in the plan if such employee made such a contribution shall be treated as an eligible employee on behalf of whom no employer contributions are made.

(C) Special rule for early participation.—If an employer elects to apply section 410(b)(4)(B) in determining whether a plan meets the requirements of section 410(b), the employer may, in determining whether the plan meets the requirements of paragraph (2), exclude from consideration all eligible employees (other than highly compensated employees) who have not met the minimum age and service requirements of section 410(a)(1)(A).

(6) Plan not disqualified if excess aggregate contributions distributed before end of following plan year.—

(A) In general.—A plan shall not be treated as failing to meet the requirements of paragraph (1) for any plan year if, before the close of the following plan year, the amount of the excess aggregate contributions for such plan year (and any income allocable to such contributions through the end of such year) is distributed (or, if forfeitable, is forfeited). Such contributions (and such income) may be distributed without regard to any other provision of law.

(B) Excess aggregate contributions.—For purposes of subparagraph (A), the term "excess aggregate contributions" means, with respect to any plan year, the excess of—

(i) the aggregate amount of the matching contributions and employee contributions (and any qualified nonelective contribution or elective contribution taken into account in computing the contribution percentage) actually made on behalf of highly compensated employees for such plan year, over

(ii) the maximum amount of such contributions permitted under the limitations of paragraph (2)(A) (determined by reducing contributions made on behalf of highly compensated employees in order of their contribution percentages beginning with the highest of such percentages).

(C) Method of distributing excess aggregate contributions.—Any distribution of the excess aggregate contributions for any plan year shall be made to highly compensated employees on the basis of the amount of contributions on behalf of, or by, each such employee. Forfeitures of excess aggregate contributions may not be allocated to participants whose contributions are reduced under this paragraph.

(D) Coordination with subsection (k) and 402(g).—The determination of the amount of excess aggregate contributions with respect to a plan shall be made after—

(i) first determining the excess deferrals (within the meaning of section 402 (g)), and

(ii) then determining the excess contributions under subsection (k).

(7) Treatment of distributions.—

(A) Additional tax of section 72(t) not applicable.—No tax shall be imposed under section 72(t) on any amount required to be distributed under paragraph (6).

(B) Exclusion of employee contributions.—Any distribution attributable to employee contributions shall not be included in gross income except to the extent attributable to income on such contributions.

(8) Highly compensated employee.—For purposes of this subsection, the term "highly compensated employee" has the meaning given to such term by section 414(q).

(9) Regulations.—The Secretary shall prescribe such regulations as may be necessary to carry out the purposes of this subsection and subsection (k), including regulations permitting appropriate aggregation of plans and contributions.

(10) Alternative method of satisfying tests.—A defined contribution plan shall be treated as meeting the requirements of paragraph (2) with respect to matching contributions if the plan—

(A) meets the contribution requirements of subparagraph (B) of subsection (k)(11),

(B) meets the exclusive plan requirements of subsection (k)(11)(C), and

(C) meets the vesting requirements of section 408(p)(3).

(11) Additional alternative method of satisfying tests.—

(A) In general.—A defined contribution plan shall be treated as meeting the requirements of paragraph (2) with respect to matching contributions if the plan—

(i) meets the contribution requirements of subparagraph (B) or (C) or subsection (k)(12),

(ii) meets the notice requirements of subsection k(12)(D), and

(iii) meets the requirements of subparagraph (B)

(B) Limitation on matching contributions.—The requirements of this subparagraph are met if—

(i) matching contributions on behalf of any employee may not be made with respect to an employee's contributions or elective deferrals in excess of 6 percent of the employee's compensation,

(ii) the rate of an employer's matching contribution does not increase as the rate of an employee's contributions or elective deferrals increase, and

(iii) the matching contribution with respect to any highly compensated employee at any rate of an employee contribution or rate of elective deferral is not greater than that with respect to an employee who is not a highly compensated employee.

(12) Alternative method for automatic contribution arrangements.—A defined contribution plan shall be treated as meeting the requirements of paragraph (2) with respect to matching contributions if the plan—

(A) is a qualified automatic contribution arrangement (as defined in subsection (k)(13)), and

(B) meets the requirements of paragraph (11)(B).

(13) Cross reference.—

For excise tax on certain excess contributions, see section 4979.

(n) Coordination with qualified domestic relations orders.—The Secretary shall prescribe such rules or regulations as may be necessary to coordinate the requirements of subsection (a)(13)(B) and section 414(p) (and the regulations issued by the Secretary of Labor thereunder) with the other provisions of this chapter.

(o) Cross reference.—

For exemption from tax of a trust qualified under this section, see section 501(a).

§ 402. Taxability of beneficiary of employees' trust

(a) Taxability of beneficiary of exempt trust.—Except as otherwise provided in this section, any amount actually distributed to any distributee by any employees' trust described in section 401(a) which is exempt from tax under section 501(a) shall be taxable to the distributee, in the taxable year of the distributee in which distributed, under section 72 (relating to annuities).

(b) Taxability of beneficiary of nonexempt trust.—

(1) Contributions.—Contributions to an employees' trust made by an employer during a taxable year of the employer which ends with or within a taxable year of the trust for which the trust is not exempt from tax under section 501(a) shall be included in the gross income of the employee in accordance with section 83 (relating to property transferred in connection with performance of services), except that the value of the employee's interest in the trust shall be substituted for the fair market value of the property for purposes of applying such section.

(2) Distributions.—The amount actually distributed or made available to any distributee by any trust described in paragraph (1) shall be taxable to the distributee, in the taxable year in which so distributed or made available, under section 72 (relating to annuities), except that distributions of income of such trust before the annuity starting date (as defined in section 72(c)(4)) shall be included in the gross income of the employee without regard to section 72(e)(5) (relating to amounts not received as annuities).

(3) Grantor trusts.—A beneficiary of any trust described in paragraph (1) shall not be considered the owner of any portion of such trust under subpart E of part I of subchapter J (relating to grantors and others treated as substantial owners).

(4) Failure to meet requirements of section 410(b).—

(A) Highly compensated employees.—If one of the reasons a trust is not exempt from tax under section 501(a) is the failure of the plan of which it is a part to meet the requirements of section 401(a)(26) or 410(b), then a highly compensated employee shall, in lieu of the amount determined under paragraph (1) or (2) include in gross income for the taxable year with or within which the taxable year of the trust ends an amount equal to the vested accrued benefit of such employee (other than the employee's investment in the contract) as of the close of such taxable year of the trust.

(B) Failure to meet coverage tests.—If a trust is not exempt from tax under section 501(a) for any taxable year solely because such trust is part of a plan which fails to meet the requirements of section 401(a)(26) or 410(b), paragraphs (1) and (2) shall not apply by reason of such failure to any employee who was not a highly compensated employee during—

(i) such taxable year, or

(ii) any preceding period for which service was creditable to such employee under the plan.

(C) Highly compensated employee.—For purposes of this paragraph, the term "highly compensated employee" has the meaning given such term by section 414(q).

(c) Rules applicable to rollovers from exempt trusts.—

(1) Exclusion from income.—If—

(A) any portion of the balance to the credit of an employee in a qualified trust is paid to the employee in an eligible rollover distribution,

(B) the distributee transfers any portion of the property received in such distribution to an eligible retirement plan, and

(C) in the case of a distribution of property other than money, the amount so transferred consists of the property distributed,

then such distribution (to the extent so transferred) shall not be includible in gross income for the taxable year in which paid.

(2) Maximum amount which may be rolled over.—In the case of any eligible rollover distribution, the maximum amount transferred to which paragraph (1) applies shall not exceed the portion of such distribution which is includible in gross income (determined without regard to paragraph (1)). The preceding sentence shall not apply to such distribution to the extent—

(A) such portion is transferred in a direct trustee-to-trustee transfer to a qualified trust or to an annuity contract described in section 403(b) and such trust or contract provides for separate accounting for amounts so transferred (and earnings thereon), including separately accounting for the portion of such distribution which is includible in gross income and the portion of such distribution which is not so includible, or

(B) such portion is transferred to an eligible retirement plan described in clause (i) or (ii) of paragraph (8)(B).

In the case of a transfer described in subparagraph (A) or (B), the amount transferred shall be treated as consisting first of the portion of such distribution that is includible in gross income (determined without regard to paragraph (1)).

(3) Transfer must be made within 60 days of receipt.—

(A) In general.—Except as provided in subparagraph (B), paragraph (1) shall not apply to any transfer of a distribution made after the 60th day following the day on which the distributee received the property distributed.

(B) Hardship exception.—The Secretary may waive the 60-day requirement under subparagraph (A) where the failure to waive such requirement would be against equity or good conscience, including casualty, disaster, or other events beyond the reasonable control of the individual subject to such requirement.

(4) Eligible rollover distribution.—For purposes of this subsection, the term "eligible rollover distribution" means any distribution to an employee of all or any portion of the balance to the credit of the employee in a qualified trust; except that such term shall not include—

(A) any distribution which is one of a series of substantially equal periodic payments (not less frequently than annually) made—

(i) for the life (or life expectancy) of the employee or the joint lives (or joint life expectancies) of the employee and the employee's designated beneficiary, or

(ii) for a specified period of 10 years or more,

(B) any distribution to the extent such distribution is required under section 401(a)(9), and

(C) any distribution which is made upon hardship of the employee.

If all or any portion of a distribution during 2009 is treated as an eligible rollover distribution but would not be so treated if the minimum distribution requirements under section 401(a)(9) had applied during 2009, such distribution shall not be treated as an eligible rollover distribution for purposes of section 401(a)(31) or 3405(c) or subsection (f) of this section.

(5) Transfer treated as rollover contribution under section 408.—For purposes of this title, a transfer to an eligible retirement plan described in clause (i) or (ii) of paragraph (8)(B) resulting in any portion of a distribution being excluded from gross income under paragraph (1) shall be treated as a rollover contribution described in section 408(d)(3).

(6) Sales of distributed property.—For purposes of this subsection—

(A) Transfer of proceeds from sale of distributed property treated as transfer of distributed property.—The transfer of an amount equal to any portion of the proceeds from the sale of property received in the distribution shall be treated as the transfer of property received in the distribution.

(B) Proceeds attributable to increase in value.—The excess of fair market value of property on sale over its fair market value on distribution shall be treated as property received in the distribution.

(C) Designation where amount of distribution exceeds rollover contribution.—In any case where part or all of the distribution consists of property other than money—

(i) the portion of the money or other property which is to be treated as attributable to amounts not included in gross income, and

(ii) the portion of the money or other property which

is to be treated as included in the rollover contribution, shall be determined on a ratable basis unless the taxpayer designates otherwise. Any designation under this subparagraph for a taxable year shall be made not later than the time prescribed by law for filing the return for such taxable year (including extensions thereof). Any such designation, once made, shall be irrevocable.

(D) Nonrecognition of gain or loss.—No gain or loss shall be recognized on any sale described in subparagraph (A) to the extent that an amount equal to the proceeds is transferred pursuant to paragraph (1).

(7) Special rule for frozen deposits.—

(A) In general.—The 60-day period described in paragraph (3) shall not—

(i) include any period during which the amount transferred to the employee is a frozen deposit, or

(ii) end earlier than 10 days after such amount ceases to be a frozen deposit.

(B) Frozen deposits.—For purposes of this subparagraph, the term "frozen deposit" means any deposit which may not be withdrawn because of—

(i) the bankruptcy or insolvency of any financial institution, or

(ii) any requirement imposed by the State in which such institution is located by reason of the bankruptcy or insolvency (or threat thereof) of 1 or more financial institutions in such State.

A deposit shall not be treated as a frozen deposit unless on at least 1 day during the 60-day period described in paragraph (3) (without regard to this paragraph) such deposit is described in the preceding sentence.

(8) Definitions.—For purposes of this subsection—

(A) Qualified trust.—The term "qualified trust" means an employees' trust described in section 401(a) which is exempt from tax under section 501(a).

(B) Eligible retirement plan.—The term "eligible retirement plan" means—

(i) an individual retirement account described in section 408(a),

(ii) an individual retirement annuity described in section 408(b) (other than an endowment contract),

(iii) a qualified trust,

(iv) an annuity plan described in section 403(a),

(v) an eligible deferred compensation plan described in section 457(b) which is maintained by an eligible employer described in section 457(e)(1)(A), and

(vi) an annuity contract described in section 403(b).

If any portion of an eligible rollover distribution is attributable to payments or distributions from a designated Roth account (as defined in section 402A), an eligible retirement plan with respect to such portion shall include only another designated Roth account and a Roth IRA.

(9) Rollover where spouse receives distribution after death of employee.—If any distribution attributable to an employee is paid to the spouse of the employee after the employee's death, the preceding provisions of this subsection shall apply to such distribution in the same manner as if the spouse were the employee.

(10) Separate accounting.—Unless a plan described in clause (v) of paragraph (8)(B) agrees to separately account for amounts rolled into such plan from eligible retirement plans not described in such clause, the plan described in such clause may not accept transfers or rollovers from such retirement plans.

(11) Distributions to inherited individual retirement plan of nonspouse beneficiary.—

(A) In general.—If, with respect to any portion of a distribution from an eligible retirement plan described in paragraph (8)(B)(iii) of a deceased employee, a direct trustee-to-trustee transfer is made to an individual retirement plan described in clause (i) or (ii) of paragraph (8)(B) established for the purposes of receiving the distribution on behalf of an individual who is a designated beneficiary (as defined by section 401(a)(9)(E)) of the employee and who is not the surviving spouse of the employee—

(i) the transfer shall be treated as an eligible rollover distribution,

(ii) the individual retirement plan shall be treated as an inherited individual retirement account or individual retirement annuity (within the meaning of section 408(d) (3) (C)) for purposes of this title, and

(iii) section 401(a)(9)(B) (other than clause (iv) thereof) shall apply to such plan.

(B) Certain trusts treated as beneficiaries.—For purposes of this paragraph, to the extent provided in rules prescribed by the Secretary, a trust maintained for the benefit of one or more designated beneficiaries shall be treated in the same manner as a designated beneficiary.

(d) Taxability of beneficiary of certain foreign situs trusts.—For purposes of subsections (a), (b), and (c), a stock bonus, pension, or profit-sharing trust which would qualify for exemption from tax under section 501(a) except for the fact that it is a trust created or organized outside the United States shall be treated as if it were a trust exempt from tax under section 501(a).

(e) Other rules applicable to exempt trusts.—

(1) Alternate payees.—

(A) Alternate payee treated as distributee.—For purposes of subsection (a) and section 72, an alternate payee who is the spouse or former spouse of the participant shall be treated as the distributee of any distribution or payment made to the alternate payee under a qualified domestic relations order (as defined in section 414(p)).

(B) Rollovers.—If any amount is paid or distributed to an alternate payee who is the spouse or former spouse of the participant by reason of any qualified domestic relations order (within the meaning of section 414(p)), subsection (c) shall apply to such distribution in the same manner as if such alternate payee were the employee.

(2) Distributions by United States to nonresident aliens.—The amount includible under subsection (a) in the gross income of a nonresident alien with respect to a distribution made by the United States in respect of services performed by an employee of the United States shall not exceed an amount which bears the same ratio to the amount includible in gross income without regard to this paragraph as—

(A) the aggregate basic pay paid by the United States to such employee for such services, reduced by the amount of such basic pay which was not includible in gross income by reason of being from sources without the United States, bears to

(B) the aggregate basic pay paid by the United States to such employee for such services.

In the case of distributions under the civil service retirement laws, the term "basic pay" shall have the meaning provided in section 8331(3) of title 5, United States Code.

(3) Cash or deferred arrangements.—For purposes of this title, contributions made by an employer on behalf of an employee to a trust which is a part of a qualified cash or deferred arrangement (as defined in section 401(k)(2)) or which is part of a salary reduction agreement under section 403(b) shall not be treated as distributed or made available to the employee nor as contributions made to the trust by the employee merely because the arrangement includes provisions under which the employee has an election whether the contribution will be made to the trust or received by the employee in cash.

(4) Net unrealized appreciation.—

(A) Amounts attributable to employee contributions.—For purposes of subsection

(a) and section 72, in the case of a distribution other than a lump-sum distribution, the amount actually distributed to any distributee from a trust described in subsection (a) shall not include any net unrealized appreciation in securities of the employer corporation attributable to amounts contributed by the employee (other than deductible employee contributions within the meaning of section 72(o)(5)). This subparagraph shall not apply to a distribution to which subsection (c) applies.

(B) Amounts attributable to employer contributions.—For purposes of subsection (a) and section 72, in the case of any lump-sum distribution which includes securities of the employer corporation, there shall be excluded from gross income the net unrealized appreciation attributable to that part of the distribution which consists of securities of the employer corporation. In accordance with rules prescribed by the Secretary, a taxpayer may elect, on the return of tax on which a lump-sum distribution is required to be included, not to have this subparagraph apply to such distribution.

(C) Determination of amounts and adjustments.—For purposes of subparagraphs (A) and (B), net unrealized appreciation and the resulting adjustments to basis shall be determined in accordance with regulations prescribed by the Secretary.

(D) Lump-sum distribution.—For purposes of this paragraph—

(i) In general.—The term "lump sum distribution" means the distribution or payment within one taxable year of the recipient of the balance to the credit of an employee which becomes payable to the recipient—

(I) on account of the employee's death,

(II) after the employee attains age 59½,

(III) on account of the employee's separation from service, or

(IV) after the employee has become disabled (within the meaning of section 72(m)(7)),

from a trust which forms a part of a plan described in section 401(a) and which is exempt from tax under section 501 or from a plan described in section 403(a). Subclause (III) of this clause shall be applied only with respect to an individual who is an employee without regard to section 401(c)(1), and subclause (IV) shall be applied only with respect to an employee within the meaning of section 401 (c)(l). For purposes of this clause, a distribution to two more more trusts shall be treated as a distribution to one recipient. For purposes of this paragraph, the balance to the credit of the employee does not include the accumulated deductible employee contributions under the plan (within the meaning of section 72(o)(5)).

(ii) Aggregation of certain trusts and plans. For purposes of determining the balance to the credit of an employee under clause (i)—

(I) all trusts which are part of a plan shall be treated as a single trust, all pension plans maintained by the employer shall be treated as a single plan, all profit-sharing plans maintained by the employer shall be treated as a single plan, and all stock bonus plans maintained by the employer shall be treated as a single plan, and

(II) trusts which are not qualified trusts under section 401 (a) and annuity contracts which do not satisfy the requirements of section 404(a)(2) shall not be taken into account.

(iii) Community property laws. The provisions of this paragraph shall be applied without regard to community property laws.

(iv) Amounts subject to penalty. This paragraph shall not apply to amounts described in subparagraph (A) of section 72 (m)(5) to the extent that section 72(m)(5) applies to such amounts.

(v) Balance to credit of employee not to include amounts payable under qualified domestic relations order. For purposes of this paragraph, the balance to the credit of an employee shall not include any amount payable to an alternate payee under a qualified domestic relations order (within the meaning of section 414(p)).

(vi) Transfers to cost-of-living arrangement not treated as distribution. For purposes of this paragraph, the balance to the credit of an employee under a defined contribution plan shall not include any amount transferred from such defined contribution plan to a qualified cost-of-living arrangement (within the meaning of section 415(k)(2)) under a defined benefit plan.

(vii) Lump-sum distributions of alternate payees. If any distribution or payment of the balance to the credit of an employee would be treated as a lump-sum distribution, then, for purposes of this paragraph, the payment under a qualified domestic relations order (within the meaning of section 414(p)) of the balance to the credit of an alternate payee who is the spouse or former spouse of the employee shall be treated as a lump-sum distribution. For purposes of this clause, the balance to the credit of the alternate payee shall not include any amount payable to the employee.

(E) Definitions relating to securities.—For purposes of this paragraph—

(i) Securities.—The term "securities" means only shares of stock and bonds or debentures issued by a corporation with interest coupons or in registered form.

(ii) Securities of the employer.—The term "securities of the employer corporation" includes securities of a parent or subsidiary corporation (as defined in subsections (e) and (f) of section 424) of the employer corporation.

*__(6) Direct trustee-to-trustee transfers.__—Any amount transferred in a direct trustee-to-trustee transfer in accordance with section 401(a)(31) shall not be includible in gross income for the taxable year of such transfer.

(f) Written explanation to recipients of distributions eligible for rollover treatment.—

(1) In general.—The plan administrator of any plan shall, within a reasonable period of time before making an eligible rollover distribution, provide a written explanation to the recipient—

(A) of the provisions under which the recipient may have the distribution directly transferred to an eligible retirement plan,

(B) of the provision which requires the withholding of tax on the distribution if it is not directly transferred to an eligible retirement plan,

(C) of the provisions under which the distribution will not be subject to tax if transferred to an eligible retirement plan within 60 days after the date on which the recipient received the distribution,

(D) if applicable, of the provisions of subsections (d) and (e) of this section, and

(E) of the provisions under which distributions from the eligible retirement plan receiving the distribution may be subject to restrictions and tax consequences which are different from those applicable to distributions from the plan making such distribution.

(2) Definitions.—For purposes of this subsection—

(A) Eligible rollover distribution.—The term "eligible rollover distribution" has the same meaning as when used in subsection (c) of this section, paragraph (4) of section 403(a), subparagraph (A) of section 403(b)(8), or subparagraph (A) of section 457(e)(16). Such term shall include any distribution to a designated beneficiary which would be treated as an eligible rollover distribution by reason of subsection (c)(11), or section 403(a)(4)(B), 403(b)(8)(B), or 457(e)(16)(B), if the requirements of subsection (c)(11) were satisfied.

(B) Eligible retirement plan.—The term "eligible retirement plan" has the meaning given such term by subsection (c)(8)(B).

(g) Limitation on exclusion for elective deferrals.—

(1) In general.—

(A) Limitation.—Notwithstanding subsections (e)(3) and (h)(1)(B), the elective deferrals of any individual for any taxable year shall be included in such individual's gross income to the extent the amount of such deferrals for the taxable year exceeds the applicable dollar amount. The preceding sentence shall not apply to the portion of such excess as does not exceed the designated Roth contributions of the individual for the taxable year.

(B) Applicable dollar amount.—For purposes of subparagraph (A), the applicable dollar amount shall be the amount determined in accordance with the following table:

For taxable years beginning in calendar year:	The applicable dollar amount:
2002	$11,000
2003	$12,000
2004	$13,000
2005	$14,000
2006 or thereafter	$15,000**

*Editorial comment: There is no subsection (e)(5).

**Editorial comment: The indexed amount for 2013 and 2014 is $17,500.

(C) Catch-up contributions.—In addition to subparagraph (A), in the case of an eligible participant (as defined in section 414(v)), gross income shall not include elective deferrals in excess of the applicable dollar amount under subparagraph (B) to the extent that the amount of such elective deferrals does not exceed the applicable dollar amount under section 414(v)(2)(B)(i) for the taxable year (without regard to the treatment of the elective deferrals by an applicable employer plan under section 414(v)).

(2) Distribution of excess deferrals.—

(A) In general.—If any amount (hereinafter in this paragraph referred to as "excess deferrals") is included in the gross income of an individual under paragraph (1) (or would be included but for the last sentence thereof) for any taxable year—

(i) not later than the 1st March 1 following the close of the taxable year, the individual may allocate the amount of such excess deferrals among the plans under which the deferrals were made and may notify each such plan of the portion allocated to it, and

(ii) not later than the 1st April 15 following the close of the taxable year, each such plan may distribute to the individual the amount allocated to it under clause (i) (and any income allocable to such amount through the end of such taxable year).

The distribution described in clause (ii) may be made notwithstanding any other provision of law.

(B) Treatment of distribution under section 401(k).—Except to the extent provided under rules prescribed by the Secretary, notwithstanding the distribution of any portion of an excess deferral from a plan under subparagraph (A)(ii), such portion shall, for purposes of applying section 401(k)(3)(A)(ii), be treated as an employer contribution.

(C) Taxation of distribution.—In the case of a distribution to which subparagraph (A) applies—

(i) except as provided in clause (ii), such distribution shall not be included in gross income, and

(ii) any income on the excess deferral shall, for purposes of this chapter, be treated as earned and received in the taxable year in which such income is distributed.

No tax shall be imposed under section 72(t) on any distribution described in the preceding sentence.

(D) Partial distributions.—If a plan distributes only a portion of any excess deferral and income allocable thereto, such portion shall be treated as having been distributed ratably from the excess deferral and the income.

(3) Elective deferrals.—For purposes of this subsection, the term "elective deferrals" means, with respect to any taxable year, the sum of—

(A) any employer contribution under a qualified cash or deferred arrangement (as defined in section 401(k)) to the extent not includible in gross income for the taxable year under subsection (e)(3) (determined without regard to this subsection),

(B) any employer contribution to the extent not includible in gross income for the taxable year under subsection (h)(1)(B) (determined without regard to this subsection),

(C) any employer contribution to purchase an annuity contract under section 403(b) under a salary reduction agreement (within the meaning of section 3121(a)(5)(D)), and

(D) any elective employer contribution under section 408(p)(2)(A)(i).

An employer contribution shall not be treated as an elective deferral described in subparagraph (C) if under the salary reduction agreement such contribution is made pursuant to a one-time irrevocable election made by the employee at the time of initial eligibility to participate in the agreement or is made pursuant to a similar arrangement involving a one-time irrevocable election specified in regulations.

(4) Cost-of-living adjustment.—In the case of taxable years beginning after December 31, 2006, the Secretary shall adjust the $15,000* amount under paragraph (1)(B) at the same time and in the same manner as under section 415(d), except that the base period shall be the calendar quarter beginning July 1, 2005, and any increase under this paragraph which is not a multiple of $500 shall be rounded to the next lowest multiple of $500.

*Editorial comment: The indexed amount for 2013 and 2014 is $17,500.

(5) Disregard of community property laws.—This subsection shall be applied without regard to community property laws.

(6) Coordination with section 72—For purposes of applying section 72, any amount includible in gross income for any taxable year under this subsection but which is not distributed from the plan during such taxable year shall not be treated as investment in the contract.

(7) Special rule for certain organizations.—

(A) In general.—In the case of a qualified employee of a qualified organization, with respect to employer contributions described in paragraph (3)(C) made by such organization, the limitation of paragraph (1) for any taxable year shall be increased by whichever of the following is the least:

(i) $3,000,

(ii) $15,000 reduced by the sum of—

(I) the amounts not included in gross income for prior taxable years by reason of this paragraph, plus

(II) the aggregate amount of designated Roth contributions (as defined in section 402A(c)) permitted for prior taxable years by reason of this paragraph, or

(iii) the excess of $5,000 multiplied by the number of years of service of the employee with the qualified organization over the employer contributions described in paragraph (3) made by the organization on behalf of such employee for prior taxable years (determined in the manner prescribed by the Secretary).

(B) Qualified organization.—For purposes of this paragraph, the term "qualified organization" means any educational organization, hospital, home health service agency, health and welfare service agency, church, or convention or association of churches. Such term includes any organization described in section 414(e) (3)(B) (ii). Terms used in this subparagraph shall have the same meaning as when used in section 415 (c)(4) (as in effect before the enactment of the Economic Growth and Tax Relief Reconciliation Act of 2001).

(C) Qualified employee.—For purposes of this paragraph, the term "qualified employee" means any employee who has completed 15 years of service with the qualified organization.

(D) Years of service.—For purposes of this paragraph, the term "years of service" has the meaning given such term by section 403(b).

(8) Matching contributions on behalf of self-employed individuals not treated as elective employer contributions.—Except as provided in section 401(k)(3)(D)(ii), any matching contribution described in section 401(m)(4)(A) which is made on behalf of a self-employed individual (as defined in section 401(c)) shall not be treated as an elective employer contribution under a qualified cash or deferred arrangement (as defined in section 401(k)) for purposes of this title.

(h) Special rules for simplified employee pensions.—For purposes of this chapter—

(1) In general.—Except as provided in paragraph (2), contributions made by an employer on behalf of an employee to an individual retirement plan pursuant to a simplified employee pension (as defined in section 408(k))—

(A) shall not be treated as distributed or made available to the employee or as contributions made by the employee, and

(B) if such contributions are made pursuant to an arrangement under section 408(k)(6) under which an employee may elect to have the employer make contributions to the simplified employee pension on behalf of the employee, shall not be treated as distributed or made available or as contributions made by the employee merely because the simplified employee pension includes provisions for such election.

(2) Limitations on employer contributions.—Contributions made by an employer to a simplified employee pension with respect to an employee for any year shall be treated as distributed or made available to such employee and as contributions made by the employee to the extent such contributions exceed the lesser of—

(A) 25 percent of the compensation (within the meaning of section 414(s)) from such employer includible in the employee's gross income for the year (determined without regard to the employer contributions to the simplified employee pension), or

(B) the limitation in effect under section 415 (c)(1)(A), reduced in the case of any highly compensated employee (within the meaning of section 414(q)) by the amount taken into account with respect to such employee under section 408(k)(3)(D).

(3) Distributions.—Any amount paid or distributed out of an individual retirement plan pursuant to a simplified employee pension shall be included in gross income by the payee or distributee, as the case may be, in accordance with the provisions of section 408(d).

(i) Treatment of self-employed individuals.—For purposes of this section, except as otherwise provided in subparagraph (A) of subsection (d)(4), the term "employee" includes a self-employed individual (as defined in section 401(c)(1)(B)) and the employer of such individual shall be the person treated as his employer under section 401(c)(4).

(j) Effect of disposition of stock by plan on net unrealized appreciation.—

(1) In general.—For purposes of subsection (e)(4), in the case of any transaction to which this subsection applies, the determination of net unrealized appreciation shall be made without regard to such transaction.

(2) Transaction to which subsection applies.—This subsection shall apply to any transaction in which—

(A) the plan trustee exchanges the plan's securities of the employer corporation for other such securities, or

(B) the plan trustee disposes of securities of the employer corporation and uses the proceeds of such disposition to acquire securities of the employer corporation within 90 days (or such longer period as the Secretary may prescribe), except that this subparagraph shall not apply to any employee with respect to whom a distribution of money was made during the period after such disposition and before such acquisition.

(k) Treatment of simple retirement accounts.—Rules similar to the rules of paragraphs (1) and (3) of subsection (h) shall apply to contributions and distributions with respect to a simple retirement account under section 408(p).

(l) Distributions from governmental plans for health and long-term care insurance.—

(1) In general.—In the case of an employee who is an eligible retired public safety officer who makes the election described in paragraph (6) with respect to any taxable year of such employee, gross income of such employee for such taxable year does not include any distribution from an eligible retirement plan maintained by the employer described in pararaph (4)(B) to the extent that the aggregate amount of such distributions does not exceed the amount paid by such employee for qualified health insurance premiums for such taxable year.

(2) Limitation.—The amount which may be excluded from gross income for the taxable year by reason of paragraph (1) shall not exceed $3,000.

(3) Distributions must otherwise be includible.—

(A) In general.—An amount shall be treated as a distribution for purposes of paragraph (1) only to the extent that such amount would be includible in gross income without regard to paragraph (1).

(B) Application of section 72.—Notwithstanding section 72, in determining the extent to which an amount is treated as a distribution for purposes of subparagraph (A), the aggregate amounts distributed from an eligible retirement plan in a taxable year (up to the amount excluded under paragraph (1)) shall be treated as includible in gross income (without regard to subparagraph (A)) to the extent that such amount does not exceed the aggregate amount which would have been so includible if all amounts to the credit of the eligible public safety officer in all eligible retirement plans maintained by the employer described in paragraph (4)(B) were distributed during such taxable year and all such plans were treated as 1 contract for purposes of determining under section 72 the aggregate amount which would have been so includable. Proper adjustments shall be made in applying section 72 to other distributions in such taxable year and subsequent taxable years.

(4) Definitions.—For purposes of this subsection—

(A) Eligible retirement plan.—For purposes of paragraph (1), the term "eligible retirement plan" means a governmental plan (within the meaning of section 414(d)) which is described in clause (iii), (iv), (v), or (vi) of subsection (c)(8)(B).

(B) Eligible retired public safety officer.—The term "eligible retired public safety officer" means an individual who, by reason of disability or attainment of normal retirement age, is separated from service as a public safety officer with the employer who maintains the eligible retirement plan from which distributions subject to paragraph (1) are made.

(C) Public safety officer.—The term "public safety officer" shall have the same meaning given such term by section 1204(9)(A) of the Omnibus Crime Control and Safe Streets Act of 1968 (42 U.S.C. 3796b(9)(A)).

(D) Qualified health insurance premiums.—The term "qualified health insurance premiums" means premiums for coverage for the eligible retired public safety officer, his spouse, and dependents, (as defined in section 152), by an accident or health plan or qualified long-term care insurance contract (as defined in section 7702B(b)).

(5) Special rules.—For purposes of this subsection—

(A) Direct payment to insurer required.—Paragraph (1) shall only apply to a distribution if payment of the premiums is made directly to the provider of the accident or health plan or qualified long-term care insurance contract by deduction from a distribution from the eligible retirement plan.

(B) Related plans treated as 1.—All eligible retirement plans of an employer shall be treated as a single plan.

(6) Election described.—

(A) In general.—For purposes of paragraph (1), an election is described in this paragraph if the election is made by an employee after separation from service with respect to amounts not distributed from an eligible retirement plan to have amounts from such plan distributed in order to pay for qualified health insurance premiums.

(B) Special rule.—Aplan shall not be treated as violating the requirements of section 401, or as engaging in a prohibited transaction for purposes of section 503(b), merely because it provides for an election with respect to amounts that are otherwise distributable under the plan or merely because of a distribution made pursuant to an election described in subparagraph (A).

(7) Coordination with medical expense deduction.— The amounts excluded from gross income under paragraph (1) shall not be taken into account under section 213.

(8) Coordination with deduction for health insurance costs of self-employed individuals.—The amounts excluded from gross income under paragraph (1) shall not be taken into account under section 162(l).

Editorial Notes

Section 1122(h) of Pub.L. 99–514 provided that:

"**(1) In general.**—Except as otherwise provided in this subsection, the amendments made by this section [amending this section and sections 72, 403, and 408 of this title] shall apply to amounts distributed after December 31, 1986, in taxable years ending after such date.

"**(3) Special rule for individuals who attained age 50 before January 1, 1986.**—

"**(A) In general.**—In the case of a lump-sum distribution to which this paragraph applies—

"**(i)** the existing capital gains provisions shall continue to apply, and

"**(ii)** the requirement of subparagraph (B) of section 402 (e)(4) of the Internal Revenue Code of 1986 [subsec. (e)(4) (B) of this section] (as amended by subsection (a)) that the distribution be received after attaining age 59½ shall not apply.

"**(B) Computation of tax.**—If subparagraph (A) applies to any lump-sum distribution of any taxpayer for any taxable year, the tax imposed by section 1 of the Internal Revenue Code of 1986 [section 1 of this title] on such taxpayer for such taxable year shall be equal to the sum of—

"**(i)** the tax imposed by such section 1 on the taxable income of the taxpayer (reduced by the portion of such lump-sum distribution to which clause (ii) applies), plus

"**(ii)** 20 percent of the portion of such lump-sum distribution to which the existing capital gains provisions continue to apply by reason of this paragraph.

"**(C) lump-sum distributions to which paragraph applies.**—This paragraph shall apply to any lump-sum distribution if—

"**(i)** such lump-sum distribution is received by an individual who has attained age 50 before January 1, 1986, and

"**(ii)** the taxpayer makes an election under this paragraph.

Not more than 1 election may be made under this paragraph with respect to an employee. An election under this subparagraph shall be treated as an election under section 402(e)(4)(B) of such Code [subsec. (e)(4)(B) of this section] with respect to any other lump-sum distribution.

"**(4) 5-year phase-out of capital gains treatment.**—

"**(A)** Notwithstanding the amendment made by subsection (b), if the taxpayer elects the application of this paragraph with respect to any distribution after December 31, 1986, and before January 1, 1992, the phase-out percentage of the amount which would have been treated, without regard to this subparagraph, as long-term capital gain under the existing capital gains provisions shall be treated as long-term capital gain.

"(B) For purposes of this paragraph—

In the case of distributions during calendar year:	The phase-out percentage is:
1987	100
1988	95
1989	75
1990	50
1991	25

"(C) No more than 1 election may be made under this paragraph with respect to an employee. An election under this paragraph shall be treated as an election under section 402(e)(4)(B) of the Internal Revenue Code of 1986 [subsec. (e)(4)(B) of this section] with respect to any other lump sum distribution.

"(5) **Election of 10-year averaging.**—An individual who has attained age 50 before January 1, 1986, and elects the application of paragraph (3) or section 402(e)(1) of the Internal Revenue Code of 1986 [subsec. (e)(1) of this section] (as amended by this Act) may elect to have such section applied by substituting "10 times" for "5 times" and "$^1/_{10}$" for "$^1/_5$" in subparagraph (B) thereof. For purposes of the preceding sentence, section 402(e)(1) of such Code [subsec. (e)(1) of this section] shall be applied by using the rate of tax in effect under section 1 of the Internal Revenue Code of 1954 [section 1 of this title prior to the revision and redesignation as the Internal Revenue Code of 1986 by Pub.L. 99–514] for taxable years beginning during 1986.

"(6) **Existing capital gain provisions.**—For purposes of paragraphs (3) and (4), the term 'existing capital gains provisions' means the provisions of paragraph (2) of section 402(a) of the Internal Revenue Code of 1954 [subsec. (a)(2) of this section] (as in effect on the day before the date of the enactment of this Act) and paragraph (2) of section 403(a) of such Code [section 403(a)(2) of this title] (as so in effect).

§ 402A. Optional treatment of elective deferrals as Roth contributions

(a) General rule.—If an applicable retirement plan includes a qualified Roth contribution program—

(1) any designated Roth contribution made by an employee pursuant to the program shall be treated as an elective deferral for purposes of this chapter, except that such contribution shall not be excludable from gross income, and

(2) such plan (and any arrangement which is part of such plan) shall not be treated as failing to meet any requirement of this chapter solely by reason of including such program.

(b) Qualified Roth contribution program.—For purposes of this section—

(1) In general.—The term "qualified Roth contribution program" means a program under which an employee may elect to make designated Roth contributions in lieu of all or a portion of elective deferrals the employee is otherwise eligible to make under the applicable retirement plan.

(2) Separate accounting required.—A program shall not be treated as a qualified Roth contribution program unless the applicable retirement plan—

(A) establishes separate accounts ("designated Roth account") for the designated Roth contributions of each employee and any earnings properly allocable to the contributions, and

(B) maintains separate recordkeeping with respect to each account.

(c) Definitions and rules relating to designated Roth contributions.—For purposes of this section—

(1) Designated Roth contribution.—The term "designated Roth contribution" means any elective deferral which—

(A) is excludable from gross income of an employee without regard to this section, and

(B) the employee designates (at such time and in such manner as the Secretary may prescribe) as not being so excludable.

(2) Designation limits.—The amount of elective deferrals which an employee may designate under paragraph (1) shall not exceed the excess (if any) of—

(A) the maximum amount of elective deferrals excludable from gross income of the employee for the taxable year (without regard to this section), over

(B) the aggregate amount of elective deferrals of the employee for the taxable year which the employee does not designate under paragraph (1).

(3) Rollover contributions.—

(A) In general.—A rollover contribution of any payment or distribution from a designated Roth account which is otherwise allowable under this chapter may be made only if the contribution is to—

(i) another designated Roth account of the individual from whose account the payment or distribution was made, or

(ii) a Roth IRA of such individual.

(B) Coordination with limit.—Any rollover contribution to a designated Roth account under subparagraph (A) shall not be taken into account for purposes of paragraph (1).

(4) Taxable rollovers to designated Roth accounts.—

(A) In general.—Notwithstanding sections 402(c), 403(b)(8), and 457(e)(16), in the case of any distribution to which this paragraph applies—

(i) there shall be included in gross income any amount which would be includible were it not part of a qualified rollover contribution,

(ii) section 72(t) shall not apply, and

(iii) unless the taxpayer elects not to have this clause apply, any amount required to be included in gross income for any taxable year beginning in 2010 by reason of this paragraph shall be so included ratably over the 2-taxable-year period beginning with the first taxable year beginning in 2011.

Any election under clause (iii) for any distributions during a taxable year may not be changed after the due date for such taxable year.

(B) Distributions to which paragraph applies.—In the case of an applicable retirement plan which includes a qualified Roth contribution program, this paragraph shall apply to a distribution from such plan other than from a designated Roth account which is contributed in a qualified rollover contribution (within the meaning of section 408A(e)) to the designated Roth account maintained under such plan for the benefit of the individual to whom the distribution is made.

(C) Coordination with limit.—Any distribution to which this paragraph applies shall not be taken into account for purposes of paragraph (1).

(D) Other rules.—The rules of subparagraphs (D), (E), and (F) of section 408A(d)(3) (as in effect for taxable years beginning after 2009) shall apply for purposes of this paragraph.

(E) Special rule for certain transfers.—In the case of an applicable retirement plan which includes a qualified Roth contribution program—

(i) the plan may allow an individual to elect to have the plan transfer any amount not otherwise distributable under the plan to a designated Roth account maintained for the benefit of the individual,

(ii) such transfer shall be treated as a distribution to which this paragraph applies which was contributed in a qualified rollover contribution (within the meaning of section 408A(e)) to such account, and

(iii) the plan shall not be treated as violating the provisions of section 401(k)(2)(B)(i), 403(b)(7)(A)(i), 403(b)(11), or 457(d)(1)(A), or of section 8433 of title 5, United States Code, solely by reason of such transfer.

(d) Distribution rules.—For purposes of this title—

(1) Exclusion.—Any qualified distribution from a designated Roth account shall not be includible in gross income.

(2) Qualified distribution.—For purposes of this subsection—

(A) In general.—The term "qualified distribution" has the meaning given such term by section 408A(d)(2)(A) (without regard to clause (iv) thereof).

(B) Distributions within nonexclusion period.—A payment or distribution from a designated Roth account shall not be treated as a qualified distribution if such payment or distribution is made within the 5-taxable-year period beginning with the earlier of—

(i) the first taxable year for which the individual made a designated Roth contribution to any designated Roth account established for such individual under the same applicable retirement plan, or

(ii) if a rollover contribution was made to such designated Roth account from a designated Roth account previously established for such individual under another applicable retirement plan, the first taxable year for which the individual made a designated Roth contribution to such previously established account.

(C) Distributions of excess deferrals and contributions and earnings thereon.—The term "qualified distribution" shall not include any distribution of any excess deferral under section 402(g)(2) or any excess contribution under section 401(k)(8), and any income on the excess deferral or contribution.

(3) Treatment of distributions of certain excess deferrals.—Notwithstanding section 72, if any excess deferral under section 402(g)(2) attributable to a designated Roth contribution is not distributed on or before the 1st April 15 following the close of the taxable year in which such excess deferral is made, the amount of such excess deferral shall—

(A) not be treated as investment in the contract, and

(B) be included in gross income for the taxable year in which such excess is distributed.

(4) Aggregation rules.—Section 72 shall be applied separately with respect to distributions and payments from a designated Roth account and other distributions and payments from the plan.

(e) Other definitions.—For purposes of this section—

(1) Applicable retirement plan.—The term "applicable retirement plan" means—

(A) an employees' trust described in section 401(a) which is exempt from tax under section 501(a),

(B) a plan under which amounts are contributed by an individual's employer for an annuity contract described in section 403(b), and

(C) an eligible deferred compensation plan (as defined in section 457(b)) of an eligible employer described in section 457(e)(1)(A).

(2) Elective deferral.—The term "elective deferral" means—

(A) any elective deferral described in subparagraph (A) or (C) of section 402(g)(3), and

(B) any elective deferral of compensation by an individual under an eligible deferred compensation plan (as defined in section 457(b) of an eligible employer described in section 457(e)(1)(A).

§ 403. Taxation of employee annuities

(a) Taxability of beneficiary under a qualified annuity plan.—

(1) Distributee taxable under section 72.—If an annuity contract is purchased by an employer for an employee under a plan which meets the requirements of section 404(a)(2) (whether or not the employer deducts the amounts paid for the contract under such section), the amount actually distributed to any distributee under the contract shall be taxable to the distributee (in the year in which so distributed) under section 72 (relating to annuities).

(2) Special rule for health and long-term care insurance.—To the extent provided in section 402 (l), paragraph (1) shall not apply to the amount distributed under the contract which is otherwise includible in gross income under this subsection.

(3) Self-employed individuals.—For purposes of this subsection, the term "employee" includes an individual who is an employee within the meaning of section 401(c)(1), and the employer of such individual is the person treated as his employer under section 401(c)(4).

(4) Rollover amounts.—

(A) General rule.—If—

(i) any portion of the balance to the credit of an employee in an employee annuity described in paragraph (1) is paid to him in an eligible rollover distribution [within the meaning of section 402(c)(4)],

(ii) the employee transfers any portion of the property he receives in such distribution to an eligible retirement plan, and

(iii) in the case of a distribution of property other than money, the amount so transferred consists of the property distributed,

then such distribution (to the extent so transferred) shall not be includible in gross income for the taxable year in which paid.

(B) Certain rules made applicable.—The rules of paragraphs (2) through (7) and (9) and (11) of section 402(c) and section 402(f) shall apply for purposes of subparagraph (A).

(5) Direct trustee-to-trustee transfer.—Any amount transferred in a direct trustee-to-trustee transfer in accordance with section 401(a)(31) shall not be includible in gross income for the taxable year of such transfer.

(b) Taxability of beneficiary under annuity purchased by section 501(c)(3) organization or public school.—

(1) General rule.—If—

(A) an annuity contract is purchased—

(i) for an employee by an employer described in section 501(c)(3) which is exempt from tax under section 501(a),

(ii) for an employee (other than an employee described in clause (i)), who performs services for an educational organization described in section 170(b)(1)(A)(ii), by an employer which is a State, a political subdivision of a State, or an agency or instrumentality of any one or more of the foregoing, or

(iii) for the minister described in section 414 (e)(5)(A) by the minister or by an employer,

(B) such annuity contract is not subject to subsection (a),

(C) the employee's rights under the contract are nonforfeitable, except for failure to pay future premiums,

(D) except in the case of a contract purchased by a church, such contract is purchased under a plan which meets the nondiscrimination requirements of paragraph (12), and

(E) in the case of a contract purchased under a salary reduction agreement, the contract meets the requirement of section 401(a)(30),

then contributions and other additions by such employer for such annuity contract shall be excluded from the gross income of the employee for the taxable year to the extent that the aggregate of such contributions and additions (when expressed as an annual addition (within the meaning of section 415(c)(2))) does not exceed the applicable limit under section 415. The amount actually distributed to any distributee under such contract shall be taxable to the distributee (in the year in which so distributed) under section 72 (relating to annuities). For purposes of applying the rules of this subsection to contributions and other additions by an employer for a taxable year, amounts transferred to a contract described in this paragraph by reason of a rollover contribution described in paragraph (8) of this subsection or section 408(d)(3)(A)(ii) shall not be considered by such employer.

* * *

(2) Special rule for health and long-term care insurance.—To the extent provided in section 402(l), paragraph (1) shall not apply to the amount distributed under the contract which is otherwise includible in gross income under this subsection.

(3) Includible compensation.—For purposes of this subsection, the term "includible compensation" means, in the case of any employee, the amount of compensation which is received from the employer described in paragraph (1) (A), and which is includible in gross income (computed without regard to section 911) for the most recent period (ending not later than the close of the taxable year) which under paragraph (4) may be counted as one year of service, and which precedes the taxable year by no more than five years. Such term does not include any amount contributed by the employer for any annuity contract to which this subsection applies. Such term includes—

(A) any elective deferral (as defined in section 402(g)(3)), and

(B) any amount which is contributed or deferred by the employer at the election of the employee and which is not includible in the gross income of the employee by reason of section 125, 132(f)(4), or 457.

(4) Years of service.—In determining the number of years of service for purposes of this subsection, there shall be included—

(A) one year for each full year during which the individual was a full-time employee of the organization purchasing the annuity for him, and

(B) a fraction of a year (determined in accordance with regulations prescribed by the Secretary) for each full year during which such individual was a part-time employee of such organization and for each part of a year during which such individual was a full-time or part-time employee of such organization.

In no case shall the number of years of service be less than one.

(5) Application to more than one annuity contract.—If for any taxable year of the employee this subsection applies to 2 or more annuity contracts purchased by the employer, such contracts shall be treated as one contract.

* * *

***(8) Rollover amounts.**—

(A) General rule.—If—

(i) any portion of the balance to the credit of an employee in an annuity contract described in paragraph (1) is paid to him in a rollover distribution [within the meaning of section 402(e)(4)],

(ii) the employee transfers any portion of the property he receives in such distribution to an eligible retirement plan described in section 402(c)(8)(B), and

(iii) in the case of a distribution of property other than money, the property so transferred consists of the property distributed,

then such distribution (to the extent so transferred) shall not be includible in gross income for the taxable year in which paid.

(B) Certain rules made applicable.—Rules similar to the rules of paragraphs (2) through (7) and (9) and (11) of section 402(c) and section 402 (f) shall apply for purposes of subparagraph (A), except that section 402(f) shall be applied to the payor in lieu of the plan administrator.

* * *

(11) Requirement that distributions not begin before age 59½, severance from employment,

*Editorial comment: There is no paragraph (6).

death, or disability.—This subsection shall not apply to any annuity contract unless under such contract distributions attributable to contributions made pursuant to a salary reduction agreement (within the meaning of section 402(g)(3)(C)) may be paid only—

(A) when the employee attains age 59½, has a severance from employment, dies, or becomes disabled (within the meaning of section 72(m)(7)),

(B) in the case of hardship, or

(C) for distributions to which section 72(t)(2)(G) applies.

Such contract may not provide for the distribution of any income attributable to such contributions in the case of hardship.

(12) Nondiscrimination requirements.—

(A) In general.—For purposes of paragraph (1)(D), a plan meets the nondiscrimination requirements of this paragraph if—

(i) with respect to contributions not made pursuant to a salary reduction agreement, such plan meets the requirements of paragraphs (4), (5), (17), and (26) of section 401(a), section 401(m), and section 410(b) in the same manner as if such plan were described in section 401(a), and

(ii) all employees of the organization may elect to have the employer make contributions of more than $200 pursuant to a salary reduction agreement if any employee of the organization may elect to have the organization make contributions for such contracts pursuant to such agreement.

For purposes of clause (i), a contribution shall be treated as not made pursuant to a salary reduction agreement if under the agreement it is made pursuant to a 1-time irrevocable election made by the employee at the time of initial eligibility to participate in the agreement or is made pursuant to a similar arrangement involving a one-time irrevocable election specified in regulations. For purposes of clause (ii), there may be excluded any employee who is a participant in an eligible deferred compensation plan (within the meaning of section 457) or a qualified cash or deferred arrangement of the organization or another annuity contract described in this subsection. Any nonresident alien described in section 410(b)(3)(C) may also be excluded. Subject to the conditions applicable under section 410(b)(4), there may be excluded for purposes of this subparagraph employees who are students performing services described in section 3121(b)(10) and employees who normally work less than 20 hours per week.

(B) Church.—For purposes of paragraph (1)(D), the term "church" has the meaning given to such term by section 3121(w)(3)(A). Such term shall include any qualified church-controlled organization (as defined in section 3121(w)(3)(B)).

(C) State and local governmental plans.—For purposes of paragraph (1)(D), the requirements of subparagraph (A)(i) (other than those relating to section 401(a)(17)) shall not apply to a governmental plan (within the meaning of section 414(d)) maintained by a State or local government or political subdivision thereof (or agency or instrumentality thereof).

(13) Trustee-to-trustee transfers to purchase permissive service credit.—No amount shall be includible in gross income by reason of a direct trustee-to-trustee transfer to a defined benefit governmental plan (as defined in section 414(d)) if such transfer is—

(A) for the purchase of permissive service credit (as defined in section 415(n)(3)(A)) under such plan, or

(B) a repayment to which section 415 does not apply by reason of subsection (k)(3) thereof.

(14) Death benefits under USERRA-qualified active military service.—This subsection shall not apply to an annuity contract unless such contract meets the requirements of section 401(a)(37).

(c) Taxability of beneficiary under nonqualified annuities or under annuities purchased by exempt organizations.—Premiums paid by an employer for an annuity contract which is not subject to subsection (a) shall be included in the gross income of the employee in accordance with section 83 (relating to property transferred in connection with performance of services), except that the value of such contract shall be substituted for the fair market value of the property for purposes of applying such section. The preceding sentence shall not apply to that portion of the premiums paid which is excluded from gross income under subsection (b). In the case of any portion of any contract which is attributable to premiums to which this subsection applies, the amount actually paid or made available under such contract to any beneficiary which is attributable to such premiums shall be taxable to the beneficiary (in the year in which so paid or made available) under section 72 (relating to annuities).

§ 404. Deduction for contributions of an employer to an employees' trust or annuity plan and compensation under a deferred-payment plan

(a) General rule.—If contributions are paid by an employer to or under a stock bonus, pension, profit-sharing, or annuity plan, or if compensation is paid or accrued on account of any employee under a plan deferring the receipt of such compensation, such contributions or compensation shall not be deductible under this chapter; but, if they would otherwise be deductible, they shall be deductible under this section, subject, however, to the following limitations as to the amounts deductible in any year:

(1) Pension trusts.—

(A) In general.—In the taxable year when paid, if the contributions are paid into a pension trust (other than a trust to which paragraph (3) applies), and if such taxable year ends within or with a taxable year of the trust for which the trust is exempt under section 501(a), in the case of a defined benefit plan other than a multiemployer plan, in an amount determined under subsection (o), and in the case of any other plan in an amount determined as follows:

(i) the amount necessary to satisfy the minimum funding standard provided by section 412(a) for plan years ending within or with such taxable year (or for any prior plan year), if such amount is greater than the amount determined under clause (ii) or (iii) (whichever is applicable with respect to the plan),

(ii) the amount necessary to provide with respect to all of the employees under the trust the remaining unfunded cost of their past and current service credits distributed as a level amount, or a level percentage of compensation, over the remaining future service of each such employee, as determined under regulations prescribed by the Secretary, but if such remaining unfunded cost with respect to any 3 individuals is more than 50 percent of such remaining unfunded cost, the amount of such unfunded cost attributable to such individuals shall be distributed over a period of at least 5 taxable years.

(iii) an amount equal to the normal cost of the plan, as determined under regulations prescribed by the Secretary, plus, if past service or other supplementary pension or annuity credits are provided by the plan, an amount necessary to amortize the unfunded costs attributable to such credits in equal annual payments (until fully amortized) over 10 years, as determined under regulations prescribed by the Secretary.

In determining the amount deductible in such year under the foregoing limitations the funding method and the actuarial assumptions used shall be those used for such year under section 431, and the maximum amount deductible for such year shall be an amount equal to the full funding limitation for such year determined under section 431.

(B) Special rule in case of certain amendments.—In the case of a multiemployer plan which the Secretary of Labor finds to be collectively bargained which makes an election under this subparagraph (in such manner and at such time as may be provided under regulations prescribed by the Secretary), if the full funding limitation determined under section 431(c)(6) for such year is zero, if as a result of any plan amendment applying to such plan year, the amount determined under section 431(c)(6)(A)(ii) exceeds the amount determined under section 431(c)(6)(A)(i), and if the funding method and the actuarial assumptions used are those used for such year under section 431, the maximum amount deductible in such year under the limitations of this paragraph shall be an amount equal to the lesser of—

(i) the full funding limitation for such year determined by applying section 431(c)(6) but increasing the amount referred to in subparagraph (A) thereof by the decrease in the present value of all unamortized liabilities resulting from such amendment, or

(ii) the normal cost under the plan reduced by the amount necessary to amortize in equal annual installments over 10 years (until fully amortized) the decrease described in clause (i).

In the case of any election under this subparagraph, the amount deductible under the limitations of this paragraph with respect to any of the plan years following the plan year for which such election was made shall be determined as provided under such regulations as may be prescribed by the Secretary to carry out the purposes of this subparagraph.

(C) Certain collectively-bargained plans.—In the case of a plan which the Secretary of Labor finds to be collectively bargained, established or maintained by an employer doing business in not less than 40 States and engaged in the trade or business of furnishing or selling services described in section 168(i)(10)(C), with respect to which the rates have been established or approved by a State or political sub-division thereof, by any agency or instrumentality of the United States, or by a public service or public utility commission or other similar body of any State or political subdivision thereof, and in the case of any employer which is a member of a controlled group with such employer, subparagraph (B) shall be applied by substituting for the words "plan amendment" the words "plan amendment or increase in benefits payable under title II of the Social Security Act." For purposes of this subparagraph, the term "controlled group" has the meaning provided by section 1563(a), determined without regard to section 1563(a)(4) and (e)(3)(C).

(D) Amount determined on basis of unfunded current liability.—In the case of a defined benefit plan which is a multiemployer plan, except as provided in regulations, the maximum amount deductible under the limitations of this paragraph shall not be less than the excess (if any) of—

(i) 140 percent of the current liability of the plan determined under section 431(c)(6)(D), over

(ii) the value of the plan's assets determined under section 431(c)(2).

(E) Carryover.—Any amount paid in a taxable year in excess of the amount deductible in such year under the foregoing limitations shall be deductible in the succeeding taxable years in order of time to the extent of the difference between the amount paid and deductible in each such succeeding year and the maximum amount deductible for such year under the foregoing limitations.

(2) Employees' annuities.—In the taxable year when paid, in an amount determined in accordance with paragraph (1), if the contributions are paid toward the purchase of retirement annuities, or retirement annuities and medical benefits as described in section 401(h), and such purchase is a part of a plan which meets the requirements of section 401(a)(3), (4), (5), (6), (7), (8), (9), (11), (12), (13), (14), (15), (16), (17), (19), (20), (22), (26), (27), (31), and (37) and, if applicable, the requirements of section 401(a)(10) and of section 401(d), and if refunds of premiums, if any, are applied within the current taxable year or next succeeding taxable year towards the purchase of such retirement annuities, or such retirement annuities and medical benefits.

(3) Stock bonus and profit-sharing trusts.—

(A) Limits on deductible contributions.—

(i) In general.—In the taxable year when paid, if the contributions are paid into a stock bonus or profit-sharing trust, and if such taxable year ends within or with a taxable year of the trust with respect to which the trust is exempt under section 501(a), in an amount not in excess of the greater of—

(I) 25 percent of the compensation otherwise paid or accrued during the taxable year to the beneficiaries under the stock bonus or profit-sharing plan, or

(II) the amount such employer is required to contribute to such trust under section 401(k)(11) for such year.

(ii) Carryover of excess contributions.—Any amount paid into the trust in any taxable year in excess of the limitation of clause (i) (or the corresponding provision of prior law) shall be deductible in the succeeding taxable years in order of time, but the amount so deductible under this clause in any 1 such succeeding taxable year together with the amount allowable under clause (i) shall not exceed the amount described in subclause (I) or (II) of clause (i), whichever is greater, with respect to such taxable year.

(iii) Certain retirement plans excluded.—For purposes of this subparagraph, the term "stock bonus or profit-sharing trust" shall not include any trust designed to provide benefits upon retirement and covering a period of years, if under the plan the amounts to be contributed by the employer can be determined actuarially as provided in paragraph (1).

(iv) 2 or more trusts treated as 1 trust.—If the contributions are made to 2 or more stock bonus or profit-sharing trusts, such trusts shall be considered a single trust for purposes of applying the limitations in this subparagraph.

(v) Defined contribution plans subject to the funding standards.—Except as provided by the Secretary, a defined contribution plan which is subject to the funding standards of section 412 shall be treated in the same manner as a stock bonus or profit-sharing plan for purposes of this subparagraph.

(B) Profit-sharing plan of affiliated group.—In the case of a profit-sharing plan, or a stock bonus plan in which contributions are determined with reference to profits, of a group of corporations which is an affiliated group within the meaning of section 1504, if any member of such affiliated group is prevented from making a contribution which it would otherwise have made under the plan, by reason of having no current or accumulated earnings or profits or because such earnings or profits are less than the contributions which it would otherwise have made, then so much of the contribution which such member was so prevented from making may be made, for the benefit of the employees of such member, by the other members of the group, to the extent of current or accumulated earnings or profits, except that such contribution by each such other member shall be limited, where the group does not file a consolidated return, to that proportion of its total current and accumulated earnings or profits remaining after adjustment for its contribution deductible without regard to this subparagraph which the total prevented contribution bears to the total current and accumulated earnings or profits of all the members of the group remaining after adjustment for all contributions deductible without regard to this subparagraph. Contributions made under the preceding sentence shall be deductible under subparagraph (A) of this paragraph by the employer making such contribution, and, for the purpose of determining amounts which may be carried forward and deducted under the second sentence of subparagraph (A) of this paragraph in succeeding taxable years, shall be deemed to have been made by the employer on behalf of whose employees such contributions were made.

(4) Trusts created or organized outside the United States.—If a stock bonus, pension, or profit-sharing trust would qualify for exemption under section 501(a) except for the fact that it is a trust created or organized outside the United States, contributions to such a trust by an employer which is a resident, or corporation, or other entity of the United States, shall be deductible under the preceding paragraphs.

(5) Other plans.—If the plan is not one included in paragraph (1), (2), or (3), in the taxable year in which an amount attributable to the contribution is includible in the gross income of employees participating in the plan, but, in the case of a plan in which more than one employee participates only if separate accounts are maintained for each employee. For purposes of this section, any vacation pay which is treated as deferred compensation shall be deductible for the taxable year of the employer in which paid to the employee.

(6) Time when contributions deemed made.—For purposes of paragraphs (1), (2), and (3), a taxpayer shall be deemed to have made a payment on the last day of the preceding taxable year if the payment is on account of such taxable year and is made not later than the time prescribed by law for filing the return for such taxable year (including extensions thereof).

(7) Limitation on deductions where combination of defined contribution plan and defined benefit plan.—

(A) In general.—If amounts are deductible under the foregoing paragraphs of this subsection (other than paragraph (5)) in connection with 1 or more defined contribution plans and 1 or more defined benefit plans or in connection with trusts or plans described in 2 or more of such paragraphs, the total amount deductible in a taxable year under such plans shall not exceed the greater of—

(i) 25 percent of the compensation otherwise paid or accrued during the taxable year to the beneficiaries under such plans, or

(ii) the amount of contributions made to or under the defined benefit plans to the extent such contributions do not exceed the amount of employer contributions necessary to satisfy the minimum funding standard provided by section 412 with respect to any such defined benefit plans for the plan year which ends with or within such taxable year (or for any prior plan year).

A defined contribution plan which is a pension plan shall not be treated as failing to provide definitely determinable benefits merely by limiting employer contributions to amounts deductible under this section. In the case of a defined benefit plan which is a single employer plan, the amount necessary to satisfy the minimum funding standard provided by section 412 shall not be less than the excess (if any) of the plan's funding target (as defined in section 430(d)(1)) over the value of the plan's assets (as determined under section 430(g)(3)).

(B) Carryover of contributions in excess of the deductible limit.—Any amount paid under the plans in any taxable year in excess of the limitation of subparagraph (A) shall be deductible in the succeeding taxable years in order of time, but the amount so deductible under this subparagraph in any 1 such succeeding taxable year together with the amount allowable under subparagraph (A) shall not exceed 25 percent of the compensation otherwise paid or accrued during such taxable year to the beneficiaries under the plans.

(C) Paragraph not to apply in certain cases.—

(i) Beneficiary test.—This paragraph shall not have the effect of reducing the amount otherwise deductible under paragraphs (1), (2), and (3), if no employee is a beneficiary under more than 1 trust or under a trust and an annuity plan.

(ii) Elective deferrals.—If, in connection with 1 or more defined contribution plans and 1 or more defined benefit plans, no amounts (other than elective deferrals (as defined in section 402(g)(3))) are contributed to any of the defined contribution plans for the taxable year, then subparagraph (A) shall not apply with respect to any of such defined contribution plans and defined benefit plans.

(iii) Limitation.—In the case of employer contributions to 1 or more defined contribution plans—

(I) if such contributions do not exceed 6 percent of the compensation otherwise paid or accrued during the taxable year to the beneficiaries under such plans, this paragraph shall not apply to such contributions or to employer contributions to the defined benefit plans to which this paragraph would otherwise apply by reason of contributions to the defined contribution plans, and

(II) if such contributions exceed 6 percent of such compensation, this paragraph shall be applied by only taking into account such contributions to the extent of such excess.

For purposes of this clause, amounts carried over from preceding taxable years under subparagraph (B) shall be treated as employer contributions to 1 or more defined contributions plans to the extent attributable to employer contributions to such plans in such preceding taxable years.

(iv) Guaranteed plans.—In applying this paragraph, any single-employer plan covered under section 4021 of the Employee Retirement Income Security Act of 1974 shall not be taken into account.

(v) Multiemployer plans.—In applying this paragraph, any multiemployer plan shall not be taken into account.

(D) Insurance contract plans.—For purposes of this paragraph, a plan described in section 412(e)(3) shall be treated as a defined benefit plan.

(8) Self-employed individuals.—In the case of a plan included in paragraph (1), (2), or (3) which provides contributions or benefits for employees some or all of whom are employees within the meaning of section 401(c)(1), for purposes of this section—

(A) the term "employee" includes an individual who is an employee within the meaning of section 401(c)(1), and the employer of such individual is the person treated as his employer under section 401(c)(4);

(B) the term "earned income" has the meaning assigned to it by section 401(c)(2);

(C) the contributions to such plan on behalf of an individual who is an employee within the meaning of section 401(c)(1) shall be considered to satisfy the conditions of section 162 or 212 to the extent that such contributions do not exceed the earned income of such individual (determined without regard to the deductions allowed by this section) derived from the trade or business with respect to which such plan is established, and to the extent that such contributions are not allocable (determined in accordance with regulations prescribed by the Secretary) to the purchase of life, accident, health, or other insurance; and

(D) any reference to compensation shall, in the case of an individual who is an employee within the meaning of section 401(c)(1), be considered to be a reference to the earned income of such individual (determined without regard to the deduction allowed by this section) derived from the trade or business with respect to which the plan is established.

(9) Certain contributions to employee stock ownership plans.—

(A) Principal payments.—Notwithstanding the provisions of paragraphs (3) and (7), if contributions are paid into a trust which forms a part of an employee stock ownership plan (as described in section 4975(e)(7)), and such contributions are, on or before the time prescribed in paragraph (6), applied by the plan to the repayment of the principal of a loan incurred for the purpose of acquiring qualifying employer securities (as described in section 4975(e)(8)), such contributions shall be deductible under this paragraph for the taxable year determined under paragraph (6). The amount deductible under this paragraph shall not, however, exceed

25 percent of the compensation otherwise paid or accrued during the taxable year to the employees under such employee stock ownership plan. Any amount paid into such trust in any taxable year in excess of the amount deductible under this paragraph shall be deductible in the succeeding taxable years in order of time to the extent of the difference between the amount paid and deductible in each such succeeding year and the maximum amount deductible for such year under the preceding sentence.

(B) Interest payment.—Notwithstanding the provisions of paragraphs (3) and (7), if contributions are made to an employee stock ownership plan (described in subparagraph (A)) and such contributions are applied by the plan to the repayment of interest on a loan incurred for the purpose of acquiring qualifying employer securities (as described in subparagraph (A)), such contributions shall be deductible for the taxable year with respect to which such contributions are made as determined under paragraph (6).

(C) S corporations.—This paragraph shall not apply to an S corporation.

(D) Qualified gratuitous transfers.—A qualified gratuitous transfer (as defined in section 664(g)(1)) shall have no effect on the amount or amounts otherwise deductible under paragraph (3) or (7) or under this paragraph.

(10) Contributions by certain ministers to retirement income accounts.—In the case of contributions made by a minister described in section 414(e)(5) to a retirement income account described in section 403(b)(9) and not by a person other than such minister, such contributions—

(A) shall be treated as made to a trust which is exempt from tax under section 501(a) and which is part of a plan which is described in section 401(a), and

(B) shall be deductible under this subsection to the extent such contributions do not exceed the limit on elective deferrals under section 402 (g) or the limit on annual additions under section 415.

For purposes of this paragraph, all plans in which the minister is a participant shall be treated as one plan.

(11) Determinations relating to deferred compensation.—For purposes of determining under this section—

(A) whether compensation of an employee is deferred compensation, and

(B) when deferred compensation is paid,

no amount shall be treated as received by the employee, or paid, until it is actually received by the employee.

(12) Definition of compensation.—For purposes of paragraphs (3), (7), (8), and (9), and subsection (h)(1)(C), the term "compensation" shall include amounts treated as "participant's compensation" under subparagraph (C) or (D) of section 415(c)(3).

(b) Method of contributions, etc., having the effect of a plan; certain deferred benefits.—

(1) Method of contributions, etc., having the effect of a plan.—If—

(A) there is no plan, but

(B) there is a method or arrangement of employer contributions or compensation which has the effect of a stock bonus, pension, profit-sharing, or annuity plan, or other plan deferring the receipt of compensation (including a plan described in paragraph (2)),

subsection (a) shall apply as if there were such a plan.

(2) Plans providing certain deferred benefits.—

(A) In general.—For purposes of this section, any plan providing for deferred benefits (other than compensation) for employees, their spouses, or their dependents shall be treated as a plan deferring the receipt of compensation. In the case of such a plan, for purposes of this section, the determination of when an amount is includible in gross income shall be made without regard to any provisions of this chapter excluding such benefits from gross income.

(B) Exception for certain benefits.—Subparagraph (A) shall not apply to any benefit provided through a welfare benefit fund (as defined in section 419(e)).

(c) Certain negotiated plans.—If contributions are paid by an employer—

(1) under a plan under which such contributions are held in trust for the purpose of paying (either from principal or income or both) for the benefit of employees and their families and dependents at least medical or hospital care, or pensions on retirement or death of employees; and

(2) such plan was established prior to January 1, 1954, as a result of an agreement between employee representatives and the Government of the United States during a period of Government operation, under seizure powers, of a major part of the productive facilities of the industry in which such employer is engaged,

such contributions shall not be deductible under this section nor be made nondeductible by this section, but the deductibility thereof shall be governed solely by section 162 (relating to trade or business expenses). For purposes of this chapter and subtitle B, in the case of any individual who before July 1, 1974, was a participant in a plan described in the preceding sentence—

(A) such individual, if he is or was an employee within the meaning of section 401 (c)(1), shall be treated (with respect to service covered by the plan) as being an employee other than an employee within the meaning of section 401(c)(1) and as being an employee of a participating employer under the plan,

(B) earnings derived from service covered by the plan shall be treated as not being earned income within the meaning of section 401(c)(2), and

(C) such individual shall be treated as an employee of a participating employer under the plan with respect to service before July 1, 1975, covered by the plan.

Section 277 (relating to deductions incurred by certain membership organizations in transactions with members) does not apply to any trust described in this subsection. The first and third sentences of this subsection shall have no application with respect to amounts contributed to a trust on or after any date on which such trust is qualified for exemption from tax under section 501(a).

(d) Deductibility of payments of deferred compensation, etc., to independent contractors.—If a plan would be described in so much of subsection (a) as precedes paragraph (1) thereof (as modified by subsection (b)) but for the fact that there is no employer-employee relationship, the contributions or compensation—

(1) shall not be deductible by the payor thereof under this chapter, but

(2) shall (if they would be deductible under this chapter but for paragraph (1)) be deductible under this subsection for the taxable year in which an amount attributable to the contribution or compensation is includible in the gross income of the persons participating in the plan.

(e) Contributions allocable to life insurance protection for self-employed individuals.—In the case of a self-employed individual described in section 401(c)(1), contributions which are allocable (determined under regulations prescribed by the Secretary) to the purchase of life, accident, health, or other insurance shall not be taken into account under paragraph (1), (2), or (3) of subsection (a).

***(g) Certain employer liability payments considered as contributions.**—

(1) In general.—For purposes of this section, any amount paid by an employer under section 4041(b), 4062, 4063, or 4064, or part 1 of subtitle E of title IV of the Employee Retirement Income Security Act of 1974 shall be treated as a contribution to which this section applies by such employer to or under a stock bonus, pension, profit-sharing, or annuity plan.

(2) Controlled group deductions.—In the case of a payment described in paragraph (1) made by an entity which is liable because it is a member of a commonly controlled group of corporations, trades, or businesses, within the meaning of subsection (b) or (c) of section 414, the fact that the entity did not directly employ participants of the plan with respect to which the liability payment was made shall not affect the deductibility of a payment which otherwise satisfies the conditions of section 162 (relating to trade or business expenses) or section 212 (relating to expenses for the production of income).

(3) Timing of deduction of contributions.—

(A) In general.—Except as otherwise provided in this paragraph, any payment described in paragraph (1) shall (subject to the last sentence of subsection (a)(1)(A)) be deductible under this section when paid.

(B) Contributions under standard terminations.—Subparagraph (A) shall not apply (and subsection (a)(1)(A) shall apply) to any payments described in paragraph (1) which are paid to terminate a plan under section 4041(b) of the Employee Retirement Income Security Act of 1974 to the extent such payments result

*Editorial comment: There is no subsection (f).

in the assets of the plan being in excess of the total amount of benefits under such plan which are guaranteed by the Pension Benefit Guaranty Corporation under section 4022 of such Act.

(C) Contributions to certain trusts.—Subparagraph (A) shall not apply to any payment described in paragraph (1) which is made under section 4062(c) of such Act and such payment shall be deductible at such time as may be prescribed in regulations which are based on principles similar to the principles of subsection (a)(1)(A).

(4) References to Employee Retirement Income Security Act of 1974.—For purposes of this subsection, any reference to a section of the Employee Retirement Income Security Act of 1974 shall be treated as a reference to such section as in effect on the date of the enactment of the Retirement Protection Act of 1994.

(h) Special rules for simplified employee pensions.—

(1) In general.—Employer contributions to a simplified employee pension shall be treated as if they are made to a plan subject to the requirements of this section. Employer contributions to a simplified employee pension are subject to the following limitations:

(A) Contributions made for a year are deductible—

(i) in the case of a simplified employee pension maintained on a calendar year basis, for the taxable year with or within which the calendar year ends, or

(ii) in the case of a simplified employee pension which is maintained on the basis of the taxable year of the employer, for such taxable year.

(B) Contributions shall be treated for purposes of this subsection as if they were made for a taxable year if such contributions are made on account of such taxable year and are made not later than the time prescribed by law for filing the return for such taxable year (including extensions thereof).

(C) The amount deductible in a taxable year for a simplified employee pension shall not exceed 25 percent of the compensation paid to the employees during the calendar year ending with or within the taxable year (or during the taxable year in the case of a taxable year described in subparagraph (A)(ii)). The excess of the amount contributed over the amount deductible for a taxable year shall be deductible in the succeeding taxable years in order of time, subject to the 25 percent limit of the preceding sentence.

(2) Effect on certain trusts.—For any taxable year for which the employer has a deduction under paragraph (1), the otherwise applicable limitations in subsection (a)(3)(A) shall be reduced by the amount of the allowable deductions under paragraph (1) with respect to participants in the trust subject to subsection (a)(3)(A).

(3) Coordination with subsection (a)(7).—For purposes of subsection (a)(7), a simplified employee pension shall be treated as if it were a separate stock bonus or profit-sharing trust.

***(j) Special rules relating to application with section 415.**—

(1) No deduction in excess of section 415 limitation.—In computing the amount of any deduction allowable under paragraph (1), (2), (3), (4), (7), or (9) of subsection (a) for any year—

(A) in the case of a defined benefit plan, there shall not be taken into account any benefits for any year in excess of any limitation on such benefits under section 415 for such year, or

(B) in the case of a defined contribution plan, the amount of any contributions otherwise taken into account shall be reduced by any annual additions in excess of the limitation under section 415 for such year.

(2) No advance funding of cost-of-living adjustments.—For purposes of clause (i), (ii) or (iii) of subsection (a)(1)(A), and in computing the full funding limitation, there shall not be taken into account any adjustments under section 415(d)(1) for any year before the year for which such adjustment first takes effect.

(k) Deduction for dividends paid on certain employer securities.—

(1) General rule.—In the case of a C corporation, there shall be allowed as a deduction for a taxable year the amount of any applicable dividend paid in cash by such corporation with respect to applicable employer securities. Such deduction

*Editorial comment: There is no subsection (i).

shall be in addition to the deductions allowed under subsection (a).

(2) Applicable dividend.—For purposes of this subsection—

(A) In general.—The term "applicable dividend" means any dividend which in accordance with the plan provisions—

(i) is paid in cash to the participants in the plan or their beneficiaries.

(ii) is paid to the plan and is distributed in cash to participants in the plan or their beneficiaries not later than 90 days after the close of the plan year in which paid,

(iii) is, at the election of such participants or their beneficiaries—

(I) payable as provided in clause (i) or (ii), or

(II) paid to the plan and reinvested in qualifying employer securities, or

(iv) is used to make payments on a loan described in subsection (a)(9) the proceeds of which were used to acquire the employer securities (whether or not allocated to participants) with respect to which the dividend is paid.

(B) Limitation on certain dividends.—A dividend described in subparagraph (A)(iv) which is paid with respect to any employer security which is allocated to a participant shall not be treated as an applicable dividend unless the plan provides that employer securities with a fair market value of not less than the amount of such dividend are allocated to such participant for the year which (but for subparagraph (A)) such dividend would have been allocated to such participant.

(3) Applicable employer securities.—For purposes of this subsection, the term "applicable employer securities" means, with respect to any dividend, employer securities which are held on the record date for such dividend by an employee stock ownership plan which is maintained by—

(A) the corporation paying such dividend, or

(B) any other corporation which is a member of a controlled group of corporations (within the meaning of section 409(l)(4)) which includes such corporation.

(4) Time for deduction.—

(A) In general.—The deduction under paragraph (1) shall be allowable in the taxable year of the corporation in which the dividend is paid or distributed to a participant or his beneficiary.

(B) Reinvestment dividends.—For purposes of subparagraph (A), an applicable dividend reinvested pursuant to clause (iii)(II) of paragraph (2)(A) shall be treated as paid in the taxable year of the corporation in which such dividend is reinvested in qualifying employer securities or in which the election under clause (iii) of paragraph (2)(A) is made, whichever is later.

(C) Repayment of loans.—In the case of an applicable dividend described in clause (iii) of paragraph (2)(A), the deduction under paragraph (1) shall be allowable in the taxable year of the corporation in which such dividend is used to repay the loan described in such clause.

(5) Other rules.—For purposes of this subsection—

(A) Disallowance of deduction.—The Secretary may disallow the deduction under paragraph (1) for any dividend if the Secretary determines that such dividend constitutes, in substance, an avoidance or evasion of taxation.

(B) Plan qualification.—A plan shall not be treated as violating the requirements of section 401, 409, or 4975(e)(7), or as engaging in a prohibited transaction for purposes of section 4975(d)(3), merely by reason of any payment or distribution described in paragraph (2)(A).

(6) Definitions.—For purposes of this subsection—

(A) Employer securities.—The term "employer securities" has the meaning given such term by section 409(1).

(B) Employee stock ownership plan.—The term "employee stock ownership plan" has the meaning given such term by section 4975(e)(7). Such term includes a tax credit employee stock ownership plan (as defined in section 409).

(7) Full vesting.—In accordance with section 411, an applicable dividend described in clause (iii)(II) of paragraph (2)(A) shall be subject to the requirements of section 411(a)(1).

(l) Limitation on amount of annual compensation taken into account.—For purposes of applying the limitations of this section, the amount of annual compensation of each employee taken into account under the plan for any year shall not exceed

$200,000.* The Secretary shall adjust the $200,000* amount at the same time, and by the same amount, as any adjustment under section 401 (a)(17)(B). For purposes of clause (i), (ii), or (iii) of subsection (a)(1)(A), and in computing the full funding limitation, any adjustment under the preceding sentence shall not be taken into account for any year before the year for which such adjustment first takes effect.

(m) Special rules for simple retirement accounts.—

(1) In general.—Employer contributions to a simple retirement account shall be treated as if they are made to a plan subject to the requirements of this section.

(2) Timing.—

(A) Deduction.—Contributions described in paragraph (1) shall be deductible in the taxable year of the employer with or within which the calendar year for which the contributions were made ends.

(B) Contributions after end of year.—For purposes of this subsection, contributions shall be treated as made for a taxable year if they are made on account of the taxable year and are made not later than the time prescribed by law for filing the return for the taxable year (including extensions thereof).

(n) Elective deferrals not taken into account for purposes of deduction limits.—Elective deferrals (as defined in section 402(g)(3)) shall not be subject to any limitation contained in paragraph (3), (7), or (9) of subsection (a), or paragraph (1)(C) of subsection (h), and such elective deferrals shall not be taken into account in applying any such limitation to any other contributions.

(o) Deduction limit for single-employer plans—For purposes of subsection (a)(1)(A)—

(1) In general.—In the case of a defined benefit plan to which subsection (a)(1)(A) applies (other than a multiemployer plan), the amount determined under this subsection for any taxable year shall be equal to the greater of—

(A) the sum of the amounts determined under paragraph (2) with respect to each plan year ending with or within the taxable year, or

(B) the sum of the minimum required contributions under section 430 for such plan years.

*Editorial comment: The $200,000 amount is subject to indexing. For 2013 the indexed amount is $255,000, and for 2014 is $260,000.

(2) Determination of amount.—

(A) In general.—The amount determined under this paragraph for any plan year shall be equal to the excess (if any) of

(i) the sum of—

(I) the funding target for the plan year,

(II) the target normal cost for the plan year, and

(III) the cushion amount for the plan year, over

(ii) the value (determined under section 430(g)(2)) of the assets of the plan which are held by the plan as of the valuation date for the plan year.

(B) Special rule for certain employers.—If section 430(i) does not apply to a plan for a plan year, the amount determined under subparagraph (A)(i) for the plan year shall in no event be less than the sum of—

(i) the funding target for the plan year (determined as if section 430(i) applied to the plan), plus

(ii) the target normal cost for the plan year (as so determined).

(3) Cushion amount.—For purposes of paragraph (2)(A)(i)(III)—

(A) In general.—The cushion amount for any plan year is the sum of—

(i) 50 percent of the funding target for the plan year, and

(ii) the amount by which the funding target for the plan year would increase if the plan were to take into account—

(I) increases in compensation which are expected to occur in succeeding plan years, or

(II) if the plan does not base benefits for service to date on compensation, increases in benefits which are expected to occur in succeeding plan years (determined on the basis of the average annual increase in benefits over the 6 immediately preceding plan years).

(B) Limitations.—

(i) In general.—In making the computation under subparagraph (A)(ii), the plan's actuary shall assume that the limitations under subsection (l) and section 415(b) shall apply.

(ii) Expected increases.—In the case of a plan year during which a plan is covered under section 4021 of the Employee Retirement Income Security Act of 1974, the plan's actuary may, notwithstanding subsection (l), take into account increases in the limitations which are expected to occur in succeeding plan years.

(4) Special rules for plans with 100 or fewer participants.—

(A) In general.—For purposes of determining the amount under paragraph (3) for any plan year, in the case of a plan which has 100 or fewer participants for the plan year, the liability of the plan attributable to benefit increases for highly compensated employees (as defined in section 414(q)) resulting from a plan amendment which is made or becomes effective, whichever is later, within the last 2 years shall not be taken into account in determining the target liability.

(B) Rule for determining number of participants.—For purposes of determining the number of plan participants, all defined benefit plans maintained by the same employer (or any member of such employer's controlled group (within the meaning of section 412(f)(4))) shall be treated as one plan, but only participants of such member or employer shall be taken into account.

(5) Special rule for terminating plans.—In the case of a plan which, subject to section 4041 of the Employee Retirement Income Security Act of 1974, terminates during the plan year, the amount determined under paragraph (2) shall in no event be less than the amount required to make the plan sufficient for benefit liabilities (within the meaning of section 4041(d) of such Act).

(6) Actuarial assumptions.—Any computation under this subsection for any plan year shall use the same actuarial assumptions which are used for the plan year under section 430.

(7) Definitions.—Any term used in this subsection which is also used in section 430 shall have the same meaning given such term by section 430.

* * *

§ 408. Individual retirement accounts

(a) Individual retirement account.—For purposes of this section, the term "individual retirement account" means a trust created or organized in the United States for the exclusive benefit of an individual or his beneficiaries, but only if the written governing instrument creating the trust meets the following requirements:

(1) Except in the case of a rollover contribution described in subsection (d)(3), in section 402(c), 403(a)(4), 403(b)(8), or 457(e)(16), no contribution will be accepted unless it is in cash, and contributions will not be accepted for the taxable year on behalf of any individual in excess of the amount in effect for such taxable year under section 219(b)(1)(A).

(2) The trustee is a bank (as defined in subsection (n)) or such other person who demonstrates to the satisfaction of the Secretary that the manner in which such other person will administer the trust will be consistent with the requirements of this section.

(3) No part of the trust funds will be invested in life insurance contracts.

(4) The interest of an individual in the balance in his account is nonforfeitable.

(5) The assets of the trust will not be commingled with other property except in a common trust fund or common investment fund.

(6) Under regulations prescribed by the Secretary, rules similar to the rules of section 401(a)(9) and the incidental death benefit requirements of section 401(a) shall apply to the distribution of the entire interest of an individual for whose benefit the trust is maintained.

(b) Individual retirement annuity.—For purposes of this section, the term "individual retirement annuity" means an annuity contract, or an endowment contract (as determined under regulations prescribed by the Secretary), issued by an insurance company which meets the following requirements:

(1) The contract is not transferable by the owner.

(2) Under the contract—

(A) the premiums are not fixed,

(B) the annual premium on behalf of any individual will not exceed the dollar amount in effect under section 219(b)(1)(A), and

(C) any refund of premiums will be applied before the close of the calendar year following the year of the refund toward the payment of future premiums or the purchase of additional benefits.

(3) Under regulations prescribed by the Secretary, rules similar to the rules of section 401(a)(9) and the incidental death benefit requirements of section 401(a) shall apply to the distribution of the entire interest of the owner.

(4) The entire interest of the owner is nonforfeitable.

Such term does not include such an annuity contract for any taxable year of the owner in which it is disqualified on the application of subsection (e) or for any subsequent taxable year. For purposes of this subsection, no contract shall be treated as an endowment contract if it matures later than the taxable year in which the individual in whose name such contract is purchased attains age 70½; if it is not for the exclusive benefit of the individual in whose name it is purchased or his beneficiaries; or if the aggregate annual premiums under all such contracts purchased in the name of such individual for any taxable year exceed the dollar amount in effect under section 219(b)(1)(A).

(c) Accounts established by employers and certain associations of employees.—A trust created or organized in the United States by an employer for the exclusive benefit of his employees or their beneficiaries, or by an association of employees (which may include employees within the meaning of section 401(c)(1)) for the exclusive benefit of its members or their beneficiaries, shall be treated as an individual retirement account (described in subsection (a)), but only if the written governing instrument creating the trust meets the following requirements:

(1) The trust satisfies the requirements of paragraphs (1) through (6) of subsection (a).

(2) There is a separate accounting for the interest of each employee or member (or spouse of an employee or member).

The assets of the trust may be held in a common fund for the account of all individuals who have an interest in the trust.

(d) Tax treatment of distributions.—

(1) In general.—Except as otherwise provided in this subsection, any amount paid or distributed out of an individual retirement plan shall be in cluded in gross income by the payee or distributee, as the case may be, in the manner provided under section 72.

(2) Special rules for applying section 72.—For purposes of applying section 72 to any amount described in paragraph (1)—

(A) all individual retirement plans shall be treated as 1 contract,

(B) all distributions during any taxable year shall be treated as 1 distribution, and

(C) the value of the contract, income on the contract, and investment in the contract shall be computed as of the close of the calendar year in which the taxable year begins.

For purposes of subparagraph (C), the value of the contract shall be increased by the amount of any distributions during the calendar year.

(3) Rollover contribution.—An amount is described in this paragraph as a rollover contribution if it meets the requirements of subparagraphs (A) and (B).

(A) In general.—Paragraph (1) does not apply to any amount paid or distributed out of an individual retirement account or individual retirement annuity to the individual for whose benefit the account or annuity is maintained if—

(i) the entire amount received (including money and any other property) is paid into an individual retirement account or individual retirement annuity (other than an endowment contract) for the benefit of such individual not later than the 60th day after the day on which he receives the payment or distribution; or

(ii) the entire amount received (including money and any other property) is paid into an eligible retirement plan for the benefit of such individual not later than the 60th day after the date on which the payment or distribution is received, except that the maximum amount which may be paid into such plan may not exceed the portion of the amount received which is includible in gross income (determined without regard to this paragraph).

For purposes of clause (ii), the term "eligible retirement plan" means an eligible retirement plan described in clause (iii), (iv), (v), or (vi) of section 402(c)(8)(B).

(B) Limitation.—This paragraph does not apply to any amount described in subparagraph (A)(i) received by an individual from an individual retirement account or individual retirement annuity if at any time during the 1-year period ending on the day of such receipt such individual received any other amount described in that subparagraph from an individual retirement account or an individual retirement annuity which was not includible in his gross income because of the application of this paragraph.

(C) Denial of rollover treatment for inherited accounts, etc.—

(i) In general.—In the case of an inherited individual retirement account or individual retirement annuity—

(I) this paragraph shall not apply to any amount received by an individual from such an account or annuity (and no amount transferred from such account or annuity to another individual retirement account or annuity shall be excluded from gross income by reason of such transfer), and

(II) such inherited account or annuity shall not be treated as an individual retirement account or annuity for purposes of determining whether any other amount is a rollover contribution.

(ii) Inherited individual retirement account or annuity.—An individual retirement account or individual retirement annuity shall be treated as inherited if—

(I) the individual for whose benefit the account or annuity is maintained acquired such account by reason of a death of another individual, and

(II) such individual was not the surviving spouse of such other individual.

(D) Partial rollovers permitted.—

(i) In general.—If any amount paid or distributed out of an individual retirement account or individual retirement annuity would meet the requirements of subparagraph (A) but for the fact that the entire amount was not paid into an eligible plan as required by clause (i) or (ii) of subparagraph (A), such amount shall be treated as meeting the requirements of subparagraph (A) to the extent it is paid into an eligible plan referred to in such clause not later than the 60th day referred to in such clause.

(ii) Eligible plan.—For purposes of clause (i), the term "eligible plan" means any account, annuity, contract, or plan referred to in subparagraph (A).

(E) Denial of rollover treatment for required distributions.—This paragraph shall not apply to any amount to the extent such amount is required to be distributed under subsection (a)(6) or (b)(3).

(F) Frozen deposits.—For purposes of this paragraph, rules similar to the rules of section 402(c)(7) (relating to frozen deposits) shall apply.

(G) Simple retirement accounts.—In the case of any payment or distribution out of a simple retirement account (as defined in subsection (p)) to which section 72(t)(6) applies, this paragraph shall not apply unless such payment or distribution is paid into another simple retirement account.

(H) Application of section 72.—

(i) In general.—If—

(I) a distribution is made from an individual retirement plan, and

(II) a rollover contribution is made to an eligible retirement plan described in section 402(c)(8)(B)(iii), (iv), (v), or (vi) with respect to all or part of such distribution,

then, notwithstanding paragraph (2), the rules of clause (ii) shall apply for purposes of applying section 72.

(ii) Applicable rules.—In the case of a distribution described in clause (i)—

(I) section 72 shall be applied separately to such distribution,

(II) notwithstanding the pro rata allocation of income on, and investment in, the contract to distributions under section 72, the portion of such distribution rolled over to an eligible retirement plan described in clause (i) shall be treated as from income on the contract (to the extent of the aggregate income on the contract from all individual retirement plans of the distributee), and

(III) appropriate adjustments shall be made in applying section 72 to other distributions in such taxable year and subsequent taxable years.

(I) Waiver of 60-day requirement.—The Secretary may waive the 60-day requirement under subparagraphs (A) and (D) where the failure to waive such requirement would be against equity or good conscience, including casualty, disaster, or other events beyond the reasonable control of the individual subject to such requirement.

(4) Contributions returned before due date of return.—Paragraph (1) does not apply to the distribution of any contribution paid during a taxable year to an individual retirement account or for an individual retirement annuity if—

(A) such distribution is received on or before the day prescribed by law (including extensions of time) for filing such individual's return for such taxable year,

(B) no deduction is allowed under section 219 with respect to such contribution, and

(C) such distribution is accompanied by the amount of net income attributable to such contribution.

In the case of such a distribution, for purposes of section 61, any net income described in subparagraph (C) shall be deemed to have been earned and receivable in the taxable year in which such contribution is made.

(5) Distributions of excess contributions after due date for taxable year and certain excess rollover contributions.—

(A) In general.—In the case of any individual, if the aggregate contributions (other than rollover contributions) paid for any taxable year to an individual retirement account or for an individual retirement annuity do not exceed the dollar amount in effect under section 219(b)(1)(A), paragraph (1) shall not apply to the distribution of any such contribution to the extent that such contribution exceeds the amount allowable as a deduction under section 219 for the taxable year for which the contribution was paid—

(i) if such distribution is received after the date described in paragraph (4),

(ii) but only to the extent that no deduction has been allowed under section 219 with respect to such excess contribution.

If employer contributions on behalf of the individual are paid for the taxable year to a simplified employee pension, the dollar limitation of the preceding sentence shall be increased by the lesser of the amount of such contributions or the dollar limitation in effect under section 415(c)(1)(A) for such taxable year.

(B) Excess rollover contributions attributable to erroneous information.—If—

(i) the taxpayer reasonably relies on information supplied pursuant to subtitle F for determining the amount of a rollover contribution, but

(ii) the information was erroneous,

subparagraph (A) shall be applied by increasing the dollar limit set forth therein by that portion of the excess contribution which was attributable to such information. For purposes of this paragraph, the amount allowable as a deduction under section 219 shall be computed without regard to section 219(g).

(6) Transfer of account incident to divorce.—The transfer of an individual's interest in an individual retirement account or an individual retirement annuity to his spouse or former spouse under a divorce or separation instrument described in subparagraph (A) of section 71(b)(2) is not to be considered a taxable transfer made by such individual notwithstanding any other provision of this subtitle, and such interest at the time of the transfer is to be treated as an individual retirement account of such spouse, and not of such individual. Thereafter such account or annuity for purposes of this subtitle is to be treated as maintained for the benefit of such spouse.

(7) Special rules for simplified employee pensions or simple retirement accounts.—

(A) Transfer or rollover of contributions prohibited until deferral test met.—Notwithstanding any other provision of this subsection or section 72(t), paragraph (1) and section 72(t)(1) shall apply to the transfer or distribution from a simplified employee pension of any contribution under a salary reduction arrangement described in subsection (k)(6) (or any income allocable thereto) before a determination as to whether the requirements of subsection (k)(6)(A)(iii) are met with respect to such contribution.

(B) Certain exclusions treated as deductions.—For purposes of paragraphs (4) and (5) and section 4973, any amount excludable or excluded from gross income under section 402(h) or 402(k) shall be treated as an amount allowable or allowed as a deduction under section 219.

(8) Distributions for charitable purposes.—

(A) In general.—So much of the aggregate amount of qualified charitable distributions with respect to a taxpayer made during any taxable year which does not exceed $100,000 shall not be includible in gross income of such taxpayer for such taxable year.

(B) Qualified charitable distribution.—For purposes of this paragraph, the term "qualified charitable distribution" means any distribution from an individual retirement plan (other than a plan described in subsection (k) or (p))—

(i) which is made directly by the trustee to an organization described in section 170(b)(1)(A) (other than any organization described in section 509(a)(3) or any fund or account described in section 4966(d)(2)), and

(ii) which is made on or after the date that the individual for whose benefit the plan is maintained has attained age 70½.

A distribution shall be treated as a qualified charitable distribution only to the extent that the distribution would be includible in gross income without regard to subparagraph (A).

(C) Contributions must be otherwise deductible.—For purposes of this paragraph, a distribution to an organization described in subparagraph (B)(i) shall be treated as a qualified charitable distribution only if a deduction for the entire distribution would be allowable under section 170 (determined without regard to subsection (b) thereof and his paragraph).

(D) Application of section 72.—Notwithstanding section 72, in determining the extent to which a distribution is a qualified charitable distribution, the entire amount of the distribution shall be treated as includible in gross income without regard to subparagraph (A) to the extent that such amount does not exceed the aggregate amount which would have been so includible if all amounts in all individual retirement plans of the individual were distributed during such taxable year and all such plans were treated as 1 contract for purposes of determining under section 72 the aggregate amount which would have been so includible. Proper adjustments shall be made in applying section 72 to other distributions in such taxable year and subsequent taxable years.

(E) Denial of deduction.—Qualified charitable distributions which are not includible in gross income pursuant to subparagraph (A) shall not be taken into account in determining the deduction under section 170.

(F) Termination.—This paragraph shall not apply to distributions made in taxable years beginning after December 31, 2013.*

(9) Distribution for health savings account funding.—

(A) In general.—In the case of an individual who is an eligible individual (as defined in section 223(c)) and who elects the application of this paragraph for a taxable year, gross income of the individual for the taxable year does not include a qualified HSA funding distribution to the extent such distribution is otherwise includible in gross income.

(B) Qualified HSA funding distribution.—For purposes of this paragraph, the term "qualified HSA funding distribution" means a distribution from an individual retirement plan (other than a plan described in subsection (k) or (p)) of the employee to the extent that such distribution is contributed to the health savings account of the individual in a direct trustee-to-trustee transfer.

(C) Limitations.—

(i) Maximum dollar limitation.—The amount excluded from gross income by subparagraph (A) shall not exceed the excess of—

(I) the annual limitation under section 223(b) computed on the basis of the type of coverage under the high deductible health plan covering the individual at the time of the qualified HSA funding distribution, over

(II) in the case of a distribution described in clause (ii)(II), the amount of the earlier qualified HSA funding distribution.

(ii) One-time transfer.—

(I) In general.—Except as provided in subclause (II), an individual may make an election under subparagraph (A) only for one qualified HSA funding distribution during the lifetime of the individual. Such an election, once made, shall be irrevocable.

(II) Conversion from self-only to family coverage.—If a qualified HSA funding distribution is made during a month in a taxable year during which an individual has self-only coverage under a high deductible health plan as of the first day of the month, the individual may elect to make an additional qualified HSA funding distribution during a subsequent month in such taxable year during which the individual has family coverage under a high deductible health plan as of the first day of the subsequent month.

(D) Failure to maintain high deductible health plan coverage.—

(i) In general.—If, at any time during the testing period, the individual is not an

*Editorial comment: At the present time, this section has not been extended. There is pending legislation in the Senate, *The Tax Extenders Act of 2013 (S. 1859)*, that would extend Section 408(d)(8)(F) until December 31, 2014.

eligible individual, then the aggregate amount of all contributions to the health savings account of the individual made under subparagraph (A)—

(I) shall be includible in the gross income of the individual for the taxable year in which occurs the first month in the testing period for which such individual is not an eligible individual, and

(II) the tax imposed by this chapter for any taxable year on the individual shall be increased by 10 percent of the amount which is so includible.

(ii) Exception for disability or death.—Subclauses (I) and (II) of clause (i) shall not apply if the individual ceased to be an eligible individual by reason of the death of the individual or the individual becoming disabled (within the meaning of section 72(m)(7)).

(iii) Testing period.—The term "testing period" means the period beginning with the month in which the qualified HSA funding distribution is contributed to a health savings account and ending on the last day of the 12th month following such month.

(E) Application of section 72.—Notwithstanding section 72, in determining the extent to which an amount is treated as otherwise includible in gross income for purposes of subparagraph (A), the aggregate amount distributed from an individual retirement plan shall be treated as includible in gross income to the extent that such amount does not exceed the aggregate amount which would have been so includible if all amounts from all individual retirement plans were distributed. Proper adjustments shall be made in applying section 72 to other distributions in such taxable year and subsequent taxable years.

(e) Tax treatment of accounts and annuities.—

(1) Exemption from tax.—Any individual retirement account is exempt from taxation under this subtitle unless such account has ceased to be an individual retirement account by reason of paragraph (2) or (3). Notwithstanding the preceding sentence, any such account is subject to the taxes imposed by section 511 (relating to imposition of tax on unrelated business income of charitable; etc. organizations).

(2) Loss of exemption of account where employee engages in prohibited transaction.—

(A) In general.—If, during any taxable year of the individual for whose benefit any individual retirement account is established, that individual or his beneficiary engages in any transaction prohibited by section 4975 with respect to such account, such account ceases to be an individual retirement account as of the first day of such taxable year. For purposes of this paragraph—

(i) the individual for whose benefit any account was established is treated as the creator of such account, and

(ii) the separate account for any individual within an individual retirement account maintained by an employer or association of employees is treated as a separate individual retirement account.

(B) Account treated as distributing all its assets.—In any case in which any account ceases to be an individual retirement account by reason of subparagraph (A) as of the first day of any taxable year, paragraph (1) of subsection (d) applies as if there were a distribution on such first day in an amount equal to the fair market value (on such first day) of all assets in the account (on such first day).

(3) Effect of borrowing on annuity contract.—If during any taxable year the owner of an individual retirement annuity borrows any money under or by use of such contract, the contract ceases to be an individual retirement annuity as of the first day of such taxable year. Such owner shall include in gross income for such year an amount equal to the fair market value of such contract as of such first day.

(4) Effect of pledging account as security.—If, during any taxable year of the individual for whose benefit an individual retirement account is established, that individual uses the account or any portion thereof as security for a loan, the portion so used is treated as distributed to that individual.

(5) Purchase of endowment contract by individual retirement account.—If the assets of an individual retirement account or any part of such assets are used to purchase an endowment contract for the benefit of the individual for whose benefit the account is established—

(A) to the extent that the amount of the assets involved in the purchase are not attributable to the purchase of life insurance, the purchase is treated as a rollover contribution described in subsection (d)(3), and

(B) to the extent that the amount of the assets involved in the purchase are attributable to the purchase of life, health, accident, or other insurance, such amounts are treated as distributed to that individual (but the provisions of subsection (f) do not apply).

(6) Commingling individual retirement account amounts in certain common trust funds and common investment funds.—Any common trust fund or common investment fund of individual retirement account assets which is exempt from taxation under this subtitle does not cease to be exempt on account of the participation or inclusion of assets of a trust exempt from taxation under section 501(a) which is described in section 401(a).

(g) Community property laws.—This section shall be applied without regard to any community property laws.

(h) Custodial accounts.—For purposes of this section, a custodial account shall be treated as a trust if the assets of such account are held by a bank (as defined in subsection (n)) or another person who demonstrates, to the satisfaction of the Secretary, that the manner in which he will administer the account will be consistent with the requirements of this section, and if the custodial account would, except for the fact that it is not a trust, constitute an individual retirement account described in subsection (a). For purposes of this title, in the case of a custodial account treated as a trust by reason of the preceding sentence, the custodian of such account shall be treated as the trustee thereof.

* * *

(j) Increase in maximum limitations for simplified employee pensions.—In the case of any simplified employee pension, subsections (a)(1) and (b)(2) of this section shall be applied by increasing the amounts contained therein by the amount of the limitation in effect under section 415(c)(1)(A).

(k) Simplified employee pension defined.—

(1) In general.—For purposes of this title, the term "simplified employee pension" means an individual retirement account or individual retirement annuity—

(A) with respect to which the requirements of paragraphs (2), (3), (4), and (5) of this subsection are met, and

(B) if such account or annuity is part of a top-heavy plan (as defined in section 416), with respect to which the requirements of section 416(c)(2) are met.

(2) Participation requirements.—This paragraph is satisfied with respect to a simplified employee pension for a year only if for such year the employer contributes to the simplified employee pension of each employee who—

(A) has attained age 21,

(B) has performed service for the employer during at least 3 of the immediately preceding 5 years, and

(C) received at least $450* in compensation (within the meaning of section 414(q)(4)) from the employer for the year.

For purposes of this paragraph, there shall be excluded from consideration employees described in subparagraph (A) or (C) of section 410(b)(3). For purposes of any arrangement described in subsection (k)(6), any employee who is eligible to have employer contributions made on the employee's behalf under such arrangement shall be treated as if such a contribution was made.

(3) Contributions may not discriminate in favor of the highly compensated, etc.—

(A) In general.—The requirements of this paragraph are met with respect to a simplified employee pension for a year if for such year the contributions made by the employer to simplified employee pensions for his employees do not discriminate in favor of any highly compensated employee (within the meaning of section 414(q)).

(B) Special rules.—For purposes of subparagraph (A), there shall be excluded from consideration employees described in subparagraph (A) or (C) of section 410(b)(3).

(C) Contributions must bear uniform relationship to total compensation.—For purposes of subparagraph (A), and except as provided in subparagraph (D), employer contributions to simplified employee

*Editorial comment: The indexed amount for 2013 is $550 and for 2014 is $550.

pensions (other than contributions under an arrangement described in paragraph (6)) shall be considered discriminatory unless contributions thereto bear a uniform relationship to the compensation (not in excess of the first $200,000)* of each employee maintaining a simplified employee pension.

(D) Permitted disparity.—For purposes of subparagraph (C), the rules of section 401(l)(2) shall apply to contributions to simplified employee pensions (other than contributions under an arrangement described in paragraph (6)).

(4) Withdrawals must be permitted.—A simplified employee pension meets the requirements of this paragraph only if—

(A) employer contributions thereto are not conditioned on the retention in such pension of any portion of the amount contributed, and

(B) there is no prohibition imposed by the employer on withdrawals from the simplified employee pension.

(5) Contributions must be made under written allocation formula.—The requirements of this paragraph are met with respect to a simplified employee pension only if employer contributions to such pension are determined under a definite written allocation formula which specifies—

(A) the requirements which an employee must satisfy to share in an allocation, and

(B) the manner in which the amount allocated is computed.

(6) Employee may elect salary reduction arrangement.—

(A) Arrangements which qualify—

(i) In general.—A simplified employee pension shall not fail to meet the requirements of this subsection for a year merely because, under the terms of the pension, an employee may elect to have the employer make payments—

(I) as elective employer contributions to the simplified employee pension on behalf of the employee, or

(II) to the employee directly in cash.

(ii) 50 percent of eligible employees must elect.—Clause (i) shall not apply to a simplified employee pension unless an election described in clause (i)(I) is made or is in effect with respect to not less than 50 percent of the employees of the employer eligible to participate.

(iii) Requirements relating to deferral percentage.—Clause (i) shall not apply to a simplified employee pension for any year unless the deferral percentage for such year of each highly compensated employee eligible to participate is not more than the product of—

(I) the average of the deferral percentages for such year of all employees (other than highly compensated employees) eligible to participate, multiplied by

(II) 1.25.

(iv) Limitations on elective deferrals.—Clause (i) shall not apply to a simplified employee pension unless the requirements of section 401(a)(30) are met.

(B) Exception where more than 25 employees.—This paragraph shall not apply with respect to any year in the case of a simplified employee pension maintained by an employer with more than 25 employees who were eligible to participate (or would have been required to be eligible to participate if a pension was maintained) at any time during the preceding year.

(C) Distributions of excess contributions.—

(i) In general.—Rules similar to the rules of section 401(k)(8) shall apply to any excess contribution under this paragraph. Any excess contribution under a simplified employee pension shall be treated as an excess contribution for purposes of section 4979.

(ii) Excess contribution.—For purposes of clause (i), the term "excess contribution" means, with respect to a highly compensated employee, the excess of elective employer contributions under this paragraph over the maximum amount of such contributions allowable under subparagraph (A)(iii).

(D) Deferral percentage.—For purposes of this paragraph, the deferral percentage for an employee for a year shall be the ratio of—

*Editorial comment: The $200,000 amount is subject to indexing. For 2013 the indexed amount is $255,000, and for 2014 is $260,000.

(i) the amount of elective employer contributions actually paid over to the simplified employee pension on behalf of the employee for the year, to

(ii) the employee's compensation (not in excess of the first $200,000)* for the year.

(E) Exception for state and local and tax-exempt pensions.—This paragraph shall not apply to a simplified employee pension maintained by—

(i) a State or local government or political subdivision thereof, or any agency or instrumentality thereof, or

(ii) an organization exempt from tax under this title.

(F) Exception where pension does not meet requirements necessary to insure distribution of excess contributions.—This paragraph shall not apply with respect to any year for which the simplified employee pension does not meet such requirements as the Secretary may prescribe as are necessary to insure that excess contributions are distributed in accordance with subparagraph (C), including—

(i) reporting requirements, and

(ii) requirements which, notwithstanding paragraph (4), provide that contributions (and any income allocable thereto) may not be withdrawn from a simplified employee pension until a determination has been made that the requirements of subparagraph (A)(iii) have been met with respect to such contributions.

(G) Highly compensated employee.—For purposes of this paragraph, the term "highly compensated employee" has the meaning given such term by section 414(q).

(H) Termination.—This paragraph shall not apply to years beginning after December 31, 1996. The preceding sentence shall not apply to a simplified employee pension of an employer if the terms of simplified employee pensions of such employer, as in effect on December 31, 1996, provide that an employee may make the election described in subparagraph (A).

(7) Definitions.—For purposes of this subsection and subsection (1)—

(A) Employee, employer, or owner-employee.—The terms "employee," "employer," and "owner-employee" shall have the respective meanings given such terms by section 401(c).

(B) Compensation.—Except as provided in paragraph (2)(C), the term "compensation" has the meaning given such term by section 414(s).

(C) Year.—The term "year" means—

(i) the calendar year, or

(ii) if the employer elects, subject to such terms and conditions as the Secretary may prescribe, to maintain the simplified employee pension on the basis of the employer's taxable year.

(8) Cost-of-living adjustment.—The Secretary shall adjust the $450** amount in paragraph (2)(C) at the same time and in the same manner as under section 415(d) and shall adjust the $200,000* amount in paragraphs (3)(C) and (6)(D)(ii) at the same time, and by the same amount, as any adjustment under section 401(a)(17)(B), except that any increase in the $450** amount which is not a multiple of $50 shall be rounded to the next lowest multiple of $50.

(9) Cross reference.—

For excise tax on certain excess contributions, see section 4979.

(l) Simplified employer reports.—

(1) In general.—An employer who makes a contribution on behalf of an employee to a simplified employee pension shall provide such simplified reports with respect to such contributions as the Secretary may require by regulations. The reports required by this subsection shall be filed at such time and in such manner, and information with respect to such contributions shall be furnished to the employee at such time and in such manner, as may be required by regulations.

(2) Simple retirement accounts.

(A) No employer reports. Except as provided in this paragraph, no report shall be required under this section by an employer maintaining a qualified salary reduction arrangement under section (p).

(B) Summary description.—The trustee of any simple retirement account established

*Editorial comment: The $200,000 amount is subject to indexing. For 2013, the indexed amount is $255,000, and for 2014 is $260,000.

**Editorial comment: The indexed amount for 2013 is $550 and for 2014 is $550.

pursuant to a qualified salary reduction arrangement under subsection (p) and the issuer of an annuity established under such an arrangement shall provide to the employer maintaining the arrangement, each year a description containing the following information:

(i) The name and address of the employer and the trustee or issuer.

(ii) The requirements for eligibility for participation.

(iii) The benefits provided with respect to the arrangement.

(iv) The time and method of making elections with respect to the arrangement.

(v) The procedures for, and effects of, withdrawals (including rollovers) from the arrangement.

(C) Employee notification.—The employer shall notify each employee immediately before the period for which an election described in subsection (p)(5)(C) may be made of the employee's opportunity to make such election. Such notice shall include a copy of the description described in subparagraph (B).

(m) Investment in collectibles treated as distributions.—

(1) In general.—The acquisition by an individual retirement account or by an individually-directed account under a plan described in section 401(a) of any collectible shall be treated (for purposes of this section and section 402) as a distribution from such account in an amount equal to the cost to such account of such collectible.

(2) Collectible defined.—For purposes of this subsection, the term "collectible" means—

(A) any work of art,

(B) any rug or antique,

(C) any metal or gem,

(D) any stamp or coin,

(E) any alcoholic beverage, or

(F) any other tangible personal property specified by the Secretary for purposes of this subsection.

(3) Exception for certain coins and bullion.—For purposes of this subsection, the term "collectible" shall not include—

(A) any coin which is—

(i) a gold coin described in paragraph (7), (8), (9), or (10) of section 5112(a) of title 31, United States Code,

(ii) a silver coin described in section 5112(e) of title 31, United States Code,

(iii) a platinum coin described in section 5112(k) of title 31, United States Code, or

(iv) a coin issued under the laws of any State, or

(B) any gold, silver, platinum, or palladium bullion of a fineness equal to or exceeding the minimum fineness that a contract market (as described in section 7 of the Commodity Exchange Act, 7 U.S.C. 7) requires for metals which may be delivered in satisfaction of a regulated futures contract,

if such bullion is in the physical possession of a trustee described under subsection (a) of this section.

* * *

(o) Definitions and rules relating to nondeductible contributions to individual retirement plans.—

(1) In general.—Subject to the provisions of this subsection, designated nondeductible contributions may be made on behalf of an individual to an individual retirement plan.

(2) Limits on amounts which may be contributed.—

(A) In general.—The amount of the designated nondeductible contributions made on behalf of any individual for any taxable year shall not exceed the nondeductible limit for such taxable year.

(B) Nondeductible limit.—For purposes of this paragraph—

(i) In general.—The term "nondeductible limit" means the excess of—

(I) the amount allowable as a deduction under section 219 (determined without regard to section 219(g)), over

(II) the amount allowable as a deduction under section 219 (determined with regard to section 219(g)).

(ii) Taxpayer may elect to treat deductible contributions as nondeductible.—If a taxpayer elects not to deduct an amount which (without regard to this clause) is allowable as a deduction under section 219 for any taxable year, the nondeductible limit for such taxable year shall be increased by such amount.

(C) Designated nondeductible contributions.—

(i) In general.—For purposes of this paragraph, the term "designated nondeductible contribution" means any contribution to an individual retirement plan for the taxable year which is designated (in such manner as the Secretary may prescribe) as a contribution for which a deduction is not allowable under section 219.

(ii) Designation.—Any designation under clause (i) shall be made on the return of tax imposed by chapter 1 for the taxable year.

(3) Time when contributions made.—In determining for which taxable year a designated nondeductible contribution is made, the rule of section 219(f)(3) shall apply.

(4) Individual required to report amount of designated nondeductible contributions.—

(A) In general.—Any individual who—

(i) makes a designated nondeductible contribution to any individual retirement plan for any taxable year, or

(ii) receives any amount from any individual retirement plan for any taxable year,

shall include on his return of the tax imposed by chapter 1 for such taxable year and any succeeding taxable year (or on such other form as the Secretary may prescribe for any such taxable year) information described in subparagraph (B).

(B) Information required to be supplied.—The following information is described in this subparagraph:

(i) The amount of designated nondeductible contributions for the taxable year.

(ii) The amount of distributions from individual retirement plans for the taxable year.

(iii) The excess (if any) of—

(I) the aggregate amount of designated nondeductible contributions for all preceding taxable years, over

(II) the aggregate amount of distributions from individual retirement plans which was excludable from gross income for such taxable years.

(iv) The aggregate balance of all individual retirement plans of the individual as of the close of the calendar year in which the taxable year begins.

(v) Such other information as the Secretary may prescribe.

(C) Penalty for reporting contributions not made.—

For penalty where individual reports designated nondeductible contributions not made, see section 6693(b).

(p) Simple retirement accounts.—

(1) In general.—For purposes of this title, the term "simple retirement account" means an individual retirement plan (as defined in section 7701(l)(37))—

(A) with respect to which the requirements of paragraphs (3), (4), and (5) are met; and

(B) with respect to which the only contributions allowed are contributions under a qualified salary reduction arrangement.

(2) Qualified salary reduction arrangement.—

(A) In general.—For purposes of this subsection, the term "qualified salary reduction arrangement" means a written arrangement of an eligible employer under which—

(i) an employee eligible to participate in the arrangement may elect to have the employer make payments—

(I) as elective employer contributions to a simple retirement account on behalf of the employee, or

(II) to the employee directly in cash,

(ii) the amount which an employee may elect under clause (i) for any year is required to be expressed as a percentage of compensation and may not exceed a total of the applicable dollar amount for any year,

(iii) the employer is required to make a matching contribution to the simple retirement account for any year in an amount equal to so much of the amount the employee elects under clause (i)(I) as does not exceed the applicable percentage of compensation for the year, and

(iv) no contributions may be made other than contributions described in clause (i) or (iii).

(B) Employer may elect 2-percent nonelective contribution.—

(i) In general.—An employer shall be treated as meeting the requirements of subparagraph (A)(iii) for any year if, in lieu of the contributions described in such clause, the employer elects to make nonelective contributions of 2 percent of compensation for each employee who is eligible to participate in the arrangement and who has at least $5,000 of compensation from the employer for the year. If an employer makes an election under this subparagraph for any year, the employer shall notify employees of such election within a reasonable period of time before the 60-day period for such year under paragraph (5)(C).

(ii) Compensation limitation.—The compensation taken into account under clause (i) for any year shall not exceed the limitation in effect for such year under section 401(a)(17).

(C) Definitions.—For purposes of this subsection—

(i) Eligible employer.—

(I) In general.—The term "eligible employer" means, with respect to any year, an employer which had no more than 100 employees who received at least $5,000 of compensation from the employer for the preceding year.

(II) 2-year grace period.—An eligible employer who establishes and maintains a plan under this subsection for 1 or more years and who fails to be an eligible employer for any subsequent year shall be treated as an eligible employer for the 2 years following the last year the employer was an eligible employer. If such failure is due to any acquisition, disposition, or similar transaction involving an eligible employer, the preceding sentence shall not apply.

(ii) Applicable percentage.—

(I) In general.—The term "applicable percentage" means 3 percent.

(II) Election of lower percentage.—An employer may elect to apply a lower percentage (not less than 1 percent) for any year for all employees eligible to participate in the plan for such year if the employer notifies the employees of such lower percentage within a reasonable period of time before the 60-day election period for such year under paragraph (5)(C). An employer may not elect a lower percentage under this subclause for any year if that election would result in the applicable percentage being lower than 3 percent in more than 2 of the years in the 5-year period ending with such year.

(III) Special rule for years arrangement not in effect.—If any year in the 5-year period described in subclause (II) is a year prior to the first year for which any qualified salary reduction arrangement is in effect with respect to the employer (or any predecessor), the employer shall be treated as if the level of the employer matching contribution was at 3 percent of compensation for such prior year.

(D) Arrangement may be only plan of employer.—

(i) In general.—An arrangement shall not be treated as a qualified salary reduction arrangement for any year if the employer (or any predecessor employer) maintained a qualified plan with respect to which contributions were made, or benefits were accrued, for service in any year in the period beginning with the year such arrangement became effective and ending with the year for which the determination is being made. If only individuals other than employees described in subparagraph (A) of section 410(b)(3) are eligible to participate in such arrangement, then the preceding sentence shall be applied without regard to any qualified plan in which only employees so described are eligible to participate.

(ii) Qualified plan.—For purposes of this subparagraph, the term "qualified plan" means a plan, contract, pension, or trust described in subparagraph (A) or (B) of section 219(g)(5).

(E) Applicable dollar amount; cost-of-living adjustment.—

(i) In general.—For purposes of subparagraph (A)(ii), the applicable dollar amount shall be the amount determined in accordance with the following table:

For years beginning in calendar year:	The applicable dollar amount:
2002	$7,000
2003	$8,000
2004	$9,000
2005 or thereafter	$10,000*

(ii) Cost-of-living adjustment.—In the case of a year beginning after December 31, 2005, the Secretary shall adjust the $10,000 amount under clause (i) at the same time and in the same manner as under section 415(d), except that the base period taken into account shall be the calendar quarter beginning July 1, 2004, and any increase under this subparagraph which is not a multiple of $500 shall be rounded to the next lower multiple of $500.

(3) Vesting requirements.—The requirements of this paragraph are met with respect to a simple retirement account if the employee's rights to any contribution to the simple retirement account are nonforfeitable. For purposes of this paragraph, rules similar to the rules of subsection (k)(4) shall apply.

(4) Participation requirements.—

(A) In general.—The requirements of this paragraph are met with respect to any simple retirement account for a year only if, under the qualified salary reduction arrangement, all employees of the employer who—

(i) received at least $5,000 in compensation from the employer during any 2 preceding years, and

(ii) are reasonably expected to receive at least $5,000 in compensation during the year,

are eligible to make the election under paragraph (2)(A)(i) or receive the nonelective contribution described in paragraph (2)(B).

(B) Excludable employees.—An employer may elect to exclude from the requirement under subparagraph (A) employees described in section 410(b)(3).

(5) Administrative requirements.—The requirements of this paragraph are met with respect to any simple retirement account if, under the qualified salary reduction arrangement—

(A) an employer must—

(i) make the elective employer contributions under paragraph (2)(A)(i) not later than the close of the 30-day period following the last day of the month with respect to which the contributions are to be made; and

(ii) make the matching contributions under paragraph (2)(A)(iii) or the nonelective contributions under paragraph (2)(B) not later than the date described in section 404(m)(2)(B),

(B) an employee may elect to terminate participation in such arrangement at any time during the year, except that if an employee so terminates, the arrangement may provide that the employee may not elect to resume participation until the beginning of the next year, and

(C) each employee eligible to participate may elect, during the 60-day period before the beginning of any year (and the 60-day period before the first day such employee is eligible to participate), to participate in the arrangement, or to modify the amounts subject to such arrangement, for such year.

(6) Definitions.—For purposes of this subsection—

(A) Compensation.—

(i) In general.—The term "compensation" means amounts described in paragraphs (3) and (8) of section 6051(a). For purposes of the preceding sentence, amounts described in section 6051(a)(3) shall be determined without regard to section 3401(a)(3).

---

*Editorial comment: The $10,000 amount is subject to indexing beginning in 2006. For 2013 and 2014, the indexed amount is $12,000.

(ii) Self-employed.—In the case of an employee described in subparagraph (B), the term "compensation" means net earnings from self-employment determined under section 1402(a) without regard to any contribution under this subsection. The preceding sentence shall be applied as if the term "trade or business" for purposes of section 1402 included service described in section 1402(c)(6).

(B) Employee.—The term "employee" includes an employee as defined in section 401(c)(1).

(C) Year.—The term "year" means the calendar year.

(7) Use of designated financial institution.—A plan shall not be treated as failing to satisfy the requirements of this subsection or any other provision of this title merely because the employer makes all contributions to the individual retirement accounts or annuities of a designated trustee or issuer. The preceding sentence shall not apply unless each plan participant is notified in writing (either separately or as part of the notice under subsection (1)(2)(C)) that the participant's balance may be transferred without cost or penalty to another individual account or annuity in accordance with subsection (d)(3)(G).

(8) Coordination with maximum limitation under subsection (a).—In the case of any simple retirement account, subsections (a)(1) and (b)(2) shall be applied by substituting "the sum of the dollar amount in effect under paragraph (2)(A)(ii) of this subsection and the employer contribution required under subparagraph (A)(iii) or (B)(i) of paragraph (2) of this subsection, whichever is applicable "for the dollar amount in effect under section 219(b)(1)(A)."

(9) Matching contributions on behalf of self-employed individuals not treated as elective employer contributions.—Any matching contribution described in paragraph (2)(A)(iii) which is made on behalf of a self-employed individual (as defined in section 401(c)) shall not be treated as an elective employer contribution to a simple retirement account for purposes of this title.

(10) Special rules for acquisitions, dispositions, and similar transactions.—

(A) In general.—An employer which fails to meet any applicable requirement by reason of an acquisition, disposition, or similar transaction shall not be treated as failing to meet such requirement during the transition period if—

(i) the employer satisfies requirements similar to the requirements of section 410 (b) (6)(C)(i)(II), and

(ii) the qualified salary reduction arrangement maintained by the employer would satisfy the requirements of this subsection after the transaction if the employer which maintained the arrangement before the transaction had remained a separate employer.

(B) Applicable requirement.—For purposes of this paragraph, the term "applicable requirement" means—

(i) the requirement under paragraph (2) (A)(i) that an employer be an eligible employer,

(ii) the requirement under paragraph (2) (D) that an arrangement be the only plan of an employer, and

(iii) the participation requirements under paragraph (4).

(C) Transition period.—For purposes of this paragraph, the term "transition period" means the period beginning on the date of any transaction described in subparagraph (A) and ending on the last day of the second calendar year following the calendar year in which such transaction occurs.

(q) Deemed IRAs under qualified employer plans.—

(1) General rule.—If—

(A) a qualified employer plan elects to allow employees to make voluntary employee contributions to a separate account or annuity established under the plan, and

(B) under the terms of the qualified employer plan, such account or annuity meets the applicable requirements of this section or section 408A for an individual retirement account or annuity,

then such account or annuity shall be treated for purposes of this title in the same manner as an individual retirement plan and not as a qualified employer plan (and contributions to such account or annuity as contributions to an individual retirement plan and not to the qualified employer plan). For purposes of subparagraph (B), the requirements of subsection (a)(5) shall not apply.

(2) Special rules for qualified employer plans.—For purposes of this title, a qualified employer plan shall not fail to meet any requirement of this title solely by reason of establishing and maintaining a program described in paragraph (1).

(3) Definitions.—For purposes of this subsection—

(A) Qualified employer plan.—The term "qualified employer plan" has the meaning given such term by section 72(p)(4)(A)(i), except that such term shall not include an eligible deferred compensation plan (as defined in section 457(b)) of an eligible employer described in section 457(e)(1)(A).

(B) Voluntary employee contribution.—The term "voluntary employee contribution" means any contribution (other than a mandatory contribution within the meaning of section 411 (c)(2)(C))—

(i) which is made by an individual as an employee under a qualified employer plan which allows employees to elect to make contributions described in paragraph (1), and

(ii) with respect to which the individual has designated the contribution as a contribution to which this subsection applies.

(r) Cross references.—

(1) For tax on excess contributions in individual retirement accounts or annuities, see section 4973.

(2) For tax on certain accumulations in individual retirement accounts or annuities, see section 4974.

§ 408A. Roth IRAs*

(a) General rule.—Except as provided in this section, a Roth IRA shall be treated for purposes of this title in the same manner as an individual retirement plan.

(b) Roth IRA.—For purposes of this title, the term "Roth IRA" means an individual retirement plan (as defined in section 7701(a)(37)) which is designated (in such manner as the Secretary may prescribe) at the time of establishment of the plan as a Roth IRA. Such designation shall be made in such manner as the Secretary may prescribe.

(c) Treatment of contributions.—

(1) No deduction allowed.—No deduction shall be allowed under section 219 for a contribution to a Roth IRA.

(2) Contribution limit.—The aggregate amount of contributions for any taxable year to all Roth IRAs maintained for the benefit of an individual shall not exceed the excess (if any) of—

(A) the maximum amount allowable as a deduction under section 219 with respect to such individual for such taxable year (computed without regard to subsection (d)(1) or (g) of such section), over

(B) the aggregate amount of contributions for such taxable year to all other individual retirement plans (other than Roth IRAs) maintained for the benefit of the individual.

(3) Limits based on modified adjusted gross income—

(A) Dollar limit.—The amount determined under paragraph (2) for any taxable year shall not exceed an amount equal to the amount determined under paragraph (2)(A) for such taxable year, reduced (but not below zero) by the amount which bears the same ratio to such amount as—

(i) the excess of—

(I) the taxpayer's adjusted gross income for such taxable year, over

(II) the applicable dollar amount, bears to

(ii) $15,000 ($10,000 in the case of a joint return or a married individual filing a separate return).

The rules of subparagraphs (B) and (C) of section 219(g)(2) shall apply to any reduction under this subparagraph.

*Editorial comment: See additional coverage on IRAs in Sec. 219.

(B) Rollover from eligible retirement plan.—A taxpayer shall not be allowed to make a qualified rollover contribution to a Roth IRA from an eligible retirement plan (as defined in section 402(c)(8)(B)) during any taxable year if, for any taxable year of the distribution to which such contribution relates—

(i) the taxpayer's adjusted gross income for such taxable year exceeds $100,000, or

(ii) the taxpayer is a married individual filing a separate return.

This subparagraph shall not apply to a qualified rollover contribution from a Roth IRA or to a qualified rollover contribution from a designated Roth account which is a rollover contribution described in section 402A(c)(3)(A).

(C) Definitions.—For purposes of this paragraph—

(i) adjusted gross income shall be determined in the same manner as under section 219(g)(3), except that any amount included in gross income under subsection (d)(3) shall not be taken into account, and

(ii) the applicable dollar amount is—

(I) in the case of a taxpayer filing a joint return, $150,000,*

(II) in the case of any other taxpayer (other than a married individual filing a separate return), $95,000,* and

(III) in the case of a married individual filing a separate return, zero.

(D) Inflation adjustment.—In the case of any taxable year beginning in a calendar year after 2006, the dollar amounts in subclauses (I) and (II) of subparagraph (C)(ii) shall each be increased by an amount equal to—

(i) such dollar amount, multiplied by

(ii) the cost-of-living adjustment determined under section 1(f)(3) for the calendar year in which the taxable year begins, determined by substituting "calendar year 2005" for "calendar year 1992" in subparagraph (B) thereof.

Any increase determined under the preceding sentence shall be rounded to the nearest multiple of $1,000.

(E) Marital status.—Section 219(g)(4) shall apply for purposes of this paragraph.

(4) Contributions permitted after age 70½.—Contributions to a Roth IRA may be made even after the individual for whom the account is maintained has attained age 70½.

(5) Mandatory distribution rules not to apply before death.—Notwithstanding subsections (a)(6) and (b)(3) of section 408 (relating to required distributions), the following provisions shall not apply to any Roth IRA:

(A) Section 401(a)(9)(A).

(B) The incidental death benefit requirements of section 401(a).

(6) Rollover contributions.—

(A) In general.—No rollover contribution may be made to a Roth IRA unless it is a qualified rollover contribution.

(B) Coordination with limit.—A qualified rollover contribution shall not be taken into account for purposes of paragraph (2).

(7) Time when contributions made.—For purposes of this section, the rule of section 219(f)(3) shall apply.

(d) Distribution rules.—For purposes of this title—

(1) Exclusion.—Any qualified distribution from a Roth IRA shall not be includible in gross income.

(2) Qualified distribution.—For purposes of this subsection—

(A) In general.—The term "qualified distribution" means any payment or distribution—

(i) made on or after the date on which the individual attains age 59½,

(ii) made to a beneficiary (or to the estate of the individual) on or after the death of the individual,

(iii) attributable to the individual's being disabled (within the meaning of section 72(m)(7)), or

(iv) which is a qualified special purpose distribution.

(B) Distributions within nonexclusion period.—A payment or distribution from a Roth IRA shall not be treated as a qualified

*Editorial comment: The indexed amounts for 2013 are $178,000 and $112,000 respectively and for 2014 are $181,000 and $114,000 respectively.

distribution under subparagraph (A) if such payment or distribution is made within the 5-taxable year period beginning with the 1st taxable year for which the individual made a contribution to a Roth IRA (or such individual's spouse made a contribution to a Roth IRA) established for such individual.

(C) Distributions of excess contributions and earnings.—The term "qualified distribution" shall not include any distribution of any contribution described in section 408(d)(4) and any net income allocable to the contribution.

(3) Rollovers from an eligible retirement plan other than a Roth IRA.—

(A) In general.—Notwithstanding sections 402(c), 403(b)(8), 408(d)(3), and 457(e)(16), in the case of any distribution to which this paragraph applies—

(i) there shall be included in gross income any amount which would be includible were it not part of a qualified rollover contribution,

(ii) section 72(t) shall not apply, and

(iii) unless the taxpayer elects not to have this clause apply, any amount required to be included in gross income for any taxable year beginning in 2010 by reason of this paragraph shall be so included ratably over the 2-taxable-year period beginning with the first taxable year beginning in 2011.

Any election under clause (iii) for any distributions during a taxable year may not be changed after the due date for such taxable year.

(B) Distributions to which paragraph applies.—This paragraph shall apply to a distribution from an eligible retirement plan (as defined by section 408(c)(8)(B)). This paragraph shall not apply to a distribution which is a qualified rollover contribution from a Roth IRA or a qualified rollover from a designated Roth IRA account which is a rollover contribution described in section 402A(c)(3)(A) maintained for the benefit of an individual which is contributed to a Roth IRA maintained for the benefit of such individual in a qualified rollover contribution.

(C) Conversions.—The conversion of an individual retirement plan (other than a Roth IRA) to a Roth IRA shall be treated for purposes of this paragraph as a distribution to which this paragraph applies.

(D) Additional reporting requirements.—Trustees of Roth IRA, trustees of individual retirement plans, persons subject to section 6047 (d)(1), or all of the foregoing persons, whichever is appropriate, shall include such additional information in reports required under section 408(i) or 6047 as the Secretary may require to ensure that amounts required to be included in gross income under subparagraph (A) are so included.

(E) Special rules for contributions to which 2-year averaging applies.—In the case of a qualified rollover contribution to a Roth IRA of a distribution to which subparagraph (A)(iii) applied, the following rules shall apply:

(i) Acceleration of inclusion.—

(I) In general.—The amount otherwise required to be included in gross income for any taxable year beginning in 2010 or the first taxable year in the 2-year period under subparagraph (A)(iii) shall be increased by the aggregate distributions from Roth IRAs for such taxable year which are allocable under paragraph (4) to the portion of such qualified rollover contribution required to be included in gross income under subparagraph (A)(i).

(II) Limitation on aggregate amount included.—The amount required to be included in gross income for any taxable year under subparagraph (A)(iii) shall not exceed the aggregate amount required to be included in gross income under subparagraph (A)(iii) for all taxable years in the 2-year period (without regard to subclause (I)) reduced by amounts included for all preceding taxable years.

(ii) Death of distributee.—

(I) In general.—If the individual required to include amounts in gross income under such subparagraph dies before all of such amounts are included, all remaining amounts shall be included in gross income for the taxable year which includes the date of death.

(II) Special rule for surviving spouse.—If the spouse of the individual described in subclause (I) acquires the individual's entire interest in any Roth IRA to which such qualified rollover contribution is properly allocable, the spouse may elect to treat the remaining amounts described in subclause (I) as includible in the spouse's gross income in the taxable years of the spouse ending with or within the taxable years of such individual in which such amounts would otherwise have been includible. Any such election may not be made or changed after the due date for the spouse's taxable year which includes the date of death.

(F) Special rule for applying section 72.—

(i) In general.—If—

(I) any portion of a distribution from a Roth IRA is properly allocable to a qualified rollover contribution described in this paragraph, and

(II) such distribution is made within the 5-taxable year period beginning with the taxable year in which such contribution was made,

then section 72(t) shall be applied as if such portion were includible in gross income.

(ii) Limitation.—Clause (i) shall apply only to the extent of the amount of the qualified rollover contribution includible in gross income under subparagraph (A)(i).

(4) Aggregation and ordering rules.—

(A) Aggregation rules.—Section 408(d)(2) shall be applied separately with respect to Roth IRAs and other individual retirement plans.

(B) Ordering rules.—For purposes of applying this section and section 72 to any distribution from a Roth IRA, such distribution shall be treated as made—

(i) from contributions to the extent that the amount of such distribution, when added to all previous distributions from the Roth IRA, does not exceed the aggregate contributions to the Roth IRA, and

(ii) from such contributions in the following order:

(I) Contributions other than qualified rollover contributions to which paragraph (3) applies.

(II) Qualified rollover contributions to which paragraph (3) applies on a first-in, first-out basis.

Any distribution allocated to a qualified rollover contribution under clause (ii)(II) shall be allocated first to the portion of such contribution required to be included in gross income.

(5) Qualified special purpose distribution.—For purposes of this section, the term "qualified special purpose distribution" means any distribution to which subparagraph (F) of section 72(t)(2) applies.

(6) Taxpayer may make adjustments before due date.—

(A) In general.—Except as provided by the Secretary, if, on or before the due date for any taxable year, a taxpayer transfers in a trustee-to-trustee transfer any contribution to an individual retirement plan made during such taxable year from such plan to any other individual retirement plan, then, for purposes of this chapter, such contribution shall be treated as having been made to the transferee plan (and not the transferor plan).

(B) Special rules.—

(i) Transfer of earnings.—Subparagraph (A) shall not apply to the transfer of any contribution unless such transfer is accompanied by any net income allocable to such contribution.

(ii) No deduction.—Subparagraph (A) shall apply to the transfer of any contribution only to the extent no deduction was allowed with respect to the contribution to the transferor plan.

(7) Due date.—For purposes of this subsection, the due date for any taxable year is the date prescribed by law (including extensions of time) for filing the taxpayer's return for such taxable year.

(e) Qualified rollover contribution.—For purposes of this section—

(1) In general.—The term "qualified rollover contribution" means a rollover contribution—

(A) to a Roth IRA from another such account,

(B) from an eligible retirement plan, but only if—

(i) in the case of an individual retirement plan, such rollover contribution meets the requirements of section 408(d)(3), and

(ii) in the case of any eligible retirement plan (as defined in section 402(c)(8)(B) other than clauses (i) and (ii) thereof), such rollover contribution meets the requirement of section 402(c), 403(b)(8), or 457(e)(16), as applicable.

For purposes of section 408(d)(3)(B), there shall be disregarded any qualified rollover contribution from an individual retirement plan (other than a Roth IRA) to a Roth IRA.

(2) Military death gratuity.—

(A) In general.—The term "qualified rollover contribution" includes a contribution to a Roth IRA maintained for the benefit of an individual made before the end of the 1-year period beginning on the date on which such individual receives an amount under section 1477 of title 10, United States Code, or section 1967 of title 38 of such Code, with respect to a person, to the extent that such contribution does not exceed—

(i) the sum of the amounts received during such period by such individual under such sections with respect to such person, reduced by

(ii) the amounts so received which were contributed to a Coverdell education savings account under section 530(d)(9).

(B) Annual limit on number of rollovers not to apply.—Section 408(d)(3)(B) shall not apply with respect to amounts treated as a rollover by subparagraph (A).

(C) Application of section 72.—For purposes of applying section 72 in the case of a distribution which is not a qualified distribution, the amount treated as a rollover by reason of subparagraph (A) shall be treated as investment in the contract.

(f) Individual retirement plan.—For purposes of this section—

(1) a simplified employee pension or a simple retirement account may not be designated as a Roth IRA, and

(2) contributions to any such pension or account shall not be taken into account for purposes of subsection (c)(2)(B).

§ 409. Qualifications for tax credit employee stock ownership plans

(a) Tax credit employee stock ownership plan defined.—Except as otherwise provided in this title, for purposes of this title, the term "tax credit employee stock ownership plan" means a defined contribution plan which—

(1) meets the requirements of section 401(a),

(2) is designed to invest primarily in employer securities, and

(3) meets the requirements of subsections (b), (c), (d), (e), (f), (g), (h) and (*o*) of this section.

(b) Required allocation of employer securities.—

(1) In general.—A plan meets the requirements of this subsection if—

(A) the plan provides for the allocation for the plan year of all employer securities transferred to it or purchased by it (because of the requirements of section 41(c)(1)(B)) to the accounts of all participants who are entitled to share in such allocation, and

(B) for the plan year the allocation to each participant so entitled is an amount which bears substantially the same proportion to the amount of all such securities allocated to all such participants in the plan for that year as the amount of compensation paid to such participant during that year bears to the compensation paid to all such participants during that year.

(2) Compensation in excess of $100,000 disregarded.—For purposes of paragraph (1), compensation of any participant in excess of the first $100,000 per year shall be disregarded.

(3) Determination of compensation.—For purposes of this subsection, the amount of compensation paid to a participant for any period is the amount of such participant's compensation (within the meaning of section 415(c)(3)) for such period.

(4) Suspension of allocation in certain cases.—Notwithstanding paragraph (1), the allocation to the account of any participant which is attributable to the basic employee plan credit or the credit allowed under section 41 (relating to the employee stock ownership credit) may be extended over whatever period may be necessary to comply with the requirements of section 415.

(c) Participants must have nonforfeitable rights.—A plan meets the requirements of this subsection only if it provides that each participant has a nonforfeitable right to any employer security allocated to his account.

(d) Employer securities must stay in the plan.—A plan meets the requirements of this subsection only if it provides that no employer security allocated to a participant's account under subsection (b) (or allocated to a participant's account in connection with matched employer and employee contributions) may be distributed from that account before the end of the 84th month beginning after the month in which the security is allocated to the account. To the extent provided in the plan, the preceding sentence shall not apply in the case of—

(1) death, disability, separation from service, or termination of the plan;

(2) a transfer of a participant to the employment of an acquiring employer from the employment of the selling corporation in the case of a sale to the acquiring corporation of substantially all of the assets used by the selling corporation in a trade or business conducted by the selling corporation, or

(3) with respect to the stock of a selling corporation, a disposition of such selling corporation's interest in a subsidiary when the participant continues employment with such subsidiary.

This subsection shall not apply to any distribution required under section 401(a)(9) or to any distribution or reinvestment required under section 401(a)(28).

(e) Voting rights.—

(1) In general.—A plan meets the requirements of this subsection if it meets the requirements of paragraph (2) or (3), whichever is applicable.

(2) Requirements where employer has a registration-type class of securities.—If the employer has a registration-type class of securities, the plan meets the requirements of this paragraph only if each participant or beneficiary in the plan is entitled to direct the plan as to the manner in which securities of the employer which are entitled to vote and are allocated to the account of such participant or beneficiary are to be voted.

(3) Requirement for other employers.—If the employer does not have a registration-type class of securities, the plan meets the requirements of this paragraph only if each participant or beneficiary in the plan is entitled to direct the plan as to the manner in which voting rights under securities of the employer which are allocated to the account of such participant or beneficiary are to be exercised with respect to any corporate matter which involves the voting of such shares with respect to the approval or disapproval of any corporate merger or consolidation, recapitalization, reclassification, liquidation, dissolution, sale of substantially all assets of a trade or business, or such similar transaction as the Secretary may prescribe in regulations.

(4) Registration-type class of securities defined.—For purposes of this subsection, the term "registration-type class of securities" means—

(A) a class of securities required to be registered under section 12 of the Securities Exchange Act of 1934, and

(B) a class of securities which would be required to be so registered except for the exemption from registration provided in subsection (g)(2)(H) of such section 12.

(5) 1 vote per participant.—A plan meets the requirements of paragraph (3) with respect to an issue if—

(A) the plan permits each participant 1 vote with respect to such issue, and

(B) the trustee votes the shares held by the plan in the proportion determined after application of subparagraph (A).

(f) Plan must be established before employer's due date.—

(1) In general.—A plan meets the requirements of this subsection only if it is established on or before the due date (including any extension of such date) for the filing of the employer's tax return for the first taxable year of the employer for which an employee plan credit is claimed by the employer with respect to the plan.

(2) Special rule for first year.—A plan which otherwise meets the requirements of this section shall not be considered to have failed to meet the requirements of section 401(a) merely because it was not established by the close of the first taxable year of the employer for which an employee plan credit is claimed by the employer with respect to the plan.

(g) Transferred amounts must stay in plan even though investment credit is redetermined or recaptured.—A plan meets the requirement of this subsection only if it provides that amounts which are transferred to the plan (because of the requirements of section 48(n)(1) or 41(c)(1)(B)) shall remain in the plan (and, if allocated under the plan, shall remain so allocated) even though part or all of the employee plan credit or the credit allowed under section 41 (relating to employee stock ownership credit) is recaptured or redetermined. For purposes of the preceding sentence, the references to section 48 (n)(1) and the employee plan credit shall refer to such section and credit as in effect before the enactment of the Tax Reform Act of 1984.

(h) Right to demand employer securities; put option.—

(1) In general.—A plan meets the requirements of this subsection if a participant who is entitled to a distribution from the plan—

(A) has a right to demand that his benefits be distributed in the form of employer securities, and

(B) if the employer securities are not readily tradable on an established market, has a right to require that the employer repurchase employer securities under a fair valuation formula.

(2) Plan may distribute cash in certain cases.

(A) In general.—A plan which otherwise meets the requirements of this subsection or of section 4975(e)(7) shall not be considered to have failed to meet the requirements of section 401(a) merely because under the plan the benefits may be distributed in cash or in the form of employer securities.

(B) Exception for certain plans restricted from distributing securities.—

(i) In general.—A plan to which this subparagraph applies shall not be treated as failing to meet the requirements of this subsection or section 401(a) merely because it does not permit a participant to exercise the right described in paragraph (1)(A) if such plan provides that the participant entitled to a distribution has a right to receive the distribution in cash, except that such plan may distribute employer securities subject to a requirement that such securities may be resold to the employer under terms which meet the requirements of paragraph (1)(B).

(ii) Applicable plans.—This subparagraph shall apply to a plan which otherwise meets the requirements of this subsection or section 4975(e)(7) and which is established and maintained by—

(I) an employer whose charter or bylaws restrict the ownership of substantially all outstanding employer securities to employees or to a trust described in section 401(a), or

(II) an S corporation.

* * *

(4) Put option period.—An employer shall be deemed to satisfy the requirements of paragraph (1)(B) if it provides a put option for a period of at least 60 days following the date of distribution of stock of the employer and, if the put option is not exercised within such 60-day period, for an additional period of at least 60 days in the following plan year (as provided in regulations promulgated by the Secretary).

(5) Payment requirement for total distribution.—If an employer is required to repurchase employer securities which are distributed to the employee as part of a total distribution, the requirements of paragraph (1)(B) shall be treated as met if—

(A) the amount to be paid for the employer securities is paid in substantially equal periodic payments (not less frequently than annually) over a period beginning not later than 30 days after the exercise of the put option described in paragraph (4) and not exceeding 5 years, and

(B) there is adequate security provided and reasonable interest paid on the unpaid amounts referred to in subparagraph (A).

For purposes of this paragraph, the term "total distribution" means the distribution within 1 taxable year to the recipient of the balance to the credit of the recipient's account.

(6) Payment requirement for installment distributions.—If an employer is required to repurchase employer securities as part of an installment distribution, the requirements of paragraph (1)(B) shall be treated as met if the amount to be paid for the employer securities is paid not later than 30 days after the exercise of the put option described in paragraph (4).

(7) Exception where employee elected diversification.—Paragraph (1)(A) shall not apply with respect to the portion of the participant's account which the employee elected to have reinvested under section 401(a)(28)(B) or subparagraph (B) or (C) of section 401(a)(35).

(i) Reimbursement for expenses of establishing and administering plan.—A plan which otherwise meets the requirements of this section shall not be treated as failing to meet such requirements merely because it provides that—

(1) Expenses of establishing plan.—As reimbursement for the expenses of establishing the plan, the employer may withhold from amounts due the plan for the taxable year for which the plan is established (or the plan may pay) so much of the amounts paid or incurred in connection with the establishment of the plan as does not exceed the sum of—

(A) 10 percent of the first $100,000 which the employer is required to transfer to the plan for that taxable year under section 41(c)(1)(B), and

(B) 5 percent of any amount so required to be transferred in excess of the first $100,000; and

(2) Administrative expenses.—As reimbursement for the expenses of administering the plan, the employer may withhold from amounts due the plan (or the plan may pay) so much of the amounts paid or incurred during the taxable year as expenses of administering the plan as does not exceed the lesser of—

(A) the sum of—

(i) 10 percent of the first $100,000 of the dividends paid to the plan with respect to stock of the employer during the plan year ending with or within the employer's taxable year, and

(ii) 5 percent of the amount of such dividends in excess of $100,000 or

(B) $100,000.

(j) Conditional contributions to the plan.—A plan which otherwise meets the requirements of this section shall not be treated as failing to satisfy such requirements (or as failing to satisfy the requirements of section 401(a) of this title or of section 403(c)(1) of the Employee Retirement Income Security Act of 1974) merely because of the return of a contribution (or a provision permitting such a return) if—

(1) the contribution to the plan is conditioned on a determination by the Secretary that such plan meets the requirements of this section,

(2) the application for a determination described in paragraph (1) is filed with the Secretary not later than 90 days after the date on which an employee plan credit is claimed, and

(3) the contribution is returned within 1 year after the date on which the Secretary issues notice to the employer that such plan does not satisfy the requirements of this section.

(k) Requirements relating to certain withdrawals.—Notwithstanding any other law or rule of law—

(1) the withdrawal from a plan which otherwise meets the requirements of this section by the employer of an amount contributed for purposes of the matching employee plan credit shall not be considered to make the benefits forfeitable, and

(2) the plan shall not, by reason of such withdrawal, fail to be for the exclusive benefit of participants or their beneficiaries,

if the withdrawn amounts were not matched by employee contributions or were in excess of the limitations of section 415. Any withdrawal described in the preceding sentence shall not be considered to violate the provisions of section 403(c)(1) of the Employee Retirement Income Security Act of 1974. For purposes of this subsection, the reference to the matching employee plan credit shall refer to such credit as in effect before the enactment of the Tax Reform Act of 1984.

(l) Employer securities defined.—For purposes of this section—

(1) In general.—The term "employer securities" means common stock issued by the employer (or by a corporation which is a member of the same controlled group) which is readily tradable on an established securities market.

(2) Special rule where there is no readily tradable common stock.—If there is no common stock which meets the requirements of paragraph (1), the term "employer securities" means common stock issued by the employer (or by a corporation which is a member of the same controlled group) having a combination of voting power and dividend rights equal to or in excess of—

(A) that class of common stock of the employer (or of any other such corporation) having the greatest voting power, and

(B) that class of common stock of the employer (or of any other such corporation) having the greatest dividend rights.

(3) Preferred stock may be issued in certain cases.—Noncallable preferred stock shall be treated as employer securities if such stock is convertible at any time into stock which meets the requirements of paragraph (1) or (2) (whichever is applicable) and if such conversion is at a conversion price which (as of the date of the acquisition by the tax credit employee stock ownership plan) is reasonable. For purposes of the preceding sentence, under regulations prescribed by the Secretary, preferred stock shall be treated as noncallable if after the call there will be a reasonable opportunity for a conversion which meets the requirements of the preceding sentence.

(4) Application to controlled group of corporations.—

(A) In general.—For purposes of this subsection, the term "controlled group of corporations" has the meaning given to such term by section 1563(a) (determined without regard to subsections (a)(4) and (e)(3)(C) of section 1563).

(B) Where common parent owns at least 50 percent of first tier subsidiary.—For purposes of subparagraph (A), if the common parent owns directly stock possessing at least 50 percent of the voting power of all classes of stock and at least 50 percent of each class of nonvoting stock in a first tier subsidiary, such subsidiary (and all other corporations below it in the chain which would meet the 80 percent test of section 1563(a) if the first tier subsidiary were the common parent) shall be treated as includible corporations.

(C) Where common parent owns 100 percent of first tier subsidiary.—For purposes of subparagraph (A), if the common parent owns directly stock possessing all of the voting power of all classes of stock and all of the non-voting stock, in a first tier subsidiary, and if the first tier subsidiary owns directly stock possessing at least 50 percent of the voting power of all classes of stock, and at least 50 percent of each class of nonvoting stock, in a second tier subsidiary of the common parent, such second tier subsidiary (and all other corporations below it in the chain which would meet the 80 percent test of section 1563(a) if the second tier subsidiary were the common parent) shall be treated as includible corporations.

(5) Nonvoting common stock may be acquired in certain cases.—Nonvoting common stock of an employer described in the second sentence of section 401(a)(22) shall be treated as employer securities if an employer has a class of non-voting common stock outstanding and the specific shares that the plan acquires have been issued and outstanding for at least 24 months.

(m) Nonrecognition of gain or loss on contribution of employer securities to tax credit employee stock ownership plan.—No gain or loss shall be recognized to the taxpayer with respect to the transfer of employer securities to a tax credit employee stock ownership plan maintained by the taxpayer to the extent that such transfer is required under section 41(c)(1)(B), or subparagraph (A) or (B) of section 48(n)(1).

(n) Securities received in certain transactions.—

(1) In general.—A plan to which section 1042 applies and an eligible worker-owned cooperative (within the meaning of section 1042(c)) shall provide that no portion of the assets of the plan or cooperative attributable to (or allocable in lieu of) employer securities acquired by the plan or cooperative in a sale to which section 1042 applies may accrue (or be allocated directly or indirectly under any plan of the employer meeting the requirements of section 401(a))—

(A) during the nonallocation period, for the benefit of—

(i) any taxpayer who makes an election under section 1042(a) with respect to employer securities,

(ii) any individual who is related to the taxpayer (within the meaning of section 267 (b)), or

(B) for the benefit of any other person who owns (after application of section 318(a)) more than 25 percent of—

(i) any class of outstanding stock of the corporation which issued such employer securities or of any corporation which is a member of the same controlled group of corporations (within the meaning of subsection (1)(4)) as such corporation, or

(ii) the total value of any class of outstanding stock of any such corporation.

For purposes of subparagraph (B), section 318 (a) shall be applied without regard to the employee trust exception in paragraph (2)(B)(i).

(2) Failure to meet requirements.—If a plan fails to meet the requirements of paragraph (1)—

(A) the plan shall be treated as having distributed to the person described in paragraph (1) the amount allocated to the account of such person in violation of paragraph (1) at the time of such allocation,

(B) the provisions of section 4979A shall apply, and

(C) the statutory period for the assessment of any tax imposed by section 4979A shall not expire before the date which is 3 years from the later of—

(i) the 1st allocation of employer securities in connection with a sale to the plan to which section 1042 applies, or

(ii) the date on which the Secretary is notified of such failure.

(3) Definitions and special rules.—For purposes of this subsection—

(A) Lineal descendants.—Paragraph (1)(A)(ii) shall not apply to any individual if—

(i) such individual is a lineal descendant of the taxpayer, and

(ii) the aggregate amount allocated to the benefit of all such lineal descendants during the nonallocation period does not exceed more than 5 percent of the employer securities (or amounts allocated in lieu thereof) held by the plan which are attributable to a sale to the plan by any person related to such descendants (within the meaning of section 267(c)(4)) in a transaction to which section 1042 applied.

(B) 25-percent shareholders.—A person shall be treated as failing to meet the stock ownership limitation under paragraph (1)(B) if such person fails such limitation—

(i) at any time during the 1-year period ending on the date of sale of qualified securities to the plan or cooperative, or

(ii) on the date as of which qualified securities are allocated to participants in the plan or cooperative.

(C) Nonallocation period.—The term "nonallocation period" means the period beginning on the date of the sale of the qualified securities and ending on the later of—

(i) the date which is 10 years after the date of sale, or

(ii) the date of the plan allocation attributable to the final payment of acquisition indebtedness incurred in connection with such sale.

(o) Distribution and payment requirements.—A plan meets the requirements of this subsection if —

(1) Distribution requirement.—

(A) In general.—The plan provides that if the participant and, if applicable pursuant to sections 401 (a)(11) and 417, with the consent of the participant's spouse elects the distribution of the participant's account balance in the plan will commence not later than 1 year after the close of the plan year—

(i) in which the participant separates from service by reason of the attainment of normal retirement age under the plan, disability, or death, or

(ii) which is the 5th plan year following the plan year in which the participant otherwise separates from service, except that this clause shall not apply if the participant is reemployed by the employer before distribution is required to begin under this clause.

(B) Exception for certain financed securities.—For purposes of this subsection, the account balance of a participant shall not include any employer securities acquired with the proceeds of the loan described in section 404(a)(9) until the close of the plan year in which such loan is repaid in full.

(C) Limited distribution period.—The plan provides that, unless the participant elects otherwise, the distribution of the participant's account balance will be in substantially equal periodic payments (not less frequently than annually) over a period not longer than the greater of—

(i) 5 years, or

(ii) in the case of a participant with an account balance in excess of $800,000,* 5 years plus 1 additional year (but not more than 5 additional years) for each $160,000** or fraction thereof by which such balance exceeds $800,000.*

(2) Cost-of-living adjustment.—The Secretary shall adjust the dollar amounts under paragraph (1)(C) at the same time and in the same manner as under section 415(d).

*Editorial comment: The indexed amount for 2013 is $1,035,000, and for 2014 is $1,050,000.

**Editorial comment: The indexed amount for 2013 is $205,000, and for 2014 is $210,000.

(p) Prohibited allocations of securities in an S corporation.—

(1) In general.—An employee stock ownership plan holding employer securities consisting of stock in an S corporation shall provide that no portion of the assets of the plan attributable to (or allocable in lieu of) such employer securities may, during a nonallocation year, accrue (or be allocated directly or indirectly under any plan of the employer meeting the requirements of section 401(a)) for the benefit of any disqualified person.

(2) Failure to meet requirements.—

(A) In general.—If a plan fails to meet the requirements of paragraph (1), the plan shall be treated as having distributed to any disqualified person the amount allocated to the account of such person in violation of paragraph (1) at the time of such allocation.

(B) Cross reference.—

For excise tax relating to violations of paragraph (1) and ownership of synthetic equity, see section 4979A.

(3) Nonallocation year.—For purposes of this subsection—

(A) In general.—The term "nonallocation year" means any plan year of an employee stock ownership plan if, at any time during such plan year—

(i) such plan holds employer securities consisting of stock in an S corporation, and

(ii) disqualified persons own at least 50 percent of the number of shares of stock in the S corporation.

(B) Attribution rules.—For purposes of subparagraph (A)—

(i) In general.—The rules of section 318 (a) shall apply for purposes of determining ownership, except that—

(I) in applying paragraph (1) thereof, the members of an individual's family shall include members of the family described in paragraph (4)(D), and

(II) paragraph (4) thereof shall not apply.

(ii) Deemed-owned shares.—Notwithstanding the employee trust exception in section 318(a)(2)(B)(i), an individual shall be treated as owning deemed-owned shares of the individual.

Solely for purposes of applying paragraph (5), this subparagraph shall be applied after the attribution rules of paragraph (5) have been applied.

(4) Disqualified person.—For purposes of this subsection—

(A) In general.—The term "disqualified person" means any person if—

(i) the aggregate number of deemed-owned shares of such person and the members of such person's family is at least 20 percent of the number of deemed-owned shares of stock in the S corporation, or

(ii) in the case of a person not described in clause (i), the number of deemed-owned shares of such person is at least 10 percent of the number of deemed-owned shares of stock in such corporation.

(B) Treatment of family members.—In the case of a disqualified person described in subparagraph (A)(i), any member of such person's family with deemed-owned shares shall be treated as a disqualified person if not otherwise treated as a disqualified person under subparagraph (A).

(C) Deemed-owned shares.—

(i) In general.—The term "deemed-owned shares" means, with respect to any person—

(I) the stock in the S corporation constituting employer securities of an employee stock ownership plan which is allocated to such person under the plan, and

(II) such person's share of the stock in such corporation which is held by such plan but which is not allocated under the plan to participants.

(ii) Person's share of unallocated stock.—For purposes of clause (i)(II), a person's share of unallocated S corporation stock held by such plan is the amount of unallocated stock which would be allocated to such person if the unallocated stock were allocated to all participants in the same proportions as the most recent stock allocation under the plan.

(D) Member of family.—For purposes of this paragraph, the term "member of the family" means, with respect to any individual—

(i) the spouse of the individual,

(ii) an ancestor or lineal descendant of the individual or the individual's spouse

(iii) a brother or sister of the individual or the individual's spouse and any lineal descendant of the brother or sister, and

(iv) the spouse of any individual described in clause (ii) or (iii).

A spouse of an individual who is legally separated from such individual under a decree of divorce or separate maintenance shall not be treated as such individual's spouse for purposes of this subparagraph.

(5) Treatment of synthetic equity.—For purposes of paragraphs (3) and (4), in the case of a person who owns synthetic equity in the S corporation, except to the extent provided in regulations, the shares of stock in such corporation on which such synthetic equity is based shall be treated as outstanding stock in such corporation and deemed-owned shares of such person if such treatment of synthetic equity of 1 or more such person results in—

(A) the treatment of any person as a disqualified person, or

(B) the treatment of any year as a nonallocation year.

For purposes of this paragraph, synthetic equity shall be treated as owned by a person in the same manner as stock is treated as owned by a person under the rules of paragraphs (2) and (3) of section 318(a). If, without regard to this paragraph, a person is treated as a disqualified person or a year is treated as a nonallocation year, this paragraph shall not be construed to result in the person or year not being so treated.

(6) Definitions.—For purposes of this subsection—

(A) Employee stock ownership plan.—The term "employee stock ownership plan" has the meaning given such term by section 4975(e)(7).

(B) Employer securities.—The term "employer security" has the meaning given such term by section 409(1).

(C) Synthetic equity.—The term "synthetic equity" means any stock option, warrant, restricted stock, deferred issuance stock right, or similar interest or right that gives the holder the right to acquire or receive stock of the S corporation in the future. Except to the extent provided in regulations, synthetic equity also includes a stock appreciation right, phantom stock unit, or similar right to a future cash payment based on the value of such stock or appreciation in such value.

(7) Regulations and guidance.—

(A) In general.—The Secretary shall prescribe such regulations as may be necessary to carry out the purposes of this subsection.

(B) Avoidance or evasion.—The Secretary may, by regulation or other guidance of general applicability, provide that a nonallocation year occurs in any case in which the principal purpose of the ownership structure of an S corporation constitutes an avoidance or evasion of this subsection.

(q) Cross references.—

(1) For requirements for allowance of employee plan credit, see section 48(n).

(2) For assessable penalties for failure to meet requirements of this section, or for failure to make contributions required with respect to the allowance of an employee plan credit or employee stock ownership credit, see section 6699.

(3) For requirements for allowance of an employee stock ownership credit, see section 41.

§ 409A. Inclusion in gross income of deferred compensation under nonqualified deferred compensation plans—

(a) Rules relating to constructive receipt.—

(1) Plan failures.—

(A) Gross income inclusion.—

(i) In general.—If at any time during a taxable year a nonqualified deferred compensation plan—

(I) fails to meet the requirements of paragraphs (2), (3), and (4), or

(II) is not operated in accordance with such requirements,

all compensation deferred under the plan for the taxable year and all preceding taxable years shall be includible in gross income for the taxable year to the extent not subject to a substantial risk of forfeiture and not previously included in gross income.

(ii) Application only to affected participants.—Clause (i) shall only apply with respect to all compensation deferred under the plan for participants with respect to whom the failure relates.

(B) Interest and additional tax payable with respect to previously deferred compensation.—

(i) In general.—If compensation is required to be included in gross income under subparagraph (A) for a taxable year, the tax imposed by this chapter for the taxable year shall be increased by the sum of—

(I) the amount of interested determined under clause (ii), and

(II) an amount equal to 20 percent of the compensation which is required to be included in gross income.

(ii) Interest.—For purposes of clause (i), the interest determined under this clause for any taxable year is the amount of interest at the underpayment rate plus 1 percentage point on the underpayments that would have occurred had the deferred compensation been includible in gross income for the taxable year in which first deferred or, if later, the first taxable year in which such deferred compensation is not subject to a substantial risk of forfeiture.

(2) Distributions.—

(A) In general.—The requirements of this paragraph are met if the plan provides that compensation deferred under the plan may not be distributed earlier than—

(i) separation from service as determined by the Secretary (except as provided in subparagraph (B)(i)),

(ii) the date the participant becomes disabled (within the meaning of subparagraph (C)),

(iii) death,

(iv) a specified time (or pursuant to a fixed schedule) specified under the plan at the date of the deferral of such compensation,

(v) to the extent provided by the Secretary, a change in the ownership or effective control of the corporation, or in the ownership of a substantial portion of the assets of the corporation, or

(vi) the occurrence of an unforeseeable emergency.

(B) Special rules.—

(i) Specified employees.—In the case of any specified employee, the requirement of subparagraph (A)(i) is met only if distributions may not be made before the date which is 6 months after the date of separation from service (or, if earlier, the date of death of the employee). For purposes of the preceding sentence, a specified employee is a key employee (as defined in section 416(i) without regard to paragraph (5) thereof) of a corporation any stock in which is publicly traded on an established securities market or otherwise.

(ii) Unforeseeable emergency.—For purposes of subparagraph (A)(vi)—

(I) In general.—The term "unforeseeable emergency" means a severe financial hardship to the participant resulting from an illness or accident of the participant, the participant's spouse, or a dependent (as defined in section 152(a)) of the participant, loss of the participant's property due to casualty, or other similar extraordinary and unforeseeable circumstances arising as a result of events beyond the control of the participant.

(II) Limitation on distributions.—The requirement of subparagraph (A)(vi) is met only if, as determined under regulations of the Secretary, the amounts distributed with respect to an emergency do not exceed the amounts necessary to satisfy such emergency plus amounts necessary to pay taxes reasonably anticipated as a result of the distribution, after taking into account the extent to which such hardship is or may be relieved through reimbursement or compensation by insurance or otherwise or by liquidation of the participant's assets (to the extent the liquidation of such assets would not itself cause severe financial hardship).

(C) Disabled.—For purposes of subparagraph (A)(ii), a participant shall be considered disabled if the participant—

(i) is unable to engage in any substantial gainful activity by reason of any medically determinable physical or mental impairment which can be expected to result in death or can be expected to last for a continuous period of not less than 12 months, or

(ii) is, by reason of any medically determinable physical or mental impairment which can be expected to result in death or can be expected to last for a continuous period of not less than 12 months, receiving income replacement benefits for a period of not less than 3 months under an accident and health plan covering employees of the participant's employer.

(3) Acceleration of benefits.—The requirements of this paragraph are met if the plan does not permit the acceleration of the time or schedule of any payment under the plan, except as provided in regulations by the Secretary.

(4) Elections.—

(A) In general.—The requirements of this paragraph are met if the requirements of subparagraphs (B) and (C) are met.

(B) Initial deferral decision.—

(i) In general.—The requirements of this subparagraph are met if the plan provides that compensation for services performed during a taxable year may be deferred at the participant's election only if the election to defer such compensation is made not later than the close of the preceding taxable year or at such other time as provided in regulations.

(ii) First year of eligibility.—In the case of the first year in which a participant becomes eligible to participate in the plan, such election may be made with respect to services to be performed subsequent to the election within 30 days after the date the participant becomes eligible to participate in such plan.

(iii) Performance-based compensation.—In the case of any performance-based compensation based on services performed over a period of at least 12 months, such election may be made no later than 6 months before the end of the period.

(C) Changes in time and form of distribution.—The requirements of this subparagraph are met if, in the case of a plan which permits under a subsequent election a delay in a payment or a change in the form of payment—

(i) the plan requires that such election may not take effect until at least 12 months after the date on which the election is made,

(ii) in the case of an election related to a payment not described in clause (ii), (iii), or (vi) of paragraph (2)(A), the plan requires that the payment with respect to which such election is made be deferred for a period of not less than 5 years from the date such payment would otherwise have been made, and

(iii) the plan requires that any election related to a payment described in paragraph (2)(A)(iv) may not be made less than 12 months prior to the date of the first scheduled payment under such paragraph.

(b) Rules relating to funding.—

(1) Offshore property in a trust.—In the case of assets set aside (directly or indirectly) in a trust (or other arrangement determined by the Secretary) for purposes of paying deferred compensation under a nonqualified deferred compensation plan, for purposes of section 83 such assets shall be treated as property transferred in connection with the performance of services whether or not such assets are available to satisfy claims of general creditors—

(A) at the time set aside if such assets (or such trust or other arrangement) are located outside of the United States, or

(B) at the time transferred if such assets (or such trust or other arrangement) are subsequently transferred outside of the United States.

This paragraph shall not apply to assets located in a foreign jurisdiction if substantially all of the services to which the nonqualified deferred compensation relates are performed in such jurisdiction.

(2) Employer's financial health.—In the case of compensation deferred under a nonqualified deferred compensation plan, there is a transfer of property within the meaning of section 83 with respect to such compensation as of the earlier of—

(A) the date on which the plan first provides that assets will become restricted to the provision of benefits under the plan in connection with a change in the employer's financial health, or

(B) the date on which assets are so restricted, whether or not such assets are available to satisfy claims of general creditors.

(3) Treatment of employer's defined benefit plan during restricted period.—

(A) In general.—If

(i) during any restricted period with respect to a single-employer defined benefit plan, assets are set aside or reserved (directly or indirectly) in a trust (or other arrangement as determined by the Secretary) or transferred to such a trust or other arrangement for purposes of paying deferred compensation of an applicable covered employee under a nonqualified deferred compensation plan of the plan sponsor or member of a controlled group which includes the plan sponsor, or

(ii) a nonqualified deferred compensation plan of the plan sponsor or member of a controlled group which includes the plan sponsor provides that assets will become restricted to the provision of benefits under the plan to an applicable covered employee in connection with such restricted period (or other similar financial measure determined by the Secretary) with respect to the defined benefit plan, or assets are so restricted,

such assets shall, for purposes of section 83, be treated as property transferred in connection with the performance of services whether or not such assets are available to satisfy claims of general creditors. Clause (i) shall not apply with respect to any assets which are so set aside before the restricted period with respect to the defined benefit plan.

(B) Restricted period.—For purposes of this section, the term "restricted period" means, with respect to any plan described in subparagraph (A)—

(i) any period during which the plan is in at-risk status (as defined in section 430(i));

(ii) any period the plan sponsor is a debtor in a case under title 11, United States Code, or similar Federal or State law, and

(iii) the 12-month period beginning on the date which is 6 months before the termination date of the plan if, as of the termination date, the plan is not sufficient for benefit liabilities (within the meaning of section 4041 of the Employee Retirement Income Security Act of 1974).

(C) Special rule for payment of taxes on deferred compensation included in income.—If an employer provides directly or indirectly for the payment of any Federal, State, or local income taxes with respect to any compensation required to be included in gross income by reason of this paragraph—

(i) interest shall be imposed under subsection (a)(1)(B)(i)(I) on the amount of such payment in the same manner as if such payment was part of the deferred compensation to which it relates,

(ii) such payment shall be taken into account in determining the amount of the additional tax under subsection (a)(1) (B)(i)(II) in the same manner as if such payment was part of the deferred compensation to which it relates, and

(iii) no deduction shall be allowed under this title with respect to such payment.

(D) Other definitions.—For purposes of this section—

(i) Applicable covered employee.—The term "applicable covered employee" means any—

(I) covered employee of a plan sponsor,

(II) covered employee of a member of a controlled group which includes the plan sponsor, and

(III) former employee who was a covered employee at the time of termination of employment with the plan sponsor or a member of a controlled group which includes the plan sponsor.

(ii) Covered employee.—The term "covered employee" means an individual described in section 162(m)(3) or an individual subject to the requirements of section 16(a) of the Securities Exchange Act of 1934.

(4) Income inclusion for offshore trusts and employer's financial health.—For each taxable year that assets treated as transferred under this subsection remain set aside in a trust or other arrangement subject to paragraph (1), (2), or (3), any increase in value in, or earnings with respect to, such assets shall be treated as an additional transfer of property under this subsection (to the extent not previously included in income).

(5) Interest on tax liability payable with respect to transferred property.—

(A) In general.—If amounts are required to be included in gross income by reason of paragraph (1), (2), or (3) for a taxable year, the tax imposed by this chapter for such taxable year shall be increased by the sum of—

(i) the amount of interest determined under subparagraph (B), and

(ii) an amount equal to 20 percent of the amounts required to be included in gross income.

(B) Interest.—For purposes of subparagraph (A), the interest determined under this subparagraph for any taxable year is the amount of interest at the underpayment rate plus 1 percentage point on the underpayments that would have occurred had the amounts so required to be included in gross income by paragraph (1), (2), or (3) been includible in gross income for the taxable year in which first deferred or, if later, the first taxable year in which such amounts are not subject to a substantial risk of forfeiture.

(c) No inference on earlier income inclusion or requirement of later inclusion.—Nothing in this section shall be construed to prevent the inclusion of amounts in gross income under any other provision of this chapter or any other rule of law earlier than the time provided in this section. Any amount included in gross income under this section shall not be required to be included in gross income under any other provision of chapter or any other rule of law later than the time provided in this section.

(d) Other definitions and special rules.—For purposes of this section:

(1) Nonqualified deferred compensation plan.—The term "nonqualified deferred compensation plan" means any plan that provides for the deferral of compensation, other than—

(A) a qualified employer plan, and

(B) any bona fide vacation leave, sick leave, compensatory time, disability pay, or death benefit plan.

(2) Qualified employer plan.—The term "qualified employer plan" means—

(A) any plan, contract, pension, account, or trust described in subparagraph (A) or (B) of section 219(g)(5) (without regard to subparagraph (A)(iii)),

(B) any eligible deferred compensation plan (within the meaning of section 457(b)), and

(C) any plan described in section 415(m).

(3) Plan includes arrangements, etc.—The term "plan" includes any agreement or arrangement, including an agreement or arrangement that includes one person.

(4) Substantial risk of forfeiture.—The rights of a person to compensation are subject to a substantial risk of forfeiture if such person's rights to such compensation are conditioned upon the future performance of substantial services by any individual.

(5) Treatment of earnings.—References to deferred compensation shall be treated as including references to income (wither actual or notional) attributable to such compensation or such income.

(6) Aggregation rules.—Except as provided by the Secretary, rules similar to the rules of subsection (b) and (c) of section 414 shall apply.

(e) Regulations.—The Secretary shall prescribe such regulations as may be necessary or appropriate to carry out the purposes of this section, including regulations—

(1) providing for the determination of amounts of deferral in the case of a nonqualified deferred compensation plan which is a defined benefit plan,

(2) relating to changes in the ownership and control of a corporation or assets of a corporation for purposes of subsection (a)(2)(A)(v),

(3) exempting arrangements from the application of subsection (b) if such arrangements will not result in an improper deferral of United States tax and will not result in assets being effectively beyond the reach of creditors,

(4) defining financial health for purposes of subsection (b)(2), and

(5) disregarding a substantial risk of forfeiture in cases where necessary to carry out the purposes of this section.

SUBPART B—SPECIAL RULES

§ 410. Minimum participation standards

(a) Participation.—

(1) Minimum age and service conditions.—

(A) General rule.—A trust shall not constitute a qualified trust under section 401(a) if the plan of which it is a part requires, as a condition of participation in the plan, that an employee complete a period of service with the employer or employers maintaining the plan extending beyond the later of the following dates—

(i) the date on which the employee attains the age of 21; or

(ii) the date on which he completes 1 year of service.

(B) Special rules for certain plans.—

(i) In the case of any plan which provides that after not more than 2 years of service each participant has a right to 100 percent of his accrued benefit under the plan which is nonforfeitable (within the meaning of section 411) at the time such benefit accrues, clause (ii) of subparagraph (A) shall be applied by substituting "2 years of service" for "1 year of service."

(ii) In the case of any plan maintained exclusively for employees of an educational institution (as defined in section 170(b)(1) (A)(ii)) by an employer which is exempt from tax under section 501(a) which provides that each participant having at least 1 year of service has a right to 100 percent of his accrued benefit under the plan which is nonforfeitable (within the meaning of section 411) at the time such benefit accrues, clause (i) of subparagraph (A) shall be applied by substituting "26" for "21." This clause shall not apply to any plan to which clause (i) applies.

(2) Maximum age conditions.—A trust shall not constitute a qualified trust under section 401(a) if the plan of which it is a part excludes from participation (on the basis of age) employees who have attained a specified age.

(3) Definition of year of service.—

(A) General rule.—For purposes of this subsection, the term "year of service" means a 12-month period during which the employee has not less than 1,000 hours of service. For purposes of this paragraph, computation of any 12-month period shall be made with reference to the date on which the employee's employment commenced, except that, under regulations prescribed by the Secretary of Labor, such computation may be made by reference to the first day of a plan year in the case of an employee who does not complete 1,000 hours of service during the 12-month period beginning on the date his employment commenced.

(B) Seasonal industries.—In the case of any seasonal industry where the customary period of employment is less than 1,000 hours during a calendar year, the term "year of service" shall be such period as may be determined under regulations prescribed by the Secretary of Labor.

(C) Hours of service.—For purposes of this subsection, the term "hour of service" means a time of service determined under regulations prescribed by the Secretary of Labor.

(D) Maritime industries.—For purposes of this subsection, in the case of any maritime industry, 125 days of service shall be treated as 1,000 hours of service. The Secretary of Labor may prescribe regulations to carry out this subparagraph.

(4) Time of participation.—A plan shall be treated as not meeting the requirements of paragraph (1) unless it provides that any employee who has satisfied the minimum age and service requirements specified in such paragraph, and who is otherwise entitled to participate in the plan, commences participation in the plan no later than the earlier of—

(A) the first day of the first plan year beginning after the date on which such employee satisfied such requirements, or

(B) the date 6 months after the date on which he satisfied such requirements,

unless such employee was separated from the service before the date referred to in subparagraph (A) or (B), whichever is applicable.

(5) Breaks in service.—

(A) General rule.—Except as otherwise provided in subparagraphs (B), (C), and (D), all years of service with the employer or employers maintaining the plan shall be taken into account in computing the period of service for purposes of paragraph (1).

(B) Employees under 2-year 100 percent vesting.—In the case of any employee who has any 1-year break in service (as defined in section 411(a)(6)(A)) under a plan to which the service requirements of clause (i) of paragraph (1)(B) apply, if such employee has not satisfied such requirements, service before such break shall not be required to be taken into account.

(C) 1-year break in service.—In computing an employee's period of service for purposes of paragraph (1) in the case of any participant who has any 1-year break in service (as defined in section 411(a)(6)(A)), service before such break shall not be required to be taken into account under the plan until he has completed a year of service (as defined in paragraph (3)) after his return.

(D) Nonvested participants.—

(i) In general.—For purposes of paragraph (1), in the case of a nonvested participant, years of service with the employer or employers maintaining the plan before any period of consecutive 1-year breaks in service shall not be required to be taken into account in computing the period of service if the number of consecutive 1-year breaks in service within such period equals or exceeds the greater of—

(I) 5, or

(II) the aggregate number of years of service before such period.

(ii) Years of service not taken into account.—If any years of service are not required to be taken into account by reason of a period of breaks in service to which clause (i) applies, such years of service shall not be taken into account in applying clause (i) to a subsequent period of breaks in service.

(iii) Nonvested participant defined.—For purposes of clause (i), the term "nonvested participant" means a participant who does not have any nonforfeitable right under the plan to an accrued benefit derived from employer contributions.

(E) Special rule for maternity or paternity absences.—

(i) General rule.—In the case of each individual who is absent from work for any period—

(I) by reason of the pregnancy of the individual,

(II) by reason of the birth of a child of the individual,

(III) by reason of the placement of a child with the individual in connection with the adoption of such child by such individual, or

(IV) for purposes of caring for such child for a period beginning immediately following such birth or placement,

the plan shall treat as hours of service, solely for purposes of determining under this paragraph whether a 1-year break in service (as defined in section 411(a)(6)(A)) has occurred, the hours described in clause (ii).

(ii) Hours treated as hours of service.—The hours described in this clause are—

(I) the hours of service which otherwise would normally have been credited to such individual but for such absence, or

(II) in any case in which the plan is unable to determine the hours described in subclause (I), 8 hours of service per day of such absence,

except that the total number of hours treated as hours of service under this clause by reason of any such pregnancy or placement shall not exceed 501 hours.

(iii) Year to which hours are credited.—The hours described in clause (ii) shall be treated as hours of service as provided in this subparagraph—

(I) only in the year in which the absence from work begins, if a participant would be prevented from incurring a 1-year break in service in such year solely because the period of absence is treated as hours of service as provided in clause (i); or

(II) in any other case, in the immediately following year.

(iv) Year defined.—For purposes of this subparagraph, the term "year" means the period used in computations pursuant to paragraph (3).

(v) Information required to be filed.—A plan shall not fail to satisfy the requirements of this subparagraph solely because it provides that no credit will be given pursuant to this subparagraph unless the individual furnishes to the plan administrator such timely information as the plan may reasonably require to establish—

(I) that the absence from work is for reasons referred to in clause (i), and

(II) the number of days for which there was such an absence.

(b) Minimum coverage requirements.—

(1) In general.—A trust shall not constitute a qualified trust under section 401(a) unless such trust is designated by the employer as part of a plan which meets 1 of the following requirements:

(A) The plan benefits at least 70 percent of employees who are not highly compensated employees.

(B) The plan benefits—

(i) a percentage of employees who are not highly compensated employees which is at least 70 percent of

(ii) the percentage of highly compensated employees benefiting under the plan.

(C) The plan meets the requirements of paragraph (2).

(2) Average benefit percentage test.—

(A) In general.—A plan shall be treated as meeting the requirements of this paragraph if—

(i) the plan benefits such employees as qualify under a classification set up by the employer and found by the Secretary not to be discriminatory in favor of highly compensated employees, and

(ii) the average benefit percentage for employees who are not highly compensated employees is at least 70 percent of the average benefit percentage for highly compensated employees.

(B) Average benefit percentage.—For purposes of this paragraph, the term "average benefit percentage" means, with respect to any group, the average of the benefit percentages calculated separately with respect to each employee in such group (whether or not a participant in any plan).

(C) Benefit percentage.—For purposes of this paragraph—

(i) In general.—The term "benefit percentage" means the employer-provided contribution or benefit of an employee under all qualified plans maintained by the employer, expressed as a percentage of such employee's compensation (within the meaning of section 414(s)).

(ii) Period for computing percentage.—At the election of an employer, the benefit percentage for any plan year shall be computed on the basis of contributions or benefits for—

(I) such plan year, or

(II) any consecutive plan year period (not greater than 3 years) which ends with such plan year and which is specified in such election.

An election under this clause, once made, may be revoked or modified only with the consent of the Secretary.

(D) Employees taken into account.—For purposes of determining who is an employee for purposes of determining the average benefit percentage under subparagraph (B)—

(i) except as provided in clause (ii), paragraph (4)(A) shall not apply, or

(ii) if the employer elects, paragraph (4)(A) shall be applied by using the lowest age and service requirements of all qualified plans maintained by the employer.

(E) Qualified plan.—For purposes of this paragraph, the term "qualified plan" means any plan which (without regard to this subsection) meets the requirements of section 401(a).

(3) Exclusion of certain employees.—For purposes of this subsection, there shall be excluded from consideration—

(A) employees who are included in a unit of employees covered by an agreement which the Secretary of Labor finds to be a collective bargaining between employee representatives and one or more employers, if there is evidence that retirement benefits were the subject of good faith bargaining between such employee representatives and such employer or employers,

(B) in the case of a trust established or maintained pursuant to an agreement which the Secretary of Labor finds to be a collective bargaining agreement between air pilots represented in accordance with title II of the Railway Labor Act and one or more employers, all employees not covered by such agreement, and

(C) employees who are nonresident aliens and who receive no earned income (within the meaning of section 911(d)(2)) from the employer which constitutes income from sources within the United States (within the meaning of section 861(a)(3)).

Subparagraph (A) shall not apply with respect to coverage of employees under a plan pursuant to an agreement under such subparagraph. For purposes of subparagraph (B), management pilots who are not represented in accordance with title II of the Railway Labor Act shall be treated as covered by a collective bargaining agreement described in such subparagraph if the management pilots manage the flight operations of air pilots who are so represented and the management pilots are, pursuant to the terms of the agreement, included in the group of employees benefiting under the trust described in such subparagraph. Subparagraph (B) shall not apply in the case of a plan which provides contributions or benefits for employees whose principal duties are not customarily performed aboard an aircraft in flight (other than management pilots described in the preceding sentence).

(4) Exclusion of employees not meeting age and service requirements.—

(A) In general.—If a plan—

(i) prescribes minimum age and service requirements as a condition of participation, and

(ii) excludes all employees not meeting such requirements from participation, then such employees shall be excluded from consideration for purposes of this subsection.

(B) Requirements may be met separately with respect to excluded group.—If employees not meeting the minimum age or service requirements of subsection (a)(1) (without regard to subparagraph (b) thereof) are covered under a plan of the employer which meets the requirements of paragraph (1) separately with respect to such employees, such employees may be excluded from consideration in determining whether any plan of the employer meets the requirements of paragraph (1).

(C) Requirements not treated as being met before entry date.—An employee shall not be treated as meeting the age and service requirements described in this paragraph until the first date on which, under the plan, any employee with the same age and service would be eligible to commence participation in the plan.

(5) Line of business exception.—

(A) In general.—If, under section 414(r), an employer is treated as operating separate lines of business for a year, the employer may apply the requirements of this subsection for such year separately with respect to employees in each separate line of business.

(B) Plan must be nondiscriminatory.—Subparagraph (A) shall not apply with respect to any plan maintained by an employer unless such plan benefits such employees as qualify under a classification set up by the employer and found by the Secretary not to be discriminatory in favor of highly compensated employees.

(6) Definitions and special rules.—For purposes of this subsection—

(A) Highly compensated employee.—The term "highly compensated employee" has the meaning given such term by section 414(q).

(B) Aggregation rules.—An employer may elect to designate—

(i) 2 or more trusts,

(ii) 1 or more trusts and 1 or more annuity plans, or

(iii) 2 or more annuity plans,

as part of 1 plan intended to qualify under section 401(a) to determine whether the requirements of this subsection are met with respect to such trusts or annuity plans. If an employer elects to treat any trust or annuity plans as 1 plan under this subparagraph, such trusts or annuity plans shall be treated as 1 plan for purposes of section 401(a)(4).

(C) Special rules for certain dispositions or acquisitions.—

(i) In general.—If a person becomes, or ceases to be, a member of a group described in subsection (b), (c), (m), or (o) of section 414, then the requirements of this subsection shall be treated as having been met during the transition period with respect to any plan covering employees of such person or any other member of such group if—

(I) such requirements were met immediately before each such change, and

(II) the coverage under such plan is not significantly changed during the transition period (other than by reason of the change in members of a group) or such plan meets such other requirements as the Secretary may prescribe by regulation.

(ii) Transition period.—For purposes of clause (i), the term "transition period" means the period—

(I) beginning on the date of the change in members of a group, and

(II) ending on the last day of the 1st plan year beginning after the date of such change.

(D) Special rule for certain employee stock ownership plans.—A trust which is part of a tax credit employee stock ownership plan which is the only plan of an employer intended to qualify under section 410(a) shall not be treated as not a qualified trust under section 401(a) solely because it fails to meet the requirements of this subsection if—

(i) such plan benefits 50 percent or more of all the employees who are eligible under a nondiscriminatory classification under the plan, and

(ii) the sum of the amounts allocated to each participant's account for the year does not exceed 2 percent of the compensation of that participant for the year.

(E) Eligibility to contribute.—In the case of contributions which are subject to section 401(k) or 401(m), employees who are eligible to contribute (or elect to have contributions made on their behalf) shall be treated as benefiting under the plan (other than for purposes of paragraph (2)(A)(ii)).

(F) Employers with only highly compensated employees.—A plan maintained by an employer which has no employees other than highly compensated employees for any year shall be treated as meeting the requirements of this subsection for such year.

(G) Regulations.—The Secretary shall prescribe such regulations as may be necessary or appropriate to carry out the purposes of this subsection.

(c) Application of participation standards to certain plans.—

(1) The provisions of this section (other than paragraph (2) of this subsection) shall not apply to—

(A) a governmental plan (within the meaning of section 414(d)),

(B) a church plan (within the meaning of section 414(e)) with respect to which the election provided by subsection (d) of this section has not been made,

(C) a plan which has not at any time after September 2, 1974, provided for employer contributions, and

(D) a plan established and maintained by a society, order, or association described in section 501(c)(8) or (9) if no part of the contributions to or under such plan are made by employers of participants in such plan.

(2) A plan described in paragraph (1) shall be treated as meeting the requirements of this section for purposes of section 401(a) except that in the case of a plan described in subparagraphs (B), (C), or (D) of paragraph (1), this paragraph shall apply only if such plan meets the requirements of section 401(a) (3) as in effect on September 1, 1974.

* * *

§ 411. Minimum vesting standards

(a) General rule.—A trust shall not constitute a qualified trust under section 401(a) unless the plan of which such trust is a part provides that an employee's right to his normal retirement benefit is nonforfeitable upon the attainment of normal retirement age (as defined in paragraph (8)) and in addition satisfies the requirements of paragraphs (1), (2), and (11) of this subsection and the requirements of subsection (b)(3), and also satisfies, in the case of a defined benefit plan, the requirements of subsection (b)(1) and, in the case of a defined contribution plan, the requirements of subsection (b)(2).

(1) Employee contributions.—A plan satisfies the requirements of this paragraph if an employee's rights in his accrued benefit derived from his own contributions are nonforfeitable.

(2) Employer contributions.—

(A) Defined benefit plans.—

(i) In general.—In the case of a defined benefit plan, a plan satisfies the requirements of this paragraph if it satisfies the requirements of clause (ii) or (iii).

(ii) 5-year vesting.—A plan satisfies the requirements of this clause if an employee who has completed at least 5 years of service has a nonforfeitable right to 100 percent of the employee's accrued benefit derived from employer contributions.

(iii) 3- to 7-year vesting.—A plan satisfies the requirements of this clause if an employee has a nonforfeitable right to a percentage of the employee's accrued benefit derived from employer contributions determined under the following table:

Years of service:	The nonforfeitable percentage is:
3	20
4	40
5	60
6	80
7 or more	100

(B) Defined contribution plans.—

(i) In general.—In the case of a defined contribution plan, a plan satisfies the requirements of this paragraph if it satisfies the requirements of clause (ii) or (iii).

(ii) 3-year vesting.—A plan satisfies the requirements of this clause if an employee who has completed at least 3 years of service has a nonforfeitable right to 100 percent of the employee's accrued benefit derived from employer contributions.

(iii) 2 to 6 year vesting.—A plan satisfies the requirements of this clause if an employee has a nonforfeitable right to a percentage of the employee's accrued benefit derived from employer contributions determined under the following table:

Years of service:	The nonforfeitable percentage is:
2	20
3	40
4	60
5	80
6 or more	100

(3) Certain permitted forfeitures, suspensions, etc.—For purposes of this subsection—

(A) Forfeiture on account of death.—A right to an accrued benefit derived from employer contributions shall not be treated as forfeitable solely because the plan provides that it is not payable if the participant dies (except in the case of a survivor annuity which is payable as provided in section 401(a)(11)).

(B) Suspension of benefits upon reemployment of retiree.—A right to an accrued benefit derived from employer contributions shall not be treated as forfeitable solely because the plan provides that the payment of benefits is suspended for such period as the employee is employed, subsequent to the commencement of payment of such benefits—

(i) in the case of a plan other than a multiemployer plan, by the employer who maintains the plan under which such benefits were being paid; and

(ii) in the case of a multiemployer plan, in the same industry, the same trade or craft, and the same geographic area covered by the plan as when such benefits commenced.

The Secretary of Labor shall prescribe such regulations as may be necessary to carry out the purposes of this subparagraph, including regulations with respect to the meaning of the term "employed".

(C) Effect of retroactive plan amendments.—A right to an accrued benefit derived from employer contributions shall not be treated as forfeitable solely because plan amendments may be given retroactive application as provided in section 412(d)(2).

(D) Withdrawal of mandatory contribution.—

(i) A right to an accrued benefit derived from employer contributions shall not be treated as forfeitable solely because the plan provides that, in the case of a participant who does not have a nonforfeitable right to at least 50 percent of his accrued benefit derived from employer contributions, such accrued benefit may be forfeited on account of the withdrawal by the participant of any amount attributable to the benefit derived from mandatory contributions (as defined in subsection (c)(2)(C)) made by such participant.

(ii) Clause (i) shall not apply to a plan unless the plan provides that any accrued benefit forfeited under a plan provision described in such clause shall be restored upon repayment by the participant of the full amount of the withdrawal described in such clause plus, in the case of a defined benefit plan, interest. Such interest shall be computed on such amount at the rate determined for purposes of subsection (c)(2)(C) on the date of such repayment (computed annually from the date of such withdrawal). The plan provision required under this clause may provide that such repayment must be made (I) in the case of a withdrawal on account of separation from service, before the earlier of 5 years after the first date on which the participant is subsequently re-employed by the employer, or the close of the first period of 5 consecutive 1-year breaks in service commencing after the withdrawal; or (II) in the case of any other withdrawal, 5 years after the date of the withdrawal.

(iii) In the case of accrued benefits derived from employer contributions which accrued before September 2, 1974, a right to such accrued benefit derived from employer contributions shall not be treated as forfeitable solely because the plan provides that an amount of such accrued benefit may be forfeited on account of the withdrawal by the participant of an amount attributable to the benefit derived from mandatory contributions (as defined in subsection (c)(2)(C)) made by such participant before September 2, 1974 if such amount forfeited is proportional to such amount withdrawn. This clause shall not apply to any plan to which any mandatory contribution is made after September 2, 1974. The Secretary shall prescribe such regulations as may be necessary to carry out the purposes of this clause.

(iv) For purposes of this subparagraph, in the case of any class-year plan, a withdrawal of employee contributions shall be treated as a withdrawal of such contributions on a plan year by plan year basis in succeeding order of time.

(v) For nonforfeitability where the employee has a nonforfeitable right to at least 50 percent of his accrued benefit, see section 401(a)(19).

(E) Cessation of contributions under a multiemployer plan.—A right to an accrued benefit derived from employer contributions under a multiemployer plan shall not be treated as forfeitable solely because the plan provides that benefits accrued as a result of service with the participant's employer before the employer had an obligation to contribute under the plan may not be payable if the employer ceases contributions to the multiemployer plan.

(F) Reduction and suspension of benefits by a multiemployer plan.—A participant's right to an accrued benefit derived from employer contributions under a multiemployer plan shall not be treated as forfeitable solely because—

(i) the plan is amended to reduce benefits under section 418D or under section 4281 of the Employee Retirement Income Security Act of 1974, or

(ii) benefit payments under the plan may be suspended under section 418E or under section 4281 of the Employee Retirement Income Security Act of 1974.

(G) Treatment of matching contributions forfeited by reason of excess deferral or contribution or permissable withdrawal.—A matching contribution (within the meaning of section 401(m)) shall not be treated as forfeitable merely because such contribution is forfeitable if the contribution to which the matching contribution relates is treated as an excess contribution under section 401(k)(8)(B), an excess deferral under section 402(g)(2)(A), a permissable withdrawal under section 414(w), or an excess aggregate contribution under section 401(m)(6)(B).

(4) Service included in determination of nonforfeitable percentage.—In computing the period of service under the plan for purposes of determining the nonforfeitable percentage under paragraph (2), all of an employee's years of service with the employer or employers maintaining the plan shall be taken into account, except that the following may be disregarded:

(A) years of service before age 18;

(B) years of service during a period for which the employee declined to contribute to a plan requiring employee contributions;

(C) years of service with an employer during any period for which the employer did not maintain the plan or a predecessor plan (as defined under regulations prescribed by the Secretary);

(D) service not required to be taken into account under paragraph (6);

(E) years of service before January 1, 1971, unless the employee has had at least 3 years of service after December 31, 1970;

(F) years of service before the first plan year to which this section applies, if such service would have been disregarded under the rules of the plan with regard to breaks in service as in effect on the applicable date; and

(G) in the case of a multiemployer plan, years of service—

(i) with an employer after—

(I) a complete withdrawal of that employer from the plan (within the meaning of section 4203 of the Employee Retirement Income Security Act of 1974), or

(II) to the extent permitted in regulations prescribed by the Secretary, a partial withdrawal described in section 4205(b)(2)(A)(i) of such Act in conjunction with the decertification of the collective bargaining representative, and

(ii) with any employer under the plan after the termination date of the plan under section 4048 of such Act.

(5) Year of service.—

(A) General rule.—For purposes of this subsection, except as provided in subparagraph (C), the term "year of service" means a calendar year, plan year, or other 12-consecutive month period designated by the plan (and not prohibited under regulations prescribed by the Secretary of Labor) during which the participant has completed 1,000 hours of service.

(B) Hours of service.—For purposes of this subsection, the term "hours of service" has the meaning provided by section 410(a)(3)(C).

(C) Seasonal industries.—In the case of any seasonal industry where the customary period of employment is less than 1,000 hours during a calendar year, the term "year of service" shall be such period as may be determined under regulations prescribed by the Secretary of Labor.

(D) Maritime industries.—For purposes of this subsection, in the case of any maritime industry, 125 days of service shall be treated as 1,000 hours of service. The Secretary of Labor may prescribe regulations to carry out the purposes of this subparagraph.

(6) Breaks in service.—

(A) Definition of 1-year break in service.—For purposes of this paragraph, "1-year break in service" means a calendar year, plan year, or other 12-consecutive-month period designated by the plan (and not prohibited under regulations prescribed by the Secretary of Labor) during which the participant has not completed more than 500 hours of service.

(B) 1 year of service after 1-year break in service.—For purposes of paragraph (4), in the case of any employee who has any 1-year break in service, years of service before such break shall not be required to be taken into account until he has completed a year of service after his return.

(C) 5 consecutive 1-year breaks in service under defined contribution plan.—For purposes of paragraph (4), in the case of any participant in a defined contribution plan, or an insured defined benefit plan which satisfies the requirements of subsection (b)(1)(F), who has 5 consecutive 1-year breaks in service, years of service after such 5-year period shall not be required to be taken into account for purposes of determining the nonforfeitable percentage of his accrued benefit derived from employer contributions which accrued before such 5-year period.

(D) Nonvested participants.—

(i) In general.—For purposes of paragraph (4), in the case of a nonvested participant, years of service with the employer or employers maintaining the plan before any period of consecutive 1-year breaks in service shall not be required to be taken into account if the number of consecutive 1-year breaks in service within such period equals or exceeds the greater of—

(I) 5, or

(II) the aggregate number of years of service before such period.

(ii) Years of service not taken into account.—If any years of service are not required to be taken into account by reason of a period of breaks in service to which clause (i) applies, such years of service shall not be taken into account in applying clause (i) to a subsequent period of breaks in service.

(iii) Nonvested participant defined.—For purposes of clause (i), the term "nonvested participant" means a participant who does not have any nonforfeitable right under the plan to an accrued benefit derived from employer contributions.

(E) Special rule for maternity or paternity absences.—

(i) General rule.—In the case of each individual who is absent from work for any period—

(I) by reason of the pregnancy of the individual,

(II) by reason of the birth of a child of the individual,

(III) by reason of the placement of a child with the individual in connection with the adoption of such child by such individual, or

(IV) for purposes of caring for such child for a period beginning immediately following such birth or placement,

the plan shall treat as hours of service, solely for purposes of determining under this paragraph whether a 1-year break in service has occurred, the hours described in clause (ii).

(ii) Hours treated as hours of service.—The hours described in this clause are—

(I) the hours of service which otherwise would normally have been credited to such individual but for such absence, or

(II) in any case in which the plan is unable to determine the hours described in subclause (I), 8 hours of service per day of absence,

except that the total number of hours treated as hours of service under this clause by reason of any such pregnancy or placement shall not exceed 501 hours.

(iii) Year to which hours are credited.—The hours described in clause (ii) shall be treated as hours of service as provided in this subparagraph—

(I) only in the year in which the absence from work begins, if a participant would be prevented from incurring a 1-year break in service in such year solely because the period of absence is treated as hours of service as provided in clause (i); or

(II) in any other case, in the immediately following year.

(iv) Year defined.—For purposes of this subparagraph, the term "year" means the period used in computations pursuant to paragraph (5).

(v) Information required to be filed.—A plan shall not fail to satisfy the requirements of this subparagraph solely because it provides that no credit will be given pursuant to this subparagraph unless the individual furnishes to the plan administrator such timely information as the plan may reasonably require to establish—

(I) that the absence from work is for reasons referred to in clause (i), and

(II) the number of days for which there was such an absence.

(7) Accrued benefit.—

(A) In general.—For purposes of this section, the term "accrued benefit" means—

(i) in the case of a defined benefit plan, the employee's accrued benefit determined under the plan and, except as provided in subsection (c)(3), expressed in the form of an annual benefit commencing at normal retirement age, or

(ii) in the case of a plan which is not a defined benefit plan, the balance of the employee's account.

(B) Effect of certain distributions.—Notwithstanding paragraph (4), for purposes of determining the employee's accrued benefit under the plan, the plan may disregard service performed by the employee with respect to which he has received—

(i) a distribution of the present value of his entire nonforfeitable benefit if such distribution was in an amount (not more than the dollar limit under section 411(a)(11)(A)) permitted under regulations prescribed by the Secretary, or

(ii) a distribution of the present value of his nonforfeitable benefit attributable to such service which he elected to receive.

Clause (i) of this subparagraph shall apply only if such distribution was made on termination of the employee's participation in the plan. Clause (ii) of this subparagraph shall apply only if such distribution was made on termination of the employee's participation in the plan or under such other circumstances as may be provided under regulations prescribed by the Secretary.

(C) Repayment of subparagraph (B) distributions.—For purposes of determining the employee's accrued benefit under a plan, the plan may not disregard service as provided in subparagraph (B) unless the plan provides an opportunity for the participant to repay the full amount of the distribution described in such subparagraph (B) with, in the case of a defined benefit plan, interest at the rate determined for purposes of subsection (c)(2)(C) and provides that upon such repayment the employee's accrued benefit shall be recomputed by taking into account service so disregarded. This subparagraph shall apply only in the case of a participant who—

(i) received such a distribution in any plan year to which this section applies, which distribution was less than the present value of his accrued benefit,

(ii) resumes employment covered under the plan, and

(iii) repays the full amount of such distribution with, in the case of a defined benefit plan, interest at the rate determined for purposes of subsection (c)(2)(C).

The plan provision required under this subparagraph may provide that such repayment must be made (I) in the case of a withdrawal on account of separation from service, before the earlier of 5 years after the first date on which the participant is subsequently re-employed by the employer, or the close of the first period of 5 consecutive 1-year breaks in service commencing after the withdrawal; or (II) in the case of any other withdrawal, 5 years after the date of the withdrawal.

(D) Accrued benefit attributable to employee contributions.—The accrued benefit of an employee shall not be less than the amount determined under subsection (c)(2)(B) with respect to the employee's accumulated contributions.

(8) Normal retirement age.—For purposes of this section, the term "normal retirement age" means the earlier of—

(A) the time a plan participant attains normal retirement age under the plan, or

(B) the later of—

(i) the time a plan participant attains age 65, or

(ii) the 5th anniversary of the time a plan participant commenced participation in the plan.

(9) Normal retirement benefit.—For purposes of this section, the term "normal retirement benefit" means the greater of the early retirement benefit under the plan, or the benefit under the plan commencing at normal retirement age. The normal retirement benefit shall be determined without regard to—

(A) medical benefits, and

(B) disability benefits not in excess of the qualified disability benefit.

For purposes of this paragraph, a qualified disability benefit is a disability benefit provided by a plan which does not exceed the benefit which would be provided for the participant if he separated from the service at normal retirement age. For purposes of this paragraph, the early retirement benefit under a plan shall be determined without regard to any benefits commencing before benefits payable under title II of the Social Security Act become payable which—

(i) do not exceed such social security benefits, and

(ii) terminate when such social security benefits commence.

(10) Changes in vesting schedule.—

(A) General rule.—A plan amendment changing any vesting schedule under the plan shall be treated as not satisfying the requirements of paragraph (2) if the nonforfeitable percentage of the accrued benefit derived from employer contributions (determined as of the later of the date such amendment is adopted, or the date such amendment becomes effective) of any employee who is a participant in the plan is less than such nonforfeitable percentage computed under the plan without regard to such amendment.

(B) Election of former schedule.—A plan amendment changing any vesting schedule under the plan shall be treated as not satisfying the requirements of paragraph (2) unless each participant having not less than 3 years of service is permitted to elect, within a reasonable period after the adoption of such amendment, to have his nonforfeitable percentage computed under the plan without regard to such amendment.

(11) Restrictions on certain mandatory distributions.—

(A) In general.—If the present value of any nonforfeitable accrued benefit exceeds $5,000, a plan meets the requirements of this paragraph only if such plan provides that such benefit may not be immediately distributed without the consent of the participant.

(B) Determination of present value.—For purposes of subparagraph (A), the present value shall be calculated in accordance with section 417(e)(3).

(C) Dividend distributions of ESOPs arrangement.—This paragraph shall not apply to any distribution of dividends to which section 404(k) applies.

(D) Special rule for rollover contributions.—A plan shall not fail to meet the requirements of this paragraph if, under the terms of the plan, the present value of the nonforfeitable accrued benefit is determined without regard to that portion of such benefit which is attributable to rollover contributions (and earnings allocable thereto). For purposes of this subparagraph, the term "rollover contributions" means any rollover contribution under sections 402(c), 403(a)(4), 403(b)(8), 408(d)(3)(A)(ii), and 457(e)(16).

***(13) Special rules for plans computing accrued benefits by reference to hypothetical account balance or equivalent amounts.**—

(A) In general.—An applicable defined benefit plan shall not be treated as failing to meet—

(i) subject to paragraph (2) [subparagraph (B)], the requirements of subsection (a)(2), or

(ii) the requirements of subsection (c) or section 417(e) with respect to contributions other than employee contributions,

solely because the present value of the accrued benefit (or any portion thereof) of any participant is, under the terms of the plan, equal to the amount expressed as the balance in the hypothetical account described in paragraph (3) [subparagraph (C)] or as an accumulated percentage of the participant's final average compensation.

(B) 3-year vesting.— In the case of an applicable defined benefit plan, such plan shall be treated as meeting the requirements of subsection (a)(2) only if an employee who has completed at least 3 years of service has a nonforfeitable right to 100 percent of the employee's accrued benefit derived from employer contributions.

(C) Applicable defined benefit plan and related rules.—For purposes of this subsection—

(i) In general.—The term "applicable defined benefit plan" means a defined benefit plan under which the accrued benefit (or any portion thereof) is calculated as the balance of a hypothetical account maintained for the participant or as an accumulated percentage of the participant's final average compensation.

(ii) Regulations to include similar plans.—The Secretary shall issue regulations which include in the definition of an applicable defined benefit plan any defined benefit plan (or any portion of such a plan) which has an effect similar to an applicable defined benefit plan.

* * *

§ 412. Minimum funding standards

(a) Requirement to meet minimum funding standard.—

(1) In general.—A plan to which this section applies shall satisfy the minimum funding standard applicable to the plan for any plan year.

(2) Minimum funding standard.—For purposes of paragraph (1), a plan shall be treated as satisfying the minimum funding standard for a plan year if—

(A) in the case of a defined benefit plan which is not a multiemployer plan, the employer makes contributions to or under the plan for the plan year which, in the aggregate,

*Editorial comment: This is no subsection (a)(12).

are not less than the minimum required contribution determined under section 430 for the plan for the plan year,

(B) in the case of a money purchase plan which is not a multiemployer plan, the employer makes contributions to or under the plan for the plan year which are required under the terms of the plan, and

(C) in the case of a multiemployer plan, the employers make contributions to or under the plan for any plan year which, in the aggregate, are sufficient to ensure that the plan does not have an accumulated funding deficiency under section 431 as of the end of the plan year.

(b) Liability for contributions.—

(1) In general.—Except as provided in paragraph (2), the amount of any contribution required by this section (including any required installments under paragraphs (3) and (4) of section 430(j)) shall be paid by the employer responsible for making contributions to or under the plan.

(2) Joint and several liability where employer member of controlled group.—If the employer referred to in paragraph (1) is a member of a controlled group, each member of such group shall be jointly and severally liable for payment of such contributions.

(3) Multiemployer plans in critical status.—Paragraph 1 shall not apply in the case of a multiemployer plan for any plan year in which the plan is in critical status pursuant to section 432. This paragraph shall only apply if the plan sponsor adopts a rehabilitation plan in accordance with section 432(e) and complies with such rehabilitation plan (and any modifications of the plan).

(c) Variance from minimum funding standards.—

(1) Waiver in case of business hardship.—

(A) In general.—If—

(i) an employer is (or in the case of a multiemployer plan, 10 percent or more of the number of employers contributing to or under the plan are) unable to satisfy the minimum funding standard for a plan year without temporary substantial business hardship (substantial business hardship in the case of a multiemployer plan), and

(ii) application of the standard would be adverse to the interests of plan participants in the aggregate,

the Secretary may, subject to subparagraph (C), waive the requirements of subsection (a) for such year with respect to all or any portion of the minimum funding standard. The Secretary shall not waive the minimum funding standard with respect to a plan for more than 3 of any 15 (5 of any 15 in the case of a multiemployer plan) consecutive plan years.

(B) Effects of waiver.—If a waiver is granted under subparagraph (A) for any plan year—

(i) in the case of a defined benefit plan which is not a multiemployer plan, the minimum required contribution under section 430 for the plan year shall be reduced by the amount of the waived funding deficiency and such amount shall be amortized as required under section 430(e), and

(ii) in the case of a multiemployer plan, the funding standard account shall be credited under section 431(b)(3)(C) with the amount of the waived funding deficiency and such amount shall be amortized as required under section 431(b)(2)(C).

(C) Waiver of amortized portion not allowed.—The Secretary may not waive under subparagraph (A) any portion of the minimum funding standard under subsection (a) for a plan year which is attributable to any waived funding deficiency for any preceding plan year.

(2) Determination of business hardship.—For purposes of this subsection, the factors taken into account in determining temporary substantial business hardship (substantial business hardship in the case of a multiemployer plan) shall include (but shall not be limited to) whether or not—

(A) the employer is operating at an economic loss,

(B) there is substantial unemployment or underemployment in the trade or business and in the industry concerned,

(C) the sales and profits of the industry concerned are depressed or declining, and

(D) it is reasonable to expect that the plan will be continued only if the waiver is granted.

(3) Waived funding deficiency.—For purposes of this section and part III of this subchapter, the term "waived funding deficiency" means the portion of the minimum funding standard under subsection (a) (determined without regard to the waiver) for a plan year waived by the Secretary and not satisfied by employer contributions.

(4) Security for waivers for single-employer plans.—

(A) Security may be required.—

(i) In general.—Except as provided in subparagraph (C), the Secretary may require an employer maintaining a defined benefit plan which is a single-employer plan (within the meaning of section 4001(a)(15) of the Employee Retirement Income Security Act of 1974) to provide security to such plan as a condition for granting or modifying a waiver under paragraph (1).

(ii) Special rules.—Any security provided under clause (i) may be perfected and enforced only by the Pension Benefit Guaranty Corporation, or at the direction of the Corporation, by a contributing sponsor (within the meaning of section 4001(a)(13) of the Employee Retirement Income Security Act of 1974), or a member of such sponsor's controlled group (within the meaning of section 4001(a)(14) of such Act).

(B) Consultation with the Pension Benefit Guaranty Corporation.—Except as provided in subparagraph (C), the Secretary shall, before granting or modifying a waiver under this subsection with respect to a plan described in subparagraph (A)(i)—

(i) provide the Pension Benefit Guaranty Corporation with—

(I) notice of the completed application for any waiver or modification, and

(II) an opportunity to comment on such application within 30 days after receipt of such notice, and

(ii) consider—

(I) any comments of the Corporation under clause (i)(II), and

(II) any views of any employee organization (within the meaning of section 3(4) of the Employee Retirement Income Security Act of 1974) representing participants in the plan which are submitted in writing to the Secretary in connection with such application.

Information provided to the Corporation under this subparagraph shall be considered tax return information and subject to the safeguarding and reporting requirements of section 6103(p).

(C) Exception for certain waivers.—

(i) In general.—The preceding provisions of this paragraph shall not apply to any plan with respect to which the sum of—

(I) the aggregate unpaid minimum required contributions (within the meaning of section 4971(c)(4)) for the plan year and all preceding plan years, and

(II) the present value of all waiver amortization installments determined for the plan year and succeeding plan years under section 430(e)(2),

is less than $100,000.

(ii) Treatment of waivers for which applications are pending.—The amount described in clause (i)(I) shall include any increase in such amount which would result if all applications for waivers of the minimum funding standard under this subsection which are pending with respect to such plan were denied.

(5) Special rules for single-employer plans.—

(A) Application must be submitted before date 2 and ½ months after close of year.—In the case of a defined benefit plan which is not a multiemployer plan, no waiver may be granted under this subsection with respect to any plan for any plan year unless an application therefore is submitted to the Secretary not later than the 15th day of the 3rd month beginning after the close of such plan year.

(B) Special rule if employer is member of controlled group.—In the case of a defined benefit plan which is not a multiemployer plan, if an employer is a member of a controlled group, the temporary substantial business hardship requirements of paragraph (1) shall be treated as met only if such requirements are met—

(i) with respect to such employer, and

(ii) with respect to the controlled group of which such employer is a member (determined by treating all members of such group as a single employer).

The Secretary may provide that an analysis of a trade or business or industry of a member need not be conducted if the Secretary determines such analysis is not necessary because the taking into account of such member would not significantly affect the determination under this paragraph.

(6) Advance notice.—

(A) In general.—The Secretary shall, before granting a waiver under this subsection, require each applicant to provide evidence satisfactory to the Secretary that the applicant has provided notice of the filing of the application for such waiver to each affected party (as defined in section 4001(a)(21) of the Employee Retirement Income Security Act of 1974). Such notice shall include a description of the extent to which the plan is funded for benefits which are guaranteed under title IV of the Employee Retirement Income Security Act of 1974 and for benefit liabilities.

(B) Consideration of relevant information.—The Secretary shall consider any relevant information provided by a person to whom notice was given under subparagraph (A).

(7) Restriction on plan amendments.—

(A) In general.—No amendment of a plan which increases the liabilities of the plan by reason of any increase in benefits, any change in the accrual of benefits, or any change in the rate at which benefits become nonforfeitable under the plan shall be adopted if a waiver under this subsection or an extension of time under section 431(d) is in effect with respect to the plan, or if a plan amendment described in subsection (d)(2) has been made at any time in the preceding 12 months (24 months in the case of a multiemployer plan). If a plan is amended in violation of the preceding sentence, any such waiver, or extension of time, shall not apply to any plan year ending on or after the date on which such amendment is adopted.

(B) Exception.—Subparagraph (A) shall not apply to any plan amendment which—

(i) the Secretary determines to be reasonable and which provides for only de minimis increases in the liabilities of the plan,

(ii) only repeals an amendment described in subsection (d)(2), or

(iii) is required as a condition of qualification under part I of subchapter D, of chapter 1.

(d) Miscellaneous rules.—

(1) Change in method or year.—If the funding method, the valuation date, or a plan year for a plan is changed, the change shall take effect only if approved by the Secretary.

(2) Certain retroactive plan amendments.—For purposes of this section, any amendment applying to a plan year which—

(A) is adopted after the close of such plan year but no later than 2 and ½ months after the close of the plan year (or, in the case of a multiemployer plan, no later than 2 years after the close of such plan year),

(B) does not reduce the accrued benefit of any participant determined as of the beginning of the first plan year to which the amendment applies, and

(C) does not reduce the accrued benefit of any participant determined as of the time of adoption except to the extent required by the circumstances,

shall, at the election of the plan administrator, be deemed to have been made on the first day of such plan year. No amendment described in this paragraph which reduces the accrued benefits of any participant shall take effect unless the plan administrator files a notice with the Secretary notifying him of such amendment and the Secretary has approved such amendment, or within 90 days after the date on which such notice was filed, failed to disapprove such amendment. No amendment described in this subsection shall be approved by the Secretary unless the Secretary determines that such amendment is necessary because of a temporary substantial business hardship (as determined under subsection (c)(2)) or a substantial business hardship (as so determined) in the case of a multiemployer plan and that a waiver under subsection (c) (or, in the case of a multiemployer plan, any extension of the amortization period under section 431(d)) is unavailable or inadequate.

(3) Controlled group.—For purposes of this section, the term "controlled group" means any group treated as a single employer under subsection (b), (c), (m), or (o) of section 414.

(e) Plans to which section applies.—

(1) In general.—Except as provided in paragraphs (2) and (4), this section applies to a plan if, for any plan year beginning on or after the effective date of this section for such plan under the Employee Retirement Income Security Act of 1974—

(A) such plan included a trust which qualified (or was determined by the Secretary to have qualified) under section 401(a), or

(B) such plan satisfied (or was determined by the Secretary to have satisfied) the requirements of section 403(a).

(2) Exceptions.—This section shall not apply to—

(A) any profit-sharing or stock bonus plan,

(B) any insurance contract plan described in paragraph (3),

(C) any governmental plan (within the meaning of section 414(d)),

(D) any church plan (within the meaning of section 414(e)) with respect to which the election provided by section 410(d) has not been made,

(E) any plan which has not, at any time after September 2, 1974, provided for employer contributions, or

(F) any plan established and maintained by a society, order, or association described in section 501(c)(8) or (9), if no part of the contributions to or under such plan are made by employers of participants in such plan.

No plan described in subparagraph (C), (D), or (F) shall be treated as a qualified plan for purposes of section 401(a) unless such plan meets the requirements of section 401(a)(7) as in effect on September 1, 1974.

(3) Certain insurance contract plans.—A plan is described in this paragraph if—

(A) the plan is funded exclusively by the purchase of individual insurance contracts,

(B) such contracts provide for level annual premium payments to be paid extending not later than the retirement age for each individual participating in the plan, and commencing with the date the individual became a participant in the plan (or, in the case of an increase in benefits, commencing at the time such increase becomes effective),

(C) benefits provided by the plan are equal to the benefits provided under each contract at normal retirement age under the plan and are guaranteed by an insurance carrier (licensed under the laws of a State to do business with the plan) to the extent premiums have been paid,

(D) premiums payable for the plan year, and all prior plan years, under such contracts have been paid before lapse or there is reinstatement of the policy,

(E) no rights under such contracts have been subject to a security interest at any time during the plan year, and

(F) no policy leans are outstanding at any time during the plan year.

A plan funded exclusively by the purchase of group insurance contracts which is determined under regulations prescribed by the Secretary to have the same characteristics as contracts described in the preceding sentence shall be treated as a plan described in this paragraph.

(4) Certain terminated multiemployer plans.—This section applies with respect to a terminated multiemployer plan to which section 4021 of the Employee Retirement Income Security Act of 1974 applies until the last day of the plan year in which the plan terminates (within the meaning of section 4041A(a)(2) of such Act).

* * *

§ 414. Definitions and special rules

* * *

(f) Multiemployer plan.—

(1) Definition.—For purposes of this part, the term "multiemployer plan" means a plan—

(A) to which more than one employer is required to contribute,

(B) which is maintained pursuant to one or more collective bargaining agreements between one or more employee organizations and more than one employer, and

(C) which satisfies such other requirements as the Secretary of Labor may prescribe by regulation.

* * *

(i) Defined contribution plan.—For purposes of this part, the term "defined contribution plan" means a plan which provides for an individual account for each participant and for benefits based solely on the amount contributed to the participant's account, and any income, expenses, gains and losses, and any forfeitures of accounts of other participants which may be allocated to such participant's account.

(j) Defined benefit plan.—For purposes of this part, the term "defined benefit plan" means any plan which is not a defined contribution plan.

(k) Certain plans.—A defined benefit plan which provides a benefit derived from employer contributions which is based partly on the balance of the separate account of a participant shall—

(1) for purposes of section 410 (relating to minimum participation standards), be treated as a defined contribution plan,

(2) for purposes of sections 72(d) (relating to treatment of employee contributions as separate contract), 411(a)(7)(A) (relating to minimum vesting standards), 415 (relating to limitations on benefits and contributions under qualified plans), and 401(m) (relating to nondiscrimination tests for matching requirements and employee contributions) be treated as consisting of a defined contribution plan to the extent benefits are based on the separate account of a participant and as a defined benefit plan with respect to the remaining portion of benefits under the plan, and

(3) for purposes of section 4975 (relating to tax on prohibited transactions), be treated as a defined benefit plan.

* * *

(p) Qualified domestic relations order defined.—For purposes of this subsection and section 401(a)(13)—

(1) In general.—

(A) Qualified domestic relations order.—The term "qualified domestic relations order" means a domestic relations order—

(i) which creates or recognizes the existence of an alternate payee's right to, or assigns to an alternate payee the right to, receive all or a portion of the benefits payable with respect to a participant under a plan, and

(ii) with respect to which the requirements of paragraphs (2) and (3) are met.

(B) Domestic relations order.—The term "domestic relations order" means any judgment, decree, or order (including approval of a property settlement agreement) which—

(i) relates to the provision of child support, alimony payments, or marital property rights to a spouse, former spouse, child, or other dependent of a participant, and

(ii) is made pursuant to a State domestic relations law (including a community property law).

(2) Order must clearly specify certain facts.—A domestic relations order meets the requirements of this paragraph only if such order clearly specifies—

(A) the name and the last known mailing address (if any) of the participant and the name and mailing address of each alternate payee covered by the order,

(B) the amount or percentage of the participant's benefits to be paid by the plan to each such alternate payee, or the manner in which such amount or percentage is to be determined,

(C) the number of payments or period to which such order applies, and

(D) each plan to which such order applies.

* * *

(q) Highly compensated employee.—

(1) In general.—The term "highly compensated employee" means any employee who—

(A) was a 5-percent owner at any time during the year or the preceding year, or

(B) for the preceding year—

(i) had compensation from the employer in excess of $80,000,* and

(ii) if the employer elects the application of this clause for such preceding year, was in the top-paid group of employees for such preceding year.

The Secretary shall adjust the $80,000* amount under subparagraph (B) at the same time and in the same manner as under section 415(d), except that the base period shall be the calendar quarter ending September 30, 1996.

(2) 5-percent owner.—An employee shall be treated as a 5-percent owner for any year if at any time

*Editorial comment: The indexed amount for 2013 and 2014 is $115,000.

during such year such employee was a 5-percent owner (as defined in section 416(i)(1)) of the employer.

(3) Top-paid group.—An employee is in the top-paid group of employees for any year if such employee is in the group consisting of the top 20 percent of the employees when ranked on the basis of compensation paid during such year.

(4) Compensation.—For purposes of this subsection, the term "compensation" has the meaning given such term by section 415(c)(3).

(5) Excluded employees.—For purposes of subsection (r) and for purposes of determining the number of employees in the top-paid group, the following employees shall be excluded—

(A) employees who have not completed 6 months of service,

(B) employees who normally work less than 17½ hours per week,

(C) employees who normally work during not more than 6 months during any year,

(D) employees who have not attained age 21, and

(E) except to the extent provided in regulations, employees who are included in a unit of employees covered by an agreement which the Secretary of Labor finds to be a collective bargaining agreement between employee representatives and the employer.

Except as provided by the Secretary, the employer may elect to apply subparagraph (A), (B), (C), or (D) by substituting a shorter period of service, smaller number of hours or months, or lower age for the period of service, number of hours or months, or age (as the case may be) than that specified in such subparagraph.

(6) Former employees.—A former employee shall be treated as a highly compensated employee if—

(A) such employee was a highly compensated employee when such employee separated from service, or

(B) such employee was a highly compensated employee at any time after attaining age 55.

(7) Coordination with other provisions.—Subsections (b), (c), (m), (n), and (o) shall be applied before the application of this subsection.

* * *

(r) Special rules for separate line of business.—

(1) In general.—For purposes of sections 129(d)(8) and 410(b), an employer shall be treated as operating separate lines of business during any year if the employer for bona fide business reasons operates separate lines of business.

(2) Line of business must have 50 employees, etc.—A line of business shall not be treated as separate under paragraph (1) unless—

(A) such line of business has at least 50 employees who are not excluded under subsection (q)(5),

(B) the employer notifies the Secretary that such line of business is being treated as separate for purposes of paragraph (1), and

(C) such line of business meets guidelines prescribed by the Secretary or the employer receives a determination from the Secretary that such line of business may be treated as separate for purposes of paragraph (1).

(3) Safe harbor rule.—

(A) In general.—The requirements of subparagraph (C) of paragraph (2) shall not apply to any line of business if the highly compensated employee percentage with respect to such line of business is—

(i) not less than one-half, and

(ii) not more than twice,

the percentage which highly compensated employees are of all employees of the employer. An employer shall be treated as meeting the requirements of clause (i) if at least 10 percent of all highly compensated employees of the employer perform services solely for such line of business.

(B) Determination may be based on preceding year.—The requirements of subparagraph (A) shall be treated as met with respect to any line of business if such requirements were met with respect to such line of business for the preceding year and if—

(i) no more than a de minimis number of employees were shifted to or from the line of business after the close of the preceding year, or

(ii) the employees shifted to or from the line of business after the close of the preceding year contained a substantially proportional number of highly compensated employees.

(4) Highly compensated employee percentage defined.—For purposes of this subsection, the term "highly compensated employee percentage" means the percentage which highly compensated employees performing services for the line of business are of all employees performing services for the line of business.

(5) Allocation of benefits to line of business.—For purposes of this subsection, benefits which are attributable to services provided to a line of business shall be treated as provided by such line of business.

(6) Headquarters personnel, etc.—The Secretary shall prescribe rules providing for—

(A) the allocation of headquarters personnel among the lines of business of the employer, and

(B) the treatment of other employees providing services for more than 1 line of business of the employer or not in lines of business meeting the requirements of paragraph (2).

(7) Separate operating units.—For purposes of this subsection, the term "separate line of business" includes an operating unit in a separate geographic area separately operated for a bona fide business reason.

(8) Affiliated service groups.—This subsection shall not apply in the case of any affiliated service group (within the meaning of section 414(m)).

(s) Compensation.—For purposes of any applicable provision—

(1) In general.—Except as provided in this subsection, the term "compensation" has the meaning given such term by section 415(c)(3).

(2) Employer may elect not to treat certain deferrals as compensation.—An employer may elect not to include as compensation any amount which is contributed by the employer pursuant to a salary reduction agreement and which is not includible in the gross income of an employee under section 125, 132(f)(4), 402(e)(3), 402(h), or 403(b).

(3) Alternative determination of compensation.—The Secretary shall by regulation provide for alternative methods of determining compensation which may be used by an employer, except that such regulations shall provide that an employer may not use an alternative method if the use of such method discriminates in favor of highly compensated employees (within the meaning of subsection (q)).

(4) Applicable provision.—For purposes of this subsection, the term "applicable provision" means any provision which specifically refers to this subsection.

(t) Application of controlled group rules to certain employee benefits.—

(1) In general.—All employees who are treated as employed by a single employer under subsection (b), (c), or (m) shall be treated as employed by a single employer for purposes of an applicable section. The provisions of subsection (o) shall apply with respect to the requirements of an applicable section.

(2) Applicable section.—For purposes of this subsection, the term "applicable section" means section 79, 106, 117(d), 120, 125, 127, 129, 132, 137, 274(j), 505, or 4090A.

* * *

(v) Catch-up contributions for individuals age 50 or over.—

(1) In general.—An applicable employer plan shall not be treated as failing to meet any requirement of this title solely because the plan permits an eligible participant to make additional elective deferrals in any plan year.

(2) Limitation of amount of additional deferrals.—

(A) In general.—A plan shall not permit additional elective deferrals under paragraph (1) for any year in an amount greater than the lesser of—

(i) the applicable dollar amount, or

(ii) the excess (if any) of—

(I) the participant's compensation (as defined in section 415(c)(3)) for the year, over

(II) any other elective deferrals of the participant for such year which are made without regard to this subsection.

(B) Applicable dollar amount.—For purposes of this paragraph—

(i) In the case of an applicable employer plan other than a plan described in section 401(k)(11) or 408(p), the applicable dollar amount shall be determined in accordance with the following table:

For taxable years beginning in:	The applicable dollar amount is:
2002	$1,000
2003	$2,000
2004	$3,000
2005	$4,000
2006 or thereafter	$5,000*

(ii) In the case of an applicable employer plan described in section 401(k)(11) or 408(p), the applicable dollar amount shall be determined in accordance with the following table:

For taxable years beginning in:	The applicable dollar amount is:
2002	$500
2003	$1,000
2004	$1,500
2005	$2,000
2006 or thereafter	$2,500**

(C) Cost-of-living adjustment.—In the case of a year beginning after December 31, 2006, the Secretary shall adjust annually the $5,000* amount in subparagraph (B)(i) and the $2,500** amount in subparagraph (B)(ii) for increases in the cost-of-living at the same time and in the same manner as adjustments under section 415(d); except that the base period taken into account shall be the calendar quarter beginning July 1, 2005, and any increase under this subparagraph which is not a multiple of $500 shall be rounded to the next lower multiple of $500.

(D) Aggregation of plans.—For purposes of this paragraph, plans described in clauses (i), (ii), and (iv) of paragraph (6)(A) that are maintained by the same employer (as determined under subsection (b), (c), (m) or (o)) shall be treated as a single plan, and plans described in clause (iii) of paragraph (6)(A) that are maintained by the same employer shall be treated as a single plan.

(3) Treatment of contributions.—In the case of any contribution to a plan under paragraph (1)—

(A) such contribution shall not, with respect to the year in which the contribution is made—

(i) be subject to any otherwise applicable limitation contained in section 401(a)(30), 402(h), 403(b), 408, 415(c), and 457(b)(2) (determined without regard to section 457(b)(3)), or

(ii) be taken into account in applying such limitations to other contributions or benefits under such plan or any other such plan, and

(B) except as provided in paragraph (4), such plan shall not be treated as failing to meet the requirements of section 401(a)(4), 401(k)(3), 401(k)(11), 403(b)(12), 408(k), 410(b), or 416 by reason of the making of (or the right to make) such contribution.

(4) Application of nondiscrimination rules.—

(A) In general.—An applicable employer plan shall be treated as failing to meet the nondiscrimination requirements under section 401(a)(4) with respect to benefits, rights, and features unless the plan allows all eligible participants to make the same election with respect to the additional elective deferrals under this subsection.

(B) Aggregation.—For purposes of subparagraph (A), all plans maintained by employers who are treated as a single employer under subsection (b), (c), (m), or (o) of section 414 shall be treated as 1 plan, except that a plan described in clause (i) of section 410(b)(6)(C) shall not be treated as a plan of the employer until the expiration of the transition period with respect to such plan (as determined under clause (ii) or such section).

(5) Eligible participant.—For purposes of this subsection, the term "eligible participant" means a participant in a plan—

(A) who would attain age 50 by the end of the taxable year,

(B) with respect to whom no other elective deferrals may (without regard to this subsection) be made to the plan for the plan (or other applicable) year by reason of the application of any limitation or other restriction described in paragraph (3) or comparable limitation or restriction contained in the terms of the plan.

(6) Other definitions and rules.—For purposes of this subsection—

(A) Applicable employer plan.—The term "applicable employer plan" means—

(i) an employees' trust described in section 401(a) which is exempt from tax under section 501(a),

*Editorial comment: The indexed amount for 2013 and 2014 is $5,500.

**Editorial comment: The indexed amount for 2013 and 2014 remains at $2,500.

(ii) a plan under which amounts are contributed by an individual's employer for annuity contract described in section 403(b),

(iii) an eligible deferred compensation plan under section 457 of an eligible employer described in section 457(e)(l)(A), and

(iv) an arrangement meeting the requirements of section 408(k) or (p).

(B) Elective deferral.—The term "elective deferral" has the meaning given such term by subsection (u)(2)(C).

(C) Exception for section 457 plans.—This subsection shall not apply to a participant for any year for which a higher limitation applies to the participant under section 457(b)(3).

* * *

§ 415. Limitations on benefits and contribution under qualified plans

(a) General rule.—

(1) Trusts.—A trust which is a part of a pension, profit-sharing, or stock bonus plan shall not constitute a qualified trust under section 401(a) if—

(A) in the case of a defined benefit plan, the plan provides for the payment of benefits with respect to a participant which exceed the limitation of subsection (b), or

(B) in the case of a defined contribution plan, contributions and other additions under the plan with respect to any participant for any taxable year exceed the limitation of subsection (c).

(2) Section applies to certain annuities and accounts.—In the case of—

(A) an employee annuity plan described in section 403(a),

(B) an annuity contract described in section 403(b), or

(C) a simplified employee pension described in section 408(k),

such a contract, plan, or pension shall not be considered to be described in section 403(a), 403(b), or 408(k), as the case may be, unless it satisfies the requirements of subparagraph (A) or subparagraph (B) of paragraph (1), whichever is appropriate, and has not been disqualified under subsection (g). In the case of an annuity contract described in section 403 (b), the preceding sentence shall apply only to the portion of the annuity contract which exceeds the limitation of subsection (b) or the limitation of subsection (c), whichever is appropriate.

(b) Limitation for defined benefit plans.—

(1) In general.—Benefits with respect to a participant exceed the limitation of this subsection if, when expressed as an annual benefit (within the meaning of paragraph (2)), such annual benefit is greater than the lesser of—

(A) $160,000*, or

(B) 100 percent of the participant's average compensation for his high 3 years.

(2) Annual benefit.—

(A) In general.—For purposes of paragraph (1), the term "annual benefit" means a benefit payable annually in the form of a straight life annuity (with no ancillary benefits) under a plan to which employees do not contribute and under which no rollover contributions (as defined in sections 402(c), 403(a)(4), 408(d)(3), and 457 (e)(16)) are made.

(B) Adjustment for certain other forms of benefit.—If the benefit under the plan is payable in any form other than the form described in subparagraph (A), or if the employees contribute to the plan or make rollover contributions (as defined in sections 402(c), 403(a)(4), 408(d)(3), and 457(e)(16)), the determinations as to whether the limitation described in paragraph (1) has been satisfied shall be made, in accordance with regulations prescribed by the Secretary, by adjusting such benefit so that it is equivalent to the benefit described in subparagraph (A). For purposes of this subparagraph, any ancillary benefit which is not directly related to retirement income benefits shall not be taken into account; and that portion of any joint and survivor annuity which constitutes a qualified joint and survivor annuity (as defined in section 417) shall not be taken into account.

(C) Adjustment to $160,000* limit where benefit begins before age 62.—If the retirement income benefit under the plan begins

*Editorial comment: The indexed amount for 2013 is $205,000, and for 2014 is $210,000.

before age 62, the determination as to whether the $160,000* limitation set forth in paragraph (1)(A) has been satisfied shall be made, in accordance with regulations prescribed by the Secretary, by reducing the limitation of paragraph (1)(A) so that such limitation (as so reduced) equals an annual benefit (beginning when such retirement income benefit begins) which is equivalent to a $160,000* annual benefit beginning at age 62.

(D) Adjustment to $160,000* limit where benefit begins after age 65.—If the retirement income benefit under the plan begins after age 65, the determination as to whether the $160,000* limitation set forth in paragraph (1)(A) has been satisfied shall be made, in accordance with regulations prescribed by the Secretary, by increasing the limitation of paragraph (1)(A) so that such limitation (as so increased) equals an annual benefit (beginning when such retirement income benefit begins) which is equivalent to a $160,000* annual benefit beginning at age 65.

(E) Limitation on certain assumptions.—

(i) For purposes of adjusting any limitation under subparagraph (C) and, except as provided in clause (ii), for purposes of adjusting any benefit under subparagraph (B), the interest rate assumption shall not be less than the greater of 5 percent or the rate specified in the plan.

(ii) For purposes of adjusting any benefit under subparagraph (B) for any form of benefit subject to section 417(e)(3), the interest rate assumption shall not be less than the greatest of—

(I) 5.5 percent,

(II) the rate that provides a benefit of not more than 105 percent of the benefit that would be provided if the applicable interest rate (as defined in section 417(e)(3)) were the interest rate assumption, or

(III) the rate specified under the plan.

(iii) For purposes of adjusting any limitation under subparagraph (D), the interest rate assumption shall not be greater than the lesser of 5 percent or the rate specified in the plan.

*Editorial comment: The indexed amount for 2013 is $205,000, and for 2014 is $210,000.

(iv) For purposes of this subsection, no adjustments under subsection (d)(1) shall be taken into account before the year for which such adjustment first takes effect.

(v) For purposes of adjusting any benefit or limitation under subparagraph (B), (C), or (D), the mortality table used shall be the applicable mortality table (within meaning of section 417(e)(3)(B)).

(vi) In the case of a plan maintained by an eligible employer (as defined in section 408(p)(2)(C)(i)), clause (ii) shall be applied without regard to subclause (II) thereof.

****(G) Special limitation for qualified police or firefighters.**—In the case of a qualified participant, subparagraph (C) of this paragraph shall not apply.

(H) Qualified participant defined.—For purposes of subparagraph (G), the term "qualified participant" means a participant—

(i) in a defined benefit plan which is maintained by a State, Indian tribal government (as defined in section 7701(a)(40)), or any political subdivision thereof,

(ii) with respect to whom the period of service taken into account in determining the amount of the benefit under such defined benefit plan includes at least 15 years of service of the participant—

(I) as a full-time employee of any police department or fire department which is organized and operated by the State, Indian tribal government (as so defined), or any political subdivision maintaining such defined benefit plan to provide police protection, firefighting services, or emergency medical services for any area within the jurisdiction of such State, Indian tribal government (as so defined), or any political subdivision, or

(II) as a member of the Armed Forces of the United States.

(I) Exemption for survivor and disability benefits provided under governmental plans.—Subparagraph (C) of this paragraph and paragraph (5) shall not apply to—

(i) income received from a governmental plan (as defined in section 414(d)) as a

**Editorial comment: There is no subparagraph (F).

pension, annuity, or similar allowance as the result of the recipient becoming disabled by reason of personal injuries or sickness, or

(ii) amounts received from a governmental plan by the beneficiaries, survivors, or the estate of an employee as the result of the death of the employee.

(3) Average compensation for high 3 years.—For purposes of paragraph (1), a participant's high 3 years shall be the period of consecutive calendar years (not more than 3) during which the participant had the greatest aggregate compensation from the employer. In the case of an employee within the meaning of section 401(c)(1), the preceding sentence shall be applied by substituting for "compensation from the employer" the following: "the participant's earned income (within the meaning of section 401(c)(2) but determined without regard to any exclusion under section 911)."

(4) Total annual benefits not in excess of $10,000.—Notwithstanding the preceding provisions of this subsection, the benefits payable with respect to a participant under any defined benefit plan shall be deemed not to exceed the limitation of this subsection if—

(A) the retirement benefits payable with respect to such participant under such plan and under all other defined benefit plans of the employer do not exceed $10,000 for the plan year, or for any prior plan year, and

(B) the employer has not at any time maintained a defined contribution plan in which the participant participated.

(5) Reduction for participation or service of less than 10 years.—

(A) Dollar limitation.—In the case of an employee who has less than 10 years of participation in a defined benefit plan, the limitation referred to in paragraph (1)(A) shall be the limitation determined under such paragraph (without regard to this paragraph) multiplied by a fraction—

(i) the numerator of which is the number of years (or part thereof) of participation in the defined benefit plan of the employer, and

(ii) the denominator of which is 10.

(B) Compensation and benefits limitations.—The provisions of subparagraph (A) shall apply to the limitations under paragraphs (1)(B) and (4), except that such subparagraph shall be applied with respect to years of service with an employer rather than years of participation in a plan.

(C) Limitation on reduction.—In no event shall subparagraph (A) or (B) reduce the limitations referred to in paragraphs (1) and (4) to an amount less than $^{1}/_{10}$ of such limitation (determined without regard to this paragraph).

(D) Application to changes in benefit structure.—To the extent provided in regulations, subparagraph (A) shall be applied separately with respect to each change in the benefit structure of a plan.

(6) Computation of benefits and contributions.—The computation of—

(A) benefits under a defined contribution plan, for purposes of section 401(a)(4),

(B) contributions made on behalf of a participant in a defined benefit plan, for purposes of section 401(a)(4), and

(C) contributions and benefits provided for a participant in a plan described in section 414(k), for purposes of this section

shall not be made on a basis inconsistent with regulations prescribed by the Secretary.

* * *

(8) Social security retirement age defined.—For purposes of this subsection, the term "social security retirement age" means the age used as the retirement age under section 216(1) of the Social Security Act, except that such section shall be applied—

(A) without regard to the age increase factor, and

(B) as if the early retirement age under section 216(1)(2) of such Act were 62.

(9) Special rule for commercial airline pilots.—

(A) In general.—Except as provided in subparagraph (B), in the case of any participant who is a commercial airline pilot, if, as of the time of the participant's retirement, regulations prescribed by the Federal Aviation Administration require an individual to separate from service as a commercial airline pilot after attaining any age occurring on or after age 60 and before age 62, paragraph (2)(C) shall be applied by substituting such age for age 62.

(B) Individuals who separate from service before age 60.—If a participant described in subparagraph (A) separates from service before age 60, the rules of paragraph (2)(C) shall apply.

(10) Special rule for state, Indian tribal, and local government plans.—

(A) Limitation to equal accrued benefit.—In the case of a plan maintained for its employees by any State or political subdivision thereof, or by any agency or instrumentality of the foregoing, or a governmental plan described in the last sentence of section 414(d) (relating to plans of Indian tribal governments), the limitation with respect to a qualified participant under this subsection shall not be less than the accrued benefit of the participant under the plan (determined without regard to any amendment of the plan made after October 14, 1987).

(B) Qualified participant.—For purposes of this paragraph, the term "qualified participant" means a participant who first became a participant in the plan maintained by the employer before January 1, 1990.

(C) Election.—

(i) In general.—This paragraph shall not apply to any plan unless each employer maintaining the plan elects before the close of the 1st plan year beginning after December 31, 1989, to have this subsection (other than paragraph (2)(G)).

(ii) Revocation of election.—An election under clause (i) may be revoked not later than the last day of the third plan year beginning after the date of the enactment of this clause. The revocation shall apply to all plan years to which the election applied and to all subsequent plan years. Any amount paid by a plan in a taxable year ending after the revocation shall be includible in income in such taxable year under the rules of this chapter in effect for such taxable year, except that, for purposes of applying the limitations imposed by this section, any portion of such amount which is attributable to any taxable year during which the election was in effect shall be treated as received in such taxable year.

(11) Special limitation rule for governmental plans.—In the case of a governmental plan (as defined in section 414(d)) or a multiemployer plan [as defined in section 414(f)], subparagraph (B) of paragraph (1) shall not apply. Subparagraph (B) of paragraph (1) shall not apply to a plan maintained by an organization described in section 3121(w)(3)(A) except with respect to highly compensated benefits. For purposes of this paragraph, the term "highly compensated benefits" means any benefits accrued for an employee in any year on or after the first year in which such employee is a highly compensated employee (as defined in section 414(q)) of the organization described in section 3121(w)(3)(A). For purposes of applying paragraph (1)(B) to highly compensated benefits, all benefits of the employee otherwise taken into account (without regard to this paragraph) shall be taken into account.

(c) Limitation for defined contribution plans.—

(1) In general.—Contributions and other additions with respect to a participant exceed the limitation of this subsection if, when expressed as an annual addition (within the meaning of paragraph (2)) to the participant's account, such annual addition is greater than the lesser of—

(A) $40,000*, or

(B) 100 percent of the participant's compensation.

(2) Annual addition.—For purposes of paragraph (1), the term "annual addition" means the sum for any year of—

(A) employer contributions,

(B) the employee contributions, and

(C) forfeitures.

For the purposes of this paragraph, employee contributions under subparagraph (B) are determined without regard to any rollover contributions (as defined in sections 402(c), 403(a)(4), 403(b)(8), 408(d)(3), and 457(e)(16)) without regard to employee contributions to a simplified employee pension which are excludable from gross income under section 408(k)(6). Subparagraph (B) of paragraph (1) shall not apply to any contribution for medical benefits (within the meaning of section 419A(f)(2)), after separation from service which is treated as an annual addition.

*Editorial comment: The indexed amount for 2013 is $51,000, and for 2014 is $52,000.

(3) Participant's compensation.—For purposes of paragraph (1)—

(A) In general.—The term "participant's compensation" means the compensation of the participant from the employer for the year.

(B) Special rule for self-employed individuals.—In the case of an employee within the meaning of section 401(c)(1), subparagraph (A) shall be applied by substituting "the participant's earned income (within the meaning of section 401(c)(2) but determined without regard to any exclusion under section 911)" for "compensation of the participant from the employer."

(C) Special rules for permanent and total disability.—In the case of a participant in any defined contribution plan—

(i) who is permanently and totally disabled (as defined in section 22(e)(3)),

(ii) who is not a highly compensated employee (within the meaning of section 414(q)), and

(iii) with respect to whom the employer elects, at such time and in such manner as the Secretary may prescribe, to have this subparagraph apply,

the term "participant's compensation" means the compensation the participant would have received for the year if the participant was paid at the rate of compensation paid immediately before becoming permanently and totally disabled. This subparagraph shall apply only if contributions made with respect to amounts treated as compensation under this subparagraph are nonforfeitable when made. If a defined contribution plan provides for the continuation of contributions on behalf of all participants described in clause (i) for a fixed or determinable period, this subparagraph shall be applied without regard to clauses (ii) and (iii).

(D) Certain deferrals included.—The term "participant's compensation" shall include—

(i) any elective deferral (as defined in section 402(g)(3)), and

(ii) any amount which is contributed or deferred by the employer at the election of the employee and which is not includible in the gross income of the employee by reason of section 125, 132(f)(4), or 457.

(E) Annuity contracts.—In the case of an annuity contract described in section 403(b), the term "participant's compensation" means the participant's includible compensation determined under section 403(b)(3).

***(6) Special rule for employee stock ownership plan.**—If no more than one-third of the employer contributions to an employee stock ownership plan (as described in section 4975(e)(7)) for a year which are deductible under paragraph (9) of section 404(a) are allocated to highly compensated employees (within the meaning of section 414(q)), the limitations imposed by this section shall not apply to—

(A) forfeitures of employer securities (within the meaning of section 409) under such an employee stock ownership plan if such securities were acquired with the proceeds of a loan (as described in section 404(a)(9)(A)), or

(B) employer contributions to such an employee stock ownership plan which are deductible under section 404(a)(9)(B) and charged against the participant's account.

The amount of any qualified gratuitous transfer (as defined in section 664(g)(1)) allocated to a participant for any limitation year shall not exceed the limitations imposed by this section, but such amount shall not be taken into account in determining whether any other amount exceeds the limitations imposed by this section.

* * *

(d) Cost-of-living adjustments.—

(1) In general.—The Secretary shall adjust annually—

(A) the $160,000** amount in subsection (b)(1)(A),

(B) in the case of a participant who separated from service, the amount taken into account under subsection (b)(1)(B), and

(C) the $40,000*** amount in subsection (c)(1)(A), for increases in the cost-of-living in accordance with regulations prescribed by the Secretary.

---

*Editorial comment: There is no paragraphs (4) and (5).

**Editorial comment: The indexed amount for 2013 is $205,000, and for 2014 is $210,000.

***Editorial comment: The indexed amount for 2013 is $51,000, and for 2014 is $52,000.

(2) Method.—The regulations prescribed under paragraph (1) shall provide for—

(A) an adjustment with respect to any calendar year based on the increase in the applicable index for the calendar quarter ending September 30 of the preceding calendar year over such index for the base period, and

(B) adjustment procedures which are similar to the procedures used to adjust benefit amounts under section 215(i)(2)(A) of the Social Security Act.

(3) Base period—For purposes of paragraph (2)—

(A) $160,000* amount.—The base period taken into account for purposes of paragraph (1)(A) is the calendar quarter beginning July 1, 2001.

(B) Separations after December 31, 1994.—The base period taken into account for purposes of paragraph (1)(B) with respect to individuals separating from service with the employer after December 31, 1994, is the calendar quarter beginning July 1 of the calendar year preceding the calendar year in which such separation occurs.

(C) Separations before January 1, 1995.—The base period taken into account for purposes of paragraph (1)(B) with respect to individuals separating from service with the employer before January 1, 1995, is the calendar quarter beginning October 1 of the calendar year preceding the calendar year in which such separation occurs.

(D) $40,000 amount.**—The base period taken into account for purposes of paragraph (1)(C) is the calendar quarter beginning July 1, 2001.

(4) Rounding.—

(A) $160,000* amount.—Any increase under subparagraph (A) of paragraph (1) which is not a multiple of $5,000 shall be rounded to the next lowest multiple of $5,000.

(B) $40,000 amount.**—Any increase under subparagraph (C) of paragraph (1) which is not a multiple of $1,000 shall be rounded to the next lowest multiple of $1,000.

***(f) **Combining of plans.**—

(1) In general.—For purposes of applying the limitations of subsections (b), (c), and (e)—

(A) all defined benefit plans (whether or not terminated) of an employer are to be treated as one defined benefit plan, and

(B) all defined contribution plans (whether or not terminated) of an employer are to be treated as one defined contribution plan.

(2) Exception for multiemployer plans.—Notwithstanding paragraph (1) and subsection (g), a multiemployer plan (as defined in section 414(f)) shall not be combined or aggregated—

(A) with any other plan which is not a multiemployer plan for purposes of applying subsection (b)(1)(B) to such other plan, or

(B) with any other multiemployer plan for purposes of applying the limitations established in this section.

(g) Aggregation of plans.—Except as provided in subsection (f)(3), the Secretary, in applying the provisions of this section to benefits or contributions under more than one plan maintained by the same employer, and to any trusts, contracts, accounts, or bonds referred to in subsection (a)(2), with respect to which the participant has the control required under section 414(b) or (c), as modified by subsection (h), shall, under regulations prescribed by the Secretary, disqualify one or more trusts, plans, contracts, accounts, or bonds, or any combination thereof until such benefits or contributions do not exceed the limitations contained in this section. In addition to taking into account such other factors as may be necessary to carry out the purposes of subsection (f), the regulations prescribed under this paragraph shall provide that no plan which has been terminated shall be disqualified until all other trusts, plans, contracts, accounts, or bonds have been disqualified.

(h) 50 percent control.—For purposes of applying subsections (b) and (c) of section 414 to this section, the phrase "more than 50 percent" shall be substituted for the phrase "at least 80 percent" each place it appears in section 1563(a)(1).

* * *

*Editorial comment: The indexed amount for 2013 is $205,000, and for 2014 is $210,000.

**Editorial comment: The indexed amount for 2013 is $51,000, and for 2014 is $52,000.

***Editorial comment: There is no subsection (e).

(j) Regulations; definition of year.—The Secretary shall prescribe such regulations as may be necessary to carry out the purposes of this section, including, but not limited to, regulations defining the term "year" for purposes of any provision of this section.

(k) Special rules.—

(1) Defined benefit plan and defined contribution plan.—For purposes of this title, the term "defined contribution plan" or "defined benefit plan" means a defined contribution plan (within the meaning of section 414(i)) or a defined benefit plan (within the meaning of section 414(j)), whichever applies, which is—

(A) a plan described in section 401(a) which includes a trust which is exempt from tax under section 501(a),

(B) an annuity plan described in section 403(a),

(C) an annuity contract described in section 403(b), or

(D) a simplified employee pension.

(2) Contributions to provide cost-of-living protection under defined benefit plans.—

(A) In general.—In the case of a defined benefit plan which maintains a qualified cost-of-living arrangement—

(i) any contribution made directly by an employee under such an arrangement shall not be treated as an annual addition for purposes of subsection (c), and

(ii) any benefit under such arrangement which is allocable to an employer contribution which was transferred from a defined contribution plan and to which the requirements of subsection (c) were applied shall, for purposes of subsection (b), be treated as a benefit derived from an employee contribution (and subsection (c) shall not again apply to such contribution by reason of such transfer).

(B) Qualified cost-of-living arrangement defined.—For purposes of this paragraph, the term "qualified cost-of-living arrangement" means an arrangement under a defined benefit plan which—

(i) provides a cost-of-living adjustment to a benefit provided under such plan or a separate plan subject to the requirements of section 412, and

(ii) meets the requirements of subparagraphs (C), (D), (E), and (F) and such other requirements as the Secretary may prescribe.

(C) Determination of amount of benefit.—An arrangement meets the requirement of this subparagraph only if the cost-of-living adjustment of participants is based—

(i) on increases in the cost-of-living after the annuity starting date, and

(ii) on average cost-of-living increases determined by reference to 1 or more indexes prescribed by the Secretary, except that the arrangement may provide that the increase for any year will not be less than 3 percent of the retirement benefit (determined without regard to such increase).

(D) Arrangement elective; time for election.—An arrangement meets the requirements of this subparagraph only if it is elective, it is available under the same terms to all participants, and it provides that such election may at least be made in the year in which the participant—

(i) attains the earliest retirement age under the defined benefit plan (determined without regard to any requirement of separation from service), or

(ii) separates from service.

(E) Nondiscrimination requirements.—An arrangement shall not meet the requirements of this subparagraph if the Secretary finds that a pattern of discrimination exists with respect to participation.

(F) Special rules for key employees.—

(i) In general.—An arrangement shall not meet the requirements of this paragraph if any key employee is eligible to participate.

(ii) Key employee.—For purposes of this subparagraph, the term "key employee" has the meaning given such term by section 416 (i)(1), except that in the case of a plan other than a top-heavy plan (within the meaning of section 416(g)), such term shall not include an individual who is a key employee solely by reason of section 416(i) (1)(A)(i).

(3) Repayments of cashouts under governmental plans.—In the case of any repayment of contributions (including interest thereon) to the governmental plan with respect to any amount previously refunded upon a forfeiture of service credit under the plan or under another governmental plan maintained by a State or local government employer within the same State, any such repayment shall not be taken into account for purposes of this section.

(4) Special rules for sections 403(b) and 408.—For purposes of this section, any annuity contract described in section 403(b) for the benefit of a participant shall be treated as a defined contribution plan maintained by each employer with respect to which the participant has the control required under subsection (b) or (c) of section 414 (as modified by subsection (h)). For purposes of this section, any contribution by an employer to a simplified employee pension plan for an individual for a taxable year shall be treated as an employer contribution to a defined contribution plan for such individual for such year.

(l) Treatment of certain medical benefits.—

(1) In general.—For purposes of this section, contributions allocated to any individual medical benefit account which is part of a pension or annuity plan shall be treated as an annual addition to a defined contribution plan for purposes of subsection (c). Subparagraph (B) of subsection (c)(1) shall not apply to any amount treated as an annual addition under the preceding sentence.

(2) Individual medical benefit account.—For purposes of paragraph (1), the term "individual medical benefit account" means any separate account—

(A) which is established for a participant under a pension or annuity plan, and

(B) from which benefits described in section 401(h) are payable solely to such participant, his spouse, or his dependents.

* * *

§ 416. Special rules for top-heavy plans

(a) General rule.—A trust shall not constitute a qualified trust under section 401(a) for any plan year if the plan of which it is a part is a top-heavy plan for such plan year unless such plan meets—

(1) the vesting requirements of subsection (b), and

(2) the minimum benefit requirements of subsection (c).

(b) Vesting requirements.—

(1) In general.—A plan satisfies the requirements of this subsection if it satisfies the requirements of either of the following subparagraphs:

(A) 3-year vesting.—A plan satisfies the requirements of this subparagraph if an employee who has completed at least 3 years of service with the employer or employers maintaining the plan has a nonforfeitable right to 100 percent of his accrued benefit derived from employer contributions.

(B) 6-year graded vesting.—A plan satisfies the requirements of this subparagraph if an employee has a nonforfeitable right to a percentage of his accrued benefit derived from employer contributions determined under the following table:

Years of service	The nonforfeitable percentage is:
2	20
3	40
4	60
5	80
6 or more	100

(2) Certain rules made applicable.—Except to the extent inconsistent with the provisions of this subsection, the rules of section 411 shall apply for purposes of this subsection.

(c) Plan must provide minimum benefits.—

(1) Defined benefit plans.—

(A) In general.—A defined benefit plan meets the requirements of this subsection if the accrued benefit derived from employer contributions of each participant who is a non-key employee, when expressed as an annual retirement benefit, is not less than the applicable percentage of the participant's average compensation for years in the testing period.

(B) Applicable percentage.—For purposes of subparagraph (A), the term "applicable percentage" means the lesser of—

(i) 2 percent multiplied by the number of years of service with the employer, or

(ii) 20 percent.

(C) Years of service.—For purposes of this paragraph—

(i) In general.—Except as provided in clause (ii) or (iii), years of service shall be determined under the rules of paragraphs (4), (5), and (6) of section 411(a).

(ii) Exception for years during which plan was not top-heavy.—A year of service with the employer shall not be taken into account under this paragraph if—

(I) the plan was not a top-heavy plan for any plan year ending during such year of service, or

(II) such year of service was completed in a plan year beginning before January 1, 1984.

(iii) Exception for plan under which no key employee (or former key employee) benefits for plan year.—For purposes of determining an employee's years of service with the employer, any service with the employer shall be disregarded to the extent that such service occurs during a plan year when the plan benefits (within the meaning of section 410(b)) no key employee or former key employee.

(D) Average compensation for high 5 years.—For purposes of this paragraph—

(i) In general.—A participant's testing period shall be the period of consecutive years (not exceeding 5) during which the participant had the greatest aggregate compensation from the employer.

(ii) Year must be included in year of service.—The years taken into account under clause (i) shall be properly adjusted for years not included in a year of service.

(iii) Certain years not taken into ac count.—Except to the extent provided in the plan, a year shall not be taken into account under clause (i) if—

(I) such year ends in a plan year beginning before January 1, 1984, or

(II) such year begins after the close of the last year in which the plan was a top-heavy plan.

(E) Annual retirement benefit.—For purposes of this paragraph, the term "annual retirement benefit" means a benefit payable annually in the form of a single life annuity (with no ancillary benefits) beginning at the normal retirement age under the plan.

(2) Defined contribution plans.—

(A) In general.—A defined contribution plan meets the requirements of the subsection if the employer contribution for the year for each participant who is a non-key employee is not less than 3 percent of such participant's compensation (within the meaning of section 415). Employer matching contributions (as defined in section 401(m)(4)(A)) shall be taken into account for purposes of this subparagraph (and any reduction under this sentence shall not be taken into account in determining whether section 401(k)(4)(A) applies).

(B) Special rule where maximum contribution less than 3 percent.—

(i) In general.—The percentage referred to in subparagraph (A) for any year shall not exceed the percentage at which contributions are made (or required to be made) under the plan for the year for the key employee for whom such percentage is the highest for the year.

(ii) Treatment of aggregation groups.—

(I) For purposes of this subparagraph, all defined contribution plans required to be included in an aggregation group under subsection (g)(2)(A)(i) shall be treated as one plan.

(II) This subparagraph shall not apply to any plan required to be included in an aggregation group if such plan enables a defined benefit plan required to be included in such group to meet the requirements of section 401(a)(4) or 410.

* * *

(e) Plan must meet requirements without taking into account social security and similar contributions and benefits.—A top-heavy plan shall not be treated as meeting the requirement of subsection (b) or (c) unless such plan meets such requirement without taking into account contributions or benefits under chapter 2 (relating to tax on self-employment income), chapter 21 (relating to Federal Insurance Contributions Act), title II of the Social Security Act, or any other Federal or State law.

(f) Coordination where employer has 2 or more plans.—The Secretary shall prescribe such regulations as may be necessary or appropriate to carry out the purposes of this section where the employer has 2 or more plans including (but not limited to) regulations to prevent inappropriate omissions or required duplication of minimum benefits or contributions.

(g) Top-heavy plan defined.—For purposes of this section—

(1) In general.—

(A) Plans not required to be aggregated.—Except as provided in subparagraph (B), the term "top-heavy plan" means, with respect to any plan year—

(i) any defined benefit plan if, as of the determination date, the present value of the cumulative accrued benefits under the plan for key employees exceeds 60 percent of the present value of the cumulative accrued benefits under the plan for all employees, and

(ii) any defined contribution plan if, as of the determination date, the aggregate of the accounts of key employees under the plan exceeds 60 percent of the aggregate of the accounts of all employees under such plan.

(B) Aggregated plans.—Each plan of an employer required to be included in an aggregation group shall be treated as a top-heavy plan if such group is a top-heavy group.

(2) Aggregation.—For purposes of this subsection—

(A) Aggregation group.—

(i) Required aggregation.—The term "aggregation group" means—

(I) each plan of the employer in which a key employee is a participant, and

(II) each other plan of the employer which enables any plan described in subclause (I) to meet the requirements of section 401(a)(4) or 410.

(ii) Permissive aggregation.—The employer may treat any plan not required to be included in an aggregation group under clause (i) as being part of such group if such group would continue to meet the requirements of sections 401(a)(4) and 410 with such plan being taken into account.

(B) Top-heavy group.—The term "top-heavy group" means any aggregation group if—

(i) the sum (as of the determination date) of—

(I) the present value of the cumulative accrued benefits for key employees under all defined benefit plans included in such group, and

(II) the aggregate of the accounts of key employees under all defined contribution plans included in such group,

(ii) exceeds 60 percent of a similar sum determined for all employees.

(3) Distributions during last year before determination date taken into account.—

(A) In general.—For purposes of determining—

(i) the present value of the cumulative accrued benefit for any employee, or

(ii) the amount of the account of any employee,

such present value or amount shall be increased by the aggregate distributions made with respect to such employee under the plan during the 1-year period ending on the determination date. The preceding sentence shall also apply to distributions under a terminated plan which if it had not been terminated would have been required to be included in an aggregation group.

(B) 5-year period in case of in-service distribution.—In the case of any distribution made for a reason other than severance from employment, death, or disability, subparagraph (A) shall be applied by substituting "5-year period" for "1-year period."

(4) Other special rules.—For purposes of this subsection—

(A) Rollover contributions to plan not taken into account.—Except to the extent provided in regulations, any rollover contribution (or similar transfer) initiated by the employee and made after December 31, 1983, to a plan shall not be taken into account with respect to the transferee plan for purposes of determining whether such plan is a top-heavy plan (or whether any aggregation group which includes such plan is a top-heavy group).

(B) Benefits not taken into account if employee ceases to be key employee.—If any individual is a non-key employee with respect to any plan for any plan year, but such individual was a key employee with respect to such plan for any prior plan year, any accrued benefit for such employee (and the account of such employee) shall not be taken into account.

(C) Determination date.—The term "determination date" means, with respect to any plan year—

(i) the last day of the preceding plan year, or

(ii) in the case of the first plan year of any plan, the last day of such plan year.

(D) Years.—To the extent provided in regulations, this section shall be applied on the basis of any year specified in such regulations in lieu of plan years.

(E) Benefits not taken into account if employee not employed for last year before determination date.—If any individual has not performed services for the employer maintaining the plan at any time during the 1-year period ending on the determination date, any accrued benefit for such individual (and the account of such individual) shall not be taken into account.

(F) Accrued benefits treated as accruing ratably.—The accrued benefit of any employee (other than a key employee) shall be determined—

(i) under the method which is used for accrual purposes for all plans of the employer, or

(ii) if there is no method described in clause (i), as if such benefit accrued not more rapidly than the slowest accrual rate permitted under section 411(b)(1)(C).

(G) Simple retirement accounts.—The term "top-heavy plan" shall not include a simple retirement account under section 408(p).

(H) Cash or deferred arrangements using alternative methods of meeting nondiscrimination requirements.—The term "top-heavy plan" shall not include a plan which consists solely of—

(i) a cash or deferred arrangement which meets the requirements of section 401(k)(12) or 401(k)(13), and

(ii) matching contributions with respect to which the requirements of section 401 (m)(11) or 401(m)(12) are met.

If, but for this subparagraph, a plan would be treated as a top-heavy plan because it is a member of an aggregation group which is a top-heavy plan group, contributions under the plan may be taken into account in determining whether any other plan in the group meets the requirements of subsection (c)(2).

* * *

*__(i) Definitions.__—For purposes of this section—

(1) Key employee.—

(A) In general.—The term "key employee" means an employee who, at any time during the plan year is—

(i) an officer of the employer having an annual compensation greater than $130,000,**

(ii) a 5-percent owner of the employer, or

(iii) a 1-percent owner of the employer having an annual compensation from the employer of more than $150,000.

For purposes of clause (i), no more than 50 em ployees (or, if lesser, the greater of 3 or 10 percent of the employees) shall be treated as officers. In the case of plan years beginning after December 31, 2002, the $130,000** amount in clause (i) shall be adjusted at the same time and in the same manner as under section 415(d), except that the base period shall be the calendar quarter beginning July 1, 2001, and any increase under this sentence which is not a multiple of $5,000 shall be rounded to the next lower multiple of $5,000. Such term shall not include any officer or employee of an entity referred to in section 414(d) (relating to governmental plans). For purposes of determining the number of officers taken into account under clause (i), employees described in section 414 (q)(5) shall be excluded.

(B) Percentage owners.—

(i) 5-percent owner.—For purposes of this paragraph, the term "5-percent owner" means—

(I) if the employer is a corporation, any person who owns (or is considered as owning within the meaning of section 318) more than 5 percent of the outstanding stock of the corporation or stock possessing more than 5 percent of the total combined voting power of all stock of the corporation, or

(II) if the employer is not a corporation, any person who owns more than 5 percent of the capital or profits interest in the employer.

*Editorial comment: There is no subsection (h).

**Editorial comment: The indexed amount for 2013 is $165,000, and for 2014 is $170,000.

(ii) 1-percent owner.—For purposes of this paragraph, the term "1 -percent owner" means any person who would be described in clause (i) if "1 percent" were substituted for "5 percent" each place it appears in clause (i).

(iii) Constructive ownership rules.—For purposes of this subparagraph—

(I) subparagraph (C) of section 318(a)(2) shall be applied by substituting "5 percent" for "50 percent," and

(II) in the case of any employer which is not a corporation, ownership in such employer shall be determined in accordance with regulations prescribed by the Secretary which shall be based on principles similar to the principles of secion 318 (as modified by subclause (I)).

(C) Aggregation rules do not apply for purposes of determining ownership in the employer.—The rules of subsections (b), (c), and (m) of section 414 shall not apply for purposes of determining ownership in the employer.

(D) Compensation.—For purposes of this paragraph, the term "compensation" has the meaning given such term by section 414(q)(4).

(2) Non-key employee.—The term "non-key employee" means any employee who is not a key employee.

(3) Self-employed individuals.—In the case of a self-employed individual described in section 401(c)(1)—

(A) such individual shall be treated as an employee, and

(B) such individual's earned income (within the meaning of section 401(c)(2)) shall be treated as compensation.

(4) Treatment of employees covered by collective bargaining agreements.—The requirements of subsections (b), (c), and (d) shall not apply with respect to any employee included in a unit of employees covered by an agreement which the Secretary of Labor finds to be a collective bargaining agreement between employee representatives and 1 or more employers if there is evidence that retirement benefits were the subject of good faith bargaining between such employee representatives and such employer or employers.

(5) Treatment of beneficiaries.—The terms "employee" and "key employee" include their beneficiaries.

(6) Treatment of simplified employee pensions.—

(A) Treatment as defined contribution plans.—A simplified employee pension shall be treated as a defined contribution plan.

(B) Election to have determinations based on employer contributions.—In the case of a simplified employee pension, at the election of the employer, paragraphs (1)(A)(ii) and (2)(B) of subsection (g) shall be applied by taking into account aggregate employer contributions in lieu of the aggregate of the accounts of employees.

* * *

*SUBPART C—SPECIAL RULES FOR MULTIEMPLOYER PLANS**

*SUBPART D—TREATMENT OF WELFARE BENEFIT FUNDS**

*SUBPART E—TREATMENT OF TRANSFERS TO RETIREE HEALTH ACCOUNTS**

PART II—CERTAIN STOCK OPTIONS.

Editorial Summary

Stock Options

Subchapter D of Chapter D (Secs. 421–424)

Congress has long recognized the utility of providing incentives to the management of an entity in the form of stock ownership. This has been implemented through the beneficial tax treatment provided for stock options. From the viewpoint of the employee, the ideal tax treatment would be deferral of recognized gain until the wherewithal to pay occurs (i.e., the related stock is sold by the employee) and taxation of such recognized gain at preferentially-treated capital gain rates.

Over the years, a variety of tax treatments have existed for stock options with a variety of statutory requirements in order to qualify for a particular tax treatment.

*Omitted

Sections 421 and 422 contain the statutory provisions for stock options. Section 421 provides the general rule that if the stock option qualifies under Sec. 422(a), gross income is not recognized to the employee at exercise date for the difference between the exercise price and the amount paid for the stock by the employee [see Sec. 421(a)].

Section 422, entitled Incentive Stock Options, was added by the Economic Recovery Tax Act of 1981 and reinstated favorable tax treatment for stock options [see Sec. 422(a)]. In order to receive favorable treatment, the stock option must qualify as an incentive stock option [see Sec. 422(b)] and certain holding period requirements must be satisfied [see Sec. 422(a)(1) and (2)].

§ 421. General Rules

(a) Effect of qualifying transfer.—If a share of stock is transferred to an individual in a transfer in respect of which the requirements of section 422(a) or 423(a) are met—

(1) no income shall result at the time of the transfer of such share to the individual upon his exercise of the option with respect to such share;

(2) no deduction under section 162 (relating to trade or business expenses) shall be allowable at any time to the employer corporation, a parent or subsidiary corporation of such corporation, or a corporation issuing or assuming a stock option in a transaction to which section 424(a) applies, with respect to the share so transferred; and

(3) no amount other than the price paid under the option shall be considered as received by any of such corporations for the share so transferred.

(b) Effect of disqualifying disposition.—If the transfer of a share of stock to an individual pursuant to his exercise of an option would otherwise meet the requirements of section 422(a) or 423(a) except that there is a failure to meet any of the holding period requirements of section 422(a)(l) or 423(a)(l), then any increase in the income of such individual or deduction from the income of his employer corporation for the taxable year in which such exercise occurred attributable to such disposition, shall be treated as an increase in income or a deduction from income in the taxable year of such individual or of such employer corporation in which such disposition occurred. No amount shall be required to be deducted and withheld under chapter 24 with respect to any increase in income attributable to a disposition described in the preceding sentence.

(c) Exercise by estate.—

(1) In general.—If an option to which this part applies is exercised after the death of the employee by the estate of the decedent, or by a person who acquired the right to exercise such option by bequest or inheritance or by reason of the death of the decedent, the provisions of subsection (a) shall apply to the same extent as if the option had been exercised by the decedent, except that—

(A) the holding period and employment requirements of sections 422(a) or 423(a) shall not apply, and

(B) any transfer by the estate of stock acquired shall be considered a disposition of such stock for purposes of section 423(c).

(2) Deduction for estate tax.—If an amount is required to be included under section 423(c) in gross income of the estate of the deceased employee or of a person described in paragraph (1), there shall be allowed to the estate or such person a deduction with respect to the estate tax attributable to the inclusion in the taxable estate of the deceased employee of the net value for estate tax purposes of the option. For this purpose, the deduction shall be determined under section 691(c) as if the option acquired from the deceased employee were an item of gross income in respect of the decedent under section 691 and as if the amount includible in gross income under section 423(c) were an amount included in gross income under section 691 in respect of such item of gross income.

(3) Basis of shares acquired.—In the case of a share of stock acquired by the exercise of an option to which paragraph (1) applies—

(A) the basis of such share shall include so much of the basis of the option as is attributable to such share; except that the basis of such share shall be reduced by the excess (if any) of (i) the amount which would have been includible in gross income under section 423(c) if the employee had exercised the option on the date of his death and had held the share acquired pursuant to such exercise at the time of his death, over (ii) the amount which is includible in gross income under such section; and

(B) the last sentence of section 423(c) shall apply only to the extent that the amount includible in gross income under such section exceeds so much of the basis of the option as is attributable to such share.

(d) Certain sales to comply with conflict-of-interest requirements.—If—

(1) a share of stock is transferred to an eligible person (as defined in section 1043(b)(1)) pursuant to such person's exercise of an option to which this part applies, and

(2) such share is disposed of by such person pursuant to a certificate of divestiture (as define in section 1043(b)(2)),

such disposition shall be treated as meeting the requirements of section 422(a)(1) or 423(a)(1), whichever is applicable.

§ 422. Incentive stock options

(a) In general.—Section 421(a) shall apply with respect to the transfer of a share of stock to an individual pursuant to his exercise of an incentive stock option if—

(1) no disposition of such share is made by him within 2 years from the date of the granting of the option nor within 1 year after the transfer of such share to him, and

(2) at all times during the period beginning on the date of the granting of the option and ending on the day 3 months before the date of such exercise, such individual was an employee of either the corporation granting such option, a parent or subsidiary corporation of such corporation, or a corporation or a parent or subsidiary corporation of such corporation issuing or assuming a stock option in a transaction to which section 424(a) applies.

(b) Incentive stock option.—For purposes of this part, the term "incentive stock option" means an option granted to an individual for any reason connected with his employment by a corporation, if granted by the employer corporation or its parent or subsidiary corporation, to purchase stock of any of such corporations, but only if—

(1) the option is granted pursuant to a plan which includes the aggregate number of shares which may be issued under options and the employees (or class of employees) eligible to receive options, and which is approved by the stockholders of the granting corporation within 12 months before or after the date such plan is adopted;

(2) such option is granted within 10 years from the date such plan is adopted, or the date such plan is approved by the stockholders, whichever is earlier;

(3) such option by its terms is not exercisable after the expiration of 10 years from the date such option is granted;

(4) the option price is not less than the fair market value of the stock at the time such option is granted;

(5) such option by its terms is not transferable by such individual otherwise than by will or the laws of descent and distribution, and is exercisable, during his lifetime, only by him; and

(6) such individual, at the time the option is granted, does not own stock possessing more than 10 percent of the total combined voting power of all classes of stock of the employer corporation or of its parent or subsidiary corporation.

Such term shall not include any option if (as of the time the option is granted) the terms of such option provide that it will not be treated as an incentive stock option.

(c) Special rules.—

(1) Good faith efforts to value stock.—If a share of stock is transferred pursuant to the exercise by an individual of an option which would fail to qualify as an incentive stock option under subsection (b) because there was a failure in an attempt, made in good faith, to meet the requirement of subsection (b)(4), the requirement of subsection (b)(4) shall be considered to have been met. To the extent provided in regulations by the Secretary, a similar rule shall apply for purposes of subsection (d).

(2) Certain disqualifying dispositions where amount realized is less than value at exercise.—If—

(A) an individual who has acquired a share of stock by the exercise of an incentive stock option makes a disposition of such share within either of the periods described in subsection (a)(1), and

(B) such disposition is a sale or exchange with respect to which a loss (if sustained) would be recognized to such individual,

then the amount which is includible in the gross income of such individual, and the amount which is deductible from the income of his employer corporation, as compensation attributable to the exercise of such option shall not exceed the excess (if any) of the amount realized on such sale or exchange over the adjusted basis of such share.

* * *

(4) Permissible provisions.—An option which meets the requirements of subsection (b) shall be treated as an incentive stock option even if—

(A) the employee may pay for the stock with stock of the corporation granting the option,

(B) the employee has a right to receive property at the time of exercise of the option, or

(C) the option is subject to any condition not inconsistent with the provisions of subsection (b).

Subparagraph (B) shall apply to a transfer of property (other than cash) only if section 83 applies to the property so transferred.

(5) 10-percent shareholder rule.—Subsection (b)(6) shall not apply if at the time such option is granted the option price is at least 110 percent of the fair market value of the stock subject to the option and such option by its terms is not exercisable after the expiration of 5 years from the date such option is granted.

(6) Special rule when disabled.—For purposes of subsection (a)(2), in the case of an employee who is disabled (within the meaning of section 22 (e)(3)), the 3-month period of subsection (a)(2) shall be 1 year.

(7) Fair market value.—For purposes of this section, the fair market value of stock shall be determined without regard to any restriction other than a restriction which, by its terms, will never lapse.

(d) $100,000 per year limitation.—

(1) In general.—To the extent that the aggregate fair market value of stock with respect to which incentive stock options (determined without regard to this subsection) are exercisable for the 1st time by any individual during any calendar year (under all plans of the individual's employer corporation and its parent and subsidiary corporations) exceeds $100,000, such options shall be treated as options which are not incentive stock options.

(2) Ordering rule.—Paragraph (1) shall be applied by taking options into account in the order in which they were granted.

(3) Determination of fair market value.—For purposes of paragraph (1), the fair market value of any stock shall be determined as of the time the option with respect to such stock is granted.

* * *

SUBCHAPTER E—ACCOUNTING PERIODS AND METHODS OF ACCOUNTING

PART I—ACCOUNTING PERIODS

Editorial Summary

Accounting Periods

Subchapter E of Chapter 1 (Secs. 441–444)

Two factors that impact on the calculation of taxable income and the related tax liability are the accounting period (see Secs. 441–444) and the accounting method [see Secs. 446–448]. Recognizing the significance of these two factors, Congress has imposed substantial statutory constraints on each of these factors.

Section 441 provides that the taxable income and the related tax liability must be calculated for the taxpayer's taxable year. Generally, the taxable year is a twelve-month period. Exceptions are provided for a short-period return [see Sec. 443(b)(3)] and for a 52–53 week return [see Sec. 441(f)]. The taxable year may be a calendar year or it may be a fiscal year.

Limitations exist on freedom of choice in selecting the taxable year-end. These limitations vary depending on the type of taxpayer. The regular corporate taxpayer generally has more flexibility than do other types of taxpayers or tax reporters (e.g., individual, partnership, S corporation, personal service corporation). [see Secs. 706(b) (i.e., partnership); 441(i), (i.e., personal service corporation); and 1378, (i.e., S corporation)]. A general concept that applies to all of these types of taxpayers is that the IRS will permit the accounting period selected by the taxpayer if there is a sound business purpose (e.g., natural business year) for the selection. However, IRS policy is restrictive in terms of what constitutes such a sound business purpose.

The Revenue Act of 1987 provides the opportunity for partnerships, S corporations, and personal service corporations to elect a taxable year other than the required taxable year [see Sec. 444(a)]. However, this freedom to elect is subject to certain parameters [see Sec. 444(b)]. Partnerships and S corporations may be required to make additional tax liability payments as provided under Sec. 7519. Personal service corporations may have their salary deductions limited as provided under Sec. 280H.

A short-period return (i.e., a return for a period of less than 12 months) may occur for a number of reasons. Included are the return for the initial accounting period, a return associated with a change in the taxable year [see Sec. 442], and the final return (e.g., death of the individual taxpayer, complete liquidation of a corporation). In certain cases, the taxpayer is required under Sec. 443(b) to annualize the taxable income for the short period (i.e., gross up the taxable income as if the return had been for a full year). Annualization is required in order that tax avoidance not be achieved through avoiding the effect of the progressive tax rates. Section 443(e) provides a listing of various types of taxable income or tax liability determinations in which annualization is not required.

§ 441. Period for computation of taxable income

(a) Computation of taxable income.—Taxable income shall be computed on the basis of the taxpayer's taxable year.

(b) Taxable year.—For purposes of this subtitle, the term "taxable year" means—

(1) the taxpayer's annual accounting period, if it is a calendar year or a fiscal year;

(2) the calendar year, if subsection (g) applies;

(3) the period for which the return is made, if a return is made for a period of less than 12 months; or

(4) in the case of a DISC filing a return for a period of at least 12 months, the period determined under subsection (h).

(c) Annual accounting period.—For purposes of this subtitle, the term "annual accounting period" means the annual period on the basis of which the taxpayer regularly computes his income in keeping his books.

(d) Calendar year.—For purposes of this subtitle, the term "calendar year" means a period of 12 months ending on December 31.

(e) Fiscal year.—For purposes of this subtitle, the term "fiscal year" means a period of 12 months ending on the last day of any month other than December. In the case of any taxpayer who has made the election provided by subsection (f), the term means the annual period (varying from 52 to 53 weeks) so elected.

(f) Election of year consisting of 52–53 weeks.—

(1) General rule.—A taxpayer who, in keeping his books, regularly computes his income on the basis of an annual period which varies from 52 to 53 weeks and ends always on the same day of the week and ends always—

(A) on whatever date such same day of the week last occurs in a calendar month, or

(B) on whatever date such same day of the weeks falls which is nearest to the last day of a calendar month,

may (in accordance with the regulations prescribed under paragraph (3)) elect to compute his taxable income for purposes of this subtitle on the basis of such annual period. This paragraph shall apply to taxable years ending after the date of the enactment of this title.

(2) Special rules for 52–53-week year.—

(A) Effective dates.—In any case in which the effective date or the applicability of any provision of this title is expressed in terms of taxable years beginning, including, or ending with reference to a specified date which is the first or last day of a month, a taxable year described in paragraph (1) shall (except for purposes of the computation under section 15) be treated—

(i) as beginning with the first day of the calendar month beginning nearest to the first day of such taxable year, or

(ii) as ending with the last day of the calendar month ending nearest to the last day of such taxable year,

as the case may be.

* * *

(3) Special rule for partnerships, S corporations, and personal service corporations.—The Secretary may by regulation provide terms and conditions for the application of this subsection to a partnership, S corporation, or personal service corporation (within the meaning of section 441(i)(2)).

(4) Regulations.—The Secretary shall prescribe such regulations as he deems necessary for the application of this subsection.

(g) No books kept; no accounting period.—Except as provided in section 443 (relating to returns for periods of less than 12 months), the taxpayer's taxable year shall be the calendar year if—

(1) the taxpayer keeps no books;

(2) the taxpayer does not have an annual accounting period; or

(3) the taxpayer has an annual accounting period, but such period does not qualify as a fiscal year.

* * *

(i) Taxable year of personal service corporations.—

(1) In general.—For purposes of this subtitle, the taxable year of any personal service corporation shall be the calendar year unless the corporation establishes, to the satisfaction of the Secretary, a business purpose for having a different period for its taxable year. For purposes of this paragraph, any deferral of income to shareholders shall not be treated as a business purpose.

(2) Personal service corporation.—For purposes of this subsection, the term "personal service corporation" has the meaning given such term by section 269A(b)(1), except that section 269A(b)(2) shall be applied—

(A) by substituting "any" for "more than 10 percent", and

(B) by substituting "any" for "50 percent or more in value" in section 318(a)(2)(C).

A corporation shall not be treated as a personal service corporation unless more than 10 percent of the stock (by value) in such corporation is held by employee-owners (within the meaning of section 269A(b)(2), as modified by the preceding sentence). If a corporation is a member of an affiliated group filing a consolidated return, all members of such group shall be taken into account in determining whether such corporation is a personal service corporation.

§ 442. Change of annual accounting period

If a taxpayer changes his annual accounting period, the new accounting period shall become the taxpayer's taxable year only if the change is approved by the Secretary. For purposes of this subtitle, if a taxpayer to whom section 441(g) applies adopts an annual accounting period (as defined in section 441(c)) other than a calendar year, the taxpayer shall be treated as having changed his annual accounting period.

§ 443. Returns for a period of less than 12 months

(a) Returns for short period.—A return for a period of less than 12 months (referred to in this section as "short period") shall be made under any of the following circumstances:

(1) Change of annual accounting period.—When the taxpayer, with the approval of the Secretary, changes his annual accounting period. In such a case, the return shall be made for the short period beginning on the day after the close of the former taxable year and ending at the close of the day before the day designated as the first day of the new taxable year.

(2) Taxpayer not in existence for entire taxable year.—When the taxpayer is in existence during only part of what would otherwise be his taxable year.

(b) Computation of tax on change of annual accounting period.—

(1) General rule.—If a return is made under paragraph (1) of subsection (a), the taxable income for the short period shall be placed on an annual basis by multiplying the modified taxable income for such short period by 12, dividing the result by the number of months in the short period. The tax shall be the same part of the tax computed on the annual basis as the number of months in the short period is of 12 months.

(2) Exception.—

(A) Computation based on 12-month period.—If the taxpayer applies for the benefits of this paragraph and establishes the amount of his taxable income for the 12-month period described in subparagraph (B), computed as if that period were a taxable year and under the law applicable to that year, then the tax for the short period, computed under paragraph (1), shall be reduced to the greater of the following:

(i) an amount which bears the same ratio to the tax computed on the taxable income for the 12-month period as the modified taxable income computed on the basis of the short period bears to the modified taxable income for the 12-month period; or

(ii) the tax computed on the modified taxable income for the short period.

The taxpayer (other than a taxpayer to whom subparagraph (B)(ii) applies) shall compute the tax and file his return without the application of this paragraph.

(B) 12-month period.—The 12-month period referred to in subparagraph (A) shall be—

(i) the period of 12 months beginning on the first day of the short period, or

(ii) the period of 12 months ending at the close of the last day of the short period, if at the end of the 12 months referred to in clause (i) the taxpayer is not in existence or (if a corporation) has theretofore disposed of substantially all of its assets.

(C) Application for benefits.—Application for the benefits of this paragraph shall be made in such manner and at such time as the regulations prescribed under subparagraph (D) may require; except that the time so prescribed shall not be later than the time (including extensions) for filing the return for the first taxable year which ends on or after the day which is 12 months after the first day of the short period. Such application, in case the return was filed without regard to this paragraph, shall be considered a claim for credit or refund with respect to the amount by which the tax is reduced under this paragraph.

(D) Regulations.—The Secretary shall prescribe such regulations as he deems necessary for the application of this paragraph.

(3) Modified taxable income defined.—For purposes of this subsection the term "modified taxable income" means, with respect to any period, the gross income for such period minus the deductions allowed by this chapter for such period (but, in the case of a short period, only the adjusted amount of the deductions for personal exemptions).

(c) Adjustment in deduction for personal exemption.—In the case of a taxpayer other than a corporation, if a return is made for a short period by reason of subsection (a)(1) and if the tax is not computed under subsection (b)(2), then the exemptions allowed as a deduction under section 151 (and any deduction in lieu thereof) shall be reduced to amounts which bear the same ratio to the full exemptions as the number of months in the short period bears to 12.

(d) Adjustment in computing minimum tax and tax preferences.—If a return is made for a short period by reason of subsection (a)—

(1) the alternative minimum taxable income for the short period shall be placed on an annual basis by multiplying such amount by 12 and dividing the result by the number of months in the short period, and

(2) the amount computed under paragraph (1) of section 55(a) shall bear the same relation to the tax computed on the annual basis as the number of months in the short period bears to 12.

(e) Cross references.—

For inapplicability of subsection (b) in computing—

(1) Accumulated earnings tax, see section 536.

(2) Personal holding company tax, see section 546.

* * *

§ 444. Election of taxable year other than required taxable year

(a) General rule.—Except as otherwise provided in this subsection, a partnership, S corporation, or personal service corporation may elect to have a taxable year other than the required taxable year.

(b) Limitations on taxable years which may be elected.—

(1) In general.—Except as provided in paragraphs (2) and (3), an election may be made under subsection (a) only if the deferral period of the taxable year elected is not longer than 3 months.

(2) Changes in taxable year.—Except as provided in paragraph (3), in the case of an entity changing a taxable year, an election may be made under subsection (a) only if the deferral period of the taxable year elected is not longer than the shorter of—

(A) 3 months, or

(B) the deferral period of the taxable year which is being changed.

(3) Special rule for entities retaining 1986 taxable years.—In the case of an entity's 1st taxable year beginning after December 31, 1986, an entity may elect a taxable year under subsection (a) which is the same as the entity's last taxable year beginning in 1986.

(4) Deferral period.—For purposes of this subsection, except as provided in regulations, the term "deferral period" means, with respect to any taxable year of the entity, the months between—

(A) the beginning of such year, and

(B) the close of the 1st required taxable year ending within such year.

(c) Effect of election.—If an entity makes an election under subsection (a), then—

(1) in the case of a partnership or S corporation, such entity shall make the payments required by section 7519, and

(2) in the case of a personal service corporation, such corporation shall be subject to the deduction limitations of section 280H.

(d) Elections.—

(1) Person making election.—An election under subsection (a) shall be made by the partnership, S corporation, or personal service corporation.

(2) Period of election.—

(A) In general.—Any election under subsection (a) shall remain in effect until the partnership, S corporation, or personal service corporation changes its taxable year or otherwise terminates such election. Any change to a required taxable year may be made without the consent of the Secretary.

(B) No further election.—If an election is terminated under subparagraph (A) or paragraph (3)(A), the partnership, S corporation, or personal service corporation may not make another election under subsection (a).

(3) Tiered structures, etc.—

(A) In general.—Except as otherwise provided in this paragraph—

(i) no election may be under subsection (a) with respect to any entity which is part of a tiered structure, and

(ii) an election under subsection (a) with respect to any entity shall be terminated if such entity becomes part of a tiered structure.

(B) Exceptions for structures consisting of certain entities with same taxable year.—Subparagraph (A) shall not apply to any tiered structure which consists only of partnerships or S corporations (or both) all of which have the same taxable year.

(e) Required taxable year.—For purposes of this section, the term "required taxable year" means the taxable year determined under section 706(b), 1378, or 441(i) without taking into account any taxable year which is allowable by reason of business purposes. Solely for purposes of the preceding sentence, sections 706(b), 1378, and 441(i) shall be treated as in effect for taxable years beginning before January 1, 1987.

(f) Personal service corporation.—For purposes of this section, the term "personal service corporation" has the meaning given to such term by section 441(i)(2).

(g) Regulations.—The Secretary shall prescribe such regulations as may be necessary to carry out the provisions of this section, including regulations to prevent the avoidance of subsection (b)(2)(B) or (d)(2)(B) through the change in form of an entity.

PART II—METHODS OF ACCOUNTING

Subpart

Editorial Summary

Accounting Method

Subchapter E of Chapter 1 (Secs. 446–448, 481, 482)

The method of accounting for the taxpayer is to be in accordance with that used in computing income for book purposes [see Sec. 446(a)]. This appears to require symmetry between the method of accounting used for tax purposes and for accounting (i.e., financial reporting) purposes. Thus, associated with audited financial statements for which an unqualified opinion is issued, this would require that the accounting methods be in accordance with generally accepted accounting principles. As discussed subsequently, this is not the statutory requirement. In fact, situations exist in which an accounting method that is in accordance with generally accepted accounting principles will not be acceptable for tax purposes.

The key to assigning the proper interpretation to the statutory language is the term "books." If the taxpayer maintains only a single set of books, then, in general, symmetry will exist in terms of the accounting methods for accounting purposes and tax purposes (i.e., for the rather obvious reason that only a single set of accounting methods will be used). However, this apparent symmetry can be avoided by maintaining one set of books for accounting purposes and another set for tax purposes.

Methods of accounting normally used are the cash method, the accrual method, or the hybrid method (i.e., a variant of the cash and accrual methods) [see Sec. 446(c)]. Two caveats are necessary with the previous sentence. First, statutory restrictions produce the result that the cash method for tax purposes will not produce exactly the same result as the cash method for accounting purposes, and the accrual method for tax purposes will not produce exactly the same result as the accrual method for accounting purposes. Second, statutory limitations restrict the taxpayer's ability to use the cash method and the hybrid method [see Secs. 447(a), 448(a)].

A short phrase that appears in Sec. 446(b) gives the IRS substantial discretionary power with respect to accounting methods. This is the phrase "clearly reflect income." This phrase served as the statutory authority for the Supreme Court decision in *Thor Power Tool Co.* [79-1 USTC ¶ 9139, 43 AFTR2d 79-362, 99 S.Ct. 773 (USSC, 1979)] in which the taxpayer's method of accounting was held to be invalid even though it was in accordance with generally accepted accounting principles. Further support for this authority for the IRS in the case of related entities is provided in Sec. 482.

Extensions of or variances from the three aforementioned methods of accounting appear in Secs. 451–460. These are covered in the subsequent editorial summary.

Special adjustments may be required if the taxpayer changes from one accounting method to another. These appear in Sec. 481.

SUBPART A—METHODS OF ACCOUNTING IN GENERAL

§ 446. General rule for methods of accounting

(a) General rule.—Taxable income shall be computed under the method of accounting on the basis of which the taxpayer regularly computes his income in keeping his books.

(b) Exceptions.—If no method of accounting has been regularly used by the taxpayer, or if the method used does not clearly reflect income, the computation of taxable income shall be made under such method as, in the opinion of the Secretary, does clearly reflect income.

(c) Permissible methods.—Subject to the provisions of subsections (a) and (b), a taxpayer may compute taxable income under any of the following methods of accounting—

(1) the cash receipts and disbursements method;

(2) an accrual method;

(3) any other method permitted by this chapter; or

(4) any combination of the foregoing methods permitted under regulations prescribed by the Secretary.

(d) Taxpayer engaged in more than one business.—A taxpayer engaged in more than one trade or business may, in computing taxable income, use a different method of accounting for each trade or business.

(e) Requirement respecting change of accounting method.—Except as otherwise expressly provided in this chapter, a taxpayer who changes the method of accounting on the basis of which he regularly computes his income in keeping his books shall, before computing his taxable income under the new method, secure the consent of the Secretary.

(f) Failure to request change of method of accounting.—If the taxpayer does not file with the Secretary a request to change the method of accounting, the absence of the consent of the Secretary to a change in the method of accounting shall not be taken into account—

(1) to prevent the imposition of any penalty, or the addition of any amount to tax, under this title, or

(2) to diminish the amount of such penalty or addition to tax.

§ 447. Method of accounting for corporations engaged in farming

(a) General rule.—Except as otherwise provided by law, the taxable income from farming of—

(1) a corporation engaged in the trade or business of farming, or

(2) a partnership engaged in the trade or business of farming, if a corporation is a partner in such partnership,

shall be computed on an accrual method of accounting. This section shall not apply to the trade or business of operating a nursery or sod farm or to the raising or harvesting of trees (other than fruit and nut trees).

(b) Preproductive period expenses.—
For rules requiring capitalization of certain preproductive period expenses, see section 263A.

(c) Exception for certain corporations.—For purposes of subsection (a), a corporation shall be treated as not being a corporation if it is—

(1) an S corporation, or

(2) a corporation the gross receipts of which meet the requirements of subsection (d).

(d) Gross receipts requirements.—

(1) In general.—A corporation meets the requirements of this subsection if, for each prior taxable year beginning after December 31, 1975, such corporation (and any predecessor corporation) did not have gross receipts exceeding $1,000,000. For purposes of the preceding sentence, all corporations which are members of the same controlled group of corporations (within the meaning of section 1563(a)) shall be treated as 1 corporation.

(2) Special rules for family corporations.—

(A) In general.—In the case of a family corporation, paragraph (1) shall be applied—

(i) by substituting "December 31, 1985," for "December 31, 1975," and

(ii) by substituting "$25,000,000" for "$1,000,000."

(B) Gross receipts test.—

(i) Controlled groups.—Notwithstanding the last sentence of paragraph (1), in the case of a family corporation—

(I) except as provided by the Secretary, only the applicable percentage of gross receipts of any other member of any controlled group of corporations of which such corporation is a member shall be taken into account, and

(II) under regulations, gross receipts of such corporation or of another member of such group shall not be taken into account by such corporation more than once.

(ii) Pass-thru entities.—For purposes of paragraph (1), if a family corporation holds directly or indirectly any interest in a partnership, estate, trust or other pass-thru entity, such corporation shall take into account its proportionate share of the gross receipts of such entity.

(iii) Applicable percentage.—For purposes of clause (i), the term "applicable percentage" means the percentage equal to a fraction—

(I) the numerator of which is the fair market value of the stock of another corporation held directly or indirectly as of the close of the taxable year by the family corporation, and

(II) the denominator of which is the fair market value of all stock of such corporation as of such time.

For purposes of this clause, the term "stock" does not include stock described in section 1563(c)(1).

(C) Family corporation.—For purposes of this section, the term "family corporation" means—

(i) any corporation if at least 50 percent of the total combined voting power of all classes of stock entitled to vote, and at least 50 percent of all other classes of stock of the corporation, are owned by members of the same family, and

(ii) any corporation described in subsection (h).

* * *

(g) Certain annual accrual accounting methods.—

(1) In general.—Notwithstanding subsection (a) or section 263A, if—

(A) for its 10 taxable years ending with its first taxable year beginning after December 31, 1975, a corporation or qualified partnership used an annual accrual method of accounting with respect to its trade or business of farming,

(B) such corporation or qualified partnership raises crops which are harvested not less than 12 months after planting, and

(C) such corporation or qualified partnership has used such method of accounting for all taxable years intervening between its first taxable year beginning after December 31, 1975, and the taxable year,

such corporation or qualified partnership may continue to employ such method of accounting for the taxable year with respect to its qualified farming trade or business.

(2) Annual accrual method of accounting defined.—For purposes of paragraph (1), the term "annual accrual method of accounting" means a method under which revenues, costs, and expenses are computed on an accrual method of accounting and the preproductive period expenses incurred during the taxable year are charged to harvested crops or deducted in determining the taxable income for such years.

(3) Certain nonrecognition transfers.—For purposes of this subsection, if—

(A) a corporation acquired substantially all the assets of a qualified farming trade or business from another corporation in a transaction in which no gain or loss was recognized to the transferor or transferee corporation, or

(B) a qualified partnership acquired substantially all the assets of a qualified farming trade or business from one of its partners in a transaction to which section 721 applies,

the transferee corporation or qualified partnership shall be deemed to have computed its taxable income on an annual accrual method of accounting during the period for which the transferor corporation or partnership computed its taxable income from such trade or business on an annual accrual method.

(4) Qualified partnership defined.—For purposes of this subsection—

(A) Qualified partnership.—The term "qualified partnership" means a partnership which is engaged in a qualified farming trade or business and each of the partners of which is a corporation other than—

(i) an S corporation, or

(ii) a personal holding company (within the meaning of section 542(a)).

(B) Qualified farming trade or business.—

(i) In general.—The term "qualified farming trade or business" means the trade or business of farming—

(I) sugar cane,

(II) any plant with a preproductive period (as defined in section 263A(e)(3)) of 2 years or less, and

(III) any other plant (other than any citrus or almond tree) if an election by the corporation under this subparagraph is in effect.

In the case of a partnership and for purposes of paragraph (3)(A), subclauses (II) and (III) shall not apply.

(ii) Effect of election.—For purposes of paragraphs (1) and (2) of section 263A(e), any election under this subparagraph shall be treated as if it were an election under subsection (d)(3) of section 263A.

(iii) Election.—Unless the Secretary otherwise consents, an election under this subparagraph may be made only for the corporation's 1st taxable year which begins after December 31, 1986, and during which the corporation engages in a farming business. Any such election, once made, may be revoked only with the consent of the Secretary.

(h) Exception for certain closely held corporations.—

(1) In general.—A corporation is described in this subsection if, on October 4, 1976, and at all times thereafter—

(A) members of 2 families (within the meaning of subsection (e)(1)) have owned (directly or through the application of subsection (e)) at least 65 percent of the total combined voting power of all classes of stock of such corporation entitled to vote, and at least 65 percent of the total number of shares of all other classes of stock of such corporation; or

(B)(i) members of 3 families (within the meaning of subsection (e)(1)) have owned (directly or through the application of subsection (e)) at least 50 percent of the total combined voting power of all classes of stock of such corporation entitled to vote, and at least 50 percent of the total number of shares of all other classes of stock of such corporation; and

(ii) substantially all of the stock of such corporation which is not so owned (directly or through the application of subsection (e)) by members of such 3 families is owned directly—

(I) by employees of the corporation or members of their families (within the meaning of section 267(c)(4)), or

(II) by a trust for the benefit of the employees of such corporation which is described in section 401(a) and which is exempt from taxation under section 501(a).

(2) Stock held by employees, etc.—For purposes of this subsection, stock which—

(A) is owned directly by employees of the corporation or members of their families (within the meaning of section 267(c)(4)) or by a trust described in paragraph (1)(B)(ii)(II), and

(B) was acquired on or after October 4, 1976, from the corporation or from a member of a family which, on October 4, 1976, was described in subparagraph (A) or (B)(i) of paragraph (1),

shall be treated as owned by a member of a family which, on October 4, 1976, was described in subparagraph (A) or (B)(i) of paragraph (1).

(3) Corporation must be engaged in farming.—This subsection shall apply only in the case of a corporation which was, on October 4, 1976, and at all times thereafter, engaged in the trade or business of farming.

(i) Suspense account for family corporations.—

(1) In general.—If any family corporation is required by this section to change its method of accounting for any taxable year (hereinafter in this subsection referred to as the "year of the change"), notwithstanding subsection (f), such corporation shall establish a suspense account under this subsection in lieu of taking into account adjustments under section 481(a) with respect to amounts included in the suspense account.

(2) Initial opening balance.—The initial opening balance of the account described in paragraph (1) shall be the lesser of—

(A) the net adjustments which would have been required to be taken into account under section 481 but for this subsection, or

(B) the amount of such net adjustments determined as of the beginning of the taxable year preceding the year of change.

If the amount referred to in subparagraph (A) exceeds the amount referred to in subparagraph (B), notwithstanding paragraph (1), such excess shall be included in gross income in the year of the change.

(3) Inclusion where corporation ceases to be a family corporation.—

(A) In general.—If the corporation ceases to be a family corporation during any taxable year, the amount in the suspense account (after taking into account prior reductions) shall be included in gross income for such taxable year.

(B) Special rule for certain transfers.—For purposes of subparagraph (A), any transfer in a corporation after December 15, 1987, shall be treated as a transfer to a person whose ownership could not qualify such corporation as a family corporation unless it is a transfer—

(i) to a member of the family of the transferor, or

(ii) in the case of a corporation described in subsection (h), to a member of a family which on December 15, 1987, held stock in such corporation which qualified the corporation under subsection (h).

(4) Subchapter transactions.—The application of this subsection with respect to a taxpayer which is a party to any transaction with respect to which there is nonrecognition of gain or loss to any party by reason of subchapter C shall be determined under regulations prescribed by the Secretary.

(5) Termination.—

(A) In general.—No suspense account may be established under this subsection by any corporation required by this section to change its method of accounting for any taxable year ending after June 8, 1997.

* * *

§ 448. Limitation on use of cash method of accounting

(a) General rule.—Except as otherwise provided in this section, in the case of a—

(1) C corporation,

(2) partnership which has a C corporation as a partner, or

(3) tax shelter,

taxable income shall not be computed under the cash receipts and disbursements method of accounting.

(b) Exceptions.—

(1) Farming business.—Paragraphs (1) and (2) of subsection (a) shall not apply to any farming business.

(2) Qualified personal service corporations.—Paragraphs (1) and (2) of subsection (a) shall not apply to a qualified personal service corporation, and such a corporation shall be treated as an individual for purposes of determining whether paragraph (2) of subsection (a) applies to any partnership.

(3) Entities with gross receipts of not more than $5,000,000.—Paragraphs (1) and (2) of subsection (a) shall not apply to any corporation or partnership for any taxable year if, for all prior taxable years beginning after December 31, 1985, such entity (or any predecessor) met the $5,000,000 gross receipts test of subsection (c).

(c) $5,000,000 gross receipts test.—For purposes of this section—

(1) In general.—A corporation or partnership meets the $5,000,000 gross receipts test of this subsection for any prior taxable year if the average annual gross receipts of such entity for the 3-taxable-year period ending with such prior taxable year does not exceed $5,000,000.

(2) Aggregation rules.—All persons treated as a single employer under subsection (a) or (b) of section 52 or subsection (m) or (o) of section 414 shall be treated as one person for purposes of paragraph (1).

(3) Special rules.—For purposes of this subsection—

(A) Not in existence for entire 3-year period.—If the entity was not in existence for the entire 3–year period referred to in paragraph (1), such paragraph shall be applied on the basis of the period during which such entity (or trade or business) was in existence.

(B) Short taxable years.—Gross receipts for any taxable year of less than 12 months shall be annualized by multiplying the gross receipts for the short period by 12 and dividing the result by the number of months in the short period.

(C) Gross receipts.—Gross receipts for any taxable year shall be reduced by returns and allowances made during such year.

(D) Treatment of predecessors.—Any reference in this subsection to an entity shall include a reference to any predecessor of such entity.

(d) Definitions and special rules.—For purposes of this section—

(1) Farming business.—

(A) In general.—The term "farming business" means the trade or business of farming (within the meaning of section 263A(e)(4)).

(B) Timber and ornamental trees.—The term "farming business" includes the raising, harvesting, or growing of trees to which section 263A(c)(5) applies.

(2) Qualified personal service corporation.—The term "qualified personal service corporation" means any corporation—

(A) substantially all of the activities of which involve the performance of services in the fields of health, law, engineering, architecture, accounting, actuarial science, performing arts, or consulting, and

(B) substantially all of the stock of which (by value) is held directly (or indirectly through 1 or more partnerships, S corporations, or qualified personal service corporations not described in paragraph (2) or (3) of subsection (a)) by—

(i) employees performing services for such corporation in connection with the activities involving a field referred to in subparagraph (A),

(ii) retired employees who had performed such services for such corporation,

(iii) the estate of any individual described in clause (i) or (ii), or

(iv) any other person who acquired such stock by reason of the death of an individual described in clause (i) or (ii) (but only for the 2-year period beginning on the date of the death of such individual).

To the extent provided in regulations which shall be prescribed by the Secretary, indirect holdings through a trust shall be taken into account under subparagraph (B).

(3) Tax shelter defined.—The term "tax shelter" has the meaning given such term by section 461(i)(3) (determined after application of paragraph (4) thereof). An S corporation shall not be treated as a tax shelter for purposes of this section merely by reason of being required to file a notice of exemption from registration with a State agency described in section 461(i)(3)(A), but only if there is a requirement applicable to all corporations offering securities for sale in the State that to be exempt from such registration the corporation must file such a notice.

(4) Special rules for application of paragraph (2).—For purposes of paragraph (2)—

(A) community property laws shall be disregarded,

(B) stock held by a plan described in section 401(a) which is exempt from tax under section 501(a) shall be treated as held by an employee described in paragraph (2)(B)(i), and

(C) at the election of the common parent of an affiliated group (within the meaning of section 1504(a)), all members of such group may be treated as 1 taxpayer for purposes of paragraph (2)(B) if 90 percent or more of the activities of such group involve the performance of services in the same field described in paragraph (2)(A).

(5) Special rule for services.—In the case of any person using an accrual method of accounting with respect to amounts to be received for the performance of services by such person, such person shall not be required to accrue any portion of such amounts which (on the basis of experience) will not be collected. This paragraph shall not apply to any amount if interest is required to be paid on such amount or there is any penalty for failure to timely pay such amount.

(6) Treatment of certain trusts subject to tax on unrelated business income.—For purposes of this section, a trust subject to tax under section 511(b) shall be treated as a C corporation with respect to its activities constituting an unrelated trade or business.

(7) Coordination with section 481.—In the case of any taxpayer required by this section to change its method of accounting for any taxable year—

(A) such change shall be treated as initiated by the taxpayer,

(B) such change shall be treated as made with the consent of the Secretary, and

(C) the period for taking into account the adjustments under section 481 by reason of such change—

(i) except as provided in clause (ii), shall not exceed 4 years, and

(ii) in the case of a hospital, shall be 10 years.

(8) Use of related parties, etc.—The Secretary shall prescribe such regulations as may be necessary to prevent the use of related parties, pass-thru entities, or intermediaries to avoid the application of this section.

SUBPART B—TAXABLE YEAR FOR WHICH ITEMS OF GROSS INCOME INCLUDED

Editorial Summary

Special Accounting Methods: Income

Subchapter E of Chapter 1 (Secs. 451–460)

The general methods of accounting were covered in the previous editorial summary. Several of the special accounting methods for the reporting of income deal with organizations involved in very specific types of activities rather than being involved in transactions that permeate the general business environment (e.g., prepaid subscriptions under Sec. 455, prepaid dues under Sec. 456, sales returns for magazines, paperbacks, and records under Sec. 458). Two of the provisions, however, have a much broader impact: the installment method and the method of accounting for long-term contracts.

Prior to the Revenue Act of 1987, the installment sales provisions were divided into two major categories. Section 453A covered the installment method for dealers in personal property, whereas Sec. 453 dealt with the installment method for other situations. The Revenue Act of 1987 repealed the use of the installment method by dealers (i.e., dealers in personalty and in realty) [see Sec. 453(b)(2)(A)]. Exception treatment is provided for certain farm property, timeshares, and residential lots [see Sec. 453(1)]. However, for timeshares and residential lots, it may be necessary to pay interest on the deferred taxes [see Sec. 453(l)(3)].

Limitations on the deferral opportunity provided by the installment sales method include the deemed payment approach for related party installment sales [see Sec. 453(e)] and for the sales of depreciable property to a controlled entity [see Secs. 453(g), 1239(b)], recognition of gain that would be classified as ordinary income under the depreciation recapture rules [see Secs. 453(i), 1245, 1250] in the year of the installment sale, and recognition of gain on revolving credit plans and stock and securities traded on an established securities market in the year of sale [see Sec. 453(j)]. The Revenue Act of 1987 repealed the treatment of allocable installment indebtedness (which was created by the Tax Reform Act of 1986) as a deemed payment on the installment sale (i.e., Sec. 453C prior to repeal). However, the Revenue Act of 1987 created Sec. 453A which provided, in certain cases, for the payment of interest on the deferred taxes resulting from the use of the installment sales method [see Sec. 453A(a)(1)]. This Code section also provided for treating the pledging of the installment obligation as a deemed payment on the installment sale in certain cases [see Sec. 453A(a)(2)]. The Tax Relief Extension Act of 1999 provided that an accrual method taxpayer may not use the installment method (e.g., the sale of investment assets or the sale of a business [see Sec. 453(a)]. The Installment Tax Correction Act of 2000 repealed this limitation on accrual method taxpayers.

The two general accounting methods available for long-term contracts are the percentage of completion method and the completed contract method. Recognizing the revenue loss resulting from the deferral opportunity provided under the completed contract method, Congress, in the Tax Reform Act of 1986, substantially limited the ability to use the method. Unless the taxpayer qualifies for exception treatment, a hybrid method (part of the accounting effectively is under the percentage of completion method and part usually is under the completed contract method) replaces the completed contract method [see Sec. 460(a) before repeal by the Revenue Reconciliation Act of 1989].

This hybrid method associated with long-term contracts is referred to as the "percentage of completion-capitalized cost" method. Under TRA of 1986, the taxpayer was required to take into account 40 percent of the items under the contract using the percentage of completion method and the remaining 60 percent of the items could be accounted for using the completed contract method (i.e., or the taxpayer's normal method for accounting for long-term contracts) [see Sec. 460(a)(1)]. An exception to being required to use the percentage of completion—capitalized cost method was provided for certain small real estate construction contracts [see Sec. 460(e)(1)(B)]. The Revenue Act of 1987 increased the required percentage under the percentage of completion method from 40 percent to 70 percent. The Technical and Miscellaneous Revenue Act of 1988 increased the required percentage under the percentage of completion method from 70 percent to 90 percent. However, TAMRA of 1988 did provide for an additional exception for certain home construction contracts [see Sec. 460(e)(1)(A)]. If residential construction cannot satisfy the definitional requirements for *certain home construction contracts*, the 70 percent factor is used rather than the 90 percent factor [see Sec. 460(e)(5)].

The Revenue Reconciliation Act of 1989 repealed the percentage of completion—capitalized cost method. In so doing, it effectively eliminated the ability to account for any of the contract under the completed contract method except for the aforementioned exceptions for home construction contracts and small real estate construction contracts [see Sec. 460(a)].

While producing the result that generally the percentage of completion method is the only acceptable method to account for long-term contracts, the RRA of 1989 did contain a de minimis rule. This permits the taxpayer to elect to delay the recognition of revenues and the related costs until cumulative contract costs are at least 10 percent of the estimated contract costs [see Sec. 460(b)(5)].

To further limit tax deferral opportunities associated with the use of either the percentage of completion method or the percentage of completion-capitalized cost method, the Tax Reform Act of 1986 created a look-back method under which a determination is made of whether the Federal income taxes paid with respect to the contract in each year of the contract were more or less than the amount that would have been paid if the actual costs and contract price had been used rather than the anticipated contract price and costs [Secs. 460(b)(2)]. This determination is made in the year the contract is completed. Interest is then applied to the calculated underpayment or overpayment. Although this procedure could result in a payment by the government to the taxpayer, in most cases it probably results in additional tax liability.

Exceptions to the use of the percentage of completion method and the look-back method are provided for small long-term construction contracts and certain home construction contracts [see Sec. 460(e)].

§ 451. General rule for taxable year of inclusion

(a) General rule.—The amount of any item of gross income shall be included in the gross income for the taxable year in which received by the taxpayer, unless, under the method of accounting used in computing taxable income, such amount is to be properly accounted for as of a different period.

(b) Special rule in case of death.—In the case of the death of a taxpayer whose taxable income is computed under an accrual method of accounting, any amount accrued only by reason of the death of the taxpayer shall not be included in computing taxable income for the period in which falls the date of the taxpayer's death.

(c) Special rule for employee tips.—For purposes of subsection (a), tips included in a written statement furnished an employer by an employee pursuant to section 6053(a) shall be deemed to be received at the time the written statement including such tips is furnished to the employer.

(d) Special rule for crop insurance proceeds or disaster payments.—In the case of insurance proceeds received as a result of destruction or damage to crops, a taxpayer reporting on the cash receipts and disbursements method of accounting may elect to include such proceeds in income for the taxable year following the taxable year of destruction or damage, if he establishes that, under his practice, income from such crops would have been reported in a following taxable year. For purposes of the preceding sentence, payments received under the Agricultural Act of 1949, as amended or title II of the Disaster Assistance Act of 1988, as a result of (1) destruction or damage to crops caused by drought, flood, or any other natural disaster, or (2) the inability to plant crops because of such a natural disaster shall be treated as insurance proceeds received as a result of destruction or damage to crops. An election under this subsection for any taxable year shall be made at such time and in such manner as the Secretary prescribes.

(e) Special rule for proceeds from livestock sold on account of drought, flood, or other weather-related condition.—

(1) In general.—In the case of income derived from the sale or exchange of livestock in excess of the number the taxpayer would sell if he followed his usual business practices, a taxpayer reporting on the cash receipts and disbursements method of accounting may elect to include such income for the taxable year following the taxable year in which such sale or exchange occurs if he establishes that, under his usual business practices, the sale or exchange would not have occurred in the taxable year in which it occurred if it were not for drought, flood, or other weather-related conditions, and that such conditions had resulted in the area being designated as eligible for assistance by the Federal Government.

(2) Limitation.—Paragraph (1) shall apply only to a taxpayer whose principal trade or business is farming (within the meaning of section 6420(c) (3)).

(3) Special election rules.—If section 1033(e)(2) applies to a sale or exchange of stock described in paragraph (1), the election under paragraph (1) shall be deemed valid if made during the replacement period described in such section.

* * *

(g) Treatment of interest on frozen deposits in certain financial institutions.—

(1) In general.—In the case of interest credited during any calendar year on a frozen deposit in a qualified financial institution, the amount of such interest includible in the gross income of a qualified individual shall not exceed the sum of—

(A) the net amount withdrawn by such individual from such deposit during such calendar year, and

(B) the amount of such deposit which is withdrawable as of the close of the taxable year (determined without regard to any penalty for premature withdrawals of a time deposit).

(2) Interest tested each year.—Any interest not included in gross income by reason of paragraph (1) shall be treated as credited in the next calendar year.

(3) Deferral of interest deduction.—No deduction shall be allowed to any qualified financial institution for interest not includible in gross income under paragraph (1) until such interest is includible in gross income.

(4) Frozen deposit.—For purposes of this subsection, the term "frozen deposit" means any deposit if, as of the close of the calendar year, any portion of such deposit may not be withdrawn because of—

(A) the bankruptcy or insolvency of the qualified financial institution (or threat thereof), or

(B) any requirement imposed by the State in which such institution is located by reason of the bankruptcy or insolvency (or threat thereof) of 1 or more financial institutions in the State.

(5) Other definitions.—For purposes of this subsection, the terms "qualified individual," "qualified financial institution," and "deposit" have the same respective meanings as when used in section 165(l).

(h) Special rule for cash options for receipt of qualified prizes.

(1) In general.—For purposes of this title, in the case of an individual on the cash receipts and disbursements method of accounting, a qualified prize option shall be disregarded in determining the taxable year for which any portion of the qualified prize is properly includible in gross income of the taxpayer.

(2) Qualified prize option; qualified prize.—For purposes of this subsection.—

(A) In general.—The term "qualified prize option" means an option which—

(i) entitles an individual to receive a single cash payment in lieu of receiving a qualified prize (or remaining portion thereof), and

(ii) is exercisable not later than 60 days after such individual becomes entitled to the qualified prize.

(B) Qualified prize.—The term "qualified prize" means any prize or award which—

(i) is awarded as a part of a contest, lottery, jackpot, game, or other similar arrangement,

(ii) does not relate to any past services performed by the recipient and does not require the recipient to perform any substantial future service, and

(iii) is payable over a period of at least 10 years.

(3) Partnership, etc.—The Secretary shall provide for the application of this subsection in the case of a partnership or other pass-through entity consisting entirely of individuals described in paragraph (1).

* * *

§ 453. Installment method

(a) General rule.—Except as otherwise provided in this section, income from an installment sale shall be taken into account for purposes of this title under the installment method.

(b) Installment sale defined.—For purposes of this section—

(1) In general.—The term "installment sale" means a disposition of property where at least 1 payment is to be received after the close of the taxable year in which the disposition occurs.

(2) Exceptions.—The term "installment sale" does not include—

(A) Dealer disposition.—Any dealer disposition as defined in subsection (l).

(B) Inventories of personal property.—A disposition of personal property of a kind which is required to be included in the inventory of the taxpayer if on hand at the close of the taxable year.

(c) Installment method defined.—For purposes of this section, the term "installment method" means a method under which the income recognized for any taxable year from a disposition is that proportion of the payments received in that year which the gross profit (realized or to be realized when payment is completed) bears to the total contract price.

(d) Election out.—

(1) In general.—Subsection (a) shall not apply to any disposition if the taxpayer elects to have subsection (a) not apply to such disposition.

(2) Time and manner for making election.—Except as otherwise provided by regulations, an election under paragraph (1) with respect to a disposition may be made only on or before the due date prescribed by law (including extensions) for filing the taxpayer's return of the tax imposed by this chapter for the taxable year in which the disposition occurs. Such an election shall be made in the manner prescribed by regulations.

(3) Election revocable only with consent.—An election under paragraph (1) with respect to any disposition may be revoked only with the consent of the Secretary.

(e) Second dispositions by related persons.—

(1) In general.—If—

(A) any person disposes of property to a related person (hereinafter in this subsection referred to as the "first disposition"), and

(B) before the person making the first disposition receives all payments with respect to such disposition, the related person disposes of the property (hereinafter in this subsection referred to as the "second disposition"),

then, for purposes of this section, the amount realized with respect to such second disposition shall be treated as received at the time of the second disposition by the person making the first disposition.

(2) 2-year cutoff for property other than marketable securities.—

(A) In general.—Except in the case of marketable securities, paragraph (1) shall apply only if the date of the second disposition is not more than 2 years after the date of the first disposition.

(B) Substantial diminishing of risk of ownership.—The running of the 2-year period set forth in subparagraph (A) shall be suspended with respect to any property for any period during which the related person's risk of loss with respect to the property is substantially diminished by—

(i) the holding of a put with respect to such property (or similar property),

(ii) the holding by another person of a right to acquire the property, or

(iii) a short sale or any other transaction.

(3) Limitation on amount treated as received.—The amount treated for any taxable year as received by the person making the first disposition by reason of paragraph (1) shall not exceed the excess of—

(A) the lesser of—

(i) the total amount realized with respect to any second disposition of the property occurring before the close of the taxable year, or

(ii) the total contract price for the first disposition, over

(B) the sum of—

(i) the aggregate amount of payments received with respect to the first disposition before the close of such year, plus

(ii) the aggregate amount treated as received with respect to the first disposition for prior taxable years by reason of this subsection.

(4) Fair market value where disposition is not sale or exchange.—For purposes of this subsection, if the second disposition is not a sale or exchange, an amount equal to the fair market value of the property disposed of shall be substituted for the amount realized.

(5) Later payments treated as receipt of tax paid amounts.—If paragraph (1) applies for any taxable year, payments received in subsequent taxable years by the person making the first disposition shall not be treated as the receipt of payments with respect to the first disposition to the extent that the aggregate of such payments does not exceed the amount treated as received by reason of paragraph (1).

(6) Exception for certain dispositions.—For purposes of this subsection—

(A) Reacquisitions of stock by issuing corporation not treated as first dispositions.—Any sale or exchange of stock to the issuing corporation shall not be treated as a first disposition.

(B) Involuntary conversions not treated as second dispositions.—A compulsory or involuntary conversion (within the meaning of section 1033) and any transfer thereafter shall not be treated as a second disposition if the first disposition occurred before the threat or imminence of the conversion.

(C) Dispositions after death.—Any transfer after the earlier of—

(i) the death of the person making the first disposition, or

(ii) the death of the person acquiring the property in the first disposition,

and any transfer thereafter shall not be treated as a second disposition.

(7) Exception where tax avoidance not a principal purpose.—This subsection shall not apply to a second disposition (and any transfer thereafter) if it is established to the satisfaction of the Secretary that neither the first disposition nor the second disposition had as one of its principal purposes the avoidance of Federal income tax.

(8) Extension of statute of limitations.—The period for assessing a deficiency with respect to a first disposition (to the extent such deficiency is attributable to the application of this subsection) shall not expire before the day which is 2 years after the date on which the person making the first disposition furnishes (in such manner as the Secretary may by regulations prescribe) a notice that there was a second disposition of the property to which this subsection may have applied. Such deficiency may be assessed notwithstanding the provisions of any law or rule of law which would otherwise prevent such assessment.

(f) Definitions and special rules.—For purposes of this section—

(1) Related person.—Except for purposes of subsections (g) and (h), the term "related person" means—

(A) a person whose stock would be attributed under section 318(a) (other than paragraph (4) thereof) to the person first disposing of the property, or

(B) a person who bears a relationship described in section 267(b) to the person first disposing of the property.

(2) Marketable securities.—The term "marketable securities" means any security for which, as of the date of the disposition, there was a market on an established securities market or otherwise.

(3) Payment.—Except as provided in paragraph (4), the term "payment" does not include the receipt of evidences of indebtedness of the person acquiring the property (whether or not payment of such indebtedness is guaranteed by another person).

(4) Purchaser evidences of indebtedness payable on demand or readily tradable.—Receipt of a bond or other evidence of indebtedness which—

(A) is payable on demand, or

(B) is readily tradable,

shall be treated as receipt of payment.

(5) Readily tradable defined.—For purposes of paragraph (4), the term "readily tradable" means a bond or other evidence of indebtedness which is issued—

(A) with interest coupons attached or in registered form (other than one in registered form which the taxpayer establishes will not be readily tradable in an established securities market), or

(B) in any other form designed to render such bond or other evidence of indebtedness readily tradable in an established securities market.

(6) Like-kind exchanges.—In the case of any exchange described in section 1031(b)—

(A) the total contract price shall be reduced to take into account the amount of any property permitted to be received in such exchange without recognition of gain,

(B) the gross profit from such exchange shall be reduced to take into account any amount not recognized by reason of section 1031(b), and

(C) the term "payment," when used in any provision of this section other than subsection (b)(1), shall not include any property permitted to be received in such exchange without recognition of gain.

Similar rules shall apply in the case of an exchange which is described in section 356(a) and is not treated as a dividend.

(7) Depreciable property.—The term "depreciable property" means property of a character which (in the hands of the transferee) is subject to the allowance for depreciation provided in section 167.

(8) Payments to be received defined.—The term "payments to be received" includes—

(A) the aggregate amount of all payments which are not contingent as to amount, and

(B) the fair market value of any payments which are contingent as to amount.

(g) Sale of depreciable property to controlled entity.—

(1) In general.—In the case of an installment sale of depreciable property between related persons—

(A) subsection (a) shall not apply,

(B) for purposes of this title—

(i) except as provided in clause (ii), all payments to be received shall be treated as received in the year of the disposition, and

(ii) in the case of any payments which are contingent as to amount but with respect to which the fair market value may not be reasonably ascertained, the basis shall be recovered ratably, and

(C) the purchaser may not increase the basis of any property acquired in such sale by any amount before the time such amount is includible in the gross income of the seller.

(2) Exception where tax avoidance not a principal purpose.—Paragraph (1) shall not apply if it is established to the satisfaction of the Secretary that the disposition did not have as one of its principal purposes the avoidance of Federal income tax.

(3) Related persons.—For purposes of this subsection, the term "related persons" has the meaning given to such term by section 1239(b), except that such term shall include 2 or more partnerships having a relationship to each other described in section 707(b)(1)(B).

(h) Use of installment method by shareholders in certain liquidations.—

(1) Receipt of obligations not treated as receipt of payment.—

(A) In general.—If, in a liquidation to which section 331 applies, the shareholder receives (in exchange for the shareholder's stock) an installment obligation acquired in respect of a sale or exchange by the corporation during the 12-month period beginning on the date a plan of complete liquidation is adopted and the liquidation is completed during such 12-month period, then, for purposes of this section, the receipt of payments under such obligation (but not the receipt of such obligation) by the shareholder shall be treated as the receipt of payment for the stock.

(B) Obligations attributable to sale of inventory must result from bulk sale.—Subparagraph (A) shall not apply to an installment obligation acquired in respect of a sale or exchange of—

(i) stock in trade of the corporation,

(ii) other property of a kind which would properly be included in the inventory of the corporation if on hand at the close of the taxable year, and

(iii) property held by the corporation primarily for sale to customers in the ordinary course of its trade or business,

unless such sale or exchange is to 1 person in 1 transaction and involves substantially all of such property attributable to a trade or business of the corporation.

(C) Special rule where obligor and shareholder are related persons.—If the obligor of any installment obligation and the shareholder are married to each other or are related persons (within the meaning of section 1239(b)), to the extent such installment obligation is attributable to the disposition by the corporation of depreciable property—

(i) subparagraph (A) shall not apply to such obligation, and

(ii) for purposes of this title, all payments to be received by the shareholder shall be deemed received in the year the shareholder receives the obligation.

(D) Coordination with subsection (e)(1)(A).—For purposes of subsection (e)(1)(A), disposition of property by the corporation shall be treated also as disposition of such property by the shareholder.

(E) Sales by liquidating subsidiaries.—For purposes of subparagraph (A), in the case of a controlling corporate shareholder (within the meaning of section 368(c)) of a selling corporation, an obligation acquired in respect of a sale or exchange by the selling corporation shall be treated as so acquired by such controlling corporate shareholder. The preceding sentence shall be applied successively to each controlling corporate shareholder above such controlling corporate shareholder.

(2) Distributions received in more than 1 taxable year of shareholder.—If—

(A) paragraph (1) applies with respect to any installment obligation received by a shareholder from a corporation, and

(B) by reason of the liquidation such shareholder receives property in more than 1 taxable year,

then, on completion of the liquidation, basis previously allocated to property so received shall be reallocated for all such taxable years so that the shareholder's basis in the stock of the corporation is properly allocated among all property received by such shareholder in such liquidation.

(i) Recognition of recapture income in year of disposition.—

(1) In general.—In the case of any installment sale of property to which subsection (a) applies—

(A) notwithstanding subsection (a), any recapture income shall be recognized in the year of the disposition, and

(B) any gain in excess of the recapture income shall be taken into account under the installment method.

(2) Recapture income.—For purposes of paragraph 1, the term "recapture income" means, with respect to any installment sale, the aggregate amount which would be treated as ordinary income under section 1245 or 1250 (or so much of section 751 as relates to section 1245 or 1250) for the taxable year of the disposition if all payments to be received were received in the taxable year of disposition.

(j) Regulations.—

(1) In general.—The Secretary shall prescribe such regulations as may be necessary or appropriate to carry out the provisions of this section.

(2) Selling price not readily ascertainable.—The regulations prescribed under paragraph (1) shall include regulations providing for ratable basis recovery in transactions where the gross profit or the total contract price (or both) cannot be readily ascertained.

(k) Current inclusion in case of revolving credit plans, etc.—In the case of—

(1) any disposition of personal property under a revolving credit plan, or

(2) any installment obligation arising out of a sale of—

(A) stock or securities which are traded on an established securities market, or

(B) to the extent provided in regulations, property (other than stock or securities) of a kind regularly traded on an established market,

subsection (a) shall not apply, and, for purposes of this title, all payments to be received shall be treated as received in the year of disposition. The Secretary may provide for the application of this subsection in whole or in part for transactions in which the rules of this subsection otherwise would be avoided through the use of related parties, pass-thru entities, or intermediaries.

(l) Dealer dispositions.—For purposes of subsection (b)(2)(A)—

(1) In general.—The term "dealer disposition" means any of the following dispositions:

(A) Personal property.—Any disposition of personal property by a person who regularly sells or otherwise disposes of personal property of the same type on the installment plan.

(B) Real property.—Any disposition of real property which is held by the taxpayer for sale to customers in the ordinary course of the taxpayer's trade or business.

(2) Exceptions.—The term "dealer disposition" does not include—

(A) Farm property.—The disposition on the installment plan of any property used or produced in the trade or business of farming (within the meaning of section 2032A(e)(4) or (5)).

(B) Timeshares and residential lots.—

(i) In general.—Any dispositions described in clause (ii) on the installment plan if the taxpayer elects to have paragraph (3) apply to any installment obligations which arise from such dispositions. An election under this paragraph shall not apply with respect to an installment obligation which is guaranteed by any person other than an individual.

(ii) Dispositions to which subparagraph applies.—A disposition is described in this clause if it is a disposition in the ordinary course of the taxpayer's trade or business to an individual of—

(I) a timeshare right to use or a timeshare ownership interest in residential real property for not more than 6 weeks per year, or a right to use specified campgrounds for recreational purposes, or

(II) Any residential lot, but only if the taxpayer (or any related person) is not to make any improvements with respect to such lot.

For purposes of subclause (I), a timeshare right to use (or timeshare ownership interest in) property held by the spouse, children, grandchildren, or parents of an individual shall be treated as held by such individual.

(C) Carrying charges or interest.—Any carrying charges or interest with respect to a disposition described in subparagraph (A) or (B) which are added on the books of account of the seller to the established cash selling price of the property shall be included in the total contract price of the property and, if such charges or interest are not so included, any payments received shall be treated as applying first against such carrying charges or interest.

(3) Payment of interest on timeshares and residential lots.—

(A) In general.—In the case of any installment obligation to which paragraph (2)(B) applies, the tax imposed by this chapter for any taxable year for which payment is received on such obligation shall be increased by the amount of interest determined in the manner provided under subparagraph (B).

(B) Computation of interest.—

(i) In general.—The amount of interest referred to in subparagraph (A) for any taxable year shall be determined—

(I) on the amount of the tax for such taxable year which is attributable to the payments received during such taxable year on installment obligations to which this subsection applies,

(II) for the period beginning on the date of sale, and ending on the date such payment is received, and

(III) by using the applicable Federal rate under section 1274 (without regard to subsection (d)(2) thereof) in effect at the time of the sale compounded semiannually.

(ii) Interest not taken into account.—For purposes of clause (i), the portion of any tax attributable to the receipt of any payment shall be determined without regard to any interest imposed under subparagraph (A).

(iii) Taxable year of sale.—No interest shall be determined for any payment received in the taxable year of the disposition from which the installment obligation arises.

(C) Treatment as interest.—Any amount payable under this paragraph shall be taken into account in computing the amount of any deduction allowable to the taxpayer for interest paid or accrued during such taxable year.

§ 453A. Special rules for nondealers

(a) General rule.—In the case of an installment obligation to which this section applies—

(1) interest shall be paid on the deferred tax liability with respect to such obligation in the manner provided under subsection (c), and

(2) the pledging rules under subsection (d) shall apply.

(b) Installment obligations to which section applies.—

(1) In general.—This section shall apply to any obligation which arises from the disposition of any property under the installment method, but only if the sales price of such property exceeds $150,000.

(2) Special rule for interest payments.—For purposes of subsection (a)(1), this section shall apply to an obligation described in paragraph (1) arising during a taxable year only if—

(A) such obligation is outstanding as of the close of such taxable year, and

(B) the face amount of all such obligations held by the taxpayer which arose during, and are outstanding as of the close of, such taxable year exceeds $5,000,000.

Except as provided in regulations, all persons treated as a single employer under subsection (a) or (b) of section 52 shall be treated as one person for purposes of this paragraph and subsection (c)(4).

(3) Exception for personal use and farm property.—An installment obligation shall not be treated as described in paragraph (1) if it arises from the disposition—

(A) by an individual of personal use property (within the meaning of section 1275(b)(3)), or

(B) of any property used or produced in the trade or business of farming (within the meaning of section 2032A(e)(4) or (5)).

(4) Special rule for timeshares and residential lots.—An installment obligation shall not be treated as described in paragraph (1) if it arises from a disposition described in section 453(l)(2)(B), but the provisions of section 453(l)(3) (relating to interest payments on timeshares and residential lots) shall apply to such obligation.

(5) Sales price.—For purposes of paragraph (1), all sales or exchanges which are part of the same transaction (or a series of related transactions) shall be treated as 1 sale or exchange.

(c) Interest on deferred tax liability.—

(1) In general.—If an obligation to which this section applies is outstanding as of the close of any taxable year, the tax imposed by this chapter for such taxable year shall be increased by the amount of interest determined in the manner provided under paragraph (2).

(2) Computation of interest.—For purposes of paragraph (1), the interest for any taxable year shall be an amount equal to the product of—

(A) the applicable percentage of the deferred tax liability with respect to such obligation, multiplied by

(B) the underpayment rate in effect under section 6621(a)(2) for the month with or within which the taxable year ends.

(3) Deferred tax liability.—For purposes of this section, the term "deferred tax liability" means, with respect to any taxable year, the product of—

(A) the amount of gain with respect to an obligation which has not been recognized as of the close of such taxable year, multiplied by

(B) the maximum rate of tax in effect under section 1 or 11, whichever is appropriate, for such taxable year.

For purposes of applying the preceding sentence with respect to so much of the gain which, when recognized, will be treated as long-term capital gain, the maximum rate on net capital gain under section 1(h) or 1201 (whichever is appropriate) shall be taken into account.

(4) Applicable percentage.—For purposes of this subsection, the term "applicable percentage" means, with respect to obligations arising in any taxable year, the percentage determined by dividing—

(A) the portion of the aggregate face amount of such obligations outstanding as of the close of such taxable year in excess of $5,000,000, by

(B) the aggregate face amount of such obligations outstanding as of the close of such taxable year.

(5) Treatment as interest.—Any amount payable under this subsection shall be taken into account in computing the amount of any deduction allowable to the taxpayer for interest paid or accrued during the taxable year.

(6) Regulations.—The Secretary shall prescribe such regulations as may be necessary to carry out the provisions of this subsection including regulations providing for the application of this subsection in the case of contingent payments, short taxable years, and pass-thru entities.

(d) Pledges, etc., of installment obligations.—

(1) In general.—For purposes of section 453, if any indebtedness (hereinafter in this subsection referred to as "secured indebtedness") is secured by an installment obligation to which this section applies, the net proceeds of the secured indebtedness shall be treated as a payment received on such installment obligation as of the later of—

(A) the time the indebtedness becomes secured indebtedness, or

(B) the time the proceeds of such indebtedness are received by the taxpayer.

(2) Limitation based on total contract price.—The amount treated as received under paragraph (1) by reason of any secured indebtedness shall not exceed the excess (if any) of—

(A) the total contract price, over

(B) any portion of the total contract price received under the contract before the later of the times referred to in subparagraph (A) or (B) of paragraph (1) (including amounts previously treated as received under paragraph (1) but not including amounts not taken into account by reason of paragraph (3)).

(3) Later payments treated as receipt of tax paid amounts.—If any amount is treated as received under paragraph (1) with respect to any installment obligation, subsequent payments received on such obligation shall not be taken into account for purposes of section 453 to the extent that the aggregate of such subsequent payments does not exceed the aggregate amount treated as received under paragraph (1).

(4) Secured indebtedness.—For purposes of this subsection indebtedness is secured by an installment obligation to the extent that payment of principal or interest on such indebtedness is directly secured (under the terms of the indebtedness or any underlying arrangements) by any interest in such installment obligation. A payment shall be treated as directly secured by an interest in an installment obligation to the extent an arrangement allows the taxpayer to satisfy all or a portion of the indebtedness with the installment obligation.

(e) Regulations.—The Secretary shall prescribe such regulations as may be necessary to carry out the purposes of this section, including regulations—

(1) disallowing the use of the installment method in whole or in part for transactions in which the rules of this section otherwise would be avoided through the use of related persons, pass-thru entities, or intermediaries, and

(2) providing that the sale of an interest in a partnership or other pass-thru entity will be treated as a sale of the proportionate share of the assets of the partnership or other entity.

§ 453B. Gain or loss disposition of installment obligations

(a) General rule.—If an installment obligation is satisfied at other than its face value or distributed, transmitted, sold, or otherwise disposed of, gain or loss shall result to the extent of the difference between the basis of the obligation and—

(1) the amount realized, in the case of satisfaction at other than face value or a sale or exchange, or

(2) the fair market value of the obligation at the time of distribution, transmission, or disposition, in the case of the distribution, transmission, or disposition otherwise than by sale or exchange.

any gain or loss so resulting shall be considered as resulting from the sale or exchange of the property in respect of which the installment obligation was received.

(b) Basis of obligation.—The basis of an installment obligation shall be the excess of the face value of the obligation over an amount equal to the income which would be returnable were the obligation satisfied in full.

(c) Special rule for transmission at death.—Except as provided in section 691 (relating to recipients of income in respect of decedents), this section shall not apply to the transmission of installment obligations at death.

(d) Exception for distributions to which section 337(a) applies.—Subsection (a) shall not apply to any distribution to which section 337(a) applies.

* * *

(f) Obligation becomes unenforceable.—For purposes of this section, if any installment obligation is canceled or otherwise becomes unenforceable—

(1) the obligation shall be treated as if it were disposed of in a transaction other than a sale or exchange, and

(2) if the obligor and obligee are related persons (within the meaning of section 453(f)(1)), the fair market value of the obligation shall be treated as not less than its face amount.

(g) Transfers between spouses or incident to divorce.—In the case of any transfer described in subsection (a) of section 1041 (other than a transfer in trust)—

(1) subsection (a) of this section shall not apply, and

(2) the same tax treatment with respect to the transferred installment obligation shall apply to the transferee as would have applied to the transferor.

(h) Certain liquidating distributions by S Corporations.—If—

(1) an installment obligation is distributed by an S corporation in a complete liquidation, and

(2) receipt of the obligation is not treated as payment for the stock by reason of section 453(h)(1),

then, except for purposes of any tax imposed by Subchapter S, no gain or loss with respect to the distribution of the obligation shall be recognized by the distributing corporation. Under regulations prescribed by the Secretary, the character of the gain or loss to the shareholder shall be determined in accordance with the principles of section 1366(b).

§ 454. Obligations issued at discount

(a) Non-interest-bearing obligations issued at a discount.—If, in the case of a taxpayer owning any non-interest-bearing obligation issued at a discount and redeemable for fixed amounts increasing at stated intervals or owning an obligation described in paragraph (2) of subsection (c), the increase in the redemption price of such obligation occurring in the taxable year does not (under the method of accounting used in computing his taxable income) constitute income to him in such year, such taxpayer may, at his election made in his return for any taxable year, treat such increase as income received in such taxable year. If any such election is made with respect to any such obligation, it shall apply also to all such obligations owned by the taxpayer at the beginning of the first taxable year to which it applies and to all such obligations thereafter acquired by him and shall be binding for all subsequent taxable years, unless on application by the taxpayer the Secretary permits him, subject to such conditions as the Secretary deems necessary, to change to a different method. In the case of any such obligations owned by the taxpayer at the beginning of the first taxable year to which his election applies, the increase in the redemption price of such obligations occurring between the date of acquisition (or, in the case of an obligation described in paragraph (2) of subsection (c), the date of acquisition of the series E bond involved) and the first day of such taxable year shall also be treated as income received in such taxable year.

(b) Short-term obligations issued on discount basis.—In the case of any obligation—

(1) of the United States; or

(2) of a State or a possession of the United States, or any political subdivision of any of the foregoing, or of the District of Columbia,

which is issued on a discount basis and payable without interest at a fixed maturity date not exceeding 1 year from the date of issue, the amount of discount at which such obligation is originally sold shall not be considered to accrue until the date on which such obligation is paid at maturity, sold, or otherwise disposed of.

(c) Matured United States savings bonds.—In the case of a taxpayer who—

(1) holds a series E United States savings bond at the date of maturity, and

(2) pursuant to regulations prescribed under chapter 31 of title 31 (A) retains his investment in such series E bond in an obligation of the United States, other than a current income obligation, or (B) exchanges such series E bond for another nontransferable obligation of the United States in an exchange upon which gain or loss is not recognized because of section 1037 (or so much of section 1031 as relates to section 1037),

the increase in redemption value (to the extent not previously includible in gross income) in excess of the amount paid for such series E bond shall be includible in gross income in the taxable year in which the obligation is finally redeemed or in the taxable year of final maturity, whichever is earlier. This subsection shall not apply to a corporation, and shall not apply in the case of any taxable year for which the taxpayer's taxable income is computed under an accrual method of accounting or for which an election made by the taxpayer under subsection (a) applies.

* * *

§ 460. Special rules for long-term contracts

(a) Requirement that percentage of completion method be used.—In the case of any long-term contract, the taxable income from such contract shall be determined under the percentage of completion method (as modified by subsection (b)).

(b) Percentage of completion method.—

(1) Requirements of percentage of completion method.—Except as provided in paragraph (3), in the case of any long-term contract with respect to which the percentage of completion method is used—

(A) the percentage of completion shall be determined by comparing costs allocated to the contract under subsection (c) and incurred before the close of the taxable year with the estimated total contract costs, and

(B) upon completion of the contract (or, with respect to any amount properly taken into account after completion of the contract, when such amount is so properly taken into account), the taxpayer shall pay (or shall be entitled to receive) interest computed under the look-back method of paragraph (2).

In the case of any long-term contract with respect to which the percentage of completion method is used, except for purposes of applying the look-back method of paragraph (2), any income under the contract (to the extent not previously includible in gross income) shall be included in gross income for the taxable year following the taxable year in which the contract was completed.

For purposes of subtitle F (other than sections 6654 and 6655), any interest required to be paid by the taxpayer under subparagraph (B) shall be treated as an increase in the tax imposed by this chapter for the taxable year in which the contract is completed (or, in the case of interest payable with respect to any amount properly taken into account after completion of the contract, for the taxable year in which the amount is so properly taken into account).

(2) Look-back method.—The interest computed under the look-back method of this paragraph shall be determined by—

(A) first allocating income under the contract among taxable years before the year in which the contract is completed on the basis of the actual contract price and costs instead of the estimated contract price and costs,

(B) second, determining (solely for purposes of computing such interest) the overpayment or underpayment of tax for each taxable year referred to in subparagraph (A) which would result solely from the application of subparagraph (A), and

(C) then using the adjusted overpayment rate (as defined in paragraph (7)), compounded daily, on the overpayment or underpayment determined under subparagraph (B).

For purposes of the preceding sentence, any amount properly taken into account after completion of the contract shall be taken into account by discounting (using the Federal mid-term rate determined under section 1274(d) as of the time such amount is so properly taken into account) such amount to its value as of the completion of the contract. The taxpayer may elect with respect to any contract to have the preceding sentence not apply to such contract.

(3) Special rules.—

(A) Simplified method of cost allocation.—In the case of any long-term contract, the Secretary may prescribe a simplified procedure for allocation of costs to such contract in lieu of the method of allocation under subsection (c).

(B) Look-back method not to apply to certain contracts.—Paragraph (1)(B) shall not apply to any contract—

(i) the gross price of which (as of the completion of the contract) does not exceed the lesser of—

(I) $1,000,000 or

(II) 1 percent of the average annual gross receipts of the taxpayer for the 3 taxable years preceding the taxable year in which the contract was completed, and

(ii) which is completed within 2 years of the contract commencement date.

For purposes of this subparagraph, rules similar to the rules of subsections (e)(2) and (f)(3) shall apply.

(4) Simplified look-back method for pass-thru entities.—

(A) In general.—In the case of a pass-thru entity—

(i) the look-back method of paragraph (2) shall be applied at the entity level,

(ii) in determining overpayments and underpayments for purposes of applying paragraph (2)(B)—

(I) any increase in the income under the contract for any taxable year by reason of the allocation under paragraph (2)(A) shall be treated as giving rise to an underpayment determined by applying the highest rate for such year to such increase, and

(II) any decrease in such income for any taxable year by reason of such allocation shall be treated as giving rise to an over-payment determined by applying the highest rate for such year to such decrease, and

(iii) any interest required to be paid by the taxpayer under paragraph (2) shall be paid by such entity (and any interest entitled to be received by the taxpayer under paragraph (2) shall be paid to such entity).

(B) Exceptions.—

(i) Closely held pass-thru entities.—This paragraph shall not apply to any closely held pass-thru entity.

(ii) Foreign contracts.—This paragraph shall not apply to any contract unless substantially all of the income from such contract is from sources in the United States.

(C) Other definitions.—For purposes of this paragraph—

(i) Highest rate.—The term "highest rate" means—

(I) the highest rate of tax specified in section 11, or

(II) if at all times during the year involved more than 50 percent of the interests in the entity are held by individuals directly or through 1 or more other pass-thru entities, the highest rate of tax specified in section 1.

(ii) Pass-thru entity.—The term "pass-thru entity" means any—

(I) partnership,

(II) S corporation, or

(III) trust.

(iii) Closely held pass-thru entity.—The term "closely held pass-thru entity" means any pass-thru entity if, at any time during any taxable year for which there is income under the contract, 50 percent or more (by value) of the beneficial interests in such entity are held (directly or indirectly) by or for 5 or fewer persons. For purposes of the preceding sentence, rules similar to the constructive ownership rules of section 1563(e) shall apply.

(5) Election to use 10-percent method.—

(A) General rule.—In the case of any long-term contract with respect to which an election under this paragraph is in effect, the 10-percent method shall apply in determining the taxable income from such contract.

(B) 10-percent method.—For purposes of this paragraph—

(i) In general.—The 10-percent method is the percentage of completion method, modified so that any item which would otherwise be taken into account in computing taxable income with respect to a contract for any taxable year before the 10-percent year is taken into account in the 10-percent year.

(ii) 10–percent year.—The term "10-percent year" means the 1st taxable year as of the close of which at least 10 percent of the estimated total contract costs have been incurred.

(C) Election.—An election under this paragraph shall apply to all long-term contracts of the taxpayer which are entered into during the taxable year in which the election is made or any subsequent taxable year.

(D) Coordination with other provisions.—

(i) Simplified method of cost allocation.—This paragraph shall not apply to any taxpayer which uses a simplified procedure for allocation of costs under paragraph (3)(A).

(ii) Look-back method.—The 10-percent method shall be taken into account for purposes of applying the look-back method of paragraph (2) to any taxpayer making an election under this paragraph.

(6) Election to have look-back method not apply in de minimis cases.—

(A) Amounts taken into account after completion of contract.—Paragraph (1)(B) shall not apply with respect to any taxable year (beginning after the taxable year in which the contract is completed) if—

(i) the cumulative taxable income (or loss) under the contract as of the close of such taxable year, is within

(ii) 10 percent of the cumulative look-back taxable income (or loss) under the contract as of the close of the most recent taxable year to which paragraph (1)(B) applied (or would have applied but for subparagraph (B)).

(B) De minimis discrepancies.—Paragraph (1)(B) shall not apply in any case to which it would otherwise apply if—

(i) the cumulative taxable income (or loss) under the contract as of the close of each prior contract year, is within

(ii) 10 percent of the cumulative look-back income (or loss) under the contract as of the close of such prior contract year.

(C) Definitions.—For purposes of this paragraph—

(i) Contract year.—The term "contract year" means any taxable year for which income is taken into account under the contract.

(ii) Look-back income or loss.—The look-back income (or loss) is the amount which would be the taxable income (or loss) under the contract if the allocation method set forth in paragraph (2)(A) were used in determining taxable income.

(iii) Discounting not applicable.—The amounts taken into account after the completion of the contract shall be determined without regard to any discounting under the 2nd sentence of paragraph (2).

(D) Contracts to which paragraph applies.—This paragraph shall only apply if the taxpayer makes an election under this subparagraph. Unless revoked with the consent of the Secretary, such an election shall apply to all long-term contracts completed during the taxable year for which election is made or during any subsequent taxable year.

(7) Adjusted overpayment rate.—

(A) In general.—The adjusted overpayment rate for any interest accrual period is the overpayment rate in effect under section 6621 for the calendar year in which such interest accrual period begins.

(B) Interest accrual period.—For purposes of subparagraph (A), the term "interest accrual period" means the period—

(i) beginning on the day after the return due date for any taxable year of the taxpayer, and

(ii) ending on the return due date for the following taxable year.

For purposes of the preceding sentence, the term "return due date" means the date prescribed for filing the return of the tax imposed by this chapter (determined without regard to extensions).

(c) Allocation of costs to contract.—

(1) Direct and certain indirect costs.—In the case of a long-term contract, all costs (including research and experimental costs) which directly benefit, or are incurred by reason of, the long-term contract activities of the taxpayer shall be allocated to such contract in the same manner as costs are allocated to extended period long-term contracts under section 451 and the regulations thereunder.

(2) Costs identified under cost-plus and certain federal contracts.—In the case of a cost-plus long-term contract or a Federal long-term contract, any cost not allocated to such contract under paragraph (1) shall be allocated to such contract if such cost is identified by the taxpayer (or a related person), pursuant to the contract or Federal, State, or local law or regulation, as being attributable to such contract.

(3) Allocation of production period interest to contract.—

(A) In general.—Except as provided in subparagraphs (B) and (C), in the case of a long-term contract, interest costs shall be allocated to the contract in the same manner as interest costs are allocated to property produced by the taxpayer under section 263A(f).

(B) Production period.—In applying section 263A(f) for purposes of subparagraph (A), the production period shall be the period—

(i) beginning on the later of—

(I) the contract commencement date, or

(II) in the case of a taxpayer who uses an accrual method with respect to long-term contracts, the date by which at least 5 percent of the total estimated costs (including design and planning costs) under the contract have been incurred, and

(ii) ending on the contract completion date.

(C) Application of de minimis rule.—In applying section 263A(f) for purposes of subparagraph (A), paragraph (1)(B)(iii) of such section shall be applied on a contract-by-contract basis; except that, in the case of a taxpayer described in subparagraph (B)(i)(II) of this paragraph, paragraph (1)(B)(iii) of section 263A(f) shall be applied on a property-by-property basis.

(4) Certain costs not included.—This subsection shall not apply to any—

(A) independent research and development expenses,

(B) expenses for unsuccessful bids and proposals, and

(C) marketing, selling, and advertising expenses.

(5) Independent research and development expenses.—For purposes of paragraph (4), the term "independent research and development expenses" means any expenses incurred in the performance of research or development, except that such term shall not include—

(A) any expenses which are directly attributable to a long-term contract in existence when such expenses are incurred, or

(B) any expenses under an agreement to perform research or development.

(6) Special rule for allocation of bonus depreciation with respect to certain property.—

(A) In general.—Solely for purposes of determining the percentage of completion under subsection (b)(1)(A), the cost of qualified property shall be taken into account as a cost allocated to the contract as if subsection (k) of section 168 had not been enacted.

(B) Qualified property.—For purposes of this paragraph, the term "qualified property" means property described in section 168(k)(2) which—

(i) has a recovery period of 7 years or less, and

(ii) is placed in service after December 31, 2009, and before January 1, 2011 (January 1, 2012, in the case of property described in section 168(k)(2)(B)), or after December 31, 2012, and before January 1, 2014* (January 1, 2015,* in the case of property described in section 168(k)(2)(B)).

(d) Federal long-term contract.—For purposes of this section—

(1) In general.—The term "Federal long-term contract" means any long-term contract—

(A) to which the United States (or any agency or instrumentality thereof) is a party, or

(B) which is a subcontract under a contract described in subparagraph (A).

(2) Special rules for certain taxable entities.—For purposes of paragraph (1), the rules of section 168(h)(2)(D) (relating to certain taxable entities not treated as instrumentalities) shall apply.

(e) Exception for certain construction contracts.—

(1) In general.—Subsections (a), (b), and (c)(1) and (2) shall not apply to—

(A) any home construction contract, or

(B) any other construction contract entered into by a taxpayer—

(i) who estimates (at the time such contract is entered into) that such contract will be completed within the 2-year period beginning on the contract commencement date of such contract, and

(ii) whose average annual gross receipts for the 3 taxable years preceding the taxable

*Editorial comment: At the present time, this section has not been extended. There is pending legislation in the Senate, *The Tax Extenders Act of 2013 (S. 1859)*, that would extend Section 460(c)(6)(B)(ii) until January 1, 2015 and January 1, 2016 respectively.

year in which such contract is entered into do not exceed $10,000,000.

In the case of a home construction contract with respect to which the requirements of clauses (i) and (ii) of subparagraph (B) are not met, section 263A shall apply notwithstanding subsection (c)(4) thereof.

(2) Determination of taxpayer's gross receipts.—For purposes of paragraph (1), the gross receipts of—

(A) all trades or businesses (whether or not incorporated) which are under common control with the taxpayer (within the meaning of section 52(b)),

(B) all members of any controlled group of corporations of which the taxpayer is a member, and

(C) any predecessor of the taxpayer or a person described in subparagraph (A) or (B),

for the 3 taxable years of such persons preceding the taxable year in which the contract described in paragraph (1) is entered into shall be included in the gross receipts of the taxpayer for the period described in paragraph (1)(B). The Secretary shall prescribe regulations which provide attribution rules that take into account, in addition to the persons and entities described in the preceding sentence, taxpayers who engage in construction contracts through partnerships, joint ventures, and corporations.

(3) Controlled group of corporations.—For purposes of this subsection, the term "controlled group of corporations" has the meaning given to such term by section 1563(a), except that—

(A) "more than 50 percent" shall be substituted for "at least 80 percent" each place it appears in section 1563(a)(1), and

(B) the determination shall be made without regard to subsections (a)(4) and (e)(3)(C) of section 1563.

(4) Construction contract.—For purposes of this subsection, the term "construction contract" means any contract for the building, construction, reconstruction, or rehabilitation of, or the installation of any integral component to, or improvements of, real property.

(5) Special rule for residential construction contracts which are not home construction contracts.—In the case of any residential construction contract which is not a home construction contract, subsection (a) (as in effect on the day before the date of the enactment of the Revenue Reconciliation Act of 1989) shall apply except that such subsection shall be applied—

(A) by substituting "70 percent" for "90 percent" each place it appears, and

(B) by substituting "30 percent" for "10 percent."

(6) Definitions relating to residential construction contracts.—For purposes of this subsection—

(A) Home construction contract.—The term "home construction contract" means any construction contract if 80 percent or more of the estimated total contract costs (as of the close of the taxable year in which the contract was entered into) are reasonably expected to be attributable to activities referred to in paragraph 4 with respect to—

(i) dwelling units (as defined in section 168(e)(2)(A)(ii)) contained in buildings containing 4 or fewer dwelling units (as so defined), and

(ii) improvements to real property directly related to such dwelling units and located on the site of such dwelling units.

For purposes of clause (i), each townhouse or rowhouse shall be treated as a separate building.

(B) Residential construction contract.—The term "residential construction contract" means any contract which would be described in subparagraph (A) if clause (i) of such subparagraph reads as follows:

"(i) dwelling units (as defined in section 168(e)(2)(A)(ii)), and."

(f) Long-term contract.—For purposes of this section—

(1) In general.—The term "long-term contract" means any contract for the manufacture, building, installation, or construction of property if such contract is not completed within the taxable year in which such contract is entered into.

(2) Special rule for manufacturing contracts.—A contract for the manufacture of property shall not be treated as a long-term contract unless such contract involves the manufacture of—

(A) any unique item of a type which is not normally included in the finished goods inventory of the taxpayer, or

(B) any item which normally requires more than 12 calendar months to complete (without regard to the period of the contract).

(3) Aggregation, etc.—For purposes of this subsection, under regulations prescribed by the Secretary—

(A) 2 or more contracts which are interdependent (by reason of pricing or otherwise) may be treated as 1 contract, and

(B) a contract which is properly treated as an aggregation of separate contracts may be so treated.

(g) Contract commencement date.—For purposes of this section, the term "contract commencement date" means, with respect to any contract, the first date on which any costs (other than bidding expenses or expenses incurred in connection with negotiating the contract) allocable to such contract are incurred.

(h) Regulations.—The Secretary shall prescribe such regulations as may be necessary or appropriate to carry out the purposes of this section, including regulations to prevent the use of related parties, pass-thru entities, intermediaries, options, or other similar arrangements to avoid the application of this section.

SUBPART C—TAXABLE YEAR FOR WHICH DEDUCTIONS TAKEN

Editorial Summary

Special Accounting Methods: Deductions

Subchapter E of Chapter 1 (Secs. 461–475)

This part of Subchapter E deals with special accounting methods with respect to deductions. The coverage includes provisions which enable deductions to be taken and provisions which prevent (i.e., disallow or defer) deductions from being taken. The Code sections can be classified into four general categories:

1. General rule [see Sec. 461].
2. Special rules for certain deductions of specialized industries [see Secs. 464, 468, 468A, 468B].
3. Deduction or loss disallowance provisions [see Secs. 465, 469].
4. Inventory provisions [see Secs. 471–475].

With regard to deduction or loss disallowance provisions, several issues need to be addressed. First, to what types of taxpayers are the disallowance provisions applicable? Both the Sec. 465 at-risk provision and the Sec. 469 passive activity loss and credit provision are applicable only to certain types of taxpayers. Second, are the disallowed amounts eligible for utilization in other taxable years (i.e., do they qualify for carryback and/or carryover treatment) or are the disallowed amounts permanently lost? Both the Sec. 465 and Sec. 469 disallowed amounts may be used in other taxable years. Third, is there a statutory defined time period which limits the other taxable years in which the disallowed amounts can be utilized? Neither the Sec. 465 nor the Sec. 469 disallowed amounts is subject to such time period limitations.

The taxpayer has substantial flexibility in selecting the method of accounting for inventories to be used for tax purposes (e.g., specific identification, Fifo, Lifo). However, the IRS also is provided with substantial authority in this area through the Sec. 471 "most clearly reflecting income" standard.

In general, different methods may be used for accounting purposes and for tax purposes. However, an exception to this appears in Sec. 472, which requires symmetry between the methods for Lifo inventory.

The major benefit associated with the use of the Lifo inventory method is the potential ability to reduce taxable income through the layering of costs, starting with the most recent costs. The major disadvantage is the complexity and the related compliance cost to the taxpayer. Congress has attempted to reduce this complexity and cost for small businesses through the application of the simplified dollar-value Lifo method contained in Sec. 474.

A critical question that must be addressed for inventories, regardless of the particular method, is which costs should be included in inventory (i.e., the product cost versus the period cost issue). The uniform capitalization rules of Sec. 263A provide detailed rules on expensing versus capitalization for certain cost components.

The Revenue Reconciliation Act of 1993 requires the use of the mark to market accounting method for securities dealers which requires such dealers to recognize income before the gain is realized in a market transaction (see Sec 475).

§ 461. General rule for taxable year of deduction

(a) General rule.—The amount of any deduction or credit allowed by this subtitle shall be taken for the taxable year which is the proper taxable year under the method of accounting used in computing taxable income.

(b) Special rule in case of death.—In the case of the death of a taxpayer whose taxable income is computed under an accrual method of accounting, any amount accrued as a deduction or credit only by reason of the death of the taxpayer shall not be allowed in computing taxable income for the period in which falls the date of the taxpayer's death.

(c) Accrual of real property taxes.—

(1) In general.—If the taxable income is computed under an accrual method of accounting, then, at the election of the taxpayer, any real property tax which is related to a definite period of time shall be accrued ratably over that period.

(2) When election may be made.—

(A) Without consent.—A taxpayer may, without the consent of the Secretary, make an election under this subsection for his first taxable year in which he incurs real property taxes. Such an election shall be made not later than the time prescribed by law for filing the return for such year (including extensions thereof).

(B) With consent.—A taxpayer may, with the consent of the Secretary, make an election under this subsection at any time.

(d) Limitation on acceleration of accrual of taxes.—

(1) General rule.—In the case of a taxpayer whose taxable income is computed under an accrual method of accounting, to the extent that the time for accruing taxes is earlier than it would be but for any action of any taxing jurisdiction taken after December 31, 1960, then, under regulations prescribed by the Secretary, such taxes shall be treated as accruing at the time they would have accrued but for such action by such taxing jurisdiction.

(2) Limitation.—Under regulations prescribed by the Secretary, paragraph (1) shall be inapplicable to any item of tax to the extent that its application would (but for this paragraph) prevent all persons (including successors in interest) from ever taking such item into account.

(e) Dividends or interest paid on certain deposits or withdrawable accounts.—Except as provided in regulations prescribed by the Secretary, amounts paid to, or credited to the accounts of, depositors or holders of accounts as dividends or interest on their deposits or withdrawable accounts (if such amounts paid or credited are withdrawable on demand subject only to customary notice to withdraw) by a mutual savings bank not having capital stock represented by shares, a domestic building and loan association, or a cooperative bank shall not be allowed as a deduction for the taxable year to the extent such amounts are paid or credited for periods representing more than 12 months. Any such amount not allowed as a deduction as the result of the application of the preceding sentence shall be allowed as a deduction for such other taxable year as the Secretary determines to be consistent with the preceding sentence.

(f) Contested liabilities.—If—

(1) the taxpayer contests an asserted liability,

(2) the taxpayer transfers money or other property to provide for the satisfaction of the asserted liability,

(3) the contest with respect to the asserted liability exists after the time of the transfer, and

(4) but for the fact that the asserted liability is contested, a deduction would be allowed for the taxable year of the transfer (or for an earlier taxable year) determined after application of subsection (h),

then the deduction shall be allowed for the taxable year of the transfer. This subsection shall not apply in respect of the deduction for income, war profits, and excess profits taxes imposed by the authority of any foreign country or possession of the United States.

(g) Prepaid interest.—

(1) In general.—If the taxable income of the taxpayer is computed under the cash receipts and disbursements method of accounting, interest paid by the taxpayer which, under regulations prescribed by the Secretary, is properly allocable to any period—

(A) with respect to which the interest represents a charge for the use or forbearance of money, and

(B) which is after the close of the taxable year in which paid,

shall be charged to capital account and shall be treated as paid in the period to which so allocable.

(2) Exception.—This subsection shall not apply to points paid in respect of any indebtedness incurred in connection with the purchase or improvement of, and secured by, the principal residence of the taxpayer to the extent that, under regulations prescribed by the Secretary, such payment of points is an established business practice in the area in which such indebtedness is incurred, and the amount of such payment does not exceed the amount generally charged in such area.

(h) Certain liabilities not incurred before economic performance.—

(1) In general.—For purposes of this title, in determining whether an amount has been incurred with respect to any item during any taxable year, the all events test shall not be treated as met any earlier than when economic performance with respect to such item occurs.

(2) Time when economic performance occurs.—Except as provided in regulations prescribed by the Secretary, the time when economic performance occurs shall be determined under the following principles:

(A) Services and property provided to the taxpayer.—If the liability of the taxpayer arises out of—

(i) the providing of services to the taxpayer by another person, economic performance occurs as such person provides such services,

(ii) the providing of property to the taxpayer by another person, economic performance occurs as the person provides such property, or

(iii) the use of the property by the taxpayer, economic performance occurs as the taxpayer uses such property.

(B) Services and property provided by the taxpayer.—If the liability of the taxpayer requires the taxpayer to provide property or services, economic performance occurs as the taxpayer provides such property or services.

(C) Workers compensation and tort liabilities of the taxpayer.—If the liability of the taxpayer requires a payment to another person and—

(i) arises under any workers compensation act, or

(ii) arises out of any tort,

economic performance occurs as the payments to such person are made. Subparagraphs (A) and (B) shall not apply to any liability described in the preceding sentence.

(D) Other items.—In the case of any other liability of the taxpayer, economic performance occurs at the time determined under regulations prescribed by the Secretary.

(3) Exception for certain recurring items.—

(A) In general.—Notwithstanding paragraph (1) an item shall be treated as incurred during any taxable year if—

(i) the all events test with respect to such item is met during such taxable year (determined without regard to paragraph (1)),

(ii) economic performance with respect to such item occurs within the shorter of—

(I) a reasonable period after the close of such taxable year, or

(II) 8½ months after the close of such taxable year,

(iii) such item is recurring in nature and the taxpayer consistently treats items of such kind as incurred in the taxable year in which the requirements of clause (i) are met, and

(iv) either—

(I) such item is not a material item, or

(II) the accrual of such item in the taxable year in which the requirements of clause (i) are met results in a more proper match against income than accruing such item in the taxable year in which economic performance occurs.

(B) Financial statements considered under subparagraph (A)(iv).—In making a determination under subparagraph (A)(iv), the treatment of such item on financial statements shall be taken into account.

(C) Paragraph not to apply to workers compensation and tort liabilities.—This paragraph shall not apply to any item described in subparagraph (C) of paragraph (2).

(4) All events test.—For purposes of this subsection, the all events test is met with respect to any item if all events have occurred which determine the fact of liability and the amount of such liability can be determined with reasonable accuracy.

(5) Subsection not to apply to certain items.—This subsection shall not apply to any item for which a deduction is allowable under a provision of this title which specifically provides for a deduction for a reserve for estimated expenses.

(i) Special rules for tax shelters.—

(1) Recurring item exception not to apply.—In the case of a tax shelter, economic performance shall be determined without regard to paragraph (3) of subsection (h).

* * *

(3) Tax shelter defined.—For purposes of this subsection, the term "tax shelter" means—

(A) any enterprise (other than a C corporation) if at any time interests in such enterprise have been offered for sale in any offering required to be registered with any Federal or State agency having the authority to regulate the offering of securities for sale,

(B) any syndicate (within the meaning of section 1256(e)(3)(B)), and

(C) any tax shelter (as defined in section 6662(d)(2)(C)(ii)).

(4) Special rules for farming.—In the case of the trade or business of farming (as defined in section 464(e)), in determining whether an entity is a tax shelter, the definition of farming syndicate in section 464(c) shall be substituted for subparagraphs (A) and (B) of paragraph (3).

(5) Economic performance.—For purposes of this subsection, the term "economic performance" has the meaning given such term by subsection (h).

* * *

§ 464. Limitations on deductions for certain farming

(a) General rule.—In the case of any farming syndicate (as defined in subsection (c)), a deduction (otherwise allowable under this chapter) for amounts paid for feed, seed, fertilizer, or other similar farm supplies shall only be allowed for the taxable year in which such feed, seed, fertilizer, or other supplies are actually used or consumed, or, if later, for the taxable year for which allowable as a deduction (determined without regard to this section).

(b) Certain poultry expenses.—In the case of any farming syndicate (as defined in subsection (c))—

(1) the cost of poultry (including egg-laying hens and baby chicks) purchased for use in a trade or business (or both for use in a trade or business and for sale) shall be capitalized and deducted ratably over the lesser of 12 months or their useful life in the trade or business, and

(2) the cost of poultry purchased for sale shall be deducted for the taxable year in which the poultry is sold or otherwise disposed of.

(c) Farming syndicate defined.—

(1) In general.—For purposes of this section, the term "farming syndicate" means—

(A) a partnership or any other enterprise other than a corporation which is not an S corporation engaged in the trade or business of farming, if at any time interest in such partnership or enterprise have been offered for sale in any offering required to be registered with any Federal or State agency having authority to regulate the offering of securities for sale, or

(B) a partnership or any other enterprise other than a corporation which is not an S corporation engaged in the trade or business of farming, if more than 35 percent of the losses during any period are allocable to limited partners or limited entrepreneurs.

(2) Holdings attributable to active management.—For purposes of paragraph (1)(B), the following shall be treated as an interest which is not held by a limited partner or a limited entrepreneur:

(A) in the case of any individual who has actively participated (for a period of not less than 5 years) in the management of any trade or business of farming, any interest in a partnership or other enterprise which is attributable to such active participation,

(B) in the case of any individual whose principal residence is on a farm, any partnership or other enterprise engaged in the trade or business of farming such farm,

(C) in the case of any individual who is actively participating in the management of any trade or business of farming or who is an individual who is described in subparagraph (A) or (B), any participation in the further processing of livestock which was raised in such trade or business (or in the trade or business referred to in subparagraph (A) or (B)),

(D) in the case of an individual whose principal business activity involves active participation in the management of a trade or business of farming, any interest in any other trade or business of farming, and

(E) any interest held by a member of the family (or a spouse of any such member) of a grandparent of an individual described in subparagraph (A), (B), (C), or (D) if the interest in the partnership or the enterprise is attributable to the active participation of the individual described in subparagraph (A), (B), (C), or (D).

For purposes of subparagraph (A), where one farm is substituted for or added to another farm, both farms shall be treated as one farm. For purposes of subparagraph (E), the term "family" has the meaning given to such term by section 267(c)(4).

(d) Exception.—Subsection (a) shall not apply to any amount paid for supplies which are on hand at the close of the taxable year on account of fire, storm, or other casualty, or on account of disease or drought.

(e) Definitions.—For purposes of this section—

(1) Farming.—The term "farming" means the cultivation of land or the raising or harvesting of any agricultural or horticultural commodity including the raising, shearing, feeding, caring for, training, and management of animals. For purposes of the preceding sentence, trees (other than trees bearing fruit or nuts) shall not be treated as an agricultural or horticultural commodity.

(2) Limited entrepreneur.—The term "limited entrepreneur" means a person who—

(A) has an interest in an enterprise other than as a limited partner, and

(B) does not actively participate in the management of such enterprise.

(f) Subsections (a) and (b) to apply to certain persons prepaying 50 percent or more of certain farming expenses.—

(1) In general.—In the case of a taxpayer to whom this subsection applies, subsections (a) and (b) shall apply to the excess prepaid farm supplies of such taxpayer in the same manner as if such taxpayer were a farming syndicate.

(2) Taxpayer to whom subsection applies.—This subsection applies to any taxpayer for any taxable year if such taxpayer—

(A) does not use an accrual method of accounting,

(B) has excess prepaid farm supplies for the taxable year, and

(C) is not a qualified farm-related taxpayer.

(3) Qualified farm-related taxpayer.—

(A) In general.—For purposes of this subsection, the term "qualified farm-related taxpayer" means any farm-related taxpayer if—

(i) (I) the aggregate prepaid farm supplies for the 3 taxable years preceding the taxable year are less than 50 percent of,

(II) the aggregate deductible farming expenses (other than prepaid farm supplies) for such 3 taxable years, or

(ii) the taxpayer has excess prepaid farm supplies for the taxable year by reason of any change in business operation directly attributable to extraordinary circumstances.

(B) Farm-related taxpayer.—For purposes of this paragraph, the term "farm-related taxpayer" means any taxpayer—

(i) whose principal residence (within the meaning of section 121) is on a farm,

(ii) who has a principal occupation of farming, or

(iii) who is a member of the family (within the meaning of subsection (c)(2)(E)) of a taxpayer described in clause (i) or (ii).

(4) Definitions.—For purposes of this subsection—

(A) Excess prepaid farm supplies.—The term "excess prepaid farm supplies" means the prepaid farm supplies for the taxable year to the extent the amount of such supplies exceeds 50 percent of the deductible farming expenses for the taxable year (other than prepaid farm supplies).

(B) Prepaid farm supplies.—The term "prepaid farm supplies" means any amounts which are described in subsection (a) or (b) and would be allowable for a subsequent taxable year under the rules of subsections (a) and (b).

(C) Deductible farming expenses.—The term "deductible farming expenses" means any amount allowable as a deduction under this chapter (including any amount allowable as a deduction for depreciation or amortization) which is properly allocable to the trade or business of farming.

(g) Termination.—Except as provided in subsection (f), subsections (a) and (b) shall not apply to any taxable year beginning after December 31, 1986.

§ 465. Deductions limited to amount at risk

(a) Limitation to amount at risk.—

(1) In general.—In the case of—

(A) an individual, and

(B) a C corporation with respect to which the stock ownership requirement of paragraph (2) of section 542(a) is met,

engaged in an activity to which this section applies, any loss from such activity for the taxable year shall be allowed only to the extent of the aggregate amount with respect to which the taxpayer is at risk (within the meaning of subsection (b)) for such activity at the close of the taxable year.

(2) Deduction in succeeding year.—Any loss from an activity to which this section applies not allowed under this section for the taxable year shall be treated as a deduction allocable to such activity in the first succeeding taxable year.

(3) Special rules for applying paragraph (1)(B).—For purposes of paragraph (1)(B)—

(A) section 544(a)(2) shall be applied as if such section did not contain the phrase "or by or for his partner"; and

(B) sections 544(a)(4)(A) and 544(b)(1) shall be applied by substituting "the corporation meet the stock ownership requirements of section

542(a)(2)" for "the corporation a personal holding company."

(b) Amounts considered at risk.—

(1) In general.—For purposes of this section, a taxpayer shall be considered at risk for an activity with respect to amounts including—

(A) the amount of money and the adjusted basis of other property contributed by the taxpayer to the activity, and

(B) amounts borrowed with respect to such activity (as determined under paragraph (2)).

(2) Borrowed amounts.—For purposes of this section, a taxpayer shall be considered at risk with respect to amounts borrowed for use in an activity to the extent that he—

(A) is personally liable for the repayment of such amounts, or

(B) has pledged property, other than property used in such activity, as security for such borrowed amount (to the extent of the net fair market value of the taxpayer's interest in such property).

No property shall be taken into account as security if such property is directly or indirectly financed by indebtedness which is secured by property described in paragraph (1).

(3) Certain borrowed amounts excluded.—

(A) In general.—Except to the extent provided in regulations, for purposes of paragraph (1)(B), amounts borrowed shall not be considered to be at risk with respect to an activity if such amounts are borrowed from any person who has an interest in such activity or from a related person to a person (other than the taxpayer) having such an interest.

(B) Exceptions.—

(i) Interest as creditor.—Subparagraph (A) shall not apply to an interest as a creditor in the activity.

(ii) Interest as shareholder with respect to amounts borrowed by corporation.—In the case of amounts borrowed by a corporation from a shareholder, subparagraph (A) shall not apply to an interest as a shareholder.

(C) Related person.—For purposes of this subsection, a person (hereinafter in this paragraph referred to as the "related person") is related to any person if—

(i) the related person bears a relationship to such person specified in section 267(b) or section 707(b)(1), or

(ii) the related person and such person are engaged in trades or business under common control (within the meaning of subsections (a) and (b) of section 52).

For purposes of clause (i), in applying section 267(b) or 707(b)(1), "10 percent" shall be substituted for "50 percent."

(4) Exception.—Notwithstanding any other provision of this section, a taxpayer shall not be considered at risk with respect to amounts protected against loss through nonrecourse financing, guarantees, stop loss agreements, or other similar arrangements.

(5) Amounts at risk in subsequent years.—If in any taxable year the taxpayer has a loss from an activity to which subsection (a) applies, the amount with respect to which a taxpayer is considered to be at risk (within the meaning of subsection (b)) in subsequent taxable years with respect to that activity shall be reduced by that portion of the loss which (after the application of subsection (a)) is allowable as a deduction.

(6) Qualified nonrecourse financing treated as amount at risk.—For purposes of this section—

(A) In general.—Notwithstanding any other provision of this subsection, in the case of an activity of holding real property, a taxpayer shall be considered at risk with respect to the taxpayer's share of any qualified nonrecourse financing which is secured by real property used in such activity.

(B) Qualified nonrecourse financing.—For purposes of this paragraph, the term "qualified nonrecourse financing" means any financing—

(i) which is borrowed by the taxpayer with respect to the activity of holding real property,

(ii) which is borrowed by the taxpayer from a qualified person or represents a loan from any Federal, State, or local government or instrumentality thereof, or is guaranteed by any Federal, State, or local government,

(iii) except to the extent provided in regulations, with respect to which no person is personally liable for repayment, and

(iv) which is not convertible debt.

(C) Special rule for partnerships.—In the case of a partnership, a partner's share of any qualified nonrecourse financing of such partnership shall be determined on the basis of the partner's share of liabilities of such partnership incurred in connection with such financing (within the meaning of section 752).

(D) Qualified person defined.—For purposes of this paragraph—

(i) In general.—The term "qualified person" has the meaning given such term by section 49(a)(1)(D)(iv).

(ii) Certain commercially reasonable financing from related persons.—For purposes of clause (i), section 49(a)(1)(D)(iv) shall be applied without regard to subclause (I) thereof (relating to financing from related persons) if the financing from the related person is commercially reasonable and on substantially the same terms as loans involving unrelated persons.

(E) Activity of holding real property.—For purposes of this paragraph—

(i) Incidental personal property and services.—The activity of holding real property includes the holding of personal property and the providing of services which are incidental to making real property available as living accommodations.

(ii) Mineral property.—The activity of holding real property shall not include the holding of mineral property.

(c) Activities to which section applies.—

(1) Types of activities.—This section applies to any taxpayer engaged in the activity of—

(A) holding, producing, or distributing motion picture films or video tapes,

(B) farming (as defined in section 464(e)),

(C) leasing any section 1245 property (as defined in section 1245(a)(3)),

(D) exploring for, or exploiting, oil and gas resources as a trade or business or for the production of income, or

(E) exploring for, or exploiting, geothermal deposits (as defined in section 613(e)(2)).

(2) Separate activities.—For purposes of this section—

(A) In general.—Except as provided in subparagraph (B), a taxpayer's activity with respect to each—

(i) film or video tape,

(ii) section 1245 property which is leased or held for leasing,

(iii) farm,

(iv) oil and gas property (as defined under section 614), or

(v) geothermal property (as defined under section 614),

shall be treated as a separate activity.

(B) Aggregation rules.—

(i) Special rule for leases of section 1245 property by partnerships or S corporations.—In the case of any partnership or S corporation, all activities with respect to section 1245 properties which—

(I) are leased or held for lease, and

(II) are placed in service in any taxable year of the partnership or S corporation,

shall be treated as a single activity.

(ii) Other aggregation rules.—Rules similar to the rules of subparagraphs (B) and (C) of paragraph (3) shall apply for purposes of this paragraph.

(3) Extension to other activities.—

(A) In general.—In the case of taxable years beginning after December 31, 1978, this section also applies to each activity—

(i) engaged in by the taxpayer in carrying on a trade or business or for the production of income, and

(ii) which is not described in paragraph (1).

(B) Aggregation of activities where taxpayer actively participates in management of trade or business.—Except as provided in subparagraph (C), for purposes of this section, activities described in subparagraph (A) which constitute a trade or business shall be treated as one activity if—

(i) the taxpayer actively participates in the management of such trade or business, or

(ii) such trade or business is carried on by a partnership or an S corporation and 65 percent or more of the losses for the taxable year is allocable to persons who actively participate in the management of the trade or business.

(C) Aggregation or separation of activities under regulations.—The Secretary shall prescribe regulations under which activities described in subparagraph (A) shall be aggregated or treated as separate activities.

(D) Application of subsection (b)(3).—In the case of an activity described in subparagraph (A), subsection (b)(3) shall apply only to the extent provided in regulations prescribed by the Secretary.

(4) Exclusion for certain equipment leasing by closely-held corporations.—

(A) In general.—In the case of a corporation described in subsection (a)(1)(B) actively engaged in equipment leasing—

(i) the activity of equipment leasing shall be treated as a separate activity, and

(ii) subsection (a) shall not apply to losses from such activity.

(B) 50-percent gross receipts test.—For purposes of subparagraph (A), a corporation shall not be considered to be actively engaged in equipment leasing unless 50 percent or more of the gross receipts of the corporation for the taxable year is attributable, under regulations prescribed by the Secretary, to equipment leasing.

(C) Component members of controlled group treated as a single corporation.—For purposes of subparagraph (A), the component members of a controlled group of corporations shall be treated as a single corporation.

* * *

(6) Definitions relating to paragraphs (4) and (5).—For purposes of paragraphs (4) and (5)—

(A) Equipment leasing.—The term "equipment leasing" means—

(i) the leasing of equipment which is section 1245 property, and

(ii) the purchasing, servicing, and selling of such equipment.

(B) Leasing of master sound recordings, etc., excluded.—The term "equipment leasing" does not include the leasing of master sound recordings, and other similar contractual arrangements with respect to tangible or intangible assets associated with literary, artistic, or musical properties.

(C) Controlled group of corporations; component member.—The terms "controlled group of corporations" and "component member" have the same meanings as when used in section 1563. The determination of the taxable years taken into account with respect to any controlled group of corporations shall be made in a manner consistent with the manner set forth in section 1563.

(7) Exclusion of active businesses of qualified C corporations.—

(A) In general.—In the case of a taxpayer which is a qualified C corporation—

(i) each qualifying business carried on by such taxpayer shall be treated as a separate activity, and

(ii) subsection (a) shall not apply to losses from such business.

(B) Qualified C corporation.—For purposes of subparagraph (A), the term "qualified C corporation" means any corporation described in subparagraph (B) of subsection (a)(1) which is not—

(i) a personal holding company (as defined in section 542(a)), or

(ii) a personal service corporation (as defined in section 269A(b) but determined by substituting "5 percent" for "10 percent" in section 269A(b)(2)).

(C) Qualifying business.—For purposes of this paragraph, the term "qualifying business" means any active business if—

(i) during the entire 12-month period ending on the last day of the taxable year, such corporation had at least 1 full-time employee substantially all the services of whom were in the active management of such business,

(ii) during the entire 12-month period ending on the last day of the taxable year, such corporation had at least 3 full-time, nonowner employees substantially all of the services of whom were services directly related to such business,

(iii) the amount of the deductions attributable to such business which are allowable to the taxpayer solely by reason of sections 162 and 404 for the taxable year exceeds 15 percent of the gross income from such business for such year, and

(iv) such business is not an excluded business.

(D) Special rules for application of subparagraph (C).—

(i) Partnerships in which taxpayer is a qualified corporate partner.—In the case of an active business of a partnership, if—

(I) the taxpayer is a qualified corporate partner in the partnership, and

(II) during the entire 12-month period ending on the last day of the partnership's taxable year, there was at least 1 full-time employee of the partnership (or of a qualified corporate partner) substantially all the services of whom were in the active management of such business,

then the taxpayer's proportionate share (determined on the basis of its profits interest) of the activities of the partnership in such business shall be treated as activities of the taxpayer (and clause (i) of subparagraph (C) shall not apply in determining whether such business is a qualifying business of the taxpayer).

(ii) Qualified corporate partner.—For purposes of clause (i), the term "qualified corporate partner" means any corporation if—

(I) such corporation is a general partner in the partnership,

(II) such corporation has an interest of 10 percent or more in the profits and losses of the partnership, and

(III) such corporation has contributed property to the partnership in an amount not less than the lesser of $500,000 or 10 percent of the net worth of the corporation.

For purposes of subclause (III), any contribution of property other than money shall be taken into account at its fair market value.

(iii) Deduction for owner employee compensation not taken into account.—For purposes of clause (iii) of subparagraph (C), there shall not be taken into account any deduction in respect of compensation for personal services rendered by any employee (other than a non-owner employee) of the taxpayer or any member of such employee's family (within the meaning of section 318(a)(1)).

* * *

(E) Definitions.—For purposes of this paragraph—

(i) Non-owner employee.—The term "non-owner employee" means any employee who does not own, at any time during the taxable year, more than 5 percent in value of the outstanding stock of the taxpayer. For purposes of the preceding sentence, section 318 shall apply, except that "5 percent" shall be substituted for "50 percent" in section 318(a)(2)(C).

(ii) Excluded business.—The term "excluded business" means—

(I) equipment leasing (as defined in paragraph (6)), and

(II) any business involving the use, exploitation, sale, lease, or other disposition of master sound recordings, motion picture films, video tapes, or tangible or intangible assets associated with literary, artistic, musical, or similar properties.

* * *

(F) Affiliated group treated as 1 taxpayer.—For purposes of this paragraph—

(i) In general.—Except as provided in subparagraph (G), the component members of an affiliated group of corporations shall be treated as a single taxpayer.

(ii) Affiliated group of corporations.—The term "affiliated group of corporations" means an affiliated group (as defined in section 1504(a)) which files or is required to file consolidated income tax returns.

(iii) Component member.—The term "component member" means an includible corporation (as defined in section 1504) which is a member of the affiliated group.

(G) Loss of 1 member of affiliated group may not offset income of personal holding company or personal service corporation.—Nothing in this paragraph shall permit any loss of a member of an affiliated group to be used as an offset against the income of any other member of such group which is a personal holding company (as defined in section 542(a)) or a personal service corporation (as defined in section 269A(b) but determined by substituting "5 percent" for "10 percent" in section 269A(b)(2)).

(d) Definition of loss.—For purposes of this section, the term "loss" means the excess of the deductions allowable under this chapter for the taxable year (determined without regard to the first sentence of subsection (a)) and allocable to an activity to which this section applies over the income received or accrued by the taxpayer during the taxable year from such activity (determined without regard to subsection (e)(1)(A)).

(e) Recapture of losses where amount at risk is less than zero.—

(1) In general.—If zero exceeds the amount for which the taxpayer is at risk in any activity at the close of any taxable year—

(A) the taxpayer shall include in his gross income for such taxable year (as income from such activity) an amount equal to such excess, and

(B) an amount equal to the amount so included in gross income shall be treated as a deduction allocable to such activity for the first succeeding taxable year.

(2) Limitation.—The excess referred to in paragraph (1) shall not exceed—

(A) the aggregate amount of the reductions required by subsection (b)(5) with respect to the activity by reason of losses for all prior taxable years beginning after December 31, 1978, reduced by

(B) the amounts previously included in gross income with respect to such activity under this subsection.

* * *

§ 469. Passive activity losses and credits limited

(a) Disallowance.—

(1) In general.—If for any taxable year the taxpayer is described in paragraph (2), neither—

(A) the passive activity loss, nor

(B) the passive activity credit,

for the taxable year shall be allowed.

(2) Persons described.—The following are described in this paragraph:

(A) any individual, estate, or trust,

(B) any closely held C corporation, and

(C) any personal service corporation.

(b) Disallowed loss or credit carried to next year.—Except as otherwise provided in this section, any loss or credit from an activity which is disallowed under subsection (a) shall be treated as a deduction or credit allocable to such activity in the next taxable year.

(c) Passive activity defined.—For purposes of this section—

(1) In general.—The term "passive activity" means any activity—

(A) which involves the conduct of any trade or business, and

(B) in which the taxpayer does not materially participate.

(2) Passive activity includes any rental activity.—Except as provided in paragraph (7), the term "passive activity" includes any rental activity.

(3) Working interests in oil and gas property. —

(A) In general.—The term "passive activity" shall not include any working interest in any oil or gas property which the taxpayer holds directly or through an entity which does not limit the liability of the taxpayer with respect to such interest.

(B) Income in subsequent years.—If any taxpayer has any loss for any taxable year from a working interest in any oil or gas property which is treated as a loss which is not from a passive activity, then any net income from such property (or any property the basis of which is determined in whole or in part by reference to the basis of such property) for any succeeding taxable year shall be treated as income of the taxpayer which is not from a passive activity. If the preceding sentence applies to the net income from any property for any taxable year, any credits allowable under subpart B (other than section 27(a)) or D of part IV of subchapter A for such taxable year which are attributable to such property shall be treated as credits not from a passive activity to the extent the amount of such credits does not exceed the regular tax liability of the taxpayer for the taxable year which is allocable to such net income.

(4) Material participation not required for paragraphs (2) and (3).—Paragraphs (2) and (3) shall be applied without regard to whether or not the taxpayer materially participates in the activity.

(5) Trade or business includes research and experimentation activity.—For purposes of paragraph (1)(A), the term "trade or business" includes any activity involving research or experimentation (within the meaning of section 174).

(6) Activity in connection with trade or business or production of income.—To the extent provided in regulations, for purposes of paragraph (1)(A), the term "trade or business" includes—

(A) any activity in connection with a trade or business, or

(B) any activity with respect to which expenses are allowable as a deduction under section 212.

(7) Special rules for taxpayers in real property business.—

(A) In general.—If this paragraph applies to any taxpayer for a taxable year—

(i) paragraph (2) shall not apply to any rental real estate activity of such taxpayer for such taxable year, and

(ii) this section shall be applied as if each interest of the taxpayer in rental real estate were a separate activity.

Notwithstanding clause (ii), a taxpayer may elect to treat all interests in rental real estate as one activity. Nothing in the preceding provisions of this subparagraph shall be construed as affecting the determination of whether the taxpayer materially participates with respect to any interest in a limited partnership as a limited partner.

(B) Taxpayers to whom paragraph applies.—This paragraph shall apply to a taxpayer for a taxable year if—

(i) more than one-half of the personal services performed in trades or businesses by the taxpayer during such taxable year are performed in real property trades or businesses in which the taxpayer materially participates, and

(ii) such taxpayer performs more than 750 hours of services during the taxable year in real property trades or businesses in which the taxpayer materially participates.

In the case of a joint return, the requirements of the preceding sentence are satisfied if and only if either spouse separately satisfies such requirements. For purposes of the preceding sentence, activities in which a spouse materially participates shall be determined under subsection (h).

(C) Real property trade or business.—For purposes of this paragraph, the term "real property trade or business" means any real property development, redevelopment, construction, reconstruction, acquisition, conversion, rental, operation, management, leasing, or brokerage trade or business.

(D) Special rules for subparagraph (B).—

(i) Closely held C corporations.—In the case of a closely held C corporation, the requirements of subparagraph (B) shall be treated as met for any taxable year if more than 50 percent of the gross receipts of such corporation for such taxable year are derived from real property trades or businesses in which the corporation materially participates.

(ii) Personal services as an employee.—For purposes of subparagraph (B), personal services performed as an employee shall not be treated as performed in real property trades or businesses. The preceding sentence shall not apply if such employee is a 5-percent owner (as defined in section 416(i)(1)(B)) in the employer.

(d) Passive activity loss and credit defined.—For purposes of this section—

(1) Passive activity loss.—The term "passive activity loss" means the amount (if any) by which—

(A) the aggregate losses from all passive activities for the taxable year, exceed

(B) the aggregate income from all passive activities for such year.

(2) Passive activity credit.—The term "passive activity credit" means the amount (if any) by which—

(A) the sum of the credits from all passive activities allowable for the taxable year under—

(i) subpart D of part IV of subchapter A, or

(ii) subpart B (other than section 27(a)) of such part IV, exceeds

(B) the regular tax liability of the taxpayer for the taxable year allocable to all passive activities.

(e) Special rules for determining income or loss from a passive activity.—For purposes of this section—

(1) Certain income not treated as income from passive activity.—In determining the income or loss from any activity—

(A) In general.—There shall not be taken into account—

(i) any—

(I) gross income from interest, dividends, annuities, or royalties not derived in the ordinary course of a trade or business,

(II) expenses (other than interest) which are clearly and directly allocable to such gross income, and

(III) interest expense properly allocable to such gross income, and

(ii) gain or loss not derived in the ordinary course of a trade or business which is attributable to the disposition of property—

(I) producing income of a type described in clause (i), or

(II) held for investment.

For purposes of clause (ii), any interest in a passive activity shall not be treated as property held for investment.

(B) Return on working capital.—For purposes of subparagraph (A), any income, gain, or loss which is attributable to an investment of working capital shall be treated as not derived in the ordinary course of a trade or business.

(2) Passive losses of certain closely held corporations may offset active income.—

(A) In general.—If a closely held C corporation (other than a personal service corporation) has net active income for any taxable year, the passive activity loss of such taxpayer for such taxable year (determined without regard to this paragraph)—

(i) shall be allowable as a deduction against net active income, and

(ii) shall not be taken into account under subsection (a) to the extent so allowable as a deduction.

A similar rule shall apply in the case of any passive activity credit of the taxpayer.

(B) Net active income.—For purposes of this paragraph, the term "net active income" means the taxable income of the taxpayer for the taxable year determined without regard to—

(i) any income or loss from a passive activity, and

(ii) any item of gross income, expense, gain, or loss described in paragraph (1)(A).

(3) Compensation for personal services.—Earned income (within the meaning of section 911(d)(2)(A)) shall not be taken into account in computing the income or loss from a passive activity for any taxable year.

(4) Dividends reduced by dividends received deduction.—For purposes of paragraphs (1) and (2), income from dividends shall be reduced by the amount of any dividends received deduction under section 243, 244, or 245.

(f) Treatment of former passive activities.—For purposes of this section—

(1) In general.—If an activity is a former passive activity for any taxable year—

(A) any unused deduction allocable to such activity under subsection (b) shall be offset against the income from such activity for the taxable year,

(B) any unused credit allocable to such activity under subsection (b) shall be offset against the regular tax liability (computed after the application of paragraph (1)) allocable to such activity for the taxable year, and

(C) any such deduction or credit remaining after the application of subparagraphs (A) and (B) shall continue to be treated as arising from a passive activity.

(2) Change in status of closely held C corporation or personal service corporation.—If a taxpayer ceases for any taxable year to be a closely held C corporation or personal service corporation, this section shall continue to apply to losses and credits to which this section applied for any preceding taxable year in the same manner as if such taxpayer continued to be a closely held C corporation or personal service corporation, whichever is applicable.

(3) Former passive activity.—The term "former passive activity" means any activity which, with respect to the taxpayer—

(A) is not a passive activity for the taxable year, but

(B) was a passive activity for any prior taxable year.

(g) Dispositions of entire interest in passive activity.—If during the taxable year a taxpayer disposes of his entire interest in any passive activity (or former passive activity), the following rules shall apply:

(1) Fully taxable transaction.—

(A) In general.—If all gain or loss realized on such disposition is recognized, the excess of—

(i) any loss from such activity for such taxable year (determined after application of subsection (b)), over

(ii) any net income or gain for such taxable year from all other passive activities (determined after the application of subsection (b)),

shall be treated as a loss which is not from a passive activity.

(B) Subparagraph (A) not to apply to disposition involving related party.—If the taxpayer and the person acquiring the interest bear a relationship to each other described in section 267(b) or section 707(b)(1), then subparagraph (A) shall not apply to any loss of the taxpayer until the taxable year in which such interest is acquired (in a transaction described in subparagraph (A)) by another person who does not bear such a relationship to the taxpayer.

(C) Income from prior years.—To the extent provided in regulations, income or gain from the activity for preceding taxable years shall be taken into account under subparagraph (A)(ii) for the taxable year to the extent necessary to prevent the avoidance of this section.

(2) Disposition by death.—If an interest in the activity is transferred by reason of the death of the taxpayer—

(A) paragraph (1)(A) shall apply to losses described in paragraph (1)(A) to the extent such losses are greater than the excess (if any) of—

(i) the basis of such property in the hands of the transferee, over

(ii) the adjusted basis of such property immediately before the death of the taxpayer, and

(B) any losses to the extent of the excess described in subparagraph (A) shall not be allowed as a deduction for any taxable year.

(3) Installment sale of entire interest.—In the case of an installment sale of an entire interest in an activity to which section 453 applies, paragraph (1) shall apply to the portion of such losses for each taxable year which bears the same ratio to all such losses as the gain recognized on such sale during such taxable year bears to the gross profit from such sale (realized or to be realized when payment is completed).

(h) Material participation defined.—For purposes of this section—

(1) In general.—A taxpayer shall be treated as materially participating in an activity only if the taxpayer is involved in the operations of the activity on a basis which is—

(A) regular,

(B) continuous, and

(C) substantial.

(2) Interests in limited partnerships.—Except as provided in regulations, no interest in a limited partnership as a limited partner shall be treated as an interest with respect to which a taxpayer materially participates.

(3) Treatment of certain retired individuals and surviving spouses.—A taxpayer shall be treated as materially participating in any farming activity for a taxable year if paragraph (4) or (5) of section 2032A(b) would cause the requirements of section 2032A(b)(1)(C)(ii) to be met with respect to real property used in such activity if such taxpayer had died during the taxable year.

(4) Certain closely held C corporations and personal service corporations.—A closely held C corporation or personal service corporation shall be treated as materially participating in an activity only if—

(A) 1 or more shareholders holding stock representing more than 50 percent (by value) of the outstanding stock of such corporation materially participate in such activity, or

(B) in the case of a closely held C corporation (other than a personal service corporation), the requirements of section 465(c)(7)(C) (without regard to clause (iv)) are met with respect to such activity.

(5) Participation by spouse.—In determining whether a taxpayer materially participates, the participation of the spouse of the taxpayer shall be taken into account.

(i) $25,000 offset for rental real estate activities.—

(1) In general.—In the case of any natural person, subsection (a) shall not apply to that portion of the passive activity loss or the deduction equivalent (within the meaning of subsection (j)(5)) of the passive activity credit for any taxable year which is attributable to all rental real estate activities with respect to which such individual actively participated in such taxable year (and if any portion of such loss or credit arose in another taxable year, in such other taxable year).

(2) Dollar limitation.—The aggregate amount to which paragraph (1) applies for any taxable year shall not exceed $25,000.

(3) Phase-out of exemption.—

(A) In general.—In the case of any taxpayer, the $25,000 amount under paragraph (2) shall be reduced (but not below zero) by 50 percent of the amount by which the adjusted gross income of the taxpayer for the taxable year exceeds $100,000.

(B) Special phase-out of rehabilitation credit.—In the case of any portion of the passive activity credit for any taxable year which is attributable to the rehabilitation credit determined under section 47, subparagraph (A) shall be applied by substituting "$200,000" for "$100,000."

(C) Exception for commercial revitalization deduction.—Subparagraph (A) shall not apply to any portion of the passive activity loss for any taxable year which is attributable to the commercial revitalization deduction under section 1400I.

(D) Exception for low-income housing credit.—Subparagraph (A) shall not apply to any portion of the passive activity credit for any taxable year which is attributable to any credit determined under section 42.

(E) Ordering rules to reflect exceptions and separate phase-outs.—If subparagraph (B), (C), or (D) applies for any taxable year, paragraph (1) shall be applied—

(i) first to the portion of the passive activity loss to which subparagraph (C) does not apply.

(ii) second to the portion of such loss to which subparagraph (C) applies.

(iii) third to the portion of the passive activity credit to which subparagraph (B) or (D) does not apply,

(iv) fourth to the portion of such credit to which subparagraph (B) applies, and

(v) then to the portion of such credit to which subparagraph (D) applies.

(F) Adjusted gross income.—For purposes of this paragraph, adjusted gross income shall be determined without regard to—

(i) any amount includible in gross income under section 86,

(ii) the amounts excludable from gross income under sections 135 and 137,

(iii) the amounts allowable as a deduction under sections 199, 219, 221, and 222, and

(iv) any passive activity loss or any loss allowable by reason of subsection (c)(7).

(4) Special rule for estates.—

(A) In general.—In the case of taxable years of an estate ending less than 2 years after the date of the death of the decedent, this subsection shall apply to all rental real estate activities with respect to which such decedent actively participated before his death.

(B) Reduction for surviving spouse's exemption.—For purposes of subparagraph (A), the $25,000 amount under paragraph (2) shall be reduced by the amount of the exemption under paragraph (1) (without regard to paragraph (3)) allowable to the surviving spouse of the decedent for the taxable year ending with or within the taxable year of the estate.

(5) Married individuals filing separately.—

(A) In general.—Except as provided in subparagraph (B), in the case of any married individual filing a separate return, this subsection shall be applied by substituting—

(i) "$12,500" for "$25,000" each place it appears,

(ii) "$50,000" for "$100,000" in paragraph (3)(A), and

(iii) "$100,000" for "$200,000" in paragraph (3)(B).

(B) Taxpayers not living apart.—This subsection shall not apply to a taxpayer who—

(i) is a married individual filing a separate return for any taxable year, and

(ii) does not live apart from his spouse at all times during such taxable year.

(6) Active participation.—

(A) In general.—An individual shall not be treated as actively participating with respect to any interest in any rental real estate activity for any period if, at any time during such period, such interest (including any interest of the spouse of the individual) is less than 10 percent (by value) of all interests in such activity.

(B) No participation requirement for low-income housing, rehabilitation credit, or commercial revitalization deduction.—

Paragraphs (1) and (4)(A) shall be applied without regard to the active participation requirement in the case of—

(i) any credit determined under section 42 for any taxable year,

(ii) any rehabilitation credit determined under section 47, or

(iii) any deduction under section 14001 (relating to commercial revitalization deduction).

(C) Interest as a limited partner.—Except as provided in regulations, no interest as a limited partner in a limited partnership shall be treated as an interest with respect to which the taxpayer actively participates.

(D) Participation by spouse.—In determining whether a taxpayer actively participates, the participation of the spouse of the taxpayer shall be taken into account.

(j) Other definitions and special rules.—For purposes of this section—

(1) Closely held C corporation.—The term "closely held C corporation" means any C corporation described in section 465(a)(1)(B).

(2) Personal service corporation.—The term "personal service corporation" has the meaning given such term by section 269A(b)(1), except that section 269A(b)(2) shall be applied—

(A) by substituting "any" for "more than 10 percent," and

(B) by substituting "any" for "50 percent or more in value" in section 318(a)(2)(C).

A corporation shall not be treated as a personal service corporation unless more than 10 percent of the stock (by value) in such corporation is held by employee-owners (within the meaning of section 269A(b)(2), as modified by the preceding sentence).

(3) Regular tax liability.—The term "regular tax liability" has the meaning given such term by section 26(b).

(4) Allocation of passive activity loss and credit.—The passive activity loss and the passive activity credit (and the $25,000 amount under subsection (i)) shall be allocated to activities, and within activities, on a pro rata basis in such manner as the Secretary may prescribe.

(5) Deduction equivalent.—The deduction equivalent of credits from a passive activity for any taxable year is the amount which (if allowed as a deduction) would reduce the regular tax liability for such taxable year by an amount equal to such credits.

(6) Special rule for gifts.—In the case of a disposition of any interest in a passive activity by gift—

(A) the basis of such interest immediately before the transfer shall be increased by the amount of any passive activity losses allocable to such interest with respect to which a deduction has not been allowed by reason of subsection (a), and

(B) such losses shall not be allowable as a deduction for any taxable year.

(7) Qualified residence interest.—The passive activity loss of a taxpayer shall be computed without regard to qualified residence interest (within the meaning of section 163(h)(3)).

(8) Rental activity.—The term "rental activity" means any activity where payments are principally for the use of tangible property.

(9) Election to increase basis of property by amount of disallowed credit.—For purposes of determining gain or loss from a disposition of any property to which subsection (g)(1) applies, the transferor may elect to increase the basis of such property immediately before the transfer by an amount equal to the portion of any unused credit allowable under this chapter which reduced the basis of such property for the taxable year in which such credit arose. If the taxpayer elects the application of this paragraph, such portion of the passive activity credit of such taxpayer shall not be allowed for any taxable year.

(10) Coordination with section 280A.—If a passive activity involves the use of a dwelling unit to which section 280A(c)(5) applies for any taxable year, any income, deduction, gain, or loss allocable to such use shall not be taken into account for purposes of this section for such taxable year.

(11) Aggregation of members of affiliated groups.—Except as provided in regulations, all members of an affiliated group which files a consolidated return shall be treated as 1 corporation.

(12) Special rule for distributions by estates or trusts.—If any interest in a passive activity is distributed by an estate or trust—

(A) the basis of such interest immediately before such distribution shall be increased by the amount of any passive activity losses allocable to such interest, and

(B) such losses shall not be allowable as a deduction for any taxable year.

(k) Separate application of section in case of publicly traded partnerships.—

(1) In general.—This section shall be applied separately with respect to items attributable to each publicly traded partnership (and subsection (i) shall not apply with respect to items attributable to any such partnership). The preceding sentence shall not apply to any credit determined under section 42, or any rehabilitation credit determined under section 47, attributable to a publicly traded partnership to the extent the amount of any such credits exceeds the regular tax liability attributable to income from such partnership.

(2) Publicly traded partnership.—For purposes of this section, the term "publicly traded partnership" means any partnership if—

(A) interests in such partnership are traded on an established securities market, or

(B) interests in such partnership are readily tradable on a secondary market (or the substantial equivalent thereof).

(3) Coordination with subsection (g).—For purposes of subsection (g), a taxpayer shall not be treated as having disposed of his entire interest in an activity of a publicly traded partnership until he disposes of his entire interest in such partnership.

* * *

(l) Regulations.—The Secretary shall prescribe such regulations as may be necessary or appropriate to carry out provisions of this section, including regulations—

(1) which specify what constitutes an activity, material participation, or active participation for purposes of this section,

(2) which provide that certain items of gross income will not be taken into account in determining income or loss from any activity (and the treatment of expenses allocable to such income),

(3) requiring net income or gain from a limited partnership or other passive activity to be treated as not from a passive activity,

(4) which provide for the determination of the allocation of interest expense for purposes of this section, and

(5) which deal with changes in marital status and changes between joint returns and separate returns.

(m) Phase-in of disallowance of losses and credits for interests held before date of enactment.—

(1) In general.—In the case of any passive activity loss or passive activity credit for any taxable year beginning in calendar years 1987 through 1990, subsection (a) shall not apply to the applicable percentage of that portion of such loss (or such credit) which is attributable to pre-enactment interests.

(2) Applicable percentage.—For purposes of this subsection, the applicable percentage shall be determined in accordance with the following table:

In the case of taxable years beginning in:	The applicable percentage is:
1987	65
1988	40
1989	20
1990	10

(3) Portion of loss or credit attributable to pre-enactment interests.—For purposes of this subsection—

(A) In general.—The portion of the passive activity loss (or passive activity credit) for any taxable year which is attributable to pre-enactment interests is the lesser of—

(i) the amount of the passive activity loss (or passive activity credit) which is disallowed for the taxable year under subsection (a) (without regard to this subsection), or

(ii) the amount of the passive activity loss (or passive activity credit) which would be disallowed for the taxable year (without regard to this subsection and without regard to any amount allocable to an activity for the taxable year under subsection (b)) taking into account only pre-enactment interests.

(B) Pre-enactment interest.—

(i) In general.—The term "pre-enactment interest" means any interest in a passive activity held by a taxpayer on the date of the enactment of the Tax Reform Act of 1986, and at all times thereafter.

(ii) Binding contract exception.—For purposes of clause (i), any interest acquired after such date of enactment pursuant to a written binding contract in effect on such date, and at all times thereafter, shall be treated as held on such date.

(iii) Interest in activities.—The term "pre-enactment interest" shall not include an interest in a passive activity unless such activity was being conducted on such date of enactment. The preceding sentence shall not apply to an activity commencing after such date if—

(I) the property used in such activity is acquired pursuant to a written binding contract in effect on August 16, 1986, and at all times thereafter, or

(II) construction of property used in such activity began on or before August 16, 1986.

* * *

SUBPART D—INVENTORIES

Editorial Summary

Accounting for Inventories

Subchapter E of Chapter 1 (Secs. 471–475)

See the discussion under the Editorial Summary entitled Special Accounting Methods: Deductions, which precedes Sec. 461.

§ 471. General rule for inventories

(a) General rule.—Whenever in the opinion of the Secretary the use of inventories is necessary in order clearly to determine the income of any taxpayer, inventories shall be taken by such taxpayer on such basis as the Secretary may prescribe as conforming as nearly as may be to the best accounting practice in the trade or business and as most clearly reflecting the income.

(b) Estimates of inventory shrinkage permitted.—A method of determining inventories shall not be treated as failing to clearly reflect income solely because it utilizes estimates of inventory shrinkage that are confirmed by a physical count only after the last day of the taxable year if—

(1) the taxpayer normally does a physical count of inventories at each location on a regular and consistent basis, and

(2) the taxpayer makes proper adjustments to such inventories and to its estimating methods to the extent such estimates are greater than or less than the actual shrinkage.

(c) Cross reference.—

For rules relating to capitalization of direct and indirect costs of property, see section 263A.

§ 472. Last-in, first-out inventories

(a) Authorization.—A taxpayer may use the method provided in subsection (b) (whether or not such method has been prescribed under section 471) in inventorying goods specified in an application to use such method filed at such time and in such manner as the Secretary may prescribe. The change to, and the use of, such method shall be in accordance with such regulations as the Secretary may prescribe as necessary in order that the use of such method may clearly reflect income.

(b) Method applicable.—In inventorying goods specified in the application described in subsection (a), the taxpayer shall:

(1) Treat those remaining on hand at the close of the taxable year as being: First, those included in the opening inventory of the taxable year (in the order of acquisition) to the extent thereof; and second, those acquired in the taxable year;

(2) Inventory them at cost; and

(3) Treat those included in the opening inventory of the taxable year in which such method is first used as having been acquired at the same time and determine their cost by the average cost method.

(c) Condition.—Subsection (a) shall apply only if the taxpayer establishes to the satisfaction of the Secretary that the taxpayer has used no procedure other than that specified in paragraphs (1) and (3) of subsection (b) in inventorying such goods to ascertain the income, profit, or loss of the first taxable year for which the method described in subsection (b) is to be used, for the purpose of a report or statement covering such taxable year—

(1) to shareholders, partners, or other proprietors, or to beneficiaries, or

(2) for credit purposes.

(d) 3-year averaging for increases in inventory value.—The beginning inventory for the first taxable year for which the method described in subsection

(b) is used shall be valued at cost. Any change in the inventory amount resulting from the application of the preceding sentence shall be taken into account ratably in each of the 3 taxable years beginning with the first taxable year for which the method described in subsection (b) is first used.

(e) Subsequent inventories.—If a taxpayer, having complied with subsection (a), uses the method described in subsection (b) for any taxable year, then such method shall be used in all subsequent taxable years unless—

(1) with the approval of the Secretary a change to a different method is authorized; or,

(2) the Secretary determines that the taxpayer has used for any such subsequent taxable year some procedure other than that specified in paragraph (1) of subsection (b) in inventorying the goods specified in the application to ascertain the income, profit, or loss of such subsequent taxable year for the purpose of a report or statement covering such taxable year (A) to shareholders, partners, or other proprietors, or beneficiaries, or (B) for credit purposes; and requires a change to a method different from that prescribed in subsection (b) beginning with such subsequent taxable year or any taxable year thereafter.

If paragraph (1) or (2) of this subsection applies, the change to, and the use of, the different method shall be in accordance with such regulations as the Secretary may prescribe as necessary in order that the use of such method may clearly reflect income.

(f) Use of government price indexes in pricing inventory.—The Secretary shall prescribe regulations permitting the use of suitable published governmental indexes in such manner and circumstances as determined by the Secretary for purposes of the method described in subsection (b).

(g) Conformity rules applied on controlled group basis.—

(1) In general.—Except as otherwise provided in regulations, all members of the same group of financially related corporations shall be treated as 1 taxpayer for purposes of subsections (c) and (e)(2).

(2) Group of financially related corporations.—For purposes of paragraph (1), the term "group of financially related corporations" means—

(A) any affiliated group as defined in section 1504 determined by substituting "50 percent" for "80 percent" each place it appears in section 1504(a) and without regard to section 1504(b), and

(B) any other group of corporations which consolidate or combine for purposes of financial statements.

* * *

§ 474. Simplified dollar-value LIFO method for certain small businesses

(a) General rule.—An eligible small business may elect to use the simplified dollar-value method of pricing inventories for purposes of the LIFO method.

(b) Simplified dollar-value method of pricing inventories.—For purposes of this section—

(1) In general.—The simplified dollar-value method of pricing inventories is a dollar-value method of pricing inventories under which—

(A) the taxpayer maintains a separate inventory pool for items in each major category in the applicable Government price index, and

(B) the adjustment for each such separate pool is based on the change from the preceding taxable year in the component of such index for the major category.

(2) Applicable government price index.—The term "applicable Government price index" means—

(A) except as provided in subparagraph (B), the Producer Price Index published by the Bureau of Labor Statistics, or

(B) in the case of a retailer using the retail method, the Consumer Price Index published by the Bureau of Labor Statistics.

(3) Major category.—The term "major category" means—

(A) in the case of the Producer Price Index, any of the 2–digit standard industrial classifications in the Producer Prices Data Report, or

(B) in the case of the Consumer Price Index, any of the general expenditure categories in the Consumer Price Index Detailed Report.

(c) Eligible small business.—For purposes of this section, a taxpayer is an eligible small business for any taxable year if the average annual gross receipts of the taxpayer for the 3 preceding taxable years do not exceed $5,000,000. For purposes of the preceding sentence, rules similar to the rules of section 448(c)(3) shall apply.

(d) Special rules.—For purposes of this section—

(1) Controlled groups.—

(A) In general.—In the case of a taxpayer which is a member of a controlled group, all persons which are component members of such group shall be treated as 1 taxpayer for purposes of determining the gross receipts of the taxpayer.

(B) Controlled group defined.—For purposes of subparagraph (A), persons shall be treated as being component members of a controlled group if such persons would be treated as a single employer under section 52.

(2) Election.—

(A) In general.—The election under this section may be made without the consent of the Secretary.

(B) Period to which election applies.—The election under this section shall apply—

(i) to the taxable year for which it is made, and

(ii) to all subsequent taxable years for which the taxpayer is an eligible small business,

unless the taxpayer secures the consent of the Secretary to the revocation of such election.

(3) LIFO method.—The term "LIFO method" means the method provided by section 472(b).

(4) Transitional rules.—

(A) In general.—In the case of a year of change under this section—

(i) the inventory pools shall—

(I) in the case of the 1st taxable year to which such an election applies, be established in accordance with the major categories in the applicable Government price index, or

(II) in the case of the 1st taxable year after such election ceases to apply, be established in the manner provided by regulations under section 472;

(ii) the aggregate dollar amount of the taxpayer's inventory as of the beginning of the year of change shall be the same as the aggregate dollar value as of the close of the taxable year preceding the year of change, and

(iii) the year of change shall be treated as a new base year in accordance with procedures provided by regulations under section 472.

(B) Year of change.—For purposes of this paragraph, the year of change under this section is—

(i) the 1st taxable year to which an election under this section applies, or

(ii) in the case of a cessation of such an election, the 1st taxable year after such election ceases to apply.

§ 475. Mark to market accounting method for dealers in securities

(a) General rule.—Notwithstanding any other provision of this subpart, the following rules shall apply to securities held by a dealer in securities:

(1) Any security which is inventory in the hands of the dealer shall be included in inventory at its fair market value.

(2) In the case of any security which is not inventory in the hands of the dealer and which is held at the close of any taxable year—

(A) the dealer shall recognize gain or loss as if such security were sold for its fair market value on the last business day of such taxable year, and

(B) any gain or loss shall be taken into account for such taxable year.

Proper adjustment shall be made in the amount of any gain or loss subsequently realized for gain or loss taken into account under the preceding sentence. The Secretary may provide by regulations for the application of this paragraph at times other than the times provided in this paragraph.

(b) Exceptions.—

(1) In general.—Subsection (a) shall not apply to—

(A) any security held for investment,

(B) (i) any security described in subsection (c)(2)(C) which is acquired (including originated) by the taxpayer in the ordinary course of a trade or business of the taxpayer and which is not held for sale, and (ii) any obligation to acquire a security described in clause (i) if such obligation is entered into in the ordinary course of such trade or business and is not held for sale, and

(C) any security which is a hedge with respect to—

(i) a security to which subsection (a) does not apply, or

(ii) a position, right to income, or a liability which is not a security in the hands of the taxpayer.

To the extent provided in regulations, subparagraph (C) shall not apply to any security held by a person in its capacity as a dealer in securities.

(2) Identification required.—A security shall not be treated as described in subparagraph (A), (B), or (C) of paragraph (1), as the case may be, unless such security is clearly identified in the dealer's records as being described in such subparagraph before the close of the day on which it was acquired, originated, or entered into (or such other time as the Secretary may by regulations prescribe).

(3) Securities subsequently not exempt.—If a security ceases to be described in paragraph (1) at any time after it was identified as such under paragraph (2), subsection (a) shall apply to any changes in value of the security occurring after the cessation.

(4) Special rule for property held for investment.—To the extent provided in regulations, subparagraph (A) of paragraph (1) shall not apply to any security described in subparagraph (D) or (E) of subsection (c)(2) which is held by a dealer in such securities.

(c) Definitions.—For purposes of this section—

(1) Dealer in securities defined.—The term "dealer in securities" means a taxpayer who—

(A) regularly purchases securities from or sells securities to customers in the ordinary course of a trade or business; or

(B) regularly offers to enter into, assume, offset, assign or otherwise terminate positions in securities with customers in the ordinary course of a trade or business.

(2) Security defined.—The term "security" means any—

(A) share of stock in a corporation;

(B) partnership or beneficial ownership interest in a widely held or publicly traded partnership or trust;

(C) note, bond, debenture, or other evidence of indebtedness;

(D) interest rate, currency, or equity notional principal contract;

(E) evidence of an interest in, or a derivative financial instrument in, any security described in subparagraph (A), (B), (C), or (D), or any currency, including any option, forward contract, short position, and any similar financial instrument in such a security or currency; and

(F) position which—

(i) is not a security described in subparagraph (A), (B), (C), (D), or (E),

(ii) is a hedge with respect to such a security, and

(iii) is clearly identified in the dealer's records as being described in this subparagraph before the close of the day on which it was acquired or entered into (or such other time as the Secretary may by regulations prescribe).

Subparagraph (E) shall not include any contract to which section 1256(a) applies.

(3) Hedge.—The term "hedge" means any position which manages the dealer's risk of interest rate or price changes or currency fluctuations, including any position which is reasonably expected to become a hedge within 60 days after the acquisition of the position.

(4) Special rules for certain receivables.—

(A) In general.—Paragraph (2)(C) shall not include any nonfinancial customer paper.

(B) Non-financial customer paper.—For purposes of subparagraph (A), the term "nonfinancial customer paper" means any receivable which—

(i) is a note, bond, debenture, or other evidence of indebtedness,

(ii) arises out of the sale of nonfinancial goods or services by a person the principal activity of which is the selling or providing of nonfinancial goods or services, and

(iii) is held by such person (or a person who bears a relationship to such person described in section 267(b) or 707(b)) at all times since issue.

(d) Special rules.—For purposes of this section—

(1) Coordination with certain rules.—The rules of sections 263(g), 263A, and 1256(a) shall not apply to securities to which subsection (a) applies, and section 1091 shall not apply (and section 1092 shall apply) to any loss recognized under subsection (a).

(2) Improper identification.—If a taxpayer—

(A) identifies any security under subsection (b)(2) as being described in subsection (b)(1) and such security is not so described, or

(B) fails under subsection (c)(2)(F)(iii) to identify any position which is described in subsection (c)(2)(F) (without regard to clause (iii) thereof) at the time such identification is required,

the provisions of subsection (a) shall apply to such security or position, except that any loss under this section prior to the disposition of the security or position shall be recognized only to the extent of gain previously recognized under this section (and not previously taken into account under this paragraph) with respect to such security or position.

(3) Character of gain or loss.—

(A) In general.—Except as provided in subparagraph (B) or section 1236(b)—

(i) In general.—Any gain or loss with respect to a security under subsection (a)(2) shall be treated as ordinary income or loss.

(ii) Special rule for dispositions.—If—

(I) gain or loss is recognized with respect to a security before the close of the taxable year, and

(II) subsection (a)(2) would have applied if the security were held as of the close of the taxable year,

such gain or loss shall be treated as ordinary income or loss.

(B) Exception.—Subparagraph (A) shall not apply to any gain or loss which is allocable to a period during which—

(i) the security is described in subsection (b)(1)(C) (without regard to subsection (b)(2)),

(ii) the security is held by a person other than in connection with its activities as a dealer in securities, or

(iii) the security is improperly identified (within the meaning of subparagraph (A) or (B) of paragraph (2)).

(e) Election of mark to market for dealers in commodities.—

(1) In general.—In the case of a dealer in commodities who elects the application of this subsection, this section shall apply to commodities held by such dealer in the same manner as this section applies to securities held by a dealer in securities.

(2) Commodity.—For purposes of this subsection and subsection (f), the term "commodity" means—

(A) any commodity which is actively traded (within the meaning of section 1092(d)(l));

(B) any notional principal contract with respect to any commodity described in subparagraph (A);

(C) any evidence of an interest in, or a derivative instrument in, any commodity described in subparagraph (A) or (B), including any option, forward contract, futures contract, short position, and any similar instrument in such a commodity; and

(D) any position which—

(i) is not a commodity described in subparagraph (A), (B), or (C).

(ii) is a hedge with respect to such a commodity, and

(iii) is clearly identified in the taxpayer's records as being described in this subparagraph before the close of the day on which it was acquired or entered into (or such other time as the Secretary may by regulations prescribe).

(3) Election.—An election under this subsection may be made without the consent of the Secretary. Such an election, once made, shall apply to the taxable year for which made and all subsequent taxable years unless revoked with the consent of the Secretary.

(f) Election of mark to market for traders in securities or commodities.—

(1) Traders in securities.—

(A) In general.—In the case of a person who is engaged in a trade or business as a trader in securities and who elects to have this paragraph apply to such trade or business—

(i) such person shall recognize gain or loss on any security held in connection with such trade or business at the close of any taxable year as if such security were sold for its fair market value on the last business day of such taxable year, and

(ii) any gain or loss shall be taken into account for such taxable year.

Proper adjustment shall be made in the amount of any gain or loss subsequently realized for gain or loss taken into account under the preceding sentence. The Secretary may provide by regulations for the application of this subparagraph at times other than the times provided in this subparagraph.

(B) Exception.—Subparagraph (A) shall not apply to any security—

(i) which is established to the satisfaction of the Secretary as having no connection to the activities of such person as a trader, and

(ii) which is clearly identified in such person's records as being described in clause (i) before the close of the day on which it was acquired, originated, or entered into (or such other time as the Secretary may by regulations prescribe).

If a security ceases to be described in clause (i) at any time after it was identified as such under clause (ii), subparagraph (A) shall apply to any changes in value of the security occurring after the cessation.

(C) Coordination with section 1259.—Any security to which subparagraph (A) applies and which was acquired in the normal course of the taxpayer's activities as a trader in securities shall not be taken into account in applying section 1259 to any position to which subparagraph (A) does not apply.

(D) Other rules to apply.—Rules similar to the rules of subsections (b)(4) and (d) shall apply to securities held by a person in any trade or business with respect to which an election under this paragraph is in effect. Subsection (d)(3) shall not apply under the preceding sentence for purposes of applying sections 1402 and 7704.

(2) Traders in commodities.—In the case of a person who is engaged in a trade or business as a trader in commodities and who elects to have this paragraph apply to such trade or business, paragraph (1) shall apply to commodities held by such trader in connection with such trade or business in the same manner as paragraph (1) applies to securities held by a trader in securities.

(3) Election.—The elections under paragraphs (1) and (2) may be made separately for each trade or business and without the consent of the Secretary. Such an election, once made, shall apply to the taxable year for which made and all subsequent taxable years unless revoked with the consent of the Secretary.

(g) Regulatory authority.—The Secretary shall prescribe such regulations as may be necessary or appropriate to carry out the purposes of this section, including rules—

(1) to prevent the use of year-end transfers, related parties, or other arrangements to avoid the provisions of this section,

(2) to provide for the application of this section to any security which is a hedge which cannot be identified with a specific security, position, right to income, or liability, and

(3) to prevent the use by taxpayers of subsection (c)(4) to avoid the application of this section to a receivable that is inventory in the hands of the taxpayer (or a person who bears a relationship to the taxpayer described in section 267(b) or 707(b)).

PART III—ADJUSTMENTS

Editorial Summary

Accounting Method Adjustments
Subchapter E of Chapter 1 (Secs. 481–483)

See the discussion under the Editorial Summary entitled Accounting Method, which precedes Sec. 446.

§ 481. Adjustments required by changes in method of accounting

(a) General rule.—In computing the taxpayer's taxable income for any taxable year (referred to in this section as the "year of the change")—

(1) if such computation is under a method of accounting different from the method under which the taxpayer's taxable income for the preceding taxable year was computed, then

(2) there shall be taken into account those adjustments which are determined to be necessary solely by reason of the change in order to prevent amounts from being duplicated or omitted, except there shall not be taken into account any adjustment in respect of any taxable year to which this section does not apply unless the adjustment is attributable to a change in the method of accounting initiated by the taxpayer.

(b) Limitation on tax where adjustments are substantial.—

(1) Three year allocation.—If—

(A) the method of accounting from which the change is made was used by the taxpayer in computing his taxable income for the

2 taxable years preceding the year of the change, and

(B) the increase in taxable income for the year of the change which results solely by reason of the adjustments required by subsection (a) (2) exceeds $3,000,

then the tax under this chapter attributable to such increase in taxable income shall not be greater than the aggregate increase in the taxes under this chapter (or under the corresponding provisions of prior revenue laws) which would result if one-third of such increase in taxable income were included in taxable income for the year of the change and one-third of such increase were included for each of the 2 preceding taxable years.

(2) Allocation under new method of accounting.—If—

(A) the increase in taxable income for the year of the change which results solely by reason of the adjustments required by subsection (a)(2) exceeds $3,000, and

(B) the taxpayer establishes his taxable income (under the new method of accounting) for one or more taxable years consecutively preceding the taxable year of the change for which the taxpayer in computing taxable income used the method of accounting from which the change is made,

then the tax under this chapter attributable to such increase in taxable income shall not be greater than the net increase in the taxes under this chapter (or under the corresponding provisions of prior revenue laws) which would result if the adjustments required by subsection (a)(2) were allocated to the taxable year or years specified in subparagraph (B) to which they are properly allocable under the new method of accounting and the balance of the adjustments required by subsection (a)(2) was allocated to the taxable year of the change.

(3) Special rules for computations under paragraphs (1) and (2).—For purposes of this subsection—

(A) There shall be taken into account the increase or decrease in tax for any taxable year preceding the year of the change to which no adjustment is allocated under paragraph (1) or (2) but which is affected by a net operating loss (as defined in section 172) or by a capital loss carryback or carryover (as defined in section 1212), determined with reference to taxable years with respect to which adjustments under paragraph (1) or (2) are allocated.

(B) The increase or decrease in the tax for any taxable year for which an assessment of any deficiency, or a credit or refund of any overpayment, is prevented by any law or rule of law, shall be determined by reference to the tax previously determined (within the meaning of section 1314(a)) for such year.

* * *

(c) Adjustments under regulations.—In the case of any change described in subsection (a), the taxpayer may, in such manner and subject to such conditions as the Secretary may by regulations prescribe, take the adjustments required by subsection (a)(2) into account in computing the tax imposed by this chapter for the taxable year or years permitted under such regulations.

§ 482. Allocation of income and deductions among taxpayers

In any case of two or more organizations, trades, or businesses (whether or not incorporated, whether or not organized in the United States, and whether or not affiliated) owned or controlled directly or indirectly by the same interests, the Secretary may distribute, apportion, or allocate gross income, deductions, credits, or allowances between or among such organizations, trades, or businesses, if he determines that such distribution, apportionment, or allocation is necessary in order to prevent evasion of taxes or clearly to reflect the income of any of such organizations, trades, or businesses. In the case of any transfer (or license) of intangible property (within the meaning of section 936(h)(3)(B)), the income with respect to such transfer or license shall be commensurate with the income attributable to the intangible.

§ 483. Interest on certain deferred payments

(a) Amount constituting interest.—For purposes of this title, in the case of any payment—

(1) under any contract for the sale or exchange of any property, and

(2) to which this section applies,

there shall be treated as interest that portion of the total unstated interest under such contract which, as determined in a manner consistent with the method of computing interest under section 1272(a), is properly allocable to such payment.

(b) Total unstated interest.—For purposes of this section, the term "total unstated interest" means, with respect to a contract for the sale or exchange of property, an amount equal to the excess of—

(1) the sum of the payments to which this section applies which are due under the contract, over

(2) the sum of the present values of such payments and the present values of any interest payments due under the contract.

For purposes of the preceding sentence, the present value of a payment shall be determined under the rules of section 1274(b)(2) using a discount rate equal to the applicable Federal rate determined under section 1274(d).

(c) Payments to which subsection (a) applies.—

(1) In general.—Except as provided in subsection (d), this section shall apply to any payment on account of the sale or exchange of property which constitutes part or all of the sales price and which is due more than 6 months after the date of such sale or exchange under a contract—

(A) under which some or all of the payments are due more than 1 year after the date of such sale or exchange, and

(B) under which there is total unstated interest.

(2) Treatment of other debt instruments.—For purposes of this section, a debt instrument of the purchaser which is given in consideration for the sale or exchange of property shall not be treated as a payment, and any payment due under such debt instrument shall be treated as due under the contract for the sale or exchange.

(3) Debt instrument defined.—For purposes of this subsection, the term "debt instrument" has the meaning given such term by section 1275(a)(1).

(d) Exceptions and limitations.—

(1) Coordination with original issue discount rules.—This section shall not apply to any debt instrument for which an issue price is determined under section 1273(b) (other than paragraph (4) thereof) or section 1274.

(2) Sales prices of $3,000 or less.—This section shall not apply to any payment on account of the sale or exchange of property if it can be determined at the time of such sale or exchange that the sales price cannot exceed $3,000.

(3) Carrying charges.—In the case of the purchaser, the tax treatment of amounts paid on account of the sale or exchange of property shall be made without regard to this section if any such amounts are treated under section 163(b) as if they included interest.

(4) Certain sales of patents.—In the case of any transfer described in section 1235(a) (relating to sale or exchange of patents), this section shall not apply to any amount contingent on the productivity, use, or disposition of the property transferred.

(e) Maximum rate of interest on certain transfers of land between related parties.—

(1) In general.—In the case of any qualified sale, the discount rate used in determining the total unstated interest rate under subsection (b) shall not exceed 6 percent, compounded semiannually.

(2) Qualified sale.—For purposes of this subsection, the term "qualified sale" means any sale or exchange of land by an individual to a member of such individual's family (within the meaning of section 267(c)(4)).

(3) $500,000 limitation.—Paragraph (1) shall not apply to any qualified sale between individuals made during any calendar year to the extent that the sales price for such sale (when added to the aggregate sales price for prior qualified sales between such individuals during the calendar year) exceeds $500,000.

(4) Nonresident alien individuals.—Paragraph (1) shall not apply to any sale or exchange if any party to such sale or exchange is a nonresident alien individual.

(f) Regulations.—The Secretary shall prescribe such regulations as may be necessary or appropriate to carry out the purposes of this section including regulations providing for the application of this section in the case of—

(1) any contract for the sale or exchange of property under which the liability for, or the amount or due date of, a payment cannot be determined at the time of the sale or exchange, or

(2) any change in the liability for, or the amount or due date of, any payment (including interest) under a contract for the sale or exchange of property.

(g) Cross references.—

(1) For treatment of assumptions, see section 1274(c)(4).

(2) For special rules for certain transactions where stated principal amount does not exceed $2,800,000, see section 1274A.

(3) For special rules in case of the borrower under certain loans for personal use, see section 1275(b).

SUBCHAPTER F—EXEMPT ORGANIZATIONS

Editorial Summary

Tax Exempt Organizations

Subchapter F of Chapter 1 (Secs. 501–530)

Certain organizations are not subject to federal income taxation. These organizations are referred to as tax exempt organizations. Such status has two effects. First, it relieves the entity from having a federal tax liability. Second, it may produce the result that contributions to the organizations in the form of gifts qualify for tax-favored status under Sec. 170 (i.e., eligible for the charitable contribution deduction to the donor).

Section 501(a) exempts from federal income taxation two major categories of organizations:

1. Qualified retirement plan trusts under Sec. 401(a).
2. Section 501(c) exempt organizations.

In addition to providing tax exempt status, Sec. 501 contains provisions that result in the partial or complete loss of tax exempt status. For example, see Secs. 501(h) and 504 for expenditures to influence legislation and Sec. 501(i) for discrimination by certain social clubs. In addition, Sec. 503 provides that an exempt organization will lose its exempt status if it engages in a prohibited transaction [see the definition of a prohibited transaction in Sec. 503(b)].

The classic, and probably the most populous, type of tax exempt entity is the Sec. 501(c)(3) type of organization, which normally is described as a public charity. Classification in this category will result in the attainment of both of the benefits of tax exempt status: exemption from federal income taxation and qualification of contributions to the entity for the most beneficial treatment under Sec. 170.

However, obtaining the benefits of Sec. 501(c)(3) status must be viewed in conjunction with the effect of Sec. 509. Section 509 effectively classifies Sec. 501(c)(3) organizations into one of two categories: the public charity that one normally thinks of when referring to a Sec. 501(c)(3) organization and the private foundation. Section 509 applies a concept similar to the one applied in Sec. 1221 in defining a capital asset. Section 1221 defines what is a capital asset by specifying what is not a capital asset. Section 509 defines which Sec. 501(c)(3) organizations are private foundations by specifying which ones are not private foundations. Other negative features associated with classification as a private foundation include statutory restrictions on the activities of the entity that may result in loss of exempt status, taxation at the entity level under Secs. 4940–4948, greater reporting requirements, and the potential for more monitoring by the IRS [see Secs. 507, 508]. The Code also distinguishes between a private operating foundation and a private nonoperating foundation [see Sec. 4942(j)(3)], the operating foundation qualifying for more beneficial tax treatment than the nonoperating foundation.

Certain entities that qualify for tax exempt status under Sec. 501 may still be subject to federal income taxation with respect to part of their income. In effect, the Code dichotomizes the income of the entity into exempt income and nonexempt income. The part that is classified as nonexempt income is subject to taxation. Section 511 provides for the imposition of the tax on the unrelated business taxable income [see the definition in Sec. 512 of unrelated business income, in Sec. 513 of an unrelated trade or business, and in Sec. 514 of unrelated debt-financed income] of the tax exempt organization. The tax is computed under Sec. 11. Absent this imposition of tax on the tax exempt entity, profit-oriented ventures would be placed at a substantial disadvantage when competing with tax exempt entities.

Section 521 provides the basis for tax exempt status for farmers' cooperatives. Section 527 provides the rules for determining the tax liability of a political organization. Section 528 provides the rules for determining the tax liability of a homeowners association.

Section 529 provides for the tax-exempt status of qualified state tuition programs.

Section 530 provides for the tax-exempt status of Coverdell education savings accounts (CESAs).

PART I—GENERAL RULE

§ 501. Exemption from tax on corporations, certain trusts, etc.

(a) Exemption from taxation.—An organization described in subsection (c) or (d) or section 401(a) shall be exempt from taxation under this subtitle unless such exemption is denied under section 502 or 503.

(b) Tax on unrelated business income and certain other activities.—An organization exempt from taxation under subsection (a) shall be subject to tax to the extent provided in parts II, III, and VI of

*Omitted.

this subchapter, but (notwithstanding parts II, III, and VI of this subchapter) shall be considered an organization exempt from income taxes for the purpose of any law which refers to organizations exempt from income taxes.

(c) List of exempt organizations.—The following organizations are referred to in subsection (a):

(1) Any corporation organized under Act of Congress which is an instrumentality of the United States but only if such corporation—

(A) is exempt from Federal income taxes—

(i) under such Act as amended and supplemented before July 18, 1984, or

(ii) under this title without regard to any provision of law which is not contained in this title and which is not contained in a revenue Act, or

(B) is described in subsection (*l*).

(2) Corporations organized for the exclusive purpose of holding title to property, collecting income therefrom, and turning over the entire amount thereof, less expenses, to an organization which itself is exempt under this section. Rules similar to the rules of subparagraph (G) of paragraph (25) shall apply for purposes of this paragraph.

(3) Corporations, and any community chest, fund, or foundation, organized and operated exclusively for religious, charitable, scientific, testing for public safety, literary, or educational purposes, or to foster national or international amateur sports competition (but only if no part of its activities involve the provision of athletic facilities or equipment), or for the prevention of cruelty to children or animals, no part of the net earnings of which inures to the benefit of any private shareholder or individual, no substantial part of the activities of which is carrying on propaganda, or otherwise attempting, to influence legislation (except as otherwise provided in subsection (h)), and which does not participate in, or intervene in (including the publishing or distributing of statements), any political campaign on behalf of (or in opposition to) any candidate for public office.

(4) Civic leagues or organizations not organized for profit but operated exclusively for the promotion of social welfare, or local associations of employees, the membership of which is limited to the employees of a designated person or persons in a particular municipality, and the net earnings of which are devoted exclusively to charitable, educational, or recreational purposes.

(5) Labor, agricultural, or horticultural organizations.

(6) Business leagues, chambers of commerce, real-estate boards, boards of trade, or professional football leagues (whether or not administering a pension fund for football players), not organized for profit and no part of the net earnings of which inures to the benefit of any private shareholder or individual.

(7) Clubs organized for pleasure, recreation, and other nonprofitable purposes, substantially all of the activities of which are for such purposes and no part of the net earnings of which inures to the benefit of any private shareholder.

(8) Fraternal beneficiary societies, orders, or associations—

(A) operating under the lodge system or for the exclusive benefit of the members of a fraternity itself operating under the lodge system, and

(B) providing for the payment of life, sick, accident, or other benefits to the members of such society, order, or association or their dependents.

(9) Voluntary employees' beneficiary associations providing for the payment of life, sick, accident, or other benefits to the members of such association or their dependents or designated beneficiaries, if no part of the net earnings of such association inures (other than through such payments) to the benefit of any private shareholder or individual. For purposes of providing for the payment of sick and accident benefits to members of such an association and their dependents, the term "dependent" shall include any individual who is a child (as defined in section 152(f)(1)) of a member who as of the end of the calendar year has not attained age 27.

(10) Domestic fraternal societies, orders, or associations, operating under the lodge system—

(A) the net earnings of which are devoted exclusively to religious, charitable, scientific, literary, educational, and fraternal purposes, and

(B) which do not provide for the payment of life, sick, accident, or other benefits.

(11) Teachers' retirement fund associations of a purely local character, if—

(A) no part of their net earnings inures (other than through payment of retirement benefits) to the benefit of any private shareholder or individual, and

(B) the income consists solely of amounts received from public taxation, amounts received from assessments on the teaching salaries of members, and income in respect of investments.

* * *

(13) Cemetery companies owned and operated exclusively for the benefit of their members or which are not operated for profit; and any corporation chartered solely for the purpose of the disposal of bodies by burial or cremation which is not permitted by its charter to engage in any business not necessarily incident to that purpose, no part of the net earnings of which inures to the benefit of any private shareholder or individual.

(14)(A) Credit unions without capital stock organized and operated for mutual purposes and without profit.

(B) Corporations or associations without capital stock organized before September 1, 1957, and operated for mutual purposes and without profit for the purpose of providing reserve funds for, and insurance of, shares or deposits in—

(i) domestic building and loan associations,

(ii) cooperative banks without capital stock organized and operated for mutual purposes and without profit,

(iii) mutual savings banks not having capital stock represented by shares, or

(iv) mutual savings banks described in section 591(b).

(C) Corporations or associations organized before September 1, 1957, and operated for mutual purposes and without profit for the purpose of providing reserve funds for associations or banks described in clause (i), (ii), or (iii) of subparagraph (B); but only if 85 percent or more of the income is attributable to providing such reserve funds and to investments. This subparagraph shall not apply to any corporation or association entitled to exemption under subparagraph (B).

* * *

(16) Corporations organized by an association subject to part IV of this subchapter or members thereof, for the purpose of financing the ordinary crop operations of such members or other producers, and operated in conjunction with such association. Exemption shall not be denied any such corporation because it has capital stock, if the dividend rate of such stock is fixed at not to exceed the legal rate of interest in the State of incorporation or 8 percent per annum, whichever is greater, on the value of the consideration for which the stock was issued, and if substantially all such stock (other than nonvoting preferred stock, the owners of which are not entitled or permitted to participate, directly or indirectly, in the profits of the corporation, on dissolution or otherwise, beyond the fixed dividends) is owned by such association, or members thereof; nor shall exemption be denied any such corporation because there is accumulated and maintained by it a reserve required by State law or a reasonable reserve for any necessary purpose.

(17)(A) A trust or trusts forming part of a plan providing for the payment of supplemental unemployment compensation benefits, if—

(i) under the plan, it is impossible, at any time prior to the satisfaction of all liabilities with respect to employees under the plan, for any part of the corpus or income to be (within the taxable year or thereafter) used for, or diverted to, any purpose other than the providing of supplemental unemployment compensation benefits,

(ii) such benefits are payable to employees under a classification which is set forth in the plan and which is found by the Secretary not to be discriminatory in favor of employees who are highly compensated employees (within the meaning of section 414(q), and

(iii) such benefits do not discriminate in favor of employees who are highly compensated employees (within the meaning of section 414(q)). A plan shall not be considered discriminatory within the meaning of this clause merely because the benefits received under the plan bear a uniform relationship to the total compensation, or the basic or regular rate of compensation, of the employees covered by the plan.

(B) In determining whether a plan meets the requirements of subparagraph (A), any benefits provided under any other plan shall not be taken into consideration, except that a plan shall not be considered discriminatory—

(i) merely because the benefits under the plan which are first determined in a nondiscriminatory manner within the meaning of subparagraph (A) are then reduced by any sick, accident, or unemployment compensation benefits received under State or Federal law (or reduced by a portion of such benefits if determined in a nondiscriminatory manner), or

(ii) merely because the plan provides only for employees who are not eligible to receive sick, accident, or unemployment compensation benefits under State or Federal law the same benefits (or a portion of such benefits if determined in a nondiscriminatory manner) which such employees would receive under such laws if such employees were eligible for such benefits, or

(iii) merely because the plan provides only for employees who are not eligible under another plan (which meets the requirements of subparagraph (A)) of supplemental unemployment compensation benefits provided wholly by the employer the same benefits (or a portion of such benefits if determined in a nondiscriminatory manner) which such employees would receive under such other plan if such employees were eligible under such other plan, but only if the employees eligible under both plans would make a classification which would be nondiscriminatory within the meaning of subparagraph (A).

(C) A plan shall be considered to meet the requirements of subparagraph (A) during the whole of any year of the plan if on one day in each quarter it satisfies such requirements.

(D) The term "supplemental unemployment compensation benefits" means only—

(i) benefits which are paid to an employee because of his involuntary separation from the employment of the employer (whether or not such separation is temporary) resulting directly from a reduction in force, the discontinuance of a plant or operation, or other similar conditions, and

(ii) sick and accident benefits subordinate to the benefits described in clause (i).

(E) Exemption shall not be denied under subsection (a) to any organization entitled to such exemption as an association described in paragraph (9) of this subsection merely because such organization provides for the payment of supplemental unemployment benefits (as defined in subparagraph (D)(i)).

(18) A trust or trusts created before June 25, 1959, forming part of a plan providing for the payment of benefits under a pension plan funded only by contributions of employees, if—

(A) under the plan, it is impossible, at any time prior to the satisfaction of all liabilities with respect to employees under the plan, for any part of the corpus or income to be (within the taxable year or thereafter) used for, or diverted to, any purpose other than the providing of benefits under the plan,

(B) such benefits are payable to employees under a classification which is set forth in the plan and which is found by the Secretary not to be discriminatory in favor of employees who are highly compensated employees (within the meaning of section 414(q)),

(C) such benefits do not discriminate in favor of employees who are highly compensated employees (within the meaning of section 414(q)). A plan shall not be considered discriminatory within the meaning of this subparagraph merely because the benefits received under the plan bear a uniform relationship to the total compensation, or the basic or regular rate of compensation, of the employees covered by the plan, and

(D) in the case of a plan under which an employee may designate certain contributions as deductible—

(i) such contributions do not exceed the amount with respect to which a deduction is allowable under section 219(b)(3),

(ii) requirements similar to the requirements of section 401(k)(3)(A)(ii) are met with respect to such elective contributions,

(iii) such contributions are treated as elective deferrals for purposes of section 402(g), and

(iv) the requirements of section 401(a)(30) are met.

For purposes of subparagraph (D)(ii), rules similar to the rules of section 401(k)(8) shall apply. For purposes of section 4979, any excess contribution under clause (ii) shall be treated as an excess contribution under a cash or deferred arrangement.

(19) A post or organization of past or present members of the Armed Forces of the United States, or an auxiliary unit or society of, or a trust or foundation for, any such post or organization—

(A) organized in the United States or any of its possessions,

(B) at least 75 percent of the members of which are past or present members of the Armed Forces of the United States and substantially all of the other members of which are individuals who are cadets or are spouses, widows, widowers, ancestors, or lineal descendants of past or present members of the Armed Forces of the United States or of cadets, and

(C) no part of the net earnings of which inures to the benefit of any private shareholder or individual.

(20) An organization or trust created or organized in the United States, the exclusive function of which is to form part of a qualified group legal services plan or plans, within the meaning of section 120. An organization or trust which receives contributions because of section 120(c)(5)(C) shall not be prevented from qualifying as an organization described in this paragraph merely because it provides legal services or indemnification against the cost of legal services unassociated with a qualified group legal services plan.

(21)(A) A trust or trusts established in writing, created or organized in the United States, and contributed to by any person (except an insurance company) if—

(i) the purpose of such trust or trusts is exclusively—

(I) to satisfy, in whole or in part, the liability of such person for, or with respect to, claims for compensation for disability or death due to pneumoconiosis under Black Lung Acts;

(II) to pay premiums for insurance exclusively covering such liability; and

(III) to pay administrative and other incidental expenses of such trust in connection with the operation of the trust and the processing of claims against such person under Black Lung Acts, and

(IV) to pay accident or health benefits for retired miners and their spouses and dependents (including administrative and other incidental expenses of such trust in connection therewith) or premiums for insurance exclusively covering such benefits; and

(ii) no part of the assets of the trust may be used for, or diverted to, any purpose other than—

(I) the purposes described in clause (i),

(II) investment (but only to the extent that the trustee determines that a portion of the assets is not currently needed for the purposes described in clause (i)) in qualified investments, or

(III) payment into the Black Lung Disability Trust Fund established under section 9501, or into the general fund of the United States Treasury (other than in satisfaction of any tax or other civil or criminal liability of the person who established or contributed to the trust).

(B) No deduction shall be allowed under this chapter for any payment described in subparagraph (A)(i)(IV) from such trust.

(C) Payments described in subparagraph (A)(i)(IV) must be made from such trust during a taxable year only to the extent that the aggregate amount of such payments during such taxable year does not exceed the excess (if any), as of the close of the preceding taxable year; of—

(i) the fair market value of the assets of the trust, over

(ii) 110 percent of the present value of the liability described in subparagraph (A)(i)(I) of such person.

The determinations under the preceding sentence shall be made by an independent actuary using actuarial methods and assumptions (not inconsistent with the regulations prescribed under section 192(c)(l)(A)) each of which is reasonable and which are reasonable in the aggregate.

(D) For purposes of this paragraph:

(i) The term "Black Lung Acts" means part C of title IV of the Federal Mine Safety and Health Act of 1977, and any State law providing compensation for disability or death due to that pneumoconiosis.

(ii) The term "qualified investments" means—

(I) public debt securities of the United States,

(II) obligations of a State or local government which are not in default as to principal or interest, and

(III) time or demand deposits in a bank (as defined in section 581) or an insured credit union (within the meaning of section 101(7) of the Federal Credit Union Act, 12 U.S.C. 1752(7)) located in the United States.

(iii) The term "miner" has the same meaning as such term has when used in section 402(d) of the Black Lung Benefits Act (30 U.S.C. 902(d)).

(iv) The term "incidental expenses" includes legal, accounting, actuarial, and trustee expenses.

(22) A trust created or organized in the United States and established in writing by the plan sponsors of multiemployer plans if—

(A) the purpose of such trust is exclusively—

(i) to pay any amount described in section 4223(c) or (h) of the Employee Retirement Income Security Act of 1974, and

(ii) to pay reasonable and necessary administrative expenses in connection with the establishment and operation of the trust and the processing of claims against the trust,

(B) no part of the assets of the trust may be used for, or diverted to, any purpose other than—

(i) the purposes described in subparagraph (A), or

(ii) the investment in securities, obligations, or time or demand deposits described in clause (ii) of paragraph (21)(D),

(C) such trust meets the requirements of paragraphs (2), (3), and (4) of section 4223(b), 4223(h), or, if applicable, section 4223(c) of the Employee Retirement Income Security Act of 1974, and

(D) the trust instrument provides that, on dissolution of the trust, assets of the trust may not be paid other than to plans which have participated in the plan or, in the case of a trust established under section 4223(h) of such Act, to plans with respect to which employers have participated in the fund.

(23) Any association organized before 1880 more than 75 percent of the members of which are present or past members of the Armed Forces and a principal purpose of which is to provide insurance and other benefits to veterans or their dependents.

(24) A trust described in section 4049 of the Employee Retirement Income Security Act of 1974 (as in effect on the date of the enactment of the Single-Employer Pension Plan Amendments Act of 1986).

(25)(A) Any corporation or trust which—

(i) has no more than 35 shareholders or beneficiaries,

(ii) has only 1 class of stock or beneficial interest, and

(iii) is organized for the exclusive purposes of—

(I) acquiring real property and holding title to, and collecting income from, such property, and

(II) remitting the entire amount of income from such property (less expenses) to 1 or more organizations described in subparagraph (C) which are shareholders of such corporation or beneficiaries of such trust.

For purposes of clause (iii), the term "real property" shall not include any interest as a tenant in common (or similar interest) and shall not include any indirect interest.

(B) A corporation or trust shall be described in subparagraph (A) without regard to whether the corporation or trust is organized by 1 or more organizations described in subparagraph (C).

(C) An organization is described in this subparagraph if such organization is—

(i) a qualified pension, profit sharing, or stock bonus plan that meets the requirements of section 401(a),

(ii) a governmental plan (within the meaning of section 414(d)),

(iii) the United States, any State or political subdivision thereof, or any agency or instrumentality of any of the foregoing, or

(iv) any organization described in paragraph (3).

(D) A corporation or trust shall in no event be treated as described in subparagraph (A) unless such corporation or trust permits its shareholders or beneficiaries—

(i) to dismiss the corporation's or trust's investment adviser, following reasonable notice, upon a vote of the shareholders or beneficiaries holding a majority of interest in the corporation or trust, and

(ii) to terminate their interest in the corporation or trust by either, or both, of the following alternatives, as determined by the corporation or trust:

(I) by selling or exchanging their stock in the corporation or interest in the trust (subject to any Federal or State securities law) to any organization described in subparagraph (C) so long as the sale or exchange does not increase the number of shareholders or beneficiaries in such corporation or trust above 35, or

(II) by having their stock or interest redeemed by the corporation or trust after the shareholder or beneficiary has provided 90 days notice to such corporation or trust.

(E) **(i)** For purposes of this title—

(I) a corporation which is a qualified subsidiary shall not be treated as a separate corporation, and

(II) all assets, liabilities, and items of income, deduction, and credit of a qualified subsidiary shall be treated as assets, liabilities, and such items (as the case may be) of the corporation or trust described in subparagraph (A).

(ii) For purposes of this subparagraph, the term "qualified subsidiary" means any corporation if, at all times during the period such corporation was in existence, 100 percent of the stock of such corporation is held by the corporation or trust described in subparagraph (A).

(iii) For purposes of this subtitle, if any corporation which was a qualified subsidiary ceases to meet the requirements of clause (ii), such corporation shall be treated as a new corporation acquiring all of its assets (and assuming all of its liabilities) immediately before such cessation from the corporation or trust described in subparagraph (A) in exchange for its stock.

(F) For purposes of subparagraph (A), the term "real property" includes any personal property which is leased under, or in connection with, a lease of real property, but only if the rent attributable to such personal property (determined under the rules of section 856(d)(1)) for the taxable year does not exceed 15 percent of the total rent for the taxable year attributable to both the real and personal property leased under, or in connection with, such lease.

(G) **(i)** An organization shall not be treated as failing to be described in this paragraph merely by reason of the receipt of any otherwise disqualifying income which is incidentally derived from the holding of real property.

(ii) Clause (i) shall not apply if the amount of gross income described in such clause exceeds 10 percent of the organization's gross income for the taxable year unless the organization establishes to the satisfaction of the Secretary that the receipt of gross income described in clause (i) in excess of such limitation was inadvertent and reasonable steps are being taken to correct the circumstances giving rise to such income.

(26) Any membership organization if—

(A) such organization is established by a State exclusively to provide coverage for medical care (as defined in section 213 (d)) on a not-for-profit basis to individuals described in subparagraph (B) through—

(i) insurance issued by the organization, or

(ii) a health maintenance organization under an arrangement with the organization,

(B) the only individuals receiving such coverage through the organization are individuals—

(i) who are residents of such State, and

(ii) who, by reason of the existence or history of a medical condition—

(I) are unable to acquire medical care coverage for such condition through insurance or from a health maintenance organization, or

(II) are able to acquire such coverage only at a rate which is substantially in excess of the rate for such coverage through the membership organization,

(C) the composition of the membership in such organization is specified by such State, and

(D) no part of the net earnings of the organization inures to the benefit of any private shareholder or individual.

A spouse and any qualifying child (as defined in section 24(c)) of an individual described in subparagraph (B) (without regard to this sentence) shall be treated as described in subparagraph (B).

* * *

(29) Co-op health insurance issuers.—

(A) In general.—A qualified nonprofit health insurance issuer (within the meaning of section 1322 of the Patient Protection and Affordable Care Act) which has received a loan or grant under the CO-OP program under such section, but only with respect to periods for which the issuer is in compliance with the requirements of such section and any agreement with respect to the loan or grant.

(B) Conditions for exemption.—Subparagraph (A) shall apply to an organization only if—

(i) the organization has given notice to the Secretary, in such manner as the Secretary may by regulations prescribe, that it is applying for recognition of its status under this paragraph,

(ii) except as provided in section 1322(c)(4) of the Patient Protection and Affordable Care Act, no part of the net earnings of which inures to the benefit of any private shareholder or individual,

(iii) no substantial part of the activities of which is carrying on propaganda, or otherwise attempting, to influence legislation, and

(iv) the organization does not participate in, or intervene in (including the publishing or distributing of statements), any political campaign on behalf of (or in opposition to) any candidate for public office.

(d) Religious and apostolic organizations.—The following organizations are referred to in subsection (a): Religious or apostolic associations or corporations, if such associations or corporations have a common treasury or community treasury, even if such associations or corporations engage in business for the common benefit of the members, but only if the members thereof include (at the time of filing their returns) in their gross income their entire pro rata shares, whether distributed or not, of the taxable income of the association or corporation for such year. Any amount so included in the gross income of a member shall be treated as a dividend received.

(e) Cooperative hospital service organizations.—For purposes of this title, an organization shall be treated as an organization organized and operated exclusively for charitable purposes, if—

(1) such organization is organized and operated solely—

(A) to perform, on a centralized basis, one or more of the following services which, if performed on its own behalf by a hospital which is an organization described in subsection (c)(3) and exempt from taxation under subsection (a), would constitute activities in exercising or performing the purpose or function constituting the basis for its exemption: data processing, purchasing (including the purchasing of insurance on a group basis), warehousing, billing and collection (including the purchase of patron accounts receivable on a recourse basis), food, clinical, industrial engineering, laboratory, printing, communications, record center, and personnel (including selection, testing, training, and education of personnel) services; and

(B) to perform such services solely for two or more hospitals each of which is—

(i) an organization described in subsection (c)(3) which is exempt from taxation under subsection (a),

(ii) a constituent part of an organization described in subsection (c)(3) which is exempt from taxation under subsection (a) and which, if organized and operated as a separate entity, would constitute an organization described in subsection (c)(3), or

(iii) owned and operated by the United States, a State, the District of Columbia, or a possession of the United States, or a political subdivision or an agency or instrumentality of any of the foregoing;

(2) such organization is organized and operated on a cooperative basis and allocates or pays, within 8 1/2 months after the close of its taxable year, all net earnings to patrons on the basis of services performed for them; and

(3) if such organization has capital stock, all of such stock outstanding is owned by its patrons.

For purposes of this title, any organization which, by reason of the preceding sentence, is an organization described in subsection (c)(3) and exempt from taxation under subsection (a), shall be treated as a hospital and as an organization referred to in section 170(b)(1)(A)(iii).

(f) Cooperative service organizations of operating educational organizations.—For purposes of this title, if an organization is—

(1) organized and operated solely to hold, commingle, and collectively invest and reinvest (including arranging for and supervising the performance by independent contractors of investment services related thereto) in stocks and securities, the moneys contributed thereto by each of the members of such organization, and to collect income therefrom and turn over the entire amount thereof, less expenses, to such members,

(2) organized and controlled by one or more such members, and

(3) comprised solely of members that are organizations described in clause (ii) or (iv) of section 170(b)(1)(A)—

(A) which are exempt from taxation under subsection (a), or

(B) the income of which is excluded from taxation under section 115(a),

then such organization shall be treated as an organization organized and operated exclusively for charitable purposes.

(g) Definition of agricultural.—For purposes of subsection (c)(5), the term "agricultural" includes the art or science of cultivating land, harvesting crops or aquatic resources, or raising livestock.

(h) Expenditures by public charities to influence legislation.—

(1) General rule.—In the case of an organization to which this subsection applies, exemption from taxation under subsection (a) shall be denied because a substantial part of the activities of such organization consists of carrying on propaganda, or otherwise attempting, to influence legislation, but only if such organization normally—

(A) makes lobbying expenditures in excess of the lobbying ceiling amount for such organization for each taxable year, or

(B) makes grass roots expenditures in excess of the grass roots ceiling amount for such organization for each taxable year.

(2) Definitions.—For purposes of this subsection—

(A) Lobbying expenditures.—The term "lobbying expenditures" means expenditures for the purpose of influencing legislation (as defined in section 4911(d)).

(B) Lobbying ceiling amount.—The lobbying ceiling amount for any organization for any taxable year is 150 percent of the lobbying nontaxable amount for such organization for such taxable year, determined under section 4911.

(C) Grass roots expenditures.—The term "grass roots expenditures" means expenditures for the purpose of influencing legislation (as defined in section 4911(d) without regard to paragraph (1)(B) thereof).

(D) Grass roots ceiling amount.—The grass roots ceiling amount for any organization for any taxable year is 150 percent of the grass roots nontaxable amount for such organization for such taxable year, determined under section 4911.

(3) Organizations to which this subsection applies.—This subsection shall apply to any organization which has elected (in such manner and at such time as the Secretary may prescribe) to have the provisions of this subsection apply to such organization and which, for the taxable year which includes the date the election is made, is described in subsection (c)(3) and—

(A) is described in paragraph (4), and

(B) is not a disqualified organization under paragraph (5).

(4) Organizations permitted to elect to have this subsection apply.—An organization is described in this paragraph if it is described in—

(A) section 170(b)(1)(A)(ii) (relating to educational institutions),

(B) section 170(b)(1)(A)(iii) (relating to hospitals and medical research organizations),

(C) section 170(b)(l)(A)(iv) (relating to organizations supporting government schools),

(D) section 170(b)(1)(A)(vi) (relating to organizations publicly supported by charitable contributions),

(E) section 509(a)(2) (relating to organizations publicly supported by admissions, sales, etc.), or

(F) section 509(a)(3) (relating to organizations supporting certain types of public charities) except that for purposes of this subparagraph, section 509(a)(3) shall be applied without regard to the last sentence of section 509(a).

(5) Disqualified organizations.—For purposes of paragraph (3) an organization is a disqualified organization if it is—

(A) described in section 170(b)(1)(A)(i) (relating to churches),

(B) an integrated auxiliary of a church or of a convention or association of churches, or

(C) a member of an affiliated group of organizations (within the meaning of section 4911(f) (2)) if one or more members of such group is described in subparagraph (A) or (B).

(6) Years for which election is effective.—An election by an organization under this subsection shall be effective for all taxable years of such organization which—

(A) end after the date the election is made, and

(B) begin before the date the election is revoked by such organization (under regulations prescribed by the Secretary).

(7) No effect on certain organizations.—With respect to any organization for a taxable year for which—

(A) such organization is a disqualified organization (within the meaning of paragraph (5)), or

(B) an election under this subsection is not in effect for such organization,

nothing in this subsection or in section 4911 shall be construed to affect the interpretation of the phrase, "no substantial part of the activities of which is carrying on propaganda, or otherwise attempting, to influence legislation," under subsection (c)(3).

(8) Affiliated organizations.—

For rules regarding affiliated organizations, see section 4911(f).

(i) Prohibition of discrimination by certain social clubs.—Notwithstanding subsection (a), an organization which is described in subsection (c)(7) shall not be exempt from taxation under subsection (a) for any taxable year if, at any time during such taxable year, the charter, bylaws, or other governing instrument, of such organization or any written policy statement of such organization contains a provision which provides for discrimination against any person on the basis of race, color, or religion. The preceding sentence to the extent it relates to discrimination on the basis of religion shall not apply to—

(1) an auxiliary of a fraternal beneficiary society if such society—

(A) is described in subsection (c)(8) and exempt from tax under subsection (a), and

(B) limits its membership to the members of a particular religion, or

(2) a club which in good faith limits its membership to the members of a particular religion in order to further the teachings or principles of that religion, and not to exclude individuals of a particular race or color.

(j) Special rules for certain amateur sports organizations.—

(1) In general.—In the case of a qualified amateur sports organization—

(A) the requirement of subsection (c)(3) that no part of its activities involve the provision of athletic facilities or equipment shall not apply, and

(B) such organization shall not fail to meet the requirements of subsection (c)(3) merely because its membership is local or regional in nature.

(2) Qualified amateur sports organization defined.—For purposes of this subsection, the term "qualified amateur sports organization" means any organization organized and operated exclusively to foster national or international amateur sports competition if such organization is also organized and operated primarily to conduct national or international competition in sports or to support and develop amateur athletes for national or international competition in sports.

(k) Treatment of certain organizations providing child care.—For purposes of subsection (c)(3) of this section and sections 170(c)(2), 2055(a)(2), and 2522(a)(2), the term "educational purposes includes the providing of care of children away from their homes if—

(1) substantially all of the care provided by the organization is for purposes of enabling individuals to be gainfully employed, and

(2) the services provided by the organization are available to the general public

* * *

(m) Certain organizations providing commercial-type insurance not exempt from tax.—

(1) Denial of tax exemption where providing commercial-type insurance is substantial part of activities.—An organization described in paragraph (3) or (4) of subsection (c) shall be exempt from tax under subsection (a) only if no substantial part of its activities consists of providing commercial-type insurance.

(2) Other organizations taxed as insurance companies on insurance business.—In the case of an organization described in paragraph (3) or (4) of subsection (c) which is exempt from tax under subsection (a) after the application of paragraph (1) of this subsection—

(A) the activity of providing commercial-type insurance shall be treated as an unrelated trade or business (as defined in section 513), and

(B) in lieu of the tax imposed by section 511 with respect to such activity, such organization shall be treated as an insurance company for purposes of applying subchapter L with respect to such activity.

(3) Commercial-type insurance.—For purposes of this subsection, the term "commercial-type insurance" shall not include—

(A) insurance provided at substantially below cost to a class of charitable recipients,

(B) incidental health insurance provided by a health maintenance organization of a kind customarily provided by such organizations, and

(C) property or casualty insurance provided (directly or through an organization described in section 414(e)(3)(B)(ii)) by a church or convention or association of churches for such church or convention or association of churches,

(D) providing retirement or welfare benefits (or both) by a church or a convention or association of churches (directly or through an organization described in section 414(e)(3)(A) or 414(e)(3)(B)(ii)) for the employees (including employees described in section 414(e)(3)(B)) of such church or convention or association of churches or the beneficiaries of such employees, and

(E) charitable gift annuities.

(4) Insurance includes annuities.—For purposes of this subsection, the issuance of annuity contracts shall be treated as providing insurance.

(5) Charitable gift annuity.—For purposes of paragraph (3)(E), the term "charitable gift annuity" means an annuity if—

(A) a portion of the amount paid in connection with the issuance of the annuity is allowable as a deduction under section 170 or 2055, and

(B) the annuity is described in section 514(c)(5) (determined as if any amount paid in cash in connection with such issuance were property).

* * *

(p) Suspension of tax-exempt status of terrorist organizations.—

(1) In general.—The exemption from tax under subsection (a) with respect to any organization described in paragraph (2), and the eligibility of any organization described in paragraph (2) to apply for recognition of exemption under subsection (a), shall be suspended during the period described in paragraph (3).

(2) Terrorist organizations.—An organization is described in this paragraph if such organization is designated or otherwise individually identified.

(A) under section 212(a)(3)(B)(vi)(II) or 219 of the Immigration and Nationality Act as a terrorist organization or foreign terrorist organization,

(B) in or pursuant to an Executive order which is related to terrorism and issued under the authority of the International Emergency Economic Powers Act or section 5 of the United Nations Participation Act of 1945 for the purpose of imposing on such organization an economic or other sanction, or

(C) in or pursuant to an Executive order issued under the authority of any Federal law if—

(i) the organization is designated or otherwise individually identified in or pursuant to such Executive order as supporting or engaging in terrorist activity (as defined in section 212(a)(3)(B) of the Immigration and Nationality Act) or supporting terrorism (as defined in section 140(d)(2) of the Foreign Relations Authorization Act, Fiscal Years 1988 and 1989); and

(ii) such Executive order refers to this subsection.

(3) Period of suspension.—With respect to any organization described in paragraph (2), the period of suspension—

(A) begins on the later of—

(i) the date of the first publication of a designation or identification described in paragraph (2) with respect to such organization, or

(ii) the date of the enactment of this subsection, and

(B) ends on the first date that all designations and identifications described in paragraph (2) with respect to such organization are rescinded pursuant to the law or Executive order under which such designation or identification was made.

(4) Denial of deduction.—No deduction shall be allowed under any provision of this title, including sections 170, 545(b)(2), 556(b)(2), 642(c), 2055, 2106(a)(2), and 2522, with respect to any contribution to an organization described in paragraph (2) during the period described in paragraph (3).

(5) Denial of administrative or judicial challenge of suspension or denial of deduction.—Notwithstanding section 7428 or any other provision of law, no organization or other person may challenge a suspension under paragraph (1), a designation or identification described in paragraph (2), the period of suspension described in paragraph (3), or a denial of a deduction under paragraph (4) in any administrative or judicial proceeding relating to the Federal tax liability of such organization or other person.

(6) Erroneous designation.—

(A) In general.—If—

(i) the tax exemption of any organization described in paragraph (2) is suspended under paragraph (1),

(ii) each designation and identification described in paragraph (2) which has been made with respect to such organization is determined to be erroneous pursuant to the law or Executive order under which such designation or identification was made, and

(iii) the erroneous designations and identifications result in an overpayment of income tax for any taxable year by such organization,

credit or refund (with interest) with respect to such overpayment shall be made.

(B) Waiver of limitations.—If the credit or refund of any overpayment of tax described in subparagraph (A)(iii) is prevented at any time by the operation of any law or rule of law (including res judicata), such credit or refund may nevertheless be allowed or made if the claim therefor is filed before the close of the 1-year period beginning on the date of the last determination described in subparagraph (A)(ii).

(7) Notice of suspensions.—If the tax exemption of any organization is suspended under this subsection, the Internal Revenue Service shall update the listings of tax-exempt organizations and shall publish appropriate notice to taxpayers of such suspension and of the fact that contributions to such organization are not deductible during the period of such suspension.

(q) Special rules for credit counseling organizations.—

(1) In general.—An organization with respect to which the provision of credit counseling services is a substantial purpose shall not be exempt from tax under subsection (a) unless such organization is described in paragraph (3) or (4) of subsection (c) and such organization is organized and operated in accordance with the following requirements:

(A) The organization—

(i) provides credit counseling services tailored to the specific needs and circumstances of consumers,

(ii) makes no loans to debtors (other than loans with no fees or interest) and does not negotiate the making of loans on behalf of debtors,

(iii) provides services for the purpose of improving a consumer's credit record, credit history, or credit rating only to the extent that such services are incidental to providing credit counseling services, and

(iv) does not charge any separately stated fee for services for the purpose of improving any consumer's credit record, credit history, or credit rating.

(B) The organization does not refuse to provide credit counseling services to a consumer due to the inability of the consumer to pay, the ineligibility of the consumer for debt management plan enrollment, or the unwillingness of the consumer to enroll in a debt management plan.

(C) The organization establishes and implements a fee policy which—

(i) requires that any fees charged to a consumer for services are reasonable,

(ii) allows for the waiver of fees if the consumer is unable to pay, and

(iii) except to the extent allowed by State law, prohibits charging any fee based in whole or in part on a percentage of the consumer's debt, the consumer's payments to be made pursuant to a debt management plan, or the projected or actual savings to the consumer resulting from enrolling in a debt management plan.

(D) At all times the organization has a board of directors or other governing body—

(i) which is controlled by persons who represent the broad interests of the public, such as public officials acting in their capacities as such, persons having special knowledge or expertise in credit or financial education, and community leaders,

(ii) not more than 20 percent of the voting power of which is vested in persons who are employed by the organization or who will benefit financially, directly or indirectly, from the organization's activities (other than through the receipt of reasonable directors' fees or the repayment of consumer debt to creditors other than the credit counseling organization or its affiliates), and

(iii) not more than 49 percent of the voting power of which is vested in persons who are employed by the organization or who will benefit financially, directly or indirectly, from the organization's activities (other than through the receipt of reasonable directors' fees).

(E) The organization does not own more than 35 percent of—

(i) the total combined voting power of any corporation (other than a corporation which is an organization described in subsection (c)(3) and exempt from tax under subsection (a)) which is in the trade or business of lending money, repairing credit, or providing debt management plan services, payment processing, or similar services,

(ii) the profits interest of any partnership (other than a partnership which is an organization described in subsection (c)(3) and exempt from tax under subsection (a)) which is in the trade or business of lending money, repairing credit, or providing debt management plan services, payment processing, or similar services, and

(iii) the beneficial interest of any trust or estate (other than a trust which is an organization described in subsection (c)(3) and exempt from tax under subsection (a)) which is in the trade or business of lending money, repairing credit, or providing debt management plan services, payment processing, or similar services.

(F) The organization receives no amount for providing referrals to others for debt management plan services, and pays no amount to others for obtaining referrals of consumers.

(2) Additional requirements for organizations described in subsection (c) (3).—

(A) In general.—In addition to the requirements under paragraph (1), an organization with respect to which the provision of credit counseling services is a substantial purpose and which is described in paragraph (3) of subsection (c) shall not be exempt from tax under subsection (a) unless such organization is organized and operated in accordance with the following requirements:

(i) The organization does not solicit contributions from consumers during the initial counseling process or while the consumer is receiving services from the organization.

(ii) The aggregate revenues of the organization which are from payments of creditors of consumers of the organization and which are attributable to debt management plan services do not exceed the applicable percentage of the total revenues of the organization.

(B) Applicable percentage.—

(i) In general.—For purposes of subparagraph (A) (ii), the applicable percentage is 50 percent.

(ii) Transition rule.—Notwithstanding clause (i), in the case of an organization with respect to which the provision of credit counseling services is a substantial purpose and which is described in paragraph (3) of subsection (c) and exempt from tax under subsection (a) on the date of the enactment of this subsection, the applicable percentage is—

(I) 80 percent for the first taxable year of such organization beginning after the date which is 1 year after the date of the enactment of this subsection, and

(II) 70 percent for the second such taxable year beginning after such date, and

(III) 60 percent for the third such taxable year beginning after such date.

(3) Additional requirement for organizations described in subsection (c)(4).—In addition to the requirements under paragraph (1), an organization with respect to which the provision of credit counseling services is a substantial purpose and which is described in paragraph (4) of subsection (c) shall not be exempt from tax under subsection (a) unless such organization notifies the Secretary, in such manner as the Secretary may by regulations prescribe, that it is applying for recognition as a credit counseling organization.

(4) Credit counseling services; debt management plan services.—For purposes of this sub-section—

(A) Credit counseling services.—The term "credit counseling services" means—

(i) the providing of educational information to the general public on budgeting, personal finance, financial literacy, saving and spending practices, and the sound use of consumer credit,

(ii) the assisting of individuals and families with financial problems by providing them with counseling, or

(iii) a combination of the activities described in clauses (i) and (ii).

(B) Debt management plan services.—The term "debt management plan services" means services related to the repayment, consolidation, or restructuring of a consumer's debt, and includes the negotiation with creditors of lower interest rates, the waiver or reduction of fees, and the marketing and processing of debt management plans.

* * *

(s) Cross reference.—For nonexemption of Communist-controlled organizations, see section 11(b) of the Internal Security Act of 1950 (64 Stat 997; 50 U.S.C. 790(b)).

§ 502. Feeder organizations

(a) General rule.—An organization operated for the primary purpose of carrying on a trade or business for profit shall not be exempt from taxation under section 501 on the ground that all of its profits are payable to one or more organizations exempt from taxation under section 501.

(b) Special rule.—For purposes of this section, the term "trade or business" shall not include—

(1) the deriving of rents which would be excluded under section 512(b)(3), if section 512 applied to the organization,

(2) any trade or business in which substantially all the work in carrying on such trade or business is performed for the organization without compensation, or

(3) any trade or business which is the selling of merchandise, substantially all of which has been received by the organization as gifts or contributions.

§ 503. Requirements for exemption

(a) Denial of exemption to organizations engaged in prohibited transactions.—

(1) General rule.—

(A) An organization described in section 501(c)(17) shall not be exempt from taxation under section 501(a) if it has engaged in a prohibited transaction after December 31, 1959.

(B) An organization described in section 401(a) which is referred to in section 4975(g)(2) or (3) shall not be exempt from taxation under section 501(a) if it has engaged in a prohibited transaction after March 1, 1954.

(C) An organization described in section 501(c)(18) shall not be exempt from taxation under section 501(a) if it has engaged in a prohibited transaction after December 31, 1969.

(2) Taxable years affected.—An organization described in section 501(c) (17) or (18) or paragraph (1)(B) shall be denied exemption from taxation under section 501(a) by reason of paragraph (1) only for taxable years after the taxable year during which it is notified by the Secretary that it has engaged in a prohibited transaction, unless such organization entered into such prohibited transaction with the purpose of diverting corpus or income of the organization from its exempt purposes, and such transaction involved a substantial part of the corpus or income of such organization.

(b) Prohibited transactions.—For purposes of this section, the term "prohibited transaction" means any transaction in which an organization subject to the provisions of this section—

(1) lends any part of its income or corpus, without the receipt of adequate security and a reasonable rate of interest, to;

(2) pays any compensation, in excess of a reasonable allowance for salaries or other compensation for personal services actually rendered, to;

(3) makes any part of its services available on a preferential basis to;

(4) makes any substantial purchase of securities or any other property, for more than adequate consideration in money or money's worth, from;

(5) sells any substantial part of its securities or other property, for less than an adequate consideration in money or money's worth, to; or

(6) engages in any other transaction which results in a substantial diversion of its income or corpus to;

the creator of such organization (if a trust); a person who has made a substantial contribution to such organization; a member of the family (as defined in section 267(c)(4)) of an individual who is the creator of such trust or who has made a substantial contribution to such organization; or a corporation controlled by such creator or person through the ownership, directly or indirectly, of 50 percent or more of the total combined voting power of all classes of stock entitled to vote or 50 percent or more of the total value of shares of all classes of stock of the corporation.

(c) Future status of organizations denied exemption.—Any organization described in section 501(c)(17) or (18) or subsection (a)(1)(B) which is denied exemption under section 501(a) by reason of subsection (a) of this section, with respect to any taxable year following the taxable year in which notice of denial of exemption was received, may, under regulations prescribed by the Secretary, file claim for exemption, and if the Secretary, pursuant to such regulations, is satisfied that such organization will not knowingly again engage in a prohibited transaction, such organization shall be exempt with respect to taxable years after the year in which such claim is filed.

*__(e) Special rules.__—For purposes of subsection (b)(1), a bond, debenture, note, or certificate or other evidence of indebtedness (hereinafter in this subsection referred to as "obligation") shall not be treated as a loan made without the receipt of adequate security if—

(1) such obligation is acquired—

(A) on the market, either (i) at the price of the obligation prevailing on a national securities exchange which is registered with the Securities

*Editorial comment: There is no subsection (d).

and Exchange Commission, or (ii) if the obligation is not traded on such a national securities exchange, at a price not less favorable to the trust than the offering price for the obligation as established by current bid and asked prices quoted by persons independent of the issuer;

(B) from an underwriter, at a price (i) not in excess of the public offering price for the obligation as set forth in a prospectus or offering circular filed with the Securities and Exchange Commission, and (ii) at which a substantial portion of the same issue is acquired by persons independent of the issuer; or

(C) directly from the issuer, at a price not less favorable to the trust than the price paid currently for a substantial portion of the same issue by persons independent of the issuer;

(2) immediately following acquisition of such obligation—

(A) not more than 25 percent of the aggregate amount of obligations issued in such issue and outstanding at the time of acquisition is held by the trust, and

(B) at least 50 percent of the aggregate amount referred to in subparagraph (A) is held by persons independent of the issuer; and

(3) immediately following acquisition of the obligation, not more than 25 percent of the assets of the trust is invested in obligations of persons described in subsection (b).

(f) Loans with respect to which employers are prohibited from pledging certain assets.—Subsection (b)(1) shall not apply to a loan made by a trust described in section 401(a) to the employer (or to a renewal of such a loan or, if the loan is repayable upon demand, to a continuation of such a loan) if the loan bears a reasonable rate of interest, and if (in the case of a making or renewal)—

(1) the employer is prohibited (at the time of such making or renewal) by any law of the United States or regulation thereunder from directly or indirectly pledging, as security for such a loan, a particular class or classes of his assets the value of which (at such time) represents more than one-half of the value of all his assets;

(2) the making or renewal, as the case may be, is approved in writing as an investment which is consistent with the exempt purposes of the trust by a trustee who is independent of the employer, and no other such trustee had previously refused to give such written approval; and

(3) immediately following the making or renewal, as the case may be, the aggregate amount loaned by the trust to the employer, without the receipt of adequate security, does not exceed 25 percent of the value of all the assets of the trust.

For purposes of paragraph (2), the term "trustee" means, with respect to any trust for which there is more than one trustee who is independent of the employer, a majority of such independent trustees. For purposes of paragraph (3), the determination as to whether any amount loaned by the trust to the employer is loaned without the receipt of adequate security shall be made without regard to subsection (e).

§ 504. Status after organization ceases to qualify for exemption under section 501(c)(3) because of substantial lobbying or because of political activities

(a) General rule.—An organization which—

(1) was exempt (or was determined by the Secretary to be exempt) from taxation under section 501(a) by reason of being an organization described in section 501(c)(3), and

(2) is not an organization described in section 501(c)(3)—

(A) by reason of carrying on propaganda, or otherwise attempting, to influence legislation, or

(B) by reason of participating in, or intervening in, any political campaign on behalf of (or in opposition to) any candidate for public office,

shall not at any time thereafter be treated as an organization described in section 501(c)(4).

(b) Regulations to prevent avoidance.—The Secretary shall prescribe such regulations as may be necessary or appropriate to prevent the avoidance of subsection (a), including regulations relating to a direct or indirect transfer of all or part of the assets of an organization to an organization controlled (directly or indirectly) by the same person or persons who control the transferor organization.

(c) Churches, etc.—Subsection (a) shall not apply to any organization which is a disqualified organization within the meaning of section 501(h)(5) (relating to churches, etc.) for the taxable year immediately preceding the first taxable year for which such organization is described in paragraph (2) of subsection (a).

§ 505. Additional requirements for organizations described in paragraph (9), (17), or (20) of section 501(c)

(a) Certain requirements must be met in the case of organizations described in paragraph (9) or (20) of section 501(c).—

(1) Voluntary employees' beneficiary associations, etc.—An organization described in paragraph (9) or (20) of subsection (c) of section 501 which is part of a plan shall not be exempt from tax under section 501(a) unless such plan meets the requirements of subsection (b) of this section.

(2) Exception for collective bargaining agreements.—Paragraph (1) shall not apply to any organization which is part of a plan maintained pursuant to an agreement between employee representatives and 1 or more employers if theSecretary finds that such agreement is a collective bargaining agreement and that such plan was the subject of good faith bargaining between such employee representatives and such employer or employers.

(b) Nondiscrimination requirements.—

(1) In general.—Except as otherwise provided in this subsection, a plan meets the requirements of this subsection only if—

(A) each class of benefits under the plan is provided under a classification of employees which is set forth in the plan and which is found by the Secretary not to be discriminatory in favor of employees who are highly compensated individuals, and

(B) in the case of each class of benefits, such benefits do not discriminate in favor of employees who are highly compensated individuals.

A life insurance, disability, severance pay, or supplemental unemployment compensation benefit shall not be considered to fail to meet the requirements of subparagraph (B) merely because the benefits available bear a uniform relationship to the total compensation, or the basic or regular rate of compensation, of employees covered by the plan.

(2) Exclusion of certain employees.—For purposes of paragraph (1), there may be excluded from consideration—

(A) employees who have not completed 3 years of service,

(B) employees who have not attained age 21,

(C) seasonal employees or less than half-time employees,

(D) employees not included in this plan who are included in a unit of employees covered by an agreement between employee representatives and 1 or more employers which the Secretary finds to be a collective bargaining agreement if the class of benefits involved was the subject of good faith bargaining between such employee representatives and such employer or employers, and

(E) employees who are nonresident aliens and who receive no earned income (within the meaning of section 911(d)(2)) from the employer which constitutes income from sources within the United States (within the meaning of section 861(a)(3)).

(3) Application of subsection where other nondiscrimination rules provided.—In the case of any benefit for which a provision of this chapter other than this subsection provides nondiscrimination rules, paragraph (1) shall not apply but the requirements of this subsection shall be met only if the nondiscrimination rules so provided are satisfied with respect to such benefit.

(4) Aggregation rules.—At the election of the employer, 2 or more plans of such employer may be treated as 1 plan for purposes of this subsection.

(5) Highly compensated individual.—For purposes of this subsection, the term "highly compensated individual" has the meaning given such term by section 105(h)(5). For purposes of the preceding sentence, section 105(h)(5) shall be applied by substituting "10 percent" for "25 percent."

(6) Compensation.—For purposes of this subsection, the term "compensation" has the meaning given such term by section 414(s).

(7) Compensation limit.—A plan shall not be treated as meeting the requirements of this subsection unless under the plan the annual compensation of each employee taken into account for any year does not exceed $200,000.* The Secretary shall adjust the $200,000* amount at the same time, and by the same amount, as the adjustment under section 401(a)(17)(B). This paragraph shall not apply in determining whether the requirements of section 79(d) are met.

*Editorial comment: The $200,000 amount is subject to indexing. For 2013, the indexed amount is $255,000 and for 2014, the indexed amount is $260,000.

(c) Requirement that organization notify Secretary that it is applying for tax-exempt status.—

(1) In general.—An organization shall not be treated as an organization described in paragraph (9), (17), or (20) of section 501(c)—

(A) unless it has given notice to the Secretary, in such manner as the Secretary may by regulations prescribed, that it is applying for recognition of such status, or

(B) for any period before the giving of such notice, if such notice is given after the time prescribed by the Secretary by regulations for giving notice under this subsection.

(2) Special rule for existing organizations.—In the case of any organization in existence on July 18, 1984, the time for giving notice under paragraph (1) shall not expire before the date 1 year after such date of the enactment.

PART II—PRIVATE FOUNDATIONS

Editorial Summary

Private Foundations

Subchapter F of Chapter 1 (Secs. 507–509)

See the discussion under the Editorial Summary entitled Tax Exempt Organizations, which precedes Sec. 501.

§ 507. Termination of private foundation Status

(a) General rule.—Except as provided in subsection (b), the status of any organization as a private foundation shall be terminated only if—

(1) such organization notifies the Secretary (at such time and in such manner as the Secretary may by regulations prescribe) of its intent to accomplish such termination, or

(2) (A) with respect to such organization, there have been either willful repeated acts (or failures to act), or a willful and flagrant act (or failure to act), giving rise to liability for tax under chapter 42, and

(B) the Secretary notifies such organization that, by reason of subparagraph (A), such organization is liable for the tax imposed by subsection (c),

and either such organization pays the tax imposed by subsection (c) (or any portion not abated under subsection (g)) or the entire amount of such tax is abated under subsection (g).

(b) Special rules.—

(1) Transfer to, or operation as, public charity.—The status as a private foundation of any organization, with respect to which there have not been either willful repeated acts (or failures to act) or a willful and flagrant act (or failure to act) giving rise to liability for tax under chapter 42, shall be terminated if—

(A) such organization distributes all of its net assets to one or more organizations described in section 170(b)(1)(A) (other than in clauses (vii) and (viii)) each of which has been in existence and so described for a continuous period of at least 60 calendar months immediately preceding such distribution, or

(B)(i) such organization meets the requirements of paragraph (1), (2), or (3) of section 509(a) by the end of the 12-month period beginning with its first taxable year which begins after December 31, 1969, or for a continuous period of 60 calendar months beginning with the first day of any taxable year which begins after December 31, 1969,

(ii) such organization notifies the Secretary (in such manner as the Secretary may by regulations prescribe) before the commencement of such 12-month or 60-month period (or before the 90th day after the day on which regulations first prescribed under this subsection become final) that it is terminating its private foundation status, and

(iii) such organization establishes to the satisfaction of the Secretary (in such manner as the Secretary may by regulations prescribe) immediately after the expiration of such 12-month or 60-month period that such organization has complied with clause (i).

If an organization gives notice under subparagraph (B)(ii) of the commencement of a 60-month period and such organization fails to meet the requirements of paragraph (1), (2), or (3) of section 509(a) for the entire 60-month period, this part and chapter 42 shall not apply to such organization for any taxable year within such 60-month period for which it does meet such requirements.

(2) Transferee foundations.—For purposes of this part, in the case of a transfer of assets of any private foundation to another private foundation pursuant to any liquidation, merger, redemption, recapitalization, or other adjustment, organization, or reorganization, the transferee foundation shall not be treated as a newly created organization.

(c) Imposition of tax.—There is hereby imposed on each organization which is referred to in subsection (a) a tax equal to the lower of—

(1) the amount which the private foundation substantiates by adequate records or other corroborating evidence as the aggregate tax benefit resulting from the section 501(c)(3) status of such foundation, or

(2) the value of the net assets of such foundation.

(d) Aggregate tax benefit.—

(1) In general.—For purposes of subsection (c), the aggregate tax benefit resulting from the section 501(c)(3) status of any private foundation is the sum of—

(A) the aggregate increases in tax under chapters 1, 11, and 12 (or the corresponding provisions of prior law) which would have been imposed with respect to all substantial contributors to the foundation if deductions for all contributions made by such contributors to the foundation after February 28, 1913, had been disallowed, and

(B) the aggregate increases in tax under chapter 1 (or the corresponding provisions of prior law) which would have been imposed with respect to the income of the private foundation for taxable years beginning after December 31, 1912, if (i) it had not been exempt from tax under section 501(a) (or the corresponding provisions of prior law), and (ii) in the case of a trust, deductions under section 642(c) (or the corresponding provisions of prior law) had been limited to 20 percent of the taxable income of the trust (computed without the benefit of section 642(c) but with the benefit of section 170(b) (1)(A)), and

(C) interest on the increases in tax determined under subparagraphs (A) and (B) from the first date on which each such increase would have been due and payable to the date on which the organization ceases to be a private foundation.

(2) Substantial contributor.—

(A) Definition.—For purposes of paragraph (1), the term "substantial contributor" means any person who contributed or bequeathed an aggregate amount of more than $5,000 to the private foundation, if such amount is more than 2 percent of the total contributions and bequests received by the foundation before the close of the taxable year of the foundation in which the contribution or bequest is received by the foundation from such person. In the case of a trust, the term "substantial contributor" also means the creator of the trust.

(B) Special rules.—For purposes of subparagraph (A)—

(i) each contribution or bequest shall be valued at fair market value on the date it was received,

(ii) in the case of a foundation which is in existence on October 9, 1969, all contributions and bequests received on or before such date shall be treated (except for purposes of clause (i)) as if received on such date,

(iii) an individual shall be treated as making all contributions and bequests made by his spouse, and

(iv) any person who is a substantial contributor on any date shall remain a substantial contributor for all subsequent periods.

(C) Person ceases to be substantial contributor in certain cases.—

(i) In general.—A person shall cease to be treated as a substantial contributor with respect to any private foundation as of the close of any taxable year of such foundation if—

(I) during the 10-year period ending at the close of such taxable year such person (and all related persons) have not made any contribution to such private foundation,

(II) at no time during such 10-year period was such person (or any related person) a foundation manager of such private foundation, and

(III) the aggregate contributions made by such person (and related persons) are determined by the Secretary to be insignificant when compared to the aggregate amount of contributions to such foundation by one other person.

For purposes of subclause (III), appreciation on contributions while held by the foundation shall be taken into account.

(ii) **Related person.**—For purposes of clause (i), the term "related person" means, with respect to any person, any other person who would be a disqualified person (within the meaning of section 4946) by reason of his relationship to such person. In the case of a contributor which is a corporation, the term also includes any officer or director of such corporation.

(3) **Regulations.**—For purposes of this section, the determination as to whether and to what extent there would have been any increase in tax shall be made in accordance with regulations prescribed by the Secretary.

(e) Value of assets.—For purposes of subsection (c), the value of the net assets shall be determined at whichever time such value is higher: (1) the first day on which action is taken by the organization which culminates in its ceasing to be a private foundation, or (2) the date on which it ceases to be a private foundation.

(f) Liability in case of transfers of assets from private foundation.—For purposes of determining liability for the tax imposed by subsection (c) in the case of assets transferred by the private foundation, such tax shall be deemed to have been imposed on the first day on which action is taken by the organization which culminates in its ceasing to be a private foundation.

(g) Abatement of taxes.—The Secretary may abate the unpaid portion of the assessment of any tax imposed by subsection (c), or any liability in respect thereof, if—

(1) the private foundation distributes all of its net assets to one or more organizations described in section 170(b)(1)(A) (other than in clauses (vii) and (viii)) each of which has been in existence and so described for a continuous period of at least 60 calendar months, or

(2) following the notification prescribed in section 6104(c) to the appropriate State officer, such State officer within one year notifies the Secretary, in such manner as the Secretary may by regulations prescribe, that corrective action has been initiated pursuant to State law to insure that the assets of such private foundation are preserved for such charitable or other purposes specified in section 501(c)(3) as may be ordered or approved by a court of competent jurisdiction, and upon completion of the corrective action, the Secretary receives certification from the appropriate State officer that such action has resulted in such preservation of assets.

§ 508. Special rules with respect to section 501(c)(3) organizations

(a) New organizations must notify Secretary that they are applying for recognition of section 501(c)(3) status.—Except as provided in subsection (c), an organization organized after October 9, 1969, shall not be treated as an organization described in section 501(c)(3)—

(1) unless it has given notice to the Secretary, in such manner as the Secretary may by regulations prescribe, that it is applying for recognition of such status, or

(2) for any period before the giving of such notice, if such notice is given after the time prescribed by the Secretary by regulations for giving notice under this subsection.

(b) Presumption that organizations are private foundations.—Except as provided in subsection (c), any organization (including an organization in existence on October 9, 1969) which is described in section 501(c)(3) and which does not notify the Secretary, at such time and in such manner as the Secretary may by regulations prescribe, that it is not a private foundation shall be presumed to be a private foundation.

(c) Exceptions.—

(1) **Mandatory exceptions.**—Subsections (a) and (b) shall not apply to—

(A) churches, their integrated auxiliaries, and conventions or associations of churches, or

(B) any organization which is not a private foundation (as defined in section 509(a)) and the gross receipts of which in each taxable year are normally not more than $5,000.

(2) **Exceptions by regulations.**—The Secretary may by regulations exempt (to the extent and subject to such conditions as may be prescribed in such regulations) from the provisions of subsection (a) or (b) or both—

(A) educational organizations described in section 170(b)(1)(A)(ii), and

(B) any other class of organizations with respect to which the Secretary determines that full compliance with the provisions of subsections (a) and (b) is not necessary to the efficient administration of the provisions of this title relating to private foundations.

(d) Disallowance of certain charitable, etc., deductions.—

(1) Gift or bequest to organizations subject to section 507(c) tax.—No gift or bequest made to an organization upon which the tax provided by section 507(c) has been imposed shall be allowed as a deduction under section 170, 545(b)(2), 642(c), 2055, 2106(a)(2), or 2522, if such gift or bequest is made—

(A) by any person after notification is made under section 507(a), or

(B) by a substantial contributor (as defined in section 507(d)(2)) in his taxable year which includes the first day on which action is taken by such organization which culminates in the imposition of tax under section 507(c) and any subsequent taxable year.

(2) Gift or bequest to taxable private foundation, section 4947 trust, etc.—No gift or bequest made to an organization shall be allowed as a deduction under section 170, 545(b)(2), 642(c), 2055, 2106(a)(2), or 2522, if such gift or bequest is made—

(A) to a private foundation or a trust described in section 4947 in a taxable year for which it fails to meet the requirements of subsection (e) (determined without regard to subsection (e)(2)), or

(B) to any organization in a period for which it is not treated as an organization described in section 501(c)(3) by reason of subsection (a).

(3) Exception.—Paragraph (1) shall not apply if the entire amount of the unpaid portion of the tax imposed by section 507(c) is abated by the Secretary under section 507(g).

(e) Governing instruments.—

(1) General rule.—A private foundation shall not be exempt from taxation under section 501(a) unless its governing instrument includes provisions the effects of which are—

(A) to require its income for each taxable year to be distributed at such time and in such manner as not to subject the foundation to tax under section 4942, and

(B) to prohibit the foundation from engaging in any act of self-dealing (as defined in section 4941(d)), from retaining any excess business holdings (as defined in section 4943(c)), from making any investments in such manner as to subject the foundation to tax under section 4944, and from making any taxable expenditures (as defined in section 4945(d)).

* * *

(f) Additional provisions relating to sponsoring organizations.— A sponsoring organization (as defined in section 4966(d)(1)) shall give notice to the Secretary (in such manner as the Secretary may provide) whether such organization maintains or intends to maintain donor advised funds (as defined in section 4966(d)(2)) and the manner in which such organization plans to operate such funds.

§ 509. Private foundation defined

(a) General rule.—For purposes of this title, the term "private foundation" means a domestic or foreign organization described in section 501(c)(3) other than—

(1) an organization described in section 170(b)(1)(A) (other than in clauses (vii) and (viii));

(2) an organization which—

(A) normally receives more than one-third of its support in each taxable year from any combination of—

(i) gifts, grants, contributions, or membership fees, and

(ii) gross receipts from admissions, sales of merchandise, performance of services, or furnishing of facilities, in an activity which is not an unrelated trade or business (within the meaning of section 513), not including such receipts from any person, or from any bureau or similar agency of a governmental unit (as described in section 170(c)(1)), in any taxable year to the extent such receipts exceed the greater of $5,000 or 1 percent of the organization's support in such taxable year,

from persons other than disqualified persons (as defined in section 4946) with respect to the organization, from governmental units described in section 170(c)(1), or from organizations described in section 170(b)(1)(A) (other than in clauses (vii) and (viii)), and

(B) normally receives not more than one-third of its support in each taxable year from the sum of—

(i) gross investment income (as defined in subsection (e)) and

(ii) the excess (if any) of the amount of the unrelated business taxable income (as defined in section 512) over the amount of the tax imposed by section 511;

(3) an organization which—

(A) is organized, and at all times thereafter is operated, exclusively for the benefit of, to perform the functions of, or to carry out the purposes of one or more specified organizations described in paragraph (1) or (2),

(B) is—

(i) operated, supervised, or controlled by one or more organizations described in paragraph (1) or (2),

(ii) supervised or controlled in connection with one or more such organizations, or

(iii) operated in connection with one or more such organizations, and

(C) is not controlled directly or indirectly by one or more disqualified persons (as defined in section 4946) other than foundation managers and other than one or more organizations described in paragraph (1) or (2); and

(4) an organization which is organized and operated exclusively for testing for public safety.

For purposes of paragraph (3), an organization described in paragraph (2) shall be deemed to include an organization described in section 501(c)(4), (5), or (6) which would be described in paragraph (2) if it were an organization described in section 501(c)(3).

(b) Continuation of private foundation status.—For purposes of this title, if an organization is a private foundation (within the meaning of subsection (a)) on October 9, 1969, or becomes a private foundation on any subsequent date, such organization shall be treated as a private foundation for all periods after October 9, 1969, or after such subsequent date, unless its status as such is terminated under section 507.

(c) Status of organization after termination of private foundation status.—For purposes of this part, an organization the status of which as a private foundation is terminated under section 507 shall (except as provided in section 507(b)(2)) be treated as an organization created on the day after the date of such termination.

(d) Definition of support.—For purposes of this part and chapter 42, the term "support" includes (but is not limited to)—

(1) gifts, grants, contributions, or membership fees,

(2) gross receipts from admissions, sales of merchandise, performance of services, or furnishing of facilities in any activity which is not an unrelated trade or business (within the meaning of section 513),

(3) net income from unrelated business activities, whether or not such activities are carried on regularly as a trade or business,

(4) gross investment income (as defined in subsection (e)),

(5) tax revenues levied for the benefit of an organization and either paid to or expended on behalf of such organization, and

(6) the value of services or facilities (exclusive of services or facilities generally furnished to the public without charge) furnished by a governmental unit referred to in section 170(c)(1) to an organization without charge.

Such term does not include any gain from the sale or other disposition of property which would be considered as gain from the sale or exchange of a capital asset, or the value of exemption from any Federal, State, or local tax or any similar benefit.

(e) Definition of gross investment income.—For purposes of subsection (d), the term "gross investment income" means the gross amount of income from interest, dividends, payments with respect to securities loans (as defined in section 512(a)(5)), rents, and royalties, but not including any such income to the extent included in computing the tax imposed by section 511. Such term shall also include income from sources similar to those in the preceding sentence.

(f) Requirements for supporting organizations. —

(1) Type III supporting organizations.—For purposes of subsection (a)(3)(B)(iii), an organization shall not be considered to be operated in connection with any organization described in paragraph (1) or (2) of subsection (a) unless such organization meets the following requirements:

(A) Responsiveness.—For each taxable year beginning after the date of the enactment of this subsection, the organization provides to each supported organization such information as the Secretary may require to ensure that such organization is responsive to the needs or demands of the supported organization.

(B) **Foreign supported organizations.**—

(i) **In general.**—The organization is not operated in connection with any supported organization that is not organized in the United States.

(ii) **Transition rule for existing organizations.**—If the organization is operated in connection with an organization that is not organized in the United States on the date of the enactment of this subsection, clause (i) shall not apply until the first day of the third taxable year of the organization beginning after the date of the enactment of this subsection.

(2) **Organizations controlled by donors.**—

(A) **In general.**—For purposes of subsection (a)(3)(B), an organization shall not be considered to be—

(i) operated, supervised, or controlled by any organization described in paragraph (1) or (2) of subsection (a), or

(ii) operated in connection with any organization described in paragraph (1) or (2) of subsection (a),

if such organization accepts any gift or contribution from any person described in subparagraph (B).

(B) **Person described.**—A person is described in this subparagraph if, with respect to a supported organization of an organization described in subparagraph (A), such person is—

(i) a person (other than an organization described in paragraph (1), (2), or (4) of section 509(a)) who directly or indirectly controls, either alone or together with persons described in clauses (ii) and (iii), the governing body of such supported organization,

(ii) a member of the family (determined under section 4958(f)(4)) of an individual described in clause (i), or

(iii) a 35-percent controlled entity (as defined in section 4958(f)(3) by substituting "persons described in clause (i) or (ii) of section 509(f)(2)(B)" for "persons described in subparagraph (A) or (B) of paragraph (1)" in subparagraph (A)(i) thereof).

(3) **Supported organization.**—For purposes of this subsection, the term "supported organization" means, with respect to an organization described in subsection (a)(3), an organization described in paragraph (1) or (2) of subsection (a)—

(A) for whose benefit the organization described in subsection (a)(3) is organized and operated, or

(B) with respect to which the organization performs the functions of, or carries out the purposes of.

PART III—TAXATION OF BUSINESS INCOME OF CERTAIN EXEMPT ORGANIZATIONS

Editorial Summary

Unrelated Business Income Tax

Subchapter F of Chapter 1 (Secs. 511–515)

See the discussion under the Editorial Summary entitled Tax Exempt Organizations, which precedes Sec. 501.

§ 511. Imposition of tax on unrelated business income of charitable, etc., organizations

(a) Charitable, etc., organizations taxable at corporation rates.—

(1) **Imposition of tax.**—There is hereby imposed for each taxable year on the unrelated business taxable income (as defined in section 512) of every organization described in paragraph (2) a tax computed as provided in section 11. In making such computation for purposes of this section, the term "taxable income" as used in section 11 shall be read as "unrelated business taxable income".

(2) **Organizations subject to tax.**—

(A) **Organizations described in sections 401(a) and 501(c).**—The tax imposed by paragraph (1) shall apply in the case of any organization (other than a trust described in subsection (b) or an organization described in section 501(c)(1)) which is exempt, except as provided in this part or part II (relating to private foundations), from taxation under this subtitle by reason of section 501(a).

(B) **State colleges and universities.**—The tax imposed by paragraph (1) shall apply in the case of any college or university which is an agency or instrumentality of any government or any political subdivision thereof, or which is owned or operated by a government or any political subdivision thereof, or by any agency or instrumentality of one or more governments or political subdivisions. Such tax shall also apply in the case of any corporation wholly owned by one or more such colleges or universities.

(b) Tax on charitable, etc., trusts.—

(1) Imposition of tax.—There is hereby imposed for each taxable year on the unrelated business taxable income of every trust described in paragraph (2) a tax computed as provided in section 1(e). In making such computation for purposes of this section, the term "taxable income" as used in section 1 shall be read as "unrelated business taxable income" as defined in section 512.

(2) Charitable, etc., trusts subject to tax.—The tax imposed by paragraph (1) shall apply in the case of any trust which is exempt, except as provided in this part or part II (relating to private foundations), from taxation under this subtitle by reason of section 501(a) and which, if it were not for such exemption, would be subject to sub chapter J (sec. 641 and following, relating to estates, trusts, beneficiaries, and decedents).

(c) Special rule for section 501(c)(2) corporations.—If a corporation described in section 501(c)(2)—

(1) pays any amount of its net income for a taxable year to an organization exempt from taxation under section 501(a) (or which would pay such an amount but for the fact that the expenses of collecting its income exceed its income), and

(2) such corporation and such organization file a consolidated return for the taxable year,

such corporation shall be treated, for purposes of the tax imposed by subsection (a), as being organized and operated for the same purposes as such organization, in addition to the purposes described in section 501(c)(2).

§ 512. Unrelated business taxable income

(a) Definition.—For purposes of this title—

(1) General rule.—Except as otherwise provided in this subsection, the term "unrelated business taxable income" means the gross income derived by any organization from any unrelated trade or business (as defined in section 513) regularly carried on by it, less the deductions allowed by this chapter which are directly connected with the carrying on of such trade or business, both computed with the modifications provided in subsection (b).

* * *

(3) Special rules applicable to organizations described in paragraph (7), (9), (17), or (20) of section 501(c).—

(A) General rule.—In the case of an organization described in paragraph (7), (9), (17), or (20) of section 501(c), the term "unrelated business taxable income" means the gross income (excluding any exempt function income), less the deductions allowed by this chapter which are directly connected with the production of the gross income (excluding exempt function income), both computed with the modifications provided in paragraphs (6), (10), (11), and (12) of subsection (b). For purposes of the preceding sentence, the deductions provided by sections 243, 244, and 245 (relating to dividends received by corporations) shall be treated as not directly connected with the production of gross income.

(B) Exempt function income.—For purposes of subparagraph (A), the term "exempt function income" means the gross income from dues, fees, charges, or similar amounts paid by members of the organization as consideration for providing such members or their dependents or guests goods, facilities, or services in furtherance of the purposes constituting the basis for the exemption of the organization to which such income is paid. Such term also means all income (other than an amount equal to the gross income derived from any unrelated trade or business regularly carried on by such organization computed as if the organization were subject to paragraph (1)), which is set aside—

(i) for a purpose specified in section 170(c)(4), or

(ii) in the case of an organization described in paragraph (9), (17), or (20) of section 501(c), to provide for the payment of life, sick, accident, or other benefits,

including reasonable costs of administration directly connected with a purpose described in clause (i) or (ii). If during the taxable year, an amount which is attributable to income so set aside is used for a purpose other than that described in clause (i) or (ii), such amount shall be included, under subparagraph (A), in unrelated business taxable income for the taxable year.

(C) Applicability to certain corporations described in section 501(c) (2).—In the case of a corporation described in section 501(c)(2), the income of which is payable to an organization described in paragraph (7), (9), (17), or (20) of section 501(c), subparagraph (A) shall apply as if such corporation were the organization to which the income is payable. For purposes of the preceding sentence, such corporation shall be treated as having exempt function income for a taxable year only if it files a consolidated return with such organization for such year.

(D) Nonrecognition of gain.—If property used directly in the performance of the exempt function of an organization described in paragraph (7), (9), (17), or (20) of section 501(c) is sold by such organization, and within a period beginning 1 year before the date of such sale, and ending 3 years after such date, other property is purchased and used by such organization directly in the performance of its exempt function, gain (if any) from such sale shall be recognized only to the extent that such organization's sales price of the old property exceeds the organization's cost of purchasing the other property. For purposes of this subparagraph, the destruction in whole or in part, theft, seizure, requisition, or condemnation of property, shall be treated as the sale of such property, and rules similar to the rules provided by subsections (b), (c), (e), and (j) of section 1034 (as in effect on the day before the date of enactment of the Taxpayer Relief Act of 1997) shall apply.

(E) Limitation on amount of set aside in the case of organizations described in paragraph (9), (17), or (20) of section 501(c).—

(i) In general.—In the case of any organization described in paragraph (9), (17), or (20) of section 501(c), a set-aside for any purpose specified in clause (ii) of subparagraph (B) may be taken into account under subparagraph (B) only to the extent that such set-aside does not result in an amount of assets set aside for such purpose in excess of the account limit determined under section 419A (without regard to subsection (f)(6) thereof) for the taxable year (not taking into account any reserve described in section 419A(c)(2)(A) for post-retirement medical benefits).

(ii) Treatment of existing reserves for post-retirement medical or life insurance benefits.—

(I) Clause (i) shall not apply to any income attributable to an existing reserve for post-retirement medical or life insurance benefits.

(II) For purposes of subclause (I), the term "reserve for post-retirement medical or life insurance benefits" means the greater of the amount of assets set aside for purposes of post-retirement medical or life insurance benefits to be provided to covered employees as of the close of the last plan year ending before the date of the enactment of the Tax Reform Act of 1984 or on July 18, 1984.

(III) All payments during plan years ending on or after the date of the enactment of the Tax Reform Act of 1984 of post-retirement medical benefits or life insurance benefits shall be charged against the reserve referred to in subclause (II). Except to the extent provided in regulations prescribed by the Secretary, all plans of an employer shall be treated as 1 plan for purposes of the preceding sentence.

(iii) Treatment of tax exempt organizations.—This subparagraph shall not apply to any organization if substantially all of the contributions to such organization are made by employers who were exempt from tax under this chapter throughout the 5-taxable year period ending with the taxable year in which the contributions are made.

(4) Special rule applicable to organizations described in section 501(c)(19).—In the case of an organization described in section 501(c)(19), the term "unrelated business taxable income" does not include any amount attributable to payments for life, sick, accident, or health insurance with respect to members of such organizations or their dependents which is set aside for the purpose of providing for the payment of insurance benefits or for a purpose specified in section 170(c)(4). If an amount set aside under the preceding sentence is used during the taxable year for a purpose other than a purpose described in the preceding sentence, such amount shall be included, under paragraph (1), in unrelated business taxable income for the taxable year.

(5) Definition of payments with respect to securities loans.—

(A) The term "payments with respect to securities loans" includes all amounts received in respect of a security (as defined in section 1236(c)) transferred by the owner to another person in a transaction to which section 1058 applies (whether or not title to the security remains in the name of the lender) including—

(i) amounts in respect of dividends, interest, or other distributions,

(ii) fees computed by reference to the period beginning with the transfer of securities by the owner and ending with the transfer of identical securities back to the transferor by the transferee and the fair market value of the security during such period,

(iii) income from collateral security for such loan, and

(iv) income from the investment of collateral security.

(B) Subparagraph (A) shall apply only with respect to securities transferred pursuant to an agreement between the transferor and the transferee which provides for—

(i) reasonable procedures to implement the obligation of the transferee to furnish to the transferor, for each business day during such period, collateral with a fair market value not less than the fair market value of the security at the close of business on the preceding business day,

(ii) termination of the loan by the transferor upon notice of not more than 5 business days, and

(iii) return to the transferor of securities identical to the transferred securities upon termination of the loan.

(b) Modifications.—The modifications referred to in subsection (a) are the following:

(1) There shall be excluded all dividends, interest, payments with respect to securities loans (as defined in section (a)(5)), amounts received or accrued as consideration for entering into agreements to make loans, and annuities, and all deductions directly connected with such income.

(2) There shall be excluded all royalties (including overriding royalties) whether measured by production or by gross or taxable income from the property, and all deductions directly connected with such income.

(3) In the case of rents—

(A) Except as provided in subparagraph (B), there shall be excluded—

(i) all rents from real property (including property described in section 1245(a)(3)(C)), and

(ii) all rents from personal property (including for purposes of this paragraph as personal property any property described in section 1245(a)(3) (B)) leased with such real property, if the rents attributable to such personal property are an incidental amount of the total rents received or accrued under the lease, determined at the time the personal property is placed in service.

(B) Subparagraph (A) shall not apply—

(i) if more than 50 percent of the total rent received or accrued under the lease is attributable to personal property described in subparagraph (A)(ii), or

(ii) if the determination of the amount of such rent depends in whole or in part on the income or profits derived by any person from the property leased (other than an amount based on a fixed percentage or percentages of receipts or sales).

(C) There shall be excluded all deductions directly connected with rents excluded under subparagraph (A).

(4) Notwithstanding paragraph (1), (2), (3), or (5), in the case of debt-financed property (as defined in section 514) there shall be included, as an item of gross income derived from an unrelated trade or business, the amount ascertained under section 514(a)(1), and there shall be allowed, as a deduction, the amount ascertained under section 514(a)(2).

(5) There shall be excluded all gains or losses from the sale, exchange, or other disposition of property other than—

(A) stock in trade or other property of a kind which would properly be includible in inventory if on hand at the close of the taxable year, or

(B) property held primarily for sale to customers in the ordinary course of the trade or business.

There shall also be excluded all gains or losses recognized, in connection with the organization's investment activities, from the lapse or termination of options to buy or sell securities (as defined in section 1236(c)) or real property and all gains or losses from the forfeiture of good-faith deposits (that are consistent with established business practice) for the purchase, sale, or lease of real property in connection with the organization's investment activities. This paragraph shall not apply with respect to the cutting of timber which is considered, on the application of section 631, as a sale or exchange of such timber.

(6) The net operating loss deduction provided in section 172 shall be allowed, except that—

(A) the net operating loss for any taxable year, the amount of the net operating loss carry-back or carryover to any taxable year, and the net operating loss deduction for any taxable year shall be determined under section 172 without taking into account any amount of income or deduction which is excluded under this part in computing the unrelated business taxable income; and

(B) the terms "preceding taxable year" and "preceding taxable years" as used in section 172 shall not include any taxable year for which the organization was not subject to the provisions of this part.

(7) There shall be excluded all income derived from research for (A) the United States, or any of its agencies or instrumentalities, or (B) any State or political subdivision thereof; and there shall be excluded all deductions directly connected with such income.

(8) In the case of a college, university, or hospital, there shall be excluded all income derived from research performed for any person, and all deductions directly connected with such income.

(9) In the case of an organization operated primarily for purposes of carrying on fundamental research the results of which are freely available to the general public, there shall be excluded all income derived from research performed for any person, and all deductions directly connected with such income.

(10) In the case of any organization described in section 511(a), the deduction allowed by section 170 (relating to charitable etc. contributions and gifts) shall be allowed (whether or not directly connected with the carrying on of the trade or business), but shall not exceed 10 percent of the unrelated business taxable income computed without the benefit of this paragraph.

(11) In the case of any trust described in section 511(b), the deduction allowed by section 170 (relating to charitable etc. contributions and gifts) shall be allowed (whether or not directly connected with the carrying on of the trade or business), and for such purpose a distribution made by the trust to a beneficiary described in section 170 shall be considered as a gift or contribution. The deduction allowed by this paragraph shall be allowed with the limitations prescribed in section 170(b)(1)(A) and (B) determined with reference to the unrelated business taxable income computed without the benefit of this paragraph (in lieu of with reference to adjusted gross income).

(12) Except for purposes of computing the net operating loss under section 172 and paragraph (6), there shall be allowed a specific deduction of $1,000. In the case of a diocese, province of a religious order, or a convention or association of churches, there shall also be allowed, with respect to each parish, individual church, district, or other local unit, a specific deduction equal to the lower of—

(A) $1,000, or

(B) the gross income derived from any unrelated trade or business regularly carried on by such local unit.

(13) Special rules for certain amounts received from controlled entities.—

(A) In general.—If an organization (in this paragraph referred to as the "controlling organization") receives or accrues (directly or indirectly) a specified payment from another entity which it controls (in this paragraph referred to as the "controlled entity"), notwithstanding paragraphs (1), (2), and (3), the controlling organization shall include such payment as an item of gross income derived from an unrelated trade or business to the extent such payment reduces the net unrelated income of the controlled entity (or increases any net unrelated loss of the controlled entity). There shall be allowed all deductions of the controlling organization directly connected with amounts treated as derived from an unrelated trade or business under the preceding sentence.

(B) Net unrelated income or loss.—For purposes of this paragraph—

(i) Net unrelated income.—The term "net unrelated income" means—

(I) in the case of a controlled entity which is not exempt from tax under section 501(a), the portion of such entity's taxable income which would be unrelated business taxable income if such entity were exempt from tax under section 501(a) and had the same exempt purposes as the controlling organization, or

(II) in the case of a controlled entity which is exempt from tax under section 501 (a), the amount of the unrelated business taxable income of the controlled entity.

(ii) Net unrelated loss.—The term "net unrelated loss" means the net operating loss adjusted under rules similar to the rules of clause (i).

(C) Specified payment.—For purposes of this paragraph, the term "specified payment" means any interest, annuity, royalty, or rent.

(D) Definition of control.—For purposes of this paragraph—

(i) Control.—The term "control" means—

(I) in the case of a corporation, ownership (by vote or value) of more than 50 percent of the stock in such corporation,

(II) in the case of a partnership, ownership of more than 50 percent of the profits interests or capital interests in such partnership, or

(III) in any other case, ownership of more than 50 percent of the beneficial interests in the entity.

(ii) Constructive ownership.—Section 318 (relating to constructive ownership of stock) shall apply for purposes of determining ownership of stock in a corporation. Similar principles shall apply for purposes of determining ownership of interests in any other entity.

(E) Paragraph to apply only to certain excess payments.—

(i) In general.—Subparagraph (A) shall apply only to the portion of a qualifying specified payment received or accrued by the controlling organization that exceeds the amount which would have been paid or accrued if such payment met the requirements prescribed under section 482.

(ii) Addition to tax for valuation misstatements.—The tax imposed by this chapter on the controlling organization shall be increased by an amount equal to 20 percent of the larger of—

(I) such excess determined without regard to any amendment or supplement to a return of tax, or

(II) such excess determined with regard to all such amendments and supplements.

(iii) Qualifying specified payment.—The term "qualifying specified payment" means a specified payment which is made pursuant to—

(I) a binding written contract in effect on the date of the enactment of this subparagraph, or

(II) a contract which is a renewal, under substantially similar terms, of a contract described in subclause (I).

(iv) Termination.—This subparagraph shall not apply to payments received or accrued after December 31, 2013.*

(v) Related persons.—The Secretary shall prescribe such rules as may be necessary or appropriate to prevent avoidance of the purposes of this paragraph through the use of related persons.

****(15)** Except as provided in paragraph (4), in the case of a trade or business—

(A) which consists of providing services under license issued by a Federal regulatory agency,

(B) which is carried on by a religious order or by an educational organization described in section 170(b)(1)(A)(ii) maintained by such religious order, and which was so carried on before May 27, 1959, and

(C) less than 10 percent of the net income of which for each taxable year is used for activities which are not related to the purpose constituting the basis for the religious order's exemption,

*Editorial comment: At the present time, this section has not been extended. There is pending legislation in the Senate, *The Tax Extenders Act of 2013 (S. 1859)*, that would extend Section 512(b)(13)(E)(iv) until December 31, 2014.

**Editorial comment: There is no paragraph 14.

there shall be excluded all gross income derived from such trade or business and all deductions directly connected with the carrying on of such trade or business, so long as it is established to the satisfaction of the Secretary that the rates or other charges for such services are competitive with rates or other charges charged for similar services by persons not exempt from taxation.

(16) (A) Notwithstanding paragraph (5)(B), there shall be excluded all gains or losses from the sale, exchange, or other disposition of any real property described in subparagraph (B) if—

(i) such property was acquired by the organization from—

(I) a financial institution described in section 581 or 591(a) which is in conservatorship or receivership, or

(II) the conservator or receiver of such an institution (or any government agency or corporation succeeding to the rights or interests of the conservator or receiver),

(ii) such property is designated by the organization within the 9-month period beginning on the date of its acquisition as property held for sale, except that not more than one-half (by value determined as of such date) of property acquired in a single transaction may be so designated,

(iii) such sale, exchange, or disposition occurs before the later of—

(I) the date which is 30 months after the date of the acquisition of such property, or

(II) the date specified by the Secretary in order to assure an orderly disposition of property held by persons described in subparagraph (A), and

(iv) while such property was held by the organization, the aggregate expenditures on improvements and development activities included in the basis of the property are (or were) not in excess of 20 percent of the net selling price of such property.

(B) Property is described in this subparagraph if it is real property which—

(i) was held by the financial institution at the time it entered into conservatorship or receivership, or

(ii) was foreclosure property (as defined in section 514(c)(9)(H)(v)) which secured indebtedness held by the financial institution at such time.

For purposes of this subparagraph, real property includes an interest in a mortgage.

* * *

(c) Special rules for partnerships.—

(1) In general.—If a trade or business regularly carried on by a partnership of which an organization is a member is an unrelated trade or business with respect to such organization, such organization in computing its unrelated business taxable income shall, subject to the exceptions, additions, and limitations contained in subsection (b), include its share (whether or not distributed) of the gross income of the partnership from such unrelated trade or business and its share of the partnership deductions directly connected with such gross income.

(2) Special rule where partnership year is different from organization's year.—If the taxable year of the organization is different from that of the partnership, the amounts to be included or deducted in computing the unrelated business taxable income under paragraph (1) shall be based upon the income and deductions of the partnership for any taxable year of the partnership ending within or with the taxable year of the organization.

* * *

(e) Special rules applicable to S corporations.—

(1) In general.—If an organization described in section 1361(c)(2)(A)(vi) or 1361(c)(6) holds stock in an S corporation—

(A) such interest shall be treated as an interest in an unrelated trade or business; and

(B) notwithstanding any other provision of this part—

(i) all items of income, loss, or deduction taken into account under section 1366(a), and

(ii) any gain or loss on the disposition of the stock in the S corporation

shall be taken into account in computing the unrelated business taxable income of such organization.

(2) Basis reduction.—Except as provided in regulations, for purposes of paragraph (1), the basis of any stock acquired by purchase (as defined in section 1361(e)(1)(C)) shall be reduced by the amount of any dividends received by the organization with respect to the stock.

(3) Exception for ESOPs.—This subsection shall not apply to employer securities (within the meaning of section 409(1)) held by an employee stock ownership plan described in section 4975(e)(7).

§ 513. Unrelated trade or business

(a) General rule.—The term "unrelated trade or business" means, in the case of any organization subject to the tax imposed by section 511, any trade or business the conduct of which is not substantially related (aside from the need of such organization for income or funds or the use it makes of the profits derived) to the exercise or performance by such organization of its charitable, educational, or other purpose or function constituting the basis for its exemption under section 501 (or, in the case of an organization described in section 511(a)(2)(B), to the exercise or performance of any purpose or function described in section 501(c)(3)), except that such term does not include any trade or business—

(1) in which substantially all the work in carrying on such trade or business is performed for the organization without compensation; or

(2) which is carried on, in the case of an organization described in section 501(c)(3) or in the case of a college or university described in section 511(a)(2)(B), by the organization primarily for the convenience of its members, students, patients, officers, or employees, or, in the case of a local association of employees described in section 501(c)(4) organized before May 27, 1969, which is the selling by the organization of items of work-related clothes and equipment and items normally sold through vending machines, through food dispensing facilities, or by snack bars, for the convenience of its members at their usual places of employment; or

(3) which is the selling of merchandise, substantially all of which has been received by the organization as gifts or contributions.

(b) Special rule for trusts.—The term "unrelated trade or business" means, in the case of—

(1) a trust computing its unrelated business taxable income under section 512 for purposes of section 681; or

(2) a trust described in section 401(a), or section 501(c)(17), which is exempt from tax under section 501(a);

any trade or business regularly carried on by such trust or by a partnership of which it is a member.

(c) Advertising, etc., activities.—For purposes of this section, the term "trade or business" includes any activity which is carried on for the production of income from the sale of goods or the performance of services. For purposes of the preceding sentence, an activity does not lose identity as a trade or business merely because it is carried on within a larger aggregate of similar activities or within a larger complex of other endeavors which may, or may not, be related to the exempt purposes of the organization. Where an activity carried on for profit constitutes an unrelated trade or business, no part of such trade or business shall be excluded from such classification merely because it does not result in profit.

(d) Certain activities of trade shows, state fairs, etc.—

(1) General rule.—The term "unrelated trade or business" does not include qualified public entertainment activities of an organization described in paragraph (2)(C), or qualified convention and trade show activities of an organization described in paragraph (3)(C).

(2) Qualified public entertainment activities.—For purposes of this subsection—

(A) Public entertainment activity.—The term "public entertainment activity" means any entertainment or recreational activity of a kind traditionally conducted at fairs or expositions promoting agricultural and educational purposes, including, but not limited to, any activity one of the purposes of which is to attract the public to fairs or expositions or to promote the breeding of animals or the development of products or equipment.

(B) Qualified public entertainment activity.—The term "qualified public entertainment activity" means a public entertainment activity which is conducted by a qualifying organization described in subparagraph (C) in—

(i) conjunction with an international, national, State, regional, or local fair or exposition,

(ii) accordance with the provisions of State law which permit the activity to be operated or conducted solely by such an organization, or by an agency, instrumentality, or political subdivision of such State, or

(iii) accordance with the provisions of State law which permit such an organization to be granted a license to conduct not more than 20 days of such activity on payment to the State of a lower percentage of the revenue from such licensed activity than the State requires from organizations not described in section 501(c)(3), (4), or (5).

(C) Qualifying organization.—For purposes of this paragraph, the term "qualifying organization" means an organization which is described in section 501(c)(3), (4), or (5) which regularly conducts, as one of its substantial exempt purposes, an agricultural and educational fair or exposition.

(3) Qualified convention and trade show activities.—

(A) Convention and trade show activity.—The term "convention and trade show activity" means any activity of a kind traditionally conducted at conventions, annual meetings, or trade shows, including, but not limited to, any activity one of the purposes of which is to attract persons in an industry generally (without regard to membership in the sponsoring organization) as well as members of the public to the show for the purpose of displaying industry products or to stimulate interest in, and demand for, industry products or services, or to educate persons engaged in the industry in the development of new products and services or new rules and regulations affecting the industry.

(B) Qualified convention and trade show activity.—The term "qualified convention and trade show activity" means a convention and trade show activity carried out by a qualifying organization described in subparagraph (C) in conjunction with an international, national, State, regional, or local convention, annual meeting, or show conducted by an organization described in subparagraph (C) if one of the purposes of such organization in sponsoring the activity is the promotion and stimulation of interest in, and demand for, the products and services of that industry in general or to educate persons in attendance regarding new developments or products and services related to the exempt activities of the organization, and the show is designed to achieve such purpose through the character of the exhibits and the extent of the industry products displayed.

(C) Qualifying organization.—For purposes of this paragraph, the term "qualifying organization" means an organization described in section 501(c)(3), (4), (5), or (6) which regularly conducts as one of its substantial exempt purposes a show which stimulates interest in, and demand for, the products of a particular industry or segment of such industry or which educates persons in attendance regarding new developments or products and services related to the exempt activities of the organization.

(4) Such activities not to affect exempt status.—An organization described in section 501(c)(3), (4), or (5) shall not be considered as not entitled to the exemption allowed under section 501(a) solely because of qualified public entertainment activities conducted by it.

(e) Certain hospital services.—In the case of a hospital described in section 170(b)(1)(A)(iii), the term "unrelated trade or business" does not include the furnishing of one or more of the services described in section 501(e)(1)(A) to one or more hospitals described in section 170(b)(1)(A)(iii) if—

(1) such services are furnished solely to such hospitals which have facilities to serve not more than 100 inpatients;

(2) such services, if performed on its own behalf by the recipient hospital, would constitute activities in exercising or performing the purpose or function constituting the basis for its exemption; and

(3) such services are provided at a fee or cost which does not exceed the actual cost of providing such services, such cost including straight line depreciation and a reasonable amount for return on capital goods used to provide such services.

(f) Certain bingo games.—

(1) In general.—The term "unrelated trade or business" does not include any trade or business which consists of conducting bingo games.

(2) Bingo game defined.—For purposes of paragraph (1), the term "bingo game" means any game of bingo—

(A) of a type in which usually—

(i) the wagers are placed,

(ii) the winners are determined, and

(iii) the distribution of prizes or other property is made,

in the presence of all persons placing wagers in such game,

(B) the conducting of which is not an activity ordinarily carried out on a commercial basis, and

(C) the conducting of which does not violate any State or local law.

(g) Certain pole rentals.—In the case of a mutual or cooperative telephone or electric company, the term "unrelated trade or business" does not include engaging in qualified pole rentals (as defined in section 501(c)(12)(D)).

(h) Certain distributions of low cost articles without obligation to purchase and exchanges and rentals of member lists.—

(1) In general.—In the case of an organization which is described in section 501 and contributions to which are deductible under paragraph (2) or (3) of section 170(c), the term "unrelated trade or business" does not include—

(A) activities relating to the distribution of low cost articles if the distribution of such articles is incidental to the solicitation of charitable contributions, or

(B) any trade or business which consists of—

(i) exchanging with another such organization names and addresses of donors to (or members of) such organization, or

(ii) renting such names and addresses to another such organization.

(2) Low cost article defined.—For purposes of this subsection—

(A) In general.—The term "low cost article" means any article which has a cost not in excess of $5* to the organization which distributes such item (or on whose behalf such item is distributed).

(B) Aggregation rule.—If more than 1 item is distributed by or on behalf of an organization to a single distributee in any calendar year, the aggregate of the items so distributed in such calendar year to such distributee shall be treated as 1 article for purposes of subparagraph (A).

(C) Indexation of $5 amount.*—In the case of any taxable year beginning in a calendar year after 1987, the $5 amount in subparagraph (A) shall be increased by an amount equal to—

(i) $5, multiplied by

(ii) the cost-of-living adjustment determined under section 1(f)(3) for the calendar year in which the taxable year begins, by substituting "calendar year 1987" for "calendar year 1992" in subparagraph (B) thereof.

(3) Distribution which is incidental to the solicitation of charitable contributions described.—For purposes of this subsection, any distribution of low cost articles by an organization shall be treated as a distribution incidental to the solicitation of charitable contributions only if—

(A) such distribution is not made at the request of the distributee,

(B) such distribution is made without the express consent of the distributee, and

(C) the articles so distributed are accompanied by—

(i) a request for a charitable contribution (as defined in section 170(c)) by the distributee to such organization, and

(ii) a statement that the distributee may retain the low cost article regardless of whether such distributee makes a charitable contribution to such organization.

(i) Treatment of certain sponsorship payments.—

(1) In general.—The term "unrelated trade or business" does not include the activity of soliciting and receiving qualified sponsorship payments.

(2) Qualified sponsorship payments.—For purposes of this subsection—

(A) In general.—The term "qualified sponsorship payment" means any payment made by any person engaged in a trade or business with respect to which there is no arrangement or expectation that such person will receive any substantial return benefit other than the use of acknowledgment of the name or logo (or product lines) of such person's trade or business in connection with the activities of the organization that receives such payment. Such a use or acknowledgment does not include advertising such person's products or services (including messages containing qualitative or comparative language, price information, or other indications of savings or value, an endorsement, or an inducement to purchase, sell, or use such products or services).

(B) Limitations.—

(i) Contingent payments.—The term "qualified sponsorship payment" does not include any payment if the amount of such

* Editorial comment: The indexed amount for 2013 is $10.20 and for 2014 is $10.40.

payment is contingent upon the level of attendance at one or more events, broadcast ratings, or other factors indicating the degree of public exposure to one or more events.

(ii) Safe harbor does not apply to periodicals and qualified convention and trade show activities.—The term "qualified sponsorship payment" does not include—

(I) any payment which entitles the payor to the use of acknowledgment of the name or logo (or product lines) of the payor's trade or business in regularly scheduled and printed material published by or on behalf of the payee organization that is not related to and primarily distributed in connection with a specific event conducted by the payee organization, or

(II) any payment made in connection with any qualified convention or trade show activity (as defined in subsection (d)(3)(B)).

(3) Allocation of portions of single payment.—For purposes of this subsection, to the extent that a portion of a payment would (if made as a separate payment) be a qualified sponsorship payment, such portion of such payment and the other portion of such payment shall be treated as separate payments.

(j) Debt management plan services.—The term "unrelated trade or business" includes the provision of debt management plan services (as defined in section § 501(q)(4)(B)) by any organization other than an organization which meets the requirements of section § 501(q).

§ 514. Unrelated debt-financed income

(a) Unrelated debt-financed income and deductions.—In computing under section 512 the unrelated business taxable income for any taxable year—

(1) Percentage of income taken into account.—There shall be included with respect to each debt-financed property as an item of gross income derived from an unrelated trade or business an amount which is the same percentage (but not in excess of 100 percent) of the total gross income derived during the taxable year from or on account of such property as (A) the average acquisition indebtedness (as defined in subsection (c)(7)) for the taxable year with respect to the property is of (B) the average amount (determined under regulations prescribed by the Secretary) of the adjusted basis of such property during the period it is held by the organization during such taxable year.

(2) Percentage of deductions taken into account.—There shall be allowed as a deduction with respect to each debt-financed property an amount determined by applying (except as provided in the last sentence of this paragraph) the percentage derived under paragraph (1) to the sum determined under paragraph (3). The percentage derived under this paragraph shall not be applied with respect to the deduction of any capital loss resulting from the carryback or carryover of net capital losses under section 1212.

(3) Deductions allowable.—The sum referred to in paragraph (2) is the sum of the deductions under this chapter which are directly connected with the debt-financed property or the income therefrom, except that if the debt-financed property is of a character which is subject to the allowance for depreciation provided in section 167, the allowance shall be computed only by use of the straight-line method.

(b) Definition of debt-financed property.—

(1) In general.—For purposes of this section, the term "debt-financed property" means any property which is held to produce income and with respect to which there is an acquisition indebtedness (as defined in subsection (c)) at any time during the taxable year (or, if the property was disposed of during the taxable year, with respect to which there was an acquisition indebtedness at any time during the 12-month period ending with the date of such disposition), except that such term does not include—

(A) (i) any property substantially all the use of which is substantially related (aside from the need of the organization for income or funds) to the exercise or performance by such organization of its charitable, educational, or other purpose or function constituting the basis for its exemption under section 501 (or, in the case of an organization described in section 511(a)(2) (B), to the exercise or performance of any purpose or function designated in section 501(c) (3)), or

(ii) any property to which clause (i) does not apply, to the extent that its use is so substantially related;

(B) except in the case of income excluded under section 512(b)(5), any property to the extent that the income from such property is taken into account in computing the gross income of any unrelated trade or business;

(C) any property to the extent that the income from such property is excluded by reason of the provisions of paragraph (7), (8), or (9) of section 512(b) in computing the gross income of any unrelated trade or business;

(D) any property to the extent that it is used in any trade or business described in paragraph (1), (2), or (3) of section 513(a); or

(E) any property the gain or loss from the sale, exchange, or other disposition of which would be excluded by reason of the provisions of section 512(b)(19) in computing the gross income of any trade or business.

For purposes of subparagraph (A), substantially all the use of a property shall be considered to be substantially related to the exercise or performance by an organization of its charitable, educational, or other purpose or function constituting the basis for its exemption under section 501 if such property is real property subject to a lease to a medical clinic entered into primarily for purposes which are substantially related (aside from the need of such organization for income or funds or the use it makes of the rents derived) to the exercise or performance by such organization of its charitable, educational, or other purpose or function constituting the basis for its exemption under section 501.

(2) Special rule for related uses.—For purposes of applying paragraphs (1)(A), (C), and (D), the use of any property by an exempt organization which is related to an organization shall be treated as use by such organization.

(3) Special rules when land is acquired for exempt use within 10 years.—

(A) Neighborhood land.—If an organization acquires real property for the principal purpose of using the land (commencing within 10 years of the time of acquisition) in the manner described in paragraph (1)(A) and at the time of acquisition the property is in the neighborhood of other property owned by the organization which is used in such manner, the real property acquired for such future use shall not be treated as debt-financed property so long as the organization does not abandon its intent to so use the land within the 10-year period. The preceding sentence shall not apply for any period after the expiration of the 10-year period, and shall apply after the first 5 years of the 10-year period only if the organization establishes to the satisfaction of the Secretary that it is reasonably certain that the land will be used in the described manner before the expiration of the 10-year period.

(B) Other cases.—If the first sentence of subparagraph (A) is inapplicable only because—

(i) the acquired land is not in the neighborhood referred to in subparagraph (A), or

(ii) the organization (for the period after the first 5 years of the 10-year period) is unable to establish to the satisfaction of the Secretary that it is reasonably certain that the land will be used in the manner described in paragraph (1) (A) before the expiration of the 10-year period,

but the land is converted to such use by the organization within the 10-year period, the real property (subject to the provisions of subparagraph (D)) shall not be treated as debt-financed property for any period before such conversion. For purposes of this subparagraph, land shall not be treated as used in the manner described in paragraph (1)(A) by reason of the use made of any structure which was on the land when acquired by the organization.

(C) Limitations.—Subparagraphs (A) and (B)—

(i) shall apply with respect to any structure on the land when acquired by the organization, or to the land occupied by the structure, only if (and so long as) the intended future use of the land in the manner described in paragraph (1)(A) requires that the structure be demolished or removed in order to use the land in such manner;

(ii) shall not apply to structures erected on the land after the acquisition of the land; and

(iii) shall not apply to property subject to a lease which is a business lease (as defined in this section immediately before the enactment of the Tax Reform Act of 1976).

(D) Refund of taxes when subparagraph (B) applies.—If an organization for any taxable year has not used land in the manner to satisfy the actual use condition of subparagraph (B) before the time prescribed by law (including extensions thereof) for filing the return for such taxable year, the tax for such year shall be computed without regard to the application of subparagraph (B), but if and when such use condition is satisfied, the provisions of subparagraph (B) shall then be applied to such taxable year. If the actual use condition of subparagraph (B) is satisfied for any taxable year after such time for filing the return, and if credit or refund of any overpayment for the taxable year resulting from the satisfaction of such use condition is prevented at the close of the taxable year in which the use condition is satisfied, by the operation of any law or rule of law (other than Chapter 74, relating to closing agreements and compromises), credit or refund of such overpayment may nevertheless be allowed or made if claim therefor is filed before the expiration of 1 year after the close of the taxable year in which the use condition is satisfied.

(E) Special rule for churches.—In applying this paragraph to a church or convention or association of churches, in lieu of the 10-year period referred to in subparagraphs (A) and (B) a 15-year period shall be applied, and subparagraphs (A) and (B)(ii) shall apply whether or not the acquired land meets the neighborhood test.

(c) Acquisition indebtedness.—

(1) General rule.—For purposes of this section, the term "acquisition indebtedness" means, with respect to any debt-financed property, the unpaid amount of—

(A) the indebtedness incurred by the organization in acquiring or improving such property;

(B) the indebtedness incurred before the acquisition or improvement of such property if such indebtedness would not have been incurred but for such acquisition or improvement; and

(C) the indebtedness incurred after the acquisition or improvement of such property if such indebtedness would not have been incurred but for such acquisition or improvement and the incurrence of such indebtedness was reasonably foreseeable at the time of such acquisition or improvement.

(2) Property acquired subject to mortgage, etc.—For purposes of this subsection—

(A) General rule.—Where property (no matter how acquired) is acquired subject to a mortgage or other similar lien, the amount of the indebtedness secured by such mortgage or lien shall be considered as an indebtedness of the organization incurred in acquiring such property even though the organization did not assume or agree to pay such indebtedness.

(B) Exceptions.—Where property subject to a mortgage is acquired by an organization by bequest or devise, the indebtedness secured by the mortgage shall not be treated as acquisition indebtedness during a period of 10 years following the date of the acquisition. If an organization acquires property by gift subject to a mortgage which was placed on the property more than 5 years before the gift, which property was held by the donor more than 5 years before the gift, the indebtedness secured by such mortgage shall not be treated as acquisition indebtedness during a period of 10 years following the date of such gift. This subparagraph shall not apply if the organization, in order to acquire the equity in the property by bequest, devise, or gift, assumes and agrees to pay the indebtedness secured by the mortgage, or if the organization makes any payment for the equity in the property owned by the decedent or the donor.

(C) Liens for taxes or assessments.—Where State law provides that—

(i) a lien for taxes, or

(ii) a lien for assessments,

made by a State or a political subdivision thereof attaches to property prior to the time when such taxes or assessments become due and payable, then such lien shall be treated as similar to a mortgage (within the meaning of subparagraph (A)) but only after such taxes or assessments become due and payable and the organization has had an opportunity to pay such taxes or assessments in accordance with State law.

(3) Extension of obligations.—For purposes of this section, an extension, renewal, or refinancing of an obligation evidencing a pre-existing indebtedness shall not be treated as the creation of a new indebtedness.

(4) Indebtedness incurred in performing exempt purpose.—For purposes of this section, the term "acquisition indebtedness" does not include indebtedness the incurrence of which is inherent in the performance or exercise of the purpose or function constituting the basis of the organization's exemption, such as the indebtedness incurred by a credit union described in section 501(c)(14) in accepting deposits from its members.

(5) Annuities.—For purposes of this section, the term "acquisition indebtedness" does not include an obligation to pay an annuity which—

(A) is the sole consideration (other than a mortgage to which paragraph (2)(B) applies) issued in exchange for property if, at the time of the exchange, the value of the annuity is less than

90 percent of the value of the property received in the exchange,

(B) is payable over the life of one individual in being at the time the annuity is issued, or over the lives of two individuals in being at such time, and

(C) is payable under a contract which—

(i) does not guarantee a minimum amount of payments or specify a maximum amount of payments, and

(ii) does not provide for any adjustment of the amount of the annuity payments by reference to the income received from the transferred property or any other property.

(6) Certain federal financing.—

(A) In general.—For purposes of this section, the term "acquisition indebtedness" does not include—

(i) an obligation, to the extent that it is insured by the Federal Housing Administration, to finance the purchase, rehabilitation, or construction of housing for low and moderate income persons, or

(ii) indebtedness incurred by a small business investment company licensed after the date of the enactment of the American Jobs Creation Act of 2004 under the Small Business Investment Act of 1958 if such indebtedness is evidenced by a debenture—

(I) issued by such company under section 303(a) of such Act, and

(II) held or guaranteed by the Small Business Administration.

(B) Limitation.—Subparagraph (A)(ii) shall not apply with respect to any small business investment company during any period that—

(i) any organization which is exempt from tax under this title (other than a governmental unit) owns more than 25 percent of the capital or profits interest in such company, or

(ii) organizations which are exempt from tax under this title (including governmental units other than any agency or instrumentality of the United States) own, in the aggregate, 50 percent or more of the capital or profits interest in such company.

(7) Average acquisition indebtedness.—For purposes of this section, the term "average acquisition indebtedness" for any taxable year with respect to a debt-financed property means the average amount, determined under regulations prescribed by the Secretary, of the acquisition indebtedness during the period the property is held by the organization during the taxable year, except that for the purpose of computing the percentage of any gain or loss to be taken into account on a sale or other disposition of debt-financed property, such term means the highest amount of the acquisition indebtedness with respect to such property during the 12-month period ending with the date of the sale or other disposition.

(8) Securities subject to loans.—For purposes of this section—

(A) payments with respect to securities loans (as defined in section 512(a)(5)) shall be deemed to be derived from the securities loaned and not from collateral security or the investment of collateral security from such loans,

(B) any deductions which are directly connected with collateral security for such loan, or with the investment of collateral security, shall be deemed to be deductions which are directly connected with the securities loaned, and

(C) an obligation to return collateral security shall not be treated as acquisition indebtedness (as defined in paragraph (1)).

(9) Real property acquired by a qualified organization.—

(A) In general.—Except as provided in subparagraph (B), the term "acquisition indebtedness" does not, for purposes of this section, include indebtedness incurred by a qualified organization in acquiring or improving any real property. For purposes of this paragraph, an interest in a mortgage shall in no event be treated as real property.

(B) Exceptions.—The provisions of subparagraph (A) shall not apply in any case in which—

(i) the price for the acquisition or improvement is not a fixed amount determined as of the date of the acquisition or the completion of the improvement;

(ii) the amount of any indebtedness or any other amount payable with respect to such indebtedness, or the time for making any payment of any such amount, is dependent, in whole or in part, upon any revenue, income, or profits derived from such real property;

(iii) the real property is at any time after the acquisition leased by the qualified organization to the person selling such property to such organization or to any person who bears a relationship described in section 267(b) or 707(b) to such person;

(iv) the real property is acquired by a qualified trust from, or is at any time after the acquisition leased by such trust to, any person who—

(I) bears a relationship which is described in subparagraph (C), (E), or (G) of section 4975(e)(2) to any plan with respect to which such trust was formed, or

(II) bears a relationship which is described in subparagraph (F) or (H) of section 4975(e)(2) to any person described in subclause (I);

(v) any person described in clause (iii) or (iv) provides the qualified organization with financing in connection with the acquisition or improvement; or

(vi) the real property is held by a partnership unless the partnership meets the requirements of clauses (i) through (v) and unless—

(I) all of the partners of the partnership are qualified organizations,

(II) each allocation to a partner of the partnership which is a qualified organization is a qualified allocation (within the meaning of section 168(h)(6)), or

(III) such partnership meets the requirements of subparagraph (E).

For purposes of subclause (I) of clause (vi), an organization shall not be treated as a qualified organization if any income of such organization would be unrelated business taxable income.

(C) Qualified organization.—For purposes of this paragraph, the term "qualified organization" means—

(i) an organization described in section 170(b)(1)(A)(ii) and its affiliated support organizations described in section 509(a)(3);

(ii) any trust which constitutes a qualified trust under section 401;

(iii) an organization described in section 501(c)(25); or

(iv) a retirement income account described in section 403(b)(9).

(D) Other pass-thru entities; tiered entities.—Rules similar to the rules of subparagraph (B)(vi) shall also apply in the case of any pass-thru entity other than a partnership and in the case of tiered partnerships and other entities.

(E) Certain allocations permitted.—

(i) In general.—A partnership meets the requirements of this subparagraph if—

(I) the allocation of items to any partner which is a qualified organization cannot result in such partner having a share of the overall partnership income for any taxable year greater than such partner's share of the overall partnership loss for the taxable year for which such partner's loss share will be the smallest, and

(II) each allocation with respect to the partnership has substantial economic effect within the meaning of section 704(b)(2).

For purposes of this clause, items allocated under section 704(c) shall not be taken into account.

(ii) Special rules.—

(I) Chargebacks.—Except as provided in regulations, a partnership may without violating the requirements of this subparagraph provide for chargebacks with respect to disproportionate losses previously allocated to qualified organizations and disproportionate income previously allocated to other partners. Any chargeback referred to in the preceding sentence shall not be at a ratio in excess of the ratio under which the loss or income (as the case may be) was allocated.

(II) Preferred rates of return, etc.—To the extent provided in regulations, a partnership may without violating the requirements of this subparagraph provide for reasonable preferred returns or reasonable guaranteed payments.

(iii) Regulations.—The Secretary shall prescribe such regulations as may be necessary to carry out the purposes of this subparagraph, including regulations which may provide for exclusion or segregation of items.

(F) Special rules for organizations described in section 501(c)(25).—

(i) In general.—In computing under section 512 the unrelated business taxable income of a disqualified holder of an interest in an organization described in section 501(c)(25), there shall be taken into account—

(I) as gross income derived from an unrelated trade or business, such holder's pro rata share of the items of income described in clause (ii)(I) of such organization, and

(II) as deductions allowable in computing unrelated business taxable income, such holder's pro rata share of the items of deduction described in clause (ii)(II) of such organization.

Such amounts shall be taken into account for the taxable year of the holder in which (or with which) the taxable year of such organization ends.

(ii) Description of amounts.—For purposes of clause (i)—

(I) gross income is described in this clause to the extent such income would (but for this paragraph) be treated under subsection (a) as derived from an unrelated trade or business, and

(II) any deduction is described in this clause to the extent it would (but for this paragraph) be allowable under subsection (a)(2) in computing unrelated business taxable income.

(iii) Disqualified holder.—For purposes of this subparagraph, the term "disqualified holder" means any shareholder (or beneficiary) which is not described in clause (i) or (ii) of subparagraph (C).

(G) Special rules for purposes of the exceptions.—Except as otherwise provided by regulations—

(i) Small leases disregarded.—For purposes of clauses (iii) and (iv) of subparagraph (B), a lease to a person described in such clause (iii) or (iv) shall be disregarded if no more than 25 percent of the leasable floor space in a building (or complex of buildings) is covered by the lease and if the lease is on commercially reasonable terms.

(ii) Commercially reasonable financing.—Clause (v) of subparagraph (B) shall not apply if the financing is on commercially reasonable terms.

(H) Qualifying sales by financial institutions.—

(i) In general.—In the case of a qualifying sale by a financial institution, except as provided in regulations, clauses (i) and (ii) of subparagraph (B) shall not apply with respect to financing provided by such institution for such sale.

(ii) Qualifying sale.—For purposes of this clause, there is a qualifying sale by a financial institution if—

(I) a qualified organization acquires property described in clause (iii) from a financial institution and any gain recognized by the financial institution with respect to the property is ordinary income,

(II) the stated principal amount of the financing provided by the financial institution does not exceed the amount of the outstanding indebtedness (including accrued but unpaid interest) of the financial institution with respect to the property described in clause (iii) immediately before the acquisition referred to in clause (iii) or (v), which-ever is applicable, and

(III) the present value (determined as of the time of the sale and by using the applicable Federal rate determined under section 1274(d)) of the maximum amount payable pursuant to the financing that is determined by reference to the revenue, income, or profits derived from the property cannot exceed 30 percent of the total purchase price of the property (including the contingent payments).

(iii) Property to which subparagraph applies.—Property is described in this clause if such property is foreclosure property, or is real property which—

(I) was acquired by the qualified organization from a financial institution which is in conservatorship or receivership, or from the conservator or receiver of such an institution, and

(II) was held by the financial institution at the time it entered into conservatorship or receivership.

(iv) Financial institution.—For purposes of this subparagraph, the term "financial institution" means—

(I) any financial institution described in section 581 or 591(a),

(II) any other corporation which is a direct or indirect subsidiary of an institution referred to in subclause (I) but only if, by virtue of being affiliated with such institution, such other corporation is subject to supervision and examination by a Federal or State agency which regulates institutions referred to in subclause (I), and

(III) any person acting as a conservator or receiver of an entity referred to in subclause (I) or (II) (or any government agency or corporation succeeding to the rights or interest of such person).

(v) Foreclosure property.—For purposes of this subparagraph, the term "foreclosure property" means any real property acquired by the financial institution as the result of having bid on such property at foreclosure, or by operation of an agreement or process of law, after there was a default (or a default was imminent) on indebtedness which such property secured.

(d) Basis of debt-financed property acquired in corporate liquidation.—For purposes of this subtitle, if the property was acquired in a complete or partial liquidation of a corporation in exchange for its stock, the basis of the property shall be the same as it would be in the hands of the transferor corporation, increased by the amount of gain recognized to the transferor corporation upon such distribution and by the amount of any gain to the organization which was included, on account of such distribution, in unrelated business taxable income under subsection (a).

(e) Allocation rules.—Where debt-financed property is held for purposes described in subsection (b)(1)(A), (B), (C), or (D) as well as for other purposes, proper allocation shall be made with respect to basis, indebtedness, and income and deductions. The allocations required by this section shall be made in accordance with regulations prescribed by the Secretary to the extent proper to carry out the purposes of this section.

(f) Personal property leased with real property.—For purposes of this section, the term "real property" includes personal property of the lessor leased by it to a lessee of its real estate if the lease of such personal property is made under, or in connection with, the lease of such real estate.

(g) Regulations.—The Secretary shall prescribe such regulations as may be necessary or appropriate to carry out the purposes of this section, including regulations to prevent the circumvention of any provision of this section through the use of segregated asset accounts.

§ 515. Taxes of foreign countries and possessions of the United States

The amount of taxes imposed by foreign countries and possessions of the United States shall be allowed as a credit against the tax of an organization subject to the tax imposed by section 511 to the extent provided in section 901; and in the case of the tax imposed by section 511, the term "taxable income" as used in section 901 shall be read as "unrelated business taxable income."

PART IV—FARMERS' COOPERATIVES

Editorial Summary

Tax Liability of Farmers' Cooperatives

Subchapter F of Chapter 1 (Sec. 521)

See the discussion under the Editorial Summary entitled Tax Exempt Organizations, which precedes Sec. 501.

§ 521. Exemption of farmers' cooperatives from tax

(a) Exemption from tax.—A farmers' cooperative organization described in subsection (b)(1) shall be exempt from taxation under this subtitle except as otherwise provided in part I of subchapter T (sec. 1381 and following). Notwithstanding part I of subchapter T (sec. 1381 and following), such an organization shall be considered an organization exempt from income taxes for purposes of any law which refers to organizations exempt from income taxes.

(b) Applicable rules.—

(1) Exempt farmers' cooperatives.—The farmers' cooperatives exempt from taxation to the extent provided in subsection (a) are farmers', fruit growers', or like associations organized and operated on a cooperative basis (A) for the purpose of marketing the products of members or other producers, and turning back to them the proceeds of sales, less the necessary marketing expenses, on the basis of either the quantity or the value of the products furnished by them, or (B) for the purpose of purchasing supplies and equipment for the use of members or other persons, and turning over such supplies and equipment to them at actual cost, plus necessary expenses.

(2) Organizations having capital stock.—Exemption shall not be denied any such association because it has capital stock, if the dividend rate of such stock is fixed at not to exceed the legal rate of interest in the State of incorporation or 8 percent per annum, whichever is greater, on the value of the consideration for which the stock was issued, and if substantially all such stock (other than nonvoting preferred stock, the owners of which are not entitled or permitted to participate, directly or indirectly, in the profits of the association, upon dissolution or otherwise, beyond the fixed dividends) is owned by producers who market their products or purchase their supplies and equipment through the association.

(3) Organizations maintaining reserve.—Exemption shall not be denied any such association because there is accumulated and maintained by it a reserve required by State law or a reasonable reserve for any necessary purpose.

(4) Transactions with nonmembers.—Exemption shall not be denied any such association which markets the products of nonmembers in an amount the value of which does not exceed the value of the products marketed for members, or which purchases supplies and equipment for nonmembers in an amount the value of which does not exceed the value of the supplies and equipment purchased for members, provided the value of the purchases made for persons who are neither members nor producers does not exceed 15 percent of the value of all its purchases.

(5) Business for the United States.—Business done for the United States or any of its agencies shall be disregarded in determining the right to exemption under this section.

(6) Netting of losses.—Exemption shall not be denied any such association because such association computes its net earnings for purposes of determining any amount available for distribution to patrons in the manner described in paragraph (1) of section 1388(j).

(7) Cross reference.—For treatment of value-added processing involving animals, see section 1388(k).

PART V—SHIPOWNERS' PROTECTION AND INDEMNITY ASSOCIATIONS*

PART VI—POLITICAL ORGANIZATIONS

Editorial Summary

Tax Liability of Political Organizations

Subchapter F of Chapter 1 (Sec. 527)

See the discussion under the Editorial Summary entitled Tax Exempt Organizations, which precedes Sec. 501.

§ 527. Political organizations

(a) General rule.—A political organization shall be subject to taxation under this subtitle only to the extent provided in this section. A political organization shall be considered an organization exempt from income taxes for the purpose of any law which refers to organizations exempt from income taxes.

(b) Tax imposed.—

(1) In general.—A tax is hereby imposed for each taxable year on the political organization taxable income of every political organization. Such tax shall be computed by multiplying the political organization taxable income by the highest rate of tax specified in section 11(b).

(2) Alternative tax in case of capital gains.—If for any taxable year any political organization has a net capital gain, then, in lieu of the tax imposed by paragraph (1), there is hereby imposed a tax (if such a tax is less than the tax imposed by paragraph (1)) which shall consist of the sum of—

(A) a partial tax, computed as provided by paragraph (1), on the political organization taxable income determined by reducing such income by the amount of such gain, and

(B) an amount determined as provided in section 1201(a) on such gain.

(c) Political organization taxable income defined.—

(1) Taxable income defined.—For purposes of this section, the political organization taxable

*Omitted.

income of any organization for any taxable year is an amount equal to the excess (if any) of—

(A) the gross income for the taxable year (excluding any exempt function income), over

(B) the deductions allowed by this chapter which are directly connected with the production of the gross income (excluding exempt function income), computed with the modifications provided in paragraph (2).

(2) Modifications.—For purposes of this subsection—

(A) there shall be allowed a specific deduction of $100,

(B) no net operating loss deduction shall be allowed under section 172, and

(C) no deduction shall be allowed under part VIII of subchapter B (relating to special deductions for corporations).

(3) Exempt function income.—For purposes of this subsection, the term "exempt function income" means any amount received as—

(A) a contribution of money or other property,

(B) membership dues, a membership fee or assessment from a member of the political organization,

(C) proceeds from a political fundraising or entertainment event, or proceeds from the sale of political campaign materials, which are not received in the ordinary course of any trade or business, or

(D) proceeds from the conducting of any bingo game (as defined in section 513(f)(2)),

to the extent such amount is segregated for use only for the exempt function of the political organization.

(d) Certain uses not treated as income to candidate.—For purposes of this title, if any political organization—

(1) contributes any amount to or for the use of any political organization which is treated as exempt from tax under subsection (a) of this section,

(2) contributes any amount to or for the use of any organization described in paragraph (1) or (2) of section 509(a) which is exempt from tax under section 501(a), or

(3) deposits any amount in the general fund of the Treasury or in the general fund of any State or local government,

such amount shall be treated as an amount not diverted for the personal use of the candidate or any other person. No deduction shall be allowed under this title for the contribution or deposit of any amount described in the preceding sentence.

(e) Other definitions.—For purposes of this section—

(1) Political organization.—The term "political organization" means a party, committee, association, fund, or other organization (whether or not incorporated) organized and operated primarily for the purpose of directly or indirectly accepting contributions or making expenditures, or both, for an exempt function.

(2) Exempt function.—The term "exempt function" means the function of influencing or attempting to influence the selection, nomination, election, or appointment of any individual to any Federal, State, or local public office or office in a political organization, or the election of Presidential or Vice-Presidential electors, whether or not such individual or electors are selected, nominated, elected, or appointed. Such term includes the making of expenditures relating to an office described in the preceding sentence which, if incurred by the individual, would be allowable as a deduction under section 162(a).

(3) Contributions.—The term "contributions" has the meaning given to such term by section 271(b)(2).

(4) Expenditures.—The term "expenditures" has the meaning given to such term by section 271(b)(3).

(f) Exempt organization which is not political organization must include certain amounts in gross income.—

(1) In general.—If an organization described in section 501(c) which is exempt from tax under section 501(a) expends any amount during the taxable year directly (or through another organization) for an exempt function (within the meaning of subsection (e)(2)), then, notwithstanding any other provision of law, there shall be included in the gross income of such organization for the taxable year, and shall be subject to tax under subsection (b) as if it constituted political organization taxable income, an amount equal to the lesser of—

(A) the net investment income of such organization for the taxable year, or

(B) the aggregate amount so expended during the taxable year for such an exempt function.

(2) Net investment income.—For purposes of this subsection, the term "net investment income" means the excess of—

(A) the gross amount of income from interest, dividends, rents, and royalties, plus the excess (if any) of gains from the sale or exchange of assets over the losses from the sale or exchange of assets, over

(B) the deductions allowed by this chapter which are directly connected with the production of the income referred to in subparagraph (A).

For purposes of the preceding sentence, there shall not be taken into account items taken into account for purposes of the tax imposed by section 511 (relating to tax on unrelated business income).

(3) Certain separate segregated funds.—For purposes of this subsection and subsection (e)(1), a separate segregated fund (within the meaning of section 610 of title 18 or of any similar State statute, or within the meaning of any State statute which permits the segregation of dues monies for exempt functions (within the meaning of subsection (e)(2))) which is maintained by an organization described in section 501(c) which is exempt from tax under section 501(a) shall be treated as a separate organization.

(g) Treatment of newsletter funds.—

(1) In general.—For purposes of this section, a fund established and maintained by an individual who holds, has been elected to, or is a candidate (within the meaning of paragraph (3)) for nomination or election to, any Federal, State, or local elective public office, for use by such individual exclusively for the preparation and circulation of such individual's newsletter shall, except as provided in paragraph (2), be treated as if such fund constituted a political organization.

(2) Additional modifications.—In the case of any fund described in paragraph (1)—

(A) the exempt function shall be only the preparation and circulation of the newsletter, and

(B) the specific deduction provided by subsection (c)(2)(A) shall not be allowed.

(3) Candidate.—For purposes of paragraph (1), the term "candidate" means, with respect to any Federal, State, or local elective public office, an individual who—

(A) publicly announces that he is a candidate for nomination or election to such office, and

(B) meets the qualifications prescribed by law to hold such office.

(h) Special rule for principal campaign committees.—

(1) In general.—In the case of a political organization, which is a principal campaign committee, paragraph (1) of subsection (b) shall be applied by substituting "the appropriate rates" for "the highest rate".

(2) Principal campaign committee defined.—

(A) In general.—For purposes of this subsection, the term "principal campaign committee" means the political committee designated by a candidate for Congress as his principal campaign committee for purposes of—

(i) section 302(e) of the Federal Election Campaign Act of 1971 (2 U.S.C. 432(e)), and

(ii) this subsection.

(B) Designation.—A candidate may have only 1 designation in effect under subparagraph (A)(ii) at any time and such designation—

(i) shall be made at such time and in such manner as the Secretary may prescribe by regulations, and

(ii) once made, may be revoked only with the consent of the Secretary.

Nothing in this subsection shall be construed to require any designation where there is only one political committee with respect to a candidate.

PART VII—CERTAIN HOMEOWNERS ASSOCIATIONS

Editorial Summary

Tax Liability of Homeowners Associations

Subchapter F of Chapter 1 (Sec. 528)

See the discussion under the Editorial Summary entitled Tax Exempt Organizations, which precedes Sec. 501.

§ 528. Certain homeowners associations

(a) General rule.—A homeowners association (as defined in subsection (c)) shall be subject to taxation under this subtitle only to the extent provided in this section. A homeowners association shall be considered an organization exempt from income taxes for the purpose of any law which refers to organizations exempt from income taxes.

(b) Tax imposed.—A tax is hereby imposed for each taxable year on the homeowners association taxable income of every homeowners association. Such tax shall be equal to 30 percent of the homeowners association taxable income (32 percent of such income in the case of a timeshare association).

(c) Homeowners association defined.—For purposes of this section—

(1) Homeowners association.—The term "homeowners association" means an organization which is a condominium management association or a residential real estate management association, or a timeshare association if—

(A) such organization is organized and operated to provide for the acquisition, construction, management, maintenance, and care of association property,

(B) 60 percent or more of the gross income of such organization for the taxable year consists solely of amounts received as membership dues, fees, or assessments from—

(i) owners of residential units in the case of a condominium management association,

(ii) owners of residences or residential lots in the case of a residential real estate management association, or

(iii) owners of timeshare rights to use, or timeshare ownership interests in, association property in the case of a timeshare association,

(C) 90 percent or more of the expenditures of the organization for the taxable year are expenditures for the acquisition, construction, management, maintenance, and care of association property and, in the case of a timeshare association, for activities provided to or on behalf of members of the association,

(D) no part of the net earnings of such organization inures (other than by acquiring, constructing, or providing management, maintenance, and care of association property, and other than by a rebate of excess membership dues, fees, or assessments) to the benefit of any private shareholder or individual, and

(E) such organization elects (at such time and in such manner as the Secretary by regulations prescribes) to have this section apply for the taxable year.

(2) Condominium management association.—The term "condominium management association" means any organization meeting the requirement of subparagraph (A) of paragraph (1) with respect to a condominium project substantially all of the units of which are used by individuals for residences.

(3) Residential real estate management association.—The term "residential real estate management association" means any organization meeting the requirements of subparagraph (A) of paragraph (1) with respect to a subdivision, development, or similar area substantially all the lots or buildings of which may only be used by individuals for residences.

(4) Timeshare association.—The term "timeshare association" means any organization (other than a condominium management association) meeting the requirement of subparagraph (A) of paragraph (1) if any member thereof holds a timeshare right to use, or a timeshare ownership interest in, real property constituting association property.

(5) Association property.—The term "association property" means—

(A) property held by the organization,

(B) property commonly held by the members of the organization,

(C) property within the organization privately held by the members of the organization, and

(D) property owned by a governmental unit and used for the benefit of residents of such unit.

In the case of a timeshare association, such term includes property in which the timeshare association, or members of the association, have rights arising out of recorded easements, covenants, or other recorded instruments to use property related to the timeshare project.

(d) Homeowners association taxable income defined.—

(1) Taxable income defined.—For purposes of this section, the homeowners association taxable income of any organization for any taxable year is an amount equal to the excess (if any) of—

(A) the gross income for the taxable year (excluding any exempt function income), over

(B) the deductions allowed by this chapter which are directly connected with the production of the gross income (excluding exempt function income), computed with the modifications provided in paragraph (2).

(2) Modifications.—For purposes of this subsection—

(A) there shall be allowed a specific deduction of $100,

(B) no net operating loss deduction shall be allowed under section 172, and

(C) no deduction shall be allowed under part VIII of subchapter B (relating to special deductions for corporations).

(3) Exempt function income.—For purposes of this subsection, the term "exempt function income" means any amount received as membership dues, fees, or assessments from—

(A) owners of condominium housing units in the case of a condominium management association,

(B) owners of real property in the case of a residential real estate management association, or

(C) owners of timeshare rights to use, or timeshare ownership interests in, real property in the case of a timeshare association.

PART VIII—HIGHER EDUCATION SAVINGS ENTITIES

Editorial Summary

Qualified Tuition Programs and Coverdell Education Savings Accounts

Subchapter F of Chapter 1 (Secs. 529 and 530)

Most states now have qualified tuition programs. Under such programs, parents can prepay their child's college tuition. The Tax Relief Reconciliation Act of 2001 expanded qualified tuition programs to apply to private educational institutions as well as public educational institutions. Distributions made after December 31, 2003 from such a plan maintained by an entity other than the state for qualified higher education expenses are eligible for exclusion from gross income.

Section 529(a) provides that such programs are tax-exempt. Thus, the earnings of such programs (except for any unrelated business income) are not subject to federal income taxation.

Such programs must be established for the purpose of paying qualified higher education expenses [Sec. 529(b)(1)]. Such expenses include tuition, fees, books, supplies, and equipment required for enrollment or attendance at a college or university [Sec. 529(e)(3)]. The American Recovery and Reinvestment Tax Act of 2009 broadens qualified expenses by providing that expenses paid or incurred in 2009 and 2010 include the cost of computer technology or equipment and Internet access and related services used by a beneficiary at an eligible educational institution.

The earnings of the contributed funds, including the discount on tuition charged to participants, are not included in gross income provided that the contributions and earnings are used for qualified higher education expenses [Sec. 529(c)(3)(B)]. A different result occurs if funds are used for nonqualified expenses. That is, the excess distributed over the amount used to pay qualified higher education expenses is included in the gross income of the student (not the parent) using an annuity-type calculation to distinguish between contributions and income [Sec. 529(c)(3)(A)]. If the parent receives a refund, the excess of the amount refunded over the amount contributed by the parent is included in the parent's gross income.

Tax legislation in 2001 changed the name of education IRAs to the more appropriate Coverdell Education Savings Account (CESA). Other 2001 tax legislation increased the annual contribution ceiling from $500 to $2,000 [Sec. 530(b)(1)]. Distributions from a CESA used to pay qualified education expenses of the designated beneficiary are tax-free [Sec. 530(d)(1)(A)]. To the extent the distributions during a tax year exceed qualified education expenses, part of the excess is treated as a return of capital (the contributions) and part is treated as a distribution of earnings under Sec. 72 annuity sales.

§ 529. Qualified state tuition programs

(a) General rule.—A qualified tuition program shall be exempt from taxation under this subtitle. Notwithstanding the preceding sentence, such program shall be subject to the taxes imposed by section 511 (relating to imposition of tax on unrelated business income of charitable organizations).

(b) Qualified tuition program.—For purposes of this section—

(1) In general.—The term "qualified tuition program" means a program established and maintained by a State or agency or instrumentality thereof or by 1 or more eligible educational institutions—

(A) under which a person—

(i) may purchase tuition credits or certificates on behalf of a designated beneficiary which entitle the beneficiary to the waiver or payment of qualified higher education expenses of the beneficiary, or

(ii) in the case of a program established and maintained by a State or agency or instrumentality thereof, may make contributions to an account which is established for the purpose of meeting the qualified higher education expenses of the designated beneficiary of the account, and

(B) which meets the other requirements of this subsection.

Except to the extent provided in regulations, a program established and maintained by 1 or more eligible educational institutions shall not be treated as a qualified tuition program unless such program provides that amounts are held in a qualified trust and such program has received a ruling or determination that such program meets the applicable requirements for a qualified tuition program. For purposes of the preceding sentence, the term "qualified trust" means a trust which is created or organized in the United States for the exclusive benefit of designated beneficiaries and with respect to which the requirements of paragraphs (2) and (5) of section 408(a) are met.

(2) Cash contributions.—A program shall not be treated as a qualified tuition program unless it provides that purchases or contributions may only be made in cash.

(3) Separate accounting.—A program shall not be treated as a qualified tuition program unless it provides separate accounting for each designated beneficiary.

(4) No investment direction.—A program shall not be treated as a qualified tuition program unless it provides that any contributor to, or designated beneficiary under, such program may not directly or indirectly direct the investment of any contributions to the program (or any earnings thereon).

(5) No pledging of interest as security.—A program shall not be treated as a qualified tuition program if it allows any interest in the program or any portion thereof to be used as security for a loan.

(6) Prohibition on excess contributions.—A program shall not be treated as a qualified tuition program unless it provides adequate safeguards to prevent contributions on behalf of a designated beneficiary in excess of those necessary to provide for the qualified higher education expenses of the beneficiary.

(c) Tax treatment of designated beneficiaries and contributors.—

(1) In general.—Except as otherwise provided in this subsection, no amount shall be includible in gross income of—

(A) a designated beneficiary under a qualified tuition program, or

(B) a contributor to such program on behalf of a designated beneficiary,

with respect to any distribution or earnings under such program.

(2) Gift tax treatment of contributions.—For purposes of chapters 12 and 13—

(A) In general.—Any contribution to a qualified tuition program on behalf of any designated beneficiary—

(i) shall be treated as a completed gift to such beneficiary which is not a future interest in property, and

(ii) shall not be treated as a qualified transfer under section 2503(e).

(B) Treatment of excess contributions.—If the aggregate amount of contributions described in subparagraph (A) during the calendar year by a donor exceeds the limitation for such year under section 2503(b), such aggregate amount shall, at the election of the donor, be taken into account for purposes of such section ratably over the 5-year period beginning with such calendar year.

(3) Distributions.—

(A) In general.—Any distribution under a qualified tuition program shall be includible in the gross income of the distributee in the manner as provided under section 72(b) to the extent not excluded from gross income under any other provision of this chapter.

(B) Distributions for qualified higher education expenses.—For purposes of this paragraph—

(i) In-kind distributions.—No amount shall be includible in gross income under subparagraph (A) by reason of a distribution which consists of providing a benefit to the distributee which, if paid for by the distributee, would constitute payment of a qualified higher education expense.

(ii) Cash distributions.—In the case of distribution not described in clause (i), if—

(I) such distributions do not exceed the qualified higher education expenses (reduced by expenses described in clause (i)), no amount shall be includible in gross income, and

(II) in any other case, the amount otherwise includible in gross income shall be reduced by an amount which bears the same ratio to such amount as such expenses bear to such distributions.

***(iii) Exception for institutional programs.**—In the case of any taxable year beginning before January 1, 2004, clauses (i) and (ii) shall not apply with respect to any distribution during such taxable year under a qualified tuition program established and maintained by 1 or more eligible educational institutions.

(iv) Treatment as distributions.—Any benefit furnished to a designated beneficiary under a qualified tuition program shall be treated as a distribution to the beneficiary for purposes of this paragraph.

(v) Coordination with HOPE and lifetime learning credits.—The total amount of qualified higher education expenses with respect to an individual for the taxable year shall be reduced—

(I) as provided in section 25A(g)(2), and

(II) by the amount of such expenses which were taken into account in determining the credit allowed to the taxpayer or any other person under section 25A.

(vi) Coordination with education individual retirement accounts.—If, with respect to an individual for any taxable year—

(I) the aggregate distributions to which clauses (i) and (ii) and section 530(d)(2)(A) apply, exceed

(II) the total amount of qualified higher education expenses otherwise taken into account under clauses (i) and (ii) (after the application of clause (v)) for such year,

the taxpayer shall allocate such expenses among such distributions for purposes of determining the amount of the exclusion under clauses (i) and (ii) and section 530(d)(2)(A).

(C) Change in beneficiaries or programs.—

(i) Rollovers.—Subparagraph (A) shall not apply to that portion of any distribution which, within 60 days of such distribution, is transferred—

(I) to another qualified tuition program for the benefit of the designated beneficiary, or

(II) to the credit of another designated beneficiary under a qualified tuition program who is a member of the family of the designated beneficiary with respect to which the distribution was made.

(ii) Change in designated beneficiaries.—Any change in the designated beneficiary of an interest in a qualified tuition program shall not be treated as a distribution for purposes of subparagraph (A) if the new beneficiary is a member of the family of the old beneficiary.

(iii) Limitation on certain rollovers.—Clause (i)(I) shall not apply to any transfer if such transfer occurs within 12 months from the date of a previous transfer to any qualified tuition program for the benefit of the designated beneficiary.

(D) Operating rules.—For purposes of applying section 72—

(i) to the extent provided by the Secretary, all qualified tuition programs of which an individual is a designated beneficiary shall be treated as one program,

(ii) except to the extent provided by the Secretary, all distributions during a taxable year shall be treated as one distribution, and

(iii) except to the extent provided by the Secretary, the value of the contract, income on the contract, and investment in the contract shall be computed as of the close of the calendar year in which the taxable year begins.

(4) Estate tax treatment.—

(A) In general.—No amount shall be includible in the gross estate of any individual for purposes of chapter 11 by reason of an interest in a qualified tuition program.

*Editorial comment: Note that the exclusion treatment on distributions did not apply to the plans of private educational institutions until after December 31, 2003.

(B) Amounts includible in estate of designated beneficiary in certain cases.—Subparagraph (A) shall not apply to amounts distributed on account of the death of a beneficiary.

(C) Amounts includible in estate of donor making excess contributions.—In the case of a donor who makes the election described in paragraph (2)(B) and who dies before the close of the 5-year period referred to in such paragraph, notwithstanding subparagraph (A), the gross estate of the donor shall include the portion of such contributions properly allocable to periods after the date of death of the donor.

(5) Other gift tax rules.—For purposes of chapters 12 and 13—

(A) Treatment of distributions.—Except as provided in subparagraph (B), in no event shall a distribution from a qualified tuition program be treated as a taxable gift.

(B) Treatment of designation of new beneficiary.—The taxes imposed by chapters 12 and 13 shall apply to a transfer by reason of a change in the designated beneficiary under the program (or a rollover to the account of a new beneficiary) unless the new beneficiary is—

(i) assigned to the same generation as (or a higher generation than) the old beneficiary (determined in accordance with section 2651), and

(ii) a member of the family of the old beneficiary.

(6) Additional tax.—The tax imposed by section 530(d)(4) shall apply to any payment or distribution from a qualified tuition program in the same manner as such tax applies to a payment or distribution from a Coverdell education savings account. This paragraph shall not apply to any payment or distribution in any taxable year beginning before January 1, 2004, which is includible in gross income but used for qualified higher education expenses of the designated beneficiary.

(d) Reports.—Each officer or employee having control of the qualified tuition program or their designee shall make such reports regarding such program to the Secretary and to designated beneficiaries with respect to contributions, distributions, and such other matters as the Secretary may require. The reports required by this subsection shall be filed at such time and in such manner and furnished to such individuals at such time and in such manner as may be required by the Secretary.

(e) Other definitions and special rules.—For purposes of this section—

(1) Designated beneficiary.—The term "designated beneficiary" means—

(A) the individual designated at the commencement of participation in the qualified tuition program as the beneficiary of amounts paid (or to be paid) to the program,

(B) in the case of a change in beneficiaries described in subsection (c)(3)(C), the individual who is the new beneficiary, and

(C) in the case of an interest in a qualified tuition program purchased by a State or local government (or agency or instrumentality thereof) or an organization described in section 501(c)(3) and exempt from taxation under section 501(a) as part of a scholarship program operated by such government or organization, the individual receiving such interest as a scholarship.

(2) Member of family.—The term "member of the family" means, with respect to any designated beneficiary—

(A) the spouse of such beneficiary,

(B) an individual who bears a relationship to such beneficiary which is described in subparagraphs (A) through (G) of section 152(d)(2),

(C) the spouse of any individual described in subparagraph (B), and

(D) any first cousin of such beneficiary.

(3) Qualified higher education expenses.—

(A) In general.—The term "qualified higher education expenses" means—

(i) tuition, fees, books, supplies, and equipment required for the enrollment or attendance of a designated beneficiary at an eligible educational institution;

(ii) expenses for special needs services in the case of a special needs beneficiary which are incurred in connection with such enrollment or attendance, and

(iii) expenses paid or incurred in 2009 or 2010 for the purchase of any computer technology or equipment (as defined in section 170(e)(6)(F)(i)) or Internet access and related services, if such technology, equipment, or services are to be used by the beneficiary and the beneficiary's family during any of the years the beneficiary is enrolled at an eligible educational institution.

Clause (iii) shall not include expenses for computer software designed for sports, games, or hobbies unless the software is predominantly educational in nature.

(B) Room and board included for students who are at least half-time.—

(i) In general.—In the case of an individual who is an eligible student (as defined in section 25A(b)(3)) for any academic period, such term shall also include reasonable costs for such period (as determined under the qualified tuition program) incurred by the designated beneficiary for room and board while attending such institution. For purposes of subsection (b)(6), a designated beneficiary shall be treated as meeting the requirements of this clause.

(ii) Limitation.—The amount treated as qualified higher education expenses by reason of the preceding clause (i) shall not exceed—

(I) the allowance (applicable to the student) for room and board included in the cost of attendance (as defined in section 472 of the Higher Education Act of 1965 (20 U.S.C. 108711), as in effect on the date of the enactment of the Economic Growth and Tax Relief Reconciliation Act of 2001) as determined by the eligible educational institution for such period, or

(II) if greater, the actual invoice amount the student residing in housing owned or operated by the eligible educational institution is charged by such institution for room and board costs for such period.

(4) Application of section 514.—An interest in a qualified State tuition program shall not be treated as debt for purposes of section 514.

(5) Eligible educational institution.—The term "eligible educational institution" means an institution—

(A) which is described in section 481 of the Higher Education Act of 1965 (20 U.S.C. 1088), as in effect on the date of the enactment of this paragraph, and

(B) which is eligible to participate in a program under title IV of such Act.

(f) Regulations.—Notwithstanding any other provision of this section, the Secretary shall prescribe such regulations as may be necessary or appropriate to carry out the purposes of this section and to prevent abuse of such purposes, including regulations under chapters 11, 12, and 13 of this title.

§ 530. Coverdell education savings accounts

(a) General rule.—A Coverdell education savings account shall be exempt from taxation under this subtitle. Notwithstanding the preceding sentence, the Coverdell education savings account shall be subject to the taxes imposed by section 511 (relating to imposition of tax on unrelated business income of charitable organizations).

(b) Definitions and special rules.—For purposes of this section—

(1) Coverdell education savings account.—The term "Coverdell education savings account" means a trust created or organized in the United States exclusively for the purpose of paying the qualified education expenses of an individual who is the designated beneficiary of the trust (and designated as a "Coverdell education savings account" at the time created or organized), but only if the written governing instrument creating the trust meets the following requirements:

(A) No contribution will be accepted—

(i) unless it is in cash,

(ii) after the date on which such beneficiary attains age 18, or

(iii) except in the case of rollover contributions, if such contribution would result in aggregate contributions for the taxable year exceeding $2,000.

(B) The trustee is a bank (as defined in section 408(n)) or another person who demonstrates to the satisfaction of the Secretary that the manner in which that person will administer the trust will be consistent with the requirements of this section or who has so demonstrated with respect to any individual retirement plan.

(C) No part of the trust assets will be invested in life insurance contracts.

(D) The assets of the trust shall not be commingled with other property except in a common trust fund or common investment fund.

(E) Except as provided in subsection (d)(7), any balance to the credit of the designated beneficiary on the date on which the beneficiary attains age 30 shall be distributed within 30 days after such date to the beneficiary or, if the beneficiary dies before attaining age 30, shall be distributed within 30 days after the date of death of such beneficiary.

The age limitation in subparagraphs (A)(ii) and (E) and paragraphs (5) and (6) of subsection (d) shall not apply to any designated beneficiary with special needs (as determined under regulations prescribed by the Secretary).

(2) Qualified education expenses.—

(A) In general.—The term "qualified education expenses" means—

(i) qualified higher education expenses (as defined in section 529(e)(3)), and

(ii) qualified elementary and secondary education expenses (as defined in paragraph (3)).

(B) Qualified tuition programs.—Such term shall include any contribution to a qualified tuition program (as defined in section 529 (b)) on behalf of the designated beneficiary (as defined in section 529(e)(1)); but there shall be no increase in the investment in the contract for purposes of applying section 72 by reason of any portion of such contribution which is not includible in gross income by reason of subsection (d)(2).

(3) Qualified elementary and secondary education expenses.—

(A) In general.—The term "qualified elementary and secondary education expenses" means—

(i) expenses for tuition, fees, academic tutoring, special needs services in the case of a special needs beneficiary, books, supplies, and other equipment which are incurred in connection with the enrollment or attendance of the designated beneficiary of the trust as an elementary or secondary school student at a public, private, or religious school,

(ii) expenses for room and board, uniforms, transportation, and supplementary items and services (including extended day programs) which are required or provided by a public, private, or religious school in connection with such enrollment or attendance, and

(iii) expenses for the purchase of any computer technology or equipment (as defined in section 170(e)(6)(F)(i)) or Internet access and related services, if such technology, equipment, or services are to be used by the beneficiary and the beneficiary's family during any of the years the beneficiary is in school.

Clause (iii) shall not include expenses for computer software designed for sports, games, or hobbies unless the software is predominantly educational in nature.

(B) School.—The term "school" means any school which provides elementary education or secondary education (kindergarten through grade 12), as determined under State law.

(4) Time when contributions deemed made.—An individual shall be deemed to have made a contribution to a Coverdell education savings account on the last day of the preceding taxable year if the contribution is made on account of such taxable year and is made not later than the time prescribed by law for filing the return for such taxable year (not including extensions thereof).

(c) Reduction in permitted contributions based on adjusted gross income.—

(1) In general.—In the case of a contributor who is an individual, the maximum amount the contributor could otherwise make to an account under this section shall be reduced by an amount which bears the same ratio to such maximum amount as—

(A) the excess of—

(i) the contributor's modified adjusted gross income for such taxable year, over

(ii) $95,000 ($190,000 in the case of a joint return), bears to

(B) $15,000 ($30,000 in the case of a joint return).

(2) Modified adjusted gross income.—For purposes of paragraph (1), the term "modified adjusted gross income" means the adjusted gross income of the taxpayer for the taxable year increased by any amount excluded from gross income under section 911, 931, or 933.

(d) Tax treatment of distributions.—

(1) In general.—Any distribution shall be includible in the gross income of the distributee in the manner as provided in section 72.

(2) Distributions for qualified education expenses.—

(A) In general.—No amount shall be includible in gross income under paragraph (1) if the qualified education expenses of the designated beneficiary during the taxable year are not less than the aggregate distributions during the taxable year.

(B) Distributions in excess of expenses.—If such aggregate distributions exceed such expenses during the taxable year, the amount otherwise includible in gross income under paragraph (1) shall be reduced by the amount which bears the same ratio to the amount which would be includible in gross income under paragraph (1) (without regard to this subparagraph) as the qualified education expenses bear to such aggregate distributions.

(C) Coordination with HOPE and lifetime learning credits and qualified tuition programs.—For purposes of subparagraph (A)—

(i) Credit coordination.—The total amount of qualified education expenses with respect to an individual for the taxable year shall be reduced—

(I) as provided in section 25A(g)(2), and

(II) by the amount of such expenses which were taken into account in determining the credit allowed to the taxpayer or any other person under section 25A.

(ii) Coordination with qualified tuition programs.—If, with respect to an individual for any taxable year—

(I) The aggregate distributions during such year to which subparagraph (A) and section 529(c)(3)(B) apply, exceed

(II) the total amount of qualified education expenses (after the application of clause (i)) for such year,

the taxpayer shall allocate such expenses among such distributions for purposes of determining the amount of the exclusion under subparagraph (A) and section 529(c)(3)(B).

(D) Disallowance of excluded amounts as deduction, credit, or exclusion.—No deduction, credit, or exclusion shall be allowed to the taxpayer under any other section of this chapter for any qualified education expenses to the extent taken into account in determining the amount of the exclusion under this paragraph.

(3) Special rules for applying estate and gift taxes with respect to account.—Rules similar to the rules of paragraphs (2), (4), and (5) of section 529(c) shall apply for purposes of this section.

(4) Additional tax for distributions not used for educational expenses.—

(A) In general.—The tax imposed by this chapter for any taxable year on any taxpayer who receives a payment or distribution from a Coverdell education savings account which is includible in gross income shall be increased by 10 percent of the amount which is so includible.

(B) Exceptions.—Subparagraph (A) shall not apply if the payment or distribution is—

(i) made to a beneficiary (or to the estate of the designated beneficiary) on or after the death of the designated beneficiary,

(ii) attributable to the designated beneficiary's being disabled (within the meaning of section 72(m)(7)),

(iii) made on account of a scholarship, allowance, or payment described in section 25A(g)(2) received by the designated beneficiary to the extent the amount of the payment or distribution does not exceed the amount of the scholarship, allowance, or payment,

(iv) made on account of the attendance of the designated beneficiary at the United States Military Academy, the United States Naval Academy, the United States Air Force Academy, the United States Coast Guard Academy, or the United States Merchant Marine Academy, to the extent that the amount of the payment or distribution does not exceed the costs of advanced education (as defined by section 2005(e)(3) of title 10, United States Code, as in effect on the date of the enactment of this section) attributable to such attendance, or

(v) an amount which is includible in gross income solely by application of paragraph (2)(C)(i)(II) for the taxable year.

(C) Contributions returned before certain date.—Subparagraph (A) shall not apply to the distribution of any contribution made during a taxable year on behalf of the designated beneficiary if—

(i) such distribution is made before the first day of the sixth month of the taxable year following the taxable year, and

(ii) such distribution is accompanied by the amount of net income attributable to such excess contribution.

Any net income described in clause (ii) Shall be included in gross income for the taxable year in which such excess contribution was made.

(5) Rollover contributions.—Paragraph (1) shall not apply to any amount paid or distributed from a Coverdell education savings account to the extent that the amount received is paid, not later than the 60th day after the date of such payment or distribution, into another Coverdell education savings account for the benefit of the same beneficiary or a member of the family (within the meaning of section 529(e)(2)) of such beneficiary who has not attained age 30 as of such date. The preceding sentence shall not apply to any payment or distribution if it applied to any prior payment or distribution during the 12-month period ending on the date of the payment or distribution.

(6) Change in beneficiary.—Any change in the beneficiary of a Coverdell education savings account shall not be treated as a distribution for purposes of paragraph (1) if the new beneficiary is a member of the family (as so defined) of the old beneficiary and has not attained age 30 as of the date of such change.

(7) Special rules for death and divorce.—Rules similar to the rules of paragraphs (7) and (8) of section 220(f) shall apply. In applying the preceding sentence, members of a family (as so defined) of the designated beneficiary shall be treated in the same manner as the spouse under such paragraph (8).

(8) Deemed distribution on required distribution date.—In any case in which a distribution is required under subsection (b)(l)(E), any balance to the credit of a designated beneficiary as of the close of the 30-day period referred to in such subsection for making such distribution shall be deemed distributed at the close of such period.

(9) Military death gratuity.—

(A) In general.—For purposes of this section, the term "rollover contribution" includes a contribution to a Coverdell education savings account made before the end of the 1-year period beginning on the date on which the contributor receives an amount under section 1477 of title 10, United States Code, or section 1967 of title 38 of such Code, with respect to a person, to the extent that such contribution does not exceed—

(i) the sum of the amounts received during such period by such contributor under such sections with respect to such person, reduced by

(ii) the amounts so received which were contributed to a Roth IRA under section 408A(e)(2) or to another Coverdell education savings account.

(B) Annual limit on number of rollovers not to apply.—The last sentence of paragraph (5) shall not apply with respect to amounts treated as a rollover by subparagraph (A).

(C) Application of section 72.—For purposes of applying section 72 in the case of a distribution which is includible in gross income under paragraph (1), the amount treated as a rollover by reason of subparagraph (A) shall be treated as investment in the contract.

(e) Tax treatment of accounts.—Rules similar to the rules of paragraphs (2) and (4) of section 408 (e) shall apply to any Coverdell education savings account.

(f) Community property laws.—This section shall be applied without regard to any community property laws.

(g) Custodial accounts.—For purposes of this section, a custodial account shall be treated as a trust if the assets of such account are held by a bank (as defined in section 408(n)) or another person who demonstrates, to the satisfaction of the Secretary, that the manner in which he will administer the account will be consistent with the requirements of this section, and if the custodial account would, except for the fact that it is not a trust, constitute an account described in subsection (b)(1). For purposes of this title, in the case of a custodial account treated as a trust by reason of the preceding sentence, the custodian of such account shall be treated as the trustee thereof.

(h) Reports.—The trustee of a Coverdell education saving account shall make such reports regarding such account to the Secretary and to the beneficiary of the account with respect to contributions, distributions, and such other matters as the Secretary may require. The reports required by this subsection shall be filed at such time and in such manner and furnished to such individuals at such time and in such manner as may be required.

SUBCHAPTER G—CORPORATIONS USED TO AVOID INCOME TAX ON SHAREHOLDERS

PART I—CORPORATIONS IMPROPERLY ACCUMULATING SURPLUS

Editorial Summary

Accumulated Earnings Tax

Subchapter G of Chapter 1 (Secs. 531–537, 561–563, 565)

From a tax perspective, the major disadvantage of the corporate form is the potential for double taxation (i.e., tax is levied on the taxable income of the corporation, and tax is levied at the shareholder level upon the receipt of dividends). Two techniques exist for avoiding this double taxation. First, the corporation can attempt to reduce its taxable income to zero through a variety of types of payments to shareholders that are deductible in calculating corporate taxable income (e.g., salaries and other compensation to shareholder/employees, lease rental payments for assets owned outside the corporation by shareholders, and interest payments on loans made by shareholders to the corporation). All of these payments are subject to the requirement of being "reasonable." If not, the IRS can disallow all, or part of, the deduction at the corporate level and treat the distribution to the shareholder as a dividend. In addition, if the loans are excessive with respect to the equity of the corporation, the loans can be reclassified as equity under Sec. 385. This likewise results in the deduction for the interest payments being disallowed at the corporate level and the reclassification of the interest income as dividend income at the shareholder level.

The second option available for avoiding double taxation is for the corporation not to distribute dividends. In the short run, this will avoid taxation at the shareholder level in the form of dividend income. In the long run, either return of capital and related capital gain treatment can be achieved (i.e., stock redemption, corporate liquidation, or stock sale), or the second tier of federal income taxation at the shareholder level can be avoided completely through the shareholder retaining the stock until death (i.e., the beneficiaries basis for the stock will be stepped-up to the fair market value). In recognition of this potential ability to avoid, or at least reduce the impact of, double taxation, Congress enacted a penalty tax termed the accumulated earnings tax.

The purpose of the accumulated earnings tax is to motivate the corporation to make dividend distributions of earnings that it cannot justify as being reasonable needs of the business. Prior to the Revenue Reconciliation Act of 1990, the rate of the penalty tax on accumulated taxable income of 28 percent was the same as the maximum statutory rate that was applicable at the shareholder level if dividends were distributed. However, while RRA of 1990 increased the maximum statutory rate in Sec. 1 from 28 percent to 31 percent, it did not change the accumulated earnings tax rate of 28 percent. Whether this was intended by Congress or was an oversight which would be corrected as part of technical corrections legislation was never addressed. Note that some commentators have suggested that the logic for the 28 percent rate was that this is the same as the alternative rate on net capital gain. In either case, the reduction in tax rates for the individual taxpayer by the Tax Reform Act of 1986 should lessen the motivation for the unjustified retention of earnings at the corporate level. The issue of the appropriate rate has been effectively resolved by the Revenue Reconciliation Act of 1993 which set the accumulated earnings tax rate as equal to the highest individual tax rate (i.e., 39.6 percent) [see Sec. 531]. The Tax Relief Reconciliation Act of 2001 changed the statutory language from 39.6% to "the highest rate of tax under section 1(c)" [e.g., 39.1% in 2001, 38.6% in 2002 and 2003, and 37.6% in 2004 and 2005]. The Jobs and Growth Tax Relief Reconciliation Act of 2003 changed the statutory language from "the highest tax rate under section 1(c)" to "15 percent" in accordance with the beneficial treatment provided certain dividends by the Act [see Sec. 301(f)(4)]. The American Taxpayer Relief Act of 2012 increased the rate from 15 percent to 20 percent.

Two situations exist for which the penalty tax is not applicable. First, earnings can be retained for the reasonable needs of the business [see Sec. 537]. Second, a limited amount of "unjustified" earnings can be retained under a materiality provision in Sec. 535(c) (i.e., either $150,000 or $250,000). In addition, even if neither of these situations is applicable, the penalty tax will not apply unless the purpose of the unreasonable accumulation is to avoid tax [see Sec. 533]. Therefore, although not specifically limited by the Code to closely held corporations [see Sec. 532(c)], the penalty tax typically is levied on closely held corporations.

The name "accumulated earnings tax" is somewhat of a misnomer in that the penalty tax is not levied on accumulated earnings but instead is levied on accumulated taxable income [see Secs. 531, 535]. The starting point for calculating the potential penalty tax is the taxable income of the corporation for the taxable year. Certain adjustments are made to convert taxable income to accumulated taxable income [see Sec. 535(b)]. Thus, a corporation with substantial "unjustified" accumulated earnings may not be subject to the penalty tax for the current taxable year because the critical issue is the taxable income variable rather than the accumulated earnings variable.

The penalty tax can be eliminated through the distribution of dividends [see Sec. 535(a)]. Dividends can take a variety of forms including dividends paid during the taxable year, dividends paid during the 2½-month period following the

*Omitted.

close of the taxable year, and consent dividends [see Secs. 561, 563, 565].

The accumulated earnings tax is not self-assessing. It applies only if assessed by the IRS. However, this should not lead to false complacency caused by thinking that tax planning is not required to avoid the penalty tax.

The accumulated earnings tax is not applicable if the personal holding company tax [see Sec. 541] applies or to a corporation exempt from tax under Sec. 501. Likewise, the accumulated earnings tax is not applicable to a corporation which has elected S corporation status under Sec. 1362.

The accumulated earnings tax model can be depicted as follows:

	Taxable income
±	Adjustments
=	Adjusted taxable income
–	Accumulated earnings credit
–	Dividends paid
=	Accumulated taxable income
×	Rate
=	Accumulated earnings tax liability

§ 531. Imposition of accumulated earnings tax

In addition to other taxes imposed by this chapter, there is hereby imposed for each taxable year on the accumulated taxable income (as defined in section 535) of every corporation described in section 532, an accumulated earnings tax equal to 20 percent of the accumulated taxable income.

§ 532. Corporations subject to accumulated earnings tax

(a) General rule.—The accumulated earnings tax imposed by section 531 shall apply to every corporation (other than those described in subsection (b)) formed or availed of for the purpose of avoiding the income tax with respect to its shareholders or the shareholders of any other corporation, by permitting earnings and profits to accumulate instead of being divided or distributed.

(b) Exceptions.—The accumulated earnings tax imposed by section 531 shall not apply to—

(1) a personal holding company (as defined in section 542),

(2) a corporation exempt from tax under subchapter F (section 501 and following), or

(3) a passive foreign investment company (as defined in section 1297).

(c) Application determined without regard to number of shareholders.—The application of this part to a corporation shall be determined without regard to the number of shareholders of such corporation.

§ 533. Evidence of purpose to avoid income tax

(a) Unreasonable accumulation determinative of purpose.—For purposes of section 532, the fact that the earnings and profits of a corporation are permitted to accumulate beyond the reasonable needs of the business shall be determinative of the purpose to avoid the income tax with respect to shareholders, unless the corporation by the preponderance of the evidence shall prove to the contrary.

(b) Holding or investment company.—The fact that any corporation is a mere holding or investment company shall be prima facie evidence of the purpose to avoid the income tax with respect to shareholders.

§ 534. Burden of proof

(a) General rule.—In any proceeding before the Tax Court involving a notice of deficiency based in whole or in part on the allegation that all or any part of thc carnings and profits have been permitted to accumulate beyond the reasonable needs of the business, the burden of proof with respect to such allegation shall—

(1) if notification has not been sent in accordance with subsection (b), be on the Secretary, or

(2) if the taxpayer has submitted the statement described in subsection (c), be on the Secretary with respect to the grounds set forth in such statement in accordance with the provisions of such subsection.

(b) Notification by Secretary.—Before mailing the notice of deficiency referred to in subsection (a), the Secretary may send by certified mail or registered mail a notification informing the taxpayer that the proposed notice of deficiency includes an amount with respect to the accumulated earnings tax imposed by section 531.

(c) Statement by taxpayer.—Within such time (but not less than 30 days) after the mailing of the notification described in subsection (b) as the Secretary may prescribe by regulations, the taxpayer may submit a statement of the grounds (together with facts sufficient to show the basis thereof) on which the taxpayer relies to establish that all or any part of the earnings and profits have not been permitted to accumulate beyond the reasonable needs of the business.

* * *

§ 535. Accumulated taxable income

(a) Definition.—For purposes of this subtitle, the term "accumulated taxable income" means the taxable income, adjusted in the manner provided in subsection (b), minus the sum of the dividends paid deduction (as defined in section 561) and the accumulated earnings credit (as defined in subsection (c)).

(b) Adjustments to taxable income.—For purposes of subsection (a), taxable income shall be adjusted as follows:

(1) Taxes.—There shall be allowed as a deduction Federal income and excess profits taxes and income, war profits, and excess profits taxes of foreign countries and possessions of the United States (to the extent not allowable as a deduction under section 275(a)(4)), accrued during the taxable year or deemed to be paid by a domestic corporation under section 902(a) or 960(a)(1) for the taxable year, but not including the accumulated earnings tax imposed by section 531, the personal holding company tax imposed by section 541, or the taxes imposed by corresponding sections of a prior income tax law.

(2) Charitable contributions.—The deduction for charitable contributions provided under section 170 shall be allowed without regard to section 170 (b)(2).

(3) Special deductions disallowed.—The special deductions for corporations provided in part VIII (except section 248) of subchapter B (section 241 and following, relating to the deduction for dividends received by corporations, etc.) shall not be allowed.

(4) Net operating loss.—The net operating loss deduction provided in section 172 shall not be allowed.

(5) Capital losses.—

(A) In general.—Except as provided in subparagraph (B), there shall be allowed as a deduction an amount equal to the net capital loss for the taxable year (determined without regard to paragraph (7)(A)).

(B) Recapture of previous deductions for capital gains.—The aggregate amount allowable as a deduction under subparagraph (A) for any taxable year shall be reduced by the lesser of—

(i) the nonrecaptured capital gains deductions, or

(ii) the amount of the accumulated earnings and profits of the corporation as of the close of the preceding taxable year.

(C) Nonrecaptured capital gains deductions.—For purposes of subparagraph (B), the term "nonrecaptured capital gains deductions" means the excess of—

(i) the aggregate amount allowable as a deduction under paragraph (6) for preceding taxable years beginning after July 18, 1984, over

(ii) the aggregate of the reductions under subparagraph (B) for preceding taxable years.

(6) Net capital gains.—

(A) In general.—There shall be allowed as a deduction—

(i) the net capital gain for the taxable year (determined with the application of paragraph (7)), reduced by

(ii) the taxes attributable to such net capital gain.

(B) Attributable taxes.—For purposes of subparagraph (A), the taxes attributable to the net capital gain shall be an amount equal to the difference between—

(i) the taxes imposed by this subtitle (except the tax imposed by this part) for the taxable year, and

(ii) such taxes computed for such year without including in taxable income the net capital gain for the taxable year (determined without the application of paragraph (7)).

(7) Capital loss carryovers.—

(A) Unlimited carryforward.—The net capital loss for any taxable year shall be treated as a short-term capital loss in the next taxable year.

(B) Section 1212 inapplicable.—No allowance shall be made for the capital loss carryback or carryforward provided in section 1212.

(8) Special rules for mere holding or investment companies.—In the case of a mere holding or investment company—

(A) Capital loss deduction, etc., not allowed.—Paragraphs (5) and (7)(A) shall not apply.

(B) Deduction for certain offsets.—There shall be allowed as a deduction the net short-term capital gain for the taxable year to the extent such gain does not exceed the amount of any capital loss carryover to such taxable year under section 1212 (determined without regard to paragraph (7)(B)).

(C) Earnings and profits.—For purposes of subchapter C, the accumulated earnings and profits at any time shall not be less than they would be if this subsection had applied to the computation of earnings and profits for all taxable years beginning after July 18, 1984.

* * *

(c) Accumulated earnings credit.—

(1) General rule.—For purposes of subsection (a), in the case of a corporation other than a mere holding or investment company the accumulated earnings credit is (A) an amount equal to such part of the earnings and profits for the taxable year as are retained for the reasonable needs of the business, minus (B) the deduction allowed by subsection (b)(6). For purposes of this paragraph, the amount of the earnings and profits for the taxable year which are retained is the amount by which the earnings and profits for the taxable year exceed the dividends paid deduction (as defined in section 561) for such year.

(2) Minimum credit.—

(A) In general.—The credit allowable under paragraph (1) shall in no case be less than the amount by which $250,000 exceeds the accumulated earnings and profits of the corporation at the close of the preceding taxable year.

(B) Certain service corporations.—In the case of a corporation the principal function of which is the performance of services in the field of health, law, engineering, architecture, accounting, actuarial science, performing arts, or consulting, subparagraph (A) shall be applied by substituting "$150,000" for "$250,000."

(3) Holding and investment companies.—In the case of a corporation which is a mere holding or investment company, the accumulated earnings credit is the amount (if any) by which $250,000 exceeds the accumulated earnings and profits of the corporation at the close of the preceding taxable year.

(4) Accumulated earnings and profits.—For purposes of paragraphs (2) and (3), the accumulated earnings and profits at the close of the preceding taxable year shall be reduced by the dividends which under section 563(a) (relating to dividends paid after the close of the taxable year) are considered as paid during such taxable year.

(5) Cross reference.—

For denial of credit provided in paragraph (2) or (3) where multiple corporations are formed to avoid tax, see section 1551, and for limitation on such credit in the case of certain controlled corporations, see section 1561.

* * *

§ 536. Income not placed on annual basis

Section 443(b) (relating to computation of tax on change of annual accounting period) shall not apply in the computation of the accumulated earnings tax imposed by section 531.

§ 537. Reasonable needs of the business

(a) General rule.—For purposes of this part, the term "reasonable needs of the business" includes—

(1) the reasonably anticipated needs of the business,

(2) the section 303 redemption needs of the business, and

(3) the excess business holdings redemption needs of the business.

(b) Special rules.—For purposes of subsection (a)—

(1) Section 303 redemption needs.—The term "section 303 redemption needs" means, with respect to the taxable year of the corporation in which a shareholder of the corporation died or any taxable year thereafter, the amount needed (or reasonably anticipated to be needed) to make a redemption of stock included in the gross estate of the decedent (but not in excess of the maximum amount of stock to which section 303(a) may apply).

* * *

(3) Obligations incurred to make redemptions.—In applying paragraphs (1) and (2), the discharge of any obligation incurred to make a redemption described in such paragraphs shall be treated as the making of such redemption.

(4) Product liability loss reserves.—The accumulation of reasonable amounts for the payment of reasonably anticipated product liability losses (as defined in section 172(f)), as determined under regulations prescribed by the Secretary, shall be treated as accumulated for the reasonably anticipated needs of the business.

(5) No inference as to prior taxable years.—The application of this part to any taxable year before the first taxable year specified in paragraph (1) shall be made without regard to the fact that distributions in redemption coming within the terms of such paragraphs were subsequently made.

PART II—PERSONAL HOLDING COMPANIES

Editorial Summary

Personal Holding Company Tax

Subchapter G of Chapter 1 (Secs. 541–547, 561–565)

In addition to the accumulated earnings tax [see Sec. 531], another penalty tax that may be levied on the corporation is the personal holding company tax. Prior to the Revenue Reconciliation Act of 1990, the rate for this penalty tax was the same as the maximum rate for the individual taxpayer (i.e., 28 percent for 1988 and thereafter) [see Sec. 541]. However, while RRA of 1990 increased the maximum statutory rate in Section 1 from 28 percent to 31 percent, it did not change the personal holding company tax rate from 28 percent. Whether this was intended by Congress or was an oversight which would be corrected as part of technical corrections legislation was never addressed. Note that some commentators have suggested that the logic for the 28 percent rate was that this is the same as the alternative rate on net capital gain. In either case, viewed from the combined perspective of the shareholder and the corporation, this penalty tax should always be avoided. The issue of the appropriate rate has been effectively resolved by the Revenue Reconciliation Act of 1993 which set the personal holding company tax rate as equal to the highest individual tax rate (i.e., 39.6 percent) [see Sec. 541]. The Tax Relief Reconciliation Act of 2001 changed the statutory language from 39.6% to "the highest rate of tax under section 1(c)" [e.g., 39.1% in 2001, 38.6% in 2002 and 2003, and 37.6% in 2004 and 2005]. The Jobs and Growth Tax Relief Reconciliation Act of 2003 changed the statutory language from "the highest tax rate under section 1(c)" to "15 percent" in accordance with the beneficial treatment provided certain dividends by the Act [see Sec. 301(f)(4)]. The American Taxpayer Relief Act of 2012 increased the rate from 15 percent to 20 percent.

The personal holding company tax is self-assessing. Therefore, unlike the accumulated earnings tax, there is no opportunity to forego dividend distributions based on the hope that the penalty tax will not be assessed by the IRS.

Two techniques are available for avoiding the application of the personal holding company tax. First, classification as a personal holding company can be avoided. Section 542 provides that a corporation will be classified as a personal holding company only if *both* a stock ownership test (i.e., applying constructive ownership rules in Sec. 544) and an income test are satisfied. Thus, from a planning perspective, the objective is to violate at least one of these two tests. For the closely held corporation, it may be impossible, in light of the constructive ownership rules, to violate the stock ownership test. In this case, the only available avoidance option is to structure the income flows such that less than 60 percent of the adjusted ordinary gross income [see Sec. 543(b)(2)] is personal holding company income [see Sec. 543(a)].

The second avoidance technique is to reduce undistributed personal holding company income to zero [see Sec. 545]. The starting point for calculating undistributed personal holding company income is the corporate taxable income for the taxable year. Taxable income is adjusted for various items specified in Sec. 545(b). If the result is zero or less, there is no personal holding company tax liability. If the result is positive, however, personal holding company tax liability will result unless adequate dividend distributions are made that reduce undistributed personal holding company income to zero [see Secs. 545(a), 562].

The timing and types of dividend distributions include the following [see Secs. 547, 561–565]:

1. Dividends paid during the taxable year.
2. Consent dividends for the taxable year.
3. Dividends paid within 2½ months after the close of the taxable year, subject to the 20 percent limit contained in Sec. 563(b).
4. Dividend carryover to the taxable year.
5. Deficiency dividend paid after a personal holding company deficiency has been assessed.

In certain cases, the amount of the required dividend distribution required to eliminate any personal holding company tax liability for the taxable year can be minimized through the recognition of the interaction of dividends paid on various personal holding company Code sections. For example, the most obvious impact is that the dividends paid are deductible in calculating undistributed personal holding company income. However, the payment of a lesser amount of dividends may result in adjusted income from rents [see Sec. 543(a)(2)] not being classified as personal holding company income, thereby enabling the corporation to avoid being classified as a personal holding company by not satisfying the income test of Sec. 542(a)(1).

The personal holding company tax model can be depicted as follows:

	Taxable income
±	Adjustments
=	Adjusted taxable income
−	Dividends paid

= Undistributed personal holding company income
× Rate
= Personal holding company tax liability

§ 541. Imposition of personal holding company tax

In addition to other taxes imposed by this chapter, there is hereby imposed for each taxable year on the undistributed personal holding company income (as defined in section 545) of every personal holding company (as defined in section 542) a personal holding company tax equal to 20 percent of the undistributed personal holding company income.

§ 542. Definition of personal holding company

(a) General rule.—For purposes of this subtitle, the term "personal holding company" means any corporation (other than a corporation described in subsection (c)) if—

(1) Adjusted ordinary gross income requirement.—At least 60 percent of its adjusted ordinary gross income (as defined in section 543(b)(2)) for the taxable year is personal holding company income (as defined in section 543(a)), and

(2) Stock ownership requirement.—At any time during the last half of the taxable year more than 50 percent in value of its outstanding stock is owned, directly or indirectly, by or for not more than 5 individuals. For purposes of this paragraph, an organization described in section 401(a), 501(c)(17), or 509(a) or a portion of a trust permanently set aside or to be used exclusively for the purposes described in section 642(c) or a corresponding provision of a prior income tax law shall be considered an individual.

(b) Corporations filing consolidated returns.—

(1) General rule.—In the case of an affiliated group of corporations filing or required to file a consolidated return under section 1501 for any taxable year, the adjusted ordinary gross income requirement of subsection (a)(1) of this section shall, except as provided in paragraphs (2) and (3), be applied for such year with respect to the consolidated adjusted ordinary gross income and the consolidated personal holding company income of the affiliated group. No member of such an affiliated group shall be considered to meet such adjusted ordinary gross income requirement unless the affiliated group meets such requirement.

(2) Ineligible affiliated group.—Paragraph (1) shall not apply to an affiliated group of corporations if—

(A) any member of the affiliated group of corporations (including the common parent corporation) derived 10 percent or more of its adjusted ordinary gross income for the taxable year from sources outside the affiliated group, and

(B) 80 percent or more of the amount described in subparagraph (A) consists of personal holding company income (as defined in section 543).

For purposes of this paragraph, section 543 shall be applied as if the amount described in subparagraph (A) were the adjusted ordinary gross income of the corporation.

(3) Excluded corporations.—Paragraph (1) shall not apply to an affiliated group of corporations if any member of the affiliated group (including the common parent corporation) is a corporation excluded from the definition of personal holding company under subsection (c).

(4) Certain dividend income received by a common parent.—In applying paragraph (2)(A) and (B), personal holding company income and adjusted ordinary gross income shall not include dividends received by a common parent corporation from another corporation if—

(A) the common parent corporation owns, directly or indirectly, more than 50 percent of the outstanding voting stock of such other corporation, and

(B) such other corporation is not a personal holding company for the taxable year in which the dividends are paid.

* * *

(c) Exceptions.—The term "personal holding company" as defined in subsection (a) does not include—

(1) a corporation exempt from tax under subchapter F (sec. 501 and following);

(2) a bank as defined in section 581, or a domestic building and loan association within the meaning of section 7701(a)(19);

(3) a life insurance company;

(4) a surety company;

* * *

(6) a lending or finance company if—

(A) 60 percent or more of its ordinary gross income (as defined in section 543(b)(1)) is derived directly from the active and regular conduct of a lending or finance business;

(B) the personal holding company income for the taxable year (computed without regard to income described in subsection (d)(3) and income derived directly from the active and regular conduct of a lending or finance business, and computed by including as personal holding company income the entire amount of the gross income from rents, royalties, produced film rents, and compensation for use of corporate property by shareholders) is not more than 20 percent of the ordinary gross income;

(C) the sum of the deductions which are directly allocable to the active and regular conduct of its lending or finance business equals or exceeds the sum of—

(i) 15 percent of so much of the ordinary gross income derived therefrom as does not exceed $500,000, plus

(ii) 5 percent of so much of the ordinary gross income derived therefrom as exceeds $500,000; and

(D) the loans to a person who is a shareholder in such company during the taxable year by or for whom 10 percent or more in value of its outstanding stock is owned directly or indirectly (including, in the case of an individual, stock owned by members of his family as defined in section 544(a)(2)), outstanding at any time during such year do not exceed $5,000 in principal amount;

* * *

§ 543. Personal holding company income

(a) General rule.—For purposes of this subtitle, the term "personal holding company income" means the portion of the adjusted ordinary gross income which consists of:

(1) Dividends, etc.—Dividends, interest, royalties (other than mineral, oil, or gas royalties or copyright royalties), and annuities. This paragraph shall not apply to—

(A) interest constituting rent (as defined in subsection (b)(3)),

* * *

(C) active business computer software royalties (within the meaning of subsection (d)), and

(D) interest received by a broker or dealer (within the meaning of section 3(a)(4) or (5) of the Securities and Exchange Act of 1934) in connection with—

(i) any securities or money market instruments held as property described in section 1221(1),

(ii) margin accounts, or

(iii) any financing for a customer secured by securities or money market instruments.

(2) Rents.—The adjusted income from rents; except that such adjusted income shall not be included if—

(A) such adjusted income constitutes 50 percent or more of the adjusted ordinary gross income, and

(B) the sum of—

(i) the dividends paid during the taxable year (determined under section 562),

(ii) the dividends considered as paid on the last day of the taxable year under section 563(d) (as limited by the second sentence of section 563(b)), and

(iii) the consent dividends for the taxable year (determined under section 565),

equals or exceeds the amount, if any, by which the personal holding company income for the taxable year (computed without regard to this paragraph and paragraph (6), and computed by including as personal holding company income copyright royalties and the adjusted income from mineral, oil, and gas royalties) exceeds 10 percent of the ordinary gross income.

(3) Mineral, oil, and gas royalties.—The adjusted income from mineral, oil, and gas royalties; except that such adjusted income shall not be included if—

(A) such adjusted income constitutes 50 percent or more of the adjusted ordinary gross income,

(B) the personal holding company income for the taxable year (computed without regard to this paragraph, and computed by including as personal holding company income copyright royalties and the adjusted income from rents) is not more than 10 percent of the ordinary gross income, and

(C) the sum of the deductions which are allowable under section 162 (relating to trade or business expenses) other than—

(i) deductions for compensation for personal services rendered by the shareholders, and

(ii) deductions which are specifically allowable under sections other than section 162,

equals or exceeds 15 percent of the adjusted ordinary gross income.

(4) Copyright royalties.—Copyright royalties; except that copyright royalties shall not be included if—

(A) such royalties (exclusive of royalties received for the use of, or right to use, copyrights or interests in copyrights on works created in whole, or in part, by any shareholder) constitute 50 percent or more of the ordinary gross income,

(B) the personal holding company income for the taxable year computed—

(i) without regard to copyright royalties, other than royalties received for the use of, or right to use, copyrights or interests in copyrights in works created in whole, or in part, by any shareholder owning more than 10 percent of the total outstanding capital stock of the corporation,

(ii) without regard to dividends from any corporation in which the taxpayer owns at least 50 percent of all classes of stock entitled to vote and at least 50 percent of the total value of all classes of stock and which corporation meets the requirements of this subparagraph and subparagraphs (A) and (C), and

(iii) by including as personal holding company income the adjusted income from rents and the adjusted income from mineral, oil, and gas royalties,

is not more than 10 percent of the ordinary gross income, and

(C) the sum of the deductions which are properly allocable to such royalties and which are allowable under section 162, other than—

(i) deductions for compensation for personal services rendered by the shareholders,

(ii) deductions for royalties paid or accrued, and

(iii) deductions which are specifically allowable under sections other than section 162,

equals or exceeds 25 percent of the amount by which the ordinary gross income exceeds the sum of the royalties paid or accrued and the amounts allowable as deductions under section 167 (relating to depreciation) with respect to copyright royalties.

For purposes of this subsection, the term "copyright royalties" means compensation, however designated, for the use of, or the right to use, copyrights in works protected by copyright issued under title 17 of the United States Code and to which copyright protection is also extended by the laws of any country other than the United States of America by virtue of any international treaty, convention, or agreement, or interests in any such copyrighted works, and includes payments from any person for performing rights in any such copyrighted work and payments (other than produced film rents as defined in paragraph (5)(B)) received for the use of, or right to use, films. For purposes of this paragraph, the term "shareholder" shall include any person who owns stock within the meaning of section 544. This paragraph shall not apply to active business computer software royalties

(5) Produced film rents.—

(A) Produced film rents; except that such rents shall not be included if such rents constitute 50 percent or more of the ordinary gross income.

(B) For purposes of this section, the term "produced film rents" means payments received with respect to an interest in a film for the use of, or right to use, such film, but only to the extent that such interest was acquired before substantial completion of production of such film. In the case of a producer who actively participates in the production of the film, such term includes an interest in the proceeds or profits from the film, but only to the extent such interest is attributable to such active participation.

(6) Use of corporate property by shareholder.—

(A) Amounts received as compensation (however designated and from whomever received) for the use of, or the right to use, tangible property of the corporation in any case where, at any time during the taxable year,

25 percent or more in value of the outstanding stock of the corporation is owned, directly or indirectly, by or for an individual entitled to the use of the property (whether such right is obtained directly from the corporation or by means of a sublease or other arrangement).

(B) Subparagraph (A) shall apply only to a corporation which has personal holding company income in excess of 10 percent of its ordinary gross income.

(C) For purposes of the limitation in subparagraph (B), personal holding company income shall be computed—

(i) without regard to subparagraph (A) or paragraph (2),

(ii) by excluding amounts received as compensation for the use of (or right to use) intangible property (other than mineral, oil, or gas royalties or copyright royalties) if a substantial part of the tangible property used in connection with such intangible property is owned by the corporation and all such tangible and intangible property is used in the active conduct of a trade or business by an individual or individuals described in subparagraph (A), and

(iii) by including copyright royalties and adjusted income from mineral, oil, and gas royalties.

(7) Personal service contracts.—

(A) Amounts received under a contract under which the corporation is to furnish personal services; if some person other than the corporation has the right to designate (by name or by description) the individual who is to perform the services, or if the individual who is to perform the services is designated (by name or by description) in the contract; and

(B) amounts received from the sale or other disposition of such a contract.

This paragraph shall apply with respect to amounts received for services under a particular contract only if at some time during the taxable year 25 percent or more in value of the outstanding stock of the corporation is owned, directly or indirectly, by or for the individual who has performed, is to perform, or may be designated (by name or by description) as the one to perform, such services.

(8) Estates and trusts.—Amounts includible in computing the taxable income of the corporation under part I of subchapter J (sec. 641 and following, relating to estates, trusts, and beneficiaries).

(b) Definitions.—For purposes of this part—

(1) Ordinary gross income.—The term "ordinary gross income" means the gross income determined by excluding—

(A) all gains from the sale or other disposition of capital assets and

(B) all gains (other than those referred to in subparagraph (A)) from the sale or other disposition of property described in section 1231(b).

(2) Adjusted ordinary gross income.—The term "adjusted ordinary gross income" means the ordinary gross income adjusted as follows:

(A) Rents.—From the gross income from rents (as defined in the second sentence of paragraph (3) of this subsection) subtract the amount allowable as deductions for—

(i) exhaustion, wear and tear, obsolescence, and amortization of property other than tangible personal property which is not customarily retained by any one lessee for more than three years,

(ii) property taxes,

(iii) interest, and

(iv) rent,

to the extent allocable, under regulations prescribed by the Secretary, to such gross income from rents. The amount subtracted under this subparagraph shall not exceed such gross income from rents.

(B) Mineral royalties, etc.—From the gross income from mineral, oil, and gas royalties described in paragraph (4), and from the gross income from working interests in an oil or gas well, subtract the amount allowable as deductions for—

(i) exhaustion, wear and tear, obsolescence, amortization, and depletion,

(ii) property and severance taxes,

(iii) interest, and

(iv) rent,

to the extent allocable, under regulations prescribed by the Secretary, to such gross income from royalties or such gross income from working interests in oil or gas wells. The amount subtracted under this subparagraph with respect to royalties shall not exceed the gross income from such royalties, and the amount subtracted under this subparagraph with respect to working interests shall not exceed the gross income from such working interests.

(C) Interest.—There shall be excluded—

(i) interest received on a direct obligation of the United States held for sale to customers in the ordinary course of trade or business by a regular dealer who is making a primary market in such obligations, and

(ii) interest on a condemnation award, a judgment, and a tax refund.

(D) Certain excluded rents.—From the gross income consisting of compensation described in subparagraph (D) of paragraph (3) subtract the amount allowable as deductions for the items described in clauses (i), (ii), (iii), and (iv) of subparagraph (A) to the extent allocable, under regulations prescribed by the Secretary, to such gross income. The amount subtracted under this subparagraph shall not exceed such gross income.

(3) Adjusted income from rents.—The term "adjusted income from rents" means the gross income from rents, reduced by the amount subtracted under paragraph (2)(A) of this subsection. For purposes of the preceding sentence, the term "rents" means compensation, however designated, for the use of, or right to use, property, and the interest on debts owed to the corporation, to the extent such debts represent the price for which real property held primarily for sale to customers in the ordinary course of its trade or business was sold or exchanged by the corporation; but such term does not include—

(A) amounts constituting personal holding company income under subsection (a)(6),

(B) copyright royalties (as defined in subsection (a)(4)),

(C) produced film rents (as defined in subsection (a)(5)(B)),

(D) compensation, however designated, for the use of, or the right to use, any tangible personal property manufactured or produced by the taxpayer, if during the taxable year the taxpayer is engaged in substantial manufacturing or production of tangible personal property of the same type, or

(E) active business computer software royalties (as defined in subsection (d)).

(4) Adjusted income from mineral, oil, and gas royalties.—The term "adjusted income from mineral, oil, and gas royalties" means the gross income from mineral, oil, and gas royalties (including production payments and overriding royalties), reduced by the amount subtracted under paragraph (2) (B) of this subsection in respect of such royalties.

* * *

(d) Active business computer software royalties.—

(1) In general.—For purposes of this section, the term "active business computer software royalties" means any royalties—

(A) received by any corporation during the taxable year in connection with the licensing of computer software, and

(B) with respect to which the requirements of paragraphs (2), (3), (4), and (5) are met.

(2) Royalties must be received by corporation actively engaged in computer software business.—The requirements of this paragraph are met if the royalties described in paragraph (1)—

(A) are received by a corporation engaged in the active conduct of the trade or business of developing, manufacturing, or producing computer software, and

(B) are attributable to computer software which—

(i) is developed, manufactured, or produced by such corporation (or its predecessor) in connection with the trade or business described in subparagraph (A), or

(ii) is directly related to such trade or business.

(3) Royalties must constitute at least 50 percent of income.—The requirements of this paragraph are met if the royalties described in paragraph (1) constitute at least 50 percent of the ordinary gross income of the corporation for the taxable year.

(4) Deductions under sections 162 and 174 relating to royalties must equal or exceed 25 percent of ordinary gross income.—

(A) In general.—The requirements of this paragraph are met if—

(i) the sum of the deductions allowable to the corporation under sections 162, 174, and

195 for the taxable year which are properly allocable to the trade or business described in paragraph (2) equals or exceeds 25 percent of the ordinary gross income of such corporation for such taxable year, or

(ii) the average of such deductions for the 5-taxable year period ending with such taxable year equals or exceeds 25 percent of the average ordinary gross income of such corporation for such period.

If a corporation has not been in existence during the 5-taxable year period described in clause (ii), then the period of existence of such corporation shall be substituted for such 5-taxable year period.

(B) Deductions allowable under section 162.—For purposes of subparagraph (A), a deduction shall not be treated as allowable under section 162 if it is specifically allowable under another section.

(C) Limitation on allowable deductions.—For purposes of subparagraph (A), no deduction shall be taken into account with respect to compensation for personal services rendered by the 5 individual shareholders holding the largest percentage (by value) of the outstanding stock of the corporation. For purposes of the preceding sentence—

(i) individuals holding less than 5 percent (by value) of the stock of such corporation shall not be taken into account, and

(ii) stock deemed to be owned by a shareholder solely by attribution from a partner under section 544(a)(2) shall be disregarded.

(5) Dividends must equal or exceed excess of personal holding company income over 10 percent of ordinary gross income.—

(A) In general.—The requirements of this paragraph are met if the sum of—

(i) the dividends paid during the taxable year (determined under section 562),

(ii) the dividends considered as paid on the last day of the taxable year under section 563(d) (as limited by the second sentence of section 563(b)), and

(iii) the consent dividends for the taxable year (determined under section 565),

equals or exceeds the amount, if any, by which the personal holding company income for the taxable year exceeds 10 percent of the ordinary gross income of such corporation for such taxable year.

(B) Computation of personal holding company income.—For purposes of this paragraph, personal holding company income shall be computed—

(i) without regard to amounts described in subsection (a)(1)(C),

(ii) without regard to interest income during any taxable year—

(I) which is in the 5-taxable year period beginning with the later of the 1st taxable year of the corporation or the 1st taxable year in which the corporation conducted the trade or business described in paragraph (2)(A), and

(II) during which the corporation meets the requirements of paragraphs (2), (3), and (4), and

(iii) by including adjusted income from rents and adjusted income from mineral, oil, and gas royalties (within the meaning of paragraphs (2) and (3) of subsection (a)).

(6) Special rules for affiliated group members.—

(A) In general.—In any case in which—

(i) the taxpayer receives royalties in connection with the licensing of computer software, and

(ii) another corporation which is a member of the same affiliated group as the taxpayer meets the requirements of paragraphs (2), (3), (4), and (5) with respect to such computer software,

the taxpayer shall be treated as having met such requirements.

(B) Affiliated group.—For purposes of this paragraph, the term "affiliated group" has the meaning given such term by section 1504(a).

§ 544. Rules for determining stock ownership

(a) Constructive ownership.—For purposes of determining whether a corporation is a personal holding company, insofar as such determination is based on stock ownership under section 542(a)(2), section 543(a)(7), section 543(a)(6), or section 543(a)(4)—

(1) Stock not owned by individual.—Stock owned, directly or indirectly, by or for a corporation, partnership, estate, or trust shall be considered as being owned proportionately by its shareholders, partners, or beneficiaries.

(2) Family and partnership ownership.—An individual shall be considered as owning the stock owned, directly or indirectly, by or for his family or by or for his partner. For purposes of this paragraph, the family of an individual includes only his brothers and sisters (whether by the whole or half blood), spouse, ancestors, and lineal descendants.

(3) Options.—If any person has an option to acquire stock, such stock shall be considered as owned by such person. For purposes of this paragraph, an option to acquire such an option, and each one of a series of such options, shall be considered as an option to acquire such stock.

(4) Application of family-partnership and option rules.—Paragraphs (2) and (3) shall be applied—

(A) for purposes of the stock ownership requirement provided in section 542(a)(2), if, but only if, the effect is to make the corporation a personal holding company;

(B) for purposes of section 543(a)(7) (relating to personal service contracts), of section 543(a)(6) (relating to use of property by shareholders), or of section 543(a)(4) (relating to copyright royalties), if, but only if, the effect is to make the amounts therein referred to includible under such paragraph as personal holding company income.

(5) Constructive ownership as actual ownership.—Stock constructively owned by a person by reason of the application of paragraph (1) or (3) shall, for purposes of applying paragraph (1) or (2), be treated as actually owned by such person; but stock constructively owned by an individual by reason of the application of paragraph (2) shall not be treated as owned by him for purposes of again applying such paragraph in order to make another the constructive owner of such stock.

(6) Option rule in lieu of family and partnership rule.—If stock may be considered as owned by an individual under either paragraph (2) or (3) it shall be considered as owned by him under paragraph (3).

(b) Convertible securities.—Outstanding securities convertible into stock (whether or not convertible during the taxable year) shall be considered as outstanding stock—

(1) for purposes of the stock ownership requirement provided in section 542(a)(2), but only if the effect of the inclusion of all such securities is to make the corporation a personal holding company;

(2) for purposes of section 543(a)(7) (relating to personal service contracts), but only if the effect of the inclusion of all such securities is to make the amounts therein referred to includible under such paragraph as personal holding company income;

(3) for purposes of section 543(a)(6) (relating to the use of property by shareholders), but only if the effect of the inclusion of all such securities is to make the amounts therein referred to includible under such paragraph as personal holding company income; and

(4) for purposes of section 543(a)(4) (relating to copyright royalties), but only if the effect of the inclusion of all such securities is to make the amounts therein referred to includible under such paragraph as personal holding company income.

The requirement in paragraphs (1), (2), (3), and (4) that all convertible securities must be included if any are to be included shall be subject to the exception that, where some of the outstanding securities are convertible only after a later date than in the case of others, the class having the earlier conversion date may be included although the others are not included, but no convertible securities shall be included unless all outstanding securities having a prior conversion date are also included.

§ 545. Undistributed personal holding company income

(a) Definition.—For purposes of this part, the term "undistributed personal holding company income" means the taxable income of a personal holding company adjusted in the manner provided in subsections (b), (c), and (d), minus the dividends paid deduction as defined in section 561. In the case of a personal holding company which is a foreign corporation, not more than 10 percent in value of the outstanding stock of which is owned (within the meaning of section 958(a)) during the last half of the taxable year by United States persons, the term "undistributed personal holding company income" means the amount determined by multiplying the undistributed personal holding company income (determined without regard to this sentence) by the percentage in value of its outstanding stock which is the greatest percentage in value of its outstanding stock so owned by United States persons on any one day during such period.

(b) Adjustments to taxable income.—For the purposes of subsection (a), the taxable income shall be adjusted as follows:

(1) Taxes.—There shall be allowed as a deduction Federal income and excess profits taxes and income, war profits and excess profits taxes of foreign countries and possessions of the United States (to the extent not allowable as a deduction under section 275(a)(4)), accrued during the taxable year or deemed to be paid by a domestic corporation under section 902(a) or 960(a)(l) for the taxable year, but not including the accumulated earnings tax imposed by section 531, the personal holding company tax imposed by section 541, or the taxes imposed by corresponding sections of a prior income tax law.

(2) Charitable contributions.—The deduction for charitable contributions provided under section 170 shall be allowed, but in computing such deduction the limitations in section 170(b)(1)(A), (B), and (D) shall apply, and section 170(b)(2) and (d)(1) shall not apply. For purposes of this paragraph, the term "contribution base" when used in section 170(b)(1) means the taxable income computed with the adjustments (other than the 10-percent limitation) provided in section 170(b)(2) and (d)(1) and without deduction of the amount disallowed under paragraph (6) of this subsection.

(3) Special deductions disallowed.—The special deductions for corporations provided in part VIII (except section 248) of subchapter B (section 241 and following, relating to the deduction for dividends received by corporations, etc.) shall not be allowed.

(4) Net operating loss.—The net operating loss deduction provided in section 172 shall not be allowed, but there shall be allowed as a deduction the amount of the net operating loss (as defined in section 172(c)) for the preceding taxable year computed without the deductions provided in part VIII (except section 248) of subchapter B.

(5) Net capital gains.—There shall be allowed as a deduction the net capital gain for the taxable year, minus the taxes imposed by this subtitle attributable to such net capital gain. The taxes attributable to such net capital gain shall be an amount equal to the difference between—

(A) the taxes imposed by this subtitle (except the tax imposed by this part) for such year, and

(B) such taxes computed for such year without including such net capital gain in taxable income.

(6) Expenses and depreciation applicable to property of the taxpayer.—The aggregate of the deductions allowed under section 162 (relating to trade or business expenses) and section 167 (relating to depreciation), which are allocable to the operation and maintenance of property owned or operated by the corporation, shall be allowed only in an amount equal to the rent or other compensation received for the use of, or the right to use, the property, unless it is established (under regulations prescribed by the Secretary) to the satisfaction of the Secretary—

(A) that the rent or other compensation received was the highest obtainable, or, if none was received, that none was obtainable;

(B) that the property was held in the course of a business carried on bona fide for profit; and

(C) either that there was reasonable expectation that the operation of the property would result in a profit, or that the property was necessary to the conduct of the business.

(7) Special rule for capital gains and losses of foreign corporations.—In the case of a foreign corporation, paragraph (5) shall be applied by taking into account only gains and losses which are effectively connected with the conduct of a trade or business within the United States and are not exempt from tax under treaty.

* * *

§ 546. Income not placed on annual basis

Section 443(b) (relating to computation of tax on change of annual accounting period) shall not apply in the computation of the personal holding company tax imposed by section 541.

§ 547. Deduction for deficiency dividends

(a) General rule.—If a determination (as defined in subsection (c)) with respect to a taxpayer establishes liability for personal holding company tax imposed by section 541 (or by a corresponding provision of a prior income tax law) for any taxable year, a deduction shall be allowed to the taxpayer for the amount of deficiency dividends (as defined in subsection (d)) for the purpose of determining the personal holding company tax for such year, but not for the purpose of determining interest, additional amounts, or assessable penalties computed with respect to such personal holding company tax.

(b) Rules for application of section.—

(1) Allowance of deduction.—The deficiency dividend deduction shall be allowed as of the date the claim for the deficiency dividend deduction is filed.

(2) Credit or refund.—If the allowance of a deficiency dividend deduction results in an overpayment of personal holding company tax for any taxable year, credit or refund with respect to such overpayment shall be made as if on the date of the determination 2 years remained before the expiration of the period of limitation on the filing of claim for refund for the taxable year to which the overpayment relates. No interest shall be allowed on a credit or refund arising from the application of this section.

(c) Determination.—For purposes of this section, the term "determination" means—

(1) a decision by the Tax Court or a judgment, decree, or other order by any court of competent jurisdiction, which has become final;

(2) a closing agreement made under section 7121; or

(3) under regulations prescribed by the Secretary, an agreement signed by the Secretary and by, or on behalf of, the taxpayer relating to the liability of such taxpayer for personal holding company tax.

(d) Deficiency dividends.—

(1) Definition.—For purposes of this section, the term "deficiency dividends" means the amount of the dividends paid by the corporation on or after the date of the determination and before filing claim under subsection (e), which would have been includible in the computation of the deduction for dividends paid under section 561 for the taxable year with respect to which the liability for personal holding company tax exists, if distributed during such taxable year. No dividends shall be considered as deficiency dividends for purposes of subsection (a) unless distributed within 90 days after the determination.

(2) Effect on dividends paid deduction.—

(A) For taxable year in which paid.—Deficiency dividends paid in any taxable year (to the extent of the portion thereof taken into account under subsection (a) in determining personal holding company tax) shall not be included in the amount of dividends paid for such year for purposes of computing the dividends paid deduction for such year and succeeding years.

(B) For prior taxable year.—Deficiency dividends paid in any taxable year (to the extent of the portion thereof taken into account under subsection (a) in determining personal holding company tax) shall not be allowed for purposes of section 563(b) in the computation of the dividends paid deduction for the taxable year preceding the taxable year in which paid.

(e) Claim required.—No deficiency dividend deduction shall be allowed under subsection (a) unless (under regulations prescribed by the Secretary) claim therefor is filed within 120 days after the determination.

(f) Suspension of statute of limitations and stay of collection.—

(1) Suspension of running of statute.—If the corporation files a claim, as provided in subsection (e), the running of the statute of limitations provided in section 6501 on the making of assessments, and the bringing of distraint or a proceeding in court for collection, in respect of the deficiency and all interest, additional amounts, or assessable penalties, shall be suspended for a period of 2 years after the date of the determination.

(2) Stay of collection.—In the case of any deficiency with respect to the tax imposed by section 541 established by a determination under this section—

(A) the collection of the deficiency and all interest, additional amounts, and assessable penalties shall, except in cases of jeopardy, be stayed until the expiration of 120 days after the date of the determination, and

(B) if claim for deficiency dividend deduction is filed under subsection (e), the collection of such part of the deficiency as is not reduced by the deduction for deficiency dividends provided in subsection (a) shall be stayed until the date the claim is disallowed (in whole or in part), and if disallowed in part collection shall be made only with respect to the part disallowed.

No distraint or proceeding in court shall be begun for the collection of an amount the collection of which is stayed under subparagraph (A) or (B) during the period for which the collection of such amount is stayed.

(g) Deduction denied in case of fraud, etc.—No deficiency dividend deduction shall be allowed under subsection (a) if the determination contains a finding that any part of the deficiency is due to fraud with intent to evade tax, or to wilful failure to file an income tax return within the time prescribed by law or prescribed by the Secretary in pursuance of law.

PART III—FOREIGN PERSONAL HOLDING COMPANIES*

PART IV—DEDUCTION FOR DIVIDENDS PAID

Editorial Summary

Deduction for Dividends Paid: Accumulated Earnings Tax and Personal Holding Company Tax

Subchapter G of Chapter 1 (Secs. 561–565)

It is important to distinguish the deduction for dividends paid in Sec. 561 from the dividends received deduction in Sec. 243. Both relate to corporations. However, the Sec. 243 deduction is available to a corporate shareholder who is receiving dividends whereas the Sec. 561 dividends paid deduction is available to the corporation who is making the distribution. Another key difference is that the Sec. 243 deduction relates to the calculation of the regular corporate tax liability whereas the Sec. 561 deduction relates to the calculation of penalty tax liabilities (i.e., the accumulated earnings tax and the personal holding company tax).

The purpose of both of the aforementioned penalty taxes is to penalize the taxpayer because the earnings of the corporation are not distributed to the shareholders. Thus, both penalty taxes can be avoided if the earnings are distributed in the form of dividends.

Two issues that are addressed in the related Code sections are the form of the dividend and the timing of the distribution. Eligible forms include the following (see Secs. 561, 564, 565, and 547):

1. Cash dividend.
2. Property dividend.
3. Consent dividend.
4. Dividend carryover (for personal holding company only).
5. Deficiency dividend (for personal holding company only).

With respect to timing, the dividends may be paid as follows [see Secs. 561(a), 563, 565, and 547]:

1. During the taxable year.
2. Within 2½ months after the close of the taxable year (100 percent can be paid during this period for purposes of the accumulated earnings tax whereas only 20 percent of the amount actually paid during the taxable year will count for purposes of the personal holding company tax).
3. For a consent dividend, the consent may be filed at any time not later than the due date of the corporation's income tax return for the taxable year.
4. For a deficiency dividend, see the provisions contained in Sec. 547 with respect to a "determination."

§ 561. Definition of deduction for dividends paid

(a) General rule.—The deduction for dividends paid shall be the sum of—

(1) the dividends paid during the taxable year,

(2) the consent dividends for the taxable year (determined under section 565), and

(3) in the case of a personal holding company, the dividend carryover described in section 564.

(b) Special rules applicable.—In determining the deduction for dividends paid, the rules provided in section 562 (relating to rules applicable in determining dividends eligible for dividends paid deduction) and section 563 (relating to dividends paid after the close of the taxable year) shall be applicable.

§ 562. Rules applicable in determining dividends eligible for dividends paid deduction

(a) General rule.—For purposes of this part, the term "dividend" shall, except as otherwise provided in this section, include only dividends described in section 316 (relating to definition of dividends for purposes of corporate distributions).

(b) Distributions in liquidation.—

(1) Except in the case of a personal holding company described in section 542—

(A) in the case of amounts distributed in liquidation, the part of such distribution which is properly chargeable to earnings and profits accumulated after February 28, 1913, shall be treated as a dividend for purposes of computing the dividends paid deduction, and

*Omitted.

(B) in the case of a complete liquidation occurring within 24 months after the adoption of a plan of liquidation, any distribution within such period pursuant to such plan shall, to the extent of the earnings and profits (computed without regard to capital losses) of the corporation for the taxable year in which such distribution is made, be treated as a dividend for purposes of computing the dividends paid deduction.

For purposes of subparagraph (A), a liquidation includes a redemption of stock to which section 302 applies. Except to the extent provided in regulations, the preceding sentence shall not apply in the case of any mere holding or investment company which is not a regulated investment company.

(2) In the case of a complete liquidation of a personal holding company, occurring within 24 months after the adoption of a plan of liquidation, the amount of any distribution within such period pursuant to such plan shall be treated as a dividend for purposes of computing the dividends paid deduction, to the extent that such amount is distributed to corporate distributees and represents such corporate distributees' allocable share of the undistributed personal holding company income for the taxable year of such distribution computed without regard to this paragraph and without regard to subparagraph (B) of section 316(b)(2).

(c) Preferential dividends.—Except in the case of a publicly offered regulated investment company (as defined in section 67(c)(2)(B)), the amount of any distribution shall not be considered as a dividend for purposes of computing the dividends paid deduction, unless such distribution is pro rata, with no preference to any share of stock as compared with other shares of the same class, and with no preference to one class of stock as compared with another class except to the extent that the former is entitled (without reference to waivers of their rights by shareholders) to such preference. In the case of a distribution by a regulated investment company (other than a publicly offered regulated investment company (as so defined)) to a shareholder who made an initial investment of at least $10,000,000 in such company, such distribution shall not be treated as not being pro rata or as being preferential solely by reason of an increase in the distribution by reason of reductions in administrative expenses of the company.

(d) Distributions by a member of an affiliated group.—In the case where a corporation which is a member of an affiliated group of corporations filing or required to file a consolidated return for a taxable year is required to file a separate personal holding company schedule for such taxable year, a distribution by such corporation to another member of the affiliated group shall be considered as a dividend for purposes of computing the dividends paid deduction if such distribution would constitute a dividend under the other provisions of this section to a recipient which is not a member of an affiliated group.

* * *

§ 563. Rules relating to dividends paid after close of taxable year

(a) Accumulated earnings tax.—In the determination of the dividends paid deduction for purposes of the accumulated earnings tax imposed by section 531, a dividend paid after the close of any taxable year and on or before the 15th day of the third month following the close of such taxable year shall be considered as paid during such taxable year.

(b) Personal holding company tax.—In the determination of the dividends paid deduction for purposes of the personal holding company tax imposed by section 541, a dividend paid after the close of any taxable year and on or before the 15th day of the third month following the close of such taxable year shall, to the extent the taxpayer elects in its return for the taxable year, be considered as paid during such taxable year. The amount allowed as a dividend by reason of the application of this subsection with respect to any taxable year shall not exceed either—

(1) The undistributed personal holding company income of the corporation for the taxable year, computed without regard to this subsection, or

(2) 20 percent of the sum of the dividends paid during the taxable year, computed without regard to this subsection.

(c) Dividends considered as paid on last day of taxable year.—For the purpose of applying section 562(a), with respect to distributions under subsection (a) or (b) of this section, a distribution made after the close of a taxable year and on or before the 15th day of the third month following the close of the taxable year shall be considered as made on the last day of such taxable year.

§ 564. Dividend carryover

(a) General rule.—For purposes of computing the dividends paid deduction under section 561, in the case of a personal holding company the dividend carryover for any taxable year shall be the dividend carryover to such taxable year, computed as provided in subsection (b), from the two preceding taxable years.

(b) Computation of dividend carryover.—The dividend carryover to the taxable year shall be determined as follows:

(1) For each of the 2 preceding taxable years there shall be determined the taxable income computed with the adjustments provided in section 545 (whether or not the taxpayer was a personal holding company for either of such preceding taxable years), and there shall also be determined for each such year the deduction for dividends paid during such year as provided in section 561 (but determined without regard to the dividend carryover to such year).

(2) There shall be determined for each such taxable year whether there is an excess of such taxable income over such deduction for dividends paid or an excess of such deduction for dividends paid over such taxable income, and the amount of each such excess.

(3) If there is an excess of such deductions for dividends paid over such taxable income for the first preceding taxable year, such excess shall be allowed as a dividend carryover to the taxable year.

(4) If there is an excess of such deduction for dividends paid over such taxable income for the second preceding taxable year, such excess shall be reduced by the amount determined in paragraph (5), and the remainder of such excess shall be allowed as a dividend carryover to the taxable year.

(5) The amount of the reduction specified in paragraph (4) shall be the amount of the excess of the taxable income, if any, for the first preceding taxable year over such deduction for dividends paid, if any, for the first preceding taxable year.

§ 565. Consent dividends

(a) General rule.—If any person owns consent stock (as defined in subsection (f)(1)) in a corporation on the last day of the taxable year of such corporation, and such person agrees, in a consent filed with the return of such corporation in accordance with regulations prescribed by the Secretary, to treat as a dividend the amount specified in such consent, the amount so specified shall, except as provided in subsection (b), constitute a consent dividend for purposes of section 561 (relating to the deduction for dividends paid).

(b) Limitations.—A consent dividend shall not include—

(1) an amount specified in a consent which, if distributed in money, would constitute, or be part of, a distribution which would be disqualified for purposes of the dividends paid deduction under section 562(c) (relating to preferential dividends), or

(2) an amount specified in a consent which would not constitute a dividend (as defined in section 316) if the total amounts specified in consents filed by the corporation had been distributed in money to shareholders on the last day of the taxable year of such corporation.

(c) Effect of consent.—The amount of a consent dividend shall be considered, for purposes of this title—

(1) as distributed in money by the corporation to the shareholder on the last day of the taxable year of the corporation, and

(2) as contributed to the capital of the corporation by the shareholder on such day.

(d) Consent dividends and other distributions.—If a distribution by a corporation consists in part of consent dividends and in part of money or other property, the entire amount specified in the consents and the amount of such money or other property shall be considered together for purposes of applying this title.

* * *

(f) Definitions.—

(1) Consent stock.—Consent stock, for purposes of this section, means the class or classes of stock entitled, after the payment of preferred dividends, to a share in the distribution (other than in complete or partial liquidation) within the taxable year of all the remaining earnings and profits, which share constitutes the same proportion of such distribution regardless of the amount of such distribution.

(2) Preferred dividends.—Preferred dividends, for purposes of this section, means a distribution (other than in complete or partial liquidation), limited in amount, which must be made on any class of stock before a further distribution (other than in complete or partial liquidation) of earnings and profits may be made within the taxable year.

SUBCHAPTER H—BANKING INSTITUTIONS*

SUBCHAPTER I—NATURAL RESOURCES

PART I—DEDUCTIONS

Editorial Summary

Depletion Deduction

Subchapter I of Chapter 1 (Secs. 611–616)

The process of writing off the cost of a long-lived asset is termed depreciation (or cost recovery), amortization, or depletion, depending on the type of asset. Tangible property is depreciated (e.g., machinery, equipment, furniture, fixtures, building); intangible property is amortized (e.g., patents, leaseholds); and natural resources are depleted (e.g., oil wells, coal mines).

The Code provides two methods for computing the depletion deduction: cost depletion and percentage depletion. For each taxable year, the depletion deduction is calculated under both methods, and the taxpayer uses the method which produces the larger deduction.

Under cost depletion, the cumulative deductions over the life of the asset are limited to the taxpayer's cost basis or other adjusted basis for the property (see Sec. 612). No such limitation applies for percentage depletion. That is, percentage depletion can be deducted even after the basis has been reduced to zero. Note that such depletion deducted after the basis is zero is a tax preference under Sec. 57. In addition, a statutory ceiling on the amount of percentage depletion that can be deducted for the taxable year is prescribed in Sec. 613(a).

The statutory rates for percentage depletion, which range from 5 percent to 22 percent, appear in Sec. 613(b). Note, also, that special limitations for calculating percentage depletion and the related statutory ceiling for oil and gas wells appear in Sec. 613A.

§ 611. Allowance of deduction for depletion

(a) General rule.—In the case of mines, oil and gas wells, other natural deposits, and timber, there shall be allowed as a deduction in computing taxable income a reasonable allowance for depletion and for depreciation of improvements, according to the peculiar conditions in each case; such reasonable allowance in all cases to be made under regulations prescribed by the Secretary. For purposes of this part, the term "mines" includes deposits of waste or residue, the extraction of ores or minerals from which is treated as mining under section 613(c). In any case in which it is ascertained as a result of operations or of development work that the recoverable units are greater or less than the prior estimate thereof, then such prior estimate (but not the basis for depletion) shall be revised and the allowance under this section for subsequent taxable years shall be based on such revised estimate.

(b) Special rules.—

(1) Leases.—In the case of a lease, the deduction under this section shall be equitably apportioned between the lessor and lessee.

(2) Life tenant and remainderman.—In the case of property held by one person for life with remainder to another person, the deduction under this section shall be computed as if the life tenant were the absolute owner of the property and shall be allowed to the life tenant.

(3) Property held in trust.—In the case of property held in trust, the deduction under this section shall be apportioned between the income beneficiaries and the trustee in accordance with the pertinent provisions of the instrument creating the trust, or, in the absence of such provisions, on the basis of the trust income allocable to each.

(4) Property held by estate.—In the case of an estate, the deduction under this section shall be apportioned between the estate and the heirs, legatees, and devisees on the basis of the income of the estate allocable to each.

(c) Cross reference.—

For other rules applicable to depreciation of improvements, see section 167.

*Omitted

§ 612. Basis for cost depletion

Except as otherwise provided in this subchapter, the basis on which depletion is to be allowed in respect of any property shall be the adjusted basis provided in section 1011 for the purpose of determining the gain upon the sale or other disposition of such property.

§ 613. Percentage depletion

(a) General rule.—In the case of the mines, wells, and other natural deposits listed in subsection (b), the allowance for depletion under section 611 shall be the percentage, specified in subsection (b), of the gross income from the property excluding from such gross income an amount equal to any rents or royalties paid or incurred by the taxpayer in respect of the property. Such allowance shall not exceed 50 percent (100 percent in the case of oil and gas properties) of the taxpayer's taxable income from the property (computed without allowance for depletion and without the deduction under section 199). For purposes of the preceding sentence, the allowable deductions taken into account with respect to expenses of mining in computing the taxable income from the property shall be decreased by an amount equal to so much of any gain which (1) is treated under section 1245 (relating to gain from disposition of certain depreciable property) as ordinary income, and (2) is properly allocable to the property. In no case shall the allowance for depletion under section 611 be less than it would be if computed without reference to this section.

(b) Percentage depletion rates.—The mines, wells, and other natural deposits, and the percentages, referred to in subsection (a) are as follows:

(1) 22 percent—

(A) sulphur and uranium; and

(B) if from deposits in the United States—anorthosite, clay, laterite, and nephelite syenite (to the extent that alumina and aluminum compounds are extracted therefrom), asbestos, bauxite, celestite, chromite, corundum, fluorspar, graphite, ilmenite, kyanite, mica, olivine, quartz crystals (radio grade), rutile, block steatite talc, and zircon, and ores of the following metals: antimony, beryllium, bismuth, cadmium, cobalt, columbium, lead, lithium, manganese, mercury, molybdenum, nickel, platinum and platinum group metals, tantalum, thorium, tin, titanium, tungsten, vanadium, and zinc.

(2) 15 percent—If from deposits in the United States—

(A) gold, silver, copper, and iron ore, and

(B) oil shale (except shale described in paragraph (5)).

(3) 14 percent—

(A) metal mines (if paragraph (1)(B) or (2)(A) does not apply), rock asphalt, and vermiculite; and

(B) if paragraph (1)(B), (5), or (6)(B) does not apply, ball clay, bentonite, china clay, sagger clay, and clay used or sold for use for purposes dependent on its refractory properties.

(4) 10 percent—asbestos (if paragraph (1)(B) does not apply), brucite, coal, lignite, perlite, sodium chloride, and wollastonite.

(5) 7½ percent—clay and shale used or sold for use in the manufacture of sewer pipe or brick, and clay, shale, and slate used or sold for use as sintered or burned lightweight aggregates.

(6) 5 percent—

(A) gravel, peat, pumice, sand, scoria, shale (except shale described in paragraph (2)(B) or (5)), and stone (except stone described in paragraph (7));

(B) clay used, or sold for use, in the manufacture of drainage and roofing tile, flower pots, and kindred products; and

(C) if from brine wells—bromine, calcium chloride, and magnesium chloride.

(7) 14 percent—all other minerals, including, but not limited to, aplite, barite, borax, calcium carbonates, diatomaceous earth, dolomite, feldspar, fullers earth, garnet, gilsonite, granite, limestone, magnesite, magnesium carbonates, marble, mollusk shells (including clam shells and oyster shells), phosphate rock, potash, quartzite, slate, soapstone, stone (used or sold for use by the mine owner or operator as dimension stone or ornamental stone), thenardite, tripoli, trona, and (if paragraph (1)(B) does not apply) bauxite, flake graphite, fluorspar, lepidolite, mica, spodumene, and talc (including pyrophyllite), except that, unless sold on bid in direct competition with a bona fide bid to sell a mineral listed in paragraph (3), the percentage shall be 5 percent for any such other mineral (other than slate to which paragraph (5) applies) when used, or sold for use, by the mine owner or operator as rip rap, ballast, road material, rubble, concrete aggregates, or for similar purposes. For purposes of this paragraph, the term "all other minerals" does not include—

(A) soil, sod, dirt, turf, water, or mosses;

(B) minerals from sea water, the air, or similar inexhaustible sources; or

(C) oil and gas wells.

For the purposes of this subsection, minerals (other than sodium chloride) extracted from brines pumped from a saline perennial lake within the United States shall not be considered minerals from an inexhaustible source.

(c) Definition of gross income from property.—For purposes of this section—

(1) Gross income from the property.—The term "gross income from the property" means, in the case of a property other than an oil or gas well, and other than a geothermal deposit the gross income from mining.

(2) Mining.—The term "mining" includes not merely the extraction of the ores or minerals from the ground but also the treatment processes considered as mining described in paragraph (4) (and the treatment processes necessary or incidental thereto), and so much of the transportation of ores or minerals (whether or not by common carrier) from the point of extraction from the ground to the plants or mills in which such treatment processes are applied thereto as is not in excess of 50 miles unless the Secretary finds that the physical and other requirements are such that the ore or mineral must be transported a greater distance to such plants or mills.

(3) Extraction of the ores or minerals from the ground.—The term "extraction of the ores or minerals from the ground" includes the extraction by mine owners or operators of ores or minerals from the waste or residue of prior mining. The preceding sentence shall not apply to any such extraction of the mineral or ore by a purchaser of such waste or residue or of the rights to extract ores or minerals therefrom.

* * *

(d) Denial of percentage depletion in case of oil and gas wells.—Except as provided in section 613A, in the case of any oil or gas well, the allowance for depletion shall be computed without reference to this section.

(e) Percentage depletion for geothermal deposits.—

(1) In general.—In the case of geothermal deposits located in the United States or in a possession of the United States, for purposes of subsection (a)—

(A) such deposits shall be treated as listed in subsection (b), and

(B) 15 percent shall be deemed to be the percentage specified in subsection (b).

(2) Geothermal deposit defined.—For purposes of paragraph (1), the term "geothermal deposit" means a geothermal reservoir consisting of natural heat which is stored in rocks or in an aqueous liquid or vapor (whether or not under pressure). Such a deposit shall in no case be treated as a gas well for purposes of this section or section 613A, and this section shall not apply to a geothermal deposit which is located outside the United States or its possessions.

(3) Percentage depletion not to include lease bonuses, etc.—In the case of any geothermal deposit, the term "gross income from the property" shall, for purposes of this section, not include any amount described in section 613A(d)(5).

§ 613A. Limitations on percentage depletion in case of oil and gas wells

(a) General rule.—Except as otherwise provided in this section, the allowance for depletion under section 611 with respect to any oil or gas well shall be computed without regard to section 613.

(b) Exemption for certain domestic gas wells.—

(1) In general.—The allowance for depletion under section 611 shall be computed in accordance with section 613 with respect to—

(A) regulated natural gas, and

(B) natural gas sold under a fixed contract, and 22 percent shall be deemed to be specified in subsection (b) of section 613 for purposes of subsection (a) of that section.

(2) Natural gas from geopressured brine.—The allowance for depletion under section 611 shall be computed in accordance with section 613 with respect to any qualified natural gas from geopressured brine, and 10 percent shall be deemed to be specified in subsection (b) of section 613 for purposes of subsection (a) of such section.

* * *

(c) Exemption for independent producers and royalty owners.—

(1) In general.—Except as provided in subsection (d), the allowance for depletion under section 611 shall be computed in accordance with section 613 with respect to—

(A) so much of the taxpayer's average daily production of domestic crude oil as does not exceed the taxpayer's depletable oil quantity; and

(B) so much of the taxpayer's average daily production of domestic natural gas as does not exceed the taxpayer's depletable natural gas quantity;

and 15 percent shall be deemed to be specified in subsection (b) of section 613 for purposes of subsection (a) of that section.

* * *

(d) Limitations on application of subsection (c).—

(1) Limitation based on taxable income.—The deduction for the taxable year attributable to the application of subsection (c) shall not exceed 65 percent of the taxpayer's taxable income for the year computed without regard to—

(A) any depletion on production from an oil or gas property which is subject to the provisions of subsection (c),

(B) any deduction allowable under section 199,

(C) any net operating loss carryback to the taxable year under section 172,

(D) any capital loss carryback to the taxable year under section 1212, and

(E) in the case of a trust, any distributions to its beneficiary, except in the case of any trust where any beneficiary of such trust is a member of the family (as defined in section 267(c)(4)) of a settlor who created inter vivos and testamentary trusts for members of the family and such settlor died within the last six days of the fifth month in 1970, and the law in the jurisdiction in which such trust was created requires all or a portion of the gross or net proceeds of any royalty or other interest in oil, gas, or other mineral representing any percentage depletion allowance to be allocated to the principal of the trust.

If an amount is disallowed as a deduction for the taxable year by reason of application of the preceding sentence, the disallowed amount shall be treated as an amount allowable as a deduction under subsection (c) for the following taxable year, subject to the application of the preceding sentence to such taxable year. For purposes of basis adjustments and determining whether cost depletion exceeds percentage depletion with respect to the production from a property, any amount disallowed as a deduction on the application of this paragraph shall be allocated to the respective properties from which the oil or gas was produced in proportion to the percentage depletion otherwise allowable to such properties under subsection (c).

* * *

§ 616. Development expenditures

(a) In general.—Except as provided in subsections (b) and (d), there shall be allowed as a deduction in computing taxable income all expenditures paid or incurred during the taxable year for the development of a mine or other natural deposit (other than an oil or gas well) if paid or incurred after the existence of ores or minerals in commercially marketable quantities has been disclosed. This section shall not apply to expenditures for the acquisition or improvement of property of a character which is subject to the allowance for depreciation provided in section 167, but allowances for depreciation shall be considered, for purposes of this section, as expenditures.

(b) Election of taxpayer.—At the election of the taxpayer, made in accordance with regulations prescribed by the Secretary, expenditures described in subsection (a) paid or incurred during the taxable year shall be treated as deferred expenses and shall be deductible on a ratable basis as the units of produced ores or minerals benefited by such expenditures are sold. In the case of such expenditures paid or incurred during the development stage of the mine or deposit, the election shall apply only with respect to the excess of such expenditures during the taxable year over the net receipts during the taxable year from the ores or minerals produced from such mine or deposit. The election under this subsection, if made, must be for the total amount of such expenditures, or the total amount of such excess, as the case may be, with respect to the mine or deposit, and shall be binding for such taxable year.

(c) Adjusted basis of mine or deposit.—The amount of expenditures which are treated under subsection (b) as deferred expenses shall be taken into account in computing the adjusted basis of the mine or deposit, except that such amount, and the adjustments to basis provided in section 1016(a)(9), shall be disregarded in determining the adjusted basis of the property for the purpose of computing a deduction for depletion under section 611.

(d) Special rules for foreign development.—In the case of any expenditures paid or incurred with respect to the development of a mine or other natural deposit (other than an oil, gas, or geothermal well) located outside of the United States—

(1) subsections (a) and (b) shall not apply, and

(2) such expenditures shall—

(A) at the election of the taxpayer, be included in adjusted basis for purposes of computing the amount of any deduction allowable under section 611 (without regard to section 613), or

(B) if subparagraph (A) does not apply, be allowed as a deduction ratably over the 10-taxable year period beginning with the taxable year in which such expenditures were paid or incurred.

(e) Cross reference.—

For election of 10-year amortization of expenditures allowable as a deduction under subsection (a), see section 59(e).

* * *

PART II—EXCLUSIONS FROM GROSS INCOME*

PART III—SALES AND EXCHANGES

Editorial Summary

Capital Asset Treatment for Timber, Coal, or Domestic Iron Ore

Subchapter I of Chapter 1 (Sec. 631)

Absent the election available under Sec. 631, two types of disposal transactions associated with timber, coal, or domestic iron ore may produce potentially undesirable tax consequences for the taxpayer. These are (1) a sale or exchange transaction and (2) a royalty transaction.

In order to qualify for capital gain treatment, the asset being disposed of generally must be a capital asset (see Sec. 1221). Inventory is not a capital asset [see Sec. 1221(1)]. Therefore, if the taxpayer is considered to be a dealer (i.e., the timber, coal, or domestic iron ore is inventory), then the recognized gain on the sale or exchange of an asset is classified as ordinary income rather than as capital gain.

Rather than a straightforward sale or exchange transaction, the form of the consideration received by the taxpayer may be royalties. In order to qualify for capital gain treatment, the form of the transaction generally must be a sale or exchange (see Sec. 1222). Therefore, the normal treatment of the receipt of royalty income is to classify it as ordinary income rather than as capital gain.

With respect to timber, coal, and domestic iron ore, Sec. 631 provides the taxpayer with the ability to avoid the capital gain/ordinary income controversy that could result in association with both of the aforementioned types of transactions and to thereby qualify for capital gain treatment.

Note the following provisions with respect to the application of Sec. 631:

1. The long-term holding period requirement for capital assets must be satisfied.

2. The taxpayer must retain an economic interest in the timber, coal, or domestic iron ore being disposed of [except for treatment under Sec. 631 (a)].

3. The date of disposal (i.e., the deemed sale), for purposes of calculating the capital gain or loss, shall be the date the timber is cut or the coal or domestic iron ore is mined. Note, however, that for timber the fair market value used in the deemed sales transaction is that on the first day of the tax year the timber is cut rather than that on the cutting date.

Therefore, the potential for ordinary income treatment does still exist with respect to all of the total proceeds if required items 1 and 2 above are not satisfied, or with respect to part of the total proceeds under item 3 above (e.g., the portion of the proceeds that relates to value changes between that on the first day of the tax year the timber is cut and that on the date the timber is sold).

§ 631. Gain or loss in the case of timber, coal, or domestic iron ore

(a) Election to consider cutting as sale or exchange.—If the taxpayer so elects on his return for a taxable year, the cutting of timber (for sale or for use in the taxpayer's trade or business) during such year by the taxpayer who owns, or has a contract right to cut, such timber (providing he has owned such timber or has held such contract right on the first day of such year and for a period of more than 1 year before such cutting) shall be considered as a sale or exchange of such timber cut during such year. If such election has been made, gain or loss to the taxpayer shall be recognized in an amount equal to the difference between the fair market value of such

*Omitted.

timber, and the adjusted basis for depletion of such timber in the hands of the taxpayer. Such fair market value shall be the fair market value as of the first day of the taxable year in which such timber is cut, and shall thereafter be considered as the cost of such cut timber to the taxpayer for all purposes for which such cost is a necessary factor. If a taxpayer makes an election under this subsection, such election shall apply with respect to all timber which is owned by the taxpayer or which the taxpayer has a contract right to cut and shall be binding on the taxpayer for the taxable year for which the election is made and for all subsequent years, unless the Secretary, on showing of undue hardship, permits the taxpayer to revoke his election; such revocation, however, shall preclude any further elections under this subsection except with the consent of the Secretary. For purposes of this subsection and subsection (b), the term "timber" includes evergreen trees which are more than 6 years old at the time severed from the roots and are sold for ornamental purposes.

(b) Disposal of timber with a retained economic interest.—In the case of the disposal of timber held for more than 1 year before such disposal, by the owner thereof under any form or type of contract by virtue of which such owner either retains an economic interest in such timber or makes an outright sale of such timber, the difference between the amount realized from the disposal of such timber and the adjusted depletion basis thereof, shall be considered as though it were a gain or loss, as the case may be, on the sale of such timber. In determining the gross income, the adjusted gross income, or the taxable income of the lessee, the deductions allowable with respect to rents and royalties shall be determined without regard to the provisions of this subsection. In the case of disposal of timber with a retained economic interest, the date of disposal of such timber shall be deemed to be the date such timber is cut, but if payment is made to the owner under the contract before such timber is cut the owner may elect to treat the date of such payment as the date of disposal of such timber. For purposes of this subsection, the term "owner" means any person who owns an interest in such timber, including a sublessor and a holder of a contract to cut timber.

(c) Disposal of coal or domestic iron ore with a retained economic interest.—In the case of the disposal of coal (including lignite), or iron ore mined in the United States held for more than 1 year before such disposal, by the owner thereof under any form of contract by virtue of which such owner retains an economic interest in such coal or iron ore, the difference between the amount realized from the disposal of such coal or iron ore and the adjusted depletion basis thereof plus the deductions disallowed for the taxable year under section 272 shall be considered as though it were a gain or loss, as the case may be, on the sale of such coal or iron ore. If for the taxable year of such gain or loss the maximum rate of tax imposed by this chapter on any net capital gain is less than such maximum rate for ordinary income, such owner shall not be entitled to the allowance for percentage depletion provided in section 613 with respect to such coal or iron ore. This subsection shall not apply to income realized by any owner as a co-adventurer, partner, or principal in the mining of such coal or iron ore, and the word "owner" means any person who owns an economic interest in coal or iron ore in place, including a sublessor. The date of disposal of such coal or iron ore shall be deemed to be the date such coal or iron ore is mined. In determining the gross income, the adjusted gross income, or the taxable income of the lessee, the deductions allowable with respect to rents and royalties shall be determined without regard to the provisions of this subsection. This subsection shall have no application, for purposes of applying subchapter G, relating to corporations used to avoid income tax on shareholders (including the determinations of the amount of the deductions under section 535(b)(6) or section 545(b)(5)). This subsection shall not apply to any disposal of iron ore or coal—

(1) to a person whose relationship to the person disposing of such iron ore or coal would result in the disallowance of losses under section 267 or 707(b), or

(2) to a person owned or controlled directly or indirectly by the same interests which own or control the person disposing of such iron ore or coal.

PART IV—MINERAL PRODUCTION PAYMENTS*

PART V—CONTINENTAL SHELF AREAS*

*Omitted.

SUBCHAPTER J—ESTATES, TRUSTS, BENEFICIARIES, AND DECEDENTS

PART I—ESTATES, TRUSTS, AND BENEFICIARIES

SUBPART A—GENERAL RULES FOR TAXATION OF ESTATES AND TRUSTS

Editorial Summary

Income Taxation of Trusts and Estates: General Subchapter J of Chapter 1 (Secs. 641–645)

Trusts are subject to income taxation under Sec. 641. An estate is subject to income taxation under the same section. In addition, an estate is subject to estate taxation under Sec. 2001. The income tax rates of trusts and estates appear in Sec. 1(e).

The basic tax model for the income taxation of a trust or estate is as follows:

	Income
–	Exclusions
=	Gross income
–	Deductions
=	Taxable income
×	Rates
=	Tentative tax liability
–	Credits
=	Tax liability

Under the general rule of Sec. 641(b), the taxable income of a trust or estate is to be computed in the same manner as that of the individual taxpayer, except as otherwise provided in Subchapter J. Thus, the orientation should be one of identifying differences with respect to the components in the tax model. A factor that complicates the computation of the tax liability is the existence of another party who may be the taxpayer rather than the trust or estate; that is, the beneficiary of the trust or estate. The existence of the two parties, the trust or estate and the beneficiary, may result in the allocation of various items between the two parties.

Section 642 contains some of the differences with respect to particular items for the individual taxpayer and the trust or estate. Section 642(c) introduces the concept of dichotomizing between the treatment of trusts that are required to distribute to beneficiaries all of its income currently (i.e., a simple trust) and those trusts that are not required to do so (i.e., a complex trust) under the governing instrument.

Section 643 contains the definition of various terms that are requisite to understanding other Code sections in Subchapter J. Section 644 provides that, in general, the taxable year of a trust shall be the calendar year. Section 645 permits an election to be made under which a revocable trust can be treated as part of the estate rather than as a separate trust.

§ 641. Imposition of tax

(a) Application of tax.—The tax imposed by section 1(e) shall apply to the taxable income of estates or of any kind of property held in trust, including—

(1) income accumulated in trust for the benefit of unborn or unascertained persons or persons with contingent interests, and income accumulated or held for future distribution under the terms of the will or trust;

(2) income which is to be distributed currently by the fiduciary to the beneficiaries, and income collected by a guardian of an infant which is to be held or distributed as the court may direct;

(3) income received by estates of deceased persons during the period of administration or settlement of the estate; and

(4) income which, in the discretion of the fiduciary, may be either distributed to the beneficiaries or accumulated.

(b) Computation and payment.—The taxable income of an estate or trust shall be computed in the same manner as in the case of an individual, except as otherwise provided in this part. The tax shall be computed on such taxable income and shall be paid by the fiduciary. ***

(c) Special rules for taxation of electing small business trusts.—

(1) In general.—For purposes of this chapter—

(A) the portion of any electing small business trust which consists of stock in 1 or more S corporations shall be treated as a separate trust, and

(B) the amount of the tax imposed by this chapter on such separate trust shall be determined with the modifications of paragraph (2).

(2) Modifications.—For purposes of paragraph (1), the modifications of this paragraph are the following:

(A) Except as provided in section 1(h), the amount of the tax imposed by section 1(e) shall be determined by using the highest rate of tax set forth in section 1(e).

(B) The exemption amount under section 55(d) shall be zero.

(C) The only items of income, loss, deduction, or credit to be taken into account are the following:

(i) The items required to be taken into account under section 1366.

(ii) Any gain or loss from the disposition of stock in an S corporation.

(iii) To the extent provided in regulations, State or local income taxes or administrative expenses to the extent allocable to items described in clauses (i) and (ii).

(iv) Any interest expense paid or accrued on indebtedness incurred to acquire stock in an S corporation.

No deduction or credit shall be allowed for any amount not described in this paragraph, and no item described in this paragraph shall be apportioned to any beneficiary.

(D) No amount shall be allowed under paragraph (1) or (2) of section 1211(b).

(3) Treatment of remainder of trust and distributions.—For purposes of determining—

(A) the amount of the tax imposed by this chapter on the portion of any electing small business trust not treated as a separate trust under paragraph (1), and

(B) the distributable net income of the entire trust,

the items referred to in paragraph (2)(C) shall be excluded. Except as provided in the preceding sentence, this subsection shall not affect the taxation of any distribution from the trust.

(4) Treatment of unused deductions where termination of separate trust.—If a portion of an electing small business trust ceases to be treated as a separate trust under paragraph (1), any carryover or excess deduction of the separate trust which is referred to in section 642(h) shall be taken into account by the entire trust.

(5) Electing small business trust.—For purposes of this subsection, the term "electing small business trust" has the meaning given such term by section 1361(e)(1).

§ 642. Special rules for credits and deductions

(a) Foreign tax credit allowed.—An estate or trust shall be allowed the credit against tax for taxes imposed by foreign countries and possessions of the United States, to the extent allowed by section 901, only in respect of so much of the taxes described in such section as is not properly allocable under such section to the beneficiaries.

(b) Deduction for personal exemption.—

(1) Estates.—An estate shall be allowed a deduction of $600.

(2) Trusts.—

(A) In general.—Except as otherwise provided in this paragraph, a trust shall be allowed a deduction of $100.

(B) Trusts distributing income currently.—A trust which, under its governing instrument, is required to distribute all of its income currently shall be allowed a deduction of $300.

(C) Disability trusts.—

(i) In general.—A qualified disability trust shall be allowed a deduction equal to the exemption amount under section 151(d), determined—

(I) by treating such trust as an individual described in section 151(d)(3)(C)(iii), and

(II) by applying section 67(e) (without the reference to section 642(b)) for purposes of determining the adjusted gross income of the trust.

(ii) Qualified disability trust.—For purposes of clause (i), the term "qualified disability trust" means any trust if—

(I) such trust is a disability trust described in subsection (c)(2)(B)(iv) of section 1917 of the Social Security Act (42 U.S.C. 1396p), and

(II) all of the beneficiaries of the trust as of the close of the taxable year are determined by the Commissioner of Social Security to have been disabled (within the meaning of section 1614(a)(3) of the Social Security Act, 42 U.S.C. 1382c(a)(3)) for some portion of such year.

A trust shall not fail to meet the requirements of subclause (II) merely because the corpus of the trust may revert to a person who is not so disabled after the trust ceases to have any beneficiary who is so disabled.

(3) Deductions in lieu of personal exemption.—The deductions allowed by this subsection shall be in lieu of the deductions allowed under section 151 (relating to deduction for personal exemption).

(c) Deduction for amounts paid or permanently set aside for a charitable purpose.—

(1) General rule.—In the case of an estate or trust (other than a trust meeting the specifications of subpart B), there shall be allowed as a deduction in computing its taxable income (in lieu of the deduction allowed by section 170(a), relating to deduction for charitable, etc., contributions and gifts) any amount of the gross income, without limitation, which pursuant to the terms of the governing instrument is, during the taxable year, paid for a purpose specified in section 170(c) (determined without regard to section 170(c)(2)(A)). If a charitable contribution is paid after the close of such taxable year and on or before the last day of the year following the close of such taxable year, then the trustee or administrator may elect to treat such contribution as paid during such taxable year. The election shall be made at such time and in such manner as the Secretary prescribes by regulations.

(2) Amounts permanently set aside.—In the case of an estate, and in the case of a trust (other than a trust meeting the specifications of subpart B) required by the terms of its governing instrument to set aside amounts which was—

(A) created on or before October 9, 1969, if—

(i) an irrevocable remainder interest is transferred to or for the use of an organization described in section 170(c), or

(ii) the grantor is at all times after October 9, 1969, under a mental disability to change the terms of the trust; or

(B) established by a will executed on or before October 9, 1969, if—

(i) the testator dies before October 9, 1972, without having republished the will after October 9, 1969, by codicil or otherwise,

(ii) the testator at no time after October 9, 1969, had the right to change the portions of the will which pertain to the trust, or

(iii) the will is not republished by codicil or otherwise before October 9, 1972, and the testator is on such date and at all times thereafter under a mental disability to republish the will by codicil or otherwise,

there shall also be allowed as a deduction in computing its taxable income any amount of the gross income, without limitation, which pursuant to the terms of the governing instrument is, during the taxable year, permanently set aside for a purpose specified in section 170(c), or is to be used exclusively for religious, charitable, scientific, literary, or educational purposes, or for the prevention of cruelty to children or animals, or for the establishment, acquisition, maintenance, or operation of a public cemetery not operated for profit. In the case of a trust, the preceding sentence shall apply only to gross income earned with respect to amounts transferred to the trust before October 9, 1969, or transferred under a will to which subparagraph (B) applies.

(3) Pooled income funds.—In the case of a pooled income fund (as defined in paragraph (5)), there shall also be allowed as a deduction in computing its taxable income any amount of the gross income attributable to gain from the sale of a capital asset held for more than 6 months, without limitation, which pursuant to the terms of the governing instrument is, during the taxable year, permanently set aside for a purpose specified in section 170(c).

(4) Adjustments.—To the extent that the amount otherwise allowable as a deduction under this subsection consists of gain described in section 1202(a), proper adjustment shall be made for any exclusion allowable to the estate or trust under section 1202. In the case of a trust, the deduction allowed by this subsection shall be subject to section 681 (relating to unrelated business income).

(5) Definition of pooled income fund.—For purposes of paragraph (3), a pooled income fund is a trust—

(A) to which each donor transfers property, contributing an irrevocable remainder interest in such property to or for the use of an organization described in section 170(b)(1)(A) (other than in clauses (vii) or (viii)), and retaining an income interest for the life of one or more beneficiaries (living at the time of such transfer),

(B) in which the property transferred by each donor is commingled with property transferred by other donors who have made or make similar transfers,

(C) which cannot have investments in securities which are exempt from the taxes imposed by this subtitle,

(D) which includes only amounts received from transfers which meet the requirements of this paragraph,

(E) which is maintained by the organization to which the remainder interest is contributed and of which no donor or beneficiary of an income interest is a trustee, and

(F) from which each beneficiary of an income interest receives income, for each year for which he is entitled to receive the income interest referred to in subparagraph (A), determined by the rate of return earned by the trust for such year.

For purposes of determining the amount of any charitable contribution allowable by reason of a transfer of property to a pooled fund, the value of the income interest shall be determined on the basis of the highest rate of return earned by the fund for any of the 3 taxable years immediately preceding the taxable year of the fund in which the transfer is made. In the case of funds in existence less than 3 taxable years preceding the taxable year of the fund in which a transfer is made, the rate of return shall be deemed to be 6 percent per annum, except that the Secretary may prescribe a different rate of return.

(6) Taxable private foundations.—In the case of a private foundation which is not exempt from taxation under section 501(a) for the taxable year, the provisions of this subsection shall not apply and the provisions of section 170 shall apply.

(d) Net operating loss deduction.—The benefit of the deduction for net operating losses provided by section 172 shall be allowed to estates and trusts under regulations prescribed by the Secretary.

(e) Deduction for depreciation and depletion.—An estate or trust shall be allowed the deduction for depreciation and depletion only to the extent not allowable to beneficiaries under sections 167(d) and 611(b).

(f) Amortization deductions.—The benefit of the deductions for amortization provided by sections 169 and 197 shall be allowed to estates and trusts in the same manner as in the case of an individual. The allowable deduction shall be apportioned between the income beneficiaries and the fiduciary under regulations prescribed by the Secretary.

(g) Disallowance of double deductions.—Amounts allowable under section 2053 or 2054 as a deduction in computing the taxable estate of a decedent shall not be allowed as a deduction (or as an offset against the sales price of property in determining gain or loss) in computing the taxable income of the estate or of any other person, unless there is filed, within the time and in the manner and form prescribed by the Secretary, a statement that the amounts have not been allowed as deductions under section 2053 or 2054 and a waiver of the right to have such amounts allowed at any time as deductions under section 2053 or 2054. Rules similar to the rules of the preceding sentence shall apply to amounts which may be taken into account under section 2621(a)(2) or 2622(b). This subsection shall not apply with respect to deductions allowed under part II (relating to income in respect of decedents).

(h) Unused loss carryovers and excess deductions on termination available to beneficiaries.—If on the termination of an estate or trust, the estate or trust has—

(1) a net operating loss carryover under section 172 or a capital loss carryover under section 1212, or

(2) for the last taxable year of the estate or trust deductions (other than the deductions allowed under subsections (b) or (c)) in excess of gross income for such year,

then such carryover or such excess shall be allowed as a deduction, in accordance with regulations prescribed by the Secretary, to the beneficiaries succeeding to the property of the estate or trust.

* * *

§ 643. Definitions applicable to subparts A, B, C, and D

(a) Distributable net income.—For purposes of this part, the term "distributable net income" means, with respect to any taxable year, the taxable income of the estate or trust computed with the following modifications—

(1) Deduction for distributions.—No deduction shall be taken under sections 651 and 661 (relating to additional deductions).

(2) Deduction for personal exemption.—No deduction shall be taken under section 642(b) (relating to deduction for personal exemptions).

(3) Capital gains and losses.—Gains from the sale or exchange of capital assets shall be excluded to the extent that such gains are allocated to corpus and are not (A) paid, credited, or required to be distributed to any beneficiary during the taxable year, or (B) paid, permanently set aside, or to be used for the purposes specified in section 642(c). Losses from the sale or exchange of capital assets shall be excluded, except to the extent such losses are taken into account in determining the amount of gains from the sale or exchange of capital assets which are paid, credited, or required to be distributed to any beneficiary during the taxable year. The exclusion under section 1202 shall not be taken into account.

(4) Extraordinary dividends and taxable stock dividends.—For purposes only of subpart B (relating to trusts which distribute current income only), there shall be excluded those items of gross income constituting extraordinary dividends or taxable stock dividends which the fiduciary, acting in good faith, does not pay or credit to any beneficiary by reason of his determination that such dividends are allocable to corpus under the terms of the governing instrument and applicable local law.

(5) Tax-exempt interest.—There shall be included any tax-exempt interest to which section 103 applies, reduced by any amounts which would be deductible in respect of disbursements allocable to such interest but for the provisions of section 265 (relating to disallowance of certain deductions).

* * *

(7) Abusive transactions.—The Secretary shall prescribe such regulations as may be necessary or appropriate to carry out the purposes of this part, including regulations to prevent avoidance of such purposes.

* * *

(b) Income.—For purposes of this subpart and subparts B, C, and D, the term "income", when not preceded by the words "taxable," "distributable net," "undistributed net," or "gross," means the amount of income of the estate or trust for the taxable year determined under the terms of the governing instrument and applicable local law. Items of gross income constituting extraordinary dividends or taxable stock dividends which the fiduciary, acting in good faith, determines to be allocable to corpus under the terms of the governing instrument and applicable local law shall not be considered income.

(c) Beneficiary.—For purposes of this part, the term "beneficiary" includes heir, legatee, devisee.

(d) Coordination with back-up withholding.—Except to the extent otherwise provided in regulations, this subchapter shall be applied with respect to payments subject to withholding under section 3406—

(1) by allocating between the estate or trust and its beneficiaries any credit allowable under section 31(c) (on the basis of their respective shares of any such payment taken into account under this subchapter),

(2) by treating each beneficiary to whom such credit is allocated as if an amount equal to such credit has been paid to him by the estate or trust, and

(3) by allowing the estate or trust a deduction in an amount equal to the credit so allocated to beneficiaries.

(e) Treatment of property distributed in kind. —

(1) Basis of beneficiary.—The basis of any property received by a beneficiary in a distribution from an estate or trust shall be—

(A) the adjusted basis of such property in the hands of the estate or trust immediately before the distribution, adjusted for

(B) any gain or loss recognized to the estate or trust on the distribution.

(2) Amount of distribution.—In the case of any distribution of property (other than cash), the amount taken into account under sections 661(a)(2) and 662(a)(2) shall be the lesser of—

(A) the basis of such property in the hands of the beneficiary (as determined under paragraph (1)), or

(B) the fair market value of such property.

(3) Election to recognize gain.—

(A) In general.—In the case of any distribution of property (other than cash) to which an election under this paragraph applies—

(i) paragraph (2) shall not apply,

(ii) gain or loss shall be recognized by the estate or trust in the same manner as if such property had been sold to the distributee at its fair market value, and

(iii) the amount taken into account under sections 661(a)(2) and 662(a)(2) shall be the fair market value of such property.

(B) Election.—Any election under this paragraph shall apply to all distributions made by the estate or trust during a taxable year and shall be made on the return of such estate or trust for such taxable year.

Any such election, once made, may be revoked only with the consent of the Secretary.

(4) Exception for distributions described in section 663(a).—This subsection shall not apply to any distribution described in section 663(a).

(f) Treatment of multiple trusts.—For purposes of this subchapter, under regulations prescribed by the Secretary, 2 or more trusts shall be treated as 1 trust if—

(1) such trusts have substantially the same grantor or grantors and substantially the same primary beneficiary or beneficiaries, and

(2) a principal purpose of such trusts is the avoidance of the tax imposed by this chapter.

For purposes of the preceding sentence, a husband and wife shall be treated as 1 person.

(g) Certain payments of estimated tax treated as paid by beneficiary.—

(1) In general.—In the case of a trust—

(A) the trustee may elect to treat any portion of a payment of estimated tax made by such trust for any taxable year of the trust as a payment made by a beneficiary of such trust,

(B) any amount so treated shall be treated as paid or credited to the beneficiary on the last day of such taxable year, and

(C) for purposes of subtitle F, the amount so treated—

(i) shall not be treated as a payment of estimated tax made by the trust, but

(ii) shall be treated as a payment of estimated tax made by such beneficiary on January 15 following the taxable year.

(2) Time for making election.—An election under paragraph (1) shall be made on or before the 65th day after the close of the taxable year of the trust and in such manner as the Secretary may prescribe.

(3) Extension to last year of estate.—In the case of a taxable year reasonably expected to be the last taxable year of an estate—

(A) any reference in this subsection to a trust shall be treated as including a reference to an estate, and

(B) the fiduciary of the estate shall be treated as the trustee.

* * *

§ 644. Taxable year of trusts

(a) In general.—For purposes of this subtitle, the taxable year of any trust shall be the calendar year.

(b) Exception for trusts exempt from tax and charitable trusts.—Subsection (a) shall not apply to a trust exempt from taxation under section 501(a) or to a trust described in section 4947(a)(1).

§ 645. Certain revocable trusts treated as part of estate

(a) General rule.—For purposes of this subtitle, if both the executor (if any) of an estate and the trustee of a qualified revocable trust elect the treatment provided in this section, such trust shall be treated and taxed as part of such estate (and not as a separate trust) for all taxable years of the estate ending after the date of the decedent's death and before the applicable date.

(b) Definitions.—For purposes of subsection (a)—

(1) Qualified revocable trust.—The term "qualified revocable trust" means any trust (or portion thereof) which was treated under section 676 as owned by the decedent of the estate referred to in subsection (a) by reason of a power in the grantor (determined without regard to section 672(e)).

(2) Applicable date.—The term "applicable date" means—

(A) if no return of tax imposed by chapter 11 is required to be filed, the date which is 2 years after the date of the decedent's death, and

(B) if such a return is required to be filed, the date which is 6 months after the date of the final determination of the liability for tax imposed by chapter 11.

(c) Election.—The election under subsection (a) shall be made not later than the time prescribed for filing the return of tax imposed by this chapter for the first taxable year of the estate (determined with regard to extensions) and, once made, shall be irrevocable.

* * *

SUBPART B—TRUSTS WHICH DISTRIBUTE CURRENT INCOME ONLY

Editorial Summary

Income Taxation of Trusts and Estates: Simple Subchapter J of Chapter 1 (Secs. 651, 652)

A simple trust is one that under the governing instrument is required to distribute all of its income currently and may not distribute corpus. A key tax question for a trust is who (i.e., the trust or the beneficiary) is effectively taxed on the income that is distributed to the beneficiary. If the trust must include the income in its gross income and is not allowed a deduction for the distribution of the income to the beneficiary, then entity theory is being applied. Conversely, if the trust must include the income in its gross income and is allowed a deduction for the distribution of the income to the beneficiary, then aggregate or proprietary theory is being applied (i.e., the trust is merely a conduit with the beneficiary being the taxpayer). Section 651 provides that aggregate or proprietary theory is appropriate for the simple trust in providing that a deduction is permitted the trust for the distribution of its current income. However, this apparent simplicity is made more complex by the Sec. 651(b) provision, which limits the deduction to the distributable net income (DNI) of the trust for the taxable year. DNI is defined in Sec. 643(a).

Section 652 covers the effect of the distribution on the beneficiary. Under the general rule, the beneficiary of a simple trust must include in gross income the current income of the trust, whether it is distributed or not. If the DNI ceiling in Sec. 651(b) limits the amount of the deduction to the trust, the inclusion in the gross income of the beneficiary also will be limited by the DNI ceiling (i.e., symmetry between the deduction to the trust and the inclusion to the beneficiary). Since the trust is viewed as a conduit in this case, the character of the amounts included by the beneficiary shall have the same character to him or her that they had to the trust. Such amounts are allocated among beneficiaries using a pro-rata approach.

The taxable year of the trust (see Sec. 645) and the taxable year of the beneficiaries may not be the same. Section 652(c) provides an inclusion rule for the beneficiary that is similar to the inclusion rule for a partner with respect to a partnership [see Sec. 706(a)]. That is, a beneficiary will include his or her share of the income from the trust for the trust taxable year ending within or with his taxable year.

Example: Z Trust has two beneficiaries, A and B. The taxable year ends are as follows:

Z Trust	June 30
A	December 31
B	June 30

For the initial taxable year of the trust, July 1, 20X0—June 30, 20X1, the income allocable to A is $6,000 and the income allocable to B is $4,000. On A's tax return for 20X0 (i.e., January 1, 20X0—December 31, 20X0), he will report no income from the trust because the trust taxable year has not ended by December 31, 20X0. On B's tax return for 20X0 (i.e., the fiscal year July 1, 20X0—June 30, 20X1), she will report income from the trust of $4,000 because a trust taxable year did end *with* her taxable year (i.e., June 30, 20X1). On A's tax return for 20X1 (i.e., January 1, 20X1—December 31, 20X1), he will report income from the trust of $6,000 because a trust taxable year did end *within* his taxable year.

§ 651. Deduction for trusts distributing current income only

(a) Deduction.—In the case of any trust the terms of which—

(1) provide that all of its income is required to be distributed currently, and

(2) do not provide that any amounts are to be paid, permanently set aside, or used for the purposes specified in section 642(c) (relating to deduction for charitable, etc., purposes),

there shall be allowed as a deduction in computing the taxable income of the trust the amount of the income for the taxable year which is required to be distributed currently. This section shall not apply in any taxable year in which the trust distributes amounts other than amounts of income described in paragraph (1).

(b) Limitation on deduction.—If the amount of income required to be distributed currently exceeds the distributable net income of the trust for the taxable year, the deduction shall be limited to the amount of the distributable net income. For this purpose, the computation of distributable net income shall not include items of income which are not included in the gross income of the trust and the deductions allocable thereto.

§ 652. Inclusion of amounts in gross income of beneficiaries of trusts distributing current income only

(a) Inclusion.—Subject to subsection (b), the amount of income for the taxable year required to be distributed currently by a trust described in section 651 shall be included in the gross income of the beneficiaries to whom the income is required to be distributed, whether distributed or not. If such amount exceeds the distributable net income, there shall be included in the gross income of each beneficiary an amount which bears the same ratio to distributable net income as the amount of income required to be distributed to such beneficiary bears to the amount of income required to be distributed to all beneficiaries.

(b) Character of amounts.—The amounts specified in subsection (a) shall have the same character in the hands of the beneficiary as in the hands of the trust. For this purpose, the amounts shall be treated as consisting of the same proportion of each class of items entering into the computation of distributable net income of the trust as the total of each class bears to the total distributable net income of the trust, unless the terms of the trust specifically allocate different classes of income to different beneficiaries. In the application of the preceding sentence, the items of deduction entering into the computation of distributable net income shall be allocated among the items of distributable net income in accordance with regulations prescribed by the Secretary.

(c) Different taxable years.—If the taxable year of a beneficiary is different from that of the trust, the amount which the beneficiary is required to include in gross income in accordance with the provisions of this section shall be based upon the amount of income of the trust for any taxable year or years of the trust ending within or with his taxable year.

SUBPART C—ESTATES AND TRUSTS WHICH MAY ACCUMULATE INCOME OR WHICH DISTRIBUTE CORPUS

Editorial Summary

Income Taxation of Trusts and Estates: Complex

Subchapter J of Chapter 1 (Secs. 661–664)

A complex trust is one that under its governing instrument is not required to distribute all of its income currently and may distribute corpus. A key tax question for a trust is who (i.e., the trust or the beneficiary) is effectively taxed on the income that is distributed to the beneficiary. If the trust must include the income in its gross income and is not allowed a deduction for the distribution of the income to the beneficiary, then entity theory is being applied. Conversely, if the trust must include the income in its gross income and is allowed a deduction for the distribution of the income to the beneficiary, then aggregate or proprietary theory is being applied (i.e., the trust is merely a conduit with the beneficiary being the taxpayer). Section 661 provides that aggregate or proprietary theory is appropriate for the complex trust in providing that a deduction is permitted the trust for the summation of the amount of its current income that is required to be distributed currently, plus any other amounts that are properly paid or credited or required to be distributed. Section 661(b) limits the deduction to the distributable net income (DNI) of the trust for the taxable year. DNI is defined in Sec. 643(a). In addition, another limitation on the deduction to the trust appears in Sec. 661(c).

Section 662 covers the effect of the distribution on the beneficiary. Under the general rule, the beneficiary of a complex trust must include in gross income the amount of the current income of the trust that is required to be distributed currently, whether it is distributed or not, plus all other amounts properly paid, credited, or required to be distributed to the beneficiary for the taxable year. If the DNI ceiling in Sec. 661(b) limits the amount of the deduction to the trust, the inclusion in the gross income of the beneficiary also will be limited by the DNI ceiling (i.e., symmetry between the deduction to the trust and the inclusion to the beneficiary). Since the trust is viewed as a conduit in this case, the character of the amounts included by the beneficiary shall have the same character to him or her that they had to the trust. Such amounts are allocated among the beneficiaries using a pro-rata approach unless the terms of the governing instrument allocate different classes of income to different beneficiaries.

The taxable year of the trust and the beneficiaries may not be the same. Section 662(c) provides an inclusion rule for the beneficiary that is similar to the inclusion rule for a partner with respect to a partnership [see Sec. 706(a)]. Additional discussion on this topic is in the Editorial Summary entitled Income Taxation of Trusts and Estates: Simple, which precedes Sec. 651.

Section 663 contains special rules that impact on the aforementioned Secs. 661 and 662 results. Section 664 provides special rules for charitable remainder trusts.

§ 661. Deduction for estates and trusts accumulating income or distributing corpus

(a) Deduction.—In any taxable year there shall be allowed as a deduction in computing the taxable income of an estate or trust (other than a trust to which subpart B applies), the sum of—

(1) any amount of income for such taxable year required to be distributed currently (including any amount required to be distributed which may be paid out of income or corpus to the extent such amount is paid out of income for such taxable year); and

(2) any other amounts properly paid or credited or required to be distributed for such taxable year;

but such deduction shall not exceed the distributable net income of the estate or trust.

(b) Character of amounts distributed.—The amount determined under subsection (a) shall be treated as consisting of the same proportion of each class of items entering into the computation of distributable net income of the estate or trust as the total of each class bears to the total distributable net income of the estate or trust in the absence of the allocation of different classes of income under the specific terms of the governing instrument. In the application of the preceding sentence, the items of deduction entering into the computation of distributable net income (including the deduction allowed under section 642(c)) shall be allocated among the items of distributable net income in accordance with regulations prescribed by the Secretary.

(c) Limitation on deduction.—No deduction shall be allowed under subsection (a) in respect of any portion of the amount allowed as a deduction under that subsection (without regard to this subsection) which is treated under subsection (b) as consisting of any item of distributable net income which is not included in the gross income of the estate or trust.

§ 662. Inclusion of amounts in gross income of beneficiaries of estates and trusts accumulating income or distributing corpus

(a) Inclusion.—Subject to subsection (b), there shall be included in the gross income of a beneficiary to whom an amount specified in section 661(a) is paid, credited, or required to be distributed (by an estate or trust described in section 661), the sum of the following amounts:

(1) Amounts required to be distributed currently.—The amount of income for the taxable year required to be distributed currently to such beneficiary, whether distributed or not. If the amount of income required to be distributed currently to all beneficiaries exceeds the distributable net income (computed without the deduction allowed by section 642(c), relating to deduction for charitable, etc., purposes) of the estate or trust, then, in lieu of the amount provided in the preceding sentence, there shall be included in the gross income of the beneficiary an amount which bears the same ratio to distributable net income (as so computed) as the amount of income required to be distributed currently to such beneficiary bears to the amount required to be distributed currently to all beneficiaries. For purposes of this section, the phrase "the amount of income for the taxable year required to be distributed currently" includes any amount required to be paid out of income or corpus to the extent such amount is paid out of income for such taxable year.

(2) Other amounts distributed.—All other amounts properly paid, credited, or required to be distributed to such beneficiary for the taxable year. If the sum of—

(A) the amount of income for the taxable year required to be distributed currently to all beneficiaries, and

(B) all other amounts properly paid, credited, or required to be distributed to all beneficiaries

exceeds the distributable net income of the estate or trust, then, in lieu of the amount provided in the preceding sentence, there shall be included in the gross income of the beneficiary an amount which bears the same ratio to distributable net income (reduced by the amounts specified in (A)) as the other amounts properly paid, credited or required to be distributed to the beneficiary bear to the other amounts properly paid, credited, or required to be distributed to all beneficiaries.

(b) Character of amounts.—The amounts determined under subsection (a) shall have the same character in the hands of the beneficiary as in the hands of the estate or trust. For this purpose, the amounts shall be treated as consisting of the same proportion of each class of items entering into the computation of distributable net income as the total of each class bears to the total distributable net income of the estate or trust unless the terms of the governing instrument specifically allocate different classes of income to different beneficiaries. In the application of the preceding sentence, the items of deduction entering into the computation of distributable net income (including the deduction allowed under section 642(c)) shall be allocated among the items of distributable net income in accordance with regulations prescribed by the Secretary. In the application of this subsection to the amount determined under paragraph (1) of subsection (a), distributable net income shall be computed without regard to any portion of the deduction under section 642(c) which is not attributable to income of the taxable year.

(c) Different taxable years.—If the taxable year of a beneficiary is different from that of the estate or trust, the amount to be included in the gross income of the beneficiary shall be based on the distributable net income of the estate or trust and the amounts properly paid, credited, or required to be distributed to the beneficiary during any taxable year or years of the estate or trust ending within or with his taxable year.

§ 663. Special rules applicable to sections 661 and 662

(a) Exclusions.—There shall not be included as amounts falling within section 661(a) or 662(a)—

(1) Gifts, bequests, etc.—Any amount which, under the terms of the governing instrument, is properly paid or credited as a gift or bequest of a specific sum of money or of specific property and which is paid or credited all at once or in not more than 3 installments. For this purpose an amount which can be paid or credited only from the income of the estate or trust shall not be considered as a gift or bequest of a specific sum of money.

(2) Charitable, etc., distributions.—Any amount paid or permanently set aside or otherwise qualifying for the deduction provided in section 642(c) (computed without regard to sections 508(d), 681, and 4948(c)(4)).

(3) Denial of double deduction.—Any amount paid, credited, or distributed in the taxable year, if section 651 or section 661 applied to such amount for a preceding taxable year of an estate or trust because credited or required to be distributed in such preceding taxable year.

(b) Distributions in first sixty-five days of taxable year.—

(1) General rule.—If within the first 65 days of any taxable year of an estate or a trust, an amount is properly paid or credited, such amount shall be considered paid or credited on the last day of the preceding taxable year.

(2) Limitation.—Paragraph (1) shall apply with respect to any taxable year of an estate or a trust only if the executor of such estate or the fiduciary of such trust (as the case may be) elects, in such manner and at such time as the Secretary prescribes by regulations, to have paragraph (1) apply for such taxable year.

(c) Separate shares treated as separate trusts.—For the sole purpose of determining the amount of distributable net income in the application of sections 661 and 662, in the case of a single trust having more than one beneficiary, substantially separate and independent shares of different beneficiaries in the trust shall be treated as separate trusts. Rules similar to the rules of the preceding provisions of this subsection shall apply to treat substantially separate and independent shares of different beneficiaries in an estate having more than 1 beneficiary as separate estates. The existence of such substantially separate and independent shares and the manner of treatment as separate trusts or estates, including the application of subpart D, shall be determined in accordance with regulations prescribed by the Secretary.

§ 664. Charitable remainder trusts

(a) General rule.—Notwithstanding any other provision of this subchapter, the provisions of this section shall, in accordance with regulations prescribed by the Secretary, apply in the case of a charitable remainder annuity trust and a charitable remainder unitrust.

(b) Character of distributions.—Amounts distributed by a charitable remainder annuity trust or by a charitable remainder unitrust shall be considered as having the following characteristics in the hands of a beneficiary to whom is paid the annuity described in subsection (d)(1)(A) or the payment described in subsection (d)(2)(A):

(1) First, as amounts of income (other than gains, and amounts treated as gains, from the sale or other disposition of capital assets) includible in gross income to the extent of such income of the trust for the year and such undistributed income of the trust for prior years;

(2) Second, as a capital gain to the extent of the capital gain of the trust for the year and the undistributed capital gain of the trust for prior years;

(3) Third, as other income to the extent of such income of the trust for the year and such undistributed income of the trust for prior years; and

(4) Fourth, as a distribution of trust corpus.

For purposes of this section, the trust shall determine the amount of its undistributed capital gain on a cumulative net basis.

(c) Taxation of trusts.—

(1) Income tax.—A charitable remainder annuity trust and a charitable remainder unitrust shall, for any taxable year, not be subject to any tax imposed by this subtitle.

(2) Excise tax.—

(A) In general.—In the case of a charitable remainder annuity trust or a charitable remainder unitrust which has unrelated business taxable income (within the meaning of section 512, determined as if part III of subchapter F applied to such trust) for a taxable year, there is hereby imposed on such trust or unitrust an excise tax equal to the amount of such unrelated business taxable income.

(B) Certain rules to apply.—The tax imposed by subparagraph (A) shall be treated as imposed by chapter 42 for purposes of this title other than subchapter E of chapter 42.

(C) Tax court proceedings.—For purposes of this paragraph, the references in section 6212(c)(1) to section 4940 shall be deemed to include references to this paragraph.

(d) Definitions.—

(1) Charitable remainder annuity trust.—For purposes of this section, a charitable remainder annuity trust is a trust—

(A) from which a sum certain (which is not less than 5 percent nor more than 50 percent of the initial net fair market value of all property placed in trust) is to be paid, not less often than annually, to one or more persons (at least one of which is not an organization described in section 170(c) and, in the case of individuals, only to an individual who is living at the time of the creation of the trust) for a term of years (not in excess of 20 years) or for the life or lives of such individual or individuals,

(B) from which no amount other than the payments described in subparagraph (A) and other than qualified transfers described in subparagraph (C) may be paid to or for the use of any person other than an organization described in section 170(c),

(C) following the termination of the payments described in subparagraph (A), the remainder interest is to be transferred to, or for the use of, an organization described in section 170(c) or is to be retained by the trust for such a use or, to the extent the remainder interest is in qualified employer securities (as defined in subsection (g)(4)), all or part of such securities are to be transferred to an employee stock ownership plan (as defined in section 4975(e)(7)) in a qualified gratuitous transfer (as defined by subsection (g)), and

(D) the value (determined under section 7520) of such remainder interest is at least 10 percent of the initial net fair market value of all property placed in the trust.

(2) Charitable remainder unitrust.—For purposes of this section, a charitable remainder unitrust is a trust—

(A) from which a fixed percentage (which is not less than 5 percent nor more than 50 percent) of the net fair market value of its assets, valued annually, is to be paid, not less often than annually, to one or more persons (at least one of which is not an organization described in section 170(c) and, in the case of individuals, only to an individual who is living at the time of the creation of the trust) for a term of years (not in excess of 20 years) or for the life or lives of such individual or individuals,

(B) from which no amount other than the payments described in subparagraph (A) and other than qualified gratuitous transfers described in subparagraph (C) may be paid to or for the use of any person other than an organization described in section 170(c),

(C) following the termination of the payments described in subparagraph (A), the remainder interest in the trust is to be transferred to, or for the use of, an organization described in section 170(c) or is to be retained by the trust for such a use or, to the extent the remainder interest is in qualified employer securities (as defined in subsection (g)(4)), all or part of such securities are to be transferred to an employee stock ownership plan (as defined in section 4975(e)(7)) in a qualified gratuitous transfer (as defined by subsection (g)), and

(D) with respect to each contribution of property to the trust, the value (determined under section 7520) of such remainder interest in such property is at least 10 percent of the net fair market value of such property as of the date such property is contributed to the trust.

(3) Exception.—Notwithstanding the provisions of paragraphs (2)(A) and (B), the trust instrument may provide that the trustee shall pay the income beneficiary for any year—

(A) the amount of the trust income, if such amount is less than the amount required to be distributed under paragraph (2)(A), and

(B) any amount of the trust income which is in excess of the amount required to be distributed under paragraph (2)(A), to the extent that (by reason of subparagraph (A)) the aggregate of the amounts paid in prior years was less than the aggregate of such required amounts.

(4) Severance of certain additional contributions.—If—

(A) any contribution is made to a trust which before the contribution is a charitable remainder unitrust, and

(B) such contribution would (but for this paragraph) result in such trust ceasing to be a charitable unitrust by reason of paragraph (2)(D),

such contribution shall be treated as a transfer to a separate trust under regulations prescribed by the Secretary.

(e) Valuation for purposes of charitable contribution.—For purposes of determining the amount of any charitable contribution, the remainder interest of a charitable remainder annuity trust or charitable remainder unitrust shall be computed on the basis that an amount equal to 5 percent of the net fair market value of its assets (or a greater amount, if required under the terms of the trust instrument) is to be distributed each year.

(f) Certain contingencies permitted.—

(1) General rule.—If a trust would, but for a qualified contingency, meet the requirements of paragraph (1)(A) or (2)(A) of subsection (d), such trust shall be treated as meeting such requirements.

(2) Value determined without regard to qualified contingency.—For purposes of determining the amount of any charitable contribution (or the actuarial value of any interest), a qualified contingency shall not be taken into account.

(3) Qualified contingency.—For purposes of this subsection, the term "qualified contingency" means any provision of a trust which provides that, upon the happening of a contingency, the payments described in paragraph (1)(A) or (2)(A) of subsection (d) (as the case may be) will terminate not later than such payments would otherwise terminate under the trust.

* * *

SUBPART D—TREATMENT OF EXCESS DISTRIBUTIONS BY TRUSTS

Editorial Summary

Income Taxation of Trusts and Estates: Distributions

Subchapter J of Chapter 1 (Secs. 665–667)

As covered in Subpart B (see Secs. 651 and 652) and Subpart C (see Secs. 661 and 662), the determination of who will ultimately pay Federal income taxes associated with a trust (i.e., the trust or the beneficiary) may be affected by the distribution policy of the trust. This area can be extremely complex. Factors that impact on this complexity include the following:

1. Whether the trust is a simple trust (see Subpart B) or a complex trust (see Subpart C).

2. The trust distributes earnings, part or all of which previously have been taxed to the trust.

3. The trust distributes earnings, part or all of which previously have been taxed to the beneficiaries.

4. The trust distributes earnings which relate to both items 2 and 3 above.

Subpart D (Secs. 665–667) contains provisions for dealing with the taxation of distributions.

§ 665. Definitions applicable to subpart D

(a) Undistributed net income.—For purposes of this subpart, the term "undistributed net income" for any taxable year means the amount by which the distributable net income of the trust for such taxable year exceeds the sum of—

(1) the amounts for such taxable year specified in paragraphs (1) and (2) of section 661(a), and

(2) the amount of taxes imposed on the trust attributable to such distributable net income.

(b) Accumulation distribution.—For purposes of this subpart, except as provided in subsection (c), the term "accumulation distribution" means, for any taxable year of the trust, the amount by which—

(1) the amounts specified in paragraph (2) of section 661(a) for such taxable year, exceed

(2) distributable net income for such year reduced (but not below zero) by the amounts specified in paragraph (1) of section 661(a).

For purposes of section 667 (other than subsection (c) thereof, relating to multiple trusts), the amounts specified in paragraph (2) of section 661(a) shall not include amounts properly paid, credited, or required to be distributed to a beneficiary from a trust (other than a foreign trust) as income accumulated before the birth of such beneficiary or before such beneficiary attains the age of 21. If the amounts properly paid, credited, or required to be distributed by the trust for the taxable year do not exceed the income of the trust for such year, there shall be no accumulation distribution for such year.

(c) Exception for accumulation distributions from certain domestic trusts.—For purposes of this subpart—

(1) In general.—In the case of a qualified trust, any distribution in any taxable year beginning after the date of the enactment of this subsection shall be computed without regard to any undistributed net income.

(2) Qualified trust.—For purposes of this subsection, the term "qualified trust" means any trust other than—

(A) a foreign trust (or, except as provided in regulations, a domestic trust which at any time was a foreign trust), or

(B) a trust created before March 1, 1984, unless it is established that the trust would not be aggregated with other trusts under section 643(f) if such section applied to such trust.

(d) Taxes imposed on the trust.—For purposes of this subpart—

(1) In general.—The term "taxes imposed on the trust" means the amount of the taxes which are imposed for any taxable year of the trust under this chapter (without regard to this subpart or part IV of subchapter A) and which, under regulations prescribed by the Secretary, are properly allocable to the undistributed portions of distributable net income and gains in excess of losses from sales or exchanges of capital assets. The amount determined in the preceding sentence shall be reduced by any amount of such taxes deemed distributed under section 666(b) and (c) to any beneficiary.

* * *

(e) Preceding taxable year.—For purposes of this subpart—

(1) In the case of a foreign trust created by a United States person, the term "preceding taxable year" does not include any taxable year of the trust to which this part does not apply.

(2) In the case of a preceding taxable year with respect to which a trust qualified, without regard to this subpart, under the provisions of subpart B, for purposes of the application of this subpart to such trust for such taxable year, such trust shall, in accordance with regulations prescribed by the Secretary, be treated as a trust to which subpart C applies.

§ 666. Accumulation distribution allocated to preceding years

(a) Amount allocated.—In the case of a trust which is subject to subpart C, the amount of the accumulation distribution of such trust for a taxable year shall be deemed to be an amount within the meaning of paragraph (2) of section 661(a) distributed on the last day of each of the preceding taxable years, commencing with the earliest of such years, to the extent that such amount exceeds the total of any undistributed net income for all earlier preceding taxable years. The amount deemed to be distributed in any such preceding taxable year under the preceding sentence shall not exceed the undistributed net income for such preceding taxable year. For purposes of this subsection, undistributed net income for each of such preceding taxable years shall be computed without regard to such accumulation distribution and without regard to any accumulation distribution determined for any succeeding taxable year.

(b) Total taxes deemed distributed.—If any portion of an accumulation distribution for any taxable year is deemed under subsection (a) to be an amount within the meaning of paragraph (2) of section 661(a) distributed on the last day of any preceding taxable year, and such portion of such distribution is not less than the undistributed net income for such preceding taxable year, the trust shall be deemed to have distributed on the last day of such preceding taxable year an additional amount within the meaning of paragraph (2) of section 661(a). Such additional amount shall be equal to the taxes (other than the tax imposed by section 55) imposed on the trust for such preceding taxable year attributable to the undistributed net income. For purposes of this subsection, the undistributed net income and the taxes imposed on the trust for such preceding taxable year attributable to such undistributed net income shall be computed without regard to such accumulation distribution and without regard to any accumulation distribution determined for any succeeding taxable year.

(c) Pro rata portion of taxes deemed distributed.—If any portion of an accumulation distribution for any taxable year is deemed under subsection (a) to be an amount within the meaning of paragraph (2) of section 661(a) distributed on the last day of any preceding taxable year and such portion of the accumulation distribution is less than the undistributed net income for such preceding taxable year, the trust shall be deemed to have distributed on the last day of such preceding taxable year an additional amount within the meaning of paragraph (2) of section 661(a). Such additional amount shall be equal to the taxes (other than the tax imposed by section 55) imposed on the trust for such taxable year attributable to the undistributed net income multiplied by the ratio of the portion of the accumulation distribution to the undistributed net income of the trust for such year. For purposes of this subsection, the undistributed net income and the taxes imposed on the trust for such preceding taxable year attributable to such undistributed net income shall be computed without regard to the accumulation distribution and without regard to any accumulation distribution determined for any succeeding taxable year.

(d) Rule when information is not available.—If adequate records are not available to determine the proper application of this subpart to an amount distributed by a trust, such amount shall be deemed to be an accumulation distribution consisting of undistributed net income earned during the earliest preceding taxable year of the trust in which it can be established that the trust was in existence.

(e) Denial of refund to trusts and beneficiaries.—No refund or credit shall be allowed to a trust or a beneficiary of such trust for any preceding taxable year by reason of a distribution deemed to have been made by such trust in such year under this section.

§ 667. Treatment of amounts deemed distributed by trust in preceding years

(a) General rule.—The total of the amounts which are treated under section 666 as having been distributed by a trust in a preceding taxable year shall be included in the income of a beneficiary of the trust when paid, credited, or required to be distributed to the extent that such total would have been included in the income of such beneficiary under section 662(a)(2) (and, with respect to any tax-exempt interest to which section 103 applies, under section 662(b)) if such total had been paid to such beneficiary on the last day of such preceding taxable year. The tax imposed by this subtitle on a beneficiary for a taxable year in which any such amount is included in his income shall be determined only as provided in this section and shall consist of the sum of—

(1) a partial tax computed on the taxable income reduced by an amount equal to the total of such amounts, at the rate and in the manner as if this section had not been enacted,

(2) a partial tax determined as provided in subsection (b) of this section, and

* * *

(b) Tax on distribution.—

(1) In general.—The partial tax imposed by subsection (a)(2) shall be determined—

(A) by determining the number of preceding taxable years of the trust on the last day of which an amount is deemed under section 666(a) to have been distributed,

(B) by taking from the 5 taxable years immediately preceding the year of the accumulation distribution the 1 taxable year for which the beneficiary's taxable income was the highest and the 1 taxable year for which his taxable income was the lowest,

(C) by adding to the beneficiary's taxable income for each of the 3 taxable years remaining after the application of subparagraph (B) an amount determined by dividing the amount deemed distributed under section 666 and required to be included in income under subsection (a) by the number of preceding taxable years determined under subparagraph (A), and

(D) by determining the average increase in tax for the 3 taxable years referred to in subparagraph (C) resulting from the application of such subparagraph.

The partial tax imposed by subsection (a)(2) shall be the excess (if any) of the average increase in tax determined under subparagraph (D), multiplied by the number of preceding taxable years determined under subparagraph (A), over the amount of taxes (other than the amount of taxes described in section 665(d)(2)) deemed distributed to the beneficiary under sections 666(b) and (c).

(2) Treatment of loss years.—For purposes of paragraph (1), the taxable income of the beneficiary for any taxable year shall be deemed to be not less than zero.

(3) Certain preceding taxable years not taken into account.—For purposes of paragraph (1), if the amount of the undistributed net income deemed distributed in any preceding taxable year of the trust is less than 25 percent of the amount of the accumulation distribution divided by the number of preceding taxable years to which the accumulation distribution is allocated under section 666(a), the number of preceding taxable years of the trust with respect to which an amount is deemed distributed to a beneficiary under section 666(a) shall be determined without regard to such year.

(4) Effect of other accumulation distributions.—In computing the partial tax under paragraph (1) for any beneficiary, the income of such beneficiary for each of his prior taxable years shall include amounts previously deemed distributed to such beneficiary in such year under section 666 as a result of prior accumulation distributions (whether from the same or another trust).

(5) Multiple distributions in the same taxable year.—In the case of accumulation distributions made from more than one trust which are includible in the income of a beneficiary in the same taxable year, the distributions shall be deemed to have been made consecutively in whichever order the beneficiary shall determine.

(6) Adjustment in partial tax for estate and generation-skipping transfer taxes attributable to partial tax.—

(A) In general.—The partial tax shall be reduced by an amount which is equal to the pre-death portion of the partial tax multiplied by a fraction—

(i) the numerator of which is that portion of the tax imposed by chapter 11 or 13, as the case may be, which is attributable (on a proportionate basis) to amounts included in the accumulation distribution, and

(ii) the denominator of which is the amount of the accumulation distribution which is subject to the tax imposed by chapter 11 or 13, as the case may be.

(B) Partial tax determined without regard to this paragraph.—For purposes of this paragraph, the term "partial tax" means the partial tax imposed by subsection (a)(2) determined under this subsection without regard to this paragraph.

(C) Pre-death portion.—For purposes of this paragraph, the pre-death portion of the partial tax shall be an amount which bears the same ratio to the partial tax as the portion of the accumulation distribution which is attributable to the period before the date of the death of the decedent or the date of the generation-skipping transfer bears to the total accumulation distribution.

(c) Special rule for multiple trusts.—

(1) In general.—If, in the same prior taxable year of the beneficiary in which any part of the accumulation distribution from a trust (hereinafter in this paragraph referred to as "third trust") is deemed under section 666(a) to have been distributed to such beneficiary, some part of prior distributions by each of 2 or more other trusts is deemed under section 666(a) to have been distributed to such beneficiary, then subsections (b) and (c) of section 666 shall not apply with respect to such part of the accumulation distribution from such third trust.

(2) Accumulation distributions from trust not taken into account unless they equal or exceed $1,000.—For purposes of paragraph (1), an accumulation distribution from a trust to a beneficiary shall be taken into account only if such distribution, when added to any prior accumulation distributions from such trust which are deemed under section 666(a) to have been distributed to such beneficiary for the same prior taxable year of the beneficiary, equals or exceeds $1,000.

* * *

SUBPART E—GRANTORS AND OTHERS TREATED AS SUBSTANTIAL OWNERS

Editorial Summary

Grantor Trusts

Subchapter J of Chapter 1 (Secs. 671–678)

Under Subchapter J, a trust is generally treated as a separate taxable entity (i.e., entity theory is applied) [see Sec. 641]. However, at times, the application of the distribution rules (e.g., actual distributions and deemed distributions) results in treating the trust as a conduit (i.e., aggregate or proprietary theory is applied) [e.g., see Secs. 651 and 652]. Unfortunately, from a complexity perspective, all too often in the taxation of trusts, Subchapter J adopts a combined entity theory and aggregate theory approach.

In addition to the earnings of the trust being taxed to the trust or to the beneficiary of the trust, a third possibility exists. The earnings may be taxed to the grantor of the trust. In this case, effectively the trust is ignored and the taxation occurs at the level of the person who created the trust (see Sec. 671).

In deciding whether the tax determination should be made at the trust level or at the grantor level, the keys are whether the grantor has the "power to control beneficial enjoyment" [see Sec. 674(a)], whether the grantor retains a reversionary interest in the trust [see Sec. 673(a)], whether the grantor has certain administrative powers (see Sec. 675), whether the grantor has the power to revoke [see Sec. 676(a)], or whether the income of the trust can be for the benefit of the grantor [see Sec. 677(a)].

§ 671. Trust income, deductions, and credits attributable to grantors and others as substantial owners

Where it is specified in this subpart that the grantor or another person shall be treated as the owner of any portion of a trust, there shall then be included in computing the taxable income and credits of the grantor or the other person those items of income, deductions, and credits against tax of the trust which are attributable to that portion of the trust to the extent that such items would be taken into account under this chapter in computing taxable income or credits against the tax of an individual. Any remaining portion of the trust shall be subject to subparts A through D. No items of a trust shall be included in computing the taxable income and credits of the grantor or of any other person solely on the grounds of his dominion and control over the trust under section 61 (relating to definition of gross income) or any other provision of this title, except as specified in this subpart.

§ 672. Definitions and rules

(a) Adverse party.—For purposes of this subpart, the term "adverse party" means any person having a substantial beneficial interest in the trust which would be adversely affected by the exercise or nonexercise of the power which he possesses respecting the trust. A person having a general power of appointment over the trust property shall be deemed to have a beneficial interest in the trust.

(b) Nonadverse party.—For purposes of this subpart, the term "nonadverse party" means any person who is not an adverse party.

(c) Related or subordinate party.—For purposes of this subpart, the term "related or subordinate party" means any nonadverse party who is—

(1) the grantor's spouse if living with the grantor;

(2) any one of the following: The grantor's father, mother, issue, brother or sister; an employee of the grantor; a corporation or any employee of a corporation in which the stock holdings of the grantor and the trust are significant from the viewpoint of voting control; a subordinate employee of a corporation in which the grantor is an executive.

For purposes of subsection (f) and sections 674 and 675, a related or subordinate party shall be presumed to be subservient to the grantor in respect of the exercise or nonexercise of the powers conferred on him unless such party is shown not to be subservient by a preponderance of the evidence.

(d) Rule where power is subject to condition precedent.—A person shall be considered to have a power described in this subpart even though the exercise of the power is subject to a precedent giving of notice or takes effect only on the expiration of a certain period after the exercise of the power.

(e) Grantor treated as holding any power or interest of grantor's spouse.—

(1) In general.—For purposes of this subpart, a grantor shall be treated as holding any power or interest held by—

(A) any individual who was the spouse of the grantor at the time of the creation of such power or interest, or

(B) any individual who became the spouse of the grantor after the creation of such power or interest, but only with respect to periods after such individual became the spouse of the grantor.

(2) Marital status.—For purposes of paragraph (1)(A), an individual legally separated from his spouse under a decree of divorce or of separate maintenance shall not be considered as married.

* * *

§ 673. Reversionary interests

(a) General rule.—The grantor shall be treated as the owner of any portion of a trust in which he has a reversionary interest in either the corpus or the income therefrom, if, as of the inception of that portion of the trust, the value of such interest exceeds 5 percent of the value of such portion.

(b) Reversionary interest taking effect at death of minor lineal descendant beneficiary.—In the case of any beneficiary who—

(1) is a lineal descendant of the grantor, and

(2) holds all of the present interests in any portion of a trust, the grantor shall not be treated under subsection (a) as the owner of such portion solely by reason of a reversionary interest in such portion which takes effect upon the death of such beneficiary before such beneficiary attains age 21.

(c) Special rule for determining value of reversionary interest.—For purposes of subsection (a), the value of the grantor's reversionary interest shall be determined by assuming the maximum exercise of discretion in favor of the grantor.

(d) Postponement of date specified for reacquisition.—Any postponement of the date specified for the reacquisition of possession or enjoyment of the reversionary interest shall be treated as a new transfer in trust commencing with the date on which the postponement is effective and terminating with the date prescribed by the postponement. However, income for any period shall not be included in the income of the grantor by reason of the preceding sentence if such income would not be so includible in the absence of such postponement.

§ 674. Power to control beneficial enjoyment

(a) General rule.—The grantor shall be treated as the owner of any portion of a trust in respect of which the beneficial enjoyment of the corpus or the income therefrom is subject to a power of disposition, exercisable by the grantor or a nonadverse party, or both, without the approval or consent of any adverse party.

(b) Exceptions for certain powers.—Subsection (a) shall not apply to the following powers regardless of by whom held:

(1) Power to apply income to support of a dependent.—A power described in section 677(b) to the extent that the grantor would not be subject to tax under that section.

(2) Power affecting beneficial enjoyment only after occurrence of event.—A power, the exercise of which can only affect the beneficial enjoyment of the income for a period commencing after the occurrence of an event such that a grantor would not be treated as the owner under section 673 if the power were a reversionary interest; but the grantor may be treated as the owner after the occurrence of the event unless the power is relinquished.

(3) Power exercisable only by will.—A power exercisable only by will, other than a power in the grantor to appoint by will the income of the trust where the income is accumulated for such disposition by the grantor or may be so accumulated in the discretion of the grantor or a nonadverse party, or both, without the approval or consent of any adverse party.

(4) Power to allocate among charitable beneficiaries.—A power to determine the beneficial enjoyment of the corpus or the income therefrom if the corpus or income is irrevocably payable for a purpose specified in section 170(c) (relating to definition of charitable contributions) or to an employee stock ownership plan (as defined in section 4975(e)(7)) in a qualified gratuitous transfer (as defined in section 664(g)(1)).

(5) Power to distribute corpus.—A power to distribute corpus either—

(A) to or for a beneficiary or beneficiaries or to or for a class of beneficiaries (whether or not income beneficiaries) provided that the power is limited by a reasonably definite standard which is set forth in the trust instrument; or

(B) to or for any current income beneficiary, provided that the distribution of corpus must be chargeable against the proportionate share of corpus held in trust for the payment of income to the beneficiary as if the corpus constituted a separate trust.

A power does not fall within the powers described in this paragraph if any person has a power to add to the beneficiary or beneficiaries or to a class of beneficiaries designated to receive the income or corpus, except where such action is to provide for after-born or after-adopted children.

(6) Power to withhold income temporarily.—A power to distribute or apply income to or for any current income beneficiary or to accumulate the income for him, provided that any accumulated income must ultimately be payable—

(A) to the beneficiary from whom distribution or application is withheld, to his estate, or to his appointees (or persons named as alternate takers in default of appointment) provided that such beneficiary possesses a power of appointment which does not exclude from the class of possible appointees any person other than the beneficiary, his estate, his creditors, or the creditors of his estate, or

(B) on termination of the trust, or in conjunction with a distribution of corpus which is augmented by such accumulated income, to the current income beneficiaries in shares which have been irrevocably specified in the trust instrument.

Accumulated income shall be considered so payable although it is provided that if any beneficiary does not survive a date of distribution which could reasonably have been expected to occur within the beneficiary's lifetime, the share of the deceased beneficiary is to be paid to his appointees or to one or more designated alternate takers (other than the grantor or the grantor's estate) whose shares have been irrevocably specified. A power does not fall within the powers described in this paragraph if any person has a power to add to the beneficiary or beneficiaries or to a class of beneficiaries designated to receive the income or corpus except where such action is to provide for after-born or after-adopted children.

(7) Power to withhold income during disability of a beneficiary.—A power exercisable only during—

(A) the existence of a legal disability of any current income beneficiary, or

(B) the period during which any income beneficiary shall be under the age of 21 years,

to distribute or apply income to or for such beneficiary or to accumulate and add the income to corpus. A power does not fall within the powers described in this paragraph if any person has a power to add to the beneficiary or beneficiaries or to a class of beneficiaries designated to receive the income or corpus, except where such action is to provide for after-born or after-adopted children.

(8) Power to allocate between corpus and income.—A power to allocate receipts and disbursements as between corpus and income, even though expressed in broad language.

(c) Exception for certain powers of independent trustees.—Subsection (a) shall not apply to a power solely exercisable (without the approval or consent of any other person) by a trustee or trustees, none of whom is the grantor, and no more than half of whom are related or subordinate parties who are subservient to the wishes of the grantor—

(1) to distribute, apportion, or accumulate income to or for a beneficiary or beneficiaries, or to, for, or within a class of beneficiaries; or

(2) to pay out corpus to or for a beneficiary or beneficiaries or to or for a class of beneficiaries (whether or not income beneficiaries).

A power does not fall within the powers described in this subsection if any person has a power to add to the beneficiary or beneficiaries or to a class of beneficiaries designated to receive the income or corpus, except where such action is to provide for after-born or after-adopted children. For periods during which an individual is the spouse of the grantor (within the meaning of section 672(e)(2)), any reference in this subsection to the grantor shall be treated as including a reference to such individual.

(d) Power to allocate income if limited by a standard.—Subsection (a) shall not apply to a power solely exercisable (without the approval or consent of any other person) by a trustee or trustees, none of whom is the grantor or spouse living with the grantor, to distribute, apportion, or accumulate income to or for a beneficiary or beneficiaries, or to, for, or within a class of beneficiaries, whether or not the conditions of paragraph (6) or (7) of subsection (b) are satisfied, if such power is limited by a reasonably definite external standard which is set forth in the trust instrument. A power does not fall within the powers described in this subsection if any person has a power to add to the beneficiary or beneficiaries or to a class of beneficiaries designated to receive the income or corpus except where such action is to provide for after-born or after-adopted children.

§ 675. Administrative powers

The grantor shall be treated as the owner of any portion of a trust in respect of which—

(1) Power to deal for less than adequate and full consideration.—A power exercisable by the grantor or a nonadverse party, or both, without the approval or consent of any adverse party enables the grantor or any person to purchase, exchange, or otherwise deal with or dispose of the corpus or the income therefrom for less than an adequate consideration in money or money's worth.

(2) Power to borrow without adequate interest or security.—A power exercisable by the grantor or a nonadverse party, or both, enables the grantor to borrow the corpus or income, directly or indirectly, without adequate interest or without adequate security except where a trustee (other than the grantor) is authorized under a general lending power to make loans to any person without regard to interest or security.

(3) Borrowing of the trust funds.—The grantor has directly or indirectly borrowed the corpus or income and has not completely repaid the loan, including any interest, before the beginning of the taxable year. The preceding sentence shall not apply to a loan which provides for adequate interest and adequate security, if such loan is made by a trustee other than the grantor and other than a related or subordinate trustee subservient to the grantor. For periods during which an individual is the spouse of the grantor (within the meaning of section 672(e)(2)), any reference in this paragraph to the grantor shall be treated as including a reference to such individual.

(4) General powers of administration.—A power of administration is exercisable in a nonfiduciary capacity by any person without the approval or consent of any person in a fiduciary capacity. For purposes of this paragraph, the term "power of administration" means any one or more of the following powers: (A) a power to vote or direct the voting of stock or other securities of a corporation in which the holdings of the grantor and the trust are significant from the viewpoint of voting control; (B) a power to control the investment of the trust funds either by directing investments or reinvestments, or by vetoing proposed investments or reinvestments, to the extent that the trust funds consist of stocks or securities of corporations in which the holdings of the grantor and the trust are significant from the viewpoint of voting control; or (C) a power to reacquire the trust corpus by substituting other property of an equivalent value.

§ 676. Power to revoke

(a) General rule.—The grantor shall be treated as the owner of any portion of a trust, whether or not he is treated as such owner under any other provision of this part, where at any time the power to revest in the grantor title to such portion is exercisable by the grantor or a non-adverse party, or both.

(b) Power affecting beneficial enjoyment only after occurrence of event.—Subsection (a) shall not apply to a power the exercise of which can only affect the beneficial enjoyment of the income for a period commencing after the occurrence of an event such that a grantor would not be treated as the owner under section 673 if the power were a reversionary interest. But the grantor may be treated as the owner after the occurrence of such event unless the power is relinquished.

§ 677. Income for benefit of grantor

(a) General rule.—The grantor shall be treated as the owner of any portion of a trust, whether or not he is treated as such owner under section 674, whose income without the approval or consent of any adverse party is, or, in the discretion of the grantor or a nonadverse party, or both, may be—

(1) distributed to the grantor or the grantor's spouse;

(2) held or accumulated for future distribution to the grantor or the grantor's spouse; or

(3) applied to the payment of premiums on policies of insurance on the life of the grantor or the grantor's spouse (except policies of insurance irrevocably payable for a purpose specified in section 170(c) (relating to definition of charitable contributions)).

This subsection shall not apply to a power the exercise of which can only affect the beneficial enjoyment of the income for a period commencing after the occurrence of an event such that the grantor would not be treated as the owner under section 673 if the power were a reversionary interest; but the grantor may be treated as the owner after the occurrence of the event unless the power is relinquished.

(b) Obligations of support.—Income of a trust shall not be considered taxable to the grantor under subsection (a) or any other provision of this chapter merely because such income in the discretion of another person, the trustee, or the grantor acting as trustee or co-trustee, may be applied or distributed for the support or maintenance of a beneficiary (other than the grantor's spouse) whom the grantor is legally obligated to support or maintain, except to the extent that such income is so applied or distributed. In cases where the amounts so applied or distributed are paid out of corpus or out of other than income for the taxable year, such amounts shall be considered to be an amount paid or credited within the meaning of paragraph (2) of section 661 (a) and shall be taxed to the grantor under section 662.

§ 678. Person other than grantor treated as substantial owner

(a) General rule.—A person other than the grantor shall be treated as the owner of any portion of a trust with respect to which:

(1) such person has a power exercisable solely by himself to vest the corpus or the income therefrom in himself, or

(2) such person has previously partially released or otherwise modified such a power and after the release or modification retains such control as would, within the principles of sections 671 to 677, inclusive, subject a grantor of a trust to treatment as the owner thereof.

(b) Exception where grantor is taxable.—Subsection (a) shall not apply with respect to a power over income, as originally granted or thereafter modified, if the grantor of the trust or a transferor (to whom section 679 applies) is otherwise treated as the owner under the provisions of this subpart other than this section.

(c) Obligations of support.—Subsection (a) shall not apply to a power which enables such person, in the capacity of trustee or co-trustee, merely to apply the income of the trust to the support or maintenance of a person whom the holder of the power is obligated to support or maintain except to the extent that such income is so applied. In cases where the amounts so applied or distributed are paid out of corpus or out of other than income of the taxable year, such amounts shall be considered to be an amount paid or credited within the meaning of paragraph (2) of section 661(a) and shall be taxed to the holder of the power under section 662.

(d) Effect of renunciation or disclaimer.—Subsection (a) shall not apply with respect to a power which has been renounced or disclaimed within a reasonable time after the holder of the power first became aware of its existence.

(e) Cross Reference.—

For provision under which beneficiary of trust is treated as owner of the portion of the trust which consists of stock in an S corporation, see section 1361(d).

* * *

SUBPART F—MISCELLANEOUS

Editorial Summary
Miscellaneous Estate and Trust Provisions
Subchapter J of Chapter 1 (Secs. 681 and 682)

Subpart F (Secs. 681 and 682) deals with two provisions not covered elsewhere in Subchapter J. Section 642(c) contains the general rule for the charitable contribution deduction of an estate or trust. Section 681 contains a special limitation on the charitable contribution deduction with respect to income of a taxable year, which is allocable to the unrelated business income of a trust. Section 682 provides for the inclusion in the gross income of the former wife of the income of a so-called "alimony trust."

§ 681. Limitation on charitable deduction

(a) Trade or business income.—In computing the deduction allowable under section 642(c) to a trust, no amount otherwise allowable under section 642(c) as a deduction shall be allowed as a deduction with respect to income of a taxable year which is allocable to its unrelated business income for such year. For purposes of the preceding sentence, the term "unrelated business income" means an amount equal to the amount which, if such trust were exempt from tax under section 501(a) by reason of section 501(c)(3), would be computed as its unrelated business taxable income under section 512 (relating to income derived from certain business activities and from certain property acquired with borrowed funds).

(b) Cross reference.—

For disallowance of certain charitable, etc., deductions otherwise allowable under section 642(c), see sections 508(d) and 4948(c)(4).

§ 682. Income of an estate or trust in case of divorce, etc.

(a) Inclusion in gross income of wife.—There shall be included in the gross income of a wife who is divorced or legally separated under a decree of divorce or of separate maintenance (or who is separated from her husband under a written separation agreement) the amount of the income of any trust which such wife is entitled to receive and which, except for this section, would be includible in the gross income of her husband, and such amount shall not, despite any other provision of this subtitle, be includible in the gross income of such husband. This subsection shall not apply to that part of any such income of the trust which the terms of the decree, written separation agreement, or trust instrument fix, in terms of an amount of money or a portion of such income, as a sum which is payable for the support of minor children of such husband. In case such income is less than the amount specified in the decree, agreement, or instrument, for the purpose of applying the preceding sentence, such income, to the extent of such sum payable for such support, shall be considered a payment for such support.

(b) Wife considered a beneficiary.—For purposes of computing the taxable income of the estate or trust and the taxable income of a wife to whom subsection (a) applies, such wife shall be considered as the beneficiary specified in this part.

(c) Cross reference.—

For definitions of "husband" and "wife," as used in this section, see section 7701(a)(17).

* * *

PART II—INCOME IN RESPECT OF DECEDENTS

Editorial Summary

Income in Respect of a Decedent

Subchapter J of Chapter 1 (Sec. 691)

Property that is included in the decedent's estate tax return generally will receive a stepped-up basis to the beneficiary (i.e., fair market value) [see Sec. 1014(a)]. Thus, any untaxed appreciation on the property is never subject to income taxation if, under the decedent's method of accounting, it is not reported on the final income tax return of the decedent. Section 691 reduces this tax avoidance opportunity by providing that certain amounts that had been earned but not recognized at the time of the decedent's death will be included on someone's income tax return. This "someone" could be either the estate or a beneficiary. The character of the income to the estate or a beneficiary will be the same as it would have been in the hands of the decedent.

Since such income is reported on the income tax return of the estate or a beneficiary and the estate tax return of the decedent's estate, such income is being subjected to double taxation. Section 691(c), in recognizing this inequity, provides that the estate or beneficiary who includes the income in gross income is permitted to take a deduction for the estate taxes that are paid associated with such income. Such deduction is permitted in the taxable year that such income in respect of a decedent is reported on the income tax return.

§ 691. Recipients of income in respect of decedents

(a) Inclusion in gross income.—

(1) General rule.—The amount of all items of gross income in respect of a decedent which are not properly includible in respect of the taxable period in which falls the date of his death or a prior period (including the amount of all items of gross income in respect of a prior decedent, if the right to receive such amount was acquired by reason of the death of the prior decedent or by bequest, devise, or inheritance from the prior decedent) shall be included in the gross income, for the taxable year when received, of:

(A) the estate of the decedent, if the right to receive the amount is acquired by the decedent's estate from the decedent;

(B) the person who, by reason of the death of the decedent, acquires the right to receive the amount, if the right to receive the amount is not acquired by the decedent's estate from the decedent; or

(C) the person who acquires from the decedent the right to receive the amount by bequest, devise, or inheritance, if the amount is received after a distribution by the decedent's estate of such right.

(2) Income in case of sale, etc.—If a right, described in paragraph (1), to receive an amount is transferred by the estate of the decedent or a person who received such right by reason of the death of the decedent or by bequest, devise, or inheritance from the decedent, there shall be included in the gross income of the estate or such person, as the case may be, for the taxable period in which the transfer occurs, the fair market value of such right at the time of such transfer plus the amount by which any consideration for the transfer exceeds such fair market value. For purposes of this paragraph, the term "transfer" includes sale, exchange, or other disposition, or the satisfaction of an installment obligation at other than face value, but does not include transmission at death to the estate of the decedent or a transfer to a person pursuant to the right of such person to receive such amount by reason of the death of the decedent or by bequest, devise, or inheritance from the decedent.

(3) Character of income determined by reference to decedent.—The right, described in paragraph (1), to receive an amount shall be treated, in the hands of the estate of the decedent or any person who acquired such right by reason of the death of the decedent, or by bequest, devise, or inheritance from the decedent, as if it had been acquired by the estate or such person in the transaction in which the right to receive the income was originally derived and the amount includible in gross income under paragraph (1) or (2) shall be considered in the hands of the estate or such person to have the character which it would have had in the hands of the decedent if the decedent had lived and received such amount.

(4) Installment obligations acquired from decedent.—In the case of an installment obligation reportable by the decedent on the installment method under section 453, if such obligation is acquired by the decedent's estate from the decedent or by any person by reason of the death of the decedent or by bequest, devise, or inheritance from the decedent—

(A) an amount equal to the excess of the face amount of such obligation over the basis of the obligation in the hands of the decedent (determined under section 453B) shall, for the purpose of paragraph (1), be considered as an item of gross income in respect of the decedent; and

(B) such obligation shall, for purposes of paragraphs (2) and (3), be considered a right to receive an item of gross income in respect of the decedent, but the amount includible in gross income under paragraph (2) shall be reduced by an amount equal to the basis of the obligation in the hands of the decedent (determined under section 453B).

(5) Other rules relating to installment obligations.—

(A) In general.—In the case of an installment obligation reportable by the decedent on the installment method under section 453, for purposes of paragraph (2)—

(i) the second sentence of paragraph (2) shall be applied by inserting "(other than the obligor)" after "or a transfer to a person,"

(ii) any cancellation of such an obligation shall be treated as a transfer, and

(iii) any cancellation of such an obligation occurring at the death of the decedent shall be treated as a transfer by the estate of the decedent (or, if held by a person other than the decedent before the death of the decedent, by such person).

(B) Face amount treated as fair market value in certain cases.—In any case to which the first sentence of paragraph (2) applies by reason of subparagraph (A), if the decedent and the obligor were related persons (within the meaning of section 453(f)(1)), the fair market value of the installment obligation shall be treated as not less than its face amount.

(C) Cancellation includes becoming unenforceable.—For purposes of subparagraph (A), an installment obligation which becomes unenforceable shall be treated as if it were canceled.

(b) Allowance of deductions and credit.—The amount of any deduction specified in section 162, 163, 164, 212, or 611 (relating to deductions for expenses, interest, taxes, and depletion) or credit specified in section 27 (relating to foreign tax credit), in respect of a decedent which is not properly allowable to the decedent in respect of the taxable period in which falls the date of his death, or a prior period, shall be allowed:

(1) Expenses, interest, and taxes.—In the case of a deduction specified in section 162, 163, 164, or 212 and a credit specified in section 27, in the taxable year when paid—

(A) to the estate of the decedent; except that

(B) if the estate of the decedent is not liable to discharge the obligation to which the deduction or credit relates, to the person who, by reason of the death of the decedent or by bequest, devise, or inheritance acquires, subject to such obligation, from the decedent an interest in property of the decedent.

(2) Depletion.—In the case of the deduction specified in section 611, to the person described in subsection (a)(1)(A), (B), or (C) who, in the manner described therein, receives the income to which the deduction relates, in the taxable year when such income is received.

(c) Deduction for estate tax.—

(1) Allowance of deduction.—

(A) **General rule.**—A person who includes an amount in gross income under subsection (a) shall be allowed, for the same taxable year, as a deduction an amount which bears the same ratio to the estate tax attributable to the net value for estate tax purposes of all the items described in subsection (a)(1) as the value for estate tax purposes of the items of gross income or portions thereof in respect of which such person included the amount in gross income (or the amount included in gross income, whichever is lower) bears to the value for estate tax purposes of all the items described in subsection (a)(1).

(B) **Estates and trusts.**—In the case of an estate or trust, the amount allowed as a deduction under subparagraph (A) shall be computed by excluding from the gross income of the estate or trust the portion (if any) of the items described in subsection (a)(1) which is properly paid, credited, or to be distributed to the beneficiaries during the taxable year.

(2) **Method of computing deduction.**—For purposes of paragraph (1)—

(A) The term "estate tax" means the tax imposed on the estate of the decedent or any prior decedent under section 2001 or 2101, reduced by the credits against such tax.

(B) The net value for estate tax purposes of all the items described in subsection (a)(1) shall be the excess of the value for estate tax purposes of all the items described in subsection (a)(1) over the deductions from the gross estate in respect of claims which represent the deductions and credit described in subsection (b). Such net value shall be determined with respect to the provisions of section 421(c)(2), relating to the deduction for estate tax with respect to stock options to which part II of subchapter D applies.

(C) The estate tax attributable to such net value shall be an amount equal to the excess of the estate tax over the estate tax computed without including in the gross estate such net value.

(3) **Special rule for generation-skipping transfers.**—In the case of any tax imposed by chapter 13 on a taxable termination or a direct skip occurring as a result of the death of the transferor, there shall be allowed a deduction (under principles similar to the principles of this subsection) for the portion of such tax attributable to items of gross income of the trust which were not properly includible in the gross income of the trust for periods before the date of such termination.

(4) **Coordination with capital gain provisions.**—For purposes of sections 1(h), 1201, 1202, and 1211, the amount taken into account with respect to any item described in subsection (a)(1) shall be reduced (but not below zero) by the amount of the deduction allowable under paragraph (1) of this subsection with respect to such item.

(d) Amounts received by surviving annuitant under joint and survivor annuity contract.—

(1) **Deduction for estate tax.**—For purposes of computing the deduction under subsection (c)(1)(A), amounts received by a surviving annuitant—

(A) as an annuity under a joint and survivor annuity contract where the decedent annuitant died after December 31, 1953, and after the annuity starting date (as defined in section 72(c)(4)), and

(B) during the surviving annuitant's life expectancy period,

shall, to the extent included in gross income under section 72, be considered as amounts included in gross income under subsection (a).

(2) **Net value for estate tax purposes.**—In determining the net value for estate tax purposes under subsection (c)(2)(B) for purposes of this subsection, the value for estate tax purposes of the items described in paragraph (1) of this subsection shall be computed—

(A) by determining the excess of the value of the annuity at the date of the death of the deceased annuitant over the total amount excludable from the gross income of the surviving annuitant under section 72 during the surviving annuitant's life expectancy period, and

(B) by multiplying the figure so obtained by the ratio which the value of the annuity for estate tax purposes bears to the value of the annuity at the date of the death of the deceased.

(3) **Definitions.**—For purposes of this subsection—

(A) The term "life expectancy period" means the period beginning with the first day of the first period for which an amount is received by the surviving annuitant under the contract and ending with the close of the taxable year with or in which falls the termination of the life expectancy of the surviving annuitant. For purposes of this subparagraph, the life expectancy of the surviving annuitant shall be determined, as of the date of the death of the deceased annuitant, with reference to actuarial tables prescribed by the Secretary.

(B) The surviving annuitant's expected return under the contract shall be computed, as of the death of the deceased annuitant, with reference to actuarial tables prescribed by the Secretary.

(e) Cross reference.—

For application of this section to income in respect of a deceased partner, see section 753.

Editorial Summary

Cancellation of Income Taxes for Deceased Members of the U.S. Armed Forces

Subchapter J of Chapter 1 (Sec. 692)

If a member of the U.S. Armed Forces is in active service and dies (1) while serving in a combat zone, (2) while outside a combat zone while performing military duties directly in support of military operations in a combat zone, or (3) at any place as the result of wounds, injury, or disease associated with (1) or (2) above, the decedent's Federal income tax liability is cancelled. Such cancellation applies to the tax year in which death occurred and for any prior tax year ending on or after the first day of service in a combat zone [Sec. 692(a)].

A similar provision applies to deceased victims of certain terrorist attacks [Sec. 692(b)] and to astronauts who die in the line of duty [Sec. 692(d)(5)].

* * *

§ 692. Income taxes of members of Armed Forces, astronauts, and victims of certain terrorist attacks on death

(a) General rule.—In the case of any individual who dies while in active service as a member of the Armed Forces of the United States, if such death occurred while serving in a combat zone (as determined under section 112) or as a result of wounds, disease, or injury occurred while so serving—

(1) any tax imposed by this subtitle shall not apply with respect to the taxable year in which falls the date of his death, or with respect to any prior taxable year ending on or after the first day he so served in a combat zone after June 24, 1950; and

(2) any tax under this subtitle and under the corresponding provisions of prior revenue laws for taxable years preceding those specified in paragraph (1) which is unpaid at the date of his death (including interest, additions to the tax, and additional amounts) shall not be assessed, and if assessed the assessment shall be abated, and if collected shall be credited or refunded as an overpayment.

(b) Individuals in missing status.—For purposes of this section, in the case of an individual who was in a missing status within the meaning of section 6013(f)(3)(A), the date of his death shall be treated as being not earlier than the date on which a determination of his death is made under section 556 of title 37 of the United States Code. Except in the case of the combat zone designated for purposes of the Vietnam conflict, the preceding sentence shall not cause subsection (a)(1) to apply for any taxable year beginning more than 2 years after the date designated under section 112 as the date of termination of combatant activities in a combat zone.

(c) Certain military or civilian employees of the United States dying as a result of injuries sustained overseas.—

(1) In general.—In the case of any individual who dies while a military or civilian employee of the United States, if such death occurs as a result of wounds or injury which was incurred while the individual was a military or civilian employee of the United States and which was incurred outside the United States in a terroristic or military action, any tax imposed by this subtitle shall not apply—

(A) with respect to the taxable year in which falls the date of his death, and

(B) with respect to any prior taxable year in the period beginning with the last taxable year ending before the taxable year in which the wounds or injury were incurred.

(2) Terroristic or military action.—For purposes of paragraph (1), the term "terroristic or military action" means—

(A) any terroristic activity which a preponderance of the evidence indicates was directed against the United States or any of its allies, and

(B) any military action involving the Armed Forces of the United States and resulting from violence or aggression against the United States or any of its allies (or threat thereof).

For purposes of the preceding sentence, the term "military action" does not include training exercises.

(3) Treatment of multinational forces.—For purposes of paragraph (2), any multinational force in which the United States is participating shall be treated as an ally of the United States.

(d) Individuals dying as a result of certain attacks.—

(1) In general.—In the case of a specified terrorist victim, any tax imposed by this chapter shall not apply—

(A) with respect to the taxable year in which falls the date of death, and

(B) with respect to any prior taxable year in the period beginning with the last taxable year ending before the taxable year in which the wounds, injury, or illness referred to in paragraph (3) were incurred.

(2) $10,000 minimum benefit.—If, but for this paragraph, the amount of tax not imposed by paragraph (1) with respect to a specified terrorist victim is less than $10,000, then such victim shall be treated as having made a payment against the tax imposed by this chapter for such victim's last taxable year in an amount equal to the excess of $10,000 over the amount of tax not so imposed.

(3) Taxation of certain benefits.—Subject to such rules as the Secretary may prescribe, paragraph (1) shall not apply to the amount of any tax imposed by this chapter which would be computed by only taking into account the items of income, gain, or other amounts attributable to—

(A) deferred compensation which would have been payable after death if the individual had died other than as a specified terrorist victim, or

(B) amounts payable in the taxable year which would not have been payable in such taxable year but for an action taken after September 11, 2001.

(4) Specified terrorist victim.—For purposes of this subsection, the term "specified terrorist victim" means any decedent—

(A) who dies as a result of wounds or injury incurred as a result of the terrorist attacks against the United States on April 19, 1995, or September 11, 2001, or

(B) who dies as a result of illness incurred as a result of an attack involving anthrax occurring on or after September 11, 2001, and before January 1, 2002.

Such term shall not include any individual identified by the Attorney General to have been a participant or conspirator in any such attack or a representative of such an individual.

(5) Relief with respect to astronauts.—The provisions of this subsection shall apply to any astronaut whose death occurs in the line of duty, except that paragraph (3)(B) shall be applied by using the date of death of the astronaut rather than September 11, 2001.

· IRC Subchapter K - 701-777 govern Partnerships
· 761(a) definition of a partnership
· Revenue Procedure 2003-99
· Characteristics to be a limited partnership
· 7704(d) defines qualified sources for MLP double taxation rules
* 721 Nonrecognition of g/L on contribution
* 721(a) Gen rule of nonrecognition for part & p'ships
* 722 Basis of contributing partner's interest
723 basis for partnership after contribution
709(a) treatment for organization/syndication fees
709(b) deduction of organization fees
752(a) increase in partner liability ↑ basis
752(b) decrease in partner liabilities ↓ basis

731(a)(1) extent of g/L recognized on distribution
707(c)(2) capitalization of certain service charges
724 Classification of g/L on certain prop
703(b) elections for accounting methods
703(a)(2) deductions not allowed for p'ship
702 separately stated items
702(b) classification & determination of p'ship income & expenses
704(b) determinations of distributive share
704(c) depreciation deduction on contributed property → ceiling rule
704(d) basis limitation on loss deductions
707(a) entity concept transaction between partner & p'ship

SUBCHAPTER K—PARTNERS AND PARTNERSHIPS

PART I—DETERMINATION OF TAX LIABILITY

Editorial Summary

Partnerships: General Tax Treatment

Subchapter K of Chapter 1 (Secs. 701–709)

For tax purposes, a partnership [see Sec. 761(a)] is treated as a conduit. As such, the partnership is merely a tax reporter rather than being a taxpayer. The partnership tax return serves an informational purpose. The data appearing on the partnership return ultimately is reported on the returns of the partners [see Sec. 701]. This conduit approach is an application of aggregate or proprietary theory as contrasted with entity theory, which is applicable for the corporation.

Each partner must report his or her distributive share of the partnership items of income, deduction, and credit. Each item that receives some special tax treatment at the partner level is segregated on the partnership return and reported to the partner with the identity maintained [see Sec. 702]. Items of income and deduction that do not require separate treatment are aggregated as taxable income (or more descriptively, as bottom line income) in accordance with Sec. 703(a) on the partnership return and the distributive share is reported to each partner.

The distributive share of a partner is determined in accordance with the partnership agreement [see Sec. 704(a)]. If the partnership agreement contains no provision for sharing profits and losses, then each partner will share in accordance with his or her interest in the partnership [see Sec. 704(b)]. The partnership agreement may contain a different percentage for sharing profits than for sharing losses (i.e., a provision quite often found in limited partnership agreements). The Code contains two overrides in terms of the profit and loss sharing agreement contained in the partnership agreement. First, Sec. 704(c) provides that precontribution appreciation or depreciation (i.e., the difference between the basis and the fair market value of property contributed by the partner to the partnership) shall be allocated to the contributing partner. Note that a variety of types of transactions will trigger partial or complete recognition of such precontribution appreciation or depreciation including sale of the contributed property, depreciation deductions, or distribution within 7 years of the contribution date of such property to a partner other than the contributing partner [but see the exception in Sec. 704(c)(2)]. Second, Sec. 704(b)(2) provides that the allocation under the partnership agreement will be followed only if it has substantial economic effect. Very detailed regulations under Sec. 704 interpret "substantial economic effect."

Two sets of basis rules are important in partnership taxation. The partnership needs to know the basis for its assets (i.e., frequently referred to as the "inside basis"). The normal basis rules which appear in Secs. 1011–1023 are applicable. In addition, Sec. 723 covers the basis for property contributed by the partner to the partnership. The partner also needs to know the basis for his interest in the partnership (i.e., frequently referred to as the "outside basis"). Section 705 is the relevant Code section for this determination. Liabilities of the partnership impact on the calculation of the "outside basis" [see Sec. 752]. By so doing, the partners have the tax avoidance concept of leverage available to them (subject to the limitations contained in Sec. 465 and Sec. 469).

The "outside basis" and the distributive share provisions interact with respect to partnership losses. The "outside basis" serves as a ceiling on the amount of a partner's distributive share of partnership losses that may be deducted on the partner's return. Any amount of loss that cannot be deducted in the current taxable year because of this limitation is placed in a suspense account and carried forward to be deducted in subsequent taxable years when the "outside basis" is adequate to absorb the loss [see Sec. 704(d)]. In additional to being logical, this ceiling treatment results because the "outside basis" cannot be less than zero.

Two other Code sections must be considered in permitting the partner to deduct his or her share of partnership losses on his or her tax return. These are the Sec. 465 at-risk provisions and the Sec. 469 passive activity loss provisions.

While the general theoretical framework that is applied for partnership taxation is aggregate or proprietary theory, the partnership taxation provisions are made more complex by the application of entity theory in certain circumstances. For purposes of the making of tax elections, the partnership is considered a separate entity. Section 703(b) provides that, subject to three exceptions, the elections are to be made at the partnership level rather than at the partner level.

One of the elections a taxpayer must make is the choice of a taxable year [see Sec. 441]. Section 706 provides specific rules that limit the choice for a partnership (i.e., the majority interest and principal partner rules). However, a partnership can choose a taxable year that is not in accordance with either of these provisions if a business purpose can be established to the satisfaction of the IRS for doing so or if an election can be made under Sec. 444. Also, note that the regulations under Sec. 706(b)(1)(B)(iii) reject the calendar year option mentioned in the Code in favor of the greater revenue generating least aggregate deferral method.

The choice of taxable year impacts on the timing of the partner's reporting of his or her distributive share. According to Sec. 706(a), a partner includes his or her distributive share and any guaranteed payments [see Sec. 707(c)] in gross income for the partnership taxable year which ends with or

within his or her taxable year. Thus, if the partner is a calendar-year taxpayer and the partnership is able to elect a fiscal year, tax deferral can result.

Another illustration of the exception application of entity theory for the partnership is the general rule in Sec. 707. Under this provision, if a partner engages in a transaction with the partnership as a nonpartner, the transaction will be taxed accordingly. However, the general rule is subject to a loss disallowance rule and a reclassification of capital gain as ordinary income rule for transactions between a partner and a controlled partnership.

Section 708, in dealing with the continuity of life issue with respect to the partnership, adopts a combination of the entity theory and aggregate theory approaches. A mere change in the identity of a partner will not in itself result in the termination of the partnership. However, if during a 12-month period there is a sale or exchange of a majority (i.e., at least 50 percent) of the partnership interests in capital and profits, then a termination will occur [see Sec. 708(b)(1)(B)]. Note that the calculation is a cumulative one during the 12-month period.

Example: The ABC partnership has three partners (A, B and C) who each own a one-third interest. A sells his interest to D on August 3, 19X1. A termination of the partnership does not occur at this time because the majority rule has not been satisfied. On January 10, 19X2, D sells the interest he acquired from A to E. Termination of the partnership does not occur at this time because the cumulative change is still only one-third (i.e., B and C's ownership interests have not changed). On February 7, 19X2, B sells his interest to F. Termination of the partnership occurs on February 7, 19X2, because the majority rule has been satisfied (i.e., A's one-third interest plus B's one-third interest is greater than 50 percent).

In addition to the majority interest rule, the partnership also will terminate if no part of any business, financial operation, or venture of the partnership continues to be carried on by any of its partners in a partnership [see Sec. 708(b)(1)(A)]. From the viewpoint of a partner, a termination usually is viewed as negative (e.g., the closing of the taxable year may produce a bunching of income problems at the partner level).

Section 709 provides for the treatment of organization costs (i.e., capital expenditures which may be deducted up to $5,000 (but subject to phaseout) with the balance being amortized over a 180-month period) and syndication fees (i.e., capital expenditures).

§ 701. Partners, not partnership, subject to tax

A partnership as such shall not be subject to the income tax imposed by this chapter. Persons carrying on business as partners shall be liable for income tax only in their separate or individual capacities.

§ 702. Income and credits of partner

(a) General rule.—In determining his income tax, each partner shall take into account separately his distributive share of the partnership's—

(1) gains and losses from sales or exchanges of capital assets held for not more than 1 year,

(2) gains and losses from sales or exchanges of capital assets held for more than 1 year,

(3) gains and losses from sales or exchanges of property described in section 1231 (relating to certain property used in a trade or business and involuntary conversions),

(4) charitable contributions (as defined in section 170(c)),

(5) dividends with respect to which section 1(h)(11) or part VIII of subchapter B applies,

(6) taxes, described in section 901, paid or accrued to foreign countries and to possessions of the United States,

(7) other items of income, gain, loss, deduction, or credit, to the extent provided by regulations prescribed by the Secretary, and

(8) taxable income or loss, exclusive of items requiring separate computation under other paragraphs of this subsection.

(b) Character of items constituting distributive share.—The character of any item of income, gain, loss, deduction, or credit included in a partner's distributive share under paragraphs (1) through (7) of subsection (a) shall be determined as if such item were realized directly from the source from which realized by the partnership, or incurred in the same manner as incurred by the partnership.

(c) Gross income of a partner.—In any case where it is necessary to determine the gross income of a partner for purposes of this title, such amount shall include his distributive share of the gross income of the partnership.

(d) Cross reference.—

For rules relating to procedures for determining the tax treatment of partnership items see subchapter C of chapter 63 (section 6221 and following).

§ 703. Partnership computations

(a) Income and deductions.—The taxable income of a partnership shall be computed in the same manner as in the case of an individual except that—

(1) the items described in section 702(a) shall be separately stated, and

(2) the following deductions shall not be allowed to the partnership:

(A) the deductions for personal exemptions provided in section 151,

(B) the deduction for taxes provided in section 164(a) with respect to taxes, described in section 901, paid or accrued to foreign countries and to possessions of the United States,

(C) the deduction for charitable contributions provided in section 170,

(D) the net operating loss deduction provided in section 172,

(E) the additional itemized deductions for individuals provided in part VII of subchapter B (sec. 211 and following), and

(F) the deduction for depletion under section 611 with respect to oil and gas wells.

(b) Elections of the partnership.—Any election affecting the computation of taxable income derived from a partnership shall be made by the partnership, except that any election under—

(1) subsection (b)(5) or (c)(3) of section 108 (relating to income from discharge of indebtedness),

(2) section 617 (relating to deduction and recapture of certain mining exploration expenditures), or

(3) section 901 (relating to taxes of foreign countries and possessions of the United States),

shall be made by each partner separately.

§ 704. Partner's distributive share

(a) Effect of partnership agreement.—A partner's distributive share of income, gain, loss, deduction, or credit shall, except as otherwise provided in this chapter, be determined by the partnership agreement.

(b) Determination of distributive share.—A partner's distributive share of income, gain, loss, deduction, or credit (or item thereof) shall be determined in accordance with the partner's interest in the partnership (determined by taking into account all facts and circumstances), if—

(1) the partnership agreement does not provide as to the partner's distributive share of income, gain, loss, deduction, or credit (or item thereof), or

(2) the allocation to a partner under the agreement of income, gain, loss, deduction, or credit (or item thereof) does not have substantial economic effect.

(c) Contributed property.—

(1) In general.—Under regulations prescribed by the Secretary—

(A) income, gain, loss, and deduction with respect to property contributed to the partnership by a partner shall be shared among the partners so as to take account of the variation between the basis of the property to the partnership and its fair market value at the time of contribution,

(B) if any property so contributed is distributed (directly or indirectly) by the partnership (other than to the contributing partner) within 7 years of being contributed—

(i) the contributing partner shall be treated as recognizing gain or loss (as the case may be) from the sale of such property in an amount equal to the gain or loss which would have been allocated to such partner under subparagraph (A) by reason of the variation described in subparagraph (A) if the property had been sold at its fair market value at the time of the distribution,

(ii) the character of such gain or loss shall be determined by reference to the character of the gain or loss which would have resulted if such property had been sold by the partnership to the distributee, and

(iii) appropriate adjustments shall be made to the adjusted basis of the contributing partner's interest in the partnership and to the adjusted basis of the property distributed to reflect any gain or loss recognized under this subparagraph, and

(C) if any property so contributed has a built-in loss—

(i) such built-in loss shall be taken into account only in determining the amount of items allocated to the contributing partner, and

(ii) except as provided in regulations, in determining the amount of items allocated to other partners, the basis of the contributed property in the hands of the partnership shall be treated as being equal to its fair market value at the time of contribution.

For purposes of subparagraph (C), the term "built-in loss" means the excess of the adjusted basis of the property (determined without regard to subparagraph (C)(ii)) over its fair market value at the time of contribution.

(2) Special rule for distributions where gain or loss would not be recognized outside partnerships.—Under regulations prescribed by the Secretary, if—

(A) property contributed by a partner (hereinafter referred to as the "contributing partner") is distributed by the partnership to another partner, and

(B) other property of a like kind (within the meaning of section 1031) is distributed by the partnership to the contributing partner not later than the earlier of—

(i) the 180th day after the date of the distribution described in subparagraph (A), or

(ii) the due date (determined with regard to extensions) for the contributing partner's return of the tax imposed by this chapter for the taxable year in which the distribution described in subparagraph (A) occurs,

then to the extent of the value of the property described in subparagraph (B), paragraph (1)(B) shall be applied as if the contributing partner had contributed to the partnership the property described in subparagraph (B).

(3) Other rules.—Under regulations prescribed by the Secretary, rules similar to the rules of paragraph (1) shall apply to contributions by a partner (using the cash receipts and disbursements method of accounting) of accounts payable and other accrued but unpaid items. Any reference in paragraph (1) or (2) to the contributing partner shall be treated as including a reference to any successor of such partner.

(d) Limitation on allowance of losses.—A partner's distributive share of partnership loss (including capital loss) shall be allowed only to the extent of the adjusted basis of such partner's interest in the partnership at the end of the partnership year in which such loss occurred. Any excess of such loss over such basis shall be allowed as a deduction at the end of the partnership year in which such excess is repaid to the partnership.

(e) Family partnerships.—

(1) Recognition of interest created by purchase or gift.—A person shall be recognized as a partner for purposes of this subtitle if he owns a capital interest in a partnership in which capital is a material income-producing factor, whether or not such interest was derived by purchase or gift from any other person.

(2) Distributive share of donee includible in gross income.—In the case of any partnership interest created by gift, the distributive share of the donee under the partnership agreement shall be includible in his gross income, except to the extent that such share is determined without allowance of reasonable compensation for services rendered to the partnership by the donor, and except to the extent that the portion of such share attributable to donated capital is proportionately greater than the share of the donor attributable to the donor's capital. The distributive share of a partner in the earnings of the partnership shall not be diminished because of absence due to military service.

(3) Purchase of interest by member of family.—For purposes of this section, an interest purchased by one member of a family from another shall be considered to be created by gift from the seller, and the fair market value of the purchased interest shall be considered to be donated capital. The "family" of any individual shall include only his spouse, ancestors, and lineal descendants, and any trusts for the primary benefit of such persons.

(f) Cross reference.—

For rules in the case of the sale, exchange, liquidation, or reduction of a partner's interest, see section 706(c)(2).

§ 705. Determination of basis of partner's interest

(a) General rule.—The adjusted basis of a partner's interest in a partnership shall, except as provided in subsection (b), be the basis of such interest determined under section 722 (relating to contributions to a partnership) or section 742 (relating to transfers of partnership interests)—

(1) increased by the sum of his distributive share for the taxable year and prior taxable years of —

(A) taxable income of the partnership as determined under section 703(a),

(B) income of the partnership exempt from tax under this title, and

(C) the excess of the deductions for depletion over the basis of the property subject to depletion;

(2) decreased (but not below zero) by distributions by the partnership as provided in section 733 and by the sum of his distributive share for the taxable year and prior taxable years of—

(A) losses of the partnership, and

(B) expenditures of the partnership not deductible in computing its taxable income and not properly chargeable to capital account; and

(3) decreased (but not below zero) by the amount of the partner's deduction for depletion for any partnership oil and gas property to the extent such deduction does not exceed the proportionate share of the adjusted basis of such property allocated to such partner under section 613A(c)(7)(D).

(b) Alternative rule.—The Secretary shall prescribe by regulations the circumstances under which the adjusted basis of a partner's interest in a partnership may be determined by reference to his proportionate share of the adjusted basis of partnership property upon a termination of the partnership.

§ 706. Taxable years of partner and partnership

(a) Year in which partnership income is includible.— In computing the taxable income of a partner for a taxable year, the inclusions required by section 702 and section 707(c) with respect to a partnership shall be based on the income, gain, loss, deduction, or credit of the partnership for any taxable year of the partnership ending within or with the taxable year of the partner.

(b) Taxable year.—

(1) Partnership's taxable year.—

(A) Partnership treated as taxpayer.—The taxable year of a partnership shall be determined as though the partnership were a taxpayer.

(B) Taxable year determined by reference to partners.—Except as provided in subparagraph (C), a partnership shall not have a taxable year other than—

(i) the majority interest taxable year (as defined in paragraph (4)),

(ii) if there is no taxable year described in clause (i), the taxable year of all the principal partners of the partnership, or

(iii) if there is no taxable year described in clause (i) or (ii), the calendar year unless the Secretary by regulations prescribes another period.

(C) Business purpose.—A partnership may have a taxable year not described in subparagraph (B) if it establishes, to the satisfaction of the Secretary, a business purpose therefor. For purposes of this subparagraph, any deferral of income to partners shall not be treated as a business purpose.

(2) Partner's taxable year.—A partner may not change to a taxable year other than that of a partnership in which he is a principal partner unless he establishes, to the satisfaction of the Secretary, a business purpose therefor.

(3) Principal partner.—For the purpose of this subsection, a principal partner is a partner having an interest of 5 percent or more in partnership profits or capital.

(4) Majority interest taxable year; limitation on required changes.—

(A) Majority interest taxable year defined.—For purposes of paragraph (1)(B)(i)—

(i) In general.—The term "majority interest taxable year" means the taxable year (if any) which, on each testing day, constituted the taxable year of 1 or more partners having (on such day) an aggregate interest in partnership profits and capital of more than 50 percent.

(ii) Testing days.—The testing days shall be—

(I) the 1st day of the partnership taxable year (determined without regard to clause (i)), or

(II) the days during such representative period as the Secretary may prescribe.

(B) Further change not required for 3 years.—Except as provided in regulations necessary to prevent the avoidance of this section, if, by reason of paragraph (1)(B)(i), the taxable year of a partnership is changed, such partnership shall not be required to change to another taxable year for either of the 2 taxable years following the year of change.

(5) Application with other sections.—Except as provided in regulations, for purposes of determining the taxable year to which a partnership is required to change by reason of this subsection, changes in taxable years of other persons required by this subsection, section 441(i), section 584(h), section 644, or section 1378(a) shall be taken into account.

(c) Closing of partnership year.—

(1) General rule.—Except in the case of a termination of a partnership and except as provided in paragraph (2) of this subsection, the taxable year of a partnership shall not close as the result of the death of a partner, the entry of a new partner, the liquidation of a partner's interest in the partnership, or the sale or exchange of a partner's interest in the partnership.

(2) Treatment of dispositions.—

(A) Disposition of entire interest.—The taxable year of a partnership shall close with respect to a partner whose entire interest in the partnership terminates (whether by reason of death, liquidation, or otherwise).

(B) Disposition of less than entire interest.—The taxable year of a partnership shall not close (other than at the end of a partnership's taxable year as determined under subsection (b)(1)) with respect to a partner who sells or exchanges less than his entire interest in the partnership or with respect to a partner whose interest is reduced (whether by entry of a new partner, partial liquidation of a partner's interest, gift, or otherwise).

(d) Determination of distributive share when partner's interest changes.—

(1) In general.—Except as provided in paragraphs (2) and (3), if during any taxable year of the partnership there is a change in any partner's interest in the partnership, each partner's distributive share of any item of income, gain, loss, deduction, or credit of the partnership for such taxable year shall be determined by the use of any method prescribed by the Secretary by regulations which takes into account the varying interests of the partners in the partnership during such taxable year.

(2) Certain cash basis items prorated over period to which attributable.—

(A) In general.—If during any taxable year of the partnership there is a change in any partner's interest in the partnership, then (except to the extent provided in regulations) each partner's distributive share of any allocable cash basis item shall be determined—

(i) by assigning the appropriate portion of such item to each day in the period to which it is attributable, and

(ii) by allocating the portion assigned to any such day among the partners in proportion to their interests in the partnership at the close of such day.

(B) Allocable cash basis item.—For purposes of this paragraph, the term "allocable cash basis item" means any of the following items with respect to which the partnership uses the cash receipts and disbursements method of accounting:

(i) Interest.

(ii) Taxes.

(iii) Payments for services or for the use of property.

(iv) Any other item of a kind specified in regulations prescribed by the Secretary as being an item with respect to which the application of this paragraph is appropriate to avoid significant misstatements of the income of the partners.

(C) Items attributable to periods not within taxable year.—If any portion of any allocable cash basis item is attributable to—

(i) any period before the beginning of the taxable year, such portion shall be assigned under subparagraph (A)(i) to the first day of the taxable year, or

(ii) any period after the close of the taxable year, such portion shall be assigned under subparagraph (A)(i) to the last day of the taxable year.

(D) Treatment of deductible items attributable to prior periods.—If any portion of a deductible cash basis item is assigned under subparagraph (C)(i) to the first day of any taxable year—

(i) such portion shall be allocated among persons who are partners in the partnership during the period to which such portion is attributable in accordance with their varying interests in the partnership during such period, and

(ii) any amount allocated under clause (i) to a person who is not a partner in the partnership on such first day shall be capitalized by the partnership and treated in the manner provided for in section 755.

(3) Items attributable to interest in lower tier partnership prorated over entire taxable year.—If—

(A) during any taxable year of the partnership there is a change in any partner's interest in the partnership (hereinafter in this paragraph referred to as the "upper tier partnership"), and

(B) such partnership is a partner in another partnership (hereinafter in this paragraph referred to as the "lower tier partnership"),

then (except to the extent provided in regulations) each partner's distributive share of any item of the upper tier partnership attributable to the lower tier partnership shall be determined by assigning the appropriate portion (determined by applying principles similar to the principles of subparagraphs (C) and (D) of paragraph (2)) of each such item to the appropriate days during which the upper tier partnership is a partner in the lower tier partnership and by allocating the portion assigned to any such day among the partners in proportion to their interests in the upper tier partnership at the close of such day.

(4) Taxable year determined without regard to subsection (c)(2)(A).—For purposes of this subsection, the taxable year of a partnership shall be determined without regard to subsection (c)(2)(A).

§ 707. Transactions between partner and partnership

(a) Partner not acting in capacity as partner.—

(1) In general.—If a partner engages in a transaction with a partnership other than in his capacity as a member of such partnership, the transaction shall, except as otherwise provided in this section, be considered as occurring between the partnership and one who is not a partner.

(2) Treatment of payments to partners for property or services.—Under regulations prescribed by the Secretary—

(A) Treatment of certain services and transfers of property.—If—

(i) a partner performs services for a partnership or transfers property to a partnership,

(ii) there is a related direct or indirect allocation and distribution to such partner, and

(iii) the performance of such services (or such transfer) and the allocation and distribution, when viewed together, are properly characterized as a transaction occurring between the partnership and a partner acting other than in his capacity as a member of the partnership,

such allocation and distribution shall be treated as a transaction described in paragraph (1).

(B) Treatment of certain property transfers.—If—

(i) there is a direct or indirect transfer of money or other property by a partner to a partnership,

(ii) there is a related direct or indirect transfer of money or other property by the partnership to such partner (or another partner), and

(iii) the transfers described in clauses (i) and (ii), when viewed together, are properly characterized as a sale or exchange of property,

such transfers shall be treated either as a transaction described in paragraph (1) or as a transaction between 2 or more partners acting other than in their capacity as members of the partnership.

(b) Certain sales or exchanges of property with respect to controlled partnerships.—

(1) Losses disallowed.—No deduction shall be allowed in respect of losses from sales or exchanges of property (other than an interest in the partnership), directly or indirectly, between—

(A) a partnership and a person owning, directly or indirectly, more than 50 percent of the capital interest, or the profits interest, in such partnership, or

(B) two partnerships in which the same persons own, directly or indirectly, more than 50 percent of the capital interests or profits interests.

In the case of a subsequent sale or exchange by a transferee described in this paragraph, section 267(d) shall be applicable as if the loss were disallowed under section 267(a)(1). For purposes of section 267(a)(2), partnerships described in subparagraph (B) of this paragraph shall be treated as persons specified in section 267(b).

(2) Gains treated as ordinary income.—In the case of a sale or exchange, directly or indirectly, of property, which in the hands of the transferee, is property other than a capital asset as defined in section 1221—

(A) between a partnership and a person owning, directly or indirectly, more than 50 percent of the capital interest, or profits interest, in such partnership, or

(B) between two partnerships in which the same persons own, directly or indirectly, more than 50 percent of the capital interests or profits interests,

any gain recognized shall be considered as ordinary income.

(3) Ownership of a capital or profits interest.—For purposes of paragraphs (1) and (2) of this subsection, the ownership of a capital or profits interest in a partnership shall be determined in accordance with the rules for constructive ownership of stock provided in section 267(c) other than paragraph (3) of such section.

(c) Guaranteed payments.—To the extent determined without regard to the income of the partnership, payments to a partner for services or the use of capital shall be considered as made to one who is not a member of the partnership, but only for the purposes of section 61(a) (relating to gross income) and, subject to section 263, for purposes of section 162(a) (relating to trade or business expenses).

§ 708. Continuation of partnership

(a) General rule.—For purposes of this subchapter, an existing partnership shall be considered as continuing if it is not terminated.

(b) Termination.—

(1) General rule.—For purposes of subsection (a), a partnership shall be considered as terminated only if—

(A) no part of any business, financial operation, or venture of the partnership continues to be carried on by any of its partners in a partnership, or

(B) within a 12-month period there is a sale or exchange of 50 percent or more of the total interest in partnership capital and profits.

(2) Special rules.—

(A) Merger or consolidation.—In the case of the merger or consolidation of two or more partnerships, the resulting partnership shall, for purposes of this section, be considered the continuation of any merging or consolidating partnership whose members own an interest of more than 50 percent in the capital and profits of the resulting partnership.

(B) Division of a partnership.—In the case of a division of a partnership into two or more partnerships, the resulting partnerships (other than any resulting partnership the members of which had an interest of 50 percent or less in the capital and profits of the prior partnership) shall, for purposes of this section, be considered a continuation of the prior partnership.

§ 709. Treatment of organization and syndication fees

(a) General rule.—Except as provided in subsection (b), no deduction shall be allowed under this chapter to the partnership or to any partner for any amounts paid or incurred to organize a partnership or to promote the sale of (or to sell) an interest in such partnership.

(b) Deduction of organization fees.—

(1) Allowance of deduction.—If a partnership elects the application of this subsection (in accordance with regulations prescribed by the Secretary) with respect to any organizational expenses—

(A) the partnership shall be allowed a deduction for the taxable year in which the partnership begins business in an amount equal to the lessor of—

(i) the amount of organizational expenses with respect to the partnership, or

(ii) $5,000, reduced (but not below zero) by the amount by which such organizational expenses exceed $50,000, and

(B) the remainder of such organizational expenses shall be allowed as a deduction ratably over the 180-month period beginning with the month in which the partnership begins business.

(2) Dispositions before close of amortization period.—In any case in which a partnership is liquidated before the end of the period to which paragraph (1)(B) applies, any deferred expenses attributable to the partnership which were not allowed as a deduction by reason of this section may be deducted to the extent allowable under section 165.

(3) Organizational expenses defined.—The organizational expenses to which paragraph (1) applies, are expenditures which—

(A) are incident to the creation of the partnership;

(B) are chargeable to capital account; and

(C) are of a character which, if expended incident to the creation of a partnership having an ascertainable life, would be amortized over such life.

PART II—CONTRIBUTIONS, DISTRIBUTIONS, AND TRANSFERS

SUBPART A—CONTRIBUTIONS TO A PARTNERSHIP

Editorial Summary

Partnership Contributions

Subchapter K of Chapter 1 (Secs. 721–724)

Aggregate or proprietary theory governs the tax treatment of contributions of property by the partner to the partnership in exchange for an interest in the partnership. The contribution is treated as a nontaxable exchange with no recognition of realized gain or loss at the partner or partnership level [see Sec. 721(a)]. The partner's basis for his partnership interest (i.e., "outside basis") is a carryover basis and the partnership's basis for the contributed assets (i.e., "inside basis") is a carryover basis [see Secs. 722, 723].

For the nonrecognition treatment to apply, property must be contributed by the partner. No control requirements are applicable as is the case for corporate contributions under Sec. 351. If part or all of the partnership interest is received by the partner in exchange for services, however, the partnership interest received for services performed or to be performed by the partner is taxable to the partner. In addition, liabilities of the partner that are assumed by the partnership may result in the recognition of gain at the partner level [see Sec. 752(b)]. Finally, nonrecognition of gain treatment will not apply if the partnership is an investment company as defined under Sec. 351 [see Sec. 721(b)].

While the "inside basis" for contributed property under Sec. 723 is a carryover basis [adjusted for gain recognized under Sec. 721(b)], the classification (i.e., capital or ordinary) of gains or losses on subsequent dispositions of the property by the partnership is determined at the partnership level. Section 724 contains exceptions for unrealized receivables, inventory items, and property which was capital loss property in the hands of the contributing partner. The exception (i.e., taint) for inventory and capital loss property is temporary in that it apples only for a 5-year period whereas the exception for unrealized receivables is permanent.

§ 721. Nonrecognition of gain or loss on contribution

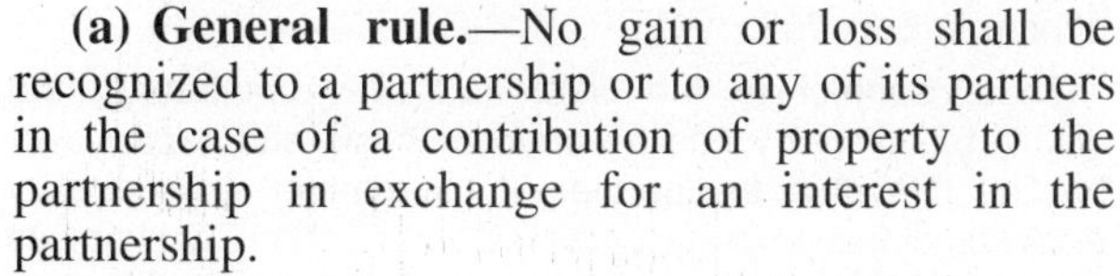

(a) General rule.—No gain or loss shall be recognized to a partnership or to any of its partners in the case of a contribution of property to the partnership in exchange for an interest in the partnership.

(b) Special rule.—Subsection (a) shall not apply to gain realized on a transfer of property to a partnership which would be treated as an investment company (within the meaning of section 351) if the partnership were incorporated.

(c) Regulations relating to certain transfers to partnerships.—The Secretary may provide by regulations that subsection (a) shall not apply to gain realized on the transfer of property to a partnership if such gain, when recognized, will be includible in the gross income of a person other than a United States person.

(d) Transfers of intangibles.—

For regulatory authority to treat intangibles transferred to a partnership as sold, see section 367(d)(3).

§ 722. Basis of contributing partner's interest

The basis of an interest in a partnership acquired by a contribution of property, including money, to the partnership shall be the amount of such money and the adjusted basis of such property to the contributing partner at the time of the contribution increased by the amount (if any) of gain recognized under section 721(b) to the contributing partner at such time.

§ 723. Basis of property contributed to partnership

The basis of property contributed to a partnership by a partner shall be the adjusted basis of such property to the contributing partner at the time of the contribution increased by the amount (if any) of gain recognized under section 721(b) to the contributing partner at such time.

§ 724. Character of gain or loss on contributed unrealized receivables, inventory items, and capital loss property

(a) Contributions of unrealized receivables.—In the case of any property which—

(1) was contributed to the partnership by a partner, and

(2) was an unrealized receivable in the hands of such partner immediately before such contribution,

any gain or loss recognized by the partnership on the disposition of such property shall be treated as ordinary income or ordinary loss, as the case may be.

(b) Contributions of inventory items.—In the case of any property which—

(1) was contributed to the partnership by a partner, and

(2) was an inventory item in the hands of such partner immediately before such contribution,

any gain or loss recognized by the partnership on the disposition of such property during the 5-year period beginning on the date of such contribution shall be treated as ordinary income or ordinary loss, as the case may be.

(c) Contributions of capital loss property.—In the case of any property which—

(1) was contributed by a partner to the partnership, and

(2) was a capital asset in the hands of such partner immediately before such contribution,

any loss recognized by the partnership on the disposition of such property during the 5-year period beginning on the date of such contribution shall be treated as a loss from the sale of a capital asset to the extent that, immediately before such contribution, the adjusted basis of such property in the hands of the partner exceeded the fair market value of such property.

(d) Definitions.—For purposes of this section—

(1) Unrealized receivable.—The term "unrealized receivable" has the meaning given such term by section 751(c) (determined by treating any reference to the partnership as referring to the partner).

(2) Inventory item.—The term "inventory item" has the meaning given such term by section 751(d) (determined by treating any reference to the partnership as referring to the partner and by applying section 1231 without regard to any holding period therein provided).

(3) Substituted basis property.—

(A) In general.—If any property described in subsection (a), (b), or (c) is disposed of in a nonrecognition transaction, the tax treatment which applies to such property under such subsection shall also apply to any substituted basis property resulting from such transaction. A similar rule shall also apply in the case of a series of non-recognition transactions.

(B) Exception for stock in C corporation.—Subparagraph (A) shall not apply to any stock in a C corporation received in an exchange described in section 351.

SUBPART B—DISTRIBUTIONS BY A PARTNERSHIP

Editorial Summary

Partnership Distributions: Nonliquidating

Subchapter K of Chapter 1 (Secs. 731–737, 754, 755)

Since the nonliquidating partnership distribution rules apply aggregate or proprietary theory, the general rule is that such distributions do not produce recognized gain or loss. An exception is provided in Sec. 731(a)(1) that if the amount of money distributed to a partner exceeds his or her basis for the partnership interest (i.e., "outside basis"), then gain is recognized to the partner to the extent of the excess. In addition, two exceptions are provided in Sec. 731(c) with respect to Sec. 736 payments (but not applicable to nonliquidating distributions) and to Sec. 751 assets.

The "outside basis" of the partner is reduced by the partnership's basis for the property distributed to the partner. In addition, Sec. 733 provides that the "outside basis" of the partner may not be reduced below zero as the result of the distribution. If no gain is recognized by the partner on the distribution, Sec. 732(a)(1) provides that the basis of the distributed property to the partner is a carryover basis. However, this is subject to the limitation that such carryover basis cannot exceed the "outside basis" of the recipient partner [see Sec. 732(a)(2)]. If such an excess asset basis does exist, this excess will be permanently wasted unless an election is made or is in effect under Sec. 754, which operationally activates the optional adjustment to basis provision of Sec. 734. The related basis allocation rules appear in Sec. 755.

Thus, subject to the Sec. 732(a)(2) limitations, the distributed property has a carryover basis and a carryover holding period to the partner. If the partner subsequently disposes of this property in a taxable transaction, gain or loss is recognized to the partner, and in general, the classification (i.e., capital or ordinary) is determined at the partner level. However, Sec. 735 provides exception treatment for unrealized receivables and inventory items. The exception (i.e., taint) for inventory is temporary in that it applies only for a 5-year period whereas the exception for unrealized receivables is permanent.

Editorial Summary

Partnership Distributions: Liquidating

Subchapter K of Chapter 1 (Secs. 731–736, 754, 755)

A liquidating distribution differs from a nonliquidating distribution in that in a liquidating distribution a partner terminates his or her interest as a partner. The tax treatment is similar, however, in that aggregate or proprietary theory is applied in Sec. 731(a) for a liquidating distribution. Therefore, realized gain is recognized to the partner only if money is received that exceeds the outside basis of the partner.

A difference does exist with respect to the treatment of realized losses. While the statutory objective is not to have losses recognized at the time of the distribution, in one limited circumstance the loss must be recognized. This occurs if the only property received by the partner is money and/or Sec. 751 property, that is, unrealized receivables as defined in Sec. 751(c) and inventory as defined in Sec. 751(d)(2), and the partner's outside basis exceeds the partnership's basis for the assets distributed to the partner. If any other assets are received by the partner, any realized loss is not recognized.

The general nonrecognition of realized gain or loss is accomplished through the basis the partner assigns to the property received under Sec. 732(b). The partner's outside basis is reduced by the money received. The partner then assigns his or her remaining outside basis to the other assets received. Section 732(c) contains the rules for the allocation of the remaining outside basis among the assets received.

If the partner subsequently disposes of the distributed property in a taxable transaction, gain or loss is recognized to the partner, and in general, the classification (i.e., capital or ordinary) is determined at the partner level. However, Sec. 735 provides exception treatment for unrealized receivables and inventory items. The exception (i.e., taint) for inventory is temporary in that it applies only for a 5-year period whereas the exception for unrealized receivables is permanent.

The statutory objective of nonrecognition and the related basis assignment rules for the partner produce the result that "lost" basis (i.e., the partner's outside basis is less than the partnership's basis for the assets distributed) or "found" basis (i.e., the partner's outside basis is greater than the partnership's basis for the assets distributed) may occur. This "lost" or "found" basis will be permanent unless an election is made or is in effect under Sec. 754 or unless there is a substantial basis reduction with respect to the distribution [Section 734(d)]. Under the Sec. 754 election, Sec. 734 is activated which results in the basis of partnership assets being increased by the amount of the "lost" basis or decreased by the amount of the "found" basis. The rules for the basis allocation appear in Sec. 755.

Exceptions to the general rules for liquidating distributions are contained in Sec. 736 (relating to a retiring partner or a deceased partner's successor) and Sec. 751 (relating to the distribution of "hot" assets). Section 736 provides flexibility to the partners with respect to classification for capital or ordinary treatment (i.e., is the payment a property payment or an income payment). As previously discussed, payments for the partner's interest in the partnership qualify for capital gain or loss treatment. To the extent the liquidating payments to this partner are treated as Sec. 736(b) payments, this is the result that occurs. However, to the extent that the liquidating payments to the partner are treated as Sec. 736(a) payments, the recipient partner has ordinary income and the payment by the partnership is treated as a distributive share or as a guaranteed payment (i.e., partnership has an ordinary deduction). Section 736(a) payments consist of payments for unrealized receivables and for unstated goodwill in excess of basis. Thus, the character of the gain to the recipient partner can be dependent on whether or not goodwill is stated (i.e., covered by the partnership agreement) or unstated.

The flexibility to label payments to a retiring partner or a deceased partner's successor in interest as an income payment or as a property payment is restricted by the Revenue Reconciliation Act of 1993. In order for payments to be labeled as income payments, both of the following additional requirements must be satisfied [see Sec. 736(b)(3)].

1. The retiring or deceased partner was a general partner.
2. Capital is not a material income-producing factor for the partnership.

Thus, the flexibility would exist for an accounting firm or a law firm, but would not exist for a hardware store or for a limited partner.

§ 731. Extent of recognition of gain or loss on distribution

(a) Partners.—In the case of a distribution by a partnership to a partner—

(1) gain shall not be recognized to such partner, except to the extent that any money distributed exceeds the adjusted basis of such partner's interest in the partnership immediately before the distribution, and

(2) loss shall not be recognized to such partner, except that upon a distribution in liquidation of a partner's interest in a partnership where no property other than that described in subparagraph (A) or (B) is distributed to such partner, loss shall be recognized to the extent of the excess of the adjusted basis of such partner's interest in the partnership over the sum of—

(A) any money distributed, and

(B) the basis to the distributee, as determined under section 732, of any unrealized receivables (as defined in section 751(c)) and inventory (as defined in section 751(d)).

Any gain or loss recognized under this subsection shall be considered as gain or loss from the sale or exchange of the partnership interest of the distributee partner.

(b) Partnerships.—No gain or loss shall be recognized to a partnership on a distribution to a partner of property, including money.

(c) Treatment of marketable securities.—

(1) In general.—For purposes of subsection (a)(1) and section 737—

(A) the term "money" includes marketable securities, and

(B) such securities shall be taken into account at their fair market value as of the date of the distribution.

(2) Marketable securities.—For purposes of this subsection:

(A) In general.—The term "marketable securities" means financial instruments and foreign currencies which are, as of the date of the distribution, actively traded (within the meaning of section 1092(d)(1)).

(B) Other property.—Such term includes—

(i) any interest in—

(I) a common trust fund, or

(II) a regulated investment company which is offering for sale or has outstanding any redeemable security (as defined in section 2(a)(32) of the Investment Company Act of 1940) of which it is the issuer,

(ii) any financial instrument which, pursuant to its terms or any other arrangement, is readily convertible into, or exchangeable for, money or marketable securities,

(iii) any financial instrument the value of which is determined substantially by reference to marketable securities,

(iv) except to the extent provided in regulations prescribed by the Secretary, any interest in a precious metal which, as of the date of the distribution, is actively traded (within the meaning of section 1092(d)(1)) unless such metal was produced, used, or held in the active conduct of a trade or business by the partnership,

(v) except as otherwise provided in regulations prescribed by the Secretary, interests in any entity if substantially all of the assets of such entity consist (directly or indirectly) of marketable securities, money, or both, and

(vi) to the extent provided in regulations prescribed by the Secretary, any interest in an entity not described in clause (v) but only to the extent of the value of such interest which is attributable to marketable securities, money, or both.

(C) Financial instrument.—The term "financial instrument" includes stocks and other equity interests, evidences of indebtedness, options, forward or futures contracts, notional principal contracts, and derivatives.

(3) Exceptions.—

(A) In general.—Paragraph (1) shall not apply to the distribution from a partnership of a marketable security to a partner if—

(i) the security was contributed to the partnership by such partner, except to the extent that the value of the distributed security is attributable to marketable securities or money contributed (directly or indirectly) to the entity to which the distributed security relates,

(ii) to the extent provided in regulations prescribed by the Secretary, the property was not a marketable security when acquired by such partnership, or

(iii) such partnership is an investment partnership and such partner is an eligible partner thereof.

(B) Limitation on gain recognized.—In the case of a distribution of marketable securities to a partner, the amount taken into account under paragraph (1) shall be reduced (but not below zero) by the excess (if any) of—

(i) such partner's distributive share of the net gain which would be recognized if all of the marketable securities of the same class and issuer as the distributed securities held by the partnership were sold (immediately before the transaction to which the distribution relates) by the partnership for fair market value, over

(ii) such partner's distributive share of the net gain which is attributable to the marketable securities of the same class and issuer as the distributed securities held by the partnership immediately after the transaction, determined by using the same fair market value as used under clause (i).

Under regulations prescribed by the Secretary, all marketable securities held by the partnership may be treated as marketable securities of the same class and issuer as the distributed securities.

(C) Definitions relating to investment partnerships.—For purposes of subparagraph (A)(iii):

(i) Investment partnership.—The term "investment partnership" means any partnership which has never been engaged in a trade or business and substantially all of the assets (by value) of which have always consisted of—

(I) money,

(II) stock in a corporation,

(III) notes, bonds, debentures, or other evidences of indebtedness,

(IV) interest rate, currency, or equity notional principal contracts,

(V) foreign currencies,

(VI) interests in or derivative financial instruments (including options, forward or futures contracts, short positions, and similar financial instruments) in any asset described in any other subclause of this clause or in any commodity traded on or subject to the rules of a board of trade or commodity exchange,

(VII) other assets specified in regulations prescribed by the Secretary, or

(VIII) any combination of the foregoing.

(ii) Exception for certain activities.—A partnership shall not be treated as engaged in a trade or business by reason of—

(I) any activity undertaken as an investor, trader, or dealer in any asset described in clause (i), or

(II) any other activity specified in regulations prescribed by the Secretary.

(iii) Eligible partner.—

(I) In general.—The term "eligible partner" means any partner who, before the date of the distribution, did not contribute to the partnership any property other than assets described in clause (i).

(II) Exception for certain nonrecognition transactions.—The term "eligible partner" shall not include the transferor or transferee in a nonrecognition transaction involving a transfer of any portion of an interest in a partnership with respect to which the transferor was not an eligible partner.

(iv) Look-thru of partnership tiers.—Except as otherwise provided in regulations prescribed by the Secretary—

(I) a partnership shall be treated as engaged in any trade or business engaged in by, and as holding (instead of a partnership interest) a proportionate share of the assets of, any other partnership in which the partnership holds a partnership interest, and

(II) a partner who contributes to a partnership an interest in another partnership shall be treated as contributing a proportionate share of the assets of the other partnership.

If the preceding sentence does not apply under such regulations with respect to any interest held by a partnership in another partnership, the interest in such other partnership shall be treated as if it were specified in a subclause of clause (i).

(4) Basis of securities distributed.—

(A) In general.—The basis of marketable securities with respect to which gain is recognized by reason of this subsection shall be—

(i) their basis determined under section 732, increased by

(ii) the amount of such gain.

(B) Allocation of basis increase.—Any increase in basis attributable to the gain described in subparagraph (A)(ii) shall be allocated to marketable securities in proportion to their respective amounts of unrealized appreciation before such increase.

(5) Subsection disregarded in determining basis of partner's interest in partnership and of basis of partnership property.—Sections 733 and 734 shall be applied as if no gain were recognized, and no adjustment were made to the basis of property, under this subsection.

(6) Character of gain recognized.—In the case of a distribution of a marketable security which is an unrealized receivable (as defined in section 751(c)) or an inventory item (as defined in section 751(d)), any gain recognized under this subsection shall be treated as ordinary income to the extent of any increase in the basis of such security attributable to the gain described in paragraph (4)(A)(ii).

(7) Regulations.—The Secretary shall prescribe such regulations as may be necessary or appropriate to carry out the purposes of this subsection, including regulations to prevent the avoidance of such purposes.

(d) Exceptions.—This section shall not apply to the extent otherwise provided by section 736 (relating to payments to a retiring partner or a deceased partner's successor in interest), section 751 (relating to unrealized receivables and inventory items), and section 737 (relating to recognition of precontribution gain in case of certain distributions).

§ 732. Basis of distributed property other than money

(a) Distributions other than in liquidation of a partner's interest.—

(1) General rule.—The basis of property (other than money) distributed by a partnership to a partner other than in liquidation of the partner's interest shall, except as provided in paragraph (2), be its adjusted basis to the partnership immediately before such distribution.

(2) Limitation.—The basis to the distributee partner of property to which paragraph (1) is applicable shall not exceed the adjusted basis of such partner's interest in the partnership reduced by any money distributed in the same transaction.

(b) Distributions in liquidation.—The basis of property (other than money) distributed by a partnership to a partner in liquidation of the partner's interest shall be an amount equal to the adjusted basis of such partner's interest in the partnership reduced by any money distributed in the same transaction.

(c) Allocation of basis.—

(1) In general.—The basis of distributed properties to which subsection (a)(2) or (b) is applicable shall be allocated—

(A)(i) first to any unrealized receivables (as defined in section 751(c)) and inventory items (as defined in section 751(d)) in an amount equal to the adjusted basis of each such property to the partnership, and

(ii) if the basis to be allocated is less than the sum of the adjusted bases of such properties to the partnership, then, to the extent any decrease is required in order to have the adjusted bases of such properties equal the basis to be allocated, in the manner provided in paragraph (3), and

(B) to the extent of any basis remaining after the allocation under subparagraph (A), to other distributed properties—

(i) first by assigning to each such other property such other property's adjusted basis to the partnership, and

(ii) then, to the extent any increase or decrease in basis is required in order to have the adjusted bases of such other distributed properties equal such remaining basis, in the manner provided in paragraph (2) or (3), whichever is appropriate.

(2) Methods of allocating increase.—Any increase required under paragraph (1)(B) shall be allocated among the properties—

(A) first to properties with unrealized appreciation in proportion to their respective amounts of unrealized appreciation before such increase (but only to the extent of each property's unrealized appreciation), and

(B) then, to the extent such increase is not allocated under subparagraph (A), in proportion to their respective fair market values.

(3) Method of allocating decrease.—Any decrease required under paragraph (1)(A) or (1)(B) shall be allocated—

(A) first to properties with unrealized depreciation in proportion to their respective amounts of unrealized depreciation before such decrease (but only to the extent of each property's unrealized depreciation), and

(B) then, to the extent such decrease is not allocated under subparagraph (A), in proportion to their respective adjusted bases (as adjusted under subparagraph (A)).

(d) Special partnership basis to transferee.—For purposes of subsections (a), (b), and (c), a partner who acquired all or a part of his interest by a transfer with respect to which the election provided in section 754 is not in effect, and to whom a distribution of property (other than money) is made with respect to the transferred interest within 2 years after such transfer, may elect, under regulations prescribed by the Secretary, to treat as the adjusted partnership basis of such property the adjusted basis such property would have if the adjustment provided in section 743(b) were in effect with respect to the partnership property. The Secretary may by regulations require the application of this subsection in the case of a distribution to a transferee partner, whether or not made within 2 years after the transfer, if at the time of the transfer the fair market value of the partnership property (other than money) exceeded 110 percent of its adjusted basis to the partnership.

(e) Exception.—This section shall not apply to the extent that a distribution is treated as a sale or exchange of property under section 751(b) (relating to unrealized receivables and inventory items).

(f) Corresponding adjustment to basis of assets of a distributed corporation controlled by a corporate partner.

(1) In general.—If—

(A) a corporation (hereafter in this subsection referred to as the "corporate partner") receives a distribution from a partnership of stock in another corporation (hereafter in this subsection referred to as the "distributed corporation"),

(B) the corporate partner has control of the distributed corporation immediately after the distribution or at any time thereafter, and

(C) the partnership's adjusted basis in such stock immediately before the distribution exceeded the corporate partner's adjusted basis in such stock immediately after the distribution,

then an amount equal to such excess shall be applied to reduce (in accordance with subsection (c)) the basis of property held by the distributed corporation at such time (or, if the corporate partner does not control the distributed corporation at such time, at the time the corporate partner first has such control).

(2) Exception for certain distributions before control acquired.—Paragraph (1) shall not apply to any distribution of stock in the distributed corporation if—

(A) the corporate partner does not have control of such corporation immediately after such distribution, and

(B) the corporate partner establishes to the satisfaction of the Secretary that such distribution was not part of a plan or arrangement to acquire control of the distributed corporation.

(3) Limitations on basis reduction.—

(A) In general.—The amount of the reduction under paragraph (1) shall not exceed the amount by which the sum of the aggregate adjusted bases of the property and the amount of money of the distributed corporation exceeds the corporate partner's adjusted basis in the stock of the distributed corporation.

(B) Reduction not to exceed adjusted basis of property. No reduction under paragraph (1) in the basis of any property shall exceed the adjusted basis of such property (determined without regard to such reduction).

(4) Gain recognition where reduction limited.—If the amount of any reduction under paragraph (1) (determined after the application of paragraph (3)(A)) exceeds the aggregate adjusted bases of the property of the distributed corporation—

(A) such excess shall be recognized by the corporate partner as long-term capital gain, and

(B) the corporate partner's adjusted basis in the stock of the distributed corporation shall be increased by such excess.

(5) Control.—For purposes of this subsection, the term "control" means ownership of stock meeting the requirements of section 1504(a)(2).

(6) Indirect distributions.—For purposes of paragraph (1), if a corporation acquires (other than in a distribution from a partnership) stock the basis of which is determined (by reason of being distributed from a partnership) in whole or in part by reference to subsection (a)(2) or (b), the corporation shall be treated as receiving a distribution of such stock from a partnership.

(7) Special rule for stock in controlled corporation.—If the property held by a distributed corporation is stock in a corporation which the distributed corporation controls, this subsection shall be applied to reduce the basis of the property of such controlled corporation. This subsection shall be reapplied to any property of any controlled corporation which is stock in a corporation which it controls.

(8) Regulations.—The Secretary shall prescribe such regulations as may be necessary to carry out the purposes of this subsection, including regulations to avoid double counting and to prevent the abuse of such purposes.

§ 733. Basis of distributee partner's interest

In the case of a distribution by a partnership to a partner other than in liquidation of a partner's interest, the adjusted basis to such partner of his interest in the partnership shall be reduced (but not below zero) by—

(1) the amount of any money distributed to such partner, and

(2) the amount of the basis to such partner of distributed property other than money, as determined under section 732.

§ 734. Adjustment to basis of undistributed partnership property where section 754 election or substantial basis reduction

(a) General rule.—The basis of partnership property shall not be adjusted as the result of a distribution of property to a partner unless the election, provided in section 754 (relating to optional adjustment to basis of partnership property), is in effect with respect to such partnership or unless there is a substantial basis reduction with respect to such distribution.

(b) Method of adjustment.—In the case of a distribution of property to a partner by a partnership with respect to which the election provided in section 754 is in effect or with respect to which there is a substantial basis reduction, the partnership shall—

(1) increase the adjusted basis of partnership property by—

(A) the amount of any gain recognized to the distributee partner with respect to such distribution under section 731(a)(1), and

(B) in the case of distributed property to which section 732(a)(2) or (b) applies, the excess of the adjusted basis of the distributed property to the partnership immediately before the distribution (as adjusted by section 732(d)) over the basis of the distributed property to the distributee, as determined under section 732, or

(2) decrease the adjusted basis of partnership property by—

(A) the amount of any loss recognized to the distributee partner with respect to such distribution under section 731(a)(2), and

(B) in the case of distributed property to which section 732(b) applies, the excess of the basis of the distributed property to the distributee, as determined under section 732, over the adjusted basis of the distributed property to the partnership immediately before such distribution (as adjusted by section 732(d)).

Paragraph (1)(B) shall not apply to any distributed property which is an interest in another partnership with respect to which the election provided in section 754 is not in effect.

(c) Allocation of basis.—The allocation of basis among partnership properties where subsection (b) is applicable shall be made in accordance with the rules provided in section 755.

(d) Substantial basis reduction.—

(1) In general.—For purposes of this section, there is a substantial basis reduction with respect to a distribution if the sum of the amounts described in subparagraphs (A) and (B) of subsection (b)(2) exceeds $250,000.

(2) Regulations.—For regulations to carry out this subsection, see section 743(d)(2).

(e) Exception for securitization partnerships.—For purposes of this section, a securitization partnership (as defined in section 743(f)) shall not be treated as having a substantial basis reduction with respect to any distribution of property to a partner.

§ 735. Character of gain or loss on disposition of distributed property

(a) Sale or exchange of certain distributed property.—

(1) Unrealized receivables.—Gain or loss on the disposition by a distributee partner of unrealized receivables (as defined in section 751(c)) distributed by a partnership, shall be considered as ordinary income or as ordinary loss, as the case may be.

(2) Inventory items.—Gain or loss on the sale or exchange by a distributee partner of inventory items (as defined in section 751(d)) distributed by a partnership shall, if sold or exchanged within

5 years from the date of the distribution, be considered as ordinary income or as ordinary loss, as the case may be.

(b) Holding period for distributed property.—In determining the period for which a partner has held property received in a distribution from a partnership (other than for purposes of subsection (a)(2)), there shall be included the holding period of the partnership, as determined under section 1223, with respect to such property.

(c) Special rules.—

(1) Waiver of holding periods contained in section 1231.—For purposes of this section, section 751(d) (defining inventory item) shall be applied without regard to any holding period in section 1231(b).

(2) Substituted basis property.—

(A) In general.—If any property described in subsection (a) is disposed of in a nonrecognition transaction, the tax treatment which applies to such property under such subsection shall also apply to any substituted basis property resulting from such transaction. A similar rule shall also apply in the case of a series of nonrecognition transactions.

(B) Exception for stock in C corporation.—Subparagraph (A) shall not apply to any stock in a C corporation received in an exchange described in section 351.

§ 736. Payments to a retiring partner or a deceased partner's successor in interest

(a) Payments considered as distributive share or guaranteed payment.—Payments made in liquidation of the interest of a retiring partner or a deceased partner shall, except as provided in subsection (b), be considered—

(1) as a distributive share to the recipient of partnership income if the amount thereof is determined with regard to the income of the partnership, or

(2) as a guaranteed payment described in section 707(c) if the amount thereof is determined without regard to the income of the partnership.

(b) Payments for interest in partnership.—

(1) General rule.—Payments made in liquidation of the interest of a retiring partner or a deceased partner shall, to the extent such payments (other than payments described in paragraph (2)) are determined, under regulations prescribed by the Secretary, to be made in exchange for the interest of such partner in partnership property, be considered as a distribution by the partnership and not as a distributive share or guaranteed payment under subsection (a).

(2) Special rules.—For purposes of this subsection, payments in exchange for an interest in partnership property shall not include amounts paid for—

(A) unrealized receivables of the partnership (as defined in section 751(c)), or

(B) good will of the partnership, except to the extent that the partnership agreement provides for a payment with respect to good will.

(3) Limitation on application of paragraph (2).—Paragraph (2) shall apply only if—

(A) capital is not a material income-producing factor for the partnership, and

(B) the retiring or deceased partner was a general partner in the partnership.

§ 737. Recognition of precontribution gain in case of certain distributions to contributing partner

(a) General rule.—In the case of any distribution by a partnership to a partner, such partner shall be treated as recognizing gain in an amount equal to the lesser of—

(1) the excess (if any) of (A) the fair market value of property (other than money) received in the distribution over (B) the adjusted basis of such partner's interest in the partnership immediately before the distribution reduced (but not below zero) by the amount of money received in the distribution, or

(2) the net precontribution gain of the partner.

Gain recognized under the preceding sentence shall be in addition to any gain recognized under section 731. The character of such gain shall be determined by reference to the proportionate character of the net precontribution gain.

(b) Net precontribution gain.—For purposes of this section, the term "net precontribution gain" means the net gain (if any) which would have been recognized by the distributee partner under section 704(c)(1)(B) if all property which—

(1) had been contributed to the partnership by the distributee partner within 7 years of the distribution, and

(2) is held by such partnership immediately before the distribution,

had been distributed by such partnership to another partner.

(c) Basis rules.—

(1) Partner's interest.—The adjusted basis of a partner's interest in a partnership shall be increased by the amount of any gain recognized by such partner under subsection (a). For purposes of determining the basis of the distributed property (other than money), such increase shall be treated as occurring immediately before the distribution.

(2) Partnership's basis in contributed property.—Appropriate adjustments shall be made to the adjusted basis of the partnership in the contributed property referred to in subsection (b) to reflect gain recognized under subsection (a).

(d) Exceptions.—

(1) Distributions of previously contributed property.—If any portion of the property distributed consists of property which had been contributed by the distributee partner to the partnership, such property shall not be taken into account under subsection (a)(1) and shall not be taken into account in determining the amount of the net precontribution gain. If the property distributed consists of an interest in an entity, the preceding sentence shall not apply to the extent that the value of such interest is attributable to property contributed to such entity after such interest had been contributed to the partnership.

(2) Coordination with section 751.—This section shall not apply to the extent section 751(b) applies to such distribution.

(e) Marketable securities treated as money.—For treatment of marketable securities as money for purposes of this section, see section 731(c).

SUBPART C—TRANSFERS OF INTERESTS IN A PARTNERSHIP

Editorial Summary

Transfers of an Interest in a Partnership Subchapter K of Chapter 1 (Secs. 741–743)

The sale or exchange of some or all of a partnership interest by a partner is a taxable event to the transferor partner [see Sec. 741]. The amount of the recognized gain is the difference between the amount realized and the partner's basis for his or her partnership interest (i.e., "outside basis") or part thereof.

As discussed in previous Editorial Summaries of Subchapter K, in certain circumstances entity theory is applied and in other circumstances aggregate or proprietary theory is applied (i.e., the partnership is a conduit). If aggregate or proprietary theory is applied to the sale of the partnership interest, then the partner would be treated as if selling his or her *pro rata* share of the individual assets of the partnership. Conversely, if entity theory is applied to the sale of the partnership interest, then the partner would be treated as actually selling an asset appropriately labeled "partnership interest." Generally, the sale of the former would result in classification of the gain or loss, consisting of both ordinary income and capital gain or loss components, whereas the sale of the latter would be classified as capital gain or loss.

The initial approach taken by Sec. 741 is to adopt the entity theory, and thereby classify the recognized gain or loss as capital gain or loss. However, an exception is provided with respect to Sec. 751 property (see the Editorial Summary entitled Section 751 Property, which precedes Sec. 751). Thus, the resultant classification of the recognized gain or loss is as capital gain or loss subject to the ordinary income override provision contained in Sec. 751.

Section 742 provides that if a partnership interest is acquired in a transaction other than in the form of a capital contribution by a partner, the "outside basis" of the partner is to be determined under the general basis rules contained in Subchapter O. Other ways of obtaining a partnership interest include purchase, exchange, gift, and inheritance. If the form of the transaction is a capital contribution, then Sec. 742 is not applicable and the "outside basis" is determined instead under Sec. 722 (see the Editorial Summary entitled Partnership Contributions, which precedes Sec. 721).

Section 743 is the operational Code section which is activated for the optional adjustment to the basis of the partnership assets if the election is made by the partnership under Sec. 754. Note that the election under Sec. 754 also activates the operational Code section Sec. 734 for the optional adjustment to the basis of partnership assets associated with partnership distributions (see the Editorial Summary entitled Partnership Distributions: Liquidating, which precedes Sec. 731). The amount of the basis adjustment under Sec. 743 is the difference between the acquiring partner's "outside basis" and his or her *pro rata* share of partnership assets (i.e., "inside basis"). Note that such basis adjustment can be either positive (i.e., the partner's "outside basis" exceeds the partner's share of "inside basis") or negative (i.e., the partner's "outside basis" is less than the partner's share of "inside basis"). Obviously, there would be no personal desire for the partner to have the partnership make the Sec. 754 election if it is going to produce a negative basis adjustment. However, the Sec. 754 election is a continuing election (see Sec. 754). Therefore, the partnership may have elected Sec. 754 at an earlier date. In addition, if there is a substantial built-in loss, the downward basis adjustment is mandatory [see Secs. 743(a) and 743(b)].

§ 741. Recognition and character of gain or loss on sale or exchange

In the case of a sale or exchange of an interest in a partnership, gain or loss shall be recognized to the transferor partner. Such gain or loss shall be considered as gain or loss from the sale or exchange of a capital asset, except as otherwise provided in section 751 (relating to unrealized receivables and inventory).

§ 742. Basis of transferee partner's interest

The basis of an interest in a partnership acquired other than by contribution shall be determined under part II of subchapter O (sec. 1011 and following).

§ 743. Optional adjustment to basis of partnership property

(a) General rule.—The basis of partnership property shall not be adjusted as the result of a transfer of an interest in a partnership by sale or exchange or on the death of a partner unless the election provided by section 754 (relating to optional adjustment to basis of partnership property) is in effect with respect to such partnership or unless the partnership has a substantial built-in loss immediately after such transfer.

(b) Adjustment to basis of partnership property.—In the case of a transfer of an interest in a partnership by sale or exchange or upon the death of a partner, a partnership with respect to which the election provided in section 754 is in effect or which has a substantial built-in loss immediately after such transfer shall—

(1) increase the adjusted basis of the partnership property by the excess of the basis to the transferee partner of his interest in the partnership over his proportionate share of the adjusted basis of the partnership property, or

(2) decrease the adjusted basis of the partnership property by the excess of the transferee partner's proportionate share of the adjusted basis of the partnership property over the basis of his interest in the partnership.

Under regulations prescribed by the Secretary, such increase or decrease shall constitute an adjustment to the basis of partnership property with respect to the transferee partner only. A partner's proportionate share of the adjusted basis of partnership property shall be determined in accordance with his interest in partnership capital and, in the case of property contributed to the partnership by a partner, section 704(c) (relating to contributed property) shall apply in determining such share. In the case of an adjustment under this subsection to the basis of partnership property subject to depletion, any depletion allowable shall be determined separately for the transferee partner with respect to his interest in such property.

(c) Allocation of basis.—The allocation of basis among partnership properties where subsection (b) is applicable shall be made in accordance with the rules provided in section 755.

(d) Substantial built-in loss.—

(1) In general.—For purposes of this section, a partnership has a substantial built-in loss with respect to a transfer of an interest in a partnership if the partnership's adjusted basis in the partnership property exceeds by more than $250,000 the fair market value of such property.

(2) Regulations.—The Secretary shall prescribe such regulations as may be appropriate to carry out the purposes of paragraph (1) and section 734(d), including regulations aggregating related partnerships and disregarding property acquired by the partnership in an attempt to avoid such purposes.

(e) Alternative rules for electing investment partnerships.—

(1) No adjustment of partnership basis.—For purposes of this section, an electing investment partnership shall not be treated as having a substantial built-in loss with respect to any transfer occurring while the election under paragraph (6)(A) is in effect.

(2) Loss deferral for transferee partner.—In the case of a transfer of an interest in an electing investment partnership, the transferee partner's distributive share of losses (without regard to gains) from the sale or exchange of partnership property shall not be allowed except to the extent that it is established that such losses exceed the loss (if any) recognized by the transferor (or any prior transferor to the extent not fully offset by a prior disallowance under this paragraph) on the transfer of the partnership interest.

(3) No reduction in partnership basis.—Losses disallowed under paragraph (2) shall not decrease the transferee partner's basis in the partnership interest.

(4) Effect of termination of partnership.—This subsection shall be applied without regard to any termination of a partnership under section 708(b)(1)(B).

(5) Certain basis reductions treated as losses.—In the case of a transferee partner whose basis in property distributed by the partnership is reduced under section 732(a)(2), the amount of the loss recognized by the transferor on the transfer of the partnership interest which is taken into account under paragraph (2) shall be reduced by the amount of such basis reduction.

(6) Electing investment partnership.—For purposes of this subsection, the term "electing investment partnership" means any partnership if—

(A) the partnership makes an election to have this subsection apply,

(B) the partnership would be an investment company under section 3(a)(1)(A) of the Investment Company Act of 1940 but for an exemption under paragraph (1) or (7) of section 3(c) of such Act,

(C) such partnership has never been engaged in a trade or business,

(D) substantially all of the assets of such partnership are held for investment,

(E) at least 95 percent of the assets contributed to such partnership consist of money,

(F) no assets contributed to such partnership had an adjusted basis in excess of fair market value at the time of contribution,

(G) all partnership interests of such partnership are issued by such partnership pursuant to a private offering before the date which is 24 months after the date of the first capital contribution to such partnership,

(H) the partnership agreement of such partnership has substantive restrictions on each partner's ability to cause a redemption of the partner's interest, and

(I) the partnership agreement of such partnership provides for a term that is not in excess of 15 years.

The election described in subparagraph (A), once made, shall be irrevocable except with the consent of the Secretary.

(7) Regulations.—The Secretary shall prescribe such regulations as may be appropriate to carry out the purposes of this subsection, including regulations for applying this subsection to tiered partnerships.

(f) Exception for securitization partnerships.—

(1) No adjustment of partnership basis.—For purposes of this section, a securitization partnership shall not be treated as having a substantial built-in loss with respect to any transfer.

(2) Securitization partnership.—For purposes of paragraph (1), the term "securitization partnership" means any partnership the sole business activity of which is to issue securities which provide for a fixed principal (or similar) amount and which are primarily serviced by the cash flows of a discrete pool (either fixed or revolving) of receivables or other financial assets that by their terms convert into cash in a finite period, but only if the sponsor of the pool reasonably believes that the receivables and other financial assets comprising the pool are not acquired so as to be disposed of.

SUBPART D—PROVISIONS COMMON TO OTHER SUBPARTS

Editorial Summary

Section 751 Property and Effect of Liabilities on Basis

Subchapter K of Chapter 1 (Secs. 741, 751, 752)

Gain or loss recognized by the partner on the sale of a partnership interest or the receipt of a partnership distribution generally qualifies for capital gain or loss treatment under Secs. 731 and 741. However, the absence of any restrictions on the classification of the recognized gain as capital gain would enable the partner to use the partnership to achieve the tax avoidance technique of conversion (i.e., converting what would be ordinary income into capital gain).

Section 751 overrides the general classification treatment of Secs. 731 and 741 for Sec. 751 property (also referred to as "hot" assets or "tainted" assets). Thus, Sec. 751 treatment applies to both actual sales of the partner's partnership interest and to deemed sales (i.e., under Sec. 751, certain asset distributions to the partner are restructured and treated as sales). The recognized gain on such sales of Sec. 751 property is classified as ordinary income. The Sec. 751

concept and related calculations probably are the most complex in Subchapter K.

Section 751 property consists of unrealized receivables and substantially appreciated inventory. Note that unrealized receivables are defined more broadly in Sec. 751(c) than merely being the receivables of the partnership which have not been recorded as income under the partnership's method of accounting. Also, note that inventory, as defined in Sec. 751(d)(2), includes more than the stock in trade of the partnership. Items satisfying this definition of inventory are not automatically subject to Sec. 751 treatment. To be classified as Sec. 751 property, the inventory must be substantially appreciated as defined in Sec. 751(d)(1).

Note that the Revenue Reconciliation Act of 1993 modified the definition of substantial appreciation. Prior to RRA of 1993, to be substantially appreciated, (1) the fair market value of the inventory must exceed 120 percent of the adjusted basis of the inventory and (2) the fair market value of the inventory must exceed 10 percent of the fair market value of all partnership property (excluding money). RRA of 1993 repealed the second requirement. In addition, it added a new second requirement that for purposes of calculating the first requirement (i.e., the 120 percent provision), any inventory, for which the principal purpose of acquiring it was to avoid the substantial appreciation requirement, shall be excluded from the calculation [see Sec. 751(d)(1)(A) and (B)].

The following example briefly illustrates the complexity and methodology of Sec. 751.

Example. The ABC partnership has three partners (A, B, and C) who each own a one-third interest. The balance sheet of the partnership is as follows:

Assets	Basis	FMV
Cash	$15,000	$15,000
Inventory	15,000	45,000
Land (investment)	15,000	30,000
	$45,000	$90,000

Capital		
A	$15,000	$30,000
B	15,000	30,000
C	15,000	30,000
	$45,000	$90,000

A receives the land in liquidation of his partnership interest.

Absent Sec. 751, the following tax consequences would occur. Although the fair market value of the land received exceeds A's outside basis of $15,000, Sec. 731(a)(1) provides that A would recognize no gain at the time of the liquidating distribution. Instead, under Sec. 732(b), A would assign his outside basis of $15,000 to the land. If A subsequently were to sell the land for $30,000, he would recognize a capital gain of $15,000 ($30,000 amount realized – $15,000 basis). Upon sale of the inventory by the partnership (i.e., now the BC partnership), B and C would each recognize $15,000 of ordinary income. While each partner ultimately would recognize $15,000, A's recognition is capital gain whereas that of B and C is ordinary income. If capital gains were beneficially taxed, the liquidating distribution could be used to achieve tax avoidance depending on who received the capital gain and who received the ordinary income.

Section 751(b) is designed to prevent this tax avoidance opportunity through the operation of the disproportionate distribution rules. In essence, the assumption is made that A receives his pro rata share of Sec. 751 property (i.e., inventory in this case) and not—Sec. 751 property (i.e., the cash and the land in this case).

Assets	A's share	Actually Received	Deemed Received
Sec. 751 property	$15,000	$-0-	$15,000
Not-Sec. 751 property	15,000	30,000	(15,000)
	$30,000	$30,000	$-0-

A received less than his share of Sec. 751 property. Therefore, he is deemed to receive $15,000 (adjusted basis of $5,000) of inventory. He then is deemed to have sold the inventory to the partnership for $15,000 in exchange for the excess not-Sec. 751 property. Therefore, he will recognize ordinary income of $10,000 ($15,000 – $5,000) and have a basis for the excess not-Sec. 751 property deemed purchased of $15,000. A's outside is now $10,000 ($15,000 outside basis – $5,000 adjusted basis of inventory deemed received).

The partnership (i.e., now BC) is deemed to have exchanged the excess not-Sec. 751 property (i.e., $15,000 of land) for the $15,000 of Sec. 751 property (i.e., inventory). B and C would each recognize a capital gain of $3,750 [($15,000 – $7,500)/2] and would each increase their outside basis by $3,750. The partnership's basis for the purchased inventory is $15,000.

On the actual distribution of the land to A, he will recognize no gain under Sec. 731(a)(1). He will assign a basis of $10,000 to the land, an amount equal to his remaining outside basis [see Sec. 732(b)]. Therefore, after the liquidating distribution is complete, A will have the following assets:

Assets	Basis	FMV
Land	$25,000	$30,000

If A were to subsequently sell the land for $30,000, he would recognize a capital gain of $5,000 ($30,000 – $25,000).

After the liquidating distribution to A, the partnership balance sheet would be as follows:

Assets	Basis	FMV
Cash	$15,000	$15,000
Inventory	25,000	45,000
	$40,000	$60,000

Capital		
B	$18,750	$30,000
C	18,750	30,000
	$37,500	$60,000

Note that the inside basis does not equal the outside basis. This occurs because A assigned a basis of $10,000 to the land under Sec. 732(b) when the inside basis for the land to the partnership was only $7,500 ($15,000 original inside basis – $7,500 deemed sold to A).

On the subsequent sale of the inventory for $45,000, B and C will each recognize ordinary income of $10,000 [($45,000 – $25,000)/2]. If the cash were then distributed to B and C in liquidation of the partnership, B and C would each recognize a capital gain of $1,250 [$30,000 cash received – $28,750 ($18,750 outside basis + $10,000 increase on sale of inventory)].

Thus, the overall results can be summarized as follows:

	A	B	C
Ordinary Income			
On deemed sale by A	$10,000		
Sale of inventory by BC partnership		$10,000	$10,000
Capital Gain			
On deemed sale by BC partnership		3,750	3,750
Sale of land by A	5,000		
On final liquidation of AB partnership		1,250	1,250
	$15,000	$15,000	$15,000

While the results produced by Sec. 751, as illustrated in the example, are logical, one sometimes must go nearly around the world to get the intended result!

Section 705 contains the rules for calculating the basis of a partner's interest in the partnership (i.e., "outside basis") (see the Editorial Summary entitled Partnerships: General Tax Treatment, which precedes Sec. 701). Section 752 contains the specific rules for the effect of liabilities on "outside basis."

The partner's "outside basis" is increased by his or her share of partnership liability increases. Likewise, the partner's "outside basis" is decreased by his or her share of partnership liability decreases. If the partnership assumes a liability of the partner, the "outside basis" of that partner decreases. Conversely, if a partner assumes a liability of the partnership, the "outside basis" of that partner increases.

With respect to liabilities, a partner's "outside basis" cannot be decreased below zero. Thus, liability decreases under such a circumstance can result in recognition of gain at the partner level.

§ 751. Unrealized receivables and inventory items

(a) Sale or exchange of interest in partnership.—The amount of any money, or the fair market value of any property, received by a transferor partner in exchange for all or a part of his interest in the partnership attributable to—

(1) unrealized receivables of the partnership, or

(2) inventory items of the partnership,

shall be considered as an amount realized from the sale or exchange of property other than a capital asset.

(b) Certain distributions treated as sales or exchanges.—

(1) General rule.—To the extent a partner receives in a distribution—

(A) partnership property which is—

(i) unrealized receivables, or

(ii) inventory items which have appreciated substantially in value,

in exchange for all or a part of his interest in other partnership property (including money), or

(B) partnership property (including money) other than property described in subparagraph (A)(i) or (ii) in exchange for all or a part of his interest in partnership property described in subparagraph (A)(i) or (ii),

such transactions shall, under regulations prescribed by the Secretary, be considered as a sale or exchange of such property between the distributee and the partnership (as constituted after the distribution).

(2) Exceptions.—Paragraph (1) shall not apply to—

(A) a distribution of property which the distributee contributed to the partnership, or

(B) payments, described in section 736(a), to a retiring partner or successor in interest of a deceased partner.

(3) Substantial appreciation.—For purposes of paragraph (1)—

(A) In general.—Inventory items of the partnership shall be considered to have appreciated substantially in value if their fair market value exceeds 120 percent of the adjusted basis to the partnership of such property.

(B) Certain property excluded.—For purposes of subparagraph (A), there shall be excluded any inventory property if a principal purpose for acquiring such property was to avoid the provisions of this subsection relating to inventory items.

(c) Unrealized receivables.—For purposes of this subchapter, the term "unrealized receivables" includes, to the extent not previously includible in income under the method of accounting used by the partnership, any rights (contractual or otherwise) to payment for—

(1) goods delivered, or to be delivered, to the extent the proceeds therefrom would be treated as amounts received from the sale or exchange of property other than a capital asset, or

(2) services rendered, or to be rendered.

For purposes of this section and sections 731, 732, and 741 (but not for purposes of section 736), such term also includes mining property (as defined in section 617(f)(2)), stock in a DISC (as described in section 992(a)), section 1245 property (as defined in section 1245(a)(3)), stock in certain foreign corporations (as described in section 1248), section 1250 property (as defined in section 1250(c)), farm land (as defined in section 1252(a)), franchises, trademarks, or trade names (referred to in section 1253(a)), and an oil, gas, or geothermal property (described in section 1254) but only to the extent of the amount which would be treated as gain to which section 617(d)(1), 995(c), 1245(a), 1248(a), 1250(a), 1252(a), 1253(a), or 1254(a) would apply if (at the time of the transaction described in this section or sections 731, 732, or 741, as the case may be) such property had been sold by the partnership at its fair market value. For purposes of this section and sections 731, 732, and 741 (but not for purposes of section 736), such term also includes any market discount bond (as defined in section 1278) and any short-term obligation (as defined in section 1283) but only to the extent of the amount which would be treated as ordinary income if (at the time of the transaction described in this section or section 731, 732, or 741, as the case may be) such property had been sold by the partnership.

(d) Inventory items.—For purposes of this subchapter, the term "inventory items" means—

(1) property of the partnership of the kind described in section 1221(1),

(2) any other property of the partnership which, on sale or exchange by the partnership, would be considered property other than a capital asset and other than property described in section 1231, and

(3) any other property held by the partnership which, if held by the selling or distributee partner, would be considered property of the type described in paragraph (1) or (2).

* * *

(f) Special rules in the case of tiered partnerships, etc.—In determining whether property of a partnership is—

(1) an unrealized receivable, or

(2) an inventory item,

such partnership shall be treated as owning its proportionate share of the property of any other partnership in which it is a partner. Under regulations, rules similar to the rules of the preceding sentence shall also apply in the case of interests in trusts.

§ 752. Treatment of certain liabilities

(a) Increase in partner's liabilities.—Any increase in a partner's share of the liabilities of a partnership, or any increase in a partner's individual liabilities by reason of the assumption by such partner of partnership liabilities, shall be considered as a contribution of money by such partner to the partnership.

(b) Decrease in partner's liabilities.—Any decrease in a partner's share of the liabilities of a partnership, or any decrease in a partner's individual liabilities by reason of the assumption by the partnership of such individual liabilities, shall be considered as a distribution of money to the partner by the partnership.

(c) Liability to which property is subject.—For purposes of this section, a liability to which property is subject shall, to the extent of the fair market value of such property, be considered as a liability of the owner of the property.

(d) Sale or exchange of an interest.—In the case of a sale or exchange of an interest in a partnership, liabilities shall be treated in the same manner as liabilities in connection with the sale or exchange of property not associated with partnerships.

§ 753. Partner receiving income in respect of decedent

The amount includible in the gross income of a successor in interest of a deceased partner under section 736(a) shall be considered income in respect of a decedent under section 691.

§ 754. Manner of electing optional adjustment to basis of partnership property

If a partnership files an election, in accordance with regulations prescribed by the Secretary, the basis of partnership property shall be adjusted, in the case of a distribution of property, in the manner provided in section 734 and, in the case of a transfer of a partnership interest, in the manner provided in section 743. Such an election shall apply with respect to all distributions of property by the partnership and to all transfers of interests in the partnership during the taxable year with respect to which such election was filed and all subsequent taxable years. Such election may be revoked by the partnership, subject to such limitations as may be provided by regulations prescribed by the Secretary.

§ 755. Rules for allocation of basis

(a) General rule.—Any increase or decrease in the adjusted basis of partnership property under section 734(b) (relating to the optional adjustment to the basis of undistributed partnership property) or section 743(b) (relating to the optional adjustment to the basis of partnership property in the case of a transfer of an interest in a partnership) shall, except as provided in subsection (b), be allocated—

(1) in a manner which has the effect of reducing the difference between the fair market value and the adjusted basis of partnership properties, or

(2) in any other manner permitted by regulations prescribed by the Secretary.

(b) Special rule.—In applying the allocation rules provided in subsection (a), increases or decreases in the adjusted basis of partnership property arising from a distribution of, or a transfer of an interest attributable to, property consisting of—

(1) capital assets and property described in section 1231 (b), or

(2) any other property of the partnership,

shall be allocated to partnership property of a like character except that the basis of any such partnership property shall not be reduced below zero. If, in the case of a distribution, the adjustment to basis of property described in paragraph (1) or (2) is prevented by the absence of such property or by insufficient adjusted basis for such property, such adjustment shall be applied to subsequently acquired property of a like character in accordance with regulations prescribed by the Secretary.

(c) No allocation of basis decrease to stock of corporate partner.—In making an allocation under subsection (a) of any decrease in the adjusted basis of partnership property under section 734(b)—

(1) no allocation may be made to stock in a corporation (or any person related (within the meaning of sections 267(b) and 707(b)(1)) to such corporation) which is a partner in the partnership, and

(2) any amount not allocable to stock by reason of paragraph (1) shall be allocated under subsection (a) to other partnership property.

Gain shall be recognized to the partnership to the extent that the amount required to be allocated under paragraph (2) to other partnership property exceeds the aggregated adjusted basis of such other property immediately before the allocation required by paragraph (2).

PART III—DEFINITIONS

Editorial Summary

Partnerships: Definitions

Subchapter K of Chapter 1 (Sec. 761)

See the discussion under the Editorial Summary entitled Partnerships: General Tax Treatment, which precedes Sec. 701.

§ 761. Terms defined

(a) Partnership.—For purposes of this subtitle, the term "partnership" includes a syndicate, group, pool, joint venture, or other unincorporated organization through or by means of which any business, financial operation, or venture is carried on, and which is not, within the meaning of this title, a corporation or a trust or estate. Under regulations the Secretary may, at the election of all the members of an unincorporated organization, exclude such organization from the application of all or part of this subchapter, if it is availed of—

(1) for investment purposes only and not for the active conduct of a business,

(2) for the joint production, extraction, or use of property, but not for the purpose of selling services or property produced or extracted, or

(3) by dealers in securities for a short period for the purpose of underwriting, selling, or distributing a particular issue of securities,

if the income of the members of the organization may be adequately determined without the computation of partnership taxable income.

(b) Partner.—For purposes of this subtitle, the term "partner" means a member of a partnership.

(c) Partnership agreement.—For purposes of this subchapter, a partnership agreement includes any modifications of the partnership agreement made prior to, or at, the time prescribed by law for the filing of the partnership return for the taxable year (not including extensions) which are agreed to by all the partners, or which are adopted in such other manner as may be provided by the partnership agreement.

(d) Liquidation of a partner's interest.—For purposes of this subchapter, the term "liquidation of a partner's interest" means the termination of a partner's entire interest in a partnership by means of a distribution, or a series of distributions, to the partner by the partnership.

(e) Distributions of partnership interests treated as exchanges.—Except as otherwise provided in regulations, for purposes of—

(1) section 708 (relating to continuation of partnership),

(2) section 743 (relating to optional adjustment to basis of partnership property), and

(3) any other provision of this subchapter specified in regulations prescribed by the Secretary,

any distribution of an interest in a partnership (not otherwise treated as an exchange) shall be treated as an exchange.

(f) Qualified joint venture.—

(1) In general—In the case of a qualified joint venture conducted by a husband and wife who file a joint return for the taxable year, for purposes of this title—

(A) such joint venture shall not be treated as a partnership,

(B) all items of income, gain, loss, deduction, and credit shall be divided between the spouses in accordance with their respective interests in the venture, and

(C) each spouse shall take into account such spouse's respective share of such items as if they were attributable to a trade or business conducted by such spouse as a sole proprietor.

(2) Qualified joint venture.—For purposes of paragraph (1), the term 'qualified joint venture' means any joint venture involving the conduct of a trade or business if—

(A) the only members of such joint venture are a husband or wife,

(B) both spouses materially participate (within the meaning of section 469(h) without regard to paragraph (5) thereof) in such trade or business, and

(C) both spouses elect the application of this subsection.

(g) Cross reference.—

For rules in the case of the sale, exchange, liquidation, or reduction of a partner's interest, see sections 704(b) and 706(c)(2).

Editorial Summary

Electing Large Partnerships

Subchapter K of Chapter 1 (Secs. 771–777)

The Taxpayer Relief Act of 1997 provides the statutory authority for large partnerships to use a simplified reporting system (see Sec. 771). Rather than applying the normal conduit approach, an electing partnership may treat many otherwise "separately stated items" as part of the calculation of partnership taxable income (see Secs. 772, 773, and 774).

A partnership is classified as a large partnership if it has at least 100 partners during the preceding tax year [see Sec. 775(a)]. For this purpose, a service partner is not counted in satisfying this minimum number of partners test [see Sec. 775(b)(1)]. In addition, service partnerships generally are not eligible to make the election [see Sec. 775(b)(2)].

Special rules apply for large partnerships with oil and gas activities (see Sec. 776).

PART IV—SPECIAL RULES FOR ELECTING LARGE PARTNERSHIPS

§ 771. Application of subchapter to electing large partnerships

The preceding provisions of this subchapter to the extent inconsistent with the provisions of this part shall not apply to an electing large partnership and its partners.

§ 772. Simplified flow-through

(a) General rule.—In determining the income tax of a partner of an electing large partnership, such partner shall take into account separately such partner's distributive share of the partnership's—

(1) taxable income or loss from passive loss limitation activities,

(2) taxable income or loss from other activities,

(3) net capital gain (or net capital loss)—

(A) to the extent allocable to passive loss limitation activities, and

(B) to the extent allocable to other activities,

(4) tax-exempt interest,

(5) applicable net AMT adjustment separately computed for—

(A) passive loss limitation activities, and

(B) other activities,

(6) general credits,

(7) low-income housing credit determined under section 42,

(8) rehabilitation credit determined under section 47,

(9) foreign income taxes,

(10) the credit allowable under section 29, and

(11) other items to the extent that the Secretary determines that the separate treatment of such items is appropriate.

(b) Separate computations.—In determining the amounts required under subsection (a) to be separately taken into account by any partner, this section and section 773 shall be applied separately with respect to such partner by taking into account such partner's distributive share of the items of income, gain, loss, deduction, or credit of the partnership.

(c) Treatment at partner level.—

(1) In general.—Except as provided in this subsection, rules similar to the rules of section 702(b) shall apply to any partner's distributive share of the amounts referred to in subsection (a).

(2) Income or loss from passive loss limitation activities.—For purposes of this chapter, any partner's distributive share of any income or loss described in subsection (a)(1) shall be treated as an item of income or loss (as the case may be) from the conduct of a trade or business which is a single passive activity (as defined in section 469). A similar rule shall apply to a partner's distributive share of amounts referred to in paragraphs (3)(A) and (5)(A) of subsection (a).

(3) Income or loss from other activities.—

(A) In general.—For purposes of this chapter, any partner's distributive share of any income or loss described in subsection (a)(2) shall be treated as an item of income or expense (as the case may be) with respect to property held for investment.

(B) Deductions for loss not subject to section 67.—The deduction under section 212 for any loss described in subparagraph (A) shall not be treated as a miscellaneous itemized deduction for purposes of section 67.

(4) Treatment of net capital gain or loss.—For purposes of this chapter, any partner's distributive share of any gain or loss described in subsection (a)(3) shall be treated as a long-term capital gain or loss, as the case may be.

(5) Minimum tax treatment.—In determining the alternative minimum taxable income of any partner, such partner's distributive share of any applicable net AMT adjustment shall be taken into account in lieu of making the separate adjustments provided in sections 56, 57, and 58 with respect to the items of the partnership. Except as provided in regulations, the applicable net AMT adjustment shall be treated, for purposes of section 53, as an adjustment or item of tax preference not specified in section 53(d)(1)(B)(ii).

(6) General credits.—A partner's distributive share of the amount referred to in paragraph (6) of subsection (a) shall be taken into account as a current year business credit.

(d) Operating rules.—For purposes of this section—

(1) Passive loss limitation activity.—The term "passive loss limitation activity" means—

(A) any activity which involves the conduct of a trade or business, and

(B) any rental activity.

For purposes of the preceding sentence, the term "trade or business" includes any activity treated as a trade or business under paragraph (5) or (6) of section 469(c).

(2) Tax-exempt interest.—The term "tax-exempt interest" means interest excludable from gross income under section 103.

(3) Applicable net AMT adjustment.—

(A) In general.—The applicable net AMT adjustment is—

(i) with respect to taxpayers other than corporations, the net adjustment determined by using the adjustments applicable to individuals, and

(ii) with respect to corporations, the net adjustment determined by using the adjustments applicable to corporations.

(B) Net adjustment.—The term "net adjustment" means the net adjustment in the items attributable to passive loss activities or other activities (as the case may be) which would result if such items were determined with the adjustments of sections 56, 57, and 58.

(4) Treatment of certain separately stated items.—

(A) Exclusion for certain purposes.—In determining the amounts referred to in paragraphs (1) and (2) of subsection (a), any net capital gain or net capital loss (as the case may be), and any item referred to in subsection (a)(11), shall be excluded.

(B) Allocation rules.—The net capital gain shall be treated—

(i) as allocable to passive loss limitation activities to the extent the net capital gain does not exceed the net capital gain determined by only taking into account gains and losses from sales and exchanges of property used in connection with such activities, and

(ii) as allocable to other activities to the extent such gain exceeds the amount allocated under clause (i).

A similar rule shall apply for purposes of allocating any net capital loss.

(C) Net capital loss.—The term "net capital loss" means the excess of the losses from sales or exchanges of capital assets over the gains from sales or exchange of capital assets.

(5) General credits.—The term "general credits" means any credit other than the low-income housing credit, the rehabilitation credit, the foreign tax credit, and the credit allowable under section 29.

(6) Foreign income taxes.—The term "foreign income taxes" means taxes described in section 901 which are paid or accrued to foreign countries and to possessions of the United States.

(e) Special rule for unrelated business tax.—In the case of a partner which is an organization subject to tax under section 511, such partner's distributive share of any items shall be taken into account separately to the extent necessary to comply with the provisions of section 512(c)(1).

(f) Special rules for applying passive loss limitations.—If any person holds an interest in an electing large partnership other than as a limited partner—

(1) paragraph (2) of subsection (c) shall not apply to such partner, and

(2) such partner's distributive share of the partnership items allocable to passive loss limitation activities shall be taken into account separately to the extent necessary to comply with the provisions of section 469.

The preceding sentence shall not apply to any items allocable to an interest held as a limited partner.

§ 773. Computations at partnership level

(a) General rule.—

(1) Taxable income.—The taxable income of an electing large partnership shall be computed in the same manner as in the case of an individual except that—

(A) the items described in section 772(a) shall be separately stated, and

(B) the modifications of subsection (b) shall apply.

(2) Elections.—All elections affecting the computation of the taxable income of an electing large partnership or the computation of any credit of an electing large partnership shall be made by the partnership; except that the election under section 901, and any election under section 108, shall be made by each partner separately.

(3) Limitations, etc.—

(A) In general.—Except as provided in subparagraph (B), all limitations and other provisions affecting the computation of the taxable income of an electing large partnership or the computation of any credit of an electing large partnership shall be applied at the partner level (and not at the partnership level).

(B) Certain limitations applied at partner level.—The following provisions shall be applied at the partner level (and not at the partnership level):

(i) Section 68 (relating to overall limitation on itemized deductions).

(ii) Sections 49 and 465 (relating to at risk limitations).

(iii) Section 469 (relating to limitation on passive activity losses and credits).

(iv) Any other provision specified in regulations.

(4) Coordination with other provisions.—Paragraphs (2) and (3) shall apply notwithstanding any other provision of this chapter other than this part.

(b) Modifications to determination of taxable income.—In determining the taxable income of an electing large partnership—

(1) Certain deductions not allowed.—The following deductions shall not be allowed:

(A) The deduction for personal exemptions provided in section 151.

(B) The net operating loss deduction provided in section 172.

(C) The additional itemized deductions for individuals provided in part VII of subchapter B (other than section 212 thereof).

(2) Charitable deductions.—In determining the amount allowable under section 170, the limitation of section 170(b)(2) shall apply.

(3) Coordination with section 67.—In lieu of applying section 67, 70 percent of the amount of the miscellaneous itemized deductions shall be disallowed.

(c) Special rules for income from discharge of indebtedness.—If an electing large partnership has income from the discharge of any indebtedness—

(1) such income shall be excluded in determining the amounts referred to in section 772(a), and

(2) in determining the income tax of any partner of such partnership—

(A) such income shall be treated as an item required to be separately taken into account under section 772(a), and

(B) the provisions of section 108 shall be applied without regard to this part.

§ 774. Other modifications

(a) Treatment of certain optional adjustments, etc.—In the case of an electing large partnership—

(1) computations under section 773 shall be made without regard to any adjustment under section 743(b) or 108(b), but

(2) a partner's distributive share of any amount referred to in section 772(a) shall be appropriately adjusted to take into account any adjustment under section 743(b) or 108(b) with respect to such partner.

(b) Credit recapture determined at partnership level.—

(1) In general.—In the case of an electing large partnership—

(A) any credit recapture shall be taken into account by the partnership, and

(B) the amount of such recapture shall be determined as if the credit with respect to which the recapture is made had been fully utilized to reduce tax.

(2) Method of taking recapture into account.—An electing large partnership shall take into account a credit recapture by reducing the amount of the appropriate current year credit to the extent thereof, and if such recapture exceeds the amount of such current year credit, the partnership shall be liable to pay such excess.

(3) Dispositions not to trigger recapture.—No credit recapture shall be required by reason of any transfer of an interest in an electing large partnership.

(4) Credit recapture.—For purposes of this subsection, the term "credit recapture" means any increase in tax under section 42(j) or 50(a).

(c) Partnership not terminated by reason of change in ownership.—Subparagraph (B) of section 708(b)(1) shall not apply to an electing large partnership.

(d) Partnership entitled to certain credits.—The following shall be allowed to an electing large partnership and shall not be taken into account by the partners of such partnership:

(1) The credit provided by section 34.

(2) Any credit or refund under section 852(b)(3)(D) or 857(b)(3)(D).

(e) Treatment of REMIC residuals.—For purposes of applying section 860E(e)(6) to any electing large partnership—

(1) all interests in such partnership shall be treated as held by disqualified organizations,

(2) in lieu of applying subparagraph (C) of section 860E(e)(6), the amount subject to tax under section 860E(e)(6) shall be excluded from the gross income of such partnership, and

(3) subparagraph (D) or section 860E(e)(6) shall not apply.

(f) Special rules for applying certain installment sale rules.—In the case of an electing large partnership—

(1) the provisions of sections 453(1)(3) and 453A shall be applied at the partnership level, and

(2) in determining the amount of interest payable under such sections, such partnership shall be treated as subject to tax under this chapter at the highest rate of tax in effect under section 1 or 11.

§ 775. Electing large partnership defined

(a) General rule.—For purposes of this part—

(1) In general.—The term "electing large partnership" means, with respect to any partnership taxable year, any partnership if—

(A) the number of persons who were partners in such partnership in the preceding partnership taxable year equaled or exceeded 100, and

(B) such partnership elects the application of this part.

To the extent provided in regulations, a partnership shall cease to be treated as an electing large partnership for any partnership taxable year if in such taxable year fewer than 100 persons were partners in such partnership.

(2) Election.—The election under this subsection shall apply to the taxable year for which made and all subsequent taxable years unless revoked with the consent of the Secretary.

(b) Special rules for certain service partnerships.—

(1) Certain partners not counted.—For purposes of this section, the term "partner" does not include any individual performing substantial services in connection with the activities of the partnership and holding an interest in such partnership, or an individual who formerly performed substantial services in connection with such activities and who held an interest in such partnership at the time the individual performed such services.

(2) Exclusion.—For purposes of this part, an election under subsection (a) shall not be effective with respect to any partnership if substantially all the partners of such partnership—

(A) are individuals performing substantial services in connection with the activities of such partnership or are personal service corporations (as defined in section 269(A)(b)) the owner-employees (as defined in section 269(A)(b)) of which perform such substantial services,

(B) are retired partners who had performed such substantial services, or

(C) are spouses of partners who are performing (or had previously performed) such substantial services.

(3) Special rules for lower tier partnerships.—For purposes of this subsection, the activities of a partnership shall include the activities of any other partnership in which the partnership owns directly an interest in the capital and profits of at least 80 percent.

(c) Exclusion of commodity pools.—For purposes of this part, an election under subsection (a) shall not be effective with respect to any partnership the principal activity of which is the buying and selling of commodities (not described in section 1221(1)), or options, futures, or forwards with respect to such commodities.

(d) Secretary may rely on treatment on return.—If, on the partnership return of any partnership, such partnership is treated as an electing large partnership, such treatment shall be binding on such partnership and all partners of such partnership but not on the Secretary.

§ 776. Special rules for partnerships holding oil and gas properties

(a) Computation of percentage depletion.—In the case of an electing large partnership, except as provided in subsection (b)—

(1) the allowance for depletion under section 611 with respect to any partnership oil or gas property shall be computed at the partnership level without regard to any provision of section 613A requiring such allowance to be computed separately by each partner,

(2) such allowance shall be determined without regard to the provisions of section 613A(c) limiting the amount of production for which percentage depletion is allowable and without regard to paragraph (1) of section 613A(d), and

(3) paragraph (3) of section 705(a) shall not apply.

(b) Treatment of certain partners.—

(1) In general.—In the case of a disqualified person, the treatment under this chapter of such person's distributive share of any item of income, gain, loss, deduction, or credit attributable to any partnership oil or gas property shall be determined without regard to this part. Such person's distributive share of any such items shall be excluded for purposes of making determinations under sections 772 and 773.

(2) Disqualified person.—For purposes of paragraph (1), the term "disqualified person" means with respect to any partnership taxable year—

(A) any person referred to in paragraph (2) or (4) of section 613A(d) for such person's taxable year in which such partnership taxable year ends, and

(B) any other person if such person's average daily production of domestic crude oil and natural gas for such person's taxable year in which such partnership taxable year ends exceeds 500 barrels.

(3) Average daily production.—For purposes of paragraph (2), a person's average daily production of domestic crude oil and natural gas for any taxable year shall be computed as provided in section 613A(c)(2)—

(A) by taking into account all production of domestic crude oil and natural gas (including such person's proportionate share of any production of a partnership),

(B) by treating 6,000 cubic feet of natural gas as a barrel of crude oil, and

(C) by treating as 1 person all persons treated as 1 taxpayer under section 613A(c)(8) or among whom allocations are required under such section.

§ 777. Regulations

The Secretary shall prescribe such regulations as may be appropriate to carry out the purposes of this part.

SUBCHAPTER L—INSURANCE COMPANIES*

SUBCHAPTER M—REGULATED INVESTMENT COMPANIES* AND REAL ESTATE INVESTMENT TRUSTS*

*Omitted.

SUBCHAPTER N—TAX BASED ON INCOME FROM SOURCES WITHIN OR WITHOUT THE UNITED STATES

PART I—DETERMINATION OF SOURCES OF INCOME*
PART II—NONRESIDENT ALIENS AND FOREIGN CORPORATIONS*
PART III—INCOME FROM SOURCES WITHOUT THE UNITED STATES

Editorial Summary

Foreign Tax Credit and Foreign Earned Income Exclusion

Subchapter N of Chapter 1 (Secs. 901, 904, 905, 911)

A taxpayer working in a foreign country may be subject to additional living costs when compared with that he or she would incur if living in the United States. In addition, the taxpayer may be subject to income taxation in the foreign country.

In recognition of the aforementioned adverse consequences and in attempting to aid American businesses that do business abroad, the taxpayer has the choice of taking a credit for foreign taxes, as calculated under Secs. 901 and 904, or a deduction for the foreign taxes paid under Sec. 164(a). Section 275(a)(4)(A) disallows the deduction if the taxpayer elects the Sec. 901 foreign tax credit treatment.

Section 904(a) limits the amount of the foreign tax credit for taxpayers living in high tax countries to what the tax would have been on the foreign taxable income if U.S. tax rates were applied. The formula for the limit is as follows:

$$\frac{\textit{Foreign source TI}}{\text{Worldwide TI}} \times \text{U.S. tax before FTC}$$

Section 911 provides that certain taxpayers [see the bona fide residence test under Sec. 911(d)(1)(A) and the physical presence in the foreign country test under Sec. 911(d)(1)(B)] who have foreign-earned income may elect to exclude, subject to a statutory ceiling, such income and certain housing costs [as defined in Sec. 911(c)]. The annual statutory ceiling on the amount of the foreign earned income exclusion is $80,000 [Sec. 911(b)(2)(A)] with the indexed amount for 2012 being $95,100 and for 2013 being $97,600. A taxpayer who elects exclusion treatment is not eligible to take a foreign tax credit or deduction on the same income [see Sec. 911(d)(6) which denies such a double benefit]. The Sec. 911 exclusion remains in effect until revoked. The election can be revoked for any taxable year after the taxable year for which the election was made. However, this revocation election is a long-run decision. That is, the revocation election applies not only to the current taxable year, but also to future taxable years (i.e., another Sec. 911 exclusion election cannot be made until the sixth taxable year after the revocation year).

Both the credit and the exclusion are subject to statutory limitations. The limitations on the amount of the foreign tax credit appear in Sec. 904. The limitations on the amount of the foreign earned income exclusion appear in Sec. 911(b)(2), and those on the housing cost exclusion appear in Sec. 911(c).

SUBPART A—FOREIGN TAX CREDIT

§ 901. Taxes of foreign countries and of possessions of United States

(a) Allowance of credit.—If the taxpayer chooses to have the benefits of this subpart, the tax imposed by this chapter shall, subject to the limitation of section 904, be credited with the amounts provided in the applicable paragraph of subsection (b) plus, in the case of a corporation, the taxes deemed to have been paid under sections 902 and 960. Such choice for any taxable year may be made or changed at any time before the expiration of the period prescribed for making a claim for credit or refund of the tax imposed by this chapter for such taxable year. The credit shall not be allowed against any tax treated as a tax not imposed by this chapter under section 26(b).

*Omitted.

(b) Amount allowed.—Subject to the limitation of section 904, the following amounts shall be allowed as the credit under subsection (a):

(1) Citizens and domestic corporations.—In the case of a citizen of the United States and of a domestic corporation, the amount of any income, war profits, and excess profits taxes paid or accrued during the taxable year to any foreign country or to any possession of the United States; and

(2) Resident of the United States or Puerto Rico.—In the case of a resident of the United States and in the case of an individual who is a bona fide resident of Puerto Rico during the entire taxable year, the amount of any such taxes paid or accrued during the taxable year to any possession of the United States; and

(3) Alien resident of the United States or Puerto Rico.—In the case of an alien resident of the United States and in the case of an alien individual who is a bona fide resident of Puerto Rico during the entire taxable year, the amount of any such taxes paid or accrued during the taxable year to any foreign country; and

(4) Nonresident alien individuals and foreign corporations.—In the case of any nonresident alien individual not described in section 876 and in the case of any foreign corporation, the amount determined pursuant to section 906; and

(5) Partnerships and estates.—In the case of any person described in paragraph (1), (2), (3), or (4), who is a member of a partnership or a beneficiary of an estate or trust, the amount of his proportionate share of the taxes (described in such paragraph) of the partnership or the estate or trust paid or accrued during the taxable year to a foreign country or to any possession of the United States, as the case may be.

* * *

(j) Denial of foreign tax credit, etc., with respect to certain foreign countries.—

(1) In general.—Notwithstanding any other provision of this part—

(A) no credit shall be allowed under subsection (a) for any income, war profits, or excess profits taxes paid or accrued (or deemed paid under section 902 or 960) to any country if such taxes are with respect to income attributable to a period during which this subsection applies to such country, and

(B) subsections (a), (b), and (c) of section 904 and sections 902 and 960 shall be applied separately with respect to income attributable to such a period from sources within such country.

(2) Countries to which subsection applies.—

(A) In general.—This subsection shall apply to any foreign country—

(i) the government of which the United States does not recognize, unless such government is otherwise eligible to purchase defense articles or services under the Arms Export Control Act,

(ii) with respect to which the United States has severed diplomatic relations,

(iii) with respect to which the United States has not severed diplomatic relations but does not conduct such relations, or

(iv) which the Secretary of State has, pursuant to section 6(j) of the Export Administration Act of 1979, as amended, designated as a foreign country which repeatedly provides support for acts of international terrorisms.

(B) Period for which subsection applies.—This subsection shall apply to any foreign country described in subparagraph (A) during the period—

(i) beginning on the later of—

(I) January 1, 1987, or

(II) 6 months after such country becomes a country described in subparagraph (A), and

(ii) ending on the date the Secretary of State certifies to the Secretary of the Treasury that such country is no longer described in subparagraph (A).

(C) Special rule for South Africa.—

(i) In general.—In addition to any period during which this subsection would otherwise apply to South Africa, this subsection shall apply to South Africa during the period—

(I) beginning on January 1, 1988, and

(II) ending on the date the Secretary of State certifies to the Secretary of the Treasury that South Africa meets the requirements of section 311(a) of the Comprehensive Anti-Apartheid Act of 1986 (as in effect on the date of the enactment of this subparagraph).

(ii) South Africa defined.—For purposes of clause (i), the term "South Africa" has the meaning given to such term by paragraph (6) of section 3 of the Comprehensive Anti-Apartheid Act of 1986 (as so in effect).

(3) Taxes allowed as a deduction.—Sections 275 and 78 shall not apply to any tax which is not allowable as a credit under subsection (a) by reason of this subsection.

(4) Regulations.—The Secretary shall prescribe such regulations as may be necessary or appropriate to carry out the purposes of this subsection, including regulations which treat income paid through 1 or more entities as derived from a foreign country to which this subsection applies if such income was, without regard to such entities, derived from such country.

* * *

§ 904. Limitation on credit

(a) Limitation.—The total amount of the credit taken under section 901(a) shall not exceed the same proportion of the tax against which such credit is taken which the taxpayer's taxable income from sources without the United States (but not in excess of the taxpayer's entire taxable income) bears to his entire taxable income for the same taxable year.

(b) Taxable income for purpose of computing limitation.—

(1) Personal exemptions.—For purposes of subsection (a), the taxable income in the case of an individual, estate, or trust shall be computed without any deduction for personal exemptions under section 151 or 642(b).

(2) Capital gains.—For purposes of this section—

(A) In general.—Taxable income from sources outside the United States shall include gain from the sale or exchange of capital assets only to the extent of foreign source capital gain net income.

(B) Special rules where capital gain rate differential.—In the case of any taxable year for which there is a capital gain rate differential—

(i) in lieu of applying subparagraph (A), the taxable income from sources outside the United States shall include gain from the sale or exchange of capital assets only in an amount equal to foreign source capital gain net income reduced by the rate differential portion of foreign source net capital gain,

(ii) the entire taxable income shall include gain from the sale or exchange of capital assets only in an amount equal to capital gain net income reduced by the rate differential portion of net capital gain, and

(iii) for purposes of determining taxable income from sources outside the United States, any net capital loss (and any amount which is a short-term capital loss under section 1212(a)) from sources outside the United States to the extent taken into account in determining capital gain net income for the taxable year shall be reduced by an amount equal to the rate differential portion of the excess of net capital gain from sources within the United States over net capital gain.

(C) Coordination with capital gains rates.—The Secretary may by regulations modify the application of this paragraph and paragraph (3) to the extent necessary to properly reflect any capital gain rate differential under section 1(h) or 1201(a) and the computation of net capital gain.

(3) Definitions.—For purposes of this subsection—

(A) Foreign source capital gain net income.—The term "foreign source capital gain net income" means the lesser of—

(i) capital gain net income from sources without the United States, or

(ii) capital gain net income.

(B) Foreign source net capital gain.—The term "foreign source net capital gain" means the lesser of—

(i) net capital gain from sources without the United States, or

(ii) net capital gain.

(C) Section 1231 gains.—The term "gain from the sale or exchange of capital assets" includes any gain so treated under section 1231.

(D) Capital gain rate differential.—There is a capital gain rate differential for any taxable year if—

(i) in the case of a taxpayer other than a corporation, subsection (h) of section 1 applies to such taxable year, or

(ii) in the case of a corporation, any rate of tax imposed by section 11, 511, or 831(a) or (b) (whichever applies) exceeds the alternative rate of tax under section 1201(a) (determined without regard to the last sentence of section 11(b)).

(E) Rate differential portion.—

(i) In general.—The rate differential portion of foreign source net capital gain, net capital gain, or the excess of net capital gain from sources within the United States over net capital gain, as the case may be, is the same proportion of such amount as—

(I) the excess of the highest applicable tax rate over the alternative tax rate, bears to

(II) the highest applicable tax rate.

(ii) Highest applicable tax rate.—For purposes of clause (i), the term "highest applicable tax rate" means—

(I) in the case of a taxpayer other than a corporation, the highest rate of tax set forth in subsection (a), (b), (c), (d), or (e) of section 1 (whichever applies), or

(II) in the case of a corporation, the highest rate of tax specified in section 11 (b).

(iii) Alternative tax rate.—For purposes of clause (i), the term "alternative tax rate" means—

(I) in the case of a taxpayer other than a corporation, the alternative rate of tax determined under section 1(h), or

(II) in the case of a corporation, the alternative rate of tax under section 1201(a).

* * *

(c) Carryback and carryover of excess tax paid.—Any amount by which all taxes paid or accrued to foreign countries or possessions of the United States for any taxable year for which the taxpayer chooses to have the benefits of this subpart exceed the limitation under subsection (a) shall be deemed taxes paid or accrued to foreign countries or possessions of the United States in the first preceding taxable year and in any of the first 10 succeeding taxable years, in that order and to the extent not deemed taxes paid or accrued in a prior taxable year, in the amount by which the limitation under subsection (a) for such preceding or succeeding taxable year exceeds the sum of the taxes paid or accrued to foreign countries or possessions of the United States for such preceding or succeeding taxable year and the amount of the taxes for any taxable year earlier than the current taxable year which shall be deemed to have been paid or accrued in such preceding or subsequent taxable year (whether or not the taxpayer chooses to have the benefits of this subpart with respect to such earlier taxable year). Such amount deemed paid or accrued in any year may be availed of only as a tax credit and not as a deduction and only if the taxpayer for such year chooses to have the benefits of this subpart as to taxes paid or accrued for that year to foreign countries or possessions of the United States.

* * *

(j) Certain individuals exempt.—

(1) In general.—In the case of an individual to whom this subsection applies for any taxable year—

(A) the limitation of subsection (a) shall not apply,

(B) no taxes paid or accrued by the individual during such taxable year may be deemed paid or accrued under subsection (c) in any other taxable year, and

(C) no taxes paid or accrued by the individual during any other taxable year may be deemed paid or accrued under subsection (c) in such taxable year.

(2) Individuals to whom subsection applies.—This subsection shall apply to an individual for any taxable year if—

(A) the entire amount of such individual's gross income for the taxable year from sources without the United States consists of qualified passive income,

(B) the amount of the creditable foreign taxes paid or accrued by the individual during the taxable year does not exceed $300 ($600 in the case of a joint return), and

(C) such individual elects to have this subsection apply for the taxable year.

(3) Definitions.—For purposes of this subsection—

(A) Qualified passive income.—The term "qualified passive income" means any item of gross income if—

(i) such item of income is passive income (as defined in subsection (d)(2)(A) without regard to clause (iii) thereof), and

(ii) such item of income is shown on a payee statement furnished to the individual.

(B) Creditable foreign taxes.—The term "creditable foreign taxes" means any taxes for which a credit is allowable under section 901;

except that such term shall not include any tax unless such tax is shown on a payee statement furnished to such individual.

(C) Payee statement.—The term "payee statement" has the meaning given to such term by section 6724(d)(2).

(D) Estate and trusts not eligible.—This subsection shall not apply to any estate or trust.

(k) Cross references.—

* * *

(2) For modification of limitation under subsection (a) for purposes of determining the amount of credit which can be taken against the alternative minimum tax, see section 59(a).

§ 905. Applicable rules

(a) Year in which credit taken.—The credits provided in this subpart may, at the option of the taxpayer and irrespective of the method of accounting employed in keeping his books, be taken in the year in which the taxes of the foreign country or the possession of the United States accrued, subject, however, to the conditions prescribed in subsection (c). If the taxpayer elects to take such credits in the year in which the taxes of the foreign country or the possession of the United States accrued, the credits for all subsequent years shall be taken on the same basis, and no portion of any such taxes shall be allowed as a deduction in the same or any succeeding year.

(b) Proof of credits.—The credits provided in this subpart shall be allowed only if the taxpayer establishes to the satisfaction of the Secretary—

(1) the total amount of income derived from sources without the United States, determined as provided in part I,

(2) the amount of income derived from each country, the tax paid or accrued to which is claimed as a credit under this subpart, such amount to be determined under regulations prescribed by the Secretary, and

(3) all other information necessary for the verification and computation of such credits.

(c) Adjustments to accrued taxes.—

(1) In general.—If—

(A) accrued taxes when paid differ from the amounts claimed as credits by the taxpayer,

(B) accrued taxes are not paid before the date 2 years after the close of the taxable year to which such taxes relate, or

(C) any tax paid is refunded in whole or in part,

the taxpayer shall notify the Secretary, who shall redetermine the amount of the tax for the year or years affected. The Secretary may prescribe adjustments to the pools of post-1986 foreign income taxes and the pools of post-1986 undistributed earnings under sections 902 and 960 in lieu of the redetermination under the preceding sentence.

(2) Special rules for taxes not paid within 2 years.—

(A) In general.—Except as provided in subparagraph (B), in making the redetermination under paragraph (1), no credit shall be allowed for accrued taxes not paid before the date referred to in subparagraph (B) of paragraph (1).

(B) Taxes subsequently paid.—Any such taxes if subsequently paid—

(i) shall be taken into account—

(I) in the case of taxes deemed paid under section 902 or section 960, for the taxable year in which paid (and no redetermination shall be made under this section by reason of such payment), and

(II) in any other case, for the taxable year to which such taxes relate, and

(ii) shall be translated as provided in section 986(a)(2)(A).

(3) Adjustments—The amount of tax (if any) due on any redetermination under paragraph (1) shall be paid by the taxpayer on notice and demand by the Secretary, and the amount of tax overpaid (if any) shall be credited or refunded to the taxpayer in accordance with subchapter B of chapter 66 (section 6511 et seq.).

(4) Bond requirements.—In the case of any tax accrued but not paid, the Secretary, as a condition precedent to the allowance of the credit provided in this subpart, may require the taxpayer to give a bond, with sureties satisfactory to and approved by the Secretary, in such sum as the Secretary may require, conditioned on the payment by the taxpayer of any amount of tax found due on any such redetermination. Any such bond shall contain such further conditions as the Secretary may require.

(5) Other special rules.—In any redetermination under paragraph (1) by the Secretary of the amount of tax due from the taxpayer for the year or years affected by a refund, the amount of the taxes refunded for which credit has been allowed under this section shall be reduced by the amount of any tax described in section 901 imposed by the foreign country or possession of the United States with respect to such refund; but no credit under this subpart, or deduction under section 164, shall be allowed for any taxable year with respect to any such tax imposed on the refund. No interest shall be assessed or collected on any amount of tax due on any redetermination by the Secretary, resulting from a refund to the taxpayer, for any period before the receipt of such refund, except to the extent interest was paid by the foreign country or possession of the United States on such refund for such period.

* * *

SUBPART B—EARNED INCOME OF CITIZENS OR RESIDENTS OF UNITED STATES

Editorial Summary

Foreign Earned Income Exclusion

Subchapter N of Chapter 1 (Sec. 911)

See the discussion under the Editorial Summary entitled Foreign Tax Credit and Foreign Earned Income Exclusion, which precedes Sec. 901.

§ 911. Citizens or residents of the United States living abroad

(a) Exclusion from gross income.—At the election of a qualified individual (made separately with respect to paragraphs (1) and (2)), there shall be excluded from the gross income of such individual, and exempt from taxation under this subtitle, for any taxable year—

(1) the foreign earned income of such individual, and

(2) the housing cost amount of such individual.

(b) Foreign earned income.—

(1) Definition.—For purposes of this section—

(A) In general.—The term "foreign earned income" with respect to any individual means the amount received by such individual from sources within a foreign country or countries which constitute earned income attributable to services performed by such individual during the period described in subparagraph (A) or (B) of subsection (d)(1), whichever is applicable.

(B) Certain amounts not included in foreign earned income.—The foreign earned income for an individual shall not include amounts—

(i) received as a pension or annuity,

(ii) paid by the United States or an agency thereof to an employee of the United States or an agency thereof,

(iii) included in gross income by reason of section 402(b) (relating to taxability of beneficiary of nonexempt trust) or section 403(c) (relating to taxability of beneficiary under a nonqualified annuity), or

(iv) received after the close of the taxable year following the taxable year in which the services to which the amounts are attributable are performed.

(2) Limitation on foreign earned income.—

(A) In general.—The foreign earned income of an individual which may be excluded under subsection (a)(1) for any taxable year shall not exceed the amount of foreign earned income computed on a daily basis at an annual rate equal to the exclusion amount for the calendar year in which such taxable year begins.

(B) Attribution to year in which services are performed.—For purposes of applying subparagraph (A), amounts received shall be considered received in the taxable year in which the services to which the amounts are attributable are performed.

(C) Treatment of community income.—In applying subparagraph (A) with respect to amounts received from services performed by a husband or wife which are community income under community property laws applicable to such income, the aggregate amount which may be excludable from the gross income of such husband and wife under subsection (a)(1) for any taxable year shall equal the amount which would be so excludable if such amounts did not constitute community income.

(D) Exclusion amount.—

(i) In general.—The exclusion amount for any calendar year is the exclusion amount determined in accordance with the following table (as adjusted by clause (ii)):

For calendar year:	The exclusion amount is
1998	$72,000
1999	74,000
2000	76,000
2001	78,000
2002 and thereafter	80,000*

(ii) Inflation adjustment.—In the case of any taxable year beginning in a calendar year after 2005, the $80,000 amount in clause (i) shall be increased by an amount equal to the product of—

(I) such dollar amount, and

(II) the cost-of-living adjustment determined under section 1(f)(3) for the calendar year in which the taxable year begins, determined by substituting "2004" for "1992" in subparagraph (B) thereof.

If any increase determined under the preceding sentence is not a multiple of $100, such increase shall be rounded to the next lowest multiple of $100.

(c) Housing cost amount.—For purposes of this section—

(1) In general.—The term "housing cost amount" means an amount equal to the excess of—

(A) the housing expenses of an individual for the taxable year to the extent such expenses do not exceed the amount determined under paragraph (2), over

(B) an amount equal to the product of—

(i) 16 percent of the amount (computed on a daily basis) in effect under subsection (b)(2)(D) for the calendar year in which such taxable year begins, multiplied by

(ii) the number of days of such taxable year within the applicable period described in subparagraph (A) or (B) of subsection (d)(1).

(2) Limitation.—

(A) In general.—The amount determined under this paragraph is an amount equal to the product of—

(i) 30 percent (adjusted as may be provided under subparagraph (B)) of the amount (computed on a daily basis) in effect under subsection (b)(2)(D) for the calendar year in which the taxable year of the individual begins, multiplied by

(ii) the number of days of such taxable year within the applicable period described in subparagraph (A) or (B) of subsection (d)(1).

(B) Regulations.—The Secretary may issue regulations or other guidance providing for the adjustment of the percentage under subparagraph (A)(i) on the basis of geographic differences in housing costs relative to housing costs in the United States.

(3) Housing expenses.—

(A) In general.—The term "housing expenses" means the reasonable expenses paid or incurred during the taxable year by or on behalf of an individual for housing for the individual (and, if they reside with him, for his spouse and dependents) in a foreign country. The term—

(i) includes expenses attributable to the housing (such as utilities and insurance), but

(ii) does not include interest and taxes of the kind deductible under section 163 or 164 or any amount allowable as a deduction under section 216(a).

Housing expenses shall not be treated as reasonable to the extent such expenses are lavish or extravagant under the circumstances.

(B) Second foreign household.—

(i) In general.—Except as provided in clause (ii), only housing expenses incurred with respect to that abode which bears the closest relationship to the tax home of the individual shall be taken into account under paragraph (1).

(ii) Separate household for spouse and dependents.—If an individual maintains a separate abode outside the United States for his spouse and dependents and they do not reside with him because of living conditions which are dangerous, unhealthful, or otherwise adverse, then—

(I) the words "if they reside with him" in subparagraph (A) shall be disregarded, and

*Editorial comment: This amount is indexed for inflation beginning in 2006. For 2013, the indexed amount is $97,600 and for 2014 the indexed amount is $99,200.

(II) the housing expenses incurred with respect to such abode shall be taken into account under paragraph (1).

(4) Special rules where housing expenses not provided by employer.—

(A) In general.—To the extent the housing cost amount of any individual for any taxable year is not attributable to employer provided amounts, such amount shall be treated as a deduction allowable in computing adjusted gross income to the extent of the limitation of subparagraph (B).

(B) Limitation.—For purposes of subparagraph (A), the limitation of this subparagraph is the excess of—

(i) the foreign earned income of the individual for the taxable year, over

(ii) the amount of such income excluded from gross income under subsection (a) for the taxable year.

(C) 1-year carryover of housing amounts not allowed by reason of subparagraph (B).—

(i) In general.—The amount not allowable as a deduction for any taxable year under subparagraph (A) by reason of the limitation of subparagraph (B) shall be treated as a deduction allowable in computing adjusted gross income for the succeeding taxable year (and only for the succeeding taxable year) to the extent of the limitation of clause (ii) for such succeeding taxable year.

(ii) Limitation.—For purposes of clause (i), the limitation of this clause for any taxable year is the excess of—

(I) the limitation of subparagraph (B) for such taxable year, over

(II) amounts treated as a deduction under subparagraph (A) for such taxable year.

(D) Employer provided amounts.—For purposes of this paragraph, the term "employer provided amounts" means any amount paid or incurred on behalf of the individual by the individual's employer which is foreign earned income included in the individual's gross income for the taxable year (without regard to this section).

(E) Foreign earned income.—For purposes of this paragraph, an individual's foreign earned income for any taxable year shall be determined without regard to the limitation of subparagraph (A) of subsection (b)(2).

(d) Definitions and special rules.—For purposes of this section—

(1) Qualified individual.—The term "qualified individual" means an individual whose tax home is in a foreign country and who is—

(A) a citizen of the United States and establishes to the satisfaction of the Secretary that he has been a bona fide resident of a foreign country or countries for an uninterrupted period which includes an entire taxable year, or

(B) a citizen or resident of the United States and who, during any period of 12 consecutive months, is present in a foreign country or countries during at least 330 full days in such period.

(2) Earned income.—

(A) In general.—The term "earned income" means wages, salaries, or professional fees, and other amounts received as compensation for personal services actually rendered, but does not include that part of the compensation derived by the taxpayer for personal services rendered by him to a corporation which represents a distribution of earnings or profits rather than a reasonable allowance as compensation for the personal services actually rendered.

(B) Taxpayer engaged in trade or business.—In the case of a taxpayer engaged in a trade or business in which both personal services and capital are material income-producing factors, under regulations prescribed by the Secretary, a reasonable allowance as compensation for the personal services rendered by the taxpayer, not in excess of 30 percent of his share of the net profits of such trade or business, shall be considered as earned income.

(3) Tax home.—The term "tax home" means, with respect to any individual, such individual's home for purposes of section 162(a)(2) (relating to traveling expenses while away from home). An individual shall not be treated as having a tax home in a foreign country for any period for which his abode is within the United States.

(4) Waiver of period of stay in foreign country.—Notwithstanding paragraph (1), an individual who—

(A) is a bona fide resident of, or is present in, a foreign country for any period,

(B) leaves such foreign country after August 31, 1978—

(i) during any period during which the Secretary determines, after consultation with the Secretary of State or his delegate, that individuals were required to leave such foreign country because of war, civil unrest, or similar adverse conditions in such foreign country which precluded the normal conduct of business by such individuals, and

(ii) before meeting the requirements of such paragraph (1), and

(C) establishes to the satisfaction of the Secretary that such individual could reasonably have been expected to have met such requirements but for the conditions referred to in clause (i) of subparagraph (B),

shall be treated as a qualified individual with respect to the period described in subparagraph (A) during which he was a bona fide resident of, or was present in, the foreign country, and in applying subsections (b)(2)(A), (c)(1)(B)(ii), and (c)(2)(A)(ii) with respect to such individual, only the days within such period shall be taken into account.

(5) Test of bona fide residence.—If—

(A) an individual who has earned income from sources within a foreign country submits a statement to the authorities of that country that he is not a resident of that country, and

(B) such individual is held not subject as a resident of that country to the income tax of that country by its authorities with respect to such earnings,

then such individual shall not be considered a bona fide resident of that country for purposes of paragraph (1)(A).

(6) Denial of double benefits.—No deduction or exclusion from gross income under this subtitle or credit against the tax imposed by this chapter (including any credit or deduction for the amount of taxes paid or accrued to a foreign country or possession of the United States) shall be allowed to the extent such deduction, exclusion, or credit is properly allocable to or chargeable against amounts excluded from gross income under subsection (a).

(7) Aggregate benefit cannot exceed foreign earned income.—The sum of the amount excluded under subsection (a) and the amount deducted under subsection (c)(4)(A) for the taxable year shall not exceed the individual's foreign earned income for such year.

(8) Limitation on income earned in restricted country.—

(A) In general.—If travel (or any transaction in connection with such travel) with respect to any foreign country is subject to the regulations described in subparagraph (B) during any period—

(i) the term "foreign earned income" shall not include any income from sources within such country attributable to services performed during such period,

(ii) the term "housing expenses" shall not include any expenses allocable to such period for housing in such country or for housing of the spouse or dependents of the taxpayer in another country while the taxpayer is present in such country, and

(iii) an individual shall not be treated as a bona fide resident of, or as present in, a foreign country for any day during which such individual was present in such country during such period.

(B) Regulations.—For purposes of this paragraph, regulations are described in this subparagraph if such regulations—

(i) have been adopted pursuant to the Trading With the Enemy Act (50 U.S.C. App. 1 et seq.), or the International Emergency Economic Powers Act (50 U.S.C. 1701 et seq.), and

(ii) include provisions generally prohibiting citizens and residents of the United States from engaging in transactions related to travel to, from, or within a foreign country.

(C) Exception.—Subparagraph (A) shall not apply to any individual during any period in which such individual's activities are not in violation of the regulations described in subparagraph (B).

(9) Regulations.—The Secretary shall prescribe such regulations as may be necessary or appropriate to carry out the purposes of this section, including regulations providing rules—

(A) for cases where a husband and wife each have earned income from sources outside the United States, and

(B) for married individuals filing separate returns.

(e) Election.—

(1) In general.—An election under subsection (a) shall apply to the taxable year for which made and to all subsequent taxable years unless revoked under paragraph (2).

(2) Revocation.—A taxpayer may revoke an election made under paragraph (1) for any taxable year after the taxable year for which such election was made. Except with the consent of the Secretary, any taxpayer who makes such a revocation for any taxable year may not make another election under this section for any subsequent taxable year before the 6th taxable year after the taxable year for which such revocation was made.

(f) Determination of tax liability.—

(1) In general.—If, for any taxable year, any amount is excluded from gross income of a taxpayer under subsection (a), then, notwithstanding sections 1 and 55—

(A) if such taxpayer has taxable income for such taxable year, the tax imposed by section 1 for such taxable year shall be equal to the excess (if any) of—

(i) the tax which would be imposed by section 1 for such taxable year if the taxpayer's taxable income were increased by the amount excluded under subsection (a) for such taxable year, over

(ii) the tax which would be imposed by section 1 for such taxable year if the taxpayer's taxable income were equal to the amount excluded under subsection (a) for such taxable year, and

(B) if such taxpayer has a taxable excess (as defined in section 55(b)(1)(A)(ii)) for such taxable year, the amount determined under the first sentence of section 55(b)(1)(A)(i) for such taxable year shall be equal to the excess (if any) of—

(i) the amount which would be determined under such sentence for such taxable year (subject to the limitation of section 55(b)(3)) if the taxpayer's taxable excess (as so defined) were increased by the amount excluded under subsection (a) for such taxable year, over

(ii) the amount which would be determined under such sentence for such taxable year if the taxpayer's taxable excess (as so defined) were equal to the amount excluded under subsection (a) for such taxable year.

(2) Special rules.—

(A) Regular tax.—In applying section 1(h) for purposes of determining the tax under paragraph (1)(A)(i) for any taxable year in which, without regard to this subsection, the taxpayer's net capital gain exceeds taxable income (hereafter in this subparagraph referred to as the capital gain excess)—

(i) the taxpayer's net capital gain (determined without regard to section 1(h)(11)) shall be reduced (but not below zero) by such capital gain excess,

(ii) the taxpayer's qualified dividend income shall be reduced by so much of such capital gain excess as exceeds the taxpayer's net capital gain (determined without regard to section 1(h)(11) and the reduction under clause (i)), and

(iii) adjusted net capital gain, unrecaptured section 1250 gain, and 28-percent rate gain shall each be determined after increasing the amount described in section 1(h)(4)(B) by such capital gain excess.

(B) Alternative minimum tax.—In applying section 55(b)(3) for purposes of determining the tax under paragraph (1)(B)(i) for any taxable year in which, without regard to this subsection, the taxpayer's net capital gain exceeds the taxable excess (as defined in section 55(b)(1)(A)(ii))—

(i) the rules of subparagraph (A) shall apply, except that such subparagraph shall be applied by substituting "the taxable excess (as defined in section 55(b)(1)(A)(ii))" for "taxable income," and

(ii) the reference in section 55(b)(3)(B) to the excess described in section 1(h)(1)(B) shall be treated as a reference to such excess as determined under the rules of subparagraph (A) for purposes of determining the tax under paragraph (1)(A)(i).

(C) Definitions.—Terms used in this paragraph which are also used in section 1(h) shall have the respective meanings given such terms by section 1(h), except that in applying subparagraph (B) the adjustments under part IV of subchapter A shall be taken into account.

* * *

*SUBPART C—TAXATION OF FOREIGN SALES CORPORATIONS**

*SUBPART D—POSSESSIONS OF THE UNITED STATES**

*SUBPART E—QUALIFYING FOREIGN TRADE INCOME**

*SUBPART F—CONTROLLED FOREIGN CORPORATIONS**

*SUBPART G—EXPORT TRADE CORPORATIONS**

*SUBPART H—[REPEALED]**

*SUBPART I—ADMISSIBILITY OF DOCUMENTATION MAINTAINED IN FOREIGN COUNTRIES**

*SUBPART J—FOREIGN CURRENCY TRANSACTIONS**

PART IV—DOMESTIC INTERNATIONAL SALES CORPORATIONS*

PART V—INTERNATIONAL BOYCOTT DETERMINATIONS*

*Omitted.

SUBCHAPTER O—GAIN OR LOSS ON DISPOSITION OF PROPERTY

Editorial Summary

Property Transactions: General

Subchapter O of Chapter 1 (Secs. 1001–1092)

From an overview perspective, Subchapter O deals with the following issues:

1. Has a transaction taken place that is subject to taxation?

A sale, exchange, or other disposition must occur before a taxable property transaction has occurred [see Sec. 1001]. The mere increase or decrease in the fair market value of an asset is not subject to taxation.

2. What is the adjusted basis of the property that is being sold, exchanged, or otherwise disposed of?

In determining the adjusted basis of property, consideration must be given to how the property was acquired.

Acquisition method	Basis calculation
Purchase	Cost (i.e. fair market value) [Sec. 1012]
Taxable exchange	Fair market value
Nontaxable exchange	Adjusted basis of property given + Adjusted basis of boot given + Gain recognized – FMV of boot received – Loss recognized or FMV of property received – Realized gain not recognized + Realized loss not recognized
Inheritance	FMV at date of death or FMV 6 months after death [Sec. 1014]
Gift	Gain basis: Donor's adjusted basis + gift tax paid on appreciation Loss basis: Lower of gain basis or FMV at date of gift [Sec. 1015]
Personal use property converted to business use	Gain basis: Adjusted basis at conversion date Loss basis: Lower of gain basis or FMV at conversion date

Once the initial basis is determined, it must be increased by capital expenditures [see Sec. 263] and decreased by allowable deductions such as depreciation [see Sec. 167], cost recovery [see Sec. 168], limited expensing [see Sec. 179], amortization [see Secs. 169, 174, 178, 197, 248], and depletion [see Secs. 611, 613].

3. What is the realized gain or loss?

The realized gain is the excess of the amount realized (i.e., net proceeds or inflows) over the adjusted basis of the property transferred, whereas the realized loss is the excess of the adjusted basis over the amount realized. The term "realized" represents the potentially taxable amount [see Sec. 1001].

4. What is the recognized gain or loss?

The term "recognized" represents the amount that actually is included in gross income (i.e., taxed). Under the general rule, realized gains and losses are recognized [see Sec. 1001 (c)]. However, numerous exceptions exist. First, the realized gain or loss may be deferred or postponed [see Secs. 1031–1045 in Subchapter O, 351 in Subchapter C, 721 in Subchapter K]. In working with the deferral rules, caution must be exercised in ascertaining whether the deferral provision is elective or mandatory. Second, the realized gain may be excluded [see Sec. 121 in Subchapter B]. Third, the realized loss may be disallowed [see Sec. 262 in Subchapter B for losses on personal use property, Sec. 267 in Subchapter B for losses on related party transactions, Sec. 269 in Subchapter B for losses on acquisitions made to evade or avoid income tax].

5. What is the basis of property received?

The basis of the property received in a property transaction is dependent on how the property was acquired. See the discussion in category 2 above. It is important to distinguish between an amount that has been disallowed and an amount that has been deferred. The deferred amount will impact on the basis of the property received, whereas the disallowed amount will not. For example, if loss is deferred in a Sec. 1031 like-kind exchange, the fair market value of the property received is increased by the deferred loss in calculating the basis of the like-kind property received. However, if loss is disallowed on the sale of a personal use residence, the basis of a replacement residence is merely the purchase price (i.e., the purchase price is not increased by the disallowed loss in calculating the basis of the replacement residence).

*Omitted.

PART I—DETERMINATION OF AMOUNT OF AND RECOGNITION OF GAIN OR LOSS

§ 1001. Determination of amount of and recognition of gain or loss

(a) Computation of gain or loss.—The gain from the sale or other disposition of property shall be the excess of the amount realized therefrom over the adjusted basis provided in section 1011 for determining gain, and the loss shall be the excess of the adjusted basis provided in such section for determining loss over the amount realized.

(b) Amount realized.—The amount realized from the sale or other disposition of property shall be the sum of any money received plus the fair market value of the property (other than money) received. In determining the amount realized—

(1) there shall not be taken into account any amount received as reimbursement for real property taxes which are treated under section 164(d) as imposed on the purchaser, and

(2) there shall be taken into account amounts representing real property taxes which are treated under section 164(d) as imposed on the taxpayer if such taxes are to be paid by the purchaser.

(c) Recognition of gain or loss.—Except as otherwise provided in this subtitle, the entire amount of the gain or loss, determined under this section, on the sale or exchange of property shall be recognized.

(d) Installment sales.—Nothing in this section shall be construed to prevent (in the case of property sold under contract providing for payment in installments) the taxation of that portion of any installment payment representing gain or profit in the year in which such payment is received.

(e) Certain term interests.—

(1) In general.—In determining gain or loss from the sale or other disposition of a term interest in property, that portion of the adjusted basis of such interest which is determined pursuant to section 1014, 1015, or 1041 (to the extent that such adjusted basis is a portion of the entire adjusted basis of the property) shall be disregarded.

(2) Term interest in property defined.—For purposes of paragraph (1), the term "term interest in property" means—

(A) a life interest in property,

(B) an interest in property for a term of years, or

(C) an income interest in a trust.

(3) Exception.—Paragraph (1) shall not apply to a sale or other disposition which is a part of a transaction in which the entire interest in property is transferred to any person or persons.

PART II—BASIS RULES OF GENERAL APPLICATION

Editorial Summary

Property Transactions: Basis

Subchapter O of Chapter 1 (Secs. 1011–1019)

See the discussion under the Editorial Summary entitled Property Transactions: General, which precedes Sec. 1001.

Several of the provisions discussed in the aforementioned Editorial Summary require additional comment. Included are the following:

1. Use of the alternate valuation date and amount for inherited property.

2. Death-bed gifts associated with inherited property.

3. Property acquired by gift before January 1, 1977.

4. Gifts or other transfers between spouses.

The primary valuation date for inherited property is the date of decedent's death and the alternate valuation date is 6 months after the decedent's death [see Secs. 1014(a) and 2032(a)]. The alternate valuation date can be used only if the executor elects to use it for estate tax purposes. The election is available to the executor only if the election results in a decrease in *both* the estate tax liability and the value of the gross estate [see Sec. 2032(c)].

Section 1014(e) is intended to eliminate the step-up in basis associated with so-called "death-bed" gifts.

Example: N owns stock with a basis of $2,000 and a fair market value of $7,000. N gives the stock to U who is terminally ill. Three months later N inherits the stock from U. At the date of U's death, the fair market value of the stock is $8,000. Under the general rule [see Sec. 1014(a)], N's basis for the inherited stock would be $8,000. However, the limitation imposed by the death-bed gift rule results in N's basis being only $2,000 [see Sec. 1014(e)].

In order for the death-bed gift limitation to apply, the time period between the date of the gift and the date of decedent's death must not be greater than one year.

The gain basis formula for gift property appearing in the previous Editorial Summary applies only for gifts made after December 31, 1976 [see Sec. 1015(d)(6)]. If the gift was made before January 1, 1977, the formula for the gain basis to the donee is as follows:

Donor's basis
\+ Gift tax paid
= Donee's basis

However, the addition of the gift tax paid is permitted only to the extent that it does not cause the summation to exceed the fair market value of the property at the date of the gift [see Sec. 1015(d)(1)(A)].

Transfers of property between spouses do not produce recognition (i.e., recognition of gain or loss) [see Sec. 1041(a)]. Therefore, the basis of the property to the transferee spouse stays the same as the transferor spouse's basis [see Secs. 1015(e) and 1041(b)].

Although generally not part of Subchapter O, the basis for an ownership interest for a partnership, C corporation, and S corporation are important tax concepts and can be used to illustrate the relationship between basis and the use of aggregate versus entity theory. Components that may impact on the basis of an ownership interest included investments (and disinvestments), profits and losses, and liabilities.

Basis for Partnership Interest (Secs. 705, 722, and 752)

Decrease	Increase
Disinvestment	Investment
Share of losses	Share of profits
Share of partnership liability decrease	Share of partnership liability increase

Basis for S Corporation Stock (Secs. 358 and 1367)

Decrease	Increase
Disinvestment	Investment
Share of losses	Share of profits

Basis for C Corporation Stock (Sec. 358)

Decrease	Increase
Disinvestment (exclude dividend distributions)	Investment

For the partnership, aggregate theory applies to all three components. For the S Corporation, aggregate theory applies to only two of the components. Liabilities not affecting stock basis is logical since the liability is that of the corporation rather than that of the shareholder. For the C corporation, only one of the three components affects stock basis. The liabilities are those of the corporation rather than those of the shareholder. Likewise, the profits and losses are those of the corporation, since the corporation is subject to taxation.

Note that if an ownership interest is purchased in the marketplace from an owner, then Subchapter O does apply to the basis for the acquisition (i.e., under Sec. 1014, the basis is the cost). Also note that for the C corporation and the S corporation, a carryover stock basis (i.e., aggregate theory) applies rather than a fair market value basis (i.e., entity theory) associated with the assets contributed by a shareholder only if the control requirement is satisfied [Sec. 351 and Sec. 368(c)].

§ 1011. Adjusted basis for determining gain or loss

(a) General rule.—The adjusted basis for determining the gain or loss from the sale or other disposition of property, whenever acquired, shall be the basis (determined under section 1012 or other applicable sections of this subchapter and subchapters C (relating to corporate distributions and adjustments), K (relating to partners and partnerships), and P (relating to capital gains and losses)), adjusted as provided in section 1016.

(b) Bargain sale to a charitable organization.—If a deduction is allowable under section 170 (relating to charitable contributions) by reason of a sale, then the adjusted basis for determining the gain from such sale shall be that portion of the adjusted basis which bears the same ratio to the adjusted basis as the amount realized bears to the fair market value of the property.

§ 1012. Basis of property—cost

(a) In general.—The basis of property shall be the cost of such property, except as otherwise provided in this subchapter and subchapters C (relating to corporate distributions and adjustments), K (relating to partners and partnerships), and P (relating to capital gains and losses).

(b) Special rule for apportioned real estate taxes.—The cost of real property shall not include any amount in respect of real property taxes which are treated under section 164(d) as imposed on the taxpayer.

(c) Determinations by account.—

(1) In general.—In the case of the sale, exchange, or other disposition of a specified security on or after the applicable date, the conventions prescribed by regulations under this section shall be applied on an account by account basis.

(2) Application to certain funds.—

(A) In general.—Except as provided in subparagraph (B), any stock for which an average basis method is permissible under section 1012 which is acquired before January 1, 2012, shall be treated as a separate account from any such stock acquired on or after such date.

(B) Election fund for treatment as single account.—If a fund described in subparagraph (A) elects to have this subparagraph apply with respect to one or more of its stockholders—

(i) subparagraph (A) shall not apply with respect to any stock in such fund held by such stockholders, and

(ii) all stock in such fund which is held by such stockholders shall be treated as covered securities described in section 6045(g)(3) without regard to the date of the acquisition of such stock.

A rule similar to the rule of the preceding sentence shall apply with respect to a broker holding such stock as a nominee.

(3) Definitions.—For purposes of this section, the terms "specified security" and "applicable date" shall have the meaning given such terms in section 6045(g).

(d) Average basis for stock acquired pursuant to a dividend reinvestment plan.—

(1) In general.—In the case of any stock acquired after December 31, 2010, in connection with a dividend reinvestment plan, the basis of such stock while held as part of such plan shall be determined using one of the methods which may be used for determining the basis of stock in an open-end fund.

(2) Treatment after transfer.—In the case of the transfer to another account of stock to which paragraph (1) applies, such stock shall have a cost basis in such other account equal to its basis in the dividend reinvestment plan immediately before such transfer (properly adjusted for any fees or other charges taken into account in connection with such transfer).

(3) Separate accounts; election for treatment as single account.—Rules similar to the rules of subsection (c)(2) shall apply for purposes of this subsection.

(4) Dividend reinvestment plan.—For purposes of this subsection—

(A) In general.—The term "dividend reinvestment plan" means any arrangement under which dividends on any stock are reinvested in stock identical to the stock with respect to which the dividends are paid.

(B) Initial stock acquisition treated as acquired in connection with plan.—Stock shall be treated as acquired in connection with a dividend reinvestment plan if such stock is acquired pursuant to such plan or if the dividends paid on such stock are subject to such plan.

§ 1013. Basis of property included in inventory

If the property should have been included in the last inventory, the basis shall be the last inventory value thereof.

§ 1014. Basis of property acquired from a decedent

(a) In general.—Except as otherwise provided in this section, the basis of property in the hands of a person acquiring the property from a decedent or to whom the property passed from a decedent shall, if not sold, exchanged, or otherwise disposed of before the decedent's death by such person, be—

(1) the fair market value of the property at the date of the decedent's death,

(2) in the case of an election under either section 2032 or section 811(j) of the Internal Revenue Code of 1939 where the decedent died after October 21, 1942, its value at the applicable valuation date prescribed by those sections,

(3) in the case of an election under section 2032A, its value determined under such section, or

(4) to the extent of the applicability of the exclusion described in section 2031(c), the basis in the hands of the decedent.

(b) Property acquired from the decedent.—For purposes of subsection (a), the following property shall be considered to have been acquired from or to have passed from the decedent:

(1) Property acquired by bequest, devise, or inheritance, or by the decedent's estate from the decedent;

(2) Property transferred by the decedent during his lifetime in trust to pay the income for life to or on the order or direction of the decedent, with the right reserved to the decedent at all times before his death to revoke the trust;

(3) In the case of decedents dying after December 31, 1951, property transferred by the decedent during his lifetime in trust to pay the income for life to or on the order or direction of the decedent with the right reserved to the decedent at all times before his death to make any change in the enjoyment thereof through the exercise of a power to alter, amend, or terminate the trust;

(4) Property passing without full and adequate consideration under a general power of appointment exercised by the decedent by will;

* * *

(6) In the case of decedents dying after December 31, 1947, property which represents the surviving spouse's one-half share of community property held by the decedent and the surviving spouse under the community property laws of any State, or possession of the United States or any foreign country, if at least one-half of the whole of the community interest in such property was includible in determining the value of the decedent's gross estate under chapter 11 of subtitle B (section 2001 and following, relating to estate tax) or section 811 of the Internal Revenue Code of 1939;

* * *

(9) In the case of decedents dying after December 31, 1953, property acquired from the decedent by reason of death, form of ownership, or other conditions (including property acquired through the exercise or non-exercise of a power of appointment), if by reason thereof the property is required to be included in determining the value of the decedent's gross estate under chapter 11 of subtitle B or under the Internal Revenue Code of 1939. In such case, if the property is acquired before the death of the decedent, the basis shall be the amount determined under subsection (a) reduced by the amount allowed to the taxpayer as deductions in computing taxable income under this subtitle or prior income tax laws for exhaustion, wear and tear, obsolescence, amortization, and depletion on such property before the death of the decedent. Such basis shall be applicable to the property commencing on the death of the decedent. This paragraph shall not apply to—

(A) annuities described in section 72;

(B) property to which paragraph (5) would apply if the property had been acquired by bequest; and

(C) property described in any other paragraph of this subsection.

(10) Property includible in the gross estate of the decedent under section 2044 (relating to certain property for which marital deduction was previously allowed). In any such case, the last 3 sentences of paragraph (9) shall apply as if such property were described in the first sentence of paragraph (9).

(c) Property representing income in respect of a decedent.—This section shall not apply to property which constitutes a right to receive an item of income in respect of a decedent under section 691.

* * *

(e) Appreciated property acquired by decedent by gift within 1 year of death.—

(1) In general.—In the case of a decedent dying after December 31, 1981, if—

(A) appreciated property was acquired by the decedent by gift during the 1-year period ending on the date of the decedent's death, and

(B) such property is acquired from the decedent by (or passes from the decedent to) the donor of such property (or the spouse of such donor),

the basis of such property in the hands of such donor (or spouse) shall be the adjusted basis of such property in the hands of the decedent immediately before the death of the decedent.

(2) Definitions.—For purposes of paragraph (1)—

(A) Appreciated property.—The term "appreciated property" means any property if the fair market value of such property on the day it was transferred to the decedent by gift exceeds its adjusted basis.

(B) Treatment of certain property sold by estate.—In the case of any appreciated property described in subparagraph (A) of paragraph (1) sold by the estate of the decedent or by a trust of which the decedent was the grantor, rules similar to the rules of paragraph (1) shall apply to the extent the donor of such property (or the spouse of such donor) is entitled to the proceeds from such sale.

§ 1015. Basis of property acquired by gifts and transfers in trust

(a) Gifts after December 31, 1920.—If the property was acquired by gift after December 31, 1920, the basis shall be the same as it would be in the hands of the donor or the last preceding owner by whom it was not acquired by gift, except that if such basis (adjusted for the period before the date of the gift as provided in section 1016) is greater than the fair market value of the property at the time of the gift, then for the purpose of determining loss the basis shall be such fair market value. If the facts necessary to determine the basis in the hands of the donor or the last preceding owner are unknown to the donee, the Secretary shall, if possible, obtain such facts from such donor or last preceding owner, or any other person cognizant thereof. If the Secretary finds it impossible to obtain such facts, the basis in the hands of such donor or last preceding owner shall be the fair market value of such property as found by the Secretary as of the date or approximate date at which, according to the best information that the Secretary is able to obtain, such property was acquired by such donor or last preceding owner.

(b) Transfer in trust after December 31, 1920.—If the property was acquired after December 31, 1920, by a transfer in trust (other than by a transfer in trust by a gift, bequest, or devise), the basis shall be the same as it would be in the hands of the grantor increased in the amount of gain or decreased in the amount of loss recognized to the grantor on such transfer under the law applicable to the year in which the transfer was made.

(c) Gift or transfer in trust before January 1, 1921.—If the property was acquired by gift or transfer in trust on or before December 31, 1920, the basis shall be the fair market value of such property at the time of such acquisition.

(d) Increased basis for gift tax paid.—

(1) In general.—If—

(A) the property is acquired by gift on or after September 2, 1958, the basis shall be the basis determined under subsection (a), increased (but not above the fair market value of the property at the time of the gift) by the amount of gift tax paid with respect to such gift, or

(B) the property was acquired by gift before September 2, 1958, and has not been sold, exchanged, or otherwise disposed of before such date, the basis of the property shall be increased on such date by the amount of gift tax paid with respect to such gift, but such increase shall not exceed an amount equal to the amount by which the fair market value of the property at the time of the gift exceeded the basis of the property in the hands of the donor at the time of the gift.

(2) Amount of tax paid with respect to gift.—For purposes of paragraph (1), the amount of gift tax paid with respect to any gift is an amount which bears the same ratio to the amount of gift tax paid under chapter 12 with respect to all gifts made by the donor for the calendar year (or preceding calendar period) in which such gift is made as the amount of such gift bears to the taxable gifts (as defined in section 2503(a) but computed without the deduction allowed by section 2521) made by the donor during such calendar year or period. For purposes of the preceding sentence, the amount of any gift shall be the amount included with respect to such gift in determining (for the purposes of section 2503(a)) the total amount of gifts made during the calendar year or period, reduced by the amount of any deduction allowed with respect to such gift under section 2522 (relating to charitable deduction) or under section 2523 (relating to marital deduction).

(3) Gifts treated as made one-half by each spouse.—For purposes of paragraph (1), where the donor and his spouse elected, under section 2513 to have the gift considered as made one-half by each, the amount of gift tax paid with respect to such gift under chapter 12 shall be the sum of the amounts of tax paid with respect to each half of such gift (computed in the manner provided in paragraph (2)).

(4) Treatment as adjustment to basis.—For purposes of section 1016(b), an increase in basis under paragraph (1) shall be treated as an adjustment under section 1016(a).

* * *

(6) Special rule for gifts made after December 31, 1976.—

(A) In general.—In the case of any gift made after December 31, 1976, the increase in basis provided by this subsection with respect to any gift for the gift tax paid under chapter 12 shall be an amount (not in excess of the amount of tax so paid) which bears the same ratio to the amount of tax so paid as—

(i) the net appreciation in value of the gift, bears to

(ii) the amount of the gift.

(B) Net appreciation.—For purposes of paragraph (1), the net appreciation in value of any gift is the amount by which the fair market value of the gift exceeds the donor's adjusted basis immediately before the gift.

(e) Gifts between spouses.—In the case of any property acquired by gift in a transfer described in section 1041(a), the basis of such property in the hands of the transferee shall be determined under section 1041(b)(2) and not this section.

§ 1016. Adjustments to basis

(a) General rule.—Proper adjustment in respect of the property shall in all cases be made—

(1) for expenditures, receipts, losses, or other items, properly chargeable to capital account, but no such adjustment shall be made—

(A) for taxes or other carrying charges described in section 266, or

(B) for expenditures described in section 173 (relating to circulation expenditures),

for which deductions have been taken by the taxpayer in determining taxable income for the taxable year or prior taxable years;

(2) in respect of any period since February 28, 1913, for exhaustion, wear and tear, obsolescence, amortization, and depletion, to the extent of the amount—

(A) allowed as deductions in computing taxable income under this subtitle or prior income tax laws, and

(B) resulting (by reason of the deductions so allowed) in a reduction for any taxable year of the taxpayer's taxes under this subtitle (other than chapter 2, relating to tax on self-employment income), or prior income, war-profits, or excess-profits tax laws,

but not less than the amount allowable under this subtitle or prior income tax laws. Where no method has been adopted under section 167 (relating to depreciation deduction), the amount allowable shall be determined under the straight line method. * * *

(4) in the case of stock (to the extent not provided for in the foregoing paragraphs) for the amount of distributions previously made which, under the law applicable to the year in which the distribution was made, either were tax-free or were applicable in reduction of basis (not including distributions made by a corporation which was classified as a personal service corporation under the provisions of the Revenue Act of 1918 (40 Stat. 1057), or the Revenue Act of 1921 (42 Stat. 227), out of its earnings or profits which were taxable in accordance with the provisions of section 218 of the Revenue Act of 1918 or 1921);

(5) in the case of any bond (as defined in section 171(d)) the interest on which is wholly exempt from the tax imposed by this subtitle, to the extent of the amortizable bond premium disallowable as a deduction pursuant to section 171(a)(2), and in the case of any other bond (as defined in section 171(d)) to the extent of the deductions allowable pursuant to section 171(a)(1) (or the amount applied to reduce interest payments under section 171(e)(2)) with respect thereto;

(6) in the case of any municipal bond (as defined in section 75(b)), to the extent provided in section 75(a)(2);

(7) in the case of a residence the acquisition of which resulted, under section 1034 (as in effect on the day before the date of enactment of the Taxpayer Relief Act of 1997), in the nonrecognition of any part of the gain realized on the sale, exchange, or involuntary conversion of another residence, to the extent provided in section 1034(e) (as so in effect);

* * *

(9) for amounts allowed as deductions as deferred expenses under section 616(b) (relating to certain expenditures in the development of mines) and resulting in a reduction of the taxpayer's taxes under this subtitle, but not less than the amounts allowable under such section for the taxable year and prior years;

* * *

(11) for deductions to the extent disallowed under section 268 (relating to sale of land with unharvested crops), notwithstanding the provisions of any other paragraph of this subsection;

* * *

(14) for amounts allowed as deductions as deferred expenses under section 174(b)(1) (relating to research and experimental expenditures) and resulting in a reduction of the taxpayers' taxes under this subtitle, but not less than the amounts allowable under such section for the taxable year and prior years;

(15) for deductions to the extent disallowed under section 272 (relating to disposal of coal or domestic iron ore), notwithstanding the provisions of any other paragraph of this subsection;

* * *

(17) to the extent provided in section 1367 in the case of stock of, and indebtedness owed to, shareholders of an S corporation;

* * *

(19) to the extent provided in section 50(c), in the case of expenditures with respect to which a credit has been allowed under section 38;

(20) for amounts allowed as deductions under section 59(e) (relating to optional 10-year writeoff of certain tax preferences);

* * *

(22) in the case of qualified replacement property, the acquisition of which resulted under section 1042 in the nonrecognition of any part of the gain realized on the sale or exchange of any property, to the extent provided in section 1042(d);

(23) in the case of property the acquisition of which resulted under section 1043, 1044, 1045, or 1397B in the nonrecognition of any part of the gain realized on the sale of other property, to the extent provided in section 1043(c), 1044(d), 1045(b)(3), or 1397B(b)(4) as the case may be;

(24) to the extent provided in section 179A(e)(6)(A),

(25) to the extent provided in section 30(e)(1),

(26) to the extent provided in sections 23(g) and 137(e),

(27) in the case of a residence with respect to which a credit was allowed under section 1400C, to the extent provided in section 1400C(h),

(28) in the case of a facility with respect to which a credit was allowed under section 45F, to the extent provided in section 45F(f)(1).

* * *

(b) Substituted basis.—Whenever it appears that the basis of property in the hands of the taxpayer is a substituted basis, then the adjustments provided in subsection (a) shall be made after first making in respect of such substituted basis proper adjustments of a similar nature in respect of the period during which the property was held by the transferor, donor, or grantor, or during which the other property was held by the person for whom the basis is to be determined. A similar rule shall be applied in the case of a series of substituted bases.

(c) Increase in basis of property on which additional estate tax is imposed.—

(1) Tax imposed with respect to entire interest.—If an additional estate tax is imposed under section 2032A(c)(1) with respect to any interest in property and the qualified heir makes an election under this subsection with respect to the imposition of such tax, the adjusted basis of such interest shall be increased by an amount equal to the excess of—

(A) the fair market value of such interest on the date of the decedent's death (or the alternate valuation date under section 2032, if the executor of the decedent's estate elected the application of such section), over

(B) the value of such interest determined under section 2032A(a).

(2) Partial dispositions.—

(A) In general.—In the case of any partial disposition for which an election under this subsection is made, the increase in basis under paragraph (1) shall be an amount—

(i) which bears the same ratio to the increase which would be determined under paragraph (1) (without regard to this paragraph) with respect to the entire interest, as

(ii) the amount of the tax imposed under section 2032A(c)(1) with respect to such disposition bears to the adjusted tax difference attributable to the entire interest (as determined under section 2032A(c)(2)(B)).

(B) Partial disposition.—For purposes of subparagraph (A), the term "partial disposition" means any disposition or cessation to which subsection (c)(2)(D), (h)(1)(B), or (i)(1)(B) of section 2032A applies.

(3) Time adjustment made.—Any increase in basis under this subsection shall be deemed to have occurred immediately before the disposition or cessation resulting in the imposition of the tax under section 2032A(c)(1).

(4) Special rule in the case of substituted property.—If the tax under section 2032A(c)(1) is imposed with respect to qualified replacement property (as defined in section 2032A(h)(3)(B)) or qualified exchange property (as defined in section 2032A(i)(3)), the increase in basis under paragraph (1) shall be made by reference to the property involuntarily converted or exchanged (as the case may be).

(5) Election.—

(A) In general.—An election under this subsection shall be made at such time and in such manner as the Secretary shall by regulations prescribe. Such an election, once made, shall be irrevocable.

(B) Interest on recaptured amount.—If an election is made under this subsection with respect to any additional estate tax imposed under section 2032A(c)(1), for purposes of section 6601 (relating to interest on underpayments), the last date prescribed for payment of such tax shall be deemed to be the last date prescribed for payment of the tax imposed by section 2001 with respect to the estate of the decedent (as determined for purposes of section 6601).

* * *

(e) Cross references.—

For treatment of separate mineral interests as one property, see section 614.

* * *

§ 1017. Discharge of indebtedness

(a) General rule.—If—

(1) an amount is excluded from gross income under subsection (a) of section 108 (relating to discharge of indebtedness), and

(2) under subsection (b)(2)(E), (b)(5), or (c)(1) of section 108, any portion of such amount is to be applied to reduce basis,

then such portion shall be applied in reduction of the basis of any property held by the taxpayer at the beginning of the taxable year following the taxable year in which the discharge occurs.

(b) Amount and properties determined under regulations.—

(1) In general.—The amount of reduction to be applied under subsection (a) (not in excess of the portion referred to in subsection (a)), and the particular properties the bases of which are to be reduced, shall be determined under regulations prescribed by the Secretary.

(2) Limitation in Title 11 case or insolvency.—In the case of a discharge to which subparagraph (A) or (B) of section 108(a)(1) applies, the reduction in basis under subsection (a) of this section shall not exceed the excess of—

(A) the aggregate of the bases of the property held by the taxpayer immediately after the discharge, over

(B) the aggregate of the liabilities of the taxpayer immediately after the discharge.

The preceding sentence shall not apply to any reduction in basis by reason of an election under section 108(b)(5).

(3) Certain reductions may only be made in the basis of depreciable property.—

(A) In general.—Any amount which under subsection (b)(5) or (c)(1) of section 108 is to be applied to reduce basis shall be applied only to reduce the basis of depreciable property held by the taxpayer.

(B) Depreciable property.—For purposes of this section, the term "depreciable property" means any property of a character subject to the allowance for depreciation, but only if a basis reduction under subsection (a) will reduce the amount of depreciation or amortization which otherwise would be allowable for the period immediately following such reduction.

(C) Special rule for partnership interests.—For purposes of this section, any interest of a partner in a partnership shall be treated as depreciable property to the extent of such partner's proportionate interest in the depreciable property held by such partnership. The preceding sentence shall apply only if there is a corresponding reduction in the partnership's basis in depreciable property with respect to such partner.

(D) Special rule in case of affiliated group.—For purposes of this section, if—

(i) a corporation holds stock in another corporation (hereinafter in this subparagraph referred to as the "subsidiary"), and

(ii) such corporations are members of the same affiliated group which file a consolidated return under section 1501 for the taxable year in which the discharge occurs,

then such stock shall be treated as depreciable property to the extent that such subsidiary consents to a corresponding reduction in the basis of its depreciable property.

(E) Election to treat certain inventory as depreciable property.—

(i) In general.—At the election of the taxpayer, for purposes of this section, the term "depreciable property" includes any real property which is described in section 1221(1).

(ii) Election.—An election under clause (i) shall be made on the taxpayer's return for the taxable year in which the discharge occurs or at such other time as may be permitted in regulations prescribed by the Secretary. Such an election, once made, may be revoked only with the consent of the Secretary.

(F) Special rules for qualified real property business indebtedness.—In the case of any amount which under section 108(c)(1) is to be applied to reduce basis—

(i) depreciable property shall only include depreciable real property for purposes of subparagraphs (A) and (C),

(ii) subparagraph (E) shall not apply, and

(iii) in the case of property taken into account under section 108(c)(2)(B), the reduction with respect to such property shall be made as of the time immediately before disposition if earlier than the time under subsection (a).

(4) Special rules for qualified farm indebtedness.—

(A) In general.—Any amount which under subsection (b)(2)(E) of section 108 is to be applied to reduce basis and which is attributable to an amount excluded under subsection (a)(1)(C) of section 108—

(i) shall be applied only to reduce the basis of qualified property held by the taxpayer, and

(ii) shall be applied to reduce the basis of qualified property in the following order:

(I) First the basis of qualified property which is depreciable property.

(II) Second the basis of qualified property which is land used or held for use in the trade or business of farming.

(III) Then the basis of other qualified property.

(B) Qualified property.—For purposes of this paragraph, the term "qualified property" has the meaning given to such term by section 108(g)(3)(C).

(C) Certain rules made applicable.—Rules similar to the rules of subparagraphs (C), (D), and (E) of paragraph (3) shall apply for purposes of this paragraph and section 108(g).

(c) Special rules.—

(1) Reduction not to be made in exempt property.—In the case of an amount excluded from gross income under section 108(a)(1)(A), no reduction in basis shall be made under this section in the basis of property which the debtor treats as exempt property under section 522 of title 11 of the United States Code.

(2) Reductions in basis not treated as dispositions.—For purposes of this title, a reduction in basis under this section shall not be treated as a disposition.

(d) Recapture of reductions.—

(1) In general.—For purposes of sections 1245 and 1250—

(A) any property the basis of which is reduced under this section and which is neither section 1245 property nor section 1250 property shall be treated as section 1245 property, and

(B) any reduction under this section shall be treated as a deduction allowed for depreciation.

(2) Special rule for section 1250.—For purposes of section 1250(b), the determination of what would have been the depreciation adjustments under the straight line method shall be made as if there had been no reduction under this section.

§ 1019. Property on which lessee has made improvements

Neither the basis nor the adjusted basis of any portion of real property shall, in the case of the lessor of such property, be increased or diminished on account of income derived by the lessor in respect of such property and excludable from gross income under section 109 (relating to improvements by lessee on lessor's property). If an amount representing any part of the value of real property attributable to buildings erected or other improvements made by a lessee in respect of such property was included in gross income of the lessor for any taxable year beginning before January 1, 1942, the basis of each portion of such property shall be properly adjusted for the amount so included in gross income.

* * *

§ 1022. Treatment of property acquired from a decedent dying after December 31, 2009*

(a) In general.—Except as otherwise provided in this section—

*Editorial comment: This section applies for property acquired from a decedent dying after December 31, 2009 and before January 1, 2011. See Sec. 1022(a)(1). However, Sec. 1022 will not apply for decedents dying in 2010 if the executor elects to have the estate tax apply for a decedent dying in 2010. If this election is made, then Sec. 1014 will apply rather than Sec. 1022. Subsequent legislation treated Sec. 1022 as if never enacted.

(1) property acquired from a decedent dying after December 31, 2009, shall be treated for purposes of this subtitle as transferred by gift, and

(2) the basis of the person acquiring property from such a decedent shall be the lesser of—

(A) the adjusted basis of the decedent, or

(B) the fair market value of the property at the date of the decedent's death.

(b) Basis increase for certain property.—

(1) In general.—In the case of property to which this subsection applies, the basis of such property under subsection (a) shall be increased by its basis increase under this subsection.

(2) Basis increase.—For purposes of this subsection—

(A) In general.—The basis increase under this subsection for any property is the portion of the aggregate basis increase which is allocated to the property pursuant to this section.

(B) Aggregate basis increase.—In the case of any estate, the aggregate basis increase under this subsection is $1,300,000.

(C) Limit increased by unused built-in losses and loss carryovers.—The limitation under subparagraph (B) shall be increased by—

(i) the sum of the amount of any capital loss carryover under section 1212(b), and the amount of any net operating loss carryover under section 172, which would (but for the decedent's death) be carried from the decedent's last taxable year to a later taxable year of the decedent, plus

(ii) the sum of the amount of any losses that would have been allowable under section 165 if the property acquired from the decedent had been sold at fair market value immediately before the decedent's death.

(3) Decedent nonresidents who are not citizens of the United States.—In the case of a decedent nonresident not a citizen of the United States—

(A) paragraph (2)(B) shall be applied by substituting "$60,000"* for "$1,300,000,"* and

(B) paragraph (2)(C) shall not apply.

(c) Additional basis increase for property acquired by surviving spouse.—

(1) In general.—In the case of property to which this subsection applies and which is qualified spousal property, the basis of such property under subsection (a) (as increased under subsection (b)) shall be increased by its spousal property basis increase.

(2) Spousal property basis increase.—For purposes of this subsection—

(A) In general.—The spousal property basis increase for property referred to in paragraph (1) is the portion of the aggregate spousal property basis increase which is allocated to the property pursuant to this section.

(B) Aggregate spousal property basis increase.—In the case of any estate, the aggregate spousal property basis increase is $3,000,000.

(3) Qualified spousal property.—For purposes of this subsection, the term "qualified spousal property" means—

(A) outright transfer property, and

(B) qualified terminable interest property.

(4) Outright transfer property.—For purposes of this subsection—

(A) In general.—The term "outright transfer property" means any interest in property acquired from the decedent by the decedent's surviving spouse.

(B) Exception.—Subparagraph (A) shall not apply where, on the lapse of time, on the occurrence of an event or contingency, or on the failure of an event or contingency to occur, an interest passing to the surviving spouse will terminate or fail—

(i) (I) if an interest in such property passes or has passed (for less than an adequate and full consideration in money or money's worth) from the decedent to any person other than such surviving spouse (or the estate of such spouse), and

(II) if by reason of such passing such person (or his heirs or assigns) may possess or enjoy any part of such property after such termination or failure of the interest so passing to the surviving spouse, or

(ii) if such interest is to be acquired for the surviving spouse, pursuant to directions of the decedent, by his executor or by the trustee of a trust.

For purposes of this subparagraph, an interest shall not be considered as an interest which will terminate or fail merely because it is the ownership of a bond, note, or similar contractual obligation, the discharge of which would not have the effect of an annuity for life or for a term.

(C) Interest of spouse conditional on survival for limited period.—For purposes of this paragraph, an interest passing to the surviving spouse shall not be considered as an interest which will terminate or fail on the death of such spouse if—

(i) such death will cause a termination or failure of such interest only if it occurs within a period not exceeding 6 months after the decedent's death, or only if it occurs as a result of a common disaster resulting in the death of the decedent and the surviving spouse, or only if it occurs in the case of either such event, and

(ii) such termination or failure does not in fact occur.

(5) Qualified terminable interest property.—For purposes of this subsection—

(A) In general.—The term "qualified terminable interest property" means property—

(i) which passes from the decedent, and

(ii) in which the surviving spouse has a qualifying income interest for life.

(B) Qualifying income interest for life.—The surviving spouse has a qualifying income interest for life if—

(i) the surviving spouse is entitled to all the income from the property, payable annually or at more frequent intervals, or has a usufruct interest for life in the property, and

(ii) no person has a power to appoint any part of the property to any person other than the surviving spouse.

Clause (ii) shall not apply to a power exercisable only at or after the death of the surviving spouse. To the extent provided in regulations, an annuity shall be treated in a manner similar to an income interest in property (regardless of whether the property from which the annuity is payable can be separately identified).

(C) Property includes interest therein.—The term "property" includes an interest in property.

(D) Specific portion treated as separate property.—A specific portion of property shall be treated as separate property. For purposes of the preceding sentence, the term "specific portion" only includes a portion determined on a fractional or percentage basis.

(d) Definitions and special rules for application of subsections (b) and (c).—

(1) Property to which subsections (b) and (c) apply.—

(A) In general.—The basis of property acquired from a decedent may be increased under subsection (b) or (c) only if the property was owned by the decedent at the time of death.

(B) Rules relating to ownership.—

(i) Jointly held property.—In the case of property which was owned by the decedent and another person as joint tenants with right of survivorship or tenants by the entirety—

(I) if the only such other person is the surviving spouse, the decedent shall be treated as the owner of only 50 percent of the property,

(II) in any case (to which subclause (I) does not apply) in which the decedent furnished consideration for the acquisition of the property, the decedent shall be treated as the owner to the extent of the portion of the property which is proportionate to such consideration, and

(III) in any case (to which subclause (I) does not apply) in which the property has been acquired by gift, bequest, devise, or inheritance by the decedent and any other person as joint tenants with right of survivorship and their interests are not otherwise specified or fixed by law, the decedent shall be treated as the owner to the extent of the value of a fractional part to be determined by dividing the value of the property by the number of joint tenants with right of survivorship.

(ii) Revocable trusts.—The decedent shall be treated as owning property transferred by the decedent during life to a qualified revocable trust (as defined in section 645(b)(l)).

(iii) Powers of appointment.—The decedent shall not be treated as owning any property by reason of holding a power of appointment with respect to such property.

(iv) Community property.—Property which represents the surviving spouse's one-half share of community property held by the decedent and the surviving spouse under the community property laws of any State or possession of the United States or any foreign country shall be treated for purposes of this section as owned by, and acquired from, the decedent if at least one-half of the whole of the community interest in such property is treated as owned by, and acquired from, the decedent without regard to this clause.

(C) Property acquired by decedent by gift within 3 years of death.—

(i) In general.—Subsections (b) and (c) shall not apply to property acquired by the decedent by gift or by inter vivos transfer for less than adequate and full consideration in money or money's worth during the 3-year period ending on the date of the decedent's death.

(ii) Exception for certain gifts from spouse.—Clause (i) shall not apply to property acquired by the decedent from the decedent's spouse unless, during such 3-year period, such spouse acquired the property in whole or in part by gift or by inter vivos transfer for less than adequate and full consideration in money or money's worth.

(D) Stock of certain entities.—Subsections (b) and (c) shall not apply to—

(i) stock or securities of a foreign personal holding company,

(ii) stock of a DISC or former DISC,

(iii) stock of a foreign investment company, or

(iv) stock of a passive foreign investment company unless such company is a qualified electing fund (as defined in section 1295) with respect to the decedent.

(2) Fair market value limitation.—The adjustments under subsections (b) and (c) shall not increase the basis of any interest in property acquired from the decedent above its fair market value in the hands of the decedent as of the date of the decedent's death.

(3) Allocation rules.—

(A) In general.—The executor shall allocate the adjustments under subsections (b) and (c) on the return required by section 6018.

(B) Changes in allocation.—Any allocation made pursuant to subparagraph (A) may be changed only as provided by the Secretary.

(4) Inflation adjustment of basis adjustment amounts.—

(A) In general.—In the case of decedents dying in a calendar year after 2010, the $1,300,000, $60,000, and $3,000,000 dollar amounts in subsections (b) and (c)(2)(B) shall each be increased by an amount equal to the product of—

(i) such dollar amount, and

(ii) the cost-of-living adjustment determined under section 1(f)(3) for such calendar year, determined by substituting "2009" for "1992" in subparagraph (B) thereof.

(B) Rounding.—If any increase determined under subparagraph (A) is not a multiple of—

(i) $100,000 in the case of the $1,300,000 amount,

(ii) $5,000 in the case of the $60,000 amount, and

(iii) $250,000 in the case of the $3,000,000 amount,

such increase shall be rounded to the next lowest multiple thereof.

(e) Property acquired from the decedent.—For purposes of this section, the following property shall be considered to have been acquired from the decedent:

(1) Property acquired by bequest, devise, or inheritance, or by the decedent's estate from the decedent.

(2) Property transferred by the decedent during his lifetime—

(A) to a qualified revocable trust (as defined in section 645(b)(1)), or

(B) to any other trust with respect to which the decedent reserved the right to make any change in the enjoyment thereof through the exercise of a power to alter, amend, or terminate the trust.

(3) Any other property passing from the decedent by reason of death to the extent that such property passed without consideration.

(f) Coordination with section 691.—This section shall not apply to property which constitutes a right to receive an item of income in respect of a decedent under section 691.

(g) Certain liabilities disregarded.—

(1) In general.—In determining whether gain is recognized on the acquisition of property—

(A) from a decedent by a decedent's estate or any beneficiary other than a tax-exempt beneficiary, and

(B) from the decedent's estate by any beneficiary other than a tax-exempt beneficiary, and in determining the adjusted basis of such property, liabilities in excess of basis shall be disregarded.

(2) Tax-exempt beneficiary.—For purposes of paragraph (1), the term "tax-exempt beneficiary" means—

(A) the United States, any State or political subdivision thereof, any possession of the United States, any Indian tribal government (within the meaning of section 7871), or any agency or instrumentality of any of the foregoing,

(B) an organization (other than a cooperative described in section 521) which is exempt from tax imposed by chapter 1,

(C) any foreign person or entity (within the meaning of section 168(h)(2)), and

(D) to the extent provided in regulations, any person to whom property is transferred for the principal purpose of tax avoidance.

(h) Regulations.—The Secretary shall prescribe such regulations as may be necessary to carry out the purposes of this section.

* * *

PART III—COMMON NONTAXABLE EXCHANGES

Editorial Summary

Property Transactions: Nontaxable Exchanges

Subchapter O of Chapter 1 (Secs. 1031–1045)

See the discussion under the Editorial Summary entitled Property Transactions: General, which precedes Sec. 1001.

§ 1031. Exchange of property held for productive use or investment

(a) Nonrecognition of gain or loss from exchanges solely in kind.—

(1) In general.—No gain or loss shall be recognized on the exchange of property held for productive use in a trade or business or for investment if such property is exchanged solely for property of like kind which is to be held either for productive use in a trade or business or for investment.

(2) Exception.—This subsection shall not apply to any exchange of—

(A) stock in trade or other property held primarily for sale,

(B) stocks, bonds, or notes,

(C) other securities or evidences of indebtedness or interest,

(D) interests in a partnership,

(E) certificates of trust or beneficial interests, or

(F) choses in action.

For purposes of this section, an interest in a partnership which has in effect a valid election under section 761(a) to be excluded from the application of all of subchapter K shall be treated as an interest in each of the assets of such partnership and not as an interest in a partnership.

(3) Requirement that property be identified and that exchange be completed not more than 180 days after transfer of exchanged property.—For purposes of this subsection, any property received by the taxpayer shall be treated as property which is not like-kind property if—

(A) such property is not identified as property to be received in the exchange on or before the day which is 45 days after the date on which the taxpayer transfers the property relinquished in the exchange, or

(B) such property is received after the earlier of—

(i) the day which is 180 days after the date on which the taxpayer transfers the property relinquished in the exchange, or

(ii) the due date (determined with regard to extension) for the transferor's return of the tax imposed by this chapter for the taxable year in which the transfer of the relinquished property occurs.

(b) Gain from exchanges not solely in kind.—If an exchange would be within the provisions of subsection (a), of section 1035(a), of section 1036(a), or of section 1037(a), if it were not for the fact that the property received in exchange consists not only of property permitted by such provisions to be received without the recognition of gain, but also of other property or money, then the gain, if any, to the recipient shall be recognized, but in an amount not in excess of the sum of such money and the fair market value of such other property.

(c) Loss from exchanges not solely in kind.—If an exchange would be within the provisions of subsection (a), of section 1035(a), of section 1036(a), or of section 1037(a), if it were not for the fact that the property received in exchange consists not only of property permitted by such provisions to be received without the recognition of gain or loss, but also of other property or money, then no loss from the exchange shall be recognized.

(d) Basis.—If property was acquired on an exchange described in this section, section 1035(a), section 1036(a), or section 1037(a), then the basis shall be the same as that of the property exchanged, decreased in the amount of any money received by the taxpayer and increased in the amount of gain or decreased in the amount of loss to the taxpayer that was recognized on such exchange. If the property so acquired consisted in part of the type of property permitted by this section, section 1035(a), section 1036(a), or section 1037(a), to be received without the recognition of gain or loss, and in part of other property, the basis provided in this subsection shall be allocated between the properties (other than money) received, and for the purpose of the allocation there shall be assigned to such other property an amount equivalent to its fair market value at the date of the exchange. For purposes of this section, section 1035(a), and section 1036(a), where as part of the consideration to the taxpayer another party to the exchange assumed a liability of the taxpayer or acquired from the taxpayer property subject to a liability, such assumption or acquisition (in the amount of the liability) shall be considered as money received by the taxpayer on the exchange.

(e) Exchanges of livestock of different sexes.—For purposes of this section, livestock of different sexes are not property of a like kind.

(f) Special rules for exchanges between related persons.—

(1) In general.—If—

(A) a taxpayer exchanges property with a related person,

(B) there is nonrecognition of gain or loss to the taxpayer under this section with respect to the exchange of such property (determined without regard to this subsection), and

(C) before the date 2 years after the date of the last transfer which was part of such exchange—

(i) the related person disposes of such property, or

(ii) the taxpayer disposes of the property received in the exchange from the related person which was of like kind to the property transferred by the taxpayer,

there shall be no nonrecognition of gain or loss under this section to the taxpayer with respect to such exchange; except that any gain or loss recognized by the taxpayer by reason of this subsection shall be taken into account as of the date on which the disposition referred to in subparagraph (C) occurs.

(2) Certain dispositions not taken into account.—For purposes of paragraph (1)(C), there shall not be taken into account any disposition—

(A) after the earlier of the death of the taxpayer or the death of the related person,

(B) in a compulsory or involuntary conversion (within the meaning of section 1033) if the exchange occurred before the threat or imminence of such conversion, or

(C) with respect to which it is established to the satisfaction of the Secretary that neither the exchange nor such disposition had as one of its principal purposes the avoidance of Federal income tax.

(3) Related person.—For purposes of this subsection, the term "related person" means any person bearing a relationship to the taxpayer described in section 267(b) or 707(b)(1).

(4) Treatment of certain transactions.—This section shall not apply to any exchange which is part of a transaction (or series of transactions) structured to avoid the purposes of this subsection.

(g) Special rule where substantial diminution of risk.—

(1) In general.—If paragraph (2) applies to any property for any period, the running of the period set forth in subsection (f)(1)(C) with respect to such property shall be suspended during such period.

(2) Property to which subsection applies.— This paragraph shall apply to any property for any period during which the holder's risk of loss with respect to the property is substantially diminished by—

(A) the holding of a put with respect to such property,

(B) the holding by another person of a right to acquire such property, or

(C) a short sale or any other transaction.

(h) Special rules for foreign real and personal property.—For purposes of this section—

(1) Real property.—Real property located in the United States and real property located outside the United States are not property of a like kind.

(2) Personal property.—

(A) In general.—Personal property used predominantly within the United States and personal property used predominantly outside the United States are not property of a like kind.

(B) Predominant use.—Except as provided in subparagraphs (C) and (D), the predominant use of any property shall be determined based on—

(i) in the case of the property relinquished in the exchange, the 2-year period ending on the date of such relinquishment, and

(ii) in the case of the property acquired in the exchange, the 2-year period beginning on the date of such acquisition.

(C) Property held for less than 2 years.— Except in the case of an exchange which is part of a transaction (or series of transactions) structured to avoid the purposes of this subsection—

(i) only the periods the property was held by the person relinquishing the property (or any related person) shall be taken into account under subparagraph (B)(i), and

(ii) only the periods the property was held by the person acquiring the property (or any related person) shall be taken into account under subparagraph (B)(ii).

(D) Special rule for certain property.— Property described in any subparagraph of section 168(g)(4) shall be treated as used predominantly in the United States.

(i) Special rules for mutual ditch, reservoir, or irrigation company stock.— For purposes of subsection (a)(2)(B), the term "stocks" shall not include shares in a mutual ditch, reservoir, or irrigation company if at the time of the exchange—

(1) the mutual ditch, reservoir, or irrigation company is an organization described in section 501(c)(12)(A) (determined without regard to the percentage of its income that is collected from its members for the purpose of meeting losses and expenses), and

(2) the shares in such company have been recognized by the highest court of the State in which such company was organized or by applicable State statute as constituting or representing real property or an interest in real property.

§ 1032. Exchange of stock for property

(a) Nonrecognition of gain or loss.—No gain or loss shall be recognized to a corporation on the receipt of money or other property in exchange for stock (including treasury stock) of such corporation. No gain or loss shall be recognized by a corporation with respect to any lapse or acquisition of an option, or with respect to a securities futures contract (as defined in section 1234B), to buy or sell its stock (including treasury stock).

(b) Basis.—

For basis of property acquired by a corporation in certain exchanges for its stock, see section 362.

§ 1033. Involuntary conversions

(a) General rule.—If property (as a result of its destruction in whole or in part, theft, seizure, or requisition or condemnation or threat or imminence thereof) is compulsorily or involuntarily converted—

(1) Conversion into similar property.—Into property similar or related in service or use to the property so converted, no gain shall be recognized.

(2) Conversion into money.—Into money or into property not similar or related in service or use to the converted property, the gain (if any) shall be recognized except to the extent hereinafter provided in this paragraph:

(A) Nonrecognition of gain.—If the taxpayer during the period specified in subparagraph (B), for the purpose of replacing the property so converted, purchases other property similar or related in service or use to the property so converted, or purchases stock in the acquisition of control of a corporation owning such other property, at the election of the taxpayer the gain shall be recognized only to the extent that the amount realized upon such conversion (regardless of whether such amount is received in one or more taxable years) exceeds the cost of such other property or such stock. Such election shall be made at such time and in such manner as the Secretary may by regulations prescribe. For purposes of this paragraph—

(i) no property or stock acquired before the disposition of the converted property shall be considered to have been acquired for the purpose of replacing such converted property unless held by the taxpayer on the date of such disposition; and

(ii) the taxpayer shall be considered to have purchased property or stock only if, but for the provisions of subsection (b) of this section, the unadjusted basis of such property or stock would be its cost within the meaning of section 1012.

(B) Period within which property must be replaced.—The period referred to in subparagraph (A) shall be the period beginning with the date of the disposition of the converted property, or the earliest date of the threat or imminence of requisition or condemnation of the converted property, whichever is the earlier, and ending—

(i) 2 years after the close of the first taxable year in which any part of the gain upon the conversion is realized, or

(ii) subject to such terms and conditions as may be specified by the Secretary, at the close of such later date as the Secretary may designate on application by the taxpayer. Such application shall be made at such time and in such manner as the Secretary may by regulations prescribe.

(C) Time for assessment of deficiency attributable to gain upon conversion.—If a taxpayer has made the election provided in subparagraph (A), then—

(i) the statutory period for the assessment of any deficiency, for any taxable year in which any part of the gain on such conversion is realized, attributable to such gain shall not expire prior to the expiration of 3 years from the date the Secretary is notified by the taxpayer (in such manner as the Secretary may by regulations prescribe) of the replacement of the converted property or of an intention not to replace, and

(ii) such deficiency may be assessed before the expiration of such 3-year period notwithstanding the provisions of section 6212(c) or the provisions of any other law or rule of law which would otherwise prevent such assessment.

(D) Time for assessment of other deficiencies attributable to election.—If the election provided in subparagraph (A) is made by the taxpayer and such other property or such stock was purchased before the beginning of the last taxable year in which any part of the gain upon such conversion is realized, any deficiency, to the extent resulting from such election, for any taxable year ending before such last taxable year may be assessed (notwithstanding the provisions of section 6212(c) or 6501 or the provisions of any other law or rule of law which would otherwise prevent such assessment) at any time before the expiration of the period within which a deficiency for such last taxable year may be assessed.

(E) Definitions.—For purposes of this paragraph—

(i) Control.—The term "control" means the ownership of stock possessing at least 80 percent of the total combined voting power of all classes of stock entitled to vote and at least 80 percent of the total number of shares of all other classes of stock of the corporation.

(ii) Disposition of the converted property.—The term "disposition of the converted property" means the destruction, theft, seizure, requisition, or condemnation of the converted property, or the sale or exchange of such property under threat or imminence of requisition or condemnation.

(b) Basis of property acquired through involuntary conversion.—

(1) Conversions described in subsection (a)(1).—If the property was acquired as the result of a compulsory or involuntary conversion described in subsection (a)(1), the basis shall be the same as in the case of the property so converted—

(A) decreased in the amount of any money received by the taxpayer which was not expended in accordance with the provisions of law (applicable to the year in which such conversion was made) determining the taxable status of the gain or loss upon such conversion, and

(B) increased in the amount of gain or decreased in the amount of loss to the taxpayer recognized upon such conversion under the law applicable to the year in which such conversion was made.

(2) Conversions described in subsection (a)(2).—In the case of property purchased by the taxpayer in a transaction described in subsection (a)(2) which resulted in the nonrecognition of any part of the gain realized as the result of a compulsory or involuntary conversion, the basis shall be the cost of such property decreased in the amount of the gain not so recognized; and if the property purchased consists of more than 1 piece of property, the basis determined under this sentence shall be allocated to the purchased properties in proportion to their respective costs.

(3) Property held by corporation the stock of which is replacement property.—

(A) In general.—If the basis of stock in a corporation is decreased under paragraph (2), an amount equal to such decrease shall also be applied to reduce the basis of property held by the corporation at the time the taxpayer acquired control (as defined in subsection (a)(2)(E)) of such corporation.

(B) Limitation.—Subparagraph (A) shall not apply to the extent that it would (but for this subparagraph) require a reduction in the aggregate adjusted bases of the property of the corporation below the taxpayer's adjusted basis of the stock in the corporation (determined immediately after such basis is decreased under paragraph (2)).

(C) Allocation of basis reduction.—The decrease required under subparagraph (A) shall be allocated—

(i) first to property which is similar or related in service or use to the converted property,

(ii) second to depreciable property (as defined in section 1017(b)(3)(B)) not described in clause (i), and

(iii) then to other property.

(D) Special rules.—

(i) Reduction not to exceed adjusted basis of property.—No reduction in the basis of any property under this paragraph shall exceed the adjusted basis of such property (determined without regard to such reduction).

(ii) Allocation of reduction among properties.—If more than 1 property is described in a clause of subparagraph (C), the reduction under this paragraph shall be allocated among such property in proportion to the adjusted bases of such property (as so determined).

(c) Property sold pursuant to reclamation laws.—For purposes of this subtitle, if property lying within an irrigation project is sold or otherwise disposed of in order to conform to the acreage limitation provisions of Federal reclamation laws, such sale or disposition shall be treated as an involuntary conversion to which this section applies.

(d) Livestock destroyed by disease.—For purposes of this subtitle, if livestock are destroyed by or on account of disease, or are sold or exchanged because of disease, such destruction or such sale or exchange shall be treated as an involuntary conversion to which this section applies.

(e) Livestock sold on account of drought, flood, or other weather-related conditions.—

(1) In general.—For purposes of this subtitle, the sale or exchange of livestock (other than poultry) held by a taxpayer for draft, breeding, or dairy purposes in excess of the number the taxpayer would sell if he followed his usual business practices shall be treated as an involuntary conversion to which this section applies if such livestock are sold or exchanged by the taxpayer solely on account of drought, flood, or other weather-related conditions.

(2) Extension of replacement period.—

(A) In general.—In the case of drought, flood, or other weather-related conditions described in paragraph (1) which result in the area being designated as eligible for assistance by the Federal Government, subsection (a)(2)

(B) shall be applied with respect to any converted property by substituting "4 years" for "2 years."

(B) Further extension by Secretary.—The Secretary may extend on a regional basis the period for replacement under this section (after the application of subparagraph (A)) for such additional time as the Secretary determines appropriate if the weather-related conditions which resulted in such application continue for more than 3 years.

(f) Replacement of livestock with other farm property where there has been environmental contamination.—For purposes of subsection (a), if, because of drought, flood, or other weather-related conditions, or soil contamination or other environmental contamination, it is not feasible for the taxpayer to reinvest the proceeds from compulsorily or involuntarily converted livestock in property similar or related in use to the livestock so converted, other property (including real property in the case of soil contamination or other environmental contamination) used for farming purposes shall be treated as property similar or related in service or use to the livestock so converted.

(g) Condemnation of real property held for productive use in trade or business or for investment.—

(1) Special rule.—For purposes of subsection (a), if real property (not including stock in trade or other property held primarily for sale) held for productive use in trade or business or for investment is (as the result of its seizure, requisition, or condemnation, or threat or imminence thereof) compulsorily or involuntarily converted, property of a like kind to be held either for productive use in trade or business or for investment shall be treated as property similar or related in service or use to the property so converted.

(2) Limitation.—Paragraph (1) shall not apply to the purchase of stock in the acquisition of control of a corporation described in subsection (a)(2)(A).

(3) Election to treat outdoor advertising displays as real property.—

(A) In general.—A taxpayer may elect, at such time and in such manner as the Secretary may prescribe, to treat property which constitutes an outdoor advertising display as real property for purposes of this chapter. The election provided by this subparagraph may not be made with respect to any property with respect to which an election under section 179(a) (relating to election to expense certain depreciable business assets) is in effect.

(B) Election.—An election made under subparagraph (A) may not be revoked without the consent of the Secretary.

(C) Outdoor advertising display.—For purposes of this paragraph, the term "outdoor advertising display" means a rigidly assembled sign, display, or device permanently affixed to the ground or permanently attached to a building or other inherently permanent structure constituting, or used for the display of, a commercial or other advertisement to the public.

(D) Character of replacement property.—For purposes of this subsection, an interest in real property purchased as replacement property for a compulsorily or involuntarily converted outdoor advertising display defined in subparagraph (C) (and treated by the taxpayer as real property) shall be considered property of a like kind as the property converted without regard to whether the taxpayer's interest in the replacement property is the same kind of interest the taxpayer held in the converted property.

(4) Special rule.—In the case of a compulsory or involuntary conversion described in paragraph (1), subsection (a)(2)(B)(i) shall be applied by substituting "3 years" for "2 years."

(h) Special rules for property damaged by Federally declared disasters.—

(1) Principal residences.—If the taxpayer's principal residence or any of its contents is compulsorily or involuntarily converted as a result of a federally declared disaster—

(A) Treatment of insurance proceeds.—

(i) Exclusion for unscheduled personal property.—No gain shall be recognized by reason of the receipt of any insurance proceeds for personal property which was part of such contents and which was not scheduled property for purposes of such insurance.

(ii) Other proceeds treated as common fund.—In the case of any insurance proceeds (not described in clause (i)) for such residence or contents—

(I) such proceeds shall be treated as received for the conversion of a single item of property, and

(II) any property which is similar or related in service or use to the residence so converted (or contents thereof) shall be treated for purposes of subsection (a)(2) as property similar or related in service or use to such single item of property.

(B) Extension of replacement period.—Subsection (a)(2)(B) shall be applied with respect to any property so converted by substituting "4 years" for "2 years."

(2) Trade or business and investment property.—If a taxpayer's property held for productive use in a trade or business or for investment located in a disaster area and compulsorily or involuntarily converted as a result of a federally declared disaster, tangible property of a type held for productive use in a trade or business shall be treated for purposes of subsection (a) as property similar or related in service or use to the property so converted.

(3) Federally declared disaster; disaster area.—The terms "federally declared disaster" and "disaster area" shall have the respective meaning given such terms by section 165(h)(3)(C).

(4) Principal residence.—For purposes of this subsection, the term "principal residence" has the same meaning as when used in section 121, except that such term shall include a residence not treated as a principal residence solely because the taxpayer does not own the residence.

(i) Replacement property must be acquired from unrelated person in certain cases.—

(1) In general.—If the property which is involuntarily converted is held by a taxpayer to which this subsection applies, subsection (a) shall not apply if the replacement property or stock is acquired from a related person. The preceding sentence shall not apply to the extent that the related person acquired the replacement property or stock from an unrelated person during the period applicable under subsection (a)(2)(B).

(2) Taxpayers to which subsection applies.—This subsection shall apply to—

(A) a C corporation,

(B) a partnership in which 1 or more C corporations own, directly or indirectly (determined in accordance with section 707(b) (3)), more than 50 percent of the capital interest, or profits interest, in such partnership at the time of the involuntary conversion, and

(C) any other taxpayer if, with respect to property which is involuntarily converted during the taxable year, the aggregate of the amount of realized gain on such property on which there is realized gain exceeds $100,000.

In the case of a partnership, subparagraph (C) shall apply with respect to the partnership and with respect to each partner. A similar rule shall apply in the case of an S corporation and its shareholders.

(3) Related person.—For purposes of this subsection, a person is related to another person if the person bears a relationship to the other person described in section 267(b) or 707(b)(1).

* * *

(k) Cross references.—

(1) For determination of the period for which the taxpayer has held property involuntarily converted, see section 1223.

(2) For treatment of gains from involuntary conversions as capital gains in certain cases, see section 1231(a).

(3) For exclusion from gross income of gain from involuntary conversion of principal residence, see section 121.

§ 1035. Certain exchanges of insurance Policies

(a) General rules.—No gain or loss shall be recognized on the exchange of—

(1) a contract of life insurance for another contract of life insurance or for an endowment or annuity contract, or for a qualified long-term care insurance contract;

(2) a contract of endowment insurance (A) for another contract of endowment insurance which provides for regular payments beginning at a date not later than the date payments would have begun under the contract exchanged, or (B) for an annuity contract, or (C) for a qualified long-term care insurance contract;

(3) an annuity contract for an annuity contract or for a qualified long-term care insurance contract, or

(4) a qualified long-term care insurance contract for a qualified long-term care insurance contract.

(b) Definitions.—For the purpose of this section—

(1) Endowment contract.—A contract of endowment insurance is a contract with an insurance company which depends in part on the life expectancy of the insured, but which may be payable in full in a single payment during his life.

(2) Annuity contract.—An annuity contract is a contract to which paragraph (1) applies but which may be payable during the life of the annuitant only in installments. For purposes of the preceding sentences, a contract shall not fail to be treated as an annuity contract solely because a qualified long-term care insurance contract is part of or a rider on such contract.

(3) Life insurance contract.—A contract of life insurance is a contract to which paragraph (1) applies but which is not ordinarily payable in full during the life of the insured. For purposes of the preceding sentences, a contract shall not fail to be treated as an annuity contract solely because a qualified long-term care insurance contract is part of or a rider on such contract.

(c) Exchanges involving foreign persons.—To the extent provided in regulations, subsection (a) shall not apply to any exchange having the effect of transferring property to any person other than a United States person.

(d) Cross references.—

(1) For rules relating to recognition of gain or loss where an exchange is not solely in kind, see subsections (b) and (c) of section 1031.

(2) For rules relating to the basis of property acquired in an exchange described in subsection (a), see subsection (d) of section 1031.

§ 1036. Stock for stock of same corporation

(a) General rule.—No gain or loss shall be recognized if common stock in a corporation is exchanged solely for common stock in the same corporation, or if preferred stock in a corporation is exchanged solely for preferred stock in the same corporation.

(b) Nonqualified preferred stock not treated as stock.—For purposes of this section, nonqualified preferred stock (as defined in section 351(g)(2)) shall be treated as property other than stock.

(c) Cross references.—

(1) For rules relating to recognition of gain or loss where an exchange is not solely in kind, see subsections (b) and (c) of section 1031.

(2) For rules relating to the basis of property acquired in an exchange described in subsection (a), see subsection (d) of section 1031.

* * *

§ 1038. Certain reacquisitions of real property

(a) General rule.—If—

(1) a sale of real property gives rise to indebtedness to the seller which is secured by the real property sold, and

(2) the seller of such property reacquires such property in partial or full satisfaction of such indebtedness,

then, except as provided in subsections (b) and (d), no gain or loss shall result to the seller from such reacquisition, and no debt shall become worthless or partially worthless as a result of such reacquisition.

(b) Amount of gain resulting.—

(1) In general.—In the case of a reacquisition of real property to which subsection (a) applies, gain shall result from such reacquisition to the extent that—

(A) the amount of money and the fair market value of other property (other than obligations of the purchaser) received, prior to such reacquisition, with respect to the sale of such property, exceeds

(B) the amount of the gain on the sale of such property returned as income for periods prior to such reacquisition.

(2) Limitation.—The amount of gain determined under paragraph (1) resulting from a reacquisition during any taxable year beginning after the date of the enactment of this section shall not exceed the amount by which the price at which the real property was sold exceeded its adjusted basis, reduced by the sum of—

(A) the amount of the gain on the sale of such property returned as income for periods prior to the reacquisition of such property, and

(B) the amount of money and the fair market value of other property (other than obligations of the purchaser received with respect to the sale of such property) paid or transferred by the seller in connection with the reacquisition of such property.

For purposes of this paragraph, the price at which real property is sold is the gross sales price reduced by the selling commissions, legal fees, and other expenses incident to the sale of such property which are properly taken into account in determining gain or loss on such sale.

(3) Gain recognized.—Except as provided in this section, the gain determined under this subsection resulting from a reacquisition to which subsection (a) applies shall be recognized, notwithstanding any other provision of this subtitle.

(c) Basis of reacquired real property.—If subsection (a) applies to the reacquisition of any real property, the basis of such property upon such reacquisition shall be the adjusted basis of the indebtedness to the seller secured by such property (determined as of the date of reacquisition), increased by the sum of—

(1) the amount of the gain determined under subsection (b) resulting from such reacquisition, and

(2) the amount described in subsection (b)(2)(B).

If any indebtedness to the seller secured by such property is not discharged upon the reacquisition of such property, the basis of such indebtedness shall be zero.

(d) Indebtedness treated as worthless prior to reacquisition.—If, prior to a reacquisition of real property to which subsection (a) applies, the seller has treated indebtedness secured by such property as having become worthless or partially worthless—

(1) such seller shall be considered as receiving, upon the reacquisition of such property, an amount equal to the amount of such indebtedness treated by him as having become worthless, and

(2) the adjusted basis of such indebtedness shall be increased (as of the date of reacquisition) by an amount equal to the amount so considered as received by such seller.

(e) Principal residences.—If—

(1) subsection (a) applies to a reacquisition of real property with respect to the sale of which gain was not recognized under section 121 (relating to gain on sale of principal residence); and

(2) within 1 year after the date of the reacquisition of such property by the seller, such property is resold by him,

then, under regulations prescribed by the Secretary, subsections (b), (c), and (d) of this section shall not apply to the reacquisition of such property and, for purposes of applying section 121, the resale of such property shall be treated as a part of the transaction constituting the original sale of such property.

*__(g) Acquisition by estate, etc., of seller.__—Under regulations prescribed by the Secretary, if an installment obligation is indebtedness to the seller which is described in subsection (a), and if such obligation is, in the hands of the taxpayer, an obligation with respect to which section 691(a)(4)(B) applies, then—

(1) for purposes of subsection (a), acquisition of real property by the taxpayer shall be treated as reacquisition by the seller, and

(2) the basis of the real property acquired by the taxpayer shall be increased by an amount equal to the deduction under section 691(c) which would (but for this subsection) have been allowable to the taxpayer with respect to the gain on the exchange of the obligation for the real property.

§ 1040. Transfer of certain farm, etc., real property

(a) General rule.—If the executor of the estate of any decedent transfers to a qualified heir (within the meaning of section 2032A(e)(1)) any property with respect to which an election was made under section 2032A, then gain on such transfer shall be recognized to the estate only to the extent that, on the date of such transfer, the fair market value of such property exceeds the value of such property for purposes of chapter 11 (determined without regard to section 2032A).

(b) Similar rule for certain trusts.—To the extent provided in regulations prescribed by the Secretary, a rule similar to the rule provided in subsection (a) shall apply where the trustee of a trust (any portion of which is included in the gross estate of the decedent) transfers property with respect to which an election was made under section 2032A.

(c) Basis of property acquired in transfer described in subsection (a) or (b).—The basis of property acquired in a transfer with respect to which gain realized is not recognized by reason of subsection (a) or (b) shall be the basis of such property immediately before the transfer increased by the amount of the gain recognized to the estate or trust on the transfer.

§ 1041. Transfers of property between spouses or incident to divorce

(a) General rule.—No gain or loss shall be recognized on a transfer of property from an individual to (or in trust for the benefit of)—

*Editorial comment: There is no subsection (f).

(1) a spouse, or

(2) a former spouse, but only if the transfer is incident to the divorce.

(b) Transfer treated as gift; transferee has transferor's basis.—In the case of any transfer of property described in subsection (a)—

(1) for purposes of this subtitle, the property shall be treated as acquired by the transferee by gift, and

(2) the basis of the transferee in the property shall be the adjusted basis of the transferor.

(c) Incident to divorce.—For purposes of subsection (a)(2), a transfer of property is incident to the divorce if such transfer—

(1) occurs within 1 year after the date on which the marriage ceases, or

(2) is related to the cessation of the marriage.

(d) Special rule where spouse is nonresident alien.—Subsection (a) shall not apply if the spouse (or former spouse) of the individual making the transfer is a nonresident alien.

(e) Transfers in trust where liability exceeds basis.—Subsection (a) shall not apply to the transfer of property in trust to the extent that—

(1) the sum of the amount of the liabilities assumed, plus the amount of the liabilities to which the property is subject, exceeds

(2) the total of the adjusted basis of the property transferred.

Proper adjustment shall be made under subsection (b) in the basis of the transferee in such property to take into account gain recognized by reason of the preceding sentence.

§ 1042. Sales of stock to employee stock ownership plans or certain cooperatives

(a) Nonrecognition of gain.—If—

(1) the taxpayer or executor elects in such form as the Secretary may prescribe the application of this section with respect to any sale of qualified securities,

(2) the taxpayer purchases qualified replacement property within the replacement period, and

(3) the requirements of subsection (b) are met with respect to such sale,

then the gain (if any) on such sale which would be recognized as long-term capital gain shall be recognized only to the extent that the amount realized on such sale exceeds the cost to the taxpayer of such qualified replacement property.

(b) Requirements to qualify for nonrecognition.—A sale of qualified securities meets the requirements of this subsection if—

(1) Sale to employee organizations.—The qualified securities are sold to—

(A) an employee stock ownership plan (as defined in section 4975(e)(7)), or

(B) an eligible worker-owned cooperative.

(2) Plan must hold 30 percent of stock after sale.—The plan or cooperative referred to in paragraph (1) owns (after application of section 318(a)(4)), immediately after the sale, at least 30 percent of—

(A) each class of outstanding stock of the corporation (other than stock described in section 1504(a)(4)) which issued the qualified securities, or

(B) the total value of all outstanding stock of the corporation (other than stock described in section 1504(a)(4)).

(3) Written statement required.—

(A) In general.—The taxpayer files with the Secretary the written statement described in subparagraph (B).

(B) Statement.—A statement is described in this subparagraph if it is a verified written statement of—

(i) the employer whose employees are covered by the plan described in paragraph (1), or

(ii) any authorized officer of the cooperative described in paragraph (1),

consenting to the application of sections 4978 and 4979A with respect to such employer or cooperative.

(4) 3-year holding period.—The taxpayer's holding period with respect to the qualified securities is at least 3 years (determined as of the time of the sale).

(c) Definitions; special rules.—For purposes of this section—

(1) Qualified securities.—The term "qualified securities" means employer securities (as defined in section 409(*l*)) which—

(A) are issued by a domestic C corporation that has no stock outstanding that is readily tradable on an established securities market, and

(B) were not received by the taxpayer in—

(i) a distribution from a plan described in section 401(a), or

(ii) a transfer pursuant to an option or other right to acquire stock to which section 83, 422, or 423 applied (or to which section 422 or 424 (as in effect on the day before the date of the enactment of the Revenue Reconciliation Act of 1990) applied).

(2) Eligible worker-owned cooperative.—The term "eligible worker-owned cooperative" means any organization—

(A) to which part I of subchapter T applies,

(B) a majority of the membership of which is composed of employees of such organization,

(C) a majority of the voting stock of which is owned by members,

(D) a majority of the board of directors of which is elected by the members on the basis of 1 person 1 vote, and

(E) a majority of the allocated earnings and losses of which are allocated to members on the basis of—

(i) patronage,

(ii) capital contributions, or

(iii) some combination of clauses (i) and (ii).

(3) Replacement period.—The term "replacement period" means the period which begins 3 months before the date on which the sale of qualified securities occurs and which ends 12 months after the date of such sale.

(4) Qualified replacement property.—

(A) In general.—The term "qualified replacement property" means any security issued by a domestic operating corporation which—

(i) did not, for the taxable year preceding the taxable year in which such security was purchased, have passive investment income (as defined in section 1362(d)(3)(C)) in excess of 25 percent of the gross receipts of such corporation for such preceding taxable year, and

(ii) is not the corporation which issued the qualified securities which such security is replacing or a member of the same controlled group of corporations (within the meaning of section 1563(a)(1)) as such corporation.

For purposes of clause (i), income which is described in section 954(c)(3) (as in effect immediately before the Tax Reform Act of 1986) shall not be treated as passive investment income.

(B) Operating corporation.—For purposes of this paragraph—

(i) In general.—The term "operating corporation" means a corporation more than 50 percent of the assets of which were, at the time the security was purchased or before the close of the replace-ment period, used in the active conduct of the trade or business.

* * *

(C) Controlling and controlled corporations treated as 1 corporation.—

(i) In general.—For purposes of applying this paragraph, if—

(I) the corporation issuing the security owns stock representing control of 1 or more other corporations,

(II) 1 or more other corporations own stock representing control of the corporation issuing the security, or

(III) both,

then all such corporations shall be treated as 1 corporation.

(ii) Control.—For purposes of clause (i), the term "control" has the meaning given such term by section 304(c). In determining control, there shall be disregarded any qualified replacement property of the taxpayer with respect to the section 1042 sale being tested.

(D) Security defined.—For purposes of this paragraph, the term "security" has the meaning given such term by section 165(g)(2), except that such term shall not include any security issued by a government or political subdivision thereof.

(5) Securities sold by underwriter.—No sale of securities by an underwriter to an employee stock ownership plan or eligible worker-owned cooperative in the ordinary course of his trade or business as an underwriter, whether or not guaranteed, shall be treated as a sale for purposes of subsection (a).

(6) Time for filing election.—An election under subsection (a) shall be filed not later than the last day prescribed by law (including extensions thereof) for filing the return of tax imposed by this chapter for the taxable year in which the sale occurs.

(7) Section not to apply to gain of C corporation.—Subsection (a) shall not apply to any gain on the sale of any qualified securities which is includible in the gross income of any C corporation.

(d) Basis of qualified replacement property.—The basis of the taxpayer in qualified replacement property purchased by the taxpayer during the replacement period shall be reduced by the amount of gain not recognized by reason of such purchase and the application of subsection (a). If more than one item of qualified replacement property is purchased, the basis of each of such items shall be reduced by an amount determined by multiplying the total gain not recognized by reason of such purchase and the application of subsection (a) by a fraction—

(1) the numerator of which is the cost of such item of property, and

(2) the denominator of which is the total cost of all such items of property.

Any reduction in basis under this subsection shall not be taken into account for purposes of section 1278(a)(2)(A)(ii) (relating to definition of market discount).

(e) Recapture of gain on disposition of qualified replacement property.—

(1) In general.—If a taxpayer disposes of any qualified replacement property, then, notwithstanding any other provision of this title, gain (if any) shall be recognized to the extent of the gain which was not recognized under subsection (a) by reason of the acquisition by such taxpayer of such qualified replacement property.

(2) Special rule for corporations controlled by the taxpayer.—If—

(A) a corporation issuing qualified replacement property disposes of a substantial portion of its assets other than in the ordinary course of its trade or business, and

(B) any taxpayer owning stock representing control (within the meaning of section 304(c)) of such corporation at the time of such disposition holds any qualified replacement property of such corporation at such time,

then the taxpayer shall be treated as having disposed of such qualified replacement property at such time.

(3) Recapture not to apply in certain cases.—Paragraph (1) shall not apply to any transfer of qualified replacement property—

(A) in any reorganization (within the meaning of section 368) unless the person making the election under subsection (a)(1) owns stock representing control in the acquiring or acquired corporation and such property is substituted basis property in the hands of the transferee,

(B) by reason of the death of the person making such election,

(C) by gift, or

(D) in any transaction to which section 1042(a) applies.

(f) Statute of limitations.—If any gain is realized by the taxpayer on the sale or exchange of any qualified securities and there is in effect an election under subsection (a) with respect to such gain, then—

(1) the statutory period for the assessment of any deficiency with respect to such gain shall not expire before the expiration of 3 years from the date the Secretary is notified by the taxpayer (in such manner as the Secretary may by regulations prescribe) of—

(A) the taxpayer's cost of purchasing qualified replacement property which the taxpayer claims results in nonrecognition of any part of such gain,

(B) the taxpayer's intention not to purchase qualified replacement property within the replacement period, or

(C) a failure to make such purchase within the replacement period, and

(2) such deficiency may be assessed before the expiration of such 3-year period notwithstanding the provisions of any other law or rule of law which would otherwise prevent such assessment.

* * *

§ 1043. Sale of property to comply with conflict-of-interest requirements

(a) Nonrecognition of gain.—If an eligible person sells any property pursuant to a certificate of divestiture, at the election of the taxpayer, gain from such sale shall be recognized only to the extent that the amount realized on such sale exceeds the cost (to the extent not previously taken into account under this subsection) of any permitted property purchased by the taxpayer during the 60-day period beginning on the date of such sale.

(b) Definitions.—For purposes of this section—

(1) Eligible person.—The term "eligible person" means—

(A) an officer or employee of the executive branch, or a judicial officer, of the Federal Government, but does not mean a special Government employee as defined in section 202 of title 18, United States Code, and

(B) any spouse or minor or dependent child whose ownership of any property is attributable under any statute, regulation, rule, Judicial Canon, or executive order referred to in paragraph (2) to a person referred to in subparagraph (A).

(2) Certificate of divestiture.—The term "certificate of divestiture" means any written determination—

(A) that states that divestiture of specific property is reasonably necessary to comply with any Federal conflict of interest statute, regulation, rule, judicial canon, or executive order (including section 208 of title 18, United States Code), or requested by a congressional committee as a condition of confirmation,

(B) that has been issued by the President or the Director of the Office of Government Ethics, in the case of executive branch officers or employees, or by the Judicial Conference of the United States (or its designee), in the case of judicial officers and

(C) that identifies the specific property to be divested.

(3) Permitted property.—The term "permitted property" means any obligation of the United States or any diversified investment fund approved by regulations issued by the Office of Government Ethics.

(4) Purchase.—The taxpayer shall be considered to have purchased any permitted property if, but for subsection (c), the unadjusted basis of such property would be its cost within the meaning of section 1012.

(5) Special rule for trusts.—For purposes of this section, the trustee of a trust shall be treated as an eligible person with respect to property which is held in the trust if—

(A) any person referred to in paragraph (1)(A) has a beneficial interest in the principal or income of the trust, or

(B) any person referred to in paragraph (1)(B) has a beneficial interest in the principal or income of the trust and such interest is attributable under any statute, regulation, rule, judicial canon, or executive order referred to in paragraph (2) to a person referred to in paragraph (1)(A).

(6) Judicial officer.—The term "judicial officer" means the Chief Justice of the United States, the Associate Justices of the Supreme Court, and the judges of the United States courts of appeals, United States district courts, including the district courts in Guam, the Northern Mariana Islands, and the Virgin Islands, Court of Appeals for the Federal Circuit, Court of International Trade, Tax Court, Court of Federal Claims, Court of Appeals for Veterans Claims, United States Court of Appeals for the Armed Forces, and any court created by Act of Congress, the judges of which are entitled to hold office during good behavior.

(c) Basis adjustments.—If gain from the sale of any property is not recognized by reason of subsection (a), such gain shall be applied to reduce (in the order acquired) the basis for determining gain or loss of any permitted property which is purchased by the taxpayer during the 60-day period described in subsection (a).

§ 1044. Rollover of publicly traded securities gain into specialized small business investment companies

(a) Nonrecognition of gain.—In the case of the sale of any publicly traded securities with respect to which the taxpayer elects the application of this section, gain from such sale shall be recognized only to the extent that the amount realized on such sale exceeds—

(1) the cost of any common stock or partnership interest in a specialized small business investment company purchased by the taxpayer during the 60–day period beginning on the date of such sale, reduced by

(2) any portion of such cost previously taken into account under this section.

This section shall not apply to any gain which is treated as ordinary income for purposes of this subtitle.

(b) Limitations.—

(1) Limitation on individuals.—In the case of an individual, the amount of gain which may be excluded under subsection (a) for any taxable year shall not exceed the lesser of—

(A) $50,000, or

(B) $500,000, reduced by the amount of gain excluded under subsection (a) for all preceding taxable years.

(2) Limitation on C corporations.—In the case of a C corporation, the amount of gain which may be excluded under subsection (a) for any taxable year shall not exceed the lesser of—

(A) $250,000, or

(B) $1,000,000, reduced by the amount of gain excluded under subsection (a) for all preceding taxable years.

(3) Special rules for married individuals.—For purposes of this subsection—

(A) Separate returns.—In the case of a separate return by a married individual, paragraph (1) shall be applied by substituting "$25,000" for "$50,000" and "$250,000" for "$500,000."

(B) Allocation of gain.—In the case of any joint return, the amount of gain excluded under subsection (a) for any taxable year shall be allocated equally between the spouses for purposes of applying this subsection to subsequent taxable years.

(C) Marital status.—For purposes of this subsection, marital status shall be determined under section 7703.

(4) Special rules for C corporation.—For purposes of this subsection—

(A) all corporations which are members of the same controlled group of corporations (within the meaning of section 52(a)) shall be treated as 1 taxpayer, and

(B) any gain excluded under subsection (a) by a predecessor of any C corporation shall be treated as having been excluded by such C corporation.

(c) Definitions and special rules.—For purposes of this section—

(1) Publicly traded securities.—The term "publicly traded securities" means securities which are traded on an established securities market.

(2) Purchase.—The taxpayer shall be considered to have purchased any property if, but for subsection (d), the unadjusted basis of such property would be its cost within the meaning of section 1012.

(3) Specialized small business investment company.—The term "specialized small business investment company" means any partnership or corporation which is licensed by the Small Business Administration under section 301(d) of the Small Business Investment Act of 1958 (as in effect on May 13, 1993).

(4) Certain entities not eligible.—This section shall not apply to any estate, trust, partnership, or S corporation.

(d) Basis adjustments.—If gain from any sale is not recognized by reason of subsection (a), such gain shall be applied to reduce (in the order acquired) the basis for determining gain or loss of any common stock or partnership interest in any specialized small business investment company which is purchased by the taxpayer during the 60-day period described in subsection (a). This subsection shall not apply for purposes of section 1202.

§ 1045. Rollover of gain from qualified small business stock to another qualified small business stock

(a) Nonrecognition of gain.—In the case of any sale of qualified small business stock held by a taxpayer other than a corporation for more than 6 months and with respect to which such taxpayer elects the application of this section, gain from such sale shall be recognized only to the extent that the amount realized on such sale exceeds—

(1) the cost of any qualified small business stock purchased by the taxpayer during the 60-day period beginning on the date of such sale, reduced by

(2) any portion of such cost previously taken into account under this section.

This section shall not apply to any gain which is treated as ordinary income for purposes of this title.

(b) Definitions and special rules.—For purposes of this section—

(1) Qualified small business stock.—The term "qualified small business stock" has the meaning given such term by section 1202(c).

(2) Purchase.—A taxpayer shall be treated as having purchased any property if, but for paragraph (3), the unadjusted basis of such property in the hands of the taxpayer would be its cost (within the meaning of section 1012).

(3) Basis adjustments.—If gain from any sale is not recognized by reason of subsection (a), such gain shall be applied to reduce (in the order acquired) the basis for determining gain or loss of any qualified small business stock which is purchased by the taxpayer during the 60-day period described in subsection (a).

(4) Holding period.—For purposes of determining whether the nonrecognition of gain under subsection (a) applies to stock which is sold—

(A) the taxpayer's holding period for such stock and the stock referred to in subsection (a)(1) shall be determined without regard to section 1223, and

(B) only the first 6 months of the taxpayer's holding period for the stock referred to in subsection (a)(1) shall be taken into account for purposes of applying section 1202(c)(2).

(5) Certain rules to apply.—Rules similar to the rules of subsections (f), (g), (h), (i), (j), and (k) of section 1202 shall apply.

PART IV—SPECIAL RULES

Editorial Summary

Property Transactions: Purchase Price Allocations Subchapter O of Chapter 1 (Secs. 1053–1060)

A lump-sum purchase price must be allocated among the assets acquired. Typically, this allocation is made in accordance with the purchase agreement.

A problem frequently encountered with the purchase of a trade or business is the treatment of a purchase price in excess of the fair market value of the identifiable assets. Typically, such excess is labeled goodwill or going-concern value. From the viewpoint of the seller, this label is beneficial because such assets are classified as capital assets (see Sec. 1221). However, from the perspective of the buyer, such labeling historically produced negative tax consequences. That is, since goodwill or going-concern value has an indefinite life, such amounts could not be deducted (i.e., amortized). Thus, it was in the buyer's interest to minimize the amount of the purchase price that was assigned to goodwill or going-concern value.

One method for doing this was for the amount, or a substantial portion thereof, to be assigned to a covenant not to compete. The buyer could amortize the covenant over its life. However, from the viewpoint of the seller, the covenant is not a capital asset and therefore produces ordinary income rather than capital gain treatment.

The Revenue Reconciliation Act of 1993 (RRA of 1993) has modified this tax difference for the buyer between the treatment of goodwill and a covenant not to compete. Since both are Sec. 197 intangibles [see Sec. 197(d)], the amortization period is a statutory 15-year period regardless of the actual life.

Note that from a legal perspective, there still are benefits to the buyer of the covenant treatment.

Another method that has been used to counter the goodwill problem is to initially value the goodwill along with other assets at the time of purchase. Then, any remaining excess is allocated *pro rata* among all of the assets, including goodwill.

Example: P purchases the assets of a trade or business from S for $600,000. Appraisals result in the assets being valued as follows:

Current assets	$100,000
Fixed assets	300,000
Intangibles excluding goodwill	75,000
Goodwill	25,000
	$500,000

Applying the *pro rata* approach would result in the $100,000 excess of the purchase price over the fair market value of the identifiable assets being allocated as follows:

Current assets (20 percent)	$ 20,000
Fixed assets (60 percent)	60,000
Intangibles excluding goodwill (15 percent)	15,000
Goodwill (5 percent)	5,000
	$100,000

Therefore, the basis for the assets would be as follows:

Current assets ($100,000 + $20,000)	$120,000
Fixed assets ($300,000 + $60,000)	360,000
Intangibles excluding goodwill ($75,000 + $15,000)	90,000
Goodwill ($25,000 + $5,000)	30,000
	$600,000

The Tax Reform Act of 1986 requires that the residual method be used for the asset allocation in the case of the purchase of the assets of a trade or business (see Sec. 1060). Referring to the example, the amount allocated to goodwill would be $125,000 (i.e., purchase price of $600,000 – $475,000 fair market value of identifiable assets, excluding goodwill).

Therefore, the basis for the assets would be as follows:

Current assets	$100,000
Fixed assets	300,000
Intangibles excluding goodwill	75,000
Goodwill ($25,000 + $100,000)	125,000
	$600,000

RRA of 1993 replaced the term goodwill in the Sec. 1060 statutory language with Sec. 197 intangibles.

* * *

§ 1053. Property acquired before March 1, 1913

In the case of property acquired before March 1, 1913, if the basis otherwise determined under this subtitle, adjusted (for the period before March 1,

1913) as provided in section 1016, is less than the fair market value of the property as of March 1, 1913, then the basis for determining gain shall be such fair market value. In determining the fair market value of stock in a corporation as of March 1, 1913, due regard shall be given to the fair market value of the assets of the corporation as of that date.

* * *

§ 1059. Corporate shareholder's basis in stock reduced by nontaxed portion of extraordinary dividends

(a) General rule.—If any corporation receives any extraordinary dividend with respect to any share of stock and such corporation has not held such stock for more than 2 years before the dividend announcement date—

(1) Reduction in basis.—The basis of such corporation in such stock shall be reduced (but not below zero) by the nontaxed portion of such dividends.

(2) Amounts in excess of basis.—If the nontaxed portion of such dividends exceeds such basis, such excess shall be treated as gain from the sale or exchange of such stock for the taxable year in which the extraordinary divided is received.

(b) Nontaxed portion.—For purposes of this section—

(1) In general.—The nontaxed portion of any dividend is the excess (if any) of—

(A) the amount of such dividend, over

(B) the taxable portion of such dividend.

(2) Taxable portion.—The taxable portion of any dividend is—

(A) the portion of such dividend includible in gross income, reduced by

(B) the amount of any deduction allowable with respect to such dividend under section 243, 244, or 245.

(c) Extraordinary dividend defined.—For purposes of this section—

(1) In general.—The term "extraordinary dividend" means any dividend with respect to a share of stock if the amount of such dividend equals or exceeds the threshold percentage of the taxpayer's adjusted basis in such share of stock.

(2) Threshold percentage.—The term "threshold percentage" means—

(A) 5 percent in the case of stock which is preferred as to dividends, and

(B) 10 percent in the case of any other stock.

(3) Aggregation of dividends.—

(A) Aggregation within 85-day period.—All dividends—

(i) which are received by the taxpayer (or a person described in subparagraph (C)) with respect to any share of stock, and

(ii) which have ex-dividend dates within the same period of 85 consecutive days, shall be treated as 1 dividend.

(B) Aggregation within 1 year where dividends exceed 20 percent of adjusted basis.— All dividends—

(i) which are received by the taxpayer (or a person described in subparagraph (C)) with respect to any share of stock, and

(ii) which have ex-dividend dates during the same period of 365 consecutive days,

shall be treated as extraordinary dividends if the aggregate of such dividends exceeds 20 percent of the taxpayer's adjusted basis in such stock (determined without regard to this section).

(C) Substituted basis transactions.—In the case of any stock, a person is described in this subparagraph if—

(i) the basis of such stock in the hands of such person is determined in whole or in part by reference to the basis of such stock in the hands of the taxpayer, or

(ii) the basis of such stock in the hands of the taxpayer is determined in whole or in part by reference to the basis of such stock in the hands of such person.

(4) Fair market value determination.—If the taxpayer establishes to the satisfaction of the Secretary the fair market value of any share of stock as of the day before the ex-dividend date, the taxpayer may elect to apply paragraphs (1) and (3) by substituting such value for the taxpayer's adjusted basis.

(d) Special rules.—For purposes of this section—

(1) Time for reduction.—Any reduction in basis under subsection (a)(1) shall be treated as occurring at the beginning of the ex-dividend date of the extraordinary dividend to which the reduction relates.

(2) Distributions in kind.—To the extent any dividend consists of property other than cash, the amount of such dividend shall be treated as the fair market value of such property (as of the date of the distribution) reduced as provided in section 301(b)(2).

(3) Determination of holding period.—For purposes of determining the holding period of stock under subsection (a), rules similar to the rules of paragraphs (3) and (4) of section 246(c) shall apply; except that "2 years" shall be substituted for the number of days specified in subparagraph (B) of section 246(c)(3).

(4) Ex-dividend date.—The term "ex-dividend date" means the date on which the share of stock becomes ex-dividend.

(5) Dividend announcement date.—The term "dividend announcement date" means, with respect to any dividend, the date on which the corporation declares, announces, or agrees to the amount or payment of such dividend, whichever is the earliest.

(6) Exception where stock held during entire existence of corporation.—

(A) In general.—Subsection (a) shall not apply to any extraordinary dividend with respect to any share of stock of a corporation if—

(i) such stock was held by the taxpayer during the entire period such corporation was in existence, and

(ii) except as provided in regulations, no earnings and profits of such corporation were attributable to transfers of property from (or earnings and profits of) a corporation which is not a qualified corporation.

(B) Qualified corporation.—For purposes of subparagraph (A), the term "qualified corporation" means any corporation (including a predecessor corporation)—

(i) with respect to which the taxpayer holds directly or indirectly during the entire period of such corporation's existence at least the same ownership interest as the taxpayer holds in the corporation distributing the extraordinary dividend, and

(ii) which has no earnings and profits—

(I) which were earned by, or

(II) which are attributable to gain on property which accrued during a period the corporation holding the property was,

a corporation not described in clause (i).

(C) Application of paragraph.—This paragraph shall not apply to any extraordinary dividend to the extent such application is inconsistent with the purposes of this section.

(e) Special rules for certain distributions.—

(1) Treatment of partial liquidations and certain redemptions.—Except as otherwise provided in regulations—

(A) Redemptions.—In the case of any redemption of stock—

(i) which is part of a partial liquidation (within the meaning of section 302(e)) of the redeeming corporation,

(ii) which is not pro rata as to all shareholders, or

(iii) which would not have been treated (in whole or in part) as a dividend if—

(I) any options had not been taken into account under section 318(a)(4), or

(II) section 304(a) had not applied,

any amount treated as a dividend with respect to such redemption shall be treated as an extraordinary dividend to which paragraphs (1) and (2) of subsection (a) apply without regard to the period the taxpayer held such stock. In the case of a redemption described in clause (iii), only the basis in the stock redeemed shall be taken into account under subsection (a).

(B) Reorganizations, etc.—An exchange described in section 356 which is treated as a dividend shall be treated as a redemption of stock for purposes of applying subparagraph (A).

(2) Qualifying dividends.—

(A) In general.—Except as provided in regulations, the term "extraordinary dividend" does not include any qualifying dividend (within the meaning of section 243).

(B) Exception.—Subparagraph (A) shall not apply to any portion of a dividend which is attributable to earnings and profits which—

(i) were earned by a corporation during a period it was not a member of the affiliated group, or

(ii) are attributable to gain on property which accrued during a period the corporation holding the property was not a member of the affiliated group.

(3) **Qualified preferred dividends.**—

(A) **In general.**—In the case of 1 or more qualified preferred dividends with respect to any share of stock—

(i) this section shall not apply to such dividends if the taxpayer holds such stock for more than 5 years, and

(ii) if the taxpayer disposes of such stock before it has been held for more than 5 years, the aggregate reduction under subsection (a)(1) with respect to such dividends shall not be greater than the excess (if any) of—

(I) the qualified preferred dividends paid with respect to such stock during the period the taxpayer held such stock, over

(II) the qualified preferred dividends which would have been paid during such period on the basis of the stated rate of return.

(B) **Rate of return.**—For purposes of this paragraph—

(i) **Actual rate of return.**—The actual rate of return shall be the rate of return for the period for which the taxpayer held the stock, determined—

(I) by only taking into account dividends during such period, and

(II) by using the lesser of the adjusted basis of the taxpayer in such stock or the liquidation preference of such stock.

(ii) **Stated rate of return.**—The stated rate of return shall be the annual rate of the qualified preferred dividend payable with respect to any share of stock (expressed as a percentage of the amount described in clause (i)(II)).

(C) **Definitions and special rules.**—For purposes of this paragraph—

(i) **Qualified preferred dividend.**—The term "qualified preferred dividend" means any fixed dividend payable with respect to any share of stock which—

(I) provides for fixed preferred dividends payable not less frequently than annually, and

(II) is not in arrears as to dividends at the time the taxpayer acquires the stock.

Such term shall not include any dividend payable with respect to any share of stock if the actual rate of return on such stock exceeds 15 percent.

(ii) **Holding period.**—In determining the holding period for purposes of subparagraph (A)(ii), subsection (d)(3) shall be applied by substituting "5 years" for "2 years."

(f) **Treatment of dividends on certain preferred stock.**—

(1) **In general.**—Any dividend with respect to disqualified preferred stock shall be treated as an extraordinary dividend to which paragraphs (1) and (2) of subsection (a) apply without regard to the period the taxpayer held the stock.

(2) **Disqualified preferred stock.**—For purposes of this subsection, the term "disqualified preferred stock" means any stock which is preferred as to dividends if—

(A) when issued, such stock has a dividend rate which declines (or can reasonably be expected to decline) in the future,

(B) the issue price of such stock exceeds its liquidation rights or its stated redemption price, or

(C) such stock is otherwise structured—

(i) to avoid the other provisions of this section, and

(ii) to enable corporate shareholders to reduce tax through a combination of dividend received deductions and loss on the disposition of the stock.

(g) **Regulations.**—The Secretary shall prescribe such regulations as may be appropriate to carry out the purposes of this section, including regulations—

(1) providing for the application of this section in the case of stock dividends, stock splits, reorganizations, and other similar transactions, in the case of stock held by pass-thru entities, and in the case of consolidated groups, and

(2) providing that the rules of subsection (f) shall apply in the case of stock which is not preferred as to dividends in cases where stock is structured to avoid the purposes of this section.

* * *

§ 1060. Special allocation rules for certain asset acquisitions

(a) General rule.—In the case of any applicable asset acquisition, for purposes of determining both—

(1) the transferee's basis in such assets, and

(2) the gain or loss of the transferor with respect to such acquisition,

the consideration received for such assets shall be allocated among such assets acquired in such acquisition in the same manner as amounts are allocated to assets under section 338(b)(5). If in connection with an applicable asset acquisition, the transferee and transferor agree in writing as to the allocation of any consideration, or as to the fair market value of any of the assets, such agreement shall be binding on both the transferee and transferor unless the Secretary determines that such allocation (or fair market value) is not appropriate.

(b) Information required to be furnished to secretary.—Under regulations, the transferor and transferee in an applicable asset acquisition shall, at such times and in such manner as may be provided in such regulations, furnish to the Secretary the following information:

(1) The amount of the consideration received for the assets which is allocated to section 197 intangibles.

(2) Any modification of the amount described in paragraph (1).

(3) Any other information with respect to other assets transferred in such acquisition as the Secretary deems necessary to carry out the provisions of this section.

(c) Applicable asset acquisition.—For purposes of this section, the term "applicable asset acquisition" means any transfer (whether directly or indirectly)—

(1) of assets which constitute a trade or business, and

(2) with respect to which the transferee's basis in such assets is determined wholly by reference to the consideration paid for such assets.

A transfer shall not be treated as failing to be an applicable asset acquisition merely because section 1031 applies to a portion of the assets transferred.

(d) Treatment of certain partnership transactions.—In the case of a distribution of partnership property or a transfer of an interest in a partnership—

(1) the rules of subsection (a) shall apply but only for purposes of determining the value of section 197 intangibles for purposes of applying section 755, and

(2) if section 755 applies, such distribution or transfer (as the case may be) shall be treated as an applicable asset acquisition for purposes of subsection (b).

(e) Information required in case of certain transfers of interests in entities.—

(1) In general.—If—

(A) a person who is a 10-percent owner with respect to any entity transfers an interest in such entity, and

(B) in connection with such transfer, such owner (or a related person) enters into an employment contract, covenant not to compete, royalty or lease agreement, or other agreement with the transferee,

such owner and the transferee shall, at such time and in such manner as the Secretary may prescribe, furnish such information as the Secretary may require.

(2) 10-percent owner.—For purposes of this subsection—

(A) In general.—The term "10-percent owner" means, with respect to any entity, any person who holds 10 percent or more (by value) of the interests in such entity immediately before the transfer.

(B) Constructive ownership.—Section 318 shall apply in determining ownership of stock in a corporation. Similar principles shall apply in determining the ownership of interests in any other entity.

(3) Related person.—For purposes of this subsection, the term "related person" means any person who is related (within the meaning of section 267(b) or 707(b)(1)) to the 10-percent owner.

(f) Cross reference.—

For provisions relating to penalties for failure to file a return required by this section, see section 6721.

* * *

PART V—CHANGES TO EFFECTUATE F.C.C. POLICY*

PART VI—EXCHANGES IN OBEDIENCE TO S.E.C. ORDERS*

PART VII—WASH SALES; STRADDLES

Editorial Summary

Property Transactions: Wash Sales and Straddles

Section O of Chapter 1 (Secs. 1091, 1092)

Both the wash sale rules and the straddle rules limit the ability of the taxpayer to deduct losses by effectively looking at the economic substance of the transaction rather than merely the transaction form.

The wash sales rules are limited in scope in that they apply only to stock and securities. In addition, the loss deduction is disallowed only if the wash sale occurs within a 60-day time period (i.e., the related acquisition occurs within 30 days before or 30 days after the sale transaction [see Sec.1091 (a)]).

The straddle rules prohibit the taxpayer from recognizing loss on a completed transaction if the taxpayer has an offsetting unrealized gain associated with the other side of the straddle position [see Sec. 1092(a)].

Neither the wash sale nor straddle rules result in a permanent disallowance of the loss. Rather, the statutory intent is one of postponement. For the wash sale, the disallowed loss is added to the basis of the replacement stock or securities [see Sec. 1091(d)]. In the case of a straddle, the realized loss effectively is permitted to be recognized at the same time that the unrealized gain is recognized [see Sec. 1092(a)(1)].

§ 1091. Loss from wash sales of stock or securities

(a) Disallowance of loss deduction.—In the case of any loss claimed to have been sustained from any sale or other disposition of shares of stock or securities where it appears that, within a period beginning 30 days before the date of such sale or disposition and ending 30 days after such date, the taxpayer has acquired (by purchase or by an exchange on which the entire amount of gain or loss was recognized by law), or has entered into a contract or option so to acquire, substantially identical stock or securities, then no deduction shall be allowed under section 165 unless the taxpayer is a dealer in stock or securities and the loss is sustained in a transaction made in the ordinary course of such business. For purposes of this section, the term "stock or securities" shall, except as provided in regulations, include contracts or options to acquire or sell stock or securities.

(b) Stock acquired less than stock sold.—If the amount of stock or securities acquired (or covered by the contract or option to acquire) is less than the amount of stock or securities sold or otherwise disposed of, then the particular shares of stock or securities the loss from the sale or other disposition of which is not deductible shall be determined under regulations prescribed by the Secretary.

(c) Stock acquired not less than stock sold.—If the amount of stock or securities acquired (or covered by the contract or option to acquire) is not less than the amount of stock or securities sold or otherwise disposed of, then the particular shares of stock or securities the acquisition of which (or the contract or option to acquire which) resulted in the nondeductibility of the loss shall be determined under regulations prescribed by the Secretary.

(d) Unadjusted basis in case of wash sale of stock.—If the property consists of stock or securities the acquisition of which (or the contract or option to acquire which) resulted in the nondeductibility (under this section or corresponding provisions of prior internal revenue laws) of the loss from the sale or other disposition of substantially identical stock or securities, then the basis shall be the basis of the stock or securities so sold or disposed of, increased or decreased, as the case may be, by the difference, if any, between the price at which the property was acquired and the price at which such substantially identical stock or securities were sold or otherwise disposed of.

(e) Certain short sales of stock or securities and securities futures contracts to sell.—Rules similar to the rules of subsection (a) shall apply to any loss realized on the closing of a short sale of (or the sale, exchange, or termination of a securities futures contract to sell) stock or securities if, within a period beginning 30 days before the date of such closing and ending 30 days after such date—

(1) substantially identical stock or securities were sold, or

(2) another short sale of (or securities futures contract to sell) substantially identical stock or securities was entered into.

For purposes of this subsection, the term "securities futures contract" has the meaning provided by section 1234B(c).

*Omitted.

(f) Cash settlement.—This section shall not fail to apply to a contract or option to acquire or sell stock or securities solely by reason of the fact that the contract or option settles in (or could be settled in) cash or property other than such stock or securities.

§ 1092. Straddles

(a) Recognition of loss in case of straddles, etc.—

(1) Limitation on recognition of loss.—

(A) In general.—Any loss with respect to 1 or more positions shall be taken into account for any taxable year only to the extent that the amount of such loss exceeds the unrecognized gain (if any) with respect to 1 or more positions which were offsetting positions with respect to 1 or more positions from which the loss arose.

(B) Carryover of loss.—Any loss which may not be taken into account under subparagraph (A) for any taxable year shall, subject to the limitations under subparagraph (A), be treated as sustained in the succeeding taxable year.

(2) Special rule for identified straddles.—

(A) In general.—In the case of any straddle which is an identified straddle—

(i) paragraph (1) shall not apply with respect to positions comprising the identified straddle,

(ii) if there is any loss with respect to any position of the identified straddle, the basis of each of the offsetting positions in the identified straddle shall be increased by an amount which bears the same ratio to the loss as the unrecognized gain with respect to such offsetting position bears to the aggregate unrecognized gain with respect to all such offsetting positions,

(iii) if the application of clause (ii) does not result in an increase in the basis of any offsetting position in the identified straddle, the basis of each of the offsetting positions in the identified straddle shall be increased in a manner which—

(I) is reasonable, consistent with the purposes of this paragraph, and consistently applied by the taxpayer, and

(II) results in an aggregate increase in the basis of such offsetting positions which is equal to the loss described in clause (ii), and

(iv) any loss described in clause (ii) shall not otherwise be taken into account for purposes of this title.

(B) Identified straddle.—The term "identified straddle" means any straddle—

(i) which is clearly identified on the taxpayer's records as an identified straddle before the earlier of—

(I) the close of the day on which the straddle is acquired, or

(II) such time as the Secretary may prescribe by regulations.

(ii) to the extent provided by regulations, the value of each position of which (in the hands of the taxpayer immediately before the creation of the straddle) is not less than the basis of such position in the hands of the taxpayer at the time the straddle is created, and

(iii) which is not part of a larger straddle.

A straddle shall be treated as clearly identified for purposes of clause (i) only if such identification includes an identification of the positions in the straddle which are offsetting with respect to other positions in the straddle.

(C) Application to liabilities and obligations.—Except as otherwise provided by the Secretary, rules similar to the rules of clauses (ii) and (iii) of subparagraph (A) shall apply for purposes of this paragraph with respect to any position which is, or has been, a liability or obligation.

(D) Regulations.—The Secretary shall prescribe such regulations or other guidance as may be necessary or appropriate to carry out the purposes of this paragraph. Such regulations or other guidance may specify the proper methods for clearly identifying a straddle as an identified straddle (and for identifying the positions comprising such straddle), the rules for the application of this section to a taxpayer which fails to comply with those identification requirements, the rules for the application of this section to a position which is or has been a liability or obligation, methods of loss allocation which satisfy the requirements of subparagraph (A)(iii), and the ordering rules in cases where a taxpayer disposes (or otherwise ceases to be the holder) of any part of any position which is part of an identified straddle.

(3) Unrecognized gain.—For purposes of this subsection—

(A) In general.—The term "unrecognized gain" means—

(i) in the case of any position held by the taxpayer as of the close of the taxable year, the amount of gain which would be taken into account with respect to such position if such position were sold on the last business day of such taxable year at its fair market value, and

(ii) in the case of any position with respect to which, as of the close of the taxable year, gain has been realized but not recognized, the amount of gain so realized.

(B) Special rule for identified straddles.—For purposes of paragraph (2)(A)(ii), the unrecognized gain with respect to any offsetting position shall be the excess of the fair market value of the position at the time of the determination over the fair market value of the position at the time the taxpayer identified the position in an identified straddle.

(C) Reporting of gain.—

(i) In general.—Each taxpayer shall disclose to the Secretary, at such time and in such manner and form as the Secretary may prescribe by regulations—

(I) each position (whether or not part of a straddle) with respect to which, as of the close of the taxable year, there is unrecognized gain, and

(II) the amount of such unrecognized gain.

(ii) Reports not required in certain cases.—Clause (i) shall not apply—

(I) to any position which is part of an identified straddle,

(II) to any position which, with respect to the taxpayer, is property described in paragraph (1) or (2) of section 1221 or to any position which is part of a hedging transaction (as defined in section 1256 (e)), or

(III) with respect to any taxable year if no loss on a position (including a regulated futures contract) has been sustained during such taxable year or if the only loss sustained on such position is a loss described in subclause (II).

(b) Regulations.—

(1) In general.—The Secretary shall prescribe such regulations with respect to gain or loss on positions which are a part of a straddle as may be appropriate to carry out the purposes of this section and section 263(g). To the extent consistent with such purposes, such regulations shall include rules applying the principles of subsections (a) and (d) of section 1091 and of subsections (b) and (d) of section 1233.

(2) Regulations relating to mixed straddles.—

(A) Elective provisions in lieu of section 1233(d) principles.—The regulations prescribed under paragraph (1) shall provide that—

(i) the taxpayer may offset gains and losses from positions which are part of mixed straddles—

(I) by straddle-by-straddle identification, or

(II) by the establishment (with respect to any class of activities) of a mixed straddle account for which gains and losses would be recognized (and offset) on a periodic basis,

(ii) such offsetting will occur before the application of section 1256, and section 1256 (a)(3) will only apply to net gain or net loss attributable to section 1256 contracts, and

(iii) the principles of section 1233(d) shall not apply with respect to any straddle identified under clause (i)(I) or part of an account established under clause (i)(II).

(B) Limitation on net gain or net loss from mixed straddle account.—In the case of any mixed straddle account referred to in subparagraph (A)(i)(II)—

(i) Not more than 50 percent of net gain may be treated as long-term capital gain.—In no event shall more than 50 percent of the net gain from such account for any taxable year be treated as long-term capital gain.

(ii) Not more than 40 percent of net loss may be treated as short-term capital loss.—In no event shall more than 40 percent of the net loss from such account for any taxable year be treated as short-term capital loss.

(C) Authority to treat certain positions as mixed straddles.—The regulations prescribed under paragraph (1) may treat as a mixed straddle positions not described in section 1256(d)(4).

(D) Timing and character authority.—The regulations prescribed under paragraph (1) shall include regulations relating to the timing and character of gains and losses in case of straddles where at least 1 position is ordinary and at least 1 position is capital.

(c) Straddle defined.—For purposes of this section—

(1) In general.—The term "straddle" means offsetting positions with respect to personal property.

(2) Offsetting positions.—

(A) In general.—A taxpayer holds offsetting positions with respect to personal property if there is a substantial diminution of the taxpayer's risk of loss from holding any position with respect to personal property by reason of his holding 1 or more other positions with respect to personal property (whether or not of the same kind).

(B) Special rule for identified straddles.—In the case of any position which is not part of an identified straddle (within the meaning of subsection (a)(2)(B)), such position shall not be treated as offsetting with respect to any position which is part of an identified straddle.

(3) Presumption.—

(A) In general.—For purposes of paragraph (2), 2 or more positions shall be presumed to be offsetting if—

(i) the positions are in the same personal property (whether established in such property or a contract for such property),

(ii) the positions are in the same personal property, even though such property may be in a substantially altered form,

(iii) the positions are in debt instruments of a similar maturity or other debt instruments described in regulations prescribed by the Secretary,

(iv) the positions are sold or marketed as offsetting positions (whether or not such positions are called a straddle, spread, butterfly, or any similar name),

(v) the aggregate margin requirement for such positions is lower than the sum of the margin requirements for each such position (if held separately), or

(vi) there are such other factors (or satisfaction of subjective or objective tests) as the Secretary may by regulations prescribe as indicating that such positions are offsetting.

For purposes of the preceding sentence, 2 or more positions shall be treated as described in clause (i), (ii), (iii), or (vi) only if the value of 1 or more of such positions ordinarily varies inversely with the value of 1 or more other such positions.

(B) Presumption may be rebutted.—Any presumption established pursuant to subparagraph (A) may be rebutted.

* * *

(d) Definitions and special rules.—For purposes of this section—

(1) Personal property.—The term "personal property" means any personal property of a type which is actively traded.

(2) Position.—The term "position" means an interest (including a futures or forward contract or option) in personal property.

(3) Special rules for stock.—For purposes of paragraph (1)—

(A) In general.—In the case of stock, the term "personal property" includes stock only if—

(i) such stock is of a type which is actively traded and at least 1 of the positions offsetting such stock is a position with respect to such stock or substantially similar or related property, or

(ii) such stock is of a corporation formed or availed of to take positions in personal property which offset positions taken by any shareholder.

(B) Rule for application.—For purposes of determining whether subsection (e) applies to any transaction with respect to stock described in subparagraph (A)(ii), all includible corporations of an affiliated group (within the meaning of section 1504(a)) shall be treated as 1 taxpayer.

(4) Positions held by related persons, etc.—

(A) In general.—In determining whether 2 or more positions are offsetting, the taxpayer shall be treated as holding any position held by a related person.

(B) Related person.—For purposes of subparagraph (A), a person is a related person to the taxpayer if with respect to any period during which a position is held by such person, such person—

(i) is the spouse of the taxpayer, or

(ii) files a consolidated return (within the meaning of section 1501) with the taxpayer for any taxable year which includes a portion of such period.

(C) Certain flowthrough entities.—If part or all of the gain or loss with respect to a position held by a partnership, trust, or other entity would properly be taken into account for purposes of this chapter by a taxpayer, then, except to the extent otherwise provided in regulations, such position shall be treated as held by the taxpayer.

* * *

(7) Special rules for foreign currency.—

(A) Position to include interest in certain debt.—For purposes of paragraph (2), an obligor's interest in a nonfunctional currency denominated debt obligation is treated as a position in the nonfunctional currency.

(B) Actively traded requirement.—For purposes of paragraph (1), foreign currency for which there is an active interbank market is presumed to be actively traded.

(8) Special rules for physically settled positions.—For purposes of subsection (a), if a taxpayer settles a position which is part of a straddle by delivering property to which the position relates (and such position, if terminated, would result in a realization of a loss), then such taxpayer shall be treated as if such taxpayer—

(A) terminated the position for its fair market value immediately before the settlement, and

(B) sold the property so delivered by the taxpayer at its fair market value.

(e) Exception for hedging transactions.—This section shall not apply in the case of any hedging transaction (as defined in section 1256(e)).

(f) Treatment of gain or loss and suspension of holding period where taxpayer grantor of qualified covered call option.—If a taxpayer holds any stock and grants a qualified covered call option to purchase such stock with a strike price less than the applicable stock price—

(1) Treatment of loss.—Any loss with respect to such option shall be treated as long-term capital loss if, at the time such loss is realized, gain on the sale or exchange of such stock would be treated as long-term capital gain.

(2) Suspension of holding period.—The holding period of such stock shall not include any period during which the taxpayer is the grantor of such option.

* * *

PART VIII—DISTRIBUTIONS PURSUANT TO BANK HOLDING COMPANY ACT*

*Omitted.

SUBCHAPTER P—CAPITAL GAINS AND LOSSES

Editorial Summary

Property Transactions: Classification of Gain or Loss

Subchapter P of Chapter 1 (Secs. 1201–1288)

If the realized gain or loss is recognized, it must be classified. The two possible classifications are ordinary and capital.

Prior to the Tax Reform Act of 1986, substantial tax benefit could result from being able to classify gains as capital. However, this Act repealed both the 60 percent capital gain deduction under Sec. 1202 for the individual and the 28 percent alternative tax for the corporation under Sec. 1201.

For the individual, the Tax Reform Act of 1986 created Sec. 1 (j) [now Sec. 1(h)], effective for taxable years beginning after December 31, 1986. Section 1(j) provided for an alternative tax with a rate of 28 percent. In 1987, this rate could produce beneficial results in that the maximum rate on ordinary income was 38.5 percent. For 1988–1990, however, the 28 percent alternative tax rate was the same as the 28 percent maximum statutory rate on ordinary income. The Revenue Reconciliation Act of 1990 (RRA of 1990) restored beneficial tax treatment for long-term capital gains. Section 1(h) now contains the alternative tax calculation (maximum rate of 28 percent) for net capital gains [see Sec. 1222(11)]. Since the highest tax rate for the individual taxpayer, as the result of RRA of 1990, was 31 percent, the alternative tax could once again result in tax savings. The Revenue Reconciliation Act of 1993 increased the potential tax savings associated with the alternative tax by adding a 36 percent and a 39.6 percent regular tax rate [see Sec. 1].

The Taxpayer Relief Act of 1997 (TRA of 1997) expanded the beneficial treatment of the alternative tax by replacing the 28 percent alternative tax rate with the following alternative tax rates: 10 percent, 20 percent, and 28 percent. For tax years beginning after December 31, 2000, if a 5-year holding period requirement is satisfied, the following additional rates are provided: 8 percent and 18 percent. [See Sec. 1(h).]

The IRS Restructuring and Reform Act of 1998 repealed the 18-month holding period requirement created by TRA of 1997 in order to be eligible for the 10% or 20% rates. Henceforth, the 28% rate applies only to Sec. 1202 gain and collectible gain. A new 25% rate applies to unrecaptured Sec. 1250 gain.

The Tax Relief Reconciliation Act of 2001, while not modifying the alternative rates for net capital gain, did impact the utility of the alternative tax calculation. The ordinary income rates are being reduced over a six-year period beginning in 2001 (see Sec. 1). This rate reduction will decrease the beneficial results of the alternative tax calculation.

The Jobs and Growth Tax Relief Reconciliation Act of 2003 accelerated the reduction of the lower tax rates on ordinary income [see Sec. 1]. In addition, the Act lowered the 20% capital gains rate to 15% and the 10% capital gains rate to 5% or 0% [see Sec. 1(h)].

The American Taxpayer Relief Act of 2012 increased the 15 percent rate to 20 percent for certain high-income taxpayers (i.e., are in the 39.6 percent tax bracket). See Sec. 1(h).

The Revenue Reconciliation Act of 1993 (RRA of 1993) provided for the exclusion from gross income of 50 percent of capital gains from certain small business stock. This provision applies only to the noncorporate taxpayer [see Sec. 1202(a)]. The exclusion is subject to an annual statutory dollar ceiling and to a lifetime ceiling per issuer [see Sec. 1202(b)(1)].

For the corporation, the Tax Reform Act of 1986 replaced the 28 percent alternative tax rate with a 34 percent alternative tax rate in Sec. 1201, effective for taxable years beginning after December 31, 1986. Since the Act reduced the corporate tax rate on ordinary income to 34 percent, however, no benefit resulted from the application of this alternative tax rate to corporate taxable gains. The Revenue Reconciliation Act of 1993 (RRA of 1993) increased the maximum corporate tax rate to 35 percent [see Sec. 11]. However, RRA of 1993 also increased the alternative tax rate for corporations to 35 percent [see Sec. 1201]. Thus, a corporation cannot presently benefit from the use of the Sec. 1201 alternative tax. In the future, if the tax rates on ordinary income are increased above 35 percent, the 35 percent alternative tax rate will again produce beneficial results (assuming it is not likewise increased). The retention of the alternative tax provision in the Code in Sec. 1201 supports the likelihood that Congress expects such rate increases to occur.

The Tax Reform Act of 1986 only slightly modified the treatment of capital losses for the individual. If a net capital loss results, $3,000 of it may be offset against ordinary income [see Sec. 1211 (b)]. Any excess capital loss can be carried over indefinitely with the identity maintained (i.e., short-term as short-term and long-term as long-term) under Sec. 1212(b). Whether the loss is short-term or long-term, one dollar of deduction against ordinary income reduces the available capital loss by one dollar. However, note that the Technical and Miscellaneous Revenue Act of 1988 produces the result that the amount available for carryback and carryforward purposes may be different than the net capital loss reduced by the capital loss deduction [see Sec. 1212(b)(2)].

For the corporate taxpayer, capital losses can be offset only against capital gains [see Sec. 1211(a)]. Therefore, if a net capital loss results for the current taxable year, none of it can be offset against ordinary income, regardless of the amount of ordinary income. From a planning perspective, this creates two objectives. First, try to structure the transaction such that the loss is ordinary rather than capital. If the first objective cannot be achieved, try to have capital gains available against which the capital losses can be offset. A net capital loss can be carried back for three years and carried forward for five years [see Sec. 1212(a)].

The definition of a capital asset appears in Sec. 1221. However, Sec. 1221 does not define what is a capital asset. Rather, it defines what is *not* a capital asset. Eight categories of

*Omitted.

items are listed as not being capital assets. The last three of these categories were added by the Tax Relief Extension Act of 1999. Therefore, if a particular item is not includible in one of the eight categories, then the general result is that the item is appropriately classified as a capital asset. However, this general treatment is subject to statutory exception in that particular Code sections are determinative with respect to certain assets:

1. Short sales [see Sec. 1233].
2. Options [see Sec. 1234].
3. Patents [see Sec. 1235].
4. Securities dealers [see Sec. 1236].
5. Real property subdivided for sale [see Sec. 1237].
6. Related-party sales [see Sec. 1239].
7. Lease cancellations [see Sec. 1241].
8. Small business stock [see Secs. 1242–1244].
9. Farm land [see Sec. 1252].
10. Franchises, trademarks, and trade names [see Sec. 1253].
11. Section 1256 contracts [see Sec. 1256].
12. Bonds and other debt instruments [see Secs. 1271–1288].

Section 1221(a)(2) provides that depreciable personal property and real property used in a trade or business are not capital assets. Initially, such property appears to receive adverse treatment because it is used in a trade or business (i.e., such property, which is held for personal use, is a capital asset). However, the opposite is true. That is, by classifying the property as not being a capital asset, losses on sales, exchanges, or other dispositions qualify for ordinary loss rather than capital loss treatment. Beneficial treatment on the gain side is provided by Sec. 1231, which provides that such gains will be treated as long-term capital gains.

Several limiting provisions are applicable to Sec. 1221(a)(2) property. First, the beneficial Sec. 1231 treatment is available only to the net gain on Sec. 1231 property. The ideal treatment would be for the losses on Sec. 1231 property to receive ordinary loss treatment and the gains to receive long-term capital gain treatment. In effect, however, Sec. 1231(a) requires that such gains and losses be netted and that only the net gain qualifies for long-term capital gain treatment. Second, in order to reduce the ability of taxpayers to avoid the adverse effect of this netting requirement by structuring transactions such that Sec. 1231 losses occur in one taxable year and Sec. 1231 gains occur in a different taxable year, Sec. 1231(c) contains a five-year look-back rule, which has the effect of classifying what otherwise would be treated as long-term capital gain as ordinary income.

From a beneficial perspective, Sec. 1231 contains two sets of netting rules. While the second set (discussed in the preceding paragraph) potentially reduces the beneficial Sec. 1231 gain treatment, the first set provides that certain Sec. 1231 property is subject to a separate netting which enables ordinary loss treatment to result that does not have to be offset against Sec. 1231 gain in the second netting [see Sec. 1231(a)(4)(C)].

The depreciation recapture provisions (e.g., Secs. 1245 and 1250) also reduce the beneficial Sec. 1231 treatment. In general, Sec. 1245 applies to depreciable personalty, and Sec. 1250 applies to depreciable realty. In certain circumstances, however, Sec. 1245 also applies to certain depreciable realty. Section 1245 is referred to as a "full" recapture provision because all the depreciation deducted [see Sec. 1245(a)(2)(A)] is subject to recapture, whereas Sec. 1250 is referred to as a "partial" recapture provision because only the "additional" depreciation deducted [see Sec. 1250(b)(1)] is subject to recapture.

The complexity of Sec. 1250 results from the variety of legislative amendments that have occurred since the original enactment of Sec. 1250 in 1964. In calculating Sec. 1250 recapture, one must consider the statutory provisions that were effective when the property was *placed in service* and the years during which depreciation was deducted. The statutory time periods are as follows:

1. Depreciation deducted prior to 1964.

No depreciation recapture because the Sec. 1250 provisions were not yet enacted.

2. Depreciation deducted after December 31, 1963, and before January 1, 1970.

Additional depreciation is subject to recapture. However, the recapture percentage (i.e., 100 percent) is reduced one percent for every month that the property is held more than 20 months. Since all such property that the taxpayer now disposes of will have been held more than 120 months, the recapture will be zero.

3. Depreciation deducted after December 31, 1969, and before January 1, 1976.

Additional depreciation is subject to recapture. If the property is residential rental property however, the recapture percentage (i.e., 100 percent) is reduced one percent for every month that the property is held more than 100 months [see Sec. 168(e)(2)(A)]. If the property is nonresidential realty, the recapture percentage remains at 100 percent.

4. Depreciation deducted after December 31, 1975, and before January 1, 1981.

Additional depreciation is subject to recapture. Regardless of whether the property is residential or nonresidential, the recapture percentage remains at 100 percent.

5. Depreciation deducted after December 31, 1980, and before January 1, 1987.

For property placed in service prior to January 1, 1981 and for residential rental property placed in service after December 31, 1980, the period 4 rules continue to apply. For nonresidential property placed in service after December 31, 1980, if the depreciation is calculated under the statutory percentage method (an accelerated method) of Sec. 168 ACRS, the property is classified as Sec. 1245 recovery property and is subject to "full" recapture under Sec. 1245.

6. Depreciation deducted after December 31, 1986.

No recapture is possible for property placed in service after December 31, 1986, because straight line depreciation must be used. However, for property placed in service prior to January 1, 1987, the period 5 rules continue to apply.

Also see the recapture provision under Sec. 291 for corporations.

The above provisions represent the general rules. For specific types of buildings (e.g., low-income housing,

Sec. 167(k) [prior to repeal by RRA of 1990] rehabilitations), different recapture rules are in effect.

The various terms associated with capital gains and losses have special meanings (refer to the definitions in Sec. 1222).

PART I—TREATMENT OF CAPITAL GAINS

§ 1201. Alternative tax for corporations

(a) General rule.—If for any taxable year a corporation has a net capital gain and any rate of tax imposed by section 11, 511, or 831(a) or (b) (whichever is applicable) exceeds 35 percent (determined without regard to the last 2 sentences of section 11(b)(1)), then, in lieu of any such tax, there is hereby imposed a tax (if such tax is less than the tax imposed by such sections) which shall consist of the sum of—

(1) a tax computed on the taxable income reduced by the amount of the net capital gain, at the rates and in the manner as if this subsection had not been enacted, plus

(2) a tax of 35 percent of the net capital gain (or, if less, taxable income).

(b) Special rate for qualified timber gains.—

(1) In general.—If, for any taxable year ending after the date of the enactment of the Food, Conservation, and Energy Act of 2008 and beginning on or before the date which is 1 year after such date, a corporation has both a net capital gain and qualified timber gain—

(A) subsection (a) shall apply to such corporation for the taxable year without regard to whether the applicable tax rate exceeds 35 percent, and

(B) the tax computed under subsection (a)(2) shall be equal to the sum of—

(i) 15 percent of the least of—

(I) qualified timber gain,

(II) net capital gain, or

(III) taxable income, plus

(ii) 35 percent of the excess (if any) of taxable income over the sum of the amounts for which a tax was determined under subsection (a)(1) and clause (i).

(2) Qualified timber gain.—For purposes of this section, the term "qualified timber gain" means, with respect to any taxpayer for any taxable year, the excess (if any) of—

(A) the sum of the taxpayer's gains described in subsections (a) and (b) of section 631 for such year, over

(B) the sum of the taxpayer's losses described in such subsections for such year.

For purposes of subparagraphs (A) and (B), only timber held more than 15 years shall be taken into account.

(3) Computation for taxable years in which rate first applies or ends.—In the case of any taxable year which includes either of the dates set forth in paragraph (1), the qualified timber gain for such year shall not exceed the qualified timber gain properly taken into account for—

(A) in the case of the taxable year including the date of the enactment of the Food, Conservation, and Energy Act of 2008, the portion of the year after such date, and

(B) in the case of the taxable year including the date which is 1 year after such date of enactment, the portion of the year on or before such later date.

* * *

§ 1202. Partial exclusion for gain from certain small business stock

(a) Exclusion.—

(1) In general.—In the case of a taxpayer other than a corporation, gross income shall not include 50 percent of any gain from the sale or exchange of qualified small business stock held for more than 5 years.

(2) Empowerment zone businesses.—

(A) In general.—In the case of qualified small business stock acquired after the date of the enactment of this paragraph in a corporation which is a qualified business entity (as defined in section 1397C(b)) during substantially all of the taxpayer's holding period for such stock, paragraph (1) shall be applied by substituting "60 percent" for "50 percent."

(B) Certain rules to apply.—Rules similar to the rules of paragraphs (5) and (7) of section 1400B(b) shall apply for purposes of this paragraph.

(C) Gain after 2018 not qualified.—Subparagraph (A) shall not apply to gain attributable to periods after December 31, 2018.

(D) Treatment of DC zone.—The District of Columbia Enterprise Zone shall not be treated as an empowerment zone for purposes of this paragraph.

(3) Special rules for 2009 and certain periods in 2010.—In the case of qualified small business stock acquired after the date of the enactment of this paragraph and on or before the date of the enactment of the Creating Small Business Jobs Act of 2010.

(A) paragraph (1) shall be applied by substituting "75 percent" for "50 percent," and

(B) paragraph (2) shall not apply.

In the case of any stock which would be described in the preceding sentence (but for this sentence), the acquisition date for purposes of this subsection shall be the first day on which such stock was held by the taxpayer determined after the application of section 1223.

(4) 100 percent exclusion for stock acquired during certain periods in 2010, 2011, 2012, and 2013.*—In the case of qualified small business stock acquired after the date of the enactment of the Creating Small Business Jobs Act of 2010 and before January 1, 2014*—

(A) paragraph (1) shall be applied by substituting "100 percent" for "50 percent,"

(B) paragraph (2) shall not apply, and

(C) paragraph (7) of section 57(a) shall not apply.

In the case of any stock which would be described in the preceding sentence (but for this sentence), the acquisition date for purposes of this subsection shall be the first day on which such stock was held by the taxpayer determined after the application of section 1223.

(b) Per-issuer limitation on taxpayer's eligible gain.—

(1) In general.—If the taxpayer has eligible gain for the taxable year from 1 or more dispositions of stock issued by any corporation, the aggregate amount of such gain from dispositions of stock issued by such corporation which may be taken into account under subsection (a) for the taxable year shall not exceed the greater of—

(A) $10,000,000 reduced by the aggregate amount of eligible gain taken into account by the taxpayer under subsection (a) for prior taxable years and attributable to dispositions of stock issued by such corporation, or

(B) 10 times the aggregate adjusted bases of qualified small business stock issued by such corporation and disposed of by the taxpayer during the taxable year.

For purposes of subparagraph (B), the adjusted basis of any stock shall be determined without regard to any addition to basis after the date on which such stock was originally issued.

(2) Eligible gain.—For purposes of this subsection, the term "eligible gain" means any gain from the sale or exchange of qualified small business stock held for more than 5 years.

(3) Treatment of married individuals.—

(A) Separate returns.—In the case of a separate return by a married individual, paragraph (1)(A) shall be applied by substituting "$5,000,000" for "$10,000,000."

(B) Allocation of exclusion.—In the case of any joint return, the amount of gain taken into account under subsection (a) shall be allocated equally between the spouses for purposes of applying this subsection to subsequent taxable years.

(C) Marital status.—For purposes of this subsection, marital status shall be determined under section 7703.

(c) Qualified small business stock.—For purposes of this section—

(1) In general.—Except as otherwise provided in this section, the term "qualified small business stock" means any stock in a C corporation which is originally issued after the date of the enactment of the Revenue Reconciliation Act of 1993, if—

(A) as of the date of issuance, such corporation is a qualified small business, and

(B) except as provided in subsections (f) and (h), such stock is acquired by the taxpayer at its original issue (directly or through an underwriter)—

(i) in exchange for money or other property (not including stock), or

(ii) as compensation for services provided to such corporation (other than services performed as an underwriter of such stock).

(2) Active business requirement; etc.—

(A) In general.—Stock in a corporation shall not be treated as qualified small business stock unless, during substantially all of the taxpayer's holding period for such stock, such corporation

*Editorial comment: At the present time, this section has not been extended. There is pending legislation in the Senate, *The Tax Extenders Act of 2013 (S. 1859)*, that would extend the heading of Section 1202(a)(4) until 2014. This would also extend 1202(a)(4) until January 1, 2015.

meets the active business requirements of subsection (e) and such corporation is a C corporation.

(B) Special rule for certain small business investment companies.—

(i) Waiver of active business requirement.—Notwithstanding any provision of subsection (e), a corporation shall be treated as meeting the active business requirements of such subsection for any period during which such corporation qualifies as a specialized small business investment company.

(ii) Specialized small business investment company.—For purposes of clause (i), the term "specialized small business investment company" means any eligible corporation (as defined in subsection (e)(4)) which is licensed to operate under section 301(d) of the Small Business Investment Act of 1958 (as in effect on May 13, 1993).

(3) Certain purchases by corporation of its own stock.—

(A) Redemptions from taxpayer or related person.— Stock acquired by the taxpayer shall not be treated as qualified small business stock if, at any time during the 4-year period beginning on the date 2 years before the issuance of such stock, the corporation issuing such stock purchased (directly or indirectly) any of its stock from the taxpayer or from a person related (within the meaning of section 267(b) or 707(b)) to the taxpayer.

(B) Significant redemptions.—Stock issued by a corporation shall not be treated as qualified business stock if, during the 2-year period beginning on the date 1 year before the issuance of such stock, such corporation made 1 or more purchases of its stock with an aggregate value (as of the time of the respective purchases) exceeding 5 percent of the aggregate value of all of its stock as of the beginning of such 2-year period.

(C) Treatment of certain transactions.—If any transaction is treated under section 304(a) as a distribution in redemption of the stock of any corporation, for purposes of subparagraphs (A) and (B), such corporation shall be treated as purchasing an amount of its stock equal to the amount treated as such a distribution under section 304(a).

(d) Qualified small business.—For purposes of this section—

(1) In general.—The term "qualified small business" means any domestic corporation which is a C corporation if—

(A) the aggregate gross assets of such corporation (or any predecessor thereof) at all times on or after the date of the enactment of the Revenue Reconciliation Act of 1993 and before the issuance did not exceed $50,000,000,

(B) the aggregate gross assets of such corporation immediately after the issuance (determined by taking into account amounts received in the issuance) do not exceed $50,000,000, and

(C) such corporation agrees to submit such reports to the Secretary and to shareholders as the Secretary may require to carry out the purposes of this section.

(2) Aggregate gross assets.—

(A) In general.—For purposes of paragraph (1), the term "aggregate gross assets" means the amount of cash and the aggregate adjusted bases of other property held by the corporation.

(B) Treatment of contributed property.—For purposes of subparagraph (A), the adjusted basis of any property contributed to the corporation (or other property with a basis determined in whole or in part by reference to the adjusted basis of property so contributed) shall be determined as if the basis of the property contributed to the corporation (immediately after such contribution) were equal to its fair market value as of the time of such contribution.

(3) Aggregation rules.—

(A) In general.—All corporations which are members of the same parent-subsidiary controlled group shall be treated as 1 corporation for purposes of this subsection.

(B) Parent-subsidiary controlled group.—For purposes of subparagraph (A), the term "parent-subsidiary controlled group" means any controlled group of corporations as defined in section 1563(a)(1), except that—

(i) "more than 50 percent" shall be substituted for "at least 80 percent" each place it appears in section 1563(a)(1), and

(ii) section 1563(a)(4) shall not apply.

(e) Active business requirement.—

(1) In general.—For purposes of subsection (c)(2), the requirements of this subsection are met by a corporation for any period if during such period—

(A) at least 80 percent (by value) of the assets of such corporation are used by such corporation in the active conduct of 1 or more qualified trades or businesses, and

(B) such corporation is an eligible corporation.

(2) Special rule for certain activities.—For purposes of paragraph (1), if, in connection with any future qualified trade or business, a corporation is engaged in—

(A) start-up activities described in section 195(c)(1)(A),

(B) activities resulting in the payment or incurring of expenditures which may be treated as research and experimental expenditures under section 174, or

(C) activities with respect to in-house research expenses described in section 41(b)(4),

assets used in such activities shall be treated as used in the active conduct of a qualified trade or business. Any determination under this paragraph shall be made without regard to whether a corporation has any gross income from such activities at the time of the determination.

(3) Qualified trade or business.—For purposes of this subsection, the term "qualified trade or business" means any trade or business other than—

(A) any trade or business involving the performance of services in the fields of health, law, engineering, architecture, accounting, actuarial science, performing arts, consulting, athletics, financial services, brokerage services, or any trade or business where the principal asset of such trade or business is the reputation or skill of 1 or more of its employees,

(B) any banking, insurance, financing, leasing, investing, or similar business,

(C) any farming business (including the business of raising or harvesting trees),

(D) any business involving the production or extraction of products of a character with respect to which a deduction is allowable under section 613 or 613A, and

(E) any business of operating a hotel, motel, restaurant, or similar business.

(4) Eligible corporation.—For purposes of this subsection, the term "eligible corporation" means any domestic corporation; except that such term shall not include—

(A) a DISC or former DISC,

(B) a corporation with respect to which an election under section 936 is in effect or which has a direct or indirect subsidiary with respect to which such an election is in effect,

(C) a regulated investment company, real estate investment trust, REMIC, and

(D) a cooperative.

(5) Stock in other corporations.—

(A) Look-thru in case of subsidiaries.—For purposes of this subsection, stock and debt in any subsidiary corporation shall be disregarded and the parent corporation shall be deemed to own its ratable share of the subsidiary's assets, and to conduct its ratable share of the subsidiary's activities.

(B) Portfolio stock or securities.—A corporation shall be treated as failing to meet the requirements of paragraph (1) for any period during which more than 10 percent of the value of its assets (in excess of liabilities) consists of stock or securities in other corporations which are not subsidiaries of such corporation (other than assets described in paragraph (6)).

(C) Subsidiary.—For purposes of this paragraph, a corporation shall be considered a subsidiary if the parent owns more than 50 percent of the combined voting power of all classes of stock entitled to vote, or more than 50 percent in value of all outstanding stock, of such corporation.

(6) Working capital.—For purposes of paragraph (1)(A), any assets which—

(A) are held as a part of the reasonably required working capital needs of a qualified trade or business of the corporation, or

(B) are held for investment and are reasonably expected to be used within 2 years to finance research and experimentation in a qualified trade or business or increases in working capital needs of a qualified trade or business,

shall be treated as used in the active conduct of a qualified trade or business. For periods after the corporation has been in existence for at least 2 years, in no event may more than 50 percent of the assets of the corporation qualify as used in the active conduct of a qualified trade or business by reason of this paragraph.

(7) Maximum real estate holdings.—A corporation shall not be treated as meeting the requirements of paragraph (1) for any period during which more than 10 percent of the total value of its assets consists of real property which is not used in the active conduct of a qualified trade or business. For purposes of the preceding sentence, the ownership of, dealing in, or renting of real property shall not be treated as the active conduct of a qualified trade or business.

(8) Computer software royalties.—For purposes of paragraph (1), rights to computer software which produces active business computer software royalties (within the meaning of section 543(d)(1)) shall be treated as an asset used in the active conduct of a trade or business.

(f) Stock acquired on conversion of other stock.—If any stock in a corporation is acquired solely through the conversion of other stock in such corporation which is qualified small business stock in the hands of the taxpayer—

(1) the stock so acquired shall be treated as qualified small business stock in the hands of the taxpayer, and

(2) the stock so acquired shall be treated as having been held during the period during which the converted stock was held.

(g) Treatment of pass-thru entities.—

(1) In general.—if any amount included in gross income by reason of holding an interest in a pass-thru entity meets the requirements of paragraph (2)—

(A) such amount shall be treated as gain described in subsection (a), and

(B) for purposes of applying subsection (b), such amount shall be treated as gain from a disposition of stock in the corporation issuing the stock disposed of by the pass-thru entity and the taxpayer's proportionate share of the adjusted basis of the pass-thru entity in such stock shall be taken into account.

(2) Requirements.—An amount meets the requirements of this paragraph if—

(A) such amount is attributable to gain on the sale or exchange by the pass-thru entity of stock which is qualified small business stock in the hands of such entity (determined by treating such entity as an individual) and which was held by such entity for more than 5 years, and

(B) such amount is includible in the gross income of the taxpayer by reason of the holding of an interest in such entity which was held by the taxpayer on the date on which such pass-thru entity acquired such stock and at all times thereafter before the disposition of such stock by such pass-thru entity.

(3) Limitation based on interest originally held by taxpayer.—Paragraph (1) shall not apply to any amount to the extent such amount exceeds the amount to which paragraph (1) would have applied if such amount were determined by reference to the interest the taxpayer held in the pass-thru entity on the date the qualified small business stock was acquired.

(4) Pass-thru entity.—For purposes of this subsection, the term "pass-thru entity" means—

(A) any partnership,

(B) any S corporation,

(C) any regulated investment company, and

(D) any common trust fund.

(h) Certain tax-free and other transfers.—For purposes of this section—

(1) In general.—In the case of a transfer described in paragraph (2), the transferee shall be treated as—

(A) having acquired such stock in the same manner as the transferor, and

(B) having held such stock during any continuous period immediately preceding the transfer during which it was held (or treated as held under this subsection) by the transferor.

(2) Description of transfers.—A transfer is described in this subsection if such transfer is—

(A) by gift,

(B) at death, or

(C) from a partnership to a partner of stock with respect to which requirements similar to the requirements of subsection (g) are met at the time of the transfer (without regard to the 5-year holding period requirement).

(3) Certain rules made applicable.—Rules similar to the rules of section 1244(d)(2) shall apply for purposes of this section.

(4) Incorporations and reorganizations involving nonqualified stock.—

(A) In general.—In the case of a transaction described in section 351 or a reorganization described in section 368, if qualified small business stock is exchanged for other stock which would not qualify as qualified small business stock but for this subparagraph, such other stock shall be treated as qualified small business stock acquired on the date on which the exchanged stock was acquired.

(B) Limitation.—This section shall apply to gain from the sale or exchange of stock treated as qualified small business stock by reason of subparagraph (A) only to the extent of the gain which would have been recognized at the time of the transfer described in subparagraph (A) if section 351 or 368 had not applied at such time. The preceding sentence shall not apply if the stock which is treated as qualified small business stock by reason of subparagraph (A) is issued by a corporation which (as of the time of the transfer described in subparagraph (A)) is a qualified small business.

(C) Successive application.—For purposes of this paragraph, stock treated as qualified small business stock under subparagraph (A) shall be so treated for subsequent transactions or reorganizations, except that the limitation of subparagraph (B) shall be applied as of the time of the first transfer to which such limitation applied (determined after the application of the second sentence of subparagraph (B)).

(D) Control test.—In the case of a transaction described in section 351, this paragraph shall apply only if, immediately after the transaction, the corporation issuing the stock owns directly or indirectly stock representing control (within the meaning of section 368(c)) of the corporation whose stock was exchanged.

(i) Basis rules.—For purposes of this section—

(1) Stock exchanged for property.—In the case where the taxpayer transfers property (other than money or stock) to a corporation in exchange for stock in such corporation—

(A) such stock shall be treated as having been acquired by the taxpayer on the date of such exchange, and

(B) the basis of such stock in the hands of the taxpayer shall in no event be less than the fair market value of the property exchanged.

(2) Treatment of contributions to capital.—If the adjusted basis of any qualified small business stock is adjusted by reason of any contribution to capital after the date on which such stock was originally issued, in determining the amount of the adjustment by reason of such contribution, the basis of the contributed property shall in no event be treated as less than its fair market value on the date of the contribution.

(j) Treatment of certain short positions.—

(1) In general.—If the taxpayer has an offsetting short position with respect to any qualified small business stock, subsection (a) shall not apply to any gain from the sale or exchange of such stock unless—

(A) such stock was held by the taxpayer for more than 5 years as of the first day on which there was such a short position, and

(B) the taxpayer elects to recognize gain as if such stock were sold on such first day for its fair market value.

(2) Offsetting short position.—For purposes of paragraph (1), the taxpayer shall be treated as having an offsetting short position with respect to any qualified small business stock if—

(A) the taxpayer has made a short sale of substantially identical property,

(B) the taxpayer has acquired an option to sell substantially identical property at a fixed price, or

For purposes of the preceding sentence, any reference to the taxpayer shall be treated as including a reference to any person who is related (within the meaning of section 267(b) or 707(b)) to the taxpayer.

(k) Regulations.—The Secretary shall prescribe such regulations as may be appropriate to carry out the purposes of this section, including regulations to prevent the avoidance of the purposes of this section through split-ups, shell corporations, partnerships, or otherwise.

PART II—TREATMENT OF CAPITAL LOSSES

Editorial Summary

Capital Losses

Subchapter P of Chapter 1 (Secs. 1211, 1212)

See the discussion under the Editorial Summary entitled Property Transactions: Classification of Gain or Loss, which precedes Sec. 1201.

§ 1211. Limitation on capital losses

(a) Corporations.—In the case of a corporation, losses from sales or exchanges of capital assets shall be allowed only to the extent of gains from such sales or exchanges.

(b) Other taxpayers.—In the case of a taxpayer other than a corporation, losses from sales or exchanges of capital assets shall be allowed only to the extent of the gains from such sales or exchanges, plus (if such losses exceed such gains) the lower of—

(1) $3,000 ($1,500 in the case of a married individual filing a separate return), or

(2) the excess of such losses over such gains.

§ 1212. Capital loss carrybacks and carryovers

(a) Corporations.—

(1) In general.—If a corporation has a net capital loss for any taxable year (hereinafter in this paragraph referred to as the "loss year"), the amount thereof shall be—

(A) a capital loss carryback to each of the 3 taxable years preceding the loss year, but only to the extent—

(i) such loss is not attributable to a foreign expropriation capital loss, and

(ii) the carryback of such loss does not increase or produce a net operating loss (as defined in section 172(c)) for the taxable year to which it is being carried back;

(B) except as provided in subparagraph (C), a capital loss carryover to each of the 5 taxable years succeeding the loss year; and

* * *

and shall be treated as a short-term capital loss in each such taxable year. The entire amount of the net capital loss for any taxable year shall be carried to the earliest of the taxable years to which such loss may be carried, and the portion of such loss which shall be carried to each of the other taxable years to which such loss may be carried shall be the excess, if any, of such loss over the total of the capital gain net income for each of the prior taxable years to which such loss may be carried. For purposes of the preceding sentence, the capital gain net income for any such prior taxable year shall be computed without regard to the net capital loss for the loss year or for any taxable year thereafter. In the case of any net capital loss which cannot be carried back in full to a preceding taxable year by reason of clause (ii) of subparagraph (A), the capital gain net income for such prior taxable year shall in no case be treated as greater than the amount of such loss which can be carried back to such preceding taxable year upon the application of such clause (ii).

* * *

(b) Other taxpayers.—

(1) In general.—If a taxpayer other than a corporation has a net capital loss for any taxable year—

(A) the excess of the net short-term capital loss over the net long-term capital gain for such year shall be a short-term capital loss in the succeeding taxable year, and

(B) the excess of the net long-term capital loss over the net short-term capital gain for such year shall be a long-term capital loss in the succeeding taxable year.

(2) Treatment of amounts allowed under section 1211(b)(1) or (2).—

(A) In general.—For purposes of determining the excess referred to in subparagraph (A) or (B) of paragraph (1), there shall be treated as a short-term capital gain in the taxable year an amount equal to the lesser of—

(i) the amount allowed for the taxable year under paragraph (1) or (2) of section 1211(b), or

(ii) the adjusted taxable income for such taxable year.

(B) Adjusted taxable income.—For purposes of subparagraph (A), the term "adjusted taxable income" means taxable income increased by the sum of—

(i) the amount allowed for the taxable year under paragraph (1) or (2) of section 1211(b), and

(ii) the deduction allowed for such year under section 151 or any deduction in lieu thereof.

For purposes of the preceding sentence, any excess of the deductions allowed for the taxable year over the gross income for such year shall be taken into account as negative taxable income.

* * *

PART III—GENERAL RULES FOR DETERMINING CAPITAL GAINS AND LOSSES

Editorial Summary

Capital Asset Transactions: Definitions and Holding Period

Subchapter P of Chapter 1 (Secs. 1221–1223)

See the discussion under the Editorial Summary entitled Property Transactions: Classification of Gain or Loss, which precedes Sec. 1201.

§ 1221. Capital asset defined

(a) In general.—For purposes of this subtitle, the term "capital asset" means property held by the taxpayer (whether or not connected with his trade or business), but does not include—

(1) stock in trade of the taxpayer or other property of a kind which would properly be included in the inventory of the taxpayer if on hand at the close of the taxable year, or property held by the taxpayer primarily for sale to customers in the ordinary course of his trade or business;

(2) property, used in his trade or business, of a character which is subject to the allowance for depreciation provided in section 167, or real property used in his trade or business;

(3) a copyright, a literary, musical, or artistic composition, a letter or memorandum, or similar property, held by—

(A) a taxpayer whose personal efforts created such property,

(B) in the case of a letter, memorandum, or similar property, a taxpayer for whom such property was prepared or produced, or

(C) a taxpayer in whose hands the basis of such property is determined, for purposes of determining gain from a sale or exchange, in whole or part by reference to the basis of such property in the hands of a taxpayer described in subparagraph (A) or (B);

(4) accounts or notes receivable acquired in the ordinary course of trade or business for services rendered or from the sale of property described in paragraph (1);

(5) a publication of the United States Government (including the Congressional Record) which is received from the United States Government or any agency thereof, other than by purchase at the price at which it is offered for sale to the public, and which is held by—

(A) a taxpayer who so received such publication, or

(B) a taxpayer in whose hands the basis of such publication is determined, for purposes of determining gain from a sale or exchange, in whole or in part by reference to the basis of such publication in the hands of a taxpayer described in subparagraph (A);

(6) any commodities derivative financial instrument held by a commodities derivatives dealer, unless—

(A) it is established to the satisfaction of the Secretary that such instrument has no connection to the activities of such dealer as a dealer, and

(B) such instrument is clearly identified in such dealer's records as being described in subparagraph (A) before the close of the day on which it was acquired, originated, or entered into (or such other time as the Secretary may by regulations prescribe);

(7) any hedging transaction which is clearly identified as such before the close of the day on which it was acquired, originated, or entered into (or such other time as the Secretary may by regulations prescribe); or

(8) supplies of a type regularly used or consumed by the taxpayer in the ordinary course of a trade or business of the taxpayer.

(b) Definitions and special rules.—

(1) Commodities derivative financial instruments.—For purposes of subsection (a)(6)—

(A) Commodities derivatives dealer. The term "commodities derivatives dealer" means a person which regularly offers to enter into, assume, offset, assign, or terminate positions in commodities derivative financial instruments with customers in the ordinary course of a trade or business.

(B) Commodities derivative financial instrument.—

(i) In general.—The term "commodities derivative financial instrument" means any contract or financial instrument with respect to commodities (other than a share of stock in a corporation, a beneficial interest in a partnership or trust, a note, bond, debenture, or other evidence of indebtedness, or a section 1256 contract (as defined in section 1256(b))), the value or settlement price of which is calculated by or determined by reference to a specified index.

(ii) Specified index. The term "specified index" means any one or more or any combination of—

(I) a fixed rate, price, or amount, or

(II) a variable rate, price, or amount, which is based on any current, objectively determinable financial or economic information with respect to commodities which is not within the control of any of the parties to the contract or instrument and is not unique to any of the parties' circumstances.

(2) Hedging transaction.—

(A) **In general.**—For purposes of this section, the term "hedging transaction" means any transaction entered into by the taxpayer in the normal course of the taxpayer's trade or business primarily—

(i) to manage risk of price changes or currency fluctuations with respect to ordinary property which is held or to be held by the taxpayer,

(ii) to manage risk of interest rate or price changes or currency fluctuations with respect to borrowings made or to be made, or ordinary obligations incurred or to be incurred, by the taxpayer, or

(iii) to manage such other risks as the Secretary may prescribe in regulations.

(B) Treatment of nonidentification or improper identification of hedging transactions. Notwithstanding subsection (a)(7), the Secretary shall prescribe regulations to properly characterize any income, gain, expense, or loss arising from a transaction—

(i) which is a hedging transaction but which was not identified as such in accordance with subsection (a)(7), or

(ii) which was so identified but is not a hedging transaction.

(3) Sale or exchange of self-created musical works.—At the election of the taxpayer, paragraphs (1) and (3) of subsection (a) shall not apply to musical compositions or copyrights in musical works sold or exchanged by a taxpayer described in subsection (a)(3).

(4) Regulations. The Secretary shall prescribe such regulations as are appropriate to carry out the purposes of paragraph (6) and (7) of subsection (a) in the case of transactions involving related parties.

§ 1222. Other terms relating to capital gains and losses

For purposes of this subtitle—

(1) Short-term capital gain.—The term "short-term capital gain" means gain from the sale or exchange of a capital asset held for not more than 1 year, if and to the extent such gain is taken into account in computing gross income.

(2) Short-term capital loss.—The term "short-term capital loss" means loss from the sale or exchange of a capital asset held for not more than 1 year, if and to the extent that such loss is taken into account in computing taxable income.

(3) Long-term capital gain.—The term "long-term capital gain" means gain from the sale or exchange of a capital asset held for more than 1 year, if and to the extent such gain is taken into account in computing gross income.

(4) Long-term capital loss.—The term "long-term capital loss" means loss from the sale or exchange of a capital asset held for more than 1 year, if and to the extent that such loss is taken into account in computing taxable income.

(5) Net short-term capital gain.—The term "net short-term capital gain" means the excess of short-term capital gains for the taxable year over the short-term capital losses for such year.

(6) Net short-term capital loss.—The term "net short-term capital loss" means the excess of short-term capital losses for the taxable year over the short-term capital gains for such year.

(7) Net long-term capital gain.—The term "net long-term capital gain" means the excess of long-term capital gains for the taxable year over the long-term capital losses for such year.

(8) Net long-term capital loss.—The term "net long-term capital loss" means the excess of long-term capital losses for the taxable year over the long-term capital gains for such year.

(9) Capital gain net income.—The term "capital gain net income" means the excess of the gains from sales or exchanges of capital assets over the losses from such sales or exchanges.

(10) Net capital loss.—The term "net capital loss" means the excess of the losses from sales or exchanges of capital assets over the sum allowed under section 1211. In the case of a corporation, for the purpose of determining losses under this paragraph, amounts which are short-term capital losses under section 1212(a)(l) shall be excluded.

(11) Net capital gain.—The term "net capital gain" means the excess of the net long-term capital gain for the taxable year over the net short-term capital loss for such year.

* * *

§ 1223. Holding period of property

For purposes of this subtitle—

(1) In determining the period for which the taxpayer has held property received in an exchange, there shall be included the period for which he held the property exchanged if, under this chapter, the property has, for the purpose of determining gain or loss from a sale or exchange, the same basis in whole or in part in his hands as the property exchanged, and, in the case of such exchanges after March 1, 1954, the property exchanged at the time of such exchange was a capital asset as defined in section 1221 or property described in section 1231. For purposes of this paragraph—

(A) an involuntary conversion described in section 1033 shall be considered an exchange of the property converted for the property acquired, and

(B) a distribution to which section 355 (or so much of section 356 as relates to section 355) applies shall be treated as an exchange.

(2) In determining the period for which the taxpayer has held property however acquired there shall be included the period for which such property was held by any other person, if under this chapter such property has, for the purpose of determining gain or loss from a sale or exchange, the same basis in whole or in part in his hands as it would have in the hands of such other person.

(3) In determining the period for which the taxpayer has held stock or securities the acquisition of which (or the contract or option to acquire which) resulted in the nondeductibility (under section 1091 relating to wash sales) of the loss from the sale or other disposition of substantially identical stock or securities, there shall be included the period for which he held the stock or securities the loss from the sale or other disposition of which was not deductible.

(4) In determining the period for which the taxpayer has held stock or rights to acquire stock received on a distribution, if the basis of such stock or rights is determined under section 307 (or under so much of section 1052(c) as refers to section 113(a)(23) of the Internal Revenue Code of 1939), there shall (under regulations prescribed by the Secretary) be included the period for which he held the stock in the distributing corporation before the receipt of such stock or rights upon such distribution.

(5) In determining the period for which the taxpayer has held stock or securities acquired from a corporation by the exercise of rights to acquire such stock or securities, there shall be included only the period beginning with the date on which the right to acquire was exercised.

(6) In determining the period for which the taxpayer has held a residence, the acquisition of which resulted under section 1034 (as in effect on the day before the date of enactment of the Taxpayer Relief Act of 1997) in the nonrecognition of any part of the gain realized on the sale or exchange of another residence, there shall be included the period for which such other residence had been held as of the date of such sale or exchange. For purposes of this paragraph, the term "sale or exchange" includes an involuntary conversion occurring after December 31, 1950, and before January 1, 1954.

* * *

(8) Any reference in this section to a provision of this title shall, where applicable, be deemed a reference to the corresponding provision of the Internal Revenue Code of 1939, or prior internal revenue laws.

(9) In the case of a person acquiring property from a decedent or to whom property passed from a decedent (within the meaning of section 1014 (b)), if—

(A) the basis of such property in the hands of such person is determined under section 1014, and

(B) such property is sold or otherwise disposed of by such person within 1 year after the decedent's death,

then such person shall be considered to have held such property for more than 1 year.

(10) If—

(A) property is acquired by any person in a transfer to which section 1040 applies,

(B) such property is sold or otherwise disposed of by such person within 1 year after the decedent's death, and

(C) such sale or disposition is to a person who is a qualified heir (as defined in section 2032A (e)(1)) with respect to the decedent,

then the person making such sale or other disposition shall be considered to have held such property for more than 1 year.

(11) In determining the period for which the taxpayer has held qualified replacement property (within the meaning of section 1042(b)) the acquisition of which resulted under section 1042 in the nonrecognition of any part of the gain realized on the sale of qualified securities (within the meaning of section 1042(b)), there shall be included the period for which such qualified securities had been held by the taxpayer.

(12) In determining the period for which the taxpayer has held property the acquisition of which resulted under section 1043 in the nonrecognition of any part of the gain realized on the sale of other property, there shall be included the period for which such other property has been held as of the date of such sale.

(13) Except for purposes of sections 1202(a)(2), 1202(c)(2)(A), 1400B(b), and 1400F(b), in determining the period for which the taxpayer has held property the acquisition of which resulted under section 1045 or 1397B in the nonrecognition of any part of the gain realized on the sale of other property, there shall be included the period for which such other property has been held as of the date of such sale.

(14) If the security to which a securities futures contract (as defined in section 1234B) relates (other than a contract to which 1256 applies) is acquired in satisfaction of such contract, in determining the period for which the taxpayer has held such security, there shall be included the period for which the taxpayer held such contract if such contract was a capital asset in the hands of the taxpayer.

(15) Cross references.—

For special holding period provision relating to certain partnership distributions, see section 735(b).

PART IV—SPECIAL RULES FOR DETERMINING CAPITAL GAINS AND LOSSES

Editorial Summary

Capital Asset Transactions: Special Rules

Subchapter P of Chapter 1 (Secs. 1231–1260)

See the discussion under the Editorial Summary entitled Property Transactions: Classification of Gain or Loss, which precedes Sec. 1201.

§ 1231. Property used in the trade or business and involuntary conversions

(a) General rule.—

(1) Gains exceed losses.—If—

(A) the section 1231 gains for any taxable year, exceed

(B) the section 1231 losses for such taxable year,

such gains and losses shall be treated as long-term capital gains or long-term capital losses, as the case may be.

(2) Gains do not exceed losses.—If—

(A) the section 1231 gains for any taxable year, do not exceed

(B) the section 1231 losses for such taxable year,

such gains and losses shall not be treated as gains and losses from sales or exchanges of capital assets.

(3) Section 1231 gains and losses.—For purposes of this subsection—

(A) Section 1231 gain.—The term "section 1231 gain" means—

(i) any recognized gain on the sale or exchange of property used in the trade or business, and

(ii) any recognized gain from the compulsory or involuntary conversion (as a result of destruction in whole or in part, theft or seizure, or an exercise of the power of requisition or condemnation or the threat or imminence thereof) into other property or money of—

(I) property used in the trade or business, or

(II) any capital asset which is held for more than 1 year and is held in connection with a trade or business or a transaction entered into for profit.

(B) Section 1231 loss.—The term "section 1231 loss" means any recognized loss from a sale or exchange or conversion described in subparagraph (A).

(4) Special rules.—For purposes of this subsection—

(A) In determining under this subsection whether gains exceed losses—

(i) the section 1231 gains shall be included only if and to the extent taken into account in computing gross income, and

(ii) the section 1231 losses shall be included only if and to the extent taken into account in computing taxable income, except that section 1211 shall not apply.

(B) Losses (including losses not compensated for by insurance or otherwise) on the destruction, in whole or in part, theft or seizure, or requisition or condemnation of—

(i) property used in the trade or business, or

(ii) capital assets which are held for more than 1 year and are held in connection with a trade or business or a transaction entered into for profit,

shall be treated as losses from a compulsory or involuntary conversion.

(C) In the case of any involuntary conversion (subject to the provisions of this subsection but for this sentence) arising from fire, storm, shipwreck, or other casualty, or from theft, of any—

(i) property used in the trade or business, or

(ii) any capital asset which is held for more than 1 year and is held in connection with a trade or business or a transaction entered into for profit,

this subsection shall not apply to such conversion (whether resulting in gain or loss) if during the taxable year the recognized losses from such conversions exceed the recognized gains from such conversions.

(b) Definition of property used in the trade or business.—For purposes of this section—

(1) General rule.—The term "property used in the trade or business" means property used in the trade or business, of a character which is subject to the allowance for depreciation provided in section 167, held for more than 1 year, and real property used in the trade or business, held for more than 1 year, which is not—

(A) property of a kind which would properly be includible in the inventory of the taxpayer if on hand at the close of the taxable year,

(B) property held by the taxpayer primarily for sale to customers in the ordinary course of his trade or business,

(C) a copyright, a literary, musical, or artistic composition, a letter or memorandum, or similar property, held by a taxpayer described in paragraph (3) of section 1221, or

(D) a publication of the United States Government (including the Congressional Record) which is received from the United States Government, or any agency thereof, other than by purchase at the price at which it is offered for sale to the public, and which is held by a taxpayer described in paragraph (5) of section 1221.

(2) Timber, coal, or domestic iron ore.—Such term includes timber, coal, and iron ore with respect to which section 631 applies.

(3) Livestock.—Such term includes—

(A) cattle and horses, regardless of age, held by the taxpayer for draft, breeding, dairy, or sporting purposes, and held by him for 24 months or more from the date of acquisition, and

(B) other livestock, regardless of age, held by the taxpayer for draft, breeding, dairy, or sporting purposes, and held by him for 12 months or more from the date of acquisition.

Such term does not include poultry.

(4) Unharvested crop.—In the case of an unharvested crop on land used in the trade or business and held for more than 1 year, if the crop and the land are sold or exchanged (or compulsorily or involuntarily converted) at the same time and to the same person, the crop shall be considered as "property used in the trade or business."

(c) Recapture of net ordinary losses.—

(1) In general.—The net section 1231 gain for any taxable year shall be treated as ordinary income to the extent such gain does not exceed the non-recaptured net section 1231 losses.

(2) Non-recaptured net section 1231 losses.—For purposes of this subsection, the term "non-recaptured net section 1231 losses" means the excess of—

(A) the aggregate amount of the net section 1231 losses for the 5 most recent preceding taxable years beginning after December 31, 1981, over

(B) the portion of such losses taken into account under paragraph (1) for such preceding taxable years.

(3) Net section 1231 gain.—For purposes of this subsection, the term "net section 1231 gain" means the excess of—

(A) the section 1231 gains, over

(B) the section 1231 losses.

(4) Net section 1231 loss.—For purposes of this subsection, the term "net section 1231 loss" means the excess of—

(A) the section 1231 losses, over

(B) the section 1231 gains.

(5) Special rules.—For purposes of determining the amount of the net section 1231 gain or loss for any taxable year, the rules of paragraph (4) of subsection (a) shall apply.

§ 1233. Gains and losses from short sales

(a) Capital assets.—For purposes of this subtitle, gain or loss from the short sale of property shall be considered as gain or loss from the sale or exchange of a capital asset to the extent that the property, including a commodity future, used to close the short sale constitutes a capital asset in the hands of the taxpayer.

(b) Short-term gains and holding periods.—If gain or loss from a short sale is considered as gain or loss from the sale or exchange of a capital asset under subsection (a) and if on the date of such short sale substantially identical property has been held by the taxpayer for not more than 1 year (determined without regard to the effect, under paragraph (2) of this subsection, of such short sale on the holding period), or if substantially identical property is acquired by the taxpayer after such short sale and on or before the date of the closing thereof—

(1) any gain on the closing of such short sale shall be considered as a gain on the sale or exchange of a capital asset held for not more than 1 year (notwithstanding the period of time any property used to close such short sale has been held); and

(2) the holding period of such substantially identical property shall be considered to begin (notwithstanding section 1223, relating to the holding period of property) on the date of the closing of the short sale, or on the date of a sale, gift, or other disposition of such property, whichever date occurs first. This paragraph shall apply to such substantially identical property in the order of the dates of the acquisition of such property, but only to so much of such property as does not exceed the quantity sold short.

For purposes of this subsection, the acquisition of an option to sell property at a fixed price shall be considered as a short sale, and the exercise or failure to exercise such option shall be considered as a closing of such short sale.

(c) Certain options to sell.—Subsection (b) shall not include an option to sell property at a fixed price acquired on the same day on which the property identified as intended to be used in exercising such option is acquired and which, if exercised, is exercised through the sale of the property so identified. If the option is not exercised, the cost of the option shall be added to the basis of the property with which the option is identified. This subsection shall apply only to options acquired after August 16, 1954.

(d) Long-term losses.—If on the date of such short sale substantially identical property has been held by the taxpayer for more than 1 year, any loss on the closing of such short sale shall be considered as a loss on the sale or exchange of a capital asset held for more than 1 year (notwithstanding the period of time any property used to close such short sale has been held, and notwithstanding section 1234).

(e) Rules for application of section.—

(1) Subsection (b)(1) or (d) shall not apply to the gain or loss, respectively, on any quantity of property used to close such short sale which is in excess of the quantity of the substantially identical property referred to in the applicable subsection.

(2) For purposes of subsections (b) and (d)—

(A) the term "property" includes only stocks and securities (including stocks and securities dealt with on a "when issued" basis), and commodity futures, which are capital assets in the hands of the taxpayer, but does not include any position to which section 1092(b) applies;

(B) in the case of futures transactions in any commodity on or subject to the rules of a board of trade or commodity exchange, a commodity future requiring delivery in 1 calendar month shall not be considered as property substantially identical to another commodity future requiring delivery in a different calendar month;

(C) in the case of a short sale of property by an individual, the term "taxpayer," in the application of this subsection and subsections (b) and (d), shall be read as "taxpayer or his spouse;" but an individual who is legally separated from the taxpayer under a decree of divorce or of separate maintenance shall not be considered as the spouse of the taxpayer,

(D) a securities futures contract (as defined in section 1234B) to acquire substantially identical property shall be treated as substantially identical property, and

(E) entering into a securities futures contract (as so defined) to sell shall be considered to be a short sale, and the settlement of such contract shall be considered to be the closing of such short sale.

(3) Where the taxpayer enters into 2 commodity futures transactions on the same day, one requiring delivery by him in one market and the other requiring delivery to him of the same (or substantially identical) commodity in the same calendar month in a different market, and the taxpayer subsequently closes both such transactions on the same day, subsections (b) and (d) shall have no application to so much of the commodity involved in either such transaction as does not exceed in quantity the commodity involved in the other.

(4)(A) In the case of a taxpayer who is a dealer in securities (within the meaning of section 1236)—

(i) if, on the date of a short sale of stock, substantially identical property which is a capital asset in the hands of the taxpayer has been held for not more than 1 year, and

(ii) if such short sale is closed more than 20 days after the date on which it was made,

subsection (b)(2) shall apply in respect of the holding period of such substantially identical property.

(B) For purposes of subparagraph (A)—

(i) the last sentence of subsection (b) applies; and

(ii) the term "stock" means any share or certificate of stock in a corporation, any bond or other evidence of indebtedness which is convertible into any such share or certificate, or any evidence of an interest in, or right to subscribe to or purchase, any of the foregoing.

* * *

(g) Hedging transactions.—This section shall not apply in the case of a hedging transaction in commodity futures.

(h) Short sales of property which becomes substantially worthless.—

(1) In general.—If—

(A) the taxpayer enters into a short sale of property, and

(B) such property becomes substantially worthless,

the taxpayer shall recognize gain in the same manner as if the short sale were closed when the property becomes substantially worthless. To the extent provided in regulations prescribed by the Secretary, the preceding sentence also shall apply with respect to any option with respect to property, an offsetting notional principal contract with respect to property, any futures or forward contract to delivery any property, and any other similar transaction.

(2) Statute of limitations.—If property becomes substantially worthless during a taxable year and any short sale of such property remains open at the time such property becomes substantially worthless, then—

(A) the statutory period for the assessment of any deficiency attributable to any part of the gain on such transaction shall not expire before the earlier of—

(i) the date which is 3 years after the date the Secretary is notified by the taxpayer (in such manner as the Secretary may by regulations prescribe) of the substantial worthlessness of such property, or

(ii) the date which is 6 years after the date the return for such taxable year is filed, and

(B) such deficiency may be assessed before the date applicable under subparagraph (A) notwithstanding the provisions of any other law or rule of law which would otherwise prevent such assessment.

§ 1234. Options to buy or sell

(a) Treatment of gain or loss in the case of the purchaser.—

(1) General rule.—Gain or loss attributable to the sale or exchange of, or loss attributable to failure to exercise, an option to buy or sell property shall be considered gain or loss from the sale or exchange of property which has the same character as the property to which the option relates has in the hands of the taxpayer (or would have in the hands of the taxpayer if acquired by him).

(2) Special rule for loss attributable to failure to exercise option.—For purposes of paragraph (1), if loss is attributable to failure to exercise an option, the option shall be deemed to have been sold or exchanged on the day it expired.

(3) Nonapplication of subsection.—This subsection shall not apply to—

(A) an option which constitutes property described in paragraph (1) of section 1221;

(B) in the case of gain attributable to the sale or exchange of an option, any income derived in connection with such option which, without regard to this subsection, is treated as other than gain from the sale or exchange of a capital asset; and

(C) a loss attributable to failure to exercise an option described in section 1233(c).

(b) Treatment of grantor of option in the case of stock, securities, or commodities.—

(1) General rule.—In the case of the grantor of the option, gain or loss from any closing transaction with respect to, and gain on lapse of, an option in property shall be treated as a gain or loss from the sale or exchange of a capital asset held not more than 1 year.

(2) Definitions.—For purposes of this subsection—

(A) Closing transaction.—The term "closing transaction" means any termination of the taxpayer's obligation under an option in property other than through the exercise or lapse of the option.

(B) Property.—The term "property" means stocks and securities (including stocks and securities dealt with on a "when issued" basis), commodities, and commodity futures.

(3) Nonapplication of subsection.—This subsection shall not apply to any option granted in the ordinary course of the taxpayer's trade or business of granting options.

* * *

§ 1234A. Gains or losses from certain terminations

Gain or loss attributable to the cancellation, lapse, expiration, or other termination of—

(1) a right or obligation (other than a securities futures contract, as defined in section 1234B) with respect to property which is (or on acquisition would be) a capital asset in the hands of the taxpayer, or

(2) a section 1256 contract (as defined in section 1256) not described in paragraph (1) which is a capital asset in the hands of the taxpayer,

shall be treated as gain or loss from the sale of a capital asset. The preceding sentence shall not apply to the retirement of any debt instrument (whether or not through a trust or other participation arrangement).

§ 1234B. Gains or losses from securities futures contracts

(a) Treatment of gain or loss.—

(1) In general.—Gain or loss attributable to the sale, exchange, or termination of a securities futures contract shall be considered gain or loss from the sale or exchange of property which has the same character as the property to which the contract relates has in the hands of the taxpayer (or would have in the hands of the taxpayer if acquired by the taxpayer).

(2) Nonapplication of subsection.—This subsection shall not apply to—

(A) a contract which constitutes property described in paragraph (1) or (7) of section 1221 (a), and

(B) any income derived in connection with a contract which, without regard to this subsection, is treated as other than gain from the sale or exchange of a capital asset.

(b) Short-term gains and losses.—Except as provided in the regulations under section 1092(b) or this section, or in section 1233, if gain or loss on the sale, exchange, or termination of a securities futures contract to sell property is considered as gain or loss from the sale or exchange of a capital asset, such gain or loss shall be treated as short-term capital gain or loss.

(c) Securities futures contract.—For purposes of this section, the term "securities futures contract" means any security future (as defined in section 3(a)(55)(A) of the Securities Exchange Act of 1934, as in effect on the date of the enactment of this section). The Secretary may prescribe regulations regarding the status of contracts the values of which are determined directly or indirectly by reference to any index which becomes (or ceases to be) a narrow-based security index (as defined for purposes of section 1256(g)(6)).

(d) Contracts not treated as commodity futures contracts.—For purposes of this title, a securities futures contract shall not be treated as a commodity futures contract.

(e) Regulations.—The Secretary shall prescribe such regulations as may be appropriate to provide for the proper treatment of securities futures contracts under this title.

(f) Cross reference.—

For special rules relating to dealer securities futures contracts, see section 1256.

§ 1235. Sale or exchange of patents

(a) General.—A transfer (other than by gift, inheritance, or devise) of property consisting of all substantial rights to a patent, or an undivided interest therein which includes a part of all such rights, by any holder shall be considered the sale or exchange of a capital asset held for more than 1 year, regardless of whether or not payments in consideration of such transfer are—

(1) payable periodically over a period generally coterminous with the transferee's use of the patent, or

(2) contingent on the productivity, use, or disposition of the property transferred.

(b) "Holder" defined.—For purposes of this section, the term "holder" means—

(1) any individual whose efforts created such property, or

(2) any other individual who has acquired his interest in such property in exchange for consideration in money or money's worth paid to such creator prior to actual reduction to practice of the invention covered by the patent, if such individual is neither—

(A) the employer of such creator, nor

(B) related to such creator (within the meaning of subsection (d)).

(c) Effective date.—This section shall be applicable with regard to any amounts received, or payments made, pursuant to a transfer described in subsection (a) in any taxable year to which this subtitle applies, regardless of the taxable year in which such transfer occurred.

(d) Related persons.—Subsection (a) shall not apply to any transfer, directly or indirectly, between persons specified within any one of the paragraphs of section 267(b) or persons described in section 707(b); except that, in applying section 267(b) and (c) and section 707(b) for purposes of this section—

(1) the phrase "25 percent or more" shall be substituted for the phrase "more than 50 percent" each place it appears in section 267(b) or 707(b), and

(2) paragraph (4) of section 267(c) shall be treated as providing that the family of an individual shall include only his spouse, ancestors, and lineal descendants.

* * *

§ 1236. Dealers in securities

(a) Capital gains.—Gain by a dealer in securities from the sale or exchange of any security shall in no event be considered as gain from the sale or exchange of a capital asset unless—

(1) the security was, before the close of the day on which it was acquired (or such earlier time as the Secretary may prescribe by regulations), clearly identified in the dealer's records as a security held for investment; and

(2) the security was not, at any time after the close of such day (or such earlier time), held by such dealer primarily for sale to customers in the ordinary course of his trade or business.

(b) Ordinary losses.—Loss by a dealer in securities from the sale or exchange of any security shall, except as otherwise provided in section 582(c), (relating to bond, etc., losses of banks), in no event be considered as ordinary loss if at any time after November 19, 1951, the security was clearly identified in the dealer's records as a security held for investment.

(c) Definition of security.—For purposes of this section, the term "security" means any share of stock in any corporation, certificate of stock or interest in any corporation, note, bond, debenture, or evidence of indebtedness, or any evidence of an interest in or right to subscribe to or purchase any of the foregoing.

* * *

(e) Special rule for options.—For purposes of subsection (a), any security acquired by a dealer pursuant to an option held by such dealer may be treated as held for investment only if the dealer, before the close of the day on which the option was acquired, clearly identified the option on his records as held for investment. For purposes of the preceding sentence, the term "option" includes the right to subscribe to or purchase any security.

§ 1237. Real property subdivided for sale

(a) General.—Any lot or parcel which is part of a tract of real property in the hands of a taxpayer other than a C corporation shall not be deemed to be held primarily for sale to customers in the ordinary course of trade or business at the time of sale solely because of the taxpayer having subdivided such tract for purposes of sale or because of any activity incident to such subdivision or sale, if—

(1) such tract, or any lot or parcel thereof, had not previously been held by such taxpayer primarily for sale to customers in the ordinary course of trade or business (unless such tract at such previous time would have been covered by this section) and, in the same taxable year in which the sale occurs, such taxpayer does not so hold any other real property; and

(2) no substantial improvement that substantially enhances the value of the lot or parcel sold is made by the taxpayer on such tract while held by the taxpayer or is made pursuant to a contract of sale entered into between the taxpayer and the buyer. For purposes of this paragraph, an improvement shall be deemed to be made by the taxpayer if such improvement was made by—

(A) the taxpayer or members of his family (as defined in section 267(c)(4)), by a corporation controlled by the taxpayer, an S corporation which included the taxpayer as a shareholder, or by a partnership which included the taxpayer as a partner; or

(B) a lessee, but only if the improvement constitutes income to the taxpayer; or

(C) Federal, State, or local government, or political subdivision thereof, but only if the improvement constitutes an addition to basis for the taxpayer; and

(3) such lot or parcel, except in the case of real property acquired by inheritance or devise, is held by the taxpayer for a period of 5 years.

(b) Special rules for application of section.—

(1) Gains.—If more than 5 lots or parcels contained in the same tract of real property are sold or exchanged, gain from any sale or exchange (which occurs in or after the taxable year in which the sixth lot or parcel is sold or exchanged) of any lot or parcel which comes within the provisions of paragraphs (1), (2) and (3) of subsection (a) of this section shall be deemed to be gain from the sale of property held primarily for sale to customers in the ordinary course of the trade or business to the extent of 5 percent of the selling price.

(2) Expenditures of sale.—For the purpose of computing gain under paragraph (1) of this subsection, expenditures incurred in connection with the sale or exchange of any lot or parcel shall neither be allowed as a deduction in computing taxable income, nor treated as reducing the amount realized on such sale or exchange; but so much of such expenditures as does not exceed the portion of gain deemed under paragraph (1) of this subsection to be gain from the sale of property held primarily for sale to customers in the ordinary course of trade or business shall be so allowed as a deduction, and the remainder, if any, shall be treated as reducing the amount realized on such sale or exchange.

(3) Necessary improvements.—No improvement shall be deemed a substantial improvement for purposes of subsection (a) if the lot or parcel is held by the taxpayer for a period of 10 years and if—

(A) such improvement is the building or installation of water, sewer, or drainage facilities or roads (if such improvement would except for this paragraph constitute a substantial improvement);

(B) it is shown to the satisfaction of the Secretary that the lot or parcel, the value of which was substantially enhanced by such improvement, would not have been marketable at the prevailing local price for similar building sites without such improvement; and

(C) the taxpayer elects, in accordance with regulations prescribed by the Secretary, to make no adjustment to basis of the lot or parcel, or of any other property owned by the taxpayer, on account of the expenditures for such improvements. Such election shall not make any item deductible which would not otherwise be deductible.

(c) Tract defined.—For purposes of this section, the term "tract of real property" means a single piece of real property, except that 2 or more pieces of real property shall be considered a tract if at any time they were contiguous in the hands of the taxpayer or if they would be contiguous except for the interposition of a road, street, railroad, stream, or similar property. If, following the sale or exchange of any lot or parcel from a tract of real property, no further sales or exchanges of any other lots or parcels from the remainder of such tract are made for a period of 5 years, such remainder shall be deemed a tract.

§ 1239. Gain from sale of depreciable property between certain related taxpayers

(a) Treatment of gain as ordinary income.—In the case of a sale or exchange of property, directly or indirectly, between related persons, any gain recognized to the transferor shall be treated as ordinary income if such property is, in the hands of the transferee, of a character which is subject to the allowance for depreciation provided in section 167.

(b) Related persons.—For purposes of subsection (a), the term "related persons" means—

(1) a person and all entities which are controlled entities with respect to such person,

(2) a taxpayer and any trust in which such taxpayer (or his spouse) is a beneficiary, unless such beneficiary's interest in the trust is a remote contingent interest (within the meaning of section 318(a)(3)(B)(i)), and

(3) except in the case of a sale or exchange in satisfaction of a pecuniary bequest, an executor of an estate and a beneficiary of such an estate.

(c) Controlled entity defined.—

(1) General rule.—For purposes of this section, the term "controlled entity" means, with respect to any person—

(A) a corporation more than 50 percent of the value of the outstanding stock of which is owned (directly or indirectly) by or for such person,

(B) a partnership more than 50 percent of the capital interest or profits interest in which is owned (directly or indirectly) by or for such person, and

(C) any entity which is a related person to such person under paragraph (3), (10), (11), or (12) of section 267(b).

(2) Constructive ownership.—For purposes of this section, ownership shall be determined in accordance with rules similar to the rules under section 267(c) (other than paragraph (3) thereof).

(d) Employer and related employee association.—For purposes of subsection (a), the term "related person" also includes—

(1) an employer and any person related to the employer (within the meaning of subsection (b)), and

* * *

(e) Patent applications treated as depreciable property.—For purposes of this section, a patent application shall be treated as property which, in the hands of the transferee, is of a character which is subject to the allowance for depreciation provided in section 167.

§ 1241. Cancellation of lease or distributor's agreement

Amounts received by a lessee for the cancellation of a lease, or by a distributor of goods for the cancellation of a distributor's agreement (if the distributor has a substantial capital investment in the distributorship), shall be considered as amounts received in exchange for such lease or agreement.

§ 1242. Losses on small business investment company stock

If—

(1) a loss is on stock in a small business investment company operating under the Small Business Investment Act of 1958, and

(2) such loss would (but for this section) be a loss from the sale or exchange of a capital asset,

then such loss shall be treated as an ordinary loss. For purposes of section 172 (relating to the net operating loss deduction) any amount of loss treated by reason of this section as an ordinary loss shall be treated as attributable to a trade or business of the taxpayer.

§ 1243. Loss of small business investment company

In the case of a small business investment company operating under the Small Business Investment Act of 1958, if—

(1) a loss is on stock received pursuant to the conversion privilege of convertible debentures acquired pursuant to section 304 of the Small Business Investment Act of 1958, and

(2) such loss would (but for this section) be a loss from the sale or exchange of a capital asset,

then such loss shall be treated as an ordinary loss.

§ 1244. Losses on small business stock

(a) General rule.—In the case of an individual, a loss on section 1244 stock issued to such individual or to a partnership which would (but for this section) be treated as a loss from the sale or exchange of a capital asset shall, to the extent provided in this section, be treated as an ordinary loss.

(b) Maximum amount for any taxable year.—For any taxable year the aggregate amount treated by the taxpayer by reason of this section as an ordinary loss shall not exceed—

(1) $50,000, or

(2) $100,000, in the case of a husband and wife filing a joint return for such year under section 6013.

(c) Section 1244 stock defined.—

(1) In general.—For purposes of this section, the term "section 1244 stock" means stock in a domestic corporation if—

(A) at the time such stock is issued, such corporation was a small business corporation,

(B) such stock was issued by such corporation for money or other property (other than stock and securities), and

(C) such corporation, during the period of its 5 most recent taxable years ending before the date the loss on such stock was sustained, derived more than 50 percent of its aggregate gross receipts from sources other than royalties, rents, dividends, interests, annuities, and sales or exchanges of stocks or securities.

(2) Rules for application of paragraph (1)(C).—

(A) Period taken into account with respect to new corporations.—For purposes of paragraph (1)(C), if the corporation has not been in existence for 5 taxable years ending before the date the loss on the stock was sustained, there shall be substituted for such 5-year period—

(i) the period of the corporation's taxable years ending before such date, or

(ii) if the corporation has not been in existence for 1 taxable year ending before such date, the period such corporation has been in existence before such date.

(B) Gross receipts from sales of securities.—For purposes of paragraph (1) (C), gross receipts from the sales or exchanges of stock or securities shall be taken into account only to the extent of gains therefrom.

(C) Nonapplication where deductions exceed gross income.—Paragraph (1)(C) shall not apply with respect to any corporation if, for the period taken into account for purposes of paragraph (1)(C), the amount of the deductions allowed by this chapter (other than by sections 172, 243, 244, and 245) exceeds the amount of gross income.

(3) Small business corporation defined.—

(A) In general.—For purposes of this section, a corporation shall be treated as a small business corporation if the aggregate amount of money and other property received by the corporation for stock, as a contribution to capital, and as paid-in surplus, does not exceed $1,000,000. The determination under the preceding sentence shall be made as of the time of the issuance of the stock in question but shall include amounts received for such stock and for all stock theretofore issued.

(B) Amount taken into account with respect to property.—For purposes of subparagraph (A), the amount taken into account with respect to any property other than money shall be the amount equal to the adjusted basis to the corporation of such property for determining gain, reduced by any liability to which the property was subject or which was assumed by the corporation. The determination under the preceding sentence shall be made as of the time the property was received by the corporation.

(d) Special rules.—

(1) Limitations on amount of ordinary loss.—

(A) Contributions of property having basis in excess of value.—If—

(i) section 1244 stock was issued in exchange for property,

(ii) the basis of such stock in the hands of the taxpayer is determined by reference to the basis in his hands of such property, and

(iii) the adjusted basis (for determining loss) of such property immediately before the exchange exceeded its fair market value at such time,

then in computing the amount of the loss on such stock for purposes of this section the basis of such stock shall be reduced by an amount equal to the excess described in clause (iii).

(B) Increases in basis.—In computing the amount of the loss on stock for purposes of this section, any increase in the basis of such stock (through contributions to the capital of the corporation, or otherwise) shall be treated as allocable to stock which is not section 1244 stock.

(2) Recapitalizations, changes in name, etc.—To the extent provided in regulations prescribed by the Secretary, stock in a corporation, the basis of which (in the hands of a taxpayer) is determined in whole or in part by reference to the basis in his hands of stock in such corporation which meets the requirements of subsection (c)(l) (other than subparagraph (C) thereof), or which is received in a reorganization described in section 368(a)(1)(F) in exchange for stock which meets such requirements, shall be treated as meeting such requirements. For purposes of paragraphs (1)(C) and (3)(A) of subsection (c), a successor corporation in a reorganization described in section 368(a)(1)(F) shall be treated as the same corporation as its predecessor.

(3) Relationship to net operating loss deduction.—For purposes of section 172 (relating to the net operating loss deduction), any amount of loss treated by reason of this section as an ordinary loss shall be treated as attributable to a trade or business of the taxpayer.

(4) Individual defined.—For purposes of this section, the term "individual" does not include a trust or estate.

(e) Regulations.—The Secretary shall prescribe such regulations as may be necessary to carry out the purposes of this section.

§ 1245. Gain from dispositions of certain depreciable property

(a) General rule.—

(1) Ordinary income.—Except as otherwise provided in this section, if section 1245 property is disposed of the amount by which the lower of—

(A) the recomputed basis of the property, or

(B) **(i)** in the case of a sale, exchange, or involuntary conversion, the amount realized, or

(ii) in the case of any other disposition, the fair market value of such property,

exceeds the adjusted basis of such property shall be treated as ordinary income. Such gain shall be recognized notwithstanding any other provision of this subtitle.

(2) Recomputed basis.—For purposes of this section—

(A) In general.—The term "recomputed basis" means, with respect to any property, its adjusted basis recomputed by adding thereto all adjustments reflected in such adjusted basis on account of deductions (whether in respect of the same or other property) allowed or allowable to the taxpayer or to any other person for depreciation or amortization.

(B) Taxpayer may establish amount allowed.—For purposes of subparagraph (A), if the taxpayer can establish by adequate records or other sufficient evidence that the amount allowed for depreciation or amortization for any period was less than the amount allowable, the amount added for such period shall be the amount allowed.

(C) Certain deductions treated as amortization.—Any deduction allowable under section 179, 179A, 179B, 179C, 179D, 179E, 190, 193, or 194 shall be treated as if it were a deduction allowable for amortization.

(3) Section 1245 property.—For purposes of this section, the term "section 1245 property" means any property which is or has been property of a character subject to the allowance for depreciation provided in section 167 and is either—

(A) personal property,

(B) other property (not including a building or its structural components) but only if such other property is tangible and has an adjusted basis in which there are reflected adjustments described in paragraph (2) for a period in which such property (or other property)—

(i) was used as an integral part of manufacturing, production, or extraction or of furnishing transportation, communications, electrical energy, gas, water, or sewage disposal services,

(ii) constituted a research facility used in connection with any of the activities referred to in clause (i), or

(iii) constituted a facility used in connection with any of the activities referred to in clause (i) for the bulk storage of fungible commodities (including commodities in a liquid or gaseous state),

(C) so much of any real property (other than any property described in subparagraph (B)) which has an adjusted basis in which there are reflected adjustments for amortization under section 169, 179, 179A, 179B, 179C, 179D, 179E, 185, 188 (as in effect before its repeal by the Revenue Reconciliation Act of 1990), 190, 193, or 194,

(D) a single purpose agricultural or horticultural structure (as defined in section 168(i)(13)),

(E) a storage facility (not including a building or its structural components) used in connection with the distribution of petroleum or any primary product of petroleum, or

(F) any railroad grading or tunnel bore (as defined in section 168(e)(4)).

(b) Exceptions and limitations.—

(1) Gifts.—Subsection (a) shall not apply to a disposition by gift.

(2) Transfers at death.—Except as provided in section 691 (relating to income in respect of a decedent), subsection (a) shall not apply to a transfer at death.

(3) Certain tax-free transactions.—If the basis of property in the hands of a transferee is determined by reference to its basis in the hands of the transferor by reason of the application of section 332, 351, 361, 721, or 731, then the amount of gain taken into account by the transferor under subsection (a)(1) shall not exceed the amount of gain recognized to the transferor on the transfer of such property (determined without regard to this section). Except as provided in paragraph (6), this paragraph shall not apply to a disposition to an organization (other than a cooperative described in section 521) which is exempt from the tax imposed by this chapter.

(4) Like kind exchanges; involuntary conversions, etc.—If property is disposed of and gain (determined without regard to this section) is not recognized in whole or in part under section 1031 or 1033, then the amount of gain taken into account by the transferor under subsection (a)(1) shall not exceed the sum of—

(A) the amount of gain recognized on such disposition (determined without regard to this section), plus

(B) the fair market value of property acquired which is not section 1245 property and which is not taken into account under subparagraph (A).

(5) Property distributed by a partnership to a partner.—

(A) In general.—For purposes of this section, the basis of section 1245 property distributed by a partnership to a partner shall be deemed to be determined by reference to the adjusted basis of such property to the partnership.

(B) Adjustments added back.—In the case of any property described in subparagraph (A), for purposes of computing the recomputed basis of such property the amount of the adjustments added back for periods before the distribution by the partnership shall be—

(i) the amount of the gain to which subsection (a) would have applied if such property had been sold by the partnership immediately before the distribution at its fair market value at such time, reduced by

(ii) the amount of such gain to which section 751(b) applied.

(6) Transfers to tax-exempt organization where property will be used in unrelated business.—

(A) In general.—The second sentence of paragraph (3) shall not apply to a disposition of section 1245 property to an organization described in section 511(a)(2) or 511(b)(2) if, immediately after such disposition, such organization uses such property in an unrelated trade or business (as defined in section 513).

(B) Later change in use.—If any property with respect to the disposition of which gain is not recognized by reason of subparagraph (A) ceases to be used in an unrelated trade or business of the organization acquiring such property, such organization shall be treated for purposes of this section as having disposed of such property on the date of such cessation.

(7) Timber property.—In determining, under subsection (a)(2), the recomputed basis of property with respect to which a deduction under section 194 was allowed for any taxable year, the taxpayer shall not take into account adjustments under section 194 to the extent such adjustments are attributable to the amortizable basis of the taxpayer acquired before the 10th taxable year preceding the taxable year in which gain with respect to the property is recognized.

(8) Disposition of amortizable section 197 intangibles.—

(A) In general.—If a taxpayer disposes of more than 1 amortizable section 197 intangible (as defined in section 197(c)) in a transaction or a series of related transactions, all such amortizable 197 intangibles shall be treated as 1 section 1245 property for purposes of this section.

(B) Exception.—Subparagraph (A) shall not apply to any amortizable section 197 intangible (as so defined) with respect to which the adjusted basis exceeds the fair market value.

(c) Adjustments to basis.—The Secretary shall prescribe such regulations as he may deem necessary to provide for adjustments to the basis of property to reflect gain recognized under subsection (a).

(d) Application of section.—This section shall apply notwithstanding any other provision of this subtitle.

* * *

§ 1250. Gain from dispositions of certain depreciable realty

(a) General rule.—Except as otherwise provided in this section—

(1) Additional depreciation after December 31, 1975.—

(A) In general.—If section 1250 property is disposed of after December 31, 1975, then the applicable percentage of the lower of—

(i) that portion of the additional depreciation (as defined in subsection (b) (1) or (4)) attributable to periods after December 31, 1975, in respect of the property, or

(ii) the excess of the amount realized (in the case of a sale, exchange, or involuntary conversion), or the fair market value of such property (in the case of any other disposition), over the adjusted basis of such property, shall be treated as gain which is ordinary income. Such gain shall be recognized notwithstanding any other provision of this subtitle.

(B) Applicable percentage.—For purposes of subparagraph (A), the term "applicable percentage" means—

(i) in the case of section 1250 property with respect to which a mortgage is insured under section 221(d)(3) or 236 of the National Housing Act, or housing financed or assisted by direct loan or tax abatement under similar provisions of State or local laws and with respect to which the owner is subject to the restrictions described in section 1039(b)(1)(B) (as in effect on the day before the date of the enactment of the Revenue Reconciliation Act of 1990), 100 percent minus 1 percentage point for each full month the property was held after the date the property was held 100 full months;

(ii) in the case of dwelling units which, on the average, were held for occupancy by families or individuals eligible to receive subsidies under section 8 of the United States Housing Act of 1937, as amended, or under the provisions of State or local law authorizing similar levels of subsidy for lower-income families, 100 percent minus 1 percentage point for each full month the property was held after the date the property was held 100 full months;

(iii) in the case of section 1250 property with respect to which a depreciation deduction for rehabilitation expenditures was allowed under section 167(k), 100 percent minus 1 percentage point for each full month in excess of 100 full months after the date on which such property was placed in service;

(iv) in the case of section 1250 property with respect to which a loan is made or insured under title V of the Housing Act of 1949, 100 percent minus 1 percentage point for each full month the property was held after the date the property was held 100 full months; and

(v) in the case of all other section 1250 property, 100 percent.

In the case of a building (or a portion of a building devoted to dwelling units), if, on the average, 85 percent or more of the dwelling units contained in such building (or portion thereof) are units described in clause (ii), such building (or portion thereof) shall be treated as property described in clause (ii). Clauses (i), (ii), and (iv) shall not apply with respect to the additional depreciation described in subsection (b)(4) which was allowed under section 167(k).

(2) Additional depreciation after December 31, 1969, and before January 1, 1976.—

(A) In general.—If section 1250 property is disposed of after December 31, 1969, and the amount determined under paragraph (1)(A)(ii) exceeds the amount determined under paragraph (1)(A)(i), then the applicable percentage of the lower of—

(i) that portion of the additional depreciation attributable to periods after December 31, 1969, and before January 1, 1976, in respect of the property, or

(ii) the excess of the amount determined under paragraph (1)(A)(ii) over the amount determined under paragraph (1)(A)(i),

shall also be treated as gain which is ordinary income. Such gain shall be recognized notwithstanding any other provision of this subtitle.

(B) Applicable percentage.—For purposes of subparagraph (A), the term "applicable percentage" means—

(i) in the case of section 1250 property disposed of pursuant to a written contract which was, on July 24, 1969, and at all times thereafter, binding on the owner of the property, 100 percent minus 1 percentage point for each full month the property was held after the date the property was held 20 full months;

(ii) in the case of section 1250 property with respect to which a mortgage is insured under section 221(d)(3) or 236 of the National Housing Act, or housing financed or assisted by direct loan or tax abatement under similar provisions of State or local laws, and with respect to which the owner is subject to the restrictions described in section 1039(b)(1)(B) (as in effect on the day before the date of the enactment of the Revenue Reconciliation Act of 1990), 100 percent minus 1 percentage point for each full month the property was held after the date the property was held 20 full months;

(iii) in the case of residential rental property (as defined in section 167(j)(2)(B)) other than that covered by clauses (i) and (ii), 100 percent minus 1 percentage point for each full month the property was held after the date the property was held 100 full months;

(iv) in the case of section 1250 property with respect to which a depreciation deduction for rehabilitation expenditures was allowed under section 167(k), 100 percent minus 1 percentage point for each full month in excess of 100 full months after the date on which such property was placed in service; and

(v) in the case of all other section 1250 property, 100 percent.

Clauses (i), (ii), and (iii) shall not apply with respect to the additional depreciation described in subsection (b)(4).

(3) Additional depreciation before January 1, 1970.—

(A) In general.—If section 1250 property is disposed of after December 31, 1963, and the amount determined under paragraph (1)(A)(ii) exceeds the sum of the amounts determined under paragraphs (1)(A)(i) and (2)(A)(i), then the applicable percentage of the lower of—

(i) that portion of the additional depreciation attributable to periods before January 1, 1970, in respect of the property, or

(ii) the excess of the amount determined under paragraph (1)(A)(ii) over the sum of the amounts determined under paragraphs (1)(A)(i) and (2)(A)(i),

shall also be treated as gain which is ordinary income. Such gain shall be recognized notwithstanding any other provision of this subtitle.

(B) Applicable percentage.—For purposes of subparagraph (A), the term "applicable percentage" means 100 percent minus 1 percentage point for each full month the property was held after the date on which the property was held for 20 full months.

(4) Special rule.—For purposes of this subsection, any reference to section 167(k) or 167(j)(2)(B) shall be treated as a reference to such section as in effect on the day before the date of the enactment of the Revenue Reconciliation Act of 1990.

(5) Cross reference.—

For reduction in the case of corporations on capital gain treatment under this section, see section 291(a)(1).

(b) Additional depreciation defined.—For purposes of this section—

(1) In general.—The term "additional depreciation" means, in the case of any property, the depreciation adjustments in respect of such property; except that, in the case of property held more than one year, it means such adjustments only to the extent that they exceed the amount of the depreciation adjustments which would have resulted if such adjustments had been determined for each taxable year under the straight line method of adjustment.

(2) Property held by lessee.—In the case of a lessee, in determining the depreciation adjustments which would have resulted in respect of any building erected (or other improvement made) on the leased property, or in respect of any cost of acquiring the lease, the lease period shall be treated as including all renewal periods. For purposes of the preceding sentence—

(A) the term "renewal period" means any period for which the lease may be renewed, extended, or continued pursuant to an option exercisable by the lessee, but

(B) the inclusion of renewal periods shall not extend the period taken into account by more than ⅔ of the period on the basis of which the depreciation adjustments were allowed.

(3) Depreciation adjustments.—The term "depreciation adjustments" means, in respect of any property, all adjustments attributable to periods after December 31, 1963, reflected in the adjusted basis of such property on account of deductions (whether in respect of the same or other property) allowed or allowable to the taxpayer or to any other person for exhaustion, wear and tear, obsolescence, or amortization (other than amortization under section 168 (as in effect before its repeal by the Tax Reform Act of 1976), 169, 185 (as in effect before its repeal by the Tax Reform Act of 1986), 188 (as in effect before its repeal by the Revenue Reconciliation Act of 1990), 190, or 193). For purposes of the preceding sentence, if the taxpayer can establish by adequate records or other sufficient evidence that the amount allowed as a deduction for any period was less than the amount allowable, the amount taken into account for such period shall be the amount allowed.

(4) Additional depreciation attributable to rehabilitation expenditures.—The term "additional depreciation" also means, in the case of section 1250 property with respect to which a depreciation or amortization deduction for rehabilitation expenditures was allowed under section 167(k) (as in effect on the day before the date of the enactment of the Revenue Reconciliation Act of 1990) or 191 (as in effect before its repeal by the Economic Recovery Tax Act of 1981), the depreciation or amortization adjustments allowed under such section to the extent attributable to such property, except that, in the case of such property held for more than one year after the rehabilitation expenditures so allowed were incurred, it means such adjustments only to the extent that they exceed the amount of the depreciation adjustments which would have resulted if such adjustments had been determined under the straight line method of adjustment without regard to the useful life permitted under section 167(k) (as in effect on the day before the date of the enactment of the Revenue Reconciliation Act of 1990) or 191 (as in effect before its repeal by the Economic Recovery Tax Act of 1981).

(5) Method of computing straight line adjustments.—For purposes of paragraph (1), the depreciation adjustments which would have resulted for any taxable year under the straight line method shall be determined—

(A) in the case of property to which section 168 applies, by determining the adjustments which would have resulted for such year if the taxpayer had elected the straight line method for such year using the recovery period applicable to such property, and

(B) in the case of any property to which section 168 does not apply if a useful life (or salvage value) was used in determining the amount allowable as a deduction for any taxable year, by using such life (or value).

(c) Section 1250 property.—For purposes of this section, the term "section 1250 property" means any real property (other than section 1245 property, as defined in section 1245(a)(3)) which is or has been property of a character subject to the allowance for depreciation provided in section 167.

(d) Exceptions and limitations.—

(1) Gifts.—Subsection (a) shall not apply to a disposition by gift.

(2) Transfers at death.—Except as provided in section 691 (relating to income in respect of a decedent), subsection (a) shall not apply to a transfer at death.

(3) Certain tax-free transactions.—If the basis of property in the hands of a transferee is determined by reference to its basis in the hands of the transferor by reason of the application of section 332, 351, 361, 721, or 731, then the amount of gain taken into account by the transferor under subsection (a) shall not exceed the amount of gain recognized to the transferor on the transfer of such property (determined without regard to this section). Except as provided in paragraph (9), this paragraph shall not apply to a disposition to an organization (other than a cooperative described in section 521) which is exempt from the tax imposed by this chapter.

(4) Like kind exchanges; involuntary conversions, etc.—

(A) Recognition limit.—If property is disposed of and gain (determined without regard to this section) is not recognized in whole or in part under section 1031 or 1033, then the amount of gain taken into account by the transferor under subsection (a) shall not exceed the greater of the following:

(i) the amount of gain recognized on the disposition (determined without regard to this section), increased as provided in subparagraph (B), or

(ii) the amount determined under subparagraph (C).

(B) Increase for certain stock.—With respect to any transaction, the increase provided by this subparagraph is the amount equal to the fair market value of any stock purchased in a corporation which (but for this paragraph) would result in nonrecognition of gain under section 1033(a)(2)(A).

(C) Adjustment where insufficient section 1250 property is acquired.—With respect to any transaction, the amount determined under this subparagraph shall be the excess of—

(i) the amount of gain which would (but for this paragraph) be taken into account under subsection (a), over

(ii) the fair market value (or cost in the case of a transaction described in section 1033(a)(2)) of the section 1250 property acquired in the transaction.

(D) Basis of property acquired.—In the case of property purchased by the taxpayer in a transaction described in section 1033(a)(2), in applying section 1033(b)(2), such sentence shall be applied—

(i) first solely to section 1250 properties and to the amount of gain not taken into account under subsection (a) by reason of this paragraph, and

(ii) then to all purchased properties to which such sentence applies and to the remaining gain not recognized on the transaction as if the cost of the section 1250 properties were the basis of such properties computed under clause (i).

In the case of property acquired in any other transaction to which this paragraph applies, rules consistent with the preceding sentence shall be applied under regulations prescribed by the Secretary.

(E) Additional depreciation with respect to property disposed of.—In the case of any transaction described in section 1031 or 1033, the additional depreciation in respect of the section 1250 property acquired which is attributable to the section 1250 property disposed of shall be an amount equal to the amount of the gain which was not taken into account under subsection (a) by reason of the application of this paragraph.

(5) Property distributed by a partnership to a partner.—

(A) In general.—For purposes of this section, the basis of section 1250 property distributed by a partnership to a partner shall be deemed to be determined by reference to the adjusted basis of such property to the partnership.

(B) Additional depreciation.—In respect of any property described in subparagraph (A), the additional depreciation attributable to periods before the distribution by the partnership shall be—

(i) the amount of the gain to which subsection (a) would have applied if such property had been sold by the partnership immediately before the distribution at its fair market value at such time and the applicable percentage for the property had been 100 percent, reduced by

(ii) if section 751(b) applied to any part of such gain, the amount of such gain to which section 751(b) would have applied if the applicable percentage for the property had been 100 percent.

(6) Transfers to tax-exempt organization where property will be used in unrelated business.—

(A) In general.—The second sentence of paragraph (3) shall not apply to a disposition of section 1250 property to an organization described in section 511(a)(2) or 511(b)(2) if, immediately after such disposition, such organization uses such property in an unrelated trade or business (as defined in section 513).

(B) Later change in use.—If any property with respect to the disposition of which gain is not recognized by reason of subparagraph (A) ceases to be used in an unrelated trade or business of the organization acquiring such property, such organization shall be treated for purposes of this section as having disposed of such property on the date of such cessation.

(7) Foreclosure dispositions.—If any section 1250 property is disposed of by the taxpayer pursuant to a bid for such property at foreclosure or by operation of an agreement or of process of law after there was a default on indebtedness which such property secured, the applicable percentage referred to in paragraph (1)(B), (2)(B), or (3)(B) of subsection (a), as the case may be, shall be determined as if the taxpayer ceased to hold such property on the date of the beginning of the proceedings pursuant to which the disposition occurred, or, in the event there are no proceedings, such percentage shall be determined as if the taxpayer ceased to hold such property on the date, determined under regulations prescribed by the Secretary, on which such operation of an agreement or process of law, pursuant to which the disposition occurred, began.

(e) Holding period.—For purposes of determining the applicable percentage under this section, the provisions of section 1223 shall not apply, and the holding period of section 1250 property shall be determined under the following rules:

(1) Beginning of holding period.—The holding period of section 1250 property shall be deemed to begin—

(A) in the case of property acquired by the taxpayer, on the day after the date of acquisition, or

(B) in the case of property constructed, reconstructed, or erected by the taxpayer, on the first day of the month during which the property is placed in service.

(2) **Property with transferred basis.**—If the basis of property acquired in a transaction described in paragraph (1), (2), or (3) of subsection (d) is determined by reference to its basis in the hands of the transferor, then the holding period of the property in the hands of the transferee shall include the holding period of the property in the hands of the transferor.

(f) **Special rules for property which is substantially improved.**—

(1) **Amount treated as ordinary income.**—If, in the case of a disposition of section 1250 property, the property is treated as consisting of more than one element by reason of paragraph (3), then the amount taken into account under subsection (a) in respect of such section 1250 property as ordinary income shall be the sum of the amounts determined under paragraph (2).

(2) **Ordinary income attributable to an element.**—For purposes of paragraph (1), the amount taken into account for any element shall be the sum of a series of amounts determined for the periods set forth in subsection (a), with the amount for any such period being determined by multiplying—

(A) the amount which bears the same ratio to the lower of the amounts specified in clause (i) or (ii) of subsection (a)(l)(A), in clause (i) or (ii) of subsection (a)(2)(A), or in clause (i) or (ii) of subsection (a)(3) (A), as the case may be, for the section 1250 property as the additional depreciation for such element attributable to such period bears to the sum of the additional depreciation for all elements attributable to such period, by

(B) the applicable percentage for such element for such period.

For purposes of this paragraph, determinations with respect to any element shall be made as if it were a separate property.

(3) **Property consisting of more than one element.**—In applying this subsection in the case of any section 1250 property, there shall be treated as a separate element—

(A) each separate improvement,

(B) if, before completion of section 1250 property, units thereof (as distinguished from improvements) were placed in service, each such unit of section 1250 property, and

(C) the remaining property which is not taken into account under subparagraphs (A) and (B).

(4) **Property which is substantially improved.**—For purposes of this subsection—

(A) **In general.**—The term "separate improvement" means each improvement added during the 36-month period ending on the last day of any taxable year to the capital account for the property, but only if the sum of the amounts added to such account during such period exceeds the greatest of—

(i) 25 percent of the adjusted basis of the property,

(ii) 10 percent of the adjusted basis of the property, determined without regard to the adjustments provided in paragraphs (2) and (3) of section 1016(a), or

(iii) $5,000.

For purposes of clauses (i) and (ii), the adjusted basis of the property shall be determined as of the beginning of the first day of such 36-month period, or of the holding period of the property (within the meaning of subsection (e)), whichever is the later.

(B) **Exception.**—Improvements in any taxable year shall be taken into account for purposes of subparagraph (A) only if the sum of the amounts added to the capital account for the property for such taxable year exceeds the greater of—

(i) $2,000, or

(ii) one percent of the adjusted basis referred to in subparagraph (A) (ii), determined, however, as of the beginning of such taxable year.

For purposes of this section, if the amount added to the capital account for any separate improvement does not exceed the greater of clause (i) or (ii), such improvement shall be treated as placed in service on the first day, of a calendar month, which is closest to the middle of the taxable year.

(C) **Improvement.**—The term "improvement" means, in the case of any section 1250 property, any addition to capital account for such property after the initial acquisition or after completion of the property.

(g) **Adjustments to basis.**—The Secretary shall prescribe such regulations as he may deem necessary to provide for adjustments to the basis of property to reflect gain recognized under subsection (a).

(h) Application of section.—This section shall apply notwithstanding any other provision of this subtitle.

§ 1252. Gain from disposition of farm land

(a) General rule.—

(1) Ordinary income.—Except as otherwise provided in this section, if farm land which the taxpayer has held for less than 10 years is disposed of during a taxable year beginning after December 31, 1969, the lower of—

(A) the applicable percentage of the aggregate of the deductions allowed under sections 175 (relating to soil and water conservation expenditures) and 182 (as in effect on the day before the date of the enactment of the Tax Reform Act of 1986) for expenditures made by the taxpayer after December 31, 1969, with respect to the farm land or

(B) the excess of—

(i) the amount realized (in the case of a sale, exchange, or involuntary conversion), or the fair market value of the farm land (in the case of any other disposition), over

(ii) the adjusted basis of such land,

shall be treated as ordinary income. Such gain shall be recognized notwithstanding any other provision of this subtitle.

(2) Farm land.—For purposes of this section, the term "farm land" means any land with respect to which deductions have been allowed under sections 175 (relating to soil and water conservation expenditures) or 182 (relating to expenditures by farmers for clearing land).

(3) Applicable percentage.—For purposes of this section—

If the farm land is disposed of—	The applicable percentage is—
Within 5 years after the date it was acquired	100 percent
Within the sixth year after it was acquired	80 percent
Within the seventh year after it was acquired	60 percent
Within the eighth year after it was acquired	40 percent
Within the ninth year after it was acquired	20 percent
10 years or more years after it was acquired	0 percent

(b) Special rules.—Under regulations prescribed by the Secretary, rules similar to the rules of section 1245 shall be applied for purposes of this section.

§ 1253. Transfers of franchises, trademarks, and trade names

(a) General rule.—A transfer of a franchise, trademark, or trade name shall not be treated as a sale or exchange of a capital asset if the transferor retains any significant power, right, or continuing interest with respect to the subject matter of the franchise, trademark, or trade name.

(b) Definitions.—For purposes of this section—

(1) Franchise.—The term "franchise" includes an agreement which gives one of the parties to the agreement the right to distribute, sell, or provide goods, services, or facilities, within a specified area.

(2) Significant power, right, or continuing interest.—The term "significant power, right, or continuing interest" includes, but is not limited to, the following rights with respect to the interest transferred:

(A) A right to disapprove any assignment of such interest, or any part thereof.

(B) A right to terminate at will.

(C) A right to prescribe the standards of quality of products used or sold, or of services furnished, and of the equipment and facilities used to promote such products or services.

(D) A right to require that the transferee sell or advertise only products or services of the transferor.

(E) A right to require that the transferee purchase substantially all of his supplies and equipment from the transferor.

(F) A right to payments contingent on the productivity, use, or disposition of the subject matter of the interest transferred, if such payments constitute a substantial element under the transfer agreement.

(3) Transfer.—The term "transfer" includes the renewal of a franchise, trademark, or trade name.

(c) Treatment of contingent payments by transferor.—Amounts received or accrued on account of a transfer, sale, or other disposition of a franchise, trademark, or trade name which are contingent on the productivity, use, or disposition of the franchise, trademark, or trade name transferred shall be treated as amounts received or accrued from the sale or other disposition of property which is not a capital asset.

(d) Treatment of payments by transferee.—

(1) Contingent serial payments.—

(A) In general.—Any amount described in subparagraph (B) which is paid or incurred during the taxable year on account of a transfer, sale, or other disposition of a franchise, trademark, or trade name shall be allowed as a deduction under section 162(a) (relating to trade or business expenses).

(B) Amounts to which paragraph applies.—An amount is described in this subparagraph if it—

(i) is contingent on the productivity, use, or disposition of the franchise, trademark, or trade name, and

(ii) is paid as part of a series of payments—

(I) which are payable not less frequently than annually throughout the entire term of the transfer agreement, and

(II) which are substantially equal in amount (or payable under a fixed formula).

(2) Other payments.—Any amount paid or incurred on account of a transfer, sale, or other disposition of a franchise, trademark, or trade name to which paragraph (1) does not apply shall be treated as an amount chargeable to capital account.

(3) Renewals, etc.—For purposes of determining the term of a transfer agreement under this section, there shall be taken into account all renewal options (and any other period for which the parties reasonably expect the agreement to be renewed).

§ 1254. Gain from disposition of interest in oil, gas, geothermal, or other mineral properties

(a) General rule.—

(1) Ordinary income.—If any section 1254 property is disposed of, the lesser of—

(A) the aggregate amount of—

(i) expenditures which have been deducted by the taxpayer or any person under section 263, 616, or 617 with respect to such property and which, but for such deduction, would have been included in the adjusted basis of such property, and

(ii) the deductions for depletion under section 611 which reduced the adjusted basis of such property, or

(B) the excess of—

(i) in the case of—

(I) a sale, exchange, or involuntary conversion, the amount realized, or

(II) in the case of any other disposition, the fair market value of such property, over

(ii) the adjusted basis of such property,

shall be treated as gain which is ordinary income. Such gain shall be recognized notwithstanding any other provision of this subtitle.

(2) Disposition of portion of property.—For purposes of paragraph (1)—

(A) In the case of the disposition of a portion of section 1254 property (other than an undivided interest), the entire amount of the aggregate expenditures or deductions described in paragraph (1)(A) with respect to such property shall be treated as allocable to such portion to the extent of the amount of the gain to which paragraph (1) applies.

(B) In the case of the disposition of an undivided interest in a section 1254 property (or a portion thereof), a proportionate part of the expenditures or deductions described in paragraph (1)(A) with respect to such property shall be treated as allocable to such undivided interest to the extent of the amount of the gain to which paragraph (1) applies.

This paragraph shall not apply to any expenditures to the extent the taxpayer establishes to the satisfaction of the Secretary that such expenditures do not relate to the portion (or interest therein) disposed of.

(3) Section 1254 property.—The term "section 1254 property" means any property (within the meaning of section 614) if—

(A) any expenditures described in paragraph (1)(A) are properly chargeable to such property, or

(B) the adjusted basis of such property includes adjustments for deductions for depletion under section 611.

(4) Adjustment for amounts included in gross income under section 617(b)(1)(A).—The amount of the expenditures referred to in paragraph (1)(A)(i) shall be properly adjusted for amounts included in gross income under section 617(b)(1)(A).

(b) Special rules under regulations.—Under regulations prescribed by the Secretary—

(1) rules similar to the rule of subsection (g) of section 617 and to the rules of subsections (b) and (c) of section 1245 shall be applied for purposes of this section; and

(2) in the case of the sale or exchange of stock in an S corporation, rules similar to the rules of section 751 shall be applied to that portion of the excess of the amount realized over the adjusted basis of the stock which is attributable to expenditures referred to in subsection (a)(1)(A) of this section.

* * *

§ 1258. Recharacterization of gain from certain financial transactions

(a) General rule.—In the case of any gain—

(1) which (but for this section) would be treated as gain from the sale or exchange of a capital asset, and

(2) which is recognized on the disposition or other termination of any position which was held as part of a conversion transaction,

such gain (to the extent such gain does not exceed the applicable imputed income amount) shall be treated as ordinary income.

(b) Applicable imputed income amount.—For purposes of subsection (a), the term "applicable imputed income amount" means, with respect to any disposition or other termination referred to in subsection (a), an amount equal to—

(1) the amount of interest which would have accrued on the taxpayer's net investment in the conversion transaction for the period ending on the date of such disposition or other termination (or, if earlier, the date on which the requirements of subsection (c) ceased to be satisfied) at a rate equal to 120 percent of the applicable rate, reduced by

(2) the amount treated as ordinary income under subsection (a) with respect to any prior disposition or other termination of a position which was held as a part of such transaction.

The Secretary shall by regulations provide for such reductions in the applicable imputed income amount as may be appropriate by reason of amounts capitalized under section 263(g), ordinary income received, or otherwise.

(c) Conversion transaction.—For purposes of this section, the term "conversion transaction" means any transaction—

(1) substantially all of the taxpayer's expected return from which is attributable to the time value of the taxpayer's net investment in such transaction, and

(2) which is—

(A) the holding of any property (whether or not actively traded), and the entering into a contract to sell such property (or substantially identical property) at a price determined in accordance with such contract, but only if such property was acquired and such contract was entered into on a substantially contemporaneous basis,

(B) an applicable straddle,

(C) any other transaction which is marketed or sold as producing capital gains from a transaction described in paragraph (1), or

(D) any other transaction specified in regulations prescribed by the Secretary.

(d) Definitions and special rules.—For purposes of this section—

(1) Applicable straddle.—The term "applicable straddle" means any straddle (within the meaning of section 1092(c)).

(2) Applicable rate.—The term "applicable rate" means—

(A) the applicable Federal rate determined under section 1274(d) (compounded semiannually) as if the conversion transaction were a debt instrument, or

(B) if the term of the conversion transaction is indefinite, the Federal short-term rates in effect under section 6621(b) during the period of the conversion transaction (compounded daily).

(3) Treatment of built-in losses.—

(A) In general.—If any position with a built-in loss becomes part of a conversion transaction—

(i) for purposes of applying this subtitle to such position for periods after such position becomes part of such transaction, such position shall be taken into account at its fair market value as of the time it became part of such transaction, except that

(ii) upon the disposition or other termination of such position in a transaction in which gain or loss is recognized, such built-in loss shall be recognized and shall have a character determined without regard to this section.

(B) Built-in loss.—For purposes of subparagraph (A), the term "built-in loss" means the loss (if any) which would have been realized if the position had been disposed of or otherwise terminated at its fair market value as of the time such position became part of the conversion transaction.

(4) Position taken into account at fair market value.—In determining the taxpayer's net investment in any conversion transaction, there shall be included the fair market value of any position which becomes part of such transaction (determined as of the time such position became part of such transaction).

(5) Special rule for options dealers and commodities traders.—

(A) In general.—Subsection (a) shall not apply to transactions—

(i) of an options dealer in the normal course of the dealer's trade or business of dealing in options, or

(ii) of a commodities trader in the normal course of the trader's trade or business of trading section 1256 contracts.

(B) Definitions.—For purposes of this paragraph—

(i) Options dealer.—The term "options dealer" has the meaning given such term by section 1256(g)(8).

(ii) Commodities trader.—The term "commodities trader" means any person who is a member (or, except as otherwise provided in regulations, is entitled to trade as a member) of a domestic board of trade which is designated as a contract market by the Commodity Futures Trading Commission.

(C) Limited partners and limited entrepreneurs.—In the case of any gain from a transaction recognized by an entity which is allocable to a limited partner or limited entrepreneur (within the meaning of section 464(e)(2)), subparagraph (A) shall not apply if—

(i) substantially all of the limited partner's (or limited entrepreneur's) expected return from the entity is attributable to the time value of the partner's (or entrepreneur's) net investment in such entity,

(ii) the transaction (or the interest in the entity) was marketed or sold as producing capital gains treatment from a transaction described in subsection (c)(1), or

(iii) the transaction (or the interest in the entity) is a transaction (or interest) specified in regulations prescribed by the Secretary.

§ 1259. Constructive sales treatment for appreciated financial positions

(a) In general.—If there is a constructive sale of an appreciated financial position—

(1) the taxpayer shall recognize gain as if such position were sold, assigned, or otherwise terminated at its fair market value on the date of such constructive sale (and any gain shall be taken into account for the taxable year which includes such date), and

(2) for purposes of applying this title for periods after the constructive sale—

(A) proper adjustment shall be made in the amount of any gain or loss subsequently realized with respect to such position for any gain taken into account by reason of paragraph (1), and

(B) the holding period of such position shall be determined as if such position were originally acquired on the date of such constructive sale.

(b) Appreciated financial position.—For purposes of this section—

(1) In general.—Except as provided in paragraph (2), the term "appreciated financial position" means any position with respect to any stock, debt instrument, or partnership interest if there would be gain were such position sold, assigned, or otherwise terminated at its fair market value.

(2) Exceptions.—The term "appreciated financial position" shall not include—

(A) any position with respect to debt if—

(i) the position unconditionally entitles the holder to receive a specified principal amount,

(ii) the interest payments (or other similar amounts) with respect to such position meet the requirements of clause (i) of section 860G(a) (1)(B), and

(iii) such position is not convertible (directly or indirectly) into stock of the issuer or any related person,

(B) any hedge with respect to a position described in subparagraph (A), and

(C) any position which is marked to market under any provision of this title or the regulations thereunder.

(3) Position.—The term "position" means an interest, including a futures or forward contract, short sale, or option.

(c) Constructive sale.—For purposes of this section—

(1) In general.—A taxpayer shall be treated as having made a constructive sale of an appreciated financial position if the taxpayer (or a related person)—

(A) enters into a short sale of the same or substantially identical property,

(B) enters into an offsetting notional principal contract with respect to the same or substantially identical property,

(C) enters into a futures or forward contract to deliver the same or substantially identical property,

(D) in the case of an appreciated financial position that is a short sale or a contract described in subparagraph (B) or (C) with respect to any property, acquires the same or substantially identical property, or

(E) to the extent prescribed by the Secretary in regulations, enters into 1 or more other transactions (or acquires 1 or more positions) that have substantially the same effect as a transaction described in any of the preceding subparagraphs.

(2) Exception for sales of nonpublicly traded property.—A taxpayer shall not be treated as having made a constructive sale solely because the taxpayer enters into a contract for sale of any stock, debt instrument, or partnership interest which is not a marketable security (as defined in section 453(f)) if the contract settles within 1 year after the date such contract is entered into.

(3) Exception for certain closed transactions.—

(A) In general.—In applying this section, there shall be disregarded any transaction (which would otherwise cause a constructive sale) during the taxable year if—

(i) such transaction is closed on or before the end of the 30th day after the close of such taxable year,

(ii) the taxpayer holds the appreciated financial position throughout the 60-day period beginning on the date such transaction is closed, and

(iii) at no time during such 60-day period is the taxpayer's risk of loss with respect to such position reduced by reason of a circumstance which would be described in section 246(c)(4) if references to stock included references to such position.

(B) Treatment of certain closed transactions where risk of loss on appreciated financial position diminished.—If—

(i) a transaction, which would otherwise cause a constructive sale of an appreciated financial position, is closed during the taxable year or during the 30 days thereafter, and

(ii) another transaction is entered into during the 60-day period beginning on the date the transaction referred to in clause (i) is closed—

(I) which would (but for this subparagraph) cause the requirement of subparagraph (A)(iii) not to be met with respect to the transaction described in clause (i) of this subparagraph,

(II) which is closed on or before the 30th day after the close of the taxable year in which the transaction referred to in clause (i) occurs, and

(III) which meets the requirements of clauses (ii) and (iii) of subparagraph (A),

the transaction referred to in clause (ii) shall be disregarded for purposes of determining whether the requirements of subparagraph (A)(iii) are met with respect to the transaction described in clause (i).

(4) Related person.—A person is related to another person with respect to a transaction if—

(A) the relationship is described in section 267(b) or 707(b), and

(B) such transaction is entered into with a view toward avoiding the purposes of this section.

(d) Other definitions.—For purposes of this section—

(1) Forward contract.—The term "forward contract" means a contract to deliver a substantially fixed amount of property (including cash) for a substantially fixed price.

(2) Offsetting notional principal contract.—The term "offsetting notional principal contract" means, with respect to any property, an agreement which includes—

(A) a requirement to pay (or provide credit for) all or substantially all of the investment yield (including appreciation) on such property for a specified period, and

(B) a right to be reimbursed for (or receive credit for) all or substantially all of any decline in the value of such property.

(e) Special rules.—

(1) Treatment of subsequent sale of position which was deemed sold.—If—

(A) there is a constructive sale of any appreciated financial position,

(B) such position is subsequently disposed of, and

(C) at the time of such disposition, the transaction resulting in the constructive sale of such position is open with respect to the taxpayer or any related person,

solely for purposes of determining whether the taxpayer has entered into a constructive sale of any other appreciated financial position held by the taxpayer, the taxpayer shall be treated as entering into such transaction immediately after such disposition. For purposes of the preceding sentence, an assignment or other termination shall be treated as a disposition.

(2) Certain trust instruments treated as stock.—For purposes of this section, an interest in a trust which is actively traded (within the meaning of section 1092(d)(1)) shall be treated as stock unless substantially all (by value) of the property held by the trust is debt described in subsection (b)(2)(A).

(3) Multiple positions in property.—If a taxpayer holds multiple positions in property, the determination of whether a specific transaction is a constructive sale and, if so, which appreciated financial position is deemed sold shall be made in the same manner as actual sales.

(f) Regulations.—The Secretary shall prescribe such regulations as may be necessary or appropriate to carry out the purposes of this section.

§ 1260. Gains from constructive ownership transactions

(a) In general.—If the taxpayer has gain from a constructive ownership transaction with respect to any financial asset and such gain would (without regard to this section) be treated as a long-term capital gain—

(1) such gain shall be treated as ordinary income to the extent that such gain exceeds the net underlying long-term capital gain, and

(2) to the extent such gain is treated as a long-term capital gain after the application of paragraph (1), the determination of the capital gain rate (or rates) applicable to such gain under section 1(h) shall be determined on the basis of the respective rate (or rates) that would have been applicable to the net underlying long-term capital gain.

(b) Interest charge on deferral of gain recognition.—

(1) In general.—If any gain is treated as ordinary income for any taxable year by reason of subsection (a)(1), the tax imposed by this chapter for such taxable year shall be increased by the amount of interest determined under paragraph (2) with respect to each prior taxable year during any portion of which the constructive ownership transaction was open. Any amount payable under this paragraph shall be taken into account in computing the amount of any deduction allowable to the taxpayer for interest paid or accrued during such taxable year.

(2) Amount of interest.—The amount of interest determined under this paragraph with respect to a prior taxable year is the amount of interest which would have been imposed under section 6601 on the underpayment of tax for such year which would have resulted if the gain (which is treated as ordinary income by reason of subsection (a)(1)) had been included in gross income in the taxable years in which it accrued (determined by treating the income as accruing at a constant rate equal to the applicable Federal rate as in effect on the day the transaction closed). The period during which such interest shall accrue shall end on the due date (without extensions) for the return of tax imposed by this chapter for the taxable year in which such transaction closed.

(3) Applicable Federal rate.—For purposes of paragraph (2), the applicable Federal rate is the applicable Federal rate determined under section 1274(d) (compounded semiannually) which would apply to a debt instrument with a term equal to the period the transaction was open.

(4) No credits against increase in tax.—Any increase in tax under paragraph (1) shall not be treated as tax imposed by this chapter for purposes of determining—

(A) the amount of any credit allowable under this chapter, or

(B) the amount of the tax imposed by section 55.

(c) Financial assets.—For purposes of this section—

(1) In general.—The term "financial asset" means—

(A) any equity interest in any pass-thru entity, and

(B) to the extend provided in regulations—

(i) any debt instrument, and

(ii) any stock in a corporation which is not a pass-thru entity.

(2) Pass-thru entity.—For purposes of paragraph (1), the term "pass-thru entity" means—

(A) a regulated investment company,

(B) a real estate investment trust,

(C) an S corporation,

(D) a partnership,

(E) a trust,

(F) a common trust fund,

(G) a passive foreign investment company (as defined in section 1297 without regard to subsection (d) thereof), and

(H) a REMIC.

(d) Constructive ownership transaction.—For purposes of this section—

(1) In general.—The taxpayer shall be treated as having entered into a constructive ownership transaction with respect to any financial asset if the taxpayer—

(A) holds a long position under a notional principal contract with respect to the financial asset,

(B) enters into a forward or futures contract to acquire the financial asset,

(C) is the holder of a call option, and is the grantor of a put option, with respect to the financial asset and such options have substantially equal strike prices and substantially contemporaneous maturity dates, or

(D) to the extent provided in regulations prescribed by the Secretary, enters into one or more other transactions (or acquires one or more positions) that have substantially the same effect as a transaction described in any of the preceding subparagraphs.

(2) Exception for positions which are marked to market.—This section shall not apply to any constructive ownership transaction if all of the positions which are part of such transaction are marked to market under any provision of this title or the regulations thereunder.

(3) Long position under notional principal contract.—A personal shall be treated as holding a long position under a notional principal contract with respect to any financial asset if such person—

(A) has the right to be paid (or receive credit for) all or substantially all of the investment yield (including appreciation) on such financial asset for a specified period, and

(B) is obligated to reimburse (or provide credit for) all or substantially all of any decline in the value of such financial asset.

(4) Forward contract.—The term "forward contract" means any contract to acquire in the future (or provide or receive credit for the future value of) any financial asset.

(e) Net underlying long-term capital gain.—For purposes of this section, in the case of any constructive ownership transaction with respect to any financial asset, the term "net underlying long-term capital gain" means the aggregate net capital gain that the taxpayer would have had if—

(1) the financial asset had been acquired for fair market value on the date such transaction was opened and sold for fair market value on the date such transaction was closed, and

(2) only gains and losses that would have resulted from the deemed ownership under paragraph (1) were taken into account.

The amount of the net underlying long-term capital gain with respect to any financial asset shall be treated as zero unless the amount thereof is established by clear and convincing evidence.

(f) Special rule where taxpayer takes delivery.—Except as provided in regulations prescribed by the Secretary, if a constructive ownership transaction is closed by reason of taking delivery, this section shall be applied as if the taxpayer had sold all the contracts, options, or other positions which are part of such transaction for fair market value on the closing date. The amount of gain recognized under the preceding sentence shall not exceed the amount of gain treated as ordinary income under subsection (a). Proper adjustments shall be made in the amount of any gain or loss subsequently realized for gain recognized and treated as ordinary income under this subsection.

(g) Regulations.—The Secretary shall prescribe such regulations as may be necessary or appropriate to carry out the purposes of this section, including regulations—

(1) to permit taxpayers to mark to market constructive ownership transactions in lieu of applying this section, and

(2) to exclude certain forward contracts which do not convey substantially all of the economic return with respect to a financial asset.

PART V—SPECIAL RULES FOR BONDS AND OTHER DEBT INSTRUMENTS

Editorial Summary

Capital Asset Transactions: Special Rules for Bonds and Other Debt Instruments

Subchapter P of Chapter 1 (Secs. 1271–1288)

See the discussion under the Editorial Summary entitled Property Transactions: Classification of Gain or Loss, which precedes Sec. 1201.

SUBPART A—ORIGINAL ISSUE DISCOUNT

§ 1271. Treatment of amounts received on retirement or sale or exchange of debt instruments

(a) General rule.—For purposes of this title—

(1) Retirement.—Amounts received by the holder on retirement of any debt instrument shall be considered as amounts received in exchange therefor.

(2) Ordinary income on sale or exchange where intention to call before maturity.—

(A) In general.—If at the time of original issue there was an intention to call a debt instrument before maturity, any gain realized on the sale or exchange thereof which does not exceed an amount equal to—

(i) the original issue discount, reduced by

(ii) the portion of original issue discount previously includible in the gross income of any holder (without regard to subsection (a)(7) or (b)(4) of section 1272 (or the corresponding provisions of prior law)),

shall be treated as ordinary income.

(B) Exceptions.—This section shall not apply to—

(i) any tax-exempt obligation, or

(ii) any holder who has purchased the debt instrument at a premium.

(3) Certain short-term government obligations.—

(A) In general.—On the sale or exchange of any short-term Government obligation, any gain realized which does not exceed an amount equal to the ratable share of the acquisition discount shall be treated as ordinary income.

(B) Short-term government obligation.—For purposes of this paragraph, the term "short-term Government obligation" means any obligation of the United States or any of its possessions, or of a State or any political subdivision thereof, or of the District of Columbia, which has a fixed maturity date not more than 1 year from the date of issue. Such term does not include any tax-exempt obligation.

(C) Acquisition discount.—For purposes of this paragraph, the term "acquisition discount" means the excess of the stated redemption price at maturity over the taxpayer's basis for the obligation.

(D) Ratable share.—For purposes of this paragraph, except as provided in subparagraph (E), the ratable share of the acquisition discount is an amount which bears the same ratio to such discount as—

(i) the number of days which the taxpayer held the obligation, bears to

(ii) the number of days after the date the taxpayer acquired the obligation and up to (and including) the date of its maturity.

(E) Election of accrual on basis of constant interest rate.—At the election of the taxpayer with respect to any obligation, the ratable share of the acquisition discount is the portion of the acquisition discount accruing while the taxpayer held the obligation determined (under regulations prescribed by the Secretary) on the basis of—

(i) the taxpayer's yield to maturity based on the taxpayer's cost of acquiring the obligation, and

(ii) compounding daily.

An election under this subparagraph, once made with respect to any obligation, shall be irrevocable.

(4) Certain short-term nongovernment obligations.—

(A) In general.—On the sale or exchange of any short-term nongovernment obligation, any gain realized which does not exceed an amount equal to the ratable share of the original issue discount shall be treated as ordinary income.

(B) Short-term nongovernment obligation.—For purposes of this paragraph, the term "short-term nongovernment obligation" means any obligation which—

(i) has a fixed maturity date not more than 1 year from the date of the issue, and

(ii) is not a short-term Government obligation (as defined in paragraph (3)(B) without regard to the last sentence thereof).

(C) Ratable share.—For purposes of this paragraph, except as provided in subparagraph (D), the ratable share of the original issue discount is an amount which bears the same ratio to such discount as—

(i) the number of days which the taxpayer held the obligation, bears to

(ii) the number of days after the date of original issue and up to (and including) the date of its maturity.

(D) Election of accrual on basis of constant interest rate.—At the election of the taxpayer with respect to any obligation, the ratable share of the original issue discount is the portion of the original issue discount accruing while the taxpayer held the obligation determined (under regulations prescribed by the Secretary) on the basis of—

(i) the yield to maturity based on the issue price of the obligation, and

(ii) compounding daily.

Any election under this subparagraph, once made with respect to any obligation, shall be irrevocable.

(b) Exception for certain obligations.—

(1) In general.—This section shall not apply to—

(A) any obligation issued by a natural person before June 9, 1997, and

(B) any obligation issued before July 2, 1982, by an issuer which is not a corporation and is not a government or political subdivision thereof.

(2) Termination.—Paragraph (1) shall not apply to any obligation purchased (within the meaning of section 1272(d)(1)) after June 8, 1997.

(c) Transition rules.—

(1) Special rule for certain obligations issued before January 1, 1955.—Paragraph (1) of subsection (a) shall apply to a debt instrument issued before January 1, 1955, only if such instrument was issued with interest coupons or in registered form, or was in such form on March 1, 1954.

(2) Special rule for certain obligations with respect to which original issue discount not currently includible.—

(A) In general.—On the sale or exchange of debt instruments issued by a government or political subdivision thereof after December 31, 1954, and before July 2, 1982, or by a corporation after December 31, 1954, and on or before May 27, 1969, any gain realized which does not exceed—

(i) an amount equal to the original issue discount, or

(ii) if at the time of original issue there was no intention to call the debt instrument before maturity, an amount which bears the same ratio to the original issue discount as the number of complete months that the debt instrument was held by the taxpayer bears to the number of complete months from the date of original issue to the date of maturity,

shall be considered as ordinary income.

(B) Subsection (a)(2)(A) not to apply.—Subsection (a)(2)(A) shall not apply to any debt instrument referred to in subparagraph (A) of this paragraph.

(C) **Cross reference.**—

For current inclusion of original issue discount, see section 1272.

(d) Double inclusion in income not required.—This section and sections 1272 and 1286 shall not require the inclusion of any amount previously includible in gross income.

§ 1272. Current inclusion in income of original issue discount

(a) Original issue discount on debt instruments issued after July 1, 1982, included in income on basis of constant interest rate.—

(1) General rule.—For purposes of this title, there shall be included in the gross income of the holder of any debt instrument having original issue discount issued after July 1, 1982, an amount equal to the sum of the daily portions of the original issue discount for each day during the taxable year on which such holder held such debt instrument.

(2) Exceptions.—Paragraph (1) shall not apply to—

(A) Tax-exempt obligations.—Any tax-exempt obligation.

(B) United States savings bonds.—Any United States savings bond.

(C) Short-term obligations.—Any debt instrument which has a fixed maturity date not more than 1 year from the date of issue.

(D) Obligations issued by natural persons before March 2, 1984.—Any obligation issued by a natural person before March 2, 1984.

(E) Loans between natural persons.—

(i) In general.—Any loan made by a natural person to another natural person if—

(I) such loan is not made in the course of a trade or business of the lender, and

(II) the amount of such loan (when increased by the outstanding amount of prior loans by such natural person to such other natural person) does not exceed $10,000.

(ii) Clause (i) not to apply where tax avoidance a principal purpose.—Clause (i) shall not apply if the loan has as 1 of its principal purposes the avoidance of any Federal tax.

(iii) Treatment of husband and wife.—For purposes of this subparagraph, a husband and wife shall be treated as 1 person. The preceding sentence shall not apply where the spouses lived apart at all times during the taxable year in which the loan is made.

(3) Determination of daily portions.—For purposes of paragraph (1), the daily portion of the original issue discount on any debt instrument shall be determined by allocating to each day in any accrual period its ratable portion of the increase during such accrual period in the adjusted issue price of the debt instrument. For purposes of the preceding sentence, the increase in the adjusted issue price for any accrual period shall be an amount equal to the excess (if any) of—

(A) the product of—

(i) the adjusted issue price of the debt instrument at the beginning of such accrual period, and

(ii) the yield to maturity (determined on the basis of compounding at the close of each accrual period and properly adjusted for the length of the accrual period), over

(B) the sum of the amounts payable as interest on such debt instrument during such accrual period.

(4) Adjusted issue price.—For purposes of this subsection, the adjusted issue price of any debt instrument at the beginning of any accrual period is the sum of—

(A) the issue price of such debt instrument, plus

(B) the adjustments under this subsection to such issue price for all periods before the first day of such accrual period.

(5) Accrual period.—Except as otherwise provided in regulations prescribed by the Secretary, the term "accrual period" means a 6-month period (or shorter period from the date of original issue of the debt instrument) which ends on a day in the calendar year corresponding to the maturity date of the debt instrument or the date 6 months before such maturity date.

(6) Determination of daily portions where principal subject to acceleration.—

(A) In general.—In the case of any debt instrument to which this paragraph applies, the daily portion of the original issue discount shall be determined by allocating to each day in any accrual period its ratable portion of the excess (if any) of—

(i) the sum of (I) the present value determined under subparagraph (B) of all remaining payments under the debt instrument as of the close of such period, and (II) the payments during the accrual period of amounts included in the stated redemption price of the debt instrument, over

(ii) the adjusted issue price of such debt instrument at the beginning of such period.

(B) Determination of present value.—For purposes of subparagraph (A), the present value shall be determined on the basis of—

(i) the original yield to maturity (determined on the basis of compounding at the close of each accrual period and properly adjusted for the length of the accrual period),

(ii) events which have occurred before the close of the accrual period, and

(iii) a prepayment assumption determined in the manner prescribed by regulations.

(C) Debt instruments to which paragraph applies.—This paragraph applies to—

(i) any regular interest in a REMIC or qualified mortgage held by a REMIC,

(ii) any other debt instrument if payments under such debt instrument may be accelerated by reason of prepayments of other obligations securing such debt instrument (or, to the extent provided in regulations, by reason of other events), or

(iii) any pool of debt instruments the yield on which may be affected by reason of prepayments (or to the extent provided in regulations, by reason of other events).

To the extent provided in regulations prescribed by the Secretary, in the case of a small business engaged in the trade or business of selling tangible personal property at retail, clause (iii) shall not apply to debt instruments incurred in the ordinary course of such trade or business while held by such business.

(7) Reduction where subsequent holder pays acquisition premium.—

(A) Reduction.—For purposes of this subsection, in the case of any purchase after its original issue of a debt instrument to which this subsection applies, the daily portion for any day shall be reduced by an amount equal to the amount which would be the daily portion for such day (without regard to this paragraph) multiplied by the fraction determined under subparagraph (B).

(B) Determination of fraction.—For purposes of subparagraph (A), the fraction determined under this subparagraph is a fraction—

(i) the numerator of which is the excess (if any) of—

(I) the cost of such debt instrument incurred by the purchaser, over

(II) the issue price of such debt instrument, increased by the portion of original issue discount previously includible in the gross income of any holder (computed without regard to this paragraph), and

(ii) the denominator of which is the sum of the daily portions for such debt instrument for all days after the date of such purchase and ending on the stated maturity date (computed without regard to this paragraph).

(b) Ratable inclusion retained for corporate debt instruments issued before July 2, 1982.—

(1) General rule.—There shall be included in the gross income of the holder of any debt instrument issued by a corporation after May 27, 1969, and before July 2, 1982—

(A) the ratable monthly portion of original issue discount, multiplied by

(B) the number of complete months (plus any fractional part of a month determined under paragraph (3)) such holder held such debt instrument during the taxable year.

(2) Determination of ratable monthly portion.—Except as provided in paragraph (4), the ratable monthly portion of original issue discount shall equal—

(A) the original issue discount, divided by

(B) the number of complete months from the date of original issue to the stated maturity date of the debt instruments.

(3) Month defined.—For purposes of this subsection—

(A) Complete month.—A complete month commences with the date of original issue and the corresponding day of each succeeding calendar month (or the last day of a calendar month in which there is no corresponding day).

(B) Transfers during month.—In any case where a debt instrument is acquired on any day other than a day determined under subparagraph

(A), the ratable monthly portion of original issue discount for the complete month (or partial month) in which such acquisition occurs shall be allocated between the transferor and the transferee in accordance with the number of days in such complete (or partial) month each held the debt instrument.

(4) Reduction where subsequent holder pays acquisition premium.—

(A) Reduction.—For purposes of this subsection, the ratable monthly portion of original issue discount shall not include its share of the acquisition premium.

(B) Share of acquisition premium.—For purposes of subparagraph (A), any month's share of the acquisition premium is an amount (determined at the time of the purchase) equal to—

(i) the excess of—

(I) the cost of such debt instrument incurred by the holder, over

(II) the issue price of such debt instrument, increased by the portion of original issue discount previously includible in the gross income of any holder (computed without regard to this paragraph),

(ii) divided by the number of complete months (plus any fractional part of a month) from the date of such purchase to the stated maturity date of such debt instrument.

(c) Exceptions.—This section shall not apply to any holder—

(1) who has purchased the debt instrument at a premium, or

(2) which is a life insurance company to which section 811(b) applies.

(d) Definition and special rule.—

(1) Purchase defined.—For purposes of this section, the term "purchase" means—

(A) any acquisition of a debt instrument, where

(B) the basis of the debt instrument is not determined in whole or in part by reference to the adjusted basis of such debt instrument in the hands of the person from whom acquired.

(2) Basis adjustment.—The basis of any debt instrument in the hands of the holder thereof shall be increased by the amount included in his gross income pursuant to this section.

§ 1273. Determination of amount of original issue discount

(a) General rule.—For purposes of this subpart—

(1) In general.—The term "original issue discount" means the excess (if any) of—

(A) the stated redemption price at maturity, over

(B) the issue price.

(2) Stated redemption price at maturity.—The term "stated redemption price at maturity" means the amount fixed by the last modification of the purchase agreement and includes interest and other amounts payable at that time (other than any interest based on a fixed rate, and payable unconditionally at fixed periodic intervals of 1 year or less during the entire term of the debt instrument).

(3) ¼ of 1 percent de minimis rule.—If the original issue discount determined under paragraph (1) is less than—

(A) ¼ of 1 percent of the stated redemption price at maturity, multiplied by

(B) the number of complete years to maturity, then the original issue discount shall be treated as zero.

(b) Issue price.—For purposes of this subpart—

(1) Publicly offered debt instruments not issued for property.—In the case of any issue of debt instruments—

(A) publicly offered, and

(B) not issued for property,

the issue price is the initial offering price to the public (excluding bond houses and brokers) at which price a substantial amount of such debt instruments was sold.

(2) Other debt instruments not issue for property.—In the case of any issue of debt instruments not issued for property and not publicly offered, the issue price of each such instrument is the price paid by the first buyer of such debt instrument.

(3) Debt instruments issued for property where there is public trading.—In the case of a debt instrument which is issued for property and which—

(A) is part of an issue a portion of which is traded on an established securities market, or

(B)

(i) is issued for stock or securities which are traded on an established securities market, or

(ii) to the extent provided in regulations, is issued for property (other than stock or securities) of a kind regularly traded on an established market,

the issue price of such debt instrument shall be the fair market value of such property.

(4) Other cases.—Except in any case—

(A) to which paragraph (1), (2), or (3) of this subsection applies, or

(B) to which section 1274 applies,

the issue price of a debt instrument which is issued for property shall be the stated redemption price at maturity.

(5) Property.—In applying this subsection, the term "property" includes services and the right to use property, but such term does not include money.

(c) Special rules for applying subsection (b).—For purposes of subsection (b)—

(1) Initial offering price; price paid by the first buyer.—The terms "initial offering price" and "price paid by the first buyer" include the aggregate payments made by the purchaser under the purchase agreement, including modifications thereof.

(2) Treatment of investment units.—In the case of any debt instrument and an option, security, or other property issued together as an investment unit—

(A) the issue price for such unit shall be determined in accordance with the rules of this subsection and subsection (b) as if it were a debt instrument,

(B) the issue price determined for such unit shall be allocated to each element of such unit on the basis of the relationship of the fair market value of all elements in such unit, and

(C) the issue price of any debt instrument included in such unit shall be the portion of the issue price of the unit allocated to the debt instrument under subparagraph (B).

§ 1274. Determination of issue price in the case of certain debt instruments issued for property

(a) In general.—In the case of any debt instrument to which this section applies, for purposes of this subpart, the issue price shall be—

(1) where there is adequate stated interest, the stated principal amount, or

(2) in any other case, the imputed principal amount.

(b) Imputed principal amount.—For purposes of this section—

(1) In general.—Except as provided in paragraph (3), the imputed principal amount of any debt instrument shall be equal to the sum of the present values of all payments due under such debt instrument.

(2) Determination of present value.—For purposes of paragraph (1), the present value of a payment shall be determined in the manner provided by regulations prescribed by the Secretary—

(A) as of the date of the sale or exchange, and

(B) by using a discount rate equal to the applicable Federal rate, compounded semiannually.

(3) Fair market value rule in potentially abusive situations.—

(A) In general.—In the case of any potentially abusive situation, the imputed principal amount of any debt instrument received in exchange for property shall be the fair market value of such property adjusted to take into account other consideration involved in the transaction.

(B) Potentially abusive situation defined.—For purposes of subparagraph (A), the term "potentially abusive situation" means—

(i) a tax shelter (as defined in section 6662 (d)(2)(C)(iii), and

(ii) any other situation which, by reason of—

(I) recent sales transactions,

(II) nonrecourse financing,

(III) financing with a term in excess of the economic life of the property, or

(IV) other circumstances,

is of a type which the Secretary specifies by regulations as having potential for tax avoidance.

(c) Debt instruments to which section applies.—

(1) In general.—Except as otherwise provided in this subsection, this section shall apply to any debt instrument given in consideration for the sale or exchange of property if—

(A) the stated redemption price at maturity for such debt instrument exceeds—

(i) where there is adequate stated interest, the stated principal amount, or

(ii) in any other case, the imputed principal amount of such debt instrument determined under subsection (b), and

(B) some or all of the payments due under such debt instrument are due more than 6 months after the date of such sale or exchange.

(2) Adequate stated interest.—For purposes of this section, there is adequate stated interest with respect to any debt instrument if the stated principal amount for such debt instrument is less than or equal to the imputed principal amount of such debt instrument determined under subsection (b).

(3) Exceptions.—This section shall not apply to—

(A) Sales for $1,000,000 or less of farms by individuals or small businesses.—

(i) In general.—Any debt instrument arising from the sale or exchange of a farm (within the meaning of section 6420(c)(2))—

(I) by an individual, estate, or testamentary trust,

(II) by a corporation which as of the date of the sale or exchange is a small business corporation (as defined in section 1244(c)(3)), or

(III) by a partnership which as of the date of the sale or exchange meets requirements similar to those of section 1244(c)(3).

(ii) $1,000,000 limitation.—Clause (i) shall apply only if it can be determined at the time of the sale or exchange that the sales price cannot exceed $1,000,000. For purposes of the preceding sentence, all sales and exchanges which are part of the same transaction (or a series of related transactions) shall be treated as 1 sale or exchange.

(B) Sales of principal residences.—Any debt instrument arising from the sale or exchange by an individual of his principal residence (within the meaning of section 121).

(C) Sales involving total payments of $250,000 or less.—

(i) In general.—Any debt instrument arising from the sale or exchange of property if the sum of the following amounts does not exceed $250,000:

(I) the aggregate amount of the payments due under such debt instrument and all other debt instruments received as consideration for the sale or exchange, and

(II) the aggregate amount of any other consideration to be received for the sale or exchange.

(ii) Consideration other than debt instrument taken into account at fair market value.—For purposes of clause (i), any consideration (other than a debt instrument) shall be taken into account at its fair market value.

(iii) Aggregation of transactions.—For purposes of this subparagraph, all sales and exchanges which are part of the same transaction (or a series of related transactions) shall be treated as 1 sale or exchange.

(D) Debt instruments which are publicly traded or issued for publicly traded property.—Any debt instrument to which section 1273(b)(3) applies.

(E) Certain sales of patents.—In the case of any transfer described in section 1235(a) (relating to sale or exchange of patents), any amount contingent on the productivity, use, or disposition of the property transferred.

(F) Sales or exchanges to which section 483(e) applies.—Any debt instrument to the extent section 483(e) (relating to certain land transfers between related persons) applies to such instrument.

(4) Exception for assumptions.—If any person—

(A) in connection with the sale or exchange of property, assumes any debt instrument, or

(B) acquires any property subject to any debt instrument,

in determining whether this section or section 483 applies to such debt instrument, such assumption (or such acquisition) shall not be taken into account unless the terms and conditions of such debt instrument are modified (or the nature of the transaction is changed) in connection with the assumption (or acquisition).

(d) Determination of applicable federal rate.—For purposes of this section—

(1) Applicable federal rate.—

(A) In general.—

In the case of a debt instrument with a term of:	The applicable Federal rate is:
Not over 3 years	The Federal short-term rate
Over 3 years but not over 9 years	The Federal mid-term rate
Over 9 years	The Federal long-term rate

(B) Determination of rates.—During each calendar month, the Secretary shall determine the Federal short-term rate, mid-term rate, and long-term rate which shall apply during the following calendar month.

(C) Federal rate for any calendar month.—For purposes of this paragraph—

(i) Federal short-term rate.—The Federal short-term rate shall be the rate determined by the Secretary based on the average market yield (during any 1-month period selected by the Secretary and ending in the calendar month in which the determination is made) on outstanding marketable obligations of the United States with remaining periods to maturity of 3 years or less.

(ii) Federal mid-term and long-term rates.—The Federal mid-term and long-term rate shall be determined in accordance with the principles of clause (i).

(D) Lower rate permitted in certain cases.—The Secretary may by regulations permit a rate to be used with respect to any debt instrument which is lower than the applicable Federal rate if the taxpayer establishes to the satisfaction of the Secretary that such lower rate is based on the same principles as the applicable Federal rate and is appropriate for the term of such instrument.

(2) Lowest 3-month rate applicable to any sale or exchange.—

(A) In general.—In the case of any sale or exchange, the applicable Federal rate shall be the lowest 3-month rate.

(B) Lowest 3-month rate.—For purposes of subparagraph (A), the term "lowest 3-month rate" means the lowest of the applicable Federal rates in effect for any month in the 3- calendar-month period ending with the 1st calendar month in which there is a binding contract in writing for such sale or exchange.

(3) Term of debt instrument.—In determining the term of a debt instrument for purposes of this subsection, under regulations prescribed by the Secretary, there shall be taken into account options to renew or extend.

(e) 110 Percent rate where sale-leaseback involved.—

(1) In general.—In the case of any debt instrument to which this subsection applies, the discount rate used under subsection (b)(2)(B) or section 483(b) shall be 110 percent of the applicable Federal rate, compounded semiannually.

(2) Lower discount rates shall not apply.—Section 1274A shall not apply to any debt instrument to which this subsection applies.

(3) Debt instruments to which this subsection applies.—This subsection shall apply to any debt instrument given in consideration for the sale or exchange of any property if, pursuant to a plan, the transferor or any related person leases a portion of such property after such sale or exchange.

§ 1274A. Special rules for certain transactions where stated principal amount does not exceed $2,800,000*

(a) Lower discount rate.—In the case of any qualified debt instrument, the discount rate used for purposes of sections 483 and 1274 shall not exceed 9 percent, compounded semiannually.

(b) Qualified debt instrument defined.—For purposes of this section, the term "qualified debt instrument" means any debt instrument given in consideration for the sale or exchange of property (other than new section 38 property within the meaning of section 48(b), as in effect on the day before the date of the enactment of the Revenue Reconciliation Act of 1990) if the stated principal amount of such instrument does not exceed $2,800,000.*

(c) Election to use cash method where stated principal amount does not exceed $2,000,000.**—

*Editorial comment: The indexed amount for 2013 is $5,468,200, and for 2014 is $5,557,200.

**Editorial comment: The indexed amount for 2013 is $3,905,900, and for 2014 is $3,969,500.

(1) In general.—In the case of any cash method debt instrument—

(A) section 1274 shall not apply, and

(B) interest on such debt instrument shall be taken into account by both the borrower and the lender under the cash receipts and disbursements method of accounting.

(2) Cash method debt instrument.—For purposes of paragraph (1), the term "cash method debt instrument" means any qualified debt instrument if—

(A) the stated principal amount does not exceed $2,000,000,*

(B) the lender does not use an accrual method of accounting and is not a dealer with respect to the property sold or exchanged,

(C) section 1274 would have applied to such instrument but for an election under this subsection, and

(D) an election under this subsection is jointly made with respect to such debt instrument by the borrower and lender.

(3) Successors bound by election.—

(A) In general.—Except as provided in subparagraph (B), paragraph (1) shall apply to any successor to the borrower or lender with respect to a cash method debt instrument.

(B) Exception where lender transfers debt instrument to accrual method taxpayer.—If the lender (or any successor) transfers any cash method debt instrument to a taxpayer who uses an accrual method of accounting, this paragraph shall not apply with respect to such instrument for periods after such transfer.

(4) Fair market value rule in potentially abusive situations.—In the case of any cash method debt instrument, section 483 shall be applied as if it included provisions similar to the provisions of section 1274(b)(3).

(d) Other special rules.—

(1) Aggregation rules.—For purposes of this section—

(A) all sales or exchanges which are part of the same transaction (or a series of related transactions) shall be treated as 1 sale or exchange, and

(B) all debt instruments arising from the same transaction (or a series of related transactions) shall be treated as 1 debt instrument.

(2) Inflation adjustments.—

(A) In general.—In the case of any debt instrument arising out of a sale or exchange during any calendar year after 1989, each dollar amount contained in the preceding provisions of this section shall be increased by the inflation adjustment for such calendar year. Any increase under the preceding sentence shall be rounded to the nearest multiple of $100 (or, if such increase is a multiple of $50, such increase shall be increased to the nearest multiple of $100).

(B) Inflation adjustment.—For purposes of subparagraph (A), the inflation adjustment for any calendar year is the percentage (if any) by which—

(i) the CPI for the preceding calendar year exceeds

(ii) the CPI for calendar year 1988.

For purposes of the preceding sentence, the CPI for any calendar year is the average of the Consumer Price Index as of the close of the 12-month period ending on September 30 of such calendar year.

(e) Regulations.—The Secretary shall prescribe such regulations as may be necessary to carry out the purposes of this subsection, including—

(1) regulations coordinating the provisions of this section with other provisions of this title,

(2) regulations necessary to prevent the avoidance of tax through the abuse of the provisions of subsection (c), and

(3) regulations relating to the treatment of transfers of cash method debt instruments.

§ 1275. Other definitions and special rules

(a) Definitions.—For purposes of this subpart—

(1) Debt instrument.—

(A) In general.—Except as provided in subparagraph (B), the term "debt instrument" means a bond, debenture, note, or certificate or other evidence of indebtedness.

(B) Exception for certain annuity contracts.—The term "debt instrument" shall not include any annuity contract to which section 72 applies and which—

*Editorial comment: The indexed amount for 2013 is $3,905,900, and for 2014 is $3,969,500.

(i) depends (in whole or in substantial part) on the life expectancy of 1 or more individuals, or

(ii) is issued by an insurance company subject to tax under subchapter L (or by an entity described in section 501(c) and exempt from tax under section 501(a) which would be subject to tax under subchapter L were it not so exempt)—

(I) in a transaction in which there is no consideration other than cash or another annuity contract meeting the requirements of this clause,

(II) pursuant to the exercise of an election under an insurance contract by a beneficiary thereof on the death of the insured party under such contract, or

(III) in a transaction involving a qualified pension or employee benefit plan.

(2) Issue date.—

(A) Publicly offered debt instruments.—In the case of any debt instrument which is publicly offered, the term "date of original issue" means the date on which the issue was first issued to the public.

(B) Issues not publicly offered and not issued for property.—In the case of any debt instrument to which section 1273(b)(2) applies, the term "date of original issue" means the date on which the debt instrument was sold by the issuer.

(C) Other debt instruments.—In the case of any debt instrument not described in subparagraph (A) or (B), the term "date of original issue" means the date on which the debt instrument was issued in a sale or exchange.

(3) Tax-exempt obligation.—The term "tax-exempt obligation" means any obligation if—

(A) the interest on such obligation is not includible in gross income under section 103, or

(B) the interest on such obligation is exempt from tax (without regard to the identity of the holder) under any other provision of law.

(4) Treatment of obligations distributed by corporations.—Any debt obligation of a corporation distributed by such corporation with respect to its stock shall be treated as if it had been issued by such corporation for property.

(b) Treatment of borrower in the case of certain loans for personal use.—

(1) Sections 1274 and 483 not to apply.—In the case of the obligor under any debt instrument given in consideration for the sale or exchange of property, sections 1274 and 483 shall not apply if such property is personal use property.

(2) Original issue discount deducted on cash basis in certain cases.—In the case of any debt instrument, if—

(A) such instrument—

(i) is incurred in connection with the acquisition or carrying of personal use property, and

(ii) has original issue discount (determined after the application of paragraph (1)), and

(B) the obligor under such instrument uses the cash receipts and disbursements method of accounting,

notwithstanding section 163(e), the original issue discount on such instrument shall be deductible only when paid.

(3) Personal use property.—For purposes of this subsection, the term "personal use property" means any property substantially all of the use of which by the taxpayer is not in connection with a trade or business of the taxpayer or an activity described in section 212. The determination of whether property is described in the preceding sentence shall be made as of the time of issuance of the debt instrument.

(c) Information requirements.—

(1) Information required to be set forth on instrument.—

(A) In general.—In the case of any debt instrument having original issue discount, the Secretary may by regulations require that—

(i) the amount of the original issue discount, and

(ii) the issue date,

be set forth on such instrument.

(B) Special rule for instruments not publicly offered.—In the case of any issue of debt instruments not publicly offered, the regulations prescribed under subparagraph (A) shall not require the information to be set forth on the debt instrument before any disposition of such instrument by the first buyer.

(2) Information required to be submitted to secretary.—In the case of any issue of publicly offered debt instruments having original issue discount, the issuer shall (at such time and in such manner as the Secretary shall by regulation prescribe) furnish the Secretary the following information:

(A) The amount of the original issue discount.

(B) The issue date.

(C) Such other information with respect to the issue as the Secretary may by regulations require.

For purposes of the preceding sentence, any person who makes a public offering of stripped bonds (or stripped coupons) shall be treated as the issuer of a publicly offered debt instrument having original issue discount.

(3) Exceptions.—This subsection shall not apply to any obligation referred to in section 1272(a)(2) (relating to exceptions from current inclusion of original issue discount).

* * *

SUBPART B—MARKET DISCOUNT ON BONDS

§ 1276. Disposition gain representing accrued market discount treated as ordinary income

(a) Ordinary income.—

(1) In general.—Except as otherwise provided in this section, gain on the disposition of any market discount bond shall be treated as ordinary income to the extent it does not exceed the accrued market discount on such bond. Such gain shall be recognized notwithstanding any other provision of this subtitle.

(2) Dispositions other than sales, etc.—For purposes of paragraph (1), a person disposing of any market discount bond in any transaction other than a sale, exchange, or involuntary conversion shall be treated as realizing an amount equal to the fair market value of the bond.

(3) Treatment of partial principal payments.—

(A) In general.—Any partial principal payment on a market discount bond shall be included in gross income as ordinary income to the extent such payment does not exceed the accrued market discount on such bond.

(B) Adjustment.—If subparagraph (A) applies to any partial principal payment on any market discount bond, for purposes of applying this section to any disposition of (or subsequent partial principal payment on) such bond, the amount of accrued market discount shall be reduced by the amount of such partial principal payment included in gross income under subparagraph (A).

(4) Gain treated as interest for certain purposes.—Except for purposes of sections 103, 871(a), 881, 1441, 1442, and 6049 (and such other provisions as may be specified in regulations), any amount treated as ordinary income under paragraph (1) or (3) shall be treated as interest for purposes of this title.

(b) Accrued market discount.—For purposes of this section—

(1) Ratable accrual.—Except as otherwise provided in this subsection or subsection (c), the accrued market discount on any bond shall be an amount which bears the same ratio to the market discount on such bond as—

(A) the number of days which the taxpayer held the bond, bears to

(B) the number of days after the date the taxpayer acquired the bond and up to (and including) the date of its maturity.

(2) Election of accrual on basis of constant interest rate (in lieu of ratable accrual).—

(A) In general.—At the election of the taxpayer with respect to any bond, the accrued market discount on such bond shall be the aggregate amount which would have been includible in the gross income of the taxpayer under section 1272(a) (determined without regard to paragraph (2) thereof) with respect to such bond for all periods during which the bond was held by the taxpayer if such bond had been—

(i) originally issued on the date on which such bond was acquired by the taxpayer,

(ii) for an issue price equal to the basis of the taxpayer in such bond immediately after its acquisition.

(B) Coordination where bond has original issue discount.—In the case of any bond having original issue discount, for purposes of applying subparagraph (A)—

(i) the stated redemption price at maturity of such bond shall be treated as equal to its revised issue price, and

(ii) the determination of the portion of the original issue discount which would have been includible in the gross income of the taxpayer under section 1272(a) shall be made under regulations prescribed by the Secretary.

(C) Election irrevocable.—An election under subparagraph (A), once made with respect to any bond, shall be irrevocable.

(3) Special rule where partial principal payments.—In the case of a bond the principal of which may be paid in 2 or more payments, the amount of accrued market discount shall be determined under regulations prescribed by the Secretary.

(c) Treatment of nonrecognition transactions.—Under regulations prescribed by the Secretary—

(1) Transferred basis property.—If a market discount bond is transferred in a nonrecognition transaction and such bond is transferred basis property in the hands of the transferee, for purposes of determining the amount of the accrued market discount with respect to the transferee—

(A) the transferee shall be treated as having acquired the bond on the date on which it was acquired by the transferor for an amount equal to the basis of the transferor, and

(B) proper adjustments shall be made for gain recognized by the transferor on such transfer (and for any original issue discount or market discount included in the gross income of the transferor).

(2) Exchanged basis property.—If any market discount bond is disposed of by the taxpayer in a nonrecognition transaction and paragraph (1) does not apply to such transaction, any accrued market discount determined with respect to the property disposed of to the extent not theretofore treated as ordinary income under subsection (a)—

(A) shall be treated as accrued market discount with respect to the exchanged basis property received by the taxpayer in such transaction if such property is a market discount bond, and

(B) shall be treated as ordinary income on the disposition of the exchanged basis property received by the taxpayer in such exchange if such property is not a market discount bond.

(3) Paragraph (1) to apply to certain distributions by corporations or partnerships.—For purposes of paragraph (1), if the basis of any market discount bond in the hands of a transferee is determined under section 732(a), or 732(b), such property shall be treated as transferred basis property in the hands of such transferee.

(d) Special rules.—Under regulations prescribed by the Secretary—

(1) rules similar to the rules of subsection (b) of section 1245 shall apply for purposes of this section; except that—

(A) paragraph (1) of such subsection shall not apply,

(B) an exchange qualifying under section 354(a), 355(a), or 356(a) (determined without regard to subsection (a) of this section) shall be treated as an exchange described in paragraph (3) of such subsection, and

(C) paragraph (3) of section 1245(b) shall be applied as if it did not contain a reference to section 351, and

(2) appropriate adjustments shall be made to the basis of any property to reflect gain recognized under subsection (a).

§ 1277. Deferral of interest deduction allocable to accrued market discount

(a) General rule.—Except as otherwise provided in this section, the net direct interest expense with respect to any market discount bond shall be allowed as a deduction for the taxable year only to the extent that such expense exceeds the portion of the market discount allocable to the days during the taxable year on which such bond was held by the taxpayer (as determined under the rules of section 1276(b)).

(b) Disallowed deduction allowed for later years.—

(1) Election to take into account in later year where net interest income from bond.—

(A) In general.—If—

(i) there is net interest income for any taxable year with respect to any market discount bond, and

(ii) the taxpayer makes an election under this subparagraph with respect to such bond,

Any disallowed interest expense with respect to such bond shall be treated as interest paid or accrued by the taxpayer during such taxable year to the extent such disallowed interest expense does not exceed the net interest income with respect to such bond.

(B) Determination of disallowed interest expense.—For purposes of subparagraph (A), the amount of the disallowed interest expense—

(i) shall be determined as of the close of the preceding taxable year, and

(ii) shall not include any amount previously taken into account under subparagraph (A).

(C) Net interest income.—For purposes of this paragraph, the term "net interest income" means the excess of the amount determined under paragraph (2) of subsection (c) over the amount determined under paragraph (1) of subsection (c).

(2) Remainder of disallowed interest expense allowed for year of disposition.—

(A) In general.—Except as otherwise provided in this paragraph, the amount of the disallowed interest expense with respect to any market discount bond shall be treated as interest paid or accrued by the taxpayer in the taxable year in which such bond is disposed of.

(B) Nonrecognition transactions.—If any market discount bond is disposed of in a nonrecognition transaction—

(i) the disallowed interest expense with respect to such bond shall be treated as interest paid or accrued in the year of disposition only to the extent of the amount of gain recognized on such disposition, and

(ii) the disallowed interest expense with respect to such property (to the extent not so treated) shall be treated as disallowed interest expense—

(I) in the case of a transaction described in section 1276(c)(1), of the transferee with respect to the transferee basis property, or

(II) in the case of a transaction described in section 1276(c)(2), with respect to the exchanged basis property.

(C) Disallowed interest expense reduced for amounts previously taken into account under paragraph (1).—For purposes of this paragraph, the amount of the disallowed interest expense shall not include any amount previously taken into account under paragraph (1).

(3) Disallowed interest expense.—For purposes of this subsection, the term "disallowed interest expense" means the aggregate amount disallowed under subsection (a) with respect to the market discount bond.

(c) Net direct interest expense.—For purposes of this section, the term "net direct interest expense" means, with respect to any market discount bond, the excess (if any) of—

(1) the amount of interest paid or accrued during the taxable year on indebtedness which is incurred or continued to purchase or carry such bond, over

(2) the aggregate amount of interest (including original issue discount) includible in gross income for the taxable year with respect to such bond.

* * *

§ 1278. Definitions and special rules

(a) In general.—For purposes of this part—

(1) Market discount bond.—

(A) In general.—Except as provided in subparagraph (B), the term "market discount bond" means any bond having market discount.

(B) Exceptions.—The term "market discount bond" shall not include—

(i) Short-term obligations.—Any obligation with a fixed maturity date not exceeding 1 year from the date of issue.

(ii) United States savings bonds.—Any United States savings bond.

(iii) Installment obligations.—Any installment obligation to which section 453B applies.

(C) Section 1277 not applicable to tax-exempt obligations.—For purposes of section 1277, the term "market discount bond" shall not include any tax-exempt obligation (as defined in section 1275(a)(3)).

(D) Treatment of bonds acquired at original issue.—

(i) In general.—Except as otherwise provided in this subparagraph or in regulations, the term "market discount bond" shall not include any bond acquired by the taxpayer at its original issue.

(ii) Treatment of bonds acquired for less than issue price.—Clause (i) shall not apply to any bond if—

(I) the basis of the taxpayer in such bond is determined under section 1012, and

(II) such basis is less than the issue price of such bond determined under subpart A of this part.

(iii) Bonds acquired in certain reorganizations.—Clause (i) shall not apply to any bond issued pursuant to a plan of reorganization (within the meaning of section 368(a)(1)) in exchange for another bond having market discount. Solely for purposes of section 1276, the preceding sentence shall not apply if such other bond was issued on or before July 18, 1984 (the date of the enactment of section 1276) and if the bond issued pursuant to such plan of reorganization has the same term and the same interest rate as such other bond had.

(iv) Treatment of certain transferred basis property.—For purposes of clause (i), if the adjusted basis of any bond in the hands of the taxpayer is determined by reference to the adjusted basis of such bond in the hands of a person who acquired such bond at its original issue, such bond shall be treated as acquired by the taxpayer at its original issue.

(2) Market discount.—

(A) In general.—The term "market discount" means the excess (if any) of—

(i) the stated redemption price of the bond at maturity, over

(ii) the basis of such bond immediately after its acquisition by the taxpayer.

(B) Coordination where bond has original issue discount.—In the case of any bond having original issue discount, for purposes of subparagraph (A), the stated redemption price of such bond at maturity shall be treated as equal to its revised issue price.

(C) De minimis rule.—If the market discount is less than ¼ of 1 percent of the stated redemption price of the bond at maturity multiplied by the number of complete years to maturity (after the taxpayer acquired the bond), then the market discount shall be considered to be zero.

(3) Bond.—The term "bond" means any bond, debenture, note, certificate, or other evidence of indebtedness.

(4) Revised issue price.—The term "revised issue price" means the sum of—

(A) the issue price of the bond, and

(B) the aggregate amount of the original issue discount includible in the gross income of all holders for periods before the acquisition of the bond by the taxpayer (determined without regard to section 1272(a)(7) or (b)(4)) or, in the case of a tax-exempt obligation, the aggregate amount of the original issue discount which accrued in the manner provided by section 1272(a) (determined without regard to paragraph (7) thereof) during periods before the acquisition of the bond by the taxpayer.

(5) Original issue discount, etc.—The terms "original issue discount," "stated redemption price at maturity," and "issue price" have the respective meanings given such terms by subpart A of this part.

(b) Election to include market discount currently.—

(1) In general.—If the taxpayer makes an election under this subsection—

(A) sections 1276 and 1277 shall not apply, and

(B) market discount on any market discount bond shall be included in the gross income of the taxpayer for the taxable years to which it is attributable (as determined under the rules of subsection (b) of section 1276).

Except for purposes of sections 103, 871(a), 881, 1441, 1442, and 6049 (and such other provisions as may be specified in regulations), any amount included in gross income under subparagraph (B) shall be treated as interest for purposes of this title.

(2) Scope of election.—An election under this subsection shall apply to all market discount bonds acquired by the taxpayer on or after the 1st day of the 1st taxable year to which such election applies.

(3) Period to which election applies.—An election under this subsection shall apply to the taxable year for which it is made and for all subsequent taxable years, unless the taxpayer secures the consent of the Secretary to the revocation of such election.

(4) Basis adjustment.—The basis of any bond in the hands of the taxpayer shall be increased by the amount included in gross income pursuant to this subsection.

(c) Regulations.—The Secretary shall prescribe such regulations as may be necessary to carry out the purposes of this subpart, including regulations providing proper adjustments in the case of a bond the principal of which may be paid in 2 or more payments.

SUBPART C—DISCOUNT ON SHORT—TERM OBLIGATIONS

§ 1281. Current inclusion in income of discount on certain short-term obligations

(a) General rule.—In the case of any short-term obligation to which this section applies, for purposes of this title—

(1) there shall be included in the gross income of the holder an amount equal to the sum of the daily portions of the acquisition discount for each day during the taxable year on which such holder held such obligation, and

(2) any interest payable on the obligation (other than interest taken into account in determining the amount of the acquisition discount) shall be included in gross income as it accrues.

(b) Short-term obligations to which section applies.—

(1) In general.—This section shall apply to any short-term obligation which—

(A) is held by a taxpayer using an accrual method of accounting,

(B) is held primarily for sale to customers in the ordinary course of the taxpayer's trade or business,

(C) is held by a bank (as defined in section 581),

(D) is held by a regulated investment company or a common trust fund,

(E) is identified by the taxpayer under section 1256(e)(2) as being part of a hedging transaction, or

(F) is a stripped bond or stripped coupon held by the person who stripped the bond or coupon (or by any other person whose basis is determined by reference to the basis in the hands of such person).

(2) Treatment of obligations held by pass-thru entities.—

(A) In general.—This section shall apply also to—

(i) any short-term obligation which is held by a pass-thru entity which is formed or availed of for purposes of avoiding the provisions of this section, and

(ii) any short-term obligation which is acquired by a pass-thru entity (not described in clause (i)) during the required accrual period.

(B) Required accrual period.—For purposes of subparagraph (A), the term "required accrual period" means the period—

(i) which begins with the first taxable year for which the ownership test of subparagraph (C) is met with respect to the pass-thru entity (or a predecessor), and

(ii) which ends with the first taxable year after the taxable year referred to in clause (i) for which the ownership test of subparagraph (C) is not met and with respect to which the Secretary consents to the termination of the required accrual period.

(C) Ownership test.—The ownership test of this subparagraph is met for any taxable year if, on at least 90 days during the taxable year, 20 percent or more of the value of the interests in the pass-thru entity are held by persons described in paragraph (1) or by other pass-thru entities to which subparagraph (A) applies.

(D) Pass-thru entity.—The term "pass-thru entity" means any partnership, S corporation, trust, or other pass-thru entity.

(c) Cross reference.—

For special rules limiting the application of this section to original issue discount in the case of nongovernmental obligations, see section 1283(c).

§ 1282. Deferral of interest deduction allocable to accrued discount

(a) General rule.—Except as otherwise provided in this section, the net direct interest expense with respect to any short-term obligation shall be allowed as a deduction for the taxable year only to the extent such expense exceeds the sum of—

(1) the daily portions of the acquisition discount for each day during the taxable year on which the taxpayer held such obligation, and

(2) the amount of any interest payable on the obligation (other than interest taken into account in determining the amount of the acquisition discount) which accrues during the taxable year while the taxpayer held such obligation (and is not included in the gross income of the taxpayer for such taxable year by reason of the taxpayer's method of accounting).

(b) Section not to apply to obligations to which section 1281 applies.—

(1) In general.—This section shall not apply to any short-term obligation to which section 1281 applies.

(2) Election to have section 1281 apply to all obligations.—

(A) In general.—A taxpayer may make an election under this paragraph to have section 1281 apply to all short-term obligations acquired by the taxpayer on or after the 1st day of the 1st taxable year to which such election applies.

(B) Period to which election applies.—An election under this paragraph shall apply to the taxable year for which it is made and for all subsequent taxable years, unless the taxpayer secures the consent of the Secretary to the revocation of such election.

(c) Certain rules made applicable.—Rules similar to the rules of subsections (b) and (c) of section 1277 shall apply for purposes of this section.

(d) Cross reference.—

For special rules limiting the application of this section to original issue discount in the case of nongovernmental obligations, see section 1283(c).

§ 1283. Definitions and special rules

(a) Definitions.—For purposes of this subpart—

(1) Short-term obligation.—

(A) In general.—Except as provided in subparagraph (B), the term "short-term obligation" means any bond, debenture, note, certificate, or other evidence of indebtedness which has a fixed maturity date not more than 1 year from the date of issue.

(B) Exceptions for tax-exempt obligations.—The term "short-term obligation" shall not include any tax-exempt obligation (as defined in section 1275(a)(3)).

(2) Acquisition discount.—The term "acquisition discount" means the excess of—

(A) the stated redemption price at maturity (as defined in section 1273), over

(B) the taxpayer's basis for the obligation.

(b) Daily portion.—For purposes of the subpart—

(1) Ratable accrual.—Except as otherwise provided in this subsection, the daily portion of the acquisition discount is an amount equal to—

(A) the amount of such discount, divided by

(B) the number of days after the day on which the taxpayer acquired the obligation and up to (and including) the day of its maturity.

(2) Election of accrual on basis of constant interest rate (in lieu of ratable accrual).—

(A) In general.—At the election of the taxpayer with respect to any obligation, the daily portion of the acquisition discount for any day is the portion of the acquisition discount accruing on such day determined (under regulations prescribed by the Secretary) on the basis of—

(i) the taxpayer's yield to maturity based on the taxpayer's cost of acquiring the obligation, and

(ii) compounding daily.

(B) Election irrevocable.—An election under subparagraph (A), once made with respect to any obligation, shall be irrevocable.

(c) Special rules for nongovernmental obligations.—

(1) In general.—In the case of any short-term obligation which is not a short-term Government obligation (as defined in section 1271(a)(3)(B))—

(A) sections 1281 and 1282 shall be applied by taking into account original issue discount in lieu of acquisition discount, and

(B) appropriate adjustments shall be made in the application of subsection (b) of this section.

(2) Election to have paragraph (1) not apply.—

(A) In general.—A taxpayer may make an election under this paragraph to have paragraph (1) not apply to all obligations acquired by the taxpayer on or after the first day of the first taxable year to which such election applies.

(B) Period to which election applies.—An election under this paragraph shall apply to the taxable year for which it is made and for all subsequent taxable years, unless the taxpayer secures the consent of the Secretary to the revocation of such election.

(d) Other special rules.—

(1) Basis adjustments.—The basis of any short-term obligation in the hands of the holder thereof shall be increased by the amount included in his gross income pursuant to section 1281.

(2) Double inclusion in income not required.—Section 1281 shall not require the inclusion of any amount previously includible in gross income.

(3) Coordination with other provisions.—Section 454(b) and paragraphs (3) and (4) of section 1271(a) shall not apply to any short-term obligation to which section 1281 applies.

SUBPART D—MISCELLANEOUS PROVISIONS

§ 1286. Tax treatment of stripped bonds

(a) Inclusion in income as if bond and coupons were original issue discount bonds.—If any person purchases after July 1, 1982, a stripped bond or a stripped coupon, then such bond or coupon while held by such purchaser (or by any other person whose basis is determined by reference to the basis in the hands of such purchaser) shall be treated for purposes of this part as a bond originally issued on the purchase date and having an original issue discount equal to the excess (if any) of—

(1) the stated redemption price at maturity (or, in the case of coupon, the amount payable on the due date of such coupon), over

(2) such bond's or coupon's ratable share of the purchase price.

For purposes of paragraph (2), ratable shares shall be determined on the basis of their respective fair market values on the date of purchase.

(b) Tax treatment of person stripping bond.—For purposes of this subtitle, if any person strips 1 or more coupons from a bond and after July 1, 1982, disposes of the bond or such coupon—

(1) such person shall include in gross income an amount equal to the sum of—

(A) the interest accrued on such bond while held by such person and before the time such coupon or bond was disposed of (to the extent such interest has not theretofore been included in such person's gross income), and

(B) the accrued market discount on such bond determined as of the time such coupon or bond was disposed of (to the extent such discount has not theretofore been included in such person's gross income),

(2) the basis of the bond and coupons shall be increased by the amount included in gross income under paragraph (1),

(3) the basis of the bond and coupons immediately before the disposition (as adjusted pursuant to paragraph (2)) shall be allocated among the items retained by such person and the items disposed of by such person on the basis of their respective fair market values, and

(4) for purposes of subsection (a), such person shall be treated as having purchased on the date of such disposition each such item which he retains for an amount equal to the basis allocated to such item under paragraph (3).

A rule similar to the rule of paragraph (4) shall apply in the case of any person whose basis in any bond or coupon is determined by reference to the basis of the person described in the preceding sentence.

(c) Retention of existing law for stripped bonds purchased before July 2, 1982.—If a bond issued at any time with interest coupons—

(1) is purchased after August 16, 1954, and before January 1, 1958, and the purchaser does not receive all the coupons which first become payable more than 12 months after the date of the purchase, or

(2) is purchased after December 31, 1957, and before July 2, 1982, and the purchaser does not receive all the coupons which first become payable after the date of the purchase,

then the gain on the sale or other disposition of such bond by such purchaser (or by a person whose basis is determined by reference to the basis in the hands of such purchaser) shall be considered as ordinary income to the extent that the fair market value (determined as of the time of the purchase) of the bond with coupons attached exceeds the purchase price. If this subsection and section 1271(a)(2)(A) apply with respect to gain realized on the sale or exchange of any evidence of indebtedness, then section 1271(a) (2)(A) shall apply with respect to that part of the gain to which this subsection does not apply.

(d) Special rules for tax-exempt obligations.—

(1) In general.—In the case of any tax-exempt obligation (as defined in section 1275(a)(3)) from which 1 or more coupons have been stripped—

(A) the amount of the original issue discount determined under subsection (a) with respect to any stripped bond or stripped coupon—

(i) shall be treated as original issue discount on a tax-exempt obligation to the extent such discount does not exceed the tax-exempt portion of such discount, and

(ii) shall be treated as original issue discount on an obligation which is not a tax-exempt obligation to the extent such discount exceeds the tax-exempt portion of such discount,

(B) subsection (b)(1)(A) shall not apply, and

(C) subsection (b)(2) shall be applied by increasing the basis of the bond or coupon by the sum of—

(i) the interest accrued but not paid before such bond or coupon was disposed of (and not previously reflected in basis), plus

(ii) the amount included in gross income under subsection (b)(1)(B).

(2) Tax-exempt portion.—For purposes of paragraph (1), the tax-exempt portion of the original issue discount determined under subsection (a) is the excess of—

(A) the amount referred to in subsection (a)(1), over

(B) an issue price which would produce a yield to maturity as of the purchase date equal to the lower of—

(i) the coupon rate of interest on the obligation from which the coupons were separated, or

(ii) the yield to maturity (on the basis of the purchase price) of the stripped obligation or coupon.

The purchaser of any stripped obligation or coupon may elect to apply clause (i) by substituting "original yield to maturity of" for "coupon rate of interest on."

(e) Definitions and special rules.—For purposes of this section—

(1) Bond.—The term "bond" means a bond, debenture, note, or certificate or other evidence of indebtedness.

(2) Stripped bond.—The term "stripped bond" means a bond issued at any time with interest coupons where there is a separation in ownership between the bond and any coupon which has not yet become payable.

(3) Stripped coupon.—The term "stripped coupon" means any coupon relating to a stripped bond.

(4) Stated redemption price at maturity.—The term "stated redemption price at maturity" has the meaning given such term by section 1273(a)(2).

(5) Coupon.—The term "coupon" includes any right to receive interest on a bond (whether or not evidenced by a coupon). This paragraph shall apply for purposes of subsection (c) only in the case of purchases after July 1, 1982.

(6) Purchase.—The term "purchase" has the meaning given such term by section 1272(d)(1).

(f) Treatment of stripped interests in bond and preferred stock funds, etc.—In the case of an account or entity substantially all of the assets of which consist of bonds, preferred stock, or a combination thereof, the Secretary may by regulations provide that rules similar to the rules of this section and section 305(e), as appropriate, shall apply to interests in such account or entity to which (but for this subsection) this section or section 305(e), as the case may be, would not apply.

(g) Regulation authority.—The Secretary may prescribe regulations providing that where, by reason of varying rates of interest, put or call options, or other circumstances, the tax treatment under this section does not accurately reflect the income of the holder of a stripped coupon or stripped bond, or of the person disposing of such bond or coupon, as the case may be, for any period, such treatment shall be modified to require that the proper amount of income be included for such period.

§ 1287. Denial of capital gain treatment for gains on certain obligations not in registered form

(a) In general.—If any registration-required obligation is not in registered form, any gain on the sale or other disposition of such obligation shall be treated as ordinary income (unless the issuance of such obligation was subject to tax under section 4701).

(b) Definitions.—For purposes of subsection (a)—

(1) Registration-required obligation.—The term "registration-required obligation" has the meaning given to such term by section 163(f)(2).

(2) **Registered form.**—The term "registered form" has the same meaning as when used in section 163(f).

§ 1288. Treatment of original issue discount on tax-exempt obligations

(a) General rule.—Original issue discount on any tax-exempt obligation shall be treated as accruing—

(1) for purposes of section 163, in the manner provided by section 1272(a) (determined without regard to paragraph (7) thereof), and

(2) for purposes of determining the adjusted basis of the holder, in the manner provided by section 1272(a) (determined with regard to paragraph (7) thereof).

(b) Definitions and special rules.—For purposes of this section—

(1) **Original issue discount.**—The term "original issue discount" has the meaning given to such term by section 1273(a) without regard to paragraph (3) thereof. In applying section 483 or 1274, under regulations prescribed by the Secretary, appropriate adjustments shall be made to the applicable Federal rate to take into account the tax exemption for interest on the obligation.

(2) **Tax-exempt obligation.**—The term "tax-exempt obligation" has the meaning given to such term by section 1275(a)(3).

(3) **Short-term obligations.**—In applying this section to obligations with maturity of 1 year or less, rules similar to the rules of section 1283(b) shall apply.

* * *

PART VI—TREATMENT OF CERTAIN PASSIVE FOREIGN INVESTMENT COMPANIES*

SUBCHAPTER Q—READJUSTMENT OF TAX BETWEEN YEARS AND SPECIAL LIMITATIONS

PART I—INCOME AVERAGING

Editorial Summary

Income Averaging for Farmers

Subchapter Q (Sec. 1301)

Section 1301 provides a procedure by which farmers can elect to average farm income over a 3-year period and thereby reduce their tax liability.

§ 1301. Averaging of farm income

(a) In general.—At the election of an individual engaged in a farming business or fishing business, the tax imposed by section 1 for such taxable year shall be equal to the sum of—

(1) a tax computed under such section on taxable income reduced by elected farm income, plus

(2) the increase in tax imposed by section 1 which would result if taxable income for each of the 3 prior taxable years were increased by an amount equal to one-third of the elected farm income.

Any adjustment under this section for any taxable year shall be taken into account in applying this section for any subsequent taxable year.

(b) Definitions.—In this section—

(1) **Elected farm income.**—

(A) **In general.**—The term "elected farm income" means so much of the taxable income for the taxable year—

(i) which is attributable to any farming business or fishing business; and

*Omitted.

(ii) which is specified in the election under subsection (a).

(B) **Treatment of gains.**—For purposes of subparagraph (A), gain from the sale or other disposition of property (other than land) regularly used by the taxpayer in such a farming business for a substantial period shall be treated as attributable to such a farming business or fishing business.

(2) **Individual.**—The term "individual" shall not include any estate or trust.

(3) **Farming business.**—The term "farming business" has the meaning given such term by section 263A(e)(4).

(4) **Fishing business.**—The term "fishing business" means the conduct of commercial fishing as defined in section 3 of the Magnuson-Stevens Fishery Conservation and Management Act (16 U.S.C. 1802).

(c) **Regulations.**—The Secretary shall prescribe such regulations as may be appropriate to carry out the purposes of this section, including regulation regarding—

(1) the order and manner in which items of income, gain, deduction, or loss, or limitations on tax, shall be taken into account in computing the tax imposed by this chapter on the income of any taxpayer to whom this section applies for any taxable year, and

(2) the treatment of any short taxable year.

PART II—MITIGATION OF EFFECT OF LIMITATIONS AND OTHER PROVISIONS

Editorial Summary

Mitigation of Limitations

Subchapter Q (Secs. 1311–1314)

Sections 1311–1314 permit error corrections that otherwise would not be permitted under the Code.

§ 1311. Correction of error

(a) **General rule.**—If a determination (as defined in section 1313) is described in one or more of the paragraphs of section 1312 and, on the date of the determination, correction of the effect of the error referred to in the applicable paragraph of section 1312 is prevented by the operation of any law or rule of law, other than this part and other than section 7122 (relating to compromises), then the effect of the error shall be corrected by an adjustment made in the amount and in the manner specified in section 1314.

(b) **Conditions necessary for adjustment.**—

(1) **Maintenance of an inconsistent position.**—Except in cases described in paragraphs (3)(B) and (4) of section 1312, an adjustment shall be made under this part only if—

(A) in case the amount of the adjustment would be credited or refunded in the same manner as an overpayment under section 1314, there is adopted in the determination a position maintained by the Secretary, or

(B) in case the amount of the adjustment would be assessed and collected in the same manner as a deficiency under section 1314, there is adopted in the determination a position maintained by the taxpayer with respect to whom the determination is made,

and the position maintained by the Secretary in the case described in subparagraph (A) or maintained by the taxpayer in the case described in subparagraph (B) is inconsistent with the erroneous inclusion, exclusion, omission, allowance, disallowance, recognition, or nonrecognition, as the case may be.

(2) **Correction not barred at time of erroneous action.**—

(A) **Determination described in section 1312(3)(B).**—In the case of a determination described in section 1312(3)(B) (relating to certain exclusions from income), adjustment shall be made under this part only if assessment of a deficiency for the taxable year in which the item is includible or against the related taxpayer was not barred, by any law or rule of law, at the time the Secretary first maintained, in a notice of deficiency sent pursuant to section 6212 or before the Tax Court, that the item described in section 1312 (3)(B) should be included in the gross income of the taxpayer for the taxable year to which the determination relates.

(B) **Determination described in section 1312(4).**—In the case of a determination described in section 1312(4) (relating to disallowance of certain deductions and credits), adjustment shall be made under this part only if credit or refund of the overpayment attributable to the deduction or credit described in such section which should have been allowed to the taxpayer or related taxpayer was not barred, by any law or rule of law, at the time the taxpayer first maintained before the Secretary or before the Tax Court, in writing, that he was entitled to such deduction or credit for the taxable year to which the determination relates.

(3) Existence of relationship.—In case the amount of the adjustment would be assessed and collected in the same manner as a deficiency (except for cases described in section 1312(3)(B)), the adjustment shall not be made with respect to a related taxpayer unless he stands in such relationship to the taxpayer at the time the latter first maintains the inconsistent position in a return, claim for refund, or petition (or amended petition) to the Tax Court for the taxable year with respect to which the determination is made, or if such position is not so maintained, then at the time of the determination.

§ 1312. Circumstances of adjustment

The circumstances under which the adjustment provided in section 1311 is authorized are as follows:

(1) Double inclusion of an item of gross income.—The determination requires the inclusion in gross income of an item which was erroneously included in the gross income of the taxpayer for another taxable year or in the gross income of a related taxpayer.

(2) Double allowance of a deduction or credit.—The determination allows a deduction or credit which was erroneously allowed to the taxpayer for another taxable year or to a related taxpayer.

(3) Double exclusion of an item of gross income.—

(A) Items included in income.—The determination requires the exclusion from gross income of an item included in a return filed by the taxpayer or with respect to which tax was paid and which was erroneously excluded or omitted from the gross income of the taxpayer for another taxable year, or from the gross income of a related taxpayer; or

(B) Items not included in income.—The determination requires the exclusion from gross income of an item not included in a return filed by the taxpayer and with respect to which the tax was not paid but which is includible in the gross income of the taxpayer for another taxable year or in the gross income of a related taxpayer.

(4) Double disallowance of a deduction or credit.—The determination disallows a deduction or credit which should have been allowed to, but was not allowed to, the taxpayer for another taxable year, or to a related taxpayer.

(5) Correlative deductions and inclusions for trusts or estates and legatees, beneficiaries, or heirs.—The determination allows or disallows any of the additional deductions allowable in computing the taxable income of estates or trusts, or requires or denies any of the inclusions in the computation of taxable income of beneficiaries, heirs, or legatees, specified in subparts A to E, inclusive (secs. 641 and following, relating to estates, trusts and beneficiaries) of part I of subchapter J of this chapter, or corresponding provisions of prior internal revenue laws, and the correlative inclusion or deduction, as the case may be, has been erroneously excluded, omitted, or included, or disallowed, omitted, or allowed, as the case may be, in respect of the related taxpayer.

(6) Correlative deductions and credits for certain related corporations.—The determination allows or disallows a deduction (including a credit) in computing the taxable income (or, as the case may be, net income, normal tax net income, or surtax net income) of a corporation, and a correlative deduction or credit has been erroneously allowed, omitted, or disallowed, as the case may be, in respect of a related taxpayer described in section 1313(c)(7).

(7) Basis of property after erroneous treatment of a prior transaction.—

(A) General rule.—The determination determines the basis of property, and in respect of any transaction on which such basis depends, or in respect of any transaction which was erroneously treated as affecting such basis, there occurred, with respect to a taxpayer described in subparagraph (B) of this paragraph, any of the errors described in subparagraph (C) of this paragraph.

(B) Taxpayers with respect to whom the erroneous treatment occurred.—The taxpayer with respect to whom the erroneous treatment occurred must be—

(i) the taxpayer with respect to whom the determination is made,

(ii) a taxpayer who acquired title to the property in the transaction and from whom, mediately or immediately, the taxpayer with respect to whom the determination is made derived title, or

(iii) a taxpayer who had title to the property at the time of the transaction and from whom, mediately or immediately, the taxpayer with respect to whom the determination is made derived title, if the basis of the property in the hands of the taxpayer with respect to whom the determination is made is determined under section 1015(a) (relating to the basis of property acquired by gift).

(C) Prior erroneous treatment.—With respect to a taxpayer described in subparagraph (B) of this paragraph—

(i) there was an erroneous inclusion in, or omission from, gross income,

(ii) there was an erroneous recognition, or nonrecognition, of gain or loss, or

(iii) there was an erroneous deduction of an item properly chargeable to capital account or an erroneous charge to capital account of an item properly deductible.

§ 1313. Definitions

(a) Determination.—For purposes of this part, the term "determination" means—

(1) a decision by the Tax Court or a judgment, decree, or other order by any court of competent jurisdiction, which has become final;

(2) a closing agreement made under section 7121;

(3) a final disposition by the Secretary of a claim for refund. For purposes of this part, a claim for refund shall be deemed finally disposed of by the Secretary—

(A) as to items with respect to which the claim was allowed, on the date of allowance of refund or credit or on the date of mailing notice of disallowance (by reason of offsetting items) of the claim for refund, and

(B) as to items with respect to which the claim was disallowed, in whole or in part, or as to items applied by the Secretary in reduction of the refund or credit, on expiration of the time for instituting suit with respect thereto (unless suit is instituted before the expiration of such time); or

(4) under regulations prescribed by the Secretary, an agreement for purposes of this part, signed by the Secretary and by any person, relating to the liability of such person (or the person for whom he acts) in respect of a tax under this subtitle for any taxable period.

(b) Taxpayer.—Notwithstanding section 7701(a)(14), the term "taxpayer" means any person subject to a tax under the applicable revenue law.

(c) Related taxpayer.—For purposes of this part, the term "related taxpayer" means a taxpayer who, with the taxpayer with respect to whom a determination is made, stood, in the taxable year with respect to which the erroneous inclusion, exclusion, omission, allowance, or disallowance was made, in one of the following relationships:

(1) husband and wife,

(2) grantor and fiduciary,

(3) grantor and beneficiary,

(4) fiduciary and beneficiary, legatee, or heir,

(5) decedent and decedent's estate,

(6) partner, or

(7) member of an affiliated group of corporations (as defined in section 1504).

§ 1314. Amount and method of adjustment

(a) Ascertainment of amount of adjustment.—In computing the amount of an adjustment under this part there shall first be ascertained the tax previously determined for the taxable year with respect to which the error was made. The amount of the tax previously determined shall be the excess of—

(1) the sum of—

(A) the amount shown as the tax by the taxpayer on his return (determined as provided in section 6211(b)(1), (3), and (4), relating to the definition of deficiency), if a return was made by the taxpayer and an amount was shown as the tax by the taxpayer thereon, plus

(B) the amounts previously assessed (or collected without assessment) as a deficiency, over—

(2) the amount of rebates, as defined in section 6211(b)(2), made.

There shall then be ascertained the increase or decrease in tax previously determined which results solely from the correct treatment of the item which was the subject of the error (with due regard given to the effect of the item in the computation of gross income, taxable income, and other matters under this subtitle). A similar computation shall be made for any other taxable year affected, or treated as affected, by a net operating loss deduction (as defined in section 172) or by a capital loss carryback or carryover (as defined in section 1212), determined with reference to the taxable year with respect to which the error was made. The amount so ascertained (together with any amounts wrongfully collected as additions to the tax or interest, as a result of such error) for each taxable year shall be the amount of the adjustment for that taxable year.

(b) Method of adjustment.—The adjustment authorized in section 1311 (a) shall be made by assessing and collecting, or refunding or crediting, the amount thereof in the same manner as if it were a deficiency determined by the Secretary with respect to the taxpayer as to whom the error was made or an overpayment claimed by such taxpayer, as the case may be, for the taxable year or years with respect to which an amount is ascertained under subsection (a), and as if on the date of the determination one year remained before the expiration of the periods of limitation upon assessment or filing claim for refund for such taxable year or years. If, as a result of a determination described in section 1313(a)(4), an adjustment has been made by the assessment and collection of a deficiency or the refund or credit of an overpayment, and subsequently such determination is altered or revoked, the amount of the adjustment ascertained under subsection (a) of this section shall be redetermined on the basis of such alteration or revocation and any overpayment or deficiency resulting from such redetermination shall be refunded or credited, or assessed and collected, as the case may be, as an adjustment under this part. In the case of an adjustment resulting from an increase or decrease in a net operating loss or net capital loss which is carried back to the year of adjustment, interest shall not be collected or paid for any period prior to the close of the taxable year in which the net operating loss or net capital loss arises.

(c) Adjustment unaffected by other items.—The amount to be assessed and collected in the same manner as a deficiency, or to be refunded or credited in the same manner as an overpayment, under this part, shall not be diminished by any credit or set-off based upon any item other than the one which was the subject of the adjustment. The amount of the adjustment under this part, if paid, shall not be recovered by a claim or suit for refund or suit for erroneous refund based upon any item other than the one which was the subject of the adjustment.

(d) Periods for which adjustments may be made.—No adjustment shall be made under this part in respect of any taxable year beginning prior to January 1, 1932.

* * *

[PART III—REPEALED]*

[PART IV—REPEALED]*

PART V—CLAIM OF RIGHT

Editorial Summary

Claim of Right Doctrine

Subchapter Q of Chapter 1 (Sec. 1341)

Under the claim of right doctrine, if the taxpayer has an unrestricted claim, amounts actually or constructively received must be included in the taxpayer's gross income. Section 1341 deals with the tax treatment to the taxpayer when he or she is required to repay such an amount. The taxpayer, of course, is eligible to take a deduction in the current taxable year (i.e., the year of repayment) for the amount repaid. However, if the taxpayer's marginal tax rate in the year of repayment is less than it was in the year included in gross income, the taxpayer would suffer a negative cash flow impact when the effect of the inclusion and deduction are netted. To mitigate this impact, Sec. 1341, in effect, permits the current period tax liability to be reduced by an amount equal to the additional tax liability that resulted in the year the item was included in gross income. Note that Sec. 1341 treatment is available only if the deduction available to the taxpayer in calculating current period taxable income is greater than $3,000 (i.e., a materiality concept) [see Sec. 1341(a)(3)].

§ 1341. Computation of tax where taxpayer restores substantial amount held under claim of right

(a) General rule.—If—

(1) an item was included in gross income for a prior taxable year (or years) because it appeared

*Omitted.

that the taxpayer had an unrestricted right to such item;

(2) a deduction is allowable for the taxable year because it was established after the close of such prior taxable year (or years) that the taxpayer did not have an unrestricted right to such item or to a portion of such item; and

(3) the amount of such deduction exceeds $3,000,

then the tax imposed by this chapter for the taxable year shall be the lesser of the following:

(4) the tax for the taxable year computed with such deduction; or

(5) an amount equal to—

(A) the tax for the taxable year computed without such deduction, minus

(B) the decrease in tax under this chapter (or the corresponding provisions of prior revenue laws) for the prior taxable year (or years) which would result solely from the exclusion of such item (or portion thereof) from gross income for such prior taxable year (or years).

* * *

(b) Special rules.—

(1) If the decrease in tax ascertained under subsection (a)(5)(B) exceeds the tax imposed by this chapter for the taxable year (computed without the deduction) such excess shall be considered to be a payment of tax on the last day prescribed by law for the payment of tax for the taxable year, and shall be refunded or credited in the same manner as if it were an overpayment for such taxable year.

(2) Subsection (a) does not apply to any deduction allowable with respect to an item which was included in gross income by reason of the sale or other disposition of stock in trade of the taxpayer (or other property of a kind which would properly have been included in the inventory of the taxpayer if on hand at the close of the prior taxable year) or property held by the taxpayer primarily for sale to customers in the ordinary course of his trade or business. This paragraph shall not apply if the deduction arises out of refunds or repayments with respect to rates made by a regulated public utility (as defined in section 7701(a)(33) without regard to the limitation contained in the last two sentences thereof) if such refunds or repayments are required to be made by the Government, political subdivision, agency, or instrumentality referred to in such section, or by an order of a court, or are made in settlement of litigation or under threat or imminence of litigation.

(3) If the tax imposed by this chapter for the taxable year is the amount determined under subsection (a)(5), then the deduction referred to in subsection (a)(2) shall not be taken into account for any purpose of this subtitle other than this section.

(4) For purposes of determining whether paragraph (4) or paragraph (5) of subsection (a) applies—

(A) in any case where the deduction referred to in paragraph (4) of subsection (a) results in a net operating loss, such loss shall, for purposes of computing the tax for the taxable year under such paragraph (4), be carried back to the same extent and in the same manner as is provided under section 172; and

(B) in any case where the exclusion referred to in paragraph (5)(B) of subsection (a) results in a net operating loss or capital loss for the prior taxable year (or years), such loss shall, for purposes of computing the decrease in tax for the prior taxable year (or years) under such paragraph (5) (B), be carried back and carried over to the same extent and in the same manner as is provided under section 172 or section 1212, except that no carryover beyond the taxable year shall be taken into account.

(5) For purposes of this chapter, the net operating loss described in paragraph (4)(A) of this subsection, or the net operating loss or capital loss described in paragraph (4)(B) of this subsection, as the case may be, shall (after the application of paragraph (4) or (5)(B) of subsection (a) for the taxable year) be taken into account under section 172 or 1212 for taxable years after the taxable year to the same extent and in the same manner as—

(A) a net operating loss sustained for the taxable year, if paragraph (4) of subsection (a) applied, or

(B) a net operating loss or capital loss sustained for the prior taxable year (or years), if paragraph (5)(B) of subsection (a) applied.

[PART VI—REPEALED]*

PART VII—RECOVERIES OF FOREIGN EXPROPRIATION LOSSES*

[SUBCHAPTER R—REPEALED]*

*Omitted.

SUBCHAPTER S—TAX TREATMENT OF S CORPORATIONS AND THEIR SHAREHOLDERS

PART I—IN GENERAL

Editorial Summary

S Corporations: General

Subchapter S of Chapter 1 (Secs. 1361–1363)

An S corporation is a corporation for which the tax treatment is similar to that of the partnership (refer to Subchapter K). That is, in general, conduit theory applies and the tax liability is assessed at the shareholder level rather than at the corporation level.

The S corporation treatment is elective [see Sec. 1361(a)]. The statutory requirements that must be satisfied in order to be eligible to make the election appear in Sec. 1361. Note that some of the requirements relate to the shareholders of the corporation, while others relate to the corporation itself. These statutory requirements serve a dual purpose. In addition to serving as initial eligibility requirements, they also serve as maintenance requirements. That is, to keep the election in effect, the requirements must continue to be satisfied.

In order that benefit not result from a retroactive election, the election must be made within the first two and one-half months of the current taxable year in order to be effective for the current taxable year [see Sec. 1362(b)(1)]. Otherwise, the election is effective for the following taxable year [see Secs. 1362(b)(2), 1362(b)(3)]. However, see Sec. 1362(b)(5) which provides the authority for the IRS to treat a late election or an incomplete election as a timely made election and Sec. 1362(f) which provides the authority for the IRS to treat an inadvertent invalid election as a valid election. To prevent shareholder disagreements regarding the tax liability being that of the corporation versus that of the shareholders, unanimous consent is required in order to make the election [see Sec. 1362(a)(2)].

Making the S corporation election generally does not produce any adverse (i.e., recognition) tax consequences. However, if the entity has been operating as a C corporation and has been using the LIFO inventory method, the S election does trigger LIFO recapture for the last C corporation tax year. Such LIFO recapture does result in a basis increase for inventory of the S corporation [see Sec. 1363(d)].

The S corporation can revert to C corporation (i.e., a regular corporation) status in two ways [see Sec. 1362(d)]. The shareholders of the corporation can revoke the election, which requires the consent of more than fifty percent of the shareholders. The revocation can be effective at the beginning of the current taxable year, at the beginning of the next taxable year, or at a prospective date, depending on when the revocation election is made and the intent of the shareholders. In addition to a voluntary revocation, the election can be involuntarily terminated as a result of the violation of one of the maintenance requirements or the 25 percent passive investment income provision in Sec. 1362(d)(3). Note that the latter termination provision is applicable only if the S corporation has some C corporation earnings and profits. Involuntary termination by violating a maintenance requirement is effective on the date of violation, whereas that under the passive investment income test is effective on the first day of the fourth year of the violation of this test (i.e., the test has been violated for the three previous years). Involuntary termination by violating a maintenance requirement produces a short taxable year problem (i.e., an S corporation short period and a C corporation short period). For the short periods, the income, deductions, and credits must be assigned to the S corporation short period and the C corporation short period. A pro-rata allocation approach will be used unless an election is made to use the actual data in the tax accounting records [see Sec. 1362(e)(2) and (3)].

Both revocation and termination usually result in the corporation being locked-out from having another S corporation election made for a period of five years [see Sec. 1362(g)]. However, see Sec. 1362(f) with respect to inadvertent terminations.

§ 1361. S corporation defined

(a) S corporation defined.—

(1) In general.—For purposes of this title, the term "S corporation" means, with respect to any taxable year, a small business corporation for which an election under section 1362(a) is in effect for such year.

(2) C corporation.—For purposes of this title, the term "C corporation" means, with respect to any taxable year, a corporation which is not an S corporation for such year.

(b) Small business corporation.—

(1) In general.—For purposes of this subchapter, the term "small business corporation" means a domestic corporation which is not an ineligible corporation and which does not—

(A) have more than 100 shareholders,

(B) have as a shareholder a person (other than an estate, a trust described in subsection (c)

(2), or an organization described in subsection (c)(6)) who is not an individual,

(C) have a nonresident alien as a shareholder, and

(D) have more than 1 class of stock.

(2) Ineligible corporation defined.—For purposes of paragraph (1), the term "ineligible corporation" means any corporation which is—

(A) a financial institution which uses the reserve method of accounting for bad debts described in section 585,

(B) an insurance company subject to tax under subchapter L,

(C) a corporation to which an election under section 936 applies, or

(D) a DISC or former DISC.

(3) Treatment of certain wholly owned subsidiaries.

(A) In general.—Except as provided in regulations prescribed by the Secretary, for purposes of this title—

(i) a corporation which is a qualified subchapter S subsidiary shall not be treated as a separate corporation, and

(ii) all assets, liabilities, and items of income, deduction, and credit of a qualified subchapter S subsidiary shall be treated as assets, liabilities, and such items (as the case may be) of the S corporation.

(B) Qualified subchapter S subsidiary.—For purposes of this paragraph, the term "qualified subchapter S subsidiary" means any domestic corporation which is not an ineligible corporation (as defined in paragraph (2)), if—

(i) 100 percent of the stock of such corporation is held by the S corporation, and

(ii) the S corporation elects to treat such corporation as a qualified subchapter S subsidiary.

(C) Treatment of terminations of qualified subchapter S subsidiary status.—

(i) In general.—For purposes of this title, if any corporation which was a qualified subchapter S subsidiary ceases to meet the requirements of subparagraph (B), such corporation shall be treated as a new corporation acquiring all of its assets (and assuming all of its liabilities) immediately before such cessation from the S corporation in exchange for its stock.

(ii) Termination by reason of sale of stock.—If the failure to meet the requirements of subparagraph (B) is by reason of the sale of stock of a corporation which is a qualified subchapter S subsidiary, the sale of such stock shall be treated as if—

(I) the sale were a sale of an undivided interest in the assets of such corporation (based on the percentage of the corporation's stock sold), and

(II) the sale were followed by an acquisition by such corporation of all of its assets (and the assumption by such corporation of all of its liabilities) in a transaction to which section 351 applies.

(D) Election after termination.—If a corporation's status as a qualified subchapter S subsidiary terminates, such corporation (and any successor corporation) shall not be eligible to make—

(i) an election under subparagraph (B)(ii) to be treated as a qualified subchapter S subsidiary, or

(ii) an election under section 1362(a) to be treated as an S corporation,

before its 5th taxable year which begins after the 1st taxable year for which such termination was effective, unless the Secretary consents to such election.

(E) Information returns.—Except to the extent provided by the Secretary, this paragraph shall not apply to part III of subchapter A of Chapter 61 (relating to information returns).

(c) Special rules for applying subsection (b).—

(1) Members of a family treated as 1 shareholder.—

(A) In general.—For purposes of subsection (b)(1)(A), there shall be treated as one shareholder—

(i) a husband and wife (and their estates), and

(ii) all members of a family (and their estates).

(B) Members of a family.—For purposes of this paragraph—

(i) In general.—The term "members of a family" means the common ancestor, any lineal descendant of such common ancestor, and any spouse or former spouse of such common ancestor or any such lineal descendant.

(ii) Common ancestor.—An individual shall not be considered to be a common ancestor if, on the applicable date, the individual is more than 6 generations removed from the youngest generation of shareholders who would (but for this subparagraph) be members of the family. For purposes of the preceding sentence, a spouse (or former spouse) shall be treated as being of the same generation as the individual to whom such spouse is (or was) married.

(iii) Applicable date.—The term "applicable date" means the latest of—

(I) the date the election under section 1362(a) is made,

(II) the earliest date that an individual described in clause (i) holds stock in the S corporation, or

(III) October 22, 2004.

(C) Effect of adoption, etc.—Any legally adopted child of an individual, any child who is lawfully placed with an individual for legal adoption by the individual, and any eligible foster child of an individual (within the meaning of section 152(f)(1)(C), shall be treated as a child of such individual by blood..

(2) Certain trusts permitted as shareholders.—

(A) In general.—For purposes of subsection (b)(1)(B), the following trusts may be shareholders:

(i) A trust all of which is treated (under subpart E of part I of subchapter J of this chapter) as owned by an individual who is a citizen or resident of the United States.

(ii) A trust which was described in clause (i) immediately before the death of the deemed owner and which continues in existence after such death, but only for the 2-year period beginning on the day of the deemed owner's death.

(iii) A trust with respect to stock transferred to it pursuant to the terms of a will, but only for the 2-year period beginning on the day on which such stock is transferred to it.

(iv) A trust created primarily to exercise the voting power of stock transferred to it.

(v) An electing small business trust.

(vi) In the case of a corporation which is a bank (as defined in section 581) or a depository institution holding company (as defined in section 3(w)(1) of the Federal Deposit Insurance Act (12 U.S.C. 1813(w)(1)), a trust which constitutes an individual retirement account under section 408(a), including one designated as a Roth IRA under section 408A, but only to the extent of the stock held by such trust in such bank or company as of the date of the enactment of this clause.

This subparagraph shall not apply to any foreign trust.

(B) Treatment as shareholders.—For purposes of subsection (b)(1)—

(i) In the case of a trust described in clause (i) of subparagraph (A), the deemed owner shall be treated as the shareholder.

(ii) In the case of a trust described in clause (ii) of subparagraph (A), the estate of the deemed owner shall be treated as the shareholder.

(iii) In the case of a trust described in clause (iii) of subparagraph (A), the estate of the testator shall be treated as the shareholder.

(iv) In the case of a trust described in clause (iv) of subparagraph (A), each beneficiary of the trust shall be treated as a shareholder.

(v) In the case of a trust described in clause (v) of subparagraph (A), each potential current beneficiary of such trust shall be treated as a shareholder; except that, if for any period there is no potential current beneficiary of such trust, such trust shall be treated as the shareholder during such period.

(vi) In the case of a trust described in clause (vi) of subparagraph (A), the individual for whose benefit the trust was created shall be treated as a shareholder.

(3) Estate of individual in bankruptcy may be shareholder.—For purposes of subsection (b)(1)(B), the term "estate" includes the estate of an individual in a case under title 11 of the United States Code.

(4) Differences in common stock voting rights disregarded.—For purposes of subsection (b)(l)(D), a corporation shall not be treated as having more than 1 class of stock solely because there are differences in voting rights among the shares of common stock.

(5) Straight debt safe harbor.—

(A) In general.—For purposes of subsection (b)(1)(D), straight debt shall not be treated as a second class of stock.

(B) Straight debt defined.—For purposes of this paragraph, the term "straight debt" means any written unconditional promise to pay on demand or on a specified date a sum certain in money if—

(i) the interest rate (and interest payment dates) are not contingent on profits, the borrower's discretion, or similar factors,

(ii) there is no convertibility (directly or indirectly) into stock, and

(iii) the creditor is an individual (other than a nonresident alien), an estate, a trust described in paragraph (2), or a person which is actively and regularly engaged in the business of lending money.

(C) Regulations.—The Secretary shall prescribe such regulations as may be necessary or appropriate to provide for the proper treatment of straight debt under this subchapter and for the coordination of such treatment with other provisions of this title.

(6) Certain exempt organizations permitted as shareholders.—For purposes of subsection (1)(B), an organization which is—

(A) described in section 401(a) or 501(c)(3), and

(B) exempt from taxation under section 501(a),

may be a shareholder in an S corporation.

(d) Special rule for qualified subchapter S trust.—

(1) In general.—In the case of a qualified subchapter S trust with respect to which a beneficiary makes an election under paragraph (2)—

(A) such trust shall be treated as a trust described in subsection (c)(2)(A)(i),

(B) for purposes of section 678(a), the beneficiary of such trust shall be treated as the owner of that portion of the trust which consists of stock in an S corporation with respect to which the election under paragraph (2) is made, and

(C) for purposes of applying sections 465 and 469 to the beneficiary of the trust, the disposition of the S corporation stock by the trust shall be treated as a disposition by such beneficiary.

(2) Election.—

(A) In general.—A beneficiary of a qualified subchapter S trust (or his legal representative) may elect to have this subsection apply.

(B) Manner and time of election.—

(i) Separate election with respect to each corporation.—An election under this paragraph shall be made separately with respect to each corporation the stock of which is held by the trust.

(ii) Elections with respect to successive income beneficiaries.—If there is an election under this paragraph with respect to any beneficiary, an election under this paragraph shall be treated as made by each successive beneficiary unless such beneficiary affirmatively refuses to consent to such election.

(iii) Time, manner, and form of election.—Any election, or refusal, under this paragraph shall be made in such manner and form, and at such time, as the Secretary may prescribe.

(C) Election irrevocable.—An election under this paragraph, once made, may be revoked only with the consent of the Secretary.

(D) Grace period.—An election under this paragraph shall be effective up to 15 days and 2 months before the date of the election.

(3) Qualified subchapter S trust.—For purposes of this subsection, the term "qualified subchapter S trust" means a trust—

(A) the terms of which require that—

(i) during the life of the current income beneficiary, there shall be only 1 income beneficiary of the trust,

(ii) any corpus distributed during the life of the current income beneficiary may be distributed only to such beneficiary,

(iii) the income interest of the current income beneficiary in the trust shall terminate on the earlier of such beneficiary's death or the termination of the trust, and

(iv) upon the termination of the trust during the life of the current income beneficiary, the trust shall distribute all of its assets to such beneficiary, and

(B) all of the income (within the meaning of section 643(b)) of which is distributed (or required to be distributed) currently to 1 individual who is a citizen or resident of the United States.

A substantially separate and independent share of a trust within the meaning of section 663(c) shall be treated as a separate trust for purposes of this subsection and subsection (c).

(4) Trust ceasing to be qualified.—

(A) Failure to meet requirements of paragraph (3)(A).—If a qualified subchapter S trust ceases to meet any requirement of paragraph (3)(A), the provisions of this subsection shall not apply to such trust as of the date it ceases to meet such requirement.

(B) Failure to meet requirements of paragraph (3)(B).—If any qualified subchapter S trust ceases to meet any requirement of paragraph (3)(B) but continues to meet the requirements of paragraph (3)(A), the provisions of this subsection shall not apply to such trust as of the first day of the first taxable year beginning after the first taxable year for which it failed to meet the requirements of paragraph (3)(B).

(e) Electing small business trust defined.—

(1) Electing small business trust.—For purposes of this section—

(A) In general.—Except as provided in subparagraph (B), the term "electing small business trust" means any trust if—

(i) such trust does not have as a beneficiary any person other than (I) an individual, (II) an estate, (III) an organization described in paragraph (2), (3), (4), or (5) of section 170(c), or (IV) an organization described in section 170(c)(1) which holds a contingent interest in such trust and is not a potential current beneficiary,

(ii) no interest in such trust was acquired by purchase, and

(iii) an election under this subsection applies to such trust.

(B) Certain trusts not eligible.—The term "electing small business trust" shall not include—

(i) any qualified subchapter S trust (as defined in subsection (d)(3)) if an election under subsection (d)(2) applies to any corporation the stock of which is held by such trust,

(ii) any trust exempt from tax under this subtitle, and

(iii) any charitable remainder annuity trust or charitable remainder unitrust (as defined in section 664(d)).

(C) Purchase.—For purposes of subparagraph (A), the term "purchase" means any acquisition if the basis of the property acquired is determined under section 1012.

(2) Potential current beneficiary.—For purposes of this section, the term "potential current beneficiary" means, with respect to any period, any person who at any time during such period is entitled to, or at the discretion of any person may receive, a distribution from the principal or income of the trust (determined without regard to any power of appointment to the extent such power remains unexercised at the end of such period). If a trust disposes of all of the stock which it holds in an S corporation, then, with respect to such corporation, the term "potential current beneficiary" does not include any person who first met the requirements of the preceding sentence during the 1-year period ending on the date of such disposition.

(3) Election.—An election under this subsection shall be made by the trustee. Any such election shall apply to the taxable year of the trust for which made and all subsequent taxable years of such trust unless revoked with the consent of the Secretary.

(4) Cross reference.—**For special treatment of electing small business trusts, see section 641(c).**

(f) Restricted bank director stock.—

(1) In general.—Restricted bank director stock shall not be taken into account as outstanding stock of the S corporation in applying this subchapter (other than section 1368(f)).

(2) Restricted bank director stock.—For purposes of this subsection, the term "restricted bank director stock" means stock in a bank (as defined in section 581) or a depository institution holding company (as defined in section 3(w)(1) of the Federal Deposit Insurance Act (12 U.S.C. 1813(w)(1)), if such stock—

(A) is required to be held by an individual under applicable Federal or State law in order to permit such individual to serve as a director, and

(B) is subject to an agreement with such bank or company (or a corporation which controls (within the meaning of section 368(c)) such bank or company) pursuant to which the holder is required to sell back such stock (at the same price as the individual acquired such stock) upon ceasing to hold the office of director.

(3) Cross reference.—**For treatment of certain distributions with respect to restricted bank director stock, see section 1368(f).**

* * *

§ 1362. Election; revocation; termination

(a) Election.—

(1) In general.—Except as provided in subsection (g), a small business corporation may elect, in accordance with the provisions of this section, to be an S corporation.

(2) All shareholders must consent to election.—An election under this subsection shall be valid only if all persons who are shareholders in such corporation on the day on which such election is made consent to such election.

(b) When made.—

(1) In general.—An election under subsection (a) may be made by a small business corporation for any taxable year—

(A) at any time during the preceding taxable year, or

(B) at any time during the taxable year and on or before the 15th day of the 3rd month of the taxable year.

(2) Certain elections made during 1st 2½ months treated as made for next taxable year.—If—

(A) an election under subsection (a) is made for any taxable year during such year and on or before the 15th day of the 3rd month of such year, but

(B) either—

(i) on 1 or more days in such taxable year before the day on which the election was made the corporation did not meet the requirements of subsection (b) of section 1361, or

(ii) 1 or more of the persons who held stock in the corporation during such taxable year and before the election was made did not consent to the election,

then such election shall be treated as made for the following taxable year.

(3) Election made after 1st 2½ months treated as made for following taxable year.—If—

(A) a small business corporation makes an election under subsection (a) for any taxable year, and

(B) such election is made after the 15th day of the 3rd month of the taxable year and on or before the 15th day of the 3rd month of the following taxable year,

then such election shall be treated as made for the following taxable year.

(4) Taxable years of 2½ months or less.—For purposes of this subsection, an election for a taxable year made not later than 2 months and 15 days after the first day of the taxable year shall be treated as timely made during such year.

(5) Authority to treat late elections, etc., as timely.—If—

(A) an election under subsection (a) is made for any taxable year (determined without regard to paragraph (3)) after the date prescribed by this subsection for making such election for such taxable year or no such election is made for any taxable year, and

(B) the Secretary determines that there was reasonable cause for the failure to timely make such election,

the Secretary may treat such an election as timely made for such taxable year (and paragraph (3) shall not apply).

(c) Years for which effective.—An election under subsection (a) shall be effective for the taxable year of the corporation for which it is made and for all succeeding taxable years of the corporation, until such election is terminated under subsection (d).

(d) Termination.—

(1) By revocation.—

(A) In general.—An election under subsection (a) may be terminated by revocation.

(B) More than one-half of shares must consent to revocation.—An election may be revoked only if shareholders holding more than one-half of the shares of stock of the corporation on the day on which the revocation is made consent to the revocation.

(C) When effective.—Except as provided in subparagraph (D)—

(i) a revocation made during the taxable year and on or before the 15th day of the 3rd month thereof shall be effective on the 1st day of such taxable year, and

(ii) a revocation made during the taxable year but after such 15th day shall be effective on the 1st day of the following taxable year.

(D) Revocation may specify prospective date.—If the revocation specifies a date for revocation which is on or after the day on which the revocation is made, the revocation shall be effective on and after the date so specified.

(2) By corporation ceasing to be small business corporation.—

(A) In general.—An election under subsection (a) shall be terminated whenever (at any time on or after the 1st day of the 1st taxable year for which the corporation is an S corporation) such corporation ceases to be a small business corporation.

(B) When effective.—Any termination under this paragraph shall be effective on and after the date of cessation.

(3) Where passive investment income exceeds 25 percent of gross receipts for 3 consecutive taxable years and corporation has accumulated earnings and profits.—

(A) Termination.—

(i) In general.—An election under subsection (a) shall be terminated whenever the corporation—

(I) has accumulated earnings and profits at the close of each of 3 consecutive taxable years, and

(II) has gross receipts for each of such taxable years more than 25 percent of which are passive investment income.

(ii) When effective.—Any termination under this paragraph shall be effective on and after the first day of the first taxable year beginning after the third consecutive taxable year referred to in clause (i).

(iii) Years taken into account.—A prior taxable year shall not be taken into account under clause (i) unless—

(I) such taxable year began after December 31, 1981, and

(II) the corporation was an S corporation for such taxable year.

(B) Gross receipts from the sales of certain assets.—For purposes of this paragraph—

(i) in the case of dispositions of capital assets (other than stock and securities), gross receipts from such dispositions shall be taken into account only to the extent of the capital gain net income therefrom, and

(ii) in the case of sales or exchanges of stocks or securities, gross receipts shall be taken into account only to the extent of the gains therefrom.

(C) Passive investment income defined.—For purposes of this paragraph—

(i) In general.—Except as otherwise provided in this subparagraph, the term "passive investment income" means gross receipts derived from royalties, rents, dividends, interest, and annuities.

(ii) Exception for interest on notes from sales of inventory.—The term "passive investment income" shall not include interest on any obligation acquired in the ordinary course of the corporation's trade or business from its sale of property described in section 1221(1).

(iii) Treatment of certain lending or finance companies.—If the S corporation meets the requirements of section 542(c)(6) for the taxable year, the term "passive investment income" shall not include gross receipts for the taxable year which are derived directly from the active and regular conduct of a lending or finance business (as defined in section 542(d)(1)).

(iv) Treatment of certain dividends.—If an S corporation holds stock in a C corporation meeting the requirements of section 1504(a)(2), the term "passive investment income" shall not include dividends from such C corporation to the extent such dividends are attributable to the earnings and profits of such C corporation derived from the active conduct of a trade or business.

* * *

(e) Treatment of S termination year.—

(1) In general.—In the case of an S termination year, for purposes of this title—

(A) S short year.—The portion of such year ending before the 1st day for which the termination is effective shall be treated as a short taxable year for which the corporation is an S corporation.

(B) C short year.—The portion of such year beginning on such 1st day shall be treated as a short taxable year for which the corporation is a C corporation.

(2) Pro rata allocation.—Except as provided in paragraph (3) and subparagraphs (C) and (D) of paragraph (6), the determination of which items are to be taken into account for each of the short taxable years referred to in paragraph (1) shall be made—

(A) first by determining for the S termination year—

(i) the amount of each of the items of income, loss, deduction, or credit described in section 1366(a)(1)(A), and

(ii) the amount of the nonseparately computed income or loss, and

(B) then by assigning an equal portion of each amount determined under subparagraph (A) to each day of the S termination year.

(3) Election to have items assigned to each short taxable year under normal tax accounting rules.—

(A) In general.—A corporation may elect to have paragraph (2) not apply.

(B) Shareholders must consent to election.—An election under this subsection shall be valid only if all persons who are shareholders in the corporation at any time during the S short year and all persons who are shareholders in the corporation on the first day of the C short year consent to such election.

(4) S termination year.—For purposes of this subsection, the term "S termination year" means any taxable year of a corporation (determined without regard to this subsection) in which a termination of an election made under subsection (a) takes effect (other than on the 1st day thereof).

(5) Tax for C short year determined on annualized basis.—

(A) In general.—The taxable income for the short year described in subparagraph (B) of paragraph (1) shall be placed on an annual basis by multiplying the taxable income for such short year by the number of days in the S termination year and by dividing the result by the number of days in the short year. The tax shall be the same part of the tax computed on the annual basis as the number of days in such short year is of the number of days in the S termination year.

(B) Section 443(d) to apply.—Subsection (d) of section 443 shall apply to the short taxable year described in subparagraph (B) of paragraph (1).

(6) Other special rules.—For purposes of this title—

(A) Short years treated as 1 year for carryover purposes.—The short taxable year described in subparagraph (A) of paragraph (1) shall not be taken into account for purposes of determining the number of taxable years to which any item may be carried back or carried forward by the corporation.

(B) Due date for S year.—The due date for filing the return for the short taxable year described in subparagraph (A) of paragraph (1) shall be the same as the due date for filing the return for the short taxable year described in subparagraph (B) of paragraph (1) (including extensions thereof).

(C) Paragraph (2) not to apply to items resulting from section 338.—Paragraph (2) shall not apply with respect to any item resulting from the application of section 338.

(D) Pro rata allocation for S termination year not to apply if 50-percent change in ownership.—Paragraph (2) shall not apply to an S termination year if there is a sale or exchange of 50 percent or more of the stock in such corporation during such year.

(f) Inadvertent invalid elections or terminations.—If—

(1) an election under subsection (a) or section 1361(b)(3)(B)(ii) by any corporation—

(A) was not effective for the taxable year for which made (determined without regard to subsection (b)(2)) by reason of a failure to meet the requirements of section 1361(b) or to obtain shareholder consents, or

(B) was terminated under paragraph (2) or (3) of subsection (d) or section 1361(b)(3)(C),

(2) the Secretary determines that the circumstances resulting in such ineffectiveness or termination were inadvertent,

(3) no later than a reasonable period of time after discovery of the circumstances resulting in such ineffectiveness or termination, steps were taken—

(A) so that the corporation for which the election was made or the termination occurred is a small business corporation or a qualified subchapter S subsidiary, as the case may be, or

(B) to acquire the required shareholder consents, and

(4) the corporation for which the election was made or the termination occurred, and each person who was a shareholder in such corporation at any time during the period specified pursuant to this subsection, agrees to make such adjustments (consistent with the treatment of the corporation as an S corporation or a qualified subchapter S subsidiary, as the case may be) as may be required by the Secretary with respect to such period,

then, notwithstanding the circumstances resulting in such ineffectiveness or termination, such corporation shall be treated as an S corporation or a qualified subchapter S subsidiary, as the case may be during the period specified by the Secretary.

(g) Election after termination.—If a small business corporation has made an election under subsection (a) and if such election has been terminated under subsection (d), such corporation (and any successor corporation) shall not be eligible to make an election under subsection (a) for any taxable year before its 5th taxable year which begins after the 1st taxable year for which such termination is effective, unless the Secretary consents to such election.

§ 1363. Effect of election on corporation

(a) General rule.—Except as otherwise provided in this subchapter, an S corporation shall not be subject to the taxes imposed by this chapter.

(b) Computation of corporation's taxable income.—The taxable income of an S corporation shall be computed in the same manner as in the case of an individual, except that—

(1) the items described in section 1366(a)(1)(A) shall be separately stated,

(2) the deductions referred to in section 703(a)(2) shall not be allowed to the corporation,

(3) section 248 shall apply, and

(4) section 291 shall apply if the S corporation (or any predecessor) was a C corporation for any of the 3 immediately preceding taxable years.

(c) Elections of the S corporation.—

(1) In general.—Except as provided in paragraph (2), any election affecting the computation of items derived from an S corporation shall be made by the corporation.

(2) Exceptions.—In the case of an S corporation, elections under the following provisions shall be made by each shareholder separately—

(A) section 617 (relating to deduction and recapture of certain mining exploration expenditures), and

(B) section 901 (relating to taxes of foreign countries and possessions of the United States).

(d) Recapture of LIFO benefits.—

(1) In general.—If—

(A) an S corporation was a C corporation for the last taxable year before the first taxable year for which the election under section 1362(a) was effective, and

(B) the corporation inventoried goods under the LIFO method for such last taxable year,

the LIFO recapture amount shall be included in the gross income of the corporation for such last taxable year (and appropriate adjustments to the basis of inventory shall be made to take into account the amount included in gross income under this paragraph).

(2) Additional tax payable in installments.—

(A) In general.—Any increase in the tax imposed by this chapter by reason of this subsection shall be payable in 4 equal installments.

(B) Date for payment of installments.—The first installment under subparagraph (A) shall be paid on or before the due date (determined without regard to extensions) for the return of the tax imposed by this chapter for the last taxable year for which the corporation was a C corporation and the 3 succeeding installments shall be paid on or before the due date (as so determined) for the corporation's return for the 3 succeeding taxable years.

(C) No interest for period of extension.—Notwithstanding section 6601(b), for purposes of section 6601, the date prescribed for the payment of each installment under this paragraph shall be determined under this paragraph.

(3) LIFO recapture amount.—For purposes of this subsection, the term "LIFO recapture amount" means the amount (if any) by which—

(A) the inventory amount of the inventory asset under the first-in, first-out method authorized by section 471, exceeds

(B) the inventory amount of such assets under the LIFO method.

For purposes of the preceding sentence, inventory amounts shall be determined as of the close of the last taxable year referred to in paragraph (1).

(4) Other definitions.—For purposes of this subsection—

(A) LIFO method.—The term "LIFO method" means the method authorized by section 472.

(B) Inventory assets.—The term "inventory assets" means stock in trade of the corporation, or other property of a kind which would properly be included in the inventory of the corporation if on hand at the close of the taxable year.

(C) Method of determining inventory amount.—The inventory amount of assets under a method authorized by section 471 shall be determined—

(i) if the corporation uses the retail method of valuing inventories under section 472, by using such method, or

(ii) if clause (i) does not apply, by using cost or market, whichever is lower.

(D) Not treated as member of affiliated group.—Except as provided in regulations, the corporation referred to in paragraph (1) shall not be treated as a member of an affiliated group with respect to the amount included in gross income under paragraph (1).

(5) Special rule.—Sections 1367(a)(2)(D) and 1371(c)(1) shall not apply with respect to any increase in the tax imposed by reason of this subsection.

PART II—TAX TREATMENT OF SHAREHOLDERS

Editorial Summary

Tax Treatment of S Corporation Shareholders

Subchapter S of Chapter 1 (Secs. 1366–1368, 1377, 1378)

The general objective of the statutory provisions is that the individual shareholders should be taxed as if the corporation did not exist (i.e., conduit theory). Therefore, all income, deduction, and credit items are classified into two categories under Sec. 1366. Items that will receive special treatment at the shareholder level (e.g. capital gains, charitable contributions) are placed in one category, and each shareholder reports his or her respective share of *each* of these items. All other items are grouped together in the second category in the calculation of corporate taxable income (or probably more appropriately described as bottom line income). Each shareholder reports his or her respective share of this amount. The "respective share" is determined using a per share/per day approach [see Sec. 1377(a)]. Section 1378 defines the permitted taxable year of an S corporation. See Sec. 444 for exceptions to the permitted taxable year rules.

In a limited number of circumstances, conduit theory does not completely apply and the corporation is subject to taxation (i.e., moves from the status of merely being a tax reporter to that of actually being a taxpayer). If tax liability is assessed at the corporate level, the related pass-through item to the shareholders is reduced by the amount of the tax [Sec. 1366 (f)(2) and (3)]. See Secs. 1371(d), 1374, and 1375; also the Editorial Summary entitled Taxation at the Corporate Level, which precedes Sec. 1371.

The shareholder needs to know the basis of his or her stock for several reasons. First, the basis is needed to calculate the shareholder's gain or loss if the stock is sold or otherwise disposed of in a taxable transaction. Second, the basis is needed in determining the tax consequence of a distribution to the shareholder [see Sec. 1368]. Third, the basis serves as a ceiling on the amount of losses the shareholder can pass through from the S corporation and deduct on his or her individual return [see Sec. 1366(d)(1)]. (Note that

Sec. 1366(d)(1)(B) provides that if the shareholder has made loans to the corporation, the shareholder can continue to deduct losses even after the stock basis is zero to the extent of the basis of the loans.) To the extent that a shareholder cannot deduct losses that have been passed through to him or her by the S corporation because of this limitation, the losses qualify for carryover treatment [see Sec. 1366(d)(2)].

Factors that impact on the shareholder's stock basis include the following [see Sec. 1367]:

1. Investment in the stock.

2. Share of taxable income and share of positive special items.

3. Share of tax-exempt income.

4. Withdrawals or distributions.

5. Share of negative taxable income and share of negative special items.

6. Nondeductible expenses that are not chargeable to the capital account.

Note that a basic difference exists between the above basis account and the "outside basis" of a partner [see Secs. 705, 752]. Liabilities of the corporation do not impact on the shareholder basis account.

Distributions, in general, do not produce income to the shareholder [see Sec. 1368]. Instead, the shareholder reduces the stock basis by the amount of the distribution. If the amount of the distribution exceeds the stock basis, the excess qualifies for capital gain treatment. The mechanics of the distribution sequence become more complex if the S corporation has C corporation earnings and profits. In this case, the sequence and related tax consequence are as follows:

Accumulated adjustments account (AAA)	Tax-free
Earnings and profits	Taxable as ordinary income
Stock basis	Tax-free
Excess over stock basis	Capital gain

Note that the AAA for this purpose is, in effect, a subsidiary account of the stock basis account. Therefore, when the AAA is reduced associated with a distribution, the stock basis is reduced by the same amount.

If the S corporation has C corporation earnings and profits, the shareholders may elect to reverse the location of earnings and profits and AAA in the distribution sequence [see Sec. 1368(e)(3)]. In order to make this election, all shareholders (to whom the S corporation makes a distribution during the taxable year) must consent. Factors motivating this reversal election include the following:

1. The shareholders would like to report ordinary income at the shareholder level (e.g., to offset losses or be taxed at lower tax rates than future tax rates).

2. The distribution treated in this fashion will reduce earnings and profits to zero, and thereby alleviate potential adverse tax consequences for the S corporation [e.g., the passive tax liability at the corporate level under Sec. 1375 or the termination of the S election associated with passive income under Sec. 1362(d)(3)].

In addition to a distribution of assets having the potential for producing recognition at the shareholder level, recognized gain can occur at the corporate level as a result of the distribution. This result will occur if the property distributed to the shareholder is appreciated property (i.e., fair market value of the property exceeds the adjusted basis) [see Sec. 311(b)].

§ 1366. Pass-thru of items to shareholders

(a) Determination of shareholder's tax liability.—

(1) In general.—In determining the tax under this chapter of a shareholder for the shareholder's taxable year in which the taxable year of the S corporation ends (or for the final taxable year of a shareholder who dies, or of a trust or estate which terminates, before the end of the corporation's taxable year), there shall be taken into account the shareholder's pro rata share of the corporation's—

(A) items of income (including tax-exempt income), loss, deduction, or credit the separate treatment of which could affect the liability for tax of any shareholder, and

(B) nonseparately computed income or loss.

For purposes of the preceding sentence, the items referred to in subparagraph (A) shall include amounts described in paragraph (4) or (6) of section 702(a).

(2) Nonseparately computed income or loss defined.—For purposes of this subchapter, the term "nonseparately computed income or loss" means gross income minus the deductions allowed to the corporation under this chapter, determined by excluding all items described in paragraph (1)(A).

(b) Character passed thru.—The character of any item included in a shareholder's pro rata share under paragraph (1) of subsection (a) shall be determined as if such item were realized directly from the source from which realized by the corporation, or incurred in the same manner as incurred by the corporation.

(c) Gross income of a shareholder.—In any case where it is necessary to determine the gross income of a shareholder for purposes of this title, such gross income shall include the shareholder's pro rata share of the gross income of the corporation.

(d) Special rules for losses and deductions.—

(1) Cannot exceed shareholder's basis in stock and debt.—The aggregate amount of losses and deductions taken into account by a shareholder under subsection (a) for any taxable year shall not exceed the sum of—

(A) the adjusted basis of the shareholder's stock in the S corporation (determined with regard to paragraphs (1) and (2)(A) of section 1367(a) for the taxable year), and

(B) the shareholder's adjusted basis of any indebtedness of the S corporation to the shareholder (determined without regard to any adjustment under paragraph (2) of section 1367(b) for the taxable year).

(2) Indefinite carryover of disallowed losses and deductions.—

(A) In general.—Except as provided in subparagraph (B), any loss or deduction which is disallowed for any taxable year by reason of paragraph (1) shall be treated as incurred by the corporation in the succeeding taxable year with respect to that shareholder.

(B) Transfers of stock between spouses or incident to divorce.—In the case of any transfer described in section 1041(a) of stock of an S corporation, any loss or deduction described in subparagraph (A) with respect to such stock shall be treated as incurred by the corporation in the succeeding taxable year with respect to the transferee.

(3) Carryover of disallowed losses and deductions to post-termination transition period.—

(A) In general.—If for the last taxable year of a corporation for which it was an S corporation a loss or deduction was disallowed by reason of paragraph (1), such loss or deduction shall be treated as incurred by the shareholder on the last day of any post-termination transition period.

(B) Cannot exceed shareholder's basis in stock.—The aggregate amount of losses and deductions taken into account by a shareholder under subparagraph (A) shall not exceed the adjusted basis of the shareholder's stock in the corporation (determined at the close of the last day of the post-termination transition period and without regard to this paragraph).

(C) Adjustment in basis of stock.—The shareholder's basis in the stock of the corporation shall be reduced by the amount allowed as a deduction by reason of this paragraph.

(D) At-risk limitations.—To the extent that any increase in adjusted basis described in subparagraph (B) would have increased the shareholder's amount at risk under section 465 if such increase had occurred on the day preceding the commencement of the post-termination transition period, rules similar to the rules described in subparagraphs (A) through (C) shall apply to any losses disallowed by reason of section 465(a).

(4) Application of limitation on charitable contributions.—In the case of any charitable contribution of property to which the second sentence of section 1367(a)(2) applies, paragraph (1) shall not apply to the extent of the excess (if any) of—

(A) the shareholder's pro rata share of such contribution, over

(B) the shareholder's pro rata share of the adjusted basis of such property.

(e) Treatment of family group.—If an individual who is a member of the family (within the meaning of section 704(e)(3)) of one or more shareholders of an S corporation renders services for the corporation or furnishes capital to the corporation without receiving reasonable compensation therefor, the Secretary shall make such adjustments in the items taken into account by such individual and such shareholders as may be necessary in order to reflect the value of such services or capital.

(f) Special rules.—

(1) Subsection (a) not to apply to credit allowable under section 34.—Subsection (a) shall not apply with respect to any credit allowable under section 34 (relating to certain uses of gasoline and special fuels.

(2) Treatment of tax imposed on built-in gains.—If any tax is imposed under section 1374 for any taxable year on an S corporation, for purposes of subsection (a), the amount so imposed shall be treated as a loss sustained by the S corporation during such taxable year. The character of such loss shall be determined by allocating the loss proportionately among the recognized built-in gains giving rise to such tax.

(3) Reduction in pass-thru for tax imposed on excess net passive income.—If any tax is imposed under section 1375 for any taxable year on an S corporation, for purposes of subsection (a), each item of passive investment income shall be reduced by an amount which bears the same ratio to the amount of such tax as—

(A) the amount of such item, bears to

(B) the total passive investment income for the taxable year.

§ 1367. Adjustments to basis of stock of shareholders, etc.

(a) General rule.—

(1) Increases in basis.—The basis of each shareholder's stock in an S corporation shall be increased for any period by the sum of the following items determined with respect to that shareholder for such period:

(A) the items of income described in subparagraph (A) of section 1366(a)(1),

(B) any nonseparately computed income determined under subparagraph (B) of section 1366(a)(1), and

(C) the excess of the deductions for depletion over the basis of the property subject to depletion.

(2) Decreases in basis.—The basis of each shareholder's stock in an S corporation shall be decreased for any period (but not below zero) by the sum of the following items determined with respect to the shareholder for such period:

(A) distributions by the corporation which were not includible in the income of the shareholder by reason of section 1368,

(B) the items of loss and deduction described in subparagraph (A) of section 1366(a)(1),

(C) any nonseparately computed loss determined under subparagraph (B) of section 1366(a)(1),

(D) any expense of the corporation not deductible in computing its taxable income and not properly chargeable to capital account, and

(E) the amount of the shareholder's deduction for depletion for any oil and gas property held by the S corporation to the extent such deduction does not exceed the proportionate share of the adjusted basis of such property allocated to such shareholder under section 613A(c)(11)(B).

The decrease under subparagraph (B) by reason of a charitable contribution (as defined in section 170(c)) of property shall be the amount equal to the shareholder's pro rata share of the adjusted basis of such property. The preceding sentence shall not apply to contributions made in taxable years beginning after December 31, 2013.*

(b) Special rules.—

(1) Income items.—An amount which is required to be included in the gross income of a shareholder and shown on his return shall be taken into account under subparagraph (A) or (B) of subsection (a)(1) only to the extent such amount is included in the shareholder's gross income on his return, increased or decreased by any adjustment of such amount in a redetermination of the shareholder's tax liability.

(2) Adjustments in basis of indebtedness.—

(A) Reduction of basis.—If for any taxable year the amounts specified in subparagraphs (B), (C), (D), and (E) of subsection (a)(2) exceed the amount which reduces the shareholder's basis to zero, such excess shall be applied to reduce (but not below zero) the shareholder's basis in any indebtedness of the S corporation to the shareholder.

(B) Restoration of basis.—If for any taxable year beginning after December 31, 1982, there is a reduction under subparagraph (A) in the shareholder's basis in the indebtedness of an S corporation to a shareholder, any net increase (after the application of paragraphs (1) and (2) of subsection (a)) for any subsequent taxable year shall be applied to restore such reduction in basis before any of it may be used to increase the shareholder's basis in the stock of the S corporation.

(3) Coordination with sections 165(g) and 166(d).—This section and section 1366 shall be applied before the application of sections 165(g) and 166(d) to any taxable year of the shareholder or the corporation in which the security or debt becomes worthless.

(4) Adjustments in case of inherited stock.—

(A) In general.—If any person acquires stock in an S corporation by reason of the death of a

*Editorial comment: At the present time, this section has not been extended. There is pending legislation in the Senate, *The Tax Extenders Act of 2013 (S. 1859)*, that would extend Section 1367(a)(2) until December 31, 2014.

decedent or by bequest, devise, or inheritance, section 691 shall be applied with respect to any item of income of the S corporation in the same manner as if the decedent had held directly his pro rata share of such item.

(B) Adjustments to basis.—The basis determined under section 1014 of any stock in an S corporation shall be reduced by the portion of the value of the stock which is attributable to items constituting income in respect of the decedent.

§ 1368. Distributions

(a) General rule.—A distribution of property made by an S corporation with respect to its stock to which (but for this subsection) section 301(c) would apply shall be treated in the manner provided in subsection (b) or (c), whichever applies.

(b) S corporation having no earnings and profits.—In the case of a distribution described in subsection (a) by an S corporation which has no accumulated earnings and profits—

(1) Amount applied against basis.—The distribution shall not be included in gross income to the extent that it does not exceed the adjusted basis of the stock.

(2) Amount in excess of basis.—If the amount of the distribution exceeds the adjusted basis of the stock, such excess shall be treated as gain from the sale or exchange of property.

(c) S corporation having earnings and profits.—In the case of a distribution described in subsection (a) by an S corporation which has accumulated earnings and profits—

(1) Accumulated adjustments account.—That portion of the distribution which does not exceed the accumulated adjustments account shall be treated in the manner provided by subsection (b).

(2) Dividend.—That portion of the distribution which remains after the application of paragraph (1) shall be treated as a dividend to the extent it does not exceed the accumulated earnings and profits of the S corporation.

(3) Treatment of remainder.—Any portion of the distribution remaining after the application of paragraph (2) of this subsection shall be treated in the manner provided by subsection (b).

Except to the extent provided in regulations, if the distributions during the taxable year exceed the amount in the accumulated adjustments account at the close of the taxable year, for purposes of this subsection, the balance of such account shall be allocated among such distributions in proportion to their respective sizes.

(d) Certain adjustments taken into account.—Subsections (b) and (c) shall be applied by taking into account (to the extent proper)—

(1) the adjustments to the basis of the shareholder's stock described in section 1367, and

(2) the adjustments to the accumulated adjustments account which are required by subsection (e)(1).

In the case of any distributions made during any taxable year, the adjusted basis of the stock shall be determined with regard to the adjustments provided in paragraph (1) of section 1367(a) for the taxable year.

(e) Definitions and special rules.—For purposes of this section—

(1) Accumulated adjustments account.—

(A) In general.—Except as otherwise provided in this paragraph, the term "accumulated adjustments account" means an account of the S corporation which is adjusted for the S period in a manner similar to the adjustments under section 1367 (except that no adjustment shall be made for income (and related expenses) which is exempt from tax under this title and the phrase "(but not below zero)" shall be disregarded in section 1367(a)(2)) and no adjustment shall be made for Federal taxes attributable to any taxable year in which the corporation was a C corporation.

(B) Amount of adjustment in the case of redemptions.—In the case of any redemption which is treated as an exchange under section 302(a) or 303(a), the adjustment in the accumulated adjustments account shall be an amount which bears the same ratio to the balance in such account as the number of shares redeemed in such redemption bears to the number of shares of stock in the corporation immediately before such redemption.

(C) Net loss for year disregarded.—

(i) In general.—In applying this section to distributions made during any taxable year, the amount in the accumulated adjustments account as of the close of such taxable year shall be determined without regard to any net negative adjustment for such taxable year.

(ii) Net negative adjustment.—For purposes of clause (i), the term "net negative adjustment" means, with respect to any taxable year, the excess (if any) of—

(I) the reductions in the account for the taxable year (other than for distributions), over

(II) the increases in such account for such taxable year.

(2) S period.—The term "S period" means the most recent continuous period during which the corporation has been an S corporation. Such period shall not include any taxable year beginning before January 1, 1983.

(3) Election to distribute earnings first.—

(A) In general.—An S corporation may, with the consent of all of its affected shareholders, elect to have paragraph (1) of subsection (c) not apply to all distributions made during the taxable year for which the election is made.

(B) Affected shareholder.—For purposes of subparagraph (A), the term "affected shareholder" means any shareholder to whom a distribution is made by the S corporation during the taxable year.

(f) Restricted bank director stock.—If a director receives a distribution (not in part or in full payment in exchange for stock) from an S corporation with respect to any restricted bank director stock (as defined in section 1361(f)), the amount of such distribution—

(1) shall be includible in gross income of the director, and

(2) shall be deductible by the corporation for the taxable year of such corporation in which or with which ends the taxable year in which such amount is included in the gross income of the director.

PART III—SPECIAL RULES

Editorial Summary

Taxation at the Corporation Level

Subchapter S of Chapter 1 (Secs. 1371–1375)

In accordance with conduit theory, taxation occurs at the shareholder level rather than at the S corporation level. In three circumstances, however, tax can be levied at the corporate level. First, Sec. 1374 imposes a tax at the corporate level on certain built-in gains. The Tax Reform Act of 1986 severely limited the ability of C corporations to avoid double taxation (i.e., taxation at both the corporate level and the shareholder level) at the time of liquidation through the application of Secs. 336 and 337. Prior to the Act, the general rule of these Code sections was that the liquidation was not taxable at the corporate level. Recognizing that the S corporation provisions would provide a technique for the C corporation to avoid taxation at the time of liquidation, Sec. 1374 was enacted as part of the Tax Reform Act of 1986 to remove the motivation for C corporations to elect S corporation status prior to liquidation. Since Sec. 1374 is intended to serve this limited purpose, it is not applicable to an S corporation that has had the election in effect for all the taxable years of the corporation [see Sec. 1374(c)(1)].

The effective date for the Sec. 1374 tax is for taxable years beginning after December 31, 1986, but only if the first taxable year for which the corporation is an S corporation is pursuant to an election made after December 31, 1986. In addition, the tax is not applicable in the following circumstances:

1. Corporation qualifies for the transitional rules for a small, closely-held corporation (see the presentation in the Editorial Summary entitled Corporate Liquidations: Effect on Corporation, which precedes Sec. 336). Note that the transitional period has expired.

2. The disposition of the assets is not a taxable transaction (e.g., a Sec. 332 liquidation of a subsidiary).

While the primary statutory intent of Sec. 1374 is to tax built-in gains associated with the liquidation of an S corporation, recognized built-in gains are not defined so restrictively as to limit the application of the Sec. 1374 tax to liquidations. Instead, the taxable disposition in the ordinary course of business during the recognition period is subject to the Sec. 1374 tax to the extent of the built-in gain. The recognition period is a 10-year period which commences with the first day of the first taxable year for which the corporation is an S corporation [see Secs. 1374(d)(3) and (7)].

The tax liability at the S corporation level under Sec. 1374 is calculated by multiplying the net recognized built-in gains [see Sec. 1374(d)(2)] for the taxable year by the highest tax rate specified in Sec. 11(b) (i.e., presently 35 percent) [see Sec. 1374(b)(1)]. In making this calculation, net operating loss carryforwards under Sec. 172 and business credit carryforwards under Sec. 39 may be used. However, the intent of Sec. 1374 is that the tax liability at the corporate level should not exceed the tax liability that would result if the S corporation were a C corporation. Therefore, the previous tax liability calculation is subject to the following statutory ceiling [see Sec. 1374(d)(2)(A)(ii)]:

Taxable income × Highest tax rate specified in Sec. 11(b)

For this purpose, taxable income is calculated as if the corporation were a C corporation [subject to the limitations in Sec. 1375(b)(1)(B)]. Net operating loss carryforwards under

Sec. 172 and business credit carryforwards under Sec. 39 may be used.

The following formula can be used to calculate the corporate tax liability under Sec. 1375:

Excess net passive income × Highest rate of tax specified in Sec. 11(b) = Tax Liability*

ENPI = [PII – 25 percent (GR)]/PII × NPII

PII = Passive investment income

GR = Gross receipts

NPII = Net passive investment income

*Subject to the following statutory ceiling:
Taxable income × Highest rate of tax specified in Sec. 11(b).

For this purpose, taxable income is calculated as if the corporation were a C corporation [subject to the limitations in Sec. 1375(b)(1)(B)].

The S corporation also can be subject to investment tax credit recapture [see Sec. 1371(d)]. The potential recapture is associated with investment tax credit that was taken by the corporation prior to the S corporation election. Thus, if the corporation has never been a C corporation, recapture will not occur at the S corporation level.

If tax liability is assessed at the corporate level, the related pass-through item to the shareholders is reduced by the amount of the tax (see Sec. 1366; also the Editorial Summary entitled Tax Treatment of S Corporation Shareholders, which precedes Sec. 1366).

§ 1371. Coordination with subchapter C

(a) Application of subchapter C rules.—In general.—Except as otherwise provided in this title, and except to the extent inconsistent with this subchapter, subchapter C shall apply to an S corporation and its shareholders.

(b) No carryover between C year and S year.—

(1) From C year to S year.—No carryforward, and no carryback, arising for a taxable year for which a corporation is a C corporation may be carried to a taxable year for which such corporation is an S corporation.

(2) No carryover from S year.—No carryforward, and no carryback, shall arise at the corporate level for a taxable year for which a corporation is an S corporation.

(3) Treatment of S year as elapsed year.—Nothing in paragraphs (1) and (2) shall prevent treating a taxable year for which a corporation is an S corporation as a taxable year for purposes of determining the number of taxable years to which an item may be carried back or carried forward.

(c) Earnings and profits.—

(1) In general.—Except as provided in paragraphs (2) and (3) and subsection (d)(3), no adjustment shall be made to the earnings and profits of an S corporation.

(2) Adjustments for redemptions, liquidations, reorganizations, divisives, etc.—In the case of any transaction involving the application of subchapter C to any S corporation, proper adjustment to any accumulated earnings and profits of the corporation shall be made.

(3) Adjustments in case of distributions treated as dividends under section 1368(c) (2).—Paragraph (1) shall not apply with respect to that portion of a distribution which is treated as a dividend under section 1368(c)(2).

(d) Coordination with investment credit recapture.—

(1) No recapture by reason of election.—Any election under section 1362 shall be treated as a mere change in the form of conducting a trade or business for purposes of the second sentence of section 50(a)(4).

(2) Corporation continues to be liable.—Notwithstanding an election under section 1362, an S corporation shall continue to be liable for any increase in tax under section 49(b) or 50(a) attributable to credits allowed for taxable years for which such corporation was not an S corporation.

(3) Adjustment to earnings and profits for amount of recapture.—Paragraph (1) of subsection (c) shall not apply to any increase in tax under section 49(b) or 50(a) for which the S corporation is liable.

(e) Cash distributions during post-termination transition period.—

(1) In general.—Any distribution of money by a corporation with respect to its stock during a post-termination transition period shall be applied against and reduce the adjusted basis of the stock, to the extent that the amount of the distribution does not exceed the accumulated adjustments account (within the meaning of section 1368(e)).

(2) Election to distribute earnings first.—An S corporation may elect to have paragraph (1) not apply to all distributions made during a post-termination transition period described in section 1377(b)(1)(A). Such election shall not be effective unless all shareholders of the S corporation to whom distributions are made by the S corporation during such post-termination transition period consent to such election.

§ 1372. Partnership rules to apply for fringe benefit purposes

(a) General rule.—For purposes of applying the provisions of this subtitle which relate to employee fringe benefits—

(1) the S corporation shall be treated as a partnership, and

(2) any 2-percent shareholder of the S corporation shall be treated as a partner of such partnership.

(b) 2-percent shareholder defined.—For purposes of this section, the term "2-percent shareholder" means any person who owns (or is considered as owning within the meaning of section 318) on any day during the taxable year of the S corporation more than 2 percent of the outstanding stock of such corporation or stock possessing more than 2 percent of the total combined voting power of all stock of such corporation.

§ 1373. Foreign income

(a) S corporation treated as partnership, etc.—For purposes of subparts A and F of part III, and part V, of subchapter N (relating to income from sources without the United States)—

(1) an S corporation shall be treated as a partnership, and

(2) the shareholders of such corporation shall be treated as partners of such partnership.

(b) Recapture of overall foreign loss.—For purposes of section 904(f) (relating to recapture of overall foreign loss), the making or termination of an election to be treated as an S corporation shall be treated as a disposition of the business.

§ 1374. Tax imposed on certain built-in gains

(a) General rule.—If for any taxable year beginning in the recognition period an S corporation has a net recognized built-in gain, there is hereby imposed a tax (computed under subsection (b)) on the income of such corporation for such taxable year.

(b) Amount of tax.—

(1) In general.—The amount of the tax imposed by subsection (a) shall be computed by applying the highest rate of tax specified in section 11(b) to the net recognized built-in gain of the S corporation for the taxable year.

(2) Net operating loss carryforwards from C years allowed.—Notwithstanding section 1371(b)(1), any net operating loss carryforward arising in a taxable year for which the corporation was a C corporation shall be allowed for purposes of this section as a deduction against the net recognized built-in gain of the S corporation for the taxable year. For purposes of determining the amount of any such loss which may be carried to subsequent taxable years, the amount of the net recognized built-in gain shall be treated as taxable income. Rules similar to the rules of the preceding sentences of this paragraph shall apply in the case of a capital loss carryforward arising in a taxable year for which the corporation was a C corporation.

(3) Credits.—

(A) In general.—Except as provided in subparagraph (B), no credit shall be allowable under part IV of subchapter A of this chapter (other than under section 34) against the tax imposed by subsection (a).

(B) Business credit carryforwards from C years allowed.—Notwithstanding section 1371(b)(1), any business credit carryforward under section 39 arising in a taxable year for which the corporation was a C corporation shall be allowed as a credit against the tax imposed by subsection (a) in the same manner as if it were imposed by section 11. A similar rule shall apply in the case of the minimum tax credit under section 53 to the extent attributable to taxable years for which the corporation was a C corporation.

(4) Coordination with section 1201(a).—For purposes of section 1201(a)—

(A) the tax imposed by subsection (a) shall be treated as if it were imposed by section 11, and

(B) the amount of the net recognized built-in gain shall be treated as the taxable income.

(c) Limitations.—

(1) Corporations which were always S corporations.—Subsection (a) shall not apply to any corporation if an election under section 1362(a) has been in effect with respect to such corporation for each of its taxable years. Except as provided in regulations, an S corporation and any predecessor corporation shall be treated as 1 corporation for purposes of the preceding sentence.

(2) Limitation on amount of recognized built-in gains.—The amount of the net recognized built-in gains taken into account under this section for any taxable year shall not exceed the excess (if any) of—

(A) the net unrealized built-in gain, over

(B) the net recognized built-in gains for prior taxable years beginning in the recognition period.

(d) Definitions and special rules.—For purposes of this section—

(1) Net unrealized built-in gain.—The term "net unrealized built-in gain" means the amount (if any) by which—

(A) the fair market value of the assets of the S corporation as of the beginning of its 1st taxable year for which an election under section 1362(a) is in effect, exceeds

(B) the aggregate adjusted bases of such assets at such time.

(2) Net recognized built-in gain.—

(A) In general.—The term "net recognized built-in gain" means, with respect to any taxable year in the recognition period, the lesser of—

(i) the amount which would be the taxable income of the S corporation for such taxable year if only recognized built-in gains and recognized built-in losses were taken into account, or

(ii) such corporation's taxable income for such taxable year (determined as provided in section 1375(b)(1)(B)).

(B) Carryover.—If, for any taxable year described in subparagraph (A), the amount referred to in clause (i) of subparagraph (A) exceeds the amount referred to in clause (ii) of subparagraph (A), such excess shall be treated as a recognized built-in gain in the succeeding taxable year. The preceding sentence shall apply only in the case of a corporation treated as an S corporation by reason of an election made on or after March 31, 1988.

(3) Recognized built-in gain.—The term "recognized built-in gain" means any gain recognized during the recognition period on the disposition of any asset except to the extent that the S corporation establishes that—

(A) such asset was not held by the S corporation as of the beginning of the 1st taxable year for which it was an S corporation, or

(B) such gain exceeds the excess (if any) of—

(i) the fair market value of such asset as of the beginning of such 1st taxable year, over

(ii) the adjusted basis of the asset as of such time.

(4) Recognized built-in losses.—The term "recognized built-in loss" means any loss recognized during the recognition period on the disposition of any asset to the extent that the S corporation establishes that—

(A) such asset was held by the S corporation as of the beginning of the 1st taxable year referred to in paragraph (3), and

(B) such loss does not exceed the excess of—

(i) the adjusted basis of such asset as of the beginning of such 1st taxable year, over

(ii) the fair market value of such asset as of such time.

(5) Treatment of certain built-in items—

(A) Income items.—Any item of income which is properly taken into account during the recognition period but which is attributable to periods before the 1st taxable year for which the corporation was an S corporation shall be treated as a recognized built-in gain for the taxable year in which it is properly taken into account.

(B) Deduction items.—Any amount which is allowable as a deduction during the recognition period (determined without regard to any carryover) but which is attributable to periods before the 1st taxable year referred to in subparagraph (A) shall be treated as a recognized built-in loss for the taxable year for which it is allowable as a deduction.

(C) Adjustment to net unrealized built-in gain.—The amount of the net unrealized built-in gain shall be properly adjusted for amounts which would be treated as recognized built-in gains or losses under this paragraph if such amounts were properly taken into account (or allowable as a deduction) during the recognition period.

(6) Treatment of certain property.—If the adjusted basis of any asset is determined (in whole or in part) by reference to the adjusted basis of any other asset held by the S corporation as of the beginning of the 1st taxable year referred to in paragraph (3)—

(A) such asset shall be treated as held by the S corporation as of the beginning of such 1st taxable year, and

(B) any determination under paragraph (3)(B) or (4)(B) with respect to such asset shall be made by reference to the fair market value and adjusted basis of such other asset as of the beginning of such 1st taxable year.

(7) Recognition period.—

(A) In general.—The term "recognition period" means the 10-year period beginning with the 1st day of the 1st taxable year for which the corporation was an S corporation.

(B) Special rules for 2009, 2010, and 2011.—No tax shall be imposed on the net recognized built-in gain of an S corporation—

(i) in the case of any taxable year beginning in 2009 or 2010, if the 7th taxable year in the recognition period preceded such taxable year, or

(ii) in the case of any taxable year beginning in 2011, if the 5th year in the recognition period preceded such taxable year.

The preceding sentence shall be applied separately with respect to any amount to which paragraph (8) applies.

(C) Special rule for 2012 and 2013.*—For purposes of determining the net recognized built-in-gain for taxable years beginning in 2012 or 2013,* subparagraphs (A) and (D) shall be applied by substituting "5-year" for "10-year".

(D) Special rule for distributions to shareholders.—For purposes of applying this section to any amount includible in income by reason of distributions to shareholders pursuant to section 593(e)—

(i) subparagraph (A) shall be applied without regard to the phrase "10-year", and

(ii) subparagraph (B) shall not apply.

(E) Installment sales.—If an S corporation sells an asset and reports the income from the sale using the installment method under section 453, the treatment of all payments received shall be governed by the provisions of this paragraph applicable to the taxable year in which such sale was made.

(8) Treatment of transfer of assets from C Corporation to S Corporation.—

(A) In general.—Except to the extent provided in regulations, if—

(i) an S corporation acquires any asset, and

(ii) the S corporation's basis in such asset is determined (in whole or in part) by reference to the basis of such asset (or any other property) in the hands of a C corporation,

then a tax is hereby imposed on any net recognized built-in gain attributable to any such assets for any taxable year beginning in the recognition period. The amount of such tax shall be determined under the rules of this section as modified by subparagraph (B).

(B) Modifications.—For purposes of this paragraph, the modifications of this subparagraph are as follows:

(i) In general.—The preceding paragraphs of this subsection shall be applied by taking into account the day on which the assets were acquired by the S corporation in lieu of the beginning of the 1st taxable year for which the corporation was an S corporation.

(ii) Subsection (c)(1) not to apply.—Subsection (c)(1) shall not apply.

(9) Reference to 1st taxable year.—Any reference in this section to the 1st taxable year for which the corporation was an S corporation shall be treated as a reference to the 1st taxable year for which the corporation was an S corporation pursuant to its most recent election under section 1362.

(e) Regulations.—The Secretary shall prescribe such regulations as may be necessary to carry out the purposes of this section including regulations providing for the appropriate treatment of successor corporations.

§ 1375. Tax imposed when passive investment income of corporation having accumulated earnings and profits exceeds 25 percent of gross receipts

(a) General rule.—If for the taxable year an S corporation has—

(1) accumulated earnings and profits at the close of such taxable year, and

(2) gross receipts more than 25 percent of which are passive investment income,

then there is hereby imposed a tax on the income of such corporation for such taxable year. Such tax shall be computed by multiplying the excess net passive income by the highest rate of tax specified in section 11(b).

(b) Definitions.—For purposes of this section—

(1) Excess net passive income.—

(A) In general.—Except as provided in subparagraph (B), the term "excess net passive income" means an amount which bears the

*Editorial comment: At the present time, this section has not been extended. There is pending legislation in the Senate, *The Tax Extenders Act of 2013 (S. 1859)*, that would extend Section 1374(d)(7)(C) until 2014.

same ratio to the net passive income for the taxable year as—

(i) the amount by which the passive investment income for the taxable year exceeds 25 percent of the gross receipts for the taxable year, bears to

(ii) the passive investment income for the taxable year.

(B) Limitation.—The amount of the excess net passive income for any taxable year shall not exceed the amount of the corporation's taxable income for such taxable year as determined under section 63(a)—

(i) without regard to the deductions allowed by part VIII of subchapter B (other than the deduction allowed by section 248, relating to organization expenditures), and

(ii) without regard to the deduction under section 172.

(2) Net passive income.—The term "net passive income" means—

(A) passive investment income, reduced by

(B) the deductions allowable under this chapter which are directly connected with the production of such income (other than deductions allowable under section 172 and part VIII of subchapter B).

(3) Passive investment income; etc.—The terms "passive investment income" and "gross receipts" shall have the same respective meanings as when used in paragraph (3) of section 1362(d).

(4) Coordination with section 1374.—Notwithstanding paragraph (3), the amount of passive investment income shall be determined by not taking into account any recognized built-in gain or loss of the S corporation for any taxable year in the recognition period. Terms used in the preceding sentence shall have the same respective meanings as when used in section 1374.

(c) Credits not allowable.—No credit shall be allowed under part IV of subchapter A of this chapter (other than section 34) against the tax imposed by subsection (a).

(d) Waiver of tax in certain cases.—If the S corporation establishes to the satisfaction of the Secretary that—

(1) it determined in good faith that it had no accumulated earnings and profits at the close of a taxable year, and

(2) during a reasonable period of time after it was determined that it did have accumulated earnings and profits at the close of such taxable year such earnings and profits were distributed,

the Secretary may waive the tax imposed by subsection (a) for such taxable year.

PART IV—DEFINITIONS; MISCELLANEOUS

Editorial Summary

Definition of Shareholder's Pro Rata Share and Corporate Taxable Year

Subchapter S of Chapter 1 (Secs. 1377–1379)

See the discussion under the Editorial Summary entitled Tax Treatment of S Corporation Shareholders, which precedes Sec. 1366.

§ 1377. Definitions and special rule

(a) Pro rata share.—For purposes of this subchapter—

(1) In general.—Except as provided in paragraph (2), each shareholder's pro rata share of any item for any taxable year shall be the sum of the amounts determined with respect to the shareholder—

(A) by assigning an equal portion of such item to each day of the taxable year, and

(B) then by dividing that portion pro rata among the shares outstanding on such day.

(2) Election to terminate year.—

(A) In general.—Under regulations prescribed by the Secretary, if any shareholder terminates the shareholder's interest in the corporation during the taxable year and all affected shareholders and the corporation agree to the application of this paragraph, paragraph (1) shall be applied to the affected shareholders as if the taxable year consisted of 2 taxable years the first of which ends on the date of the termination.

(B) Affected shareholders.—For purposes of subparagraph (A), the term "affected shareholders" means the shareholder whose interest is terminated and all shareholders to whom such shareholder has transferred shares during the taxable year. If such shareholder has transferred shares to the corporation, the term "affected shareholders" shall include all persons who are shareholders during the taxable year.

(b) Post-termination transition period.—

(1) In general.—For purposes of this subchapter, the term "post-termination transition period" means—

(A) the period beginning on the day after the last day of the corporation's last taxable year as an S corporation and ending on the later of—

(i) the day which is 1 year after such last day, or

(ii) the due date for filing the return for such last year as an S corporation (including extensions),

(B) the 120-day period beginning on the date of any determination pursuant to an audit of the taxpayer which follows the termination of the corporation's election and which adjusts a subchapter S item of income, loss, or deduction of the corporation arising during the S period (as defined in section 1368(e)(2)), and

(C) the 120-day period beginning on the date of a determination that the corporation's election under section 1362(a) had terminated for a previous taxable year.

(2) Determination defined.—For purposes of paragraph (1), the term "determination" means—

(A) a determination as defined in section 1313(a), or

(B) an agreement between the corporation and the Secretary that the corporation failed to qualify as an S corporation.

(3) Special rules for audit related post-termination transition periods.—

(A) No application to carryovers.—Paragraph (1)(B) shall not apply for purposes of section 1366(d)(3).

(B) Limitation on application to distributions.—Paragraph (1)(B) shall apply to a distribution described in section 1371(e) only to the extent that the amount of such distribution does not exceed the aggregate increase (if any) in the accumulated adjustments account (within the meaning of section 1368(e)) by reason of the adjustments referred to in such paragraph.

(c) Manner of making elections, etc.—Any election under this subchapter, and any revocation under section 1362(d)(1), shall be made in such manner as the Secretary shall by regulations prescribe.

§ 1378. Taxable year of S corporation

(a) General rule.—For purposes of this subtitle, the taxable year of an S corporation shall be a permitted year.

(b) Permitted year defined.—For purposes of this section, the term "permitted year" means a taxable year which—

(1) is a year ending December 31, or

(2) is any other accounting period for which the corporation establishes a business purpose to the satisfaction of the Secretary.

For purposes of paragraph (2), any deferral of income to shareholders shall not be treated as a business purpose.

§ 1379. Transitional rules on enactment

(a) Old elections.—Any election made under section 1372(a) (as in effect before the enactment of the Subchapter S Revision Act of 1982) shall be treated as an election made under section 1362.

(b) References to prior law included.—Any references in this title to a provision of this subchapter shall, to the extent not inconsistent with the purposes of this subchapter, include a reference to the corresponding provision as in effect before the enactment of the Subchapter S Revision Act of 1982.

(c) Distributions of undistributed taxable income.—If a corporation was an electing small business corporation for the last preenactment year, subsections (f) and (d) of section 1375 (as in effect before the enactment of the Subchapter S Revision Act of 1982) shall continue to apply with respect to distributions of undistributed taxable income for any taxable year beginning before January 1, 1983.

(d) Carryforwards.—If a corporation was an electing small business corporation for the last preenactment year and is an S corporation for the 1st postenactment year, any carryforward to the 1st postenactment year which arose in a taxable year for which the corporation was an electing small business corporation shall be treated as arising in the 1st postenactment year.

(e) Preenactment and postenactment years defined.—For purposes of this subsection—

(1) Last preenactment year.—The term "last preenactment year" means the last taxable year of a corporation which begins before January 1, 1983.

(2) 1st postenactment year.—The term "1st postenactment year" means the 1st taxable year of a corporation which begins after December 31, 1982.

SUBCHAPTER T—COOPERATIVES AND THEIR PATRONS*

SUBCHAPTER U—DESIGNATION AND TREATMENT OF EMPOWERMENT ZONES, ENTERPRISE COMMUNITIES, AND RURAL INVESTMENT AREAS*

SUBCHAPTER V—TITLE 11 CASES*

SUBCHAPTER W—DISTRICT OF COLUMBIA ENTERPRISE ZONE*

SUBCHAPTER X—DESIGNATION OF RENEWAL COMMUNITIES*

SUBCHAPTER Y—NEW YORK LIBERTY ZONE BENEFITS*

CHAPTER 2—TAX ON SELF-EMPLOYMENT INCOME

Editorial Summary

Self—Employment Tax

Chapter 2 (Secs. 1401–1403)

A tax is imposed on self-employment income as defined in Sec. 1402. The tax consists of two components: (1) the Social Security tax (i.e., old age, survivors, and disability insurance) and (2) the Medicare tax (i.e., hospital insurance). The rates to be applied and the ceiling on the covered income is as follows:

Self-Employment Tax
Rates and Ceilings

	Rates			Ceiling		
	2012	2013	2014	2012	2013	2014
Social Security Tax	10.4%***	12.4%	12.4%	$110,100	$113,700	$117,000
Medicare Tax	2.9%	2.9%	2.9%	None	None	None

§ 1401. Rate of tax

(a) Old-age, survivors, and disability insurance.**—In addition to other taxes, there shall be imposed for each taxable year, on the self-employment income of every individual, a tax equal to the following percent of the amount of the self-employment income for such taxable year:

In the case of a taxable year Beginning after:	And before:	Percent:
December 31, 1983	January 1, 1988	11.40
December 31, 1987	January 1, 1990	12.12
December 31, 1989		12.40

(b) Hospital insurance.—

(1) In general.—In addition to the tax imposed by the preceding subsection, there shall be imposed for each taxable year, on the self-employment income of every individual, a tax equal to the following percent of the amount of the self-employment income for such taxable year:

In the case of a taxable year Beginning after:	And before:	Percent:
December 31, 1983	January 1, 1985	2.60
December 31, 1984	January 1, 1986	2.70
December 31, 1985		2.90

(2) Additional tax.—

(A) In general.—In addition to the tax imposed by paragraph (1) and the preceding subsection, there is hereby imposed on every taxpayer (other than a corporation, estate, or trust) for each taxable year beginning after December 31, 2012, a tax equal to 0.9 percent of the self-employment income for such taxable year which is in excess of—

(i) in the case of a joint return, $250,000,

(ii) in the case of a married taxpayer (as defined in section 7703) filing a separate return, 1/2 of the dollar amount determined under clause (i), and

(iii) in any other case, $200,000.

(B) Coordination with FICA.—The amounts under clause (i), (ii), or (iii) (whichever is applicable) of subparagraph (A) shall be reduced (but not below zero) by the amount of wages taken into account in determining the tax imposed under section 3121(b)(2) with respect to the taxpayer.

(c) Relief from taxes in cases covered by certain international agreements.—During any period in which there is in effect an agreement entered into pursuant to section 233 of the Social Security Act with any foreign country, the self-employment income of an individual shall be exempt from the taxes

*Omitted.

**Editorial comment: The ceiling on self-employment income subject to the Social Security tax is $113,700 in 2013, and $117,000 in 2014.

***Editorial comment: The normal rate for 2014 is 12.4%, unchanged from 2013. However, for 2011 and 2012, the rate was reduced to 10.4%.

imposed by this section to the extent that such self-employment income is subject under such agreement to taxes or contributions for similar purposes under the social security system of such foreign country.

§ 1402. Definitions

(a) Net earnings from self-employment.—The term "net earnings from self-employment" means the gross income derived by an individual from any trade or business carried on by such individual, less the deductions allowed by this subtitle which are attributable to such trade or business, plus his distributive share (whether or not distributed) of income or loss described in section 702(a)(8) from any trade or business carried on by a partnership of which he is a member; except that in computing such gross income and deductions and such distributive share of partnership ordinary income or loss—

(1) there shall be excluded rentals from real estate and from personal property leased with the real estate (including such rentals paid in crop shares, and including payments under section 1233 (2) of the Food Security Act of 1985 [16 U.S.C. 3833(2)] to individuals receiving benefits under section 202 or 223 of the Social Security Act) together with the deductions attributable thereto, unless such rentals are received in the course of a trade or business as a real estate dealer; except that the preceding provisions of this paragraph shall not apply to any income derived by the owner or tenant of land if (A) such income is derived under an arrangement, between the owner or tenant and another individual, which provides that such other individual shall produce agricultural or horticultural commodities (including livestock, bees, poultry, and fur-bearing animals and wildlife) on such land, and that there shall be material participation by the owner or tenant (as determined without regard to any activities of an agent of such owner or tenant) in the production or the management of the production of such agricultural or horticultural commodities, and (B) there is material participation by the owner or tenant (as determined without regard to any activities of an agent of such owner or tenant) with respect to any such agricultural or horticultural commodity;

(2) there shall be excluded dividends on any share of stock, and interest on any bond, debenture, note, or certificate, or other evidence of indebtedness, issued with interest coupons or in registered form by any corporation (including one issued by a government or political subdivision thereof), unless such dividends and interest are received in the course of a trade or business as a dealer in stocks or securities;

(3) there shall be excluded any gain or loss—

(A) which is considered as gain or loss from the sale or exchange of a capital asset,

(B) from the cutting of timber, or the disposal of timber, coal, or iron ore, if section 631 applies to such gain or loss, or

(C) from the sale, exchange, involuntary conversion, or other disposition of property if such property is neither—

(i) stock in trade or other property of a kind which would properly be includible in inventory if on hand at the close of the taxable year, nor

(ii) property held primarily for sale to customers in the ordinary course of the trade or business;

(4) the deduction for net operating losses provided in section 172 shall not be allowed;

(5) if—

(A) any of the income derived from a trade or business (other than a trade or business carried on by a partnership) is community income under community property laws applicable to such income, all of the gross income and deductions attributable to such trade or business shall be treated as the gross income and deductions of the husband unless the wife exercises substantially all of the management and control of such trade or business, in which case all of such gross income and deductions shall be treated as the gross income and deductions of the wife; and

(B) any portion of a partner's distributive share of the ordinary income or loss from a trade or business carried on by a partnership is community income or loss under the community property laws applicable to such share, all of such distributive share shall be included in computing the net earnings from self-employment of such partner, and no part of such share shall be taken into account in computing the net earnings from self-employment of the spouse of such partner;

(6) a resident of Puerto Rico shall compute his net earnings from self-employment in the same manner as a citizen of the United States but without regard to section 933;

(7) the deduction for personal exemptions provided in section 151 shall not be allowed;

(8) an individual who is a duly ordained, commissioned, or licensed minister of a church or a member of a religious order shall compute his net earnings from self-employment derived from the performance of service described in subsection (c)(4) without regard to section 107 (relating to rental value of parsonages), section 119 (relating to meals and lodging furnished for the convenience of the employer), and section 911 (relating to citizens or residents of the United States living abroad), but shall not include in such net earnings from self-employment the rental value of any parsonage or any parsonage allowance (whether or not excludable under section 107) provided after the individual retires, or any other retirement benefit received by such individual from a church plan (as defined in section 414(e) after the individual retires;

(9) the exclusion from gross income provided by section 931 shall not apply;

(10) there shall be excluded amounts received by a partner pursuant to a written plan of the partnership, which meets such requirements as are prescribed by the Secretary, and which provides for payments on account of retirement, on a periodic basis, to partners generally or to a class or classes of partners, such payments to continue at least until such partner's death, if—

(A) such partner rendered no services with respect to any trade or business carried on by such partnership (or its successors) during the taxable year of such partnership (or its successors), ending within or with his taxable year, in which such amounts were received, and

(B) no obligation exists (as of the close of the partnership's taxable year referred to in subparagraph (A) from the other partners to such partner except with respect to retirement payments under such plan, and

(C) such partner's share, if any, of the capital of the partnership has been paid to him in full before the close of the partnership's taxable year referred to in subparagraph (A);

(11) the exclusion from gross income provided by section 911(a)(1) shall not apply;

(12) in lieu of the deduction provided by section 164(f) (relating to deduction for one-half of self-employment taxes), there shall be allowed a deduction equal to the product of—

(A) the taxpayer's net earnings from self-employment for the taxable year (determined without regard to this paragraph), and

(B) one-half of the sum of the rates imposed by subsections (a) and (b) of section 1401 for such year (determined without regard to the rate imposed under paragraph 2 of section 1401(b));

(13) there shall be excluded the distributive share of any item of income or loss of a limited partner, as such, other than guaranteed payments described in section 707(c) to that partner for services actually rendered to or on behalf of the partnership to the extent that those payments are established to be in the nature of remuneration for those services;

(14) in the case of church employee income, the special rules of subsection (j)(1) shall apply;

(15) in the case of a member of an Indian tribe, the special rules of section 7873 (relating to income derived by Indians from exercise of fishing rights) shall apply;

(16) the deduction provided by section 199 shall not be allowed; and

(17) notwithstanding the preceding provision of this subsection, each spouse's share of income or loss from a qualified joint venture shall be taken into account as provided in section 761(f) in determining net earnings from self-employment of such spouse.

If the taxable year of a partner is different from that of the partnership, the distributive share which he is required to include in computing his net earnings from self-employment shall be based on the ordinary income or loss of the partnership for any taxable year of the partnership ending within or with his taxable year. In the case of any trade or business which is carried on by an individual or by a partnership and in which, if such trade or business were carried on exclusively by employees, the major portion of the services would constitute agricultural labor as defined in section 3121(g)—

(i) in the case of an individual, if the gross income derived by him from such trade or business is not more than the upper limit, the net earnings from self-employment derived by him from such trade or business may, at his option, be deemed to be 66⅔ percent of such gross income; or

(ii) in the case of an individual, if the gross income derived by him from such trade or business is more than the upper limit and the net earnings from self-employment derived by him from such trade or business (computed under this subsection without regard to this sentence) are less than the lower limit, the net earnings from self-employment derived by him from such trade or business may, at his option, be deemed to be the lower limit; and

(iii) in the case of a member of a partnership, if his distributive share of the gross income of the partnership derived from such trade or business (after such gross income has been reduced by the sum of all payments to which section 707(c) applies) is not more than the upper limit, his distributive share of income described in section 702(a)(8) derived from such trade or business may, at his option, be deemed to be an amount equal to 66⅔ percent of his distributive share of such gross income (after such gross income has been so reduced); or

(iv) in the case of a member of a partnership, if his distributive share of the gross income of the partnership derived from such trade or business (after such gross income has been reduced by the sum of all payments to which section 707(c) applies) is more than the upper limit and his distributive share (whether or not distributed) of income described in section 702(a)(8) derived from such trade or business (computed under this subsection without regard to this sentence) is less than the lower limit, his distributive share of income described in section 702 (a)(8) derived from such trade or business may, at his option, be deemed to be the lower limit.

For purposes of the preceding sentence, gross income means—

(v) in the case of any such trade or business in which the income is computed under a cash receipts and disbursements method, the gross receipts from such trade or business reduced by the cost or other basis of property which was purchased and sold in carrying on such trade or business, adjusted (after such reduction) in accordance with the provisions of paragraphs (1) through (7) and paragraph (9) of this subsection; and

(vi) in the case of any such trade or business in which the income is computed under an accrual method, the gross income from such trade or business, adjusted in accordance with the provisions of paragraphs (1) through (7) and paragraph (9) of this subsection;

and, for purposes of such sentence, if an individual (including a member of a partnership) derives gross income from more than one such trade or business, such gross income (including his distributive share of the gross income of any partnership derived from any such trade or business) shall be deemed to have been derived from one trade or business.

The preceding sentence and clauses (i) through (iv) of the second preceding sentence shall also apply in the case of any trade or business (other than a trade or business specified in such second preceding sentence) which is carried on by an individual who is self-employed on a regular basis as defined in subsection (h), or by a partnership of which an individual is a member on a regular basis as defined in subsection (h), but only if such individual's net earnings from self-employment as determined without regard to this sentence in the taxable year are less than the lower limit and less than 66⅔ percent of the sum (in such taxable year) of such individual's gross income derived from all trades or businesses carried on by him and his distributive share of the income or loss from all trades or businesses carried on by all the partnerships of which he is a member; except that this sentence shall not apply to more than 5 taxable years in the case of any individual, and in no case in which an individual elects to determine the amount of his net earnings from self-employment for a taxable year under the provisions of the two preceding sentences with respect to a trade or business to which the second preceding sentence applies and with respect to a trade or business to which this sentence applies shall such net earnings for such year exceed the lower limit.

(b) Self-employment income.—The term "self-employment income" means the net earnings from self-employment derived by an individual (other than a nonresident alien individual, except as provided by an agreement under section 233 of the Social Security Act) during any taxable year; except that such term shall not include—

(1) in the case of the tax imposed by section 1401 (a), that part of the net earnings from self-employment which is in excess of (i) an amount equal to the contribution and benefit base (as determined under section 230 of the Social Security Act) which is effective for the calendar year in which such taxable year begins, minus (ii) the amount of the wages paid to such individual during such taxable years; or

(2) the net earnings from self-employment, if such net earnings for the taxable year are less than $400.

For purposes of paragraph (1), the term "wages" (A) includes such remuneration paid to an employee for services included under an agreement entered into pursuant to the provisions of section 3212(*l*) (relating to coverage of citizens of the United States who are employees of foreign affiliates of American employers), as would be wages under section 3121(a) if such services constituted employment under section 3121 (b), and (B) includes compensation which is subject to the tax imposed by section 3201 or 3211. An individual who is not a citizen of the United States but who is a resident of the Commonwealth of Puerto Rico, the Virgin Islands, Guam, or American Samoa shall not, for purposes of this chapter be considered to be a nonresident alien individual. In the case of church employee income, the special rules of subsection (j)(2) shall apply for purposes of paragraph (2).

(c) Trade or business.—The term "trade or business," when used with reference to self-employment income or net earnings from self-employment, shall have the same meaning as when used in section 162 (relating to trade or business expenses), except that such term shall not include—

(1) the performance of the functions of a public office, other than the functions of a public office of a State or a political subdivision thereof with respect to fees received in any period in which the functions are performed in a position compensated solely on a fee basis and in which such functions are not covered under an agreement entered into by such State and the Commissioner of Social Security pursuant to section 218 of the Social Security Act;

(2) the performance of service by an individual as an employee, other than—

(A) service described in section 3121(b) (14) (B) performed by an individual who has attained the age of 18,

(B) service described in section 3121(b)(16),

(C) service described in section 3121(b)(11), (12), or (15) performed in the United States (as defined in section 3121(e)(2)) by a citizen of the United States, except service which constitutes "employment" under section 3121(y),

(D) service described in paragraph (4) of this subsection,

(E) service performed by an individual as an employee of a State or a political subdivision thereof in a position compensated solely on a fee basis with respect to fees received in any period in which such service is not covered under an agreement entered into by such State and the Commissioner of Social Security pursuant to section 218 of the Social Security Act,

(F) service described in section 3121(b)(20), and

(G) service described in section 3121(b) (8) (B);

(3) the performance of service by an individual as an employee or employee representative as defined in section 3231;

(4) the performance of service by a duly ordained, commissioned, or licensed minister of a church in the exercise of his ministry or by a member of a religious order in the exercise of duties required by such order;

(5) the performance of service by an individual in the exercise of his profession as a Christian Science practitioner; or

(6) the performance of service by an individual during the period for which an exemption under subsection (g) is effective with respect to him.

The provisions of paragraph (4) or (5) shall not apply to service (other than service performed by a member of a religious order who has taken a vow of poverty as a member of such order) performed by an individual unless an exemption under subsection (e) is effective with respect to him.

(d) Employee and wages.—The term "employee" and the term "wages" shall have the same meaning as when used in chapter 21 (sec. 3101 and following, relating to Federal Insurance Contributions Act).

(e) Ministers, members of religious orders, and Christian Science practitioners.—

(1) Exemption.—Subject to paragraph (2), any individual who is (A) a duly ordained, commissioned, or licensed minister of a church or a member of a religious order (other than a member of a religious order who has taken a vow of poverty as a member of such order) or (B) a Christian Science practitioner, upon filing an application (in such form and manner, and with such official, as may be prescribed by regulations made under this chapter) together with a statement that either he is conscientiously opposed to, or because of religious principles he is opposed to, the acceptance (with respect to services performed by him as such minister, member, or practitioner) of any public insurance which makes payments in the event of death, disability, old age, or retirement or makes payments toward the cost of, or provides services for, medical care (including the benefits of any insurance system established by the Social Security Act) and, in the case of an individual described in subparagraph (A), that he has informed the ordaining, commissioning, or licensing body of the church or order that he is opposed to such insurance, shall receive an exemption from the tax imposed by this chapter with respect to services performed by him as such minister, member, or practitioner. Notwithstanding the preceding sentence, an exemption may not be granted to an individual under this subsection if he had filed an effective waiver certificate under this section as it was in effect before its amendment in 1967.

(2) Verification of application.—The Secretary may approve an application for an exemption filed pursuant to paragraph (1) only if the Secretary has verified that the individual applying for the exemption is aware of the grounds on which the individual may receive an exemption pursuant to this subsection and that the individual seeks exemption on such grounds. The Secretary (or the Commissioner of Social Security under an agreement with the Secretary) shall make such verification by such means as prescribed in regulations.

(3) Time for filing application.—Any individual who desires to file an application pursuant to paragraph (1) must file such application on or before whichever of the following dates is later: (A) the due date of the return (including any extension thereof) for the second taxable year for which he has net earnings from self-employment (computed without regard to subsections (c)(4) and (c)(5) of $400 or more, any part of which was derived from the performance of service described in subsection (c)(4) or (c)(5); or (B) the due date of the return (including any extension thereof) for his second taxable year ending after 1967.

(4) Effective date of exemption.—An exemption received by an individual pursuant to this subsection shall be effective for the first taxable year for which he has net earnings from self-employment (computed without regard to subsections (c)(4) and (c)(5) of $400 or more, any part of which was derived from the performance of service described in subsection (c)(4) or (c)(5), and for all succeeding taxable years. An exemption received pursuant to this subsection shall be irrevocable.

(f) Partner's taxable year ending as the result of death.—In computing a partner's net earnings from self-employment for his taxable year which ends as a result of his death (but only if such taxable year ends within, and not with, the taxable year of the partnership), there shall be included so much of the deceased partner's distributive share of the partnership's ordinary income or loss for the partnership taxable year as is not attributable to an interest in the partnership during any period beginning on or after the first day of the first calendar month following the month in which such partner died. For purposes of this subsection—

(1) in determining the portion of the distributive share which is attributable to any period specified in the preceding sentence, the ordinary income or loss of the partnership shall be treated as having been realized or sustained ratably over the partnership taxable year; and

(2) the term "deceased partner's distributive share" includes the share of his estate or of any other person succeeding, by reason of his death, to rights with respect to his partnership interest.

(g) Members of certain religious faiths.—

(1) Exemption.—Any individual may file an application (in such form and manner, and with such official, as may be prescribed by regulations under this chapter) for an exemption from the tax imposed by this chapter if he is a member of a recognized religious sect or division thereof and is an adherent of established tenets or teachings of such sect or division by reason of which he is conscientiously opposed to acceptance of the benefits of any private or public insurance which makes payments in the event of death, disability, old-age, or retirement or makes payments toward the cost of, or provides services for, medical care (including the benefits of any insurance system established by the Social Security Act). Such exemption may be granted only if the application contains or is accompanied by—

(A) such evidence of such individual's membership in, and adherence to the tenets or teachings of, the sect or division thereof as the Secretary may require for purposes of determining such individual's compliance with the preceding sentence, and

(B) his waiver of all benefits and other payments under titles II and XVIII of the Social Security Act on the basis of his wages and self-employment income as well as all such benefits and other payments to him on the basis of the wages and self-employment income of any other person,

and only if the Commissioner of Social Security finds that—

(C) such sect or division thereof has the established tenets or teachings referred to in the preceding sentence,

(D) it is the practice, and has been for a period of time which he deems to be substantial, for members of such sect or division thereof to make provision for their dependent members which in his judgment is reasonable in view of their general level of living, and

(E) such sect or division thereof has been in existence at all times since December 31, 1950.

An exemption may not be granted to any individual if any benefit or other payment referred to in subparagraph (B) became payable (or, but for section 203 or 222(b) of the Social Security Act, would have become payable) at or before the time of the filing of such waiver.

(2) Period for which exemption effective.—An exemption granted to any individual pursuant to this subsection shall apply with respect to all taxable years beginning after December 31, 1950, except that such exemption shall not apply for any taxable year—

(A) beginning (i) before the taxable year in which such individual first met the requirements of the first sentence of paragraph (1), or (ii) before the time as of which the Commissioner of Social Security finds that the sect or division thereof of which such individual is a member met the requirements of subparagraphs (C) and (D), or

(B) ending (i) after the time such individual ceases to meet the requirements of the first sentence of paragraph (1), or (ii) after the time as of which the Commissioner of Social Security finds that the sect or division thereof of which he is a member ceases to meet the requirements of subparagraph (C) or (D).

(3) Subsection to apply to certain church employees.—This subsection shall apply with respect to services which are described in subparagraph (B) of section 3121(b)(8) (and are not described in subparagraph (A) of such section).

(h) Regular basis.—An individual shall be deemed to be self-employed on a regular basis in a taxable year, or to be a member of a partnership on a regular basis in such year, if he had net earnings from self-employment, as defined in the first sentence of subsection (a), of not less than $400 in at least two of the three consecutive taxable years immediately preceding such taxable year from trades or businesses carried on by such individual or such partnership.

(i) Special rules for options and commodities dealers.—

(1) In general.—Notwithstanding subsection (a)(3)(A), in determining the net earnings from self-employment of any options dealer or commodities dealer, there shall not be excluded any gain or loss (in the normal course of the taxpayer's activity of dealing in or trading section 1256 contracts) from section 1256 contracts or property related to such contracts.

(2) Definitions.—For purposes of this subsection—

(A) Options dealer.—The term "options dealer" has the meaning given such term by section 1256(g)(8).

(B) Commodities dealer.—The term "commodities dealer" means a person who is actively engaged in trading section 1256 contracts and is registered with a domestic board of trade which is designated as a contract market by the Commodities Futures Trading Commission.

(C) Section 1256 contracts.—The term "section 1256 contract" has the meaning given to such term by section 1256(b).

(j) Special rules for certain church employee income.—

(1) Computation of net earnings.—In applying subsection (a)—

(A) church employee income shall not be reduced by any deduction;

(B) church employee income and deductions attributable to such income shall not be taken into account in determining the amount of other net earnings from self-employment.

(2) Computation of self-employment income.—

(A) Separate application of subsection (b)(2).—Paragraph (2) of subsection (b) shall be applied separately—

(i) to church employee income, and

(ii) to other net earnings from self-employment.

(B) $100 floor.—In applying paragraph (2) of subsection (b) to church employee income, "$100" shall be substituted for "$400."

(3) Coordination with subsection (a)(12).—Paragraph (1) shall not apply to any amount allowable as a deduction under subsection (a)(12), and paragraph (1) shall be applied before determining the amount so allowable.

(4) Church employee income defined.—For purposes of this section, the term "church employee income" means gross income for services which are described in section 3121(b)(8)(B) (and are not described in section 3121(b)(8)(A)).

§ 1403. Miscellaneous provisions

(a) Title of chapter.—This chapter may be cited as the "Self-Employment Contributions Act of 1954".

(b) Cross references.—

(1) For provisions relating to returns, see section 6017.

(2) For provisions relating to collection of taxes in Virgin Islands, Guam, American Samoa, and Puerto Rico, see section 7651.

CHAPTER 2A—UNEARNED INCOME MEDICARE CONTRIBUTION

§ 1411. Imposition of tax

(a) In general.—
Except as provided in subsection (e)—

(1) Application to individuals.—In the case of an individual, there is hereby imposed (in addition to any other tax imposed by this subtitle) for each taxable year a tax equal to 3.8 percent of the lesser of—

(A) net investment income for such taxable year, or

(B) the excess (if any) of—

(i) the modified adjusted gross income for such taxable year, over

(ii) the threshold amount.

(2) Application to estates and trusts.—In the case of an estate or trust, there is hereby imposed (in addition to any other tax imposed by this subtitle) for each taxable year a tax of 3.8 percent of the lesser of—

(A) the undistributed net investment income for such taxable year, or

(B) the excess (if any) of—

(i) the adjusted gross income (as defined in section 67(e)) for such taxable year, over

(ii) the dollar amount at which the highest tax bracket in section 1(e) begins for such taxable year.

(b) Threshold amount.—For purposes of this chapter, the term "threshold amount" means—

(1) in the case of a taxpayer making a joint return under section 6013 or a surviving spouse (as defined in section 2(a)), $250,000,

(2) in the case of a married taxpayer (as defined in section 7703) filing a separate return, ½ of the dollar amount determined under paragraph (1), and

(3) in any other case, $200,000.

(c) Net investment income.—For purposes of this chapter—

(1) In general.—The term "net investment income" means the excess (if any) of—

(A) the sum of—

(i) gross income from interest, dividends, annuities, royalties, and rents, other than such income which is derived in the ordinary course of a trade or business not described in paragraph (2),

(ii) other gross income derived from a trade or business described in paragraph (2), and

(iii) net gain (to the extent taken into account in computing taxable income) attributable to the disposition of property other than property held in a trade or business not described in paragraph (2), over

(B) the deductions allowed by this subtitle which are properly allocable to such gross income or net gain.

(2) Trades and businesses to which tax applies.—A trade or business is described in this paragraph if such trade or business is—

(A) a passive activity (within the meaning of section 469) with respect to the taxpayer, or

(B) a trade or business of trading financial instruments or commodities (as defined in section 475(e)(2)).

(3) Income on investment of working capital subject to tax.—A rule similar to the rule of section 469(e)(1)(B) shall apply for purposes of this subsection.

(4) Exception for certain active interests in partnerships and S corporations.—In the case of a disposition of an interest in a partnership or S corporation—

(A) gain from such disposition shall be taken into account under clause (iii) of paragraph (1)(A) only to the extent of the net gain which would be so taken into account by the transferor if all property of the partnership or S corporation were sold for fair market value immediately before the disposition of such interest, and

(B) a rule similar to the rule of subparagraph (A) shall apply to a loss from such disposition.

(5) Exception for distributions from qualified plans.—The term "net investment income" shall not include any distribution from a plan or arrangement described in section 401(a), 403(a), 403(b), 408, 408A, or 457(b).

(6) Special rule.—Net investment income shall not include any item taken into account in determining self-employment income for such taxable year on which a tax is imposed by section 1401(b).

(d) Modified adjusted gross income.—For purposes of this chapter, the term "modified adjusted gross income" means adjusted gross income increased by the excess of—

(1) the amount excluded from gross income under section 911(a)(1), over

(2) the amount of any deductions (taken into account in computing adjusted gross income) or exclusions disallowed under section 911(d)(6) with respect to the amounts described in paragraph (1).

(e) Nonapplication of section.—This section shall not apply to—

(1) a nonresident alien, or

(2) a trust all of the unexpired interest in which are devoted to one or more of the purposes described in section 170(c)(2)(B).

CHAPTER 3—WITHHOLDING OF TAX ON NONRESIDENT ALIENS AND FOREIGN CORPORATIONS*

CHAPTER 4—RULES APPLICABLE TO RECOVERY OF EXCESSIVE PROFITS ON GOVERNMENT CONTRACTS*

CHAPTER 5—TAX ON TRANSFERS TO AVOID INCOME TAX*

---

*Omitted.

CHAPTER 6—CONSOLIDATED RETURNS

SUBCHAPTER A—RETURNS AND PAYMENT OF TAX

Editorial Summary

Consolidated Returns

Subchapter A of Chapter 6 (Secs. 1501–1504)

The consolidated return area is a classic illustration of the Congress delegating legislative authority to the Treasury Department. In Secs. 1501–1504, Congress establishes that the filing of a consolidated return is a privilege available only to an affiliated group of corporations, defines an affiliated group, and delegates to the Secretary of the Treasury the authority to promulgate legislative regulations for consolidated returns.

Affiliated group status is available only for the parent-subsidiary relationship [see Sec. 1504]. Therefore, if the ownership relationship is brother-sister, the filing of a consolidated return is not permitted. Compare this with parent-subsidiary and brother-sister ownership relationships that will produce controlled group status under Sec. 1563.

The 80 percent ownership test is a dual test. That is, both a voting power and a value requirement must be satisfied. Compare this with the Sec. 1563 test for controlled groups under which the test is satisfied if either the voting power or the value test is satisfied.

§ 1501. Privilege to file consolidated returns

An affiliated group of corporations shall, subject to the provisions of this chapter, have the privilege of making a consolidated return with respect to the income tax imposed by chapter 1 for the taxable year in lieu of separate returns. The making of a consolidated return shall be upon the condition that all corporations which at any time during the taxable year have been members of the affiliated group consent to all the consolidated return regulations prescribed under section 1502 prior to the last day prescribed by law for the filing of such return. The making of a consolidated return shall be considered as such consent. In the case of a corporation which is a member of the affiliated group for a fractional part of the year, the consolidated return shall include the income of such corporation for such part of the year as it is a member of the affiliated group.

§ 1502. Regulations

The Secretary shall prescribe such regulations as he may deem necessary in order that the tax liability of any affiliated group of corporations making a consolidated return and of each corporation in the group, both during and after the period of affiliation, may be returned, determined, computed, assessed, collected, and adjusted, in such manner as clearly to reflect the income-tax liability and the various factors necessary for the determination of such liability, and in order to prevent avoidance of such tax liability. In carrying out the preceding sentence, the Secretary may prescribe rules that are different from the provisions of chapter 1 that would apply if such corporations filed separate returns.

§ 1503. Computation and payment of tax

(a) General rule.—In any case in which a consolidated return is made or is required to be made, the tax shall be determined, computed, assessed, collected, and adjusted in accordance with the regulations under section 1502 prescribed before the last day prescribed by law for the filing of such return.

* * *

(d) Dual consolidated loss.—

(1) In general.—The dual consolidated loss for any taxable year of any corporation shall not be allowed to reduce the taxable income of any other member of the affiliated group for the taxable year or any other taxable year.

(2) Dual consolidated loss.—For purposes of this section—

(A) In general.—Except as provided in subparagraph (B), the term "dual consolidated loss" means any net operating loss of a domestic corporation which is subject to an income tax of a foreign country on its income without regard to whether such income is from sources in or outside of such foreign country, or is subject to such a tax on a residence basis.

(B) Special rule where loss not used under foreign law.—To the extent provided in regulations, the term "dual consolidated loss" shall not include any loss which, under the foreign income tax law, does not offset the income of any foreign corporation.

(3) Treatment of losses of separate business units.—To the extent provided in regulations, any loss of a separate unit of a domestic corporation shall be subject to the limitations of this subsection in the same manner as if such unit were a wholly owned subsidiary of such corporation.

(4) Income on assets acquired after the loss.—The Secretary shall prescribe such regulations as may be necessary or appropriate to prevent the avoidance of the purposes of this subsection by contributing assets to the corporation with the dual consolidated loss after such loss was sustained.

(e) Special rule for determining adjustments to basis.—

(1) In general.—Solely for purposes of determining gain or loss on the disposition of intragroup stock and the amount of any inclusion by reason of an excess loss account, in determining the adjustments to the basis of such intragroup stock on account of the earnings and profits of any member of an affiliated group for any consolidated year (and in determining the amount in such account)—

(A) such earnings and profits shall be determined as if section 312 were applied for such taxable year (and all preceding consolidated years of the member with respect to such group) without regard to subsections (k) and (n) thereof, and

(B) earnings and profits shall not include any amount excluded from gross income under section 108 to the extent the amount so excluded was not applied to reduce tax attributes (other than basis in property).

(2) Definitions.—For purposes of this subsection—

(A) Intragroup stock.—The term "intragroup stock" means any stock which—

(i) is in a corporation which is or was a member of an affiliated group of corporations, and

(ii) is held by another corporation which is or was a member of such group.

Such term includes any other property the basis of which is determined (in whole or in part) by reference to the basis of stock described in the preceding sentence.

(B) Consolidated year.—The term "consolidated year" means any taxable year for which the affiliated group makes a consolidated return.

(C) Application of section 312(n)(7) not affected.—The reference in paragraph (1) to subsection (n) of section 312 shall be treated as not including a reference to paragraph (7) of such subsection.

(3) Adjustments.—Under regulations prescribed by the Secretary, proper adjustments shall be made in the application of paragraph (1)—

(A) in the case of any property acquired by the corporation before consolidation, for the difference between the adjusted basis of such property for purposes of computing taxable income and its adjusted basis for purposes of computing earnings and profits, and

(B) in the case of any property, for any basis adjustment under section 50(c).

(4) Elimination of election to reduce basis of indebtedness.—Nothing in the regulations prescribed under section 1502 shall permit any reduction in the amount otherwise included in gross income by reason of an excess loss account if such reduction is on account of a reduction in the basis of indebtedness.

(f) Limitation on use of group losses to offset income of subsidiary paying preferred dividends.—

(1) In general.—In the case of any subsidiary distributing during any taxable year dividends on any applicable preferred stock—

(A) no group loss item shall be allowed to reduce the disqualified separately computed income of such subsidiary for such taxable year, and

(B) no group credit item shall be allowed against the tax imposed by this chapter on such disqualified separately computed income.

(2) Group items.—For purposes of this subsection—

(A) Group loss item.—The term "group loss item" means any of the following items of any other member of the affiliated group which includes the subsidiary:

(i) Any net operating loss and any net operating loss carryover or carryback under section 172.

(ii) Any loss from the sale or exchange of any capital asset and any capital loss carryover or carryback under section 1212.

(B) Group credit item.—The term "group credit item" means any credit allowable under part IV of subchapter A of chapter 1 (other than section 34) to any other member of the affiliated group which includes the subsidiary and any carryover or carryback of any such credit.

(3) Other definitions.—For purposes of this subsection—

(A) Disqualified separately computed income.—The term "disqualified separately computed income" means the portion of the separately computed taxable income of the subsidiary which does not exceed the dividends distributed by the subsidiary during the taxable year on applicable preferred stock.

(B) Separately computed taxable income.—The term "separately computed taxable income" means the separate taxable income of the subsidiary for the taxable year determined—

(i) by taking into account gains and losses from the sale or exchange of a capital asset and section 1231 gains and losses,

(ii) without regard to any net operating loss or capital loss carryover or carryback, and

(iii) with such adjustments as the Secretary may prescribe.

(C) Subsidiary.—The term "subsidiary" means any corporation which is a member of an affiliated group filing a consolidated return other than the common parent.

(D) Applicable preferred stock.—The term "applicable preferred stock" means stock described in section 1504(a)(4) in the subsidiary which is—

(i) issued after November 17, 1989, and

(ii) held by a person other than a member of the same affiliated group as the subsidiary.

(4) Regulations.—The Secretary shall prescribe such regulations as may be necessary or appropriate to carry out the provisions of this subsection, including regulations—

(A) to prevent the avoidance of this subsection through the transfer of built-in losses to the subsidiary,

(B) to provide rules for cases in which the subsidiary owns (directly or indirectly) stock in another member of the affiliated group, and

(C) to provide for the application of this subsection where dividends are not paid currently, where the redemption and liquidation rights of the applicable preferred stock exceed the issue price for such stock, or where the stock is otherwise structured to avoid the purpose of this subsection.

§ 1504. Definitions

(a) Affiliated group defined.—For purposes of this subtitle—

(1) In general.—The term "affiliated group" means—

(A) 1 or more chains of includible corporations connected through stock ownership with a common parent corporation which is an includible corporation, but only if—

(B)(i) the common parent owns directly stock meeting the requirements of paragraph (2) in at least 1 of the other includible corporations, and

(ii) stock meeting the requirements of paragraph (2) in each of the includible corporations (except the common parent) is owned directly by 1 or more of the other includible corporations.

(2) 80-percent voting and value test.—The ownership of stock of any corporation meets the requirements of this paragraph if it—

(A) possesses at least 80 percent of the total voting power of the stock of such corporation, and

(B) has a value equal to at least 80 percent of the total value of the stock of such corporation.

(3) 5 years must elapse before reconsolidation.—

(A) In general.—If—

(i) a corporation is included (or required to be included) in a consolidated return filed by an affiliated group for a taxable year which includes any period after December 31, 1984, and

(ii) such corporation ceases to be a member of such group in a taxable year beginning after December 31, 1984,

with respect to periods after such cessation, such corporation (and any successor of such corporation) may not be included in any consolidated return filed by the affiliated group (or by another affiliated group with the same common parent or a successor of such common parent) before the 61st month beginning after its first taxable year in which it ceased to be a member of such affiliated group.

(B) Secretary may waive application of subparagraph (A).—The Secretary may waive the application of subparagraph (A) to any corporation for any period subject to such conditions as the Secretary may prescribe.

(4) Stock not to include certain preferred stock.—For purposes of this subsection, the term "stock" does not include any stock which—

(A) is not entitled to vote,

(B) is limited and preferred as to dividends and does not participate in corporate growth to any significant extent,

(C) has redemption and liquidation rights which do not exceed the issue price of such stock (except for a reasonable redemption or liquidation premium), and

(D) is not convertible into another class of stock.

(5) Regulations.—The Secretary shall prescribe such regulations as may be necessary or appropriate to carry out the purposes of this subsection, including (but not limited to) regulations—

(A) which treat warrants, obligations convertible into stock, and other similar interests as stock, and stock as not stock,

(B) which treat options to acquire or sell stock as having been exercised,

(C) which provide that the requirements of paragraph (2)(B) shall be treated as met if the affiliated group, in reliance on a good faith determination of value, treated such requirements as met,

(D) which disregard an inadvertent ceasing to meet the requirements of paragraph (2)(B) by reason of changes in relative values of different classes of stock,

(E) which provide that transfers of stock within the group shall not be taken into account in determining whether a corporation ceases to be a member of an affiliated group, and

(F) which disregard changes in voting power to the extent such changes are disproportionate to related changes in value.

(b) Definition of "includible corporation."—As used in this chapter, the term "includible corporation" means any corporation except—

(1) Corporations exempt from taxation under section 501.

(2) Insurance companies subject to taxation under section 801.

(3) Foreign corporations.

(4) Corporations with respect to which an election under section 936 (relating to possession tax credit) is in effect for the taxable year.

*(6) Regulated investment companies and real estate investment trusts subject to tax under subchapter M of chapter 1.

(7) A DISC (as defined in section 992(a)(1)).

(8) An S corporation.

* * *

SUBCHAPTER B—RELATED RULES

PART I—IN GENERAL

§ 1551. Disallowance of the benefits of the graduated corporate rates and accumulated earnings credit

(a) In general.—If—

(1) any corporation transfers, on or after January 1, 1951, and on or before June 12, 1963, all or part of its property (other than money) to a transferee corporation,

(2) any corporation transfers, directly or indirectly, after June 12, 1963, all or part of its property (other than money) to a transferee corporation, or

*Editorial comment: There is no subsection (b)(5).

(3) five or fewer individuals who are in control of a corporation transfer, directly or indirectly, after June 12, 1963, property (other than money) to a transferee corporation,

and the transferee corporation was created for the purpose of acquiring such property or was not actively engaged in business at the time of such acquisition, and if after such transfer the transferor or transferors are in control of such transferee corporation during any part of the taxable year of such transferee corporation, then for such taxable year of such transferee corporation the Secretary may (except as may be otherwise determined under subsection (c)) disallow the benefits of the rates contained in section 11(b) which are lower than the highest rate specified in such section, or the accumulated earnings credit provided in paragraph (2) or (3) of section 535(c), unless such transferee corporation shall establish by the clear preponderance of the evidence that the securing of such benefits or credit was not a major purpose of such transfer.

(b) Control.—For purposes of subsection (a), the term "control" means—

(1) With respect to a transferee corporation described in subsection (a)(1) or (2), the ownership by the transferor corporation, its shareholders, or both, of stock possessing at least 80 percent of the total combined voting power of all classes of stock entitled to vote or at least 80 percent of the total value of shares of all classes of the stock; or

(2) With respect to each corporation described in subsection (a)(3), the ownership by the five or fewer individuals described in such subsection of stock possessing—

(A) at least 80 percent of the total combined voting power of all classes of stock entitled to vote or at least 80 percent of the total value of shares of all classes of the stock of each corporation, and

(B) more than 50 percent of the total combined voting power of all classes of stock entitled to vote or more than 50 percent of the total value of shares of all classes of stock of each corporation, taking into account the stock ownership of each such individual only to the extent such stock ownership is identical with respect to each such corporation.

For purposes of this subsection, section 1563(e) shall apply in determining the ownership of stock.

(c) Authority of the Secretary under this section.—The provisions of section 269(c), and the authority of the Secretary under such section, shall, to the extent not inconsistent with the provisions of this section, be applicable to this section.

§ 1552. Earnings and profits

(a) General rule.—Pursuant to regulations prescribed by the Secretary the earnings and profits of each member of an affiliated group required to be included in a consolidated return for such group filed for a taxable year shall be determined by allocating the tax liability of the group for such year among the members of the group in accord with whichever of the following methods the group shall elect in its first consolidated return filed for such a taxable year:

(1) The tax liability shall be apportioned among the members of the group in accordance with the ratio which that portion of the consolidated taxable income attributable to each member of the group having taxable income bears to the consolidated taxable income.

(2) The tax liability of the group shall be allocated to the several members of the group on the basis of the percentage of the total tax which the tax of such member if computed on a separate return would bear to the total amount of the taxes for all members of the group so computed.

(3) The tax liability of the group (excluding the tax increases arising from the consolidation) shall be allocated on the basis of the contribution of each member of the group to the consolidated taxable income of the group. Any tax increases arising from the consolidation shall be distributed to the several members in direct proportion to the reduction in tax liability resulting to such members from the filing of the consolidated return as measured by the difference between their tax liabilities determined on a separate return basis and their tax liabilities based on their contributions to the consolidated taxable income.

(4) The tax liability of the group shall be allocated in accord with any other method selected by the group with the approval of the Secretary.

(b) Failure to elect.—If no election is made in such first return, the tax liability shall be allocated among the several members of the group pursuant to the method prescribed in subsection (a)(1).

PART II—CERTAIN CONTROLLED CORPORATIONS

Editorial Summary

Controlled Group of Corporations

Subchapter B of Chapter 6 (Secs. 1561–1563)

The ability to elect to file a consolidated return under Sec. 1501 provides the taxpayer with a potential tax opportunity. If the taxpayer who otherwise qualifies perceives that the election to consolidate would not be beneficial, the election is not made.

On the other hand, the mere achieving of controlled group status under Sec. 1563 produces potential tax detriments rather than tax opportunities. If it appears that the ownership structure is going to produce the result of controlled group status under Sec. 1563, consideration should be given to seeing that the ownership structure provides the taxpayer with the opportunity to elect to file a consolidated return (i.e., the Sec. 1504 requirements for affiliated group status are satisfied).

The statutory intent associated with Sec. 1561 is to prevent tax avoidance through the establishment of more than one corporation. If common ownership is present in terms of a set of corporations, the opportunity exists to reduce the tax liability (i.e., regular and/or penalty taxes) of the business venture or ventures when compared with operating as one corporation. Such tax avoidance opportunities are prevented by the statutory limitations contained in Sec. 1561, which provide that for certain tax benefits, the set of corporations will be limited to the same benefit that would be available to one corporation. The following tax benefits are included:

1. The beneficial tax rates under Sec. 11.
2. The accumulated earnings credit under Sec. 535.
3. The alternative minimum tax exemption under Sec. 55.

Section 1561 imposes limitation only on the there above items. However, other Code sections impose specific limitations on other tax benefits if controlled group status is present.

The common ownership test contained in Sec. 1563 is a voting power test or a value test. Contrast this with the requirement in Sec. 1504 that both a voting power and a value test be satisfied for classification as an affiliated group and thereby eligible to elect to file a consolidated return.

For classification as a controlled group under Sec. 1563, any one of the following ownership structures will suffice:

1. Parent-subsidiary.
2. Brother-sister.
3. Combined (i.e., both the parent-subsidiary and the brother-sister relationships are present).

Note that only the parent-subsidiary structure can result in eligibility to file a consolidated return under Sec. 1501.

The parent-subsidiary common ownership test requires that an 80 percent voting power or value test be satisfied in terms of the parent corporation's stock ownership of the subsidiary corporation. For the brother-sister ownership structure, two tests had to be satisfied. In making this calculation, the five largest shareholders (i.e., individuals, estates, or trusts applying constructive ownership rules) of the corporations being tested for controlled group status are counted. The tests are as follows:

1. At least 80 percent voting power or value.
2. Greater than 50 percent voting power or value, taking into account for each shareholder the least common ownership (i.e., the smallest ownership of each shareholder in the corporations being tested) in the corporations being tested for controlled group status.

A controversy in terms of the mechanical application of the first test and the concept of common ownership was resolved by the Supreme Court in *Vogel Fertilizer Co.*, 82–1 USTC ¶ 9134, 49 AFTR2d 82-491, 102 S.Ct. 821 (USSC, 1982). The Court ruled that the regulations on this point were invalid. The Court concluded that for a shareholder to be counted with respect to the first test, he must have some stock ownership in each of the corporations being tested for controlled group membership. Thus, from a planning perspective, it may be possible to avoid controlled group status by eliminating the stock ownership of a shareholder who has only a small amount of stock.

The American Jobs Creation Act of 2004 repealed the first test. Note, however, that Sec. 1563(f)(5) retains the first test for all other uses of the term "controlled group" (i.e., except for determining brother-sister status under Sec. 1563(a)(2)).

In ascertaining the presence of controlled group status, the determination initially is made for the largest possible set of corporations. If this set is not a controlled group, the size of the set is reduced and the tests are again applied. Note that a particular corporation may not be a component member of more than one controlled group (i.e., overlapping groups exist). Section 1563(b)(4) provides that a particular corporation will not be treated as a component member of more than one controlled group.

§ 1561. Limitations on certain multiple tax benefits in the case of certain controlled corporations

(a) General rule.—The component members of a controlled group of corporations on a December 31 shall, for their taxable years which include such December 31, be limited for purposes of this subtitle to—

(1) amounts in each taxable income bracket in the tax table in section 11(b)(1) which do not aggregate more than the maximum amount in such bracket to which a corporation which is not a component member of a controlled group is entitled,

(2) one $250,000 ($150,000 if any component member is a corporation described in section 535 (c)(2)(B)) amount for purposes of computing the accumulated earnings credit under section 535(c) (2) and (3),

(3) one $40,000 exemption amount for purposes of computing the amount of the minimum tax, and

(4) one $2,000,000 amount for purposes of computing the tax imposed by section 59A.

The amounts specified in paragraph (1), the amount specified in paragraph (3), the amount specified in paragraph (4) shall be divided equally among the component members of such group on such December 31 unless all of such component members consent (at such time and in such manner as the Secretary shall by regulations prescribe) to an apportionment plan providing for an unequal allocation of such amounts. The amounts specified in paragraph (2) shall be divided equally among the component members of such group on such December 31 unless the Secretary prescribes regulations permitting an unequal allocation of such amounts. Notwithstanding paragraph (1), in applying the last 2 sentences of section 11(b) to such component members, the taxable income of all such component members shall be taken into account and any increase in tax under such last 2 sentences shall be divided among such component members in the same manner as amounts under paragraph (1). In applying section 55(d)(3), the alternative minimum taxable income of all component members shall be taken into account and any decrease in the exemption amount shall be allocated to the component members in the same manner as under paragraph (3).

(b) Certain short taxable years.—If a corporation has a short taxable year which does not include a December 31 and is a component member of a controlled group of corporations with respect to such taxable year, then for purposes of this subtitle—

(1) the amount in each taxable income bracket in the tax table in section 11(b), and

(2) the amount to be used in computing the accumulated earnings credit under section 535(c) (2) and (3),

of such corporation for such taxable year shall be the amount specified in subsection (a)(1) or (2), as the case may be, divided by the number of corporations which are component members of such group on the last day of such taxable year. For purposes of the preceding sentence, section 1563(b) shall be applied as if such last day were substituted for December 31.

§ 1563. Definitions and special rules

(a) Controlled group of corporations.—For purposes of this part, the term "controlled group of corporations" means any group of—

(1) Parent-subsidiary controlled group.—One or more chains of corporations connected through stock ownership with a common parent corporation if—

(A) stock possessing at least 80 percent of the total combined voting power of all classes of stock entitled to vote or at least 80 percent of the total value of shares of all classes of stock of each of the corporations, except the common parent corporation, is owned (within the meaning of subsection (d) (1)) by one or more of the other corporations; and

(B) the common parent corporation owns (within the meaning of subsection (d) (1)) stock possessing at least 80 percent of the total combined voting power of all classes of stock entitled to vote or at least 80 percent of the total value of shares of all classes of stock of at least one of the other corporations, excluding, in computing such voting power or value, stock owned directly by such other corporations.

(2) Brother-sister controlled group.—Two or more corporations if 5 or fewer persons who are individuals, estates, or trusts own (within the meaning of subsection (d)(2)) stock possessing more than 50 percent of the total combined voting power of all classes of stock entitled to vote or more than 50 percent of the total value of shares of all classes of stock of each corporation, taking into account the stock ownership of each such person only to the extent such stock ownership is identical with respect to each such corporation.

(3) Combined group.—Three or more corporations each of which is a member of a group of corporations described in paragraph (1) or (2), and one of which—

(A) is a common parent corporation included in a group of corporations described in paragraph (1), and also

(B) is included in a group of corporations described in paragraph (2).

* * *

(b) Component member.—

(1) General rule.—For purposes of this part, a corporation is a component member of a controlled group of corporations on a December 31 of any taxable year (and with respect to the taxable year which includes such December 31) if such corporation—

(A) is a member of such controlled group of corporations on the December 31 included in such year and is not treated as an excluded member under paragraph (2), or

(B) is not a member of such controlled group of corporations on the December 31 included in such year but is treated as an additional member under paragraph (3).

(2) Excluded members.—A corporation which is a member of a controlled group of corporations on December 31 of any taxable year shall be treated as an excluded member of such group for the taxable year including such December 31 if such corporation—

(A) is a member of such group for less than one-half the number of days in such taxable year which precede such December 31,

(B) is exempt from taxation under section 501(a) (except a corporation which is subject to tax on its unrelated business taxable income under section 511) for such taxable year,

(C) is a foreign corporation subject to tax under section 881 for such taxable year,

(D) is an insurance company subject to taxation under section 801 (other than an insurance company which is a member of a controlled group described in subsection (a)(4)), or

(E) is a franchised corporation, as defined in subsection (f)(4).

(3) Additional members.—A corporation which—

(A) was a member of a controlled group of corporations at any time during a calendar year,

(B) is not a member of such group on December 31 of such calendar year, and

(C) is not described, with respect to such group, in subparagraph (B), (C), (D), or (E) of paragraph (2),

shall be treated as an additional member of such group on December 31 for its taxable year including such December 31 if it was a member of such group for one-half (or more) of the number of days in such taxable year which precede such December 31.

(4) Overlapping groups.—If a corporation is a component member of more than one controlled group of corporations with respect to any taxable year, such corporation shall be treated as a component member of only one controlled group. The determination as to the group of which such corporation is a component member shall be made under regulations prescribed by the Secretary which are consistent with the purposes of this part.

(c) Certain stock excluded.—

(1) General rule.—For purposes of this part, the term "stock" does not include—

(A) nonvoting stock which is limited and preferred as to dividends,

(B) treasury stock, and

(C) stock which is treated as "excluded stock" under paragraph (2).

(2) Stock treated as "excluded stock."—

(A) Parent-subsidiary controlled group.—For purposes of subsection (a) (1), if a corporation (referred to in this paragraph as "parent corporation") owns (within the meaning of subsections (d)(1) and (e)(4)), 50 percent or more of the total combined voting power of all classes of stock entitled to vote or 50 percent or more of the total value of shares of all classes of stock in another corporation (referred to in this paragraph as "subsidiary corporation"), the following stock of the subsidiary corporation shall be treated as excluded stock—

(i) stock in the subsidiary corporation held by a trust which is part of a plan of deferred compensation for the benefit of the employees of the parent corporation or the subsidiary corporation,

(ii) stock in the subsidiary corporation owned by an individual (within the meaning of subsection (d)(2)) who is a principal stockholder or officer of the parent corporation. For purposes of this clause, the term "principal stockholder" of a corporation means an individual who owns (within the meaning of subsection (d)(2)) 5 percent or more of the total combined voting power of all classes of stock entitled to vote or 5 percent or more of the total value of shares of all classes of stock in such corporation,

(iii) stock in the subsidiary corporation owned (within the meaning of subsection (d) (2)) by an employee of the subsidiary corporation if such stock is subject to conditions which run in favor of such parent (or subsidiary) corporation and which substantially restrict or limit the employee's right (or if the employee constructively owns such stock, the direct owner's right) to dispose of such stock, or

(iv) stock in the subsidiary corporation owned (within the meaning of subsection (d)(2)) by an organization (other than the parent corporation) to which section 501 (relating to certain educational and charitable organizations which are exempt from tax) applies and which is controlled directly or indirectly by the parent corporation or subsidiary corporation, by an individual, estate, or trust that is a principal stockholder (within the meaning of clause (ii)) of the parent corporation, by an officer of the parent corporation, or by any combination thereof.

(B) Brother-sister controlled group.—For purposes of subsection (a)(2), if 5 or fewer persons who are individuals, estates, or trusts (referred to in this subparagraph as "common owners") own (within the meaning of subsection (d)(2)), 50 percent or more of the total combined voting power of all classes of stock entitled to vote or 50 percent or more of the total value of shares of all classes of stock in a corporation, the following stock of such corporation shall be treated as excluded stock—

(i) stock in such corporation held by an employees' trust described in section 401(a) which is exempt from tax under section 501 (a), if such trust is for the benefit of the employees of such corporation,

(ii) stock in such corporation owned (within the meaning of subsection (d) (2)) by an employee of the corporation if such stock is subject to conditions which run in favor of any of such common owners (or such corporation) and which substantially restrict or limit the employee's right (or if the employee constructively owns such stock, the direct owner's right) to dispose of such stock. If a condition which limits or restricts the employee's right (or the direct owner's right) to dispose of such stock also applies to the stock held by any of the common owners pursuant to a bona fide reciprocal stock purchase arrange-ment, such condition shall not be treated as one which restricts or limits the employee's right to dispose of such stock, or

(iii) stock in such corporation owned (within the meaning of subsection (d) (2)) by an organization to which section 501 (relating to certain educational and charitable organizations which are exempt from tax) applies and which is controlled directly or indirectly by such corporation, by an individual, estate, or trust that is a principal stockholder (within the meaning of subparagraph (A)(ii)) of such corporation, by an officer of such corporation, or by any combination thereof.

(d) Rules for determining stock ownership.—

(1) Parent-subsidiary controlled group.—For purposes of determining whether a corporation is a member of a parent-subsidiary controlled group of corporations (within the meaning of subsection (a) (1)), stock owned by a corporation means—

(A) stock owned directly by such corporation, and

(B) stock owned with the application of paragraphs (1), (2), and (3) of subsection (e).

(2) Brother-sister controlled group.—For purposes of determining whether a corporation is a member of a brother-sister controlled group of corporations (within the meaning of subsection (a) (2)), stock owned by a person who is an individual, estate, or trust means—

(A) stock owned directly by such person, and

(B) stock owned with the application of subsection (e).

(e) Constructive ownership.—

(1) Options.—If any person has an option to acquire stock, such stock shall be considered as owned by such person. For purposes of this paragraph, an option to acquire such an option, and each one of a series of such options, shall be considered as an option to acquire such stock.

(2) Attribution from partnerships.—Stock owned, directly or indirectly, by or for a partnership shall be considered as owned by any partner having an interest of 5 percent or more in either the capital or profits of the partnership in proportion to his interest in capital or profits, whichever such proportion is the greater.

(3) Attribution from estates or trusts.—

(A) Stock owned, directly or indirectly, by or for an estate or trust shall be considered as owned by any beneficiary who has an actuarial interest of 5 percent or more in such stock, to the extent of such actuarial interest. For purposes of this subparagraph, the actuarial interest of each beneficiary shall be determined by assuming the maximum exercise of discretion by the fiduciary in favor of such beneficiary and the maximum use of such stock to satisfy his rights as a beneficiary.

(B) Stock owned, directly or indirectly, by or for any portion of a trust of which a person is considered the owner under subpart E of part I of subchapter J (relating to grantors and others treated as substantial owners) shall be considered as owned by such person.

(C) This paragraph shall not apply to stock owned by any employees' trust described in section 401(a) which is exempt from tax under section 501(a).

(4) Attribution from corporations.—Stock owned, directly or indirectly, by or for a corporation shall be considered as owned by any person who owns (within the meaning of subsection (d)) 5 percent or more in value of its stock in that proportion which the value of the stock which such person so owns bears to the value of all the stock in such corporation.

(5) Spouse.—An individual shall be considered as owning stock in a corporation owned, directly or indirectly, by or for his spouse (other than a spouse who is legally separated from the individual under a decree of divorce whether interlocutory or final, or a decree of separate maintenance), except in the case of a corporation with respect to which each of the following conditions is satisfied for its taxable year—

(A) The individual does not, at any time during such taxable year, own directly any stock in such corporation;

(B) The individual is not a director or employee and does not participate in the management of such corporation at any time during such taxable year;

(C) Not more than 50 percent of such corporation's gross income for such taxable year was derived from royalties, rents, dividends, interest, and annuities; and

(D) Such stock in such corporation is not, at any time during such taxable year, subject to conditions which substantially restrict or limit the spouse's right to dispose of such stock and which run in favor of the individual or his children who have not attained the age of 21 years.

(6) Children, grandchildren, parents, and grandparents.—

(A) Minor children.—An individual shall be considered as owning stock owned, directly or indirectly, by or for his children who have not attained the age of 21 years, and, if the individual has not attained the age of 21 years, the stock owned, directly or indirectly, by or for his parents.

(B) Adult children and grandchildren.—An individual who owns (within the meaning of subsection (d)(2), but without regard to this subparagraph) more than 50 percent of the total combined voting power of all classes of stock entitled to vote or more than 50 percent of the total value of shares of all classes of stock in a corporation shall be considered as owning the stock in such corporation owned, directly or indirectly, by or for his parents, grandparents, grandchildren, and children who have attained the age of 21 years.

(C) Adopted child.—For purposes of this section, a legally adopted child of an individual shall be treated as a child of such individual by blood.

(f) Other definitions and rules.—

(1) Employee defined.—For purposes of this section the term "employee" has the same meaning such term is given by paragraphs (1) and (2) of section 3121(d).

(2) Operating rules.—

(A) In general.—Except as provided in subparagraph (B), stock constructively owned by a person by reason of the application of paragraph (1), (2), (3), (4), (5), or (6) of subsection (e) shall, for purposes of applying such paragraphs, be treated as actually owned by such person.

(B) Members of family.—Stock constructively owned by an individual by reason of the application of paragraph (5) or (6) of subsection (e) shall not be treated as owned by him for purposes of again applying such paragraphs in order to make another the constructive owner of such stock.

(3) Special rules.—For purposes of this section—

(A) If stock may be considered as owned by a person under subsection (e)(1) and under any other paragraph of subsection (e), it shall be considered as owned by him under subsection (e)(1).

(B) If stock is owned (within the meaning of subsection (d)) by two or more persons, such stock shall be considered as owned by the person whose ownership of such stock results in the corporation being a component member of a controlled group. If by reason of the preceding sentence, a corporation would (but for this sentence) become a component member of two controlled groups, it shall be treated as a component member of one controlled group. The determination as to the group of which such corporation is a component member shall be made under regulations prescribed by the Secretary which are consistent with the purposes of this part.

(C) If stock is owned by a person within the meaning of subsection (d) and such ownership results in the corporation being a component member of a controlled group, such stock shall not be treated as excluded stock under subsection (c)(2), if by reason of treating such stock as excluded stock the result is that such corporation is not a component member of a controlled group of corporations.

(4) Franchised corporation.—If—

(A) a parent corporation (as defined in subsection (c)(2)(A)), or a common owner (as defined in subsection (c)(2)(B)), of a corporation which is a member of a controlled group of corporations is under a duty (arising out of a written agreement) to sell stock of such corporation (referred to in this paragraph as "franchised corporation") which is franchised to sell the products of another member, or the common owner, of such controlled group;

(B) such stock is to be sold to an employee (or employees) of such franchised corporation pursuant to a bona fide plan designed to eliminate the stock ownership of the parent corporation or of the common owner in the franchised corporation;

(C) such plan—

(i) provides a reasonable selling price for such stock, and

(ii) requires that a portion of the employee's share of the profits of such corporation (whether received as compensation or as a dividend) be applied to the purchase of such stock (or the purchase of notes, bonds, debentures or other similar evidence of indebtedness of such franchised corporation held by such parent corporation or common owner);

(D) such employee (or employees) owns directly more than 20 percent of the total value of shares of all classes of stock in such franchised corporation;

(E) more than 50 percent of the inventory of such franchised corporation is acquired from members of the controlled group, the common owner, or both; and

(F) all of the conditions contained in subparagraphs (A), (B), (C), (D), and (E) have been met for one-half (or more) of the number of days preceding the December 31 included within the taxable year (or if the taxable year does not include December 31, the last day of such year) of the franchised corporation,

then such franchised corporation shall be treated as an excluded member of such group, under subsection (b)(2), for such taxable year.

(5) Brother-sister controlled group definition for provisions other than this part.—

(A) In general.—Except as specifically provided in an applicable provision, subsection (a)(2) shall be applied to an applicable provision as if it read as follows:

(2) "Brother-sister controlled group."—Two or more corporations if 5 or fewer persons who are individuals, estates, or trusts own (within the meaning of subsection (d)(2)) stock possessing—

(A) "at least 80 percent of the total combined voting power of all classes of stock entitled to vote, or at least 80 percent of the total value of shares of all classes of stock, of each corporation, and

(B) "more than 50 percent of the total combined voting power of all classes of stock entitled to vote or more than 50 percent of the total value of shares of all classes of stock of each corporation, taking into account the stock ownership of each such person only to the extent such stock ownership is identical with respect to each such corporation."

(B) Applicable provision.—For purposes of this paragraph, an applicable provision is any provision of law (other than this part) which incorporates the definition of controlled group of corporations under subsection (a).

SUBTITLE B—ESTATE AND GIFT TAXES

CHAPTER 11—ESTATE TAX

SUBCHAPTER A—ESTATES OF CITIZENS OR RESIDENTS

PART I—TAX IMPOSED

Editorial Summary

Estate Tax: General

Subchapter A of Chapter 11 (Secs. 2001–2002)

The estate tax is an excise tax which is levied on the right to transfer property at the death of the taxpayer [see Sec. 2001(a)]. The basic estate tax model is as follows:

Gross estate
− Deductions
= Taxable estate
+ Post-1976 taxable gifts
= Tax base for estate tax
× Rates
= Tentative estate tax liability
− Adjustment for transfer tax liability on post-1976 gifts
− Credits
= Estate tax liability

The first noteworthy aspect associated with the estate tax model is the relationship between the gift tax and the estate tax. Prior to the effect of the Tax Reform Act of 1976, the gift tax and the estate tax were separate tax structures. Since both are transfer-type taxes, Congress in the 1976 Act created a unified gift and estate tax structure. Therefore, transfers during life (i.e., gifts) and transfers at death (i.e., estate) are viewed cumulatively. In general, therefore, taxpayers for whom the following situations apply should be subject to the same total transfer tax liability:

1. All transfers are made as gifts during the taxpayer's life.

2. All transfers are made at death through the taxpayer's estate.

3. Some transfers are made as gifts during the taxpayer's life, and some transfers are made at death through the taxpayer's estate.

However, although the general statutory objective is a unified transfer tax structure, differences do exist in the statutory treatment of transfers during life and transfers at death. Therefore, perfect horizontal equity does not exist with respect to the three illustrative taxpayers.

Various items are excludable in calculating the amount of the gross estate. This topic is presented in a later Editorial Summary.

The tax rates for the estate tax and the gift tax appear in Sec. 2001(c). The lowest rate is 18 percent, and the highest rate was 55 percent.

Tax legislation in the early 1980s provided for the gradual reduction of the top estate tax rates. One such reduction was supposed to occur in 1988. However, the Revenue Act of 1987, in addition to delaying the year in which the maximum rate is reduced to 50 percent (i.e., from 1988 to 1993), provided for the phaseout of the graduated tax rates (i.e., the beneficial rates) and the unified credit [see Sec. 2001(c)(2)]. The Revenue Reconciliation Act of 1993 made permanent the estate tax rate schedule that was in effect for 1992. Therefore, the 53 and 55 percent rates were no longer scheduled to be reduced to 50 percent.

The Tax Relief Reconciliation Act of 2001 provided for a reduction in the estate tax rates using a phased approach [see Sec. 2001(c)(1) and Sec. 2001(c)(2)]. By 2007, the highest rate will have been reduced to 45 percent.

The Tax Relief Reconciliation Act of 2001 provides for the repeal of the estate tax in 2010 for one year. Note, however, the executor could elect to have an estate tax apply for 2010 in order to have a step-up in basis rather than a carryover basis for the estate assets (see §1022). Congress reenacted the estate tax for decedents dying after 2010 in the Tax Relief Act of 2010.

The American Taxpayer Relief Act of 2012 modified the estate tax rates. The lowest rate is 18 percent and the highest rate is 40 percent.

§ 2001. Imposition and rate of tax

(a) Imposition.—A tax is hereby imposed on the transfer of the taxable estate of every decedent who is a citizen or resident of the United States.

*Omitted.

(b) Computation of tax.—The tax imposed by this section shall be the amount equal to the excess (if any) of—

(1) a tentative tax computed under subsection (c) on the sum of—

(A) the amount of the taxable estate, and

(B) the amount of the adjusted taxable gifts, over

(2) the aggregate amount of tax which would have been payable under chapter 12 with respect to gifts made by the decedent after December 31, 1976, if the modifications described in subsection (g) had been applicable at the time of such gifts.

For purposes of paragraph (1)(B), the term "adjusted taxable gifts" means the total amount of the taxable gifts (within the meaning of section 2503) made by the decedent after December 31, 1976, other than gifts which are includible in the gross estate of the decedent.

(c) Rate schedule.—

If the amount with respect to which the tentative tax is to be computed is:	The tentative tax is:
Not over $10,000	18 percent of such amount.
Over $10,000 but not over $20,000	$1,800, plus 20 percent of the excess of such amount over $10,000.
Over $20,000 but not over $40,000	$3,800, plus 22 percent of the excess of such amount over $20,000.
Over $40,000 but not over $60,000	$8,200, plus 24 percent of the excess of such amount over $40,000.
Over $60,000 but not over $80,000	$13,000, plus 26 percent of the excess of such amount over $60,000.
Over $80,000 but not over $100,000	$18,200, plus 28 percent of the excess of such amount over $80,000.
Over $100,000 but not over $150,000	$23,800, plus 30 percent of the excess of such amount over $100,000.
Over $150,000 but not over $250,000	$38,800, plus 32 percent of the excess of such amount over $150,000.
Over $250,000 but not over $500,000	$70,800, plus 34 percent of the excess of such amount over $250,000.
Over $500,000 but not over $750,000	$155,800, plus 37 percent of the excess of such amount over $500,000.
Over $750,000 but not over $1,000,000	$248,300, plus 39 percent of the excess of such amount over $750,000.
Over $1,000,000	$345,800, plus 40 percent of the excess of such amount over $1,000,000.

(d) Adjustment for gift tax paid by spouse.—For purposes of subsection (b) (2), if—

(1) the decedent was the donor of any gift one-half of which was considered under section 2513 as made by the decedent's spouse, and

(2) the amount of such gift is includible in the gross estate of the decedent,

any tax payable by the spouse under chapter 12 on such gift (as determined under section 2012(d)) shall be treated as a tax payable with respect to a gift made by the decedent.

(e) Coordination of sections 2513 and 2035.—If—

(1) the decedent's spouse was the donor of any gift one-half of which was considered under section 2513 as made by the decedent, and

(2) the amount of such gift is includible in the gross estate of the decedent's spouse by reason of section 2035,

such gift shall not be included in the adjusted taxable gifts of the decedent for purposes of subsection (b) (1)(B), and the aggregate amount determined under subsection (b)(2) shall be reduced by the amount (if any) determined under subsection (d) which was treated as a tax payable by the decedent's spouse with respect to such gift.

(f) Valuation of gifts.—

(1) In general.—If the time has expired under section 6501 within which a tax may be assessed under chapter 12 (or under corresponding provisions of prior laws) on—

(A) the transfer of property by gift made during a preceding calendar period (as defined in section 2502(b)), or

(B) an increase in taxable gifts required under section 2701(d),

the value thereof shall, for purposes of computing the tax under this chapter, be the value as finally determined for purposes of chapter 12.

(2) Final determination.—For purposes of paragraph (1), a value shall be treated as finally determined for purposes of chapter 12 if—

(A) the value is shown on a return under such chapter and such value is not contested by the Secretary before the expiration of the time referred to in paragraph (1) with respect to such return,

(B) in a case not described in subparagraph (A), the value is specified by the Secretary and such value is not timely contested by the taxpayer, or

(C) the value is determined by a court or pursuant to a settlement agreement with the Secretary.

For purposes of subparagraph (A), the value of an item shall be treated as shown on a return if the item is disclosed in the return, or in a statement attached to the return, in a manner adequate to apprise the Secretary of the nature of such item.

(g) Modifications to gift tax payable to reflect different tax rates.—For purposes of applying subsection (b)(2) with respect to 1 or more gifts, the rates of tax under subsection (c) in effect at the decedent's death shall, in lieu of the rates of tax in effect at the time of such gifts, be used both to compute—

(1) the tax imposed by chapter 12 with respect to such gifts, and

(2) the credit allowed against such tax under section 2505, including in computing—

(A) the applicable credit amount under section 2505(a)(1), and

(B) the sum of the amounts allowed as a credit for all preceding periods under section 2505(a)(2).

§ 2002. Liability for payment

The tax imposed by this chapter shall be paid by the executor.

PART II—CREDITS AGAINST TAX

Editorial Summary

Estate Tax: Credits

Subchapter A of Chapter 11 (Secs. 2010–2016)

The estate tax credits are designed to achieve several purposes. The unified credit and the related exemption amount in Sec. 2010 can be viewed in terms of the concept of materiality. Transfers, both during life and at death, should be subject to the transfer tax only if they exceed a particular amount. Although this application of the materiality concept was stated in terms of a credit against the tax liability (i.e., $192,800 beginning in 1987), from a planning perspective, it was more logical to think of it in terms of an equivalent exemption. The equivalent exemption for 1987 was $600,000.

Note that the unified credit, as the term is supposed to indicate, is applicable to both lifetime transfers and transfers at death. That is, for 1987 and thereafter, a total credit of $192,800 was available to reduce the gift tax and the estate tax liability. Therefore, if the credit was consumed through lifetime gifts, no tax benefit would be available at the time of the taxpayer's death for death transfers.

The Revenue Act of 1987 provided that not all taxpayers are eligible for the unified credit. This was accomplished by providing for the phaseout of the unified credit once the amount of taxable transfers rose above a certain level [see Sec. 2001 (c)(2) prior to repeal].

The Taxpayer Relief Act of 1997 (TRA of 1997) provided for a phased in increase in the equivalent exemption amount (with the statutory language now referring to an "applicable exclusion amount"). For 2001, the amount was $675,000. The phase-in was to be completed in 2006 with the amount being $1,000,000 for that year and thereafter [see Sec. 2010(c)].

The relationship between the equivalent exemption amount [now called the applicable exclusion amount in Sec. 2010(c)] and the unified transfer tax credit amount was scheduled to be as follows during this transition.

Year	Applicable Exclusion Amount	Unified Transfer Tax Credit
1998	$625,000	$202,050
1999	650,000	211,300
2000 and 2001	675,000	220,550
2002 and 2003	700,000	229,800
2004	850,000	287,300
2005	950,000	326,300
2006 or thereafter	1,000,000	345,800

The Tax Relief Reconciliation Act of 2001 modified this phase-in as follows:

Year	Unified Transfer Tax Credit	Applicable Exclusion Amount
2002–2003	$345,800	$1,000,000
2004–2005	555,800	1,500,000
2006, 2007, and 2008	780,800	2,000,000

Note, however, that the Act freezes the applicable exclusion amount for the gift tax at $1,000,000 [Sec. 2505(a)(1)].

The Tax Relief Act of 2010 once again unified the unified transfer tax credit for the estate tax and the gift tax. For 2011, the credit is $1,730,800 and the related exclusion amount is $5 million. These amounts are indexed for inflation starting in 2012. For 2012, the indexed credit amount is $1,772,800 and the indexed amount for the exclusion is $5,120,000. For 2013, the indexed credit amount is $2,045,800 and the indexed amount for the exclusion is $5.25 million. For 2014, the indexed credit amount is $2,081,800 and the indexed amount for the exclusion is $5.34 million.

Note that Sec. 2010(c)(4) and (5) provide for the portability of any unused exclusion amount of the first spouse to die to the estate of the second spouse to die.

Sections 2011, 2012, and 2014 are intended to prevent transfers from being subject to a transfer tax twice. Section 2011 provides a credit for death taxes paid to a state, and Sec. 2014 provides a credit for death taxes paid to a foreign country. Note, however, that Sec. 2011(b) imposes a ceiling on the amount of this credit. Therefore, the amount of state death taxes paid may exceed the amount of the credit. Likewise, Sec. 2014(b) imposes a ceiling on the amount of the foreign death tax credit, which relates the credit to property situated in the foreign country. As indicated in the estate tax model presented in the previous Editorial Summary, post-1976 taxable gifts must be included (i.e., the gross-up concept) in the calculation of the estate tax liability. Section 2012 provides a credit to offset the liability that has been imposed on any other lifetime transfer that has been subjected to transfer tax liability and which is included in the gross estate. Section 2012(e) specifically provides that the Sec. 2012 credit is not to apply for transfer tax paid on gifts made after December 31, 1976. This exception to credit treatment is logical in that Sec. 2001(b) provides an adjustment designed to negate double taxation on post-1976 gifts. Note that Sec. 2012 contains a ceiling on the amount of the credit.

The credit in Sec. 2013 also is designed to prevent a transfer tax from being applied more than once with respect to property included in an estate. In this case, however, the credit relates to property being included in the estate of more than one taxpayer (e.g., property is included in the estate of taxpayer A and in the estate of taxpayer B, A's beneficiary, who dies shortly after A). This credit has two parameters: one relating to the time period between the deaths of the taxpayers involved and the other setting a statutory ceiling on the amount of the credit.

The Tax Relief Reconciliation Act of 2001 provides for the repeal of the state death tax credit using a phased approach [see Sec. 2011(b)(2) and (f)] with the repeal fully effective by 2005.

§ 2010. Unified credit against estate tax

(a) General rule.—A credit of the applicable credit amount shall be allowed to the estate of every decedent against the tax imposed by section 2001.

(b) Adjustment to credit for certain gifts made before 1977.—The amount of the credit allowable under subsection (a) shall be reduced by an amount equal to 20 percent of the aggregate amount allowed as a specific exemption under section 2521 (as in effect before its repeal by the Tax Reform Act of 1976) with respect to gifts made by the decedent after September 8, 1976.

(c) Applicable credit amount.—

(1) In general.—For purposes of this section, the applicable credit amount is the amount of the tentative tax which would be determined under section 2001(c) if the amount with respect to which such tentative tax is to be computed were equal to the applicable exclusion amount.

(2) Applicable exclusion amount.—For purposes of this subsection, the applicable exclusion amount is the sum of—

(A) the basic exclusion amount, and

(B) in the case of a surviving spouse, the deceased spousal unused exclusion amount.

(3) Basic exclusion amount.—

(A) In general.—For purposes of this subsection, the basic exclusion amount is $5,000,000.*

(B) Inflation adjustment.—In the case of any decedent dying in a calendar year after 2011, the dollar amount in subparagraph (A) shall be increased by an amount equal to—

(i) such dollar amount, multiplied by

(ii) the cost-of-living adjustment determined under section 1(f)(3) for such calendar year by substituting "calendar year 2010" for "calendar year 1992" in subparagraph (B) thereof.

If any amount as adjusted under the preceding sentence is not a multiple of $10,000, such amount shall be rounded to the nearest multiple of $10,000.

(4) Deceased spousal unused exclusion amount.—For purposes of this subsection, with respect to a surviving spouse of a deceased spouse dying after December 31, 2010, the term "deceased spousal unused exclusion amount" means the lesser of—

(A) the basic exclusion amount, or

(B) the excess of—

(i) the applicable exclusion amount of the last such deceased spouse of such surviving spouse, over

(ii) the amount with respect to which the tentative tax is determined under section 2001 (b)(1) on the estate of such deceased spouse.

(5) Special rules.—

(A) Election required.—A deceased spousal unused exclusion amount may not be taken into account by a surviving spouse under paragraph (2) unless the executor of the estate of the deceased spouse files an estate tax return on which such amount is computed and makes an election on such return that such amount may be so taken into account. Such election, once made, shall be irrevocable. No election may be made under this subparagraph if such return is filed after the time prescribed by law (including extensions) for filing such return.

*Editorial comment: The indexed exclusion amount for 2014 is $5,340,000.

(B) Examination of prior returns after expiration of period of limitations with respect to deceased spousal unused exclusion amount.—Notwithstanding any period of limitation in section 6501, after the time has expired under section 6501 within which a tax may be assessed under chapter 11 or 12 with respect to a deceased spousal unused exclusion amount, the Secretary may examine a return of the deceased spouse to make determinations with respect to such amount for purposes of carrying out this subsection.

(6) Regulations.—The Secretary shall prescribe such regulations as may be necessary or appropriate to carry out this subsection.

(d) Limitation based on amount of tax.—The amount of the credit allowed by subsection (a) shall not exceed the amount of the tax imposed by section 2001.

§ 2011. Credit for State death taxes*

(a) In general.—The tax imposed by section 2001 shall be credited with the amount of any estate, inheritance, legacy, or succession taxes actually paid to any State or the District of Columbia, in respect of any property included in the gross estate (not including any such taxes paid with respect to the estate of a person other than the decedent).

(b) Amount of credit.—**(1) In general.**—Except as provided in paragraph (2), the credit allowed by this section shall not exceed the appropriate amount stated in the following table:

If the adjusted taxable estate is:	The maximum tax credit shall be:
Not over $90,000	8/10ths of 1% of the amount by which the taxable estate exceeds $40,000.
Over $90,000 but not over $140,000	$400 plus 1.6% of the excess over $90,000.
Over $140,000 but not over $240,000	$1,200 plus 2.4% of the excess over $140,000.
Over $240,000 but not over $440,000	$3,600 plus 3.2% of the excess over $240,000.
Over $440,000 but not over $640,000	$10,000 plus 4% of the excess over $440,000.
Over $640,000 but not over $840,000	$18,000 plus 4.8% of the excess over $640,000.
Over $840,000 but not over $1,040,000	$27,600 plus 5.6% of the excess over $840,000.
Over $1,040,000 but not over $1,540,000	$38,800 plus 6.4% of the excess over $1,040,000.
Over $1,540,000 but not over $2,040,000	$70,800 plus 7.2% of the excess over $1,540,000.
Over $2,040,000 but not over $2,540,000	$106,800 plus 8% of the excess over $2,040,000.
Over $2,540,000 but not over $3,040,000	$146,800 plus 8.8% of the excess over $2,540,000.
Over $3,040,000 but not over $3,540,000	$190,800 plus 9.6% of the excess over $3,040,000.
Over $3,540,000 but not over $4,040,000	$238,800 plus 10.4% of the excess over $3,540,000.
Over $4,040,000 but not over $5,040,000	$290,800 plus 11.2% of the excess over $4,040,000.
Over $5,040,000 but not over $6,040,000	$402,800 plus 12% of the excess over $5,040,000.
Over $6,040,000 but not over $7,040,000	$522,800 plus 12.8% of the excess over $6,040,000.
Over $7,040,000 but not over $8,040,000	$650,800 plus 13.6% of the excess over $7,040,000.
Over $8,040,000 but not over $9,040,000	$786,800 plus 14.4% of the excess over $8,040,000.
Over $9,040,000 but not over $10,040,000	$930,800 plus 15.2% of the excess over $9,040,000.
Over $10,040,000	$1,082,800 plus 16% of the excess over $10,040,000.

(2) Reduction of maximum credit.—

(A) In general.—In the case of estates of decedents dying after December 31, 2001, the credit allowed by this section shall not exceed the applicable percentage of the credit otherwise determined under paragraph (1).

(B) Applicable percentage.—

In the case of estates of decedents dying during:	The applicable percentage is:
2002	75 percent
2003	50 percent
2004	25 percent

(3) Adjusted taxable estate.—For purposes of this section, the term "adjusted taxable estate" means the taxable estate reduced by $60,000.

(c) Period of limitations on credit.—The credit allowed by this section shall include only such taxes as were actually paid and credit therefor claimed within 4 years after the filing of the return required by section 6018, except that—

(1) If a petition for redetermination of a deficiency has been filed with the Tax Court within the time prescribed in section 6213(a), then within such 4-year period or before the expiration of

*Editorial comment: This section is repealed for estates of decedents dying after December 31, 2004 [see Sec. 2011(f)].

60 days after the decision of the Tax Court becomes final.

(2) If, under section 6161 or 6166, an extension of time has been granted for payment of the tax shown on the return, or of a deficiency, then within such 4-year period or before the date of the expiration of the period of the extension.

(3) If a claim for refund or credit of an overpayment of tax imposed by this chapter has been filed within the time prescribed in section 6511, then within such 4-year period or before the expiration of 60 days from the date of mailing by certified mail or registered mail by the Secretary to the taxpayer of a notice of the disallowance of any part of such claim, or before the expiration of 60 days after a decision by any court of competent jurisdiction becomes final with respect to a timely suit instituted upon such claim, whichever is later.

Refund based on the credit may (despite the provisions of sections 6511 and 6512) be made if claim therefor is filed within the period above provided. Any such refund shall be made without interest.

(d) Limitation in cases involving deduction under section 2053(d).—In any case where a deduction is allowed under section 2053(d) for an estate, succession, legacy, or inheritance tax imposed by a State or the District of Columbia upon a transfer for public, charitable, or religious uses described in section 2055 or 2106(a)(2), the allowance of the credit under this section shall be subject to the following conditions and limitations:

(1) The taxes described in subsection (a) shall not include any estate, succession, legacy, or inheritance tax for which such deduction is allowed under section 2053(d).

(2) The credit shall not exceed the lesser of—

(A) the amount stated in subsection (b) on an adjusted taxable estate determined by allowing such deduction authorized by section 2053(d), or

(B) that proportion of the amount stated in subsection (b) on an adjusted taxable estate determined without regard to such deduction authorized by section 2053(d) as (i) the amount of the taxes described in subsection (a), as limited by the provisions of paragraph (1) of this subsection, bears to (ii) the amount of the taxes described in subsection (a) before applying the limitation contained in paragraph (1) of this subsection.

(3) If the amount determined under subparagraph (B) of paragraph (2) is less than the amount determined under subparagraph (A) of that paragraph, then for purposes of subsection (d) such lesser amount shall be the maximum credit provided by subsection (b).

(e) Limitation based on amount of tax.—The credit provided by this section shall not exceed the amount of the tax imposed by section 2001, reduced by the amount of the unified credit provided by section 2010.

(f) Termination.—This section shall not apply to the estates of decedents dying after December 31, 2004.

§ 2012. Credit for gift tax

(a) In general.—If a tax on a gift has been paid under chapter 12 (sec. 2501 and following), or under corresponding provisions of prior laws, and thereafter on the death of the donor any amount in respect of such gift is required to be included in the value of the gross estates of the decedent for purposes of this chapter, then there shall be credited against the tax imposed by section 2001 the amount of the tax paid on a gift under chapter 12, or under corresponding provisions of prior laws, with respect to so much of the property which constituted the gift as is included in the gross estate, except that the amount of such credit shall not exceed an amount which bears the same ratio to the tax imposed by section 2001 (after deducting from such tax the unified credit provided by section 2010) as the value (at the time of the gift or at the time of the death, whichever is lower) of so much of the property which constituted the gift as is included in the gross estate bears to the value of the entire gross estate reduced by the aggregate amount of the charitable and marital deductions allowed under sections 2055, 2056, and 2106(a)(2).

(b) Valuation reductions.—In applying, with respect to any gift, the ratio stated in subsection (a), the value at the time of the gift or at the time of the death, referred to in such ratio, shall be reduced—

(1) by such amount as will properly reflect the amount of such gift which was excluded in determining (for purposes of section 2503(a)), or of corresponding provisions of prior laws, the total amount of gifts made during the calendar quarter (or calendar year if the gift was made before January 1, 1971) in which the gift was made;

(2) if a deduction with respect to such gift is allowed under section 2056(a) (relating to marital deduction), then by the amount of such value, reduced as provided in paragraph (1); and

(3) if a deduction with respect to such gift is allowed under sections 2055 or 2106(a)(2) (relating to charitable deduction), then by the amount of such value, reduced as provided in paragraph (1) of this subsection.

(c) Where gift considered made one-half by spouse.—Where the decedent was the donor of the gift but, under the provisions of section 2513, or corresponding provisions of prior laws, the gift was considered as made one-half by his spouse—

(1) the term "the amount of the tax paid on a gift under chapter 12", as used in subsection (a), includes the amounts paid with respect to each half of such gift, the amount paid with respect to each being computed in the manner provided in subsection (d); and

(2) in applying, with respect to such gift, the ratio stated in subsection (a), the value at the time of the gift or at the time of the death, referred to in such ratio, includes such value with respect to each half of such gift, each such value being reduced as provided in paragraph (1) of subsection (b).

(d) Computation of amount of gift tax paid.—

(1) Amount of tax.—For purposes of subsection (a), the amount of tax paid on a gift under chapter 12, or under corresponding provisions of prior laws, with respect to any gift shall be an amount which bears the same ratio to the total tax paid for the calendar quarter (or calendar year if the gift was made before January 1, 1971) in which the gift was made as the amount of such gift bears to the total amount of taxable gifts (computed without deduction of the specific exemption) for such quarter or year.

(2) Amount of gift.—For purposes of paragraph (1), the "amount of such gift" shall be the amount included with respect to such gift in determining (for the purposes of section 2503(a), or of corresponding provisions of prior laws) the total amount of gifts made during such quarter or year, reduced by the amount of any deduction allowed with respect to such gift under section 2522, or under corresponding provisions of prior laws (relating to charitable deduction), or under section 2523 (relating to marital deduction).

(e) Section inapplicable to gifts made after December 31, 1976.—No credit shall be allowed under this section with respect to the amount of any tax paid under chapter 12 on any gift made after December 31, 1976.

§ 2013. Credit for tax on prior transfers

(a) General rule.—The tax imposed by section 2001 shall be credited with all or a part of the amount of the Federal estate tax paid with respect to the transfer of property (including property passing as a result of the exercise or non-exercise of a power of appointment) to the decedent by or from a person (herein designated as a "transferor") who died within 10 years before, or within 2 years after, the decedent's death. If the transferor died within 2 years of the death of the decedent, the credit shall be the amount determined under subsections (b) and (c). If the transferor predeceased the decedent by more than 2 years, the credit shall be the following percentage of the amount so determined—

(1) 80 percent, if within the third or fourth years preceding the decedent's death;

(2) 60 percent, if within the fifth or sixth years preceding the decedent's death;

(3) 40 percent, if within the seventh or eighth years preceding the decedent's death; and

(4) 20 percent, if within the ninth or tenth years preceding the decedent's death.

(b) Computation of credit.—Subject to the limitation prescribed in subsection (c), the credit provided by this section shall be an amount which bears the same ratio to the estate tax paid (adjusted as indicated hereinafter) with respect to the estate of the transferor as the value of the property transferred bears to the taxable estate of the transferor (determined for purposes of the estate tax) decreased by any death taxes paid with respect to such estate. For purposes of the preceding sentence, the estate tax paid shall be the Federal estate tax paid increased by any credits allowed against such estate tax under section 2012, or corresponding provisions of prior laws, on account of gift tax, and for any credits allowed against such estate tax under this section on account of prior transfers where the transferor acquired property from a person who died within 10 years before the death of the decedent.

(c) Limitation on credit.—

(1) In general.—The credit provided in this section shall not exceed the amount by which—

(A) the estate tax imposed by section 2001 or section 2101 (after deducting the credits provided for in sections 2010, 2012, and 2014) computed without regard to this section, exceeds

(B) such tax computed by excluding from the decedent's gross estate the value of such property transferred and, if applicable, by making the adjustment hereinafter indicated.

If any deduction is otherwise allowable under section 2055 or section 2106(a) (2) (relating to charitable deduction) then, for the purpose of the computation indicated in subparagraph (B), the amount of such deduction shall be reduced by that part of such deduction which the value of such property transferred bears to the decedent's entire gross estate reduced by the deductions allowed under sections 2053 and 2054, or section 2106(a) (l) (relating to deduction for expenses, losses, etc.). For purposes of this section, the value of such property transferred shall be the value as provided for in subsection (d) of this section.

(2) Two or more transferors.—If the credit provided in this section relates to property received from 2 or more transferors, the limitation provided in paragraph (1) of this subsection shall be computed by aggregating the value of the property so transferred to the decedent. The aggregate limitation so determined shall be apportioned in accordance with the value of the property transferred to the decedent by each transferor.

(d) Valuation of property transferred.—The value of property transferred to the decedent shall be the value used for the purpose of determining the Federal estate tax liability of the estate of the transferor but—

(1) there shall be taken into account the effect of the tax imposed by section 2001 or 2101, or any estate, succession, legacy, or inheritance tax, on the net value to the decedent of such property;

(2) where such property is encumbered in any manner, or where the decedent incurs any obligation imposed by the transferor with respect to such property, such encumbrance or obligation shall be taken into account in the same manner as if the amount of a gift to the decedent of such property was being determined; and

(3) if the decedent was the spouse of the transferor at the time of the transferor's death, the net value of the property transferred to the decedent shall be reduced by the amount allowed under section 2056 (relating to marital deductions) as a deduction from the gross estate of the transferor.

(e) Property defined.—For purposes of this section, the term "property" includes any beneficial interest in property, including a general power of appointment (as defined in section 2041).

(f) Treatment of additional tax imposed under section 2032A.—If section 2032A applies to any property included in the gross estate of the transferor and an additional tax is imposed with respect to such property under section 2032A(c) before the date which is 2 years after the date of the decedent's death, for purposes of this section—

(1) the additional tax imposed by section 2032A(c) shall be treated as a Federal estate tax payable with respect to the estate of the transferor; and

(2) the value of such property and the amount of the taxable estate of the transferor shall be determined as if section 2032A did not apply with respect to such property.

§ 2014. Credit for foreign death taxes

(a) In general.—The tax imposed by section 2001 shall be credited with the amount of any estate, inheritance, legacy, or succession taxes actually paid to any foreign country in respect of any property situated within such foreign country and included in the gross estate (not including any such taxes paid with respect to the estate of a person other than the decedent). The determination of the country within which property is situated shall be made in accordance with the rules applicable under subchapter B (sec. 2101 and following) in determining whether property is situated within or without the United States.

(b) Limitations on credit.—The credit provided in this section with respect to such taxes paid to any foreign country—

(1) shall not, with respect to any such tax, exceed an amount which bears the same ratio to the amount of such tax actually paid to such foreign country as the value of property which is—

(A) situated within such foreign country,

(B) subjected to such tax, and

(C) included in the gross estate

bears to the value of all property subjected to such tax; and

(2) shall not, with respect to all such taxes, exceed an amount which bears the same ratio to the tax imposed by section 2001 (after deducting from such tax the credits provided by sections 2010 and 2012) as the value of property which is—

(A) situated within such foreign country,

(B) subjected to the taxes of such foreign country, and

(C) included in the gross estate

bears to the value of the entire gross estate reduced by the aggregate amount of the deductions allowed under sections 2055 and 2056.

(c) Valuation of property.—

(1) The values referred to in the ratio stated in subsection (b)(1) are the values determined for purposes of the tax imposed by such foreign country.

(2) The values referred to in the ratio stated in subsection (b)(2) are the values determined under this chapter; but, in applying such ratio, the value of any property described in subparagraphs (A), (B), and (C) thereof shall be reduced by such amount as will properly reflect, in accordance with regulations prescribed by the Secretary, the deductions allowed in respect of such property under sections 2055 and 2056 (relating to charitable and marital deductions).

(d) Proof of credit.—The credit provided in this section shall be allowed only if the taxpayer establishes to the satisfaction of the Secretary—

(1) the amount of taxes actually paid to the foreign country,

(2) the amount and date of each payment thereof,

(3) the description and value of the property in respect of which such taxes are imposed, and

(4) all other information necessary for the verification and computation of the credit.

(e) Period of limitation.—The credit provided in this section shall be allowed only for such taxes as were actually paid and credit therefor claimed within 4 years after the filing of the return required by section 6018, except that—

(1) If a petition for redetermination of a deficiency has been filed with the Tax Court within the time prescribed in section 6213(a), then within such 4-year period or before the expiration of 60 days after the decision of the Tax Court becomes final.

(2) If, under section 6161, an extension of time has been granted for payment of the tax shown on the return, or of a deficiency, then within such 4-year period or before the date of the expiration of the period of the extension.

Refund based on such credit may (despite the provisions of sections 6511 and 6512) be made if claim therefor is filed within the period above provided. Any such refund shall be made without interest.

(f) Additional limitation in cases involving a deduction under section 2053(d).—In any case where a deduction is allowed under section 2053(d) for an estate, succession, legacy, or inheritance tax imposed by and actually paid to any foreign country upon a transfer by the decedent for public, charitable, or religious uses described in section 2055, the property described in subparagraphs (A), (B), and (C) of paragraphs (1) and (2) of subsection (b) of this section shall not include any property in respect of which such deduction is allowed under section 2053 (d).

(g) Possession of United States deemed a foreign country.—For purposes of the credits authorized by this section, each possession of the United States shall be deemed to be a foreign country.

(h) Similar credit required for certain alien residents.—Whenever the President finds that—

(1) a foreign country, in imposing estate, inheritance, legacy, or succession taxes, does not allow to citizens of the United States resident in such foreign country at the time of death a credit similar to the credit allowed under subsection (a),

(2) such foreign country, when requested by the United States to do so has not acted to provide such a similar credit in the case of citizens of the United States resident in such foreign country at the time of death, and

(3) it is in the public interest to allow the credit under subsection (a) in the case of citizens or subjects of such foreign country only if it allows such a similar credit in the case of citizens of the United States resident in such foreign country at the time of death,

the President shall proclaim that, in the case of citizens or subjects of such foreign country dying while the proclamation remains in effect, the credit under subsection (a) shall be allowed only if such foreign country allows such a similar credit in the case of citizens of the United States resident in such foreign country at the time of death.

§ 2015. Credit for death taxes on remainders

Where an election is made under section 6163(a) to postpone payment of the tax imposed by section 2001 or 2101, such part of any estate, inheritance, legacy, or succession taxes allowable as a credit under section 2014, as is attributable to a reversionary or remainder interest may be allowed as a credit against the tax attributable to such interest, subject to the limitations on the amount of the credit contained in such sections, if such part is paid, and credit therefor claimed, at any time before the expiration of the time for payment of the tax imposed by section 2001 or 2101 as postponed and extended under section 6163.

§ 2016. Recovery of taxes claimed as credit

If any tax claimed as a credit under section 2014 is recovered from any foreign country, the executor, or any other person or persons recovering such amount, shall give notice of such recovery to the Secretary at such time and in such manner as may be required by regulations prescribed by him, and the Secretary shall (despite the provisions of section 6501) redetermine the amount of the tax under this chapter and the amount, if any, of the tax due on such redetermination, shall be paid by the executor or such person or persons, as the case may be, on notice and demand. No interest shall be assessed or collected on any amount of tax due on any redetermination by the Secretary resulting from a refund to the executor of tax claimed as a credit under Section 2014, for any period before the receipt of such refund, except to the extent interest was paid by the foreign country on such refund.

PART III—GROSS ESTATE

Editorial Summary

Estate Tax: The Gross Estate

Subchapter A of Chapter 11 (Secs. 2031–2046)

Section 2031, which contains the general rule for determining what is included in the decedent's gross estate, appears to take a more limited perspective than does Sec. 61, which defines what is to be included in a taxpayer's gross income for income tax purposes. The approach taken by Sec. 2031 is that property is to be included in the gross estate only if so provided in Part III (i.e., Secs. 2031–2046). Although the approach is different, the result is much the same in that the Code sections in Part III are very inclusive in terms of the assets to be included in the gross estate.

A critical factor with respect to the gross estate is the value at which the assets are included. Section 2031 provides that assets are to be included at the fair market value at the date of the death of the decedent. Section 2032 provides an alternate valuation in providing that the executor of the estate can elect to value the assets at the fair market value six months after the death of the decedent. This election must be made for the total estate and cannot be made asset by asset. Since the purpose of this alternate valuation is to enable the executor to reduce the potential transfer tax liability if the included assets decrease in value during the six month period, Sec. 2032(c) provides that the election can be made only if it has the effect of reducing both the gross estate and the estate tax liability. This irrevocable election is available only if the estate is required to file an estate tax return. Section 2032A provides special valuation rules for certain real property used in farming or in a closely held trade or business.

Sections 2033–2046 contain the specific rules for determining what assets are to be included in the gross estate.

§ 2031. Definition of gross estate

(a) General.—The value of the gross estate of the decedent shall be determined by including to the extent provided for in this part, the value at the time of his death of all property, real or personal, tangible or intangible, wherever situated.

(b) Valuation of unlisted stock and securities.—In the case of stock and securities of a corporation the value of which, by reason of their not being listed on an exchange and by reason of the absence of sales thereof, cannot be determined with reference to bid and asked prices or with reference to sales prices, the value thereof shall be determined by taking into consideration, in addition to all other factors, the value of stock or securities of corporations engaged in the same or a similar line of business which are listed on an exchange.

* * *

§ 2032. Alternate valuation

(a) General.—The value of the gross estate may be determined, if the executor so elects, by valuing all the property included in the gross estate as follows:

(1) In the case of property distributed, sold, exchanged, or otherwise disposed of, within 6 months after the decedent's death such property shall be valued as of the date of distribution, sale, exchange, or other disposition.

(2) In the case of property not distributed, sold, exchanged, or otherwise disposed of, within 6 months after the decedent's death such property shall be valued as of the date 6 months after the decedent's death.

(3) Any interest or estate which is affected by mere lapse of time shall be included at its value as of the time of death (instead of the later date) with adjustment for any difference in its value as of the later date not due to mere lapse of time.

(b) Special rules.—No deduction under this chapter of any item shall be allowed if allowance for such item is in effect given by the alternate valuation provided by this section. Wherever in any other subsection or section of this chapter reference is made to the value of property at the time of the decedent's death, such reference shall be deemed to refer to the value of such property used in determining the value of the gross estate. In case of an election made by the executor under this section, then—

(1) for purposes of the charitable deduction under section 2055 or 2106(a) (2), any bequest, legacy, devise, or transfer enumerated therein, and

(2) for the purpose of the marital deduction under section 2056, any interest in property passing to the surviving spouse,

shall be valued as of the date of the decedent's death with adjustment for any difference in value (not due to mere lapse of time or the occurrence or nonoccurrence of a contingency) of the property as of the date 6 months after the decedent's death (substituting, in the case of property distributed by the executor or trustee, or sold, exchanged, or otherwise disposed of, during such 6-month period, the date thereof).

(c) Election must decrease gross estate and estate tax.—No election may be made under this section with respect to an estate unless such election will decrease—

(1) the value of the gross estate, and

(2) the sum of the tax imposed by this chapter and the tax imposed by chapter 13 with respect to property includible in the decedent's gross estate (reduced by credits allowable against such taxes).

(d) Election.—

(1) In general.—The election provided for in this section shall be made by the executor on the return of the tax imposed by this chapter. Such election, once made, shall be irrevocable.

(2) Exception.—No election may be made under this section if such return is filed more than 1 year after the time prescribed by law (including extensions) for filing such return.

§ 2032A. Valuation of certain farm, etc., real property

(a) Value based on use under which property qualifies.—

(1) General rule.—If—

(A) the decedent was (at the time of his death) a citizen or resident of the United States, and

(B) the executor elects the application of this section and files the agreement referred to in subsection (d)(2),

then, for purposes of this chapter, the value of qualified real property shall be its value for the use under which it qualifies, under subsection (b), as qualified real property.

(2) Limit on aggregate reduction in fair market value.—The aggregate decrease in the value of qualified real property taken into account for purposes of this chapter which results from the application of paragraph (1) with respect to any decedent shall not exceed $750,000.

(3) Inflation adjustment.—In the case of estates of decedents dying in a calendar year after 1998, the $750,000 amount contained in paragraph (2) shall be increased by an amount equal to--

(A) $750,000, multiplied by

(B) the cost-of-living adjustment determined under section 1(f)(3) for such calendar year by substituting "calendar year 1997" for "calendar year 1992" in subparagraph (B) thereof.

If any amount as adjusted under the preceding sentence is not a multiple of $10,000, such amount shall be rounded to the next lowest multiple of $10,000.

(b) Qualified real property.*—

(1) In general.—For purposes of this section, the term "qualified real property" means real property located in the United States which was acquired from or passed from the decedent to a qualified heir of the decedent and which, on the date of the decedent's death, was being used for a qualified use by the decedent or a member of the decedent's family, but only if—

(A) 50 percent or more of the adjusted value of the gross estate consists of the adjusted value of real or personal property which—

(i) on the date of the decedent's death, was being used for a qualified use by the decedent or a member of the decedent's family, and

*Editorial comment: For an estate of a descendant dying in calendar year 2014, if the executor makes the 2032A election for qualified real property, the aggregate decrease in the value of the property cannot exceed $1,090,000.

(ii) was acquired from or passed from the decedent to a qualified heir of the decedent.

(B) 25 percent or more of the adjusted value of the gross estate consists of the adjusted value of real property which meets the requirements of subparagraphs (A)(ii) and (C),

(C) during the 8-year period ending on the date of the decedent's death there have been periods aggregating 5 years or more during which—

(i) such real property was owned by the decedent or a member of the decedent's family and used for a qualified use by the decedent or a member of the decedent's family, and

(ii) there was material participation by the decedent or a member of the decedent's family in the operation of the farm or other business, and

(D) such real property is designated in the agreement referred to in subsection (d)(2).

(2) Qualified use.—For purposes of this section, the term "qualified use" means the devotion of the property to any of the following:

(A) use as a farm for farming purposes, or

(B) use in a trade or business other than the trade or business of farming.

(3) Adjusted value.—For purposes of paragraph (1), the term "adjusted value" means—

(A) in the case of the gross estate, the value of the gross estate for purposes of this chapter (determined without regard to this section), reduced by any amounts allowable as a deduction under paragraph (4) of section 2053(a), or

(B) in the case of any real or personal property, the value of such property for purposes of this chapter (determined without regard to this section), reduced by any amounts allowable as a deduction in respect of such property under paragraph (4) of section 2053(a).

(4) Decedents who are retired or disabled.—

(A) In general.—If, on the date of the decedent's death, the requirements of paragraph (1)(C)(ii) with respect to the decedent for any property are not met, and the decedent—

(i) was receiving old-age benefits under title II of the Social Security Act for a continuous period ending on such date, or

(ii) was disabled for a continuous period ending on such date,

then paragraph (1)(C)(ii) shall be applied with respect to such property by substituting "the date on which the longer of such continuous periods began" for "the date of the decedent's death" in paragraph (1)(C).

(B) Disabled defined.—For purposes of subparagraph (A), an individual shall be disabled if such individual has a mental or physical impairment which renders him unable to materially participate in the operation of the farm or other business.

(C) Coordination with recapture.—For purposes of subsection (c)(6)(B)(i), if the requirements of paragraph (1)(C)(ii) are met with respect to any decedent by reason of subparagraph (A), the period ending on the date on which the continuous period taken into account under subparagraph (A) began shall be treated as the period immediately before the decedent's death.

(5) Special rules for surviving spouses.—

(A) In general.—If property is qualified real property with respect to a decedent (hereinafter in this paragraph referred to as the "first decedent") and such property was acquired from or passed from the first decedent to the surviving spouse of the first decedent, for purposes of applying this subsection and subsection (c) in the case of the estate of such surviving spouse, active management of the farm or other business by the surviving spouse shall be treated as material participation by such surviving spouse in the operation of such farm or business.

(B) Special rule.—For the purposes of subparagraph (A), the determination of whether property is qualified real property with respect to the first decedent shall be made without regard to subparagraph (D) of paragraph (1) and without regard to whether an election under this section was made.

(C) Coordination with paragraph (4).—In any case in which to do so will enable the requirements of paragraph (1)(C)(ii) to be met with respect to the surviving spouse, this subsection and subsection (c) shall be applied by taking into account any application of paragraph (4).

(c) Tax treatment of dispositions and failures to use for qualified use.—

(1) Imposition of additional estate tax.—If, within 10 years after the decedent's death and before the death of the qualified heir—

(A) the qualified heir disposes of any interest in qualified real property (other than by a disposition to a member of his family), or

(B) the qualified heir ceases to use for the qualified use the qualified real property which was acquired (or passed) from the decedent,

then, there is hereby imposed an additional estate tax.

(2) Amount of additional tax.—

(A) In general.—The amount of the additional tax imposed by paragraph (1) with respect to any interest shall be the amount equal to the lesser of—

(i) the adjusted tax difference attributable to such interest, or

(ii) the excess of the amount realized with respect to the interest (or, in any case other than a sale or exchange at arm's length, the fair market value of the interest) over the value of the interest determined under subsection (a).

(B) Adjusted tax difference attributable to interest.—For purposes of subparagraph (A), the adjusted tax difference attributable to an interest is the amount which bears the same ratio to the adjusted tax difference with respect to the estate (determined under subparagraph (C)) as—

(i) the excess of the value of such interest for purposes of this chapter (determined without regard to subsection (a)) over the value of such interest determined under subsection (a), bears to

(ii) a similar excess determined for all qualified real property.

(C) Adjusted tax difference with respect to the estate.—For purposes of subparagraph (B), the term "adjusted tax difference with respect to the estate" means the excess of what would have been the estate tax liability but for subsection (a) over the estate tax liability. For purposes of this subparagraph, the term "estate tax liability" means the tax imposed by section 2001 reduced by the credits allowable against such tax.

(D) Partial dispositions.—For purposes of this paragraph, where the qualified heir disposes of a portion of the interest acquired by (or passing to) such heir (or a predecessor qualified heir) or there is a cessation of use of such a portion—

(i) the value determined under subsection (a) taken into account under subparagraph (A)(ii) with respect to such portion shall be its pro rata share of such value of such interest, and

(ii) the adjusted tax difference attributable to the interest taken into account with respect to the transaction involving the second or any succeeding portion shall be reduced by the amount of the tax imposed by this subsection with respect to all prior transactions involving portions of such interest.

(E) Special rule for disposition of timber.—In the case of qualified woodland to which an election under subsection (e)(13)(A) applies, if the qualified heir disposes of (or severs) any standing timber on such qualified woodland—

(i) such disposition (or severance) shall be treated as a disposition of a portion of the interest of the qualified heir in such property, and

(ii) the amount of the additional tax imposed by paragraph (1) with respect to such disposition shall be an amount equal to the lesser of—

(I) the amount realized on such disposition (or, in any case other than a sale or exchange at arm's length, the fair market value of the portion of the interest disposed or severed), or

(II) the amount of additional tax determined under this paragraph (without regard to this subparagraph) if the entire interest of the qualified heir in the qualified woodland had been disposed of, less the sum of the amount of the additional tax imposed with respect to all prior transactions involving such woodland to which this subparagraph applied.

For purposes of the preceding sentence, the disposition of a right to sever shall be treated as the disposition of the standing timber. The amount of additional tax imposed under paragraph (1) in any case in which a qualified heir disposes of his entire interest in the qualified woodland shall be reduced by any amount determined under this subparagraph with respect to such woodland.

(3) Only 1 additional tax imposed with respect to any 1 portion.—In the case of an interest acquired from (or passing from) any decedent, if subparagraph (A) or (B) of paragraph (1) applies to any portion of an interest, subparagraph (B) or (A), as the case may be, of paragraph (1) shall not apply with respect to the same portion of such interest.

(4) Due date.—The additional tax imposed by this subsection shall become due and payable on the day which is 6 months after the date of the disposition or cessation referred to in paragraph (1).

(5) Liability for tax; furnishing of bond.—The qualified heir shall be personally liable for the additional tax imposed by this subsection with respect to his interest unless the heir has furnished bond which meets the requirements of subsection (e)(11).

(6) Cessation of qualified use.—For purposes of paragraph (1)(B), real property shall cease to be used for the qualified use if—

(A) such property ceases to be used for the qualified use set forth in subparagraph (A) or (B) of subsection (b)(2) under which the property qualified under subsection (b), or

(B) during any period of 8 years ending after the date of the decedent's death and before the date of the death of the qualified heir, there had been periods aggregating more than 3 years during which—

(i) in the case of periods during which the property was held by the decedent, there was no material participation by the decedent or any member of his family in the operation of the farm or other business, and

(ii) in the case of periods during which the property was held by any qualified heir, there was no material participation by such qualified heir or any member of his family in the operation of the farm or other business.

(7) Special rules.—

(A) No tax if use begins within 2 years.—If the date on which the qualified heir begins to use the qualified real property (hereinafter in this subparagraph referred to as the commencement date) is before the date 2 years after the decedent's death—

(i) no tax shall be imposed under paragraph (1) by reason of the failure by the qualified heir to so use such property before the commencement date, and

(ii) the 10-year period under paragraph (1) shall be extended by the period after the decedent's death and before the commencement date.

(B) Active management by eligible qualified heir treated as material participation.—For purposes of paragraph (6)(B)(ii), the active management of a farm or other business by—

(i) an eligible qualified heir, or

(ii) a fiduciary of an eligible qualified heir described in clause (ii) or (iii) of subparagraph (C),

shall be treated as material participation by such eligible qualified heir in the operation of such farm or business. In the case of an eligible qualified heir described in clause (ii), (iii), or (iv) of subparagraph (C), the preceding sentence shall apply only during periods during which such heir meets the requirements of such clause.

(C) Eligible qualified heir.—For purposes of this paragraph, the term "eligible qualified heir" means a qualified heir who—

(i) is the surviving spouse of the decedent,

(ii) has not attained the age of 21,

(iii) is disabled (within the meaning of subsection (b)(4)(B)), or

(iv) is a student.

(D) Student.—For purposes of subparagraph (C), an individual shall be treated as a student with respect to periods during any calendar year if (and only if) such individual is a student (within the meaning of section 152(f)(2)) for such calendar year.

(E) Certain rents treated as qualified use.—For purposes of this subsection, a surviving spouse or lineal descendant of the decedent shall not be treated as failing to use qualified real property in a qualified use solely because such spouse or descendant rents such property to a member of the family of such spouse or descendant on a net cash basis. For purposes of the preceding sentence, a legally adopted child of an individual shall be treated as the child of such individual by blood.

(8) Qualified conservation contribution is not a disposition.—A qualified conservation contribution (as defined in section 170(h)) by gift or otherwise shall not be deemed a disposition under subsection (c)(1)(A).

(d) Election; agreement.—

(1) Election.—The election under this section shall be made on the return of the tax imposed by section 2001. Such election shall be made in such manner as the Secretary shall by regulations prescribe. Such an election, once made, shall be irrevocable.

(2) Agreement.—The agreement referred to in this paragraph is a written agreement signed by each person in being who has an interest (whether or not in possession) in any property designated in such agreement consenting to the application of subsection (c) with respect to such property.

(3) Modification of election and agreement to be permitted.—The Secretary shall prescribe procedures which provide that in any case in which the executor makes an election under paragraph (1) (and submits the agreement referred to in paragraph (2)) within the time prescribed therefor, but—

(A) the notice of election, as filed, does not contain all required information, or

(B) signatures of 1 or more persons required to enter into the agreement described in paragraph (2) are not included on the agreement as filed, or the agreement does not contain all required information,

the executor will have a reasonable period of time (not exceeding 90 days) after notification of such failures to provide such information or signatures.

(e) Definitions; special rules.—For purposes of this section—

(1) Qualified heir.—The term "qualified heir" means, with respect to any property, a member of the decedent's family who acquired such property (or to whom such property passed) from the decedent. If a qualified heir disposes of any interest in qualified real property to any member of his family, such member shall thereafter be treated as the qualified heir with respect to such interest.

(2) Member of family.—The term "member of the family" means, with respect to any individual, only—

(A) an ancestor of such individual,

(B) the spouse of such individual,

(C) a lineal descendant of such individual, of such individual's spouse, or of a parent of such individual, or

(D) the spouse of any lineal descendant described in subparagraph (C).

For purposes of the preceding sentence, a legally adopted child of an individual shall be treated as the child of such individual by blood.

(3) Certain real property included.—In the case of real property which meets the requirements of subparagraph (C) of subsection (b)(1), residential buildings and related improvements on such real property occupied on a regular basis by the owner or lessee of such real property or by persons employed by such owner or lessee for the purpose of operating or maintaining such real property, and roads, buildings, and other structures and improvements functionally related to the qualified use shall be treated as real property devoted to the qualified use.

(4) Farm.—The term "farm" includes stock, dairy, poultry, fruit, furbearing animal, and truck farms, plantations, ranches, nurseries, ranges, greenhouses or other similar structures used primarily for the raising of agricultural or horticultural commodities, and orchards and woodlands.

(5) Farming purposes.—The term "farming purposes" means—

(A) cultivating the soil or raising or harvesting any agricultural or horticultural commodity (including the raising, shearing, feeding, caring for, training, and management of animals) on a farm;

(B) handling, drying, packing, grading, or storing on a farm any agricultural or horticultural commodity in its unmanufactured state, but only if the owner, tenant, or operator of the farm regularly produces more than one-half of the commodity so treated; and

(C) **(i)** the planting, cultivating, caring for, or cutting of trees, or

(ii) the preparation (other than milling) of trees for market.

(6) Material participation.—Material participation shall be determined in a manner similar to the manner used for purposes of paragraph (1) of section 1402(a) (relating to net earnings from self-employment).

(7) Method of valuing farms.—

(A) In general.—Except as provided in subparagraph (B), the value of a farm for farming purposes shall be determined by dividing—

(i) the excess of the average annual gross cash rental for comparable land used for farming purposes and located in the locality of such farm over the average annual State and local real estate taxes for such comparable land, by

(ii) the average annual effective interest rate for all new Federal Land Bank loans.

For purposes of the preceding sentence, each average annual computation shall be made on the basis of the 5 most recent calendar years ending before the date of the decedent's death.

(B) Value based on net share rental in certain cases.—

(i) In general.—If there is no comparable land from which the average annual gross cash rental may be determined but there is comparable land from which the average net share rental may be determined, subparagraph (A)(i) shall be applied by substituting "average annual net share rental" for "average annual gross cash rental."

(ii) Net share rental.—For purposes of this paragraph, the term "net share rental" means the excess of—

(I) the value of the produce received by the lessor of the land on which such produce is grown, over

(II) the cash operating expenses of growing such produce which, under the lease, are paid by the lessor.

(C) Exception.—The formula provided by subparagraph (A) shall not be used—

(i) where it is established that there is no comparable land from which the average annual gross cash rental may be determined and that there is no comparable land from which the average net share rental may be determined, or

(ii) where the executor elects to have the value of the farm for farming purposes determined under paragraph (8).

(8) Method of valuing closely held business interests, etc.—In any case to which paragraph (7)(A) does not apply, the following factors shall apply in determining the value of any qualified real property:

(A) The capitalization of income which the property can be expected to yield for farming or closely held business purposes over a reasonable period of time under prudent management using traditional cropping patterns for the area, taking into account soil capacity, terrain configuration, and similar factors,

(B) The capitalization of the fair rental value of the land for farmland or closely held business purposes,

(C) Assessed land values in a State which provides a differential or use value assessment law for farmland or closely held business,

(D) Comparable sales of other farm or closely held business land in the same geographical area far enough removed from a metropolitan or resort area so that nonagricultural use is not a significant factor in the sales price, and

(E) Any other factor which fairly values the farm or closely held business value of the property.

(9) Property acquired from decedent.—Property shall be considered to have been acquired from or to have passed from the decedent if—

(A) such property is so considered under section 1014(b) (relating to basis of property acquired from a decedent),

(B) such property is acquired by any person from the estate, or

(C) such property is acquired by any person from a trust (to the extent such property is includible in the gross estate of the decedent).

(10) Community property.—If the decedent and his surviving spouse at any time held qualified real property as community property, the interest of the surviving spouse in such property shall be taken into account under this section to the extent necessary to provide a result under this section with respect to such property which is consistent with the result which would have obtained under this section if such property had not been community property.

(11) Bond in lieu of personal liability.—If the qualified heir makes written application to the Secretary for determination of the maximum amount of the additional tax which may be imposed by subsection (c) with respect to the qualified heir's interest, the Secretary (as soon as possible, and in any event within 1 year after the making of such application) shall notify the heir of such maximum amount. The qualified heir, on furnishing a bond in such amount and for such period as may be required, shall be discharged from personal liability for any additional tax imposed by subsection (c) and shall be entitled to a receipt or writing showing such discharge.

(12) Active management.—The term "active management" means the making of the management decisions of a business (other than the daily operating decisions).

(13) Special rules for woodlands.—

(A) In general.—In the case of any qualified woodland with respect to which the executor elects to have this subparagraph apply, trees growing on such woodland shall not be treated as a crop.

(B) Qualified woodland.—The term "qualified woodland" means any real property which—

(i) is used in timber operations, and

(ii) is an identifiable area of land such as an acre or other area for which records are normally maintained in conducting timber operations.

(C) Timber operations.—The term "timber operations" means—

(i) the planting, cultivating, caring for, or cutting of trees, or

(ii) the preparation (other than milling) of trees for market.

(D) Election.—An election under subparagraph (A) shall be made on the return of the tax imposed by section 2001. Such election shall be made in such manner as the Secretary shall by regulations prescribe. Such an election, once made, shall be irrevocable.

(14) Treatment of replacement property acquired in section 1031 or 1033 transactions.—

(A) In general.—In the case of any qualified replacement property, any period during which there was ownership, qualified use, or material participation with respect to the replaced property by the decedent or any member of his family shall be treated as a period during which there was such ownership, use, or material participation (as the case may be) with respect to the qualified replacement property.

(B) Limitation.—Subparagraph (A) shall not apply to the extent that the fair market value of the qualified replacement property (as of the date of its acquisition) exceeds the fair market value of the replaced property (as of the date of its disposition).

(C) Definitions.—For purposes of this paragraph—

(i) Qualified replacement property.—The term "qualified replacement property" means any real property which is—

(I) acquired in an exchange which qualifies under section 1031, or

(II) the acquisition of which results in the nonrecognition of gain under section 1033.

Such term shall only include property which is used for the same qualified use as the replaced property was being used before the exchange.

(ii) Replaced property.—The term "replaced property" means—

(I) the property transferred in the exchange which qualifies under section 1031, or

(II) the property compulsorily or involuntarily converted (within the meaning of section 1033).

(f) Statute of limitations.—If qualified real property is disposed of or ceases to be used for a qualified use, then—

(1) the statutory period for the assessment of any additional tax under subsection (c) attributable to such disposition or cessation shall not expire before the expiration of 3 years from the date the Secretary is notified (in such manner as the Secretary may by regulations prescribe) of such disposition or cessation (or if later in the case of an involuntary conversion or exchange to which subsection (h) or (i) applies, 3 years from the date the Secretary is notified of the replacement of the converted property or of an intention not to replace or of the exchange of property), and

(2) such additional tax may be assessed before the expiration of such 3-year period notwithstanding the provisions of any other law or rule of law which would otherwise prevent such assessment.

(g) Application of this section and section 6324B to interests in partnerships, corporations, and trusts.—The Secretary shall prescribe regulations setting forth the application of this section and section 6324B in the case of an interest in a partnership, corporation, or trust which, with respect to the decedent, is an interest in a closely held business (within the meaning of paragraph (1) of section 6166(b)). For purposes of the preceding sentence, an interest in a discretionary trust all the beneficiaries of which are qualified heirs shall be treated as a present interest.

(h) Special rules for involuntary conversions of qualified real property.—

(1) Treatment of converted property.—

(A) In general.—If there is an involuntary conversion of an interest in qualified real property—

(i) no tax shall be imposed by subsection (c) on such conversion if the cost of the qualified replacement property equals or exceeds the amount realized on such conversion, or

(ii) if clause (i) does not apply, the amount of the tax imposed by subsection (c) on such conversion shall be the amount determined under subparagraph (B).

(B) Amount of tax where there is not complete reinvestment.—The amount determined under this subparagraph with respect to any involuntary conversion is the amount of the tax which (but for this subsection) would have been imposed on such conversion reduced by an amount which—

(i) bears the same ratio to such tax, as

(ii) the cost of the qualified replacement property bears to the amount realized on the conversion.

(2) Treatment of replacement property.—For purposes of subsection (c)—

(A) any qualified replacement property shall be treated in the same manner as if it were a portion of the interest in qualified real property which was involuntarily converted; except that with respect to such qualified replacement property the 10-year period under paragraph (1) of subsection (c) shall be extended by any period, beyond the 2-year period referred to in section 1033(a)(2)(B)(i), during which the qualified heir was allowed to replace the qualified real property,

(B) any tax imposed by subsection (c) on the involuntary conversion shall be treated as a tax imposed on a partial disposition, and

(C) paragraph (6) of subsection (c) shall be applied—

(i) by not taking into account periods after the involuntary conversion and before the acquisition of the qualified replacement property, and

(ii) by treating material participation with respect to the converted property as material participation with respect to the qualified replacement property.

(3) Definitions and special rules.—For purposes of this subsection—

(A) Involuntary conversion.—The term "involuntary conversion" means a compulsory or involuntary conversion within the meaning of section 1033.

(B) Qualified replacement property.—The term "qualified replacement property" means—

(i) in the case of an involuntary conversion described in section 1033(a)(1), any real property into which the qualified real property is converted, or

(ii) in the case of an involuntary conversion described in section 1033(a) (2), any real property purchased by the qualified heir during the period specified in section 1033 (a)(2)(B) for purposes of replacing the qualified real property.

Such term only includes property which is to be used for the qualified use set forth in subparagraph (A) or (B) of subsection (b)(2) under which the qualified real property qualified under subsection (a).

(4) Certain rules made applicable.—The rules of the last sentence of section 1033(a)(2)(A) shall apply for purposes of paragraph (3)(B)(ii).

(i) Exchanges of qualified real property.—

(1) Treatment of property exchanged.—

(A) Exchanges solely for qualified exchange property.—If an interest in qualified real property is exchanged solely for an interest in qualified exchange property in a transaction which qualifies under section 1031, no tax shall be imposed by subsection (c) by reason of such exchange.

(B) Exchanges where other property received.—If an interest in qualified real property is exchanged for an interest in qualified exchange property and other property in a transaction which qualifies under section 1031, the amount of the tax imposed by subsection (c) by reason of such exchange shall be the amount of tax which (but for this subparagraph) would have been imposed on such exchange under subsection (c)(1), reduced by an amount which—

(i) bears the same ratio to such tax, as

(ii) the fair market value of the qualified exchange property bears to the fair market value of the qualified real property exchanged.

For purposes of clause (ii) of the preceding sentence, fair market value shall be determined as of the time of the exchange.

(2) Treatment of qualified exchange property.—For purposes of subsection (c)—

(A) any interest in qualified exchange property shall be treated in the same manner as if it were a portion of the interest in qualified real property which was exchanged,

(B) any tax imposed by subsection (c) by reason of the exchange shall be treated as a tax imposed on a partial disposition, and

(C) paragraph (6) of subsection (c) shall be applied by treating material participation with respect to the exchanged property as material participation with respect to the qualified exchange property.

(3) Qualified exchange property.—For purposes of this subsection, the term "qualified exchange property" means real property which is to be used for the qualified use set forth in subparagraph (A) or (B) of subsection (b)(2) under which the real property exchanged therefor originally qualified under subsection (a).

§ 2033. Property in which the decedent had an interest

The value of the gross estate shall include the value of all property to the extent of the interest therein of the decedent at the time of his death.

§ 2034. Dower or curtesy interests

The value of the gross estate shall include the value of all property to the extent of any interest therein of the surviving spouse, existing at the time of the decedent's death as dower or curtesy, or by virtue of a statute creating an estate in lieu of dower or curtesy.

§ 2035. Adjustments for certain gifts made within 3 years of decedent's death

(a) Inclusion of certain property in gross estate.—If—

(1) the decedent made a transfer (by trust or otherwise) of an interest in any property, or relinquished a power with respect to any property, during the 3-year period ending on the date of the decedent's death, and

(2) the value of such property (or an interest therein) would have been included in the decedent's gross estate under section 2036, 2037, 2038, or 2042 if such transferred interest or relinquished power had been retained by the decedent on the date of his death, the value of the gross estate shall include the value of any property (or interest therein) which would have been so included.

(b) Inclusion of gift tax on gifts made during 3 years before decedent's death.—The amount of the gross estate (determined without regard to this subsection) shall be increased by the amount of any tax paid under chapter 12 by the decedent or his estate on any gift made by the decedent or his spouse during the 3-year period ending on the date of the decedent's death.

(c) Other rules relating to transfers within 3 years of death.—

(1) In general.—For purposes of—

(A) section 303(b) (relating to distributions in redemption of stock to pay death taxes),

(B) section 2032A (relating to special valuation of certain farms, etc., real property), and

(C) subchapter C of chapter 64 (relating to lien for taxes),

the value of the gross estate shall include the value of all property to the extent of any interest therein of which the decedent has at any time made a transfer, by trust or otherwise, during the 3-year period ending on the date of the decedent's death.

(2) Coordination with section 6166.—An estate shall be treated as meeting the 35 percent of adjusted gross estate requirement of section 6166(a)(1) only if the estate meets such requirement both with and without the application of paragraph (1).

(3) Marital and small transfers.—Paragraph (1) shall not apply to any transfer (other than a transfer with respect to a life insurance policy) made during a calendar year to any donee if the decedent was not required by section 6019 (other than by reason of section 6019(2)) to file any gift tax return for such year with respect to transfers to such donee.

(d) Exception.—Subsection (a) shall not apply to any bona fide sale for an adequate and full consideration in money or money's worth.

(e) Treatment of certain transfers from revocable trusts.—For purposes of this section and section 2038, any transfer from any portion of a trust during any period that such portion was treated under section 676 as owned by the decedent by reason of a power in the grantor (determined without regard to section 672(e)) shall be treated as a transfer made directly by the decedent.

§ 2036. Transfers with retained life estate

(a) General rule.—The value of the gross estate shall include the value of all property to the extent of any interest therein of which the decedent has at any time made a transfer (except in case of a bona fide sale for an adequate and full consideration in money or money's worth), by trust or otherwise, under which he has retained for his life or for any period not ascertainable without reference to his death or for any period which does not in fact end before his death—

(1) the possession or enjoyment of, or the right to the income from, the property, or

(2) the right, either alone or in conjunction with any person, to designate the persons who shall possess or enjoy the property or the income therefrom.

(b) Voting rights.—

(1) In general.—For purposes of subsection (a)(1), the retention of the right to vote (directly or indirectly) shares of stock of a controlled corporation shall be considered to be a retention of the enjoyment of transferred property.

(2) Controlled corporation.—For purposes of paragraph (1), a corporation shall be treated as a controlled corporation if, at any time after the transfer of the property and during the 3-year period ending on the date of the decedent's death, the decedent owned (with the application of section 318), or had the right (either alone or in conjunction with any person) to vote, stock possessing at least 20 percent of the total combined voting power of all classes of stock.

(3) Coordination with section 2035.—For purposes of applying section 2035 with respect to paragraph (1), the relinquishment or cessation of voting rights shall be treated as a transfer of property made by the decedent.

* * *

§ 2037. Transfers taking effect at death

(a) General rule.—The value of the gross estate shall include the value of all property to the extent of any interest therein of which the decedent has at any time after September 7, 1916, made a transfer (except in case of a bona fide sale for an adequate and full consideration in money or money's worth), by trust or otherwise, if—

(1) possession or enjoyment of the property can, through ownership of such interest, be obtained only by surviving the decedent, and

(2) the decedent has retained a reversionary interest in the property (but in the case of a transfer made before October 8, 1949, only if such reversionary interest arose by the express terms of the instrument of transfer), and the value of such reversionary interest immediately before the death of the decedent exceeds 5 percent of the value of such property.

(b) Special rules.—For purposes of this section, the term "reversionary interest" includes a possibility that property transferred by the decedent—

(1) may return to him or his estate, or

(2) may be subject to a power of disposition by him,

but such term does not include a possibility that the income alone from such property may return to him or become subject to a power of disposition by him. The value of a reversionary interest immediately before the death of the decedent shall be determined (without regard to the fact of the decedent's death) by usual methods of valuation, including the use of tables of mortality and actuarial principles, under regulations prescribed by the Secretary. In determining the value of a possibility that property may be subject to a power of disposition by the decedent, such possibility shall be valued as if it were a possibility that such property may return to the decedent or his estate. Notwithstanding the foregoing, an interest so transferred shall not be included in the decedent's gross estate under this section if possession or enjoyment of the property could have been obtained by any beneficiary during the decedent's life through the exercise of a general power of appointment (as defined in section 2041) which in fact was exercisable immediately before the decedent's death.

§ 2038. Revocable transfers

(a) In general.—The value of the gross estate shall include the value of all property—

(1) Transfers after June 22, 1936.—To the extent of any interest therein of which the decedent has at any time made a transfer (except in case of a bona fide sale for an adequate and full consideration in money or money's worth), by trust or otherwise, where the enjoyment thereof was subject at the date of his death to any change through the exercise of a power (in whatever capacity exercisable) by the decedent alone or by the decedent in conjunction with any other person (without regard to when or from what source the decedent acquired such power), to alter, amend, revoke, or terminate, or where any such power is relinquished during the 3-year period ending on the date of the decedent's death.

(2) Transfers on or before June 22, 1936.—To the extent of any interest therein of which the decedent has at any time made a transfer (except in case of a bona fide sale for an adequate and full consideration in money or money's worth), by trust or otherwise, where the enjoyment thereof was subject at the date of his death to any change through the exercise of a power, either by the decedent alone or in conjunction with any person, to alter, amend, or revoke, or where the decedent relinquished any such power during the 3-year period ending on the date of the decedent's death. Except in the case of transfers made after June 22, 1936, no interest of the decedent of which he has made a transfer shall be included in the gross estate under paragraph (1) unless it is includible under this paragraph.

(b) Date of existence of power.—For purposes of this section, the power to alter, amend, revoke, or terminate shall be considered to exist on the date of the decedent's death even though the exercise of the power is subject to a precedent giving of notice or even though the alteration, amendment, revocation, or termination takes effect only on the expiration of a stated period after the exercise of the power, whether or not on or before the date of the decedent's death notice has been given or the power has been exercised. In such cases proper adjustment shall be made representing the interests which would have been excluded from the power if the decedent had lived, and for such purpose, if the notice has not been given or the power has not been exercised on or before the date of his death, such notice shall be considered to have been given, or the power exercised, on the date of his death.

§ 2039. Annuities

(a) General.—The gross estate shall include the value of an annuity or other payment receivable by any beneficiary by reason of surviving the decedent under any form of contract or agreement entered into after March 3, 1931 (other than as insurance under policies on the life of the decedent), if, under such contract or agreement, an annuity or other payment was payable to the decedent, or the decedent possessed the right to receive such annuity or payment, either alone or in conjunction with another for his life or for any period not ascertainable without reference to his death or for any period which does not in fact end before his death.

(b) Amount includible.—Subsection (a) shall apply to only such part of the value of the annuity or other payment receivable under such contract or agreement as is proportionate to that part of the purchase price therefor contributed by the decedent. For purposes of this section, any contribution by the decedent's employer or former employer to the purchase price of such contract or agreement (whether or not to an employee's trust or fund forming part of a pension, annuity, retirement, bonus or profit sharing plan) shall be considered to be contributed by the decedent if made by reason of his employment.

§ 2040. Joint interests

(a) General rule.—The value of the gross estate shall include the value of all property to the extent of the interest therein held as joint tenants with right of survivorship by the decedent and any other person, or as tenants by the entirety by the decedent and spouse, or deposited, with any person carrying on the banking business, in their joint names and payable to either or the survivor, except such part thereof as may be shown to have originally belonged to such other person and never to have been received or acquired by the latter from the decedent for less than an adequate and full consideration in money or money's worth: *Provided*, That where such property or any part thereof, or part of the consideration with which such property was acquired, is shown to have been at any time acquired by such other person from the decedent for less than an adequate and full consideration in money or money's worth, there shall be excepted only such part of the value of such property as is proportionate to the consideration furnished by such other person: *Provided further*, That where any property has been acquired by gift, bequest, devise, or inheritance, as a tenancy by the entirety by the decedent and spouse, then to the extent of one-half of the value thereof, or, where so acquired by the decedent and any other person as joint tenants with right of survivorship and their interests are not otherwise specified or fixed by law, then to the extent of the value of a fractional part to be determined by dividing the value of the property by the number of joint tenants with right of survivorship.

(b) Certain joint interests of husband and wife.—

(1) Interests of spouse excluded from gross estate.—Notwithstanding subsection (a), in the case of any qualified joint interest, the value included in the gross estate with respect to such interest by reason of this section is one-half of the value of such qualified joint interest.

(2) Qualified joint interest defined.—For purposes of paragraph (1), the term "qualified joint interest" means any interest in property held by the decedent and the decedent's spouse as—

(A) tenants by the entirety, or

(B) joint tenants with right of survivorship, but only if the decedent and the spouse of the decedent are the only joint tenants.

§ 2041. Powers of appointment

(a) In general.—The value of the gross estate shall include the value of all property.

(1) Powers of appointment created on or before October 21, 1942.—To the extent of any property with respect to which a general power of appointment created on or before October 21, 1942, is exercised by the decedent—

(A) by will, or

(B) by a disposition which is of such nature that if it were a transfer of property owned by the decedent, such property would be includible in the decedent's gross estate under sections 2035 to 2038, inclusive;

but the failure to exercise such a power or the complete release of such a power shall not be deemed an exercise thereof. If a general power of appointment created on or before October 21, 1942, has been partially released so that it is no longer a general power of appointment, the exercise of such power shall not be deemed to be the exercise of a general power of appointment if—

(i) such partial release occurred before November 1, 1951, or

(ii) the donee of such power was under a legal disability to release such power on October 21, 1942, and such partial release occurred not later than 6 months after the termination of such legal disability.

(2) Powers created after October 21, 1942.—To the extent of any property with respect to which the decedent has at the time of his death a general power of appointment created after October 21, 1942, or with respect to which the decedent has at any time exercised or released such a power of appointment by a disposition which is of such nature that if it were a transfer of property owned by the decedent, such property would be includible in the decedent's gross estate under sections 2035 to 2038, inclusive. For purposes of this paragraph (2), the power of appointment shall be considered to exist on the date of the decedent's death even though the exercise of the power is subject to a precedent giving of notice or even though the exercise of the power takes effect only on the expiration of a stated period after its exercise, whether or not on or before the date of the decedent's death notice has been given or the power has been exercised.

(3) Creation of another power in certain cases.—To the extent of any property with respect to which the decedent—

(A) by will, or

(B) by a disposition which is of such nature that if it were a transfer of property owned by the decedent such property would be includible in the decedent's gross estate under section 2035, 2036, or 2037,

exercises a power of appointment created after October 21, 1942, by creating another power of appointment which under the applicable local law can be validly exercised so as to postpone the vesting of any estate or interest in such property, or suspend the absolute ownership or power of alienation of such property, for a period ascertainable without regard to the date of the creation of the first power.

(b) Definitions.—For purposes of subsection (a)—

(1) General power of appointment.—The term "general power of appointment" means a power which is exercisable in favor of the decedent, his estate, his creditors, or the creditors of his estate; except that—

(A) A power to consume, invade, or appropriate property for the benefit of the decedent which is limited by an ascertainable standard relating to the health, education, support, or maintenance of the decedent shall not be deemed a general power of appointment.

(B) A power of appointment created on or before October 21, 1942, which is exercisable by the decedent only in conjunction with another person shall not be deemed a general power of appointment.

(C) In the case of a power of appointment created after October 21, 1942, which is exercisable by the decedent only in conjunction with another person—

(i) If the power is not exercisable by the decedent except in conjunction with the creator of the power—such power shall not be deemed a general power of appointment.

(ii) If the power is not exercisable by the decedent except in conjunction with a person having a substantial interest in the property, subject to the power, which is adverse to exercise of the power in favor of the decedent—such power shall not be deemed a general power of appointment. For the purposes of this clause a person who, after the death of the decedent, may be possessed of a power of appointment (with respect to the property subject to the decedent's power) which he may exercise in his own favor shall be deemed as having an interest in the property and such interest shall be deemed adverse to such exercise of the decedent's power.

(iii) If (after the application of clauses (i) and (ii)) the power is a general power of appointment and is exercisable in favor of such other person—such power shall be deemed a general power of appointment only in respect of a fractional part of the property subject to such power, such part to be determined by dividing the value of such property by the number of such persons (including the decedent) in favor of whom such power is exercisable.

For purposes of clauses (ii) and (iii), a power shall be deemed to be exercisable in favor of a person if it is exercisable in favor of such person, his estate, his creditors, or the creditors of his estate.

(2) Lapse of power.—The lapse of a power of appointment created after October 21, 1942, during the life of the individual possessing the power shall be considered a release of such power. The preceding sentence shall apply with respect to the lapse of powers during any calendar year only to the extent that the property, which could have been appointed by exercise of such lapsed powers, exceeded in value, at the time of such lapse, the greater of the following amounts:

(A) $5,000, or

(B) 5 percent of the aggregate value, at the time of such lapse, of the assets out of which, or the proceeds of which, the exercise of the lapsed powers could have been satisfied.

(3) Date of creation of power.—For purposes of this section, a power of appointment created by a will executed on or before October 21, 1942, shall be considered a power created on or before such date if the person executing such will dies before July 1, 1949, without having republished such will, by codicil or otherwise, after October 21, 1942.

§ 2042. Proceeds of life insurance

The value of the gross estate shall include the value of all property—

(1) Receivable by the executor.—To the extent of the amount receivable by the executor as insurance under policies on the life of the decedent.

(2) Receivable by other beneficiaries.—To the extent of the amount receivable by all other beneficiaries as insurance under policies on the life of the decedent with respect to which the decedent possessed at his death any of the incidents of ownership, exercisable either alone or in conjunction with any other person. For purposes of the preceding sentence, the term "incident of ownership" includes a reversionary interest (whether arising by the express terms of the policy or other instrument or by operation of law) only if the value of such reversionary interest exceeded 5 percent of the value of the policy immediately before the death of the decedent. As used in this paragraph, the term "reversionary interest" includes a possibility that the policy, or the proceeds of the policy, may return to the decedent or his estate, or may be subject to a power of disposition by him. The value of a reversionary interest at any time shall be determined (without regard to the fact of the decedent's death) by usual methods of valuation, including the use of tables of mortality and actuarial principles, pursuant to regulations prescribed by the Secretary. In determining the value of a possibility that the policy or proceeds thereof may be subject to a power of disposition by the decedent, such possibility shall be valued as if it were a possibility that such policy or proceeds may return to the decedent or his estate.

§ 2043. Transfers for insufficient consideration

(a) In general.—If any one of the transfers, trusts, interests, rights, or powers enumerated and described in sections 2035 to 2038, inclusive, and section 2041 is made, created, exercised, or relinquished for a consideration in money or money's worth, but is not a bona fide sale for an adequate and full consideration in money or money's worth, there shall be included in the gross estate only the excess of the fair market value at the time of death of the property otherwise to be included on account of such transaction, over the value of the consideration received therefor by the decedent.

(b) Marital rights not treated as consideration.—

(1) In general.—For purposes of this chapter, a relinquishment or promised relinquishment of dower or curtesy, or of a statutory estate created in lieu of dower or curtesy, or of other marital rights in the decedent's property or estate, shall not be considered to any extent a consideration "in money or money's worth."

(2) Exception.—For purposes of section 2053 (relating to expenses, indebtedness, and taxes), a transfer of property which satisfies the requirements of paragraph (1) of section 2516 (relating to certain property settlements) shall be considered to be made for an adequate and full consideration in money or money's worth.

§ 2044. Certain property for which marital deduction was previously allowed

(a) General rule.—The value of the gross estate shall include the value of any property to which this section applies in which the decedent had a qualifying income interest for life.

(b) Property to which this section applies.—This section applies to any property if—

(1) a deduction was allowed with respect to the transfer of such property to the decedent—

(A) under section 2056 by reason of subsection (b)(7) thereof, or

(B) under section 2523 by reason of subsection (f) thereof, and

(2) section 2519 (relating to dispositions of certain life estates) did not apply with respect to a disposition by the decedent of part or all of such property.

(c) Property treated as having passed from decedent.—For purposes of this chapter and chapter 13, property includible in the gross estate of the decedent under subsection (a) shall be treated as property passing from the decedent.

§ 2045. Prior interests

Except as otherwise specifically provided by law, sections 2034 to 2042, inclusive, shall apply to the transfers, trusts, estates, interests, rights, powers, and relinquishment of powers, as severally enumerated and described therein, whenever made, created, arising, existing, exercised, or relinquished.

§ 2046. Disclaimers

For provisions relating to the effect of a qualified disclaimer for purposes of this chapter, see section 2518.

PART IV—TABLE ESTATE

Editorial Summary

Estate Tax: The Taxable Estate

Subchapter A of Chapter 11 (Secs. 2051–2058)

The Editorial Summary on the estate tax entitled Estate Tax: General (which precedes Sec. 2001) contains the basic tax model for the estate tax. Sections 2051–2058 deal with the deductions that are permitted in converting the gross estate into the taxable estate.

Note that the marital deduction in Sec. 2056 provides a simple methodology for reducing the decedent's estate tax liability to zero. If all of the decedent's assets are left to the spouse, the taxable estate will be zero. However, such an approach may produce two negative tax effects. First, other available deduction and credit opportunities are effectively foregone. Second, due to the progressive nature of the estate tax rates, subjecting the assets to taxation in one estate (i.e., that of the spouse) rather than in two estates may result in an overall increase in the estate tax liability.

§ 2051. Definition of taxable estate

For purposes of the tax imposed by section 2001, the value of the taxable estate shall be determined by deducting from the value of the gross estate the deductions provided for in this part.

§ 2053. Expenses, indebtedness, and taxes

(a) General rule.—For purposes of the tax imposed by section 2001, the value of the taxable estate shall be determined by deducting from the value of the gross estate such amounts—

(1) for funeral expenses,

(2) for administration expenses,

(3) for claims against the estate, and

(4) for unpaid mortgages on, or any indebtedness in respect of, property where the value of the decedent's interest therein, undiminished by such mortgage or indebtedness, is included in the value of the gross estate,

as are allowable by the laws of the jurisdiction, whether within or without the United States, under which the estate is being administered.

(b) Other administration expenses.—Subject to the limitations in paragraph (1) of subsection (c), there shall be deducted in determining the taxable estate amounts representing expenses incurred in administering property not subject to claims which is included in the gross estate to the same extent such amounts would be allowable as a deduction under subsection (a) if such property were subject to claims, and such amounts are paid before the expiration of the period of limitation for assessment provided in section 6501.

(c) Limitations.—

(1) Limitations applicable to subsections (a) and (b).—

(A) Consideration for claims.—The deduction allowed by this section in the case of claims against the estate, unpaid mortgages, or any indebtedness shall, when founded on a promise or agreement, be limited to the extent that they were contracted bona fide and for an adequate and full consideration in money or money's worth; except that in any case in which any such claim is founded on a promise or agreement of the decedent to make a contribution or gift to or for the use of any donee described in section 2055 for the purposes specified therein, the deduction for such claims shall not be so limited, but shall be limited to the extent that it would be allowable as a deduction under section 2055 if such promise or agreement constituted a bequest.

(B) Certain taxes.—Any income taxes on income received after the death of the decedent, or property taxes not accrued before his death, or any estate, succession, legacy, or inheritance taxes, shall not be deductible under this section.

(C) Certain claims by remaindermen.—No deduction shall be allowed under this section for a claim against the estate by a remainderman relating to any property described in section 2044.

(D) Section 6166 interest.—No deduction shall be allowed under this section for any interest payable under section 6601 on any unpaid portion of the tax imposed by section 2001 for the period during which an extension of time for payment of such tax is in effect under section 6166.

(2) Limitations applicable only to subsection (a).—In the case of the amounts described in subsection (a), there shall be disallowed the amount by which the deductions specified therein exceed the value, at the time of the decedent's death, of property subject to claims, except to the extent that such deductions represent amounts paid before the date prescribed for the filing of the estate tax return. For purposes of this section, the term "property subject to claims" means property includible in the gross estate of the decedent which, or the avails of which, would under the applicable law, bear the burden of the payment of such deductions in the final adjustment and settlement of the estate, except that the value of the property shall be reduced by the amount of the deduction under section 2054 attributable to such property.

(d) Certain state and foreign death taxes.—

(1) In general.—Notwithstanding the provisions of subsection (c)(1)(B), for purposes of the tax imposed by section 2001, the value of the taxable estate may be determined, if the executor so elects before the expiration of the period of limitation for assessment provided in section 6501, by deducting from the value of the gross estate the amount (as determined in accordance with regulations prescribed by the Secretary) of any estate, succession, legacy, or inheritance tax imposed by and actually paid to any foreign country, in respect of any property situated within such foreign country and included in the gross estate of a citizen or resident of the United States, upon a transfer by the decedent for public, charitable, or religious uses described in section 2055. The determination under this paragraph of the country within which property is situated shall be made in accordance with the rules applicable under subchapter B (sec. 2101 and following) in determining whether property is situated within or without the United States. Any election under this paragraph shall be exercised in accordance with regulations prescribed by the Secretary.

(2) Condition for allowance of deduction.—No deduction shall be allowed under paragraph (1) for a State death tax or a foreign death tax specified therein unless the decrease in the tax imposed by section 2001 which results from the deduction provided in paragraph (1) will inure solely for the benefit of the public, charitable, or religious transferees described in section 2055 or section 2106(a)(2). In any case where the tax imposed by section 2001 is equitably apportioned among all the transferees of property included in the gross estate, including those described in sections 2055 and 2106(a)(2) (taking into account any exemptions, credits, or deductions allowed by this chapter), in determining such decrease, there shall be disregarded any decrease in the Federal estate tax which any transferees other than those described in sections 2055 and 2106(a)(2) are required to pay.

(3) Effect on credits for state and foreign death taxes of deduction under this subsection.—

(A) Election.—An election under this subsection shall be deemed a waiver of the right to claim a credit, against the Federal estate tax, under a death tax convention with any foreign country for any tax or portion thereof in respect of which a deduction is taken under this subsection.

(B) Cross references.—

See section 2014(f) for the effect of a deduction taken under this subsection on the credit for foreign death taxes.

(e) Marital rights.—

For provisions treating certain relinquishments of marital rights as consideration in money or money's worth, see section 2043(b)(2).

§ 2054. Losses

For purposes of the tax imposed by section 2001, the value of the taxable estate shall be determined by deducting from the value of the gross estate losses incurred during the settlement of estates arising from fires, storms, shipwrecks, or other casualties, or from theft, when such losses are not compensated for by insurance or otherwise.

§ 2055. Transfers for public, charitable, and religious uses

(a) In general.—For purposes of the tax imposed by section 2001, the value of the taxable estate shall be determined by deducting from the value of the gross estate the amount of all bequests, legacies, devises, or transfers—

(1) to or for the use of the United States, any State, any political subdivision thereof, or the District of Columbia, for exclusively public purposes;

(2) to or for the use of any corporation organized and operated exclusively for religious, charitable, scientific, literary, or educational purposes, including the encouragement of art, or to foster national or international amateur sports competition (but only if no part of its activities involve the provision of athletic facilities or equipment), and the prevention of cruelty to children or animals, no part of the net earnings of which inures to the benefit of any private stockholder or individual, which is not disqualified for tax exemption under section 501(c)(3) by reason of attempting to influence legislation, and which does not participate in, or intervene in (including the publishing or distributing of statements), any political campaign on behalf of (or in opposition to) any candidate for public office;

(3) to a trustee or trustees, or a fraternal society, order, or association operating under the lodge system, but only if such contributions or gifts are to be used by such trustee or trustees, or by such fraternal society, order, or association, exclusively for religious, charitable, scientific, literary, or educational purposes, or for the prevention of cruelty to children or animals, such trust, fraternal society, order, or association would not be disqualified for tax exemption under section 501(c)(3) by reason of attempting to influence legislation, and such trustee or trustees, or such fraternal society, order, or association, does not participate in, or intervene in (including the publishing or distributing of statements), any political campaign on behalf of (or in opposition to) any candidate for public office;

(4) to or for the use of any veterans' organization incorporated by Act of Congress, or of its departments or local chapters or posts, no part of the net earnings of which inures to the benefit of any private shareholder or individual, or

(5) to an employee stock ownership plan if such transfer qualified as a qualified gratuitous transfer of qualified employer securities within the meaning of section 664(g).

For purposes of this subsection, the complete termination before the date prescribed for the filing of the estate tax return of a power to consume, invade, or appropriate property for the benefit of an individual before such power has been exercised by reason of the death of such individual or for any other reason shall be considered and deemed to be a qualified disclaimer with the same full force and effect as though he had filed such qualified disclaimer. Rules similar to the rules of section 501(j) shall apply for purposes of paragraph (2).

(b) Powers of appointment.—Property includible in the decedent's gross estate under section 2041 (relating to powers of appointment) received by a donee described in this section shall, for purposes of this section, be considered a bequest of such decedent.

(c) Death taxes payable out of bequests.—If the tax imposed by section 2001, or any estate, succession, legacy, or inheritance taxes, are, either by the terms of the will, by the law of the jurisdiction under which the estate is administered, or by the law of the jurisdiction imposing the particular tax, payable in whole or in part out of the bequests, legacies, or devises otherwise deductible under this section, then the amount deductible under this section shall be the amount of such bequests, legacies, or devises reduced by the amount of such taxes.

(d) Limitation on deduction.—The amount of the deduction under this section for any transfer shall not exceed the value of the transferred property required to be included in the gross estate.

(e) Disallowance of deductions in certain cases.—

(1) No deduction shall be allowed under this section for a transfer to or for the use of an organization or trust described in section 508(d) or 4948(c)(4) subject to the conditions specified in such sections.

(2) Where an interest in property (other than an interest described in section 170(f)(3)(B)) passes or has passed from the decedent to a person, or for a use, described in subsection (a), and an interest (other than an interest which is extinguished upon the decedent's death) in the same property passes or has passed (for less than an adequate and full consideration in money or money's worth) from the decedent to a person, or for a use, not described in subsection (a), no deduction shall be allowed under this section for the interest which passes or has passed to the person, or for the use, described in subsection (a) unless—

(A) in the case of a remainder interest, such interest is in a trust which is a charitable remainder annuity trust or a charitable remainder unitrust (described in section 664) or a pooled income fund (described in section 642(c)(5)), or

(B) in the case of any other interest, such interest is in the form of a guaranteed annuity or is a fixed percentage distributed yearly of the fair market value of the property (to be determined yearly).

(3) Reformations to comply with paragraph (2).—

(A) In general.—A deduction shall be allowed under subsection (a) in respect of any qualified reformation.

(B) Qualified reformation.—For purposes of this paragraph, the term "qualified reformation" means a change of a governing instrument by reformation, amendment, construction, or otherwise which changes a reformable interest into a qualified interest but only if—

(i) any difference between—

(I) the actuarial value (determined as of the date of the decedent's death) of the qualified interest, and

(II) the actuarial value (as so determined) of the reformable interest,

does not exceed 5 percent of the actuarial value (as so determined) of the reformable interest,

(ii) in the case of—

(I) a charitable remainder interest, the nonremainder interest (before and after the qualified reformation) terminated at the same time, or

(II) any other interest, the reformable interest and the qualified interest are for the same period, and

(iii) such change is effective as of the date of the decedent's death.

A nonremainder interest (before reformation) for a term of years in excess of 20 years shall be treated as satisfying subclause (I) of clause (ii) if such interest (after reformation) is for a term of 20 years.

(C) Reformable interest.—For purposes of this paragraph—

(i) In general.—The term "reformable interest" means any interest for which a deduction would be allowable under subsection (a) at the time of the decedent's death but for paragraph (2).

(ii) Beneficiary's interest must be fixed.— The term "reformable interest" does not include any interest unless, before the remainder vests in possession, all payments to persons other than an organization described in subsection (a) are expressed either in specified dollar amounts or a fixed percentage of the fair market value of the property. For purposes of determining whether all such payments are expressed as a fixed percentage of the fair market value of the property, section 664(d)(3) shall be taken into account.

(iii) Special rule where timely commencement of reformation.—Clause (ii) shall not apply to any interest if a judicial proceeding is commenced to change such interest into a qualified interest not later than the 90th day after—

(I) if an estate tax return is required to be filed, the last date (including extensions) for filing such return, or

(II) if no estate tax return is required to be filed, the last date (including extensions) for filing the income tax return for the 1st taxable year for which such a return is required to be filed by the trust.

(iv) Special rule for will executed before January 1, 1979, etc.—In the case of any interest passing under a will executed before January 1, 1979, or under a trust created before such date, clause (ii) shall not apply.

(D) Qualified interest.—For purposes of this paragraph, the term "qualified interest" means an interest for which a deduction is allowable under subsection (a).

(E) Limitation.—The deduction referred to in subparagraph (A) shall not exceed the amount of the deduction which would have been allowable for the reformable interest but for paragraph (2).

(F) Special rule where income beneficiary dies.—If (by reason of the death of any individual, or by termination or distribution of a trust in accordance with the terms of the trust instrument) by the due date for filing the estate tax return (including any extension thereof) a reformable interest is in a wholly charitable trust or passes directly to a person or for a use described in subsection (a), a deduction shall be allowed for such reformable interest as if it had met the requirements of paragraph (2) on the date of the decedent's death. For purposes of the preceding sentence, the term "wholly charitable trust" means a charitable trust which, upon the allowance of a deduction, would be described in section 4947(a)(1).

(G) Statute of limitations.—The period for assessing any deficiency of any tax attributable to the application of this paragraph shall not expire before the date 1 year after the date on which the Secretary is notified that such reformation has occurred (or other proceeding pursuant to subparagraph (J)) has occurred.

(H) Regulations.—The Secretary shall prescribe such regulations as may be necessary to carry out the purposes of this paragraph, including regulations providing such adjustments in the application of the provisions of section 508 (relating to special rules relating to section 501(c)(3) organizations), subchapter J (relating to estates, trusts, beneficiaries, and decedents), and chapter 42 (relating to private foundations) as may be necessary by reason of the qualified reformation.

(I) Reformations permitted in case of remainder interests in residence or farm, pooled income funds, etc.—The Secretary shall prescribe regulations (consistent with the provisions of this paragraph) permitting reformations in the case of any failure—

(i) to meet the requirements of section 170 (f)(3)(B) (relating to remainder interests in personal residence or farm, etc.), or

(ii) to meet the requirements of section 642 (c)(5).

(J) Void or reformed trust in cases of insufficient remainder interests.—In the case of a trust that would qualify (or could be reformed to qualify pursuant to subparagraph (B)) but for failure to satisfy the requirement of paragraph (1)(D) or (2)(D) or section 664(d), such trust may be—

(i) declared null and void ab initio, or

(ii) changed by reformation, amendment, or otherwise to meet such requirement by reducing the payout rate or the duration (or both) of any noncharitable beneficiary's interest to the extent necessary to satisfy such requirement,

pursuant to a proceeding that is commenced within the period required in subparagraph (C)(iii). In a case described in clause (i), no deduction shall be allowed under this title for any transfer to the trust and any transactions entered into by the trust prior to being declared void shall be treated as entered into by the transferor.

(4) Works of art and their copyrights treated as separate properties in certain cases.—

(A) In general.—In the case of a qualified contribution of a work of art, the work of art and the copyright on such work of art shall be treated as separate properties for purposes of paragraph (2).

(B) Work of art defined.—For purposes of this paragraph, the term "work of art" means any tangible personal property with respect to which there is a copyright under Federal law.

(C) Qualified contribution defined.—For purposes of this paragraph, the term "qualified contribution" means any transfer of property to a qualified organization if the use of the property by the organization is related to the purpose or function constituting the basis for its exemption under section 501.

(D) Qualified organization defined.—For purposes of this paragraph, the term "qualified organization" means any organization described in section 501(c)(3) other than a private foundation (as defined in section 509). For purposes of the preceding sentence, a private operating foundation (as defined in section 4942(j)(3)) shall not be treated as a private foundation.

(5) Contributions to donor advised funds.—A deduction otherwise allowed under subsection (a) for any contribution to a donor advised fund (as defined in section 4966(d)(2)) shall only be allowed if—

(A) the sponsoring organization (as defined in section 4966(d)(1)) with respect to such donor advised fund is not—

(i) described in paragraph (3) or (4) of subsection (a), or

(ii) a type III supporting organization (as defined in section 4943(f)(5)(A)) which is not a functionally integrated type III supporting organization (as defined in section 4943 (f)(5)(B)), and

(B) the taxpayer obtains a contemporaneous written acknowledgment (determined under rules similar to the rules of section 170(f)(8) (C)) from the sponsoring organization (as so defined) of such donor advised fund that such organization has exclusive legal control over the assets contributed.

(f) Special rule for irrevocable transfers of easements in real property.—A deduction shall be allowed under subsection (a) in respect of any transfer of a qualified real property interest (as defined in section 170(h)(2)(C)) which meets the requirements of section 170(h) (without regard to paragraph (4)(A) thereof).

(g) Cross reference.—

(1) For option as to time for valuation for purpose of deduction under this section, see section 2032.

* * *

§ 2056. Bequests, etc., to surviving spouse

(a) Allowance of marital deduction.—For purposes of the tax imposed by section 2001, the value of the taxable estate shall, except as limited by subsection (b), be determined by deducting from the value of the gross estate an amount equal to the value of any interest in property which passes or has passed from the decedent to his surviving spouse, but only to the extent that such interest is included in determining the value of the gross estate.

(b) Limitation in the case of life estate or other terminable interest.—

(1) General rule.—Where, on the lapse of time, on the occurrence of an event or contingency, or on the failure of an event or contingency to occur, an interest passing to the surviving spouse will terminate or fail, no deduction shall be allowed under this section with respect to such interest—

(A) if an interest in such property passes or has passed (for less than an adequate and full consideration in money or money's worth) from the decedent to any person other than such surviving spouse (or the estate of such spouse); and

(B) if by reason of such passing such person (or his heirs or assigns) may possess or enjoy any part of such property after such termination or failure of the interest so passing to the surviving spouse;

and no deduction shall be allowed with respect to such interest (even if such deduction is not disallowed under subparagraphs (A) and (B))—

(C) if such interest is to be acquired for the surviving spouse, pursuant to directions of the decedent, by his executor or by the trustee of a trust.

For purposes of this paragraph, an interest shall not be considered as an interest which will terminate or fail merely because it is the ownership of a bond, note, or similar contractual obligation, the discharge of which would not have the effect of an annuity for life or for a term.

(2) Interest in unidentified assets.—Where the assets (included in the decedent's gross estate) out of which, or the proceeds of which, an interest passing to the surviving spouse may be satisfied include a particular asset or assets with respect to which no deduction would be allowed if such asset or assets passed from the decedent to such spouse, then the value of such interest passing to such spouse shall, for purposes of subsection (a), be reduced by the aggregate value of such particular assets.

(3) Interest of spouse conditional on survival for limited period.—For purposes of this subsection, an interest passing to the surviving spouse shall not be considered as an interest which will terminate or fail on the death of such spouse if—

(A) such death will cause a termination or failure of such interest only if it occurs within a period not exceeding 6 months after the decedent's death, or only if it occurs as a result of a common disaster resulting in the death of the decedent and the surviving spouse, or only if it occurs in the case of either such event; and

(B) such termination or failure does not in fact occur.

(4) Valuation of interest passing to surviving spouse.—In determining for purposes of subsection (a) the value of any interest in property passing to the surviving spouse for which a deduction is allowed by this section—

(A) there shall be taken into account the effect which the tax imposed by section 2001, or any estate, succession, legacy, or inheritance tax, has on the net value to the surviving spouse of such interest; and

(B) where such interest or property is encumbered in any manner, or where the surviving spouse incurs any obligation imposed by the decedent with respect to the passing of such interest, such encumbrance or obligation shall be taken into account in the same manner as if the amount of a gift to such spouse of such interest were being determined.

(5) Life estate with power of appointment in surviving spouse.—In the case of an interest in property passing from the decedent, if his surviving spouse is entitled for life to all the income from the entire interest, or all the income from a specific portion thereof, payable annually or at more frequent intervals, with power in the surviving spouse to appoint the entire interest, or such specific portion (exercisable in favor of such surviving spouse, or of the estate of such surviving spouse, or in favor of either, whether or not in each case the power is exercisable in favor of others), and with no power in any other person to appoint any part of the interest, or such specific portion, to any person other than the surviving spouse—

(A) the interest or such portion thereof so passing shall, for purposes of subsection (a), be considered as passing to the surviving spouse, and

(B) no part of the interest so passing shall, for purposes of paragraph (1) (A), be considered as passing to any person other than the surviving spouse.

This paragraph shall apply only if such power in the surviving spouse to appoint the entire interest, or such specific portion thereof, whether exercisable by will or during life, is exercisable by such spouse alone and in all events.

(6) Life insurance or annuity payments with power of appointment in surviving spouse.—In the case of an interest in property passing from the decedent consisting of proceeds under a life insurance, endowment, or annuity contract, if under the terms of the contract such proceeds are payable in installments or are held by the insurer subject to an agreement to pay interest thereon (whether the proceeds, on the termination of any interest payments, are payable in a lump sum or in annual or more frequent installments), and such installment or interest payments are payable annually or at more frequent intervals, commencing not later than 13 months after the decedent's death, and all amounts, or a specific portion of all such amounts, payable during the life of the surviving spouse are payable only to such spouse, and such spouse has the power to appoint all amounts, or such specific portion, payable under such contract (exercisable in favor of such surviving spouse, or of the estate of such surviving spouse, or in favor of either, whether or not in each case the power is exercisable in favor of others), with no power in any other person to appoint such amounts to any person other than the surviving spouse—

(A) such amounts shall, for purposes of subsection (a), be considered as passing to the surviving spouse, and

(B) no part of such amounts shall, for purposes of paragraph (1)(A), be considered as passing to any person other than the surviving spouse.

This paragraph shall apply only if, under the terms of the contract, such power in the surviving spouse to appoint such amounts, whether exercisable by will or during life, is exercisable by such spouse alone and in all events.

(7) Election with respect to life estate for surviving spouse.—

(A) In general.—In the case of qualified terminable interest property—

(i) for purposes of subsection (a), such property shall be treated as passing to the surviving spouse, and

(ii) for purposes of paragraph (1)(A), no part of such property shall be treated as passing to any person other than the surviving spouse.

(B) Qualified terminable interest property defined.—For purposes of this paragraph—

(i) In general.—The term "qualified terminable interest property" means property—

(I) which passes from the decedent,

(II) in which the surviving spouse has a qualifying income interest for life, and

(III) to which an election under this paragraph applies.

(ii) Qualifying income interest for life.—The surviving spouse has a qualifying income interest for life if—

(I) the surviving spouse is entitled to all the income from the property, payable annually or at more frequent intervals, or has a usufruct interest for life in the property, and

(II) no person has a power to appoint any part of the property to any person other than the surviving spouse.

Subclause (II) shall not apply to a power exercisable only at or after the death of the surviving spouse. To the extent provided in regulations, an annuity shall be treated in a manner similar to an income interest in property (regardless of whether the property from which the annuity is payable can be separately identified).

(iii) Property includes interest therein.—The term "property" includes an interest in property.

(iv) Specific portion treated as separate property.—A specific portion of property shall be treated as separate property.

(v) Election.—An election under this paragraph with respect to any property shall be made by the executor on the return of tax imposed by section 2001. Such an election, once made, shall be irrevocable.

(C) Treatment of survivor annuities.—In the case of an annuity included in the gross estate of the decedent under section 2039 (or, in the case of an interest in an annuity arising under the community property laws of a State, included in the gross estate of the decedent under section 2033) where only the surviving spouse has the right to receive payments before the death of such surviving spouse—

(i) the interest of such surviving spouse shall be treated as a qualifying income interest for life, and

(ii) the executor shall be treated as having made an election under this subsection with respect to such annuity unless the executor otherwise elects on the return of tax imposed by section 2001.

An election under clause (ii), once made, shall be irrevocable.

(8) Special rule for charitable remainder trusts.—

(A) In general.—If the surviving spouse of the decedent is the only beneficiary of a qualified charitable remainder trust who is not a charitable beneficiary nor an ESOP beneficiary, paragraph (1) shall not apply to any interest in such trust which passes or has passed from the decedent to such surviving spouse.

(B) Definitions.—For purposes of subparagraph (A)—

(i) Charitable beneficiary.—The term "charitable beneficiary" means any beneficiary which is an organization described in section 170(c).

(ii) ESOP beneficiary.—The term "ESOP beneficiary" means any beneficiary which is an employee stock ownership plan (as defined in section 4975(e)(7)) that holds a remainder interest in qualified employer securities (as defined in section 664(g)(4)) to be transferred to such plan in a qualified gratuitous transfer (as defined in section 664 (g)(1)).

(iii) Qualified charitable remainder trust.—The term "qualified charitable remainder trust" means a charitable remainder annuity trust or a charitable remainder unitrust (described in section 664).

(9) Denial of double deduction.—Nothing in this section or any other provision of this chapter shall allow the value of any interest in property to be deducted under this chapter more than once with respect to the same decedent.

(10) Specific portion.—For purposes of paragraphs (5), (6), and (7)(B)(iv), the term "specific portion" only includes a portion determined on a fractional or percentage basis.

(c) Definition.—For purposes of this section, an interest in property shall be considered as passing from the decedent to any person if and only if—

(1) such interest is bequeathed or devised to such person by the decedent;

(2) such interest is inherited by such person from the decedent;

(3) such interest is the dower or curtesy interest (or statutory interest in lieu thereof) of such person as surviving spouse of the decedent;

(4) such interest has been transferred to such person by the decedent at any time;

(5) such interest was, at the time of the decedent's death, held by such person and the decedent (or by them and any other person) in joint ownership with right of survivorship;

(6) the decedent had a power (either alone or in conjunction with any person) to appoint such interest and if he appoints or has appointed such interest to such person, or if such person takes such interest in default on the release or nonexercise of such power; or

(7) such interest consists of proceeds of insurance on the life of the decedent receivable by such person.

Except as provided in paragraph (5) or (6) of subsection (b), where at the time of the decedent's death it is not possible to ascertain the particular person or persons to whom an interest in property may pass from the decedent, such interest shall, for purposes of subparagraphs (A) and (B) of subsection (b)(1), be considered as passing from the decedent to a person other than the surviving spouse.

(d) Disallowance of marital deduction where surviving spouse not United States citizen.—

(1) In general.—Except as provided in paragraph (2), if the surviving spouse of the decedent is not a citizen of the United States—

(A) no deduction shall be allowed under subsection (a), and

(B) section 2040(b) shall not apply.

(2) Marital deduction allowed for certain transfers in trust.—

(A) In general.—Paragraph (1) shall not apply to any property passing to the surviving spouse in a qualified domestic trust.

(B) Special rule.—If any property passes from the decedent to the surviving spouse of the decedent, for purposes of subparagraph (A), such property shall be treated as passing to such spouse in a qualified domestic trust if—

(i) such property is transferred to such a trust before the date on which the return of the tax imposed by this chapter is made, or

(ii) such property is irrevocably assigned to such a trust under an irrevocable assignment made on or before such date which is enforceable under local law.

(3) Allowance of credit to certain spouses.—If—

(A) property passes to the surviving spouse of the decedent (hereinafter in this paragraph referred to as the "first decedent"),

(B) without regard to this subsection, a deduction would be allowable under subsection (a) with respect to such property, and

(C) such surviving spouse dies and the estate of such surviving spouse is subject to the tax imposed by this chapter,

the Federal estate tax paid (or treated as paid under section 2056A(b)(7)) by the first decedent with respect to such property shall be allowed as a credit under section 2013 to the estate of such surviving spouse and the amount of such credit shall be determined under such section without regard to when the first decedent died and without regard to subsection (d)(3) of such section.

(4) Special rule where resident spouse becomes citizen.—Paragraph (1) shall not apply if—

(A) the surviving spouse of the decedent becomes a citizen of the United States before the day on which the return of the tax imposed by this chapter is made, and

(B) such spouse was a resident of the United States at all times after the date of the death of the decedent and before becoming a citizen of the United States.

(5) **Reformations permitted.**—

(A) **In general.**—In the case of any property with respect to which a deduction would be allowable under subsection (a) but for this subsection, the determination of whether a trust is a qualified domestic trust shall be made—

(i) as of the date on which the return of the tax imposed by this chapter is made, or

(ii) if a judicial proceeding is commenced on or before the due date (determined with regard to extensions) for filing such return to change such trust into a trust which is a qualified domestic trust, as of the time when the changes pursuant to such proceeding are made.

(B) **Statute of limitations.**—If a judicial proceeding described in subparagraph (A)(ii) is commenced with respect to any trust, the period for assessing any deficiency of tax attributable to any failure of such trust to be a qualified domestic trust shall not expire before the date 1 year after the date on which the Secretary is notified that the trust has been changed pursuant to such judicial proceeding or that such proceeding has been terminated.

§ 2056A. Qualified domestic trust

(a) **Qualified domestic trust defined.**—For purposes of this section and section 2056(d), the term "qualified domestic trust" means, with respect to any decedent, any trust if—

(1) the trust instrument—

(A) except as provided in regulations prescribed by the Secretary, requires that at least 1 trustee of the trust be an individual citizen of the United States or a domestic corporation, and

(B) provides that no distribution (other than a distribution of income) may be made from the trust unless a trustee who is an individual citizen of the United States or a domestic corporation has the right to withhold from such distribution the tax imposed by this section on such distribution.

(2) such trust meets such requirements as the Secretary may by regulations prescribe to ensure the collection of any tax imposed by subsection (b), and

(3) an election under this section by the executor of the decedent applies to such trust.

(b) **Tax treatment of trust.**—

(1) **Imposition of estate tax.**—There is hereby imposed an estate tax on—

(A) any distribution before the date of the death of the surviving spouse from a qualified domestic trust, and

(B) the value of the property remaining in a qualified domestic trust on the date of the death of the surviving spouse.

(2) **Amount of tax.**—

(A) **In general.**—In the case of any taxable event, the amount of the estate tax imposed by paragraph (1) shall be the amount equal to—

(i) the tax which would have been imposed under section 2001 on the estate of the decedent if the taxable estate of the decedent had been increased by the sum of—

(I) the amount involved in such taxable event, plus

(II) the aggregate amount involved in previous taxable events with respect to qualified domestic trusts of such decedent, reduced by

(ii) the tax which would have been imposed under section 2001 on the estate of the decedent if the taxable estate of the decedent had been increased by the amount referred to in clause (i)(II).

(B) **Tentative tax where tax of decedent not finally determined.**—

(i) **In general.**—If the tax imposed on the estate of the decedent under section 2001 is not finally determined before the taxable event, the amount of the tax imposed by paragraph (1) on such event shall be determined by using the highest rate of tax in effect under section 2001 as of the date of the decedent's death.

(ii) **Refund of excess when tax finally determined.**—If—

(I) the amount of the tax determined under clause (i), exceeds

(II) the tax determined under subparagraph (A) on the basis of the final determination of the tax imposed by section 2001 on the estate of the decedent, such excess shall be allowed as a credit or refund (with interest) if claim therefor is filed not later than 1 year after the date of such final determination.

(C) Special rule where decedent has more than 1 qualified domestic trust.—If there is more than 1 qualified domestic trust with respect to any decedent, the amount of the tax imposed by paragraph (1) with respect to such trusts shall be determined by using the highest rate of tax in effect under section 2001 as of the date of the decedent's death (and the provisions of paragraph (3)(B) shall not apply) unless, pursuant to a designation made by the decedent's executor, there is 1 person—

(i) who is an individual citizen of the United States or a domestic corporation and is responsible for filing all returns of tax imposed under paragraph (1) with respect to such trusts and for paying all tax so imposed, and

(ii) who meets such requirements as the Secretary may by regulations prescribe.

(3) Certain lifetime distributions exempt from tax.—

(A) Income distributions.—No tax shall be imposed by paragraph (1)(A) on any distribution of income to the surviving spouse.

(B) Hardship exemption.—No tax shall be imposed by paragraph (1)(A) on any distribution to the surviving spouse on account of hardship.

(4) Tax where trust ceases to qualify.—If any qualified domestic trust ceases to meet the requirements of paragraphs (1) and (2) of subsection (a), the tax imposed by paragraph (1) shall apply as if the surviving spouse died on the date of such cessation.

(5) Due date.—

(A) Tax on distributions.—The estate tax imposed by paragraph (1)(A) shall be due and payable on the 15th day of the 4th month following the calendar year in which the taxable event occurs; except that the estate tax imposed by paragraph (1)(A) on distributions during the calendar year in which the surviving spouse dies shall be due and payable not later than the date on which the estate tax imposed by paragraph (1)(B) is due and payable.

(B) Tax at death of spouse.—The estate tax imposed by paragraph (1)(B) shall be due and payable on the date 9 months after the date of such death.

(6) Liability for tax.—Each trustee shall be personally liable for the amount of the tax imposed by paragraph (1). Rules similar to the rules of section 2204 shall apply for purposes of the preceding sentence.

(7) Treatment of tax.—For purposes of section 2056(d), any tax paid under paragraph (1) shall be treated as a tax paid under section 2001 with respect to the estate of the decedent.

(8) Lien for tax.—For purposes of section 6324, any tax imposed by paragraph (1) shall be treated as an estate tax imposed under this chapter with respect to a decedent dying on the date of the taxable event (and the property involved shall be treated as the gross estate of such decedent).

(9) Taxable event.—The term "taxable event" means the event resulting in tax being imposed under paragraph (1).

(10) Certain benefits allowed.—

(A) In general.—If any property remaining in the qualified domestic trust on the date of the death of the surviving spouse is includible in the gross estate of such spouse for purposes of this chapter (or would be includible if such spouse were a citizen or resident of the United States), any benefit which is allowable (or would be allowable if such spouse were a citizen or resident of the United States) with respect to such property to the estate of such spouse under section 2014, 2032, 2032A, 2055, 2056, 2058, or 6166 shall be allowed for purposes of the tax imposed by paragraph (1)(B).

(B) Section 303.—If the estate of the surviving spouse meets the requirements of section 303 with respect to any property described in subparagraph (A), for purposes of section 303, the tax imposed by paragraph (1)(B) with respect to such property shall be treated as a Federal estate tax payable with respect to the estate of the surviving spouse.

(C) Section 6161(a)(2).—The provisions of section 6161(a)(2) shall apply with respect to the tax imposed by paragraph (1)(B), and the reference in such section to the executor shall be treated as a reference to the trustees of the trust.

(11) Special rule where distribution tax paid out of trust.—For purposes of this subsection, if any portion of the tax imposed by paragraph (1)(A) with respect to any distribution is paid out of the trust, an amount equal to the portion so paid shall be treated as a distribution described in paragraph (1)(A).

(12) Special rule where spouse becomes citizen.—If the surviving spouse of the decedent becomes a citizen of the United States and if—

(A) such spouse was a resident of the United States at all times after the date of the death of the decedent and before such spouse becomes a citizen of the United States,

(B) no tax was imposed by paragraph (1)(A) with respect to any distribution before such spouse becomes such a citizen, or

(C) such spouse elects—

(i) to treat any distribution on which tax was imposed by paragraph (1)(A) as a taxable gift made by such spouse for purposes of—

(I) section 2001, and

(II) determining the amount of the tax imposed by section 2501 on actual taxable gifts made by such spouse during the year in which the spouse becomes a citizen or any subsequent year, and

(ii) to treat any reduction in the tax imposed by paragraph (1)(A) by reason of the credit allowable under section 2010 with respect to the decedent as a credit allowable to such surviving spouse under section 2505 for purposes of determining the amount of the credit allowable under section 2505 with respect to taxable gifts made by the surviving spouse during the year in which the spouse becomes a citizen or any subsequent year,

paragraph (1)(A) shall not apply to any distributions after such spouse becomes such a citizen (and paragraph (1)(B) shall not apply).

(13) Coordination with section 1015.—For purposes of section 1015, any distribution on which tax is imposed by paragraph (1)(A) shall be treated as a transfer by gift, and any tax paid under paragraph (1)(A) shall be treated as a gift tax.

(14) Coordination with terminable interest rules.—Any interest in a qualified domestic trust shall not be treated as failing to meet the requirements of paragraph (5) or (7) of section 2056(b) merely by reason of any provision of the trust instrument permitting the withholding from any distribution of an amount to pay the tax imposed by paragraph (1) on such distribution.

(15) No tax on certain distributions.—No tax shall be imposed by paragraph (1) on any distribution to the surviving spouse to the extent such distribution is to reimburse such surviving spouse for any tax imposed by subtitle A on any item of income of the trust to which such surviving spouse is not entitled under the terms of the trust.

(c) Definitions.—For purposes of this section—

(1) Property includes interest therein.—The term "property" includes an interest in property.

(2) Income.—Except as provided in regulations, the term "income" has the meaning given to such term by section 643(b).

(3) Trust.—To the extent provided in regulations prescribed by the Secretary, the term "trust" includes other arrangements which have substantially the same effect as a trust.

(d) Election.—An election under this section with respect to any trust shall be made by the executor on the return of the tax imposed by section 2001. Such an election, once made, shall be irrevocable. No election may be made under this section on any return if such return is filed more than one year after the time prescribed by law (including extensions) for filing such return.

(e) Regulations.—The Secretary shall prescribe such regulations as may be necessary or appropriate to carry out the purposes of this section, including regulations under which there may be treated as a qualified domestic trust any annuity or other payment which is includible in the decedent's gross estate and is by its terms payable for life or a term of years.

§ 2058. State death taxes

(a) Allowance of deduction.—For purposes of the tax imposed by section 2001, the value of the taxable estate shall be determined by deducting from the value of the gross estate the amount of any estate, inheritance, legacy, or succession taxes actually paid to any State or the District of Columbia, in respect of any property included in the gross estate (not including any such taxes paid with respect to the estate of a person other than the decedent).

(b) Period of limitations.—The deduction allowed by this section shall include only such taxes as were actually paid and deduction therefor claimed before the later of—

(1) 4 years after the filing of the return required by section 6108, or

(2) if—

(A) a petition for redetermination of a deficiency has been filed with the Tax Court within the time prescribed in section 6213(a), the expiration of 60 days after the decision of the Tax Court becomes final,

(B) an extension of time has been granted under section 6161 or 6166 for payment of the tax shown on the return, or of a deficiency, the date of the expiration of the period of the extension, or

(C) a claim for refund or credit of an overpayment of tax imposed by this chapter has been filed within the time prescribed in section 6511, the latest of the expiration of—

(i) 60 days from the date of mailing by certified mail or registered mail by the Secretary to the taxpayer of a notice of the disallowance of any part of such claim,

(ii) 60 days after a decision by any court of competent jurisdiction becomes final with respect to a timely suit instituted upon such claim, or

(iii) 2 years after a notice of the waiver of disallowance is filed under section 6532(a)(3).

Notwithstanding sections 6511 and 6512, refund based on the deduction may be made if the claim for refund is filed within the period provided in the preceding sentence. Any such refund shall be made without interest.

SUBCHAPTER B—ESTATES OF NONRESIDENTS NOT CITIZENS*

SUBCHAPTER C—MISCELLANEOUS

Editorial Summary

Special Estate Tax Rates for Combat-Zone Related, Etc. Deaths

Subchapter C of Chapter 11 (Sec. 2201)

A special estate tax rate schedule is provided for members of the U.S. Armed Forces (1) who were killed in action while serving in a combat zone or (2) died as the result of wounds, disease, or injury suffered while serving in a combat zone [Sec. 2201(a) and (b)(1)]. This special tax rate schedule also applies to individuals whose death resulted from certain terrorist attacks [Sec. 2201(b)(2)], and to astronauts who die in the line of duty [Sec. 2201(b)(3)].

This special tax rate schedule contains tax rates that are substantially lower than the estate tax rates contained in Sec. 2201(c).

§ 2201. Combat zone-related deaths of members of the Armed Forces, deaths of astronauts, and deaths of victims of certain terrorist attacks

(a) **In general.**—Unless the executor elects not to have this section apply, in applying sections 2001 and 2101 to the estate of a qualified decedent, the rate schedule set forth in subsection (c) shall be deemed to be the rate schedule set forth in section 2001(c).

(b) **Qualified decedent.**—For purposes of this section, the term "qualified decedent" means—

(1) any citizen or resident of the United States dying while in active service of the Armed Forces of the United States, if such decedent—

(A) was killed in action while serving in a combat zone, as determined under section 112 (c), or

(B) died as a result of wounds, disease, or injury suffered while serving in a combat zone (as determined under section 112(c)), and while in the line of duty, by reason of a hazard to which such decedent was subjected as an incident of such service,

(2) any specified terrorist victim (as defined in section 692(d)(4)), and

*Omitted.

(3) any astronaut whose death occurs in the line of duty.

(c) Rate schedule.—

If the amount with respect to which the tentative tax to be computed is:	**The tentative tax is:**
Not over $150,000	1 percent of the amount by which such amount exceeds $100,000.
Over $150,000 but not over $200,000	$500 plus 2 percent of the excess over $150,000.
Over $200,000 but not over $300,000	$1,500 plus 3 percent of the excess over $200,000.
Over $300,000 but not over $500,000	$4,500 plus 4 percent of the excess over $300,000.
Over $500,000 but not over $700,000	$12,500 plus 5 percent of the excess over $500,000.
Over $700,000 but not over $900,000	$22,500 plus 6 percent of the excess over $700,000.
Over $900,000 but not over $1,100,000	$34,500 plus 7 percent of the excess over $900,000.
Over $1,100,000 but not over $1,600,000	$48,500 plus 8 percent of the excess over $1,100,000.
Over $1,600,000 but not over $2,100,000	$88,500 plus 9 percent of the excess over $1,600,000.
Over $2,100,000 but not over $2,600,000	$133,500 plus 10 percent of the excess over $2,100,000.
Over $2,600,000 but not over $3,100,000	$183,500 plus 11 percent of the excess over $2,600,000.
Over $3,100,000 but not over $3,600,000	$238,500 plus 12 percent of the excess over $3,100,000.
Over $3,600,000 but not over $4,100,000	$298,500 plus 13 percent of the excess over $3,600,000.
Over $4,100,000 but not over $5,100,000	$363,500 plus 14 percent of the excess over $4,100,000.
Over $5,100,000 but not over $6,100,000	$503,500 plus 15 percent of the excess over $5,100,000.
Over $6,100,000 but not over $7,100,000	$653,500 plus 16 percent of the excess over $6,100,000.
Over $7,100,000 but not over $8,100,000	$813,500 plus 17 percent of the excess over $7,100,000.
Over $8,100,000 but not over $9,100,000	$983,500 plus 18 percent of the excess over $8,100,000.
Over $9,100,000 but not over $10,100,000	$1,163,500 plus 19 percent of the excess over $9,100,000.
Over $10,100,000	$1,353,500 plus 20 percent of the excess over $10,100,000.

(d) Determination of unified credit.—In the case of an estate to which this section applies, subsection (a) shall not apply in determining the credit under section 2010.

* * *

CHAPTER 12—GIFT TAX

SUBCHAPTER A—DETERMINATION OF TAX LIABILITY

Editorial Summary

Gift Tax: General

Subchapter A of Chapter 12 (Secs. 2501–2505)

The gift tax is an excise tax imposed on the donor on the right to transfer property during the taxpayer's life [see Sec. 2501(a)]. As presented in the Editorial Summary on the estate tax entitled Estate Tax: General (which precedes Sec. 2001), the general intent of the Tax Reform Act of 1976 was to create a unified transfer tax system (i.e., applicable to both transfers during life and transfers at death). Thus, in dealing with the gift tax structure, one must be aware of the interrelationships with the estate tax structure.

The basic tax model for the gift tax is as follows:

	Gross gifts
–	Per donee annual exclusion of $13,000
–	Deductions
=	Taxable gifts for the current period
+	Prior periods' taxable gifts
=	Total taxable gifts
×	Rates
=	Tentative gift tax liability
–	Gift tax paid on prior periods' taxable gifts (actual or deemed amount)
–	Unified credit
=	Gift tax liability

The gift tax liability must be calculated annually under Sec. 2501. The gift tax rates are progressive [see Secs. 2502, 2001(c)]. If the gift tax liability were not a cumulative lifetime calculation, the taxpayer would be able to reduce his total gift tax liability by spreading the gifts over a period of years when compared with making all or a substantial portion of the gifts in one or a few taxable years. In addition, horizontal equity would not be achieved with respect to two taxpayers who chose the two different gift patterns mentioned in the previous sentence. Therefore, as the model indicates, the gift tax liability calculation is a cumulative lifetime calculation. Note that it still is possible to reduce the overall gift tax liability by spreading through the use of other model components.

The provision for the gift tax rates appears in Sec. 2502. Due to the unified estate and gift tax structure objective, however, the gift tax rates and the estate tax rates are the same. Therefore, the gift tax rates in Sec. 2502(a)(2) are the same as the estate tax rates in Sec. 2001(c). Refer to the presentation on the transfer tax rates in the Editorial Summary on the estate tax entitled Estate Tax: General (which precedes Sec. 2001).

Section 2503 defines a taxable gift, and Sec. 2504 defines taxable gifts for the preceding calendar periods. Note that Sec. 2503(b), in providing for the annual $10,000 (indexed for inflation; 2006 through 2008 amount is $12,000, and 2009, 2010, 2011, and 2012 amount is $13,000; and for 2013 and 2014 is $14,000) per donee annual exclusion, requires that the gift be of a present interest rather than a future interest. Section 2503(e), in effect, increases the amount of this annual exclusion for qualified transfers for educational expenses and medical expenses.

The statutory authority for the unified credit appears in Sec. 2505. Refer to the discussion of the unified credit in the Editorial Summary on the estate tax entitled Estate Tax: Credits (which precedes Sec. 2010). Note that the unified credit amount for the gift tax was frozen at $345,800 (i.e., applicable exclusion amount of $1,000,000) beginning in 2004.

The Tax Relief Act of 2010 once again unifies the unified transfer tax credit for the estate tax and the gift tax. For 2011, the credit is $1,730,800 and the related exclusion amount is $5 million. These amounts are indexed for inflation starting in 2012. For 2012, the indexed credit amount is $1,772,800 and the indexed amount for the exclusion is $5,120,000. For 2013, the indexed credit amount is $2,045,800 and the indexed amount for the exclusion is $5.25 million. For 2014, the indexed credit amount is $2,081,800 and the indexed amount for the exclusion is $5.34 million.

§ 2501. Imposition of tax

(a) Taxable transfers.—

(1) General rule.—A tax, computed as provided in section 2502, is hereby imposed for each calendar year on the transfer of property by gift during such calendar year by any individual, resident or nonresident.

(2) Transfers of intangible property.—Except as provided in paragraph (3), paragraph (1) shall not apply to the transfer of intangible property by a nonresident not a citizen of the United States.

(3) Exception.—

(A) Certain individuals.—Paragraph (2) shall not apply in the case of a donor to whom section 877(b) applies for the taxable year which includes the date of the transfer.

(B) Credit for foreign gift taxes.—The tax imposed by this section solely by reason of this paragraph shall be credited with the amount of any gift tax actually paid to any foreign country in respect of any gift which is taxable under this section solely by reason of this paragraph.

(4) Transfers to political organizations.—Paragraph (1) shall not apply to the transfer of money or other property to a political organization (within the meaning of section 527(e) (1)) for the use of such organization.

* * *

(b) Certain residents of possessions considered citizens of the United States.—A donor who is a citizen of the United States and a resident of a possession thereof shall, for purposes of the tax imposed by this chapter, be considered a "citizen" of the United States within the meaning of that term wherever used in this title unless he acquired his United States citizenship solely by reason of (1) his being a citizen of such possession of the United States, or (2) his birth or residence within such possession of the United States.

(c) Certain residents of possessions considered nonresidents not citizens of the United States.—A donor who is a citizen of the United States and a resident of a possession thereof shall, for purposes of the tax imposed by this chapter, be considered a "nonresident not a citizen of the United States" within the meaning of that term wherever used in this title, but only if such donor acquired his United States citizenship solely by reason of (1) his being a citizen of such possession of the United States, or (2) his birth or residence within such possession of the United States.

(d) Cross references.—

(1) For increase in basis of property acquired by gift for gift tax paid, see section 1015(d).

(2) For exclusion of transfers of property outside the United States by a nonresident who is not a citizen of the United States, see section 2511(a).

§ 2502. Rate of tax

(a) Computation of tax.—

(1) In general.—The tax imposed by section 2501 for each calendar year shall be an amount equal to the excess of—

(A) a tentative tax, computed under paragraph (2), on the aggregate sum of the taxable gifts for such calendar year and for each of the preceding calendar periods, over

(B) a tentative tax, computed under paragraph (2), on the aggregate sum of the taxable gifts for each of the preceding calendar periods.

(2) Rate schedule.—

If the amount with respect to which the tentative tax to be computed is:	The tentative tax is:
Not over $10,000	18% of such amount
Over $10,000 but not over $20,000	$1,800, plus 20% of the excess over $10,000
Over $20,000 but not over $40,000	$3,800, plus 22% of the excess over $20,000
Over $40,000 but not over $60,000	$8,200, plus 24% of the excess over $40,000
Over $60,000 but not over $80,000	$13,000, plus 26% of the excess over $60,000
Over $80,000 but not over $100,000	$18,200, plus 28% of the excess over $80,000
Over $100,000 but not over $150,000	$23,800, plus 30% of the excess over $100,000
Over $150,000 but not over $250,000	$38,800, plus 32% of the excess over $150,000
Over $250,000 but not over $500,000	$70,800, plus 34% of the excess over $250,000
Over $500,000	$155,800, plus 35% of the excess over $500,000

(b) Preceding calendar period.—Whenever used in this title in "connection with the gift" tax imposed by this chapter, the term preceding calendar period means—

(1) calendar years 1932 and 1970 and all calendar years intervening between calendar year 1932 and calendar year 1970,

(2) the first calendar quarter of calendar year 1971 and all calendar quarters intervening between such calendar quarter and the first calendar quarter of calendar year 1982, and

(3) all calendar years after 1981 and before the calendar year for which the tax is being computed.

For purposes of paragraph (1), the term "calendar year 1932" includes only that portion of such year after June 6, 1932.

(c) Tax to be paid by donor.—The tax imposed by section 2501 shall be paid by the donor.

§ 2503. Taxable gifts

(a) General definition.—The term "taxable gifts" means the total amount of gifts made during the calendar year, less the deductions provided in subchapter C (section 2522 and following).

(b) Exclusion from gifts.—

(1) In general.—In the case of gifts (other than gifts of future interests in property) made to any person by the donor during the calendar year, the first $10,000* of such gifts to such person shall not, for purposes of subsection (a), be included in the total amount of gifts made during such year. Where there has been a transfer to any person of a present interest in property, the possibility that such interest may be diminished by the exercise of a power shall be disregarded in applying this subsection, if no part of such interest will at any time pass to any other person.

(2) Inflation adjustment.—In the case of gifts made in a calendar year after 1998, the $10,000* amount contained in paragraph (1) shall be increased by an amount equal to—

(A) $10,000, multiplied by

(B) the cost-of-living adjustment determined under section 1(f)(3) for such calendar year by substituting "calendar year 1997" for "calendar year 1992" in subparagraph (B) thereof.

If any amount as adjusted under the preceding sentence is not a multiple of $1,000, such amount shall be rounded to the next lowest multiple of $1,000.

(c) Transfer for the benefit of minor.—No part of a gift to an individual who has not attained the age of 21 years on the date of such transfer shall be considered a gift of a future interest in property for purposes of subsection (b) if the property and the income therefrom—

(1) may be expended by, or for the benefit of, the donee before his attaining the age of 21 years, and

(2) will to the extent not so expended—

(A) pass to the donee on his attaining the age of 21 years, and

(B) in the event the donee dies before attaining the age of 21 years, be payable to the estate of the donee or as he may appoint under a general power of appointment as defined in section 2514(c).

* Editorial comment: The amount is indexed for inflation. For 2008, the amount is $12,000, and for 2009, 2010, 2011, and 2012 the amount is $13,000. For 2013 and 2014, the indexed amount is $14,000.

****(e) Exclusion for certain transfers for educational expenses or medical expenses.**—

(1) In general.—Any qualified transfer shall not be treated as a transfer of property by gift for purposes of this chapter.

(2) Qualified transfer.—For purposes of this subsection, the term "qualified transfer" means any amount paid on behalf of an individual—

(A) as tuition to an educational organization described in section 170(b)(1)(A)(ii) for the education or training of such individual, or

(B) to any person who provides medical care (as defined in section 213(d)) with respect to such individual as payment for such medical care.

(f) Waiver of certain pension rights.—If any individual waives, before the death of a participant, any survivor benefit, or right to such benefit, under section 401(a)(11) or 417, such waiver shall not be treated as a transfer of property by gift for purposes of this chapter.

(g) Treatment of certain loans of artworks.—

(1) In general.—For purposes of this subtitle, any loan of a qualified work of art shall not be treated as a transfer (and the value of such qualified work of art shall be determined as if such loan had not been made) if—

(A) such loan is to an organization described in section 501(c)(3) and exempt from tax under section 501(c) (other than a private foundation), and

(B) the use of such work by such organization is related to the purpose or function constituting the basis for its exemption under section 501.

(2) Definitions.—For purposes of this section—

(A) Qualified work of art.—The term "qualified work of art" means any archaeological, historic, or creative tangible personal property.

(B) Private foundation.—The term "private foundation" has the meaning given such term by section 509, except that such term shall not include any private operating foundation (as defined in section 4942(j)(3)).

** Editorial comment: There is no subsection (d).

§ 2504. Taxable gifts for preceding calendar periods

(a) In general.—In computing taxable gifts for preceding calendar periods for purposes of computing the tax for any calendar year—

(1) there shall be treated as gifts such transfers as were considered to be gifts under the gift tax laws applicable to the calendar period in which the transfers were made,

(2) there shall be allowed such deductions as were provided for under such laws, and

(3) the specific exemption in the amount (if any) allowable under section 2521 (as in effect before its repeal by the Tax Reform Act of 1976) shall be applied in all computations in respect of preceding calendar periods ending before January 1, 1977, for purposes of computing the tax for any calendar year.

(b) Exclusions from gifts for preceding calendar periods.—In the case of gifts made to any person by the donor during preceding calendar periods, the amount excluded, if any, by the provisions of gift tax laws applicable to the periods in which the gifts were made shall not, for purposes of subsection (a), be included in the total amount of the gifts made during such preceding calendar periods.

(c) Valuation of gifts.—If the time has expired under section 6501 within which a tax may be assessed under this Chapter 12 (or under corresponding provisions of prior laws) on—

(1) the transfer of property by gift made during a preceding calendar period (as defined in section 2502(b)), or

(2) an increase in taxable gifts required under section 2701(d),

the value thereof shall, for purposes of computing tax under this chapter, be the value as finally determined (within the meaning of section 2001(f)(2)) for purposes of this chapter.

(d) Net gifts.—The term "net gifts" as used in corresponding provisions of prior laws shall be read as "taxable gifts for purposes of this chapter.

§ 2505. Unified credit against gift tax

(a) General rule.—In the case of a citizen or resident of the United States, there shall be allowed as a credit against the tax imposed by section 2501 for each calendar year an amount equal to—

(1) the applicable credit amount in effect under section 2010(c) which would apply if the donor died as of the end of the calendar year, reduced by

(2) the sum of the amounts allowable as a credit to the individual under this section for all preceding calendar periods.

For purposes of applying paragraph (2) for any calendar year, the rates of tax in effect under section 2502(a)(2) for such calendar year shall, in lieu of the rates of tax in effect for preceding calendar periods, be used in determining the amounts allowable as a credit under this section for all preceding calendar periods.

(b) Adjustment to credit for certain gifts made before 1977.—The amount allowable under subsection (a) shall be reduced by an amount equal to 20 percent of the aggregate amount allowed as a specific exemption under section 2521 (as in effect before its repeal by the Tax Reform Act of 1976) with respect to gifts made by the individual after September 8, 1976.

(c) Limitation based on amount of tax.—The amount of the credit allowed under subsection (a) for any calendar year shall not exceed the amount of the tax imposed by section 2501 for such calendar year.

SUBCHAPTER B—TRANSFERS

Editorial Summary

Gift Tax: Transfers

Subchapter B of Chapter 12 (Secs. 2511–2519)

Sections 2511–2519 deals with transfers that are subject to the gift tax and the related valuation. Section 2512 provides the general rule that the value of the gift is the fair market value of the property transferred by gift. If the transaction is a part gift/part sale, the value of the gift is the excess of the fair market value of the property over the selling price of the property.

Two of the Code sections provide special treatment for a husband and wife. Section 2516 provides that certain property settlements associated with a divorce will not be treated as a taxable gift. Section 2513 allows a married couple to elect to treat a gift made out of the separate property of one of the spouses as if it were made one-half by each spouse. This can be particularly beneficial with respect to the $10,000 (indexed for inflation; 2009, 2010, 2011, and

2012 amount is $13,000; and for 2013 and 2014 is $14,000) per donee annual exclusion. In addition, this splitgift concept is beneficial in that spouses file separate gift tax returns.

§ 2511. Transfers in general

(a) Scope.—Subject to the limitations contained in this chapter, the tax imposed by section 2501 shall apply whether the transfer is in trust or otherwise, whether the gift is direct or indirect, and whether the property is real or personal, tangible or intangible; but in the case of a nonresident not a citizen of the United States, shall apply to a transfer only if the property is situated within the United States.

(b) Intangible property.—For purposes of this chapter, in the case of a nonresident not a citizen of the United States who is excepted from the application of section 2501(a)(2)—

(1) shares of stock issued by a domestic corporation, and

(2) debt obligations of—

(A) a United States person, or

(B) the United States, a State or any political subdivision thereof, or the District of Columbia,

which are owned and held by such nonresident shall be deemed to be property situated within the United States.

§ 2512. Valuation of gifts

(a) If the gift is made in property, the value thereof at the date of the gift shall be considered the amount of the gift.

(b) Where property is transferred for less than an adequate and full consideration in money or money's worth, then the amount by which the value of the property exceeded the value of the consideration shall be deemed a gift, and shall be included in computing the amount of gifts made during the calendar year.

§ 2513. Gift by husband or wife to third party

(a) Considered as made one-half by each.—

(1) In general.—A gift made by one spouse to any person other than his spouse shall, for the purposes of this chapter, be considered as made one-half by him and one-half by his spouse, but only if at the time of the gift each spouse is a citizen or resident of the United States. This paragraph shall not apply with respect to a gift by a spouse of an interest in property if he creates in his spouse a general power of appointment, as defined in section 2514(c), over such interest. For purposes of this section, an individual shall be considered as the spouse of another individual only if he is married to such individual at the time of the gift and does not remarry during the remainder of the calendar year.

(2) Consent of both spouses.—Paragraph (1) shall apply only if both spouses have signified (under the regulations provided for in subsection (b)) their consent to the application of paragraph (1) in the case of all such gifts made during the calendar year by either while married to the other.

(b) Manner and time of signifying consent.—

(1) Manner.—A consent under this section shall be signified in such manner as is provided under regulations prescribed by the Secretary.

(2) Time.—Such consent may be so signified at any time after the close of the calendar year in which the gift was made, subject to the following limitations—

(A) The consent may not be signified after the 15th day of April following the close of such year, unless before such 15th day no return has been filed for such year by either spouse, in which case the consent may not be signified after a return for such year is filed by either spouse.

(B) The consent may not be signified after a notice of deficiency with respect to the tax for such year has been sent to either spouse in accordance with section 6212(a).

(c) Revocation of consent.—Revocation of a consent previously signified shall be made in such manner as is provided under regulations prescribed by the Secretary, but the right to revoke a consent previously signified with respect to a calendar year—

(1) shall not exist after the 15th day of April following the close of such year if the consent was signified on or before such 15th day; and

(2) shall not exist if the consent was not signified until after such 15th day.

(d) Joint and several liability for tax.—If the consent required by subsection (a)(2) is signified with respect to a gift made in any calendar year, the liability with respect to the entire tax imposed by this chapter of each spouse for such year shall be joint and several.

§ 2514. Powers of appointment

(a) Powers created on or before October 21, 1942.—An exercise of a general power of appointment created on or before October 21, 1942, shall be deemed a transfer of property by the individual possessing such power; but the failure to exercise such a power or the complete release of such a power shall not be deemed an exercise thereof. If a general power of appointment created on or before October 21, 1942, has been partially released so that it is no longer a general power of appointment, the subsequent exercise of such power shall not be deemed to be the exercise of a general power of appointment if—

(1) such partial release occurred before November 1, 1951, or

(2) the donee of such power was under a legal disability to release such power on October 21, 1942, and such partial release occurred not later than six months after the termination of such legal disability.

(b) Powers created after October 21, 1942.—The exercise or release of a general power of appointment created after October 21, 1942, shall be deemed a transfer of property by the individual possessing such power.

(c) Definition of general power of appointment.—For purposes of this section, the term "general power of appointment" means a power which is exercisable in favor of the individual possessing the power (hereafter in this subsection referred to as the "possessor"), his estate, his creditors, or the creditors of his estate; except that—

(1) A power to consume, invade, or appropriate property for the benefit of the possessor which is limited by an ascertainable standard relating to the health, education, support, or maintenance of the possessor shall not be deemed a general power of appointment.

(2) A power of appointment created on or before October 21, 1942, which is exercisable by the possessor only in conjunction with another person shall not be deemed a general power of appointment.

(3) In the case of a power of appointment created after October 21, 1942, which is exercisable by the possessor only in conjunction with another person—

(A) if the power is not exercisable by the possessor except in conjunction with the creator of the power—such power shall not be deemed a general power of appointment;

(B) if the power is not exercisable by the possessor except in conjunction with a person having a substantial interest, in the property subject to the power, which is adverse to exercise of the power in favor of the possessor—such power shall not be deemed a general power of appointment. For the purposes of this subparagraph a person who, after the death of the possessor, may be possessed of a power of appointment (with respect to the property subject to the possessor's power) which he may exercise in his own favor shall be deemed as having an interest in the property and such interest shall be deemed adverse to such exercise of the possessor's power;

(C) if (after the application of subparagraphs (A) and (B)) the power is a general power of appointment and is exercisable in favor of such other person—such power shall be deemed a general power of appointment only in respect of a fractional part of the property subject to such power, such part to be determined by dividing the value of such property by the number of such persons (including the possessor) in favor of whom such power is exercisable.

For purposes of subparagraphs (B) and (C), a power shall be deemed to be exercisable in favor of a person if it is exercisable in favor of such person, his estate, his creditors, or the creditors of his estate.

(d) Creation of another power in certain cases.—If a power of appointment created after October 21, 1942, is exercised by creating another power of appointment which, under the applicable local law, can be validly exercised so as to postpone the vesting of any estate or interest in the property which was subject to the first power, or suspend the absolute ownership or power of alienation of such property, for a period ascertainable without regard to the date of the creation of the first power, such exercise of the first power shall, to the extent of the property subject to the second power, be deemed a transfer of property by the individual possessing such power.

(e) Lapse of power.—The lapse of a power of appointment created after October 21, 1942, during the life of the individual possessing the power shall be considered a release of such power. The rule of the preceding sentence shall apply with respect to the lapse of powers during any calendar year only to the extent that the property which could have been appointed by exercise of such lapsed powers exceeds in value the greater of the following amounts:

(1) $5,000, or

(2) 5 percent of the aggregate value of the assets out of which, or the proceeds of which, the exercise of the lapsed powers could be satisfied.

(f) Date of creation of power.—For purposes of this section a power of appointment created by a will executed on or before October 21, 1942, shall be considered a power created on or before such date if the person executing such will dies before July 1, 1949, without having republished such will, by codicil or otherwise, after October 21, 1942.

§ 2515. Treatment of generation-skipping transfer tax

In the case of any taxable gift which is a direct skip (within the meaning of chapter 13), the amount of such gift shall be increased by the amount of any tax imposed on the transferor under chapter 13 with respect to such gift.

§ 2516. Certain property settlements

Where husband and wife enter into a written agreement relative to their marital and property rights and divorce occurs within the 3-year period beginning on the date 1 year before such agreement is entered into (whether or not such agreement is approved by the divorce decree), any transfers of property or interests in property made pursuant to such agreement—

(1) to either spouse in settlement of his or her marital or property rights, or

(2) to provide a reasonable allowance for the support of issue of the marriage during minority,

shall be deemed to be transfers made for a full and adequate consideration in money or money's worth.

§ 2518. Disclaimers

(a) General rule.—For purposes of this subtitle, if a person makes a qualified disclaimer with respect to any interest in property, this subtitle shall apply with respect to such interest as if the interest had never been transferred to such person.

(b) Qualified disclaimer defined.—For purposes of subsection (a), the term "qualified disclaimer" means an irrevocable and unqualified refusal by a person to accept an interest in property but only if—

(1) such refusal is in writing,

(2) such writing is received by the transferor of the interest, his legal representative, or the holder of the legal title to the property to which the interest relates not later than the date which is 9 months after the later of—

(A) the day on which the transfer creating the interest in such person is made, or

(B) the day on which such person attains age 21,

(3) such person has not accepted the interest or any of its benefits, and

(4) as a result of such refusal, the interest passes without any direction on the part of the person making the disclaimer and passes either—

(A) to the spouse of the decedent, or

(B) to a person other than the person making the disclaimer.

(c) Other rules.—For purposes of subsection (a)—

(1) Disclaimer of undivided portion of interest.—A disclaimer with respect to an undivided portion of an interest which meets the requirements of the preceding sentence shall be treated as a qualified disclaimer of such portion of the interest.

(2) Powers.—A power with respect to property shall be treated as an interest in such property.

(3) Certain transfers treated as disclaimers.—A written transfer of the transferor's entire interest in the property—

(A) which meets requirements similar to the requirements of paragraphs (2) and (3) of subsection (b), and

(B) which is to a person or persons who would have received the property had the transferor made a qualified disclaimer (within the meaning of subsection (b)),

shall be treated as a qualified disclaimer.

§ 2519. Dispositions of certain life estates

(a) General rule.—For purposes of this chapter and Chapter 11, any disposition of all or part of a qualifying income interest for life in any property to which this section applies shall be treated as a transfer of all interests in such property other than the qualifying income interest.

(b) Property to which this subsection applies.—This section applies to any property if a deduction was allowed with respect to the transfer of such property to the donor—

(1) under section 2056 by reason of subsection (b)(7) thereof, or

(2) under section 2523 by reason of subsection (f) thereof.

SUBCHAPTER C—DEDUCTIONS

Editorial Summary

Gift Tax: Deductions

Subchapter C of Chapter 12 (Secs. 2522–2524)

In terms of the basic gift tax model presented in the Editorial Summary on the gift tax, entitled Gift Tax: General (which precedes Sec. 2501), charitable contributions made by the taxpayer are included in the gross gifts category. Such charitable contributions obviously should not be subject to the gift tax. Section 2522 provides that such gifts are deductible in calculating the taxable gifts for the current period. Note, however, that the definition of a qualifying charitable contribution in Sec. 170(c) for income tax purposes is not exactly the same as the definition in Sec. 2522.

Section 2523 provides a marital deduction for gifts between spouses. This is consistent with the marital deduction associated with the estate tax in Sec. 2056 and with the nonrecognition provision in Sec. 1041 for property transactions between spouses for income tax purposes.

§ 2522. Charitable and similar gifts

(a) Citizens or residents.—In computing taxable gifts for the calendar year, there shall be allowed as a deduction in the case of a citizen or resident the amount of all gifts made during such year to or for the use of—

(1) the United States, any State, or any political subdivision thereof, or the District of Columbia, for exclusively public purposes;

(2) a corporation, or trust, or community chest, fund, or foundation, organized and operated exclusively for religious, charitable, scientific, literary, or educational purposes, or to foster national or international amateur sports competition (but only if no part of its activities involve the provision of athletic facilities or equipment), including the encouragement of art and the prevention of cruelty to children or animals, no part of the net earnings of which inures to the benefit of any private shareholder or individual, which is not disqualified for tax exemption under section 501(c) (3) by reason of attempting to influence legislation, and which does not participate in, or intervene in (including the publishing or distributing of statements), any political campaign on behalf of (or in opposition to) any candidate for public office;

(3) a fraternal society, order, or association, operating under the lodge system, but only if such gifts are to be used exclusively for religious, charitable, scientific, literary, or educational purposes, including the encouragement of art and the prevention of cruelty to children or animals;

(4) posts or organizations of war veterans, or auxiliary units or societies of any such posts or organizations, if such posts, organizations, units, or societies are organized in the United States or any of its possessions, and if no part of their net earnings inures to the benefit of any private shareholder or individual.

Rules similar to the rules of section 501(j) shall apply for purposes of paragraph (2).

(b) Nonresidents.—In the case of a nonresident not a citizen of the United States, there shall be allowed as a deduction the amount of all gifts made during such year to or for the use of—

(1) the United States, any State, or any political subdivision thereof, or the District of Columbia, for exclusively public purposes;

(2) a domestic corporation organized and operated exclusively for religious, charitable, scientific, literary, or educational purposes, including the encouragement of art and the prevention of cruelty to children or animals, no part of the net earnings of which inures to the benefit of any private shareholder or individual, which is not disqualified for tax exemption under section 501(c)(3) by reason of attempting to influence legislation, and which does not participate in, or intervene in (including the publishing or distributing of statements), any political campaign on behalf of (or in opposition to) any candidate for public office;

(3) a trust, or community chest, fund, or foundation, organized and operated exclusively for religious, charitable, scientific, literary, or educational purposes, including the encouragement of art and the prevention of cruelty to children or animals, no substantial part of the activities of which is carrying on propaganda, or otherwise attempting, to influence legislation, and which does not participate in, or intervene in (including the publishing or distributing of statements), any political campaign on behalf of (or in opposition to) any candidate for public office; but only if such gifts are to be used within the United States exclusively for such purposes;

(4) a fraternal society, order, or association, operating under the lodge system, but only if such gifts are to be used within the United States exclusively for religious, charitable, scientific, literary, or educational purposes, including the encouragement of art and the prevention of cruelty to children or animals;

(5) posts or organizations of war veterans, or auxiliary units or societies of any such posts or organizations, if such posts, organizations, units, or societies are organized in the United States or any of its possessions, and if no part of their net earnings inures to the benefit of any private shareholder or individual.

(c) Disallowance of deductions in certain cases.—

(1) No deduction shall be allowed under this section for a gift to or for the use of an organization or trust described in section 508(d) or 4948(c) (4) subject to the conditions specified in such sections.

(2) Where a donor transfers an interest in property (other than an interest described in section 170(f)(3)(B)) to a person, or for a use, described in subsection (a) or (b) and an interest in the same property is retained by the donor, or is transferred or has been transferred (for less than an adequate and full consideration in money or money's worth) from the donor to a person, or for a use, not described in subsection (a) or (b), no deduction shall be allowed under this section for the interest which is, or has been transferred to the person, or for the use, described in subsection (a) or (b), unless—

(A) in the case of a remainder interest, such interest is in a trust which is a charitable remainder annuity trust or a charitable remainder unitrust (described in section 664) or a pooled income fund (described in section 642(c)(5)), or

(B) in the case of any other interest, such interest is in the form of a guaranteed annuity or is a fixed percentage distributed yearly of the fair market value of the property (to be determined yearly).

(3) Rules similar to the rules of section 2055(e)(4) shall apply for purposes of paragraph (2).

(4) Reformations to comply with paragraph (2).—

(A) In general.—A deduction shall be allowed under subsection (a) in respect of any qualified reformation (within the meaning of section 2055(e)(3)(B)).

(B) Rules similar to section 2055(e)(3) to apply.—For purposes of this paragraph, rules similar to the rules of section 2055(e)(3) shall apply.

(5) Contributions to donor advised funds.— A deduction otherwise allowed under subsection (a) for any contribution to a donor advised fund (as defined in section 4966(d)(2)) shall only be allowed if—

(A) the sponsoring organization (as defined in section 4966(d)(1)) with respect to such donor advised fund is not—

(i) described in paragraph (3) or (4) of subsection(a), or

(ii) a type III supporting organization (as defined in section 4943(f)(5)(A)) which is not a functionally integrated type III supporting organization (as defined in section 4943(f)(5)(B)), and

(B) the taxpayer obtains a contemporaneous written acknowledgment (determined under rules similar to the rules of section 170(f)(8)(C)) from the sponsoring organization (as so defined) of such donor advised fund that such organization has exclusive legal control over the assets contributed.

(d) Special rule for irrevocable transfers of easements in real property.—A deduction shall be allowed under subsection (a) in respect of any transfer of a qualified real property interest (as defined in section 170(h)(2)(C)) which meets the requirements of section 170(h) (without regard to paragraph (4)(A) thereof).

(e) Special rules for fractional gifts.—

(1) Denial of deduction in certain cases.—

(A) In general.—No deduction shall be allowed for a contribution of an undivided portion of a taxpayer's entire interest in tangible personal property unless all interests in the property are held immediately before such contribution by—

(i) the taxpayer, or

(ii) the taxpayer and the donee.

(B) Exceptions.—The Secretary may, by regulation, provide for exceptions to subparagraph (A) in cases where all persons who hold an interest in the property make proportional contributions of an undivided portion of the entire interest held by such persons.

(2) Recapture of deduction in certain cases; addition to tax.—

(A) In general.—The Secretary shall provide for the recapture of an amount equal to any deduction allowed under this section (plus interest) with respect to any contribution of an undivided portion of a taxpayer's entire interest in tangible personal property—

(i) in any case in which the donor does not contribute all of the remaining interests in such property to the donee (or, if such donee is no longer in existence, to any person described in section 170(c)) on or before the earlier of—

(I) the date that is 10 years after the date of the initial fractional contribution, or

(II) the date of the death of the donor, and

(ii) in any case in which the donee has not, during the period beginning on the date of the initial fractional contribution and ending on the date described in clause (i)—

(I) had substantial physical possession of the property, and

(II) used the property in a use which is related to a purpose or function constituting the basis for the organizations' exemption under section 501.

(B) Addition to tax.—The tax imposed under this chapter for any taxable year for which there is a recapture under subparagraph (A) shall be increased by 10 percent of the amount so recaptured.

(C) Initial fractional contribution.—For purposes of this paragraph, the term "initial fractional contribution" means, with respect to any donor, the first gift of an undivided portion of the donor's entire interest in any tangible personal property for which a deduction is allowed under subsection (a) or (b).

* * *

§ 2523. Gift to spouse

(a) Allowance of deduction.—Where a donor transfers during the calendar year by gift an interest in property to a donee who at the time of the gift is the donor's spouse, there shall be allowed as a deduction in computing taxable gifts for the calendar year an amount with respect to such interest equal to its value.

(b) Life estate or other terminable interest.—Where, on the lapse of time, on the occurrence of an event or contingency, or on the failure of an event or contingency to occur, such interest transferred to the spouse will terminate or fail, no deduction shall be allowed with respect to such interest—

(1) if the donor retains in himself, or transfers or has transferred (for less than an adequate and full consideration in money or money's worth) to any person other than such donee spouse (or the estate of such spouse), an interest in such property, and if by reason of such retention or transfer the donor (or his heirs or assigns) or such person (or his heirs or assigns) may possess or enjoy any part of such property after such termination or failure of the interest transferred to the donee spouse; or

(2) if the donor immediately after the transfer to the donee spouse has a power to appoint an interest in such property which he can exercise (either alone or in conjunction with any person) in such manner that the appointee may possess or enjoy any part of such property after such termination or failure of the interest transferred to the donee spouse. For purposes of this paragraph, the donor shall be considered as having immediately after the transfer to the donee spouse such power to appoint even though such power cannot be exercised until after the lapse of time, upon the occurrence of an event or contingency, or on the failure of an event or contingency to occur.

An exercise or release at any time by the donor, either alone or in conjunction with any person, of a power to appoint an interest in property, even though not otherwise a transfer, shall, for purposes of paragraph (1), be considered as a transfer by him. Except as provided in subsection (e), where at the time of the transfer it is impossible to ascertain the particular person or persons who may receive from the donor an interest in property so transferred by him, such interest shall, for purposes of paragraph (1), be considered as transferred to a person other than the donee spouse.

(c) Interest in unidentified assets.—Where the assets out of which, or the proceeds of which, the interest transferred to the donee spouse may be satisfied include a particular asset or assets with respect to which no deduction would be allowed if such asset or assets were transferred from the donor to such spouse, then the value of the interest transferred to such spouse shall, for purposes of subsection (a), be reduced by the aggregate value of such particular assets.

(d) Joint interests.—If the interest is transferred to the donee spouse as sole joint tenant with the donor or as tenant by the entirety, the interest of the donor in the property which exists solely by reason of the possibility that the donor may survive the donee spouse, or that there may occur a severance of the tenancy, shall not be considered for purposes of subsection (b) as an interest retained by the donor in himself.

(e) Life estate with power of appointment in donee spouse.—Where the donor transfers an interest in property, if by such transfer his spouse is entitled for life to all of the income from the entire interest, or all the income from a specific portion thereof, payable annually or at more frequent intervals, with power in the donee spouse to appoint the entire interest, or such specific portion (exercisable in favor of such donee spouse, or of the estate of such donee spouse, or in favor of either, whether or not in each case the power is exercisable in favor of others), and with no power in any other person to appoint any part of such interest, or such portion, to any person other than the donee spouse—

(1) the interest, or such portion, so transferred shall, for purposes of subsection (a) be considered as transferred to the donee spouse, and

(2) no part of the interest, or such portion, so transferred shall, for purposes of subsection (b)(l), be considered as retained in the donor or transferred to any person other than the donee spouse.

This subsection shall apply only if, by such transfer, such power in the donee spouse to appoint the interest, or such portion, whether exercisable by will or during life, is exercisable by such spouse alone and in all events. For purposes of this subsection, the term "specific portion" only includes a portion determined on a fractional or percentage basis.

(f) Election with respect to life estate for donee spouse.—

(1) In general.—In the case of qualified terminable interest property—

(A) for purposes of subsection (a), such property shall be treated as transferred to the donee spouse, and

(B) for purposes of subsection (b)(1), no part of such property shall be considered as retained in the donor or transferred to any person other than the donee spouse.

(2) Qualified terminable interest property.—For purposes of this subsection, the term "qualified terminable interest property" means any property—

(A) which is transferred by the donor spouse,

(B) in which the donee spouse has a qualifying income interest for life, and

(C) to which an election under this subsection applies.

(3) Certain rules made applicable.—For purposes of this subsection, rules similar to the rules of clauses (ii), (iii), and (iv) of section 2056(b)(7)(B) shall apply and the rules of section 2056(b)(10) shall apply.

(4) Election.—

(A) Time and manner.—An election under this subsection with respect to any property shall be made on or before the date prescribed by section 6075(b) for filing a gift tax return with respect to the transfer (determined without regard to section 6019(2)) and shall be made in such manner as the Secretary shall by regulations prescribe.

(B) Election irrevocable.—An election under this subsection, once made, shall be irrevocable.

(5) Treatment of interest retained by donor spouse.—

(A) In general.—In the case of any qualified terminable interest property—

(i) such property shall not be includible in the gross estate of the donor spouse, and

(ii) any subsequent transfer by the donor spouse of an interest in such property shall not be treated as a transfer for purposes of this chapter.

(B) Subparagraph (A) not to apply after transfer by donee spouse.—Subparagraph

(A) shall not apply with respect to any property after the donee spouse is treated as having transferred such property under section 2519, or such property is includible in the donee spouse's gross estate under section 2044.

(6) Treatment of joint and survivor annuities.—In the case of a joint and survivor annuity where only the donor spouse and donee spouse have the right to receive payments before the death of the last spouse to die—

(A) the donee spouse's interest shall be treated as a qualifying income interest for life,

(B) the donor spouse shall be treated as having made an election under this subsection with respect to such annuity unless the donor spouse otherwise elects on or before the date specified in paragraph (4)(A),

(C) paragraph (5) and section 2519 shall not apply to the donor spouse's interest in the annuity, and

(D) if the donee spouse dies before the donor spouse, no amount shall be includible in the gross estate of the donee spouse under section 2044 with respect to such annuity.

An election under subparagraph (B), once made, shall be irrevocable.

(g) Special rule for charitable remainder trusts.—

(1) In general.—If, after the transfer, the donee spouse is the only noncharitable beneficiary (other than the donor) of a qualified charitable remainder trust, subsection (b) shall not apply to the interest in such trust which is transferred to the donee spouse.

(2) Definitions.—For purposes of paragraph (1), the terms "noncharitable beneficiary" and "qualified charitable remainder trust" have the meanings given to such terms by section 2056(b)(8)(B).

(h) Denial of double deduction.—Nothing in this section or any other provision of this chapter shall allow the value of any interest in property to be deducted under this chapter more than once with respect to the same donor.

(i) Disallowance of marital deduction where spouse not citizen.*—If the spouse of the donor is not a citizen of the United States—

(1) no deduction shall be allowed under this section,

(2) section 2503(b) shall be applied with respect to gifts which are made by the donor to such spouse and with respect to which a deduction would be allowable under this section but for paragraph (1) by substituting "$100,000" for "$10,000," and

(3) the principles of sections 2515 and 2515A (as such sections were in effect before their repeal by the Economic Recovery Tax Act of 1981) shall apply, except that the provisions of such section 2515 providing for an election shall not apply.

This subsection shall not apply to any transfer resulting from the acquisition of rights under a joint and survivor annuity described in subsection (f)(6).

§ 2524. Extent of deductions

The deductions provided in sections 2522 and 2523 shall be allowed only to the extent that the gifts therein specified are included in the amount of gifts against which such deductions are applied.

* Editorial Comment: For calendar year 2014, the first $145,000 of gifts made to a spouse that is not a citizen are not included in the total amount of taxable gifts.

CHAPTER 13—TAX ON GENERATION-SKIPPING TRANSFERS

Subchapter

- A. Tax imposed.
- B. Generation-skipping transfers.
- C. Taxable amount.
- D. GST exemption.
- E. Applicable rate; inclusion ratio.
- F. Other definitions and special rules.
- G. Administration.

Editorial Summary
Tax on Generation-Skipping Transfers
Subchapters A–G of Chapter 13
(Secs. 2601–2663)

The Tax Reform Act of 1986 modified the tax imposed on generation-skipping transfers. The basic tax model for generation-skipping transfers consists of the following components:

Value of property received by transferee
– Deductions
= Taxable amount
× Rates
= Tentative tax liability
– Credits
= Tax liability

The intent of Chapter 13 is to limit the ability to avoid transfer taxes (i.e., gift tax and estate tax) through transfers to the generation below the generation of the taxpayer (e.g., transfer by grandparents to grandchildren, life estates to taxpayer's children with remainder interest to grandchildren). Included are Sec. 2612(a) taxable terminations, Sec. 2612(b) taxable distributions, and Sec. 2612(c) direct skips.

Section 2631 provides a lifetime generation-skipping tax exemption of $5 million* per grantor, and Sec. 2632 contains the rules for allocating the exemption among transfers. In addition, a transitional rule was in effect for pre-1990 transfers for direct skips to grandchildren, which provided a $2 million exclusion per grandchild. Section 2611(b)(1) excludes from the generation-skipping tax any transfer, other than a direct skip, from a trust to the extent the transfer was subject to the gift tax or estate with respect to a person in the first generation below that of the grantor. Also excluded are lifetime transfers that would not be subject to gift tax under the Sec. 2503(e) provision for transfers for educational or medical expenses [see Sec. 2611(b)(2)] or would not have been subject to gift tax based on the Sec. 2503(b) $10,000 per donee annual exclusion (indexed for inflation; 2009 through 2012 is $13,000, and is $14,000 for 2013 and 2014). Section 2611(b)(3) excludes from the generation-skipping tax any transfer to the extent the property has previously been subject to the generation-skipping tax, the transferee in the prior transfer is a member of the same or lower generation as the current transferee, and such transfers do not have the effect of tax avoidance. Finally, if the parents of a grandchild are deceased at the time of the transfer, the transfer to a grandchild will not be subject to the generation-skipping tax because the grandchild will be treated as the generation below the transferor grandparent rather than the second such generation [see Sec. 2612(c)(2)].

Section 2624(a) provides that the primary valuation date is the date of the generation-skipping transfer. However, Secs. 2624(b) and (c) provide alternate valuation dates for certain direct skips and taxable terminations occurring at death. The value is reduced by any consideration for the property paid by the transferee.

The deductions that are available for the three types of transfers subject to the generation-skipping tax differ. Section 2621(a)(2) permits deductions for taxable distributions for any expense incurred by the transferee with respect to the determination, collection, or refund of the generation-skipping tax. Section 2622(a)(2) permits deductions for taxable terminations for expenses similar to those provided in Sec. 2053. Section 2623 does not provide any deductions for direct skips.

Section 2641 provides that the *applicable rate* is the product of the maximum estate tax rate under Sec. 2001 (i.e., 40 percent for 2013) times the inclusion ratio. The inclusion ratio is defined in Sec. 2642.

Only one credit is available associated with the generation-skipping tax. This is the credit for certain generation-skipping taxes paid to a state [see Sec. 2604]. The credit is limited to 5 percent of the tax imposed under Sec. 2601.

The identity of the party who is responsible for the generation-skipping tax depends on the type of transfer as indicated below [see Sec. 2603].

Type of Transfer	Imposed on
Taxable distribution	Transferee
Taxable termination or direct skip (from a trust)	Trustee
Direct skip (other)	Transferor

The Tax Relief Reconciliation Act of 2001 repeals the Tax on Generation-Skipping Transfers effective for such transfers after December 31, 2009 for one year (see Sec. 2664). In the Tax Relief Act of 2010, Congress reenacted the Tax on Generation-Skipping Transfers effective for 2011.

The lifetime generation–skipping tax exemption has been increased to $5 million* per grantor.

* Editorial comment: The indexed amount for 2014 is $5.34 million.

SUBCHAPTER A—TAX IMPOSED

§ 2601. Tax imposed

A tax is hereby imposed on every generation-skipping transfer (within the meaning of subchapter B).

§ 2602. Amount of tax

The amount of the tax imposed by section 2601 is—

(1) the taxable amount (determined under subchapter C), multiplied by

(2) the applicable rate (determined under subchapter E).

§ 2603. Liability for tax

(a) Personal liability.—

(1) Taxable distributions.—In the case of a taxable distribution, the tax imposed by section 2601 shall be paid by the transferee.

(2) Taxable termination.—In the case of a taxable termination or a direct skip from a trust, the tax shall be paid by the trustee.

(3) Direct skip.—In the case of a direct skip (other than a direct skip from a trust), the tax shall be paid by the transferor.

(b) Source of tax.—Unless otherwise directed pursuant to the governing instrument by specific reference to the tax imposed by this chapter, the tax imposed by this chapter on a generation-skipping transfer shall be charged to the property constituting such transfer.

(c) Cross reference.—

For provisions making estate and gift tax provisions with respect to transferee liability, liens, and related matters applicable to the tax imposed by section 2601, see section 2661.

§ 2604. Credit for certain state taxes*

(a) General rule.—If a generation-skipping transfer (other than a direct skip) occurs at the same time as and as a result of the death of an individual, a credit against the tax imposed by section 2601 shall be allowed in an amount equal to the generation-skipping transfer tax actually paid to any State in respect to any property included in the generation-skipping transfer.

(b) Limitation.—The aggregate amount allowed as a credit under this section with respect to any transfer shall not exceed 5 percent of the amount of the tax imposed by section 2601 on such transfer.

(c) Termination.—This section shall not apply to the generation-skipping transfers after December 31, 2004.

SUBCHAPTER B—GENERATION-SKIPPING TRANSFERS

Editorial Summary

Generation-Skipping Transfers: Types

Subchapter B of Chapter 13 (Secs. 2611–2613)

See the discussion under the Editorial Summary entitled Tax on Generation-Skipping Transfers, which precedes Sec. 2601.

§ 2611. Generation-skipping transfer defined

(a) In general.—For purposes of this chapter, the term "generation-skipping transfer" means—

(1) a taxable distribution,

(2) a taxable termination, and

(3) a direct skip.

(b) Certain transfers excluded.—The term "generation-skipping transfer" does not include—

(1) any transfer which, if made inter vivos by an individual, would not be treated as a taxable gift by reason of section 2503(e) (relating to exclusion of certain transfers for educational or medical expenses), and

(2) any transfer to the extent—

(A) the property transferred was subject to a prior tax imposed under this chapter,

(B) the transferee in the prior transfer was assigned to the same generation as (or a lower generation than) the generation assignment of the transferee in this transfer, and

(C) such transfers do not have the effect of avoiding tax under this chapter with respect to any transfer.

* Editorial comment: See the termination date in Sec. 2604(c).

§ 2612. Taxable termination; taxable distribution; direct skip

(a) Taxable termination.—

(1) General rule.—For purposes of this chapter, the term "taxable termination" means the termination (by death, lapse of time, release of power, or otherwise) of an interest in property held in a trust unless—

(A) immediately after such termination, a non-skip person has an interest in such property, or

(B) at no time after such termination may a distribution (including distributions on termination) be made from such trust to a skip person.

(2) Certain partial terminations treated as taxable.—If, upon the termination of an interest in property held in trust by reason of the death of a lineal descendant of the transferor, a specified portion of the trust's assets are distributed to 1 or more skip persons (or 1 or more trusts for the exclusive benefit of such persons), such termination shall constitute a taxable termination with respect to such portion of the trust property.

(b) Taxable distribution.—For purposes of this chapter, the term "taxable distribution" means any distribution from a trust to a skip person (other than a taxable termination or a direct skip).

(c) Direct skip.—For purposes of this chapter—

(1) In general.—The term "direct skip" means a transfer subject to a tax imposed by chapter 11 or 12 of an interest in property to a skip person.

(2) Look-thru rules not to apply.—Solely for purposes of determining whether any transfer to a trust is a direct skip, the rules of section 2651(f)(2) shall not apply.

§ 2613. Skip person and non-skip person defined

(a) Skip person.—For purposes of this chapter, the term "skip person" means—

(1) a natural person assigned to a generation which is 2 or more generations below the generation assignment of the transferor, or

(2) a trust—

(A) if all interests in such trust are held by skip persons, or

(B) if—

(i) there is no person holding an interest in such trust, and

(ii) at no time after such transfer may a distribution (including distributions on termination) be made from such trust to a non-skip person.

(b) Non-skip person.—For purposes of this chapter, the term "non-skip person" means any person who is not a skip person.

SUBCHAPTER C—TAXABLE AMOUNT

Editorial Summary

Generation-Skipping Transfers:

Taxable Amount

Subchapter C of Chapter 13 (Secs. 2621–2624)

See the discussion under the Editorial Summary entitled Tax on Generation-Skipping Transfers, which precedes Sec. 2601.

§ 2621. Taxable amount in case of taxable distribution

(a) In general.—For purposes of this chapter, the taxable amount in the case of any taxable distribution shall be—

(1) the value of the property received by the transferee, reduced by

(2) any expense incurred by the transferee in connection with the determination, collection, or refund of the tax imposed by this chapter with respect to such distribution.

(b) Payment of GST tax treated as taxable distribution.—For purposes of this chapter, if any of the tax imposed by this chapter with respect to any taxable distribution is paid out of the trust, an amount equal to the portion so paid shall be treated as a taxable distribution.

§ 2622. Taxable amount in case of taxable termination

(a) In general.—For purposes of this chapter, the taxable amount in the case of a taxable termination shall be—

(1) the value of all property with respect to which the taxable termination has occurred, reduced by

(2) any deduction allowed under subsection (b).

(b) Deduction for certain expenses.—For purposes of subsection (a), there shall be allowed a deduction similar to the deduction allowed by section 2053 (relating to expenses, indebtedness, and taxes) for amounts attributable to the property with respect to which the taxable termination has occurred.

§ 2623. Taxable amount in case of direct skip

For purposes of this chapter, the taxable amount in the case of a direct skip shall be the value of the property received by the transferee.

§ 2624. Valuation

(a) General rule.—Except as otherwise provided in this chapter, property shall be valued as of the time of the generation-skipping transfer.

(b) Alternate valuation and special use valuation elections apply to certain direct skips.—In the case of any direct skip of property which is included in the transferor's gross estate, the value of such property for purposes of this chapter shall be the same as its value for purposes of chapter 11 (determined with regard to sections 2032 and 2032A).

(c) Alternate valuation election permitted in the case of taxable terminations occurring at death.—If 1 or more taxable terminations with respect to the same trust occur at the same time as and as a result of the death of an individual, an election may be made to value all of the property included in such terminations in accordance with section 2032.

(d) Reduction for consideration provided by transferee.—For purposes of this chapter, the value of the property transferred shall be reduced by the amount of any consideration provided by the transferee.

SUBCHAPTER D—GST EXEMPTION

Editorial Summary

Generation-Skipping Transfers: Exemption

Subchapter D of Chapter 13 (Secs. 2631, 2632)

See the discussion under the Editorial Summary entitled Tax on Generation-Skipping Transfers, which precedes Sec. 2601.

§ 2631. GST exemption

(a) General rule.—For purposes of determining the inclusion ratio, every individual shall be allowed a GST exemption amount which may be allocated by such individual (or his executor) to any property with respect to which such individual is the transferor.

(b) Allocations irrevocable.—Any allocation under subsection (a), once made, shall be irrevocable.

(c) GST exemption amount.—For purposes of subsection (a), the GST exemption amount for any calendar year shall be equal to the applicable exclusion amount under section 2010(c) for such calendar year.

§ 2632. Special rules for allocation of GST exemption

(a) Time and manner of allocation.—

(1) Time.—Any allocation by an individual of his GST exemption under section 2631(a) may be made at any time on or before the date prescribed for filing the estate tax return for such individual's estate (determined with regard to extensions), regardless of whether such a return is required to be filed.

(2) Manner.—The Secretary shall prescribe by forms or regulations the manner in which any allocation referred to in paragraph (1) is to be made.

(b) Deemed allocation to certain lifetime direct skips.—

(1) In general.—If any individual makes a direct skip during his lifetime, any unused portion of such individual's GST exemption shall be allocated to the property transferred to the extent necessary to make the inclusion ratio for such property zero. If the amount of the direct skip exceeds such unused portion, the entire unused portion shall be allocated to the property transferred.

(2) Unused portion.—For purposes of paragraph (1), the unused portion of an individual's GST exemption is that portion of such exemption which has not previously been allocated by such individual (or treated as allocated under paragraph or subsection (c)(1).

(3) Subsection not to apply in certain cases.—An individual may elect to have this subsection not apply to a transfer.

(c) Deemed allocation to certain lifetime transfers to GST trusts.—

(1) In general.—If any individual makes an indirect skip during such individual's lifetime, any unused portion of such individual's GST exemption shall be allocated to the property transferred to the extent necessary to make the inclusion ratio for such property zero. If the amount of the indirect skip exceeds such unused portion, the entire unused portion shall be allocated to the property transferred.

(2) Unused portion.—For purposes of paragraph (1), the unused portion of an individual's GST exemption is that portion of such exemption which has not previously been—

(A) allocated by such individual,

(B) treated as allocated under subsection (b) with respect to a direct skip occurring during or before the calendar year in which the indirect skip is made, or

(C) treated as allocated under paragraph (1) with respect to a prior indirect skip.

(3) Definitions.—

(A) Indirect skip.—For purposes of this subsection, the term "indirect skip" means any transfer of property (other than a direct skip) subject to the tax imposed by chapter 12 made to a GST trust.

(B) GST trust.—The term "GST trust" means a trust that could have a generation-skipping transfer with respect to the transferor unless—

(i) the trust instrument provides that more than 25 percent of the trust corpus must be distributed to or may be withdrawn by one or more individuals who are non-skip persons—

(I) before the date that the individual attains age 46,

(II) on or before one or more dates specified in the trust instrument that will occur before the date that such individual attains age 46, or

(III) upon the occurrence of an event that, in accordance with regulations prescribed by the Secretary, may reasonably be expected to occur before the date that such individual attains age 46,

(ii) the trust instrument provides that more than 25 percent of the trust corpus must be distributed to or may be withdrawn by one or more individuals who are non-skip persons and who are living on the date of death or another person identified in the instrument (by name or by class) who is more than 10 years older than such individuals,

(iii) the trust instrument provides that, if one or more individuals who are non-skip persons die on or before a date or event described in clause (i) or (ii), more than 25 percent of the trust corpus either must be distributed to the estate or estates of one or more of such individuals or is subject to a general power of appointment exercisable by one or more of such individuals,

(iv) the trust is a trust any portion of which would be included in the gross estate of a non-skip person (other than the transferor) if such person died immediately after the transfer,

(v) the trust is a charitable lead annuity trust (within the meaning of section 2642(e)(3)(A)) or a charitable remainder annuity trust or a charitable remainder unitrust (within the meaning of section 664(d)), or

(vi) the trust is a trust with respect to which a deduction was allowed under section 2522 for the amount of an interest in the form of the right to receive annual payments of a fixed percentage of the net fair market value of the trust property (determined yearly) and which is required to pay principal to a non-skip person if such person is alive when the yearly payments for which the deduction was allowed terminate.

For purposes of this subparagraph, the value of transferred property shall not be considered to be includible in the gross estate of a non-skip person or subject to a right of withdrawal by reason of such person holding a right to withdraw so much of such property as does not exceed the amount referred to in section 2503(b) with respect to any transferor, and it shall be assumed that powers of appointment held by non-skip persons will not be exercised.

(4) Automatic allocations to certain GST trusts.—For purposes of this subsection, an indirect skip to which section 2642(f) applies shall be deemed to have been made only at the close of the estate tax inclusion period. The fair market value of such transfer shall be the fair market value of the trust property at the close of the estate tax inclusion period.

(5) Applicability and effect.—

(A) In general.—An individual—

(i) may elect to have this subsection not apply to—

(I) an indirect skip, or

(II) any or all transfers made by such individual to a particular trust, and

(ii) may elect to treat any trust as a GST trust for purposes of this subsection with respect to any or all transfers made by such individual to such trust.

(B) Elections.—

(i) Elections with respect to indirect skips.—An election under subparagraph (A)(i)(I) shall be deemed to be timely if filed on a timely filed gift tax return for the calendar year in which the transfer was made or deemed to have been made pursuant to paragraph (4) or on such later date or dates as may be prescribed by the Secretary.

(ii) Other elections.—An election under clause (i)(II) or (ii) of subparagraph (A) may be made on a timely filed gift tax return for the calendar year for which the election is to become effective.

(d) Retroactive allocations.—

(1) In general.—If—

(A) a non-skip person has an interest or a future interest in a trust to which any transfer has been made,

(B) such person—

(i) is a lineal descendant of a grandparent of the transferor or of a grandparent of the transferor's spouse or former spouse, and

(ii) is assigned to a generation below the generation assignment of the transferor, and

(C) such person predeceases the transferor, then the transferor may make an allocation of any of such transferor's unused GST exemption to any previous transfer or transfers to the trust on a chronological basis.

(2) Special rules.—If the allocation under paragraph (1) by the transferor is made on a gift tax return filed on or before the date prescribed by section 6075(b) for gifts made within the calendar year within which the non-skip person's death occurred—

(A) the value of such transfer or transfers for purposes of section 2642(a) shall be determined as if such allocation had been made on a timely filed gift tax return for each calendar year within which each transfer was made,

(B) such allocation shall be effective immediately before such death, and

(C) the amount of the transferor's unused GST exemption available to be allocated shall be determined immediately before such death.

(3) Future interest.—For purposes of this subsection, a person has a future interest in a trust if the trust may permit income or corpus to be paid to such person on a date or dates in the future.

(e) Allocation of unused GST exemption.—

(1) In general.—Any portion of an individual's GST exemption which has not been allocated within the time prescribed by subsection (a) shall be deemed to be allocated as follows—

(A) first, to property which is the subject of a direct skip occurring at such individual's death, and

(B) second, to trusts with respect to which such individual is the transferor and from which a taxable distribution or a taxable termination might occur at or after such individual's death.

(2) Allocation within categories.—

(A) In general.—The allocation under paragraph (1) shall be made among the properties described in subparagraph (A) thereof and the trusts described in subparagraph (B) thereof, as the case may be, in proportion to the respective amounts (at the time of allocation) of the nonexempt portions of such properties or trusts.

(B) Nonexempt portion.—For purposes of subparagraph (A), the term "nonexempt portion" means the value (at the time of allocation) of the property or trust, multiplied by the inclusion ratio with respect to such property or trust.

SUBCHAPTER E—APPLICABLE RATE; INCLUSION RATIO

Editorial Summary

Generation-Skipping Transfers: Rates

Subchapter E of Chapter 13 (Secs. 2641, 2642)

See the discussion under the Editorial Summary entitled Tax on Generation-Skipping Transfers, which precedes Sec. 2601.

§ 2641. Applicable rate

(a) General rule.—For purposes of this chapter, the term "applicable rate" means, with respect to any generation-skipping transfer, the product of—

(1) the maximum Federal estate tax rate, and

(2) the inclusion ratio with respect to the transfer.

(b) Maximum federal estate tax rate.—For purposes of subsection (a), the term "maximum Federal estate tax rate" means the maximum rate imposed by section 2001 on the estates of decedents dying at the time of the taxable distribution, taxable termination, or direct skip, as the case may be.

§ 2642. Inclusion ratio

(a) Inclusion ratio defined.—For purposes of this chapter—

(1) In general.—Except as otherwise provided in this section, the inclusion ratio with respect to any property transferred in a generation-skipping transfer shall be the excess (if any) of 1 over—

(A) except as provided in subparagraph (B), the applicable fraction determined for the trust from which such transfer is made, or

(B) in the case of a direct skip, the applicable fraction determined for such skip.

(2) Applicable fraction.—For purposes of paragraph (1), the applicable fraction is a fraction—

(A) the numerator of which is the amount of the GST exemption allocated to the trust (or in the case of a direct skip, allocated to the property transferred in such skip), and

(B) the denominator of which is—

(i) the value of the property transferred to the trust (or involved in the direct skip), reduced by

(ii) the sum of—

(I) any Federal estate tax or State death tax actually recovered from the trust attributable to such property, and

(II) any charitable deduction allowed under section 2055 or 2522 with respect to such property.

(3) Severing of trusts.—

(A) In general.—If a trust is severed in a qualified severance, the trusts resulting from such severance shall be treated as separate trusts thereafter for purposes of this chapter.

(B) Qualified severance.—For purposes of subparagraph (A)—

(i) In general.—The term "qualified severance" means the division of a single trust and the creation (by any means available under the governing instrument or under local law) of two or more more trusts if—

(I) the single trust was divided on a fractional basis, and

(II) the terms of the new trusts, in the aggregate, provide for the same succession of interests of beneficiaries as are provided in the original trust.

(ii) Trusts with inclusion ratio greater than zero.—If a trust has an inclusion ratio of greater than zero and less than 1, a severance is a qualified severance only if the single trust is divided into two trusts, one of which receives a fractional share of the total value of all trust assets equal to the applicable fraction of the single trust immediately before the severance. In such case, the trust receiving such fractional share shall have an inclusion ratio of zero and the other trust shall have an inclusion ratio of 1.

(iii) Regulations.—The term "qualified severance" includes any other severance permitted under regulations prescribed by the Secretary.

(C) Timing and manner of severances.—A severance pursuant to this paragraph may be made at any time. The Secretary shall prescribe by forms or regulations the manner in which the qualified severance shall be reported to the Secretary.

(b) Valuation rules, etc.—Except as provided in subsection (f)—

(1) Gifts for which gift tax return filed or deemed allocation made.—If the allocation of the GST exemption to any property is made on a gift tax return filed on or before the date prescribed by section 6075(b) or is deemed to be made under section 2632(b)(1) or (c)(l)—

(A) the value of such property for purposes of subsection (a) shall be its value as finally determined for purposes of chapter 12 (within the meaning of section 2001(f)(2)), or, in the case of an allocation deemed to have been made at the close of an estate tax inclusion period, its value at the time of the close of the estate tax inclusion period, and

(B) such allocation shall be effective on and after the date of such transfer, or, in the case of an allocation deemed to have been made at the close of an estate tax inclusion period, on and after the close of such estate tax inclusion period.

(2) Transfers and allocations at or after death.—

(A) Transfers at death.—If property is transferred as a result of the death of the transferor, the value of such property for purposes of subsection (a) shall be its value for purposes of chapter 11; except that, if the requirements prescribed by the Secretary respecting allocation of post-death changes in value are not met, the value of such property shall be determined as of the time of the distribution concerned.

(B) Allocations to property transferred at death of transferor.—Any allocation to property transferred as a result of the death of the transferor shall be effective on and after the death of the transferor.

(3) Allocations to inter vivos transfers not made on timely filed gift tax return.—If any allocation of the GST exemption to any property not transferred as a result of the death of the transferor is not made on a gift tax return filed on or before the date prescribed by section 6075(b) and is not deemed to be made under section 2632(b)(1)—

(A) the value of such property for purposes of subsection (a) shall be determined as of the time such allocation is filed with the Secretary, and

(B) such allocation shall be effective on and after the date on which such allocation is filed with the Secretary.

(4) QTIP trusts.—If the value of property is included in the estate of a spouse by virtue of section 2044, and if such spouse is treated as the transferor of such property under section 2652(a), the value of such property for purposes of subsection (a) shall be its value for purposes of chapter 11 in the estate of such spouse.

(c) Treatment of certain direct skips which are non-taxable gifts.—

(1) In general.—In the case of a direct skip which is a nontaxable gift, the inclusion ratio shall be zero.

(2) Exception for certain transfers in trust.—Paragraph (1) shall not apply to any transfer to a trust for the benefit of an individual unless—

(A) during the life of such individual, no portion of the corpus or income of the trust may be distributed to (or for the benefit of) any person other than such individual, and

(B) if the trust does not terminate before the individual dies, the assets of such trust will be includible in the gross estate of such individual.

Rules similar to the rules of section 2652(c)(3) shall apply for purposes of subparagraph (A).

(3) Nontaxable gift.—For purposes of this subsection, the term "nontaxable gift" means any transfer of property to the extent such transfer is not treated as a taxable gift by reason of—

(A) section 2503(b) (taking into account the application of section 2513), or

(B) section 2503(e).

(d) Special rules where more than 1 transfer made to trust.—

(1) In general.—If a transfer of property is made to a trust in existence before such transfer, the applicable fraction for such trust shall be recomputed as of the time of such transfer in the manner provided in paragraph (2).

(2) Applicable fraction.—In the case of any such transfer, the recomputed applicable fraction is a fraction—

(A) the numerator of which is the sum of—

(i) the amount of the GST exemption allocated to property involved in such transfer, plus

(ii) the nontax portion of such trust immediately before such transfer, and

(B) the denominator of which is the sum of—

(i) the value of the property involved in such transfer reduced by the sum of—

(I) any Federal estate tax or State death tax actually recovered from the trust attributable to such property, and

(II) any charitable deduction allowed under section 2055 or 2522 with respect to such property, and

(ii) the value of all of the property in the trust (immediately before such transfer).

(3) Nontax portion.—For purposes of paragraph (2), the term "nontax portion" means the product of—

(A) the value of all of the property in the trust, and

(B) the applicable fraction in effect for such trust.

(4) Similar recomputation in case of certain late allocations.—If—

(A) any allocation of the GST exemption to property transferred to a trust is not made on a timely filed gift tax return required by section 6019, and

(B) there was a previous allocation with respect to property transferred to such trust,

the applicable fraction for such trust shall be recomputed as of the time of such allocation under rules similar to the rules of paragraph (2).

(e) Special rules for charitable lead annuity trusts.—

(1) In general.—For purposes of determining the inclusion ratio for any charitable lead annuity trust, the applicable fraction shall be a fraction—

(A) the numerator of which is the adjusted GST exemption, and

(B) the denominator of which is the value of all of the property in such trust immediately after the termination of the charitable lead annuity.

(2) Adjusted GST exemption.—For purposes of paragraph (1), the adjusted GST exemption is an amount equal to the GST exemption allocated to the trust increased by interest determined—

(A) at the interest rate used in determining the amount of the deduction under section 2055 or 2522 (as the case may be) for the charitable lead annuity, and

(B) for the actual period of the charitable lead annuity.

(3) Definitions.—For purposes of this subsection—

(A) Charitable lead annuity trust.—The term "charitable lead annuity trust" means any trust in which there is a charitable lead annuity.

(B) Charitable lead annuity.—The term "charitable lead annuity" means any interest in the form of a guaranteed annuity with respect to which a deduction was allowed under section 2055 or 2522 (as the case may be).

(4) Coordination with subsection (d).—Under regulations, appropriate adjustments shall be made in the application of subsection (d) to take into account the provisions of this subsection.

(f) Special rules for certain inter vivos transfers.—Except as provided in regulations—

(1) In general.—For purposes of determining the inclusion ratio, if—

(A) an individual makes an inter vivos transfer of property, and

(B) the value of such property would be includible in the gross estate of such individual under chapter 11 if such individual died immediately after making such transfer (other than by reason of section 2035),

any allocation of GST exemption to such property shall not be made before the close of the estate tax inclusion period (and the value of such property shall be determined under paragraph (2)). If such transfer is a direct skip, such skip shall be treated as occurring as of the close of the estate tax inclusion period.

(2) Valuation.—In the case of any property to which paragraph (1) applies, the value of such property shall be—

(A) if such property is includible in the gross estate of the transferor (other than by reason of section 2035), its value for purposes of chapter 11, or

(B) if subparagraph (A) does not apply, its value as of the close of the estate tax inclusion period (or, if any allocation of GST exemption to such property is not made on a timely filed gift tax return for the calendar year in which such period ends, its value as of the time such allocation is filed with the Secretary).

(3) Estate tax inclusion period.—For purposes of this subsection, the term "estate tax inclusion period" means any period after the transfer described in paragraph (1) during which the value of the property involved in such transfer would be includible in the gross estate of the transferor under chapter 11 if he died. Such period shall in no event extend beyond the earlier of—

(A) the date on which there is a generation-skipping transfer with respect to such property, or

(B) the date of the death of the transferor.

(4) Treatment of spouse.—Except as provided in regulations, any reference in this subsection to an individual or transferor shall be treated as including a reference to the spouse of such individual or transferor.

(5) Coordination with subsection (d).—Under regulations, appropriate adjustments shall be made in the application of subsection (d) to take into account the provisions of this subsection.

(g) Relief provisions.—

(1) Relief from late elections.—

(A) In general.—The Secretary shall by regulation prescribe such circumstances and procedures under which extensions of time will be granted to make—

(i) an allocation of GST exemption described in paragraph (1) or (2) of subsection (b), and

(ii) an election under subsection (b)(3) or (c)(5) of section 2632.

Such regulations shall include procedures for requesting comparable relief with respect to transfers made before the date of the enactment of this paragraph.

(B) Basis for determinations.—In determining whether to grant relief under this paragraph, the Secretary shall take into account all relevant circumstances, including evidence of intent contained in the trust instrument or instrument of transfer and such other factors as the Secretary deems relevant. For purposes of determining whether to grant relief under this paragraph, the time for making the allocation (or election) shall be treated as if not expressly prescribed by statute.

(2) Substantial compliance.—An allocation of GST exemption under section 2632 that demonstrates an intent to have the lowest possible inclusion ratio with respect to a transfer or a trust shall be deemed to be an allocation of so much of the transferor's unused GST exemption as produces the lowest possible inclusion ratio. In determining whether there has been substantial compliance, all relevant circumstances shall be taken into account, including evidence of intent contained in the trust instrument or instrument of transfer and such other factors as the Secretary deems relevant.

SUBCHAPTER F—OTHER DEFINITIONS AND SPECIAL RULES

Editorial Summary

Generation-Skipping Transfers: Other Definitions and Special Rules

Subchapter F of Chapter 13 (Secs. 2651–2654)

See the discussion under the Editorial Summary entitled Tax on Generation-Skipping Transfers, which precedes Sec. 2601.

§ 2651. Generation assignment

(a) In general.—For purposes of this chapter, the generation to which any person (other than the transferor) belongs shall be determined in accordance with the rules set forth in this section.

(b) Lineal descendants.—

(1) In general.—An individual who is a lineal descendant of a grandparent of the transferor shall be assigned to that generation which results from comparing the number of generations between the grandparent and such individual with the number of generations between the grandparent and the transferor.

(2) On spouse's side.—An individual who is a lineal descendant of a grandparent of a spouse (or former spouse) of the transferor (other than such spouse) shall be assigned to that generation which results from comparing the number of generations between such grandparent and such individual with the number of generations between such grandparent and such spouse.

(3) Treatment of legal adoptions, etc.—For purposes of this subsection—

(A) Legal adoptions.—A relationship by legal adoption shall be treated as a relationship by blood.

(B) Relationships by half-blood.—A relationship by the half-blood shall be treated as a relationship of the whole-blood.

(c) Marital relationship.—

(1) Marriage to transferor.—An individual who has been married at any time to the transferor shall be assigned to the transferor's generation.

(2) Marriage to other lineal descendants.—An individual who has been married at any time to an individual described in subsection (b) shall be assigned to the generation of the individual so described.

(d) Persons who are not lineal descendants.—An individual who is not assigned to a generation by reason of the foregoing provisions of this section shall be assigned to a generation on the basis of the date of such individual's birth with—

(1) an individual born not more than 12½ years after the date of the birth of the transferor assigned to the transferor's generation,

(2) an individual born more than 12½ years but not more than 37½ years after the date of the birth of the transferor assigned to the first generation younger than the transferor, and

(3) similar rules for a new generation every 25 years.

(e) Special rule for persons with a deceased parent.—

(1) In general.—For purposes of determining whether any transfer is a generation-skipping transfer, if—

(A) an individual is a descendant of a parent of the transferor (or the transferor's spouse or former spouse), and

(B) such individual's parent who is a lineal descendant of the parent of the transferor (or the transferor's spouse or former spouse) is dead at the time the transfer (from which an interest of such individual is established or derived) is subject to a tax imposed by chapter 11 or 12 upon the transferor (and if there shall be more than 1 such time, then at the earliest such time),

such individual shall be treated as if such individual were a member of the generation which is 1 generation below the lower of the transferor's generation or the generation assignment of the youngest living ancestor of such individual who is also a descendant of the parent of the transferor (or the transferor's spouse or former spouse), and the generation assignment of any descendant of such individual shall be adjusted accordingly.

(2) Limited application of subsection to collateral heirs.—This subsection shall not apply with respect to a transfer to any individual who is not a lineal descendant of the transferor (or the transferor's spouse or former spouse) if, at the time of the transfer, such transferor has any living lineal descendant.

(f) Other special rules.—

(1) Individuals assigned to more than 1 generation.—Except as provided in regulations, an individual who, but for this subsection, would be assigned to more than 1 generation shall be assigned to the youngest such generation.

(2) Interests through entities.—Except as provided in paragraph (3), if an estate, trust, partnership, corporation, or other entity has an interest in property, each individual having a beneficial interest in such entity shall be treated as having an interest in such property and shall be assigned to a generation under the foregoing provisions of this subsection.

(3) Treatment of certain charitable organizations and governmental entities.—Any—

(A) organization described in section 511(a)(2),

(B) charitable trust described in section 511(b)(2), and

(C) governmental entity,

shall be assigned to the transferor's generation.

§ 2652. Other definitions

(a) Transferor.—For purposes of this chapter—

(1) In general.—Except as provided in this subsection or section 2653(a), the term "transferor" means—

(A) in the case of any property subject to the tax imposed by chapter 11, the decedent, and

(B) in the case of any property subject to the tax imposed by chapter 12, the donor.

An individual shall be treated as transferring any property with respect to which such individual is the transferor.

(2) Gift-splitting by married couples.—If, under section 2513, one-half of a gift is treated as made by an individual and one-half of such gift is treated as made by the spouse of such individual, such gift shall be so treated for purposes of this chapter.

(3) Special election for qualified terminable interest property.—In the case of—

(A) any trust with respect to which a deduction is allowed to the decedent under section 2056 by reason of subsection (b)(7) thereof, and

(B) any trust with respect to which a deduction to the donor spouse is allowed under section 2523 by reason of subsection (f) thereof,

the estate of the decedent or the donor spouse, as the case may be, may elect to treat all the property in such trust for purposes of this chapter as if the election to be treated as qualified terminable interest property had not been made.

(b) Trust and trustee.—

(1) Trust.—The term "trust" includes any arrangement (other than an estate) which, although not a trust, has substantially the same effect as a trust.

(2) Trustee.—In the case of an arrangement which is not a trust but which is treated as a trust under this subsection, the term "trustee" shall mean the person in actual or constructive possession of the property subject to such arrangement.

(3) Examples.—Arrangements to which this subsection applies include arrangements involving life estates and remainders, estates for years, and insurance and annuity contracts.

(c) Interest.—

(1) In general.—A person has an interest in property held in trust if (at the time the determination is made) such person—

(A) has a right (other than a future right) to receive income or corpus from the trust,

(B) is a permissible current recipient of income or corpus from the trust and is not described in section 2055(a), or

(C) is described in section 2055(a) and the trust is—

(i) a charitable remainder annuity trust,

(ii) a charitable remainder unitrust within the meaning of section 664, or

(iii) a pooled income fund within the meaning of section 642(c)(5).

(2) Certain interests disregarded.—For purposes of paragraph (1), an interest which is used primarily to postpone or avoid any tax imposed by this chapter shall be disregarded.

(3) Certain support obligations disregarded.—The fact that income or corpus of the trust may be used to satisfy an obligation of support arising under State law shall be disregarded in determining whether a person has an interest in the trust, if—

(A) such use is discretionary, or

(B) such use is pursuant to the provisions of any State law substantially equivalent to the Uniform Gifts to Minors Act.

(d) Executor.—For purposes of this chapter, the term "executor" has the meaning given such term by section 2203.

§ 2653. Taxation of multiple skips

(a) General rule.—For purposes of this chapter, if—

(1) there is a generation-skipping transfer of any property, and

(2) immediately after such transfer such property is held in trust,

for purposes of applying this chapter (other than section 2651) to subsequent transfers from the portion of such trust attributable to such property, the trust will be treated as if the transferor of such property were assigned to the first generation above the highest generation of any person who has an interest in such trust immediately after the transfer.

(b) Trust retains inclusion ratio.—

(1) In general.—Except as provided in paragraph (2), the provisions of subsection (a) shall not affect the inclusion ratio determined with respect to any trust. Under regulations prescribed by the Secretary, notwithstanding the preceding sentence, proper adjustment shall be made to the inclusion ratio with respect to such trust to take into account any tax under this chapter borne by such trust which is imposed by this chapter on the transfer described in subsection (a).

(2) Special rule for pour-over trust.—

(A) In general.—If the generation-skipping transfer referred to in subsection (a) involves the transfer of property from 1 trust to another trust (hereinafter in this paragraph referred to as the "pour-over trust"), the inclusion ratio for the pour-over trust shall be determined by treating the nontax portion of such distribution as if it were a part of a GST exemption allocated to such trust.

(B) Nontax portion.—For purposes of subparagraph (A), the nontax portion of any distribution is the amount of such distribution multiplied by the applicable fraction which applies to such distribution.

§ 2654. Special rules

(a) Basis adjustment.—

(1) In general.—Except as provided in paragraph (2), if property is transferred in a generation-skipping transfer, the basis of such property shall be increased (but not above the fair market value of such property) by an amount equal to that portion of the tax imposed by section 2601 (computed without regard to section 2604) with respect to the transfer which is attributable to the excess of the fair market value of such property over its adjusted basis immediately before the transfer. The preceding shall be applied after any basis adjustment under section 1015 with respect to the transfer.

(2) Certain transfers at death.—If property is transferred in a taxable termination which occurs at the same time as and as a result of the death of an individual, the basis of such property shall be adjusted in a manner similar to the manner provided under section 1014(a); except that, if the inclusion ratio with respect to such property is less than 1, any increase or decrease in basis shall be limited by multiplying such increase or decrease (as the case may be) by the inclusion ratio.

(b) Certain trusts treated as separate trusts.—For purposes of this chapter—

(1) the portions of a trust attributable to transfers from different transferors shall be treated as separate trusts, and

(2) substantially separate and independent shares of different beneficiaries in a trust shall be treated as separate trusts.

Except as provided in the preceding sentence, nothing in this chapter shall be construed as authorizing a single trust to be treated as 2 or more trusts. For purposes of this subsection, a trust shall be treated as part of an estate during any period that the trust is so treated under section 645.

(c) Disclaimers.—For provisions relating to the effect of a qualified disclaimer for purposes of this chapter, see section 2518.

(d) Limitation on personal liability of trustee.—A trustee shall not be personally liable for any increase in the tax imposed by section 2601 which is attributable to the fact that—

(1) section 2642(c) (relating to exemption of certain nontaxable gifts) does not apply to a transfer to the trust which was made during the life of the transferor and for which a gift tax return was not filed, or

(2) the inclusion ratio with respect to the trust is greater than the amount of such ratio as computed on the basis of the return on which was made (or was deemed made) an allocation of the GST exemption to property transferred to such trust.

The preceding sentence shall not apply if the trustee has knowledge of facts sufficient reasonably to conclude that a gift tax return was required to be filed or that the inclusion ratio was erroneous.

SUBCHAPTER G—ADMINISTRATION

Editorial Summary

Generation-Skipping Transfers: Administration

Subchapter G of Chapter 13 (Secs. 2661–2664)

See the discussion under the Editorial Summary entitled Tax on Generation-Skipping Transfers, which precedes Sec. 2601.

§ 2661. Administration

Insofar as applicable and not inconsistent with the provisions of this chapter—

(1) except as provided in paragraph (2), all provisions of subtitle F (including penalties) applicable to the gift tax, to chapter 12, or to section 2501, are hereby made applicable in respect of the generation-skipping transfer tax, this chapter, or section 2601, as the case may be, and

(2) in the case of a generation-skipping transfer occurring at the same time as and as a result of the death of an individual, all provisions of subtitle F (including penalties) applicable to the estate tax, to chapter 11, or to section 2001 are hereby made applicable in respect of the generation-skipping transfer tax, this chapter, or section 2601 (as the case may be).

§ 2662. Return requirements

(a) In general.—The Secretary shall prescribe by regulations the person who is required to make the return with respect to the tax imposed by this chapter and the time by which any such return must be filed. To the extent practicable, such regulations shall provide that—

(1) the person who is required to make such return shall be the person liable under section 2603(a) for payment of such tax, and

(2) the return shall be filed—

(A) in the case of a direct skip (other than from a trust), on or before the date on which an estate or gift tax return is required to be filed with respect to the transfer, and

(B) in all other cases, on or before the 15th day of the 4th month after the close of the taxable year of the person required to make such return in which such transfer occurs.

(b) Information returns.—The Secretary may by regulations require a return to be filed containing such information as he determines to be necessary for purposes of this chapter.

§ 2663. Regulations

The Secretary shall prescribe such regulations as may be necessary or appropriate to carry out the purposes of this chapter, including—

(1) such regulations as may be necessary to coordinate the provisions of this chapter with the recapture tax imposed under section 2032A(c), and

(2) regulations (consistent with the principles of chapters 11 and 12) providing for the application of this chapter in the case of transferors who are nonresidents not citizens of the United States, and

(3) regulations providing for such adjustments as may be necessary to the application of this chapter in the case of any arrangement which, although not a trust, is treated as a trust under section 2652(b).

CAUTION: FUTURE EFFECTIVE DATE

§ 2664. Termination*

This chapter shall not apply to generation-skipping transfers after December 31, 2009.

* Editorial comment: The Tax of Generation-Skipping Transfers is repealed for such transfers after December 31, 2009. Section 2664 is repealed by the Tax Relief Act of 2010. Thus, Congress has reenacted the Tax on Generation-Skipping Transfers effective for 2011, 2012, and subsequent years.

CHAPTER 14—SPECIAL VALUATION RULES

Editorial Summary

Special Valuation Rules

Chapter 14 (Secs. 2701–2704)

With the repeal of the estate freeze provisions contained in Sec. 2036(c) by the Revenue Reconciliation Act of 1990, Congress adopted a more direct approach for preventing tax avoidance through the use of the estate freeze strategy. Included are the valuation of the following:

1. Retained interests in corporations (see Sec. 2701).
2. Retained interests in partnerships (see Sec. 2701).
3. Split temporal interests in property.
4. Retained interests in trusts (see Sec. 2702).
5. Transfers under options, agreements, or buy-sell arrangements at less than fair market value (see Sec. 2703).
6. Lapsing of voting or liquidation rights in a family-controlled entity (see Sec. 2704).

Prior to the enactment of the estate freeze provision in Sec. 2036(c) by the Revenue Act of 1987, it was possible for an older family member to transfer property (e.g., a business) during his or her life and reduce the unified transfer taxes (i.e., gift taxes during life and estate taxes at death) when compared with either making a complete gift of the property or transferring the property as part of the decedent's estate. This was accomplished by having the older family member transfer an interest in the property to a younger family member (e.g., a gift) while retaining a residual interest in the property. This could be structured in such a way that the transferor could retain control and collect income while the transferee received the benefit of the property's appreciation in value. By effectively understating (or minimizing) the fair market value of the interest transferred and effectively overstating (or maximizing) the fair market value of the interest retained, the gift taxes on the initial transfer could be minimized. Then, at death, the estate taxes could be minimized because of the transfers made during life.

The estate freeze strategy which was contained in Sec. 2036(c) was designed to negate the aforementioned tax avoidance technique. Initially, the approach taken was to include the post transfer appreciation in the transferor's estate if the transferor retained a disproportionately large share of income or other rights in the property. This was modified in the Technical and Miscellaneous Revenue Act of 1988 to provide that if the transferor retained any interest or share in the income or rights in the property, the disproportionate appreciation test was automatically met and the post-transfer appreciation was included in the transferor's estate. Such appreciation was included even if it resulted entirely from the efforts of the transferees.

The more direct approach taken by Secs. 2701–2704 is to emphasize a more accurate gift tax valuation of the initial transfer rather than on the estate tax valuation at the transferor's death. The general assumption made by the Code is that the value of the retained interest is zero. This is accompanied by the open-ended statute of limitations on such transfers unless certain data with respect to the transfer is adequately disclosed on the tax return [see Sec. 6501(c)(9)].

§ 2701. Special valuation rules in case of transfers of certain interests in corporations or partnerships

(a) Valuation rules.—

(1) In general.—Solely for purposes of determining whether a transfer of an interest in a corporation or partnership to (or for the benefit of) a member of the transferor's family is a gift (and the value of such transfer), the value of any right—

(A) which is described in subparagraph (A) or (B) of subsection (b)(1), and

(B) which is with respect to any applicable retained interest that is held by the transferor or an applicable family member immediately after the transfer,

shall be determined under paragraph (3). This paragraph shall not apply to the transfer of any interest for which market quotations are readily available (as of the date of transfer) on an established securities market.

(2) Exceptions for marketable retained interests, etc.—Paragraph (1) shall not apply to any right with respect to an applicable retained interest if—

(A) market quotations are readily available (as of the date of the transfer) for such interest on an established securities market,

(B) such interest is of the same class as the transferred interest, or

(C) such interest is proportionally the same as the transferred interest, without regard to nonlapsing differences in voting power (or, for a partnership, nonlapsing differences with respect to management and limitations on liability).

Subparagraph (C) shall not apply to any interest in a partnership if the transferor or an applicable family member has the right to alter the liability of the transferee of the transferred property. Except as provided by the Secretary, any difference described in subparagraph (C) which lapses by reason of any Federal or State law shall be treated as a nonlapsing difference for purposes of such subparagraph.

(3) Valuation of rights to which paragraph (1) applies.—

(A) In general.—The value of any right described in paragraph (1), other than a distribution right which consists of a right to receive a qualified payment, shall be treated as being zero.

(B) Valuation of certain qualified payments.—If—

(i) any applicable retained interest confers a distribution right which consists of the right to a qualified payment, and

(ii) there are 1 or more liquidation, put, call, or conversion rights with respect to such interest,

the value of all such rights shall be determined as if each liquidation, put, call, or conversion right were exercised in the manner resulting in the lowest value being determined for all such rights.

(C) Valuation of qualified payments where no liquidation, etc. rights.—In the case of an applicable retained interest which is described in subparagraph (B)(i) but not subparagraph (B)(ii), the value of the distribution right shall be determined without regard to this section.

(4) Minimum valuation of junior equity.—

(A) In general.—In the case of a transfer described in paragraph (1) of a junior equity interest in a corporation or partnership, such interest shall in no event be valued at an amount less than the value which would be determined if the total value of all of the junior equity interests in the entity were equal to 10 percent of the sum of—

(i) the total value of all of the equity interests in such entity, plus

(ii) the total amount of indebtedness of such entity to the transferor (or an applicable family member).

(B) Definitions.—For purposes of this paragraph—

(i) Junior equity interest.—The term "junior equity interest" means common stock or, in the case of a partnership, any partnership interest under which the rights as to income and capital (or, to the extent provided in regulations, the rights as to either income or capital) are junior to the rights of all other classes of equity interests.

(ii) Equity interest.—The term "equity interest" means stock or any interest as a partner, as the case may be.

(b) Applicable retained interests.—For purposes of this section—

(1) In general.—The term "applicable retained interest" means any interest in an entity with respect to which there is—

(A) a distribution right, but only if, immediately before the transfer described in subsection (a)(1), the transferor and applicable family members hold (after application of subsection (e)(3)) control of the entity, or

(B) a liquidation, put, call, or conversion right.

(2) Control.—For purposes of paragraph (1)—

(A) Corporations.—In the case of a corporation, the term "control" means the holding of at least 50 percent (by vote or value) of the stock of the corporation.

(B) Partnerships.—In the case of a partnership, the term "control" means—

(i) the holding of at least 50 percent of the capital or profits interests in the partnership, or

(ii) in the case of a limited partnership, the holding of any interest as a general partner.

(C) Applicable family member.—For purposes of this subsection, the term "applicable family member" includes any lineal descendant of any parent of the transferor or the transferor's spouse.

(c) Distribution and other rights; qualified payments.—For purposes of this section—

(1) Distribution right.—

(A) In general.—The term "distribution right" means—

(i) a right to distributions from a corporation with respect to its stock, and

(ii) a right to distributions from a partnership with respect to a partner's interest in the partnership.

(B) Exceptions.—The term "distribution right" does not include—

(i) a right to distributions with respect to any interest which is junior to the rights of the transferred interest,

(ii) any liquidation, put, call, or conversion right, or

(iii) any right to receive any guaranteed payment described in section 707(c) of a fixed amount.

(2) Liquidation, etc. rights.—

(A) In general.—The term "liquidation, put, call, or conversion right" means any liquidation, put, call, or conversion right, or any similar right, the exercise or nonexercise of which affects the value of the transferred interest.

(B) Exception for fixed rights.—

(i) In general.—The term "liquidation, put, call, or conversion right" does not include any right which must be exercised at a specific time and at a specific amount.

(ii) Treatment of certain rights.—If a right is assumed to be exercised in a particular manner under subsection (a)(3)(B), such right shall be treated as so exercised for purposes of clause (i).

(C) Exception for certain rights to convert.—The term "liquidation, put, call, or conversion right" does not include any right which—

(i) is a right to convert into a fixed number (or a fixed percentage) of shares of the same class of stock in a corporation as the transferred stock in such corporation under subsection (a)(1) (or stock which would be of the same class but for nonlapsing differences in voting power),

(ii) is nonlapsing,

(iii) is subject to proportionate adjustments for splits, combinations, reclassifications, and similar changes in the capital stock, and

(iv) is subject to adjustments similar to the adjustments under subsection (d) for accumulated but unpaid distributions.

A rule similar to the rule of the preceding sentence shall apply for partnerships.

(3) Qualified payment.—

(A) In general.—Except as otherwise provided in this paragraph, the term "qualified payment" means any dividend payable on a periodic basis under any cumulative preferred stock (or a comparable payment under any partnership interest) to the extent that such dividend (or comparable payment) is determined at a fixed rate.

(B) Treatment of variable rate payments.—For purposes of subparagraph (A), a payment shall be treated as fixed as to rate if such payment is determined at a rate which bears a fixed relationship to a specified market interest rate.

(C) Elections.—

(i) In general.—Payments under any interest held by a transferor which (without regard to this subparagraph) are qualified payments shall be treated as qualified payments unless the transferor elects not to treat such payments as qualified payments. Payments described in the preceding sentence which are held by an applicable family member shall be treated as qualified payments only if such member elects to treat such payments as qualified payments.

(ii) Election to have interest treated as qualified payment.—A transferor or applicable family member holding any distribution right which (without regard to this subparagraph) is not a qualified payment may elect to treat such right as a qualified payment, to be paid in the amounts and at the times specified in such election. The preceding sentence shall apply only to the extent that the amounts and times so specified are not inconsistent with the underlying legal instrument giving rise to such right.

(iii) Elections irrevocable.—Any election under this subparagraph with respect to an interest shall, once made, be irrevocable.

(d) Transfer tax treatment of cumulative but unpaid distributions.—

(1) In general.—If a taxable event occurs with respect to any distribution right to which subsection (a)(3)(B) or (C) applied, the following shall be increased by the amount determined under paragraph (2):

(A) The taxable estate of the transferor in the case of a taxable event described in paragraph (3)(A)(i).

(B) The taxable gifts of the transferor for the calendar year in which the taxable event occurs in the case of a taxable event described in paragraph (3)(A)(ii) or (iii).

(2) Amount of increase.—

(A) In general.—The amount of the increase determined under this paragraph shall be the excess (if any) of—

(i) the value of the qualified payments payable during the period beginning on the date of the transfer under subsection (a)(1) and ending on the date of the taxable event determined as if—

(I) all such payments were paid on the date payment was due, and

(II) all such payments were reinvested by the transferor as of the date of payment at a yield equal to the discount rate used in determining the value of the applicable retained interest described in subsection (a)(1), over

(ii) the value of such payments paid during such period computed under clause (i) on the basis of the time when such payments were actually paid.

(B) Limitation on amount of increase.—

(i) In general.—The amount of the increase under subparagraph (A) shall not exceed the applicable percentage of the excess (if any) of—

(I) the value (determined as of the date of the taxable event) of all equity interests in the entity which are junior to the applicable retained interest, over

(II) the value of such interests (determined as of the date of the transfer to which subsection (a)(1) applied).

(ii) Applicable percentage.—For purposes of clause (i), the applicable percentage is the percentage determined by dividing—

(I) the number of shares in the corporation held (as of the date of the taxable event) by the transferor which are applicable retained interests of the same class, by

(II) the total number of shares in such corporation (as of such date) which are of the same class as the class described in subclause (I).

A similar percentage shall be determined in the case of interests in a partnership.

(iii) Definition.—For purposes of this subparagraph, the term "equity interest" has the meaning given such term by subsection (a)(4)(B).

(C) Grace period.—For purposes of subparagraph (A), any payment of any distribution during the 4-year period beginning on its due date shall be treated as having been made on such due date.

(3) Taxable events.—For purposes of this subsection—

(A) In general.—The term "taxable event" means any of the following:

(i) The death of the transferor if the applicable retained interest conferring the distribution right is includible in the estate of the transferor.

(ii) The transfer of such applicable retained interest.

(iii) At the election of the taxpayer, the payment of any qualified payment after the period described in paragraph (2)(C), but only with respect to such payment.

(B) Exception where spouse is transferee.—

(i) Deathtime transfers.—Subparagraph (A)(i) shall not apply to any interest includible in the gross estate of the transferor if a deduction with respect to such interest is allowable under section 2056 or 2106(a)(3).

(ii) Lifetime transfers.—A transfer to the spouse of the transferor shall not be treated as a taxable event under subparagraph (A)(ii) if such transfer does not result in a taxable gift by reason of—

(I) any deduction allowed under section 2523 or the exclusion under section 2503(b), or

(II) consideration for the transfer provided by the spouse.

(iii) Spouse succeeds to treatment of transferor.—If an event is not treated as a taxable event by reason of this subparagraph, the transferee spouse or surviving spouse (as the case may be) shall be treated in the same manner as the transferor in applying this subsection with respect to the interest involved.

(4) Special rules for applicable family members.—

(A) Family member treated in same manner as transferor.—For purposes of this subsection, an applicable family member shall be treated in the same manner as the transferor with respect to any distribution right retained by such family member to which subsection (a)(3)(B) or (C) applied.

(B) Transfer to applicable family member.—In the case of a taxable event described in paragraph (3)(A)(ii) involving the transfer of an applicable retained interest to an applicable family member (other than the spouse of the transferor), the applicable family member shall be treated in the same manner as the transferor in applying this subsection to distributions accumulating with respect to such interest after such taxable event.

(C) Transfer to transferors.—In the case of a taxable event described in paragraph (3)(A)(ii) involving a transfer of an applicable retained interest from an applicable family member to a transferor, this subsection shall continue to apply to the transferor during any period the transferor holds such interest.

(5) Transfer to include termination.—For purposes of this subsection, any termination of an interest shall be treated as a transfer.

(e) Other definitions and rules.—For purposes of this section—

(1) Member of the family.—The term "member of the family" means, with respect to any transferor—

(A) the transferor's spouse,

(B) a lineal descendant of the transferor or the transferor's spouse, and

(C) the spouse of any such descendant.

(2) Applicable family member.—The term "applicable family member" means, with respect to any transferor—

(A) the transferor's spouse,

(B) an ancestor of the transferor or the transferor's spouse, and

(C) the spouse of any such ancestor.

(3) Attribution of indirect holdings and transfers.—An individual shall be treated as holding any interest to the extent such interest is held indirectly by such individual through a corporation, partnership, trust, or other entity. If any individual is treated as holding any interest by reason of the preceding sentence, any transfer which results in such interest being treated as no longer held by such individual shall be treated as a transfer of such interest.

(4) Effect of adoption.—A relationship by legal adoption shall be treated as a relationship by blood.

(5) Certain changes treated as transfers.—Except as provided in regulations, a contribution to capital or a redemption, recapitalization, or other change in the capital structure of a corporation or partnership shall be treated as a transfer of an interest in such entity to which this section applies if the taxpayer or an applicable family member—

(A) receives an applicable retained interest in such entity pursuant to such transaction, or

(B) under regulations, otherwise holds, immediately after such transaction, an applicable retained interest in such entity.

This paragraph shall not apply to any transaction (other than a contribution to capital) if the interests in the entity held by the transferor, applicable family members, and members of the transferor's family before and after the transaction are substantially identical.

(6) Adjustments.—Under regulations prescribed by the Secretary, if there is any subsequent transfer, or inclusion in the gross estate, of any applicable retained interest which was valued under the rules of subsection (a), appropriate adjustments shall be made for purposes of Chapter 11, 12, or 13 to reflect the increase in the amount of any prior taxable gift made by the transferor or decedent by reason of such valuation or to reflect the application of subsection (d).

(7) Treatment as separate interests.—The Secretary may by regulation provide that any applicable retained interest shall be treated as 2 or more separate interests for purposes of this section.

§ 2702. Special valuation rules in case of transfers of interests in trusts

(a) Valuation rules.—

(1) In general.—Solely for purposes of determining whether a transfer of an interest in trust to (or for the benefit of) a member of the transferor's family is a gift (and the value of such transfer), the value of any interest in such trust retained by the transferor or any applicable family member (as defined in section 2701(e)(2)) shall be determined as provided in paragraph (2).

(2) Valuation of retained interests.—

(A) In general.—The value of any retained interest which is not a qualified interest shall be treated as being zero.

(B) Valuation of qualified interest.—The value of any retained interest which is a qualified interest shall be determined under section 7520.

(3) Exceptions.—

(A) In general.—This subsection shall not apply to any transfer—

(i) if such transfer is an incomplete gift,

(ii) if such transfer involves the transfer of an interest in trust all the property in which consists of a residence to be used as a personal residence by persons holding term interests in such trust, or

(iii) to the extent the regulations provide that such transfer is not inconsistent with the purposes of this section.

(B) Incomplete gift.—For purposes of subparagraph (A), the term "incomplete gift" means any transfer which would not be treated as a gift whether or not consideration was received for such transfer.

(b) Qualified interest.—For purposes of this section, the term "qualified interest" means—

(1) any interest which consists of the right to receive fixed amounts payable not less frequently than annually,

(2) any interest which consists of the right to receive amounts which are payable not less frequently than annually and are a fixed percentage of the fair market value of the property in the trust (determined annually), and

(3) any noncontingent remainder interest if all of the other interests in the trust consist of interests described in paragraph (1) or (2).

(c) Certain property treated as held in trust.—For purposes of this section—

(1) In general.—The transfer of an interest in property with respect to which there is 1 or more term interests shall be treated as a transfer of an interest in a trust.

(2) Joint purchases.—If 2 or more members of the same family acquire interests in any property described in paragraph (1) in the same transaction (or a series of related transactions), the person (or persons) acquiring the term interests in such property shall be treated as having acquired the entire property and then transferred to the other persons the interests acquired by such other persons in the transaction (or series of transactions). Such transfer shall be treated as made in exchange for the consideration (if any) provided by such other persons for the acquisition of their interests in such property.

(3) Term interest.—The term "term interest" means—

(A) a life interest in property, or

(B) an interest in property for a term of years.

(4) Valuation rule for certain term interests.—If the nonexercise of rights under a term interest in tangible property would not have a substantial effect on the valuation of the remainder interest in such property—

(A) subparagraph (A) of subsection (a)(2) shall not apply to such term interest, and

(B) the value of such term interest for purposes of applying subsection (a)(1) shall be the amount which the holder of the term interest establishes as the amount for which such interest could be sold to an unrelated third party.

(d) Treatment of transfers of interests in portion of trust.—In the case of a transfer of an income or remainder interest with respect to a specified portion of the property in a trust, only such portion shall be taken into account in applying this section to such transfer.

(e) Member of the family.—For purposes of this section, the term "member of the family" shall have the meaning given such term by section 2704(c)(2).

§ 2703. Certain rights and restrictions disregarded

(a) General rule.—For purposes of this subtitle, the value of any property shall be determined without regard to—

(1) any option, agreement, or other right to acquire or use the property at a price less than the fair market value of the property (without regard to such option, agreement, or right), or

(2) any restriction on the right to sell or use such property.

(b) Exceptions.—Subsection (a) shall not apply to any option, agreement, right, or restriction which meets each of the following requirements:

(1) It is a bona fide business arrangement.

(2) It is not a device to transfer such property to members of the decedent's family for less than full and adequate consideration in money or money's worth.

(3) Its terms are comparable to similar arrangements entered into by persons in an arms' length transaction.

§ 2704. Treatment of certain lapsing rights and restrictions

(a) Treatment of lapsed voting or liquidation rights.—

(1) In general.—For purposes of this subtitle, if—

(A) there is a lapse of any voting or liquidation right in a corporation or partnership, and

(B) the individual holding such right immediately before the lapse and members of such individual's family hold, both before and after the lapse, control of the entity,

such lapse shall be treated as a transfer by such individual by gift, or a transfer which is includible in the gross estate of the decedent, whichever is applicable, in the amount determined under paragraph (2).

(2) Amount of transfer.—For purposes of paragraph (1), the amount determined under this paragraph is the excess (if any) of—

(A) the value of all interests in the entity held by the individual described in paragraph (1) immediately before the lapse (determined as if the voting and liquidation rights were nonlapsing), over

(B) the value of such interests immediately after the lapse.

(3) Similar rights.—The Secretary may by regulations apply this subsection to rights similar to voting and liquidation rights.

(b) Certain restrictions on liquidation disregarded.—

(1) In general.—For purposes of this subtitle, if—

(A) there is a transfer of an interest in a corporation or partnership to (or for the benefit of) a member of the transferor's family, and

(B) the transferor and members of the transferor's family hold, immediately before the transfer, control of the entity,

any applicable restriction shall be disregarded in determining the value of the transferred interest.

(2) Applicable restriction.—For purposes of this subsection, the term "applicable restriction" means any restriction—

(A) which effectively limits the ability of the corporation or partnership to liquidate, and

(B) with respect to which either of the following applies:

(i) The restriction lapses, in whole or in part, after the transfer referred to in paragraph (1).

(ii) The transferor or any member of the transferor's family, either alone or collectively, has the right after such transfer to remove, in whole or in part, the restriction.

(3) Exceptions.—The term "applicable restriction" shall not include—

(A) any commercially reasonable restriction which arises as part of any financing by the corporation or partnership with a person who is not related to the transferor or transferee, or a member of the family of either, or

(B) any restriction imposed, or required to be imposed, by any Federal or State law.

(4) Other restrictions.—The Secretary may by regulations provide that other restrictions shall be disregarded in determining the value of the transfer of any interest in a corporation or partnership to a member of the transferor's family if such restriction has the effect of reducing the value of the transferred interest for purposes of this subtitle but does not ultimately reduce the value of such interest to the transferee.

(c) Definitions and special rules.—For purposes of this section—

(1) Control.—The term "control" has the meaning given such term by section 2701(b)(2).

(2) Member of the family.—The term "member of the family" means, with respect to an individual—

(A) such individual's spouse,

(B) any ancestor or lineal descendant of such individual or such individual's spouse,

(C) any brother or sister of the individual, and

(D) any spouse of any individual described in subparagraph (B) or (C).

(3) Attribution.—The rule of section 2701(e)(3) shall apply for purposes of determining the interests held by any individual.

SUBTITLE C—EMPLOYMENT TAXES*
SUBTITLE D—MISCELLANEOUS EXCISE TAXES

Chapter
31. Retail excise taxes.*
32. Manufacturers excise taxes.*
33. Facilities and services.*
34. Documentary stamp taxes.*
35. Taxes on wagering.*
36. Certain other excise taxes.*
37. Sugar, coconut and palm oil.*
38. Environmental taxes.*
39. Registration—required obligations.*

Chapter
40. General provisions relating to occupational taxes.*
41. Public charities.
42. Private foundations and certain other tax-exempt organizations.
43. Qualified pension, etc., plans.
44. Qualified investment entities.*
45. Windfall profit tax on domestic crude oil.*
46. Golden parachute payments.
47. Certain large group Health Plans.*

*   *   *

*Omitted

CHAPTER 41—PUBLIC CHARITIES

Editorial Summary

Tax on Certain Lobbying Expenditures of Public Charities

Chapter 41 (Secs. 4911, 4912)

Certain organizations are not subject to federal income taxation. These organizations are referred to as tax exempt organizations. See the discussion under the Editorial Summary entitled Tax Exempt Organizations, which precedes Sec. 501.

Tax exempt organizations generally are not permitted to engage in lobbying activities. Doing so can result in the loss of tax exempt status. However, certain tax exempt organizations are permitted to engage in lobbying activities on a limited basis [see Sec. 501(h)]. If the expenditures for such permitted lobbying activities exceed the amount permitted by the statute, two results can occur. First, such excess expenditures can result in the forfeiture of tax exempt status if the lobbying expenditures ceiling is exceeded [Sec. 501(h)(1)]. The lobbying expenditures ceiling is 150 percent of the lobbying nontaxable amount [Sec. 4911(c)(2)]. Second, even if the lobbying expenditures ceiling is not exceeded, a tax is imposed on the excess lobbying expenditures at a 25 percent rate [Sec. 4911(a)(1)]. Excess lobbying expenditures are the excess of the lobbying expenditures over the lobbying nontaxable amount [Sec. 4911(c)(2)].

A Sec. 501(c)(3) organization that makes disqualifying lobbying expenditures is subject to a 5 percent tax on the lobbying expenditures for the tax year [Sec. 4912(a)]. A matching tax may be levied on the management of the organization [Sec. 4912(b)].

§ 4911. Tax on excess expenditures to influence legislation

(a) Tax imposed.—

(1) In general.—There is hereby imposed on the excess lobbying expenditures of any organization to which this section applies a tax equal to 25 percent of the amount of the excess lobbying expenditures for the taxable year.

(2) Organizations to which this section applies.—This section applies to any organization with respect to which an election under section 501(h) (relating to lobbying expenditures by public charities) is in effect for the taxable year.

(b) Excess lobbying expenditures.—For purposes of this section, the term "excess lobbying expenditures" means, for a taxable year, the greater of—

(1) the amount by which the lobbying expenditures made by the organization during the taxable year exceed the lobbying nontaxable amount for such organization for such taxable year, or

(2) the amount by which the grass roots expenditures made by the organization during the taxable year exceed the grass roots nontaxable amount for such organization for such taxable year.

(c) Definitions.—For purposes of this section—

(1) Lobbying expenditures.—The term "lobbying expenditures" means expenditures for the purpose of influencing legislation (as defined in subsection (d)).

(2) Lobbying nontaxable amount.—The lobbying nontaxable amount for any organization for any taxable year is the lesser of (A) $1,000,000 or (B) the amount determined under the following table:

If the exempt purpose expenditures are—	The lobbying nontaxable amount is—
Not over $500,000	20 percent of the exempt purpose expenditures.
Over $500,000 but not over $1,000,000	$100,000, plus 15 percent of the excess of the exempt purpose expenditures over $500,000.
Over $1,000,000 but not over $1,500,000	$175,000 plus 10 percent of the the excess of the exempt purpose expenditures over $1,000,000.
Over $1,500,000	$225,000 plus 5 percent of the excess of the exempt purpose expenditures over $1,500,000.

(3) Grass roots expenditures.—The term "grass roots expenditures" means expenditures for the purpose of influencing legislation (as defined in subsection (d) without regard to paragraph (1)(B) thereof).

(4) Grass roots nontaxable amount.—The grass roots nontaxable amount for any organization for any taxable year is 25 percent of the lobbying nontaxable amount (determined under paragraph (2)) for such organization for such taxable year.

(d) Influencing legislation.—

(1) General rule.—Except as otherwise provided in paragraph (2), for purposes of this section, the term "influencing legislation" means—

(A) any attempt to influence any legislation through an attempt to affect the opinions of the general public or any segment thereof, and

(B) any attempt to influence any legislation through communication with any member or employee of a legislative body, or with any government official or employee who may participate in the formulation of the legislation.

(2) Exceptions.—For purposes of this section, the term "influencing legislation," with respect to an organization, does not include—

(A) making available the results of nonpartisan analysis, study, or research;

(B) providing of technical advice or assistance (where such advice would otherwise constitute the influencing of legislation) to a governmental body or to a committee or other subdivision thereof in response to a written request by such body or subdivision, as the case may be;

(C) appearances before, or communications to, any legislative body with respect to a possible decision of such body which might affect the existence of the organization, its powers and duties, tax-exempt status, or the deduction of contributions to the organization;

(D) communications between the organization and its bona fide members with respect to legislation or proposed legislation of direct interest to the organization and such members, other than communications described in paragraph (3); and

(E) any communication with a government official or employee, other than—

(i) a communication with a member or employee of a legislative body (where such communication would otherwise constitute the influencing of legislation), or

(ii) a communication the principal purpose of which is to influence legislation.

(3) Communications with members.—

(A) A communication between an organization and any bona fide member of such organization to directly encourage such member to communicate as provided in paragraph (1)(B) shall be treated as a communication described in paragraph (1)(B).

(B) A communication between an organization and any bona fide member of such organization to directly encourage such member to urge persons other than members to communicate as provided in either subparagraph (A) or subparagraph (B) of paragraph (1) shall be treated as a communication described in paragraph (1)(A).

(e) Other definitions and special rules.—For purposes of this section—

(1) Exempt purpose expenditures.—

(A) In general.—The term "exempt purpose expenditures" means, with respect to any organization for any taxable year, the total of the amounts paid or incurred by such organization to accomplish purposes described in section 170(c)(2)(B) (relating to religious, charitable, educational, etc., purposes).

(B) Certain amounts included.—The term "exempt purpose expenditures" includes—

(i) administrative expenses paid or incurred for purposes described in section 170(c)(2)(B), and

(ii) amounts paid or incurred for the purpose of influencing legislation (whether or not for purposes described in section 170(c)(2)(B)).

(C) Certain amounts excluded.—The term "exempt purpose expenditures" does not include amounts paid or incurred to or for—

(i) a separate fundraising unit of such organization, or

(ii) one or more other organizations, if such amounts are paid or incurred primarily for fundraising.

(2) Legislation.—The term "legislation" includes action with respect to Acts, bills, resolutions, or similar items by the Congress, any State legislature, any local council, or similar governing body, or by the public in a referendum, initiative, constitutional amendment, or similar procedure.

(3) Action.—The term "action" is limited to the introduction, amendment, enactment, defeat, or repeal of Acts, bills, resolutions, or similar items.

(4) Depreciation, etc., treated as expenditures.—In computing expenditures paid or incurred for the purpose of influencing legislation (within the meaning of subsection (b)(1) or (b)(2)) or exempt purpose expenditures (as defined in paragraph (1)), amounts properly chargeable to capital account shall not be taken into account. There shall be taken into account a reasonable allowance for exhaustion, wear and tear, obsolescence, or amortization. Such allowance shall be computed only on the basis of the straight-line method of depreciation. For purposes of this section, a determination of whether an amount is properly chargeable to capital account shall be made on the basis of the principles that apply under subtitle A to amounts which are paid or incurred in a trade or business.

(f) Affiliated organizations.—

(1) In general.—Except as otherwise provided in paragraph (4), if for a taxable year two or more organizations described in section 501(c)(3) are members of an affiliated group of organizations as defined in paragraph (2), and an election under section 501(h) is effective for at least one such organization for such year, then—

(A) the determination as to whether excess lobbying expenditures have been made and the determination as to whether the expenditure limits of section 501(h)(1) have been exceeded shall be made as though such affiliated group is one organization,

(B) if such group has excess lobbying expenditures, each such organization as to which an election under section 501(h) is effective for such year shall be treated as an organization which has excess lobbying expenditures in an amount which equals such organization's proportionate share of such group's excess lobbying expenditures,

(C) if the expenditure limits of section 501(h)(1) are exceeded, each such organization as to which an election under section 501(h) is effective for such year shall be treated as an organization which is not described in section 501(c)(3) by reason of the application of 501(h), and

(D) subparagraphs (C) and (D) of subsection (d)(2), paragraph (3) or subsection (d), and clause (i) of subsection (e)(1)(C) shall be applied as if such affiliated group were one organization.

(2) Definition of affiliation.—For purposes of paragraph (1), two organizations are members of an affiliated group of organizations but only if—

(A) the governing instrument of one such organization requires it to be bound by decisions of the other organization on legislative issues, or

(B) the governing board of one such organization includes persons who—

(i) are specifically designated representatives of another such organization or are members of the governing board, officers, or paid executive staff members of such other organization, and

(ii) by aggregating their votes, have sufficient voting power to cause or prevent action on legislative issues by the first such organization.

(3) Different taxable years.—If members of an affiliated group of organizations have different taxable years, their expenditures shall be computed for purposes of this section in a manner to be prescribed by regulations promulgated by the Secretary.

(4) Limited control.—If two or more organizations are members of an affiliated group of organizations (as defined in paragraph (2) without regard to subparagraph (B) thereof), no two members of such affiliated group are affiliated (as defined in paragraph (2) without regard to subparagraph (A) thereof), and the governing instrument of no such organization requires it to be bound by decisions of any of the other such organizations on legislative issues other than as to action with respect to Acts, bills, resolutions, or similar items by the Congress, then—

(A) in the case of any organization whose decisions bind one or more members of such affiliated group, directly or indirectly, the determination as to whether such organization has paid or incurred excess lobbying expenditures and the determination as to whether such organization has exceeded the expenditure limits of section 501(h)(1) shall be made as though such organization has paid or incurred those amounts paid or incurred by such members of such affiliated group to influence legislation with respect to Acts, bills, resolutions, or similar items by the Congress, and

(B) in the case of any organization to which subparagraph (A) does not apply, but which is a member of such affiliated group, the determination as to whether such organization has paid or incurred excess lobbying expenditures and the determination as to whether such organization has exceeded the expenditure limits of section 501(h)(1) shall be made as though such organization is not a member of such affiliated group.

§ 4912. Tax on disqualifying lobbying expenditures of certain organizations

(a) Tax on organization.—If an organization to which this section applies is not described in section 501(c)(3) for any taxable year by reason of making lobbying expenditures, there is hereby imposed a tax on the lobbying expenditures of such organization for such taxable year equal to 5 percent of the amount of such expenditures. The tax imposed by this subsection shall be paid by the organization.

(b) On management.—If tax is imposed under subsection (a) on the lobbying expenditures of any organization, there is hereby imposed on the agreement of any organization manager to the making of any such expenditures, knowing that such expenditures are likely to result in the organization not being described in section 501(c)(3), a tax equal to 5 percent of the amount of such expenditures, unless such agreement is not willful and is due to reasonable cause. The tax imposed by this subsection shall be paid by any manager who agreed to the making of the expenditures.

(c) Organizations to which section applies.—

(1) In general.—Except as provided in paragraph (2), this section shall apply to any organization which was exempt (or was determined by the Secretary to be exempt) from taxation under section 501(a) by reason of being an organization described in section 501(c)(3).

(2) Exceptions.—This section shall not apply to any organization—

(A) to which an election under section 501(h) applies,

(B) which is a disqualified organization (within the meaning of section 501(h)(5)), or

(C) which is a private foundation.

(d) Definitions.—

(1) Lobbying expenditures.—The term "lobbying expenditure" means any amount paid or incurred by the organization in carrying on propaganda, or otherwise attempting to influence legislation.

(2) Organization manager.—The term "organization manager" has the meaning given to such term by section 4955(f)(2).

(3) Joint and several liability.—If more than 1 person is liable under subsection (b), all such persons shall be jointly and severally liable under such subsection.

CHAPTER 42—PRIVATE FOUNDATIONS AND CERTAIN OTHER TAX-EXEMPT ORGANIZATIONS

Subchapter

* * *

*Omitted

SUBCHAPTER D—FAILURE BY CERTAIN CHARITABLE ORGANIZATIONS TO MEET CERTAIN QUALIFICATION REQUIREMENTS

Editorial Summary

Intermediate Sanctions

Subchapter D of Chapter 42 (Sec. 4958)

Prior to 1996, the IRS had only two options available for dealing with exempt organizations (other than private foundations) engaging in prohibited transactions. First, it could attempt to subject part or all of the organization's income to Federal income tax. Second, it could revoke the exempt status of the organization. For private foundations, an additional option was available. The IRS could impose certain taxes on private foundations for engaging in so-called prohibited transactions.

Tax legislation enacted in 1996 added another option to the IRS toolbox—**intermediate sanctions**—for so-called public charities. The intermediate sanctions take the form of excise taxes imposed on disqualified persons (any individuals who are in a position to exercise substantial influence over the affairs of the organization) who engaged in *excess benefit transactions* and on exempt organization managers who participate in such a transaction knowing that it is improper. Such excess benefit transactions include transactions in which a disqualified person engages in a non-fair market value transaction with the exempt organization or receives unreasonable compensation.

§ 4958. Taxes on excess benefit transactions

(a) Initial taxes.—

(1) On the disqualified person.—There is hereby imposed on each excess benefit transaction a tax equal to 25 percent of the excess benefit. The tax imposed by this paragraph shall be paid by any disqualified person referred to in subsection (f)(1) with respect to such transaction.

(2) On the management.—In any case in which a tax is imposed by paragraph (1), there is hereby imposed on the participation of any organization manager in the excess benefit transaction, knowing that it is such a transaction, a tax equal to 10 percent of the excess benefit, unless such participation is not willful and is due to reasonable cause. The tax imposed by this paragraph shall be paid by any organization manager who participated in the excess benefit transaction.

(b) Additional tax on the disqualified person.—In any case in which an initial tax is imposed by subsection (a)(l) on an excess benefit transaction and the excess benefit involved in such transaction is not corrected within the taxable period, there is hereby imposed a tax equal to 200 percent of the excess benefit involved. The tax imposed by this subsection shall be paid by any disqualified person referred to in subsection (f)(1) with respect to such transaction.

(c) Excess benefit transaction; excess benefit.—For purposes of this section—

(1) Excess benefit transaction.—

(A) In general.—The term "excess benefit transaction" means any transaction in which an economic benefit is provided by an applicable tax-exempt organization directly or indirectly to or for the use of any disqualified person if the value of the economic benefit provided exceeds the value of the consideration (including the performance of services) received for providing such benefit. For purposes of the preceding sentence, an economic benefit shall not be treated as consideration for the performance of services unless such organization clearly indicated its intent to so treat such benefit.

(B) Excess benefit.—The term "excess benefit" means the excess referred to in subparagraph (A).

(2) Special rules for donor advised funds.—In the case of any donor advised fund (as defined in section 4966(d)(2))—

(A) the term "excess benefit transaction" includes any grant, loan, compensation, or other similar payment from such fund to a person described in subsection (f)(7) with respect to such fund, and

(B) the term "excess benefit" includes, with respect to any transaction described in subparagraph (A), the amount of any such grant, loan, compensation, or other similar payment.

(3) Special rules for supporting organizations.—

(A) In general.—In the case of any organization described in section 509(a)(3)—

(i) the term "excess benefit transaction" includes—

(I) any grant, loan, compensation, or other similar payment provided by such organization to a person described in subparagraph (B), and

(II) any loan provided by such organization to a disqualified person (other than an organization described in subparagraph (C)(ii)), and

(ii) the term "excess benefit" includes, with respect to any transaction described in clause (i), the amount of any such grant, loan, compensation, or other similar payment.

(B) Person described.—A person is described in this subparagraph if such person is—

(i) a substantial contributor to such organization,

(ii) a member of the family (determined under section 4958(f)(4)) of an individual described in clause (i), or

(iii) a 35-percent controlled entity (as defined in section 4958(f)(3) by substituting "persons described in clause (i) or (ii) of section 4958(c)(3)(B)" for "persons described in subparagraph (A) or (B) of paragraph (1)" in subparagraph (A)(i) thereof).

(C) Substantial contributor.—For purposes of this paragraph—

(i) In general.—The term "substantial contributor" means any person who contributed or bequeathed an aggregate amount of more than $5,000 to the organization, if such amount is more than 2 percent of the total contributions and bequests received by the organization before the close of the taxable year of the organization in which the contribution or bequest is received by the organization from such person. In the case of a trust, such term also means the creator of the trust. Rules similar to the rules of subparagraphs (B) and (C) of section 507(d)(2) shall apply for purposes of this subparagraph.

(ii) Exception.—Such term shall not include—

(I) any organization described in paragraph (1), (2), or (4) of section 509(a), and

(II) any organization which is treated as described in such paragraph (2) by reason of the last sentence of section 509(a) and which is a supported organization (as defined in section 509(f)(3)) of the organization to which subparagraph (A) applies.

(4) Authority to include certain other private inurement.—To the extent provided in regulations prescribed by the Secretary, the term "excess benefit transaction" includes any transaction in which the amount of any economic benefit provided to or for the use of a disqualified person is determined in whole or in part by the revenues of 1 or more activities of the organization but only if such transaction results in inurement not permitted under paragraph (3) or (4) of section 501(c), as the case may be. In the case of any such transaction, the excess benefit shall be the amount of the inurement not so permitted.

(d) Special rules.—For purposes of this section—

(1) Joint and several liability.—If more than 1 person is liable for any tax imposed by subsection (a) or subsection (b), all such persons shall be jointly and severally liable for such tax.

(2) Limit for management.—With respect to any 1 excess benefit transaction, the maximum amount of the tax imposed by subsection (a)(2) shall not exceed $20,000.

(e) Applicable tax-exempt organization.—For purposes of this subchapter, the term "applicable tax-exempt organization" means—

(1) any organization which (without regard to any excess benefit) would be described in paragraph (3), (4), or (29) of section 501(c) and exempt from tax under section 501(a), and

(2) any organization which was described in paragraph (1) at any time during the 5-year period ending on the date of the transaction.

Such term shall not include a private foundation (as defined in section 509(a)).

(f) Other definitions.—For purposes of this section—

(1) Disqualified person.—The term "disqualified person" means, with respect to any transaction—

(A) any person who was, at any time during the 5-year period ending on the date of such transaction, in a position to exercise substantial influence over the affairs of the organization,

(B) a member of the family of an individual described in subparagraph (A),

(C) a 35-percent controlled entity,

(D) any person who is described in subparagraph (A), (B), or (C) with respect to an organization described in section 509(a)(3) and organized and operated exclusively for the benefit of, to perform the functions of, or to carry out the purposes of the applicable tax-exempt organization,

(E) which involves a donor advised fund (as defined in section 4966(d)(2)), any person who is described in paragraph (7) with respect to such donor advised fund (as so defined), and

(F) which involves a sponsoring organization (as defined in section 4966(d)(1)), any person who is described in paragraph (8) with respect to such sponsoring organization (as so defined).

(2) Organization manager.—The term "organization manager" means, with respect to any applicable tax-exempt organization, any officer, director, or trustee of such organization (or any individual having powers or responsibilities similar to those of officers, directors, or trustees of the organization).

(3) 35-percent controlled entity.—

(A) In general.—The term "35-percent controlled entity" means—

(i) a corporation in which persons described in subparagraph (A) or (B) of paragraph (1) own more than 35 percent of the total combined voting power,

(ii) a partnership in which such persons own more than 35 percent of the profits interest, and

(iii) a trust or estate in which such persons own more than 35 percent of the beneficial interest.

(B) Constructive ownership rules.—Rules similar to the rules of paragraphs (3) and (4) of section 4946(a) shall apply for purposes of this paragraph.

(4) Family members.—The members of an individual's family shall be determined under section 4946(d); except that such members also shall include the brothers and sisters (whether by the whole or half blood) of the individual and their spouses.

(5) Taxable period.—The term "taxable period" means, with respect to any excess benefit transaction, the period beginning with the date on which the transaction occurs and ending on the earliest of—

(A) the date of mailing a notice of deficiency under section 6212 with respect to the tax imposed by subsection (a)(1), or

(B) the date on which the tax imposed by subsection (a)(1) is assessed.

(6) Correction.—The terms "correction" and "correct" mean, with respect to any excess benefit transaction, undoing the excess benefit to the extent possible, and taking any additional measures necessary to place the organization in a financial position not worse than that in which it would be if the disqualified person were dealing under the highest fiduciary standards, except that in the case of any correction of an excess benefit transaction described in subsection (c)(2), no amount repaid in a manner prescribed by the Secretary may be held in any donor advised fund.

(7) Donors and donor advisors.—For purposes of paragraph (1)(E), a person is described in this paragraph if such person—

(A) is described in section 4966(d)(2)(A)(iii),

(B) is a member of the family of an individual described in subparagraph (A), or

(C) is a 35-percent controlled entity (as defined in paragraph (3) by substituting "persons described in subparagraph (A) or (B) of paragraph (7)" for "persons described in subparagraph (A) or (B) of paragraph (1)" in subparagraph (A)(i) thereof).

(8) Investment advisors.—For purposes of paragraph (1)(F)—

(A) In general.—A person is described in this paragraph if such person—

(i) is an investment advisor,

(ii) is a member of the family of an individual described in clause (i), or

(iii) is a 35-percent controlled entity (as defined in paragraph (3) by substituting "persons described in clause (i) or (ii) of paragraph (8)(A)" for "persons described in subparagraph (A) or (B) of paragraph (1)" in subparagraph (A)(i) thereof).

(B) Investment advisor defined.—For purposes of subparagraph (A), the term "investment advisor" means, with respect to any sponsoring organization (as defined in section 4966(d)(1)), any person (other than an employee of such organization) compensated by such organization for managing the investment of, or providing investment advice with respect to, assets maintained in donor advised funds (as defined in section 4966(d)(2)) owned by such organization.

* * *

CHAPTER 43—QUALIFIED PENSION, ETC., PLANS

Editorial Summary

Tax on Qualified Plans

Chapter 43 (Secs. 4971–4980G)

In order to receive the beneficial treatment of a qualified retirement plan, Subchapter D of Chapter 1 imposes qualification and maintenance requirements. Included are provisions on discrimination, coverage, participation, vesting, contributions, funding, distributions, and prohibited transactions. Failure to satisfy the statutory requirements can produce two potential negative results. First, beneficial tax consequences can be lost by the plan not receiving qualified plan status [see Subchapter D of Chapter 1]. Second, various excise taxes can be imposed. Such excise tax provisions appear in Chapter 43.

§ 4971. Taxes on failure to meet minimum funding standards

(a) Initial tax.—If at any time during any taxable year an employer maintains a plan to which section 412 applies, there is hereby imposed for the taxable year a tax equal to—

(1) in the case of a single-employer plan, 10 percent of the aggregate unpaid minimum required contributions for all plan years remaining unpaid as of the end of any plan year ending with or within the taxable year, and

(2) in the case of a multiemployer plan, 5 percent of the accumulated funding deficiency determined under section 431 as of the end of any plan year ending with or within the taxable year.

(b) Additional tax.—If—

(1) a tax is imposed under subsection (a)(1) on any unpaid minimum required contribution and such amount remains unpaid as of the close of the taxable period, or

(2) a tax is imposed under subsection (a)(2) on any accumulated funding deficiency and the accumulated funding deficiency is not corrected within the taxable period,

there is hereby imposed a tax equal to 100 percent of the unpaid minimum required contribution or accumulated funding deficiency, whichever is applicable, to the extent not so paid or corrected.

(c) Definitions.—For purposes of this section—

(1) Accumulated funding deficiency.— The term "accumulated funding deficiency" has the meaning given to such term by section 431.

(2) Correct.— The term "correct" means, with respect to an accumulated funding deficiency, the contribution, to or under the plan, of the amount necessary to reduce such accumulated funding deficiency as of the end of a plan year in which such deficiency arose to zero.

(3) Taxable period.— The term "taxable period" means, with respect to an accumulated funding deficiency, or unpaid minimum required distribution, whichever is applicable, the period beginning with the end of a plan year in which there is an accumulated funding deficiency or unpaid minimum required contribution, whichever is applicable and ending on the earlier of—

(A) the date of mailing of a notice of deficiency with respect to the tax imposed by subsection (a), or

(B) the date on which the tax imposed by subsection (a) is assessed.

(4) Unpaid minimum required contribution.—

(A) In general.—The term "unpaid minimum required contribution" means, with respect to any plan year, any minimum required contribution under section 430 for the plan year which is not paid on or before the due date (as determined under section 430 (j)(1)) for the plan year.

(B) Ordering rule.—Any payment to or under a plan for any plan year shall be allocated first to unpaid minimum required contributions for all preceding plan years on a first-in, first-out basis and then to the minimum required contribution under section 430 for the plan year.

(d) Notification of the Secretary of Labor.—Before issuing a notice of deficiency with respect to the tax imposed by subsection (a) or (b), the Secretary shall notify the Secretary of Labor and provide him a reasonable opportunity (but not more than 60 days)—

(1) to require the employer responsible for contributing to or under the plan to eliminate the accumulated funding deficiency or unpaid minimum required contribution, whichever is applicable, or

(2) to comment on the imposition of such tax.

In the case of a multiemployer plan which is in reorganization under section 418, the same notice and opportunity shall be provided to the Pension Benefit Guaranty Corporation.

(e) Liability for tax.—

(1) In general.—Except as provided in paragraph (2), the tax imposed by subsection (a), (b), or (f) shall be paid by the employer responsible for contributing to or under the plan the amount described in section 412(a)(2).

(2) Joint and several liability where employer member of controlled group.—

(A) In general.—In the case of a plan other than a multiemployer plan, if the employer referred to in paragraph (1) is a member of a controlled group, each member of such group shall be jointly and severally liable for the tax imposed by subsection (a), (b), (f), or (g).

(B) Controlled group.—For purposes of subparagraph (A), the term "controlled group" means any group treated as a single employer under subsection (b), (c), (m), or (o) of section 414.

(f) Failure to pay liquidity shortfall.—

(1) In general.—In the case of a plan to which section 430(j)(4) applies, there is hereby imposed a tax of 10 percent of the excess (if any) of—

(A) the amount of the liquidity shortfall for any quarter, over

(B) the amount of such shortfall which is paid by the required installment under section 430(j) for such quarter (but only if such installment is paid on or before the due date for such installment).

(2) Additional tax.—If the plan has a liquidity shortfall as of the close of any quarter and as of the close of each of the following 4 quarters, there is hereby imposed a tax equal to 100 percent of the amount on which tax was imposed by paragraph (1) for such first quarter.

(3) Definitions and special rule.—

(A) Liquidity shortfall; quarter.—For purposes of this subsection, the terms "liquidity shortfall" and "quarter" have the respective meanings given such terms by section 412(m)(5).

(B) Special rule.—If the tax imposed by paragraph (2) is paid with respect to any liquidity shortfall for any quarter, no further tax shall be imposed by this subsection on such shortfall for such quarter.

(4) Waiver by Secretary.—If the taxpayer establishes to the satisfaction of the Secretary that—

(A) the liquidity shortfall described in paragraph (1) was due to reasonable cause and not willful neglect, and

(B) reasonable steps have been taken to remedy such liquidity shortfall,

the Secretary may waive all or part of the tax imposed by this subsection.

* * *

(h) Cross references.—

For disallowance of deduction for taxes paid under this section, see section 275.

* * *

§ 4972. Tax on nondeductible contributions to qualified employer plans

(a) Tax imposed.—In the case of any qualified employer plan, there is hereby imposed a tax equal to 10 percent of the nondeductible contributions under the plan (determined as of the close of the taxable year of the employer).

(b) Employer liable for tax.—The tax imposed by this section shall be paid by the employer making the contributions.

(c) Nondeductible contributions.—For purposes of this section—

(1) In general.—The term "nondeductible contributions" means, with respect to any qualified employer plan, the sum of—

(A) the excess (if any) of—

(i) the amount contributed for the taxable year by the employer to or under such plan, over

(ii) the amount allowable as a deduction under section 404 for such contributions (determined without regard to subsection (e) thereof), and

(B) the amount determined under this subsection for the preceding taxable year reduced by the sum of—

(i) the portion of the amount so determined returned to the employer during the taxable year, and

(ii) the portion of the amount so determined deductible under section 404 for the taxable year (determined without regard to subsection (e) thereof).

(2) Ordering rule for section 404.—For purposes of paragraph (1), the amount allowable as a deduction under section 404 for any taxable year shall be treated as—

(A) first from carryforwards to such taxable year from preceding taxable years (in order of time), and

(B) then from contributions made during such taxable year.

(3) Contributions which may be returned to employer.—In determining the amount of nondeductible contributions for any taxable year, there shall not be taken into account any contribution for such taxable year which is distributed to the employer in a distribution described in section 4980(c)(2)(B)(ii) if such distribution is made on or before the last day on which a contribution may be made for such taxable year under section 404(a)(6).

(4) Special rule for self-employed individuals.—For purposes of paragraph (1), if—

(A) the amount which is required to be contributed to a plan under section 412 on behalf of an individual who is an employee (within the meaning of section 401(c)(1)), exceeds

(B) the earned income (within the meaning of section 404(a)(8)) of such individual derived from the trade or business with respect to which such plan is established,

such excess shall be treated as an amount allowable as a deduction under section 404.

(5) Pre–1987 contributions.—The term "nondeductible contribution" shall not include any contribution made for a taxable year beginning before January 1, 1987.

(6) Exceptions.—In determining the amount of nondeductible contributions for any taxable year, there shall not be taken into account—

(A) so much of the contributions to 1 or more defined contribution plans which are not deductible when contributed solely because of section 404(a)(7) as does not exceed the amount of contributions described in section 401(m)(4)(A), or

(i) the amount of contributions not in excess of 6 percent of compensation (within the meaning of section 404(a) and as adjusted under section 404(a)(12)) paid or accrued (during the taxable year for which the contributions were made) to beneficiaries under the plans, or

(ii) the amount of contributions described in section 401(m)(4)(A), or

(B) so much of the contributions to a simple retirement account (within the meaning of section 408(p)) or a simple plan (within the meaning of section 401(k)(11)) which are not deductible when contributed solely because such contributions are not made in connection with a trade or business of the employer.

For purposes of subparagraph (A), the deductible limits under section 404(a)(7) shall first be applied to amounts contributed to a defined benefit plan and then to amounts described in subparagraph (A). Subparagraph (B) shall not apply to contributions made on behalf of the employer or a member of the employer's family (as defined in section 447(e)(1)).

(7) Defined benefit plan exception.—In determining the amount of nondeductible contributions for any taxable year, an employer may elect for such year not to take into account any contributions to a defined benefit plan except to the extent that such contributions except, in the case of a multiemployer plan, to the extent that such contributions exceed the full-funding limitation (as defined in section 431(c)(6)). For purposes of this paragraph, the deductible limits under section 404(a)(7) shall first be applied to amounts contributed to defined contribution plans and then to amounts described in this paragraph. If an employer makes an election under this paragraph for a taxable year, paragraph (6) shall not apply to such employer for such taxable year.

(d) Definitions.—For purposes of this section—

(1) Qualified employer plan.—

(A) In general.—The term "qualified employer plan" means—

(i) any plan meeting the requirements of section 401(a) which includes a trust exempt from tax under section 501(a),

(ii) an annuity plan described in section 403(a),

(iii) any simplified employee pension (within the meaning of section 408(k)), and

(iv) any simple retirement account (within the meaning of section 408(p)).

(B) Exemption for governmental and tax exempt plans.—The term "qualified employer plan" does not include a plan described in subparagraph (A) or (B) of section 4980(c)(1).

(2) Employer.— In the case of a plan which provides contributions or benefits for employees some or all of whom are self-employed individuals within the meaning of section 401(c)(1), the term "employer" means the person treated as the employer under section 401(c)(4).

§ 4973. Tax on excess contributions to certain tax-favored accounts and annuities

(a) Tax imposed.—In the case of—

(1) an individual retirement account (within the meaning of section 408(a)),

(2) an Archer MSA (within the meaning of section 220(d)),

(3) an individual retirement annuity (within the meaning of section 408(b)), a custodial account treated as an annuity contract under section 403(b)(7)(A) (relating to custodial accounts for regulated investment company stock),

(4) a Coverdell education savings account (as defined in section 530), or

(5) a health savings account (within the meaning of section 223(d)),

there is imposed for each taxable year a tax in an amount equal to 6 percent of the amount of the excess contributions to such individual's accounts or annuities (determined as of the close of the taxable year). The amount of such tax for any taxable year shall not exceed 6 percent of the value of the account or annuity (determined as of the close of the taxable year). In the case of an endowment contract described in section 408(b), the tax imposed by this section does not apply to any amount allocable to life, health, accident, or other insurance under such contract. The tax imposed by this subsection shall be paid by such individual.

(b) Excess contributions.—For purposes of this section, in the case of individual retirement accounts or individual retirement annuities, the term "excess contributions" means the sum of—

(1) the excess (if any) of—

(A) the amount contributed for the taxable year to the accounts or for the annuities (other than a contribution to a Roth IRA or a rollover contribution described in section 402(c), 403(a)(4), 403(b)(8), 408(d)(3), or 457(e)(16)), over

(B) the amount allowable as a deduction under section 219 for such contributions, and

(2) the amount determined under this subsection for the preceding taxable year reduced by the sum of—

(A) the distributions out of the account for the taxable year which were included in the gross income of the payee under section 408(d)(l),

(B) the distributions out of the account for the taxable year to which section 408(d) (5) applies, and

(C) the excess (if any) of the maximum amount allowable as a deduction under section 219 for the taxable year over the amount contributed (determined without regard to section 219(f)(6)) to the accounts or for the annuities (including the amount contributed to a Roth IRA) for the taxable year.

For purposes of this subsection, any contribution which is distributed from the individual retirement account or the individual retirement annuity in a distribution to which section 408(d)(4) applies shall be treated as an amount not contributed. For purposes of paragraphs (1)(B) and (2)(C), the amount allowable as a deduction under section 219 shall be computed without regard to section 219(g).

(c) Section 403(b) contracts.—For purposes of this section, in the case of a custodial account referred to in subsection (a)(3), the term "excess contributions" means the sum of—

(1) the excess (if any) of the amount contributed for the taxable year to such account (other than a rollover contribution described in section 403(b)(8) or 408(d)(3)(A)(iii)), over the lesser of the amount excludable from gross income under section 403(b) or the amount permitted to be contributed under the limitations contained in section 415 (or under whichever such section is applicable, if only one is applicable), and

(2) the amount determined under this subsection for the preceding taxable year, reduced by—

(A) the excess (if any) of the lesser of (i) the amount excludable from gross income under section 403(b) or (ii) the amount permitted to be contributed under the limitations contained in section 415 over the amount contributed to the account for the taxable year (or under whichever such section in applicable, if only one is applicable), and

(B) the sum of the distributions out of the account (for all prior taxable years) which are included in gross income under section 72(e).

(d) Excess contributions to Archer MSAs.—For purposes of this section, in the case of Archer MSAs (within the meaning of section 220(d)), the term "excess contributions" means the sum of—

(1) the aggregate amount contributed for the taxable year to the accounts (other than rollover contributions described in section 220(f)(5) which is neither excludable from gross income under section 106(b) nor allowable as a deduction under section 220 for such year, and

(2) the amount determined under this subsection for the preceding taxable year, reduced by the sum of—

(A) the distributions out of the accounts which were included in gross income under section 220(f)(2), and

(B) the excess (if any) of—

(i) the maximum amount allowable as a deduction under section 220(b)(1) (determined without regard to section 106(b)) for the taxable year, over

(ii) the amount contributed to the accounts for the taxable year.

For purposes of this subsection, any contribution which is distributed out of the Archer MSA in a distribution to which section 220(f)(3) or section 138(c)(3) applies shall be treated as an amount not contributed.

(e) Excess contributions to Coverdell education savings accounts.—For purposes of this section—

(1) In general.—In the case of Coverdell education savings accounts maintained for the benefit of any 1 beneficiary, the term "excess contributions" means the sum of—

(A) the amount by which the amount contributed for the taxable year to such accounts exceeds $2,000 (or, if less, the sum of the maximum amounts permitted to be contributed under section 530(c) by the contributors to such accounts for such year), and

(B) the amount determined under this subsection for the preceding taxable year, reduced by the sum of—

(i) the distributions out of the accounts for the taxable year (other than rollover distributions), and

(ii) the excess (if any) of the maximum amount which may be contributed to the accounts for the taxable year over the amount contributed to the accounts for the taxable year.

(2) Special rules.—For purposes of paragraph (1), the following contributions shall not be taken into account:

(A) Any contribution which is distributed out of the Coverdell education savings account in a distribution to which section 530(d)(4)(C) applies.

(B) Any rollover contribution.

(f) Excess contributions to Roth IRAs.—For purposes of this section, in the case of contributions to a Roth IRA (within the meaning of section 408A(b)), the term "excess contributions" means the sum of—

(1) the excess (if any) of—

(A) the amount contributed for the taxable year to Roth IRAs (other than a qualified rollover contribution described in section 408A(e)), over

(B) the amount allowable as a contribution under sections 408A (c)(2) and (c)(3), and

(2) the amount determined under this subsection for the preceding taxable year, reduced by the sum of—

(A) the distributions out of the accounts for the taxable year, and

(B) the excess (if any) of the maximum amount allowable as a contribution under sections 408A (c)(2) and (c)(3) for the taxable year over the amount contributed by the individual to all individual retirement plans for the taxable year.

For purposes of this subsection, any contribution which is distributed from a Roth IRA in a distribution described in section 408(d)(4) shall be treated as an amount not contributed.

(g) Excess contributions to health savings accounts.—For purposes of this section, in the case of health savings accounts (within the meaning of section 223(d)), the term "excess contributions" means the sum of—

(1) the aggregate amount contributed for the taxable year to the accounts (other than a rollover contribution described in section 220(f)(5) or 223(f)(5)) which is neither excludable from gross income under section 106(d) nor allowable as a deduction under section 223 for such year, and

(2) the amount determined under this subsection for the preceding taxable year, reduced by the sum of—

(A) the distributions out of the accounts which were included in gross income under section 223(f)(2), and

(B) the excess (if any) of—

(i) the maximum amount allowable as a deduction under section 223(b) (determined without regard to section 106(d)) for the taxable year, over

(ii) the amount contributed to the accounts for the taxable year.

For purposes of this subsection, any contribution which is distributed out of the health savings account in a distribution to which section 223(f)(3) applies shall be treated as an amount not contributed.

(d) Waiver of tax in certain cases.—If the taxpayer establishes to the satisfaction of the Secretary that—

(1) the shortfall described in subsection (a) in the amount distributed during any taxable year was due to reasonable error, and

(2) reasonable steps are being taken to remedy the shortfall,

the Secretary may waive the tax imposed by subsection (a) for the taxable year.

§ 4974. Excise tax on certain accumulations in qualified retirement plans

(a) General rule.—If the amount distributed during the taxable year of the payee under any qualified retirement plan or any eligible deferred compensation plan (as defined in section 457(b)) is less than the minimum required distribution for such taxable year, there is hereby imposed a tax equal to 50 percent of the amount by which such minimum required distribution exceeds the actual amount distributed during the taxable year. The tax imposed by this section shall be paid by the payee.

(b) Minimum required distribution.—For purposes of this section, the term "minimum required distribution" means the minimum amount required to be distributed during a taxable year under section 401(a)(9), 403(b)(10), 408(a)(6), 408(b)(3), or 457(d)(2), as the case may be, as determined under regulations prescribed by the Secretary.

(c) Qualified retirement plan.—For purposes of this section, the term "qualified retirement plan" means—

(1) a plan described in section 401(a) which includes a trust exempt from tax under section 501(a),

(2) an annuity plan described in section 403(a),

(3) an annuity contract described in section 403(b),

(4) an individual retirement account described in section 408(a), or

(5) an individual retirement annuity described in section 408(b).

Such term includes any plan, contract, account, or annuity which, at any time, has been determined by the Secretary to be such a plan, contract, account, or annuity.

§ 4975. Tax on prohibited transactions

(a) Initial taxes on disqualified person.—There is hereby imposed a tax on each prohibited transaction. The rate of tax shall be equal to 15 percent of the amount involved with respect to the prohibited transaction for each year (or part thereof) in the taxable period. The tax imposed by this subsection shall be paid by any disqualified person who participates in the prohibited transaction (other than a fiduciary acting only as such).

(b) Additional taxes on disqualified person.—In any case in which an initial tax is imposed by subsection (a) on a prohibited transaction and the transaction is not corrected within the taxable period, there is hereby imposed a tax equal to 100 percent of the amount involved. The tax imposed by this subsection shall be paid by any disqualified person who participated in the prohibited transaction (other than a fiduciary acting only as such).

(c) Prohibited transaction.—

(1) General rule.—For purposes of this section, the term "prohibited transaction" means any direct or indirect—

(A) sale or exchange, or leasing, of any property between a plan and a disqualified person;

(B) lending of money or other extension of credit between a plan and a disqualified person;

(C) furnishing of goods, services, or facilities between a plan and a disqualified person;

(D) transfer to, or use by or for the benefit of, a disqualified person of the income or assets of a plan;

(E) act by a disqualified person who is a fiduciary whereby he deals with the income or assets of a plan in his own interest or for his own account; or

(F) receipt of any consideration for his own personal account by any disqualified person who is a fiduciary from any party dealing with the plan in connection with a transaction involving the income or assets of the plan.

(2) Special exemption.—The Secretary shall establish an exemption procedure for purposes of this subsection. Pursuant to such procedure, he may grant a conditional or unconditional exemption of any disqualified person or transaction, orders of disqualified persons or transactions, from all or part of the restrictions imposed by paragraph (1) of this subsection. Action under this subparagraph may be taken only after consultation and coordination with the Secretary of Labor. The Secretary may not grant an exemption under this paragraph unless he finds that such exemption is—

(A) administratively feasible,

(B) in the interests of the plan and of its participants and beneficiaries, and

(C) protective of the rights of participants and beneficiaries of the plan.

Before granting an exemption under this paragraph, the Secretary shall require adequate notice to be given to interested persons and shall publish notice in the Federal Register of the pendency of such exemption and shall afford interested persons an opportunity to present views. No exemption may be granted under this paragraph with respect to a transaction described in subparagraph (E) or (F) of paragraph (1) unless the Secretary affords an opportunity for a hearing and makes a determination on the record with respect to the findings required under subparagraphs (A), (B), and (C) of this paragraph, except that in lieu of such hearing the Secretary may accept any record made by the Secretary of Labor with respect to an application for exemption under section 408(a) of title I of the Employee Retirement Income Security Act of 1974.

(3) Special rule for individual retirement accounts.—An individual for whose benefit an individual retirement account is established and his beneficiaries shall be exempt from the tax imposed by this section with respect to any transaction concerning such account (which would otherwise be taxable under this section) if, with respect to such transaction, the account ceases to be an individual retirement account by reason of the application of section 408(e)(2)(A) or if section 408(e)(4) applies to such account.

(4) Special rule for Archer MSAs.—An individual for whose benefit an Archer MSA (within the meaning of section 220(d)) is established shall be exempt from the tax imposed by this section with respect to any transaction concerning such account (which would otherwise be taxable under this section) if section 220(e)(2) applies to such transaction.

(5) Special rule for Coverdell education savings accounts.—Any individual for whose benefit an education individual retirement account is established and any contributor to such account shall be exempt from the tax imposed by this section with respect to any transaction concerning such account (which would otherwise be taxable under this section) if section 530(d) applies with respect to such transaction.

(6) Special rule for health savings account.—An individual for whose benefit a health savings account (within the meaning of section 223(d)) is established shall be exempt from the tax imposed by this section with respect to any transaction concerning such account (which would otherwise be taxable under this section) if, with respect to such transaction, the account ceases to be a health savings account by reason of the application of section 223(e)(2) to such account.

(d) Exemptions.—Except as provided in subsection (f)(6), the prohibitions provided in subsection (c) shall not apply to—

(1) any loan made by the plan to a disqualified person who is a participant or beneficiary of the plan if such loan—

(A) is available to all such participants or beneficiaries on a reasonably equivalent basis,

(B) is not made available to highly compensated employees, officers, or shareholders in an amount greater than the amount made available to other employees,

(C) is made in accordance with specific provisions regarding such loans set forth in the plan,

(D) bears a reasonable rate of interest, and

(E) is adequately secured;

(2) any contract, or reasonable arrangement, made with a disqualified person for office space, or legal, accounting, or other services necessary for the establishment or operation of the plan, if no more than reasonable compensation is paid therefor;

(3) any loan to a leveraged employee stock ownership plan (as defined in subsection (e)(7)), if —

(A) such loan is primarily for the benefit of participants and beneficiaries of the plan, and

(B) such loan is at a reasonable rate of interest, and any collateral which is given to a disqualified person by the plan consists only of qualifying employer securities (as defined in subsection (e)(8));

(4) the investment of all or part of a plan's assets in deposits which bear a reasonable interest rate in a bank or similar financial institution supervised by the United States or a State, if such bank or other institution is a fiduciary of such plan and if—

(A) the plan covers only employees of such bank or other institution and employees of affiliates of such bank or other institution, or

(B) such investment is expressly authorized by a provision of the plan or by a fiduciary (other than such bank or institution or affiliates thereof) who is expressly empowered by the plan to so instruct the trustee with respect to such investment;

(5) any contract for life insurance, health insurance, or annuities with one or more insurers which are qualified to do business in a State if the plan pays no more than adequate consideration, and if each such insurer or insurers is—

(A) the employer maintaining the plan, or

(B) a disqualified person which is wholly owned (directly or indirectly) by the employer establishing the plan, or by any person which is a disqualified person with respect to the plan, but only if the total premiums and annuity considerations written by such insurers for life insurance, health insurance, or annuities for all plans (and their employers) with respect to which such insurers are disqualified persons (not including premiums or annuity considerations written by the employer maintaining the plan) do not exceed 5 percent of the total premiums and annuity considerations written for all lines of insurance in that year by such insurers (not including premiums or annuity considerations written by the employer maintaining the plan);

(6) the provision of any ancillary service by a bank or similar financial institution supervised by the United States or a State, if such service is provided at not more than reasonable compensation, if such bank or other institution is a fiduciary of such plan, and if—

(A) such bank or similar financial institution has adopted adequate internal safeguards which assure that the provision of such ancillary service is consistent with sound banking and financial practice, as determined by Federal or State supervisory authority, and

(B) the extent to which such ancillary service is provided is subject to specific guidelines issued by such bank or similar financial institution (as determined by the Secretary after consultation with Federal and State supervisory authority), and under such guidelines the bank or similar financial institution does not provide such ancillary service—

(i) in an excessive or unreasonable manner, and

(ii) in a manner that would be inconsistent with the best interests of participants and beneficiaries of employee benefit plans;

(7) the exercise of a privilege to convert securities, to the extent provided in regulations of the Secretary, but only if the plan receives no less than adequate consideration pursuant to such conversion;

(8) any transaction between a plan and a common or collective trust fund or pooled investment fund maintained by a disqualified person which is a bank or trust company supervised by a State or Federal agency or between a plan and a pooled investment fund of an insurance company qualified to do business in a State if—

(A) the transaction is a sale or purchase of an interest in the fund,

(B) the bank, trust company, or insurance company receives not more than reasonable compensation, and

(C) such transaction is expressly permitted by the instrument under which the plan is maintained, or by a fiduciary (other than the bank, trust company, or insurance company, or an affiliate thereof) who has authority to manage and control the assets of the plan;

(9) receipt by a disqualified person of any benefit to which he may be entitled as a participant or beneficiary in the plan, so long as the benefit is computed and paid on a basis which is consistent with the terms of the plan as applied to all other participants and beneficiaries;

(10) receipt by a disqualified person of any reasonable compensation for services rendered, or for the reimbursement of expenses properly and actually incurred, in the performance of his duties with the plan, but no person so serving who already receives full-time pay from an employer or an association of employers, whose employees are participants in the plan or from an employee organization whose members are participants in such plan shall receive compensation from such fund, except for reimbursement of expenses properly and actually incurred;

(11) service by a disqualified person as a fiduciary in addition to being an officer, employee, agent, or other representative of a disqualified person;

(12) the making by a fiduciary of a distribution of the assets of the trust in accordance with the terms of the plan if such assets are distributed in the same manner as provided under section 4044 of title IV of the Employee Retirement Income Security Act of 1974 (relating to allocation of assets);

(13) any transaction which is exempt from section 406 of such Act by reason of section 408(e) of such Act (or which would be so exempt if such section 406 applied to such transaction) or which is exempt from section 406 of such Act by reason of section 408(b)(12) of such Act;

(14) any transaction required or permitted under part 1 of subtitle E of title IV or section 4223 of the Employee Retirement Income Security Act of 1974, but this paragraph shall not apply with respect to the application of subsection (c)(1)(E) or (F);

(15) a merger of multiemployer plans, or the transfer of assets or liabilities between multiemployer plans, determined by the Pension Benefit Guaranty Corporation to meet the requirements of section 4231 of such Act, but this paragraph shall not apply with respect to the application of subsection (c)(1)(E) or (F),

(16) a sale of stock held by a trust which constitutes an individual retirement account under section 408(a) to the individual for whose benefit such account is established if—

(A) such stock is in a bank (as defined in section 581),

(B) such stock is held by such trust as of the date of the enactment of this paragraph,

(C) such sale is pursuant to an election under section 1362(a) by such bank,

(D) such sale is for fair market value at the time of sale (as established by an independent appraiser) and the terms of the sale are otherwise at least as favorable to such trust as the terms that would apply on a sale to an unrelated party,

(E) such trust does not pay any commissions, costs, or other expenses in connection with the sale,

(F) the stock is sold in a single transaction for cash not later than 120 days after the S corporation election is made.

(17) Any transaction in connection with the provision of investment advice described in subsection (e)(3)(B) to a participant or beneficiary in a plan that permits such participant or beneficiary to direct the investment of plan assets in an individual account, if—

(A) the transaction is—

(i) the provision of the investment advice to the participant or beneficiary of the plan with respect to a security or other property available as an investment under the plan,

(ii) the acquisition, holding, or sale of a security or other property available as an investment under the plan pursuant to the investment advice, or

(iii) the direct or indirect receipt of fees or other compensation by the fiduciary adviser or an affiliate thereof (or any employee, agent, or registered representative of the fiduciary adviser or affiliate) in connection with the provision of the advice or in connection with an acquisition, holding, or sale of a security or other property available as an investment under the plan pursuant to the investment advice; and

(B) the requirements of subsection (f)(8) are met,

(18) any transaction involving the purchase or sale of securities, or other property (as determined by the Secretary of Labor), between a plan and a disqualified person (other than a fiduciary described in subsection (e)(3)) with respect to a plan if—

(A) the transaction involves a block trade,

(B) at the time of the transaction, the interest of the plan (together with the interests of any other plans maintained by the same plan sponsor), does not exceed 10 percent of the aggregate size of the block trade,

(C) the terms of the transaction, including the price, are at least as favorable to the plan as an arm's length transaction, and

(D) the compensation associated with the purchase and sale is not greater than the compensation associated with an arm's length transaction with an unrelated party,

(19) any transaction involving the purchase or sale of securities, or other property (as determined by the Secretary of Labor), between a plan and a disqualified person if—

(A) the transaction is executed through an electronic communication network, alternative trading system, or similar execution system or trading venue subject to regulation and oversight by—

(i) the applicable Federal regulating entity, or

(ii) such foreign regulatory entity as the Secretary of Labor may determine by regulation,

(B) either—

(i) the transaction is effected pursuant to rules designed to match purchases and sales at the best price available through the execution system in accordance with applicable rules of the Securities and Exchange Commission or other relevant governmental authority, or

(ii) neither the execution system nor the parties to the transaction take into account the identity of the parties in the execution of trades,

(C) the price and compensation associated with the purchase and sale are not greater than the price and compensation associated with an arm's length transaction with an unrelated party,

(D) if the disqualified person has an ownership interest in the system or venue described in subparagraph (A), the system or venue has been authorized by the plan sponsor or other independent fiduciary for transactions described in this paragraph, and

(E) not less than 30 days prior to the initial transaction described in this paragraph executed through any system or venue described in subparagraph (A), a plan fiduciary is provided written or electronic notice of the execution of such transaction through such system or venue,

(20) transactions described in subparagraph (A), (B), and (D) of subsection (c)(1) between a plan and a person that is a disqualified person other than a fiduciary (or an affiliate) who has or exercises any discretionary authority or control with respect to the investment of the plan assets involved in the transaction or renders investment advice (within the meaning of subsection (e)(3)(B)) with respect to those assets, solely by reason of providing services to the plan or solely by reason of a relationship to such a service provider described in subparagraph (F), (G), (H), or (I) of subsection (e)(2), or both, but only if in connection with such transaction the plan receives no less, nor pays no more, than adequate consideration,

(21) any foreign exchange transactions, between a bank or broker-dealer (or any affiliate of either) and a plan (as defined in this section) with respect to which such bank or broker-dealer (or affiliate) is a trustee, custodian, fiduciary, or other disqualified person, if—

(A) the transaction is in connection with the purchase, holding, or sale of securities or other investment assets (other than a foreign exchange transaction unrelated to any other investment in securities or other investment assets),

(B) at the time the foreign exchange transaction is entered into, the terms of the transaction are not less favorable to the plan than the terms generally available in comparable arm's length foreign exchange transactions between unrelated parties, or the terms afforded by the bank or broker-dealer (or any affiliate of either) in comparable arm's-length foreign exchange transactions involving unrelated parties,

(C) the exchange rate used by such bank or broker-dealer (or affiliate) for a particular foreign exchange transaction does not deviate by more than 3 percent from the interbank bid and asked rates for transactions of comparable size and maturity at the time of the transaction as displayed on an independent service that reports rates of exchange in the foreign currency market for such currency, and

(D) the bank or broker-dealer (or any affiliate of either) does not have investment discretion, or provide investment advice, with respect to the transaction,

(22) any transaction described in subsection (c)(1)(A) involving the purchase and sale of a security between a plan and any other account managed by the same investment manager, if—

(A) the transaction is a purchase or sale, for no consideration other than cash payment against prompt delivery of a security for which market quotations are readily available,

(B) the transaction is effected at the independent current market price of the security (within the meaning of section 270.17a-7(b) of title 17, Code of Federal Regulations),

(C) no brokerage commission, fee (except for customary transfer fees, the fact of which is disclosed pursuant to subparagraph (D)), or other remuneration is paid in connection with the transaction,

(D) a fiduciary (other than the investment manager engaging in the cross-trades or any affiliate) for each plan participating in the transaction authorizes in advance of any cross-trades (in a document that is separate from any other written agreement of the parties) the investment manager to engage in cross trades at the investment manager's discretion, after such fiduciary has received disclosure regarding the conditions under which cross trades may take place (but only if such disclosure is separate from any other agreement or disclosure involving the asset management relationship), including the written policies and procedures of the investment manager described in subparagraph (H),

(E) each plan participating in the transaction has assets of at least $100,000,000, except that if the assets of a plan are invested in a master trust containing the assets of plans maintained by employers in the same controlled group (as defined in section 407(d)(7) of the Employee Retirement Income Security Act of 1974), the master trust has assets of at least $100,000,000,

(F) the investment manager provides to the plan fiduciary who authorized cross trading under subparagraph (D) a quarterly report detailing all cross trades executed by the investment manager in which the plan participated during such quarter, including the following information, as applicable: (i) the identity of each security bought or sold; (ii) the number of shares or units traded; (iii) the parties involved in the cross-trade; and (iv) trade price and the method used to establish the trade price,

(G) the investment manager does not base its fee schedule on the plan's consent to cross trading, and no other service (other than the investment opportunities and cost savings available through a cross trade) is conditioned on the plan's consent to cross trading,

(H) the investment manager has adopted, and cross-trades are effected in accordance with, written cross-trading policies and procedures that are fair and equitable to all accounts participating in the cross-trading program, and that include a description of the manager's pricing policies and procedures, and the manager's policies and procedures for allocating cross trades in an objective manner among accounts participating in the crosstrading program, and

(I) the investment manager has designated an individual responsible for periodically reviewing such purchases and sales to ensure compliance with the written policies and procedures described in subparagraph (H), and following such review, the individual shall issue an annual written report no later than 90 days following the period to which it relates signed under penalty of perjury to the plan fiduciary who authorized cross trading under subparagraph (D) describing the steps performed during the course of the review, the level of compliance, and any specific instances of non-compliance.

The written report shall also notify the plan fiduciary of the plan's right to terminate participation in the investment manager's cross-trading program at any time, or

(23) except as provided in subsection (f)(11), a transaction described in subparagraph (A), (B), (C), or (D) of subsection (c)(1) in connection with the acquisition, holding, or disposition of any security or commodity, if the transaction is corrected before the end of the correction period.

(e) Definitions.—

(1) Plan.—For purposes of this section, the term "plan" means—

(A) a trust described in section 401(a) which forms a part of a plan, or a plan described in section 403(a), which trust or plan is exempt from tax under section 501(a),

(B) an individual retirement account described in section 408(a),

(C) an individual retirement annuity described in section 408(b),

(D) an Archer MSA described in section 220(d),

(E) a health savings account described in section 223(d),

(F) a Coverdell education savings account described in section 530, or

(G) a trust, plan, account, or annuity which, at any time, has been determined by the Secretary to be described in any preceding subparagraph of this paragraph.

(2) Disqualified person.—For purposes of this section, the term "disqualified person" means a person who is—

(A) a fiduciary;

(B) a person providing services to the plan;

(C) an employer any of whose employees are covered by the plan;

(D) an employee organization any of whose members are covered by the plan;

(E) an owner, direct or indirect, of 50 percent or more of—

(i) the combined voting power of all classes of stock entitled to vote or the total value of shares of all classes of stock of a corporation,

(ii) the capital interest or the profits interest of a partnership, or

(iii) the beneficial interest of a trust or unincorporated enterprise,

which is an employer or an employee organization described in subparagraph (C) or (D);

(F) a member of the family (as defined in paragraph (6)) of any individual described in subparagraph (A), (B), (C), or (E);

(G) a corporation, partnership, or trust or estate of which (or in which) 50 percent or more of—

(i) the combined voting power of all classes of stock entitled to vote or the total value of shares of all classes of stock of such corporation,

(ii) the capital interest or profits interest of such partnership, or

(iii) the beneficial interest of such trust or estate,

is owned directly or indirectly, or held by persons described in subparagraph (A), (B), (C), (D), or (E);

(H) an officer, director (or an individual having powers or responsibilities similar to those of officers or directors), a 10 percent or more shareholder, or a highly compensated employee (earning 10 percent or more of the yearly wages of an employer) of a person described in subparagraph (C), (D), (E), or (G); or

(I) a 10 percent or more (in capital or profits) partner or joint venturer of a person described in subparagraph (C), (D), (E), or (G).

The Secretary, after consultation and coordination with the Secretary of Labor or his delegate, may by regulation prescribe a percentage lower than 50 percent for subparagraphs (E) and (G) and lower than 10 percent for subparagraphs (H) and (I).

(3) Fiduciary.—For purposes of this section, the term "fiduciary" means any person who—

(A) exercises any discretionary authority or discretionary control respecting management of such plan or exercises any authority or control respecting management or disposition of its assets,

(B) renders investment advice for a fee or other compensation, direct or indirect, with respect to any moneys or other property of such plan, or has any authority or responsibility to do so, or

(C) has any discretionary authority or discretionary responsibility in the administration of such plan.

such term includes any person designated under section 405(c)(1)(B) of the Employee Retirement Income Security Act of 1974.

(4) Stockholdings.—For purposes of paragraphs (2)(E)(i) and (G)(i) there shall be taken into account indirect stockholdings which would be taken into account under section 267(c), except that, for purposes of this paragraph, section 267(c)(4) shall be treated as providing that the members of the family of an individual are the members within the meaning of paragraph (6).

(5) Partnerships; trusts.—For purposes of paragraphs (2)(E)(ii) and (iii), (G)(ii) and (iii), and (I) the ownership of profits or beneficial interests shall be determined in accordance with the rules for constructive ownership of stock provided in section 267(c) (other than paragraph (3) thereof), except that section 267(c)(4) shall be treated as providing that the members of the family of an individual are the members within the meaning of paragraph (6).

(6) Member of family.—For purposes of paragraph (2)(F), the family of any individual shall include his spouse, ancestor, lineal descendant, and any spouse of a lineal descendant.

(7) Employee stock ownership plan.—The term "employee stock ownership plan" means a defined contribution plan—

(A) which is a stock bonus plan which is qualified, or a stock bonus and a money purchase plan both of which are qualified under section 401(a), and which are designed to invest primarily in qualifying employer securities; and

(B) which is otherwise defined in regulations prescribed by the Secretary.

A plan shall not be treated as an employee stock ownership plan unless it meets the requirements of section 409(h), section 409(o), and, if applicable, section 409(n), 409(p), and section 664(g) and, if the employer has a registration-type class of securities (as defined in section 409(e)(4)), it meets the requirements of section 409(e).

(8) Qualifying employer security.—The term "qualifying employer security" means any employer security within the meaning of section 409(1). If any moneys or other property of a plan are invested in shares of an investment company registered under the Investment Company Act of 1940, the investment shall not cause that investment company or that investment company's investment adviser or principal underwriter to be treated as a fiduciary or a disqualified person for purposes of this section, except when an investment company or its investment adviser or principal underwriter acts in connection with a plan covering employees of the investment company, its investment adviser, or its principal underwriter.

(9) Section made applicable to withdrawal liability payment funds.—For purposes of this section—

(A) In general.—The term "plan" includes a trust described in section 501(c)(22).

(B) Disqualified person.—In the case of any trust to which this section applies by reason of subparagraph (A), the term "disqualified person" includes any person who is a disqualified person with respect to any plan to which such trust is permitted to make payments under section 4223 of the Employee Retirement Income Security Act of 1974.

(f) Other definitions and special rules.—For purposes of this section—

(1) Joint and several liability.—If more than one person is liable under subsection (a) or (b) with respect to any one prohibited transaction, all such persons shall be jointly and severally liable under such subsection with respect to such transaction.

(2) Taxable period.—The term "taxable period" means, with respect to any prohibited transaction, the period beginning with the date on which the prohibited transaction occurs and ending on the earliest of—

(A) the date of mailing a notice of deficiency with respect to the tax imposed by subsection (a) under section 6212,

(B) the date on which the tax imposed by subsection (a) is assessed, or

(C) the date on which correction of the prohibited transaction is completed.

(3) Sale or exchange; encumbered property.—A transfer of real or personal property by a disqualified person to a plan shall be treated as a sale or exchange if the property is subject to a mortgage or similar lien which the plan assumes or if it is subject to a mortgage or similar lien which a disqualified person placed on the property within the 10-year period ending on the date of the transfer.

(4) Amount involved.—The term "amount involved" means, with respect to a prohibited transaction, the greater of the amount of money and the fair market value of the other property given or the amount of money and the fair market value of the other property received; except that, in the case of services described in paragraphs (2) and (10) of subsection (d) the amount involved shall be only the excess compensation. For purposes of the preceding sentence, the fair market value—

(A) in the case of the tax imposed by subsection (a), shall be determined as of the date on which the prohibited transaction occurs; and

(B) in the case of the tax imposed by subsection (b), shall be the highest fair market value during the taxable period.

(5) Correction.—The terms "correction" and "correct" mean, with respect to a prohibited transaction, undoing the transaction to the extent possible, but in any case placing the plan in a financial position not worse than that in which it would be if the disqualified person were acting under the highest fiduciary standards.

(6) Exemptions not to apply to certain transactions.—

(A) In general.—In the case of a trust described in section 401(a) which is part of a plan providing contributions or benefits for employees some or all of whom are owner-employees (as defined in section 401(c)(3)), the exemptions provided by subsection (d) (other than paragraphs (9) and (12)) shall not apply to a transaction in which the plan directly or indirectly—

(i) lends any part of the corpus or income of the plan to,

(ii) pays any compensation for personal services rendered to the plan to, or

(iii) acquires for the plan any property from, or sells any property to,

any such owner-employee, a member of the family (as defined in section 267(c)(4)) of any such owner-employee, or any corporation in which any such owner-employee owns, directly or indirectly, 50 percent or more of the total combined voting power of all classes of stock entitled to vote or 50 percent or more of the total value of shares of all classes of stock of the corporation.

(B) Special rules for shareholder-employees, etc.—

(i) In general.—For purposes of subparagraph (A), the following shall be treated as owner-employees:

(I) A shareholder-employee.

(II) A participant or beneficiary of an individual retirement plan (as defined in section 7701 (a)(37)).

(III) An employer or association of employees which establishes such an individual retirement plan under section 408(c).

(ii) Exception for certain transactions involving shareholder-employees.—Subparagraph (A)(iii) shall not apply to a transaction which consists of a sale of employer securities to an employee stock ownership plan (as defined in subsection (e)(7)) by a shareholder-employee, a member of the family (as defined in section 267(c)(4)) of such shareholder-employee, or a corporation in which such a shareholder-employee owns stock representing a 50 percent or greater interest described in subparagraph (A).

(iii) Loan exception.—For purposes of subparagraph (A)(i), the term "owner-employee" shall only include a person described in subclause (II) or (III) of clause (i).

(C) Shareholder-employee.—For purposes of subparagraph (B), the term "shareholder-employee" means an employee or officer of an S corporation who owns (or is considered as owning within the meaning of section 318(a)(l)) more than 5 percent of the outstanding stock of the corporation on any day during the taxable year of such corporation.

(7) S corporation repayment of loans for qualifying employer securities.—A plan shall not be treated as violating the requirements of section 401 or 409 or subsection (e)(7), or as engaging in a prohibited transaction for purposes of subsection (d)(3), merely by reason of any distribution (as described in section 1368(a)) with respect to S corporation stock that constitutes qualifying employer securities, which in accordance with the plan provisions is used to make payments on a loan described in subsection (d)(3) the proceeds of which were used to acquire such qualifying employer securities (whether or not allocated to participants). The preceding sentence shall not apply in the case of a distribution which is paid with respect to any employer security which is allocated to a participant unless the plan provides that employer securities with a fair market value of not less than the amount of such distribution are allocated to such participant for the year which (but for the preceding sentence) such distribution would have been allocated to such participant.

* * *

(g) Application of section.—This section shall not apply—

(1) in the case of a plan to which a guaranteed benefit policy (as defined in section 401(b)(2)(B) of the Employee Retirement Income Security Act of 1974) is issued, to any assets of the insurance company, insurance service, or insurance organization merely because of its issuance of such policy;

(2) to a governmental plan (within the meaning of section 414(d)); or

(3) to a church plan (within the meaning of section 414(e)) with respect to which the election provided by section 410(d) has not been made.

In the case of a plan which invests in any security issued by an investment company registered under the Investment Company Act of 1940, the assets of such plan shall be deemed to include such security but shall not, by reason of such investment, be deemed to include any assets of such company.

(h) Notification of Secretary of Labor.—Before sending a notice of deficiency with respect to the tax imposed by subsection (a) or (b), the Secretary shall notify the Secretary of Labor and provide him a reasonable opportunity to obtain a correction of the prohibited transaction or to comment on the imposition of such tax.

* * *

§ 4977. Tax on certain fringe benefits provided by an employer

(a) Imposition of tax.—In the case of an employer to whom an election under this section applies for any calendar year, there is hereby imposed a tax for such calendar year equal to 30 percent of the excess fringe benefits.

(b) Excess fringe benefits.—For purposes of subsection (a), the term "excess fringe benefits" means, with respect to any calendar year—

(1) the aggregate value of the fringe benefits provided by the employer during the calendar year which were not includible in gross income under paragraphs (1) and (2) of section 132(a), over

(2) 1 percent of the aggregate amount of compensation—

(A) which was paid by the employer during such calendar year to employees, and

(B) was includible in gross income for purposes of chapter 1.

(c) Effect of election on section 132(a).—If—

(1) an election under this section is in effect with respect to an employer for any calendar year, and

(2) at all times on or after January 1, 1984, and before the close of the calendar year involved, substantially all of the employees of the employer were entitled to employee discounts on goods or services provided by the employer in 1 line of business,

for purposes of paragraphs (1) and (2) of section 132(a) (but not for purposes of section 132(h)), all employees of any line of business of the employer which was in existence on January 1, 1984, shall be treated as employees of the line of business referred to in paragraph (2).

(d) Period of election.—An election under this section shall apply to the calendar year for which made and all subsequent calendar years unless revoked by the employer.

(e) Treatment of controlled groups.—All employees treated as employed by a single employer under subsection (b), (c), or (m) of section 414 shall be treated as employed by a single employer for purposes of this section.

(f) Section to apply only to employment within the United States.—Except as otherwise provided in regulations, this section shall apply only with respect to employment within the United States.

* * *

§ 4979. Tax on certain excess contributions

(a) General rule.—In the case of any plan, there is hereby imposed a tax for the taxable year equal to 10 percent of the sum of—

(1) any excess contributions under such plan for the plan year ending in such taxable year, and

(2) any excess aggregate contributions under the plan for the plan year ending in such taxable year.

(b) Liability for tax.—The tax imposed by subsection (a) shall be paid by the employer.

(c) Excess contributions.—For purposes of this section, the term "excess contributions" has the meaning given such term by sections 401(k)(8)(B), 408(k)(6)(C), and 501(c)(18).

(d) Excess aggregate contribution.—For purposes of this section, the term "excess aggregate contribution" has the meaning given to such term by section 401(m)(6)(B). For purposes of determining excess aggregate contributions under an annuity contract described in section 403(b), such contract shall be treated as a plan described in subsection (e)(l).

(e) Plan.—For purposes of this section, the term "plan" means—

(1) a plan described in section 401(a) which includes a trust exempt from tax under section 501(a),

(2) any annuity plan described in section 403(a),

(3) any annuity contract described in section 403(b),

(4) a simplified employee pension of an employer which satisfies the requirements of section 408(k), and

(5) a plan described in section 501(c)(18).

Such term includes any plan which, at any time, has been determined by the Secretary to be such a plan.

(f) No tax where excess distributed within specified period after close of year.—

(1) In general.—No tax shall be imposed under this section on any excess contribution or excess aggregate contribution, as the case may be, to the extent such contribution (together with any income allocable thereto through the end of the plan year for which the contribution is made) is distributed (or, if forfeitable, is forfeited) before the close of the first 2½ months (6 months in the case of an excess contribution or excess aggregate contribution to an eligible automatic contribution arrangement (as defined in section 414(w)(3)) of the following plan year.

(2) Year of inclusion.—Any amount distributed as provided in paragraph (1) shall be treated as earned and received by the recipient in the recipient's taxable year in which such distributions were made.

(A) De minimis distributions.—If the total excess contributions and excess aggregate contributions distributed to a recipient under a plan for any plan year are less than $100, such distributions (and any income allocable thereto) shall be treated as earned and received by the recipient in his taxable year in which such distributions were made.

* * *

§ 4980C. Requirements for issuers of qualified long-term care insurance contracts

(a) General rule.—There is hereby imposed on any person failing to meet the requirements of subsection (c) or (d) a tax in the amount determined under subsection (b).

(b) Amount.—

(1) In general.—The amount of the tax imposed by subsection (a) shall be $100 per insured for each day any requirement of subsection (c) or (d) is not met with respect to each qualified long-term care insurance contract.

(2) Waiver.—In the case of a failure which is due to reasonable cause and not to willful neglect, the Secretary may waive part or all of the tax imposed by subsection (a) to the extent that payment of the tax would be excessive relative to the failure involved.

(c) Responsibilities.— The requirements of this subsection are as follows:

(1) Requirements of model provisions.—

(A) Model regulation.—The following requirements of the model regulation must be met:

(i) Section 13 (relating to application forms and replacement coverage).

(ii) Section 14 (relating to reporting requirements), except that the issuer shall also report at least annually the number of claims denied during the reporting period for each class of business (expressed as a percentage of claims denied), other than claims denied for failure to meet the waiting period or because of any applicable preexisting condition.

(iii) Section 20 (relating to filing requirements for marketing).

(iv) Section 21 (relating to standards for marketing), including inaccurate completion of medical histories, other than sections 21C(1) and 21C(6) thereof, except that—

(I) in addition to such requirements, no person shall, in selling or offering to sell a qualified long-term care insurance contract, misrepresent a material fact; and

(II) no such requirements shall include a requirement to inquire or identify whether a prospective applicant or enrollee for long-term care insurance has accident and sickness insurance.

(v) Section 22 (relating to appropriateness of recommended purchase).

(vi) Section 24 (relating to standard format outline of coverage).

(vii) Section 25 (relating to requirement to deliver shopper's guide).

(B) Model act.—The following requirements of the model Act must be met:

(i) Section 6F (relating to right to return), except that such section shall also apply to denials of applications and any refund shall be made within 30 days of the return or denial.

(ii) Section 6G (relating to outline of coverage).

(iii) Section 6H (relating to requirements for certificates under group plans).

(iv) Section 61 (relating to policy summary).

(v) Section 6J (relating to monthly reports on accelerated death benefits).

(vi) Section 7 (relating to incontestability period).

(C) Definitions.—For purposes of this paragraph, the terms "model regulation" and "model Act" have the meanings given such terms by section 7702(B)(g)(2)(B).

(2) Delivery of policy.—If an application for a qualified long-term care insurance contract (or for a certificate under such a contract for a group) is approved, the issuer shall deliver to the applicant (or policyholder or certificate holder) the contract (or certificate) of insurance not later than 30 days after the date of the approval.

(3) Information on denials of claims.—If a claim under a qualified long-term care insurance contract is denied, the issuer shall, within 60 days of the date of a written request by the policyholder or certificate holer (or representative)—

(A) provide a written explanation of the reasons for the denial, and

(B) make available all information directly relating to such denial.

(d) Disclosure.—The requirements of this subsection are met if the issuer of a long-term care insurance policy discloses in such policy and in the outline of coverage required under subsection (c)(1)(B)(ii) that the policy is intended to be a qualified long-term care insurance contract under section 7702B(b).

(e) Qualified long-term care insurance contract defined.—For purposes of this section, the term "qualified long-term care insurance contract" has the meaning given such term by section 7702B.

(f) Coordination with state requirements.— If a State imposes any requirement which is more stringent than the analogous requirement imposed by this section or section 7702B(g), the requirement imposed by this section or section 7702B(g) shall be treated as met if the more stringent State requirement is met.

§ 4980D. Failure to meet certain group health plan requirements

(a) General rule.—There is hereby imposed a tax on any failure of a group health plan to meet the requirements of chapter 100 (relating to group health plans requirements).

(b) Amount of tax.—

(1) In general.—The amount of the tax imposed by subsection (a) on any failure shall be $100 for each day in the noncompliance period with respect to each individual to whom such failure relates.

(2) Noncompliance period.—For purposes of this section, the term "noncompliance period" means, with respect to any failure, the period—

(A) beginning on the date such failure first occurs, and

(B) ending on the date such failure is corrected.

(3) Minimum tax for noncompliance period where failure discovered after notice of examination.—Notwithstanding paragraphs (1) and (2) of subsection (c)—

(A) In general.—In the case of 1 or more failures with respect to an individual—

(i) which are not corrected before the date a notice of examination of income tax liability is sent to the employer, and

(ii) which occurred or continued during the period under examination,

the amount of tax imposed by subsection (a) by reason of such failures with respect to such individual shall not be less than the lesser of $2,500 or the amount of tax which would be imposed by subsection (a) without regard to such paragraphs.

(B) Higher minimum tax where violations are more than de minimis.—To the extent violations for which any person is liable under subsection (e) for any year are more than de minimis, subparagraph (A) shall be applied by substituting "$15,000" for "$2,500" with respect to such person.

(C) Exception for church plans.—This paragraph shall not apply to any failure under a church plan (as defined in section 414(e)).

(c) Limitations on amount of tax.—

(1) Tax not to apply where failure not discovered exercising reasonable diligence.— No tax shall be imposed by subsection (a) on any failure during any period for which it is established to the satisfaction of the Secretary that the person otherwise liable for such tax did not know, and exercising reasonable diligence would not have known, that such failure existed.

(2) Tax not to apply to failures corrected within certain periods.—No tax shall be imposed by subsection (a) on any failure if—

(A) such failure was due to reasonable cause and not to willful neglect, and

(B)(i) in the case of a plan other than a church plan (as defined in section 414(e)), such failure is corrected during the 30-day period beginning on the 1st date the person otherwise liable for such tax knew, or exercising reasonable diligence would have known, that such failure existed, and

(ii) in the case of a church plan (as so defined), such failure is corrected before the close of the correction period (determined under the rules of section 414(e)(4)(C)).

(3) Overall limitation for unintentional failures.—In the case of failures which are due to reasonable cause and not to willful neglect—

(A) Single employer plans.—

(i) In general.—In the case of failures with respect to plans other than specified multiple employer health plans, the tax imposed by subsection (a) for failures during the taxable year of the employer shall not exceed the amount equal to the lesser of—

(I) 10 percent of the aggregate amount paid or incurred by the employer (or predecessor employer) during the preceding taxable year for group health plans, or

(II) $500,000.

(ii) Taxable years in the case of certain controlled groups.—For purposes of this subparagraph, if not all persons who are treated as a single employer for purposes of this section have the same taxable year, the taxable years taken into account shall be determined under principles similar to the principles of section 1561.

(B) Specified multiple employer health plans.—

(i) In general.—In the case of failures with respect to a specified multiple employer health plan, the tax imposed by subsection (a) for failures during the taxable year of the trust forming part of such plan shall not exceed the amount equal to the lesser of—

(I) 10 percent of the amount paid or incurred by such trust during such taxable year to provide medical care (as defined in section 9832(d)(3)) directly or through insurance, reimbursement, or otherwise, or

(II) $500,000.

For purposes of the preceding sentence, all plans of which the same trust forms a part shall be treated as 1 plan.

(ii) Special rule for employers required to pay tax.—If an employer is assessed a tax imposed by subsection (a) by reason of a failure with respect to a specified multiple employer health plan, the limit shall be determined under subparagraph (A) (and not under this subparagraph) and as if such plan were not a specified multiple employer health plan.

(4) Waiver by Secretary.—In the case of a failure which is due to reasonable cause and not to willful neglect, the Secretary may waive part or all of the tax imposed by subsection (a) to the extent that the payment of such tax would be excessive relative to the failure involved.

(d) Tax not to apply to certain insured small employer plans.—

(1) In general.—In the case of a group health plan of a small employer which provides health insurance coverage solely through a contract with a health insurance issuer, no tax shall be imposed by this section on the employer on any failure (other than a failure attributable to section 9811) which is solely because of the health insurance coverage offered by such issuer.

(2) Small employer.—

(A) In general.—For purposes of paragraph (1), the term "small employer" means, with respect to a calendar year and a plan year, an employer who employed an average of at least 2 but not more than 50 employees on business days during the preceding calendar year and who employs at least 2 employees on the first day of the plan year. For purposes of the preceding sentence, all persons treated as a single employer under subsection (b), (c), (m), or (o) of section 414 shall be treated as 1 employer.

(B) Employers not in existence in preceding year.—In the case of an employer which was not in existence throughout the preceding calendar year, the determination of whether such employer is a small employer shall be based on the average number of employees that it is reasonably expected such employer will employ on business days in the current calendar year.

(C) Predecessors.—Any reference in this paragraph to an employer shall include a reference to any predecessor of such employer.

(3) Health insurance coverage; health insurance issuer.—For purposes of paragraph (1), the terms "health insurance coverage" and "health insurance issuer" have the respective meanings given such terms by section 9832.

(e) Liability for tax.—The following shall be liable for the tax imposed by subsection (a) on a failure:

(1) Except as otherwise provided in this subsection, the employer.

(2) In the case of a multiemployer plan, the plan.

(3) In the case of a failure under section 9803 (relating to guaranteed renewability) with respect to a plan described in subsection (f)(2)(B), the plan.

(f) Definitions.—For purposes of this section—

(1) Group health plan.—The term "group health plan" has the meaning given such term by section 9832(a).

(2) Specified multiple employer health plan.—The term "specified multiple employer health plan" means a group health plan which is—

(A) any multiemployer plan, or

(B) any multiple employer welfare arrangement (as defined in section 3(40) of the Employee Retirement Income Security Act of 1974, as in effect on the date of the enactment of this section).

(3) Correction.—A failure of a group health plan shall be treated as corrected if—

(A) such failure is retroactively undone to the extent possible, and

(B) the person to whom the failure relates is placed in a financial position which is as good as such person would have been in had such failure not occurred.

§ 4980E. Failure of employer to make comparable medical savings account contributions

(a) General rule.—In the case of an employer who makes a contribution to the Archer MSA of any employee with respect to coverage under a high deductible health plan of the employer during a calendar year, there is hereby imposed a tax on the failure of such employer to meet the requirements of subsection (d) for such calendar year.

(b) Amount of tax.—The amount of the tax imposed by subsection (a) on any failure for any calendar year is the amount equal to 35 percent of the aggregate amount contributed by the employer to Archer MSAs of employees for taxable years of such employees ending with or within such calendar year.

(c) Waiver by Secretary.—In the case of a failure which is due to reasonable cause and not to willful neglect, the Secretary may waive part or all of the tax imposed by subsection (a) to the extent that the payment of such tax would be excessive relative to the failure involved.

(d) Employer required to make comparable MSA contributions for all participating employees.—

(1) In general.—An employer meets the requirements of this subsection for any calendar year if the employer makes available comparable contributions to the Archer MSAs of all comparable participating employees for each coverage period during such calendar year.

(2) Comparable contributions.—

(A) In general.—For purposes of paragraph (1), the term "comparable contributions" means contributions—

(i) which are the same amount, or

(ii) which are the same percentage of the annual deductible limit under the high deductible health plan covering the employees.

(B) Part-year employees.—In the case of an employee who is employed by the employer for only a portion of the calendar year, a contribution to the Archer MSA of such employee shall be treated as comparable if it is an amount which bears the same ratio to the comparable amount (determined without regard to this subparagraph) as such portion bears to the entire calendar year.

(3) Comparable participating employees.—For purposes of paragraph (1), the term "comparable participating employees" means all employees—

(A) who are eligible individuals covered under any high deductible health plan of the employer, and

(B) who have the same category of coverage.

For purposes of subparagraph (B), the categories of coverage are self-only and family coverage.

(4) Part-time employees.—

(A) In general.—Paragraph (3) shall be applied separately with respect to part-time employees and other employees.

(B) Part-time employee.—For purposes of subparagraph (A), the term "part-time employee" means any employee who is customarily employed for fewer than 30 hours per week.

(e) Controlled groups.—For purposes of this section, all persons treated as a single employer under subsection (b), (c), (m), or (o) section 414 shall be treated as 1 employer.

(f) Definitions.—Terms used in this section which are also used in section 220 have the respective meanings given such terms in section 220.

* * *

§ 4980G. Failure of employer to make comparable health savings account contributions

(a) General rule.—In the case of an employer who makes a contribution to the health savings account of any employee during a calendar year, there is hereby imposed a tax on the failure of such employer to meet the requirements of subsection (b) for such calendar year.

(b) Rules and requirements.—Rules and requirements similar to the rules and requirements of section 4980E shall apply for purposes of this section.

(c) Regulations.—The Secretary shall issue regulations to carry out the purposes of this section, including regulations providing special rules for employers who make contributions to Archer MSAs and health savings accounts during the calendar year.

(d) Exception.—For purposes of applying section 4980E to a contribution to a health savings account of an employee who is not a highly compensated employee (as defined in section 414(q)), highly compensated employees shall not be treated as comparable participating employees.

* * *

CHAPTER 46—GOLDEN PARACHUTE PAYMENTS

Editorial Summary

Tax on Golden Parachute Payments

Chapter 46 (Sec. 4999)

The decade of the 1980s frequently is characterized as the decade of the acceleration of the corporate acquisition movement. A frequently applied technique to protect the management of the acquired company when terminated by the acquiring company is the presence of contractual provisions which provide for substantial salary-type payments associated with the termination. Congress, in the Deficit Reduction Act of 1984, provided two potential negative tax results associated with such payments, which are labeled golden parachute payments.

Section 280G of Subchapter B of Chapter 1 defines a golden parachute payment and disallows the deduction for the payment to the extent of any excess parachute payment as defined in Sec. 280G(b). Thus, the impact in this case is on the payor. Section 4999 of Chapter 46 imposes a 20 percent excise tax on the excess parachute payment. Thus, in this case, the impact is on the recipient.

§ 4999. Golden parachute payments

(a) Imposition of tax.—There is hereby imposed on any person who receives an excess parachute payment a tax equal to 20 percent of the amount of such payment.

(b) Excess parachute payment defined.—For purposes of this section, the term "excess parachute payment" has the meaning given to such term by section 280G(b).

(c) Administrative provisions.—

(1) Withholding.—In the case of any excess parachute payment which is wages (within the meaning of section 3401) the amount deducted and withheld under section 3402 shall be increased by the amount of the tax imposed by this section on such payment.

(2) Other administrative provisions.—For purposes of subtitle F, any tax imposed by this section shall be treated as a tax imposed by subtitle A.

* * *

SUBTITLE E—ALCOHOL, TOBACCO, AND CERTAIN OTHER EXCISE TAXES

*Omitted.

CHAPTER 54—GREENMAIL

Editorial Summary

Tax on Greenmail Payments

Chapter 54 (Sec. 5881)

Golden parachute payments are associated with protecting the management of an acquired company in a corporate acquisition. See the discussion under the Editorial Summary entitled Tax on Golden Parachute Payments which precedes Sec. 4999. Greenmail payments are associated with payments made in redemption of its stock by the corporation to a taxpayer who is attempting to acquire the corporation in a hostile takeover.

Prior to the Revenue Act of 1987, the redemption transaction to the taxpayer who had attempted the hostile takeover qualified for taxation as a capital gain (or as ordinary income if the taxpayer qualified for dealer status). The Revenue Act of 1987 does not modify this basic tax treatment for such a taxpayer. However, it does, in addition, impose a 50 percent nondeductible excise tax on the realized gain for the taxpayer who receives greenmail payments [see Sec. 5881(a)].

§ 5881. Greenmail

(a) Imposition of tax.—There is hereby imposed on any person who receives greenmail a tax equal to 50 percent of gain or other income of such person by reason of such receipt.

(b) Greenmail.—For purposes of this section, the term "greenmail" means any consideration transferred by a corporation (or any person acting in concert with such corporation) to directly or indirectly acquire stock of such corporation from any shareholder if—

(1) such shareholder held such stock (as determined under section 1223) for less than 2 years before entering into the agreement to make the transfer,

(2) at some time during the 2-year period ending on the date of such acquisition—

(A) such shareholder,

(B) any person acting in concert with such shareholder, or

(C) any person who is related to such shareholder or person described in subparagraph (B),

made or threatened to make a public tender offer for stock of such corporation, and

(3) such acquisition is pursuant to an offer which was not made on the same terms to all shareholders.

For purposes of the preceding sentence, payments made in connection with, or in transactions related to, an acquisition shall be treated as paid in such acquisition.

(c) Other definitions.—For purposes of this section—

(1) Public tender offer.—The term "public tender offer" means any offer to purchase or otherwise acquire stock or assets in a corporation if such offer was or would be required to be filed or registered with any Federal or State agency regulating securities.

(2) Related person.—A person is related to another person if the relationship between such persons would result in the disallowance of losses under section 267 or 707(b).

(d) Tax applies whether or not amount recognized.—The tax imposed by this section shall apply whether or not the gain or other income referred to in subsection (a) is recognized.

(e) Administrative provisions.—For purposes of the deficiency procedures of subtitle F, any tax imposed by this section shall be treated as a tax imposed by subtitle A.

SUBTITLE F—PROCEDURE AND ADMINISTRATION

CHAPTER 61—INFORMATION AND RETURNS

SUBCHAPTER A—RETURNS AND RECORDS

Editorial Summary

Information and Returns

Subchapter A of Chapter 61 (Secs. 6001–6081)

Chapter 61 begins the procedure and administration portion of the Code. It applies to income taxes, estate taxes, and gift taxes. It covers the records that the taxpayer must maintain, filing requirements for tax returns and various information returns, filing status, and signature requirements.

PART I—RECORDS, STATEMENTS, AND SPECIAL RETURNS

§ 6001. Notice or regulations requiring records, statements, and special returns

Every person liable for any tax imposed by this title, or for the collection thereof, shall keep such records, render such statements, make such returns, and comply with such rules and regulations as the Secretary may from time to time prescribe. Whenever in the judgment of the Secretary it is necessary, he may require any person, by notice served upon such person or by regulations, to make such returns, render such statements, or keep such records, as the Secretary deems sufficient to show whether or not such person is liable for tax under this title. The only records which an employer shall be required to keep under this section in connection with charged tips shall be charge receipts, records necessary to comply with section 6053(c), and copies of statements furnished by employees under section 6053(a).

PART II—TAX RETURNS OR STATEMENTS

Editorial Summary

Requirement for Filing a Tax Return

Subchapter A of Chapter 61 (Secs. 6011–6019)

See the discussion under the Editorial Summary entitled Information and Returns, which precedes Sec. 6001.

*Omitted.

SUBPART A—GENERAL REQUIREMENT

§ 6011. General requirement of return, statement, or list

(a) General rule.—When required by regulations prescribed by the Secretary any person made liable for any tax imposed by this title, or with respect to the collection thereof, shall make a return or statement according to the forms and regulations prescribed by the Secretary. Every person required to make a return or statement shall include therein the information required by such forms or regulations.

* * *

SUBPART B—INCOME TAX RETURNS

§ 6012. Persons required to make returns of income

(a) General rule.—Returns with respect to income taxes under subtitle A shall be made by the following:

(1)(A) Every individual having for the taxable year gross income which equals or exceeds the exemption amount, except that a return shall not be required of an individual—

(i) who is not married (determined by applying section 7703), is not a surviving spouse (as defined in section 2(a)), is not a head of a household (as defined in section 2(b)), and for the taxable year has gross income of less than the sum of the exemption amount plus the basic standard deduction applicable to such an individual,

(ii) who is a head of a household (as so defined) and for the taxable year has gross income of less than the sum of the exemption amount plus the basic standard deduction applicable to such an individual,

(iii) who is a surviving spouse (as so defined) and for the taxable year has gross income of less than the sum of the exemption amount plus the basic standard deduction applicable to such an individual, or

(iv) who is entitled to make a joint return and whose gross income, when combined with the gross income of his spouse, is, for the taxable year, less than the sum of twice the exemption amount plus the basic standard deduction applicable to a joint return, but only if such individual and his spouse, at the close of the taxable year, had the same household as their home.

Clause (iv) shall not apply if for the taxable year such spouse makes a separate return or any other taxpayer is entitled to an exemption for such spouse under section 151(c).

(B) The amount specified in clause (i), (ii), or (iii) of subparagraph (A) shall be increased by the amount of 1 additional standard deduction (within the meaning of section 63(c)(3)) in the case of an individual entitled to such deduction by reason of section 63(f)(1)(A) (relating to individuals age 65 or more), and the amount specified in clause (iv) of subparagraph (A) shall be increased by the amount of the additional standard deduction for each additional standard deduction to which the individual or his spouse is entitled by reason of section 63(f)(1).

(C) The exception under subparagraph (A) shall not apply to any individual—

(i) who is described in section 63(c)(5) and who has—

(I) income (other than earned income) in excess of the amount in effect under section 63(c)(5)(A) plus the additional standard deduction (if any) to which the individual is entitled, or

(II) total gross income in excess of the standard deduction, or

(ii) for whom the standard deduction is zero under section 63(c)(6).

(D) For purposes of this subsection—

(i) The terms "standard deduction," "basic standard deduction" and "additional standard deduction" have the respective meanings given such terms by section 63(c).

(ii) The term "exemption amount" has the meaning given such term by section 151(d). In the case of an individual described in section 151(d)(2), the exemption amount shall be zero.

(2) Every corporation subject to taxation under subtitle A;

(3) Every estate the gross income of which for the taxable year is $600 or more;

(4) Every trust having for the taxable year any taxable income, or having gross income of $600 or over, regardless of the amount of taxable income;

(5) Every estate or trust of which any beneficiary is a nonresident alien;

* * *

(8) Every individual who receives payments during the calendar year in which the taxable year begins under section 3507 (relating to advance payment of earned income credit).

* * *

except that subject to such conditions, limitations, and exceptions and under such regulations as may be prescribed by the Secretary, nonresident alien individuals subject to the tax imposed by section 871 and foreign corporations subject to the tax imposed by section 881 may be exempted from the requirement of making returns under this section.

(b) Returns made by fiduciaries and receivers.—

(1) Returns of decedents.—If an individual is deceased, the return of such individual required under subsection (a) shall be made by his executor, administrator, or other person charged with the property of such decedent.

(2) Persons under a disability.—If an individual is unable to make a return required under subsection (a), the return of such individual shall be made by a duly authorized agent, his committee, guardian, fiduciary or other person charged with the care of the person or property of such individual. The preceding sentence shall not apply in the case of a receiver appointed by authority of law in possession of only a part of the property of an individual.

(3) Receivers, trustees and assignees for corporations.—In a case where a receiver, trustee in a case under title 11 of the United States Code, or assignee, by order of a court of competent jurisdiction, by operation of law or otherwise, has possession of or holds title to all or substantially all the property or business of a corporation, whether or not such property or business is being operated, such receiver, trustee, or assignee shall make the return of income for such corporation in the same manner and form as corporations are required to make such returns.

(4) Returns of estates and trusts.—Returns of an estate, a trust, or an estate of an individual under chapter 7 or 11 of title 11 of the United States Code shall be made by the fiduciary thereof.

(5) Joint fiduciaries.—Under such regulations as the Secretary may prescribe, a return made by one of two or more joint fiduciaries shall be sufficient compliance with the requirements of this section. A return made pursuant to this paragraph shall contain a statement that the fiduciary has sufficient knowledge of the affairs of the person for whom the return is made to enable him to make the return, and that the return is, to the best of his knowledge and belief, true and correct.

(6) IRA share of partnership income.—In the case of a trust which is exempt from taxation under section 408(e), for purposes of this section, the trust's distributive share of items of gross income and gain of any partnership to which subchapter C or D of chapter 63 applies shall be treated as equal to the trust's distributive share of the taxable income of such partnership.

(c) Certain income earned abroad or from sale of residence.—For purposes of this section, gross income shall be computed without regard to the exclusion provided for in section 121 (relating to gain from sale of principal residence) and without regard to the exclusion provided for in section 911 (relating to citizens or residents of United States living abroad).

(d) Tax-exempt interest required to be shown on return.—Every person required to file a return under this section for the taxable year shall include on such return the amount of interest received or accrued during the taxable year which is exempt from the tax imposed by chapter 1.

(e) Consolidated returns.—

For provisions relating to consolidated returns by affiliated corporations, see chapter 6.

§ 6013. Joint returns of income tax by husband and wife

(a) Joint returns.—A husband and wife may make a single return jointly of income taxes under subtitle A, even though one of the spouses has neither gross income nor deductions, except as provided below:

(1) no joint return shall be made if either the husband or wife at any time during the taxable year is a nonresident alien;

(2) no joint return shall be made if the husband and wife have different taxable years; except that if such taxable years begin on the same day and end on different days because of the death of either or both, then the joint return may be made with respect to the taxable year of each. The above exception shall not apply if the surviving spouse remarries before the close of his taxable year, nor if the taxable year of either spouse is a fractional part of a year under section 443(a)(l);

(3) in the case of death of one spouse or both spouses the joint return with respect to the decedent may be made only by his executor or administrator; except that in the case of the death of one spouse the joint return may be made by the surviving spouse with respect to both himself and the decedent if no return for the taxable year has been made by the decedent, no executor or administrator has been appointed, and no executor or administrator is appointed before the last day prescribed by law for filing the return of the surviving spouse. If an executor or administrator of the decedent is appointed after the making of the joint return by the surviving spouse, the executor or administrator may disaffirm such joint return by making, within 1 year after the last day prescribed by law for filing the return of the surviving spouse, a separate return for the taxable year of the decedent with respect to which the joint return was made, in which case the return made by the survivor shall constitute his separate return.

(b) Joint return after filing separate return.—

(1) In general.—Except as provided in paragraph (2), if an individual has filed a separate return for a taxable year for which a joint return could have been made by him and his spouse under subsection (a) and the time prescribed by law for filing the return for such taxable year has expired, such individual and his spouse may nevertheless make a joint return for such taxable year. A joint return filed by the husband and wife under this subsection shall constitute the return of the husband and wife for such taxable year, and all payments, credits, refunds, or other repayments made or allowed with respect to the separate return of either spouse for such taxable year shall be taken into account in determining the extent to which the tax based upon the joint return has been paid. If a joint return is made under this subsection, any election (other than the election to file a separate return) made by either spouse in his separate return for such taxable year with respect to the treatment of any income, deduction, or credit of such spouse shall not be changed in the making of the joint return where such election would have been irrevocable if the joint return had not been made. If a joint return is made under this subsection after the death of either spouse, such return with respect to the decedent can be made only by his executor or administrator.

(2) Limitations for making of election.—The election provided for in paragraph (1) may not be made—

(A) unless there is paid in full at or before the time of the filing of the joint return the amount shown as tax upon such joint return; or

(B) after the expiration of 3 years from the last date prescribed by law for filing the return for such taxable year (determined without regard to any extension of time granted to either spouse); or

(C) after there has been mailed to either spouse, with respect to such taxable year, a notice of deficiency under section 6212, if the spouse, as to such notice, files a petition with the Tax Court within the time prescribed in section 6213; or

(D) after either spouse has commenced a suit in any court for the recovery of any part of the tax for such taxable year; or

(E) after either spouse has entered into a closing agreement under section 7121 with respect to such taxable year, or after any civil or criminal case arising against either spouse with respect to such taxable year has been compromised under section 7122.

(3) When return deemed filed.—

(A) Assessment and collection.—For purposes of section 6501 (relating to periods of limitations on assessment and collection), and for purposes of section 6651 (relating to delinquent returns), a joint return made under this subsection shall be deemed to have been filed—

(i) Where both spouses filed separate returns prior to making the joint return—on the date the last separate return was filed (but not earlier than the last date prescribed by law for filing the return of either spouse);

(ii) Where only one spouse filed a separate return prior to the making of the joint return, and the other spouse had less than the exemption amount of gross income for such taxable year—on the date of the filing of such separate return (but not earlier than the last date prescribed by law for the filing of such separate return); or

(iii) Where only one spouse filed a separate return prior to the making of the joint return, and the other spouse had gross income of the exemption amount or more for such taxable year—on the date of the filing of such joint return.

For purposes of this subparagraph, the term "exemption amount" has the meaning given to such term by section 151(d). For purposes of clauses (ii) and (iii), if the spouse whose gross income is being compared to the exemption amount is 65 or over, such clauses shall be applied by substituting "the sum of the exemption amount and the additional standard deduction under section 63(c)(2) by reason of section 63(f)(1)(A)" for "the exemption amount."

(B) Credit or refund.—For purposes of section 6511, a joint return made under this subsection shall be deemed to have been filed on the last date prescribed by law for filing the return for such taxable year (determined without regard to any extension of time granted to either spouse).

(4) Additional time for assessment.—If a joint return is made under this subsection, the periods of limitations provided in sections 6501 and 6502 on the making of assessments and the beginning of levy or a proceeding in court for collection shall with respect to such return include one year immediately after the date of the filing of such joint return (computed without regard to the provisions of paragraph (3)).

(5) Additions to the tax and penalties.—

(A) Coordination with part II of subchapter A of chapter 68.—For purposes of part II of subchapter A of chapter 68, where the sum of the amounts shown as tax on the separate returns of each spouse is less than the amount shown as tax on the joint return made under this subsection—

(i) such sum shall be treated as the amount shown on the joint return,

(ii) any negligence (or disregard of rules or regulations) on either separate return shall be treated as negligence (or such disregard) on the joint return, and

(iii) any fraud on either separate return shall be treated as fraud on the joint return.

(B) Criminal penalty.—For purposes of section 7206(1) and (2) and section 7207 (relating to criminal penalties in the case of fraudulent returns) the term "return" includes a separate return filed by a spouse with respect to a taxable year for which a joint return is made under this subsection after the filing of such separate return.

(c) Treatment of joint return after death of either spouse.—For purposes of sections 15, 443, and 7851(a)(1)(A), where the husband and wife have different taxable years because of the death of either spouse, the joint return shall be treated as if the taxable years of both spouses ended on the date of the closing of the surviving spouse's taxable year.

(d) Special rules.—For purposes of this section—

(1) the status as husband and wife of two individuals having taxable years beginning on the same day shall be determined—

(A) if both have the same taxable year—as of the close of such year; or

(B) if one dies before the close of the taxable year of the other—as of the time of such death;

(2) an individual who is legally separated from his spouse under a decree of divorce or of separate maintenance shall not be considered as married; and

(3) if a joint return is made, the tax shall be computed on the aggregate income and the liability with respect to the tax shall be joint and several.

***(f) Joint return where individual is in missing status.**—For purposes of this section and subtitle A—

(1) Election by spouse.—If—

(A) an individual is in a missing status (within the meaning of paragraph (3)) as a result of service in a combat zone (as determined for purposes of section 112), and

(B) the spouse of such individual is otherwise entitled to file a joint return for any taxable year which begins on or before the day which is 2 years after the date designated under section 112 as the date of termination of combatant activities in such zone.

then such spouse may elect under subsection (a) to file a joint return for such taxable year. With respect to service in the combat zone designated for purposes of the Vietnam conflict, such election may be made for any taxable year while an individual is in missing status.

(2) Effect of election.—If the spouse of an individual described in paragraph (1)(A) elects to file a joint return under subsection (a) for a taxable year, then, until such election is revoked—

(A) such election shall be valid even if such individual died before the beginning of such year, and

*Editorial comment: There is no subsection (e).

(B) except for purposes of section 692 (relating to income taxes of members of the Armed Forces, astronauts, and victims of certain terrorist attacks on death), the income tax liability of such individual, his spouse, and his estate shall be determined as if he were alive throughout the taxable year.

(3) Missing status.—For purposes of this subsection—

(A) Uniformed services.—A member of a uniformed service (within the meaning of section 101(3) of title 37 of the United States Code) is in a missing status for any period for which he is entitled to pay and allowances under section 552 of such title 37.

(B) Civilian employees.—An employee (within the meaning of section 5561(2) of title 5 of the United States Code) is in a missing status for any period for which he is entitled to pay and allowances under section 5562 of such title 5.

(4) Making of election; revocation.—An election described in this subsection with respect to any taxable year may be made by filing a joint return in accordance with subsection (a) and under such regulations as may be prescribed by the Secretary. Such an election may be revoked by either spouse on or before the due date (including extensions) for such taxable year, and, in the case of an executor or administrator, may be revoked by disaffirming as provided in the last sentence of subsection (a)(3).

* * *

§ 6015. Relief from joint and several liability on joint return

(a) In general.—Notwithstanding section 6013(d)(3)—

(1) an individual who has made a joint return may elect to seek relief under the procedures prescribed under subsection (b), and

(2) if such individual is eligible to elect the application of subsection (c), such individual may, in addition to any election under paragraph (1), elect to limit such individual's liability for any deficiency with respect to such joint return in the manner prescribed under subsection (c).

Any determination under this section shall be made without regard to community property laws.

(b) Procedures for relief from liability applicable to all joint filers.—

(1) In general.—Under procedures prescribed by the Secretary, if—

(A) a joint return has been made for a taxable year,

(B) on such return there is an understatement of tax attributable to erroneous items of 1 individual filing the joint return,

(C) the other individual filing the joint return establishes that in signing the return he or she did not know, and had no reason to know, that there was such understatement,

(D) taking into account all the facts and circumstances, it is inequitable to hold the other individual liable for the deficiency in tax for such taxable year attributable to such understatement, and

(E) the other individual elects (in such form as the Secretary may prescribe) the benefits of this subsection not later than the date which is 2 years after the date the Secretary has begun collection activities with respect to the individual making the election,

then the other individual shall be relieved of liability for tax (including interest, penalties, and other amounts) for such taxable year to the extent such liability is attributable to such understatement.

(2) Apportionment of relief.—If an individual who, but for paragraph (1)(C), would be relieved of liability under paragraph (1), establishes that in signing the return such individual did not know, and had no reason to know, the extent of such understatement, then such individual shall be relieved of liability for tax (including interest, penalties, and other amounts) for such taxable year to the extent that such liability is attributable to the portion of such understatement of which such individual did not know and had no reason to know.

(3) Understatement.—For purposes of this subsection, the term "understatement" has the meaning given to such term by section 6662(d)(2) (A).

(c) Procedures to limit liability for taxpayers no longer married or taxpayers legally separated or not living together.—

(1) In general.—Except as provided in this subsection, if an individual who has made a joint return for any taxable year elects the application of this subsection, the individual's liability for any deficiency which is assessed with respect to the return shall not exceed the portion of such deficiency properly allocable to the individual under subsection (d).

(2) Burden of proof.—Except as provided in subparagraph (A)(ii) or (C) of paragraph (3), each individual who elects the application of this subsection shall have the burden of proof with respect to establishing the portion of any deficiency allocable to such individual.

(3) Election.—

(A) Individuals eligible to make election.—

(i) In general.—An individual shall only be eligible to elect the application of this subsection if—

(I) at the time such election is filed, such individual is no longer married to, or is legally separated from, the individual with whom such individual filed the joint return to which the election relates, or

(II) such individual was not a member of the same household as the individual with whom such joint return was filed at any time during the 12-month period ending on the date such election is filed.

(ii) Certain taxpayers ineligible to elect.—If the Secretary demonstrates that assets were transferred between individuals filing a joint return as part of a fraudulent scheme by such individuals, an election under this subsection by either individual shall be invalid (and section 6013(d)(3) shall apply to the joint return).

(B) Time for election.—An election under this subsection for any taxable year may be made at any time after a deficiency for such year is asserted but not later than 2 years after the date on which the Secretary has begun collection activities with respect to the individual making the election.

(C) Election not valid with respect to certain deficiencies.—If the Secretary demonstrates than an individual making an election under this subsection had actual knowledge, at the time such individual signed the return, of any item giving rise to a deficiency (or portion thereof) which is not allocable to such individual under subsection (d), such election shall not apply to such deficiency (or portion). This subparagraph shall not apply where the individual with actual knowledge establishes that such individual signed the return under duress.

(4) Liability increased by reason of transfers of property to avoid tax.—

(A) In general.—Notwithstanding any other provision of this subsection, the portion of the deficiency for which the individual electing the application of this subsection is liable (without regard to this paragraph) shall be increased by the value of any disqualified asset transferred to the individual.

(B) Disqualified asset.—For purposes of this paragraph—

(i) In general.—The term "disqualified asset" means any property or right to property transferred to an individual making the election under this subsection with respect to a joint return by the other individual filing such joint return if the principal purpose of the transfer was the avoidance of tax or payment of tax.

(ii) Presumption.—

(I) In general.—For purposes of clause (i), except as provided in subclause (II), any transfer which is made after the date which is 1 year before the date on which the 1st letter of proposed deficiency which allows the taxpayer an opportunity for administrative review in the Internal Revenue Service Office of Appeals is sent shall be presumed to have as its principal purpose the avoidance of tax or payment of tax.

(II) Exceptions.—Subclause (I) shall not apply to any transfer pursuant to a decree of divorce or separate maintenance or a written instrument incident to such a decree or to any transfer which an individual establishes did not have as its principal purpose the avoidance of tax or payment of tax.

(d) Allocation of deficiency.—For purposes of subsection (c)—

(1) In general.—The portion of any deficiency on a joint return allocated to an individual shall be the amount which bears the same ratio to such deficiency as the net amount of items taken into account in computing the deficiency and allocable to the individual under paragraph (3) bears to the net amount of all items taken into account in computing the deficiency.

(2) Separate treatment of certain items.—If a deficiency (or portion thereof) is attributable to—

(A) the disallowance of a credit, or

(B) any tax (other than tax imposed by section 1 or 55) required to be included with the joint return,

and such item is allocated to 1 individual under paragraph (3), such deficiency (or portion) shall be allocated to such individual. Any such item shall not be taken into account under paragraph (1).

(3) Allocation of items giving rise to the deficiency.—For purposes of this subsection—

(A) In general.—Except as provided in paragraphs (4) and (5), any item giving rise to a deficiency on a joint return shall be allocated to individuals filing the return in the same manner as it would have been allocated if the individuals had filed separate returns for the taxable year.

(B) Exception where other spouse benefits.—Under rules prescribed by the Secretary, an item otherwise allocable to an individual under subparagraph (A) shall be allocated to the other individual filing the joint return to the extent the item gave rise to a tax benefit on the joint return to the other individual.

(C) Exception for fraud.—The Secretary may provide for an allocation of any item in a manner not prescribed by subparagraph (A) if the Secretary establishes that such allocation is appropriate due to fraud of 1 or both individuals.

(4) Limitations on separate returns disregarded.—If an item of deduction or credit is disallowed in its entirety solely because a separate return is filed, such disallowance shall be disregarded and the item shall be computed as if a joint return had been filed and then allocated between the spouses appropriately. A similar rule shall apply for purposes of section 86.

(5) Child's liability.—If the liability of a child of a taxpayer is included on a joint return, such liability shall be disregarded in computing the separate liability of either spouse and such liability shall be allocated appropriately between the spouses.

(e) Petition for review by tax court.—

(1) In general.—In the case of an individual against whom a deficiency has been asserted and who elects to have subsection (b) or (c) apply, or in the case of an individual who requests equitable relief under subsection (f)—

(A) In general.—In addition to any other remedy provided by law, the individual may petition the Tax Court (and the Tax Court shall have jurisdiction) to determine the appropriate relief available to the individual under this section if such petition is filed—

(i) at any time after the earlier of—

(I) the date the Secretary mails, by certified or registered mail to the taxpayer's last known address, notice of the Secretary's final determination of relief available to the individual, or

(II) the date which is 6 months after the date such election is filed or request is made with the Secretary, and

(ii) not later than the close of the 90th day after the date described in clause (i)(I).

(B) Restrictions applicable to collection of assessment.—

(i) In general.—Except as otherwise provided in section 6851 or 6861, no levy or proceeding in court shall be made, begun, or prosecuted against the individual making an election under subsection (b) or (c) or requesting equitable relief under subsection (f) for collection of any assessment to which such election relates until the close of the 90th day referred to in subparagraph (A)(ii), or, if a petition has been filed with the Tax Court under subparagraph (A), until the decision of the Tax Court has become final. Rules similar to the rules of section 7485 shall apply with respect to the collection of such assessment.

(ii) Authority to enjoin collection actions.—Notwithstanding the provisions of section 7421(a), the beginning of such levy or proceeding during the time the prohibition under clause (i) is in force may be enjoined by a proceeding in the proper court, including the Tax Court. The Tax Court shall have no jurisdiction under this subparagraph to enjoin any action or proceeding unless a timely petition has been filed under subparagraph (A) and then only in respect of the amount of the assessment to which the election under subsection (b) or (c) relates or to which the request under subsection (f) relates.

(2) Suspension of running of period of limitations.—The running of the period of limitations in section 6502 on the collection of the assessment to which the petition under paragraph (1)(A) relates shall be suspended—

(A) for the period during which the Secretary is prohibited by paragraph (1)(B) from collecting by levy or a proceeding in court and for 60 days thereafter, and

(B) if a waiver under paragraph (5) is made, from the date the claim for relief was filed until 60 days after the wavier is filed with the Secretary.

(3) Limitation on tax court jurisdiction.—If a suit for refund is begun by either individual filing the joint return pursuant to section 6532—

(A) the Tax Court shall lose jurisdiction of the individual's action under this section to whatever extent jursidiction is acquired by the district court or the United States Court of Federal Claims over the taxable years that are the subject of the suit for refund, and

(B) the court acquiring jurisdiction shall have jurisdiction over the petition filed under this subsection.

(4) Notice to other spouse.—The Tax Court shall establish rules which provide the individual filing a joint return but not making the election under subsection (b) or (c) or the request for equitable relief under subsection (f) with adequate notice and an opportunity to become a party to a proceeding under either such subsection.

(5) Waiver.—An individual who elects the application of subsection (b) or (c) or who requests equitable relief under subsection (f) (and who agrees with the Secretary's determination of relief) may waive in writing at any time the restrictions in paragraph (1)(B) with respect to collection of the outstanding assessment (whether or not a notice of the Secretary's final determination of relief has been mailed).

(f) Equitable relief.—Under procedures prescribed by the Secretary, if—

(1) taking into account all the facts and circumstances, it is inequitable to hold the individual liable for any unpaid tax or any deficiency (or any portion of either), and

(2) relief is not available to such individual under subsection (b) or (c),

(3) the Secretary may relieve such individual of such liability.

(g) Credits and refunds.—

(1) In general.—Except as provided in paragraphs (2) and (3), notwithstanding any other law or rule of law (other than section 6511, 6512(b), 7121, or 7122), credit or refund shall be allowed or made to the extent attributable to the application of this section.

(2) Res judicata.—In the case of any election under subsection (b) or (c) or of any request for equitable relief under subsection (f), if a decision of a court in any prior proceeding for the same taxable year has become final, such decision shall be conclusive except with respect to the qualification of the individual for relief which was not an issue in such proceeding. The exception contained in the preceding sentence shall not apply if the court determines that the individual participated meaningfully in such prior proceeding.

(3) Credit and refund not allowed under subsection (c).—No credit or refund shall be allowed as a result of an election under subsection (c).

(h) Regulations.—The Secretary shall prescribe such regulations as are necessary to carry out the provisions of this section, including—

(1) regulations providing methods for allocation of items other than the methods under subsection (d)(3), and

(2) regulations providing the opportunity for an individual to have notice of, and an opportunity to participate in, any administrative proceeding with respect to an election made under subsection (b) or (c) or a request for equitable relief made under subsection (f) by the other individual filing the joint return.

* * *

SUBPART C—ESTATE AND GIFT TAX RETURNS

§ 6018. Estate tax returns

(a) Returns by executor.—

(1) Citizens or residents.—In all cases where the gross estate at the death of a citizen or resident exceeds the basic exclusion amount in effect under section 2010(c) for the calendar year which includes the date of death, the executor shall make a return with respect to the estate tax imposed by subtitle B.

(2) Nonresidents not citizens of the United States.—In the case of the estate of every nonresident not a citizen of the United States if that part of the gross estate which is situated in the United States exceeds $60,000, the executor shall make a return with respect to the estate tax imposed by subtitle B.

(3) Adjustment for certain gifts.—The amount applicable under paragraph (1) and the amount set forth in paragraph (2) shall each be reduced (but not below zero) by the sum of—

(A) the amount of the adjusted taxable gifts (within the meaning of section 2001(b)) made by the decedent after December 31, 1976, plus

(B) the aggregate amount allowed as a specific exemption under section 2521 (as in effect before its repeal by the Tax Reform Act of 1976) with respect to gifts made by the decedent after September 8, 1976.

(b) Returns by beneficiaries.—If the executor is unable to make a complete return as to any part of the gross estate of the decedent, he shall include in his return a description of such part and the name of every person holding a legal or beneficial interest therein. Upon notice from the Secretary such person shall in like manner make a return as to such part of the gross estate.

* * *

§ 6019. Gift tax returns

(a) In general.—Any individual who in any calendar year makes any transfer by gift other than—

(1) a transfer which under subsection (b) or (e) of section 2503 is not to be included in the total amount of gifts for such year,

(2) a transfer of an interest with respect to which a deduction is allowed under section 2523, or

(3) a transfer with respect to which a deduction is allowed under section 2522 but only if—

(A) (i) such transfer is of the donor's entire interest in the property transferred, and

(ii) no other interest in such property is or has been transferred (for less than adequate and full consideration in money or money's worth) from the donor to a person, or for a use, not described in subsection (a) or (b) of section 2522, or

(B) such transfer is described in section 2522(d),

shall make a return for such year with respect to the gift tax imposed by subtitle B.

(b) Statements to be furnished to certain persons.—Every person required to make a return under subsection (a) shall furnish to each person whose name is required to be set forth in such return (other than the person required to make such return) a written statement showing—

(1) the name, address, and phone number of the person required to make such return, and

(2) the information specified in such return with respect to property received by the person required to receive such statement.

The written statement required under the preceding sentence shall be furnished not later than 30 days after the date that the return required by subsection (a) is filed.

SUBPART D—MISCELLANEOUS PROVISIONS *

PART III—INFORMATION RETURNS

Editorial Summary

Information Returns

Subchapter A of Chapter 61 (Secs. 6031–6053)

See the discussion under the Editorial Summary entitled Information and Returns, which precedes Sec. 6001.

SUBPART A—INFORMATION CONCERNING PERSONS SUBJECT TO SPECIAL PROVISIONS

§ 6031. Return of partnership income

(a) General rule.—Every partnership (as defined in section 761(a)) shall make a return for each taxable year, stating specifically the items of its gross income and the deductions allowable by subtitle A, and such other information for the purpose of carrying out the provisions of subtitle A as the Secretary may by forms and regulations prescribe, and shall include in the return the names and addresses of the individuals who would be entitled to share in the taxable income if distributed and the amount of the distributive share of each individual.

(b) Copies to partners.—Each partnership required to file a return under subsection (a) for any partnership taxable year shall (on or before the day on which the return for such taxable year was required to be filed) furnish to each person who is a partner or who holds an interest in such partnership as a nominee for another person at any time during such taxable year a copy of such information required to be shown on such return as may be required by regulations. In the case of an electing large partnership (as defined in section 775), such information shall be furnished on or before the first March 15 following the close of such taxable year.

(c) Nominee reporting.—Any person who holds an interest in a partnership as a nominee for another person—

(1) shall furnish to the partnership, in the manner prescribed by the Secretary, the name and address of such other person, and any other information for such taxable year as the Secretary may by form and regulation prescribe, and

(2) shall furnish in the manner prescribed by the Secretary such other person the information provided by such partnership under subsection (b).

(d) Separate statement of items of unrelated business taxable income.—In the case of any partnership regularly carrying on a trade or business (within the meaning of section 512(c)(1)), the information required under subsection (b) to be furnished to its partners shall include such information as is necessary to enable each partner to compute its distributive share of partnership income or loss from such trade or business in accordance with section 512(a)(1), but without regard to the modifications described in paragraphs (8) through (15) of section 512(b).

(e) Foreign partnerships.—

(1) Exception for foreign partnership.—Except as provided in paragraph (2), the preceding provisions of this section shall not apply to a foreign partnership.

(2) Certain foreign partnerships required to file return.—Except as provided in regulations prescribed by the Secretary, this section shall apply to a foreign partnership for any taxable year if for such year, such partnership has—

(A) gross income derived from sources within the United States, or

(B) gross income which is effectively connected with the conduct of a trade or business within the United States.

The Secretary may provide simplified filing procedures for foreign partnerships to which this section applies.

*Omitted.

(f) Electing investment partnerships.—In the case of any electing investment partnership (as defined in section 743(e)(6)), the information required under subsection (b) to be furnished to any partner to whom section 743(e)(2) applies shall include such information as is necessary to enable the partner to compute the amount of losses disallowed under section 743(e).

* * *

§ 6033. Returns by exempt organizations

(a) Organizations required to file.—

(1) In general.—Except as provided in paragraph (3), every organization exempt from taxation under section 501(a) shall file an annual return, stating specifically the items of gross income, receipts, and disbursements, and such other information for the purpose of carrying out the internal revenue laws as the Secretary may by forms or regulations prescribe, and shall keep such records, render under oath such statements, make such other returns, and comply with such rules and regulations as the Secretary may from time to time prescribe; except that, in the discretion of the Secretary, any organization described in section 401(a) may be relieved from stating in its return any information which is reported in returns filed by the employer which established such organization.

(2) Being a party to certain reportable transactions.—Every tax-exempt entity described in section 4965(c) shall file (in such form and manner and at such time as determined by the Secretary) a disclosure of—

(A) such entity's being a party to any prohibited tax shelter transaction (as defined in section 4965(e)), and

(B) the identity of any other party to such transaction which is known by such tax-exempt entity.

(3) Exceptions from filing.—

(A) Mandatory exceptions.—Paragraph (1) shall not apply to—

(i) churches, their integrated auxiliaries, and conventions or associations of churches,

(ii) any organization (other than a private foundation, as defined in section 509(a)) described in subparagraph (C), the gross receipts of which in each taxable year are normally not more than $5,000, or

(iii) the exclusively religious activities of any religious order.

(B) Discretionary exceptions.—The Secretary may relieve any organization required under paragraph (1) (other than an organization described in section 509(a)(3)) to file an information return from filing such a return where he determines that such filing is not necessary to the efficient administration of the internal revenue laws.

(C) Certain organizations.—The organizations referred to in subparagraph (A)(ii) are—

(i) a religious organization described in section 501(c)(3);

(ii) an educational organization described in section 170(b)(1)(A)(ii);

(iii) a charitable organization, or an organization for the prevention of cruelty to children or animals, described in section 501(c)(3), if such organization is supported, in whole or in part, by funds contributed by the United States or any State or political subdivision thereof, or is primarily supported by contributions of the general public;

(iv) an organization described in section 501(c)(3), if such organization is operated, supervised, or controlled by or in connection with a religious organization described in clause (i);

(v) an organization described in section 501(c)(8); and

(vi) an organization described in section 501(c)(1), if such organization is a corporation wholly owned by the United States or any agency or instrumentality thereof, or a wholly owned subsidiary of such a corporation.

(b) Certain organizations described in section 501(c)(3).—Every organization described in section 501(c)(3) which is subject to the requirements of subsection (a) shall furnish annually information, at such time and in such manner as the Secretary may by forms or regulations prescribe, setting forth—

(1) its gross income for the year,

(2) its expenses attributable to such income and incurred within the year,

(3) its disbursements within the year for the purposes for which it is exempt,

(4) a balance sheet showing its assets, liabilities, and net worth as of the beginning of such year,

(5) the total of the contributions and gifts received by it during the year, and the names and addresses of all substantial contributors,

(6) the names and addresses of its foundation managers (within the meaning of section 4946(b)(1)) and highly compensated employees,

(7) the compensation and other payments made during the year to each individual described in paragraph (6),

(8) in the case of an organization with respect to which an election under section 501(h) is effective for the taxable year, the following amounts for such organization for such taxable year:

(A) the lobbying expenditures (as defined in section 4911(c)(1)),

(B) the lobbying nontaxable amount (as defined in section 4911(c)(2)),

(C) the grass roots expenditures (as defined in section 4911(c)(3)), and

(D) the grass roots nontaxable amount (as defined in section 4911(c)(4)),

(9) such other information with respect to direct or indirect transfers to, and other direct or indirect transactions and relationships with, other organizations described in section 501(c) (other than paragraph (3) thereof) or section 527 as the Secretary may require to prevent—

(A) diversion of funds from the organization's exempt purpose, or

(B) misallocation of revenues or expenses,

(10) the respective amounts (if any) of the taxes imposed on the organization, or any organization manager of the organization, during the taxable year under any of the following provisions (and the respective amounts (if any) of reimbursements paid by the organization during the taxable year with respect to taxes imposed on any such organization manager under any of such provisions):

(A) section 4911 (relating to tax on excess expenditures to influence legislation),

(B) section 4912 (relating to tax on disqualifying lobbying expenditures of certain organizations),

(C) section 4955 (relating to taxes on political expenditures of section 501(c)(3) organizations), except to the extent that, by reason of section 4962, the taxes imposed under such section are not required to be paid or are credited or refunded, and

(D) section 4959 (relating to taxes on failure by hospital organizations).

(11) the respective amounts (if any) of—

(A) the taxes imposed with respect to the organization on any organization manager, or any disqualified person, during the taxable year under section 4958 (relating to taxes on private excess benefit from certain charitable organizations), and

(B) reimbursements paid by the organization during the taxable year with respect to taxes imposed under such section, except to the extent that, by reason of section 4962, the taxes imposed under such section are not required to be paid or are credited or refunded,

(12) such other information as the Secretary may require with respect to any excess benefit transaction (as defined in section 4958),

(13) such information with respect to disqualified persons as the Secretary may prescribe,

(14) such information as the Secretary may require with respect to disaster relief activities, including the amount and use of qualified contributions to which section 1400S(a) applies,

(15) in the case of an organization to which the requirements of section 501(r) apply for the taxable year—

(A) a description of how the organization is addressing the needs identified in each community health needs assessment conducted under section 501(r)(3) and a description of any such needs that are not being addressed together with the reasons why such needs are not being addressed, and

(B) the audited financial statements of such organization (or, in the case of an organization the financial statements of which are included in a consolidated financial statement with other organizations, such consolidated financial statement).

(16) such other information for purposes of carrying out the internal revenue laws as the Secretary may require.

For purposes of paragraph (8), if section 4911(f) applies to the organization for the taxable year, such organization shall furnish the amounts with respect to the affiliated group as well as with respect to such organization.

(c) Additional provisions relating to private foundations.—In the case of an organization which is a private foundation (within the meaning of section 509(a))—

(1) the Secretary shall by regulations provide that the private foundation shall include in its annual return under this section such information (not required to be furnished by subsection (b) or the forms or regulations prescribed thereunder) as would have been required to be furnished under section 6056 (relating to annual reports by private foundations) as such section 6056 was in effect on January 1, 1979, and

(2) the foundation managers shall furnish copies of the annual return under this section to such State officials, at such times, and under such conditions, as the Secretary may by regulations prescribe.

Nothing in paragraph (1) shall require the inclusion of the name and address of any recipient (other than a disqualified person within the meaning of section 4946) of 1 or more charitable gifts or grants made by the foundation to such recipient as an indigent or needy person if the aggregate of such gifts or grants made by the foundation to such recipient during the year does not exceed $1,000.

(d) Section to apply to nonexempt charitable trusts and nonexempt private foundations.—The following organizations shall comply with the requirements of this section in the same manner as organizations described in section 501(c)(3) which are exempt from tax under section 501(a):

(1) Nonexempt charitable trusts.—A trust described in section 4947(a)(1) (relating to nonexempt charitable trusts).

(2) Nonexempt private foundations.—A private foundation which is not exempt from tax under section 501(a).

(e) Special rules relating to lobbying activities.—

(1) Reporting requirements.—

(A) In general.—If this subsection applies to an organization for any taxable year, such organization—

(i) shall include on any return required to be filed under subsection (a) for such year information setting forth the total expenditures of the organization to which section 162(e)(1) applies and the total amount of the dues or other similar amounts paid to the organization to which such expenditures are allocable, and

(ii) except as provided in paragraphs (2)(A)(i) and (3), shall, at the time of assessment or payment of such dues or other similar amounts, provide notice to each person making such payment which contains a reasonable estimate of the portion of such dues or other similar amounts to which such expenditures are so allocable.

(B) Organizations to which subsection applies.—

(i) In general.—This subsection shall apply to any organization which is exempt from taxation under this subtitle other than an organization described in section 501(c)(3).

(ii) Special rule for in-house expenditures.—This subsection shall not apply to the in-house expenditures (within the meaning of section 162(e)(5)(B)(ii)) of an organization for a taxable year if such expenditures do not exceed $2,000. In determining whether a taxpayer exceeds the $2,000 limit under this clause, there shall not be taken into account overhead costs otherwise allocable to activities described in subparagraphs (A) and (D) of section 162(e)(1).

(C) Allocation.—For purposes of this paragraph—

(i) In general.—Expenditures to which section 162(e)(1) applies shall be treated as paid out of dues or other similar amounts to the extent thereof.

(ii) Carryover of lobbying expenditures in excess of dues.—If expenditures to which section 162(e)(1) applies exceed the dues or other similar amounts for any taxable year, such excess shall be treated as expenditures to which section 162(e)(1) applies which are paid or incurred by the organization during the following taxable year.

(2) Tax imposed where organization does not notify.—

(A) In general.—If an organization—

(i) elects not to provide the notices described in paragraph (1)(A) for any taxable year, or

(ii) fails to include in such notices the amount allocable to expenditures to which section 162(e)(1) applies (determined on the basis of actual amounts rather than the reasonable estimates under paragraph (1)(A)(ii)),

then there is hereby imposed on such organization for such taxable year a tax in an amount equal to the product of the highest rate of tax imposed by section 11 for the taxable year and the aggregate amount not included in such notices by reason of such election or failure.

(B) Waiver where future adjustments made.—The Secretary may waive the tax imposed by subparagraph (A)(ii) for any taxable year if the organization agrees to adjust its estimates under paragraph (1)(A)(ii) for the following taxable year to correct any failures.

(C) Tax treated as income tax.—For purposes of this title, the tax imposed by subparagraph (A) shall be treated in the same manner as a tax imposed by chapter 1 (relating to income taxes).

(3) Exception where dues generally nondeductible.—Paragraph (1)(A) shall not apply to an organization which establishes to the satisfaction of the Secretary that substantially all of the dues or other similar amounts paid by persons to such organization are not deductible without regard to section 162(e).

* * *

(m) Additional information required from CO-OP insurers.—An organization described in section 501(c)(29) shall include on the return required under subsection (a) the following information:

(1) The amount of the reserves required by each State in which the organization is licensed to issue qualified health plans.

(2) The amount of reserves on hand.

(n) Cross references.—

For provisions relating to statements, etc., regarding exempt status of organizations, see section 6001.

For reporting requirements as to certain liquidations, dissolutions, terminations, and contractions, see section 6043(b).

For provisions relating to penalties for failure to file a return required by this section, see section 6652(c).

For provisions relating to information required in connection with certain plans of deferred compensation, see section 6058.

* * *

§ 6037. Return of S corporation

(a) In general.—Every S corporation shall make a return for each taxable year, stating specifically the items of its gross income and the deductions allowable by subtitle A, the names and addresses of all persons owning stock in the corporation at any time during the taxable year, the number of shares of stock owned by each shareholder at all times during the taxable year, the amount of money and other property distributed by the corporation during the taxable year to each shareholder, the date of each such distribution, each shareholder's pro rata share of each item of the corporation for the taxable year, and such other information, for the purpose of carrying out the provisions of subchapter S of chapter 1, as the Secretary may by forms and regulations prescribe. Any return filed pursuant to this section shall, for purposes of chapter 66 (relating to limitations), be treated as a return filed by the corporation under section 6012.

(b) Copies to shareholders.—Each S corporation required to file a return under subsection (a) for any taxable year shall (on or before the day on which the return for such taxable year was filed) furnish to each person who is a shareholder at any time during such taxable year a copy of such information shown on such return as may be required by regulations.

* * *

§ 6039D. Returns and records with respect to certain fringe benefit plans

(a) In general.—Every employer maintaining a specified fringe benefit plan during any year beginning after December 31, 1984, for any portion of which the applicable exclusion applies, shall file a return (at such time and in such manner as the Secretary shall by regulations prescribe) with respect to such plan showing for such year—

(1) the number of employees of the employer,

(2) the number of employees of the employer eligible to participate under the plan,

(3) the number of employees participating under the plan,

(4) the total cost of the plan during the year,

(5) the name, address, and taxpayer identification number of the employer and the type of business in which the employer is engaged, and

(6) the number of highly compensated employees among the employees described in paragraphs (1), (2), and (3).

(b) Recordkeeping requirement.—Each employer maintaining a specified fringe benefit plan during any year shall keep such records as may be necessary for purposes of determining whether the requirements of the applicable exclusion are met.

(c) Additional information when required by the Secretary.—Any employer—

(1) who maintains a specified fringe benefit plan during any year for which a return is required under subsection (a), and

(2) who is required by the Secretary to file an additional return for such year,

shall file such additional return. Such additional return shall be filed at such time and in such manner as the Secretary shall prescribe and shall contain such information as the Secretary shall prescribe.

(d) Definitions and special rules.—For purposes of this section—

(1) Specified fringe benefit plan.—The term "specified fringe benefit plan" means any plan under section 79, 105, 106, 120, 125, 127, 129, or 137.

(2) Applicable exclusion.—The term "applicable exclusion" means, with respect to any specified fringe benefit plan, the section specified under paragraph (1) under which benefits under such plan are excludable from gross income.

* * *

SUBPART B—INFORMATION CONCERNING TRANSACTIONS WITH OTHER PERSONS

§ 6041. Information at source

(a) Payments of $600 or more.—All persons engaged in a trade or business and making payment in the course of such trade or business to another person, of rent, salaries, wages, premiums, annuities, compensations, remunerations, emoluments, or other fixed or determinable gains, profits, and income (other than payments to which section 6042(a)(1), 6044(a)(1), 6047(e), 6049(a), or 6050N(a) applies, and other than payments with respect to which a statement is required under the authority of section 6042(a)(2), 6044(a)(2), or 6045), of $600 or more in any taxable year, or, in the case of such payments made by the United States, the officers or employees of the United States having information as to such payments and required to make returns in regard thereto by the regulations hereinafter provided for, shall render a true and accurate return to the Secretary, under such regulations and in such form and manner and to such extent as may be prescribed by the Secretary, setting forth the amount of such gains, profits, and income, and the name and address of the recipient of such payment.

* * *

(c) Recipient to furnish name and address.—When necessary to make effective the provisions of this section, the name and address of the recipient of income shall be furnished upon demand of the person paying the income.

(d) Statements to be furnished to persons with respect to whom information is required.—Every person required to make a return under subsection (a) shall furnish to each person with respect to whom such a return is required a written statement showing—

(1) the name and address of the person required to make such return, and

(2) the aggregate amount of payments to the person required to be shown on the return.

The written statement required under the preceding sentence shall be furnished to the person on or before January 31 of the year following the calendar year for which the return under subsection (a) was required to be made. To the extent provided in regulations prescribed by the Secretary, this subsection shall also apply to persons required to make returns under subsection (b).

(e) Section does not apply to certain tips.—This section shall not apply to tips with respect to which section 6053(a) (relating to reporting of tips) applies.

(f) Section does not apply to certain health arrangements.—This section shall not apply to any payment for medical care (as defined in section 231(d)) made under—

(1) a flexible spending arrangement (as define in section 106(c)(2)), or

(2) a health reimbursement arrangement which is treated as employer-provided coverage under an accident or health plan for purposes of section 106.

(g) Nonqualified deferred compensation.—Subsection (a) shall apply to—

(1) any deferrals for the year under a nonqualified deferred compensation plan (within the meaning of section 409A(d)), whether or not paid, except that this paragraph shall not apply to deferrals which are required to be reported under section 6051(a)(13) (without regard to any de minimis exception), and

(2) any amount includible under section 409A and which is not treated as wages under section 3401(a).

§ 6041A. Returns regarding payments of remuneration for services and direct sales

(a) Returns regarding remuneration for services. If—

(1) any service-recipient engaged in a trade or business pays in the course of such trade or business during any calendar year remuneration to any person for services performed by such person, and

(2) the aggregate of such remuneration paid to such person during such calendar year is $600 or more,

then the service-recipient shall make a return, according to the forms or regulations prescribed by the Secretary, setting forth the aggregate amount of such payments and the name and address of the recipient of such payments. For purposes of the preceding sentence, the term "service-recipient" means the person for whom the service is performed.

(b) Direct sales of $5,000 or more.—

(1) In general.—If—

(A) any person engaged in a trade or business in the course of such trade or business during any calendar year sells consumer products to any buyer on a buy-sell basis, a deposit-commission basis, or any similar basis which the Secretary prescribes by regulations, for resale (by the buyer or any other person) in the home or otherwise than in a permanent retail establishment, and

(B) the aggregate amount of the sales to such buyer during such calendar year is $5,000 or more,

then such person shall make a return, according to the forms or regulations prescribed by the Secretary, setting forth the name and address of the buyer to whom such sales are made.

(2) Definitions.—For purposes of paragraph (1)—

(A) Buy-sell basis.—A transaction is on a buy-sell basis if the buyer performing the services is entitled to retain part or all of the difference between the price at which the buyer purchases the product and the price at which the buyer sells the product as part or all of the buyer's remuneration for the services, and

(B) Deposit-commission basis.—A transaction is on a deposit-commission basis if the buyer performing the services is entitled to retain part or all of a purchase deposit paid by the consumer in connection with the transaction as part or all of the buyer's remuneration for the services.

(c) Certain services not included.—No return shall be required under subsection (a) or (b) if a statement with respect to the services is required to be furnished under section 6051, 6052, or 6053.

(d) Applications to governmental units.—

(1) Treated as persons.—The term "person" includes any governmental unit (and any agency or instrumentality thereof).

(2) Special rules.—In the case of any payment by a governmental entity or any agency or instrumentality thereof—

(A) subsection (a) shall be applied without regard to the trade or business requirement contained therein, and

(B) any return under this section shall be made by the officer or employee having control of the payment or appropriately designated for the purpose of making such return.

(3) Payments to corporations by federal executive agencies.—

(A) In general.—Notwithstanding any regulation prescribed by the Secretary before the date of the enactment of this paragraph, subsection (a) shall apply to remuneration paid to a corporation by any Federal executive agency (as defined in section 6050M(b)).

(B) Exception.—Subparagraph (A) shall not apply to—

(i) services under contracts described in section 6050M(e)(3) with respect to which the requirements of section 6050M(e)(2) are met, and

(ii) such other services as the Secretary may specify in regulations prescribed after the date of the enactment of this paragraph.

(e) Statements to be furnished to persons with respect to whom information is required to be furnished.—Every person required to make a return under subsection (a) or (b) shall furnish to each person whose name is required to be set forth in such return a written statement showing—

(1) the name and address of the person required to make such return, and

(2) in the case of subsection (a), the aggregate amount of payments to the person required to be shown on such return.

The written statement required under the preceding sentence shall be furnished to the person on or before January 31 of the year following the calendar year for which the return under subsection (a) was made.

(f) Recipient to furnish name, address, and identification number; inclusion on return.—

(1) Furnishing of information.—Any person with respect to whom a return or statement is required under this section to be made by another person shall furnish to such other person his name, address, and identification number at such time and in such manner as the Secretary may prescribe by regulations.

(2) Inclusion on return.— The person to whom an identification number is furnished under paragraph (1) shall include such number on any return which such person is required to file under this section and to which such identification number relates.

* * *

SUBPART C—INFORMATION REGARDING WAGES PAID EMPLOYEES

* * *

§ 6053. Reporting of tips

(a) Reports by employees.—Every employee who, in the course of his employment by an employer, receives in any calendar month tips which are wages (as defined in section 3121(a) or section 3401(a)) or which are compensation (as defined in section 3231(e)) shall report all such tips in one or more written statements furnished to his employer on or before the 10th day following such month. Such statements shall be furnished by the employee under such regulations, at such other times before such 10th day, and in such form and manner, as may be prescribed by the Secretary.

(b) Statements furnished by employers.—If the tax imposed by section 3101 or section 3201 (as the case may be) with respect to tips reported by an employee pursuant to subsection (a) exceeds the tax which can be collected by the employer pursuant to section 3102 or section 3202 (as the case may be), the employer shall furnish to the employee a written statement showing the amount of such excess. The statement required to be furnished pursuant to this subsection shall be furnished at such time, shall contain such other information, and shall be in such form as the Secretary may by regulations prescribe. When required by such regulations, a duplicate of any such statement shall be filed with the Secretary.

(c) Reporting requirements relating to certain large food or beverage establishments.—

(1) Report to Secretary.—In the case of a large food or beverage establishment, each employer shall report to the Secretary, at such time and manner as the Secretary may prescribe by regulation, the following information with respect to each calendar year:

(A) The gross receipts of such establishment from the provision of food and beverages (other than nonallocable receipts).

(B) The aggregate amount of charge receipts (other than nonallocable receipts).

(C) The aggregate amount of charged tips shown on such charge receipts.

(D) The sum of—

(i) the aggregate amount reported by employees to the employer under subsection (a), plus

(ii) the amount the employer is required to report under section 6051 with respect to service charges of less than 10 percent.

(E) With respect to each employee, the amount allocated to such employee under paragraph (3).

(2) Furnishing of statement to employees.— Each employer described in paragraph (1) shall furnish, in such manner as the Secretary may prescribe by regulations, to each employee of the large food or beverage establishment a written statement for each calendar year showing the following information:

(A) The name and address of such employer.

(B) The name of the employee.

(C) The amount allocated to the employee under paragraph (3) for all payroll periods ending within the calendar year.

Any statement under this paragraph shall be furnished to the employee during January of the calendar year following the calendar year for which such statement is made.

(3) Employee allocation of 8 percent of gross receipts.—

(A) In general.—For purposes of paragraphs (1)(E) and (2)(C), the employer of a large food or beverage establishment shall allocate (as tips for purposes of the requirements of this subsection) among employees performing services during any payroll period who customarily receive tip income an amount equal to the excess of—

(i) 8 percent of the gross receipts (other than nonallocable receipts) of such establishment for the payroll period, over

(ii) the aggregate amount reported by such employees to the employer under subsection (a) for such period.

(B) Method of allocation.—The employer shall allocate the amount under subparagraph (A)—

(i) on the basis of a good faith agreement by the employer and the employees, or

(ii) in the absence of an agreement under clause (i), in the manner determined under regulations prescribed by the Secretary.

(C) The Secretary may lower the percentage required to be allocated.—Upon the petition of the employer or the majority of employees of such employer, the Secretary may reduce (but not below 2 percent) the percentage of gross receipts required to be allocated under subparagraph (A) where he determines that the percentage of gross receipts constituting tips is less than 8 percent.

(4) Large food or beverage establishment.—For purposes of this subsection, the term "large food or beverage establishment" means any trade or business (or portion thereof)—

(A) which provides food or beverages,

(B) with respect to which the tipping of employees serving food or beverages by customers is customary, and

(C) which normally employed more than 10 employees on a typical business day during the preceding calendar year.

For purposes of subparagraph (C), rules similar to the rules of subsections (a) and (b) of section 52 shall apply under regulations prescribed by the Secretary, and an individual who owns 50 percent or more in value of the stock of the corporation operating the establishment shall not be treated as an employee.

(5) Employer not to be liable for wrong allocations.—The employer shall not be liable to any person if any amount is improperly allocated under paragraph (3)(B) if such allocation is done in accordance with the regulations prescribed under paragraph (3)(B).

(6) Nonallocable receipts defined.—For purposes of this subsection, the term "nonallocable receipts" means receipts which are allocable to—

(A) carryout sales, or

(B) services with respect to which a service charge of 10 percent or more is added.

(7) Application to new businesses.—The Secretary shall prescribe regulations for the application of this subsection to new businesses.

*[SUBPART D—REPEALED]**

*SUBPART E—REGISTRATION OF AND INFORMATION CONCERNING PENSION, ETC., PLANS**

*SUBPART F—INFORMATION CONCERNING INCOME TAX RETURN PREPARERS**

PART IV—SIGNING AND VERIFYING OF RETURNS AND OTHER DOCUMENTS*

PART V—TIME FOR FILING RETURNS AND OTHER DOCUMENTS

Editorial Summary

Filing Due Dates

Subchapter A of Chapter 61 (Secs. 6072, 6075)

See the discussion under the Editorial Summary entitled Information and Returns, which precedes Sec. 6001.

* * *

§ 6072. Time for filing income tax returns

(a) General rule.—In the case of returns under section 6012, 6013, 6017, or 6031 (relating to income tax under subtitle A), returns made on the basis of the calendar year shall be filed on or before the 15th day of April following the close of the calendar year and returns made on the basis of a fiscal year shall be filed on or before the 15th day of the fourth month following the close of the fiscal year, except as otherwise provided in the following subsections of this section.

(b) Returns of corporations.—Returns of corporations under section 6012 made on the basis of the calendar year shall be filed on or before the 15th day of March following the close of the calendar year, and such returns made on the basis of a fiscal year shall be filed on or before the 15th day of the third month following the close of the fiscal year. Returns required for a taxable year by section 6011(e)(2) (relating to returns of a DISC) shall be filed on or before the fifteenth day of the ninth month following the close of the taxable year.

(c) Returns by certain nonresident alien individuals and foreign corporations.—Returns made by nonresident alien individuals (other than those whose wages are subject to withholding under chapter 24) and foreign corporations (other than those having an office or place of business in the United States or a former FSC (as defined in section 922 as in effect before its repeal by the FSC Repeal and Extraterritorial Income Exclusion Act of 2000) under section 6012 on the basis of a calendar year shall be filed on or before the 15th day of June following the close of the calendar year and such returns made on the basis of a fiscal year shall be filed on or before the 15th day of the 6th month following the close of the fiscal year.

* * *

§ 6075. Time for filing estate and gift tax returns

(a) Estate tax returns.—Returns made under section 6018(a) (relating to estate taxes) shall be filed within 9 months after the date of the decedent's death.

(b) Gift tax returns.—

(1) General rule.—Returns made under section 6019 (relating to gift taxes) shall be filed on or before the 15th day of April following the close of the calendar year.

(2) Extension where taxpayer granted extension for filing income tax return.—Any extension of time granted the taxpayer for filing the return of income taxes imposed by subtitle A for any taxable year which is a calendar year shall be deemed to be also an extension of time granted the taxpayer for filing the return under section 6019 for such calendar year.

(3) Coordination with due date for estate tax return.—Notwithstanding paragraphs (1) and (2), the time for filing the return made under section 6019 for the calendar year which includes the date of death of the donor shall not be later than the time (including extensions) for filing the return made under section 6018 (relating to estate tax returns) with respect to such donor.

* * *

*Omitted.

PART VI—EXTENSION OF TIME FOR FILING RETURNS

Editorial Summary

Filing Due Dates: Extensions

Subchapter A of Chapter 61 (Sec. 6081)

See the discussion under the Editorial Summary entitled Information and Returns, which precedes Sec. 6001.

§ 6081. Extension of time for filing returns

(a) General rule.—The Secretary may grant a reasonable extension of time for filing any return, declaration, statement, or other document required by this title or by regulations. Except in the case of taxpayers who are abroad, no such extension shall be for more than 6 months.

(b) Automatic extension for corporation income tax returns.—An extension of 3 months for the filing of the return of income taxes imposed by subtitle A shall be allowed any corporation if, in such manner and at such time as the Secretary may by regulations prescribe, there is filed on behalf of such corporation the form prescribed by the Secretary, and if such corporation pays, on or before the date prescribed for payment of the tax, the amount properly estimated as its tax; but this extension may be terminated at any time by the Secretary by mailing to the taxpayer notice of such termination at least 10 days prior to the date for termination fixed in such notice.

* * *

PART VII—PLACE FOR FILING RETURNS OR OTHER DOCUMENTS*

PART VIII—DESIGNATION OF INCOME TAX PAYMENTS TO PRESIDENTIAL ELECTION CAMPAIGN FUNDS*

SUBCHAPTER B—MISCELLANEOUS PROVISIONS

Editorial Summary

Disclosure for Quid Pro Quo Contributions

Subchapter B of Chapter 61 (Sec. 6115)

Section 170 provides for the deductions of charitable contributions. One of the issues in determining the amount of a charitable contribution is to determine the value of the contribution. If a quid pro quo contribution (taxpayer receives a benefit from the charitable organization) is made by the taxpayer, the value of the contribution must be reduced by the value of the benefit. Section 6115 requires that the charitable organization (1) disclose to the taxpayer an estimate of the value of the benefit received by the taxpayer and (2) inform the taxpayer that the value of the contribution must be reduced by the benefit received in calculating the Sec. 170 deduction. This disclosure is required if the value of the quid pro quo contribution exceeds $75 [Sec. 6115(a)].

* * *

§ 6115. Disclosure related to quid pro quo contributions

(a) Disclosure requirement.—If an organization described in section 170(c) (other than paragraph (1) thereof) receives a quid pro quo contribution in excess of $75, the organization shall, in connection with the solicitation or receipt of the contribution, provide a written statement which—

(1) informs the donor that the amount of the contribution that is deductible for Federal income tax purposes is limited to the excess of the amount of any money and the value of any property other than money contributed by the donor over the value of the goods or services provided by the organization, and

(2) provides the donor with a good faith estimate of the value of such goods or services.

(b) Quid pro quo contribution.— For purposes of this section, the term "quid pro quo contribution" means a payment made partly as a contribution and partly in consideration for goods or services provided to the payor by the donee organization. A quid pro quo contribution does not include any payment made to an organization, organized exclusively for religious purposes, in return for which the taxpayer receives solely an intangible religious benefit that generally is not sold in a commercial transaction outside the donative context.

* * *

*Omitted.

CHAPTER 62—TIME AND PLACE FOR PAYING TAX

SUBCHAPTER A—PLACE AND DUE DATE FOR PAYMENT OF TAX

Editorial Summary

Due Dates and Extension of Time for Payment of Tax

Subchapters A and B of Chapter 62 (Secs. 6151, 6161–6166)

Chapter 62 applies to income taxes, estate taxes, and gift taxes. It deals with the topics of due dates and extensions of payment.

Sections 6072 and 6075 in Subchapter A of Chapter 61 contain the general due dates for each of these types of returns. Section 6081 provides the taxpayer with the ability to obtain extensions with respect to the return due date. Note that some of the extensions are automatic and some can be obtained only with IRS permission.

The Code sections in Subchapter B of Chapter 62 deal with a different aspect of extensions. That is, the extension is on the due date for the payment of the tax liability (see sec. 6151) rather than on the due date for filing the return. Note that some of the extensions are general purpose (e.g., Sec. 6161), whereas others are available only in specific circumstances (e.g., Sec. 6166, which applies only if the estate consists largely of an interest in a closely held business).

§ 6151. Time and place for paying tax shown on returns

(a) General rule.—Except as otherwise provided in this subchapter, when a return of tax is required under this title or regulations, the person required to make such return shall, without assessment or notice and demand from the Secretary, pay such tax to the internal revenue officer with whom the return is filed, and shall pay such tax at the time and place fixed for filing the return (determined without regard to any extension of time for filing the return).

(b) Exceptions.—

(1) Income tax not computed by taxpayer.—If the taxpayer elects under section 6014 not to show the tax on the return, the amount determined by the Secretary as payable shall be paid within 30 days after the mailing by the Secretary to the taxpayer of a notice stating such amount and making demand therefor.

(2) Use of government depositaries.—For authority of the Secretary to require payments to Government depositaries, see section 6302(c).

(c) Date fixed for payment of tax.—In any case in which a tax is required to be paid on or before a certain date, or within a certain period, any reference in this title to the date fixed for payment of such tax shall be deemed a reference to the last day fixed for such payment (determined without regard to any extension of time for paying the tax).

* * *

SUBCHAPTER B—EXTENSIONS OF TIME FOR PAYMENT

§ 6161. Extension of time for paying tax

(a) Amount determined by taxpayer on return.—

(1) General rule.—The Secretary, except as otherwise provided in this title, may extend the time for payment of the amount of the tax shown, or required to be shown, on any return or declaration required under authority of this title (or any installment thereof), for a reasonable period not to exceed 6 months (12 months in the case of estate tax) from the date fixed for payment thereof. Such extension may exceed 6 months in the case of a taxpayer who is abroad.

(2) Estate tax.—The Secretary may, for reasonable cause, extend the time for payment of—

(A) any part of the amount determined by the executor as the tax imposed by chapter 11, or

(B) any part of any installment under section 6166 (including any part of a deficiency prorated to any installment under such section),

for a reasonable period not in excess of 10 years from the date prescribed by section 6151(a) for payment of the tax (or, in the case of an amount referred to in subparagraph (B), if later, not beyond the date which is 12 months after the due date for the last installment).

(b) Amount determined as deficiency.—

(1) Income, gift, and certain other taxes.—Under regulations prescribed by the Secretary, the Secretary may extend the time for the payment of the amount determined as a deficiency of a tax imposed by chapter 1, 12, 41, 42, 43, 44, or 45 for a period not to exceed 18 months from the date fixed for the payment of the deficiency, and in exceptional cases, for a further period not to exceed 12 months. An extension under this paragraph may be granted only where it is shown to the satisfaction of the Secretary that payment of a deficiency upon the date fixed for the payment thereof will result in undue hardship to the taxpayer in the case of a tax imposed by chapter 1, 41, 42, 43, 44, or 45, or to the donor in the case of a tax imposed by chapter 12.

(2) Estate tax.—Under regulations prescribed by the Secretary, the Secretary may, for reasonable cause, extend the time for the payment of any deficiency of a tax imposed by chapter 11 for a reasonable period not to exceed 4 years from the date otherwise fixed for the payment of the deficiency.

(3) No extension for certain deficiencies.—No extension shall be granted under this subsection for any deficiency if the deficiency is due to negligence, to intentional disregard of rules and regulations, or to fraud with intent to evade tax.

* * *

(d) Cross references.—

(1) Period of limitation.—

For extension of the period of limitation in case of an extension under subsection (a)(2) or subsection (b)(2), see section 6503(d).

* * *

§ 6163. Extension of time for payment of estate tax on value of reversionary or remainder interest in property

(a) Extension permitted.—If the value of a reversionary or remainder interest in property is included under chapter 11 in the value of the gross estate, the payment of the part of the tax under chapter 11 attributable to such interest may, at the election of the executor, be postponed until 6 months after the termination of the precedent interest or interests in the property, under such regulations as the Secretary may prescribe.

(b) Extension for reasonable cause.—At the expiration of the period of postponement provided for in subsection (a), the Secretary may, for reasonable cause, extend the time for payment for a reasonable period or periods not in excess of 3 years from the expiration of the period of postponement provided in subsection (a).

* * *

§ 6166. Extension of time for payment of estate tax where estate consists largely of interest in closely held business

(a) 5-year deferral; 10-year installment payment.—

(1) In general.—If the value of an interest in a closely held business which is included in determining the gross estate of a decedent who was (at the date of his death) a citizen or resident of the United States exceeds 35 percent of the adjusted gross estate, the executor may elect to pay part or all of the tax imposed by section 2001 in 2 or more (but not exceeding 10) equal installments.

(2) Limitation.— The maximum amount of tax which may be paid in installments under this subsection shall be an amount which bears the same ratio to the tax imposed by section 2001 (reduced by the credits against such tax) as—

(A) the closely held business amount, bears to

(B) the amount of the adjusted gross estate.

(3) Date for payment of installments.—If an election is made under paragraph (1), the first installment shall be paid on or before the date selected by the executor which is not more than 5 years after the date prescribed by section 6151(a) for payment of the tax, and each succeeding installment shall be paid on or before the date which is 1 year after the date prescribed by this paragraph for payment of the preceding installment.

(b) Definitions and special rules.—

(1) Interest in closely held business.—For purposes of this section, the term "interest in a closely held business" means—

(A) an interest as a proprietor in a trade or business carried on as a proprietorship;

(B) an interest as a partner in a partnership carrying on a trade or business, if—

(i) 20 percent or more of the total capital interest in such partnership is included in determining the gross estate of the decedent, or

(ii) such partnership had 45 or fewer partners; or

(C) stock in a corporation carrying on a trade or business if—

(i) 20 percent or more in value of the voting stock of such corporation is included in determining the gross estate of the decedent, or

(ii) such corporation had 45 or fewer shareholders.

(2) Rules for applying paragraph (1).—For purposes of paragraph (1)—

(A) Time for testing.—Determinations shall be made as of the time immediately before the decedent's death.

(B) Certain interests held by husband and wife.—Stock or a partnership interest which—

(i) is community property of a husband and wife (or the income from which is community income) under the applicable community property law of a State, or

(ii) is held by a husband and wife as joint tenants, tenants by the entirety, or tenants in common,

shall be treated as owned by one shareholder or one partner, as the case may be.

(C) Indirect ownership.—Property owned, directly or indirectly, by or for a corporation, partnership, estate, or trust shall be considered as being owned proportionately by or for its shareholders, partners, or beneficiaries. For purposes of the preceding sentence, a person shall be treated as a beneficiary of any trust only if such person has a present interest in the trust.

(D) Certain interests held by members of decedent's family.—All stock and all partnership interests held by the decedent or by any member of his family (within the meaning of section 267(c)(4)) shall be treated as owned by the decedent.

(3) Farmhouses and certain other structures taken into account.—For purposes of the 35-percent requirement of subsection (a)(1), an interest in a closely held business which is the business of farming includes an interest in residential buildings and related improvements on the farm which are occupied on a regular basis by the owner or lessee of the farm or by persons employed by such owner or lessee for purposes of operating or maintaining the farm.

(4) Value.—For purposes of this section, value shall be value determined for purposes of chapter 11 (relating to estate tax).

(5) Closely held business amount.—For purposes of this section, the term "closely held business amount" means the value of the interest in a closely held business which qualifies under subsection (a)(1).

(6) Adjusted gross estate.—For purposes of this section, the term, "adjusted gross estate" means the value of the gross estate reduced by the sum of the amounts allowable as a deduction under section 2053 or 2054. Such sum shall be determined on the basis of the facts and circumstances in existence on the date (including extensions) for filing the return of tax imposed by section 2001 (or, if earlier, the date on which such return is filed).

(7) Partnership interests and stock which is not readily tradable.—

(A) In general.—If the executor elects the benefits of this paragraph (at such time and in such manner as the Secretary shall by regulations prescribe), then—

(i) for purposes of paragraph (1)(B)(i) or (1)(C)(i) (whichever is appropriate) and for purposes of subsection (c), any capital interest in a partnership and any non-readily-tradable stock which (after the application of paragraph (2)) is treated as owned by the decedent shall be treated as included in determining the value of the decedent's gross estate,

(ii) the executor shall be treated as having selected under subsection (a)(3) the date prescribed by section 6151(a), and

(iii) For purposes of applying section 6601(j), the 2-percent portion (as defined in such section) shall be treated as being zero.

(B) Non-readily-tradable stock defined.—For purposes of this paragraph, the term "non-readily-tradable stock" means stock for which, at the time of the decedent's death, there was no market on a stock exchange or in an over-the-counter market.

(8) Stock in holding company treated as business company stock in certain cases.—

(A) In general.—If the executor elects the benefits of this paragraph, then—

(i) Holding company stock treated as business company stock.—For purposes of this section, the portion of the stock of any holding company which represents direct ownership (or indirect ownership through 1 or more other holding companies) by such company in a business company shall be deemed to be stock in such business company.

(ii) 5-year deferral for principal not to apply.—The executor shall be treated as having selected under subsection (a)(3) the date prescribed by section 6151(a).

(iii) 2-percent interest rate not to apply.—For purposes of applying section 6601(j), the 2-percent portion (as defined in such section) shall be treated as being zero.

(B) All stock must be non-readily-tradable stock.—

(i) In general.—No stock shall be taken into account for purposes of applying this paragraph unless it is non-readily-tradable stock (within the meaning of paragraph (7)(B)).

(ii) Special application where only holding company stock is non-readily-tradable stock.—If the requirements of clause (i) are not met, but all of the stock of each holding company takes into account is non-readily-tradable, then this paragraph shall apply, but subsection (a)(1) shall be applied by substituting "5" for "10."

(C) Application of voting stock requirement of paragraph (1)(C)(i).—For purposes of clause (i) of paragraph (1)(C), the deemed stock resulting from the application of subparagraph (A) shall be treated as voting stock to the extent that voting stock in the holding company owns directly (or through the voting stock of 1 or more other holding companies) voting stock in the business company.

(D) Definitions.—For purposes of this paragraph—

(i) Holding company.—The term "holding company" means any corporation holding stock in another corporation.

(ii) Business company.—The term "business company" means any corporation carrying on a trade or business.

(9) Deferral not available for passive assets.—

(A) In general.—For purposes of subsection (a)(1) and determining the closely held business amount (but not for purposes of subsection (g)), the value of any interest in a closely held business shall not include the value of that portion of such interest which is attributable to passive assets held by the business.

(B) Passive asset defined.—For purposes of this paragraph—

(i) In general.—The term "passive asset" means any asset other than an asset used in carrying on a trade or business.

(ii) Stock treated as passive asset.—The term "passive asset" includes any stock in another corporation unless—

(I) such stock is treated as held by the decedent by reason of an election under paragraph (8), and

(II) such stock qualified under subsection (a)(1).

(iii) Exception for active corporations.—If—

(I) a corporation owns 20 percent or more in value of the voting stock of another corporation, or such other corporation has 15 or fewer shareholders, and

(II) 80 percent or more of the value of the assets of each such corporation is attributable to assets used in carrying on a trade or business,

then such corporations shall be treated as 1 corporation for purposes of clause (ii). For purposes of applying subclause (II) to the corporation holding the stock of the other corporation, such stock shall not be taken into account.

(10) Stock in qualifying lending and finance business treated as stock in an active trade or business company.—

(A) In general.—If the executor elects the benefits of this paragraph, then—

(i) Stock in qualifying lending and finance business treated as stock in an active trade or business company.—For purposes of this section, any asset used in a qualifying lending and finance business shall be treated as an asset which is used in carrying on a trade or business.

(ii) 5-year deferral for principal not to apply.—The executor shall be treated as having selected under subsection (a)(3) the date prescribed by section 6151(a).

(iii) 5 equal installments allowed.—For purposes of applying subsection (a)(1), "5" shall be substituted for "10."

(B) Definitions.—For purposes of this paragraph—

(i) Qualifying lending and finance business.—The term "qualifying lending and finance business" means a lending and finance business, if—

(I) based on all the facts and circumstances immediately before the date of the decedent's death, there was substantial activity with respect to the lending and finance business, or

(II) during at least 3 of the 5 taxable years ending before the date of the decedent's death, such business had at least 1 full-time employee substantially all of whose services were the active management of such business, 10 full-time, nonowner employees substantially all of whose services were directly related to such business, and $5,000,000 in gross receipts from activities described in clause (ii).

(ii) Lending and finance business.—The term "lending and finance business" means a trade or business of—

(I) making loans,

(II) purchasing or discounting accounts receivable, notes, or installment obligations,

(III) engaging in rental and leasing of real and tangible personal property, including entering into leases and purchasing, servicing, and disposing of leases and leased assets,

(IV) rendering services or making facilities available in the ordinary course of a lending or finance business, and

(V) rendering services or making facilities available in connection with activities described in subclauses (I) through (IV) carried on by the corporation rendering services or making facilities available, or another corporation which is a member of the same affiliated group (as defined in section 1504 without regard to section 1504(b)(3)).

(iii) Limitation.—The term "qualifying lending and financing business" shall not include any interest in an entity, if the stock or debt of such entity or a controlled group (as defined in section 267(f)(1)) of which such entity was a member was readily tradable on an established securities market or secondary market (as defined by the Secretary) at any time within 3 years before the date of the decedent's death.

(c) Special rule for interests in 2 or more closely held businesses.—For purposes of this section, interests in 2 or more closely held businesses, with respect to each of which there is included in determining the value of the decedent's gross estate 20 percent or more of the total value of each such business, shall be treated as an interest in a single closely held business. For purposes of the 20-percent requirement of the preceding sentence, an interest in a closely held business which represents the surviving spouse's interest in property held by the decedent and the surviving spouse as community property or as joint tenants, tenants by the entirety, or tenants in common shall be treated as having been included in determining the value of the decedent's gross estate.

(d) Election.—Any election under subsection (a) shall be made not later than the time prescribed by section 6075(a) for filing the return of tax imposed by section 2001 (including extensions thereof), and shall be made in such manner as the Secretary shall by regulations prescribe. If an election under subsection (a) is made, the provisions of this subtitle shall apply as though the Secretary were extending the time for payment of the tax.

(e) Proration of deficiency to installments.—If an election is made under subsection (a) to pay any part of the tax imposed by section 2001 in installments and a deficiency has been assessed, the deficiency shall (subject to the limitation provided by subsection (a)(2)) be prorated to the installments payable under subsection (a). The part of the deficiency so prorated to any installment the date for payment of which has not arrived shall be collected at the same time as, and as a part of, such installment. The part of the deficiency so prorated to any installment the date for payment of which has arrived shall be paid upon notice and demand from the Secretary. This subsection shall not apply if the deficiency is due to negligence, to intentional disregard of rules and regulations, or to fraud with intent to evade tax.

(f) Time for payment of interest.—If the time for payment of any amount of tax has been extended under this section—

(1) Interest for first 5 years.—Interest payable under section 6601 of any unpaid portion of such amount attributable to the first 5 years after the date prescribed by section 6151(a) for payment of the tax shall be paid annually.

(2) Interest for periods after first 5 years.—Interest payable under section 6601 on any unpaid portion of such amount attributable to any period after the 5-year period referred to in paragraph (1) shall be paid annually at the same time as, and as a part of, each installment payment of the tax.

(3) Interest in the case of certain deficiencies.—In the case of a deficiency to which subsection (e) applies which is assessed after the close of the 5-year period referred to in paragraph (1), interest attributable to such 5-year period, and interest assigned under paragraph (2) to any installment the date for payment of which has arrived on or before the date of the assessment of the deficiency, shall be paid upon notice and demand from the Secretary.

(4) Selection of shorter period.—If the executor has selected a period shorter than 5 years under subsection (a)(3), such shorter period shall be substituted for 5 years in paragraphs (1), (2), and (3) of this subsection.

(g) Acceleration of payment.—

(1) Disposition of interest; withdrawal of funds from business.—

(A) If—

(i) **(I)** any portion of an interest in a closely held business which qualifies under subsection (a)(1) is distributed, sold, exchanged, or otherwise disposed of, or

(II) money and other property attributable to such an interest is withdrawn from such trade or business, and

(ii) the aggregate of such distributions, sales, exchanges, or other dispositions and withdrawals equals or exceeds 50 percent of the value of such interest,

then the extension of time for payment of tax provided in subsection (a) shall cease to apply, and the unpaid portion of the tax payable in installments shall be paid upon notice and demand from the Secretary.

(B) In the case of a distribution in redemption of stock to which section 303 (or so much of section 304 as relates to section 303) applies—

(i) the redemption of such stock, and the withdrawal of money and other property distributed in such redemption, shall not be treated as a distribution or withdrawal for purposes of subparagraph (A), and

(ii) for purposes of subparagraph (A), the value of the interest in the closely held business shall be considered to be such value reduced by the value of the stock redeemed.

This subparagraph shall apply only if, on or before the date prescribed by subsection (a)(3) for the payment of the first installment which becomes due after the date of the distribution (or, if earlier, on or before the day which is 1 year after the date of the distribution), there is paid an amount of the tax imposed by section 2001 not less than the amount of money and other property distributed.

(C) Subparagraph (A)(i) does not apply to an exchange of stock pursuant to a plan of reorganization described in subparagraph (D), (E), or (F) of section 368(a)(1) nor to an exchange to which section 355 (or so much of section 356 as relates to section 355) applies; but any stock received in such an exchange shall be treated for purposes of subparagraph (A)(i) as an interest qualifying under subsection (a)(1).

(D) Subparagraph (A)(i) does not apply to a transfer of property of the decedent to a person entitled by reason of the decedent's death to receive such property under the decedent's will, the applicable law of descent and distribution, or a trust created by the decedent. A similar rule shall apply in the case of a series of subsequent transfers of the property by reason of death so long as each transfer is to a member of the family (within the meaning of section 267(c)(4)) of the transferor in such transfer.

(E) Changes in interest in holding company.—If any stock in a holding company is treated as stock in a business company by reason of subsection (b)(8)(A)—

(i) any disposition of any interest in such stock in such holding company which was included in determining the gross estate of the decedent, or

(ii) any withdrawal of any money or other property from such holding company attributable to any interest included in determining the gross estate of the decedent,

shall be treated for purposes of subparagraph (a) as a disposition of (or a withdrawal with respect to) the stock qualifying under subsection (a)(1).

(F) Changes in interest in business company.—If any stock in a holding company is treated as stock in a business company by reason of subsection (b)(8)(A)—

(i) any disposition of any interest in such stock in the business company by such holding company, or

(ii) any withdrawal of any money or other property from such business company attributable to such stock by such holding company owning such stock,

shall be treated for purposes of subparagraph (a) as a disposition of (or a withdrawal with respect to) the stock qualifying under subsection (a)(1).

(2) Undistributed income of estate.—

(A) If an election is made under this section and the estate has undistributed net income for any taxable year ending on or after the due date for the first installment, the executor shall, on or before the date prescribed by law for filing the income tax return for such taxable year (including extensions thereof), pay an amount equal to such undistributed net income in liquidation of the unpaid portion of the tax payable in installments.

(B) For purposes of subparagraph (A), the undistributed net income of the estate for any taxable year is the amount by which the distributable net income of the estate for such taxable year (as defined in section 643) exceeds the sum of—

(i) the amounts for such taxable year specified in paragraphs (1) and (2) of section 661(a) (relating to deductions for distributions, etc.);

(ii) the amount of tax imposed for the taxable year on the estate under chapter 1; and

(iii) the amount of the tax imposed by section 2001 (including interest) paid by the executor during the taxable year (other than any amount paid pursuant to this paragraph).

(C) For purposes of this paragraph, if any stock in a corporation is treated as stock in another corporation by reason of subsection (b)(8)(A), any dividends paid by such other corporation to the corporation shall be treated as paid to the estate of the decedent to the extent attributable to the stock qualifying under subsection (a)(1).

(3) Failure to make payment of principal or interest.—

(A) In general.—Except as provided in subparagraph (B), if any payment of principal or interest under this section is not paid on or before the date fixed for its payment by this section (including any extension of time), the unpaid portion of the tax payable in installments shall be paid upon notice and demand from the Secretary.

(B) Payment within 6 months.—If any payment of principal or interest under this section is not paid on or before the date determined under subparagraph (A) but is paid within 6 months of such date—

(i) the provisions of subparagraph (A) shall not apply with respect to such payment,

(ii) the provisions of section 6601(j) shall not apply with respect to the determination of interest on such payment, and

(iii) there is imposed a penalty in an amount equal to the product of—

(I) 5 percent of the amount of such payment, multiplied by

(II) the number of months (or fractions thereof) after such date and before payment is made.

The penalty imposed under clause (iii) shall be treated in the same manner as a penalty imposed under Subchapter B of chapter 68.

(h) Election in case of certain deficiencies.—

(1) In general.—If—

(A) a deficiency in the tax imposed by section 2001 is assessed,

(B) the estate qualifies under subsection (a)(1), and

(C) the executor has not made an election under subsection (a),

the executor may elect to pay the deficiency in installments. This subsection shall not apply if the deficiency is due to negligence, to intentional disregard of rules and regulations, or to fraud with intent to evade tax.

(2) Time of election.—An election under this subsection shall be made not later than 60 days after issuance of notice and demand by the Secretary for the payment of the deficiency, and shall be made in such manner as the Secretary shall by regulations prescribe.

(3) Effect of election on payment.—If an election is made under this subsection, the deficiency shall (subject to the limitation provided by subsection (a)(2)) be prorated to the installments which would have been due if an election had been timely made under subsection (a) at the time the estate tax return was filed. The part of the deficiency so prorated to any installment the date for payment of which would have arrived shall be paid at the time of the making of the election under this subsection. The portion of the deficiency so prorated to installments the date for payment of which would not have so arrived shall be paid at the time such installments would have been due if such an election had been made.

(i) Special rule for certain direct skips.—To the extent that an interest in a closely held business is the subject of a direct skip (within the meaning of section 2612(c)) occurring at the same time as and as a result of the decedent's death, then for purposes of this section any tax imposed by section 2601 on the transfer of such interest shall be treated as if it were additional tax imposed by section 2001.

(j) Regulations.—The Secretary shall prescribe such regulations as may be necessary to the application of this section.

* * *

CHAPTER 63—ASSESSMENT

SUBCHAPTER A—IN GENERAL*

SUBCHAPTER B—DEFICIENCY PROCEDURES IN THE CASE OF INCOME, ESTATE, GIFT, AND CERTAIN EXCISE TAXES

Editorial Summary

Assessment of Tax Liability

Subchapters B, C, and D of Chapter 63 (Secs. 6211–6231)

In terms of the income, estate, and gift tax structure, the general rule is that the tax is self-assessing (i.e., the taxpayer is required to calculate and pay the tax liability). The major exception to this self-assessment concept is the Sec. 531 accumulated earnings tax.

Subchapter B provides a deficiency procedure whereby the IRS can assess the taxpayer for the amount of tax liability it calculates for the taxpayer in excess of the amount calculated by the taxpayer on the tax return. In addition to the calculation methodology, rules covering the rights and duties of the taxpayer and of the IRS are provided.

Subchapter C deals with the tax treatment of partnership items. Section 6221 applies entity rather than conduit theory in providing that under the general rule the tax treatment is to be determined at the partnership level rather than at the partner level. Since the taxpayer is the partner rather than the partnership, each partner must report his or her share of the partnership items on his or her return. If a partner decides to take a position inconsistent with the partnership return, the inconsistency must be disclosed in the tax return of the partner [see Sec. 6222(b)]. Section 6229 provides the statutory period for assessing a deficiency on a partner with respect to the partnership.

§ 6211. Definition of a deficiency

(a) In general.— For purposes of this title in the case of income, estate, and gift taxes imposed by subtitles A and B and excise taxes imposed by chapters 41, 42, 43, 44, and 45 the term "deficiency" means the amount by which the tax imposed by subtitle A or B, or chapter 41, 42, 43, 44, or 45 exceeds the excess of—

(1) the sum of

(A) the amount shown as the tax by the taxpayer upon his return, if a return was made by the taxpayer and an amount was shown as the tax by the taxpayer thereon, plus

(B) the amounts previously assessed (or collected without assessment) as a deficiency, over—

(2) the amount of rebates, as defined in subsection (b)(2), made.

(b) Rules for application of subsection (a).—For purposes of this section—

(1) The tax imposed by subtitle A and the tax shown on the return shall both be determined without regard to payments on account of estimated tax, without regard to the credit under section 31,

*Omitted.

without regard to the credit under section 33, and without regard to any credits resulting from the collection of amounts assessed under section 6851 or 6852 (relating to termination assessments).

(2) The term "rebate" means so much of an abatement, credit, refund, or other repayment, as was made on the ground that the tax imposed by subtitle A or B or Chapter 41, 42, 43, or 44 was less than the excess of the amount specified in subsection (a)(1) over the rebates previously made.

(3) The computation by the Secretary, pursuant to section 6014, of the tax imposed by chapter 1 shall be considered as having been made by the taxpayer and the tax so computed considered as shown by the taxpayer upon his return.

(4) For purposes of subsection (a)—

CAUTION: FUTURE EFFECTIVE DATE

Section 6211(b)(4)(A) is amended by the Patient Protection and Affordable Care Act of 2010 effective for taxable years ending after 12/31/2013.

(A) any excess of the sum of the credits allowable under sections 24(d), 25A by reason of subsection (i)(6) thereof, 32, 34, 35, 36, 36A, 36B, 36C, 53(e), 168(k)(4), 6428, and 6431 over the tax imposed by subtitle A (determined without regard to such credits), and

(B) any excess of the sum of such credits as shown by the taxpayer on his return over the amount shown as the tax by the taxpayer on such return (determined without regard to such credits), shall be taken into account as negative amounts of tax.

(c) Coordination with subchapters C and D.— In determining the amount of any deficiency for purposes of this subchapter, adjustments to partnership items shall be made only as provided in subchapters C and D.

§ 6212. Notice of deficiency

(a) In general.—If the Secretary determines that there is a deficiency in respect of any tax imposed by subtitles A or B or chapter 41, 42, 43, 44, or 45, he is authorized to send notice of such deficiency to the taxpayer by certified mail or registered mail. Such notice shall include a notice to the taxpayer of the taxpayer's right to contact a local office of the taxpayer advocate and the location and phone number of the appropriate office.

(b) Address for notice of deficiency.—

(1) Income and gift taxes and certain excise taxes.—In the absence of notice to the Secretary under section 6903 of the existence of a fiduciary relationship, notice of a deficiency in respect of a tax imposed by subtitle A, chapter 12, chapter 41, chapter 42, chapter 43, chapter 44, or chapter 45, if mailed to the taxpayer at his last known address, shall be sufficient for purposes of subtitle A, chapter 12, chapter 41, chapter 42, chapter 43, chapter 44, chapter 45, and this chapter even if such taxpayer is deceased, or is under a legal disability, or, in the case of a corporation, has terminated its existence.

(2) Joint income tax return.—In the case of a joint income tax return filed by husband and wife, such notice of deficiency may be a single joint notice, except that if the Secretary has been notified by either spouse that separate residences have been established, then, in lieu of the single joint notice, a duplicate original of the joint notice shall be sent by certified mail or registered mail to each spouse at his last known address.

(3) Estate tax.—In the absence of notice to the Secretary under section 6903 of the existence of a fiduciary relationship, notice of a deficiency in respect of a tax imposed by Chapter 11, if addressed in the name of the decedent or other person subject to liability and mailed to his last known address, shall be sufficient for purposes of chapter 11 and of this chapter.

(c) Further deficiency letters restricted.—

(1) General rule.—If the Secretary has mailed to the taxpayer a notice of deficiency as provided in subsection (a), and the taxpayer files a petition with the Tax Court within the time prescribed in section 6213(a), the Secretary shall have no right to determine any additional deficiency of income tax for the same taxable year, of gift tax for the same calendar year, of estate tax in respect of the taxable estate of the same decedent, of Chapter 41 tax for the same taxable year, of chapter 43 tax for the same taxable year, of Chapter 44 tax for the same taxable year, of section 4940 tax for the same taxable year, or of Chapter 42 tax (other than under section 4940) with respect to any act (or failure to act) to which such petition relates, or of chapter 45 tax for the same taxable period, except in the case of fraud, and except as provided in section 6214(a) (relating to assertion of greater deficiencies before the Tax Court), in section 6213(b)(1) (relating to mathematical or clerical errors), in section 6851 or 6852 (relating to termination assessments), or in section 6861(c) (relating to the making of jeopardy assessments).

(2) Cross references—

For assessment as a deficiency notwithstanding the prohibition of further deficiency letters, in the case of—

(A) Deficiency attributable to change of treatment with respect to itemized deductions, see section 63(e)(3).

(B) Deficiency attributable to gain on involuntary conversion, see section 1033(a)(2)(C) and (D).

(C) Deficiency attributable to activities not engaged in for profit, see section 183(e)(4).

* * *

(d) Authority to rescind notice of deficiency with taxpayer's consent.—The Secretary may, with the consent of the taxpayer, rescind any notice of deficiency mailed to the taxpayer. Any notice so rescinded shall not be treated as a notice of deficiency for purposes of subsection (c)(1) (relating to further deficiency letters restricted), section 6213(a) (relating to restrictions applicable to deficiencies; petition to Tax Court), and section 6512(a) (relating to limitations in case of petition to Tax Court), and the taxpayer shall have no right to file a petition with the Tax Court based on such notice. Nothing in this subsection shall affect any suspension of the running of any period of limitations during any period during which the rescinded notice was outstanding.

§ 6213. Restrictions applicable to deficiencies; petition to Tax Court

(a) Time for filing petition and restriction on assessment.— Within 90 days, or 150 days if the notice is addressed to a person outside the United States, after the notice of deficiency authorized in section 6212 is mailed (not counting Saturday, Sunday, or a legal holiday in the District of Columbia as the last day), the taxpayer may file a petition with the Tax Court for a redetermination of the deficiency. Except as otherwise provided in section 6851, 6852, or 6861 no assessment of a deficiency in respect of any tax imposed by subtitle A, or B, chapters 41, 42, 43, 44, or 45 and no levy or proceeding in court for its collection shall be made, begun, or prosecuted until such notice has been mailed to the taxpayer, nor until the expiration of such 90-day or 150-day period, as the case may be, nor, if a petition has been filed with the Tax Court, until the decision of the Tax Court has become final. Notwithstanding the provisions of section 7421(a), the making of such assessment or the beginning of such proceeding or levy during the time such prohibition is in force may be enjoined by a proceeding in the proper court, including the Tax Court, and a refund may be ordered by such court of any amount collected within the period during which the Secretary is prohibited from collecting by levy or through a proceeding in court under the provisions of this subsection. The Tax Court shall have no jurisdiction to enjoin any action or proceeding or order any refund under this subsection unless a timely petition for a redetermination of the deficiency has been filed and then only in respect of the deficiency that is the subject of such petition. Any petition filed with the Tax Court on or before the last day specified for filing such petition by the Secretary in the notice of deficiency shall be treated as timely filed.

(b) Exceptions to restrictions on assessment.—

(1) Assessments arising out of mathematical or clerical errors.—If the taxpayer is notified that, on account of a mathematical or clerical error appearing on the return, an amount of tax in excess of that shown on the return is due, and that an assessment of the tax has been or will be made on the basis of what would have been the correct amount of tax but for the mathematical or clerical error, such notice shall not be considered as a notice of deficiency for the purposes of subsection (a) (prohibiting assessment and collection until notice of the deficiency has been mailed), or of section 6212 (c)(1) (restricting further deficiency letters), or of section 6512(a) (prohibiting credits or refunds after petition to the Tax Court), and the taxpayer shall have no right to file a petition with the Tax Court based on such notice, nor shall such assessment or collection be prohibited by the provisions of subsection (a) of this section. Each notice under this paragraph shall set forth the error alleged and an explanation thereof.

(2) Abatement of assessment of mathematical or clerical errors.—

(A) Request for abatement.—Notwithstanding section 6404(b), a taxpayer may file with the Secretary within 60 days after notice is sent under paragraph (1) a request for an abatement of any assessment specified in such notice, and upon receipt of such request, the Secretary shall abate the assessment. Any reassessment of the tax with respect to which an abatement is made under this subparagraph shall be subject to the deficiency procedures prescribed by this subchapter.

(B) Stay of collection.—In the case of any assessment referred to in paragraph (1), notwithstanding paragraph (1), no levy or proceeding in court for the collection of such assessment shall be made, begun, or prosecuted during the period in which such assessment may be abated under this paragraph.

(3) Assessments arising out of tentative carryback or refund adjustments.—If the Secretary determines that the amount applied, credited, or refunded under section 6411 is in excess of the overassessment attributable to the carryback or the amount described in section 1341(b)(1) with respect to which such amount was applied, credited, or refunded, he may assess without regard to the provisions of paragraph (2) the amount of the excess as a deficiency as if it were due to a mathematical or clerical error appearing on the return.

(4) Assessment of amount paid.—Any amount paid as a tax or in respect of a tax may be assessed upon the receipt of such payment notwithstanding the provisions of subsection (a). In any case where such amount is paid after the mailing of a notice of deficiency under section 6212, such payment shall not deprive the Tax Court of jurisdiction over such deficiency determined under section 6211 without regard to such assessment.

(c) Failure to file petition.— If the taxpayer does not file a petition with the Tax Court within the time prescribed in subsection (a), the deficiency, notice of which has been mailed to the taxpayer, shall be assessed, and shall be paid upon notice and demand from the Secretary.

(d) Waiver of restrictions.—The taxpayer shall at any time (whether or not a notice of deficiency has been issued) have the right, by a signed notice in writing filed with the Secretary, to waive the restrictions provided in subsection (a) on the assessment and collection of the whole or any part of the deficiency.

* * *

(g) Definitions.— For purposes of this section—

(1) Return.— The term "return" includes any return, statement, schedule, or list, and any amendment or supplement thereto, filed with respect to any tax imposed by subtitle A or B, or chapter 41, 42, 43, or 44.

(2) Mathematical or clerical error.— The term "mathematical or clerical error" means—

(A) an error in addition, subtraction, multiplication, or division shown on any return,

(B) an incorrect use of any table provided by the Internal Revenue Service with respect to any return if such incorrect use is apparent from the existence of other information on the return,

(C) an entry on a return of an item which is inconsistent with another entry of the same or another item on such return,

(D) an omission of information which is required to be supplied on the return to substantiate an entry on the return,

(E) an entry on a return of a deduction or credit in an amount which exceeds a statutory limit imposed by subtitle A or B, or chapter 41, 42, 43, or 44, if such limit is expressed—

(i) as a specified monetary amount, or

(ii) as a percentage, ratio, or fraction,

and if the items entering into the application of such limit appear on such return,

(F) an omission of a correct taxpayer identification number required under section 32 (relating to the earned income credit) to be included on a return,

(G) an entry on a return claiming the credit under section 32 with respect to net earnings from self-employment described in section 32 (c)(2)(A) to the extent the tax imposed by section 1401 (relating to self-employment tax) on such net earnings has not been paid,

(H) an omission of a correct TIN required under section 21 (relating to expenses for household and dependent care services necessary for gainful employment) or section 151 (relating to allowance of deductions for personal exemptions),

(I) an omission of a correct TIN required under section 24(e) (relating to child tax credit) to be included on a return,

(J) an omission of a correct TIN required under section 25A(g)(1) (relating to higher education tuition and related expenses) to be included on a return,

(K) an omission of information required by section 32(k)(2) (relating to taxpayers making improper prior claims of earned income credit),

(L) the inclusion on a return of a TIN required to be included on the return under section 21, 24, 32, or 6428 if—

(i) such TIN is of an individual whose age affects the amount of the credit under such section, and

(ii) the computation of the credit on the return reflects the treatment of such individual as being of an age different from the individual's age based on such TIN,

(M) the entry on the return claiming the credit under section 32 with respect to a child if, according to the Federal Case Registry of Child

Support Orders established under section 453(h) of the Social Security Act, the taxpayer is a noncustodial parent of such child,

(N) an omission of the reduction required under section 36A(c) with respect to the credit allowed under section 36A or an omission of the correct social security account number required under section 36A(d)(1)(B),

(O) an omission of any increase required under section 36(f) with respect to the recapture of a credit allowed under section 36, and

(P) an entry on a return claiming the credit under section 36 if—

(i) the Secretary obtains information from the person issuing the TIN of the taxpayer that indicates that the taxpayer does not meet the age requirement of section 36(b)(4),

(ii) information provided to the Secretary by the taxpayer on an income tax return for at least one of the 2 preceding taxable years is inconsistent with eligibility for such credit, or

(iii) the taxpayer fails to attach to the return the form described in section 36(d)(4).

A taxpayer shall be treated as having omitted a correct TIN for purposes of the preceding sentence if information provided by the taxpayer on the return with respect to the individual whose TIN was provided differs from the information the Secretary obtains from the person issuing the TIN.

* * *

SUBCHAPTER C—TAX TREATMENT OF PARTNERSHIP ITEMS

Editorial Summary

Assessment of Tax Liability: Partnerships

Subchapter C of Chapter 63 (Secs. 6221–6231)

See the discussion under the Editorial Summary entitled Assessment of Tax Liability, which precedes Sec. 6211.

§ 6221. Tax treatment determined at partnership level

Except as otherwise provided in this subchapter, the tax treatment of any partnership item (and the applicability of any penalty, addition to tax, or additional amount which relates to an adjustment to a partnership item) shall be determined at the partnership level.

§ 6222. Partner's return must be consistent with partnership return or secretary notified of inconsistency

(a) In general.—A partner shall, on the partner's return, treat a partnership item in a manner which is consistent with the treatment of such partnership item on the partnership return.

(b) Notification of inconsistent treatment.—

(1) In general.—In the case of any partnership item, if—

(A) (i) the partnership has filed a return but the partner's treatment on his return is (or may be) inconsistent with the treatment of the item on the partnership return, or

(ii) the partnership has not filed a return, and

(B) the partner files with the Secretary a statement identifying the inconsistency,

subsection (a) shall not apply to such item.

(2) Partner receiving incorrect information.—A partner shall be treated as having complied with subparagraph (B) of paragraph (1) with respect to a partnership item if the partner—

(A) demonstrates to the satisfaction of the Secretary that the treatment of the partnership item on the partner's return is consistent with the treatment of the item on the schedule furnished to the partner by the partnership, and

(B) elects to have this paragraph apply with respect to that item.

* * *

§ 6229. Period of limitations for making assessments

(a) General rule.—Except as otherwise provided in this section, the period for assessing any tax imposed by subtitle A with respect to any person which is attributable to any partnership item (or affected item) for a partnership taxable year shall not expire before the date which is 3 years after the later of—

(1) the date on which the partnership return for such taxable year was filed, or

(2) the last day for filing such return for such year (determined without regard to extensions).

(b) Extension by agreement.—

(1) In general.—The period described in subsection (a) (including an extension period under this subsection) may be extended—

(A) with respect to any partner, by an agreement entered into by the Secretary and such partner, and

(B) with respect to all partners, by an agreement entered into by the Secretary and the tax matters partner (or any other person authorized by the partnership in writing to enter into such an agreement),

before the expiration of such period.

(2) Special rule with respect to debtors in title 11 cases.—Notwithstanding any other law or rule of law, if an agreement is entered into under paragraph (1)(B) and the agreement is signed by a person who would be the tax matters partner but for the fact that, at the time that the agreement is executed, the person is a debtor in a bankruptcy proceeding under title 11 of the United States Code, such agreement shall be binding on all partners in the partnership unless the Secretary has been notified of the bankruptcy proceeding in accordance with regulations prescribed by the Secretary.

(3) Coordination with section 6501(c)(4).—Any agreement under section 6501 (c)(4) shall apply with respect to the period described in subsection (a) only if the agreement expressly provides that such agreement applies to tax attributable to partnership items.

(c) Special rule in case of fraud, etc.—

(1) False return.—If any partner has, with the intent to evade tax, signed or participated directly or indirectly in the preparation of a partnership return which includes a false or fraudulent item—

(A) in the case of partners so signing or participating in the preparation of the return, any tax imposed by subtitle A which is attributable to any partnership item (or affected item) for the partnership taxable year to which the return relates may be assessed at any time, and

(B) in the case of all other partners, subsection (a) shall be applied with respect to such return by substituting "6 years" for "3 years."

(2) Substantial omission of income.—If any partnership omits from gross income an amount properly includible therein and such amount is described in clause (i) or (ii) of section 6501(e)(1)(A), subsection (a) shall be applied by substituting "6 years" for "3 years."

(3) No return.—In the case of a failure by a partnership to file a return for any taxable year, any tax attributable to a partnership item (or affected item) arising in such year may be assessed at any time.

(4) Return filed by secretary.—For purposes of this section, a return executed by the Secretary under subsection (b) of section 6020 on behalf of the partnership shall not be treated as a return of the partnership.

* * *

(f) Special rules.—

(1) Items becoming nonpartnership items.—If, before the expiration of the period otherwise provided in this section for assessing any tax imposed by subtitle A with respect to the partnership items of a partner for the partnership taxable year, such items become nonpartnership items by reason of 1 or more of the events described in subsection (b) of section 6231, the period for assessing any tax imposed by subtitle A which is attributable to such items (or any item affected by such items) shall not expire before the date which is 1 year after the date on which the items become nonpartnership items. The period described in the preceding sentence (including any extension period under this sentence) may be extended with respect to any partnership by agreement entered into by the Secretary and such partner.

(2) Special rule for partial settlement agreements.—If a partner enters into a settlement agreement with the Secretary or the Attorney General (or his delegate) with respect to the treatment of some of the partnership items in dispute for a partnership taxable year but other partnership items for such year remain in dispute, the period of limitations for assessing any tax attributable to the settled items shall be determined as if such agreement had not been entered into.

(g) Period of limitations for penalties.—The provisions of this section shall apply also in the case of any addition to tax or an additional amount imposed under subchapter A of chapter 68 which arises with respect to any tax imposed under subtitle A in the same manner as if such addition or additional amount were a tax imposed by subtitle A.

* * *

§ 6231. Definitions and special rules

(a) Definitions.—For purposes of this subchapter—

(1) Partnership.—

(i) In general.—The term "partnership" shall not include any partnership having 10 or fewer partners each of whom is an individual (other than a nonresident alien), a C corporation, or an estate of a deceased partner. For purposes of the preceding sentence, a husband and wife (and their estates) shall be treated as 1 partner.

(ii) Election to have subchapter apply.—A partnership (within the meaning of subparagraph (A)) may for any taxable year elect to have clause (i) not apply. Such election shall apply for such taxable year and all subsequent taxable years unless revoked with the consent of the Secretary.

(2) Partner.—The term "partner" means—

(A) a partner in the partnership, and

(B) any other person whose income tax liability under subtitle A is determined in whole or in part by taking into account directly or indirectly partnership items of the partnership.

(3) Partnership item.—The term "partnership item" means, with respect to a partnership, any item required to be taken into account for the partnership's taxable year under any provision of subtitle A to the extent regulations prescribed by the Secretary provide that, for purposes of this subtitle, such item is more appropriately determined at the partnership level than at the partner level.

(4) Nonpartnership item.—The term "nonpartnership item" means an item which is (or is treated as) not a partnership item.

(5) Affected item.—The term "affected item" means any item to the extent such item is affected by a partnership item.

(6) Computational adjustment.—The term "computational adjustment" means the change in the tax liability of a partner which properly reflects the treatment under this subchapter of a partnership item. All adjustments required to apply the results of a proceeding with respect to a partnership under this subchapter to an indirect partner shall be treated as computational adjustments.

(7) Tax matters partner.—The tax matters partner of any partnership is—

(A) the general partner designated as the tax matters partner as provided in regulations, or

(B) if there is no general partner who has been so designated, the general partner having the largest profits interest in the partnership at the close of the taxable year involved (or, where there is more than 1 such partner, the 1 of such partners whose name would appear first in an alphabetical listing).

If there is no general partner designated under subparagraph (A) and the Secretary determines that it is impracticable to apply subparagraph (B), the partner selected by the Secretary shall be treated as the tax matters partner. The Secretary shall, within 30 days of selecting a tax matters partner under the preceding sentence, notify all partners required to receive notice under section 6223(a) of the name and address of the person selected.

(8) Notice partner.—The term "notice partner" means a partner who, at the time in question, would be entitled to notice under subsection (a) of section 6223 (determined without regard to subsections (b)(2) and (e)(1)(B) thereof).

(9) Pass-thru partner.—The term "pass-thru partner" means a partnership, estate, trust, S corporation, nominee, or other similar person through whom other persons hold an interest in the partnership with respect to which proceedings under this subchapter are conducted.

(10) Indirect partner.—The term "indirect partner" means a person holding an interest in a partnership through 1 or more pass-thru partners.

(11) 5-percent group.—A 5-percent group is a group of partners who for the partnership taxable year involved had profits interests which aggregated 5 percent or more.

(12) Husband and wife.—Except to the extent otherwise provided in regulations, a husband and wife who have a joint interest in a partnership shall be treated as 1 person.

(b) Items cease to be partnership items in certain cases.—

(1) In general.—For purposes of this subchapter, the partnership items of a partner for a partnership taxable year shall become nonpartnership items as of the date—

(A) the Secretary mails to such partner a notice that such items shall be treated as nonpartnership items,

(B) the partner files suit under section 6228(b) after the Secretary fails to allow an administrative adjustment request with respect to any of such items,

(C) the Secretary or the Attorney General (or his delegate) enters into a settlement agreement with the partner with respect to such items, or

(D) such change occurs under subsection (e) of section 6223 (relating to effect of Secretary's failure to provide notice) or under subsection (c) of this section.

* * *

CHAPTER 64—COLLECTION*

CHAPTER 65—ABATEMENTS, CREDITS, AND REFUNDS

Subchapter
A. Procedure in general.*
B. Rules of Special application.

SUBCHAPTER A—PROCEDURE IN GENERAL*

SUBCHAPTER B—RULES OF SPECIAL APPLICATION

* * *

§ 6428. 2008 recovery rebates for individuals

(a) In general.—In the case of an eligible individual, there shall be allowed as a credit against the tax imposed by subtitle A for the first taxable year beginning in 2008 an amount equal to the lesser of—

(1) net income tax liability, or

(2) $600 ($1,200 in the case of a joint return).

(b) Special rules.—

(1) In general.—In the case of a taxpayer described in paragraph (2)—

(A) the amount determined under subsection (a) shall not be less than $300 ($600 in the case of a joint return), and

(B) the amount determined under subsection (a) (after the application of subparagraph (A)) shall be increased by the product of $300 multiplied by the number of qualifying children (within the meaning of section 24(c)) of the taxpayer.

(2) Taxpayer described.—A taxpayer is described in this paragraph if the taxpayer—

(A) has qualifying income of at least $3,000, or

(B) has—

(i) net income tax liability which is greater than zero, and

(ii) gross income which is greater than the sum of the basic standard deduction plus the exemption amount (twice the exemption amount in the case of a joint return).

(c) Treatment of credit.—The credit allowed by subsection (a) shall be treated as allowed by subpart C of part IV of subchapter A of chapter 1.

(d) Limitation based on adjusted gross income.—The amount of the credit allowed by subsection (a) (determined without regard to this subsection and subsection (f)) shall be reduced (but not below zero) by 5 percent of so much of the taxpayer's adjusted gross income as exceeds $75,000 ($150,000 in the case of a joint return).

(e) Definitions.—For purposes of this section—

(1) Qualifying income.—The term "qualifying income" means—

(A) earned income,

(B) social security benefits (within the meaning of section 86(d)), and

(C) any compensation or pension received under chapter 11, chapter 13, or chapter 15 of title 38, United States Code.

(2) Net income tax liability.—The term "net income tax liability" means the excess of—

(A) the sum of the taxpayer's regular tax liability (within the meaning of section 26(b)) and the tax imposed by section 55 for the taxable year, over

(B) the credits allowed by part IV (other than section 24 and subpart C thereof) of subchapter A of chapter 1.

(3) Eligible individual.—The term "eligible individual" means any individual other than—

(A) any nonresident alien individual,

(B) any individual with respect to whom a deduction under section 151 is allowable to another taxpayer for a taxable year beginning in the calendar year in which the individual's taxable year begins, and,

(C) an estate or trust.

(4) Earned income.—The term "earned income" has the meaning set forth in section 32(c)(2) except that such term shall not include net earnings from self-employment which are not taken into account in computing taxable income.

*Omitted.

(5) Basic standard deduction; exemption amount.—The terms "basic standard deduction" and "exemption amount" shall have the same respective meanings as when used in section 6012(a).

(f) Coordination with advance refunds of credit.—

(1) In general.—The amount of credit which would (but for this paragraph) be allowable under this section shall be reduced (but not below zero) by the aggregate refunds and credits made or allowed to the taxpayer under subsection (g). Any failure to so reduce the credit shall be treated as arising out of a mathematical or clerical error and assessed according to section 6213(b)(1).

(2) Joint returns.—In the case of a refund or credit made or allowed under subsection (g) with respect to a joint return, half of such refund or credit shall be treated as having been made or allowed to each individual filing such return.

(g) Advance refunds and credits.—

(1) In general.—Each individual who was an eligible individual for such individual's first taxable year beginning in 2007 shall be treated as having made a payment against the tax imposed by chapter 1 for such first taxable year in an amount equal to the advance refund amount for such taxable year.

(2) Advance refund amount.—For purposes of paragraph (1), the advance refund amount is the amount that would have been allowed as a credit under this section for such first taxable year if this section (other than subsection (f) and this subsection) had applied to such taxable year.

(3) Timing of payments.—The Secretary shall, subject to the provisions of this title, refund or credit any overpayment attributable to this section as rapidly as possible. No refund or credit shall be made or allowed under this subsection after December 31, 2008.

(4) No interest.—No interest shall be allowed on any overpayment attributable to this section.

(h) Identification number requirement.—

(1) In general.—No credit shall be allowed under subsection (a) to an eligible individual who does not include on the return of tax for the taxable year—

(A) such individual's valid identification number,

(B) in the case of a joint return, the valid identification number of such individual's spouse, and

(C) in the case of any qualifying child taken into account under subsection (b)(I)(B), the valid identification number of such qualifying child.

(2) Valid identification number.—For purposes of paragraph (1), the term "valid identification number" means a social security number issued to an individual by the Social Security Administration. Such term shall not include a TIN issued by the Internal Revenue Service.

(3) Special rule for members of the Armed Forces.—Paragraph (1) shall not apply to a joint return where at least 1 spouse was a member of the Armed Forces of the United States at any time during the taxable year.

§ 6429. Advance payment of portion of increased child credit for 2003

(a) In general.—Each taxpayer who was allowed a credit under section 24 on the return for the taxpayer's first taxable year beginning in 2002 shall be treated as having made a payment against the tax imposed by chapter 1 for such taxable year in an amount equal to the child tax credit refund amount (if any) for such taxable year.

(b) Child tax credit refund amount.—For purposes of this section, the child tax credit refund amount is the amount by which the aggregate credits allowed under part IV of subchapter A of chapter 1 for such first taxable year would have been increased if—

(1) the per child amount under section 24(a)(2) for such year were $1,000,

(2) only qualifying children (as defined in section 24(c)) of the taxpayer for such year who had not attained age 17 as of December 31, 2003, were taken into account, and

(3) section 24(d)(1)(B)(ii) did not apply

(c) Timing of payments.—In the case of any overpayment attributable to this section, the Secretary shall, subject to the provisions of this title, refund or credit such overpayment as rapidly as possible and, to the extent practicable, before October 1, 2003. No refund or credit shall be made or allowed under this section after December 31, 2003.

(d) Coordination with child tax credit.—

(1) **In general.**—The amount of credit which would (but for this subsection and section 26) be allowed under section 24 for the taxpayer's first taxable year beginning in 2003 shall be reduced (but not below zero) by the payments made to the taxpayer under this section. Any failure to so reduce the credit shall be treated as arising out of a mathematical or clerical error and assessed according to section 6213(b)(1).

(2) **Joint returns.**—In the case of a payment under this section with respect to a joint return, half of such payment shall be treated as having been made to each individual filing such return.

(e) **No interest.**—No interest shall be allowed on any overpayment attributable to this section.

CHAPTER 66—LIMITATIONS

Editorial Summary

Limitations on Assessments, Collections, Credits, and Refunds

Subchapters A and B of Chapter 66 (Secs. 6501–6513)

The tax liability or tax refund rights of the taxpayer do not remain open indefinitely. Likewise, the rights of the IRS with respect to assessment and collection do not remain open indefinitely. Instead, these time periods are limited by statutory provisions. Subchapters A and B define these time periods and the factors that can result in the suspension of the running of the time period.

SUBCHAPTER A—LIMITATIONS ON ASSESSMENT AND COLLECTION

§ 6501. Limitations on assessment and collection

(a) **General rule.**— Except as otherwise provided in this section, the amount of any tax imposed by this title shall be assessed within 3 years after the return was filed (whether or not such return was filed on or after the date prescribed) or, if the tax is payable by stamp, at any time after such tax became due and before the expiration of 3 years after the date on which any part of such tax was paid, and no proceeding in court without assessment for the collection of such tax shall be begun after the expiration of such period. For purposes of this chapter, the term "return" means the return required to be filed by the taxpayer (and does not include a return of any person from whom the taxpayer has received an item of income, gain, loss, deduction, or credit).

(b) **Time return deemed filed.**—

(1) **Early return.**— For purposes of this section, a return of tax imposed by this title, except tax imposed by chapter 3, 21 or 24, filed before the last day prescribed by law or by regulations promulgated pursuant to law for the filing thereof, shall be considered as filed on such last day.

* * *

(c) **Exceptions.**—

(1) **False return.**— In the case of a false or fraudulent return with the intent to evade tax, the tax may be assessed, or a proceeding in court for collection of such tax may be begun without assessment, at any time.

(2) **Willful attempt to evade tax.**— In case of a willful attempt in any manner to defeat or evade tax imposed by this title (other than tax imposed by subtitle A or B), the tax may be assessed, or a proceeding in court for the collection of such tax may be begun without assessment, at any time.

(3) **No return.**—In the case of failure to file a return, the tax may be assessed, or a proceeding in court for the collection of such tax may be begun without assessment, at any time.

(4) **Extension by agreement.**—

*Omitted.

(A) **In general.**— Where before the expiration of the time prescribed in this section for the assessment of any tax imposed by this title, except the estate tax provided in chapter 11, both the Secretary and the taxpayer have consented in writing to its assessment after such time, the tax may be assessed at any time prior to the expiration of the period agreed upon. The period so agreed upon may be extended by subsequent agreements in writing made before the expiration of the period previously agreed upon.

(B) **Notice to taxpayer of right to refuse or limit extension.**— The Secretary shall notify the taxpayer of the taxpayer's right to refuse to extend the period of limitations, or to limit such extension to particular issues or to a particular period of time, on each occasion when the taxpayer is requested to provide such consent.

* * *

(7) **Special rule for certain amended returns.**—Where, within the 60-day period ending on the day on which the time prescribed in this section for the assessment of any tax imposed by subtitle A for any taxable year would otherwise expire, the Secretary receives a written document signed by the taxpayer showing that the taxpayer owes an additional amount of such tax for such taxable year, the period for the assessment of such additional amount shall not expire before the day 60 days after the day on which the Secretary receives such document.

(8) **Failure to notify Secretary of certain foreign transfers.**— In the case of any information which is required to be reported to the Secretary under section 6038, 6038A, 6038B, 6046, 6046A, or 6048, the time for assessment of any tax imposed by this title with respect to any event or period to which such information relates shall not expire before the date which is 3 years after the date on which the Secretary is furnished the information required to be reported under such section.

(9) **Gift tax on certain gifts not shown on return.**— If any gift of property the value of which (or any increase in taxable gifts required under section 2701(d) which) is required to be shown on a return of tax imposed by chapter 12 (without regard to section 2503(b)), and is not shown on such return, any tax imposed by chapter 12 on such gift may be assessed, or a proceeding in court for the collection of such tax may be begun without assessment, at any time. The preceding sentence shall not apply to any item which is disclosed in such return, or in a statement attached to the return, in a manner adequate to apprise the Secretary of the nature of such item.

(10) **Listed transactions.**—If a taxpayer fails to include on any return or statement for any taxable year any information with respect to a listed transaction (as defined in section 6707A(c)(2)) which is required under section 6011 to be included with such return or statement, the time for assessment of any tax imposed by this title with respect to such transaction shall not expire before the date which is 1 year after the earlier of—

(A) the date on which the Secretary is furnished the information so required, or

(B) the date that a material advisor meets the requirements of section 6112 with respect to a request by the Secretary under section 6112(b) relating to such transaction with respect to such taxpayer.

(d) **Request for prompt assessment.**—Except as otherwise provided in subsection (c), (e), or (f), in the case of any tax (other than the tax imposed by chapter 11 of subtitle B, relating to estate taxes) for which return is required in the case of a decedent, or by his estate during the period of administration, or by a corporation, the tax shall be assessed, and any proceeding in court without assessment for the collection of such tax shall be begun, within 18 months after written request therefor (filed after the return is made and filed in such manner and such form as may be prescribed by regulations of the Secretary) by the executor, administrator, or other fiduciary representing the estate of such decedent, or by the corporation, but not after the expiration of 3 years after the return was filed. This subsection shall not apply in the case of a corporation unless—

(1)(A) such written request notifies the Secretary that the corporation contemplates dissolution at or before the expiration of such 18-month period, (B) the dissolution is in good faith begun before the expiration of such 18-month period, and (C) the dissolution is completed;

(2)(A) such written request notifies the Secretary that a dissolution has in good faith been begun, and (B) the dissolution is completed; or

(3) a dissolution has been completed at the time such written request is made.

(e) **Substantial omission of items.**—Except as otherwise provided in subsection (c)—

(1) **Income taxes.**—In the case of any tax imposed by subtitle A—

(A) General rule.—If the taxpayer omits from gross income an amount properly includible therein which is in excess of 25 percent of the amount of gross income stated in the return, the tax may be assessed, or a proceeding in court for the collection of such tax may be begun without assessment, at any time within 6 years after the return was filed. For purposes of this subparagraph—

(i) In the case of a trade or business, the term "gross income" means the total of the amounts received or accrued from the sale of goods or services (if such amounts are required to be shown on the return) prior to diminution by the cost of such sales or services; and

(ii) In determining the amount omitted from gross income, there shall not be taken into account any amount which is omitted from gross income stated in the return if such amount is disclosed in the return, or in a statement attached to the return, in a manner adequate to apprise the Secretary of the nature and amount of such item.

(B) Constructive dividends.—If the taxpayer omits from gross income an amount properly includible therein under section 951(a), the tax may be assessed, or a proceeding in court for the collection of such tax may be begun without assessment, at any time within 6 years after the return was filed.

(2) Estate and gift taxes.—In the case of a return of estate tax under chapter 11 or a return of gift tax under chapter 12, if the taxpayer omits from the gross estate or from the total amount of the gifts made during the period for which the return was filed items includible in such gross estate or such total gifts, as the case may be, as exceed in amount 25 percent of the gross estate stated in the return or the total amount of gifts stated in the return, the tax may be assessed, or a proceeding in court for the collection of such tax may be begun without assessment, at any time within 6 years after the return was filed. In determining the items omitted from the gross estate or the total gifts, there shall not be taken into account any item which is omitted from the gross estate or from the total gifts stated in the return if such item is disclosed in the return, or in a statement attached to the return, in a manner adequate to apprise the Secretary of the nature and amount of such item.

* * *

(f) Personal holding company tax.—If a corporation which is a personal holding company for any taxable year fails to file with its return under chapter 1 for such year a schedule setting forth—

(1) the items of gross income and adjusted ordinary gross income, described in section 543, received by the corporation during such year, and

(2) the names and addresses of the individuals who owned, within the meaning of section 544 (relating to rules for determining stock ownership), at any time during the last half of such year more than 50 percent in value of the outstanding capital stock of the corporation,

the personal holding company tax for such year may be assessed, or a proceeding in court for the collection of such tax may be begun without assessment, at any time within 6 years after the return for such year was filed.

(g) Certain income tax returns of corporations.—

(1) Trusts or partnerships.—If a taxpayer determines in good faith that it is a trust or partnership and files a return as such under subtitle A, and if such taxpayer is thereafter held to be a corporation for the taxable year for which the return is filed, such return shall be deemed the return of the corporation for purposes of this section.

* * *

(h) Net operating loss or capital loss carrybacks.—In the case of a deficiency attributable to the application to the taxpayer of a net operating loss carryback or a capital loss carryback (including deficiencies which may be assessed pursuant to the provisions of section 6213(b)(3)), such deficiency may be assessed at any time before the expiration of the period within which a deficiency for the taxable year of the net operating loss or net capital loss which results in such carryback may be assessed.

* * *

§ 6502. Collection after assessment

(a) Length of period.—Where the assessment of any tax imposed by this title has been made within the period of limitation properly applicable thereto, such tax may be collected by levy or by a proceeding in court, but only if the levy is made or the proceeding begun—

(1) within 10 years after the assessment of the tax, or

(2) if—

(A) there is an installment agreement between the taxpayer and the Secretary, prior to the date which is 90 days after the expiration of any period for collection agreed upon in writing by the Secretary and the taxpayer at the time the installment agreement was entered into, or

(B) there is a release of levy under section 6343 after such 10-year period, prior to the expiration of any period for collection agreed upon in writing by the Secretary and the taxpayer before such release.

If a timely proceeding in court for the collection of a tax is commenced, the period during which such tax may be collected by levy shall be extended and shall not expire until the liability for the tax (or a judgment against the taxpayer arising from such liability) is satisfied or becomes unenforceable.

(b) Date when levy is considered made.—The date on which a levy on property or rights to property is made shall be the date on which the notice of seizure provided in section 6335(a) is given.

§ 6503. Suspension of running of period of limitation

(a) Issuance of statutory notice of deficiency.—

(1) General rule.—The running of the period of limitations provided in section 6501 or 6502 (or section 6229, but only with respect to a deficiency described in paragraph (2)(A) or (3) of section 6230(a)) on the making of assessments or the collection by levy or a proceeding in court, in respect of any deficiency as defined in section 6211 (relating to income, estate, gift and certain excise taxes), shall (after the mailing of a notice under section 6212(a)) be suspended for the period during which the Secretary is prohibited from making the assessment or from collecting by levy or a proceeding in court (and in any event, if a proceeding in respect of the deficiency is placed on the docket of the Tax Court, until the decision of the Tax Court becomes final), and for 60 days thereafter.

(2) Corporation joining in consolidated income tax return.—If a notice under section 6212(a) in respect of a deficiency in tax imposed by subtitle A for any taxable year is mailed to a corporation, the suspension of the running of the period of limitations provided in paragraph (1) of this subsection shall apply in the case of corporations with which such corporation made a consolidated income tax return for such taxable year.

(b) Assets of taxpayer in control or custody of court.—The period of limitations on collection after assessment prescribed in section 6502 shall be suspended for the period the assets of the taxpayer are in the control or custody of the court in any proceeding before any court of the United States or of any State or of the District of Columbia, and for 6 months thereafter.

(c) Taxpayer outside United States.—The running of the period of limitations on collection after assessment prescribed in section 6502 shall be suspended for the period during which the taxpayer is outside the United States if such period of absence is for a continuous period of at least 6 months. If the preceding sentence applies and at the time of the taxpayer's return to the United States the period of limitations on collection after assessment prescribed in section 6502 would expire before the expiration of 6 months from the date of his return, such period shall not expire before the expiration of such 6 months.

(d) Extensions of time for payment of estate tax.—The running of the period of limitations for collection of any tax imposed by chapter 11 shall be suspended for the period of any extension of time for payment granted under the provisions of section 6161(a)(2) or (b)(2) or under the provisions of section 6163 or 6166.

(e) Extensions of time for payment of tax attributable to recoveries of foreign expropriation losses.—The running of the period of limitations for collection of the tax attributable to a recovery of a foreign expropriation loss (within the meaning of section 6167(f)) shall be suspended for the period of any extension of time for payment under subsection (a) or (b) of section 6167.

* * *

SUBCHAPTER B—LIMITATIONS ON CREDIT OR REFUND

Editorial Summary

Limitations on Credits and Refunds

Subchapter B of Chapter 66 (Secs. 6511, 6513)

See the discussion under the Editorial Summary entitled Limitations on Assessments, Collections, Credits, and Refunds, which precedes Sec. 6501.

§ 6511. Limitations on credit or refund

(a) Period of limitation on filing claim.—Claim for credit or refund of an overpayment of any tax imposed by this title in respect of which tax the taxpayer is required to file a return shall be filed by the taxpayer within 3 years from the time the return was filed or 2 years from the time the tax was paid, whichever of such periods expires the later, or if no return was filed by the taxpayer, within 2 years from the time the tax was paid. Claim for credit or refund of an overpayment of any tax imposed by this title which is required to be paid by means of a stamp shall be filed by the taxpayer within 3 years from the time the tax was paid.

(b) Limitation on allowance of credits and refunds.—

(1) Filing of claim within prescribed period.—No credit or refund shall be allowed or made after the expiration of the period of limitation prescribed in subsection (a) for the filing of a claim for credit or refund, unless a claim for credit or refund is filed by the taxpayer within such period.

(2) Limit on amount of credit or refund.—

(A) Limit where claim filed within 3-year period.—If the claim was filed by the taxpayer during the 3-year period prescribed in subsection (a), the amount of the credit or refund shall not exceed the portion of the tax paid within the period, immediately preceding the filing of the claim, equal to 3 years plus the period of any extension of time for filing the return. If the tax was required to be paid by means of a stamp, the amount of the credit or refund shall not exceed the portion of the tax paid within the 3 years immediately preceding the filing of the claim.

(B) Limit where claim not filed within 3-year period.—If the claim was not filed within such 3-year period, the amount of the credit or refund shall not exceed the portion of the tax paid during the 2 years immediately preceding the filing of the claim.

(C) Limit if no claim filed.—If no claim was filed, the credit or refund shall not exceed the amount which would be allowable under subparagraph (A) or (B), as the case may be, if claim was filed on the date the credit or refund is allowed.

(c) Special rules applicable in case of extension of time by agreement.—If an agreement under the provisions of section 6501(c)(4) extending the period for assessment of a tax imposed by this title is made within the period prescribed in subsection (a) for the filing of a claim for credit or refund—

(1) Time for filing claim.—The period for filing claim for credit or refund or for making credit or refund if no claim is filed, provided in subsections (a) and (b)(1), shall not expire prior to 6 months after the expiration of the period within which an assessment may be made pursuant to the agreement or any extension thereof under section 6501(c)(4).

(2) Limit on amount.—If a claim is filed, or a credit or refund is allowed when no claim was filed, after the execution of the agreement and within 6 months after the expiration of the period within which an assessment may be made pursuant to the agreement or any extension thereof, the amount of the credit or refund shall not exceed the portion of the tax paid after the execution of the agreement and before the filing of the claim or the making of the credit or refund, as the case may be, plus the portion of the tax paid within the period which would be applicable under subsection (b)(2) if a claim had been filed on the date the agreement was executed.

(3) Claims not subject to special rule.—This subsection shall not apply in the case of a claim filed, or credit or refund allowed if no claim is filed, either—

(A) prior to the execution of the agreement or

(B) more than 6 months after the expiration of the period within which an assessment may be made pursuant to the agreement or any extension thereof.

(d) Special rules applicable to income taxes.—

(1) Seven-year period of limitation with respect to bad debts and worthless securities.—If the claim for credit or refund relates to an overpayment of tax imposed by subtitle A on account of—

(A) The deductibility by the taxpayer, under section 166 or section 832(c), of a debt as a debt which became worthless, or, under section 165(g), of a loss from worthlessness of a security, or

(B) The effect that the deductibility of a debt or loss described in subparagraph (A) has on the application to the taxpayer of a carryover,

in lieu of the 3-year period of limitation prescribed in subsection (a), the period shall be 7 years from the date prescribed by law for filing the return for the year with respect to which the claim is made. If the claim for credit or refund relates to an overpayment on account of the effect that the deductibility of such a debt or loss has on the application to the taxpayer of a carryback, the period shall be either 7 years from the date prescribed by law for filing the return for the year of the net operating loss which results in such carryback or the period prescribed in paragraph (2) of this subsection, whichever expires the later. In the case of a claim described in this paragraph the amount of the credit or refund may exceed the portion of the tax paid within the period prescribed in subsection (b)(2) or (c), whichever is applicable, to the extent of the amount of the overpayment attributable to the deductibility of items described in this paragraph.

(2) Special period of limitation with respect to net operating loss or capital loss carrybacks.—

(A) Period of limitation.—If the claim for credit or refund relates to an overpayment attributable to a net operating loss carryback or a capital loss carryback, in lieu of the 3-year period of limitation prescribed in subsection (a), the period shall be that period which ends 3 years after the time prescribed by law for filing the return (including extensions thereof) for the taxable year of the net operating loss or net capital loss which results in such carryback, or the period prescribed in subsection (c) in respect of such taxable year, whichever expires later. In the case of such a claim, the amount of the credit or refund may exceed the portion of the tax paid within the period provided in subsection (b)(2) or (c), whichever is applicable, to the extent of the amount of the overpayment attributable to such carryback.

(B) Applicable rules.—

(i) In general.—If the allowance of a credit or refund of an overpayment of tax attributable to a net operating loss carryback or a capital loss carryback is otherwise prevented by the operation of any law or rule of law other than section 7122 (relating to compromises), such credit or refund may be allowed or made, if claim therefor is filed within the period provided in subparagraph (A) of this paragraph.

(ii) Tentative carryback adjustments.—If the allowance of an application, credit, or refund of a decrease in tax determined under section 6411(b) is otherwise prevented by the operation of any law or rule of law other than section 7122, such application, credit, or refund may be allowed or made if application for a tentative carryback adjustment is made within the period provided in section 6411(a).

(iii) Determinations by courts to be conclusive.—In the case of any such claim for credit or refund or any such application for a tentative carryback adjustment, the determination by any court, including the Tax Court, in any proceeding in which the decision of the court has become final, shall be conclusive except with respect to—

(I) the net operating loss deduction and the effect of such deduction, and

(II) the determination of a short-term capital loss and the effect of such short-term capital loss, to the extent that such deduction or short-term capital loss is affected by a carryback which was not an issue in such proceeding.

(3) Special rules relating to foreign tax credit.—

(A) Special period of limitation with respect to foreign taxes paid or accrued.—If the claim for credit or refund relates to an overpayment attributable to any taxes paid or accrued to any foreign country or to any possession of the United States for which credit is allowed against the tax imposed by subtitle A in accordance with the provisions of section 901 or the provisions of any treaty to which the United States is a party, in lieu of the 3-year period of limitation prescribed in subsection (a), the period shall be 10 years from the date prescribed by law for filing the return for the year in which such taxes were actually paid or accrued.

(B) Exception in the case of foreign taxes paid or accrued.—In the case of a claim described in subparagraph (A), the amount of the credit or refund may exceed the portion of the tax paid within the period provided in subsection (b) or (c), whichever is applicable, to the extent of the amount of the overpayment attributable to the allowance of a credit for the taxes described in subparagraph (A).

(4) Special period of limitation with respect to certain credit carrybacks.—

(A) Period of limitation.—If the claim for credit or refund relates to an overpayment attributable to a credit carryback, in lieu of the 3-year period of limitation prescribed in subsection (a), the period shall be that period which ends 3 years after the time prescribed by law for filing the return (including extensions thereof) for the taxable year of the unused credit which results in such carryback (or, with respect to any portion of a credit carryback from a taxable year attributable to a net operating loss carryback, capital loss carryback, or other credit carryback from a subsequent taxable year, the period shall be that period which ends 3 years after the time prescribed by law for filing the return, including extensions thereof, for such subsequent taxable year) or the period prescribed in subsection (c) in respect of such taxable year, whichever expires later. In the case of such a claim, the amount of the credit or refund may exceed the portion of the tax paid within the period provided in subsection (b)(2) or (c), whichever is applicable, to the extent of the amount of the overpayment attributable to such carryback.

(B) Applicable rules.—If the allowance of a credit or refund of an overpayment of tax attributable to a credit carryback is otherwise prevented by the operation of any law or rule of law other than section 7122, relating to compromises, such credit or refund may be allowed or made, if claim therefor is filed within the period provided in subparagraph (A) of this paragraph. In the case of any such claim for credit or refund, the determination by any court, including the Tax Court, in any proceeding in which the decision of the court has become final, shall not be conclusive with respect to any credit, and the effect of such credit, to the extent that such credit is affected by a credit carryback which was not in issue in such proceeding.

(C) Credit carryback defined.—For purposes of this paragraph, the term "credit carryback" means any business carryback under section 39 and any research credit carryback under section 30(g)(2).

* * *

§ 6513. Time return deemed filed and tax considered paid

(a) Early return or advance payment of tax.—For purposes of section 6511, any return filed before the last day prescribed for the filing thereof shall be considered as filed on such last day. For purposes of section 6511(b)(2) and (c) and section 6512, payment of any portion of the tax made before the last day prescribed for the payment of the tax shall be considered made on such last day. For purposes of this subsection, the last day prescribed for filing the return or paying the tax shall be determined without regard to any extension of time granted the taxpayer and without regard to any election to pay the tax in installments.

(b) Prepaid income tax.—For purposes of section 6511 or 6512—

(1) Any tax actually deducted and withheld at the source during any calendar year under chapter 24 shall, in respect of the recipient of the income, be deemed to have been paid by him on the 15th day of the fourth month following the close of his taxable year with respect to which such tax is allowable as a credit under section 31.

(2) Any amount paid as estimated income tax for any taxable year shall be deemed to have been paid on the last day prescribed for filing the return under section 6012 for such taxable year (determined without regard to any extension of time for filing such return).

(3) Any tax withheld at the source under chapter 3 shall, in respect of the recipient of the income, be deemed to have been paid by such recipient on the last day prescribed for filing the return under section 6012 for the taxable year (determined without regard to any extension of time for filing) with respect to which such tax is allowable as a credit under section 1462. For this purpose, any exemption granted under section 6012 from the requirement of filing a return shall be disregarded.

(c) Return and payment of social security taxes and income tax withholding.—Notwithstanding subsection (a), for purposes of section 6511 with respect to any tax imposed by chapter 3 ,21, or 24—

(1) If a return for any period ending with or within a calendar year is filed before April 15 of the succeeding calendar year, such return shall be considered filed on April 15 of such succeeding calendar year; and

(2) If a tax with respect to remuneration or other amount paid during any period ending with or within a calendar year is paid before April 15 of the succeeding calendar year, such tax shall be considered paid on April 15 of such succeeding calendar year.

(d) Overpayment of income tax credited to estimated tax.—If any overpayment of income tax is, in accordance with section 6402(b), claimed as a credit against estimated tax for the succeeding taxable year, such amount shall be considered as a payment of the income tax for the succeeding taxable year (whether or not claimed as a credit in the return of estimated tax for such succeeding taxable year), and no claim for credit or refund of such overpayment shall be allowed for the taxable year in which the overpayment arises.

* * *

SUBCHAPTER C—MITIGATION OF EFFECT OF PERIOD OF LIMITATIONS*

SUBCHAPTER D—PERIODS OF LIMITATION IN JUDICIAL PROCEEDINGS*

CHAPTER 67—INTEREST

Subchapter
- A. Interest on underpayments.
- B. Interest on overpayments.
- C. Determination of interest rate; compounding of interest.

Editorial Summary

Interest on Underpayments and Overpayments

Subchapters A, B, and C of Chapter 67 (Secs. 6601–6622)

Subchapter A provides the procedure for assessing interest charges on the underpayment of the taxpayer's tax liability, whereas Subchapter B provides the procedure for the IRS to pay interest to the taxpayer with respect to the overpayment of the taxpayer's tax liability. Subchapter C provides the rules for calculating the amount of the interest. Note that the starting date for interest due the IRS is not the same as the starting date for interest due the taxpayer. Also note that the interest rate on underpayments exceeds the interest rate on overpayments by 1 percentage point if the taxpayer is a corporation [see Sec. 6621(a)].

SUBCHAPTER A—INTEREST ON UNDERPAYMENTS

§ 6601. Interest on underpayment, nonpayment, or extensions of time for payment, of tax

(a) General rule.—If any amount of tax imposed by this title (whether required to be shown on a return, or to be paid by stamp or by some other method) is not paid on or before the last date prescribed for payment, interest on such amount at the underpayment rate established under section 6621 shall be paid for the period from such last date to the date paid.

(b) Last date prescribed for payment.—For purposes of this section, the last date prescribed for payment of the tax shall be determined under chapter 62 with the application of the following rules:

(1) Extensions of time disregarded.—The last date prescribed for payment shall be determined without regard to any extension of time for payment or any installment agreement entered into under section 6159.

(2) Installment payments.—In the case of an election under section 6156(a) to pay the tax in installments—

(A) The date prescribed for payment of each installment of the tax shown on the return shall be determined under section 6156(b), and

*Omitted.

(B) The last date prescribed for payment of the first installment shall be deemed the last date prescribed for payment of any portion of the tax not shown on the return.

* * *

(4) Accumulated earnings tax.—In the case of the tax imposed by section 531 for any taxable year, the last date prescribed for payment shall be deemed to be the due date (without regard to extensions) for the return of tax imposed by subtitle A for such taxable year.

(5) Last date for payment not otherwise prescribed.—In the case of taxes payable by stamp and in all other cases in which the last date for payment is not otherwise prescribed, the last date for payment shall be deemed to be the date the liability for tax arises (and in no event shall be later than the date notice and demand for the tax is made by the Secretary).

(c) Suspension of interest in certain income, estate, gift, and certain excise tax cases.—In the case of a deficiency as defined in section 6211 (relating to income, estate, gift, and certain excise taxes), if a waiver of restrictions under section 6213(d) on the assessment of such deficiency has been filed, and if notice and demand by the Secretary for payment of such deficiency is not made within 30 days after the filing of such waiver, interest shall not be imposed on such deficiency for the period beginning immediately after such 30th day and ending with the date of notice and demand and interest shall not be imposed during such period on any interest with respect to such deficiency for any prior period. In the case of a settlement under section 6224(c) which results in the conversion of partnership items to nonpartnership items pursuant to section 6231(b)(1)(C), the preceding sentence shall apply to a computational adjustment resulting from such settlement in the same manner as if such adjustment were a deficiency and such settlement were a waiver referred to in the preceding sentence.

(d) Income tax reduced by carryback or adjustment for certain unused deductions.—

(1) Net operating loss or capital loss carryback.—If the amount of any tax imposed by subtitle A is reduced by reason of a carryback of a net operating loss or net capital loss, such reduction in tax shall not affect the computation of interest under this section for the period ending with the filing date for the taxable year in which the net operating loss or net capital loss arises.

(2) Foreign tax credit carrybacks.—If any credit allowed for any taxable year is increased by reason of a carryback of tax paid or accrued to foreign countries or possessions of the United States, such increase shall not affect the computation of interest under this section for the period ending with the filing date for the taxable year in which such taxes were in fact paid or accrued, or, with respect to any portion of such credit carryback from a taxable year attributable to a net operating loss carryback or a capital loss carryback from a subsequent taxable year, such increase shall not affect the computation of interest under this section for the period ending with the filing date for such subsequent taxable year.

(3) Certain credit carrybacks.—

(A) In general.—If any credit allowed for any taxable year is increased by reason of a credit carryback, such increase shall not affect the computation of interest under this section for the period ending with the filing date for the taxable year in which the credit carryback arises, or, with respect to any portion of a credit carryback from a taxable year attributable to a net operating loss carryback, capital loss carryback, or other credit carryback from a subsequent taxable year, such increase shall not affect the computation of interest under this section for the period ending with the filing date for such subsequent taxable year.

(B) Credit carryback defined.—For purposes of this paragraph, the term "credit carryback" has the meaning given such term by section 6511 (d)(4)(C).

(4) Filing date.—For purposes of this subsection, the term "filing date" has the meaning given to such term by section 6611(f)(4)(A).

(e) Applicable rules.—Except as otherwise provided in this title—

(1) Interest treated as tax.—Interest prescribed under this section on any tax shall be paid upon notice and demand, and shall be assessed, collected, and paid in the same manner as taxes. Any reference in this title (except subchapter B of chapter 63, relating to deficiency procedures) to any tax imposed by this title shall be deemed also to refer to interest imposed by this section on such tax.

(2) Interest on penalties, additional amounts, or additions to the tax.—

(A) In general.—Interest shall be imposed under subsection (a) in respect of any assessable penalty, additional amount, or addition to the tax (other than an addition to tax imposed under section 6651(a)(1) or 6653 or under part II of subchapter A of chapter 68) only if such assessable penalty, additional amount, or addition to the tax is not paid within 10 days from the date of notice and demand therefor, and in such case interest shall be imposed only for the period from the date of the notice and demand to the date of payment.

(B) Interest on certain additions to tax.—Interest shall be imposed under this section with respect to any addition to tax imposed by section 6651(a)(1) or 6653 or under part II of subchapter A of chapter 68 for the period which—

(i) begins on the date on which the return of the tax with respect to which such addition to tax is imposed is required to be filed (including any extensions), and

(ii) ends on the date of payment of such addition to tax.

(3) Payments made within 10 days after notice and demand.—If notice and demand is made for payment of any amount, and if such amount is paid within 10 days after the date of such notice and demand, interest under this section on the amount so paid shall not be imposed for the period after the date of such notice and demand.

(f) Satisfaction by credits.—If any portion of a tax is satisfied by credit of an overpayment, then no interest shall be imposed under this section on the portion of the tax so satisfied for any period during which, if the credit had not been made, interest would have been allowable with respect to such overpayment. The preceding sentence shall not apply to the extent that section 6621 (d) applies.

(g) Limitation on assessment and collection.—Interest prescribed under this section on any tax may be assessed and collected at any time during the period within which the tax to which such interest relates may be collected.

(h) Exception as to estimated tax.—This section shall not apply to any failure to pay any estimated tax required to be paid by section 6654 or 6655.

(i) Exception as to Federal unemployment tax.—This section shall not apply to any failure to make a payment of tax imposed by section 3301 for a calendar quarter or other period within a taxable year required under authority of section 6157.

(j) 2-percent rate on certain portion of estate tax extended under section 6166.—

(1) In general.—If the time for payment of an amount of tax imposed by chapter 11 is extended as provided in section 6166, then in lieu of the annual rate provided by subsection (a)—

(A) interest on the 2-percent portion of such amount shall be paid at the rate of 2 percent, and

(B) interest on so much of such amount as exceeds the 2-percent portion shall be paid at a rate equal to 45 percent of the annual rate provided by subsection (a).

For purposes of this subsection, the amount of any deficiency which is prorated to installments payable under section 6166 shall be treated as an amount of tax payable in installments under such section.

(2) 2-percent portion.—For purposes of this subsection, the term "2-percent portion" means the lesser of—

(A)(i) the amount of the tentative tax which would be determined under the rate schedule set forth in section 2001(c) if the amount with respect to which such tentative tax is to be computed were the sum of $1,000,000* and the applicable exclusion amount in effect under section 2010(c), reduced by

(ii) the applicable credit amount in effect under section 2010(c), or

(B) the amount of the tax imposed by chapter 11 which is extended as provided in section 6166.

(3) Inflation adjustment.—In the case of estates of decedents dying in a calendar year after 1998, the $1,000,000* amount contained in paragraph (2)(A) shall be increased by an amount equal to—

(A) $1,000,000,* multiplied by

(B) the cost-of-living adjustment determined under section 1(f)(3) for such calendar year by substituting "calendar year 1997" for "calendar year 1992" in subparagraph (B) thereof.

If any amount as adjusted under the preceding sentence is not a multiple of $10,000, such amount shall be rounded to the next lowest multiple of $10,000.

(4) Treatment of payments.—If the amount of tax imposed by chapter 11 which is extended as provided in section 6166 exceeds the 2-percent

*Editorial comment: The indexed amount for 2013 is $1,430,000 and for 2014 is $1,450,000.

portion, any payment of a portion of such amount shall, for purposes of computing interest for periods after such payment, be treated as reducing the 2-percent portion by an amount which bears the same ratio to the amount of such payment as the amount of the 2-percent portion (determined without regard to this paragraph) bears to the amount of the tax which is extended as provided in section 6166.

* * *

SUBCHAPTER B—INTEREST ON OVERPAYMENTS

Editorial Summary

Interest on Overpayments

Subchapter B of Chapter 67 (Sec. 6611)

See the discussion under the Editorial Summary entitled Interest on Underpayments and Overpayments, which precedes Sec. 6601.

§ 6611. Interest on overpayments

(a) Rate.—Interest shall be allowed and paid upon any overpayment in respect of any internal revenue tax at the overpayment rate established under section 6621.

(b) Period.—Such interest shall be allowed and paid as follows:

(1) Credits.—In the case of a credit, from the date of the overpayment to the due date of the amount against which the credit is taken.

(2) Refunds.—In the case of a refund, from the date of the overpayment to a date (to be determined by the Secretary) preceding the date of the refund check by not more than 30 days, whether or not such refund check is accepted by the taxpayer after tender of such check to the taxpayer. The acceptance of such check shall be without prejudice to any right of the taxpayer to claim any additional overpayment and interest thereon.

(3) Late returns.—Notwithstanding paragraph (1) or (2) in the case of a return of tax which is filed after the last date prescribed for filing such return (determined with regard to extensions), no interest shall be allowed or paid for any day before the date on which the return is filed.

* * *

(e) Disallowance of interest on certain overpayments.—

(1) Refunds within 45 days after return is filed.—If any overpayment of tax imposed by this title is refunded within 45 days after the last day prescribed for filing the return of such tax (determined without regard to any extension of time for filing the return) or, in the case of a return filed after such last date, is refunded within 45 days after the date the return is filed, no interest shall be allowed under subsection (a) on such overpayment.

(2) Refunds after claim for credit or refund.—If—

(A) the taxpayer files a claim for a credit or refund for any overpayment of tax imposed by this title, and

(B) such overpayment is refunded within 45 days after such claim is filed,

no interest shall be allowed on such overpayment from the date the claim is filed until the day the refund is made.

(3) IRS initiated adjustments.—If an adjustment initiated by the Secretary, results in a refund or credit of an overpayment, interest on such overpayment shall be computed by subtracting 45 days from the number of days interest would otherwise be allowed with respect to such overpayment.

(f) Refund of income tax caused by carryback or adjustment for certain unused deductions.—

(1) Net operating loss or capital loss carryback.—For purposes of subsection (a), if any overpayment of tax imposed by subtitle A results from a carryback of a net operating loss or net capital loss, such overpayment shall be deemed not to have been made prior to the filing date for the taxable year in which such net operating loss or net capital loss arises.

(2) Foreign tax credit carrybacks.—For purposes of subsection (a), if any overpayment of tax imposed by subtitle A results from a carryback of tax paid or accrued to foreign countries or possessions of the United States, such overpayment shall be deemed not to have been made before the filing date for the taxable year in which such taxes were in fact paid or accrued, or, with respect to any portion of such credit carryback from a taxable year attributable to a net operating loss carryback or a capital loss carryback from a subsequent taxable year, such overpayment shall be deemed not to have been made before the filing date for such subsequent taxable year.

(3) Certain credit carrybacks.—

(A) In general.—For purposes of subsection (a), if any overpayment of tax imposed by subtitle A results from a credit carryback, such overpayment shall be deemed not to have been made before the filing date for the taxable year in which such credit carryback arises, or, with respect to any portion of a credit carryback from a taxable year attributable to a net operating loss carryback, capital loss carryback, or other credit carryback from a subsequent taxable year, such overpayment shall be deemed not to have been made before the filing date for such subsequent taxable year.

(B) Credit carryback defined.—For purposes of this paragraph, the term "credit carryback" has the meaning given such term by section 6511 (d)(4)(C).

(g) No interest until return in processible form.—

(1) For purposes of subsections (b)(3) and (e), a return shall not be treated as filed until it is filed in processible form.

(2) For purposes of paragraph (1), a return is in a processible form if—

(A) such return is filed on a permitted form, and

(B) such return contains—

(i) the taxpayer's name, address, and identifying number and the required signature, and

(ii) sufficient required information (whether on the return or on required attachments) to permit the mathematical verification of tax liability shown on the return.

* * *

* * *

SUBCHAPTER C—DETERMINATION OF INTEREST RATE; COMPOUNDING OF INTEREST

Editorial Summary

Calculation of Interest on Underpayments and Overpayments

Subchapter C of Chapter 67 (Secs. 6621, 6622)

See the discussion under the Editorial Summary entitled Interest on Underpayments and Overpayments, which precedes Sec. 6601.

§ 6621. Determination of rate of interest

(a) General rule.—

(1) Overpayment rate.—The overpayment rate established under this section shall be the sum of—

(A) the Federal short-term rate determined under subsection (b), plus

(B) 3 percentage points (2 percentage points in the case of a corporation).

To the extent that an overpayment of tax by a corporation for any taxable period (as defined in subsection (c)(3), applied by substituting "overpayment" for "underpayment") exceeds $10,000, subparagraph (B) shall be applied by substituting "0.5 percentage point" for "2 percentage points."

(2) Underpayment rate.—The underpayment rate established under this section shall be the sum of—

(A) the Federal short-term rate determined under subsection (b), plus

(B) 3 percentage points.

(b) Federal short-term rate.—For purposes of this section—

(1) General rule.—The Secretary shall determine the Federal short-term rate for the first month in each calendar quarter.

(2) Period during which rate applies.—

(A) In general.—Except as provided in subparagraph (B), the Federal short-term rate determined under paragraph (1) for any month shall apply during the first calendar quarter beginning after such month.

(B) Special rule for individual estimated tax.—In determining the addition to tax under section 6654 for failure to pay estimated tax for any taxable year, the Federal short-term rate which applies during the 3rd month following such taxable year shall also apply during the first 15 days of the 4th month following such taxable year.

(3) Federal short-term rate.—The Federal short-term rate for any month shall be the Federal short-term rate determined during such month by the Secretary in accordance with section 1274(d). Any such rate shall be rounded to the nearest full percent (or, if a multiple of ½ of 1 percent, such rate shall be increased to the next highest full percent).

(c) Increase in underpayment rate for large corporate underpayments.—

(1) In general.—For purposes of determining the amount of interest payable under section 6601 on any large corporate underpayment for periods after the applicable date, paragraph (2) of subsection (a) shall be applied by substituting "5 percentage points" for "3 percentage points."

(2) Applicable date.—For purposes of this subsection—

(A) In general.—The applicable date is the 30th day after the earlier of—

(i) the date on which the 1st letter of proposed deficiency which allows the taxpayer an opportunity for administrative review in the Internal Revenue Service Office of Appeals is sent, or

(ii) the date on which the deficiency notice under section 6212 is sent.

The preceding sentence shall be applied without regard to any such letter or notice which is withdrawn by the Secretary.

(B) Special rules.—

(i) Nondeficiency procedures.—In the case of any underpayment of any tax imposed by this title to which the deficiency procedures do not apply, subparagraph (A) shall be applied by taking into account any letter or notice provided by the Secretary which notifies the taxpayer of the assessment or proposed assessment of the tax.

(ii) Exception where amounts paid in full.—For purposes of subparagraph (A), a letter or notice shall be disregarded if, during the 30-day period beginning on the day on which it was sent, the taxpayer makes a payment equal to the amount shown as due in such letter or notice, as the case may be.

(iii) Exception for letters or notices involving small amounts.—For purposes of this paragraph, any letter or notice shall be disregarded if the amount of the deficiency or proposed deficiency (or the assessment or proposed assessment) set forth in such letter or notice is not greater than $100,000 (determined by not taking into account any interest, penalties, or additions to tax).

(3) Large corporate underpayment.—For purposes of this subsection—

(A) In general.—The term "large corporate underpayment" means any underpayment of a tax by a C corporation for any taxable period if the amount of such underpayment for such period exceeds $100,000.

(B) Taxable period.—For purposes of subparagraph (A), the term "taxable period" means—

(i) in the case of any tax imposed by subtitle A, the taxable year, or

(ii) in the case of any other tax, the period to which the underpayment relates.

(d) Elimination of interest on overlapping periods of tax overpayments and underpayments.—To the extent that, for any period, interest is payable under subchapter A and allowable under subchapter B on equivalent underpayments and overpayments by the same taxpayer of tax imposed by this title, the net rate of interest under this section on such amounts shall be zero for such period.

§ 6622. Interest compounded daily

(a) General rule.—In computing the amount of any interest required to be paid under this title or sections 1961(c)(1) or 2411 of title 28, United States Code, by the Secretary or by the taxpayer, or any other amount determined by reference to such amount of interest, such interest and such amount shall be compounded daily.

(b) Exception for penalty for failure to file estimated tax.—Subsection (a) shall not apply for purposes of computing the amount of any addition to tax under section 6654 or 6655.

SUBCHAPTER D—NOTICE REQUIREMENTS

§ 6631. Notice requirements

The Secretary shall include with each notice to an individual taxpayer which includes an amount of interest required to be paid by such taxpayer under this title information with respect to the section of this title under which the interest is imposed and a computation of the interest.

CHAPTER 68—ADDITIONS TO THE TAX, ADDITIONAL AMOUNTS, AND ASSESSABLE PENALTIES

Editorial Summary

Penalties on Taxpayer

Subchapter A of Chapter 68

(Secs. 6651, 6654, 6662–6665)

Failure to file a tax return on time or to appropriately calculate and pay the tax liability as required by the Code can result in the taxpayer being assessed interest. In addition, the potential exists that penalties may also be assessed. Subchapter A identifies the circumstances under which penalties are applicable and the rules for calculating the amount of the penalty. See Subchapter B for penalties imposed on the tax return preparer.

SUBCHAPTER A—ADDITIONS TO THE TAX AND ADDITIONAL AMOUNTS

PART I—GENERAL PROVISIONS

§ 6651. Failure to file tax return or to pay tax

(a) Addition to the tax.—In case of failure—

(1) to file any return required under authority of subchapter A of chapter 61 (other than part III thereof), subchapter A of chapter 51 (relating to distilled spirits, wines, and beer), or of subchapter A of chapter 52 (relating to tobacco, cigars, cigarettes, and cigarette papers and tubes), or of subchapter A of chapter 53 (relating to machine guns and certain other firearms), on the date prescribed therefor (determined with regard to any extension of time for filing), unless it is shown that such failure is due to reasonable cause and not due to willful neglect, there shall be added to the amount required to be shown as tax on such return 5 percent of the amount of such tax if the failure is for not more than 1 month, with an additional 5 percent for each additional month or fraction thereof during which such failure continues, not exceeding 25 percent in the aggregate;

(2) to pay the amount shown as tax on any return specified in paragraph (1) on or before the date prescribed for payment of such tax (determined with regard to any extension of time for payment), unless it is shown that such failure is due to reasonable cause and not due to willful neglect, there shall be added to the amount shown as tax on such return 0.5 percent of the amount of such tax if the failure is for not more than 1 month, with an additional 0.5 percent for each additional month or fraction thereof during which such failure continues, not exceeding 25 percent in the aggregate; or

(3) to pay any amount in respect of any tax required to be shown on a return specified in paragraph (1) which is not so shown (including an assessment made pursuant to section 6213(b)) within 10 days of the date of the notice and demand therefor, unless it is shown that such failure is due to reasonable cause and not due to willful neglect, there shall be added to the amount of tax stated in such notice and demand 0.5 percent of the amount of such tax if the failure is for not more than 1 month, with an additional 0.5 percent for each additional month or fraction thereof during which such failure continues, not exceeding 25 percent in the aggregate.

In the case of a failure to file a return of tax imposed by chapter 1 within 60 days of the date prescribed for filing of such return (determined with regard to any extensions of time for filing), unless it is shown that such failure is due to reasonable cause and not due to willful neglect, the addition to tax under paragraph (1) shall not be less than the lesser of $135 or 100 percent of the amount required to be shown as tax on such return.

*Omitted.

(b) Penalty imposed on net amount due.—For purposes of—

(1) subsection (a)(1), the amount of tax required to be shown on the return shall be reduced by the amount of any part of the tax which is paid on or before the date prescribed for payment of the tax and by the amount of any credit against the tax which may be claimed on the return,

(2) subsection (a)(2), the amount of tax shown on the return shall, for purposes of computing the addition for any month, be reduced by the amount of any part of the tax which is paid on or before the beginning of such month and by the amount of any credit against the tax which may be claimed on the return, and

(3) subsection (a)(3), the amount of tax stated in the notice and demand shall, for the purpose of computing the addition for any month, be reduced by the amount of any part of the tax which is paid before the beginning of such month.

(c) Limitations and special rule.—

(1) Additions under more than one paragraph.—With respect to any return, the amount of the addition under paragraph (1) of subsection (a) shall be reduced by the amount of the addition under paragraph (2) of subsection (a) for any month (or fraction thereof) to which an addition to tax applies under both paragraphs (1) and (2). In any case described in the last sentence of subsection (a), the amount of the addition under paragraph (1) of subsection (a) shall not be reduced under the preceding sentence below the amount provided in such last sentence.

(2) Amount of tax shown more than amount required to be shown.—If the amount required to be shown as tax on a return is less than the amount shown as tax on such return, subsections (a)(2) and (b)(2) shall be applied by substituting such lower amount.

(d) Increase in penalty for failure to pay tax in certain cases.—

(1) In general.—In the case of each month (or fraction thereof) beginning after the day described in paragraph (2) of this subsection, paragraphs (2) and (3) of subsection (a) shall be applied by substituting "1 percent" for "0.5 percent" each place it appears.

(2) Description.—For purposes of paragraph (1), the day described in this paragraph is the earlier of—

(A) the day 10 days after the date on which notice is given under section 6331(d), or

(B) the day on which notice and demand for immediate payment is given under the last sentence of section 6331(a).

* * *

(f) Increase in penalty for fraudulent failure to file.—If any failure to file any return is fraudulent, paragraph (1) of subsection (a) shall be applied—

(1) by substituting "15 percent" for "5 percent" each place it appears, and

(2) by substituting "75 percent" for "25 percent."

* * *

§ 6654. Failure by individual to pay estimated income tax

CAUTION: FUTURE EFFECTIVE DATE

Section 6654(a) is amended by the Patient Protection and Affordable Care Act of 2010 effective for taxable years beginning after 12/31/2012.

(a) Addition to the tax.—Except as otherwise provided in this section, in the case of any underpayment of estimated tax by an individual, there shall be added to the tax under chapter 1 and the tax under chapter 2 for the taxable year an amount determined by applying—

(1) the underpayment rate established under section 6621,

(2) to the amount of the underpayment,

(3) for the period of the underpayment.

(b) Amount of underpayment; period of underpayment.—For purposes of subsection (a)—

(1) Amount.—The amount of the underpayment shall be the excess of—

(A) the required installment, over

(B) the amount (if any) of the installment paid on or before the due date for the installment.

(2) Period of underpayment.—The period of the underpayment shall run from the due date for the installment to whichever of the following dates is the earlier—

(A) the 15th day of the 4th month following the close of the taxable year, or

(B) with respect to any portion of the underpayment, the date on which such portion is paid.

(3) Order of crediting payments.—For purposes of paragraph (2)(B), a payment of estimated tax shall be credited against unpaid required installments in the order in which such installments are required to be paid.

(c) Number of required installments; due dates.—For purposes of this section—

(1) Payable in 4 installments.—There shall be 4 required installments for each taxable year.

(2) Time for payment of installments.—

In the case of the following required installments	The due date is:
1st	April 15
2nd	June 15
3rd	September 15
4th	January 15 of the following taxable year.

(d) Amount of required installments.—For purposes of this section—

(1) Amount.

(A) In general.—Except as provided in paragraph (2), the amount of any required installment shall be 25 percent of the required annual payment.

(B) Required annual payment.—For purposes of subparagraph (A), the term "required annual payment" means the lesser of—

(i) 90 percent of the tax shown on the return for the taxable year (or, if no return is filed, 90 percent of the tax for such year), or

(ii) 100 percent of the tax shown on the return of the individual for the preceding taxable year.

Clause (ii) shall not apply if the preceding taxable year was not a taxable year of 12 months or if the individual did not file a return for such preceding taxable year.

(C) Limitation on use of preceding year's tax.—

(i) In general.—If the adjusted gross income shown on the return of the individual for the preceding taxable year beginning in any calendar year exceeds $150,000, clause (ii) of subparagraph (B) shall be applied by substituting the applicable percentage for "100 percent." For purposes of the preceding sentence, the applicable percentage shall be determined in accordance with the following table:

If the preceding taxable year begins in:	The applicable percentage is:
1998	105
1999	108.6
2000	110
2001	112
2002 or thereafter	110

This clause shall not apply in the case of a preceding taxable year beginning in calendar year 1997.

(ii) Separate returns.—In the case of a married individual (within the meaning of section 7703) who files a separate return for the taxable year for which the amount of the installment is being determined, clause (i) shall be applied by substituting "$75,000" for "$150,000."

(iii) Special rule.—In the case of an estate or trust, adjusted gross income shall be determined as provided in section 67(e).

(D) Special rule for 2009.—

(i) In general.—Notwithstanding subparagraph (C), in the case of any taxable year beginning in 2009, clause (ii) of subparagraph (B) shall be applied to any qualified individual by substituting "90 percent" for "100 percent".

(ii) Qualified individual.—For purposes of this subparagraph, the term "qualified individual" means any individual if—

(I) the adjusted gross income shown on the return of such individual for the preceding taxable year is less than $500,000, and

(II) such individual certifies that more than 50 percent of the gross income shown on the return of such individual for the preceding taxable year was income from a small business.

A certification under subclause (II) shall be in such form and manner and filed at such time as the Secretary may by regulations prescribe.

(iii) Income from a small business.—For purposes of clause (ii), income from a small business means, with respect to any individual, income from a trade or business the average number of employees of which was less than 500 employees for the calendar year ending with or within the preceding taxable year of the individual.

(iv) Separate returns.—In the case of a married individual (within the meaning of section 7703) who files a separate return for the taxable year for which the amount of the installment is being determined, clause (ii)(I) shall be applied by substituting "$250,000" for "$500,000".

(v) Estates and trusts.—In the case of an estate or trust, adjusted gross income shall be determined as provided in section 67(e).

(2) Lower required installment where annualized income installment is less than amount determined under paragraph (1).—

(A) In general.—In the case of any required installment, if the individual establishes that the annualized income installment is less than the amount determined under paragraph (1)—

(i) the amount of such required installment shall be the annualized income installment, and

(ii) any reduction in a required installment resulting from the application of this subparagraph shall be recaptured by increasing the amount of the next required installment determined under paragraph (1) by the amount of such reduction (and by increasing subsequent required installments to the extent that the reduction has not previously been recaptured under this clause).

(B) Determination of annualized income installment.—In the case of any required installment, the annualized income installment is the excess (if any) of—

(i) an amount equal to the applicable percentage of the tax for the taxable year computed by placing on an annualized basis the taxable income, alternative minimum taxable income, and adjusted self-employment income for months in the taxable year ending before the due date for the installment, over

(ii) the aggregate amount of any prior required installments for the taxable year.

(C) Special rules.—For purposes of this paragraph—

(i) Annualization.—The taxable income, alternative minimum taxable income, and adjusted self-employment income shall be placed on an annualized basis under regulations prescribed by the Secretary.

(ii) Applicable percentage.—

In the case of the following required installments:	The applicable percentage is:
1st	22.5
2nd	45
3rd	67.5
4th	90

(iii) Adjusted self-employment income.—The term "adjusted self-employment income" means self-employment income (as defined in section 1402(b)); except that section 1402(b) shall be applied by placing wages (within the meaning of section 1402(b)) for months in the taxable year ending before the due date for the installment on an annualized basis consistent with clause (i).

* * *

(e) Exceptions.—

(1) Where tax is small amount.—No addition to tax shall be imposed under subsection (a) for any taxable year if the tax shown on the return for such taxable year (or, if no return is filed, the tax), reduced by the credit allowable under section 31, is less than $1,000.

(2) Where no tax liability for preceding taxable year.—No addition to tax shall be imposed under subsection (a) for any taxable year if—

(A) the preceding taxable year was a taxable year of 12 months,

(B) the individual did not have any liability for tax for the preceding taxable year, and

(C) the individual was a citizen or resident of the United States throughout the preceding taxable year.

(3) Waiver in certain cases.—

(A) In general.—No addition to tax shall be imposed under subsection (a) with respect to any underpayment to the extent the Secretary determines that by reason of casualty, disaster, or other unusual circumstances the imposition of such addition to tax would be against equity and good conscience.

(B) Newly retired or disabled individuals.—No addition to tax shall be imposed under subsection (a) with respect to any underpayment if the Secretary determines that—

(i) the taxpayer—

(I) retired after having attained age 62, or

(II) became disabled,

in the taxable year for which estimated payments were required to be made or in the taxable year preceding such taxable year, and

(ii) such underpayment was due to reasonable cause and not to willful neglect.

CAUTION: FUTURE EFFECTIVE DATE

Section 6654(f) is amended by the Patient Protection and Affordable Care Act of 2010 effective for taxable years beginning after 12/31/2012.

(f) Tax computed after application of credits against tax.—For purposes of this section, the term "tax" means—

(1) the tax imposed by chapter 1 (other than any increase in such tax by reason of section 143(m)), plus

(2) the tax imposed by chapter 2, minus

(3) the credits against tax provided by part IV of subchapter A of chapter 1, other than the credit against tax provided by section 31 (relating to tax withheld on wages).

(g) Application of section in case of tax withheld on wages.—

(1) In general.—For purposes of applying this section, the amount of the credit allowed under section 31 for the taxable year shall be deemed a payment of estimated tax, and an equal part of such amount shall be deemed paid on each due date for such taxable year, unless the taxpayer establishes the dates on which all amounts were actually withheld, in which case the amounts so withheld shall be deemed payments of estimated tax on the dates on which such amounts were actually withheld.

(2) Separate application.—The taxpayer may apply paragraph (1) separately with respect to—

(A) wage withholding, and

(B) all other amounts withheld for which credit is allowed under section 31.

(h) Special rule where return filed on or before January 31.—If, on or before January 31 of the following taxable year, the taxpayer files a return for the taxable year and pays in full the amount computed on the return as payable, then no addition to tax shall be imposed under subsection (a) with respect to any underpayment of the 4th required installment for the taxable year.

* * *

(k) Fiscal years and short years.—

(1) Fiscal years.—In applying this section to a taxable year beginning on any date other than January 1, there shall be substituted, for the months specified in this section, the months which correspond thereto.

(2) Short taxable year.—This section shall be applied to taxable years of less than 12 months in accordance with regulations prescribed by the Secretary

* * *

PART II—ACCURACY-RELATED AND FRAUD PENALTIES

§ 6662. Imposition of accuracy-related penalty on underpayments

(a) Imposition of penalty.—If this section applies to any portion of an underpayment of tax required to be shown on a return, there shall be added to the tax an amount equal to 20 percent of the portion of the underpayment to which this section applies.

(b) Portion of underpayment to which section applies.—This section shall apply to the portion of any underpayment which is attributable to 1 or more of the following:

(1) Negligence or disregard of rules or regulations.

(2) Any substantial understatement of income tax.

(3) Any substantial valuation misstatement under chapter 1.

(4) Any substantial overstatement of pension liabilities.

(5) Any substantial estate or gift tax valuation understatement.

(6) Any disallowance of claimed tax benefits by reason of a transaction lacking economic substance (within the meaning of section 7701(o)) or failing to meet the requirements of any similar rule of law.

(7) Any undisclosed foreign financial asset understatement.

This section shall not apply to any portion of an underpayment on which a penalty is imposed under section 6663. Except as provided in paragraph (1) or (2)(B) of section 6662A(e), this section shall not apply to the portion of any underpayment which is attributable to a reportable transaction understatement on which a penalty is imposed under section 6662A.

(c) Negligence.—For purposes of this section, the term "negligence" includes any failure to make a reasonable attempt to comply with the provisions of this title, and the term "disregard" includes any careless, reckless, or intentional disregard.

(d) Substantial understatement of income tax.—

(1) Substantial understatement.—

(A) In general.—For purposes of this section, there is a substantial understatement of income tax for any taxable year if the amount of the understatement for the taxable year exceeds the greater of—

(i) 10 percent of the tax required to be shown on the return for the taxable year, or

(ii) $5,000.

(B) Special rule for corporations.—In the case of a corporation other than an S corporation or a personal holding company (as defined in section 542), there is a substantial understatement of income tax for any taxable year if the amount of the understatement for the taxable year exceeds the lesser of—

(i) 10 percent of the tax required to be shown on the return for the taxable year (or, if greater, $10,000), or

(ii) $10,000,000.

(2) Understatement.—

(A) In general.—For purposes of paragraph (1), the term "understatement" means the excess of—

(i) the amount of the tax required to be shown on the return for the taxable year, over

(ii) the amount of the tax imposed which is shown on the return, reduced by any rebate (within the meaning of section 6211(b)(2)).

The excess under the preceding sentence shall be determined without regard to items to which section 6662A applies.

(B) Reduction for understatement due to position of taxpayer or disclosed item.—The amount of the understatement under subparagraph (A) shall be reduced by that portion of the understatement which is attributable to—

(i) the tax treatment of any item by the taxpayer if there is or was substantial authority for such treatment, or

(ii) any item if—

(I) the relevant facts affecting the item's tax treatment are adequately disclosed in the return or in a statement attached to the return, and

(II) there is a reasonable basis for the tax treatment of such item by the taxpayer.

For purposes of clause (ii)(II), in no event shall a corporation be treated as having a reasonable basis for its tax treatment of an item attributable to a multiple-party financing transaction if such treatment does not clearly reflect the income of the corporation.

(C) Reduction not to apply to tax shelters.—

(i) In general.—Subparagraph (B) shall not apply to any item attributable to a tax shelter.

(ii) Tax shelter.—For purposes of clause (i), the term "tax shelter" means—

(I) a partnership or other entity,

(II) any investment plan or arrangement, or

(III) any other plan or arrangement,

if a significant purpose of such partnership, entity, plan, or arrangement is the avoidance or evasion of Federal income tax.

(3) Secretarial list.—The Secretary may prescribe a list of positions which the Secretary believes do not meet 1 or more of the standards specified in paragraph (2)(B)(i), section 6664(d)(2), and section 6694(a)(l). Such list (and any revisions thereof) shall be published in the Federal Register or the Internal Revenue Bulletin.

(e) Substantial valuation misstatement under chapter 1.—

(1) In general.—For purposes of this section, there is a substantial valuation misstatement under chapter 1 if—

(A) the value of any property (or the adjusted basis of any property) claimed on any return of tax imposed by chapter 1 is 150 percent or more of the amount determined to be the correct amount of such valuation or adjusted basis (as the case may be), or

(B)(i) the price for any property or services (or for the use of property) claimed on any such return in connection with any transaction between persons described in section 482 is 200 percent or more (or 50 percent or less) of the amount determined under section 482 to be the correct amount of such price, or

(ii) the net section 482 transfer price adjustment for the taxable year exceeds the lesser of $5,000,000 or 10 percent of the taxpayer's gross receipts.

(2) Limitation.—No penalty shall be imposed by reason of subsection (b)(3) unless the portion of the underpayment for the taxable year attributable to substantial valuation misstatements under chapter 1 exceeds $5,000 ($10,000 in the case of a corporation other than an S corporation or a personal holding company (as defined in section 542)).

(3) Net section 482 transfer price adjustment.—For purposes of this subsection—

(A) In general.—The term "net section 482 transfer price adjustment" means, with respect to any taxable year, the net increase in taxable income for the taxable year (determined without regard to any amount carried to such taxable year from another taxable year) resulting from adjustments under section 482 in the price for any property or services (or for the use of property).

(B) Certain adjustments excluded in determining threshold.—For purposes of determining whether the threshold requirements of paragraph (1)(B)(ii) are met, the following shall be excluded:

(i) Any portion of the net increase in taxable income referred to in subparagraph (A) which is attributable to any redetermination of a price if—

(I) it is established that the taxpayer determined such price in accordance with a specific pricing method set forth in the regulations prescribed under section 482 and that the taxpayer's use of such method was reasonable.

(II) the taxpayer has documentation (which was in existence as of the time of filing the return) which sets forth the determination of such price in accordance with such a method and which establishes that the use of such method was reasonable, and

(III) the taxpayer provides such documentation to the Secretary within 30 days of a request for such documentation.

(ii) Any portion of the net increase in taxable income referred to in subparagraph (A) which is attributable to a redetermination of price where such price was not determined in accordance with such a specific pricing method if—

(I) the taxpayer establishes that none of such pricing methods was likely to result in a price that would clearly reflect income, the taxpayer used another pricing method to determine such price, and such other pricing method was likely to result in a price that would clearly reflect income,

(II) the taxpayer has documentation (which was in existence as of the time of filing the return) which sets forth the determination of such price in accordance with such other method and which establishes that the requirements of subclause (I) were satisfied, and

(III) the taxpayer provides such documentation to the Secretary within 30 days of request for such documentation.

(iii) Any portion of such net increase which is attributable to any transaction solely between foreign corporations unless, in the case of any such corporations, the treatment of such transaction affects the determination of income from sources within the United States or taxable income effectively connected with the conduct of a trade or business within the United States.

(C) Special rule.—If the regular tax (as defined in section 55(c)) imposed by chapter 1 on the taxpayer is determined by reference to an amount other than taxable income, such amount shall be treated as the taxable income of such taxpayer for purposes of this paragraph.

(D) Coordination with reasonable cause exception.—For purposes of section 6664(c), the taxpayer shall not be treated as having reasonable cause for any portion of an underpayment attributable to a net section 482 transfer price adjustment unless such taxpayer meets the requirements of clause (i), (ii), or (iii) of subparagraph (B) with respect to such portion.

(f) Substantial overstatement of pension liabilities.—

(1) In general.—For purposes of this section, there is a substantial overstatement of pension liabilities if the actuarial determination of the liabilities taken into account for purposes of computing the deduction under paragraph (1) or (2) of section 404(a) is 200 percent or more of the amount determined to be the correct amount of such liabilities.

(2) Limitation.—No penalty shall be imposed by reason of subsection (b)(4) unless the portion of the underpayment for the taxable year attributable to substantial overstatements of pension liabilities exceeds $1,000.

(g) Substantial estate or gift tax valuation understatement.—

(1) In general.—For purposes of this section, there is a substantial estate or gift tax valuation understatement if the value of any property claimed on any return of tax imposed by subtitle B is 65 percent or less of the amount determined to be the correct amount of such valuation.

(2) Limitation.—No penalty shall be imposed by reason of subsection (b)(5) unless the portion of the underpayment attributable to substantial estate or gift tax valuation understatements for the taxable period (or, in the case of the tax imposed by chapter 11, with respect to the estate of the decedent) exceeds $5,000.

(h) Increase in penalty in case of gross valuation misstatements.—

(1) In general.—To the extent that a portion of the underpayment to which this section applies is attributable to one or more gross valuation misstatements, subsection (a) shall be applied with respect to such portion by substituting "40 percent" for "20 percent."

(2) Gross valuation misstatements.—The term "gross valuation misstatements" means—

(A) any substantial valuation misstatement under chapter 1 as determined under subsection (e) by substituting—

(i) in paragraph (1)(A), "200 percent" for "150 percent,"

(ii) in paragraph (1)(B)(i)—

(I) "400 percent" for "200 percent," and

(II) "25 percent" for "50 percent," and

(iii) in paragraph (1)(B)(ii)—

(I) "$20,000,000" for "$5,000,000," and

(II) "20 percent" for "10 percent."

(B) any substantial overstatement of pension liabilities as determined under subsection (f) by substituting "400 percent" for "200 percent," and

(C) any substantial estate or gift tax valuation understatement as determined under subsection (g) by substituting "40 percent" for "65 percent."

(i) Increase in penalty in case of nondisclosed noneconomic substance transactions.—

(1) In general.—In the case of any portion of an underpayment which is attributable to one or more nondisclosed noneconomic substance transactions, subsection (a) shall be applied with respect to such portion by substituting "40 percent" for "20 percent".

(2) Nondisclosed noneconomic substance transactions.—For purposes of this subsection, the term "nondisclosed noneconomic substance transaction" means any portion of a transaction described in subsection (b)(6) with respect to which the relevant facts affecting the tax treatment are not adequately disclosed in the return nor in a statement attached to the return.

(3) Special rule for amended returns.—In no event shall any amendment or supplement to a return of tax be taken into account for purposes of this subsection if the amendment or supplement is filed after the earlier of the date the taxpayer is first contacted by the Secretary regarding the examination of the return or such other date as is specified by the Secretary.

§ 6662A. Imposition of accuracy-related penalty on understatements with respect to reportable transactions

(a) Imposition of penalty.—If a taxpayer has a reportable transaction understatement for any taxable year, there shall be added to the tax an amount equal to 20 percent of the amount of such understatement.

(b) Reportable transaction understatement.—For purposes of this section—

(1) In general.—The term "reportable transaction understatement" means the sum of—

(A) the product of—

(i) the amount of the increase (if any) in taxable income which results from a difference between the proper tax treatment of an item to which this section applies and the taxpayer's treatment of such item (as shown on the taxpayer's return of tax), and

(ii) the highest rate of tax imposed by section 1 (section 11 in the case of a taxpayer which is a corporation), and

(B) the amount of the decrease (if any) in the aggregate amount of credits determined under subtitle A which results from a difference between the taxpayer's treatment of an item to which this section applies (as shown on the taxpayer's return of tax) and the proper tax treatment of such item.

For purposes of subparagraph (A), any reduction of the excess of deductions allowed for the taxable year over gross income for such year, and any reduction in the amount of capital losses which would (without regard to section 1211) be allowed for such year, shall be treated as an increase in taxable income.

(2) Items to which section applies.—This section shall apply to any item which is attributable to—

(A) any listed transaction, and

(B) any reportable transaction (other than a listed transaction) if a significant purpose of such transaction is the avoidance or evasion of Federal income tax.

(c) Higher penalty for nondisclosed listed and other avoidance transactions.—Subsection (a) shall be applied by substituting "30 percent" for "20 percent" with respect to the portion of any reportable transaction understatement with respect to which the requirement of section 6664(d)(2)(A) is not met.

(d) Definitions of reportable and listed transactions.—For purposes of this section, the terms "reportable transaction" and "listed transaction" have the respective meanings given to such terms by section 6707A(c).

(e) Special rules.—

(1) Coordination with penalties, etc., on other understatements.—In the case of an understatement (as defined in section 6662(d)(2))—

(A) the amount of such understatement (determined without regard to this paragraph) shall be increased by the aggregate amount of reportable transaction understatements for purposes of determining whether such understatement is a substantial understatement under section 6662(d)(1), and

(B) the addition to tax under section 6662(a) shall apply only to the excess of the amount of the substantial understatement (if any) after the application of subparagraph (A) over the aggregate amount of reportable transaction understatements.

(2) Coordination with other penalties.—

(A) Coordination with fraud penalty.—This section shall not apply to any portion of an understatement on which a penalty is imposed under section 6663.

(B) Coordination with certain increased underpayment penalties.—This section shall not apply to any portion of an understatement on which a penalty is imposed under section 6662 if the rate of the penalty is determined under subsection (h) or (i) of section 6662.

(3) Special rule for amended returns.—Except as provided in regulations, in no event shall any tax treatment included with an amendment or supplement to a return of tax be taken into account in determining the amount of any reportable transaction understatement if the amendment or supplement is filed after the earlier of the date the taxpayer is first contacted by the Secretary regarding the examination of the return or such other date as is specified by the Secretary.

§ 6663. Imposition of fraud penalty

(a) Imposition of penalty.—If any part of any underpayment of tax required to be shown on a return is due to fraud, there shall be added to the tax an amount equal to 75 percent of the portion of the underpayment which is attributable to fraud.

(b) Determination of portion attributable to fraud.—If the Secretary establishes that any portion of an underpayment is attributable to fraud, the entire underpayment shall be treated as attributable to fraud, except with respect to any portion of the underpayment which the taxpayer establishes (by a preponderance of the evidence) is not attributable to fraud.

(c) Special rule for joint returns.—In the case of a joint return, this section shall not apply with respect to a spouse unless some part of the underpayment is due to the fraud of such spouse.

§ 6664. Definitions and special rules

(a) Underpayment.—For purposes of this part, the term "underpayment" means the amount by which any tax imposed by this title exceeds the excess of—

(1) the sum of—

(A) the amount shown as the tax by the taxpayer on his return, plus

(B) amounts not so shown previously assessed (or collected without assessment), over

(2) the amount of rebates made.

For purposes of paragraph (2), the term "rebate" means so much of an abatement, credit, refund, or other repayment, as was made on the ground that the tax imposed was less than the excess of the amount specified in paragraph (1) over the rebates previously made.

(b) Penalties applicable only where return filed.—The penalties provided in this part shall apply only in cases where a return of tax is filed (other than a return prepared by the Secretary under the authority of section 6020(b)).

(c) Reasonable cause exception for underpayments.—

(1) In general.—No penalty shall be imposed under section 6662 or 6663 with respect to any portion of an underpayment if it is shown that there was a reasonable cause for such portion and that the taxpayer acted in good faith with respect to such portion.

(2) Exception.—Paragraph (1) shall not apply to any portion of an underpayment which is attributable to one or more transactions described in section 6662(b)(6).

(3) Special rule for certain valuation overstatements.—In the case of any underpayment attributable to a substantial or gross valuation overstatement under chapter 1 with respect to charitable deduction property, paragraph (1) shall not apply. The preceding sentence shall not apply to a substantial valuation overstatement under chapter 1—

(A) the claimed value of the property was based on a qualified appraisal made by a qualified appraiser, and

(B) in addition to obtaining such appraisal, the taxpayer made a good faith investigation of the value of the contributed property.

(4) Definitions.—For purposes of this subsection—

(A) Charitable deduction property.—The term "charitable deduction property" means any property contributed by the taxpayer in a contribution for which a deduction was claimed under section 170. For purposes of paragraph (2), such term shall not include any securities for which (as of the date of the contribution) market quotations are readily available on an established securities market.

(B) Qualified appraisal.—The term "qualified appraisal" has the meaning given such term by section 1701(f)(11)(E)(i).

(C) Qualified appraiser.—The term "qualified appraiser" has the meaning given such term by section 170(f)(11)(E)(ii).

(d) Reasonable cause exception for reportable transaction understatements—

(1) In general.—No penalty shall be imposed under section 6662A with respect to any portion of a reportable transaction understatement if it is shown that there was a reasonable cause for such portion and that the taxpayer acted in good faith with respect to such portion.

(2) Exception.—Paragraph (1) shall not apply to any portion of a reportable transaction understatement which is attributable to one or more transactions described in section 6662(b)(6).

(3) Special rules.—Paragraph (1) shall not apply to any reportable transaction understatement unless—

(A) the relevant facts affecting the tax treatment of the item are adequately disclosed in accordance with the regulations prescribed under section 6011.

(B) there is or was substantial authority, for such treatment, and

(C) the taxpayer reasonably believed that such treatment was more likely than not the proper treatment.

A taxpayer failing to adequately disclose in accordance with section 6011 shall be treated as meeting the requirements of subparagraph (A) if the penalty for such failure was rescinded under section 6707A(d).

(4) Rules relating to reasonable belief.—For purposes of paragraph (3)(C)—

(A) In general.—A taxpayer shall be treated as having a reasonable belief with respect to the tax treatment of an item only if such belief—

(i) is based on the facts and law that exist at the time the return of tax which includes such tax treatment is filed, and

(ii) relates solely to the taxpayer's chances of success on the merits of such treatment and does not take into account the possibility that a return will not be audited, such treatment will not be raised on audit, or such treatment will be resolved through settlement if it is raised.

(B) Certain opinions may not be relied upon.—

(i) In general.—An opinion of a tax advisor may not be relied upon to establish the reasonable belief of a taxpayer if—

(I) the tax advisor is described in clause (ii), or

(II) the opinion is described in clause (iii).

(ii) Disqualified tax advisors.—A tax advisor is described in this clause if the tax advisor—

(I) is a material advisor (within the meaning of section 6111(b)(1)) and participates in the organization, management, promotion, or sale of the transaction or is related (within the meaning of section 267 (b) or 707(b)(1)) to any person who so participates,

(II) is compensated directly or indirectly by a material advisor with respect to the transaction,

(III) has a fee arrangement with respect to the transaction which is contingent on all or part of the intended tax benefits from the transaction being sustained, or

(IV) as determined under regulations prescribed by the Secretary, has a disqualifying financial interest with respect to the transaction.

(iii) Disqualified opinions.—For purposes of clause (i), an opinion is disqualified if the opinion—

(I) is based on unreasonable factual or legal assumptions (including assumptions as to future events),

(II) unreasonably relies on representations, statements, findings, or agreements of the taxpayer or any other person,

(III) does not identify and consider all relevant facts, or

(IV) fails to meet any other requirement as the Secretary may prescribe.

PART III—APPLICABLE RULES

§ 6665. Applicable rules

(a) Additions treated as tax.—Except as otherwise provided in this title—

(1) the additions to the tax, additional amounts, and penalties provided by this chapter shall be paid upon notice and demand and shall be assessed, collected, and paid in the same manner as taxes; and

(2) any reference in this title to "tax" imposed by this title shall be deemed also to refer to the additions to the tax, additional amounts, and penalties provided by this chapter.

(b) Procedure for assessing certain additions to tax.—For purposes of subchapter B of chapter 63 (relating to deficiency procedures for income, estate, gift, and certain excise taxes), subsection (a) shall not apply to any addition to tax under section 6651, 6654, or 6655; except that it shall apply—

(1) in the case of an addition described in section 6651, to that portion of such addition which is attributable to a deficiency in tax described in section 6211; or

(2) to an addition described in section 6654 or 6655, if no return is filed for the taxable year.

SUBCHAPTER B—ASSESSABLE PENALTIES

Part

* * *

*Omitted

Editorial Summary

Penalties on Tax Return Preparer

Subchapter B of Chapter 68 (Secs. 6694–6703)

Subchapter A imposes penalties on the taxpayer. Subchapter B imposes penalties on the tax return preparer.

§ 6694. Understatement of taxpayer's liability by tax return preparer

(a) Understatements due to unreasonable positions.—

(1) In general.— If a tax return preparer—

(A) prepares any return or claim of refund with respect to which any part of an understatement of liability is due to a position described in paragraph (2), and

(B) knew (or reasonably should have known) of the position,

such tax return preparer shall pay a penalty with respect to each such return or claim in an amount equal to the greater of $1,000 or 50 percent of the income derived (or to be derived) by the tax return preparer with respect to the return or claim.

(2) Unreasonable position.—

(A) In general.—Except as otherwise provided in this paragraph, a position is described in this paragraph unless there is or was substantial authority for the position.

(B) Disclosed positions.—If the position was disclosed as provided in section 6662(d)(2)(B)(iii)(I) and is not a position to which subparagraph (C) applies, the position is described in this paragraph unless there is a reasonable basis for the position.

(C) Tax shelters and reportable transaction.—If the position is with respect to a tax shelter (as defined in section 6662(d)(2)(C)(ii)) or a reportable transaction to which section 6662A applies, the position is described in this paragraph unless it is reasonable to believe that the position would more likely than not be sustained on its merits.

(3) Reasonable cause exception.—No penalty shall be imposed under this subsection if it is shown that there is reasonable cause for the understatement and the tax return preparer acted in good faith.

(b) Understatement due to willful or reckless conduct.—

(1) In general.—Any tax return preparer who prepares any return or claim for refund with respect to which any part of an understatement of liability is due to a conduct described in paragraph (2) shall pay a penalty with respect to each such return or claim in an amount equal to the greater of—

(A) $5,000, or

(B) 50 percent of the income derived (or to be derived) by the tax return preparer with respect to the return or claim.

(2) Willful or reckless conduct.—Conduct described in this paragraph is conduct by the tax return preparer which is—

(A) a willful attempt in any manner to understate the liability for tax on the return or claim, or

(B) a reckless or intentional disregard of rules or regulations.

(3) Reduction in penalty.—The amount of any penalty payable by any person by reason of this subsection for any return or claim for refund shall be reduced by the amount of the penalty paid by such person by reason of subsection (a).

(c) Extension of period of collection where preparer pays 15 percent of penalty.—

(1) In general.—If, within 30 days after the day on which notice and demand of any penalty under subsection (a) or (b) is made against any person who is a tax return preparer, such person pays an amount which is not less than 15 percent of the amount of such penalty and files a claim for refund of the amount so paid, no levy or proceeding in court for the collection of the remainder of such penalty shall be made, begun, or prosecuted until the final resolution of a proceeding begun as provided in paragraph (2). Notwithstanding the provisions of section 7421(a), the beginning of such proceeding or levy during the time such prohibition is in force may be enjoined by a proceeding in the proper court. Nothing in this paragraph shall be construed to prohibit any counterclaim for the remainder of such penalty in a proceeding begun as provided in paragraph (2).

(2) Preparer must bring suit in district court to determine his liability for penalty.—If, within 30 days after the day on which his claim for refund of any partial payment of any penalty under subsection (a) or (b) is denied (or, if earlier, within 30 days after the expiration of 6 months after the day on which he filed the claim for refund), the income tax return preparer fails to begin a proceeding in the appropriate United States district court for the determination of his liability for such penalty, paragraph (1) shall cease to apply with respect to such penalty, effective on the day following the close of the applicable 30-day period referred to in this paragraph.

(3) Suspension of running of period of limitations on collection.—The running of the period of limitations provided in section 6502 on the collection by levy or by a proceeding in court in respect of any penalty described in paragraph (1) shall be suspended for the period during which the Secretary is prohibited from collecting by levy or a proceeding in court.

(d) Abatement of penalty where taxpayer's liability not understated.—If at any time there is a final administrative determination or a final judicial decision that there was no understatement of liability in the case of any return or claim for refund with respect to which a penalty under subsection (a) or (b) has been assessed, such assessment shall be abated, and if any portion of such penalty has been paid the amount so paid shall be refunded to the person who made such payment as an overpayment of tax without regard to any period of limitations which, but for this subsection, would apply to the making of such refund.

(e) Understatement of liability defined.—For purposes of this section, the term "understatement of liability" means any understatement of the net amount payable with respect to any tax imposed by this title or any overstatement of the net amount creditable or refundable with respect to any such tax. Except as otherwise provided in subsection (d), the determination of whether or not there is an understatement of liability shall be made without regard to any administrative or judicial action involving the taxpayer.

(f) Cross reference.—

For definition of tax return preparer, see section 7701(a)(36).

§ 6695. Other assessable penalties with respect to the preparation of tax returns for other persons

(a) Failure to furnish copy to taxpayer.—Any person who is a tax return preparer with respect to any return or claim for refund who fails to comply with section 6107(a) with respect to such return or claim shall pay a penalty of $50 for such failure, unless it is shown that such failure is due to reasonable cause and not due to willful neglect. The maximum penalty imposed under this subsection on any person with respect to documents filed during any calendar year shall not exceed $25,000.

(b) Failure to sign return.—Any person who is a tax return preparer with respect to any return or claim for refund, who is required by regulations prescribed by the Secretary to sign such return or claim, and who fails to comply with such regulations with respect to such return or claim, shall pay a penalty of $50 for such failure, unless it is shown that such failure is due to reasonable cause and not due to willful neglect. The maximum penalty imposed under this subsection on any person with respect to documents filed during any calendar year shall not exceed $25,000.

(c) Failure to furnish identifying number.—Any person who is a tax return preparer with respect to any return or claim for refund and who fails to comply with section 6109(a)(4) with respect to such return or claim shall pay a penalty of $50 for such failure, unless it is shown that such failure is due to reasonable cause and not due to willful neglect. The maximum penalty imposed under this subsection on any person with respect to documents filed during any calendar year shall not exceed $25,000.

(d) Failure to retain copy or list.—Any person who is a tax return preparer with respect to any return or claim for refund who fails to comply with section 6107(b) with respect to such return or claim shall pay a penalty of $50 for each such failure, unless it is shown that such failure is due to reasonable cause and not due to willful neglect. The maximum penalty imposed under this subsection on any person with respect to any return period shall not exceed $25,000.

(e) Failure to file correct information returns.—Any person required to make a return under section 6060 who fails to comply with the requirements of such section shall pay a penalty of $50 for—

(1) each failure to file a return as required under such section, and

(2) each failure to set forth an item in the return as required under such section,

unless it is shown that such failure is due to reasonable cause and not due to willful neglect. The maximum penalty imposed under this subsection on any person with respect to any return period shall not exceed $25,000.

(f) Negotiation of check.—Any person who is a tax return preparer who endorses or otherwise negotiates (directly or through an agent) any check made in respect of the taxes imposed by this title which is issued to a taxpayer (other than the tax return preparer) shall pay a penalty of $500 with respect to each such check. The preceding sentence shall not apply with respect to the deposit by a bank (within the meaning of section 581) of the full amount of the check in the taxpayer's account in such bank for the benefit of the taxpayer.

(g) Failure to be diligent in determining eligibility for earned income credit.—Any person who is a tax preparer with respect to any return or claim for refund who fails to comply with due diligence requirements imposed by the Secretary by regulations with respect to determining eligibility for, or the amount of, the credit allowable by section 32 shall pay a penalty of $100 for each such failure.

* * *

§ 6696. Rules applicable with respect to sections 6694, 6695, and 6695A

(a) Penalties to be additional to any other penalties.—The penalties provided by section 6694, 6695, and 6695A shall be in addition to any other penalties provided by law.

(b) Deficiency procedures not to apply.—Subchapter B of chapter 63 (relating to deficiency procedures for income, estate, gift, and certain excise taxes) shall not apply with respect to the assessment or collection of the penalties provided by sections 6694, 6695, and 6695A.

(c) Procedure for claiming refund.—Any claim for credit or refund of any penalty paid under section 6694, 6695, or 6695A shall be filed in accordance with regulations prescribed by the Secretary.

(d) Periods of limitation.—

(1) Assessment.—The amount of any penalty under section 6694(a), 6695, or 6695A shall be assessed within 3 years after the return or claim for refund with respect to which the penalty is assessed was filed, and no proceeding in court without assessment for the collection of such tax shall be begun after the expiration of such period. In the case of any penalty under section 6694(b), the penalty may be assessed, or a proceeding in court for the collection of the penalty may be begun without assessment, at any time.

(2) Claim for refund.—Except as provided in section 6694(d), any claim for refund of an overpayment of any penalty assessed under section 6694, 6695, or 6695A shall be filed within 3 years from the time the penalty was paid.

(e) Definitions.—For purposes of sections 6694, 6695, and 6695A—

(1) Return.—The term "return" means any return of any tax imposed by this title.

(2) Claim for refund.—The term "claim for refund" means a claim for refund of, or credit against, any tax imposed by this title.

* * *

§ 6701. Penalties for aiding and abetting understatement of tax liability

(a) Imposition of penalty.—Any person—

(1) who aids or assists in, procures, or advises with respect to, the preparation or presentation of any portion of a return, affidavit, claim, or other document,

(2) who knows (or has reason to believe) that such portion will be used in connection with any material matter arising under the internal revenue laws, and

(3) who knows that such portion (if so used) would result in an understatement of the liability for tax of another person, shall pay a penalty with respect to each such document in the amount determined under subsection (b).

(b) Amount of penalty.—

(1) In general.—Except as provided in paragraph (2), the amount of the penalty imposed by subsection (a) shall be $1,000.

(2) Corporations.—If the return, affidavit, claim, or other document relates to the tax liability of a corporation, the amount of the penalty imposed by subsection (a) shall be $10,000.

(3) Only 1 penalty per person per period.—If any person is subject to a penalty under subsection (a) with respect to any document relating to any taxpayer for any taxable period (or where there is no taxable period, any taxable event), such person shall not be subject to a penalty under subsection (a) with respect to any other document relating to such taxpayer for such taxable period (or event).

(c) Activities of subordinates.—

(1) In general.—For purposes of subsection (a), the term "procures" includes—

(A) ordering (or otherwise causing) a subordinate to do an act, and

(B) knowing of, and not attempting to prevent, participation by a subordinate in an act.

(2) Subordinate.—For purposes of paragraph (1), the term "subordinate" means any other person (whether or not a director, officer, employee, or agent of the taxpayer involved) over whose activities the person has direction, supervision, or control.

(d) Taxpayer not required to have knowledge.—Subsection (a) shall apply whether or not the understatement is with the knowledge or consent of the persons authorized or required to present the return, affidavit, claim, or other document.

(e) Certain actions not treated as aid or assistance.—For purposes of subsection (a)(1), a person furnishing typing, reproducing, or other mechanical assistance with respect to a document shall not be treated as having aided or assisted in the preparation of such document by reason of such assistance.

(f) Penalty in addition to other penalties.—

(1) In general.—Except as provided by paragraphs (2) and (3), the penalty imposed by this section shall be in addition to any other penalty provided by law.

(2) Coordination with return preparer penalties.—No penalty shall be assessed under subsection (a) or (b) of section 6694 on any person with respect to any document for which a penalty is assessed on such person under subsection (a).

(3) Coordination with section 6700.—No penalty shall be assessed under section 6700 on any person with respect to any document for which a penalty is assessed on such person under subsection (a).

§ 6702. Frivolous income tax return

(a) Civil penalty for frivolous tax returns.—A person shall pay a penalty of $5,000 if—

(1) such person files what purports to be a return of a tax imposed by this title but which—

(A) does not contain information on which the substantial correctness of the self-assessment may be judged, or

(B) contains information that on its face indicates that the self-assessment is substantially incorrect, and

(2) the conduct referred to in paragraph (1)—

(A) is based on a position which the Secretary has identified as frivolous under subsection (c), or

(B) reflects a desire to delay or impede the administration of Federal tax laws.

(b) Civil penalty for specified frivolous submissions.—

(1) Imposition of penalty.—Except as provided in paragraph (3), any person who submits a specified frivolous submission shall pay a penalty of $5,000.

(2) Specified frivolous submission.—For purposes of this section—

(A) Specified frivolous submission.—The term "specified frivolous submission" means a specified submission if any portion of such submission—

(i) is based on a position which the Secretary has identified as frivolous under subsection (c), or

(ii) reflects a desire to delay or impede the administration of Federal tax laws.

(B) Specified submission.—The term "specified submission" means—

(i) a request for a hearing under—

(I) section 6320 (relating to notice and opportunity for hearing upon filing of notice of lien), or

(II) section 6330 (relating to notice and opportunity for hearing before levy), and

(ii) an application under—

(I) section 6159 (relating to agreements for payment of tax liability in installments),

(II) section 7122 (relating to compromises), or

(III) section 7811 (relating to taxpayer assistance orders).

(3) Opportunity to withdraw submission.—If the Secretary provides a person with notice that a submission is a specified frivolous submission and such person withdraws such submission within 30 days after such notice, the penalty imposed under paragraph (1) shall not apply with respect to such submission.

(c) Listing of frivolous positions.—The Secretary shall prescribe (and periodically revise) a list of positions which the Secretary has identified as being frivolous for purposes of this subsection. The Secretary shall not include in such list any position that the Secretary determines meets the requirement of section 6662(d)(2)(B)(ii)(II).

(d) Reduction of penalty.—The Secretary may reduce the amount of any penalty imposed under this section if the Secretary determines that such reduction would promote compliance with and administration of the Federal tax laws.

(e) Penalties in addition to other penalties.—The penalties imposed by this section shall be in addition to any other penalty provided by law.

§ 6703. Rules applicable to penalties under sections 6700, 6701, and 6702

(a) Burden of proof.—In any proceeding involving the issue of whether or not any person is liable for a penalty under section 6700, 6701, or 6702, the burden of proof with respect to such issue shall be on the Secretary.

(b) Deficiency procedures not to apply.—Subchapter B of chapter 63 (relating to deficiency procedures) shall not apply with respect to the assessment or collection of the penalties provided by sections 6700, 6701, and 6702.

(c) Extension of period of collection where person pays 15 percent of penalty.—

(1) In general.—If, within 30 days after the day on which notice and demand of any penalty under section 6700 or 6701 is made against any person, such person pays an amount which is not less than 15 percent of the amount of such penalty and files a claim for refund of the amount so paid, no levy or proceeding in court for the collection of the remainder of such penalty shall be made, begun, or prosecuted until the final resolution of a proceeding begun as provided in paragraph (2). Notwithstanding the provisions of section 7421(a), the beginning of such proceeding or levy during the time such prohibition is in force may be enjoined by a proceeding in the proper court. Nothing in this paragraph shall be construed to prohibit any counterclaim for the remainder of such penalty in a proceeding begun as provided in paragraph (2).

(2) Person must bring suit in district court to determine his liability for penalty.—If, within 30 days after the day on which his claim for refund of any partial payment of any penalty under section 6700 or 6701 is denied (or, if earlier, within 30 days after the expiration of 6 months after the day on which he filed the claim for refund), the person fails to begin a proceeding in the appropriate United States district court for the determination of his liability for such penalty, paragraph (1) shall cease to apply with respect to such penalty, effective on the day following the close of the applicable 30-day period referred to in this paragraph.

(3) Suspension of running of period of limitations on collection.—The running of the period of limitations provided in section 6502 on the collection by levy or by a proceeding in court in respect of any penalty described in paragraph (1) shall be suspended for the period during which the Secretary is prohibited from collecting by levy or a proceeding in court.

* * *

CHAPTER 69—GENERAL PROVISIONS RELATING TO STAMPS*

CHAPTER 70—JEOPARDY, RECEIVERSHIPS, ETC.*

CHAPTER 71—TRANSFEREES AND FIDUCIARIES*

CHAPTER 72—LICENSING AND REGISTRATION*

CHAPTER 73—BONDS*

CHAPTER 74—CLOSING AGREEMENTS AND COMPROMISES*

CHAPTER 75—CRIMES, OTHER OFFENSES, AND FORFEITURES

Editorial Summary

Criminal Penalties

Subchapter A of Chapter 75 (Secs. 7201–7207, 7216, 7217)

Failure to determine, report, and pay one's tax liability can result in both civil and criminal penalties. Subchapter A deals with the criminal penalties. Such penalties are applicable only if tax evasion, willful failure, or fraud is involved on the part of the taxpayer.

Criminal penalties also apply to a tax return preparer for unlawful disclosures of information associated with the preparation of returns.

*Omitted

SUBCHAPTER A—CRIMES

PART I—GENERAL PROVISIONS

§ 7201. Attempt to evade or defeat tax

Any person who willfully attempts in any manner to evade or defeat any tax imposed by this title or the payment thereof shall, in addition to other penalties provided by law, be guilty of a felony and, upon conviction thereof, shall be fined not more than $100,000 ($500,000 in the case of a corporation), or imprisoned not more than 5 years, or both, together with the costs of prosecution.

§ 7202. Willful failure to collect or pay over tax

Any person required under this title to collect, account for, and pay over any tax imposed by this title who willfully fails to collect or truthfully account for and pay over such tax shall, in addition to other penalties provided by law, be guilty of a felony and, upon conviction thereof, shall be fined not more than $10,000, or imprisoned not more than 5 years, or both, together with the costs of prosecution.

§ 7203. Willful failure to file return, supply information, or pay tax

Any person required under this title to pay any estimated tax or tax, or required by this title or by regulations made under authority thereof to make a return, keep any records, or supply any information, who willfully fails to pay such estimated tax or tax, make such return, keep such records, or supply such information, at the time or times required by law or regulations, shall, in addition to other penalties provided by law, be guilty of a misdemeanor and, upon conviction thereof, shall be fined not more than $25,000 ($100,000 in the case of a corporation), or imprisoned not more than 1 year, or both, together with the costs of prosecution. In the case of any person with respect to whom there is a failure to pay any estimated tax, this section shall not apply to such person with respect to such failure if there is no addition to tax under section 6654 or 6655 with respect to such failure.

§ 7204. Fraudulent statement or failure to make statement to employees

In lieu of any other penalty provided by law (except the penalty provided by section 6674) any person required under the provisions of section 6051 to furnish a statement who willfully furnishes a false or fraudulent statement or who willfully fails to furnish a statement in the manner, at the time, and showing the information required under section 6051, or regulations prescribed thereunder, shall, for each such offense, upon conviction thereof, be fined not more than $1,000, or imprisoned not more than 1 year, or both.

§ 7205. Fraudulent withholding exemption certificate or failure to supply information

(a) Withholding on wages.—Any individual required to supply information to his employer under section 3402 who willfully supplies false or fraudulent information, or who willfully fails to supply information thereunder which would require an increase in the tax to be withheld under section 3402, shall, in addition to any other penalty provided by law, upon conviction thereof, be fined not more than $1,000, or imprisoned not more than 1 year, or both.

(b) Backup withholding on interest and dividends.—If any individual willfully makes a false certification under paragraph (1) or (2)(C) of section 3406(d), then such individual shall, in addition to any other penalty provided by law, upon conviction thereof, be fined not more than $1,000, or imprisoned not more than 1 year, or both.

§ 7206. Fraud and false statements

Any person who—

(1) Declaration under penalties of perjury.—Willfully makes and subscribes any return, statement, or other document, which contains or is verified by a written declaration that it is made under the penalties of perjury, and which he does not believe to be true and correct as to every material matter; or

(2) Aid or assistance.—Willfully aids or assists in, or procures, counsels, or advises the preparation or presentation under, or in connection with any matter arising under, the internal revenue laws, of a return, affidavit, claim, or other document, which is fraudulent or is false as to any material matter, whether or not such falsity or fraud is with the knowledge or consent of the person authorized or required to present such return, affidavit, claim, or document; or

(3) Fraudulent bonds, permits, and entries.—Simulates or falsely or fraudulently executes or signs any bond, permit, entry, or other document required by the provisions of the internal revenue laws, or by any regulation made in pursuance thereof, or procures the same to be falsely or fraudulently executed, or advises, aids in, or connives at such execution thereof; or

(4) Removal or concealment with intent to defraud.—Removes, deposits, or conceals, or is concerned in removing, depositing, or concealing, any goods or commodities for or in respect whereof any tax is or shall be imposed, or any property upon which levy is authorized by section 6331, with intent to evade or defeat the assessment or collection of any tax imposed by this title; or

(5) Compromises and closing agreements.—In connection with any compromise under section 7122, or offer of such compromise, or in connection with any closing agreement under section 7121, or offer to enter into any such agreement, willfully—

(A) Concealment of property.—Conceals from any officer or employee of the United States any property belonging to the estate of a taxpayer or other person liable in respect of the tax, or

(B) Withholding, falsifying, and destroying records.—Receives, withholds, destroys, mutilates, or falsifies any book, document, or record, or makes any false statement, relating to the estate or financial condition of the taxpayer or other person liable in respect of the tax;

shall be guilty of a felony and, upon conviction thereof, shall be fined not more than $100,000 ($500,000 in the case of a corporation), or imprisoned not more than 3 years, or both, together with the costs of prosecution.

§ 7207. Fraudulent returns, statements, or other documents

Any person who willfully delivers or discloses to the Secretary any list, return, account, statement, or other document, known by him to be fraudulent or to be false as to any material matter, shall be fined not more than $10,000 ($50,000 in the case of a corporation), or imprisoned not more than 1 year, or both. Any person required pursuant to subsection (b) of section 6047 or pursuant to subsection (d) of section 6104 to furnish any information to the Secretary or any other person who willfully furnishes to the Secretary or such other person any information known by him to be fraudulent or to be false as to any material matter shall be fined not more than $10,000 ($50,000 in the case of a corporation), or imprisoned not more than 1 year, or both.

* * *

§ 7216. Disclosure or use of information by preparers of returns

(a) General rule.—Any person who is engaged in the business of preparing, or providing services in connection with the preparation of, returns of the tax imposed by chapter 1, or any person who for compensation prepares any such return for any other person, and who knowingly or recklessly—

(1) discloses any information furnished to him for, or in connection with, the preparation of any such return, or

(2) uses any such information for any purpose other than to prepare, or assist in preparing, any such return,

shall be guilty of a misdemeanor, and, upon conviction thereof, shall be fined not more than $1,000, or imprisoned not more than 1 year, or both, together with the costs of prosecution.

(b) Exceptions.—

(1) Disclosure.—Subsection (a) shall not apply to a disclosure of information if such disclosure is made—

(A) pursuant to any other provision of this title, or

(B) pursuant to an order of a court.

(2) Use.—Subsection (a) shall not apply to the use of information in the preparation of, or in connection with the preparation of, State and local tax returns and declarations of estimated tax of the person to whom the information relates.

(3) Regulations.—Subsection (a) shall not apply to a disclosure or use of information which is permitted by regulations prescribed by the Secretary under this section. Such regulations shall permit (subject to such conditions as such regulations shall provide) the disclosure or use of information for quality or peer reviews.

§ 7217. Prohibition on executive branch influence over taxpayer audits and other investigations

(a) Prohibition.—It shall be unlawful for any applicable person to request, directly or indirectly, any officer or employee of the Internal Revenue Service to conduct or terminate an audit or other investigation of any particular taxpayer with respect to the tax liability of such taxpayer.

(b) Reporting requirement.—Any officer or employee of the Internal Revenue Service receiving any request prohibited by subsection (a) shall report the receipt of such request to the Treasury Inspector General for Tax Administration.

(c) Exceptions.—Subsection (a) shall not apply to any written request made—

(1) to an applicable person by or on behalf of the taxpayer and forwarded by such applicable person to the Internal Revenue Service,

(2) by an applicable person for disclosure of return or return information under section 6103 if such request is made in accordance with the requirements of such section, or

(3) by the Secretary of the Treasury as a consequence of the implementation of a change in tax policy.

(d) Penalty.—Any person who willfully violates subsection (a) or fails to report under subsection (b) shall be punished upon conviction by a fine in any amount not exceeding $5,000, or imprisonment of not more than 5 years, or both, together with the costs of prosecution.

(e) Applicable person.—For purposes of this section, the term "applicable person" means—

(1) the President, the Vice President, any employee of the executive office of the President, and any employee of the executive office of the Vice President, and

(2) any individual (other than the Attorney General of the United States) serving in a position specified in section 5312 of title 5, United States Code.

* * *

PART II—PENALTIES APPLICABLE TO CERTAIN TAXES**

SUBCHAPTER B—OTHER OFFENSES*

SUBCHAPTER C—FORFEITURES*

SUBCHAPTER D—MISCELLANEOUS PENALTY AND FORFEITURE PROVISIONS*

CHAPTER 76—JUDICIAL PROCEEDINGS

* * *

SUBCHAPTER C—THE TAX COURT

Editorial Summary

The Tax Court

Subchapter C of chapter 76 (Secs. 7441–7663)

The Tax Court is one of the three courts of original jurisdiction for Federal tax cases. The organization, procedure, and jurisdiction of the Tax Court is presented.

*Omitted.

PART I—ORGANIZATION AND JURISDICTION

§ 7441. Status

There is hereby established, under article I of the Constitution of the United States, a court of record to be known as the United States Tax Court. The members of the Tax Court shall be the chief judge and the judges of the Tax Court.

§ 7442. Jurisdiction

The Tax Court and its divisions shall have such jurisdiction as is conferred on them by this title, by chapters 1, 2, 3, and 4 of the Internal Revenue Code of 1939, by title II and title III of the Revenue Act of 1926 (44 Stat. 10–87), or by laws enacted subsequent to February 26, 1926.

§ 7443. Membership

(a) Number.—The Tax Court shall be composed of 19 members.

(b) Appointment.—Judges of the Tax Court shall be appointed by the President, by and with the advice and consent of the Senate, solely on the grounds of fitness to perform the duties of the office.

(c) Salary.—

(1) Each judge shall receive salary at the same rate and in the same installments as judges of the district courts of the United States.

(2) For rate of salary and frequency of installment see section 135, title 28, United States Code, and section 5505, title 5, United States Code.

(d) Expenses for travel and subsistence.—Judges of the Tax Court shall receive necessary traveling expenses, and expenses actually incurred for subsistence while traveling on duty and away from their designated stations, subject to the same limitations in amount as are now or may hereafter be applicable to the United States Court of International Trade.

(e) Term of office.—The term of office of any judge of the Tax Court shall expire 15 years after he takes office.

(f) Removal from office.—Judges of the Tax Court may be removed by the President, after notice and opportunity for public hearing, for inefficiency, neglect of duty, or malfeasance in office, but for no other cause.

(g) Disbarment of removed judges.—A judge of the Tax Court removed from office in accordance with subsection (f) shall not be permitted at any time to practice before the Tax Court.

§ 7443A. Special trial judges

(a) Appointment.—The chief judge may, from time to time, appoint special trial judges who shall proceed under such rules and regulations as may be promulgated by the Tax Court.

(b) Proceedings which may be assigned to special trial judges.—The chief judge may assign—

(1) any declaratory judgment proceeding,

(2) any proceeding under section 7463,

(3) any proceeding where neither the amount of the deficiency placed in dispute (within the meaning of section 7463) nor the amount of any claimed overpayment exceeds $50,000,

(4) any proceeding under section 6320 or 6330,

(5) any proceeding under section 7436(c),

(6) any proceeding under section 7623(b)(4), and

(7) any other proceeding which the chief judge may designate,

to be heard by the special trial judges of the court.

(c) Authority to make court decision.—The court may authorize a special trial judge to make the decision of the court with respect to any proceeding described in paragraph (1), (2), (3), (4), (5), or (6) of subsection (b), subject to such conditions and review as the court may provide.

(d) Salary.—Each special trial judge shall receive salary—

(1) at a rate equal to 90 percent of the rate for judges of the Tax Court, and

(2) in the same installments as such judges.

(e) Expenses for travel and subsistence.—Subsection (d) of section 7443 shall apply to special trial judges subject to such rules and regulations as may be promulgated by the Tax Court.

§ 7444. Organization

(a) Seal.—The Tax Court shall have a seal which shall be judicially noticed.

(b) Designation of chief judge.—The Tax Court shall at least biennially designate a judge to act as chief judge.

(c) Divisions.—The chief judge may from time to time divide the Tax Court into divisions of one or more judges, assign the judges of the Tax Court thereto, and in case of a division of more than one judge, designate the chief thereof. If a division, as a result of a vacancy or the absence or inability of a judge assigned thereto to serve thereon, is composed of less than the number of judges designated for the division, the chief judge may assign other judges to the division or direct the division to proceed with the transaction of business without awaiting any additional assignment of judges thereto.

(d) Quorum.—A majority of the judges of the Tax Court or of any division thereof shall constitute a quorum for the transaction of the business of the Tax Court or of the division, respectively. A vacancy in the Tax Court or in any division thereof shall not impair the powers nor affect the duties of the Tax Court or division nor of the remaining judges of the Tax Court or division, respectively.

§ 7445. Offices

The principal office of the Tax Court shall be in the District of Columbia, but the Tax Court or any of its divisions may sit at any place within the United States.

§ 7446. Times and places of sessions

The times and places of the sessions of the Tax Court and of its divisions shall be prescribed by the chief judge with a view to securing reasonable opportunity to taxpayers to appear before the Tax Court or any of its divisions, with as little inconvenience and expense to taxpayers as is practicable.

* * *

PART II—PROCEDURE

§ 7451. Fee for filing petition

The Tax Court is authorized to impose a fee in an amount not in excess of $60 to be fixed by the Tax Court for the filing of any petition for the redetermination of a deficiency or for a declaratory judgment under part IV of this subchapter or under section 7428 or for judicial review under section 6226 or section 6228(a).

§ 7452. Representation of parties

The Secretary shall be represented by the Chief Counsel for the Internal Revenue Service or his delegate in the same manner before the Tax Court as he has heretofore been represented in proceedings before such Court. The taxpayer shall continue to be represented in accordance with the rules of practice prescribed by the Court. No qualified person shall be denied admission to practice before the Tax Court because of his failure to be a member of any profession or calling.

§ 7453. Rules of practice, procedure, and evidence

Except in the case of proceedings conducted under section 7436(c) or 7463, the proceedings of the Tax Court and its divisions shall be conducted in accordance with such rules of practice and procedure (other than rules of evidence) as the Tax Court may prescribe and in accordance with the rules of evidence applicable in trials without a jury in the United States District Court of the District of Columbia.

§ 7454. Burden of proof in fraud, foundation manager, and transferee cases

(a) Fraud.—In any proceeding involving the issue whether the petitioner has been guilty of fraud with intent to evade tax, the burden of proof in respect of such issue shall be upon the Secretary.

(b) Foundation managers.—In any proceeding involving the issue whether a foundation manager (as defined in section 4946(b)) has "knowingly" participated in an act of self-dealing (within the meaning of section 4941), participated in an investment which jeopardizes the carrying out of exempt purposes (within the meaning of section 4944), or agreed to the making of a taxable expenditure (within the meaning of section 4945), or whether the trustee of a trust described in section 501(c)(21) has "knowingly" participated in an act of self-dealing (within the meaning of section 4951) or agreed to the making of a taxable expenditure (within the meaning of section 4952), or whether an organization manager (as defined in section 4955(f)(2)) has "knowingly" agreed to the making of a political expenditure (within the meaning of section 4955), or whether an organization manager (as defined in section 4912(d)(2)) has "knowingly" agreed to the making of disqualifying lobbying expenditures within the meaning of section 4912(b), the burden of proof in respect of such issue shall be upon the Secretary.

(c) Cross reference.—

For provisions relating to burden of proof as to transferee liability, see section 6902(a).

* * *

§ 7463. Disputes involving $50,000 or less

(a) In general.—In the case of any petition filed with the Tax Court for a redetermination of a deficiency where neither the amount of the deficiency placed in dispute, nor the amount of any claimed overpayment, exceeds—

(1) $50,000 for any one taxable year, in the case of the taxes imposed by subtitle A,

(2) $50,000, in the case of the tax imposed by chapter 11,

(3) $50,000 for any one calendar year, in the case of the tax imposed by chapter 12, or

(4) $50,000 for any 1 taxable period (or, if there is no taxable period, taxable event) in the case of any tax imposed by subtitle D which is described in section 6212(a) (relating to a notice of deficiency),

at the option of the taxpayer concurred in by the Tax Court or a division thereof before the hearing of the case, proceedings in the case shall be conducted under this section. Notwithstanding the provisions of section 7453, such proceedings shall be conducted in accordance with such rules of evidence, practice, and procedure as the Tax Court may prescribe. A decision, together with a brief summary of the reasons therefor, in any such case shall satisfy the requirements of sections 7459(b) and 7460.

(b) Finality of decisions.—A decision entered in any case in which the proceedings are conducted under this section shall not be reviewed in any other court and shall not be treated as a precedent for any other case.

(c) Limitation of jurisdiction.—In any case in which the proceedings are conducted under this section, notwithstanding the provisions of sections 6214(a) and 6512(b), no decision shall be entered redetermining the amount of a deficiency, or determining an overpayment, except with respect to amounts placed in dispute within the limits described in subsection (a) and with respect to amounts conceded by the parties.

(d) Discontinuance of proceedings.—At any time before a decision entered in a case in which the proceedings are conducted under this section becomes final, the taxpayer or the Secretary may request that further proceedings under this section in such case be discontinued. The Tax Court, or the division thereof hearing such case, may, if it finds that (1) there are reasonable grounds for believing that the amount of the deficiency placed in dispute, or the amount of an overpayment, exceeds the applicable jurisdictional amount described in subsection (a), and (2) the amount of such excess is large enough to justify granting such request, discontinue further proceedings in such case under this section. Upon any such discontinuance, proceedings in such case shall be conducted in the same manner as cases to which the provisions of sections 6214(a) and 6512(b) apply.

(e) Amount of deficiency in dispute.—For purposes of this section, the amount of any deficiency placed in dispute includes additions to the tax, additional amounts, and penalties imposed by chapter 68, to the extent that the procedures described in subchapter B of chapter 63 apply.

(f) Additional cases in which proceedings may be conducted under this section.—At the option of the taxpayer concurred in by the Tax Court or a division thereof before the hearing of the case, proceedings may be conducted under this section (in the same manner as a case described in subsection (a)) in the case of—

(1) a petition to the Tax Court under section 6015(e) in which the amount of relief sought does not exceed $50,000, and

(2) an appeal under section 6330(d)(1)(A) to the Tax Court of a determination in which the unpaid tax does not exceed $50,000.

* * *

SUBCHAPTER D—COURT REVIEW OF TAX COURT DECISIONS

Editorial Summary

Appellate Courts

Subchapter D of chapter 76 (Secs. 7482, 7483, 7491)

Tax Court decisions are subject to two levels of appeal. The first is to the Circuit Courts of Appeal which consists of 11 circuits identified by number, the circuit for the District of Columbia, and the Federal Circuit which hears cases originating in the Court of Federal Claims (previously the Claims Court). The second level of appeal (i.e., from the Circuit Courts of Appeal) is to the Supreme Court. In most tax cases, the Supreme Court denies the Writ of Certiorari. In the few instances that the Supreme Court grants the Writ, it usually is to resolve conflicts among the Circuit Courts of Appeal.

* * *

§ 7482. Courts of review

(a) Jurisdiction.—

(1) In general.—The United States Courts of Appeals (other than the United States Court of Appeals for the Federal Circuit) shall have exclusive jurisdiction to review the decisions of the Tax Court, except as provided in section 1254 of Title 28 of the United States Code, in the same manner and to the same extent as decisions of the district courts in civil actions tried without a jury; and the judgment of any such court shall be final, except that it shall be subject to review by the Supreme Court of the United States upon certiorari, in the manner provided in section 1254 of Title 28 of the United States Code.

(2) Interlocutory orders.—

(A) In general.—When any judge of the Tax Court includes in an interlocutory order a statement that a controlling question of law is involved with respect to which there is a substantial ground for difference of opinion and that an immediate appeal from that order may materially advance the ultimate termination of the litigation, the United States Court of Appeals may, in its discretion, permit an appeal to be taken from such order, if application is made to it within 10 days after the entry of such order. Neither the application for nor the granting of an appeal under this paragraph shall stay proceedings in the Tax Court, unless a stay is ordered by a judge of the Tax Court or by the United States Court of Appeals which has jurisdiction of the appeal or a judge of that court.

(B) Order treated as tax court decision.—For purposes of subsections (b) and (c), an order described in this paragraph shall be treated as a decision of the Tax Court.

(C) Venue for review of subsequent proceedings.—If a United States Court of Appeals permits an appeal to be taken from an order described in subparagraph (A), except as provided in subsection (b)(2), any subsequent review of the decision of the Tax Court in the proceeding shall be made by such Court of Appeals.

(3) Certain orders entered under section 6213(a).—An order of the Tax Court which is entered under authority of section 6213(a) and which resolves a proceeding to restrain assessment or collection shall be treated as a decision of the Tax Court for purposes of this section and shall be subject to the same review by the United States Court of Appeals as a similar order of a district court.

(b) Venue.—

(1) In general.—Except as otherwise provided in paragraphs (2) and (3), such decisions may be reviewed by the United States Court of Appeals for the circuit in which is located—

(A) in the case of a petitioner seeking redetermination of tax liability other than a corporation, the legal residence of the petitioner,

(B) in the case of a corporation seeking redetermination of tax liability, the principal place of business or principal office or agency of the corporation, or, if it has no principal place of business or principal office or agency in any judicial circuit, then the office to which was made the return of the tax in respect of which the liability arises,

(C) in the case of a person seeking a declaratory decision under section 7476, the principal place of business, or principal office or agency of the employer,

(D) in the case of an organization seeking a declaratory decision under section 7428, the principal office or agency of the organization,

(E) in the case of a petition under section 6226, 6228(a), 6247, or 6252, the principal place of business of the partnership, or

(F) in the case of a petition under section 6234(c)—

(i) the legal residence of the petitioner if the petitioner is not a corporation, and

(ii) the place or office applicable under subparagraph (B) if the petitioner is a corporation.

If for any reason no subparagraph of the preceding sentence applies, then such decisions may be reviewed by the Court of Appeals for the District of Columbia. For purposes of this paragraph, the legal residence, principal place of business, or principal office or agency referred to herein shall be determined as of the time the petition seeking redetermination of tax liability was filed with the Tax Court or as of the time the petition seeking a declaratory decision under section 7428 or 7476, or the petition under section 6226, 6228(a), or 6234(c), was filed with the Tax Court.

(2) By agreement.—Notwithstanding the provisions of paragraph (1), such decisions may be reviewed by any United States Court of Appeals which may be designated by the Secretary and the taxpayer by stipulation in writing.

(3) Declaratory judgment actions relating to status of certain governmental obligations.—In the case of any decision of the Tax Court in a proceeding under section 7478, such decision may only be reviewed by the Court of Appeals for the District of Columbia.

(c) Powers.—

(1) To affirm, modify, or reverse.—Upon such review, such courts shall have power to affirm or, if the decision of the Tax Court is not in accordance with law, to modify or to reverse the decision of the Tax Court, with or without remanding the case for a rehearing, as justice may require.

(2) To make rules.—Rules for review of decisions of the Tax Court shall be those prescribed by the Supreme Court under section 2072 of Title 28 of the United States Code.

(3) To require additional security.—Nothing in section 7483 shall be construed as relieving the petitioner from making or filing such undertakings as the court may require as a condition of or in connection with the review.

(4) To impose penalties.—The United States Court of Appeals and the Supreme Court shall have power to require the taxpayer to pay to the United States a penalty in any case where the decision of the Tax Court is affirmed and it appears that the appeal was instituted or maintained primarily for delay or that the taxpayer's position in the appeal is frivolous or groundless.

§ 7483. Notice of appeal

Review of a decision of the Tax Court shall be obtained by filing a notice of appeal with the clerk of the Tax Court within 90 days after the decision of the Tax Court is entered. If a timely notice of appeal is filed by one party, any other party may take an appeal by filing a notice of appeal within 120 days after the decision of the Tax Court is entered.

* * *

SUBCHAPTER E—BURDEN OF PROOF

§ 7491. Burden of proof

(a) Burden shifts where taxpayer produces credible evidence.—

(1) General rule.—If, in any court proceeding, a taxpayer introduces credible evidence with respect to any factual issue relevant to ascertaining the liability of the taxpayer for any tax imposed by subtitle A or B, the Secretary shall have the burden of proof with respect to such issue.

(2) Limitations.—Paragraph (1) shall apply with respect to an issue only if—

(A) the taxpayer has compiled with the requirements under this title to substantiate any item,

(B) the taxpayer has maintained all records required under this title and has cooperated with reasonable requests by the Secretary for witnesses, information, documents, meetings, and interviews, and

(C) in the case of a partnership, corporation, or trust, the taxpayer is described in section 7430(c)(4)(A)(ii).

(3) Coordination.—Paragraph (1) shall not apply to any issue if any other provision of this title provides for a specific burden of proof with respect to such issue.

(b) Use of statistical information on unrelated taxpayers.—In the case of an individual taxpayer, the Secretary shall have the burden of proof in any court proceeding with respect to any item of income which was reconstructed by the Secretary solely through the use of statistical information on unrelated taxpayers.

(c) Penalties.—Notwithstanding any other provision of this title, the Secretary shall have the burden of production in any court proceeding with respect to the liability of any individual for any penalty, addition to tax, or additional amount imposed by this title.

* * *

CHAPTER 77—MISCELLANEOUS PROVISIONS

* * *

§ 7508. Time for performing certain acts postponed by reason of service in combat zone or contingency operation

(a) Time to be disregarded.—In the case of an individual serving in the Armed Forces of the United States, or serving in support of such Armed Forces, in an area designated by the President of the United States by Executive order as a "combat zone" for purposes of section 112, or when deployed outside the United States away from the individual's permanent duty station while participating in an operation designated by the Secretary of Defense as a contingency operation (as defined in section 101(a)(13) of title 10, United States Code) or which became such a contingency operation by operation of law, at any time during the period designated by the President by Executive order as the period of combatant activities in such zone for purposes of such section or at any time during the period of such contingency operation, or hospitalized as a result of injury received while serving in such an area or operation during such time, the period of service in such area or operation, plus the period of continuous qualified hospitalization attributable to such injury, and the next 180 days thereafter, shall be disregarded in determining, under the internal revenue laws, in respect of any tax liability (including any interest, penalty, additional amount, or addition to the tax) of such individual—

(1) Whether any of the following acts was performed within the time prescribed therefore:

(A) Filing any return of income, estate, or gift tax (except income tax withheld at source and income tax imposed by subtitle C or any law superseded thereby);

(B) Payment of any income, estate, or gift tax (except income tax withheld at source and income tax imposed by subtitle C or any law superseded thereby) or any installment thereof or of any other liability to the United States in respect thereof;

(C) Filing a petition with the Tax Court for redetermination of a deficiency, or for review of a decision rendered by the Tax Court;

(D) Allowance of a credit or refund of any tax;

(E) Filing a claim for credit or refund of any tax;

(F) Bringing suit upon any such claim for credit or refund;

(G) Assessment of any tax;

(H) Giving or making any notice or demand for the payment of any tax, or with respect to any liability to the United States in respect of any tax;

(I) Collection, by the Secretary, by levy or otherwise, of the amount of any liability in respect of any tax;

(J) Bringing suit by the United States, or any officer on its behalf, in respect of any liability in respect of any tax; and

(K) Any other act required or permitted under the internal revenue laws specified by the Secretary;

(2) The amount of any credit or refund.

(b) Special rule for overpayments.—

(1) In general.—Subsection (a) shall not apply for purposes of determining the amount of interest on any overpayment of tax.

(2) Special rules.—If an individual is entitled to the benefits of subsection (a) with respect to any return and such return is timely filed (determined after the application of such subsection), subsections (b)(3) and (e) of section 6611 shall not apply.

(c) Application to spouse.—The provisions of this section shall apply to the spouse of any individual entitled to the benefits of subsection (a). Except in the case of the combat zone designated for purposes of the Vietnam conflict, the preceding sentence shall not cause this section to apply for any spouse for any taxable year beginning more than 2 years after the date designated under section 112 as the date of termination of combatant activities in a combat zone.

(d) Missing status.—The period of service in the area or contingency operation referred to in subsection (a) shall include the period during which an individual entitled to benefits under subsection (a) is in a missing status, within the meaning of section 6013(f)(3).

(e) Exceptions.—

(1) Tax in jeopardy; cases under Title 11 of the United States Code and receiverships; and transferred assets.—Notwithstanding the provisions of subsection (a), any action or proceeding authorized by section 6851 (regardless of the taxable year for which the tax arose), chapter 70, or 71, as well as any other action or proceeding authorized by law in connection therewith, may be taken, begun, or prosecuted. In any other case in which the Secretary determines that collection of the amount of any assessment would be jeopardized by delay, the provisions of subsection (a) shall not operate to stay collection of such amount by levy or otherwise as authorized by law. There shall be excluded from any amount assessed or collected pursuant to this paragraph the amount of interest, penalty, additional amount, and addition to the tax, if any, in respect of the period disregarded under subsection (a). In any case to which this paragraph relates, if the Secretary is required to give any notice to or make any demand upon any person, such requirement shall be deemed to be satisfied if the notice or demand is prepared and signed, in any case in which the address of such person last known to the Secretary is in an area for which United States post offices under instructions of the Postmaster General are not, by reason of the combatant activities, accepting mail for delivery at the time the notice or demand is signed. In such case the notice or demand shall be deemed to have been given or made upon the date it is signed.

(2) Action taken before ascertainment of right to benefits.—The assessment or collection of any internal revenue tax or of any liability to the United States in respect of any internal revenue tax, or any action or proceeding by or on behalf of the United States in connection therewith, may be made, taken, begun, or prosecuted in accordance with law, without regard to the provisions of subsection (a), unless prior to such assessment, collection, action, or proceeding it is ascertained that the person concerned is entitled to the benefits of subsection (a).

(f) Treatment of individuals performing Desert Shield services.—

(1) In general.—Any individual who performed Desert Shield services (and the spouse of such individual) shall be entitled to the benefits of this section in the same manner as if such services were services referred to in subsection (a).

(2) Desert Shield services.—For purposes of this subsection, the term "Desert Shield services" means any services in the Armed Forces of the United States or in support of such Armed Forces if—

(A) such services are performed in the area designated by the President pursuant to this subparagraph as the "Persian Gulf Desert Shield area," and

(B) Such services are performed during the period beginning on August 2, 1990, and ending on the date on which any portion of the area referred to in subparagraph (A) is designated by the President as a combat zone pursuant to section 112.

(g) Qualified hospitalization.—For purposes of subsection (a), the term "qualified hospitalization" means—

(1) any hospitalization outside the United States, and

(2) any hospitalization inside the United States, except that not more than 5 years of hospitalization may be taken into account under this paragraph.

Paragraph (2) shall not apply for purposes of applying this section with respect to the spouse of an individual entitled to the benefits of subsection (a).

* * *

Editorial Summary

Election of Taxable Year: Required Payments

Chapter 77 (Sec. 7519)

The Revenue Act of 1987 provides the partnership and the S corporation with additional flexibility in selecting a taxable year by making an election under Sec. 444 (see the discussion under the Editorial Summary entitled Accounting Periods, which precedes Sec. 441). However, as a condition for making the election under Sec. 444, the partnership or corporation must agree to make certain *required payments* [see Sec. 7519(a)].

§ 7519. Required payments for entities electing not to have required taxable year

(a) General rule.—This section applies to a partnership or S corporation for any taxable year, if—

(1) an election under section 444 is in effect for the taxable year, and

(2) the required payment determined under subsection (b) for such taxable year (or any preceding taxable year) exceeds $500.

(b) Required payment.—For purposes of this section, the term "required payment" means, with respect to any applicable election year of a partnership or S corporation, an amount equal to—

(1) the excess of the product of—

(A) the applicable percentage of the adjusted highest section 1 rate, multiplied by

(B) the net base year income of the entity, over

(2) the net required payment balance.

For purposes of paragraph (1)(A), the term "adjusted highest section 1 rate" means the highest rate of tax in effect under section 1 as of the end of the base year plus 1 percentage point (or, in the case of applicable election years beginning in 1987, 36 percent).

(c) Refund of payments.—

(1) In general.—If, for any applicable election year, the amount determined under subsection (b)(2) exceeds the amount determined under subsection (b)(1), the entity shall be entitled to a refund of such excess for such year.

(2) Termination of elections, etc.—If—

(A) an election under section 444 is terminated effective with respect to any year, or

(B) the entity is liquidated during any year, the entity shall be entitled to a refund of the net required payment balance.

(3) Date on which refund payable.—Any refund under this subsection shall be payable on the later of—

(A) April 15 of the calendar year following—

(i) in the case of the year referred to in paragraph (1), the calendar year in which it begins,

(ii) in the case of the year referred to in paragraph (2), the calendar year in which it ends, or

(B) the day 90 days after the day on which claim therefor is filed with the Secretary.

(d) Net base year income.—For purposes of this section—

(1) In general.—An entity's net base year income shall be equal to the sum of—

(A) the deferral ratio multiplied by the entity's net income for the base year, plus

(B) the excess (if any) of—

(i) the deferral ratio multiplied by the aggregate amount of applicable payments made by the entity during the base year, over

(ii) the aggregate amount of such applicable payments made during the deferral period of the base year.

For purposes of this paragraph, the term "deferral ratio" means the ratio which the number of months in the deferral period of the base year bears to the number of months in the partnership's or S corporation's taxable year.

(2) Net income.—Net income is determined by taking into account the aggregate amount of the following items—

(A) Partnerships.—In the case of a partnership, net income shall be the amount (not below zero) determined by taking into account the aggregate amount of the partnership's items described in section 702(a) (other than credits and tax-exempt income).

(B) S corporations.—In the case of an S corporation, net income shall be the amount (not below zero) determined by taking into account the aggregate amount of the S corporation's items described in section 1366(a) (other than credits and tax-exempt income). If the S corporation was a C corporation for the base year, its taxable income for such year shall be treated as its net income for such year (and such corporation shall be treated as an S corporation for such taxable year for purposes of paragraph (3)).

(C) Certain limitations disregarded.—For purposes of subparagraph (A) or (B), any limitation on the amount of any item described in either such paragraph which may be taken into account for purposes of computing the taxable income of a partner or shareholder shall be disregarded.

(3) Applicable payments.—

(A) In general.—The term "applicable payment" means amounts paid by a partnership or S corporation which are includible in gross income of a partner or shareholder.

(B) Exceptions.—The term "applicable payment" shall not include any—

(i) gain from the sale or exchange of property between the partner or shareholder and the partnership or S corporation, and

(ii) dividend paid by the S corporation.

(4) Applicable percentage.—The applicable percentage is the percentage determined in accordance with the following table:

If the applicable election year of the partnership or S corporation begins during:	The applicable percentage is:
1987	25
1988	50
1989	75
1990 or thereafter	100

Notwithstanding the preceding provisions of this paragraph, the applicable percentage for any partnership or S corporation shall be 100 percent unless more than 50 percent of such entity's net income for the short taxable year which would have resulted if the entity had not made an election under section 444 would have been allocated to partners or shareholders who would have been entitled to the benefits of section 806(e)(2)(C) of the Tax Reform Act of 1986 with respect to such income.

(5) Treatment of guaranteed payments.—

(A) In general.—Any guaranteed payment by a partnership shall not be treated as an applicable subparagraph (A), the term "guaranteed payment" means any payment referred to in section 707(c).

(B) Guaranteed payment.—For purposes of subparagraph (A), the term "guaranteed payment" means any payment referred to in section 707(c).

(e) Other definitions and special rules.—For purposes of this section—

(1) Deferral period.—The term "deferral period" has the meaning given to such term by section 444(b)(4).

(2) Years.—

(A) Base year.—The term "base year" means, with respect to any applicable election year, the taxable year of the partnership or S corporation preceding such applicable election year.

(B) Applicable election year.—The term "applicable election year" means any taxable year of a partnership or S corporation with respect to which an election is in effect under section 444.

(3) Requirement of reporting.—Each partnership or S corporation which makes an election under section 444 shall include on any required return or statement such information as the

Secretary shall prescribe as is necessary to carry out the provisions of this section.

(4) Net required payment balance.—The term "net required payment balance" means the excess (if any) of—

(A) the aggregate of the required payments under this section for all preceding applicable election years, over

(B) the aggregate amount allowable as a refund to the entity under subsection (c) for all preceding applicable election years.

(f) Administrative provisions.—

(1) In general.—Except as otherwise provided in this subsection or in regulations prescribed by the Secretary, any payment required by this section shall be assessed and collected in the same manner as if it were a tax imposed by subtitle C.

(2) Due date.—The amount of any payment required by this section shall be paid on or before April 15 of the calendar year following the calendar year in which the applicable election year begins (or such later date as may be prescribed by the Secretary).

(3) Interest.—For purposes of determining interest, any payment required by this section shall be treated as a tax; except that no interest shall be allowed with respect to any refund of a payment made under this section.

(4) Penalties.—

(A) In general.—In the case of any failure by any person to pay on the date prescribed therefor any amount required by this section, there shall be imposed on such person a penalty of 10 percent of the underpayment. For purposes of the preceding sentence, the term "underpayment" means the excess of the amount of the payment required under this section over the amount (if any) of such payment paid on or before the date prescribed therefor. No penalty shall be imposed under this subparagraph on any failure which is shown to be due to reasonable course and not willful neglect.

(B) Negligence and fraud penalties made applicable.—For purposes of part II of subchapter A of chapter 68, any payment required by this section shall be treated as a tax.

(C) Willful failure.—If any partnership or S corporation willfully fails to comply with the requirements of this section, section 444 shall cease to apply with respect to such partnership or S corporation.

(g) Regulations.—The Secretary shall prescribe such regulations as may be necessary or appropriate to carry out the provisions of this section and section 280H, including regulations providing for appropriate adjustments in the application of this section and sections 280H and 444 in cases where—

(1) 2 or more applicable election years begin in the same calendar year, or

(2) the base year is a taxable year of less than 12 months.

* * *

CHAPTER 78—DISCOVERY OF LIABILITY AND ENFORCEMENT OF TITLE*
CHAPTER 79—DEFINITIONS

Editorial Summary
Definitions
Chapter 79 (Secs. 7701–7704)

The Code contains thousands of definitions. Most of the definitions appear in the particular Code section or set of Code sections to which they relate. However, certain terms appear many times in different parts of the Code. Such terms are defined in Sec. 7701. Section 7702B defines long-term care insurance. In addition, an individual's marital status affects the tax consequences of a number of Code provisions. Thus, the determination of marital status is defined in Sec. 7703. Section 7704 provides the rules under which a publicly-traded partnership will be treated as a corporation.

§ 7701. Definitions

(a) When used in this title, where not otherwise distinctly expressed or manifestly incompatible with the intent thereof—

(1) Person.—The term "person" shall be construed to mean and include an individual, a trust, estate, partnership, association, company or corporation.

(2) Partnership and partner.—The term "partnership" includes a syndicate, group, pool, joint venture, or other unincorporated organization, through or by means of which any business, financial operation, or venture is carried on, and which is not, within the meaning of this title, a trust or estate or a corporation; and the term "partner" includes a member in such a syndicate, group, pool, joint venture, or organization.

(3) Corporation.—The term "corporation" includes associations, joint-stock companies, and insurance companies.

(4) Domestic.—The term "domestic" when applied to a corporation or partnership means created or organized in the United States or under the law of the United States or of any State unless, in the case of a partnership, the Secretary provides otherwise by regulations.

(5) Foreign.—The term "foreign" when applied to a corporation or partnership means a corporation or partnership which is not domestic.

(6) Fiduciary.—The term "fiduciary" means a guardian, trustee, executor, administrator, receiver, conservator, or any person acting in any fiduciary capacity for any person.

(7) Stock.—The term "stock" includes shares in an association, joint-stock company, or insurance company.

(8) Shareholder.—The term "shareholder" includes a member in an association, joint-stock company, or insurance company.

(9) United States.—The term "United States" when used in a geographical sense includes only the States and the District of Columbia.

(10) State.—The term "State" shall be construed to include the District of Columbia, where such construction is necessary to carry out provisions of this title.

(11) Secretary of the Treasury and Secretary.—

(A) Secretary of the Treasury.—The term "Secretary of the Treasury" means the Secretary of the Treasury, personally, and shall not include any delegate of his.

(B) Secretary.—The term "Secretary" means the Secretary of the Treasury or his delegate.

* * *

(13) Commissioner.—The term "Commissioner" means the Commissioner of Internal Revenue.

(14) Taxpayer.—The term "taxpayer" means any person subject to any internal revenue tax.

* * *

(17) Husband and wife.—As used in sections 682 and 2516, if the husband and wife therein referred to are divorced, wherever appropriate to the meaning of such sections, the term "wife" shall be read "former wife" and the term "husband" shall be read "former husband;" and, if the payments described in such sections are made by or on behalf of the wife or former wife to the husband or former husband instead of vice versa, wherever appropriate to the meaning of such sections, the term "husband" shall be read "wife" and the term "wife" shall be read "husband."

* * *

(20) Employee.—For the purpose of applying the provisions of section 79 with respect to

---
*Omitted.

group-term life insurance purchased for employees, for the purpose of applying the provisions of sections 104, 105, and 106, with respect to accident and health insurance or accident and health plans, and for the purpose of applying the provisions of subtitle A with respect to contributions to or under a stock bonus, pension, profit-sharing, or annuity plan, and with respect to distributions under such a plan, or by a trust forming part of such a plan, and for purposes of applying section 125 with respect to cafeteria plans, the term "employee" shall include a full-time life insurance salesman who is considered an employee for the purpose of chapter 21, or in the case of services performed before January 1, 1951, who would be considered an employee if his services were performed during 1951.

* * *

(23) Taxable year.—The term "taxable year" means the calendar year, or the fiscal year ending during such calendar year, upon the basis of which the taxable income is computed under subtitle A. "Taxable year" means, in the case of a return made for a fractional part of a year under the provisions of subtitle A or under regulations prescribed by the Secretary, the period for which such return is made.

(24) Fiscal year.—The term "fiscal year" means an accounting period of 12 months ending on the last day of any month other than December.

(25) Paid or incurred, paid or accrued.—The terms "paid or incurred" and "paid or accrued" shall be construed according to the method of accounting upon the basis of which the taxable income is computed under subtitle A.

(26) Trade or business.—The term "trade or business" includes the performance of the functions of a public office.

(27) Tax Court.—The term "Tax Court" means the United States Tax Court.

(28) Other terms.—Any term used in this subtitle with respect to the application of, or in connection with, the provisions of any other subtitle of this title shall have the same meaning as in such provisions.

* * *

(36) Tax return preparer.—

(A) In general.—The term "tax return preparer" means any person who prepares for compensation, or who employs one or more persons to prepare for compensation, any return of tax imposed by this title or any claim for refund of tax imposed by this title. For purposes of the preceding sentence, the preparation of a substantial portion of a return or claim for refund shall be treated as if it were the preparation of such return or claim for refund.

(B) Exceptions.—A person shall not be a "tax return preparer" merely because such person—

(i) furnishes typing, reproducing, or other mechanical assistance,

(ii) prepares a return or claim for refund of the employer (or of an officer or employee of the employer) by whom he is regularly and continuously employed,

(iii) prepares as a fiduciary a return or claim for refund for any person, or

(iv) prepares a claim for refund for a taxpayer in response to any notice of deficiency issued to such taxpayer or in response to any waiver of restriction after the commencement of an audit of such taxpayer or another taxpayer if a determination in such audit of such other taxpayer directly or indirectly affects the tax liability of such taxpayer.

(37) Individual retirement plan.—The term "individual retirement plan" means—

(A) an individual retirement account described in section 408(a), and

(B) an individual retirement annuity described in section 408(b).

(38) Joint return.—The term "joint return" means a single return made jointly under section 6013 by a husband and wife.

* * *

(42) Substituted basis property.—The term "substituted basis property" means property which is—

(A) transferred basis property, or

(B) exchanged basis property.

(43) Transferred basis property.—The term "transferred basis property" means property having a basis determined under any provision of subtitle A (or under any corresponding provision of prior income tax law) providing that the basis shall be determined in whole or in part by reference to the basis in the hands of the donor, grantor, or other transferor.

(44) Exchanged basis property.—The term "exchanged basis property" means property having a basis determined under any provision of subtitle A (or under any corresponding provision of prior income tax law) providing that the basis shall be determined in whole or in part by reference to other property held at any time by the person for whom the basis is to be determined.

(45) Nonrecognition transaction.—The term "nonrecognition transaction" means any disposition of property in a transaction in which gain or loss is not recognized in whole or in part for purposes of subtitle A.

* * *

(48) Off-highway vehicles.—

(A) Off-highway transportation vehicles.—

(i) In general.—A vehicle shall not be treated as a highway vehicle if such vehicle is specially designed for the primary function of transporting a particular type of load other than over the public highway and because of this special design such vehicle's capability to transport a load over the public highway is substantially limited or impaired.

(ii) Determination of vehicle's design.—For purposes of clause (i), a vehicle's design is determined solely on the basis of its physical characteristics.

(iii) Determination of substantial limitation or impairment.—For purposes of clause (i), in determining whether substantial limitation or impairment exists, account may be taken of factors such as the size of the vehicle, whether such vehicle is subject to the licensing, safety, and other requirements applicable to highway vehicles, and whether such vehicle can transport a load at a sustained speed of at least 25 miles per hour. It is immaterial that a vehicle can transport a greater load off the public highway than such vehicle is permitted to transport over the public highway.

(B) Nontransportation trailers and semitrailers.—A trailer or semitrailer shall not be treated as a highway vehicle if it is specially designed to function only as an enclosed stationary shelter for the carrying on of an off-highway function at an off-highway site.

* * *

§ 7702B. Treatment of qualified long-term care insurance

(a) In general.—For purposes of this title—

(1) a qualified long-term care insurance contract shall be treated as an accident and health insurance contract,

(2) amounts (other than policyholder dividends, as defined in section 808, or premium refunds) received under a qualified long-term care insurance contract shall be treated as amounts received for personal injuries and sickness and shall be treated as reimbursement for expenses actually incurred for medical care (as defined in section 213(d)),

(3) any plan of an employer providing coverage under a qualified long-term care insurance contract shall be treated as an accident and health plan with respect to such coverage,

(4) except as provided in subsection (e)(3), amounts paid for a qualified long-term care insurance contract providing the benefits described in subsection (b)(2)(A) shall be treated as payments made for insurance for purposes of section 213(d)(1)(D), and

(5) a qualified long-term care insurance contract shall be treated as a guaranteed renewable contract subject to the rules of section 816(e).

(b) Qualified long-term care insurance contract.—For purposes of this title—

(1) In general.—The term "qualified long-term care insurance contract" means any insurance contract if—

(A) the only insurance protection provided under such contract is coverage of qualified long-term care services,

(B) such contract does not pay or reimburse expenses incurred for services or items to the extent that such expenses are reimbursable under title XVIII of the Social Security Act or would be so reimbursable but for the application of a deductible or coinsurance amount,

(C) such contract is guaranteed renewable,

(D) such contract does not provide for a cash surrender value or other money that can be—

(i) paid, assigned, or pledged as collateral for a loan, or

(ii) borrowed,

other than as provided in subparagraph (E) or paragraph (2)(C),

(E) all refunds of premiums, and all policyholder dividends or similar amounts, under such contract are to be applied as a reduction in future premiums or to increase future benefits, and

(F) such contract meets the requirements of subsection (g).

(2) Special rules.—

(A) Per diem, etc. payments permitted.—A contract shall not fail to be described in subparagraph (A) or (B) of paragraph (1) by reason of payments being made on a per diem or other periodic basis without regard to the expenses incurred during the period to which the payments relate.

(B) Special rules relating to Medicare.—

(i) Paragraph (1)(B) shall not apply to expenses which are reimbursable under title XVIII of the Social Security Act only as a secondary payor.

(ii) No provision of law shall be construed or applied so as to prohibit the offering of a qualified long-term care insurance contract on the basis that the contract coordinates its benefits with those provided under such title.

(C) Refunds of premiums.—Paragraph (1)(E) shall not apply to any refund on the death of the insured, or on a complete surrender or cancellation of the contract, which cannot exceed the aggregate premiums paid under the contract. Any refund on a complete surrender or cancellation of the contract shall be includible in gross income to the extent that any deduction or exclusion was allowable with respect to the premiums.

(c) Qualified long-term care services.—For purposes of this section—

(1) In general.—The term "qualified long-term care services" means necessary diagnostic, preventive, therapeutic, curing, treating, mitigating, and rehabilitative services, and maintenance or personal care services, which—

(A) are required by a chronically ill individual, and

(B) are provided pursuant to a plan of care prescribed by a licensed health care practitioner.

(2) Chronically ill individual.—

(A) In general.—The term "chronically ill individual" means any individual who has been certified by a licensed health care practitioner as—

(i) being unable to perform (without substantial assistance from another individual) at least 2 activities of daily living for a period of at least 90 days due to a loss of functional capacity,

(ii) having a level of disability similar (as determined under regulations prescribed by the Secretary in consultation with the Secretary of Health and Human Services) to the level of disability described in clause (i), or

(iii) requiring substantial supervision to protect such individual from threats to health and safety due to severe cognitive impairment.

Such term shall not include any individual otherwise meeting the requirements of the preceding sentence unless within the preceding 12-month period a licensed health care practitioner has certified that such individual meets such requirements.

(B) Activities of daily living.—For purposes of subparagraph (A), each of the following is an activity of daily living:

(i) Eating.

(ii) Toileting.

(iii) Transferring.

(iv) Bathing.

(v) Dressing.

(vi) Continence.

A contract shall not be treated as a qualified long-term care insurance contract unless the determination of whether an individual is a chronically ill individual described in subparagraph (A)(i) takes into account at least 5 of such activities.

(3) Maintenance or personal care services.—The term "maintenance or personal care services" means any care the primary purpose of which is the provision of needed assistance with any of the disabilities as a result of which the individual is a chronically ill individual (including the protection from threats to health and safety due to severe cognitive impairment).

(4) Licensed health care practitioner.—The term "licensed health care practitioner" means any physician (as defined in section 1861(r)(1) of the Social Security Act) and any registered professional nurse, licensed social worker, or other individual who meets such requirements as may be prescribed by the Secretary.

(d) Aggregate payments in excess of limits.—

(1) In general.—If the aggregate of—

(A) the periodic payments received for any period under all qualified long-term care insurance contracts which are treated as made for qualified long-term care services for an insured, and

(B) the periodic payments received for such period which are treated under section 101(g) as paid by reason of the death of such insured,

exceeds the per diem limitation for such period, such excess shall be includible in gross income without regard to section 72. A payment shall not be taken into account under subparagraph (B) if the insured is a terminally ill individual (as defined in section 101 (g)) at the time the payment is received.

(2) Per diem limitation.—For purposes of paragraph (1), the per diem limitation for any period is an amount equal to the excess (if any) of—

(A) the greater of—

(i) the dollar amount in effect for such period under paragraph (4), or

(ii) the costs incurred for qualified long-term care services provided for the insured for such period, over

(B) the aggregate payments received as reimbursements (through insurance or otherwise) for qualified long-term care services provided for the insured during such period.

(3) Aggregation rules.—For purposes of this subsection—

(A) all persons receiving periodic payments described in paragraph (1) with respect to the same insured shall be treated as 1 person, and

(B) the per diem limitation determined under paragraph (2) shall be allocated first to the insured and any remaining limitation shall be allocated among the other such persons in such manner as the Secretary shall prescribe.

(4) Dollar amount.—The dollar amount in effect under this subsection shall be $175* per day (or the equivalent amount in the case of payments on another periodic basis).

(5) Inflation adjustment.—In the case of a calendar year after 1997, the dollar amount contained in paragraph (4) shall be increased at the same time and in the same manner as amounts are increased pursuant to section 213(d)(10).

(6) Periodic payments.—For purposes of this subsection, the term "periodic payment" means any payment (whether on a periodic basis or otherwise) made without regard to the extent of the costs incurred by the payee for qualified long-term care services.

(e) Treatment of coverage provided as part of a life insurance contract or annuity contract.—Except as otherwise provided in regulations prescribed by the Secretary, in the case of any long-term care insurance coverage (whether or not qualified) provided by a rider on or as part of a life insurance contract or an annuity contract—

(1) In general.—This title shall apply as if the portion of the contract providing such coverage is a separate contract.

(2) Denial of deduction under section 213.—No deduction shall be allowed under section 213 (a) for any payment made for coverage under a qualified long-term care insurance contract if such payment is made as a charge against the cash surrender value of a life insurance contract or the cash value of an annuity contract.

(3) Portion defined.—For purposes of this subsection, the term "portion" means only the terms and benefits under a life insurance contract or annuity contact that are in addition to the terms and benefits under the contract without regard to long-term care insurance coverage.

(4) Annuity contracts to which paragraph (1) does not apply.—For purposes of this subsection, none of the following shall be treated as an annuity contract:

(A) A trust described in section 401(a) which is exempt from tax under section 501(a).

(B) A contract—

(i) purchased by a trust described in subparagraph (A),

(ii) purchased as part of a plan described in section 403(a),

(iii) described in section 403(b),

(iv) provided for employees of a life insurance company under a plan described in section 818(a)(3), or

*Editorial comment: The indexed amount for 2013 is $320 and for 2014 is $330.

(v) from an individual retirement account or an individual retirement annuity.

(C) A contract purchased by an employer for the benefit of the employee (or the employee's spouse).

Any dividend described in section 404(k) which is received by a participant or beneficiary shall, for purposes of this paragraph, be treated as paid under a separate contract to which subparagraph (B)(i) applies.

(f) Treatment of certain state-maintained plans.—

(1) In general.—If—

(A) an individual receives coverage for qualified long-term care services under a State long-term care plan, and

(B) the terms of such plan would satisfy the requirements of subsection (b) were such plan an insurance contract,

such plan shall be treated as a qualified long-term care insurance contract for purposes of this title.

(2) State long-term care plan.—For purposes of paragraph (1), the term "State long-term care plan" means any plan—

(A) which is established and maintained by a State or an instrumentality of a State,

(B) which provides coverage only for qualified long-term care services, and

(C) under which such coverage is provided only to—

(i) employees and former employees of a State (or any political subdivision or instrumentality of a State),

(ii) the spouses of such employees, and

(iii) individuals bearing a relationship to such employees or spouses which is described in any of subparagraphs (A) through (G) of section 152(d)(2).

* * *

§ 7703. Determination of marital status

(a) General rule.—For purposes of part V of subchapter B of chapter 1 and those provisions of this title which refer to this subsection—

(1) the determination of whether an individual is married shall be made as of the close of his taxable year; except that if his spouse dies during his taxable year such determination shall be made as of the time of such death; and

(2) an individual legally separated from his spouse under a decree of divorce or of separate maintenance shall not be considered as married.

(b) Certain married individuals living apart.—For purposes of these provisions of this title which refer to this subsection, if—

(1) an individual who is married (within the meaning of subsection (a)) and who files a separate return maintains as his home a household which constitutes for more than one-half of the taxable year the principal place of abode of a child (within the meaning of section 152(f)(1)) with respect to whom such individual is entitled to a deduction for the taxable year under section 151 (or would be so entitled but for section 152(e)),

(2) such individual furnishes over one-half of the cost of maintaining such household during the taxable year, and

(3) during the last 6 months of the taxable year, such individual's spouse is not a member of such household,

such individual shall not be considered as married.

§ 7704. Certain publicly traded partnerships treated as corporations

(a) General rule.—For purposes of this title, except as provided in subsection (c), a publicly traded partnership shall be treated as a corporation.

(b) Publicly traded partnership.—For purposes of this section, the term "publicly traded partnership" means any partnership if—

(1) interests in such partnership are traded on an established securities market, or

(2) interests in such partnership are readily tradable on a secondary market (or the substantial equivalent thereof).

(c) Exception for partnerships with passive-type income.—

(1) In general.—Subsection (a) shall not apply to any publicly traded partnership for any taxable year if such partnership met the gross income requirements of paragraph (2) for such taxable year and each preceding taxable year beginning after December 31, 1987, during which the partnership (or any predecessor) was in existence. For purposes of the preceding sentence, a partnership shall not be treated as being in existence during any period before the 1st taxable year in which such partnership (or a predecessor) was a publicly traded partnership.

(2) Gross income requirements.—A partnership meets the gross income requirements of this paragraph for any taxable year if 90 percent or more of the gross income of such partnership for such taxable year consists of qualifying income.

(3) Exception not to apply to certain partnerships which could qualify as regulated investment companies.—This subsection shall not apply to any partnership which would be described in section 851(a) if such partnership were a domestic corporation. To the extent provided in regulations, the preceding sentence shall not apply to any partnership a principal activity of which is the buying and selling of commodities (not described in section 1221(1)), or options, futures, or forwards with respect to commodities.

(d) Qualifying income.—For purposes of this section—

(1) In general.—Except as otherwise provided in this subsection, the term "qualifying income" means—

(A) interest,

(B) dividends,

(C) real property rents,

(D) gain from the sale or other disposition of real property (including property described in section 1221(1)),

(E) income and gains derived from the exploration, development, mining or production, processing, refining, transportation (including pipelines transporting gas, oil, or products thereof), or the marketing of any mineral or natural resource (including fertilizer, geothermal energy, and timber), industrial source carbon dioxide, or the transportation or storage of any fuel described in subsection (b), (c), (d), or (e) of section 6426, or any alcohol fuel defined in section 6426(b)(4)(A) or any biodiesel fuel as defined in section 40A(d)(1),

(F) any gain from the sale or disposition of a capital asset (or property described in section 1231(b)) held for the production of income described in any of the foregoing subparagraphs of this paragraph, and

(G) in the case of a partnership described in the second sentence of subsection (c)(3), income and gains from commodities (not described in section 1221(1)) or futures, forwards, and options with respect to commodities.

For purposes of subparagraph (E), the term "mineral or natural resource" means any product of a character with respect to which a deduction for depletion is allowable under section 611; except that such term shall not include any product described in subparagraph (A) or (B) of section 613(b)(7).

(2) Certain interest not qualified.—Interest shall not be treated as qualifying income if—

(A) such interest is derived in the conduct of a financial or insurance business, or

(B) such interest would be excluded from the term "interest" under section 856(f).

(3) Real property rent.—The term "real property rent" means amounts which would qualify as rent from real property under section 856(d) if—

(A) such section were applied without regard to paragraph (2)(C) thereof (relating to independent contractor requirements), and

(B) stock owned, directly or indirectly, by or for a partner would not be considered as owned under section 318(a)(3)(A) by the partnership unless 5 percent or more (by value) of the interests in such partnership are owned, directly or indirectly, by or for such partner.

(4) Certain income qualifying under regulated investment company or real estate trust provisions.—The term "qualifying income" also includes any income which would qualify under section 851(b)(2)(A) or 856(c)(2).

(5) Special rule for determining gross income from certain real property sales.—In the case of the sale or other disposition of real property described in section 1221(1), gross income shall not be reduced by inventory costs.

(e) Inadvertent terminations.—If—

(1) a partnership fails to meet the gross income requirements of subsection (c)(2),

(2) the Secretary determines that such failure was inadvertent,

(3) no later than a reasonable time after the discovery of such failure, steps are taken so that such partnership once more meets such gross income requirements, and

(4) such partnership agrees to make such adjustments (including adjustments with respect to the partners) or to pay such amounts as may be required by the Secretary with respect to such period, then, notwithstanding such failure, such entity shall be treated as continuing to meet such gross income requirements for such period.

(f) Effect of becoming corporation.—As of the 1st day that a partnership is treated as a corporation under this section, for purposes of this title, such partnership shall be treated as—

(1) transferring all of its assets (subject to its liabilities) to a newly formed corporation in exchange for the stock of the corporation, and

(2) distributing such stock to its partners in liquidation of their interests in the partnership.

* * *

CHAPTER 80—GENERAL RULES

SUBCHAPTER A—APPLICATION OF INTERNAL REVENUE LAWS

Editorial Summary

Authority to Promulgate Regulations

Subchapter A of Chapter 80 (Sec. 7805)

Statutory authority exists for two types of regulations. First, the Secretary of the Treasury can issue regulations based on the legislative authority to do so contained in a particular Code section. For an example, refer to Sec. 1502 regarding the authority to issue regulations associated with consolidated tax returns. Such regulations are referred to as legislative regulations.

Regulations also are issued to interpret Code sections for which no such legislative authority is provided in the related Code section or sections. Such regulations are issued under the general authority provided to the Treasury Department in Sec. 7805 and are referred to as interpretative regulations.

* * *

§ 7805. Rules and regulations

(a) Authorization.—Except where such authority is expressly given by this title to any person other than an officer or employee of the Treasury Department, the Secretary shall prescribe all needful rules and regulations for the enforcement of this title, including all rules and regulations as may be necessary by reason of any alteration of law in relation to internal revenue.

(b) Retroactivity of regulations or rulings.—The Secretary may prescribe the extent, if any, to which any ruling or regulation, relating to the internal revenue laws, shall be applied without retroactive effect.

(c) Preparation and distribution of regulations, forms, stamps, and other matters.—The Secretary shall prepare and distribute all the instructions, regulations, directions, forms, blanks, stamps, and other matters pertaining to the assessment and collection of internal revenue.

(d) Manner of making elections prescribed by Secretary.—Except to the extent otherwise provided by this title, any election under this title shall be made at such time and in such manner as the Secretary shall prescribe.

(e) Temporary regulations.—

(1) Issuance.—Any temporary regulation issued by the Secretary shall also be issued as a proposed regulation.

(2) 3-year duration.—Any temporary regulation shall expire within 3 years after the date of issuance of such regulation.

* * *

SUBCHAPTER B—EFFECTIVE DATE AND RELATED PROVISIONS

Editorial Summary

Effect of Treaties

Subchapter B of Chapter 80 (Sec. 7852)

Prior to the Technical and Miscellaneous Revenue Act of 1988, treaties took precedence over the provisions of the Internal Revenue Code. However, TAMRA of 1988 provided that neither was to have precedence [see Sec. 7852(d)].

§ 7852. Other applicable rules

* * *

(d) Treaty obligations.—

(1) In general.—For purposes of determining the relationship between a provision of a treaty and any law of the United States affecting revenue, neither the treaty nor the law shall have preferential status by reason of its being a treaty or law.

(2) Savings clause for 1954 treaties.—No provision of this title (as in effect without regard to any amendment thereto enacted after August 16, 1954) shall apply in any case where its application would be contrary to any treaty obligation of the United States in effect on August 16, 1954.

* * *

SUBCHAPTER C—PROVISIONS AFFECTING MORE THAN ONE SUBTITLE

Editorial Summary

Imputed Interest on Loans with Below-Market Interest Rates

Subchapter C of Chapter 80 (Sec. 7872)

Prior to 1984, it was possible for taxpayers to achieve certain tax avoidance objectives through the use of loans for which the interest rate was less than the market rate of interest or for which the interest rate was zero. While the issue had been litigated by the Internal Revenue Service, the decisions (i.e., with respect to both the income tax and the gift tax) consistently had been for the taxpayer. However, in 1984 in *Dickman vs. Comm.* the taxpayer was treated as having made a gift (i.e., and thereby subject to the gift tax) for an interest-free loan between family members.

In the Deficit Reduction Act of 1984, Congress added Sec. 7872 to the Code. In so doing, Congress provided for the potential of both a gift tax and an income tax liability for loans not charging a market rate of interest [see Sec. 7872(a)]. Such loans are recharacterized as arms-length transactions in which some or all of the following factors may be present:

1. The lender is treated as having made a loan to the borrower in exchange for a note requiring the payment of interest at a statutory rate,
2. The borrower is treated as having paid interest at the statutory rate, and
3. The lender is treated as having made a gift to the borrower of such "imputed interest."

Section 7872 applies to the following types of loans [see Sec. 7872(c)(1)]:

1. Gift loans (e.g., between family members).
2. Compensation-related loans (i.e., between an employer and an employee or an independent contractor and a person for whom the independent contractor provides services).
3. Corporation-shareholder loans (i.e., between a corporation and one of its shareholders).
4. Tax avoidance loans (i.e., a principal purpose is tax avoidance).
5. Other interest-free or below-market loans as provided by regulations.

Even though an interest-free or below-market loan is included in one of these categories, it may not be necessary to impute interest, or if it is necessary to do so, the amount of the imputed interest may be limited. This may result from the application of materiality provisions or provisions which relate to the use of the loan proceeds [see Sec. 7872(c)(2), (3) and (d)].

Loans are classified in two categories: term loans and demand loans [see Sec. 7872(e)(1)]. A key difference with respect to this classification is the interest rate to use in making the imputed interest calculation [see Sec. 7872(f)(2)]. If other imputed interest Code sections apply, Sec. 7872 is not applicable [see Sec. 7872(f)(8)].

The effect of a loan with a below-market interest rate on the two parties to the transaction can be summarized as follows:

Type of Loan		Lender	Borrower
Gift	Step 1	Interest income	Interest expense
	Step 2	Gift made	Gift received
Compensation-related	Step 1	Interest income	Interest expense
	Step 2	Compensation expense	Compensation income
Corporation-shareholder	Step 1	Interest income	Interest expense
	Step 2	Dividend paid	Dividend income

* * *

§ 7872. Treatment of loans with below-market interest rates

(a) Treatment of gift loans and demand loans.—

(1) In general.—For purposes of this title, in the case of any below-market loan to which this section applies and which is a gift loan or a demand loan, the foregone interest shall be treated as—

(A) transferred from the lender to the borrower, and

(B) retransferred by the borrower to the lender as interest.

(2) Time when transfers made.—Except as otherwise provided in regulations prescribed by the Secretary, any forgone interest attributable to periods during any calendar year shall be treated as transferred (and retransferred) under paragraph (1) on the last day of such calendar year.

(b) Treatment of other below-market loans.—

(1) In general.—For purposes of this title, in the case of any below-market loan to which this section applies and to which subsection (a)(1) does not apply, the lender shall be treated as having transferred on the date the loan was made (or, if later, on the first day on which this section applies to such loan), and the borrower shall be treated as having received on such date, cash in an amount equal to the excess of—

(A) the amount loaned, over

(B) the present value of all payments which are required to be made under the terms of the loan.

(2) Obligation treated as having original issue discount.—For purposes of this title—

(A) In general.—Any below-market loan to which paragraph (1) applies shall be treated as having original issue discount in an amount equal to the excess described in paragraph (1).

(B) Amount in addition to other original issue discount.—Any original issue discount which a loan is treated as having by reason of subparagraph (A) shall be in addition to any other original issue discount on such loan (determined without regard to subparagraph (A)).

(c) Below-market loans to which section applies.—

(1) In general.—Except as otherwise provided in this subsection and subsection (g), this section shall apply to—

(A) Gifts.—Any below-market loan which is a gift loan.

(B) Compensation-related loans.—Any below-market loan directly or indirectly between—

(i) an employer and an employee, or

(ii) an independent contractor and a person for whom such independent contractor provides services.

(C) Corporation-shareholder loans.—Any below-market loan directly or indirectly between a corporation and any shareholder of such corporation.

(D) Tax avoidance loans.—Any below-market loan 1 of the principal purposes of the interest arrangements of which is the avoidance of any Federal tax.

(E) Other below-market loans.—To the extent provided in regulations, any below-market loan which is not described in subparagraph (A), (B), (C), or (F) if the interest arrangements of such loan have a significant effect on any Federal tax liability of the lender or the borrower.

(F) Loans to qualified continuing care facilities.—Any loan to any qualified continuing care facility pursuant to a continuing care contract.

(2) $10,000 de minimis exception for gift loans between individuals.—

(A) In general.—In the case of any gift loan directly between individuals, this section shall not apply to any day on which the aggregate outstanding amount of loans between such individuals does not exceed $10,000.

(B) De minimis exception not to apply to loans attributable to acquisition of income-producing assets.—Subparagraph (A) shall not apply to any gift loan attributable to the purchase or carrying of income-producing assets.

(C) Cross reference.—

For limitation on amount treated as interest where loans do not exceed $100,000, see subsection (d)(1).

(3) $10,000 de minimis exception for compensation-related and corporate-shareholder loans.—

(A) In general.—In the case of any loan described in subparagraph (B) or (C) of paragraph (1), this section shall not apply to any day on which the aggregate outstanding amount of loans between the borrower and lender does not exceed $10,000.

(B) Exception not to apply where 1 of principal purposes is tax avoidance.—Subparagraph (A) shall not apply to any loan the interest arrangements of which have as 1 of their principal purposes the avoidance of any Federal tax.

(d) Special rules for gift loans.—

(1) Limitation on interest accrual for purposes of income taxes where loans do not exceed $100,000.—

(A) In general.—For purposes of subtitle A, in the case of a gift loan directly between individuals, the amount treated as retransferred by the borrower to the lender as of the close of any year shall not exceed the borrower's net investment income for such year.

(B) Limitation not to apply where 1 of principal purposes is tax avoidance.—Subparagraph (A) shall not apply to any loan the interest arrangements of which have as 1 of their principal purposes the avoidance of any Federal tax.

(C) Special rule where more than 1 gift loan outstanding.—For purposes of subparagraph (A), in any case in which a borrower has outstanding more than 1 gift loan, the net investment income of such borrower shall be allocated among such loans in proportion to the respective amounts which would be treated as retransferred by the borrower without regard to this paragraph.

(D) Limitation not to apply where aggregate amount of loans exceed $100,000.—This paragraph shall not apply to any loan made by a lender to a borrower for any day on which the aggregate outstanding amount of loans between the borrower and lender exceeds $100,000.

(E) Net investment income.—For purposes of this paragraph—

(i) In general.—The term "net investment income" has the meaning given such term by section 163(d)(4).

(ii) De minimis rule.—If the net investment income of any borrower for any year does not exceed $1,000, the net investment income of such borrower for such year shall be treated as zero.

(iii) Additional amounts treated as interest.—In determining the net investment income of a person for any year, any amount which would be included in the gross income of such person for such year by reason of section 1272 if such section applied to all deferred payment obligations shall be treated as interest received by such person for such year.

(iv) Deferred payment obligations.—The term "deferred payment obligation" includes any market discount bond, short-term obligation, United States savings bond, annuity, or similar obligation.

(2) Special rule for gift tax.—In the case of any gift loan which is a term loan, subsection (b)(1) (and not subsection (a)) shall apply for purposes of chapter 12.

(e) Definitions of below-market loan and foregone interest.—For purposes of this section—

(1) Below-market loan.—The term "below-market loan" means any loan if—

(A) in the case of a demand loan, interest is payable on the loan at a rate less than the applicable Federal rate, or

(B) in the case of a term loan, the amount loaned exceeds the present value of all payments due under the loan.

(2) Forgone interest.—The term "forgone interest" means, with respect to any period during which the loan is outstanding, the excess of—

(A) the amount of interest which would have been payable on the loan for the period if interest accrued on the loan at the applicable Federal rate and were payable annually on the day referred to in subsection (a)(2), over

(B) any interest payable on the loan properly allocable to such period.

(f) Other definitions and special rules.—For purposes of this section—

(1) Present value.—The present value of any payment shall be determined in the manner provided by regulations prescribed by the Secretary—

(A) as of the date of the loan, and

(B) by using a discount rate equal to the applicable Federal rate.

(2) Applicable federal rate.—

(A) Term loans.—In the case of any term loan, the applicable Federal rate shall be the applicable Federal rate in effect under section 1274(d) (as of the day on which the loan was made), compounded semiannually.

(B) Demand loans.—In the case of a demand loan, the applicable Federal rate shall be the Federal short-term rate in effect under section 1274(d) for the period for which the amount of forgone interest is being determined, compounded semiannually.

(3) Gift loan.—The term "gift loan" means any below-market loan where the forgoing of interest is in the nature of a gift.

(4) Amount loaned.—The term "amount loaned" means the amount received by the borrower.

(5) Demand loan.—The term "demand loan" means any loan which is payable in full at any time on the demand of the lender. Such term also includes (for purposes other than determining the applicable Federal rate under paragraph (2)) any loan if the benefits of the interest arrangements of such loan are not transferable and are conditioned on the future performance of substantial services by an individual. To the extent provided in regulations, such term also includes any loan with an indefinite maturity.

(6) Term loan.—The term "term loan" means any loan which is not a demand loan.

(7) Husband and wife treated as 1 person.—A husband and wife shall be treated as 1 person.

(8) Loans to which section 483, 643(i), or 1274 applies.—This section shall not apply to any loan to which section 483, 643(i), or 1274 applies.

(9) No withholding.—No amount shall be withheld under chapter 24 with respect to—

(A) any amount treated as transferred or retransferred under subsection (a), and

(B) any amount treated as received under subsection (b).

(10) Special rule for term loans.—If this section applies to any term loan on any day, this section shall continue to apply to such loan notwithstanding paragraphs (2) and (3) of subsection (c). In the case of a gift loan, the preceding sentence shall only apply for purposes of chapter 12.

(11) Time for determining rate applicable to employee relocation loans.—

(A) In general.—In the case of any term loan made by an employer to an employee the proceeds of which are used by the employee to purchase a principal residence (within the meaning of section 121), the determination of the applicable Federal rate shall be made as of the date the written contract to purchase such residence was entered into.

(B) Paragraph only to apply to cases to which section 217 applies.—Subparagraph (A) shall only apply to the purchase of a principal residence in connection with the commencement of work by an employee or a change in the principal place of work of an employee to which section 217 applies.

(g) Exception for certain loans to qualified continuing care facilities.—

(1) In general.—This section shall not apply for any calendar year to any below-market loan made by a lender to a qualified continuing care facility pursuant to a continuing care contract if the lender (or the lender's spouse) attains age 65 before the close of such year.

(2) $90,000 limit.*—Paragraph (1) shall apply only to the extent that the aggregate outstanding amount of any loan to which such paragraph applies (determined without regard to this paragraph), when added to the aggregate outstanding amount of all other previous loans between the lender (or the lender's spouse) and any qualified continuing care facility to which paragraph (1) applies, does not exceed $90,000.*

(3) Continuing care contract.—For purposes of this section, the term "continuing care contract" means a written contract between an individual and a qualified continuing care facility under which—

(A) the individual or individual's spouse may use a qualified continuing care facility for their life or lives,

(B) the individual or individual's spouse—

(i) will first—

(I) reside in a separate, independent living unit with additional facilities outside such unit for the providing of meals and other personal care, and

(II) not require long-term nursing care, and

(ii) then will be provided long-term and skilled nursing care as the health of such individual or individual's spouse requires, and

(C) no additional substantial payment is required if such individual or individual's spouse requires increased personal care services or long-term and skilled nursing care.

(4) Qualified continuing care facility.—

(A) In general.—For purposes of this section, the term "qualified continuing care facility" means 1 or more facilities—

(i) which are designed to provide services under continuing care contracts, and

---

*Editorial comment: The indexed amount for 2006 is $163,300. If new section 7872(h) applies, section 7872(g) will no longer apply. New section 7872(h) does not have a dollar limit. So after 2006 the IRS will no longer issue an indexed amount for the $90,000 amount in section 7872(g)(2).

(ii) substantially all of the residents of which are covered by continuing care contracts.

(B) Substantially all facilities must be owned or operated by borrower.—A facility shall not be treated as a qualified continuing care facility unless substantially all facilities which are used to provide services which are required to be provided under a continuing care contract are owned or operated by the borrower.

(C) Nursing homes excluded.—The term "qualified continuing care facility" shall not include any facility which is of a type which is traditionally considered a nursing home.

(5) Adjustment of limit for inflation.—

(A) In general.—In the case of any loan made during any calendar year after 1986 to which paragraph (1) applies, the dollar amount in paragraph (2) shall be increased by the inflation adjustment for such calendar year. Any increase under the preceding sentence shall be rounded to the nearest multiple of $100 (or, if such increase is a multiple of $50, such increase shall be increased to the nearest multiple of $100).

(B) Inflation adjustment.—For purposes of subparagraph (A), the inflation adjustment for any calendar year is the percentage (if any) by which—

(i) the CPI for the preceding calendar year exceeds

(ii) the CPI for calendar year 1985.

For purposes of the preceding sentence, the CPI for any calendar year is the average of the Consumer Price Index as of the close of the 12-month period ending on September 30 of such calendar year.

(6) Suspension of application.—Paragraph (1) shall not apply for any calendar year to which subsection (h) applies.

(h) Exception for loans to qualified continuing care facilities.—

(1) In general.—This section shall not apply for any calendar year to any below-market loan owed by a facility which on the last day of such year is a qualified continuing care facility, if such loan was made pursuant to a continuing care contract and if the lender (or the lender's spouse) attains age 62 before the close of such year.

(2) Continuing care contract.—For purposes of this section, the term "continuing care contract" means a written contract between an individual and a qualified continuing care facility under which—

(A) the individual or individual's spouse may use a qualified continuing care facility for their life or lives,

(B) the individual or individual's spouse will be provided with housing, as appropriate for the health of such individual or individual's spouse—

(i) in an independent living unit (which has additional available facilities outside such unit for the provision of meals and other personal care), and

(ii) in an assisted living facility or a nursing facility, as is available in the continuing care facility, and

(C) the individual or individual's spouse will be provided assisted living or nursing care as the health of such individual or individual's spouse requires, and as is available in the continuing care facility.

The Secretary shall issue guidance which limits such term to contracts which provide only facilities, care, and services described in this paragraph.

(3) Qualified continuing care facility.—

(A) In general.—For purposes of this section, the term "qualified continuing care facility" means 1 or more facilities—

(i) which are designed to provide services under continuing care contracts,

(ii) which include an independent living unit, plus an assisted living or nursing facility, or both, and

(iii) substantially all of the independent living unit residents of which are covered by continuing care contracts.

(B) Nursing homes excluded.—The term "qualified continuing care facility" shall not include any facility which is of a type which is traditionally considered a nursing home.

(i) Regulations.—

(1) In general.—The Secretary shall prescribe such regulations as may be necessary or appropriate to carry out the purposes of this section, including—

(A) regulations providing that where, by reason of varying rates of interest, conditional interest payments, waivers of interest, disposition of the lender's or borrower's interest in the loan, or other circumstances, the provisions of this section do not carry out the purposes of this section, adjustments to the provisions of this section will be made to the extent necessary to carry out the purposes of this section,

(B) regulations for the purpose of assuring that the positions of the borrower and lender are consistent as to the application (or nonapplication) of this section, and

(C) regulations exempting from the application of this section any class of transactions the interest arrangements of which have no significant effect on any Federal tax liability of the lender or the borrower.

(2) Estate tax coordination.—Under regulations prescribed by the Secretary, any loan which is made with donative intent and which is a term loan shall be taken into account for purposes of chapter 11 in a manner consistent with the provisions of subsection (b).

* * *

SUBTITLE G—THE JOINT COMMITTEE ON TAXATION*

SUBTITLE H—FINANCING OF PRESIDENTIAL ELECTION CAMPAIGNS*

SUBTITLE I—TRUST FUND CODE*

*Omitted.

FEDERAL
TAX REGULATIONS

TITLE 26—INTERNAL REVENUE, 1986

CODE OF FEDERAL REGULATIONS

Chapter 1—Internal Revenue Service, Department of the Treasury

Subchapter A—Income Tax

Part 1. Income Tax; Taxable Years Beginning after December 31, 1953

*Omitted.

INCOME TAX REGULATIONS

*Omitted.

*Omitted.

Subchapter B—Estate and Gift Taxes

Part 20. Estate Tax; Estates of Decedents Dying after August 16, 1954

Part 25. Gift Tax; Gifts Made after December 31, 1954

Subchapter C—Employment Taxes

Subchapter F—Procedure and Administration

Part 301. Procedure and Administration

Subchapter H—Internal Revenue Practice

*Omitted.

PART 1—INCOME TAX; TAXABLE YEARS BEGINNING AFTER DECEMBER 31, 1953

* * *

NORMAL TAXES AND SURTAXES

DETERMINATION OF TAX LIABILITY

Tax on Individuals

* * *

§ 1.1(i)–1T Questions and answers relating to the tax on unearned income certain minor children (temporary).

In General

Q–1. To whom does section 1(i)* apply?

A–1. Section 1(i)* applies to any child who is under 14** years of age at the close of the taxable year, who has at least one living parent at the close of the taxable year, and who recognizes over $1,000 of unearned income during the taxable year.

Q–2. What is the effective date of section 1(i)?*

A–2. Section 1(i)* applies to taxable years of the child beginning after December 31, 1986.

Computation of Tax

Q–3. What is the amount of tax imposed by section 1 on a child to whom section 1(i)* applies?

A–3. In the case of a child to whom section 1(i)* applies, the amount of tax imposed by section 1 equals the greater of (A) the tax imposed by section 1 without regard to section 1(i)* or (B) the sum of the tax that would be imposed by section 1 if the child's taxable income was reduced by the child's net unearned income, plus the child's share of the allocable parental tax.

Q–4. What is the allocable parental tax?

A–4. The allocable parental tax is the excess of (A) the tax that would be imposed by section 1 on the sum of the parent's taxable income plus the net unearned income of all children of such parent to whom section 1(i)* applies, over (B) the tax imposed by section 1 on the parent's taxable income. Thus, the allocable parental tax is not computed with reference to unearned income of a child over 14** or a child under 14** with less than $1,000 of unearned income. See A–10 through A–13 for rules regarding the determination of the parent(s) whose taxable income is taken into account under section 1(i).* See A–14 for rules regarding the determination of children of the parent whose net unearned income is taken into account under section 1(i).*

Q–5. What is the child's share of the allocable parental tax?

A–5. The child's share of the allocable parental tax is an amount that bears the same ratio to the total allocable parental tax as the child's net unearned income bears to the total net unearned income of all children of such parent to whom section 1(i)* applies. See A-14.

Example (1). During 1988, D, and a 12-year-old, receives $5,000 of unearned income and no earned income. D has no itemized deductions and is not eligible for a personal exemption. D's parents have two other children, E, a 15 year old, and F, a 10 year old. E has $10,000 of unearned income and F has $100 of unearned income. D's parents file a joint return for 1988 and report taxable income of $70,000. Neither D's nor his parent's taxable income is attributable to net capital gain. D's tax liability for 1988, determined without regard to section l(i), * is $675 on $4,500 of taxable income ($5,000 less $500 allowable standard deduction). In applying section 1(i), D's tax would be equal to the sum of (A) the tax that would be imposed on D's taxable income if it were reduced by any net unearned income, plus (B) D's share of the allocable parental tax. Only D's unearned income is taken into account in determining the allocable parental tax because E is over 14** and F has less than $1,000 of unearned income. See A–4. D's net unearned income is $4,000 ($4,500 taxable unearned income less $500). The tax imposed on D's taxable income as reduced by

*Editorial comment: The Regulations do not reflect the numbering change made by the Revenue Reconciliation Act of 1990. The reference now should be Sec. 1(g).

**Editorial comment: The Regulations do not reflect the effect of the Small Business and Work Opportunity Tax Act of 2007 which increased the age 14 provision to age 19 (age 24 if a full-time student).

D's net unearned income is $75 ($500 × 15%). The allocable parental tax is $1,225, the excess of $16,957.50 (the tax on $74,000, the parent's taxable income plus D's net unearned income) over $15,732.50 (the tax on $70,000, the parent's taxable income). See A–4. Thus, D's tax under section 1(i)(1)(B)* is $1,300 ($1,225 + $75). Since this amount is greater than the amount of D's tax liability as determined without regard to section 1(i),* the amount of tax imposed on D for 1988 is $1,300. See A–3.

Example (2). H and W have 3 children, A, B, and C, who are all under 14** years of age. For the taxable year 1988, H and W file a joint return and report taxable income of $129,750. The tax imposed by section 1 on H and W is $35,355. A has $5,000 of net unearned income and B and C each have $2,500 of net unearned income during 1988. The allocable parental tax imposed on A, B, and C's combined net unearned income of $10,000 is $3,300. This tax is the excess of $38,655, which is the tax imposed by section 1 on $139,750 ($129,750 + 10,000), over $35,355 (the tax imposed by section 1 on H and W's taxable income of $129,750). See A–4. Each child's share of the allocable parental tax is an amount that bears the same ratio to the total allocable parental tax as the child's net unearned income bears to the total net unearned income of A, B, and C. Thus, A's share of the allocable parental tax is $1,650 (5,000 ÷ 10,000 × 3,300) and B and C's share of the tax is $825 (2,500 ÷ 10,000 × 3,300) each. See A–5.

Definition of Net Unearned Income

Q–6. What is net unearned income?

A–6. Net unearned income is the excess of the portion of adjusted gross income for the taxable year that is not "earned income" as defined in section 911(d)(2) (income that is not attributable to wages, salaries, or other amounts received as compensation for personal services), over the sum of the standard deduction amount provided for under section 63(c)(5)(A) ($500 for 1987 and 1988; adjusted for inflation thereafter), plus the greater of (A) $500 (adjusted for inflation after 1988) or (B) the amount of allowable itemized deductions that are directly connected with the production of unearned income. A child's net unearned income for any taxable year shall not exceed the child's taxable income for such year.

Example (3). A is a child who is under 14** years of age at the end of the taxable year 1987. Both of A's parents are alive at this time. During 1987, A receives $3,000 of interest from a bank savings account and earns $1,000 from a paper route and performing odd jobs. A has no itemized deductions for 1987. A's standard deduction is $1,000, which is an amount equal to A's earned income for 1987. Of this amount, $500 is applied against A's unearned income and the remaining $500 is applied against A's earned income. Thus, A's $500 of taxable earned income ($1,000 less the remaining $500 of the standard deduction) is taxed without regard to section 1 (i)*; A has $2,500 of taxable unearned income ($3,000 gross unearned income less $500 of the standard deduction) of which $500 is taxed without regard to section 1(i).* The remaining $2,000 of taxable unearned income is A's net unearned income and is taxed under section l(i).*

Example (4). B is a child who is subject to tax under section 1(i).* B has $400 of earned income and $2,000 of unearned income. B has itemized deductions of $800 (net of the 2 percent of adjusted gross income (AGI) floor on miscellaneous itemized deductions under section 67) of which $200 are directly connected with the production of unearned income. The amount of itemized deductions that B may apply against unearned income is equal to the greater of $500 or the deductions directly connected with the production of unearned income. See A–6. Thus, $500 of B's itemized deductions are applied against the $2,000 of unearned income and the remaining $300 of deductions are applied against earned income. As a result, B has taxable earned income of $100 and taxable unearned income of $1,500. Of these amounts, all of the earned income and $500 of the unearned income are taxed without regard to section l(i).* The remaining $1,000 of unearned income is net unearned income and is taxed under section 1(i).*

Unearned Income Subject to Tax Under Section 1(i)*

Q–7. Will a child be subject to tax under section 1(i)* on net unearned income (as defined in section 1(i)* (4) and A–6 of this section) that is attributable to property transferred to the child prior to 1987?

A–7. Yes. The tax imposed by section l(i)* on a child's net unearned income applies to any net unearned income of the child for taxable years beginning after December 31, 1986, regardless of when the underlying assets were transferred to the child.

Q–8. Will a child be subject to tax under section 1(i)* on net unearned income that is attributable to gifts from persons other than the child's parents or attributable to assets resulting from the child's earned income?

A–8. Yes. The tax imposed by section 1(i)* applies to all net unearned income of the child, regardless of the source of the assets that produced such income. Thus, the rules of section 1(i)* apply to income attributable to gifts not only from the parents but also from any other source, such as the child's grandparents. section 1(i)* also applies to unearned income derived with respect to assets resulting from earned income of the child, such as interest earned on bank deposits.

Example (5). A is a child who is under 14** years of age at the end of the taxable year beginning on January 1, 1987. Both of A's

*Editorial comment: The Regulations do not reflect the numbering change made by the Revenue Reconciliation Act of 1990. The reference now should be Sec. 1(g).

**Editorial comment: The Regulations do not reflect the effect of the Small Business and Work Opportunity Tax Act of 2007 which increased the age 14 provision to age 19 (age 24 if a full-time student).

parents are alive at the end of the taxable year. During 1987, A receives $2,000 in interest from his bank account and $1,500 from a paper route. Some of the interest earned by A from the bank account is attributable to A's paper route earnings that were deposited in the account. The balance of the account is attributable to cash gifts from A's parents and grandparents and interest earned prior to 1987. Some cash gifts were received by A prior to 1987. A has no itemized deductions and is eligible to be claimed as a dependent on his parent's return. Therefore, for the taxable year 1987, A's standard deduction is $1,500, the amount of A's earned income. Of this standard deduction amount, $500 is allocated against unearned income and $1,000 is allocated against earned income. A's taxable unearned income is $1,500 of which $500 is taxed without regard to section 1(i).* The remaining taxable unearned income of $1,000 is net unearned income and is taxed under section 1(i).* The fact that some of A's unearned income is attributable to interest on principal created by earned income and gifts from persons other than A's parents or that some of the unearned income is attributable to property transferred to A prior to 1987, will not affect the tax treatment of this income under section 1(i).* See A–8.

Q–9. For purposes of section 1(i), does income which is not earned income (as defined in section 911(d)(2)) include social security benefits or pension benefits that are paid to the child?

A–9. Yes. For purposes of section 1(i), earned income (as defined in section 911(d)(2)) does not include any social security or pension benefits paid to the child. Thus, such amounts are included in unearned income to the extent they are includible in the child's gross income.

Determination of the Parent's Taxable Income

Q–10. If a child's parents file a joint return, what is the taxable income that must be taken into account by the child in determining tax liability under section 1(i)?*

A–10. In the case of parents who file a joint return, the parental taxable income to be taken into account in determining the tax liability of a child is the total taxable income shown on the joint return.

Q–11. If a child's parents are married and file separate tax returns, which parent's taxable income must be taken into account by the child in determining tax liability under section 1(i)?*

A–11. For purposes of determining the tax liability of a child under section 1(i)* where such child's parents are married and file separate tax returns, the parent whose taxable income is the greater of the two for the taxable year shall be taken into account.

*Editorial comment: The Regulations do not reflect the numbering change made by the Revenue Reconciliation Act of 1990. The reference now should be Sec. 1(g).

Q–12. If the parents of a child are divorced, legally separated, or treated as not married under section 7703(b), which parent's taxable income is taken into account in computing the child's tax liability?

A–12. If the child's parents are divorced, legally separated, or treated as not married under section 7703(b), the taxable income of the custodial parent (within the meaning of section 152(e)) of the child is taken into account under section 1(i)* in determining the child's tax liability.

Q–13. If a parent whose taxable income must be taken into account in determining a child's tax liability under section 1(i)* files a joint return with a spouse who is not a parent of the child, what taxable income must the child take into account?

A–13. The amount of a parent's taxable income that a child must take into account for purposes of section 1(i)* where the parent files a joint return with a spouse who is not a parent of the child is the total taxable income shown on such joint return.

Children of the Parent

Q–14. In determining a child's share of the allocable parental tax, is the net unearned income of legally adopted children, children related to such child by half-blood, or children from a prior marriage of the spouse of such child's parent taken into account in addition to the natural children of such child's parent?

A–14. Yes. In determining a child's share of the allocable parental tax, the net unearned income of all children subject to tax under section l(i)* and who use the same parent's taxable income as such child to determine their tax liability under section 1(i)* must be taken into account. Such children are taken into account regardless of whether they are adopted by the parent, related to such child by half-blood, or are children from a prior marriage of the spouse of such child's parent.

Rules Regarding Income From a Trust or Similar Instrument

Q–15. Will the unearned income of a child who is subject to section 1(i)* that is attributable to gifts given to the child under the Uniform Gift to Minors Act (UGMA) be subject to tax under section 1(i)?*

A–15. Yes. A gift under the UGMA vests legal title to the property in the child although an adult custodian is given certain rights to deal with the property until the child attains majority. Any unearned income attributable to such a gift is the child's unearned income and is subject to tax under section 1(i),* whether distributed to the child or not.

Q–16. Will a child who is a beneficiary of a trust be required to take into account the income of a trust in determining the child's tax liability under section 1(i)?*

A–16. The income of a trust must be taken into account for purposes of determining the tax liability of a beneficiary who is subject to section 1(i)* only to the extent it is included in the child's gross income for the taxable year under sections 652(a) or 662(a). Thus, income from a trust for the fiscal taxable year of a trust ending during 1987, that is included in the gross income of a child who is subject to section 1(i)* and who has a calendar taxable year, will be subject to tax under section 1(i)* for the child's 1987 taxable year.

Subsequent Adjustments

Q–17. What effect will a subsequent adjustment to a parent's taxable income have on the child's tax liability if such parent's taxable income was used to determine the child's tax liability under section 1(i)* for the same taxable year?

A–17. If the parent's taxable income is adjusted and if, for the same taxable year as the adjustment, the child paid tax determined under section 1(i)* with reference to that parent's taxable income, then the child's tax liability under section 1(i)* must be recomputed using the parent's taxable income as adjusted.

Q–18. In the case where more than one child who is subject to section 1(i)* uses the same parent's taxable income to determine their allocable parental tax, what effect will a subsequent adjustment to the net unearned income of one child have on the other child's share of the allocable parental tax?

A–18. If, for the same taxable year, more than one child uses the same parent's taxable income to determine their share of the allocable parental tax and a subsequent adjustment is made to one or more of such children's net unearned income, each child's share of the allocable parental tax must be recomputed using the combined net unearned income of all such children as adjusted.

Q–19. If a recomputation of a child's tax under section 1(i),* as a result of an adjustment to the taxable income of the child's parents or another child's net unearned income, results in additional tax being imposed by section 1(i)* on the child, is, the child subject to interest and penalties on such additional tax?

A–19. Any additional tax resulting from an adjustment to the taxable income of the child's parents or the net unearned income of another child shall be treated as an underpayment of tax and interest shall be imposed on such underpayment as provided in section 6601. However, the child shall not be liable for any penalties on the underpayment resulting from additional tax being imposed under section 1(i)* due to such an adjustment.

Example (6). D and M are the parents of C, a child under the age of 14.** D and M file a joint return for 1988 and report taxable income of $69,900. C has unearned income of $3,000 and no itemized deductions for 1988. C properly reports a total tax liability of $635 for 1988. This amount is the sum of the allocable parental tax of $560 on C's net unearned income of $2,000 (the excess of $3,000 over the sum of $500 standard deduction and the first $500 of taxable unearned income) plus $75 (the tax imposed on C's first $500 of taxable unearned income). See A–3. One year later, D and M's 1988 tax return is adjusted on audit by adding an additional $1,000 of taxable income. No adjustment is made to the amount reported as C's net unearned income for 1988. However, the adjustment to D and M's taxable income causes C's tax liability under section 1(i)* for 1988 to be increased by $50 as a result of the phase-out of the 15 percent rate bracket. See A–20. In addition to this further tax liability, C will be liable for interest on the $50. However, C will not have to pay any penalty on the delinquent amount.

Miscellaneous Rules

Q–20. Does the phase-out of the parent's 15 percent rate bracket and personal exemptions under section 1(g),*** if applicable, have any effect on the calculation of the allocable parental tax imposed on a child's net unearned income under section 1(i)?*

*Editorial comment: The Regulations do not reflect the numbering change made by the Revenue Reconciliation Act of 1990. The reference now should be Sec. 1(g).

**Editorial comment: The Regulations do not reflect the effect of the Small Business and Work Opportunity Tax Act of 2007 which increased the age 14 provision to age 19 (age 24 if a full-time student).

***Editorial comment: The Regulations do not reflect the repeal of the phase-out of the 15 percent tax bracket by the Revenue Reconciliation Act of 1990. In addition, RRA of 1990 relocated the phase-out of the personal and dependency exemption deductions from Sec. 1(g) to Sec. 151(d)(3). The Regulations do not reflect the effect of the Revenue Reconciliation Act of 1990 which provides for the phase out of the personal exemption and dependency deductions. RRA of 1990 relocated the phaseout. The Regulations do not reflect the repeal of the phaseout of the personal exemption and dependency deductions (which begins in 2006 and is completed in 2010) by the Tax Relief Reconciliation Act of 2001. So commencing in 2010, the full amount of the personal exemption and dependency deduction was available without reduction. The Regulations do not reflect the reinstatement of the phaseout for personal exemption and dependency deductions by the American Taxpayer Relief Act of 2012.

A–20. Yes. Any phase-out of the parent's 15 percent rate bracket or personal exemptions under section 1(g)* is given full effect in determining the tax that would be imposed on the sum of the parent's taxable income and the total net unearned income of all children of the parent. Thus, any additional tax on a child's net unearned income resulting from the phase-out of the 15 percent rate bracket and the personal exemptions is reflected in the tax liability of the child.

Q–21. For purposes of calculating a parent's tax liability or the allocable parental tax imposed on a child, are other phase-outs, limitations, or floors on deductions or credits, such as the phase-out of the $25,000 passive loss allowance for rental real estate activities under section 469(i)(3) or the 2 percent of AGI floor on miscellaneous itemized deductions under section 67, affected by the addition of a child's net unearned income to the parent's taxable income?

A–21. No. A child's net unearned income is not taken into account in computing any deduction or credit for purposes of determining the parent's tax liability or the child's allocable parental tax. Thus, for example, although the amounts allowable to the parent as a charitable contribution deduction, medical expense deduction, section 212 deduction, or a miscelaneous itemized deduction are affected by the amount of the parent's adjusted gross income, the amount of these deductions that is allowed does not change as a result of the application of section 1(i)** because the amount of the parent's adjusted gross income does not include the child's net unearned income. Similarly, the amount of itemized deductions that is allowed to a child does not change as a result of section 1(i)** because section 1(i) ** only affects the amount of tax liability and not the child's adjusted gross income.

Q–22. If a child is unable to obtain information concerning the tax return of the child's parents directly from such parents, how may the child obtain information from the parent's tax return which is necessary to determine the child's tax liability under section 1(i)?**

A–22. Under section 6103(e)(l)(A)(iv), a return of a parent shall, upon written request be open to inspection or disclosure to a child of that individual (or the child's legal representative) to the extent necessary to comply with section 1(i).** Thus, a child may request the Internal Revenue Service to disclose sufficient tax information about the parent to the child so that the child can properly file his or her return.

* * *

§ 1.2–2 Definitions and special rules.

(a) Surviving spouse. **(1)** If a taxpayer is eligible to file a joint return under the Internal Revenue Code of 1954 without regard to section 6013(a)(3) thereof for the taxable year in which his spouse dies, his return for each of the next 2 taxable years following the year of the death of the spouse shall be treated as a joint return for all purposes if all three of the following requirements are satisfied:

(i) He has not remarried before the close of the taxable year the return for which is sought to be treated as a joint return, and

(ii) He maintains as his home a household which constitutes for the taxable year the principal place of abode as a member of such household of a person who is (whether by blood or adoption) a son, stepson, daughter, or stepdaughter of the taxpayer, and

(iii) He is entitled for the taxable year to a deduction under section 151 (relating to deductions for dependents) with respect to such son, stepson, daughter, or stepdaughter.

(2) See paragraphs (c)(1) and (d) of this section for rules for the determination of when the taxpayer maintains as his home a household which constitutes for the taxable year the principal place of abode, as a member of such household, of another person.

(3) If the taxpayer does not qualify as a surviving spouse he may nevertheless qualify as a head of a household if he meets the requirements of § 1.2–2(b).

(4) The following example illustrates the provisions relating to a surviving spouse:

Example: Assume that the taxpayer meets the requirements of this paragraph for the years 1967 through 1971, and that the

*Editorial comment: The Regulations do not reflect the repeal of the phase-out of the 15 percent tax bracket by the Revenue Reconciliation Act of 1990. In addition, RRA of 1990 relocated the phase-out of the personal and dependency exemption deductions from Sec. 1(g) to Sec. 151(d)(3). The Regulations do not reflect the effect of the Revenue Reconciliation Act of 1990 which provides for the phase out of the personal exemption and dependency deductions. RRA of 1990 relocated the phaseout. The Regulations do not reflect the repeal of the phaseout of the personal exemption and dependency deductions (which begins in 2006 and is completed in 2010) by the Tax Relief Reconciliation Act of 2001. So commencing in 2010, the full amount of the personal exemption and dependency deduction is available without reduction. The Regulations do not reflect the reinstatement of the phaseout for personal exemption and dependency deductions by the American Taxpayer Relief Act of 2012.

**Editorial comment: The Regulations do not reflect the numbering change made by the Revenue Reconciliation Act of 1990. The reference now should be Sec. 1(g).

taxpayer, whose wife died during 1966 while married to him, remarried in 1968. In 1969, the taxpayer's second wife died while married to him, and he remained single thereafter. For 1967 the taxpayer will qualify as a surviving spouse, provided that neither the taxpayer nor the first wife was a nonresident alien at any time during 1966 and that she (immediately prior to her death) did not have a taxable year different from that of the taxpayer. For 1968 the taxpayer does not qualify as a surviving spouse because he remarried before the close of the taxable year. The taxpayer will qualify as a surviving spouse for 1970 and 1971, provided that neither the taxpayer nor the second wife was a nonresident alien at any time during 1969 and that she (immediately prior to her death) did not have a taxable year different from that of the taxpayer. On the other hand, if the taxpayer, in 1969, was divorced or legally separated from his second wife, the taxpayer will not qualify as a surviving spouse for 1970 or 1971, since he could not have filed a joint return for 1969 (the year in which his second wife died).

(b) Head of household. (1) A taxpayer shall be considered the head of a household if, and only if, he is not married at the close of his taxable year, is not a surviving spouse (as defined in paragraph (a) of this section, and (i) maintains as his home a household which constitutes for such taxable year the principal place of abode, as a member of such household, of at least one of the individuals described in subparagraph (3), or (ii) maintains (whether or not as his home) a household which constitutes for such taxable year the principal place of abode of one of the individuals described in subparagraph (4).

(2) Under no circumstances shall the same person be used to qualify more than one taxpayer as the head of a household for the same taxable year.

(3) Any of the following persons may qualify the taxpayer as a head of a household:

*__(i)__ A son, stepson, daughter, or stepdaughter of the taxpayer, or a descendant of a son or daughter of the taxpayer. For the purpose of determining whether any of the stated relationships exist, a legally adopted child of a person is considered a child of such person by blood. If any such person is not married at the close of the taxable year of the taxpayer, the taxpayer may qualify as the head of a household by reason of such person even though the taxpayer may not claim a deduction for such person under section 151, for example, because the taxpayer does not furnish more than half of the support of such person. However, if any such person is married at the close of the taxable year of the taxpayer, the taxpayer may qualify as the head of a household by reason of such person only if the taxpayer is entitled to a deduction for such person under section 151 and the regulations thereunder. In applying the preceding sentence there shall be disregarded any such person for whom a deduction is allowed under section 151 only by reason of section 152(c) (relating to persons covered by a multiple support agreement).

(ii) Any other person who is a dependent of the taxpayer, if the taxpayer is entitled to a deduction for the taxable year for such person under section 151 and paragraphs (3) through (8) of section 152(a) and the regulations thereunder. Under section 151 the taxpayer may be entitled to a deduction for any of the following persons:

(a) His brother, sister, stepbrother, or stepsister;

(b) His father or mother, or an ancestor of either;

(c) His stepfather or stepmother;

(d) A son or a daughter of his brother or sister;

(e) A brother or sister of his father or mother; or

(f) His son-in-law, daughter-in-law, father-in-law, mother-in-law, brother-in-law, or sister-in-law;

if such person has a gross income of less than the amount determined pursuant to § 1.151–2 applicable to the calendar year in which the taxable year of the taxpayer begins, if the taxpayer supplies more than one-half of the support of such person for such calendar year and if such person does not make a joint return with his spouse for the taxable year beginning in such calendar year. The taxpayer may not be considered to be a head of a household by reason of any person for whom a deduction is allowed under section 151 only by reason of sections 152(a)(9), 152(a)(10), or 152(c) (relating to persons not related to the taxpayer, persons receiving institutional care, and persons covered by multiple support agreements).

(4) The father or mother of the taxpayer may qualify the taxpayer as a head of a household, but only if the taxpayer is entitled to a deduction for the taxable year for such father or mother under section 151 (determined without regard to section 152(c)). For example, an unmarried taxpayer who maintains a home for his widowed mother may not qualify as the head of a household by reason of his maintenance of a home for his mother if his mother has gross income equal to or in excess of the amount determined pursuant to § 1.151–2 applicable to the calendar year in which the taxable year of the taxpayer begins, or if he does not furnish more than one-half of the support of his mother for such calendar year. For this purpose, a person who legally adopted the taxpayer is considered the father or mother of the taxpayer.

*Editorial comment: The Regulations do not reflect the change made by the Working Families Tax Relief Act of 2004 which now requires dependency status for a child in order to qualify for head of household status.

(5) For the purpose of this paragraph, the status of the taxpayer shall be determined as of the close of the taxpayer's taxable year. A taxpayer shall be considered as not married if at the close of his taxable year he is legally separated from his spouse under a decree of divorce or separate maintenance, or if at any time during the taxable year the spouse to whom the taxpayer is married at the close of his taxable year was a nonresident alien. A taxpayer shall be considered married at the close of his taxable year if his spouse (other than a spouse who is a nonresident alien) dies during such year.

(6) If the taxpayer is a nonresident alien during any part of the taxable year he may not qualify as a head of a household even though he may comply with the other provisions of this paragraph. See the regulations prescribed under section 871 for a definition of nonresident alien.

(c) Household. (1) In order for a taxpayer to be considered as maintaining a household by reason of any individual described in paragraph (a)(1) or (b)(3) of this section, the household must actually constitute the home of the taxpayer for his taxable year. A physical change in the location of such home will not prevent a taxpayer from qualifying as a head of a household. Such home must also constitute the principal place of abode of at least one of the persons specified in such paragraph (a)(1) or (b)(3) of this section. It is not sufficient that the taxpayer maintain the household without being its occupant. The taxpayer and such other person must occupy the household for the entire taxable year of the taxpayer. However, the fact that such other person is born or dies within the taxable year will not prevent the taxpayer from qualifying as a head of household if the household constitutes the principal place of abode of such other person for the remaining or preceding part of such taxable year. The taxpayer and such other person will be considered as occupying the house-hold for such entire taxable year notwithstanding temporary absences from the household due to special circumstances. A nonpermanent failure to occupy the common abode by reason of illness, education, business, vacation, military service, or a custody agreement under which a child or stepchild is absent for less than 6 months in the taxable year of the taxpayer, shall be considered temporary absence due to special circumstances. Such absence will not prevent the taxpayer from being considered as maintaining a household if **(i)** it is reasonable to assume that the taxpayer or such other person will return to the household, and **(ii)** the taxpayer continues to maintain such household or a substantially equivalent household in anticipation of such return.

(2) In order for a taxpayer to be considered as maintaining a household by reason of any individual described in paragraph (b)(4) of this section, the household must actually constitute the principal place of abode of the taxpayer's dependent father or mother, or both of them. It is not, however, necessary for the purposes of such subparagraph for the taxpayer also to reside in such place of abode. A physical change in the location of such home will not prevent a taxpayer from qualifying as a head of a household. The father or mother of the taxpayer, however, must occupy the household for the entire taxable year of the taxpayer. They will be considered as occupying the household for such entire year notwithstanding temporary absences from the household due to special circumstances. For example, a nonpermanent failure to occupy the household by reason of illness or vacation shall be considered temporary absence due to special circumstances. Such absence will not prevent the taxpayer from qualifying as the head of a household if (i) it is reasonable to assume that such person will return to the household, and (ii) the taxpayer continues to maintain such household or a substantially equivalent household in anticipation of such return. However, the fact that the father or mother of the taxpayer dies within the year will not prevent the taxpayer from qualifying as a head of a household if the household constitutes the principal place of abode of the father or mother for the preceding part of such taxable year.

(d) Cost of maintaining a household. A taxpayer shall be considered as maintaining a household only if he pays more than one-half the cost thereof for his taxable year. The cost of maintaining a household shall be the expenses incurred for the mutual benefit of the occupants thereof by reason of its operation as the principal place of abode of such occupants for such taxable year. The cost of maintaining a household shall not include expenses otherwise incurred. The expenses of maintaining a household include property taxes, mortgage interest, rent, utility charges, upkeep and repairs, property insurance, and food consumed on the premises. Such expenses do not include the cost of clothing, education, medical treatment, vacations, life insurance, and transportation. In addition, the cost of maintaining a household shall not include any amount which represents the value of services rendered in the household by the taxpayer or by a person qualifying the taxpayer as a head of a household or as a surviving spouse.

(e) Certain married individuals living apart. For taxable years beginning after December 31, 1969, an individual who is considered as not married under section 143(b) shall be considered as not married for purposes of determining whether he or she qualifies as a single individual, a married individual, a head of household or a surviving spouse under sections 1 and 2 of the Code.

* * *

Credits Against Tax

Credits Allowable

§ 1.25–1T Credit for interest paid on certain home mortgages (temporary).

(a) In general. Section 25 permits States and political subdivisions to elect to issue mortgage credit certificates in lieu of qualified mortgage bonds. An individual who holds a qualified mortgage credit certificate (as defined in § 1.25–3T) is entitled to a credit against his Federal income taxes. The amount of the credit depends upon (1) the amount of mortgage interest paid or accrued during the year and (2) the applicable certificate credit rate. See § 1.25–2T. The amount of the deduction under section 163 for interest paid or accrued during any taxable year is reduced by the amount of the credit allowable under section 25 for such year. See § 1.163–6T. The holder of a qualified mortgage credit certificate may be entitled to additional withholding allowances. See section 3402(m) and the regulations thereunder.

(b) Definitions. For purposes of §§ 1.25–2T through 1.25–8T and this section, the following definitions apply:

(1) Mortgage. The term "mortgage" includes deeds of trust, conditional sales contracts, pledges, agreements to hold title in escrow, and any other form of owner financing.

(2) State. **(i)** The term "State" includes a possession of the United States and the District of Columbia.

(ii) Mortgage credit certificates issued by or on behalf of any State or political subdivision ("governmental unit") by constituted authorities empowered to issue such certificates are the certificates of such governmental unit.

(3) Qualified home improvement loan. The term "qualified home improvement loan" has the meaning given that term under section 103A(1)(6) and the regulations thereunder.

(4) Qualified rehabilitation loan. The term "qualified rehabilitation loan" has the meaning given that term under section 103A(l)(7)(A) and the regulations thereunder.

(5) Single-family and owner-occupied residences. The terms "single-family" and "owneroccupied" have the meaning given those terms under section 103A(1)(9) and the regulations thereunder.

(6) Constitutional home rule city. The term "constitutional home rule city" means, with respect to any calendar year, any political subdivision of a State which, under a State constitution which was adopted in 1970 and effective on July 1, 1971, had home rule powers on the 1st day of the calendar year.

(7) Targeted area residence. The term "targeted area residence" has the meaning given that term under section 103A(k) and the regulations thereunder.

(8) Acquisition cost. The term "acquisition cost" has the meaning given that term under section 103A(1)(5) and the regulations thereunder.

(9) Average area purchase price. The term "average area purchase price" has the meaning given that term under subparagraphs (2), (3), and (4) of section 103A(f) and the regulations thereunder. For purposes of this paragraph (b)(9), all determinations of average area purchase price shall be made with respect to residences as that term is defined in section 103A and the regulations thereunder.

(10) Total proceeds. The "total proceeds" of an issue is the sum of the products determined by multiplying—

(i) The certified indebtedness amount of each mortgage credit certificate issued pursuant to such issue, by

(ii) The certificate credit rate specified in such certificate.

Each qualified mortgage credit certificate program shall be treated as a separate issue of mortgage credit certificates.

(11) Residence. The term "residence" includes stock held by a tenant-stockholder in a cooperative housing corporation (as those terms are defined in section 216(b)(1) and (2)). It does not include property such as an appliance, a piece of furniture, a radio, *etc.*, which, under applicable local law, is not a fixture. The term also includes any manufactured home which has a minimum of 400 square feet of living space and a minimum width in excess of 102 inches and which is of a kind customarily used at a fixed location. The preceding sentence shall not apply for purposes of determining the average area purchase price for single-family residences, nor shall it apply for purposes of determining the State ceiling amount. The term "residence" does not, however, include recreational vehicles, campers, and other similar vehicles.

(12) Related person. The term "related person" has the meaning given that term under section 103(b)(6)(C)(i) and § 1.103–10(e)(1).

(13) Date of issue. A mortgage credit certificate is considered issued on the date on which a closing agreement is signed with respect to the certified indebtedness amount.

(c) Affidavits. For purposes of §§ 1.25–1T through 1.25–8T, an affidavit filed in connection with the requirements of §§ 1.25–1T through 1.25–8T shall be made under penalties of perjury. Applicants for mortgage credit certificates who are required by a lender or the issuer to sign affidavits must be informed that any fraudulent statement will result in (1) the revocation of the individual's mortgage credit certificate, and (2) a $10,000 penalty under section 6709. Other persons required by a lender or an issuer to provide affidavits must receive similar notice. A person may not rely on an affidavit where that person knows or has reason to know that the information contained in the affidavit is false.

§ 1.25–2T Amount of credit (temporary).

(a) In general. Except as otherwise provided, the amount of the credit allowable for any taxable year to an individual who holds a qualified mortgage credit certificate is equal to the product of the certificate credit rate (as defined in paragraph (b)) and the amount of the interest paid or accrued by the taxpayer during the taxable year on the certified indebtedness amount (as defined in paragraph (c)).

(b) Certificate credit rate— (1) In general. For purposes of §§ 1.25–1T through 1.25–8T, the term "certificate credit rate" means the rate specified by the issuer on the mortgage credit certificate. The certificate credit rate shall not be less than 10 percent nor more than 50 percent.

(2) Limitation in certain States. **(i)** In the case of a State which— **(A)** Has a State ceiling for the calendar year in which an election is made that exceeds 20 percent of the average annual aggregate principal amount of mortgages executed during the immediately preceding 3 calendar years for single-family owner-occupied residences located within the jurisdiction of such State, or

(B) Issued qualified mortgage bonds in an aggregate amount less than $150 million for calendar year 1983.

the certificate credit rate for any mortgage credit certificate issued under such program shall not exceed 20 percent unless the issuing authority submits a plan to the Commissioner to ensure that the weighted average of the certificate credit rates in such mortgage credit certificate program does not exceed 20 percent and the Commissioner approves such plan. For purposes of determining the average annual aggregate principal amount of mortgages executed during the immediately preceding 3 calendar years for single family owner-occupied residences located within the jurisdiction of such State, an issuer may rely upon the amount published by the Treasury Department for such calendar years. An issuer may rely on a different amount from that safe-harbor limitation where the issuer has made a more accurate and comprehensive determination of that amount. The weighted average of the certificate credit rates in a mortgage credit certificate program is determined by dividing the sum of the products obtained by multiplying the certificate credit rate of each certificate by the certified indebtedness amount with respect to that certificate by the sum of the certified indebtedness amounts of the certificates issued. See section 103A(g) and the regulations thereunder for the definition of the term "State ceiling".

(ii) The following example illustrates the application of this paragraph (b)(2):

Example. City Z issues four qualified mortgage credit certificates pursuant to its qualified mortgage credit certificate program. H receives a certificate with a certificate credit rate of 30 percent and a certified indebtedness amount of $50,000. I receives a certificate with a certificate credit rate of 25 percent and a certified indebtedness amount of $100,000. J and K each receive certificates with certificate credit rates of 10 percent; their certified indebtedness amounts are $50,000 and $100,000, respectively. The weighted average of the certificate credit rates is determined by dividing the sum of the products obtained by multiplying the certificate credit rate of each certificate by the certified indebtedness amount with respect to that certificate ((.3 × $50,000) + (.25 × $100,000) + (.1 × $50,000) + (.1 × $100,000)) by the sum of the certified indebtedness amounts of the certificates issued ($50,000 + $100,000 + $50,000 + $100,000). Thus, the weighted average of the certificate credit rates is 18.33 percent ($55,000/$300,000).

(c) Certified indebtedness amount—(1) In general. The term "certified indebtedness amount" means the amount of indebtedness which is—

(i) Incurred by the taxpayer—

(A) To acquire his principal residence, § 1.25–2T(c)(1)(i)

(B) As a qualified home improvement loan, or

(C) As a qualified rehabilitation loan, and

(ii) Specified in the mortgage credit certificate.

(2) Example. The following example illustrates the application of this paragraph:

Example. On March 1, 1986, State X, pursuant to its qualified mortgage credit certificate program, provides a mortgage credit certificate to B. State X specifies that the maximum amount of the mortgage loan for which B may claim a credit is $65,000. On March 15, B purchases for $67,000 a single-family dwelling for use as his principal residence. B obtains from Bank M a mortgage loan for $60,000. State X, or Bank M acting on behalf of State X, indicates on B's mortgage credit certificate that the certified indebtedness amount of B's loan is $60,000. B may claim a credit under section 25(e) based on this amount.

(d) Limitation on credit— (1) Limitation where certificate credit rate exceeds 20 percent. **(i)** If the certificate credit rate of any mortgage credit certificate exceeds 20 percent, the allowed to the taxpayer by section 25(a)(1) for any year shall not exceed $2,000. Any amount denied under this paragraph (d)(1) may not be carried forward under section 25(e)(1) and paragraph (d)(2) of this section.

(ii) If two or more persons hold interests in any residence, the limitation of paragraph (d)(l)(i) shall be allocated among such persons in proportion to their respective interests in the residence.

(2) Carryforward of unused credit. **(i)** If the credit allowable under section 25(a) and § 1.25–2T for any taxable year exceeds the applicable tax limit for that year, the excess (the "unused credit") will be a carryover to each of the 3 succeeding taxable years and, subject to the limitations of paragraph (d)(2)(ii), will be added to the credit allowable by section 25(a) and § 1.25–2T for that succeeding year.

(ii) The amount of the unused credit for any taxable year (the "unused credit year") which may be taken into account under this paragraph (d)(2) for any subsequent taxable year may not exceed the amount by which the applicable tax limit for that subsequent taxable year exceeds the sum of (A) the amount of the credit allowable under section 25(a) and § 1.25–1T for the current taxable year, and (B) the sum of the unused credits which, by reason of this paragraph (d)(2), are carried to that subsequent taxable year and are attributable to taxable years before the unused credit year. Thus, if by reason of this paragraph (d)(2), unused credits from 2 prior taxable years are carried forward to a subsequent taxable year, the unused credit from the earlier of those 2 prior years must be taken into account before the unused credit from the later of those 2 years is taken into account.

(iii) For purposes of this paragraph (d)(2) the term "applicable tax limit" means the limitation imposed by section 26(a) for the taxable year reduced by the sum of the credits allowable for that year under section 21, relating to expenses for household and dependent care services necessary for gainful employment, section 22, relating to the credit for the elderly and the permanently disabled, section 23, relating to the residential energy credit, and section 24, relating to contributions to candidates for public office. The limitation imposed by section 26(a) for any taxable year is equal to the taxpayer's tax liability (as defined in section 26(b)) for that year.

(iv) The following examples illustrate the application of this paragraph (d)(2):

Example (1). (i) B, a calendar year taxpayer, holds a qualified mortgage credit certificate. For 1986 B's applicable tax limit (*i.e.,* tax liability) is $1,100. The amount of the credit under section 25(a) and § 1.25–2T for 1986 is $1,700. For 1986 B is not entitled to any of the credits described in sections 21 through 24. Under § 1.25–2T(d)(2), B's unused credit for 1986 is $600, and B is entitled to carry forward that amount to the 3 succeeding years.

(ii) For 1987 B's applicable tax limit is $1,500, the amount of the credit under section 25(a) and § 1.25–2T is $1,700, and the unused credit is $200. For 1988 B's applicable tax limit is $2,000, the amount of the credit under section 25(a) and § 1.25–2T is $1,300, and there is no unused credit. For 1987 and 1988 B is not entitled to any of the credits described in sections 21 through 24. No portion of the unused credit for 1986 may be used in 1987. For 1988 B is entitled to claim a credit of $2,000 under section 25(a) and § 1.25–2T, consisting of a $1,300 credit for 1988, the $600 unused credit for 1986, and $100 of the $200 unused credit for 1987. In addition, B may carry forward the remaining unused credit for 1987 ($100) to 1989 and 1990.

Example (2). The facts are the same as in Example (1) except that for 1988 B is entitled to a credit of $400 under section 23. B's applicable tax limit for 1988 is $1,600 ($2,000 less $400). For 1988 B is entitled to claim a credit of $1,600 under section 25(a) and § 1.25–2T, consisting of a $1,300 credit for 1988 and $300 of the unused credit for 1986. In addition, B may carry forward the remaining unused credits of $300 for 1986 to 1989 and of $200 for 1987 to 1989 and 1990.

* * *

COMPUTATION OF TAXABLE INCOME

Definition of Gross Income, Adjusted Gross Income, and Taxable Income

§ 1.61–1 Gross income.

(a) General definition. Gross income means all income from whatever source derived, unless excluded by law. Gross income includes income realized in any form, whether in money, property, or services. Income may be realized, therefore, in the form of services, meals, accommodations, stock, or other property, as well as in cash. Section 61 lists the more common items of gross income for purposes of illustration. For purposes of further illustration, § 1.61–14 mentions several miscellaneous items of gross income not listed specifically in section 61. Gross income, however, is not limited to the items so enumerated.

(b) Cross references. Cross references to other provisions of the Code are to be found throughout the regulations under section 61. The purpose of these cross references is to direct attention to the more common items which are included in or excluded from gross income entirely, or treated in some special manner. To the extent that another section of the Code or of the regulations thereunder, provides specific treatment for any item of income, such other provision shall apply notwithstanding section 61 and the regulations thereunder. The cross references do not cover all possible items.

* * *

§ 1.61–2 Compensation for services, including fees, commissions, and similar items.

(a) In general. (1) Wages, salaries, commissions paid salesmen, compensation for services on the basis of a percentage of profits, commissions on insurance premiums, tips, bonuses (including Christmas bonuses), termination or severance pay, rewards, jury fees, marriage fees and other contributions received by a clergyman for services, pay of persons in the military or naval forces of the United States, retired pay of employees, pensions, and retirement allowances are income to the recipients unless excluded by law.* * *

(c) Payment to charitable, etc., organization on behalf of person rendering services. The value of services is not includible in gross income when such services are rendered directly and gratuitously to an organization described in section 170(c). Where, however, pursuant to an agreement or understanding, services are rendered to a person for the benefit of an organization described in section 170(c) and an amount for such services is paid to such organization by the person to whom the services are rendered, the amount so paid constitutes income to the person performing the services.

(d) Compensation paid other than in cash—(1) In general. Except as otherwise provided in paragraph (d)(6)(i) of this section (relating to certain property transferred after June 30, 1969), if services are paid for in property, the fair market value of the property taken in payment must be included in income as compensation. If services are paid for in exchange for other services, the fair market value of such other services taken in payment must be included in income as compensation. If the services are rendered at a stipulated price, such price will be presumed to be the fair market value of the compensation received in the absence of evidence to the contrary.* * *

(3) Meals and living quarters. The value of living quarters or meals which an employee receives in addition to his salary constitutes gross income unless they are furnished for the convenience of the employer and meet the conditions specified in section 119 and the regulations thereunder. For the treatment of rental value of parsonages or rental allowance paid to ministers, see section 107 and the regulations thereunder;* * *

* * *

§ 1.61–3 Gross income derived from business.

(a) In general. In a manufacturing, merchandising, or mining business, "gross income" means the total sales, less the cost of goods sold, plus any income from investments and from incidental or outside operations or sources. Gross income is determined without subtraction of depletion allowances based on a percentage of income to the extent that it exceeds cost depletion which may be required to be included in the amount of inventoriable costs as provided in § 1.471–11 and without subtraction of selling expenses, losses or other items not ordinarily used in computing costs of goods sold or amounts which are of a type for which a deduction would be disallowed under section 162(c), (f), or (g) in the case of a business expense. The cost of goods sold should be determined in accordance with the method of accounting consistently used by the taxpayer. Thus, for example, an amount cannot be taken into account in the computation of cost of goods sold any earlier than the taxable year in which economic performance occurs with respect to the amount [see § 1.446–1(c)(1)(ii)].

* * *

§ 1.61–6 Gains derived from dealings in property.

(a) In general. Gain realized on the sale or exchange of property is included in gross income, unless excluded by law. For this purpose property includes tangible items, such as a building, and intangible items, such as goodwill. Generally, the gain is the excess of the amount realized over the unrecovered cost or other basis for the property sold or exchanged. The specific rules for computing the amount of gain or loss are contained in section 1001 and the regulations thereunder. When a part of a larger property is sold, the cost or other basis of the entire property shall be equitably apportioned among the several parts, and the gain realized or loss sustained on the part of the entire property sold is the difference between the selling price and the cost or other basis allocated to such part. The sale of each part is treated as a separate transaction and gain or loss shall be computed separately on each part. Thus, gain or loss shall be determined at the time of sale of each part and not deferred until the entire property has been disposed of. This rule may be illustrated by the following examples:

Example (1). A, a dealer in real estate, acquires a 10-acre tract for $10,000, which he divides into 20 lots. The $10,000 cost must be equitably apportioned among the lots so that on the sale of each A can determine his taxable gain or deductible loss.

Example (2). B purchases for $25,000 property consisting of a used car lot and adjoining filling station. At the time, the fair market value of the filling station is $15,000 and the fair market value of the used car lot is $10,000. Five years later B sells the filling station for $20,000 at a time when $2,000 has been properly allowed as depreciation thereon. B's gain on this sale is $7,000, since $7,000 is the amount by which the selling price of the filling station exceeds the portion of the cost equitably allocable to the filling station at the time of purchase reduced by the depreciation properly allowed.

(b) Nontaxable exchanges. Certain realized gains or losses on the sale or exchange of property are not "recognized", that is, are not included in or deducted from gross income at the time the transaction occurs. Gain or loss from such sales or exchanges is generally recognized at some later time. Examples of such sales or exchanges are the following:

(1) Certain formations, reorganizations, and liquidations of corporations, see sections 331, 333, 337, 351, 354, 355, and 361;

(2) Certain formations and distributions of partnerships, see sections 721 and 731;

(3) Exchange of certain property held for productive use or investment for property of like kind, see section 1031;

(4) A corporation's exchange of its stock for property, see section 1032;

(5) Certain involuntary conversions of property if replaced, see section 1033;

(6) Sale or exchange of residence if replaced, see section 1034;

(7) Certain exchanges of insurance policies and annuity contracts, see section 1035; and

(8) Certain exchanges of stock for stock in the same corporation, see section 1036.

* * *

§ 1.61–7 Interest.

(a) In general. As a general rule, interest received by or credited to the taxpayer constitutes gross income and is fully taxable. Interest income includes interest on savings or other bank deposits; interest on coupon bonds; interest on an open account, a promissory note, a mortgage, or a corporate bond or debenture; the interest portion of a condemnation award; usurious interest (unless by State law it is automatically converted to a payment on the principal); interest on legacies; interest on life insurance proceeds held under an agreement to pay interest thereon; and interest on refunds of Federal taxes. For rules determining the taxable year in which interest, including interest accrued or constructively received, is included in gross income, see section 451 and the regulations thereunder.* * *

(b) Interest on Government obligations— (1) Wholly tax-exempt interest. Interest upon the obligations of a State, Territory, or a possession of the United States, or any political subdivision of any of the foregoing, or of the District of Columbia, is wholly exempt from tax. Interest on certain United States obligations issued before March 1, 1941, is exempt from tax to the extent provided in the acts of Congress authorizing the various issues. See section 103 and the regulations thereunder.

* * *

(3) **Fully taxable interest.** In general, interest on United States obligations issued on or after March 1, 1941, and obligations issued by any agency or instrumentality of the United States after that date, is fully taxable; but see section 103 and the regulations thereunder. A taxpayer using the cash receipts and disbursements method of accounting who owns United States savings bonds issued at a discount has an election as to when he will report the interest; see section 454 and the regulations thereunder.

(c) Obligations bought at a discount; bonds bought when interest defaulted or accrued. When notes, bonds, or other certificates of indebtedness are issued by a corporation or the Government at a discount and are later redeemed by the debtor at the face amount, the original discount is interest, except as otherwise provided by law. See also paragraph (b) of this section for the rules relating to Government bonds. If a taxpayer purchases bonds when interest has been defaulted or when the interest has accrued but has not been paid, any interest which is in arrears but has accrued at the time of purchase is not income and is not taxable as interest if subsequently paid. Such payments are returns of capital which reduce the remaining cost basis. Interest which accrues after the date of purchase, however, is taxable interest income for the year in which received or accrued (depending on the method of accounting used by the taxpayer).

* * *

§ 1.61–8 Rents and royalties.

(a) In general. Gross income includes rentals received or accrued for the occupancy of real estate or the use of personal property. * * * Gross income includes royalties. Royalties may be received from books, stories, plays, copyrights, trademarks, formulas, patents, and from the exploitation of natural resources, such as coal, gas, oil, copper, or timber. Payments received as a result of the transfer of patent rights may under some circumstances constitute capital gain instead of ordinary income. See section 1235 and the regulations thereunder. For special rules for certain income from natural resources, see subchapter I (section 611 and following), chapter 1 of the Code, and the regulations thereunder.

(b) Advance rentals; cancellation payments. Except as provided in section 467 and the regulations thereunder and except as otherwise provided by the Commissioner in published guidance (see § 601.601(d)(2) of this chapter), gross income includes advance rentals, which must be included in income for the year of receipt regardless of the period covered or the method of accounting employed. An amount received by a lessor from a lessee for cancelling a lease constitutes gross income for the year in which it is received, since it is essentially a substitute for rental payments. As to amounts received by a lessee for the cancellation of a lease, see section 1241 and the regulations thereunder.

(c) Expenditures by lessee. As a general rule, if a lessee pays any of the expenses of his lessor such payments are additional rental income of the lessor. If a lessee places improvements on real estate which constitute, in whole or in part, a substitute for rent, such improvements constitute rental income to the lessor. Whether or not improvements made by a lessee result in rental income to the lessor in a particular case depends upon the intention of the parties, which may be indicated either by the terms of the lease or by the surrounding circumstances. For the exclusion from gross income of income (other than rent) derived by a lessor of real property on the termination of a lease, representing the value of such property attributable to buildings erected or other improvements made by a lessee, see section 109 and the regulations thereunder.* * *

§ 1.61–9 Dividends.

(a) In general. Except as otherwise specifically provided, dividends are included in gross income under sections 61 and 301. For the principal rules with respect to dividends includible in gross income, see section 316 and the regulations thereunder. * * *

(b) Dividends in kind; stock dividends; stock redemptions. Gross income includes dividends in property other than cash, as well as cash dividends. For amounts to be included in gross income when distributions of property are made, see section 301 and the regulations thereunder. A distribution of stock, or rights to acquire stock, in the corporation making the distribution is not a dividend except under the circumstances described in section 305(b). However, the term "dividend" includes a distribution of stock, or rights to acquire stock, in a corporation other than the corporation making the distribution. * * * For rules determining when amounts received in exchanges under section 354 or exchanges and distributions under section 355 shall be treated as dividends, see section 356 and the regulations thereunder.

(c) Dividends on stock sold. When stock is sold, and a dividend is both declared and paid after the sale, such dividend is not gross income to the seller. When stock is sold after the declaration of a dividend and after the date as of which the seller becomes entitled to the dividend, the dividend ordinarily is income to the seller. When stock is sold between the time of declaration and the time of payment of the dividend, and the sale takes place at such time that the purchaser becomes entitled to the dividend, the dividend ordinarily is income to him. The fact that the purchaser may have included the amount of the dividend in his purchase price in contemplation of receiving the dividend does not exempt him from tax. Nor can the purchaser deduct the added amount he advanced to the seller in anticipation of the dividend. That added amount is merely part of the purchase price of the stock. In some cases, however, the purchaser may be considered to be the recipient of the dividend even though he has not received the legal title to the stock itself and does not himself receive the dividend. For example, if the seller retains the legal title to the stock as trustee solely for the purpose of securing the payment of the purchase price, with the understanding that he is to apply the dividends received from time to time in reduction of the purchase price, the dividends are considered to be income to the purchaser.

§ 1.61–10 Alimony and separate maintenance payments; annuities; income from life insurance and endowment contracts.

(a) In general. Alimony and separate maintenance payments, annuities, and income from life insurance and endowment contracts in general constitute gross income, unless excluded by law. Annuities paid by religious, charitable, and educational corporations are generally taxable to the same extent as other annuities.* * *

(b) Cross references. For the detailed rules relating to—

(1) Alimony and separate maintenance payments, see section 71 and the regulations thereunder;

(2) Annuities, certain proceeds of endowment and life insurance contracts, see section 72 and the regulations thereunder;

(3) Life insurance proceeds paid by reason of death of insured, employees' death benefits, see section 101 and the regulations thereunder;

(4) Annuities paid by employees' trusts, see section 402 and the regulations thereunder;

(5) Annuities purchased for employee by employer, see section 403 and the regulations thereunder.

§ 1.61–11 Pensions.

(a) In general. Pensions and retirement allowances paid either by the Government or by private persons constitute gross income unless excluded by law. Usually, where the taxpayer did not contribute to the cost of a pension and was not taxable on his employer's contributions, the full amount of the pension is to be included in his gross income. But see sections 72, 402, and 403, and the regulations thereunder. When amounts are received from other types of pensions, a portion of the payment may be excluded from gross income. Under some circumstances, amounts distributed from a pension plan in excess of the employee's contributions may constitute long-term capital gain, rather than ordinary income.

* * *

§ 1.61–12 Income from discharge of indebtedness.

(a) In general. The discharge of indebtedness, in whole or in part, may result in the realization of income. If, for example, an individual performs services for a creditor, who in consideration thereof cancels the debt, the debtor realizes income in the amount of the debt as compensation for his services. A taxpayer may realize income by the payment or purchase of his obligations at less than their face value. In general, if a shareholder in a corporation which is indebted to him gratuitously forgives the debt, the transaction amounts to a contribution to the capital of the corporation to the extent of the principal of the debt.

* * *

§ 1.61–13 Distributive share of partnership gross income; income in respect of a decedent; income from an interest in an estate or trust.

(a) In general. A partner's distributive share of partnership gross income (under section 702(c)) constitutes gross income to him. Income in respect of a decedent (under section 691) constitutes gross income to the recipient. Income from an interest in an estate or trust constitutes gross income under the detailed rules of part I (section 641 and following), subchapter J, chapter 1 of the Code. In many cases, these sections also determine who is to include in his gross income the income from an estate or trust.

* * *

§ 1.61–14 Miscellaneous items of gross income.

(a) In general. In addition to the items enumerated in section 61(a), there are many other kinds of gross income. For example, punitive damages such as treble damages under the antitrust laws and exemplary damages for fraud are gross income. Another person's payment of the taxpayer's income taxes constitutes gross income to the taxpayer unless excluded by law. Illegal gains constitute gross income. Treasure trove, to the extent of its value in United States currency, constitutes gross income for the taxable year in which it is reduced to undisputed possession.

* * *

§ 1.61–21 Taxation of fringe benefits

(a) Fringe benefits— (1) In general. Section 61(a)(1) provides that, except as otherwise provided in subtitle A of the Internal Revenue Code of 1986, gross income includes compensation for services, including fees, commissions, fringe benefits, and similar items. For an outline of the regulations under this section relating to fringe benefits, see paragraph (a)(7) of this section. Examples of fringe benefits include: an employer-provided automobile, a flight on an employer-provided aircraft, an employer-provided free or discounted commercial airline flight, an employer-provided vacation, an employer-provided discount on property or services, an employer-provided membership in a country club or other social club, and an employer-provided ticket to an entertainment or sporting event.

(2) Fringe benefits excluded from income. To the extent that a particular fringe benefit is specifically excluded from gross income pursuant to another section of subtitle A of the Internal Revenue Code of 1986, that section shall govern the treatment of that fringe benefit. Thus, if the requirements of the governing section are satisfied, the fringe benefits may be excludable from gross income. Examples of excludable fringe benefits include qualified tuition reductions provided to an employee (section 117(d)); meals or lodging furnished to an employee for the convenience of the employer (section 119); benefits provided under a dependent care assistance program (section 129); and no-additional-cost services, qualified employee discounts, working condition fringes, and de minimis fringes (section 132). Similarly, the value of the use by an employee of an employer-provided vehicle or a flight provided to an employee on an employer-provided aircraft may be excludable from income under section 105 (because, for example, the transportation is provided for medical reasons) if and to the extent that the requirements of that section are satisfied. Section 134 excludes from gross income "qualified military benefits." An example of a benefit that is not a qualified military benefit is the personal use of an employer-provided vehicle. The fact that another section of subtitle A of the Internal Revenue Code addresses the taxation of a particular fringe benefit will not preclude section 61 and the regulations thereunder from applying, to the extent that they are not inconsistent with such other section. For example, many fringe benefits specifically addressed in other sections of subtitle A of the Internal Revenue Code are excluded from gross income only to the extent that they do not exceed specific dollar or percentage limits, or only if certain other requirements are met. If the limits are exceeded or the requirements are not met, some or all of the fringe benefit may be includible in gross income pursuant to section 61. See paragraph (b)(3) of this section.

(3) Compensation for services. A fringe benefit provided in connection with the performance of services shall be considered to have been provided as compensation for such services. Refraining from the performance of services (such as pursuant to a covenant not to compete) is deemed to be the performance of services for purposes of this section.

(4) Person to whom fringe benefit is taxable— (i) In general. A taxable fringe benefit is included in the income of the person performing the services in connection with which the fringe benefit is furnished. Thus, a fringe benefit may be taxable to a person even though that person did not actually receive the fringe benefit. If a fringe benefit is furnished to someone other than the service provider such benefit is considered in this section as furnished to the service provider, and use by the other person is considered use by the service provider. For example, the provision of an automobile by an employer to an employee's spouse in connection with the performance of services by the employee is taxable to the employee. The automobile is considered available to the employee and use by the employee's spouse is considered use by the employee.

(ii) All persons to whom benefits are taxable referred to as employees. The person to whom a fringe benefit is taxable need not be an employee of the provider of the fringe benefit, but may be, for example, a partner, director, or an independent contractor. For convenience, the term "employee" includes any person performing services in connection with which a fringe benefit is furnished, unless otherwise specifically provided in this section.

(5) Provider of a fringe benefit referred to as an employer. The "provider" of a fringe benefit is that person for whom the services are performed, regardless of whether that person actually provides the fringe benefit to the recipient. The provider of a fringe benefit need not be the employer of the recipient of the fringe benefit, but may be, for example, a client or customer of the employer or of an independent contractor. For convenience, the term "employer" includes any provider of a fringe benefit in connection with payment for the performance of services, unless otherwise specifically provided in this section.

(6) Effective date. Except as otherwise provided, this section is effective as of January 1, 1989, with respect to fringe benefits provided after December 31, 1988.

* * *

(b) Valuation of fringe benefits—(1) In general. An employee must include in gross income the amount by which the fair market value of the fringe benefit exceeds the sum of—

(i) The amount, if any, paid for the benefit by or on behalf of the recipient, and

(ii) The amount, if any, specifically excluded from gross income by some other section of subtitle A of the Internal Revenue Code of 1986.

Therefore, for example, if the employee pays fair market value for what is received, no amount is includible in the gross income of the employee. In general, the determination of the fair market value of a fringe benefit must be made before subtracting out the amount, if any, paid for the benefit and the amount, if any, specifically excluded from gross income by another section of subtitle A. See paragraphs (d)(2)(ii) and (e)(1)(iii) of this section.

(2) Fair market value. In general, fair market value is determined on the basis of all the facts and circumstances. Specifically, the fair market value of a fringe benefit is the amount that an individual would have to pay for the particular fringe benefit in an arm's-length transaction. Thus, for example, the effect of any special relationship that may exist between the employer and the employee must be disregarded. Similarly, an employee's subjective perception of the value of a fringe benefit is not relevant to the determination of the fringe benefit's fair market value nor is the cost incurred by the employer determinative of its fair market value. For special rules relating to the valuation of certain fringe benefits, see paragraph (c) of this section.

(3) Exclusion from income based on cost. If a statutory exclusion phrased in terms of cost applies to the provision of a fringe benefit, section 61 does not require the inclusion in the recipient's gross income of the difference between the fair market value and the excludable cost of that fringe benefit. For example, section 129 provides an exclusion from an employee's gross income for amounts contributed by an employer to a dependent care assistance program for employees. Even if the fair market value of the dependent care assistance exceeds the employer's cost, the excess is not subject to inclusion under section 61 and this section. However, if the statutory cost exclusion is a limited amount, the fair market value of the fringe benefit attributable to any excess cost is subject to inclusion. This would be the case, for example, where an employer pays or incurs a cost of more than $5,000 to provide dependent care assistance to an employee.

(4) Fair market value of the availability of an employer-provided vehicle—(i) In general. If the vehicle special valuation rules of paragraph (d), (e), or (f) of this section do not apply with respect to an employer-provided vehicle, the value of the availability of that vehicle is determined under the general valuation principles set forth in this section. In general, that value equals the amount that an individual would have to pay in an arm's-length transaction to lease the same or comparable vehicle on the same or comparable conditions in the geographic area in which the vehicle is available for use. An example of a comparable condition is the amount of time that the vehicle is available to the employee for use, e.g., a one-year period. Unless the employee can substantiate that the same or comparable vehicle could have been leased on a cents-per-mile basis, the value of the availability of the vehicle cannot be computed by applying a cents-per-mile rate to the number of miles the vehicle is driven.

(ii) Certain equipment excluded. The fair market value of a vehicle does not include the fair market value of any specialized equipment not susceptible to personal use or any telephone that is added to or carried in the vehicle, provided that the presence of that equipment or telephone is necessitated by, and attributable to, the business needs of the employer. However, the value of specialized equipment must be included, if the employee to whom the vehicle is available uses the specialized equipment in a trade or business of the employee other than the employee's trade or business of being an employee of the employer.

* * *

(c) Special valuation rule—(1) In general. Paragraphs (d) through (k) of this section provide special valuation rules that may be used under certain circumstances for certain commonly provided fringe benefits. For general rules relating to the valuation of fringe benefits not eligible for valuation under the special valuation rules or fringe benefits with respect to which the special valuation rules are not used, see paragraph (b) of this section.

(2) Use of the special valuation rules—(i) For benefits provided before January 1, 1993. The special valuation rules may be used for income tax, employment tax, and reporting purposes. The employer has the option to use any of the special valuation rules. However, an employee may only use a special valuation rule if the employer uses the rule. Moreover, an employee may only use the special rule that the employer uses to value the benefit provided; the employee may not use another special rule to value that benefit. The employee may always use general valuation rules based on facts and circumstances (see paragraph (b) of this section) even if the employer uses a special rule. If a special rule is used, it must be used for all purposes. If an employer properly uses a special rule and the employee uses the special rule, the employee must include in gross income the amount determined by the employer under the special rule reduced by the sum of—

(A) Any amount reimbursed by the employee to the employer, and

(B) Any amount excludable from income under another section of subtitle A of the Internal Revenue Code of 1986. If an employer properly uses a special rule and properly determines the amount of an employee's working condition fringe under section 132 and § 1.132–5 (under the general rule or under a special rule), and the employee uses the special valuation rule, the employee must include in gross income the amount determined by the employer less any amount reimbursed by the employee to the employer. The employer and employee may use the special rules to determine the amount of the reimbursement due the employer by the employee. Thus, if an employee reimburses an employer for the value of a benefit as determined under a special valuation rule, no amount is includible in the employee's gross income with respect to the benefit. The provisions of this paragraph are effective for benefits provided before January 1, 1993.

(ii) For benefits provided after December 31, 1992. The special valuation rules may be used for income tax, employment tax, and reporting purposes. The employer has the option to use any of the special valuation rules. An employee may use a special valuation rule only if the employer uses that rule or the employer does not meet the condition of paragraph (c)(3)(ii)(A) of this section, but one of the other conditions of paragraph (c)(3)(ii) of this section is met. The employee may always use general valuation rules based on facts and circumstances (see paragraph (b) of this section) even if the employer uses a special rule. If a special rule is used, it must be used for all purposes. If an employer properly uses a special rule and the employee uses the special rule, the employee must include in gross income the amount determined by the employer under the special rule reduced by the sum of—

(A) Any amount reimbursed by the employee to the employer; and

(B) Any amount excludable from income under another section of subtitle A of the Internal Revenue Code of 1986. If an employer properly uses a special rule and properly determines the amount of an employee's working condition fringe under section 132 and § 1.132–5 (under the general rule or under a special rule), and the employee uses the special valuation rule, the employee must include in gross income the amount determined by the employer less any amount reimbursed by the employee to the employer. The employer and employee may use the special rules to determine the amount of the reimbursement due the employer by the employee. Thus, if an employee reimburses an employer for the value of a benefit as determined under a special valuation rule, no amount is includible in the employee's gross income with respect to the benefit. The provisions of this paragraph are effective for benefits provided after December 31, 1992.

* * *

(3) Additional rules for using special valuation— (i) Election to use special valuation rules for benefits provided before January 1, 1993. A particular special valuation rule is deemed to have been elected by the employer (and, if applicable, by the employee), if the employer (and, if applicable, the employee) determines the value of the fringe benefit provided by applying the special valuation rule and treats that value as the fair market value of the fringe benefit for income, employment tax, and reporting purposes. Neither the employer nor the employee must notify the Internal Revenue Service of the election. The provisions of this paragraph are effective for benefits provided before January 1, 1993.

(ii) Conditions on the use of special valuation rules for benefits provided after December 31, 1992. Neither the employer nor the employee may use a special valuation rule to value a benefit provided after December 31, 1992, unless one of the following conditions is satisfied—

(A) The employer treats the value of the benefit as wages for reporting purposes within the time for filing the returns for the taxable year (including extensions) in which the benefit is provided;

(B) The employee includes the value of the benefit in income within the time for filing the returns for the taxable year (including extensions) in which the benefit is provided;

(C) The employee is not a control employee as defined in paragraphs (f)(5) and (f)(6) of this section; or

(D) The employer demonstrates a good faith effort to treat the benefit correctly for reporting purposes.

* * *

(5) Valuation formulae contained in the special valuation rules. The valuation formula contained in the special valuation rules are provided only for use in connection with those rules. Thus, when a special valuation rule is properly applied to a fringe benefit, the Commissioner will accept the value calculated pursuant to the rule as the fair market value of that fringe benefit. However, when a special valuation rule is not properly applied to a fringe benefit (see, for example, paragraph (g)(13) of this section), or when a special valuation rule is used to value a fringe benefit by a taxpayer not entitled to use the rule, the fair market value of that fringe benefit may not be determined by reference to any value calculated under any special valuation rule. Under the circumstances described in the preceding sentence, the fair market value of the fringe benefit must be determined pursuant to the general valuation rules of paragraph (b) of this section.

(6) Modification of the special valuation rules. The Commissioner may, to the extent necessary for tax administration, add, delete, or modify any special valuation rule, including the valuation formulae contained herein, on a prospective basis by regulation, revenue ruling or revenue procedure.

* * *

§ 1.62–1T Adjusted gross income (temporary).

(a) Basis for determining the amount of certain deductions. The term "adjusted gross income" means the gross income computed under section 61 minus such of the deductions allowed by chapter 1 of the Code as are specified in section 62(a). Adjusted gross income is used as the basis for determining the following:*

(1) The limitation on the amount of miscellaneous itemized deductions (under section 67),

(2) The limitation on the amount of the deduction for casualty losses (under section 165(h)(2)),

(3) The limitation on the amount of the deduction for charitable contributions (under section 170(b)(1)),

(4) The limitation on the amount of the deduction for medical and dental expenses (under section 213),

(5) The limitation on the amount of the deduction for qualified retirement contributions for active participants in certain pension plans (under section 219(g)), and

*Editorial comment: The Regulations do not reflect the phase-out of the personal exemption and dependency deductions in Sec. 151(d)(3) or the phase-out of certain itemized deductions in Sec. 68 provided for in the Revenue Reconciliation Act of 1990. Both of these phase-outs are based on adjusted gross income. The Regulations also do not reflect the "phase-out of the phase-out" in Sec. 151(d)(3) and in Sec. 68(f) provided for in the Tax Relief Reconciliation Act of 2001. So commencing in 2010, the full amount of the personal exemption and dependency deduction is available without reduction. The Regulations do not reflect the reinstatement of the phaseout for personal exemption and dependency deductions by the American Taxpayer Relief Act of 2012. Likewise, the Regulations do not reflect the adjusted gross income ceiling on the educational savings bonds exclusion in Sec. 135 provided for in the Technical and Miscellaneous Revenue Act of 1988.

(6) The phase-out of the exemption from the disallowance of passive activity losses and credits (under section 469(i)(3)).

(b) Double deduction not permitted. Section 62(a) merely specifies which of the deductions provided in chapter 1 of the Code shall be allowed in computing adjusted gross income. It does not create any new deductions. The fact that a particular item may be described in more than one of the paragraphs under section 62(a) does not permit the item to be deducted twice in computing adjusted gross income or taxable income.

* * *

(d) Expenses directly related to a trade or business. For the purpose of the deductions specified in section 62, the performance of personal services as an employee does not constitute the carrying on of a trade or business, except as otherwise expressly provided. The practice of a profession, not as an employee, is considered the conduct of a trade or business within the meaning of such section. To be deductible for the purposes of determining adjusted gross income, expenses must be those directly, and not those merely remotely, connected with the conduct of a trade or business. For example, taxes are deductible in arriving at adjusted gross income only if they constitute expenditures directly attributable to a trade or business or to property from which rents or royalties are derived. Thus, property taxes paid or incurred on real property used in a trade or business are deductible, but state taxes on net income are not deductible even though the taxpayer's income is derived from the conduct of a trade or business.

(e) Reimbursed and unreimbursed employee expenses—(1) In general. Expenses paid or incurred by an employee that are deductible from gross income under part VI in computing taxable income (determined without regard to section 67) and for which the employee is reimbursed by the employer, its agent, or third party (for whom the employee performs a benefit as an employee of the employer) under an express agreement for reimbursement or pursuant to an express expense allowance arrangement may be deducted from gross income in computing adjusted gross income.

* * *

(g) Moving expenses.*** For taxable years beginning after December 31, 1986, a taxpayer described in section 217(a) shall not take into account the deduction described in section 217 relating to moving expenses in computing adjusted gross income under section 62 even if the taxpayer is reimbursed for his or her moving expenses. Such a taxpayer shall include the amount of any reimbursement for moving expenses in income pursuant to section 82. The deduction described in section 217 shall be taken into account in computing the taxable income of the taxpayer under section 63. Pursuant to section 67(b)(6), the 2-percent floor described in section 67(a) does not apply to moving expenses.***

* * *

§ 1.63–1 Change of treatment with respect to the zero bracket amount* and itemized deductions.

(a) In general. An individual who files a return on which the individual itemizes deductions in accordance with section 63(g)** may later make a change of treatment by recomputing taxable income for the taxable year to which that return relates without itemizing deductions. Similarly, an individual who files a return on which the individual computes taxable income without itemizing deductions may later make a change of treatment by itemizing deductions in accordance with section 63(g)** in recomputing taxable income for the taxable year to which that return relates.

(b) No extension of time for claiming credit or refund. A change of treatment described in paragraph (a) of this section does not extend the period of time prescribed in section 6511 within which the taxpayer may make a claim for credit or refund of tax.

(c) Special requirements if spouse filed separate return—(1) Requirements. If the spouse of the taxpayer filed a separate return for a taxable year corresponding to the taxable year of the taxpayer, the taxpayer may not make a change of treatment described in paragraph (a) of this section for that year unless—

(i) The spouse makes a change of treatment on the separate return consistent with the change of treatment sought by the taxpayer; and

(ii) The taxpayer and the taxpayer's spouse file a consent in writing to the assessment of any deficiency of either spouse to the extent attributable to

*Editorial comment: The Tax Reform Act of 1986 replaced the zero bracket amount with the standard deduction.

**Editorial comment: Now Sec. 63(e).

***Editorial comment: Subsequent legislation provides that moving expenses are classified as a deduction for AGI. See Sec. 62(a)(15).

the change of treatment, even though the assessment of the deficiency would otherwise be prevented by the operation of any law or rule of law. The consent must be filed with the district director for the district in which the taxpayer applies for the change of treatment, and the period during which a deficiency may be assessed shall be established by agreement of the spouses and the district director.

(2) Corresponding taxable year. A taxable year of one spouse corresponds to a taxable year of the other spouse if both taxable years end in the same calendar year. If the taxable year of one spouse ends with death, however, the corresponding taxable year of the surviving spouse is that in which the death occurs.

* * *

§ 1.67–1T 2-Percent floor on miscellaneous itemized deductions (temporary).

(a) Type of expenses subject to the floor—
(1) In general. With respect to individuals, section 67 disallows deductions for miscellaneous itemized deductions (as defined in paragraph (b) of this section) in computing taxable income (i.e., so-called "below-the-line" deductions) to the extent that such otherwise allowable deductions do not exceed 2 percent of the individual's adjusted gross income (as defined in section 62 and the regulations thereunder). Examples of expenses that, if otherwise deductible, are subject to the 2-percent floor include but are not limited to—

(i) Unreimbursed employee expenses, such as expenses for transportation, travel fares and lodging while away from home, business meals and entertainment, continuing education courses, subscriptions to professional journals, union or professional dues, professional uniforms, job hunting, and the business use of the employee's home,

(ii) Expenses for the production or collection of income for which a deduction is otherwise allowable under section 212(1) and (2), such as investment advisory fees, subscriptions to investment advisory publications, certain attorneys' fees, and the cost of safe deposit boxes,

(iii) Expenses for the determination of any tax for which a deduction is otherwise allowable under section 212(3), such as tax counsel fees and appraisal fees, and

(iv) Expenses for an activity for which a deduction is otherwise allowable under section 183.

See section 62 with respect to deductions that are allowable in computing adjusted gross income (i.e., so-called "above-the-line" deductions).

(2) Other limitations. Except as otherwise provided in paragraph (d) of this section, to the extent that any limitation or restriction is placed on the amount of a miscellaneous itemized deduction, that limitation shall apply prior to the application of the 2-percent floor. For example, in the case of an expense for food or beverages, only 80 percent* of which is allowable as a deduction because of the limitations provided in section 274(n), the otherwise deductible 80 percent* of the expense is treated as a miscellaneous itemized deduction and is subject to the 2-percent limitation of section 67.

* * *

Items Specifically Included in Gross Income

* * *

§ 1.71–1T Alimony and separate maintenance payments (temporary).

(a) In general.

Q–1. What is the income tax treatment of alimony or separate maintenance payments?

A–1. Alimony or separate maintenance payments are, under section 71, included in the gross income of the payee spouse and, under section 215, allowed as a deduction from the gross income of the payor spouse.

Q–2. What is an alimony or separate maintenance payment?

A–2. An alimony or separate maintenance payment is any payment received by or on behalf of a spouse

*Editorial comment: The Regulations do not reflect the effect of the Revenue Reconciliation Act of 1993 which changed the 80% to 50%.

(which for this purpose includes a former spouse) of the payor under a divorce or separation instrument that meets all of the following requirements:

(a) The payment is in cash (see A–5).

(b) The payment is not designated as a payment which is excludable from the gross income of the payee and nondeductible by the payor (see A–8).

(c) In the case of spouses legally separated under a decree of divorce or separate maintenance, the spouses are not members of the same household at the time the payment is made (see A–9).

(d) The payor has no liability to continue to make any payment after the death of the payee (or to make any payment as a substitute for such payment)* * * (see A–10).

(e) The payment is not treated as child support (see A–15).

* * *

Q–3. In order to be treated as alimony or separate maintenance payments, must the payments be "periodic" as that term was defined prior to enactment of the Tax Reform Act of 1984 or be made in discharge of a legal obligation of the payor to support the payee arising out of a marital or family relationship?

A–3. No. The Tax Reform Act of 1984 replaces the old requirements with the requirements described in A–2 above. Thus, the requirements that alimony or separate maintenance payments be "periodic" and be made in discharge of a legal obligation to support arising out of a marital or family relationship have been eliminated.

Q–4. Are the instruments described in section 71(a) of prior law the same as divorce or separation instruments described in section 71, as amended by the Tax Reform Act of 1984?

A–4. Yes.

(b) Specific requirements.

Q–5. May alimony or separate maintenance payments be made in a form other than cash?

A–5. No. Only cash payments (including checks and money orders payable on demand) qualify as alimony or separate maintenance payments. Transfers of services or property (including a debt instrument of a third party or an annuity contract), execution of a debt instrument by the payor, or the use of property of the payor do not qualify as alimony or separate maintenance payments.

Q–6. May payments of cash to a third party on behalf of a spouse qualify as alimony or separate maintenance payments if the payments are pursuant to the terms of a divorce or separation instrument?

A–6. Yes. Assuming all other requirements are satisfied, a payment of cash by the payor spouse to a third party under the terms of the divorce or separation instrument will qualify as a payment of cash which is received "on behalf of a spouse". For example, cash payments of rent, mortgage, tax, or tuition liabilities of the payee spouse made under the terms of the divorce or separation instrument will qualify as alimony or separate maintenance payments. Any payments to maintain property owned by the payor spouse and used by the payee spouse (including mortgage payments, real estate taxes and insurance premiums) are not payments on behalf of a spouse even if those payments are made pursuant to the terms of the divorce or separation instrument. Premiums paid by the payor spouse for term or whole life insurance on the payor's life made under the terms of the divorce or separation instrument will qualify as payments on behalf of the payee spouse to the extent that the payee spouse is the owner of the policy.

Q–7. May payments of cash to a third party on behalf of a spouse qualify as alimony or separate maintenance payments if the payments are made to the third party at the written request of the payee spouse?

A–7. Yes. For example, instead of making an alimony or separate maintenance payment directly to the payee, the payor spouse may make a cash payment to a charitable organization if such payment is pursuant to the written request, consent or ratification of the payee spouse. Such request, consent or ratification must state that the parties intend the payment to be treated as an alimony or separate maintenance payment to the payee spouse subject to the rules of section 71, and must be received by the payor spouse prior to the date of filing of the payor's first return of tax for the taxable year in which the payment was made.

Q–8. How may spouses designate that payments otherwise qualifying as alimony or separate maintenance payments shall be excludable from the gross income of the payee and nondeductible by the payor?

A–8. The spouses may designate that payments otherwise qualifying as alimony or separate maintenance payments shall be nondeductible by the payor and excludable from gross income by the payee by so providing in a divorce or separation instrument (as defined in section 71(b)(2)). If the spouses have executed a written separation agreement (as described in section 71(b)(2)(B)), any writing signed by both spouses which designates otherwise qualifying alimony or separate maintenance payments as nondeductible and excludable and which refers to the written separation agreement will be treated as a written separation agreement (and thus a divorce or separation instrument) for purposes of the preceding sentence. If the spouses are subject to temporary support orders (as described in section 71(b)(2)(C), the designation of otherwise qualifying alimony or separate payments as nondeductible and excludable must be made in the original or a subsequent temporary support order. A copy of the instrument containing the designation of payments as not alimony or separate maintenance payments must be attached to the payee's first filed return of tax (Form 1040) for each year in which the designation applies.

Q–9. What are the consequences if, at the time a payment is made, the payor and payee spouses are members of the same household?

A–9. Generally, a payment made at the time when the payor and payee spouses are members of the same household cannot qualify as an alimony or separate maintenance payment if the spouses are legally separated under a decree of divorce or of separate maintenance. For purposes of the preceding sentence, a dwelling unit formerly shared by both spouses shall not be considered two separate households even if the spouses physically separate themselves within the dwelling unit. The spouses will not be treated as members of the same household if one spouse is preparing to depart from the household of the other spouse, and does depart not more than one month after the date the payment is made. If the spouses are not legally separated under a decree of divorce or separate maintenance, a payment under a written separation agreement or a decree described in section 71(b)(2)(C) may qualify as an alimony or separate maintenance payment notwithstanding that the payor and payee are members of the same household at the time the payment is made.

Q–10. Assuming all other requirements relating to the qualification of certain payments as alimony or separate maintenance payments are met, what are the consequences if the payor spouse is required to continue to make the payments after the death of the payee spouse?

A–10. None of the payments before (or after) the death of the payee spouse qualify as alimony or separate maintenance payments.

* * *

Q–13. What are the consequences if the payor spouse is required to make one or more payments (in cash or property) after the death of the payee spouse as a substitute for the continuation of pre-death payments which would otherwise qualify as alimony or separate maintenance payments?

A–13. If the payor spouse is required to make any such substitute payments, none of the otherwise qualifying payments will qualify as alimony or separate maintenance payments. The divorce or separation instrument need not state, however, that there is no liability to make any such substitute payment.

Q–14. Under what circumstances will one or more payments (in cash or property) which are to occur after the death of the payee spouse be treated as a substitute for the continuation of payments which would otherwise qualify as alimony or separate maintenance payments?

A–14. To the extent that one or more payments are to begin to be made, increase in amount, or become accelerated in time as a result of the death of the payee spouse, such payments may be treated as a substitute for the continuation of payments terminating on the death of the payee spouse which would otherwise qualify as alimony or separate maintenance payments. The determination of whether or not such payments are a substitute for the continuation of payments which would otherwise qualify as alimony or separate maintenance payments, and of the amount of the otherwise qualifying alimony or separate maintenance payments for which any such payments are a substitute, will depend on all of the facts and circumstances.

Example (1). Under the terms of a divorce decree, A is obligated to make annual alimony payments to B of $30,000, terminating on the earlier of the expiration of 6 years or the death of B. B maintains custody of the minor children of A and B. The decree provides that at the death of B, if there are minor children of A and B remaining, A will be obligated to make annual payments of $10,000 to a trust, the income and corpus of which are to be used for the benefit of the children until the youngest child attains the age of majority. These facts indicate that A's liability to make annual $10,000 payments in trust for the benefit of his minor children upon the death of B is a substitute for $10,000 of the $30,000 annual payments to B. Accordingly, $10,000 of each of the $30,000 annual payments to B will not qualify as alimony or separate maintenance payments.

Example (2). Under the terms of a divorce decree, A is obligated to make annual alimony payments to B of $30,000, terminating on the earlier of the expiration of 15 years or the death of B. The divorce decree provides that if B dies before the expiration of the 15 year period, A will pay to B's estate the difference between the total amount that A would have paid had B survived, minus the amount actually paid. For example, if B dies at the end of the 10th year in which payments are made, A will pay to

B's estate $150,000 ($450,000–$300,000). These facts indicate that A's liability to make a lump sum payment to B's estate upon the death of B is a substitute for the full amount of each of the annual $30,000 payments to B. Accordingly, none of the annual $30,000 payments to B will qualify as alimony or separate maintenance payments. The result would be the same if the lump sum payable at B's death were discounted by an appropriate interest factor to account for the prepayment.

(c) Child support payments.

Q–15. What are the consequences of a payment which the terms of the divorce or separation instrument fix as payable for the support of a child of the payor spouse?

A–15. A payment which under the terms of the divorce or separation instrument is fixed (or treated as fixed) as payable for the support of a child of the payor spouse does not qualify as an alimony or separate maintenance payment. Thus, such a payment is not deductible by the payor spouse or includible in the income of the payee spouse.

Q–16. When is a payment fixed (or treated as fixed) as payable for the support of a child of the payor spouse?

A–16. A payment is fixed as payable for the support of a child of the payor spouse if the divorce or separation instrument specifically designates some sum or portion (which sum or portion may fluctuate) as payable for the support of a child of the payor spouse. A payment will be treated as fixed as payable for the support of a child of the payor spouse if the payment is reduced (a) on the happening of a contingency relating to a child of the payor, or (b) at a time which can clearly be associated with such a contingency. A payment may be treated as fixed as payable for the support of a child of the payor spouse even if other separate payments specifically are designated as payable for the support of a child of the payor spouse.

Q–17. When does a contingency relate to a child of the payor?

A–17. For this purpose, a contingency relates to a child of the payor if it depends on any event relating to that child, regardless of whether such event is certain or likely to occur. Events that relate to a child of the payor include the following: the child's attaining a specified age or income level, dying, marrying, leaving school, leaving the spouse's household, or gaining employment.

Q–18. When will a payment be treated as to be reduced at a time which can clearly be associated with the happening of a contingency relating to a child of the payor?

A–18. There are two situations, described below, in which payments which would otherwise qualify as alimony or separate maintenance payments will be presumed to be reduced at a time clearly associated with the happening of a contingency relating to a child of the payor. In all other situations, reductions in payments will not be treated as clearly associated with the happening of a contingency relating to a child of the payor.

The first situation referred to above is where the payments are to be reduced not more than 6 months before or after the date the child is to attain the age of 18, 21, or local age of majority. The second situation is where the payments are to be reduced on two or more occasions which occur not more than one year before or after a different child of the payor spouse attains a certain age between the ages of 18 and 24, inclusive. The certain age referred to in the preceding sentence must be the same for each such child, but need not be a whole number of years.

The presumption in the two situations described above that payments are to be reduced at a time clearly associated with the happening of a contingency relating to a child of the payor may be rebutted (either by the Service or by taxpayers) by showing that the time at which the payments are to be reduced was determined independently of any contingencies relating to the children of the payor. The presumption in the first situation will be rebutted conclusively if the reduction is a complete cessation of alimony or separate maintenance payments during the sixth post-separation year (described in A-21) or upon the expiration of a 72-month period. The presumption may also be rebutted in other circumstances, for example, by showing that alimony payments are to be made for a period customarily provided in the local jurisdiction, such as a period equal to one-half the duration of the marriage.

Example: A and B are divorced on July 1, 1985, when their children, C (born July 15, 1970) and D (born September 23, 1972), are 14 and 12, respectively. Under the divorce decree, A is to make alimony payments to B of $2,000 per month. Such payments are to be reduced to $1,500 per month on January 1, 1991 and to $1,000 per month on January 1, 1995. On January 1, 1991, the date of the first reduction in payments, C will be 20 years 5 months and 17 days old. On January 1, 1995, the date of the second reduction in payments, D will be 22 years 3 months and 9 days old. Each of the reductions in payments is to occur not more than one year before or after a different child of A attains the age of 21 years and 4 months. (Actually, the reductions are to occur not more than one year before or after C and D attain any of the ages 21 years 3 months and 9 days through 21 years 5 months and 17 days). Accordingly, the reductions will be presumed to clearly be associated with the happening of a contingency relating to C and D. Unless this presumption is rebutted, payments under the divorce decree equal to the sum of the reduction ($1,000 per month) will be treated as fixed for the support of the children of A and therefore will not qualify as alimony or separate maintenance payments.

(d) Excess front-loading rules.*

* * *

§ 1.72–1 Introduction.

(a) General principle. Section 72 prescribes rules relating to the inclusion in gross income of amounts received under a life insurance, endowment, or annuity contract unless such amounts are specifically excluded from gross income under other provisions of chapter 1 of the Code. In general, these rules provide that amounts subject to the provisions of section 72 are includible in the gross income of the recipient except to the extent that they are considered to represent a reduction or return of premiums or other consideration paid.

* * *

§ 1.72–3 Excludable amounts not income.

In general, amounts received under contracts described in paragraph (a)(1) of § 1.72–2 are not to be included in the income of the recipient to the extent that such amounts are excludable from gross income as the result of the application of section 72 and the regulations thereunder.

§ 1.72–4 Exclusion ratio.**

(a) General rule. (1)(i) To determine the proportionate part of the total amount received each year as an annuity which is excludable from the gross income of a recipient in the taxable year of receipt (other than amounts received under * * *(b) certain annuities described in section 72(*o*) and § 1.22–1), an exclusion ratio is to be determined for each contract. In general, this ratio is determined by dividing the investment in the contract as found under § 1.72–6 by the expected return under such contract as found under § 1.72–5. Where a single consideration is given for a particular contract which provides for two or more annuity elements, an exclusion ratio shall be determined for the contract as a whole by dividing the investment in such contract by the aggregate of the expected returns under all the annuity elements provided thereunder.* * *

(ii) The exclusion ratio for the particular contract is then applied to the total amount received as an annuity during the taxable year by each recipient.* * * Any excess of the total amount received as an annuity during the taxable year over the amount determined by the application of the exclusion ratio to such total amount shall be included in the gross income of the recipient for the taxable year of receipt.

(2) The principles of subparagraph (1) may be illustrated by the following example:

Example. Taxpayer A purchased an annuity contract providing for payments of $100 per month for a consideration of $12,650. Assuming that the expected return under this contract is $16,000, the exclusion ratio to be used by A is $12,650 ÷ $16,000; or 79.1 percent (79.06 rounded to the nearest tenth). If 12 such monthly payments are received by A during his taxable year, the total amount he may exclude from his gross income in such year is $949.20 ($1,200 × 79.1 percent). The balance of $250.80 ($1,200 less $949.20) is the amount to be included in gross income. If A instead received only five such payments during the year, he should exclude $395.50 ($500 × 79.1 percent) of the total amounts received.

* * *

§ 1.73–1 Services of child.

(a) Compensation for personal services of a child shall, regardless of the provisions of State law relating to who is entitled to the earnings of the child, and regardless of whether the income is in fact received by the child, be deemed to be the gross income of the child and not the gross income of the parent of the child. Such compensation, therefore, shall be included in the gross income of the child and shall be reflected in the return rendered by or for such child. The income of a minor child is not required to be included in the gross income of the parent for income tax purposes. For requirements for making the return by such child, or for such child by his guardian, or other person charged with the care of his person or property, see section 6012.

*Editorial comment: The Regulations do not reflect the changes made in the front-loading rules by the Tax Reform Act of 1986. See Sec. 71(f).

**Editorial comment: The Regulations do not reflect the provision for qualified employer retirement plan annuities added in the Small Business Job Protection Act of 1996. See Sec. 72(d).

(b) In the determination of taxable income or adjusted gross income, as the case may be, all expenditures made by the parent or the child attributable to amounts which are includible in the gross income of the child and not of the parent solely by reason of section 73 are deemed to have been paid or incurred by the child. In such determination, the child is entitled to take deductions not only for expenditures made on his behalf by his parent which would be commonly considered as business expenses, but also for other expenditures such as charitable contributions made by the parent in the name of the child and out of the child's earnings.

(c) For purposes of section 73, the term "parent" includes any individual who is entitled to the services of the child by reason of having parental rights and duties in respect of the child.* * *

§ 1.74–1 Prizes and awards.

(a) Inclusion in gross income. **(1)** Section 74(a) requires the inclusion in gross income of all amounts received as prizes and awards, unless such prizes or awards qualify as an exclusion from gross income under subsection (b), or unless such prize or award is a scholarship or fellowship grant excluded from gross income by section 117. Prizes and awards which are includible in gross income include (but are not limited to) amounts received from radio and television giveaway shows, door prizes, and awards in contests of all types, as well as any prizes and awards from an employer to an employee in recognition of some achievement in connection with his employment.

(2) If the prize or award is not made in money but is made in goods or services, the fair market value of the goods or services is the amount to be included in income.

(b) Exclusion from gross income.* Section 74(b) provides an exclusion from gross income of any amount received as a prize or award, if (1) such prize or award was made primarily in recognition of past achievements of the recipient in religious, charitable, scientific, educational, artistic, literary, or civic fields; (2) the recipient was selected without any action on his part to enter the contest or proceedings; and (3) the recipient is not required to render substantial future services as a condition to receiving the prize or award. Thus, such awards as the Nobel prize and the Pulitzer prize would qualify for the exclusion. Section 74(b) does not exclude prizes or awards from an employer to an employee in recognition of some achievement in connection with his employment.

(c) Scholarships and fellowship grants. See section 117 and the regulations thereunder for provisions relating to scholarships and fellowship grants.

* * *

§ 1.79–1 Group-term life insurance—general rules.

(a) What is group-term life insurance? Life insurance is not group-term life insurance for purposes of section 79 unless it meets the following conditions: **(1)** It provides a general death benefit that is excludable from gross income under section 101(a).

(2) It is provided to a group of employees.

(3) It is provided under a policy carried directly or indirectly by the employer.

(4) The amount of insurance provided to each employee is computed under a formula that precludes individual selection. This formula must be based on factors such as age, years of service, compensation, or position. This condition may be satisfied even if the amount of insurance provided is determined under a limited number of alternative schedules that are based on the amount each employee elects to contribute. However, the amount of insurance provided under each schedule must be computed under a formula that precludes individual selection.

* * *

§ 1.79–2 Exceptions to the rule of inclusion.

(a) In general. **(1)** Section 79(b) provides exceptions for the cost of group-term life insurance provided under certain policies otherwise described in section 79(a). The policy or policies of group-term life insurance which are described in section 79(a) but which qualify for one of the exceptions set forth in section 79(b) are described in paragraphs (b) through (d) of this section. Paragraph (b) of this

*Editorial comment: The Regulations do not reflect the changes made by the Tax Reform Act of 1986. See Sec. 74(b)(3).

section discusses the exception provided in section 79(b)(1); paragraph (c) of this section discusses the exception provided in section 79(b)(2); and paragraph (d) of this section discusses the exception provided in section 79(b)(3).

(2) (i) If a policy of group-term life insurance qualifies for an exception provided by section 79(b), then the amount equal to the cost of such insurance is excluded from the application of the provisions of section 79(a).

(ii) If a policy, or portion of a policy of group-term life insurance qualifies for an exception provided by section 79(b), the amount (if any) paid by the employee toward the purchase of such insurance is not to be taken into account as an amount referred to in section 79(a)(2). In the case of a policy or policies of group-term life insurance which qualify for an exception provided by section 79(b)(1) or (3), the amount paid by the employee which is not to be taken into account as an amount referred to in section 79(a)(2) is the amount paid by the employee for the particular policy or policies of group-term life insurance which qualify for an exception provided under such section. If the exception provided in section 79(b)(2) is applicable only to a portion of the group-term life insurance on the employee's life, the amount considered to be paid by the employee toward the purchase of such portion is the amount equal to the excess of the cost of such portion of the insurance over the amount otherwise includible in the employee's gross income with respect to the group-term life insurance on his life carried directly or indirectly by such employer.

(iii) The rules of this subparagraph may be illustrated by the following example:

Example. A is an employee of X Corporation and is also an employee of Y Corporation, a subsidiary of X Corporation. A is provided, under a separate plan arranged by each of his employers, group-term life insurance on his life. During his taxable year, under the group-term life insurance plan of X Corporation, A is provided $60,000 of group-term life insurance on his life, and A pays $360.00 toward the purchase of such insurance. Under the group-term life insurance plan of Y Corporation, A is provided $65,000 of group-term life insurance on his life, but does not pay any part of the cost of such insurance. At the beginning of his taxable year, A terminates his employment with the X Corporation after he has reached the retirement age with respect to such employer, and the policy carried by the X Corporation qualifies for the exception provided by section 79(b)(1). For that taxable year, the cost of the group-term life insurance on A's life which is provided under the plan of X Corporation is not taken into account in determining the amount includible in A's gross income under section 79(a), and A may not take into account as an amount described in section 79(a)(2) the $360.00 he pays toward the purchase of such insurance.

(b) Retired and disabled employees— (1) In general. Section 79(b)(1) provides an exception for the cost of group-term life insurance on the life of an individual which is provided under a policy or policies otherwise described in section 79(a) if the individual has terminated his employment (as defined in subparagraph (2) of this paragraph) with such employer and either has reached the retirement age with respect to such employer (as defined in subparagraph (3) of this paragraph), or has become disabled (as defined in subparagraph (4)(i) of this paragraph). If an individual who has terminated his employment attains retirement age or has become disabled during his taxable year, or if an employee who has attained retirement age or has become disabled terminates his employment during the taxable year, the exception provided by section 79(b)(1) applies only to the portion of the cost of group-term life insurance which is provided subsequent to the happening of the last event which qualifies the policy of insurance on the employee's life for the exception provided in such section.

(2) Termination of employment. For purposes of section 79(b)(1), an individual has terminated his employment with an employer providing such individual group-term life insurance when such individual no longer renders services to that employer as an employee of such employer.

* * *

(c) Employer or charity a beneficiary— (1) General rule. Section 79(b)(2) provides an exception with respect to the amounts referred to in section 79 (a) for the cost of any portion of the group-term life insurance on the life of an employee provided during part or all of the taxable year of the employee under which the employer is directly or indirectly the beneficiary, or under which a person described in section 170(c) (relating to definition of charitable contributions) is the sole beneficiary, for the entire period during such taxable year for which the employee receives such insurance.

(2) Employer is a beneficiary. For purposes of section 79(b)(2) and subparagraph (1) of this paragraph, the determination of whether the employer is directly or indirectly the beneficiary under a policy or policies of group-term life insurance depends upon the facts and circumstances of the particular case. Such determination is not made solely with regard to whether the employer possesses all the incidents of ownership in the policy. Thus, for example, if the employer is the nominal beneficiary under a policy of group-term life insurance on the life of his employee but there is an arrangement whereby the employer is required to pay over all (or a portion) of the proceeds of such policy to the employee's estate or his beneficiary, the employer is not considered a beneficiary under such policy (or such portion of the policy).

(3) Charity a beneficiary. (i) For purposes of section 79(b)(2) and subparagraph (1) of this paragraph, a person described in section 170(c) is a beneficiary under a policy providing group-term life insurance if such person is designated the beneficiary under the policy by any assignment or designation of beneficiary under the policy which, under the law of the jurisdiction which is applicable to the policy, has the effect of making such person the beneficiary under such policy (whether or not such designation is revocable during the taxable year). Such a designation may be made by the employee with respect to any portion of the group-term life insurance on his life. However, no deduction is allowed under section 170, relating to charitable, etc., contributions and gifts, with respect to any such assignment or designation.

(ii) A person described in section 170(c) must be designated the sole beneficiary under the policy or portion of the policy. Such requirement is satisfied if the person described in section 170(c) is the beneficiary under such policy or portion of the policy, and there is no contingent or similar beneficiary under such policy or such portion other than a person described in section 170(c). A general "preference beneficiary clause" in a policy governing payment where there is no designated beneficiary in existence at the death of the employee will not of itself be considered to create a contingent or similar beneficiary. A person described in section 170(c) may be designated the beneficiary under a portion of the policy if such person is designated the sole beneficiary under a beneficiary designation which is expressed, for example, as a fraction of the amount of insurance on the insured's life.

* * *

(d) Insurance contracts purchased under qualified employee plans. (1) Section 79(b)(3) provides an exception with respect to the cost of any group-term life insurance which is provided under a life insurance contract purchased as a part of a plan described in section 403(a), or purchased by a trust described in section 401(a) which is exempt from tax under section 501(a) if the proceeds of such contract are payable directly or indirectly to a participant in such trust or to a beneficiary of such participant. The provisions of section 72(m)(3) and § 1.72–16 apply to the cost of such group-term life insurance, and, therefore, no part of such cost is excluded from the gross income of the employee by reason of the provisions of section 79.

(2) Whether the life insurance protection on an employee's life is provided under a qualified employee plan referred to in subparagraph (1) of this paragraph depends upon the provisions of such plan. In determining whether a pension, profit-sharing, stock bonus, or annuity plan satisfies the requirements for qualification set forth in sections 401(a) or 403(a), only group-term life insurance which is provided under such plan is taken into account.

§ 1.79–3 Determination of amount equal to cost of group-term life insurance.

(a) In general. This section prescribes the rules for determining the amount equal to the cost of group-term life insurance on an employee's life which is to be included in his gross income pursuant to the rule of inclusion set forth in section 79(a). Such amount is determined by—

(1) Computing the cost of the portion of the group-term life insurance on the employee's life to be taken into account (determined in accordance with the rules set forth in paragraph (b) of this section) for each "period of coverage" (as defined in paragraph (c) of this section) and aggregating the costs so determined, then

(2) Reducing the amount determined under subparagraph (1) of this paragraph by the amount determined in accordance with the rules set forth in paragraph (e) of this section, relating to the amount paid by the employee toward the purchase of group-term life insurance.

(b) Determination of the portion of the group-term life insurance on the employee's life to be taken into account. (1) For each "period of coverage" (as defined in paragraph (c) of this section), the portion of the group-term life insurance to be taken into account in computing the amount includible in an employee's gross income for purposes of paragraph (a)(1) of this section is the sum of the proceeds payable upon the death of the employee under each policy, or portion of a policy, of group-term life insurance on such employee's life to which the rule of inclusion set forth in section 79(a) applies, less $50,000 of such insurance. Thus, the amount of any proceeds payable under a policy, or portion of a policy, which qualifies for one of the exceptions to the rule of inclusion provided by section 79(b) is not taken into account. For the regulations relating to such exceptions to the rule of inclusion, see § 1.79–2.

(2) For purposes of making the computation required by subparagraph (1) of this paragraph in any case in which the amount payable under the policy, or portion thereof, varies during the period of coverage, the amount payable under such policy during such period is considered to be the average of the amount payable under such policy at the beginning and the end of such period.

(3)(i) For purposes of making the computation required by subparagraph (1) of this paragraph in any case in which the amount payable under the policy is not payable as a specific amount upon the death of the employee in full discharge of the liability of the insurer, and such form of payment is not one of alternative methods of payment, the amount payable under such policy is the present value of the agreement by the insurer under the policy to make the payments to the beneficiary or beneficiaries entitled to such amounts upon the employee's death. For each period of coverage, such present value is to be determined as if the first and last day of such period is the date of death of the employee.

(ii) The present value of the agreement by the insurer under the policy to make payments shall be determined by the use of the mortality tables and interest rate employed by the insurer with respect to such a policy in calculating the amount held by the insurer (as defined in section 101(d)(2)), unless the Commissioner otherwise determines that a particular mortality table and interest rate, representative of the mortality table and interest rate used by commercial insurance companies with respect to such policies, shall be used to determine the present value of the policy for purposes of this subdivision.

(iii) For purposes of making the computation required by subdivision (i) of this subparagraph in any case in which it is necessary to determine the age of an employee's beneficiary and such beneficiary remains the same (under the policy, or the portion of the policy, with respect to which the determination of the present value of the agreement of the insurer to pay benefits is being made) for the entire period during the employee's taxable year for which such policy is in effect, the age of such beneficiary is such beneficiary's age at his nearest birthday on June 30th of the calendar year.

(iv) If the policy of group-term life insurance on the employee's life is such that the present value of the agreement by the insurer under the policy to pay benefits cannot be determined by the rules prescribed in this subparagraph, the taxpayer may submit with his return a computation of such present value, consistent with the actuarial and other assumptions set forth in this subparagraph, showing the appropriate factors applied in his case. Such computation shall be subject to the approval of the Commissioner upon examination of such return.

(c) Period of coverage. For purposes of this section, the phrase "period of coverage" means any one calendar month period, or part thereof, during the employee's taxable year during which the employee is provided group-term life insurance on his life to which the rule of inclusion set forth in section 79(a) applies. The phrase "part thereof" as used in the preceding sentence means any continuous period which is less than the one calendar month period referred to in the preceding sentence for which premiums are charged by the insurer.

(d) The cost of the portion of the group-term life insurance on an employee's life. **(1)** This paragraph sets forth the rules for determining the cost, for each period of coverage, of the portion of the group-term life insurance on the employee's life to be taken into account in computing the amount includible in the employee's gross income for purposes of paragraph (a)(1) of this section. The portion of the group-term life insurance on the employee's life to be taken into account is determined in accordance with the provisions of paragraph (b) of this section. Table 1, which is set forth in subparagraph (2) of this paragraph, determines the cost for each $1,000 of such portion of the group-term life insurance on the employee's life for each one-month period. The cost of the portion of the group-term life insurance on the employee's life for each period of coverage of one month is obtained by multiplying the number of thousand dollars of such insurance computed to the nearest tenth which is provided during such period by the appropriate amount set forth in Table 1. In any case in which group-term life insurance is provided for a period of coverage of less than one month, the amount set forth in Table 1 is prorated over such period of coverage.

(2) For the cost of group-term life insurance provided after June 30, 1999, the following table sets forth the cost of $1,000 of group-term life insurance for one month, computed on the basis of 5-year age brackets.* * * For purposes of Table I, the age of the employee is the employee's attained age on the last day of the employee's taxable year.

TABLE 1—UNIFORM PREMIUMS FOR $1,000 OF GROUP-TERM LIFE INSURANCE PROTECTION

5-year age bracket	Cost per $1,000 of protection for 1-month period
Under 25	$0.05
25 to 29	.06
30 to 34	.08
35 to 39	.09
40 to 44	.10
45 to 49	.15
50 to 54	.23
55 to 59	.43
60 to 64	.66
65 to 69	1.27
70 and above	2.06

(3) The net premium cost of group-term life insurance as provided in Table 1 of subparagraph (2) of this paragraph applies only to the cost of group-term life insurance subject to the rule of inclusion set forth in section 79(a). Therefore, such net premium cost is not applicable to the determination of the cost of group-term life insurance provided under a policy which is not subject to such rule of inclusion.

* * *

(f) Amount paid by the employee toward the purchase of group-term life insurance. **(1)** Except as otherwise provided in subparagraph (2) of this paragraph, if an employee pays any amount toward the purchase of group-term life insurance provided for a taxable year which is subject to the rule of inclusion set forth in paragraph (a)(2) of § 1.79–1, the sum of all such amounts is the amount referred to in section 79(a)(2) and paragraph (a)(2) of this section. The rule of the preceding sentence applies even though the payments made by the employee are made with respect to a period of coverage during which no portion of the group-term life insurance on his life is taken into account under paragraph (b)(1) of this section.

(2) In determining the amount paid by the employee for purposes of section 79(a)(2) and paragraph (a)(2) of this section, there is not taken into account any amounts paid by the employee for group-term life insurance provided (or to be provided) for a different taxable year (other than amounts applicable to regular pay periods extending into the next taxable year). Thus, for example, if part of an employee's payment during a taxable year represents a prepayment for insurance to be provided after his retirement, such part does not reduce the amount includible in his gross income for the current taxable year. Furthermore, in determining such amount, there is not taken into account any amount paid by an employee toward the purchase of groupterm life insurance which qualifies for one of the exceptions described in section 79(b). The amount paid by an employee toward the purchase of group-term life insurance which qualifies for one of the exceptions described in section 79(b) is determined under the rules of paragraph (a)(2) of § 1.79–2.

(3) If payments are made by the employer and his employees to provide group-term life insurance which is subject to the rule of inclusion set forth in section 79(a) as well as to provide other benefits for the employees, and if the amount paid by the employee toward the purchase of such insurance cannot be determined by the provisions of the policy or plan under which such benefits are provided, then the determination of the portion of the cost of group-term life insurance (computed in accordance with the provisions of this section) which is attributable to the contributions of the employee shall be made in accordance with the provisions of this subparagraph. The amount paid by the employee toward the purchase of all the group-term life insurance on his life for his taxable year (or for the portion of his taxable year if such portion is the basis of the computation) under such group policy shall be an amount determined first by ascertaining the total amount paid by all employees who are covered for multiple benefits which is allocable toward the purchase of group-term life insurance on their lives for the year, and then by ascertaining the pro rata portion of such total amount attributable to the individual employee. The total amount paid by all employees who are covered for multiple benefits which is allocable toward the purchase of group-term life insurance on their lives with respect to such year shall be an amount which bears the same ratio to the total amount paid by all employees for multiple benefits with respect to such year as the aggregate premiums paid to the insurer for group-term life insurance on such employees' lives with respect to such year bears to the aggregate premiums paid to the insurer for such multiple benefits with respect to such year. The pro rata portion of such total amount attributable to the individual employee for the cost of group-term life insurance on his life shall be an amount which bears the same ratio to the total amount paid by all employees which is allocable toward the purchase of group-term insurance on their lives with respect to such year as the amount of group-term life insurance on the life of the employee at a specified time during the year, as determined by the employer, bears to the total amount of group-term life insurance on the lives of all employees insured for such multiple benefits at such time.

* * *

§ 1.82–1 Payments for or reimbursements of expenses of moving from one residence to another residence attributable to employment or self-employment.

(a) Reimbursements in gross income—(1) In general. Any amount received or accrued, directly or indirectly, by an individual as a payment for or reimbursement of expenses of moving from one residence to another residence attributable to employment or self-employment is includible in gross income under section 82 as compensation for services in the taxable year received or accrued. For rules relating to the year a deduction may be allowed for expenses of moving from one residence to another residence, see section 217 and the regulations thereunder.

(2) Amounts received or accrued as reimbursement or payment. For purposes of this section, amounts are considered as being received or accrued by an individual as reimbursement or payment whether received in the form of money, property, or services. A cash basis taxpayer will include amounts in gross income under section 82 when they are received or treated as received by him. Thus, for example, if an employer moves an employee's household goods and personal effects from the employee's old resident to his new residence using the employer's facilities, the employee is considered as having received a payment in the amount of the fair market value of the services furnished at the time the services are furnished by the employer. If the employer pays a mover for moving the employee's household goods and personal effects, the employee is considered as having received the payment at the time the employer pays the mover, rather than at the time the mover moves the employee's household goods and personal effects. Where an employee receives a loan or advance from an employer to enable him to pay his moving expenses, the employee will not be deemed to have received a reimbursement of moving expenses until such time as he accounts to his employer if he is not required to repay such loan or advance and if he makes such accounting within a reasonable time. Such loan or advance will be deemed to be a reimbursement of moving expenses at the time of such accounting to the extent used by the employee for such moving expenses.

(3) Direct or indirect payments or reimbursements. For purposes of this section amounts are considered as being received or accrued whether received directly (paid or provided to an individual by an employer, a client, a customer, or similar person) or indirectly (paid to a third party on behalf of an individual by an employer, a client, a customer, or similar person). Thus, if an employer pays a mover for the expenses of moving an employee's household goods and personal effects from one residence to another residence, the employee has indirectly received a payment which is includible in his gross income under section 82.

(4) Expenses of moving from one residence to another residence. An expense of moving from one residence to another residence is any expenditure, cost, loss, or similar item paid or incurred in connection with a move from one residence to another residence. Moving expenses include (but are not limited to) any expenditure, cost, loss, or similar item directly or indirectly resulting from the acquisition, sale, or exchange of property, the transportation of goods or property, or travel (by the taxpayer or any other person) in connection with a change in residence. Such expenses include items described in section 217(b) (relating to the definition of moving expenses), irrespective of the dollar limitations contained in section 217(b)(3) and the conditions contained in section 217(c), as well as items not described in section 217(b), such as a loss sustained on the sale or exchange of personal property, storage charges, taxes, or expenses of refitting rugs or draperies.

(5) Attributable to employment or self-employment. Any amount received or accrued from an employer, a client, a customer, or similar person in connection with the performance of services for such employer, client, customer, or similar person, is attributable to employment or self-employment. Thus, for example, if an employer reimburses an employee for a loss incurred on the sale of the employee's house, reimbursement is attributable to the performance of services if made because of the employer-employee relationship. Similarly, if an employer in order to prevent an employee's sustaining a loss on a sale of a house acquires the property from the employee at a price in excess of fair market value, the employee is considered to have received a payment attributable to employment to the extent that such payment exceeds the fair market value of the property.

* * *

§ 1.83–1 Property transferred in connection with the performance of services.

(a) Inclusion in gross income— (1) General rule. Section 83 provides rules for the taxation of property transferred to an employee or independent contractor (or beneficiary thereof) in connection with the performance of services by such employee or independent contractor. In general, such property is not taxable under section 83(a) until it has been transferred (as defined in § 1.83–3(a)) to such person and become substantially vested (as defined in § 1.83–3(b)) in such person. In that case, the excess of—

(i) The fair market value of such property (determined without regard to any lapse restriction, as defined in § 1.83—3(i)) at the time that the property becomes substantially vested, over

(ii) The amount (if any) paid for such property, shall be included as compensation in the gross income of such employee or independent contractor for the taxable year in which the property becomes substantially vested. Until such property becomes substantially vested, the transferor shall be regarded as the owner of such property, and any income from such property received by the employee or independent contractor (or beneficiary thereof) or the right to the use of such property by the employee or independent contractor constitutes additional compensation and shall be included in the gross income of such employee or independent contractor for the taxable year in which such income is received or such use is made available. This paragraph applies to a transfer of property in connection with the performance of services even though the transferor is not the person for whom such services are performed.

* * *

(b) Subsequent sale, forfeiture, or other disposition of nonvested property. (1) If substantially nonvested property (that has been transferred in connection with the performance of services) is subsequently sold or otherwise disposed of to a third party in an arm's length transaction while still substantially nonvested, the person who performed such services shall realize compensation in an amount equal to the excess of—

(i) The amount realized on such sale or other disposition, over

(ii) The amount (if any) paid for such property.

Such amount of compensation is includible in his gross income in accordance with his method of accounting. Two preceding sentences also apply when the person disposing of the property has received it in a non-arm's length transaction described in paragraph (c) of this section. In addition, section 83(a) and paragraph (a) of this section shall thereafter cease to apply with respect to such property.

(2) If substantially nonvested property that has been transferred in connection with the performance of services to the person performing such services is forfeited while still substantially nonvested and held by such person, the difference between the amount paid (if any) and the amount received upon forfeiture (if any) shall be treated as an ordinary gain or loss. This paragraph (b)(2) does not apply to property to which § 1.83–2(a) applies.

(3) This paragraph (b) shall not apply to, and no gain shall be recognized on, any sale, forfeiture, or other disposition described in this paragraph to the extent that any property received in exchange therefor is substantially nonvested. Instead, section 83 and this section shall apply with respect to such property received (as if it were substituted for the property disposed of).

(c) Dispositions of nonvested property not at arm's length. If substantially nonvested property (that has been transferred in connection with the performance of services) is disposed of in a transaction which is not at arm's length and the property remains substantially nonvested, the person who performed such services realizes compensation equal in amount to the sum of any money and the fair market value of any substantially vested property received in such disposition. Such amount of compensation is includible in his gross income in accordance with his method of accounting. However, such amount of compensation shall not exceed the fair market value of the property disposed of at the time of disposition (determined without regard to any lapse restriction), reduced by the amount paid for such property. In addition, section 83 and these regulations shall continue to apply with respect to such property, except that any amount previously includible in gross income under this paragraph (c) shall thereafter be treated as an amount paid for such property. For example, if in 1971 an employee pays $50 for a share of stock which has a fair market value of $100 and is substantially nonvested at that time and later in 1971 (at a time when the property still has a fair market value of $100 and is still substantially nonvested) the employee disposes of, in a transaction not at arm's length, the share of stock to his wife for $10, the employee realizes compensation of $10 in 1971. If in 1972, when the share of stock has a fair market value of $120, it becomes substantially vested, the employee realizes additional compensation in 1972 in the amount of $60 (the $120 fair market value of the stock less both the $50 price paid for the stock and the $10 taxed as compensation in 1971). For purposes of this paragraph, if substantially nonvested property has been transferred to a person other than the person who performed the services, and the transferee dies holding the property while the property is still substantially nonvested and while the person who performed the services is alive, the transfer which results by reason of the death of such transferee is a transfer not at arm's length.

(d) Certain transfers upon death. If substantially nonvested property has been transferred in connection with the performance of services and the person who performed such services dies while the property is still substantially nonvested, any income realized on or after such death with respect to such property under this section is income in respect of a decedent to which the rules of section 691 apply. In such a case the income in respect of such property shall be taxable under section 691 (except to the extent not includible under section 101(b)) to the estate or beneficiary of the person who performed the services, in accordance with section 83 and the regulations thereunder.* * *

(e) Forfeiture after substantial vesting. If a person is taxable under section 83(a) when the property transferred becomes substantially vested and thereafter the person's beneficial interest in such property is nevertheless forfeited pursuant to a lapse restriction, any loss incurred by such person (but not by a beneficiary of such person) upon such forfeiture shall be an ordinary loss to the extent the basis in such property has been increased as a result of the recognition of income by such person under section 83(a) with respect to such property.

(f) Examples. The provisions of this section may be illustrated by the following examples:

Example (1). On November 1, 1978, X corporation sells to E, an employee, 100 shares of X corporation stock at $10 per share. At the time of such sale the fair market value of the X corporation stock is $100 per share. Under the terms of the sale each share of stock is subject to a substantial risk of forfeiture which will not lapse until November 1, 1988. Evidence of this restriction is stamped on the face of E's stock certificates, which are therefore nontransferable (within the meaning of § 1.83–3(d)). Since in 1978 E's stock is substantially nonvested, E does not include any of such amount in his gross income as compensation in 1978. On November 1, 1988, the fair market value of the X corporation stock is $250 per share. Since the X corporation stock becomes substantially vested in 1988, E must include $24,000 (100 shares of X corporation stock × $250 fair market value per share less $10 price paid by E for each share) as compensation for 1988. Dividends paid by X to E on E's stock after it was transferred to E on November 1, 1973, are taxable to E as additional compensation during the period E's stock is substantially nonvested and are deductible as such by X.

Example (2). Assume the facts are the same as in example (1), except that on November 1, 1985, each share of stock of X corporation in E's hands could as a matter of law be transferred to a bona fide purchaser who would not be required to forfeit the stock if the risk of forfeiture materialized. In the event, however, that the risk materializes, E would be liable in damages to X. On November 1, 1985, the fair market value of the X corporation stock is $230 per share. Since E's stock is transferable within the meaning of § 1.83–3(d) in 1985, the stock is substantially vested and E must include $22,000 (100 shares of X corporation stock × $230 fair market value per share less $10 price paid by E for each share) as compensation for 1985.

Example (3). Assume the facts are the same as in example (1) except that, in 1984 E sells his 100 shares of X corporation stock in an arm's length sale to I, an investment company, for $120 per share. At the time of this sale each share of X corporation's stock has a fair market value of $200. Under paragraph (b) of this section, E must include $11,000 (100 shares of X corporation stock × $120 amount realized per share less $10 price paid by E per share) as compensation for 1984 notwithstanding that the stock remains non-transferable and is still subject to a substantial risk of forfeiture at the time of such sale. Under § 1.83–4(b)(2), I's basis in the X corporation stock is $120 per share.

§ 1.83–2 Election to include in gross income in year of transfer.

(a) In general. If property is transferred (within the meaning of § 1.83–3(a)) in connection with the performance of services, the person performing such services may elect to include in gross income under section 83(b) the excess (if any) of the fair market value of the property at the time of transfer (determined without regard to any lapse restriction, as defined in § 1.83–3(i)) over the amount (if any) paid for such property, as compensation for services. The fact that the transferee has paid full value for the property transferred, realizing no bargain element in the transaction, does not preclude the use of the election as provided for in this section. If this election is made, the substantial vesting rules of section 83(a) and the regulations thereunder do not apply with respect to such property, and except as otherwise provided in section 83(d)(2) and the regulations thereunder (relating to the cancellation of a nonlapse restriction), any subsequent appreciation in the value of the property is not taxable as compensation to the person who performed the services. Thus, property with respect to which this election is made shall be includible in gross income as of the time of transfer, even though such property is substantially nonvested (as defined in § 1.83–3(b)) at the time of transfer, and no compensation will be includible in gross income when such property becomes substantially vested (as defined in § 1.83–3(b)). In computing the gain or loss from the subsequent sale or exchange of such property, its basis shall be the amount paid for the property increased by the amount included in gross income under section 83(b). If property for which a section 83(b) election is in effect is forfeited while substantially nonvested, such forfeiture shall be treated as a sale or exchange upon which there is realized a loss equal to the excess (if any) of—

(1) The amount paid (if any) for such property, over,

(2) The amount realized (if any) upon such forfeiture.

If such property is a capital asset in the hands of the taxpayer, such loss shall be a capital loss. A sale or other disposition of the property that is in substance a forfeiture, or is made in contemplation of a forfeiture, shall be treated as a forfeiture under the two immediately preceding sentences.

(b) Time for making election. Except as provided in the following sentence, the election referred to in paragraph (a) of this section shall be filed not later than 30 days after the date the property was transferred (or, if later, January 29, 1970) and may be filed prior to the date of transfer. Any statement filed before February 15, 1970, which was amended not later than February 16, 1970, in order to make it conform to the requirements of paragraph (e) of this section, shall be deemed a proper election under section 83(b).

(c) Manner of making election. The election referred to in paragraph (a) of this section is made by filing one copy of a written statement with the internal revenue office with whom the person who performed the services files his return. In addition, one copy of such statement shall be submitted with this income tax return for the taxable year in which such property was transferred.

(d) Additional copies. The person who performed the services shall also submit a copy of the statement referred to in paragraph (c) of this section to the person for whom the services are performed. In addition, if the person who performs the services and the transferee of such property are not the same person, the person who performs the services shall submit a copy of such statement to the transferee of the property.

(e) Content of statement. The statement shall be signed by the person making the election and shall indicate that it is being made under section 83(b) of the Code, and shall contain the following information:

(1) The name, address and taxpayer identification number of the taxpayer;

(2) A description of each property with respect to which the election is being made;

(3) The date or dates on which the property is transferred and the taxable year (for example, "calendar year 1970" or "fiscal year ending May 31, 1970") for which such election was made;

(4) The nature of the restriction or restrictions to which the property is subject;

(5) The fair market value at the time of transfer (determined without regard to any lapse restriction, as defined in § 1.83—3(i)) of each property with respect to which the election is being made;

(6) The amount (if any) paid for such property; and

(7) With respect to elections made after July 21, 1978, a statement to the effect that copies have been furnished to other persons as provided in paragraph (d) of this section.

(f) Revocability of election. An election under section 83(b) may not be revoked except with the consent of the Commissioner. Consent will be granted only in the case where the transferee is under a mistake of fact as to the underlying transaction and must be requested within 60 days of the date on which the mistake of fact first became known to the person who made the election. In any event, a mistake as to the value, or decline in the value, of the property with respect to which an election under section 83(b) has been made or a failure to perform an act contemplated at the time of transfer of such property does not constitute a mistake of fact.

§ 1.83–3 Meaning and use of certain terms.*

* * *

(b) Substantially vested and substantially nonvested property. For purposes of section 83 and the regulations thereunder, property is substantially nonvested when it is subject to a substantial risk of forfeiture, within the meaning of paragraph (c) of this section, and is nontransferable, within the meaning of paragraph (d) of this section. Property is substantially vested for such purposes when it is either transferable or not subject to a substantial risk of forfeiture.

(c) Substantial risk of forfeiture—(1) In general. For purposes of section 83 and these regulations, whether a risk of forfeiture is substantial or not depends upon the facts and circumstances. Except as set forth in paragraphs (j) and (k) of this section, a substantial risk of forfeiture exists only if rights in property that are transferred are conditioned, directly or indirectly, upon the future performance (or refraining from performance) of substantial services by any person, or upon the occurrence of a condition related to a purpose of the transfer if the possibility of forfeiture is substantial. Property is not transferred subject to a substantial risk of forfeiture if at the time of transfer the facts and circumstances demonstrate that the forfeiture condition is unlikely to be enforced. Further, property is not transferred subject to a substantial risk of forfeiture to the extent that the employer is required to pay the fair market value of a portion of such property to the employee upon the return of such property. The risk that the value of property will decline during a certain period of time does not constitute a substantial risk of forfeiture. A nonlapse restriction, standing by itself, will not result in a substantial risk of forfeiture. A restriction on the transfer of property, whether contractual or by operation of applicable law, will result in a substantial risk of forfeiture only if and to the extent that the restriction is described in paragraph (j) or (k) of this section. For this purpose, transfer restrictions that will not result in a substantial risk of forfeiture include, but are not limited to, restrictions that if violated, whether by transfer or attempted transfer of the property, would result in the forfeiture of some or all of the property, or liability by the employee for any damages, penalties, fees, or other amount.

(2) Illustrations of substantial risks of forfeiture. The regularity of the performance of services and the time spent in performing such services tend to indicate whether services required by a condition are substantial. The fact that the person performing services has the right to decline to perform such services without forfeiture may tend to establish that services are insubstantial. Where stock is transferred to an underwriter prior to a public offering and the full enjoyment of such stock is expressly or impliedly conditioned upon the successful completion of the underwriting, the stock is subject to a substantial risk of forfeiture. Where an employee receives property from an employer subject to a requirement that it be returned if the total earnings of the employer do not increase, such property is subject to a substantial risk of forfeiture. On the other hand, requirements that the property be returned to the employer if the employee is discharged for cause or for committing a crime will not be considered to result in a substantial risk of forfeiture. An enforceable requirement that the property be returned to the employer if the employee accepts a job with a competing firm will not ordinarily be considered to result in a substantial risk of forfeiture unless the particular facts and circumstances indicate to the contrary. Factors which may be taken into account in determining whether a covenant not to compete constitutes a substantial risk of forfeiture are the age of the employee, the availability of alternative employment opportunities, the likelihood of the employee's obtaining such other employment, the degree of skill possessed by the employee, the employee's health, and the practice (if any) of the employer to enforce such covenants. Similarly, rights in property transferred to a retiring employee subject to the sole requirement that it be returned unless he renders consulting services upon the request of his former employer will not be considered subject to a substantial risk of forfeiture unless he is in fact expected to perform substantial services.

* * *

(4) Examples. The rules contained in paragraph (c)(1) of this section may be illustrated by the following examples. In each example it is assumed that, if the conditions on transfer are not satisfied, the forfeiture provision will be enforced.

*Editorial comment: In general, these final regulations are effective beginning February 26, 2014.

Example (1). On November 1, 1971, corporation X transfers in connection with the performance of services to E, an employee, 100 shares of corporation X stock for $90 per share. Under the terms of the transfer, E will be subject to a binding commitment to resell the stock to corporation X at $90 per share if he leaves the employment of corporation X for any reason prior to the expiration of a 2-year period from the date of such transfer. Since E must perform substantial services for corporation X and will not be paid more than $90 for the stock, regardless of its value, if he fails to perform such services during such 2-year period, E's rights in the stock are subject to a substantial risk of forfeiture during such period.

Example (2). On November 10, 1971, corporation X transfers in connection with the performance of services to a trust for the benefit of employees, $100x. Under the terms of the trust any child of an employee who is an enrolled full-time student at an accredited educational institution as a candidate for a degree will receive an annual grant of cash for each academic year the student completes as a student in good standing, up to a maximum of four years. E, an employee, has a child who is enrolled as a full-time student at an accredited college as a candidate for a degree. Therefore, E has a beneficial interest in the assets of the trust equalling the value of four cash grants. Since E's child must complete one year of college in order to receive a cash grant, E's interest in the trust assets are subject to a substantial risk of forfeiture to the extent E's child has not become entitled to any grants.

Example (3). On November 25, 1971, corporation X gives to E, an employee, in connection with his performance of services to corporation X, a bonus of 100 shares of corporation X stock. Under the terms of the bonus arrangement E is obligated to return the corporation X stock to corporation X if he terminates his employment for any reason. However, for each year occurring after November 25, 1971, during which E remains employed with corporation X, E ceases to be obligated to return 10 shares of the corporation X stock. Since in each year occurring after November 25, 1971, for which E remains employed he is not required to return 10 shares of corporation X's stock, E's rights in 10 shares each year for 10 years cease to be subject to a substantial risk of forfeiture for each year he remains so employed.

* * *

Example (6). On April 3, 2013, Y corporation grants to Q, an officer of Y, a nonstatutory option to purchase Y common stock. Although the option is immediately exercisable, it has no readily ascertainable fair market value when it is granted. Under the option, Q has the right to purchase 100 shares of Y common stock for $10 per share, which is the fair market value of a Y share on the date of grant of the option. On August 1, 2013, Y sells its common stock in an initial public offering. Pursuant to an underwriting agreement entered into in connection with the initial public offering, Q agrees not to sell, otherwise dispose of, or hedge any Y common stock from August 1 through February 1 of 2014 ("the lock-up period"). Q exercises the option and Y shares are transferred to Q on November 15, 2013, during the lock-up period. The underwriting agreement does not impose a substantial risk of forfeiture on the Y shares acquired by Q because the provisions of the agreement do not condition Q's rights in the shares upon anyone's future performance (or refraining from performance) of substantial services or on the occurrence of a condition related to the purpose of the transfer of shares to Q. Accordingly, neither section 83(c)(3) nor the imposition of the lock-up period by the underwriting agreement precludes taxation under section 83 when the shares resulting from exercise of the option are transferred to Q.

Example (7). Assume the same facts as in Example 6, except that on August 1, 2013, Y also adopts an insider trading compliance program, under which, as applied to 2013, insiders (such as Q) may trade Y shares only during a limited number of days following each quarterly earnings release ("a trading window"). Under the program, if Q trades Y shares outside a trading window without Y's permission, Y has the right to terminate Q's employment. However, the exercise of the non-statutory options outside a trading window for Y shares is not prohibited under the insider trading compliance program. Q fully exercises the option, and Y shares are transferred to Q, on November 15, 2013. The exercise of the option occurs outside a trading window, and, on the date of exercise, Q is in possession of material nonpublic information concerning Y that would subject him to liability under Rule 10b-5 under the Securities Exchange Act of 1934 if Q sold the Y shares while in possession of such information. Neither the insider trading compliance program nor the potential liability under Rule 10b-5 impose a substantial risk of forfeiture on the Y shares acquired by Q because the provisions of the program and Rule 10b-5 do not condition Q's rights in the shares upon anyone's future performance (or refraining from performance) of substantial services or on the occurrence of a condition related to the purpose of the transfer of shares to Q. Accordingly, none of section 83(c)(3), the imposition of the trading windows by the insider trading compliance program, and the potential liability under Rule 10b-5 preclude taxation under section 83 when the shares resulting from exercise of the option are transferred to Q.

* * *

(d) Transferability of property. For purposes of section 83 and the regulations thereunder, the rights of a person in property are transferable if such person can transfer any interest in the property to any person other than the transferor of the property, but only if the rights in such property of such transferee are not subject to a substantial risk of forfeiture. Accordingly, property is transferable if the person performing the services or receiving the property can sell, assign, or pledge (as collateral for a loan, or as security for the performance of an obligation, or for any other purpose) his interest in the property to any person other than the transferor of such property and if the transferee is not required to give up the property or its value in the event the substantial risk of forfeiture materializes. On the other hand, property is not considered to be transferable merely because the person performing the services or receiving the property may designate a beneficiary to receive the property in the event of his death.

* * *

(f) Property transferred in connection with the performance of services. Property transferred to an employee or an independent contractor (or beneficiary thereof) in recognition of the performance of, or the refraining from performance of, services is considered transferred in connection with the performance of services within the meaning of section 83. The existence of other persons entitled to buy stock on the same terms and conditions as an employee, whether pursuant to a public or private offering may, however, indicate that in such circumstances a transfer to the employee is not in recognition of the performance of, or the refraining from performance of, services. The transfer of property is subject to section 83 whether such transfer is in respect of past, present, or future services.

* * *

(h) Nonlapse restriction. For purposes of section 83 and the regulations thereunder, a restriction which by its terms will never lapse (also referred to as a "nonlapse restriction") is a permanent limitation on the transferability of property—

(1) Which will require the transferee of the property to sell, or offer to sell, such property at a price determined under a formula, and

(2) Which will continue to apply to and be enforced against the transferee or any subsequent holder (other than the transferor).

A limitation subjecting the property to a permanent right of first refusal in a particular person at a price determined under a formula is a permanent nonlapse restriction. Limitations imposed by registration requirements of State or Federal security laws or similar laws imposed with respect to sales or other dispositions of stock or securities are not nonlapse restrictions. An obligation to resell or to offer to sell property transferred in connection with the performance of services to a specific person or persons at its fair market value at the time of such sale is not a nonlapse restriction. See § 1.83–5(c) for examples of nonlapse restrictions.

(i) Lapse restriction. For purposes of section 83 and the regulations thereunder, the term "lapse restriction" means a restriction other than a nonlapse restriction as defined in paragraph (h) of this section, and includes (but is not limited to) a restriction that carries a substantial risk of forfeiture.

* * *

§ 1.83–4 Special rules.

(a) Holding period. Under section 83(f), the holding period of transferred property to which section 83(a) applies shall begin just after such property is substantially vested. However, if the person who has performed the services in connection with which property is transferred has made an election under section 83(b), the holding period of such property shall begin just after the date such property is transferred. If property to which section 83 and the regulations thereunder apply is transferred at arm's length, the holding period of such property in the hands of the transferee shall be determined in accordance with the rules provided in section 1223.

(b) Basis. (1) Except as provided in paragraph (b)(2) of this section, if property to which section 83 and the regulations thereunder apply is acquired by any person (including a person who acquires such property in a subsequent transfer which is not at arm's length), while such property is still substantially nonvested, such person's basis for the property shall reflect any amount paid for such property and any amount includible in the gross income of the person who performed the services (including any amount so includible as a result of a disposition by the person who acquired such property.) Such basis shall also reflect any adjustments to basis provided under sections 1015 and 1016.

(2) If property to which § 1.83–1 applies is transferred at arm's length, the basis of the property in the hands of the transferee shall be determined under section 1012 and the regulations thereunder.

(c) Forgiveness of indebtedness treated as an amount paid. If an indebtedness that has been treated as an amount paid under § 1.83–1 (a)(1)(ii) is subsequently cancelled, forgiven or satisfied for an amount less than the amount of such indebtedness, the amount that is not, in fact, paid shall be includible in the gross income of the service provider in the taxable year in which such cancellation, forgiveness or satisfaction occurs.

§ 1.83–5 Restrictions that will never lapse.

(a) Valuation. For purposes of section 83 and the regulations thereunder, in the case of property subject to a nonlapse restriction (as defined in § 1.83–3(h)), the price determined under the formula price will be considered to be the fair market value of the property unless established to the contrary by the Commissioner, and the burden of proof shall be on the commissioner with respect to such value. If stock in a corporation is subject to a nonlapse restriction which requires the transferee to sell such stock only at a formula price based on book value, a reasonable multiple of earnings or a reasonable combination thereof, the price so determined will ordinarily be regarded as determinative of the fair market value of such property for purposes of section 83. However, in certain circumstances the formula price will not be considered to be the fair market value of property subject to such a formula price restriction, even though the formula price restriction is a substantial factor in determining such value. For example, where the formula price is the current book value of stock, the book value of the stock at some time in the future may be a more accurate measure of the value of the stock than the current book value of the stock for purposes of determining the fair market value of the stock at the time the stock becomes substantially vested.

* * *

§ 1.83–6 Deduction by employer.

(a) Allowance of deduction— (1) General rule. In the case of a transfer of property in connection with the performance of services, or a compensatory cancellation of a nonlapse restriction described in section 83(d) and § 1.83–5, a deduction is allowable under sections 162 or 212 to the person for whom such services were performed. The amount of the deduction is equal to the amount includible as compensation in the gross income of the service provider under section 83(a), (b), or (d)(2), but only to the extent such amount meets the requirements of sections 162 or 212 and the regulations thereunder. The deduction is allowed only for the taxable year of that person in which or with which ends the taxable year of the service provider in which such amount is includible as compensation. For purposes of this paragraph, any amount excluded from gross income under section 79 or section 101(b) or subchapter is considered to have been includible in gross income.

(2) Special rule. For purposes of paragraph (a)(1) of this section, the service provider is deemed to have included the amount as compensation in gross income if the person for whom the services were performed satisfies in a timely manner all requirements of section 6041 or section 6041 A, and the regulations thereunder, with respect to that amount of compensation.* * *

(3) Exceptions. Where property is substantially vested upon transfer, the deduction shall be allowed to such person in accordance with his method of accounting (in conformity with sections 446 and 461). In the case of a transfer to an employee benefit plan described in § 1.162–10(a) or a transfer to an employees' trust or annuity plan described in section 404(a)(5) and the regulations thereunder, section 83(h) and this section do not apply.

(4) Capital expenditure, etc. No deduction is allowed under section 83(h) to the extent that the transfer of property constitutes a capital expenditure, an item of deferred expense, or an amount properly includible in the value of inventory items. In the case of a capital expenditure, for example, the basis of the property to which such capital expenditure relates shall be increased at the same time and to the same extent as any amount includible in the employee's gross income in respect of such transfer. Thus, for example, no deduction is allowed to a corporation in respect of a transfer of its stock to a promoter upon its organization, notwithstanding that such promoter must include the value of such stock in his gross income in accordance with the rules under section 83.

* * *

(b) Recognition of gain or loss. Except as provided in section 1032, at the time of a transfer of property in connection with the performance of services the transferor recognizes gain to the extent that the transferor receives an amount that exceeds the transferor's basis in the property. In addition, at the time a deduction is allowed under section 83(h) and paragraph (a) of this section, gain or loss is recognized to the extent of the difference between (i) the sum of the amount paid plus the amount allowed as a deduction under section 83(h), and (ii) the sum of the taxpayer's basis in the property plus any amount recognized pursuant to the previous sentence.

(c) Forfeitures. If, under section 83(h) and paragraph (a) of this section, a deduction, an increase in basis, or a reduction of gross income was allowable (disregarding the reasonableness of the amount of compensation) in respect of a transfer of property and such property is subsequently forfeited, the amount of such deduction, increase in basis or reduction of gross income shall be includible in the gross income of the person to whom it was allowable for the taxable year of forfeiture. The basis of such property in the hands of the person to whom it is forfeited shall include any such amount includible in the gross income of such person, as well as any amount such person pays upon forfeiture.

(d) Special rules for transfers by shareholders— (1) Transfers. If a shareholder of a corporation transfers property to an employee of such corporation or to an independent contractor (or to a beneficiary thereof), in consideration of services performed for the corporation, the transaction shall be considered to be a contribution of such property to the capital of such corporation by the shareholder, and immediately thereafter a transfer of such property by the corporation to the employee or independent contractor under paragraphs (a) and (b) of this section. For purposes of this (1), such a transfer will be considered to be in consideration for services performed for the corporation if either the property transferred is substantially nonvested at the time of transfer or an amount is includible in the gross income of the employee or independent contractor at the time of transfer under § 1.83–1(a)(1) or § 1.83–2(a). In the case of such a transfer, any money or other property paid to the shareholder for such stock shall be considered to be paid to the corporation and transferred immediately thereafter by the corporation to the shareholder as a distribution to which section 302 applies. For special rules that may apply to a corporation's transfer of its own stock to any person in consideration of services performed for another corporation or partnership, see §1.1032-3. The preceding sentence applies to transfers of stock and amounts paid for such stock on or after May 16, 2000.

(2) Forfeiture. If, following a transaction described in paragraph (d)(1) of this section, the transferred property is forfeited to the shareholder, paragraph (c) of this section shall apply both with respect to the shareholder and with respect to the corporation. In addition, the corporation shall in the taxable year of forfeiture be allowed a loss (or realize a gain) to offset any gain (or loss) realized under paragraph (b) of this section. For example, if a shareholder transfers property to an employee of the corporation as compensation, and as a result the shareholder's basis of $200x in such property is allocated to his stock in such corporation and such corporation recognizes a short-term capital gain of $800x, and is allowed a deduction of $1,000x on such transfer, upon a subsequent forfeiture of the property to the shareholder, the shareholder shall take $200x into gross income, and the corporation shall take $1,000x into gross income and be allowed a short-term capital loss of $800x.

* * *

§ 1.83–7 Taxation of nonqualified stock options.

(a) In general. If there is granted to an employee or independent contractor (or beneficiary thereof) in connection with the performance of services, an option to which section 421 (relating generally to certain qualified and other options) does not apply, section 83(a) shall apply to such grant if the option has a readily ascertainable fair market value (determined in accordance with paragraph (b) of this section) at the time the option is granted. The person who performed such services realizes compensation upon such grant at the time and in the amount determined under section 83(a). If section 83(a) does not apply to the grant of such an option because the option does not have a readily ascertainable fair market value at the time of grant, sections 83(a) and 83(b) shall apply at the time the option is exercised or otherwise disposed of, even though the fair market value of such option may have become readily ascertainable before such time. If the option is exercised, sections 83(a) and 83(b) apply to the transfer of property pursuant to such exercise, and the employee or independent contractor realizes compensation upon such transfer at the time and in the amount determined under section 83(a) or 83(b). If the option is sold or otherwise disposed of in an arm's length transaction, sections 83(a) and 83(b) apply to the transfer of money or other property received in the same manner as sections 83(a) and 83 (b) would have applied to the transfer of property pursuant to an exercise of the option. The preceding sentence does not apply to a sale or other disposition of the option to a person related to the service provider that occurs on or after July 2, 2003. For this purpose, a person is related to the service provider if—

(1) The person and the service provider bear a relationship to each other that is specified in section 267(b) or 707(b)(1), subject to the modifications that the language "20 percent" is used instead of "50 percent" each place it appears in sections 267(b) and 707(b)(1), and section 267(c)(4) is applied as if the family of an individual includes the spouse of any member of the family; or

(2) The person and the service provider are engaged in trades or businesses under common control (within the meaning of section 52(a) and (b)); provided that a person is not related to the service provider if the person is the service recipient with respect to the option or the grantor of the option.

(b) Readily ascertainable defined—(1) Actively traded on an established market. Options have a value at the time they are granted, but that value is ordinarily not readily ascertainable unless the option is actively traded on an established market. If an option is actively traded on an established market, the fair market value of such option is readily ascertainable for purposes of this section by applying the rules of valuation set forth in § 20.2031–2.

(2) Not actively traded on an established market. When an option is not actively traded on an established market, it does not have a readily ascertainable fair market value unless its fair market value can otherwise be measured with reasonable accuracy. For purposes of this section, if an option is not actively traded on an established market, the option does not have a readily ascertainable fair market value when granted unless the taxpayer can show that all of the following conditions exist:

(i) The option is transferable by the optionee;

(ii) The option is exercisable immediately in full by the optionee;

(iii) The option or the property subject to the option is not subject to any restriction or condition (other than a lien or other condition to secure the payment of the purchase price) which has a significant effect upon the fair market value of the option; and

(iv) The fair market value of the option privilege is readily ascertainable in accordance with paragraph (b)(3) of this section.

* * *

Items Specifically Excluded From Gross Income

§ 1.101–1 Exclusion from gross income of proceeds of life insurance contracts payable by reason of death.

(a)(1) In general. Section 101(a)(1) states the general rule that the proceeds of life insurance policies, if paid by reason of the death of the insured, are excluded from the gross income of the recipient. Death benefit payments having the characteristics of life insurance proceeds payable by reason of death under contracts, such as workmen's compensation insurance contracts, endowment contracts, or accident and health insurance contracts, are covered by this provision. For provisions relating to death benefits paid by or on behalf of employers, see section 101(b) and § 1.101–2. The exclusion from gross income allowed by section 101(a) applies whether payment is made to the estate of the insured or to any beneficiary (individual, corporation, or partnership) and whether it is made directly or in trust. The extent to which this exclusion applies in cases where life insurance policies have been transferred for a valuable consideration is stated in section 101(a)(2) and in paragraph (b) of this section. In cases where the proceeds of a life insurance policy, payable by reason of the death of the insured, are paid other than in a single sum at the time of such death, the amounts to be excluded from gross income may be affected by the provisions of section 101(c) (relating to amounts held under agreements to pay interest) or section 101(d) (relating to amounts payable at a date later than death). See §§ 1.101–3 and 1.101–4. However, neither section 101(c) nor section 101(d) applies to a single sum payment which does not exceed the amount payable at the time of death even though such amount is actually paid at a date later than death.

* * *

(b) Transfers of life insurance policies. (1) In the case of a transfer, by assignment or otherwise, of a life insurance policy or any interest therein for a valuable consideration, the amount of the proceeds attributable to such policy or interest which is excludable from the transferee's gross income is generally limited to the sum of (i) the actual value of the consideration for such transfer, and (ii) the premiums and other amounts subsequently paid by the transferee (see section 101(a)(2) and example (1) of subparagraph (5) of this paragraph). However, this limitation on the amount excludable from the transferee's gross income does not apply (except in certain special cases involving a series of transfers), where the basis of the policy or interest transferred, for the purpose of determining gain or loss with respect to the transferee, is determinable, in whole or in part, by reference to the basis of such policy or interest in the hands of the transferor (see section 101(a)(2)(A) and examples (2) and (4) of subparagraph (5) of this paragraph). Neither does the limitation apply where the policy or interest therein is transferred to the insured, to a partner of the insured, to a partnership in which the insured is a partner, or to a corporation in which the insured is a shareholder or officer (see section 101(a)(2)(B)). For rules relating to gratuitous transfers, see subparagraph (2) of this paragraph. For special rules with respect to certain cases where a series of transfers is involved, see subparagraph (3) of this paragraph.

(2) In the case of a gratuitous transfer, by assignment or otherwise, of a life insurance policy or any interest therein, as a general rule the amount of the proceeds attributable to such policy or interest which is excludable from the transferee's gross income under section 101(a) is limited to the sum of (i) the amount which would have been excludable by the transferor (in accordance with this section) if no such transfer had taken place, and (ii) any premiums and other amounts subsequently paid by the transferee. See example (6) of subparagraph (5) of this paragraph. However, where the gratuitous transfer in question is made by or to the insured, a partner of the insured, a partnership in which the insured is a partner, or a corporation in which the insured is a shareholder or officer, the entire amount of the proceeds attributable to the policy or interest transferred shall be excludable from the transferee's gross income (see section 101(a)(2)(B) and example (7) of subparagraph (5) of this paragraph).

(3) In the case of a series of transfers, if the last transfer of a life insurance policy or an interest therein is for a valuable consideration—

(i) The general rule is that the final transferee shall exclude from gross income, with respect to the proceeds of such policy or interest therein, only the sum of—

(a) The actual value of the consideration paid by him, and

(b) The premiums and other amounts subsequently paid by him;

(ii) If the final transfer is to the insured, to a partner of the insured, to a partnership in which the insured is a partner, or to a corporation in which the insured is a shareholder or officer, the final transferee shall exclude the entire amount of the proceeds from gross income;

(iii) Except where subdivision (ii) of this subparagraph applies, if the basis of the policy or interest transferred, for the purpose of determining gain or loss with respect to the final transferee, is determinable, in whole or in part, by reference to the basis of such policy or interest therein in the hands of the transferor, the amount of the proceeds which is excludable by the final transferee is limited to the sum of—

(a) The amount which would have been excludable by his transferor if no such transfer had taken place, and

(b) Any premiums and other amounts subsequently paid by the final transferee himself.

(4) For the purposes of section 101(a)(2) and subparagraphs (1) and (3) of this paragraph, a "transfer for a valuable consideration" is any absolute transfer for value of a right to receive all or a part of the proceeds of a life insurance policy. Thus, the creation, for value, of an enforceable contractual right to receive all or a part of the proceeds of a policy may constitute a transfer for a valuable consideration of the policy or an interest therein. On the other hand, the pledging or assignment of a policy as collateral security is not a transfer for a valuable consideration of such policy or an interest therein, and section 101 is inapplicable to any amounts received by the pledgee or assignee.

(5) The application of this paragraph may be illustrated by the following examples:

Example (1). A pays premiums of $500 for an insurance policy in the face amount of $1,000 upon the life of B, and subsequently transfers the policy to C for $600. C receives the proceeds of $1,000 upon the death of B. The amount which C can exclude from his gross income is limited to $600 plus any premiums paid by C subsequent to the transfer.

Example (2). The X Corporation purchases for a single premium of $500 an insurance policy in the face amount of $1,000 upon the life of A, one of its employees, naming the X Corporation as beneficiary. The X Corporation transfers the policy to the Y Corporation in a tax-free reorganization (the policy having a basis for determining gain or loss in the hands of the Y Corporation determined by reference to its basis in the hands of the X Corporation). The Y Corporation receives the proceeds of $1,000 upon the death of A. The entire $1,000 is to be excluded from the gross income of the Y Corporation.

Example (3). The facts are the same as in example (2) except that, prior to the death of A, the Y Corporation transfers the policy to the Z Corporation for $600. The Z Corporation receives the proceeds of $1,000 upon the death of A. The amount which the Z Corporation can exclude from its gross income is limited to $600 plus any premiums paid by the Z Corporation subsequent to the transfer of the policy to it.

Example (4). The facts are the same as in example (3) except that, prior to the death of A, the Z Corporation transfers the policy to the M Corporation in a tax-free reorganization (the policy having a basis for determining gain or loss in the hands of the M Corporation determined by reference to its basis in the hands of the Z Corporation). The M Corporation receives the proceeds of $1,000 upon the death of A. The amount which the M Corporation can exclude from its gross income is limited to $600 plus any premiums paid by the Z Corporation and the M Corporation subsequent to the transfer of the policy to the Z Corporation.

Example (5). The facts are the same as in example (3) except that, prior to the death of A, the Z Corporation transfers the policy to the N Corporation, in which A is a shareholder. The N Corporation receives the proceeds of $1,000 upon the death of A.

The entire $1,000 is to be excluded from the gross income of the N Corporation.

Example (6). A pays premiums of $500 for an insurance policy in the face amount of $1,000 upon his own life, and subsequently transfers the policy to his wife B for $600. B later transfers the policy without consideration to C, who is the son of A and B. C receives the proceeds of $1,000 upon the death of A. The amount which C can exclude from his gross income is limited to $600 plus any premiums paid by B and C subsequent to the transfer of the policy to B.

Example (7). The facts are the same as in example (6) except that, prior to the death of A, C transfers the policy without consideration to A, the insured. A's estate receives the proceeds of $1,000 upon the death of A. The entire $1,000 is to be excluded from the gross income of A's estate.

* * *

§ 1.101–3 Interest payments.

(a) Applicability of section 101(c). Section 101(c) provides that if any amount excluded from gross income by section 101(a) (relating to life insurance proceeds) or section 101(b) (relating to employees' death benefits) is held under an agreement to pay interest thereon, the interest payments shall be included in gross income. This provision applies to payments made (either by an insurer or by or on behalf of an employer) of interest earned on any amount so excluded from gross income which is held without substantial diminution of the principal amount during the period when such interest payments are being made or credited to the beneficiaries or estate of the insured or the employee. For example, if a monthly payment is $100, of which $99 represents interest and $1 represents diminution of the principal amount, the principal amount shall be considered held under an agreement to pay interest thereon and the interest payment shall be included in the gross income of the recipient. Section 101(c) applies whether the election to have an amount held under an agreement to pay interest thereon is made by the insured or employee or by his beneficiaries or estate, and whether or not an interest rate is explicitly stated in the agreement. Section 101 (d), relating to the payment of life insurance proceeds at a date later than death, shall not apply to any amount to which section 101(c) applies.* * * However, both section 101(c) and section 101(d) may apply to payments received under a single life insurance contract. For provisions relating to the application of this rule to payments received under a permanent life insurance policy with a family income rider attached, see paragraph (h) of § 1.101–4.

(b) Determination of "present value". For the purpose of determining whether section 101(c) or section 101(d) applies, the present value (at the time of the insured's death) of any amount which is to be paid at a date later than death shall be determined by the use of the interest rate and mortality tables used by the insurer in determining the size of the payments to be made.

§ 1.101–4 Payment of life insurance proceeds at a date later than death.

(a) In general. (1) (i) Section 101(d) states the provisions governing the exclusion from gross income of amounts (other than those to which section 101(c) applies) received under a life insurance contract and paid by reason of the death of the insured which are paid to a beneficiary on a date or dates later than the death of the insured. However, if the amounts payable as proceeds of life insurance to which section 101(a)(1) applies cannot in any event exceed the amount payable at the time of the insured's death, such amounts are fully excludable from the gross income of the recipient (or recipients) without regard to the actual time of payment and no further determination need be made under this section. Section 101(d)(1) * * * provides an exclusion from gross income of any amount determined by a proration, under applicable regulations, of "an amount held by an insurer with respect to any beneficiary". The quoted phrase is defined in section 101(d)(2). For the regulations governing the method of computation of this proration, see paragraphs (c) through (f) of this section. The prorated amounts are to be excluded from the gross income of the beneficiary regardless of the taxable year in which they are actually received (see example (2) of subparagraph (2) of this paragraph).

* * *

(b) Amount held by an insurer. (1) For the purpose of the proration referred to in section 101(d)(1), an "amount held by an insurer with respect to any beneficiary" means an amount equal to the present value to such beneficiary (as of the date of death of the insured) of an agreement by the insurer under a life insurance policy (whether as an option or otherwise) to pay such beneficiary an amount or amounts at a date or dates later than the death of the insured (section 101(d)(2)). The present value of such agreement is to be computed as if the agreement under the life insurance policy had been entered into on the date of death of the insured, except that such value shall be determined by the use of the mortality table and interest rate used by the insurer in calculating payments to be made to the beneficiary under such agreement. Where an insurance policy provides an option for the payment of a specific amount upon the death of the insured in full discharge of the contract, such lump sum is the amount held by the insurer with respect to all beneficiaries (or their beneficiaries) under the contract. See, however, paragraph (e) of this section.

(2) In the case of two or more beneficiaries, the "amount held by the insurer" with respect to each beneficiary depends on the relationship of the different benefits payable to such beneficiaries. Where the amounts payable to two or more beneficiaries are independent of each other, the "amount held by the insurer with respect to each beneficiary" shall be determined and prorated over the periods involved independently. Thus, if a certain amount per month is to be paid to A for his life, and, concurrently, another amount per month is to be paid to B for his life, the "amount held by the insurer" shall be determined and prorated for both A and B independently, but the aggregate shall not exceed the total present value of such payments to both. On the other hand, if the obligation to pay B was contingent on his surviving A, the "amount held by the insurer" shall be considered an amount held with respect to both beneficiaries simultaneously. Furthermore, it is immaterial whether B is a named beneficiary or merely the ultimate recipient of payments for a term of years. For the special rules governing the computation of the proration of the "amount held by an insurer" in determining amounts excludable under the provisions of section 101(d), see paragraphs (c) to (f), inclusive, of this section.

(3) Notwithstanding any other provision of this section, if the policy was transferred for a valuable consideration, the total "amount held by an insurer" cannot exceed the sum of the consideration paid plus any premiums or other consideration paid subsequent to the transfer if the provisions of section 101(a)(2) and paragraph (b) of § 1.101–1 limit the excludability of the proceeds to such total.

(c) Treatment of payments for life to a sole beneficiary. If the contract provides for the payment of a specified lump sum, but, pursuant to an agreement between the beneficiary and the insurer, payments are to be made during the life of the beneficiary in lieu of such lump sum, the lump sum shall be divided by the life expectancy of the beneficiary determined in accordance with the mortality table used by the insurer in determining the benefits to be paid. However, if payments are to be made to the estate or beneficiary of the primary beneficiary in the event that the primary beneficiary dies before receiving a certain number of payments or a specified total amount, such lump sum shall be reduced by the present value (at the time of the insured's death) of amounts which may be paid by reason of the guarantee, in accordance with the provisions of paragraph (e) of this section, before making this calculation. To the extent that payments received in each taxable year do not exceed the amount found from the above calculation, they are "prorated amounts" of the "amount held by an insurer" and are excludable from the gross income of the beneficiary without regard to whether he lives beyond the life expectancy used in making the calculation. If the contract in question does not provide for the payment of a specific lump sum upon the death of the insured as one of the alternative methods of payment, the present value (at the time of the death of the insured) of the payments to be made the beneficiary, determined in accordance with the interest rate and mortality table used by the insurer in determining the benefits to be paid, shall be used in the above calculation in lieu of a lump sum.

* * *

§ 1.104–1 Compensation for injuries or 'sickness.

(a) In general. Section 104(a) provides an exclusion from gross income with respect to certain amounts* * * which are received for personal injuries or sickness, except to the extent that such amounts are attributable to (but not in excess of) deductions allowed under section 213 (relating to medical, etc., expenses) for any prior taxable year. See section 213 and the regulations thereunder.

(b) Amounts received under workmen's compensation acts. Section 104(a)(1) excludes from gross income amounts which are received by an employee under a workmen's compensation act (such as the Longshoremen's and Harbor Workers' Compensation Act, 33 U.S.C., c. 18), or under a statute in the nature of a workmen's compensation act which provides compensation to employees for personal injuries or sickness incurred in the course of employment. Section 104(a)(1) also applies to compensation which is paid under a workmen's compensation act to the survivor or survivors of a deceased employee. However, section 104(a)(1) does not apply to a retirement pension or annuity to the extent that it is determined by reference to the employee's age or length of service, or the employee's prior contributions, even though the employee's retirement is occasioned by an occupational injury or sickness. Section 104(a)(1) also does not apply to amounts which are received as compensation for a nonoccupational injury or sickness nor to amounts received as compensation for an occupational injury or sickness to the extent that they are in excess of the amount provided in the applicable workmen's compensation act or acts. See, however, §§ 1.105–1 through 1.105–5 for rules relating to exclusion of such amounts from gross income.

(c) Damages received on account of personal injuries or sickness. Section 104(a)(2) excludes from gross income the amount of any damages received (whether by suit or agreement) on account of personal injuries or sickness. The term "damages received (whether by suit or agreement)" means an amount received (other than workmen's compensation) through prosecution of a legal suit or action based upon tort or tort type rights, or through a settlement agreement entered into in lieu of such prosecution.

(d) Accident or health insurance. Section 104(a)(3) excludes from gross income amounts received through accident or health insurance for personal injuries or sickness (other than amounts received by an employee, to the extent that such amounts (1) are attributable to contributions of the employer which were not includible in the gross income of the employee, or (2) are paid by the employer). Similar treatment is also accorded to amounts received under accident or health plans and amounts received from sickness or disability funds. See section 105(e) and § 1.105–5. If, therefore, an individual purchases a policy accident or health insurance out of his own funds, amounts received thereunder for personal injuries or sickness are excludable from his gross income under section 104(a)(3). See, however, section 213 and the regulations thereunder as to the inclusion in gross income of amounts attributable to deductions allowed under section 213 for any prior taxable year. Section 104(a)(3) also applies to amounts received by an employee for personal injuries or sickness from a fund which is maintained exclusively by employee contributions. Conversely, if an employer is either the sole contributor to such a fund, or is the sole purchaser of a policy of accident or health insurance for his employees (on either a group or individual basis), the exclusion provided under section 104(a)(3) does not apply to any amounts received by his employees through such fund or insurance. If the employer and his employees contribute to a fund or purchase insurance which pays accident or health benefits to employees, section 104(a)(3) does not apply to amounts received thereunder by employees to the extent that such amounts are attributable to the employer's contributions. See § 1.105–1 for rules relating to the determination of the amount attributable to employer contributions. Although amounts paid by or on behalf of an employer to an employee for personal injuries or sickness are not excludable from the employee's gross income under section 104(a)(3), they may be excludable therefrom under section 105. See §§ 1.105–1 through 1.105–5, inclusive. For treatment of accident or health benefits paid to or on behalf of a self-employed individual by a trust described in section 401(a) which is exempt under section 501(a) or under a plan described in section 403(a), see paragraph (g) of § 1.72–15.

(e) Amounts received as pensions, etc., for certain personal injuries or sickness. (1) Section 104(a)(4) excludes from gross income amounts which are received as a pension, annuity, or similar allowance for personal injuries or sickness resulting from active service in the armed forces of any country, or in the Coast and Geodetic Survey, or the Public Health Service.* * *

§ 1.105–1 Amounts attributable to employer contributions.

(a) In general. Under section 105(a), amounts received by an employee through accident or health insurance for personal injuries or sickness must be included in his gross income to the extent that such amounts (1) are attributable to contributions of the employer which were not includible in the gross income of the employee, or (2) are paid by the employer, unless such amounts are excluded therefrom under section 105(b), (c).* * * For purposes of this section, the term "amounts received by an employee through an accident or health plan" refers to any amounts received through accident or health insurance, and also to any amounts which, under section 105(e), are treated as being so received.* * * In determining the extent to which amounts received for personal injuries or sickness by an employee through an accident or health plan are subject to the provisions of section 105(a), rather than section 104(a)(3), the provisions of paragraphs (b), (c),* * * and (e) of this section shall apply. A self-employed individual is not an employee for purposes of section 105 and §§ 1.105–1 through 1.105–5.* * * Thus, such an individual will not be treated as an employee with respect to benefits described in section 105 received from a plan in which he participates as an employee within the meaning of section 401(c)(1) at the time he, his spouse, or any of his dependents becomes entitled to receive such benefits.

(b) Noncontributory plans. All amounts received by employees through an accident or health plan which is financed solely by their employer, either by payment of premiums on an accident or health insurance policy (whether on a group or individual basis), by contributions to a fund which pays accident or health benefits, or by direct payment of the benefits under the plan, are subject to the provisions of section 105(a), except to the extent that they are excludable under section 105(b), (c).* * *

* * *

(c) Contributory plans. (1) In the case of amounts received by an employee through an accident or health plan which is financed partially by his employer and partially by contributions of the employee, section 105(a) applies to the extent that such amounts are attributable to contributions of the employer which were not includible in the employee's gross income. The portion of such amounts which is attributable to such contributions of the employer shall be determined in accordance with paragraph (d) of this section in the case of an insured plan, or paragraph (e) of this section in the case of a noninsured plan. As used in this section, the phrase "contributions of the employer" means employer contributions which were not includible in the gross income of the employee. See section 106 for the exclusion from an employee's gross income of employer contributions to accident or health plans.

* * *

(4) A determination of the portion attributable to the contributions of the employer, once made in accordance with the rules of this section, shall as to such portion be used for all purposes. For example, if an employee receives amounts under a wage continuation plan during the month of January and terminates his services during February, the portion of such amounts which is attributable to the contributions of the employer may be determined in order to provide the employee with such information at the time he is provided his Form W-2. The determination made for such purpose will also be used by the employee to report his income for his taxable year in which such amounts are received, without regard to the experience under the plan for the rest of the year.

(d) Insured plans— (1) Individual policies. If an amount is received from an insurance company by an employee under an individual policy of accident or health insurance purchased by contributions of the employer and the employee, the portion of the amount received which is attributable to the employer's contributions shall be an amount which bears the same ratio to the amount received as the portion of the premiums paid by the employer for the current policy year bears to the total premiums paid by the employer and the employee for that year. This rule may be illustrated by the following example:

Example. Employer A maintains a plan whereby he pays two-thirds of the annual premium cost on individual policies of accident and health insurance for his employees. The remainder of each employee's premium is paid by a payroll deduction from the wages of the employee. The annual premium for employee X is $24, of which $16 is paid by the employer. Thus, 16/24 or two-thirds of all amounts received by X under such insurance policy are attributable to the contributions of the employer and are subject to section 105(a), and the remaining one-third of such amounts is excludable from X's gross income under section 104(a)(3).

(2) Group policies. If the accident or health coverage is provided under or is a part of a group insurance policy purchased by contributions of the employer and of the employees, and the net premiums for such coverage for a period of at least three policy years are known at the beginning of the calendar year, the portion of any amount received by an employee which is attributable to the contributions of the employer for such coverage shall be an amount which bears the same ratio to the amount received as the portion of the net premiums contributed by the employer for the last three policy years which are known at the beginning of the calendar year, bears to the total of the net premiums contributed by the employer and all employees for such policy years. If the net premiums for such coverage for a period of at least three policy years are not known at the beginning of the calendar year but are known for at least one policy year, such determination shall be made by using the net premiums for such coverage which are known at the beginning of the calendar year. If the net premiums for such coverage are not known at the beginning of the calendar year for even one policy year, such determination shall be made by using either (i) a reasonable estimate of the net premiums for the first policy year, or (ii) if the net premiums for a policy year are ascertained during the calendar year, by using such net premiums.

* * *

(e) Noninsured plans. If the accident or health benefits are a part of a noninsured plan to which the employer and the employees contribute, and such plan has been in effect for at least three years before the beginning of the calendar year, the portion of the amount received which is attributable to the employer's contributions shall be an amount which bears the same ratio to the amount received as the contributions of the employer for the period of three calendar years next preceding the year of receipt bear to the total contributions of the employer and all the employees for such period. If, at the beginning of the calendar year of receipt, such plan has not been in effect for three years but has been in effect for at least one year, such determination shall be based upon the contributions made during the 1-year or 2-year period during which the plan has been in effect. If such plan has not been in effect for one full year at the beginning of the calendar year of receipt, such determination may be based upon the portion of the year of receipt preceding the time when the determination is made, or such determination may be made periodically (such as monthly or quarterly) and used throughout the succeeding period. For example, if an employee terminates his services on April 15, 1955, and 1955 is the first year the plan has been in effect, such determination may be based upon the contributions of the employer and the employees during the period beginning with January 1 and ending with April 15, or during the month of March, or during the quarter consisting of January, February, and March.

§ 1.105–2 Amounts expended for medical care.

Section 105(b) provides an exclusion from gross income with respect to the amounts referred to in section 105(a) (see § 1.105–1) which are paid, directly or indirectly, to the taxpayer to reimburse him for expenses incurred for the medical care (as defined in section 213(e)) of the taxpayer, his spouse, and his dependents (as defined in section 152). However, the exclusion does not apply to amounts which are attributable to (and not in excess of) deductions allowed under section 213 (relating to medical, etc., expenses) for any prior taxable year. See section 213 and the regulations thereunder. Section 105(b) applies only to amounts which are paid specifically to reimburse the taxpayer for expenses incurred by him for the prescribed medical care. Thus, section 105(b) does not apply to amounts which the taxpayer would be entitled to receive irrespective of whether or not he incurs expenses for medical care. For example, if under a wage continuation plan the taxpayer is entitled to regular wages during a period of absence from work due to sickness or injury, amounts received under such plan are not excludable from his gross income under section 105(b) even though the taxpayer may have incurred medical expenses during the period of illness.* * * If the amounts are paid to the taxpayer solely to reimburse him for expenses which he incurred for the prescribed medical care, section 105(b) is applicable even though such amounts are paid without proof of the amount of the actual expenses incurred by the taxpayer, but section 105(b) is not applicable to the extent that such amounts exceed the amount of the actual expenses for such medical care. If the taxpayer incurs an obligation for medical care, payment to the obligee in discharge of such obligation shall constitute indirect payment to the taxpayer as reimbursement for medical care. Similarly, payment to or on behalf of the taxpayer's spouse or dependents shall constitute indirect payment to the taxpayer.

§ 1.105–3 Payments unrelated to absence from work.

Section 105(c) provides an exclusion from gross income with respect to the amounts referred to in section 105(a) to the extent that such amounts (a) constitute payments for the permanent loss or permanent loss of use of a member or function of the body, or the permanent disfigurement, of the taxpayer, his spouse, or a dependent (as defined in section 152), and (b) are computed with reference to the nature of the injury without regard to the period the employee is absent from work. Loss of use or disfigurement shall be considered permanent when it may reasonably be expected to continue for the life of the individual. For purposes of section 105(c), loss or loss of use of a member or function of the body includes the loss or loss of use of an appendage of the body, the loss of an eye, the loss of substantially all of the vision of an eye, and the loss of substantially all of the hearing in one or both ears. The term "disfigurement" shall be given a reasonable interpretation in the light of all the particular facts and circumstances. Section 105(c) does not apply if the amount of the benefits is determined by reference to the period the employee is absent from work. For example, if an employee is absent from work as a result of the loss of an arm, and under the accident and health plan established by his employer, he is to receive $125 a week so long as he is absent from work for a period not in excess of 52 weeks, section 105(c) is not applicable to such payments. * * *

However, for purposes of section 105(c), it is immaterial whether an amount is paid in a lump sum or in installments. Section 105(c) does not apply to amounts which are treated as workmen's compensation under paragraph (b) of § 1.104–1, or to amounts paid by reason of the death of the employee (see section 101).

* * *

§ 1.105–5 Accident and health plans.

(a) In general. Sections 104(a)(3) and 105(b), (c),* * * exclude from gross income certain amounts received through accident or health insurance. Section 105(e) provides that for purposes of sections 104 and 105 amounts received through an accident or health plan for employees, and amounts received from a sickness and disability fund for employees maintained under the law of a State, a Territory, or the District of Columbia, shall be treated as amounts received through accident or health insurance. In general, an accident or health plan is an arrangement for the payment of amounts to employees in the event of personal injuries or sickness. A plan may cover one or more employees, and there may be different plans for different employees or classes of employees. An accident or health plan may be either insured or noninsured, and it is not necessary that the plan be in writing or that the employee's rights to benefits under the plan be enforceable. However, if the employee's rights are not enforceable, an amount will be deemed to be received under a plan only if, on the date the employee became sick or injured, the employee was covered by a plan (or a program, policy, or custom having the effect of a plan) providing for the payment of amounts to the employee in the event of personal injuries or sickness, and notice or knowledge of such plan was reasonably available to the employee. It is immaterial who makes payment of the benefits provided by the plan. For example, payment may be made by the employer, a welfare fund, a State sickness or disability benefits fund, an association of employers or employees, or by an insurance company.

(b) Self-employed individuals. Under section 105(g), a self-employed individual is not treated as an employee for purposes of section 105. Therefore, for example, benefits paid under an accident or health plan as referred to in section 105(e) to or on behalf of an individual who is self-employed in the business with respect to which the plan is established will not be treated as received through accident and health insurance for purposes of sections 104(a)(3) and 105.

* * *

§ 1.106–1 Contributions by employer to accident and health plans.

The gross income of an employee does not include contributions which his employer makes to an accident or health plan for compensation (through insurance or otherwise) to the employee for personal injuries or sickness incurred by him, his spouse, or his dependents, as defined in section 152. The employer may contribute to an accident or health plan either by paying the premium (or a portion of the premium) on a policy of accident or health insurance covering one or more of his employees, or by contributing to a separate trust or fund (including a fund referred to in section 105(e)) which provides accident or health benefits directly or through insurance to one or more of his employees. However, if such insurance policy, trust, or fund provides other benefits in addition to accident or health benefits, section 106 applies only to the portion of the employer's contribution which is allocable to accident or health benefits. See paragraph (d) of § 1.104–1 and §§ 1.105–1 through 1.105–5, inclusive, for regulations relating to exclusion from an employee's gross income of amounts received through accident or health insurance and through accident or health plans.

§ 1.107–1 Rental value of parsonages.

(a) In the case of a minister of the gospel, gross income does not include (1) the rental value of a home, including utilities, furnished to him as a part of his compensation, or (2) the rental allowance paid to him as part of his compensation to the extent such allowance is used by him to rent or otherwise provide a home. In order to qualify for the exclusion, the home or rental allowance must be provided as remuneration for services which are ordinarily the duties of a minister of the gospel.* * * Examples of specific services the performance of which will be considered duties of a minister for purposes of section 107 include the performance of sacerdotal functions, the conduct of religious worship, the administration and maintenance of religious organizations and their integral agencies, and the performance of teaching and administrative duties at theological seminaries. Also, the service performed by a qualified minister as an employee of the United States (other than as a chaplain in the Armed Forces, whose service is considered to be that of a commissioned officer in his capacity as such, and not as a minister in the exercise of his ministry), or a State, Territory, or possession of the United States, or a political subdivision of any of the foregoing, or the District of Columbia, is in the exercise of his ministry provided the service performed includes such services as are ordinarily the duties of a minister.

* * *

(c) A rental allowance must be included in the minister's gross income in the taxable year in which it is received, to the extent that such allowance is not used by him during such taxable year to rent or otherwise provide a home. Circumstances under which a rental allowance will be deemed to have been used to rent or provide a home will include cases in which the allowance is expended (1) for rent of a home, (2) for purchase of a home, and (3) for expenses directly related to providing a home. Expenses for food and servants are not considered for this purpose to be directly related to providing a home. Where the minister rents, purchases, or owns a farm or other business property in addition to a home, the portion of the rental allowance expended in connection with the farm or business property shall not be excluded from his gross income.

* * *

§ 1.109–1 Exclusion from gross income of lessor of real property of value of improvements erected by lessee.

(a) Income derived by a lessor of real property upon the termination, through forfeiture or otherwise, of the lease of such property and attributable to buildings erected or other improvements made by the lessee upon the leased property is excluded from gross income. However, where the facts disclose that such buildings or improvements represent in whole or in part a liquidation in kind of lease rentals, the exclusion from gross income shall not apply to the extent that such buildings or improvements represent such liquidation. The exclusion applies only with respect to the income realized by the lessor upon the termination of the lease and has no application to income, if any, in the form of rent, which may be derived by a lessor during the period of the lease and attributable to buildings erected or other improvements made by the lessee. It has no application to income which may be realized by the lessor upon the termination of the lease but not attributable to the value of such buildings or improvements. Neither does it apply to income derived by the lessor subsequent to the termination of the lease incident to the ownership of such buildings or improvements.

* * *

§ 1.118–1 Contributions to the capital of a corporation.

In the case of a corporation, section 118 provides an exclusion from gross income with respect to any contribution of money or property to the capital of the taxpayer. Thus, if a corporation requires additional funds for conducting its business and obtains such funds through voluntary pro rata payments by its shareholders, the amounts so received being credited to its surplus account or to a special account, such amounts do not constitute income, although there is no increase in the outstanding shares of stock of the corporation. In such a case the payments are in the nature of assessments upon, and represent an additional price paid for, the shares of stock held by the individual shareholders, and will be treated as an addition to and as a part of the operating capital of the company. Section 118 also applies to contributions to capital made by persons other than shareholders. For example, the exclusion applies to the value of land or other property contributed to a corporation by a governmental unit or by a civic group for the purpose of inducing the corporation to locate its business in a particular community, or for the purpose of enabling the corporation to expand its operating facilities. However, the exclusion does not apply to any money or property transferred to the corporation in consideration for goods or services rendered, or to subsidies paid for the purpose of inducing the taxpayer to limit production. See section 362 for the basis of property acquired by a corporation through a contribution to its capital by its stockholders or by nonstockholders.

§ 1.119–1 Meals and lodging furnished for the convenience of the employer.

(a) Meals—(1) In general. The value of meals furnished to an employee by his employer shall be excluded from the employee's gross income if two tests are met: (i) The meals are furnished on the business premises of the employer, and (ii) the meals are furnished for the convenience of the employer. The question of whether meals are furnished for the convenience of the employer is one of fact to be determined by analysis of all the facts and circumstances in each case. If the tests described in subdivisions (i) and (ii) of this subparagraph are met, the exclusion shall apply irrespective of whether under an employment contract or a statute fixing the terms of employment such meals are furnished as compensation.

(2) Meals furnished without a charge. (i) Meals furnished by an employer without charge to the employee will be regarded as furnished for the convenience of the employer if such meals are furnished for a substantial noncompensatory business reason of the employer. If an employer furnishes meals as a means of providing additional compensation to his employee (and not for a substantial noncompensatory business reason of the employer), the meals so furnished will not be regarded as furnished for the convenience of the employer. Conversely, if the employer furnishes meals to his employee for a substantial noncompensatory business reason, the meals so furnished will be regarded as furnished for the convenience of the employer, even though such meals are also furnished for a compensatory reason. In determining the reason of an employer for furnishing meals, the mere declaration that meals are furnished for a noncompensatory business reason is not sufficient to prove that meals are furnished for the convenience of the employer, but such determination will be based upon an examination of all the surrounding facts and circumstances. In subdivision (ii) of this subparagraph, there are set forth some of the substantial noncompensatory business reasons which occur frequently and which justify the conclusion that meals furnished for such a reason are furnished for the convenience of the employer. In subdivision (iii) of this subparagraph, there are set forth some of the business reasons which are considered to be compensatory and which, in the absence of a substantial noncompensatory business reason, justify the conclusion that meals furnished for such a reason are not furnished for the convenience of the employer. Generally, meals furnished before or after the working hours of the employee will not be regarded as furnished for the convenience of the employer, but see subdivision (ii)(d) and (f) of this subparagraph for some exceptions to this general rule. Meals furnished on nonworking days do not qualify for the exclusion under section 119. If the employee is required to occupy living quarters on the business premises of his employer as a condition of his employment (as defined in paragraph (b) of this section), the exclusion applies to the value of any meal furnished without charge to the employee on such premises.

(ii) (a) Meals will be regarded as furnished for a substantial noncompensatory business reason of the employer when the meals are furnished to the employee during his working hours to have the employee available for emergency call during his meal period. In order to demonstrate that meals are furnished to the employee to have the employee available for emergency call during the meal period, it must be shown that emergencies have actually occurred, or can reasonably be expected to occur, in the employer's business which have resulted, or will result, in the employer calling on the employee to perform his job during his meal period.

(b) Meals will be regarded as furnished for a substantial noncompensatory business reason of the employer when the meals are furnished to the employee during his working hours because the employer's business is such that the employee must be restricted to a short meal period, such as 30 or 45 minutes, and because the employee could not be expected to eat elsewhere in such a short meal period. For example, meals may qualify under this subdivision when the employer is engaged in a business in which the peak work load occurs during the normal lunch hours. However, meals cannot qualify under this subdivision (b) when the reason for restricting the time of the meal period is so that the employee can be let off earlier in the day.

(c) Meals will be regarded as furnished for a substantial noncompensatory business reason of the employer when the meals are furnished to the employee during his working hours because the employee could not otherwise secure proper meals within a reasonable meal period. For example, meals may qualify under this subdivision (c) when there are insufficient eating facilities in the vicinity of the employer's premises.

(d) A meal furnished to a restaurant employee or other food service employee for each meal period in which the employee works will be regarded as furnished for a substantial noncompensatory business reason of the employer, irrespective of whether the meal is furnished during, immediately before, or immediately after the working hours of the employee.

(e) If the employer furnishes meals to employees at a place of business and the reason for furnishing the meals to each of substantially all of the employees who are furnished the meals is a substantial noncompensatory business reason of the employer, the meals furnished to each other employee will also be regarded as furnished for a substantial noncompensatory business reason of the employer.

(f) If an employer would have furnished a meal to an employee during his working hours for a substantial noncompensatory business reason, a meal furnished to such an employee immediately after his working hours because his duties prevented him from obtaining a meal during his working hours will be regarded as furnished for a substantial non-compensatory business reason.

(iii) Meals will be regarded as furnished for a compensatory business reason of the employer when the meals are furnished to the employee to promote the morale or goodwill of the employee, or to attract prospective employees.

(3) Meals furnished with a charge. (i) If an employer provides meals which an employee may or may not purchase, the meals will not be regarded as furnished for the convenience of the employer. Thus, meals for which a charge is made by the employer will not be regarded as furnished for the convenience of the employer if the employee has a choice of accepting the meals and paying for them or of not paying for them and providing his meals in another manner.

(ii) If an employer furnishes an employee meals for which the employee is charged an unvarying amount (for example, by subtraction from his stated compensation) irrespective of whether he accepts the meals, the amount of such flat charge made by the employer for such meals is not, as such, part of the compensation includible in the gross income of the employee; whether the value of the meals so furnished is excludable under section 119 is determined by applying the rules of subparagraph (2) of this paragraph. If meals furnished for an unvarying amount are not furnished for the convenience of the employer in accordance with the rules of subparagraph (2) of this paragraph, the employee shall include in gross income the value of the meals regardless of whether the value exceeds or is less than the amount charged for such meals. In the absence of evidence to the contrary, the value of the meals may be deemed to be equal to the amount charged for them.

(b) Lodging. The value of lodging furnished to an employee by the employer shall be excluded from the employee's gross income if three tests are met:

(1) The lodging is furnished on the business premises of the employer,

(2) The lodging is furnished for the convenience of the employer, and

(3) The employee is required to accept such lodging as a condition of his employment.

The requirement of subparagraph (3) of this paragraph that the employee is required to accept such lodging as a condition of his employment means that he be required to accept the lodging in order to enable him properly to perform the duties of his employment. Lodging will be regarded as furnished to enable the employee properly to perform the duties of his employment when, for example, the lodging is furnished because the employee is required to be available for duty at all times or because the employee could not perform the services required of him unless he is furnished such lodging. If the tests described in subparagraphs (1), (2), and (3) of this paragraph are met, the exclusion shall apply irrespective of whether a charge is made, or whether, under an employment contract or statute fixing the terms of employment, such lodging is furnished as compensation. If the employer furnishes the employee lodging for which the employee is charged an unvarying amount irrespective of whether he accepts the lodging, the amount of the charge made by the employer for such lodging is not, as such, part of the compensation includible in the gross income of the employee; whether the value of the lodging is excludable from gross income under section 119 is determined by applying the other rules of this paragraph. If the tests described in subparagraph (1), (2), and (3) of this paragraph are not met, the employee shall include in gross income the value of the lodging regardless of whether it exceeds or is less than the amount charged. In the absence of evidence to the contrary, the value of the lodging may be deemed to be equal to the amount charged.

(c) Business premises of the employer— (1) In general. For purposes of this section, the term "business premises of the employer" generally means the place of employment of the employee. For example, meals and lodging furnished in the employer's home to a domestic servant would constitute meals and lodging furnished on the business premises of the employer. Similarly, meals furnished to cowhands while herding their employer's cattle on leased land would be regarded as furnished on the business premises of the employer.

(2) Certain camps. For taxable years beginning after December 31, 1981, in the case of an individual who is furnished lodging by or on behalf of his employer in a camp (as defined in paragraph (d) of this section) in a foreign country (as defined in

§ 1.911—2(h)), the camp shall be considered to be part of the business premises of the employer.

(d) Camp defined—**(1) In general.** For the purposes of paragraph (c)(2) of this section, a camp is lodging that is all of the following:

(i) Provided by or on behalf of the employer for the convenience of the employer because the place at which the employee renders services is in a remote area where satisfactory housing is not available to the employee on the open market within a reasonable commuting distance of that place;

(ii) Located, as near as practicable, in the vicinity of the place at which the employee renders services; and

(iii) Furnished in a common area or enclave which is not available to the general public for lodging or accommodations and which normally accommodates ten or more employees.

(2) Satisfactory housing. For purposes of paragraph (d)(1)(i) of this section, facts and circumstances that may be relevant in determining whether housing available to the employee is satisfactory include, but are not limited to, the size and condition of living space and the availability and quality of utilities such as water, sewers or other waste disposal facilities, electricity, or heat. The general environment in which housing is located (e.g. climate, prevalence of insects, etc.) does not of itself make housing unsatisfactory. The general environment is relevant, however, if housing is inadequate to protect the occupants from environmental conditions. The individual employee's income level is not relevant in determining whether housing is satisfactory; it may, however, be relevant in determining whether satisfactory housing is available to the employee (see paragraph (d)(3)(i)(B) of this section).

(3) Availability of satisfactory housing—**(i) Facts and circumstances.** For purposes of paragraph (d)(1)(i) of this section, facts and circumstances to be considered in determining whether satisfactory housing is available to the employee on the open market include but are not limited to:

(A) The number of housing units available on the open market in relation to the number of housing units required for the employer's employees;

(B) The cost of housing available on the open market;

(C) The quality of housing available on the open market; and

(D) The presence of warfare or civil insurrection within the area where housing would be available which would subject U.S. citizens to unusual risk of personal harm or property loss.

(ii) Presumptions. Satisfactory housing will generally be considered to be unavailable to the employee on the open market if either of the following conditions is satisfied:

(A) The foreign government requires the employer to provide housing for its employees other than housing available on the open market; or

(B) An unrelated person awarding work to the employer requires that the employer's employees occupy housing specified by such unrelated person.

The condition of either paragraph (d)(3)(ii)(A) or (B) of this section is not satisfied if the requirement described therein and imposed either by a foreign government or unrelated person applies primarily to U.S. employers and not to a significant number of third country employers or applies primarily to employers of U.S. employees and not to a significant number of employers of third country employees.

(4) Reasonable commuting distance. For purposes of paragraph (d)(1)(i) of this section, in determining whether a commuting distance is reasonable, the accessibility of the place at which the employee renders services due to geographic factors, the quality of the roads, the customarily available transportation, and the usual travel time (at the time of day such travel would be required) to the place at which the employee renders services shall be taken into account.

(5) Common area or enclave. A cluster of housing units does not satisfy paragraph (d)(1)(iii) of this section if it is adjacent to or surrounded by substantially similar housing available to the general public. Two or more common areas or enclaves that house employees who work on the same project (for example, a highway project) are considered to be one common area or enclave in determining whether they normally accommodate ten or more employees.

(e) Rules. The exclusion provided by section 119 applies only to meals and lodging furnished in kind by or on behalf of an employer to his employee. If the employee has an option to receive additional compensation in lieu of meals or lodging in kind, the value of such meals and lodging is not excludable from gross income under section 119. However, the mere fact that an employee, at his option, may decline to accept meals tendered in kind will not of itself require inclusion of the value thereof in gross income. Cash allowances for meals or lodging received by an employee are includible in gross income to the extent that such allowances constitute compensation.

(f) Examples. The provisions of section 119 may be illustrated by the following examples:

Example (1). A waitress who works from 7 a.m. to 4 p.m. is furnished without charge two meals a work day. The employer encourages the waitress to have her breakfast on his business premises before starting work, but does not require her to have breakfast there. She is required, however, to have her lunch on such premises. Since the waitress is a food service employee and works during the normal breakfast and lunch periods, the waitress is permitted to exclude from her gross income both the value of the breakfast and the value of the lunch.

Example (2). The waitress in example (1) is allowed to have meals on the employer's premises without charge on her days off. The waitress is not permitted to exclude the value of such meals from her gross income.

Example (3). A bank teller who works from 9 a.m. to 5 p.m. is furnished his lunch without charge in a cafeteria which the bank maintains on its premises. The bank furnishes the teller such meals in order to limit his lunch period to 30 minutes since the bank's peak work load occurs during the normal lunch period. If the teller had to obtain his lunch elsewhere, it would take him considerably longer than 30 minutes for lunch, and the bank strictly enforces the 30-minute time limit. The bank teller may exclude from his gross income the value of such meals obtained in the bank cafeteria.

* * *

Example (6). An employee of an institution is given the choice of residing at the institution free of charge, or of residing elsewhere and receiving a cash allowance in addition to his regular salary. If he elects to reside at the institution, the value to the employee of the lodging furnished by the employer will be includible in the employee's gross income because his residence at the institution is not required in order for him to perform properly the duties of his employment.

Example (7). A construction worker is employed at a construction project at a remote job site in Alaska. Due to the inaccessibility of facilities for the employees who are working at the job site to obtain food and lodging and the prevailing weather conditions, the employer is required to furnish meals and lodging to the employee at the camp site in order to carry on the construction project. The employee is required to pay $40 a week for the meals and lodging. The weekly charge of $40 is not, as such, part of the compensation includible in the gross income of the employee, and under paragraphs (a) and (b) of this section the value of the meals and lodging is excludable from his gross income.

Example (8). A manufacturing company provides a cafeteria on its premises at which its employees can purchase their lunch. There is no other eating facility located near the company's premises, but the employee can furnish his own meal by bringing his lunch. The amount of compensation which any employee is required to include in gross income is not reduced by the amount charged for the meals, and the meals are not considered to be furnished for the convenience of the employer.

Example (9). A hospital maintains a cafeteria on its premises where all of its 230 employees may obtain a meal during their working hours. No charge is made for these meals. The hospital furnishes such meals in order to have each of 210 of the employees available for any emergencies that may occur, and it is shown that each such employee is at times called upon to perform services during his meal period. Although the hospital does not require such employees to remain on the premises during meal periods, they rarely leave the hospital during their meal period. Since the hospital furnishes meals to each of substantially all of its employees in order to have each of them available for emergency call during his meal period, all of the hospital employees who obtain their meals in the hospital cafeteria may exclude from their gross income the value of such meals.

* * *

§ 1.121–3 Reduced maximum exclusion for taxpayers failing to meet certain requirements.

(a) In general. In lieu of the limitation under section 121(b) and §1.121–2, a reduced maximum exclusion limitation may be available for a taxpayer who sells or exchanges property used as the taxpayer's principal residence but fails to satisfy the ownership and use requirements described in §1.121–1(a) and (c) or the 2-year limitation described in §1.12–2(b).

(b) Primary reason for sale or exchange. In order for a taxpayer to claim a reduced maximum exclusion under section 121(c), the sale or exchange must be by reason of a change in place of employment, health, or unforeseen circumstances. If a safe harbor described in this section applies, a sale or exchange is deemed to be by reason of a change in place of employment, health, or unforeseen circumstances. If a safe harbor described in this section does not apply, a sale or exchange is by reason of a change in place of employment, health, or unforeseen circumstances only if the primary reason for the sale or exchange is a change in place of employment (within the meaning of paragraph (c) of this section), health (within the meaning of paragraph (d) of this section), or unforeseen circumstances (within the meaning of paragraph (e) of this section). Whether the requirements of this section are satisfied depends upon all the facts and circumstances. Factors that may be relevant in determining the taxpayer's primary reason for the sale or exchange include (but are not limited to) the extent to which—

(1) The sale or exchange and the circumstances giving rise to the sale or exchange are proximate in time;

(2) The suitability of the property as the taxpayer's principal residence materially changes;

(3) The taxpayer's financial ability to maintain the property materially changes;

(4) The taxpayer uses the property as the taxpayer's residence during the period of the taxpayer's ownership of the property;

(5) The circumstances giving rise to the sale or exchange are not reasonably foreseeable when the taxpayer begins using the property as the taxpayer's principal residence; and

(6) The circumstances giving rise to the sale or exchange occur during the period of the taxpayer's ownership and use of the property as the taxpayer's principal residence.

(c) Sale or exchange by reason of a change in place of employment— (1) In general. A sale or exchange is by reason of a change in place of employment if, in the case of a qualified individual described in paragraph (f) of this section, the primary reason for the sale or exchange is a change in the location of the individual's employment.

(2) Distance safe harbor. A sale or exchange is deemed to be a change in place of employment (within the meaning of paragraph (c)(1) of this section) if—

(i) The change in place of employment occurs during the period of the taxpayer's ownership and use of the property as the taxpayer's principal residence; and

(ii) The qualified individual's new place of employment is at least 50 miles farther from the residence sold or exchanged than was the former place of employment, or, if there was no former place of employment, the distance between the individual's new place of employment and the residence sold or exchanged is at least 50 miles.

(3) Employment. For purposes of this paragraph (c), *employment* includes the commencement of employment with a new employer, the continuation of employment with the same employer, and the commencement or continuation of self-employment.

(4) Examples. The following examples illustrate the rules of this paragraph (c):

Example (1). A is unemployed and owns a townhouse that she has owned and used as her principal residence since 2003. In 2004 A obtains a job that is 54 miles from her townhouse, and she sells the townhouse. Because the distance between A's new place of employment and the townhouse is at least 50 miles, the sale is within the safe harbor of paragraph (c)(2) of this section and A is entitled to claim a reduced maximum exclusion under section 121(c)(2).

Example (2). B is an officer in the United States Air Force stationed in Florida. B purchases a house in Florida in 2002. In May 2003 B moves out of his house to take a 3-year assignment in Germany. B sells his house in January 2004. Because B's new place of employment in Germany is at least 50 miles farther from the residence sold than is B's former place of employment in Florida, the sale is within the safe harbor of paragraph (c)(2) of this section and B is entitled to claim a reduced maximum exclusion under section 121(c)(2).

Example (3). C is employed by Employer R at R's Philadelphia office. C purchases a house in February 2002 that is 35 miles from R's Philadelphia office. In May 2003 C begins a temporary assignment at R's Wilmington office that is 72 miles from C's house, and moves out of the house. In June 2005 C is assigned to work in R's London office, and as a result, sells her house in August 2005. The sale of the house is not within the safe harbor of paragraph (c)(2) of this section by reason of the change in place of employment from Philadelphia to Wilmington because the Wilmington office is not 50 miles farther from C's house than is the Philadelphia office. Furthermore, the sale is not within the safe harbor by reason of the change in place of employment to London because C is not using the house as her principal residence when she moves to London. However, C is entitled to claim a reduced maximum exclusion under section 121 (c)(2) because, under the facts and circumstances, the primary reason for the sale is the change in C's place of employment.

Example (4). In July 2003 D buys a condominium that is 5 miles from her place of employment and uses it as her principal residence. In February 2004 D, who works as an emergency medicine physician, obtains a job that is located 51 miles from D's condominium. D may be called in to work unscheduled hours and, when called, must be able to arrive at work quickly. Therefore, D sells her condominium and buys a townhouse that is 4 miles from her new place of employment. Because D's new place of employment is only 46 miles farther from the condominium than is D's former place of employment, the sale is not within the safe harbor of paragraph (c)(2) of this section. However, D is entitled to claim a reduced maximum exclusion under section 121(c)(2) because, under the facts and circumstances, the primary reason for the sale is the change in D's place of employment.

(d) Sale or exchange by reason of health— (1) In general. A sale or exchange is by reason of health if the primary reason for the sale or exchange is to obtain, provide, or facilitate the diagnosis, cure, mitigation, or treatment of disease, illness, or injury of a qualified individual described in paragraph (f) of this section, or to obtain or provide medical or personal care for a qualified individual suffering from a disease, illness, or injury. A sale or exchange that is merely beneficial to the general health or well-being of the individual is not a sale or exchange by reason of health.

(2) Physician's recommendation safe harbor. The primary reason for the sale or exchange is deemed to be health if the physician (as defined in section 213(d)(4)) recommends a change of residence for reasons of health (as defined in paragraph (d)(1) of this section).

(3) Examples. The following examples illustrate the rules of this paragraph (d):

Example (1). In 2003 A buys a house that she uses as her principal residence. A is injured in an accident and is unable to care for herself. As a result, A sells her house in 2004 and moves in with her daughter so that the daughter can provide the care that A requires as a result of her injury. Because, under the facts and circumstances, the primary reason for the sale of A's house is A's health, A is entitled to claim a reduced maximum exclusion under section 121(c)(2).

Example (2). H's father has a chronic disease. In 2003 H and W purchase a house that they use as their principal residence. In 2004 H and W sell their house in order to move into the house of H's father so that they can provide the care he requires as a result of his disease. Because, under the facts and circumstances, the primary reason for the sale of their house is the health of H's father, H and W are entitled to claim a reduced maximum exclusion under section 121(c)(2).

Example (3). H and W purchase a house in 2003 that they use as their principal residence. Their son suffers from a chronic illness that requires regular medical care. Later that year their doctor recommends that their son begin a new treatment that is available at a medical facility 100 miles away from their residence. In 2004 H and W sell their house to be closer to the medical facility. Because, under the facts and circumstances, the primary reason for the sale is to facilitate the treatment of their son's chronic illness, H and W are entitled to claim a reduced maximum exclusion under section 121(c)(2).

Example (4). B, who has chronic asthma, purchases a house in Minnesota in 2003 that he uses as his principal residence. B's doctor tells B that moving to a warm, dry climate would mitigate B's asthma symptoms. In 2004 B sells his house and moves to Arizona to relieve his asthma symptoms. The sale is within the safe harbor of paragraph (d)(2) of this section and B is entitled to claim a reduced maximum exclusion under section 121(c)(2).

Example (5). In 2003 H and W purchase a house in Michigan that they use as their principal residence. H's doctor tells H that he should get more exercise, but H is not suffering from any diseases that can be treated or mitigated by exercise. In 2004 H and W sell their house and move to Florida so that H can increase his general level of exercise by playing golf year-round. Because the sale of the house is merely beneficial to H's general health, the sale of the house is not by reason of H's health. H and W are not entitled to claim a reduced maximum exclusion under section 121(c)(2).

(e) Sale or exchange by reason of unforeseen circumstances— (1) In general. A sale or exchange is by reason of unforeseen circumstances if the primary reason for the sale or exchange is the occurrence of an event that the taxpayer could not reasonably have anticipated before purchasing and occupying the residence. A sale or exchange by reason of unforeseen circumstances (other than a sale or exchange deemed to be by reason of unforeseen circumstances under paragraph (e)(2) or (3) of this section) does not qualify for the reduced maximum exclusion if the primary reason for the sale or exchange is a preference for a different residence or an improvement in financial circumstances.

(2) Specific event safe harbors. The primary reason for the sale or exchange is deemed to be unforeseen circumstances (within the meaning of paragraph (e)(1) of this section) if any of the events specified in paragraphs (e)(2)(i) through (iii) of this section occur during the period of the taxpayer's ownership and use of the residence as the taxpayer's principal residence—

(i) The involuntary conversion of the residence;

(ii) Natural or man-made disasters or acts of war or terrorism resulting in a casualty to the residence (without regard to deductibility under section 165(h));

(iii) In the case of a qualified individual described in paragraph (f) of this section—

(A) Death;

(B) The cessation of employment as a result of which the individual is eligible for unemployment compensation (as defined in section 85(b));

(C) A change in employment or self-employment status that results in the taxpayer's inability to pay housing costs and reasonable basic living expenses for the taxpayer's household (including amounts for food, clothing, medical expenses, taxes, transportation, court-ordered payments, and expenses reasonably necessary to the production of income, but not for the maintenance of an affluent or luxurious standard of living):

(D) Divorce or legal separation under a decree of divorce or separate maintenance; or

(E) Multiple births resulting from the same pregnancy; or

(3) Designation of additional events as unforeseen circumstances. The Commissioner may designate other events or situations as unforeseen circumstances in published guidance of general applicability and may issue rulings addressed to specific taxpayers identifying other events or situations as unforeseen circumstances with regard to those taxpayers (see § 601.601(d)(2) of this chapter).

(4) Examples. The following examples illustrate the rules of this paragraph (e):

Example (1). In 2003 A buys a house in California. After A begins to use the house as her principal residence, an earthquake causes damage to A's house. A sells the house in 2004. The sale is within the safe harbor of paragraph (e)(2)(ii) of this section and A is entitled to claim a reduced maximum exclusion under section 121(c)(2).

Example (2). H works as a teacher and W works as a pilot. In 2003 H and W buy a house that they use as their principal residence. Later that year W is furloughed from her job for six months. H and W are unable to pay their mortgage during the period W is furloughed. H and W sell their house in 2004. The sale is within the safe harbor of paragraph (e)(2)(iii)(C) of this section and H and W are entitled to claim a reduced maximum exclusion under section 121(c)(2).

Example (3). In 2003 H and W buy a two-bedroom condominium that they use as their principal residence. In 2004 W gives birth to twins and H and W sell their condominium and buy a four-bedroom house. The sale is within the safe harbor of paragraph (e)(2)(iii)(E) of this section, and H and W are entitled to claim a reduced maximum exclusion under section 121(c)(2).

Example (4). B buys a condominium in 2003 and uses it as his principal residence. B's monthly condominium fee is $X. Three months after B moves into the condominium, the condominium association decides to replace the building's roof and heating system. Six months later, B's monthly condominium fee doubles. B sells the condominium in 2004 because B is unable to pay the new condominium fee along with the monthly mortgage payment. The safe harbors of paragraph (e)(2) of this section do not apply. However, under the facts and circumstances, the primary reason for the sale is unforeseen circumstances, and B is entitled to claim a reduced maximum exclusion under section 121(c)(2).

Example (5). In 2003 C buys a house that he uses as his principal residence. The property is located on a heavily traveled road. C sells the property in 2004 because C is disturbed by the traffic. The safe harbors of paragraph (e)(2) of this section do not apply. Under the facts and circumstances, the traffic is not an unforeseen circumstance because C could reasonably have anticipated the traffic at the time he purchased and occupied the house. Consequently, the sale of the house is not by reason of unforeseen circumstances and C is not entitled to claim a reduced maximum exclusion under section 121(c)(2).

Example (6). In 2003 D and her fiance E buy a house and live in it as their principal residence. In 2004 D and E cancel their wedding plans and E moves out of the house. Because D cannot afford to make the monthly mortgage payments alone, D and E sell the house in 2004. The safe harbors of paragraph (e)(2) of this section do not apply. However, under the facts and circumstances, the primary reason for the sale, the broken engagement, is an unforeseen circumstance because D and E could not reasonably have anticipated the broken engagement at the time they purchased and occupied the house. Consequently, the sale is by reason of unforeseen circumstances and D and E are each entitled to claim a reduced maximum exclusion under section 121(c)(2).

Example (7). In 2003 F buys a small condominium that she uses as her principal residence. In 2005 F receives a promotion and a large increase in her salary. F sells the condominium in 2004 and purchases a house because she can now afford the house. The safe harbors of paragraph (e)(2) of this section do not apply. Under the facts and circumstances, the primary reason for the sale of the house, F's salary increase, is an improvement in F's financial circumstances. Under paragraph (e)(1) of this section, an improvement in financial circumstances, even if the result of unforeseen circumstances, does not qualify for the reduced maximum exclusion by reason of unforeseen circumstances under section 121(c)(2).

Example (8). In April 2003 G buys a house that he uses as his principal residence. G sells his house in October 2004 because the house has greatly appreciated in value, mortgage rates have substantially decreased, and G can afford a bigger house. The safe harbors of paragraph (e)(2) of this section do not apply. Under the facts and circumstances, the primary reasons for the sale of the house, the changes in G's house value and in the mortgage rates, are an improvement in G's financial circumstances. Under paragraph (e)(1) of this section, an improvement in financial circumstances, even if the result of unforeseen circumstances, does not qualify for the reduced maximum exclusion by reason of unforeseen circumstances under section 121(c)(2).

Example (9). H works as a police officer for City X. In 2003 H buys a condominium that he uses as his principal residence. In 2004 H is assigned to City X's K-9 unit and is required to care for the police service dog at his home. Because H's condominium association does not permit H to have a dog in his condominium, in 2004 he sells the condominium and buys a house. The safe harbors of paragraph (e)(2) of this section do not apply. However, under the facts and circumstances, the primary reason for the sale, H's assignment to the K-9 unit, is an unforeseen circumstance because H could not reasonably have anticipated his assignment to the K-9 unit at the time he purchased and occupied the condominium. Consequently, the sale of the condominium is by reason of unforeseen circumstances and H is entitled to claim a reduced maximum exclusion under section 12(c)(2).

Example (10). In 2003, J buys a small house that she uses as her principal residence. After J wins the lottery, she sells the small house in 2004 and buys a bigger, more expensive house. The safe harbors of paragraph (e)(2) of this section do not apply. Under the facts and circumstances, the primary reason for the sale of the house, winning the lottery, is an improvement in J's financial circumstances. Under paragraph (e)(1) of this section, an improvement in financial circumstances, even if the result of unforeseen circumstances, does not qualify for the reduced maximum exclusion under section 12(c)(2).

(f) Qualified individual. For purposes of this section, qualified individual means—

(1) The taxpayer;

(2) The taxpayer's spouse;

(3) A co-owner of the residence;

(4) A person whose principal place of abode is in the same household as the taxpayer; or

(5) For purposes of paragraph (d) of this section, a person bearing a relationship specified in sections 152(a)(1) through 152(a)(8) (without regard to qualification as a dependent) to a qualified individual described in paragraphs (f)(1) through (4) of this section, or a descendant of the taxpayer's grandparent.

(g) Computation of reduced maximum exclusion.—**(1)** The reduced maximum exclusion is computed by multiplying the maximum dollar limitation of $250,000 ($500,000 for certain joint filers) by a fraction. The numerator of the fraction is the shortest of the period of time that the taxpayer owned the property during the 5-year period ending on the date of the sale or exchange; the period of time that the taxpayer used the property as the taxpayer's principal residence during the 5-year period ending on the date of the sale or exchange; or the period of time between the date of a prior sale or exchange of property for which the taxpayer excluded gain under section 121 and the date of the current sale or exchange. The numerator of the fraction may be expressed in days or months. The denominator of the fraction is 730 days or 24 months (depending on the measure of time used in the numerator).

(2) Examples. The following examples illustrate the rules of this paragraph (g):

Example (1). Taxpayer A purchases a house that she uses as her principal residence. Twelve months after the purchase, A sells the house due to a change in place of her employment. A has not excluded gain under section 121 on a prior sale or exchange of property within the last 2 years. A is eligible to exclude up to $125,000 of the gain from the sale of her house (12/24 × $250,000).

Example (2). **(i)** Taxpayer H owns a house that he has used as his principal residence since 1996. On January 15, 1999, H and W marry and W begins to use H's house as her principal residence. On January 15, 2000, H sells the house due to a change in W's place of employment. Neither H nor W has excluded gain under section 121 on a prior sale or exchange of property within the last 2 years.

(ii) Because H and W have not each used the house as their principal residence for at least 2 years during the 5-year period preceding its sale, the maximum dollar limitation amount that may be claimed by H and W will not be $500,000, but the sum of each spouse's limitation amount determined on a separate basis as if they had not been married. (See §1.121–2(a)(3)(ii).)

(iii) H is eligible to exclude up to $250,000 of gain because he meets the requirements of section 121. W is not eligible to exclude the maximum dollar limitation amount. Instead, because the sale of the house is due to a change in place of employment, W is eligible to claim a reduced maximum exclusion of up to $125,000 of the gain (365/730 × $250,000). Therefore, H and W are eligible to exclude up to $375,000 of gain ($250,000 + $125,000) from the sale of the house.

* * *

§ 1.121–5 Suspension of 5-year period for certain members of the uniformed services and Foreign Service.

(a) In general. Under section 121(d)(9), a taxpayer who is serving (or whose spouse is serving) on qualified official extended duty as a member of the uniformed services or Foreign Service of the United States may elect to suspend the running of the 5-year period of ownership and use during such service but for not more than 10 years. The election does not suspend the running of the 5-year period for any period during which the running of the 5-year period with respect to any other property of the taxpayer is suspended by an election under section 121(d)(9).

(b) Manner of making election. The taxpayer makes the election under section 121(d)(9) and this section by filing a return for the taxable year of the sale or exchange of the taxpayer's principal residence that does not include the gain in the taxpayer's gross income.

(c) Application of election to closed years. A taxpayer who would otherwise qualify under §§ 1.121–1 through 1.121–4 to exclude gain from a sale or exchange of a principal residence on or after May 7, 1997, may elect to apply section 121(d)(9) and this section for any years for which a claim for refund is barred by operation of any law or rule of law by filing an amended return before November 11, 2004.

(d) Example. The provisions of this section are illustrated by the following example:

Example. B purchases a house in Virginia in 2003 that he uses as his principal residence for 3 years. For 8 years, from 2006 through 2014, B serves on qualified official extended duty as a member of the Foreign Service of the United States in Brazil. In 2015 B sells the house. B did not use the house as his principal residence for 2 of the 5 years preceding the sale. Under section 121(d)(9) and this section, however, B may elect to suspend the running of the 5-year period of ownership and use during his 8-year period of service with the Foreign Service in Brazil. If B makes the election, the 8-year period is not counted in determining whether B used the house for 2 of the 5 years preceding the sale. Therefore, B may exclude the gain from the sale of the house under section 121.

* * *

§ 1.127–1 Amounts received under a qualified educational assistance program.

(a) Exclusion from gross income.* The gross income of an employee does not include—

(1) Amounts paid to, or on behalf of the employee under a qualified educational assistance program described in § 1.127–2, or

(2) The value of education provided to the employee under such a program.

(b) Disallowance of excluded amounts as credit or deduction. Any amount excluded from the gross income of an employee under paragraph (a) of this section shall not be allowed as a credit or deduction to such employee under any other provision of this part.

(c) Amounts received under a nonqualified program. Any amount received under an educational assistance program that is not a "qualified program" described in § 1.127–2 will not be excluded from gross income under paragraph (a) of this section. All or part of the amounts received under such a nonqualified program may, however, be excluded under section 117 or deducted under section 162 or section 212 (as the case may be), if the requirements of such section are satisfied.

(d) Definitions. For rules relating to the meaning of the terms "employee" and "employer", see paragraph (h) of § 1.127–2.

(e) Effective date.* This section is effective for taxable years of the employee beginning after December 31, 1978, and before January 1, 1984.

§ 1.127–2 Qualified educational assistance program.

(a) In general. A qualified educational assistance program is a plan established and maintained by an employer under which the employer provides educational assistance to employees. To be a qualified program, the requirements described in paragraphs (b) through (g) of this section must be satisfied. It is not required that a program be funded or that the employer apply to the Internal Revenue Service for a determination that the plan is a qualified program. However, under § 601.201 (relating to rulings and determination letters), an employer may request that the Service determine whether a plan is a qualified program.

(b) Separate written plan. The program must be a separate written plan of the employer. This requirement means that the terms of the program must be set forth in a separate document or documents providing only educational assistance within the meaning of paragraph (c) of this section. The requirement for a separate plan does not, however, preclude an educational assistance program from being part of a more comprehensive employer plan that provides a choice of nontaxable benefits to employees.

(c) Educational assistance—(1) In general. The benefits provided under the program must consist solely of educational assistance. The term "educational assistance" means—.

(i) The employer's payment of expenses incurred by or on behalf of an employee for education, or

(ii) The employer's provision of education to an employee.

(2) Alternative benefits. Benefits will not be considered to consist solely of educational assistance if the program, in form or in actual operation, provides employees with a choice between educational assistance and other remuneration includible in the employee's gross income.

(3) Certain benefits not considered educational assistance. The term "educational assistance" does not include the employer's payment for, or provision of—

(i) Tools or supplies (other than textbooks) that the employee may retain after completing a course of instruction,

*Editorial comment: The Regulations do not include the effect of Public Law 99–514 which imposed a $5,250 per individual ceiling on the exclusion (or P.L. 98–611 which earlier had imposed a $5,000 ceiling). See Sec. 127(a)(2). In addition, note that under the sunset legislation concept, Sec. 127 terminated for taxable years beginning after December 31, 1994. However, Sec. 127 was reinstated by the Small Business Job Protection Act of 1996 for tax years beginning after 1994 with a termination date of tax years beginning after May 31, 1997 (with courses beginning before July 1, 1997). The Taxpayer Relief Act of 1997 reinstated the exclusion with the termination date being for expenses paid with respect to courses beginning after May 31, 2000. The Tax Relief Extension Act of 1999 extended the exclusion with the termination date being for expenses paid with respect to courses beginning after December 31, 2001. Section 127 did not apply, however, to any graduate-level course beginning after June 30, 1996. The Tax Relief Reconciliation Act of 2001 made the education assistance exclusion permanent and extended the exclusion to include graduate as well as undergraduate education.

(ii) Meals, lodging, or transportation, or

(iii) Education involving sports, games, or hobbies, unless such education involves the business of the employer or is required as part of a degree program. The phrase "sports, games, or hobbies" does not include education that instructs employees how to maintain and improve health so long as such education does not involve the use of athletic facilities or equipment and is not recreational in nature.

(4) Education defined. As used in section 127, § 1.127–1, and this section, the term "education" includes any form of instruction or training that improves or develops the capabilities of an individual. Education paid for or provided under a qualified program may be furnished directly by the employer, either alone or in conjunction with other employers, or through a third party such as an educational institution. Education is not limited to courses that are job related or part of a degree program.

(d) Exclusive benefit. The program may benefit only the employees of the employer, including, at the employer's option, individuals who are employees within the meaning of paragraph (h)(1) of this section. A program that provides benefits to spouses or dependents of employees is not a qualified program within the meaning of this section.

(e) Prohibited discrimination—(1) Eligibility for benefits. The program must benefit the employer's employees generally. Among those benefited may be employees who are officers, shareholders, self-employed or highly compensated. A program is not for the benefit of employees generally, however, if the program discriminates in favor of employees described in the preceding sentence (or in favor of their spouses and dependents who are themselves employees) in requirements relating to eligibility for benefits. Thus, although a program need not provide benefits for all employees, it must benefit those employees who qualify under a classification of employees that does not discriminate in favor of the employees with respect to whom discrimination is prohibited. The classification of employees to be considered benefited will consist of that group of employees who are actually eligible for educational assistance under the program, taking into account the eligibility requirements set forth in the written plan, the eligibility requirements reflected in the types of educational assistance available under the program, and any other conditions that may affect the availability of benefits under the program. Thus, for example, if an employer's plan provides that all employees are eligible for educational assistance, yet limits that assistance to courses of study leading to post-graduate degrees in fields relating to the employer's business, then only those employees able to pursue such a course of study are considered actually eligible for educational assistance under the program. Whether any classification of employees discriminates in favor of employees with respect to whom discrimination is prohibited will generally be determined by applying the same standards as are applied under section 410(b)(1)(B) (relating to qualified pension, profit-sharing and stock bonus plans), without regard to section 401(a)(5). For purposes of making this determination, there shall be excluded from consideration employees not covered by the program who are included in a unit of employees covered by an agreement which the Secretary of Labor finds to be a collective bargaining agreement between employee representatives and one or more employers, if the Internal Revenue Service finds that educational assistance benefits were the subject of good faith bargaining between the employee representatives and the employer or employers. For purposes of determining whether such bargaining occurred, it is not material that the employees are not covered by another educational assistance program or that the employer's present program was not considered in the bargaining.

(2) Factors not considered in determining the existence of prohibited discrimination. A program shall not be considered discriminatory under this paragraph (e) merely because—

(i) Different types of educational assistance available under the program are utilized to a greater degree by employees with respect to whom discrimination is prohibited than by other employees, or

(ii) With respect to a course of study for which benefits are otherwise available, successful completion of the course, attaining a particular course grade, or satisfying a reasonable condition subsequent (such as remaining employed for one year after completing the course) are required or considered in determining the availability of benefits.

(f) Benefit limitation—(1) In general. Under section 127(b)(3), a program is a qualified program for a program year only if no more than 5% of the amounts paid or incurred by the employer for educational assistance benefits during the year are provided to the limitation class described in subparagraph (2). For purposes of this paragraph (f), the program year must be specified in the written plan as either the calendar year or the taxable year of the employer.

(2) Limitation class. The limitation class consists of—

(i) Shareholders. Individuals who, on any day of the program year, own more than 5% of the total number of shares of outstanding stock of the employer, or

(ii) Owners. In the case of an employer's trade or business which is not incorporated, individuals who, on any day of the program year, own more than 5% of the capital or profits interest in the employer, and

(iii) Spouses or dependents. Individuals who are spouses or dependents of shareholders or owners described in subdivision (i) or (ii). For purposes of determining stock ownership, the attribution rules described in paragraph (h)(4) of this section apply. The regulations prescribed under section 414(c) are applicable in determining an individual's interest in the capital or profits of an unincorporated trade or business.

(g) Notification of employees. A program is not a qualified program unless employees eligible to participate in the program are given reasonable notice of the terms and availability of the program.

(h) Definitions. For purposes of this section and §1.127–1—

(1) Employee. The term "employee" includes—

(i) A retired disabled or laid-off employee,

(ii) A present employee who is on leave, as, for example, in the Armed Forces of the United States, or

(iii) An individual who is self-employed within the meaning of section 401(c)(1).

(2) Employer. An individual who owns the entire interest in an unincorporated trade or business shall be treated as his or her own employer. A partnership is treated as the employer of each partner who is an employee within the meaning of section 401(c)(l).

(3) Officer. An officer is an individual who is an officer within the meaning of regulations prescribed under section 414(c).

(4) Shareholder. The term "shareholder" includes an individual who is a shareholder as determined by the attribution rules under section 1563(d) and (e), without regard to section 1563(e)(3)(C).

(5) Highly compensated. The term "highly compensated" has the same meaning as it does for purposes of section 410(b)(1)(B).

(i) Substantiation. An employee receiving payments under a qualified educational assistance program must be prepared to provide substantiation to the employer such that it is reasonable to believe that payments or reimbursements made under the program constitute educational assistance within the meaning of paragraph (c) of this section.

* * *

§ 1.132–1 Exclusion from gross income for certain fringe benefits.

(a) In general. Gross income does not include any fringe benefit which qualifies as a—

(1) No-additional-cost service,

(2) Qualified employee discount,

(3) Working condition fringe, or

(4) De minimis fringe.*

Special rules apply with respect to certain on-premises gyms and other athletic facilities (§ 1.132–1(e)), demonstration use of employer-provided automobiles by full-time automobile salesmen (§ 1.132–5(o)), parking provided to an employee on or near the business premises of the employer (§ 1.132–5(p)), and on-premises eating facilities (§ 1.132–7).

(b) Definition of employee— (1) No-additional cost services and qualified employee discounts. For purposes of section 132(a)(1) (relating to no-additional-cost services) and section 132(a)(2) (relating to qualified employee discounts), the term "employee" with respect to a line of business of an employer means—

(i) Any individual who is currently employed by the employer in the line of business,

(ii) Any individual who was formerly employed by the employer in the line of business and who separated from service with the employer in the line of business by reason of retirement or disability, and

(iii) Any widow or widower of an individual who died while employed by the employer in the line of business or who separated from service with the

*Editorial comment: The Regulations do not reflect the effect of the Energy Policy Act of 1992 which added Sec. 132(a)(5) on the "qualified transportation fringe," the Revenue Reconciliation Act of 1993 which added Sec. 132(a)(6) on the "qualified moving expense reimbursement, the Tax Relief Reconciliation Act of 2001 which added §132(a)(7) on "qualified retirement planning services," or the Military Family Tax Relief Act of 2003 which added § 132(a)(8) on "qualified military base realignment and closure fringe."

employer in the line of business by reason of retirement or disability.

For purposes of this paragraph (b)(l), any partner who performs services for a partnership is considered employed by the partnership. In addition, any use by the spouse or dependent child (as defined in paragraph (b)(5) of this section) of the employee will be treated as use by the employee. For purposes of section 132(a)(1) (relating to no-additional-cost services), any use of air transportation by a parent of an employee (determined without regard to section 132(f)(1)(B) and paragraph (b)(l)(iii) of this section) will be treated as use by the employee.

(2) Working condition fringes. For purposes of section 132(a)(3) (relating to working condition fringes), the term "employee" means—

(i) Any individual who is currently employed by the employer,

(ii) Any partner who performs services for the partnership,

(iii) Any director of the employer, and

(iv) Any independent contractor who performs services for the employer.

Notwithstanding anything in this paragraph (b)(2) to the contrary, an independent contractor who performs services for the employer cannot exclude the value of parking or the use of consumer goods provided pursuant to a product testing program under § 1.132–5(n); in addition, any director of the employer cannot exclude the value of the use of consumer goods provided pursuant to a product testing program under § 1.132–5(n).

(3) On-premises athletic facilities. For purposes of section 132(h)(5) (relating to on-premises athletic facilities), the term "employee" means—

(i) Any individual who is currently employed by the employer,

(ii) Any individual who was formerly employed by the employer and who separated from service with the employer by reason of retirement or disability, and

(iii) Any widow or widower of an individual who died while employed by the employer or who separated from service with the employer by reason of retirement or disability.

For purposes of this paragraph (b)(3), any partner who performs services for a partnership is considered employed by the partnership. In addition, any use by the spouse or dependent child (as defined in paragraph (b)(5) of this section) of the employee will be treated as use by the employee.

(4) De minimis fringes. For purposes of section 132(a)(4) (relating to de minimis fringes), the term "employee" means any recipient of a fringe benefit.

(5) Dependent child. The term "dependent child" means any son, stepson, daughter, or stepdaughter of the employee who is a dependent of the employee, or both of whose parents are deceased and who has not attained age 25. Any child to whom section 152(e) applies will be treated as the dependent of both parents.

(c) Special rules for employers—Effect of section 414. All employees treated as employed by a single employer under section 414(b), (c), (m), or (o) will be treated as employed by a single employer for purposes of this section. Thus, employees of one corporation that is part of a controlled group of corporations may under certain circumstances be eligible to receive section 132 benefits from the other corporations that comprise the controlled group. However, the aggregation of employers described in this paragraph (c) does not change the other requirements for an exclusion, such as the line of business requirement. Thus, for example, if a controlled group of corporations consists of two corporations that operate in different lines of business, the corporations are not treated as operating in the same line of business even though the corporations are treated as one employer.

(d) Customers not to include employees. For purposes of section 132 and the regulations thereunder, the term "customer" means any customer who is not an employee. However, the preceding sentence does not apply to section 132(c)(2) (relating to the gross profit percentage for determining a qualified employee discount). Thus, an employer that provides employee discounts cannot exclude sales made to employees in determining the aggregate sales to customers.

(e) Treatment of on-premises athletic facilities—(1) In general. Gross income does not include the value of any on-premises athletic facility provided by an employer to its employees. For purposes of section 132(h)(5) and this paragraph (e), the term "on-premises athletic facility" means any gym or other athletic facility (such as a pool, tennis court, or golf course)—

(i) Which is located on the premises of the employer, (ii) Which is operated by the employer, and (iii) Substantially all of the use of which during the calendar year is by employees of the employer, their spouses, and their dependent children.

For purposes of paragraph (e)(1)(iii) of this section, the term "dependent children" has the same meaning as the plural of the term "dependent child" in paragraph (b)(5) of this section. The exclusion of this paragraph (e) does not apply to any athletic facility if access to the facility is made available to the general public through the sale of memberships, the rental of the facility, or a similar arrangement.

(2) Premises of the employer. The athletic facility need not be located on the employer's business premises. However, the athletic facility must be located on premises of the employer. The exclusion provided in this paragraph (e) applies whether the premises are owned or leased by the employer; in addition, he exclusion is available even if the employer is not a named lessee on the lease so long as the employer pays reasonable rent. The exclusion provided in this paragraph (e) does not apply to any athletic facility that is a facility for residential use. Thus, for example, a resort with accompanying athletic facilities (such as tennis courts, pool, and gym) would not qualify for the exclusion provided in this paragraph (e). An athletic facility is considered to be located on the employer's premises if the facility is located on the premises of a voluntary employees' beneficiary association funded by the employer.

(3) Application of rules to membership in an athletic facility. The exclusion provided in this paragraph (e) does not apply to any membership in an athletic facility (including health clubs or country clubs) unless the facility is owned (or leased) and operated by the employer and substantially all the use of the facility is by employees of the employer, their spouses, and their dependent children. Therefore, membership in a health club or country club not meeting the rules provided in this paragraph (e) would not qualify for the exclusion.

(4) Operation by the employer. An employer is considered to operate the athletic facility if the employer operates the facility through its own employees, or if the employer contracts out to another to operate the athletic facility. For example, if an employer hires an independent contractor to operate the athletic facility for the employer's employees, the facility is considered to be operated by the employer. In addition, if an athletic facility is operated by more than one employer, it is considered to be operated by each employer. For purposes of paragraph (e)(1)(iii) of this section, substantially all of the use of a facility that is operated by more than one employer must be by employees of the various employers, their spouses, and their dependent children. Where the facility is operated by more than one employer, an employer that pays rent either directly to the owner of the premises or to a sublessor of the premises is eligible for the exclusion. If an athletic facility is operated by a voluntary employees' beneficiary association funded by an employer, the employer is considered to operate the facility.

(5) Nonapplicability of nondiscrimination rules. The nondiscrimination rules of section 132 and § 1.132–8 do not apply to on-premises athletic facilities.

(f) Nonapplicability of section 132 in certain cases— (1) Tax treatment provided for in another section. If the tax treatment or a particular fringe benefit is expressly provided for in another section of Chapter 1 of the Internal Revenue Code of 1986, section 132 and the applicable regulations (except for section 132(e) and the regulations thereunder) do not apply to such fringe benefit. For example, because section 129 provides an exclusion from gross income for amounts paid or incurred by an employer for dependent care assistance for an employee, the exclusions under section 132 and this section do not apply to the provision by an employer to an employee of dependent care assistance. Similarly, because section 117(d) applies to tuition reductions, the exclusions under section 132 do not apply to free or discounted tuition provided to an employee by an organization operated by the employer, whether the tuition is for study at or below the graduate level. Of course, if the amounts paid by the employer are for education relating to the employee's trade or business of being an employee of the employer so that, if the employee paid for the education, the amount paid could be deducted under section 162, the costs of the education may be eligible for exclusion as a working condition fringe.

(2) Limited statutory exclusions. If another section of Chapter 1 of the Internal Revenue Code of 1986 provides an exclusion from gross income based on the cost of the benefit provided to the employee and such exclusion is a limited amount, section 132 and the regulations thereunder may apply to the extent the cost of the benefit exceeds the statutory exclusion.

* * *

§ 1.132–2 No-additional-cost services.

(a) In general— (1) Definition. Gross income does not include the value of a no-additional-cost service. A "no-additional-cost service" is any service provided by an employer to an employee for the employee's personal use if—

(i) The service is offered for sale by the employer to its customers in the ordinary course of the line of business of the employer in which the employee performs substantial services, and

(ii) The employer incurs no substantial additional cost in providing the service to the employee (including foregone revenue and excluding any amount paid by or on behalf of the employee for the service).

For rules relating to the line of business limitation, see § 1.132–4. For purposes of this section, a service will not be considered to be offered for sale by the employer to its customers if that service is primarily provided to employees and not to the employer's customers.

(2) Excess capacity services. Services that are eligible for treatment as no-additional-cost services include excess capacity services such as hotel accommodations; transportation by aircraft, train, bus, subway, or cruise line; and telephone services. Services that are not eligible for treatment as no-additional-cost services are non-excess capacity services such as the facilitation by a stock brokerage firm of the purchase of stock. Employees who receive non-excess capacity services may, however, be eligible for a qualified employee discount of up to 20 percent of the value of the service provided. See § 1.132–3.

(3) Cash rebates. The exclusion for a no-additional-cost service applies whether the service is provided at no charge or at a reduced price. The exclusion also applies if the benefit is provided through a partial or total cash rebate of an amount paid for the service.

(4) Applicability of nondiscrimination rules. The exclusion for a no-additional-cost service applies to highly compensated employees only if the service is available on substantially the same terms to each member of a group of employees that is defined under a reasonable classification set up by the employer that does not discriminate in favor of highly compensated employees. See § 1.132–8.

(5) No substantial additional cost— (i) In general. The exclusion for a no-additional-cost service applies only if the employer does not incur substantial additional cost in providing the service to the employee. For purposes of the preceding sentence, the term "cost" includes revenue that is forgone because the service is provided to an employee rather than a nonemployee. (For purposes of determining whether any revenue is forgone, it is assumed that the employee would not have purchased the service unless it were available to the employee at the actual price charged to the employee.) Whether an employer incurs substantial additional cost must be determined without regard to any amount paid by the employee for the service. Thus, any reimbursement by the employee for the cost of providing the service does not affect the determination of whether the employer incurs substantial additional cost.

(ii) Labor intensive services. An employer must include the cost of labor incurred in providing services to employees when determining whether the employer has incurred substantial additional cost. An employer incurs substantial additional cost, whether non-labor costs are incurred, if a substantial amount of time is spent by the employer or its employees in providing the service to employees. This would be the result whether the time spent by the employer or its employees in providing the services would have been "idle," or if the services were provided outside normal business hours. An employer generally incurs no substantial additional cost, however, if the services provided to the employee are merely incidental to the primary service being provided by the employer. For example, the in-flight services of a flight attendant and the cost of in-flight meals provided to airline employees traveling on a space-available basis are merely incidental to the primary service being provided (i.e., air transportation). Similarly, maid service provided to hotel employees renting hotel rooms on a space-available basis is merely incidental to the primary service being provided (i.e., hotel accommodations).

(6) Payments for telephone service. Payment made by an entity subject to the modified final judgment (as defined in section 559(c)(5) of the Tax Reform Act of 1984) of all or part of the cost of local telephone service provided to an employee by a person other than an entity subject to the modified final judgment shall be treated as telephone service provided to the employee by the entity making the payment for purposes of this section. The preceding sentence also applies to a rebate of the amount paid by the employee for the service and payment to the person providing the service. This paragraph (a)(6) applies only to services and employees described in § 1.132–4(c). For a special line of business rule relating to such services and employees, see § 1.132–4(c).

(b) Reciprocal agreements. For purposes of the exclusion from gross income for a no-additional-cost service, an exclusion is available to an employee of one employer for a no-additional-cost service provided by an unrelated employer only if all of the following requirements are satisfied—

(1) The service provided to such employee by the unrelated employer is the same type of service generally provided to nonemployee customers by both the line of business in which the employee works and the line of business in which the service is provided to such employee (so that the employee would be permitted to exclude from gross income the value of the service if such service were provided directly by the employee's employer);

(2) Both employers are parties to a written reciprocal agreement under which a group of employees of each employer, all of whom perform substantial services in the same line of business, may receive no-additional-cost services from the other employer; and

(3) Neither employer incurs any substantial additional cost (including forgone revenue) in providing such service to the employees of the other employer, or pursuant to such agreement. If one employer receives a substantial payment from the other employer with respect to the reciprocal agreement, the paying employer will be considered to have incurred a substantial additional cost pursuant to the agreement, and consequently services performed under the reciprocal agreement will not qualify for exclusion as no-additional-cost services.

(c) Example. The rules of this section are illustrated by the following example:

Example. Assume that a commercial airline permits its employees to take personal flights on the airline at no charge and receive reserved seating. Because the employer forgoes potential revenue by permitting the employees to reserve seats, employees receiving such free flights are not eligible for the no-additional-cost exclusion.

* * *

§ 1.132–3 Qualified employee discounts.

(a) In general—(1) Definition. Gross income does not include the value of a qualified employee discount. A "qualified employee discount" is any employee discount with respect to qualified property or services provided by an employer to an employee for use by the employee to the extent the discount does not exceed—

(i) The gross profit percentage multiplied by the price at which the property is offered to customers in the ordinary course of the employer's line of business, for discounts on property, or

(ii) Twenty percent of the price at which the service is offered to customers, for discounts on services.

(2) Qualified property or services—(i) In general. The term "qualified property or services" means any property or services that are offered for sale to customers in the ordinary course of the line of business of the employer in which the employee performs substantial services. For rules relating to the line of business limitation, see § 1.132–4.

(ii) Exception for certain property. The term "qualified property" does not include real property and it does not include personal property (whether tangible or intangible) of a kind commonly held for investment. Thus, an employee may not exclude from gross income the amount of an employee discount provided on the purchase of securities, commodities, or currency, or of either residential or commercial real estate, whether or not the particular purchase is made for investment purposes.

(iii) Property and services not offered in ordinary course of business. The term "qualified property or services" does not include any property or services of a kind that is not offered for sale to customers in the ordinary course of the line of business of the employer. For example, employee discounts provided on property or services that are offered for sale primarily to employees and their families (such as merchandise sold at an employee store or through an employer-provided catalog service) may not be excluded from gross income. For rules relating to employer-operated eating facilities, see § 1.132–7, and for rules relating to employer-operated on-premises athletic facilities, see § 1.132–1(e).

(3) No reciprocal agreement exception. The exclusion for a qualified employee discount does not apply to property or services provided by another employer pursuant to a written reciprocal agreement that exists between employers to provide discounts on property and services to employees of the other employer.

(4) Property or services provided without charge, at a reduced price, or by rebates. The exclusion for a qualified employee discount applies whether the property or service is provided at no charge (in which case only part of the discount may be excludable as a qualified employee discount) or at a reduced price. The exclusion also applies if the benefit is provided through a partial or total cash rebate of an amount paid for the property or service.

(5) Property or services provided directly by the employer or indirectly through a third party. A qualified employee discount may be provided either directly by the employer or indirectly through a third party. For example, an employee of an appliance manufacturer may receive a qualified employee discount on the manufacturer's appliances purchased at a retail store that offers such appliances for sale to customers. The employee may exclude the amount of the qualified employee discount whether the employee is provided the appliance at no charge or purchases it at a reduced price, or whether the employee receives a partial or total cash rebate from either the employer-manufacturer or the retailer. If an employee receives additional rights associated with the property that are not provided by the employee's employer to customers in the ordinary course of the line of business in which the employee performs substantial services (such as the right to return or exchange the property or special warranty rights), the employee may only receive a qualified employee discount with respect to the property and not the additional rights. Receipt of such additional rights may occur, for example, when an employee of a manufacturer purchases property manufactured by the employee's employer at a retail outlet.

(6) Applicability of nondiscrimination rules. The exclusion for a qualified employee discount applies to highly compensated employees only if the discount is available on substantially the same terms to each member of a group of employees that is defined under a reasonable classification set up by the employer that does not discriminate in favor of highly compensated employees. See § 1.132–8.

(b) Employee discount— (1) Definition. The term "employee discount" means the excess of—

(i) The price at which the property or service is being offered by the employer for sale to customers, over

(ii) The price at which the property or service is provided by the employer to an employee for use by the employee. A transfer of property by an employee without consideration is treated as use by the employee for purposes of this section. Thus, for example, if an employee receives a discount on property offered for sale by his employer to customers and the employee makes a gift of the property to his parent, the property will be considered to be provided for use by the employee; thus, the discount will be eligible for exclusion as a qualified employee discount.

(2) Price to customers— (i) Determined at time of sale. In determining the amount of an employee discount, the price at which the property or service is being offered to customers at the time of the employee's purchase is controlling. For example, assume that an employer offers a product to customers for $20 during the first six months of a calendar year, but at the time the employee purchases the product at a discount, the price at which the product is being offered to customers is $25. In this case, the price from which the employee discount is measured is $25. Assume instead that, at the time the employee purchases the product at a discount, the price at which the product is being offered to customers is $15 and the price charged the employee is $12. The employee discount is measured from $15, the price at which the product is offered for sale to customers at the time of the employee purchase. Thus, the employee discount is $15 – $12, or $3.

(ii) Quantity discount not reflected. The price at which a property or service is being offered to customers cannot reflect any quantity discount unless the employee actually purchases the requisite quantity of the property or service.

(iii) Price to employer's customers controls. In determining the amount of an employee discount, the price at which a property or service is offered to customers of the employee's employer is controlling. Thus, the price at which the property is sold to the wholesale customers of a manufacturer will generally be lower than the price at which the same property is sold to the customers of a retailer. However, see paragraph (a)(5) of this section regarding the effect of a wholesaler providing to its employees additional rights not provided to customers of the wholesaler in the ordinary course of its business.

(iv) Discounts to discrete customer or consumer groups. Subject to paragraph (2)(ii) of this section, if an employer offers for sale property or services at one or more discounted prices to discrete customer or consumer groups, and sales at all such discounted prices comprise at least 35 percent of the employer's gross sales for a representative period, then in determining the amount of an employee discount, the price at which such property or service is being offered to customers for purposes of this section is a discounted price. The applicable discounted price is the current undiscounted price, reduced by the percentage discount at which the greatest percentage of the employer's discounted gross sales are made for such representative period. If sales at different percentage discounts equal the same percentage of the employer's gross sales, the price at which the property or service is being provided to customers may be reduced by the average of the discounts offered to each of the two groups. For purposes of this section, a representative period is the taxable year of the employer immediately preceding the taxable year in which the property or service is provided to the employee at a discount. If more than one employer would be aggregated under section 414(b), (c), (m), or (*o*), and not all of the employers have the same taxable year, the employers required to be aggregated must designate the 12-month period to be used in determining gross sales for a representative period. The 12-month period designated, however, must be used on a consistent basis.

(v) Examples. The rules provided in this paragraph (b)(2) are illustrated by the following examples:

Example (1). Assume that a wholesale employer offers property for sale to two discrete customer groups at differing prices. Assume further that during the prior taxable year of the employer, 70 percent of the employer's gross sales are made at a 15 percent discount and 30 percent at no discount. For purposes of this paragraph (b)(2), the current undiscounted price at which the property or service is being offered by the employer for sale to customers may be reduced by the 15 percent discount.

Example (2). Assume that a retail employer offers a 20 percent discount to members of the American Bar Association, a 15 percent discount to members of the American Medical Association, and a ten percent discount to employees of the Federal Government. Assume further that during the prior taxable year of the employer, sales to American Bar Association members equal 15 percent of the employer's gross sales, sales to American Medical Association members equal 20 percent of the employer's gross sales, and sales to Federal Government employees equal 25 percent of the employer's gross sales. For purposes of this paragraph (b)(2), the current undiscounted price at which the property or service is being offered by the employer for sale to customers may be reduced by the ten percent Federal Government discount.

(3) Damaged, distressed, or returned goods. If an employee pays at least fair market value for damaged, distressed, or returned property, such employee will not have income attributable to such purchase.

(c) Gross profit percentage— (1) In general— (i) General rule. An exclusion from gross income for an employee discount on qualified property is limited to the price at which the property is being offered to customers in the ordinary course of the employer's line of business, multiplied by the employer's gross profit percentage. The term "gross profit percentage" means the excess of the aggregate sales price of the property sold by the employer to customers (including employees) over the employer's aggregate cost of the property, then divided by the aggregate sales price.

(ii) Calculation of gross profit percentage. The gross profit percentage must be calculated separately for each line of business based on the aggregate sales price and aggregate cost of property in that line of business for a representative period. For purposes of this section, a representative period is the taxable year of the employer immediately preceding the taxable year in which the discount is available. For example, if the aggregate amount of sales of property in an employer's line of business for the prior taxable year was $800,000, and the aggregate cost of the property for the year was $600,000, the gross profit percentage would be 25 percent ($800,000 minus $600,000, then divided by $800,000). If two or more employers are required to aggregate under section 414(b), (c), (m), or (*o*) (aggregated employer), and if all of the aggregated employers do not share the same taxable year, then the aggregated employers must designate the 12-month period to be used in determining the gross profit percentage. The 12-month period designated, however, must be used on a consistent basis. If an employee performs substantial services in more than one line of business, the gross profit percentage of the line of business in which the property is sold determines the amount of the excludable employee discount.

(iii) Special rule for employers in their first year of existence. An employer in its first year of existence may estimate the gross profit percentage of a line of business based on its mark-up from cost. Alternatively, an employer in its first year of existence may determine the gross profit percentage by reference to an appropriate industry average.

(iv) Redetermination of gross profit percentage. If substantial changes in an employer's business indicate at any time that it is inappropriate for the prior year's gross profit percentage to be used for the current year, the employer must, within a reasonable period, redetermine the gross profit percentage for the remaining portion of the current year as if such portion of the year were the first year of the employe's existence.

(2) Line of business. In general, an employer must determine the gross profit percentage on the basis of all property offered to customers (including employees) in each separate line of business. An employer may instead select a classification of property that is narrower than the applicable line of business. However, the classification must be reasonable. For example, if an employer computes gross profit percentage according to the department in which products are sold, such classification is reasonable. Similarly, it is reasonable to compute gross profit percentage on the basis of the type of merchandise sold (such as high mark-up and low mark-up classifications). It is not reasonable, however, for an employer to classify certain low mark-up products preferred by certain employees (such as highly compensated employees) with high mark-up products or to classify certain high mark-up products preferred by other employees with low mark-up products.

(3) Generally accepted accounting principles. In general, the aggregate sales price of property must be determined in accordance with generally accepted accounting principles. An employer must compute the aggregate cost of property in the same manner in which it is computed for the employer's Federal income tax liability; thus, for example, section 263A and the regulations thereunder apply in determining the cost of property.

(d) Treatment of leased sections of department stores—(1) In general—(i) General rule. For purposes of determining whether employees of a leased section of a department store may receive qualified employee discounts at the department store and whether employees of the department store may receive qualified employee discounts at the leased section of the department store, the leased section is treated as part of the line of business of the person operating the department store, and employees of the leased section are treated as employees of the person operating the department store as well as employees of their employer. The term "leased section of a department store" means a section of a department store where substantially all of the gross receipts of the leased section are from over-the-counter sales of property made under a lease, license, or similar arrangement where it appears to the general public that individuals making such sales are employed by the department store. A leased section of a department store which, in connection with the offering of beautician services, customarily makes sales of beauty aids in the ordinary course of business is deemed to derive substantially all of its gross receipts from over-the-counter sales of property.

(ii) Calculation of gross profit percentage. For purposes of paragraph (d) of this section, when calculating the gross profit percentage of property and services sold at a department store, sales of property and services sold at the department store, as well as sales of property and services sold at the leased section, are considered. The rule provided in the preceding sentence does not apply, however, if it is more reasonable to calculate the gross profit percentage for the department store and leased section separately, or if it would be inappropriate to combine them (such as where either the department store or the leased section but not both provides employee discounts).

(2) Employees of the leased section—(i) Definition. For purposes of this paragraph (d), "employees of the leased section" means all employees who perform substantial services at the leased section of the department store regardless of whether the employees engage in over-the-counter sales of property or services. The term "employee" has the same meaning as in section 132(f) and § 1.132–1(b)(1).

(ii) Discounts offered to either department store employees or employees of the leased section. If the requirements of this paragraph (d) are satisfied, employees of the leased section may receive qualified employee discounts at the department store whether or not employees of the department store are offered discounts at the leased section. Similarly, employees of the department store may receive a qualified employee discount at the leased section whether or not employees of the leased section are offered discounts at the department store.

(e) Excess discounts. Unless excludable under a provision of the Internal Revenue Code of 1986 other than section 132(a)(2), an employee discount provided on property is excludable to the extent of the gross profit percentage multiplied by the price at which the property is being offered for sale to customers. If an employee discount exceeds the gross profit percentage, the excess discount is includible in the employee's income. For example, if the discount on employer-purchased property is 30 percent and the employer's gross profit percentage for the period in the relevant line of business is 25 percent, then 5 percent of the price at which the property is being offered for sale to customers is includible in the employee's income. With respect to services, an employee discount of up to 20 percent may be excludable. If an employee discount exceeds 20 percent, the excess discount is includible in the employee's income. For example, assume that a commercial airline provides a pass to each of its employees permitting the employees to obtain a free round-trip coach ticket with a confirmed seat to any destination the airline services. Neither the exclusion of section 132(a)(1) (relating to no-additional-cost services) nor any other statutory exclusion applies to a flight taken primarily for personal purposes by an employee under this program. However, an employee discount of up to 20 percent may be excluded as a qualified employee discount. Thus, if the price charged to customers for the flight taken is $300 (under restrictions comparable to those actually placed on travel associated with the employee airline ticket), $60 is excludable from gross income as a qualified employee discount and $240 is includible in gross income.

* * *

§ 1.132–4 Line of business limitation.

(a) In general— (1) Applicability— (i) General rule. A no-additional-cost service or a qualified employee discount provided to an employee is only available with respect to property or services that are offered for sale to customers in the ordinary course of the same line of business in which the employee receiving the property or service performs substantial services. Thus, an employee who does not perform substantial services in a particular line of business of the employer may not exclude from income under section 132(a)(1) or (a)(2) the value of services or employee discounts received on property or services in that line of business. For rules that relax the line of business requirement, see paragraphs (b) through (g) of this section.

(ii) Property and services sold to employees rather than customers. Because the property or services must be offered for sale to customers in the ordinary course of the same line of business in which the employee performs substantial services, the line of business limitation is not satisfied if the employer's products or services are sold primarily to employees of the employer, rather than to customers. Thus, for example, an employer in the banking line of business is not considered in the variety store line of business if the employer establishes an employee store that offers variety store items for sale to the employer's employees. See § 1.132–7 for rules relating to employer-operated eating facilities, and see § 1.132–1(e) for rules relating to employer-operated on-premises athletic facilities.

(iii) Performance of substantial services in more than one line of business. An employee who performs services in more than one of the employer's lines of business may only exclude no-additional-cost services and qualified employee discounts in the lines of business in which the employee performs substantial services.

(iv) Performance of services that directly benefit more than one line of business— (A) In general. An employee who performs substantial services that directly benefit more than one line of business of an employer is treated as performing substantial services in all such line of business. For example, an employee who maintains accounting records for an employer's three lines of business may receive qualified employee discounts in all three lines of business. Similarly, if an employee of a minor line of business of an employer that is significantly interrelated with a major line of business of the employer performs substantial services that directly benefit both the major and the minor lines of business, the employee is treated as performing substantial services for both the major and the minor lines of business.

(B) Examples. The rules provided in this paragraph (a)(1)(iv) are illustrated by the following examples:

Example (1). Assume that employees of units of an employer provide repair or financing services, or sell by catalog, with respect to retail merchandise sold by the employer. Such employees may be considered to perform substantial services for the retail merchandise line of business under paragraph (a)(1)(iv)(A) of this section.

Example (2). Assume that an employer operates a hospital and a laundry service. Assume further that some of the gross receipts of the laundry service line of business are from laundry services sold to customers other than the hospital employer. Only the employees of the laundry service who perform substantial services which directly benefit the hospital line of business (through the provision of laundry services to the hospital) will be treated as performing substantial services for the hospital line of business. Other employees of the laundry service line of business will not be treated as employees of the hospital line of business.

Example (3). Assume the same facts as in example (2), except that the employer also operates a chain of dry cleaning stores. Employees who perform substantial services which directly benefit the dry cleaning stores but who do not perform substantial services that directly benefit the hospital line of business will not be treated as performing substantial services for the hospital line of business.

(2) Definition— (i) In general. An employer's line of business is determined by reference to the Enterprise Standard Industrial Classification Manual (ESIC Manual) prepared by the Statistical Policy Division of the U.S. Office of Management and Budget. An employer is considered to have more than one line of business if the employer offers for sale to customers property or services in more than one two-digit code classification referred to in the ESIC Manual.

(ii) Examples. Examples of two-digit classifications are general retail merchandise stores; hotels and other lodging places; auto repair, services, and garages; and food stores.

(3) Aggregation of two-digit classifications. If, pursuant to paragraph (a)(2) of this section, an employer has more than one line of business, such lines of business will be treated as a single line of business where and to the extent that one or more of the following aggregation rules apply:

(i) If it is uncommon in the industry of the employer for any of the separate lines of business of the employer to be operated without the others, the separate lines of business are treated as one line of business.

(ii) If it is common for a substantial number of employees (other than those employees who work at the headquarters or main office of the employer) to perform substantial services for more than one line of business of the employer, so that determination of which employees perform substantial services for which line or lines of business would be difficult, then the separate lines of business of the employer in which such employees perform substantial services are treated as one line of business. For example, assume that an employer operates a delicatessen with an attached service counter at which food is sold for consumption on the premises. Assume further that most but not all employees work both at the delicatessen and at the service counter. Under the aggregation rule of this paragraph (a)(3)(ii), the delicatessen and the service counter are treated as one line of business.

(iii) If the retail operations of an employer that are located on the same premises are in separate lines of business but would be considered to be within one line of business under paragraph (a)(2) of this section if the merchandise offered for sale in such lines of business were offered for sale at a department store, then the operations are treated as one line of business. For example, assume that on the same premises an employer sells both women's apparel and jewelry. Because, if sold together at a department store, the operations would be part of the same line of business, the operations are treated as one line of business.

(b) Grandfather rule for certain retail stores—(1) In general. The line of business limitation may be relaxed under the special grandfather rule of this paragraph (b). Under this special grandfather rule, if—

(i) On October 5, 1983, at least 85 percent of the employees of one member of an affiliated group (as defined in section 1504 without regard to subsections (b)(2) and (b)(4) thereof) ("first member") were entitled to receive employee discounts at retail department stores operated by another member of the affiliated group ("second member"), and

(ii) More than 50 percent of the previous year's sales of the affiliated group are attributable to the operation of retail department stores, then, for purposes of the exclusion from gross income of a qualified employee discount, the first member is treated as engaged in the same line of business as the second member (the operator of the retail department stores). Therefore, employees of the first member of the affiliated group may exclude from income qualified employee discounts received at the retail department stores operated by the second member. However, employees of the second member of the affiliated group may not under this paragraph (b)(l) exclude any discounts received on property or services offered for sale to customers by the first member of the affiliated group.

(2) Taxable year of affiliated group. If not all of the members of an affiliated group have the same taxable year, the affiliated group must designate the 12-month period to be used in determining the "previous year's sales" (as referred to in the grandfather rule of this paragraph (b)). The 12-month period designated, however, must be used on a consistent basis.

(3) Definition of "sales." For purposes of this paragraph (b), the term "sales" means the gross receipts of an affiliated group, based upon the accounting methods used by its members.

(4) Retired and disabled employees. For purposes of this paragraph (b), an employee includes any individual who was, or whose spouse was, formerly employed by the first member of an affiliated group and who separated from service with the member by reason of retirement or disability if the second member of the group provided employee discounts to that individual on October 5, 1983.

(5) Increase of employee discount. If, after October 5, 1983, the employee discount described in this paragraph (b) is increased, the grandfather rule of this paragraph (b) does not apply to the amount of the increase. For example, if on January 1, 1989, the employee discount is increased from 10 percent to 15 percent, the grandfather rule will not apply to the additional 5 percent discount.

(c) Grandfather rule for telephone service provided to predivestiture retirees. All entities subject to the modified final judgment (as defined in section 559(c)(5) of the Tax Reform Act of 1984) shall be treated as a single employer engaged in the same line of business for purposes of determining whether telephone service provided to certain employees is a no-additional-cost service. The preceding sentence applies only in the case of an employee who by reason of retirement or disability separated before January 1, 1984, from the service of an entity subject to the modified final judgment. This paragraph (c) only applies to services provided to such employees as of January 1, 1984. For a special no-additional-cost service rule relating to such employees and such services, see § 1.132–2(a)(6).

(d) Special rule for certain affiliates of commercial airlines— (1) General rule. If a qualified affiliate is a member of an airline affiliated group and employees of the qualified affiliate who are directly engaged in providing airline-related services are entitled to no-additional-cost service with respect to air transportation provided by such other member, then, for purposes of applying § 1.132–2 (relating to no-additional-cost services with respect to such air transportation), such qualified affiliate shall be treated as engaged in the same line of business as such other member.

(2) "Airline affiliated group" defined. An "airline affiliated group" is an affiliated group (as defined in section 1504(a)) one of whose members operates a commercial airline that provides air transportation to customers on a per-seat basis.

(3) "Qualified affiliate" defined. A "qualified affiliate" is any corporation that is predominantly engaged in providing airline-related services. The term "airline-related services" means any of the following services provided in connection with air transportation:

(i) Catering,

(ii) Baggage handling,

(iii) Ticketing and reservations,

(iv) Flight planning and weather analysis, and

(v) Restaurants and gift shops located at an airport.

(e) Grandfather rule for affiliated groups operating airlines. The line of business limitation may be relaxed under the special grandfather rule of this paragraph (e). Under this special grandfather rule, if, as of September 12, 1984—

(1) An individual—

(i) Was an employee (within the meaning of § 1.132–1(b)) of one member of an affiliated group (as defined in section 1504(a)) ("first corporation"), and

(ii) Was eligible for no-additional-cost services in the form of air transportation provided by another member of such affiliated group ("second corporation"),

(2) At least 50 percent of the individuals performing services for the first corporation were, or had been employees of, or had previously performed services for, the second corporation, and

(3) The primary business of the affiliated group was air transportation of passengers, then, for purposes of applying sections 132(a)(1) and (2), with respect to no-additional-cost services and qualified employee discounts provided after December 31, 1984, for that individual by the second corporation, the first corporation is treated as engaged in the same air transportation line of business as the second corporation. For purposes of the preceding sentence, an employee of the second corporation who is performing services for the first corporation is also treated as an employee of the first corporation.

(f) Special rule for qualified air transportation organizations. A qualified air transportation organization is treated as engaged in the line of business of providing air transportation with respect to any individual who performs services for the organization if those services are performed primarily for persons engaged in providing air transportation, and are of a kind which (if performed on September 12, 1984) would qualify the individual for no-additional-cost services in the form of air transportation. The term "qualified air transportation organization" means any organization—

(1) If such organization (or a predecessor) was in existence on September 12, 1984,

(2) If such organization is—

(i) A tax-exempt organization under section (c)(6) whose membership is limited to entities engaged in the transportation by air of individuals or property for compensation or hire, or

(ii) Is a corporation all the stock of which is owned entirely by entities described in paragraph (f)(2)(i) of this section, and

(3) If such organization is operated in furtherance of the activities of its members or owners.

(g) Relaxation of line of business requirement. The line of business requirement may be relaxed under an elective grandfather rule provided in section 4977. For rules relating to the section 4977 election, see § 54.4977–1T.

(h) Line of business requirement does not expand benefits eligible for exclusion. The line of business requirement limits the benefits eligible for the no-additional-cost service and qualified employee discount exclusions to property or services provided by an employer to its customers in the ordinary course of the line of business of the employer in which the employee performs substantial services. The requirement is intended to ensure that employers do not offer, on a tax-free or reduced basis, property or services to employees that are not offered to the employer's customers, even if the property or services offered to the customers and the employees are within the same line of business (as defined in this section).

* * *

§ 1.132–5 Working condition fringes.

(a) In general—(1) Definition. Gross income does not include the value of a working condition fringe. A "working condition fringe" is any property or service provided to an employee of an employer to the extent that, if the employee paid for the property or service, the amount paid would be allowable as a deduction under section 162 or 167.

(i) A service or property offered by an employer in connection with a flexible spending account is not excludable from gross income as a working condition fringe. For purposes of the preceding sentence, a flexible spending account is an agreement (whether or not written) entered into between an employer and an employee that makes available to the employee over a time period a certain level of unspecified non-cash benefits with a pre-determined cash value.

(ii) If, under section 274 or any other section, certain substantiation requirements must be met in order for a deduction under section 162 or 167 to be allowable, then those substantiation requirements apply when determining whether a property or service is excludable as a working condition fringe.

(iii) An amount that would be deductible by the employee under a section other than section 162 or 167, such as section 212, is not a working condition fringe.

(iv) A physical examination program provided by the employer is not excludable as a working condition fringe even if the value of such program might be deductible to the employee under section 213. The previous sentence applies without regard to whether the employer makes the program mandatory to some or all employees.

(v) A cash payment made by an employer to an employee will not qualify as a working condition fringe unless the employer requires the employee to—

(A) Use the payment for expenses in connection with a specific or pre-arranged activity or undertaking for which a deduction is allowable under section 162 or 167,

(B) Verify that the payment is actually used for such expenses, and

(C) Return to the employer any part of the payment not so used.

(vi) The limitation of section 67(a) (relating to the two-percent floor on miscellaneous itemized deductions) is not considered when determining the amount of a working condition fringe. For example, assume that an employer provides a $1,000 cash advance to Employee A and that the conditions of paragraph (a)(1)(v) of this section are not satisfied. Even to the extent A uses the allowance for expenses for which a deduction is allowable under section 162 and 167, because such cash payment is not a working condition fringe, section 67(a) applies. The $1,000 payment is includible in A's gross income and subject to income and employment tax withholding. If, however, the conditions of paragraph (a)(1)(v) of this section are satisfied with respect to the payment, then the amount of A's working condition fringe is determined without regard to section 67(a). The $1,000 payment is excludable from A's gross income and not subject to income and employment tax reporting and withholding.

(2) Trade or business of the employee—(i) General. If the hypothetical payment for a property or service would be allowable as a deduction with respect to a trade or business of an employee other than the employee's trade or business of being an employee of the employer, it cannot be taken into account for purposes of determining the amount, if any, of the working condition fringe.

(ii) Examples. The rule of paragraph (a)(2)(i) of this section may be illustrated by the following examples:

Example (1). Assume that, unrelated to company X's trade or business and unrelated to employee A's trade or business of being an employee of company X, A is a member of the board of directors of company Y. Assume further that company X provides A with air transportation to a company Y board of director's meeting. A may not exclude from gross income the value of the air transportation to the meeting as a working condition fringe. A may, however, deduct such amount under section 162 if the section 162 requirements are satisfied. The result would be the same whether the air transportation was provided in the form of a flight on a commercial airline or a seat on a company X airplane.

Example (2). Assume the same facts as in example (1) except that A serves on the board of directors of company Z and company Z regularly purchases a significant amount of goods and services from company X. Because of the relationship between Company Z and A's employer, A's membership on Company Z's board of directors is related to A's trade or business of being an employee of Company X. Thus, A may exclude from gross income the value of air transportation to board meetings as a working condition fringe.

Example (3). Assume the same facts as in example (1) except that A serves on the board of directors of a charitable organization. Assume further that the service by A on the charity's board is substantially related to company X's trade or business. In this case,

A may exclude from gross income the value of air transportation to board meetings as a working condition fringe.

Example (4). Assume the same facts as in example (3) except that company X also provides A with the use of a company X conference room which A uses for monthly meetings relating to the charitable organization. Also assume that A uses company X's copy machine and word processor each month in connection with functions of the charitable organization. Because of the substantial business benefit that company X derives from A's service on the board of the charity, A may exclude as a working condition fringe the value of the use of company X property in connection with the charitable organization.

(b) Vehicle allocation rules— (1) In general— (i) General rule. In general, with respect to an employer-provided vehicle, the amount excludable as a working condition fringe is the amount that would be allowable as a deduction under section 162 or 167 if the employee paid for the availability of the vehicle. For example, assume that the value of the availability of an employer-provided vehicle for a full year is $2,000, without regard to any working condition fringe (i.e., assuming all personal use). Assume further that the employee drives the vehicle 6,000 miles for his employer's business and 2,000 miles for reasons other than the employer's business. In this situation, the value of the working condition fringe is $2,000 multiplied by a fraction, the numerator of which is the business-use mileage (6,000 miles) and the denominator of which is the total mileage (8,000 miles). Thus, the value of the working condition fringe is $1,500. The total amount includible in the employee's gross income on account of the availability of the vehicle is $500 ($2,000–$1,500). For purposes of this section, the term "vehicle" has the meaning given the term in § 1.61–21(e)(2). Generally, when determining the amount of an employee's working condition fringe, miles accumulated on the vehicle by all employees of the employer during the period in which the vehicle is available to the employee are considered. For example, assume that during the year in which the vehicle is available to the employee in the above example, other employees accumulate 2,000 additional miles on the vehicle (while the employee is not in the automobile). In this case, the value of the working condition fringe is $2,000 multiplied by a fraction, the numerator of which is the business-use mileage by the employee (including all mileage (business and personal) accumulated by other employees) (8,000 miles) and the denominator of which is the total mileage (including all mileage accumulated by other employees) (10,000 miles). Thus, the value of the working condition fringe is $1,600; the total amount includible in the employee's gross income on account of the availability of the vehicle is $400 ($2,000–$1,600). If, however, substantially all of the use of the automobile by other employees in the employer's business is limited to a certain period, such as the last three months of the year, the miles driven by the other employees during that period would not be considered when determining the employee's working condition fringe exclusion. Similarly, miles driven by other employees are not considered if the pattern of use of the employer-provided automobiles is designed to reduce Federal taxes. For example, assume that an employer provides employees A and B each with the availability of an employer-provided automobile and that A uses the automobile assigned to him 80 percent for the employer's business and that B uses the automobile assigned to him 30 percent for the employer's business. If A and B alternate the use of their assigned automobiles each week in such a way as to achieve a reduction in federal taxes, then the employer may count only miles placed on the automobile by the employee to whom the automobile is assigned when determining each employee's working condition fringe.

(ii) Use by an individual other than the employee. For purposes of this section, if the availability of a vehicle to an individual would be taxed to an employee, use of the vehicle by the individual is included in references to use by the employee.

(iii) Provision of an expensive vehicle for personal use. If an employer provides an employee with a vehicle that an employee may use in part for personal purposes, there is no working condition fringe exclusion with respect to the personal miles driven by the employee; if the employee paid for the availability of the vehicle, he would not be entitled to deduct under section 162 or 167 any part of the payment attributable to personal miles. The amount of the inclusion is not affected by the fact that the employee would have chosen the availability of a less expensive vehicle. Moreover, the result is the same even though the decision to provide an expensive rather than an inexpensive vehicle is made by the employer for bona fide noncompensatory business reasons.

(iv) Total value inclusion. In lieu of excluding the value of a working condition fringe with respect of an automobile, an employer using the automobile lease valuation rule of § 1.61–21(d) may include in an employee's gross income the entire Annual Lease Value of the automobile. Any deduction allowable to the employee under section 162 or 167 with respect to the automobile may be taken on the employee's income tax return. The total inclusion rule of this paragraph (b)(1)(iv) is not available if the employer is valuing the use or availability of a vehicle under general valuation principles or a special valuation rule other than the automobile lease valuation rule. See §§ 1.162–25 and 1.162–25T for rules relating to the employee's deduction.

(v) Shared usage. In calculating the working condition fringe benefit exclusion with respect to a vehicle provided for use by more than one employee, an employer shall compute the working condition fringe in a manner consistent with the allocation of the value of the vehicle under section 1.61–21(c)(2)(ii)(B).

(2) Use of different employer-provided vehicles. The working condition fringe exclusion must be applied on a vehicle-by-vehicle basis. For example, assume that automobile Y is available to employee D for 3 days in January and for 5 days in March, and automobile Z is available to D for a week in July. Assume further that the Daily Lease Value, as defined in § 1.61–21(d)(4)(ii), of each automobile is $50. For the eight days of availability of Y in January and March, D uses Y 90 percent for business (by mileage). During July, D uses Z 60 percent for business (by mileage). The value of the working condition fringe is determined separately for each automobile. Therefore, the working condition fringe for Y is $360 ($400 × .90) leaving an income inclusion of $40. The working condition fringe for Z is $210 ($350 × .60), leaving an income inclusion of $140. If the value of the availability of an automobile is determined under the Annual Lease Value rule for one period and Daily Lease Value rule for a second period (see § 1.61–21(d)), the working condition fringe exclusion must be calculated separately for the two periods.

(3) Provision of a vehicle and chauffeur services— (i) General rule. In general, with respect to the value of chauffeur services provided by an employer, the amount excludable as a working condition fringe is the amount that would be allowable as a deduction under section 162 and 167 if the employee paid for the chauffeur services. The working condition fringe with respect to a chauffeur is determined separately from the working condition fringe with respect to the vehicle. An employee may exclude from gross income the excess of the value of the chauffeur services over the value of the chauffeur services for personal purposes (such as commuting) as determined under § 1.61–21(b)(5). See § 1.61–21(b)(5) for additional rules and examples concerning the valuation of chauffeur services. See § 1.132–5(m)(5) for rules relating to an exclusion from gross income for the value of bodyguard/chauffeur services. When determining whether miles placed on the vehicle are for the employer's business, miles placed on the vehicle by a chauffeur between the chauffeur's residence and the place at which the chauffeur picks up (or drops off) the employee are with respect to the employee (but not the chauffeur) considered to be miles placed on the vehicle for the employer's business and thus eligible for the working condition fringe exclusion. Thus, because miles placed on the vehicle by a chauffeur between the chauffeur's residence and the place at which the chauffeur picks up (or drops off) the employee are not considered business miles with respect to the chauffeur, the value of the availability of the vehicle for commuting is includible in the gross income of the chauffeur. For general and special rules concerning the valuation of thc use of employer-provided vehicles, see paragraphs (b) through (f) of § 1.61–21.

(ii) Examples. The rules of paragraph (b)(3)(i) of this section are illustrated by the following examples:

Example (1). Assume that an employer makes available to an employee an automobile and a chauffeur. Assume further that the value of the chauffeur services determined in accordance with § 1.61–21 is $30,000 and that the chauffeur spends 30 percent of each workday driving the employee for personal purposes. There may be excluded from the employee's income 70 percent of $30,000, or $21,000, leaving an income inclusion with respect to the chauffeur services of $9,000.

Example (2). Assume that the value of the availability of an employer-provided vehicle for a year is $4,850 and that the value of employer-provided chauffeur services with respect to the vehicle for the year is $20,000. Assume further that 40 percent of the miles placed on the vehicle are for the employer's business and that 60 percent are for other purposes. In addition, assume that the chauffeur spends 25 percent of each workday driving the employee for personal purposes (i.e., 2 hours). The value of the chauffeur services includible in the employee's income is 25 percent of $20,000, or $5,000. The excess of $20,000 over $5,000 or $15,000 is excluded from the employee's income as a working condition fringe. The amount excludable as a working condition fringe with respect to the vehicle is 40 percent of $4,850, or $1,940 and the amount includible is $4,850–$1,940, or $2,910.

(c) Applicability of substantiation requirements of sections 162 and 274(d)— (1) In general. The value of property or services provided to an employee may not be excluded from the employee's gross income as a working condition fringe, by either the employer or the employee, unless the applicable substantiation requirements of either section 274(d) or section 162 (whichever is applicable) and the regulations thereunder are satisfied. The substantiation requirements of section 274(d) apply to an employee even if the requirements of section 274 do not apply to the employee's employer for deduction purposes (such as when the employer is a tax-exempt organization or a governmental unit).

(2) Section 274(d) requirements. The substantiation requirements of section 274(d) are satisfied by "adequate records or sufficient evidence corroborating the [employee's] own statement". Therefore, such records or evidence provided by the employee, and relied upon the employer to the extent permitted by the regulations promulgated under section 274(d), will be sufficient to substantiate a working condition fringe exclusion.

(d) Safe harbor substantiation rules—(1) In general. Section 1.274–6T provides that the substantiation requirements of section 274(d) and the regulations thereunder may be satisfied, in certain circumstances, by using one or more of the safe harbor rules prescribed in § 1.274–6T. If the employer uses one of the safe harbor rules prescribed in § 1.274–6T during a period with respect to a vehicle (as defined in § 1.61–21(e)(2)), that rule must be used by the employer to substantiate a working condition fringe exclusion with respect to that vehicle during the period. An employer that is exempt from Federal income tax may still use one of the safe harbor rules (if the requirements of that section are otherwise met during a period) to substantiate a working condition fringe exclusion with respect to a vehicle during the period. If the employer uses one of the methods prescribed in § 1.274–6T during a period with respect to an employer-provided vehicle, that method may be used by an employee to substantiate a working condition fringe exclusion with respect to the same vehicle during the period, as long as the employee includes in gross income the amount allocated to the employee pursuant to § 1.274–6T and this section. (See § 1.61–21(c)(2) for other rules concerning when an employee must include in income the amount determined by the employer.) If, however, the employer uses the safe harbor rule prescribed in § 1.274–6T(a)(2) or (3) and the employee without the employer's knowledge uses the vehicle for purposes other than de minimis personal use (in the case of the rule prescribed in § 1.274–6T(a)(2)), or for purposes other than de minimis personal use and commuting (in the case of the rule prescribed in § 1.274–6T(a)(3)), then the employees must include an additional amount in income for the unauthorized use of the vehicle.

(2) Period for use of safe harbor rules. The rules prescribed in this paragraph (d) assume that the safe harbor rules prescribed in § 1.274-6T are used for a one-year period. Accordingly, references to the value of the availability of a vehicle, amounts excluded as a working condition fringe, etc., are based on a one-year period. If the safe harbor rules prescribed in § 1.274-6T are used for a period of less than a year, the amounts referred to in the previous sentence must be adjusted accordingly. For purposes of this section, the term "personal use" has the same meaning as prescribed in § 1.274–6T(e)(5).

(e) Safe harbor substantiation rule for vehicles not used for personal purposes. For a vehicle described in § 1.274–6T(a)(2) (relating to certain vehicles not used for personal purposes), the working condition fringe exclusion is equal to the value of the availability of the vehicle if the employer uses the method prescribed in § 1.274–6T(a)(2).

(f) Safe harbor substantiation rule for vehicles not available to employees for personal use other than commuting. For a vehicle described in § 1.274–6T(a)(3) (relating to certain vehicles not used for personal purposes other than commuting), the working condition fringe exclusion is equal to the value of the availability of the vehicle for purposes other than commuting if the employer uses the method prescribed in § 1.274–6T(a)(3). This rule applies only if the special rule for valuing commuting use, as prescribed in § 1.61–21(f), is used and the amount determined under the special rule is either included in the employee's income or reimbursed by the employee.

(g) Safe harbor substantiation rule for vehicles used in connection with the business of farming that are available to employees for personal use—(1) In general. For a vehicle described in § 1.274–6T(b) (relating to certain vehicles used in connection with the business of farming), the working condition fringe exclusion is calculated by multiplying the value of the availability of the vehicle by 75 percent.

(2) Vehicles available to more than one individual. If the vehicle is available to more than one individual, the employer must allocate the gross income inclusion attributable to the vehicle (25 percent of the value of the availability of the vehicle) among the employees (and other individuals whose use would not be attributed to an employee) to whom the vehicle was available. This allocation must be done in a reasonable manner to reflect the personal use of the vehicle by the individuals. An amount that would be allocated to a sole proprietor reduces the amounts that may be allocated to employees but is otherwise to be disregarded for purposes of this paragraph (g). For purposes of this paragraph (g), the value of the availability of a vehicle may be calculated as if the vehicle were available to only one employee continuously and without regard to any working condition fringe exclusion.

(3) Examples. The following examples illustrate a reasonable allocation of gross income with respect to an employer-provided vehicle between two employees:

Example (1). Assume that two farm employees share the use of a vehicle that for a calendar year is regularly used directly in connection with the business of farming and qualifies for use of the rule in § 1.274–6T(b). Employee A uses the vehicle in the morning directly in connection with the business of farming and employee B uses the vehicle in the afternoon directly in connection with the business of farming. Assume further that employee B takes the vehicle home in the evenings and on weekends. The employer should allocate all the income attributable to the availability of the vehicle to employee B.

Example (2). Assume that for a calendar year, farm employees C and D share the use of a vehicle that is regularly used directly in connection with the business of farming and qualifies for use of the rule in § 1.274–6T(b). Assume further that the employees alternate taking the vehicle home in the evening and alternate the availability of the vehicle for personal purposes on weekends. The employer should allocate the income attributable to the availability of the vehicle for personal use (25 percent of the value of the availability of the vehicle) equally between the two employees.

Example (3). Assume the same facts as in example (2) except that C is the sole proprietor of the farm. Based on these facts, C should allocate the same amount of income to D as was allocated to D in example (2). No other income attributable to the availability of the vehicle for personal use should be allocated.

(h) Qualified nonpersonal use vehicles. (1) In general. Except as provided in paragraph (h)(2) of this section, 100 percent of the value of the use of a qualified nonpersonal use vehicle (as described in § 1.274–5T(k)) is excluded from gross income as a working condition fringe, provided that, in the case of a vehicle described in paragraph (k)(3) through (8) of that section, the use of the vehicle conforms to the requirements of that paragraph.

(2) Shared usage of qualified nonpersonal use vehicles. In general, a working condition fringe under paragraph (h) of this section is available to the driver and all passengers of a qualified nonpersonal use vehicle. However, a working condition fringe under this paragraph (h) is available only with respect to the driver and not with respect to any passengers of a qualified nonpersonal use vehicle described in § 1.274—5T(k)(2)(ii)(L) or (P). In this case, the passengers must comply with provisions of this section (excluding this paragraph (h)) to determine the applicability of the working condition fringe exclusion. For example, if an employer provides a passenger bus with a capacity of 25 passengers to its employees for purposes of transporting employees to and/or from work, the driver of the bus may exclude from gross income as a working condition fringe 100 percent of the value of the use of the vehicle. The value of the commuting use of the employer-provided bus by the employee-passengers is includible in their gross incomes. See § 1.61–21(f) for a special rule to value the commuting-only use of employer–provided vehicles.

(i) [Reserved].

(j) Application of section 280F. In determining the amount, if any, of an employee's working condition fringe, section 280F and the regulations thereunder do not apply. For example, assume that an employee has available for a calendar year an employer-provided automobile with a fair market value of $28,000. Assume further that the special rule provided in § 1.61–21(d) is used yielding an Annual Lease Value, as defined in § 1.61–21(d), of $7,750, and that all of the employee's use of the automobile is for the employer's business. The employee would be entitled to exclude as a working condition fringe the entire Annual Lease Value, despite the fact that if the employee paid for the availability of the automobile, an income inclusion would be required under § 1.280F–6(d)(1). This paragraph (j) does not affect the applicability of section 280F to the employer with respect to such employer-provided automobile, nor does it affect the applicability of section 274 to either the employer or the employee. For rules concerning substantiation of an employee's working condition fringe, see paragraph (c) of this section.

(k) Aircraft allocation rule. In general, with respect to a flight on an employer-provided aircraft, the amount excludable as a working condition fringe is the amount that would be allowable as a deduction under section 162 or 167 if the employee paid for the flight on the aircraft. For example, if employee P and P's spouse fly on P's employer's airplane primarily for business reasons of P's employer so that P could deduct the expenses relating to the trip to the extent of P's payments, the value of the flights is excludable from gross income as a working condition fringe. However, if P's children accompany P on the trip primarily for personal reasons, the value of the flights by P's children are includible in P's gross income. See § 1.61–21(g) for special rules for valuing personal flights on employer-provided aircraft.

(l) [Reserved].

(m) Employer-provided transportation for security concerns— (1) In general. The amount of a working condition fringe exclusion with respect to employer-provided transportation is the amount that would be allowable as a deduction under section 162 or 167 if the employee paid for the transportation. Generally, if an employee pays for transportation taken for primarily personal purposes, the employee may not deduct any part of the amount paid. Thus, the employee may not generally exclude the value of employer-provided transportation as a working condition fringe if such transportation is primarily personal. If, however, for bona fide business-oriented security concerns, the employee purchases transportation that provides him or her with additional security, the employee may generally deduct the excess of the amount actually paid for the transportation over the amount the employee would have paid for the same mode of transportation absent the bona fide business-oriented security concerns. This is the case whether or not the employee would have taken the same mode of transportation absent the bona fide business-oriented security concerns. With respect to a vehicle, the phrase "the same mode of transportation" means use of the same vehicle without the additional security aspects, such as bullet-proof glass. With respect to air transportation, the phrase "the same mode of transportation" means comparable air transportation. These same rules apply to the determination of an employee's working condition fringe exclusion. For example, if an employer provides an employee with a vehicle for commuting and, because of bona fide business-oriented security concerns, the vehicle is specially designed for security, then the employee may exclude from gross income the value of the special security design as a working condition fringe. The employee may not exclude the value of the commuting from income as a working condition fringe because commuting is a nondeductible personal expense. Similarly, if an employee travels on a personal trip in an employer-provided aircraft for bona fide business-oriented security concerns, the employee may exclude the excess, if any, of the value of the flight over the amount the employee would have paid for the same mode of transportation, but for the bona fide business-oriented security concerns. However, if an independent security study meeting the requirements of paragraph (m)(2)(v) of this section has been performed with respect to a government employee, the government employee may exclude the value of the personal use (other than commuting) of the employer-provided vehicle that the security study determines to be reasonable and necessary for local transportation. Because personal travel is a nondeductible expense, the employee may not exclude the total value of the trip as a working condition fringe.

(2) Demonstration of bona fide business-oriented security concerns— (i) In general. For the purposes of this paragraph (m), a bona fide business-oriented security concern exists only if the facts and circumstances establish a specific basis for concern regarding the safety of the employee. A generalized concern for an employee's safety is not a bona fide business-oriented security concern. Once a bona fide business-oriented security concern is determined to exist with respect to a particular employee, the employer must periodically evaluate the situation for purposes of determining whether the bona fide business-oriented security concern still exists. Example of factors indicating a specific basis for concern regarding the safety of an employee are—

(A) A threat of death or kidnapping of, or serious bodily harm to, the employee or a similarly situated employee because of either employee's status as an employee of the employer; or

(B) A recent history of violent terrorist activity (such as bombings) in the geographic area in which the transportation is provided, unless that activity is focused on a group of individuals which does not include the employee (or a similarly situated employee of an employer), or occurs to a significant degree only in a location within the geographic area where the employee does not travel.

(ii) Establishment of overall security program. Notwithstanding anything in paragraph (m)(2)(i) of this section to the contrary, no bona fide business-oriented security concern will be deemed to exist unless the employee's employer establishes to the satisfaction of the Commissioner than an overall security program has been provided with respect to the employee involved. An overall security program is deemed to exist if the requirements of paragraph (m)(2)(iv) of this section are satisfied (relating to an independent security study).

(iii) Overall security program— (A) Defined. An overall security program is one in which security is provided to protect the employee on a 24-hour basis. The employee must be protected while at the employee's residence, while commuting to and from the employee's workplace, and while at the employee's workplace. In addition, the employee must be protected while traveling both at home and away from home, whether for business or personal purposes. An overall security program must include the provision of a bodyguard/chauffeur who is trained in evasive driving techniques; an automobile specially equipped for security; guards, metal detectors, alarms, or similar methods of controlling access to the employee's workplace and residence; and, in appropriate cases, flights on the employer's aircraft for business and personal reasons.

(B) Application. There is no overall security program when, for example, security is provided at the employee's workplace but not at the employee's residence. In addition, the fact that an employer requires an employee to travel on the employer's aircraft, or in an employer-provided vehicle that contains special security features, does not alone constitute an overall security program. The preceding sentence applies regardless of the existence of a corporate or other resolution requiring the employee to travel in the employer's aircraft or vehicle for personal as well as business reasons.

(iv) Effect of an independent security study. An overall security program with respect to an employee is deemed to exist if the conditions of this paragraph (m)(2)(iv) are satisfied:

(A) A security study is performed with respect to the employer and the employee (or a similarly situated employee of the employer) by an independent security consultant;

(B) The security study is based on an objective assessment of all facts and circumstances;

(C) The recommendation of the security study is that an overall security program (as defined in paragraph (m)(2)(iii) of this section) is not necessary and the recommendation is reasonable under the circumstances; and

(D) The employer applies the specific security recommendations contained in the security study to the employee on a consistent basis.

The value of transportation-related security provided pursuant to a security study that meets the requirements of this paragraph (m)(2)(iv) may be excluded from income if the security study conclusions are reasonable and, but for the bona fide business-oriented security concerns, the employee would not have had such security. No exclusion from income applies to security provided by the employer that is not recommended in the security study. Security study conclusions may be reasonable even if, for example, it is recommended that security be limited to certain geographic areas, as in the case in which air travel security is provided only in certain foreign countries.

(v) Independent security study with respect to government employees. For purposes of establishing the existence of an overall security program under paragraph (m)(2)(ii) of this section with respect to a particular government employee, a security study conducted by the government employer (including an agency or instrumentality thereof) will be treated as a security study pursuant to paragraph (m)(2)(iv) of this section if, in lieu of the conditions of paragraphs (m)(2)(iv)(A) through (D) of this section, the following conditions are satisfied:

(A) The security study is conducted by a person expressly designated by the government employer as having the responsibility and independent authority to determine both the need for employer-provided security and the appropriate protective services in response to that determination;

(B) The security study is conducted in accordance with written internal procedures that require an independent and objective assessment of the facts and circumstances, such as the nature of the threat to the employee, the appropriate security response to that threat, an estimate of the length of time protective services will be necessary, and the extent to which employer-provided transportation may be necessary during the period of protection;

(C) With respect to employer-provided transportation, the security study evaluates the extent to which personal use, including commuting, by the employee and the employee's spouse and dependents may be necessary during the period of protection and makes a recommendation as to what would be considered reasonable personal use during that period; and

(D) The employer applies the specific security recommendations contained in the study to the employee on a consistent basis.

(3) Application of security rules to spouses and dependents— (i) In general. If a bona fide business-oriented security concern exists with respect to an employee (because, for example, threats are made on the life of an employee), the bona fide business-oriented security concern is deemed to exist with respect to the employee's spouse and dependents to the extent provided in this paragraph (m)(3).

(ii) Certain transportation. If a working condition fringe exclusion is available under this paragraph (m) for transportation in a vehicle or aircraft provided for a bona fide business-oriented security concern with respect to an employee, the requirements of this paragraph (m) are deemed to be satisfied with respect to transportation in the same vehicle or aircraft provided at the same time to the employee's spouse and dependent children.

(iii) Other. Except as provided in paragraph (m)(3)(ii) of this section, a bona fide business-oriented security concern is deemed to exist for the spouse and dependent children of the employer only if the requirements of paragraph (m)(2)(iii) or (iv) of this section are applied independently to such spouse and dependent children.

(iv) Spouses and dependents of government employees. The security rules of this paragraph (m)(3) apply to the spouse and dependents of a government employee. However, the value of local vehicle transportation provided to the government employee's spouse and dependents for personal purposes, other than commuting, during the period that a bona fide business-oriented security concern exists with respect to the government employee will not be included in the government employee's gross income if the personal use is determined to be reasonable and necessary by the security study described in paragraph (m)(2)(v) of this section.

(4) Working condition safe harbor for travel on employer-provided aircraft. Under the safe harbor rule of this paragraph (m)(4), if, for a bona fide business-oriented security concern, the employer requires that an employee travel on an employer-provided aircraft for a personal trip, the employer and the employee may exclude from the employee's gross income, as a working condition fringe, the excess value of the aircraft trip over the safe harbor airfare without having to show what method of transportation the employee would have flown but for the bona fide business-oriented security concern. For purposes of the safe harbor rule of this paragraph (m)(4), the value of the safe harbor airfare is determined under the non-commercial flight valuation rule of § 1.61–21(g) (regardless of whether the employer or employee elects to use such valuation rule) by multiplying an aircraft multiple of 200-percent by the applicable cents-per-mile rates and the number of miles in the flight and then adding the applicable terminal charge. The value of the safe harbor airfare determined under this paragraph (m)(4) must be included in the employee's income (to the extent not reimbursed by the employee) regardless of whether the employee or the employer uses the special valuation rule of § 1.61–21(g). The excess of the value of the aircraft trip over this amount may be excluded from gross income as a working condition fringe. If, for a bona fide business-oriented security concern, the employer requires that an employee's spouse and dependents travel on an employer-provided aircraft for a personal trip, the special rule of this paragraph (m)(4) is available to exclude the excess value of the aircraft trips over the safe harbor airfares.

(5) Bodyguard/chauffeur provided for a bona fide business-oriented security concern. If an employer provides an employee with vehicle transportation and a bodyguard/chauffeur for a bona fide business-oriented security concern, and but for the bona fide business-oriented security concern the employee would not have had a bodyguard or a chauffeur, then the entire value of the services of the bodyguard/chauffeur is excludable from gross income as a working condition fringe. For purposes of this section, a bodyguard/chauffeur must be trained in evasive driving techniques. An individual who performs services as a driver for an employee is not a bodyguard/chauffeur if the individual is not trained in evasive driving techniques. Thus, no part of the value of the services of such an individual is excludable from gross income under this paragraph (m)(5). (See paragraph (b)(3) of this section for rules relating to the determination of the working condition fringe exclusion for chauffeur services.)

(6) Special valuation rule for government employees. If transportation is provided to a government employee for commuting during the period that a bona fide business-oriented security concern under § 1.132–5(m) exists, the commuting use may be valued by reference to the values set forth in § 1.61–21(e)(l)(i) or (f)(3) (vehicle cents-per-mile or commuting valuation of $1.50 per one-way commute, respectively) without regard to the additional requirements contained in § 1.61–21(e) or (f) and is deemed to have met the requirements of § 1.61–21(c).

(7) Government employer and employee defined. For purposes of this paragraph (m), "government employer" includes any Federal, State, or local government unit, and any agency or instrumentality thereof. A "government employee" is any individual who is employed by the government employer.

(8) Examples. The provisions of this paragraph (m) may be illustrated by the following examples:

Example (1). Assume that in response to several death threats on the life of A, the president of X, a multinational company, X establishes an overall security program for A, including an alarm system at A's home and guards at A's workplace, the use of a vehicle that is specially equipped with alarms, bulletproof glass, and armor plating, and a bodyguard/chauffeur. Assume further that A is driven for both personal and business reasons in the vehicle. Also, assume that but for the bona fide business-oriented security concerns, no part of the overall security program would have been provided to A. With respect to the transportation provided for security reasons, A may exclude as a working condition fringe the value of the special security features of the vehicle and the value attributable to the bodyguard/chauffeur. Thus, if the value of the specially equipped vehicle is $40,000, and the value of the vehicle without the security features is $25,000, A may determine A's inclusion in income attributable to the vehicle as if the vehicle were worth $25,000. A must include in income the value of the availability of the vehicle for personal use.

Example (2). Assume that B is the chief executive officer of Y, a multinational corporation. Assume further that there have been kidnapping attempts and other terrorist activities in the foreign countries in which B performs services and that at least some of such activities have been directed against B or similarly situated employees. In response to these activities, Y provides B with an overall security program, including an alarm system at B's home and bodyguards at B's workplace, a bodyguard/chauffeur, and a vehicle specially designed for security during B's overseas travels. In addition, assume that Y requires B to travel in Y's airplane for business and personal trips taken to, from, and within these foreign countries. Also, assume that but for bona fide business-oriented security concerns, no part of the overall security program would have been provided to B. B may exclude as a working condition fringe the value of the special security features of the automobile and the value attributable to the bodyguards and the bodyguard/chauffeur. B may also exclude the excess, if any, of the value of the flights over the amount A would have paid for the same mode of transportation but for the security concerns. As an alternative to the preceding sentence, B may use the working condition safe harbor described in paragraph (m)(4) of this section and exclude as a working condition fringe the excess, if any, of the value of personal flights in the Y airplane over the safe harbor airfare determined under the method described in paragraph (m)(4) of this section. If this alternative is used, B must include in income the value of the availability of the vehicle for personal use and the value of the safe harbor.

Example (3). Assume the same facts as in example (2) except that Y also requires B to travel in Y's airplane within the United States, and provides B with a chauffeur-driven limousine for business and personal travel in the United States. Assume further that Y also requires B's spouse and dependents to travel in Y's airplane for personal flights in the United States. If no bona fide business-oriented security concern exists with respect to travel in the United States, B may not exclude from income any portion of the value of the availability of the chauffeur or limousine for personal use in the United States. Thus, B must include in income the value of the availability of the vehicle and chauffeur for personal use. In addition, B may not exclude any portion of the value attributable to personal flights by B or B's spouse and dependents on Y's airplane. Thus, B must include in income the value attributable to the personal use of Y's airplane. See § 1.61–21 for rules relating to the valuation of an employer-provided vehicle and chauffeur, and personal flights on employer-provided airplanes.

Example (4). Assume that company Z retains an independent security consultant to perform a security study with respect to its chief executive officer. Assume further that, based on an objective assessment of the facts and circumstances, the security consultant reasonably recommends that 24-hour protection is not necessary but that the employee be provided security at his workplace and for ground transportation, but not for air transportation. If company Z follows the recommendations on a consistent basis, an overall security program will be deemed to exist with respect to the workplace and ground transportation security only.

Example (5). Assume the same facts as in example (4) except that company Z only provides the employee security while commuting to and from work, but not for any other ground transportation. Because the recommendations of the independent security study are not applied on a consistent basis, and overall security program will not be deemed to exist. Thus, the value of commuting to and from work is not excludable from income. However, the value of a bodyguard with professional security training who does not provide chauffeur or other personal services to the employee or any member of the employee's family may be excludable as a working condition fringe if such expense would be otherwise allowable as a deduction by the employee under section 162 or 167.

Example (6). J is a United States District Judge. At the beginning of a 3-month criminal trial in J's court, a member of J's family receives death threats. M, the division (within government agency W) responsible for evaluating threats and providing protective services to the Federal judiciary, directs its threat analysis unit to conduct a security study with respect to J and J's family. The study is conducted pursuant to internal written procedures that require an independent and objective assessment of any threats to members of the Federal judiciary and their families, a statement of the requisite security response, if any, to a particular threat (including the form of transportation to be furnished to the employee as part of the security program), and a description of the circumstances under which local transportation for the employee and the employee's spouse and dependents may be necessary for personal reasons during the time protective services are provided. M's study concludes that a bona fide business-oriented security concern exists with respect to J and J's family and determines that 24-hour protection of J and J's family is not necessary, but that protection is necessary during the course of the criminal trial whenever J or J's family is away from home. Consistent with that recommendation, J is transported every day in a government vehicle for both personal and business reasons and is accompanied by two bodyguard/chauffeurs who have been trained in evasive driving techniques. In addition, J's spouse is driven to and from work and J's children are driven to and from school and occasional school activities. Shortly after the trial is concluded, M's threat analysis unit determines that J and J's family no longer need special protection because the danger posed by the threat no longer exists and, accordingly, vehicle transportation is no longer provided. Because the security study conducted by M complies with the conditions of § 1.132–5(m)(2)(v), M has satisfied the requirement for an independent security study and an overall security program with respect to J is deemed to exist. Thus, with respect to the transportation provided for security concerns, J may exclude as a working condition fringe the value of any special security features of the government vehicle and the value attributable to the two bodyguard/chauffeurs. See Example (1) of this paragraph (m)(8). The value of vehicle transportation provided to J and J's family for personal reasons, other than commuting, may also be excluded during the period of protection, because its provision was consistent with the recommendation of the security study.

Example (7). Assume the same facts as in Example (6) and that J's one-way commute between home and work is 10 miles. Under paragraph (m)(6) of this section, the Federal Government may value transportation provided to J for commuting purposes pursuant to the value set forth in either the vehicle cents-per-mile rule of § 1.61–21(e) or the commuting valuation rule of § 1.61–21(f). Because the commuting valuation rule yields the least amount of taxable income to J under the circumstances, W values the transportation provided to J for commuting at $1.50 per one-way commute, even though J is a control employee within the meaning of § 1.61–21(f)(6).

(n) Product testing—(1) In general. The fair market value of the use of consumer goods, which are manufactured for sale to nonemployees, for product testing and evaluation by an employee of the manufacturer outside the employer's workplace, is excludable from gross income as a working condition fringe if—

(i) Consumer testing and evaluation of the product is an ordinary and necessary business expense of the employer;

(ii) Business reasons necessitate that the testing and evaluation of the product be performed off the employer's business premises by employees (i.e., the testing and evaluation cannot be carried out adequately in the employer's office or in laboratory testing facilities);

(iii) The product is furnished to the employee for purposes of testing and evaluation;

(iv) The product is made available to the employee for no longer than necessary to test and evaluate its performance and (to the extent not exhausted) must be returned to the employer at completion of the testing and evaluation period;

(v) The employer imposes limits on the employee's use of the product that significantly reduce the value of any personal benefit to the employee; and

(vi) The employee must submit detailed reports to the employer on the testing and evaluation. The length of the testing and evaluation period must be reasonable in relation to the product being tested.

(2) Employer-imposed limits. The requirement of paragraph (n)(1)(v) of this section is satisfied if—

(i) The employer places limits on the employee's ability to select among different models or varieties of the consumer product that is furnished for testing and evaluation purposes; and

(ii) The employer generally prohibits use of the product by persons other than the employee and, in appropriate cases, requires the employee, to purchase or lease at the employee's own expense the same type of product as that being tested (so that personal use by the employee's family will be limited). In addition, any charge by the employer for the personal use by an employee of a product being tested shall be taken into account in determining whether the requirement of paragraph (n)(1)(v) of this section is satisfied.

(3) Discriminating classifications. If an employer furnishes products under a testing and evaluation program only, or presumably, to certain classes of employees (such as highly compensated employees, as defined in § 1.132–8(g)), this fact may be relevant when determining whether the products are furnished for testing and evaluation purposes or for compensation purposes, unless the employer can show a business reason for the classification of employees to whom the products are furnished (e.g., that automobiles are furnished for testing and evaluation by an automobile manufacturer to its design engineers and supervisory mechanics).

(4) Factors that negate the existence of a product testing program. If an employer fails to tabulate and examine the results of the detailed reports submitted by employees within a reasonable period of time after expiration of the testing period, the program will not be considered a product testing program for purposes of the exclusion of this paragraph (n). Existence of one or more of the following factors may also establish that the program is not a bona fide product testing program for purposes of the exclusion of this paragraph (n):

(i) The program is in essence a leasing program under which employees lease the consumer goods from the employer for a fee;

(ii) The nature of the product and other considerations are insufficient to justify the testing program; or

(iii) The expense of the program outweighs the benefits to be gained from testing and evaluation.

(5) Failure to meet the requirements of this paragraph (n). The fair market value of the use of property for product testing and evaluation by an employee outside the employee's workplace, under a product testing program that does not meet all of the requirements of this paragraph (n), is not excludable from gross income as a working condition fringe under this paragraph (n).

(6) Example. The rules of this paragraph (n) may be illustrated by the following example:

Example. Assume that an employer that manufactures automobiles establishes a product testing program under which 50 of its 5,000 employees test and evaluate the automobiles for 30 days. Assume further that the 50 employees represent a fair cross-section of all of the employees of the employer, such employees submit detailed reports to the employer on the testing and evaluation, the employer tabulates and examines the test results within a reasonable time, and the use of the automobiles is restricted to the employees. If the employer imposes the limits described in paragraph (n)(2) of this section, the employees may exclude the value of the use of the automobile during the testing and evaluation period.

(o) Qualified automobile demonstration use—(1) In general. The value of qualified automobile demonstration use is excludable from gross income as a working condition fringe. "Qualified automobile demonstration use" is any use of a demonstration automobile by a full-time automobile salesman in the sales area in which the automobile dealer's sales office is located if—

(i) Such use if provided primarily to facilitate the salesman's performance of services for the employer; and

(ii) There are substantial restrictions on the personal use of the automobile by the salesman.

(2) Full-time automobile salesman—

(i) Defined. The term "full-time automobile salesman" means any individual who—

(A) Is employed by an automobile dealer;

(B) Customarily spends at least half of a normal business day performing the functions of a floor salesperson or sales manager;

(C) Directly engages in substantial promotion and negotiation of sales to customers;

(D) Customarily works a number of hours considered full-time in the industry (but at a rate not less than 1,000 hours per year); and

(E) Derives at least 25 percent of his or her gross income from the automobile dealership directly as a result of the activities described in paragraphs (o)(2)(i) (B) and (C) of this section.

For purposes of paragraph (o)(2)(i)(E) of this section, income is not considered to be derived directly as a result of activities described in paragraphs (o)(2)(i) (B) and (C) of this section to the extent that the income is attributable to an individual's ownership interest in the dealership. An individual will not be considered to engage in direct sales activities if the individual's sales-related activities are substantially limited to review of sales price offers from customers. An individual, such as the general manager of an automobile dealership, who receives a sales commission on the sale of an automobile is not a full-time automobile salesman unless the requirements of this paragraph (o)(2)(i) are met. The exclusion provided in this paragraph (o) is available to an individual who meets the definition of this paragraph (o)(2)(i) whether the individual performs services in addition to those described in this paragraph (o)(2)(i). For example, an individual who is an owner of the automobile dealership but who otherwise meets the requirements of this paragraph (o)(2)(i) may exclude from gross income the value of qualified automobile demonstration use. However, the exclusion of this paragraph (o) is not available to owners of large automobile dealerships who do not customarily engage in significant sales activities.

(ii) Use by an individual other than a full-time automobile salesman. Personal use of a demonstration automobile by an individual other than a full-time automobile salesman is not treated as a working condition fringe. Therefore, any personal use, including commuting use, of a demonstration automobile by a part-time salesman, automobile mechanic, or other individual who is not a full-time automobile salesman is not "qualified automobile demonstration use" and thus not excludable from gross income. This is the case whether or not the personal use is within the sales area (as defined in paragraph (o)(5) of this section).

(3) Demonstration automobile. The exclusion provided in this paragraph (o) applies only to qualified use of a demonstration automobile. A demonstration automobile is an automobile that is—

(i) Currently in the inventory of the automobile dealership; and

(ii) Available for test drives by customers during the normal business hours of the employee.

(4) Substantial restrictions on personal use. Substantial restrictions on the personal use of a demonstration automobile exist when all of the following conditions are satisfied:

(i) Use by individuals other than the full-time automobile salesmen (e.g., the salesman's family) is prohibited;

(ii) Use for personal vacation trips is prohibited;

(iii) The storage of personal possessions in the automobile is prohibited; and

(iv) The total use by mileage of the automobile by the salesman outside the salesman's normal working hours is limited.

(5) Sales area—(i) In general. Qualified automobile demonstration use consists of use in the sales area in which the automobile dealer's sales office is located. The sales area is the geographic area surrounding the automobile dealer's sales office from which the office regularly derives customers.

(ii) Sales area safe harbor. With respect to a particular full-time salesman, the automobile dealer's sales area may be treated as the area within a radius of the larger of—

(A) 75 miles or

(B) The one-way commuting distance (in miles) of the particular salesman from the dealer's sales office.

(6) Applicability of substantiation requirements of sections 162 and 274(d). Notwithstanding anything in this section to the contrary, the value of the use of a demonstration automobile may not be excluded from gross income as a working condition fringe, by either the employer or the employee, unless, with respect to the restrictions of paragraph (o)(4) of this section, the substantiation requirements of section 274(d) and the regulations thereunder are satisfied. See § 1.132–5(c) for general and safe harbor rules relating to the applicability of the substantiation requirements of section 274(d).

(7) Special valuation rules. See § 1.61–21(d)(6)(ii) for special rules that may be used to value the availability of demonstration automobiles.

(p) Parking—(1) In general. The value of parking provided to an employee on or near the business premises of the employer is excludable from gross income as a working condition fringe under the special rule of this paragraph (p). If the rules of this paragraph (p) are satisfied, the value of parking is excludable from gross income whether the amount paid by the employee for parking would be deductible under section 162. The working condition fringe exclusion applies whether the employer owns or rents the parking facility or parking space.

(2) Reimbursement of parking expenses. A reimbursement to the employee of the ordinary and necessary expenses of renting a parking space on or near the business premises of the employer is excludable from gross income as a working condition fringe, if, but for the parking expense, the employee would not have been entitled to receive and retain such amount from the employer. If, however, an employee is entitled to retain a general transportation allowance or a similar benefit whether or not the employee has parking expenses, no portion of that allowance is excludable from gross income under this paragraph (p) even if it is used for parking expenses.

(3) Parking on residential property. With respect to an employee, this paragraph (p) does not apply to any parking facility or space located on property owned or leased by the employee for residential purposes.

* * *

(q) Nonapplicability of nondiscrimination rules. Except to the extent provided in paragraph (n)(3) of this section (relating to discriminating classifications of a product testing program), the non-discrimination rules of section 132(h)(1) and § 1.132–8 do not apply in determining the amount, if any, of a working condition fringe.

(r) Volunteers—(1) In general. Solely for purposes of section 132(d) and paragraph (a)(1) of this section, a bona fide volunteer (including a director or officer) who performs services for an organization exempt from tax under section 501(a), or for a government employer (as defined in paragraph (m)(7) of this section), is deemed to have a profit motive under section 162.

(2) Limit on application of this paragraph. This paragraph (r) shall not be used to support treatment of the bona fide volunteer as having a profit motive for purposes of any provision of the Internal Revenue Code of 1986 (Code) other than section 132(d). Nothing in this paragraph (r) shall be interpreted as determining the employment status of a bona fide volunteer for purposes of any section of the Code other than section 132(d).

(3) Definitions—(i) Bona fide volunteer. For purposes of this paragraph (r), an individual is considered a "bona fide volunteer" if the individual does not have a profit motive for purposes of section 162. For example, an individual is considered a "bona fide volunteer" if the total value of the benefits provided with respect to the volunteer services is substantially less than the total value of the volunteer services the individual provides to an exempt organization or government employer.

(ii) Liability insurance coverage for a bona fide volunteer. For purposes of this paragraph (r), the receipt of liability insurance coverage by a volunteer, or an exempt organization or government employer's undertaking to indemnify the volunteer for liability, does not by itself confer a profit motive on the volunteer, provided the insurance coverage or indemnification relates to acts performed by the volunteer in the discharge of duties, or the performance of services, on behalf of the exempt organization or government employer.

(4) Example. The following example illustrates the provisions of paragraph (r) of this section.

Example. A is a manager and full-time employee of P, a tax-exempt organization described in section 501 (c)(3). B is a member of P's board of directors. Other than $25 to defray expenses for attending board meetings, B receives no compensation for serving as a director and does not have a profit motive. Therefore, B is a bona fide volunteer by application of paragraph (r)(3)(i) of this section and is deemed to have a profit motive under paragraph (r)(1) of this section for purposes of section 132(d). In order to provide liability insurance coverage, P purchases a policy that covers actions arising from A's and B's activities performed as part of their duties to P. The value of the policy and payments made to or on behalf of A under the policy are excludable for A's gross income as a working condition fringe, because A has a profit motive under section 162 and would be able to deduct payments for liability insurance coverage had he paid for it himself. The receipt of liability insurance coverage by B does not confer a profit motive on B by application of paragraph (r)(3)(ii) of this section. Thus, the value of the policy and payments made to or on behalf of B under the policy are excludable from B's income as a working condition fringe. For the year in which the liability insurance coverage is provided to A and B, P may exclude the value of the benefit on the Form W–2 it issues to A or on any Form 1099 it might otherwise issue to B.

* * *

(s) Application of section 274(a)(3)—(1) In general. If an employer's deduction under section 162(a) for dues paid or incurred for membership in any club organized for business, pleasure, recreation, or other social purpose is disallowed by section 274(a)(3), the amount, if any, of an employee's working condition fringe benefit relating to an employer-provided membership in the club is determined without regard to the application of section 274(a) to the employee. To be excludable as a working condition fringe benefit, however, the amount must otherwise qualify for deduction by the employee under section 162(a). If an employer treats the amount paid or incurred for membership in any club organized for business, pleasure, recreation, or other social purpose as compensation under section 274(e)(2), then the expense is deductible by the employer as compensation and no amount may be excluded from the employee's gross income as a working condition fringe benefit. See § 1.274-2(f) (2)(iii)(A).

(2) Treatment of tax-exempt employers. In the case of an employer exempt from taxation under subtitle A of the Internal Revenue Code, any reference in this paragraph (s) to a deduction disallowed by section 274(a)(3) shall be treated as a reference to the amount which would be disallowed as a deduction by section 274(a)(3) to the employer if the employer were not exempt from taxation under subtitle A of the Internal Revenue Code.

(3) Examples. The following examples illustrate this paragraph (s):

Example 1. Assume that Company X provides Employee B with a country club membership for which it paid $20,000. B substantiates, within the meaning of paragraph (c) of this section, that the club was used 40 percent for business purposes. The business use of the club (40 percent) may be considered a working condition fringe benefit, notwithstanding that the employer's deduction for the dues allocable to the business use is disallowed by section 274(a)(3), if X does not treat the club membership as compensation under section 274(e)(2). Thus, B may exclude from gross income $8,000 (40 percent of the club dues, which reflect B's business use). X must report $12,000 as wages subject to withholding and payment of employment taxes (60 percent of the value of the club dues, which reflects B's personal use). B must include $12,000 in gross income. X may deduct as compensation the amount it paid for the club dues which reflects B's personal use provided the amount satisfies the other requirements for a salary or compensation deduction under section 162.

Example 2. Assume the same facts as Example 1 except that Company X treats the $20,000 as compensation to B under section 274(e)(2). No portion of the $20,000 will be considered a working condition fringe benefit because the section 274(a)(3) disallowance will apply to B. Therefore, B must include $20,000 in gross income.

(t) Application of section 274(m)(3)—(1) In general. If an employer's deduction under section 162(a) for amounts paid or incurred for the travel expenses of a spouse, dependent, or other individual accompanying an employee is disallowed by section 274(m)(3), the amount, if any, of the employee's working condition fringe benefit relating to the employer-provided travel is determined without regard to the application of section 274(m)(3). To be excludable as a working condition fringe benefit, however, the amount must otherwise qualify for deduction by the employee under section 162(a). The amount will qualify for deduction and for exclusion as a working condition fringe benefit if it can be adequately shown that the spouse's, dependent's, or other accompanying individual's presence on the employee's business trip has a bona fide business purpose and if the employee substantiates the travel within the meaning of paragraph (c) of this section. If the travel does not qualify as a working condition fringe benefit, the employee must include in gross income as a fringe benefit the value of the employer's payment of travel expenses with respect to a spouse, dependent, or other individual accompanying the employee on business travel. See §§ 1.61–21(a)(4) and 1.162–2(c). If an employer treats as compensation under section 274(e)(2) the amount paid or incurred for the travel expenses of a spouse, dependent, or other individual accompanying an employee, then the expense is deductible by the employer as compensation and no amount may be excluded from the employee's gross income as a working condition fringe benefit. See § 1.274–2(f) (2)(iii)(A).

(2) Treatment of tax-exempt employers. In the case of an employer exempt from taxation under subtitle A of the Internal Revenue Code, any reference in this paragraph (t) to a deduction disallowed by section 274(m)(3) shall be treated as a reference to the amount which would be disallowed as a deduction by section 274(m)(3) to the employer if the employer were not exempt from taxation under subtitle A of the Internal Revenue Code.

§ 1.132–6 De minimis fringes.

(a) In general. Gross income does not include the value of a de minimis fringe provided to an employee. The term "de minimis fringe" means any property or service the value of which is (after taking into account the frequency with which similar fringes are provided by the employer to the employer's employees) so small as to make accounting for it unreasonable or administratively impracticable.

(b) Frequency—(1) Employee-measured frequency. Generally, the frequency with which similar fringes are provided by the employer to the employer's employees is determined by reference to the frequency with which the employer provides the fringes to each individual employee. For example, if an employer provides a free meal in kind to one employee on a daily basis, but not to any other employee, the value of the meals is not de minimis with respect to that one employee even though with respect to the employer's entire workforce the meals are provided "infrequently."

(2) Employer-measured frequency. Notwithstanding the rule of paragraph (b)(1) of this section, except for purposes of applying the special rules of paragraph (d)(2) of this section, where it would be administratively difficult to determine frequency with respect to individual employees, the frequency with which similar fringes are provided by the employer to the employer's employees is determined by reference to the frequency with which the employer provides the fringes to the workforce as a whole. Therefore, under this rule, the frequency with which any individual employee receives such a fringe benefit is not relevant and in some circumstances, the de minimis fringe exclusion may apply with respect to a benefit even though a particular employee receives the benefit frequently. For example, if an employer exercises sufficient control and imposes significant restrictions on the personal use of a company copying machine so that at least 85 percent of the use of the machine is for business purposes, any personal use of the copying machine by particular employees is considered to be a de minimis fringe.

(c) Administrability. Unless excluded by a provision of chapter 1 of the Internal Revenue Code of 1986 other than section 132(a)(4), the value of any fringe benefit that would not be unreasonable or administratively impracticable to account for is includible in the employee's gross income. Thus, except as provided in paragraph (d)(2) of this section, the provision of any cash fringe benefit is never excludable under section 132(a) as a de minimis fringe benefit. Similarly except as otherwise provided in paragraph (d) of this section, a cash equivalent fringe benefit (such as a fringe benefit provided to an employee through the use of a gift certificate or charge or credit card) is generally not excludable under section 132(a) even if the same property or service acquired (if provided in kind) would be excludable as a de minimis fringe benefit. For example, the provision of cash to an employee for a theatre ticket that would itself be excludable as a de minimis fringe (see paragraph (e)(1) of this section) is not excludable as a de minimis fringe.

(d) Special rules—(1) Transit passes. A public transit pass provided at a discount to defray an employee's commuting costs may be excluded from the employee's gross income as a de minimis fringe if such discount does not exceed $21 in any month. The exclusion provided in this paragraph (d)(1) also applies to the provision of tokens or fare cards that enable an individual to travel on the public transit system if the value of such tokens and fare cards in any month does not exceed by more than $21 the amount the employee paid for the tokens and farecards for such month. Similarly, the exclusion of this paragraph (d)(1) applies to the provision of a voucher or similar instrument that is exchangeable solely for tokens, farecards, or other instruments that enable the employee to use the public transit system if the value of such vouchers and other instruments in any month does not exceed $21. The exclusion of this paragraph (d)(1) also applies to reimbursements made by an employer to an employee after December 31, 1988, to cover the cost of commuting on a public transit system, provided the employee does not receive more than $21 in such reimbursements for commuting costs in any given month. The reimbursement must be made under a bona fide reimbursement arrangement. A reimbursement arrangement will be treated as bona fide if the employer establishes appropriate procedures for verifying on a periodic basis that the employee's use of public transportation for commuting is consistent with the value of the benefit provided by the employer for that purpose. The amount of in-kind public transit commuting benefits and reimbursements provided during any month that are excludable under this paragraph (d)(1) is limited to $21. For months ending before July 1, 1991, the amount is $15 per month. The exclusion provided in this paragraph (d)(l) does not apply to the provision of any benefit to defray public transit expenses incurred for personal travel other than commuting.

(2) Occasional meal money or local transportation fare—(i) General rule. Meals, meal money or local transportation fare provided to an employee is excluded as a de minimis fringe benefit if the benefit provided is reasonable and is provided in a manner that satisfies the following three conditions:

(A) Occasional basis. The meals, meal money or local transportation fare is provided to the employee on an occasional basis. Whether meal money or local transportation fare is provided to an employee on an occasional basis will depend upon the frequency i.e. the availability of the benefit and regularity with which the benefit is provided by the employer to the employee. Thus, meals, meal money, or local transportation fare or a combination of such benefits provided to an employee on a regular or routine basis is not provided on an occasional basis.

(B) Overtime. The meals, meal money or local transportation fare is provided to an employee because overtime work necessitates an extension of the employee's normal work schedule. This condition does not fail to be satisfied merely because the circumstances giving rise to the need for overtime work are reasonably foreseeable.

(C) Meal money. In the case of a meal or meal money, the meal or meal money is provided to enable the employee to work overtime. Thus, for example, meals provided on the employer's premises that are consumed during the period that the employee works overtime or meal money provided for meals consumed during such period satisfy this condition.

In no event shall meal money or local transportation fare calculated on the basis of the number of hours worked (e.g., $1.00 per hour for each hour over eight hours) be considered a de minimis fringe benefit.

(ii) Applicability of other exclusions for certain meals and for transportation provided for security concerns. The value of meals furnished to an employee, an employee's spouse, or any of the employee's dependents by or on behalf of the employee's employer for the convenience of the employer is excluded from the employee's gross income if the meals are furnished on the business premises of the employer (see section 119). (For purposes of the exclusion under section 119, the definitions of an employee under § 1.132–1(b) do not apply.) If, for a bona fide business-oriented security concern, an employer provides an employee vehicle transportation that is specially designed for security (for example, the vehicle is equipped with bulletproof glass and armor plating), and the conditions of § 1.132–5(m) are satisfied, the value of the special security design is excludable from gross income as a working condition fringe if the employee would not have had such special security design but for the bona fide business-oriented security concern.

(iii) Special rule for employer-provided transportation provided in certain circumstances. (A) Partial exclusion of value. If an employer provides transportation (such as taxi fare) to an employee for use in commuting to and/or from work because or unusual circumstances and because, based on the facts and circumstances, it is unsafe for the employee to use other available means of transportation, the excess of the value of each one-way trip over $1.50 per one-way commute is excluded from gross income. The rule of this paragraph (d)(2)(iii) is not available to a control employee as defined in § 1.61–21(f)(5) and (6).

(B) "Unusual circumstances". Unusual circumstances are determined with respect to the employee receiving the transportation and are based on all facts and circumstances. An example of unusual circumstances would be when an employee is asked to work outside of his normal work hours (such as being called to the workplace at 1:00 a.m. when the employee normally works from 8:00 a.m. to 4:00 p.m.). Another example of unusual circumstances is a temporary change in the employee's work schedule (such as working from 12 midnight to 8:00 a.m. rather than from 8:00 a.m. to 4:00 p.m. for a two-week period).

(C) "Unsafe conditions". Factors indicating whether it is unsafe for an employee to use other available means of transportation are the history of crime in the geographic area surrounding the employee's workplace or residence and the time of day during which the employee must commute.

(3) Use of special rules or examples to establish a general rule. The special rules provided in this paragraph (d) or examples provided in paragraph (e) of this section may not be used to establish any general rule permitting exclusion as a de minimis fringe. For example, the fact that $252 (i.e., $21 per month for 12 months) worth of public transit passes can be excluded from gross income as a de minimis fringe in 1992 does not mean that any fringe benefit with a value equal to or less than $252 may be excluded as a de minimis fringe. As another example, the fact that the commuting use of an employer-provided vehicle more than one day a month is an example of a benefit not excludable as a de minimis fringe (see paragraph (e)(2) of this section) does not mean that the commuting use of a vehicle up to 12 times per year is excludable from gross income as a de minimis fringe.

(4) Benefits exceeding value and frequency limits. If a benefit provided to an employee is not de minimis because either the value or frequency exceeds a limit provided in this paragraph (d), no amount of the benefit is considered to be a de minimis fringe. For example, if in 1992, an employer provides a $50 monthly public transit pass, the entire $50 must be included in income, not just the excess value over $21.

(e) Examples—(1) Benefits excludable from income. Examples of de minimis fringe benefits are occasional typing of personal letters by a company secretary; occasional personal use of an employer's copying machine, provided that the employer exercises sufficient control and imposes significant restrictions on the personal use of the machine so that at least 85 percent of the use of the machine is for business purposes; occasional cocktail parties, group meals, or picnics for employees and their guests; traditional birthday or holiday gifts of property (not cash) with a low fair market value; occasional theater or sporting event tickets; coffee, doughnuts, and soft drinks; local telephone calls; and flowers, fruit, books, or similar property provided to employees under special circumstances (e.g., on account of illness, outstanding performance, or family crisis).

(2) Benefits not excludable as de minimis fringes. Examples of fringe benefits that are not excludable from gross income as de minimis fringes are: season tickets to sporting or theatrical event; the commuting use of an employer-provided automobile or other vehicle more than one day a month; membership in a private country club or athletic facility, regardless of the frequency with which the employee uses the facility; employer-provided group-term life insurance on the life of the spouse or child of an employee; and use of employer-owned or leased facilities (such as an apartment, hunting lodge, boat, etc.) for a weekend. Some amount of the value of certain of these fringe benefits may be excluded from income under other statutory provisions, such as the exclusion for working condition fringes. See § 1.132–5.

(f) Nonapplicability of nondiscrimination rules. Except to the extent provided in § 1.132–7, the nondiscrimination rules of section 132(h)(1) and § 1.132–8 do not apply in determining the amount, if any, of a de minimis fringe. Thus, a fringe benefit may be excludable as a de minimis fringe even if the benefit is provided exclusively to highly compensated employees of the employer.

* * *

§ 1.132–7 Employer-operated eating facilities.

(a) In general—(1) Condition for exclusion—(i) General rule. The value of meals provided to employees at an employer-operated eating facility for employees is excludable from gross income as a de minimis fringe only if on an annual basis, the revenue from the facility equals or exceeds the direct operating costs of the facility.

(ii) Additional condition for highly compensated employees. With respect to any highly compensated employee, an exclusion is available under this section only if the condition set out in paragraph (a)(1)(i) of this section is satisfied and access to the facility is available on substantially the same terms to each member of a group of employees that is defined under a reasonable classification set up by the employer that does not discriminate in favor of highly compensated employees. See § 1.132–8. For purposes of this paragraph (a)(1)(ii), each dining room or cafeteria in which meals are served is treated as a separate eating facility, whether each such dining room or cafeteria has its own kitchen or other food-preparation area.

(2) Employer-operated eating facility for employees. An employer-operated eating facility for employees is a facility that meets all of the following conditions—

(i) The facility is owned or leased by the employer,

(ii) The facility is operated by the employer,

(iii) The facility is located on or near the business premises of the employer, and

(iv) The meals furnished at the facility are provided during, or immediately before or after, the employee's workday.

For purposes of this section, the term "meals" means food, beverages, and related services provided at the facility. If an employer can reasonably determine the number of meals that are excludable from income by the recipient employees under section 119, the employer may, in determining whether the requirement of paragraph (a)(1)(i) of this section is satisfied, disregard all costs and revenues attributable to such meals provided to such employees. If an employer can reasonably determine the number of meals received by volunteers who receive food and beverages at a hospital, free or at a discount, the employer may, in determining whether the requirement of paragraph (a)(1)(i) of this section is satisfied, disregard all costs and revenues attributable to such meals provided to such volunteers. If an employer charges non-employees a greater amount than employees, in determining whether the requirement of paragraph (a)(1)(i) of this section is satisfied, the employer must disregard all costs and revenues attributable to such meals provided to such nonemployees.

(3) Operation by the employer. If an employer contracts with another to operate an eating facility for its employees, the facility is considered to be operated by the employer for purposes of this section. If an eating facility is operated by more than one employer, it is considered to be operated by each employer.

(4) Example. The provisions of this paragraph (a)(2) may be illustrated by the following example:

Example (1). Assume that a not-for-profit hospital system maintains cafeterias for the use of its employees and volunteers. Only the employees are charged for food service at the cafeteria and the policy of the hospital is to charge the employees only for the costs of food, beverage and labor directly attributable to the meal. Most of the cafeterias within the system furnish more free meals to volunteers than they serve paid meals to employees. For purposes of this paragraph, as long as the employer can accurately determine the number of meals received free or at a discount by volunteers, the employer may disregard all the costs and revenues attributable to such meals provided to volunteers. Therefore, for purposes of this paragraph, the costs of the hospital system for furnishing meals to employees who pay for them are the costs to be compared to determine if the revenues from the facility equal or exceed direct operating costs of the facility's service to employees.

(b) Direct operating costs—(1) In general. For purposes of this section, the direct operating costs of an eating facility are—

(i) The cost of food and beverages, and

(ii) The cost of labor for personnel whose services relating to the facility are performed primarily on the premises of the eating facility. Direct operating costs do not include the labor cost attributable to personnel whose services relating to the facility are not performed primarily on the premises of the eating facility. Thus, for example, the labor costs attributable to cooks, waiters, and waitresses are included in direct operating costs, but the labor cost attributable to a manager of an eating facility whose services relating to the facility are not primarily performed on the premises of the eating facility is not included in direct operating costs. If an employee performs services relating to the facility both on and off the premises of the eating facility, only the portion of the total labor cost of the employee relating to the facility that bears the same proportion to such total labor cost as time spent on the premises bears to total time spent performing services relating to the facility is included in direct operating costs. For example, assume that 60 percent of the services of a cook in the above example are not related to the eating facility. Only 40 percent of the total labor cost of the cook is includible in direct operating costs. For purposes of this section, labor costs include all compensation required to be reported on a Form W-2 for income tax purposes and related employment taxes paid by the employer. In determining the direct operating costs of an eating facility, the employer may include as part of the facility, vending machines that are provided by the employer and located on the same premises as the other eating facilities operated by the employer.

(2) Multiple dining rooms or cafeterias. The direct operating costs test may be applied separately for each dining room or cafeteria. Alternatively, the direct operating costs test may be applied with respect to all the eating facilities operated by the employer.

(3) Payment to operator of facility. If an employer contracts with another to operate an eating facility for its employees, the direct operating costs of the facility consist both of direct operating costs, if any, incurred by the employer and the amount paid to the operator of the facility to the extent that such amount is attributable to what would be direct operating costs if the employer operated the facility directly.

(c) Valuation of non-excluded meals provided at an employer-operated eating facility for employees. If the exclusion for meals provided at an employer-operated eating facility for employees is not available, the recipient of meals provided at such facility must include in income the amount by which the fair market value of the meals provided exceeds the sum of—

(1) The amount, if any, paid for the meals, and

(2) The amount, if any, specifically excluded by another section of chapter 1 of this subtitle.

For special valuation rules relating to such meals, see § 1.61–21(j).

* * *

§ 1.132–8 Fringe benefit nondiscrimination rules.

(a) Application of nondiscrimination rules—(1) General rule. A highly compensated employee who receives a no-additional cost service, a qualified employee discount or a meal provided at an employer-operated eating facility for employees shall not be permitted to exclude such benefit from his or her income unless the benefit is available on substantially the same terms to:

(i) All employees of the employer; or

(ii) A group of employees of the employer which is defined under a reasonable classification set up by the employer that does not discriminate in favor of highly compensated employees. See paragraph (f) of this section for the definition of a highly compensated employee.

(2) Consequences of discrimination— (i) In general. If an employer maintains more than one fringe benefit program, i.e., either different fringe benefits being provided to the same group of employees, or different classifications of employees or the same fringe benefit being provided to two or more classifications of employees, the nondiscrimination requirements of section 132 will generally be applied separately to each such program. Thus, a determination that one fringe benefit program discriminates in favor of highly compensated employees generally will not cause other fringe benefit programs covering the same highly compensated employees to be treated as discriminatory. If the fringe benefits provided to a highly compensated individual do not satisfy the nondiscrimination rules provided in this section, such individual shall be unable to exclude from gross income any portion of the benefit. For example, if an employer offers a 20 percent discount (which otherwise satisfies the requirements for a qualified employee discount) to all non-highly compensated employees and a 35 percent discount to all highly compensated employees, the entire value of the 35 percent discount (not just the excess over 20 percent) is includible in the gross income and wages of the highly compensated employees who make purchases at a discount.

(ii) Exception—(A) Related fringe benefit programs. If one of a group of fringe benefit programs discriminates in favor of highly compensated employees, no related fringe benefit provided to such highly compensated employees under any other fringe benefit program may be excluded from the gross income of such highly compensated employees. For example, assume a department store provides a 20 percent merchandise discount to all employees under one fringe benefit program. Assume further that under a second fringe benefit program, the department store provides an additional 15 percent merchandise discount to a group of employees defined under a classification which discriminates in favor of highly compensated employees. Because the second fringe benefit program is discriminatory, the 15 percent merchandise discount provided to the highly compensated employees is not a qualified employee discount. In addition, because the 20 percent merchandise discount provided under the first fringe benefit program is related to the fringe benefit provided under the second fringe benefit program, the 20 percent merchandise discount provided the highly compensated employees is not a qualified employee discount. Thus, the entire 35 percent merchandise discount provided to the highly compensated employees is includible in such employees' gross incomes.

(B) Employer-operated eating facilities for employees. For purposes of paragraph (a)(2)(ii)(A) of this section, meals at different employer-operated eating facilities for employees are not related fringe benefits, so that a highly compensated employee may exclude from gross income the value of a meal at a nondiscriminatory facility even though any meals provided to him or her at a discriminatory facility cannot be excluded.

(3) Scope of the nondiscrimination rules provided in this section. The nondiscrimination rules provided in this section apply only to fringe benefits provided pursuant to section 132(a)(1), (a)(2), and (e)(2). These rules have no application to any other employee benefit that may be subject to nondiscrimination requirements under any other section of the Code.

(b) Aggregation of employees— (1) Section 132 (a)(1) and (2). For purposes of determining whether the exclusions for no-additional-cost services and qualified employee discounts are available to highly compensated employees, the nondiscrimination rules of this section are applied by aggregating the employees of all related employers (as defined in § 1.132–1(c)), except that employees in different lines of business (as defined in § 1.132–4) are not to be aggregated. Thus, in general, for purposes of this section, the term "employees of the employer" refers to all employees of the employer and any other entity that is a member of a group described in sections 414(b), (c), (m), or (o) and that performs services within the same line of business as the employer which provides the particular fringe benefit. Employees in different lines of business will be aggregated, however, if the line of business limitation has been relaxed pursuant to paragraphs (b) through (g) of § 1.132–4.

(2) Section 132(e)(2). For purposes of determining whether the exclusions for meals provided at employer-operated eating facilities are available to highly compensated, the nondiscrimination rules of this section are applied by aggregating the employees of all related employers (as defined in § 1.132—1(c)) who regularly work at or near the premises on which the eating facility is located, except that employees in different lines of business (as defined in § 1.132–4) are not to be aggregated. The nondiscrimination rules of this section are applied separately to each eating facility. Each dining room or cafeteria in which meals are served is treated as a separate eating facility, regardless of whether each such dining room or cafeteria has its own kitchen or other food-preparation area.

(3) Classes of employees who may be excluded. For purposes of applying the nondiscrimination rules of this section to a particular fringe benefit program, there may be excluded from consideration employees who may be excluded from consideration under section 89(h),* as enacted by the Tax Reform Act of 1986, Pub.L. 99–514, 100 Stat. 2085 (1986) and amended by the Technical and Miscellaneous Revenue Act of 1988, Pub.L. 100–647, 102 Stat. 3342 (1988).

(c) Availability on substantially the same terms—(1) General rule. The determination of whether a benefit is available on substantially the same terms shall be made upon the basis of the facts and circumstances of each situation. In general, however, if any one of the terms or conditions governing the availability of a particular benefit to one or more employees varies from any one of the terms or conditions governing the availability of a benefit made available to one or more other employees, such benefit shall not be considered to be available on substantially the same terms except to the extent otherwise provided in paragraph (c)(2) of this section. For example, if a department store provides a 20 percent qualified employee discount to all of its employees on all merchandise, the substantially the same terms requirement will be satisfied. Similarly, if the discount provided to all employees is 30 percent on certain merchandise (such as apparel), and 20 percent on all other merchandise, the substantially the same terms requirement will be satisfied. However, if a department store provides a 20 percent qualified employee discount to all employees, but as to the employees in certain departments, the discount is available upon hire, and as to the remaining departments, the discount is only available when an employee has completed a specified term of services, the 20 percent discount is not available on substantially the same terms to all of the employees of the employer. Similarly, if a greater discount is given to employees with more seniority, full-time work status, or a particular job description, such benefit (i.e., the discount) would not be available to all employees eligible for the discount on substantially the same terms, except to the extent otherwise provided in paragraph (c)(2) of this section. These examples also apply to no-additional-cost services. Thus, if an employer charges non-highly compensated employees for a no-additional-cost service and does not charge highly compensated employees (or charges highly compensated employees a lesser amount), the substantially the same terms requirement will not be satisfied.

(2) Certain terms relating to priority. Certain fringe benefits made available to employees are available only in limited quantities that may be insufficient to meet employee demand. This situation may occur either because of employer policy (such as where an employer determines that only a certain number of units of a specific product will be made available to employees each year) or because of the nature of the fringe benefit (such as where an employer provides a no-additional-cost transportation service that is limited to the number of seats available just before departure). Under these circumstances, an employer may find it necessary to establish some method of allocating the limited fringe benefits among the employees eligible to receive the fringe benefits. The employer may establish the priorities described below.

(i) Priority on a first come, first served, or similar basis. A benefit shall not fail to be treated as available to a group of employees on substantially

*Editorial comment: The Regulations do not reflect the effect of the Energy Policy Act of 1992 which added Sec. 132(a)(5) on the "qualified transportation fringe," the Revenue Reconciliation Act of 1993 which added Sec. 132(a)(6) on the "qualified moving expense reimbursement," or subsequent legislation which added Sec. 132(a)(7) on qualified retirement planning services.

the same terms merely because the employer allocates the benefit among such employees on a "first come, first served" or lottery basis, provided that the same notice of the terms of availability is given to all employees in the group and the terms under which the benefit is provided to employees within the group are otherwise the same with respect to all employees. For purposes of the preceding sentence, a program that gives priority to employees who are the first to submit written requests for the benefit will constitute priority on a "first come, first served" basis. Similarly, if the employer regularly engages in the practice of allocating benefits on a priority basis to employees demonstrating a critical need, such benefit shall not fail to be treated as available on substantially the same terms to all of the employees with respect to whom such priority status is available as long as the determination is based upon uniform and objective criteria which have been communicated to all employees in the group of eligible employees. An example of a critical need would be priority transportation given to an employee in the event of a medical emergency involving the employee (or a member of the employee's immediate family) or a recent death in the employee's immediate family. Frustrated vacation plans or forfeited deposits would not be treated as giving rise to particularly critical needs.

(ii) Priority on the basis of seniority. Solely for purposes of § 1.132–8, a benefit shall not fail to be treated as available to a group of employees of the employer on substantially the same terms merely because the employer allocates the benefit among such employees on a seniority basis provided that:

(A) The same notice of the terms of availability is given to all employees in the group; and

(B) The average value of the benefit provided for each nonhighly compensated employee is at least 75% of that provided for each highly compensated employee. For purposes of this test, the average value of the benefit provided for each nonhighly compensated (highly compensated) employee is determined by taking the sum of the fair market values of such benefit provided to all the nonhighly compensated (highly compensated) employees, determined in accordance with § 1.61–21, and then dividing that sum by the total number of nonhighly compensated (highly compensated) employees of the employer. For purposes of determining the average value of the benefit provided for each employee, all employee's of the employer are counted, including those who are not eligible to receive the benefit from the employer.

(d) Testing for discrimination.

(1) Classification test. In the event that a benefit described in section 132(a)(1), (a)(2) or (e)(2) is not available on substantially the same terms to all of the employees of the employer, no exclusion shall be available to a highly compensated employee for such benefit unless the program under which the benefit is provided satisfies the nondiscrimination standards set forth in this section. The nondiscrimination standard of this section will be satisfied only if the benefit is available on substantially the same terms to a group of employees of the employer which is defined under a reasonable classification established by thc cmployer that does not discriminate in favor of highly compensated employees. The determination of whether a particular classification is discriminatory will generally depend upon the facts and circumstances involved, based upon principles similar to those applied for purposes of section 410(b)(2)(A)(i) or, for years commencing prior to January 1, 1988, section 410(b)(1) (B). Thus, in general, except as otherwise provided in this section, if a benefit is available on substantially the same terms to a group of employees which, when compared with all of the other employees of the employer, constitutes a nondiscriminatory classification under section 410(b)(2)(A)(i) (or, if applicable, section 410(b)(1)(B)), it shall be deemed to be nondiscriminatory.

(2) Classifications that are per se discriminatory. A classification that, on its face, makes fringe benefits available principally to highly compensated employees is per se discriminatory. In addition, a classification that is based on either an amount or rate of compensation is per se discriminatory if it favors those with the higher amount or rate of compensation. On the other hand, a classification that is based on factors such as seniority, full-time vs. part-time employment, or job description is not per se discriminatory but may be discriminatory as applied to the workforce of a particular employer.

(3) Former employees. When determining whether a classification is discriminatory, former employees shall be tested separately from other employees of the employer. Therefore, a classification is not discriminatory solely because the employer does not make fringe benefits available to any former employee. Whether a classification of former employees discriminates in favor of highly compensated employees will depend upon the particular facts and circumstances.

(4) Restructuring of benefits. For purposes of testing whether a particular group of employees would constitute a discriminatory classification for purposes of this section, an employer may restructure its fringe benefit program as described in this paragraph. If a fringe benefit is provided to more than one group of employees, and one or more such groups would constitute a discriminatory classification if considered by itself, then for purposes of this section, the employer may restructure its fringe benefit program so that all or some of the members of such group may be aggregated with another group, provided that each member of the restructured group will have available to him or her the same benefit upon the same terms and conditions. For example, assume that all highly compensated employees of an employer have fewer than five years of service and all nonhighly compensated employees have over five years of service. If the employer provided a five percent discount to employees with under five years of service and a ten percent discount to employees with over five years of service, the discount program available to the highly compensated employees would not satisfy the nondiscriminatory classification test; however, as a result of the rule described in this paragraph (d)(4), the employer could structure the program to consist of a five percent discount for all employees and a five percent additional discount for nonhighly compensated employees.

(5) Employer-operated eating facilities for employees— (i) General rule. If access to an employer-operated eating facility for employees is available to a classification of employees that discriminates in favor of highly compensated employees, then the classification will not be treated as discriminating in favor of highly compensated employees unless the facility is used by one or more executive group employees more than a de minimis amount.

(ii) Executive group employee. For purposes of this paragraph (d)(5), an employee is an "executive group employee" if the definition of paragraph (f)(1) of this section is satisfied. For purposes of identifying such employees, the phrase "top one percent of the employees" is substituted for the phrase "top ten percent of the employees" in section 414(q)(4) (relating to the definition of "top-paid group").

(e) Cash bonuses or rebates. A cash bonus or rebate provided to an employee by an employer that is determined with reference to the value of employer-provided property or services purchased by the employee, is treated as an equivalent employee discount. For example, assume a department store provides a 20 percent merchandise discount to all employees under a fringe benefit program. In addition, assume that the department store provides cash bonuses to a group of employees defined under a classification which discriminates in favor of highly compensated employees. Assume further that such cash bonuses equal 15 percent of the value of merchandise purchased by each employee. This arrangement is substantively identical to the example described in paragraph (e)(2)(i) of this section concerning related fringe benefit programs. Thus, both the 20 percent merchandise discount and the 15 percent cash bonus provided to the highly compensated employees are includible in such employees' gross incomes.

* * *

(f) Highly compensated employee*—(1) Government and nongovernment employees. A highly compensated employee of any employer is any employee who, during the year or the preceding year—

(i) Was a 5-percent owner,

(ii) Received compensation from the employer in excess of $75,000,

(iii) Received compensation from the employer in excess of $50,000 and was in the top-paid group of employees for such year, or

(iv) Was at any time an officer and received compensation greater than 150 percent of the amount in effect under section 415(c)(1)(A) for such year.

For purposes of determining whether an employee is a highly compensated employee, the rules of sections 414(q), (s), and (t) apply.

(2) Former employees. A former employee shall be treated as a highly compensated employee if—

(i) The employee was a highly compensated employee when the employee separated from service, or

(ii) The employee was a highly compensated employee at any time after attaining age 55.

* * *

*Editorial comment: The Regulations do not reflect the changes made by the Small Business Job Protection Act of 1996. See Sec. 414(q).

Deductions for Personal Exemptions

§ 1.151–1 Deductions for personal exemptions.*

(a) In general. (1) In computing taxable income, an individual is allowed a deduction for the exemptions specified in section 151. Such exemptions are: (i) The exemptions for an individual taxpayer and spouse (the so-called personal exemptions); (ii) the additional exemptions for a taxpayer attaining the age of 65 years and spouse attaining the age of 65 years (the so-called old-age exemptions);** (iii) the additional exemptions for a blind taxpayer and a blind spouse;** and (iv) the exemptions for dependents of the taxpayer.

* * *

(b) Exemptions for individual taxpayer and spouse (so-called personal exemptions). Section 151(b) allows an exemption for the taxpayer and an additional exemption for the spouse of the taxpayer if a joint return is not made by the taxpayer and his spouse, and if the spouse, for the calendar year in which the taxable year of the taxpayer begins, has no gross income and is not the dependent of another taxpayer. Thus, a husband is not entitled to an exemption for his wife on his separate return for the taxable year beginning in a calendar year during which she has any gross income (though insufficient to require her to file a return). Since, in the case of a joint return, there are two taxpayers (although under section 6013 there is only one income for the two taxpayers on such return, *i.e.,* their aggregate income), two exemptions are allowed on such return, one for each taxpayer spouse. If in any case a joint return is made by the taxpayer and his spouse, no other person is allowed an exemption for such spouse even though such other person would have been entitled to claim an exemption for such spouse as a dependent if such joint return had not been made.

* * *

§ 1.151–2 Additional exemptions for dependents.

(a) Section 151(e)*** allows to a taxpayer an exemption for each dependent (as defined in section 152) whose gross income (as defined in section 61) for the calendar year in which the taxable year of the taxpayer begins is less than the amount provided in section 151(e)(1)(A)*** applicable to the taxable year of the taxpayer, or who is a child of the taxpayer and who—

(1) The taxable year of the taxpayer begins, or

(2) Is a student, as defined in paragraph (b) of § 1.151–3.

No exemption shall be allowed under section 151(e)*** for any dependent who has made a joint return with his spouse under section 6013 for the taxable year beginning in the calendar year in which the taxable year of the taxpayer begins.

§ 1.151–3 Definitions.

(a) Child.**** For purposes of sections 151(e),*** 152, and the regulations thereunder, the term "child" means a son, stepson, daughter, stepdaughter, adopted son, adopted daughter, or for taxable years beginning after December 31, 1958, a child who is a member of an individual's household if the child was placed with the individual by an authorized placement agency for legal adoption pursuant to a formal application filed by the individual with the agency (see paragraph (c)(2) of § 1.152–2), or, for taxable years beginning after December 31, 1969, a foster child (if such foster child satisfies the requirements set forth in paragraph (b) of § 1.152–1 with respect to the taxpayer) of the taxpayer.

(b) Student. For purposes of section 151(e)*** and section 152(d), and the regulations thereunder, the term "student" means an individual who during

*Editorial comment: The Regulations do not reflect the effect of the Revenue Reconciliation Act of 1990 which provides for the phase-out of the personal exemption and dependency deductions. The Regulations do not reflect the repeal of the phaseout of the personal exemption deduction (which begins in 2006 and is completed in 2010) by the Tax Relief Reconciliation Act of 2001. So commencing in 2010, the full amount of the personal exemption and dependency deduction is available without reduction. The Regulations do not reflect the reinstatement of the phaseout for personal exemption and dependency deductions by the American Taxpayer Relief Act of 2012.

**Editorial comment: The Regulations do not reflect thechanges made by Tax Reform Act of 1986 which deleted these items as personal exemptions and transferred them to the standard deduction category. See Sec. 63(c)(3).

***Editorial comment: The Regulations do not reflect the numbering changes made by the Tax Reform Act of 1986. The reference should now be Sec. 151(c).

****Editorial comment: The Regulations do not reflect the changes made by the Working Families Tax Relief Act of 2004 to the definition of a child. See Secs. 152(c) and (f).

each of 5 calendar months during the calendar year in which the taxable year of the taxpayer begins is a full-time student at an educational institution or is pursuing a full-time course of institutional on-farm training under the supervision of an accredited agent of an educational institution or of a state or political subdivision of a State.* * * A full-time student is one who is enrolled for some part of 5 calendar months for the number of hours or courses which is considered to be full-time attendance. The 5 calendar months need not be consecutive. School attendance exclusively at night does not constitute full-time attendance. However, full-time attendance at an educational institution may include some attendance at night in connection with a full-time course of study.

(c) Educational institution. For purposes of sections 151(e)* and 152, and the regulations thereunder, the term "educational institution" means a school maintaining a regular faculty and established curriculum, and having an organized body of students in attendance. It includes primary and secondary schools, colleges, universities, normal schools, technical schools, mechanical schools, and similar institutions, but does not include noneducational institutions, on-the-job training, correspondence schools, night schools, and so forth.

* * *

§ 1.152–1 General definition of a dependent.**

(a)(1) For purposes of the income taxes imposed on individuals by chapter 1 of the Code, the term "dependent" means any individual described in paragraphs (1) through (10) of section 152(a) over half of whose support, for the calendar year in which the taxable year of the taxpayer begins, was received from the taxpayer.

(2)(i) For purposes of determining whether or not an individual received, for a given calendar year, over half of his support from the taxpayer, there shall be taken into account the amount of support received from the taxpayer as compared to the entire amount of support which the individual received from all sources, including support which the individual himself supplied. The term "support" includes food, shelter, clothing, medical and dental care, education, and the like. Generally, the amount of an item of support will be the amount of expense incurred by the one furnishing such item. If the item of support furnished an individual is in the form of property or lodging, it will be necessary to measure the amount of such item of support in terms of its fair market value.

(ii) In computing the amount which is contributed for the support of an individual, there must be included any amount which is contributed by such individual for his own support, including income which is ordinarily excludable from gross income, such as benefits received under the Social Security Act (42 U.S.C. ch. 7).* * *

(iii)(a) For purposes of determining the amount of support furnished for a child (or children) by a taxpayer for a given calendar year, an arrearage payment made in a year subsequent to a calendar year for which there is an unpaid liability shall not be treated as paid either during that calendar year or in the year of payment, but no amount shall be treated as an arrearage payment to the extent that there is an unpaid liability (determined without regard to such payment) with respect to the support of a child for the taxable year of payment; and

(b) Similarly, payments made prior to any calendar year (whether or not made in the form of a lump sum payment in settlement of the parent's liability for support) shall not be treated as made during such calendar year, but payments made during any calendar year from amounts set aside in trust by a parent in a prior year, shall be treated as made during the calendar year in which paid.

(b) Section 152(a)(9) applies to any individual (other than an individual who at any time during the taxable year was the spouse, determined without regard to section 153, of the taxpayer) who lives with the taxpayer and is a member of the taxpayer's household during the entire taxable year of the taxpayer. An individual is not a member of the taxpayer's household if at any time during the taxable year of the taxpayer the relationship between such individual and the taxpayer is in violation of local law. It is not necessary under section 152(a)(9)

*Editorial comment: The Regulations do not reflect the numbering changes made by the Tax Reform Act of 1986. The reference should now be Sec. 151(c).

**Editorial comment: The Regulations do not reflect the changes made by the Working Families Tax Relief Act of 2004 which changed the definition of a dependent from someone who meets the five statutory tests contained in Secs. 151 and 152 to being (1) a qualifying child or (2) a qualifying relative. See Sec. 152(a).

that the dependent be related to the taxpayer. For example, foster children may qualify as dependents. It is necessary, however, that the taxpayer both maintain and occupy the household. The taxpayer and dependent will be considered as occupying the household for such entire taxable year notwithstanding temporary absences from the household due to special circumstances. A nonpermanent failure to occupy the common abode by reason of illness, education, business, vacation, military service, or a custody agreement under which the dependent is absent for less than six months in the taxable year of the taxpayer, shall be considered temporary absence due to special circumstances. The fact that the dependent dies during the year shall not deprive the taxpayer of the deduction if the dependent lived in the household for the entire part of the year preceding his death. Likewise, the period during the taxable year preceding the birth of an individual shall not prevent such individual from qualifying as a dependent under section 152(a)(9). Moreover, a child who actually becomes a member of the taxpayer's household during the taxable year shall not be prevented from being considered a member of such household for the entire taxable year, if the child is required to remain in a hospital for a period following its birth, and if such child would otherwise have been a member of the taxpayer's household during such period.

(c) In the case of a child of the taxpayer who is under 19 or who is a student,* the taxpayer may claim the dependency exemption for such child provided he has furnished more than one-half of the support of such child for the calendar year in which the taxable year of the taxpayer begins, even though the income of the child for such calendar year may be equal to or in excess of the amount determined pursuant to § 1.151–2 applicable to such calendar year. In such a case, there may be two exemptions claimed for the child: One on the parent's (or stepparent's) return, and one on the child's return.** In determining whether the taxpayer does in fact furnish more than one-half of the support of an individual who is a child, as defined in paragraph (a) of § 1.151–3, of the taxpayer and who is a student, as defined in paragraph (b) of § 1.151–3, a special rule regarding scholarships applies. Amounts received as scholarships, as defined in paragraph (a) of § 1.117–3, for study at an educational institution shall not be considered in determining whether the taxpayer furnishes more than one-half the support of such individual. For example, A has a child who receives a $1,000 scholarship to the X college for 1 year. A contributes $500, which constitutes the balance of the child's support for that year. A may claim the child as a dependent, as the $1,000 scholarship is not counted in determining the support of the child. * * *

§ 1.152–2 Rules relating to general definition of dependent.***

(a)(1) Except as provided in subparagraph (2) of this paragraph, to qualify as a dependent an individual must be a citizen or resident of the United States or be a resident of* * * Canada, or Mexico, or, for taxable years beginning after December 31, 1971, a national of the United States, at some time during the calendar year in which the taxable year of the taxpayer begins.* * *

(2)(i) For any taxable year beginning after December 31, 1957, a taxpayer who is a citizen, or, for any taxable year beginning after December 31, 1971, a national, of the United States is permitted under section 152(b)(3)(B) to treat as a dependent his legally adopted child who lives with him, as a member of his household, for the entire taxable year and who, but for the citizenship, nationality, or residence requirements of section 152(b)(3) and subparagraph (1) of this paragraph, would qualify as a dependent of the taxpayer for such taxable year.

(ii) Under section 152(b)(3)(B) and this subparagraph, it is necessary that the taxpayer both maintain and occupy the household. The taxpayer and his legally adopted child will be considered as occupying the household for the entire taxable year of the taxpayer notwithstanding temporary absences from the household due to special circumstances. A nonpermanent failure to occupy the common abode by reason of illness, education, business, vacation, military service, or a custody agreement under which the legally adopted child is absent for less than six months in the taxable year of the taxpayer shall be considered temporary absence due to special circumstances. The fact that a legally

*Editorial comment: The Regulations do not reflect the changes made to Sec. 152 by the Working Families Tax Relief Act of 2004. See Sec. 152(C)(3)(A) and Sec. 152(d)(1)(B).

**Editorial comment: The Regulations do not reflect the effect of the Tax Reform Act of 1986. See Sec. 151(d)(2).

***Editorial comment: The Regulations do not reflect the changes made to Sec. 152 by the Working Families Tax Relief Act of 2004.

adopted child dies during the year shall not deprive the taxpayer of the deduction if the child lived in the household for the entire part of the year preceding his death. The period during the taxable year preceding the birth of a child shall not prevent such child from qualifying as a dependent under this subparagraph. Moreover, a legally adopted child who actually becomes a member of the taxpayer's household during the taxable year shall not be prevented from being considered a member of such household for the entire taxable year, if the child is required to remain in a hospital for a period following its birth and if such child would otherwise have been a member of the taxpayer's household during such period.

(iii) For purposes of section 152(b)(3)(B) and this subparagraph, any child whose legal adoption by the taxpayer (a citizen or national of the United States) becomes final at any time before the end of the taxable year of the taxpayer shall not be disqualified as a dependent of such taxpayer by reason of his citizenship, nationality, or residence, provided the child lived with the taxpayer and was a member of the taxpayer's household for the entire taxable year in which the legal adoption became final. For example, A, a citizen of the United States who makes his income tax returns on the basis of the calendar year, is employed in Brazil by an agency of the United States Government. In October 1958 he takes into his household C, a resident of Brazil who is not a citizen of the United States, for the purpose of initiating adoption proceedings. C lives with A and is a member of his household for the remainder of 1958 and for the entire calendar year 1959. On July 1, 1959, the adoption proceedings were completed and C became the legally adopted child of A. If C otherwise qualifies as a dependent, he may be claimed as a dependent by A for 1959.

(b) A payment to a wife which is includible in her gross income under section 71 or section 682 shall not be considered a payment by her husband for the support of any dependent.

(c)(1) For purposes of determining the existence of any of the relationships specified in section 152(a) or (b)(1), a legally adopted child of an individual shall be treated as a child of such individual by blood.

(2) For any taxable year beginning after December 31, 1958, a child who is a member of an individual's household also shall be treated as a child of such individual by blood if the child was placed with the individual by an authorized placement agency for legal adoption pursuant to a formal application filed by the individual with the agency. For purposes of this subparagraph an authorized placement agency is any agency which is authorized by a State, the District of Columbia, a possession of the United States, a foreign country, or a political subdivision of any of the foregoing to place children for adoption. A taxpayer who claims as a dependent a child placed with him for adoption shall attach to his income tax return a statement setting forth the name of the child for whom the dependency deduction is claimed, the name and address of the authorized placement agency, and the date the formal application was filed with the agency.

(3) The application of this paragraph may be illustrated by the following example:

Example. On March 1, 1959, D, a resident of the United States, made formal application to an authorized child placement agency for the placement of E, a resident of the United States, with him for legal adoption. On June 1, 1959, E was placed with D for legal adoption. During the year 1959 E received over one-half of his support from D. D may claim E as a dependent for 1959. Since E was a resident of the United States, his qualification as a dependent is in no way based on the provisions of section 152(b)(3)(B). Therefore, it is immaterial that E was not a member of D's household during the entire taxable year.

(4) For purposes of determining the existence of any of the relationships specified in section 152(a) or (b)(1), a foster child of an individual (if such foster child satisfies the requirements set forth in paragraph (b) of § 1.152–1 with respect to such individual) shall, for taxable years beginning after December 31, 1969, be treated as a child of such individual by blood. For purposes of this subparagraph, a foster child is a child who is in the care of a person or persons (other than the parents or adopted parents of the child) who care for the child as their own child. Status as a foster child is not dependent upon or affected by the circumstances under which the child became a member of the household.

(d) In the case of a joint return it is not necessary that the prescribed relationship exist between the person claimed as a dependent and the spouse who furnishes the support; it is sufficient if the prescribed relationship exists with respect to either spouse. Thus, a husband and wife making a joint return may claim as a dependent a daughter of the wife's brother (wife's niece) even though the husband is the one who furnishes the chief support. The relationship of affinity once existing will not terminate by divorce or the death of a spouse. For example, a widower may continue to claim his deceased wife's father (his father-in-law) as a dependent provided he meets the other requirements of section 151.

§ 1.152–3 Multiple support agreements.

(a) Section 152(c)* provides that a taxpayer shall be treated as having contributed over half of the support of an individual for the calendar year (in cases where two or more taxpayers contributed to the support of such individual) if—

(1) No one person contributed over half of the individual's support,

(2) Each member of the group which collectively contributed more than half of the individual would have been entitled to claim the individual as a dependent but for the fact that he did not contribute more than one-half of such support,

(3) The member of the group claiming the individual as a dependent contributed more than 10 percent of the individual's support, and

(4) Each other person in the group who contributed more than 10 percent of such support furnishes to the taxpayer claiming the dependent a written declaration that such other person will not claim the individual as a dependent for any taxable year beginning in such calendar year.

(b) Application of the rule contained in paragraph (a) of this section may be illustrated by the following examples:

Example (1). During the taxable year, brothers A, B, C, and D contributed the entire support of their mother in the following percentages: A, 30 percent; B, 20 percent; C, 29 percent; and D, 21 percent. Any one of the brothers, except for the fact that he did not contribute more than half of her support, would have been entitled to claim his mother as a dependent. Consequently, any one of the brothers could claim a deduction for the exemption of the mother if he obtained a written declaration (as provided in paragraph (a)(4) of this section) from each of the other brothers is attached to his income tax return. Even though A and D together contributed more than one-half the support of the mother, A, if he wished to claim his mother as a dependent, would be required to obtain written declarations from B, C, and D, since each of those three contributed more than 10 percent of the support and, but for the failure to contribute more than half of the mother's support, would have been entitled to claim his mother as a dependent.

* * *

(c) The member of a group of contributors who claim an individual as a dependent under the multiple support agreement provisions of section 152(c) must attach to his income tax return for the year of the deduction a written declaration from each of the other persons who contributed more than 10 percent of the support of such individual and who, but for the failure to contribute more than half of the support of the individual, would have been entitled to claim the individual as a dependent. The written declaration required by this paragraph may be made on Form 2120. Any declaration made other than on Form 2120 shall conform to the substance of Form 2120. The taxpayer claiming the individual as a dependent should be prepared to furnish other information, when required, which will substantiate his right to claim such individual as a dependent. Such information may include a statement showing the names of all contributors (whether or not members of the group described in section 152(c)) and the amount contributed by each to the support of the claimed dependent.

* * *

§ 1.152–4T Dependency exemption in the case of a child of divorced parent, etc. (temporary).**

(a) In general.

Q–1. Which parent may claim the dependency exemption in the case of a child of divorced or separated parents?

A–1. Provided the parents together would have been entitled to the dependency exemption had they been married and filing a joint return, the parent having custody of a child for the greater portion of the year (the custodial parent) will generally be entitled to the dependency exemption. This rule applies to parents not living together during the last 6 months of the calendar year, as well as those divorced or separated under a separation agreement.

Q–2. Are there any exceptions to the general rule in A-1?

A–2. Yes, there are three exceptions. The general rule does not apply (i) if a multiple support agreement is in effect (see section 152(c)), (ii) if a decree or agreement executed prior to January 1, 1985 provides that the custodial parent has agreed to release his or her claim to the dependency exemption to the noncustodial parent and the noncustodial parent provides at least $600 of support to the child

*Editorial comment: The Regulations do not reflect the numbering changes made by the Working Families Tax Relief Act of 2004. The reference should now be Sec. 152(d)(3).

**Editorial comment: The Regulations do not reflect the changes made by the Working Families Tax Relief Act of 2004. See Sec. 152(e).

(see section 152(e)(4)), or (iii) if the custodial parent relinquishes the exemption in the manner described in A–3.

Q–3. How may the exemption for a dependent child be claimed by a noncustodial parent?

A–3. A noncustodial parent may claim the exemption for a dependent child only if the noncustodial parent attaches to his/her income tax return for the year of the exemption a written declaration from the custodial parent stating that he/she will not claim the child as a dependent for the taxable year beginning in such calendar year. The written declaration may be made on a form to be provided by the Service for this purpose. Once the Service has released the form, any declaration made other than on the official form shall conform to the substance of such form.

Q–4. For what period may a custodial parent release to the noncustodial parent a claim to the exemption for a dependent child?

A–4. The exemption may be released for a single year, for a number of specified years (for example, alternate years), or for all future years, as specified in the declaration. If the exemption is released for more than one year, the original release must be attached to the return of the noncustodial spouse and a copy of such release must be attached to his/her return for each succeeding taxable year for which he/she claims the dependency exemption.

Q–5. May only the custodial parent claim a deduction under section 213(d) for medical expenses paid by the parent or an income exclusion under section 105(b) for medical expenses paid by an employer for a dependent child?

A–5. No. Under the new rules, if a child receives over half of his support during the calendar year from his parents who are divorced or legally separated under a decree of divorce or separate maintenance, or who are separated under a written separation agreement, that child will be treated as a dependent of both parents for purposes of sections 105(b) and 213(d). Thus, a parent can deduct medical expenses paid by that parent for a child even though a dependency exemption for the child is claimed by the other parent. The special rule of sections 105(b) and 213(d) does not apply where over half of the support of a child is treated as having been received from a person under the provisions of section 152(c) (relating to multiple support agreements).

Q–6. When does section 152(e), as amended by the Tax Reform Act of 1984, become effective?

A–6. Section 152(e), as amended, is effective with respect to dependency exemptions for taxable years beginning after December 31, 1984.

* * *

Itemized Deductions for Individuals and Corporations

§ 1.162–1 Business expenses.

(a) In general. Business expenses deductible from gross income include the ordinary and necessary expenditures directly connected with or pertaining to the taxpayer's trade or business, except items which are used as the basis for a deduction or a credit under provisions of law other than section 162. The cost of goods purchased for resale, with proper adjustment for opening and closing inventories, is deducted from gross sales in computing gross income. See paragraph (a) of § 1.161–3. Among the items included in business expenses are management expenses, commissions (but see section 263 and the regulations thereunder), labor, supplies, incidental repairs, operating expenses of automobiles used in the trade or business, traveling expenses while away from home solely in the pursuit of a trade or business (see § 1.162–2), advertising and other selling expenses, together with insurance premiums against fire, storm, theft, accident, or other similar losses in the case of a business, and rental for the use of business property. No such item shall be included in business expenses, however, to the extent that it is used by the taxpayer in computing the cost of property included in its inventory or used in determining the gain or loss basis of its plant, equipment, or other property.* * * A deduction for an expense paid or incurred after December 30, 1969, which would otherwise be allowable under section 162 shall not be denied on the grounds that allowance of such deduction would frustrate a sharply defined public policy. See section 162(c), (f), and (g) and the regulations thereunder. The full amount of the allowable deduction for ordinary and necessary expenses in carrying on a business is deductible, even though such expenses exceed the gross income derived during the taxable year from such business.* * *

§ 1.162–2 Traveling expenses.

(a) Traveling expenses include travel fares, meals and lodging, and expenses incident to travel such as expenses for sample rooms, telephone and telegraph, public stenographers, etc. Only such traveling expenses as are reasonable and necessary in the conduct of the taxpayer's business and directly attributable to it may be deducted. If the trip is undertaken for other than business purposes, the travel fares and expenses incident to travel are personal expenses and the meals and lodging are living expenses. If the trip is solely on business, the reasonable and necessary traveling expenses, including travel fares, meals and lodging, and expenses incident to travel, are business expenses. For the allowance of traveling expenses as deductions in determining adjusted gross income, see section 62(2)(B) and the regulations thereunder.

(b)(1) If a taxpayer travels to a destination and while at such destination engages in both business and personal activities, traveling expenses to and from such destination are deductible only if the trip is related primarily to the taxpayer's trade or business. If the trip is primarily personal in nature, the traveling expenses to and from the destination are not deductible even though the taxpayer engages in business activities while at such destination. However, expenses while at the destination which are properly allocable to the taxpayer's trade or business are deductible even though the traveling expenses to and from the destination are not deductible.

(2) Whether a trip is related primarily to the taxpayer's trade or business or is primarily personal in nature depends on the facts and circumstances in each case. The amount of time during the period of the trip which is spent on personal activity compared to the amount of time spent on activities directly relating to the taxpayer's trade or business is an important factor in determining whether the trip is primarily personal. If, for example, a taxpayer spends one week while at a destination on activities which are directly related to his trade or business and subsequently spends an additional five weeks for vacation or other personal activities, the trip will be considered primarily personal in nature in the absence of a clear showing to the contrary.

(c) Where a taxpayer's wife accompanies him on a business trip, expenses attributable to her travel are not deductible unless it can be adequately shown that the wife's presence on the trip has a bona fide business purpose. The wife's performance of some incidental service does not cause her expenses to qualify as deductible business expenses. The same rules apply to any other members of the taxpayer's family who accompany him on such a trip.

(d) Expenses paid or incurred by a taxpayer in attending a convention or other meeting may constitute an ordinary and necessary business expense under section 162 depending upon the facts and circumstances of each case. No distinction will be made between self-employed persons and employees. The fact that an employee uses vacation or leave time or that his attendance at the convention is voluntary will not necessarily prohibit the allowance of the deduction. The allowance of deductions for such expenses will depend upon whether there is a sufficient relationship between the taxpayer's trade of business and his attendance at the convention or other meeting so that he is benefiting or advancing the interests of his trade or business by such attendance. If the convention is for political, social or other purposes unrelated to the taxpayer's trade or business, the expenses are not deductible.

(e) Commuters' fares are not considered as business expenses and are not deductible.

* * *

§ 1.162–3 Materials and supplies.*

(a) In general—(1) Non-incidental materials and supplies. Except as provided in paragraphs (d), (e), and (f) of this section, amounts paid to acquire or produce materials and supplies (as defined in paragraph (c) of this section) are deductible in the taxable year in which the materials and supplies are first used in the taxpayer's operations or are consumed in the taxpayer's operations.

(2) Incidental materials and supplies. Amounts paid to acquire or produce incidental materials and supplies (as defined in paragraph (c) of this section) that are carried on hand and for which no record of consumption is kept or of which physical inventories at the beginning and end of the taxable year are not taken, are deductible in the taxable year in which these amounts are paid, provided taxable income is clearly reflected.

(b) Coordination with other provisions of the Internal Revenue Code. Nothing in this section changes the treatment of any amount that is

*Editorial comment: In general, these final regulations apply to taxable years beginning on or after January 1, 2014.

specifically provided for under any provision of the Internal Revenue Code (Code) or regulations other than section 162(a) or section 212 and the regulations under those sections. For example, see § 1.263(a)–3, which requires taxpayers to capitalize amounts paid to improve tangible property and section 263A and the regulations under section 263A, which require taxpayers to capitalize the direct and allocable indirect costs, including the cost of materials and supplies, of property produced by the taxpayer and property acquired for resale. See also §1.471-1, which requires taxpayers to include in inventory certain materials and supplies.

(c) Definitions— (1) Materials and supplies. For purposes of this section, materials and supplies means tangible property that is used or consumed in the taxpayer's operations that is not inventory and that—

(i) Is a component acquired to maintain, repair, or improve a unit of tangible property (as determined under §1.263(a)–3(e)) owned, leased, or serviced by the taxpayer and that is not acquired as part of any single unit of tangible property;

(ii) Consists of fuel, lubricants, water, and similar items, reasonably expected to be consumed in 12 months or less, beginning when used in the taxpayer's operations;

(iii) Is a unit of property as determined under §1.263(a)–3(e) that has an economic useful life of 12 months or less, beginning when the property is used or consumed in the taxpayer's operations;

(iv) Is a unit of property as determined under §1.263(a)–3(e) that has an acquisition cost or production cost (as determined under section 263A) of $200 or less (or other amount as identified in published guidance in the Federal Register or in the Internal Revenue Bulletin (see §601.601(d)(2)(ii)(b) of this chapter); or

(v) Is identified in published guidance in the Federal Register or in the Internal Revenue Bulletin (see §601.601(d)(2)(ii)(b) of this chapter) as materials and supplies for which treatment is permitted under this section.

(2) Rotable and temporary spare parts. For purposes of this section, rotable spare parts are materials and supplies under paragraph (c)(1)(i) of this section that are acquired for installation on a unit of property, removable from that unit of property, generally repaired or improved, and either reinstalled on the same or other property or stored for later installation. Temporary spare parts are materials and supplies under paragraph (c)(1)(i) of this section that are used temporarily until a new or repaired part can be installed and then are removed and stored for later installation.

(3) Standby emergency spare parts. Standby emergency spare parts are materials and supplies under paragraph (c)(1)(i) of this section that are—

(i) Acquired when particular machinery or equipment is acquired (or later acquired and set aside for use in particular machinery or equipment);

(ii) Set aside for use as replacements to avoid substantial operational time loss caused by emergencies due to particular machinery or equipment failure;

(iii) Located at or near the site of the installed related machinery or equipment so as to be readily available when needed;

(iv) Directly related to the particular machinery or piece of equipment they serve;

(v) Normally expensive;

(vi) Only available on special order and not readily available from a vendor or manufacturer;

(vii) Not subject to normal periodic replacement;

(viii) Not interchangeable in other machines or equipment;

(ix) Not acquired in quantity (generally only one is on hand for each piece of machinery or equipment); and

(x) Not repaired and reused.

(4) Economic useful life. (i) General rule. The economic useful life of a unit of property is not necessarily the useful life inherent in the property but is the period over which the property may reasonably be expected to be useful to the taxpayer or, if the taxpayer is engaged in a trade or business or an activity for the production of income, the period over which the property may reasonably be expected to be useful to the taxpayer in its trade or business or for the production of income, as applicable. See §1.167(a)–1(b) for the factors to be considered in determining this period.

(d) Election to capitalize and depreciate certain materials and supplies— (1) In general. A taxpayer may elect to treat as a capital expenditure and to treat as an asset subject to the allowance for depreciation the cost of any rotable spare part, temporary spare part, or standby emergency spare part as defined in paragraph (c)(3) or (c)(4) of this section. Except as specified in paragraph (d)(2) of this section, an election made under this paragraph (d) applies to amounts paid during the taxable year to acquire or produce any rotable, temporary, or standby emergency spare part to which paragraph (a) of this section would apply (but for the election under this paragraph (d)). Any property for which this election is made shall not be treated as a material or a supply.

(e) Optional method of accounting for rotable and temporary spare parts— (1) In general. This paragraph (e) provides an optional method of accounting for rotable and temporary spare parts (the optional method for rotable parts). A taxpayer may use the optional method for rotable parts, instead of the general rule under paragraph (a)(3) of this section, to account for its rotable and temporary spare parts as defined in paragraph (c)(2) of this section. A taxpayer that uses the optional method for rotable parts must use this method for all of its pools of rotable and temporary spare parts used in the same trade or business and for which it uses this method for its books and records. If a taxpayer uses the optional method for rotable and temporary spare parts for pools of rotable or temporary spare parts for which the taxpayer does not use the optional method for its book and records, then the taxpayer must use the optional method for all its pools of rotable spare parts in the same trade or business. The optional method for rotable parts is a method of accounting under section 446(a). Under the optional method for rotable parts, the taxpayer must apply the rules in this paragraph (e) to each rotable or temporary spare part (part) upon the taxpayer's initial installation, removal, repair, maintenance or improvement, reinstallation, and disposal of each part.

§ 1.162–4 Repairs.*

(a) In general. A taxpayer may deduct amounts paid for repairs and maintenance to tangible property if the amounts paid are not otherwise required to be capitalized. For the election to capitalize amounts paid for repair and maintenance consistent with the taxpayer's books and records, see §1.263(a)-3(n).

§ 1.162–5 Expenses for education.

(a) General rule. Expenditures made by an individual for education (including research undertaken as part of his educational program) which are not expenditures of a type described in paragraph (b)(2) or (3) of this section are deductible as ordinary and necessary business expenses (even though the education may lead to a degree) if the education—

(1) Maintains or improves skills required by the individual in his employment or other trade or business, or

(2) Meets the express requirements of the individual's employer, or the requirements of applicable law or regulations, imposed as a condition to the retention by the individual of an established employment relationship, status, or rate of compensation.

(b) Nondeductible educational expenditures— (1) In general. Educational expenditures described in subparagraphs (2) and (3) of this paragraph are personal expenditures or constitute an inseparable aggregate of personal and capital expenditures and, therefore, are not deductible as ordinary and necessary business expenses even though the education may maintain or improve skills required by the individual in his employment or other trade or business or may meet the express requirements of the individual's employer or of applicable law or regulations.

(2) Minimum educational requirements. (i) The first category of nondeductible educational expenses within the scope of subparagraph (1) of this paragraph are expenditures made by an individual for education which is required of him in order to meet the minimum educational requirements for qualification in his employment or other trade or business. The minimum education necessary to qualify for a position or other trade or business must be determined from a consideration of such factors as the requirements of the employer, the applicable law and regulations, and the standards of the profession, trade, or business involved. The fact that an individual is already performing service in an employment status does not establish that he has met the minimum educational requirements for qualification in that employment. Once an individual has met the minimum educational requirements for qualification in his employment or other trade or business (as in effect when he enters the employment or trade or business), he shall be treated as continuing to meet those requirements even though they are changed.

(ii) The minimum educational requirements for qualification of a particular individual in a position in an educational institution is the minimum level of education (in terms of aggregate college hours or

*Editorial comment: In general, these final regulations apply to taxable years beginning on or after January 1, 2014.

degree) which under the applicable laws or regulations, in effect at the time this individual is first employed in such position, is normally required of an individual initially being employed in such a position. If there are no normal requirements as to the minimum level of education required for a position in an educational institution, then an individual in such a position shall be considered to have met the minimum educational requirements for qualification in that position when he becomes a member of the faculty of the educational institution. The determination of whether an individual is a member of the faculty of an educational institution must be made on the basis of the particular practices of the institution. However, an individual will ordinarily be considered to be a member of the faculty of an institution if (a) he has tenure or his years of service are being counted toward obtaining tenure; (b) the institution is making contributions to a retirement plan (other than Social Security or a similar program) in respect of his employment; or (c) he has a vote in faculty affairs.

* * *

(3) Qualification for new trade or business. **(i)** The second category of nondeductible educational expenses within the scope of subparagraph (1) of this paragraph are expenditures made by an individual for education which is part of a program of study being pursued by him which will lead to qualifying him in a new trade or business. In the case of an employee, a change of duties does not constitute a new trade or business if the new duties involve the same general type of work as is involved in the individual's present employment. For this purpose, all teaching and related duties shall be considered to involve the same general type of work. The following are examples of changes in duties which do not constitute new trades or businesses:

(a) Elementary to secondary school classroom teacher.

(b) Classroom teacher in one subject (such as mathematics) to classroom teacher in another subject (such as science).

(c) Classroom teacher to guidance counselor.

(d) Classroom teacher to principal.

(ii) The application of this subparagraph to individuals other than teachers may be illustrated by the following examples:

Example (1). A, a self-employed individual practicing a profession other than law, for example, engineering, accounting, etc., attends law school at night and after completing his law school studies receives a bachelor of laws degree. The expenditures made by A in attending law school are nondeductible because this course of study qualifies him for a new trade or business.

Example (2). Assume the same facts as in example (1) except that A has the status of an employee rather than a self-employed individual, and that his employer requires him to obtain a bachelor of laws degree. A intends to continue practicing his nonlegal profession as an employee of such employer. Nevertheless, the expenditures made by A in attending law school are not deductible since this course of study qualifies him for a new trade or business.

Example (3). B, a general practitioner of medicine, takes a 2-week course reviewing new developments in several specialized fields of medicine. B's expenses for the course are deductible because the course maintains or improves skills required by him in his trade or business and does not qualify him for a new trade or business.

Example (4). C, while engaged in the private practice of psychiatry, undertakes a program of study and training at an accredited psychoanalytic institute which will lead to qualifying him to practice psychoanalysis. C's expenditures for such study and training are deductible because the study and training maintains or improves skills required by him in his trade or business and does not qualify him for a new trade or business.

(c) Deductible educational expenditures—(1) Maintaining or improving skills. The deduction under the category of expenditures for education which maintains or improves skills required by the individual in his employment or other trade or business includes refresher courses or courses dealing with current developments as well as academic or vocational courses provided the expenditures for the courses are not within either category of nondeductible expenditures described in paragraph (b)(2) or (3) of this section.

(2) Meeting requirements of employer. An individual is considered to have undertaken education in order to meet the express requirements of his employer, or the requirements of applicable law or regulations, imposed as a condition to the retention by the taxpayer of his established employment relationship, status, or rate of compensation only if such requirements are imposed for a bona fide business purpose of the individual's employer. Only the minimum education necessary to the retention by the individual of his established employment relationship, status, or rate of compensation may be considered as undertaken to meet the express requirements of the taxpayer's employer. However, education in excess of such minimum education may qualify as education undertaken in order to maintain or improve the skills required by the taxpayer in his employment or other trade or business (see subparagraph (1) of this paragraph). In no event, however, is a deduction allowable for expenditures for education which, even though for education required by the employer or applicable law or regulations, are within one of the categories of nondeductible expenditures described in paragraph (b)(2) and (3) of this section.

* * *

(e) Travel away from home. **(1)** If an individual travels away from home primarily to obtain education the expenses of which are deductible under this section, his expenditures for travel, meals, and lodging while away from home are deductible. However, if as an incident of such trip the individual engages in some personal activity such as sightseeing, social visiting, or entertaining, or other recreation, the portion of the expenses attributable to such personal activity constitutes nondeductible personal or living expenses and is not allowable as a deduction. If the individual's travel away from home is primarily personal, the individual's expenditures for travel, meals and lodging (other than meals and lodging during the time spent in participating in deductible education pursuits) are not deductible. Whether a particular trip is primarily personal or primarily to obtain education the expenses of which are deductible under this section depends upon all the facts and circumstances of each case. An important factor to be taken into consideration in making the determination is the relative amount of time devoted to personal activity as compared with the time devoted to educational pursuits. The rules set forth in this paragraph are subject to the provisions of section 162(a)(2), relating to deductibility of certain traveling expenses, and section 274(c) and (d), relating to allocation of certain foreign travel expenses and substantiation required, respectively, and the regulations thereunder.

(2) Examples. The application of this subsection may be illustrated by the following examples:

Example (1). A, a self-employed tax practitioner, decides to take a 1-week course in new developments in taxation, which is offered in City X, 500 miles away from his home. His primary purpose in going to X is to take the course, but he also takes a side trip to City Y (50 miles from X) for 1 day, takes a sightseeing trip while in X, and entertains some personal friends. A's transportation expenses to City X and return to his home are deductible but his transportation expenses to City Y are not deductible. A's expenses for meals and lodging while away from home will be allocated between his educational pursuits and his personal activities. Those expenses which are entirely personal, such as sightseeing and entertaining friends, are not deductible to any extent.

Example (2). The facts are the same as in example (1) except that A's primary purpose in going to City X is to take a vacation. This purpose is indicated by several factors, one of which is the fact that he spends only 1 week attending the tax course and devotes 5 weeks entirely to personal activities. None of A's transportation expenses are deductible and his expenses for meals and lodging while away from home are not deductible to the extent attributable to personal activities. His expenses for meals and lodging allocable to the week attending the tax course are, however, deductible.

* * *

§ 1.162–6 Professional expenses.

A professional man may claim as deductions the cost of supplies used by him in the practice of his profession, expenses paid or accrued in the operation and repair of an automobile used in making professional calls, dues to professional societies and subscriptions to professional journals, the rent paid or accrued for office rooms, the cost of the fuel, light, water, telephone, etc., used in such offices, and the hire of office assistance. Amounts currently paid or accrued for books, furniture, and professional instruments and equipment, the useful life of which is short, may be deducted.

§ 1.162–7 Compensation for personal Services.

(a) There may be included among the ordinary and necessary expenses paid or incurred in carrying on any trade or business a reasonable allowance for salaries or other compensation for personal services actually rendered. The test of deductibility in the case of compensation payments is whether they are reasonable and are in fact payments purely for services.

(b) The test set forth in paragraph (a) of this section and its practical application may be further stated and illustrated as follows: **(1)** Any amount paid in the form of compensation, but not in fact as the purchase price of services, is not deductible. An ostensible salary paid by a corporation may be a distribution of a dividend on stock. This is likely to occur in the case of a corporation having few shareholders, practically all of whom draw salaries. If in such a case the salaries are in excess of those ordinarily paid for similar services and the excessive payments correspond or bear a close relationship to the stockholdings of the officers or employees, it would seem likely that the salaries are not paid wholly for services rendered, but that the excessive payments are a distribution of earnings upon the stock. An ostensible salary may be in part payment for property. This may occur, for example, where a partnership sells out to a corporation, the former partners agreeing to continue in the service of the corporation. In such a case it may be found that the salaries of the former partners are not merely for services, but in part constitute payment for the transfer of their business.

(2) The form or method of fixing compensation is not decisive as to deductibility. While any form of contingent compensation invites scrutiny as a possible distribution of earnings of the enterprise, it does not follow that payments on a contingent basis are to be treated fundamentally on any basis different from that applying to compensation at a flat rate. Generally speaking, if contingent compensation is paid pursuant to a free bargain between the employer and the individual made before the services are rendered, not influenced by any consideration on the part of the employer other than that of securing on fair and advantageous terms the services of the individual, it should be allowed as a deduction even though in the actual working out of the contract it may prove to be greater than the amount which would ordinarily be paid.

(3) In any event the allowance for the compensation paid may not exceed what is reasonable under all the circumstances. It is, in general, just to assume that reasonable and true compensation is only such amount as would ordinarily be paid for like services by like enterprises under like circumstances. The circumstances to be taken into consideration are those existing at the date when the contract for services was made, not those existing at the date when the contract is questioned.

* * *

§ 1.162–8 Treatment of excessive compensation.

The income tax liability of the recipient in respect of an amount ostensibly paid to him as compensation, but not allowed to be deducted as such by the payor, will depend upon the circumstances of each case. Thus, in the case of excessive payments by corporations, if such payments correspond or bear a close relationship to stockholdings, and are found to be a distribution of earnings or profits, the excessive payments will be treated as a dividend. If such payments constitute payment for property, they should be treated by the payor as a capital expenditure and by the recipient as part of the purchase price. In the absence of evidence to justify other treatment, excessive payments for salaries or other compensation for personal services will be included in gross income of the recipient.

§ 1.162–9 Bonuses to employees.

Bonuses to employees will constitute allowable deductions from gross income when such payments are made in good faith and as additional compensation for the services actually rendered by the employees, provided such payments, when added to the stipulated salaries, do not exceed a reasonable compensation for the services rendered. It is immaterial whether such bonuses are paid in cash or in kind or partly in cash and partly in kind. Donations made to employees and others, which do not have in them the element of compensation or which are in excess of reasonable compensation for services, are not deductible from gross income.

§ 1.162–10 Certain employee benefits.

(a) In general. Amounts paid or accrued by a taxpayer on account of injuries received by employees and lump sum amounts paid or accrued as compensation for injuries, are proper deductions as ordinary and necessary expenses. Such deductions are limited to the amount not compensated for by insurance or otherwise. Amounts paid or accrued within the taxable year for dismissal wages, unemployment benefits, guaranteed annual wages, vacations, or a sickness, accident, hospitalization, medical expense, recreational, welfare, or similar benefit plan, are deductible under section 162(a) if they are ordinary and necessary expenses of the trade or business.* * *

§ 1.162–11 Rentals.*

(a) Acquisition of a leasehold. If a leasehold is acquired for business purposes for a specified sum, the purchaser may take as a deduction in his return an aliquot part of such sum each year, based on the number of years the lease has to run. Taxes paid by a tenant to or for a landlord for business property are additional rent and constitute a deductible item to the tenant and taxable income to the landlord, the amount of the tax being deductible by the latter. For disallowance of deduction for income taxes paid by a lessee corporation pursuant to a lease arrangement with the lessor corporation, see section 110 and the regulations thereunder. See section 178 and the regulations thereunder for rules governing the effect

*Editorial comment: In general, these final regulations apply to taxable years beginning on or after January 1, 2014.

to be given renewal options in amortizing the costs incurred after July 28, 1958 of acquiring a lease. See § 1.197-2 for rules governing the amortization of costs to acquire limited interests in section 197 intangibles.

(b) Improvements by lessee on lessor's property—(1) In general. The cost to a taxpayer of erecting buildings or making permanent improvements on property of which the taxpayer is a lessee is a capital expenditure. For the rules regarding improvements to leased property when the improvements are tangible property, see §1.263(a)-3(f). For the rules regarding depreciation or amortization deductions for leasehold improvements, see §1.167(a)-4.

(c) Improvements by lessee on lessor's property. **(1)** The cost to a lessee of erecting buildings or making permanent improvements on property of which he is the lessee is a capital investment, and is not deductible as a business expense. If the estimated useful life in the hands of the taxpayer of the building erected or of the improvements made, determined without regard to the terms of the lease, is longer than the remaining period of the lease, an annual deduction may be made from gross income of an amount equal to the total cost of such improvements divided by the number of years remaining in the term of the lease, and such deduction shall be in lieu of a deduction for depreciation. If, on the other hand, the useful life of such buildings or improvements in the hands of the taxpayer is equal to or shorter than the remaining period of the lease, this deduction shall be computed under the provisions of section 167 (relating to depreciation).

(2) If the lessee began improvements on leased property before July 28, 1958, or if the lessee was on such date and at all times thereafter under a binding legal obligation to make such improvements, the matter of spreading the cost of erecting buildings or making permanent improvements over the term of the original lease, together with the renewal period or periods depends upon the facts in the particular case, including the presence or absence of an obligation of renewal and the relationship between the parties. As a general rule, unless the lease has been renewed or the facts show with reasonable certainty that the lease will be renewed, the cost or other basis of the lease, or the cost of improvements shall be spread only over the number of years the lease has to run without taking into account any right of renewal. The provisions of this subparagraph may be illustrated by the following examples:

Example (1). A subsidiary corporation leases land from its parent at a fair rental for a 25-year period. The subsidiary erects on the land valuable factory buildings having an estimated useful life of 50 years. These facts show with reasonable certainty that the lease will be renewed, even though the lease contains no option of renewal. Therefore, the cost of the buildings shall be depreciated over the estimated useful life of the buildings in accordance with section 167 and the regulations thereunder.

Example (2). A retail merchandising corporation leases land at a fair rental from an unrelated lessor for the longest period that the lessor is willing to lease the land (30 years). The lessee erects on the land a department store having an estimated useful life of 40 years. These facts do not show with reasonable certainty that the lease will be renewed. Therefore, the cost of the building shall be spread over the remaining term of the lease. An annual deduction may be made of an amount equal to the cost of the building divided by the number of years remaining in the term of the lease, and such deduction shall be in lieu of a deduction for depreciation.

(3) See section 178 and the regulations thereunder for rules governing the effect to be given renewal options where a lessee begins improvements on leased property after July 28, 1958, other than improvements which on such date and at all times thereafter, the lessee was under a binding legal obligation to make.

* * *

§ 1.162–15 Contributions, dues, etc.

(a) Contributions to organizations described in section 170—(1) In general. No deduction is allowable under section 162(a) for a contribution or gift by an individual or a corporation if any part thereof is deductible under section 170. For example, if a taxpayer makes a contribution of $5,000 and only $4,000 of this amount is deductible under section 170(a) (whether because of the percentage limitation under either section 170(b)(1) or (2), the requirement as to time of payment, or both) no deduction is allowable under section 162(a) for the remaining $1,000.

(2) Scope of limitations. The limitations provided in section 162(b) and this paragraph apply only to payments which are in fact contributions or gifts to organizations described in section 170. For example, payments by a transit company to a local hospital (which is a charitable organization within the meaning of section 170) in consideration of a binding obligation on the part of the hospital to provide hospital services and facilities for the company's employees are not contributions or gifts within the meaning of section 170 and may be deductible under section 162(a) if the requirements of section 162(a) are otherwise satisfied.

(b) Other contributions. Donations to organizations other than those described in section 170 which bear a direct relationship to the taxpayer's business and are made with a reasonable expectation of a financial return commensurate with the amount of the donation may constitute allowable deductions as business expenses, provided the donation is not made for a purpose for which a deduction is not allowable by reason of the provisions of paragraph (b)(1)(i) or (c) of § 1.162–20. For example, a transit company may donate a sum of money to an organization (of a class not referred to in section 170) intending to hold a convention in the city in which it operates, with a reasonable expectation that the holding of such convention will augment its income through a greater number of people using its transportation facilities.

(c) Dues. Dues and other payments to an organization, such as a labor union or a trade association, which otherwise meet the requirements of the regulations under section 162, are deductible in full. For limitations on the deductibility of dues and other payments, see paragraph (b) and (c) of § 1.162–20.

* * *

§ 1.162–17 Reporting and substantiation of certain business expenses of employees.

(a) Introductory. The purpose of the regulations in this section is to provide rules for the reporting of information on income tax returns by taxpayers who pay or incur ordinary and necessary business expenses in connection with the performance of services as an employee and to furnish guidance as to the type of records which will be useful in compiling such information and in its substantiation, if required. The rules prescribed in this section do not apply to expenses paid or incurred for incidentals, such as office supplies for the employer or local transportation in connection with an errand. Employees incurring such incidental expenses are not required to provide substantiation for such amounts. The term "ordinary and necessary business expenses" means only those expenses which are ordinary and necessary in the conduct of the taxpayer's business and are directly attributable to such business. The term does not include nondeductible personal, living or family expenses.

(b) Expenses for which the employee is required to account to his employer—(1) Reimbursements equal to expenses. The employee need not report on his tax return (either itemized or in total amount) expenses for travel, transportation, entertainment, and similar purposes paid or incurred by him solely for the benefit of his employer for which he is required to account and does account to his employer and which are charged directly or indirectly to the employer (for example, through credit cards) or for which the employee is paid through advances, reimbursements, or otherwise, provided the total amount of such advances, reimbursements, and charges is equal to such expenses. In such a case the taxpayer need only state in his return that the total of amounts charged directly or indirectly to his employer through credit cards or otherwise and received from the employer as advances or reimbursements did not exceed the ordinary and necessary business expenses paid or incurred by the employee.

(2) Reimbursements in excess of expenses. In case the total of amounts charged directly or indirectly to the employer and received from the employer as advances, reimbursements, or otherwise, exceeds the ordinary and necessary business expenses paid or incurred by the employee and the employee is required to and does account to his employer for such expenses, the taxpayer must include such excess in income and state on his return that he has done so.

(3) Expenses in excess of reimbursements. If the employee's ordinary and necessary business expenses exceed the total of the amounts charged directly or indirectly to the employer and received from the employer as advances, reimbursements, or otherwise, and the employee is required to and does account to his employer for such expenses, the taxpayer may make the statement in his return required by subparagraph (1) of this paragraph unless he wishes to claim a deduction for such excess. If, however, he wishes to secure a deduction for such excess, he must submit a statement showing the following information as part of his tax return:

(i) The total of any charges paid or borne by the employer and of any other amounts received from the employer for payment of expenses whether by means of advances, reimbursements or otherwise; and

(ii) The nature of his occupation, the number of days away from home on business, and the total amount of ordinary and necessary business expenses paid or incurred by him (including those charged directly or indirectly to the employer through credit cards or otherwise) broken down into such broad categories as transportation, meals and lodging while away from home overnight, entertainment expenses, and other business expenses.

(4) To "account" to his employer as used in this section means to submit an expense account or other required written statement to the employer showing the business nature and the amount of all the employee's expenses (including those charged directly or indirectly to the employer through credit cards or otherwise) broken down into such broad categories as transportation, meals and lodging while away from home overnight, entertainment expenses, and other business expenses. For this purpose, the Commissioner in his discretion may approve reasonable business practices under which mileage, per diem in lieu of subsistence, and similar allowances providing for ordinary and necessary business expenses in accordance with a fixed scale may be regarded as equivalent to an accounting to the employer.

(c) Expenses for which the employee is not required to account to his employer. If the employee is not required to account to his employer for his ordinary and necessary business expenses, e.g., travel, transportation, entertainment, and similar items, or, though required, fails to account for such expenses, he must submit, as a part of his tax return, a statement showing the following information:

(1) The total of all amounts received as advances or reimbursements from his employer in connection with the ordinary and necessary business expenses of the employee, including amounts charged directly or indirectly to the employer through credit cards or otherwise; and

(2) The nature of his occupation, the number of days away from home on business, and the total amount of ordinary and necessary business expenses paid or incurred by him (including those charged directly or indirectly to the employer through credit cards or otherwise) broken down into such broad categories as transportation, meals and lodging while away from home overnight, entertainment expenses, and other business expenses.

* * *

§ 1.162–18 Illegal bribes and kickbacks.

(a) Illegal payments to government officials or employees— (1) In general. No deduction shall be allowed under section 162(a) for any amount paid or incurred, directly or indirectly, to an official or employee of any government, or of any agency or other instrumentality of any government, if—

(i) In the case of a payment made to an official or employee of a government other than a foreign government described in subparagraph (3)(ii) or (iii) of this paragraph, the payment constitutes an illegal bribe or kickback, or

(ii) In the case of a payment made to an official or employee of a foreign government described in subparagraph (3)(ii) or (iii) of this paragraph, the making of the payment would be unlawful under the laws of the United States (if such laws were applicable to the payment and to the official or employee at the time the expenses were paid or incurred).

No deduction shall be allowed for an accrued expense if the eventual payment thereof would fall within the prohibition of this section. The place where the expenses are paid or incurred is immaterial. For purposes of subdivision (ii) of this subparagraph, lawfulness, or unlawfulness of the payment under the laws of the foreign country is immaterial.

* * *

§ 1.162–21 Fines and penalties.

(a) In general. No deduction shall be allowed under section 162(a) for any fine or similar penalty paid to—

(1) The government of the United States, a State, a territory or possession of the United States, the District of Columbia, or the Commonwealth of Puerto Rico;

(2) The government of a foreign country; or

(3) A political subdivision of, or corporation or other entity serving as an agency or instrumentality of, any of the above.

(b) Definition. (1) For purposes of this section a fine or similar penalty includes an amount—

(i) Paid pursuant to conviction or a plea of guilty or *nolo contendere* for a crime (felony or misdemeanor) in a criminal proceeding;

(ii) Paid as a civil penalty imposed by Federal, State, or local law, including additions to tax and additional amounts and assessable penalties imposed by chapter 68 of the Internal Revenue Code of 1954;

(iii) Paid in settlement of the taxpayer's actual or potential liability for a fine or penalty (civil or criminal); or

(iv) Forfeited as collateral posted in connection with a proceeding which could result in imposition of such a fine or penalty.

(2) The amount of a fine or penalty does not include legal fees and related expenses paid or incurred in the defense of a prosecution or civil action arising from a violation of the law imposing the fine or civil penalty, nor court costs assessed against the taxpayer, or stenographic and printing charges. Compensatory damages (including damages under section 4A of the Clayton Act (15 U.S.C. 15a), as amended) paid to a government do not constitute a fine or penalty.

(c) Examples. The application of this section may be illustrated by the following examples:

Example (1). M Corp. was indicted under section 1 of the Sherman Anti-Trust Act (15 U.S.C. 1) for fixing and maintaining prices of certain electrical products. M Corp. was convicted and was fined $50,000. The United States sued M Corp. under section 4A of the Clayton Act (15 U.S.C. 15a) for $100,000, the amount of the actual damages resulting from the price fixing of which M Corp. was convicted. Pursuant to a final judgment entered in the civil action M Corp. paid the United States $100,000 in damages. Section 162(f) precludes M Corp. from deducting the fine of $50,000 as a trade or business expense. Section 162(f) does not preclude it from deducting the $100,000 paid to the United States as actual damages.

Example (2). N Corp. was found to have violated 33 U.S.C. 1321(b)(3) when a vessel it operated discharged oil in harmful quantities into the navigable waters of the United States. A civil penalty under 33 U.S.C. 1321 (b)(6) of $5,000 was assessed against N Corp. with respect to the discharge. N Corp. paid $5,000 to the Coast Guard in payment of the civil penalty. Section 162(f) precludes N Corp. from deducting the $5,000 penalty.

Example (3). O Corp., a manufacturer of motor vehicles, was found to have violated 42 U.S.C. 1857f–2(a)(1) by selling a new motor vehicle which was not covered by the required certificate of conformity. Pursuant to 42 U.S.C. 1857f–4, O Corp. was required to pay, and did pay, a civil penalty of $10,000. In addition, pursuant to 42 U.S.C. 1857f–5a(c)(1), O Corp. was required to expend, and did expend, $500 in order to remedy the nonconformity of that motor vehicle. Section 162(f) precludes O Corp. from deducting the $10,000 penalty as a trade or business expense, but does not preclude it from deducting the $500 which it expended to remedy the nonconformity.

Example (4). P Corp. was the operator of a coal mine in which occurred a violation of a mandatory safety standard prescribed by the Federal Coal Mine Health and Safety Act of 1969 (30 U.S.C. 801 et seq.). Pursuant to 30 U.S.C. 819(a), a civil penalty of $10,000 was assessed against P Corp., and P Corp. paid the penalty. Section 162(f) precludes P Corp. from deducting the $10,000 penalty.

Example (5). Q Corp., a common carrier engaged in interstate commerce by railroad, hauled a railroad car which was not equipped with efficient hand brakes, in violation of 45 U.S.C. 11. Q Corp. was found to be liable for a penalty of $250 pursuant to 45 U.S.C. 13. Q Corp. paid that penalty. Section 162(f) precludes Q Corp. from deducting the $250 penalty.

Example (6). R Corp. owned and operated on the highways of State X a truck weighing in excess of the amount permitted under the law of State X. R Corp. was found to have violated the law and was assessed a fine of $85 which it paid to State X. Section 162(f) precludes R Corp. from deducting the amount so paid.

Example (7). S Corp. was found to have violated a law of State Y which prohibited the emission into the air of particulate matter in excess of a limit set forth in a regulation promulgated under that law. The Environmental Quality Hearing Board of State Y assessed a fine of $500 against S Corp. The fine was payable to State Y, and S Corp. paid it. Section 162(f) precludes S Corp. from deducting the $500 fine.

Example (8). T Corp. was found by a magistrate of City Z to be operating in such city an apartment building which did not conform to a provision of the city housing code requiring operable fire escapes on apartment buildings of that type. Upon the basis of the magistrate's finding, T Corp. was required to pay, and did pay, a fine of $200 to City Z. Section 162(f) precludes T Corp. from deducting the $200 fine.

§ 1.162–22 Treble damage payments under the antitrust laws.

(a) In general. In the case of a taxpayer who after December 31, 1969, either is convicted in a criminal action of a violation of the Federal antitrust laws or enters a plea of guilty or *nolo contendere* to an indictment or information charging such a violation, and whose conviction or plea does not occur in a new trial following an appeal of a conviction on or before such date, no deduction shall be allowed under section 162(a) for two-thirds of any amount paid or incurred after December 31, 1969, with respect to—

(1) Any judgment for damages entered against the taxpayer under section 4 of the Clayton Act (15 U.S.C. 15), as amended, on account of such violation or any related violation of the Federal antitrust laws, provided such related violation occurred prior to the date of the final judgment of such conviction, or

(2) Settlement of any action brought under such section 4 on account of such violation or related violation.

* * *

§ 1.162–25 Deductions with respect to noncash fringe benefits.

(a) [Reserved]

(b) Employee. If an employer provides the use of a vehicle (as defined in § 1.61–21(e)(2)) to an employee as a noncash fringe benefit and includes the entire value of the benefit in the employee's gross income without taking into account any exclusion for a working condition fringe allowable under section 132 and the regulations thereunder, the employee may deduct that value multiplied by the percentage of the total use of the vehicle that is in connection with the employer's trade or business (business value). For taxable years beginning before January 1, 1990, the employee may deduct the business value from gross income in determining adjusted gross income. For taxable years beginning on or after January 1, 1990, the employee may deduct the business value only as a miscellaneous itemized deduction in determining taxable income, subject to the 2-percent floor provided in section 67. If the employer determines the value of the noncash fringe benefit under a special accounting rule that allows the employer to treat the value of benefits provided during the last two months of the calendar year or any shorter period as paid during the subsequent calendar year, then the employee must determine the deduction allowable under this paragraph (b) without regard to any use of the benefit during those last two months or any shorter period. The employee may not use a cent-per-mile valuation method to determine the deduction allowable under this paragraph (b).

§ 1.162–25T Deductions with respect to noncash fringe benefits (temporary).

(a) Employer. If an employer includes the value of a noncash fringe benefit in an employee's gross income, the employer may not deduct this amount as compensation for services, but rather may deduct only the costs incurred by the employer in providing the benefit to the employee. The employer may be allowed a cost recovery deduction under section 168 or a deduction under section 179 for an expense not chargeable to capital account, or, if the noncash fringe benefit is property leased by the employer, a deduction for the ordinary and necessary business expense of leasing the property.

(b) [Reserved]

(c) Examples. The following examples illustrate the provisions of this section.

Example (1). On January 1, 1986, X Company owns and provides the use of an automobile with a fair market value of $20,000 to E, an employee, for the entire calendar year. Both X and E compute taxable income on the basis of the calendar year. Seventy percent of the use of the automobile by E is in connection with X's trade or business. If X uses the special rule provided in § 1.61–2T for valuing the availability of the automobile and takes into account the amount excludable as a working condition fringe, X would include $1,680 ($5,600, the Annual Lease Value, less 70 percent of $5,600) in E's gross income for 1986. X may not deduct the amount included in E's income as compensation for services. X may, however, determine a cost recovery deduction under section 168, subject to the limitations under section 280F, for taxable year 1986.

Example (2). The facts are the same as in example (1), except that X includes $5,600 in E's gross income, the value of the noncash fringe benefit without taking into account the amount excludable as a working condition fringe. X may not deduct that amount as compensation for services, but may determine a cost recovery deduction under section 168, subject to the limitations under section 280F. For purposes of determining adjusted gross income, E may deduct $3,920 ($5,600 multiplied by the percent of business use).

* * *

§ 1.163–1 Interest deduction in general.

(a) Except as otherwise provided in sections 264 to 267, inclusive, interest paid or accrued within the taxable year on indebtedness shall be allowed as a deduction in computing taxable income.* For rules relating to interest on certain deferred payments, see section 483 and the regulations thereunder.

(b) Interest paid by the taxpayer on a mortgage upon real estate of which he is the legal or equitable owner, even though the taxpayer is not directly liable upon the bond or note secured by such mortgage, may be deducted as interest on his indebtedness. Pursuant to the provisions of section 163(c), any annual or periodic rental payment made by a taxpayer on or after January 1, 1962, under a redeemable ground rent, as defined in section 1055(c) and paragraph (b) of § 1.1055–1, is required to be treated as interest on an indebtedness secured by a mortgage and, accordingly, may be deducted by the taxpayer as interest on his indebtedness. Section 163(c) has no application in respect of any annual or periodic rental payment made prior to January 1, 1962, or pursuant to an arrangement which does not constitute a "redeemable ground rent" as defined in section 1055(c) and paragraph (b) of § 1.1055–1. * * *

§ 1.163–2 Installment purchases where interest charge is not separately stated.

(a) In general. (1) Whenever there is a contract with a seller for the purchase of personal property providing for payment of part or all of the

*Editorial comment: This Regulation does not reflect the interest deduction disallowance provisions modified or added by the Tax Reform Act of 1986. See Reg.Sec. 1.163–9T.

purchase price in installments and there is a separately stated carrying charge (including a finance charge, service charge, and the like) but the actual interest charge cannot be ascertained, a portion of the payments made during the taxable year under the contract shall be treated as interest and is deductible under section 163 and this section. Section 163(b) contains a formula, described in paragraph (b) of this section, in accordance with which the amount of interest deductible in the taxable year must be computed. This formula is designed to operate automatically in the case of any installment purchase, without regard to whether payments under the contract are made when due or are in default. For applicable limitations when an obligation to pay is terminated, see paragraph (c) of this section.

* * *

(b) Computation. The portion of any such payments to be treated as interest shall be equal to 6 percent of the average unpaid balance under the contract during the taxable year. For purposes of this computation, the average unpaid balance under the contract is the sum of the unpaid balance outstanding on the first day of each month beginning during the taxable year, divided by 12.

(c) Limitations. The amount treated as interest under section 163(b) and this section for any taxable year shall not exceed the amount of the payments made under the contract during the taxable year nor the aggregate carrying charges properly attributable to each contract for such taxable year. In computing the amount to be treated as interest if the obligation to pay is terminated as, for example, in the case of a repossession of the property, the unpaid balance on the first day of the month during which the obligation is terminated shall be zero.

* * *

§ 1.163–9T Personal interest (temporary).*

(a) In general. No deduction under any provision of Chapter 1 of the Internal Revenue Code shall be allowed for personal interest paid or accrued during the taxable year by a taxpayer other than a corporation.

*Editorial comment: The Regulations do not reflect the deduction for interest on education loans permitted by the Taxpayer Relief Act of 1997. See Sec. 221.

(b) Personal interest— (1) Definition. For purposes of this section, personal interest is any interest expense other than—

(i) Interest paid or accrued on indebtedness properly allocable (within the meaning of § 1.163–8T) to the conduct of trade or business (other than the trade or business of performing services as an employee).

(ii) Any investment interest (within the meaning of section 163(d)(3)).

(iii) Any interest that is taken into account under section 469 in computing income or loss from a passive activity of the taxpayer.

(iv) Any qualified residence interest (within the meaning of section 163(h)(3) and § 1.163–10T), and

(v) Any interest payable under section 6601 with respect to the unpaid portion of the tax imposed by section 2001 for the period during which an extension of time for payment of such tax is in effect under section 6163, 6166, or 6166A (as in effect before its repeal by the Economic Recovery Tax Act of 1981).

(2) Interest relating to taxes— (i) In general. Except as provided in paragraph (b)(2)(iii) of this section, personal interest includes interest—

(A) Paid on underpayments of individual Federal, State or local income taxes and on indebtedness used to pay such taxes (within the meaning of § 1.163–8T), regardless of the source of the income generating the tax liability;

(B) Paid under section 453(e)(4)(B) (interest on deferred tax resulting from certain installment sales) and section 1291(c) (interest on deferred tax attributable to passive foreign investment companies); or

(C) Paid by a trust, S corporation, or other pass-through entity on underpayments of State or local income taxes and on indebtedness used to pay such taxes.

(ii) Example: A, an individual, owns stock of an S corporation. On its return for 1987, the corporation underreports its taxable income. Consequently, A underreports A's share of that income on A's tax return. In 1989, A pays the resulting deficiency plus interest to the Internal Revenue Service. The interest paid by A in 1989 on the tax deficiency is personal interest, notwithstanding the fact that the additional tax liability may have arisen out of income from a trade or business. The result would be the same if A's business had been operated as a sole proprietorship.

(iii) Certain other taxes. Personal interest does not include interest—

(A) Paid with respect to sales, excise and similar taxes that are incurred in connection with a trade or business or an investment activity;

(B) Paid by an S corporation with respect to an underpayment of income tax from a year in which the S corporation was a C corporation or with respect to an underpayment of the taxes imposed by sections 1374 or 1375, or similar provision of State law; or

(C) Paid by a transferee under section 6901 (tax liability resulting from transferred assets), or a similar provision of State law, with respect to a C corporation's underpayment of income tax.

(3) Cross references. See § 1.163–8T for rules for determining the allocation of interest expense to various activities. See § 1.163–10T for rules concerning qualified residence interest.

(c) Effective date— (1) In general. The provisions of this section are effective for taxable years beginning after December 31, 1986.

* * *

§ 1.164–1 Deduction for taxes.

(a) In general. Only the following taxes shall be allowed as a deduction under this section for the taxable year within which paid or accrued, according to the method of accounting used in computing taxable income:

(1) State and local, and foreign, real property taxes.

(2) State and local personal property taxes.

(3) State and local, and foreign, income, war profits, and excess profits taxes.

(4) State and local general sales taxes.*

(5) State and local taxes on the sale of gasoline, diesel fuel, and other motor fuels.*

In addition, there shall be allowed as a deduction under this section State and local and foreign taxes not described in subparagraphs (1) through (5) of this paragraph which are paid or accrued within the taxable year in carrying on a trade or business or an activity described in section 212 (relating to expenses for production of income). For example, dealers or investors in securities and dealers or investors in real estate may deduct State stock transfer and real estate transfer taxes, respectively, under section 164, to the extent they are expenses incurred in carrying on a trade or business or an activity for the production of income. In general, taxes are deductible only by the person upon whom they are imposed. However, see § 1.164–5 in the case of certain taxes paid by the consumer. Also, in the case of a qualified State individual income tax (as defined in section 6362 and the regulations thereunder) which is determined by reference to a percentage of the Federal income tax (pursuant to section 6362(c)), an accrual method taxpayer shall use the cash receipts and disbursements method to compute the amount of his deduction therefor. Thus, the deduction under section 164 is in the amount actually paid with respect to the qualified tax, rather than the amount accrued with respect thereto, during the taxable year even though the taxpayer uses the accrual method of accounting for other purposes. * * *

§ 1.164–2 Deduction denied in case of certain taxes.

This section and § 1.275 describe certain taxes for which no deduction is allowed. In the case of taxable years beginning before January 1, 1964, the denial is provided for by section 164(b) (prior to being amended by section 207 of the Revenue Act of 1964 (78 Stat. 40)). In the case of taxable years beginning after December 31, 1963, the denial is governed by sections 164 and 275. No deduction is allowed for the following taxes:

(a) Federal income taxes. Federal income taxes, including the taxes imposed by section 3101, relating to the tax on employees under the Federal Insurance Contributions Act (Chapter 21 of the Code); sections 3201 and 3211, relating to the taxes on railroad employees and railroad employee representatives; section 3402, relating to the tax withheld at source on wages; and by corresponding provisions of prior internal revenue laws.

*Editorial comment: The Regulations do not reflect the disallowance of these deductions imposed by the Tax Reform Act of 1986 (item 4) and prior legislation (item 5). Likewise, the Regulations do not reflect the sales tax deduction election option provided in the American Jobs Creation Act of 2004 and extended through 2007 by the Tax Relief and Health Care Act of 2006. See Sec. 164(b)(5). Likewise, the Regulations do not reflect the effect of the Tax Extenders and AMT Relief Act of 2008 which extended this provision through 2009. The Tax Relief Act of 2010 extended this provision through 2012. The American Taxpayer Relief Act of 2012 did reinstate the sales tax paid deduction option for 2013. The American Recovery and Reinvestment Tax Act of 2009 permits a deduction for sales taxes paid on a qualified motor vehicle in 2009 as a component of the standard deduction. Congress did not extend this provision in the Tax Relief Act of 2010 or other 2010 tax legislation. See Sec. 164 (a)(6) and Sec. 63(c)(1)(E).

(b) Federal war profits and excess profits taxes. Federal war profits and excess profits taxes including those imposed by Title II of the Revenue Act of 1917 (39 Stat. 1000), Title III of the Revenue Act of 1918 (40 Stat. 1088), Title III of the Revenue Act of 1921 (42 Stat. 271), section 216 of the National Industrial Recovery Act (48 Stat. 208), section 702 of the Revenue Act of 1934 (48 Stat. 770), Subchapter D, Chapter 1 of the Internal Revenue Code of 1939, and Subchapter E, Chapter 2 of the Internal Revenue Code of 1939.

(c) Estate and gift taxes. Estate, inheritance, legacy, succession, and gift taxes.

(d) Foreign income, war profits, and excess profits taxes. Income, war profits, and excess profits taxes imposed by the authority of any foreign country or possession of the United States, if the taxpayer chooses to take to any extent the benefits of section 901, relating to the credit for taxes of foreign countries and possessions of the United States.

(e) Real property taxes. Taxes on real property, to the extent that section 164(d) and § 1.164–6 require such taxes to be treated as imposed on another taxpayer.

* * *

(g) Taxes for local benefits. Except as provided in § 1.164–4, taxes assessed against local benefits of a kind tending to increase the value of the property assessed.

* * *

§ 1.164–4 Taxes for local benefits.

(a) So-called taxes for local benefits referred to in paragraph (g) of § 1.164–2, more properly assessments, paid for local benefits such as street, sidewalk, and other like improvements, imposed because of and measured by some benefit inuring directly to the property against which the assessment is levied are not deductible as taxes. A tax is considered assessed against local benefits when the property subject to the tax is limited to property benefited. Special assessments are not deductible, even though an incidental benefit may inure to the public welfare. The real property taxes deductible are those levied for the general public welfare by the proper taxing authorities at a like rate against all property in the territory over which such authorities have jurisdiction.* * * For treatment of assessments for local benefits as adjustments to the basis of property, see section 1016(a)(1) and the regulations thereunder.

(b)(1) Insofar as assessments against local benefits are made for the purpose of maintenance or repair or for the purpose of meeting interest charges with respect to such benefits, they are deductible. In such cases, the burden is on the taxpayer to show the allocation of the amounts assessed to the different purposes. If the allocation cannot be made, none of the amount so paid is deductible.

* * *

§ 1.164–6 Apportionment of taxes on real property between seller and purchaser.

(a) Scope. Except as provided otherwise in section 164(f) and § 1.164–8, when real property is sold, section 164(d)(1) governs the deduction by the seller and the purchaser of current real property taxes. Section 164(d)(1) performs two functions: (1) It provides a method by which a portion of the taxes for the real property tax year in which the property is sold may be deducted by the seller and a portion by the purchaser; and (2) it limits the deduction of the seller and the purchaser to the portion of the taxes corresponding to the part of the real property tax year during which each was the owner of the property. These functions are accomplished by treating a portion of the taxes for the real property tax year in which the property is sold as imposed on the seller and a portion as imposed on the purchaser. To the extent that the taxes are treated as imposed on the seller and the purchaser, each shall be allowed a deduction, under section 164(a), in the taxable year such tax is paid or accrued, or treated as paid or accrued under section 164(d)(2)(A) or (D) and this section. No deduction is allowed for taxes on real property to the extent that they are imposed on another taxpayer, or are treated as imposed on another taxpayer under section 164(d). For the election to accrue real property taxes ratably see section 461(c) and the regulations thereunder.

(b) Application of rule of apportionment.(1)(i) For purposes of the deduction provided by section 164 (a), if real property is sold during any real property tax year, the portion of the real property tax properly allocable to that part of the real property tax year which ends on the day before the date of the sale shall be treated as a tax imposed on the seller, and the portion of such tax properly allocable to that part of such real property tax year which begins on the date of the sale shall be treated as a tax imposed on the purchased. For definition of "real property tax year" see paragraph (c) of this section. This rule shall apply whether or not the seller and the purchaser apportion such tax. The rule of apportionment contained in section 164(d)(1) applies even though the same real property is sold more than once during the real property tax year. (See paragraph (d)(5) of this section for rule requiring inclusion in gross income of excess deductions.)

* * *

(3) The provisions of this paragraph may be illustrated by the following examples:

Example (1). The real property tax year in County R is April 1 to March 31. A, the owner on April 1, 1954, of real property located in County R sells the real property to B on June 30, 1954. B owns the real property from June 30, 1954, through March 31, 1955. The real property tax for the real property tax year April 1, 1954–March 31, 1955 is $365. For purposes of section 164(a), $90 (90/365 × $365, April 1, 1954-June 29, 1954) of the real property tax is treated as imposed on A, the seller, and $275 (275/365 × $365, June 30, 1954–March 31, 1955) of such real property tax is treated as imposed on B, the purchaser.

* * *

§ 1.165–1 Losses.

(a) Allowance of deduction. Section 165(a) provides that, in computing taxable income under section 63, any loss actually sustained during the taxable year and not made good by insurance or some other form of compensation shall be allowed as a deduction subject to any provision of the internal revenue laws which prohibits or limits the amount of the deduction. This deduction for losses sustained shall be taken in accordance with section 165 and the regulations thereunder.* * *

(b) Nature of loss allowable. To be allowable as a deduction under section 165(a), a loss must be evidenced by closed and completed transactions, fixed by identifiable events, and, except as otherwise provided in section 165(h) and § 1.165–11, relating to disaster losses, actually sustained during the taxable year. Only a bona fide loss is allowable. Substance and not mere form shall govern in determining a deductible loss.

(c) Amount deductible. **(1)** The amount of loss allowable as a deduction under section 165(a) shall not exceed the amount prescribed by § 1.1011–1 as the adjusted basis for determining the loss from the sale or other disposition of the property involved. In the case of each such deduction claimed, therefore, the basis of the property must be properly adjusted as prescribed by § 1.1011–1 for such items as expenditures, receipts, or losses, properly chargeable to capital account, and for such items as depreciation, obsolescence, amortization, and depletion, in order to determine the amount of loss allowable as a deduction.* * *

(2) The amount of loss recognized upon the sale or exchange of property shall be determined for purposes of section 165(a) in accordance with § 1.1002–1.

(3) A loss from the sale or exchange of a capital asset shall be allowed as a deduction under section 165(a) but only to the extent allowed in section 1211 (relating to limitation on capital losses) and section 1212 (relating to capital loss carrybacks and carryovers), and in the regulations under those sections.

(4) In determining the amount of loss actually sustained for purposes of section 165(a), proper adjustment shall be made for any salvage value and for any insurance or other compensation received.

(d) Year of deduction. **(1)** A loss shall be allowed as a deduction under section 165(a) only for the taxable year in which the loss is sustained. For this purpose, a loss shall be treated as sustained during the taxable year in which the loss occurs as evidenced by closed and completed transactions and as fixed by identifiable events occurring in such taxable year. For provisions relating to situations where a loss attributable to a disaster will be treated as sustained in the taxable year immediately preceding the taxable year in which the disaster actually occurred, see section 165(h) and § 1.165–11.

(2)(i) If a casualty or other event occurs which may result in a loss and, in the year of such casualty or event, there exists a claim for reimbursement with respect to which there is a reasonable prospect of recovery, no portion of the loss with respect to which reimbursement may be received is sustained, for purposes of section 165, until it can be ascertained with reasonable certainty whether or not such reimbursement will be received. Whether a reasonable prospect of recovery exists with respect to a claim for reimbursement of a loss is a question of fact to be determined upon an examination of all facts and circumstances. Whether or not such reimbursement will be received may be ascertained with reasonable certainty, for example, by a settlement of the claim, by an adjudication of the claim, or by an abandonment of the claim. When a taxpayer claims that the taxable year in which a loss is sustained is fixed by his abandonment of the claim for reimbursement, he must be able to produce objective evidence of his having abandoned the claim, such as the execution of a release.

(ii) If in the year of the casualty or other event a portion of the loss is not covered by a claim for reimbursement with respect to which there is a reasonable prospect of recovery, then such portion of the loss is sustained during the taxable year in which the casualty or other event occurs. For example, if property having an adjusted basis of $10,000 is completely destroyed by fire in 1961, and if the taxpayer's only claim for reimbursement consists of an insurance claim for $8,000 which is settled in 1962, the taxpayer sustains a loss of $2,000 in 1961. However, if the taxpayer's automobile is completely destroyed in 1961 as a result of the negligence of another person and there exists a reasonable prospect of recovery on a claim for the full value of the automobile against such person, the taxpayer does not sustain any loss until the taxable year in which the claim is adjudicated or otherwise settled. If the automobile had an adjusted basis of $5,000 and the taxpayer secures a judgment of $4,000 in 1962, $1,000 is deductible for the taxable year 1962. If in 1963 it becomes reasonably certain that only $3,500 can ever be collected on such judgment, $500 is deductible for the taxable year 1963.

(iii) If the taxpayer deducted a loss in accordance with the provisions of this paragraph and in a subsequent taxable year receives reimbursement for such loss, he does not recompute the tax for the taxable year in which the deduction was taken but includes the amount of such reimbursement in his gross income for the taxable year in which received, subject to the provisions of section 111, relating to recovery of amounts previously deducted.

(3) Any loss arising from theft shall be treated as sustained during the taxable year in which the taxpayer discovers the loss (see § 1.165–8, relating to theft losses). However, if in the year of discovery there exists a claim for reimbursement with respect to which there is a reasonable prospect of recovery, no portion of the loss with respect to which reimbursement may be received is sustained, for purposes of section 165, until the taxable year in which it can be ascertained with reasonable certainty whether or not such reimbursement will be received.

* * *

(e) Limitation on losses of individuals. In the case of an individual, the deduction for losses granted by section 165(a) shall, subject to the provisions of section 165(c) and paragraph (a) of this section, be limited to:

(1) Losses incurred in a trade or business;

(2) Losses incurred in any transaction entered into for profit, though not connected with a trade or business; and

(3) Losses of property not connected with a trade or business and not incurred in any transaction entered into for profit, if such losses arise from fire, storm, shipwreck, or other casualty, or from theft, and if the loss involved has not been allowed for estate tax purposes in the estate tax return. For additional provisions pertaining to the allowance of casualty and theft losses, see §§ 1.165–7 and 1.165–8, respectively.

For special rules relating to an election by a taxpayer to deduct disaster losses in the taxable year immediately preceding the taxable year in which the disaster occurred, see section 165(h) and § 1.165–11.

§ 1.165–2 Obsolescence of nondepreciable property.

(a) Allowance of deduction. A loss incurred in a business or in a transaction entered into for profit and arising from the sudden termination of the usefulness in such business or transaction of any nondepreciable property, in a case where such business or transaction is discontinued or where such property is permanently discarded from use therein, shall be allowed as a deduction under section 165(a) for the taxable year in which the loss is actually sustained. For this purpose, the taxable year in which the loss is sustained is not necessarily the taxable year in which the overt act of abandonment, or the loss of title to the property, occurs.

(b) Exceptions. This section does not apply to losses sustained upon the sale or exchange of property, losses sustained upon the obsolescence or worthlessness of depreciable property, casualty losses, or losses reflected in inventories required to be taken under section 471. The limitations contained in sections 1211 and 1212 upon losses from the sale or exchange of capital assets do not apply to losses allowable under this section.

* * *

§ 1.165–4 Decline in value of stock.

(a) Deduction disallowed. No deduction shall be allowed under section 165(a) solely on account of a decline in the value of stock owned by the taxpayer when the decline is due to a fluctuation in the market price of the stock or to other similar cause. A mere shrinkage in the value of stock owned by the taxpayer, even though extensive, does not give rise to a deduction under section 165(a) if the stock has any recognizable value on the date claimed as the date of loss. No loss for a decline in the value of stock owned by the taxpayer shall be allowed as a deduction under section 165(a) except insofar as the loss is recognized under § 1.1002–1 upon the sale or exchange of the stock and except as otherwise provided in § 1.165–5 with respect to stock which becomes worthless during the taxable year.

* * *

§ 1.165–5 Worthless securities.

(a) Definition of security. As used in section 165(g) and this section, the term "security" means:

(1) A share of stock in a corporation;

(2) A right to subscribe for, or to receive, a share of stock in a corporation; or

(3) A bond, debenture, note, or certificate, or other evidence of indebtedness to pay a fixed or determinable sum of money, which has been issued with interest coupons or in registered form by a domestic or foreign corporation or by any government or political subdivision thereof.

(b) Ordinary loss. If any security which is not a capital asset becomes wholly worthless during the taxable year, the loss resulting therefrom may be deducted under section 165(a) as an ordinary loss.

(c) Capital loss. If any security which is a capital asset becomes wholly worthless at any time during the taxable year, the loss resulting therefrom may be deducted under section 165(a) but only as though it were a loss from a sale or exchange, on the last day of the taxable year, of a capital asset. See section 165(g)(1). The amount so allowed as a deduction shall be subject to the limitations upon capital losses described in paragraph (c)(3) of § 1.165–1.

* * *

§ 1.165–7 Casualty losses.

(a) In general— (1) Allowance of deduction. Except as otherwise provided in paragraphs (b)(4) and (c) of this section, any loss arising from fire, storm, shipwreck, or other casualty is allowable as a deduction under section 165(a) for the taxable year in which the loss is sustained. However, see § 1.165–6, relating to farming losses, and § 1.165–11, relating to an election by a taxpayer to deduct disaster losses in the taxable year immediately preceding the taxable year in which the disaster occurred. The manner of determining the amount of a casualty loss allowable as a deduction in computing taxable income under section 63 is the same whether the loss has been incurred in a trade or business or in any transaction entered into for profit, or whether it has been a loss of property not connected with a trade or business and not incurred in any transaction entered into for profit. The amount of a casualty loss shall be determined in accordance with paragraph (b) of this section. For other rules relating to the treatment of deductible casualty losses, see § 1.1231–1, relating to the involuntary conversion of property.

(2) Method of valuation. (i) In determining the amount of loss deductible under this section, the fair market value of the property immediately before and immediately after the casualty shall generally be ascertained by competent appraisal. This appraisal must recognize the effects of any general market decline affecting undamaged as well as damaged property which may occur simultaneously with the casualty, in order that any deduction under this section shall be limited to the actual loss resulting from damage to the property.

(ii) The cost of repairs to the property damaged is acceptable as evidence of the loss of value if the taxpayer shows that (a) the repairs are necessary to restore the property to its condition immediately before the casualty, (b) the amount spent for such repairs is not excessive, (c) the repairs do not care for more than the damage suffered, and (d) the value of the property after the repairs does not as a result of the repairs exceed the value of the property immediately before the casualty.

(3) Damage to automobiles. An automobile owned by the taxpayer, whether used for business purposes or maintained for recreation or pleasure, may be the subject of a casualty loss, including those losses specifically referred to in subparagraph (1) of this paragraph. In addition, a casualty loss occurs when an automobile owned by the taxpayer is damaged and when:

(i) The damage results from the faulty driving of the taxpayer or other person operating the automobile but is not due to the willful act or willful negligence of the taxpayer or of one acting in his behalf or

(ii) The damage results from the faulty driving of the operator of the vehicle with which the automobile of the taxpayer collides.

(4) Application to inventories. This section does not apply to a casualty loss reflected in the inventories of the taxpayer. For provisions relating to inventories, see section 471 and the regulations thereunder.

(5) Property converted from personal use. In the case of property which originally was not used in the trade or business or for income-producing purposes and which is thereafter converted to either of such uses, the fair market value of the property on the date of conversion, if less than the adjusted basis of the property at such time, shall be used, after making proper adjustments in respect of basis, as the basis for determining the amount of loss under paragraph (b)(1) of this section. See paragraph (b) of § 1.165–9, and § 1.167(g)–1.

(6) Theft losses. A loss which arises from theft is not considered a casualty loss for purposes of this section. See § 1.165–8, relating to theft losses.

(b) Amount deductible—(1) General rule. In the case of any casualty loss whether or not incurred in a trade or business or in any transaction entered into for profit, the amount of loss to be taken into account for purposes of section 165(a) shall be the lesser of either—

(i) The amount which is equal to the fair market value of the property immediately before the casualty reduced by the fair market value of the property immediately after the casualty; or

(ii) The amount of the adjusted basis prescribed in § 1.1011–1 for determining the loss from the sale or other disposition of the property involved.

However, if property used in a trade or business or held for the production of income is totally destroyed by casualty, and if the fair market value of such property immediately before the casualty is less than the adjusted basis of such property, the amount of the adjusted basis of such property shall be treated as the amount of the loss for purposes of section 165(a).

(2) Aggregation of property for computing loss. (i) A loss incurred in a trade or business or in any transaction entered into for profit shall be determined under subparagraph (1) of this paragraph by reference to the single, identifiable property damaged or destroyed. Thus, for example, in determining the fair market value of the property before and after the casualty in a case where damage by casualty has occurred to a building and ornamental or fruit trees used in a trade or business, the decrease in value shall be measured by taking the building and trees into account separately, and not together as an integral part of the realty, and separate losses shall be determined for such building and trees.

(ii) In determining a casualty loss involving real property and improvements thereon not used in a trade or business or in any transaction entered into for profit, the improvements (such as buildings and ornamental trees and shrubbery) to the property damaged or destroyed shall be considered an integral part of the property, for purposes of subparagraph (1) of this paragraph, and no separate basis need be apportioned to such improvements.

(3) Examples. The application of this paragraph may be illustrated by the following examples:

Example (1). In 1956 B purchases for $3,600 an automobile which he uses for nonbusiness purposes. In 1959 the automobile is damaged in an accidental collision with another automobile. The fair market value of B's automobile is $2,000 immediately before the collision and $1,500 immediately after the collision. B receives insurance proceeds of $300 to cover the loss. The amount of the deduction allowable under section 165(a) for the taxable year 1959 is $200, computed as follows:

Value of automobile immediately before casualty	$2,000
Less: Value of automobile immediately after casualty	1,500
Value of property actually destroyed	500
Loss to be taken into account for purposes of section 165(a): Lesser amount of property actually destroyed ($500) or adjusted basis of property ($3,600)	500
Less: Insurance received	300
Deduction allowable	200

Example (2). In 1958 A purchases land containing an office building for the lump sum of $90,000. The purchase price is allocated between the land ($18,000) and the building ($72,000) for purposes of determining basis. After the purchase A planted trees and ornamental shrubs on the grounds surrounding the building. In 1961 the land, building, trees, and shrubs are damaged by hurricane. At the time of the casualty the adjusted basis of the land is $18,000 and the adjusted basis of the building is $66,000. At that time the trees and shrubs have an adjusted basis of $1,200. The fair market value of the land and building immediately before the casualty is $18,000 and $70,000, respectively, and immediately after the casualty is $18,000 and $52,000, respectively. The fair market value of the trees and shrubs immediately before the casualty is $2,000 and immediately after the casualty is $400. In 1961 insurance of $5,000 is received to cover the loss to the building. A has no other gains or losses in 1961 subject to section 1231 and § 1.1231–1. The amount of the deduction allowable under section 165(a) with respect to the building for the taxable year 1961 is $13,000, computed as follows:

Value of property immediately before casualty.	$70,000
Less: Value of property immediately after casualty	52,000
Value of property actually destroyed......	18,000
Less: Insurance received	5,000
Loss to be taken into account for purposes of section 165(a): Lesser amount of property actually destroyed ($18,000) or adjusted basis of property ($66,000)	18,000
Less: Insurance received	5,000
Deduction allowable......	13,000

The amount of the deduction allowable under section 165(a) with respect to the trees and shrubs for the taxable year 1961 is $1,200, computed as follows:

Value of property immediately before casualty	$2,000
Less: Value of property immediately after casualty	$400
Value of property actually destroyed......	1,600
Loss to be taken into account for purposes of section 165(a): Lesser amount of property actually destroyed ($1,600) or adjusted basis of property ($1,200)	1,200

Example (3). Assume the same facts as in example (2) except that A purchases land containing a house instead of an office building. The house is used as his private residence. Since the property is used for personal purposes, no allocation of the purchase price is necessary for the land and house. Likewise, no individual determination of the fair market values of the land, house, trees, and shrubs is necessary. The amount of the deduction allowable under section 165(a) with respect to the land, house, trees, and shrubs for the taxable year 1961 is $14,600, computed as follows:

Value of property immediately before casualty.	$90,000
Less: Value of property immediately after casualt	70,400
Value of property actually destroyed......	19,600
Loss to be taken into account for purposes of section 165(a): Lesser amount of property actually destroyed ($19,600) or adjusted basis of property ($91,200)	19,600
Less: Insurance received	5,000
Deduction allowable......	14,600

(4) Limitation on certain losses sustained by individuals after December 31, 1963.* **(i)** Pursuant to section 165(c)(3), the deduction allowable under section 165(a) in respect of a loss sustained—

(a) After December 31, 1963, in a taxable year ending after such date,

(b) In respect of property not used in a trade or business or for income producing purposes, and

(c) From a single casualty

shall be limited to that portion of the loss which is in excess of $100. The nondeductibility of the first $100 of loss applies to a loss sustained after December 31, 1963, without regard to when the casualty occurred. Thus, if property not used in a trade or business or for income producing purposes is damaged or destroyed by a casualty which occurred prior to January 1, 1964, and loss resulting therefrom is sustained after December 31, 1963, the $100 limitation applies.

(ii) The $100 limitation applies separately in respect of each casualty and applies to the entire loss sustained from each casualty. Thus, if as a result of a particular casualty occurring in 1964, a taxpayer sustains in 1964 a loss of $40 and in 1965 a loss of $250, no deduction is allowable for the loss sustained in 1964 and the loss sustained in 1965 must be reduced by $60 ($100 – $40). The determination of whether damage to, or destruction of, property resulted from a single casualty or from two or more separate casualties will be made upon the basis of the particular facts of each case. However, events which are closely related in origin generally give rise to a single casualty. For example, if a storm damages a taxpayer's residence and his automobile parked in his driveway, any loss sustained results from a single casualty. Similarly, if a hurricane causes high waves, all wind and flood damage to a taxpayer's property caused by the hurricane and the waves results from a single casualty.

* * *

(iv) If a loss is sustained in respect of property used partially for business and partially for nonbusiness purposes, the $100 limitation applies only to that portion of the loss properly attributable to the nonbusiness use. For example, if a taxpayer sustains a $1,000 loss in respect of an automobile which he uses 60 percent for business and 40 percent for nonbusiness, the loss is allocated 60 percent to business use and 40 percent to nonbusiness use. The $100 limitation applies to the portion of the loss allocable to the nonbusiness loss.

(c) Loss sustained by an estate. A casualty loss of property not connected with a trade or business and not incurred in any transaction entered into for profit which is sustained during the settlement of an estate shall be allowed as a deduction under sections 165(a) and 641(b) in computing the taxable income of the estate if the loss has not been allowed under section 2054 in computing the taxable estate of the

*Editorial comment: The Regulations do not include the effect of Sec. 165(h)(2).

decedent and if the statement has been filed in accordance with § 1.642(g)–1. See section 165(c)(3).

(d) Loss treated as though attributable to a trade or business. For the rule treating a casualty loss not connected with a trade or business as though it were a deduction attributable to a trade or business for purposes of computing a net operating loss, see paragraph (a)(3)(iii) of § 1.172–3.

* * *

§ 1.165–8 Theft losses.

(a) Allowance of deduction. **(1)** Except as otherwise provided in paragraphs (b) and (c) of this section, any loss arising from theft is allowable as a deduction under section 165(a) for the taxable year in which the loss is sustained. See section 165(c)(3).

(2) A loss arising from theft shall be treated under section 165(a) as sustained during the taxable year in which the taxpayer discovers the loss. See section 165(e). Thus, a theft loss is not deductible under section 165(a) for the taxable year in which the theft actually occurs unless that is also the year in which the taxpayer discovers the loss. However, if in the year of discovery there exists a claim for reimbursement with respect to which there is a reasonable prospect of recovery, see paragraph (d) of § 1.165–1.

* * *

(b) Loss sustained by an estate. A theft loss of property not connected with a trade or business and not incurred in any transaction entered into for profit which is discovered during the settlement of an estate, even though the theft actually occurred during a taxable year of the decedent, shall be allowed as a deduction under sections 165(a) and 641(b) in computing the taxable income of the estate if the loss has not been allowed under section 2054 in computing the taxable estate of the decedent and if the statement has been filed in accordance with § 1.642(g)–1. See section 165(c)(3). For purposes of determining the year of deduction, see paragraph (a)(2) of this section.

(c) Amount deductible.* The amount deductible under this section in respect of a theft loss shall be determined consistently with the manner prescribed in § 1.165–7 for determining the amount of casualty loss allowable as a deduction under section 165(a). In applying the provisions of paragraph (b) of § 1.165–7 for this purpose, the fair market value of the property immediately after the theft shall be considered to be zero. In the case of a loss sustained after December 31, 1963, in a taxable year ending after such date, in respect of property not used in a trade or business or for income producing purposes, the amount deductible shall be limited to that portion of the loss which is in excess of $100. For rules applicable in applying the $100 limitation, see paragraph (b)(4) of § 1.165–7. For other rules relating to the treatment of deductible theft losses, see § 1.1231–1, relating to the involuntary conversion of property.

(d) Definition. For purposes of this section the term "theft" shall be deemed to include, but shall not necessarily be limited to, larceny, embezzlement, and robbery.

(e) Application to inventories. This section does not apply to a theft loss reflected in the inventories of the taxpayer. For provisions relating to inventories, see section 471 and the regulations thereunder.

(f) Example. The application of this section may be illustrated by the following example:

Example. In 1955 B, who makes her return on the basis of the calendar year, purchases for personal use a diamond brooch costing $4,000. On November 30, 1961, at which time it has a fair market value of $3,500, the brooch is stolen; but B does not discover the loss until January 1962. The brooch was fully insured against theft. A controversy develops with the insurance company over its liability in respect of the loss. However, in 1962, B has a reasonable prospect of recovery of the fair market value of the brooch from the insurance company. The controversy is settled in March 1963, at which time B receives $2,000 in insurance proceeds to cover the loss from theft. No deduction for the loss is allowable for 1961 or 1962; but the amount of the deduction allowable under section 165(a) for the taxable year 1963 is $1,500, computed as follows:

Value of property immediately before theft	$3,500
Less: Value of property immediately after the theft	0
Balance	3,500
Loss to be taken into account for purposes of section 165(a): ($3,500 but not to exceed adjusted basis of $4,000 at time of theft)	$3,500
Less: Insurance received in 1963	2,000
Deduction allowable for 1963	1,500

§ 1.165–9 Sale of residential property.

(a) Losses not allowed. A loss sustained on the sale of residential property purchased or constructed by the taxpayer for use as his personal residence and so used by him up to the time of the sale is not deductible under section 165(a).

(b) Property converted from personal use. (1) If property purchased or constructed by the taxpayer for

*Editorial comment: The Regulations do not include the effect of Sec. 165(h)(2).

use as his personal residence is, prior to its sale, rented or otherwise appropriated to income-producing purposes and is used for such purposes up to the time of its sale, a loss sustained on the sale of the property shall be allowed as a deduction under section 165(a).

(2) The loss allowed under this paragraph upon the sale of the property shall be the excess of the adjusted basis prescribed in § 1.1011–1 for determining loss over the amount realized from the sale. For this purpose, the adjusted basis for determining loss shall be the lesser of either of the following amounts, adjusted as prescribed in § 1.1011–1 for the period subsequent to the conversion of the property to income-producing purposes:

(i) The fair market value of the property at the time of conversion, or

(ii) The adjusted basis for loss, at the time of conversion, determined under § 1.1011–1 but without reference to the fair market value.

(3) For rules relating to casualty losses of property converted from personal use, see paragraph (a)(5) of § 1.165–7. To determine the basis for depreciation in the case of such property, see § 1.167(g)-1. For limitations on the loss from the sale of a capital asset, see paragraph (c)(3) of § 1.165–1.

(c) Examples. The application of paragraph (b) of this section may be illustrated by the following examples:

Example (1). Residential property is purchased by the taxpayer in 1943 for use as his personal residence at a cost of $25,000, of which $15,000 is allocable to the building. The taxpayer uses the property as his personal residence until January 1, 1952, at which time its fair market value is $22,000, of which $12,000 is allocable to the building. The taxpayer rents the property from January 1, 1952, until January 1, 1955, at which time it is sold for $16,000. On January 1, 1952, the building has an estimated useful life of 20 years. It is assumed that the building has no estimated salvage value and that there are no adjustments in respect of basis other than depreciation, which is computed on the straight-line method. The loss to be taken into account for purposes of section 165(a) for the taxable year 1955 is $4,200, computed as follows:

Basis of property at time of conversion for purposes of this section (that is, the lesser of $25,000 cost or $22,000 fair market value)	$22,000
Less: Depreciation allowable from January 1, 1952, to January 1, 1955 (3 years at 5 percent based on $12,000, the value of the building at time of conversion, as prescribed by § 1.167(g)–1)	1,800
Adjusted basis prescribed in § 1.1011–1 for determining loss on sale of the property	20,200
Less: Amount realized on sale	16,000
Loss to be taken into account for purposes of section 165(a)	4,200

In this example the value of the building at the time of conversion is used as the basis for computing depreciation. See example (2) of this paragraph wherein the adjusted basis of the building is required to be used for such purpose.

* * *

§ 1.165–10 Wagering losses.

Losses sustained during the taxable year on wagering transactions shall be allowed as a deduction but only to the extent of the gains during the taxable year from such transactions. In the case of a husband and wife making a joint return for the taxable year, the combined losses of the spouses from wagering transactions shall be allowed to the extent of the combined gains of the spouses from wagering transactions.

§ 1.165–11 Election in respect of losses attributable to a disaster.

(a) In general. Section 165(h)* provides that a taxpayer who has sustained a disaster loss which is allowable as a deduction under section 165(a) may, under certain circumstances, elect to deduct such loss for the taxable year immediately preceding the taxable year in which the disaster actually occurred.

(b) Loss subject to election. The election provided by section 165(h)* and paragraph (a) of this section applies only to a loss:

(1) Arising from a disaster resulting in a determination referred to in subparagraph (2) of this paragraph and occurring—

(i) After December 31, 1971, or

(ii) After December 31, 1961, and before January 1, 1972, and during the period following the close of a particular taxable year of the taxpayer and on or before the due date for filing the income tax return for that taxable year (determined without regard to any extension of time granted the taxpayer for filing such return);

(2) Occurring in an area subsequently determined by the President of the United States to warrant assistance by the Federal Government under the Disaster Relief Act of 1974; and

(3) Constituting a loss otherwise allowable as a deduction for the year in which the loss occurred under section 165(a) and the provisions of §§ 1.165–1 through 1.165–10 which are applicable to such losses.

*Editorial comment: The reference is now Sec. 165(i).

(c) Amount of loss to which election applies. The amount of the loss to which section 165(h)* and this section apply shall be the amount of the loss sustained during the period specified in paragraph (b)(1) of this section computed in accordance with the provisions of section 165 and those provisions of §§ 1.165–1 through 1.165–10 which are applicable to such losses. However, for purposes of making such computation, the period specified in paragraph (b)(1) of this section shall be deemed to be a taxable year.

(d) Scope and effect of election. An election made pursuant to section 165(h)* and this section in respect of a loss arising from a particular disaster shall apply to the entire loss sustained by the taxpayer from such disaster during the period specified in paragraph (b)(1) of this section in the area specified in paragraph (b)(2) of this section. If such an election is made, the disaster to which the election relates will be deemed to have occurred in the taxable year immediately preceding the taxable year in which the disaster actually occurred, and the loss to which the election applies will be deemed to have been sustained in such preceding taxable year.

(e) Time and manner of making election. An election to claim a deduction with respect to a disaster loss described in paragraph (b) of this section for the taxable year immediately preceding the taxable year in which the disaster actually occurred must be made by filing a return, an amended return, or a claim for refund clearly showing that the election provided by section 165(h)* has been made. In general, the return or claim should specify the date or dates of the disaster which gave rise to the loss, and the city, town, county, and State in which the property which was damaged or destroyed was located at the time of the disaster. An election in respect of a loss arising from a particular disaster occurring after December 31, 1971, must be made on or before the later of (1) the due date for filing the income tax return (determined without regard to any extension of time granted the taxpayer for filing such return) for the taxable year in which the disaster actually occurred, or (2) the due date of filing the income tax return (determined with regard to any extension of time granted the taxpayer for filing such return) for the taxable year immediately preceding the taxable year in which the disaster actually occurred. Such election shall be irrevocable after the later of (1) 90 days after the date on which the election was made, or (2) March 6, 1973. No revocation of such election shall be effective unless the amount of any credit or refund which resulted from such election is paid to the Internal Revenue Service within the revocation period described in the preceding sentence. However, in the case of a revocation made before receipt by the taxpayer of a refund claimed pursuant to such election, the revocation shall be effective if the refund is repaid within 30 calendar days after such receipt. An election in respect of a loss arising from a particular disaster occurring after December 31, 1961, and before January 1, 1972, must be made on or before the later of (1) the 15th day of the third month following the month in which falls the date prescribed for the filing of the income tax return (determined without regard to any extension of time granted the taxpayer for filing such return) for the taxable year immediately preceding the taxable year in which the disaster actually occurred, or (2) the due date for filing the income tax return (determined with regard to any extension of time granted the taxpayer for filing such return) for the taxable year immediately preceding the taxable year in which the disaster actually occurred. Such election shall be irrevocable after the date by which it must be made.

* * *

§ 1.166–1 Bad debts.

(a) Allowance of deduction. Section 166 provides that, in computing taxable income under section 63, a deduction shall be allowed in respect of bad debts owed to the taxpayer. For this purpose, bad debts shall, subject to the provisions of section 166 and the regulations thereunder, be taken into account either as—

(1) A deduction in respect of debts which become worthless in whole or in part; or as

(2) A deduction for a reasonable addition to a reserve for bad debts.**

* * *

(c) Bona fide debt required. Only a bona fide debt qualifies for purposes of section 166. A bona fide debt is a debt which arises from a debtor-creditor relationship based upon a valid and enforceable obligation to pay a fixed or determinable sum of

*Editorial comment: The reference is now Sec. 165(i).

**Editorial comment: The Regulations do not reflect the repeal of the reserve method by the Tax Reform Act of 1986.

money. A debt arising out of the receivables of an accrual method taxpayer is deemed to be an enforceable obligation for purposes of the preceding sentence to the extent that the income such debt represents have been included in the return of income for the year for which the deduction as a bad debt is claimed or for a prior taxable year. For example, a debt arising out of gambling receivables that are unenforceable under state or local law, which an accrual method taxpayer includes in income under section 61, is an enforceable obligation for purposes of this paragraph. A gift or contribution to capital shall not be considered a debt for purposes of section 166. The fact that a bad debt is not due at the time of deduction shall not of itself prevent its allowance under section 166. * * *

(d) Amount deductible—(1) General rule. Except in the case of a deduction for a reasonable addition to a reserve for bad debts, the basis for determining the amount of deduction under section 166 in respect of a bad debt shall be the same as the adjusted basis prescribed by § 1.1011–1 for determining the loss from the sale or other disposition of property.* * *

(2) Specific cases. Subject to any provision of section 166 and the regulations thereunder which provides to the contrary, the following amounts are deductible as bad debts:

(i) Notes or accounts receivable. **(a)** If, in computing taxable income, a taxpayer values his notes or accounts receivable at their fair market value when received, the amount deductible as a bad debt under section 166 in respect of such receivables shall be limited to such fair market value even though it is less than their face value.

(b) A purchaser of accounts receivable which become worthless during the taxable year shall be entitled under section 166 to a deduction which is based upon the price he paid for such receivables but not upon their face value.

(ii) Bankruptcy claim. Only the difference between the amount received in distribution of the assets of a bankrupt and the amount of the claim may be deducted under section 166 as a bad debt.

(iii) Claim against decedent's estate. The excess of the amount of the claim over the amount received by a creditor of a decedent in distribution of the assets of the decedent's estate may be considered a worthless debt under section 166.

(e) Prior inclusion in income required. Worthless debts arising from unpaid wages, salaries, fees, rents, and similar items of taxable income shall not be allowed as a deduction under section 166 unless the income such items represent has been included in the return of income for the year for which the deduction as a bad debt is claimed or for a prior taxable year.

(f) Recovery of bad debts. Any amount attributable to the recovery during the taxable year of a bad debt, or of a part of a bad debt, which was allowed as a deduction from gross income in a prior taxable year shall be included in gross income for the taxable year of recovery, except to the extent that the recovery is excluded from gross income under the provisions of § 1.111–1, relating to the recovery of certain items previously deducted or credited.* * *

(g) Worthless securities. (1) Section 166 and the regulations thereunder do not apply to a debt which is evidenced by a bond, debenture, note, or certificate, or other evidence of indebtedness, issued by a corporation or by a government or political subdivision thereof, with interest coupons or in registered form. See section 166(e). For provisions allowing the deduction of a loss resulting from the worthlessness of such a debt, see § 1.165–5.

* * *

§ 1.166–2 Evidence of worthlessness.

(a) General rule. In determining whether a debt is worthless in whole or in part the district director will consider all pertinent evidence, including the value of the collateral, if any, securing the debt and the financial condition of the debtor.

(b) Legal action not required. Where the surrounding circumstances indicate that a debt is worthless and uncollectible and that legal action to enforce payment would in all probability not result in the satisfaction of execution on a judgment, a showing of these facts will be sufficient evidence of the worthlessness of the debt for purposes of the deduction under section 166.

(c) Bankruptcy—(1) General rule. Bankruptcy is generally an indication of the worthlessness of at least a part of an unsecured and unpreferred debt.

(2) Year of deduction. In bankruptcy cases a debt may become worthless before settlement in some instances; and in others, only when a settlement in bankruptcy has been reached. In either case, the mere fact that bankruptcy proceedings instituted against the debtor are terminated in a later year, thereby confirming the conclusion that the debt is worthless, shall not authorize the shifting of the deduction under section 166 to such later year.

* * *

§ 1.166–3 Partial or total worthlessness.

(a) Partial worthlessness—(1) Applicable to specific debts only. A deduction under section 166(a)(2) on account of partially worthless debts shall be allowed with respect to specific debts only.

(2) Charge-off required. **(i)** If, from all the surrounding and attending circumstances, the district director is satisfied that a debt is partially worthless, the amount which has become worthless shall be allowed as a deduction under section 166(a)(2) but only to the extent charged off during the taxable year.

(ii) If a taxpayer claims a deduction for a part of a debt for the taxable year within which that part of the debt is charged off and the deduction is disallowed for that taxable year, then, in a case where the debt becomes partially worthless after the close of that taxable year, a deduction under section 166(a)(2) shall be allowed for a subsequent taxable year but not in excess of the amount charged off in the prior taxable year plus any amount charged off in the subsequent taxable year. In such instance, the charge-off in the prior taxable year shall, if consistently maintained as such, be sufficient to that extent to meet the charge-off requirement of section 166(a)(2) with respect to the subsequent taxable year.

(iii) Before a taxpayer may deduct a debt in part, he must be able to demonstrate to the satisfaction of the district director the amount thereof which is worthless and the part thereof which has been charged off.

(b) Total worthlessness. If a debt becomes wholly worthless during the taxable year, the amount thereof which has not been allowed as a deduction from gross income for any prior taxable year shall be allowed as a deduction for the current taxable year.

* * *

§ 1.166–5 Nonbusiness debts.

(a) Allowance of deduction as capital loss. (1) The loss resulting from any nonbusiness debt's becoming partially or wholly worthless within the taxable year shall not be allowed as a deduction under either section 166(a) or section 166(c) in determining the taxable income of a taxpayer other than a corporation. See section 166(d)(1)(A).

(2) If, in the case of a taxpayer other than a corporation, a nonbusiness debt becomes wholly worthless within the taxable year, the loss resulting therefrom shall be treated as a loss from the sale or exchange, during the taxable year, of a capital asset held for not more than 1 year (6 months for taxable years beginning before 1977; 9 months for taxable years beginning in 1977). Such a loss is subject to the limitations provided in section 1211, relating to the limitation on capital losses, and section 1212, relating to the capital loss carryover, and in the regulations under those sections. A loss on a nonbusiness debt shall be treated as sustained only if and when the debt has become totally worthless, and no deduction shall be allowed for a nonbusiness debt which is recoverable in part during the taxable year.

(b) Nonbusiness debt defined. For purposes of section 166 and this section, a nonbusiness debt is any debt other than—

(1) A debt which is created, or acquired, in the course of a trade or business of the taxpayer, determined without regard to the relationship of the debt to a trade or business of the taxpayer at the time when the debt becomes worthless; or

(2) A debt the loss from the worthlessness of which is incurred in the taxpayer's trade or business.

The question whether a debt is a nonbusiness debt is a question of fact in each particular case. The determination of whether the loss on a debt's becoming worthless has been incurred in a trade or business of the taxpayer shall, for this purpose, be made in substantially the same manner for determining whether a loss has been incurred in a trade or business for purposes of section 165(c)(1). For purposes of subparagraph (2) of this paragraph, the character of the debt is to be determined by the relation which the loss resulting from the debt's becoming worthless bears to the trade or business of the taxpayer. If that relation is a proximate one in the conduct of the trade or business in which the taxpayer is engaged at the time the debt becomes worthless, the debt comes within the exception provided by that subparagraph. The use to which the borrowed funds are put by the debtor is of no consequence in making a determination under this paragraph. For purposes of section 166 and this section, a nonbusiness debt does not include a debt described in section 165(g)(2)(C). See § 1.165–5, relating to losses on worthless securities.

(c) Guaranty of obligations. For provisions treating a loss sustained by a guarantor of obligations as a loss resulting from the worthlessness of a debt, see §§ 1.166–8 and 1.166–9.

(d) Examples. The application of this section may be illustrated by the following examples involving a case where A, an individual who is engaged in the grocery business and who makes his return on the basis of the calendar year, extends credit to B in 1955 on an open account:

Example (1). In 1956 A sells the business but retains the claim against B. The claim becomes worthless in A's hands in 1957. A's loss is not controlled by the nonbusiness debt provisions, since the original consideration has been advanced by A in his trade or business.

Example (2). In 1956 A sells the business to C but sells the claim against B to the taxpayer, D. The claim becomes worthless in D's hands in 1957. During 1956 and 1957, D is not engaged in any trade or business. D's loss is controlled by the nonbusiness debt provisions even though the original consideration has been advanced by A in his trade or business, since the debt has not been created or acquired in connection with a trade or business of D and since in 1957 D is not engaged in a trade or business incident to the conduct of which a loss from the worthlessness of such claim is a proximate result.

Example (3). In 1956 A dies, leaving the business, including the accounts receivable, to his son, C, the taxpayer. The claim against B becomes worthless in C's hands in 1957. C's loss is not controlled by the nonbusiness debt provisions. While C does not advance any consideration for the claim, or create or acquire it in connection with his trade or business, the loss is sustained as a proximate incident to the conduct of the trade or business in which he is engaged at the time the debt becomes worthless.

Example (4). In 1956 A dies, leaving the business to his son, C, but leaving the claim against B to his son, D, the taxpayer. The claim against B becomes worthless in D's hands in 1957. During 1956 and 1957, D is not engaged in any trade or business. D's loss is controlled by the nonbusiness debt provisions even though the original consideration has been advanced by A in his trade or business, since the debt has not been created or acquired in connection with a trade or business of D and since in 1957 D is not engaged in a trade or business incident to the conduct of which a loss from the worthlessness of such claim is a proximate result.

Example (5). In 1956 A dies; and, while his executor, C, is carrying on the business, the claim against B becomes worthless in 1957. The loss sustained by A's estate is not controlled by the nonbusiness debt provisions. While C does not advance any consideration for the claim on behalf of the estate, or create or acquire it in connection with a trade or business in which the estate is engaged, the loss is sustained as a proximate incident to the conduct of the trade or business in which the estate is engaged at the time the debt becomes worthless.

Example (6). In 1956, A, in liquidating the business, attempts to collect the claim against B but finds that it has become worthless. A's loss is not controlled by the nonbusiness debt provisions, since the original consideration has been advanced by A in his trade or business and since a loss incurred in liquidating a trade or business is a proximate incident to the conduct thereof.

§ 1.166–6 Sale of mortgaged or pledged property.

(a) Deficiency deductible as bad debt—(1) Principal amount. If mortgaged or pledged property is lawfully sold (whether to the creditor or another purchaser) for less than the amount of the debt, and the portion of the indebtedness remaining unsatisfied after the sale is wholly or partially uncollectible, the mortgagee or pledgee may deduct such amount under section 166(a)(to the extent that it constitutes capital or represents an item the income from which has been returned by him) as a bad debt for the taxable year in which it becomes wholly worthless or is charged off as partially worthless. See § 1.166–3.

(2) Accrued interest. Accrued interest may be included as part of the deduction allowable under this paragraph, but only if it has previously been returned as income.

* * *

§ 1.166–9 Losses of guarantors, endorsers, and indemnitors incurred, on agreements made after december 31, 1975, in taxable years beginning after such date.

(a) Payment treated as worthless business debt. This paragraph applies to taxpayers who, after December 31, 1975, enter into an agreement in the course of their trade or business to act as (or in a manner essentially equivalent to) a guarantor, endorser, or indemnitor of (or other secondary obligor upon) a debt obligation. Subject to the provisions of paragraphs (c), (d), and (e) of this section, a payment of principal or interest made during a taxable year beginning after December 31, 1975, by the taxpayer in discharge of part or all of the taxpayer's obligation as a guarantor, endorser, or indemnitor is treated as a business debt becoming worthless in the taxable year in which the payment is made or in the taxable year described in paragraph (e)(2) of this section. Neither section 163 (relating to interest) nor section 165 (relating to losses) shall apply with respect to such a payment.

(b) Payment treated as worthless nonbusiness debt. This paragraph applies to taxpayers (other than corporations) who, after December 31, 1975, enter into a transaction for profit, but not in the course of their trade or business, to act as (or in a manner essentially equivalent to) a guarantor, endorser, or indemnitor of (or other secondary obligor upon) a debt obligation. Subject to the provisions of paragraphs (c), (d), and (e) of this section, a payment of principal or interest made during a taxable year beginning after December 31, 1975, by the taxpayer in discharge of part or all of the taxpayer's obligation as a guarantor, endorser, or indemnitor is treated as a worthless nonbusiness debt in the taxable year in which the payment is made or in the taxable year described in paragraph (e)(2) of this section. Neither section 163 nor section 165 shall apply with respect to such a payment.

(c) Obligations issued by corporations. No treatment as a worthless debt is allowed with respect to a payment made by the taxpayer in discharge of part or all of the taxpayer's obligation as a guarantor, endorser, or indemnitor of an obligation issued by a corporation if, on the basis of the facts and circumstances at the time the obligation was entered into, the payment constitutes a contribution to capital by a shareholder. The rule of this paragraph (c) applies to payments whenever made (see paragraph (f) of this section).

(d) Certain payments treated as worthless debts. A payment in discharge of part or all of taxpayer's agreement to act as guarantor, endorser, or indemnitor of an obligation is to be treated as a worthless debt only if—

(1) The agreement was entered into in the course of the taxpayer's trade or business or a transaction for profit;

(2) There was an enforceable legal duty upon the taxpayer to make the payment (except that legal action need not have been brought against the taxpayer); and

(3) The agreement was entered into before the obligation became worthless (or partially worthless in the case of an agreement entered into in the course of the taxpayer's trade or business). See §§ 1.166–2 and 1.166–3 for rules on worthless and partially worthless debts. For purposes of this paragraph (d)(3), an agreement is considered as entered into before the obligation became worthless (or partially worthless) if there was a reasonable expectation on the part of the taxpayer at the time the agreement was entered into that the taxpayer would not be called upon to pay the debt (subject to such agreement) without full reimbursement from the issuer of the obligation.

(e) Special rules—(1) Reasonable consideration required. Treatment as a worthless debt of a payment made by a taxpayer in discharge of part or all of the taxpayer's agreement to act as a guarantor, endorser, or indemnitor of an obligation is allowed only if the taxpayer demonstrates that reasonable consideration was received for entering into the agreement. For purposes of this paragraph (e)(1), reasonable consideration is not limited to direct consideration in the form of cash or property. Thus, where a taxpayer can demonstrate that the agreement was given without direct consideration in the form of cash or property but in accordance with normal business practice or for a good faith business purpose, worthless debt treatment is allowed with respect to a payment in discharge of part or all of the agreement if the conditions of this section are met. However, consideration received from a taxpayer's spouse or any individual listed in section 152(a) must be direct consideration in the form of cash or property.

(2) Right of subrogation. With respect to a payment made by a taxpayer in discharge of part or all of the taxpayer's agreement to act as a guarantor, endorser, or indemnitor where the agreement provides for a right of subrogation or other similar right against the issuer, treatment as a worthless debt is not allowed until the taxable year in which the right of subrogation or other similar right becomes totally worthless (or partially worthless in the case of an agreement which arose in the course of the taxpayer's trade or business).

* * *

§ 1.170A–1 Charitable, etc., contributions and gifts; allowance of deduction.

(a) Allowance of deduction. Any charitable contribution, as defined in section 170(c), actually paid during the taxable year is allowable as a deduction in computing taxable income irrespective of the method of accounting employed or of the date on which the contribution is pledged. However, charitable contributions by corporations may under certain circumstances be deductible even though not paid during the taxable year as provided in section 170(a)(2) and § 1.170A–11. For rules relating to recordkeeping and return requirements in support of deductions for charitable contributions* * *see § 1.170A–13. The deduction is subject to the limitations of section 170(b) and § 1.170A–8 or § 1.170A–11. Subject to the provisions of section 170(d) and §§ 1.170A–10 and 1.170A–11, certain excess charitable contributions made by individuals and corporations shall be treated as paid in certain succeeding taxable years.* * * For rules relating to the determination of, and the deduction for, amounts paid to maintain certain students as members of the taxpayer's household and treated under section 170(g) as paid for the use of an organization described in section 170(c)(2), (3), or (4), see § 1.170A–2. For the reduction of any charitable contributions for interest on certain indebtedness, see section 170(f)(5) and § 1.170A–3. For a special rule relating to the computation of the amount of the deduction with respect to a charitable contribution of certain ordinary income or capital gain property, see section 170(e) and §§ 1.170A–4 and § 1.170A–4A. For rules for postponing the time for deduction of a charitable contribution of a future interest in tangible personal property, see section 170(a)(3) and § 1.170A–5. For rules with respect to transfers in trust and of partial interests in property, see section 170(e), section 170(f)(2) and (3), §§ 1.170A–4, § 1.170A–6, and § 1.170A–7. For definition of the term "section 170(b)(1)(A) organization," see § 1.170A–9. For valuation of a remainder interest in real property, see section 170(f)(4) and the regulations thereunder. The deduction for charitable contributions is subject to verification by the district director.

(b) Time of making contribution. Ordinarily, a contribution is made at the time delivery is effected. The unconditional delivery or mailing of a check which subsequently clears in due course will constitute an effective contribution on the date of delivery or mailing. If a taxpayer unconditionally delivers or mails a properly endorsed stock certificate to a charitable donee or the donee's agent, the gift is completed on the date of delivery or, if such certificate is received in the ordinary course of the mails, on the date of mailing. If the donor delivers the stock certificate to his bank or broker as the donor's agent, or to the issuing corporation or its agent, for transfer into the name of the donee, the gift is completed on the date the stock is transferred on the books of the corporation. For rules relating to the date of payment of a contribution consisting of a future interest in tangible personal property, see section 170(a)(3) and § 1.170A–5.

(c) Value of a contribution in property. **(1)** If a charitable contribution is made in property other than money, the amount of the contribution is the fair market value of the property at the time of the contribution reduced as provided in section 170(e)(1) and paragraph (a) of § 1.170A–4, or section 170(e)(3) and paragraph (c) of § 1.170A–4A.

(2) The fair market value is the price at which the property would change hands between a willing buyer and a willing seller, neither being under any compulsion to buy or sell and both having reasonable knowledge of relevant facts. If the contribution is made in property of a type which the taxpayer sells in the course of his business, the fair market value is the price which the taxpayer would have received if he had sold the contributed property in the usual market in which he customarily sells, at the time and place of the contribution and, in the case of a contribution of goods in quantity, in the quantity contributed. The usual market of a manufacturer or other producer consists of the wholesalers or other distributors to or through whom he customarily sells, but if he sells only at retail the usual market consists of his retail customers.

(3) If a donor makes a charitable contribution of property, such as stock in trade, at a time when he could not reasonably have been expected to realize its usual selling price, the value of the gift is not the usual selling price but is the amount for which the quantity of property contributed would have been sold by the donor at the time of the contribution.

(4) Any costs and expenses pertaining to the contributed property which were incurred in taxable years preceding the year of contribution and are properly reflected in the opening inventory for the year of contribution must be removed from inventory and are not a part of the cost of goods sold for purposes of determining gross income for the year of contribution. Any costs and expenses pertaining to the contributed property which are incurred in the year of contribution and would, under the method of accounting used, be properly reflected in the cost of goods sold for such year are to be treated as part of the costs of goods sold for such year. If costs and expenses incurred in producing or acquiring the contributed property are, under the method of accounting used, properly deducted under section 162 or other section of the Code, such costs and expenses will be allowed as deductions for the taxable year in which they are paid or incurred whether or not such year is the year of the contribution. Any such costs and expenses which are treated as part of the cost of goods sold for the year of contribution, and any such costs and expenses which are properly deducted under section 162 or other section of the Code, are not to be treated under any section of the Code as resulting in any basis for the contributed property. Thus, for example, the contributed property has no basis for purposes of determining under section 170(e)(1)(A) and paragraph (a) of § 1.170A–4 the amount of gain which would have been recognized if such property had been sold by the donor at its fair market value at the time of its contribution. The amount of any charitable contribution for the taxable year is not to be reduced by the amount of any costs or expenses pertaining to the contributed property which was properly deducted under section 162 or other section of the Code for any taxable year preceding the year of the contribution. This subparagraph applies only to property which was held by the taxpayer for sale in the course of a trade or business. The application of this subparagraph may be illustrated by the following examples:

Example (1). In 1970, A, an individual using the calendar year as the taxable year and the accrual method of accounting, contributed to a church property from inventory having a fair market value of $600. The closing inventory at the end of 1969 properly included $400 of costs attributable to the acquisition of such property, and in 1969 A properly deducted under section 162 $50 of administrative and other expenses attributable to such property. Under section 170(e)(1)(A) and paragraph (a) of § 1.170A–4, the amount of the charitable contribution allowed for 1970 is $400 ($600–[$600–$400]). Pursuant to this subparagraph, the cost of goods sold to be used in determining gross income for 1970 may not include the $400 which was included in opening inventory for that year.

Example (2). The facts are the same as in example (1) except that the contributed property was acquired in 1970 at a cost of $400. The $400 cost of the property is included in determining the cost of goods sold for 1970, and $50 is allowed as a deduction for that year under section 162. A is not allowed any deduction under section 170 for the contributed property, since under section 170(e)(1)(A) and paragraph (a) of § 1.170A–4 the amount of the charitable contribution is reduced to zero ($600–[$600–$0]).

Example (3). In 1970, B, an individual using the calendar year as the taxable year and the accrual method of accounting, contributed to a church property from inventory having a fair market value of $600. Under § 1.471–3(c), the closing inventory at the end of 1969 properly included $450 costs attributable to the production of such property, including $50 of administrative and other indirect expenses which, under his method of accounting, was properly added to inventory rather than deducted as a business expense. Under section 170(e)(1)(A) and paragraph (a) of § 1.170A–4, the amount of the charitable contribution allowed for 1970 is $450 ($600–[$600–$450]). Pursuant to this subparagraph, the cost of goods sold to be used in determining gross income for 1970 may not include the $450 which was included in opening inventory for that year.

Example (4). The facts are the same as in example (3) except that the contributed property was produced in 1970 at a cost of $450, including $50 of administrative and other indirect expenses. The $450 cost of the property is included in determining the cost of goods sold for 1970. B is not allowed any deduction under section 170 for the contributed property, since under section 170(e)(1)(A) and paragraph (a) of § 1.170A–4 the amount of the charitable contribution is reduced to zero ($600–[$600–$0]).

Example (5). In 1970, C, a farmer using the cash method of accounting and the calendar year as the taxable year, contributed to a church a quantity of grain which he had raised having a fair market value of $600. In 1969, C paid expenses of $450 in raising the property which he properly deducted for such year under section 162. Under section 170(e)(1)(A) and paragraph (a) of § 1.170A–4, the amount of the charitable contribution in 1970 is reduced to zero ($600–[$600–$0]). Accordingly, C is not allowed any deduction under section 170 for the contributed property.

Example (6). The facts are the same as in example (5) except that the $450 expenses incurred in raising the contributed property were paid in 1970. The result is the same as in example (5), except the amount of $450 is deductible under section 162 for 1970.

(5) Transfers of property to an organization described in section 170(c) which bear a direct relationship to the taxpayer's trade or business and which are made with a reasonable expectation of financial return commensurate with the amount of the transfer may constitute allowable deductions as trade or business expenses rather than as charitable contributions. See section 162 and the regulations thereunder.

* * *

(e) Transfers subject to a condition or power. If as of the date of a gift a transfer for charitable purposes is dependent upon the performance of some act or the happening of a precedent event in order that it might become effective, no deduction is allowable unless the possibility that the charitable transfer will not become effective is so remote as to be negligible. If an interest in property passes to, or is vested in, charity on the date of the gift and the interest would be defeated by the subsequent performance of some act or the happening of some event, the possibility of occurrence of which appears on the date of the gift to be so remote as to be negligible, the deduction is allowable. For example, A transfers land to a city government for as long as the land is used by the city for a public park. If on the date of the gift the city does plan to use the land for a park and the possibility that the city will not use the land for a public park is so remote as to be negligible, A is entitled to a deduction under section 170 for his charitable contribution.

* * *

(g) Contributions of services. No deduction is allowable under section 170 for a contribution of services. However, unreimbursed expenditures made incident to the rendition of services to an organization contributions to which are deductible may constitute a deductible contribution. For example, the cost of a uniform without general utility which is required to be worn in performing donated services is deductible. Similarly, out-of-pocket transportation expenses necessarily incurred in performing donated services are deductible. Reasonable expenditures for meals and lodging necessarily incurred while away from home in the course of performing donated services also are deductible. For the purposes of this paragraph, the phrase "while away from home" has the same meaning as that phrase is used for purposes of section 162 and the regulations thereunder.

* * *

§ 1.170A–4 Reduction in amount of charitable contributions of certain appreciated property.

(a) Amount of reduction. Section 170(e)(1) requires that the amount of the charitable contribution which would be taken into account under section 170(a) without regard to section 170(e) shall be reduced before applying the percentage limitations under section 170(b)—

(1) In the case of a contribution by an individual or by a corporation of ordinary income property, as defined in paragraph (b)(1) of this section, by the amount of gain (hereinafter in this section referred to as ordinary income) which would have been recognized as gain which is not long-term capital gain if the property had been sold by the donor at its fair market value at the time of its contribution to the charitable organization,

(2) In the case of a contribution by an individual of section 170(e) capital gain property, as defined in paragraph (b)(2) of this section, by 50 percent* of the amount of gain (hereinafter in this section referred to as long-term capital gain) which would have been recognized as long-term capital gain if the property had been sold by the donor at its fair market value at the time of its contribution to the charitable organization, and

(3) In the case of a contribution by a corporation of section 170(e) capital gain property, as defined in paragraph (b)(2) of this section, by 62½ percent* of the amount of gain (hereinafter in this section referred to as long-term capital gain) which would have been recognized as long-term capital gain if the property had been sold by the donor at its fair market value at the time of its contribution to the charitable organization.

Section 170(e)(1) and this paragraph do not apply to reduce the amount of the charitable contribution where, by reason of the transfer of the contributed property, ordinary income or capital gain is recognized by the donor in the same taxable year in which the contribution is made. Thus, where income or gain is recognized under section 453(d) upon the transfer of an installment obligation to a charitable organization, or under section 454(b) upon the transfer of an obligation issued at a discount to such an organization, or upon the assignment of income to such an organization, section 170(e)(1) and this paragraph do not apply if recognition of the income or gain occurs in the same taxable year in which the contribution is made. Section 170(e)(1) and this paragraph apply to a charitable contribution of an interest in ordinary income property or section 170(e) capital gain property which is described in paragraph (b) of § 1.170A–6, or paragraph (b) of § 1.170A–7. For purposes of applying section 170(e)(1) and this paragraph it is immaterial whether the charitable contribution is made "to" the charitable organization or whether it is made "for the use of" the charitable organization. See § 1.170A–8(a)(2).

(b) Definitions and other rules. For purposes of this section—

(1) Ordinary income property. The term "ordinary income property" means property any portion of the gain on which would not have been long term capital gain if the property had been sold by the donor at its fair market value at the time of its contribution to the charitable organization. Such term includes, for example, property held by the donor primarily for sale to customers in the ordinary course of his trade or business, a work of art created by the donor, a manuscript prepared by the donor, letters and memorandums prepared by or for the donor, a capital asset held by the donor for not more than 1 year (6 months for taxable years beginning before 1977; 9 months for taxable years beginning in 1977), and stock described in section 306(a), 341(a), or 1248(a) to the extent that, after applying such section, gain on its disposition would not have been long-term capital gain. The term does not include an income interest in respect of which a deduction is allowed under section 170(f)(2)(B) and paragraph (c) of § 1.170A–6.

*Editorial comment: The Regulations do not reflect the effect of the Tax Reform Act of 1986 which has increased this percentage to 100 percent. Likewise, the Regulations do not reflect the third option provided in Sec. 170(e)(1)(B)(iii) which requires a 100 percent negative adjustment associated with the charitable contribution of certain intangible property held for the long-term holding period [change made in the American Jobs Creation Act of 2004].

(2) Section 170(e) capital gain property. The term "section 170(e) capital gain property" means property any portion of the gain on which would have been treated as long-term capital gain if the property had been sold by the donor at its fair market value at the time of its contribution to the charitable organization and which—

(i) Is contributed to or for the use of a private foundation, as defined in section 509(a) and the regulations thereunder, other than a private foundation described in section 170(b)(1)(E),

(ii) Constitutes tangible personal property contributed to or for the use of a charitable organization, other than a private foundation to which subdivision (i) of this subparagraph applies, which is put to an unrelated use by the charitable organization within the meaning of subparagraph (3) of this paragraph, or

(iii) Constitutes property not described in subdivision (i) or (ii) of this subparagraph which is 30-percent capital gain property to which an election under paragraph (d)(2) of § 1.170A–8 applies.

For purposes of this subparagraph a fixture which is intended to be severed from real property shall be treated as tangible personal property.

(3) Unrelated use— (i) In general. The term "unrelated use" means a use which is unrelated to the purpose or function constituting the basis of the charitable organization's exemption under section 501 or, in the case of a contribution of property to a governmental unit, the use of such property by such unit for other than exclusively public purposes. For example, if a painting contributed to an educational institution is used by that organization for educational purposes by being placed in its library for display and study by art students, the use is not an unrelated use; but if the painting is sold and the proceeds used by the organization for educational purposes, the use of the property is an unrelated use. If furnishings contributed to a charitable organization are used by it in its offices and buildings in the course of carrying out its functions, the use of the property is not an unrelated use. If a set or collection of items of tangible personal property is contributed to a charitable organization or governmental unit, the use of the set or collection is not an unrelated use if the donee sells or otherwise disposes of only an insubstantial portion of the set or collection. The use by a trust of tangible personal property contributed to it for the benefit of a charitable organization is an unrelated use if the use by the trust is one which would have been unrelated if made by the charitable organization.

(ii) Proof of use. For purposes of applying subparagraph (2)(ii) of this paragraph, a taxpayer who makes a charitable contribution of tangible personal property to or for the use of a charitable organization or governmental unit may treat such property as not being put to an unrelated use by the donee if—

(a) He establishes that the property is not in fact put to an unrelated use by the donee, or

(b) At the time of the contribution or at the time the contribution is treated as made, it is reasonable to anticipate that the property will not be put to an unrelated use by the donee. In the case of a contribution of tangible personal property to or for the use of a museum, if the object donated is of a general type normally retained by such museum or other museums for museum purposes, it will be reasonable for the donor to anticipate, unless he has actual knowledge to the contrary, that the object will not be put to an unrelated use by the donee, whether or not the object is later sold or exchanged by the donee.

(4) Property used in trade or business. For purposes of applying subparagraphs (1) and (2) of this paragraph, property which is used in the trade or business, as defined in section 1231(b), shall be treated as a capital asset, except that any gain in respect of such property which would have been recognized if the property had been sold by the donor at its fair market value at the time of its contribution to the charitable organization shall be treated as ordinary income to the extent that such gain would have constituted ordinary income by reason of the application of section 617(d)(1), 1245(a), 1250(a), 1251(c), 1252(a), or 1254(a).

* * *

(c) Allocation of basis and gain— (1) In general. Except as provided in subparagraph (2) of this paragraph—

(i) If a taxpayer makes a charitable contribution of less than his entire interest in appreciated property, whether or not the transfer is made in trust, as, for example, in the case of a transfer of appreciated property to a pooled income fund described in section 642(c)(5) and § 1.642(c)–5, and is allowed a deduction under section 170 for a portion of the fair market value of such property, then for purposes of applying the reduction rules of section 170(e)(1) and this section to the contributed portion of the property the taxpayer's adjusted basis in such property at the time of the contribution shall be allocated under section 170(e)(2) between the contributed portion of the property and the non-contributed portion.

(ii) The adjusted basis of the contributed portion of the property shall be that portion of the adjusted basis of the entire property which bears the same ratio to the total adjusted basis as the fair market value of the contributed portion of the property bears to the fair market value of the entire property.

(iii) The ordinary income and the long-term capital gain which shall be taken into account in applying section 170(e)(1) and paragraph (a) of this section to the contributed portion of the property shall be the amount of gain which would have been recognized as ordinary income and long-term capital gain if such contributed portion had been sold by the donor at its fair market value at the time of its contribution to the charitable organization.

(2) Bargain sale. (i) Section 1011(b) and § 1.1011–2 apply to bargain sales of property to charitable organizations. For purposes of applying the reduction rules of section 170(e)(1) and this section to the contributed portion of the property in the case of a bargain sale, there shall be allocated under section 1011(b) to the contributed portion of the property that portion of the adjusted basis of the entire property that bears the same ratio to the total adjusted basis as the fair market value of the contributed portion of the property bears to the fair market value of the entire property. For purposes of applying section 170(e)(1) and paragraph (a) of this section to the contributed portion of the property in such a case, there shall be allocated to the contributed portion the amount of gain that is not recognized on the bargain sale but that would have been recognized if such contributed portion had been sold by the donor at its fair market value at the time of its contribution to the charitable organization.

(ii) The term "bargain sale," as used in this subparagraph, means a transfer of property which is in part a sale or exchange of the property and in part a charitable contribution, as defined in section 170(c), of the property.

(3) Ratio of ordinary income and capital gain. For purposes of applying subparagraphs (1)(iii) and (2)(i) of this paragraph, the amount of ordinary income (or long-term capital gain) which would have been recognized if the contributed portion of the property had been sold by the donor at its fair market value at the time of its contribution shall be that amount which bears the same ratio to the ordinary income (or long-term capital gain) which would have been recognized if the entire property had been sold by the donor at its fair market value at the time of its contribution as (i) the fair market value of the contributed portion at such time bears to (ii) the fair market value of the entire property at such time. In the case of a bargain sale, the fair market value of the contributed portion for purposes of subdivision (i) is the amount determined by subtracting from the fair market value of the entire property the amount realized on the sale.

(4) Donee's basis of property acquired. The adjusted basis of the contributed portion of the property, as determined under subparagraph (1) or (2) of this paragraph, shall be used by the donee in applying to the contributed portion such provisions as section 514(a)(1), relating to adjusted basis of debt-financed property; section 1015(a), relating to basis of property acquired by gift; section 4940(c)(4), relating to capital gains and losses in determination of net investment income; and section 4942(f)(2)(B), relating to net short-term capital gain in determination of tax on failure to distribute income. The fair market value of the contributed portion of the property at the time of the contribution shall not be used by the donee as the basis of such contributed portion.

(d) Illustrations.* The application of this section may be illustrated by the following examples:

Example (1). (a) On July 1, 1970, C, an individual, makes the following charitable contributions, all of which are made to a church except in the case of the stock (as indicated):

Property	Fair market value	Adjusted basis	Recognized gain sold
Ordinary income property	$50,000	$35,000	$15,000
Property which, if sold, would produce long-term capital gain:			
(1) Stock held more than 6 months contributed to—			
(i) A church	25,000	21,000	4,000
(ii) A private foundation not described in section 170(b)(1)(E)	15,000	10,000	5,000
(2) Tangible personal property held more than 6 months (put to unrelated use by church)	12,000	6,000	6,000
Total	102,000	72,000	30,000

(b) After making the reductions required by paragraph (a) of this section, the amount of charitable contributions allowed (before application of section 170(b) limitations) is as follows:

Property	Fair market value	Reduction	Contribution allowed
Ordinary income property	$50,000	$15,000	$35,000
Property which, if sold, would produce long-term capital gain:			
(1) Stock contributed to—			
(i) The church	25,000	.....	25,000
(ii) The private foundation	15,000	2,500	12,500
(2) Tangible personal property	12,000	3,000	9,000
Total	102,000	20,500	81,500

(c) If C were a corporation, rather than an individual, the amount of charitable contributions allowed (before application of section 170(b) limitation) would be as follows:

Property	Fair market value	Reduction	Contribution allowed
Ordinary income property	$50,000	$15,000	$35,000
Property which, if sold, would produce long-term capital gain:			
(1) Stock contributed to—			
(i) The church	25,000	.....	25,000
(ii) The private foundation	15,000	3,125	11,875
(2) Tangible personal property	12,000	3,750	8,250
Total	102,000	21,875	80,125

Example (2). On March 1, 1970, D, an individual, contributes to a church intangible property to which section 1245 applies which has a fair market value of $60,000 and an adjusted basis of $10,000. At the time of the contribution D has used the property in his business for more than 6 months. If the property had been sold by D at its fair market value at the time of its contribution, it is assumed that under section 1245 $20,000 of the gain of $50,000 would have been treated as ordinary income and $30,000 would have been long-term capital gain. Under paragraph (a)(1) of this section, D's contribution of $60,000 is reduced by $20,000.

Example (3). The facts are the same as in example (2) except that the property is contributed to a private foundation not described in section 170(b)(1)(E). Under paragraph (a)(1) and (2) of this section, D's contribution is reduced by $35,000 (100 percent of the ordinary income of $20,000 and 50 percent of the long-term capital gain of $30,000).

Example (4). (a) In 1971, E, an individual calendar-year taxpayer, contributes to a church stock held for more than 6 months which has a fair market value of $90,000 and an adjusted basis of $10,000. In 1972, E also contributes to a church stock held for more than 6 months which has a fair market value of $20,000 and an adjusted basis of $10,000. E's contribution base for 1971 is $200,000; and for 1972, is $150,000. E makes no other charitable contributions for these 2 taxable years.

(b) For 1971 the amount of the contribution which may be taken into account under section 170(a) is limited by section 170(b)(1)(D)(i) to $60,000 ($200,000 × 30%), and A is allowed a deduction for $60,000. Under section 170(b)(1)(D)(ii), E has a $30,000 carryover to 1972 of 30-percent capital gain property, as defined in paragraph (d)(3) of § 1.170A–8. For 1972 the amount of the charitable contributions deduction is $45,000 (total contributions of $50,000 [$30,000 + $20,000] but not to exceed 30% of $150,000).

(c) Assuming, however, that in 1972 E elects under section 170(b)(1)(D)(iii) and paragraph (d)(2) of § 1.170A–8 to have section 170(e)(1)(B) apply to his contributions and carryovers of 30-percent capital gain property, he must apply section 170(d)(1) as if section 170(e)(1)(B) had applied to the contribution for 1971. If section 170(e)(1)(B) had applied in 1971 to his contributions of 30-percent capital gain property, E's contribution would have been reduced from $90,000 to $50,000, the reduction of $40,000 being 50 percent of the gain of $80,000 ($90,000–$10,000) which would have been recognized as long-term capital gain if the property had been sold by E at its fair market value at the time of its contribution to the church. Accordingly, by taking the election into account, E has no carryover of 30-percent capital gain property to 1972 since the charitable contributions deduction of $60,000 allowed for 1971 in respect of that property exceeds the reduced contribution of $50,000 for 1971 which may be taken into account by reason of the election. The charitable contributions deduction of $60,000 allowed for 1971 is not reduced by reason of the election.

(d) Since by reason of the election E is allowed under paragraph (a)(2) of this section a charitable contributions deduction for 1972 of $15,000 ($20,000–[($20,000–$10,000) × 50%]) and since the $30,000 carryover from 1971 is eliminated, it would not be to E's advantage to make the election under section 170(b)(1)(D)(iii) in 1972.

Example (5). In 1970, F, an individual calendar-year taxpayer, sells to a church for $4,000 ordinary income property with a fair market value of $10,000 and an adjusted basis of $4,000. F's contribution base for 1970 is $20,000, and F makes no other charitable contributions in 1970. Thus, F makes a charitable contribution to the church of $6,000 ($10,000 – $4,000 amount realized), which is 60% of the value of the property. The amount realized on the bargain sale is 40% ($4,000/$ 10,000) of the value of the property. In applying section 1011(b) to the bargain sale, adjusted basis in the amount of $1,600 ($4,000 adjusted basis × 40%) is allocated under § 1.1011–2(b) to the non-contributed portion of the property, and F recognizes $2,400 ($4,000 amount realized less $1,600 adjusted basis) of ordinary income. Under paragraphs (a)(1) and (c)(2)(i) of this section, F's contribution of $6,000 is reduced by $3,600 ($6,000 – [$4,000 adjusted basis × 60%]) (i.e., the amount of ordinary income that would have been recognized on the contributed portion had the property been sold). The reduced contribution of $2,400 consists of the portion ($4,000 × 60%) of the adjusted basis not allocated to the noncontributed portion of the property. That is, the reduced contribution consists of the portion of the adjusted basis allocated to the contributed portion. Under sections 1012 and 1015(a) the basis of the property to the church is $6,400 ($4,000 + $2,400).

Example (6). In 1970, G, an individual calendar-year taxpayer, sells to a church for $6,000 ordinary income property with a fair market value of $10,000 and an adjusted basis of $4,000. G's contribution base for 1970 is $20,000, and G makes no other charitable contributions in 1970. Thus, G makes a charitable contribution to the church of $4,000 ($10,000 – $6,000 amount realized), which is 40% of the value of the property. The amount realized on the bargain sale is 60% ($6,000/$ 10,000) of the value of the property. In applying section 1011 (b) to the bargain sale, adjusted basis in the amount of $2,400 ($4,000 adjusted basis × 60%) is allocated under § 1.1011–2(b) to the noncontributed portion of the property, and G recognizes $3,600 ($6,000 amount realized less $2,400 adjusted basis) of ordinary income. Under paragraphs (a)(1) and (c)(2)(i) of this section, G's contribution of $4,000 is reduced by $2,400 ($4,000–[$4,000 adjusted basis × 40%]) (i.e., the amount of ordinary income that would have been recognized on the contributed portion had the property been sold). The reduced contribution of $1,600 consist of the portion ($4,000 × 40%) of the adjusted basis not allocated to the noncontributed portion of the property. That is, the reduced contribution consists of the portion of the adjusted basis allocated to the contributed portion. Under sections 1012 and 1015(a) the basis of the property to the church is $7,600 ($6,000 + $1,600).

Example (7). In 1970, H, an individual calendar-year taxpayer, sells to a church for $2,000 stock held for not more than 6 months which has an adjusted basis of $4,000 and a fair market value of $10,000. H's contribution base for 1970 is $20,000, and H makes no other charitable contributions in 1970. Thus, H makes a charitable contribution to the church of $8,000 ($10,000 – $2,000 amount realized), which is 80% of the value of the property. The amount realized on the bargain sale is 20% ($2,000/$ 10,000) of the value of the property. In applying section 1011 (b) to the bargain sale, adjusted basis in the amount of $800 ($4,000 adjusted basis × 20%) is allocated under § 1.1011–2(b) to the noncontributed portion of the property, and H recognizes $1,200 ($2,000 amount realized less $800 adjusted basis) of ordinary income. Under paragraphs (a)(1) and (c)(2)(i) of this section, H's contribution of $8,000 is reduced by $4,800 ($8,000 – [$4,000 adjusted basis × 80%]) (i.e., the amount of ordinary income that would have been recognized on the contributed portion had the property been sold). The reduced contribution of $3,200 consists of the portion ($4,000 × 80%) of the adjusted basis not allocated to the noncontributed portion of the property. That is, the reduced contribution consists of the portion of the adjusted basis allocated to the contributed portion. Under sections 1012 and 1015(a) the basis of the property to the church is $5,200 ($2,000 + $3,200).

Example (8). In 1970, F, an individual calendar-year taxpayer, sells for $4,000 to a private foundation not described in section 170(b)(1)(E) property to which section 1245 applies which has a fair market value of $10,000 and an adjusted basis of $4,000. F's contribution base for 1970 is $20,000, and F makes no other charitable contributions in 1970. At the time of the bargain sale, F has used the property in his business for more than 6 months. Thus F makes a charitable contribution of $6,000 ($10,000 – $4,000 amount realized), which is 60% of the value of the property. The amount realized on the bargain sale is 40% ($4,000/$10,000) of the value of the property. If the property had been sold by F at its fair market value at the time of its contribution, it is assumed that under section 1245 $4,000 of the gain of $6,000 ($10,000 – $4,000 adjusted basis) would have been treated as ordinary income and $2,000 would have been long-term capital gain. In applying section 1011(b) to the bargain sale, adjusted basis in the amount of $1,600 ($4,000 adjusted basis × 40%) is allocated under § 1.1011-2(b) to the noncontributed portion of the property, and F's recognized gain of $2,400 ($4,000 amount realized less $1,600 adjusted basis) consists of $1,600 ($4,000 × 40%) of ordinary income and $800 ($2,000 × 40%) of long-term capital gain. Under paragraphs (a) and (c)(2)(i) of this section, F's contribution of $6,000 is reduced by $3,000 (the sum of $2,400 ($4,000 × 60%) of ordinary income and $600 ([$2,000 × 60%] × 50%) of long-term capital gain) (i.e., the amount of gain that would have been recognized on the contributed portion had the property been sold). The reduced contribution of $3,000 consists of $2,400 ($4,000 × 60%) of adjusted basis and $600 ([$2,000 × 60%] × 50%) of long-term capital gain not used as a reduction under paragraph (a)(2) of this section. Under sections 1012 and 1015(a) the basis of the property to the private foundation is $6,400 ($4,000 + $2,400).

Example (9). On January 1, 1970, A, an individual, transfers to a charitable remainder annuity trust described in section 664(d)(1) stock which he has held for more than 6 months and which has a fair market value of $250,000 and an adjusted basis of $50,000, an irrevocable remainder interest in the property being contributed to a private foundation not described in section 170(b)(1)(E). The trusts provides that an annuity of $12,500 a year is payable to A at the end of each year for 20 years. By reference to Table B of § 20.203–10(f) of this chapter (Estate Tax Regulations) the figure in column (2) opposite 20 years is 11.4699. Therefore, under § 1.664–2 the fair market value of the gift of the remainder interest to charity is $106,626.25 ($250,000 – [$12,500 × 11.4699]). Under paragraph (c)(1)(ii) of this section, the adjusted basis allocated to the contributed portion of the property is $21,325.25 × ($50,000 × $106,626.25/$250,000). Under paragraphs (a)(2) and (c)(1) of this section, A's contribution is reduced by $42,650.50 (50 percent × [$106,626.25 – $21,325.25]) to $63,975.75 ($106,626.25 – $42,650.50). If, however, the irrevocable remainder interest in the property had been contributed to a section 170(b)(1)(A) organization, A's contribution of $106,626.25 would not be reduced under paragraph (a) of this section.

Example (10). (a) On July 1, 1970, B, a calendar-year individual taxpayer, sells to a church for $75,000 intangible property to which section 1245 applies which has a fair market value of $250,000 and an adjusted basis of $75,000. Thus, B makes a charitable contribution to the church of $175,000 ($250,000 – $75,000 amount realized), which is 70% ($175,000/$250,000) of the value of the property, the amount realized on the bargain sale is 30% ($75,000/$250,000) of the value of the property. At the time of the bargain sale, B has used the property in his business for more than 6 months. B's contribution base for 1970 is $500,000, and B makes no other charitable contributions in 1970. If the property had been sold by B at its fair market value at the time of its contribution, it is assumed that under section 1245 $105,000 of the gain of $175,000 ($250,000 – $75,000 adjusted basis) would have been treated as ordinary income and $70,000 would have been long-term capital gain. In applying section 1011(b) to the bargain sale, adjusted basis in the amount of $22,500 ($75,000 adjusted basis × 30%) is allocated under

§ 1.1011–2(b) to the noncontributed portion of the property and B's recognized gain of $52,500 ($75,000 amount realized less $22,500 adjusted basis) consists of $31,500 ($105,000 × 30%) of ordinary income and $21,000 ($70,000 × 30%) of long-term capital gain.

(b) Under paragraphs (a)(1) and (c)(2)(i) of this section B's contribution of $175,000 is reduced by $73,500 ($105,000 × 70%) (i.e., the amount of ordinary income that would have been recognized on the contributed portion had the property been sold). The reduced contribution of $101,500 consists of $52,500 [$75,000 × 70%] of adjusted basis allocated to the contributed portion of the property and $49,000 [$70,000 × 70%] of long-term capital gain allocated to the contributed portion. Under sections 1012 and 1015(a) the basis of the property to the church is $127,500 ($75,000 + $52,500).

* * *

§ 1.170A–4A Special rule for the deduction of certain charitable contributions of inventory and other property.

(a) Introduction. Section 170(e)(3) provides a special rule for the deduction of certain qualified contributions of inventory and certain other property. To be treated as a "qualified contribution", a contribution must meet the restrictions and requirements of section 170(e)(3)(A) and paragraph (b) of this section. Paragraph (b)(1) of this section describes the corporations whose contributions may be subject to this section, the exempt organizations to which these contributions may be made, and the kinds of property which may be contributed. Under paragraph (b)(2) of this section, the use of the property must be related to the purpose or function constituting the ground for the exemption of the organization to which the contribution is made. Also, the property must be used for the care of the ill, needy, or infants. Under paragraph (b)(3) of this section, the recipient organization may not, except as there provided, require or receive in exchange money, property, or services for the transfer or use of property contributed under section 170(e)(3). Under paragraph (b)(4) of this section, the recipient organization must provide the contributing taxpayer with a written statement representing that the organization intends to comply with the restrictions set forth in paragraph (b)(2) and (3) of this section on the use and transfer of the property. Under paragraph (b)(5) of this section, the contributed property must conform to any applicable provisions of the Federal Food, Drug, and Cosmetic Act (as amended), and the regulations thereunder, at the date of contribution and for the immediately preceding 180 days. Paragraph (c) of this section provides the rules for determining the amount of reduction of the charitable contribution under section 170(e)(3). In general, the amount of the reduction is equal to one-half of the amount of gain (other than gain described in paragraph (d) of this section) which would not have been long-term capital gain if the property had been sold by the donor-taxpayer at fair market value at the date of contribution. If, after this reduction, the amount of the deduction would be more than twice the basis of the contributed property, the amount of the deduction is accordingly further reduced under paragraph (c)(1) of this section. The basis of contributed property which is inventory is determined under paragraph (c)(2) of this section, and the donor's cost of goods sold for the year of contribution must be adjusted under paragraph (c)(3) of this section. Under paragraph (d) of this section, a deduction is not allowed for any amount which, if the property had been sold by the donor-taxpayer, would have been gain to which the recapture provisions of section 617, 1245, 1250, 1251, or 1252 would have applied. For purposes of section 170(e)(3) of rules of § 1.170A–4 apply where not inconsistent with the rules of this section.

(b) Qualified contributions— (1) In general. A contribution of property qualifies under section 170(e)(3) of this section only if it is a charitable contribution—

(i) By a corporation, other than a corporation which is an electing small business corporation within the meaning of section 1371(b);

(ii) To an organization described in section 501(c)(3) and exempt under section 501(a), other than a private foundation, as defined in section 509 (a), which is not an operating foundation, as defined in section 4942(j)(e);

(iii) Of property described in section 1221(1) or (2);

(iv) Which contribution meets the restrictions and requirements of paragraph (b)(2) through (5) of this section.

(2) Restrictions on use of contributed property. In order for the contribution to qualify under this section, the contributed property is subject to the following restrictions in use. If the transferred property is used or transferred by the donee organization (or by any subsequent transferee that furnished to the donee organization the written statement described in paragraph (b)(4)(ii) of this section) in a manner inconsistent with the requirements of subdivision (i) or (ii) of this paragraph (b)(2) or the requirements of paragraph (b)(3) of this section, the donor's deduction is reduced to the amount allowable under section 170 of the regulations thereunder, determined without regard to section 170(e)(3) of this section. If, however, the donor establishes that, at the time of the contribution, the donor reasonably anticipated that the property would be used in a manner consistent with those requirements, then the donor's deduction is not reduced.

(i) Requirement of use for exempt purpose. The use of the property must be related to the purpose or function constituting the ground for exemption under section 501(c)(3) of the organization to which the contribution is made. The property may not be used in connection with any activity which gives rise to unrelated trade or business income, as defined in sections 512 and 513 and the regulations thereunder.

(ii) Requirement of use for care of the ill, needy, or infants— **(A)** In general. The property must be used for the care of the ill, needy, or infants, as defined in this subdivision (ii). The property itself must ultimately either be transferred to (or for the use of) the ill, needy, or infants for their care or be retained for their care. No other person may use the contributed property except as incidental to primary use in the care of the ill, needy, or infants. The organization may satisfy the requirement of this subdivision by transferring the property to a relative, custodian, parent or guardian of the ill or needy individual or infant, or to any other individual if it makes a reasonable effort to ascertain that the property will ultimately be used primarily for the care of the ill or needy individual, or infant, and not for the primary benefit of any other person. The recipient organization may transfer the property to another exempt organization within the jurisdiction of the United States which meets the description contained in paragraph (b)(1)(ii) of this section, or to an organization not within the jurisdiction of the United States that, but for the fact that it is not within the jurisdiction of the United States, would be described in paragraph (b)(1)(ii) of this section. If an organization transfers the property to another organization, the transferring organization must obtain a written statement from the transferee organization as set forth in paragraph (b)(4) of this section. If the property is ultimately transferred to, or used for the benefit of, ill or needy persons, or infants, not within the jurisdiction of the United States, the organization which so transfers the property outside the jurisdiction of the United States must necessarily be a corporation. See section 170(c)(2) and § 1.170A–11(a). For purposes of this subdivision, if the donee-organization charges for its transfer of contributed property (other than a fee allowed by paragraph (b)(3)(ii) of this section), the requirement of this subdivision is not met. See paragraph (b)(3) of this section.

(B) Definition of the ill. An ill person is a person who requires medical care within the meaning of § 1.213–1(e). Examples of ill persons include a person suffering from physical injury, a person with a significant impairment of a bodily organ, a person with an existing handicap, whether from birth or later injury, a person suffering from malnutrition, a person with a disease, sickness, or infection which significantly impairs physical health, a person partially or totally incapable of self-care (including incapacity due to old age). A person suffering from mental illness is included if the person is hospitalized or institutionalized for the mental disorder, or, although the person is non-hospitalized or noninstitutionalized, if the person's mental illness constitutes a significant health impairment.

(C) Definition of care of the ill. Care of the ill means alleviation or cure of an existing illness and includes care of the physical, mental, or emotional needs of the ill.

(D) Definition of the needy. A needy person is a person who lacks the necessities of life, involving physical, mental, or emotional well-being, as a result of poverty or temporary distress. Examples of needy persons include a person who is financially impoverished as a result of low income and lack of financial resources, a person who temporarily lacks food or shelter (and the means to provide for it), a person who is the victim of a natural disaster (such as fire or flood), a person who is the victim of a civil disaster (such as a civil disturbance), a person who is temporarily not self-sufficient as a result of a sudden and severe personal or family crisis (such as a person who is the victim of a crime of violence or who has been physically abused), a person who is a refugee or immigrant and who is experiencing language, cultural, or financial difficulties, a minor child who is not self-sufficient and who is not cared for by a parent or guardian, and a person who is not self-sufficient as a result of previous institutionalization (such as a former prisoner or a former patient in a mental institution).

(E) Definition of care of the needy. Care of the needy means alleviation or satisfaction of an existing need. Since a person may be needy in some respects and not needy in other respects, care of the needy must relate to the particular need which causes the person to be needy. For example, a person whose temporary need arises from a natural disaster may need temporary shelter and food but not recreational facilities.

(F) Definition of infant. An infant is a minor child (as determined under the laws of the jurisdiction in which the child resides).

(G) Definition of care of an infant. Care of an infant means performance of parental functions and provision for the physical, mental, and emotional needs of the infant.

(3) Restrictions on transfer of contributed property— (i) In general. Except as otherwise provided in subdivision (ii) of this paragraph (b)(3), a contribution will not qualify under this section, if the donee-organization or any transferee of the donee-organization requires or receives any money, property, or services for the transfer or use of property contributed under section 170(e)(3). For example, if an organization provides temporary shelter for a fee, and also provides free meals to ill or needy individuals, or infants using food contributed under this section the contribution of food is subject to this section (if the other requirements of this section are met). However, the fee charged by the organization for the shelter may not be increased merely because meals are served to the ill or needy individuals or infants.

(ii) Exception. A contribution may qualify under this section if the donee-organization charges a fee to another organization in connection with its transfer of the donated property, if—

(A) The fee is small or nominal in relation to the value of the transferred property and is not determined by this value; and

(B) The fee is designed to reimburse the donee-organization for its administrative, warehousing, or other similar costs.

For example, if a charitable organization (such as a food bank) accepts surplus food to distribute to other charities which give the food to needy persons, a small fee may be charged to cover administrative, warehousing, and other similar costs. This fee may be charged on the basis of the total number of pounds of food distributed to the transferee charity but not on the basis of the value of the food distributed. The provisions of this subdivision (ii) do not apply to a transfer of donated property directly from an organization to ill or needy individuals, or infants.

(4) Requirement of a written statement— (i) Furnished to taxpayer. In the case of any contribution made on or after March 3, 1982, the donee-organization must furnish to the taxpayer a written statement which—

(A) Describes the contributed property, stating the date of its receipt;

(B) Represents that the property will be used in compliance with section 170(e)(3) and paragraphs (b)(2) and (3) of this section;

(C) Represents that the donee-organization meets the requirements of paragraph (b)(1)(ii) of this section; and

(D) Represents that adequate books and records will be maintained, and made available to the Internal Revenue Service upon request.

The written statement must be furnished within a reasonable period after the contribution, but not later than the date (including extensions) by which the donor is required to file a United States corporate income tax return for the year in which the contribution was made. The books and records described in (D) of this subdivision (i) need not trace the receipt and disposition of specific items of donated property if they disclose compliance with the requirements by reference to aggregate quantities of donated property. The books and records are adequate if they reflect total amounts received and distributed (or used), and outline the procedure used for determining that the ultimate recipient of the property is an ill or needy individual, or infant. However, the books and records need not reflect the names of the ultimate individual recipients or the property distributed to (or used by) each one.

(ii) Furnished to transferring organization. If an organization that received a contribution under this section transfers the contributed property to another organization on or after March 3, 1982, the transferee organization must furnish to the transferring organization a written statement which contains the information required in paragraph (b)(4)(i)(A), (B) and (D) of this section. The statement must also represent that the transferee organization meets the requirements of paragraph (b)(1)(ii) of this section (or, in the case of a transferee organization which is a foreign organization not within the jurisdiction of the United States, that, but for such fact, the organization would meet the requirements of paragraph (b)(1)(ii) of this section). The written statement must be furnished within a reasonable period after the transfer.

* * *

(c) Amount of reduction—(1) In general. Section 170(e)(3)(B) requires that the amount of the charitable contribution subject to this section which would be taken into account under section 170(a), without regard to section 170(e), must be reduced before applying the percentage limitations under section 170(b). The amount of the first reduction is equal to one-half of the amount of gain which would not have been long-term capital gain if the property had been sold by the donor-taxpayer at its fair market value on the date of its contribution, excluding, however, any amount described in paragraph (d) of this section. If the amount of the charitable contribution which remains after this reduction exceeds twice the basis of the contributed property, then the amount of the charitable contribution is reduced a second time to an amount which is equal to twice the amount of the basis of the property.

(2) Basis of contributed property which is inventory. For the purposes of this section, notwithstanding the rules of § 1.170A–1(c)(4), the basis of contributed property which is inventory must be determined under the donor's method of accounting for inventory for purposes of United States income tax. The donor must use as the basis of the contributed item the inventoriable carrying cost assigned to any similar item not included in closing inventory. For example, under the LIFO dollar value method of accounting for inventory, where there has been an invasion of a prior year's layer, the donor may choose to treat the item contributed as having a basis of the unit's cost with reference to the layer(s) of prior year(s) cost or with reference to the current year cost.

(3) Adjustment to cost of goods sold. Notwithstanding the rules of § 1.170A–1(c)(4), the donor of the property which is inventory contributed under this section must make a corresponding adjustment to cost of goods sold by decreasing the cost of goods sold by the lesser of the fair market value of the contributed item or the amount of basis determined under paragraph (c)(2) of this section.

(4) Examples. The rules of this paragraph (c) may be illustrated by the following examples:

Example (1). During 1978 corporation X, a calendar year taxpayer, makes a qualified contribution of women's coats which were section 1221(1) property. The fair market value of the property at the date of contribution is $1,000, and the basis of the property is $200. The amount of the charitable contribution which would be taken into account under section 170(a) is the fair market value ($1,000). The amount of gain which would not have been long-term capital gain if the property had been sold is $800 ($1,000 – $200). The amount of the contribution is reduced by one-half the amount which would not have been capital gain if the property had been sold ($800/2 = $400).

After this reduction, the amount of the contribution which may be taken into account is $600 ($1,000 – $400). A second reduction is made in the amount of the charitable contribution because this amount (as first reduced to $600) is more than $400 which is an amount equal to twice the basis of the property. The amount of the further reduction is $200 [$600 – (2 × $200)], and the amount of the contribution as finally reduced is $400 [$1,000 – ($400 + $200)]. X would also have to decrease its cost of goods sold for the year of contribution by $200.

Example (2). Assume the same facts as set forth in example (1) except that the basis of the property is $600. The amount of the first reduction is $200 (($1,000 – $600)/2).

As reduced, the amount of the contribution which may be taken into account is $800 ($1,000 – $200). There is no second reduction because $800 is less than $1,200 which is twice the basis of the property. However, X would have to decrease its cost of goods sold for the year of contribution by $600.

(d) Recapture excluded. A deduction is not allowed under section 170(e)(3) or this section for any amount which, if the property had been sold by the donor-taxpayer on the date of its contribution for an amount equal to its fair market value, would have been treated as ordinary income under section 617, 1245, 1250, 1251, or 1252. Thus, before making either reduction required by section 170(e)(3)(B) and paragraph (c) of this section, the fair market value of the contributed property must be reduced by the amount of gain that would have been recognized (if the property had been sold) as ordinary income under section 617, 1245, 1250, 1251, or 1252.

* * *

§ 1.170A–8 Limitations on charitable deductions by individuals.*

(a) Percentage limitations—(1) In general. An individual's charitable contributions deduction is subject to 20-, 30-, and 50-percent limitations unless the individual qualifies for the unlimited charitable contributions deduction under section 170(b)(1)(C). For a discussion of these limitations and examples of their application, see paragraphs (b) through (f) of this section. If a husband and wife make a joint return, the deduction for contributions is the aggregate of the contributions made by the spouses, and the limitations in section 170(b) and this section are based on the aggregate contribution base of the spouses. A charitable contribution by an individual to or for the use of an organization described in section 170(c) may be deductible even though all, or some portion, of the funds of the organization may be used in foreign countries for charitable or educational purposes.

(2) "To" or "for the use of" defined. For purposes of section 170, a contribution of an income interest in property, whether or not such contributed interest is transferred in trust, for which a deduction is allowed under section 170(f)(2)(B) or (3)(A) shall be considered as made "for the use of" rather than "to" the charitable organization. A contribution of a remainder interest in property, whether or not such contributed interest is transferred in trust, for which a deduction is allowed under section 170(f)(2)(A) or (3)(A), shall be considered as made "to" the charitable organization except that, if such interest is transferred in trust and, pursuant to the terms of the trust instrument, the interest contributed is, upon termination of the predecessor estate, to be held in trust for the benefit of such organization, the contribution shall be considered as made "for the use of" such organization. Thus, for example, assume that A transfers property to a charitable remainder annuity trust described in section 664(d)(1) which is required to pay to B for life an annuity equal to 5 percent of the initial fair market value of the property transferred in trust. The trust instrument provides that after B's death the remainder interest in the trust is to be transferred to M Church or, in the event M Church is not an organization described in section 170(c) when the amount is to be irrevocably transferred to such church, to an organization which is described in section 170(c) at that time. The contribution by A of the remainder interest shall be considered as made "to" M Church. However, if in the trust instrument A had directed that after B's death the remainder interest is to be held in trust for the benefit of M Church, the contribution shall be considered as made "for the use of" M Church. This subparagraph does not apply to the contribution of a partial interest in property, or of an undivided portion of such partial interest, if such partial interest is the donor's entire interest in the property and such entire interest was not created to avoid section 170(f)(2) or (3)(A). See paragraph (a)(2) of §1.170A–6 and paragraphs (a)(2)(i) and (b)(1) of §1.170A–7.

(b) 50-percent limitation. An individual may deduct charitable contributions made during a taxable year to any one or more section 170(b)(1)(A) organizations, as defined in §1.170A–9, to the extent that such contributions in the aggregate do not exceed 50 percent of his contribution base, as defined in section 170(b)(1)(F) and paragraph (e) of this section, for the taxable year. However, see paragraph (d) of this section for a limitation on the amount of charitable contributions of 30-percent capital gain property. To qualify for the 50-percent limitation the contributions must be made "to," and not merely "for the use of," one of the specified organizations. A contribution to an organization referred to in section 170(c)(2), other than a section 170(b)(1)(A) organization, will not qualify for the 50-percent limitation even though such organization makes the contribution available to an organization which is a section 170(b)(1)(A) organization. For provisions relating to the carryover of contributions in excess of 50-percent of an individual's contribution base see section 170(d)(1) and paragraph (b) of §1.170A–10.

(c) 20-percent limitation. (1) An individual may deduct charitable contributions made during a taxable year—

(i) To any one or more charitable organizations described in section 170(c) other than section 170(b)(1)(A) organizations, as defined in §1.170A–9, and,

(ii) For the use of any charitable organization described in section 170(c), to the extent that such contributions in the aggregate do not exceed the

*Editorial comment: The Regulations do not include the effect of the Deficit Reduction Act of 1984 [see Sec. 170(b)] and the Tax Reform Act of 1986 (see Sec. 170(e)).

lesser of the limitations under subparagraph (2) of this paragraph.

(2) For purposes of subparagraph (1) of this paragraph the limitations are—

(i) 20 percent of the individual's contribution base, as defined in paragraph (e) of this section, for the taxable year, or

(ii) The excess of 50 percent of the individual's contribution base, as so defined, for the taxable year over the total amount of the charitable contributions allowed under section 170(b)(1)(A) and paragraph (b) of this section, determined by first reducing the amount of such contributions under section 170(e)(1) and paragraph (a) of §1.170A–4 but without applying the 30-percent limitation under section 170(b)(1)(D)(i) and paragraph (d)(1) of this section.

However, see paragraph (d) of this section for a limitation on the amount of charitable contributions of 30-percent capital gain property. If an election under section 170(b)(1)(D)(iii) and paragraph (d)(2) of this section applies to any contributions of 30-percent capital gain property made during the taxable year or carried over to the taxable year, the amount allowed for the taxable year under paragraph (b) of this section with respect to such contributions for purposes of applying subdivision (ii) of this subparagraph shall be the reduced amount of such contributions determined by applying paragraph (d)(2) of this section.

(d) 30-percent limitation—(1) In general. An individual may deduct charitable contributions of 30-percent capital gain property, as defined in subparagraph (3) of this paragraph, made during a taxable year to or for the use of any charitable organization described in section 170(c) to the extent that such contributions in the aggregate do not exceed 30-percent of his contribution base, as defined in paragraph (e) of this section, subject, however, to the 50- and 20-percent limitations prescribed by paragraphs (b) and (c) of this section. For purposes of applying the 50-percent and 20-percent limitations described in paragraphs (b) and (c) of this section, charitable contributions of 30-percent capital gain property paid during the taxable year, and limited as provided by this subparagraph, shall be taken into account after all other charitable contributions paid during the taxable year. For provisions relating to the carryover of certain contributions of 30-percent capital gain property in excess of 30-percent of an individual's contribution base, see section 170(b)(1) (D)(ii) and paragraph (c) of §1.170A–10.

(2) Election by an individual to have section 170(e)(1)(B) apply to contributions—(i) In general. **(a)** An individual may elect under section 170(b)(1)(D)(iii) for any taxable year to have the reduction rule of section 170(e)(1)(B) and paragraph (a) of §1.170A–4 apply to all his charitable contributions of 30-percent capital gain property made during such taxable year or carried over to such taxable year from a taxable year beginning after December 31, 1969. If such election is made such contributions shall be treated as contributions of section 170(e) capital gain property in accordance with paragraph (b)(2)(iii) of §1.170A–4. The election may be made with respect to contributions of 30-percent capital gain property carried over to the taxable year even though the individual has not made any contribution of 30-percent capital gain property in such year. If such an election is made, section 170(b)(1)(D)(i) and (ii) and subparagraph (1) of this paragraph shall not apply to such contributions made during such year. However, such contributions must be reduced as required under section 170(e)(1)(B) and paragraph (a) of §1.170A–4.

(b) If there are carryovers to such taxable year of charitable contributions of 30-percent capital gain property made in preceding taxable years beginning after December 31, 1969, the amount of such contributions in each such preceding year shall be reduced as if section 170(e)(1)(B) had applied to them in the preceding year and shall be carried over to the taxable year and succeeding taxable years under section 170(d)(1) and paragraph (b) of §1.170A–10 as contributions of property other than 30-percent capital gain property. For purposes of applying the immediately preceding sentence, the percentage limitations under section 170(b) for the preceding taxable year and for any taxable years intervening between such year and the year of the election shall not be redetermined and the amount of any deduction allowed for such years under section 170 in respect of the charitable contributions of 30-percent capital gain property in the preceding taxable year shall not be redetermined. However, the amount of the deduction so allowed under section 170 in the preceding taxable year must be subtracted from the reduced amount of the charitable contributions made in such year in order to determine the excess amount which is carried over from such year under section 170(d)(1). If the amount of the deduction so allowed in the preceding taxable year equals or exceeds the reduced amount of the charitable contributions, there shall be no carryover from such year to the year of the election.

(c) An election under this subparagraph may be made for each taxable year in which charitable contributions of 30-percent capital gain property are made or to which they are carried over under section 170(b)(1)(D)(ii). If there are also carryovers under section 170(d)(1) to the year of the election by reason of an election made under this subparagraph for a previous taxable year, such carryovers under section 170(d)(l) shall not be redetermined by reason of the subsequent election.

(ii) Husband and wife making joint return. If a husband and wife make a joint return of income for a contribution year and one of the spouses elects under this subparagraph in a later year when he files a separate return, or if a spouse dies after a contribution year for which a joint return is made, any excess contribution of 30-percent capital gain property which is carried over to the election year from the contribution year shall be allocated between the husband and wife as provided in paragraph (d)(4)(i) and (iii) of §1.170A–10. If a husband and wife file separate returns in a contribution year, any election under this subparagraph in a later year when a joint return is filed shall be applicable to any excess contributions of 30-percent capital gain property of either taxpayer carried over from the contribution year to the election year. The immediately preceding sentence shall also apply where two single individuals are subsequently married and file a joint return. A remarried individual who filed a joint return with his former spouse for a contribution year and thereafter files a joint return with his present spouse shall treat the carryover to the election year as provided in paragraph (d)(4)(ii) of §1.170A–10.

(iii) Manner of making election. The election under subdivision (i) of this subparagraph shall be made by attaching to the income tax return for the election year a statement indicating that the election under section 170(b)(1)(D)(iii) and this subparagraph is being made. If there is a carryover to the taxable year of any charitable contributions of 30-percent capital gain property from a previous taxable year or years, the statement shall show a recomputation, in accordance with this subparagraph and §1.170A–4, of such carryover, setting forth sufficient information with respect to the previous taxable year or any intervening year to show the basis of the recomputation. The statement shall indicate the district director, or the director of the internal revenue service center, with whom the return for the previous taxable year or years was filed, the name or names in which such return or returns were filed, and whether each such return was a joint or separate return.

(3) 30-percent capital gain property defined. If there is a charitable contribution of a capital asset which, if it were sold by the donor at its fair market value at the time of its contribution, would result in the recognition of gain all, or any portion, of which would be long-term capital gain and if the amount of such contribution is not required to be reduced under section 170(e)(1)(B) and §1.170A–4(a)(2), such capital asset shall be treated as "30-percent capital gain property" for purposes of section 170 and the regulations thereunder. For such purposes any property which is property used in the trade or business, as defined in section 1231(b), shall be treated as a capital asset. However, see paragraph (b)(4) of §1.170A–4. For the treatment of such property as section 170(e) capital gain property, see paragraph (b)(2)(iii) of §1.170A–4.

(e) Contribution base defined. For purposes of section 170 the term "contribution base" means adjusted gross income under section 62, computed without regard to any net operating loss carryback to the taxable year under section 172. See section 170(b)(1)(F).

(f) Illustrations. The application of this section may be illustrated by the following examples:

Example (1). B, an individual, reports his income on the calendar-year basis and for 1970 has a contribution base of $100,000. During 1970 he makes charitable contributions of $70,000 in cash, of which $40,000 is given to section 170(b)(1)(A) organizations and $30,000 is given to other organizations described in section 170(c). Accordingly, B is allowed a charitable contributions deduction of $50,000 (50% of $100,000), which consists of the $40,000 contributed to section 170(b)(1)(A) organizations and $10,000 of the $30,000 contributed to the other organizations. Under paragraph (c) of this section, only $10,000 of the $30,000 contributed to the other organizations is allowed as a deduction since such contribution of $30,000 is allowed to the extent of the lesser of $20,000 (20% of $100,000) or $10,000 ([50% of $100,000]–$40,000 (contributions allowed under section 170(b)(1)(A) and paragraph (b) of this section)). Under section 170 (b)(1)(D)(ii) and (d)(1) and §1.170A–10, B is not allowed a carryover to 1971 or to any other taxable year for any of the $20,000 ($30,000–$10,000) not deductible under section 170(b)(1)(B) and paragraph (c) of this section.

Example (2). C, an individual, reports his income on the calendar-year basis and for 1970 has a contribution base of $100,000. During 1970 he makes charitable contributions of $40,000 in 30-percent capital gain property to section 170(b)(1)(A) organizations and of $30,000 in cash to other organizations described in section 170(c). The 20-percent limitation in section 170(b)(1)(B) and paragraph (c) of this section is applied before the 30-percent limitation in section 170(b)(1)(D)(i) and paragraph (d) of this section; accordingly section 170(b)(1)(B)(ii) limits the deduction for the $30,000 cash contribution to $10,000 ([50% of $100,000] – $40,000). The amount of the contribution of 30-percent capital gain property is limited by section 170(b)(1)(D)(i) and paragraph (d) of this section to $30,000 (30% of $100,000). Accordingly, C's charitable contributions deduction for 1970 is limited to $40,000 ($10,000 + $30,000). Under section 170(b)(1)(D)(ii) and paragraph (c) of §1.170A–10, C is allowed a carryover to 1971 of $10,000 ($40,000–$30,000) in respect of his contributions of 30-percent capital gain property. C is not allowed a carryover to 1971 or to any other taxable year for any of the $20,000 cash ($30,000 – $10,000) not deductible under section 170(b)(1)(B) and paragraph (c) of this section.

Example (3). (a) D, an individual, reports his income on the calendar-year basis and for 1970 has a contribution base of $100,000. During 1970 he makes charitable contributions of $70,000 in cash, of which $40,000 is given to section 170(b)(1)(A) organizations and $30,000 is given to other organizations described in section 170(c). During 1971 D makes charitable contributions to a section 170(b)(l)(A) organization of $12,000, consisting of cash of $1,000 and $11,000 in 30-percent capital gain property. His contribution base for 1971 is $10,000.

(b) For 1970, D is allowed a charitable contributions deduction of $50,000 (50% of $100,000), which consists of the $40,000 contributed to section 170(b)(1)(A) organizations and $10,000 of the $30,000 contributed to the other organizations. Under paragraph (c) of this section, only $10,000 of the $30,000 contributed to the other organizations is allowed as a deduction since such contribution of $30,000 is allowed to the extent of the lesser of $20,000 (20% of $100,000) or $10,000 ([50% of $100,000] – $40,000 (contributions allowed under section 170(b)(1)(A) and paragraph (b) of this section)). D is not allowed a carryover to 1971 or to any other taxable year for any of the $20,000 ($30,000 – $10,000) not deductible under section 170(b)(1)(B) and paragraph (c) of this section.

(c) For 1971, D is allowed a charitable contributions deduction of $4,000, consisting of $1,000 cash and $3,000 of the 30-percent capital gain property (30% of $10,000). Under section 170(b)(1)(D)(ii) and paragraph (c) of §1.170A–10, D is allowed a carryover to 1972 of $8,000 ($11,000–$3,000) in respect of his contribution of 30-percent capital gain property in 1971.

* * *

Example (9). (a) In 1970, A, a calendar-year individual taxpayer, makes a charitable contribution to a church of 30-percent capital gain property having a fair market value of $60,000 and an adjusted basis of $10,000. A's contribution base for 1970 is $50,000, and he makes no other charitable contributions in that year. A does not elect for 1970 under paragraph (d)(2) of this section to have section 170(e)(1)(B) apply to such contribution. Accordingly, under section 170(b)(1)(D)(i) and paragraph (d) of this section, A is allowed a charitable contributions deduction for 1970 of $15,000 (30% of $50,000). Under section 170(b)(1)(D)(ii) and paragraph (c) of §1.170A–10, A is allowed a carryover to 1971 of $45,000 ($60,000–$15,000) for his contribution of 30-percent capital gain property.

(b) In 1971, A makes a charitable contribution to a church of 30-percent capital gain property having a fair market value of $11,000 and an adjusted basis of $10,000. A's contribution base for 1971 is $60,000, and he makes no other charitable contributions in that year. A elects for 1971 under paragraph (d)(2) of this section to have section 170(e)(1)(B) and §1.170A–4 apply to his contribution of $11,000 in that year and to his carryover of $45,000 from 1970. Accordingly, he is required to recompute his carryover from 1970 as if section 170(e)(1)(B) had applied to his contribution of 30-percent capital gain property in that year.

(c) If section 170(e)(1)(B) had applied in 1970 to his contribution of 30-percent capital gain property, A's contribution would have been reduced from $60,000 to $35,000, the reduction of $25,000 being 50 percent of the gain of $50,000 ($60,000 – $10,000) which would have been recognized as long-term capital gain if the property had been sold by A at its fair market value at the time of the contribution in 1970. Accordingly, by taking the election under paragraph (d)(2) of this section into account, A has a recomputed carryover to 1971 of $20,000 ($35,000 – $15,000) of his contribution of 30-percent capital gain property in 1970. However, A's charitable contributions deduction of $15,000 allowed for 1970 is not recomputed by reason of the election.

(d) Pursuant to the election for 1971, the contribution of 30-percent capital gain property for 1971 is reduced from $11,000 to $10,500, the reduction of $500 being 50 percent of the gain of $1,000 ($11,000 – $10,000) which would have been recognized as long-term capital gain if the property had been sold by A at its fair market value at the time of its contribution in 1971.

(e) Accordingly, A is allowed a charitable contributions deduction for 1971 of $30,000 (total contributions of $30,500 [$20,000 + $10,500] but not to exceed 50% of $60,000).

(f) Under section 170(d)(l) and paragraph (b) of §1.170A–10, A is allowed a carryover of $500 ($30,500 – $30,000) to 1972 and the 3 succeeding taxable years. The $500 carryover, which by reason of the election is no longer treated as a contribution of 30-percent capital gain property, is treated as carried over under paragraph (b) of §1.170A–10 from 1970 since in 1971 current year contributions are deducted before contributions which are carried over from preceding taxable years.

* * *

§ 1.170A–10 Charitable contributions carryovers of individuals.*

(a) In general. **(1)** Section 170(d)(1), relating to carryover of charitable contributions in excess of 50 percent of contribution base, and section 170(b)(1)(D)(ii), relating to carryover of charitable contributions in excess of 30 percent of contribution base, provide for excess charitable contributions carryovers by individuals of charitable contributions to section 170(b)(1)(A) organizations described in § 1.170A–9. These carryovers shall be determined as provided in paragraphs (b) and (c) of this section. No excess charitable contributions carryover shall be allowed with respect to contributions "for the use of," rather than "to," section 170(b)(1)(A) organizations or with respect to

*Editorial comment: The Regulations do not reflect the effect of the Deficit Reduction Act of 1984 and the Tax Reform Act of 1986. See Sec. 170(d)(1).

contributions "to" or "for the use of" organizations which are not section 170(b)(1)(A) organizations. See §1.170A–8(a)(2) for definitions of "to" or "for the use of" a charitable organization.

(2) The carryover provisions apply with respect to contributions made during a taxable year in excess of the applicable percentage limitation even though the taxpayer elects under section 144* to take the standard deduction in that year instead of itemizing the deduction allowable in computing taxable income for that year.

(3) For provisions requiring a reduction of the excess charitable contribution computed under paragraph (b)(1) or (c)(1) of this section when there is a net operating loss carryover to the taxable year, see paragraph (d)(l) of this section.

(4) The provisions of section 170(b)(1)(D)(ii) and (d)(1) and this section do not apply to contributions by an estate; nor do they apply to a trust unless the trust is a private foundation which, pursuant to §1.642(c)–4, is allowed a deduction under section 170 subject to the provisions applicable to individuals.

(b) 50-percent charitable contributions carryover of individuals—(1) Computation of excess of charitable contributions made in a contribution year. Under section 170(d)(1), subject to certain conditions and limitations, the excess of—

(i) The amount of the charitable contributions made by an individual in a taxable year (hereinafter) in this paragraph referred to as the "contribution year" to section 170(b)(1)(A) organizations described in §1.170A–9, over

(ii) 50 percent of his contribution base, as defined in section 170(b)(1)(F), for such contribution year, shall be treated as a charitable contribution paid by him to a section 170(b)(1)(A) organization in each of the 5 taxable years immediately succeeding the contribution year in order of time. However, such excess to the extent it consists of contributions of 30-percent capital gain property, as defined in §1.170A–8(d)(3), shall be subject to the rules of section 170(b)(1) (D)(ii) and paragraph (c) of this section in the years to which it is carried over. A charitable contribution made in a taxable year beginning before January 1, 1970, to a section 170(b)(1)(A) organization and carried over to a taxable year beginning after December 31, 1969, under section 170(b)(5) (before its amendment by the Tax Reform Act of 1969) shall be treated in such taxable year beginning after December 31, 1969, as a charitable contribution of cash subject to the limitations of this paragraph, whether or not such carryover consists of contributions of 30-percent capital gain property or of ordinary income property described in §1.170A–4 (b)(1). For purposes of applying this paragraph and paragraph (c) of this section, such a carryover from a taxable year beginning before January 1, 1970, which is so treated as paid to a section 170(b)(1)(A) organization in a taxable year beginning after December 31, 1969, shall be treated as paid to such an organization under section 170(d)(1) and this section. The provisions of this subparagraph may be illustrated by the following examples:

Example (1). Assume that H and W (husband and wife) have a contribution base for 1970 of $50,000 and for 1971 of $40,000 and file a joint return for each year. Assume further that in 1970 they make a charitable contribution in cash of $26,500 to a church and $1,000 to X (not a section 170(b)(1)(A) organization) and in 1971 they make a charitable contribution in cash of $19,000 to a church and $600 to X. They may claim a charitable contributions deduction of $25,000 in 1970, and the excess of $26,500 (contribution to the church) over $25,000 (50 percent of contribution base), or $1,500, constitutes a charitable contributions carryover which shall be treated as a charitable contribution paid by them to a section 170(b)(1)(A) organization in each of the 5 succeeding taxable years in order of time. No carryover is allowed with respect to the $1,000 contribution made to X in 1970. Since 50 percent of their contribution base for 1971 ($20,000) exceeds the charitable contributions of $19,000 made by them in 1971 to section 170(b)(1)(A) organizations (computed without regard to section 170(b)(1)(D)(ii) and (d)(1) and this section), the portion of the 1970 carryover equal to such excess of $1,000 ($20,000 minus $19,000) is treated, pursuant to the provisions of subparagraph (2) of this paragraph, as paid to a section 170(b)(1)(A) organization in 1971; the remaining $500 constitutes an unused charitable contributions carryover. No deduction for 1971, and no carryover, are allowed with respect to the $600 contribution made to X in 1971.

Example (2). Assume the same facts as in example (1) except that H and W have a contribution base for 1971 of $42,000. Since 50 percent of their contribution base for 1971 ($21,000) exceeds by $2,000 the charitable contribution of $19,000 made by them in 1971 to the section 170(b)(1)(A) organization (computed without regard to section 170(b)(1)(D)(ii) and (d)(1) and this section), the full amount of the 1970 carryover of $1,500 is treated, pursuant to the provisions of subparagraph (2) of this paragraph, as paid to a section 170(b)(1)(A) organization in 1971. They may also claim a charitable contribution of $500 ($21,000 – $20,500[$19,000 + $1,500]) with respect to the gift to X in 1971. No carryover is allowed with respect to the $100 ($600–$500) of the contribution to X which is not deductible in 1971.

(2) Determination of amount treated as paid in taxable years succeeding contribution year. In applying the provisions of subparagraph (1) of this

*Editorial comment: See Sec. 63 rather than Sec. 144.

paragraph, the amount of the excess computed in accordance with the provisions of such subparagraph and paragraph (d)(1) of this section which is to be treated as paid in any one of the 5 taxable years immediately succeeding the contribution year to a section 170(b)(1)(A) organization shall not exceed the lesser of the amounts computed under subdivisions (i) to (iii), inclusive, of this subparagraph:

(i) The amount by which 50 percent of the taxpayer's contribution base for such succeeding taxable year exceeds the sum of—

(a) The charitable contributions actually made (computed without regard to the provisions of section 170(b)(1)(D)(ii) and (d)(1) and this section) by the taxpayer in such succeeding taxable year to section 170(b)(1)(A) organizations, and

(b) The charitable contributions, other than contributions of 30-percent capital gain property, made to section 170(b)(1)(A) organizations in taxable years preceding the contribution year which, pursuant to the provisions of section 170(d)(1) and this section, are treated as having been paid to a section 170(b)(1)(A) organization in such succeeding year.

(ii) In the case of the first taxable year succeeding the contribution year, the amount of the excess charitable contribution in the contribution year, computed under subparagraph (1) of this paragraph and paragraph (d)(1) of this section.

(iii) In the case of the second, third, fourth, and fifth taxable years succeeding the contribution year, the portion of the excess charitable contribution in the contribution year, computed under subparagraph (1) of this paragraph and paragraph (d)(1) of this section, which has not been treated as paid to a section 170(b)(1)(A) organization in a year intervening between the contribution year and such succeeding taxable year.

For purposes of applying subdivision (i)(a) of this subparagraph, the amount of charitable contributions of 30-percent capital gain property actually made in a taxable year succeeding the contribution year shall be determined by first applying the 30-percent limitation of section 170(b)(1)(D)(i) and paragraph (d) of §1.170A–8. If a taxpayer, in any one of the 4 taxable years succeeding a contribution year, elects under section 144* to take the standard deduction instead of itemizing the deductions allowable in computing taxable income, there shall be treated as paid (but not allowable as a deduction) in such standard deduction year the lesser of the amounts determined under subdivisions (i) to (iii), inclusive, of this subparagraph.* * *

(c) 30-percent charitable contributions carryover of individuals—(1) Computation of excess of charitable contributions made in a contribution year. Under section 170(b)(1)(D)(ii), subject to certain conditions and limitations, the excess of—

(i) The amount of the charitable contributions of 30-percent capital gain property, as defined in §1.170A–8(d)(3), made by an individual in a taxable year (hereinafter in this paragraph referred to as the "contribution year") to section 170(b)(1)(A) organizations described in §1.170A–9, over

(ii) 30 percent of his contribution base for such contribution year,

shall, subject to section 170(b)(1)(A) and paragraph (b) of §1.170A–8, be treated as a charitable contribution of 30-percent capital gain property paid by him to a section 170(b)(1)(A) organization in each of the 5 taxable years immediately succeeding the contribution year in order of time. In addition, any charitable contribution of 30-percent capital gain property which is carried over to such years under section 170(d)(1) and paragraph (b) of this section shall also be treated as though it were a carryover of 30-percent capital gain property under section 170(b)(1)(D)(ii) and this paragraph. The provisions of this subparagraph may be illustrated by the following examples:

Example (1). Assume that H and W (husband and wife) have a contribution base for 1970 of $50,000 and for 1971 of $40,000 and file a joint return for each year. Assume further that in 1970 they contribute $20,000 cash and $13,000 of 30-percent capital gain property to a church, and that in 1971 they contribute $5,000 cash and $10,000 of 30-percent capital gain property to a church. They may claim a charitable contributions deduction of $25,000 in 1970 and the excess of $33,000 (contributed to the church) over $25,000 (50 percent of contribution base), or $8,000, constitutes a charitable contributions carryover which shall be treated as a charitable contribution of 30-percent capital gain property paid by them to a section 170(b)(1)(A) organization in each of the 5 succeeding taxable years in order of time. Since 30 percent of their contribution base for 1971 ($12,000) exceeds the charitable contributions of 30-percent capital gain property ($10,000) made by them in 1971 to section 170(b)(1)(A) organizations (computed without regard to section 170(b)(1)(D)(ii) and (d)(1) and this section), the portion of the 1970 carryover equal to such excess of $2,000 ($12,000–$10,000) is treated, pursuant to the provisions of subparagraph (2) of this paragraph, as paid to a section 170(b)(1)(A) organization in 1971; the remaining $6,000 constitutes an unused charitable contributions carryover in respect of 30-percent capital gain property from 1970.

Example (2). Assume the same facts as in example (1) except the $33,000 of charitable contributions in 1970 are all 30-percent capital gain property. Since their charitable contributions in 1970 exceed 30 percent of their contribution base ($15,000) by $18,000

*Editorial comment: See Sec. 63 rather than Sec. 144.

($33,000–$15,000), they may claim a charitable contributions deduction of $15,000 in 1970, and the excess of $33,000 over $15,000, or $18,000, constitutes a charitable contributions carryover which shall be treated as a charitable contribution of 30-percent capital gain property paid by them to a section 170(b)(1)(A) organization in each of the 5 succeeding taxable years in order of time. Since they are allowed to treat only $2,000 of their 1970 contribution as paid in 1971, they have a remaining unused charitable contributions carryover of $16,000 in respect of 30-percent capital gain property from 1970.

(2) Determination of amount treated as paid in taxable years succeeding contribution year. In applying the provisions of subparagraph (1) of this paragraph, the amount of the excess computed in accordance with the provisions of such subparagraph and paragraph (d)(1) of this section which is to be treated as paid in any one of the 5 taxable years immediately succeeding the contribution year to a section 170(b)(1)(A) organization shall not exceed the least of the amounts computed under subdivisions (i) to (iv), inclusive, of this subparagraph:

(i) The amount by which 30 percent of the taxpayer's contribution base for such succeeding taxable year exceeds the sum of—

(a) The charitable contributions of 30-percent capital gain property actually made (computed without regard to the provisions of section 170(b)(1)(D)(ii) and (d)(1) and this section) by the taxpayer in such succeeding taxable year to section 170(b)(1)(A) organizations, and

(b) The charitable contributions of 30-percent capital gain property made to section 170(b)(1)(A) organizations in taxable years preceding the contribution year, which, pursuant to the provisions of section 170(b)(1)(D)(ii) and (d)(1) and this section, are treated as having been paid to a section 170(b)(1)(A) organization in such succeeding year.

(ii) The amount by which 50 percent of the taxpayer's contribution base for such succeeding taxable year exceeds the sum of—

(a) The charitable contributions actually made (computed without regard to the provisions of section 170(b)(1)(D)(ii) and (d)(1) and this section) by the taxpayer in such succeeding taxable year to section 170(b)(1)(A) organizations,

(b) The charitable contributions of 30-percent capital gain property made to section 170(b)(1)(A) organizations in taxable years preceding the contribution year which, pursuant to the provisions of section 170(b)(1)(D)(ii) and (d)(1) and this section, are treated as having been paid to a section 170(b)(1)(A) organization in such succeeding year, and

(c) The charitable contributions, other than contributions of 30-percent capital gain property, made to section 170(b)(1)(A) organizations which, pursuant to the provisions of section 170(d)(1) and paragraph (b) of this section, are treated as having been paid to a section 170(b)(1)(A) organization in such succeeding year.

(iii) In the case of the first taxable year succeeding the contribution year, the amount of the excess charitable contribution of 30-percent capital gain property in the contribution year, computed under subparagraph (1) of this paragraph and paragraph (d)(l) of this section.

(iv) In the case of the second, third, fourth, and fifth succeeding taxable years succeeding the contribution year, the portion of the excess charitable contribution of 30-percent capital gain property in the contribution year (computed under subparagraph (1) of this paragraph and paragraph (d)(1) of this section) which has not been treated as paid to a section 170(b)(1)(A) organization in a year intervening between the contribution year and such succeeding taxable year.

For purposes of applying subdivisions (i) and (ii) of this subparagraph, the amount of charitable contributions of 30-percent capital gain property actually made in a taxable year succeeding the contribution year shall be determined by first applying the 30-percent limitation of section 170(b)(1)(D)(i) and paragraph (d) of §1.170A–8. If a taxpayer, in any one of the four taxable years succeeding a contribution year, elects under section 144* to take the standard deduction instead of itemizing the deductions allowable in computing taxable income, there shall be treated as paid (but not allowable as a deduction) in the standard deduction year the least of the amounts determined under subdivisions (i) to (iv), inclusive, of this subparagraph. * * *

(d) Adjustments—(1) Effect of net operating loss carryovers on carryover of excess contributions. An individual having a net operating loss carryover from a prior taxable year which is available as a deduction in a contribution year must apply the special rule of section 170(d)(1)(B) and this subparagraph in computing the excess described in paragraph (b)(1) or (c)(1) of this section for such contribution year. In determining the amount of excess charitable contributions that shall be treated

*Editorial comment: See Sec. 63 rather than Sec. 144.

as paid in each of the 5 taxable years succeeding the contribution year, the excess charitable contributions described in paragraph (b)(1) or (c)(1) of this section must be reduced by the amount by which such excess reduces taxable income (for purposes of determining the portion of a net operating loss which shall be carried to taxable years succeeding the contribution year under the second sentence of section 172(b)(2)) and increases the net operating loss which is carried to a succeeding taxable year. In reducing taxable income under the second sentence of section 172(b)(2), an individual who has made charitable contributions in the contribution year to both section 170(b)(l)(A) organizations, as defined in §1.170A–9, and to organizations which are not section 170(b)(1)(A) organizations must first deduct contributions made to the section 170(b)(1)(A) organizations from his adjusted gross income computed without regard to his net operating loss deduction before any of the contributions made to organizations which are not section 170(b)(1)(A) organizations may be deducted from such adjusted gross income. Thus, if the excess of the contributions made in the contribution year to section 170(b)(1)(A) organizations over the amount deductible in such contribution year is utilized to reduce taxable income (under the provisions of section 172(b)(2)) for such year, thereby serving to increase the amount of the net operating loss carryover to a succeeding year or years, no part of the excess charitable contributions made in such contribution year shall be treated as paid in any of the 5 immediately succeeding taxable years. If only a portion of the excess charitable contributions is so used, the excess charitable contributions shall be reduced only to that extent. The provisions of this subparagraph may be illustrated by the following examples:

Example (1). B, an individual, reports his income on the calendar year basis and for the year 1970 has adjusted gross income (computed without regard to any net operating loss deduction) of $50,000. During 1970 he made charitable contributions of cash in the amount of $30,000 all of which were to section 170(b)(1)(A) organizations. B has a net operating loss carryover from 1969 of $50,000. In the absence of the net operating loss deduction B would have been allowed a deduction for charitable contributions of $25,000. After the application of the net operating loss deduction, B is allowed no deduction for charitable contributions, and there is (before applying the special rule of section 170(d)(1)(B) and this subparagraph) a tentative excess charitable contribution of $30,000. For purposes of determining the net operating loss which remains to be carried over to 1971, B computes his taxable income for 1970 under section 172(b)(2) by deducting the $25,000 charitable contribution. After the $50,000 net operating loss carryover is applied against the $25,000 of taxable income for 1970 (computed in accordance with section 172 (b)(2), assuming no deductions other than the charitable contributions deduction are applicable in making such computation), there remains a $25,000 net operating loss carryover to 1971. Since the application of the net operating loss carryover of $50,000 from 1969 reduces the 1970 adjusted gross income (for purposes of determining 1970 tax liability) to zero, no part of the $25,000 of charitable contributions in that year is deductible under section 170(b)(1). However, in determining the amount of the excess charitable contributions which shall be treated as paid in taxable years 1971, 1972, 1973, 1974, and 1975, the $30,000 must be reduced to $5,000 by the portion of the excess charitable contributions ($25,000) which was used to reduce taxable income for 1970 (as computed for purposes of the second sentence of section 172(b)(2)) and which thereby served to increase the net operating loss carryover to 1971 from zero to $25,000.

Example (2). Assume the same facts as in example (1), except that B's total charitable contributions of $30,000 in cash made during 1970 consisted of $25,000 to section 170(b)(1)(A) organizations and $5,000 to organizations other than section 170(b)(1)(A) organizations. Under these facts there is a tentative excess charitable contribution of $25,000, rather than $30,000 as in example (1). For purposes of determining the net operating loss which remains to be carried over to 1971, B computes his taxable income for 1970 under section 172(b)(2) by deducting the $25,000 of charitable contributions made to section 170(b)(1)(A) organizations. Since the excess charitable contribution of $25,000 determined in accordance with paragraph (b)(1) of this section was used to reduce taxable income for 1970 (as computed for purposes of the second sentence of section 172(b)(2)) and thereby served to increase the net operating loss carryover to 1971 from zero to $25,000, no part of such excess charitable contributions made in the contribution year shall be treated as paid in any of the five immediately succeeding taxable years. No carryover is allowed with respect to the $5,000 of charitable contributions made in 1970 to organizations other than section 170(b)(1)(A) organizations.

Example (3). Assume the same facts as in example (1), except that B's total contributions of $30,000 made during 1970 were of 30-percent capital gain property. Under these facts there is a tentative excess charitable contribution of $30,000. For purposes of determining the net operating loss which remains to be carried over to 1971, B computes his taxable income for 1970 under section 172(b)(2)(B) by deducting the $15,000 (30% of $50,000) contribution of 30-percent capital gain property which would have been deductible in 1970 absent the net operating loss deduction. Since $15,000 of the excess charitable contribution of $30,000 determined in accordance with paragraph (c)(1) of this section was used to reduce taxable income for 1970 (as computed for purposes of the second sentence of section 172(b)(2)) and thereby served to increase the net operating loss carryover to 1971 from zero to $15,000, only $15,000 ($30,000 – $15,000) of such excess shall be treated as paid in taxable years 1971, 1972, 1973, 1974, and 1975.

(2) Effect of net operating loss carryback to contribution year. The amount of the excess contribution for a contribution year computed as provided in paragraph (b)(1) or (c)(1) of this section and subparagraph (1) of this paragraph shall not be increased because a net operating loss carryback is available as a deduction in the contribution year. Thus, for example, assuming that in 1970 there is an excess contribution of $50,000 (determined as provided in paragraph (b)(1) of this section) which is to be carried to the 5 succeeding taxable years and that in 1973 the taxpayer has a net operating loss which may be carried back to 1970, the excess contribution of $50,000 for 1970 is not increased by reason of the fact that the adjusted gross income for 1970 (on which such excess contribution was based) is subsequently decreased by the carryback of the net operating loss from 1973. In addition, in determining under the provisions of section 172(b)(2) the amount of the net operating loss for any year subsequent to the contribution year which is a carryback or carryover to taxable years succeeding the contribution year, the amount of contributions made to section 170(b)(1)(A) organizations shall be limited to the amount of such contributions which did not exceed 50 percent or, in the case of 30-percent capital gain property, 30 percent of the donor's contribution base, computed without regard to any of the modifications referred to in section 172(d), for the contribution year. Thus, for example, assume that the taxpayer has a net operating loss in 1973 which is carried back to 1970 and in turn to 1971 and that he has made charitable contributions in 1970 to section 170(b)(1)(A) organizations. In determining the maximum amount of such charitable contributions which may be deducted in 1970 for purposes of determining the taxable income for 1970 which is deducted under section 172(b)(2) from the 1973 loss in order to ascertain the amount of such loss which is carried back to 1971, the 50-percent limitation of section 170(b)(1)(A) is based upon the adjusted gross income for 1970 computed without taking into account the net operating loss carryback from 1973 and without making any of the modifications specified in section 172(d).

(3) Effect of net operating loss carryback to taxable years succeeding the contribution year. The amount of the charitable contribution from a preceding taxable year which is treated as paid, as provided in paragraph (b)(2) or (c)(2) of this section, in a current taxable year (hereinafter referred to in this subparagraph as the "deduction year") shall not be reduced because a net operating loss carryback is available as a deduction in the deduction year. In addition, in determining under the provisions of section 172(b)(2) the amount of the net operating loss for any taxable year subsequent to the deduction year which is a carryback or carryover to taxable years succeeding the deduction year, the amount of contributions made to section 170(b)(1)(A) organizations in the deduction year shall be limited to the amount of such contributions, which were actually made in such year and those which were treated as paid in such year, which did not exceed 50 percent or, in the case of 30-percent capital gain property, 30 percent of the donor's contribution base, computed without regard to any of the modifications referred to in section 172(d), for the deduction year.

* * *

§ 1.170A–11 Limitation on, and carryover of, contributions by corporations.

(a) In general. The deduction by a corporation in any taxable year for charitable contributions, as defined in section 170(c), is limited to 5 percent of its taxable income for the year, computed without regard to—

(1) The deduction under section 170 for charitable contributions,

(2) The special deductions for corporations allowed under part VIII (except section 248), subchapter B, chapter 1 of the Code,

(3) Any net operating loss carryback to the taxable year under section 172, and

(4) Any capital loss carryback to the taxable year under section 1212(a)(1).

A charitable contribution by a corporation to a trust, chest, fund, or foundation described in section 170(c)(2) is deductible under section 170 only if the contribution is to be used in the United States or its possessions exclusively for religious, charitable, scientific, literary, or educational purposes or for the prevention of cruelty to children or animals. For the purposes of section 170, amounts excluded from the gross income of a corporation under section 114, relating to sports programs conducted for the American National Red Cross, are not to be considered contributions or gifts.

(b) Election by corporations on an accrual method. **(1)** A corporation reporting its taxable income on an accrual method may elect to have a charitable contribution treated as paid during the taxable year, if payment is actually made on or before the 15th day of the third month following the close of such year and if, during such year, its board of directors authorizes the charitable contribution. * * *

(2) The election must be made at the time the return for the taxable year is filed, by reporting the contribution on the return. There shall be attached to the return when filed a written declaration stating that the resolution authorizing the contribution was adopted by the board of directors during the taxable year. For taxable years beginning before January 1,

2003, the declaration shall be verified by a statement signed by an officer authorized to sign the return that it is made under the penalties of perjury, and there shall also be attached to the return when filed a copy of the resolution of the board of directors authorizing the contribution. For taxable years beginning after December 31, 2002, the declaration must also include the date of the resolution, the declaration shall be verified by signing the return, and a copy of the resolution of the board of directors authorizing the contribution is a record the taxpayer must retain and keep available for inspection in the manner required by §1.6001–1(e).

(c) Charitable contributions carryover of corporations—(1) In general. Subject to the reduction provided in subparagraph (2) of this paragraph, any charitable contributions made by a corporation in a taxable year (hereinafter in this paragraph referred to as the "contribution year") in excess of the amount deductible in such contribution year under the 5-percent limitation of section 170(b)(2) are deductible in each of the five succeeding taxable years in order of time, but only to the extent of the lesser of the following amounts:

(i) The excess of the maximum amount deductible for such succeeding taxable year under the 5-percent limitation of section 170(b)(2) over the sum of the charitable contributions made in that year plus the aggregate of the excess contributions which were made in taxable years before the contribution year and which are deductible under this paragraph in such succeeding taxable year; or

(ii) In the case of the first taxable year succeeding the contribution year, the amount of the excess charitable contributions, and in the case of the second, third, fourth, and fifth taxable years succeeding the contribution year, the portion of the excess charitable contributions not deductible under this subparagraph for any taxable year intervening between the contribution year and such succeeding taxable year.

This paragraph applies to excess charitable contributions by a corporation, whether or not such contributions are made to, or for the use of, the donee organization and whether or not such organization is a section 170(b)(1)(A) organization, as defined in §1.170A–9. * * * The application of this subparagraph may be illustrated by the following example:

Example. A corporation which reports its income on the calendar year basis makes a charitable contribution of $20,000 in 1970. Its taxable income (determined without regard to any deduction for charitable contributions) for 1970 is $100,000. Accordingly, the charitable contributions deduction for that year is limited to $5,000 (5 percent of $100,000). The excess charitable contribution not deductible in 1970 ($15,000) is a carryover to 1971. The corporation has taxable income (determined without regard to any deduction for charitable contributions) of $150,000 in 1971 and makes a charitable contribution of $5,000 in that year. For 1971 the corporation may deduct as a charitable contribution the amount of $7,500 (5 percent of $150,000). This amount consists of the $5,000 contribution made in 1971 and of the $2,500 carried over from 1970. The remaining $12,500 carried over from 1970 and not allowable as a deduction for 1971 because of the 5-percent limitation may be carried over to 1972. The corporation has taxable income (determined without regard to any deduction for charitable contributions) of $200,000 in 1972 and makes a charitable contribution of $5,000 in that year. For 1972 the corporation may deduct the amount of $10,000 (5 percent of $200,000). This amount consists of the $5,000 contributed in 1972, and $5,000 of the $12,500 carried over from 1970 to 1972. The remaining $7,500 of the carryover from 1970 is available for purposes of computing the charitable contributions carryover from 1970 to 1973, 1974, and 1975.

(2) Effect of net operating loss carryovers on carryover of excess contributions. A corporation having a net operating loss carryover from any taxable year must apply the special rule of section 170(d)(2)(B) and this subparagraph before computing under subparagraph (1) of this paragraph the excess charitable contributions carryover from any taxable year. In determining the amount of excess charitable contributions that may be deducted in accordance with subparagraph (1) of this paragraph in taxable years succeeding the contribution year, the excess of the charitable contributions made by a corporation in the contributions year over the amount deductible in such year must be reduced by the amount by which such excess reduces taxable in–come for purposes of determining the net operating loss carryover (under the second sentence of section 172(b)(2)) and increases a net operating loss carry–over to a succeeding taxable year. Thus, if the excess of the contributions made in a taxable year over the amount deductible in the taxable year is utilized to reduce taxable income (under the provisions of section 172(b)(2)) for such year, thereby serving to increase the amount of the net operating loss carryover to a succeeding taxable year or years, no charitable contributions carryover will be allowed. If only a portion of the excess charitable contributions is so used, the charitable contributions carryover will be reduced only to that extent. The application of this subparagraph may be illustrated by the following example:

Example. A corporation, which reports its income on the calendar year basis, makes a charitable contribution of $10,000 during 1971. Its taxable income for 1971 is $80,000 (computed without regard to any net operating loss deduction and computed in accordance with section 170(b)(2) without regard to any deduction for charitable contributions). The corporation has a net operating loss carryover from 1970 of $80,000. In the absence of the net operating loss deduction the corporation would have been allowed a deduction for charitable contributions of $4,000 (5 percent of $80,000). After the application of the net operating loss deduction the corporation is allowed no deduction for charitable contributions, and there is a tentative charitable contribution carryover from 1971 of $10,000. For purposes of determining the net operating loss carryover to 1972 the corporation computes its taxable income for 1971 under section 172(b)(2) by deducting the $4,000 charitable contribution. Thus, after the $80,000 net operating loss carryover is applied against the $76,000 of taxable income for 1971 (computed in accordance with section 172(b)(2)), there remains a $4,000 net operating loss carryover to 1972. Since the application of the net operating loss carryover of $80,000 from 1970 reduces the taxable income for 1971 to zero, no part of the $10,000 of charitable contributions in that year is deductible under section 170(b)(2). However, in determining the amount of the allowable charitable contributions carryover from 1971 to 1972, 1973, 1974, 1975, and 1976, the $10,000 must be reduced by the portion thereof ($4,000) which was used to reduce taxable income for 1971 (as computed for purposes of the second sentence of section 172(b)(2)) and which thereby served to increase the net operating loss carryover from 1970 to 1972 from zero to $4,000.

(3) Effect of net operating loss carryback to contribution year. The amount of the excess contribution for a contribution year computed as provided in subparagraph (1) of this paragraph shall not be increased because a net operating loss carryback is available as a deduction in the contribution year. In addition, in determining under the provisions of section 172(b)(2) the amount of the net operating loss for any year subsequent to the contribution year which is a carryback or carryover to taxable years succeeding the contribution year, the amount of any charitable contributions shall be limited to the amount of such contributions which did not exceed 5 percent of the donor's taxable income, computed as provided in paragraph (a) of this section and without regard to any of the modifications referred to in section 172(d), for the contribution year. For illustrations see paragraph (d)(2) of §1.170A–10.

(4) Effect of net operating loss carryback to taxable year succeeding the contribution year. The amount of the charitable contribution from a preceding taxable year which is deductible (as provided in this paragraph) in a current taxable year (hereinafter referred to in this subparagraph as the "deduction year") shall not be reduced because a net operating loss carryback is available as a deduction in the deduction year. In addition, in determining under the provisions of section 172(b)(2) the amount of the net operating loss for any taxable year subsequent to the deduction year which is a carryback or a carryover to taxable years succeeding the deduction year, the amount of contributions made in the deduction year shall be limited to the amount of such contributions, which were actually made in such year and those which were deductible in such year under section 170(d)(2), which did not exceed 5 percent of the donor's taxable income, computed as provided in paragraph (a) of this section and without regard to any of the modifications referred to in section 172(d), for the deduction year.

(5) Year contribution is made. For purposes of this paragraph, contributions made by a corporation in a contribution year include contributions which, in accordance with the provisions of section 170(a)(2) and paragraph (b) of this section, are considered as paid during such contribution year.

* * *

§ 1.170A–13 Recordkeeping and return requirements for deductions for charitable contributions.*

(a) Charitable contributions of money made in taxable years beginning after December 31, 1982—(1) In general. If a taxpayer makes a charitable contribution of money in a taxable year beginning after December 31, 1982, the taxpayer shall maintain for each contribution one of the following:

(i) A cancelled check.

(ii) A receipt from the donee charitable organization showing the name of the donee, the date of the contribution, and the amount of the contribution. A letter or other communication from the donee charitable organization acknowledging receipt of a contribution and showing the date and amount of the contribution constitutes a receipt for purposes of this paragraph (a).

(iii) In the absence of a canceled check or receipt from the donee charitable organization, other reliable written records showing the name of the donee, the date of the contribution, and the amount of the contribution.

(2) Special rules— (i) Reliability of records. The reliability of the written records described in 'paragraph (a)(1)(iii) of this section is to be

*Editorial comment: The Regulations now include the effect of the Revenue Reconciliation Act of 1993 on Sec. 170(f)(8). See Sec. 1.170A–13(f).

determined on the basis of all of the facts and circumstances of a particular case. In all events, however, the burden shall be on the taxpayer to establish reliability. Factors indicating that the written records are reliable include, but are not limited to:

(A) The contemporaneous nature of the writing evidencing the contribution.

(B) The regularity of the taxpayer's recordkeeping procedures. For example, a contemporaneous diary entry stating the amount and date of the donation and the name of the donee charitable organization made by a taxpayer who regularly makes such diary entries would generally bc considered reliable.

(C) In the case of a contribution of a small amount, the existence of any written or other evidence from the donee charitable organization evidencing receipt of a donation that would not otherwise constitute a receipt under paragraph (a)(1)(ii) of this section (including an emblem, button, or other token traditionally associated with a charitable organization and regularly given by the organization to persons making cash donations).

(ii) Information stated in income tax return. The information required by paragraph (a)(1)(iii) of this section shall be stated in taxpayer's income tax return if required by the return form or its in–structions.

* * *

(b) Charitable contributions of property other than money made in taxable years beginning after December 31, 1982—(1) In general. Except in the case of certain charitable contributions of property made after December 31, 1984, to which paragraph (c) of this section applies, any taxpayer who makes a charitable contribution of property other than money in a taxable year beginning after December 31, 1982, shall maintain for each contribution a receipt from the donee showing the following information:

(i) The name of the donee.

(ii) The date and location of the contribution.

(iii) A description of the property in detail reasonably sufficient under the circumstances. Although the fair market value of the property is one of the circumstances to be taken into account in determining the amount of detail to be included on the receipt, such value need not be stated on the receipt.

A letter or other written communication from the donee acknowledging receipt of the contribution, showing the date of the contribution, and containing the required description of the property contributed constitutes a receipt for purposes of this paragraph. A receipt is not required if the contribution is made in circumstances where it is impractical to obtain a receipt (e.g., by depositing property at a charity's unattended drop site). In such cases, however, the taxpayer shall maintain reliable written records with respect to each item of donated property that include the information required by paragraph (b)(2)(ii) of this section.

(2) Special rules—(i) Reliability of records. The rules described in paragraph (a)(2)(i) of this section also apply to this paragraph (b) for determining the reliability of the written records described in paragraph (b)(1) of this section.

(ii) Content of records. The written records described in paragraph (b)(1) of this section shall include the following information and such information shall be stated in the taxpayers income tax return if required by the return form or its instructions:

(A) The name and address of the donee organization to which the contribution was made.

(B) The date and location of the contribution.

(C) A description of the property in detail reasonable under the circumstances (including the value of the property), and, in the case of securities, the name of the issuer, the type of security, and whether or not such security is regularly traded on a stock exchange or in an over-the-counter market.

(D) The fair market value of the property at the time the contribution was made, the method utilized in determining the fair market value, and, if the valuation was determined by appraisal, a copy of the signed report of the appraiser.

(E) In the case of property to which section 170(e) applies, the cost or other basis, adjusted as provided by section 1016, the reduction by reason of section 170(e)(1) in the amount of the charitable contribution otherwise taken into account, and the manner in which such reduction was determined. A taxpayer who elects under paragraph (d)(2) of §1.170A–8 to apply section 170(e)(1) to contributions and carryovers of 30 percent capital gain property shall maintain a written record indicating the years for which the election was made and showing the contributions in the current year and carryovers from preceding years to which it applies. For the definition of the term "30-percent capital gain property," see paragraph (d)(3) of §1.170A–8.

(F) If less than the entire interest in the property is contributed during the taxable year, the total amount claimed as a deduction for the taxable year due to the contribution of the property, and the amount claimed as a deduction in any prior year or years for contributions of other interests in such property, the name and address of each organization to which any such contribution was made, the place where any such property which is tangible property is located or kept, and the name of any person, other than the organization to which the property giving rise to the deduction was contributed, having actual possession of the property.

(G) The terms of any agreement or understanding entered into by or on behalf of the taxpayer which relates to the use, sale, or other disposition of the property contributed, including for example, the terms of any agreement or understanding which—.

(1) Restricts temporarily or permanently the donee's right to use or dispose of the donated property,

(2) Reserves to, or confers upon, anyone (other than the donee organization or an organization participating with the donee organization in cooperative fundraising) any right to the income from the donated property or to the possession of the property, including the right to vote donated securities, to acquire the property by purchase or otherwise, or to designate the person having such income, possession, or right to acquire, or

(3) Earmarks donated property for a particular use.

(3) Deductions in excess of $500 claimed for a charitable contribution of property other than money—(i) In general. In addition to the information required under paragraph (b)(2)(ii) of this section, if a taxpayer makes a charitable contribution of property other than money in a taxable year beginning after December 31, 1982, and claims a deduction in excess of $500 in respect of the contribution of such item, the taxpayer shall maintain written records that include the following information with respect to such item of donated property, and shall state such information in his or her income tax return if required by the return form or its instructions:

(A) The manner of acquisition, as for example by purchase, gift, bequest, inheritance, or exchange, and the approximate date of acquisition of the property by the taxpayer or, if the property was created, produced, or manufactured by or for the taxpayer, the approximate date the property was substantially completed.

(B) The cost or other basis, adjusted as provided by section 1016, of property, other than publicly traded securities, held by the taxpayer for a period of less than 12 months (6 months for property contributed in taxable years beginning after December 31, 1982, and on or before June 6, 1988, immediately preceding the date on which the contribution was made and, when the information is available, of property, other than publicly traded securities, held for a period of 12 months or more (6 months or more for property contributed in taxable years beginning after December 31, 1982, and on or before June 6, 1988, preceding the date on which the contribution was made.

(ii) Information on acquisition date or cost basis not available. If the return form or its instructions require the taxpayer to provide information on either the acquisition date of the property or the cost basis as described in paragraph (b)(3)(i)(A) and (B), respectively, of this section, and the taxpayer has reasonable cause for not being able to provide such information, the taxpayer shall attach an explanatory statement to the return. If a taxpayer has reasonable cause for not being able to provide such information, the taxpayer shall not be disallowed a charitable contribution deduction under section 170 for failure to comply with paragraph (b)(3)(i)(A) and (B) of the section.

* * *

(c) Deductions in excess of $5,000 for certain charitable contributions of property made after December 31, 1984—(1) General rule—(i) In general. This paragraph applies to any charitable contribution made after December 31, 1984, by an individual, closely held corporation, personal service corporation, partnership, or S corporation of an item of property (other than money and publicly traded securities to which §1.170A–13(c)(7)(xi)(B) does not apply if the amount claimed or reported as a deduction under section 170 with respect to such item exceeds $5,000. This paragraph also applies to charitable contributions by C corporations (as defined in section 1361(a)(2) of the Code) to the extent described in paragraph (c)(2)(ii) of this section. No deduction under section 170 shall be allowed with respect to a charitable contribution to which this paragraph applies unless the substantiation requirements described in paragraph (c)(2) of this section are met. For purposes of this paragraph (c), the amount claimed or reported as a deduction for an item of property is the aggregate amount claimed or reported as a deduction for a charitable contribution under section 170 for such items of property and all similar items of property (as defined in paragraph (c)(7)(iii) of this section) by the same donor for the same taxable year (whether or not donated to the same donee).

(ii) Special rule for property to which section 170(e)(3) or (4) applies. For purposes of this paragraph (c), in computing the amount claimed or reported as a deduction for donated property to which section 170(e)(3) or (4) applies (pertaining to certain contributions of inventory and scientific equipment) there shall be taken into account only the amount claimed or reported as a deduction in excess of the amount which would have been taken into account for tax purposes by the donor as costs of goods sold if the donor had sold the contributed property to the donee. For example, assume that a donor makes a contribution from inventory of clothing for the care of the needy to which section 170(e)(3) applies. The cost of the property to the donor was $5,000, and, pursuant to section 170(e)(3)(B), the donor claims a charitable contribution deduction of $8,000 with respect to the property. Therefore, $3,000 ($8,000 – $5,000) is the amount taken into account for purposes of determining whether the $5,000 threshold of this paragraph (c)(l) is met.

(2) Substantiation requirements—(i) In general. Except as provided in paragraph (c)(2)(ii) of this section, a donor who claims or reports a deduction with respect to a charitable contribution to which this paragraph (c) applies must comply with the following three requirements:

(A) Obtain a qualified appraisal (as defined in paragraph (c)(3) of this section) for such property contributed. If the contributed property is a partial interest, the appraisal shall be of the partial interest.

(B) Attach a fully completed appraisal summary (as defined in paragraph (c)(4) of this section) to the tax return (or, in the case of a donor that is a partnership or S corporation, the information return) on which the deduction for the contribution is first claimed (or reported) by the donor.

(C) Maintain records containing the information required by paragraph (b)(2)(ii) of this section.

(ii) Special rules for certain nonpublicly traded stock, certain publicly traded securities, and contributions by certain C corporations.—(A) In cases described in paragraph (c)(2)(ii)(B) of this section, a qualified appraisal is not required, and only a partially completed appraisal summary form (as described in paragraph (c)(4)(iv)(A) of this section) is required to be attached to the tax or information return specified in paragraph (c)(2)(i)(B) of this section. However, in all cases donors must maintain records containing the information required by paragraph (b)(2)(ii) of this section.

(B) This paragraph (c)(2)(ii) applies in each of the following cases:

(1) The contribution of nonpublicly traded stock, if the amount claimed or reported as a deduction for the charitable contribution of such stock is greater than $5,000 but does not exceed $10,000;

(2) The contribution of a security to which paragraph (c)(7)(xi)(B) of this section applies; and

(3) The contribution of an item of property or of similar items of property described in paragraph (c)(1) of this section made after June 6, 1988, by a C corporation (as defined in section 1361(a)(2) of the Code), other than a closely held corporation or a personal service corporation.

(3) Qualified appraisal—(i) In general. For purposes of this paragraph (c), the term "qualified appraisal" means an appraisal document that—

(A) Relates to an appraisal that is made not earlier than 60 days prior to the date of contribution of the appraised property nor later than the date specified in paragraph (c)(3)(iv)(B) of this section;

(B) Is prepared, signed, and dated by a qualified appraiser (within the meaning of paragraph (c)(5) of this section);

(C) Includes the information required by paragraph (c)(3)(ii) of this section; and

(D) Does not involve an appraisal fee prohibited by paragraph (c)(6) of this section.

(ii) Information included in qualified appraisal. A qualified appraisal shall include the following information:

(A) A description of the property in sufficient detail for a person who is not generally familiar with the type of property to ascertain that the property that was appraised is the property that was (or will be) contributed;

(B) In the case of tangible property, the physical condition of the property;

(C) The date (or expected date) of contribution to the donee;

(D) The terms of any agreement or understanding entered into (or expected to be entered into) by or on behalf of the donor or donee that relates to the use, sale, or other disposition of the property contributed, including, for example, the terms of any agreement or understanding that—

(1) Restricts temporarily or permanently a donee's right to use or dispose of the donated property,

(2) Reserves to, or confers upon, anyone (other than a donee organization or an organization participating with a donee organization in cooperative fundraising) any right to the income from the contributed property or to the possession of the property, including the right to vote donated securities, to acquire the property by purchase or otherwise, or to designate the person having such income, possession, or right to acquire, or

(3) Earmarks donated property for a particular use;

(E) The name, address, and (if a taxpayer identification number is otherwise required by section 6109 and the regulations thereunder) the identifying number of the qualified appraiser; and, if the qualified appraiser is acting in his or her capacity as a partner in a partnership, an employee of any person (whether an individual, corporation, or partnership), or an independent contractor engaged by a person other than the donor, the name, address, and taxpayer identification number (if a number is otherwise required by section 6109 and the regulations thereunder) of the partnership or the person who employs or engages the qualified appraiser;

(F) The qualifications of the qualified appraiser who signs the appraisal, including the appraiser's background, experience, education, and membership, if any, in professional appraisal associations;

(G) A statement that the appraisal was prepared for income tax purposes;

(H) The date (or dates) on which the property was appraised;

(I) The appraised fair market value (within the meaning of §1.170A–1(c)(2)) of the property on the date (or expected date) of contribution;

(J) The method of valuation used to determine the fair market value, such as the income approach, the market–data approach, and the replacement-cost-less-depreciation approach; and

(K) The specific basis for the valuation, such as specific comparable sales transactions or statistical sampling, including a justification for using sampling and an explanation of the sampling procedure employed.

(iii) Effect of signature of the qualified appraiser. Any appraiser who falsely or fraudulently overstates the value of the contributed property referred to in a qualified appraisal or appraisal summary (as defined in paragraphs (c)(3) and (4), respectively, of this section) that the appraiser has signed may be subject to a civil penalty under section 6701 for aiding and abetting an understatement of tax liability and, moreover, may have appraisals disregarded pursuant to 31 U.S.C. 330(c).

(iv) Special rules—**(A)** Number of qualified appraisals. For purposes of paragraph (c)(2)(i)(A) of this section, a separate qualified appraisal is required for each item of property that is not included in a group of similar items of property. See paragraph (c)(7)(iii) of this section for the definition of similar items of property. Only one qualified appraisal is required for a group of similar items of property contributed in the same taxable year of the donor, although a donor may obtain separate qualified appraisals for each item of property. A qualified appraisal prepared with respect to a group of similar items of property shall provide all the information required by paragraph (c)(3)(ii) of this section for each item of similar property, except that the appraiser may select any items whose aggregate value is appraised at $100 or less and provide a group description of such items.

(B) Time of receipt of qualified appraisal. The qualified appraisal must be received by the donor before the due date (including extensions) of the return on which a deduction is first claimed (or reported in the case of a donor that is a partnership or S corporation) under section 170 with respect to the donated property, or, in the case of a deduction first claimed (or reported) on an amended return, the date on which the return is filed.

(C) Retention of qualified appraisal. The donor must retain the qualified appraisal in the donor's records for so long as it may be relevant in the administration of any internal revenue law.

(D) Appraisal disregarded pursuant to 31 U.S.C. 330(c). If an appraisal is disregarded pursuant to 31 U.S.C. 330(c) it shall have no probative effect as to the value of the appraised property. Such appraisal will, however, otherwise constitute a "qualified appraisal" for purposes of this paragraph (c) if the appraisal summary includes the declaration described in paragraph (c)(4)(ii)(L)(2) and the taxpayer had no knowledge that such declaration was false as of the time described in paragraph (c)(4)(i)(B) of this section.

(4) Appraisal summary—(i) In general. For purposes of this paragraph (c), except as provided in paragraph (c)(4)(iv)(A) of this section, the term "appraisal summary" means a summary of a qualified appraisal that—

(A) Is made on the form prescribed by the Internal Revenue Service;

(B) Is signed and dated (as described in paragraph (c)(4)(iii) of this section) by the donee (or presented to the donee for signature in cases described in paragraph (c)(4)(iv)(C)(2) of this section);

(C) Is signed and dated by the qualified appraiser (within the meaning of paragraph (c)(5) of this section) who prepared the qualified appraisal (within the meaning of paragraph (c)(3) of this section); and

(D) Includes the information required by paragraph (c)(4)(ii) of this section.

(ii) Information included in an appraisal summary. An appraisal summary shall include the following information:

(A) The name and taxpayer identification number of the donor (social security number if the donor is an individual or employer identification number if the donor is a partnership or corporation);

(B) A description of the property in sufficient detail for a person who is not generally familiar with the type of property to ascertain that the property that was appraised is the property that was contributed;

(C) In the case of tangible property, a brief summary of the overall physical condition of the property at the time of the contribution;

(D) The manner of acquisition (e.g., purchase, exchange, gift, or bequest) and the date of acquisition of the property by the donor, or, if the property was created, produced, or manufactured by or for the donor, a statement to that effect and the approximate date the property was substantially completed;

(E) The cost or other basis of the property adjusted as provided by section 1016;

(F) The name, address, and taxpayer identification number of the donee;

(G) The date the donee received the property;

(H) For charitable contributions made after June 6, 1988, a statement explaining whether or not the charitable contribution was made by means of a bargain sale and the amount of any consideration received from the donee for the contribution;

(I) The name, address, and (if a taxpayer identification number is otherwise required by section 6109 and the regulations thereunder) the identifying number of the qualified appraiser who signs the appraisal summary and of other persons as required by paragraph (c)(3)(ii)(E) of this section;

(J) The appraised fair market value of the property on the date of contribution;

(K) The declaration by the appraiser described in paragraph (c)(5)(i) of this section;

(L) A declaration by the appraiser stating that—

(1) The fee charged for the appraisal is not of a type prohibited by paragraph (c)(6) of this section; and

(2) Appraisals prepared by the appraiser are not being disregarded pursuant to 31 U.S.C. 330(c) on the date the appraisal summary is signed by the appraiser; and

(M) Such other information as may be specified by the form.

(iii) Signature of the original donee. The person who signs the appraisal summary for the donee shall be an official authorized to sign the tax or information returns of the donee, or a person specifically authorized to sign appraisal summaries by an official authorized to sign the tax or information returns of such donee. In the case of a donee that is a governmental unit, the person who signs the appraisal summary for such donee shall be the official authorized by such donee to sign appraisal summaries. The signature of the donee on the appraisal summary does not represent concurrence in the appraised value of the contributed property. Rather, it represents acknowledgment of receipt of the property described in the appraisal summary on the date specified in the appraisal summary and that the donee understands the information reporting requirements imposed by §6050L and §1.6050L–1.

In general, §1.6050L–1 requires the donee to file an information return with the Internal Revenue Service in the event the donee sells, exchanges, consumes, or otherwise disposes of the property (or any portion thereof) described in the appraisal summary within 2 years after the date of the donor's contribution of such property.

(iv) Special rules—**(A)** Content of appraisal summary required in certain cases. With respect to contributions of nonpublicly traded stock described in paragraph (c)(2)(ii)(B)(1) of this section, contributions of securities described in paragraph (c)(7)(xi)(B) of this section, and contributions by C corporations described in paragraph (c)(2)(ii)(B)(3) of this section, the term "appraisal summary" means a document that—

(1) Complies with the requirements of paragraph (c)(4)(i)(A) and (B) of this section,

(2) Includes the information required by paragraph (c)(4)(ii)(A) through (H) of this section,

(3) Includes the amount claimed or reported as a charitable contribution deduction, and

(4) In the case of securities described in paragraph (c)(7)(xi)(B) of this section, also includes the pertinent average trading price (as described in paragraph (c)(7)(xi)(B)(2)(iii) of this section).

(B) Number of appraisal summaries. A separate appraisal summary for each item of property described in paragraph (c)(1) of this section must be attached to the donor's return. If, during the donor's taxable year, the donor contributes similar items of property described in paragraph (c)(1) of this section to more than one donee, the donor shall attach to the donor's return a separate appraisal summary for each donee. See paragraph (c)(7)(iii) of this section for the definition of similar items of property. If, however, during the donor's taxable year, a donor contributes similar items of property described in paragraph (c)(1) of this section to the same donee, the donor may attach to the donor's return a single appraisal summary with respect to all similar items of property contributed to the same donee. Such an appraisal summary shall provide all the information required by paragraph (c)(4)(ii) of this section for each item of property, except that the appraiser may select any items whose aggregate value is appraised at $100 or less and provide a group description for such items.

(C) Manner of acquisition, cost basis and donee's signature. **(1)** If a taxpayer has reasonable cause for being unable to provide the information required by paragraph (c)(4)(ii)(D) and (E) of this section (relating to the manner of acquisition and basis of the contributed property), an appropriate explanation should be attached to the appraisal summary. The taxpayer's deduction will not be disallowed simply because of the inability (for reasonable cause) to provide these items of information.

(2) In rare and unusual circumstances in which it is impossible for the taxpayer to obtain the signature of the donee on the appraisal summary as required by paragraph (c)(4)(i)(B) of this section, the taxpayer's deduction will not be disallowed for that reason provided that the taxpayer attaches a statement to the appraisal summary explaining, in detail, why it was not possible to obtain the donee's signature. For example, if the donee ceases to exist as an entity subsequent to the date of the contribution and prior to the date when the appraisal summary must be signed, and the donor acted reasonably in not obtaining the donee's signature at the time of the contribution, relief under this paragraph (c)(4)(iv)(C)(2) would generally be appropriate.

(D) Information excluded from certain appraisal summaries. The information required by paragraph (c)(4)(i)(C), paragraph (c)(4)(ii)(D), (E), (H) through (M), and paragraph (c)(4)(iv)(A)(3), and the average trading price referred to in paragraph (c)(4)(iv)(A)(4) of this section do not have to be included on the appraisal summary at the time it is signed by the donee or a copy is provided to the donee pursuant to paragraph (c)(4)(iv)(E) of this section.

(E) Statement to be furnished by donors to donees. Every donor who presents an appraisal summary to a donee for signature after June 6, 1988, in order to comply with paragraph (c)(4)(i)(B) of this section shall furnish a copy of the appraisal summary to such donee.

(F) Appraisal summary required to be provided to partners and S corporation shareholders. If the donor is a partnership or S corporation, the donor shall provide a copy of the appraisal summary to every partner or shareholder, respectively, who receives an allocation of a charitable contribution deduction under section 170 with respect to the property described in the appraisal summary.

(G) Partners and S corporation shareholders. A partner of a partnership or shareholder of an S corporation who receives an allocation of a deduction under section 170 for a charitable contribution of property to which this paragraph (c) applies must attach a copy of the partnership's or S corporation's appraisal summary to the tax return on which the deduction for the contribution is first claimed. If such appraisal summary is not attached, the partner's or shareholder's deduction shall not be allowed except as provided for in paragraph (c)(4)(iv)(H) of this section.

(H) Failure to attach appraisal summary. In the event that a donor fails to attach to the donor's return an appraisal summary as required by paragraph (c)(2)(i)(B) of this section, the Internal Revenue Service may request that the donor submit the appraisal summary within 90 days of the request. If such a request is made and the donor complies with the request within the 90-day period, the deduction under section 170 shall not be disallowed for failure to attach the appraisal summary, provided that the donor's failure to attach the appraisal summary was a good faith omission and the requirements of paragraph (c)(3) and (4) of this section are met (including the completion of the qualified appraisal prior to the date specified in paragraph (c)(3)(iv)(B) of this section).

(5) Qualified appraiser—(i) In general. The term "qualified appraiser" means an individual (other than a person described in paragraph (c)(5)(iv) of this section) who includes on the appraisal summary (described in paragraph (c)(4) of this section), a declaration that—

(A) The individual either holds himself or herself out to the public as an appraiser or performs appraisals on a regular basis;

(B) Because of the appraiser's qualifications as described in the appraisal (pursuant to paragraph (c)(3)(ii)(F) of this section), the appraiser is qualified to make appraisals of the type of property being valued;

(C) The appraiser is not one of the persons described in paragraph (c)(5)(iv) of this section; and

(D) The appraiser understands that an intentionally false or fraudulent overstatement of the value of the property described in the qualified appraisal or appraisal summary may subject the appraiser to a civil penalty under section 6701 for aiding and abetting an understatement of tax liability, and, moreover, the appraiser may have appraisals disregarded pursuant to 31 U.S.C. 330(c) (see paragraph (c)(3)(iii) of this section).

(ii) Exception. An individual is not a qualified appraiser with respect to a particular donation, even if the declaration specified in paragraph (c)(5)(i) of this section is provided in the appraisal summary, if the donor had knowledge of facts that would cause a reasonable person to expect the appraiser falsely to overstate the value of the donated property (e.g., the donor and the appraiser make an agreement concerning the amount at which the property will be valued and the donor knows that such amount exceeds the fair market value of the property).

(iii) Numbers of appraisers. More than one appraiser may appraise the donated property. If more than one appraiser appraises the property, the donor does not have to use each appraiser's appraisal for purposes of substantiating the charitable contribution deduction pursuant to this paragraph (c). If the donor uses the appraisal of more than one appraiser, or if two or more appraisers contribute to a single appraisal, each appraiser shall comply with the requirements of this paragraph (c), including signing the qualified appraisal and appraisal summary as required by paragraphs (c)(3)(i)(B) and (c)(4)(i)(C) of this section, respectively.

(iv) Qualified appraiser exclusions. The following persons cannot be qualified appraisers with respect to particular property:

(A) The donor or the taxpayer who claims or reports a deductions under section 170 for the contribution of the property that is being appraised.

(B) A party to the transaction in which the donor acquired the property being appraised (i.e., the person who sold, exchanged, or gave the property to the donor, or any person who acted as an agent for the transferor or for the donor with respect to such sale, exchange, or gift), unless the property is donated within 2 months of the date of acquisition and its appraised value does not exceed its acquisition price.

(C) The donee of the property.

(D) Any person employed by any of the foregoing persons (e.g., if the donor acquired a painting from an art dealer, neither the art dealer nor persons employed by the dealer can be qualified appraisers with respect to that painting).

(E) Any person related to any of the foregoing persons under section 267(b), or, with respect to appraisals made after June 6, 1988, married to a person who is in a relationship described in section 267(b) with any of the foregoing persons.

(F) An appraiser who is regularly used by any person described in paragraph (c)(5)(iv)(A), (B), or (C) of this section and who does not perform a majority of his or her appraisals made during his or her taxable year for other persons.

(6) Appraisal fees—(i) In general. Except as otherwise provided in paragraph (c)(6)(ii) of this section, no part of the fee arrangement for a qualified appraisal can be based, in effect, on a percentage (or set of percentages) of the appraised value of the property. If a fee arrangement for an appraisal is based in whole or in part on the amount of the appraised value of the property, if any, that is allowed as a deduction under section 170, after Internal Revenue Service examination or otherwise, it shall be treated as a fee based on a percentage of the appraised value of the property. For example, an appraiser's fee that is subject to reduction by the same percentage as the appraised value may be reduced by the Internal Revenue Service would be treated as a fee that violates this paragraph (c)(6).

(ii) Exception. Paragraph (c)(6)(i) of this section does not apply to a fee paid to a generally recognized association that regulates appraisers provided all of the following requirements are met:

(A) The association is not organized for profit and no part of the net earnings of the association inures to the benefit of any private shareholder or individual (these terms have the same meaning as in section 501(c)),

(B) The appraiser does not receive any compensation from the association or any other persons for making the appraisal, and

(C) The fee arrangement is not based in whole or in part on the amount of the appraised value of the donated property, if any, that is allowed as a deduction under section 170 after Internal Revenue Service examination or otherwise.

(7) Meaning of terms. For purposes of this paragraph (c)—

(i) Closely held corporation. The term "closely held corporation" means any corporation (other than an S corporation) with respect to which the stock ownership requirement of paragraph (2) of section 542(a) of the Code is met.

(ii) Personal service corporation. The term "personal service corporation" means any corporation (other than an S corporation) which is a service organization (within the meaning of section 414(m)(3) of the Code).

(iii) Similar items of property. The phrase "similar items of property" means property of the same generic category or type, such as stamp collections (including philatelic supplies and books on stamp collecting), coin collections (including numismatic supplies and books on coin collecting), lithographs, paintings, photographs, books, nonpublicly traded stock, nonpublicly traded securities other than nonpublicly trade stock, land, buildings, clothing, jewelry, furniture, electronic equipment, household appliances, toys, everyday kitchenware, china, crystal, or silver. For example, if a donor claims on her return for the year deductions of $2,000 for books given by her to College A, $2,500 for books given by her to College B, and $900 for books given by her to College C, the $5,000 threshold of paragraph (c)(1) of this section is exceeded. Therefore, the donor must obtain a qualified appraisal for the books and attach to her return three appraisal summaries for the books donated to A, B, and C. For rules regarding the number of qualified appraisals and appraisal summaries required when similar items of property are contributed, see paragraphs (c)(3)(iv)(A) and (c)(4)(iv)(B), respectively, of this section.

(iv) Donor. The term "donor" means a person or entity (other than an organization described in section 170(c) to which the donated property was previously contributed) that makes a charitable contribution of property.

(v) Donee. The term "donee" means—

(A) Except as provided in paragraph (c)(7)(v)(B) and (C) of this section, an organization described in section 170(c) to which property is contributed,

(B) Except as provided in paragraph (c)(7)(v)(C) of this section, in the case of a charitable contribution of property placed in trust for the benefit of an organization described in section 170(c), the trust, or

(C) In the case of a charitable contribution of property placed in trust for the benefit of an organization described in section 170(c) made on or before June 6, 1988, the beneficiary that is an organization described in section 170(c), or if the trust has assumed the duties of a donee by signing the appraisal summary pursuant to paragraph (c)(4)(i)(B) of this section, the trust.

In general, the term, refers only to the original donee. However, with respect to paragraph (c)(3)(ii)(D), the last sentence of paragraph (c)(4)(iii), and paragraph (c)(5)(iv)(C) of this section, the term “donee” means the original donee and all successor donees in cases where the original donee transfers the contributed property to a successor donee after July 5, 1988.

(vi) Original donee. The term “original donee” means the donee to or for which property is initially donated by a donor.

(vii) Successor donee. The term “successor donee” means any donee of property other than its original donee (i.e., a transferee of property for less than fair market value from an original donee or another successor donee).

(viii) Fair market value. For the meaning of the term “fair market value,” see section 1.170A–1(c)(2).

(ix) Nonpublicly traded securities. The term “nonpublicly traded securities” means securities (within the meaning of section 165(g)(2) of the Code) which are not publicly traded securities as defined in paragraph (c)(7)(xi) of this section.

(x) Nonpublicly traded stock. The term “nonpublicly traded stock” means any stock of a corporation (evidence by a stock certificate) which is not a publicly traded security. The term stock does not include a debenture or any other evidence of indebtedness.

(xi) Publicly traded securities—(A) In general. Except as provided in paragraph (c)(7)(xi)(C) of this section, the term “publicly traded securities” means securities (within the meaning of section 165(g)(2) of the Code) for which (as of the date of the contribution) market quotations are readily available on an established securities market. For purposes of this section, market quotations are readily available on an established securities market with respect to a security if:

(1) The security is listed on the New York Stock Exchange, the American Stock Exchange, or any city or regional exchange in which quotations are published on a daily basis, including foreign securities listed on a recognized foreign, national, or regional exchange in which quotations are published on a daily basis;

(2) The security is regularly traded in the national or regional over-the-counter market, for which published quotations are available; or

(3) The security is a share of an open–end investment company (commonly known as a mutual fund) registered under the Investment Company Act of 1940, as amended (15 U.S.C. 80a–1 to 80b–2), for which quotations are published on a daily basis in a newspaper of general circulation throughout the United States.

(If the market value of an issue of a security is reflected only on an interdealer quotation system, the issue shall not be considered to be publicly traded unless the special rule described in paragraph (c)(7)(xi)(B) of this section is satisfied.)

(B) Special rule—**(1)** In general. An issue of a security that does not satisfy the requirements of paragraph (c)(7)(xi)(A)(1), (2), or (3) of this section shall nonetheless be considered to have market quotations readily available on an established securities market for purposes of paragraph (c)(7)(xi)(A) of this section if all of the following five requirements are met:

(i) The issue is regularly traded during the computational period (as defined in paragraph (c)(7)(xi) (B)(2)(iv) of this section) in a market that is reflected by the existence of an interdealer quotation system for the issue,

(ii) The issuer or an agent of the issuer computes the average trading price (as defined in paragraph (c)(7)(xi)(B)(2)(iii) of this section) for the issue for the computational period,

(iii) The average trading price and total volume of the issue during the computational period are published in a newspaper of general circulation throughout the United States not later than the last day of the month following the end of the calendar quarter in which the computational period ends,

(iv) The issuer or its agent keeps books and records that list for each transaction during the computational period involving each issue covered by this procedure the date of the settlement of the transaction, the name and address of the broker or dealer making the market in which the transaction occurred, and the trading price and volume, and

(v) The issuer or its agent permits the Internal Revenue Service to review the books and records described in paragraph (c)(7)(xi)(B)(1)(iv) of this section with respect to transactions during the computational period upon giving reasonable notice to the issuer or agent.

(2) Definitions. For purposes of this paragraph (c)(7)(xi)(B)—

(i) Issue of a security. The term “issue of a security” means a class of debt securities with the same obligor and identical terms except as to their relative denominations (amounts) or a class of stock having identical rights.

(ii) Interdealer quotation system. The term "interdealer quotation system" means any system of general circulation to brokers and dealers that regularly disseminates quotations of obligations by two or more identified brokers or dealers, who are not related to either the issuer of the security or to the issuer's agent, who compute the average trading price of the security. A quotation sheet prepared and distributed by a broker or dealer in the regular course of its business and containing only quotations of such broker or dealer is not an interdealer quotation system.

(iii) Average trading price. The term "average trading price" means the mean price of all transactions (weighted by volume), other than original issue or redemption transactions, conducted through a United States office of a broker or dealer who maintains a market in the issue of the security during the computational period. For this purpose, bid and asked quotations are not taken into account.

(iv) Computational period. For calendar quarters beginning on or after June 6, 1988, the term "computational period" means weekly during October through December (beginning with the first Monday in October and ending with the first Sunday following the last Monday in December) and monthly during January through September (beginning January 1). For calendar quarters beginning before June 6, 1988, the term "computational period" means weekly during October through December and monthly during January through September.

(C) Exception. Securities described in paragraph (c)(7)(xi)(A) or (B) of this section shall not be considered publicly traded securities if—

(1) The securities are subject to any restrictions that materially affect the value of the securities to the donor or prevent the securities from being freely traded, or

(2) If the amount claimed or reported as a deduction with respect to the contribution of the securities is different than the amount listed in the market quotations that are readily available on an established securities market pursuant to paragraph (c)(7)(xi)(A) or (B) of this section.

(D) Market quotations and fair market value. The fair market value of a publicly traded security, as defined in this paragraph (c)(7)(xi), is not necessarily equal to its market quotation, its average trading price (as defined in paragraph (c)(7)(xi)(B)(2)(iii) of this section), or its face value, if any. See section 1.170A–1(c)(2) for the definition of "fair market value."

* * *

(e) [Reserved]

(f) Substantiation of charitable contributions of $250 or more.

(1) through (10) [Reserved]

(11) Contributions made by payroll deduction—(i) Form of substantiation. A contribution made by means of withholding from a taxpayer's wages and payment by the taxpayer's employer to a donee organization may be substantiated, for purposes of section 170(f)(8), by both—

(A) A pay stub, Form W–2, or other document furnished by the employer that sets forth the amount withheld by the employer for the purpose of payment to a donee organization; and

(B) A pledge card or other document prepared by or at the direction of the donee organization that includes a statement to the effect that the organization does not provide goods or services in whole or partial consideration for any contributions made to the organization by payroll deduction.

(ii) Application of $250 threshold. For the purpose of applying the $250 threshold provided in section 170(f)(8)(A) to contributions made by the means described in paragraph (f)(11)(i) of this section, the amount withheld from each payment of wages to a taxpayer is treated as a separate contribution.

(12) Distributing organizations as donees. An organization described in section 170(c), or an organization described in 5 CFR 950.105 (a Principal Combined Fund Organization for purposes of the Combined Federal Campaign) and acting in that capacity, that receives a payment made as a contribution is treated as a donee organization solely for purposes of section 170(f)(8), even if the organization (pursuant to the donor's instructions or otherwise) distributes the amount received to one or more organizations described in section 170(c). This paragraph (f)(12) does not apply, however, to a case in which the distributee organization provides goods or services as part of a transaction structured with a view to avoid taking the goods or services into account in determining the amount of the deduction to which the donor is entitled under section 170.

(13) through (15) [Reserved]

(16) Effective date. Paragraphs (f)(11) and (12) of this section apply to contributions made on or after January 1, 1994.

* * *

§ 1.171–1 Amortizable bond premium.

(a) In general. Under section 171, bond premium is amortizable by the owner of the bond (as defined in §1.171–4) in accordance with subparagraph (1) or (2) of this paragraph as follows:

(1) Amortization of bond premium is mandatory with respect to—

(i) Fully tax–exempt bonds (the interest on which is excludable from gross income), whether the owner is a corporation, individual, or other taxpayer; and

(ii) Partially tax–exempt bonds owned by a corporation.

(2) Amortization of bond premium is optional, at the election of the taxpayer, with respect to—

(i) Fully taxable bonds, whether the owner is a corporation, individual, or other taxpayer; and

(ii) Partially tax–exempt bonds owned by taxpayers other than corporations.

(b) Operation. **(1)** In the case of a fully tax–exempt bond, the amortizable bond premium for the taxable year is simply an adjustment to the basis or adjusted basis of the bond. Thus, if such premium is $1, the basis or adjusted basis of the bond is reduced by $1. No deduction is allowable on account of such amortizable bond premium. See paragraph (b)(2) of §1.171–2 for treatment of bonds with alternative call dates.

(2) In the case of a fully taxable bond to which section 171 is applicable, the amortizable bond premium is applied both as an adjustment to the basis or adjusted basis of the bond and as a deduction in computing taxable income. For the disallowance of a deduction in certain cases, see paragraph (a)(3) of §1.171–2.

(3) In the case of a partially tax exempt bond, the amortizable bond premium for the taxable year is used for the following purposes:

(i) As an adjustment to the basis or adjusted basis of the bond;

(ii) As a deduction in computing taxable income;

(iii) In the case of individuals, estates, or trusts, as a reduction of the amount which would otherwise be taken into account in computing the credit against the tax provided under section 35; or

(iv) In the case of corporations, as a reduction of the amount allowed under section 242 as a deduction in computing taxable income.

(4) The application of the provisions of subparagraph (3) of this paragraph relating to a partially tax–exempt bond may be illustrated by the following example:

Example. In the case of an individual who has elected to amortize the premium on a partially tax–exempt bond, if the interest on such bond with an adjusted basis of $1,024 is $30 for the taxable year, and the amortizable bond premium thereon is $4 for the taxable year, then the $30 is included in gross income, the $4 is allowable as a deduction, the adjusted basis of $1,024 is reduced by $4 to $1,020, and a credit amounting to $0.78 (3 percent of $30 minus $4) is allowed against the tax for such taxable year. In the case of a corporation, which is required to amortize the premium on such bond, no credit is allowed against the tax, but the deduction under section 242 on account of the interest is $26 ($30 minus $4).

(5) In the case where no specific deduction is permitted under section 171(a) for amortization of bond premium as such, * * * because the taxpayer elects under section 144* to take the standard deduction, it shall be deemed, if the taxpayer has elected to amortize bond premium in accordance with the provisions of section 171, that the deduction for amortization of bond premium has been allowed for the purpose of determining the adjusted basis of the bond.

* * *

§ 1.171–2 Determination of bond premium.

(a) In general. **(1)** Except as otherwise provided in this section, bond premium on any bond to which section 171 applies is the excess of the amount of the basis (for determining loss on sale or exchange under section 1011) of the bond over the amount payable at maturity or, in the case of a callable bond, the earlier call date. For determination of applicable call date, see paragraph (b) of this section.

*Editorial comment: See Sec. 63 rather than Sec. 144.

(2) (i) * * * If a wholly taxable bond described in section 171(c)(1)(B) is acquired after December 31, 1957, the amortizable bond premium shall be computed by reference to the amount payable on maturity, or if it results in a smaller amortizable bond premium attributable to the period of earlier call date, the computation shall be made by reference to the amount payable on the earlier call date. For purposes of this subdivision, the date of acquisition of a bond shall be the date such bond was ordered under a firm commitment to buy and not the date the bond was delivered to the taxpayer. For determining whether an earlier call date is a date more than 3 years after the date of original issue, consideration will be given to the terms under which a bond is issued.

(ii) The application of the provisions of subdivision (i) of this subparagraph may be illustrated by the following examples:

* * *

Example (2). On January 1, 1958, the taxpayer (who is on a calendar year basis) pays $1,200 for a $1,000 wholly taxable bond which matures on December 31, 1977. The bond is callable on January 1, 1963, at $1,165. The premium computed with reference to the maturity date of the bond is $200. The premium computed with reference to the earlier call date is $35. Although the premium amortized ratably to maturity would yield a deduction of $10 for each year ($200 divided by 20 years), under section 171(b)(1)(B)(ii) the deduction for each taxable year for the period before January 1, 1963, will be $7 ($35 divided by 5 years). If the bond is not called, the deduction for each taxable year in the period from 1963 through 1977 will be $11 ($165 divided by 15 years). If the earliest call date in this example had been January 1, 1961, instead of January 1, 1963, the premium amortized ratably to maturity would be used to obtain a deduction of $10 per year since this would be less than the premium amortized ratably to earlier call date of $11.67 ($35 divided by 3, the number of years to the earliest call date).

* * *

§ 1.172–1 Net operating loss deduction.

(a) Allowance of deduction. Section 172(a) allows as a deduction in computing taxable income for any taxable year subject to the Code the aggregate of the net operating loss carryovers and net operating loss carrybacks to such taxable year. This deduction is referred to as the net operating loss deduction. The net operating loss is the basis for the computation of the net operating loss carryovers and net operating loss carrybacks and ultimately for the net operating loss deduction itself. The net operating loss deduction shall not be disallowed for any taxable year merely because the taxpayer has no income from a trade or business for the taxable year.

(b) Steps in computation of net operating loss deduction. The three steps to be taken in the ascertainment of the net operating loss deduction for any taxable year subject to the Code are as follows:

(1) Compute the net operating loss for any preceding or succeeding taxable year from which a net operating loss may be carried over or carried back to such taxable year.

(2) Compute the net operating loss carryovers to such taxable year from such preceding taxable years and the net operating loss carrybacks to such taxable year from such succeeding taxable years.

(3) Add such net operating loss carryovers and carrybacks in order to determine the net operating loss deduction for such taxable year.

(c) Statement with tax return. Every taxpayer claiming a net operating loss deduction for any taxable year shall file with his return for such year a concise statement setting forth the amount of the net operating loss deduction claimed and all material and pertinent facts relative thereto, including a detailed schedule showing the computation of the net operating loss deduction.

(d) Ascertainment of deduction dependent upon net operating loss carryback. If the taxpayer is entitled in computing his net operating loss deduction to a carryback which he is not able to ascertain at the time his return is due, he shall compute the net operating loss deduction on his return without regard to such net operating loss carryback. When the taxpayer ascertains the net operating loss carryback, he may within the applicable period of limitations file a claim for credit or refund of the overpayment, if any, resulting from the failure to compute the net operating loss deduction for the taxable year with the inclusion of such carryback; or he may file an application under the provisions of section 6411 for a tentative carryback adjustment.

(e) Law applicable to computations.

(1) In determining the amount of any net operating loss carryback or carryover to any taxable year, the necessary computations involving any other taxable year shall be made under the law applicable to such other taxable year.

(2) The net operating loss for any taxable year shall be determined under the law applicable to that year without regard to the year to which it is to be carried and in which, in effect, it is to be deducted as part of the net operating loss deduction.

(3) The amount of the net operating loss deduction which shall be allowed for any taxable year shall be determined under the law applicable to that year.

(f) Electing small business corporations. In determining the amount of the net operating loss deduction of any corporation, there shall be disregarded the net operating loss of such corporation for any taxable year for which such corporation was an electing small business corporation under subchapter S (section 1371 and following), chapter 1 of the Code. In applying section 172(b)(1) and (2) to a net operating loss sustained in a taxable year in which the corporation was not an electing small business corporation, a taxable year in which the corporation was an electing small business corporation is counted as a taxable year to which such net operating loss is carried back or over. However, the taxable income for such year as determined under section 172(b)(2) is treated as if it were zero for purposes of computing the balance of the loss available to the corporation as a carryback or carryover to other taxable years in which the corporation is not an electing small business corporation. See section 1374 and the regulations thereunder for allowance of a deduction to shareholders for a net operating loss sustained by an electing small business corporation.

(g) Husband and wife. The net operating loss deduction of a husband and wife shall be determined in accordance with this section, but subject also to the provisions of §1.172–7.

§ 1.172–2 Net operating loss in case of a corporation.

(a) Modification of deductions. A net operating loss is sustained by a corporation in any taxable year if and to the extent that, for such year, there is an excess of deductions allowed by chapter 1 of the Code over gross income computed thereunder. In determining the excess of deductions over gross income for such purpose—

(1) Items not deductible. No deduction shall be allowed under—

(i) Section 172 for the net operating loss deduction, and

* * *

(2) Dividends received. The 85-percent* limitation provided by section 246(b) shall not apply to the deductions otherwise allowed under—

(i) Section 243(a) in respect of dividends received from domestic corporations,

(ii) Section 244 in respect of dividends received on preferred stock of public utilities, and

(iii) Section 245 in respect of dividends received from foreign corporations; and

(3) Dividends paid. The deduction granted by Section 247 in respect of dividends paid on the preferred stock of public utilities shall be computed without regard to subsection (a)(1)(B) of Section 247.

(b) Example. The following example illustrates the application of paragraph (a):

Example. For the calendar year 1981, the X Corporation has a gross income of $400,000 and total deductions allowed by chapter 1 of the Code of $375,000 exclusive of any net operating loss deduction and exclusive of any deduction for dividends received or paid. Corporation X in 1981 received $100,000 of dividends entitled to the benefits of section 243(a). These dividends are included in Corporation X's $400,000 gross income. Corporation X has no other deductions to which section 172(d) applies. On the basis of these facts, Corporation X has a net operating loss for the year 1981 of $60,000, computed as follows:

Deductions for 1981	$375,000
Plus: Deduction for dividends received, computed without regard to the limitation provided in section 246(b) (85% of $100,000)	85,000
Total	460,000
Less: Gross income for 1981 (including $100,000 dividends)	400,000
Net operating loss for 1981	60,000

* * *

§ 1.172–3 Net operating loss in case of a taxpayer other than a corporation.

(a) Modification of deductions. A net operating loss is sustained by a taxpayer other than a corporation in any taxable year beginning after December 31, 1953, if and to the extent that, for such year there is an

*Editorial comment: The Regulations do not include the effect of the Tax Reform Act of 1986 which reduced the percentage to 80 percent or the Revenue Act of 1987 which reduced the percentage to 70 percent in certain cases.

excess of deductions allowed by chapter 1 of the Internal Revenue Code over gross income computed thereunder. In determining the excess of deductions over gross income for such purpose—

(1) Items not deductible. No deduction shall be allowed under—

(i) Section 151 for the personal exemptions or under any other section which grants a deduction in lieu of the deductions allowed by section 151,

(ii) Section 172 for the net operating loss deduction, and

(iii) Section 1202 in respect of the net long-term capital gain.*

(2) Capital losses. (i) The amount deductible on account of business capital losses shall not exceed the sum of the amount includible on account of business capital gains and that portion of nonbusiness capital gains which is computed in accordance with paragraph (c) of this section.

(ii) The amount deductible on account of nonbusiness capital losses shall not exceed the amount includible on account of nonbusiness capital gains.

(3) Nonbusiness deductions—(i) Ordinary deductions. Ordinary nonbusiness deductions shall be taken into account without regard to the amount of business deductions and shall be allowed in full to the extent, but not in excess, of that amount which is the sum of the ordinary nonbusiness gross income and the excess of nonbusiness capital gains over nonbusiness capital losses. See paragraph (c) of this section. For purposes of section 172, nonbusiness deductions and income are those deductions and that income which are not attributable to, or derived from, a taxpayer's trade or business. Wages and salary constitute income attributable to the taxpayer's trade or business for such purposes.

(ii) Sale of business property. Any gain or loss on the sale or other disposition of property which is used in the taxpayer's trade or business and which is of a character that is subject to the allowance for depreciation provided in section 167, or of real property used in the taxpayer's trade or business, shall be considered, for purposes of section 172(d)(4), as attributable to, or derived from, the taxpayer's trade or business. Such gains and losses are to be taken into account fully in computing a net operating loss without regard to the limitation on nonbusiness deductions. Thus, a farmer who sells at a loss land used in the business of farming may, in computing a net operating loss, include in full the deduction otherwise allowable with respect to such loss, without regard to the amount of his nonbusiness income and without regard to whether he is engaged in the trade or business of selling farms. Similarly, an individual who sells at a loss machinery which is used in his trade or business and which is of a character that is subject to the allowance for depreciation may, in computing the net operating loss, include in full the deduction otherwise allowable with respect to such loss.

(iii) Casualty losses. Any deduction allowable under section 165(c)(3) for losses of property not connected with a trade or business shall not be considered, for purposes of section 172(d)(4), to be a nonbusiness deduction but shall be treated as a deduction attributable to the taxpayer's trade or business.

(iv) Self-employed retirement plans. Any deduction allowed under section 404, relating to contributions of an employer to an employees' trust or annuity plan, or under section 405(c), relating to contributions to a bond purchase plan, to the extent attributable to contributions made on behalf of an individual while he is an employee within the meaning of section 401(c)(1), shall not be treated, for purposes of section 172(d)(4), as attributable to, or derived from, the taxpayer's trade or business, but shall be treated as a nonbusiness deduction.

(v) Limitation. The provisions of this subparagraph shall not be construed to permit the deduction of items disallowed by subparagraph (1) of this paragraph.

(b) Treatment of capital loss carryovers. Because of the distinction between business and nonbusiness capital gains and losses, a taxpayer who has a capital loss carryover from a preceding taxable year, includible by virtue of section 1212 among the capital losses for the taxable year in issue, is required to determine how much of such capital loss carryover is a business capital loss and how much is a nonbusiness capital loss. In order to make this determination, the taxpayer shall first ascertain what proportion of the net capital loss for such preceding taxable year was attributable to an excess of business capital losses over business capital gains for such year, and what proportion was attributable to an excess of nonbusiness capital losses over

*Editorial comment: The Regulations do not include the effect of the Tax Reform Act of 1986 which repealed the Sec. 1202 capital gain deduction. The Regulations also do not include the effect of the Revenue Reconciliation Act of 1993 which created the new Sec. 1202 exclusion. See Sec. 172(d)(2)(B).

nonbusiness capital gains. The same proportion of the capital loss carryover from such preceding taxable year shall be treated as a business capital loss and a nonbusiness capital loss, respectively. In order to determine the composition (business—nonbusiness) of a net capital loss for a taxable year, for purposes of this paragraph, if such net capital loss is computed under paragraph (b) of §1.1212–1 and takes into account a capital loss carryover from a preceding taxable year, the composition (business—nonbusiness) of the net capital loss for such preceding taxable year must also be determined. For purposes of this paragraph, the term "capital loss carryover" means the sum of the short-term and long-term capital loss carryovers from such year. This paragraph may be illustrated by the following examples:

Example (1). (i) A, an individual, has $5,000 ordinary taxable income (computed without regard to the deductions for personal exemptions) for the calendar year 1954 and also has the following capital gains and losses for such year: Business capital gains of $2,000; business capital losses of $3,200; nonbusiness capital gains of $1,000; and nonbusiness capital losses of $1,200.

(ii) A's net capital loss for the taxable year 1954 is $400, computed as follows:

Capital losses	$4,400
Capital gains	3,000
Excess of capital losses over capital gains	1,400
Less: $1,000 of such ordinary taxable income	1,000
Net capital loss for 1954	400

(iii) A's capital losses for 1954 exceeded his capital gains for such year by $1,400. Since A's business capital losses for 1954 exceeded his business capital gains for such year by $1,200, 6/7ths ($1,200/$1,400) of A's net capital loss for 1954 is attributable to an excess of his business capital losses over his business capital gains for such year. Similarly, 1/7th of the net capital loss is attributable to the excess of nonbusiness capital losses over nonbusiness capital gains. Since the capital loss carryover for 1954 to 1955 is $400, 6/7ths of $400, or $342.86, shall be treated as a business capital loss in 1955; and 1/7th of $400, or $57.14, as a nonbusiness capital loss.

Example (2). (i) A, an individual who is computing a net operating loss for the calendar year 1966, has a capital loss carryover from 1965 of $8,000. In order to apply the provisions of this paragraph, A must determine what portion of the $8,000 carryover is attributable to the excess of business capital losses over business capital gains and what portion thereof is attributable to the excess of nonbusiness capital losses over nonbusiness capital gains. For 1965, A had $10,000 ordinary taxable income (computed without regard to the deductions for personal exemptions), and a short-term capital loss carryover of $6,000 from 1964. In order to determine the composition (business—nonbusiness) of the $8,000 carryover from 1965, A first determines that of the $6,000 carryover from 1964, $5,000 is a business capital loss and $1,000 is a nonbusiness capital loss. This must be done since, under paragraph (b) of §1.1212–1, the net capital loss for 1965 is computed by taking into account the capital loss carryover from 1964. A's capital gains and losses for 1965 are as follows:

	65	Carried over from 1964
Business capital gains	$2,000	0
Business capital losses	3,000	$5,000
Nonbusiness capital gains	4,000	0
Nonbusiness capital losses	6,000	1,000

(ii) A's net capital loss for the taxable year 1965 is $8,000, computed as follows:

Capital losses (including carryovers)	$15,000
Capital gains	6,000
Excess of capital losses over capital gains	9,000
Less: $1,000 of such ordinary taxable income	1,000
Net capital loss for 1965	8,000

(iii) A's capital losses, including carryovers, for 1965 exceeded his capital gains for such year by $9,000. Since A's business capital losses for 1965 exceeded his business capital gains for such year by $6,000, 2/3rds ($6,000/$9,000) of A's net capital loss for 1965 is attributable to an excess of his business capital losses over his business capital gains for such year. Similarly, 1/3rd of the net capital loss is attributable to the excess of nonbusiness capital losses over nonbusiness capital gains. Since the total capital loss carryover from 1965 to 1966 is $8,000, 2/3rds of $8,000, or $5,333.33, shall be treated as a business capital loss in 1966; and 1/3rd of $8,000, or $2,666.67, as a nonbusiness capital loss.

(c) Determination of portion of nonbusiness capital gains available for the deduction of business capital losses. In the computation of a net operating loss a taxpayer other than a corporation must use his nonbusiness capital gains for the deduction of his nonbusiness capital losses. Any amount not necessary for this purpose shall then be used for the deduction of any excess of ordinary nonbusiness deductions over ordinary nonbusiness gross income. The remainder, computed by applying the excess ordinary nonbusiness deductions against the excess nonbusiness capital gains, shall be treated as nonbusiness capital gains and used for the purpose of determining the deductibility of business capital losses under paragraph (a)(2)(i) of this section. This principle may be illustrated by the following example:

Example. (1) A, an individual, has a total nonbusiness gross income of $20,500 computed as follows:

Ordinary gross income	$7,500
Capital gains	13,000
Total gross income	20,500

(2) A also has total nonbusiness deductions of $16,000, computed as follows:

Ordinary deduction	$9,000
Capital loss	7,000
Total deductions	16,000

(3) The portion of nonbusiness capital gains to be used for the purpose of determining the deductibility of business capital losses is $4,500, computed as follows:

Nonbusiness capital gains		$13,000
Less: Nonbusiness capital loss		7,000
Excess to be taken into account for purposes of paragraph (a)(3)(i) of this section		6,000
Ordinary nonbusiness deductions	$9,000	
Less: Ordinary nonbusiness gross income	7,500	
		1,500
Portion of nonbusiness capital gains to be used for purposes of paragraph (a)(2)(i) of this section		4,500

(d) Joint net operating loss of husband and wife. In the case of a husband and wife, the joint net operating loss for any taxable year for which a joint return is filed is to be computed on the basis of the combined income and deductions of both spouses, and the modifications prescribed in paragraph (a) of this section are to be computed as if the combined income and deductions of both spouses were the income and deductions of one individual.

(e) Illustration of computation of net operating loss of a taxpayer other than a corporation—(1) Facts. For the calendar year 1954 A, an individual, has gross income of $483,000 and allowable deductions of $540,000. The latter amount does not include the net operating loss deduction or any deduction on account of the sale or exchange of capital assets. Included in gross income are business capital gains of $50,000 and ordinary nonbusiness income of $10,000. Included among the deductions are ordinary nonbusiness deductions of $12,000 and a deduction of $600 for his personal exemption. A has a business capital loss of $60,000 in 1954. A has no other items of income or deductions to which section 172(d) applies.

(2) Computation. On the basis of these facts, A has a net operating loss for 1954 of $104,400, computed as follows:

Deductions for 1954 (as specified in first sentence of subparagraph (1))		$540,000
Plus: Amount of business capital loss ($60,000) to extent such amount does not exceed business capital gains ($50,000)		50,000
Total		590,000
Less: Excess of ordinary nonbusiness deductions over ordinary nonbusiness gross income ($12,000 minus $10,000)	$2,000	
Deduction for personal exemption	600	
		$2,600
Deductions for 1954 adjusted as required by section 172(d)		587,400
Gross income for 1954		483,000
Net operating loss for 1954		104,400

§ 1.172–4 Net operating loss carrybacks and net operating loss carryovers.*

(a) General provisions—(1) Years to which loss may be carried—(i) In general. In order to compute the net operating loss deduction the taxpayer must first determine the part of any net operating losses for any preceding or succeeding taxable years which are carrybacks or carryovers to the taxable year in issue.

(ii) General rule for carrybacks and carryovers. Except as provided in section 172(b)(1)(C), (D), (E), (F), (G), (H), (I), and (J), paragraphs (a)(1)(iii), (iv), (v), and (vi) of this section, and §1.172–10(a), a net operating loss shall be carried back to the 3 preceding taxable years and carried over to the 15 succeeding taxable years (5 succeeding taxable years for a loss sustained in a taxable year ending before January 1, 1976).

* * *

(b) Portion of net operating loss which is a carryback or a carryover to the taxable year in issue. (1) A net operating loss shall first be carried to the earliest of the several taxable years for which such loss is allowable as a carryback or a carryover, and shall then be carried to the next earliest of such several taxable years, etc. Except as provided in §1.172–9, the entire net operating loss shall be carried back to such earliest year.

(2) The portion of the loss which shall be carried to any of such several taxable years subsequent to the earliest taxable year is the excess of such net operating loss over the sum of the taxable incomes (computed as provided in §1.172–5) for all of such several taxable years preceding such subsequent taxable year.

* * *

§ 1.172–5 Taxable income which is subtracted from net operating loss to determine carryback or carryover.

(a) Taxable year subject to the Internal Revenue Code of 1954. The taxable income for any

*Editorial comment: The Regulations do not reflect the change in the carryback and carryover periods made by the Taxpayer Relief Act of 1997. See Sec. 172(b)(1). The Regulations also do not reflect the change in the carryback period for 2001 and 2002 made by the Job Creation and Worker Assistance Act of 2002. See §172(b)(1)(H). The Regulations do not reflect the change in the carryback period for small businesses made by the American Recovery and Reinvestment Tax Act of 2009 for 2008 NOLs. Finally, the Regulations do not reflect the change in the carryback period made by the Worker, Homeownership, and Business Assistance Act of 2009. See Sec. 172(b)(1)(H).

taxable year subject to the Internal Revenue Code of 1954 which is subtracted from the net operating loss for any other taxable year to determine the portion of such net operating loss which is a carryback or a carryover to a particular taxable year is computed with the modifications prescribed in this paragraph. These modifications shall be made independently of, and without reference to, the modifications required by §§1.172–2(a) and 1.172–3(a) for purposes of computing the net operating loss itself.

(1) Modifications applicable to unincorporated taxpayers only. In the case of a taxpayer other than a corporation, in computing taxable income and adjusted gross income—

(i) No deduction shall be allowed under section 151 for the personal exemptions (or under any other section which grants a deduction in lieu of the deductions allowed by section 151) and under section 1202* in respect of the net long-term capital gain.

(ii) The amount deductible on account of losses from sales or exchanges of capital assets shall not exceed the amount includible on account of gains from sales or exchanges of capital assets.

(2) Modifications applicable to all taxpayers. In the case either of a corporation or of a taxpayer other than a corporation—

(i) Net operating loss deduction. The net operating loss deduction for such taxable year shall be computed by taking into account only such net operating losses otherwise allowable as carrybacks or carryovers to such taxable year as were sustained in taxable years preceding the taxable year in which the taxpayer sustained the net operating loss from which the taxable income is to be deducted. Thus, for such purposes, the net operating loss for the loss year or any taxable year thereafter shall not be taken into account.

Example. The taxpayer's income tax returns are made on the basis of the calendar year. In computing the net operating loss deduction for 1954, the taxpayer has a carryover from 1952 of $9,000, a carryover from 1953 of $6,000, a carryback from 1955 of $18,000, and a carryback from 1956 of $10,000, or an aggregate of $43,000 in carryovers and carrybacks. Thus, the net operating loss deduction for 1954, for purposes of determining the tax liability for 1954, is $43,000. However, in computing the taxable income for 1954 which is subtracted from the net operating loss for 1955 for the purpose of determining the portion of such loss which may be carried over to subsequent taxable years, the net operating loss deduction for 1954 is $15,000, that is, the aggregate of the $9,000 carryover from 1952 and the $6,000 carryover from 1953. In computing the net operating loss deduction for such purpose, the $18,000 carryback from 1955 and the $10,000 carryback from 1956 are disregarded. In computing the taxable income for 1954, however, which is subtracted from the net operating loss for 1956 for the purpose of determining the portion of such loss which may be carried over to subsequent taxable years, the net operating loss deduction for 1954 is $33,000, that is, the aggregate of the $9,000 carryover from 1952, the $6,000 carryover from 1953, and the $18,000 carryback from 1955. In computing the net operating loss deduction for such purpose, the $10,000 carryback from 1956 is disregarded.

(ii) Recomputation of percentage limitations. Unless otherwise specifically provided in this subchapter, any deduction which is limited in amount to a percentage of the taxpayer's taxable income or adjusted gross income shall be recomputed upon the basis of the taxable income or adjusted gross income, as the case may be, determined with the modifications prescribed in this paragraph. Thus, in the case of an individual the deduction for medical expenses would be recomputed after making all the modifications prescribed in this paragraph, whereas the deduction for charitable contributions would be determined without regard to any net operating loss carryback but with regard to any other modifications so prescribed. See, however, the regulations under paragraph (g) of §1.170–2 (relating to charitable contributions carryover of individuals) and paragraph (c) of §1.170–3 (relating to charitable contributions carryover of corporations) for special rules regarding charitable contributions in excess of the percentage limitations which may be treated as paid in succeeding taxable years.

Example (1). For the calendar year 1954 the taxpayer, an individual, files a return showing taxable income of $4,800, computed as follows:

Salary		$5,000
Net long-term capital gain		4,000
Total gross income		9,000
Less: Deduction allowed by section 1202* in respect of net long-term capital gain		2,000
Adjusted gross income		7,000
Less:		
Deduction for personal exemption	$600	
Deduction for medical expense ($410 actually paid but allowable only to extent in excess of 3 percent of adjusted gross income)	200	
Deduction for charitable contributions ($2,000 actually paid but allowable only to extent not in excess of 20 percent of adjusted gross income)	$1,400	
		$2,200
Taxable income		4,800

*Editorial comment: The Regulations do not include the effect of the Tax Reform Act of 1986 which repealed the Sec. 1202 capital gain deduction. The Regulations also do not include the effect of the Revenue Reconciliation Act of 1993 which created the new Sec. 1202 exclusion.

In 1955 the taxpayer undertakes the operation of a trade or business and sustains therein a net operating loss of $3,000. Under section 172(b)(2), it is determined that the entire $3,000 is a carryback to 1954. In 1956 he sustains a net operating loss of $10,000 in the operation of the business. In determining the amount of the carryover of the 1956 loss to 1957, the taxable income for 1954 as computed under this paragraph is $3,970, determined as follows:

Salary		$5,000
Net long-term capital gain		4,000
Total gross income		9,000
Less: Deduction for carryback of 1955 net operating loss		3,000
Adjusted gross income		6,000
Less:		
Deduction for medical expense ($410 actually paid but allowable only to extent in excess of 3 percent of adjusted gross income as modified under this paragraph)	$230	
Deduction for charitable contributions ($2,000 actually paid but allowable only to extent not in excess of 20 percent of adjusted gross income determined with all the modifications prescribed in this paragraph other than the net operating loss carryback)	1,800	
		2,030
Taxable income		3,970

Example (2). For the calendar year 1959 the taxpayer, an individual, files a return showing taxable income of $5,700, computed as follows:

Salary		$5,000
Net long-term capital gain		4,000
Total gross income		9,000
Less: Deduction allowed by section 1202* in respect of net long-term capital gain		2,000
Adjusted gross income		7,000
Less:		
Deduction for personal exemption	$600	
Standard deduction allowed by section 141	$700	
		$1,300
Taxable income		5,700

In 1960 the taxpayer undertakes the operation of a trade or business and sustains therein a net operating loss of $4,700. In 1961 he sustains a net operating loss of $10,000 in the operation of the business. Under section 172(b)(2), it is determined that the entire amount of each loss, $4,700 and $10,000, is a carryback to 1959. In determining the amount of the carryover of the 1961 loss to 1962, the taxable income for 1959 as computed under this paragraph is $3,870, determined as follows:

Salary	$5,000
Net long-term capital gain	4,000
Total gross income	9,000
Less: Deduction for carryback of 1960 net operating loss	4,700
Adjusted gross income	4,300
Less: Standard deduction	430
Taxable income	3,870

(iii) Minimum limitation. The taxable income, as modified under this paragraph, shall in no case be considered less than zero.

* * *

§ 1.183–1 Activities not engaged in for profit.

(a) In general. Section 183 provides rules relating to the allowance of deductions in the case of activities (whether active or passive in character) not engaged in for profit by individuals and electing small business corporations, creates a presumption that an activity is engaged in for profit if certain requirements are met, and permits the taxpayer to elect to postpone determination of whether such presumption applies until he has engaged in the activity for at least 5 taxable years, or, in certain cases, 7 taxable years. Whether an activity is engaged in for profit is determined under section 162 and section 212(1) and (2) except insofar as section 183(d) creates a presumption that the activity is engaged in for profit. If deductions are not allowable under sections 162 and 212(1) and (2), the deduction allowance rules of section 183(b) and this section apply. Pursuant to section 641(b), the taxable income of an estate or trust is computed in the same manner as in the case of an individual, with certain exceptions not here relevant. Accordingly, where an estate or trust engages in an activity or activities which are not for profit, the rules of section 183 and this section apply in computing the allowable deductions of such trust or estate. No inference is to be drawn from the provisions of section 183 and the regulations thereunder that any activity of a corporation (other than an electing small business corporation) is or is not a business or engaged in for profit. * * * For the definition of an activity not engaged in for profit, see §1.183–2. For rules relating to the election contained in section 183(e), see §1.183–3.

*Editorial comment: The Regulations do not include the effect of the Tax Reform Act of 1986 which repealed the Sec. 1202 capital gain deduction. The Regulations also do not include the effect of the Revenue Reconciliation Act of 1993 which created the new Sec. 1202 exclusion.

(b) Deductions allowable—(1) Manner and extent. If an activity is not engaged in for profit, deductions are allowable under section 183(b) in the following order and only to the following extent—

(i) Amounts allowable as deductions during the taxable year under chapter 1 of the Code without regard to whether the activity giving rise to such amounts was engaged in for profit are allowable to the full extent allowed by the relevant sections of the Code, determined after taking into account any limitations or exceptions with respect to the allowability of such amounts. For example, the allowability–of–interest expenses incurred with respect to activities not engaged in for profit is limited by the rules contained in section 163(d).

(ii) Amounts otherwise allowable as deductions during the taxable year under chapter 1 of the Code, but only if such allowance does not result in an adjustment to the basis of property, determined as if the activity giving rise to such amounts was engaged in for profit, are allowed only to the extent the gross income attributable to such activity exceeds the deductions allowed or allowable under subdivision (i) of this subparagraph.

(iii) Amounts otherwise allowable as deductions for the taxable year under chapter 1 of the Code which result in (or if otherwise allowed would have resulted in) an adjustment to the basis of property, determined as if the activity giving rise to such deductions was engaged in for profit, are allowed only to the extent the gross income attributable to such activity exceeds the deductions allowed or allowable under subdivisions (i) and (ii) of this subparagraph. Deductions falling within this subdivision include such items as depreciation, partial losses with respect to property, partially worthless debts, amortization, and amortizable bond premium.

(2) Rule for deductions involving basis adjustments—(i) In general. If deductions are allowed under subparagraph (1)(iii) of this paragraph, and such deductions are allowed with respect to more than one asset, the deduction allowed with respect to each asset shall be determined separately in accordance with the computation set forth in subdivision (ii) of this subparagraph.

(ii) Basis adjustment fraction. The deduction allowed under subparagraph (1)(iii) of this paragraph is computed by multiplying the amount which would have been allowed, had the activity been engaged in for profit, as a deduction with respect to each particular asset which involves a basis adjustment, by the basis adjustment fraction—

(a) The numerator of which is the total of deductions allowable under subparagraph (1)(iii) of this paragraph, and

(b) The denominator of which is the total of deductions which involve basis adjustments which would have been allowed with respect to the activity had the activity been engaged in for profit.

The amount resulting from this computation is the deduction allowed under subparagraph (1)(iii) of this paragraph with respect to the particular asset. The basis of such asset is adjusted only to the extent of such deduction.

(3) Examples. The provisions of subparagraphs (1) and (2) of this paragraph may be illustrated by the following examples:

Example (1). A, an individual, maintains a herd of dairy cattle, which is an "activity not engaged in for profit" within the meaning of section 183(c). A sold milk for $1,000 during the year. During the year A paid $300 State taxes on gasoline used to transport the cows, milk, etc., and paid $1,200 for feed for the cows. For the year A also had a casualty loss attributable to this activity of $500. A determines the amount of his allowable deductions under section 183 as follows:

(i) First, A computes his deductions allowable under subparagraph (1)(i) of this paragraph as follows:

State gasoline taxes specifically allowed under section 164(a)(5) without regard to whether the activity is engaged in for profit	$300
Casualty loss specifically allowed under section 165(c)(3) without regard to whether the activity is engaged in for profit ($500 less $100 limitation)	400
Deductions allowable under subparagraph (1)(i) of this paragraph	700

(ii) Second, A computes his deductions allowable under subparagraph (1)(ii) of this paragraph (deductions which would be allowed under chapter 1 of the Code if the activity were engaged in for profit and which do not involve basis adjustments) as follows:

Maximum amount of deductions allowable under subparagraph (1)(ii) of this paragraph:

Income from milk sales	$1,000
Gross income from activity	1,000
Less: Deductions allowable under subparagraph (1)(i) of this paragraph	700
Maximum amount of deductions allowable under subparagraph (1)(ii) of this paragraph	300
Feed for cows	1,200
Deduction allowed under subparagraph (1)(ii) of this paragraph	300

$900 of the feed expense is not allowed as a deduction under section 183 because the total feed expense ($1,200) exceeds the maximum amount of deductions allowable under subparagraph (1)(ii) of this paragraph ($300). In view of these circumstances, it is not necessary to determine deductions allowable under subparagraph (1)(iii) of this paragraph which would be allowable under chapter 1 of the Code if the activity were engaged in for profit and which involve basis adjustment (the $100 of casualty loss not allowable under subparagraph (1)(i) of this paragraph because of the limitation in section 165(c)(3)) because none of such amount will be allowed as a deduction under section 183.

Example (2). Assume the same facts as in example (1), except that A also had income from sales of hay grown on the farm of $1,200 and that depreciation of $750 with respect to a barn, and $650 with respect to a tractor would have been allowed with respect to the activity had it been engaged in for profit. A determines the amount of his allowable deductions under section 183 as follows:

(i) First, A computes his deductions allowable under subparagraph (1)(i) of this paragraph as follows:

State gasoline taxes specifically allowed under section 164(a)(5) without regard to whether the activity is engaged in for profit	$300
Casualty loss specifically allowed under section 165(c)(3) without regard to whether the activity is engaged in for profit ($500 less $100 limitation)	400
Deductions allowable under subparagraph (1)(i) of this paragraph	700

(ii) Second, A computes his deductions allowable under subparagraph (l)(ii) of this paragraph (deductions which would be allowable under chapter 1 of the Code if the activity were engaged in for profit and which do not involve basis adjustments) as follows:

Maximum amount of deductions allowable under subparagraph (1)(ii) of this paragraph:

Income from milk sales	$1,000
Income from hay sales	1,200
Gross income from activity	2,200
Less: Deductions allowable under subparagraph (1)(i) of this paragraph	700
Maximum amount of deductions allowable under subparagraph (1)(ii) of this paragraph	1,500
Feed for cows	1,200

The entire $1,200 of expenses relating to feed for cows is allowable as a deduction under subparagraph (1)(ii) of this paragraph, since it does not exceed the maximum amount of deductions allowable under such subparagraph.

(iii) Last, A computes the deductions allowable under subparagraph (1)(iii) of this paragraph (deductions which would be allowable under chapter 1 of the Code if the activity were engaged in for profit and which involve basis adjustments) as follows:

Maximum amount of deductions allowable under subparagraph (1)(iii) of this paragraph:

Gross income from farming		$2,200
Less: Deductions allowed under subparagraph (1)(i) of this paragraph	$700	
Deductions allowed under subparagraph (1)(ii) of this paragraph	1,200	1,900
Maximum amount of deductions allowable under subparagraph (1)(iii) of this paragraph		300

(iv) Since the total of A's deductions under chapter 1 of the Code (determined as if the activity was engaged in for profit) which involve basis adjustments ($750 with respect to barn, $650 with respect to tractor, and $100 with respect to limitation on casualty loss) exceeds the maximum amount of the deductions allowable under subparagraph (1)(iii) of this paragraph ($300), A computes his allowable deductions with respect to such assets as follows:

A first computes his basis adjustment fraction under subparagraph (2)(ii) of this paragraph as follows:

The numerator of the fraction is the maximum of deductions allowable under subparagraph (1)(iii) of this paragraph which involve basis adjustments	$300
The denominator of the fraction is the total of deductions that involve basis adjustments which would have been allowed with respect to the activity had the activity been engaged in for profit	1,500

The basis adjustment fraction is then applied to the amount of each deduction which would have been allowable if the activity were engaged in for profit and which involves a basis adjustment as follows:

Depreciation allowed with respect to barn (300/1,500 × $750)	$150
Depreciation allowed with respect to tractor (300/1,500 × $650)	130
Deduction allowed with respect to limitation on casualty loss (300/1,500 × $100)	20

The basis of the barn and of the tractor are adjusted only by the amount of depreciation actually allowed under section 183 with respect to each (as determined by the above computation). The basis of the asset with regard to which the casualty loss was suffered is adjusted only to the extent of the amount of the casualty loss actually allowed as a deduction under subparagraph (1)(i) and (iii) of this paragraph.

(4) Rule for capital gains and losses—(i) In general. For purposes of section 183 and the regulations thereunder, the gross income from any activity not engaged in for profit includes the total of all capital gains attributable to such activity determined without regard to the section 1202 deduction.* Amounts attributable to an activity not engaged in for profit which would be allowable as a deduction under section 1202,* without regard to section 183, shall be allowable as a deduction under section

*Editorial comment: The Regulations do not include the effect of the Tax Reform Act of 1986 which repealed the Sec. 1202 capital gain deduction. The Regulations also do not include the effect of the Revenue Reconciliation Act of 1993 which created the new Sec. 1202 exclusion.

183(b)(1) in accordance with the rules stated in this subparagraph.

(ii) Cases where deduction not allowed under section 183. No deduction is allowable under section 183(b)(1) with respect to capital gains attributable to an activity not engaged in for profit if—

(a) Without regard to section 183 and the regulations thereunder, there is no excess of net long-term capital gain over net short-term capital loss for the year, or

(b) There is no excess of net long-term capital gain attributable to the activity over net short-term capital loss attributable to the activity.

* * *

(c) Presumption that activity is engaged in for profit—(1) In general. If for—

(i) Any 2 of 7 consecutive taxable years, in the case of an activity which consists in major part of the breeding, training, showing, or racing of horses, or

(ii) Any 2* of 5 consecutive taxable years, in the case of any other activity, the gross income derived from an activity exceeds the deductions attributable to such activity which would be allowed or allowable if the activity were engaged in for profit, such activity is presumed, unless the Commissioner establishes to the contrary, to be engaged in for profit.* * *. Such presumption applies with respect to the second profit year and all years subsequent to the second profit year within the 5- or 7-year period beginning with the first profit year. This presumption arises only if the activity is substantially the same activity for each of the relevant taxable years, including the taxable year in question. If the taxpayer does not meet the requirements of section 183(d) and this paragraph, no inference that the activity is not engaged in for profit shall arise by reason of the provisions of section 183. For purposes of this paragraph, a net operating loss deduction is not taken into account as a deduction. For purposes of this subparagraph a short taxable year constitutes a taxable year.

(2) Examples. The provisions of subparagraph (1) of this paragraph may be illustrated by the following examples, in each of which it is assumed that the taxpayer has not elected, in accordance with section 183(e), to postpone determination of whether the presumption described in section 183(d) and this paragraph is applicable.

Example (1). For taxable years 1970–74, A, an individual who uses the cash receipts and disbursement method of accounting and the calendar year as the taxable year, is engaged in the activity of farming. In taxable years 1971, 1973, and 1974, A's deductible expenditures with respect to such activity exceed his gross income from the activity. In taxable years 1970 and 1972 A has income from the sale of farm produce of $30,000 for each year. In each of such years A had expenses for feed for his livestock of $10,000, depreciation of equipment of $10,000, and fertilizer cost of $5,000 which he elects to take as a deduction. A also has a net operating loss carryover to taxable year 1970 of $6,000. A is presumed, for taxable years 1972, 1973, and 1974, to have engaged in the activity of farming for profit, since for 2 years of a 5-consecutive-year period the gross income from the activity ($30,000 for each year) exceeded the deductions (computed without regard to the net operating loss) which are allowable in the case of the activity ($25,000 for each year).

* * *

(3) Activity which consists in major part of the breeding, training, showing, or racing of horses. For purposes of this paragraph an activity consists in major part of the breeding, training, showing, or racing of horses for the taxable year if the average of the portion of expenditures attributable to breeding, training, showing, and racing of horses for the 3 taxable years preceding the taxable year (or, in the case of an activity which has not been conducted by the taxpayer for 3 years, for so long as it has been carried on by him) was at least 50 percent of the total expenditures attributable to the activity for such prior taxable years.

* * *

(d) Activity defined—(1) Ascertainment of activity. In order to determine whether, and to what extent, section 183 and the regulations thereunder apply, the activity or activities of the taxpayer must be ascertained. For instance, where the taxpayer is engaged in several undertakings, each of these may be a separate activity, or several undertakings may constitute one activity. In ascertaining the activity or activities of the taxpayer, all the facts and circumstances of the case must be taken into account. Generally, the most significant facts and circumstances in making this determination are the degree of organizational and economic interrelationship of various undertakings, the business purpose

*Editorial comment: The Regulations do not include the effect of the Tax Reform Act of 1986 which increased the 2 out of 5-year period to a 3 out of 5-year period. See § 183(d).

which is (or might be) served by carrying on the various undertakings separately or together in a trade or business or in an investment setting, and the similarity of various undertakings. Generally, the Commissioner will accept the characterization by the taxpayer of several undertakings either as a single activity or as separate activities. The taxpayer's characterization will not be accepted, however, when it appears that his characterization is artificial and cannot be reasonably supported under the facts and circumstances of the case. If the taxpayer engages in two or more separate activities, deductions and income from each separate activity are not aggregated either in determining whether a particular activity is engaged in for profit or in applying section 183. Where land is purchased or held primarily with the intent to profit from increase in its value, and the taxpayer also engages in farming on such land, the farming and the holding of the land will ordinarily be considered a single activity only if the farming activity reduces the net cost of carrying the land for its appreciation in value. Thus, the farming and holding of the land will be considered a single activity only if the income derived from farming exceeds the deductions attributable to the farming activity which are not directly attributable to the holding of the land (that is, deductions other than those directly attributable to the holding of the land such as interest on a mortgage secured by the land, annual property taxes attributable to the land and improvements, and depreciation of improvements to the land).

(2) Rules for allocation of expenses. If the taxpayer is engaged in more than one activity, an item of deduction or income may be allocated between two or more of these activities. Where property is used in several activities, and one or more of such activities is determined not to be engaged in for profit, deductions relating to such property must be allocated between the various activities on a reasonable and consistently applied basis.

(3) Example. The provisions of this paragraph may be illustrated by the following example:

Example. (i) A, an individual, owns a small house located near the beach in a resort community. Visitors come to the area for recreational purposes during only 3 months of the year. During the remaining 9 months of the year houses such as A's are not rented. Customarily, A arranges that the house will be leased for 2 months of 3–month recreational season to vacationers and reserves the house for his own vacation during the remaining month of the recreational season. In 1971, A leases the house for 2 months for $1,000 per month and actually uses the house for his own vacation during the other month of the recreational season. For 1971, the expenses attributable to the house are $1,200 interest, $600 real estate taxes, $600 maintenance, $300 utilities, and $1,200 which would have been allowed as depreciation had the activity been engaged in for profit. Under these facts and circumstances, A is engaged in a single activity, holding the beach house primarily for personal purposes, which is an "activity not engaged in for profit" within the meaning of section 183(c). See paragraph (b)(9) of §1.183–2.

(ii) Since the $1,200 of interest and the $600 of real estate taxes are specifically allowable as deductions under sections 163 and 164(a) without regard to whether the beach house activity is engaged in for profit, no allocation of these expenses between the uses of the beach house is necessary. However, since section 262 specifically disallows personal, living, and family expenses as deductions, the maintenance and utilities expenses and the depreciation from the activity must be allocated between the rental use and the personal use of the beach house. Under the particular facts and circumstances, 2/3 (2 months of rental use over 3 months of total use) of each of these expenses are allocated to the rental use, and 1/3 (1 month of personal use over 3 months of total use) of each of these expenses are allocated to the personal use as follows:

	Rental use 2/3— expenses allocable to section 183(b)(2)	Personal use 1/3— expenses allocable to section 262
Maintenance expense $600	$400	$200
Utilities expense $300	200	100
Depreciation $1,200	800	400
Total	1,400	700

The $700 of expenses and depreciation allocated to the personal use of the beach house are disallowed as a deduction under section 262. In addition, the allowability of each of the expenses and the depreciation allocated to section 183(b)(2) is determined under paragraph (b)(1)(ii) and (iii) of this section. Thus, the maximum amount allowable as a deduction under section 183(b)(2) is $200 ($2,000 gross income from activity, less $1,800 deductions under section 183(b)(1)). Since the amounts described in section 183(b)(2) ($1,400) exceed the maximum amount allowable ($200), and since the amounts described in paragraph (b)(1)(ii) of this section ($600) exceed such maximum amount allowable ($200), none of the depreciation (an amount described in paragraph (b)(1)(iii) of this section) is allowable as a deduction.

(e) Gross income from activity not engaged in for profit defined. For purposes of section 183 and the regulations thereunder, gross income derived from an activity not engaged in for profit includes the total of all gains from the sale, exchange, or other disposition of property, and all other gross receipts derived from such activity. Such gross income shall include, for instance, capital gains, and rents received for the use of property which is held in connection with the activity. The taxpayer may determine gross income from any activity by subtracting the cost of goods sold from the gross receipts so long as he consistently does so and follows generally accepted methods of accounting in determining such gross income.

(f) Rule for electing small business corporations. Section 183 and this section shall be applied at the corporate level in determining the allowable deductions of an electing small business corporation.

§ 1.183–2 Activity not engaged in for profit defined.

(a) In general. For purposes of section 183 and the regulations thereunder, the term "activity not engaged in for profit" means any activity other than one with respect to which deductions are allowable for the taxable year under section 162 or under paragraph (1) or (2) of section 212. Deductions are allowable under section 162 for expenses of carrying on activities which constitute a trade or business of the taxpayer and under section 212 for expenses incurred in connection with activities engaged in for the production or collection of income or for the management, conservation, or maintenance of property held for the production of income. Except as provided in section 183 and §1.183–1, no deductions are allowable for expenses incurred in connection with activities which are not engaged in for profit. Thus, for example, deductions are not allowable under section 162 or 212 for activities which are carried on primarily as a sport, hobby, or for recreation. The determination whether an activity is engaged in for profit is to be made by reference to objective standards, taking into account all of the facts and circumstances of each case. Although a reasonable expectation of profit is not required, the facts and circumstances must indicate that the taxpayer entered into the activity, or continued the activity, with the objective of making a profit. In determining whether such an objective exists, it may be sufficient that there is a small chance of making a large profit. Thus it may be found that an investor in a wildcat oil well who incurs very substantial expenditures is in the venture for profit even though the expectation of a profit might be considered unreasonable. In determining whether an activity is engaged in for profit, greater weight is given to objective facts than to the taxpayer's mere statement of his intent.

(b) Relevant factors. In determining whether an activity is engaged in for profit, all facts and circumstances with respect to the activity are to be taken into account. No one factor is determinative in making this determination. In addition, it is not intended that only the factors described in this paragraph are to be taken into account in making the determination, or that a determination is to be made on the basis that the number of factors (whether or not listed in this paragraph) indicating a lack of profit objective exceeds the number of factors indicating a profit objective, or vice versa. Among the factors which should normally be taken into account are the following:

(1) Manner in which the taxpayer carries on the activity. The fact that the taxpayer carries on the activity in a businesslike manner and maintains complete and accurate books and records may indicate that the activity is engaged in for profit. Similarly, where an activity is carried on in a manner substantially similar to other activities of the same nature which are profitable, a profit motive may be indicated. A change of operating methods, adoption of new techniques or abandonment of unprofitable methods in a manner consistent with an intent to improve profitability may also indicate a profit motive.

(2) The expertise of the taxpayer or his advisors. Preparation for the activity by extensive study of its accepted business, economic, and scientific practices, or consultation with those who are expert therein, may indicate that the taxpayer has a profit motive where the taxpayer carries on the activity in accordance with such practices. Where a taxpayer has such preparation or procures such expert advice, but does not carry on the activity in accordance with such practices, a lack of intent to derive profit may be indicated unless it appears that the taxpayer is attempting to develop new or superior techniques which may result in profits from the activity.

(3) The time and effort expended by the taxpayer in carrying on the activity. The fact that the taxpayer devotes much of his personal time and effort to carrying on an activity, particularly if the activity does not have substantial personal or recreational aspects, may indicate an intention to derive a profit. A taxpayer's withdrawal from another occupation to devote most of his energies to the activity may also be evidence that the activity is engaged in for profit. The fact that the taxpayer devotes a limited amount of time to an activity does not necessarily indicate a lack of profit motive where the taxpayer employs competent and qualified persons to carry on such activity.

(4) Expectation that assets used in activity may appreciate in value. The term "profit" encompasses appreciation in the value of assets, such as land, used in the activity. Thus, the taxpayer may intend to derive a profit from the operation of the activity, and may also intend that, even if no profit from current operations is derived, an overall profit will result when appreciation in the value of land used in the activity is realized since income from the activity together with the appreciation of land will exceed expenses of operation. See, however, paragraph (d) of §1.183–1 for definition of an activity in this connection.

(5) The success of the taxpayer in carrying on other similar or dissimilar activities. The fact that the taxpayer has engaged in similar activities in the past and converted them from unprofitable to profitable enterprises may indicate that he is engaged in the present activity for profit, even though the activity is presently unprofitable.

(6) The taxpayer's history of income or losses with respect to the activity. A series of losses during the initial or start-up stage of an activity may not necessarily be an indication that the activity is not engaged in for profit. However, where losses continue to be sustained beyond the period which customarily is necessary to bring the operation to profitable status such continued losses, if not explainable, as due to customary business risks or reverses, may be indicative that the activity is not being engaged in for profit. If losses are sustained because of unforeseen or fortuitous circumstances which are beyond the control of the taxpayer, such as drought, disease, fire, theft, weather damages, other involuntary conversions, or depressed market conditions, such losses would not be an indication that the activity is not engaged in for profit. A series of years in which net income was realized would of course be strong evidence that the activity is engaged in for profit.

(7) The amount of occasional profits, if any, which are earned. The amount of profits in relation to the amount of losses incurred, and in relation to the amount of the taxpayer's investment and the value of the assets used in the activity, may provide useful criteria in determining the taxpayer's intent. An occasional small profit from an activity generating large losses, or from an activity in which the taxpayer has made a large investment, would not generally be determinative that the activity is engaged in for profit. However, substantial profit, though only occasional, would generally be indicative that an activity is engaged in for profit, where the investment or losses are comparatively small. Moreover, an opportunity to earn a substantial ultimate profit in a highly speculative venture is ordinarily sufficient to indicate that the activity is engaged in for profit even though losses or only occasional small profits are actually generated.

(8) The financial status of the taxpayer. The fact that the taxpayer does not have substantial income or capital from sources other than the activity may indicate that an activity is engaged in for profit. Substantial income from sources other than the activity (particularly if the losses from the activity generate substantial tax benefits) may indicate that the activity is not engaged in for profit especially if there are personal or recreational elements involved.

(9) Elements of personal pleasure or recreation. The presence of personal motives in carrying on of an activity may indicate that the activity is not engaged in for profit, especially where there are recreational or personal elements involved. On the other hand, a profit motivation may be indicated where an activity lacks any appeal other than profit. It is not, however, necessary that an activity be engaged in with the exclusive intention of deriving a profit or with the intention of maximizing profits. For example, the availability of other investments which would yield a higher return, or which would be more likely to be profitable, is not evidence that an activity is not engaged in for profit. An activity will not be treated as not engaged in for profit merely because the taxpayer has purposes or motivations other than solely to make a profit. Also, the fact that the taxpayer derives personal pleasure from engaging in the activity is not sufficient to cause the activity to be classified as not engaged in for profit if the activity is in fact engaged in for profit as evidenced by other factors whether or not listed in this paragraph.

(c) Examples. The provisions of this section may be illustrated by the following examples:

Example (1). The taxpayer inherited a farm from her husband in an area which was becoming largely residential, and is now nearly all so. The farm had never made a profit before the taxpayer inherited it, and the farm has since had substantial losses in each year. The decedent from whom the taxpayer inherited the farm was a stockbroker, and he also left the taxpayer substantial stock holdings which yield large income from dividends. The taxpayer lives on an area of the farm which is set aside exclusively for living purposes. A farm manager is employed to operate the farm, but modern methods are not used in operating the farm. The taxpayer was born and raised on a farm, and expresses a strong preference for living on a farm. The taxpayer's activity of farming, based on all the facts and circumstances, could be found not to be engaged in for profit.

Example (2). The taxpayer is a wealthy individual who is greatly interested in philosophy. During the past 30 years he has written and published at his own expense several pamphlets, and he has engaged in extensive lecturing activity, advocating and disseminating his ideas. He has made a profit from these activities in only occasional years, and the profits in those years were small in relation to the amounts of the losses in all other years. The taxpayer has very sizable income from securities (dividends and capital gains) which constitutes the principal source of his livelihood. The activity of lecturing, publishing pamphlets, and disseminating his ideas is not an activity engaged in by the taxpayer for profit.

Example (3). The taxpayer, very successful in the business of retailing soft drinks, raises dogs and horses. He began raising a particular breed of dogs many years ago in the belief that the breed was in danger of declining, and he has raised and sold the dogs in each year since. The taxpayer recently began raising and racing thoroughbred horses. The losses from the taxpayer's dog and horse activities have increased in magnitude over the years, and he has not made a profit on these operations during any of the last 15 years. The taxpayer generally sells the dogs only to friends, does not advertise the dogs for sale, and shows the dogs only infrequently. The taxpayer races his horses only at the "prestige" tracks at which he combines his racing activities with social and recreational activities. The horse and dog operations are conducted at a large residential property on which the taxpayer also lives, which includes substantial living quarters and attractive recreational facilities for the taxpayer and his family. Since (i) the activity of raising dogs and horses and racing the horses is of a sporting and recreational nature, (ii) the taxpayer has substantial income from his business activities of retailing soft drinks, (iii) the horse and dog operations are not conducted in a businesslike manner, and (iv) such operations have a continuous record of losses, it could be determined that the horse and dog activities of the taxpayer are not engaged in for profit.

Example (4). The taxpayer inherited a farm of 65 acres from his parents when they died 6 years ago. The taxpayer moved to the farm from his house in a small nearby town, and he operates it in the same manner as his parents operated the farm before they died. The taxpayer is employed as a skilled machine operator in a nearby factory, for which he is paid approximately $8,500 per year. The farm has not been profitable for the past 15 years because of rising costs of operating farms in general, and because of the decline in the price of the produce of this farm in particular. The taxpayer consults the local agent of the State agricultural service from time to time, and the suggestions of the agent have generally been followed. The manner in which the farm is operated by the taxpayer is substantially similar to the manner in which farms of similar size, and which grow similar crops in the area, are operated. Many of these other farms do not make profits. The taxpayer does much of the required labor around the farm himself, such as fixing fences, planting crops, etc. The activity of farming could be found, based on all the facts and circumstances, to be engaged in by the taxpayer for profit.

Example (5). A, an independent oil and gas operator, frequently engages in the activity of searching for oil on undeveloped and unexplored land which is not near proven fields. He does so in a manner substantially similar to that of others who engage in the same activity. The chances, based on the experience of A and others who engaged in this activity, are strong that A will not find a commercially profitable oil deposit when he drills on land not established geologically to be proven oil bearing land. However, on the rare occasions that these activities do result in discovering a well, the operator generally realizes a very large return from such activity. Thus, there is a small chance that A will make a large profit from his soil exploration activity. Under these circumstances, A is engaged in the activity of oil drilling for profit.

Example (6). C, a chemist, is employed by a large chemical company and is engaged in a wide variety of basic research projects for his employer. Although he does no work for his employer with respect to the development of new plastics, he has always been interested in such development and has outfitted a workshop in his home at his own expense which he uses to experiment in the field. He has patented several developments at his own expense but as yet has realized no income from his inventions or from such patents. C conducts his research on a regular, systematic basis, incurs fees to secure consultation on his projects from time to time, and makes extensive efforts to "market" his developments. C has devoted substantial time and expense in an effort to develop a plastic sufficiently hard, durable, and malleable that it could be used in lieu of sheet steel in many major applications, such as automobile bodies. Although there may be only a small chance that C will invent new plastics, the return from any such development would be so large that it induces C to incur the costs of his experimental work. C is sufficiently qualified by his background that there is some reasonable basis for his experimental activities. C's experimental work does not involve substantial personal or recreational aspects and is conducted in an effort to find practical applications for his work. Under these circumstances, C may be found to be engaged in the experimental activities for profit.

* * *

Additional Itemized Deductions for Individuals

* * *

§ 1.212–1 Nontrade or nonbusiness expenses.

(a) An expense may be deducted under section 212 only if—

(1) It has been paid or incurred by the taxpayer during the taxable year (i) for the production or collection of income which, if and when realized, will be required to be included in income for Federal income tax purposes, or (ii) for the management, conservation, or maintenance of property held for the production of such income, or (iii) in connection with the determination, collection, or refund of any tax; and

(2) It is an ordinary and necessary expense for any of the purposes stated in subparagraph (1) of this paragraph.

(b) The term "income" for the purpose of section 212 includes not merely income of the taxable year but also income which the taxpayer has realized in a prior taxable year or may realize in subsequent taxable years; and is not confined to recurring income but applies as well to gains from the disposition of property. For example, if defaulted bonds, the interest from which if received would be includible in income, are purchased with the expectation of realizing capital gain on their resale, even though no current yield thereon is anticipated, ordinary and necessary expenses thereafter paid or incurred in connection with such bonds are deductible. Similarly, ordinary and necessary expenses paid or incurred in the management, conservation, or maintenance of a building devoted to rental purposes are deductible notwithstanding that there is actually no income therefrom in the taxable year, and regardless of the manner in which or the purpose for which the property in question was acquired. Expenses paid or incurred in managing, conserving, or maintaining property held for investment may be deductible under section 212 even though the property is not currently productive and there is no likelihood that the property will be sold at a profit or will otherwise be productive of income and even though the property is held merely to minimize a loss with respect thereto.

* * *

(d) Expenses, to be deductible under section 212, must be "ordinary and necessary". Thus, such expenses must be reasonable in amount and must bear a reasonable and proximate relation to the production or collection of taxable income or to the management, conservation, or maintenance of property held for the production of income.

(e) A deduction under section 212 is subject to the restrictions and limitations in part IX (section 261 and following), subchapter B, chapter 1 of the Code, relating to items not deductible. Thus, no deduction is allowable under section 212 for any amount allocable to the production or collection of one or more classes of income which are not includible in gross income, or for any amount allocable to the management, conservation, or maintenance of property held for the production of income which is not included in gross income. See section 265. Nor does section 212 allow the deduction of any expenses which are disallowed by any of the provisions of subtitle A of the Code, even though such expenses may be paid or incurred for one of the purposes specified in section 212.

(f) Among expenditures not allowable as deductions under section 212 are the following: Commuter's expenses; expenses of taking special courses or training; expenses for improving personal appearance; the cost of rental of a safe–deposit box for storing jewelry and other personal effects; expenses such as those paid or incurred in seeking employment or in placing oneself in a position to begin rendering personal services for compensation, campaign expenses of a candidate for public office, bar examination fees and other expenses paid or incurred in securing admission to the bar, and corresponding fees and expenses paid or incurred by physicians, dentists, accountants, and other taxpayers for securing the right to practice their respective professions. See, however, section 162 and the regulations thereunder.

(g) Fees for services of investment counsel, custodial fees, clerical help, office rent, and similar expenses paid or incurred by a taxpayer in connection with investments held by him are deductible under section 212 only if (1) they are paid or incurred by the taxpayer for the production or collection of income or for the management, conservation, or maintenance of investments held by him for the production of income; and (2) they are ordinary and necessary under all the circumstances, having regard to the type of investment and to the relation of the taxpayer to such investment.

(h) Ordinary and necessary expenses paid or incurred in connection with the management, conservation, or maintenance of property held for use as a residence by the taxpayer are not deductible. However, ordinary and necessary expenses paid or incurred in connection with the management, conservation, or maintenance of property held by the taxpayer as rental property are deductible even though such property was formerly held by the taxpayer for use as a home.

(i) Reasonable amounts paid or incurred by the fiduciary of an estate or trust on account of administration expenses, including fiduciaries' fees and expenses of litigation, which are ordinary and necessary in connection with the performance of the duties of administration are deductible under section 212, notwithstanding that the estate or trust is not engaged in a trade or business, except to the extent that such expenses are allocable to the production or collection of tax–exempt income. But see section 642 (g) and the regulations thereunder for disallowance of such deductions to an estate where such items are allowed as a deduction under section 2053 or 2054 in computing the net estate subject to the estate tax.

(j) Reasonable amounts paid or incurred for the services of a guardian or committee for a ward or minor, and other expenses of guardians and committees which are ordinary and necessary, in connection with the production or collection of income inuring to the ward or minor, or in connection with the management, conservation, or maintenance of property, held for the production of income, belonging to the ward or minor, are deductible.

(k) Expenses paid or incurred in defending or perfecting title to property, in recovering property (other than investment property and amounts of income which, if and when recovered, must be included in gross income), or in developing or improving property, constitute a part of the cost of the property and are not deductible expenses. Attorneys' fees paid in a suit to quiet title to lands are not deductible; but if the suit is also to collect accrued rents thereon, that portion of such fees is deductible which is properly allocable to the services rendered in collecting such rents. Expenses paid or incurred in protecting or asserting one's right to property of a decedent as heir or legatee, or as beneficiary under a testamentary trust, are not deductible.

(l) Expenses paid or incurred by an individual in connection with the determination, collection, or refund of any tax, whether the taxing authority be Federal, State, or municipal, and whether the tax be income, estate, gift, property, or any other tax, are deductible. Thus, expenses paid or incurred by a taxpayer for tax counsel or expenses paid or incurred in connection with the preparation of his tax returns or in connection with any proceedings involved in determining the extent of his tax liability or in contesting his tax liability are deductible.

(m) An expense (not otherwise deductible) paid or incurred by an individual in determining or contesting a liability asserted against him does not become deductible by reason of the fact that property held by him for the production of income may be required to be used or sold for the purpose of satisfying such liability.

(n) Capital expenditures are not allowable as nontrade or nonbusiness expenses. The deduction of an item otherwise allowable under section 212 will not be disallowed simply because the taxpayer was entitled under subtitle A of the Code to treat such item as a capital expenditure, rather than to deduct it as an expense. For example, see section 266. Where, however, the item may properly be treated only as a capital expenditure or where it was properly so treated under an option granted in subtitle A of the Code, no deduction is allowable under section 212; and this is true regardless of whether any basis adjustment is allowed under any other provision of the Code.

(o) The provisions of section 212 are not intended in any way to disallow expenses which would otherwise be allowable under section 162 and the regulations thereunder. Double deductions are not permitted. Amounts deducted under one provision of the Internal Revenue Code of 1954 cannot again be deducted under any other provision thereof.

(p) Frustration of public policy. The deduction of a payment will be disallowed under section 212 if the payment is of a type for which a deduction would be disallowed under section 162(c), (f), or (g) and the regulations thereunder in the case of a business expense.

* * *

§ 1.215–1T Alimony, etc., payments (temporary).

Q–1. What information is required by the Internal Revenue Service when an alimony or separate maintenance payment is claimed as a deduction by a payor?

A–1. The payor spouse must include on his/her first filed return of tax (Form 1040) for the taxable year in which the payment is made the payee's social security number, which the payee is required to furnish to the payor. For penalties applicable to a payor spouse who fails to include such information on his/her return of tax or to a payee spouse who fails to furnish his/her social security number to the payor spouse, see section 6676.

* * *

§ 1.217–2 Deduction for moving expenses paid or incurred in taxable years beginning after December 31, 1969.

(a) Allowance of deduction—(1) In general. Section 217(a) allows a deduction from gross income for moving expenses paid or incurred by the taxpayer during the taxable year in connection with his commencement of work as an employee or as a self-employed individual at a new principal place of work. For purposes of this section, amounts are considered as being paid or incurred by an individual whether goods or services are furnished to the taxpayer directly (by an employer, a client, a customer, or similar person) or indirectly (paid to a third party on behalf of the taxpayer by an employer, a client, a customer, or similar person). A cash basis taxpayer will treat moving expenses as being paid for purposes of section 217 and this section in the year in which the taxpayer is considered to have received such payment under section 82 and §1.82–1. No deduction is allowable under section 162 for any expenses incurred by the taxpayer in connection with moving from one residence to another residence unless such expenses are deductible under section 162 without regard to such change in residence. To qualify for the deduction under section 217 the expenses must meet the definition of the term "moving expenses" provided in section 217(b) and the taxpayer must meet the conditions set forth in section 217(c). The term "employee" as used in this section has the same meaning as in §31.3401(c)–1 of this chapter (Employment Tax Regulations). The term "self-employed individual" as used in this section is defined in paragraph (f)(1) of this section.

(2) Expenses paid in a taxable year other than the taxable year in which reimbursement representing such expenses is received. In general, moving expenses are deductible in the year paid or incurred. If a taxpayer who uses the cash receipts and disbursements method of accounting receives reimbursement for a moving expense in a taxable year other than the taxable year the taxpayer pays such expense, he may elect to deduct such expense in the taxable year that he receives such reimbursement, rather than the taxable year when he paid such expense in any case where—

(i) The expense is paid in a taxable year prior to the taxable year in which the reimbursement is received, or

(ii) The expense is paid in the taxable year immediately following the taxable year in which the reimbursement is received, provided that such expense is paid on or before the due date prescribed for filing the return (determined with regard to any extension of time for such filing) for the taxable year in which the reimbursement is received.

An election to deduct moving expenses in the taxable year that the reimbursement is received shall be made by claiming the deduction on the return, amended return, or claim for refund for the taxable year in which the reimbursement is received.

(3) Commencement of work. (i) To be deductible the moving expenses must be paid or incurred by the taxpayer in connection with his commencement of work at a new principal place of work (see paragraph (c)(3) of this section for a discussion of the term "principal place of work"). Except for those expenses described in section 217(b)(1)(C) and (D) it is not necessary for the taxpayer to have made arrangements to work prior to his moving to a new location; however, a deduction is not allowable unless employment or self-employment actually does occur. The term "commencement" includes (a) the beginning of work by a taxpayer as an employee or as a self-employed individual for the first time or after a substantial period of unemployment or part-time employment, (b) the beginning of work by a taxpayer for a different employer or in the case of a self-employed individual in a new trade or business, or (c) the beginning of work by a taxpayer for the same employer or in the case of a self-employed individual in the same trade or business at a new location. To qualify as being in connection with the commencement of work, the move must bear a reasonable proximity both in time and place to such commencement at the new principal place of work. In general, moving expenses incurred within 1 year of the date of the commencement of work are considered to be reasonably proximate in time to such commencement. Moving expenses incurred after the 1-year period may be considered reasonably proximate in time if it can be shown that circumstances existed which prevented the taxpayer from incurring the expenses of moving within the 1-year period allowed. Whether circumstances existed which prevented the taxpayer from incurring the expenses of moving within the period allowed is dependent upon the facts and circumstances of each case. The length of the delay and the fact that the taxpayer may have incurred part of the expenses of the move within the 1-year period allowed shall be taken into account in determining whether expenses incurred after such period are allowable. In general, a move is not considered to be reasonably proximate in place to the commencement of work at the new principal place of work where the distance between the taxpayer's new residence and his new principal place of work exceeds the distance between his former residence and his new principal place of work. A move to a new residence which does not satisfy this test may, however, be considered reasonably proximate in place to the commencement of work if the taxpayer can demonstrate, for example, that he is required to live at such residence as a condition of employment or that living at such residence will result in an actual decrease in commuting time or expense. For example, assume that in 1977 A is transferred by his employer to a new principal place of work and the distance between his former residence and his new principal place of work is 35 miles* greater than was the distance between his former residence and his former principal place of work. However, the distance between his new residence and his new principal place of work is 10 miles greater than was the distance between his former residence and his new principal place of work. Although the minimum distance requirement of section 217(c)(1) is met, the expenses of moving to the new residence are not considered as incurred in connection with A's commencement of work at his new principal place of work since the new residence is not proximate in place to the new place of work. If, however, A can demonstrate, for example, that he is required to live at such new residence as a condition of employment or if living at such new residence will result in an actual decrease in commuting time or expense, the expenses of the move may be considered as incurred in connection with A's commencement of work at his new principal place of work.

(ii) The provisions of subdivision (i) of this subparagraph may be illustrated by the following examples:

Example (1). Assume that A is transferred by his employer from Boston, Mass., to Washington, D.C. A moves to a new residence in Washington, D.C., and commences work on February 1, 1971. A's wife and his two children remain in Boston until June 1972 in order to allow A's children to complete their grade school education in Boston. On June 1, 1972, A sells his home in Boston and his wife and children move to the new residence in Washington, D.C. The expenses incurred on June 1, 1972, in selling the old residence and in moving A's family, their household goods, and personal effects to the new residence in Washington are allowable as a deduction although they were incurred 16 months after the date of the commencement of work by A since A has moved to and established a new residence in Washington, D.C., and thus incurred part of the total expenses of the move prior to the expiration of the 1-year period.

Example (2). Assume that A is transferred by his employer from Washington, D.C., to Baltimore, Md. A commences work on January 1, 1971, in Baltimore. A commutes from his residence in Washington to his new principal place of work in Baltimore for a period of 18 months. On July 1, 1972, A decides to move to and establish a new residence in Baltimore. None of the moving expenses otherwise allowable under section 217 may be deducted since A neither incurred the expenses within 1 year nor has shown circumstances under which he was prevented from moving within such period.

(b) Definition of moving expenses—(1) In general.** Section 217(b) defines the term "moving expenses" to mean only the reasonable expenses (i) of moving household goods and personal effects from the taxpayer's former residence to his new residence, (ii) of traveling (including meals and lodging) from the taxpayer's former residence to his new place of residence, (iii) of traveling (including meals and lodging), after obtaining employment, from the taxpayer's former residence to the general location of his new principal place of work and return, for the principal purpose of searching for a new residence, (iv) of meals and lodging while occupying temporary quarters in the general location of the new principal place of work during any period of 30 consecutive days after obtaining employment, or (v) of a nature constituting qualified residence sale, purchase, or lease expenses. Thus, the test of deductibility is whether the expenses are reasonable and are incurred for the items set forth in subdivisions (i) through (v) of this subparagraph.

(2) Reasonable expenses. (i) The term "moving expenses" includes only those expenses which are reasonable under the circumstances of the particular move. Expenses paid or incurred in excess of a reasonable amount are not deductible. Generally, expenses paid or incurred for movement of household goods and personal effects or for travel (including meals and lodging) are reasonable only to the extent that they are paid or incurred for such movement or travel by the shortest and most direct route available from the former residence to the new residence by the conventional mode or modes of transportation actually used and in the shortest period of time commonly required to travel the distance involved by such mode. Thus, if moving or travel arrangements are made to provide a circuitous route for scenic, stopover, or other similar reasons, additional expenses resulting therefrom are not deductible since they are not reasonable nor related to the commencement of work at the new principal place of work. In addition, expenses paid or incurred for meals and lodging while traveling from the former residence to the new place of residence or to

*Editorial comment: The Regulations do not include the effect of the Revenue Reconciliation Act of 1993 which increased the distance requirement from 35 to 50 miles.

**Editorial comment: The Regulations do not reflect the effect of the Revenue Reconciliation Act of 1993 which modified the definition of moving expenses. See Sec. 217(b).

the general location of the new principal place of work and return or occupying temporary quarters in the general location of the new principal place of work are reasonable only if under the facts and circumstances involved such expenses are not lavish or extravagant.

(ii) The application of this subparagraph may be illustrated by the following example:

Example. A, an employee of the M Company works and maintains his residence in Boston, Mass. Upon receiving orders from his employer that he is to be transferred to M's Los Angeles, Calif., office, A motors to Los Angeles with his family with stopovers at various cities between Boston and Los Angeles to visit friends and relatives. In addition, A detours into Mexico for sightseeing. Because of the stopovers and tour into Mexico, A's travel time and distance are increased over what they would have been had he proceeded directly to Los Angeles. To the extent that A's route of travel between Boston and Los Angeles is in a generally southwesterly direction it may be said that he is traveling by the shortest and most direct route available by motor vehicle. Since A's excursion into Mexico is away from the usual Boston–Los Angeles route, the portion of the expenses paid or incurred attributable to such excursion is not deductible. Likewise, that portion of the expenses attributable to A's delay en route in visiting personal friends and sightseeing are not deductible.

(3) Expense of moving household goods and personal effects. Expenses of moving household goods and personal effects include expenses of transporting such goods and effects from the taxpayer's former residence to his new residence, and expenses of packing, crating, and in-transit storage and insurance for such goods and effects. Such expenses also include any costs of connecting or disconnecting utilities required because of the moving of household goods, appliances, or personal effects. Expenses of storing and insuring household goods and personal effects constitute in-transit expenses if incurred within any consecutive 30-day period after the day such goods and effects are moved from the taxpayer's former residence and prior to delivery at the taxpayer's new residence. Expenses paid or incurred in moving household goods and personal effects to the taxpayer's new residence from a place other than his former residence are allowable, but only to the extent that such expenses do not exceed the amount which would be allowable had such goods and effects been moved from the taxpayer's former residence. Expenses of moving household goods and personal effects do not include, for example, storage charges (other than in-transit), costs incurred in the acquisition of property, costs incurred and losses sustained in the disposition of property, penalties for breaking leases, mortgage penalties, expenses of refitting rugs or draperies, losses sustained on the disposal of memberships in clubs, tuition fees, and similar items. The above expenses may, however, be described in other provisions of section 217(b) and if so a deduction may be allowed for them subject to the allowable dollar limitations.

(4) Expenses of traveling from the former residence to the new place of residence. Expenses of traveling from the former residence to the new place of residence include the cost of transportation and of meals and lodging en route (including the date of arrival) from the taxpayer's former residence to his new place of residence. Expenses of meals and lodging incurred in the general location of the former residence within 1 day after the former residence is no longer suitable for occupancy because of the removal of household goods and personal effects shall be considered as expenses of traveling for purposes of this subparagraph. The date of arrival is the day the taxpayer secures lodging at the new place of residence, even if on a temporary basis. Expenses of traveling from the taxpayer's former residence to his new place of residence do not include, for example, living or other expenses following the date of arrival at the new place of residence and while waiting to enter the new residence or waiting for household goods to arrive, expenses in connection with house or apartment hunting, living expenses preceding date of departure for the new place of residence (other than expenses of meals and lodging incurred within 1 day after the former residence is no longer suitable for occupancy), expenses of trips for purposes of selling property, expenses of trips to the former residence by the taxpayer pending the move by his family to the new place of residence, or any allowance for depreciation. The above expenses may, however, be described in other provisions of section 217(b) and if so a deduction may be allowed for them subject to the allowable dollar limitations. The deduction for traveling expenses from the former residence to the new place of residence is allowable for only one trip made by the taxpayer and members of his household; however, it is not necessary that the taxpayer and all members of his household travel together or at the same time.

* * *

(10) Individuals other than taxpayer. **(i)** In addition to the expenses set forth in subparagraphs (A) through (D) of section 217(b)(1) attributable to the taxpayer alone, the same type of expenses attributable to certain individuals other than the taxpayer, if paid or incurred by the taxpayer, are deductible. These other individuals must be members of the taxpayer's household, and have both the taxpayer's former residence and his new residence as their principal place of abode. A member of the taxpayer's household includes any individual residing at the tax–payer's residence who is neither a tenant nor an employee of the taxpayer. Thus, for example, a member of the taxpayer's household may not be an individual such as a servant, governess, chauffeur, nurse, valet, or personal attendant. However, for purposes of this paragraph, a tenant or employee will be considered a member of the taxpayer's household where the tenant or employee is a dependent of the taxpayer as defined in section 152.

(ii) In addition to the expenses set forth in section 217(b)(2) paid or incurred by the taxpayer attributable to property sold, purchased, or leased by the taxpayer alone, the same type of expenses paid or incurred by the taxpayer attributable to property sold, purchased, or leased by the taxpayer's spouse or by the taxpayer and his spouse are deductible providing such property is used by the taxpayer as his principal place of residence.

(c) Conditions for allowance—(1) In general. Section 217(c) provides two conditions which must be satisfied in order for a deduction of moving expenses to be allowed under section 217(a). The first is a minimum distance condition prescribed by section 217(c)(1), and the second is a minimum period of employment condition prescribed by section 217(c)(2).

(2) Minimum distance.* For purposes of applying the minimum distance condition of section 217(c)(1) all taxpayers are divided into one or the other of the following categories: Taxpayers having a former principal place of work, and taxpayers not having a former principal place of work. Included in this latter category are individuals who are seeking full-time employment for the first time either as an employee or on a self-employed basis (for example, recent high school or college graduates), or individuals who are reentering the labor force after a substantial period of unemployment or part-time employment.

(i) In the case of a taxpayer having a former principal place of work, section 217(c)(1)(A) provides that no deduction is allowable unless the distance between the former residence and the new principal place of work exceeds by at least 35 miles * * * the distance between the former residence and the former principal place of work.

(ii) In the case of a taxpayer not having a former principal place of work, section 217(c)(l)(B) provides that no deduction is allowable unless the distance between the former residence and the new principal place of work is at least 35 miles * * *.

(iii) For purposes of measuring distances under section 217(c)(1) the distance between two geographic points is measured by the shortest of the more commonly traveled routes between such points. The shortest of the more commonly traveled routes refers to the line of travel and the mode or modes of transportation commonly used to go between two geographic points comprising the shortest distance between such points irrespective of the route used by the taxpayer.

(3) Principal place of work. (i) A taxpayer's "principal place of work" usually is the place where he spends most of his working time. The principal place of work of a taxpayer who performs services as an employee is his employer's plant, office, shop, store, or other property. The principal place of work of a taxpayer who is self-employed is the plant, office, shop, store, or other property which serves as the center of his business activities. However, a taxpayer may have a principal place of work even if there is no one place where he spends a substantial portion of his working time. In such case, the taxpayer's principal place of work is the place where his business activities are centered—for example, because he reports there for work, or is required either by his employer or the nature of his employment to "base" his employment there. Thus, while a member of a railroad crew may spend most of his working time aboard a train, his principal place of work is his home terminal, station, or other such central point where he reports in, checks out, or receives instructions. The principal place of work of a taxpayer who is employed by a number of employers on a relatively short-term basis, and secures employment by means of a union hall system (such as a construction or building trades worker) would be the union hall.

(ii) Where a taxpayer has more than one employment (i.e., the taxpayer is employed by more than one employer, or is self-employed in more than one trade or business, or is an employee and is self-employed at any particular time) his principal place

*Editorial comment: The Regulations do not include the effect of the Revenue Reconciliation Act of 1993 which increased the distance requirement from 35 to 50 miles.

of work is determined with reference to his principal employment. The location of a taxpayer's principal place of work is a question of fact determined on the basis of the particular circumstances in each case. The more important factors to be considered in making this determination are (a) the total time ordinarily spent by the taxpayer at each place, (b) the degree of the taxpayer's business activity at each place, and (c) the relative significance of the financial return to the taxpayer from each place.

(iii) Where a taxpayer maintains inconsistent positions by claiming a deduction for expenses of meals and lodging while away from home (incurred in the general location of the new principal place of work) under section 162 (relating to trade or business expenses) and by claiming a deduction under this section for moving expenses incurred in connection with the commencement of work at such place of work, it will be a question of facts and circumstances as to whether such new place of work will be considered a principal place of work, and accordingly, which category of deductions he will be allowed.

(4) Minimum period of employment. (i) Under section 217(c)(2) no deduction is allowed unless—

(a) Where a taxpayer is an employee, during the 12-month period immediately following his arrival in the general location of the new principal place of work, he is a full-time employee, in such general location, during at least 39 weeks, or

(b) Where a taxpayer is a self-employed individual (including a taxpayer who is also an employee, but is unable to satisfy the requirements of the 39-week test of (a) of this subdivision (i)), during the 24-month period immediately following his arrival in the general location of the new principal place of work, he is a full-time employee or performs services as a self-employed individual on a full-time basis, in such general location, during at least 78 weeks, of which not less than 39 weeks are during the 12-month period referred to above.

Where a taxpayer works as an employee and at the same time performs services as a self-employed individual his principal employment (determined according to subdivision (i) of subparagraph (3) of this paragraph) governs whether the 39-week or 78-week test is applicable.

(ii) The 12-month period and the 39-week period set forth in subparagraph (A) of section 217(c)(2) and the 12- and 24-month periods as well as 39- and 78-week periods set forth in subparagraph (B) of such section are measured from the date of the taxpayer's arrival in the general location of the new principal place of work. Generally, date of arrival is the date of the termination of the last trip preceding the taxpayer's commencement of work on a regular basis and is not the date the taxpayer's family or household goods and effects arrive.

(iii) The taxpayer need not remain in the employ of the same employer or remain self-employed in the same trade or business for the required number of weeks. However, he must be employed in the same general location of the new principal place of work during such period. The "general location" of the new principal place of work refers to a general commutation area and is usually the same area as the "new place of residence"; see paragraph (b)(8) of this section.

(iv) Only those weeks during which the taxpayer is a full-time employee or during which he performs services as a self-employed individual on a full-time basis qualify as a week of work for purposes of the minimum period of employment condition of section 217(c)(2).

(a) Whether an employee is a full-time employee during any particular week depends upon the customary practices of the occupation in the geographic area in which the taxpayer works. Where employment is on a seasonal basis, weeks occurring in the off-season when no work is required or available may be counted as weeks of full-time employment only if the employee's contract or agreement of employment covers the off-season period and such period is less than 6 months. Thus, for example, a schoolteacher whose employment contract covers a 12-month period and who teaches on a full-time basis for more than 6 months is considered a full-time employee during the entire 12-month period. A taxpayer will be treated as a full-time employee during any week of involuntary temporary absence from work because of illness, strikes, shutouts, layoffs, natural disasters, etc. A taxpayer will, also, be treated as a full-time employee during any week in which he voluntarily absents himself from work for leave or vacation provided for in his contract or agreement of employment.

(b) Whether a taxpayer performs services as a self-employed individual on a full-time basis during any particular week depends on the practices of the trade or business in the geographic area in which the taxpayer works. For example, a self-employed dentist maintaining office hours 4 days a week is considered to perform services as a self-employed individual on a full-time basis providing it is not unusual for other self-employed dentists in the geographic area in which the taxpayer works to maintain office hours only 4 days a week. Where a trade or business is seasonal, weeks occurring during the off-season when no work is required or available may be counted as weeks of performance of services on a full-time basis only if the off-season is less than 6 months and the taxpayer performs services on a full-time basis both before and after the off-season. For example, a taxpayer who owns and operates a motel at a beach resort is considered to perform services as a self-employed individual on a full-time basis if the motel is closed for a period not exceeding 6 months during the off-season and if he performs services on a full-time basis as the operator of a motel both before and after the off-season. A taxpayer will be treated as performing services as a self-employed individual on a full-time basis during any week of involuntary temporary absence from work because of illness, strikes, natural disasters, etc.

(v) Where taxpayers file a joint return, either spouse may satisfy the minimum period of employment condition. However, weeks worked by one spouse may not be added to weeks worked by the other spouse in order to satisfy such condition. The taxpayer seeking to satisfy the minimum period of employment condition must satisfy the condition applicable to him. Thus, if a taxpayer is subject to the 39-week condition and his spouse is subject to the 78-week condition and the taxpayer satisfies the 39-week condition, his spouse need not satisfy the 78-week condition. On the other hand, if the taxpayer does not satisfy the 39-week condition, his spouse in such case must satisfy the 78-week condition.

(vi) The application of this subparagraph may be illustrated by the following examples:

Example (1). A is an electrician residing in New York City. He moves himself, his family, and his household goods and personal effects, at his own expense, to Denver where he commences employment with the M Aircraft Corporation. After working full-time for 30 weeks he voluntarily leaves his job, and he subsequently moves to and commences employment in Los Angeles, Calif., which employment lasts for more than 39 weeks. Since A was not employed in the general location of his new principal place of employment in Denver for at least 39 weeks, no deduction is allowable for moving expenses paid or incurred between New York City and Denver. A will be allowed to deduct only those moving expenses attributable to his move from Denver to Los Angeles, assuming all other conditions of section 217 are met.

Example (2). Assume the same facts as in example (1), except that A's wife commences employment in Denver at the same time as A, and that she continues to work in Denver for at least 9 weeks after A's departure for Los Angeles. Since she has met the 39-week requirement in Denver, and assuming all other requirements of section 217 are met, the moving expenses paid by A attributable to the move from New York City to Denver will be allowed as a deduction, provided A and his wife file a joint return. If A and his wife file separate returns moving expenses paid by A's wife attributable to the move from New York City to Denver will be allowed as a deduction on A's wife's return.

Example (3). Assume the same facts as in example (1), except that A's wife commences employment in Denver on the same day that A departs for Los Angeles, and continues to work in Denver for 9 weeks thereafter. Since neither A (who has worked 30 weeks) nor his wife (who has worked 9 weeks) has independently satisfied the 39-week requirement, no deduction for moving expenses attributable to the move from New York City to Denver is allowable.

(d) Rules for application of section 217(c)(2)—(1) Inapplicability of minimum period of employment condition in certain cases. Section 217(d)(1) provides that the minimum period of employment condition of section 217(c)(2) does not apply in the case of a taxpayer who is unable to meet such condition by reason of—

(i) Death or disability, or

(ii) Involuntary separation (other than for willful misconduct) from the service of an employer or separation by reason of transfer for the benefit of an employer after obtaining full-time employment in which the taxpayer could reasonably have been expected to satisfy such condition.

For purposes of subdivision (i) of this paragraph disability shall be determined according to the rules in section 72(m)(7) and §1.72–17(f). Subdivision (ii) of this subparagraph applies only where the taxpayer has obtained full-time employment in which he could reasonably have been expected to satisfy the minimum period of employment condition. A taxpayer could reasonably have been expected to satisfy the minimum period of employment condition if at the time he commences work at the new principal place of work he could have been expected, based upon the facts known to him at such time, to satisfy such condition. Thus, for example, if the taxpayer at the time of transfer was not advised by his employer that he planned to transfer him within 6 months to another principal place of work, the taxpayer could, in the absence of other factors, reasonably have been expected to satisfy the minimum employment period condition at the time of the first transfer. On the other hand, a taxpayer could not reasonably have been expected to satisfy the minimum employment condition if at the time of the commencement of the move he knew that his employer's retirement age policy would prevent his satisfying the minimum employment period condition.

(2) Election of deduction before minimum period of employment condition is satisfied. (i) Paragraph (2) of section 217(d) provides a rule which applies where a taxpayer paid or incurred, in a taxable year, moving expenses which would be deductible in that taxable year except that the minimum period of employment condition of section 217(c)(2) has not been satisfied before the time prescribed by law for filing the return for such taxable year. The rule provides that where a taxpayer has paid or incurred moving expenses and as of the date prescribed by section 6072 for filing his return for such taxable year (determined with regard to extensions of time for filing) there remains unexpired a sufficient portion of the 12-month or the 24-month period so that it is still possible for the taxpayer to satisfy the applicable period of employment condition, the taxpayer may elect to claim a deduction for such moving expenses on the return for such taxable year. The election is exercised by taking the deduction on the return.

(ii) Where a taxpayer does not elect to claim a deduction for moving expenses on the return for the taxable year in which such expenses were paid or incurred in accordance with subdivision (i) of this subparagraph and the applicable minimum period of employment condition of section 217(c)(2) (as well as all other requirements of section 217) is subsequently satisfied, the taxpayer may file an amended return or a claim for refund for the taxable year such moving expenses were paid or incurred on which he may claim a deduction under section 217.

(iii) The application of this subparagraph may be illustrated by the following examples:

Example (1). A is transferred by his employer from Boston, Massachusetts, to Cleveland, Ohio. He begins working there on November 1, 1970. Moving expenses are paid by A in 1970 in connection with this move. On April 15, 1971, when he files his income tax return for the year 1970, A has been a full-time employee in Cleveland for approximately 24 weeks. Although he has not satisfied the 39-week employment condition at this time, A may elect to claim his 1970 moving expenses on his 1970 income tax return as there is still sufficient time remaining before November 1, 1971, to satisfy such condition.

Example (2). Assume the same facts as in example (1), except that on April 15, 1971, A has voluntarily left his employer and is looking for other employment in Cleveland. A may not be sure he will be able to meet the 39-week employment condition by November 1, 1971. Thus, he may if he wishes wait until such condition is met and file an amended return claiming as a deduction the expenses paid in 1970. Instead of filing an amended return A may file a claim for refund based on a deduction for such expenses. If A fails to meet the 39-week employment condition on or before November 1, 1971, no deduction is allowable for such expenses.

Example (3). B is a self-employed accountant. He moves from Rochester, N.Y., to New York, N.Y., and begins to work there on December 1, 1970. Moving expenses are paid by B in 1970 and 1971 in connection with this move. On April 15, 1971, when he files his income tax return for the year 1970, B has been performing services as a self-employed individual on a full-time basis in New York City for approximately 20 weeks. Although he has not satisfied the 78-week employment condition at this time, A may elect to claim his 1970 moving expenses on his 1970 income tax return as there is still sufficient time remaining before December 1, 1972, to satisfy such condition. On April 15, 1972, when he files his income tax return for the year 1971, B has been performing services as a self-employed individual on a full-time basis in New York City for approximately 72 weeks. Although he has not met the 78-week employment condition at this time, B may elect to claim his 1971 moving expenses on his 1971 income tax return as there is still sufficient time remaining before December 1, 1972, to satisfy such requirement.

(3) Recapture of deduction. Paragraph (3) of section 217(d) provides a rule which applies where a taxpayer has deducted moving expenses under the election provided in section 217(d)(2) prior to satisfying the applicable minimum period of employment condition and such condition cannot be satisfied at the close of a subsequent taxable year. In such cases an amount equal to the expenses deducted must be included in the taxpayer's gross income for the taxable year in which the taxpayer is no longer able to satisfy such minimum period of employment condition. Where the taxpayer has deducted moving expenses under the election provided in section 217(d)(2) for the taxable year and subsequently files an amended return for such year on which he does not claim the deduction, such expenses are not treated as having been deducted for purposes of the recapture rule of the preceding sentence.

* * *

(f) Rules for self-employed individuals—(1) Definition. Section 217(f)(1) defines the term "self-employed individual" for purposes of section 217 to mean an individual who performs personal services either as the owner of the entire interest in an unincorporated trade or business or as a partner in a partnership carrying on a trade or business. The term "self-employed individual" does not include the semi-retired, part-time students, or other similarly situated taxpayers who work only a few hours each week. * * *

Special Deductions for Corporations

* * *

§ 1.248–1 Election to amortize organizational expenditures.

(a) In general.* **(1)** Section 248(a) provides that a corporation may elect for any taxable year beginning after December 31, 1953, to treat its organizational expenditures, as defined in subsection (b) of section 248 and in paragraph (b) of this section, as deferred expenses. A corporation which exercises such election must, at the time it makes the election, select a period of not less than 60 months, beginning with the month in which it began business, over which it will amortize its organizational expenditures. The period selected by the corporation may be equal to or greater, but not less, than 60 months, but in any event it must begin with the month in which the corporation began business. The organizational expenditures of the corporation which are treated as deferred expenses under the provisions of section 248 and this section shall then be allowed as a deduction in computing taxable income ratably over the period selected by the taxpayer. The period selected by the taxpayer in making its election may not be subsequently changed but shall be adhered to in computing taxable income for the taxable year for which the election is made and all subsequent taxable years.

(2) If a corporation exercises the election provided in section 248(a), such election shall apply to all of its expenditures which are organizational expenditures within the meaning of subsection (b) of section 248 and paragraph (b) of this section. The election shall apply, however, only with respect to expenditures incurred before the end of the taxable year in which the corporation begins business (without regard to whether the corporation files its returns on the accrual or cash method of accounting or whether the expenditures are paid in the taxable year in which they are incurred), if such expenditures are paid or incurred on or after August 16, 1954 (the date of enactment of the Internal Revenue Code of 1954).

(3) The deduction allowed under section 248 must be spread over a period beginning with the month in which the corporation begins business. The determination of the date the corporation begins business presents a question of fact which must be determined in each case in light of all the circumstances of the particular case. The words "begins business," however, do not have the same meaning as "in existence." Ordinarily, a corporation begins business when it starts the business operations for which it was organized; a corporation comes into existence on the date of its incorporation. Mere organizational activities, such as the obtaining of the corporate charter, are not alone sufficient to show the beginning of business. If the activities of the corporation have advanced to the extent necessary to establish the nature of its business operations, however, it will be deemed to have begun business. For example, the acquisition of operating assets which are necessary to the type of business contemplated may constitute the beginning of business.

(b) Organizational expenditures defined. (1) Section 248(b) defines the term "organizational expenditures." Such expenditures, for purposes of section 248 and this section, are those expenditures which are directly incident to the creation of the corporation. An expenditure, in order to qualify as an organizational expenditure, must be (i) incident to the creation of the corporation, (ii) chageable to the capital account of the corporation, and (iii) of a character which, if expended incident to the creation of a corporation having a limited life, would be amortizable over such life. An expenditure which fails to meet each of these three tests may not be considered an organizational expenditure for purposes of section 248 and this section.

(2) The following are examples of organizational expenditures within the meaning of section 248 and this section: legal services incident to the organization of the corporation, such as drafting the corporate charter, bylaws, minutes of organizational meetings, terms of original stock certificates, and the like; necessary accounting services; expenses of temporary directors and of organizational meetings of directors or stockholders; and fees paid to the State of incorporation.

(3) The following expenditures are not organizational expenditures within the meaning of section 248 and this section:

(i) Expenditures connected with issuing or selling shares of stock or other securities, such as commissions, professional fees, and printing costs. This is so

*Editorial comment: The Regulations do not reflect the effect of the American Jobs Creation Act of 2004 on organizational expenditures which provides for the opportunity to elect limited expensing (i.e., maximum of $5,000 subject to a phaseout provision) with the balance being subject to amortization over an 180-month period. See §248(a).

even where the particular issue of stock to which the expenditures relate is for a fixed term of years;

(ii) Expenditures connected with the transfer of assets to a corporation.

(4) Expenditures connected with the reorganization of a corporation, unless directly incident to the creation of a corporation, are not organizational expenditures within the meaning of section 248 and this section.

(c) Time and manner of making election. The election provided by section 248(a) and paragraph (a) of this section shall be made in a statement attached to the taxpayer's return for the taxable year in which it begins business. Such taxable year must be one which begins after December 31, 1953. The return and statement must be filed not later than the date prescribed by law for filing the return (including any extensions of time) for the taxable year in which the taxpayer begins business. The statement shall set forth the description and amount of the expenditures involved, the date such expenditures were incurred, the month in which the corporation began business, and the number of months (not less than 60 and beginning with the month in which the taxpayer began business) over which such expenditures are to be deducted ratably.

* * *

Items Not Deductible

* * *

§ 1.262–1 Personal, living, and family expenses.

(a) In general. In computing taxable income, no deduction shall be allowed, except as otherwise expressly provided in chapter 1 of the Code, for personal, living, and family expenses.

(b) Examples of personal, living, and family expenses. Personal, living, and family expenses are illustrated in the following examples:

(1) Premiums paid for life insurance by the insured are not deductible. * * *

(2) The cost of insuring a dwelling owned and occupied by the taxpayer as a personal residence is not deductible.

(3) Expenses of maintaining a household, including amounts paid for rent, water, utilities, domestic service, and the like, are not deductible. A taxpayer who rents a property for residential purposes, but incidentally conducts business there (his place of business being elsewhere) shall not deduct any part of the rent. If, however, he uses part of the house as his place of business, such portion of the rent and other similar expenses as is properly attributable to such place of business is deductible as a business expense.

(4) Losses sustained by the taxpayer upon the sale or other disposition of property held for personal, living, and family purposes are not deductible. But see section 165 and the regulations thereunder for deduction of losses sustained to such property by reason of casualty, etc.

(5) Expenses incurred in traveling away from home (which include transportation expenses, meals, and lodging) and any other transportation expenses are not deductible unless they qualify as expenses deductible under section 162, §1.162–2, and paragraph (d) of §1.162–5 (relating to trade or business expenses), section 170 and paragraph (a)(2) of § 1.170–2 or paragraph (g) of §1.170A–1 (relating to charitable contributions), section 212 and §1.212–1 (relating to expenses for production of income), section 213(e) and paragraph (e) of §1.213–1 (relating to medical expenses) or section 217(a) and paragraph (a) of §1.217–1 (relating to moving expenses). The taxpayer's costs of commuting to his place of business or employment are personal expenses and do not qualify as deductible expenses. The costs of the taxpayer's lodging not incurred in traveling away from home are personal expenses and are not deductible unless they qualify as deductible expenses under section 217. Except as permitted under section 162, 212, or 217, the costs of the taxpayer's meals not incurred in traveling away from home are personal expenses.

(6) Amounts paid as damages for breach of promise to marry, and attorney's fees and other costs of suit to recover such damages, are not deductible.

(7) Generally, attorney's fees and other costs paid in connection with a divorce, separation, or decree for support are not deductible by either the husband or the wife. However, the part of an attorney's fee and the part of the other costs paid in connection with a divorce, legal separation, written separation agreement, or a decree for support, which are properly attributable to the production or collection of amounts includible in gross income under section 71 are deductible by the wife under section 212.

* * *

(9) Expenditures made by a taxpayer in obtaining an education or in furthering his education are not deductible unless they qualify under section 162 and §1.162–5 (relating to trade or business expenses).

* * *

§ 1.263A-1 Uniform capitalization of costs.*

(a) Introduction. (1) In general. The regulations under §§1.263A-1 through 1.263A-6 provide guidance to taxpayers that are required to capitalize certain costs under section 263A. These regulations generally apply to all costs required to be capitalized under section 263A except for interest that must be capitalized under section 263A(f) and the regulations thereunder. Statutory or regulatory exceptions may provide that section 263A does not apply to certain activities or costs; however, those activities or costs may nevertheless be subject to capitalization requirements under other provisions of the Internal Revenue Code and regulations.

(2) Effective dates. (i) In general, this section and §§1.263A-2 and 1.263A-3 apply to costs incurred in taxable years beginning after December 31, 1993. In the case of property that is inventory in the hands of the taxpayer, however, these sections are effective for taxable years beginning after December 31, 1993. Changes in methods of accounting necessary as a result of the rules in this section and §§1.263A-2 and 1.263A-3 must be made under terms and conditions prescribed by the Commissioner. Under these terms and conditions, the principles of §1.263A-7 generally must be applied in revaluing inventory property.

(ii) For taxable years beginning before January 1, 1994, taxpayers must take reasonable positions on their federal income tax returns when applying section 263A. For purposes of this paragraph (a)(2)(iii), a reasonable position is a position consistent with the temporary regulations, revenue rulings, revenue procedures, notices, and announcements concerning section 263A applicable in taxable years beginning before January 1, 1994. See §601.601(d)(2)(ii)(b) of this chapter.

(3) General scope. (i) Property to which section 263A applies. Taxpayers subject to section 263A must capitalize all direct costs and certain indirect costs properly allocable to—

(A) Real property and tangible personal property produced by the taxpayer; and

(B) Real property and personal property described in section 1221(1), which is acquired by the taxpayer for resale.

(ii) Property produced. Taxpayers that produce real property and tangible personal property (producers) must capitalize all the direct costs of producing the property and the property's properly allocable share of indirect costs (described in paragraphs (e)(2)(i) and (3) of this section), regardless of whether the property is sold or used in the taxpayer's trade or business. See §1.263A-2 for rules relating to producers.

(iii) Property acquired for resale. Retailers, wholesalers, and other taxpayers that acquire property described in section 1221(1) for resale (resellers) must capitalize the direct costs of acquiring the property and the property's properly allocable share of indirect costs (described in paragraphs (e)(2)(ii) and (3) of this section). See §1.263A-3 for rules relating to resellers. See also section 263A(b)(2)(B), which excepts from section 263A personal property acquired for resale by a small reseller.

(iv) Inventories valued at market. Section 263A does not apply to inventories valued at market under either the market method or the lower of cost or market method if the market valuation used by the taxpayer generally equals the property's fair market value. For purposes of this paragraph (a)(3)(iv), the term fair market value means the price at which the taxpayer sells its inventory to its customers (e.g., as in the market value definition provided in §1.471-4(b)) less, if applicable, the direct cost of disposing of the inventory. However, section 263A does apply in determining the market value of any inventory for which market is determined with reference to replacement cost or reproduction cost. See §§ 1.471-4 and 1.471-5.

(v) Property produced in a farming business. Section 263A generally requires taxpayers engaged in a farming business to capitalize certain costs. See section 263A(d) and §1.263A-4 for rules relating to taxpayers engaged in a farming business.

(vi) Creative property. Section 263A generally requires taxpayers engaged in the production and resale of creative property to capitalize certain costs.

*Editorial comment: In general, these final regulations apply to taxable years after January 1, 2014.

(vii) Property produced or property acquired for resale by foreign persons. Section 263A generally applies to foreign persons.

(b) Exceptions. **(1) Small resellers.** See section 263A(b)(2)(B) for the $10,000,000 gross receipts exception for small resellers of personal property. See §1.263A-3(b) for rules relating to this exception. See also the exception for small resellers with de minimis production activities in §1.263A-3(a)(2)(ii) and the exception for small resellers that have property produced under contract in §1.263A-3(a)(3).

(2) Long-term contracts. Except for certain home construction contracts described in section 460(e)(1), section 263A does not apply to any property produced by the taxpayer pursuant to a long-term contract as defined in section 460(f), regardless of whether the taxpayer uses an inventory method to account for such production.

(3) Costs incurred in certain farming businesses. See section 263A(d) for an exception for costs paid or incurred in certain farming businesses. See §1.263A-4 for specific rules relating to taxpayers engaged in the trade or business of farming.

(4) Costs incurred in raising, harvesting, or growing timber. See section 263A(c)(5) for an exception for costs paid or incurred in raising, harvesting, or growing timber and certain ornamental trees. See §1.263A-4, however, for rules relating to taxpayers producing certain trees to which section 263A applies.

(5) Qualified creative expenses. See section 263A(h) for an exception for qualified creative expenses paid or incurred by certain free-lance authors, photographers, and artists.

(6) Certain not-for-profit activities. See section 263A(c)(1) for an exception for property produced by a taxpayer for use by the taxpayer other than in a trade or business or an activity conducted for profit. This exception does not apply, however, to property produced by an exempt organization in connection with its unrelated trade or business activities.

* * *

(9) Research and experimental expenditures. See section 263A(c)(2) for an exception for any research and experimental expenditure allowable as a deduction under section 174 or the regulations thereunder. Additionally, section 263A does not apply to any amount allowable as a deduction under section 59(e) with respect to qualified expenditures under section 174.

(10) Certain property that is substantially constructed. Section 263A does not apply to any property produced by a taxpayer for use in its trade or business if substantial construction occurred before March 1, 1986.

(i) For purposes of this section, substantial construction is deemed to have occurred if the lesser of—

(A) 10 percent of the total estimated costs of construction; or

(B) The greater of $10 million or 2 percent of the total estimated costs of construction, was incurred before March 1, 1986.

(ii) For purposes of this provision, the total estimated costs of construction shall be determined by reference to a reasonable estimate, on or before March 1, 1986, of such amount. Assume, for example, that on March 1, 1986, the estimated costs of constructing a facility were $150 million. Assume that before March 1, 1986, $12 million of construction costs had been incurred. Based on the above facts, substantial construction would be deemed to have occurred before March 1, 1986, because $12 million (the costs of construction incurred before such date) is greater than $10 million (the lesser of $15 million; or the greater of $10 million or $3 million). For purposes of this provision, construction costs are defined as those costs incurred after construction has commenced at the site of the property being constructed (unless the property will not be located on land and, therefore, the initial construction of the property must begin at a location other than the intended site). For example, in the case of a building, construction commences when work begins on the building, such as the excavation of the site, the pouring of pads for the building, or the driving of foundation pilings into the ground. Preliminary activities such as project engineering and architectural design do not constitute the commencement of construction, nor are such costs considered construction costs, for purposes of this paragraph (b)(10).

(11) Certain property provided incident to services. **(i) In general.** Under this paragraph (b)(11), section 263A does not apply to property that is provided to a client (or customer) incident to the provision of services by the taxpayer if the property provided to the client is—

(A) De minimis in amount; and

(B) Not inventory in the hands of the service provider.

(ii) Definition of services. For purposes of this paragraph (b)(11), services is defined with reference to its ordinary and accepted meaning under federal income tax principles. In determining whether a taxpayer is a bona-fide service provider under this paragraph (b)(11), the nature of the taxpayer's trade or business and the facts and circumstances surrounding the taxpayer's trade or business activities must be considered. Examples of taxpayers qualifying as service providers under this paragraph include taxpayers performing services in the fields of health, law, engineering, architecture, accounting, actuarial science, performing arts, or consulting.

(iii) De minimis property provided incident to services. In determining whether property provided to a client by a service provider is de minimis in amount, all facts and circumstances, such as the nature of the taxpayer's trade or business and the volume of its service activities in the trade or business, must be considered. A significant factor in making this determination is the relationship between the acquisition or direct materials costs of the property that is provided to clients and the price that the taxpayer charges its clients for its services and the property. For purposes of this paragraph (b)(11), if the acquisition or direct materials cost of the property provided to a client incident to the services is less than or equal to five percent of the price charged to the client for the services and property, the property is de minimis. If the acquisition or direct materials cost of the property exceeds five percent of the price charged for the services and property, the property may be de minimis if additional facts and circumstances so indicate.

(12) De minimis rule for certain producers with total indirect costs of $200,000 or less. See §1.263A-2(b)(3)(iv) for a de minimis rule that treats producers with total indirect costs of $200,000 or less as having no additional section 263A costs (as defined in paragraph (d)(3) of this section) for purposes of the simplified production method.

* * *

(c) General operation of section 263A— (1) Allocations. Under section 263A, taxpayers must capitalize their direct costs and a properly allocable share of their indirect costs to property produced or property acquired for resale. In order to determine these capitalizable costs, taxpayers must allocate or apportion costs to various activities, including production or resale activities. After section 263A costs are allocated to the appropriate production or resale activities, these costs are generally allocated to the items of property produced or property acquired for resale during the taxable year and capitalized to the items that remain on hand at the end of the taxable year. See however, the simplified production method and the simplified resale method in §§1.263A-2(b) and 1.263A-3(d).

(2) Otherwise deductible. (i) Any cost which (but for section 263A and the regulations thereunder) may not be taken into account in computing taxable income for any taxable year is not treated as a cost properly allocable to property produced or acquired for resale under section 263A and the regulations thereunder. Thus, for example, if a business meal deduction is limited by section 274(n) to 80 percent of the cost of the meal, the amount properly allocable to property produced or acquired for resale under section 263A is also limited to 80 percent of the cost of the meal.

(ii) The amount of any cost required to be capitalized under section 263A may not be included in inventory or charged to capital accounts or basis any earlier than the taxable year during which the amount is incurred within the meaning of §1.446-1(c)(1)(ii).

(3) Capitalize. Capitalize means, in the case of property that is inventory in the hands of a taxpayer, to include in inventory costs and, in the case of other property, to charge to a capital account or basis.

(4) Recovery of capitalized costs. Costs that are capitalized under section 263A are recovered through depreciation, amortization, cost of goods sold, or by an adjustment to basis at the time the property is used, sold, placed in service, or otherwise disposed of by the taxpayer. Cost recovery is determined by the applicable Internal Revenue Code and regulation provisions relating to use, sale, or disposition of property.

(5) Costs allocable to property sold. A cost that is allocated under this section, §1.263A-2, or §1.263A-3 entirely to property sold must be included in cost of goods sold and may not be included in determining the cost of goods on hand at the end of the taxable year.

(d) Definitions— (1) Self-constructed assets. Self-constructed assets are assets produced by a taxpayer for use by the taxpayer in its trade or business. Self-constructed assets are subject to section 263A.

(2) Section 471 costs. (i) In general. Except as otherwise provided in paragraphs (d)(2)(ii) and (iii) of this section, for purposes of the regulations under section 263A, a taxpayer's section 471 costs are the costs, other than interest, capitalized under its method of accounting immediately prior to the effective date of section 263A. Thus, although section 471 applies only to inventories, section 471 costs include any non-inventory costs, other than interest, capitalized or included in acquisition or production costs under the taxpayer's method of accounting immediately prior to the effective date of section 263A.

* * *

(3) Additional section 263A costs. Additional section 263A costs are defined as the costs, other than interest, that were not capitalized under the taxpayer's method of accounting immediately prior to the effective date of section 263A (adjusted as appropriate for any changes in methods of accounting for section 471 costs under paragraph (d)(2)(iii) of this section), but that are required to be capitalized under section 263A. For new taxpayers, additional section 263A costs are defined as the costs, other than interest, that the taxpayer must capitalize under section 263A, but which the taxpayer would not have been required to capitalize if the taxpayer had been in existence prior to the effective date of section 263A.

(4) Section 263A costs. Section 263A costs are defined as the costs that a taxpayer must capitalize under section 263A. Thus, section 263A costs are the sum of a taxpayer's section 471 costs, its additional section 263A costs, and interest capitalizable under section 263A(f).

(e) Types of costs subject to capitalization. **(1) In general.** Taxpayers subject to section 263A must capitalize all direct costs and certain indirect costs properly allocable to property produced or property acquired for resale. This paragraph (e) describes the types of costs subject to section 263A.

(2) Direct costs. **(i)** Producers. Producers must capitalize direct material costs and direct labor costs.

(A) Direct material costs. Direct materials costs include the cost of those materials that become an integral part of specific property produced and those materials that are consumed in the ordinary course of production and that can be identified or associated with particular units or groups of units of property produced. For example, a cost described in §1.162-3, relating to the cost of a material or supply, may be a direct material cost.

(B) Direct labor costs include the costs of labor that can be identified or associated with particular units or groups of units of specific property produced. For this purpose, labor encompasses full-time and part-time employees, as well as contract employees and independent contractors. Direct labor costs include all elements of compensation other than employee benefit costs described in paragraph (e)(3)(ii)(D) of this section. Elements of direct labor costs include basic compensation, overtime pay, vacation pay, holiday pay, sick leave pay (other than payments pursuant to a wage continuation plan under section 105(d) as it existed prior to its repeal in 1983), shift differential, payroll taxes, and payments to a supplemental unemployment benefit plan.

(3) Indirect costs. **(i)** In general. **(A)** Indirect costs are defined as all costs other than direct material costs and direct labor costs (in the case of property produced) or acquisition costs (in the case of property acquired for resale). Taxpayers subject to section 263A must capitalize all indirect costs properly allocable to property produced or property acquired for resale. Indirect costs are properly allocable to property produced or property acquired for resale when the costs directly benefit or are incurred by reason of the performance of production or resale activities. Indirect costs may directly benefit or be incurred by reason of the performance of production or resale activities even if the costs are calculated as a percentage of revenue or gross profit from the sale of inventory, are determined by reference to the number of units of property sold, or are incurred only upon the sale of inventory. Indirect costs may be allocable to both production and resale activities, as well as to other activities that are not subject to section 263A. Taxpayers must make a reasonable allocation of indirect costs between production, resale, and other activities.

§ 1.265–1 Expenses relating to tax-exempt income.

(a) Nondeductibility of expenses allocable to exempt income. **(1)** No amount shall be allowed as a deduction under any provision of the Code for any expense or amount which is otherwise allowable as a deduction and which is allocable to a class or classes of exempt income other than a class or classes of exempt interest income.

(2) No amount shall be allowed as a deduction under section 212 (relating to expenses for production of income) for any expense or amount which is otherwise allowable as a deduction and which is allocable to a class or classes of exempt interest income.

(b) Exempt income and nonexempt income. **(1)** As used in this section, the term "class of exempt income" means any class of income (whether or not any amount of income of such class is received or accrued) wholly exempt from the taxes imposed by subtitle A of the Code. For purposes of this section, a class of income which is considered as wholly exempt from the taxes imposed by subtitle A includes any class of income which is—

(i) Wholly excluded from gross income under any provision of subtitle A, or

(ii) Wholly exempt from the taxes imposed by subtitle A under the provisions of any other law.

(2) As used in this section the term "nonexempt income" means any income which is required to be included in gross income.

(c) Allocation of expenses to a class or classes of exempt income. Expenses and amounts otherwise allowable which are directly allocable to any class or classes of exempt income shall be allocated thereto; and expenses and amounts directly allocable to any class or classes of nonexempt income shall be allocated thereto. If an expense or amount otherwise allowable is indirectly allocable to both a class of nonexempt income and a class of exempt income, a reasonable proportion thereof determined in the light of all the facts and circumstances in each case shall be allocated to each.

(d) Statement of classes of exempt income; records. (1) A taxpayer receiving any class of exempt income or holding any property or engaging in any activity the income from which is exempt shall submit with his return as a part thereof an itemized statement, in detail, showing (i) the amount of each class of exempt income, and (ii) the amount of expenses and amounts otherwise allowable allocated to each such class (the amount allocated by apportionment being shown separately) as required by paragraph (c) of this section. If an item is apportioned between a class of exempt income and a class of nonexempt income, the statement shall show the basis of the apportionment. Such statement shall also recite that each deduction claimed in the return is not in any way attributable to a class of exempt income.

(2) The taxpayer shall keep such records as will enable him to make the allocations required by this section. See section 6001 and the regulations thereunder.

§ 1.265–2 Interest relating to tax-exempt income.

(a) In general. No amount shall be allowed as a deduction for interest on any indebtedness incurred or continued to purchase or carry obligations, the interest on which is wholly exempt from tax under subtitle A of the Code, such as municipal bonds * * *.

* * *

§ 1.267(a)–1 Deductions disallowed.

(a) Losses. Except in cases of distributions in corporate liquidations, no deduction shall be allowed for losses arising from direct or indirect sales or exchanges of property between persons who, on the date of the sale or exchange, are within any one of the relationships specified in section 267(b). See §1.267(b)–1.

* * *

(c) Scope of section. Section 267(a) requires that deductions for losses or unpaid expenses or interest described therein be disallowed even though the transaction in which such losses, expenses, or interest were incurred was a bona fide transaction. However, section 267 is not exclusive. No deduction for losses or unpaid expenses or interest arising in a transaction which is not bona fide will be allowed even though section 267 does not apply to the transaction.

§ 1.267(a)–2T Temporary regulations; questions and answers arising under the Tax Reform Act of 1984 (temporary).

(a) Introduction—(1) Scope. This section prescribes temporary question and answer regulations under section 267(a) and related provisions as amended by section 174 of the Tax Reform Act of 1984, Pub.L. No. 98–369.

(2) Effective date. Except as otherwise provided by Answer 2 or Answer 3 in paragraph (c) of this section, the effective date set forth in section 174(c) of the Tax Reform Act of 1984 applies to this section.

(b) Questions applying section 267(a)(2) and (b) generally. The following questions and answers deal with the application of section 267(a)(2) and (b) generally:

Question 1: Does section 267(a)(2) ever apply to defer the deduction of an otherwise deductible amount if the person to whom the payment is to be made properly uses the completed contract method of accounting with respect to such amount?

Answer 1: No. Section 267(a)(2) applies only if an otherwise deductible amount is owed to a related person under whose method of accounting such amount is not includible in income unless paid to such person. Regardless of when payment is made, an amount owed to a contractor using the completed contract method of accounting is includible in the income of the contractor in accordance with §1.451–3(d) in the year in which the contract is completed or in which certain disputes are resolved.

Question 2: Does section 267(a)(2) ever apply to defer the deduction of otherwise deductible original issue discount as defined in sections 163(e) and 1271 through 1275 ("the OID rules")?

Answer 2: No. Regardless of when payment is made, an amount owed to a lender that constitutes original issue discount is included in the income of the lender periodically in accordance with the OID rules. Similarly, section 267(a)(2) does not apply to defer an otherwise deductible amount to the extent section 467 or section 7872 requires periodic inclusion of such amount in the income of the person to whom payment is to be made, even though payment has not been made.

Question 3: Does section 267(a)(2) ever apply to defer the deduction of otherwise deductible unstated interest determined to exist under section 483?

Answer 3: Yes. If section 483 recharacterizes any amount as unstated interest and the other requirements of section 267(a)(2) are met, a deduction for such unstated interest will be deferred under section 267.

Question 4: Does section 267(a)(2) ever apply to defer the deduction of otherwise deductible cost recovery, depreciation, or amortization?

Answer 4: Yes, in certain cases. In general, section 267(a)(2) does not apply to defer the deduction of otherwise deductible cost recovery, depreciation, or amortization. Notwithstanding this general rule, if the other requirements of section 267(a)(2) are met, section 267(a)(2) does apply to defer deductions for cost recovery, depreciation, or amortization of an amount owed to a related person for interest or rent or for the performance or nonperformance of services, which amount the taxpayer payor capitalized or treated as a deferred expense (unless the taxpayer payor elected to capitalize or defer the amount and section 267(a)(2) would not have deferred the deduction of such amount if the taxpayer payor had not so elected). Amounts owed for services that may be subject to this provision include, for example, amounts owed for acquisition, development, or organizational services or for covenants not to compete. In applying this rule, payments made between persons described in any of the paragraphs of section 267(b) (as modified by section 267(e)) will be closely scrutinized to determine whether they are made in respect of capitalized costs (or costs treated as deferred expenses) that are subject to deferral under section 267(a)(2), or in respect of other capitalized costs not so subject.

Question 5: If a deduction in respect of an otherwise deductible amount is deferred by section 267(a)(2) and, prior to the time the amount is includible in the gross income of the person to whom payment is to be made, such person and the payor taxpayer cease to be persons specified in any of the paragraphs of section 267(b) (as modified by section 267(e)), is the deduction allowable as of the day on which the relationship ceases?

Answer 5: No. The deduction is not allowable until the day as of which the amount is includible in the gross income of the person to whom payment of the amount is made, even though the relationship ceases to exist at an earlier time.

Question 6: Do references in other sections to persons described in section 267(b) incorporate changes made to section 267(b) by section 174 of the Tax Reform Act of 1984?

Answer 6: Yes. References in other sections to persons described in section 267(b) take into account changes made to section 267(b) by section 174 of the Tax Reform Act of 1984 (without modification by section 267(e)(1)). For example, a transfer after December 31, 1983 (the effective date of the new section 267(b)(3) relationship added by the Tax Reform Act of 1984) of section 1245 class property placed in service before January 1, 1981, from one corporation to another corporation, 11 percent of the stock of which is owned by the first corporation, will not constitute recovery property (as defined in section 168) in the hands of the second corporation by reason of section 168(e)(4)(A)(i) and (D).

(c) Questions applying section 267(a) to partnerships. The following questions and answers deal with the application of section 267(a) to partnerships:

Question 1: Does section 267(a) disallow losses and defer otherwise deductible amounts at the partnership (entity) level?

Answer 1: Yes. If a loss realized by a partnership from a sale or exchange of property is disallowed under section 267(a)(1), that loss shall not enter into the computation of the partnership's taxable income. If an amount that otherwise would be deductible by a partnership is deferred by section 267(a)(2), that amount shall not enter into the computation of the partnership's taxable income until the taxable year of the partnership in which falls the day on which the amount is includible in the gross income of the person to whom payment of the amount is made.

Question 2: Does section 267(a)(1) ever apply to disallow a loss if the sale or exchange giving rise to the loss is between two partnerships even though the two partnerships are not persons specified in any of the paragraphs of section 267(b)?

Answer 2: Yes. If the other requirements of section 267(a)(1) are met, section 267(a)(1) applies to such losses arising as a result of transactions entered into after December 31, 1984 between partnerships not described in any of the paragraphs of section 267(b) as follows, and §1.267(b)–1(b) does not apply. If the two partnerships have one or more common partners (*i.e.*, if any person owns directly, indirectly, or constructively any capital or profits interest in each of such partnerships), or if any partner in either partnership and one or more partners in the other partnership are persons specified in any of the paragraphs of section 267(b) (without modification by section 267(e)), a portion of the selling partnership's loss will be disallowed under section 267(a)(l). The amount disallowed under this rule is the greater of: (1) The amount that would be disallowed if the transaction giving rise to the loss had occurred between the selling partnership and the separate partners of the purchasing partnership (in proportion to their respective interests in the purchasing partnership); or (2) the amount that would be disallowed if such transaction had occurred between the separate partners of the selling partnership (in proportion to their respective interests in the selling partnership) and the purchasing partnership. Notwithstanding the general rule of this paragraph (c) *Answer 2*, no disallowance shall occur if the amount that would be disallowed pursuant to the immediately preceding sentence is less than 5 percent of the loss arising from the sale or exchange.

Question 3: Does section 267(a)(2) ever apply to defer an otherwise deductible amount if the taxpayer payor is a partnership and the person to whom payment of such amount is to be made is a partnership even though the two partnerships are not persons specified in any of the paragraphs of section 267(b) (as modified by section 267(e))?

Answer 3: Yes. If the other requirements of section 267(a)(2) are met, section 267(a)(2) applies to such amounts arising as a result of transactions entered into after December 31, 1984 between partnerships not described in any of the paragraphs of section 267(b) (as modified by section 267(e)) as follows, and §1.267(b)–1(b) does not apply. If the two partnerships have one or more common partners (*i.e.*, if any person owns directly, indirectly, or constructively any capital or profits interest in each of such partnerships), or if any partner in either partnership and one or more partners in the other partnership are persons specified in any of the paragraphs of section 267(b) (without modification by section 267(e)), a portion of the payor partnership's otherwise allowable deduction will be deferred under section 267(a)(2). The amount deferred under this rule is the greater of: (1) The amount that would be deferred if the transaction giving rise to the otherwise allowable deduction had occurred between the payor partnership and the separate partners of the payee partnership (in proportion to their respective interests in the payee partnership); or (2) the amount that would be deferred if such transaction had occurred between the separate partners of the payor partnership (in proportion to their respective interests in the payor partnership) and the payee partnership. Notwithstanding the general rule of this paragraph (c) *Answer 3*, no deferral shall occur if the amount that would be deferred pursuant to the immediately preceding sentence is less than 5 percent of the otherwise allowable deduction.

Example. On May 1, 1985, partnership AB enters into a transaction whereby it accrues an otherwise deductible amount to partnership AC. AC is on the cash receipts and disbursements method of accounting. A holds a 5 percent capital and profits interest in AB and a 49 percent capital and profits interest in AC, and A's interest in each item of the income, gain, loss, deduction, and credit of each partnership is 5 percent and 49 percent, respectively. B and C are not related. Notwithstanding that AB and AC are not persons specified in section 267(b), 49 percent of the deduction in respect of such amount will be deferred under section 267(a)(2). The result would be the same if A held a 49 percent interest in AB and a 5 percent interest in AC. However, if A held more than 50 percent of the capital or profits interest of either AB or AC, the entire deduction in respect of such amount would be deferred under section 267(a)(2).

Question 4: What does the phrase "incurred at an annual rate not in excess of 12 percent" mean as used in section 267(e)(5)(C)(ii)?

Answer 4: The phrase refers to interest that accrues but is not includible in the income of the person to whom payment is to be made during the taxable year of the payor. Thus, in determining whether the requirements of section 267(e)(5) (providing an exception to certain provisions of section 267 for certain expenses and interest of partnerships owning low income housing) are met with respect to a transaction, the requirement of section 267(e)(5)(C)(ii) will be satisfied, even though the total interest (both stated and unstated) paid or accrued in any taxable year of the payor taxpayer exceeds 12 percent, if the interest in excess of 12 percent per annum, compounded semi–annually, on the outstanding loan balance (principal and accrued but unpaid interest) is includible in the income of the person to whom payment is to be made no later than the last day of such taxable year of the payor taxpayer.

* * *

§ 1.267(b)–1 Relationships.

(a) In general. **(1)** The persons referred to in section 267(a) and §1.267 (a) 1 are specified in section 267(b).

* * *

(b) Partnerships. **(1)** Since section 267 does not include members of a partnership and the partnership as related persons, transactions between partners and partnerships do not come within the scope of section 267. Such transactions are governed by section 707 for the purposes of which the partnership is considered to be an entity separate from the partners. See section 707 and §1.707–1. Any transaction described in section 267(a) between a partnership and a person other than a partner shall be considered as occurring between the other person and the members of the partnership separately. Therefore, if the other person and a partner are within any one of the relationships specified in section 267(b), no deductions with respect to such transactions between the other person and the partnership shall be allowed—

(i) To the related partner to the extent of his distributive share of partnership deductions for losses or unpaid expenses or interest resulting from such transactions, and

(ii) To the other person to the extent the related partner acquires an interest in any property sold to or exchanged with the partnership by such other person at a loss, or to the extent of the related partner's distributive share of the unpaid expenses or interest payable to the partnership by the other person as a result of such transaction.

(2) The provisions of this paragraph may be illustrated by the following examples:

Example (1). A, an equal partner in the ABC partnership, personally owns all the stock of M Corporation. B and C are not related to A. The partnership and all the partners use an accrual method of accounting, and are on a calendar year. M Corporation uses the cash receipts and disbursements method of accounting and is also on a calendar year. During 1956 the partnership borrowed money from M Corporation and also sold property to M Corporation, sustaining a loss on the sale. On December 31, 1956, the partnership accrued its interest liability to the M Corporation and on April 1, 1957 (more than 2½ months after the close of its taxable year), it paid the M Corporation the amount of such accrued interest. Applying the rules of this paragraph, the transactions are considered as occurring between M Corporation and the partners separately. The sale and interest transactions considered as occurring between A and the M Corporation fall within the scope of section 267 (a) and (b), but the transactions considered as occurring between partners B and C and the M Corporation do not. The latter two partners may, therefore, deduct their distributive shares of partnership deductions for the loss and the accrued interest. However, no deduction shall be allowed to A for his distributive shares of these partnership deductions. Furthermore, A's adjusted basis for his partnership interest must be decreased by the amount of his distributive share of such deductions. See section 705(a)(2).

Example (2). Assume the same facts as in example (1) of this subparagraph except that the partnership and all the partners use the cash receipts and disbursements method of accounting, and that M Corporation uses an accrual method. Assume further, that during 1956 M Corporation borrowed money from the partnership and that on a sale of property to the partnership during that year M Corporation sustained a loss. On December 31, 1956, the M Corporation accrued its interest liability on the borrowed money and on April 1, 1957 (more than 2½ months after the close of its taxable year) it paid the accrued interest to the partnership. The corporation's deduction for the accrued interest is not allowed to the extent of A's distributive share (one-third) of such interest income. M Corporation's deduction for the loss on the sale of the property to the partnership is not allowed to the extent of A's one-third interest in the purchased property.

§ 1.267(c)–1 Constructive ownership of stock.

(a) In general. **(1)** The determination of stock ownership for purposes of section 267(b) shall be in accordance with the rules in section 267(c).

(2) For an individual to be considered under section 267(c)(2) as constructively owning the stock of a corporation which is owned, directly or indirectly, by or for members of his family it is not necessary that he own stock in the corporation either directly or indirectly. On the other hand, for an individual to be considered under section 267(c)(3) as owning the stock of a corporation owned either actually, or constructively under section 267(c)(1), by or for his partner, such individual must himself actually own, or constructively own under section 267(c)(1), stock of such corporation.

(3) An individual's constructive ownership, under section 267(c)(2) or (3), of stock owned directly or indirectly by or for a member of his family, or by or for his partner, is not to be considered as actual ownership of such stock, and the individual's constructive ownership of the stock is not to be attributed to another member of his family or to another partner. However, an individual's constructive ownership, under section 267(c)(1), of stock owned directly or indirectly by or for a corporation, partnership, estate, or trust shall be considered as actual ownership of the stock, and the individual's ownership may be attributed to a member of his family or to his partner.

(4) The family of an individual shall include only his brothers and sisters, spouse, ancestors, and lineal descendants. In determining whether any of these relationships exist, full effect shall be given to a legal adoption. The term "ancestors" includes parents and grandparents, and the term "lineal descendants" includes children and grandchildren.

(b) Examples. The application of section 267(c) may be illustrated by the following examples:

Example (1). On July 1, 1957, A owned 75 percent, and AW, his wife, owned 25 percent, of the outstanding stock of the M Corporation. The M Corporation in turn owned 80 percent of the outstanding stock of the O Corporation. Under section 267(c)(1), A and AW are each considered as owning an amount of the O Corporation stock actually owned by M Corporation in proportion to their respective ownership of M Corporation stock. Therefore, A constructively owns 60 percent (75 percent of 80 percent) of the O Corporation stock and AW constructively owns 20 percent (25 percent of 80 percent) of such stock. Under the family ownership rule of section 267(c)(2), an individual is considered as constructively owning the stock actually owned by his spouse. A and AW, therefore, are each considered as constructively owning the M Corporation stock actually owned by the other. For the purpose of applying this family ownership rule, A's and AW's constructive ownership of O Corporation stock is considered as actual ownership under section 267(c)(5). Thus, A constructively owns the 20 percent of the O Corporation stock constructively owned by AW, and AW constructively owns the 60 percent of the O Corporation stock constructively owned by A. In addition, the family ownership rule may be applied to make AWF, AW's father, the constructive owner of the 25 percent of the M Corporation stock actually owned by AW. As noted above, AW's constructive ownership of 20 percent of the O Corporation stock is considered as actual ownership for purposes of applying the family ownership rule, and AWF is thereby considered the constructive owner of this stock also. However, AW's constructive ownership of the stock constructively and actually owned by A may not be considered as actual ownership for the purpose of again applying the family ownership rule to make AWF the constructive owner of these shares. The ownership of the stock in the M and O Corporations may be tabulated as follows:

	Stock ownership in M Corporation			Stock ownership in O Corporation		
Person	Actual (Percent)	Constructive (Percent)	Total under Section 267 (Percent)	Actual (Percent)	Constructive (Percent)	Total under Section 267 (Percent)
A	75	25	100	None	60—20	80
AW (A's wife)	25	75	100	None	20—60	80
AWF (AW's father)	None	25	25	None	20	20
M Corporation	....	....	....	80	None	80
O Corporation	None	None	None	....	....	....

Assuming that the M Corporation and the O Corporation make their income tax returns for calendar years, and that there was no distribution in liquidation of the M or O Corporation, and further assuming that other corporation was a personal holding company under section 542 for the calendar year 1956, no deduction is allowable with respect to losses from sales or exchanges of property made on July 1, 1957, between the two corporations. Moreover, whether or not either corporation was a personal holding company, no loss would be allowable on a sale or exchange between A or AW and either corporation. A deduction would be allowed, however, for a loss sustained in an arm's length sale or exchange between A and AWF, and between AWF and the M or O Corporation.

Example (2). On June 15, 1957, all of the stock of the N Corporation was owned in equal proportions by A and his partner, AP. Except in the case of distributions in liquidation by the N Corporation, no deduction is allowable with respect to losses from sales or exchanges of property made on June 15, 1957, between A and the N Corporation or AP and the N Corporation since each partner is considered as owning the stock owned by the other; therefore, each is considered as owning more than 50 percent in value of the outstanding stock of the N Corporation.

Example (3). On June 7, 1957, A owned no stock in X Corporation, but his wife, AW, owned 20 percent in value of the outstanding stock of X, and A's partner, AP, owned 60 percent in value of the outstanding stock of X. The partnership firm of A and AP owned no stock in X Corporation. The ownership of AW's stock is attributed to A, but not that of AP since A does not own any X Corporation stock either actually, or constructively under section 267(c)(1). A's constructive ownership of AW's stock is not the ownership required for the attribution of AP's stock. Therefore, deductions for losses from sales or exchanges of property made on June 7, 1957, between X Corporation and A or AW are allowable since neither person owned more than 50 percent in value of the outstanding stock of X, but deductions for losses from sales or exchanges between X Corporation and AP would not be allowable by section 267(a) (except for distributions in liquidation of X Corporation).

§ 1.267(d)–1 Amount of gain where loss previously disallowed.

(a) General rule. (1) If a taxpayer acquires property by purchase or exchange from a transferor who, on the transaction, sustained a loss not allowable as a deduction by reason of section 267(a)(1) * * *, then any gain realized by the taxpayer on a sale or other disposition of the property after December 31, 1953, shall be recognized only to the extent that the gain exceeds the amount of such loss as is properly allocable to the property sold or otherwise disposed of by the taxpayer.

(2) The general rule is also applicable to a sale or other disposition of property by a taxpayer when the basis of such property in the taxpayer's hands is determined directly or indirectly by reference to other property acquired by the taxpayer from a transferor through a sale or exchange in which a loss sustained by the transferor was not allowable. Therefore, section 267(d) applies to a sale or other disposition of property after a series of transactions if the basis of the property acquired in each transaction is determined by reference to the basis of the property transferred, and if the original property was acquired in a transaction in which a loss to a transferor was not allowable by reason of section 267(a)(1)* * *.

(3) The benefit of the general rule is available only to the original transferee but does not apply to any original transferee (*e.g.*, a donee) who acquired the property in any manner other than by purchase or exchange.

(4) The application of the provisions of this paragraph may be illustrated by the following examples:

Example (1). H sells to his wife, W, for $500, certain corporate stock with an adjusted basis for determining loss to him of $800. The loss of $300 is not allowable to H by reason of section 267(a)(1) and paragraph (a) of §1.267(a)–1. W later sells this stock for $1,000. Although W's realized gain is $500 ($1,000 minus $500, her basis), her recognized gain under section 267(d) is only $200, the excess of the realized gain of $500 over the loss of $300 not allowable to H. In determining capital gain or loss W's holding period commences on the date of the sale from H to W.

Example (2). Assume the same facts as in example (1) except that W later sells her stock for $300 instead of $1,000. Her recognized loss is $200 and not $500 since section 267(d) applies only to the nonrecognition of gain and does not affect basis.

Example (3). Assume the same facts as in example (1) except that W transfers her stock as a gift to X. The basis of the stock in the hands of X for the purpose of determining gain, under the provisions of section 1015, is the same as W's, or $500. If X later sells the stock for $1,000 the entire $500 gain is taxed to him.

Example (4). H sells to his wife, W, for $5,500, farmland, with an adjusted basis for determining loss to him of $8,000. The loss of $2,500 is not allowable to H by reason of section 267(a)(1) and paragraph (a) of §1.267(a)–1. W exchanges the farmland, held for investment purposes, with S, an unrelated individual, for two city lots, also held for investment purposes. The basis of the city lots in the hands of W ($5,500) is a substituted basis determined under section 1031(d) by reference to the basis of the farmland. Later W sells the city lots for $10,000. Although W's realized gain is $4,500 ($10,000 minus $5,500), her recognized gain under section 267(d) is only $2,000, the excess of the realized gain of $4,500 over the loss of $2,500 not allowable to H.

(b) Determination of basis and gain with respect to divisible property—(1) Taxpayer's basis. When the taxpayer acquires divisible property or property that consists of several items or classes of items by a purchase or exchange on which loss is not allowable to the transferor, the basis in the taxpayer's hands of a particular part, item, or class of such property shall be determined (if the taxpayer's basis for that part is not known) by allocating to the particular part, item, or class a portion of the taxpayer's basis for the entire property in the proportion that the fair market value of the particular part, item, or class bears to the fair market value of the entire property at the time of the taxpayer's acquisition of the property.

(2) Taxpayer's recognized gain. Gain realized by the taxpayer on sales or other dispositions after December 31, 1953, of a part, item, or class of the property shall be recognized only to the extent that such gain exceeds the amount of loss attributable to such part, item, or class of property not allowable to the taxpayer's transferor on the latter's sale or exchange of such property to the taxpayer.

(3) Transferor's loss not allowable. (i) The transferor's loss on the sale or exchange of a part, item, or class of the property to the taxpayer shall be the excess of the transferor's adjusted basis for determining loss on the part, item, or class of the property over the amount realized by the transferor on the sale or exchange of the part, item, or class. The amount realized by the transferor on the part, item, or class shall be determined (if such amount is not known) in the same manner that the taxpayer's basis for such part, item, or class is determined. See subparagraph (1) of this paragraph.

(ii) If the transferor's basis for determining loss on the part, item, or class cannot be determined, the transferor's loss on the particular part, item, or class transferred to the taxpayer shall be determined by allocating to the part, item, or class a portion of his loss on the entire property in the proportion that the fair market value of such part, item, or class bears to the fair market value of the entire property on the date of the taxpayer's acquisition of the entire property.

* * *

§ 1.269–1 Meaning and use of terms.

As used in section 269 and §§1.269–2 through 1.269–7—

(a) Allowance. The term "allowance" refers to anything in the internal revenue laws which has the effect of distinguishing tax liability. The term includes, among other things, a deduction, a credit, an adjustment, an exemption, or an exclusion.

(b) Evasion or avoidance. The phrase "evasion or avoidance" is not limited to cases involving criminal penalties, or civil penalties for fraud.

(c) Control. The term "control" means the ownership of stock possessing at least 50 percent of the total combined voting power of all classes of stock entitled to vote, or at least 50 percent of the total value of shares of all classes of stock of the corporation. For control to be "acquired on or after October 8, 1940", it is not necessary that all of such stock be acquired on or after October 8, 1940. Thus, if A, on October 7, 1940, and at all times thereafter, owns 40 percent of the stock of X Corporation and acquires on October 8, 1940, an additional 10 percent of such stock, an acquisition within the meaning of such phrase is made by A on October 8, 1940.* * *

(d) Person. The term "person" includes an individual, a trust, an estate, a partnership, an association, a company or a corporation.

§ 1.269–2 Purpose and scope of section 269.

(a) General. Section 269 is designed to prevent in the instances specified therein the use of the sections of the Internal Revenue Code providing deductions, credits, or allowances in evading or avoiding Federal income tax. See §1.269–3.

(b) Disallowance of deduction, credit, or other allowance. Under the Code, an amount otherwise constituting a deduction, credit, or other allowance becomes unavailable as such under certain circumstances. Characteristic of such circumstances are those in which the effect of the deduction, credit, or other allowance would be to distort the liability of the particular taxpayer when the essential nature of the transaction or situation is examined in the light of the basic purpose or plan which the deduction, credit, or other allowance was designed by the Congress to effectuate. The distortion may be evidenced, for example, by the fact that the transaction was not undertaken for reasons germane to the conduct of the business of the taxpayer, by the unreal nature of the transaction such as its sham character, or by the unreal or unreasonable relation which the deduction, credit, or other allowance bears to the transaction. The principle of law making an amount unavailable as a deduction, credit, or other allowance in cases in which the effect of making an amount so available would be to distort the liability of the taxpayer, has been judicially recognized and applied in several cases. Included in these cases are Gregory v. Helvering (1935) (293 U.S. 465; Ct. D. 911, C.B. XIV–1, 193); Griffiths v. Helvering (1939) (308 U.S. 355; Ct. D. 1431, C.B. 1940–1, 136); Higgins v. Smith (1940) (308 U.S. 473; Ct. D. 1434, C.B. 1940–1, 127); and J. D. & A. B. Spreckles Co. v. Commissioner (1940) (41 B.T.A. 370). In order to give effect to such principle, but not in limitation thereof, several provisions of the Code, for example, section 267 * * *, specify with some particularity instances in which disallowance of the deduction, credit, or other allowance is required. Section 269 is also included in such provisions of the Code. The principle of law and the particular sections of the Code are not mutually exclusive and in appropriate circumstances they may operate together or they may operate separately. See, for example, §1.269–6.

§ 1.269–3 Instances in which section 269(a) disallows a deduction, credit, or other allowance.

(a) Instances of disallowance. Section 269 specifies two instances in which a deduction, credit, or other allowance is to be disallowed. These instances, described in paragraphs (1) and (2) of section 269(a), are those in which—

(1) Any person or persons acquire, or acquired on or after October 8, 1940, directly or indirectly, control of a corporation, or

(2) Any corporation acquires, or acquired on or after October 8, 1940, directly or indirectly, property of another corporation (not controlled, directly or indirectly, immediately before such acquisition by such acquiring corporation or its stockholders), the basis of which property in the hands of the acquiring corporation is determined by reference to the basis in the hands of the transferor corporation.

In either instance the principal purpose for which the acquisition was made must have been the evasion or avoidance of Federal income tax by securing the benefit of a deduction, credit, or other allowance which such person, or persons, or corporation, would not otherwise enjoy. If this requirement is satisfied, it is immaterial by what method or by what conjunction of events the benefit was sought. Thus, an acquiring person or corporation can secure the benefit of a deduction, credit, or other allowance within the meaning of section 269 even though it is the acquired corporation that is entitled to such deduction, credit, or other allowance in the determination of its tax. If the purpose to evade or avoid

Federal income tax exceeds in importance any other purpose, it is the principal purpose. This does not mean that only those acquisitions fall within the provisions of section 269 which would not have been made if the evasion or avoidance purpose was not present. The determination of the purpose for which an acquisition was made requires a scrutiny of the entire circumstances in which the transaction or course of conduct occurred, in connection with the tax result claimed to arise therefrom.

(b) Acquisition of control; transactions indicative of purpose to evade or avoid tax. If the requisite acquisition of control within the meaning of paragraph (1) of section 269(a) exists, the transactions set forth in the following subparagraphs are among those which, in the absence of additional evidence to the contrary, ordinarily are indicative that the principal purpose for acquiring control was evasion or avoidance of Federal income tax:

(1) A corporation or other business enterprise (or the interest controlling such corporation or enterprise) with large profits acquires control of a corporation with current, past, or prospective credits, deductions, net operating losses, or other allowances and the acquisition is followed by such transfers or other action as is necessary to bring the deduction, credit, or other allowance into conjunction with the income (see further §1.269–6). This subparagraph may be illustrated by the following example:

Example. Individual A acquires all of the stock of L Corporation which has been engaged in the business of operating retail drug stores. At the time of the acquisition, L Corporation has net operating loss carryovers aggregating $100,000 and its net worth is $100,000. After the acquisition, L Corporation continues to engage in the business of operating retail drug stores but the profits attributable to such business after the acquisition are not sufficient to absorb any substantial portion of the net operating loss carryovers. Shortly after the acquisition, individual A causes to be transferred to L Corporation the assets of a hardware business previously controlled by A which business produces profits sufficient to absorb a substantial portion of L Corporation's net operating loss carryovers. The transfer of the profitable business, which has the effect of using net operating loss carryovers to offset gains of a business unrelated to that which produced the losses, indicates that the principal purpose for which the acquisition of control was made is evasion or avoidance of Federal income tax.

(2) A person or persons organize two or more corporations instead of a single corporation in order to secure the benefit of * * * or multiple minimum accumulated earnings credits (see section 535(c)(2) and (3)).

(3) A person or persons with high earning assets transfer them to a newly organized controlled corporation retaining assets producing net operating losses which are utilized in an attempt to secure refunds.

(c) Acquisition of property; transactions indicative of purpose to evade or avoid tax. If the requisite acquisition of property within the meaning of paragraph (2) of section 269(a) exists, the transactions set forth in the following subparagraphs are among those which, in the absence of additional evidence to the contrary, ordinarily are indicative that the principal purpose for acquiring such property was evasion or avoidance of Federal income tax:

(1) A corporation acquires property having in its hands an aggregate carryover basis which is materially greater than its aggregate fair market value at the time of such acquisition and utilizes the property to create tax-reducing losses or deductions.

(2) A subsidiary corporation, which has sustained large net operating losses in the operation of business X and which has filed separate returns for the taxable years in which the losses were sustained, acquires high earning assets, comprising business Y, from its parent corporation. The acquisition occurs at a time when the parent would not succeed to the net operating loss carryovers of the subsidiary if the subsidiary were liquidated, and the profits of business Y are sufficient to offset a substantial portion of the net operating loss carryovers attributable to business X (see further example (3) of §1.269–6).

(d) Ownership changes to which section 382(l)(5) applies; transactions indicative of purpose to evade or avoid tax—(1) In general. Absent strong evidence to the contrary, a requisite acquisition of control or property in connection with an ownership change to which section 382(l)(5) applies is considered to be made for the principal purpose of evasion or avoidance of Federal income tax unless the corporation carries on more than an insignificant amount of an active trade or business during and subsequent to the title 11 or similar case (as defined in section 382(l)(5)(G)). The determination of whether the corporation carries on more than an insignificant amount of an active trade or business is made without regard to the continuity of business enterprise set forth in §1.368–1(d). The determination is based on all the facts and circumstances, including, for example, the amount of business assets that continue to be used, or the number of employees in the work force who continue employment, in an active trade or business (although not necessarily the historic trade or business). Where the corporation continues to utilize a significant amount of its business assets or work force, the requirement of carrying on more than an insignificant amount of an active trade or business may be met even though all trade or business activities temporarily cease for a period of time in order to address business exigencies.

* * *

(e) Relationship of section 269 to 11 U.S.C. 1129(d). In determining for purposes of section 269 of the Internal Revenue Code whether an acquisition pursuant to a plan of reorganization in a case under title 11 of the United States Code was made for the principal purpose of evasion or avoidance of Federal income tax, the fact that a governmental unit did not seek a determination under 11 U.S.C. 1129(d) is not taken into account and any determination by a court under 11 U.S.C. 1129(d) that the principal purpose of the plan is not avoidance of taxes is not controlling.

§ 1.269–4 Power of district director to allocate deduction, credit, or allowance in part.

The district director is authorized by section 269(b) to allow a part of the amount disallowed by section 269(a), but he may allow such part only if and to the extent that he determines that the amount allowed will not result in the evasion or avoidance of Federal income tax for which the acquisition was made. The district director is also authorized to use other methods to give effect to part of the amount disallowed under section 269(a), but only to such extent as he determines will not result in the evasion or avoidance of Federal income tax for which the acquisition was made. Whenever appropriate to give proper effect to the deduction, credit, or other allowance, or such part of it which may be allowed, this authority includes the distribution, apportionment, or allocation of both the gross income and the deductions, credits, or other allowances the benefit of which was sought, between or among the corporations, or properties, or parts thereof, involved, and includes the disallowance of any such deduction, credit, or other allowance to any of the taxpayers involved.

§ 1.269–5 Time of acquisition of control.

(a) In general. For purposes of section 269, an acquisition of control occurs when one or more persons acquire beneficial ownership of stock possessing at least 50 percent of the total combined voting power of all classes of stock entitled to vote or at least 50 percent of the total value of shares of all classes of stock of the corporation.

(b) Application of general rule to certain creditor acquisitions. (1) For purposes of section 269, creditors of an insolvent or bankrupt corporation (by themselves or in conjunction with other persons) acquire control of the corporation when they acquire beneficial ownership of the requisite amount of stock. Although insolvency or bankruptcy may cause the interests of creditors to predominate as a practical matter, creditor interests do not constitute beneficial ownership of the corporation's stock. Solely for purposes of section 269, creditors of a bankrupt corporation are treated as acquiring beneficial ownership of stock of the corporation no earlier than the time a bankruptcy court confirms a plan of reorganization.

(2) The provisions of this section are illustrated by the following example.

Example. Corporation L files a petition under chapter 11 of the Bankruptcy Code on January 5, 1987. A creditors' committee is formed. On February 22, 1987, and upon the request of the creditors, the bankruptcy court removes the debtor-in-possession from business management and operations and appoints a trustee. The trustee consults regularly with the creditors' committee in formulating both short-term and long-term management decisions. After three years, the creditors approve a plan of reorganization in which the outstanding stock of Corporation L is canceled and its creditors receive shares of stock constituting all of the outstanding shares. The bankruptcy court confirms the plan of reorganization on March 23, 1990, and the plan is put into effect on May 25, 1990. For purposes of section 269, the creditors acquired control of Corporation L no earlier than March 23, 1990. Similarly, the determination of whether the creditors acquired control of Corporation L with the principal purpose of evasion or avoidance of Federal income tax is made by reference to the creditors' purposes as of no earlier than March 23, 1990.

* * *

§ 1.269–7 Relationship of section 269 to sections 382 and 383 after the Tax Reform Act of 1986.

Section 269 and §§1.269–1 through 1.269–5 may be applied to disallow a deduction, credit, or other allowance notwithstanding that the utilization or amount of a deduction, credit, or other allowance is limited or reduced under section 382 or 383 and the regulations thereunder. However, the fact that the amount of taxable income or tax that may be offset by a deduction, credit, or other allowance is limited under section 382(a) or 383 and the regulations thereunder is relevant to the determination of whether the principal purpose of an acquisition is the evasion or avoidance of Federal income tax.

* * *

§ 1.274–1 Disallowance of certain entertainment, gift and travel expenses.

Section 274 disallows in whole, or in part, certain expenditures for entertainment, gifts and travel which would otherwise be allowable under chapter 1 of the Code. The requirements imposed by section 274 are in addition to the requirements for deductibility imposed by other provisions of the Code. If a deduction is claimed for an expenditure for entertainment, gifts, or travel, the taxpayer must first establish that it is otherwise allowable as a deduction under chapter 1 of the Code before the provisions of section 274 become applicable. An expenditure for entertainment, to the extent it is lavish or extravagant, shall not be allowable as a deduction. The taxpayer should then substantiate such an expenditure in accordance with the rules under section 274(d). See §1.274–5. Section 274 is a disallowance provision exclusively, and does not make deductible any expense which is disallowed under any other provision of the Code. Similarly, section 274 does not affect the includibility of an item in, or the excludability of an item from, the gross income of any taxpayer. For specific provisions with respect to the deductibility of expenditures: for an activity of a type generally considered to constitute entertainment, amusement, or recreation, and for a facility used in connection with such an activity, as well as certain travel expenses of a spouse, etc., see §1.274–2; for expenses for gifts, see §1.274–3; for expenses for foreign travel, see § 1.274–4; for expenditures deductible without regard to business activity, see §1.274–6; and for treatment of personal portion of entertainment facility, see §1.274–7.

§ 1.274–2 Disallowance of deductions for certain expenses for entertainment, amusement, recreation, or travel.

(a) General rules—(1) Entertainment activity. Except as provided in this section, no deduction otherwise allowable under chapter 1 of the Code shall be allowed for any expenditure with respect to entertainment unless the taxpayer establishes—

(i) That the expenditure was directly related to the active conduct of the taxpayer's trade or business, or

(ii) In the case of an expenditure directly preceding or following a substantial and bona fide business discussion (including business meetings at a convention or otherwise), that the expenditure was associated with the active conduct of the taxpayer's trade or business.

Such deduction shall not exceed the portion of the expenditure directly related to (or in the case of an expenditure described in subdivision (ii) of this subparagraph, the portion of the expenditure associated with) the active conduct of the taxpayer's trade or business.

(2) Entertainment facilities—(i) Expenditures paid or incurred after December 31, 1978, and not with respect to a club. Except as provided in this section with respect to a club, no deduction otherwise allowable under chapter 1 of the Code shall be allowed for any expenditure paid or incurred after December 31, 1978, with respect to a facility used in connection with entertainment.

(ii) Expenditures paid or incurred before January 1, 1979, with respect to entertainment facilities, or paid or incurred before January 1, 1994, with respect to clubs—(a) Requirements for deduction. Except as provided in this section, no deduction otherwise allowable under chapter 1 of the Code shall be allowed for any expenditure paid or incurred before January 1, 1979, with respect to a facility used in connection with entertainment, or for any expenditure paid or incurred before January 1, 1994, with respect to a club used in connection with entertainment, unless the taxpayer establishes—

(1) That the facility or club was used primarily for the furtherance of the taxpayer's trade or business, and

(2) That the expenditure was directly related to the active conduct of that trade or business.

(b) Amount of deduction. The deduction allowable under paragraph (a)(2)(ii)(a) of this section shall not exceed the portion of the expenditure directly related to the active conduct of the taxpayer's trade or business.

(iii) Expenditures paid or incurred after December 31, 1993, with respect to a club—(a) In general. No deduction otherwise allowable under chapter 1 of the Internal Revenue Code shall be allowed for amounts paid or incurred after December 31, 1993, for membership in any club organized for business, pleasure, recreation, or other social purpose. The purposes and activities of a club, and not its name, determine whether it is organized for business, pleasure, recreation, or other social purpose. Clubs organized for business, pleasure, recreation, or other social purpose include any membership organization if a principal purpose of the organization is to conduct entertainment activities for members of the organization or their guests or to provide members or their guests with access to entertainment facilities within the meaning of paragraph (e)(2) of this section. Clubs organized for business, pleasure, recreation, or other social purpose include, but are not limited to, country clubs, golf and athletic clubs, airline clubs, hotel clubs, and clubs operated to provide meals under circumstances generally considered to be conducive to business discussion.

(b) Exceptions. Unless a principal purpose of the organization is to conduct entertainment activities for members or their guests or to provide members or their guests with access to entertainment facilities, business leagues, trade associations, chambers of commerce, boards of trade, real estate boards, professional organizations (such as bar associations and medical associations), and civic or public service organizations will not be treated as clubs organized for business, pleasure, recreation, or other social purpose.

(3) Cross references. For definition of the term "entertainment", see paragraph (b)(1) of this section. For the disallowance of deductions for the cost of admission to a dinner or program any part of the proceeds of which inures to the use of a political party or political candidate, and cost of admission to an inaugural event or similar event identified with any political party or political candidate, see §1.276–1. For rules and definitions with respect to—

(i) "Directly related entertainment", see paragraph (c) of this section,

(ii) "Associated entertainment", see paragraph (d) of this section,

(iii) "Expenditures paid or incurred before January 1, 1979, with respect to entertainment facilities or before January 1, 1994, with respect to clubs", see paragraph (e) of this section, and

(iv) "Specific exceptions" to the disallowance rules of this section, see paragraph (f) of this section.

(b) Definitions—(1) Entertainment defined—(i) In general. For purposes of this section, the term "entertainment" means any activity which is of a type generally considered to constitute entertainment, amusement, or recreation, such as entertaining at night clubs, cocktail lounges, theaters, country clubs, golf and athletic clubs, sporting events, and on hunting, fishing, vacation and similar trips, including such activity relating solely to the taxpayer or the taxpayer's family. The term "entertainment" may include an activity, the cost of which is claimed as a business expense by the taxpayer, which satisfies the personal, living, or family needs of any individual, such as providing food and beverages, a hotel suite, or an automobile to a business customer or his family. The term "entertainment" does not include activities which, although satisfying personal, living, or family needs of an individual, are clearly not regarded as constituting entertainment, such as (a) supper money provided by an employer to his employee working overtime, (b) a hotel room maintained by an employer for lodging of his employees while in business travel status, or (c) an automobile used in the active conduct of trade or business even though used for routine personal purposes such as commuting to and from work. On the other hand, the providing of a hotel room or an automobile by an employer to his employee who is on vacation would constitute entertainment of the employee.

(ii) Objective test. An objective test shall be used to determine whether an activity is of a type generally considered to constitute entertainment. Thus, if an activity is generally considered to be entertainment, it will constitute entertainment for purposes of this section and section 274(a) regardless of whether the expenditure can also be described otherwise, and even though the expenditure relates to the taxpayer alone. This objective test precludes arguments such as that "entertainment" means only entertainment of others or that an expenditure for entertainment should be characterized as an expenditure for advertising or public relations. However, in applying this test the taxpayer's trade or business shall be considered. Thus, although attending a theatrical performance would generally be considered entertainment, it would not be so considered in the case of a professional theater critic, attending in his professional capacity. Similarly, if a manufacturer of dresses conducts a fashion show to introduce his products to a group of store buyers, the show would not be generally considered to constitute entertainment. However, if an appliance distributor conducts a fashion show for the wives of his retailers, the fashion show would be generally considered to constitute entertainment.

(iii) Special definitional rules—(a) In general. Except as otherwise provided in (b) or (c) of this subdivision, any expenditure which might generally be considered either for a gift or entertainment, or considered either for travel or entertainment, shall be considered an expenditure for entertainment rather than for a gift or travel.

(b) Expenditures deemed gifts. An expenditure described in (a) of this subdivision shall be deemed for a gift to which this section does not apply if it is:

(1) An expenditure for packaged food or beverages transferred directly or indirectly to another person intended for consumption at a later time.

(2) An expenditure for tickets of admission to a place of entertainment transferred to another person if the taxpayer does not accompany the recipient to the entertainment unless the taxpayer treats the expenditure as entertainment. The taxpayer may change his treatment of such an expenditure as either a gift or entertainment at any time within the period prescribed for assessment of tax as provided in section 6501 of the Code and the regulations thereunder.

(3) Such other specific classes of expenditure generally considered to be for a gift as the Commissioner, in his discretion, may prescribe.

(c) Expenditures deemed travel. An expenditure described in (a) of this subdivision shall be deemed for travel to which this section does not apply if it is:

(1) With respect to a transportation type facility (such as an automobile or an airplane), even though used on other occasions in connection with an activity of a type generally considered to constitute entertainment, to the extent the facility is used in pursuit of a trade or business for purposes of transportation not in connection with entertainment. See also paragraph (e)(3)(iii)(b) of this section for provisions covering nonentertainment expenditures with respect to such facilities.

(2) Such other specific classes of expenditure generally considered to be for travel as the Commissioner, in his discretion, may prescribe.

(2) Other definitions—(i) Expenditure. The term "expenditure" as used in this section shall include expenses paid or incurred for goods, services, facilities, and items (including items such as losses and depreciation).

(ii) Expenses for production of income. For purposes of this section, any reference to "trade or business" shall include any activity described in section 212.

(iii) Business associate. The term "business associate" as used in this section means a person with whom the taxpayer could reasonably expect to engage or deal in the active conduct of the taxpayer's trade or business such as the taxpayer's customer, client, supplier, employee, agent, partner, or professional adviser, whether established or prospective.

(c) Directly related entertainment—(1) In general. Except as otherwise provided in paragraph (d) of this section (relating to associated entertainment) or under paragraph (f) of this section (relating to business meals and other specific exceptions), no deduction shall be allowed for any expenditure for entertainment unless the taxpayer establishes that the expenditure was directly related to the active conduct of his trade or business within the meaning of this paragraph.

(2) Directly related entertainment defined. Any expenditure for entertainment, if it is otherwise allowable as a deduction under chapter 1 of the Code, shall be considered directly related to the active conduct of the taxpayer's trade or business if it meets the requirements of any one of subparagraphs (3), (4), (5), or (6) of this paragraph.

(3) Directly related in general. Except as provided in subparagraph (7) of this paragraph, an expenditure for entertainment shall be considered directly related to the active conduct of the taxpayer's trade or business if it is established that it meets all of the requirements of subdivisions (i), (ii), (iii) and (iv) of this subparagraph.

(i) At the time the taxpayer made the entertainment expenditure (or committed himself to make the expenditure), the taxpayer had more than a general expectation of deriving some income or other specific trade or business benefit (other than the goodwill of the person or persons entertained) at some indefinite future time from the making of the expenditure. A taxpayer, however, shall not be required to show that income or other business benefit actually resulted from each and every expenditure for which a deduction is claimed.

(ii) During the entertainment period to which the expenditure related, the taxpayer actively engaged in a business meeting, negotiation, discussion, or other bona fide business transaction, other than entertainment, for the purpose of obtaining such income or other specific trade or business benefit (or, at the time the taxpayer made the expenditure or committed himself to the expenditure, it was reasonable for the taxpayer to expect that he would have done so, although such was not the case solely for reasons beyond the taxpayer's control).

(iii) In light of all the facts and circumstances of the case, the principal character or aspect of the combined business and entertainment to which the expenditure related was the active conduct of the taxpayer's trade or business (or at the time the taxpayer made the expenditure or committed himself to the expenditure, it was reasonable for the taxpayer to expect that the active conduct of trade or business would have been the principal character or aspect of the entertainment, although such was not the case solely for reasons beyond the taxpayer's control). It is not necessary that more time be devoted to business than to entertainment to meet this requirement. The active conduct of trade or business is considered not to be the principal character or aspect of combined business and entertainment activity on hunting or fishing trips or on yachts and other pleasure boats unless the taxpayer clearly establishes to the contrary.

(iv) The expenditure was allocable to the taxpayer and a person or persons with whom the taxpayer engaged in the active conduct of trade or business during the entertainment or with whom the taxpayer establishes he would have engaged in such active conduct of trade or business if it were not for circumstances beyond the taxpayer's control. For expenditures closely connected with directly related entertainment, see paragraph (d)(4) of this section.

(4) Expenditures in clear business setting. An expenditure for entertainment shall be considered directly related to the active conduct of the taxpayer's trade or business if it is established that the expenditure was for entertainment occurring in a clear business setting directly in furtherance of the taxpayer's trade or business. Generally, entertainment shall not be considered to have occurred in a clear business setting unless the taxpayer clearly establishes that any recipient of the entertainment would have reasonably known that the taxpayer had no significant motive, in incurring the expenditure, other than directly furthering his trade or business. Objective rather than subjective standards will be determinative. Thus, entertainment which occurred under any circumstances described in subparagraph (7)(ii) of this paragraph ordinarily will not be considered as occurring in a clear business setting. Such entertainment will generally be considered to be socially rather than commercially motivated. Expenditures made for the furtherance of a taxpayer's trade or business in providing a "hospitality room" at a convention (described in paragraph (d)(3)(i)(b) of this section) at which goodwill is created through display or discussion of the taxpayer's products, will, however, be treated as directly related. In addition, entertainment of a clear business nature which occurred under circumstances where there was no meaningful personal or social relationship between the taxpayer and the recipients of the entertainment may be considered to have occurred in a clear business setting. For example, entertainment of business representatives and civic leaders at the opening of a new hotel or theatrical production, where the clear purpose of the taxpayer is to obtain business publicity rather than to create or maintain the goodwill of the recipients of the entertainment, would generally be considered to be in a clear business setting. Also, entertainment which has the principal effect of a price rebate in connection with the sale of the taxpayer's products generally will be considered to have occurred in a clear business setting. Such would be the case, for example, if a taxpayer owning a hotel were to provide occasional free dinners at the hotel for a customer who patronized the hotel.

(5) Expenditures for services performed. An expenditure shall be considered directly related to the active conduct of the taxpayer's trade or business if it is established that the expenditure was made directly or indirectly by the taxpayer for the benefit of an individual (other than an employee), and if such expenditure was in the nature of compensation for services rendered or was paid as a prize or award which is required to be included in gross income under section 74 and the regulations thereunder. For example, if a manufacturer of products provides a vacation trip for retailers of his products who exceed sales quotas as a prize or award which is includible in gross income, the expenditure will be considered directly related to the active conduct of the taxpayer's trade or business.

(6) Club dues, etc., allocable to business meals. An expenditure shall be considered directly related to the active conduct of the taxpayer's trade or business if it is established that the expenditure was with respect to a facility (as described in paragraph (e) of this section) used by the taxpayer for the furnishing of food or beverages under circumstances described in paragraph (f)(2)(i) of this section (relating to business meals and similar expenditures), to the extent allocable to the furnishing of such food or beverages. This paragraph (c)(6) applies to club dues paid or incurred before January 1, 1987.

(7) Expenditures generally considered not directly related. Expenditures for entertainment, even if connected with the taxpayer's trade or business, will generally be considered not directly related to the active conduct of the taxpayer's trade or business, if the entertainment occurred under circumstances where there was little or no possibility of engaging in the active conduct of trade or business. The following circumstances will generally be considered circumstances where there was little or no possibility of engaging in the active conduct of a trade or business:

(i) The taxpayer was not present;

(ii) The distractions were substantial, such as—

(a) A meeting or discussion at night clubs, theaters, and sporting events, or during essentially social gatherings such as cocktail parties, or

(b) A meeting or discussion, if the taxpayer meets with a group which includes persons other than business associates, at places such as cocktail lounges, country clubs, golf and athletic clubs, or at vacation resorts.

An expenditure for entertainment in any such case is considered not to be directly related to the active conduct of the taxpayer's trade or business unless the taxpayer clearly establishes to the contrary.

(d) Associated entertainment—(1) In general. Except as provided in paragraph (f) of this section (relating to business meals and other specific exceptions) and subparagraph (4) of this paragraph (relating to expenditures closely connected with directly related entertainment), any expenditure for entertainment which is not directly related to the active conduct of the taxpayer's trade or business will not be allowable as a deduction unless—

(i) It was associated with the active conduct of trade or business as defined in subparagraph (2) of this paragraph, and

(ii) The entertainment directly preceded or followed a substantial and bona fide business discussion as defined in subparagraph (3) of this paragraph.

(2) Associated entertainment defined. Generally, any expenditure for entertainment, if it is otherwise allowable under chapter 1 of the Code, shall be considered associated with the active conduct of the taxpayer's trade or business if the taxpayer establishes that he had a clear business purpose in making the expenditure, such as to obtain new business or to encourage the continuation of an existing business relationship. However, any portion of an expenditure allocable to a person who was not closely connected with a person who engaged in the substantial and bona fide business discussion (as defined in subparagraph (3)(i) of this paragraph) shall not be considered associated with the active conduct of the taxpayer's trade or business. The portion of an expenditure allocable to the spouse of a person who engaged in the discussion will, if it is otherwise allowable under chapter 1 of the Code, be considered associated with the active conduct of the taxpayer's trade or business.

(3) Directly preceding or following a substantial and bona fide business discussion defined—(i) Substantial and bona fide business discussion—(a) In general. Whether any meeting, negotiation or discussion constitutes a "substantial and bona fide business discussion" within the meaning of this section depends upon the facts and circumstances of each case. It must be established, however, that the taxpayer actively engaged in a business meeting, negotiation, discussion, or other bona fide business transaction, other than entertainment, for the purpose of obtaining income or other specific trade or business benefit. In addition, it must be established that such a business meeting, negotiation, discussion, or transaction was substantial in relation to the entertainment. This requirement will be satisfied if the principal character or aspect of the combined entertainment and business activity was the active conduct of business. However, it is not necessary that more time be devoted to business than to entertainment to meet this requirement.

(b) Meetings at conventions, etc. Any meeting officially scheduled in connection with a program at a convention or similar general assembly, or at a bona fide trade or business meeting sponsored and conducted by business or professional organizations, shall be considered to constitute a substantial and bona fide business discussion within the meaning of this section provided—

(1) Expenses necessary to taxpayer's attendance. The expenses necessary to the attendance of the taxpayer at the convention, general assembly, or trade or business meeting, were ordinary and necessary within the meaning of section 162 or 212;

(2) Convention program. The organization which sponsored the convention, or trade or business meeting had scheduled a program of business activities (including committee meetings or presentation of lectures, panel discussions, display of products, or other similar activities), and that such program was the principal activity of the convention, general assembly, or trade or business meeting.

(ii) Directly preceding or following. Entertainment which occurs on the same day as a substantial and bona fide business discussion (as defined in subdivision (i) of this subparagraph) will be considered to directly precede or follow such discussion. If the entertainment and the business discussion do not occur on the same day, the facts and circumstances of each case are to be considered, including the place, date and duration of the business discussion, whether the taxpayer or his business associates are from out of town, and, if so, the date of arrival and departure, and the reasons the entertainment did not take place on the day of the business discussion. For example, if a group of business associates comes from out of town to the taxpayer's place of business to hold a substantial business discussion, the entertainment of such business guests and their wives on the evening prior to, or on the evening of the day following, the business discussion would generally be regarded as directly preceding or following such discussion.

(4) Expenses closely connected with directly related entertainment. If any portion of an expenditure meets the requirements of paragraph (c)(3) of this section (relating to directly related entertainment in general), the remaining portion of the expenditure, if it is otherwise allowable under chapter 1 of the Code, shall be considered associated with the active conduct of the taxpayer's trade or business to the extent allocable to a person or persons closely connected with a person referred to in paragraph (c)(3)(iv) of this section. The spouse of a person referred to in paragraph (c)(3)(iv) of this section will be considered closely connected to such a person for purposes of this subparagraph. Thus, if a taxpayer and his wife entertain a business customer and the customer's wife under circumstances where the entertainment of the customer is considered directly related to the active conduct of the taxpayer's trade or business (within the meaning of paragraph (c)(3) of this section) the portion of the expenditure allocable to both wives will be considered associated with the active conduct of the taxpayer's trade or business under this subparagraph.

(e) Expenditures paid or incurred before January 1, 1979, with respect to entertainment facilities or before January 1, 1994, with respect to clubs—(1) In general. Any expenditure paid or in curred before January 1, 1979, with respect to a facility, or paid or incurred before January 1, 1994, with respect to a club, used in connection with entertainment shall not be allowed as a deduction except to the extent it meets the requirements of paragraph (a)(2)(ii) of this section.

(2) Facilities used in connection with entertainment—(i) In general. Any item of personal or real property owned, rented, or used by a taxpayer shall (unless otherwise provided under the rules of subdivision (ii) of this subparagraph) be considered to constitute a facility used in connection with entertainment if it is used during the taxable year for, or in connection with, entertainment (as defined in paragraph (b)(1) of this section). Examples of facilities which might be used for, or in connection with, entertainment include yachts, hunting lodges, fishing camps, swimming pools, tennis courts, bowling alleys, automobiles, airplanes, apartments, hotel suites, and homes in vacation resorts.

(ii) Facilities used incidentally for entertainment. A facility used only incidentally during a taxable year in connection with entertainment, if such use is insubstantial, will not be considered a "facility used in connection with entertainment" for purposes of this section or for purposes of the record–keeping requirements of section 274(d). See §1.274–5(c)(6)(iii).

(3) Expenditures with respect to a facility used in connection with entertainment—(i) In general. The phrase "expenditures with respect to a facility used in connection with entertainment" includes depreciation and operating costs, such as rent and utility charges (for example, water or electricity), expenses for the maintenance, preservation or protection of a facility (for example, repairs, painting, insurance charges), and salaries or expenses for subsistence paid to caretakers or watchmen. In addition, the phrase includes losses realized on the sale or other disposition of a facility.

(ii) Club dues—(a) Club dues paid or incurred before January 1, 1994. Dues or fees paid before January 1, 1994, to any social, athletic, or sporting club or organization are considered expenditures with respect to a facility used in connection with entertainment. The purposes and activities of a club or organization, and not its name, determine its character. Generally, the phrase "social, athletic, or sporting club or organization" has the same meaning for purposes of this section as that phrase had in section 4241 and the regulations thereunder, relating to the excise tax on club dues, prior to the repeal of section 4241 by section 301 of Public Law 89–44. However, for purposes of this section only, clubs operated solely to provide lunches under circumstances of a type generally considered to be conducive to business discussion, within the meaning of paragraph (f)(2)(i) of this section, will not be considered social clubs.

(b) Club dues paid or incurred after December 31, 1993. See paragraph (a)(2)(iii) of this section with reference to the disallowance of deductions for club dues paid or incurred after December 31, 1993.

(iii) Expenditures not with respect to a facility. The following expenditures shall not be considered to constitute expenditures with respect to a facility used in connection with entertainment—

(a) Out of pocket expenditures. Expenses (exclusive of operating costs and other expenses referred to in subdivision (i) of this subparagraph) incurred at the time of an entertainment activity, even though in connection with the use of facility for entertainment purposes, such as expenses for food and beverages, or expenses for catering, or expenses for gasoline and fishing bait consumed on a fishing trip;

(b) Non–entertainment expenditures. Expenses or items attributable to the use of a facility for other than entertainment purposes such as expenses for an automobile when not used for entertainment; and

(c) Expenditures otherwise deductible. Expenses allowable as a deduction without regard to their connection with a taxpayer's trade or business such as taxes, interest, and casualty losses. The provisions of this subdivision shall be applied in the case of a taxpayer which is not an individual as if it were an individual. See also §1.274–6.

(iv) Cross reference. For other rules with respect to treatment of certain expenditures for entertainment-type facilities, see §1.274–7.

(4) Determination of primary use—(i) In general. A facility used in connection with entertainment shall be considered as used primarily for the furtherance of the taxpayer's trade or business only if it is established that the primary use of the facility during the taxable year was for purposes considered ordinary and necessary within the meaning of sections 162 and 212 and the regulations thereunder. All of the facts and circumstances of each case shall be considered in determining the primary use of a facility. Generally, it is the actual use of the facility which establishes the deductibility of expenditures with respect to the facility; not its availability for use and not the taxpayer's principal purpose in acquiring the facility. Objective rather than subjective standards will be determinative. If membership entitles the member's entire family to use of a facility, such as a country club, their use will be considered in determining whether business use of the facility exceeds personal use. The factors to be considered include the nature of each use, the frequency and duration of use for business purposes as compared with other purposes, and the amount of expenditures incurred during use for business compared with amount of expenditures incurred during use for other purposes. No single standard of comparison, or quantitative measurement, as to the significance of any such factor, however, is necessarily appropriate for all classes or types of facilities. For example, an appropriate standard for determining the primary use of a country club during a taxable year will not necessarily be appropriate for determining the primary use of an airplane. However, a taxpayer shall be deemed to have established that a facility was used primarily for the furtherance of his trade or business if he establishes such primary use in accordance with subdivision (ii) or (iii) of this subparagraph. Subdivisions (ii) and (iii) of this subparagraph shall not preclude a taxpayer from otherwise establishing the primary use of a facility under the general provisions of this subdivision.

(ii) Certain transportation facilities. A taxpayer shall be deemed to have established that a facility of a type described in this subdivision was used primarily for the furtherance of his trade or business if—

(a) Automobiles. In the case of an automobile, the taxpayer establishes that more than 50 percent of mileage driven during the taxable year was in connection with travel considered to be ordinary and necessary within the meaning of section 162 or 212 and the regulations thereunder.

(b) Airplanes. In the case of an airplane, the taxpayer establishes that more than 50 percent of hours flown during the taxable year was in connection with travel considered to be ordinary and necessary within the meaning of section 162 or 212 and the regulations thereunder.

(iii) Entertainment facilities in general. A taxpayer shall be deemed to have established that—

(a) A facility used in connection with entertainment, such as a yacht or other pleasure boat, hunting lodge, fishing camp, summer home or vacation cottage, hotel suite, country club, golf club or similar social, athletic, or sporting club or organization, bowling alley, tennis court, or swimming pool, or,

(b) A facility for employees not falling within the scope of section 274(e)(2) or (5)

was used primarily for the furtherance of his trade or business if he establishes that more than 50 percent of the total calendar days of use of the facility by, or under authority of, the taxpayer during the taxable year were days of business use. Any use of a facility (of a type described in this subdivision) during one calendar day shall be considered to constitute a "day of business use" if the primary use of the facility on such day was ordinary and necessary within the meaning of section 162 or 212 and the regulations thereunder. For the purposes of this subdivision, a facility shall be deemed to have been primarily used for such purposes on any one calendar day if the facility was used for the conduct of a substantial and bona fide business discussion (as defined in paragraph (d)(3)(i) of this section) notwithstanding that the facility may also have been used on the same day for personal or family use by the taxpayer or any member of the taxpayer's family not involving entertainment of others by, or under the authority of, the taxpayer.

* * *

(g) Additional provisions of section 274—travel of spouse, dependent or others. Section 274(m)(3) provides that no deduction shall be allowed under this chapter (except section 217) for travel expenses paid or incurred with respect to a spouse, dependent, or other individual accompanying the taxpayer (or an officer or employee of the taxpayer) on business travel, unless certain conditions are met. As provided in section 274(m)(3), the term *other individual* does not include a business associate (as defined in paragraph (b)(2)(iii) of this section) who otherwise meets the requirements of sections 274(m)(3)(B) and (C).

* * *

§ 1.274–3 Disallowance of deduction for gifts.

(a) In general. No deduction shall be allowed under section 162 or 212 for any expense for a gift made directly or indirectly by a taxpayer to any individual to the extent that such expense, when added to prior expenses of the taxpayer for gifts made to such individual during the taxpayer's taxable year, exceeds $25.

(b) Gift defined—(1) In general. Except as provided in subparagraph (2) of this paragraph the term "gift", for purposes of this section, means any item excludable from the gross income of the recipient under section 102 which is not excludable from his gross income under any other provision of chapter 1 of the Code. Thus, a payment by an employer to a deceased employee's widow is not a gift, for purposes of this section, to the extent the payment constitutes an employee's death benefit excludable by the recipient under section 101(b). Similarly, a scholarship which is excludable from a recipient's gross income under section 117, and a prize or award which is excludable from a recipient's gross income under section 74(b), are not subject to the provisions of this section.

(2) Items not treated as gifts. The term "gift", for purposes of this section, does not include the following:

(i) An item having a cost to the taxpayer not in excess of $4.00 on which the name of the taxpayer is clearly and permanently imprinted and which is one of a number of identical items distributed generally by such a taxpayer.

(ii) A sign, display rack, or other promotional material to be used on the business premises of the recipient, or

(iii) In the case of a taxable year of a taxpayer ending on or after August 13, 1981, an item of tangible personal property which is awarded before January 1, 1987, to an employee of the taxpayer by reason of the employee's length of service (including an award upon retirement), productivity, or safety achievement, but only to the extent that—

(A) The cost of the item to the taxpayer does not exceed $400; or

(B) The item is a qualified plan award (as defined in paragraph (d) of this section); or

(iv) In the case of a taxable year of a taxpayer ending before August 13, 1981, an item of tangible personal property having a cost to the taxpayer not in excess of $100 which is awarded to an employee of the taxpayer by reason of the employee's length of service (including an award upon retirement) or safety achievement.

For purposes of paragraphs (b)(2)(iii) and (iv) of this section, the term "tangible personal property" does not include cash or any gift certificate other than a nonnegotiable gift certificate conferring only the right to receive tangible personal property. Thus, for example, if a nonnegotiable gift certificate entitles an employee to choose between selecting an item of merchandise or receiving cash or reducing the balance due on his account with the issuer of the gift certificate, the gift certificate is not tangible personal property for purposes of this section. To the extent that an item is not treated as a gift for purposes of this section, the deductibility of the expense of the item is not governed by this section, and the taxpayer need not take such item into account in determining whether the $25 limitation on gifts to any individual has been exceeded. For example, if an employee receives by reason of his length of service a gift of an item of tangible personal property that costs the employer $450, the deductibility of only $50 ($450 minus $400) is governed by this section, and the employer takes the $50 into account for purposes of the $25 limitation on gifts to that employee. The fact that an item is wholly or partially excepted from the applicability of this section has no effect in determining whether the value of the item is includible in the gross income of the recipient. For rules relating to the taxability to the recipient of any item described in this subparagraph, see sections 61, 74, and 102 and the regulations thereunder. For rules relating to the deductibility of employee achievement awards awarded after December 31, 1986, see section 274(j).

(c) Expense for a gift. For purposes of this section, the term "expense for a gift" means the cost of the gift to the taxpayer, other than incidental costs such as for customary engraving on jewelry, or for packaging, insurance, and mailing or other delivery. A related cost will be considered "incidental" only if it does not add substantial value to the gift. Although the cost of customary gift wrapping will be considered an incidental cost, the purchase of an ornamental basket for packaging fruit will not be considered an incidental cost of packaging if the basket has a value which is substantial in relation to the value of the fruit.

* * *

§ 1.274–5T Substantiation requirements (temporary).

(a) In general. For taxable years beginning on or after January 1, 1986, no deduction or credit shall be allowed with respect to—

(1) Traveling away from home (including meals and lodging),

(2) Any activity which is of a type generally considered to constitute entertainment, amusement, or recreation, or with respect to a facility used in connection with such an activity, including the items specified in section 274(e),

(3) Gifts defined in section 274(b), or

(4) Any listed property (as defined in section 280F(d)(4) and §1.280F–6T(b)), unless the taxpayer substantiates each element of the expenditure or use (as described in paragraph (b) of this section) in the manner provided in paragraph (c) of this section. This limitation supersedes the doctrine founded in Cohan v. Commissioner, 39 F.2d 540 (2d Cir.1930). The decision held that, where the evidence indicated a taxpayer incurred deductible travel or entertainment expenses but the exact amount could not be determined, the court should make a close approximation and not disallow the deduction entirely. Section 274(d) contemplates that no deduction or credit shall be allowed a taxpayer on the basis of such approximations or unsupported testimony of the taxpayer. For purposes of this section, the term "entertainment" means entertainment, amusement, or recreation, and use of a facility therefor; and the term "expenditure" includes expenses and items (including items such as losses and depreciation).

(b) Elements of an expenditure or use—(1) In general. Section 274(d) and this section contemplate that no deduction or credit shall be allowed for travel, entertainment, a gift, or with respect to listed property unless the taxpayer substantiates the requisite elements of each expenditure or use as set forth in this paragraph (b).

(2) Travel away from home. The elements to be proved with respect to an expenditure for travel away from home are—

(i) Amount. Amount of each separate expenditure for traveling away from home, such as cost of transportation or lodging, except that the daily cost of the traveler's own breakfast, lunch, and dinner and of expenditures incidental to such travel may be aggregated, if set forth in reasonable categories, such as for meals, for gasoline and oil, and for taxi fares;

(ii) Time. Dates of departure and return for each trip away from home, and number of days away from home spent on business;

(iii) Place. Destinations or locality of travel, described by name of city or town or other similar designation; and

(iv) Business purpose. Business reason for travel or nature of the business benefit derived or expected to be derived as a result of travel.

(3) Entertainment in general. The elements to be proved with respect to an expenditure for entertainment are—

(i) Amount. Amount of each separate expenditure for entertainment, except that such incidental items as taxi fares or telephone calls may be aggregated on a daily basis;

(ii) Time. Date of entertainment;

(iii) Place. Name, if any, address or location, and designation of type of entertainment, such as dinner or theater, if such information is not apparent from the designation of the place;

(iv) Business purpose. Business reason for the entertainment or nature of business benefit derived or expected to be derived as a result of the entertainment and, except in the case of business meals described in section 274(e)(1), the nature of any business discussion or activity;

(v) Business relationship. Occupation or other information relating to the person or persons entertained, including name, title, or other designation, sufficient to establish business relationship to the taxpayer.

(4) Entertainment directly preceding or following a substantial and bona fide business discussion. If a taxpayer claims a deduction for entertainment directly preceding or following a substantial and bona fide business discussion on the ground that such entertainment was associated with the active conduct of the taxpayer's trade or business, the elements to be proved with respect to such expenditure, in addition to those enumerated in paragraph (b)(3)(i), (ii), (iii), and (v) of this section are—

(i) Time. Date and duration of business discussion;

(ii) Place. Place of business discussion;

(iii) Business purpose. Nature of business discussion, and business reason for the entertainment or nature of business benefit derived or expected to be derived as the result of the entertainment;

(iv) Business relationship. Identification of those persons entertained who participated in the business discussion.

(5) Gifts. The elements to be proved with respect to an expenditure for a gift are—

(i) Amount. Cost of the gift to the taxpayer;

(ii) Time. Date of the gift;

(iii) Description. Description of the gift;

(iv) Business purpose. Business reason for the gift or nature of business benefit derived or expected to be derived as a result of the gift; and

(v) Business relationship. Occupation or other information relating to the recipient of the gift, including name, title, or other designation, sufficient to establish business relationship to the taxpayer.

(6) Listed property. The elements to be proved with respect to any listed property are—

(i) Amount—(A) Expenditures. The amount of each separate expenditure with respect to an item of listed property, such as the cost of acquisition, the cost of capital improvements, lease payments, the cost of maintenance and repairs, or other expenditures, and

(B) Uses. The amount of each business/investment use (as defined in §1.280F–6T(d)(3) and (e)), based on the appropriate measure (i.e., mileage for automobiles and other means of transportation and time for other listed property, unless the Commissioner approves an alternative method), and the total use of the listed property for the taxable period.

(ii) Time. Date of the expenditure or use with respect to listed property, and

(iii) Business or investment purpose. The business purpose for an expenditure or use with respect to any listed property (see §1.274–5T(c)(6)(i)(B) and (C) for special rules for the aggregation of expenditures and business use and §1.280F–6T(d)(2) for the distinction between qualified business use and business/investment use).

See also §1.274–5T(e) relating to the substantiation of business use of employer–provided listed property and §1.274–6T for special rules for substantiating the business/investment use of certain types of listed property.

(c) Rules of substantiation—(1) In general. Except as otherwise provided in this section and §1.274–6T, a taxpayer must substantiate each element of an expenditure or use (described in paragraph (b) of this section) by adequate records or by sufficient evidence corroborating his own statement. Section 274(d) contemplates that a taxpayer will maintain and produce such substantiation as will constitute proof of each expenditure or use referred to in section 274. Written evidence has considerably more probative value than oral evidence alone. In addition, the probative value of written evidence is greater the closer in time it relates to the expenditure or use. A contemporaneous log is not required, but a record of the elements of an expenditure or of a business use of listed property made at or near the time of the expenditure or use, supported by sufficient documentary evidence, has a high degree of credibility not present with respect to a statement prepared subsequent thereto when generally there is a lack of accurate recall. Thus, the corroborative evidence required to support a statement not made at or near the time of the expenditure or use must have a high degree of probative value to elevate such statement and evidence to the level of credibility reflected by a record made at or near the time of the expenditure or use supported by sufficient documentary evidence. The substantiation requirements of section 274(d) are designed to encourage taxpayers to maintain the records, together with documentary evidence, as provided in paragraph (c)(2) of this section.

(2) Substantiation by adequate records—(i) In general. To meet the "adequate records" requirements of section 274(d), a taxpayer shall maintain an account book, diary, log, statement of expense, trip sheets, or similar record (as provided in paragraph (c)(2)(ii) of this section), and documentary evidence (as provided in paragraph (c)(2)(iii) of this section) which, in combination, are sufficient to establish each element of an expenditure or use specified in paragraph (b) of this section. It is not necessary to record information in an account book, diary, log, statement of expense, trip sheet, or similar record which duplicates information reflected on a receipt so long as the account book, etc., and receipt complement each other in an orderly manner.

(ii) Account book, diary, etc. An account book, diary, log, statement of expense, trip sheet, or similar record must be prepared or maintained in such manner that each recording of an element of an expenditure or use is made at or near the time of the expenditure or use.

(A) Made at or near the time of the expenditure or use. For purposes of this section, the phrase "made at or near the time of the expenditure or use" means the elements of an expenditure or use are recorded at a time when, in relation to the use or making of an expenditure, the taxpayer has full present knowledge of each element of the expenditure or use, such as the amount, time, place, and business purpose of the expenditure and business relationship. An expense account statement which is a transcription of an account book, diary, log, or similar record prepared or maintained in accordance with the provisions of this paragraph (c)(2)(ii) shall be considered a record prepared or maintained in the manner prescribed in the preceding sentence if such expense account statement is submitted by an employee to his employer or by an independent contractor to his client or customer in the regular course of good business practice. For example, a log maintained on a weekly basis, which accounts for use during the week, shall be considered a record made at or near the time of such use.

(B) Substantiation of business purpose. In order to constitute an adequate record of business purpose within the meaning of section 274(d) and this paragraph (c)(2), a written statement of business purpose generally is required. However, the degree of substantiation necessary to establish business purpose will vary depending upon the facts and circumstances of each case. Where the business purpose is evident from the surrounding facts and circumstances, a written explanation of such business purpose will not be required. For example, in the case of a salesman calling on customers on an established sales route, a written explanation of the business purpose of such travel ordinarily will not be required. Similarly, in the case of a business meal described in section 274(e)(1), if the business purpose of such meal is evident from the business relationship to the taxpayer of the persons entertained and other surrounding circumstances, a written explanation of such business purpose will not be required.

(C) Substantiation of business use of listed property—**(1)** Degree of substantiation. In order to constitute an adequate record (within the meaning of section 274(d) and this paragraph (c)(2)(ii)), which substantiates business/investment use of listed property (as defined in §1.280F–6T(d)(3)), the record must contain sufficient information as to each element of every business/investment use. However, the level of detail required in an adequate record to substantiate business/investment use may vary depending upon the facts and circumstances. For example, a taxpayer who uses a truck for both business and personal purposes and whose only business use of a truck is to make deliveries to customers on an established route may satisfy the adequate record requirement by recording the total number of miles driven during the taxable year, the length of the delivery route once, and the date of each trip at or near the time of the trips. Alternatively, the taxpayer may establish the date of each trip with a receipt, record of delivery, or other documentary evidence.

(2) Written record. Generally, an adequate record must be written. However, a record of the business use of listed property, such as a computer or automobile, prepared in a computer memory device with the aid of a logging program will constitute an adequate record.

(D) Confidential information. If any information relating to the elements of an expenditure or use, such as place, business purpose, or business relationship, is of a confidential nature, such information need not be set forth in the account book, diary, log, statement of expense, trip sheet, or similar record, provided such information is recorded at or near the time of the expenditure or use and is elsewhere available to the district director to substantiate such element of the expenditure or use.

(iii) Documentary evidence. Documentary evidence, such as receipts, paid bills, or similar evidence sufficient to support an expenditure shall be required for—

(A) Any expenditure for lodging while traveling away from home, and

(B) Any other expenditure of $75 or more ($25 or more for expenditures before October 1, 1995) except, for transportation charges, documentary evidence will not be required if not readily available, provided, however, that the Commissioner, in his discretion, may prescribe rules waiving such requirements in circumstances where he determines it is impracticable for such documentary evidence to be required.* * * Ordinarily, documentary evidence will be considered adequate to support an expenditure if it includes sufficient information to establish the amount, date, place, and the essential character of the expenditure. For example, a hotel receipt is sufficient to support expenditures for business travel if it contains the following: name, location, date, and separate amounts for charges such as for lodging, meals, and telephone. Similarly, a restaurant receipt is sufficient to support an expenditure for a business meal if it contains the following: name and location of the restaurant, the date and amount of the expenditure, the number of people served, and, if a charge is made for an item other than meals and beverages, an indication that such is the case. A document may be indicative of only one (or part of one) element of an expenditure. Thus, a cancelled check together with a bill from the payee, ordinarily would establish the element of cost. In contrast, a cancelled check drawn payable to a named payee would not by itself support a business expenditure without other evidence showing that the check was used for a certain business purpose.

(iv) Retention of written evidence. The Commissioner may, in his discretion, prescribe rules under which an employer may dispose of the adequate records and documentary evidence submitted to him by employees who are required to, and do, make an adequate accounting to the employer (within the meaning of paragraph (f)(4) of this section) if the employer maintains adequate accounting procedures with respect to such employees (within the meaning of paragraph (f)(5) of this section).

(v) Substantial compliance. If a taxpayer has not fully substantiated a particular element of an expenditure or use, but the taxpayer establishes to the satisfaction of the district director that he has substantially complied with the "adequate records" requirements of this paragraph (c)(2) with respect to the expenditure or use, the taxpayer may be permitted to establish such element by evidence which the district director shall deem adequate.

(3) Substantiation by other sufficient evidence—(i) In general. If a taxpayer fails to establish to the satisfaction of the district director that he has substantially complied with the "adequate records" requirements of paragraph (c)(2) of this section with respect to an element of an expenditure or use, then, except as otherwise provided in this paragraph, the taxpayer must establish such element—

(A) By his own statement, whether written or oral, containing specific information in detail as to such element; and

(B) By other corroborative evidence sufficient to establish such element.

If such element is the description of a gift, or the cost or amount, time, place, or date of an expenditure or use, the corroborative evidence shall be direct evidence, such as a statement in writing or the oral testimony of persons entertained or other witnesses setting forth detailed information about such element, or the documentary evidence described in paragraph (c)(2) of this section. If such element is either the business relationship to the taxpayer of persons entertained, or the business purpose of an expenditure, the corroborative evidence may be circumstantial evidence.

(ii) Sampling—(A) In general. Except as provided in paragraph (c)(3)(ii)(B) of this section, a taxpayer may maintain an adequate record for portions of a taxable year and use that record to substantiate the business/investment use of listed property for all or a portion of the taxable year if the taxpayer can demonstrate by other evidence that the periods for which an adequate record is maintained are representative of the use for the taxable year or a portion thereof.

(B) Exception for pooled vehicles. The sampling method of paragraph (c)(3)(ii)(A) of this section may not be used to substantiate the business/investment use of an automobile or other vehicle of an employer that is made available for use by more than one employee for all or a portion of a taxable year.

(C) Examples. The following examples illustrate this paragraph (c)(3)(ii).

Example (1). A, a sole proprietor and calendar year taxpayer, operates an interior decorating business out of her home. A uses an automobile for local business travel to visit the homes or offices of clients, to meet with suppliers and other subcontractors, and to pick up and deliver certain items to clients when feasible. There is no other business use of the automobile but A and other members of her family also use the automobile for personal purposes. A maintains adequate records for the first three months of 1986 that indicate that 75 percent of the use of the automobile was in A's business. Invoices from subcontractors and paid bills indicate that A's business continued at approximately the same rate for the remainder of 1986. If other circumstances do not change (e.g., A does not obtain a second car for exclusive use in her business), the determination that the business/investment use of the automobile for the taxable year is 75 percent is based on sufficient corroborative evidence.

Example (2). The facts are the same as in example (1), except that A maintains adequate records during the first week of every month, which indicate that 75 percent of the use of the automobile is in A's business. The invoices from A's business indicate that A's business continued at the same rate during the subsequent weeks of each month so that A's weekly records are representative of each month's business use of the automobile. Thus, the determination that the business/investment use of the automobile for the taxable year is 75 percent is based on sufficient corroborative evidence.

Example (3). B, a sole proprietor and calendar year taxpayer, is a salesman in a large metropolitan area for a company that manufactures household products. For the first three weeks of each month, B uses his own automobile occasionally to travel within the metropolitan area on business. During these three weeks, B's use of the automobile for business purposes does not follow a consistent pattern from day to day or week to week. During the fourth week of each month, B delivers to his customers all the orders taken during the previous month. B's use of his automobile for business purposes, as substantiated by adequate records, is 70 percent of the total use during that fourth week. In this example, a determination based on the records maintained during that fourth week that the business/investment use of the automobile for the taxable year is 70 percent is not based on sufficient corroborative evidence because use during this week is not representative of use during other periods.

(iii) Special rules. See §1.274–6T for special rules for substantiation by sufficient corroborating evidence with respect to certain listed property.

(4) Substantiation in exceptional circumstances. If a taxpayer establishes that, by reason of the inherent nature of the situation—

(i) He was unable to obtain evidence with respect to an element of the expenditure or use which conforms fully to the "adequate records" requirements of paragraph (c)(2) of this section,

(ii) He is unable to obtain evidence with respect to such element which conforms fully to the "other sufficient evidence" requirements of paragraph (c)(3) of this section, and

(iii) He has presented other evidence, with respect to such element, which possesses the highest degree of probative value possible under the circumstances, such other evidence shall be considered to satisfy the substantiation requirements of section 274(d) and this paragraph.

(5) Loss of records due to circumstances beyond control of the taxpayer. Where the taxpayer establishes that the failure to produce adequate records is due to the loss of such records through circumstances beyond the taxpayer's control, such as destruction by fire, flood, earthquake, or other casualty, the taxpayer shall have a right to substantiate a deduction by reasonable reconstruction of his expenditures or use.

(6) Special rules—(i) Separate expenditure or use—(A) In general. For the purposes of this section, each separate payment or use by the taxpayer shall ordinarily be considered to constitute a separate expenditure. However, concurrent or repetitious expenses or uses may be substantiated as a single item. To illustrate the above rules, where a taxpayer entertains a business guest at dinner and thereafter at the theater, the payment for dinner shall be considered to constitute one expenditure and the payment for the tickets for the theater shall be considered to constitute a separate expenditure. Similarly, if during a day of business travel a taxpayer makes separate payments for breakfast, lunch, and dinner, he shall be considered to have made three separate expenditures. However, if during entertainment at a cocktail lounge the taxpayer pays separately for each serving of refreshments, the total amount expended for the refreshments will be treated as a single expenditure. A tip may be treated as a separate expenditure.

(B) Aggregation of expenditures. Except as otherwise provided in this section, the account book, diary, log, statement of expense, trip sheet, or similar record required by paragraph (c)(2)(ii) of this section shall be maintained with respect to each separate expenditure and not with respect to aggregate amounts for two or more expenditures. Thus, each expenditure for such items as lodging and air or rail travel shall be recorded as a separate item and not aggregated. However, at the option of the taxpayer, amounts expended for breakfast, lunch, or dinner, may be aggregated. A tip or gratuity which is related to an underlying expense may be aggregated with such expense. In addition, amounts expended in connection with the use of listed property during a taxable year, such as for gasoline or repairs for an automobile, may be aggregated. If these expenses are aggregated, the taxpayer must establish the date and amount, but need not prove the business purpose of each expenditure. Instead, the taxpayer may prorate the expenses based on the total business use of the listed property. For other provisions permitting recording of aggregate amounts in an account book, diary, log, statement of expense, trip sheet, or similar record, see paragraphs (b)(2)(i) and (b)(3) of this section (relating to incidental costs of travel and entertainment).

(C) Aggregation of business use. Uses which may be considered part of a single use, for example, a round trip or uninterrupted business use, may be accounted for by a single record. For example, use of a truck to make deliveries at several different locations which begins and ends at the business premises and which may include a stop at the business premises in between two deliveries may be accounted for by a single record of miles driven. In addition, use of a passenger automobile by a salesman for a business trip away from home over a period of time may be accounted for by a single record of miles traveled. De minimis personal use (such as a stop for lunch on the way between two business stops) is not an interruption of business use.

(ii) Allocation of expenditure. For purposes of this section, if a taxpayer has established the amount of an expenditure, but is unable to establish the portion of such amount which is attributable to each person participating in the event giving rise to the expenditure, such amount shall ordinarily be allocated to each participant on a pro rata basis, if such determination is material. Accordingly, the total number of persons for whom a travel or entertainment expenditure is incurred must be established in order to compute the portion of the expenditure allocable to each such person.

(iii) Primary use of a facility. Section 274(a)(1)(B) and (2)(C) deny a deduction for any expenditure paid or incurred before January 1, 1979, with respect to a facility, or paid or incurred before January 1, 1994, with respect to a club, used in connection with an entertainment activity unless the taxpayer establishes that the facility (including a club) was used primarily for the furtherance of the taxpayer's trade or business. A determination whether a facility before January 1, 1979, or a club before January 1, 1994, was used primarily for the furtherance of the taxpayer's trade or business will depend upon the facts and circumstances of each case. In order to establish that a facility was used primarily for the furtherance of his trade or business, the taxpayer shall maintain records of the use of the facility, the cost of using the facility, mileage or its equivalent (if appropriate), and such other information as shall tend to establish such primary use. Such records of use shall contain—

(A) For each use of the facility claimed to be in furtherance of the taxpayer's trade or business, the elements of an expenditure specified in paragraph (b)(3) of this section, and

(B) For each use of the facility not in furtherance of the taxpayer's trade or business, an appropriate description of such use, including cost, date, number of persons entertained, nature of entertainment and, if applicable, information such as mileage or its equivalent. A notation such as "personal use" or "family use" would, in the case of such use, be sufficient to describe the nature of entertainment.

If a taxpayer fails to maintain adequate records concerning a facility which is likely to serve the personal purposes of the taxpayer, it shall be presumed that the use of such facility was primarily personal.

(iv) Additional information. In a case where it is necessary to obtain additional information, either—

(A) To clarify information contained in records, statements, testimony, or documentary evidence submitted by a taxpayer under the provisions of paragraph (c)(2) or (c)(3) of this section, or

(B) To establish the reliability or accuracy of such records, statements, testimony, or documentary evidence,

the district director may, notwithstanding any other provision of this section, obtain such additional information by personal interview or otherwise as he determines necessary to implement properly the provisions of section 274 and the regulations thereunder.

(7) Specific exceptions. Except as otherwise prescribed by the Commissioner, substantiation otherwise required by this paragraph is not required for—

(i) Expenses described in section 274(e)(2) relating to food and beverages for employees, section 274(e)(3) relating to expenses treated as compensation, section 274(e)(8) relating to items available to the public, and section 274(e)(9) relating to entertainment sold to customers, and

(ii) Expenses described in section 274(e)(5) relating to recreational, etc., expenses for employees, except that a taxpayer shall keep such records or other evidence as shall establish that such expenses were for activities (or facilities used in connection therewith) primarily for the benefit of employees other than employees who are officers, shareholders or other owners (as defined in section 274(e)(5)), or highly compensated employees.

(d) Disclosure on returns—(1) In general. The Commissioner may, in his discretion, prescribe rules under which any taxpayer claiming a deduction or credit for entertainment, gifts, travel, or with respect to listed property, or any other person receiving advances, reimbursements, or allowances for such items, shall make disclosure on his tax return with respect to such items. The provisions of this paragraph shall apply notwithstanding the provisions of paragraph (f) of this section.

(2) Business use of passenger automobiles and other vehicles. (i) On returns for taxable years beginning after December 31, 1984, taxpayers that claim a deduction or credit with respect to any vehicle are required to answer certain questions providing information about the use of the vehicle. The information required on the tax return relates to mileage (total, business, commuting, and other personal mileage), percentage of business use, date placed in service, use of other vehicles, after–work use, whether the taxpayer has evidence to support the business use claimed on the return, and whether or not the evidence is written.

(ii) Any employer that provides the use of a vehicle to an employee must obtain information from the employee sufficient to complete the employer's tax return. Any employer that provides more than five vehicles to its employees need not include any information on its return. The employer, instead, must obtain the information from its employees, indicate on its return that it has obtained the information, and retain the information received. Any employer—

(A) That can satisfy the requirements of §1.274–6T(a)(2), relating to vehicles not used for personal purposes,

(B) That can satisfy the requirements of §1.274–6T(a)(3), relating to vehicles not used for personal purposes other than commuting, or

(C) That treats all use of vehicles by employees as personal use need not obtain information with respect to those vehicles, but instead must indicate on its return that it has vehicles exempt from the requirements of this paragraph (d)(2).

(3) Business use of other listed property. On returns for taxable years beginning after December 31, 1984, taxpayers that claim a deduction or credit with respect to any listed property other than a vehicle (for example, a yacht, airplane, or certain computers) are required to provide the following information:

(i) The date that the property was placed in service,

(ii) The percentage of business use,

(iii) Whether evidence is available to support the percentage of business use claimed on the return, and

(iv) Whether the evidence is written.

(e) Substantiation of the business use of listed property made available by an employer for use by an employee—(1) Employee—(i) In general. An employee may not exclude from gross income as a working condition fringe any amount of the value of the availability of listed property provided by an employer to the employee, unless the employee substantiates for the period of availability the amount of the exclusion in accordance with the requirements of section 274(d) and either this section or §1.274–6T.

(ii) Vehicles treated as used entirely for personal purposes. If an employer includes the value of the availability of a vehicle (as defined in §1.61–25(e)(2) in an employee's gross income without taking into account any exclusion for a working condition fringe allowable under section 132 and the regulations thereunder with respect to the vehicle, the employee must substantiate any deduction claimed under §§1.162–25 and 1.162–25T for the business/investment use of the vehicle in accordance with the requirements of section 274(d) and either this section or §1.274–6T.

(2) Employer—(i) In general. An employer substantiates its business/investment use of listed property by showing either—

(A) That, based on evidence that satisfies the requirements of section 274(d) or statements submitted by employees that summarize such evidence, all or a portion of the use of the listed property is by employees in the employer's trade or business and, if any employee used the property for personal purposes, the employer included an appropriate amount in the employee's income, or

(B) In the case of a vehicle, the employer treats all use by employees as personal use and includes an appropriate amount in the employees' income.

(ii) Reliance on employee records. For purposes of substantiating the business/investment use of listed property that an employer provides to an employee and for purposes of the information required by paragraph (d)(2) and (3) of this section, the employer may rely on adequate records maintained by the employee or on the employee's own statement if corroborated by other sufficient evidence unless the employer knows or has reason to know that the statement, records, or other evidence are not accurate. The employer must retain a copy of the adequate records maintained by the employee or the other sufficient evidence, if available. Alternatively, the employer may rely on a statement submitted by the employee that provides sufficient information to allow the employer to determine the business/investment use of the property unless the employer knows or has reason to know that the statement is not based on adequate records or on the employee's own statement corroborated by other sufficient evidence. If the employer relies on the employee's statement, the employer must retain only a copy of the statement. The employee must retain a copy of the adequate records or other evidence.

(f) Reporting and substantiation of expenses of certain employees for travel, entertainment, gifts, and with respect to listed property—(1) In general. The purpose of this paragraph is to provide rules for reporting and substantiation of certain expenses paid or incurred by employees in connection with the performance of services as employees. For purposes of this paragraph, the term "business expenses" means ordinary and necessary expenses for travel, entertainment, gifts, or with respect to listed property which are deductible under section 162, and the regulations thereunder, to the extent not disallowed by sections 262, 274(c), and 280F. Thus, the term "business expenses" does not include personal, living, or family expenses disallowed by section 262, travel expenses disallowed by section 274(c), or cost recovery deductions and credits with respect to listed property disallowed by section 280F(d)(3) because the use of such property is not for the convenience of the employer and required as a condition of employment. Except as provided in paragraph (f)(2), advances, reimbursements, or allowances for such expenditures must be reported as income by the employee.

(2) Reporting of expenses for which the employee is required to make an adequate accounting to his employer—(i) Reimbursements equal to expenses. For purposes of computing tax liability, an employee need not report on his tax return business expenses for travel, transportation, entertainment, gifts, or with respect to listed property, paid or incurred by him solely for the benefit of his employer for which he is required to, and does, make an adequate accounting to his employer (as defined in paragraph (f)(4) of this section) and which are charged directly or indirectly to the employer (for example, through credit cards) or for which the employee is paid through advances, reimbursements, or otherwise, provided that the total amount of such advances, reimbursements, and charges is equal to such expenses.

(ii) Reimbursements in excess of expenses. In case the total of the amounts charged directly or indirectly to the employer or received from the employer as advances, reimbursements, or otherwise, exceeds the business expenses paid or incurred by the employee and the employee is required to, and does, make an adequate accounting to his employer for such expenses, the employee must include such excess (including amounts received for expenditures not deductible by him) in income.

(iii) Expenses in excess of reimbursements. If an employee incurs deductible business expenses on behalf of his employer which exceed the total of the amounts charged directly or indirectly to the employer and received from the employer as advances, reimbursements, or otherwise, and the employee makes an adequate accounting to his employer, the employee must be able to substantiate any deduction for such excess with such records and supporting evidence as will substantiate each element of an expenditure (described in paragraph (b) of this section) in accordance with paragraph (c) of this section.

(3) Reporting of expenses for which the employee is not required to make an adequate accounting to his employer. If the employee is not required to make an adequate accounting to his employer for his business expenses or, though required, fails to make an adequate accounting for such expenses, he must submit, as a part of his tax return, the appropriate form issued by the Internal Revenue Service for claiming deductions for employee business expenses (e.g., Form 2106, Employee Business Expenses, for 1985) and provide the information requested on that form, including the information required by paragraph (d)(2) and (3) of this section if the employee's business expenses are with respect to the use of listed property. In addition, the employee must maintain such records and supporting evidence as will substantiate each element of an expenditure or use (described in paragraph (b) of this section) in accordance with paragraph (c) of this section.

(4) Definition of an "adequate accounting" to the employer. For purposes of this paragraph an adequate accounting means the submission to the employer of an account book, diary, log, statement of expense, trip sheet, or similar record maintained by the employee in which the information as to each element of an expenditure or use (described in paragraph (b) of this section) is recorded at or near the time of the expenditure or use, together with supporting documentary evidence, in a manner which conforms to all the "adequate records" requirements of paragraph (c)(2) of this section. An adequate accounting requires that the employee account for all amounts received from his employer during the taxable year as advances, reimbursements, or allowances (including those charged directly or indirectly to the employer through credit cards or otherwise) for travel, entertainment, gifts, and the use of listed property. The methods of substantiation allowed under paragraph (c)(4) or (c)(5) of this section also will be considered to be an adequate accounting if the employer accepts an employee's substantiation and establishes that such substantiation meets the requirements of such paragraph (c)(4) or (c)(5). For purposes of an adequate accounting, the method of substantiation allowed under paragraph (c)(3) of this section will not be permitted.

(5) Substantiation of expenditures by certain employees. An employee who makes an adequate accounting to his employer within the meaning of this paragraph will not again be required to substantiate such expense account information except in the following cases:

(i) An employee whose business expenses exceed the total of amounts charged to his employer and amounts received through advances, reimbursements or otherwise and who claims a deduction on his return for such excess,

(ii) An employee who is related to his employer within the meaning of section 267(b), but for this purpose the percentage referred to in section 267(b)(2) shall be 10 percent, and

(iii) Employees in cases where it is determined that the accounting procedures used by the employer for the reporting and substantiation of expenses by such employees are not adequate, or where it cannot be determined that such procedures are adequate. The district director will determine whether the employer's accounting procedures are adequate by considering the facts and circumstances of each case, including the use of proper internal controls. For example, an employer should require that an expense account be verified and approved by a reasonable person other than the person incurring such expenses. Accounting procedures will be considered inadequate to the extent that the employer does not require an adequate accounting from his employees as defined in paragraph (f)(4) of this section, or does not maintain such substantiation. To the extent an employer fails to maintain adequate accounting procedures he will thereby obligate his employees to substantiate separately their expense account information.

(g) Substantiation by reimbursement arrangements or per diem, mileage, and other traveling allowances. For guidance, see §1.274(d)–1. The Commissioner may, in his discretion, prescribe rules in pronouncements of general applicability under which—

(1) Reimbursement arrangements covering ordinary and necessary expenses of traveling away from home (exclusive of transportation expenses to and from destination),

(2) Per diem allowances providing for ordinary and necessary expenses of traveling away from home (exclusive of transportation costs to and from destination), and

(3) Mileage allowances providing for ordinary and necessary expenses of local travel and transportation while traveling away from home, will, if in accordance with reasonable business practice, be regarded as equivalent to substantiation by adequate records or other sufficient evidence for purposes of paragraph (c) of this section of the amount of such expenses and as satisfying, with respect to the amount of such expenses, the requirements of an adequate accounting to the employer for purposes of paragraph (f)(4) of this section. If the total allowance received exceeds the deductible expenses paid or incurred by the employee, such excess must be reported as income on the employee's return. A mileage allowance provided under paragraph (g)(3) of this section is available only to the owner of a vehicle. See paragraph (j) of this section relating to the substantiation of meal expenses while traveling away from home.

(h) Reporting and substantiation of certain reimbursements of persons other than employees—(1) In general. The purpose of this paragraph is to provide rules for the reporting and substantiation of certain expenses for travel, entertainment, gifts, or with respect to listed property paid or incurred by one person (hereinafter termed "independent contractor") in connection with services performed for another person other than an employer (hereinafter termed "client or customer") under a reimbursement or other expense allowance arrangement with such client or customer. For purposes of this paragraph, the term "business expenses" means ordinary and necessary expenses for travel, entertainment, gifts, or with respect to listed property which are deductible under section 162, and the regulations thereunder, to the extent not disallowed by sections 262 and 274(c). Thus, the term "business expenses" does not include personal, living, or family expenses disallowed by section 262 or travel expenses disallowed by section 274(c), and reimbursements for such expenditures must be reported as income by the independent contractor. For purposes of this paragraph, the term "reimbursements" means advances, allowances, or reimbursements received by an independent contractor for travel, entertainment, gifts, or with respect to listed property in connection with the performance by him of services for his client or customer, under a reimbursement or other expense allowance arrangement with his client or customer, and includes amounts charged directly or indirectly to the client or customer through credit card systems or otherwise. See paragraph (j) of this section relating to the substantiation of meal expenses while traveling away from home.

(2) Substantiation by independent contractors. An independent contractor shall substantiate, with respect to his reimbursements, each element of an expenditure (described in paragraph (b) of this section) in accordance with the requirements of paragraph (c) of this section; and, to the extent he does not so substantiate, he shall include such reimbursements in income. An independent contractor shall so substantiate a reimbursement for entertainment regardless of whether he accounts (within the meaning of paragraph (h)(3) of this section) for such entertainment.

(3) Accounting to a client or customer under section 274(e)(4)(B). Section 274(e)(4)(B) provides that section 274(a) (relating to disallowance of expenses for entertainment) shall not apply to expenditures for entertainment for which an independent contractor has been reimbursed if the independent contractor accounts to his client or customer, to the extent provided by section 274(d). For purposes of section 274(e)(4)(B), an independent contractor shall be considered to account to his client or customer for an expense paid or incurred under a reimbursement or other expense allowance arrangement with his client or customer if, with respect to such expense for entertainment, he submits to his client or customer adequate records or other sufficient evidence conforming to the requirements of paragraph (c) of this section.

(4) Substantiation by client or customer. A client or customer shall not be required to substantiate, in accordance with the requirements of paragraph (c) of this section, reimbursements to an independent contractor for travel and gifts, or for entertainment unless the independent contractor has accounted to him (within the meaning of section 274(e)(4)(B) and paragraph (h)(3) of this section) for such entertainment. If an independent contractor has so accounted to a client or customer for entertainment, the client or customer shall substantiate each element of the expenditure (as described in paragraph (b) of this section) in accordance with the requirements of paragraph (c) of this section.

(i) [Reserved].

* * *

(j)(3) Incidental expenses while traveling away from home. The Commissioner may establish a method under which a taxpayer may use a specified amount for incidental expenses paid or accrued while traveling away from home in lieu of substantiating the actual cost of incidental expenses. The taxpayer will not be relieved of the requirement to substantiate the actual cost of other travel expenses as well as the time, place, and business purpose of the travel.

(k) Exceptions for qualified nonpersonal use vehicles—(1) In general. The substantiation requirements of section 274(d) and this section do not apply to any qualified nonpersonal use vehicle (as defined in paragraph (k)(2) of this section).

(2) Qualified nonpersonal use vehicle—(i) In general. For purposes of section 274(d) and this section, the term "qualified nonpersonal use vehicle" means any vehicle which, by reason of its nature (i.e., design), is not likely to be used more than a de minimis amount for personal purposes.

(ii) List of vehicles. Vehicles which are qualified nonpersonal use vehicles include the following—

(A) Clearly marked police and fire vehicles (as defined and to the extent provided in paragraph (k)(3) of this section),

(B) Ambulances used as such or hearses used as such,

(C) Any vehicle designed to carry cargo with a loaded gross vehicle weight over 14,000 pounds,

(D) Bucket trucks ("cherry pickers"),

(E) Cement mixers,

(F) Combines,

(G) Cranes and derricks,

(H) Delivery trucks with seating only for the driver, or only for the driver plus a folding jump seat,

(I) Dump trucks (including garbage trucks),

(J) Flatbed trucks,

(K) Forklifts,

(L) Passenger buses used as such with a capacity of at least 20 passengers,

(M) Qualified moving vans (as defined in paragraph (k)(4) of this section),

(N) Qualified specialized utility repair trucks (as defined in paragraph (k)(5) of this section),

(O) Refrigerated trucks,

(P) School buses (as defined in section 4221(d)(7)(C)),

(Q) Tractors and other special purpose farm vehicles,

(R) Unmarked vehicles used by law enforcement officers (as defined in paragraph (k)(6) of this section) if the use is officially authorized, and

(S) Such other vehicles as the Commissioner may designate.

(3) Clearly marked police or fire vehicles. A police or fire vehicle is a vehicle, owned or leased by a governmental unit, or any agency or instrumentality thereof, that is required to be used for commuting by a police officer or fire fighter who, when not on a regular shift, is on call at all times, provided that any personal use (other than commuting) of the vehicle outside the limit of the police officer's arrest powers or the fire fighter's obligation to respond to an emergency is prohibited by such governmental unit. A police or fire vehicle is clearly marked if, through painted insignia or words, it is readily apparent that the vehicle is a police or fire vehicle. A marking on a license plate is not a clear marking for purposes of this paragraph (k).

(4) Qualified moving van. The term "qualified moving van" means any truck or van used by a professional moving company in the trade or business of moving household or business goods if—

(i) No personal use of the van is allowed other than for travel to and from a move site (or for de minimis personal use, such as a stop for lunch on the way between two move sites),

(ii) Personal use for travel to and from a move site is an irregular practice (i.e., not more than five times a month on average), and

(iii) Personal use is limited to situations in which it is more convenient to the employer, because of the location of the employee's residence in relation to the location of the move site, for the van not to be returned to the employer's business location.

(5) Qualified specialized utility repair truck. The term "qualified specialized utility repair truck" means any truck (not including a van or pickup truck) specifically designed and used to carry heavy tools, testing equipment, or parts if—

(i) The shelves, racks, or other permanent interior construction which has been installed to carry and store such heavy items is such that it is unlikely that the truck will be used more than a de minimis amount for personal purposes, and

(ii) The employer requires the employee to drive the truck home in order to be able to respond in emergency situations for purposes of restoring or maintaining electricity, gas, telephone, water, sewer, or steam utility services.

(6) Unmarked law enforcement vehicles—(i) In general. The substantiation requirements of section 274(d) and this section do not apply to officially authorized uses of an unmarked vehicle by a "law enforcement officer". To qualify for this exception, any personal use must be authorized by the Federal, State, county, or local governmental agency or department that owns or leases the vehicle and employs the officer, and must be incident to law-enforcement functions, such as being able to report directly from home to a stakeout or surveillance site, or to an emergency situation. Use of an unmarked vehicle for vacation or recreation trips cannot qualify as an authorized use.

(ii) Law enforcement officer. The term "law enforcement officer" means an individual who is employed on a full-time basis by a governmental unit that is responsible for the prevention or investigation of crime involving injury to persons or property (including apprehension or detention of persons for such crimes), who is authorized by law to carry firearms, execute search warrants, and to make arrests (other than merely a citizen's arrest), and who regularly carries firearms (except when it is not possible to do so because of the requirements of undercover work). The term "law enforcement officer" may include an arson investigator if the investigator otherwise meets the requirements of this paragraph (k)(6)(ii), but does not include Internal Revenue Service special agents.

(7) Trucks and vans. The substantiation requirements of section 274(d) and this section apply generally to any pickup truck or van, unless the truck or van has been specially modified with the result that it is not likely to be used more than a de minimis amount for personal purposes. For example, a van that has only a front bench for seating, in which permanent shelving that fills most of the cargo area has been installed, that constantly carries merchandise or equipment, and that has been specially painted with advertising or the company's name, is a vehicle not likely to be used more than a de minimis amount for personal purposes.

(8) Examples. The following examples illustrate the provisions of paragraph (k)(3) and (6) of this section:

Example (1). Detective C, who is a "law enforcement officer" employed by a state police department, headquartered in city M, is provided with an unmarked vehicle (equipped with radio communication) for use during off-duty hours because C must be able to communicate with headquarters and be available for duty at any time (for example, to report to a surveillance or crime site). The police department generally has officially authorized personal use of the vehicle by C but has prohibited use of the vehicle for recreational purposes or for personal purposes outside the state. Thus, C's use of the vehicle for commuting between headquarters or a surveillance site and home and for personal errands is authorized personal use as described in paragraph (k)(6)(i) of this section. With respect to these authorized uses, the vehicle is not subject to the substantiation requirements of section 274(d) and the value of these uses is not included in C's gross income.

Example (2). Detective T is a "law enforcement officer" employed by city M. T is authorized to make arrests only within M's city limits. T, along with all other officers on the force, is ordinarily on duty for eight hours each work day and on call during the other sixteen hours. T is provided with the use of a clearly marked police vehicle in which T is required to commute to his home in city M. The police department's official policy regarding marked police vehicles prohibits personal use (other than commuting) of the vehicles outside the city limits. When not using the vehicle on the job, T uses the vehicle only for commuting, personal errands on the way between work and home, and personal errands within city M. All use of the vehicle by T conforms to the requirements of paragraph (k)(3) of this section. Therefore, the value of that use is excluded from T's gross income as a working condition fringe and the vehicle is not subject to the substantiation requirements of section 274(d).

(l) Definitions. For purposes of section 274(d) and this section, the terms "automobile" and "vehicle" have the same meanings as prescribed in §1.61–21(d)(1)(ii) and §1.61–21(e)(2), respectively. Also, for purposes of section 274(d) and this section, the terms "employer," "employee," and "personal use" have the same meanings as prescribed in §1.274–6T(e).

(m) Effective date. Section 274(d), as amended by the Tax Reform Act of 1984 and Public Law 99–44, and this section (except as provided in paragraph (d)(2) and (3) of this section) apply with respect to taxable years beginning after December 31, 1985. Section 274(d) and this section apply to any deduction or credit claimed in a taxable year beginning after December 31, 1985, with respect to any listed property, regardless of the taxable year in which the property was placed in service. However, except as provided in §1.132–5(h) with respect to qualified nonpersonal use vehicles, the substantiation requirements of section 274(d) and this section do not apply to the determination of an employee's working condition fringe exclusion or to the determination under §1.162–25(b) of an employee's deduction before the date that those requirements apply, under this paragraph (m), to the employer, if the employer is taxable.

§ 1.274–6 Expenditures deductible without regard to trade or business or other income producing activity.

The provisions of §§1.274–1 through 1.274–5, inclusive, do not apply to any deduction allowable to the taxpayer without regard to its connection with the taxpayer's trade or business or other income producing activity. Examples of such items are interest, taxes such as real property taxes, and casualty losses. Thus, if a taxpayer owned a fishing camp, the taxpayer could still deduct mortgage interest and real property taxes in full even if deductions for its use are not allowable under section 274(a) and §1.274–2. In the case of a taxpayer which is not an individual, the provisions of this section shall be applied as if it were an individual. Thus, if a corporation sustains a casualty loss on an entertainment facility used in its trade or business, it could deduct the loss even though deductions for the use of the facility are not allowable.

§ 1.274–6T Substantiation with respect to certain types of listed property for taxable years beginning after 1985 (temporary).

(a) Written policy statements as to vehicles— (1) In general. Two types of written policy statements satisfying the conditions described in paragraph (a)(2) and (3) of this section, if initiated and kept by an employer to implement a policy of no personal use, or no personal use except for commuting, of a vehicle provided by the employer, qualify as sufficient evidence corroborating the taxpayer's own statement and therefore will satisfy the employer's substantiation requirements under section 274(d). Therefore, the employee need not keep a separate set of records for purposes of the employer's substantiation requirements under section 274(d) with respect to use of a vehicle satisfying these written policy statement rules. A written policy statement adopted by a governmental unit as to employee use of its vehicles is eligible for these exceptions to the section 274(d) substantiation rules. Thus, a resolution of a city council or a provision of state law or a state constitution would qualify as a written policy statement, as long as the conditions described in paragraph (a)(2) and (3) of this section are met.

(2) Vehicles not used for personal purposes—(i) Employers. A policy statement that prohibits personal use by an employee satisfies an employer's substantiation requirements under section 274(d) if all the following conditions are met—

(A) The vehicle is owned or leased by the employer and is provided to one or more employees for use in connection with the employer's trade or business,

(B) When the vehicle is not used in the employer's trade or business, it is kept on the employer's business premises, unless it is temporarily located elsewhere, for example, for maintenance or because of a mechanical failure,

(C) No employee using the vehicle lives at the employer's business premises,

(D) Under a written policy of the employer, neither an employee, nor any individual whose use would be taxable to the employee, may use the vehicle for personal purposes, except for de minimis personal use (such as a stop for lunch between two business deliveries), and

(E) The employer reasonably believes that, except for de minimis use, neither the employee, nor any individual whose use would be taxable to the employee, uses the vehicle for any personal purpose.

There must also be evidence that would enable the Commissioner to determine whether the use of the vehicle meets the preceding five conditions.

(ii) Employees. An employee, in lieu of substantiating the business/investment use of an employerprovided vehicle under §1.274–5T, may treat all use of the vehicle as business/investment use if the following conditions are met—

(A) The vehicle is owned or leased by the employer and is provided to one or more employees for use in connection with the employer's trade or business,

(B) When the vehicle is not used in the employer's trade or business, it is kept on the employer's business premises, unless it is temporarily located elsewhere, for example, for maintenance or because of a mechanical failure,

(C) No employee using the vehicle lives at the employer's business premises,

(D) Under a written policy of the employer, neither the employee, nor any individual whose use would be taxable to the employee, may use the vehicle for personal purposes, except for de minimis personal use (such as a stop for lunch between two business deliveries), and

(E) Except for de minimis personal use, neither the employee, nor any individual whose use would be taxable to the employee, uses the vehicle for any personal purpose.

There must also be evidence that would enable the Commissioner to determine whether the use of the vehicle meets the preceding five conditions.

(3) Vehicles not used for personal purposes other than commuting—(i) Employers. A policy statement that prohibits personal use by an employee, other than commuting, satisfies an employer's substantiation requirements under section 274(d) if all the following conditions are met—

(A) The vehicle is owned or leased by the employer and is provided to one or more employees for use in connection with the employer's trade or business and is used in the employer's trade or business,

(B) For bona fide noncompensatory business reasons, the employer requires the employee to commute to and/or from work in the vehicle,

(C) The employer has established a written policy under which neither the employee, nor any individual whose use would be taxable to the employee, may use the vehicle for personal purposes, other than for commuting or de minimis personal use (such as a stop for a personal errand on the way between a business delivery and the employee's home),

(D) The employer reasonably believes that, except for de minimis personal use, neither the employee, nor any individual whose use would be taxable to the employee, uses the vehicle for any personal purpose other than commuting,

(E) The employee required to use the vehicle for commuting is not a control employee (as defined in §1.61–2T(f)(5) and (6)) required to use an automobile (as defined in §1.61–2T(d)(1)(ii)), and

(F) The employer accounts for the commuting use by including in the employee's gross income the commuting value provided in §1.61–2T(f)(3) (to the extent not reimbursed by the employee).

There must be evidence that would enable the Commissioner to determine whether the use of the vehicle met the preceding six conditions.

(ii) Employees. An employee, in lieu of substantiating the business/investment use of an employer–provided vehicle under §1.274–5T, may substantiate any exclusion allowed under section 132 for a working condition fringe by including in income the commuting value of the vehicle (determined by the employer pursuant to §1.61–2T(f)(3)) if all the following conditions are met:

(A) The vehicle is owned or leased by the employer and is provided to one or more employees for use in connection with the employer's trade or business and is used in the employer's trade or business,

(B) For bona fide noncompensatory business reasons, the employer requires the employee to commute to and/or from work in the vehicle,

(C) Under a written policy of the employer, neither the employee, nor any individual whose use would be taxable to the employee, may use the vehicle for personal purposes, other than for commuting or de minimis personal use (such as a stop for a personal errand on the way between a business delivery and the employee's home),

(D) Except for de minimis personal use, neither the employee, nor any individual whose use would be taxable to the employee, uses the vehicle for any personal purpose other than commuting,

(E) The employee required to use the vehicle for commuting is not a control employee (as defined in §1.61–2T(f)(5) and (6)) required to use an automobile (as defined in §1.61—2T(d)(1)(ii)), and

(F) The employee includes in gross income the commuting value determined by the employer as provided in §1.61–2T(f)(3) (to the extent that the employee does not reimburse the employer for the commuting use).

There must also be evidence that would enable the Commissioner to determine whether the use of the vehicle met the preceding six conditions.

(b) Vehicles used in connection with the business of farming—(1) In general. If, during a taxable year or shorter period, a vehicle, not otherwise described in section 274(i), §1.274–5T(k), or paragraph (a)(2) or (3) of this section, is owned or leased by an employer and used during most of a normal business day directly in connection with the business of farming (as defined in paragraph (b)(2) of this section), the employer, in lieu of substantiating the use of the vehicle as prescribed in §1.274–5T(b)(6)(i)(B), may determine any deduction or credit with respect to the vehicle as if the business/investment use (as defined in §1.280F–6T(d)(3)(i)) and the qualified business use (as defined in §1.280F–6T(d)(2)) of the vehicle in the business of farming for the taxable year or shorter period were 75 percent plus that percentage, if any, attributable to an amount included in an employee's gross income. If the vehicle is also available for personal use by employees, the employer must include the value of that personal use in the gross income of the employees, allocated among them in the manner prescribed in §1.132–5T(g).

(2) Directly in connection with the business of farming. The phrase "directly in connection with the business of farming" means that the vehicle must be used directly in connection with the business of operating a farm (i.e., cultivating land or raising or harvesting any agricultural or horticultural commodity, or the raising, shearing, feeding, caring for, training, and management of animals) or incidental thereto (for example, trips to the feed and supply store).

(3) Substantiation by employees. If an employee is provided with the use of a vehicle to which this paragraph (b) applies, the employee may, in lieu of substantiating the business/investment use of the vehicle in the manner prescribed in §1.274–5T, substantiate any exclusion allowed under section 132 for a working condition fringe as if the business/investment use of the vehicle were 75 percent, plus that percentage, if any, determined by the employer to be attributable to the use of the vehicle by individuals other than the employee, provided that the employee includes in gross income the amount determined by the employer as includible in the employee's gross income. See §1.132–5T(g)(3) for examples illustrating the allocation of use of a vehicle among employees.

(c) Vehicles treated as used entirely for personal purposes. An employer may satisfy the substantiation requirements under section 274(d) for a taxable year or shorter period with respect to the business use of a vehicle that is provided to an employee by including the value of the availability of the vehicle during the relevant period in the employee's gross income without any exclusion for a working condition fringe with respect to the vehicle and, if required, by withholding any taxes. Under these circumstances, the employer's business/investment use of the vehicle during the relevant period is 100 percent. The employer's qualified business use of the vehicle is dependent upon the relationship of the employee to the employer (see §1.280F–6T(d)(2)).

(d) Limitation. If a taxpayer chooses to satisfy the substantiation requirements of section 274(d) and §1.274–5T by using one of the methods prescribed in paragraphs (a)(2) or (3), (b), or (c) of this section and files a return with the Internal Revenue Service for a taxable year consistent with such choice, the taxpayer may not later use another of these methods. Similarly, if a taxpayer chooses to satisfy the substantiation requirements of section 274(d) in the manner prescribed in §1.274–5T and files a return with the Internal Revenue Service for a taxable year consistent with such choice, the taxpayer may not later use a method prescribed in paragraph (a)(2) or (3), (b), or (c) of this section. This rule applies to an employee for purposes of substantiating any working condition fringe exclusion as well as to an employer. For example, if an employee excludes on his federal income tax return for a taxable year 90 percent of the value of the availability of an employer-provided automobile on the basis of records that allegedly satisfy the "adequate records" requirement of §1.274–5T(c) (2), and that requirement is not satisfied, then the employee may not satisfy the substantiation requirements of section 274(d) for the taxable year by any method prescribed in this section, but may present other corroborative evidence as prescribed in §1.274–5T(c)(3).

(e) Definitions—(1) In general. The definitions provided in this paragraph (e) apply for purposes of section 274(d), §1.274–5T, and this section.

(2) Employer and employee. The terms employer and employee"include the following:

(i) A sole proprietor shall be treated as both an employer and employee,

(ii) A partnership shall be treated as an employer of its partners, and

(iii) A partner shall be treated as an employee of the partnership.

(3) Automobile. The term "automobile" has the same meaning as prescribed in §1.61–2T(d)(1)(ii).

(4) Vehicle. The term "vehicle" has the same meaning as prescribed in §1.61–2T(e)(2).

(5) Personal use. "Personal use" by an employee of an employer-provided vehicle includes use in any trade or business other than the trade or business of being the employee of the employer providing the vehicle.

(f) Effective date. This section is effective for taxable years beginning after December 31, 1985.

§ 1.274–7 Treatment of certain expenditures with respect to entertainment–type facilities.

If deductions are disallowed under §1.274–2 with respect to any portion of a facility, such portion shall be treated as an asset which is used for personal, living, and family purposes (and not as an asset used in a trade or business). Thus, the basis of such a facility will be adjusted for purposes of computing depreciation deductions and determining gain or loss on the sale of such facility in the same manner as other property (for example, a residence) which is regarded as used partly for business and partly for personal purposes.

* * *

§ 1.280F–1T Limitations on investment tax credit and recovery deductions under section 168 for passenger automobiles and certain other listed property; overview of regulations (temporary).*

(a) In general. Section 280F(a) limits the amount of investment tax credit determined under section 46(a) and recovery deductions under section 168 for passenger automobiles. Section 280F(b) denies the investment tax credit and requires use of the straight line method of recovery for listed property that is not predominantly used in a qualified business use. In certain circumstances, section 280F(b) requires the recapture of an amount of cost recovery deductions previously claimed by the taxpayer. Section 280F(c) provides that lessees are to be subject to restrictions substantially equivalent to those imposed on owners of such property under section 280F(a) and (b). §280F(d) provides definitions and special rules; note

*Editorial comment: The Regulations do not reflect the effect of the Tax Reform Act of 1986 which repealed the investment tax credit, lowered the ceiling amounts on the cost recovery deductions, and provided for indexing. See Sec. 280F(a)(1).

that section 280F(d)(2) and (3) apply with respect to all listed property, even if the other provisions of section 280F do not affect the treatment of the property.

(b) Key to Code provisions. The following table identifies the provisions of section 280F under which regulations are provided, and lists each provision below with its corresponding regulation section:

Section 1.280F–2T	Section 1.280F–3T	Section 1.280F–4T and 1.280F–7	Section 1.280F–5T	Section 1.280F–6
(a)	(b)	(d)(2)	(c)	(d)(3)
(d)(1)	(d)(1)			(d)(4)
(d)(8)				(d)(5)
(d)(10)				(d)(6)

Sections 1.280F–2T(f) and 1.280F–4T(b) also provide special rules for improvements to passenger automobiles and other listed property that qualify as capital expenditures.

(c) Effective dates—(1) In general. This section and §§1.280F–2T through 1.280F–6T apply to property placed in service or leased after June 18, 1984, in taxable years ending after that date. Section 1.280F–7 applies to property leased after December 31, 1986, in taxable years ending after that date.

* * *

(3) Leased passenger automobiles. Section 1.280F–5T(e) generally applies to passenger automobiles leased after April 2, 1985, and before January 1, 1987, in taxable years ending after April 2, 1985.* * *

§ 1.280F–2T Limitations on recovery deductions and the investment tax credit for certain passenger automobiles (temporary).*

(a) Limitation on amount of investment tax credit—(1) General rule. The amount of the investment tax credit determined under section 46(a) for any passenger automobile shall not exceed $1,000. For a passenger automobile placed in service after December 31, 1984, the $1,000 amount shall be increased by the automobile price inflation adjustment (as defined in section 280F(d)(7)) for the calendar year in which the automobile is placed in service.

(2) Election of reduced investment tax credit. If the taxpayer elects under section 48(q)(4) to reduce the amount of the investment tax credit in lieu of adjusting the basis of the passenger automobile under section 48(q)(l), the amount of the investment tax credit for any passenger automobile shall not exceed two–thirds of the amount determined under paragraph (a)(1) of this section.

(b) Limitations on allowable recovery deductions—(1) Recovery deduction for year passenger automobile is placed in service. For the taxable year that a taxpayer places a passenger automobile in service, the allowable recovery deduction under section 168(a) shall not exceed $4,000. See paragraph (b)(3) of this section for the adjustment to this limitation.

(2) Recovery deduction for remaining taxable years during the recovery period. For any taxable year during the recovery period remaining after the year that the property is placed in service, the allowable recovery deduction under section 168(a) shall not exceed $6,000. See paragraph (b)(3) of this section for the adjustment to this limitation.

(3) Adjustment to limitation by reason of automobile price inflation adjustment. The limitations on the allowable recovery deductions prescribed in paragraph (b)(1) and (2) of this section are increased by the automobile price inflation adjustment (as defined in section 280F(d)(7)) for the calendar year in which the automobile is placed in service.

(4) Coordination with section 179. For purposes of section 280F(a) and this section, any deduction allowable under section 179 (relating to the election to expense certain depreciable trade or business assets) is treated as if that deduction were a recovery deduction under section 168. Thus, the amount of the section 179 deduction is subject to the limitations described in paragraph (b)(1) and (2) of this section.

(c) Disallowed recovery deductions allowed for years subsequent to the recovery period—(1) In general. (i) Except as otherwise provided in this paragraph (c), the "unrecovered basis" (as defined in paragraph (c)(1)(ii) of this section) of any passenger automobile is treated as a deductible expense in the first taxable year succeeding the end of the recovery period.

*Editorial comment: The Regulations do not reflect the effect of the Tax Reform Act of 1986 which repealed the investment tax credit, lowered the ceiling amounts on the cost recovery deductions, and provided for indexing. See Sec. 280F(a)(l).

(ii) The term "unrecovered basis" means the excess (if any) of—

(A) The unadjusted basis (as defined in section 168(d)(1)(A), except that there is no reduction by reason of an election to expense a portion of the basis under section 179) of the passenger automobile, over

(B) The amount of the recovery deductions (including any section 179 deduction elected by the taxpayer) which would have been allowable for taxable years in the recovery period (determined after the application of section 280F(a) and paragraph (b) of this section and as if all use during the recovery period were used described in section 168(c)(1)).

(2) Special rule when taxpayer elects to use the section 168(b)(3) optional recovery percentages. If the taxpayer elects to use the optional recovery percentages under section 168(b)(3) or must use the straight line method over the earnings and profits life (as defined and described in §1.280F–3T(f)), the second succeeding taxable year after the end of the recovery period is treated as the first succeeding taxable year after the end of the recovery period for purposes of this paragraph (c) because of the half–year convention. For example, assume a calendar-year taxpayer places in service on July 1, 1984, a passenger automobile (i.e., 3-year recovery property) and elects under section 168(b)(3) to recover its cost over 5 years using the straight line optional percentages. Based on these facts, calendar year 1990 is treated as the first succeeding taxable year after the end of the recovery period.

(3) Deduction limited to $6,000 for any taxable year. The amount that may be treated as a deductible expense under this paragraph (c) in the first taxable year succeeding the recovery period shall not exceed $6,000. Any excess shall be treated as an expense for the succeeding taxable years. However, in no event may any deduction in a succeeding taxable year exceed $6,000. The limitation on amounts deductible as an expense under this paragraph (c) with respect to any passenger automobile is increased by the automobile price inflation adjustment (as defined in section 280F(d)(7)) for the calendar year in which such automobile is placed in service.

(4) Deduction treated as a section 168 recovery deduction. Any amount allowable as an expense in a taxable year after the recovery period by reason of this paragraph (c) shall be treated as a recovery deduction allowable under section 168. However, a deduction is allowable by reason of this paragraph (c) with respect to any passenger automobile for a taxable year only to the extent that a deduction under section 168 would be allowable with respect to the automobile for that year. For example, no recovery deduction is allowable for a year during which a passenger automobile is disposed of or is used exclusively for personal purposes.

(d) Additional reduction in limitations by reason of personal use of passenger automobile or by reason of a short taxable year. See paragraph (i) of this section for rules regarding the additional reduction in the limitations prescribed by paragraphs (a) through (c) of this section by reason of the personal use of a passenger automobile or by reason of a short taxable year.

(e) Examples. The provisions of paragraphs (a) through (c) of this section may be illustrated by the following examples. For purposes of these examples, assume that all taxpayers use the calendar year and that no short taxable years are involved.

Example (1). (i) On July 1, 1984, B purchases for $45,000 and places in service a passenger automobile which is 3-year recovery property under section 168. In 1984, B does not elect under section 179 to expense a portion of the cost of the automobile. The automobile is used exclusively in B's business during taxable years 1984 through 1990.

(ii) The maximum amount of B's investment tax credit is $1,000 (i.e., the lesser of $1,000 or .06 × $45,000). B's unadjusted basis for purposes of section 168 is $44,500 (i.e., $45,000 reduced under section 48(q)(1) by $500). B selects the use of the accelerated recovery percentages under section 168(b)(1).

(iii) The maximum amount of B's recovery deduction for 1984 is $4,000 (i.e., the lesser of $4,000 or .25 × $44,500); for 1985, $6,000 (i.e., the lesser of $6,000 or .38 × $44,500); and for 1986, $6,000 (i.e., the lesser of $6,000 or .37 × $44,500).

(iv) At the beginning of taxable year 1987, B's unrecovered basis in the automobile is $28,500 (i.e., $44,500–$16,000). Under paragraph (c) of this section, B may expense $6,000 of the unrecovered basis in the automobile in 1987. This expense is treated as a recovery deduction under section 168. For taxable years 1988 through 1990, B may deduct $6,000 of the unrecovered basis per year. At the beginning of 1991, B's unrecovered basis in the automobile is $4,500. During that year, B disposes of the automobile. B is not allowed a deduction for 1991 because no deduction would be allowable under section 168 based on these facts.

Example (2). (i) On July 1, 1984, C purchases for $50,000 and places in service a passenger automobile which is 3-year recovery property under section 168. The automobile is used exclusively in C's business during taxable years 1984 through 1992. In 1984, C does not elect under section 179 to expense a portion of the automobile's cost. C elects under section 48(q)(4) to take a reduced investment tax credit in lieu of the section 48(q)(1) basis adjustment.

(ii) The maximum amount of C's investment tax credit is $666.67 (i.e., the lesser of ⅔ of $1,000 or .04 × $50,000). C's unadjusted basis for purposes of section 168 is $50,000. C elects to use the optional recovery percentages under section 168(b)(3) based on a 5-year recovery period.

(iii) The maximum amount of C's recovery deduction for 1984 is $4,000 (i.e., the lesser of $4,000 or .10 × $50,000); for taxable years 1985 through 1988, $6,000 per year (i.e., the lesser of $6,000 or .20 of $50,000). C's recovery deduction for 1989 is $5,000 (i.e., the lesser of .10 × $50,000 or $6,000).

(iv) At the beginning of taxable year 1990, C's unrecovered basis in the automobile is $17,000. Under paragraph (c) of this section, C may expense $6,000 of the unrecovered basis in the automobile in 1990, this expense is treated as a recovery deduction under section 168. For taxable years 1991 and 1992, C may deduct $6,000, and $5,000, respectively of the unrecovered basis per year.

Example (3). Assume the same facts as in example (2), except that C disposes of the passenger automobile on July 1, 1990. Under paragraph (c) of this section, C is not allowed a deduction for 1990 or for any succeeding taxable year because no deduction would be allowable under section 168 based on these facts.

Example (4). (i) On July 1, 1984, G purchases for $15,000 and places in service a passenger automobile which is 3-year recovery property under section 168. The automobile is used exclusively in G's business during taxable years 1984 through 1987. In 1984, G elects under section 179 to expense $5,000 of the cost of the property.

(ii) The maximum amount of G's investment tax credit is $600 (i.e., the lesser of .06 × $10,000 or $1,000).

(iii) G's unadjusted basis for purposes of section 168 is $9,700 (i.e., $15,000 minus the sum of $5,000 (the amount of the expense elected under section 179) and $300 (one–half of the investment tax credit under section 48(q)(1))). Under paragraph (b)(4) of this section, the allowable deduction under section 179 is treated as a recovery deduction under section 168 for purposes of this section. Thus, the maximum amount of G's section 179 deduction is $4,000 (i.e., the lesser of $4,000 or $5,000 + .25 × $9,700). G is entitled to no further recovery deduction under section 168 for 1984. The amount of G's 1985 and 1986 recovery deductions are $3,686 (i.e., the lesser of .38 × $9,700 or $6,000) and $3,589 (i.e., the lesser of .37 × $9,700 or $6,000), respectively. At the beginning of 1987, G's unrecovered basis in the automobile is $3,425 (i.e., $14,700–$11,275). Under paragraph (c) of this section, G may expense the remaining $3,425 in 1987.

Example (5). (i) On July 1, 1984, D purchases for $55,000 and places in service a passenger automobile which is 3-year recovery property under section 168. The automobile is used exclusively in D's business during taxable years 1984 through 1993. In 1984 D elects under section 179 to expense $5,000 of the cost of the property.

(ii) The maximum amount of D's investment tax credit is $1,000 (i.e., the lesser of $1,000 or .06 × $50,000).

(iii) D's unadjusted basis for purposes of section 168 is $49,500 (i.e., $55,000 minus the sum of $5,000 (the amount of the expense elected under section 179) and $500 (one–half of the investment tax credit under section 48(q)(1))). Under paragraph (b)(4) of this section, the allowable deduction under section 179 is treated as a recovery deduction under section 168 for purposes of this section. Thus, the maximum amount of D's section 179 deduction is $4,000 (i.e., the lesser of $4,000 or $5,000 + .25 × $49,500). D is entitled to no further recovery deduction under section 168 for 1984. The maximum amount of D's 1985 recovery deduction is $6,000 (i.e., the lesser of $6,000 or .38 × $49,500); and for 1986, $6,000 (i.e., the lesser of $6,000 or .37 of $49,500).

(iv) At the beginning of 1987, D's unrecovered basis is $38,500. D may expense the remaining unrecovered basis at the rate of $6,000 per year through 1992 and $2,500 in 1993.

Example (6). Assume the same facts as in example (5), except that in 1993, D uses the automobile only 60 percent in his business. Under paragraph (c)(4) of this section for 1993, D may expense $1,500 (i.e., .60 × $2,500). D is entitled to no further deductions with respect to the automobile in any later year.

Example (7). (i) On July 1, 1984, F purchases for $44,500 and places in service a passenger automobile which is 3-year recovery property under section 168. The automobile is used exclusively in F's business during taxable years 1984 through 1992. In 1984, F elects under section 179 to expense $5,000 of the cost of the property.

(ii) F elects under section 48(q)(4) to take a reduced investment tax credit in lieu of the section 48(q)(1) basis adjustment. The maximum amount of F's investment tax credit is $666.67 (i.e., the lesser of 2/3 of $1,000 or .04 × $39,500).

(iii) F's unadjusted basis for purposes of section 168 is $39,500 (i.e., $44,500–$5,000 (the amount of the expense elected under section 179)). F elects to use the optional recovery percentage under section 168(b)(3) based on a 5-year recovery period. Under paragraph (b)(4) of this section, the allowable section 179 deduction is treated as a recovery deduction under section 168 for purposes of this section. Thus, the maximum amount of F's section 179 deduction is $4,000 (i.e., the lesser of $4,000 or $5,000 + .10 × $39,500). F is entitled to no further recovery deduction under section 168 for 1984. The maximum amounts of F's recovery deductions for 1985 through 1988 are $6,000 per year (i.e., the lesser of $6,000 or .20 × $39,500). F's recovery deduction for 1989 (the first taxable year after the 5-year recovery period but the sixth recovery year for purposes of section 168) is $3,950 (i.e., the lesser of .10 × $39,500 or $6,000).

(iv) Under paragraph (c), taxable year 1990 is considered to be the first taxable year succeeding the end of the recovery period. At the beginning of taxable year 1990, F's unrecovered basis in the automobile is $12,550 (i.e., $44,500–$31,950). Under paragraph (c), F may expense $6,000 of his unrecovered basis in the automobile in 1990 and in 1991. This expense is treated as a recovery deduction under section 168. For taxable year 1992, F may expense the remaining $550 of his unrecovered basis in the automobile.

(f) Treatment of improvements that qualify as capital expenditures. An improvement to a passenger automobile that qualifies as a capital expenditure under section 263 is treated as a new item of recovery property placed in service in the year the improvement is made. However, the limitations in paragraph (b) of this section on the amount of recovery deductions allowable are determined by taking into account as a whole both the improvement and the property of which the improvement is a part. If that improvement also qualifies as an investment in new section 38 property under section 48(b) and §1.48–2(b)(2), the limitation in paragraph (a)(1) of this section on the amount of the investment tax credit for that improvement is determined by taking into account any investment tax credit previously allowed for the passenger automobile (including any prior improvement considered part of the passenger automobile). Thus, the maximum credit allowable for the automobile (including the improvement) will be $1,000 (or 2/3 of $1,000, in the case of an election to take a reduced credit under section 48(q)(4)) (adjusted under section 280F(d)(7) to reflect the automobile price inflation adjustment for the year the property of which the improvement is a part is placed in service).

(g) Treatment of section 1031 or section 1033 transactions—(1) Treatment of exchanged passenger automobile. For a taxable year in which a transaction described in section 1031 or section 1033 occurs, the unadjusted basis of an exchanged or converted passenger automobile shall cease to be taken into account in determining any recovery deductions allowable under section 168 as of the beginning of the taxable year in which the exchange or conversion occurs. Thus, no recovery deduction is allowable for the exchanged or converted automobile in the year of the exchange or conversion.

(2) Treatment of acquired passenger automobile—(i) In general. The acquired automobile is treated as new property placed in service in the year of the exchange (or in the replacement year) and that year is its first recovery year.

(ii) Limitations on recovery deductions. If the exchanged (or converted) automobile was acquired after the effective date of section 280F (as set out in §1.280F–1(c)), the basis of that automobile as determined under section 1031(d) or section 1033(b) (whichever is applicable) must be reduced for purposes of computing recovery deductions with respect to the acquired automobile (but not for purposes of determining the amount of the investment tax credit and gain or loss on the sale or other disposition of the property) by the excess (if any) of—

(A) The sum of the amounts that would have been allowable as recovery deductions with respect to the exchanged (or converted) automobile during taxable years preceding the year of the exchange (or conversion) if all of the use of the automobile during those years was use described in section 168(c), over

(B) The sum of the amounts allowable as recovery deductions during those years.

(3) Examples. The provisions of this paragraph (g) may be illustrated by the following examples:

Example (1). (i) In 1982, F purchases and places in service a passenger automobile which is 3-year recovery property under section 168. The automobile is used exclusively in F's business.

(ii) On July 1, 1984, F exchanges the passenger automobile and $1,000 cash for a new passenger automobile ("like kind" property). Under paragraph (g)(1) of this section, no recovery deduction is allowed in 1984 for the exchanged automobile. Any investment tax credit claimed with respect to that automobile is subject to recapture under section 47.

(iii) F's basis in the acquired property (as determined under section 1031(d) and F's qualified investment are $20,000. Under the provisions of paragraph (g)(2)(i) of this section, the acquired property is treated as new recovery property placed in service in 1984 to the extent of the full $20,000 of basis. The maximum amount of F's investment tax credit is limited to $1,000 (i.e., the lesser of $1,000 or .06 × $20,000). Cost recovery deductions are computed pursuant to paragraph (b) of this section.

Example (2). (i) On July 1, 1984, E purchases for $30,000 and places in service a passenger automobile which is 3-year recovery property under section 168. In 1984, E's business use percentage is 80 percent and such use constitutes his total business/investment use.

(ii) E elects under section 48(q)(4) to take a reduced investment tax credit in lieu of the section 48(q)(1) basis adjustment. The maximum amount of E's investment tax credit is $533.33 (i.e., the lesser of $^2/_3$ of $1,000 × .80 or .80 × .04 × $30,000).

(iii) E's unadjusted basis for purposes of section 168 is $30,000. E selects the use of the accelerated recovery percentages under section 168(b)(1). The maximum amount of E's recovery deduction for 1984 is $3,200 (i.e., the lesser of .80 × $4,000 or .80 × .25 × $30,000).

(iv) On June 10, 1985, E exchanges the passenger automobile and $1,000 cash for a new passenger automobile ("like kind" property). Under paragraph (g)(1) of this section, no recovery deduction is allowable in 1985 for the exchanged automobile. The investment tax credit claimed is subject to recapture under section 47. Under paragraph (g)(2)(ii) of this section, E's basis in the acquired property for purposes of computing recovery deductions under section 280F is $27,000 (i.e., $27,800 (section 1031(d) basis)—$800). The acquired automobile is used exclusively in F's business during taxable years 1985 through 1988. Under paragraph (g)(2) of this section, the acquired property is treated as new recovery property placed in service in 1985. Assume that the automobile price inflation adjustment (as described under section 280F(d)(7)) is zero. E's qualified investment in the property, as determined under §1.46–3(c)(1), is $27,800. The maximum amount of E's investment tax credit is $1,000 (i.e., the lesser of $1,000 or .06 × $27,800). E's unadjusted basis for purposes of section 168 is $26,500 (i.e., $27,000 reduced under section 48(q)(1) by $500). Cost recovery deductions are computed pursuant to paragraph (b) of this section.

(h) Other nonrecognition transactions. [Reserved]

(i) Limitation under this section applies before other limitations—(1) Personal use. The limitations imposed upon the maximum amount of the allowable investment tax credit and the allowable recovery deductions (as described in paragraphs (a) through (c) of this section) must be adjusted during any taxable year in which a taxpayer makes any use of a passenger automobile other than for business/investment use (as defined in §1.280F–6(d)(3)). The limitations on the amount of the allowable investment tax credit (as described in paragraph (a) of this section) and the allowable cost recovery deductions (as described in paragraphs (b) and (c) of this section) are redetermined by multiplying the limitations by the percentage of business/investment use (determined on an annual basis) during the taxable year.

(2) Short taxable year. The limitations imposed upon the maximum amount of the allowable recovery deductions (as described in paragraphs (a) through (c) of this section) must be adjusted during any taxable year in which a taxpayer has a short taxable year. In this case, the limitation is adjusted by multiplying the limitation that would have been applied if the taxable year were not a short taxable year by a fraction, the numerator of which is the number of months and part–months in the short taxable year and the denominator of which is 12.

(3) Examples. The provisions of this paragraph (i) may be illustrated by the following examples:

Example (1). On July 1, 1984, A purchases and places in service a passenger automobile and uses it 80 percent for business/investment use during 1984. Under paragraph (i)(1) of this section, the maximum amount of the investment tax credit that A may claim for the automobile is $800 (i.e., .80 × $1,000).

Example (2). Assume the same facts as in example (1), except that A elects under section 48(q)(4) to take a reduced investment tax credit in lieu of the section 48(q)(1) basis adjustment. Under paragraph (i)(1) of this section, the maximum amount of the investment tax credit that A may claim for the automobile is $533.33 (i.e., .80 × 2/3 × $1,000).

Example (3). On July 1, 1984, B purchases and places in service a passenger automobile and uses it 60 percent for business/investment use during 1984. Under paragraph (i)(1) of this section, the maximum amount of the investment tax credit that B may claim for the automobile is $600 (i.e., .60 × $1,000). B uses the car 70 percent for business/investment use during 1985 and 80 percent during 1986. Under paragraph (i)(1) of this section, the maximum amount of recovery deductions that B may claim for 1984, 1985, and 1986 are $2,400 (i.e., .60 .A $4,000), $4,200 (i.e., .70 × $6,000), and $4,800 (i.e, .80 × $6,000), respectively.

Example (4). Assume the same facts as in example (3) with the added facts that B's unrecovered basis at the beginning of 1987 is $6,000 and that B uses the automobile 85 percent for business/investment use during 1987. Under paragraph (i)(1) of this section, the maximum amount that B may claim as an expense for 1987 is $5,000 (i.e., .85 × $6,000).

Example (5). On August 1, 1984, C purchases and places in service a passenger automobile and uses it exclusively for business. Taxable year 1984 for C is a short taxable year which consists of 6 months. Under paragraph (i)(2) of this section, the maximum amount that C may claim as a recovery deduction for 1984 is $2,000 (i.e., 6/12 × $4,000).

Example (6). Assume the same facts as in example (5), except that C uses the passenger automobile 70 percent for business/investment use during 1984. Under paragraph (i)(1) and (2) of this section, the maximum amount that C may claim as a recovery deduction for 1984 is $1,400 (i.e., .70 × 6/12 × $4,000).

§ 1.280F–3T Limitations on recovery deductions and the investment tax credit when the business use percentage of listed property is not greater than 50 percent (temporary).*

(a) In general. Section 280F(b), generally, imposes limitations with respect to the amount allowable as an investment tax credit under section 46(a) and the amount allowable as a recovery deduction under section 168 in the case of listed property (as defined in §1.280F–6(b)) if certain business use of the property (referred to as "qualified business use") does not exceed 50 percent during a taxable year. "Qualified business use" generally means use in a trade or business, rather than use in an investment or other activity conducted for the production of income within the meaning of section 212. See §1.280F–6(d) for the distinction between "business/investment use" and "qualified business use."

(b) Limitation on the amount of investment tax credit—(1) Denial of investment tax credit when business use percentage not greater than 50 percent. Listed property is not treated as section 38 property to any extent unless the business use percentage (as defined in section 280F(d)(6) and §1.280F–6(d)(1)) is greater than 50 percent. For example, if a taxpayer uses listed property in a trade or business in the taxable year in which it is placed in service, but the business use percentage is not greater than 50 percent, no investment tax credit is allowed for that listed property. If, in the taxable year in which listed property is placed in service, the only business/investment use (as defined in §1.280F–6(d)(3)) of that property is qualified business use (as defined in §1.280F–6(d)(2)(i)), and the business use percentage is 55 percent, the investment tax credit is allowed for the 55 percent of the listed property that is treated as section 38 property. The credit allowed is unaffected by any

*Editorial comment: The Regulations do not reflect the effect of the Tax Reform Act of 1986 which repealed the investment tax credit, lowered the ceiling amounts on the cost recovery deductions, and provided for indexing. See Sec. 280F(a)(1).

increase in the business use percentage in a subsequent taxable year.

(2) Recapture of investment tax credit. Listed property ceases to be section 38 property to the extent that the business/investment use (as defined in §1.280F–6(d)(3)) for any taxable year is less than the business/investment use for the taxable year in which the property is placed in service. See §1.47–2(c). If the business use percentage (as defined in §1.280F–6(d)(1)) of listed property is greater than 50 percent for the taxable year in which the property is placed in service, and less than or equal to 50 percent for any subsequent taxable year, that property ceases to be section 38 property in its entirety in that subsequent taxable year. Under §1.47–1(c)(1)(ii)(b), the property (or a portion thereof) is treated as ceasing to be section 38 property on the first day of the taxable year in which the cessation occurs.

(c) Limitation on the method of cost recovery under section 168 when business use of property not greater than 50 percent—(1) Year of acquisition. If any listed property (as defined in §1.280F–6(b)) is not predominantly used in a qualified business use (as defined in §1.280F–6(d)(4)) in the year it is acquired, the recovery deductions allowed under section 168 for the property for that taxable year and for succeeding taxable years are to be determined using the straight line method over its earnings and profits life (as defined in paragraph (f) of this section). Additionally, the taxpayer is not entitled to make any election under section 179 with respect to the property for that year.

(2) Subsequent years. If any listed property is not subject to paragraph (c)(1) of this section because such property is predominantly used in a qualified business use (as defined in §1.280F–6(d)(4)) during the year it is acquired but is not predominantly used in a qualified business use during a subsequent taxable year, the rules of this paragraph (c)(2) apply. In such a case, the taxpayer must determine the recovery deductions allowed under section 168 for the taxable year that the listed property is not predominantly used in a qualified business use and for any subsequent taxable year as if such property was not predominantly used in a qualified business use in the year in which it was acquired and there had been no section 179 election with respect to the property. Thus, the recovery deductions allowable under section 168 for the remaining taxable years are computed by determining the applicable recovery percentage that would apply if the taxpayer had used the straight line method over the property's earnings and profits life beginning with the year the property was placed in service.

(3) Effect of rule on recovery property that is not listed property. The mandatory use of the straight line method over the property's earnings and profits life under paragraphs (d)(1) and (2) of this section does not have any effect on the proper method of cost recovery for other recovery property of that same class placed in service in the same taxable year by the taxpayer and does not constitute an election to use an optional recovery period under section 168(b)(3).

(d) Recapture of excess recovery deductions claimed—(1) In general. If paragraph (c)(2) of this section is applicable, any excess depreciation (as defined in paragraph (d)(2) of this section) must be included in the taxpayer's gross income and added to the property's adjusted basis for the first taxable year in which the property is not predominantly used in a qualified business use (as defined in §1.280F–6 (d)(4)).

(2) Definition of "excess depreciation". For purposes of this section, the term "excess depreciation" means the excess (if any) of—

(i) The amount of the recovery deductions allowable with respect to the property for taxable years before the first taxable year in which the property was not predominantly used in a qualified business use, over

(ii) The amount of the recovery deductions which would have been allowable for those years if the property had not been predominantly used in a qualified business use for the year it was acquired and there had been no section 179 election with respect to the property.

For purposes of paragraph (d)(2)(i), any deduction allowable under section 179 (relating to the election to expense certain depreciable trade or business assets) is treated as if that deduction was a recovery deduction under section 168.

(3) Recordkeeping requirement. A taxpayer must be able to substantiate the use of any listed property, as prescribed in section 274(d)(4) and §1.274–5T or §1.274–6T, for any taxable year for which recapture under section 280F(b)(3) and paragraph (d)(1) and (2) of this section may occur even if the taxpayer has fully depreciated (or expensed) the listed property in a prior year. For example, in the case of 3-year recovery property, the taxpayer shall maintain a log, journal, etc. for six years even though the taxpayer fully depreciated the property in the first three years.

* * *

§ 1.280F–4T Special rules for listed property (temporary).

(a) Limitations on allowable recovery deductions in subsequent taxable years—(1) Subsequent taxable years affected by reason of personal use in prior years. For purposes of computing the amount of the recovery deduction for "listed property" for a subsequent taxable year, the amount that would have been allowable as a recovery deduction during an earlier taxable year if all of the use of the property was use described in section 168(c) is treated as the amount of the recovery deduction allowable during that earlier taxable year. The preceding sentence applies with respect to all earlier taxable years, beginning with the first taxable year in which some or all use of the "listed property" is use described in section 168(c). For example, on July 1, 1984, B purchases and places in service listed property (other than a passenger automobile) which is 5-year recovery property under section 168. B selects the use of the accelerated percentages under section 168. B's business/investment use of the property (all of which is qualified business use as defined in section 280F(d)(6)(B) and §1.280F–6(d)(2)) in 1984 through 1988 is 80 percent, 70 percent, 60 percent, and 55 percent, respectively, and B claims recovery deductions for those years based on those percentages. B's qualified business use for the property for 1989 and taxable years thereafter increases to 100 percent. Pursuant to this rule, B may not claim a recovery deduction in 1989 (or for any subsequent taxable year) for the increase in business use because there is no adjusted basis remaining to be recovered for cost recovery purposes after 1988.

(2) Special rule for passenger automobiles. In the case of a passenger automobile that is subject to the limitations of §1.280F–2T, the amount treated as the amount that would have been allowable as a recovery deduction if all of the use of the automobile was use described in section 168(c) shall not exceed $4,000* for the year the passenger automobile is placed in service and $6,000* for each succeeding taxable year (adjusted to account for the automobile price inflation adjustment, if any, under section 280F(d)(7) and for short taxable year under §1.280F–2T(i)(2)). See, §1.280F–3T(g), Example (8).

(b) Treatment of improvements that qualify as capital expenditures—(1) In general. In the case of any improvement that qualifies as a capital expenditure under section 263 made to any listed property other than a passenger automobile, the rules of this paragraph (b) apply. See §1.280F–2T(f) for the treatment of an improvement made to a passenger automobile.

(2) Investment tax credit allowed for the improvement. If the improvement qualifies as an investment in new section 38 property under section 48(b) and §1.48–2(b), the investment tax credit for that improvement is limited by paragraph (b)(1) of §1.280F–3T, as applied to the item of listed property as a whole.

(3) Cost recovery of the improvement. The improvement is treated as a new item of recovery property. The method of cost recovery with respect to that improvement is limited by §1.280F–3T(c), as applied to the item of listed property as a whole.

* * *

§ 1.280F–6 Special rules and definitions.

(a) Deductions of employee—(1) In general. Employee use of listed property shall not be treated as business/investment use (as defined in paragraph (d)(3) of this section) for purposes of determining the amount of any credit allowable under section 38 to the employee or the amount of any recovery deduction allowable (including any deduction under section 179) to the employee unless that use is for the convenience of the employer and required as a condition of employment.

(2) "Convenience of the employer" and "condition of employment" requirements—(i) In general. The terms "convenience of the employer" and "condition of employment" generally have the same

*Editorial comment: See Sec. 280F(a)(1) for the revised amounts, which are subject to indexing, per the Tax Reform Act of 1986.

meaning for purposes of section 280F as they have for purposes of section 119 (relating to the exclusion from gross income for meals or lodging furnished for the convenience of the employer).

(ii) "Condition of employment". In order to satisfy the "condition of employment" requirement, the use of the property must be required in order for the employee to perform the duties of his or her employment properly. Whether the use of the property is so required depends on all the facts and circumstances. Thus, the employer need not explicitly require the employee to use the property. Similarly, a mere statement by the employer that the use of the property is a condition of employment is not sufficient.

(iii) "Convenience of employer". [Reserved]

(3) Employee use. For purposes of this section, the term "employee use" means any use in connection with the performance of services by the employee as an employee.

(4) Examples. The principles of this paragraph are illustrated in the following examples:

Example (1). A is employed as a courier with W, which provides local courier services. A owns and uses a motorcycle to deliver packages to downtown offices for W. W does not provide delivery vehicles and explicitly requires all of its couriers to own a car or motorcycle for use in their employment with the company. A's use of the motorcycle for delivery purposes is for the convenience of W and is required as a condition of employment.

Example (2). B is an inspector for X, a construction company with many construction sites in the local area. B is required to travel to the various construction sites on a regular basis; B uses her automobile to make these trips. Although X does not furnish B an automobile, X does not explicitly require B to use her own automobile. However, X reimburses B for any costs she incurs in traveling to the various job sites. B's use of her automobile in her employment is for the convenience of X and is required as a condition of employment.

Example (3). Assume the same facts as in example (2), except that X makes an automobile available to B who chooses to use her own automobile and receive reimbursement. B's use of her own automobile is not for the convenience of X and is not required as a condition of employment.

Example (4). C is a pilot for Y, a small charter airline. Y requires its pilots to obtain × hours of flight time annually in addition to the number of hours of flight time spent with the airline. Pilots can usually obtain these hours by flying with a military reserve unit or by flying part-time with another airline. C owns his own airplane. C's use of his airplane to obtain the required flight hours is not for the convenience of the employer and is not required as a condition of employment.

Example (5). D is employed as an engineer with Z, an engineering contracting firm. D occasionally takes work home at night rather than working late in the office. D owns and uses a computer which is virtually identical to the one she uses at the office to complete her work at home. D's use of the computer is not for the convenience of her employer and is not required as a condition of employment.

(b) Listed property—(1) In general. Except as otherwise provided in paragraph (b)(5) of this section, the term "listed property" means—

(i) Any passenger automobile (as defined in paragraph (c) of this section),

(ii) Any other property used as a means of transportation (as defined in paragraph (b)(2) of this section),

(iii) Any property of a type generally used for purposes of entertainment, recreation, or amusement, and

(iv) Any computer or peripheral equipment (as defined in section 168(i)(2)), and

(v) Any other property specified in paragraph (b)(4) of this section.

(2) "Means of transportation"—(i) In general. Except as otherwise provided in paragraph (b)(2)(ii) of this section, property used as a "means of transportation" includes trucks, buses, trains, boats, airplanes, motorcycles, and any other vehicles for transporting persons or goods.

(ii) Exception. The term "listed property" does not include any vehicle that is a qualified nonpersonal use vehicle as defined in section 274(i) and §1.274–5T(k).

(3) Property used for entertainment, etc.—(i) In general. Property of a type generally used for purposes of entertainment, recreation, or amusement includes property such as photographic, phonographic, communication, and video recording equipment.

(ii) Exception. The term "listed property" does not include any photographic, phonographics, communication, or video recording equipment of a taxpayer if the equipment is used either exclusively at the taxpayer's regular business establishment or in connection with the taxpayer's principal trade or business.

(iii) Regular business establishment. The regular business establishment of an employee is the regular business establishment of the employer of the employee. For purposes of this paragraph (b)(3), a portion of a dwelling unit is treated as a regular business establishment if the requirements of section 280A(c)(1) are met with respect to that portion.

(4) Other property. [Reserved]

(5) Exception for computers. The term "listed property" shall not include any computer (including peripheral equipment) used exclusively at a regular business establishment. For purposes of the preceding sentence, a portion of a dwelling unit shall be treated as a regular business establishment if (and only if) the requirements of section 280A(c)(1) are met with respect to that portion.

(c) Passenger automobile—(1) In general. Except as provided in paragraph (c)(3) of this section, the term "passenger automobile" means any 4-wheeled vehicle which is—

(i) Manufactured primarily for use on public streets, roads, and highways, and

(ii) Rated at 6,000 pounds gross vehicle weight or less.*

(2) Parts, etc. of automobile. The term "passenger automobile" includes any part, component, or other item that is physically attached to the automobile or is traditionally included in the purchase price of an automobile. The term does not include repairs that are not capital expenditures within the meaning of section 263.

(3) Exception for certain vehicles. The term "passenger automobile" shall not include any—

(i) Ambulance, hearse, or combination ambulance–hearse used by the taxpayer directly in a trade or business,

(ii) Vehicle used by the taxpayer directly in the trade or business of transporting persons or property for compensation or hire, or

(iii) Truck or van that is a qualified nonpersonal use vehicle as defined in §1.274–5T(k).

(d) Business use percentage—(1) In general. The term "business use percentage" means the percentage of the use of any listed property which is qualified business use as described in paragraph (d)(2) of this section.

(2) Qualified business use—(i) In general. Except as provided in paragraph (d)(2)(ii) of this section, the term "qualified business use" means any use in a trade or business of the taxpayer. The term "qualified business use" does not include use for which a deduction is allowable under section 212. Whether the amount of qualified business use exceeds 50 percent is determinative of whether the investment tax credit and the accelerated percentages under section 168 are available for listed property (or must be recaptured). See §1.280F–3T.

(ii) Exception for certain use by 5-percent owners and related persons—**(A)** In general. The term "qualified business use" shall not include—

(1) Leasing property to any 5-percent owner or related person,

(2) Use of property provided as compensation for the performance of services by a 5-percent owner or related person, or

(3) Use of property provided as compensation for the performance of services by any person not described in paragraph (d)(2)(ii)(A)(2) of this section unless an amount is properly reported by the taxpayer as income to such person and, where required, there was withholding under chapter 24.

Paragraph (d)(2)(ii)(A)(1) of this section shall apply only to the extent that the use of the listed property is by an individual who is a related party or a 5-percent owner with respect to the owner or lessee of the property.

(B) Special rule for aircraft. Paragraph (d)(2)(ii)(A) of this section shall not apply with respect to any aircraft if at least 25 percent of the total use of the aircraft during the taxable year consists of qualified business use not described in paragraph (d)(2)(ii)(A).

(C) Definitions. For purposes of this paragraph—

(1) 5-percent owner. The term "5-percent owner" means any person who is a 5-percent owner with respect to the taxpayer (as defined in section 416(i)(1)(B)(i)).

(2) Related person. The term "related person" means any person related to the taxpayer (within the meaning of section 267(b)).

(3) Business/investment use—(i) In general. The term "business/investment use" means the total business or investment use of listed property that may be taken into account for purposes of computing (without regard to section 280F(b)) the percentage of investment tax credit or cost recovery deduction for a passenger automobile or other listed property for the

*Editorial comment: The Regulations do not reflect the revised statutory language per the Tax Reform Act of 1986. See Sec. 280F (d)(5)(A).

taxable year. Whether the investment tax credit and the accelerated percentages under section 168 (as opposed to use of the straight line method of cost recovery) are available with respect to listed property or must be recaptured is determined, however, by reference to qualified business use (as defined in paragraph (d)(2) of this section) rather than by reference to business/investment use. Whether a particular use of property is a business or investment use shall generally be determined under the rules of section 162 or 212.

(ii) Entertainment use. The use of listed property for entertainment, recreation, or amusement purposes shall be treated as business use to the extent that expenses (other than interest and property tax expenses) attributable to that use are deductible after application of section 274.

(iii) Employee use. See paragraph (a) of this section for requirements to be satisfied for employee use of listed property to be considered business/investment use of the property.

(iv) Use of taxpayer's automobile by another person. Any use of the taxpayer's automobile by another person shall not be treated, for purposes of section 280F, as use in a trade or business under section 162 unless that use—

(A) Is directly connected with the business of the taxpayer,

(B) Is properly reported by the taxpayer as income to the other person and, where required, there was withholding under chapter 24, or

(C) Results in a payment of fair market rent.

For purposes of this paragraph (d)(4)(iv)(C), payment to the owner of the automobile in connection with such use is treated as the payment of rent.

(4) Predominantly used in qualified business use—(i) Definition. Property is predominantly used in a qualified business use for any taxable year if the business use percentage (as defined in paragraph (d)(1) of this section) is greater than 50 percent.

(ii) Special rule for transfers at death. Property does not cease to be used predominantly in a qualified business use by reason of a transfer at death.

(iii) Other dispositions of property. [Reserved]

(5) Examples. The following examples illustrate the principles set forth in this paragraph.

Example (1). E uses a home computer 50 percent of the time to manage her investments. The computer is listed property within the meaning of section 280F(d)(4). E also uses the computer 40 percent of the time in her part-time consumer research business. Because E's business use percentage for the computer does not exceed 50 percent, the computer is not predominantly used in a qualified business use for the taxable year. Her aggregate business/investment use for purposes of determining the percent of the total allowable straight line depreciation that she can claim is 90 percent.

Example (2). Assume that E in example (1) uses the computer 30 percent of the time to manage her investments and 60 percent of the time in her consumer research business. E's business use percentage exceeds 50 percent. Her aggregate business/investment use for purposes of determining her allowable investment tax credit and cost recovery deductions is 90 percent.

Example (3). F is the proprietor of a plumbing contracting business. F's brother is employed with F's company. As part of his compensation, F's brother is allowed to use one of the company automobiles for personal use. The use of the company automobiles by F's brother is not a qualified business use because F and F's brother are related parties within the meaning of section 267(b).

Example (4). F, in example (3), allows employees unrelated to him to use company automobiles as part of their compensation. F, however, does not include the value of these automobiles in the employees' gross income and F does not withhold with respect to the use of these automobiles. The use of the company automobiles by the employees in this case is not business/investment use.

Example (5). X Corporation owns several automobiles which its employees use for business purposes. The employees are also allowed to take the automobiles home at night. However, the fair market value of the use of the automobile for any personal purpose, e.g., commuting to work, is reported by X as income to the employee and is withheld upon by X. The use of the automobile by the employee, even for personal purposes, is a qualified business use with respect to X.

(e) Method of allocating use of property—(1) In general. For purposes of section 280F, the taxpayer shall allocate the use of any listed property that is used for more than one purpose during the taxable year to the various uses in the manner prescribed in paragraph (e)(2) and (3) of this section.

(2) Passenger automobiles and other means of transportation. In the case of a passenger automobile or any other means of transportation, the taxpayer shall allocate the use of the property on the basis of mileage. Thus, the percentage of use in a trade or business for the year shall be determined by dividing the number of miles the vehicle is driven for purposes of that trade or business during the year by the total number of miles the vehicle is driven during the year for any purpose.

(3) Other listed property. In the case of other listed property, the taxpayer shall allocate the use of that property on the basis of the most appropriate unit of time the property is actually used (rather than merely being available for use). For example, the percentage of use of a computer in a trade or business for a taxable year is determined by dividing the number of hours the computer is used for business purposes during the year by the total number of hours the computer is used for any purpose during the year.

* * *

§ 1.280H–1T Limitation on certain amounts paid to employee-owners by personal service corporations electing alternative taxable years (temporary).

(a) Introduction. This section applies to any taxable year that a personal service corporation has a section 444 election in effect (an "applicable election year"). For purposes of this section, the term "personal service corporation" has the same meaning given such term in §1.441–4T(d).

(b) Limitation on certain deductions of personal service corporations—(1) In general. If, for any applicable election year, a personal service corporation does not satisfy the minimum distribution requirement in paragraph (c) of this section, the deduction otherwise allowable under chapter 1 of the Internal Revenue Code of 1986 (the Code) for applicable amounts, as defined in paragraph (b)(4) of this section, shall not exceed the maximum deductible amount, as defined in paragraph (d) of this section.

(2) Carryover of nondeductible amounts. Any amount not allowed as a deduction in an applicable election year under paragraph (b)(1) of this section shall be allowed as a deduction in the succeeding taxable year.

(3) Disallowance inapplicable for certain purposes. The disallowance of deductions under paragraph (b)(1) of this section shall not apply for purposes of subchapter G of chapter 1 of the Code (relating to corporations used to avoid income tax on shareholders) nor for determining whether the compensation of employee-owners is reasonable. Thus, for example, in determining whether a personal service corporation is subject to the accumulated earnings tax imposed by section 531, deductions disallowed under paragraph (b)(1) of this section are treated as allowed in computing accumulated taxable income.

(4) Definition of applicable amount—(i) In general. For purposes of section 280H and the regulations thereunder, the term "applicable amount" means, with respect to a taxable year, any amount that is otherwise deductible by a personal service corporation in such year and includible at any time, directly or indirectly, in the gross income of a taxpayer that during such year is an employee-owner. Thus, an amount includible in the gross income of an employee-owner will be considered an applicable amount even though such employee owns no stock of the corporation on the date the employee includes the amount in income. See example (1) in paragraph (b)(4)(iii) of this section.

(ii) Special rule for certain indirect payments. For purposes of paragraph (b)(4)(i) of this section, amounts are indirectly includible in the gross income of an employee-owner of a personal service corporation that has made a section 444 election (an electing personal service corporation) if the amount is includible in the gross income of—

(A) The spouse (other than a spouse who is legally separated from the partner or shareholder under a decree of divorce or separate maintenance) or child (under age 14) of such employee-owner, or

(B) A corporation more than 50 percent (measured by fair market value) of which is owned in the aggregate by employee-owners (and individuals related under paragraph (b)(4)(ii)(A) of this section to such employee-owners), of the electing personal service corporation, or

(C) A partnership more than 50 percent of the profits and capital of which is owned by employee-owners (and individuals related under paragraph (b)(4)(ii)(A) of this section to such employee-owners) of the electing personal service corporation, or

(D) A trust more than 50 percent of the beneficial ownership of which is owned in the aggregate by employee-owners (and individuals related under paragraph (b)(4)(ii)(A) of this section to any such employee-owners), of the electing personal service corporation.

For purposes of this paragraph (b)(4)(ii), ownership by any person described in this paragraph (b)(4)(ii) shall be treated as ownership by the employee-owners of the electing personal service corporation. Paragraph (b)(4)(ii)(B) of this section will not apply if the corporation has made a section 444 election to use the same taxable year as that of the electing personal service corporation. Similarly, paragraph (b)(4)(ii)(C) of this section will not apply if the partnership has made a section 444 election to use the same taxable year as that of the electing personal service corporation. Notwithstanding the general effective date provision of paragraph (f) of this section, this paragraph (b)(4)(ii) is effective for amounts deductible on or after June 1, 1988.

(iii) Example. The provisions of paragraph (b)(4) of this section may be illustrated by the following examples.

Example (1). A is an employee of P, an accrual basis personal service corporation with a taxable year ending September 30. P makes a section 444 election for its taxable year beginning October 1, 1987. On October 1, 1987, A owns no stock of P; However, on March 31, 1988, A acquires 10 of the 200 outstanding shares of P stock. During the period October 1, 1987 to March 31, 1988, A earned $40,000 of compensation as an employee of P. During the period April 1, 1988 to September 30, 1988, A earned $60,000 of compensation as an employee-owner of P. If paragraph (b) of this section does not apply, P would deduct for its taxable year ended September 30, 1988 the $100,000 earned by A during such year. Based upon these facts, the $100,000 otherwise deductible amount is considered an applicable amount under this section.

Example (2). I1 and 12, calendar year individuals, are employees of PSC1, a personal service corporation that has historically used a taxable year ending January 31. I1 and 12 also own all the stock, and are employees, of PSC2, a calendar year personal service corporation. For its taxable years beginning February 1, 1987, 1988, and 1989, PSC1 has a section 444 election in effect to use a January 31 taxable year. During its taxable years beginning February 1, 1986, 1987, and 1988, PSC1 deducted $10,000, $11,000, and $12,000, respectively, that was included in PSC2's gross income. Furthermore, of the $12,000 deducted by PSC1 for its taxable year beginning February 1, 1988, $7,000 was deducted during the period June 1, 1988 to January 31, 1989. Pursuant to paragraph (b)(4)(ii)(B) of this section, the $7,000 deducted by PSC1 on or after June 1, 1988, and included in PSC2's gross income is considered an applicable amount for PSC1's taxable year beginning February 1, 1988. Amounts deducted by PSC1 prior to June 1, 1988, are not subject to paragraph (b)(4)(ii)(B) of this section.

Example (3). The facts are the same as in example (2), except that for its taxable years beginning February 1, 1987, 1988, and 1989, PSC2 has a section 444 election in effect to use a January 31 taxable year. Since both PSC1 and PSC2 have the same taxable year and both have section 444 elections in effect, paragraph (b)(4)(ii)(B) of this section does not apply to the $7,000 deducted by PSC1 for its taxable year beginning February 1, 1988.

(c) Minimum distribution requirement—(1) Determination of whether requirement satisfied—(i) In general. A personal service corporation meets the minimum distribution requirement of this paragraph (c) for an applicable election year if, during the deferral period of such taxable year, the applicable amounts (determined without regard to paragraph (b)(2) of this section) for all employee-owners in the aggregate equal or exceed the lesser of—

(A) The amount determined under the "preceding year test" (see paragraph (c)(2) of this section), or

(B) The amount determined under the "3-year average test" (see paragraph (c)(3) of this section).

The following example illustrates the application of this paragraph (c)(1)(i).

Example. Q, an accrual-basis personal service corporation, makes a section 444 election to retain a year ending January 31 for its taxable year beginning February 1, 1987. Q has 4 employee-owners, B, C, D, and E. For Q's applicable election year beginning February 1, 1987 and ending January 31, 1988, B earns $6,000 a month plus a $45,000 bonus on January 15, 1988; C earns $5,000 a month plus a $40,000 bonus on January 15, 1988; D and E each earn $4,500 a month plus a $4,000 bonus on January 15, 1988. Q meets the minimum distribution requirement for such applicable election year if the applicable amounts during the deferral period (i.e., $220,000) equal or exceed the amount determined under the preceding year test or the 3-year average test.

(ii) Employee-owner defined. For purposes of section 280H and the regulations thereunder, a person is an employee-owner of a corporation for a taxable year if—

(A) On any day of the corporation's taxable year, the person is an employee of the corporation or performs personal services for or on behalf of the corporation, even if the legal form of that person's relationship to the corporation is that of an independent contractor, and

(B) On any day of the corporation's taxable year, the person owns any outstanding stock of the corporation.

(2) Preceding year test—(i) In general. The amount determined under the preceding year test is the product of—

(A) The applicable amounts during the taxable year preceding the applicable election year (the "preceding taxable year"), divided by the number of months (but not less than one) in the preceding taxable year, multiplied by

(B) The number of months in the deferral period of the applicable election year.

(ii) Example. The provisions of paragraph (c)(2) of this section may be illustrated by the following example.

Example. R, a personal service corporation, has historically used a taxable year ending January 31. For its taxable year beginning February 1, 1987, R makes a section 444 election to retain its January 31 taxable year. R is an accrual basis taxpayer and has one employee-owner, F. For R's taxable year ending January 31, 1987, F earns $5,000 a month plus a $40,000 bonus on January 15, 1987. The amount determined under the preceding year test for R's applicable election year beginning February 1, 1987 is $91,667 ($100,000, the applicable amounts during R's taxable year ending January 31, 1987, divided by 12, the number of months in R's taxable year ending January 31, 1987, multiplied by 11, the number of months in R's deferral period for such year).

(3) 3-year average test—(i) In general. The amount determined under the 3-year average test is the applicable percentage multiplied by the adjusted taxable income for the deferral period of the applicable election year.

(ii) Applicable percentage. The term "applicable percentage" means the percentage (not in excess of 95 percent) determined by dividing—

(A) The applicable amounts during the 3 taxable years of the corporation (or, if fewer, the taxable years the corporation has been in existence) immediately preceding the applicable election year, by

(B) The adjusted taxable income of such corporation for such 3 taxable years (or, if fewer, the taxable years of existence).

(iii) Adjusted taxable income—(A) In general. The term "adjusted taxable income" means taxable income determined without regard to applicable amounts.

(B) Determination of adjusted taxable income for the deferral period of the applicable election year. Adjusted taxable income for the deferral period of the applicable election year equals the adjusted taxable income that would result if the personal service corporation filed an income tax return for the deferral period of the applicable election year under its normal method of accounting. However, a personal service corporation may make a reasonable estimate of such amount.

(C) NOL carryovers. For purposes of determining adjusted taxable income for any period, any NOL carryover shall be reduced by the amount of such carryover that is attributable to the deduction of applicable amounts. The portion of the NOL carryover attributable to the deduction of applicable amounts is the difference between the NOL carryover computed with the deduction of such amounts and the NOL carryover computed without the deduction of such amounts. For purposes of determining the adjusted taxable income for the deferral period, an NOL carryover to the applicable election year, reduced as provided in this paragraph (c)(3)(iii)(C), shall be allowed first against the income of the deferral period.

(D) Examples. The provisions of this paragraph (c)(3)(iii) may be illustrated by the following examples.

Example (1). S is a personal service corporation that has historically used a taxable year ending January 31. For its taxable year beginning February 1, 1987, S makes a section 444 election to retain its taxable year ending January 31. S does not satisfy the minimum distribution requirement for its first applicable election year, and the applicable amounts for that year exceed the maximum deductible amount by $54,000. Under paragraph (b)(2) of this section, the $54,000 excess is carried over to S's taxable year beginning February 1, 1988. Furthermore, if S continues its section 444 election for its taxable year beginning February 1, 1988, and desires to use the 3-year average test provided in this paragraph for such year, pursuant to paragraph (c)(3)(iii)(A) of this section the $54,000 will not be allowed to reduce adjusted taxable income for such year. See also section 280H(e) regarding the disallowance of net operating loss carrybacks to (or from) any taxable year of a corporation personal service election under section 444 applies.

Example (2). T, a personal service corporation with a section 444 election in effect, is determining whether it satisfies the 3-year average test for its second applicable election year. T had a net operating loss (NOL) for its first applicable election year of $45,000. The NOL resulted from $150,000 of gross income less the sum of $96,000 of salary, $45,000 of other expenses, and $54,000 of deductible applicable amounts. Pursuant to paragraph (c)(3)(iii)(C) of this section, the entire amount of the $45,000 NOL is attributable to applicable amounts since the applicable amounts deducted in arriving at the NOL (i.e., $54,000) were greater than the NOL (i.e., $45,000). Thus, for purposes of computing the adjusted taxable income for the deferral period of T's second applicable election year, the NOL carryover to that year is $0 ($45,000 NOL less $45,000 amount of NOL attributable to applicable amounts).

(d) Maximum deductible amount—(1) In general. For purposes of this section, the term "maximum deductible amount" means the sum of—

(i) The applicable amounts during the deferral period of the applicable election year, plus

(ii) An amount equal to the product of—

(A) The amount determined under paragraph (d)(1)(i) of this section divided by the number of months in the deferral period of the applicable election year, multiplied by

(B) The number of months in the nondeferral period of the applicable election year. For purposes of the preceding sentence, the term "nondeferral period" means the portion of the applicable election year that occurs after the portion of such year constituting the deferral period.

(2) Example. The provisions of paragraph (d)(1) of this section may be illustrated by the following example.

Example. U, an accrual basis personal service corporation with a taxable year ending January 31, makes a section 444 election to retain a year ending January 31 for its taxable year beginning February 1, 1987. For its applicable election year beginning February 1, 1987, U does not satisfy the minimum distribution requirement in paragraph (c) of this section. Furthermore, U has 3 employee-owners, G, H, and I. G and H have been employee–owners of U for 10 years. Although I has been an employee of U for 4 years, I did not become an employee–owner until December 1, 1987, when I acquired 5 of the 20 outstanding shares of U stock. For U's applicable election year beginning February 1, 1987, G earns $5,000 a month plus a $40,000 bonus on January 15, 1988, and H and I each earn $4,000 a month plus a $32,000 bonus on January 15, 1988. Thus, the total of the applicable amounts during the deferral period of the applicable election year beginning February 1, 1987 is $143,000. Based on these facts, U's deduction for applicable amounts is limited to $156,000, determined as follows—$143,000 (applicable amounts during the deferral period) plus $13,000 (applicable amounts during the deferral period, divided by the number of months in the deferral period, multiplied by the number of months in the nondeferral period).

(e) Special rules and definition—(1) Newly organized personal service corporations. A personal service corporation is deemed to satisfy the preceding year test and the 3-year average test for the first year of the corporation's existence.

(2) Existing corporations that become personal service corporations. If an existing corporation becomes a personal service corporation and makes a section 444 election, the determination of whether the corporation satisfies the preceding year test and the 3-year average test is made by treating the corporation as though it were a personal service corporation for each of the 3 years preceding the applicable election year.

(3) Disallowance of NOL carryback. No net operating loss carryback shall be allowed to (or from) any applicable election year of a personal service corporation.

(4) Deferral period. For purposes of section 280H and the regulations thereunder, the term "deferral period" has the same meaning as under §1.444–1T(b)(4).

(5) Examples. The provisions of this paragraph (e) may be illustrated by the following examples.

Example (1). V is a personal service corporation with a taxable year ending September 30. V makes a section 444 election for its taxable year beginning October 1, 1987, and incurs a net operating loss (NOL) for such year. Because an NOL is not allowed to be carried back from an applicable election year, V may not carry back the NOL from its first applicable election year to reduce its 1985, 1986, or 1987 taxable income.

Example (2). W, a personal service corporation, commences operations on July 1, 1990. Furthermore, for its taxable year beginning July 1, 1990, W makes a section 444 election to use a year ending September 30. Pursuant to paragraph (e)(1) of this section, W satisfies the preceding year test and the 3-year average test for its first year in existence. Thus, W may deduct, without limitation under this section, any applicable amounts for its taxable year beginning July 1, 1990.

Example (3). The facts are the same as in example (2). For its taxable year beginning October 1, 1990, W incurs an NOL and is not a personal service corporation. Furthermore, W desires to carry back the NOL to its preceding taxable year (a year that was an applicable election year). Pursuant to paragraph (e)(3) of this section, W may not carry back an NOL "to" its taxable year beginning July 1, and ending September 30, 1990, because such year was an applicable election year.

* * *

CORPORATE DISTRIBUTIONS AND ADJUSTMENTS

Distributions by Corporations

Effects on Recipients

§ 1.301–1 Rules applicable with respect to distributions of money and other property.

(a) General. Section 301 provides the general rule for treatment of distributions on or after June 22, 1954, of property by a corporation to a shareholder with respect to its stock. The term "property" is defined in section 317(a). Such distributions, except as otherwise provided in this chapter, shall be treated as provided in section 301(c). Under section 301(c), distributions may be included in gross income, applied against and reduce the adjusted basis of the stock, treated as gain from the sale or exchange of property, or (in the case of certain distributions out of increase in value accrued before March 1, 1913) may be exempt from tax. The amount of the distributions to which section 301 applies is determined in accordance with the provisions of section 301(b). The basis of property received in a distribution to which section 301 applies is determined in accordance with the provisions of section 301(d). Accordingly, except as otherwise provided in this chapter, a distribution on or after June 22, 1954, of property by a corporation to a shareholder with respect to its stock shall be included in gross income to the extent the amount distributed is considered a dividend under section 316. For examples of distributions treated otherwise, see sections 116, 301(c)(2), 301(c)(3)(B), 301(e), 302(b), 303, and 305. See also part II (relating to distributions in partial or complete liquidation), part III (relating to corporate organizations and reorganizations), and part IV (relating to insolvency reorganizations), subchapter C, chapter 1 of the Code.

(b) Time of inclusion in gross income and of determination of fair market value. A distribution made by a corporation to its shareholders shall be included in the gross income of the distributees when the cash or other property is unqualifiedly made subject to their demands. However, if such distribution is a distribution other than in cash, the fair market value of the property shall be determined as of the date of distribution without regard to whether such date is the same as that on which the distribution is includible in gross income. For example, if a corporation distributes a taxable dividend in property (the adjusted basis of which exceeds its fair market value on December 31, 1955) on December 31, 1955, which is received by, or unqualifiedly made subject to the demand of, its shareholders on January 2, 1956, the amount to be included in the gross income of the shareholders will be the fair market value of such property on December 31, 1955, although such amount will not be includible in the gross income of the shareholders until January 2, 1956.

(c) Application of section to shareholders. Section 301 is not applicable to an amount paid by a corporation to a shareholder unless the amount is paid to the shareholder in his capacity as such.

(d) Distributions to corporate shareholders. **(1)** If the shareholder is a corporation, the amount of any distribution to be taken into account under section 301(c) shall be:

(i) The amount of money distributed,

(ii) An amount equal to the fair market value of any property distributed which consists of any obligations of the distributing corporation, stock of the distributing corporation treated as property under section 305(b), or rights to acquire such stock treated as property under section 305(b), plus

(iii) In the case of a distribution not described in subdivision (iv) of this subparagraph, an amount equal to (a) the fair market value of any other property distributed or, if lesser, (b) the adjusted basis of such other property in the hands of the distributing corporation (determined immediately before the distribution and increased for any gain recognized to the distributing corporation under section 311(b), (c), or (d), or under section 341(f), 617(d), 1245(a), 1250(a), 1251(c), 1252(a), or 1254(a)), or

* * *

(2) In the case of a distribution the amount of which is determined by reference to the adjusted basis described in subparagraph (1)(iii)(b) of this paragraph:

(i) That portion of the distribution which is a dividend under section 301(c)(1) may not exceed such adjusted basis, or

(ii) If the distribution is not out of earnings and profits, the amount of the reduction in basis of the shareholder's stock, and the amount of any gain resulting from such distribution, are to be determined by reference to such adjusted basis of the property which is distributed.

* * *

(e) Adjusted basis. In determining the adjusted basis of property distributed in the hands of the distributing corporation immediately before the distribution for purposes of section 301(b)(1)(B)(ii), (b)(1) (C)(i), and (d)(2)(B), the basis to be used shall be the basis for determining gain upon a sale or exchange.

(f) Examples. The application of this section (except paragraph (n)) may be illustrated by the following examples:

Example (1). On January 1, 1955, A, an individual owned all of the stock of Corporation M with an adjusted basis of $2,000. During 1955, A received distributions from Corporation M totaling $30,000, consisting of $10,000 in cash and listed securities having a basis in the hands of Corporation M and a fair market value on the date distributed of $20,000. Corporation M's taxable year is the calendar year. As of December 31, 1954, Corporation M had earnings and profits accumulated after February 28, 1913, in the amount of $26,000, and it had no earnings and profits and no deficit for 1955. Of the $30,000 received by A, $26,000 will be treated as an ordinary dividend; the remaining $4,000 will be applied against the adjusted basis of his stock; the $2,000 in excess of the adjusted basis of his stock will either be treated as gain from the sale or exchange of property (under section 301(c)(3)(A)) or, if out of increase in value accrued before March 1, 1913, will (under section 301(c)(3)(B)) be exempt from tax. If A subsequently sells his stock in Corporation M, the basis for determining gain or loss on the sale will be zero.

Example (2). The facts are the same as in Example 1 with the exceptions that the shareholder of Corporation M is Corporation W and that the securities which were distributed had an adjusted basis to Corporation M of $15,000. The distribution received by Corporation W totals $25,000 consisting of $10,000 in cash and securities with an adjusted basis of $15,000. The total $25,000 will be treated as a dividend to Corporation W since the earnings and profits of Corporation M ($26,000) are in excess of the amount of the distribution.

* * *

(g) Reduction for liabilities.—

(1) General rule. For the purpose of section 301, no reduction shall be made for the amount of any liability, unless the liability is assumed by the shareholder within the meaning of section 357(d)

(2) No reduction below zero. Any reduction pursuant to paragraph (g)(1) of this section shall not cause the amount of the distribution to be reduced below zero.

* * *

(h) Basis. The basis of property received in the distribution to which section 301 applies shall be—

(1) If the shareholder is not a corporation, the fair market value of such property;

(2) If the shareholder is a corporation—

(i) In the case of a distribution of the obligations of the distributing corporation or of the stock of such corporation or rights to acquire such stock (if such stock or rights are treated as property under section 305(b)), the fair market value of such obligations, stock, or rights;

(ii) In the case of the distribution of any other property, except as provided in subdivision (iii) (relating to certain distributions by a foreign corporation) or subdivision (iv) (relating to certain distributions to foreign corporate distributees) of this subparagraph, whichever of the following is the lesser—

(a) The fair market value of such property; or

(b) The adjusted basis (in the hands of the distributing corporation immediately before the distribution) of such property increased in the amount of gain to the distributing corporation which is recognized under section 311 (b) (relating to distributions of LIFO inventory), section 311(c) (relating to distributions of property subject to liabilities in excess of basis), section 311(d) (relating to appreciated property used to redeem stock), section 341(f) (relating to certain sales of stock of consenting corporations), section 617(d) (relating to gain from dispositions of certain mining property), section 1245(a) or 1250(a) (relating to gain from dispositions of certain depreciable property), section 1251(c) (relating to gain from disposition of farm recapture property), section 1252(a) (relating to gain from disposition of farm land), or section 1254(a) (relating to gain from disposition of interest in natural resource recapture property);

* * *

(j) Transfers for less than fair market value. If property is transferred by a corporation to a shareholder which is not a corporation for an amount less than its fair market value in a sale or exchange, such shareholder shall be treated as having received a distribution to which section 301 applies. In such case, the amount of the distribution shall be the difference between the amount paid for the property and its fair market value. If property is transferred in a sale or exchange by a corporation to a shareholder which is a corporation, for an amount less than its fair market value and also less than its adjusted basis, such shareholder shall be treated as having received a distribution to which section 301 applies, and—

(1) Where the fair market value of the property equals or exceeds its adjusted basis in the hands of the distributing corporation the amount of the distribution shall be the excess of the adjusted basis (increased by the amount of gain recognized under section 311(b), (c), or (d), or under section 341(f), 617(d), 1245(a), 1250(a), 1251(c), 1252(a), or 1254(a) to the distributing corporation) over the amount paid for the property;

(2) Where the fair market value of the property is less than its adjusted basis in the hands of the distributing corporation, the amount of the distribution shall be the excess of such fair market value over the amount paid for the property.* * *

(k) Application of rule respecting transfers for less than fair market value. The application of paragraph (j) of this section may be illustrated by the following examples:

Example (1). On January 1, 1955, A, an individual shareholder of corporation X, purchased property from that corporation for $20. The fair market value of such property was $100, and its basis in the hands of corporation X was $25. The amount of the distribution determined under section 301(b) is $80. If A were a corporation, the amount of the distribution would be $5 (assuming that sections 311(b) and (c), 1245(a), and 1250(a) do not apply), the excess of the basis of the property in the hands of corporation X over the amount received therefor. The basis of such property to corporation A would be $25. If the basis of the property in the hands of corporation X were $10, the corporate shareholder, A, would not receive a distribution. The basis of such property to corporation A would be $20. Whether or not A is a corporation, the excess of the amount paid over the basis of the property in the hands of corporation X ($20 over $10) would be a taxable gain to corporation X.

* * *

(l) Transactions treated as distributions. A distribution to shareholders with respect to their stock is within the terms of section 301 although it takes place at the same time as another transaction if the distribution is in substance a separate transaction whether or not connected in a formal sense. This is most likely to occur in the case of a recapitalization, a reincorporation, or a merger of a corporation with a newly organized corporation having substantially no property. For example, if a corporation having only common stock outstanding, exchanges one share of newly issued common stock and one bond in the principal amount of $10 for each share of outstanding common stock, the distribution of the bonds will be a distribution of property (to the extent of their fair market value) to which section 301 applies, even though the exchange of common stock for common stock may be pursuant to a plan of reorganization under the terms of section 368(a)(1)(E) (recapitalization) and even though the exchange of common stock for common stock may be tax free by virtue of section 354.

(m) Cancellation of indebtedness. The cancellation of indebtedness of a shareholder by a corporation shall be treated as a distribution of property.

* * *

§ 1.302–1 General.

(a) Under section 302(d), unless otherwise provided in subchapter C, chapter 1 of the Code, a distribution in redemption of stock shall be treated as a distribution of property to which section 301 applies if the distribution is not within any of the provisions of section 302(b). A distribution in redemption of stock shall be considered a distribution in part or full payment in exchange for the stock under section 302(a) provided paragraph (1), (2), (3), or (4) of section 302(b) applies. Section 318(a) (relating to constructive ownership of stock) applies to all redemptions under section 302 except that in the termination of a shareholder's interest certain limitations are placed on the application of section 318(a)(1) by section 302(c)(2). The term "redemption of stock" is defined in section 317(b). * * * For special rules relating to redemption of stock to pay death taxes see section 303. For special rules relating to redemption of section 306 stock see section 306. For special rules relating to redemption of stock in partial or complete liquidation see section 331.

* * *

§ 1.302–2 Redemptions not taxable as dividends.

(a) The fact that a redemption fails to meet the requirements of paragraph (2), (3) or (4) of section 302(b) shall not be taken into account in determining whether the redemption is not essentially equivalent to a dividend under section 302(b)(1). See, however, paragraph (b) of this section. For example, if a shareholder owns only nonvoting stock of a corporation which is not section 306 stock and which is limited and preferred as to dividends and in liquidation, and one–half of such stock is redeemed, the distribution will ordinarily meet the requirements of paragraph (1) of section 302(b) but will not meet the requirements of paragraph (2), (3) or (4) of such section. The determination of whether or not a distribution is within the phrase "essentially equivalent to a dividend" (that is, having the same effect as a distribution without any redemption of stock) shall be made without regard to the earnings and profits of the corporation at the time of the distribution. For example, if A owns all the stock of a corporation and the corporation redeems part of his stock at a time when it has no earnings and profits, the distribution shall be treated as a distribution under section 301 pursuant to section 302(d).

(b)(1) The question whether a distribution in redemption of stock of a shareholder is not essentially equivalent to a dividend under section 302(b)(1) depends upon the facts and circumstances of each case. One of the facts to be considered in making this determination is the constructive stock ownership of such shareholder under section 318(a). All distributions in pro rata redemptions of a part of the stock of a corporation generally will be treated as distributions under section 301 if the corporation has only one class of stock outstanding. However, for distributions in partial liquidation, see section 302(e).* The redemption of all of one class of stock (except section 306 stock) either at one time or in a series of redemptions generally will be considered as a distribution under section 301 if all classes of stock outstanding at the time of the redemption are held in the same proportion. Distributions in redemption of stock may be treated as distributions under section 301 regardless of the provisions of the stock certificate and regardless of whether all stock being redeemed was acquired by the stockholders from whom the stock was redeemed by purchase or otherwise.

* * *

(c) In any case in which an amount received in redemption of stock is treated as a distribution of a dividend, proper adjustment of the basis of the remaining stock will be made with respect to the stock redeemed. (For adjustments to basis required for certain redemptions of corporate shareholders that are treated as extraordinary dividends, see section 1059 and the regulations thereunder.) The following examples illustrate the application of this rule:

Example (1). A, an individual, purchased all of the stock of Corporation X for $100,000. In 1955 the corporation redeems half of the stock for $150,000, and it is determined that this amount constitutes a dividend. The remaining stock of Corporation X held by A has a basis of $100,000.

Example (2). H and W, husband and wife, each own half of the stock of Corporation X. All of the stock was purchased by H for $100,000 cash. In 1950 H gave one–half of the stock to W, the stock transferred having a value in excess of $50,000. In 1955 all of the stock of H is redeemed for $150,000, and it is determined that the distribution to H in redemption of his shares constitutes the distribution of a dividend. Immediately after the transaction, W holds the remaining stock of Corporation X with a basis of $100,000.

Example (3). The facts are the same as in Example (2) with the additional facts that the outstanding stock of Corporation X consists of 1,000 shares and all but 10 shares of the stock of H is redeemed. Immediately after the transaction, H holds 10 shares of the stock of Corporation X with a basis of $50,000, and W holds 500 shares with a basis of $50,000.

§ 1.302–3 Substantially disproportionate redemption.

(a) Section 302(b)(2) provides for the treatment of an amount received in redemption of stock as an amount received in exchange for such stock if—

(1) Immediately after the redemption the shareholder owns less than 50 percent of the total combined voting power of all classes of stock as provided in section 302(b)(2)(B),

(2) The redemption is a substantially disproportionate redemption within the meaning of section 302(b)(2)(C), and

(3) The redemption is not pursuant to a plan described in section 302(b)(2)(D).

Section 318(a) (relating to constructive ownership of stock) shall apply both in making the disproportionate redemption test and in determining the percentage of stock ownership after the redemption. The requirements under section 302(b)(2) shall be applied to each shareholder separately and shall be applied only with respect to stock which is issued and outstanding in the hands of the shareholders. Section 302(b)(2) only applies to a redemption of voting stock or to a redemption of both voting stock and other stock. Section 302(b)(2) does not apply to the redemption solely of nonvoting stock (common or preferred). However, if a redemption is treated as an exchange to a particular shareholder under the terms of section 302(b)(2), such section will apply to the simultaneous redemption of nonvoting preferred stock (which is not section 306 stock) owned by such shareholder and such redemption will also be treated as an exchange. Generally, for purposes of this section, stock which does not have voting rights until the happening of an event, such as a default in the payment of dividends on preferred stock, is not voting stock until the happening of the specified event. Subsection 302(b)(2)(D) provides that a redemption will not be treated as substantially disproportionate if made pursuant to a plan the purpose or effect of which is a series of redemptions which result in the aggregate in a distribution which is not substantially disproportionate. Whether or not such a plan exists will be determined from all the facts and circumstances.

(b) The application of paragraph (a) of this section is illustrated by the following example:

Example. Corporation M has outstanding 400 shares of common stock of which A, B, C and D each own 100 shares or 25 percent. No stock is considered constructively owned by A, B, C or D under section 318. Corporation M redeems 55 shares from A, 25 shares from B, and 20 shares from C. For the redemption to be disproportionate as to any shareholder, such shareholder must own after the redemptions less than 20 percent (80 percent of 25 percent) of the 300 shares of stock then outstanding. After the redemptions, A owns 45 shares (15 percent), B owns 75 shares (25 percent), and C owns 80 shares ($26\frac{2}{3}$ percent). The distribution is disproportionate only with respect to A.

§ 1.302–4 Termination of shareholder's interest.

Section 302(b)(3) provides that a distribution in redemption of all of the stock of the corporation owned by a shareholder shall be treated as a distribution in part or full payment in exchange for the stock of such shareholder. In determining whether all of the stock of the shareholder has been redeemed, the general rule of section 302(c)(1) requires that the rules of constructive ownership provided in section 318(a) shall apply. Section 302(c)(2), however, provides that section 318(a)(1) (relating to constructive ownership of stock owned by members of a family) shall not apply where the specific requirements of section 302(c)(2) are met. The following rules shall be applicable in determining whether the specific requirements of section 302(c)(2) are met:

(a) Statement. The agreement specified in section 302(c)(2)(A)(iii) shall be in the form of a statement entitled, "STATEMENT PURSUANT TO SECTION 302(c)(2)(A)(iii) BY [INSERT NAME AND TAXPAYER IDENTIFICATION NUMBER (IF ANY) OF TAXPAYER OR RELATED PERSON, AS THE CASE MAY BE], A DISTRIBUTEE (OR RELATED PERSON) OF [INSERT NAME AND EMPLOYER IDENTIFICATION NUMBER (IF ANY) OF DISTRIBUTING CORPORATION]." The distributee must include such statement on or with the distributee's first return for the taxable year in which the distribution described in section 302(b)(3) occurs. If the distributee is a controlled foreign corporation (within the meaning of section 957), each United States shareholder (within the meaning of section 951(b)) with respect thereto must include this statement on or with its return. The distributee must represent this statement —

(1) THE DISTRIBUTEE (OR RELATED PERSON) HAS NOT ACQUIRED, OTHER THAN BY BEQUEST OR INHERITANCE, ANY INTEREST IN THE CORPORATION (AS DESCRIBED IN SECTION 302(c)(2)(A)(i)) SINCE THE DISTRIBUTION; and

(2) THE DISTRIBUTEE (OR RELATED PERSON) WILL NOTIFY THE INTERNAL REVENUE SERVICE OF ANY ACQUISITION, OTHER THAN BY BEQUEST OR INHERITANCE, OF SUCH AN INTEREST IN THE CORPORATION WITHIN 30 DAYS AFTER THE ACQUISITION, IF THE ACQUISITION OCCURS WITHIN 10 YEARS FROM THE DATE OF THE DISTRIBUTION.

(b) Substantiation information. The distributee who files an agreement under section 302(c)(2)(A)(iii) shall retain copies of income tax returns and any other records indicating fully the amount of tax which would have been payable had the redemption been treated as a distribution subject to section 301.

(c) Stock of parent, subsidiary or successor corporation redeemed. If stock of a parent corporation is redeemed, section 302(c)(2)(A), relating to acquisition of an interest in the corporation within 10 years after termination shall be applied with reference to an interest both in the parent corporation and any subsidiary of such parent corporation. If stock of a parent corporation is sold to a subsidiary in a transaction described in section 304, section 302(c)(2)(A) shall be applicable to the acquisition of an interest in such subsidiary corporation or in the parent corporation. If stock of a subsidiary corporation is redeemed, section 302(c)(2)(A) shall be applied with reference to an interest both in such subsidiary corporation and its parent. Section 302(c)(2)(A) shall also be applied with respect to an interest in a corporation which is a successor corporation to the corporation the interest in which has been terminated.

(d) Redeemed shareholder as creditor. For the purpose of section 302(c)(2)(A)(i), a person will be considered to be a creditor only if the rights of such person with respect to the corporation are not greater or broader in scope than necessary for the enforcement of his claim. Such claim must not in any sense be proprietary and must not be subordinate to the claims of general creditors. An obligation in the form of a debt may thus constitute a proprietary interest. For example, if under the terms of the instrument the corporation may discharge the principal amount of its obligation to a person by payments, the amount or certainty of which are dependent upon the earnings of the corporation, such a person is not a creditor of the corporation. Furthermore, if under the terms of the instrument the rate of purported interest is dependent upon earnings, the holder of such instrument may not, in some cases, be a creditor.

(e) Acquisition of assets pursuant to creditor's rights. In the case of a distributee to whom section 302 (b)(3) is applicable, who is a creditor after such transaction, the acquisition of the assets of the corporation in the enforcement of the rights of such creditor shall not be considered an acquisition of an interest in the corporation for purposes of section 302(c)(2) unless stock of the corporation, its parent corporation, or, in the case of a redemption of stock of a parent corporation, of a subsidiary of such corporation is acquired.

(f) Constructive ownership rules applicable. In determining whether an entire interest in the corporation has been terminated under section 302(b)(3), under all circumstances paragraphs (2), (3), (4), and (5) of section 318(a) (relating to constructive ownership of stock) shall be applicable.

(g) Avoidance of Federal income tax. Section 302(c)(2)(B) provides that section 302(c)(2)(A) shall not apply—

(1) If any portion of the stock redeemed was acquired directly or indirectly within the 10-year period ending on the date of the distribution by the distributee from a person, the ownership of whose stock would (at the time of distribution) be attributable to the distributee under section 318(a), or

(2) If any person owns (at the time of the distribution) stock, the ownership of which is attributable to the distributee under section 318(a), such person acquired any stock in the corporation directly or indirectly from the distributee within the 10-year period ending on the date of the distribution, and such stock so acquired from the distributee is not redeemed in the same transaction, unless the acquisition (described in subparagraph (1) of this paragraph) or the disposition by the distributee (described in subparagraph (2) of this paragraph) did not have as one of its principal purposes the avoidance of Federal income tax. A transfer of stock by the transferor, within the 10-year period ending on the date of the distribution, to a person whose stock would be attributable to the transferor shall not be deemed to have as one of its principal purposes the avoidance of Federal income tax merely because the transferee is in a lower income tax bracket than the transferor.

* * *

§ 1.305–1 Stock dividends.

(a) In general. Under section 305, a distribution made by a corporation to its shareholders in its stock or in rights to acquire its stock is not included in gross income except as provided in section 305(b) and the regulations promulgated under the authority of section 305(c). A distribution made by a corporation to its shareholders in its stock or rights to acquire its stock which would not otherwise be included in gross income by reason of section 305 shall not be so included merely because such distribution was made out of Treasury stock or consisted of rights to acquire Treasury stock. See section 307 for rules as to basis of stock and stock rights acquired in a distribution.

(b) Amount of distribution. (1) In general, where a distribution of stock or rights to acquire stock of a corporation is treated as a distribution of property to which section 301 applies by reason of section 305(b), the amount of the distribution, in accordance with section 301(b) and §1.301—1, is the fair market value of such stock or rights on the date of distribution. See example (1) of §1.305–2(b).

(2) Where a corporation which regularly distributes its earnings and profits, such as a regulated investment company, declares a dividend pursuant to which the shareholders may elect to receive either money or stock of the distributing corporation of equivalent value, the amount of the distribution of the stock received by any shareholder electing to receive stock will be considered to equal the amount of the money which could have been received instead. See example (2) of §1.305–2(b).

(3) For rules for determining the amount of the distribution where certain transactions, such as changes in conversion ratios or periodic redemptions, are treated as distributions under section 305(c), see examples (6), (8), (9), and (15) of §1.305–3(e).

(c) Adjustment in purchase price. A transfer of stock (or rights to acquire stock) or an increase or decrease in the conversion ratio or redemption price of stock which represents an adjustment of the price to be paid by the distributing corporation in acquiring property (within the meaning of section 317(a)) is not within the purview of section 305 because it is not a distribution with respect to its stock. For example, assume that on January 1, 1970, pursuant to a reorganization, corporation X acquires all the stock of corporation Y solely in exchange for its convertible preferred class B stock. Under the terms of the class B stock, its conversion ratio is to be adjusted in 1976 under a formula based upon the earnings of corporation Y over the 6-year period ending on December 31, 1975. Such an adjustment in 1976 is not covered by section 305.

(d) Definitions. (1) For purposes of this section and §§1.305–2 through 1.305–7, the term "stock" includes rights or warrants to acquire such stock.

(2) For purposes of §§1.305–2 through 1.305–7, the term "shareholder" includes a holder of rights or warrants or a holder of convertible securities.

§ 1.305–2 Distributions in lieu of money.

(a) In general. Under section 305(b)(1), if any shareholder has the right to an election or option with respect to whether a distribution shall be made either in money or any other property, or in stock or rights to acquire stock of the distributing corporation, then, with respect to all shareholders, the distribution of stock or rights to acquire stock is treated as a distribution of property to which section 301 applies regardless of—

(1) Whether the distribution is actually made in whole or in part in stock or in stock rights;

(2) Whether the election or option is exercised or exercisable before or after the declaration of the distribution;

(3) Whether the declaration of the distribution provides that the distribution will be made in one medium unless the shareholder specifically requests payment in the other;

(4) Whether the election governing the nature of the distribution is provided in the declaration of the distribution or in the corporate charter or arises from the circumstances of the distribution; or

(5) Whether all or part of the shareholders have the election.

(b) Examples. The application of section 305(b)(1) may be illustrated by the following examples:

Example (1). (i) Corporation X declared a dividend payable in additional shares of its common stock to the holders of its outstanding common stock on the basis of two additional shares for each share held on the record date but with the provision that, at the election of any shareholder made within a specified period prior to the distribution date, he may receive one additional share for each share held on the record date plus $12 principal amount of securities of corporation Y owned by corporation X. The fair market value of the stock of corporation X on the distribution date was $10 per share. The fair market value of $12 principal amount of securities of corporation Y on the distribution date was $11 but such securities had a cost basis to corporation X of $9.

(ii) The distribution to all shareholders of one additional share of stock of corporation X (with respect to which no election applies) for each share outstanding is not a distribution to which section 301 applies.

(iii) The distribution of the second share of stock of corporation X to those shareholders who do not elect to receive securities of corporation Y is a distribution of property to which section 301 applies, whether such shareholders are individuals or corporations. The amount of the distribution to which section 301 applies is $10 per share of stock of corporation X held on the record date (the fair market value of the stock of corporation X on the distribution date).

(iv) The distribution of securities of corporation Y in lieu of the second share of stock of corporation X to the shareholders of corporation X whether individuals or corporations, who elect to receive such securities, is also a distribution of property to which section 301 applies.

(v) In the case of the individual shareholders of corporation X who elects to receive such securities, the amount of the distribution to which section 301 applies is $11 per share of stock of corporation X held on the record date (the fair market value of the $12 principal amount of securities of corporation Y on the distribution date).

(vi) In the case of the corporate shareholders of corporation X electing to receive such securities, the amount of the distribution to which section 301 applies is $9 per share of stock of corporation X held on the record date (the basis of the securities of corporation Y in the hands of corporation X).

Example (2). On January 10, 1970, corporation X, a regulated investment company, declared a dividend of $1 per share on its common stock payable on February 11, 1970, in cash or in stock of corporation X of equivalent value determined as of January 22, 1970, at the election of the shareholder made on or before January 22, 1970. The amount of the distribution to which section 301 applies is $1 per share whether the shareholder elects to take cash or stock and whether the shareholder is an individual or a corporation. Such amount will also be used in determining the dividend paid deduction of corporation X and the reduction in earnings and profits of corporation X.

§ 1.305–3 Disproportionate distributions.

(a) In general. Under section 305(b)(2), a distribution (including a deemed distribution) by a corporation of its stock or rights to acquire its stock is treated as a distribution of property to which section 301 applies if the distribution (or a series of distributions of which such distribution is one) has the result of (1) the receipt of money or other property by some shareholders, and (2) an increase in the proportionate interests of other shareholders in the assets or earnings and profits of the corporation. Thus, if a corporation has two classes of common stock outstanding and cash dividends are paid on one class and stock dividends are paid on the other class, the stock dividends are treated as distributions to which section 301 applies.

(b) Special rules. (1) As used in section 305(b)(2), the term "a series of distributions" encompasses all distributions of stock made or deemed made by a corporation which have the result of the receipt of cash or property by some shareholders and an increase in the proportionate interests of other shareholders.

(2) In order for a distribution of stock to be considered as one of a series of distributions it is not necessary that such distribution be pursuant to a plan to distribute cash or property to some shareholders and to increase the proportionate interests of other shareholders. It is sufficient if there is an actual or deemed distribution of stock (of which such distribution is one) and as a result of such distribution or distributions some shareholders receive cash or property and other shareholders increase their proportionate interests. For example, if a corporation pays quarterly stock dividends to one class of common shareholders and annual cash dividends to another class of common shareholders the quarterly stock dividends constitute a series of distributions of stock having the result of the receipt of cash or property by some shareholders and an increase in the proportionate interests of other shareholders. This is so whether or not the stock distributions and the cash distributions are steps in an overall plan or are independent and unrelated. Accordingly, all the quarterly stock dividends are distributions to which section 301 applies.

(3) There is no requirement that both elements of section 305(b)(2) (*i.e.*, receipt of cash or property by some shareholders and an increase in proportionate interests of other shareholders) occur in the form of a distribution or series of distributions as long as the result of a distribution or distributions of stock is that some shareholders' proportionate interests increase and other shareholders in fact receive cash or property. Thus, there is no requirement that the shareholders receiving cash or property acquire the cash or property by way of a corporate distribution with respect to their shares, so long as they receive such cash or property in their capacity as shareholders, if there is a stock distribution which results in a change in the proportionate interests of some shareholders and other shareholders receive cash or property. However, in order for a distribution of property to meet the requirement of section 305(b)(2), such distribution must be made to a shareholder in his capacity as a shareholder, and must be a distribution to which section 301, 356(a)(2), 871(a)(1)(A), 881(a)(1), 852(b), or 857(b) applies. (Under section 305(d)(2), the payment of interest to a holder of a convertible debenture is treated as a distribution of property to a shareholder for purposes of section 305(b)(2).) For example if a corporation makes a stock distribution to its shareholders and, pursuant to a prearranged plan with such corporation, a related corporation purchases such stock from those shareholders who want cash, in a transaction to which section 301 applies by virtue of section 304, the requirements of section 305(b)(2) are satisfied. In addition, a distribution of property incident to an isolated redemption of stock (for example, pursuant to a tender offer) will not cause section 305(b)(2) to apply even though the redemption distribution is treated as a distribution of property to which section 301, 871(a)(1)(A), 881(a)(1), or 356(a)(2) applies.

(4) Where the receipt of cash or property occurs more than 36 months following a distribution or series of distributions of stock, or where a distribution or series of distributions of stock is made more than 36 months following the receipt of cash or property, such distribution or distributions will be presumed not to result in the receipt of cash or property by some shareholders and an increase in the proportionate interest of other shareholders, unless the receipt of cash or property and the distribution or series of distributions of stock are made pursuant to a plan. For example, if, pursuant to a plan, a corporation pays cash dividends to some shareholders on January 1, 1971 and increases the proportionate interests of other shareholders on March 1, 1974, such increases in proportionate interests are distributions to which section 301 applies.

(5) In determining whether a distribution or a series of distributions has the result of a disproportionate distribution, there shall be treated as outstanding stock of the distributing corporation (i) any right to acquire such stock (whether or not exercisable during the taxable year), and (ii) any security convertible into stock of the distributing corporation (whether or not convertible during the taxable year).

(6) In cases where there is more than one class of stock outstanding, each class of stock is to be considered separately in determining whether a shareholder has increased his proportionate interest in the assets or earnings and profits of a corporation. The individual shareholders of a class of stock will be deemed to have an increased interest if the class of stock as a whole has an increased interest in the corporation.

(c) Distributions of cash in lieu of fractional shares. **(1)** Section 305(b)(2) will not apply if—

(i) A corporation declares a dividend payable in stock of the corporation and distributes cash in lieu of fractional shares to which shareholders would otherwise be entitled, or

(ii) Upon a conversion of convertible stock or securities a corporation distributes cash in lieu of fractional shares to which shareholders would otherwise be entitled.

Provided the purpose of the distribution of cash is to save the corporation the trouble, expense, and inconvenience of issuing and transferring fractional shares (or scrip representing fractional shares), or issuing full shares representing the sum of fractional shares, and not to give any particular group of shareholders an increased interest in the assets or earnings and profits of the corporation. For purposes of paragraph (c)(1)(i) of this section, if the total amount of cash distributed in lieu of fractional shares is 5 percent or less of the total fair market value of the stock distributed (determined as of the date of declaration), the distribution shall be considered to be for such valid purpose.

(2) In a case to which subparagraph (1) of this paragraph applies, the transaction will be treated as though the fractional shares were distributed as part of the stock distribution and then were redeemed by the corporation. The treatment of the cash received by a shareholder will be determined under section 302.

(d) Adjustment in conversion ratio. (1) (i) Except as provided in subparagraph (2) of this paragraph, if a corporation has convertible stock or convertible securities outstanding (upon which it pays or is deemed to pay dividends or interest in money or other property) and distributes a stock dividend (or rights to acquire such stock) with respect to the stock into which the convertible stock or securities are convertible, an increase in proportionate interest in the assets or earnings and profits of the corporation by reason of such stock dividend shall be considered to have occurred unless a full adjustment in the conversion ratio or conversion price to reflect such stock dividend is made. Under certain circumstances, however, the application of an adjustment formula which in effect provides for a "credit" where stock is issued for consideration in excess of the conversion price may not satisfy the requirement for a "full adjustment." Thus, if under a "conversion price" antidilution formula the formula provides for a "credit" where stock is issued for consideration in excess of the conversion price (in effect as an offset against any decrease in the conversion price which would otherwise be required when stock is subsequently issued for consideration below the conversion price) there may still be an increase in proportionate interest by reason of a stock dividend after application of the formula, since any downward adjustment of the conversion price that would otherwise be required to reflect the stock dividend may be offset, in whole or in part, by the effect of prior sales made at prices above the conversion price. On the other hand, if there were no prior sales of stock above the conversion price then a full adjustment would occur upon the application of such an adjustment formula and there would be no change in proportionate interest. Similarly, if consideration is to be received in connection with the issuance of stock, such as in the case of a rights offering or a distribution of warrants, the fact that such consideration is taken into account in making the antidilution adjustment will not preclude a full adjustment. See paragraph (b) of the example in this subparagraph for a case where the application of an adjustment formula with a cumulative feature does not result in a full adjustment and where a change in proportionate interest therefore occurs. See paragraph (c) for a case where the application of an adjustment formula with a cumulative feature does result in a full adjustment and where no change in proportionate interest therefore occurs. See paragraph (d) for an application of an antidilution formula in the case of a rights offering. See paragraph (e) for a case where the application of a non-cumulative type adjustment formula will in all cases prevent a change in proportionate interest from occurring in the case of a stock dividend, because of the omission of the cumulative feature.

* * *

§ 1.305–4 Distributions of common and preferred stock.

(a) In general. Under section 305(b)(3), a distribution (or a series of distributions) by a corporation which results in the receipt of preferred stock (whether or not convertible into common stock) by some common shareholders and the receipt of common stock by other common shareholders is treated as a distribution of property to which section 301 applies. For the meaning of the term "a series of distribution," see subparagraphs (1) through (6) of §1.305–3(b).

(b) Examples. The application of section 305(b)(3) may be illustrated by the following examples:

Example (1). Corporation X is organized with two classes of common stock, class A and class B. Dividends may be paid in stock or in cash on either class of stock without regard to the medium of payment of dividends on the other class. A dividend is declared on the class A stock payable in additional shares of class A stock and a dividend is declared on class B stock payable in newly authorized class C stock which is nonconvertible and limited and preferred as to dividends. Both the distribution of class A shares and the distribution of new class C shares are distributions to which section 301 applies.

Example (2). Corporation Y is organized with one class of stock, class A common. During the year the corporation declares a dividend on the class A stock payable in newly authorized class B preferred stock which is convertible into class A stock no later than 6 months from the date of distribution at a price that is only slightly higher than the market price of class A stock on the date of distribution. Taking into account the dividend rate, redemption provisions, the marketability of the convertible stock, and the conversion price, it is reasonable to anticipate that within a relatively short period of time some shareholders will exercise their conversion rights and some will not. Since the distribution can reasonably be expected to result in the receipt of preferred stock by some common shareholders and the receipt of common stock by other common shareholders, the distribution is a distribution of property to which section 301 applies.

§ 1.305–5 Distributions on preferred stock.

(a) In general. Under section 305(b)(4), a distribution by a corporation of its stock (or rights to acquire its stock) made (or deemed made under section 305(c)) with respect to its preferred stock is treated as a distribution of property to which section 301 applies unless the distribution is made with respect to convertible preferred stock to take into account a stock dividend, stock split, or any similar event (such as the sale of stock at less than the fair market value pursuant to a rights offering) which would otherwise result in the dilution of the conversion right. For purposes of the preceding sentence, an adjustment in the conversion ratio of convertible preferred stock made solely to take into account the distribution by a closed end regulated investment company of a capital gain dividend with respect to the stock into which such stock is convertible shall not be considered a "similar event." The term "preferred stock" generally refers to stock which, in relation to other classes of stock outstanding, enjoys certain limited rights and privileges (generally associated with specified dividend and liquidation priorities) but does not participate in corporate growth to any significant extent. The distinguishing feature of "preferred stock" for the purposes of section 305(b)(4) is not its privileged position as such, but that such privileged position is limited, and that such stock does not participate in corporate growth to any significant extent. However, a right to participate which lacks substance will not prevent a class of stock from being treated as preferred stock. Thus, stock which enjoys a priority as to dividends and on liquidation but which is entitled to participate, over and above such priority, with another less privileged class of stock in earnings and profits and upon liquidation, may nevertheless be treated as preferred stock for purposes of section 305 if, taking into account all the facts and circumstances, it is reasonable to anticipate at the time a distribution is made (or is deemed to have been made) with respect to such stock that there is little or no likelihood of such stock actually participating in current and anticipated earnings and upon liquidation beyond its preferred interest. Among the facts and circumstances to be considered are the prior and anticipated earnings per share, the cash dividends per share, the book value per share, the extent of preference and of participation of each class, both absolutely and relative to each other, and any other facts which indicate whether or not the stock has a real and meaningful probability of actually participating in the earnings and growth of the corporation. The determination of whether stock is preferred for purposes of section 305 shall be made without regard to any right to convert such stock into another class of stock of the corporation. The term "preferred stock", however, does not include convertible debentures.

(b) Redemption premium—(1) In general. If a corporation issues preferred stock that may be redeemed under the circumstances described in this paragraph (b) at a price higher than the issue price, the difference (the redemption premium) is treated under section 305(c) as a constructive distribution (or series of constructive distributions) of additional stock on preferred stock that is taken into account under principles similar to the principles of section 1272(a). However, constructive distribution treatment does not result under this paragraph (b) if the redemption premium does not exceed a de minimis amount, as determined under the principles of section 1273(a)(3). For purposes of this paragraph (b), preferred stock that may be acquired by a person other than the issuer (the third person) is deemed to be redeemable under the circumstances described in this paragraph (b), and references to the issuer include the third person, if—

(i) This paragraph (b) would apply to the stock if the third person were the issuer; and

(ii) Either—

(A) The acquisition of the stock by the third person would be treated as a redemption for federal income tax purposes (under section 304 or otherwise); or

(B) The third person and the issuer are members of the same affiliated group (having the meaning for this purpose given the term by section 1504(a), except that section 1504(b) shall not apply) and a principal purpose of the arrangement for the third person to acquire the stock is to avoid the application of section 305 and paragraph (b)(1) of this section.

* * *

(c) Cross reference. For rules for applying sections 305(b)(4) and 305(c) to recapitalizations, see §1.305–7(c).

(d) Examples. The application of sections 305(b)(4) and 305(c) may be illustrated by the following examples:

Example (1). (i) Corporation T has outstanding 1,000 shares of $100 par 5-percent cumulative preferred stock and 10,000 shares of no–par common stock. The corporation is 4 years in arrears on dividends to the preferred shareholders. The issue price of the preferred stock is $100 per share. Pursuant to a recapitalization under section 368(a)(1)(E), the preferred shareholders exchange their preferred stock, including the right to dividend arrearages, on the basis of one old preferred share for 1.20 newly authorized class A preferred shares. Immediately following the recapitalization, the new class A shares are traded at $100 per share. The class A shares are entitled to a liquidation preference of $100. The preferred shareholders have increased their proportionate interest in the assets or earnings and profits of corporation T since the fair market value of 1.20 shares of class A preferred stock ($120) exceeds the issue price of the old preferred stock ($100). Accordingly, the preferred shareholders are deemed under section 305(c) to receive a distribution in the amount of $20 on each share of old preferred stock and the distribution is one to which sections 305(b)(4) and 301 apply.

(ii) The same result would occur if the fair market value of the common stock immediately following the recapitalization were $20 per share and each share of preferred stock were exchanged for one share of the new class A preferred stock and one share of common stock.

Example (2). Corporation A, a publicly held company whose stock is traded on a securities exchange (or in the over-the-counter market) has two classes of stock outstanding, common and cumulative preferred. Each share of preferred stock is convertible into .75 shares of common stock. There are no dividend arrearages. At the time of issue of the preferred stock, there was no plan or prearrangement by which it was to be exchanged for common stock. The issue price of the preferred stock is $100 per share. In order to retire the preferred stock, corporation A recapitalizes in a transaction to which section 368(a)(1)(E) applies and each share of preferred stock is exchanged for one share of common stock. Immediately after the recapitalization the common stock has a fair market value of $110 per share. Notwithstanding the fact that the fair market value of the common stock received in the exchange (determined immediately following the recapitalization) exceeds the issue price of the preferred stock surrendered, the recapitalization is not deemed under section 305(c) to result in a distribution to which sections 305(b)(4) and 301 apply since the recapitalization is not pursuant to a plan to periodically increase a shareholder's proportionate interest in the assets or earnings and profits and does not involve dividend arrearages.

Example (3). Corporation V is organized with two classes of stock, 1,000 shares of class A common and 1,000 shares of class B convertible preferred. Each share of class B stock may be converted into two shares of class A stock. Pursuant to a recapitalization under section 368(a)(1)(E), the 1,000 shares of class A stock are surrendered in exchange for 500 shares of new class A common and 500 shares of newly authorized class C common. The conversion right of class B stock is changed to one share of class A stock and one share of class C stock for each share of class B stock. The change in the conversion right is not deemed under section 305(c) to be a distribution on preferred stock to which sections 305(b)(4) and 301 apply.

Example (4)—(i) **Facts.** Corporation X is a domestic corporation with only common stock outstanding. In connection with its acquisition of Corporation T, X issues 100 shares of its 4% preferred stock to the shareholders of T, who are unrelated to X both before and after the transaction. The issue price of the preferred stock is $40 per share. Each share of preferred stock is convertible at the shareholder's election into three shares of X common stock. At the time the preferred stock is issued, the X common stock has a value of $10 per share. The preferred stock does not provide for its mandatory redemption or for redemption at the option of the holder. It is callable at the option of X at any time beginning three years from the date of issuance for $100 per share. There are no other plans, arrangements, or agreements that effectively require or are intended to compel X to redeem the stock.

(ii) **Analysis.** The preferred stock is described in the safe harbor rule of paragraph (b)(3)(ii) of this section because X and the former shareholders of T are unrelated, there are no plans, arrangements, or agreements that effectively require or are intended to compel X to redeem the stock, and calling the stock for $100 per share would not reduce the yield of the preferred stock. Therefore, the $60 per share call premium is not treated as a constructive distribution to the shareholders of the preferred stock under paragraph (b) of this section.

Example (5)—(i) Facts—(A) Corporation Y is a domestic corporation with only common stock outstanding. On January 1, 1996, Y issues 100 shares of its 10% preferred stock to a holder. The holder is unrelated to Y both before and after the stock issuance. The issue price of the preferred stock is $100 per share. The preferred stock is—

(1) Callable at the option of Y on or before January 1, 2001, at a price of $105 per share plus any accrued but unpaid dividends; and

(2) Mandatorily redeemable on January 1, 2006, at a price of $100 per share plus any accrued but unpaid dividends.

(B) The preferred stock provides that if Y fails to exercise its option to call the preferred stock on or before January 1, 2001, the holder will be entitled to appoint a majority of Y's directors. Based on all of the facts and circumstances as of the issue date, Y is likely to have the legal and financial capacity to exercise its right to redeem. There are no other facts and circumstances as of the issue data that would affect whether Y will call the preferred stock on or before January 1, 2001.

(ii) Analysis. Under paragraph (b)(3)(i) of this section, paragraph (b)(1) of this section applies because, by virtue of the change of control provision and the absence of any contrary facts, it is more likely than not that Y will exercise its option to call the preferred stock on or before January 1, 2001. The safe harbor rule of paragraph (b)(3)(ii) of this section does not apply because the provision that failure to call will cause the holder to gain control of the corporation is a plan, arrangement, or agreement that effectively requires or is intended to compel Y to redeem the preferred stock. Under paragraph (b)(4) of this section, the constructive distribution occurs over the period ending on January 1, 2001. Redemption is most likely to occur on that date, because that is the date on which the corporation minimizes the rate of return to the holder while preventing the holder from gaining control. The de minimis exception of paragraph (b)(1) of this section does not apply because the $5 per share difference between the redemption price and the issue price exceeds the amount determined under the principles of section 1273(a)(3) (5 × .0025 × $105 = $1.31). Accordingly, $5 per share, the difference between the redemption price and the issue price, is treated as a constructive distribution received by the holder on an economic accrual basis over the five-year period ending on January 1, 2001, under principles similar to the principles of section 1272(a).

Example (6). Corporation A, a publicly held company whose stock is traded on a securities exchange (or in the over-the-counter market) has two classes of stock outstanding, common and preferred. The preferred stock is nonvoting and nonconvertible, limited and preferred as to dividends, and has a fixed liquidation preference. There are no dividend arrearages. At the time of issue of the preferred stock, there was no plan or prearrangement by which it was to be exchanged for common stock. In order to retire the preferred stock, corporation A recapitalizes in a transaction to which section 368(a)(1)(E) applies and the preferred stock is exchanged for common stock. The transaction is not deemed to be a distribution under section 305(c) and sections 305(b) and 301 do not apply to the transaction. The same result would follow if the preferred stock was exchanged in any reorganization described in section 368(a)(1) for a new preferred stock having substantially the same market value and having no greater call price or liquidation preference than the old preferred stock, whether the new preferred stock has voting rights or is convertible into common stock of corporation A at a fixed ratio subject to change solely to take account of stock dividends, stock splits, or similar transactions with respect to the stock into which the preferred stock is convertible.

Example (7)—(i) Facts—(A) Corporation Z is a domestic corporation with only common stock outstanding. On January 1, 1996, Z issues 100 shares of its 10% preferred stock to C, an individual unrelated to Z both before and after the stock issuance. The issue price of the preferred stock is $100 per share. The preferred stock is—

(1) Not callable for a period of 5 years from the issue date;

(2) Callable at the option of Z on January 1, 2001, at a price of $110 per share plus any accrued but unpaid dividends;

(3) Callable at the option of Z on July 1, 2002, at a price of $120 per share plus any accrued but unpaid dividends; and

(4) Mandatorily redeemable on January 1, 2004, at a price of $150 per share plus any accrued but unpaid dividends.

(B) There are no other plans, arrangements, or agreements between Z and C concerning redemption of the stock. Moreover, there are no other facts and circumstances as of the issue date that would affect whether Z will call the preferred stock on either January 1, 2001, or July 1, 2002.

(ii) Analysis. This stock is described in paragraph (b)(2) of this section because it is mandatorily redeemable. It is also potentially described in paragraph (b)(3)(i) of this section because it is callable at the option of the issuer. The safe harbor rule of paragraph (b)(3)(ii) of this section does not apply to the option to call on January 1, 2001, because the call would reduce the yield of the stock when compared to the yield produced by the January 1, 2004, mandatory redemption feature. Moreover, absent any other facts indicating a contrary result, the fact that redemption on January 1, 2001, would produce the lowest yield indicates that redemption is most likely to occur on that date. Under paragraph (b)(4) of this section, paragraph (b)(1) of this section applies with respect to the issuer's right to call on January 1, 2001, because redemption is most likely to occur on January 1, 2001, for $110 per share. The de minimis exception of paragraph (b)(1) of this section does not apply because the $10 per share difference between the redemption price payable in 2001 and the issue price exceeds the amount determined under the principles of section 1273(a)(3) (5 × .0025 × $110 = $1.38). Accordingly, $10 per share, the difference between the redemption price and the issue price, is treated as a constructive distribution received by the holder on an economic accrual basis over the five-year period ending January 1, 2001, under principles similar to the principles of section 1272(a).

(iii) Coordination rules—(A) If Z does not exercise its option to call the preferred stock on January 1, 2001, paragraph (b)(4) of this section provides that the principles of paragraph (b) of this section must be applied to determine if any remaining constructive distribution occurs. Under paragraphs (b)(3)(i) and (b)(4) of this section, paragraph (b)(1) of this section applies because, absent any other facts indicating a contrary result, the fact that redemption on July 1, 2002, would produce a lower yield than the yield produced by the mandatory redemption feature indicates that redemption on that date is most likely to occur. The safe harbor rule of paragraph (b)(3)(ii) of this section does not apply to the option to call on July 1, 2002, because, as of January 1, 2001, a call by Z on July 1, 2002, for $120 would reduce the yield of the stock. The de minimis exception of paragraph (b)(1) of this section does not apply because the $10 per share difference between the redemption price and the issue price (revised as of the missed call date as provided by paragraph (b)(4) of this section) exceeds the amount determined under the principles of section 1273(a)(3) (1 × .0025 × $120 = $.30). Accordingly, the $10 per share of additional redemption premium that is payable on July 1, 2002, is treated as a constructive distribution received by the holder on an economic accrual basis over the period between January 1, 2001, and July 1, 2002, under principles similar to the principles of section 1272(a).

(B) If Z does not exercise its second option to call the preferred stock on July 1, 2002, then the $30 additional redemption premium that is payable on January 1, 2004, is treated as a constructive distribution under paragraphs (b)(2) and (b)(1) of this section. The de minimis exception of paragraph (b)(1) of this section does not apply because the $30 per share difference between the redemption price and the issue price (revised as of the second missed call date) exceeds the amount determined under the principles of section 1273(a)(3) (1 × .0025 × $150 = $.38). The holder is treated as receiving the constructive distribution on an economic accrual basis over the period between July 1, 2002, and January 1, 2004, under principles similar to the principles of section 1272(a).

Example (8)—(i) Facts. The facts are the same as in paragraph (i) of Example 7, except that, based on all of the facts and circumstances as of the issue date (including an expected lack of funds on the part of Z), it is unlikely that Z will exercise the right to redeem on either January 1, 2001, or July 1, 2002.

(ii) Analysis. The safe harbor rule of paragraph (b)(3)(ii) of this section does not apply to the option to call on either January 1, 2001, or July 1, 2002, because each call would reduce the yield of the stock. Under paragraph (b)(3)(i) of this section, neither option to call is more likely than not to occur, because, based on all of the facts and circumstances as of the issue date (including an expected lack of funds on the part of Z), it is not more likely than not that Z will exercise either option. However, the $50 per share redemption premium that is payable on January 1, 2004, is treated as a constructive distribution under paragraphs (b)(1) and (2) of this section, regardless of whether Z is anticipated to have sufficient funds to redeem on that date, because Z is required to redeem the stock on that date. The de minimis exception of paragraph (b)(1) of this section does not apply because the $50 per share difference between the redemption price and the issue price exceeds the amount determined under the principles of section 1273(a)(3) (8 × .0025 × $150 = $3).

Example (9). Corporation Q is organized with 10,000 shares of class A stock and 1,000 shares of class B stock. The terms of the class B stock require that the class B have a preference of $5 per share with respect to dividends and $100 per share with respect to liquidation. In addition, upon a distribution of $10 per share to the class A stock, class B participates equally in any additional dividends. The terms also provide that upon liquidation the class B stock participates equally after the class A stock receives $100 per share. Corporation Q has no accumulated earnings and profits. In 1971 it earned $10,000, the highest earnings in its history. The corporation is in an industry in which it is reasonable to anticipate a growth in earnings of 5 percent per year. In 1971 the book value of corporation Q's assets totalled $100,000. In that year the corporation paid a dividend of $5 per share to the class B stock and $.50 per share to the class A. In 1972 the corporation had no earnings and in lieu of a $5 dividend distributed one share of class B stock for each outstanding share of class B. No distribution was made to the class A stock. Since, in 1972, it was not reasonable to anticipate that the class B stock would participate in the current and anticipated earnings and growth of the corporation beyond its preferred interest, the class B stock is preferred stock and the distribution of class B shares to the class B shareholders is a distribution to which sections 305(b)(4) and 301 apply.

Example (10). Corporation P is organized with 10,000 shares of class A stock and 1,000 shares of class B stock. The terms of the class B stock require that the class B have a preference of $5 per share with respect to dividends and $100 per share with respect to liquidation. In addition, upon a distribution of $5 per share to the class A stock, class B participates equally in any additional dividends. The terms also provide that upon liquidation the class B stock participates equally after the class A receives $100 per share. Corporation P has accumulated earnings and profits of $100,000. In 1971 it earned $75,000. The corporation is in an industry in which it is reasonable to anticipate a growth in earnings of 10 percent per year. In 1971 the book value of corporation P's assets totalled $5 million. In that year the corporation paid a dividend of $5 per share to the class B stock, $5 per share to the class A stock, and it distributed an additional $1 per share to both class A and class B stock. In 1972 the corporation had earnings of $82,500. In that year it paid a dividend of $5 per share to the class B stock and $5 per share to the class A stock. In addition, the corporation declared stock dividends of one share of class B stock for every 10 outstanding shares of class B and one share of class A stock for every 10 outstanding shares of class A. Since, in 1972, it was reasonable to anticipate that both the class B stock and the class A stock would participate in the current and anticipated earnings and growth of the corporation beyond their preferred interests, neither class is preferred stock and the stock dividends are not distributions to which section 305(b)(4) applies.

* * *

§ 1.305–6 Distributions of convertible preferred.

(a) In general. (1) Under section 305(b)(5), a distribution by a corporation of its convertible preferred stock or rights to acquire such stock made or considered as made with respect to its stock is treated as a distribution of property to which section 301 applies unless the corporation establishes that such distribution will not result in a disproportionate distribution as described in §1.305–3.

(2) The distribution of convertible preferred stock is likely to result in a disproportionate distribution when both of the following conditions exist: (i) The conversion right must be exercised within a relatively short period of time after the date of distribution of the stock; and (ii) taking into account such factors as the dividend rate, the redemption provisions, the marketability of the convertible stock, and the conversion price, it may be anticipated that some shareholders will exercise their conversion rights and some will not. On the other hand, where the conversion right may be exercised over a period of many years and the dividend rate is consistent with market conditions at the time of distribution of the stock, there is no basis for predicting at what time and the extent to which the stock will be converted and it is unlikely that a disproportionate distribution will result.

(b) Examples. The application of section 305(b)(5) may be illustrated by the following examples:

Example (1). Corporation Z is organized with one class of stock, class A common. During the year the corporation declares a dividend on the class A stock payable in newly authorized class B preferred stock which is convertible into class A stock for a period of 20 years from the date of issuance. Assuming dividend rates are normal in light of existing conditions so that there is no basis for predicting the extent to which the stock will be converted, the circumstances will ordinarily be sufficient to establish that a disproportionate distribution will not result since it is impossible to predict the extent to which the class B stock will be converted into class A stock. Accordingly, the distribution of class B stock is not one to which section 301 applies.

Example (2). Corporation X is organized with one class of stock, class A common. During the year the corporation declares a dividend on the class A stock payable in newly authorized redeemable class C preferred stock which is convertible into class A common stock no later than 4 months from the date of distribution at a price slightly higher than the market price of class A stock on the date of distribution. By prearrangement with corporation X, corporation Y, an insurance company, agrees to purchase class C stock from any shareholder who does not wish to convert. By reason of this prearrangement, it is anticipated that the shareholders will either sell the class C stock to the insurance company (which expects to retain the shares for investment purposes) or will convert. As a result, some of the shareholders exercise their conversion privilege and receive additional shares of class A stock, while other shareholders sell their class C stock to corporation Y and receive cash. The distribution is a distribution to which section 301 applies since it results in the receipt of property by some shareholders and an increase in the proportionate interests of other shareholders.

§ 1.305–7 Certain transactions treated as distributions.

(a) In general. Under section 305(c), a change in conversion ratio, a change in redemption price, a difference between redemption price and issue price, a redemption which is treated as a distribution to which section 301 applies, or any transaction (including a recapitalization) having a similar effect on the interest of any shareholder may be treated as a distribution with respect to any shareholder whose proportionate interest in the earnings and profits or assets of the corporation is increased by such change, difference, redemption, or similar transaction. In general, such change, difference, redemption, or similar transaction will be treated as a distribution to which sections 305(b) and 301 apply where—

(1) The proportionate interest of any shareholder in the earnings and profits or assets of the corporation deemed to have made such distribution is increased by such change, difference, redemption, or similar transaction; and

(2) Such distribution has the result described in paragraph (2), (3), (4), or (5) of section 305(b).

Where such change, difference, redemption, or similar transaction is treated as a distribution under the provisions of this section, such distribution will be deemed made with respect to any shareholder whose interest in the earnings and profits or assets of the distributing corporation is increased thereby. Such distribution will be deemed to be a distribution of the stock of such corporation made by the corporation to such shareholder with respect to his stock. Depending upon the facts presented, the distribution may be deemed to be made in common or preferred stock. For example, where a redemption premium exists with respect to a class of preferred stock under the circumstances described in §1.305–5(b) and the other requirements of this section are also met, the distribution will be deemed made with respect to such preferred stock, in stock of the same class. Accordingly, the preferred shareholders are considered under sections 305(b)(4) and 305(c) to have received a distribution of preferred stock to which section 301 applies. See the examples in §§1.305–3(e) and 1.305–5(d) for further illustrations of the application of section 305(c).

(b) Antidilution provisions. (1) For purposes of applying section 305(c) in conjunction with section 305(b), a change in the conversion ratio or conversion price of convertible preferred stock (or securities), or in the exercise price of rights or warrants, made pursuant to a bona fide, reasonable, adjustment formula (including, but not limited to, either the so-called "market price" or "conversion price" type of formulas) which has the effect of preventing dilution of the interest of the holders of such stock (or securities) will not be considered to result in a deemed distribution of stock. An adjustment in the conversion ratio or price to compensate for cash or property distributions to other shareholders that are taxable under section 301, 356(a)(2), 871(a)(1)(A), 881(a)(1), 852(b), or 857(b) will not be considered as made pursuant to a bona fide adjustment formula.

(2) The principles of this paragraph may be illustrated by the following example:

Example. (i) Corporation U has two classes of stock outstanding, class A and class B. Each class B share is convertible into class A stock. In accordance with a bona fide, reasonable, antidilution provision, the conversion price is adjusted if the corporation transfers class A stock to anyone for a consideration that is below the conversion price.

(ii) The corporation sells class A stock to the public at the current market price but below the conversion price. Pursuant to the antidilution provision, the conversion price is adjusted downward. Such a change in conversion price will not be deemed to be a distribution under section 305(c) for the purposes of section 305(b).

(c) Recapitalizations. (1) A recapitalization (whether or not an isolated transaction) will be deemed to result in a distribution to which section 305(c) and this section apply if—

(i) It is pursuant to a plan to periodically increase a shareholder's proportionate interest in the assets or earnings and profits of the corporation, or

(ii) A shareholder owning preferred stock with dividends in arrears exchanges his stock for other stock and, as a result, increases his proportionate interest in the assets or earnings and profits of the corporation. An increase in a preferred shareholder's proportionate interest occurs in any case where the fair market value or the liquidation preference, whichever is greater, of the stock received in the exchange (determined immediately following the recapitalization), exceeds the issue price of the preferred stock surrendered.

(2) In a case to which subparagraph (1)(ii) of this paragraph applies, the amount of the distribution deemed under section 305(c) to result from the recapitalization is the lesser of (i) the amount by which the fair market value or the liquidation preference, whichever is greater, of the stock received in the exchange (determined immediately following the recapitalization) exceeds the issue price of the preferred stock surrendered, or (ii) the amount of the dividends in arrears.

(3) For purposes of applying subparagraphs (1) and (2) of this paragraph with respect to stock issued before July 12, 1973, the term "issue price of the preferred stock surrendered" shall mean the greater of the issue price or the liquidation preference (not including dividends in arrears) of the stock surrendered.

(4) For an illustration of the application of this paragraph, see example (12) of §1.305–3(e) and examples (1), (2), (3), and (6) of §1.305–5(d).

(5) For rules relating to redemption premiums on preferred stock, see §1.305–5(b).

* * *

§ 1.306–1 General.

(a) Section 306 provides, in general, that the proceeds from the sale or redemption of certain stock (referred to as "section 306 stock") shall be treated either as ordinary income or as a distribution of property to which section 301 applies. Section 306 stock is defined in section 306(c) and is usually preferred stock received either as a nontaxable dividend or in a transaction in which no gain or loss is recognized. Section 306(b) lists certain circumstances in which the special rules of section 306(a) shall not apply.

(b) (1) If a shareholder sells or otherwise disposes of section 306 stock (other than by redemption or within the exceptions listed in section 306(b)), the entire proceeds received from such disposition shall be treated as ordinary income to the extent that the fair market value of the stock sold, on the date distributed to the shareholder, would have been a dividend to such shareholder had the distributing corporation distributed cash in lieu of stock. Any excess of the amount received over the sum of the amount treated as ordinary income plus the adjusted basis of the stock disposed of, shall be treated as gain from the sale of a capital asset or noncapital asset as the case may be. No loss shall be recognized. No reduction of earnings and profits results from any disposition of stock other than a redemption. The term "disposition" under section 306(a)(1) includes, among other things, pledges of stock under certain circumstances, particularly where the pledgee can look only to the stock itself as its security.

(2) Section 306(a)(1) may be illustrated by the following examples:

Example (1). On December 15, 1954, A and B owned equally all of the stock of Corporation X which files its income tax return on a calendar year basis. On that date Corporation X distributed pro rata 100 shares of preferred stock as a dividend on its outstanding common stock. On December 15, 1954, the preferred stock had a fair market value of $10,000. On December 31, 1954, the earnings and profits of Corporation X were $20,000. The 50 shares of preferred stock so distributed to A had an allocated basis to him of $10 per share or a total of $500 for the 50 shares. Such shares had a fair market value of $5,000 when issued. A sold the 50 shares of preferred stock on July 1, 1955, for $6,000. Of this amount $5,000 will be treated as ordinary income; $500 ($6,000 minus $5,500) will be treated as gain from the sale of a capital or noncapital asset as the case may be.

Example (2). The facts are the same as in Example 1 except that A sold his 50 shares of preferred stock for $5,100. Of this amount $5,000 will be treated as ordinary income. No loss will be allowed. There will be added back to the basis of the common stock of Corporation X with respect to which the preferred stock was distributed, $400, the allocated basis of $500 reduced by the $100 received.

Example (3). The facts are the same as in example 1 except that A sold 25 of his shares of preferred stock for $2,600. Of this amount $2,500 will be treated as ordinary income. No loss will be allowed. There will be added back to the basis of the common stock of Corporation X with respect to which the preferred stock was distributed, $150, the allocated basis of $250 reduced by the $100 received.

(c) The entire amount received by a shareholder from the redemption of section 306 stock shall be treated as a distribution of property under section 301. See also section 303 (relating to distribution in redemption of stock to pay death taxes).

§ 1.306–2 Exception.

(a) If a shareholder terminates his entire stock interest in a corporation—

(1) By a sale or other disposition within the requirements of section 306(b)(1)(A), or

(2) By redemption under section 302(b)(3) (through the application of section 306(b)(1)(B)),

the amount received from such disposition shall be treated as an amount received in part or full payment for the stock sold or redeemed. In the case of a sale, only the stock interest need be terminated. In determining whether an entire stock interest has been terminated under section 306(b)(1)(A), all of the provisions of section 318(a) (relating to constructive ownership of stock) shall be applicable. In determining whether a shareholder has terminated his entire interest in a corporation by a redemption of his stock under section 302(b)(3), all of the provisions of section 318(a) shall be applicable unless the shareholder meets the requirements of section 302(c)(2) (relating to termination of all interest in the corporation). If the requirements of section 302(c)(2) are met, section 318(a)(1) (relating to members of a family) shall be inapplicable. Under all circumstances paragraphs (2), (3), (4), and (5) of section 318(a) shall be applicable.

(b) Section 306(a) does not apply to—

(1) Redemptions of section 306 stock pursuant to a partial or complete liquidation of a corporation to which part II (section 331 and following), subchapter C, chapter 1 of the Code applies,

(2) Exchanges of section 306 stock solely for stock in connection with a reorganization or in an exchange under section 351, 355, or section 1036 (relating to exchanges of stock for stock in the same corporation) to the extent that gain or loss is not recognized to the shareholder as the result of the exchange of the stock (see paragraph (d) of §1.306–3 relative to the receipt of other property), and

(3) A disposition or redemption, if it is established to the satisfaction of the Commissioner that the distribution, and the disposition or redemption, was not in pursuance of a plan having as one of its principal purposes the avoidance of Federal income tax. However, in the case of a prior or simultaneous disposition (or redemption) of the stock with respect to which the section 306 stock disposed of (or redeemed) was issued, it is not necessary to establish that the distribution was not in pursuance of such a plan. For example, in the absence of such a plan and of any other facts the first sentence of this subparagraph would be applicable to the case of dividends and isolated dispositions of section 306 stock by minority shareholders. Similarly, in the absence of such a plan and of any other facts, if a shareholder received a distribution of 100 shares of section 306 stock on his holdings of 100 shares of voting common stock in a corporation and sells his voting common stock before he disposes of his section 306 stock, the subsequent disposition of his section 306 stock would not ordinarily be considered a disposition one of the principal purposes of which is the avoidance of Federal income tax.

§ 1.306–3 Section 306 stock defined.

(a) For the purpose of subchapter C, chapter 1 of the Code, the term "section 306 stock" means stock which meets the requirements of section 306(c)(1). Any class of stock distributed to a shareholder in a transaction in which no amount is includible in the income of the shareholder or no gain or loss is recognized may be section 306 stock, if a distribution of money by the distributing corporation in lieu of such stock would have been a dividend in whole or in part. However, except as provided in section 306(g), if no part of a distribution of money by the distributing corporation in lieu of such stock would have been a dividend, the stock distributed will not constitute section 306 stock.

(b) For the purpose of section 306, rights to acquire stock shall be treated as stock. Such rights shall not be section 306 stock if no part of the distribution would have been a dividend if money had been distributed in lieu of the rights. When stock is acquired by the exercise of rights which are treated at section 306 stock, the stock acquired is section 306 stock. Upon the disposition of such stock (other than by redemption or within the exceptions listed in section 306(b)), the proceeds received from the disposition shall be treated as ordinary income to the extent that the fair market value of the stock rights, on the date distributed to the shareholder, would have been a dividend to the shareholder had the distributing corporation distributed cash in lieu of stock rights. Any excess of the amount realized over the sum of the amount treated as ordinary income plus the adjusted basis of the stock, shall be treated as gain from the sale of the stock.

(c) Section 306(c)(1)(A) provides that section 306 stock is any stock (other than common issued with respect to common) distributed to the shareholder selling or otherwise disposing thereof if, under section 305(a) (relating to distributions of stock and stock rights) any part of the distribution was not included in the gross income of the distributee.

(d) Section 306(c)(1)(B) includes in the definition of section 306 stock any stock except common stock, which is received by a shareholder in connection with a reorganization under section 368 or in a distribution or exchange under section 355 (or so much of section 356 as relates to section 355) provided the effect of the transaction is substantially the same as the receipt of a stock dividend, or the stock is received in exchange for section 306 stock. If, in a transaction to which section 356 is applicable, a shareholder exchanges section 306 stock for stock and money or other property, the entire amount of such money and of the fair market value of the other property (not limited to the gain recognized) shall be treated as a distribution of property to which section 301 applies. Common stock received in exchange for section 306 stock in a recapitalization shall not be considered section 306 stock. Ordinarily, section 306 stock includes stock which is not common stock received in pursuance of a plan of reorganization (within the meaning of section 368(a)) or received in a distribution or exchange to which section 355 (or so much of section 356 as relates to section 355) applies if cash received in lieu of such stock would have been treated as a dividend under section 356(a)(2) or would have been treated as a distribution to which section 301 applies by virtue of section 356(b) or section 302(d). The application of the preceding sentence is illustrated by the following examples:

Example (1). Corporation A, having only common stock outstanding, is merged in a statutory merger (qualifying as a reorganization under section 368(a)) with Corporation B. Pursuant to such merger, the shareholders of Corporation A received both common and preferred stock in Corporation B. The preferred stock received by such shareholders is section 306 stock.

Example (2). X and Y each own one-half of the 2,000 outstanding shares of preferred stock and one-half of the 2,000 outstanding shares of common stock of Corporation C. Pursuant to a reorganization within the meaning of section 368(a)(1)(E) (recapitalization) each shareholder exchanges his preferred stock for preferred stock of a new issue which is not substantially different from the preferred stock previously held. Unless the preferred stock exchanged was itself section 306 stock the preferred stock received is not section 306 stock.

(e) Section 306(c)(1)(C) includes in the definition of section 306 stock any stock (except as provided in section 306(c)(1)(B)) the basis of which in the hands of the person disposing of such stock, is determined by reference to section 306 stock held by such shareholder or any other person. Under this paragraph common stock can be section 306 stock. Thus, if a person owning section 306 stock in Corporation A transfers it to Corporation B which is controlled by him in exchange for common stock of Corporation B in a transaction to which section 351 is applicable, the common stock so received by him would be section 306 stock and subject to the provisions of section 306(a) on its disposition. In addition, the section 306 stock transferred is section 306 stock in the hands of Corporation B, the transferee. Section 306 stock transferred by gift remains section 306 stock in the hands of the donee. Stock received in exchange for section 306 stock under section 1036(a) (relating to exchange of stock for stock in the same corporation) or under so much of section 1031(b) as relates to section 1036(a) becomes section 306 stock and acquires, for purposes of section 306, the characteristics of the section 306 stock exchanged. The entire amount of the fair market value of the other property received in such transaction shall be considered as received upon a disposition (other than a redemption) to which section 306(a) applies. Section 306 stock ceases to be so classified if the basis of such stock is determined by reference to its fair market value on the date of the decedent–stockholder's death or the optional valuation date under section 1014.

(f) If section 306 stock which was distributed with respect to common stock is exchanged for common stock in the same corporation (whether or not such exchange is pursuant to a conversion privilege contained in section 306 stock), such common stock shall not be section 306 stock. This paragraph applies to exchanges not coming within the purview of section 306(c)(1)(B). Common stock which is convertible into stock other than common stock or into property, shall not be considered common stock. It is immaterial whether the conversion privilege is contained in the stock or in some type of collateral agreement.

(g) If there is a substantial change in the terms and conditions of any stock, then, for the purpose of this section—

(1) The fair market value of such stock shall be the fair market value at the time of distribution or the fair market value at the time of such change, whichever is higher;

(2) Such stock's ratable share of the amount which would have been a dividend if money had been distributed in lieu of stock shall be determined by reference to the time of distribution or by reference to the time of such change, whichever ratable share is higher; and

(3) Section 306(c)(2) shall be inapplicable if there would have been a dividend to any extent if money had been distributed in lieu of the stock either at the time of the distribution or at the time of such change.

* * *

§ 1.307–1 General.

(a) If a shareholder receives stock or stock rights as a distribution on stock previously held and under section 305 such distribution is not includible in gross income then, except as provided in section 307(b) and §1.307–2, the basis of the stock with respect to which the distribution was made shall be allocated between the old and new stocks or rights in proportion to the fair market values of each on the date of distribution. If a shareholder receives stock or stock rights as a distribution on stock previously held and pursuant to section 305 part of the distribution is not includible in gross income, then (except as provided in section 307(b) and §1.307–2) the basis of the stock with respect to which the distribution is made shall be allocated between (1) the old stock and (2) that part of the new stock or rights which is not includible in gross income, in proportion to the fair market values of each on the date of distribution. The date of distribution in each case shall be the date the stock or the rights are distributed to the stockholder and not the record date. The general rule will apply with respect to stock rights only if such rights are exercised or sold.

(b) The application of paragraph (a) of this section is illustrated by the following example:

Example. A taxpayer in 1947 purchased 100 shares of common stock at $100 per share and in 1954 by reason of the ownership of such stock acquired 100 rights entitling him to subscribe to 100 additional shares of such stock at $90 a share. Immediately after the issuance of the rights, each of the shares of stock in respect of which the rights were acquired had a fair market value, ex-rights, of $110 and the rights had a fair market value of $19 each. The basis of the rights and the common stock for the purpose of determining the basis for gain or loss on a subsequent sale or exercise of the rights or a sale of the old stock is computed as follows:

100 (shares) × $100 = $10,000, cost of old stock (stock in respect of which the rights were acquired).

100 (shares) × $110 = $11,000, market value of old stock.

100 (rights) × $19 = $1,900, market value of rights.

11,000/12,900 of $10,000 = $8,527.13, cost of old stock apportioned to such stock.

1,900/12,900 of $10,000 = $1,472.87, cost of old stock apportioned to rights.

If the rights are sold, the basis for determining gain or loss will be $14.7287 per right. If the rights are exercised, the basis of the new stock acquired will be the subscription price paid therefor ($90) plus the basis of the rights exercised ($14.7287 each) or $104.7287 per share. The remaining basis of the old stock for the purpose of determining gain or loss on a subsequent sale will be $85.2713 per share.

* * *

Effects On Corporation

* * *

§ 1.312–1 Adjustment to earnings and profits reflecting distributions by corporations.

(a) In general, on the distribution of property by a corporation with respect to its stock, its earnings, and profits (to the extent thereof) shall be decreased by—

(1) The amount of money,

(2) The principal amount of the obligations of such corporation issued in such distribution, and

(3) The adjusted basis of other property.

For special rule with respect to distributions to which section 312(e)* applies, see §1.312–5.

(b) The adjustment provided in section 312(a)(3) and paragraph (a)(3) of this section with respect to a distribution of property (other than money or its own obligations) shall be made notwithstanding the fact that such property has appreciated or depreciated in value since acquisition.

(c) The application of paragraphs (a) and (b) of this section may be illustrated by the following examples:

Example (1). Corporation A distributes to its sole shareholder property with a value of $10,000 and a basis of $5,000. It has $12,500 in earnings and profits. The reduction in earnings and profits by reason of such distribution is $5,000. Such is the reduction even though the amount of $10,000 is includible in the income of the shareholder (other than a corporation) as a dividend.

Example (2). The facts are the same as in example (1) above except that the property has a basis of $15,000 and the earnings and profits of the corporation are $20,000. The reduction in earnings and profits is $15,000. Such is the reduction even though only the amount of $10,000 is includible in the income of the shareholder as a dividend.

(d) In the case of a distribution of stock or rights to acquire stock a portion of which is includible in income by reason of section 305(b), the earnings and profits shall be reduced by the fair market value of such portion. No reduction shall be made if a distribution of stock or rights to acquire stock is not includible in income under the provisions of section 305.

(e) No adjustment shall be made in the amount of the earnings and profits of the issuing corporation upon a disposition of section 306 stock unless such disposition is a redemption.

*Editorial comment: The Regulations do not reflect the effect of the Tax Reform Act of 1984 which repealed Sec. 312(e).

§ 1.312–2 Distribution of inventory assets.

Section 312(b)* provides for the increase and the decrease of the earnings and profits of a corporation which distributes, with respect to its stock, inventory assets as defined in section 312(b)(2), where the fair market value of such assets exceeds their adjusted basis. The rules provided in section 312(b) (relating to distributions of certain inventory assets) shall be applicable without regard to the method used in computing inventories for the purpose of the computation of taxable income. * * *

§ 1.312–3 Liabilities.

The amount of any reductions in earnings and profits described in section 312(a) or (b) shall be (a) reduced by the amount of any liability to which the property distributed was subject and by the amount of any other liability of the corporation assumed by the shareholder in connection with such distribution, and (b) increased by the amount of gain recognized to the corporation under section 311 * * * or under section 341(f), 617(d), 1245(a), 1250(a), 1251(c), 1252(a), or 1254(a).

* * *

§ 1.312–6 Earnings and profits.

(a) In determining the amount of earnings and profits (whether of the taxable year, or accumulated since February 28, 1913, or accumulated before March 1, 1913) due consideration must be given to the facts, and, while mere bookkeeping entries increasing or decreasing surplus will not be conclusive, the amount of the earnings and profits in any case will be dependent upon the method of accounting properly employed in computing taxable income (or net income, as the case may be). For instance, a corporation keeping its books and filing its income tax returns under subchapter E, chapter 1 of the Code, on the cash receipts and disbursements basis may not use the accrual basis in determining earnings and profits; a corporation computing income on the installment basis as provided in section 453 shall, with respect to the installment transactions, compute earnings and profits on such basis; and an insurance company subject to taxation under section 831 shall exclude from earnings and profits that portion of any premium which is unearned under the provisions of section 832(b)(4) and which is segregated accordingly in the unearned premium reserve.

(b) Among the items entering into the computation of corporate earnings and profits for a particular period are all income exempted by statute, income not taxable by the Federal Government under the Constitution, as well as all items includible in gross income under section 61 or corresponding provisions of prior revenue acts. Gains and losses within the purview of section 1002 or corresponding provisions of prior revenue acts are brought into the earnings and profits at the time and to the extent such gains and losses are recognized under that section. Interest on State bonds and certain other obligations, although not taxable when received by a corporation, is taxable to the same extent as other dividends when distributed to shareholders in the form of dividends.

(c) (1) In the case of a corporation in which depletion or depreciation is a factor in the determination of income, the only depletion or depreciation deductions to be considered in the computation of the total earnings and profits are those based on cost or other basis without regard to March 1, 1913, value. In computing the earnings and profits for any period beginning after February 28, 1913, the only depletion or depreciation deductions to be considered are those based on (i) cost or other basis, if the depletable or depreciable asset was acquired subsequent to February 28, 1913, or (ii) adjusted cost or March 1, 1913, value, whichever is higher, if acquired before March 1, 1913. Thus, discovery or percentage depletion under all revenue acts for mines and oil and gas wells is not to be taken into consideration in computing the earnings and profits of a corporation. Similarly, where the basis of property in the hands of a corporation is a substituted basis, such basis, and not the fair market value of the property at the time of the acquisition by the corporation, is the basis for computing depletion and depreciation for the purpose of determining earnings and profits of the corporation.

(2) The application of subparagraph (1) of this paragraph may be illustrated by the following example:

Example. Oil producing property which A had acquired in 1949 at a cost of $28,000 was transferred to Corporation Y in December 1951, in exchange for all of its capital stock. The fair market value of the stock and of the property as of the date of the transfer was $247,000. Corporation Y, after four years' operation, effected in 1955 a cash distribution to A in the amount of $165,000. In determining the extent to which the earnings and profits of Corporation Y available for dividend distributions have been increased as the result of production and sale of oil, the depletion to be taken into account is to be computed upon the basis of $28,000 established in the nontaxable exchange in 1951 regardless of the fair market value of the property or of the stock issued in exchange therefor.

* * *

*Editorial comment: The Regulations do not reflect the effect of the Tax Reform Act of 1986 which broadened the impact of Sec. 312(b) by replacing "inventory" with "appreciated property."

§ 1.312–15 Effect of depreciation on earnings and profits.*

(a) Depreciation for taxable years beginning after June 30, 1972—(1) In general. Except as provided in subparagraph (2) of this paragraph and paragraph (c) of this section, for purposes of computing the earnings and profits of a corporation (including a real estate investment trust as defined in section 856) for any taxable year beginning after June 30, 1972, the allowance for depreciation (and amortization, if any) shall be deemed to be the amount which would be allowable for such year if the straight line method of depreciation had been used for all property for which depreciation is allowable for each taxable year beginning after June 30, 1972. Thus, for taxable years beginning after June 30, 1972, in determining the earnings and profits of a corporation, depreciation must be computed under the straight line method, notwithstanding that in determining taxable income the corporation uses an accelerated method of depreciation described in subparagraph (A), (B), or (C) of section 312(m)(2) or elects to amortize the basis of property under section 169, 184, 187, or 188, or any similar provision.* * *

(2) Exception. **(i)** If, for any taxable year beginning after June 30, 1972, a method of depreciation is used by a corporation in computing taxable income which the Secretary or his delegate has determined results in a reasonable allowance under section 167(a) and which is not a declining balance method of depreciation (described in §1.167(b)–2), the sum of the years–digits method (described in §1.167(b) –3), or any other method allowed solely by reason of the application of subsection (b)(4) or (j)(1)(C) of section 167, then the adjustment to earnings and profits for depreciation for such year shall be determined under the method so used (in lieu of the straight line method).

(ii) The Commissioner has determined that the "unit of production" (see §1.167(b)-0(b)), and the "machine hour" methods of depreciation, when properly used under appropriate circumstances, meet the requirements of subdivision (i) of this subparagraph. Thus, the adjustment to earnings and profits for depreciation (for the taxable year for which either of such methods is properly used under appropriate circumstances) shall be determined under whichever of such methods is used to compute taxable income.

(3) Determinations under straight line method. **(i)** In the case of property with respect to which an allowance for depreciation is claimed in computing taxable income, the determination of the amount which would be allowable under the straight line method shall be based on the manner in which the corporation computes depreciation in determining taxable income. Thus, if an election under §1.167 (a)–11 is in effect with respect to the property, the amount of depreciation which would be allowable under the straight line method shall be determined under §1.167(a)–11(g)(3). On the other hand, if property is not depreciated under the provisions of §1.167(a)–11, the amount of depreciation which would be allowable under the straight line method shall be determined under §1.167(b)–1. Any election made under section 167(f), with respect to reducing the amount of salvage value taken into account in computing the depreciation allowance for certain property, or any convention adopted under §1.167(a)–10(b) or §1.167(a)–11(c)(2), with respect to additions and retirements from multiple asset accounts, which is used in computing depreciation for taxable income shall be used in computing depreciation for earnings and profits purposes.

(ii) In the case of property with respect to which an election to amortize is in effect under section 169, 184, 187, or 188, or any similar provision, the amount which would be allowable under the straight line method of depreciation shall be determined under the provisions of §1.167(b)–1. Thus, the cost or other basis of the property, less its estimated salvage value, is to be deducted in equal annual amounts over the period of the estimated useful life of the property. In computing the amount of depreciation for earnings and profits purposes, a taxpayer may utilize the provisions of section 167(f) (relating to the reduction in the amount of salvage value taken into account in computing the depreciation allowance for certain property) and any convention which could have been adopted for such property under §1.167(a)–10(b) (relating to additions and retirements from multiple asset accounts).

* * *

(d) Books and records. Wherever different methods of depreciation are used for taxable income and earnings and profits purposes, records shall be maintained which show the depreciation taken for earnings and profits purposes each year and which will allow computation of the adjusted basis of the property in each account using the depreciation taken for earnings and profits purposes.

*Editorial comment: The Regulations do not reflect the effect of the Tax Reform Act of 1986 which created the alternative depreciation system for E & P purposes. See Sec. 312(k)(3).

Definitions; Constructive Ownership of Stock

§ 1.316–1 Dividends.

(a)(1) The term "dividend" for the purpose of subtitle A of the Code (except when used in subchapter L, chapter 1 of the Code, in any case where the reference is to dividends and similar distributions of insurance companies paid to policyholders as such) comprises any distribution of property as defined in section 317 in the ordinary course of business, even though extraordinary in amount, made by a domestic or foreign corporation to its shareholders out of either

(i) Earnings and profits accumulated since February 28, 1913, or

(ii) Earnings and profits of the taxable year computed without regard to the amount of the earnings and profits (whether of such year or accumulated since February 28, 1913) at the time the distribution was made.

The earnings and profits of the taxable year shall be computed as of the close of such year, without diminution by reason of any distributions made during the taxable year. For the purpose of determining whether a distribution constitutes a dividend, it is unnecessary to ascertain the amount of the earnings and profits accumulated since February 28, 1913, if the earnings and profits of the taxable year are equal to or in excess of the total amount of the distributions made within such year.

(2) Where a corporation distributes property to its shareholders on or after June 22, 1954, the amount of the distribution which is a dividend to them may not exceed the earnings and profits of the distributing corporation.

(3) The rule of (2) above may be illustrated by the following example:

Example. X and Y, individuals, each own one-half of the stock of Corporation A which has earnings and profits of $10,000. Corporation A distributes property having a basis of $6,000 and a fair market value of $16,000 to its shareholders, each shareholder receiving property with a basis of $3,000 and with a fair market value of $8,000 in a distribution to which section 301 applies. The amount taxable to each shareholder as a dividend under section 301(c) is $5,000.

* * *

(c) Except as provided in section 316(b)(1), the term "dividend" includes any distribution of property to shareholders to the extent made out of accumulated or current earnings and profits. See, however, section 331 (relating to distributions in complete or partial liquidation), * * * section 302(b) (relating to redemptions treated as amounts received from the sale or exchange of stock), and section 303 (relating to distributions in redemption of stock to pay death taxes). See also section 305(b) for certain distributions of stock or stock rights treated as distributions of property.

* * *

(e) The application of section 316 may be illustrated by the following examples:

Example (1). At the beginning of the calendar year 1955, Corporation M had an operating deficit of $200,000 and the earnings and profits for the year amounted to $100,000. Beginning on March 16, 1955, the corporation made quarterly distributions of $25,000 during the taxable year to its shareholders. Each distribution is a taxable dividend in full, irrespective of the actual or the pro rata amount of the earnings and profits on hand at any of the dates of distribution, since the total distributions made during the year ($100,000) did not exceed the total earnings and profits of the year ($100,000).

* * *

§ 1.316–2 Sources of distribution in general.

(a) For the purpose of income taxation every distribution made by a corporation is made out of earnings and profits to the extent thereof and from the most recently accumulated earnings and profits. In determining the source of a distribution, consideration should be given first, to the earnings and profits of the taxable year; second, to the earnings and profits accumulated since February 28, 1913, only in the case where, and to the extent that, the distributions made during the taxable year are not regarded as out of the earnings and profits of that year; third, to the earnings and profits accumulated before March 1, 1913, only after all the earnings and profits of the taxable year and all the earnings and profits accumulated since February 28, 1913, have been distributed; and, fourth, to sources other than earnings and profits only after the earnings and profits have been distributed.

(b) If the earnings and profits of the taxable year (computed as of the close of the year without diminution by reason of any distributions made during the year and without regard to the amount of earnings and profits at the time of the distribution) are sufficient in amount to cover all the distributions made during that year, then each distribution is a taxable dividend. See § 1.316–1. If the distributions made during the taxable year consist only of money and exceed the earnings and profits of such year, then that proportion of each distribution which the total of the earnings and profits of the year bears to the total distributions made during the year shall be regarded as out of the earnings and profits of that year. The portion of each such distribution which is not regarded as out of earnings and profits of the taxable year shall be considered a taxable dividend to the extent of the earnings and profits accumulated since February 28, 1913, and available on the date of the distribution. In any case in which it is necessary to determine the amount of earnings and profits accumulated since February 28, 1913, and the actual earnings and profits to the date of a distribution within any taxable year (whether beginning before January 1, 1936, or, in the case of an operating deficit, on or after that date) cannot be shown, the earnings and profits for the year (or accounting period, if less than a year) in which the distribution was made shall be prorated to the date of the distribution not counting the date on which the distribution was made.

(c) The provisions of the section may be illustrated by the following example:

Example. At the beginning of the calendar year 1955, Corporation M had $12,000 in earnings and profits accumulated since February 28, 1913. Its earnings and profits for 1955 amounted to $30,000. During the year it made quarterly cash distributions of $15,000 each. Of each of the four distributions made, $7,500 (that portion of $15,000 which the amount of $30,000, the total earnings and profits of the taxable year, bears to $60,000, the total distributions made during the year) was paid out of the earnings and profits of the taxable year; and of the first and second distributions, $7,500 and $4,500, respectively, were paid out of the earnings and profits accumulated after February 28, 1913, and before the taxable year, as follows:

Distributions during 1955				
Date	Amount	Portion out of earnings and profits of the taxable year	Portion out of earnings accumulated since Feb.28, 1913, and before the taxable year	Taxable amt. of each distribution
March 10	$15,000	$7,500	$7,500	$15,000
June 10	15,000	7,500	4,500	12,000
September 10	15,000	7,500	.....	7,500
December 10	15,000	7,500	.....	7,500
Total amount taxable as dividends	.....	.....	.....	42,000

(d) Any distribution by a corporation out of earnings and profits accumulated before March 1, 1913, or out of increase in value of property accrued before March 1, 1913 (whether or not realized by sale or other disposition, and, if realized, whether before, on, or after March 1, 1913), is not a dividend within the meaning of subtitle A of the Code.

* * *

§ 1.318–1 Constructive ownership of stock; introduction.

(a) For the purposes of certain provisions of chapter 1 of the Code, section 318(a) provides that stock owned by a taxpayer includes stock constructively owned by such taxpayer under the rules set forth in such section. An individual is considered to own the stock owned, directly or indirectly, by or for his spouse (other than a spouse who is legally separated from the individual under a decree of divorce or separate maintenance), and by or for his children, grandchildren, and parents. Under section 318(a)(2) and (3), constructive ownership rules are established for partnerships and partners, estates and beneficiaries, trusts and beneficiaries, and corporations and stockholders. If any person has an option to acquire stock, such stock is considered as owned by such person. The term "option" includes an option to acquire such an option and each of a series of such options.

(b) In applying section 318(a) to determine the stock ownership of any person for any one purpose—

(1) A corporation shall not be considered to own its own stock by reason of section 318(a)(3)(C);

(2) In any case in which an amount of stock owned by any person may be included in the computation more than one time, such stock shall be included only once, in the manner in which it will impute to the person concerned the largest total stock ownership; and

(3) In determining the 50-percent requirement of section 318(a)(2)(C) and (3)(C), all of the stock owned actually and constructively by the person concerned shall be aggregated.

§ 1.318–2 Application of general rules.

(a) The application of paragraph (b) of § 1.318–1 may be illustrated by the following examples:

Example (1). H, an individual, owns all of the stock of corporation A. Corporation A is not considered to own the stock owned by H in corporation A.

Example (2). H, an individual, his wife, W, and his son, S, each own one-third of the stock of the Green Corporation. For purposes of determining the amount of stock owned by H, W, or S for purposes of section 318(a)(2)(C) and (3)(C), the amount of stock held by the other members of the family shall be added pursuant to paragraph (b)(3) of § 1.318–1 in applying the 50-percent requirement of such section. H, W, or S, as the case may be, is for this purpose deemed to own 100 percent of the stock of the Green Corporation.

(b) The application of section 318(a)(1), relating to members of a family, may be illustrated by the following example:

Example. An individual, H, his wife, W, his son, S, and his grandson (S's son), G, own the 100 outstanding shares of stock of a corporation, each owning 25 shares. H, W, and S are each considered as owning 100 shares. G is considered as owning only 50 shares, that is, his own and his father's.

(c) The application of section 318(a)(2) and (3), relating to partnerships, trusts and corporations, may be illustrated by the following examples:

Example (1). A, an individual, has a 50 percent interest in a partnership. The partnership owns 50 of the 100 outstanding shares of stock of a corporation, the remaining 50 shares being owned by A. The partnership is considered as owning 100 shares. A is considered as owning 75 shares.

Example (2). A testamentary trust owns 25 of the outstanding 100 shares of stock of a corporation. A, an individual, who holds a vested remainder in the trust having a value, computed actuarially equal to 4 percent of the value of the trust property, owns the remaining 75 shares. Since the interest of A in the trust is a vested interest rather than a contingent interest (whether or not remote), the trust is considered as owning 100 shares. A is considered as owning 76 shares.

Example (3). The facts are the same as in (2), above, except that A's interest in the trust is a contingent remainder. A is considered as owning 76 shares. However, since A's interest in the trust is a remote contingent interest, the trust is not considered as owning any of the shares owned by A.

Example (4). A and B, unrelated individuals, own 70 percent and 30 percent, respectively, in value of the stock of Corporation M. Corporation M owns 50 of the 100 outstanding shares of stock of Corporation O, the remaining 50 shares being owned by A. Corporation M is considered as owning 100 shares of Corporation O, and A is considered as owning 85 shares.

* * *

§ 1.318–3 Estates, trusts, and options.

(a) For the purpose of applying section 318(a), relating to estates, property of a decedent shall be considered as owned by his estate if such property is subject to administration by the executor or administrator for the purpose of paying claims against the estate and expenses of administration notwithstanding that, under local law, legal title to such property vests in the decedent's heirs, legatees or devisees immediately upon death. The term "beneficiary" includes any person entitled to receive property of a decedent pursuant to a will or pursuant to laws of descent and distribution. A person shall no longer be considered a beneficiary of an estate when all the property to which he is entitled has been received by him, when he no longer has a claim against the estate arising out of having been a beneficiary, and when there is only a remote possibility that it will be necessary for the estate to seek the return of property or to seek payment from him by contribution or otherwise to satisfy claims against the estate or expenses of administration. When, pursuant to the preceding sentence, a person ceases to be a beneficiary, stock owned by him shall not thereafter be considered owned by the estate, and stock owned by the estate shall not thereafter be considered owned by him. The application of section 318(a) relating to estates may be illustrated by the following examples:

Example (1). (a) A decedent's estate owns 50 of the 100 outstanding shares of stock of corporation X. The remaining shares are owned by three unrelated individuals, A, B, and C, who together own the entire interest in the estate. A owns 12 shares of stock of corporation X directly and is entitled to 50 percent of the estate. B owns 18 shares directly and has a life estate in the remaining 50 percent of the estate. C owns 20 shares directly and also owns the remainder interest after B's life estate.

(b) If section 318(a)(5)(C) applies (see paragraph (c)(3) of § 1.318–4), the stock of corporation X is considered to be owned as follows: the estate is considered as owning 80 shares, 50 shares directly, 12 shares constructively through A, and 18 shares constructively through B; A is considered as owning 37 shares, 12 shares directly, and 25 shares constructively (50 percent of the 50 shares owned directly by the estate); B is considered as owning 43 shares, 18 shares directly and 25 shares constructively (50 percent of the 50 shares owned directly by the estate); C is considered as owning 20 shares directly and no shares constructively. C is not considered a beneficiary of the estate under section 318(a) since he has no direct present interest in the property held by the estate nor in the income produced by such property.

(c) If section 318(a)(5)(C) does not apply, A is considered as owning nine additional shares (50 percent of the 18 shares owned constructively by the estate through B), and B is considered as owning six additional shares (50 percent of the 12 shares owned constructively by the estate through A).

Example (2). Under the will of A, Blackacre is left to B for life, remainder to C, an unrelated individual. The residue of the estate consisting of stock of a corporation is left to D. B and D are beneficiaries of the estate under section 318(a). C is not considered a beneficiary since he has no direct present interest in Blackacre nor in the income produced by such property. The stock owned by the estate is considered as owned proportionately by B and D.

(b) For the purpose of section 318(a)(2)(B) stock owned by a trust will be considered as being owned by its beneficiaries only to the extent of the interest of such beneficiaries in the trust. Accordingly, the interest of income beneficiaries, remainder beneficiaries, and other beneficiaries will be computed on an actuarial basis. Thus, if a trust owns 100 percent of the stock of Corporation A, and if, on an actuarial basis, W's life interest in the trust is 15 percent, Y's life interest is 25 percent, and Z's remainder interest is 60 percent, under this provision W will be considered to be the owner of 15 percent of the stock of Corporation A, Y will be considered to be the owner of 25 percent of such stock, and Z will be considered to be the owner of 60 percent of such stock. The factors and methods prescribed in § 20.2031–7 of this chapter (Estate Tax Regulations) for use in ascertaining the value of an interest in property for estate tax purposes shall be used in determining a beneficiary's actuarial interest in a trust for purposes of this section. See § 20.2031–7 of this chapter (Estate Tax Regulations) for examples illustrating the use of these factors and methods.

(c) The application of section 318(a) relating to options may be illustrated by the following example:

Example. A and B, unrelated individuals, own all of the 100 outstanding shares of stock of a corporation, each owning 50 shares. A has an option to acquire 25 of B's shares and has an option to acquire a further option to acquire the remaining 25 of B's shares. A is considered as owning the entire 100 shares of stock of the corporation.

§ 1.318–4 Constructive ownership as actual ownership; exceptions.

(a) In general. Section 318(a)(5)(A) provides that, except as provided in section 318(a)(5)(B) and (C), stock constructively owned by a person by reason of the application of section 318(a)(1), (2), (3), or (4) shall be considered as actually owned by such person for purposes of applying section 318(a)(1), (2), (3), and (4). For example, if a trust owns 50 percent of the stock of corporation X, stock of corporation Y owned by corporation X which is attributed to the trust may be further attributed to the beneficiaries of the trust.

(b) Constructive family ownership. Section 318 (a)(5)(B) provides that stock constructively owned by an individual by reason of ownership by a member of his family shall not be considered as owned by him for purposes of making another family member the constructive owner of such stock under section 318 (a)(1). For example, if F and his two sons, A and B, each own one-third of the stock of a corporation, under section 318(a)(1), A is treated as owning constructively the stock owned by his father but is not treated as owning the stock owned by B. Section 318(a)(5)(B) prevents the attribution of the stock of one brother through the father to the other brother, an attribution beyond the scope of section 318(a)(1) directly.

(c) Reattribution. **(1)** Section 318(a)(5)(C) provides that stock constructively owned by a partnership, estate, trust, or corporation by reason of the application of section 318(a)(3) shall not be considered as owned by it for purposes of applying section 318(a)(2) in order to make another the constructive owner of such stock. For example, if two unrelated individuals are beneficiaries of the same trust, stock held by one which is attributed to the trust under section 318(a)(3) is not reattributed from the trust to the other beneficiary. However, stock constructively owned by reason of section 318(a)(2) may be reattributed under section 318 (a)(3). Thus, for example, if all the stock of corporations X and Y is owned by A, stock of corporation Z held by X is attributed to Y through A.

(2) Section 318(a)(5)(C) does not prevent reattribution under section 318(a)(2) of stock constructively owned by an entity under section 318(a)(3) if the stock is also constructively owned by the entity under section 318(a)(4). For example, if individuals A and B are beneficiaries of a trust and the trust has an option to buy stock from A, B is considered under section 318(a)(2)(B) as owning a proportionate part of such stock.

* * *

Corporate Liquidations

Effects on Recipients

§ 1.331–1 Corporate liquidations.

(a) Section 331 contains rules governing the extent to which gain or loss is recognized to a shareholder receiving a distribution in complete* * * liquidation of a corporation. Under section 331(a)(1),* it is provided that amounts distributed in complete liquidation of a corporation shall be treated as in full

*Editorial comment: Sec. 331(a) rather than Sec. 331(a)(1).

payment in exchange for the stock. * * * If section 331 is applicable to the distribution of property by a corporation, section 301 (relating to the effects on a shareholder of distributions of property) has no application other than to a distribution in complete liquidation to which section 316(b)(2)(B) applies. See paragraph (b)(2) of § 1.316–1.

(b) The gain or loss to a shareholder from a distribution in * * * complete liquidation is to be determined under section 1001 by comparing the amount of the distribution with the cost or other basis of the stock. The gain or loss will be recognized to the extent provided in section 1002 and will be subject to the provisions of parts I, II, and III (section 1201 and following), subchapter P, chapter 1 of the Code.

(c) A liquidation which is followed by a transfer to another corporation of all or part of the assets of the liquidating corporation or which is preceded by such a transfer may, however, have the effect of the distribution of a dividend or of a transaction in which no loss is recognized and gain is recognized only to the extent of "other property." See sections 301 and 356.

(d) In every case in which a shareholder transfers stock in exchange for property to the corporation which issued such stock, the facts and circumstances shall be reported on his return unless the property is part of a distribution made pursuant to a corporate resolution reciting that the distribution is made in liquidation of the corporation and the corporation is completely liquidated and dissolved within one year after the distribution. See section 6043 for requirements relating to returns by corporations.

(e) The provisions of this section may be illustrated by the following example:

Example. A, an individual who makes his income tax returns on the calendar year basis, owns 20 shares of stock of the P Corporation, a domestic corporation, 10 shares of which were acquired in 1951 at a cost of $1,500 and the remainder of 10 shares in December 1954 at a cost of $2,900. He receives in April 1955 a distribution of $250 per share in complete liquidation, or $2,500 on the 10 shares acquired in 1951, and $2,500 on the 10 shares acquired in December 1954. The gain of $1,000 on the shares acquired in 1951 is a long–term capital gain to be treated as provided in parts I, II, and III (section 1201 and following), subchapter P, chapter 1 of the Code. The loss of $400 on the shares acquired in 1954 is a short-term capital loss to be treated as provided in parts I, II, and III (section 1201 and following), subchapter P, chapter 1 of the Code.

§ 1.332–1 Distributions in liquidation of subsidiary corporation; general.

Under the general rule prescribed by section 331 for the treatment of distributions in liquidation of a corporation, amounts received by one corporation in complete liquidation of another corporation are treated as in full payment in exchange for stock in such other corporation, and gain or loss from the receipt of such amounts is to be determined as provided in section 1001. Section 332 excepts from the general rule property received, under certain specifically described circumstances, by one corporation as a distribution in complete liquidation of the stock of another corporation and provides for the nonrecognition of gain or loss in those cases which meet the statutory requirements. Section 367 places a limitation on the application of section 332 in the case of foreign corporations. See section 334(b) for the basis for determining gain or loss from the subsequent sale of property received upon complete liquidations such as described in this section.* * *

§ 1.332–2 Requirements for nonrecognition of gain or loss.

(a) The nonrecognition of gain or loss is limited to the receipt of such property by a corporation which is the actual owner of stock (in the liquidating corporation) possessing at least 80 percent of the total combined voting power of all classes of stock entitled to vote and the owner of at least 80 percent of the total number of shares of all other classes of stock (except nonvoting stock which is limited and preferred as to dividends). The recipient corporation must have been the owner of the specified amount of such stock on the date of the adoption of the plan of liquidation and have continued so to be at all times until the receipt of the property. If the recipient corporation does not continue qualified with respect to the ownership of stock of the liquidating corporation and if the failure to continue qualified occurs at any time prior to the completion of the transfer of all the property, the provisions for the nonrecognition of gain or loss do not apply to any distribution received under the plan.

(b) Section 332 applies only to those cases in which the recipient corporation receives at least partial payment for the stock which it owns in the liquidating corporation. If section 332 is not applicable, see section 165(g) relative to allowance of losses on worthless securities.

(c) To constitute a distribution in complete liquidation within the meaning of section 332, the distribution must be (1) made by the liquidating corporation in complete cancellation or redemption of all of its stock in accordance with a plan of liquidation, or (2) one of a series of distributions in complete cancellation or redemption of all its stock in accordance with a plan of liquidation. Where there is more than one distribution, it is essential that a status of liquidation exist at the time the first distribution is made under the plan and that such status continue until the liquidation is completed. Liquidation is completed when the liquidating corporation and the receiver or trustees in liquidation are finally divested of all the property (both tangible and intangible). A status of liquidation exists when the corporation ceases to be a going concern and its activities are merely for the purpose of winding up its affairs, paying its debts, and distributing any remaining balance to its shareholders. A liquidation may be completed prior to the actual dissolution of the liquidating corporation. However, legal dissolution of the corporation is not required. Nor will the mere retention of a nominal amount of assets for the sole purpose of preserving the corporation's legal existence disqualify the transaction.* * *

(d) If a transaction constitutes a distribution in complete liquidation within the meaning of the Internal Revenue Code of 1954 and satisfies the requirements of section 332, it is not material that it is otherwise described under the local law. If a liquidating corporation distributes all of its property in complete liquidation and if pursuant to the plan for such complete liquidation a corporation owning the specified amount of stock in the liquidating corporation receives property constituting amounts distributed in complete liquidation within the meaning of the Code and also receives other property attributable to shares not owned by it, the transfer of the property to the recipient corporation shall not be treated, by reason of the receipt of such other property, as not being a distribution (or one of a series of distributions) in complete cancellation or redemption of all of the stock of the liquidating corporation within the meaning of section 332, even though for purposes of those provisions relating to corporate reorganizations the amount received by the recipient corporation in excess of its ratable share is regarded as acquired upon the issuance of its stock or securities in a tax-free exchange as described in section 361 and the cancellation or redemption of the stock not owned by the recipient corporation is treated as occurring as a result of a tax-free exchange described in section 354.

(e) The application of these rules may be illustrated by the following example:

Example. On September 1, 1954, the M Corporation had outstanding capital stock consisting of 3,000 shares of common stock, par value $100 a share, and 1,000 shares of preferred stock, par value $100 a share, which preferred stock was limited and preferred as to dividends and had no voting rights. On that date, and thereafter until the date of dissolution of the M Corporation, the O Corporation owned 2,500 shares of common stock of the M Corporation. By statutory merger consummated on October 1, 1954, pursuant to a plan of liquidation adopted on September 1, 1954, the M Corporation was merged into the O Corporation, the O Corporation under the plan issuing stock which was received by the other holders of the stock of the M Corporation. The receipt by the O Corporation of the properties of the M Corporation is a distribution received by the O Corporation in complete liquidation of the M Corporation within the meaning of section 332, and no gain or loss is recognized as the result of the receipt of such properties.

§ 1.332–3 Liquidations completed within one taxable year.

If in a liquidation completed within one taxable year pursuant to a plan of complete liquidation, distributions in complete liquidation are received by a corporation which owns the specified amount of stock in the liquidating corporation and which continues qualified with respect to the ownership of such stock until the transfer of all the property within such year is completed (see paragraph (a) of § 1.332–2), then no gain or loss shall be recognized with respect to the distributions received by the recipient corporation. In such case no waiver or bond is required of the recipient corporation under section 332.

§ 1.332–4 Liquidations covering more than one taxable year.

(a) If the plan of liquidation is consummated by a series of distributions extending over a period of more than one taxable year, the nonrecognition of gain or loss with respect to the distributions in liquidation shall, in addition to the requirements of § 1.332–2, be subject to the following requirements:

(1) In order for the distribution in liquidation to be brought within the exception provided in section 332 to the general rule for computing gain or loss with respect to amounts received in liquidation of a corporation, the entire property of the corporation shall be transferred in accordance with a plan of liquidation, which plan shall include a statement showing the period within which the transfer of the property of the liquidating corporation to the recipient corporation is to be completed. The transfer of all the property under the liquidation must be completed within three years from the close of the taxable year during which is made the first of the series of distributions under the plan.

* * *

(b) Pending the completion of the liquidation, if there is a compliance with paragraph (a)(1), (2), and (3) of this section and § 1.332–2 with respect to the nonrecognition of gain or loss, the income and profits tax liability of the recipient corporation for each of the years covered in whole or in part by the liquidation shall be determined without the recognition of any gain or loss on account of the receipt of the distributions in liquidation. In such determination, the basis of the property or properties received by the recipient corporation shall be determined in accordance with section 334(b). However, if the transfer of the property is not completed within the three-year period allowed by section 332 or if the recipient corporation does not continue qualified with respect to the ownership of stock of the liquidating corporation as required by that section, gain or loss shall be recognized with respect to each distribution and the tax liability for each of the years covered in whole or in part by the liquidation shall be recomputed without regard to the provisions of section 332 or section 334 (b) and the amount of any additional tax due upon such recomputation shall be promptly paid.

§ 1.332–5 Distribution in liquidation as affecting minority interests.

Upon the liquidation of a corporation in pursuance of a plan of complete liquidation, the gain or loss of minority shareholders shall be determined without regard to section 332, since it does not apply to that part of distributions in liquidation received by minority shareholders.

* * *

§ 1.334–1 Basis of property received in liquidations.

(a) In general. Section 334 sets forth rules prescribing the basis of property received in a distribution in partial or complete liquidation of a corporation. The general rule of section 334 is set forth in section 334(a) to the effect that if property is received in a distribution in partial or complete liquidation and if gain or loss is recognized on the receipt of such property, then the basis of the property in the hands of the distributee shall be the fair market value of such property at the time of the distribution. Such general rule has no application to a liquidation to which section 332 * * * applies. See section 334(b) * * *.

(b) Transferor's basis. Unless section 334(b)(2) and subsection (c) of this section apply, property received by a parent corporation in a complete liquidation to which section 332 is applicable shall, under section 334(b)(1), have the same basis in the hands of the parent as its adjusted basis in the hands of the subsidiary.* * *

Effect on Corporation*

* * *

Collapsible Corporations; Foreign Personal Holding Companies*

Corporate Organizations and Reorganizations

Corporate Organizations

§ 1.351–1 Transfer to corporation controlled by transferor.

(a)(1) Section 351(a) provides, in general, for the nonrecognition of gain or loss upon the transfer by one or more persons of property to a corporation solely in exchange for stock or securities** in such corporation, if immediately after the exchange, such person or persons are in control of the corporation to which the property was transferred. As used in section 351, the phrase "one or more persons" includes individuals, trusts, estates, partnerships, associations, companies, or corporations (see section 7701(a)(l)). To be in control of the transferee corporation, such person or persons must own immediately after the transfer stock possessing at least 80 percent of the total combined voting power of all classes of stock entitled to vote and at least 80 percent of the total number of shares of all other classes of stock of such corporation (see section 368(c)). In determining control under this section, the fact that any corporate transferor distributes part or all of the stock which it receives in the exchange to its shareholders shall not be taken into account. The phrase "immediately after the exchange" does not necessarily require simultaneous exchanges by two or more persons, but comprehends a situation

*Omitted.

**Editorial comment: The Regulations do not reflect the effect of Public Law 100–239 which deleted the term "securities" from Sec. 351.

where the rights of the parties have been previously defined and the execution of the agreement proceeds with an expedition consistent with orderly procedure. For purposes of this section—

(i) Stock or securities* issued for services rendered or to be rendered to or for the benefit of the issuing corporation will not be treated as having been issued in return for property, and

(ii) Stock or securities* issued for property which is of relatively small value in comparison to the value of the stock and securities already owned (or to be received for services) by the person who transferred such property, shall not be treated as having been issued in return for property if the primary purpose of the transfer is to qualify under this section the exchanges of property by other persons transferring property.

For the purpose of section 351, stock rights or stock warrants are not included in the term "stock or securities"*

(2) The application of section 351(a) is illustrated by the following examples:

Example (1). C owns a patent right worth $25,000 and D owns a manufacturing plant worth $75,000. C and D organize the R Corporation with an authorized capital stock of $100,000. C transfers his patent right to the R Corporation for $25,000 of its stock and D transfers his plant to the new corporation for $75,000 of its stock. No gain or loss to C or D is recognized.

Example (2). B owns certain real estate which cost him $50,000 in 1930, but which has a fair market value of $200,000 in 1955. He transfers the property to the N Corporation in 1955 for 78 percent of each class of stock of the corporation having a fair market value of $200,000, the remaining 22 percent of the stock of the corporation having been issued by the corporation in 1940 to other persons for cash. B realized a taxable gain of $150,000 on this transaction.

Example (3). E, an individual, owns property with a basis of $10,000 but which has a fair market value of $18,000. E also had rendered services valued at $2,000 to Corporation F. Corporation F has outstanding 100 shares of common stock all of which are held by G. Corporation F issues 400 shares of its common stock (having a fair market value of $20,000) to E in exchange for his property worth $18,000 and in compensation for the services he has rendered worth $2,000. Since immediately after the transaction, E owns 80 percent of the outstanding stock of Corporation F, no gain is recognized upon the exchange of the property for the stock. However, E realized $2,000 of ordinary income as compensation for services rendered to Corporation F.

(3) Underwritings of stock—(i) In general. For the purpose of section 351, if a person acquires stock of a corporation from an underwriter in exchange for cash in a qualified underwriting transaction, the person who acquires stock from the underwriter is treated as transferring cash directly to the corporation in exchange for stock of the corporation and the underwriter is disregarded. A qualified underwriting transaction is a transaction in which a corporation issues stock for cash in an underwriting in which either the underwriter is an agent of the corporation or the underwriter's ownership of the stock is transitory.

(ii) Effective date. This paragraph (a)(3) is effective for qualified underwriting transactions occurring on or after May 1, 1996.

(b)(1) Where property is transferred to a corporation by two or more persons in exchange for stock or securities,* as described in paragraph (a) of this section, it is not required that the stock and securities* received by each be substantially in proportion to his interest in the property immediately prior to the transfer. However, where the stock and securities* received are received in disproportion to such interest, the entire transaction will be given tax effect in accordance with its true nature, and in appropriate cases the transaction may be treated as if the stock and securities* had first been received in proportion and then some of such stock and securities* had been used to make gifts (section 2501 and following), to pay compensation (section 61(a)(1)), or to satisfy obligations of the transferor of any kind.

(2) The application of paragraph (b)(1) of this section may be illustrated as follows:

Example (1). Individuals A and B, father and son, organize a corporation with 100 shares of common stock to which A transfers property worth $8,000 in exchange for 20 shares of stock, and B transfers property worth $2,000 in exchange for 80 shares of stock. No gain or loss will be recognized under section 351. However, if it is determined that A in fact made a gift to B, such gift will be subject to tax under section 2501 and following. Similarly, if B had rendered services to A (such services having no relation to the assets transferred or to the business of the corporation) and the disproportion in the amount of stock received constituted the payment of compensation by A to B, B will be taxable upon the fair market value of the 60 shares of stock received as compensation for services rendered, and A will realize gain or loss upon the difference between the basis to him of the 60 shares and their fair market value at the time of the exchange.

Example (2). Individuals C and D each transferred, to a newly organized corporation, property having a fair market value of $4,500 in exchange for the issuance by the corporation of 45 shares of its capital stock to each transferor. At the same time, the corporation issued to E, an individual, 10 shares of its capital stock in payment for organizational and promotional services rendered by E for the benefit of the corporation. E transferred no property to the corporation. C and D were under no obligation to pay for E's services. No gain or loss is recognized to C or D. E received compensation taxable as ordinary income to the extent of the fair market value of the 10 shares of stock received by him.

*Editorial comment: The Regulations do not reflect the effect of Public Law 100–239 which deleted the term "securities" from Sec. 351.

* * *

§ 1.351–2 Receipt of property.

(a) If an exchange would be within the provisions of section 351(a) if it were not for the fact that the property received in exchange consists not only of property permitted by such subsection to be received without the recognition of gain, but also of other property or money, then the gain, if any, to the recipient shall be recognized, but in an amount not in excess of the sum of such money and the fair market value of such other property. No loss to the recipient shall be recognized.

(b) See section 357 and the regulations pertaining to that section for applicable rules as to the treatment of liabilities as "other property" in cases subject to section 351, where another party to the exchange assumes a liability, or acquires property subject to a liability.

(c) See sections 358 and 362 and the regulations pertaining to those sections for applicable rules with respect to the determination of the basis of stock, securities, or other property received in exchanges subject to section 351.

(d) See part 1 (section 301 and following), subchapter C, chapter 1 of the Code, and the regulations thereunder for applicable rules with respect to the taxation of dividends where a distribution by a corporation of its stock or securities* in connection with an exchange subject to section 351(a) has the effect of the distribution of a taxable dividend.

* * *

Effects On Shareholders And Security Holders

§ 1.354–1 Exchanges of stock and securities in certain reorganizations.

(a) Section 354 provides that under certain circumstances no gain or loss is recognized to a shareholder who surrenders his stock in exchange for other stock or to a security holder who surrenders his securities in exchange for stock. Section 354 also provides that under certain circumstances a security holder may surrender securities and receive securities in the same principal amount or in a lesser principal amount without the recognition of gain or loss to him. The exchanges to which section 354 applies must be pursuant to a plan of reorganization as provided in section 368(a) and the stock and securities surrendered as well as the stock and securities received must be those of a corporation which is a party to the reorganization. Section 354 does not apply to exchanges pursuant to a reorganization described in section 368(a)(1)(D) unless the transferor corporation—

(1) Transfers all or substantially all of its assets to a single corporation, and

(2) Distributes all of its remaining properties (if any) and the stock, securities and other properties received in the exchange to its shareholders or security holders in pursuance of the plan of reorganization. The fact that properties retained by the transferor corporation, or received in exchange for the properties transferred in the reorganization, are used to satisfy existing liabilities not represented by securities and which were incurred in the ordinary course of business before the reorganization does not prevent the application of section 354 to an exchange pursuant to a plan of reorganization defined in section 368(a)(1)(D).

(b) Except as provided in section 354(c) and (d), section 354 is not applicable to an exchange of stock or securities if a greater principal amount of securities is received than the principal amount of securities the recipient surrenders, or if securities are received and the recipient surrenders no securities. See, however, section 356 and regulations pertaining to such section. See also section 306 with respect to the receipt of preferred stock in a transaction to which section 354 is applicable.

* * *

(d) The rules of section 354 may be illustrated by the following examples:

Example (1). Pursuant to a reorganization under section 368(a) to which Corporations T and W are parties, A, a shareholder in Corporation T, surrenders all his common stock in Corporation T in exchange for common stock of Corporation W. No gain or loss is recognized to A.

Example (2). Pursuant to a reorganization under section 368(a) to which Corporations X and Y (which are not railroad corporations) are parties, B, a shareholder in Corporation X, surrenders all his stock in X for stock and securities in Y. Section 354 does not apply to this exchange. See, however, section 356.

*Editorial comment: The Regulations do not reflect the effect of Public Law 100–239 which deleted the term "securities" from Sec. 351.

Example (3). C, a shareholder in Corporation Z (which is not a railroad corporation), surrenders all his stock in Corporation Z in exchange for securities in Corporation Z. Whether or not this exchange is in connection with a recapitalization under section 368(a)(1)(E), section 354 does not apply. See, however, section 302.

(e) For the purpose of section 354, stock rights or stock warrants are not included in the term "stock or securities."

* * *

§ 1.355–1 Distribution of stock and securities of controlled corporation.*

* * *

(b) Application of section. Section 355 provides for the separation, without recognition of gain or loss to (or the inclusion in income of) the shareholders and security holders, of one or more existing businesses formerly operated, directly or indirectly, by a single corporation (the "distributing corporation"). It applies only to the separation of existing businesses that have been in active operation for at least five years (or a business that has been in active operation for at least five years into separate businesses), and which, in general, have been owned, directly or indirectly, for at least five years by the distributing corporation. A separation is achieved through the distribution by the distributing corporation of stock, or stock and securities, of one or more subsidiaries (the "controlled corporations") to its shareholders with respect to its stock or to its security holders in exchange for its securities. The controlled corporations may be preexisting or newly created subsidiaries. Throughout the regulations under section 355, the term "distribution" refers to a distribution by the distributing corporation of stock, or stock and securities, of one or more controlled corporations, unless the context indicates otherwise. Section 355 contemplates the continued operation of the business or businesses existing prior to the separation. See § 1.355–4 for types of distributions that may qualify under section 355, including pro rata distributions and non pro rata distributions.

* * *

§ 1.355–2 Limitations.

(a) Property distributed. Section 355 applies to a distribution only if the property distributed consists solely of stock, or stock and securities, of a controlled corporation. If additional property (including an excess principal amount of securities received over securities surrendered) is received, see section 356.

(b) Independent business purpose—(1) Independent business purpose requirement. Section 355 applies to a transaction only if it is carried out for one or more corporate business purposes. A transaction is carried out for a corporate business purpose if it is motivated, in whole or substantial part, by one or more corporate business purposes. The potential for the avoidance of Federal taxes by the distributing or controlled corporations (or a corporation controlled by either) is relevant in determining the extent to which an existing corporate business purpose motivated the distribution. The principal reason for this business purpose requirement is to provide non-recognition treatment only to distributions that are incident to readjustments of corporate structures required by business exigencies and that effect only readjustments of continuing interests in property under modified corporate forms. This business purpose requirement is independent of the other requirements under section 355.

(2) Corporate business purpose. A corporate business purpose is a real and substantial non Federal tax purpose germane to the business of the distributing corporation, the controlled corporation, or the affiliated group (as defined in § 1.355–3(b)(4)(iv)) to which the distributing corporation belongs. A purpose of reducing non Federal taxes is not a corporate business purpose if (i) the transaction will effect a reduction in both Federal and non Federal taxes because of similarities between Federal tax law and the tax law of the other jurisdiction and (ii) the reduction of Federal taxes is greater than or substantially coextensive with the reduction of non Federal taxes. See examples (7) and (8) of paragraph (b)(5) of this section. A shareholder purpose (for example, the personal planning purposes of a shareholder) is not a corporate business purpose. Depending upon the facts of a particular case, however, a shareholder purpose for a transaction may be so nearly coextensive with a corporate business purpose as to preclude any distinction between them. In such a case, the transaction is carried out for one or more corporate business purposes. See example (2) of paragraph (b)(5) of this section.

*Editorial comment: The Regulations do not include the effect of the Revenue Act of 1987 and the Technical and Miscellaneous Revenue Act of 1988.

(3) Business purpose for distribution. The distribution must be carried out for one or more corporate business purposes. See example (3) of paragraph (b)(5) of this section. If a corporate business purpose can be achieved through a nontaxable transaction that does not involve the distribution of stock of a controlled corporation and which is neither impractical nor unduly expensive, then, for purposes of paragraph (b)(1) of this section, the separation is not carried out for that corporate business purpose. See examples (3) and (4) of paragraph (b)(5) of this section. For rules with respect to the requirement of a business purpose for a transfer of assets to a controlled corporation in connection with a reorganization described in section 368(a)(l)(D). See § 1.368–1(b).

(4) Business purpose as evidence of nondevice. The corporate business purpose or purposes for a transaction are evidence that the transaction was not used principally as a device for the distribution of earnings and profits within the meaning of section 355(a)(1)(B). See paragraph (d)(3)(ii) of this section.

(5) Examples. The provisions of this paragraph (b) may be illustrated by the following examples:

Example (1). Corporation X is engaged in the production, transportation, and refining of petroleum products. In 1985, X acquires all of the properties of corporation Z, which is also engaged in the production, transportation, and refining of petroleum products. In 1991, as a result of antitrust litigation, X is ordered to divest itself of all of the properties acquired from Z. X transfers those properties to new corporation Y and distributes the stock of Y pro rata to X's shareholders. In view of the divestiture order, the distribution is carried out for a corporate business purpose. See paragraph (b)(1) of this section.

Example (2). Corporation X is engaged in two businesses: The manufacture and sale of furniture and the sale of jewelry. The businesses are of equal value. The outstanding stock of X is owned equally by unrelated individuals A and B. A is more interested in the furniture business, while B is more interested in the jewelry business. A and B decide to split up the businesses and go their separate ways. A and B anticipate that the operations of each business will be enhanced by the separation because each shareholder will be able to devote his undivided attention to the business in which he is more interested and more proficient. Accordingly, X transfers the jewelry business to new corporation Y and distributes the stock of Y to B in exchange for all of B's stock in X. The distribution is carried out for a corporate business purpose, notwithstanding that it is also carried out in part for shareholder purposes. See paragraph (b)(2) of this section.

Example (3). Corporation X is engaged in the manufacture and sale of toys and the manufacture and sale of candy. The shareholders of X wish to protect the candy business from the risks and vicissitudes of the toy business. Accordingly, X transfers the toy business to new corporation Y and distributes the stock of Y to X's shareholders. Under applicable law, the purpose of protecting the candy business from the risks and vicissitudes of the toy business is achieved as soon as X transfers the toy business to Y. Therefore, the distribution is not carried out for a corporate business purpose. See paragraph (b)(3) of this section.

Example (4). Corporation X is engaged in a regulated business in State T. X owns all of the stock of corporation Y, a profitable corporation that is not engaged in a regulated business. Commission C sets the rates that X may charge its customers, based on its total income. C has recently adopted rules according to which the total income of a corporation includes the income of a business if, and only if, the business is operated, directly or indirectly, by the corporation. Total income, for this purpose, includes the income of a wholly owned subsidiary corporation but does not include the income of a parent or "brother/sister" corporation. Under C's new rule, X's total income includes the income of Y, with the result that X has suffered a reduction of the rates that it may charge its customers. It would not be impractical or unduly expensive to create in a nontaxable transaction (such as a transaction qualifying under section 351) a holding company to hold the stock of X and Y. X distributes the stock of Y to X's shareholders. The distribution is not carried out for the purpose of increasing the rates that X may charge its customers because that purpose could be achieved through a nontaxable transaction, the creation of a holding company, that does not involve the distribution of stock of a controlled corporation and which is neither impractical nor unduly expensive. See paragraph (b)(3) of this section.

Example (5). The facts are the same as in example (4), except that C has recently adopted rules according to which the total income of a corporation includes not only the income included in example (3), but also the income of any member of the affiliated group to which the corporation belongs. In order to avoid a reduction in the rates that it may charge its customers, X distributes the stock of Y to X's shareholders. The distribution is carried out for a corporate business purpose. See paragraph (b)(3) of this section.

* * *

(c) Continuity of interest requirement—(1) Requirement. Section 355 applies to a separation that effects only a readjustment of continuing interests in the property of the distributing and controlled corporations. In this regard section 355 requires that one or more persons who, directly or indirectly, were the owners of the enterprise prior to the distribution or exchange own, in the aggregate, an amount of stock establishing a continuity of interest in each of the modified corporate forms in which the enterprise is conducted after the separation. This continuity of interest requirement is independent of the other requirements under section 355.

(2) Examples.

Example (1). For more than five years, corporation X has been engaged directly in one business, and indirectly in a different business through its wholly owned subsidiary, S. The businesses are equal in value. At all times, the outstanding stock of X has been owned equally by unrelated individuals A and B. For valid business reasons, A and B cause X to distribute all of the stock of S to B in exchange for all of B's stock in X. After the transaction, A owns all the stock of X and B owns all the stock of S. The continuity of interest requirement is met because one or more persons who were the owners of X prior to the distribution (A and B) own, in the aggregate, an amount of stock establishing a continuity of interest in each of X and S after the distribution.

Example (2). Assume the same facts as in Example (1), except that pursuant to a plan to acquire a stock interest in X without acquiring, directly or indirectly, an interest in S, C purchased one-half of the X stock owned by A and immediately thereafter X distributed all of the S stock to B in exchange for all of B's stock in X. After the transactions, A owns 50 percent of X and B owns 100 percent of S. The distribution by X of all of the stock of S to B in exchange for all of B's stock in X will satisfy the continuity of interest requirement for section 355 because one or more persons who were the owners of X prior to the distribution (A and B) own, in the aggregate, an amount of stock establishing a continuity of interest in each of X and S after the distribution.

Example (3). Assume the same facts as in Examples (1) and (2), except that C purchased all of the X stock owned by A. After the transactions, neither A nor B own any of the stock of X, and B owns all the stock of S. The continuity of interest requirement is not met because the owners of X prior to the distribution (A and B) do not, in the aggregate, own an amount of stock establishing a continuity of interest in each of X and S after the distribution, i.e., although A and B collectively have retained 50 percent of their equity interest in the former combined enterprise, they have failed to continue to own the minimum stock interest in the distributing corporation, X, that would be required in order to meet the continuity of interest requirement.

* * *

(d) Device for distribution of earnings and profits—(1) In general. Section 355 does not apply to a transaction used principally as a device for the distribution of the earnings and profits of the distributing corporation, the controlled corporation, or both (a "device"). Section 355 recognizes that a tax-free distribution of the stock of a controlled corporation presents a potential for tax avoidance by facilitating the avoidance of the dividend provisions of the Code through the subsequent sale or exchange of stock of one corporation and the retention of the stock of another corporation. A device can include a transaction that effects a recovery of basis. In this paragraph (d), "exchange" includes transactions, such as redemptions, treated as exchanges under the Code. Generally, the determination of whether a transaction was used principally as a device will be made from all of the facts and circumstances, including, but not limited to, the presence of the device factors specified in paragraph (d)(2) of this section ("evidence of device"), and the presence of the nondevice factors specified in paragraph (d)(3) of this section ("evidence of nondevice"). However, if a transaction is specified in paragraph (d)(5) of this section, then it is ordinarily considered not to have been used principally as a device.

(2) Device factors—(i) In general. The presence of any of the device factors specified in this subparagraph (2) is evidence of device. The strength of this evidence depends on the facts and circumstances.

(ii) Pro rata distribution. A distribution that is pro rata or substantially pro rata among the shareholders of the distributing corporation presents the greatest potential for the avoidance of the dividend provisions of the Code and, in contrast to other types of distributions, is more likely to be used principally as a device. Accordingly, the fact that a distribution is pro rata or substantially pro rata is evidence of device.

(iii) Subsequent sale or exchange of stock—(A) In general. A sale or exchange of stock of the distributing or the controlled corporation after the distribution (a "subsequent sale or exchange") is evidence of device. Generally, the greater the percentage of the stock sold or exchanged after the distribution, the stronger the evidence of device. In addition, the shorter the period of time between the distribution and the sale or exchange, the stronger the evidence of device.

(B) Sale or exchange negotiated or agreed upon before the distribution. A subsequent sale or exchange pursuant to an arrangement negotiated or agreed upon before the distribution is substantial evidence of device.

(C) Sale or exchange not negotiated or agreed upon before the distribution. A subsequent sale or exchange not pursuant to an arrangement negotiated or agreed upon before the distribution is evidence of device.

(D) Negotiated or agreed upon before the distribution. For purposes of this subparagraph (2), a sale or exchange is always pursuant to an arrangement negotiated or agreed upon before the distribution if enforceable rights to buy or sell existed before the distribution. If a sale or exchange was discussed by the buyer and the seller before the distribution and was reasonably to be anticipated by both parties, then the sale or exchange will ordinarily be considered to be pursuant to an arrangement negotiated or agreed upon before the distribution.

(E) Exchange in pursuance of a plan of reorganization. For purposes of this subparagraph (2), if stock is exchanged for stock in pursuance of a plan of reorganization, and either no gain or loss or only an insubstantial amount of gain is recognized on the exchange, then the exchange is not treated as a subsequent sale or exchange, but the stock received in the exchange is treated as the stock surrendered in the exchange. For this purpose, gain treated as a dividend pursuant to sections 356(a)(2) and 316 shall be disregarded.

(iv) Nature and use of assets—(A) In general. The determination of whether a transaction was used principally as a device will take into account the nature, kind, amount, and use of the assets of the distributing and the controlled corporations (and corporations controlled by them) immediately after the transaction.

(B) Assets not used in a trade or business meeting the requirement of section 355(b). The existence of assets that are not used in a trade or business that satisfies the requirements of section 355(b) is evidence of device. For this purpose, assets that are not used in a trade or business that satisfies the requirements of section 355(b) include, but are not limited to, cash and other liquid assets that are not related to the reasonable needs of a business satisfying such section. The strength of the evidence of device depends on all the facts and circumstances, including, but not limited to, the ratio for each corporation of the value of assets not used in a trade or business that satisfies the requirements of section 355(b) to the value of its business that satisfies such requirements. A difference in the ratio described in the preceding sentence for the distributing and controlled corporation is ordinarily not evidence of device if the distribution is not pro rata among the shareholders of the distributing corporation and such difference is attributable to a need to equalize the value of the stock distributed and the value of the stock or securities exchanged by the distributees.

(C) Related function. There is evidence of device if a business of either the distributing or controlled corporation (or a corporation controlled by it) is (1) a "secondary business" that continues as a secondary business for a significant period after the separation, and (2) can be sold without adversely affecting the business of the other corporation (or a corporation controlled by it). A secondary business is a business of either the distributing or controlled corporation, if its principal function is to serve the business of the other corporation (or a corporation controlled by it). A secondary business can include a business transferred to a newly-created subsidiary or a business which serves a business transferred to a newly–created subsidiary. The activities of the secondary business may consist of providing property or performing services. Thus, in example (11) of § 1.35–3(c), evidence of device would be presented if the principal function of the coal mine (satisfying the requirements of the steel business) continued after the separation and the coal mine could be sold without adversely affecting the steel business. Similarly, in example (10) of § 1.355–3(c), evidence of device would be presented if the principal function of the sales operation after the separation is to sell the output from the manufacturing operation and the sales operation could be sold without adversely affecting the manufacturing operation.

(3) Nondevice factors—(i) In general. The presence of any of the nondevice factors specified in this subparagraph (3) is evidence of nondevice. The strength of this evidence depends on all of the facts and circumstances.

(ii) Corporate business purpose. The corporate business purpose for the transaction is evidence of nondevice. The stronger the evidence of device (such as the presence of the device factors specified in paragraph (d)(2) of this section), the stronger the corporate business purpose required to prevent the determination that the transaction was used principally as a device. Evidence of device presented by the transfer or retention of assets not used in a trade or business that satisfies the requirements of section 355(b) can be outweighed by the existence of a corporate business purpose for those transfers or retentions. The assessment of the strength of a corporate business purpose will be based on all of the facts and circumstances, including, but not limited to, the following factors:

(A) The importance of achieving the purpose to the success of the business;

(B) The extent to which the transaction is prompted by a person not having a proprietary interest in either corporation, or by other outside factors beyond the control of the distributing corporation; and

(C) The immediacy of the conditions prompting the transaction.

(iii) Distributing corporation publicly traded and widely held. The fact that the distributing corporation is publicly traded and has no shareholder who is directly or indirectly the beneficial owner of more than five percent of any class of stock is evidence of nondevice.

(iv) Distribution to domestic corporate shareholders. The fact that the stock of the controlled corporation is distributed to one or more domestic corporations that, if section 355 did not apply, would be entitled to a deduction under section 243(a)(1) available to corporations meeting the stock ownership requirements of section 243(c), or a deduction under section 243(c)(2) or (3) or 245(b) is evidence of nondevice.

(4) Examples. The provisions of paragraph (d)(1) through (3) of this section may be illustrated by the following examples:

Example (1). Individual A owns all of the stock of corporation X, which is engaged in the warehousing business. X owns all of the stock of corporation Y, which is engaged in the transportation business. X employs individual B, who is extremely knowledgeable of the warehousing business in general and the operations of X in particular. B has informed A that he will seriously consider leaving the company if he is not given the opportunity to purchase a significant amount of stock of X. Because of his knowledge and experience, the loss of B would seriously damage the business of X. B cannot afford to purchase any significant amount of stock of X as long as X owns Y. Accordingly, X distributes the stock of Y to A and A subsequently sells a portion of his X stock to B. However, X could have issued additional shares to B sufficient to give B an equivalent ownership interest in X. There is no other evidence of device or evidence of nondevice. In light of the fact that X could have issued additional shares to B, the sale of X stock by A is substantial evidence of device. The transaction is considered to have been used principally as a device. See paragraph (d)(1), (2)(ii), (iii)(A)(B) and (D), and (3)(i) and (ii) of this section.

Example (2). Corporation X owns and operates a fast food restaurant in State M and owns all of the stock of corporation Y, which owns and operates a fast food restaurant in State N. X and Y operate their businesses under franchises granted by D and E, respectively. X owns cash and marketable securities that exceed the reasonable needs of its business but whose value is small relative to the value of its business. E has recently changed its franchise policy and will no longer grant or renew franchises to subsidiaries (or other members of the same affiliated group) of corporations operating businesses under franchises granted by its competitors. Thus, Y will lose its franchise if it remains a subsidiary of X. The franchise is about to expire. Accordingly, X distributes the stock of Y pro rata among X's shareholders. X retains its business and transfers cash and marketable securities to Y in an amount proportional to the value of Y's business. There is no other evidence of device or evidence of nondevice. The transfer by X to Y and the retention by X of cash and marketable securities is relatively weak evidence of device because after the transfer X and Y hold cash and marketable securities in amounts proportional to the values of their businesses. The fact that the distribution is pro rata is evidence of device. A strong corporate business purpose is relatively strong evidence of nondevice. Accordingly, the transaction is considered not to have been used principally as a device. See paragraph (d)(1), (2)(ii), (iv)(A), and (B) and (3)(i) and (ii)(A), (B) and (C) of this section.

* * *

(5) Transactions ordinarily not considered as a device—(i) In general. This subparagraph (5) specifies three distributions that ordinarily do not present the potential for tax avoidance described in paragraph (d)(1) of this section. Accordingly, such distributions are ordinarily considered not to have been used principally as a device, notwithstanding the presence of any of the device factors described in paragraph (d)(2) of this section. A transaction described in paragraph (d)(5)(iii) or (iv) of this section is not protected by this subparagraph (5) from a determination that it was used principally as a device if it involves the distribution of the stock of more than one controlled corporation and facilitates the avoidance of the dividend provisions of the Code through the subsequent sale or exchange of stock of one corporation and the retention of the stock of another corporation.

(ii) Absence of earnings and profits. A distribution is ordinarily considered not to have been used principally as a device if—

(A) The distributing and controlled corporations have no accumulated earnings and profits at the beginning of their respective taxable years.

(B) The distributing and controlled corporations have no current earnings and profits as of the date of the distribution, and

(C) No distribution of property by the distributing corporation immediately before the separation would require recognition of gain resulting in current earnings and profits for the taxable year of the distribution.

(iii) Section 303(a) transactions. A distribution is ordinarily considered not to have been used principally as a device if, in the absence of section 355, with respect to each shareholder distributee, the distribution would be a redemption to which section 303(a) applied.

(iv) Section 302(a) transactions. A distribution is ordinarily considered not to have been used principally as a device if, in the absence of section 355, with respect to each shareholder distributee, the distribution would be a redemption to which section 302(a) applied. For purposes of the preceding sentence, section 302(c)(2)(A)(ii) and (iii) shall not apply.

(v) Examples. The provisions of this subparagraph (5) may be illustrated by the following examples:

* * *

Example (2). Corporation X is engaged in three businesses: a hotel business, a restaurant business, and a rental real estate business. Individuals A, B, and C own all of the stock of X. X transfers the restaurant business to new corporation Y and transfers the rental real estate business to new corporation Z. X then distributes the stock of Y and Z pro rata between B and C in exchange for all of their stock in X. In the absence of section 355, the distribution would be a redemption to which section 302(a) applied. Since this distribution involves the stock of more than one controlled corporation and facilitates the avoidance of the dividend provisions of the Code through the subsequent sale or exchange of stock in one corporation and the retention of the stock of another corporation, it is not protected by paragraph (d)(5)(i) and (iv) of this section from a determination that it was used principally as a device. Thus, the determination of whether the transaction was used principally as a device must be made from all the facts and circumstances, including the presence of the device factors and nondevice factors specified in paragraph (d)(2) and (3) of this section.

(e) Stock and securities distributed—(1) In general. Section 355 applies to a distribution only if the distributing corporation distributes—

(i) All of the stock and securities of the controlled corporation that it owns, or

(ii) At least an amount of the stock of the controlled corporation that constitutes control as defined in section 368(c). In such a case, all, or any part, of the securities of the controlled corporation may be distributed, and paragraph (e)(2) of this section shall apply.

(2) Additional rules. Where a part of either the stock or the securities of the controlled corporation is retained under paragraph (e)(1)(ii) of this section, it must be established to the satisfaction of the Commissioner that the retention by the distributing corporation was not in pursuance of a plan having as one of its principal purposes the avoidance of Federal income tax. Ordinarily, the corporate business purpose or purposes for the distribution will require the distribution of all of the stock and securities of the controlled corporation. If the distribution of all of the stock and securities of a controlled corporation would be treated to any extent as a distribution of "other property" under section 356, this fact tends to establish that the retention of stock or securities is in pursuance of a plan having as one of its principal purposes the avoidance of Federal income tax.

(f) Principal amount of securities—(1) Securities received. Section 355 does not apply to a distribution if, with respect to any shareholder or security holder, the principal amount of securities received exceeds the principal amount of securities surrendered, or securities are received but no securities are surrendered. In such cases, see section 356.

(2) Only stock received. If only stock is received in a distribution to which section 355(a)(1)(A) applies, the principal amount of the securities surrendered, if any, and the par value or stated value of the stock surrendered, if any, are not relevant to the application of that section.

(g) Period of ownership—(1) Other property. For purposes of section 355(a)(1)(A), stock of a controlled corporation acquired in a transaction in which gain or loss was recognized in whole or in part (other than a transaction described in § 1.355–3(b)(4)(iii)) within the five-year period ending on the date of the distribution shall not be treated as stock of the controlled corporation but shall be treated as "other property." See section 356. However, for purposes of section 355(a)(1)(D), the stock so acquired is stock of the controlled corporation.

(2) Example. Paragraph (g)(1) of this section may be illustrated by the following example:

Example. Corporation X has held 85 of the 100 outstanding shares of the stock of corporation Y for more than five years on the date of the distribution. Six months before that date, X purchased ten more shares. If X distributes all of its 95 shares of the stock of Y, so much of section 356 as relates to section 355 may apply to the transaction and the ten newly acquired shares are treated as other property. On the other hand, if X retains ten of the shares of the stock of Y then the application of paragraph (e) of this section must take into account all of the stock of Y, including the ten shares newly acquired by X and the five shares owned by others. Similarly, if, by the use of any agency, X acquired any of the stock of Y within the five-year period ending on the date of the distribution in a transaction in which gain or loss was recognized in whole or in part (for example, where another subsidiary of X purchased stock of Y), then that stock is treated as other property. If X had held only 75 of the 100 outstanding shares of the stock of Y for more than five years on the date of the distribution and had purchased the remaining 25 shares six months before that date, then neither section 355 nor section 356 would apply to the distribution.

(h) Active conduct of a trade or business. Section 355 applies to a distribution only if the requirements of § 1.355–3 (relating to the active conduct of a trade or business) are satisfied.

§ 1.355–3 Active conduct of a trade or business.

(a) General requirements—(1) Application of section 355. Under section 355(b)(1), a distribution of stock, or stock and securities, of a controlled corporation qualifies under section 355 only if—

(i) The distributing and the controlled corporations are each engaged in the active conduct of a trade or business immediately after the distribution (section 355(b)(1)(A)), or

(ii) Immediately before the distribution, the distributing corporation had no assets other than stock or securities of the controlled corporations, and each of the controlled corporations is engaged in the active conduct of a trade or business immediately after the distribution (section 355(b)(1)(B)). A *de minimis* amount of assets held by the distributing corporation shall be disregarded for purposes of this paragraph (a)(1)(ii).

(2) Examples. Paragraph (a)(1) of this section may be illustrated by the following examples:

Example (1). Prior to the distribution, corporation X is engaged in the active conduct of a trade or business and owns all of the stock of corporation Y, which also is engaged in the active conduct of a trade or business. X distributes all of the stock of Y to X's shareholders, and each corporation continues the active conduct of its trade or business. The active business requirement of section 355(b)(1)(A) is satisfied.

Example (2). The facts are the same as in example (1), except that X transfers all of its assets other than the stock of Y to a new corporation in exchange for all of the stock of the new corporation and then distributes the stock of both controlled corporations to X's shareholders. The active business requirement of section 355(b)(1)(B) is satisfied.

(b) Active conduct of a trade or business defined—(1) In general. Section 355(b)(2) provides rules for determining whether a corporation is treated as engaged in the active conduct of a trade or business for purposes of section 355(b)(1). Under section 355(b)(2)(A), a corporation is treated as engaged in the active conduct of a trade or business if it is itself engaged in the active conduct of a trade or business or if substantially all of its assets consist of the stock, or stock and securities, of a corporation or corporations controlled by it (immediately after the distribution) each of which is engaged in the active conduct of a trade or business.

(2) Active conduct of a trade or business immediately after distribution—(i) In general. For purposes of section 355(b), a corporation shall be treated as engaged in the "active conduct of a trade or business" immediately after the distribution if the assets and activities of the corporation satisfy the requirements and limitations described in paragraph (b)(2)(ii), (iii), and (iv) of this section.

(ii) Trade or business. A corporation shall be treated as engaged in a trade or business immediately after the distribution if a specific group of activities are being carried on by the corporation for the purpose of earning income or profit, and the activities included in such group include every operation that forms a part of, or a step in, the process of earning income or profit. Such group of activities ordinarily must include the collection of income and the payment of expenses.

(iii) Active conduct. For purposes of section 355(b), the determination whether a trade or business is actively conducted will be made from all of the facts and circumstances. Generally, the corporation is required itself to perform active and substantial management and operational functions. Generally, activities performed by the corporation itself do not include activities performed by persons outside the corporation, including independent contractors. A corporation may satisfy the requirements of this subdivision (iii) through the activities that it performs itself, even though some of its activities are performed by others. Separations of real property all or substantially all of which is occupied prior to the distribution by the distributing or the controlled corporation (or by any corporation controlled directly or indirectly by either of those corporations) will be carefully scrutinized with respect to the requirements of section 355(b) and this § 1.355–3.

(iv) Limitations. The active conduct of a trade or business does not include—

(A) The holding for investment purposes of stock, securities, land, or other property, or

(B) The ownership and operation (including leasing) of real or personal property used in a trade or business, unless the owner performs significant services with respect to the operation and management of the property.

(3) Active conduct for five-year period preceding distribution. Under section 355(b)(2)(B), a trade or business that is relied upon to meet the requirements of section 355(b) must have been actively conducted throughout the five-year period ending on the date of the distribution. For purposes of this subparagraph (3)—

(i) Activities which constitute a trade or business under the tests described in paragraph (b)(2) of this section shall be treated as meeting the requirement of the preceding sentence if such activities were actively conducted throughout the five-year period ending on the date of distribution, and

(ii) The fact that a trade or business underwent change during the five-year period preceding the distribution (for example, by the addition of new or the dropping of old products, changes in production capacity, and the like) shall be disregarded, provided that the changes are not of such a character as to constitute the acquisition of a new or different business. In particular, if a corporation engaged in the active conduct of one trade or business during that five-year period purchased, created, or otherwise acquired another trade or business in the same line of business, then the acquisition of that other business is ordinarily treated as an expansion of the original business, all of which is treated as having been actively conducted during that five-year period, unless that purchase, creation, or other acquisition effects a change of such a character as to constitute the acquisition of a new or different business.

* * *

(iii) Gain or loss recognized in certain transactions. The requirements of section 355(b)(2)(C) and (D) are intended to prevent the direct or indirect acquisition of a trade or business by a corporation in anticipation of a distribution by the corporation of that trade or business in a distribution to which section 355 would otherwise apply. A direct or indirect acquisition of a trade or business by one member of an affiliated group from another member of the group is not the type of transaction to which section 355(b)(2)(C) and (D) is intended to apply. Therefore, in applying section 355(b)(2)(C) or (D), such an acquisition, even though taxable, shall be disregarded.

(iv) Affiliated group. For purposes of this subparagraph (4), the term "affiliated group" means an affiliated group as defined in section 1504(a) (without regard to section 1504(b)), except that the term "stock" includes nonvoting stock described in section 1504(a)(4).

(5) Special rules for acquisition of a trade or business (After the Revenue Act of 1987 and Technical and Miscellaneous Revenue Act of 1988). [Reserved]

(c) Examples. The following examples illustrate section 355(b)(2)(A) and (B) and paragraph (b)(1), (2), and (3) of this section. However, a transaction that satisfies these active business requirements will qualify under section 355 only if it satisfies the other requirements of section 355(a) and (b).

Example (1). Corporation X is engaged in the manufacture and sale of soap and detergents and also owns investment securities. X transfers the investment securities to new subsidiary Y and distributes the stocks of Y to X's shareholders. Y does not satisfy the requirements of section 355(b) because the holding of investment securities does not constitute the active conduct of a trade or business. See paragraph (b)(2)(iv)(A) of this section.

Example (2). Corporation X owns, manages, and derives rental income from an office building and also owns vacant land. X transfers the land to new subsidiary Y and distributes the stock of Y to X's shareholders. Y will subdivide the land, install streets and utilities, and sell the developed lots to various homebuilders. Y does not satisfy the requirements of section 355(b) because no significant development activities were conducted with respect to the land during the five-year period ending on the date of the distribution. See paragraph (b)(3) of this section.

Example (3). Corporation X owns land on which it conducts a ranching business. Oil has been discovered in the area, and it is apparent that oil may be found under the land on which the ranching business is conducted. X has engaged in no significant activities in connection with its mineral rights. X transfers its mineral rights to new subsidiary Y and distributes the stock of Y to X's shareholders. Y will actively pursue the development of the oil producing potential of the property. Y does not satisfy the requirements of section 355(b) because X engaged in no significant exploitation activities with respect to the mineral rights during the five-year period ending on the date of the distribution. See paragraph (b)(3) of this section.

* * *

§ 1.355–4 Non pro rata distributions, etc.

Section 355 provides for nonrecognition of gain or loss with respect to a distribution whether or not (a) the distribution is pro rata with respect to all of the shareholders of the distributing corporation, (b) the distribution is pursuant to a plan of reorganization within the meaning of section 368(a)(1)(D), or (c) the shareholder surrenders stock in the distributing corporation. Under section 355, the stock of a controlled corporation may consist of common stock or preferred stock. (See, however, section 306 and the regulations thereunder.) Section 355 does not apply, however, if the substance of a transaction is merely an exchange between shareholders or security holders of stock or securities in one corporation for stock or securities in another corporation. For example, if two individuals, A and B, each own directly 50 percent of the stock of corporation X and 50 percent of the stock of corporation Y, section 355 would not apply to a transaction in which A and B transfer all of their stock of X and Y to a new corporation Z, for all of the stock of Z, and Z then distributes the stock of X to A and the stock of Y to B.

* * *

§ 1.356–1 Receipt of additional consideration in connection with an exchange.

(a) If in any exchange to which the provisions of section 354 or section 355 would apply except for the fact that there is received by the shareholders or the security holders other property (in addition to property permitted to be received without recognition of gain by such sections) or money, then—

(1) The gain, if any, to the taxpayer shall be recognized in an amount not in excess of the sum of the money and the fair market value of the other property, but,

(2) The loss, if any, to the taxpayer from the exchange or distribution shall not be recognized to any extent.

(b) For purposes of computing the gain, if any, recognized pursuant to section 356 and paragraph (a)(1) of this section, to the extent the terms of the exchange specify the other property or money that is received in exchange for a particular share of stock or security surrendered or a particular class of stock or securities surrendered, such terms shall control provided that such terms are economically reasonable. To the extent the terms of the exchange do not specify the other property or money that is received in exchange for a particular share of stock or security surrendered or a particular class of stock or securities surrendered, a pro rata portion of the other property and money received shall be treated as received in exchange for each share of stock and security surrendered, based on the fair market value of such surrendered share of stock or security.

(c) If the distribution of such other property or money by or on behalf of a corporation has the effect of the distribution of a dividend, then there shall be chargeable to each distributee (either an individual or a corporation)—

(1) As a dividend, such an amount of the gain recognized as is not in excess of the distributee's ratable share of the undistributed earnings and profits of the corporation accumulated after February 28, 1913, and

(2) As a gain from the exchange of property, the remainder of the gain so recognized.

(d) This section may be illustrated by the following examples:

Example (1). In an exchange to which the provisions of section 356 apply and to which section 354 would apply but for the receipt of property not permitted to be received without the recognition of gain or loss, A (either an individual or a corporation), received the following in exchange for a share of stock having an adjusted basis to him of $85:

One share of stock worth	$100
Cash	25
Other property (basis $25) fair market value	50
Total fair market value of consideration received	175
Adjusted basis of stock surrendered in exchange	85
Total gain	90
Gain to be recognized, limited to cash and other property received	75
A's pro rata share of earnings and profits accumulated after February 28, 1913 (taxable dividend)	30
Remainder to be treated as a gain from the exchange of property	45

Example (2). If, in example (1), A's stock had an adjusted basis to him of $200, he would have realized a loss of $25 on the exchange, which loss would not be recognized.

* * *

(e) Section 301(b)(1)(B) and section 301(d)(2) do not apply to a distribution of "other property" to a corporate shareholder if such distribution is within the provisions of section 356.

(f) See paragraph (1) of § 1.301–1 for certain transactions which are not within the scope of section 356.

* * *

§ 1.356–2 Receipt of additional consideration not in connection with an exchange.

(a) If, in a transaction to which section 355 would apply except for the fact that a shareholder (individual or corporate) receives property permitted by section 355 to be received without the recognition of gain, together with other property or money, without the surrender of any stock or securities of the distributing corporation, then the sum of the money and the fair market value of the other property as of the date of the distribution shall be treated as a distribution of property to which the rules of section 301 (other than section 301(b) and section 301(d)) apply. See section 358 for determination of basis of such other property.

(b) Paragraph (a) of this section may be illustrated by the following examples:

Example (1). Individuals A and B each own 50 of the 100 outstanding shares of common stock of Corporation X. Corporation X owns all of the stock of Corporation Y, 100 shares. Corporation X distributes to each shareholder 50 shares of the stock of Corporation Y plus $100 cash without requiring the surrender of any shares of its own stock. The $100 cash received by each is treated as a distribution of property to which the rules of section 301 apply.

Example (2). If, in the above example, Corporation X distributes 50 shares of stock of Corporation Y to A and 30 shares of such stock plus $100 cash to B without requiring the surrender of any of its own stock, the amount of cash received by B is treated as a distribution of property to which the rules of section 301 apply.

§ 1.356–3 Rules for treatment of securities as "other property".

(a) As a general rule, for purposes of section 356, the term "other property" includes securities. However, it does not include securities permitted under section 354 or section 355 to be received tax free. Thus, when securities are surrendered in a transaction to which section 354 or section 355 is applicable, the characterization of the securities received as "other property" does not include securities received where the principal amount of such securities does not exceed the principal amount of securities surrendered in the transaction. If a greater principal amount of securities is received in an exchange described in section 354 (other than subsection (c) or

(d) thereof) or section 355 over the principal amount of securities surrendered, the term "other property" includes the fair market value of such excess principal amount as of the date of the exchange. If no securities are surrendered in exchange, the term "other property" includes the fair market value, as of the date of receipt, of the entire principal amount of the securities received.

(b) The following examples illustrate the application of the above regulations:

Example (1). A, an individual, exchanged 100 shares of stock for 100 shares of stock and a security in the principal amount of $1,000 with a fair market value of $990. The amount of $990 is treated as "other property."

Example (2). B, an individual, exchanged 100 shares of stock and a security in the principal amount of $1,000 for 300 shares of stock and a security in the principal amount of $1,500. The security had a fair market value on the date of receipt of $1,575. The fair market value of the excess principal amount, or $525, is treated as "other property."

Example (3). C, an individual, exchanged a security in the principal amount of $1,000 for 100 shares of stock and a security in the principal amount of $900. No part of the security received is treated as "other property."

Example (4). D, an individual, exchanged a security in the principal amount of $1,000 for 100 shares of stock and a security in the principal amount of $1,200 with a fair market value of $1,100. The fair market value of the excess principal amount, or $183.33, is treated as "other property."

Example (5). E, an individual, exchanged a security in the principal amount of $1,000 for another security in the principal amount of $1,200 with a fair market value of $1,080. The fair market value of the excess principal amount, or $180, is treated as "other property."

Example (6). F, an individual, exchanged a security in the principal amount of $1,000 for two different securities each in the principal amount of $750. One of the securities had a fair market value of $750, the other had a fair market value of $600. One-third of the fair market value of each security ($250 and $200) is treated as "other property."

§ 1.356–4 Exchanges for section 306 stock.

If, in a transaction to which section 356 is applicable, other property or money is received in exchange for section 306 stock, an amount equal to the fair market value of the property plus the money, if any, shall be treated as a distribution of property to which section 301 is applicable. The determination of whether section 306 stock is surrendered for other property (including money) is a question of fact to be decided under all of the circumstances of each case. Ordinarily, the other property (including money) received will first be treated as received in exchange for any section 306 stock owned by a shareholder prior to such transaction. For example, if a shareholder who owns a share of common stock (having a basis to him of $100) and a share of preferred stock which is section 306 stock (having a basis to him of $100) surrenders both shares in a transaction to which section 356 is applicable for one share of common stock having a fair market value of $80 and one $100 bond having a fair market value of $100, the bond will be deemed received in exchange for the section 306 stock and it will be treated as a distribution to which section 301 is applicable to the extent of its entire fair market value ($100).

§ 1.356–5 Transactions involving gift or compensation.

With respect to transactions described in sections 354, 355, or 356, but which—

(a) Result in a gift, see section 2501 and following, and the regulations pertaining thereto, or

(b) Have the effect of the payment of compensation, see section 61(a)(1), and the regulations pertaining thereto.

* * *

§ 1.357–1 Assumption of liability.

(a) General rule. Section 357(a) does not affect the rule that liabilities assumed are to be taken into account for the purpose of computing the amount of gain or loss realized under section 1001 upon an exchange. Section 357(a) provides, subject to the exceptions and limitations specified in section 357(b) and (c), that—

(1) Liabilities assumed are not to be treated as "other property or money" for the purpose of determining the amount of realized gain which is to be recognized under section 351, 361, 371, or 374,* if the transactions would, but for the receipt of "other property or money" have been exchanges of the type described in any one of such sections; and

(2) If the only type of consideration received by the transferor in addition to that permitted to be received by section 351, 361, 371, or 374,* consists of an assumption of liabilities, the transaction, if otherwise qualified, will be deemed to be within the provisions of section 351, 361, 371, or 374.*

(b) Application of general rule. The application of paragraph (a) of this section may be illustrated by the following example:

*Editorial comment: The reference is now Sec. 351 or 361. The Regulations do not reflect the repeal of Secs. 371 and 374 by the Revenue Reconciliation Act of 1990.

Example. A, an individual, transfers to a controlled corporation property with an adjusted basis of $10,000 in exchange for stock of the corporation with a fair market value of $8,000, $3,000 cash, and the assumption by the corporation of indebtedness of A amounting to $4,000. A's gain is $5,000, computed as follows:

Stock received, fair market value	$8,000
Cash received	3,000
Liability assumed by transferee	4,000
Total consideration received	15,000
Less: Adjusted basis of property transferred	10,000
Gain realized	5,000

Assuming that the exchange falls within section 351 as a transaction in which the gain to be recognized is limited to "other property or money" received, the gain recognized to A will be limited to the $3,000 cash received, since, under the general rule of section 357(a), the assumption of the $4,000 liability does not constitute "other property."

(c) Tax avoidance purpose. The benefits of section 357(a) do not extend to any exchange involving an assumption of liabilities where it appears that the principal purpose of the taxpayer with respect to such assumption was to avoid Federal income tax on the exchange, or, if not such purpose, was not a bona fide business purpose. In such cases, the total amount of liabilities assumed or acquired pursuant to such exchange (and not merely a particular liability with respect to which the tax avoidance purpose existed) shall, for the purpose of determining the amount of gain to be recognized upon the exchange in which the liabilities are assumed or acquired, be treated as money received by the taxpayer upon the exchange. Thus, if in the example set forth in paragraph (b) of this section, the principal purpose of the assumption of the $4,000 liability was to avoid tax on the exchange, or was not a bona fide business purpose, then the amount of gain recognized would be $5,000. In any suit or proceeding where the burden is on the taxpayer to prove that an assumption of liabilities is not to be treated as "other property or money" under section 357, which is the case if the Commissioner determines that the taxpayer's purpose with respect thereto was a purpose to avoid Federal income tax on the exchange or was not a bona fide business purpose, and the taxpayer contests such determination by litigation, the taxpayer must sustain such burden by the clear preponderance of the evidence. Thus, the taxpayer must prove his case by such a clear preponderance of all the evidence that the absence of a purpose to avoid Federal income tax on the exchange, or the presence of a bona fide business purpose, is unmistakable.

*Editorial comment: The Regulations do not include the effect of P.L. 96–222. See Sec. 357(c)(3).

§ 1.357–2 Liabilities in excess of basis.*

(a) Section 357(c) provides in general that in an exchange to which section 351 (relating to a transfer to a corporation controlled by the transferor) is applicable, or to which section 361 (relating to the nonrecognition of gain or loss to corporations) is applicable by reason of a section 368(a)(1)(D) reorganization, if the sum of the amount of liabilities assumed plus the amount of liabilities to which the property is subject exceeds the total of the adjusted basis of the property transferred pursuant to such exchange, then such excess shall be considered as a gain from the sale or exchange of a capital asset or of property which is not a capital asset as the case may be. Thus, if an individual transfers, under section 351, properties having a total basis in his hands of $20,000, one of which has a basis of $10,000 but is subject to a mortgage of $30,000, to a corporation controlled by him, such individual will be subject to tax with respect to $10,000, the excess of the amount of the liability over the total adjusted basis of all the properties in his hands. The same result will follow whether or not the liability is assumed by the transferee. The determination of whether a gain resulting from the transfer of capital assets is long-term or short-term capital gain shall be made by reference to the holding period to the transferor of the assets transferred. An exception to the general rule of section 357(c) is made (1) for any exchange as to which under section 357(b) (relating to assumption of liabilities for tax–avoidance purposes) the entire amount of the liabilities is treated as money received and (2) for an exchange to which section 371 (relating to reorganizations in certain receivership and bankruptcy proceedings) or section 374 (relating to gain or loss not recognized in certain railroad reorganizations) is applicable.** and***

(b) The application of paragraph (a) of this section may be illustrated by the following examples:

Example (1). If all such assets transferred are capital assets and if half the assets (ascertained by reference to their fair market value at the time of the transfer) have been held for less than 1 year (6 months for taxable years beginning before 1977; 9 months for taxable years beginning in 1977), and the remaining half for more than 1 year (6 months for taxable years beginning before 1977; 9 months for taxable years beginning in 1977), half the excess of the amount of the liability over the total of the adjusted basis of the property transferred pursuant to the exchange shall be treated as short-term capital gain, and the remaining half shall be treated as long–term capital gain.

**Editorial comment: The Regulations do not reflect the repeal of Secs. 371 and 374 by the Revenue Reconciliation Act of 1990.

Example (2). If half of the assets (ascertained by reference to their fair market value at the time of the transfer) transferred are capital assets and half are assets other than capital assets, then half of the excess of the amount of the liability over the total of the adjusted basis of the property transferred pursuant to the exchange shall be treated as capital gain, and the remaining half shall be treated as gain from the sale or exchange of assets other than capital assets.

§ 1.358–1 Basis to distributees.

(a) In the case of an exchange or distribution to which section 354 or 355 applies in which, under the law applicable to the year in which the exchange is made, only nonrecognition property is received, the sum of the basis of all of the stock and securities in the corporation whose stock and securities are exchanged or with respect to which the distribution is made, held immediately after the transaction, plus the basis of all stock and securities received in the transaction shall be the same as the basis of all the stock and securities in such corporation held immediately before the transaction allocated in the manner described in § 1.358–2. In the case of a distribution to which section 355 applies in which, under the law applicable to the year in which the distribution is made, only nonrecognition property is received, immediately after the transaction, the sum of the basis of all the stock and securities with respect to which the distribution is made plus the basis of all stock and securities received in the distribution with respect to such stock and securities shall be the same as the basis of stock and securities with respect to which the distribution is made immediately before the transaction, allocated in the manner described in §1.358–2. In the case of an exchange to which section 351 or 361 applies in which, under the law applicable to the year in which the exchange was made, only nonrecognition property is received, the basis of all the stock and securities received in the exchange shall be the same as the basis of all property exchange therefor. If in an exchange or distribution to which section 351, 356, or 361 applies both nonrecognition property and "other property" are received, the basis of all the property except "other property" held after the transaction shall be determined as described in the preceding two sentences decreased by the sum of the money and the fair market value of the "otherproperty" (as of the date of the transaction) and increased by the sum of the amount treated as a dividend (if any) and the amount of the gain recognized on the exchange, but the term "gain" as here used does not include any portion of the recognized gain that was treated as a dividend. In any case in which a taxpayer transfers property with respect to which loss is recognized, such loss shall be reflected in determining the basis of the property received in the exchange. The basis of the "other property" is its fair market value as of the date of the transaction. See §1.460-4(k)(3)(iv)(A) for rules relating to stock basis adjustments required when a contract accounted for using the long-term contract method of accounting is transferred in a transaction described in section 351 or in are organization described in section 368(a)(1)(D) with respect to which the requirements of section 355 (or so much of section 356 as relates to section 355) are met.

(b) The application of paragraph (a) of this section may be illustrated by the following example:

Example. A purchased a share of stock in Corporation X in 1935 for $150. Since that date he has received distributions out of other than earnings and profits (as defined in section 316) totalling $60, so that his adjusted basis for the stock is $90. In a transaction qualifying under section 356, A exchanged this share for one share in Corporation Y, worth $100, cash in the amount of $10, and other property with a fair market value of $30. The exchanging had the effect of the distribution of a dividend. A's ratable share of the earnings and profits of Corporation X accumulated after February 28, 1913, was $5. A realized a gain of $50 on the exchange, but the amount recognized is limited to $40, the sum of the cash received and the fair market value of the other property. Of the gain recognized, $5 is taxable as a dividend, and $35 as a gain from the exchange of property. The basis to A of the one share of stock of Corporation Y is $90, that is, the adjusted basis of the one share of stock Corporation X ($90), decreased by the sum of the cash received ($10) and the fair market value of the other property received ($30) and increased by the sum of the amount treated as a dividend ($5) and the amount treated as a gain from the exchange of property ($35). The basis of the other property received is $30.

* * *

§ 1.358–2 Allocation of basis among nonrecognition property.*

(a) Allocation of basis in exchanges or distributions to which section 354, 355, or 356 applies. **(1)** As used in this paragraph the term *stock* means stock which is not "other property" under section 356. The term securities means securities (including, where appropriate, fractional parts of securities) which are not "other property" under section 356. Stock, or securities, as the case may be, which differ either because they are in different corporations or because the rights attributable to them differ (although they are in the same corporation) are considered different classes of stock or securities, as the case may be, for purposes of this section.

(2) **(i)** If a shareholder or security holder surrenders a share of stock or a security in an exchange

*Editorial comment: In general, these final regulations are effective after September 3, 2013.

under the terms of section 354, 355, or 356, the basis of each share of stock or security received in the exchange shall be the same as the basis of the share or shares of stock or security or securities (or allocable portions thereof) exchanged therefore (as adjusted under § 1.358–1). If more than one share of stock or security is received in exchange for one share of stock or one security, the basis of the share of stock or security surrendered shall be allocated to the shares of stock or securities received in the exchange in proportion to the fair market value of the shares of stock or securities received. If one share of stock or security is received in exchange for more than one share of stock or security or if a fraction of a share of stock or security is received, then the basis of the shares of stock or securities surrendered must be allocated to the shares of stock or securities (or allocable portions thereof) received in a manner that reflects, to the greatest extent possible, that a share of stock or security received is received in respect of shares of stock or securities that were acquired on the same date and at the same price. To the extent it is not possible to allocate basis in this manner, the basis of the shares of stock or securities surrendered must be allocated to the shares of stock or securities (or allocable portions thereof) received in a manner that minimizes the disparity in the holding periods of the surrendered shares of stock or securities whose basis is allocated to any particular share of stock or security received.

(ii) If a shareholder or security holder surrenders a share of stock or a security in an exchange under the terms of section 354, 355, or 356, and receives shares of stock or securities of more than one class, or receives "other property" or money in addition to shares of stock or securities, then, to the extent the terms of the exchange specify that shares of stock or securities of a particular class or "other property" or money is received in exchange for a particular share of stock or security or a particular class of stock or securities, for purposes of applying the rules of this section, such terms shall control provided such terms are economically reasonable. To the extent the terms of the exchange do not specify that shares of stock or securities of a particular class or "other property" or money is received in exchange for a particular share of stock or security or a particular class of stock or securities, then, for purposes of applying the rules of paragraph (a)(2)(i) of this section, a pro rata portion of the shares of stock and securities of each class received and a pro rata portion of the "other property" and money received shall be treated as received in exchange for each share of stock and security surrendered, based on the fair market value of the stock and securities surrendered.

(iii) For purposes of this section, if a shareholder or security holder surrenders a share of stock or a security in a transaction under the terms of section 354 (or so much of section 356 as relates to section 354) in which such shareholder or security holder receives no property or property (including property permitted by section 354 to be received without the recognition of gain or "other property" or money) with a fair market value less than that of the stock or securities surrendered in the transaction, such shareholder or security holder shall be treated as follows. First, the shareholder or security holder shall be treated as receiving the stock, securities, other property, and money actually received by the shareholder or security holder in the transaction and an amount of stock of the issuing corporation (as defined in § 1.368–1(b)) that has a value equal to the excess of the value of the stock or securities the shareholder or security holder surrendered in the transaction over the value of the stock, securities, other property, and money the shareholder or security holder actually received in the transaction. If the shareholder owns only one class of stock of the issuing corporation the receipt of which would be consistent with the economic rights associated with each class of stock of the issuing corporation, the stock deemed received by the shareholder pursuant to the previous sentence shall be stock of such class. If the shareholder owns multiple classes of stock of the issuing corporation the receipt of which would be consistent with the economic rights associated with each class of stock of the issuing corporation, the stock deemed received by the shareholder shall be stock of each such class owned by the shareholder immediately prior to the transaction, in proportion to the value of the stock of each such class owned by the shareholder immediately prior to the transaction. The basis of each share of stock or security deemed received and actually received shall be determined under the rules of this section. Second, the shareholder or security holder shall then be treated as surrendering all of its shares of stock and securities in the issuing corporation, including those shares of stock or securities held immediately prior to the transaction, those shares of stock or securities actually received in the transaction, and those shares of stock deemed received pursuant to the previous sentence, in a reorganization under section 368(a)(1)(E) in exchange for the shares of stock and securities of the issuing corporation that the shareholder or security holder actually holds immediately after the transaction. The basis of each share of stock and security deemed received in the reorganization under section 368(a)(1)(E) shall be determined under the rules of this section.

(iv) If a shareholder or security holder receives one or more shares of stock or one or more securities in a distribution under the terms of section 355 (or so much of section 356 as relates to section 355), the basis of each share of stock or security of the distributing corporation (as defined in §1.355-1(b)), as adjusted under §1.358-1, shall be allocated between the share of stock or security of the distributing corporation with respect to which the distribution is made and the share or shares of stock or security or securities (or allocable portions thereof) received with respect to the share of stock or security of the distributing corporation in proportion to their fair market values. If one share of stock or security is received with respect to more than one share of stock or security or if a fraction of a share of stock or security is received, then the basis of each share of stock or security of the distributing corporation must be allocated to the shares of stock or securities (or allocable portions thereof) received in a manner that reflects that, to the greatest extent possible, a share of stock or security received is received with respect to shares of stock or securities acquired on the same date and at the same price. To the extent it is not possible to allocate basis in this manner, the basis of each share of stock or security of the distributing corporation must be allocated to the shares of stock or securities (or allocable portions thereof) received in a manner that minimizes the disparity in the holding periods of the shares of stock or securities with respect to which such shares of stock or securities are received.

(v) If a shareholder or security holder receives shares of stock or securities of more than one class, or receives "other property" or money in addition to stock or securities in a distribution under the terms of section 355 (or so much of section 356 as relates to section 355), then, to the extent the terms of the distribution specify that shares of stock or securities of a particular class or "other property" or money is received with respect to a particular share of stock or security of the distributing corporation or a particular class of stock or securities of the distributing corporation, for purposes of applying the rules of this section, such terms shall control provided that such terms are economically reasonable. To the extent the terms of the distribution do not specify the shares of stock or securities of a particular class or "other property" or money is received with respect to a particular share of stock or security of the distributing corporation or a particular class of stock or securities of the distributing corporation, then, for purposes of applying the rules of this section, a pro rata portion of the shares of stock and securities of each class received and a pro rata portion of the "other property" and money received shall be treated as received with respect to each share of stock and security of the distributing corporation with respect to which the distribution is made, based on the fair market value of each such share of stock or security.

(vi) If a share of stock or a security is received in exchange for, or with respect to, more than one share of stock or security and such shares or securities were acquired on different dates or at different prices, the share of stock or security received shall be divided into segments based on the relative fair market values of the shares of stock or securities surrendered in exchange for such share or security or the relative fair market values of the shares of stock or securities with respect to which the share of stock or security is received in a distribution under the terms of section 355 (or so much of section 356 as relates to section 355)). Each segment shall have a basis determined under the rules of paragraph (a)(2) of this section and a corresponding holding period.

(vii) If a shareholder or security holder that purchased or acquired shares of stock or securities in a corporation on different dates or at different prices exchanges such shares of stock or securities under the terms of section 354, 355, or 356, or receives a distribution of shares of stock or securities under the terms of section 355 (or so much of section 356 as relates to section 355), and the shareholder or security holder is not able to identify which particular share of stock or security (or allocable portion of a share of stock or security) is received (or deemed received) in exchange for, or with respect to, a particular share of stock or security, the shareholder or security holder may designate which share of stock or security is received in exchange for, or with respect to, a particular share of stock or security, provided that such designation is consistent with the terms of the exchange or distribution (or an exchange deemed to have occurred pursuant to paragraph (a)(2)(iii) of this section), and the other rules of this section. In the case of an exchange under the terms of section 354 or 356 (including a deemed exchange as a result of the application of paragraph (a)(2)(iii) of this section), the designation must be made on or before the first date on which the basis of a share of stock or a security received (or deemed received in the reorganization under section 368(a)(1)(E) in the case of a transaction to which paragraph (a)(2)(iii) of this section applies) is relevant. In the case of an exchange or distribution under the terms of section 355 (or so much of section 356 as relates to section 355), the designation must be made on or before the first date on which the basis of a share of stock or a security of the distributing corporation or the controlled corporation (as defined in § 1.355–1(b)) is relevant. The basis of the shares or securities received in an exchange under the terms of section 354 or section 356, for example, is relevant when such shares or securities are sold or otherwise transferred. The designation will be binding for purposes of determining the Federal tax consequences of any sale or transfer of, or distribution with respect to, the shares or securities received. If the shareholder fails to make a designation in a case in which the shareholder is not able to identify which share of stock is received in exchange for, or with respect to, a particular share of stock, then the shareholder will not be able to identify which shares are sold or transferred for purposes of determining the basis of property sold or transferred under section 1012 and § 1.1012–1(c) and, instead, will be treated as selling or transferring the share received in respect of the earliest share purchased or acquired.

(viii) This paragraph (a)(2) shall not apply to determine the basis of a share of stock or security received by a shareholder or security holder in an exchange described in both section 351 and either section 354 or 356, if, in connection with the exchange—

(A) The shareholder or security holder exchanges property for stock or securities in an exchange to which neither section 354 nor section 356 applies;

(B) The shareholder or security holder exchanges property for stock or securities in a transaction for which an election to apply section 362(e)(2)(C) is in effect; or

(C) Liabilities of the shareholder or security holder are assumed.

(ix) This paragraph (a)(2) shall apply to determine the basis of a share of stock or security received by a shareholder or security holder in an exchange described in both section 1036 and section 354 or section 356.

(b) Allocation of basis in exchanges to which section 351 or 361 applies. (1) As used in this paragraph (b), the term *stock* refers only to stock which is not "other property" under section 351 or 361 and the term securities refers only to securities which are not "other property" under section 351 or 361.

(2) If in an exchange to which section 351 or 361 applies property is transferred to a corporation and the transferor receives stock or securities of more than one class or receives both stock and securities, then the basis of the property transferred (as adjusted under § 1.358–1) shall be allocated among all of the stock and securities received in proportion to the fair market values of the stock of each class and the securities of each class.

(c) Examples. The application of paragraphs (a) and (b) of this section is illustrated by the following examples:

Example (1). (i) Facts. J, an individual, acquired 20 shares of Corporation X stock on Date 1 for $3 each and 10 shares of Corporation X stock on Date 2 for $6 each. On Date 3, Corporation Y acquires the assets of Corporation X in a reorganization under section 368(a)(1)(A). Pursuant to the terms of the plan of reorganization, J receives 2 shares of Corporation Y stock in exchange for each share of Corporation X stock. Therefore, J receives 60 shares of Corporation Y stock. Pursuant to section 354, J recognizes no gain or loss on the exchange. J is not able to identify which shares of Corporation Y stock are received in exchange for each share of Corporation X stock.

(ii) Analysis. Under paragraph (a)(2)(i) of this section, J has 40 shares of Corporation Y stock each of which has a basis of $1.50 and is treated as having been acquired on Date 1 and 20 shares of Corporation Y stock each of which has a basis of $3 and is treated as having been acquired on Date 2. Under paragraph (a)(2)(vii) of this section, on or before the date on which the basis of a share of Corporation Y stock received becomes relevant, J may designate which of the shares of Corporation Y stock have a basis of $1.50 and which have a basis of $3.

Example (2). (i) Facts. The facts are the same as in *Example 1*, except that instead of receiving 2 shares of Corporation Y stock in exchange for each share of Corporation X stock, J receives 1½ shares of Corporation Y stock in exchange for each share of Corporation X stock. Therefore, J receives 45 shares of Corporation Y stock. Again, J is not able to identify which shares (or portions of shares) of Corporation Y stock are received in exchange for each share of Corporation X stock.

(ii) Analysis. Under paragraph (a)(2)(i) of this section, J has 30 shares of Corporation Y stock each of which has a basis of $2 and is treated as having been acquired on Date 1 and 15 shares of Corporation Y stock each of which has a basis of $4 and is treated as having been acquired on Date 2. Under paragraph (a)(2)(vii) of this section, on or before the date on which the basis of a share of Corporation Y stock received becomes relevant, J may designate which of the shares of Corporation Y stock received have a basis of $2 and which have a basis of $4.

Example (3). (i) Facts. J, an individual, acquired 10 shares of Class A stock of Corporation X on Date 1 for $3 each, 10 shares of Class A stock of Corporation X on Date 2 for $9 each, and 10 shares of Class B stock of Corporation X on Date 3 for $3 each. On Date 4, J surrenders all of J's shares of Class A stock in exchange for 20 shares of new Class C stock and 20 shares of new Class D stock in a reorganization under section 368(a)(1)(E). Pursuant to section 354, J recognizes no gain or loss on the exchange. On the date of the exchange, the fair market value of each share of Class A stock is $6, the fair market value of each share of Class C stock is $2, and the fair market value of each share of Class D stock is $4. The terms of the exchange do not specify that shares of Class C stock or shares of Class D stock of Corporation X are received in exchange for particular shares of Class A stock of Corporation X.

(ii) Analysis. Under paragraph (a)(2)(ii) of this section, because the terms of the exchange do not specify that shares of Class C stock or shares of Class D stock of Corporation X are received in exchange for particular shares of Class A stock of Corporation X, a pro rata portion of the shares of Class C stock and shares of Class D stock received will be treated as received in exchange for each share of Class A stock based on the fair market value of the surrendered shares of Class A stock. Therefore, J is treated as receiving one share of Class C stock and one share of Class D stock in exchange for each share of Class A stock. Under paragraph (a)(2)(i) of this section, J has 10 shares of Class C stock, each of which has a basis of $1 and is treated as having been acquired on Date 1 and 10 shares of Class C stock, each of which has a basis of $3 and is treated as having been acquired on Date 2. In addition, J has 10 shares of Class D stock, each of which has a basis of $2 and is treated as having been acquired on Date 1 and 10 shares of Class D stock, each of which has a basis of $6 and is treated as having been acquired on Date 2. J's basis in each share of Class B stock remains $3. Under paragraph (a)(2)(vii) of this section, on or before the date on which the basis of a share of Class C stock or Class D stock received becomes relevant, J may designate which of the shares of Class C stock have a basis of $1 and which have a basis of $3, and which of the shares of Class D stock have a basis of $2 and which have a basis of $6.

* * *

§ 1.358–3 Treatment of assumption of liabilities.

(a) For purposes of section 358, where a party to the exchange assumes a liability of a distributee or acquires from him property subject to a liability, the amount of such liability is to be treated as money received by the distributee upon the exchange, whether or not the assumption of liabilities resulted in a recognition of gain or loss to the taxpayer under the law applicable to the year in which the exchange was made.

(b) The application of paragraph (a) of this section may be illustrated by the following examples:

Example (1). A, an individual, owns property with an adjusted basis of $100,000 on which there is a purchase money mortgage of $25,000. On December 1, 1945, A organizes Corporation X to which he transfers the property in exchange for all the stock of Corporation X and the assumption by Corporation X of the mortgage. The capital stock of the Corporation X has a fair market value of $150,000. Under sections 351 and 357, no gain or loss is recognized to A. The basis in A's hands of the stock of Corporation X is $75,000, computed as follows:

Adjusted basis of property transferred	$100,000
Less: Amount of money received (amount of liabilities assumed)	– 25,000
Basis of Corporation X stock to A	75,000

Example (2). A, an individual, owns property with an adjusted basis of $25,000 on which there is a mortgage of $50,000. On December 1, 1954, A organizes Corporation X to which he transfers the property in exchange for all the stock of Corporation X and the assumption by Corporation X of the mortgage. The stock of Corporation X has a fair market value of $50,000. Under sections 351 and 357, gain is recognized to A in the amount of $25,000. The basis in A's hands of the stock of Corporation X is zero, computed as follows:

Adjusted basis of property transferred	$25,000
Less: Amount of money received (amount of liabilities)	– 50,000
Plus: Amount of gain recognized to taxpayer.	25,000
Basis of Corporation X stock to A	0

§ 1.358–4 Exceptions.

(a) Plan of reorganization adopted after October 22, 1968. In the case of a plan of reorganization adopted after October 22, 1968, section 358 does not apply in determining the basis of property acquired by a corporation in connection with such reorganization by the exchange of its stock or securities (or by the exchange of stock or securities of a corporation which is in control of the acquiring corporation) as the consideration in whole or in part for the transfer of the property to it. See section 362 and the regulations pertaining to that section for rules relating to basis to corporations of property acquired in such cases.

* * *

Effects On Corporation

§ 1.361–1 Nonrecognition of gain or loss to corporations.

Section 361 provides the general rule that no gain or loss shall be recognized if a corporation, a party to a reorganization, exchanges property in pursuance of the plan of reorganization solely for stock or securities in another corporation, a party to the reorganization. This provision includes only stock and securities received in connection with a reorganization defined in section 368(a). It also includes nonvoting stock and securities in a corporation, a party to a reorganization, received in a transaction to which section 368(a)(1)(C) is applicable only by reason of section 368(a)(2)(B).

§ 1.362–1 Basis to corporations.

(a) In general. Section 362 provides, as a general rule, that if property was acquired on or after June 22, 1954, by a corporation (1) in connection with a transaction to which section 351 (relating to transfer of property to corporation controlled by transferor) applies, (2) as paid-in surplus or as a contribution to capital,* * * then the basis shall be the same as it would be in the hands of the transferor, increased in the amount of gain recognized to the transferor on such transfer. (See also § 1.362–2.) See § 1.460–4(k)(3)(iv)(B)(2) for rules relating to adjustments to the basis of certain contracts accounted for using a long-term contract method of accounting that are acquired in certain transfers described in section 351 and certain reorganizations described in section 368(a).

(b) Exceptions. (1) In the case of a plan of reorganization adopted after October 22, 1968, section 362 does not apply if the property acquired in connection with such reorganization consists of stock or securities in a corporation a party to the reorganization, unless acquired by the exchange of stock or securities of the transferee (or of a corporation which is in control of the transferee) as the consideration in whole or in part for the transfer.

* * *

§ 1.362–2 Certain contributions to capital.

The following regulations shall be used in the application of section 362(c):

(a) Property deemed to be acquired with contributed money shall be that property, if any, the acquisition of which was the purpose motivating the contribution;

(b) In the case of an excess of the amount of money contributed over the cost of the property deemed to be acquired with such money (as defined in paragraph (a) of this section) such excess shall be applied to the reduction of the basis (but not below zero) of other properties held by the corporation, on the last day of the 12-month period beginning on the day the contribution is received, in the following order—

(1) All property of a character subject to an allowance for depreciation (not including any properties as to which a deduction for amortization is allowable),

(2) Property with respect to which a deduction for amortization is allowable,

(3) Property with respect to which a deduction for depletion is allowable under section 611 but not under section 613, and

(4) All other remaining properties.

The reduction of the basis of each of the properties within each of the above categories shall be made in proportion to the relative bases of such properties.

(c) With the consent of the Commissioner, the taxpayer may, however, have the basis of the various units of property within a particular category adjusted in a manner different from the general rule set forth in paragraph (b) of this section. Variations from such rule may, for example, involve adjusting the basis of only certain units of the taxpayer's property within a given category. A request for variations from the general rule should be filed by the taxpayer with its return for the taxable year for which the transfer of the property has occurred.

§ 1.362–4 Basis of loss duplication property.*

(a) Purpose and scope. (1) In general. The purpose of section 362(e)(2) and this section is to prevent the duplication of net loss in transfers to which section 351 applies, capital contributions, and paid-in surplus (each, a section 362(a) transaction). See paragraph (g) of this section for definitions of terms used in this section.

(2) Intercompany transactions. For rules relating to the application of section 362(e)(2) to transfers between members of a consolidated group on or after October 22, 2004, see §1.1502-80(h).

(b) Basis determinations under section 362(e)(2) and this section. Notwithstanding section 362(a), if a corporation (Acquiring) receives loss duplication property (as defined in paragraph (g)(1) of this section) from a person (Transferor) in a loss duplication transaction (as defined in paragraph (g)(2) of this section), Acquiring's basis in such property is equal to the basis of the property determined without regard to section 362(e)(2) and this section (as described in paragraph (g)(1)(ii) of this section), reduced by the property's allocable portion of Transferor's net built-in loss (as defined in paragraph (g)(3) of this section). If more than one Transferor transfers property to a corporation in a section 362(a) transaction, whether and the extent to which section 362(e)(2) and this section apply is determined separately for each Transferor.

(c) Exceptions. (1) Transactions in which net built-in loss is eliminated without recognition. Section 362(e)(2) does not apply to a transaction to the extent that—

(i) Without recognizing gain or loss, Transferor distributes the Acquiring stock received in the transaction; and

(ii) Upon completion of the transaction, no person holds Acquiring stock or any other asset with a basis determined, in whole or in part, by reference to Transferor's basis in the distributed Acquiring stock.

(d) Election to reduce Transferor's stock basis instead of Acquiring's asset basis. (1) In general. In lieu of making the basis reductions otherwise required under paragraph (b) of this section, Transferor and Acquiring may elect to reduce Transferor's basis in Acquiring stock that is received in the transaction without the recognition of gain or loss (the section 362(e)(2)(C) election). The section 362(e)(2)(C) election may be made protectively

*Editorial comment: In general, these final regulations are effective after September 3, 2013.

and will have no effect to the extent that property transferred in the transaction is determined not to be subject to section 362(e)(2) and this section. However, the election is irrevocable once it is made. A section 362(e)(2)(C) election is made and effective if—

(i) Prior to the filing of a Section 362(e)(2)(C) Statement (described in paragraph (d)(3)(i) of this section), Transferor and Acquiring enter into a written, binding agreement to elect to apply section 362(e)(2)(C); and

(ii) The Section 362(e)(2)(C) Statement is filed in accordance with the provisions of paragraph (d)(3) of this section.

(2) Effect of section 362(e)(2)(C) election. If a section 362(e)(2)(C) election is made and in effect—

(i) An amount equal to the portion of Transferor's net built-in loss (as defined in paragraph (g)(3) of this section) that would otherwise be applied to reduce asset basis under paragraph (b) of this section is allocated among the Acquiring shares received or deemed received in the exchange (in proportion to the value of such shares) and applied to reduce Transferor's basis (determined without regard to section 362(e)(2) and this section) in each such share; and

(ii) Acquiring's basis in loss duplication propertyreceived from Transferor in the transaction is not determined under section 362(e)(2) and this section.

* * *

Special Rule; Definitions

§ 1.368–1 Purpose and scope of exception of reorganization exchanges.

(a) Reorganizations. As used in the regulations under parts I, II, and III (section 301 and following), subchapter C, chapter 1 of the Code, the terms "reorganization" and "party to a reorganization" mean only a reorganization or a party to a reorganization as defined in subsections (a) and (b) of section 368. * * *

(b) Purpose. Under the general rule, upon the exchange of property, gain or loss must be accounted for if the new property differs in a material particular, either in kind or in extent, from the old property. The purpose of the reorganization provisions of the Code is to except from the general rule certain specifically described exchanges incident to such readjustments of corporate structures made in one of the particular ways specified in the Code, as are required by business exigencies and which effect only a readjustment of continuing interest in property under modified corporate forms. Requisite to a reorganization under the Internal Revenue Code are a continuity of the business enterprise through the issuing corporation under the modified corporate form as described in paragraph (d) of this section, and (except as provided in section 368 (a)(1)(D)) a continuity of interest as described in paragraph (e) of this section. (For rules regarding the continuity of interest requirement under section 355, see §1.355-2(c).) For purposes of this section, the term issuing corporation means the acquiring corporation (as that term is used in section 368(a)), except that, in determining whether a reorganization qualifies as a triangular reorganization (as defined in §1.358-6(b)(2)), the issuing corporation means the corporation in control of the acquiring corporation. The preceding three sentences apply to transactions occurring after January 28, 1998, except that they do not apply to any transaction occurring pursuant to a written agreement which is binding on January 28, 1998, and at all times thereafter. The continuity of business enterprise requirement is described in paragraph (d) of this section. The Code recognizes as a reorganization the amalgamation (occurring in a specified way) of two corporate enterprises under a single corporate structure if there exists among the holders of the stock and securities of either of the old corporations the requisite continuity of interest in the new corporation, but there is not a reorganization if the holders of the stock and securities of the old corporation are merely the holders of short-term notes in the new corporation. In order to exclude transactions not intended to be included, the specifications of the reorganization provisions of the law are precise. Both the terms of the specifications and their underlying assumptions and purposes must be satisfied in order to entitle the taxpayer to the benefit of the exception from the general rule. Accordingly, under the Code, a short-term purchase money note is not a security of a party to a reorganization, an ordinary dividend is to be treated as an ordinary dividend, and a sale is nevertheless to be treated as a sale even though the mechanics of a reorganization have been set up.

(c) Scope. The nonrecognition of gain or loss is prescribed for two specifically described types of exchanges, viz: The exchange that is provided for in section 354(a)(1) in which stock or securities in a corporation, a party to a reorganization, are, in pursuance of a plan of reorganization, exchanged for the stock or securities in a corporation, a party to the same reorganization; and the exchange that is provided for in section 361(a) in which a corporation, a party to a reorganization, exchanges property, in pursuance of a plan of reorganization, for stock or securities in another corporation, a party to the same reorganization. Section 368(a)(1) limits the definition of the term "reorganization" to six kinds of transactions and excludes all others. From its context, the term "a party to a reorganization" can only mean a party to a transaction specifically defined as a reorganization by section 368 (a). Certain rules respecting boot received in either of the two types of exchanges provided for in section 354 (a)(1) and section 361(a) are prescribed in sections 356, 357, and 361(b). A special rule respecting a transfer of property with a liability in excess of its basis is prescribed in section 357(c). Under section 367 a limitation is placed on all these provisions by providing that except under specified conditions foreign corporations shall not be deemed within their scope. The provisions of the Code referred to in this paragraph are inapplicable unless there is a plan of reorganization. A plan of reorganization must contemplate the bona fide execution of one of the transactions specifically described as a reorganization in section 368(a) and for the bona fide consummation of each of the requisite acts under which nonrecognition of gain is claimed. Such transaction and such acts must be an ordinary and necessary incident of the conduct of the enterprise and must provide for a continuation of the enterprise. A scheme, which involves an abrupt departure from normal reorganization procedure in connection with a transaction on which the imposition of tax is imminent, such as a mere device that puts on the form of a corporate reorganization as a disguise for concealing its real character, and the object and accomplishment of which is the consummation of a preconceived plan having no business or corporate purpose, is not a plan of reorganization.

(d) Continuity of business enterprise—(1) General rule. Continuity of business enterprise (COBE) requires that the issuing corporation (P), as defined in paragraph (b) of this section, either continue the target corporation's (T's) historic business or use a significant portion of T's historic business assets in a business. The preceding sentence applies to transactions occurring after January 28, 1998, except that it does not apply to any transaction occurring pursuant to a written agreement which is binding on January 28, 1998, and at all times thereafter. The application of this general rule to certain transactions, such as mergers of holding companies, will depend on all facts and circumstances. The policy underlying this general rule, which is to ensure that reorganizations are limited to readjustments of continuing interests in property under modified corporate form, provides the guidance necessary to make these facts and circumstances determinations.

(2) Business continuity. (i) The continuity of business enterprise requirement is satisfied if P continues T's historic business. The fact P is in the same line of business as T tends to establish the requisite continuity, but is not alone sufficient.

(ii) If T has more than one line of business, continuity of business enterprise requires only that P continue a significant line of business.

(iii) In general, a corporation's historic business is the business it has conducted most recently. However, a corporation's historic business is not one the corporation enters into as part of a plan of reorganization.

(iv) All facts and circumstances are considered in determining the time when the plan comes into existence and in determining whether a line of business is "significant."

(3) Asset continuity. (i) The continuity of business enterprise requirement is satisfied if P uses a significant portion of T's historic business assets in a business.

(ii) A corporation's historic business assets are the assets used in its historic business. Business assets may include stock and securities and intangible operating assets such as good will, patents, and trademarks, whether or not they have a tax basis.

(iii) In general, the determination of the portion of a corporation's assets considered "significant" is based on the relative importance of the assets to operation of the business. However, all other facts and circumstances, such as the net fair market value of those assets, will be considered.

(4) Acquired assets or stock held by members of the qualified group or partnerships. The following rules apply in determining whether the COBE requirement of paragraph (d)(1) of this section is satisfied:

(i) Businesses and assets of members of a qualified group. The issuing corporation is treated as holding all of the businesses and assets of all of the members of the qualified group, as defined in paragraph (d)(4)(ii) of this section.

(ii) Qualified group. A qualified group is one or more chains of corporations connected through stock ownership with the issuing corporation, but only if the issuing corporation owns directly stock meeting the requirements of section 368(c) in at least one other corporation, and stock meeting the requirements of section 368(c) in each of the corporations (except the issuing corporation) is owned directly (or indirectly as provided in paragraph (d)(4)(iii)(D) of this section) by one of the other corporations.

(iii) Partnerships.

(A) Partnership assets. Each partner of a partnership will be treated as owning the T business assets used in a business of the partnership in accordance with that partner's interest in the partnership.

(B) Partnership businesses. The issuing corporation will be treated as conducting a business of a partnership if—

(1) Members of the qualified group, in the aggregate, own an interest in the partnership representing a significant interest in that partnership business; or

(2) One or more members of the qualified group have active and substantial management functions as a partner with respect to that partnership business.

(C) Conduct of the historic T business in a partnership. If a significant historic T business is conducted in a partnership, the fact that P is treated as conducting such T business under paragraph (d)(4)(iii)(B) of this section tends to establish the requisite continuity, but is not alone sufficient.

(D) Stock attributed from certain partnerships. Solely for purposes of paragraph (d)(4)(ii) of this section, if members of the qualified group own interests in a partnership meeting requirements equivalent to section 368(c) (a section 368(c) controlled partnership), any stock owned by the section 368(c) controlled partnership shall be treated as owned by members of the qualified group. Solely for purposes of determining whether a lower-tier partnership is a section 368(c) controlled partnership, any interest in a lower-tier partnership that is owned by a section 368(c) controlled partnership shall be treated as owned by members of the qualified group.

(iv) Effective/applicability dates. Paragraphs (d)(4)(i) and (d)(4)(iii) (other than paragraph (d)(4)(iii)(D)) of this section apply to transactions occurring after January 28, 1998, except that they do not apply to any transaction occurring pursuant to a written agreement which is binding on January 28, 1998, and all the times thereafter. Paragraphs (d)(4)(ii) and (d)(4)(iii)(D) of this section apply to transactions occurring on or after October 25, 2007, except that they do not apply to any transaction occurring pursuant to a written agreement which is binding before October 25, 2007, and at all times after that.

(5) Examples. The following examples illustrate this paragraph (d). All the corporations have one class of stock outstanding. The preceding sentence and paragraph (d)(5) Example 6 and Example 8 through Example 13 apply to transactions occurring after January 28, 1998, expect they do not apply to any transaction occurring pursuant to a written agreement which is binding on January 28, 1998, and at all times thereafter. Paragraph (d))(5) Example 7, Example 14, and Example 15 apply to transactions occurring on or after October 25, 2007, except that they do not apply to any transaction occurring pursuant to a written agreement which is binding before October 25, 2007, and at all times after that. The examples read as follows:

Example (1). T conducts three lines of business: manufacture of synthetic resins, manufacture of chemicals for the textile industry, and distribution of chemicals. The three lines of business are approximately equal in value. On July 1, 1981, T sells the synthetic resin and chemicals distribution businesses to a third party for cash and marketable securities. On December 31, 1981, T transfers all of its assets to P solely for P voting stock. P continues the chemical manufacturing business without interruption. The continuity of business enterprise requirement is met. Continuity of business enterprise requires only that P continue one of T's three significant lines of business.

Example (2). P manufactures computers and T manufactures components for computers. T sells all of its output to P. On January 1, 1981, P decides to buy imported components only. On March 1, 1981, T merges into P. P continues buying imported components but retains T's equipment as a backup source of supply. The use of the equipment as a backup source of supply constitutes use of significant portion of T's historic business assets, thus establishing continuity of business enterprise. P is not required to continue T's business.

Example (3). T is a manufacturer of boys' and men's trousers. On January 1, 1978, as part of a plan of reorganization, T sold all of its assets to a third party for cash and purchased a highly diversified portfolio of stocks and bonds. As part of the plan T operates an investment business until July 1, 1981. On that date, the plan of reorganization culminates in a transfer by T of all its assets to P, a regulated investment company, solely in exchange for P voting stock. The continuity of business enterprise requirement is not met. T's investment activity is not its historic business, and the stocks and bonds are not T's historic business assets.

Example (4). T manufactures children's toys and P distributes steel and allied products. On January 1, 1981, T sells all of its assets to a third party for $100,000 cash and $900,000 in notes. On March 1, 1981, T merges into P. Continuity of business enterprise is lacking. The use of the sales proceeds in P's business is not sufficient.

Example (5). T manufactures farm machinery and P operates a lumber mill. T merges into P. P disposes of T's assets immediately after the merger as part of the plan of reorganization. P does not continue T's farm machinery manufacturing business. Continuity of business enterprise is lacking.

Example (6). Use of a significant portion of T's historic business assets by the qualified group. (i) Facts. T operates an auto parts distributorship. P owns 80 percent of the stock of a holding company (HC). HC owns 80 percent of the stock of ten subsidiaries, S-1 through S-10. S-1 through S-10 each separately operate a full service gas station. Pursuant to a plan of reorganization, T merges into P and the T shareholders receive solely P stock. As part of the plan of reorganization, P transfers T's assets to

HC, which in turn transfers some of the T assets to each of the ten subsidiaries. No one subsidiary receives a significant portion of T's historic business assets. Each of the subsidiaries will use the T assets in the operation of its full service gas station. No P subsidiary will be an auto parts distributor.

(ii) Continuity of business enterprise. Under paragraph (d)(4)(i) of this section, P is treated as conducting the ten gas station businesses of S-1 through S-10 and as holding the historic T assets used in those businesses. P is treated as holding all the assets and conducting the businesses of all of the members of the qualified group, which includes S-l through S-10 (paragraphs (d)(4)(i) and (ii) of this section). No member of the qualified group continues T's historic distributorship business. However, subsidiaries S-1 through S-10 continue to use the historic T assets in a business. Even though no one corporation of the qualified group is using a significant portion of T's historic business assets in a business, the COBE requirement of paragraph (d)(1) of this section is satisfied because, in the aggregate, the qualified group is using a significant portion of T's historic business assets in a business.

Example (7). Transfers of acquired stock to members of the qualified group-continuity of business enterprise satisfied. (i) Facts. The facts are the same as Example 6, except that, instead of P acquiring the assets of T, HC acquires all of the outstanding stock of T in exchange solely for stock of P. In addition, as part of the plan of reorganization, HC transfers 10 percent of the stock of T to each of subsidiaries S-1 through S-10. T will continue to operate an auto parts distributorship. Without regard to whether the transaction satisfies the COBE requirement, the transaction qualifies as a triangular B reorganization (as defined in §1.358-6(b)(2)(iv)).

(ii) Continuity of business enterprise. Under paragraph (d)(4)(i) of this section, P is treated as holding the assets and conducting the business of T because T is a member of the qualified group (as defined in paragraph (d)(4)(ii) of this section). The COBE requirement of paragraph (d)(1) of this section is satisfied.

Example (8). Continuation of the historic T business in a partnership satisfies continuity of business enterprise. (i) Facts. T manufactures ski boots. P owns all of the stock of S-1. S-1 owns all of the stock of S-2, and S-2 owns all of the stock of S-3. T merges into P and the T shareholders receive consideration consisting of P stock and cash. The T ski boot business is to be continued and expanded. In anticipation of this expansion, P transfers all of the T assets to S-1, S-1 transfers all of the T assets to S-2, and S-2 transfers all of the T assets to S-3. S-3 and X (an unrelated party) form a new partnership (PRS). As part of the plan of reorganization, S-3 transfers all the T assets to PRS, and S-3, in its capacity as a partner, performs active and substantial management functions for the PRS ski boot business, including making significant business decisions and regularly participating in the overall supervision, direction, and control of the employees of the ski boot business. S-3 receives a 20 percent interest in PRS. X transfers cash in exchange for an 80 percent interest in PRS.

(ii) Continuity of business enterprise. Under paragraph (d)(4)(iii)(B)(2) of this section, P is treated as conducting T's historic business because S-3 performs active and substantial management functions for the ski boot business in S-3's capacity as a partner. P is treated as holding all the assets and conducting the businesses of all of the members of the qualified group, which includes S-3 (paragraph (d)(4)(i) and (ii) of this section). The COBE requirement of paragraph (d)(1) of this section is satisfied.

Example (9). Continuation of the historic T business in a partnership does not satisfy continuity of business enterprise. (i) Facts. The facts are the same as Example 8 except that S-3 transfers the historic T business to PRS in exchange for a 1 percent interest in PRS.

(ii) Continuity of business enterprise. Under paragraph (d)(4)(iii)(B)(2) of this section, P is treated as conducting T's historic business because S-3 performs active and substantial management functions for the ski boot business in S-3's capacity as a partner. The fact that a significant historic T business is conducted in PRS, and P is treated as conducting such T business under (d)(4)(iii)(B) tends to establish the requisite continuity, but is not alone sufficient (paragraph (d)(4)(iii)(C) of this section). The COBE requirement of paragraph (d)(1) of this section is not satisfied.

Example (10). Continuation of the T historic business in a partnership satisfies continuity of business enterprise. (i) Facts. The facts are the same as Example 8 except that S-3 transfers the historic T business to PRS in exchange for a 33 $^1/_3$ percent interest in PRS, and no member of P's qualified group performs active and substantial management functions for the ski boot business operated in PRS.

(ii) Continuity of business enterprise. Under paragraph (d)(4)(iii)(B)(1) of this section, P is treated as conducting T's historic business because S-3 owns an interest in the partnership representing a significant interest in that partnership business. P is treated as holding all the assets and conducting the businesses of all of the members of the qualified group, which includes S-3 (paragraphs (d)(4)(i) and (ii) of this section). The COBE requirement of paragraph (d)(1) of this section is satisfied.

Example (11). Use of T's historic business assets in a partnership business. (i) Facts. T is a fabric distributor. P owns all of the stock of S-1. T merges into P and the T shareholders receive solely P stock. S-1 and X (an unrelated party) own interests in a partnership (PRS). As part of the plan of reorganization, P transfers all of the T assets to S-1, and S-1 transfers all of the T assets to PRS, increasing S-1's percentage interest in PRS from 5 to 33 $^1/_3$ percent. After the transfer, X owns the remaining 66 $^2/_3$ percent interest in PRS. Almost all of the T assets consist of T's large inventory of fabric, which PRS uses to manufacture sportswear. All of the T assets are used in the sportswear business. No member of P's qualified group performs active and substantial management functions for the sportswear business operated in PRS.

(ii) Continuity of business enterprise. Under paragraph (d)(4)(iii)(A) of this section, S-1 is treated as owning 33 $^1/_3$ percent of the T assets used in the PRS sportswear manufacturing business. Under paragraph (d)(4)(iii)(B)(1) of this section, P is treated as conducting the sportswear manufacturing business because S-1 owns an interest in the partnership representing a significant interest in that partnership business. P is treated as holding all the assets and conducting the businesses of all of the members of the qualified group, which includes S-1 (paragraphs (d)(4)(i) and (ii) of this section). The COBE requirement of paragraph (d)(1) of this section is satisfied.

Example (12). Aggregation of partnership interests among members of the qualified group: use of T's historic business assets in a partnership business. (i) Facts. The facts are the same as Example 11, except that S-1 transfers all the T assets to PRS, and P and X each transfer cash to PRS in exchange for partnership interests. After the transfers, P owns 11 percent, S-1 owns 22 $^1/_3$ percent and X owns 66 $^2/_3$ percent of PRS.

(ii) Continuity of business enterprise. Under paragraph (d)(4)(iii)(B)(1) of this section, P is treated as conducting the sportswear manufacturing business because members of the qualified group, in the aggregate, own an interest in the partnership representing a significant interest in that business. P is treated as owning 11 percent of the assets directly, and S-1 is treated as owning 22 $^1/_3$ percent of the assets, used in the PRS sportswear business (paragraph (d)(4)(iii)(A) of this section). P is treated as holding all the assets of all of the members of the qualified group, which includes S-1, and thus in the aggregate, P is treated as owning 33 $^1/_3$ of the T assets (paragraphs (d)(4)(i) and (ii) of this section). The COBE requirement of paragraph (d)(1) of this section is satisfied because P is treated as using a significant portion of T's historic business assets in its sportswear manufacturing business.

Example (13). Tiered partnerships: use of T's historic business assets in a partnership business. (i) Facts. T owns and manages a commercial office building in state Z. Pursuant to a plan of reorganization, T merges into P, solely in exchange for P stock, which is distributed to the T shareholders. P transfers all of the T assets to a partnership, PRS-1, which owns and operates television stations nationwide. After the transfer, P owns a 50-percent interest in PRS-1. P does not have active and substantial management functions as a partner with respect to the PRS-1 business. X, not a member of P's qualified group, owns the remaining 50-percent interest in PRS-1. PRS-1, in an effort to expand its state Z television operation, enters into a joint venture with U, an unrelated party. As part of the plan of reorganization, PRS-1 transfers all the T assets and its state Z television station to PRS-2, in exchange for a 75-percent partnership interest. U contributes cash to PRS-2 in exchange for a 25-percent partnership interest and oversees the management of the state Z television operation. PRS-1 does not actively and substantially manage PRS-2's business. PRS-2's state Z operations are moved into the acquired T office building. All of the assets that P acquired from T are used in PRS-2's business.

(ii) Continuity of business enterprise. Under paragraph (d)(4)(iii)(A) of this section, PRS-1 is treated as owning 75 percent of the T assets used in PRS-2's business. P, in turn, is treated as owning 50 percent of PRS-1's interest in the T assets. Thus, P is treated as owning 37½ percent (50 percent × 75 percent) of the T assets used in the PRS-2 business. Under paragraph (d)(4)(iii)(B)(1) of this section, P is treated as conducting PRS-2's business, the operation of the state Z television station, and under paragraph (d)(4)(iii)(A) of this section, P is treated as using 37½ percent of the historic T business assets in that business. The COBE requirement of paragraph (d)(1) of this section is satisfied because P is treated as using a significant portion of T's historic business assets in its television business.

Example (14). Transfer of acquired stock to a partnership—continuity of business enterprise satisfied. (i) Facts. Pursuant to a plan of reorganization, the T shareholders transfer all of their T stock to a subsidiary of P, S-1, solely in exchange for P stock. In addition, as part of the plan of reorganization, S-1 transfers the T stock to its subsidiary, S-2, and S-2 transfers the T stock to its subsidiary, S-3. S-2 and S-3 form a new partnership, PRS. Immediately thereafter, S-3 transfers all of the T stock to PRS in exchange for an 80 percent interest in PRS, and S-2 transfers cash to PRS in exchange for a 20 percent interest in PRS.

(ii) Continuity of business enterprise. Members of the qualified group, in the aggregate, own all of the interests in PRS. Because these interests in PRS meet requirements equivalent to section 368(c), under paragraph (d)(4)(iii)(D) of this section, the T stock owned by PRS is treated as owned by members of the qualified group. P is treated as holding all of the businesses and assets of T because T is a member of the qualified group (as defined in paragraph (d)(4)(ii) of this section). The COBE requirement of paragraph (d)(1) of this section is satisfied because P is treated as continuing T's business.

Example (15). Transfer of acquired stock to a partnership—continuity of business enterprise not satisfied. (i) Facts. The facts are the same as in Example 14, except that S-3 and U, an unrelated corporation, form a new partnership, PRS, and, immediately thereafter, S-3 transfers all of the T stock to PRS in exchange for a 50 percent interest in PRS, and U transfers cash to PRS in exchange for a 50 percent interest in PRS.

(ii) Continuity of business enterprise. Members of the qualified group, in the aggregate, own 50 percent of the interests in PRS. Because these interests in PRS do not meet requirements equivalent to section 368(c), the T stock owned by PRS is not treated as owned by members of the qualified group under paragraph (d)(4)(iii)(D) of this section. P is not treated as holding all of the businesses and assets of T because T has ceased to be a member of the qualified group (as defined in paragraph (d)(4)(ii) of this section). The COBE requirement of paragraph (d)(1) of this section is not satisfied because P is not treated as continuing T's business or using T's historic business assets in a business.

(e) Continuity of interest.—(1) General rule.

(i) The purpose of the continuity of interest requirement is to prevent transactions that resemble sales from qualifying for nonrecognition of gain or loss available to corporate reorganizations. Continuity of interest requires that in substance a substantial part of the value of the proprietary interests in the target corporation be preserved in the reorganization. A proprietary interest in the target corporation is preserved if, in a potential reorganization, it is exchanged for a proprietary interest in the issuing corporation (as defined in paragraph (b) of this section), it is exchanged by the acquiring corporation for a direct interest in the target corporation enterprise, or it otherwise continues as a proprietary interest in the target corporation. However, a proprietary interest in the target corporation is not preserved if, in connection with the potential reorganization, it is acquired by the issuing corporation for consideration other than stock of the issuing corporation, or stock of the issuing corporation furnished in exchange for a proprietary interest in the target corporation in the potential reorganization is redeemed. All facts and circumstances must be considered in determining whether, in substance, a proprietary interest in the target corporation is preserved. For purposes of the continuity of interest requirement, a mere disposition of stock of the target corporation prior to a potential reorganization to persons not related (as defined in paragraph (e)(3) of this section determined without regard to paragraph (e)(3)(i)(A) of this section) to the target corporation or to persons not related (as defined in paragraph (e)(3) of this section) to the issuing corporation is disregarded and a mere disposition of stock of the issuing corporation received in a potential reorganization to persons not related (as defined in paragraph (e)(3) of this section) to the issuing corporation is disregarded.

* * *

§ 1.368–2 Definition of terms.

(a) The application of the term "reorganization" is to be strictly limited to the specific transactions set forth in section 368(a). The term does not embrace the mere purchase by one corporation of the properties of another corporation. The preceding sentence applies to transactions occurring after January 28, 1998, except that it does not apply to any transaction occurring pursuant to a written agreement which is binding on January 28, 1998, and at all times thereafter. If the properties are transferred for cash and deferred payment obligations of the transferee evidenced by short-term notes, the transaction is a sale and not an exchange in which gain or loss is not recognized.

(b)(1)(i) Definitions. For purposes of this paragraph (b)(1), the following terms shall have the following meanings:

(A) Disregarded entity. A disregarded entity is a business entity (as defined in § 301.7701–2(a) of this chapter) that is disregarded as an entity separate from its owner for Federal income tax purposes. Examples of disregarded entities include a domestic single member limited liability company that does not elect to be classified as a corporation for Federal income tax purposes, a corporation (as defined in § 301.7701–2(b) of this chapter) that is a qualified REIT subsidiary (within the meaning of section 856 (i)(2)), and a corporation that is a qualified subchapter S subsidiary (within the meaning of section 1361(b)(3)(B)).

(B) Combining entity. A combining entity is a business entity that is a corporation (as defined in § 301.7701–2(b) of this chapter) that is not a disregarded entity.

(C) Combining unit. A combining unit is composed solely of a combining entity and all disregarded entities, if any, the assets of which are treated as owned by such combining entity for Federal income tax purposes.

(ii) Statutory merger or consolidation generally. For purposes of section 368(a)(1)(A), a statutory merger or consolidation is a transaction effected pursuant to the statute or statutes necessary to effect the merger or consolidation, in which transaction, as a result of the operation of such statute or statutes, the following events occur simultaneously at the effective time of the transaction—

(A) All of the assets (other than those distributed in the transaction) and liabilities (except to the extent such liabilities are satisfied or discharged in the transaction or are nonrecourse liabilities to which assets distributed in the transaction are subject) of each member of one or more combining units (each a transferor unit) become the assets and liabilities of one or more members of one other combining unit (the transferee unit); and

(B) The combining entity of each transferor unit ceases its separate legal existence for all purposes; provided, however, that this requirement will be satisfied even if, under applicable law, after the effective time of the transaction, the combining entity of the transferor unit (or its officers, directors, or agents) may act or be acted against, or a member of the transferee unit (or its officers, directors, or agents) may act or be acted against in the name of the combining entity of the transferor unit, provided that such actions relate to assets or obligations of the combining entity of the transferor unit that arose, or relate to activities engaged in by such entity, prior to the effective time of the transaction, and such actions are not inconsistent with the requirements of paragraph (b)(1)(ii)(A) of this section.

* * *

(2) In order for the transaction to qualify under section 368(a)(1)(A) by reason of the application of section 368(a)(2)(D), one corporation (the acquiring corporation) must acquire substantially all of the properties of another corporation (the acquired corporation) partly or entirely in exchange for stock of a corporation which is in control of the acquiring corporation (the controlling corporation), provided that (i) the transaction would have qualified under section 368(a)(1)(A) if the merger had been into the controlling corporation, and (ii) no stock of the acquiring corporation is used in the transaction. The foregoing test of whether the transaction would have qualified under section 368(a)(1)(A) if the merger had been into the controlling corporation means that the general requirements of a reorganization under section 368(a)(1)(A) (such as a business purpose, continuity of business enterprise, and continuity of interest) must be met in addition to the special requirements of section 368(a)2)(D). Under this test, it is not relevant whether the merger into the controlling corporation could have been effected pursuant to State or Federal corporation law. The term "substantially all" has the same meaning as it has in section 368(a)(1)(C). Although no stock of the acquiring corporation can be used in the transaction, there is no prohibition (other than the continuity of interest requirement) against using other property, such as cash or securities, of either the acquiring corporation or the parent or both. In addition, the controlling corporation may assume liabilities of the acquired corporation without disqualifying the transaction under section 368(a)(2) (D), and for purposes of section 357(a) the controlling corporation is considered a party to the exchange. For example, if the controlling corporation agrees to substitute its stock for stock of the acquired corporation under an outstanding employee stock option agreement, this assumption of liability will not prevent the transaction from qualifying as a reorganization under section 368(a)(2)(D) and the assumption of liability is not treated as money or other property for purposes of section 361(b). Section 368 (a) (2)(D) applies whether or not the controlling corporation (or the acquiring corporation) is formed immediately before the merger, in anticipation of the merger, or after preliminary steps have been taken to merge directly into the controlling corporation. Section 368(a)(2)(D) applies only to statutory mergers occurring after October 22, 1968.

* * *

(3) For regulations under section 368(a)(2)(E), see paragraph (j) of this section.

(c) In order to qualify as a "reorganization" under section 368(a)(1)(B), the acquisition by the acquiring corporation of stock of another corporation must be in exchange solely for all or a part of the voting stock of the acquiring corporation (or, in the case of transactions occurring after December 31, 1963, solely for all or a part of the voting stock of a corporation which is in control of the acquiring corporation), and the acquiring corporation must be in control of the other corporation immediately after the transaction. If, for example, Corporation X in one transaction exchanges nonvoting preferred stock or bonds in addition to all or a part of its voting stock in the acquisition of stock of Corporation Y, the transaction is not a reorganization under section 368(a)(1)(B). Nor is a transaction a reorganization described in section 368(a)(1)(B) if stock is acquired in exchange for voting stock both of the acquiring corporation and of a corporation which is in control of the acquiring corporation. The acquisition of stock of another corporation by the acquiring corporation solely for its voting stock (or solely for voting stock of a corporation which is in control of the acquiring corporation) is permitted tax-free even though the acquiring corporation already owns some of the stock of the other corporation. Such an acquisition is permitted tax-free in a single transaction or in a series of transactions taking place over a relatively short period of time such as 12 months. For example, Corporation A purchased 30 percent of the common stock of Corporation W (the only class of stock outstanding) for cash in 1939. On March 1, 1955, Corporation A offers to exchange its own voting stock for all the stock of Corporation W tendered within 6 months from the date of the offer. Within the 6–months' period Corporation A acquires an additional 60 percent of stock of Corporation W solely for its own voting stock, so that it owns 90 percent of the stock of Corporation W. No gain or loss is recognized with respect to the exchanges of stock of Corporation A for stock of Corporation W. For this purpose, it is immaterial whether such exchanges occurred before Corporation A acquired control (80 percent) of Corporation W or after such control was acquired. If Corporation A had acquired 80 percent of the stock of Corporation W for cash in 1939, it could likewise acquire some or all of the remainder of such stock solely in exchange for its own voting stock without recognition of gain or loss.

(d) In order to qualify as a reorganization under section 368(a)(l)(C), the transaction must be one described in subparagraph (1) or (2) of this paragraph:

(1) One corporation must acquire substantially all the properties of another corporation solely in exchange for all or a part of its own voting stock, or solely in exchange for all or a part of the voting stock of a corporation which is in control of the acquiring corporation. For example, Corporation P owns all the stock of Corporation A. All the properties of Corporation W are transferred to Corporation A either solely in exchange for voting stock of Corporation P or solely in exchange for less than 80 percent of the voting stock of Corporation A. Either of such transactions constitutes a reorganization under section 368(a)(1)(C). However, if the properties of Corporation W are acquired in exchange for voting stock of both Corporation P and Corporation A, the transaction will not constitute a reorganization under section 368(a)(1)(C). In determining whether the exchange meets the requirement of "solely for voting stock", the assumption by the acquiring corporation of liabilities of the transferor corporation, or the fact that property acquired from the transferor corporation is subject to a liability, shall be disregarded. Though such an assumption does not prevent an exchange from being solely for voting stock for the purposes of the definition of a reorganization contained in section 368(a)(l)(C), it may in some cases, however, so alter the character of the transaction as to place the transaction outside the purposes and assumptions of the reorganization provisions. Section 368(a)(1)(C) does not prevent consideration of the effect of an assumption of liabilities on the general character of the transaction but merely provides that the requirement that the exchange be solely for voting stock is satisfied if the only additional consideration is an assumption of liabilities.

(2) One corporation:

(i) Must acquire substantially all of the properties of another corporation in such manner that the acquisition would qualify under (1) above, but for the fact that the acquiring corporation exchanges money, or other property in addition to such voting stock, and

(ii) Must acquire solely for voting stock (either of the acquiring corporation or of a corporation which is in control of the acquiring corporation) properties of the other corporation having a fair market value which is at least 80 percent of the fair market value of all the properties of the other corporation.

(3) For the purposes of subparagraph (2)(ii) only, a liability assumed or to which the properties are subject is considered money paid for the properties. For example, Corporation A has properties with a fair market value of $100,000 and liabilities of $10,000. In exchange for these properties, Corporation Y transfers its own voting stock, assumes the $10,000 liabilities, and pays $8,000 in cash. The transaction is a reorganization even though a part of the properties of Corporation A is acquired for cash. On the other hand, if the properties of Corporation A worth $100,000, were subject to $50,000 in liabilities, an acquisition of all the properties, subject to the liabilities, for any consideration other than solely voting stock would not qualify as a reorganization under this section since the liabilities alone are in excess of 20 percent of the fair market value of the properties. If the transaction would qualify under either subparagraph (1) or (2) of this paragraph and also under section 368(a)(1)(D), such transaction shall not be treated as a reorganization under section 368(a)(1)(C).

* * *

(e) A "recapitalization," and therefore a reorganization, takes place if, for example:

(1) A corporation with $200,000 par value of bonds outstanding, instead of paying them off in cash, discharges them by issuing preferred shares to the bondholders;

(2) There is surrendered to a corporation for cancellation 25 percent of its preferred stock in exchange for no par value common stock;

(3) A corporation issues preferred stock, previously authorized but unissued, for outstanding common stock;

(4) An exchange is made of a corporation's outstanding preferred stock, having certain priorities with reference to the amount and time of payment of dividends and the distribution of the corporate assets upon liquidation, for a new issue of such corporation's common stock having no such rights;

(5) An exchange is made of an amount of a corporation's outstanding preferred stock with dividends in arrears for other stock of the corporation. However, if pursuant to such an exchange there is an increase in the proportionate interest of the preferred shareholders in the assets or earnings and profits of the corporation, then under § 1.305–7(c)(2), an amount equal to the lesser of (i) the amount by which the fair market value or liquidation preference, whichever is greater, of the stock received in the exchange (determined immediately following the recapitalization) exceeds the issue price of the preferred stock surrendered, or (ii) the amount of the dividends in arrears, shall be treated under section 305(c) as a deemed distribution to which sections 305(b)(4) and 301 apply.

(f) The term "a party to a reorganization" includes a corporation resulting from a reorganization, and both corporations, in a transaction qualifying as a reorganization where one corporation acquires stock or properties of another corporation. If a transaction otherwise qualifies as a reorganization, a corporation remains a party to the reorganization even though stock or assets acquired in the reorganization are transferred in a transaction described in paragraph (k) of this section. If a transaction otherwise qualifies as a reorganization, a corporation shall not cease to be a party to the reorganization solely by reason of the fact that part or all of the assets acquired in the reorganization are transferred to a partnership in which the transferor is a partner if the continuity of business enterprise requirement is satisfied. See § 1.368-1(d). The preceding three sentences apply to transactions occurring after January 28, 1998, except that they do not apply to any transaction occurring pursuant to a written agreement which is binding on January 28, 1998, and at all times thereafter. A corporation controlling an acquiring corporation is a party to the reorganization when the stock of such controlling corporation is used in the acquisition of properties. Both corporations are parties to the reorganization if, under statutory authority, Corporation A is merged into Corporation B. All three of the corporations are parties to the reorganization if, pursuant to statutory authority, Corporation C and Corporation D are consolidated into Corporation E. Both corporations are parties to the reorganization if Corporation F transfers substantially all its assets to Corporation G in exchange for all or a part of the voting stock of Corporation G. All three corporations are parties to the reorganization if Corporation H transfers substantially all its assets to Corporation K in exchange for all or a part of the voting stock of Corporation L, which is in control of Corporation K. Both corporations are parties to the reorganization if Corporation M transfers all or part of its assets to Corporation N in exchange for all or a part of the stock and securities of Corporation N, but only if (1) immediately after such transfer, Corporation M, or one or more of its shareholders (including persons who were shareholders immediately before such transfer), or any combination thereof, is in control of Corporation N, and (2) in pursuance of the plan, the stock and securities of Corporation N are transferred or distributed by Corporation M in a transaction in which gain or loss is not recognized under section 354 or 355, or is recognized only to the extent provided in section 356. Both Corporation O and Corporation P, but not Corporation S, are parties to the reorganization if Corporation O acquires stock of Corporation P from Corporation S in exchange solely for a part of the voting stock of Corporation O, if (1) the stock of Corporation P does not constitute substantially all of the assets of Corporation S, (2) Corporation S is not in control of Corporation O immediately after the acquisition, and (3) Corporation O is in control of Corporation P immediately after the acquisition.

(g) The term "plan of reorganization" has reference to a consummated transaction specifically defined as a reorganization under section 368(a). The term is not to be construed as broadening the definition of "reorganization" as set forth in section 368(a), but is to be taken as limiting the nonrecognition of gain or loss to such exchanges or distributions as are directly a part of the transaction specifically described as a reorganization in section 368(a). Moreover, the transaction, or series of transactions, embraced in a plan of reorganization must not only come within the specific language of section 368(a), but the readjustments involved in the exchanges or distributions effected in the consummation thereof must be undertaken for reasons germane to the continuance of the business of a corporation a party to the reorganization. Section 368 (a) contemplates genuine corporate reorganizations which are designed to effect a readjustment of continuing interests under modified corporate forms.

(h) As used in section 368, as well as in other provisions of the Internal Revenue Code, if the context so requires, the conjunction "or" denotes both the conjunctive and the disjunctive, and the singular includes the plural. For example, the provisions of the statute are complied with if "stock and securities" are received in exchange as well as if "stock or securities" are received.

(i) [Reserved]

(j)(1) This paragraph (j) prescribes rules relating to the application of section 368(a)(2)(E). Section 368(a)(2)(E) applies to statutory mergers occurring after December 31, 1970.

(2) Section 368(a)(2)(E) does not apply to a consolidation.

(3) A transaction otherwise qualifying under section 368(a)(1)(A) is not disqualified by reason of the fact that stock of a corporation (the controlling corporation) which before the merger was in control of the merged corporation is used in the transaction, if the conditions of section 368(a)(2)(E) are satisfied. Those conditions are as follows:

(i) In the transaction, shareholders of the surviving corporation must surrender stock in exchange for voting stock of the controlling corporation. Further, the stock so surrendered must constitute control of the surviving corporation. Control is defined in section 368(c). The amount of stock constituting control is measured immediately before the transaction. For purposes of this subdivision (i), stock in the surviving corporation which is surrendered in the transaction (by any shareholder except the controlling corporation) in exchange for consideration furnished by the surviving corporation (and not by the controlling corporation of the merged corporation) is considered not to be outstanding immediately before the transaction. For effect on "substantially all" test of consideration furnished by the surviving corporation, see paragraph (j)(3)(iii) of this section.

(ii) Except as provided in paragraph (k) of this section, the controlling corporation must control the surviving corporation immediately after the transaction.

(iii) After the transaction, the surviving corporation must hold substantially all of its own properties and substantially all of the properties of the merged corporation (other than stock of the controlling corporation distributed in the transaction). The surviving corporation may transfer such properties as provided in paragraph (k) of this section. The term "substantially all" has the same meaning as in section 368(a)(1)(C). The "substantially all" test applies separately to the merged corporation and to the surviving corporation. In applying the "substantially all" test to the surviving corporation, consideration furnished in the transaction by the surviving corporation in exchange for its stock is property of the surviving corporation which it does not hold after the transaction. In applying the "substantially all" test to the merged corporation, assets transferred from the controlling corporation to the merged corporation in pursuance of the plan of reorganization are not taken into account. Thus, for example, money transferred from the controlling corporation to the merged corporation to be used for the following purposes is not taken into account for purposes of the "substantially all" test:

(A) To pay additional consideration to shareholders of the surviving corporation;

(B) To pay dissenting shareholders of the surviving corporation;

(C) To pay creditors of the surviving corporation;

(D) To pay reorganization expenses; or

(E) To enable the merged corporation to satisfy state minimum capitalization requirements (where the money is returned to the controlling corporation as part of the transaction).

(4) The controlling corporation may assume liabilities of the surviving corporation without disqualifying the transaction under section 368(a)(2)(E). An assumption of liabilities of the surviving corporation by the controlling corporation is a contribution to capital by the controlling corporation to the surviving corporation. If, in pursuance of the plan of reorganization, securities of the surviving corporation are exchanged for securities of the controlling corporation, or for other securities of the surviving corporation, see sections 354 and 356.

(5) In applying section 368(a)(2)(E), it makes no difference if the merged corporation is an existing corporation, or is formed immediately before the merger, in anticipation of the merger, or after preliminary steps have been taken to otherwise acquire control of the surviving corporation.

(6) The following examples illustrate the application of this paragraph (j). In each of the examples, Corporation P owns all of the stock of Corporation S and, except as otherwise stated, Corporation T has outstanding 1,000 shares of common stock and no shares of any other class. In each of the examples, it is also assumed that the transaction qualifies under section 368(a)(l)(A) if the conditions of section 368 (a)(2)(E) are satisfied.

Example (1). P owns no T stock. On January 1, 1981, S merges into T. In the merger, T's shareholders surrender 950 shares of common stock in exchange for P voting stock. The holders of the other 50 shares (who dissent from the merger) are paid in cash with funds supplied by P. After the transaction, T holds all of its own assets and all of S's assets. Based on these facts, the transaction qualifies under section 368(a)(1)(A) by reason of the application of section 368(a)(2)(E). In the transaction, former shareholders of T surrender, in exchange for P voting stock, an amount of T stock (950/1,000 shares or 95 percent) which constitutes control of T.

Example (2). The facts are the same as in example (1) except that holders of 100 shares in corporation T, who dissented from the merger, are paid in cash with funds supplied by T (and not by P or S) and in the merger. T's remaining shareholders surrender 720 shares of common stock in exchange for P voting stock and 180 shares of common stock for cash supplied by P. The requirements of section 368(a)(2)(E)(ii) are satisfied since, in the transaction, former shareholders of T surrender, in exchange for P voting stock, an amount of T stock (720/900 shares or 80 percent) which constitutes control of T. The T stock surrendered in exchange for consideration furnished by T is not considered outstanding for purposes of determining whether the amount of T stock surrendered by T shareholders for P stock constitutes control of T.

Example (3). T has outstanding 1,000 shares of common stock, 100 shares of nonvoting preferred stock, and no shares of any other class. On January 1, 1981, S merges into T. Prior to the merger, as part of the transaction, T distributes its own cash in redemption of the 100 shares of preferred stock. In the transaction, T's remaining shareholders surrender their 1,000 shares of common stock in exchange for P voting stock. The requirements of section 368(a)(2)(E)(ii) are satisfied since, in the transaction, former shareholders of T surrender, in exchange for P voting stock, an amount of T stock (1,000/1,000 shares or 100 percent) which constitutes control of T. The preferred stock surrendered in exchange for consideration furnished by T is not considered outstanding for purposes of determining whether the amount of T stock surrendered by T shareholders for P stock constitutes control of T. However, the consideration furnished by T for its stock is property of T which T does not hold after the transaction for purposes of the substantially all test in paragraph (j)(3)(iii) of this section.

Example (4). On January 1, 1971, P purchased 201 shares of T's stock. On January 1, 1981, S merges into T. In the merger, T's shareholders (other than P) surrender 799 shares of T stock in exchange for P voting stock. Based on these facts, in the transaction, former shareholders of T do not surrender, in exchange for P voting stock, an amount of T stock which constitutes control of T (799/1,000 shares being less than 80 percent). Therefore, the transaction does not qualify under section 368(a)(1)(A). However, if S is a transitory corporation, formed solely for purposes of effectuating the transaction, the transaction may qualify as a reorganization described in section 368(a)(1)(B) provided all of the applicable requirements are satisfied.

Example (5). On January 1, 1971, P purchased 200 shares of T's stock. On January 1, 1981, S merges into T. Prior to the merger, as part of the transaction, T distributes its own cash in redemption of 1 share of T stock from a T shareholder other than P. In the merger, T's remaining shareholders (other than P) surrender 799 shares of T stock in exchange for P voting stock. Based on these facts, in the transaction, former shareholders of T do not surrender, in exchange for P voting stock, an amount of T stock which constitutes control of T (799/999 shares being less than 80 percent). Therefore, the transaction does not qualify under section 368(a)(l)(A). However, if S is a transitory corporation, formed for purposes of effectuating the transaction, the transaction may qualify as a reorganization described in section 368(a)(1)(B) provided all of the applicable requirements are satisfied.

Example (6). The stock of S has a value of $25,000. The stock of T has a value of $75,000. On January 1, 1984, S merges into T. In the merger, T's shareholders surrender all of their T stock in exchange for P voting stock. After the transaction, T holds all of its own assets and all of S's assets. Based on these facts, the transaction qualifies under section 368(a)(1)(A) by reason of the application of section 368(a)(2)(E). In the transaction, former shareholders of T surrender, in exchange for P voting stock, an amount of T stock (1,000/1,000 shares or 100 percent) which constitutes control of T. The stock of T received by P in exchange for P's prior interest in S is not taken into account for purposes of section 368(a)(2)(E)(ii) since the amount of T stock constituting control of T is measured before the transaction.

Example (7). The stock of T has a value of $75,000. On January 1, 1984, S merges into T. In the merger, T's shareholders surrender all of their T stock in exchange for P voting stock. As part of the transaction, P contributes $25,000 to T in exchange for new shares of T stock. None of the cash received by T is distributed or otherwise paid out to former T shareholders. After the transaction, T holds all of its own assets and all of S's assets. Based on these facts, the transaction qualifies under section 368(a)(1)(A) by reason of the application of section 368(a)(2)(E). In the transaction, former shareholders of T surrender, in exchange for P voting stock, an amount of T stock (1,000/1,000 shares or 100 percent) which constitutes control of T. The T stock received by P in exchange for its contribution to T is not taken into account for purposes of section 368(a)(2)(E)(ii) since the amount of T stock constituting control of T is measured before the transaction.

Example (8). The facts are the same as in example (7) except that, as part of the transaction, corporation R, instead of P, contributes $25,000 to T in exchange for T stock. Based on these facts, the transaction does not qualify under section 368(a)(1)(A) by reason of section 368(a)(2)(E) since P does not control T immediately after the transaction.

Example (9). T stock has a value of $75,000. P owns 500 shares (½) of that stock with a value of $37,500. The stock of S has a value of $125,000. On January 1, 1984, S merges into T. In the merger, T's shareholders (other than P) surrender their T stock in exchange for P voting stock. Based on these facts, in the transaction, former shareholders of T do not surrender, in exchange for P voting stock, an amount of T stock which constitutes control of T (500/1,000 shares being less than 80 percent). Therefore, the transaction does not qualify under section 368(a)(1)(A). The stock of T received by P in exchange for P's prior interest in S does not contribute to satisfaction of the requirement of section 368(a)(2)(E)(ii).

* * *

ACCOUNTING PERIODS AND METHODS OF ACCOUNTING

Accounting Periods

* * *

§ 1.441–1 Period for computation of taxable income.

(a) Computation of taxable income— (1) In general. Taxable income must be computed and a return must be made for a period known as the taxable year. For rules relating to methods of accounting, the taxable year for which items of gross income are included and deductions are taken, inventories, and adjustments, see parts II and III (section 446 and following), subchapter E, chapter 1 of the Internal Revenue Code, and the regulations thereunder.

(2) Length of taxable year. Except as otherwise provided in the Internal Revenue Code and the regulations thereunder (e.g., § 1.441–2 regarding 52–53-week taxable years), a taxable year may not cover a period of more than 12 calendar months.

(b) General rules and definitions. The general rules and definitions in this paragraph (b) apply for purposes of sections 441 and 442 and the regulations thereunder.

(1) Taxable year. Taxable year means—

(i) The period for which a return is made, if a return is made for a period of less than 12 months (short period). See section 443 and the regulations thereunder;

(ii) Except as provided in paragraph (b)(1)(i) of this section, the taxpayer's required taxable year (as defined in paragraph (b)(2) of this section), if applicable;

(iii) Except as provided in paragraphs (b)(1)(i) and (ii) of this section, the taxpayer's annual accounting period (as defined in paragraph (b)(3) of this section), if it is a calendar year or a fiscal year; or

(iv) Except as provided in paragraphs (b)(1)(i) and (ii) of this section, the calendar year, if the taxpayer keeps no books, does not have an annual accounting period, or has an annual accounting period that does not qualify as a fiscal year.

(2) Required taxable year— (i) In general. Certain taxpayers must use the particular taxable year that is required under the Internal Revenue Code and the regulations thereunder (the required taxable year). For example, the required taxable year is—

(A) In the case of a foreign sales corporation or domestic international sales corporation, the taxable year determined under section 441(h) and § 1.921–1T(a)(11), (b)(4), and (b)(6);

(B) In the case of a personal service corporation (PSC), the taxable year determined under section 441 (i) and § 1.441–3;

* * *

(F) In the case of certain trusts, the taxable year determined under section 644;

(G) In the case of a partnership, the taxable year determined under section 706 and § 1.706–1;

* * *

(L) In the case of an S corporation, the taxable year determined under section 1378 and § 1.1378–1; or

(M) In the case of a member of an affiliated group that makes a consolidated return, the taxable year determined under § 1.1502–76.

(ii) Exceptions. Notwithstanding paragraph (b) (2)(i) of this section, the following taxpayers may have a taxable year other than their required taxable year;

(A) 52–53-week taxable years. Certain taxpayers may elect to use a 52–53-week taxable year that ends with reference to their required taxable year. See, for example, §§ 1.441–3 (PSCs), 1.706–1 (partnerships), 1.1378–1 (S corporations), and 1.1502–76(a)(1) (members of a consolidated group).

(B) Partnerships, S corporations, and PSCs. A partnership, S corporation, or PSC may use a taxable year other than its required taxable year if the taxpayer elects to use a taxable year other than its required taxable year under section 444, elects a 52–53-week taxable year that ends with reference to its required taxable year as provided in paragraph (b)(2) (ii)(A) of this section or to a taxable year elected under section 444, or establishes a business purpose to the satisfaction of the Commissioner under section 442 (such as a grandfathered fiscal year).

* * *

(3) Annual accounting period. *Annual accounting period* means the annual period (calendar year or fiscal year) on the basis of which the taxpayer regularly computes its income in keeping its books.

(4) Calendar year. *Calendar year* means a period of 12 consecutive months ending on December 31. A taxpayer who has not established a fiscal year must make its return on the basis of a calendar year.

(5) Fiscal year—(i) Definition. *Fiscal year* means—

(A) A period of 12 consecutive months ending on the last day of any month other than December; or

(B) A 52–53-week taxable year, if such period has been elected by the taxpayer. See § 1.441–2.

(ii) Recognition. A fiscal year will be recognized only if the books of the taxpayer are kept in accordance with such fiscal year.

(6) Grandfathered fiscal year. *Grandfathered fiscal year* means a fiscal year (other than a year that resulted in a three month or less deferral of income) that a partnership or an S corporation received permission to use on or after July 1, 1974, by a letter ruling (i.e., not by automatic approval.)

(7) Books. Books include the taxpayer's regular books of account and such other records and data as may be necessary to support the entries on the taxpayer's books and on the taxpayer's return, as for example, a reconciliation of any difference between such books and the taxpayer's return. Records that are sufficient to reflect income adequately and clearly on the basis of an annual accounting period will be regarded as the keeping of books. See section 6001 and the regulations thereunder for rules relating to the keeping of books and records.

(8) Taxpayer. *Taxpayer* has the same meaning as the term person as defined in section 7701(a)(1) (e.g., an individual, trust, estate, partnership, association, or corporation) rather than the meaning of the term taxpayer as defined in section 7701(a)(14) (any person subject to tax).

(c) Adoption of taxable year—(1) In general. Except as provided in paragraph (c)(2) of this section, a new taxpayer may adopt any taxable year that satisfies the requirements of section 441 and the regulations thereunder without the approval of the Commissioner. A taxable year of a new taxpayer is adopted by filing its first Federal income tax return using that taxable year. The filing of an application for automatic extention of time to file a Federal income tax return (e.g., Form 7004, "Application for Automatic Extension of Time to File Corporation Income Tax Return"), the filing of an application for an employer identification number (i.e., Form SS-4, "Application for Employer Identification Number"), or the payment of estimated taxes, for a particular taxable year do not constitute an adoption of that taxable year.

(2) Approval required—(i) Taxpayers with required taxable years. A newly-formed partnership, S corporation, or PSC that wants to adopt a taxable year other than its required taxable year, a taxable year elected under section 444, or a 52–53-week taxable year that ends with reference to its required taxable year or a taxable year elected under section 444 must establish a business purpose and obtain the approval of the Commissioner under section 442.

(ii) Taxpayers without books. A taxpayer that must use a calendar year under section 441(g) and paragraph (f) of this section may not adopt a fiscal year without obtaining the approval of the Commissioner.

(d) Retention of taxable year. In certain cases, a partnership, S corporation, electing S corporation, or PSC will be required to change its taxable year unless it obtains the approval of the Commissioner under section 442, or makes an election under section 444, to retain its current taxable year. For example, a corporation using a June 30 fiscal year that either becomes a PSC or elects to be an S corporation and, as a result, is required to use the calendar year under section 441(i) or 1378, respectively, must obtain the approval of the Commissioner to retain its current fiscal year. Similarly, a partnership using a taxable year that corresponds to its required taxable year must obtain the approval of the Commissioner to retain such taxable year if its required taxable year changes as a result of a change in ownership. However, a partnership that previously established a business purpose to the satisfaction of the Commissioner to use a taxable year is not required to obtain the approval of the Commissioner if its required taxable year changes as a result of a change in ownership.

(e) Change of taxable year. Once a taxpayer has adopted a taxable year, such taxable year must be used in computing taxable income and making returns for all subsequent years unless the taxpayer obtains approval from the Commissioner to make a change or the taxpayer is otherwise authorized to change without the approval of the Commissioner under the Internal Revenue Code (e.g., section 444 or 859) or the regulations thereunder.

(f) Obtaining approval of the Commissioner or making a section 444 election. See § 1.442–1(b) for procedures for obtaining approval of the Commissioner (automatically or otherwise) to adopt, change, or retain an annual accounting period. See §§ 1.444–1T and 1.444–2T for qualifications, and 1.444–3T for procedures, for making an election under section 444.

§ 1.441–2 Election of taxable year consisting of 52–53 weeks.

(a) In general—(1) Election. An eligible taxpayer may elect to compute its taxable income on the basis of a fiscal year that—

(i) Varies from 52 to 53 weeks;

(ii) Ends always on the same day of the week; and

(iii) Ends always on—

(A) Whatever date this same day of the week last occurs in a calendar month; or

(B) Whatever date this same day of the week falls that is the nearest to the last day of the calendar month.

(2) Effect. In the case of a taxable year described in paragraph (a)(1)(iii)(A) of this section, the year will always end within the month and may end on the last day of the month, or as many as six days before the end of the month. In the case of a taxable year described in paragraph (a)(1)(iii)(B) of this section, the year may end on the last day of the month, or as many as three days before or three days after the last day of the month.

(3) Eligible taxpayer. A taxpayer is eligible to elect a 52–53-week taxable year if such fiscal year would otherwise satisfy the requirements of section 441 and the regulations thereunder. For example, a taxpayer that is required to use a calendar year under § 1.441–1 (b)(2)(i)(D) is not an eligible taxpayer.

(4) Example. The provisions of this paragraph (a) are illustrated by the following example:

Example. If the taxpayer elects a taxable year ending always on the last Saturday in November, then for the year 2001, the taxable year would end on November 24, 2001. On the other hand, if the taxpayer had elected a taxable year ending always on the Saturday nearest to the end of November, then for the year 2001, the taxable year would end on December 1, 2001.

(b) Procedures to elect a 52–53-week taxable year—(1) Adoption of a 52–53-week taxable year—(i) In general. A new eligible taxpayer elects a 52–53-week taxable year by adopting such year in accordance with § 1.441–1(c). A newly-formed partnership, S corporation or personal service corporation (PSC) may adopt a 52–53-week taxable year without the approval of the Commissioner if such year ends with reference to either the taxpayer's required taxable year (as defined in § 1.441–1(b)(2)) or the taxable year elected under section 444. See §§ 1.441–3, 1.706–1, and 1.1378–1. Similarly, a newly–formed specified foreign corporation (as defined in section 898(b)) may adopt a 52–53-week taxable year if such year ends with reference to the taxpayer's required taxable year, or, if the one–month deferral election under section 898(c)(l)(B) is made, with reference to the month immediately preceding the required taxable year. See § 1.1502–76 (a)(1) for special rules regarding subsidiaries adopting 52–53-week taxable years.

(ii) Filing requirement. A taxpayer adopting a 52–53-week taxable year must file with its Federal income tax return for its first taxable year a statement containing the following information—

(A) The calendar month with reference to which the 52–53-week taxable year ends;

(B) The day of the week on which the 52–53-week taxable year always will end; and

(C) Whether the 52–53-week taxable year will always end on the date on which that day of the week last occurs in the calendar month, or on the date on which that day of the week falls that is nearest to the last day of that calendar month.

(2) Change to (or from) a 52–53-week taxable year— (i) In general. An election of a 52–53-week taxable year by an existing eligible taxpayer with an established taxable year is treated as a change in annual accounting period that requires the approval of the Commissioner in accordance with § 1.442–1. Thus, a taxpayer must obtain approval to change from its current taxable year to a 52–53-week taxable year, even if such 52–53-week taxable year ends with reference to the same calendar month. Similarly, a taxpayer must obtain approval to change from a 52–53-week taxable year, or to change from one 52–53-week taxable year to another 52–53-week taxable year. However, a taxpayer may obtain approval for 52–53-week taxable year changes automatically to the extent provided in administrative procedures published by the Commissioner. See § 1.442–1(b) for procedures for obtaining such approval.

(ii) Special rules for the short period required to effect the change. If a change to or from a 52–53-week taxable year results in a short period (within the meaning of § 1.443–1(a)) of 359 days or more, or six days or less, the tax computation under § 1.443–1 (b) does not apply. If the short period is 359 days or more, it is treated as a full taxable year. If the short period is six days or less, such short period is not a separate taxable year but instead is added to and deemed a part of the following taxable year. (In the case of a change to or from a 52–53-week taxable year not involving a change of the month with reference to which the taxable year ends, the tax computation under § 1.443–1(b) does not apply because the short period will always be 359 days or more, or six days or less.) In the case of a short period which is more than six days and less than 359 days, taxable income for the short period is placed on an annual basis for purposes of § 1.443–1(b) by multiplying such income by 365 and dividing the result by the number of days in the short period. In such case, the tax for the short period is the same part of the tax computed on such income placed on an annual basis as the number of days in the short period is of 365 days (unless § 1.443–1(b)(2), relating to the alternative tax computation, applies). For an adjustment in deduction for personal exemption, see § 1.443–1 (b)(1)(v).

(3) Examples. The following examples illustrate paragraph (b)(2)(ii) of this section:

Example (1). A taxpayer having a fiscal year ending April 30, obtains approval to change to a 52–53-week taxable year ending the last Saturday in April for taxable years beginning after April 30, 2001. This change involves a short period of 362 days, from May 1, 2001, to April 27, 2002, inclusive. Because the change results in a short period of 359 days or more, it is not placed on an annual basis and is treated as a full taxable year.

Example (2). Assume the same conditions as Example 1, except that the taxpayer changes for taxable years beginning after April 30, 2002, to a taxable year ending on the Thursday nearest to April 30. This change results in a short period of two days, May 1 to May 2, 2002. Because the short period is less than seven days, tax is not separately computed. This short period is added to and deemed part of the following 52–53-week taxable year, which would otherwise begin on May 3, 2002, and end on May 1, 2003.

* * *

§ 1.441–3 Taxable year of a personal service corporation.

(a) Taxable year— (1) Required taxable year. Except as provided in paragraph (a)(2) of this section, the taxable year of a personal service corporation (PSC) (as defined in paragraph (c) of this section) must be the calendar year.

(2) Exceptions. A PSC may have a taxable year other than its required taxable year (i.e., a fiscal year) if it makes an election under section 444, elects to use a 52–53-week taxable year that ends with reference to the calendar year or a taxable year elected under section 444, or establishes a business purpose for such fiscal year and obtains the approval of the Commissioner under section 442.

(b) Adoption, change, or retention of taxable year— (1) Adoption of taxable year. A PSC may adopt, in accordance with § 1.441–1(c), the calendar year, a taxable year elected under section 444, or a 52–53-week taxable year ending with reference to the calendar year or a taxable year elected under section 444 without the approval of the Commissioner. See § 1.441–1. A PSC that wants to adopt any other taxable year must establish a business purpose and obtain the approval of the Commissioner under section 442.

(2) Change in taxable year. A PSC that wants to change its taxable year must obtain the approval of the Commissioner under section 442 or make an election under section 444. However, a PSC may obtain automatic approval for certain changes, including a change to the calendar year or to a 52–53-week taxable year ending with reference to the calendar year, pursuant to administrative procedures published by the Commissioner.

(3) Retention of taxable year. In certain cases, a PSC will be required to change its taxable year unless it obtains the approval of the Commissioner under section 442, or makes an election under section 444, to retain its current taxable year. For example, a corporation using a June 30 fiscal year that becomes a PSC and, as a result, is required to use the calendar year must obtain the approval of the Commissioner to retain its current fiscal year.

(4) Procedures for obtaining approval or making a section 444 election. See § 1.442–1(b) for procedures to obtain the approval of the Commissioner (automatically or otherwise) to adopt, change, or retain a taxable year. See §§ 1.444–1T and 1.444–2T for qualifications, and 1.444–3T for procedures, for making an election under section 444.

(5) Examples. The provisions of paragraph (b)(4) of this section may be illustrated by the following examples:

Example (1). X, whose taxable year ends on January 31, 2001, becomes a PSC for its taxable year beginning February 1, 2001, and does not obtain the approval of the Commissioner for using a fiscal year. Thus, for taxable years ending before February 1, 2001, this section does not apply with respect to X. For taxable year beginning on February 1, 2001, however, X will be required to comply with paragraph (a) of this section. Thus, unless X obtains approval of the Commissioner to use a January 31 taxable year, or makes a section 444 election, X will be required to change its taxable year to the calendar year under paragraph (b) of this section by using a short taxable year that begins on February 1, 2001, and ends on December 31, 2001. Under paragraph (b)(1) of this section, X may obtain automatic approval to change its taxable year to a calendar year. See § 1.442–1(b).

Example (2). Assume the same facts as in Example 1, except that X desires to change to a 52–53-week taxable year ending with reference to the month of December. Under paragraph (b)(1) of this section X may obtain automatic approval to make the change. See § 1.442–1(b).

(c) Personal service corporation defined— (1) In general. For purposes of this section and section 442, a taxpayer is a PSC for a taxable year only if—

(i) The taxpayer is a C corporation (as defined in section 1361(a)(2)) for the taxable year;

(ii) The principal activity of the taxpayer during the testing period is the performance of personal services;

(iii) During the testing period, those services are substantially performed by employee-owners (as defined in paragraph (g) of this section); and

(iv) Employee-owners own (as determined under the attribution rules of section 318, except that the language "any" applies instead of "50 percent" in section 318(a)(2)(C)) more than 10 percent of the fair market value of the outstanding stock in the taxpayer on the last day of the testing period.

(2) Testing period— (i) In general. Except as otherwise provided in paragraph (c)(2)(ii) of this section, the testing period for any taxable year is the immediately preceding taxable year.

(ii) New corporations. The testing period for a taxpayer's first taxable year is the period beginning on the first day of that taxable year and ending on the earlier of—

(A) The last day of that taxable year; or

(B) The last day of the calendar year in which that taxable year begins.

(3) Examples. The provisions of paragraph (c)(2)(ii) of this section may be illustrated by the following examples:

Example (1). Corporation A's first taxable year begins on June 1, 2001, and a desires to use a September 30 taxable year. However, if A is a personal service corporation, it must obtain the Commissioner's approval to use a September 30 taxable year. Pursuant to paragraph (c)(2)(ii) of this section, A's testing period for its first taxable year beginning June 1, 2001, is the period June 1, 2001 through September 30, 2001. Thus, if, based upon such testing period, A is a personal service corporation, A must obtain the Commissioner's permission to use a September 30 taxable year.

Example (2). The facts are the same as in Example 1, except that A desires to use a March 31 taxable year. Pursuant to paragraph (c)(2)(ii) of this section, A's testing period for its first taxable year beginning June 1, 2001, is the period June 1, 2001, through September 31, 2001. Thus, if, based upon such testing period, A is a personal service corporation, A must obtain the Commissioner's permission to use a March 31 taxable year.

(d) Performance of personal services—(1) Activities described in section 448(d)(2)(A). For purposes of this section, any activity of the taxpayer described in section 448(d)(2)(A) or the regulations thereunder will be treated as the performance of personal services. Therefore, any activity of the taxpayer that involves the performance of services in the fields of health, law, engineering, architecture, accounting, actuarial science, performing arts, or consulting (as such fields are defined in § 1.448–1T) will be treated as the performance of personal services for purposes of this section.

(2) Activities not described in section 448(d)(2)(A). For purposes of this section, any activity of the taxpayer not described in section 448(d)(2)(A) or the regulations thereunder will not be treated as the performance of personal services.

(e) Principal activity—(1) General rule. For purposes of this section, the principal activity of a corporation for any testing period will be the performance of personal services if the cost of the corporation's compensation (the compensation cost) for such testing period that is attributable to its activities that are treated as the performance of personal services within the meaning of paragraph (d) of this section (i.e., the total compensation for personal service activities) exceeds 50 percent of the corporation's total compensation cost for such testing period.

(2) Compensation cost—(i) Amounts included. For purposes of this section, the compensation cost of a corporation for a taxable year is equal to the sum of the following amounts allowable as a deduction, allocated to a long-term contract, or otherwise chargeable to a capital account by the corporation during such taxable year—

(A) Wages and salaries; and

(B) Any other amounts, attributable to services performed for or on behalf of the corporation by a person who is an employee of the corporation (including an owner of the corporation who is treated as an employee under paragraph (g)(2) of this section) during the testing period. Such amounts include, but are not limited to, amounts attributable to deferred compensation, commissions, bonuses, compensation includible in income under section 83, compensation for services based on a percentage of profits, and the cost of providing fringe benefits that are includible in income.

(ii) Amounts excluded. Notwithstanding paragraph (e)(2)(i) of this section, compensation cost does not include amounts attributable to a plan qualified under section 401(a) or 403(a), or to a simplified employee pension plan defined in section 408(k).

(3) Attribution of compensation cost to personal service activity—(i) Employees involved only in the performance of personal services. The compensation cost for employees involved only in the performance of activities that are treated as personal services under paragraph (d) of this section, or employees involved only in supporting the work of such employees, are considered to be attributable to the corporation's personal service activity.

(ii) Employees involved only in activities that are not treated as the performance of personal services. The compensation cost for employees involved only in the performance of activities that are not treated as personal services under paragraph (d) of this section, or for employees involved only in supporting the work of such employees, are not considered to be attributable to the corporation's personal service activity.

(iii) Other employees. The compensation cost for any employee who is not described in either paragraph (e)(3)(i) or (ii) of this section (a mixed-activity employee) is allocated as follows—

(A) Compensation cost attributable to personal service activity. That portion of the compensation cost for a mixed activity employee that is attributable to the corporation's personal service activity equals the compensation cost for that employee multiplied by the percentage of the total time worked for the corporation by that employee during the year that is attributable to activities of the corporation that are treated as the performance of personal services under paragraph (d) of this section. That percentage is to be determined by the taxpayer in any reasonable and consistent manner. Time logs are not required unless maintained for other purposes;

(B) Compensation cost not attributable to personal service activity. That portion of the compensation cost for a mixed activity employee that is not considered to be attributable to the corporation's personal service activity is the compensation cost for that employee less the amount determined in paragraph (e)(3)(iii)(A) of this section.

(f) Services substantially performed by employeeowners—(1) General rule. Personal services are substantially performed during the testing period by employee-owners of the corporation if more than 20 percent of the corporation's compensation cost for that period attributable to its activities that are treated as the performance of personal services within the meaning of paragraph (d) of this section (i.e., the total compensation for personal service activities) is attributable to personal services performed by employee-owners.

(2) Compensation cost attributable to personal services. For purposes of paragraph (f)(1) of this section—

(i) The corporation's compensation cost attributable to its activities that are treated as the performance of personal services is determined under paragraph (e)(3) of this section; and

(ii) The portion of the amount determined under paragraph (f)(2)(i) of this section that is attributable to personal services performed by employee-owners is to be determined by the taxpayer in any reasonable and consistent manner.

(3) Examples. The provisions of this paragraph (f) may be illustrated by the following examples:

Example (1). For its taxable year beginning February 1, 2001, Corp A's testing period is the taxable year ending January 31, 2000. During that testing period, A's only activity was the performance of personal services. The total compensation cost of A (including compensation cost attributable to employee-owners) for the testing period was $1,000,000. The total compensation cost attributable to employee-owners of A for the testing period was $210,000. Pursuant to paragraph (f)(1) of this section, the employee-owners of A substantially performed the personal services of A during the testing period because the compensation cost of A's employee-owners was more than 20 percent of the total compensation cost for all of A's employees (including employee-owners).

Example (2). Corp B has the same facts as corporation A in Example 1, except that during the taxable year ending January 31, 2001, B also participated in an activity that would not be characterized as the performance of personal services under this section. The total compensation cost of B (including compensation cost attributable to employee-owners) for the testing period was $1,500,000 ($1,000,000 attributable to B's personal service activity and $500,000 attributable to B's other activity). The total compensation cost attributable to employee-owners of B for the testing period was $250,000 ($210,000 attributable to B's personal service activity and $40,000 attributable to B's other activity). Pursuant to paragraph (f)(1) of this section, the employee-owners of B substantially performed the personal services of B during the testing period because more than 20 percent of B's compensation cost during the testing period attributable to its personal service activities was attributable to personal services performed by employee-owners ($210,000).

(g) Employee-owner defined—(1) General rule. For purposes of this section, a person is an employee-owner of a corporation for a testing period if—

(i) The person is an employee of the corporation on any day of the testing period; and

(ii) The person owns any outstanding stock of the corporation on any day of the testing period.

(2) Special rule for independent contractors who are owners. Any person who is an owner of the corporation within the meaning of paragraph (g)(1)(ii) of this section and who performs personal services for, or on behalf of, the corporation is treated as an employee for purposes of this section, even if the legal form of that person's relationship to the corporation is such that the person would be considered an independent contractor for other purposes.

* * *

§ 1.442–1 Change of annual accounting period.

(a) Approval of the Commissioner. A taxpayer that has adopted an annual accounting period (as defined in § 1.441–1(b)(3)) as its taxable year generally must continue to use that annual accounting period in computing its taxable income and for making its Federal income tax returns. If the taxpayer wants to change its annual accounting period and use a new taxable year, it must obtain the approval of the Commissioner, unless it is otherwise authorized to change without the approval of the Commissioner under either the Internal Revenue Code (e.g., section 444 and section 859) or the regulations thereunder (e.g., paragraph (c) of this section). In addition, as described in § 1.441–1(c) and (d), a partnership, S corporation, or personal service corporation (PSC) generally is required to secure the approval of the Commissioner to adopt or retain an annual accounting period other than its required taxable year. The manner of obtaining approval from the Commissioner to adopt, change, or retain an annual accounting period is provided in paragraph (b) of this section. However, special rules for obtaining approval may be provided in other sections.

(b) Obtaining approval—(1) Time and manner for requesting approval. In order to secure the approval of the Commissioner to adopt, change, or retain an annual accounting period, a taxpayer must file an application, generally on Form 1128, "Application To Adopt, Change, or Retain a Tax Year," with the Commissioner within such time and in such manner as is provided in administrative procedures published by the Commissioner.

(2) General requirements for approval. An adoption, change, or retention in annual accounting period will be approved where the taxpayer establishes a business purpose for the requested annual accounting period and agrees to the Commissioner's prescribed terms, conditions, and adjustments for effecting the adoption, change, or retention. In determining whether a taxpayer has established a business purpose and which terms, conditions, and adjustments will be required, consideration will be given to all the facts and circumstances relating to the adoption, change, or retention, including the tax consequences resulting therefrom. Generally, the requirement of a business purpose will be satisfied, and adjustments to neutralize any tax consequences will not be required, if the requested annual accounting period coincides with the taxpayer's required taxable year (as defined in § 1.441–1(b)(2)), ownership taxable year, or natural business year. In the case of a partnership, S corporation, electing S corporation, or PSC, deferral of income to partners, shareholders, or employee-owners will not be treated as a business purpose.

(3) Administrative procedures. The Commissioner will prescribe administrative procedures under which a taxpayer may be permitted to adopt, change, or retain an annual accounting period. These administrative procedures will describe the business purpose requirements (including an ownership taxable year and a natural business year) and the terms, conditions, and adjustments necessary to obtain approval. Such terms, conditions, and adjustments may include adjustments necessary to neutralize the tax effects of a substantial distortion of income that would otherwise result from the requested annual accounting period including: a deferral of a substantial portion of the taxpayer's income, or shifting of a substantial portion of deductions, from one taxable year to another; a similar deferral or shifting in the case of any other person, such as a beneficiary in an estate; the creation of a short period in which there is a substantial net operating loss, capital loss, or credit (including a general business credit); or the creation of a short period in which there is a substantial amount of income to offset an expiring net operating loss, capital loss, or credit. See, for example, Rev. Proc. 2002–39, 2002–22 I.R.B., procedures for obtaining the Commissioner's prior approval of an adoption, change, or retention in annual accounting period through application to the national office; Rev. Proc. 2002–37, 2002–22 I.R.B., automatic approval procedures for certain corporations; Rev. Proc. 2002–38, 2002–22 I.R.B., automatic approval procedures for partnerships, S corporations, electing S corporations, and PSCs; and Rev. Proc. 66–50, 1966–2 C.B. 1260, automatic approval procedures for individuals. For availability of Revenue Procedures and Notices, see § 601.601(d)(2) of this chapter.

(4) Taxpayers to whom section 441(g) applies. If section 441(g) and § 1.441–1 (b)(1)(iv) apply to a taxpayer, the adoption of a fiscal year is treated as a change in the taxpayer's annual accounting period under section 442. Therefore, that fiscal year can become the taxpayer's taxable year only with the approval of the Commissioner. In addition to any other terms and conditions that may apply to such a change, the taxpayer must establish and maintain books that adequately and clearly reflect income for the short period involved in the change and for the fiscal year proposed.

(c) Special rule for change of annual accounting period by subsidiary corporation. A subsidiary corporation that is required to change its annual accounting period under § 1.1502–76, relating to the taxable year of members of an affiliated group that file a consolidated return, does not need to obtain the approval of the Commissioner or file an application on Form 1128 with respect to that change.

(d) Special rule for newly married couples. **(1)** A newly married husband or wife may obtain automatic approval under this paragraph (d) to change his or her annual accounting period in order to use the annual accounting period of the other spouse so that a joint return may be filed for the first or second taxable year of that spouse ending after the date of marriage. Such automatic approval will be granted only if the newly married husband or wife adopting the annual accounting period of the other spouse files a Federal income tax return for the short period required by that change on or before the 15th day of the 4th month following the close of the short period. See section 443 and the regulations thereunder. If the due date for any such short-period return occurs before the date of marriage, the first taxable year of the other spouse ending after the date of marriage cannot be adopted under this paragraph (d). The short-period return must contain a statement at the top of page one of the return that it is filed under the authority of this paragraph (d). The newly married husband or wife need not file Form 1128 with respect to a change described in this paragraph (d). For a change of annual accounting period by a husband or wife that does not qualify under this paragraph (d), see paragraph (b) of this section.

(2) The provisions of this paragraph (d) may be illustrated by the following example:

Example. H & W marry on September 25, 2001. H is on a fiscal year ending June 30, and W is on a calendar year. H wishes to change to a calendar year in order to file joint returns with W. W's first taxable year after marriage ends on December 31, 2001. H may not change to a calendar year for 2001 since, under this paragraph (d), he would have had to file a return for the short period from July 1 to December 31, 2000, by April 16, 2001. Since the date of marriage occurred subsequent to this due date, the return could not be filed under this paragraph (d). Therefore, H cannot change to a calendar year for 2001. However, H may change to a calendar year for 2002 by filing a return under this paragraph (d) by April 15, 2002, for the short period from July 1 to December 31, 2001. If H files such a return, H and W may file a joint return for calendar year 2002 (which is W's second taxable year ending after the date of marriage).

(e) Effective date. The rules of this section are applicable for taxable years ending on or after May 17, 2002.

* * *

§ 1.443–1 Returns for periods of less than 12 months.

(a) Returns for short period. A return for a short period, that is, for a taxable year consisting of a period of less than 12 months, shall be made under any of the following circumstances:

(1) Change of annual accounting period. In the case of a change in the annual accounting period of a taxpayer, a separate return must be filed for the short period of less than 12 months beginning with the day following the close of the old taxable year and ending with the day preceding the first day of the new taxable year. However, such a return is not required for a short period of six days or less, or 359 days or more, resulting from a change from or to a 52–53-week taxable year. See section 441(f) and § 1.441–2. The computation of the tax for a short period required to effect a change of annual accounting period is described in paragraph (b) of this section. In general, a return for a short period resulting from a change of annual accounting period shall be filed and the tax paid within the time prescribed for filing a return for a tax day of the short period. For rules applicable to a subsidiary corporation which becomes a member of an affiliated group which files a consolidated return, see § 1.1502–76.

(2) Taxpayer not in existence for entire taxable year. If a taxpayer is not in existence for the entire taxable year, a return is required for the short period during which the taxpayer was in existence. For example, a corporation organized on August 1 and adopting the calendar year as its annual accounting period is required to file a return for the short period from August 1 to December 31, and returns for each calendar year thereafter. Similarly, a dissolving corporation which files its returns for the calendar year is required to file a return for the short period from January 1 to the date it goes out of existence. Income for the short period is not required to be annualized if the taxpayer is not in existence for the entire taxable year, and, in the case of a taxpayer other than a corporation, the deduction under section 151 for personal exemptions (or deductions in lieu thereof) need not be reduced under section 443(c). In general, the requirements with respect to the filing of returns and the payment of tax for a short period where the taxpayer has not been in existence for the entire taxable year are the same as for the filing of a return and the payment of tax for a taxable year of 12 months ending on the last day of the short period. Although the return of a decedent is a return for the short period beginning with the first day of his last taxable year and ending with the date of his death, the filing of a return and the payment of tax for a decedent may be made as though the decedent had lived throughout his last taxable year.

(b) Computation of tax for short period on change of annual accounting period—(1) General rule. **(i)** If a return is made for a short period resulting from a change of annual accounting period, the taxable income for the short period shall be placed on an annual basis by multiplying such income by 12 and dividing the result by the number of months in the short period. Unless section 443(b)(2) and subparagraph (2) of this paragraph apply, the tax for the short period shall be the same part of the tax computed on the annual basis as the number of months in the short period is of 12 months.

(ii) If a return is made for a short period of more than 6 days, but less than 359 days, resulting from a change from or to a 52–53-week taxable year, the taxable income for the short period shall be annualized and the tax computed on a daily basis, as provided in section 441(f)(2)(B)(iii) and paragraph (c)(5) of § 1.441–2.

(iii) For method of computation of income for a short period in the case of a subsidiary corporation required to change its annual accounting period to conform to that of its parent, see § 1.1502–76(b).

(iv) An individual taxpayer making a return for a short period resulting from a change of annual accounting period is not allowed to take the standard deduction provided in section 141* in computing his taxable income for the short period. See section 142(b)(3).

(v) In computing the taxable income of a taxpayer other than a corporation for a short period (which income is to be annualized in order to determine the tax under section 443(b)(l)) the personal exemptions allowed individuals under section 151 (and any deductions allowed other taxpayers in lieu thereof,

*Editorial comment: See Sec. 63 rather than Sec. 141.

such as the deduction under section 642(b)) shall be reduced to an amount which bears the same ratio to the full amount of the exemptions as the number of months in the short period bears to 12. In the case of the taxable income for a short period resulting from a change from or to a 52–53-week taxable year to which section 441(f)(2)(B)(iii) applies, the computation required by the preceding sentence shall be made on a daily basis, that is, the deduction for personal exemptions (or any deduction in lieu thereof) shall be reduced to an amount which bears the same ratio to the full deduction as the number of days in the short period bears to 365.

(vi) If the amount of a credit against the tax* * * is dependent upon the amount of any item of income or deduction, such credit shall be computed upon the amount of the item annualized separately in accordance with the foregoing rules. The credit so computed shall be treated as a credit against the tax computed on the basis of the annualized taxable income. In any case in which a limitation on the amount of a credit is based upon taxable income, taxable income shall mean the taxable income computed on the annualized basis.

* * *

Methods Of Accounting

§ 1.446–1 General rule for methods of accounting.

(a) General rule. (1) Section 446(a) provides that taxable income shall be computed under the method of accounting on the basis of which a taxpayer regularly computes his income in keeping his books. The term "method of accounting" includes not only the overall method of accounting of the taxpayer but also the accounting treatment of any item. Examples of such over all methods are the cash receipts and disbursements method, an accrual method, combinations of such methods, and combinations of the foregoing with various methods provided for the accounting treatment of special items. These methods of accounting for special items include the accounting treatment prescribed for research and experimental expenditures, soil and water conservation expenditures, depreciation, net operating losses, etc. Except for deviations permitted or required by such special accounting treatment, taxable income shall be computed under the method of accounting on the basis of which the taxpayer regularly computes his income in keeping his books. For requirement respecting the adoption or change of accounting method, see section 446(e) and paragraph (e) of this section.

(2) It is recognized that no uniform method of accounting can be prescribed for all taxpayers. Each taxpayer shall adopt such forms and systems as are, in his judgment, best suited to his needs. However, no method of accounting is acceptable unless, in the opinion of the Commissioner, it clearly reflects income. A method of accounting which reflects the consistent application of generally accepted accounting principles in a particular trade or business in accordance with accepted conditions or practices in that trade or business will ordinarily be regarded as clearly reflecting income, provided all items of gross income and expense are treated consistently from year to year.

(3) Items of gross income and expenditures which are elements in the computation of taxable income need not be in the form of cash. It is sufficient that such items can be valued in terms of money. For general rules relating to the taxable year for inclusion of income and for taking deductions, see sections 451 and 461, and the regulations thereunder.

(4) Each taxpayer is required to make a return of his taxable income for each taxable year and must maintain such accounting records as will enable him to file a correct return. See section 6001 and the regulations thereunder. Accounting records include the taxpayer's regular books of account and such other records and data as may be necessary to support the entries on his books of account and on his return, as for example, a reconciliation of any differences between such books and his return. The following are among the essential features that must be considered in maintaining such records:

(i) In all cases in which the production, purchase, or sale of merchandise of any kind is an income-producing factor, merchandise on hand (including finished goods, work in process, raw materials, and supplies) at the beginning and end of the year shall be taken into account in computing the taxable income of the year. (For rules relating to computation of inventories, see sections 263A, 471 and 472, and the regulations thereunder.)

(ii) Expenditures made during the year shall be properly classified as between capital and expense. For example, expenditures for such items as plant and equipment, which have a useful life extending substantially beyond the taxable year, shall be charged to a capital account and not to an expense account.

(iii) In any case in which there is allowable with respect to an asset a deduction for depreciation, amortization, or depletion, any expenditures (other than ordinary repairs) made to restore the asset or prolong its useful life shall be added to the asset account or charged against the appropriate reserve.

(b) Exceptions. (1) If the taxpayer does not regularly employ a method of accounting which clearly reflects his income, the computation of taxable income shall be made in a manner which, in the opinion of the Commissioner, does clearly reflect income.

(2) A taxpayer whose sole source of income is wages need not keep formal books in order to have an accounting method. Tax returns, copies thereof, or other records may be sufficient to establish the use of the method of accounting used in the preparation of the taxpayer's income tax returns.

(c) Permissible methods— (1) In general. Subject to the provisions of paragraphs (a) and (b) of this section, a taxpayer may compute his taxable income under any of the following methods of accounting:

(i) Cash receipts and disbursements method. Generally, under the cash receipts and disbursements method in the computation of taxable income, all items which constitute gross income (whether in the form of cash, property, or services) are to be included for the taxable year in which actually or constructively received. Expenditures are to be deducted for the taxable year in which actually made. For rules relating to constructive receipt, see § 1.451–2. For treatment of an expenditure attributable to more than one taxable year, see section 461(a) and paragraph (a)(1) of § 1.461–1.

(ii) Accrual method. (A) Generally, under an accrual method, income is to be included for the taxable year when all the events have occurred that fix the right to receive the income and the amount of the income can be determined with reasonable accuracy. Under such a method, a liability is incurred, and generally is taken into account for Federal income tax purposes, in the taxable year in which all the events have occurred that establish the fact of the liability, the amount of the liability can be determined with reasonable accuracy, and economic performance has occurred with respect to the liability. (See paragraph (a)(2)(iii)(A) of § 1.461–1 for examples of liabilities that may not be taken into account until after the taxable year incurred, and see §§ 1.461–4 through 1.461–6 for rules relating to economic performance.) Applicable provisions of the Code, the Income Tax Regulations, and other guidance published by the Secretary prescribe the manner in which a liability that has been incurred is taken into account. For example, section 162 provides that a deductible liability generally is taken into account in the taxable year incurred through a deduction from gross income. As a further example, under section 263 or 263A, a liability that relates to the creation of an asset having a useful life extending substantially beyond the close of the taxable year is taken into account in the taxable year incurred through capitalization (within the meaning of § 1.263A–1(c)(3)), and may later affect the computation of taxable income through depreciation or otherwise over a period including subsequent taxable years, in accordance with applicable Internal Revenue Code sections and related guidance.

(B) The term "liability" includes any item allowable as a deduction, cost, or expense for Federal income tax purposes. In addition to allowable deductions, the term includes any amount otherwise allowable as a capitalized cost, as a cost taken into account in computing cost of goods sold, as a cost allocable to a long-term contract, or as any other cost or expense. Thus, for example, an amount that a taxpayer expends or will expend for capital improvements to property must be incurred before the taxpayer may take the amount into account in computing its basis in the property. The term "liability" is not limited to items for which a legal obligation to pay exists at the time of payment. Thus, for example, amounts prepaid for goods or services and amounts paid without a legal obligation to do so may not be taken into account by an accrual basis taxpayer any earlier than the taxable year in which those amounts are incurred.

(C) No method of accounting is acceptable unless, in the opinion of the Commissioner, it clearly reflects income. The method used by the taxpayer in determining when income is to be accounted for will generally be acceptable if it accords with generally accepted accounting principles, is consistently used by the taxpayer from year to year, and is consistent with the Income Tax Regulations. For example, a taxpayer engaged in a manufacturing business may account for sales of the taxpayer's product when the goods are shipped, when the product is delivered or accepted, or when title to the goods passes to the customers, whether or not billed, depending on the method regularly employed in keeping the taxpayer's books.

(iii) Other permissible methods. Special methods of accounting are described elsewhere in chapter 1 of the Code and the regulations thereunder. For example, see the following sections and the regulations thereunder: Sections 61 and 162, relating to the crop method of accounting; section 453, relating to the installment method; section 460, relating to the long-term contract methods. In addition, special methods of accounting for particular items of income and expense are provided under other sections of chapter 1. For example, see section 174, relating to research and experimental expenditures, and section 175, relating to soil and water conservation expenditures.

(iv) Combinations of the foregoing methods. **(a)** In accordance with the following rules, any combination of the foregoing methods of accounting will be permitted in connection with a trade or business if such combination clearly reflects income and is consistently used. Where a combination of methods of accounting includes any special methods, such as those referred to in subdivision (iii) of this subparagraph, the taxpayer must comply with the requirements relating to such special methods. A taxpayer using an accrual method of accounting with respect to purchases and sales may use the cash method in computing all other items of income and expense. However, a taxpayer who uses the cash method of accounting in computing gross income from his trade or business shall use the cash method in computing expenses of such trade or business. Similarly, a taxpayer who uses an accrual method of accounting in computing business expenses shall use an accrual method in computing items affecting gross income from his trade or business.

(b) A taxpayer using one method of accounting in computing items of income and deductions of his trade or business may compute other items of income and deductions not connected with his trade or business under a different method of accounting.

(2) Special rules. (i) In any case in which it is necessary to use an inventory the accrual method of accounting must be used with regard to purchases and sales unless otherwise authorized under subdivision (ii) of this subparagraph.

(ii) No method of accounting will be regarded as clearly reflecting income unless all items of gross profit and deductions are treated with consistency from year to year. The Commissioner may authorize a taxpayer to adopt or change to a method of accounting permitted by this chapter although the method is not specifically described in the regulations in this part if, in the opinion of the Commissioner, income is clearly reflected by the use of such method. Further, the Commissioner may authorize a taxpayer to continue the use of a method of accounting consistently used by the taxpayer, even though not specifically authorized by the regulations in this part, if, in the opinion of the Commissioner, income is clearly reflected by the use of such method. See section 446(a) and paragraph (a) of this section, which require that taxable income shall be computed under the method of accounting on the basis of which the taxpayer regularly computes his income in keeping his books, and section 446(e) and paragraph (e) of this section, which require the prior approval of the Commissioner in the case of changes in accounting method.

* * *

(d) Taxpayer engaged in more than one business. (1) Where a taxpayer has two or more separate and distinct trades or businesses, a different method of accounting may be used for each trade or business, provided the method used for each trade or business clearly reflects the income of that particular trade or business. For example, a taxpayer may account for the operations of a personal service business on the cash receipts and disbursements method and of a manufacturing business on an accrual method, provided such businesses are separate and distinct and the methods used for each clearly reflect income. The method first used in accounting for business income and deductions in connection with each trade or business, as evidenced in the taxpayer's income tax return in which such income or deductions are first reported, must be consistently followed thereafter.

(2) No trade or business will be considered separate and distinct for purposes of this paragraph unless a complete and separable set of books and records is kept for such trade or business.

(3) If, by reason of maintaining different methods of accounting, there is a creation or shifting of profits or losses between the trades or businesses of the taxpayer (for example, through inventory adjustments, sales, purchases, or expenses) so that income of the taxpayer is not clearly reflected, the trades or businesses of the taxpayer will not be considered to be separate and distinct.

(e) Requirement respecting the adoption or change of accounting method. (1) A taxpayer filing his first return may adopt any permissible method of accounting in computing taxable income for the taxable year covered by such return. See section 446(c) and paragraph (c) of this section for permissible methods. Moreover, a taxpayer may adopt any permissible method of accounting in connection with each separate and distinct trade or business, the income from which is reported for the first time. See section 446(d) and paragraph (d) of this section. See also section 446(a) and paragraph (a) of this section.

(2) **(i)** Except as otherwise expressly provided in chapter 1 of the Code and the regulations thereunder, a taxpayer who changes the method of accounting employed in keeping his books shall, before computing his income upon such new method for purposes of taxation, secure the consent of the Commissioner. Consent must be secured whether or not such method is proper or is permitted under the Internal Revenue Code or the regulations thereunder.

(ii) **(a)** [Reserved]. For further guidance, see § 1.446–1T(e)(2)(ii)(a).

(b) [Reserved]. For further guidance, see § 1.446–1T(e)(2)(ii)(b).

(c) A change in an overall plan or system of identifying or valuing items in inventory is a change in method of accounting. Also a change in the treatment of any material item used in the overall plan for identifying or valuing items in inventory is a change in method of accounting.

(iii) A change in the method of accounting may be illustrated by the following examples:

Example (1). Although the sale of merchandise is an income producing factor, and therefore inventories are required, a taxpayer in the retail jewelry business reports his income on the cash receipts and disbursements method of accounting. A change from the cash receipts and disbursements method of accounting to the accrual method of accounting is a change in the overall plan of accounting and thus is a change in method of accounting.

Example (2). A taxpayer in the wholesale dry goods business computes its income and expenses on the accrual method of accounting and files its Federal income tax returns on such basis except for real estate taxes which have been reported on the cash receipts and disbursements method of accounting. A change in the treatment of real estate taxes from the cash receipts and disbursements method to the accrual method is a change in method of accounting because such change is a change in the treatment of a material item within his overall accounting practice.

Example (3). A taxpayer in the wholesale dry goods business computes its income and expenses on the accrual method of accounting and files its Federal income tax returns on such basis. Vacation pay has been deducted in the year in which paid because the taxpayer did not have a completely vested vacation pay plan, and, therefore, the liability for payment did not accrue until that year. Subsequently, the taxpayer adopts a completely vested vacation pay plan that changes its year for accruing the deduction from the year in which payment is made to the year in which the liability to make the payment now arises. The change for the year of deduction of the vacation pay plan is not a change in method of accounting but results, instead, because the underlying facts (that is, the type of vacation pay plan) have changed.

* * *

(3) **(i)** Except as otherwise provided under the authority of paragraph (e)(3)(ii) of this section, to secure the Commissioner's consent to a taxpayer's change in method of accounting, the taxpayer must file an application on Form 3115 with the Commissioner within 180 days after the beginning of the taxable year in which the taxpayer desires to make the change in method of accounting. To the extent applicable, the taxpayer must furnish all information requested on the Form 3115. This information includes all classes of items that will be treated differently under the new method of accounting, any amounts that will be duplicated or omitted as a result of the proposed change, and the taxpayer's computation of any adjustments necessary to prevent such duplications or omissions. The Commissioner may require such other information as may be necessary to determine whether the proposed change will be permitted. Permission to change a taxpayer's method of accounting will not be granted unless the taxpayer agrees to the Commissioner's prescribed terms and conditions for effecting the change, including the taxable year or years in which any adjustment necessary to prevent amounts from being duplicated or omitted is to be taken into account. See section 481 and the regulations thereunder, relating to certain adjustments resulting from accounting method changes, and section 472 and the regulations thereunder, relating to adjustments for changes to and from the last-in, first-out inventory method. For any Form 3115 filed on or after May 15, 1997, see § 1.446–1T(e)(i)(B).

(ii) Notwithstanding the provisions of paragraph (e)(3)(i) of this section, the Commissioner may prescribe administrative procedures under which taxpayers will be permitted to change their method of accounting. The administrative procedures shall prescribe those terms and conditions necessary to obtain the Commissioner's consent to effect the change and to prevent amounts from being duplicated or omitted. The terms and conditions that may be prescribed by the Commissioner may include terms and conditions that require the change in method of accounting to be effected on a cut-off basis or by an adjustment under section 481(a) to be taken into account in the taxable year or years prescribed by the Commissioner.

* * *

§ 1.446–1T General rule for methods of accounting (temporary).

(a) through (e)(2)(i) [Reserved]. For further guidance, see § 1.446–1(a) through (e)(2)(i).

(e)(2)(ii)(*a*) A change in the method of accounting includes a change in the overall plan of accounting for gross income or deductions or a change in the treatment of any material item used in such overall plan. Although a method of accounting may exist under this definition without the necessity of a pattern of consistent treatment of an item, in most instances a method of accounting is not established for an item without such consistent treatment. A material item is any item that involves the proper time for the inclusion of the item in income or the taking of a deduction. Changes in method of accounting include a change from the cash receipts and disbursement method to an accrual method, or vice versa, a change involving the method or basis used in the valuation of inventories (see sections 471 and 472 and the regulations under sections 471 and 472), a change from the cash or accrual method to a long–term contract method, or vice versa (see § 1.460–4), certain changes in computing depreciation or amortization (see paragraph (e)(2)(ii)(d) of this section), a change involving the adoption, use or discontinuance of any other specialized method of computing taxable income, such as the crop method, and a change where the Internal Revenue Code and regulations under the Code specifically require that the consent of the Commissioner must be obtained before adopting such a change.

(b) A change in method of accounting does not include correction of mathematical or posting errors, or errors in the computation of tax liability (such as errors in computation of the foreign tax credit, net operating loss, percentage depletion, or investment credit). Also, a change in method of accounting does not include adjustment of any item of income or deduction that does not involve the proper time for the inclusion of the item of income or the taking of a deduction. For example, corrections of items that are deducted as interest or salary, but that are in fact payments of dividends, and of items that are deducted as business expenses, but which are in fact personal expenses, are not changes in method of accounting. In addition, a change in the method of accounting does not include an adjustment with respect to the addition to a reserve for bad debts. Although such adjustment may involve the question of the proper time for the taking of a deduction, such items are traditionally corrected by adjustment in the current and future years. For the treatment of the adjustment of the addition to a bad debt reserve (for example, for banks under section 585 of the Internal Revenue Code), see the regulations under section 166 of the Internal Revenue Code. A change in the method of accounting also does not include a change in treatment resulting from a change in underlying facts. For further guidance on changes involving depreciable or amortizable assets, see paragraph (e)(2)(ii)(d) of this section and § 1.1016–3T(h).

(c) [Reserved]. For further guidance, see § 1.446–1 (e)(2)(ii)(c).

* * *

§ 1.448–1 Limitation on the use of the cash receipts and disbursements method of accounting.—(a) through (f). [Reserved]

(g) Treatment of accounting method change and timing rules for section 481(a) adjustment—(1) Treatment of change in accounting method. Notwithstanding any other procedure published prior to January 7, 1991, concerning changes from the cash method, any taxpayer to whom section 448 applies must change its method of accounting in accordance with the provisions of this paragraph (g) and paragraph (h) of this section. In the case of any taxpayer required by this section to change its method of accounting for any taxable year, the change shall be treated as a change initiated by the taxpayer. The adjustments required under section 481(a) with respect to the change in method of accounting of such a taxpayer shall not be reduced by amounts attributable to taxable years preceding the Internal Revenue Code of 1954. Paragraph (h)(2) of this section provides procedures under which a taxpayer may change to an overall accrual method of accounting for the first taxable year the taxpayer is subject to this section ("first section 448 year"). If the taxpayer complies with the provisions of paragraph (h)(2) of this section for its first section 448 year, the change shall be treated as made with the consent of the Commissioner. Paragraph (h)(3) of this section provides procedures under which a taxpayer may change to other than an overall accrual method of accounting for its first section 448 year. Unless the taxpayer complies with the provisions of paragraph (h)(2) or (h)(3) of this section for its first section 448 year, the taxpayer must comply with the provisions of paragraph (h)(4) of this section. See paragraph (h) of this section for rules to effect a change in method of accounting.

(2) Timing rules for section 481(a) adjustment— **(i)** In general. Except as otherwise provided in paragraph (g)(2)(ii) and (g)(3) of this section, a taxpayer required by this section to change from the cash method must take the net section 481(a) adjustment into account over the section 481(a) adjustment period as determined under the applicable administrative procedures issued under § 1.446–1 (e)(3)(ii) for obtaining the Commissioner's consent to a change in accounting method (for example, see Rev. Proc. 2002–9 (2002–1 C.B. 327) and Rev. Proc. 97–27 (1997–1 C.B. 680) (also see § 601.601(d)(2) of this chapter)), provided the taxpayer complies with the provisions of paragraph (h)(2) or (3) of this section for its first section 448 year.

(ii) Hospital timing rules— **(A)** In general. In the case of a hospital that is required by this section to change from the cash method, the section 481(a) adjustment shall be taken into account ratably (beginning with the year of change) over 10 years, provided the taxpayer complies with the provisions of paragraph (h)(2) or (h)(3) of this section for its first section 448 year.

(B) Definition of hospital. For purposes of paragraph (g) of this section, a hospital is an institution—

(1) Accredited by the Joint Commission of Accreditation of Hospitals (the JCAH) (or accredited or approved by a program of the qualified governmental unit in which such institution is located if the Secretary of Health and Human Services has found that the accreditation or comparable approval standards of such qualified governmental unit are essentially equivalent to those of the JCAH);

(2) Used primarily to provide, by or under the supervision of physicians, to inpatients diagnostic services and therapeutic services for medical diagnosis, treatment, and care of injured, disabled, or sick persons;

(3) Requiring every patient to be under the care and supervision of a physician; and

(4) Providing 24-hour nursing services rendered or supervised by a registered professional nurse and having a licensed practical nurse or registered nurse on duty at all times.

For purposes of this section, an entity need not be owned by or on behalf of a governmental unit or by a section 501(c)(3) organization, or operated by a section 501(c)(3) organization, in order to be considered a hospital. In addition, for purposes of this section, a hospital does not include a rest or nursing home, continuing care facility, daycare center, medical school facility, research laboratory, or ambulatory care facility.

(C) Dual function facilities. With respect to any taxpayer whose operations consist both of a hospital, and other facilities not qualifying as a hospital, the portion of the adjustment required by section 481(a) that is attributable to the hospital shall be taken into account in accordance with the rules of paragraph (g)(2) of this section relating to hospitals. The portion of the adjustment required by section 481(a) that is not attributable to the hospital shall be taken into account in accordance with the rules of paragraph (g)(2) of this section not relating to hospitals.

(iii) Untimely change in method of accounting to comply with this section. Unless a taxpayer (including a hospital and a cooperative) required by this section to change from the cash method complies with the provisions of paragraph (h)(2) or (h)(3) of this section for its first section 448 year within the time prescribed by those paragraphs, the taxpayer must take the section 481(a) adjustment into account under the provisions of any applicable administrative procedure that is prescribed by the Commissioner after January 7, 1991, specifically for purposes of complying with this section. Absent such an administrative procedure, a taxpayer must request a change under § 1.466–1(e)(3) and shall be subject to any terms and conditions (including the year of change) as may be imposed by the Commissioner.

(3) Special timing rules for section 481(a) adjustment— **(i)** Cessation of trade or business. If the taxpayer ceases to engage in the trade or business to which the section 481(a) adjustment relates, or if the taxpayer operating the trade or business terminates existence, and such cessation or termination occurs prior to the expiration of the adjustment period described in paragraph (g)(2)(i) or (ii) of this section, the taxpayer must take into account, in the taxable year of such cessation or termination, the balance of the adjustment not previously taken into account in computing taxable income. For purposes of this paragraph (g)(3)(i), the determination as to whether taxpayer has ceased to engage in the trade or business to which the section 481(a) adjustment relates, or has terminated its existence, is to be made under the principles of § 1.446–1 (e)(3)(ii) and its underlying administrative procedures.

* * *

(4) Additional rules relating to section 481(a) adjustment. In addition to the rules set forth in paragraph (g)(2) and (3) of this section, the following rules shall apply in taking the section 481(a) adjustment into account—

(i) Any net operating loss and tax credit carryforwards will be allowed to offset any positive section 481(a) adjustment,

(ii) Any net operating loss arising in the year of change or in any subsequent year that is attributable to a negative section 481(a) adjustment may be carried back to earlier taxable years in accordance with section 172, and

(iii) For purposes of determining estimated income tax payments under sections 6654 and 6655, the section 481(a) adjustment will be recognized in taxable income ratably throughout a taxable year.

(5) Outstanding section 481(a) adjustment from previous change in method of accounting. If a taxpayer changed its method of accounting to the cash method for a taxable year prior to the year the taxpayer was required by this section to change from the cash method (the section 448 year), any section 481(a) adjustment from such prior change in method of accounting that is outstanding as of the section 448 year shall be taken into account in accordance with the provisions of this paragraph (g)(5). A taxpayer shall account for any remaining portion of the prior section 481(a) adjustment outstanding as of the section 448 year by continuing to take such remaining portion into account under the provisions and conditions of the prior change in method of accounting, or, at the taxpayer's option, combining or netting the remaining portion of the prior section 481(a) adjustment with the section 481(a) adjustment required under this section, and taking into account under the provisions of this section the resulting net amount of the adjustment. Any taxpayer choosing to combine or net the section 481(a) adjustments as described in the preceding sentence shall indicate such choice on the Form 3115 required to be filed by such taxpayer under the provisions of paragraph (h) of this section.

(6) Examples. The following examples illustrate the provisions of paragraph (g) of this section:

Example (1). Y is required by this section to change from the cash method of accounting for its taxable year beginning January 1, 1987. Y changes to an overall accrual method. The adjustment required by section 481(a) to effect the change is $10,000. Y has been using the cash method for the 10–year period preceding the year of change. Y is required by paragraph (g)(2)(i) to include the section 481(a) adjustment in taxable income ratably over four consecutive taxable years, beginning with 1987, i.e., $2,500 of the section 481(a) adjustment should be included in income for each of the four years.

Example (2). The facts are the same as in example (1), except that Y is required to change from the cash method and changes to an overall accrual method of accounting for its taxable year beginning January 1, 1989. The result is the same as in example (1), except that the four–year period for ratably taking the section 481(a) adjustment into account begins with the 1989 taxable year.

Example (3). Assume that X is required by this section to change from the cash method and that it changes to an overall accrual method for its taxable year beginning January 1, 1987. The adjustment required by section 481(a) to effect the change is $10,000. X was formed on January 1, 1986, and began business operations during that year. Since X only used the cash method for one year, X is required by paragraph (g)(2)(i) of this section to include all ($10,000) of the section 481(a) adjustment in taxable income for the 1987 taxable year.

Example (4). The facts are the same as in example (1). In addition, Y previously changed from an accrual method of accounting to the cash method for its taxable year beginning January 1, 1983. As a result of that prior change, Y was required to take into account a $5,000 negative section 481(a) adjustment ratably over a ten-year period, beginning with the 1983 taxable year. As of the beginning of the 1987 taxable year $3,000 of that adjustment had not been taken into account. Y may continue to take the remaining negative $3,000 section 481(a) adjustment into account ratably over the remaining adjustment period for the prior change in method of accounting (i.e., six remaining years). Alternatively, Y may combine or net the negative $3,000 adjustment with the positive $10,000 section 481(a) adjustment required by this section, and include the resulting $7,000 amount in taxable income ratably over four consecutive taxable years, beginning with 1987. Y is not allowed to take the entire unamortized amount of the prior section 481(a) adjustment into account for its 1987 taxable year.

(h) Procedures for change in method of accounting—(1) Applicability. Paragraph (h) of this section applies to taxpayers who change from the cash method as required by this section.

Paragraph (h) of this section does not apply to a change in accounting method required by any Code section (or regulations thereunder) other than this section.

(2) Automatic rule for changes to an overall accrual method— **(i)** Timely changes in method of accounting. Notwithstanding any other available procedures to change to the accrual method of accounting, a taxpayer to whom paragraph (h) of this section applies who desires to make a change to an overall accrual method for its first section 448 year must make that change under the provisions of this paragraph (h)(2). A taxpayer changing to an overall accrual method under this paragraph (h)(2) must file a current Form 3115 by the time prescribed in paragraph (h)(2)(ii). In addition, the taxpayer must set forth on a statement accompanying the Form 3115 the period over which the section 481(a) adjustment will be taken into account and the basis for such conclusion. Moreover, the taxpayer must type or legibly print the following statement at the top of page 1 of the Form 3115: "Automatic Change to Accrual Method—Section 448." The consent of the Commissioner to the change in method of accounting is granted to taxpayers who change to an overall accrual method under this paragraph (h)(2). See paragraph (g)(2)(i), (g)(2)(ii), or (g)(3) of this section, whichever is applicable, for rules to account for the section 481(a) adjustment.

(ii) Time and manner for filing Form 3115— **(A)** In general. Except as provided in paragraph (h)(2) (ii)(B) of this section, the Form 3115 required by paragraph (h)(2)(i) must be filed no later than the due date (determined with regard to extensions) of the taxpayer's federal income tax return for the first section 448 year and must be attached to that return.

(B) Extension of filing deadline. Notwithstanding paragraph (h)(2)(ii)(A) of this section, the filing of the Form 3115 required by paragraph (h)(2)(i) shall not be considered late if such Form 3115 is attached to a timely filed amended income tax return for the first section 448 year, provided that—

(1) The taxpayer's first section 448 year is a taxable year that begins (or, pursuant to § 1.441–2T (b)(1), is deemed to begin) in 1987, 1988, 1989, or 1990.

(2) The taxpayer has not been contacted for examination, is not before appeals, and is not before a federal court with respect to an income tax issue (each as defined in applicable administrative pronouncements), unless the taxpayer also complies with any requirements for approval in those applicable administrative pronouncements, and

(3) Any amended return required by this paragraph (h)(2)(ii)(B) is filed on or before July 8, 1991.

Filing an amended return under this paragraph (h)(2) (ii)(B) does not extend the time for making any other election. Thus, for example, taxpayers that comply with this section by filing an amended return pursuant to this paragraph (h)(2)(ii)(B) may not elect out of section 448 pursuant to paragraph (i)(2) of this section.

(3) Changes to a method other than overall accrual method— **(i)** In general. A taxpayer to whom paragraph (h) of this section applies who desires to change to a special method of accounting must make that change under the provisions of this paragraph (h)(3), except to the extent other special procedures have been promulgated regarding the special method of accounting. Such a taxpayer includes taxpayers who change to both an accrual method of accounting and a special method of accounting such as a long–term contract method. In order to change an accounting method under this paragraph (h)(3), a taxpayer must submit an application for change in accounting method under the applicable administrative procedures in effect at the time of change, including the applicable procedures regarding the time and place of filing the application for change in method. Moreover, a taxpayer who changes an accounting method under this paragraph (h)(3) must type or legibly print the following statement on the top of page 1 of Form 3115: "Change to a Special Method of Accounting—Section 448." The filing of a Form 3115 by any taxpayer requesting a change of method of accounting under this paragraph (h)(3) for its taxable year beginning in 1987 will not be considered late if the form is filed with the appropriate office of the Internal Revenue Service on or before the later of: the date that is the 180th day of the taxable year of change; or September 14, 1987. If the Commissioner approves the taxpayer's application for change in method of accounting, the timing of the adjustment required under section 481(a), if applicable, will be determined under the provisions of paragraph (g)(2) (i), (g)(2)(ii), or (g)(3) of this section, whichever is applicable. If the Commissioner denies the taxpayer's application for change in accounting method, or if the taxpayer's application is untimely, the taxpayer must change to an overall accrual method of accounting under the provisions of either paragraph (h)(2) or (h)(4) of this section, whichever is applicable.

(ii) Extension of filing deadline. Notwithstanding paragraph (h)(3)(i) of this section, if the events or circumstances which under section 448 disqualify a taxpayer from using the cash method occur after the time prescribed under applicable procedures for filing the Form 3115, the filing of such form shall not be considered late if such form is filed on or before 30 days after the close of the taxable year.

(4) Untimely change in method of accounting to comply with this section. Unless a taxpayer to whom paragraph (h) of this section applies complies with the provisions of paragraph (h)(2) or (h)(3) of this section for its first section 448 year, the taxpayer must comply with the requirements of § 1.446–1 (e) (3) (including any applicable administrative procedure that is prescribed thereunder after January 7, 1991 specifically for purposes of complying with this section) in order to secure the consent of the Commissioner to change to a method of accounting that is in compliance with the provisions of this section. The taxpayer shall be subject to any terms and conditions (including the year of change) as may be imposed by the Commissioner. A taxpayer to whom section 448 applies that changes from the cash method by filing Form 3115 after January 7, 1991, will generally be subject to terms and conditions designed to place the taxpayer in a position no more favorable than a taxpayer that timely complied with this section.

(i) Effective date—(1) In general. Except as provided in paragraph (i)(2) of this section, this section applies to any taxable year beginning after December 31, 1986.

(2) Election out of section 448—(i) In general. A taxpayer may elect not to have this section apply to any (A) transaction with a related party (within the meaning of section 267(b) of the Internal Revenue Code of 1954, as in effect on October 21, 1986), (B) loan, or (C) lease, if such transaction, loan, or lease was entered into on or before September 25, 1985. Any such election described in the preceding sentence may be made separately with respect to each transaction, loan, or lease. For rules relating to the making of such election, see 26 CFR 5h.5 (temporary regulations relating to elections under the Tax Reform Act of 1986). Notwithstanding the provisions of this paragraph (i)(2), the gross receipts attributable to a transaction, loan, or lease described in this paragraph (i)(2) shall be taken into account for purposes of the $5,000,000 gross receipts test described in paragraph (f) of this section.

(ii) Special rules for loans. If the taxpayer makes an election under paragraph (i)(2)(i) of this section with respect to a loan entered into on or before September 25, 1985, the election shall apply only with respect to amounts that are attributable to the loan balance outstanding on September 25, 1985. The election shall not apply to any amounts advanced or lent after September 25, 1985, regardless of whether the loan agreement was entered into on or before such date. Moreover, any payments made on outstanding loan balances after September 25, 1985, shall be deemed to first extinguish loan balances outstanding on September 25, 1985, regardless of any contrary treatment of such loan payments by the borrower and lender.

§ 1.448–1T Limitation on the use of the cash receipts and disbursements method of accounting (temporary).

(a) Limitation on accounting method—(1) In general. This section prescribes regulations under section 448 relating to the limitation on the use of the cash receipts and disbursements method of accounting (the cash method) by certain taxpayers.

(2) Limitation rule. Except as otherwise provided in this section, the computation of taxable income using the cash method is prohibited in the case of a—

(i) C corporation,

(ii) Partnership with a C corporation as a partner, or

(iii) Tax shelter.

A partnership is described in paragraph (a)(2)(ii) of this section, if the partnership has a C corporation as a partner at any time during the partnership's taxable year beginning after December 31, 1986.

(3) Meaning of C corporation. For purposes of this section, the term "C corporation" includes any corporation that is not an S corporation. For example, a regulated investment company (as defined in section 851) or a real estate investment trust (as defined in section 856) is a C corporation for purposes of this section. In addition, a trust subject to tax under section 511(b) shall be treated, for purposes of this section, as a C corporation, but only with respect to the portion of its activities that constitute an unrelated trade or business. Similarly, for purposes of this section, a corporation that is exempt from federal income taxes under section 501 (a) shall be treated as a C corporation only with respect to the portion of its activities that constitute an unrelated trade or business. Moreover, for purposes of determining whether a partnership has a C corporation as a partner, any partnership described in paragraph (a)(2)(ii) of this section is treated as a C corporation. Thus, if partnership ABC has a partner that is a partnership with a C corporation, then, for purposes of this section, partnership ABC is treated as a partnership with a C corporation partner.

(4) Treatment of a combination of methods. For purposes of this section, the use of a method of accounting that records some, but not all, items on the cash method shall be considered the use of the cash method. Thus, a C corporation that uses a combination of accounting methods including the use of the cash method is subject to this section.

(b) Tax shelter defined—(1) In general. For purposes of this section, the term "tax shelter" means any—

(i) Enterprise (other than a C corporation) if at any time (including taxable years beginning before January 1, 1987) interests in such enterprise have been offered for sale in any offering required to be registered with any federal or state agency having the authority to regulate the offering of securities for sale,

(ii) Syndicate (within the meaning of paragraph (b)(2) of this section), or

(iii) Tax shelter within the meaning of section 6662(d)(2)(C).

(2) Requirement of registration. For purposes of paragraph (b)(1)(i) of this section, an offering is required to be registered with a federal or state agency if, under the applicable federal or state law, failure to register the offering would result in a violation of the applicable federal or state law (regardless of whether the offering is in fact registered). In addition, an offering is required to be registered with a federal or state agency if, under the applicable federal or state law, failure to file a notice of exemption from registration would result in a violation of the applicable federal or state law (regardless of whether the notice is in fact filed).

(3) Meaning of syndicate. For purposes of paragraph (b)(1)(ii) of this section, the term "syndicate" means a partnership or other entity (other than a C corporation) if more than 35 percent of the losses of such entity during the taxable year (for taxable years beginning after December 31, 1986) are allocated to limited partners or limited entrepreneurs. For purposes of this paragraph (b)(3), the term "limited entrepreneur" has the same meaning given such term in section 464(e)(2). In addition, in determining whether an interest in a partnership is held by a limited partner, or an interest in an entity or enterprise is held by a limited entrepreneur, section 464(c)(2) shall apply in the case of the trade or business of farming (as defined in paragraph (d)(2) of this section), and section 1256(e)(3)(C) shall apply in any other case. Moreover, for purposes of this paragraph (b)(3), the losses of a partnership, entity, or enterprise (the enterprise) means the excess of the deductions allowable to the enterprise over the amount of income recognized by such enterprise under the enterprise's method of accounting used for federal income tax purposes (determined without regard to this section). For this purpose, gains or losses from the sale of capital assets or section 1221 (2) assets are not taken into account.

(4) Presumed tax avoidance. For purposes of paragraph (b)(1)(iii) of this section, marketed arrangements in which persons carry on farming activities using the services of a common managerial or administrative service will be presumed to have the principal purpose of tax avoidance if such persons use borrowed funds to prepay a substantial portion of their farming expenses (e.g., payment for farm supplies that will not be used or consumed until a taxable year subsequent to the taxable year of payment).

(5) Taxable year tax shelter must change accounting method. A partnership, entity, or enterprise that is a tax shelter must change from the cash method for the later of (i) the first taxable year beginning after December 31, 1986, or (ii) the taxable year that such partnership, entity, or enterprise becomes a tax shelter.

(c) Effect of section 448 on other provisions. Nothing in section 448 shall have any effect on the application of any other provision of law that would otherwise limit the use of the cash method, and no inference shall be drawn from section 448 with respect to the application of any such provision. For example, nothing in section 448 affects the requirement of section 447 that certain corporations must use an accrual method of accounting in computing taxable income from farming, or the requirement of § 1.446–1 (c)(2) that an accrual method be used with regard to purchases and sales of inventory. Similarly, nothing in section 448 affects the authority of the Commissioner under section 446(b) to require the use of an accounting method that clearly reflects income, or the requirement under section 446(e) that a taxpayer secure the consent of the Commissioner before changing its method of accounting. For example, a taxpayer using the cash method may be required to change to an accrual method of accounting under section 446(b) because such method clearly reflects that taxpayer's income, even though the taxpayer is not prohibited by section 448 from using the cash method. Similarly, a taxpayer using an accrual method of accounting that is not prohibited by section 448 from using the cash method may not change to the cash method unless the taxpayer secures the consent of the Commissioner under section 446(e), and, in the opinion of the Commissioner, the use of the cash method clearly reflects that taxpayer's income under section 446(b).

(d) Exception for farming business— (1) In general. Except in the case of a tax shelter, this section shall not apply to any farming business. A taxpayer engaged in a farming business and a separate nonfarming business is not prohibited by this section from using the cash method with respect to the farming business, even though the taxpayer may be prohibited by this section from using the cash method with respect to the nonfarming business.

(2) Meaning of farming business. For purposes of paragraph (d) of this section, the term "farming business" means—

(i) The trade or business of farming as defined in section 263A(e)(4) (including the operation of a nursery or sod farm, or the raising or harvesting of trees bearing fruit, nuts, or other crops, or ornamental trees), or

(ii) The raising, harvesting, or growing of trees described in section 263A(c)(5) (relating to trees raised, harvested, or grown by the taxpayer other than trees described in paragraph (d)(2)(i) of this section).

Thus, for purposes of this section, the term "farming business" includes the raising of timber. For purposes of this section, the term "farming business" does not include the processing of commodities or products beyond those activities normally incident to the growing, raising or harvesting of such products. For example, assume that a C corporation taxpayer is in the business of growing and harvesting wheat and other grains. The taxpayer processes the harvested grains to produce breads, cereals, and similar food products which it sells to customers in the course of its business. Although the taxpayer is in the farming business with respect to the growing and harvesting of grain, the taxpayer is not in the farming business with respect to the processing of such grains to produce food products which the taxpayer sells to customers. Similarly, assume that a taxpayer is in the business of raising poultry or other livestock. The taxpayer uses the livestock in a meat processing operation in which the livestock are slaughtered, processed, and packaged or canned for sale to customers. Although the taxpayer is in the farming business with respect to the raising of livestock, the taxpayer is not in the farming business with respect to the meat processing operation. However, under this section the term "farming business" does include processing activities which are normally incident to the growing, raising or harvesting of agricultural products. For example, assume a taxpayer is in the business of growing fruits and vegetables. When the fruits and vegetables are ready to be harvested, the taxpayer picks, washes, inspects, and packages the fruits and vegetables for sale. Such activities are normally incident to the raising of these crops by farmers. The taxpayer will be considered to be in the business of farming with respect to the growing of fruits and vegetables, and the processing activities incident to the harvest.

(e) Exception for qualified personal service corporation— (1) In general. Except in the case of a tax shelter, this section does not apply to a qualified personal service corporation.

(2) Certain treatment for qualified personal service corporation. For purposes of paragraph (a)(2)(ii) of this section (relating to whether a partnership has a C corporation as a partner), a qualified personal service corporation shall be treated as an individual.

(3) Meaning of qualified personal service corporation. For purposes of this section, the term "qualified personal service corporation" means any corporation that meets—

(i) The function test of paragraph (e)(4) of this section, and

(ii) The ownership test of paragraph (e)(5) of this section.

(4) Function test— (i) In general. A corporation meets the function test if substantially all the corporation's activities for a taxable year involve the performance of services in one or more of the following fields—

(A) Health,

(B) Law,

(C) Engineering (including surveying and mapping),

(D) Architecture,

(E) Accounting,

(F) Actuarial science,

(G) Performing arts, or

(H) Consulting.

Substantially all of the activities of a corporation are involved in the performances of services in any field described in the preceding sentence (a qualifying field), only if 95 percent or more of the time spent by employees of the corporation, serving in their capacity as such, is devoted to the performance of services in a qualifying field. For purposes of determining whether this 95 percent test is satisfied, the performance of any activity incident to the actual performance of services in a qualifying field is considered the performance of services in that field. Activities incident to the performance of services in a qualifying field include the supervision of employees engaged in directly providing services to clients, and the performance of administrative and support services incident to such activities.

(ii) Meaning of services performed in the field of health. For purposes of paragraph (e)(4)(i)(A) of this section, the performance of services in the field of health means the provision of medical services by physicians, nurses, dentists, and other similar health–care professionals. The performance of services in the field of health does not include the provision of services not directly related to a medical field, even though the services may purportedly relate to the health of the service recipient. For example, the performance of services in the field of health does not include the operation of health clubs or health spas that provide physical exercise or conditioning to their customers.

(iii) Meaning of services performed in the field of performing arts. For purposes of paragraph (e)(4) (i) (G) of this section, the performance of services in the field of performing arts means the provision of services by actors, actresses, singers, musicians, entertainers, and similar artists in their capacity as such. The performance of services in the field of the performing arts does not include the provision of services by persons who themselves are not performing artists (e.g., persons who may manage or promote such artists, and other persons in a trade or business that relates to the performing arts). Similarly, the performance of services in the field of the performing arts does not include the provision of services by persons who broadcast or otherwise disseminate the performances of such artists to members of the public (e.g., employees of a radio station that broadcasts the performances of musicians and singers). Finally, the performance of services in the field of the performing arts does not include the provision of services by athletes.

(iv) Meaning of services performed in the field of consulting—**(A)** In general. For purposes of paragraph (e)(4)(i)(H) of this section, the performance of services in the field of consulting means the provision of advice and counsel. The performance of services in the field of consulting does not include the performance of services other than advice and counsel, such as sales or brokerage services, or economically similar services. For purposes of the preceding sentence, the determination of whether a person's services are sales or brokerage services, or economically similar services, shall be based on all the facts and circumstances of that person's business. Such facts and circumstances include, for example, the manner in which the taxpayer is compensated for the services provided (e.g., whether the compensation for the services is contingent upon the consummation of the transaction that the services were intended to effect).

(B) Examples. The following examples illustrate the provisions of paragraph (e)(4)(iv)(A) of this section. The examples do not address all types of services that may or may not qualify as consulting. The determination of whether activities not specifically addressed in the examples qualify as consulting shall be made by comparing the service activities in question to the types of service activities discussed in the examples. With respect to a corporation which performs services which qualify as consulting under this section, and other services which do not qualify as consulting, see paragraph (e)(4)(i) of this section which requires that substantially all of the corporation's activities involve the performance of services in a qualifying field.

Example (1). A taxpayer is in the business of providing economic analyses and forecasts of business prospects for its clients. Based on these analyses and forecasts, the taxpayer advises its clients on their business activities. For example, the taxpayer may analyze the economic conditions and outlook for a particular industry which a client is considering entering. The taxpayer will then make recommendations and advise the client on the prospects of entering the industry, as well as on other matters regarding the client's activities in such industry. The taxpayer provides similar services to other clients, involving, for example, economic analyses and evaluations of business prospects in different areas of the United States or in other countries, or economic analyses of overall economic trends and the provision of advice based on these analyses and evaluations. The taxpayer is considered to be engaged in the performance of services in the field of consulting.

Example (2). A taxpayer is in the business of providing services that consist of determining a client's electronic data processing needs. The taxpayer will study and examine the client's business, focusing on the types of data and information relevant to the client and the needs of the client's employees for access to this information. The taxpayer will then make recommendations regarding the design and implementation of data processing systems intended to meet the needs of the client. The taxpayer does not, however, provide the client with additional computer programming services distinct from the recommendations made by the taxpayer with respect to the design and implementation of the client's data processing systems. The taxpayer is considered to be engaged in the performance of services in the field of consulting.

Example (3). A taxpayer is in the business of providing services that consist of determining a client's management and business structure needs. The taxpayer will study the client's organization, including, for example, the departments assigned to perform specific functions, lines of authority in the managerial hierarchy, personnel hiring, job responsibility, and personnel evaluations and compensation. Based on the study, the taxpayer will then advise the client on changes in the client's management and business structure, including, for example, the restructuring of the client's departmental systems or its lines of managerial authority. The taxpayer is considered to be engaged in the performance of services in the field of consulting.

Example (4). A taxpayer is in the business of providing financial planning services. The taxpayer will study a particular client's financial situation, including, for example, the client's present income, savings and investments, and anticipated future economic and financial needs. Based on this study, the taxpayer will then assist the client in making decisions and plans regarding the client's financial activities. Such financial planning includes the design of a personal budget to assist the client in monitoring the client's financial situation, the adoption of investment strategies tailored to the client's needs, and other similar services. The taxpayer is considered to be engaged in the performance of services in the field of consulting.

Example (5). A taxpayer is in the business of executing transactions for customers involving various types of securities or commodities generally traded through organized exchanges or other similar networks. The taxpayer provides its clients with economic analyses and forecasts of conditions in various industries and businesses. Based on these analyses, the taxpayer makes recommendations regarding transactions in securities and commodities. Clients place orders with the taxpayer to trade securities or commodities based on the taxpayer's recommendations. The taxpayer's compensation for its services is typically based on the trade orders. The taxpayer is not considered to be engaged in the performance of services in the field of consulting. The taxpayer is engaged in brokerage services. Relevant to this determination is the fact that the compensation of the taxpayer for its services is contingent upon the consummation of the transaction the services were intended to effect (i.e., the execution of trade orders for its clients).

Example (6). A taxpayer is in the business of studying a client's needs regarding its data processing facilities and making recommendations to the client regarding the design and implementation of data processing systems. The client will then order computers and other data processing equipment through the taxpayer based on the taxpayer's recommendations. The taxpayer's compensation for its services is typically based on the equipment orders made by the clients. The taxpayer is not considered to be engaged in the performance of services in the field of consulting. The taxpayer is engaged in the performance of sales services. Relevant to this determination is the fact that the compensation of the taxpayer for its services is contingent upon the consummation of the transaction the services were intended to effect (i.e., the execution of equipment orders for its clients).

Example (7). A taxpayer is in the business of assisting businesses in meeting their personnel requirements by referring job applicants to employers with hiring needs in a particular area. The taxpayer may be informed by potential employers of their need for job applicants, or, alternatively, the taxpayer may become aware of the client's personnel requirements after the taxpayer studies and examines the client's management and business structure. The taxpayer's compensation for its services is typically based on the job applicants, referred by the taxpayer to the clients, who accept employment positions with the clients. The taxpayer is not considered to be engaged in the performance of services in the field of consulting. The taxpayer is involved in the performance of services economically similar to brokerage services. Relevant to this determination is the fact that the compensation of the taxpayer for its services is contingent upon the consummation of the transaction the services were intended to effect (i.e., the hiring of a job applicant by the client).

Example (8). The facts are the same as in example (7), except that the taxpayer's clients are individuals who use the services of the taxpayer to obtain employment positions. The taxpayer is typically compensated by its clients who obtain employment as a result of the taxpayer's services. For the reasons set forth in example (7), the taxpayer is not considered to be engaged in the performance of services in the field of consulting.

Example (9). A taxpayer is in the business of assisting clients in placing advertisements for their goods and services. The taxpayer analyzes the conditions and trends in the client's particular industry, and then makes recommendations to the client regarding the types of advertisements which should be placed by the client and the various types of advertising media (e.g., radio, television, magazines, etc.) which should be used by the client. The client will then purchase, through the taxpayer, advertisements in various media based on the taxpayer's recommendations. The taxpayer's compensation for its services is typically based on the particular orders for advertisements which the client makes. The taxpayer is not considered to be engaged in the performance of services in the field of consulting. The taxpayer is engaged in the performance of services economically similar to brokerage services. Relevant to this determination is the fact that the compensation of the taxpayer for its services is contingent upon the consummation of the transaction the services were intended to effect (i.e., the placing of advertisements by clients).

Example (10). A taxpayer is in the business of selling insurance (including life and casualty insurance), annuities, and other similar insurance products to various individual and business clients. The taxpayer will study the particular client's financial situation, including, for example, the client's present income, savings and investments, business and personal insurance risks, and anticipated future economic and financial needs. Based on this study, the taxpayer will then make recommendations to the client regarding the desirability of various insurance products. The client will then purchase these various insurance products through the taxpayer. The taxpayer's compensation for its services is typically based on the purchases made by the clients. The taxpayer is not considered to be engaged in the performance of services in the field of consulting. The taxpayer is engaged in the performance of brokerage or sales services. Relevant to this determination is the fact that the compensation of the taxpayer for its services is contingent upon the consummation of the transaction the services were intended to effect (i.e., the purchase of insurance products by its clients).

(5) Ownership test— (i) In general. A corporation meets the ownership test, if at all times during the taxable year, substantially all the corporation's stock, by value, is held, directly or indirectly, by—

(A) Employees performing services for such corporation in connection with activities involving a field referred to in paragraph (e)(4) of this section,

(B) Retired employees who had performed such services for such corporation,

(C) The estate of any individual described in paragraph (e)(5)(i)(A) or (B), or

(D) Any other person who acquired such stock by reason of the death of an individual described in paragraph (e)(5)(i)(A) or (B), but only for the 2-year period beginning on the date of the death of such individual.

For purposes of this paragraph (e)(5), the term "substantially all" means an amount equal to or greater than 95 percent.

(ii) Definition of employee. For purposes of the ownership test of this paragraph (e)(5), a person shall not be considered an employee of a corporation unless the services performed by that person for such corporation, based on the facts and circumstances, are more than de minimis. In addition, a person who is an employee of a corporation shall not be treated as an employee of another corporation merely by reason of the employer corporation and the other corporation being members of the same affiliated group or otherwise related.

(iii) Attribution rules. For purposes of this paragraph (e)(5), a corporation's stock is considered held indirectly by a person if, and to the extent, such person owns a proportionate interest in a partnership, S corporation, or qualified personal service corporation that owns such stock. No other arrangement or type of ownership shall constitute indirect ownership of a corporation's stock for purposes of this paragraph (e)(5). Moreover, stock of a corporation held by a trust is considered held by a person if, and to the extent, such person is treated under subpart E, part I, subchapter J, chapter 1 of the Code as the owner of the portion of the trust that consists of such stock.

(iv) Disregard of community property laws. For purposes of this paragraph (e)(5), community property laws shall be disregarded. Thus, in determining the stock ownership of a corporation, stock owned by a spouse solely by reason of community property laws shall be treated as owned by the other spouse.

(v) Treatment of certain stock plans. For purposes of this paragraph (e)(5), stock held by a plan described in section 401(a) that is exempt from tax under section 501(a) shall be treated as held by an employee described in paragraph (e)(5)(i)(A) of this section.

(vi) Special election for certain affiliated groups. For purposes of determining whether the stock ownership test of this paragraph (e)(5) has been met, at the election of the common parent of an affiliated group (within the meaning of section 1504 (a)), all members of such group shall be treated as one taxpayer if substantially all (within the meaning of paragraph (e)(4)(i) of this section) the activities of all such members (in the aggregate) are in the same field described in paragraph (e)(4)(i)(A)—(H) of this section. For rules relating to the making of the election, see 26 CFR 5h.5 (temporary regulations relating to elections under the Tax Reform Act of 1986).

(vii) Examples. The following examples illustrate the provisions of paragraph (e) of this section:

Example (11). (i) X, a C corporation, is engaged in the business of providing accounting services to its clients. These services consist of the preparation of audit and financial statements and the preparation of tax returns. For purposes of section 448, such services consist of the performance of services in the field of accounting. In addition, for purposes of section 448, the supervision of employees directly preparing the statements and returns, and the performance of all administrative and support services incident to such activities (including secretarial, janitorial, purchasing, personnel, security, and payroll services) are the performance of services in the field of accounting.

(ii) In addition, X owns and leases a portion of an office building. For purposes of this section, the following types of activities undertaken by the employees of X shall be considered as the performance of services in a field other than the field of accounting: (A) services directly relating to the leasing activities, e.g., time spent in leasing and maintaining the leased portion of the building; (B) supervision of employees engaged in directly providing services in the leasing activity; and (C) all administrative and support services incurred incident to services described in (A) and (B). The leasing activities of X are considered the performance of services in a field other than the field of accounting, regardless of whether such leasing activities constitute a trade or business under the Code. If the employees of X spend 95% or more of their time in the performance of services in the field of accounting, X satisfies the function test of paragraph (e)(4) of this section.

Example (2). Assume that Y, a C corporation, meets the function test of paragraph (e)(4) of this section. Assume further that all the employees of Y are performing services for Y in a qualifying field as defined in paragraph (e)(4) of this section. P, a partnership, owns 40%, by value, of the stock of Y. The remaining 60% of the stock of Y is owned directly by employees of Y. Employees of Y have an aggregate interest of 90% in the capital and profits of P. Thus, 96% of the stock of Y is held directly, or indirectly, by employees of Y performing services in a qualifying field. Accordingly, Y meets the ownership test of paragraph (e)(5) of this section and is a qualified personal service corporation.

Example (3). The facts are the same as in example (2), except that 40% of the stock of Y is owned by Z, a C corporation. The remaining 60% of the stock is owned directly by the employees of Y. Employees of Y own 90% of the stock, by value, of Z. Assume that Z independently qualifies as a personal service corporation. The result is the same as in example (2), i.e., 96% of the stock of Y is held, directly or indirectly, by employees of Y performing services in a qualifying field. Thus, Y is a qualified personal service corporation.

Example (4). The facts are the same as in example (3), except that Z does not independently qualify as a personal service corporation. Because Z is not a qualified personal service corporation, the Y stock owned by Z is not treated as being held indirectly by the Z shareholders. Consequently, only 60% of the stock of Y is held, directly or indirectly, by employees of Y. Thus, Y does not meet the ownership test of paragraph (e)(5) of this section, and is not a qualified personal service corporation.

Example (5). Assume that W, a C corporation, meets the function test of paragraph (e)(4) of this section. In addition, assume that all the employees of W are performing services for W in a qualifying field. Nominal legal title to 100% of the stock of W is held by employees of W. However, due solely to the operation of community property laws, 20% of the stock of W is held by spouses of such employees who themselves are not employees of W. In determining the ownership of the stock, community property laws are disregarded. Thus, Y meets the ownership test of paragraph (e)(5) of this section, and is a qualified personal service corporation.

Example (6). Assume that 90% of the stock of T, a C corporation, is directly owned by the employees of T. Spouses of T's employees directly own 5% of the stock of T. The spouses are not employees of T, and their ownership does not occur solely by operation of community property laws. In addition, 5% of the stock of T is held by trusts (other than a trust described in section 401(a) that is exempt from tax under section 501(a)), the sole beneficiaries of which are employees of T. The employees are not treated as owners of the trusts under subpart E, part I, subchapter J, chapter 1 of the Code. Since a person is not treated as owning the stock of a corporation owned by that person's spouse, or by any portion of a trust that is not treated as owned by such person under subpart E, only 90% of the stock of T is treated as held, directly or indirectly, by employees of T. Thus, T does not meet the ownership test of paragraph (e)(5) of this section, and is not a qualified personal service corporation.

Example (7). Assume that Y, a C corporation, directly owns all the stock of three subsidiaries, F, G, and H. Y is a common parent of an affiliated group within the meaning of section 1504(a) consisting of Y, F, G, and H. Y is not engaged in the performance of services in a qualifying field. Instead, Y is a holding company whose activities consist of its ownership and investment in its operating subsidiaries. Substantially all the activities of F involve the performance of services in the field of engineering. In addition, a majority of (but not substantially all) the activities of G involve the performance of services in the field of engineering; the remainder of G's services involve the performance of services in a nonqualifying field. Moreover, a majority of (but not substantially all) the activities of H involve the performance of services in the field of engineering; the remainder of H's activities involve the performance of services in the field of architecture. Nevertheless, substantially all the activities of the group consisting of Y, F, G, and H, in the aggregate, involve the performance of services in the field of engineering. Accordingly, Y elects under paragraph (e)(5)(vi) of this section to be treated as one taxpayer for determining the ownership test of paragraph (e)(5) of this section. Assume that substantially all the stock of Y (by value) is held by employees of F, G, or H who perform services in connection with a qualifying field (engineering or architecture). Thus, for purposes of determining whether any member corporation is a qualified personal service corporation, the ownership test of paragraph (e)(5) of this section has been satisfied. Since F and H satisfy the function test of paragraph (e)(4) of this section, F and H are qualified personal service corporations. However, since Y and G each fail the function test of paragraph (e)(4) of this section, neither corporation is a qualified personal service corporation.

Example (8). The facts are the same as in example (7), except that less than substantially all the activities of the group consisting of Y, F, G, and H, in the aggregate, are performed in the field of engineering. Substantially all the activities of the group consisting of Y, F, G, and H, are, in the aggregate, performed in two fields, the fields of engineering and architecture. Y may not elect to have the affiliated group treated as one taxpayer for purposes of determining whether group members meet the ownership test of paragraph (e)(5) of this section. The election is available only if substantially all the activities of the group, in the aggregate, involve the performance of services in only one qualifying field. Moreover, none of the group members are qualified personal service corporations. Y fails the function test of paragraph (e)(4) of this section because less than substantially all the activities of Y are performed in a qualifying field. In addition, F, G, and H, fail the ownership test of paragraph (e)(5) of this section because substantially all their stock is owned by Y and not by their employees. The owners of Y are not deemed to indirectly own the stock owned by Y because Y is not a qualified personal service corporation.

Example (9). (i) The facts are the same as in example (8), except that Y itself satisfies the function test of paragraph (e)(4) of this section because substantially all the activities of Y involve the performance of services in the field of engineering. In addition, assume that all employees of Y are involved in the performance of services in the field of engineering, and that all such employees own 100% of Y's stock. Moreover, assume that one–third of all the employees of Y are separately employed by F. Similarly, another one-third of the employees of Y are separately employed by G and H, respectively. None of the employees of Y are employed by more than one of Y's subsidiaries. Also, no other persons except the employees of Y are employed by any of the subsidiaries.

(ii) Y is a personal service corporation under section 448 because Y satisfies both the function and the ownership test of paragraphs (e)(4) and (5) of this section. As in example (8), Y is unable to make the election to have the affiliated group treated as one taxpayer for purposes of determining whether group members meet the ownership test of paragraph (e)(5) of this section because less than substantially all the activities, in the aggregate, of the group members are performed in one of the qualifying fields. However, because Y is a personal service corporation, the stock owned by Y is treated as indirectly owned, proportionately, by the owners of Y. Thus, the employees of F are collectively treated as owning one-third of the stock of F, G, and H. The employees of G and H are similarly treated as owning one-third of each subsidiary's stock.

(iii) F, G, and H each fail the ownership test of paragraph (e)(5) of this section because less than substantially all of each corporation's stock is owned by the employees of the respective corporation. Only one-third of each corporation's stock is owned by employees of that corporation. Thus, F, G, and H are not qualified personal service corporations.

Example (10). (i) Assume that Y, a C corporation, directly owns all the stock of three subsidiaries, F, G, and Z. Y is a common parent of an affiliated group within the meaning of section 1504(a) consisting of Y, F, and G. Z is a foreign corporation and is excluded from the affiliated group under section 1504. Assume that Y is a holding company whose activities consist of its ownership and investment in its operating subsidiaries. Substantially all the activities of F, G, and Z involve the performance of services in the field of engineering. Assume that employees of Z own one-third of the stock of Y and that none of these employees are also employees of Y, F, or G. In addition, assume that Y elects to be treated as one taxpayer for determining whether group members meet the ownership test of paragraph (e)(5) of this section. Thus, Y, F, and G are treated as one taxpayer for purposes of the ownership test.

(ii) None of the members of the group are qualified personal service corporations. Y, F, and G fail the ownership test of paragraph (e)(5) of this section because less than substantially all the stock of Y is owned by employees of either Y, F, or G. Moreover, Z fails the ownership test of paragraph (e)(5) of this section because substantially all its stock is owned by Y and not by its employees.

(6) Application of function and ownership tests. A corporation that fails the function test of paragraph (e)(4) of this section for any taxable year, or that fails the ownership test of paragraph (e)(5) of this section at any time during any taxable year, shall change from the cash method effective for the year in which the corporation fails to meet the function test or the ownership test. For example, if a personal service corporation fails the function test for taxable year 1987, such corporation must change from the cash method effective for taxable year 1987. A corporation that fails the function or ownership test for a taxable year shall not be treated as a qualified personal service corporation for any part of that taxable year.

(f) Exception for entities with gross receipts of not more than $5 million— (1) In general. Except in the case of a tax shelter, this section shall not apply to any C corporation or partnership with a C corporation as a partner for any taxable year if, for all prior taxable years beginning after December 31, 1985, such corporation or partnership (or any predecessor thereof) meets the $5,000,000 gross receipts test of paragraph (f)(2) of this section.

(2) The $5,000,000 gross receipts test— (i) In general. A corporation meets the $5,000,000 gross receipts test of this paragraph (f)(2) for any prior taxable year if the average annual gross receipts of such corporation for the 3 taxable years (or, if shorter, the taxable years during which such corporation was in existence) ending with such prior taxable year does not exceed $5,000,000. In the case of a C corporation exempt from federal income taxes under section 501(a), or a trust subject to tax under section 511(b) that is treated as a C corporation under paragraph (a)(3) of this section, only gross receipts from the activities of such corporation or trust that constitute unrelated trades or businesses are taken into account in determining whether the $5,000,000 gross receipts test is satisfied. A partnership with a C corporation as a partner meets the $5,000,000 gross receipts test of this paragraph (f)(2) for any prior taxable year if the average annual gross receipts of such partnership for the 3 taxable years (or, if shorter, the taxable years during which such partnership was in existence) ending with such prior year does not exceed $5,000,000. The gross receipts of the corporate partner are not taken into account in determining whether the partnership meets the $5,000,000 gross receipts test.

(ii) Aggregation of gross receipts. For purposes of determining whether the $5,000,000 gross receipts test has been satisfied, all persons treated as a single employer under section 52(a) or (b), or section 414 (m) or (o) (or who would be treated as a single employer under such sections if they had employees) shall be treated as one person. Gross receipts attributable to transactions between persons who are treated as a common employer under this paragraph shall not be taken into account in determining whether the $5,000,000 gross receipts test is satisfied.

(iii) Treatment of short taxable year. In the case of any taxable year of less than 12 months (a short taxable year), the gross receipts shall be annualized by (A) multiplying the gross receipts for the short period by 12 and (B) dividing the result by the number of months in the short period.

(iv) Determination of gross receipts—(A) In general. The term "gross receipts" means gross receipts of the taxable year in which such receipts are properly recognized under the taxpayer's accounting method used in that taxable year (determined without regard to this section) for federal income tax purposes. For this purpose, gross receipts include total sales (net of returns and allowances) and all amounts received for services. In addition, gross receipts include any income from investments, and from incidental or outside sources. For example, gross receipts include interest (including original issue discount and tax-exempt interest within the meaning of section 103), dividens, rents, royalties, and annuities, regardless of whether such amounts are derived in the ordinary course of the taxpayer's trade or business. Gross receipts are not reduced by cost of goods sold or by the cost of property sold if such property is described in section 1221(1), (3), (4) or (5). With respect to sales of capital assets as defined in section 1221, or sales of property described in 1221(2) (relating to property used in a trade or business), gross receipts shall be reduced by the taxpayer's adjusted basis in such property. Gross receipts do not include the repayment of a loan or similar instrument (e.g., a repayment of the principal amount of a loan held by a commercial lender). Finally, gross receipts do not include amounts received by the taxpayer with respect to sales tax or other similar state and local taxes if, under the applicable state or local law, the tax is legally imposed on the purchaser of the good or service, and the taxpayer merely collects and remits the tax to the taxing authority. If, in contrast, the tax is imposed on the taxpayer under the applicable law, then gross receipts shall include the amounts received that are allocable to the payment of such tax.

(3) Examples. The following examples illustrate the provisions of paragraph (f) of this section:

Example (1). X, a calendar year C corporation, was formed on January 1, 1986. Assume that in 1986 X has gross receipts of $15 million. For taxable year 1987, this section applies to X because in 1986, the period during which X was in existence, X has average annual gross receipts of more than $5 million.

Example (2). Y, a calendar year C corporation that is not a qualified personal service corporation, has gross receipts of $10 million, $9 million, and $4 million for taxable years 1984, 1985, and 1986, respectively. In taxable year 1986, X has average annual gross receipts for the 3-taxable-year period ending with 1986 of $7.67 million ($10 million + 9 million + 4 million/3). Thus, for taxable year 1987, this section applies and Y must change from the cash method for such year.

Example (3). Z, a C corporation which is not a qualified personal service corporation, has a 5% partnership interest in ZAB partnership, a calendar year cash method taxpayer. All other partners of ZAB partnership are individuals. Z corporation has average annual gross receipts of $100,000 for the 3-taxable-year period ending with 1986, (i.e., 1984, 1985, and 1986). The ZAB partnership has average annual gross receipts of $6 million for the same 3-taxable-year period. Since ZAB fails to meet the $5,000,000 gross receipts test for 1986, this section applies to ZAB for its taxable year beginning January 1, 1987. Accordingly, ZAB must change from the cash method for its 1987 taxable year. The gross receipts of Z corporation are not relevant in determining whether ZAB is subject to this section.

Example (4). The facts are the same as in example (3), except that during the 1987 taxable year of ZAB, the Z corporation transfers its partnership interest in ZAB to an individual. Under paragraph (a)(l) of this section, ZAB is treated as a partnership with a C corporation as a partner. Thus, this section requires ZAB to change from the cash method effective for its taxable year 1987. If ZAB later desires to change its method of accounting to the cash method for its taxable year beginning January 1, 1988 (or later), ZAB must comply with all requirements of law, including sections 446(b), 446(e), 481, to effect the change.

Example (5). X, a C corporation that is not a qualified personal service corporation, was formed on January 1, 1986, in a transaction described in section 351. In the transaction, A, an individual, contributed all of the assets and liabilities of B, a trade or business, to X, in return for the receipt of all of the outstanding stock of X. Assume that in 1986 X has gross receipts of $4 million. In 1984 and 1985, the gross receipts of B, the trade or business, were $10 million and $7 million, respectively. The gross receipts test is applied for the period during which X and its predecessor trade or business were in existence. X has average annual gross receipts for the 3-taxable-year period ending with 1986 of $7 million ($10 million + $7 million + $4 million/3). Thus, for taxable year 1987, this section applies and X must change from the cash method for such year.

* * *

§ 1.448–2T Nonaccrual of certain amounts by service providers (temporary).

(a) In general. Except as otherwise provided, this section applies to any person using an accrual method of accounting with respect to amounts to be received from the performance of services by such person. This section applies to such persons regardless of whether such persons changed their method of accounting from the cash method under section 448. For example, this section applies to a taxpayer who used an overall accrual method of accounting in taxable years prior to 1987.

(b) Nonaccrual-experience method; treatment as method of accounting. Any person to whom this section applies is not required to accrue any portion of amounts to be received from the performance of services which, on the basis of experience, will not be collected. This nonaccrual of amounts to be received for the performance of services shall be treated as a method of accounting under the Code (the nonaccrual-experience method).

(c) Method not available if interest charged on amounts due—(1) In general. The nonaccrual-experience method of accounting may not be used with respect to amounts due for which interest is required to be paid, or for which there is any penalty for failure to timely pay any amounts due. For this purpose, interest or penalties for late payment will be deemed to be charged by a taxpayer if such treatment is in accordance with the economic substance of a transaction, regardless of the characterization of the transaction by the parties, or the treatment of the transaction under state or local law. However, the offering of a discount for early payment of an amount due will not be regarded as the charging of interest or penalties for late payment under this section, if (i) the full amount due is otherwise accrued as gross income by the taxpayer at the time the services are provided, and (ii) the discount for early payment is treated as an adjustment to gross income in the year of payment, if payment is received within the time required for allowance of such discount.

(2) Example. The provisions of this paragraph (c) may be illustrated by the following example:

Example. X uses an accrual method of accounting for amounts to be received from the provision of services. For such amounts, X has two billing methods. Under one method, for amounts that are more than 90 days past due, X charges interest at a market rate until such amounts (together with interest) are paid. Under the other billing method, X charges no interest for amounts past due. X cannot use the nonaccrual-experience method of accounting with respect to any of the amounts billed under the method that charges interest on amounts that are more than 90 days past due. X may, however, use the nonaccrual-experience method with respect to the amounts billed under the method that does not charge interest for amounts past due.

(d) Method not available for certain receivables. The nonaccrual-experience method of accounting may be used only with respect to amounts earned by the taxpayer and otherwise recognized in income (an account receivable) through the performance of services by such taxpayer. For example, the nonaccrual-experience method may not be used with respect to amounts owed to the taxpayer by reason of the taxpayer's activities with respect to (1) lending money; (2) selling goods; or (3) acquiring receivables or other rights to receive payment from other persons (including persons related to the taxpayer) regardless of whether those other persons earned such amounts through the provision of services.

(e) Use of experience to estimate uncollectible amounts—(1) In general. In determining the portion of any amount due which, on the basis of experience, will not be collected, the formula prescribed by paragraph (e)(2) of this section shall be used by the taxpayer with respect to each separate trade or business of the taxpayer. No other method or formula may be used by a taxpayer in determining the uncollectible amounts under this section.

(2) Six-year moving average—(i) General rule. For any taxable year the uncollectible amount of a receivable is the amount which bears the same ratio to the account receivable outstanding at the close of the taxable year as (A) the total bad debts (with respect to accounts receivable) sustained throughout the period consisting of the taxable year and the five preceding taxable years (or, with the approval of the Commissioner, a shorter period), adjusted for recoveries of bad debts during such period, bears to (B) the sum of the accounts receivable earned throughout the entire six (or fewer) taxable year period (i.e., the total amount of sales resulting in accounts receivable throughout the period). Accounts receivable described in paragraphs (c) and (d) of this section are not taken into account in computing the ratio.

(ii) Period of less than six years. A period shorter than six years generally will be appropriate only if there is a change in the type of a substantial portion of the outstanding accounts receivable such that the risk of loss is substantially increased. A decline in the general economic conditions in the area, which substantially increases the risk of loss, is a relevant factor in determining whether a shorter period is appropriate. However, approval to use a shorter period will not be granted unless the taxpayer supplies specific evidence that the loans outstanding at the close of the taxable years for the shorter period requested are not comparable in nature and risk to loans outstanding at the close of the six taxable years. A substantial increase in a taxpayer's bad debt experience, is not, by itself, sufficient to justify the use of a shorter period. If approval is granted to use a shorter period, the experience for the excluded taxable years shall not be used for any subsequent year. A request for approval to exclude the experience of a prior taxable year shall be made in accordance with the applicable procedures for requesting a letter ruling and shall include a statement of the reasons such experience should be excluded. A request will not be considered unless it is sent to the Commissioner at least 30 days before the close of the first taxable year for which such approval is requested.

(iii) Special rule for new taxpayers. In the case of any current taxable year which is preceded by less than 5 taxable years, paragraph (e)(2)(i) of this section shall be applied by using the experience of the current year and the actual number of preceding taxable years. However, for this purpose, experience from preceding taxable years of a predecessor trade or business may be used in applying paragraph (e)(2)(i) of this section.

(3) Mechanics of nonaccrual-experience method. The nonaccrual-experience method shall be applied with respect to each account receivable of the taxpayer which is eligible for such method. With respect to a particular account receivable, the taxpayer will determine, in the manner prescribed in paragraph (e) of this section, the amount of such account receivable that is not expected to be collected. Such determination shall be made only once with respect to each account receivable, regardless of the term of such receivable. The estimated uncollectible amount shall not be recognized as gross income. Thus, the amount recognized as gross income shall be the amount that would otherwise be recognized as gross income with respect to the account receivable, less the amount which is not expected to be collected. Upon the collection of the account receivable, additional gross income shall be recognized with respect to the collection of any amount not initially expected to be collected. Similarly, no bad debt deduction under section 166 for a wholly or partially worthless account receivable shall be allowed for any amount not previously taken into income under the nonaccrual-experience method.

(4) Examples. The following examples illustrate the provisions of paragraph (e) of this section:

Example (1). X is a calendar year service provider that uses an accrual method of accounting with respect to the amounts (accounts receivable) to be received from the provision of services. X does not require the payment of interest or penalties with respect to past due accounts receivable. Assume that under this section, X adopts for taxable year 1987 the nonaccrual-experience method of accounting with respect to its accounts receivable. Further, assume that X's accounts receivable and bad debt experience for the current and five preceding taxable years is as follows:

Years	Accounts receivables	Bad debts adjusted for recoveries
1982	$ 30,000	$ 5,700
1983	40,000	7,200
1984	50,000	11,000
1985	60,000	10,200
1986	70,000	14,000
1987	80,000	16,800
	$330,000	$64,900

Thus, the ratio of the bad debts (adjusted for recoveries) for the current and five preceding taxable years to the total accounts receivable over the same period is 19.67% ($64,900/$330,000). Assume that $49,300 of the total $80,000 of accounts receivable earned throughout the taxable year 1987 are outstanding as of the close of such year. Assume further that the $49,300 of the accounts receivable outstanding as of the close of the tax year 1987 consist of 10 separate accounts receivable. The uncollectible amount of each receivable is 19.67%. The amount of these accounts receivable and the uncollectible amount of each is as follows:

	Accounts receivable	Applicable ratio	Uncollectible amount
1.	$5,200	.1967	$1,022.84
2.	7,300	.1967	1,435.91
3.	3,200	.1967	629.44
4.	4,300	.1967	845.81
5.	1,700	.1967	334.39
6.	4,000	.1967	786.80
	Accounts receivable	Applicable ratio	Uncollectible amount
7.	6,300	.1967	1,239.21
8.	8,000	.1967	1,573.60
9.	3,200	.1967	629.44
10.	6,100	.1967	1,199.87
	49,300		9,697.31

For taxable year 1987, X will not accrue as income $9,697.31 of its accounts receivable of $49,300 outstanding as of the close of the year.

Example (2). The facts are the same as in example (1). In 1988 the entire amount of account receivable number 8 becomes wholly worthless. Since in 1987 X did not accrue as income under the nonaccrual-experience method $1,573.60 of that account receivable, no deduction under section 166 is allowable with respect to that amount of the account receivable; a deduction of $6,426.40 under section 166 is allowable for 1988.

Example (3). The facts are the same as in example (1). In 1988 X collects, in full, account receivable number 5. Accordingly, in 1988 X must recognize additional gross income of $334.39, the amount of the account receivable that was initially considered uncollectible.

* * *

(f) [Reserved].

(g) Coordination of change in accounting method with section 481—(1) Taxpayers required to change their method of accounting under section 448. The provisions of this paragraph (g)(1) apply to taxpayers who under § 1.448–1T(h) change from the cash method as required by section 448 and who also change under paragraph (h) of this section to a method of accounting that includes the nonaccrual-experience method. With respect to such taxpayers, the section 481(a) adjustment resulting from the change in method of accounting to the nonaccrual-experience method shall be combined or netted with the section 481(a) adjustment applicable to the change in method of accounting required under section 448. The resulting amount shall then be taken into account in accordance with the provisions of § 1.448–1T(g) applicable to the change in method of accounting required by section 448.

(2) Taxpayers not required to change their method of accounting under section 448. The provisions of this paragraph (g)(2) apply to taxpayers who are not required by section 448 to change their method of accounting (e.g., taxpayers who were using an accrual method of accounting for taxable years preceding 1987) and who change to the nonaccrual-experience method under paragraph (h)(3) of this section. With respect to such taxpayers, the section 481(a) adjustment resulting from the change in method of accounting to the nonaccrual-experience method shall be taken into account ratably over four taxable years. The provisions of this paragraph (g)(2) shall apply to any taxpayer regardless of whether such taxpayer was required to change its method of accounting for bad debts under section 805 of the Tax Reform Act of 1986.

(h) Changes in method of accounting to nonaccrual-experience method.— (1) Automatic changes to overall accrual method. The provisions of this paragraph (h)(1) apply to taxpayers who change from the cash method as required by section 448, and change to an overall accrual method of accounting under the automatic change provisions of § 1.448–1T(h)(2). Taxpayers to whom this paragraph (h)(1) applies may automatically change their method of accounting to the nonaccrual-experience method under this paragraph (h)(1), if they otherwise qualify under this section for the use of such method. Taxpayers changing to the nonaccrual-experience method under this paragraph (h)(l) shall comply with the provisions of § 1.448–1T(h)(2). Moreover, such taxpayers shall type or legibly print the following statement at the top of page 1 of Form 3115: "Automatic Change to Nonaccrual Experience Method—Section 448." The consent of the Commissioner to the change in method of accounting is granted to taxpayers changing to the nonaccrual-experience method under this paragraph (h)(1).

(2) Changes to a method other than overall accrual method. The provisions of this paragraph (h)(2) apply to taxpayers who change from the cash method as required by section 448 and who also change to a permissible special method of accounting under § 1.448–1T(h)(3). Taxpayers to whom this paragraph (h)(2) applies may change their method of accounting to the nonaccrual-experience method under this paragraph (h)(2). Taxpayers changing to the nonaccrual-experience method under this paragraph (h)(2) shall comply with the provisions of § 1.448–1T (h)(3). Moreover, such taxpayers shall type or legibly print the following statement on the top of page 1 of Form 3115: "Change to Nonaccrual-Experience Method and Special Method of Accounting–Section 448." The consent of the Commissioner to the change in method of accounting is granted to taxpayers changing to the nonaccrual-experience method under this paragraph (h)(2).

(3) Taxpayers not required to change their method of accounting under section 448. The provisions of this paragraph (h)(3) apply to taxpayers who are not required by section 448 to change their method of accounting for the taxable year in which such taxpayers desire to adopt the nonaccrual-experience method (e.g., taxpayers who were using an accrual method of accounting for taxable years preceding 1987). Such taxpayers may automatically change their method of accounting to the nonaccrual-experience method under the provisions of this paragraph (h)(3), for their taxable year beginning in 1987, if they otherwise qualify under the provisions of this section for the use of such method. Taxpayers changing to the nonaccrual-experience method for their taxable year beginning in 1987 shall complete and file a current Form 3115. The Form 3115 shall be filed no later than the due date (including extension) of the taxpayer's federal income tax return for the year of change and shall be attached to that return. Moreover, the taxpayer shall type or legibly print the following statement at the top of page 1 of Form 3115: "Automatic Change to Nonaccrual Experience Method—Taxpayer not Required to Change Method of Accounting Under Section 448. The consent of the Commissioner to the change in method of accounting is granted to taxpayers changing to the nonaccrual-experience method for their taxable year beginning in 1987 under this paragraph (h)(3). With respect to taxpayers described in this paragraph (h)(3) who desire to change to the nonaccrual-experience method for a taxable year beginning after December 31, 1987, such taxpayers shall submit an application for change in accounting method under the administrative procedures applicable to taxpayers at the time of change, including the applicable procedures regarding the time and place of filing the application for change in method. Taxpayers described in the preceding sentence include taxpayers who were required to change their method of accounting under section 448 for an earlier taxable year, but who did not change to the nonaccrual-experience method at that time.

(i) Effective date. This section applies to any taxable year beginning after December 31, 1986.

Taxable Year For Which Items Of Gross Income Included

§ 1.451–1 General rule for taxable year of inclusion.

(a) General rule. Gains, profits, and income are to be included in gross income for the taxable year in which they are actually or constructively received by the taxpayer unless includible for a different year in accordance with the taxpayer's method of accounting. Under an accrual method of accounting, income is includible in gross income when all the events have occurred which fix the right to receive such income and the amount thereof can be determined with reasonable accuracy. Therefore, under such a method of accounting if, in the case of compensation for services, no determination can be made as to the right to such compensation or the amount thereof until the services are completed, the amount of compensation is ordinarily income for the taxable year in which the determination can be made. Under the cash receipts and disbursements method of accounting, such an amount is includible in gross income when actually or constructively received. Where an amount of income is properly accrued on the basis of a reasonable estimate and the exact amount is subsequently determined, the difference, if any, shall be taken into account for the taxable year in which such determination is made. To the extent that income is attributable to the recovery of bad debts for accounts charged off in prior years, it is includible in the year of recovery in accordance with the taxpayer's method of accounting, regardless of the date when the amounts were charged off. For treatment of bad debts and bad debt recoveries, see sections 166 and 111 and the regulations thereunder. For rules relating to the treatment of amounts received in crop shares, see section 61 and the regulations thereunder. For the year in which a partner must include his distributive share of partnership income, see section 706(a) and paragraph (a) of § 1.706–1. If a taxpayer ascertains that an item should have been included in gross income in a prior taxable year, he should, if within the period of limitation, file an amended return and pay any additional tax due. Similarly, if a taxpayer ascertains that an item was improperly included in gross income in a prior taxable year, he should, if within the period of limitation, file claim for credit or refund of any overpayment of tax arising therefrom.

(b) Special rule in case of death. **(1)** A taxpayer's taxable year ends on the date of his death. See section 443(a)(2) and paragraph (a)(2) of § 1.443–1. In computing taxable income for such year, there shall be included only amounts properly includible under the method of accounting used by the taxpayer. However, if the taxpayer used an accrual method of accounting, amounts accrued only by reason of his death shall not be included in computing taxable income for such year. If the taxpayer uses no regular accounting method, only amounts actually or constructively received during such year shall be included. (For rules relating to the inclusion of partnership income in the return of a decedent partner, see subchapter K, chapter 1 of the Code, and the regulations thereunder.)

(2) If the decedent owned an installment obligation the income from which was taxable to him under section 453, no income is required to be reported in the return of the decedent by reason of the transmission at death of such obligation. See section 453(d)(3). For the treatment of installment obligations acquired by the decedent's estate or by any person by bequest, devise, or inheritance from the decedent, see section 691(a)(4) and the regulations thereunder.

* * *

§ 1.451–2 Constructive receipt of income.

(a) General rule. Income although not actually reduced to a taxpayer's possession is constructively received by him in the taxable year during which it is credited to his account, set apart for him, or otherwise made available so that he may draw upon it at any time, or so that he could have drawn upon it during the taxable year if notice of intention to withdraw had been given. However, income is not constructively received if the taxpayer's control of its receipt is subject to substantial limitations or restrictions. Thus, if a corporation credits its employees with bonus stock, but the stock is not available to such employees until some future date, the mere crediting on the books of the corporation does not constitute receipt. In the case of interest, dividends, or other earnings (whether or not credited) payable in respect of any deposit or account in a bank, building and loan association, savings and loan association, or similar institution, the following are not substantial limitations or restrictions on the taxpayer's control over the receipt of such earnings:

(1) A requirement that the deposit or account, and the earnings thereon, must be withdrawn in multiples of even amounts;

(2) The fact that the taxpayer would, by withdrawing the earnings during the taxable year, receive earnings that are not substantially less in comparison with the earnings for the corresponding period to which the taxpayer would be entitled had he left the account on deposit until a later date (for example, if an amount equal to three months' interest must be forfeited upon withdrawal or redemption before maturity of a one year or less certificate of deposit, time deposit, bonus plan, or other deposit arrangement then the earnings payable on premature withdrawal or redemption would be substantially less when compared with the earnings available at maturity);

(3) A requirement that the earnings may be withdrawn only upon a withdrawal of all or part of the deposit or account. However, the mere fact that such institutions may pay earnings on withdrawals, total or partial, made during the last three business days of any calendar month ending a regular quarterly or semiannual earnings period at the applicable rate calculated to the end of such calendar month shall not constitute constructive receipt of income by any depositor or account holder in any such institution who has not made a withdrawal during such period;

(4) A requirement that a notice of intention to withdraw must be given in advance of the withdrawal. In any case when the rate of earnings payable in respect of such a deposit or account depends on the amount of notice of intention to withdraw that is given, earnings at the maximum rate are constructively received during the taxable year regardless of how long the deposit or account was held during the year or whether, in fact, any notice of intention to withdraw is given during the year. However, if in the taxable year of withdrawal the depositor or account holder receives a lower rate of earnings because he failed to give the required notice of intention to withdraw, he shall be allowed an ordinary loss in such taxable year in an amount equal to the difference between the amount of earnings previously included in gross income and the amount of earnings actually received. See section 165 and the regulations thereunder.

(b) Examples of constructive receipt. Amounts payable with respect to interest coupons which have matured and are payable but which have not been cashed are constructively received in the taxable year during which the coupons mature, unless it can be shown that there are no funds available for payment of the interest during such year. Dividends on corporate stock are constructively received when unqualifiedly made subject to the demand of the shareholder. However, if a dividend is declared payable on December 31 and the corporation followed its usual practice of paying the dividends by checks mailed so that the shareholders would not receive them until January of the following year, such dividends are not considered to have been constructively received in December. Generally, the amount of dividends or interest credited on savings bank deposits or to shareholders of organizations such as building and loan associations or cooperative banks is income to the depositors or shareholders for the taxable year when credited. However, if any portion of such dividends or interest is not subject to withdrawal at the time credited, such portion is not constructively received and does not constitute income to the depositor or shareholder until the taxable year in which the portion first may be withdrawn. Accordingly, if, under a bonus or forfeiture plan, a portion of the dividends or interest is accumulated and may not be withdrawn until the maturity of the plan, the crediting of such portion to the account of the shareholder or depositor does not constitute constructive receipt. In this case, such credited portion is income to the depositor or shareholder in the year in which the plan matures. * * * Accrued interest on unwithdrawn insurance policy dividends is gross income to the taxpayer for the first taxable year during which such interest may be withdrawn by him.

* * *

§ 1.451–5 Advance payments for goods and long–term contracts.

(a) Advance payment defined. (1) For purposes of this section, the term "advance payment" means any amount which is received in a taxable year by a taxpayer using an accrual method of accounting for purchases and sales or a long-term contract method of accounting (described in § 1.451–3), pursuant to, and to be applied against, an agreement:

(i) For the sale or other disposition in a future taxable year of goods held by the taxpayer primarily for sale to customers in the ordinary course of his trade or business, or

(ii) For the building, installing, constructing or manufacturing by the taxpayer of items where the agreement is not completed within such taxable year.

(2) For purposes of subparagraph (1) of this paragraph:

(i) The term "agreement" includes (a) a gift certificate that can be redeemed for goods, and (b) an agreement which obligates a taxpayer to perform activities described in subparagraph (1)(i) or (ii) of this paragraph and which also contains an obligation to perform services that are to be performed as an integral part of such activities; and

(ii) Amounts due and payable are considered "received."

(3) If a taxpayer (described in subparagraph (1) of this paragraph) receives an amount pursuant to, and to be applied against, an agreement that not only obligates the taxpayer to perform the activities described in subparagraph (1)(i) and (ii) of this paragraph, but also obligates the taxpayer to perform services that are not to be performed as an integral part of such activities, such amount will be treated as an "advance payment" (as defined in subparagraph (1) of this paragraph) only to the extent such amount is properly allocable to the obligation to perform the activities described in subparagraph (1)(i) and (ii) of this paragraph. The portion of the amount not so allocable will not be considered an "advance payment" to which this section applies. If, however, the amount not so allocable is less than 5 percent of the total contract price, such amount will be treated as so allocable except that such treatment cannot result in delaying the time at which the taxpayer would otherwise accrue the amounts attributable to the activities described in subparagraph (1)(i) and (ii) of this paragraph.

(b) Taxable year of inclusion—(1) In general. Advance payments must be included in income either—

(i) In the taxable year of receipt; or

(ii) Except as provided in paragraph (c) of this section.

(a) In the taxable year in which properly accruable under the taxpayer's method of accounting for tax purposes if such method results in including advance payments in gross receipts no later than the time such advance payments are included in gross receipts for purposes of all of his reports (including consolidated financial statements) to shareholders, partners, beneficiaries, other proprietors, and for credit purposes, or

(b) If the taxpayer's method of accounting for purposes of such reports results in advance payments (or any portion of such payments) being included in gross receipts earlier than for tax purposes, in the taxable year in which includible in gross receipts pursuant to his method of accounting for purposes of such reports.

(2) Examples. This paragraph may be illustrated by the following examples:

Example (1). S, a retailer who uses for tax purposes and for purposes of the reports referred to in subparagraph (1)(ii)(a) of this paragraph, an accrual method of accounting under which it accounts for its sales of goods when the goods are shipped, receives advance payments for such goods. Such advance payments must be included in gross receipts for tax purposes either in the taxable year the payments are received or in the taxable year such goods are shipped (except as provided in paragraph (c) of this section).

Example (2). T, a manufacturer of household furniture, is a calendar year taxpayer who uses an accrual method of accounting pursuant to which income is accrued when furniture is shipped for purposes of its financial reports (referred to in subparagraph (1)(ii)(a) of this paragraph) and an accrual method of accounting pursuant to which the income is accrued when furniture is delivered and accepted for tax purposes. See § 1.446–1(c)(1)(ii). In 1974, T receives an advance payment of $8,000 from X with respect to an order of furniture to be manufactured for X for a total price of $20,000. The furniture is shipped to X in December 1974, but it is not delivered to and accepted by X until January 1975. As a result of this contract, T must include the entire advance payment in its gross income for tax purposes in 1974 pursuant to subparagraph (1)(ii)(b) of this paragraph. T must include the remaining $12,000 of the gross contract price in its gross income in 1975 for tax purposes.

(3) Long-term contracts. In the case of a taxpayer accounting for advance payments for tax purposes pursuant to a long-term contract method of accounting under § 1.460-4, or of a taxpayer accounting for advance payments with respect to a long-term contract pursuant to an accrual method of accounting referred to in the succeeding sentence, advance payments shall be included in income in the taxable year in which properly included in gross receipts pursuant to such method of accounting (without regard to the financial reporting requirement contained in subparagraph (1)(ii) (a) or (b) of this paragraph). An accrual method of accounting to which the preceding sentence applies shall consist of any method of accounting under which the income is accrued when, and costs are accumulated until, the subject matter of the contract (or, if the subject matter of the contract consists of more than one item, an item) is shipped, delivered, or accepted.

(4) Installment method. The financial reporting requirement of subparagraph (1)(ii) (a) or (b) of this paragraph shall not be construed to prevent the use of the installment method under section 453. See § 1.446-l(c)(l)(ii).

(c) Exception for inventoriable goods. (1) (i) If a taxpayer receives an advance payment in a taxable year with respect to an agreement for the sale of goods properly includible in his inventory, or with respect to an agreement (such as a gift certificate) which can be satisfied with goods or a type of goods that cannot be identified in such taxable year, and on the last day of such taxable year the taxpayer—

(a) Is accounting for advance payments pursuant to a method described in paragraph (b)(1)(ii) of this section for tax purposes,

(b) Has received "substantial advance payments" (as defined in subparagraph (3) of this paragraph) with respect to such agreement, and

(c) Has on hand (or available to him in such year through his normal source of supply) goods of substantially similar kind and in sufficient quantity to satisfy the agreement in such year,

then all advance payments received with respect to such agreement by the last day of the second taxable year following the year in which such substantial advance payments are received, and not previously included in income in accordance with the taxpayer's accrual method of accounting, must be included in income in such second taxable year.

(ii) If advance payments are required to be included in income in a taxable year solely by reason of subdivision (i) of this subparagraph, the taxpayer must take into account in such taxable year the costs and expenditures included in inventory at the end of such year with respect to such goods (or substantially similar goods) on hand or, if no such goods are on hand by the last day of such second taxable year, the estimated cost of goods necessary to satisfy the agreement.

(iii) Subdivision (ii) of this subparagraph does not apply if the goods or type of goods with respect to which the advance payment is received are not identifiable in the year the advance payments are required to be included in income by reason of subdivision (i) of this subparagraph (for example, where an amount is received for a gift certificate).

(2) If subparagraph (1)(i) of this paragraph is applicable to advance payments received with respect to an agreement, any advance payments received with respect to such agreement subsequent to such second taxable year must be included in gross income in the taxable year of receipt. To the extent estimated costs of goods are taken into account in a taxable year pursuant to subparagraph (1)(ii) of this paragraph, such costs may not again be taken into account in another year. In addition, any variances between the costs or estimated costs taken into account pursuant to subparagraph (1)(ii) of this paragraph and the costs actually incurred in fulfilling the taxpayer's obligations under the agreement must be taken into account as an adjustment to the cost of goods sold in the year the taxpayer completes his obligations under such agreement.

(3) For purposes of subparagraph (1) of this paragraph, a taxpayer will be considered to have received "substantial advance payments" with respect to an agreement by the last day of a taxable year if the advance payments received with respect to such agreement during such taxable year plus the advance payments received prior to such taxable year pursuant to such agreement, equal or exceed the total costs and expenditures reasonably estimated as includible in inventory with respect to such agreement. Advance payments received in a taxable year with respect to an agreement (such as a gift certificate) under which the goods or type of goods to be sold are not identifiable in such year shall be treated as "substantial advance payments" when received.

(4) The application of this paragraph is illustrated by the following example:

Example. In 1971, X, a calendar year accrual method taxpayer, enters into a contract for the sale of goods (properly includible in X's inventory) with a total contract price of $100. X estimates that his total inventoriable costs and expenditures for the goods will be $50. X receives the following advance payments with respect to the contract:

1971	$35
1972	20
1973	15
1974	10
1975	10
1976	10

The goods are delivered pursuant to the customer's request in 1977. X's closing inventory for 1972 of the type of goods involved in the contract is sufficient to satisfy the contract. Since advance payments received by the end of 1972 exceed the inventoriable costs X estimates that he will incur, such payments constitute "substantial advance payments". Accordingly, all payments received by the end of 1974, the end of the second taxable year following the taxable year during which "substantial advance payments" are received, are includible in gross income for 1974. Therefore, for taxable year 1974 X must include $80 in his gross income. X must include in his cost of goods sold for 1974 the cost of such goods (or similar goods) on hand or, if no such goods are on hand, the estimated inventoriable costs necessary to satisfy the contract. Since no further deferral is allowable for such contract, X must include in his gross income for the remaining years of the contract, the advance payment received each year. Any variance between estimated costs and the costs actually incurred in fulfilling the contract is to be taken into account in 1977, when the goods are delivered. See paragraph (c)(2) of this section.

* * *

Taxable Year for Which Deductions Taken

§ 1.461–0 Table of contents.

This section lists the captions that appear in the regulations under section 461 of the Internal Revenue Code.

(1) In general.

(2) Liabilities arising under a workers compensation act or out of any tort, breach of contract, or violation of law.

(3) Rebates and refunds.

(4) Awards, prizes, and jackpots.

(5) Insurance, warranty, and service contracts.

(6) Taxes.

(7) Other liabilities.

(8) Examples.

(h) Liabilities arising under the Nuclear Waste Policy Act of 1982.

(i) [Reserved]

(j) Contingent liabilities. [Reserved]

(k) Special effective dates.

(1) In general.

(2) Long-term contracts.

(3) Payment liabilities.

(l) [Reserved]

(m) Change in method of accounting required by this section.

(1) In general.

(2) Change in method of accounting for long-term contracts and payment liabilities.

§ 1.461–5 Recurring item exception.

(a) In general.

(b) Requirements for use of the exception.

(1) General rule.

(2) Amended returns.

(3) Liabilities that are recurring in nature.

(4) Materiality requirement.

(5) Matching requirement.

(c) Types of liabilities not eligible for treatment under the recurring item exception.

(d) Time and manner of adopting the recurring item exception.

(1) In general.

(2) Change to the recurring item exception method for the first taxable year beginning after December 31, 1991.

(3) Retroactive change to the recurring item exception method.

(e) Examples.

§ 1.461–6 Economic performance when certain liabilities are assigned or are extinguished by the establishment of a fund.

(a) Qualified assignments of certain personal injury liabilities under section 130.

(b) Section 468B.

(c) Payments to other funds or persons that constitute economic performance. [Reserved]

(d) Effective dates.

§ 1.461–1 General rule for taxable year of deduction.

(a) General rule—(1) Taxpayer using cash receipts and disbursements method. Under the cash receipts and disbursements method of accounting, amounts representing allowable deductions shall, as a general rule, be taken into account for the taxable year in which paid. Further, a taxpayer using this method may also be entitled to certain deductions in the computation of taxable income which do not involve cash disbursements during the taxable year, such as the deductions for depreciation, depletion, and losses under sections 167, 611, and 165, respectively. If an expenditure results in the creation of an asset having a useful life which extends substantially beyond the close of the taxable year, such an expenditure may not be deductible, or may be deductible only in part, for the taxable year in which made. An example is an expenditure for the construction of improvements by the lessee on leased property where the estimated life of the improvements is in excess of the remaining period of the lease. In such a case, in lieu of the allowance for depreciation provided by section 167, the basis shall be amortized ratably over the remaining period of the lease. See section 178 and the regulations thereunder for rules governing the effect to be given renewal options in determining whether the useful life of the improvements exceeds the remaining term of the lease where a lessee begins improvements on leased property after July 28, 1958, other than improvements which on such date and at all times thereafter, the lessee was under a binding legal obligation to make. See section 263 and the regulations thereunder for rules relating to capital expenditures. See section 467 and the regulations thereunder for rules under which a liability arising out of the use of property pursuant to a section 467 rental agreement is taken into account.

(2) Taxpayer using an accrual method.—(i) In general. Under an accrual method of accounting, a liability (as defined in § 1.446–1(c)(1)(ii)(B)) is incurred, and generally is taken into account for Federal income tax purposes, in the taxable year in which all the events have occurred that establish the fact of the liability, the amount of the liability can be determined with reasonable accuracy, and economic performance has occurred with respect to the liability. (See paragraph (a)(2)(iii)(A) of this section for examples of liabilities that may not be taken into account until a taxable year subsequent to the taxable year incurred, and see §§ 1.461–4 through 1.461–6 for rules relating to economic performance.) Applicable provisions of the Code, the Income Tax Regulations, and other guidance published by the Secretary prescribe the manner in which a liability that has been incurred is taken into account. For example, section 162 provides that the deductible liability generally is taken into account in the taxable year incurred through a deduction from gross income. As a further example, under section 263 or 263A, a liability that relates to the creation of an asset having a useful life extending substantially beyond the close of the taxable year is taken into account in the taxable year incurred through capitalization (within the meaning of § 1.263A–1(c)(3)), and may later affect the computation of taxable income through depreciation or otherwise over a period including subsequent taxable years, in accordance with applicable Internal Revenue Code sections and guidance published by the Secretary. The principles of this paragraph (a)(2) also apply in the calculation of earnings and profits and accumulated earnings and profits.

(ii) Uncertainty as to the amount of a liability. While no liability shall be taken into account before economic performance and all of the events that fix the liability have occurred, the fact that the exact amount of the liability cannot be determined does not prevent a taxpayer from taking into account that portion of the amount of the liability which can be computed with reasonable accuracy within the taxable year. For example, A renders services to B during the taxable year for which A charges $10,000. B admits a liability to A for $6,000 but contests the remainder. B may take into account only $6,000 as an expense for the taxable year in which the services were rendered.

(iii) Alternative timing rules. **(A)** If any provision of the Code requires a liability to be taken into account in a taxable year later than the taxable year provided in paragraph (a)(2)(i) of this section, the liability is taken into account as prescribed in that Code provision. See, for example, section 267 (transactions between related parties) and section 464 (farming syndicates).

(B) If the liability of a taxpayer is subject to section 170 (charitable contributions), section 192 (black lung benefit trusts), section 194A (employer liability trusts), section 468 (mining and solid waste disposal reclamation and closing costs), or section 468A(a) (certain nuclear decommissioning costs), the liability is taken into account as determined under that section and not under section 461 or the regulations thereunder. For special rules relating to certain loss deductions, see sections 165(e), 165(i), and 165(1), relating to theft losses, disaster losses, and losses from certain deposits in qualified financial institutions.

(C) Section 461 and the regulations thereunder do not apply to any amount allowable under a provision of the Code as a deduction for a reserve for estimated expenses.

(D) Except as otherwise provided in any Internal Revenue regulations, revenue procedure, or revenue ruling, the economic performance requirement of section 461(h) and the regulations thereunder is satisfied to the extent that any amount is otherwise deductible under section 404 (employer contributions to a plan of deferred compensation), section 404A (certain foreign deferred compensation plans), or section 419 (welfare benefit funds). See § 1.461–4(d) (2)(iii).

(E) Except as otherwise provided by regulations or other published guidance issued by the Commissioner (See §601.601(b)(2) of this chapter), in the case of a liability arising out of the use of property pursuant to a section 467 rental agreement, the all events test (including economic performance) is considered met in the taxable year in which the liability is to be taken into account under section 467 and the regulations thereunder.

(3) Effect in current taxable year of improperly accounting for a liability in a prior taxable year. Each year's return should be complete in itself, and taxpayers shall ascertain the facts necessary to make a correct return. The expenses, liabilities, or loss of one year generally cannot be used to reduce the income of a subsequent year. A taxpayer may not take into account in a return for a subsequent taxable year liabilities that, under the taxpayer's method of accounting, should have been taken into account in a prior taxable year. If a taxpayer ascertains that a liability should have been taken into account in a prior taxable year, the taxpayer should, if within the period of limitation, file a claim for credit or refund of any overpayment of tax arising therefrom. Similarly, if a taxpayer ascertains that a liability was improperly taken into account in a prior taxable year, the taxpayer should, if within the period of limitation, file an amended return and pay any additional tax due. However, except as provided in section 905(c) and the regulations thereunder, if a liability is properly taken into account in an amount based on a computation made with reasonable accuracy and the exact amount of the liability is subsequently determined in a later taxable year, the difference, if any, between such amounts shall be taken into account for the later taxable year.

* * *

(b) Special rule in case of death. A taxpayer's taxable year ends on the date of his death. See section 443(a)(2) and paragraph (a)(2) of § 1.443–1. In computing taxable income for such year, there shall be deducted only amounts properly deductible under the method of accounting used by the taxpayer. However, if the taxpayer used an accrual method of accounting, no deduction shall be allowed for amounts accrued only by reason of his death. For rules relating to the inclusion of items of partnership deduction, loss, or credit in the return of a decedent partner, see subchapter K, chapter 1 of the Code, and the regulations thereunder.

(c) Accrual of real property taxes—(1) In general. If the accrual of real property taxes is proper in connection with one of the methods of accounting described in section 446(c), any taxpayer using such a method of accounting may elect to accrue any real property tax, which is related to a definite period of time, ratably over that period in the manner described in this paragraph. For example, assume that such an election is made by a calendar-year taxpayer whose real property taxes, applicable to the period from July 1, 1955, to June 30, 1956, amount to $1,200. Under section 461(c), $600 of such taxes accrue in the calendar year 1955, and the balance accrues in 1956. For special rule in the case of certain contested real property taxes in respect of which the taxpayer transfers money or other property to provide for the satisfaction of the contested tax, see § 1.461–2. For general rules relating to deductions for taxes, see section 164 and the regulations thereunder.

* * *

(5) Apportionment of taxes on real property between seller and purchaser. For apportionment of taxes on real property between seller and purchaser, see section 164(d) and the regulations thereunder.

* * *

§ 1.461–2 Contested liabilities.

(a) General rule—(1) Taxable year of deduction. If—

(i) The taxpayer contests an asserted liability,

(ii) The taxpayer transfers money or other property to provide for the satisfaction of the asserted liability,

(iii) The contest with respect to the asserted liability exists after the time of the transfer, and

(iv) But for the fact that the asserted liability is contested, a deduction would be allowed for the taxable year of the transfer (or, in the case of an accrual method taxpayer, for an earlier taxable year for which such amount would be accruable), then the deduction with respect to the contested amount shall be allowed for the taxable year of the transfer.

* * *

(3) Refunds includible in gross income. If any portion of the contested amount which is deducted under subparagraph (1) of this paragraph for the taxable year of transfer is refunded when the contest is settled, such portion is includible in gross income except as provided in § 1.111–1, relating to recovery of certain items previously deducted or credited. Such refunded amount is includible in gross income for the taxable year of receipt, or for an earlier taxable year if properly accruable for such earlier year.

(4) Examples. The provisions of this paragraph are illustrated by the following examples:

Example (1). X Corporation, which uses an accrual method of accounting, in 1964 contests $20 of a $100 asserted real property tax liability but pays the entire $100 to the taxing authority. In 1968, the contest is settled and X receives a refund of $5. X deducts $100 for the taxable year 1964, and includes $5 in gross income for the taxable year 1968 (assuming § 1.111–1 does not apply to such amount). If in 1964 X pays only $80 to the taxing authority, X deducts only $80 for 1964. The result would be the same if X Corporation used the cash method of accounting.

Example (2). Y Corporation makes its return on the basis of a calendar year and uses an accrual method of accounting. Y's real property taxes are assessed and become a lien on December 1, but are not payable until March 1 of the following year. On December 10, 1964, Y contests $20 of the $100 asserted real property tax which was assessed and became a lien on December 1, 1964. On March 1, 1965, Y pays the entire $100 to the taxing authority. In 1968, the contest is settled and Y receives a refund of $5. Y deducts $80 for the taxable year 1964, deducts $20 for the taxable year 1965, and includes $5 in gross income for the taxable year 1968 (assuming § 1.111–1 does not apply to such amount).

(b) Contest of asserted liability—Asserted liability. For purposes of paragraph (a)(**1**) of this section, the term "asserted liability" means an item with respect to which, but for the existence of any contest in respect of such item, a deduction would be allowable under an accrual method of accounting. For example, a notice of a local real estate tax assessment and a bill received for services may represent asserted liabilities.

(2) Definition of the term "contest." Any contest which would prevent accrual of a liability under section 461(a) shall be considered to be a contest in determining whether the taxpayer satisfies paragraph (a)(1)(i) of this section. A contest arises when there is a bona fide dispute as to the proper evaluation of the law or the facts necessary to determine the existence or correctness of the amount of an asserted liability. It is not necessary to institute suit in a court of law in order to contest an asserted liability. An affirmative act denying the validity or accuracy, or both, of an asserted liability to the person who is asserting such liability, such as including a written protest with payment of the asserted liability, is sufficient to commence a contest. Thus, lodging a protest in accordance with local law is sufficient to contest an asserted liability for taxes. It is not necessary that the affirmative act denying the validity or accuracy, or both, of an asserted liability be in writing if, upon examination of all the facts and circumstances, it can be established to the satisfaction of the Commissioner that a liability has been asserted and contested.

(3) Example. The provisions of this paragraph are illustrated by the following example:

Example. O Corporation makes its return on the basis of a calendar year and uses an accrual method of accounting. O receives a large shipment of typewriter ribbons from S Company on January 30, 1964, which O pays for in full on February 10, 1964. Subsequent to their receipt, several of the ribbons prove defective because of inferior materials used by the manufacturer. On August 9, 1964, O orally notifies S and demands refund of the full purchase price of the ribbons. After negotiations prove futile and a written demand is rejected by S, O institutes an action for the full purchase price. For purposes of paragraph (a)(1)(i) of this section, S has asserted a liability against O which O contests on August 9, 1964. O deducts the contested amount for 1964.

(c) Transfer to provide for the satisfaction of an asserted liability—(1) In general. A taxpayer may provide for the satisfaction of an asserted liability by transferring money or other property beyond his control **(i)** to—

(A) The person who is asserting the liability;

(B) An escrowee or trustee pursuant to a written agreement (among the escrowee or trustee, the taxpayer, and the person who is asserting the liability) that the money or other property be delivered in accordance with the settlement of the contest;

(C) An escrowee or trustee pursuant to an order of the United States or of any State or political subdivision thereof or any agency or instrumentality of the foregoing, or of a court, that the money or other property be delivered in accordance with the settlement of the contest; or

(D) A court with jurisdiction over the contest.

(ii) In order for money or other property to be beyond the control of a taxpayer, the taxpayer must relinquish all authority over the money or other property.

(iii) The following are not transfers to provide for the satisfaction of an asserted liability—

(A) Purchasing a bond to guarantee payment of the asserted liability;

(B) An entry on the taxpayer's books of account;

(C) A transfer to an account that is within the control of the taxpayer;

(D) A transfer of any indebtedness of the taxpayer or of any promise by the taxpayer to provide services or property in the future; and

(E) A transfer to a person (other than the person asserting the liability) of any stock of the taxpayer or of any stock or indebtedness of a person related to the taxpayer (as defined in section 267(b)).

(2) Examples. The provisions of this paragraph are illustrated by the following examples:

Example (1). M Corporation contests a $5,000 liability asserted against it by L Company for services rendered. To provide for the contingency that it might have to pay the liability, M establishes a separate bank account in its own name. M then transfers $5,000 from its general account to such separate account. Such transfer does not qualify as a transfer to provide for the satisfaction of an asserted liability because M has not transferred the money beyond its control.

Example (2). M Corporation contests a $5,000 liability asserted against it by L Company for services rendered. To provide for the contingency that it might have to pay the liability, M transfers $5,000 to an irrevocable trust pursuant to a written agreement among the trustee, M (the taxpayer), and L (the person who is asserting the liability) that the money shall be held until the contest is settled and then disbursed in accordance with the settlement. Such transfer qualifies as a transfer to provide for the satisfaction of an asserted liability.

(d) Contest exists after transfer. In order for a contest with respect to an asserted liability to exist after the time of transfer, such contest must be pursued subsequent to such time. Thus, the contest must have been neither settled nor abandoned at the time of the transfer. A contest may be settled by a decision, judgment, decree, or other order of any court of competent jurisdiction which has become final, or by written or oral agreement between the parties. For example, Z Corporation, which uses an accrual method of accounting, in 1964 contests a $100 asserted liability. In 1967 the contested liability is settled as being $80 which Z accrues and deducts for such year. In 1968 Z pays the $80. Section 461(f) does not apply to Z with respect to the transfer because a contest did not exist after the time of such transfer.

(e) Deduction otherwise allowed— (1) In general. The existence of the contest with respect to an asserted liability must prevent (without regard to section 461(f)) and be the only factor preventing a deduction for the taxable year of the transfer (or, in the case of an accrual method taxpayer, for an earlier taxable year for which such amount would be accruable) to provide for the satisfaction of such liability. Nothing in section 461(f) or this section shall be construed to give rise to a deduction since section 461(f) and this section relate only to the timing of deductions which are otherwise allowable under the Code.

(2) Application of economic performance rules to transfers under section 461(f). **(i)** A taxpayer using an accrual method of accounting is not allowed a deduction under section 461(f) in the taxable year of the transfer unless economic performance has occurred.

(ii) Economic performance occurs for liabilities requiring payment to another person arising out of any workers compensation act or any tort, or any other liability designated in § 1.461–4(g), as payments are made to the person to which the liability is owed. Except as provided in section 468B or the regulations thereunder, economic performance does not occur when a taxpayer transfers money or other property to a trust, an escrow account, or a court to provide for the satisfaction of an asserted workers compensation, tort, or other liability designated under § 1.461–4(g) that the taxpayer is contesting unless the trust, escrow account, or court is the person to which the liability is owed or the taxpayer's payment to the trust, escrow account, or court discharges the taxpayer's liability to the claimant. Rather, economic performance occurs in the taxable year the taxpayer transfers money or other property to the person that is asserting the workers compensation, tort, or other liability designated under § 1.461–4(g) that the taxpayer is contesting or in the taxable year that payment is made from a trust, an escrow account, or a court registry funded by the taxpayer to the person to which the liability is owed.

(3) Example. The provisions of this paragraph are illustrated by the following examples:

Example (1). A, an individual, makes a gift of certain property to B, an individual. A pays the entire amount of gift tax assessed against him but contests his liability for such tax. Section 275(a)(3) provides that gift taxes are not deductible. A does not satisfy the requirement of paragraph (a)(1)(iv) of this section since a deduction would not be allowed for the taxable year of the transfer even if A did not contest his liability for such tax.

Example (2). Corporation X is a defendant in a class action suit for tort liabilities. In 2002, X establishes a trust for the purpose of satisfying the asserted liability and transfers $10,000,000 to the trust. The trust does not satisfy the requirements of section 468B or the regulations thereunder. In 2004, the trustee pays $10,000,000 to the plaintiffs in settlement of the litigation. Under paragraph (e)(2) of this section, economic performance with respect to X's liability to the plaintiffs occurs in 2004. X may deduct the $10,000,000 payment to the plaintiffs in 2004.

(f) Treatment of money or property transferred to an escrowee, trustee, or court and treatment of any income attributable thereto. [Reserved]

* * *

§ 1.469–1T General rules (temporary).

(a) Passive activity loss and credit disallowed—

(1) In general. Except as otherwise provided in paragraph (a)(2) of this section—

(i) The passive activity loss for the taxable year shall not be allowed as a deduction; and

(ii) The passive activity credit for the taxable year shall not be allowed.

(2) Exceptions. Paragraph (a)(1) of this section shall not apply to the passive activity loss or the passive activity credit for the taxable year to the extent provided in—

(i) Section 469(i) and the rules to be contained in § 1.469–9T (relating to losses and credits attributable to certain rental real estate activities); and

(ii) Section 1.469–11T (relating to losses and credits attributable to certain pre-enactment interests in activities).

(b) Taxpayers to whom these rules apply. The rules of section 469 and the regulations thereunder generally apply to—

(1) Individuals;

(2) Trusts (other than trusts (or portions of trusts) described in section 671);

(3) Estates;

(4) Personal service corporations (within the meaning of paragraph (g)(2)(i) of this section); and

(5) Closely held corporations (within the meaning of paragraph (g)(2)(ii) of this section).

* * *

(d) Effect of section 469 and the regulations thereunder for other purposes—(1) Treatment of items of passive activity income and gain. Neither the provisions of section 469(a)(1) and paragraph (a)(1) of this section nor the characterization of items of income or deduction as passive activity gross income (within the meaning of § 1.469–2T(c)) or passive activity deductions (within the meaning of § 1.469–2T (d)) affects the treatment of any item of income or gain under any provision of the Internal Revenue Code other than section 469. The following example illustrates the application of this paragraph (d)(1):

Example. (i) In 1991, an individual's only income and loss from passive activities are a $10,000 capital gain from passive activity X and a $12,000 ordinary loss from passive activity Y. The taxpayer also has a $10,000 capital loss that is not derived from a passive activity.

(ii) Under § 1.469–2T(b), the taxpayer has a $2,000 passive activity loss for the taxable year. The only effect of section 469 and the regulations thereunder is to disallow a deduction for the taxpayer's $2,000 passive activity loss for the taxable year. Thus, the taxpayer's capital loss for the taxable year is allowed because the $10,000 capital gain from passive activity X is taken into account under section 1211(b) in computing the taxpayer's allowable capital loss for the year.

* * *

(3) Treatment of passive activity losses. Except as otherwise provided by regulations, a deduction that is disallowed for a taxable year under section 469 and the regulations thereunder is not taken into account as a deduction that is allowed for the taxable year in computing the amount subject to any tax imposed by subtitle A of the Internal Revenue Code. The following example illustrates the application of this paragraph (d)(3):

Example. An individual has a $5,000 passive activity loss for a taxable year, all of which is disallowed under paragraph (a)(1) of this section. All of the disallowed loss is allocated under paragraph (f) of this section to activities that are trades or businesses (within the meaning of section 1402(c)). Such loss is not taken into account for the taxable year in computing the taxpayer's taxable income subject to tax under section 1. In addition, under this paragraph (d)(3), such loss is not taken into account for the taxable year in computing the taxpayer's net earnings from self-employment subject to tax under section 1401.

* * *

(g) Application of these rules to C corporations—(1) In general. Except as otherwise provided in the rules to be contained in paragraph (k) of this section, section 469 and the regulations thereunder do not apply to any corporation that is not a personal service corporation or a closely held corporation for the taxable year. See paragraphs (g)(4) and (5) of this section for special rules for computing the passive activity loss and passive activity credit, respectively, of a closely held corporation.

(2) Definitions. For purposes of section 469 and the regulations thereunder—

(i) The term "personal service corporation" means a C corporation that is a personal service corporation for the taxable year (within the meaning of § 1.441–4T(d)); and

(ii) The term "closely held corporation" means a C corporation that meets the stock ownership requirements of section 542(a)(2) (taking into account the modifications in section 465(a)(3)) for the taxable year and is not a personal service corporation for such year.

* * *

(4) Modified computation of passive activity loss in the case of closely held corporations.—(i) In general. A closely held corporation's passive activity loss for the taxable year is the amount, if any, by which the corporation's passive activity deductions for the taxable year (within the meaning of § 1.469–2T(d)) exceed the sum of—

(A) The corporation's passive activity gross income for the taxable year (within the meaning of § 1.469–2T(c)); and

(B) The corporation's net active income for the taxable year.

* * *

(5) Allowance of passive activity credit of closely held corporations to extent of net active income tax liability—(i) In general. Solely for purposes of determining the amount disallowed under paragraph (a)(1)(ii) of this section, a closely held corporation's passive activity credit for the taxable year shall be reduced by such corporation's net active income tax liability for such year.

* * *

§ 1.469–5T Material participation (temporary).

(a) In general. Except as provided in paragraphs (e) and (h)(2) of this section, an individual shall be treated, for purposes of section 469 and the regulations thereunder, as materially participating in an activity for the taxable year if and only if—

(1) The individual participates in the activity for more than 500 hours during such year;

(2) The individual's participation in the activity for the taxable year constitutes substantially all of the participation in such activity of all individuals (including individuals who are not owners of interests in the activity) for such year;

(3) The individual participates in the activity for more than 100 hours during the taxable year, and such individual's participation in the activity for the taxable year is not less than the participation in the activity of any other individual (including individuals who are not owners of interests in the activity) for such year;

(4) The activity is a significant participation activity (within the meaning of paragraph (c) of this section) for the taxable year, and the individual's aggregate participation in all significant participation activities during such year exceeds 500 hours;

(5) The individual materially participated in the activity (determined without regard to this paragraph (a)(5)) for any five taxable years (whether or not consecutive) during the ten taxable years that immediately precede the taxable year;

(6) The activity is a personal service activity (within the meaning of paragraph (d) of this section), and the individual materially participated in the activity for any three taxable years (whether or not consecutive) preceding the taxable year; or

(7) Based on all of the facts and circumstances (taking into account the rules in paragraph (b) of this section), the individual participates in the activity on a regular, continuous, and substantial basis during such year.

* * *

(c) Significant participation activity.— (1) In general. For purposes of paragraph (a)(4) of this section, an activity is a significant participation activity of an individual if and only if such activity—

(i) Is a trade or business activity (within the meaning of § 1.469–1T(e)(2)) in which the individual significantly participates for the taxable year; and

(ii) Would be an activity in which the individual does not materially participate for the taxable year if material participation for such year were determined without regard to paragraph (a)(4) of this section.

(2) Significant participation. An individual is treated as significantly participating in an activity for a taxable year if and only if the individual participates in the activity for more than 100 hours during such year.

(d) Personal service activity. An activity constitutes a personal service activity for purposes of paragraph (a)(6) of this section if such activity involves the performance of personal services in—

(1) The fields of health, law, engineering, architecture, accounting, actuarial science, performing arts, or consulting; or

(2) Any other trade or business in which capital is not a material income-producing factor.

* * *

Inventories

§ 1.471–1 Need for inventories.

In order to reflect taxable income correctly, inventories at the beginning and end of each taxable year are necessary in every case in which the production, purchase, or sale of merchandise is an income-producing factor. The inventory should include all finished or partly finished goods and, in the case of raw materials and supplies, only those which have been acquired for sale or which will physically become a part of merchandise intended for sale, in which class fall containers, such as kegs, bottles, and cases, whether returnable or not, if title thereto will pass to the purchaser of the product to be sold therein. Merchandise should be included in the inventory only if title thereto is vested in the taxpayer. Accordingly, the seller should include in his inventory goods under contract for sale but not yet segregated and applied to the contract and goods out upon consignment, but should exclude from inventory goods sold (including containers), title to which has passed to the purchaser. A purchaser should include in inventory merchandise purchased (including containers), title to which has passed to him, although such merchandise is in transit or for other reasons has not been reduced to physical possession, but should not include goods ordered for future delivery, transfer of title to which has not yet been effected. (But see § 1.472–1.)

§ 1.471–2 Valuation of inventories.

(a) Section 471 provides two tests to which each inventory must conform:

(1) It must conform as nearly as may be to the best accounting practice in the trade or business, and

(2) It must clearly reflect the income.

(b) It follows, therefore, that inventory rules cannot be uniform but must give effect to trade customs which come within the scope of the best accounting practice in the particular trade or business. In order to clearly reflect income, the inventory practice of a taxpayer should be consistent from year to year, and greater weight is to be given to consistency than to any particular method of inventorying or basis of valuation so long as the method or basis used is in accord with §§ 1.471–1 through 1.471–11.

(c) The bases of valuation most commonly used by business concerns and which meet the requirements of section 471 are (1) cost and (2) cost or market, whichever is lower. (For inventories by dealers in securities, see § 1.471–5.) Any goods in an inventory which are unsalable at normal prices or unusable in the normal way because of damage, imperfections, shop wear, changes of style, odd or broken lots, or other similar causes, including second-hand goods taken in exchange, should be valued at bona fide selling prices less direct cost of disposition, whether subparagraph (1) or (2) of this paragraph is used, or if such goods consist of raw materials or partly finished goods held for use or consumption, they shall be valued upon a reasonable basis, taking into consideration the usability and the condition of the goods, but in no case shall such value be less than the scrap value. Bona fide selling price means actual offering of goods during a period ending not later than 30 days after inventory date. The burden of proof will rest upon the taxpayer to show that such exceptional goods as are valued upon such selling basis come within the classifications indicated above, and he shall maintain such records of the disposition of the goods as will enable a verification of the inventory to be made.

(d) In respect of normal goods, whichever method is adopted must be applied with reasonable consistency to the entire inventory of the taxpayer's trade or business except as to those goods inventoried under the last-in, first-out method authorized by section 472 or to animals inventoried under the elective unit, livestock-price-method authorized by § 1.471–6. See paragraph (d) of § 1.446–1 for rules permitting the use of different methods of accounting if the taxpayer has more than one trade or business. Where the taxpayer is engaged in more than one trade or business the Commissioner may require that the method of valuing inventories with respect to goods in one trade or business also be used with respect to similar goods in other trades or businesses if, in the opinion of the Commissioner, the use of such method with respect to such other goods is essential to a clear reflection of income. Taxpayers were given an option to adopt the basis of either (1) cost or (2) cost or market, whichever is lower, for their 1920 inventories. The basis properly adopted for that year or any subsequent year is controlling, and a change can now be made only after permission is secured from the Commissioner. Application for permission to change the basis of valuing inventories shall be made in writing and filed with the Commissioner as provided in paragraph (e) of § 1.446–1. Goods taken in the inventory which have been so intermingled that they cannot be identified with specific invoices will be deemed to be the goods most recently purchased or produced, and the cost thereof will be the actual cost of the goods purchased or produced during the period in which the quantity of goods in the inventory has been acquired. But see section 472 as to last-in, first-out inventories. Where the taxpayer maintains book inventories in accordance with a sound accounting system in which the respective inventory accounts are charged with the actual cost of the goods purchased or produced and credited with the value of goods used, transferred, or sold, calculated upon the basis of the actual cost of the goods acquired during the taxable year (including the inventory at the beginning of the year), the net value as shown by such inventory accounts will be deemed to be the cost of the goods on hand. The balances shown by such book inventories should be verified by physical inventories at reasonable intervals and adjusted to conform therewith.

(e) Inventories should be recorded in a legible manner, properly computed and summarized, and should be preserved as a part of the accounting records of the taxpayer. The inventories of taxpayers on whatever basis taken will be subject to investigation by the district director, and the taxpayer must satisfy the district director of the correctness of the prices adopted.

(f) The following methods, among others, are sometimes used in taking or valuing inventories, but are not in accord with the regulations in this part:

(1) Deducting from the inventory a reserve for price changes, or an estimated depreciation in the value thereof.

(2) Taking work in process, or other parts of the inventory, at a nominal price or at less than its proper value.

(3) Omitting portions of the stock on hand.

(4) Using a constant price or nominal value for so-called normal quantity of materials or goods in stock.

(5) Including stock in transit, shipped either to or from the taxpayer, the title to which is not vested in the taxpayer.

(6) Segregating indirect production costs into fixed and variable production cost classifications (as defined in § 1.471–11(b)(3)(ii)) and allocating only the variable costs to the cost of goods produced while treating fixed costs as period costs which are currently deductible. This method is commonly referred to as the "direct cost" method.

(7) Treating all or substantially all indirect production costs (whether classified as fixed or variable) as period costs which are currently deductible. This method is generally referred to as the "prime cost" method.

§ 1.471–3 Inventories at cost.

Cost means:

(a) In the case of merchandise on hand at the beginning of the taxable year, the inventory price of such goods.

(b) In the case of merchandise purchased since the beginning of the taxable year, the invoice price less trade or other discounts, except strictly cash discounts approximating a fair interest rate, which may be deducted or not at the option of the taxpayer, provided a consistent course is followed. To this net invoice price should be added transportation or other necessary charges incurred in acquiring possession of the goods. For taxpayers acquiring merchandise for resale that are subject to the provisions of section 263A, see §§ 1.263A–1 and 1.263A–3 for additional amounts that must be included in inventory costs.

(c) In the case of merchandise produced by the taxpayer since the beginning of the taxable year, (1) the cost of raw materials and supplies entering into or consumed in connection with the product, (2) expenditures for direct labor, and (3) indirect production costs incident to and necessary for the production of the particular article, including in such indirect production costs an appropriate portion of management expenses, but not including any cost of selling or return on capital, whether by way of interest or profit. See §§ 1.263A–1 and 1.263A–2 for more specific rules regarding the treatment of production costs.

(d) In any industry in which the usual rules for computation of cost of production are inapplicable, costs may be approximated upon such basis as may be reasonable and in conformity with established trade practice in the particular industry. Among such cases are: (1) Farmers and raisers of livestock (see § 1.471–6); (2) miners and manufacturers who by a single process or uniform series of processes derive a product of two or more kinds, sizes, or grades, the unit cost of which is substantially alike (see § 1.471–7); and (3) retail merchants who use what is known as the "retail method" in ascertaining approximate cost (see § 1.471–8). Notwithstanding the other rules of this section, cost shall not include an amount which is of a type for which a deduction would be disallowed under section 162(c), (f), or (g) and the regulations thereunder in the case of a business expense.

§ 1.471–4 Inventories at cost or market, whichever is lower.

(a) In general—(1) Market definition. Under ordinary circumstances and for normal goods in an inventory, market means the aggregate of the current bid prices prevailing at the date of the inventory of the basic elements of cost reflected in inventories of goods purchased and on hand, goods in process of manufacture, and finished manufactured goods on hand. The basic elements of cost include direct materials, direct labor, and indirect costs required to be included in inventories by the taxpayer (e.g., under section 263A and its underlying regulations for taxpayers subject to that section). For taxpayers to which section 263A applies, for example, the basic elements of cost must reflect all direct costs and all indirect costs properly allocable to goods on hand at the inventory date at the current bid price of those costs, including but not limited to the cost of purchasing, handling, and storage activities conducted by the taxpayer, both prior to and subsequent to acquisition or production of the goods. The determination of the current bid price of the basic elements of costs reflected in goods on hand at the inventory date must be based on the usual volume of particular cost elements purchased (or incurred) by the taxpayer.

(2) Fixed price contracts. Paragraph (a)(1) of this section does not apply to any goods on hand or in process of manufacture for delivery upon firm sales contracts (i.e., those not legally subject to cancellation by either party) at fixed prices entered into before the date of the inventory, under which the taxpayer is protected against actual loss. Any such goods must be inventoried at cost.

(3) Examples. The valuation principles in paragraph (a)(1) of this section are illustrated by the following examples:

Example (1). (i) Taxpayer A manufactures tractors. A values its inventory using cost or market, whichever is lower, under paragraph (a)(1) of this section. At the end of 1994, the cost of one of A's tractors on hand is determined as follows:

Direct materials	$ 3,000
Direct labor	4,000
Indirect costs under section 263A	3,000
Total section 263A costs (cost)	10,000

(ii) A determines that the aggregate of the current bid prices of the materials, labor, and overhead required to reproduce the tractor at the end of 1994 are as follows:

Direct materials	$ 3,100
Direct labor	4,100
Indirect costs under section 263A	3,100
Total section 263A costs (market)	10,300

(iii) In determining the lower of cost or market value of the tractor, A compares the cost of the tractor, $10,000, with the market value of the tractor, $10,300, in accordance with paragraph (c) of this section. Thus, under this section, A values the tractor at $10,000.

Example (2). (i) Taxpayer B purchases and resells several lines of shoes and is subject to section 263A. B values its inventory using cost or market, whichever is lower, under paragraph (a)(1) of this section. At the end of 1994, the cost of one pair of shoes on hand is determined as follows:

Acquisition cost	$200
Indirect costs under section 263A	10
Total section 263A costs (cost)	210

(ii) B determines the aggregate current bid prices prevailing at the end of 1994 for the elements of cost (both direct costs and indirect costs incurred prior and subsequent to acquisition of the shoes) based on the volume of the elements usually purchased (or incurred) by B as follows:

Acquisition cost	$178
Indirect costs under section 263A	12
Total § 263A costs (market)	190

(iii) In determining the lower of cost or market value of the shoes, B compares the cost of the pair of shoes, $210, with the market value of the shoes, $190, in accordance with paragraph (c) of this section. Thus, under this section, B values the shoes at $190.

(b) Inactive markets. Where no open market exists or where quotations are nominal, due to inactive market conditions, the taxpayer must use such evidence of a fair market price at the date or dates nearest the inventory as may be available, such as specific purchases or sales by the taxpayer or others in reasonable volume and made in good faith, or compensation paid for cancellation of contracts for purchase commitments. Where the taxpayer in the regular course of business has offered for sale such merchandise at prices lower than the current price as above defined, the inventory may be valued at such prices less direct cost of disposition, and the correctness of such prices will be determined by reference to the actual sales of the taxpayer for a reasonable period before and after the date of the inventory. Prices which vary materially from the actual prices so ascertained will not be accepted as reflecting the market.

(c) Comparison of cost and market. Where the inventory is valued upon the basis of cost or market, whichever is lower, the market value of each article on hand at the inventory date shall be compared with the cost of the article, and the lower of such values shall be taken as the inventory value of the article.

* * *

§ 1.471–8 Inventories of retail merchants.

(a) Retail merchants who employ what is known as the "retail method" of pricing inventories may make their returns upon that method, provided that the use of such method is designated upon the return, that accurate accounts are kept, and that such method is consistently adhered to unless a change is authorized by the Commissioner as provided in paragraph (e) of § 1.446–1. Under the retail method the total of the retail selling prices of the goods on hand at the end of the year in each department or of each class of goods is reduced to approximate cost by deducting therefrom an amount which bears the same ratio to such total as—

(1) The total of the retail selling prices of the goods included in the opening inventory plus the retail selling prices of the goods purchased during the year, with proper adjustment to such selling prices for all mark-ups and mark-downs, less

(2) The cost of the goods included in the opening inventory plus the cost of the goods purchased during the year, bears to (1).

The result should represent as accurately as may be the amounts added to the cost price of the goods to cover selling and other expenses of doing business and for the margin of profit. See § 1.263A–1T for rules regarding the computation of costs with respect to property acquired for resale.

(b) For further adjustments to be made in the case of a retail merchant using the last-in, first-out inventory method authorized by section 472, see paragraph (k) of § 1.472–1.

(c) A taxpayer maintaining more than one department in his store or dealing in classes of goods carrying different percentages of gross profit should not use a percentage of profit based upon an average of his entire business, but should compute and use in valuing his inventory the proper percentages for the respective departments or classes of goods.

(d) A taxpayer (other than one using the last-in, first-out inventory method) who previously has determined inventories in accordance with the retail method, except that, to obtain a basis of approximate cost or market, whichever is lower, has consistently and uniformly followed the practice of adjusting the retail selling prices of the goods included in the opening inventory and purchased during the taxable year for mark-ups but not for mark-downs, may continue such practice subject to the conditions prescribed in this section. The adjustments must be bona fide and consistent and uniform. Where mark-downs are not included in the adjustments, mark-ups made to cancel or correct mark-downs shall not be included; and the mark-ups included must be reduced by the mark-downs made to cancel or correct such mark-ups.

(e) In no event shall mark-downs not based on actual reduction of retail sale prices, such as mark-downs based on depreciation and obsolescence, be recognized in determining the retail selling prices of the goods on hand at the end of the taxable year.

(f) A taxpayer (other than one using the last-in, first-out inventory method) who previously has determined inventories without following the practice of eliminating mark-downs in making adjustments to retail selling prices may adopt such practice, provided permission to do so is obtained in accordance with, and subject to the terms provided by, paragraph (e) of § 1.446–1. A taxpayer filing a first return of income may adopt such practice subject to approval by the district director upon examination of the return.

(g) A taxpayer using the last-in, first-out inventory method in conjunction with retail computations must adjust retail selling prices for mark-downs as well as mark-ups, in order that there may be reflected the approximate cost of the goods on hand at the end of the taxable year regardless of market values.

* * *

§ 1.471–11 Inventories of manufacturers.*

(a) Use of full absorption method of inventory costing. In order to conform as nearly as may be possible to the best accounting practices and to clearly reflect income (as required by section 471 of the Code), both direct and indirect production costs must be taken into account in the computation of inventoriable costs in accordance with the "full absorption" method of inventory costing. Under the full absorption method of inventory costing production costs must be allocated to goods produced during the taxable year, whether sold during the taxable year or in inventory at the close of the taxable year determined in accordance with the taxpayer's method of identifying goods in inventory. Thus, the taxpayer must include as inventoriable costs all direct production costs and, to the extent provided by paragraphs (c) and (d) of this section, all indirect production costs. For purposes of this section, the term "financial reports" means financial reports (including consolidated financial statements) to shareholders, partners, beneficiaries or other proprietors and for credit purposes. See also § 1.263A–1T with respect to the treatment of production costs incurred in taxable

*Editorial comment: The Regulations do not reflect the effect of the Tax Reform Act of 1986. See Secs. 263A and 471(b).

years beginning after December 31, 1986, and before January 1, 1994. See also §§ 1.263A–1 and 1.263A–2 with respect to the treatment of production costs incurred in taxable years beginning after December 31, 1993.

* * *

§ 1.472–1 Last-in, first-out inventories.

(a) Any taxpayer permitted or required to take inventories pursuant to the provisions of section 471, and pursuant to the provisions of §§ 1.471–1 to 1.471–9, inclusive, may elect with respect to those goods specified in his application and properly subject to inventory to compute his opening and closing inventories in accordance with the method provided by section 472, this section, and § 1.472–2. Under this last-in, first-out (LIFO) inventory method, the taxpayer is permitted to treat those goods remaining on hand at the close of the taxable year as being:

(1) Those included in the opening inventory of the taxable year, in the order of acquisition and to the extent thereof, and

(2) Those acquired during the taxable year.

The LIFO inventory method is not dependent upon the character of the business in which the taxpayer is engaged, or upon the identity or want of identity through commingling of any of the goods on hand, and may be adopted by the taxpayer as of the close of any taxable year.

(b) If the LIFO inventory method is used by a taxpayer who regularly and consistently, in a manner similar to hedging on a futures market, matches purchases with sales, then firm purchases and sales contracts (*i.e.*, those not legally subject to cancellation by either party) entered into at fixed prices on or before the date of the inventory may be included in purchases or sales, as the case may be, for the purpose of determining the cost of goods sold and the resulting profit or loss, provided that this practice is regularly and consistently adhered to by the taxpayer and provided that, in the opinion of the Commissioner, income is clearly reflected thereby.

(c) A manufacturer or processor who has adopted the LIFO inventory method as to a class of goods may elect to have such method apply to the raw materials only (including those included in goods in process and in finished goods) expressed in terms of appropriate units. If such method is adopted, the adjustments are confined to costs of the raw material in the inventory and the cost of the raw material in goods in process and in finished goods produced by such manufacturer or processor and reflected in the inventory. The provisions of this paragraph may be illustrated by the following examples:

Example (1). Assume that the opening inventory had 10 units of raw material, 10 units of goods in process, and 10 units of finished goods, and that the raw material cost was 6 cents a unit, the processing cost 2 cents a unit, and overhead cost 1 cent a unit. For the purposes of this example, it is assumed that the entire amount of goods in process was 50 percent processed.

OPENING INVENTORY

	Raw material	Goods in process	Finished goods
Raw material	$0.60	$0.60	$0.60
Processing cost	.....	.10	.20
Overhead	.....	.05	.10

In the closing inventory there are 20 units of raw material, 6 units of goods in process, and 8 units of finished goods and the costs were: Raw material 10 cents, processing cost 4 cents, and overhead 1 cent.

Closing Inventory
[Based on cost and prior to adjustment]

	Raw material	Goods in process	Finished goods
Raw material	$2.00	$0.60	$0.80
Processing costs	.....	.12	.32
Overhead	.....	.03	.08
Total	2.00	.75	1.20

There were 30 units of raw material in the opening inventory and 34 units in the closing inventory. The adjustment to the closing inventory would be as follows:

Closing Inventory As Adjusted

	Raw material	Goods in process	Finished goods
Raw material:			
20 at 6 cents	$1.20	.....	.....
6 at 6 cents	.....	$0.36	.....
4 at 6 cents	.....	.....	$0.24
4 at 10 cents	.....	.....	.40
Processing costs	.....	.12	.32
Overhead	.....	.03	.08
Total	1.20	.51	1.04

[1]This excess is subject to determination of price under section 472(b)(1) and § 1.472–2. If the excess falls in goods in process, the same adjustment is applicable.

The only adjustment to the closing inventory is the cost of the raw material; the processing costs and overhead cost are not changed.

Example (2). Assume that the opening inventory had 5 units of raw material, 10 units of goods in process, and 20 units of finished goods, with the same prices as in example (1), and that the closing inventory had 20 units of raw material, 20 units of goods in process, and 10 units of finished goods, with raw material costs as in the closing inventory in example (1). The adjusted closing inventory would be as follows in so far as the raw material is concerned:

Raw material, 20 at 6 cents	$1.20
Goods in process:	
15 at 6 cents	.90
5 at 10 cents	.50
Finished goods:	
None at 6 cents	0.00
10 at 10 cents[1]	1.00

[1]This excess is subject to determination of price under section 472(b)(1) and § 1.472–2.

The 20 units of raw material in the raw state plus 15 units of raw material in goods in process make up the 35 units of raw material that were contained in the opening inventory.

(d) For the purposes of this section, raw material in the opening inventory must be compared with similar raw material in the closing inventory. There may be several types of raw materials, depending upon the character, quality, or price, and each type of raw material in the opening inventory must be compared with a similar type in the closing inventory.

* * *

(k) If a taxpayer using the retail method of pricing inventories, authorized by § 1.471–8, elects to use in connection therewith the LIFO inventory method authorized by section 472 and this section, the apparent cost of the goods on hand at the end of the year, determined pursuant to § 1.471–8, shall be adjusted to the extent of price changes therein taking place after the close of the preceding taxable year. The amount of any apparent inventory increase or decrease to be eliminated in this adjustment shall be determined by reference to acceptable price indexes established to the satisfaction of the Commissioner. Price indexes prepared by the United States Bureau of Labor Statistics which are applicable to the goods in question will be considered acceptable to the Commissioner. Price indexes which are based upon inadequate records, or which are not subject to complete and detailed audit within the Internal Revenue Service, will not be approved.

(l) If a taxpayer uses consistently the so–called "dollar-value" method of pricing inventories, or any other method of computation established to the satisfaction of the Commissioner as reasonably adaptable to the purpose and intent of section 472 and this section, and if such taxpayer elects under section 472 to use the LIFO inventory method authorized by such section, the taxpayer's opening and closing inventories shall be determined under section 472 by the use of the appropriate adaptation. See § 1.472–8 for rules relating to the use of the dollar-value method.

§ 1.472–2 Requirements incident to adoption and use of LIFO inventory method.

Except as otherwise provided in § 1.472–1 with respect to raw material computations, with respect to retail inventory computations, and with respect to other methods of computation established to the satisfaction of the Commissioner as reasonably adapted to the purpose and intent of section 472, and in § 1.472–8 with respect to the "dollar-value" method, the adoption and use of the LIFO inventory method is subject to the following requirements:

(a) The taxpayer shall file an application to use such method specifying with particularity the goods to which it is to be applied.

(b) The inventory shall be taken at cost regardless of market value.

(c) Goods of the specified type included in the opening inventory of the taxable year for which the method is first used shall be considered as having been acquired at the same time and at a unit cost equal to the actual cost of the aggregate divided by the number of units on hand. The actual cost of the aggregate shall be determined pursuant to the inventory method employed by the taxpayer under the regulations applicable to the prior taxable year with the exception that restoration shall be made with respect to any writedown to market values resulting from the pricing of former inventories.

(d) Goods of the specified type on hand as of the close of the taxable year in excess of what were on hand as of the beginning of the taxable year shall be included in the closing inventory, regardless of identification with specific invoices and regardless of specific cost accounting records, at costs determined pursuant to the provisions of subparagraph (1) or (2) of this paragraph, dependent upon the character of the transactions in which the taxpayer is engaged:

(1)(i) In the case of a taxpayer engaged in the purchase and sale of merchandise, such as a retail grocer or druggist, or engaged in the initial production of merchandise and its sale without processing, such as a miner selling his ore output without smelting or refining, such costs shall be determined—

(a) By reference to the actual cost of the goods most recently purchased or produced;

(b) By reference to the actual cost of the goods purchased or produced during the taxable year in the order of acquisition;

(c) By application of an average unit cost equal to the aggregate cost of all of the goods purchased or produced throughout the taxable year divided by the total number of units so purchased or produced, the goods reflected in such inventory increase being considered for the purposes of section 472 as having been acquired all at the same time; or

(d) Pursuant to any other proper method which, in the opinion of the Commissioner, clearly reflects income.

(ii) Whichever of the several methods of valuing the inventory increase is adopted by the taxpayer and approved by the Commissioner shall be consistently adhered to in all subsequent taxable years so long as the LIFO inventory method is used by the taxpayer.

(iii) The application of subdivisions (i) and (ii) of this subparagraph may be illustrated by the following examples:

Example (1). Suppose that the taxpayer adopts the LIFO inventory method for the taxable year 1957 with an opening inventory of 10 units at 10 cents per unit, that it makes 1957 purchases of 10 units as follows:

January	1 at	$0.11 =	$0.11
April	2 at	.12 =	.24
July	3 at	.13 =	.39
October	4 at	.14 =	.56
Totals	10		1.30

and that it has a 1957 closing inventory of 15 units. This closing inventory, depending upon the taxpayer's method of valuing inventory increases, will be computed as follows:

(a) Most recent purchases—

	10 at	$0.10	$1.00
October	4 at	.14	.56
July	1 at	.13	.13
Totals	15		1.69

(b) In order of acquisitions—

	10 at	$0.10	$1.00
January	1 at	.11	.11
April	2 at	.12	.24
July	2 at	.13	.26
Totals	15		1.61

or

(c) At an annual average—

	10 at	$0.10	$1.00
(130/10)	5 at	.13	.65
Totals	15		1.65

Example (2). Suppose that the taxpayer's closing inventory for 1958, the year following that involved in example (1) of this subdivision, reflects an inventory decrease for the year, and not an increase; suppose that there is, accordingly, a 1958 closing inventory of 13 units. Inasmuch as the decreased closing inventory will be determined wholly by reference to the 15 units reflected in the opening inventory for the year, and will be taken "in the order of acquisition" pursuant to section 472(b)(1), and inasmuch as the character of the taxpayer's opening inventory for 1958 will be dependent upon its method of valuing its 5-unit inventory increase for 1957, the closing inventory for 1958 will be computed as follows:

(a) In case the increase for 1957 was taken by reference to the most recent purchases—

From 1956	10 at	$0.10	$1.00
July 1957	1 at	.13	.13
October 1957	2 at	.14	.28
Totals	13		1.41

or

(b) In case the increase for 1957 was taken in the order of acquisition—

From 1956	10 at	$0.10	$1.00
January 1957	1 at	.11	.11
April 1957	2 at	.12	.24
Totals	13		1.35

or

(c) In case the increase for 1957 was taken on the basis of an average—

From 1956	10 at	$0.10	$1.00
From 1957	3 at	.13	.39
Totals	13		1.39

(2) In the case of a taxpayer engaged in manufacturing, fabricating, processing, or otherwise producing merchandise, such costs shall be determined:

(i) In the case of raw materials purchased or initially produced by the taxpayer, in the manner elected by the taxpayer under subparagraph (1) of this paragraph to the same extent as if the taxpayer were engaged in purchase and sale transactions; and

(ii) In the case of goods in process, regardless of the stage to which the manufacture, fabricating, or processing may have advanced, and in the case of finished goods, pursuant to any proper method which, in the opinion of the Commissioner, clearly reflects income.

(e) LIFO conformity requirement—(1) In general. The taxpayer must establish to the satisfaction of the Commissioner that the taxpayer, in ascertaining the income, profit, or loss for the taxable year for which the LIFO inventory method is first used, or for any subsequent taxable year, for credit purposes or for purposes of reports to shareholders, partners, or other proprietors, or to beneficiaries, has not used any inventory method other than that referred to in § 1.472–1 or at variance with the requirement referred to in § 1.472–2(c). See paragraph (e)(2) of this section for rules relating to the meaning of the term "taxable year" as used in this paragraph. The following are not considered at variance with the requirement of this paragraph:

(i) The taxpayer's use of an inventory method other than LIFO for purposes of ascertaining information reported as a supplement to or explanation of the taxpayer's primary presentation of the taxpayer's income, profit, or loss for a taxable year in credit statements or financial reports (including preliminary and unaudited financial reports). See paragraph (e)(3) of this section for rules relating to the reporting of supplemental and explanatory information ascertained by the use of an inventory method other than LIFO.

(ii) The taxpayer's use of an inventory method other than LIFO to ascertain the value of the taxpayer's inventory of goods on hand for purposes of reporting the value of such inventories as assets. See paragraph (e)(4) of this section for rules relating to such disclosures.

(iii) The taxpayer's use of an inventory method other than LIFO for purposes of ascertaining information reported in internal management reports. See paragraph (e)(5) of this section for rules relating to such reports.

(iv) The taxpayer's use of an inventory method other than LIFO for purposes of issuing reports or credit statements covering a period of operations that is less than the whole of a taxable year for which the LIFO method is used for Federal income tax purposes. See paragraph (e)(6) of this section for rules relating to series of interim reports.

(v) The taxpayer's use of the lower of LIFO cost or market method to value LIFO inventories for purposes of financial reports and credit statements. However, except as provided in paragraph (e)(7) of this section, a taxpayer may not use market value in lieu of cost to value inventories for purposes of financial reports or credit statements.

(vi) The taxpayer's use of a costing method or accounting method to ascertain income, profit, or loss for credit purposes or for purposes of financial reports if such costing method or accounting method is neither inconsistent with the inventory method referred to in § 1.472–1 nor at variance with the requirement referred to in § 1.472–2(c), regardless of whether such costing method or accounting method is used by the taxpayer for Federal income tax purposes. See paragraph (e)(8) of this section for examples of such costing methods and accounting methods.

(vii) For credit purposes or for purposes of financial reports, the taxpayer's treatment of inventories, after such inventories have been acquired in a transaction to which section 351 applies from a transferor that used the LIFO method with respect to such inventories, as if such inventories had the same acquisition dates and costs as in the hands of the transferor.

(viii) For credit purposes or for purposes of financial reports relating to a taxable year, the taxpayer's determination of income, profit, or loss for the taxable year by valuing inventories in accordance with the procedures described in section 472(b)(1) and (3), notwithstanding that such valuation differs from the valuation of inventories for Federal income tax purposes because the taxpayer either—

(A) Adopted such procedures for credit or financial reporting purposes beginning with an accounting period other than the taxable year for which the LIFO method was first used by the taxpayer for Federal income tax purposes, or

(B) With respect to such inventories treated a business combination for credit or financial reporting purposes in a manner different from the treatment of the business combination for Federal income tax purposes.

* * *

(3) Supplemental and explanatory information—(i) Face of the income statement. Information reported on the face of a taxpayer's financial income statement for a taxable year is not considered a supplement to or explanation of the taxpayer's primary presentation of the taxpayer's income, profit, or loss for the taxable year in credit statements or financial reports. For purposes of paragraph (e)(3) of this section, the face of an income statement does not include notes to the income statement presented on the same page as the income statement, but only if all notes to the financial income statement are presented together.

(ii) Notes to the income statement. Information reported in notes to a taxpayer's financial income statement is considered a supplement to or explanation of the taxpayer's primary presentation of income, profit, or loss for the period covered by the income statement if all notes to the financial income statement are presented together and if they accompany the income statement in a single report. If notes to an income statement are issued in a report that does not include the income statement, the question of whether the information reported therein is supplemental or explanatory is determined under the rules in paragraph (e)(3)(iv) of this section.

* * *

§ 1.472–3 Time and manner of making election.

(a) The LIFO inventory method may be adopted and used only if the taxpayer files with his income tax return for the taxable year as of the close of which the method is first to be used a statement of his election to use such inventory method. The statement shall be made on Form 970 pursuant to the instructions printed with respect thereto and to the requirements of this section, or in such other manner as may be acceptable to the Commissioner. Such statement shall be accompanied by an analysis of all inventories of the taxpayer as of the beginning and as of the end of the taxable year for which the LIFO inventory method is proposed first to be used, and also as of the beginning of the prior taxable year. In the case of a manufacturer, this analysis shall show in detail the manner in which costs are computed with respect to raw materials, goods in process, and finished goods, segregating the products (whether in process or finished goods) into natural groups on the basis of either (1) similarity in factory processes through which they pass, or (2) similarity of raw materials used, or (3) similarity in style, shape, or use of finished products. Each group of products shall be clearly described.

(b) The taxpayer shall submit for the consideration of the Commissioner in connection with the taxpayer's adoption or use of the LIFO inventory method such other detailed information with respect to his business or accounting system as may be at any time requested by the Commissioner.

(c) As a condition to the taxpayer's use of the LIFO inventory method, the Commissioner may require that the method be used with respect to goods other than those specified in the taxpayer's statement of election if, in the opinion of the Commissioner, the use of such method with respect to such other goods is essential to a clear reflection of income.

(d) Whether or not the taxpayer's application for the adoption and use of the LIFO inventory method should be approved, and whether or not such method, once adopted, may be continued, and the propriety of all computations incidental to the use of such method, will be determined by the Commissioner in connection with the examination of the taxpayer's income tax returns.

§ 1.472–4 Adjustments to be made by taxpayer.

A taxpayer may not change to the LIFO method of taking inventories unless, at the time he files his application for the adoption of such method, he agrees to such adjustments incident to the change to or from such method, or incident to the use of such method, in the inventories of prior taxable years or otherwise, as the district director upon the examination of the taxpayer's returns may deem necessary in order that the true income of the taxpayer will be clearly reflected for the years involved.

§ 1.472–5 Revocation of election.

An election made to adopt and use the LIFO inventory method is irrevocable, and the method once adopted shall be used in all subsequent taxable years, unless the use of another method is required by the Commissioner, or authorized by him pursuant to a written application therefor filed as provided in paragraph (e) of § 1.446–1.

* * *

Adjustments

* * *

Regulations Applicable to Taxable Years Beginning on or Before April 21, 1993

§ 1.482–1A Allocation of income and deductions among taxpayers.

(a) Definitions. When used in this section and in § 1.482–2—

(1) The term "organization" includes any organization of any kind, whether it be a sole proprietorship, a partnership, a trust, an estate, an association, or a corporation (as each is defined or understood in the Internal Revenue Code or the regulations thereunder), irrespective of the place where organized, where operated, or where its trade or business is conducted, and regardless of whether domestic or foreign, whether exempt, whether affiliated, or whether a party to a consolidated return.

(2) The term "trade" or "business" includes any trade or business activity of any kind, regardless of whether or where organized, whether owned individually or otherwise, and regardless of the place where carried on.

(3) The term "controlled" includes any kind of control, direct or indirect, whether legally enforceable, and however exercisable or exercised. It is the reality of the control which is decisive, not its form or the mode of its exercise. A presumption of control arises if income or deductions have been arbitrarily shifted.

(4) The term "controlled taxpayer" means any one of two or more organizations, trades, or businesses owned or controlled directly or indirectly by the same interests.

(5) The terms "group" and "group of controlled taxpayers" mean the organizations, trades, or businesses owned or controlled by the same interests.

(6) The term "true taxable income" means, in the case of a controlled taxpayer, the taxable income (or, as the case may be, any item or element affecting taxable income) which would have resulted to the controlled taxpayer, had it in the conduct of its affairs (or, as the case may be, in the particular contract, transaction, arrangement, or other act) dealt with the other member or members of the group at arm's length. It does not mean the income, the deductions, the credits, the allowances, or the item or element of income, deductions, credits, or allowances, resulting to the controlled taxpayer by reason of the particular contract, transaction, or arrangement, the controlled taxpayer, or the interests controlling it, chose to make (even though such contract, transaction, or arrangement be legally binding upon the parties thereto).

(b) Scope and purpose. **(1)** The purpose of section 482 is to place a controlled taxpayer on a tax parity with an uncontrolled taxpayer, by determining, according to the standard of an uncontrolled taxpayer, the true taxable income from the property and business of a controlled taxpayer. The interests controlling a group of controlled taxpayers are assumed to have complete power to cause each controlled taxpayer so to conduct its affairs that its transactions and accounting records truly reflect the taxable income from the property and business of each of the controlled taxpayers. If, however, this has not been done, and the taxable incomes are thereby understated, the district director shall intervene, and, by making such distributions, apportionments, or allocations as he may deem necessary of gross income, deductions, credits, or allowances, or of any item or element affecting taxable income, between or among the controlled taxpayers constituting the group, shall determine the true taxable income of each controlled taxpayer. The standard to be applied in every case is that of an uncontrolled taxpayer dealing at arm's length with another uncontrolled taxpayer.

(2) Section 482 and this section apply to the case of any controlled taxpayer, whether such taxpayer makes a separate or a consolidated return. If a controlled taxpayer makes a separate return, the determination is of its true separate taxable income. If a controlled taxpayer is a party to a consolidated return, the true consolidated taxable income of the affiliated group and the true separate taxable income of the controlled taxpayer are determined consistently with the principles of a consolidated return.

(3) Section 482 grants no right to a controlled taxpayer to apply its provisions at will, nor does it grant any right to compel the district director to apply such provisions. It is not intended (except in the case of the computation of consolidated taxable income under a consolidated return) to effect in any case such a distribution, apportionment, or allocation of gross income, deductions, credits, or allowances, or any item of gross income, deductions, credits, or allowances, as would produce a result equivalent to a computation of consolidated taxable income under subchapter A, chapter 6 of the Code.

(c) Application. Transactions between one controlled taxpayer and another will be subjected to special scrutiny to ascertain whether the common control is being used to reduce, avoid, or escape taxes. In determining the true taxable income of a controlled taxpayer, the district director is not restricted to the case of improper accounting, to the case of a fraudulent, colorable, or sham transaction, or to the case of a device designed to reduce or avoid tax by shifting or distorting income, deductions, credits, or allowances. The authority to determine true taxable income extends to any case in which either by inadvertence or design the taxable income, in whole or in part, of a controlled taxpayer, is other than it would have been had the taxpayer in the conduct of his affairs been an uncontrolled taxpayer dealing at arm's length with another uncontrolled taxpayer.

(d) Method of allocation. (1) The method of allocating, apportioning, or distributing income, deductions, credits, and allowances to be used by the district director in any case, including the form of the adjustments and the character and source of amounts allocated, shall be determined with reference to the substance of the particular transactions or arrangements which result in the avoidance of taxes or the failure to clearly reflect income. The appropriate adjustments may take the form of an increase or decrease in gross income, increase or decrease in deductions (including depreciation), increase or decrease in basis of assets (including inventory), or any other adjustment which may be appropriate under the circumstances. See § 1.482–2 for specific rules relating to methods of allocation in the case of several types of business transactions.

(2) Whenever the district director makes adjustments to the income of one member of a group of controlled taxpayers (such adjustments being referred to in this paragraph as "primary" adjustments) he shall also make appropriate correlative adjustments to the income of any other member of the group involved in the allocation. The correlative adjustment shall actually be made if the U.S. income tax liability of the other member would be affected for any pending taxable year. Thus, if the district director makes an allocation of income, he shall not only increase the income of one member of the group, but shall decrease the income of the other member if such adjustment would have an effect on the U.S. income tax liability of the other member for any pending taxable year. For the purposes of this subparagraph, a "pending taxable year" is any taxable year with respect to which the U.S. income tax return of the other member has been filed by the time the allocation is made, and with respect to which a credit or refund is not barred by the operation of any law or rule of law. If a correlative adjustment is not actually made because it would have no effect on the U.S. income tax liability of the other member involved in the allocation for any pending taxable year, such adjustment shall nevertheless be deemed to have been made for the purpose of determining the U.S. income tax liability of such member for a later taxable year, or for the purposes of determining the U.S. income tax liability of any person for any taxable year. The district director shall furnish to the taxpayer with respect to which the primary adjustment is made a written statement of the amount and nature of the correlative adjustment which is deemed to have been made. * * *

(3) In making distributions, apportionments, or allocations between two members of a group of controlled entities with respect to particular transactions, the district director shall consider the effect upon such members of an arrangement between them for reimbursement within a reasonable period before or after the taxable year if the taxpayer can establish that such an arrangement in fact existed during the taxable year under consideration. The district director shall also consider the effect of any other nonarm's length transaction between them in the taxable year which, if taken into account, would result in a setoff against any allocation which would otherwise be made, provided the taxpayer is able to establish with reasonable specificity that the transaction was not at arm's length and the amount of the appropriate arm's length charge. For purposes of the preceding sentence, the term arm's length refers to the amount which was charged or would have been charged in independent transactions with unrelated parties under the same or similar circumstances considering all the relevant facts and without regard to the rules found in § 1.482–2 by which certain charges are deemed to be equal to arm's length. For example, assume that one member of a group performs services which benefit a second member, which would in itself require an allocation to reflect an arm's length charge for the performance of such services. Assume further that the first member can establish that during the same taxable year the second member engages in other nonarm's length transactions which benefit the first member, such as by selling products to the first member at a discount, or purchasing products from the first member at a premium, or paying royalties to the first member in an excessive amount. In such case, the value of the benefits received by the first member as a result of the other activities will be set–off against the allocation which would otherwise be made. If the effect of the set-off is to change the characterization or source of the income or deductions, or otherwise distort taxable income, in such a manner as to affect the United States tax liability of any member, allocations will be made to reflect the correct amount of each category of income or deductions. In order to establish that a set-off to the adjustments proposed by the district director is appropriate, the taxpayer must notify the district director of the basis of any claimed set-off at any time before the expiration of the period ending 30 days after the date of a letter by which the district director transmits an examination report notifying the taxpayer of proposed adjustments or before July 16, 1968, whichever is later. The principles of this subparagraph may be illustrated by the following examples, in each of which it is assumed that P and S are calendar year corporations and are both members of the same group of controlled entities:

Example (1). P performs services in 1966 for the benefit of S in connection with S's manufacture and sale of a product. S does not pay P for such services in 1966, but in consideration for such services, agrees in 1966 to pay P a percentage of the amount of sales of the product in 1966 through 1970. In 1966 it appeared this agreement would provide adequate consideration for the services. No allocation will be made with respect to the services performed by P.

Example (2). P renders services to S in connection with the construction of S's factory. An arm's length charge for such services, determined under paragraph (b) of § 1.482–2, would be $100,000. During the same taxable year P makes available to S a machine to be used in such construction. P bills S $125,000 for the services, but does not bill for the use of the machine. No allocation will be made with respect to the excessive charge for services or the undercharge for the machine if P can establish that the excessive charge for services was equal to an arm's length charge for the use of the machine, and if the taxable income and income tax liabilities of P and S are not distorted.

Example (3). Assume the same facts as in example (2), except that, if P had reported $25,000 as rental income and $25,000 less service income, it would have been subject to the tax on personal holding companies. Allocations will be made to reflect the correct amounts of rental income and service income.

(4) If the members of a group of controlled taxpayers engage in transactions with one another, the district director may distribute, apportion, or allocate income, deductions, credits, or allowances to reflect the true taxable income of the individual members under the standards set forth in this section and in § 1.482–2 notwithstanding the fact that the ultimate income anticipated from a series of transactions may not be realized or is realized during a later period. For example, if one member of a controlled group sells a product at less than an arm's length price to a second member of the group in one taxable year and the second member resells the product to an unrelated party in the next taxable year, the district director may make an appropriate allocation to reflect an arm's length price for the sale of the product in the first taxable year, notwithstanding that the second member of the group had not realized any gross income from the resale of the product in the first year. Similarly, if one member of a group lends money to a second member of the group in a taxable year, the district director may make an appropriate allocation to reflect an arm's length charge for interest during such taxable year even if the second member does not realize income during such year. The provisions of this subparagraph apply even if the gross income contemplated from a series of transactions is never, in fact, realized by the other members.

(5) Section 482 may, when necessary to prevent the avoidance of taxes or to clearly reflect income, be applied in circumstances described in sections of the Code (such as section 351) providing for nonrecognition of gain or loss. See, for example, "National Securities Corporation v. Commissioner of Internal Revenue", 137 F.2d 600 (3d Cir. 1943), cert. denied 320 U.S. 794 (1943).

* * *

Regulations Applicable to Taxable Years Beginning After April 21, 1993

§ 1.482–1T Allocation of income and deductions among taxpayers.

(a) In general—(1) Purpose and scope. The purpose of section 482 is to ensure that taxpayers clearly reflect income attributable to controlled transactions, and to prevent the avoidance of taxes with respect to such transactions. Section 482 places a controlled taxpayer on a tax parity with an uncontrolled taxpayer by determining the true taxable income of the controlled taxpayer in a manner that reasonably reflects the relative economic activity undertaken by each taxpayer. This § 1.482–1T sets forth general principles and guidelines to be followed under section 482. Section 1.482–2T provides rules for the determination of the true taxable income of controlled taxpayers in specific situations, including controlled transactions involving loans or advances, services, and property. Sections 1.482–3T through 1.482–5T elaborate on the rules that apply to controlled transactions involving property.

(2) Authority to make allocations. If a controlled taxpayer has not reported its true taxable income, the district director may make allocations between or among the members of a controlled group. In such cases, the district director may allocate income, deductions, credits, allowances, basis, or any other item or element affecting taxable income (referred to as "allocations"). The appropriate allocation may take the form of an increase or decrease in any relevant amount.

* * *

§ 1.482–2A Determination of taxable income in specific situations.

(a) Loans or advances—(1) Interest on bona-fide indebtedness—(i) In general. Where one member of a group of controlled entities makes a loan or advance directly or indirectly to, or otherwise becomes a creditor of, another member of such group and either charges no interest, or charges interest at a rate which is not equal to an arm's length rate of interest (as defined in paragraph (a)(2) of this section) with respect to such loan or advance, the district directory may make appropriate allocations to reflect an arm's length rate of interest for the use of such loan or advance.

(ii) Application of paragraph (a) of this section—(A) Interest on bona fide indebtedness. Paragraph (a) of this section applies only to determine the appropriateness of the rate of interest charged on the principal amount of a bona fide indebtedness between members of a group of controlled entities, including—

(1) Loans or advances of money or other consideration (whether or not evidenced by a written instrument), and

(2) Indebtedness arising in the ordinary course of business from sales, leases, or the rendition of services by or between members of the group, or any other similar extension of credit.

(B) Alleged indebtedness. This paragraph (a) does not apply to so much of an alleged indebtedness which is not in fact a bona fide indebtedness, even if the stated rate of interest thereon would be within the safe haven rates prescribed in paragraph (a)(2)(iii) of this section. For example, paragraph (a) of this section does not apply to payments with respect to all or a portion of such alleged indebtedness where in fact all or a portion of an alleged indebtedness is a contribution to the capital of a corporation or a distribution by a corporation with respect to its shares. Similarly, this paragraph (a) does not apply to payments with respect to an alleged purchase-money debt instrument given in consideration for an alleged sale of property between two controlled entities where in fact the transaction constitutes a lease of the property. Payments made with respect to alleged indebtedness (including alleged stated interest thereon) shall be treated according to their substance. See § 1.482–2 (a)(3)(i).

(iii) Period for which interest shall be charged—(A) General rule. This paragraph (a)(1) (iii) is effective for indebtedness arising after June 30, 1988. See 26 CFR 1.482–2(a)(3) (revised as of April 1, 1988) for indebtedness arising before July 1, 1988. Except as otherwise provided in paragraphs (a)(1)(iii)(B) through (E) of this section, the period for which interest shall be charged with respect to a bona fide indebtedness between controlled entities begins on the day after the day the indebtedness arises and ends on the day the indebtedness is satisfied (whether by payment, offset, cancellation, or otherwise.) Paragraphs (a)(2)(iii)(B) through (E) of this section provide certain alternative periods during which interest is not required to be charged on certain indebtedness. These exceptions apply only to indebtedness described in paragraph (a)(1)(ii)(A)(2) of this section (relating to indebtedness incurred in the ordinary course of business from sales, services, etc., between members of the group) and not evidenced by a written instrument requiring the payment of interest. Such amounts are hereinafter referred to as "intercompany trade receivables". The period for which interest is not required to be charged on intercompany trade receivables under this paragraph (a)(1)(iii) is called the "interest-free period".

In general, an intercompany trade receivable arises at the time economic performance occurs (within the meaning of section 461(h) and the regulations thereunder) with respect to the underlying transaction between controlled entities. For purpose of this paragraph (a)(1)(iii), the term "United States" includes any possession of the United States, and the term "foreign country" excludes any possession of the United States.

(B) Exception for certain intercompany transactions in the ordinary course of business. Interest is not required to be charged on an intercompany trade receivable until the first day of the third calendar month following the month in which the intercompany trade receivable arises.

(C) Exception for trade or business of debtor member located outside the United States. In the case of an intercompany trade receivable arising from a transaction in the ordinary course of a trade or business which is actively conducted outside the United States by the debtor member, interest is not required to be charged until the first day of the fourth calendar month following the month in which such intercompany trade receivable arises.

(D) Exception for regular trade practice of creditor member or others in creditor's industry. If the creditor member or unrelated persons in the creditor member's industry, as a regular trade practice, allow unrelated parties a longer period without charging interest than that described in paragraph (a)(1)(iii)(B) or (C) of this section (whichever is applicable) with respect to transactions which are similar to transactions that give rise to intercompany trade receivables, such longer interest-free period shall be allowed with respect a comparable amount of intercompany trade receivables.

* * *

(iv) Payment; book entries. (A) Except as otherwise provided in this paragraph (a)(1)(iv), in determining the period of time for which an amount owed by one member of the group to another member is outstanding, payments or other credits to an account are considered to be applied against the earliest amount outstanding, that is, payments or credits are applied against amounts in a first–in, first-out (FIFO) order. Thus, tracing payments to individual intercompany trade receivables is generally not required in order to determine whether a particular intercompany trade receivable has been paid within the applicable interest-free period determined under paragraph (a)(1)(iii) of this section.

* * *

(B) Notwithstanding the first-in, first-out payment application rule described in paragraph (a)(1)(iv)(A) of this section, the taxpayer may apply payments or credits against amounts owed in some other order on its books in accordance with an agreement or understanding of the related parties if the taxpayer can demonstrate that either it or others in its industry, as a regular trade practice, enter into such agreements or understandings in the case of similar balances with unrelated parties.

(2) Arm's length interest rate—(i) In general. For purposes of section 482 and paragraph (a) of this section, an arm's length rate of interest shall be a rate of interest which was charged, or would have been charged, at the time the indebtedness arose, in independent transactions with or between unrelated parties under similar circumstances. All relevant factors shall be considered, including the principal amount and duration of the loan, the security involved, the credit standing of the borrower, and the interest rate prevailing at the situs of the lender or creditor for comparable loans between unrelated parties.

(ii) Funds obtained at situs of borrower. Notwithstanding the other provisions of paragraph (a)(2) of this section, if the loan or advance represents the proceeds of a loan obtained by the lender at the situs of the borrower, the arm's length rate for any taxable year shall be equal to the rate actually paid by the lender increased by an amount which reflects the costs or deductions incurred by the lender in borrowing such amounts and making such loans, unless the taxpayer establishes a more appropriate rate under the standards set forth in paragraph (a)(2)(i) of this section.

(iii) Safe haven interest rates for certain loans and advances made after May 8, 1986—**(A)** Applicability—**(1)** General rule. Except as otherwise provided in paragraph (a)(2) of this section, paragraph (a)(2)(iii)(B) of this section applies with respect to the rate of interest charged and to the amount of interest paid or accrued in any taxable year—

(i) Under a term loan or advance between members of a group of controlled entities where (except as provided in paragraph (a)(2)(iii)(A)(2)(ii)) of this section the loan or advance is entered into after May 8, 1986, and

(ii) After May 8, 1986, under a demand loan or advance between such controlled entities.

(2) Grandfather rule for existing loans. The safe haven rates prescribed in paragraph (a)(2)(iii)(B) of this section shall not apply, and the safe haven rates prescribed in 26 CFR § 1.482–2(a)(2)(iii) (revised as of April 1, 1985) shall apply to—

(i) Term loans or advances made before May 9, 1986, and

(ii) Term loans or advances made before August 7, 1986, pursuant to a binding written contract entered into before May 9, 1986.

(B) Safe haven interest rate based on applicable Federal rate. Except as otherwise provided in this paragraph (a)(2), in the case of a loan or advance between members of a group of controlled entities, an arm's length rate of interest referred to in paragraph (a)(2)(i) of this section shall be for purposes of Chapter 1 of the Code—

(1) The rate of interest actually charged if that rate is—

(i) Not less than 100 percent of the applicable Federal rate (the "lower limit"), and

(ii) Not greater than 130 percent of the applicable Federal rate (the "upper limit"), or

(2) If either no interest is charged or if the rate of interest charged is less than the lower limit, then an arm's length rate of interest shall be equal to the lower limit, compounded semiannually, or

(3) If the rate of interest charged is greater than the upper limit, then an arm's length rate of interest shall be equal to the upper limit, compounded semiannually, unless the taxpayer establishes a more appropriate compound rate of interest under paragraph (a)(2)(i) of this section. However, if the compound rate of interest actually charged is greater than the upper limit and less than the rate determined under paragraph (a)(2)(i) of this section, or if the compound rate actually charged is less than the lower limit and greater than the rate determined under paragraph (a)(2)(i) of this section, then the compound rate actually charged shall be deemed to be an arm's length rate under paragraph (a)(2)(i) of this section. In the case of any sale-leaseback described in section 1274(e), the lower limit shall be 110 percent of the applicable Federal rate, compounded semiannually.

(C) Applicable Federal rate. For purposes of paragraph (a)(2)(iii)(B) of this section, the term "applicable Federal rate" means, in the case of a loan or advance to which this section applies and having a term of—

(1) Not over 3 years, the Federal short-term rate.

(2) Over 3 years but not over 9 years, the Federal mid-term rate, or

(3) Over 9 years, the Federal long-term rate, as determined under section 1274(d) in effect on the date such loan or advance is made. In the case of any sale or exchange between controlled entities, the lower limit shall be the lowest of the applicable Federal rates in effect for any month in the 3-calendar-month period ending with the first calendar month in which there is a binding written contract in effect for such sale or exchange (the "lowest 3-month rate", as defined in section 1274 (d)(2)). In the case of a demand loan or advance to which this section applies, the "applicable Federal rate" means the Federal short-term rate determined under section 1274(d) (determined without regard to the lowest 3-month short-term rate determined under section 1274(d)(2)) in effect for each day on which any amount of such loan or advance (including unpaid accrued interest determined under paragraph (a)(2) of this section) is outstanding.

(D) Lender in business of making loans. If the lender in a loan or advance transaction to which paragraph (a)(2) of this section applies is regularly engaged in the trade or business or making loans or advances to unrelated parties, the safe haven rates prescribed in paragraph (a)(2)(iii)(B) of this section shall not apply, and the arm's length interest rate to be used shall be determined under the standards described in paragraph (a)(2)(i) of this section, including reference to the interest rates charged in such trade or business by the lender on loans or advances of a similar type made to unrelated parties at and about the time the loan or advance to which paragraph (a)(2) of this section applies was made.

(E) Foreign currency loans. The safe haven interest rates prescribed in paragraph (a)(2)(iii)(B) of this section do not apply to any loan or advance the principal or interest of which is expressed in a currency other than U.S. dollars.

(3) Coordination with interest adjustments required under certain other Code sections. If the stated rate of interest on the stated principal amount of a loan or advance between controlled entities is subject to adjustment under section 482 and is also subject to adjustment under any other section of the Code (for example, section 467, 483, 1274 or 7872), section 482 and paragraph (a) of this section may be applied to such loan or advance in addition to such other Code section. After the enactment of the Tax Reform Act of 1984, Pub.L. 98–369, and the enactment of Pub.L. 99–121, such other Code sections include sections 467, 483, 1274 and 7872. The order in which the different provisions shall be applied is as follows:

(i) First, the substance of the transaction shall be determined; for this purpose, all the relevant facts and circumstances shall be considered and any law or rule of law (assignment of income, step transaction, etc.) may apply. Only the rate of interest with respect to the stated principal amount of the bona fide indebtedness (within the meaning of paragraph (a)(1) of this section), if any, shall be subject to adjustment under section 482, paragraph (a) of this section, and any other Code section.

(ii) Second, the other Code section shall be applied to the loan or advance to determine whether any amount other than stated interest is to be treated as interest, and if so, to determine such amount according to the provisions of such other Code section.

(iii) Third, whether or not the other Code section applies to adjust the amounts treated as interest under such loan or advance, section 482 and paragraph (a) of this section may then be applied by the district director to determine whether the rate of interest charged on the loan or advance, as adjusted by any other Code section, is greater or less than an arm's length rate of interest, and if so, to make appropriate allocations to reflect an arm's length rate of interest.

(iv) Fourth, section 482 and paragraphs (b) through (e) of this section, if applicable, may be applied by the district director to make any appropriate allocations, other than an interest rate adjustment, to reflect an arm's length transaction based upon the principal amount of the loan or advance and the interest rate as adjusted under paragraph (a)(3)(i), (ii) or (iii) of this section. For example, assume that two commonly controlled taxpayers enter into a deferred payment sale of tangible property and no interest is provided, and assume also that section 483 is applied to treat a portion of the stated sales price as interest, thereby reducing the stated sales price. If after this recharacterization of a portion of the stated sales price as interest, the recomputed sales price does not reflect an arm's length sales price under the principles of paragraph (e) of this section, the district director may make other appropriate allocations (other than an interest rate adjustment) to reflect an arm's length sales price.

* * *

(b) Performance of services for another—(1) General rule. Where one member of a group of controlled entities performs marketing, managerial, administrative, technical, or other services for the benefit of, or on behalf of another member of the group without charge, or at a charge which is not equal to an arm's length charge as defined in subparagraph (3) of this paragraph, the district director may make appropriate allocations to reflect an arm's length charge for such services.

* * *

§ 1.483–1 Interest on certain deferred payments.

(a) Amount constituting interest in certain deferred payment transactions—(1) In general. Except as provided in paragraph (c) of this section, section 483 applies to a contract for the sale or exchange of property if the contract provides for one or more payments due more than 1 year after the date of the sale or exchange, and the contract does not provide for adequate stated interest. In general, a contract has adequate stated interest if the contract provides for a stated rate of interest that is at least equal to the test rate (determined under § 1.483–3) and the interest is paid or compounded at least annually. Section 483 may apply to a contract whether the contract is express (written or oral) or implied. For purposes of section 483, a sale or exchange is any transaction treated as a sale or exchange for tax purposes. In addition, for purposes of section 483, property includes debt instruments and investment units, but does not include money, services, or the right to use property. For the treatment of certain obligations given in exchange for services or the use of property, see sections 404 and 467. For purposes of this paragraph (a), money includes functional currency and, in certain circumstances, nonfunctional currency. See § 1.988–2(b)(2) for circumstances when nonfunctional currency is treated as money rather than as property.

(2) Treatment of contracts to which section 483 applies—(i) Treatment of unstated interest. If section 483 applies to a contract, unstated interest under the contract is treated as interest for tax purposes. Thus, for example, unstated interest is not treated as part of the amount realized from the sale or exchange of property (in the case of the seller), and is not included in the purchaser's basis in the property acquired in the sale or exchange.

(ii) Method of accounting for interest on contracts subject to section 483. Any stated or unstated interest on a contract subject to section 483 is taken into account by a taxpayer under the taxpayer's regular method of accounting (e.g., an accrual method or the cash receipts and disbursements method). See §§ 1.446–1, 1.451–1, and 1.461–1. For purposes of the preceding sentence, the amount of interest (including unstated interest) allocable to a payment under a contract to which section 483 applies is determined under § 1.446–2(e).

(b) Definitions—(1) Deferred payments. For purposes of the regulations under section 483, a deferred payment means any payment that constitutes all or a part of the sales price (as defined in paragraph (b)(2) of this section), and that is due more than 6 months after the date of the sale or exchange. Except as provided in section 483(c)(2) (relating to the treatment of a debt instrument of the purchaser), a payment may be made in the form of cash, stock or securities, or other property.

(2) Sales price. For purposes of section 483, the sales price for any sale or exchange is the sum of the amount due under the contract (other than stated interest) and the amount of any liability included in the amount realized from the sale or exchange. See § 1.1001–2. Thus, the sales price for any sale or exchange includes any amount of unstated interest under the contract.

(c) Exceptions to and limitations on the application of section 483—(1) In general. Sections 483(d), 1274(c)(4), and 1275(b) contain exceptions to and limitations on the application of section 483.

(2) Sales price of $3,000 or less. Section 483(d)(2) applies only if it can be determined at the time of the sale or exchange that the sales price cannot exceed $3,000, regardless of whether the sales price eventually paid for the property is less than $3,000.

(3) Other exceptions and limitations—(i) Certain transfers subject to section 1041. Section 483 does not apply to any transfer of property subject to section 1041 (relating to transfers of property between spouses or incident to divorce).

(ii) Treatment of certain obligees. Section 483 does not apply to an obligee under a contract for the sale or exchange of personal use property (within the meaning of section 1275(b)(3)) in the hands of the obligor and that evidences a below-market loan described in section 7872(c)(1).

(iii) Transactions involving certain demand loans. Section 483 does not apply to any payment under a contract that evidences a demand loan that is a below-market loan described in section 7872(c)(1).

(iv) Transactions involving certain annuity contracts. Section 483 does not apply to any payment under an annuity contract described in section 1275(a)(1)(B) (relating to annuity contracts excluded from the definition of debt instrument).

(v) Options. Section 483 does not apply to any payment under an option to buy or sell property.

(d) Assumptions. If a debt instrument is assumed, or property is taken subject to a debt instrument, in connection with a sale or exchange of property, the debt instrument is treated for purposes of section 483 in a manner consistent with the rules of § 1.1274–5.

(e) Aggregation rule. For purposes of section 483, all sales or exchanges that are part of the same transaction (or a series of related transactions) are treated as a single sale or exchange, and all contracts calling for deferred payments arising from the same transaction (or a series of related transactions) are treated as a single contract. This rule, however, generally only applies to contracts and to sales or exchanges involving a single buyer and a single seller.

(f) Effective date. This section applies to sales and exchanges that occur on or after April 4, 1994. Taxpayers, however, may rely on this section for sales and exchanges that occur after December 21, 1992, and before April 4, 1994.

* * *

CORPORATIONS USED TO AVOID INCOME TAX ON SHAREHOLDERS

Corporations Improperly Accumulating Surplus

* * *

§ 1.532–1 Corporations subject to accumulated earnings tax.

(a) General rule. **(1)** The tax imposed by section 531 applies to any domestic or foreign corporation (not specifically excepted under section 532 (b) and paragraph (b) of this section) formed or availed of to avoid or prevent the imposition of the individual income tax on its shareholders, or on the shareholders of any other corporation, by permitting earnings and profits to accumulate instead of dividing or distributing them. See section 533 and § 1.533–1, relating to evidence of purpose to avoid income tax with respect to shareholders.

(2) The tax imposed by section 531 may apply if the avoidance is accomplished through the formation or use of one corporation or a chain of corporations. For example, if the capital stock of the M Corporation is held by the N Corporation, the earnings and profits of the M Corporation would not be returned as income subject to the individual income tax until such earnings and profits of the M Corporation were distributed to the N Corporation and distributed in turn by the N Corporation to its shareholders. If either the M Corporation or the N Corporation was formed or is availed of for the purpose of avoiding or preventing the imposition of the individual income tax upon the shareholders of the N Corporation, the accumulated taxable income of the corporation so formed or availed of (M or N, as the case may be) is subject to the tax imposed by section 531.

(b) Exceptions. The accumulated earnings tax imposed by section 531 does not apply to a personal holding company (as defined in section 542), to a foreign personal holding company (as defined in section 552), or to a corporation exempt from tax under subchapter F, chapter 1 of the Code.

* * *

§ 1.533–1 Evidence of purpose to avoid income tax.

(a) In general. **(1)** The Commissioner's determination that a corporation was formed or availed of for the purpose of avoiding income tax with respect to shareholders is subject to disproof by competent evidence. Section 533(a) provides that the fact that earnings and profits of a corporation are permitted to accumulate beyond the reasonable needs of the business shall be determinative of the purpose to avoid the income tax with respect to shareholders unless the corporation, by the preponderance of the evidence, shall prove to the contrary. The burden of proving that earnings and profits have been permitted to accumulate beyond the reasonable needs of the business may be shifted to the Commissioner under section 534. See §§ 1.534–1 through 1.534–4. Section 533(b) provides that the fact that the taxpayer is a mere holding or investment company shall be prima facie evidence of the purpose to avoid income tax with respect to shareholders.

(2) The existence or nonexistence of the purpose to avoid income tax with respect to shareholders may be indicated by circumstances other than the conditions specified in section 533. Whether or not such purpose was present depends upon the particular circumstances of each case. All circumstances which might be construed as evidence of the purpose to avoid income tax with respect to shareholders cannot be outlined, but among other things, the following will be considered:

(i) Dealings between the corporation and its shareholders, such as withdrawals by the shareholders as personal loans or the expenditure of funds by the corporation for the personal benefit of the shareholders,

(ii) The investment by the corporation of undistributed earnings in assets having no reasonable connection with the business of the corporation (see § 1.537–3), and

(iii) The extent to which the corporation has distributed its earnings and profits.

The fact that a corporation is a mere holding or investment company or has an accumulation of earnings and profits in excess of the reasonable needs of the business is not absolutely conclusive against it if the taxpayer satisfies the Commissioner that the corporation was neither formed nor availed of for the purpose of avoiding income tax with respect to shareholders.

(b) General burden of proof and statutory presumptions. The Commissioner may determine that the taxpayer was formed or availed of to avoid income tax with respect to shareholders through the medium of permitting earnings and profits to accumulate. In the case of litigation involving any such determination (except where the burden of proof is on the Commissioner under section 534), the burden of proving such determination wrong by a preponderance of the evidence, together with the corresponding burden of first going forward with the evidence, is on the taxpayer under principles applicable to income tax cases generally. For the burden of proof in a proceeding before the Tax Court with respect to the allegation that earnings and profits have been permitted to accumulate beyond the reasonable needs of the business, see section 534 and §§ 1.534–2 through 1.534–4. For a definition of a holding or investment company, see paragraph (c) of this section. For determination of the reasonable needs of the business, see section 537 and §§ 1.537–1 through 1.537–3. If the taxpayer is a mere holding or investment company, and the Commissioner therefore determines that the corporation was formed or availed of for the purpose of avoiding income tax with respect to shareholders, then section 533(b) gives further weight to the presumption of correctness already arising from the Commissioner's determination by expressly providing an additional presumption of the existence of a purpose to avoid income tax with respect to shareholders. Further, if it is established (after complying with section 534 where applicable) that earnings and profits were permitted to accumulate beyond the reasonable needs of the business and the Commissioner has therefore determined that the corporation was formed or availed of for the purpose of avoiding income tax with respect to shareholders, then section 533(a) adds still more weight to the Commissioner's determination. Under such circumstances, the existence of such an accumulation is made determinative of the purpose to avoid income tax with respect to shareholders unless the taxpayer proves to the contrary by the preponderance of the evidence.

(c) Holding or investment company. A corporation having practically no activities except holding property and collecting the income therefrom or investing therein shall be considered a holding company within the meaning of section 533(b). If the activities further include, or consist substantially of, buying and selling stocks, securities, real estate, or other investment property (whether upon an outright or marginal basis) so that the income is derived not only from the investment yield but also from profits upon market fluctuations, the corporation shall be considered an investment company within the meaning of section 533(b).

* * *

§ 1.533–2 Statement required.

The corporation may be required to furnish a statement of its accumulated earnings and profits, the payment of dividends, the name and address of, and number of shares held by, each of its shareholders, the amounts that would be payable to each of the shareholders if the income of the corporation were distributed and other information required under section 6042.

§ 1.534–1 Burden of proof as to unreasonable accumulations generally.

For purposes of applying the presumption provided for in section 533(a) and in determining the extent of the accumulated earnings credit under section 535(c)(1), the burden of proof with respect to an allegation by the Commissioner that all or any part of the earnings and profits of the corporation have been permitted to accumulate beyond the reasonable needs of the business may vary under section 534 as between litigation in the Tax Court and that in any other court. In case of a proceeding in a court other than the Tax Court, see paragraph (b) of § 1.533–1.

§ 1.534–2 Burden of proof as to unreasonable accumulations in cases before the Tax Court.

(a) Burden of proof on Commissioner. Under the general rule provided in section 534(a), in any proceeding before the Tax Court involving a notice of deficiency based in whole or in part on the allegation that all or any part of the earnings and profits have been permitted to accumulate beyond the reasonable needs of the business, the burden of proof with respect to such allegation is upon the Commissioner if—

(1) A notification, as provided for in section 534 (b) and paragraph (c) of this section, has not been sent to the taxpayer; or

(2) A notification, as provided for in section 534 (b) and paragraph (c) of this section, has been sent to the taxpayer and, in response to such notification, the taxpayer has submitted a statement, as provided in section 534(c) and paragraph (d) of this section, setting forth the ground or grounds (together with facts sufficient to show the basis thereof) on which it relies to establish that all or any part of its earnings and profits have not been permitted to accumulate beyond the reasonable needs of the business. However, the burden of proof in the latter case is upon the

Commissioner only with respect to the relevant ground or grounds set forth in the statement submitted by the taxpayer, and only if such ground or grounds are supported by facts (contained in the statement) sufficient to show the basis thereof.

(b) Burden of proof on the taxpayer. The burden of proof in a Tax Court proceeding with respect to an allegation that all or any part of the earnings and profits have been permitted to accumulate beyond the reasonable needs of the business is upon the taxpayer if—

(1) A notification, as provided for in section 534 (b) and paragraph (c) of this section, has been sent to the taxpayer and the taxpayer has not submitted a statement, in response to such notification, as provided in section 534(c) and paragraph (d) of this section; or

(2) A statement has been submitted by the taxpayer in response to such notification, but the ground or grounds on which the taxpayer relies are not relevant to the allegation or, if relevant, the statement does not contain facts sufficient to show the basis thereof.

(c) Notification to the taxpayer. Under section 534(b) a notification informing the taxpayer that the proposed notice of deficiency includes an amount with respect to the accumulated earnings tax imposed by section 531 may be sent by registered mail (or by certified or registered mail, if the notification is mailed after September 2, 1958) to the taxpayer at any time before the mailing of the notice of deficiency in the case of a taxable year beginning after December 31, 1953, and ending after August 16, 1954. * * * See section 534(d) * * * with respect to a notification in the case of a jeopardy assessment.

(d) Statement by taxpayer. (1) A taxpayer who has received a notification, as provided in section 534(b) and paragraph (c) of this section, that the proposed notice of deficiency includes an amount with respect to the accumulated earnings tax imposed by section 531, may, under section 534(c), submit a statement that all or any part of the earnings and profits of the corporation have not been permitted to accumulate beyond the reasonable needs of the business. Such statement shall set forth the ground or grounds (together with facts sufficient to show the basis thereof) on which the taxpayer relies to establish that there has been no accumulation of earnings and profits beyond the reasonable needs of the business. See paragraphs (a) and (b) of this section for rules concerning the effect of the statement with respect to burden of proof. See §§ 1.537–1 to 1.537–3, inclusive, relating to reasonable needs of the business.

(2) The taxpayer's statement, under section 534 (c) and this paragraph, must be submitted to the Internal Revenue office which issued the notification (referred to in section 534(b) and paragraph (c) of this section) within 60 days after the mailing of such notification. If the taxpayer is unable, for good cause, to submit the statement within such 60-day period, an additional period not exceeding 30 days may be granted upon receipt in the Internal Revenue office concerned (before the expiration of the 60-day period provided herein) of a request from the taxpayer, setting forth the reasons for such request. See section 534(d) * * * with respect to a statement in the case of a jeopardy assessment.

* * *

§ 1.535–1 Definition.

(a) The accumulated earnings tax is imposed by section 531 on the accumulated taxable income. Accumulated taxable income is the taxable income of the corporation with the adjustments prescribed by section 535(b) and § 1.535–2, minus the sum of the dividends paid deduction and the accumulated earnings credit. See section 561 and the regulations thereunder, relating to the definition of the deduction for dividends paid, and section 535(c) and § 1.535–3, relating to the accumulated earnings credit.

* * *

§ 1.535–2 Adjustments to taxable income.

(a) Taxes—(1) United States taxes. In computing accumulated taxable income for any taxable year, there shall be allowed as a deduction the amount by which Federal income and excess profits taxes accrued during the taxable year exceed the credit provided by section 33* (relating to taxes of foreign countries and possessions of the United States), except that no deduction shall be allowed for (i) the accumulated earnings tax imposed by section 531 (or a corresponding section of a prior law), (ii) the personal holding company tax imposed by section 541 (or a corresponding section of a prior law). * * * The deduction is for taxes accrued during the taxable

*Editorial comment: See Sec. 27 rather than Sec. 33.

year, regardless of whether the corporation uses an accrual method of accounting, the cash receipts and disbursements method, or any other allowable method of accounting. In computing the amount of taxes accrued, an unpaid tax which is being contested is not considered accrued until the contest is resolved.

* * *

(b) Charitable contributions. Section 535(b)(2) provides that, in computing the accumulated taxable income of a corporation, the deduction for charitable contributions shall be computed without regard to section 170(b)(2). Thus, the amount of charitable contributions made during the taxable year not allowable as a deduction under section 170 by reason of the limitations imposed by section 170(b)(2) shall be allowed as a deduction in computing accumulated taxable income for the taxable year. However, any excess of the amount of the charitable contributions made in a prior taxable year over the amount allowed as a deduction under section 170 for such year shall not be allowed as a deduction from taxable income in computing accumulated taxable income for the taxable year.

(c) Special deductions disallowed. Sections 241 through 248 provide for the allowance of special deductions for such items as partially tax-exempt interest, certain dividends received, dividends paid on certain preferred stock of public utilities, and organizational expenses. Such special deductions, except the deduction provided by section 248 (relating to organizational expenses) shall be disallowed in computing accumulated taxable income.

(d) Net operating loss. The net operating loss deduction provided in section 172 is not allowed for purposes of computing accumulated taxable income.

(e) Capital losses. (1) Losses from sales or exchanges of capital assets during the taxable year, which are disallowed as deductions under section 1211(a) in computing taxable income, shall be allowed as deductions in computing accumulated taxable income.

(2) The computation of the capital losses allowable as a deduction in computing accumulated taxable income may be illustrated by the following example:

Example. X Corporation has capital losses of $30,000 which are disallowed under section 1211(a) for the taxable year ended December 31, 1956. This amount represents a loss of $25,000 from the sale or exchange of capital assets during the taxable year ended December 31, 1956, plus a $5,000 capital loss carryover resulting from the sale or exchange of capital assets during the taxable year ended December 31, 1955. In computing accumulated taxable income for the taxable year ended December 31, 1956, only the loss of $25,000 arising from the sale or exchange of capital assets during that taxable year will be allowed as a deduction.

(f) Long-term capital gains. (1) There is allowed as a deduction in computing accumulated taxable income, the excess of the net long-term capital gain for the taxable year over the net short-term capital loss for such year (determined without regard to the capital loss carryover provided in section 1212) minus the taxes attributable to such excess as provided by section 535(b)(6). The tax attributable to such excess is the difference between—

(i) The taxes (except the accumulated earnings tax) imposed by subtitle A of the Code for such year, and

(ii) The taxes (except the accumulated earnings tax) imposed by subtitle A computed for such year as if taxable income were reduced by the excess of the net long-term capital gain over net short-term capital loss (including the capital loss carryover to such year).

Where the tax (except the accumulated earnings tax) imposed by subtitle A includes an amount computed under section 1201(a)(2), the tax attributable to such excess is such amount computed under section 1201 (a)(2).

(2) The application of the rule in subparagraph (1) of this paragraph may be illustrated by the following example:

Example. Assume that D Corporation, for the taxable year ended December 31, 1956, has taxable income of $103,000 of which $8,000 is the excess of net long-term capital gain of $12,000 over a net short-term capital loss of $9,000. The $9,000 net short-term capital loss includes a capital loss carryover of $5,000. The amount allowable as a deduction under section 535(b)(6) and subparagraph (1) of this paragraph is $7,250, computed as follows: Net long-term capital gain less net short-term capital loss (computed without regard to the capital loss carryover) is $8,000 (that is, $12,000 net long-term capital gain less $4,000 net short-term capital loss computed without regard to the capital loss carryover of $5,000). The tax attributable to the excess of net long-term capital gain over net short-term capital loss (computed by taking the capital loss carryover into account) is $750, that is, 25 percent of such excess of $3,000, computed under section 1201 (a)(2). The difference of $7,250 ($8,000 less $750) is the amount allowable as a deduction in computing accumulated taxable income.

(3) Section 631(c) (relating to gain or loss in the case of disposal of coal or domestic iron ore) shall have no application in determining the amount of the deduction allowable under section 535(b)(6).

(g) Capital loss carrybacks and carryovers. Capital losses carried to a taxable year under section 1212(a) shall have no application for purposes of computing accumulated taxable income for such year.

§ 1.535–3 Accumulated earnings credit.

(a) In general. As provided in section 535(a) and § 1.535–1, the accumulated earnings credit, provided by section 535(c), reduces taxable income in computing accumulated taxable income. In the case of a corporation, not a mere holding or investment company, the accumulated earnings credit is determined as provided in paragraph (b) of this section and, in the case of a holding or investment company, as provided in paragraph (c) of this section.

(b) Corporation which is not a mere holding or investment company—(1) General rule. (i) In the case of a corporation, not a mere holding or investment company, the accumulated earn- ings credit is the amount equal to such part of the earnings and profits of the taxable year which is retained for the reasonable needs of the business, minus the deduction allowed by section 535(b)(6) (see paragraph (f) of § 1.535–2, relating to the deduction for long-term capital gains). In no event shall the accumulated earnings credit be less than the minimum credit provided for in section 535(c)(2) and subparagraph (2) of this paragraph. The amount of the earnings and profits for the taxable year retained is the amount by which the earnings and profits for the taxable year exceed the dividends paid deduction for such taxable year. See section 561 and §§ 1.561–1 and 1.561–2, relating to the deduction for dividends paid.

(ii) In determining whether any amount of the earnings and profits of the taxable year has been retained for the reasonable needs of the business, the accumulated earnings and profits of prior years will be taken into consideration. Thus, for example, if such accumulated earnings and profits of prior years are sufficient for the reasonable needs of the business, then any earnings and profits of the current taxable year which are retained will not be considered to be retained for the reasonable needs of the business. See section 537 and §§ 1.537–1 and 1.537–2.

(2) Minimum credit. Section 535(c)(2) provides for the allowance of a minimum accumulated earnings credit in the case of a corporation which is not a mere holding or investment company. Except as otherwise provided in section 243(b)(3) and § 1.243–5 (relating to effect of 100-percent dividends received deduction under section 243(b)) and sections 1561, 1562, and 1564 (relating to limitations on certain tax benefits in the case of certain controlled corporations), in the case of such a corporation, this minimum credit shall in no case be less than the amount by which $150,000* ($100,000 in the case of taxable years beginning before January 1, 1975) exceeds the accumulated earnings and profits of the corporation at the close of the preceding taxable year. See paragraph (d) of this section for the effect of dividends paid after the close of the taxable year in determining accumulated earnings and profits at the close of the preceding taxable year. In determining the amount of the minimum credit allowable under section 535(c)(2), the needs of the business are not taken into consideration. If the taxpayer has accumulated earnings and profits at the close of the preceding taxable year equal to or in excess of $150,000* ($100,000 in the case of taxable years beginning before January 1, 1975), the credit, if any, is determined without regard to section 535(c)(2). It is not intended that the provision for the minimum credit shall in any way create an inference that an accumulation in excess of $150,000* ($100,000 in the case of taxable years beginning before January 1, 1975) is unreasonable. The reasonable needs of the business may require the accumulation of more or less than $150,000* ($100,000 in the case of taxable years beginning before January 1, 1975), depending upon the circumstances in the case, but such needs shall not be taken into consideration to any extent in cases where the minimum accumulated earnings credit is applicable. For a discussion of the reasonable needs of the business, see section 537 and §§ 1.537–1, 1.537–2, and 1.537–3.

(3) Illustrations of accumulated earnings credit. The computation of the accumulated earnings credit provided by section 535(c) may be illustrated by the following examples:

*Editorial comment: For certain corporations, the statutory amount has been increased to $250,000. See Sec. 535(c)(2).

Example (1). The X Corporation, which is not a mere holding or investment company, has accumulated earnings and profits in the amount of $125,000 as of December 31, 1974. Thus, the minimum credit provided by section 535(c)(2) exceeds the accumulated earnings and profits of X by $25,000. It has earnings and profits for the taxable year ended December 31, 1975, in the amount of $100,000 and has a dividends paid deduction under section 561 in the amount of $30,000 so that the earnings and profits for the taxable year which are retained in the business amount to $70,000. Assume that it has been determined that the earnings and profits for the taxable year which may be retained for the reasonable needs of the business amount to $55,000 and that a deduction has been allowed under section 535 (b)(6) in the amount of $5,000. Since the amount by which $150,000 exceeds the accumulated earnings and profits at the close of the preceding taxable year is less than $50,000 ($55,000 – $5,000), the minimum credit provided by section 535(c)(2) will not apply and the accumulated earnings credit must be computed under section 535(c)(1) on the basis of the reasonable needs of the business. In this case, the accumulated earnings credit for the taxable year ended December 31, 1975, will be $50,000 computed as follows:

Earnings and profits of the taxable year determined to be retained for the reasonable needs of the business	$55,000
Less: The deduction for long-term capital gains (less applicable tax) allowed under sec. 535(b)(6)	5,000
Accumulated earnings credit allowable under sec. 535(c)(1)	50,000

Example (2). The Z Corporation which is not a mere holding or investment company, has accumulated earnings and profits in the amount of $45,000 as of December 31, 1974; it has earnings and profits for the taxable year ended December 31, 1975, in the amount of $115,000 and has a dividends paid deduction under section 561 in the amount of $10,000, so that the earnings and profits for the taxable year which are retained amount to $105,000. Assume that it has been determined that the accumulated earnings and profits of the taxable year which may be retained for the reasonable needs of the business amount to $20,000 and that no deduction is allowable for long-term capital gains under section 535(b)(6). The accumulated earnings credit allowable under section 535(c)(1) on the basis of the reasonable needs of the business is determined to be only $20,000. However, since the amount by which $150,000* exceeds the accumulated earnings and profits at the close of the preceding taxable year is more than $20,000, the minimum accumulated earnings credit provided by section 535(c)(2) is applicable. The allowable credit will be the amount by which $150,000* exceeds the accumulated earnings and profits at the close of the preceding taxable year (*i.e.*, $105,000, $150,000* less $45,000 of accumulated earnings and profits at the close of the preceding taxable year).

(c) Holding and investment companies. Section 535(c)(3) provides that, in the case of a mere holding or investment company, the accumulated earnings credit shall be the amount, if any, by which $150,000* ($100,000 in the case of taxable years beginning before January 1, 1975) exceeds the accumulated earnings and profits of the corporation at the close of the preceding taxable year. Thus, if such a corporation has accumulated earnings equal to or in excess of $150,000* ($100,000 in the case of taxable years beginning before January 1, 1975) at the close of its preceding taxable year, no accumulated earnings credit is allowable in computing the accumulated taxable income. See paragraph (c) of § 1.533–1 for a definition of a holding or investment company. For the accumulated earnings credit of a mere holding or investment company which is a member of an affiliated group which has elected the 100 percent dividends received deduction under section 243(b), see section 243(b)(3) and § 1.243–5. For the accumulated earnings credit of a mere holding or investment company which is a component member of a controlled group of corporations (as defined in section 1563), see sections 1561, 1562, and 1564.

§ 1.536–1 Short taxable tears.

Accumulated taxable income for a taxable year consisting of a period of less than 12 months shall not be placed on an annual basis for the purpose of the accumulated earnings tax imposed by section 531. In such cases accumulated taxable income shall be computed on the basis of the taxable income for such period of less than 12 months, adjusted in the manner provided by section 535(b) and § 1.535–2.

§ 1.537–1 Reasonable needs of the business.

(a) In general. The term "reasonable needs of the business" includes (1) the reasonable anticipated needs of the business (including product liability loss reserves, as defined in paragraph (f) of this section), (2) the section 303 redemption needs of the business, as defined in paragraph (c) of this section, and (3) the excess business holdings redemption needs of the business as described in paragraph (d) of this section. See paragraph (E) of this section for additional rules relating to the section 303 redemption needs and the excess business holdings redemption needs of the business. An accumulation of the earnings and profits (including the undistributed earnings and profits of prior years) is in excess of the reasonable

*Editorial comment: For certain corporations, the statutory amount has been increased to $250,000. See Sec. 535(c)(2).

needs of the business if it exceeds the amount that a prudent businessman would consider appropriate for the present business purposes and for the reasonably anticipated future needs of the business. The need to retain earnings and profits must be directly connected with the needs of the corporation itself and must be for bona fide business purposes. For purposes of this paragraph the section 303 redemption needs of the business and the excess business holdings redemption needs of the business are deemed to be directly connected with the needs of the business and for a bona fide business purpose. See § 1.537–3 for a discussion of what constitutes the business of the corporation. The extent to which earnings and profits have been distributed by the corporation may be taken into account in determining whether or not retained earnings and profits exceed the reasonable needs of the business. See § 1.537–2, relating to grounds for accumulation of earnings and profits.

(b) Reasonable anticipated needs. (1) In order for a corporation to justify an accumulation of earnings and profits for reasonably anticipated future needs, there must be an indication that the future needs of the business require such accumulation, and the corporation must have specific, definite, and feasible plans for the use of such accumulation. Such an accumulation need not be used immediately, nor must the plans for its use be consummated within a short period after the close of the taxable year, provided that such accumulation will be used within a reasonable time depending upon all the facts and circumstances relating to the future needs of the business. Where the future needs of the business are uncertain or vague, where the plans for the future use of an accumulation are not specific, definite, and feasible, or where the execution of such a plan is postponed indefinitely, an accumulation cannot be justified on the grounds of reasonably anticipated needs of the business.

(2) Consideration shall be given to reasonably anticipated needs as they exist on the basis of the facts at the close of the taxable year. Thus, subsequent events shall not be used for the purpose of showing that the retention of earnings or profits was unreasonable at the close of the taxable year if all the elements of reasonable anticipation are present at the close of such taxable year. However, subsequent events may be considered to determine whether the taxpayer actually intended to consummate or has actually consummated the plans for which the earnings and profits were accumulated. In this connection, projected expansion or investment plans shall be reviewed in the light of the facts during each year and as they exist as of the close of the taxable year. If a corporation has justified an accumulation for future needs by plans never consummated, the amount of such an accumulation shall be taken into account in determining the reasonableness of subsequent accumulations.

(c) Section 303 redemption needs of the business. (1) The term "section 303 redemption needs" means, with respect to the taxable year of the corporation in which a shareholder of the corporation died or any taxable year thereafter, the amount needed (or reasonably anticipated to be needed) to redeem stock included in the gross estate of such shareholder but not in excess of the amount necessary to effect a distribution to which section 303 applies. For purposes of this paragraph, the term "shareholder" includes an individual in whose gross estate stock of the corporation is includible upon his death for Federal estate tax purposes.

(2) This paragraph applies to a corporation to which section 303(c) would apply if a distribution described therein were made.

(3) If stock included in the gross estate of a decedent is stock of two or more corporations described in section 303(b)(2)(B), the amount needed by each such corporation for section 303 redemption purposes under this section shall, unless the particular facts and circumstances indicate otherwise, be that amount which bears the same ratio to the amount described in section 303(a) as the fair market value of such corporation's stock included in the gross estate of such decedent bears to the fair market value of all of the stock of such corporations included in the gross estate. For example, facts and circumstances indicating that the allocation prescribed by this subparagraph is not required would include notice given to the corporations by the executor or administrator of the decedent's estate that he intends to request the redemption of stock of only one of such corporations or the redemption of stock of such corporations in a ratio which is unrelated to the respective fair market values of the stock of the corporations included in the decedent's gross estate.

(4) The provisions of this paragraph apply only to taxable years ending after May 26, 1969.

* * *

§ 1.537–2 Grounds for accumulation of earnings and profits.

(a) In general. Whether a particular ground or grounds for the accumulation of earnings and profits indicate that the earnings and profits have been accumulated for the reasonable needs of the business or beyond such needs is dependent upon the particular circumstances of the case. Listed below in paragraphs (b) and (c) of this section are some of the grounds which may be used as guides under ordinary circumstances.

(b) Reasonable accumulation of earnings and profits. Although the following grounds are not exclusive, one or more of such grounds, if supported by sufficient facts, may indicate that the earnings and profits of a corporation are being accumulated for the reasonable needs of the business provided the general requirements under §§ 1.537–1 and 1.537–3 are satisfied:

(1) To provide for bona fide expansion of business or replacement of plant;

(2) To acquire a business enterprise through purchasing stock or assets;

(3) To provide for the retirement of bona fide indebtedness created in connection with the trade or business, such as the establishment of a sinking fund for the purpose of retiring bonds issued by the corporation in accordance with contract obligations incurred on issue;

(4) To provide necessary working capital for the business, such as, for the procurement of inventories;

(5) To provide for investments or loans to suppliers or customers if necessary in order to maintain the business of the corporation; or

(6) To provide for the payment of reasonably anticipated product liability losses, as defined in section 172(j), § 1.172–13(b)(1), and § 1.537–1(f).

(c) Unreasonable accumulations of earnings and profits. Although the following purposes are not exclusive, accumulations of earnings and profits to meet any one of such objectives may indicate that the earnings and profits of a corporation are being accumulated beyond the reasonable needs of the business:

(1) Loans to shareholders, or the expenditure of funds of the corporation for the personal benefit of the shareholders;

(2) Loans having no reasonable relation to the conduct of the business made to relatives or friends of shareholders, or to other persons;

(3) Loans to another corporation, the business of which is not that of the taxpayer corporation, if the capital stock of such other corporation is owned, directly or indirectly, by the shareholder or shareholders of the taxpayer corporation and such shareholder or shareholders are in control of both corporations;

(4) Investments in properties, or securities which are unrelated to the activities of the business of the taxpayer corporation; or

(5) Retention of earnings and profits to provide against unrealistic hazards.

§ 1.537–3 Business of the corporation.

(a) The business of a corporation is not merely that which it has previously carried on but includes, in general, any line of business which it may undertake.

(b) If one corporation owns the stock of another corporation and, in effect, operates the other corporation, the business of the latter corporation may be considered in substance, although not in legal form, the business of the first corporation. However, investment by a corporation of its earnings and profits in stock and securities of another corporation is not, of itself, to be regarded as employment of the earnings and profits in its business. Earnings and profits of the first corporation put into the second corporation through the purchase of stock or securities or otherwise, may, if a subsidiary relationship is established, constitute employment of the earnings and profits in its own business. Thus, the business of one corporation may be regarded as including the business of another corporation if such other corporation is a mere instrumentality of the first corporation; that may be established by showing that the first corporation owns at least 80 percent of the voting stock of the second corporation. If the taxpayer's ownership of stock is less than 80 percent in the other corporation, the determination of whether the funds are employed in a business operated by the taxpayer will depend upon the particular circumstances of the case. Moreover, the business of one corporation does not include the business of another corporation if such other corporation is a personal holding company, an investment company, or a corporation not engaged in the active conduct of a trade or business.

Personal Holding Companies

§ 1.541–1 Imposition of tax.

(a) Section 541 imposes a graduated tax* upon corporations classified as personal holding companies under section 542. This tax, if applicable, is in addition to the tax imposed upon corporations generally under section 11. Unless specifically excepted under section 542(c) the tax applies to domestic and foreign corporations and, to the extent provided by section 542(b), to an affiliated group of corporations filing a consolidated return. Corporations classified as personal holding companies are exempt from the accumulated earnings tax imposed under section 531 but are not exempt from other income taxes imposed upon corporations, generally, under any other provisions of the Code. Unlike the accumulated earnings tax imposed under section 531, the personal holding company tax imposed by section 541 applies to all personal holding companies as defined in section 542, whether or not they were formed or availed of to avoid income tax upon shareholders. See section 6501 (f) and § 301.6501(f)–1 of this chapter (Regulations on Procedure and Administration) with respect to the period of limitation on assessment of personal holding company tax upon failure to file a schedule of personal holding company income.

* * *

§ 1.542–1 General rule.

A personal holding company is any corporation (other than one specifically excepted under section 542(c)) which, for the taxable year, meets—

(a) The gross income requirement specified in section 542(a)(1) and § 1.542–2, and

(b) The stock ownership requirement specified in section 542(a)(2) and § 1.542–3.

Both requirements must be satisfied with respect to each taxable year.

§ 1.542–2 Gross income requirement.

To meet the gross income requirement it is necessary that at least 80 percent of the total gross income of the corporation for the taxable year be personal holding company income as defined in section 543 and §§ 1.543–1 and 1.543–2. For the definition of "gross income" see section 61 and §§ 1.61–1 through 1.61–14. Under such provisions gross income is not necessarily synonymous with gross receipts. Further, in the case of transactions in stocks and securities and in commodities transactions, gross income for personal holding company tax purposes shall include only the excess of gains over losses from such transactions. See section 543 (b), paragraph (b)(5) and (6) of § 1.543–1 and § 1.543–2. * * *

§ 1.542–3 Stock ownership requirement.

(a) General rule. To meet the stock ownership requirement, it is necessary that at some time during the last half of the taxable year more than 50 percent in value of the outstanding stock of the corporation be owned, directly or indirectly, by or for not more than 5 individuals. Any organization or trust to which subparagraph (1) of this paragraph applies shall be considered as one individual for purposes of this stock ownership requirement subject, however, to the exception in subparagraph (2) of this paragraph which is applicable only to taxable years beginning after December 31, 1954. Thus, if an organization or trust which is considered as an individual owns 51 percent in value of the outstanding stock of the corporation at any time during the last half of the taxable year, the stock ownership requirement will be met by ownership of the required percentage by one individual. See section 544 and §§ 1.544–1 through 1.544–7 for the determination of stock ownership.

* * *

(b) Changes in stock outstanding. It is necessary to consider any change in the stock outstanding during the last half of the taxable year, whether in the number of shares or classes of stock, or in the ownership thereof. Stock subscribed and paid for will be considered as stock outstanding, whether or not such stock is evidenced by issued certificates. Treasury stock shall not be considered as stock outstanding.

(c) Value of stock outstanding. The value of the stock outstanding shall be determined in the light of all the circumstances. The value may be determined upon the basis of the company's net worth, earning and dividend paying capacity, appreciation of assets, together with such other factors as have a bearing upon the value of the stock. If the value of the stock

*Editorial comment: The Regulations do not include the effect of the Jobs and Growth Tax Relief Reconciliation Act of 2003 which reduced the personal holding company tax rate to 15 percent. See Sec. 541. Likewise, the Regulations do not include the effect of the American Taxpayer Relief Act of 2012 which increased the tax rate from 15 percent to 20 percent.

is greatly at variance with that reflected by the corporate books, the evidence of such value should be filed with the return. In any case where there are two or more classes of stock outstanding, the total value of all the stock should be allocated among the different classes according to the relative value of each class.

* * *

§ 1.543–1 Personal holding company income.

(a) General rule. The term "personal holding company income" means the portion of the gross income which consists of the classes of gross income described in paragraph (b) of this section. See section 543(b) and § 1.543–2 for special limitations on gross income and personal holding company income in cases of gains from stocks', securities', and commodities' transactions.

(b) Definitions—(1) Dividends. The term "dividends" includes dividends as defined in section 316 and amounts required to be included in gross income under section 551 and §§ 1.551–1—1.551–2 (relating to foreign personal holding company income taxed to United States shareholders).

(2) Interest. The term "interest" means any amounts, includible in gross income, received for the use of money loaned. However, (i) interest which constitutes "rent" shall not be classified as interest but shall be classified as "rents" (see subparagraph (10) of this paragraph) * * *.

(3) Royalties (other than mineral, oil, or gas royalties or certain copyright royalties). The term "royalties" (other than mineral, oil, or gas royalties or certain copyright royalties) includes amounts received for the privilege of using patents, copyrights, secret processes and formulas, good will, trade marks, trade brands, franchises, and other like property. It does not, however, include rents. For rules relating to rents see section 543(a)(7) and subparagraph (10) of this paragraph. For rules relating to mineral, oil, or gas royalties, see section 543(a)(8) and subparagraph (11) of this paragraph. For rules relating to certain copyright royalties for taxable years beginning after December 31, 1959, see section 543(a)(9) and subparagraph (12) of this paragraph.

(4) Annuities. The term "annuities" includes annuities only to the extent includible in the computation of gross income. See section 72 and §§ 1.72–1—1.72–14 for rules relating to the inclusion of annuities in gross income.

(5) Gains from the sale or exchange of stock or securities. (i) Except in the case of regular dealers in stock or securities as provided in subdivision (ii) of this subparagraph, gross income and personal holding company income include the amount by which the gains exceed the losses from the sale or exchange of stock or securities. See section 543(b)(1) and § 1.543–2 for provisions relating to this limitation. For this purpose, there shall be taken into account all those gains includible in gross income (including gains from liquidating dividends and other distributions from capital) and all those losses deductible from gross income which are considered under chapter 1 of the Code to be gains or losses from the sale or exchange of stock or securities. The term "stock or securities" as used in section 543(a)(2) and this subparagraph includes shares or certificates of stock, stock rights or warrants, or interest in any corporation (including any joint stock company, insurance company, association, or other organization classified as a corporation by the Code), certificates of interest or participation in any profit-sharing agreement, or in any oil, gas, or other mineral property, or lease, collateral trust certificates, voting trust certificates, bonds, debentures, certificates of indebtedness, notes, car trust certificates, bills of exchange, obligations issued by or on behalf of a State, Territory, or political subdivision thereof.

(ii) In the case of "regular dealers in stock or securities" there shall not be included gains or losses derived from the sale or exchange of stock or securities made in the normal course of business. The term "regular dealer in stock or securities" means a corporation with an established place of business regularly engaged in the purchase of stock or securities and their resale to customers. However, such corporations shall not be considered as regular dealers with respect to stock or securities which are held for investment. See section 1236 and § 1.1236–1.

(6) Gains from futures transactions in commodities. Gross income and personal holding company income include the amount by which the gains exceed the losses from futures transactions in any commodity on or subject to the rules of a board of trade or commodity exchange. See § 1.543–2 for provisions relating to this limitation. In general, for the purpose of determining such excess, there are included all gains and losses on futures contracts which are speculative. However, for the purpose of determining such excess, there shall not be included gains or losses from cash transactions, or gains or losses by a producer, processor, merchant, or handler of the commodity, which arise out of bona fide hedging transactions reasonably necessary to the conduct of its business in the manner in which such business is customarily and usually conducted by others. See section 1233 and § 1.1233–1.

(7) Estates and trusts. Under section 543(a)(4) personal holding company income includes amounts includible in computing the taxable income of the corporation under Part I, subchapter J, chapter 1 of the Code (relating to estates, trusts, and beneficiaries); and any gain derived by the corporation from the sale or other disposition of any interest in an estate or trust.

(8) Personal service contracts. **(i)** Under section 543(a)(5) amounts received under a contract under which the corporation is to furnish personal services, as well as amounts received from the sale or other disposition of such contract, shall be included as personal holding company income if—

(a) Some person other than the corporation has the right to designate (by name or by description) the individual who is to perform the services, or if the individual who is to perform the services is designated (by name or by description) in the contract; and

(b) At any time during the taxable year 25 percent or more in value of the outstanding stock of the corporation is owned, directly or indirectly, by or for the individual who has performed, is to perform, or may be designated (by name or by description) as the one to perform, such services. For this purpose, the amount of stock outstanding and its value shall be determined in accordance with the rules set forth in the last two sentences of paragraph (b) and in paragraph (c) of § 1.542–3. It should be noted that the stock ownership requirement of section 543(a)(5) and this subparagraph relates to the stock ownership at any time during the taxable year. For rules relating to the determination of stock ownership, see section 544 and §§ 1.544–1 through 1.544–7.

(ii) If the contract, in addition to requiring the performance of services by a 25-percent stockholder who is designated or who could be designated (as specified in section 543(a)(5) and subdivision (i) of this subparagraph), requires the performance of services by other persons which are important and essential, then only that portion of the amount received under such contract which is attributable to the personal services of the 25-percent stockholder shall constitute personal holding company income. Incidental personal services of other persons employed by the corporation to facilitate the performance of the services by the 25-percent stockholder, however, shall not constitute important or essential services. Under section 482 gross income, deductions, credits, or allowances between or among organizations, trades, or businesses may be allocated if it is determined that allocation is necessary in order to prevent evasion of taxes or clearly to reflect the income of any such organizations, trades, or businesses.

(iii) The application of section 543(a)(5) and this subparagraph may be illustrated by the following examples:

Example (1). A, whose profession is that of an actor, owns all of the outstanding capital stock of the M Corporation. The M Corporation entered into a contract with A under which A was to perform personal services for the person or persons whom the M Corporation might designate, in consideration of which A was to receive $10,000 a year from the M Corporation. The M Corporation entered into a contract with the O Corporation in which A was designated to perform personal services for the O Corporation in consideration of which the O Corporation was to pay the M Corporation $500,000 a year. The $500,000 received by the M Corporation from the O Corporation constitutes personal holding company income.

Example (2). Assume the same facts as in example (1), except that, in addition to A's contract with the M Corporation, B, whose profession is that of a dancer and C, whose profession is that of a singer, were also under contract to the M Corporation to perform personal services for the person or persons whom the M Corporation might designate, in consideration of which they were each to receive $25,000 a year from the M Corporation. Neither B nor C were stockholders of the M Corporation. The contract entered into by the M Corporation with the O Corporation, in addition to designating that A was to perform personal services for the O Corporation, designated that B and C were also to perform personal services for the O Corporation. Although the O Corporation particularly desired the services of A for an entertainment program it planned, it also desired the services of B and C, who were prominent in their fields, to provide a good supporting cast for the program. The services of B and C required under the contract are determined to be important and essential; therefore, only that portion of the $500,000 received by the M Corporation which is attributable to the personal services of A constitutes personal holding company income. The same result would obtain although the dancer and the singer required by the contract were not designated by name but the contract gave the M Corporation discretion to select and provide the services of a singer and a dancer for the program and such services were provided.

Example (3). The N Corporation is engaged in engineering. Its entire outstanding capital stock is owned by four individuals. The N Corporation entered into a contract with the R Corporation to perform engineering services in consideration of which the R Corporation was to pay the N Corporation $50,000. The individual who was to perform the services was not designated (by name or by description) in the contract and no one but the N Corporation had the right to designate (by name or by description) such individual. The $50,000 received by the N Corporation from the R Corporation does not constitute personal holding company income.

(9) Compensation for use of property. Under section 543(a)(6) amounts received as compensation for the use of, or right to use, property of the corporation shall be included as personal holding company income if, at any time during the taxable year, 25 percent or more in value of the outstanding stock of the corporation is owned, directly or indirectly, by or for an individual entitled to the use of the property. Thus, if a shareholder who meets the stock ownership requirement of section 543(a)(6) and this subparagraph uses, or has the right to use, a yacht, residence, or other property owned by the corporation, the compensation to the corporation for such use, or right to use, the property constitutes personal holding company income. This is true even though the shareholder may acquire the use of, or the right to use, the property by means of a sublease or under any other arrangement involving parties other than the corporation and the shareholder. However, if the personal holding company income of the corporation (after excluding any such income described in section 543(a)(6) and this subparagraph, relating to compensation for use of property, and after excluding any such income described in section 543(a)(7) and subparagraph (10) of this paragraph, relating to rents) is not more than 10 percent of its gross income, compensation for the use of property shall not constitute personal holding company income. For purposes of the preceding sentence, in determining whether personal holding company income is more than 10 percent of gross income, copyright royalties constitute personal holding company income, regardless of whether such copyright royalties are excluded from personal holding company income under section 543(a)(9) and subparagraph (12)(ii) of this paragraph. For purposes of applying section 543(a)(6) and this subparagraph, the amount of stock outstanding and its value shall be determined in accordance with the rules set forth in the last two sentences of paragraph (b) and in paragraph (c) of § 1.542–3. It should be noted that the stock ownership requirement of section 543(a)(6) and this subparagraph relates to the stock outstanding at any time during the entire taxable year. For rules relating to the determination of stock ownership, see section 544 and §§ 1.544–1 through 1.544–7.

(10) Rents (including interest constituting rents). Rents which are to be included as personal holding company income consist of compensation (however designated) for the use, or right to use, property of the corporation. The term "rents" does not include amounts includible in personal holding company income under section 543(a)(6) and subparagraph (9) of this paragraph. The amounts considered as rents include charter fees, etc., for the use of, or the right to use, property, as well as interest on debts owed to the corporation (to the extent such debts represent the price for which real property held primarily for sale to customers in the ordinary course of the corporation's trade or business was sold or exchanged by the corporation). However, if the amount of the rents includible under section 543(a)(7) and this subparagraph constitutes 50 percent or more of the gross income of the corporation, such rents shall not be considered to be personal holding company income.

(11) Mineral, oil, or gas royalties. (i) The income from mineral, oil, or gas royalties is to be included as personal holding company income, unless (a) the aggregate amount of such royalties constitutes 50 percent or more of the gross income of the corporation for the taxable year and (b) the aggregate amount of deductions allowable under section 162 (other than compensation for personal services rendered by the shareholders of the corporation) equals 15 percent or more of the gross income of the corporation for the taxable year.

(ii) The term "mineral, oil, or gas royalties" means all royalties, including overriding royalties and, to the extent not treated as loans under section 636, mineral production payments, received from any interest in mineral, oil, or gas properties. The term "mineral" includes those minerals which are included within the meaning of the term "minerals" in the regulations under section 611.

(iii) The first sentence of subdivision (ii) of this subparagraph shall apply to overriding royalties received from the sublessee by the operating company which originally leased and developed the natural resource property in respect of which such overriding royalties are paid, and to mineral, oil, or gas production payments, only with respect to amounts received after September 30, 1958.

(12) Copyright royalties— (i) In general. The income from copyright royalties constitutes, generally, personal holding company income. However, for taxable years beginning after December 31, 1959, those copyright royalties which come within the definition of "copyright royalties" in section 543(a)(9) and subdivision (iv) of this subparagraph shall be excluded from personal holding company income only if the conditions set forth in subdivision (ii) of this subparagraph are satisfied.

(ii) Exclusion from personal holding company income. For taxable years beginning after December 31, 1959, copyright royalties (as defined in section 543(a)(9) and subdivision (iv) of this subparagraph) shall be excluded from personal holding company income only if the conditions set forth in (a), (b), and (c) of this subdivision are met.

(*a*) Such copyright royalties for the taxable year must constitute 50 percent or more of the corporation's gross income. For this purpose, copyright royalties shall be computed by excluding royalties received for the use of, or the right to use, copyrights or interests in copyrights in works created, in whole or in part, by any person who, at any time during the corporation's taxable year, is a shareholder.

(*b*) Personal holding company income for the taxable year must be 10 percent or less of the corporation's gross income. For this purpose, personal holding company income shall be computed by excluding (1) copyright royalties (except that there shall be included royalties received for the use of, or the right to use, copyrights or interests in copyrights in works created, in whole or in part, by any shareholder owning, at any time during the corporation's taxable year, more than 10 percent in value of the outstanding stock of the corporation), and (2) dividends from any corporation in which the taxpayer owns, on the date the taxpayer becomes entitled to the dividends, at least 50 percent of all classes of stock entitled to vote and at least 50 percent of the total value of all classes of stock, provided the corporation which pays the dividends meets the requirements of subparagraphs (A), (B), and (C) of section 543(a)(9).

(*c*) The aggregate amount of the deductions allowable under section 162 must constitute 50 percent or more of the corporation's gross income for the taxable year. For this purpose, the deductions allowable under section 162 shall be computed by excluding deductions for compensation for personal services rendered by, and deductions for copyright and other royalties to, shareholders of the corporation.

(iii) Determination of stock value and stock ownership. For purposes of section 543(a)(9) and this subparagraph, the following rules shall apply:

(*a*) The amount and value of the outstanding stock of a corporation shall be determined in accordance with the rules set forth in the last two sentences of paragraph (b) and in paragraph (c) of § 1.542–3.

(*b*) The ownership of stock shall be determined in accordance with the rules set forth in section 544 and §§ 1.544–1 through 1.544–7.

(*c*) Any person who is considered to own stock within the meaning of section 544 and §§ 1.544–1 through 1.544–7 shall be a shareholder.

(iv) Copyright royalties defined. For purposes of section 543(a)(9) and this subparagraph, the term "copyright royalties" means compensation, however designated, for the use of, or the right to use, copyrights in works protected by copyright issued under Title 17 of the United States Code (other than by reason of section 2 or 6 thereof), and to which copyright protection is also extended by the laws of any foreign country as a result of any international treaty, convention, or agreement to which the United States is a signatory. Thus, "copyright royalties" includes not only royalties from sources within the United States under protection of United States laws relating to statutory copyrights but also royalties from sources within a foreign country with respect to United States statutory copyrights protected in such foreign country by any international treaty, convention, or agreement to which the United States is a signatory. The term "copyright royalties" includes compensation for the use of, or right to use, an interest in any such copyrighted works as well as payments from any person for performing rights in any such copyrighted works.

(v) Compensation which is rent. Section 543(a)(9) and subdivisions (i) through (iv) of this subparagraph shall not apply to compensation which is "rent" within the meaning of the second sentence of section 543(a)(7).

§ 1.543–2 Limitation on gross income and personal holding company income in transactions involving stocks, securities and commodities.

(a) Under section 543(b)(1) the gains which are to be included in gross income, and in personal holding company income with respect to transactions described in section 543(a)(2) and paragraph (b)(5) of § 1.543–1, shall be the net gains from the sale or exchange of stock or securities. If there is an excess of losses over gains from such transactions, such excess (or net loss) shall not be used to reduce gross income or personal holding company income for purposes of the personal holding company tax. Similarly, under section 543(b)(2) the gains which are to be included in gross income, and in personal holding company income with respect to transactions described in section 543(a)(3) and paragraph (b)(6) of § 1.543–1, shall be the net gains from commodity transactions which reflect personal holding company income. Any excess of losses over gains from such transactions (resulting in a net loss) shall not be used to reduce gross income or personal holding company income. The capital loss carryover under section 1212 shall not be taken into account.

(b) The application of section 543(b) may be illustrated by the following examples:

Example (1). The P Corporation, not a regular dealer in stocks and securities, received rentals of $250,000 for its property from a 25-percent shareholder, and also had gains of $50,000 during the taxable year from the sale of stocks and securities. It also had losses on the sale of stocks and securities in the amount of $30,000. Accordingly, P Corporation had gross income during the taxable year of $270,000 ($250,000 plus $20,000 net gain from the sales of stocks and securities). It had personal holding company income of $20,000. (The rentals of $250,000 would not be personal holding company income under section 543(a)(6) since the personal holding company income of the corporation, $20,000 (after excluding any such income described in section 543(a)(6)), is not more than 10 percent of its gross income.)

* * *

§ 1.544–1 Constructive ownership.

(a) Rules relating to the constructive ownership of stock are provided by section 544 for the purpose of determining whether the stock ownership requirements of the following sections are satisfied:

(1) Section 542(a)(2), relating to ownership of stock by five or fewer individuals.

(2) Section 543(a)(5), relating to personal holding company income derived from personal service contracts.

(3) Section 543(a)(6), relating to personal holding company income derived from property used by shareholders.

(4) Section 543(a)(9), relating to personal holding company income derived from copyright royalties.

(b) Section 544 provides four general rules with respect to constructive ownership. These rules are:

(1) Constructive ownership by reason of indirect ownership. See section 544(a)(1) and § 1.544–2.

(2) Constructive ownership by reason of family and partnership ownership. See section 544(a)(2), (4), (5), and (6), and §§ 1.544–3, 1.544–6, and 1.544–7.

(3) Constructive ownership by reason of ownership of options. See section 544(a)(3), (4), (5), and (6), and §§ 1.544–4, 1.544–6, and 1.544–7.

(4) Constructive ownership by reason of ownership of convertible securities. See section 544(b) and § 1.544–5.

Each of the rules referred to in subparagraphs (2), (3), and (4) of this paragraph is applicable only if it has the effect of satisfying the stock ownership requirement of the section to which applicable; that is, when applied to section 542(a)(2), its effect is to make the corporation a personal holding company, or when applied to section 543(a)(5), section 543(a)(6), or section 543(a)(9), its effect is to make the amounts described in such provisions includible as personal holding company income.

(c) All forms and classes of stock, however denominated, which represent the interests of shareholders, members, or beneficiaries in the corporation shall be taken into consideration in applying the constructive ownership rules of section 544.

(d) For rules applicable in treating constructive ownership, determined by one application of section 544, as actual ownership for purposes of a second application of section 544, see section 544(a)(5) and § 1.544–6.

§ 1.544–2 Constructive ownership by reason of indirect ownership.

The following example illustrates the application of section 544(a)(1), relating to constructive ownership by reason of indirect ownership:

Example. A and B, two individuals, are the exclusive and equal beneficiaries of a trust or estate which owns the entire capital stock of the M Corporation. The M Corporation in turn owns the entire capital stock of the N Corporation. Under such circumstances the entire capital stock of both the M Corporation and the N Corporation shall be considered as being owned equally by A and B as the individuals owning the beneficial interest therein.

§ 1.544–3 Constructive ownership by reason of family and partnership ownership.

(a) The following example illustrates the application of section 544(a)(2), relating to constructive ownership by reason of family and partnership ownership.

Example. The M Corporation at some time during the last half of the taxable year, had 1,800 shares of outstanding stock, 450 of which were held by various individuals having no relationship to one another and none of whom were partners, and the remaining 1,350 were held by 51 shareholders as follows:

Relationships	Shares	Shares	Shares	Shares	Shares
An individual	(A)100	(B)20	(C)20	(D)20	(E)20
His father	(AF)10	(BF)10	(CF)10	(DF)10	(EF)10
His wife	(AW)10	(BW)40	(CW)40	(DW)40	(EW)40
His brother	(AB)10	(BB)10	(CB)10	(DB)10	(EB)10
His son	(AS)10	(BS)40	(CS)40	(DS)40	(ES)40
His daughter by former marriage (son's half-sister)	(ASHS)10	(BSHS)40	(CSHS)40	(DSHS)40	(ESHS)40
His brother's wife	(ABW)10	(BBW)10	(CBW)10	(DBW)160	(EBW)10
His wife's father	(AWF)10	(BWF)10	(CWF)110	(DWF)10	(EWF)10
His wife's brother	(AWB)10	(BWB)10	(CWB)10	(DWB)10	(EWB)10
His wife's brother's wife	(AWBW)10	(BWBW)10	(CWBW)10	(DWBW)10	(EWBW)110
Individual's partner	(AP)10	....	....	....	....

By applying the statutory rule provided in section 544(a)(2) five individuals own more than 50 percent of the outstanding stock as follows:

A (including AF, AW, AB, AS, ASHS, AP)	160
B (including BF, BW, BB, BS, BSHS)	160
CW (including C, CS, CWF, CWB)	220
DB (including D, DF, DBW)	200
EWB (including EW, EWF, EWBW)	170
Total, or more than 50 percent	910

Individual A represents the obvious case where the head of the family owns the bulk of the family stock and naturally is the head of the group. A's partner owns 10 shares of the stock. Individual B represents the case where he is still head of the group because of the ownership of stock by his immediate family. Individuals C and D represent cases where the individuals fall in groups headed in C's case by his wife and in D's case by his brother because of the preponderance of holdings on the part of relatives by marriage. Individual E represents the case where the preponderant holdings of others eliminate that individual from the group.

(b) For the restriction on the applicability of the family and partnership ownership rules of this section, see paragraph (b) of § 1.544–1. For rules relating to constructive ownership as actual ownership, see § 1.544–6.

§ 1.544–4 Options.

The shares of stock which may be acquired by reason of an option shall be considered to be constructively owned by the individual having the option to acquire such stock. * * *

§ 1.544–5 Convertible securities.

Under section 544(b) outstanding securities of a corporation such as bonds, debentures, or other corporate obligations, convertible into stock of the corporation (whether or not convertible during the taxable year) shall be considered as outstanding stock of the corporation. The consideration of convertible securities as outstanding stock is subject to the exception that, if some of the outstanding securities are convertible only after a later date than in the case of others, the class having the earlier conversion date may be considered as outstanding stock although the others are not so considered, but no convertible securities shall be considered as outstanding stock unless all outstanding securities having a prior conversion date are also so considered. For example, if outstanding securities are convertible in 1954, 1955 and 1956, those convertible in 1954 can be properly considered as outstanding stock without so considering those convertible in 1955 or 1956, and those convertible in 1954 and 1955 can be properly considered as outstanding stock without so considering those convertible in 1956. However, the securities convertible in 1955 could not be properly considered as outstanding stock without so considering those convertible in 1954 and the securities convertible in 1956 could not be properly considered as outstanding stock without so considering those convertible in 1954 and 1955. For the restriction on the applicability of the rule of this section, see paragraph (b) of § 1.544–1.

§ 1.544–6 Constructive ownership as actual ownership.

(a) General rules. (1) Stock constructively owned by a person by reason of the application of the rule provided in section 544(a)(1), relating to stock not owned by an individual, shall be considered as actually owned by such person for the purpose of again applying such rule or of applying the family and partnership rule provided in section 544(a)(2), in order to make another person the constructive owner of such stock, and

(2) Stock constructively owned by a person by reason of the application of the option rule provided in section 544(a)(3) shall be considered as actually owned by such person for the purpose of applying either the rule provided in section 544(a)(1), relating to stock not owned by an individual, or the family and partnership rule provided in section 544(a)(2) in order to make another person the constructive owner of such stock, but

(3) Stock constructively owned by an individual by reason of the application of the family and partnership rule provided in section 544(a)(2) shall not be considered as actually owned by such individual for the purpose of again applying such rule in order to make another individual the constructive owner of such stock.

(b) Examples. The application of this section may be illustrated by the following examples:

Example (1). A's wife, AW, owns all the stock of the M Corporation, which in turn owns all the stock of the O Corporation. The O Corporation in turn owns all the stock of the P Corporation. Under the rule provided in section 544(a)(1), relating to stock not owned by an individual, the stock in the P Corporation owned by the O Corporation is considered to be owned constructively by the M Corporation, the sole shareholder of the O Corporation. Such constructive ownership of the stock of the M Corporation is considered as actual ownership for the purpose of again applying such rule in order to make AW, the sole shareholder of the M Corporation, the constructive owner of the stock of the P Corporation. Similarly, the constructive ownership of the stock by AW is considered as actual ownership for the purpose of applying the family and partnership rule provided in section 544(a)(2) in order to make A the constructive owner of the stock of the P Corporation, if such application is necessary for any of the purposes set forth in paragraph (b) of § 1.544–1. But the stock thus constructively owned by A may not be considered as actual ownership for the purpose of again applying the family and partnership rule in order to make another member of A's family, for example, A's father, the constructive owner of the stock of the P Corporation.

Example (2). B, an individual, owns all the stock of the R Corporation which has an option to acquire all the stock of the S Corporation, owned by C, an individual, who is not related to B. Under the option rule provided in section 544(a)(3) the R Corporation may be considered as owning constructively the stock of the S Corporation owned by C. Such constructive ownership of the stock by the R Corporation is considered as actual ownership for the purpose of applying the rule provided in section 544(a)(1), relating to stock not owned by an individual, in order to make B, the sole shareholder of the R Corporation, the constructive owner of the stock of the S Corporation. The stock thus constructively owned by B by reason of the application of the rule provided in section 544(a)(1) likewise is considered as actual ownership for the purpose, if necessary, of applying the family and partnership rule provided in section 544(a)(2), in order to make another member of B's family, for example, B's wife, BW, the constructive owner of the stock of the S Corporation. However, the family and partnership rule could not again be applied so as to make still another individual the constructive owner of the stock of the S Corporation, that is, the stock constructively owned by BW could not be considered as actually owned by her in order to make BW's father the constructive owner of such stock by a second application of the family and partnership rule.

* * *

§ 1.545–1 Definition.

(a) Undistributed personal holding company income is the amount which is subject to the personal holding company tax imposed under section 541. Undistributed personal holding company income is the taxable income of the corporation adjusted in the manner described in section 545(b) and § 1.545–2, and section 545(c) and § 1.545–3, less the deduction for dividends paid. See part IV (section 561 and following), subchapter G, chapter 1 of the Code, and the regulations thereunder, relating to the dividends paid deduction.

* * *

§ 1.545–2 Adjustments to taxable income.

(a) Taxes— (1) General rule. (i) In computing undistributed personal holding company income for any taxable year, there shall be allowed as a deduction the amount by which Federal income and excess profits taxes accrued during the taxable year exceed the credit provided by section 33* (relating to taxes of foreign countries and possessions of the United States), * * * except that no deduction shall be allowed for (a) the accumulated earnings tax imposed by section 531 (or a corresponding section of a prior law), (b) the personal holding company tax imposed by section 541 (or a corresponding section of a prior law) * * *. The deduction is for taxes for the taxable year, determined under the accrual method of accounting, regardless of whether the corporation uses an accrual method of accounting, the cash receipts and disbursement method, or any other allowable method of accounting. In computing the amount of taxes accrued, an unpaid tax which is being contested is not considered accrued until the contest is resolved.

* * *

(b) Charitable contributions—* * *

(2) Taxable years beginning after December 31, 1969. (i) Section 545(b)(2) provides that, in computing the deduction allowable for charitable contributions for purposes of determining undistributed

*Editorial comment: See Sec. 27 rather than Sec. 33.

personal holding company income of a corporation for taxable years beginning after December 31, 1969, the limitations in section 170(b)(1)(A), (B), and (D)(i) (relating to charitable contributions by individuals) shall apply, and section 170(b)(1)(D)(ii) (relating to excess charitable contributions by individuals of certain capital gain property), section 170(b)(2) (relating to the 5-percent limitation on charitable contributions by corporations), and section 170(d) (relating to carryovers of excess contributions of individuals and corporations) shall not apply.

(ii) Although the limitations of section 170(b)(1)(A), (B), and (D)(i) are 50, 20, and 30 percent, respectively, of an individual's contribution base, these limitations are applied for purposes of section 545(b)(2) by using 50, 20, and 30 percent, respectively, of the corporation's taxable income as adjusted for purposes of section 170(b)(2), that is, the same amount of taxable income to which the 5-percent limitation applies. Thus, the term "contribution base" when used in section 170(b)(1) means the corporation's taxable income computed with the adjustments, other than the 5-percent limitation, provided in section 170(b)(2). However, a further adjustment for this purpose is that the taxable income shall also be computed without the deduction of the amount disallowed under section 545(b)(8), relating to expenses and depreciation applicable to property of the taxpayer. The carryover of charitable contributions made in a prior year, otherwise allowable as a deduction in computing taxable income to the extent provided in section 170(b)(1)(D)(ii) and (d), shall not be allowed as a deduction in computing undistributed personal holding company income for any taxable year.

(iii) See § 1.170A–8 for the rules with respect to the charitable contributions to which the 50-, 20-, and 30-percent limitations apply.

(c) Special deductions disallowed. Part VIII, Subchapter B, chapter 1 of the Code, allows corporations, in computing taxable income, special deductions for such matters as partially tax-exempt interest, certain dividends received, dividends paid on certain preferred stock of public utilities, organizational expenses, etc. See section 241. Such special deductions, except the deduction provided by section 248 (relating to organizational expenses) shall be disallowed in computing undistributed personal holding company income.

(d) Net operating loss. The net operating loss deduction provided in section 172 is not allowed for purposes of the computation of undistributed personal holding company income. For purposes of such a computation, however, there is allowed as a deduction the amount of the net operating loss (as defined in section 172(c)) for the preceding taxable year, except that, in computing undistributed personal holding company income for a taxable year beginning after December 31, 1957, the amount of such net operating loss shall be computed without the deductions provided in part VIII (section 241 and following, except section 248), subchapter B, chapter 1 of the Code.

(e) Long-term capital gains. (1) There is allowed as a deduction the excess of the net long-term capital gain for the taxable year over the net short-term capital loss for such year, minus the taxes attributable to such excess, as provided in section 545(b)(5).

(2) Section 631(c) (relating to gain or loss in the case of disposal of coal or domestic iron ore) shall have no application.

* * *

(h) Expenses and depreciation applicable to property of the taxpayer. (1) In computing undistributed personal holding company income in the case of a personal holding company which owns or operates property, section 545(b)(8) provides a specific limitation with respect to the allowance of deductions for trade or business expenses and depreciation allocable to the operation or maintenance of such property. Under this limitation, these deductions shall not be allowed in an amount in excess of the aggregate amount of the rent or other compensation received for the use of, or the right to use, the property, unless it is established to the satisfaction of the Commissioner—

(i) That the rent or other compensation received was the highest obtainable, or if none was received, that none was obtainable;

(ii) That the property was held in the course of a business carried on bona fide for profit; and

(iii) Either that there was reasonable expectation that the operation of the property would result in a profit, or that the property was necessary to the conduct of the business.

(2) The burden of proof will rest upon the taxpayer to sustain the deduction claimed. If, in computing undistributed personal holding company income, a personal holding company claims deductions for expenses and depreciation allocable to the operation and maintenance of property owned or operated by the company, in an aggregate amount in excess of the rent or other compensation received for the use of, or the right to use, the property, it shall attach to its income tax return a statement setting forth its claim for allowance of the additional deductions, together with a complete statement of the facts and circumstances pertinent to its claim and the arguments on which it relies. * * *

§ 1.545–3 Special adjustment to taxable income.

(a) In general. In computing undistributed personal holding company income for any taxable year beginning after December 31, 1963, section 545(c)(l) provides that, except as otherwise provided in section 545(c), there shall be allowed as a deduction amounts used or amounts irrevocably set aside (to the extent reasonable with reference to the size and terms of the indebtedness) during such year to pay or retire qualified indebtedness (as defined in section 545(c)(3) and paragraph (d) of this section). The reasonableness of amounts irrevocably set aside shall be determined under the rules of paragraph (g)(4) of § 1.545–2.

(b) Amounts used or irrevocably set aside— (1) In general. The deduction is allowable, in any taxable year, only for amounts used or irrevocably set aside in that year to extinguish or discharge qualified indebtedness. If amounts are set aside in 1 year, no deduction is allowable for a later year in which such amounts are actually paid. As long as all other conditions are satisfied, the aggregate amount allowable as a deduction for any taxable year includes all amounts (from whatever source) used and all amounts (from whatever source) irrevocably set aside, irrespective of whether in cash or other medium. The same item shall not be deducted more than once.

* * *

§ 1.547–1 General rule.

Section 547 provides a method under which, by virtue of dividend distributions, a corporation may be relieved from the payment of a deficiency in the personal holding company tax imposed by section 541 (or by a corresponding provision of a prior income tax law), or may be entitled to a credit or refund of a part or all of any such deficiency which has been paid. The method provided by section 547 is to allow an additional deduction for a dividend distribution (which meets the requirements of this section) in computing undistributed personal holding company income for the taxable year for which a deficiency in personal holding company tax is determined. The additional deduction for deficiency dividends will not, however, be allowed for the purpose of determining interest, additional amounts, or assessable penalties, computed with respect to the personal holding company tax prior to the allowance of the additional deduction for deficiency dividends. Such amounts remain payable as if section 547 had not been enacted.

§ 1.547–2 Requirements for deficiency dividends.

(a) In general. There are certain requirements which must be fulfilled before a deduction is allowed for a deficiency dividend under section 547 and this section. These are—

(1) The taxpayer's liability for personal holding company tax shall be determined only in the manner provided in section 547(c) and paragraph (b)(1) of this section.

(2) The deficiency dividend shall be paid by the corporation on, or within 90 days after, the date of such determination and prior to the filing of a claim under section 547(e) and paragraph (b)(2) of this section for deduction for deficiency dividends. This claim must be filed within 120 days after such determination.

(3) The deficiency dividend must be of such a nature as would have permitted its inclusion in the computation of a deduction for dividends paid under section 561 for the taxable year with respect to which the liability for personal holding company tax exists, if it had been distributed during such year. See section 562 and §§ 1.562–1 through 1.562–3. In this connection, it should be noted that under section 316 (b)(2), the term "dividend" means (in addition to the usual meaning under section 316(a)) any distribution of property (whether or not a dividend as defined in section 316(a)) made by a corporation to its shareholders, to the extent of its undistributed personal holding company income (determined under section 545 and §§ 1.545–1 and 1.545–2 without regard to section 316(b)(2)) for the taxable year in respect of which the distribution is made.

* * *

§ 1.547–3 Claim for credit or refund.

(a) If a deficiency in personal holding company tax is asserted for any taxable year, and the corporation has paid any portion of such asserted deficiency, it is entitled to a credit or refund of such payment to the extent that such payment constitutes an overpayment as the result of a deduction for a deficiency dividend as provided in section 547 and §§ 1.547–1 through 1.547–7. It should be noted that a "determination" under section 547(c) and paragraph (b)(1) of § 1.547–2, of taxpayer's liability for personal holding company tax may take place subsequent to the time the deficiency was paid. To secure credit or refund of such overpayment, the taxpayer must file a claim on Form 843 in addition to the claim for the deduction for deficiency dividends required under section 547(e) and paragraph (b)(2) of § 1.547–2.

(b) No interest shall be allowed on such credit or refund.

(c) Such credit or refund will be allowed as if, on the date of the determination under section 547(c) and paragraph (b)(1) of § 1.547–2, two years remained before the expiration of the period of limitation on the filing of claim for refund for the taxable year to which the overpayment relates.

§ 1.547–4 Effect on dividends paid deduction.

The deficiency dividends deduction shall be allowed as of the date the claim is filed. No duplication of deductions with respect to any deficiency dividends is permitted. If a corporation claims and receives the benefit of the provisions of section 547, * * * based upon a distribution of deficiency dividends, that distribution does not become a part of the dividends paid deduction under section 561. Likewise, it will not be made the basis of a dividends paid deduction under section 561 by reason of the application of section 563(b), relating to dividends paid after the close of the taxable year and on or before the 15th day of the third month following the close of such taxable year.

§ 1.547–5 Deduction denied in case of fraud or wilful failure to file timely return.

No deduction for deficiency dividends shall be allowed under section 547(a) if the determination contains a finding that any part of the deficiency is due to fraud with intent to evade tax, or to wilful failure to file an income tax return within the time prescribed by law or prescribed by the Secretary or his delegate in pursuance of law. See § 1.547–7 for effective date.

§ 1.547–6 Suspension of statute of limitations and stay of collection.

(a) Statute of limitations. If the corporation files a claim for a deduction for deficiency dividends under section 547(e) and paragraph (b)(2) of § 1.547–2, the running of the statute of limitations upon assessment, distraint, and collection in court in respect of the deficiency, and all interest, additional amounts, or assessable penalties, shall be suspended for a period of two years after the date of the determination under section 547(c) and paragraph (b)(1) of § 1.547–2.

(b) Stay of collection. If a deficiency in personal holding company tax is established by a determination under section 547(c) and paragraph (b)(1) of § 1.547–2, collection by distraint or court proceeding (except in case of jeopardy), of the deficiency and all interest, additional amounts, and assessable penalties, shall be stayed for a period of 120 days after the date of such determination, and, to the extent any part of such deficiency remains after deduction for deficiency dividends, for an additional period until the date the claim is disallowed. After such claim is allowed or rejected, either in whole or in part, the amount of the deficiency which was not eliminated by the application of section 547, together with interest, additional amounts and assessable penalties, will be assessed and collected in the usual manner.

* * *

Deduction For Dividends Paid

§ 1.561–1 Deduction for dividends paid.

(a) The deduction for dividends paid is applicable in determining accumulated taxable income under section 535, undistributed personal holding company income under section 545. * * * The deduction for dividends paid includes—

(1) The dividends paid during the taxable year;

(2) The consent dividends for the taxable year, determined as provided in section 565; and

(3) In the case of a personal holding company, the dividend carryover computed as provided in section 564.

(b) For dividends for which the dividends paid deduction is allowable, see section 562 and § 1.562–1.

As to when dividends are considered paid, see § 1.561–2.

§ 1.561–2 When dividends are considered paid.

(a) In general. (1) A dividend will be considered as paid when it is received by the shareholder. A deduction for dividends paid during the taxable year will not be permitted unless the shareholder receives the dividend during the taxable year for which the deduction is claimed. See section 563 for special rule with respect to dividends paid after the close of the taxable year.

(2) If a dividend is paid by check and the check bearing a date within the taxable year is deposited in the mails, in a cover properly stamped and addressed to the shareholder at his last known address, at such time that in the ordinary handling of the mails the check would be received by the shareholder within the taxable year, a presumption arises that the dividend was paid to the shareholder in such year.

(3) The payment of a dividend during the taxable year to the authorized agent of the shareholder will be deemed payment of the dividend to the shareholder during such year.

(4) If a corporation, instead of paying the dividend directly to the shareholder, credits the account of the shareholder on the books of the corporation with the amount of the dividend, the deduction for a dividend paid will not be permitted unless it be shown to the satisfaction of the Commissioner that such crediting constituted payment of the dividend to the shareholder within the taxable year.

(5) A deduction will not be permitted for the amount of a dividend credited during the taxable year upon an obligation of the shareholder to the corporation unless it is shown to the satisfaction of the Commissioner that such crediting constituted payment of the dividend to the shareholder within the taxable year.

(6) If the dividend is payable in obligations of the corporation, they should be entered or registered in the taxable year on the books of the corporation, in the name of the shareholder (or his nominee or transferee), and, in the case of obligations payable to bearer, should be received in the taxable year by the shareholder (or his nominee or transferee) to constitute payment of the dividend within the taxable year.

(7) In the case of a dividend from which the tax has been deducted and withheld as required by chapter 3 (section 1441 and following), of the Code the dividend is considered as paid when such deducting and withholding occur.

(b) Methods of accounting. The determination of whether a dividend has been paid to the shareholder by the corporation during its taxable year is in no way dependent upon the method of accounting regularly employed by the corporation in keeping its books or upon the method of accounting upon the basis of which the taxable income of the corporation is computed.

* * *

§ 1.562–1 Dividends for which the dividends paid deduction is allowable.

(a) General rule. Except as otherwise provided in section 562 (b) and (d), the term "dividend", for purposes of determining dividends eligible for the dividends paid deduction, refers only to a dividend described in section 316 (relating to definition of dividends for purposes of corporate distributions). No distribution, however, which is preferential within the meaning of section 562(c) and § 1.562–2 shall be eligible for the dividends paid deduction. * * * Further, for purposes of the dividends paid deduction, the term "dividend" does not include a distribution in liquidation unless the distribution is treated as a dividend under section 316(b)(2) and paragraph (b)(2) of § 1.316–1, or under section 333(e)(1) and paragraph (c) of § 1.333–4 or paragraph (c)(2), (d)(2)(ii), or (d)(2) of § 1.333–5, or qualifies under section 562(b) and paragraph (b) of this section. If a dividend is paid in property (other than money) the amount of the dividends paid deduction with respect to such property shall be the adjusted basis of the property in the hands of the distributing corporation at the time of the distribution. See paragraph (b)(2) of this section for special rules with respect to liquidating distributions by personal holding companies occurring during a taxable year of the distributing corporation beginning after December 31, 1963. Also see section 563 for special rules with respect to dividends paid after the close of the taxable year.

(b) Distributions in liquidation—(1) General rule—(i) In general. In the case of amounts distributed in liquidation by any corporation during a taxable year of such corporation beginning before January 1, 1964, or by a corporation other than a personal holding company (as defined in section 542) or a foreign personal holding company (as defined in section 552) during a taxable year of such a corporation beginning after December 31, 1963, section 562(b) makes an exception to the general rule that a deduction for dividends paid is permitted only with respect to dividends described in section 316. In order to qualify under that exception, the distribution must be one either in complete or partial liquidation of a corporation pursuant to sections 331, 332, or 333.* * * *

§ 1.562–2 Preferential dividends.

(a) Section 562(c) imposes a limitation upon the general rule that a corporation is entitled to a deduction for dividends paid with respect to all dividends which it actually pays during the taxable year. Before a corporation may be entitled to any such deduction with respect to a distribution regardless of the medium in which the distribution is made, every shareholder of the class of stock with respect to which the distribution is made must be treated the same as every other shareholder of that class, and no class of stock may be treated otherwise than in accordance with its dividend rights as a class. The limitation imposed by section 562(c) is unqualified, except in the case of an actual distribution made in connection with a consent distribution (see section 565), if the entire distribution composed of such actual distribution and consent distribution is not preferential. The existence of a preference is sufficient to prohibit the deduction regardless of the fact (1) that such preference is authorized by all the shareholders of the corporation or (2) that the part of the distribution received by the shareholder benefited by the preference is taxable to him as a dividend. A corporation will not be entitled to a deduction for dividends paid with respect to any distribution upon a class of stock if there is distributed to any shareholder of such class (in proportion to the number of shares held by him) more or less than his pro rata part of the distribution as compared with the distribution made to any other shareholder of the same class. Nor will a corporation be entitled to a deduction for dividends paid in the case of any distribution upon a class of stock if there is distributed upon such class of stock more or less than the amount to which it is entitled as compared with any other class of stock. A preference exists if any rights to preference inherent in any class of stock are violated. The disallowance, where any preference in fact exists, extends to the entire amount of the distribution and not merely to a part of such distribution. As used in this section, the term "distribution" includes a dividend as defined in Subchapter C, Chapter 1 of the Code, and a distribution in liquidation referred to in section 562(b).

(b) The application of the provisions of section 562(c) may be illustrated by the following examples:

Example (1). A, B, C, and D are the owners of all the shares of class A common stock in the M Corporation, which makes its income tax returns on a calendar year basis. With the consent of all the shareholders, the M Corporation on July 15, 1954, declared a dividend of $5 a share payable in cash on August 1, 1954, to A. On September 15, 1954, it declared a dividend of $5 a share payable in cash on October 1, 1954, to B, C, and D. No allowance for dividends paid for the taxable year 1954 is permitted to the M Corporation with respect to any part of the dividends paid on August 1, 1954, and October 1, 1954.

Example (2). The N Corporation, which makes its income tax returns on the calendar year basis, has a capital of $100,000 (consisting of 1,000 shares of common stock of a par value of $100) and earnings or profits accumulated after February 28, 1913, in the amount of $50,000. In the year 1954, the N Corporation distributes $7,500 in cancellation of 50 shares of the stock owned by three of the four shareholders of the corporation. No deduction for dividends paid is permissible under section 562(c) and paragraph (a) of this section with respect to such distribution.

Example (3). The P Corporation has two classes of stock outstanding, 10 shares of cumulative preferred, owned by E, entitled to $5 per share and on which no dividends have been paid for two years, and 10 shares of common, owned by F. On December 31, 1954, the corporation distributes a dividend of $125, $50 to E, and $75 to F. The corporation is entitled to no deduction for any part of such dividend paid, since there has been a preference to F. If, however, the corporation had distributed $100 to E and $25 to F, it would have been entitled to include $125 as a dividend paid deduction.

§ 1.562–3 Distributions by a member of an affiliated group.

A personal holding company which files or is required to file a consolidated return with other members of an affiliated group may be required to file a separate personal holding company schedule by reason of the limitations and exceptions provided in section 542(b) and § 1.542–4. Section 562(d) provides that in such case the dividends paid deduction shall be allowed to the personal holding company, with respect

*Editorial comment: The Regulations do not reflect the repeal of Sec. 333 by the Tax Reform Act of 1986.

to a distribution made to any member of the affiliated group, if such distribution would constitute a dividend if it were made to a shareholder which is not a member of the affiliated group.

§ 1.563–1 Accumulated earnings tax.

In the determination of the dividends paid deduction for purposes of the accumulated earnings tax imposed by section 531, a dividend paid after the close of any taxable year and on or before the 15th day of the third month following the close of such taxable year shall be considered as paid during such taxable year, and shall not be included in the computation of the dividends paid deduction for the year of payment. However, the rule provided in section 563(a) is not applicable to dividends paid during the first two and one-half months of the first taxable year of the corporation subject to tax under Chapter 1 of the Internal Revenue Code of 1954.

§ 1.563–2 Personal holding company tax.

In the case of a personal holding company subject to the provisions of section 541, dividends paid after the close of the taxable year and before the 15th day of the third month thereafter shall be included in the computation of the dividends paid deduction for the taxable year only if the taxpayer so elects in its return for such taxable year. The election shall be made by including such dividends in computing its dividends paid deduction. The amount of such dividends which may be included in computing the dividends paid deduction for the taxable year shall not exceed either—

(a) The undistributed personal holding company income of the corporation for the taxable year, computed without regard to this section, or

(b) In the case of a taxable year beginning after December 31, 1969, 20 percent (10 percent, in the case of a taxable year beginning before Jan. 1, 1970) of the sum of the dividends paid during the taxable year (not including consent dividends), computed without regard to this section.

In computing the amount of the dividends paid deduction allowable for any taxable year, the amount allowed by reason of section 563(b) for any preceding taxable year is considered a dividend paid in such preceding taxable year and not in the year of actual distribution. Thus, a double deduction is not allowable.

§ 1.563–3 Dividends considered as paid on last day of taxable year.

(a) General rule. Where a distribution made after the close of the taxable year is considered as paid during such taxable year, for purposes of applying section 562(a) the distribution shall be considered as made on the last day of such taxable year.

(b) Personal holding company tax. In the case of a corporation which under the law applicable to the taxable year in respect of which a distribution is made under section 563(b) and § 1.563–2 is a personal holding company under the law applicable to such taxable year, section 316(b)(2) provides that the term dividend means (in addition to the general rule under section 316(a)) any distribution to the extent of the corporation's undistributed personal holding company income (determined under section 545 without regard to distributions under section 316 (b)(2)) for such year. See paragraph (b) of § 1.316–1.

* * *

§ 1.564–1 Dividend carryover.

(a) General rule. The dividend carryover from the two preceding years, allowable only to personal holding companies, is includible in the dividends paid deduction under section 561. It is computed as follows:

(1) If, for each of the preceding two years, the deduction for dividends paid under section 561 (determined without regard to the dividend carryover to each such year) exceeds the taxable income (adjusted as provided in section 545 for purposes of determining undistributed personal holding company income) then the dividend carryover to the taxable year is the sum of both such excess amounts.

(2) If the deduction for dividends paid under section 561 for the second preceding year (determined without regard to the dividend carryover to such year) exceeds the taxable income for such year (adjusted as provided in section 545), and if the taxable income for the first preceding year (as so adjusted) exceeds the dividends paid deduction for such first preceding year (as so determined), then the dividend carryover to the taxable year shall be such excess amount for the second preceding year, less such excess amount for the first preceding year.

(3) If for the first preceding year the deduction for dividends paid under section 561 (determined without regard to the dividend carryover to such year) exceeds the taxable income (adjusted as provided in section 545) for such year, and such excess is not present in the second preceding year, then the dividend carryover to the taxable year shall be such excess amount for the first preceding year.

(b) Dividend carryover from year in which taxpayer was not a personal holding company. In computing the dividend carryover, the taxable income as adjusted under section 545 of any preceding taxable year shall be determined as if the corporation was, under the law applicable to such taxable year, a personal holding company.

* * *

(e) Computation of dividend carryover. The computation of the dividend carryover may be illustrated by the following examples:

Example (1). The X Corporation, which files its income tax returns on the calendar year basis, has taxable income, adjusted as required by section 545, in the amount of $110,000 and has a dividends paid deduction of $150,000 for the year 1954. For 1955, its taxable income, adjusted as required by section 545, is $200,000 and its dividends paid deduction is $300,000. The dividend carryover to the year 1956 is $140,000, computed as follows:

Dividends paid deduction for 1954	$150,000
Taxable income for 1954	110,000
Dividend carryover from 1954	40,000
Dividends paid deduction for 1955	300,000
Taxable income for 1955	200,000
Dividend carryover from 1955	100,000
Dividend carryover for 2 preceding taxable years, allowable as a deduction for the year 1956	140,000

Example (2). The Y Corporation, which files its income tax returns on the calendar year basis, has taxable income, adjusted as required by section 545, in the amount of $100,000 and has a dividends paid deduction of $150,000 for the year 1954. For 1955, its taxable income, adjusted as required by section 545, is $200,000 and its dividends paid deduction is $170,000. The dividend carryover to the year 1956 is $20,000 computed as follows:

Dividends paid deduction for 1954	$150,000
Taxable income for 1954	100,000
Dividend carryover from 1954	50,000
Taxable income for 1955	200,000
Dividends paid deduction for 1955	170,000
Excess of taxable income over dividends paid deduction	30,000
Dividend carryover for second preceding taxable year, allowable as a deduction for the year 1956	20,000

§ 1.565–1 General rule.

(a) Consent dividends. The dividends paid deduction, as defined in section 561, includes the consent dividends for the taxable year. A consent dividend is a hypothetical distribution (as distinguished from an actual distribution) made by:

(1) A corporation that has a reasonable basis to believe that it is subject to the accumulated earnings tax imposed in part I of subchapter G, chapter 1 of the Code, or

(2) A corporation described in part II (personal holding companies or a corporation with adjust- ed income from rents described in section 543(a)(2)(A) which utilizes the consent dividends described in section 543(a)(2)(B)(iii) to avoid personal holding company status) or part III (foreign personal holding companies) of subchapter G or in part I (regulated in vestment companies) or part II (real estate investment trusts) of Subchapter M, Chapter 1 of the Code. A consent dividend may be made by a corporation described in this paragraph to any person who owns consent stock on the last day of the taxable year of such corporation and who agrees to treat the hypothetical distribution as an actual dividend, subject to the limitations in section 565, § 1.565–2, and paragraph (c)(2) of this section, by filing a consent at the time and in the manner specified in paragraph (b) of this section.

(b) Making and filing of consents. (1) A consent shall be made on Form 972 in accordance with this section and the instructions on the form issued therewith. It may be made only by or on behalf of a person who was the actual owner on the last day of the corporation's taxable year of any class of consent stock, that is, the person who would have been required to include in gross income any dividends on such stock actually distributed on the last day of such year. Form 972 shall contain or be verified by a written declaration that it is made under the penalties of perjury. In the consent such person must agree to include in gross income for his taxable year in which or with which the taxable year of the corporation ends a specific amount as a taxable dividend.

(2) See paragraph (c) of this section and § 1.565–2 for the rules as to when all or a portion of the amount so specified will be disregarded for tax purposes.

(3) A consent may be filed at any time not later than the due date of the corporation's income tax return for the taxable year for which the dividends paid deduction is claimed. With such return, and not later than the due date thereof, the corporation must file Forms 972 duly executed by each consenting shareholder, and a return on Form 973 showing by classes the stock outstanding on the first and last days of the taxable year, the dividend rights of such stock, distributions made during the taxable year to shareholders, and giving all the other information required by the form. Form 973 shall contain or be verified by a written declaration that is made under the penalties of perjury.

(c) Taxability of amounts specified in consents. **(1)** The filing of a consent is irrevocable, and except as otherwise provided in section 565(b), § 1.565–2, and paragraph (c)(2) of this section, the full amount specified in a consent filed by a shareholder of a corporation described in paragraph (a) of this section shall be included in the gross income of the shareholder as a taxable dividend. Where the shareholder is taxable on a dividend only if received from sources within the United States, the amount specified in the consent of the shareholder shall be treated as a dividend from sources within the United States in the same manner as if the dividend has been paid in money to the shareholder on the last day of the corporation's taxable year. See paragraph (b) of this section relating to the making and filing of consents, and section 565(e) and § 1.565–5, with respect to the payment requirement in the case of nonresident aliens and foreign corporations.

(2) To the extent that the Commissioner determines that the corporation making a consent dividend is not a corporation described in paragraph (a) of this section, the amount specified in the consent is not a consent dividend and the amount specified in the consent will not be included in the gross income of the shareholder. In addition, where a corporation is described in paragraph (a)(1) but not paragraph (a)(2) of this section, to the extent that the Commissioner determines that the amount specified in a consent is larger than the amount of earnings subject to the accumulated earnings tax imposed by Part I of Subchapter G, such excess is not a consent dividend under paragraph (a) of this section and will not be included in the gross income of the shareholder.

(3) Except as provided in section 565(b), § 1.565–2 and paragraph (c)(2) of this section, once a shareholder's consent is filed, the full amount specified in such consent must be included in the shareholder's gross income as a taxable dividend, and the ground upon which a deduction for consent dividends is denied the corporation does not affect the taxability of a shareholder whose consent has been filed for the amount specified in the consent. For example, although described in part I, II, or III, of subchapter G, or part I or II of subchapter M, chapter 1 of the Code, the corporation's taxable income (as adjusted under section 535(b), 545(b), 556(b), 852(b) (2), or 857(b)(2), as appropriate) may be less than the total of the consent dividends.

* * *

§ 1.565–2 Limitations.

(a) General rule. Amounts specified in consents filed by shareholders or other beneficial owners of a corporation described in § 1.565–1(a) are not treated as consent dividends to the extent that—

(1) They would constitute a preferential dividend or

(2) They would not constitute a dividend (as defined in section 316), if distributed in money to shareholders on the last day of the taxable year of the corporation. If any portion of any amount specified in a consent filed by a shareholder of a corporation described in the preceding sentence is not treated as a consent dividend under section 565(b) and this section, it is disregarded for all tax purposes. For example, it is not taxable to the consenting shareholder, and paragraph (c) of § 1.565–1 is not applicable to this portion of the amount specified in the consent.

(b) Preferential Distribution. **(1)** A preferential distribution is an actual distribution, or a consent distribution, or a combination of the two, which involves a preference to one or more shares of stock as compared with other shares of the same class or to one class of stock as compared with any other class of stock. See section 562(c) and § 1.562–2.

(2) The application of section 565(b)(1) and § 1.565–2(b) may be illustrated by the following examples:

Example (1). The X Corporation, a personal holding company, which makes its income tax returns on the calendar year basis, has 200 shares of stock outstanding, owned by A and B in equal amounts. On December 15, 1967, the corporation distributes $600 to B and $100 to A. As a part of the same distribution, A executes a consent to include $500 in his gross income as a taxable dividend although such amount is not distributed to him. The X Corporation, assuming the other requirements of section 565 have been complied with, is entitled to a consent dividends deduction of $500. Although the consent dividend is deemed to have been paid on December 31, 1987, the last day of the taxable year of the corporation, the total amount of all distributions constitutes a single nonpreferential distribution of $1200.

Example (2). The Y corporation, a personal holding company, which makes its income tax returns on the calendar year basis, has one class of consent stock outstanding, owned in equal amounts by A, B, and C. If A and B each receive a distribution in cash of

$5,000 and C consents to include $3,000 in gross income as a taxable dividend, the combined actual and consent distribution of $13,000 is preferential. See section 562(c) and § 1.562–2(a). Similarly, if no one receives a distribution in cash, but A and B each consents to include $5,000 as a taxable dividend in gross income and C agrees to include only $3,000, the entire consent distribution is preferential.

* * *

(c) Section 316 Limitation. (1) An additional limitation under section 565(b) is that the amounts specified in consents which may be treated as consent dividends cannot exceed the amounts which would constitute a dividend (as defined in section 316) if the corporation had distributed the total specified amounts in money to shareholders on the last day of the taxable year of the corporation. If only a portion of such total would constitute a dividend, then only a corresponding portion of each specified amount is treated as a consent dividend.

(2) The application of section 565(b)(2) and § 1.565–2(c) may be illustrated by the following example:

Example. The X Corporation, a corporation described in § 1.565–(a)(1) or (2), which makes its income tax returns on the calendar year basis, has only one class of stock outstanding, owned in equal amounts by A and B. It makes no distributions during the taxable year 1987. Its earnings and profits for the calendar year 1987 amount to $8,000, there being at the beginning of such year no accumulated earnings or profits. A and B execute proper consents to include $5,000 each in their gross income as a dividend received by them on December 31, 1987. The sum of the amounts specified in the consents executed by A and B is $10,000, but if $10,000 had actually been distributed by the X corporation on December 31, 1987, only $8,000 would have constituted a dividend under section 316(a). The amount which could be considered as consent dividends in computing the dividends paid deduction for purposes of the accumulated earnings tax is limited to $8,000, or $4,000 of the $5,000 specified in each consent. The remaining $1,000 in each consent is disregarded for all tax purposes. (In the case of a personal holding company, see also the example in § 1.565–3(b).)

§ 1.565–3 Effect of consent.

(a) General Rule. The amount of the consent dividend that is described in paragraph (a) of § 1.565–1 shall be considered, for all purposes of the Code, as if it were distributed in money by the corporation to the shareholder on the last day of the taxable year of the corporation, received by the shareholder on such day, and immediately contributed by the shareholder as paid-in capital to the corporation on such day. Thus, the amount of the consent dividend will be treated by the shareholder as a dividend. The shareholder will be entitled to the dividends received deduction under section 243 or 245 with respect to such consent dividend. The basis of the shareholder's consent stock in a corporation will be increased by the amount thus treated in his hands as a dividend which he is considered as having contributed to the corporation as paid-in capital. The amount of the current dividend will also be treated as a dividend received from sources within the United States in the same manner as if the dividend had been paid in money to the shareholders. Among other effects of the consent dividend, the earnings and profits of the corporation will be decreased by the amount of the consent dividends. Moreover, if the shareholder is a corporation, its accumulated earnings and profits will be increased by the amount of the consent dividend with respect to which it makes a consent.

(b) Example. The application of section 565(c) may be illustrated by the following example:

Example. Corporation A, a personal holding company and a calendar year taxpayer, has one shareholder, individual B, whose consent to include $10,000 in his gross income for the calendar year 1987 has been timely filed. A has $8,000 of earnings and profits at the beginning of 1987. A has $10,000 of undistributed personal holding company income (determined without regard to distributions under section 316(b)(2)) for 1987. B must include $10,000 in his gross income as a taxable income and is treated as having immediately contributed $10,000 to A as paid-in capital. See section 316(b)(2).

* * *

§ 1.565–6 Definitions.

(a) Consent stock. (1) The term "consent stock" includes what is generally known as common stock. It also includes participating preferred stock, the participation rights of which are unlimited.

(2) The definition of consent stock may be illustrated by the following example:

Example. If in the case of the X Corporation, a personal holding company, there is only one class of stock outstanding, it would all be consent stock. If, on the other hand, there were two classes of stock, class A and class B, and class A was entitled to 6 percent before any distribution could be made on class B, but class B was entitled to everything distributed after class A had received its 6 percent, only class B stock would be consent stock. Similarly, if class A, after receiving its 6 percent, was to participate equally or in some fixed proportion with class B until it had received a second 6 percent, after which class B alone was entitled to any further distributions, only class B stock would be consent stock. The same result would follow if the order of preferences were class A 6 percent, then class B 6 percent, then class A a second 6 percent, either alone or in conjunction with class B, then class B the remainder. If, however, class A stock is entitled to ultimate participation without limit as to amount, then it, too, may be consent stock. For example, if class A is to receive 3 percent and then share equally or in some fixed proportion with class B in the remainder of the earnings or profits distributed, both class A stock and class B stock are consent stock.

(b) Preferred dividends. (1) The term "preferred dividends" includes all fixed amounts (whether determined by percentage of par value, a stated return expressed in a certain number of dollars per share, or otherwise) the distribution of which on any class of stock is a condition precedent to a further distribution of earnings or profits (not including a distribution in partial or complete liquidation). A distribution, though expressed in terms of a fixed amount, is not a preferred dividend, however, unless it is preferred over a subsequent distribution within the taxable year upon some class or classes of stock other than one on which it is payable.

(2) The definition of preferred dividends may be illustrated by the following example:

Example. If, in the case of the X Corporation, there are only two classes of stock outstanding, class A and class B, and class A is entitled to a distribution of 6 percent of par, after which the balance of the earnings and profits are distributable on class B exclusively, class A's 6 percent is a preferred dividend. If the order of preferences is class A $6 per share, class B $6 per share, then class A and class B in fixed proportions until class A receives $3 more per share, then class B the remainder, all of class A's $9 per share and $6 per share of the amount distributable on class B are preferred dividends. The amount which class B is entitled to receive in conjunction with the payment to class A of its last $3 per share is not a preferred dividend, because the payment of such amount is preferred over no subsequent distribution except one made on class B itself. Finally, if a distribution must be $6 on class A, $6 on class B, then on class A and class B share and share alike, the distribution on class A of $6 and the distribution on class B of $6 are both preferred dividends.

* * *

NATURAL RESOURCES

Deductions

* * *

§ 1.611–1 Allowance of deduction for depletion.

(a) Depletion of mines, oil and gas wells, other natural deposits, and timber—(1) In general. Section 611 provides that there shall be allowed as a deduction in computing taxable income in the case of mines, oil and gas wells, other natural deposits, and timber, a reasonable allowance for depletion. In the case of standing timber, the depletion allowance shall be computed solely upon the adjusted basis of the property. In the case of other exhaustible natural resources the allowance for depletion shall be computed upon either the adjusted depletion basis of the property (see section 612, relating to cost depletion) or upon a percentage of gross income from the property (see section 613, relating to percentage depletion), whichever results in the greater allowance for depletion for any taxable year. In no case will depletion based upon discovery value be allowed.

(2) See § 1.611–5 for methods of depreciation relating to improvements connected with mineral or timber properties.

(3) See paragraph (d) of this section for definition of terms.

(b) Economic interest. (1) Annual depletion deductions are allowed only to the owner of an economic interest in mineral deposits or standing timber. An economic interest is possessed in every case in which the taxpayer has acquired by investment any interest in mineral in place or standing timber and secures, by any form of legal relationship, income derived from the extraction of the mineral or severance of the timber, to which he must look for a return of his capital. For an exception in the case of certain mineral production payments, see section 636 and the regulations thereunder. A person who has no capital investment in the mineral deposit or standing timber does not possess an economic interest merely because through a contractual relation he possesses a mere economic or pecuniary advantage derived from production. For example, an agreement between the owner of an economic interest and another entitling the latter to purchase or process the product upon production or entitling the latter to compensation for extraction or cutting does not convey a depletable economic interest. Further, depletion deductions with respect to an economic interest of a corporation are allowed to the corporation and not to its shareholders.

(2) No depletion deduction shall be allowed the owner with respect to any timber, coal, or domestic iron ore that such owner has disposed of under any form of contract by virtue of which he retains an economic interest in such timber, coal, or iron ore, if such disposal is considered a sale of timber, coal, or domestic iron ore under section 631(b) or (c).

(c) Special rules—(1) In general. For the purpose of the equitable apportionment of depletion among the several owners of economic interests in a mineral deposit or standing timber, if the value of any mineral or timber must be ascertained as of any specific date for the determination of the basis for depletion, the values of such several interests therein may be determined separately, but, when determined as of the same date, shall together never exceed the value at that date of the mineral or timber as a whole.

(2) Leases. In the case of a lease, the deduction for depletion under section 611 shall be equitably apportioned between the lessor and lessee. In the case of a lease or other contract providing for the sharing of economic interests in a mineral deposit or standing timber, such deduction shall be computed by each taxpayer by reference to the adjusted basis of his property determined in accordance with sections 611 and 612, or computed in accordance with section 613, if applicable, and the regulations thereunder.

(3) Life tenant and remainderman. In the case of property held by one person for life with remainder to another person, the deduction for depletion under section 611 shall be computed as if the life tenant were the absolute owner of the property so that he will be entitled to the deduction during his life, and thereafter the deduction, if any, shall be allowed to the remainderman.

* * *

(d) Definitions. As used in this part, and the regulations thereunder, the term—

(1) "Property" means—(i) in the case of minerals, each separate economic interest owned in each mineral deposit in each separate tract or parcel of land or an aggregation or combination of such mineral interests permitted under section 614(b), (c), (d), or (e); and (ii) in the case of timber, an economic interest in standing timber in each tract or block representing a separate timber account (see paragraph (d) of § 1.611–3). For rules with respect to waste or residue of prior mining, see paragraph (c) of § 1.614–1. When, in the regulations under this part, either the word "mineral" or "timber" precedes the word "property," such adjectives are used only to classify the type of "property" involved. For further explanation of the term "property," see section 614 and the regulations thereunder.

(2) "Fair market value" of a property is that amount which would induce a willing seller to sell and a willing buyer to purchase.

(3) "Mineral enterprise" is the mineral deposit or deposits and improvements, if any, used in mining or in the production of oil and gas, and only so much of the surface of the land as is necessary for purposes of mineral extraction. The value of the mineral enterprise is the combined value of its component parts.

(4) "Mineral deposit" refers to minerals in place. When a mineral enterprise is acquired as a unit, the cost of any interest in the mineral deposit or deposits is that proportion of the total cost of the mineral enterprise which the value of the interest in the deposit or deposits bears to the value of the entire enterprise at the time of its acquisition.

(5) "Minerals" includes ores of the metals, coal, oil, gas, and all other natural metallic and nonmetallic deposits, except minerals derived from sea water, the air, or from similar inexhaustible sources. It includes but is not limited to all of the minerals and other natural deposits subject to depletion based upon a percentage of gross income from the property under section 613 and the regulations thereunder.

§ 1.611–2 Rules applicable to mines, oil and gas wells, and other natural deposits.

(a) Computation of cost depletion of mines, oil and gas wells, and other natural deposits. (1) The basis upon which cost depletion is to be allowed in respect of any mineral property is the basis provided for in section 612 and the regulations thereunder. After the amount of such basis applicable to the mineral property has been determined for the taxable year, the cost depletion for that year shall be computed by dividing such amount by the number of units of mineral remaining as of the taxable year (see subparagraph (3) of this paragraph), and by multiplying the depletion unit, so determined, by the number of units of mineral sold within the taxable year (see subparagraph (2) of this paragraph). In the selection of a unit of mineral for depletion, preference shall be given to the principal or customary unit or units paid for in the products sold, such as tons of ore, barrels of oil, or thousands of cubic feet of natural gas.

(2) As used in this paragraph, the phrase "number of units sold within the taxable year"—

(i) In the case of a taxpayer reporting income on the cash receipts and disbursements method, includes units for which payments were received within the taxable year although produced or sold prior to the taxable year, and excludes units sold but not paid for in the taxable year, and

(ii) In the case of a taxpayer reporting income on the accrual method, shall be determined from the taxpayer's inventories kept in physical quantities and in a manner consistent with his method of inventory accounting under section 471 or 472.

The phrase does not include units with respect to which depletion deductions were allowed or allowable prior to the taxable year.

(3) "The number of units of mineral remaining as of the taxable year" is the number of units of mineral remaining at the end of the year to be recovered from the property (including units recovered but not sold) plus the "number of units sold within the taxable year" as defined in this section.

(4) In the case of a natural gas well where the annual production is not metered and is not capable of being estimated with reasonable accuracy, the taxpayer may compute the cost depletion allowance in respect of such property for the taxable year by multiplying the adjusted basis of the property by a fraction, the numerator of which is equal to the decline in rock pressure during the taxable year and the denominator of which is equal to the expected total decline in rock pressure from the beginning of the taxable year to the economic limit of production. Taxpayers computing depletion by this method must keep accurate records of periodical pressure determinations.

(5) If an aggregation of two or more separate mineral properties is made during a taxable year under section 614, cost depletion for each such property shall be computed separately for that portion of the taxable year ending immediately before the effective date of the aggregation. Cost depletion with respect to the aggregated property shall be computed for that portion of the taxable year beginning on such effective date. The allowance for cost depletion for the taxable year shall be the sum of such cost depletion computations. For purposes of this paragraph, each such portion of the taxable year shall be considered as a taxable year. Similar rules shall be applied where a separate mineral property is properly removed from an existing aggregation during a taxable year. See section 614 and the regulations thereunder for rules relating to the effective date of an aggregation of mineral interests and for rules relating to the adjusted basis of an aggregation.

(6) The apportionment of the deduction among the several owners of economic interests in the mineral deposit or deposits will be made as provided in paragraph (c) of § 1.611–1.

* * *

§ 1.612–1 Basis for allowance of cost depletion.

(a) In general. The basis upon which the deduction for cost depletion under section 611 is to be allowed in respect of any mineral or timber property is the adjusted basis provided in section 1011 for the purpose of determining gain upon the sale or other disposition of such property except as provided in paragraph (b) of this section. The adjusted basis of such property is the cost or other basis determined under section 1012, relating to the basis of property, adjusted as provided in section 1016, relating to adjustments to basis, and the regulations under such sections. In the case of the sale of a part of such property, the unrecovered basis thereof shall be allocated to the part sold and the part retained.

* * *

§ 1.613–1 Percentage depletion; general rule.

(a) In general. In the case of a taxpayer computing the deduction for depletion under section 611 with respect to minerals on the basis of a percentage of gross income from the property, as defined in section 613(c) and §§ 1.613–3 and 1.613–4, the deduction shall be the percentage of the gross income as specified in section 613(b) and § 1.613–2. The deduction shall not exceed 50 percent (100 percent in the case of oil and gas properties for taxable years beginning after December 31, 1990) of the taxpayer's taxable income from the property (computed without allowance for depletion). Such taxable income shall be computed in accordance with § 1.613–5. In no case shall the deduction for depletion computed under this section be less than the deduction computed upon the cost or other basis of the property provided in section 612 and the regulations thereunder. The apportionment of the deduction between the several owners of economic interests in a mineral deposit will be made as provided in paragraph (c) of § 1.611–1. For rules with respect to "gross income from the property" and for definition of the term "mining", see §§ 1.613–3 and 1.613–4. For definitions of the terms "property", "mineral deposit", and "minerals", see paragraph (d) of § 1.611–1.

(b) Denial of percentage depletion in case of oil and gas wells. Except as otherwise provided in section 613A and the regulations thereunder, in the case of oil or gas which is produced after December 31, 1974, and to which gross income is attributable after that date, the allowance for depletion shall be computed without regard to section 613.

§ 1.613–2 Percentage depletion rates.

(a) In general. Subject to the provisions of paragraph (b) of this section and as provided in section 613(b), in the case of mines, wells, or other natural deposits, a taxpayer may deduct as an allowance for depletion under section 611 the percentages of gross income from the property. * * *

§ 1.613–3 Gross income from the property.

(a) Oil and gas wells. In the case of oil and gas wells, "gross income from the property", as used in section 613(c)(l), means the amount for which the taxpayer sells the oil or gas in the immediate vicinity of the well. If the oil or gas is not sold on the premises but is manufactured or converted into a refined product prior to sale, or is transported from the premises prior to sale, the gross income from the property shall be assumed to be equivalent to the representative market or filed price of the oil or gas before conversion or transportation.

(b) Minerals other than oil and gas—(1) In general. The term "gross income from the property," as used in section 613(c)(1), means, in the case of a mineral property other than an oil or gas property, gross income from mining. "Gross income from mining" is that amount of income which is attributable to the processes of extraction of the ores or minerals from the ground and the application of mining processes, including mining transportation. For the purpose of this section, "ordinary treatment processes" (applicable to the taxable years beginning before January 1, 1961) and "treatment processes considered as mining" (applicable to the taxable years beginning after December 31, 1960) will be referred to as "mining processes." Processes, including packaging and transportation, which do not qualify as mining will be referred to as "nonmining processes." Also for the purpose of this section, transportation which qualifies as "mining" will be referred to as "mining transportation" and transportation which does not qualify as "mining" will be referred to as "nonmining transportation." See paragraph (f) of this section for the definition of the term "mining" and paragraph (g) of this section for rules relating to nonmining processes.

* * *

§ 1.613–5 Taxable income from the pxroperty.

(a) General rule. The term "taxable income from the property (computed without allowance for depletion)", as used in section 613 and this part, means "gross income from the property" as defined in section 613(c) and §§ 1.613–3 and 1.613–4, less all allowable deductions (excluding any deduction for depletion) which are attributable to mining processes, including mining transportation, with respect to which depletion is claimed. These deductible items include operating expenses, certain selling expenses, administrative and financial overhead, depreciation, taxes deductible under section 162 or 164, losses sustained, intangible drilling and development costs, exploration and development expenditures, etc. See paragraph (c) of this section for special rules relating to discounts and to certain of these deductible items. Expenditures which may be attributable both to the mineral property upon which depletion is claimed and to other activities shall be properly apportioned to the mineral property and to such other activities. Furthermore, where a taxpayer has more than one mineral property, deductions which are not directly attributable to a specific mineral property shall be properly apportioned among the several properties. In determining the taxpayer's taxable income from the property, the amount of any particular item to be taken into account shall be determined in accordance with the principles set forth in paragraph (d)(2) and (3) of § 1.613–4.

* * *

Sales and Exchanges

§ 1.631–1 Election to consider cutting as sale or exchange.

(a) Effect of election. (1) Section 631(a) provides an election to certain taxpayers to treat the difference between the actual cost or other basis of certain timber cut during the taxable year and its fair market value as standing timber on the first day of such year as gain or loss from a sale or exchange under section 1231. Thereafter, any subsequent gain or loss shall be determined in accordance with paragraph (e) of this section.

(2) For the purposes of section 631(a) and this section, timber shall be considered cut at the time when in the ordinary course of business the quantity of timber felled is first definitely determined.

(3) The election may be made with respect to any taxable year even though such election was not made with respect to a previous taxable year. If an election has been made under the provisions of section 631 (a), or corresponding provisions of prior internal revenue laws, such election shall be binding upon the taxpayer not only for the taxable year for which the election is made but also for all subsequent taxable years, unless the Commissioner on showing by the taxpayer of undue hardship permits the taxpayer to revoke his election for such subsequent taxable years. If the taxpayer has revoked a previous election, such revocation shall preclude any further elections unless the taxpayer obtains the consent of the Commissioner.

(4) Such election shall apply with respect to all timber which the taxpayer has owned, or has had a contract right to cut, for a period of more than 1 year (6 months for taxable years beginning before 1977; 9 months for taxable years beginning in 1977) prior to when such timber is cut for sale or for use in the taxpayer's trade or business, irrespective of whether such timber or contract right was acquired before or after the election. (For purposes of the preceding sentence, the rules with respect to the holding period of property contained in section 1223 shall be applicable.) However, timber which is not cut for sale or for use in the taxpayer's trade or business (for example, firewood cut for the taxpayer's own household consumption) shall not be considered to have been sold or exchanged upon the cutting thereof.

(b) Who may make election. (1) A taxpayer who has owned, or has held a contract right to cut, timber for a period of more than 1 year (6 months for taxable years beginning before 1977; 9 months for taxable years beginning in 1977) prior to when the timber is cut may elect under section 631(a) to consider the cutting of such timber during such year for sale or for use in the taxpayer's trade or business as a sale or exchange of the timber so cut. In order to have a "contract right to cut timber" within the meaning of section 631(a) and this section, a taxpayer must have a right to sell the timber cut under the contract on his own account or to use such cut timber in his trade or business.

(2) For purposes of section 631(a) and this section, the term "timber" includes evergreen trees which are more than six years old at the time severed from their roots and are sold for ornamental purposes, such as Christmas decorations. Section 631 (a) is not applicable to evergreen trees which are sold in a live state, whether or not for ornamental purposes. Tops and other parts of standing timber are not considered as evergreen trees within the meaning of section 631(a). The term "evergreen trees" is used in its commonly accepted sense and includes pine, spruce, fir, hemlock, cedar, and other coniferous trees.

(c) Manner of making election. The election under section 631(a) must be made by the taxpayer in his income tax return for the taxable year for which the election is applicable, and such election cannot be made in an amended return for such year. The election in the return shall take the form of a computation under the provisions of section 631(a) and section 1231.

(d) Computation of gain or loss under the election. (1) If the cutting of timber is considered as a sale or exchange pursuant to an election made under section 631(a), gain or loss shall be recognized to the taxpayer in an amount equal to the difference between the adjusted basis for depletion in the hands of the taxpayer of the timber which has been cut during the taxable year and the fair market value of such timber as of the first day of the taxable year in which such timber is cut. The adjusted basis for depletion of the cut timber shall be based upon the number of units of timber cut during the taxable year which are considered to be sold or exchanged and upon the depletion unit of the timber in the timber account or accounts pertaining to the timber cut, and shall be computed in the same manner as is provided in section 611 and the regulations thereunder with respect to the computation of the allowance for depletion.

(2) The fair market value of the timber as of the first day of the taxable year in which such timber is cut shall be determined, subject to approval or revision by the district director upon examination of the taxpayer's return, by the taxpayer in the light of the most reliable and accurate information available with reference to the condition of the property as it existed at that date, regardless of all subsequent changes, such as changes in surrounding circumstances, methods of exploitation, degree of utilization, etc. The value sought will be the selling price, assuming a transfer between a willing seller and a willing buyer as of that particular day. Due consideration will be given to the factors and the principles involved in the determination of the fair market value of timber as described in the regulations under section 611.

(3) The fair market value as of the beginning of the taxable year of the standing timber cut during the year shall be considered to be the cost of such timber, in lieu of the actual cost or other basis of such timber, for all purposes for which such cost is a necessary factor. See paragraph (e) of this section.

(4) For any taxable year for which the cutting of timber is considered to be a sale or exchange of such timber under section 631(a), the timber so cut shall be considered as property used in the trade or business for the purposes of section 1231, along with other property of the taxpayer used in the trade or business as defined in section 1231(b), regardless of whether such timber is property of a kind which would properly be includible in the inventory of the taxpayer if on hand at the close of the taxable year or property held by the taxpayer primarily for sale to customers in the ordinary course of his trade or business. Whether the gain or loss considered to have resulted from the cutting of the timber will be considered to be gain or loss resulting from the sale or exchange of capital assets held for more than 1 year (6 months for taxable years beginning before 1977; 9 months for taxable years beginning in 1977) depends upon the application of section 1231 to the taxpayer for the taxable year. See section 1231 and the regulations thereunder.

(e) Computation of subsequent gain or loss. (1) In case the products of the timber are sold after cutting, either in the form of logs or lumber or in the form of manufactured products, the income from such actual sales shall be considered ordinary income. When the election under section 631(a) is in effect, the cost of standing timber cut during the taxable year is determined as if the taxpayer had purchased such timber on the first day of the taxable year. Thus, in determining the cost of the products so sold, the cost of the timber shall be the fair market value on the first day of the taxable year in which the standing timber was cut, in lieu of the actual cost or other basis of such timber.

(2) This is also the rule in case the products of the timber cut during one taxable year, with respect to which an election has been made under section 631 (a), are sold during a subsequent taxable year, whether or not the election provided in section 631 (a) is applicable with respect to such subsequent year. If the products of the timber cut during a taxable year with respect to which an election under section 631(a) was made were not sold during such year and are included in inventory at the close of such year, the fair market value as of the beginning of the year of the timber cut during the year shall be used in lieu of the actual cost of such timber in computing the closing inventory for such year and the opening inventory for the succeeding year. With respect to the costs applicable in the determination of the amount of such inventories, there shall be included the fair market value of the timber cut, the costs of cutting, logging, and all other expenses incident to the cost of converting the standing timber into the products in inventory. See section 471 and the regulations thereunder. The fact that the fair market value as of the first day of the taxable year in which the timber is cut is deemed to be the cost of such timber shall not preclude the taxpayer from computing its inventories upon the basis of cost or market, whichever is lower, if such is the method used by the taxpayer. Nor shall it preclude the taxpayer from computing its inventories under the last-in, first-out inventory method provided by section 472 if such section is applicable to, and has been elected by, the taxpayer.

§ 1.631–2 Gain or loss upon the disposal of timber under cutting contract.

(a) In general. (1) If an owner disposes of timber held for more than 1 year (6 months for taxable years beginning before 1977; 9 months for taxable years beginning in 1977) before such disposal, under any form or type of contract whereby he retains an economic interest in such timber, the disposal shall be considered to be a sale of such timber. The difference between the amounts realized from disposal of such timber in any taxable year and the adjusted basis for depletion thereof shall be considered to be a gain or loss upon the sale of such timber for such year. Such adjusted basis shall be computed in the same manner as provided in section 611 and the regulations thereunder with respect to the allowance for depletion. See paragraph (e)(2) of this section for definition of "owner". For the purpose of determining whether or not the timber disposed of was held for more than 1 year (6 months for taxable years beginning before 1977; 9 months for taxable years beginning in 1977) before such disposal the rules with respect to the holding period of property contained in section 1223 shall be applicable.

(2) In the case of such a disposal, the provisions of section 1231 apply and such timber shall be considered to be property used in the trade or business for the taxable year in which it is considered to have been sold, along with other property of the taxpayer used in the trade or business as defined in section 1231(b), regardless of whether such timber is property held by the taxpayer primarily for sale to customers in the ordinary course of his trade or business. Whether gain or loss resulting from the disposition of the timber which is considered to have been sold will be deemed to be gain or loss resulting from a sale of a capital asset held for more than 1 year (6 months for taxable years beginning before 1977; 9 months for taxable years beginning in 1977) will depend upon the application of section 1231 to the taxpayer for the taxable year.

(b) Determination of date of disposal. (1) For purposes of section 631(b) and this section, the date of disposal of timber shall be deemed to be the date such timber is cut. However, if payment is made to the owner under the contract for timber before such timber is cut the owner may elect to treat the date of payment as the date of disposal of such timber. Such election shall be effective only for purposes of determining the holding period of such timber. Neither section 631(b) nor the election thereunder has any effect on the time of reporting gain or loss. See subchapter E, chapter 1 of the Code and the regulations thereunder. See paragraph (c)(2) of this section for the effect of exercising the election with respect to the payment for timber held for 1 year (6 months for taxable years beginning before 1977; 9 months for taxable years beginning in 1977) or less. See paragraph (d) of this section for the treatment of payments received in advance of cutting.

(2) For purposes of section 631(b) and this section, the "date such timber is cut" means the date when in the ordinary course of business the quantity of timber felled is first definitely determined.

(c) Manner and effect of election to treat date of payment as the date of disposal. (1) The election to treat the date of payment as the date of disposal of timber shall be evidenced by a statement attached to the taxpayer's income tax return filed on or before the due date (including extensions thereof) for the taxable year in which the payment is received. The statement shall specify the advance payments which are subject to the election and shall identify the contract under which the payments are made. * * *

(2) Where the election to treat the date of payment as the date of disposal is made with respect to a payment made in advance of cutting, and such payment is made 1 year (6 months for taxable years beginning before 1977; 9 months for taxable years beginning in 1977) or less from the date the timber disposed of was acquired, section 631(b) shall not apply to such payment irrespective of the date such timber is cut, since the timber was not held for more than six months prior to disposal.

* * *

(e) Other rules for application of section. (1) Amounts paid by the lessee for timber or the acquisition of timber cutting rights, whether designated as such or as a rental, royalty, or bonus, shall be treated as the cost of timber and constitute part of the lessee's depletable basis of the timber, irrespective of the treatment accorded such payments in the hands of the lessor.

(2) The provisions of section 631(b) apply only to an owner of timber. An owner of timber means any person who owns an interest in timber, including a sublessor and a holder of a contract to cut timber. Such owner of timber must have a right to cut timber for sale on his own account or for use in his trade or business in order to own an interest in timber within the meaning of section 631(b).

(3) For purposes of section 631(b) and this section, the term "timber" includes evergreen trees which are more than 6 years old at the time severed from their roots and are sold for ornamental purposes such as Christmas decorations. Tops and other parts of standing timber are not considered as evergreen trees within the meaning of section 631(b). The term "evergreen trees" is used in its commonly accepted sense and includes pine, spruce, fir, hemlock, cedar, and other coniferous trees.

§ 1.631–3 Gain or loss upon the disposal of coal or domestic iron ore with a retained economic interest.

(a) In general. (1) The provisions of section 631 (c) apply to an owner who disposes of coal (including lignite), or iron ore mined in the United States, held for more than 1 year (6 months for taxable years beginning before 1977; 9 months for taxable years beginning in 1977) before such disposal under any form or type of contract whereby he retains an economic interest in such coal or iron ore. The difference between the amount realized from disposal of the coal or iron ore in any taxable year, and the adjusted depletion basis thereof plus the deductions disallowed for the taxable year under section 272, shall be gain or loss upon the sale of the coal or iron ore. See paragraph (b)(4) of this section for the definition of "owner." See paragraph (e) of this section for special rules relating to iron ore.

(2) In the case of such a disposal, the provisions of section 1231 apply, and the coal or iron ore shall be considered to be property used in the trade or business for the taxable year in which it is considered to have been sold, along with other property of the taxpayer used in the trade or business as defined in section 1231(b), regardless of whether the coal or iron ore is property held by the taxpayer primarily for sale to customers in the ordinary course of his trade or business. Whether gain or loss resulting from the disposition of the coal or iron ore which is considered to have been sold will be deemed to be gain or loss resulting from a sale of a capital asset held for more than 1 year (6 months for taxable years beginning before 1977; 9 months for taxable years beginning in 1977) will depend on the application of section 1231 to the taxpayer for the taxable year; *i.e.*, if the gains do not exceed the losses, they shall not be considered as gains and losses from sales or exchanges of capital assets but shall be treated as ordinary gains and losses.

(b) Rules for application of section. **(1)** For purposes of section 631(c) and this section, the date of disposal of the coal or iron ore shall be deemed to be the date the coal or iron ore is mined. If the coal or iron ore has been held for more than 1 year (6 months for taxable years beginning before 1977; 9 months for taxable years beginning in 1977) on the date it is mined, it is immaterial that it had not been held for more than 1 year (6 months for taxable years beginning before 1977; 9 months for taxable years beginning in 1977) on the date of the contract. There shall be no allowance for percentage depletion provided in section 613 with respect to amounts which are considered to be realized from the sale of coal or iron ore under section 631(c).

(2) The term "adjusted depletion basis" as used in section 631(c) and this section means the basis for allowance of cost depletion provided in section 612 and the regulations thereunder. Such "adjusted depletion basis" shall include exploration or development expenditures treated as deferred expenses under section 615(b) or 616(b), or corresponding provisions of prior income tax laws, and be reduced by adjustments under section 1016(a)(9) and (10), or corresponding provisions of prior income tax laws, relating to deductions of deferred expenses for exploration or development expenditures in the taxable year or any prior taxable years. The depletion unit of the coal or iron ore disposed of shall be determined under the rules provided in the regulations under section 611, relating to cost depletion.

(3) (i) In determining the gross income, the adjusted gross income, or the taxable income of the lessee, the deductions allowable with respect to rents and royalties (except rents and royalties paid by a lessee with respect to coal or iron ore disposed of by the lessee as an "owner" under section 631(c)) shall be determined without regard to the provisions of section 631(c). Thus, the amounts of rents and royalties paid or incurred by a lessee with respect to coal or iron ore shall be excluded from the lessee's gross income from the property for the purpose of determining his percentage depletion without regard to the treatment of such rents or royalties in the hands of the recipient under this section. See section 613 and the regulations thereunder.

(ii) (a) However, a lessee who is also a sublessor may dispose of coal or iron ore as an "owner" under section 631(c). Rents and royalties paid with respect to coal or iron ore disposed of by such a lessee under section 631(c) shall increase the adjusted depletion basis of the coal or iron ore and are not otherwise deductible.

(b) The provisions of this subdivision may be illustrated by the following example:

Example. B is a sublessor of a coal lease; A is the lessor; and C is the sublessee. B pays A a royalty of 50 cents per ton. C pays B a royalty of 60 cents per ton. The amount realized by B under section 631(c) is 60 cents per ton and will be reduced by the adjusted depletion basis of 50 cents per ton, leaving a gain of 10 cents per ton taxable under section 631(c).

(4) (i) The provisions of this section applies only to an owner who has disposed of coal or iron ore and retained an economic interest. For the purposes of section 631(c) and this section, the word "owner" means any person who owns an economic interest in coal or iron ore in place, including a sublessor thereof. A person who merely acquires an economic interest and has not disposed of coal or iron ore under a contract retaining an economic interest does not qualify under section 631(c). A successor to the interest of a person who has disposed of coal or iron ore under a contract by virtue of which he retained an economic interest in such coal or iron ore is also entitled to the benefits of this section. Section 631(c) and this section shall not apply with respect to any income realized by any owner as co-adventurer, partner, or principal in the mining of such coal or iron ore.

(ii) The provisions of this subparagraph may be illustrated by the following examples:

Example (1). A owns a tract of coal land in fee. A leases to B the right to mine all the coal in this tract in return for a royalty of 30 cents per ton. B subleases his right to mine coal in this tract to C, who agrees to pay A 30 cents per ton and to pay to B an additional royalty of 10 cents per ton. Section 631(c) applies to the royalties of both A and B, if the other requisites of the section have been met.

Example (2). Assume the same facts as in example (1), except that A dies leaving his royalty interest to D. D has an economic interest in the coal in place and qualifies for section 631(c) treatment with respect to his share of the royalties since he is a successor in title to A.

Example (3). Assume the same facts as in example (1), except that E agrees to pay a sum of money to C in return for 10 cents per ton on the coal mined by C. E has an economic interest, since he must look solely to the extraction of the coal for the return of his investment. However, E has not made a disposal of coal under a contract wherein he retains an economic interest, and, therefore does not qualify under section 631(c). E is entitled to depletion on his royalties.

* * *

(d) Nonapplication of section. Section 631(c) shall not affect the application of the provisions of Subchapter G, chapter 1 of the Code, relating to corporations used to avoid income tax on shareholders. For example, for the purposes of applying section 543 (relating to personal holding companies), the amounts received from a disposal of coal or iron ore subject to section 631(c) shall be considered as mineral royalties. The determination of whether an amount received under a contract to which section 631(c) applies is "personal holding company income" shall be made in accordance with section 543 and the regulations thereunder, without regard to section 631(c) or this section. See also paragraph (e) of § 1.272–1.

(e) Special rules with regard to iron ore. (1) With regard to iron ore, section 631(c) and this section apply only to amounts received or accrued in taxable years beginning after December 31, 1963, attributable to iron ore mined in such taxable years.

(2) Section 631(c) and this section apply only to disposals of iron ore mined in the United States.

(3) For the purposes of section 631(c) and this section, iron ore is any ore which is used as a source of iron, including but not limited to taconite and jaspilite.

(4) Section 631(c) shall not apply to any disposal of iron ore to a person whose relationship to the person disposing of such iron ore would result in the disallowance of losses under section 267 or 707(b).

(5) Section 631(c)(2) results in the denial of section 631(c) treatment in the case of a contract for disposal of iron ore entered into with a person owned or controlled, directly or indirectly, by the same interests which own or control the person disposing of the iron ore, even though section 631(c) treatment would not be denied under the provisions of section 631(c)(1). For example, section 631(c) treatment is denied in the case of a contract for disposal of iron ore entered into between two "brother and sister" corporations, or a parent corporation and its subsidiary. The presence or absence of control shall be determined by applying the same standards as are applied under section 482 (relating to the allocation of income and deductions between taxpayers).

* * *

ESTATES, TRUSTS, BENEFICIARIES, AND DECEDENTS

Estates, Trusts, And Beneficiaries

General Rules For Taxation Of Estates And Trusts

* * *

§ 1.641(a)–1 Imposition of tax; application of tax.

For taxable years beginning after December 31, 1970, section 641 prescribes that the taxes imposed by section 1(d),* as amended by the Tax Reform Act of 1969, shall apply to the income of estates or of any kind of property held in trust. * * * The rates of tax, the statutory provisions respecting gross income, and, with certain exceptions, the deductions and credits allowed to individuals apply also to estates and trust.

§ 1.641(a)–2 Gross income of estates and trusts.

The gross income of an estate or trust is determined in the same manner as that of an individual. Thus, the gross income of an estate or trust consists of all items of gross income received during the taxable year, including:

(a) Income accumulated in trust for the benefit of unborn or unascertained persons or persons with contingent interests;

(b) Income accumulated or held for future distribution under the terms of the will or trust;

(c) Income which is to be distributed currently by the fiduciary to the beneficiaries, and income collected by a guardian of an infant which is to be held or distributed as the court may direct;

(d) Income received by estates of deceased persons during the period of administration or settlement of the estate; and

(e) Income which, in the discretion of the fiduciary, may be either distributed to the beneficiaries or accumulated. The several classes of income enumerated in this section do not exclude others which also may come within the general purposes of section 641.

§ 1.641(b)–1 Computation and payment of tax; deductions and credits of estates and trusts.

Generally, the deductions and credits allowed to individuals are also allowed to estates and trusts. However, there are special rules for the computation of certain deductions and for the allocation between the estate or trust and the beneficiaries of certain credits and deductions. See section 642 and the regulations thereunder. In addition, an estate or trust is allowed to deduct, in computing its taxable income, the deductions provided by sections 651 and 661 and regulations thereunder, relating to distributions to beneficiaries.

§ 1.641(b)–2 Filing of returns and payment of the tax.

(a) The fiduciary is required to make and file the return and pay the tax on the taxable income of an estate or of a trust. Liability for the payment of the tax on the taxable income of an estate attaches to the person of the executor or administrator up to and after his discharge if, prior to distribution and discharge, he had notice of his tax obligations or failed to exercise due diligence in ascertaining whether or not such obligations existed.* * * Liability for the tax also follows the assets of the estate distributed to heirs, devisees, legatees, and distributees, who may be required to discharge the amount of the tax due and unpaid to the extent of the distributive shares received by them. See section 6901. The same considerations apply to trusts.

(b) The estate of an infant, incompetent, or other person under a disability, or, in general, of an individual or corporation in receivership or a corporation in bankruptcy is not a taxable entity separate from the person for whom the fiduciary is acting, in that respect differing from the estate of a deceased person or of a trust. See section 6012(b)(2) and (3) for provisions relating to the obligation of the fiduciary with respect to returns of such persons.

§ 1.641(b)–3 Termination of estates and trusts.

(a) The income of an estate of a deceased person is that which is received by the estate during the period of administration or settlement. The period of administration or settlement is the period actually required by

*Editorial comment: See Sec. 1(e) rather than Sec. 1(d).

the administrator or executor to perform the ordinary duties of administration, such as the collection of assets and the payment of debts, taxes, legacies, and bequests, whether the period required is longer or shorter than the period specified under the applicable local law for the settlement of estates. For example, where an executor who is also named as trustee under a will fails to obtain his discharge as executor, the period of administration continues only until the duties of administration are complete and he actually assumes his duties as trustee, whether or not pursuant to a court order. However, the period of administration of an estate cannot be unduly prolonged. If the administration of an estate is unreasonably prolonged, the estate is considered terminated for Federal income tax purposes after the expiration of a reasonable period for the performance by the executor of all the duties of administration. Further, an estate will be considered as terminated when all the assets have been distributed except for a reasonable amount which is set aside in good faith for the payment of unascertained or contingent liabilities and expenses (not including a claim by a beneficiary in the capacity of beneficiary). Notwithstanding the above, if the estate has joined in making a valid election under section 645 to treat a qualified revocable trust, as defined under section 645 (b)(1), as part of the estate, the estate shall not terminate under this paragraph prior to the termination of the section 645 election period. See section 645 and the regulations thereunder for rules regarding the termination of the section 645 election period.

(b) Generally, the determination of whether a trust has terminated depends upon whether the property held in trust has been distributed to the persons entitled to succeed to the property upon termination of the trust rather than upon the technicality of whether or not the trustee has rendered his final accounting. A trust does not automatically terminate upon the happening of the event by which the duration of the trust is measured. A reasonable time is permitted after such event for the trustee to perform the duties necessary to complete the administration of the trust. Thus, if under the terms of the governing instrument, the trust is to terminate upon the death of the life beneficiary and the corpus is to be distributed to the remainderman, the trust continues after the death of the life beneficiary for a period reasonably necessary to a proper winding up of the affairs of the trust. However, the winding up of a trust cannot be unduly postponed and if the distribution of the trust corpus is unreasonably delayed, the trust is considered terminated for Federal income tax purposes after the expiration of a reasonable period for the trustee to complete the administration of the trust. Further, a trust will be considered as terminated when all the assets have been distributed except for a reasonable amount which is set aside in good faith for the payment of unascertained or contingent liabilities and expenses (not including a claim by a beneficiary in the capacity of beneficiary).

(c) (1) Except as provided in subparagraph (2) of this paragraph, during the period between the occurrence of an event which causes a trust to terminate and the time when the trust is considered as terminated under this section, whether or not the income and the excess of capital gains over capital losses of the trust are to be considered as amounts required to be distributed currently to the ultimate distributee for the year in which they are received depends upon the principles stated in § 1.651(a)–2. See § 1.663–1 et seq. for application of the separate share rule.

* * *

(d) If a trust or the administration or settlement of an estate is considered terminated under this section for Federal income tax purposes (as for instance, because administration has been unduly prolonged), the gross income, deductions, and credits of the estate or trust are, subsequent to the termination, considered the gross income, deductions, and credits of the person or persons succeeding to the property of the estate or trust.

* * *

§ 1.642(b)–1 Deduction for personal exemption.

In lieu of the deduction for personal exemptions provided by section 151:

(a) An estate is allowed a deduction of $600,

(b) A trust which, under its governing instrument, is required to distribute currently all of its income for the taxable year is allowed a deduction of $300, and

(c) All other trusts are allowed a deduction of $100.

A trust which, under its governing instrument, is required to distribute all of its income currently is allowed a deduction of $300, even though it also distributes amounts other than income in the taxable year and even though it may be required to make distributions which would qualify for the charitable contributions deduction under section 642(c) (and therefore does not qualify as a "simple trust" under sections 651–652). A trust for the payment of annuity is allowed a deduction of $300 in a taxable year in which the amount of the annuity required to be paid equals or exceeds all the income of the trust for the taxable year. For the meaning of the term "income required to be distributed currently," see § 1.651(a)–2.

* * *

§ 1.642(c)–1 Unlimited deduction for amounts paid for a charitable purpose.

(a) In general. (1) Any part of the gross income of an estate, or trust which, pursuant to the terms of the governing instrument is paid (or treated under paragraph (b) of this section as paid) during the taxable year for a purpose specified in section 170(c) shall be allowed as a deduction to such estate or trust in lieu of the limited charitable contributions deduction authorized by section 170(a). In applying this paragraph without reference to paragraph (b) of this section, a deduction shall be allowed for an amount paid during the taxable year in respect of gross income received in a previous taxable year, but only if no deduction was allowed for any previous taxable year to the estate or trust, or in the case of a section 645 election, to a related estate, as defined under § 1.645–1(b), for the amount so paid.

(2) In determining whether an amount is paid for a purpose specified in section 170(c)(2) the provisions of section 170(c)(2)(A) shall not be taken into account. Thus, an amount paid to a corporation, trust, or community chest, fund, or foundation otherwise described in section 170(c)(2) shall be considered paid for a purpose specified in section 170(c) even though the corporation, trust, or community chest, fund, or foundation is not created or organized in the United States, any State, the District of Columbia, or any possession of the United States.

(3) See section 642(c)(6) and § 1.642(c)–4 for disallowance of a deduction under this section to a trust which is, or is treated under section 4947(a)(1) as though it were a private foundation (as defined in section 509(a) and the regulations thereunder) and not exempt from taxation under section 501(a).

(b) Election to treat contributions as paid in preceding taxable year—(1) In general. For purposes of determining the deduction allowed under paragraph (a) of this section, the fiduciary (as defined in section 7701(a)(6)) of an estate or trust may elect under section 642(c)(1) to treat as paid during the taxable year (whether or not such year begins before January 1, 1970) any amount of gross income received during such taxable year or any preceding taxable year which is otherwise deductible under such paragraph and which is paid after the close of such taxable year but on or before the last day of the next succeeding taxable year of the estate or trust. * * * No election shall be made, however, in respect of any amount which was deducted for any previous taxable year or which is deducted for the taxable year in which such amount is paid.

(2) Time for making election. The election under subparagraph (1) of this paragraph shall be made not later than the time, including extensions thereof, prescribed by law for filing the income tax return for the succeeding taxable year. Such election shall, except as provided in subparagraph (4) of this paragraph, become irrevocable after the last day prescribed for making it. Having made the election for any taxable year, the fiduciary may, within the time prescribed for making it, revoke the election without the consent of the Commissioner.

* * *

§ 1.642(d)–1 Net operating loss deduction.

The net operating loss deduction allowed by section 172 is available to estates and trusts generally, with the following exceptions and limitations:

(a) In computing gross income and deductions for the purposes of section 172, a trust shall exclude that portion of the income and deductions attributable to the grantor or another person under sections 671 through 678 (relating to grantors and others treated as substantial owners).

(b) An estate or trust shall not, for the purposes of section 172, avail itself of the deductions allowed by section 642(c) (relating to charitable contributions deductions) and sections 651 and 661 (relating to deductions for distributions).

§ 1.642(e)–1 Depreciation and depletion.

An estate or trust is allowed the deductions for depreciation and depletion, but only to the extent the deductions are not apportioned to beneficiaries under sections 167(h)* and 611(b). For purposes of sections 167(h)* and 611(b), the term "beneficiaries" includes charitable beneficiaries. See the regulations under those sections.

* * *

*Editorial comment: The reference is now Sec. 167(d).

§ 1.642(g)–1 Disallowance of double deductions; in general.

Amounts allowable under section 2053(a)(2) (relating to administration expenses) or under section 2054 (relating to losses during administration) as deductions in computing the taxable estate of a decedent are not allowed as deductions in computing the taxable income of the estate unless there is filed a statement, in duplicate, to the effect that the items have not been allowed as deductions from the gross estate of the decedent under section 2053 or 2054 and that all rights to have such items allowed at any time as deductions under section 2053 or 2054 are waived. The statement should be filed with the return for the year for which the items are claimed as deductions or with the district director for the internal revenue district in which the return was filed, for association with the return. The statement may be filed at any time before the expiration of the statutory period of limitation applicable to the taxable year for which the deduction is sought. Allowance of a deduction in computing an estate's taxable income is not precluded by claiming a deduction in the estate tax return, so long as the estate tax deduction is not finally allowed and the statement is filed. However, after a statement is filed under section 642(g) with respect to a particular item or portion of an item, the item cannot thereafter be allowed as a deduction for estate tax purposes since the waiver operates as a relinquishment of the right to have the deduction allowed at any time under section 2053 or 2054.

§ 1.642(g)–2 Deductions included.

It is not required that the total deductions, or the total amount of any deduction, to which section 642 (g) is applicable be treated in the same way. One deduction or portion of a deduction may be allowed for income tax purposes if the appropriate statement is filed, while another deduction or portion is allowed for estate tax purposes. Section 642(g) has no application to deductions for taxes, interest, business expenses, and other items accrued at the date of a decedent's death so that they are allowable as a deduction under section 2053(a)(3) for estate tax purposes as claims against the estate, and are also allowable under section 691(b) as deductions in respect of a decedent for income tax purposes. However, section 642(g) is applicable to deductions for interest, business expenses, and other items not accrued at the date of the decedent's death so that they are allowable as deductions for estate tax purposes only as administration expenses under section 2053(a)(2). Although deductible under section 2053(a)(3) in determining the value of the taxable estate of a decedent, medical, dental, etc., expenses of a decedent which are paid by the estate of the decedent are not deductible in computing the taxable income of the estate. See section 213(d) and the regulations thereunder for rules relating to the deductibility of such expenses in computing the taxable income of the decedent.

§ 1.642(h)–1 Unused loss carryovers on termination of an estate or trust.

(a) If, on the final termination of an estate or trust, a net operating loss carryover under section 172 or a capital loss carryover under section 1212 would be allowable to the estate or trust in a taxable year subsequent to the taxable year of termination but for the termination, the carryover or carryovers are allowed under section 642(h)(1) to the beneficiaries succeeding to the property of the estate or trust. See § 1.641(b)–3 for the determination of when an estate or trust terminates.

(b) The net operating loss carryover and the capital loss carryover are the same in the hands of a beneficiary as in the estate or trust, except that the capital loss carryover in the hands of a beneficiary which is a corporation is a short-term loss irrespective of whether it would have been a long-term or short-term capital loss in the hands of the estate or trust. The net operating loss carryover and the capital loss carryover are taken into account in computing taxable income, adjusted gross income, and the tax-imposed by section 56 (relating to the minimum tax for tax preferences). The first taxable year of the beneficiary to which the loss shall be carried over is the taxable year of the beneficiary in which or with which the estate or trust terminates. However, for purposes of determining the number of years to which a net operating loss, or a capital loss under paragraph (a) of § 1.1212–1, may be carried over by a beneficiary, the last taxable year of the estate or trust (whether or not a short taxable year) and the first taxable year of the beneficiary to which a loss is carried over each constitute a taxable year, and, in the case of a beneficiary of an estate or trust that is a corporation, capital losses carried over by the estate or trust to any taxable year of the estate or trust beginning after December 31, 1963, shall be treated as if they were incurred in the last taxable year of the estate or trust (whether or not a short taxable year). For the treatment of the net operating loss carryover when the last taxable year of the estate or trust is the last taxable year to which such loss can be carried over, see § 1.642(h)–2.

(c) The application of this section may be illustrated by the following examples:

Example (1). A trust distributes all of its assets to A, the sole remainderman, and terminates on December 31, 1954, when it has a capital loss carryover of $10,000 attributable to transactions during the taxable year 1952. A, who reports on the calendar year basis, otherwise has ordinary income of $10,000 and capital gains of $4,000 for the taxable year 1954. A would offset his capital gains of $4,000 against the capital loss of the trust and, in addition, deduct under section 1211 (b) $1,000 on his return for the taxable year 1954. The balance of the capital loss carryover of $5,000 may be carried over only to the years 1955 and 1956, in accordance with paragraph (a) of § 1.1212–1 and the rules of this section.

Example (2). A trust distributes all of its assets, one-half to A, an individual, and one-half to X, a corporation, who are the sole remaindermen, and terminates on December 31, 1966, when it has a short-term capital loss carryover of $20,000 attributable to short-term transactions during the taxable years 1964, 1965, and 1966, and a long-term capital loss carryover of $12,000 attributable to long-term transactions during such years. A, who reports on the calendar year basis, otherwise has ordinary income of $15,000, short-term capital gains of $4,000 and long-term capital gains of $6,000, for the taxable year 1966. A would offset his short-term capital gains of $4,000 against his share of the short-term capital loss carryover of the trust, $10,000 (one-half of $20,000), and, in addition deduct under section 1211 (b) $1,000 (treated as a short-term gain for purposes of computing capital loss carryovers) on his return for the taxable year 1966. A would also offset his long-term capital gains of $6,000 against his share of the long-term capital loss carryover of the trust, $6,000 (one-half of $12,000). The balance of A's share of the short-term capital loss carryover, $5,000, may be carried over as a short-term capital loss carryover to the succeeding taxable year and treated as a short-term capital loss incurred in such succeeding taxable year in accordance with paragraph (b) of § 1.1212–1. X, which also reports on the calendar year basis, otherwise has capital gains of $4,000 for the taxable year 1966. X would offset its capital gains of $4,000 against its share of the capital loss carryovers of the trust, $16,000 (the sum of one-half of each the short-term carryover and the long-term carryover of the trust), on its return for the taxable year 1966. The balance of X's share, $12,000, may be carried over as a short-term capital loss only to the years 1967, 1968, 1969, and 1970, in accordance with paragraph (a) of § 1.1212–1 and the rules of this section.

* * *

§ 1.643(a)–0 Distributable net income; deduction for distributions; in general.

The term "distributable net income" has no application except in the taxation of estates and trusts and their beneficiaries. It limits the deductions allowable to estates and trusts for amounts paid, credited, or required to be distributed to beneficiaries and is used to determine how much of an amount paid, credited, or required to be distributed to a beneficiary will be includible in his gross income. It is also used to determine the character of distributions to the beneficiaries. Distributable net income means for any taxable year, the taxable income (as defined in section 63) of the estate or trust, computed with the modifications set forth in §§ 1.643(a)–1 through 1.643(a)–7.

§ 1.643(a)–1 Deduction for distributions.

The deduction allowable to a trust under section 651 and to an estate or trust under section 661 for amounts paid, credited, or required to be distributed to beneficiaries is not allowed in the computation of distributable net income.

§ 1.643(a)–2 Deduction for personal exemption.

The deduction for personal exemption under section 642(b) is not allowed in the computation of distributable net income.

§ 1.643(a)–3 Capital gains and losses.

(a) In general. Except as provided in § 1.643(a)–6 and paragraph (b) of this section, gains from the sale or exchange of capital assets are ordinarily excluded from distributable net income and are not ordinarily considered as paid, credited, or required to be distributed to any beneficiary.

(b) Capital gains included in distributable net income. Gains from the sale or exchange of capital assets are included in distributable net income to the extent they are, pursuant to the terms of the governing instrument and applicable local law, or pursuant to a reasonable and impartial exercise of discretion by the fiduciary (in accordance with a power granted to the fiduciary by applicable local law or by the governing instrument if not prohibited by applicable local law)—

(1) Allocated to income (but if income under the state statute is defined as, or consists of, a unitrust amount, a discretionary power to allocate gains to income must also be exercised consistently and the amount so allocated may not be greater than the excess of the unitrust amount over the amount of distributable net income determined without regard to this subparagraph § 1.643(a)–3(b));

(2) Allocated to corpus but treated consistently by the fiduciary on the trust's books, records, and tax returns as part of a distribution to a beneficiary; or

(3) Allocated to corpus but actually distributed to the beneficiary or utilized by the fiduciary in determining the amount that is distributed or required to be distributed to a beneficiary.

(c) Charitable contributions included in distributable net income. If capital gains are paid, permanently set aside, or to be used for the purposes specified in section 642(c), so that a charitable deduction is allowed under that section in respect of the gains, they must be included in the computation of distributable net income.

(d) Capital losses. Losses from the sale or exchange of capital assets shall first be netted at the trust level against any gains from the sale or exchange of capital assets, except for a capital gain that is utilized under paragraph (b)(3) of this section in determining the amount that is distributed or required to be distributed to a particular beneficiary. See § 1.642 (h)–1 with respect to capital loss carryovers in the year of final termination of an estate or trust.

(e) Examples. The following examples illustrate the rules of this section:

Example (1). Under the terms of Trust's governing instrument, all income is to be paid to A for life. Trustee is given discretionary powers to invade principal for A's benefit and to deem discretionary distributions to be made from capital gains realized during the year. During Trust's first taxable year, Trust has $5,000 of dividend income and $10,000 of capital gain from the sale of securities. Pursuant to the terms of the governing instrument and applicable local law, Trustee allocates the $10,000 capital gain to principal. During the year, Trustee distributes to A $5,000, representing A's right to trust income. In addition, Trustee distributes to A $12,000, pursuant to the discretionary power to distribute principal. Trustee does not exercise the discretionary power to deem the discretionary distributions of principal as being paid from capital gains realized during the year. Therefore, the capital gains realized during the year are not included in distributable net income and the $10,000 of capital gain is taxed to the trust. In future years, Trustee must treat all discretionary distributions as not being made from any realized capital gains.

Example (2). The facts are the same as in Example 1, except that Trustee intends to follow a regular practice of treating discretionary distributions of principal as being paid first from any net capital gains realized by Trust during the year. Trustee evidences this treatment by including the $10,000 capital gain in distributable net income on Trust's federal income tax return so that it is taxed to A. This treatment of the capital gains is a reasonable exercise of Trustee's discretion. In future years Trustee must treat all discretionary distributions as being made first from any realized capital gains.

Example (3). The facts are the same as in Example 1, except that Trustee intends to follow a regular practice of treating discretionary distributions of principal as being paid from any net capital gains realized by Trust during the year from the sale of certain specified assets or a particular class of investments. This treatment of capital gains is a reasonable exercise of Trustee's discretion.

Example (4). The facts are the same as in Example 1, except that pursuant to the terms of the governing instrument (in a provision not prohibited by applicable local law), capital gains realized by Trust are allocated to income. Because the capital gains are allocated to income pursuant to the terms of the governing instrument, the $10,000 capital gain is included in Trust's distributable net income for the taxable year.

Example (5). The facts are the same as in Example 1, except that Trustee decides that discretionary distributions will be made only to the extent Trust has realized capital gains during the year and thus the discretionary distribution to A is $10,000, rather than $12,000. Because Trustee will use the amount of any realized capital gain to determine the amount of the discretionary distribution to the beneficiary, the $10,000 capital gain is included in Trust's distributable net income for the taxable year.

Example (6). Trust's assets consist of Blackacre and other property. Under the terms of Trust's governing instrument, Trustee is directed to hold Blackacre for ten years and then sell it and distribute all the sales proceeds to A. Because Trustee uses the amount of the sales proceeds that includes any realized capital gain to determine the amount required to be distributed to A, any capital gain realized from the sale of Blackacre is included in Trust's distributable net income for the taxable year.

* * *

§ 1.643(a)–4 Extraordinary dividends and taxable stock dividends.

In the case solely of a trust which qualifies under Subpart B (section 651 and following) as a "simple trust," there are excluded from distributable net income extraordinary dividends (whether paid in cash or in kind) or taxable stock dividends which are not distributed or credited to a beneficiary because the fiduciary in good faith determines that under the terms of the governing instrument and applicable local law such dividends are allocable to corpus. See section 665(e), paragraph (b) of § 1.665(e)–1, and paragraph (b) of § 1.665(e)–1A for the treatment of such dividends upon subsequent distribution.

§ 1.643(a)–5 Tax-exempt interest.

(a) There is included in distributable net income any tax-exempt interest excluded from gross income under section 103, reduced by disbursements allocable to such interest which would have been deductible under section 212 but for the provisions of section 265 (relating to disallowance of deductions allocable to tax-exempt income).

(b) If the estate or trust is allowed a charitable contributions deduction under section 642(c), the amounts specified in paragraph (a) of this section and § 1.643(a)–6 are reduced by the portion deemed to be included in income paid, permanently set aside, or to be used for the purposes specified in section 642(c). If the governing instrument specifically provides as to the source out of which amounts are paid, permanently set aside, or to be used for such charitable purposes, the specific provisions control. In the absence of specific provisions in the governing instrument, an amount to which section 642(c) applies is deemed to consist of the same proportion of each class of the items of income of the estate or trust as the total of each class bears to the total of all classes. For illustrations showing the determination of the character of an amount deductible under section 642(c), see examples (1) and (2) of § 1.662(b)–2 and paragraph (e) of § 1.662(c)–4.

* * *

§ 1.643(a)–7 Dividends.

Dividends excluded from gross income under section 116* (relating to partial exclusion of dividends received) are included in distributable net income. For this purpose, adjustments similar to those required by § 1.643(a)–5 with respect to expenses allocable to tax-exempt income and to income included in amounts paid or set aside for charitable purposes are not made. See the regulations under section 642(c).

§ 1.643(b)–1 Definition of "income."

For purposes of subparts A through D, Part I, Subchapter J, Chapter 1 of the Internal Revenue Code, "income," when not preceded by the words "taxable," "distributable net," "undistributed net," or "gross," means the amount of income of an estate or trust for the taxable year determined under the terms of the governing instrument and applicable local law. Trust provisions that depart fundamentally from traditional principles of income and principal will generally not be recognized. For example, if a trust instrument directs that all the trust income shall be paid to the income beneficiary but defines ordinary dividends and interest as principal, the trust will not be considered one that under its governing instrument is required to distribute all its income currently for purposes of section 642(b) (relating to the personal exemption) and section 651 (relating to simple trusts). Thus, items such as dividends, interest, and rents are generally allocated to income and proceeds from the sale or exchange of trust assets are generally allocated to principal. However, an allocation of amounts between income and principal pursuant to applicable local law will be respected if local law provides for a reasonable apportionment between the income and remainder beneficiaries of the total return of the trust for the year, including ordinary and taxexempt income, capital gains, and appreciation. For example, a state statute providing that income is a unitrust amount of no less than 3% and no more than 5% of the fair market value of the trust assets, whether determined annually or averaged on a multiple year basis, is a reasonable apportionment of the total return of the trust. Similarly, a state statute that permits the trustee to make adjustments between income and principal to fulfill the trustee's duty of impartiality between the income and remainder beneficiaries is generally a reasonable apportionment of the total return of the trust. Generally, these adjustments are permitted by state statutes when the trustee invests and manages the trust assets under the state's prudent investor standard, the trust describes the amount that may or must be distributed to a beneficiary by referring to the trust's income, and the trustee after applying the state statutory rules regarding the allocation of receipts and disbursements to income and principal, is unable to administer the trust impartially. Allocations pursuant to methods prescribed by such state statutes for apportioning the total return of a trust between income and principal will be respected regardless of whether the trust provides that the income must be distributed to one or more beneficiaries or may be accumulated in whole or in part, and regardless of which alternate permitted method is actually used, provided the trust complies with all requirements of the state statute for switching methods. A switch between methods of determining trust income authorized by state statute will not constitute a recognition event for purposes of section 1001 and will not result in a taxable gift from the trust's grantor or any of the trust's beneficiaries. A switch to a method not specifically authorized by state statute, but valid under state law (including a switch via judicial decision or a binding non-judicial settlement) may constitute a recognition event to the trust or its beneficiaries for purposes of section 1001 and may result in taxable gifts from the trust's grantor and beneficiaries, based on the relevant facts and circumstances. In addition, an allocation to income of all or a part of the gains from the sale or exchange of trust assets will generally be respected if the allocation is made either pursuant to the terms of the governing instrument and applicable local law, or pursuant to a reasonable and impartial exercise of a discretionary power granted to the fiduciary by applicable local law or by the governing instrument, if not prohibited by applicable local law. This section is effective for

*Editorial comment: The Regulations do not reflect the effect of the Tax Reform Act of 1986 which repealed the Sec. 116 exclusion.

taxable years of trusts and estates ending after January 2, 2004.

§ 1.643(b)–2 Dividends allocated to corpus.

Extraordinary dividends or taxable stock dividends which the fiduciary, acting in good faith, determines to be allocable to corpus under the terms of the governing instrument and applicable local law are not considered "income" for purposes of Subpart A, B, C, or D, Part I, Subchapter J, Chapter 1 of the Code. See section 643 (a)(4), § 1.643(a)–4, § 1.643(d)–2, section 665(e), paragraph (b) of § 1.665(e)–1, and paragraph (b) of § 1.665(e)–1A for the treatment of such items in the computation of distributable net income.

§ 1.643(c)–1 Definition of "beneficiary."

An heir, legatee, or devisee (including an estate or trust) is a beneficiary. A trust created under a decedent's will is a beneficiary of the decedent's estate. The following persons are treated as beneficiaries:

(a) Any person with respect to an amount used to discharge or satisfy that person's legal obligation as that term is used in § 1.662(a)–4.

(b) The grantor of a trust with respect to an amount applied or distributed for the support of a dependent under the circumstances specified in section 677(b) out of corpus or out of other than income for the taxable year of the trust.

(c) The trustee or cotrustee of a trust with respect to an amount applied or distributed for the support of a dependent under the circumstances specified in section 678(c) out of corpus or out of other than income for the taxable year of the trust.

* * *

§ 1.643(d)–2 Illustration of the provisions of section 643.

(a) The provisions of section 643 may be illustrated by the following example:

Example. (1) Under the terms of the trust instrument, the income of a trust is required to be currently distributed to W during her life. Capital gains are allocable to corpus and all expenses are charges against corpus. During the taxable year the trust has the following items of income and expenses:

Dividends from domestic corporations	$30,000
Extraordinary dividends allocated to corpus by the trustee in good faith	20,000
Taxable interest	10,000
Tax-exempt interest	10,000
Long-term capital gains	10,000
Trustee's commissions and miscellaneous expenses allocable to corpus	5,000

(2) The "income" of the trust determined under section 643(b) which is currently distributable to W is $50,000, consisting of dividends of $30,000, taxable interest of $10,000, and tax-exempt interest of $10,000. The trustee's commissions and miscellaneous expenses allocable to tax-exempt interest amount to $1,000 (10,000/50,000 × $5,000).

(3) The "distributable net income" determined under section 643(a) amounts to $45,000, computed as follows:

Dividends from domestic corporations		$30,000
Taxable interest		10,000
Nontaxable interest	$10,000	
Less: Expenses allocable thereto	1,000	
		9,000
Total		49,000
Less: Expenses ($5,000 less $1,000 allocable to tax-exempt interest)		4,000
		$45,000

In determining the distributable net income of $45,000, the taxable income of the trust is computed with the following modifications: No deductions are allowed for distributions to W and for personal exemption of the trust (section 643(a)(1) and (2)); capital gains allocable to corpus are excluded and the deduction allowable under section 1202* is not taken into account (section 643(a)(3)): the extraordinary dividends allocated to corpus by the trustee in good faith are excluded (sections 643(a)(4)); and the tax-exempt interest (as adjusted for expenses) and the dividend exclusion * of $50 are included (section 643(a)(5) and (7)).

* * *

Trusts Which Distribute Current Income Only

§ 1.651(a)–1 Simple trusts; deduction for distributions; in general.

Section 651 is applicable only to a trust the governing instruments of which:

(a) Requires that the trust distribute all of its income currently for the taxable year, and

(b) Does not provide that any amounts may be paid, permanently set aside, or used in the taxable

*Editorial comment: The Regulations do not reflect the effect of the Tax Reform Act of 1986 which has repealed both the Sec. 116 exclusion and the Sec. 1202 deduction. The Regulations also do not include the effect of the Revenue Reconciliation Act of 1993 which created the new Sec. 1202 exclusion.

year for the charitable, etc., purposes specified in section 642(c),

and does not make any distribution other than of current income. A trust to which section 651 applies is referred to in this part as a "simple" trust. Trusts subject to section 661 are referred to as "complex" trusts. A trust may be a simple trust for one year and a complex trust for another year. It should be noted that under section 651 a trust qualifies as a simple trust in a taxable year in which it is required to distribute all its income currently and makes no other distributions, whether or not distributions of current income are in fact made. On the other hand a trust is not a complex trust by reason of distributions of amounts other than income unless such distributions are in fact made during the taxable year, whether or not they are required in that year.

§ 1.651(a)–2 Income required to be distributed currently.

(a) The determination of whether trust income is required to be distributed currently depends upon the terms of the trust instrument and the applicable local law. For this purpose, if the trust instrument provides that the trustee in determining the distributable income shall first retain a reserve for depreciation or otherwise make due allowance for keeping the trust corpus intact by retaining a reasonable amount of the current income for that purpose, the retention of current income for that purpose will not disqualify the trust from being a "simple" trust. The fiduciary must be under a duty to distribute the income currently even if, as a matter of practical necessity, the income is not distributed until after the close of the trust's taxable year. For example: Under the terms of the trust instrument, all of the income is currently distributable to A. The trust reports on the calendar year basis and as a matter of practical necessity makes distribution to A of each quarter's income on the fifteenth day of the month following the close of the quarter. The distribution made by the trust on January 15, 1955, of the income for the fourth quarter of 1954 does not disqualify the trust from treatment in 1955 under section 651, since the income is required to be distributed currently. However, if the terms of a trust require that none of the income be distributed until after the year of its receipt by the trust, the income of the trust is not required to be distributed currently and the trust is not a simple trust. For definition of the term "income" see section 643(b) and § 1.643(b)–1.

(b) It is immaterial, for purposes of determining whether all the income is required to be distributed currently, that the amount of income allocated to a particular beneficiary is not specified in the instrument. For example, if the fiduciary is required to distribute all the income currently, but has discretion to "sprinkle" the income among a class of beneficiaries, or among named beneficiaries, in such amount as he may see fit, all the income is required to be distributed currently, even though the amount distributable to a particular beneficiary is unknown until the fiduciary has exercised his discretion.

(c) If in one taxable year of a trust its income for that year is required or permitted to be accumulated, and in another taxable year its income for the year is required to be distributed currently (and no other amounts are distributed), the trust is a simple trust for the latter year. For example, a trust under which income may be accumulated until a beneficiary is 21 years old, and thereafter must be distributed currently, is a simple trust for taxable years beginning after the beneficiary reaches the age of 21 years in which no other amounts are distributed.

(d) If a trust distributes property in kind as part of its requirement to distribute currently all the income as defined under section 643(b) and the applicable regulations, the trust shall be treated as having sold the property for its fair market value on the date of distribution. If no amount in excess of the amount of income as defined under section 643(b) and the applicable regulations is distributed by the trust during the year, the trust will qualify for treatment under section 651 even though property in kind was distributed as part of a distribution of all such income. This paragraph (d) applies for taxable years of trusts ending after January 2, 2004.

§ 1.651(a)–3 Distribution of amounts other than income.

(a) A trust does not qualify for treatment under section 651 for any taxable year in which it actually distributes corpus. For example, a trust which is required to distribute all of its income currently would not qualify as a simple trust under section 651 in the year of its termination since in that year actual distributions of corpus would be made.

(b) A trust, otherwise qualifying under section 651, which may make a distribution of corpus in the discretion of the trustee, or which is required under the terms of its governing instrument to make a distribution of corpus upon the happening of a specified event, will be disqualified for treatment under section 651 only for the taxable year in which an actual distribution of corpus is made. For example: Under the terms of a trust, which is required to distribute all of its income currently, half of the corpus is to be distributed to beneficiary A when he becomes 30 years of age. The trust reports on the calendar year basis. On December 28, 1954, A becomes 30 years of age and the trustee distributes half of the corpus of the trust to him on January 3, 1955. The trust will be disqualified for treatment under section 651 only for the taxable year 1955, the year in which an actual distribution of corpus is made.

(c) See section 661 and the regulations thereunder for the treatment of trusts which distribute corpus or claim the charitable contributions deduction provided by section 642(c).

§ 1.651(a)–4 Charitable purposes.

A trust is not considered to be a trust which may pay, permanently set aside, or use any amount for charitable, etc., purposes for any taxable year for which it is not allowed a charitable, etc., deduction under section 642(c). Therefore, a trust with a remainder to a charitable organization is not disqualified for treatment as a simple trust if either (a) the remainder is subject to a contingency, so that no deduction would be allowed for capital gains or other amounts added to corpus as amounts permanently set aside for a charitable, etc., purpose under section 642 (c), or (b) the trust receives no capital gains or other income added to corpus for the taxable year for which such a deduction would be allowed.

§ 1.651(a)–5 Estates.

Subpart B has no application to an estate.

§ 1.651(b)–1 Deduction for distributions to beneficiaries.

In computing its taxable income, a simple trust is allowed a deduction for the amount of income which is required under the terms of the trust instrument to be distributed currently to beneficiaries. If the amount of income required to be distributed currently exceeds the distributable net income, the deduction allowable to the trust is limited to the amount of the distributable net income. For this purpose the amount of income required to be distributed currently, or distributable net income, whichever is applicable, does not include items of trust income (adjusted for deductions allocable thereto) which are not included in the gross income of the trust. For determination of the character of the income required to be distributed currently, see § 1.652(b)–2. Accordingly, for the purposes of determining the deduction allowable to the trust under section 651, distributable net income is computed without the modifications specified in paragraphs (5), (6), and (7) of section 643(a), relating to tax-exempt interest, foreign income, and excluded dividends. For example: Assume that the distributable net income of a trust as computed under section 643(a) amounts to $99,000 but includes nontaxable income of $9,000. Then distributable net income for the purpose of determining the deduction allowable under section 651 is $90,000 ($99,000 less $9,000 nontaxable income).

§ 1.652(a)–1 Simple trusts; inclusion of amounts in income of beneficiaries.

Subject to the rules in §§ 1.652(a)–2 and 1.652 (b)–1, a beneficiary of a simple trust includes in his gross income for the taxable year the amounts of income required to be distributed to him for such year, whether or not distributed. Thus, the income of a simple trust is includible in the beneficiary's gross income for the taxable year in which the income is required to be distributed currently even though, as a matter of practical necessity, the income is not distributed until after the close of the taxable year of the trust. See § 1.642(a)(3)–2 with respect to time of receipt of dividends. See § 1.652(c)–1 for treatment of amounts required to be distributed where a beneficiary and the trust have different taxable years. The term "income required to be distributed currently" includes income required to be distributed currently which is in fact used to discharge or satisfy any person's legal obligation as that term is used in § 1.662(a)–4.

§ 1.652(a)–2 Distributions in excess of distributable net income.

If the amount of income required to be distributed currently to beneficiaries exceeds the distributable net income of the trust (as defined in section 643(a)), each beneficiary includes in his gross income an amount equivalent to his proportionate share of such distributable net income. Thus, if beneficiary A is to receive two-thirds of the trust income and B is to receive one-third, and the income required to be distributed currently is $99,000, A will receive $66,000 and B, $33,000. However, if the distributable net income, as determined under section 643 (a) is only $90,000, A will include two-thirds

($60,000) of that sum in his gross income, and B will include one-third ($30,000) in his gross income. See §§ 1.652(b)–1 and 1.652(b)–2, however, for amounts which are not includible in the gross income of a beneficiary because of their tax-exempt character.

§ 1.652(b)–1 Character of amounts.

In determining the gross income of a beneficiary, the amounts includible under § 1.652(a)–1 have the same character in the hands of the beneficiary as in the hands of the trust. For example, to the extent that the amounts specified in § 1.652(a)–1 consist of income exempt from tax under section 103, such amounts are not included in the beneficiary's gross income. Similarly, dividends distributed to a beneficiary retain their original character in the beneficiary's hands for purposes of * * * the dividend exclusion under section 116.* Also, to the extent that the amounts specified in § 1.652(a)–1 consist of "earned income" in the hands of the trust under the provisions of section 1348 such amount shall be treated under section 1348 as "earned income" in the hands of the beneficiary. Similarly, to the extent such amounts consist of an amount received as a part of a lump sum distribution from a qualified plan and to which the provisions of section 72(n) would apply in the hands of the trust, such amount shall be treated as subject to such section in the hands of the beneficiary except where such amount is deemed under section 666(a) to have been distributed in a preceding taxable year of the trust and the partial tax described in section 668(a)(2) is determined under section 668(b)(1)(B). The tax treatment of amounts determined under § 1.652(a)–1 depends upon the beneficiary's status with respect to them not upon the status of the trust. * * *

§ 1.652(b)–2 Allocation of income items.

(a) The amounts specified in § 1.652(a)–1 which are required to be included in the gross income of a beneficiary are treated as consisting of the same proportion of each class of items entering into distributable net income of the trust (as defined in section 643(a)) as the total of each class bears to such distributable net income, unless the terms of the trust specifically allocate different classes of income to different beneficiaries, or unless local law requires such an allocation. For example: Assume that under the terms of the governing instrument, beneficiary A is to receive currently one-half of the trust income and beneficiaries B and C are each to receive currently one-quarter, and the distributable net income of the trust (after allocation of expenses) consists of dividends of $10,000, taxable interest of $10,000, and tax-exempt interest of $4,000. A will be deemed to have received $5,000 of dividends, $5,000 of taxable interest, and $2,000 of tax-exempt interest; B and C will each be deemed to have received $2,500 of dividends, $2,500 of taxable interest, and $1,000 of tax-exempt interest. However, if the terms of the trust specifically allocate different classes of income to different beneficiaries, entirely or in part, or if local law requires such an allocation, each beneficiary will be deemed to have received those items of income specifically allocated to him.

(b) The terms of the trust are considered specifically to allocate different classes of income to different beneficiaries only to the extent that the allocation is required in the trust instrument, and only to the extent that it has an economic effect independent of the income tax consequences of the allocation. For example:

(1) Allocation pursuant to a provision in a trust instrument granting the trustee discretion to allocate different classes of income to different beneficiaries is not a specific allocation by the terms of the trust.

(2) Allocation pursuant to a provision directing the trustee to pay all of one income to A, or $10,000 out of the income to A, and the balance of the income to B, but directing the trustee first to allocate a specific class of income to A's share (to the extent there is income of that class and to the extent it does not exceed A's share) is not a specific allocation by the terms of the trust.

(3) Allocation pursuant to a provision directing the trustee to pay half the class of income (whatever it may be) to A, and the balance of the income to B, is a specific allocation by the terms of the trust.

§ 1.652(b)–3 Allocation of deductions.

Items of deduction of a trust that enter into the computation of distributable net income are to be allocated among the items of income in accordance with the following principles:

*Editorial comment: The Regulations do not reflect the effect of the Tax Reform Act of 1986 which repealed the Sec. 116 exclusion.

(a) All deductible items directly attributable to one class of income (except dividends excluded under section 116)* are allocated thereto. For example, repairs to, taxes on, and other expenses directly attributable to the maintenance of rental property or the collection of rental income are allocated to rental income. See § 1.642(e)–1 for treatment of depreciation of rental property. Similarly, all expenditures directly attributable to a business carried on by a trust are allocated to the income from such business. If the deductions directly attributable to a particular class of income exceed that income, the excess is applied against other classes of income in the manner provided in paragraph (d) of this section.

(b) The deductions which are not directly attributable to a specific class of income may be allocated to any item of income (including capital gains) included in computing distributable net income, but a portion must be allocated to nontaxable income (except dividends excluded under section 116)* pursuant to section 265 and the regulations thereunder. For example, if the income of a trust is $30,000 (after direct expenses), consisting equally of $10,000 of dividends, tax-exempt interest, and rents, and income commissions amount to $3,000, one-third ($1,000) of such commissions should be allocated to tax-exempt interest, but the balance of $2,000 may be allocated to the rents or dividends in such proportions as the trustee may elect. The fact that the governing instrument or applicable local law treats certain items of deduction as attributable to corpus or to income not included in distributable net income does not affect allocation under this paragraph. For instance, if in the example set forth in this paragraph the trust also had capital gains which are allocable to corpus under the terms of the trust instrument, no part of the deductions would be allocable thereto since the capital gains are excluded from the computation of distributable net income under section 643(a)(3).

(c) Examples of expenses which are considered as not directly attributable to a specific class of income are trustee's commissions, the rental of safe deposit boxes, and State income and personal property taxes.

(d) To the extent that any items of deduction which are directly attributable to a class of income exceed that class of income, they may be allocated to any other class of income (including capital gains) included in distributable net income in the manner provided in paragraph (b) of this section, except that any excess deductions attributable to tax-exempt income (other than dividends excluded under section 116)* may not be offset against any other class of income. See section 265 and the regulations thereunder. Thus, if the trust has rents, taxable interest, dividends, and tax-exempt interest, and the deductions directly attributable to the rents exceed the rental income, the excess may be allocated to the taxable interest or dividends in such proportions as the fiduciary may elect. However, if the excess deductions are attributable to the tax-exempt interest, they may not be allocated to either the rents, taxable interest, or dividends.

§ 1.652(c)–1 Different taxable years.

If a beneficiary has a different taxable year (as defined in section 441 or 442) from the taxable year of the trust, the amount he is required to include in gross income in accordance with section 652(a) and (b) is based on the income of the trust for any taxable year or years ending with or within his taxable year. This rule applies to taxable years of normal duration as well as to so-called short taxable years. Income of the trust for its taxable year or years is determined in accordance with its method of accounting and without regard to that of the beneficiary.

* * *

Estates and Trusts Which May Accumulate Income or Which Distribute Corpus

§ 1.661(a)–1 Estates and trusts accumulating income or distributing corpus; general.

Subpart C, part I, subchapter J, chapter 1 of the Code, is applicable to all decedents' estates and their beneficiaries, and to trusts and their beneficiaries other than trusts subject to the provisions of subpart B of such part I (relating to trusts which distribute current income only, or "simple" trusts). A trust which is required to distribute amounts other than

*Editorial comment: The Regulations do not reflect the effect of the Tax Reform Act of 1986 which repealed the Sec. 116 exclusion.

income during the taxable year may be subject to subpart B, and not subpart C, in the absence of an actual distribution of amounts other than income during the taxable year. See §§ 1.651(a)–1 and 1.651 (a)–3. A trust to which subpart C is applicable is referred to as a "complex" trust in this part. Section 661 has no application to amounts excluded under section 663(a).

§ 1.661(a)–2 Deduction for distributions to beneficiaries.

(a) In computing the taxable income of an estate or trust there is allowed under section 661(a) as a deduction for distributions to beneficiaries the sum of:

(1) The amount of income for the taxable year which is required to be distributed currently, and

(2) Any other amounts properly paid or credited or required to be distributed for such taxable year.

However, the total amount deductible under section 661(a) cannot exceed the distributable net income as computed under section 643(a) and as modified by section 661(c). See § 1.661(c)–1.

(b) The term "income required to be distributed currently" includes any amount required to be distributed which may be paid out of income or corpus (such as an annuity), to the extent it is paid out of income for the taxable year. See § 1.651(a)–2 which sets forth additional rules which are applicable in determining whether income of an estate or trust is required to be distributed currently.

(c) The term "any other amounts properly paid, credited, or required to be distributed" includes all amounts properly paid, credited, or required to be distributed by an estate or trust during the taxable year other than income required to be distributed currently. Thus, the term includes the payment of an annuity to the extent it is not paid out of income for the taxable year, and a distribution of property in kind (see paragraph (f) of this section). However, see section 663(a) and regulations thereunder for distributions which are not included. Where the income of an estate or trust may be accumulated or distributed in the discretion of the fiduciary, or where the fiduciary has a power to distribute corpus to a beneficiary, any such discretionary distribution would qualify under section 661(a)(2). The term also includes an amount applied or distributed for the support of a dependent of a grantor or of a trustee or cotrustee under the circumstances described in section 677(b) or section 678(c) out of corpus or out of other than income for the taxable year.

(d) The terms "income required to be distributed currently" and "any other amounts properly paid or credited or required to be distributed" also include any amount used to discharge or satisfy any person's legal obligation as that term is used in § 1.662(a)–4.

(e) The terms "income required to be distributed currently" and "any other amounts properly paid or credited or required to be distributed" include amounts paid, or required to be paid, during the taxable year pursuant to a court order or decree or under local law, by a decedent's estate as an allowance or award for the support of the decedent's widow or other dependent for a limited period during the administration of the estate. The term "any other amounts properly paid or credited or required to be distributed" does not include the value of any interest in real estate owned by a decedent, title to which under local law passes directly from the decedent to his heirs or devisees.

(f) Gain or loss is realized by the trust or estate (or the other beneficiaries) by reason of a distribution of property in kind if the distribution is in satisfaction of a right to receive a distribution of a specific dollar amount, of specific property other than that distributed, or of income as defined under section 643(b) and the applicable regulations, if income is required to be distributed currently. In addition, gain or loss is realized if the trustee or executor makes the election to recognize gain or loss under section 643 (e). This paragraph applies for taxable years of trusts and estates ending after January 2, 2004.

§ 1.661(b)–1 Character of amounts distributed; in general.

In the absence of specific provisions in the governing instrument for the allocation of different classes of income, or unless local law requires such an allocation, the amount deductible for distributions to beneficiaries under section 661(a) is treated as consisting of the same proportion of each class of items entering into the computation of distributable net income as the total of each class bears to the total distributable net income. For example, if a trust has distributable net income of $20,000, consisting of $10,000 each of taxable interest and royalties and distributes $10,000 to beneficiary A, the deduction of $10,000 allowable under section 661(a) is deemed to consist of $5,000 each of taxable interest and royalties, unless the trust instrument specifically provides for the distribution or accumulation of different classes of income or unless local law requires such an allocation. See also § 1.661(c)–1.

§ 1.661(b)–2 Character of amounts distributed when charitable contributions are made.

In the application of the rule stated in § 1.661(b)–1, the items of deduction which enter into the computation of distributable net income are allocated among the items of income which enter into the computation of distributable net income in accordance with the rules set forth in § 1.652(b)–3, except that, in the absence of specific provisions in the governing instrument, or unless local law requires a different apportionment, amounts paid, permanently set aside, or to be used for the charitable, etc., purposes specified in section 642(c) are first ratably apportioned among each class of items of income entering into the computation of the distributable net income of the estate or trust, in accordance with the rules set out in paragraph (b) of § 1.643(a)–5.

§ 1.661(c)–1 Limitation on deduction.

An estate or trust is not allowed a deduction under section 661(a) for any amount which is treated under section 661(b) as consisting of any item of distributable net income which is not included in the gross income of the estate or trust. For example, if in 1962, a trust, which reports on the calendar year basis, has distributable net income of $20,000, which is deemed to consist of $10,000 of dividends and $10,000 of tax-exempt interest, and distributes $10,000 to beneficiary A, the deduction allowable under section 661(a) (computed without regard to section 661(c)) would amount to $10,000 consisting of $5,000 of dividends and $5,000 of tax-exempt interest. The deduction actually allowable under section 661(a) as limited by section 661(c) is $4,975, since no deduction is allowable for the $5,000 of tax-exempt interest and the $25 deemed distributed out of the $50 of dividends excluded under section 116,* items of distributable net income which are not included in the gross income of the estate or trust.

§ 1.661(c)–2 Illustration of the provisions of Section 661.

The provisions of section 661 may be illustrated by the following example:

Example. (a) Under the terms of a trust, which reports on the calendar year basis, $10,000 a year is required to be paid out of income to a designated charity. The balance of the income may, in the trustee's discretion, be accumulated or distributed to beneficiary A. Expenses are allocable against income and the trust instrument requires a reserve for depreciation. During the taxable year 1955 the trustee contributes $10,000 to charity and in his discretion distributes $15,000 of income to A. The trust has the following items of income and expense for the taxable year 1955:

Dividends	$10,000
Partially tax-exempt interest	10,000
Fully tax-exempt interest	10,000
Rents	20,000
Rental expenses	2,000
Depreciation of rental property	3,000
Trustee's commissions	5,000

(b) The income of the trust for fiduciary accounting purposes is $40,000, computed as follows:

Dividends		$10,000
Partially tax-exempt interest		10,000
Fully tax-exempt interest		10,000
Rents		20,000
Total		50,000
Less:		
Rental expenses	$2,000	
Depreciation	3,000	
Trustee's commissions	5,000	
		10,000
Income as computed under section 643(b)		40,000

(c) The distributable net income of the trust as computed under section 643(a) is $30,000, determined as follows:

Rents			$20,000
Dividends			10,000
Partially tax-exempt interest			10,000
Fully tax-exempt interest		$10,000	
Less:			
Expenses allocable thereto (10,000/50,000 × $5,000)	$1,000		
Charitable contributions allocable thereto (10,000/50,000 × $10,000)	2,000		
		3,000	
			7,000
Total			47,000
Deductions:			
Rental expenses		2,000	
Depreciation of rental property		3,000	
Trustee's commissions ($5,000 less $1,000 allocated to tax-exempt interest)		4,000	
Charitable contributions ($10,000 less $2,000 allocated to tax-exempt interests)		8,000	
			17,000
Distributable net income (section 643(a))			30,000

(d) The character of the amounts distributed under section 661 (a), determined in accordance with the rules prescribed in §§ 1.661

*Editorial comment: The Regulations do not reflect the effect of the Tax Reform Act of 1986 which repealed the Sec. 116 exclusion.

(b)–1 and 1.661(b)–2 is shown by the following table (for the purpose of this allocation, it is assumed that the trustee elected to allocate the trustee's commissions to rental income except for the amount required to be allocated to tax-exempt interest):

	Rental income	Taxable dividends	Excluded dividends	Partially Tax-exempt interest	Tax-exempt interest	Total
Trust income	$20,000	$9,950	$50	$10,000	$10,000	$50,000
Less:						
Charitable contributions	4,000	2,000	......	2,000	2,000	10,000
Rental expenses	2,000	....	......	....	....	2,000
Depreciation	3,000	....	......	....	....	3,000
Trustee's commissions	4,000	....	......	....	1,000	5,000
Total deductions	13,000	2,000	0	2,000	3,000	20,000
Distributable net income	7,000	7,950	50	8,000	7,000	30,000
Amounts deemed distributed under section 661(a) before applying the limitation of section 661(c)	3,500	3,975	25	4,000	3,500	15,000

In the absence of specific provisions in the trust instrument for the allocation of different classes of income, the charitable contribution is deemed to consist of a pro rata portion of the gross amount of each items of income of the trust (except dividends excluded under section 116 *) and the trust is deemed to have distributed to A a pro rata portion (one-half) of each item of income included in distributable net income.

(e) The taxable income of the trust is $11,375 computed as follows:

Rental income		$20,000
Dividends ($10,000 less $50 exclusion)*		9,950
Partially tax-exempt interest		10,000
Gross income		39,950
Deductions:		
Rental expenses	$2,000	
Depreciation of rental property	3,000	
Trustee's commissions	4,000	
Charitable contributions	8,000	
Distributions to A	11,475	
Personal exemption	100	
		28,575
Taxable income		11,375

In computing the taxable income of the trust no deduction is allowable for the portions of the charitable contributions deduction ($2,000) and trustee's commissions ($1,000) which are treated under section 661(b) as attributable to the tax-exempt interest excludable from gross income. Also, of the dividends of $4,000 deemed to have been distributed to A under section 661(a), $25 ($^{25}/_{50}$ths of $50) * is deemed to have been distributed from the excluded dividends and is not an allowable deduction to the trust. Accordingly, the deduction allowable under section 661 is deemed to be composed of $3,500 rental income, $3,975 of dividends, and $4,000 partially tax-exempt interest. No deduction is allowable for the portion of tax-exempt interest or for the portion of the excluded dividends deemed to have been distributed to the beneficiary.

(f) The trust is entitled to the credit allowed by section 34* with respect to dividends of $5,975 ($9,950 less $3,975 distributed to A) included in gross income. Also, the trust is allowed the credit provided by section 35* with respect to partially tax-exempt interest of $6,000 ($10,000 less $4,000 deemed distributed to A) included in gross income.

(g) Dividends of $4,000 allocable to A are to be aggregated with his other dividends (if any) for purposes of the dividend exclusion under section 116* and the dividend received credit under section 34.*

§ 1.662(a)–1 Inclusion of amounts in gross income of beneficiaries of estates and complex trusts; general.

There is included in the gross income of a beneficiary of an estate or complex trust the sum of:

(1) Amounts of income required to be distributed currently to him, and

(2) All other amounts properly paid, credited, or required to be distributed to him

by the estate or trust. The preceding sentence is subject to the rules contained in § 1.662(a)–2 (relating to currently distributable income), § 1.662 (a)–3 (relating to other amounts distributed), and §§ 1.662(b)–1 and 1.662(b)–2 (relating to character of amounts). Section 662 has no application to amounts excluded under section 663(a).

§ 1.662(a)–2 Currently distributable income.

(a) There is first included in the gross income of each beneficiary under section 662(a)(1) the amount

*Editorial comment: The Regulations do not reflect the effect of the Tax Reform Act of 1986 which repealed the Sec. 116 exclusion and prior legislation which repealed the credits under Secs. 34 and 35.

of income for the taxable year of the estate or trust required to be distributed currently to him, subject to the provisions of paragraph (b) of this section. Such amount is included in the beneficiary's gross income whether or not it is actually distributed.

(b) If the amount of income required to be distributed currently to all beneficiaries exceeds the distributable net income (as defined in section 643(a) but computed without taking into account the payment, crediting, or setting aside of an amount for which a charitable contributions deduction is allowable under section 642(c)) of the estate or trust, then there is included in the gross income of each beneficiary an amount which bears the same ratio to distributable net income (as so computed) as the amount of income required to be distributed currently to the beneficiary bears to the amount required to be distributed currently to all beneficiaries.

(c) The phrase "the amount of income for the taxable year required to be distributed currently" includes any amount required to be paid out of income or corpus to the extent the amount is satisfied out of income for the taxable year. Thus, an annuity required to be paid in all events (either out of income or corpus) would qualify as income required to be distributed currently to the extent there is income (as defined in section 643(b)) not paid, credited, or required to be distributed to other beneficiaries for the taxable year. If an annuity or a portion of an annuity is deemed under this paragraph to be income required to be distributed currently, it is treated in all respects in the same manner as an amount of income actually required to be distributed currently. The phrase "the amount of income for the taxable year required to be distributed currently" also includes any amount required to be paid during the taxable year in all events (either out of income or corpus) pursuant to a court order or decree or under local law, by a decedent's estate as an allowance or award for the support of the decedent's widow or other dependent for a limited period during the administration of the estate to the extent there is income (as defined in section 643(b)) of the estate for the taxable year not paid, credited, or required to be distributed to other beneficiaries.

(d) If an annuity is paid, credited, or required to be distributed tax free, that is, under a provision whereby the executor or trustee will pay the income tax of the annuitant resulting from the receipt of the annuity, the payment of or for the tax by the executor or trustee will be treated as income paid, credited, or required to be distributed currently to the extent it is made out of income.

(e) The application of the rules stated in this section may be illustrated by the following examples:

Example (1). (1) Assume that under the terms of the trust instrument $5,000 is to be paid to X charity out of income each year; that $20,000 of income is currently distributable to A; and that an annuity of $12,000 is to be paid to B out of income or corpus. All expenses are charges against income and capital gains are allocable to corpus. During the taxable year the trust had income of $30,000 (after the payment of expenses) derived from taxable interest and made the payments to X charity and distributions to A and B as required by the governing instrument.

(2) The amounts treated as distributed currently under section 662(a)(1) total $25,000 ($20,000 to A and $5,000 to B). Since the charitable contribution is out of income the amount of income available for B's annuity is only $5,000. The distributable net income of the trust computed under section 643(a) without taking into consideration the charitable contributions deduction of $5,000 as provided by section 661(a)(1), is $30,000. Since the amounts treated as distributed currently of $25,000 do not exceed the distributable net income (as modified) of $30,000, A is required to include $20,000 in his gross income and B is required to include $5,000 in his gross income under section 662(a)(1).

Example (2). Assume the same facts as in paragraph (1) of example (1), except that the trust has, in addition, $10,000 of administration expenses, commissions, etc., chargeable to corpus. The amounts treated as distributed currently under section 662(a)(1) total $25,000 ($20,000 to A and $5,000 to B), since trust income under section 643(b) remains the same as in example (1). Distributable net income of the trust computed under section 643(a) but without taking into account the charitable contributions deduction of $5,000 as provided by section 662(a)(1) is only $20,000. Since the amounts treated as distributed currently of $25,000 exceed the distributable net income (as so computed) of $20,000, A is required to include $16,000 (20,000/25,000 of $20,000) in his gross income and B is required to include $4,000 (5,000/25,000 of $20,000) in his gross income under section 662(a)(1). Because A and B are beneficiaries of amounts of income required to be distributed currently, they do not benefit from the reduction of distributable net income by the charitable contributions deduction.

§ 1.662(a)–3 Other amounts distributed.

(a) There is included in the gross income of a beneficiary under section 662(a)(2) any amount properly paid, credited, or required to be distributed to the beneficiary for the taxable year, other than (1) income required to be distributed currently, as determined under § 1.662(a)–2, (2) amounts excluded under section 663(a) and the regulations thereunder, and (3) amounts in excess of distributable net income (see paragraph (c) of this section). An amount which is credited or required to be distributed is included in the gross income of a beneficiary whether or not it is actually distributed.

(b) Some of the payments to be included under paragraph (a) of this section are: (1) A distribution made to a beneficiary in the discretion of the fiduciary; (2) a distribution required by the terms of the governing instrument upon the happening of a specified event; (3) an annuity which is required to be paid in all events but which is payable only out of corpus; (4) a distribution of property in kind (see paragraph (f) of § 1.661(a)–2); (5) an amount applied or distributed for the support of a dependent of a grantor or a trustee or cotrustee under the circumstances specified in section 677(b) or section 678(c) out of corpus or out of other than income for the taxable year; and (6) an amount required to be paid during the taxable year pursuant to a court order or decree or under local law, by a decedent's estate as an allowance or award for the support of the decedent's widow or other dependent for a limited period during the administration of the estate which is payable only out of corpus of the estate under the order or decree or local law.

(c) If the sum of the amounts of income required to be distributed currently (as determined under § 1.662(a)–2) and other amounts properly paid, credited, or required to be distributed (as determined under paragraph (a) of this section) exceeds distributable net income (as defined in section 643(a)), then such other amounts properly paid, credited, or required to be distributed are included in gross income of the beneficiary but only to the extent of the excess of such distributable net income over the amounts of income required to be distributed currently. If the other amounts are paid, credited, or required to be distributed to more than one beneficiary, each beneficiary includes in gross income his proportionate share of the amount includible in gross income pursuant to the preceding sentence. The proportionate share is an amount which bears the same ratio to distributable net income (reduced by amounts of income required to be distributed currently) as the other amounts (as determined under paragraphs (a) and (d) of this section) distributed to the beneficiary bear to the other amounts distributed to all beneficiaries. For treatment of excess distributions by trusts, see sections 665 to 668, inclusive, and the regulations thereunder.

(d) The application of the rules stated in this section may be illustrated by the following example:

Example. The terms of a trust require the distribution annually of $10,000 of income to A. If any income remains, it may be accumulated or distributed to B, C, and D in amounts in the trustee's discretion. He may also invade corpus for the benefit of A, B, C, or D. In the taxable year, the trust has $20,000 of income after the deduction of all expenses. Distributable net income is $20,000. The trustee distributes $10,000 of income to A. Of the remaining $10,000 of income, he distributes $3,000 each to B, C, and D, and also distributes an additional $5,000 to A. A includes $10,000 in income under section 662(a)(1). The "other amounts distributed" amount of $14,000, includible in the income of the recipients to the extent of $10,000, distributable net income less the income currently distributable to A. A will include an additional $3,571 (5,000/14,000 × $10,000) in income under this section, and B, C, and D will each include $2,143 (3,000/14,000 × $10,000).

§ 1.662(a)–4 Amounts used in discharge of a legal obligation.

Any amount which, pursuant to the terms of a will or trust instrument, is used in full or partial discharge or satisfaction of a legal obligation of any person is included in the gross income of such person under section 662(a)(1) or (2), whichever is applicable, as though directly distributed to him as a beneficiary, except in cases to which section 71 (relating to alimony payments) or section 682 (relating to income of a trust in case of divorce, etc.) applies. The term "legal obligation" includes a legal obligation to support another person if, and only if, the obligation is not affected by the adequacy of the dependent's own resources. For example, a parent has a "legal obligation" within the meaning of the preceding sentence to support his minor child if under local law property or income from property owned by the child cannot be used for his support so long as his parent is able to support him. On the other hand, if under local law a mother may use the resources of a child for the child's support in lieu of supporting him herself, no obligation of support exists within the meaning of this paragraph, whether or not income is actually used for support. Similarly, since under local law a child ordinarily is obligated to support his parent only if the parent's earnings and resources are insufficient for the purpose, no obligation exists whether or not the parent's earnings and resources are sufficient. In any event the amount of trust income which is included in the gross income of a person obligated to support a dependent is limited by the extent of his legal obligation under local law. In the case of a parent's obligation to support his child, to the extent that the parent's legal obligation of support, including education, is determined under local law by the family's station in life and by the means of the parent, it is to be determined without consideration of the trust income in question.

§ 1.662(b)–1 Character of amounts; when no charitable contributions are made.

In determining the amount includible in the gross income of a beneficiary, the amounts which are determined under section 662(a) and §§ 1.662(a)–1 through 1.662(a)–4 shall have the same character in the hands of the beneficiary as in the hands of the estate or trust. The amounts are treated as consisting of the same proportion of each class of items entering into the computation of distributable net income as the total of each class bears to the total distributable net income of the estate or trust unless the terms of the governing instrument specifically allocate different classes of income to different beneficiaries, or unless local law requires such an allocation. For this purpose, the principles contained in § 1.652(b)–1 shall apply.

§ 1.662(b)–2 Character of amounts; when charitable contributions are made.

When a charitable contribution is made, the principles contained in §§ 1.652(b)–1 and 1.662(b)–1 generally apply. However, before the allocation of other deductions among the items of distributable net income, the charitable contributions deduction allowed under section 642(c) is (in the absence of specific allocation under the terms of the governing instrument or the requirement under local law of a different allocation) allocated among the classes of income entering into the computation of estate or trust income in accordance with the rules set forth in paragraph (b) of § 1.643(a)–5. In the application of the preceding sentence, for the purpose of allocating items of income and deductions to beneficiaries to whom income is required to be distributed currently, the amount of the charitable contributions deduction is disregarded to the extent that it exceeds the income of the trust for the taxable year reduced by amounts for the taxable year required to be distributed currently. The application of this section may be illustrated by the following examples (of which example (1) is illustrative of the preceding sentence):

Example (1). (a) A trust instrument provides that $30,000 of its income must be distributed currently to A, and the balance may either be distributed to B, distributed to a designated charity, or accumulated. Accumulated income may be distributed to B and to the charity. The trust for its taxable year has $40,000 of taxable interest and $10,000 of tax-exempt income, with no expenses. The trustee distributed $30,000 to A, $50,000 to charity X, and $10,000 to B.

(b) Distributable net income for the purpose of determining the character of the distribution to A is $30,000 (the charitable contributions deduction, for this purpose, being taken into account only to the extent of $20,000, the difference between the income of the trust for the taxable year, $50,000, and the amount required to be distributed currently, $30,000).

(c) The charitable contributions deduction taken into account, $20,000, is allocated proportionately to the items of income of the trust, $16,000 to taxable interest and $4,000 to tax-exempt income.

(d) Under section 662(a)(1), the amount of income required to be distributed currently to A is $30,000, which consists of the balance of these items, $24,000 of taxable interest and $6,000 of tax-exempt income.

(e) In determining the amount to be included in the gross income of B under section 662 for the taxable year, however, the entire charitable contributions deduction is taken into account, with the result that there is no distributable net income and therefore no amount to be included in gross income.

(f) See subpart D (section 665 and following), part I, subchapter J, chapter 1 of the Code for application of the throwback provisions to the distribution made to B.

Example (2). The net income of a trust is payable to A for life, with the remainder to a charitable organization. Under the terms of the trust instrument and local law capital gains are added to corpus. During the taxable year the trust receives dividends of $10,000 and realized a long-term capital gain of $10,000, for which a long-term capital gain deduction* of $5,000 is allowed under section 1202. Since under the trust instrument and local law the capital gains are allocated to the charitable organization, and since the capital gain deduction is directly attributable to the capital gain, the charitable contributions deduction and the capital gain deduction are both allocable to the capital gain, and dividends in the amount of $10,000 are allocable to A.

§ 1.662(c)–1 Different taxable years.

If a beneficiary has a different taxable year (as defined in section 441 or 442) from the taxable year of an estate or trust, the amount he is required to include in gross income in accordance with section 662(a) and (b) is based upon the distributable net income of the estate or trust and the amounts properly paid, credited, or required to be distributed to the beneficiary for any taxable year or years of the estate or trust ending with or within his taxable year. This rule applies as to so-called short taxable years as well as taxable years of normal duration. Income of an estate or trust for its taxable year or years is determined in accordance with its method of accounting and without regard to that of the beneficiary.

* * *

§ 1.662(c)–4 Illustration of the provisions of sections 661 and 662.

The provisions of sections 661 and 662 may be illustrated in general by the following example:

*Editorial comment: The Regulations do not reflect the effect of the Tax Reform Act of 1986 which repealed both the Sec. 116 exclusion and the Sec. 1202 deduction. The Regulations also do not include the effect of the Revenue Reconciliation Act of 1993 which created the new Sec. 1202 exclusion.

Example. (a) Under the terms of a testamentary trust one-half of the trust income is to be distributed currently to W, the decedent's wife, for her life. The remaining trust income may, in the trustee's discretion, either be paid to D, the grantor's daughter, paid to designated charities, or accumulated. The trust is to terminate at the death of W and the principal will then be payable to D. No provision is made in the trust instrument with respect to depreciation of rental property. Capital gains are allocable to the principal account under the applicable local law. The trust and both beneficiaries file returns on the calendar year basis. The records of the fiduciary show the following items of income and deduction for the taxable year 1955:

Rents	$50,000
Dividends of domestic corporations	50,000
Tax-exempt interest	20,000
Partially tax-exempt interest	10,000
Capital gains (long term)	20,000
Depreciation of rental property	10,000
Expenses attributable to rental income	15,400
Trustee's commissions allocable to income account	2,800
Trustee's commissions allocable to principal account	1,100

(b) The income for trust accounting purposes is $111,800, and the trustee distributes one-half ($55,900) to W and in his discretion makes a contribution of one-quarter ($27,950) to charity X and distributes the remaining one-quarter ($27,950) to D. The total of the distributions to beneficiaries is $83,850, consisting of (1) income required to be distributed currently to W of $55,900 and (2) other amounts properly paid or credited to D of $27,950. The income for trust accounting purposes of $111,800 is determined as follows:

Rents		$50,000
Dividends		50,000
Tax-exempt interest		20,000
Partially tax-exempt interest		10,000
Total		130,000
Less:		
Rental expenses	$15,400	
Trustee's commissions allocable to income account	2,800	
		18,200
Income as computed under section 643(b)		111,800

(c) The distributable net income of the trust as computed under section 643(a) is $82,750, determined as follows:

Rents			$50,000
Dividends			50,000
Partially tax-exempt interest			10,000
Tax-exempt interest	$20,000		
Less:			
Trustee's commissions allocable thereto (20,000/130,000 of $3,900)	$600		
Charitable contributions allocable thereto (20,000/130,000 of $27,950)	4,300		
		4,900	
			15,100
Total			125,100
Deductions:			
Rental expenses		15,400	
Trustee's commissions ($3,900 less $600 allocated to tax-exempt interest)		3,300	
Charitable deduction ($27,950 less $4,300 attributable to tax-exempt interest)		23,650	
			42,350
Distributable net income			82,750

In computing the distributable net income of $82,750, the taxable income of the trust was computed with the following modifications: No deductions were allowed for distributions to beneficiaries and for personal exemption of the trust (section 643(a)(1) and (2)); capital gains were excluded and no deduction under section 1202* (relating to the 50 percent deduction for long-term capital gains) was taken into account (section 643(a)(3)); and the tax-exempt interest (as adjusted for expenses and charitable contributions) and the dividend exclusion* of $50 were included (section 643(a)(5) and (7)).

(d) Inasmuch as the distributable net income of $82,750 as determined under section 643(a) is less than the sum of the amounts distributed to W and D of $83,850, the deduction allowable to the trust under section 661(a) is such distributable net income as modified under section 661(c) to exclude therefrom the items of income not included in the gross income of the trust, as follows:

Distributable net income		$82,750
Less:		
Tax-exempt interest (as adjusted for expenses and the charitable contributions)	$15,100	
Dividend exclusion allowable under section 116*	50	
		15,150
Deduction allowable under section 661(a)		67,600

(e) For the purpose of determining the character of the amounts deductible under section 642(c) and section 661(a), the trustee elected to offset the trustee's commissions (other than the portion required to be allocated to tax-exempt interest) against the rental income. The following table shows the determination of the character of the amounts deemed distributed to beneficiaries and contributed to charity.

*Editorial comment: The Regulations do not reflect the effect of the Tax Reform Act of 1986 which repealed both the Sec. 116 exclusion and the Sec. 1202 deduction.

	Rents	Taxable dividends	Excluded dividends*	Tax exempt interest	Partially tax exempt interest	Total
Trust income	$50,000	$49,950	$50	$20,000	$10,000	$130,000
Less:						
Charitable contribution	10,750	10,750	......	4,300	2,150	27,950
Rental expenses	15,400	....	......	....	....	15,400
Trustee's commissions	3,300	....	......	600	....	3,900
Total deductions	29,450	10,750	0	4,900	2,150	47,250
Amounts distributable to beneficiaries	20,550	39,200	50	15,100	7,850	82,750

The character of the charitable contribution is determined by multiplying the total charitable contribution ($27,950) by a fraction consisting of each item of trust income, respectively, over the total trust income, except that no part of the dividends excluded from gross income are deemed included in the charitable contribution. For example, the charitable contribution is deemed to consist of rents of $10,750 (50,000/130,000 × $27,950).

(f) The taxable income of the trust is $9,900 determined as follows:

Rental income		$50,000
Dividends ($50,000 less $50 exclusion)*		49,950
Partially tax-exempt interest		10,000
Capital gains		20,000
Gross income		129,950
Deductions:		
Rental expenses	$15,400	
Trustee's commissions	3,300	
Charitable contributions	23,650	
Capital gain deductions*	10,000	
Distributions to beneficiaries	67,600	
Personal exemption	100	
		120,050
Taxable income		9,900

(g) In computing the amount includible in W's gross income under section 662(a)(1), the $55,900 distribution to her is deemed to be composed of the following proportions of the items of income deemed to have been distributed to the beneficiaries by the trust (see paragraph (e) of this example):

Rents (20,550/82,750 × $55,900)	$13,882
Dividends (39,250/82,750 × $55,900)	26,515
Partially tax-exempt interest (7,850/82,750 × $55,900)	5,303
Tax-exempt interest (15,100/82,750 × $55,900)	10,200
Total	55,900

Accordingly, W will exclude $10,200 of tax-exempt interest from gross income and will receive the credits and exclusion for dividends received and for partially tax-exempt interest provided in sections 34,* 116,* and 35,* respectively, with respect to the dividends and partially tax-exempt interest deemed to have been distributed to her, her share of the dividends being aggregated with other dividends received by her for purposes of the dividend credit and exclusion. In addition, she may deduct a share of the depreciation deduction proportionate to the trust income allocable to her; that is, one-half of the total depreciation deduction, or $5,000.

(h) Inasmuch as the sum of the amount of income required to be distributed currently to W ($55,900) and the other amounts properly paid, credited, or required to be distributed to D ($27,950) exceeds the distributable net income ($82,750) of the trust as determined under section 643(a), D is deemed to have received $26,850 ($82,750 less $55,900) for income tax purposes. The character of the amounts deemed distributed to her is determined as follows:

Rents (20,550/82,750 × $26,850)	$6,668
Dividends (39,250/82,750 × $26,850)	12,735
Partially tax-exempt interest (7,850/82,750 × $26,850)	2,547
Tax-exempt interest (15,100/82,750 × $26,850)	4,900
Total	26,850

Accordingly, D will exclude $4,900 of tax-exempt interest from gross income and will receive the credits and exclusion for dividends received and for partially tax-exempt interest provided in sections 34,* 116,* and 35,* respectively, with respect to the dividends and partially tax-exempt interest deemed to have been distributed to her, her share of the dividends being aggregated with other dividends received by her for purposes of the dividend credit and exclusion. In addition, she may deduct a share of the depreciation deduction proportionate to the trust income allocable to her; that is, one-fourth of the total depreciation deduction, or $2,500.

(i) [Reserved]

(j) The remaining $2,500 of the depreciation deduction is allocated to the amount distributed to charity X and is hence nondeductible by the trust, W, or D. (See § 1.642(e)–1.)

* * *

§ 1.665(a)–0A Excess distributions by trusts; scope of subpart D.

(a) In general. (1) Subpart D (section 665 and following), part I, subchapter J, chapter 1 of the Code

*Editorial comment: The Regulations do not reflect the effect of the Tax Reform Act of 1986 which repealed both the Sec. 116 exclusion and the Sec. 1202 deduction and prior legislation which repealed the credits under Secs. 34 and 35.

as amended by the Tax Reform Act of 1969, is designed to tax the beneficiary of a trust that accumulates, rather than distributes, all or part of its income currently (*i.e.,* an accumulation trust), in most cases, as if the income had been currently distributed to the beneficiary instead of accumulated by the trusts. Accordingly, subpart D provides special rules for the treatment of amounts paid, credited, or required to be distributed by a complex trust (one that is subject to subpart C (section 661 and following) of such part I) in any year in excess of "distributable net income" (as defined in section 643 (a)) for that year. Such an excess distribution is an "accumulation distribution" (as defined in section 665(b)). The special rules of subpart D are generally inapplicable to amounts paid, credited, or required to be distributed by a trust in a taxable year in which it qualifies as a simple trust (one that is subject to subpart B (section 651 and following) of such part I). However, see § 1.665(e)–1A(b) for rules relating to the treatment of a simple trust as a complex trust.

(2) An accumulation distribution is deemed to consist of, first, "undistributed net income" (as defined in section 665(a)) of the trust from preceding taxable years, and, after all the undistributed net income for all preceding taxable years has been deemed distributed, "undistributed capital gain" (as defined in section 665 (f)) of the trust for all preceding taxable years commencing with the first year such amounts were accumulated. An accumulation distribution of undistributed capital gain is a "capital gain distribution" (as defined in section 665(g)). To the extent an accumulation distribution exceeds the "undistributed net income" and "undistributed capital gain" so determined, it is deemed to consist of corpus.

(3) The accumulation distribution is "thrown back" to the earliest "preceding taxable year" of the trust, which, in the case of distributions made for a taxable year beginning after December 31, 1973, from a trust (other than a foreign trust created by a U.S. person), is any taxable year beginning after December 31, 1968.* * *

(4) A distribution of undistributed net income (included in an accumulation distribution) and a capital gain distribution will be included in the income of the beneficiary in the year they are actually paid, credited, or required to be distributed to him. The tax on the distribution will be approximately the amount of tax the beneficiary would have paid with respect to the distribution had the income and capital gain been distributed to the beneficiary in the year earned by the trust. An additional amount equal to the "taxes imposed on the trust" for the preceding year is also deemed distributed. To prevent double taxation, however, the beneficiary receives a credit for such taxes.

* * *

(c) Examples. Where examples contained in the regulations under subpart D refer to tax rates for years after 1968, such tax rates are not necessarily the actual rates for such years, but are only used for example purposes.

(d) Applicability to estates. Subpart D does not apply to any estate.

§ 1.665(a)–1A Undistributed net income.

(a) Domestic trusts. The term "undistributed net income," in the case of a trust (other than a foreign trust created by a U.S. person) means, for any taxable year beginning after December 31, 1968, the distributable net income of the trust for that year (as determined under section 643(a)), less:

(1) The amount of income required to be distributed currently and any other amounts properly paid or credited or required to be distributed to beneficiaries in the taxable year as specified in section 661(a), and

(2) The amount of taxes imposed on the trust attributable to such distributable net income, as defined in § 1.665(d)–1A. The application of the rule in this paragraph to a taxable year of a trust in which income is accumulated may be illustrated by the following example:

Example. Under the terms of the trust, $10,000 of income is required to be distributed currently to A and the trustee has discretion to make additional distributions to A. During the taxable year 1971 the trust had distributable net income of $30,100 derived from royalties and the trustee made distributions of $20,000 to A. The taxable income of the trust is $10,000 on which a tax of $2,190 is paid. The undistributed net income of the trust for the taxable year 1971 is $7,910, computed as follows:

Distributable net income		$30,100
Less:		
Income currently distributable to A	$10,000	
Other amounts distributed to A.	10,000	
Taxes imposed on the trust attributable to the undistributed net income (see § 1.665(d)–1A)	2,190	
Total		22,190
Undistributed net income		7,910

* * *

§ 1.665(b)–1A Accumulation distributions.

(a) **In general.** (1) For any taxable year of a trust the term "accumulation distribution" means an amount by which the amounts properly paid, credited, or required to be distributed within the meaning of section 661(a)(2) (*i.e.*, all amounts properly paid, credited, or required to be distributed to the beneficiary other than income required to be distributed currently within the meaning of section 661(a)(1)) for that year exceed the distributable net income (determined under section 643(a)) of the trust, reduced (but not below zero) by the amount of income required to be distributed currently. To the extent provided in section 663(b) and the regulations thereunder, distributions made within the first 65 days following a taxable year may be treated as having been distributed on the last day of such taxable year.

(2) An accumulation distribution also includes, for a taxable year of the trust, any amount to which section 661(a)(2) and the preceding paragraph are inapplicable and which is paid, credited, or required to be distributed during the taxable year of the trust by reason of the exercise of a power to appoint, distribute, consume, or withdraw corpus of the trust or income of the trust accumulated in a preceding taxable year. No accumulation distribution is deemed to be made solely because the grantor or any other person is treated as owner of a portion of the trust by reason of an unexercised power to appoint, distribute, consume, or withdraw corpus or accumulated income of the trust. Nor will an accumulation distribution be deemed to have been made by reason of the exercise of a power that may affect only taxable income previously attributed to the holders of such power under subpart E (section 671 and following). See example 4 of paragraph (d) of this section for an example of an accumulation distribution occurring as a result of the exercise of a power of withdrawal.

(3) Although amounts properly paid or credited under section 661(a) do not exceed the income of the trust during the taxable year, an accumulation distribution may result if the amounts properly paid or credited under section 661(a)(2) exceed distributable net income reduced (but not below zero) by the amount required to be distributed currently under section 661(a)(1). This may occur, for example, when expenses, interest, taxes, or other items allocable to corpus are taken into account in determining taxable income and hence causing distributable net income to be less than the trust's income.

(b) **Payments that are accumulation distributions.** The following are some instances in which an accumulation distribution may arise:

(1) **One trust to another.** A distribution from one trust to another trust is generally an accumulation distribution. See § 1.643(c)–1. This general rule will apply regardless of whether the distribution is to an existing trust or to a newly created trust and regardless of whether the trust to which the distribution is made was created by the same person who created the trust from which the distribution is made or a different person. However, a distribution made from one trust to a second trust will be deemed an accumulation distribution by the first trust to an ultimate beneficiary of the second trust if the primary purpose of the distribution to the second trust is to avoid the capital gain distribution provisions (see section 669 and the regulations thereunder). An amount passing from one separate share of a trust to another separate share of the same trust is not an accumulation distribution. See § 1.665(g)–2A. For rules relating to the computation of the beneficiary's tax under section 668 by reason of an accumulation distribution from the second trust, see paragraphs (b)(1) and (c)(1)(i) of § 1.668(b)–1A and paragraphs (b)(1) and (c)(1)(i) of § 1.669(b)–1A.

(2) **Income accumulated during minority.** A distribution of income accumulated during the minority of the beneficiary is generally an accumulation distribution. For example, if a trust accumulates income until the beneficiary's 21st birthday, and then distributes the income to the beneficiary, such a distribution is an accumulation distribution. However, see § 1.665(b)–2A for rules governing income accumulated in taxable years beginning before January 1, 1969.

(3) **Amounts paid for support.** To the extent that amounts forming all or part of an accumulation distribution are applied or distributed for the support of a dependent under the circumstances specified in section 677(b) or section 678(c) or are used to discharge or satisfy any person's legal obligation as that term is used in § 1.662(a)–4, such amounts will be considered as having been distributed directly to the person whose obligation is being satisfied.

(c) **Payments that are not accumulation distributions—(1) Gifts, bequests, etc., described in section 663(a)(1).** A gift or bequest of a specific sum of money or of specific property described in section 663(a)(1) is not an accumulation distribution.

(2) **Charitable payments.** Any amount paid, permanently set aside, or used for the purposes specified in section 642(c) is not an accumulation distribution, even though no charitable deduction is

allowed under such section with respect to such payment.

(3) Income required to be distributed currently. No accumulation distribution will arise by reason of a payment of income required to be distributed currently even though such income exceeds the distributable net income of the trust because the payment is an amount specified in section 661(a)(1).

(d) Examples. The provisions of this section may be illustrated by the following examples:

Example (1). A trustee properly makes a distribution to a beneficiary of $20,000 during the taxable year 1976, of which $10,000 is income required to be distributed currently to the beneficiary. The distributable net income of the trust is $15,000. There is an accumulation distribution of $5,000 computed as follows:

Total distribution		$20,000
Less: Income required to be distributed currently (section 661(a)(1))		10,000
Other amounts distributed (section 661(a)(2))		10,000
Distributable net income	$15,000	
Less: Income required to be distributed currently	10,000	
Balance of distributable net income		5,000
Accumulation distribution		5,000

Example (2). Under the terms of the trust instrument, an annuity of $15,000 is required to be paid to A out of income each year and the trustee may in his discretion make distributions out of income or corpus to B. During the taxable year the trust had income of $18,000, as defined in section 643(b), and expenses allocable to corpus of $5,000. Distributable net income amounted to $13,000. The trustee distributed $15,000 of income to A and, in the exercise of his discretion, paid $5,000 to B. There is an accumulation distribution of $5,000 computed as follows:

Total distribution		$20,000
Less: Income required to be distributed currently to A (section 661(a)(1))		15,000
Other amounts distributed (section 661(a)(2))		5,000
Distributable net income	$13,000	
Less: Income required to be distributed currently to A	15,000	
Balance of distributable net income		0
Accumulation distribution to B		5,000

Example (3). Under the terms of a trust instrument, the trustee may either accumulate the trust income or make distributions to A and B. The trustee may also invade corpus for the benefit of A and B. During the taxable year, the trust had income as defined in section 643(b) of $22,000 and expenses of $5,000 allocable to corpus. Distributable net income amounts to $17,000. The trustee distributed $10,000 each to A and B during the taxable year. There is an accumulation distribution of $3,000 computed as follows:

Total distribution		$20,000
Less: Income required to be distributed currently		0
Other amounts distributed (section 661(a)(2))		20,000
Distributable net income	$17,000	
Less: Income required to be distributed currently	0	
Balance of distributable net income		17,000
Accumulation distribution		3,000

Example (4). A dies in 1974 and bequeaths one-half the residue of his estate in trust. His widow, W, is given a power, exercisable solely by her, to require the trustee to pay her each year of the trust $5,000 from corpus. W's right to exercise such power was exercisable at any time during the year but was not cumulative, so that, upon her failure to exercise it before the end of any taxable year of the trust, her right as to that year lapsed. The trust's taxable year is the calendar year. During the calendar years 1975 and 1976, W did not exercise her right and it lapsed as to those years. In the calendar years 1977 and 1978, in which years the trust had no distributable net income, she exercised her right and withdrew $4,000 in 1977 and $5,000 in 1978. No accumulation distribution was made by the trust in the calendar years 1975 and 1976. An accumulation distribution of $4,000 was made in 1977 and an accumulation distribution of $5,000 was made in 1978. The accumulation distribution for the years 1977 and 1978 is not reduced by any amount of income of the trust attributable to her under section 678 by reason of her power of withdrawal.

§ 1.665(d)–1A Taxes imposed on the trust.

(a) In general. (1) For purposes of subpart D, the term "taxes imposed on the trust" means the amount of Federal income taxes properly imposed for any taxable year on the trust that are attributable to the undistributed portions of distributable net income and gains in excess of losses from the sales or exchanges of capital assets. Except as provided in paragraph (c)(2) of this section, the minimum tax for tax preferences imposed by section 56* is not a tax attributable to the undistributed portions of distributable net income and gains in excess of losses from the sales or exchanges of capital assets. See section 56* and the regulations thereunder.

(2) In the case of a trust that has received an accumulation distribution from another trust, the term "taxes imposed on the trust" also includes the amount of taxes deemed distributed under §§ 1.666(b)–1A, 1.666(c)–1A, 1.669(d)–1A, and 1.669(e)–1A (whichever are applicable) as a result of such accumulation distribution, to the extent that they were taken into account under paragraphs (b)(2) or (c)(1)(vi) of § 1.668(b)–1A and (b)(2) or (c)(1)(vi)

*Editorial comment: The Regulations do not reflect the effect of the Tax Reform Act of 1986 which modified the minimum tax calculation under Secs. 55–59.

of § 1.669(b)–1A in computing the partial tax on such accumulation distribution. For example, assume that trust A, a calendar year trust, makes an accumulation distribution in 1975 to trust B, also on the calendar year basis, in connection with which $500 of taxes are deemed under § 1.666(b)–1A to be distributed to trust B. The partial tax on the accumulation distribution is computed under paragraph (b) of § 1.668(b)–1A (the exact method) to be $600 and all of the $500 is used under paragraph (b)(2) of § 1.668(b)–1A to reduce the partial tax to $100. The taxes imposed on trust B for 1975 will, in addition to the $100 partial tax, also include the $500 used to reduce the partial tax.

(b) Taxes imposed on the trust attributable to undistributed net income. (1) For the purpose of subpart D, the term "taxes imposed on the trust attributable to the undistributed net income" means the amount of Federal income taxes for the taxable year properly allocable to the undistributed portion of the distributable net income for such taxable year. This amount is (i) an amount that bears the same relationship to the total taxes of the trust for the year (other than the minimum tax for tax preferences imposed by section 56*), computed after the allowance of credits under section 642(a), as (a) the taxable income of the trust, other than the capital gains not included in distributable net income less their share of section 1202 deduction*, bears to (b) the total taxable income of the trust for such year or, (ii) if the alternative tax computation under section 1201(b) is used and there are no net short-term gains, an amount equal to such total taxes less the amount of the alternative tax imposed on the trust and attributable to the capital gain. Thus, for the purposes of subpart D, in determining the amount of taxes imposed on the trust attributable to the undistributed net income, that portion of the taxes paid by the trust attributable to capital gain allocable to corpus is excluded. The rule stated in this subparagraph may be illustrated by the following example, which assumes that the alternative tax computation is not used:

Example. (1) Under the terms of a trust, which reports on the calendar year basis, the income may be accumulated or distributed to A in the discretion of the trustee and capital gains are allocable to corpus. During the taxable year 1974, the trust had income of $20,000 from royalties, long-term capital gains of $10,000, and expenses of $2,000. The trustee in his discretion made a distribution of $10,000 to A. The taxes imposed on the trust for such year attributable to the undistributed net income are $2,319, determined as shown below.

(2) The distributable net income of the trust computed under section 643(a) is $18,000 (royalties of $20,000 less expenses of $2,000). The total taxes paid by the trust are $3,787, computed as follows:

Royalties		$20,000
Capital gain allocable to corpus		10,000
Gross income		30,000
Deductions:		
Expenses	$2,000	
Distributions to A	10,000	
Capital gain deduction*	5,000	
Personal exemption	100	
		17,100
Taxable income		12,900
Total income taxes		3,787

(3) Taxable income other than capital gains less the section 1202 deduction * is $7,900 ($12,900 – ($10,000 – $5,000)). Therefore, the amount of taxes imposed on the trust attributable to the undistributed net income is $2,319, computed as follows:

$3,787 (total taxes) × $7,900 (taxable income other than capital gains not included in d.n.i. less the 1202 deduction) * divided by $12,900 (taxable income)	$2,319

(2) If in any taxable year an accumulation distribution of undistributed net income is made by the trust which results in a throwback to a prior year, the taxes of the prior year imposed on the trust attributable to any remaining undistributed net income of such prior year are the taxes prescribed in subparagraph (1) of this paragraph reduced by the taxes of the prior year deemed distributed under section 666(b) or (c). The provisions of this subparagraph may be illustrated by the following example:

Example. Assume the same facts as in the example in subparagraph (1) of this paragraph. In 1975 the trust makes an accumulation distribution, of which an amount of undistributed net income is deemed distributed in 1974. Taxes imposed on the trust (in the amount of $1,000) attributable to the undistributed net income are therefore deemed distributed in such year. Consequently, the taxes imposed on the trust subsequent to the 1975 distribution attributable to the remaining undistributed net income are $1,319 ($2,319 less $1,000).

(c) Taxes imposed on the trust attributable to undistributed capital gain—(1) Regular tax. For the purpose of subpart D the term "taxes imposed on the trust attributable to undistributed capital gain" means the amount of Federal income taxes for the taxable year properly attributable to that portion of the excess of capital gains over capital losses of the

*Editorial comment: The Regulations do not reflect the effect of the Tax Reform Act of 1986 which repealed the Sec. 1202 capital gain deduction, modified the minimum tax calculation under Secs. 55–59, and modified the Sec. 1201 alternative tax on capital gains. The Regulations also do not include the effect of the Revenue Reconciliation Act of 1993 which created the new Sec. 1202 exclusion.

trust that is allocable to corpus for such taxable year. Such amount is the total of—

(i) The amount computed under subparagraph (2) of this paragraph (the minimum tax),* plus

(ii) The amount that bears the same relationship to the total taxes of the trust for the year (other than the minimum tax), computed after the allowance of credits under section 642(a), as (a) the excess of capital gains over capital losses for such year that are not included in distributable net income, computed after its share of the deduction under section 1202* (relating to the deduction for capital gains) has been taken into account, bears to the greater of (b) the total taxable income of the trust for such year, or (c) the amount of capital gains computed under (a) of this subdivision. However, if the alternative tax computation under section 1201(b) * is used and there are no net short-term gains, the amount is the amount of the alternative tax imposed on the trust and attributable to the capital gain. The application of this subparagraph may be illustrated by the following example, which assumes that the alternative tax computation is not used:

Example. Assume the same facts as in the example in paragraph (b)(1). The capital gains not included in d.n.i. are $10,000, and the deduction under section 1202* is $5,000. The amount of taxes imposed on the trust attributable to undistributed capital gain is $1,468, computed as follows:

$3,787 (total taxes) × $5,000 (capital gains not included in d.n.i. less section 1202 deductions) * divided by $12,900 (taxable income)	$1,468

(2) Minimum tax.* The term "taxes imposed on the trust attributable to the undistributed capital gain" also includes the minimum tax for tax preferences imposed on the trust by section 56 with respect to the undistributed capital gain. The amount of such minimum tax so included bears the same relation to the total amount of minimum tax imposed on the trust by section 56 for the taxable year as one-half the net capital gain (net section 1201 gain for taxable years beginning before January 1, 1977) (as defined in section 1222(11)) from such taxable year bears to the sum of the items of tax preference of the trust for such taxable year which are apportioned to the trust in accordance with § 1.58–3(a)(1).

(3) Reduction for prior distribution. If in any taxable year a capital gain distribution is made by the trust which results in a throwback to a prior year, the taxes of the prior year imposed on the trust attributable to any remaining undistributed capital gain of the prior year are the taxes prescribed in subparagraph (1) of this paragraph reduced by the taxes of the prior year deemed distributed under section 669(d) or (e). The provisions of this subparagraph may be illustrated by the following example:

Example. Assume the same facts as in the example in subparagraph (1) of this paragraph. In 1976, the trust makes a capital gain distribution, of which an amount of undistributed capital gain is deemed distributed in 1974. Taxes imposed on the trust (in the amount of $500) attributable to the undistributed capital gain are therefore deemed distributed in such year. Consequently, the taxes imposed on the trust attributable to the remaining undistributed capital gain are $968 ($1,468 less $500).

* * *

§ 1.666(a)–1A Amount allocated.

(a) In general. In the case of a trust that is subject to subpart C of part I of subchapter J of chapter 1 of the Code (relating to estates and trusts that may accumulate income or that distribute corpus), section 666(a) prescribes rules for determining the taxable years from which an accumulation distribution will be deemed to have been made and the extent to which the accumulation distribution is considered to consist of undistributed net income. In general, an accumulation distribution made in taxable years beginning after December 31, 1969, is deemed to have been made first from the earliest preceding taxable year of the trust for which there is undistributed net income.* * *

(b) Distributions by domestic trusts—(1) Taxable years beginning after December 31, 1973. An accumulation distribution made by a trust (other than a foreign trust created by a U.S. person) in any taxable year beginning after December 31, 1973, is allocated to the preceding taxable years of the trust (defined in § 1.665(e)–1A(a)(1)(ii) as those beginning after December 31, 1968) according to the amount of undistributed net income of the trust for such years. For this purpose, an accumulation distribution is first to be allocated to the earliest such preceding taxable year in which there is undistributed net income and shall then be allocated, beginning with the next earliest, to any remaining preceding taxable years of the trust. The portion of the accumulation distribution allocated to the earliest preceding taxable year is the amount of the undistributed net income for that preceding taxable year. The portion of the

*Editorial comment: The Regulations do not reflect the effect of the Tax Reform Act of 1986 which repealed the Sec. 1202 capital gain deduction, modified the minimum tax calculation under Secs. 55–59, and modified the Sec. 1201 alternative tax on capital gains. The Regulations also do not include the effect of the Revenue Reconciliation Act of 1993 which created the new Sec. 1202 exclusion.

accumulation distribution allocated to any preceding taxable year subsequent to the earliest such preceding taxable year is the excess of the accumulation distribution over the aggregate of the undistributed net income for all earlier preceding taxable years. See paragraph (d) of this section for adjustments to undistributed net income for prior distributions. The provisions of this subparagraph may be illustrated by the following example:

Example. In 1977, a domestic trust reporting on the calendar year basis makes an accumulation distribution of $33,000. Therefore, years before 1969 are ignored. In 1969, the trust had $6,000 of undistributed net income; in 1970, $4,000; in 1971, none; in 1972, $7,000; in 1973, $5,000; in 1974, $8,000; in 1975, $6,000; and $4,000 in 1976. The accumulation distribution is deemed distributed $6,000 in 1969, $4,000 in 1970, none in 1971, $7,000 in 1972, $5,000 in 1973, $8,000 in 1974, and $3,000 in 1975.

* * *

§ 1.666(b)–1A Total taxes deemed distributed.

(a) If an accumulation distribution is deemed under § 1.666(a)–1A to be distributed on the last day of a preceding taxable year and the amount is not less than the undistributed net income for such preceding taxable year, then an additional amount equal to the "taxes imposed on the trust attributable to the undistributed net income" (as defined in § 1.665(d)–1A(b)) for such preceding taxable year is also deemed distributed under section 661(a)(2). For example, a trust has undistributed net income of $8,000 for the taxable year 1974. The taxes imposed on the trust attributable to the undistributed net income are $3,032. During the taxable year 1977, an accumulation distribution of $8,000 is made to the beneficiary, which is deemed under § 1.666(a)–1A to have been distributed on the last day of 1974. The 1977 accumulation distribution is not less than the 1974 undistributed net income. Accordingly, the taxes of $3,032 imposed on the trust attributable to the undistributed net income for 1974 are also deemed to have been distributed on the last day of 1974. Thus, a total of $11,032 will be deemed to have been distributed on the last day of 1974.

(b) For the purpose of paragraph (a) of this section, the undistributed net income of any preceding taxable year and the taxes imposed on the trust for such preceding taxable year attributable to such undistributed net income are computed after taking into account any accumulation distributions of taxable years intervening between such preceding taxable year and the taxable year. See paragraph (d) of § 1.666(a)–1A.

§ 1.666(c)–1A Pro rata portion of taxes deemed distributed.

(a) If an accumulation distribution is deemed under § 1.666(a)–1A to be distributed on the last day of a preceding taxable year and the amount is less than the undistributed net income for such preceding taxable year, then an additional amount is also deemed distributed under section 661(a)(2). The additional amount is equal to the "taxes imposed on the trust attributable to the undistributed net income" (as defined in § 1.665(a)–1A(b)) for such preceding taxable year, multiplied by a fraction, the numerator of which is the amount of the accumulation distribution allocated to such preceding taxable year and the denominator of which is the undistributed net income for such preceding taxable year. See paragraph (b) of example (1) and paragraphs (c) and (f) of example (2) in § 1.666(c)–2A for illustrations of this paragraph.

(b) For the purpose of paragraph (a) of this section, the undistributed net income of any preceding taxable year and the taxes imposed on the trust for such preceding taxable year attributable to such undistributed net income are computed after taking into account any accumulation distributions of any taxable years intervening between such preceding taxable year and the taxable year. See paragraph (d) of § 1.666(a)–1A and paragraph (c) of example (1) and paragraphs (e) and (h) of example (2) in § 1.666(c)–2A.

* * *

Grantors and Others Treated as Substantial Owners

§ 1.671–1 Grantors and others treated as substantial owners; scope.

(a) Subpart E (section 671 and following), part I, subchapter J, chapter 1 of the Code, contains provisions taxing income of a trust to the grantor or another person under certain circumstances even though he is not treated as a beneficiary under subparts A through D (section 641 and following) of such part I. Sections 671 and 672 contain general provisions relating to the entire subpart. Sections 673 through 677 define the circumstances under which income of a trust is taxed to a grantor. These circumstances are in general as follows:

(1) If the grantor has retained a reversionary interest in the trust, within specified time limits (section 673);

(2) If the grantor or a nonadverse party has certain powers over the beneficial interests under the trust (section 674);

(3) If certain administrative powers over the trust exist under which the grantor can or does benefit (section 675);

(4) If the grantor or a nonadverse party has a power to revoke the trust or return the corpus to the grantor (section 676); or

(5) If the grantor or a nonadverse party has the power to distribute income to or for the benefit of the grantor or the grantor's spouse (section 677).

Under section 678, income of a trust is taxed to a person other than the grantor to the extent that he has the sole power to vest corpus or income in himself.

(b) Sections 671 through 677 do not apply if the income of a trust is taxable to a grantor's spouse under section 71 or 682 (relating respectively to alimony and separate maintenance payments, and the income of an estate or trust in the case of divorce, etc.).

(c) Except as provided in such subpart E, income of a trust is not included in computing the taxable income and credits of a grantor or another person solely on the grounds of his dominion and control over the trust. However, the provisions of subpart E do not apply in situations involving an assignment of future in- come, whether or not the assignment is to a trust. Thus, for example, a person who assigns his right to future income under an employment contract may be taxed on that income even though the assignment is to a trust over which the assignor has retained none of the controls specified in sections 671 through 677. Similarly, a bondholder who assigns his right to interest may be taxed on interest payments even though the assignment is to an uncontrolled trust. Nor are the rules as to family partnerships affected by the provisions of subpart E, even though a partnership interest is held in trust. Likewise, these sections have no application in determining the right of a grantor to deductions for payments to a trust under a transfer and leaseback arrangement. In addition, the limitation of the last sentence of section 671 does not prevent any person from being taxed on the income of a trust when it is used to discharge his legal obligation. See § 1.662 (a)–4. He is then treated as a beneficiary under subparts A through D or treated as an owner under section 677 because the income is distributed for his benefit, and not because of his dominion or control over the trust.

* * *

(f) For rules relating to the treatment of liabilities resulting on the sale or other disposition of encumbered trust property due to a renunciation of powers by the grantor or other owner, see § 1.1001–2.

§ 1.671–2 Applicable principles.

(a) Under section 671 a grantor or another person includes in computing his taxable income and credits those items of income, deduction, and credit against tax which are attributable to or included in any portion of a trust of which he is treated as the owner. Sections 673 through 678 set forth the rules for determining when the grantor or another person is treated as the owner of any portion of a trust. The rules for determining the items of income, deduction, and credit against tax that are attributable to or included in a portion of the trust are set forth in § 1.671–3.

(b) Since the principle underlying subpart E (section 671 and following), part I, subchapter J, chapter 1 of the Code, is in general that income of a trust over which the grantor or another person has retained substantial dominion or control should be taxed to the grantor or other person rather than to the trust which receives the income or to the beneficiary to whom the income may be distributed, it is ordinarily immaterial whether the income involved constitutes income or corpus for trust accounting purposes. Accordingly, when it is stated in the regulations under subpart E that "income" is attributed to the grantor or another person, the reference, unless specifically limited, is to income determined for tax purposes and not to income for trust accounting purposes. When it is intended to emphasize that income for trust accounting purposes (determined in accordance with the provisions set forth in § 1.643(b)–1), is meant, the phrase "ordinary income" is used.

(c) An item of income, deduction, or credit included in computing the taxable income and credits of a grantor or another person under section 671 is treated as if it had been received or paid directly by the grantor or other person (whether or not an individual). For example, a charitable contribution made by a trust which is attributed to the grantor (an individual) under sections 671 through 677 will be aggregated with his other charitable contributions to determine their deductibility under the limitations of section 170(b)(1). Likewise, dividends received by a trust from sources in a particular foreign country which are attributed to a grantor or another person under subpart E will be aggregated with his other income from sources within that country to determine whether the taxpayer is subject to the limitations of section 904 with respect to credit for the tax paid to that country.

(d) Items of income, deduction, and credit not attributed to or included in any portion of a trust of which the grantor or another person is treated as the owner under subpart E are subject to the provisions of subparts A through D (section 641 and following), of such part I.

(e) [Reserved] For further guidance, see §1.671–2T(e).

§ 1.671–2T Applicable principles (temporary).

(a) through (d) [Reserved]. For further guidance, see § 1.671–2(a) through (d).

(e) (1) For purposes of part I, subchapter J, chapter 1 of the Internal Revenue Code, a grantor includes any person to the extent such person either creates a trust, or directly or indirectly makes a gratuitous transfer (within the meaning of paragraph (e)(2) of this section) of property to a trust. For purposes of this section, the term property includes cash. If a person creates or funds a trust on behalf of another person, both persons are treated as grantors of the trust. (See section 6048 for reporting requirements that apply to grantors of foreign trusts.) However, a person who creates a trust but makes no gratuitous transfers to the trust is not treated as an owner of any portion of the trust under sections 671 through 677 or 679. Also, a person who funds a trust with an amount that is directly reimbursed to such person within a reasonable period of time and who makes no other transfers to the trust that constitute gratuitous transfers is not treated as an owner of any portion of the trust under sections 671 through 677 or 679. See also §1.672(f)–5(a).

(2) (i) A gratuitous transfer is any transfer other than a transfer for fair market value. A transfer of property to a trust may be considered a gratuitous transfer without regard to whether the transfer is treated as a gift for gift tax purposes.

(ii) For purposes of this paragraph (e), a transfer is for fair market value only to the extent of the value of property received from the trust, services rendered by the trust, or the right to use property of the trust. For example, rents, royalties, interest, and compensation paid to a trust are transfers for fair market value only to the extent that the payments reflect an arm's length price for the use of the property of, or for the services rendered by, the trust. For purposes of this determination, an interest in the trust is not property received from the trust. In addition, a person will not be treated as making a transfer for fair market value merely because the transferor recognizes gain on the transaction. See, for example, section 684 regarding the recognition of gain on certain transfers to foreign trusts.

(iii) For purposes of this paragraph (e), a gratuitous transfer does not include a distribution to a trust with respect to an interest held by such trust in either a trust described in paragraph (e)(3) of this section or an entity other than a trust. For example, a distribution to a trust by a corporation with respect to its stock described in section 301 is not a gratuitous transfer.

(3) A grantor includes any person who acquires an interest in a trust from a grantor of the trust if the interest acquired is an interest in certain investment trusts described in §301.7701–4(c) of this chapter, liquidating trusts described in §301.7701–4(d) of this chapter, or environmental remediation trusts described in §301.7701–4(e) of this chapter.

(4) If a gratuitous transfer is made by a partnership or corporation to a trust and is for a business purpose of the partnership or corporation, the partnership or corporation will generally be treated as the grantor of the trust. For example, if a partnership makes a gratuitous transfer to a trust in order to secure a legal obligation of the partnership to a third party unrelated to the partnership, the partnership will be treated as the grantor of the trust. However, if a partnership or a corporation makes a gratuitous transfer to a trust that is not for a business purpose of the partnership or corporation but is for the personal purposes of one or more of the partners or shareholders, the gratuitous transfer will be treated as a constructive distribution to such partners or shareholders under federal tax principles and the partners or the shareholders will be treated as the grantors of the trust. For example, if a partnership makes a gratuitous transfer to a trust that is for the benefit of a child of a partner, the gratuitous transfer will be treated as a distribution to the partner under section 731 and a subsequent gratuitous transfer by the partner to the trust.

(5) If a trust makes a gratuitous transfer of property to another trust, the grantor of the transferor trust generally will be treated as the grantor of the transferee trust. However, if a person with a general power of appointment over the transferor trust exercises that power in favor of another trust, then such person will be treated as the grantor of the transferee trust, even if the grantor of the transferor trust is treated as the owner of the transferor trust under subpart E of part I, subchapter J, chapter 1 of the Internal Revenue Code.

(6) The following examples illustrate the rules of this paragraph (e). Unless otherwise indicated, all trusts are domestic trusts and all other persons are United States persons.

The examples are as follows:

Example (1). A creates and funds a trust, T, for the benefit of her children. B subsequently makes a gratuitous transfer to T. Under paragraph (e)(l) of this section, both A and B are grantors of T.

Example (2). A makes an investment in a fixed investment trust, T, that is classified as a trust under §301.7701–4(c)(1) of this chapter. A is a grantor of T. B subsequently acquires A's entire interest in T. Under paragraph (e)(3) of this section, B is a grantor of T with respect to such interest.

Example (3). A, an attorney, creates a foreign trust, FT, on behalf of A's client, B, and transfers $100 to FT out of A's funds. A is reimbursed by B for the $100 transferred to FT. The trust instrument states that the trustee has discretion to distribute the income or corpus of FT to B, and B's children. Both A and B are treated as grantors of FT under paragraph (e)(1) of this section. In addition, B is treated as the owner of the entire trust under section 677. Because A is reimbursed for the $100 transferred to FT on behalf of B, A is not treated as transferring any property to FT. Therefore, A is not an owner of any portion of T under sections 671 through 677 regardless of whether A retained any power over or interest in T described in sections 673 through 677. A also is not treated as an owner of any portion of T under section 679. Both A and B are responsible parties for purposes of the reporting requirements in section 6048.

Example (4). A creates and funds a trust, T. A is not treated as an owner of any portion of the trust under subpart E. B holds an unrestricted power, exercisable solely by B, to withdraw certain amounts contributed to the trust before the end of the calendar year and to vest those amounts in B. B is treated as an owner of the portion of T that is subject to the withdrawal power under section 678(a)(1). However, B is not a grantor of T under paragraph (e)(1) of this section because B neither created T nor made a gratuitous transfer to T.

Example (5). A transfers cash to a trust, T, through a broker, in exchange for units in T. The units in T are not property for purposes of determining whether A has received fair market value under paragraph (e)(2)(ii) of this section. Therefore, A has made a gratuitous transfer to T, and, under paragraph (e)(1) of this section, A is a grantor of T.

Example (6). A borrows cash from T, a trust. A has not made any gratuitous transfers to T. Arm's length interest payments by A to T will not be treated as gratuitous transfers under paragraph (e)(2)(ii) of this section. Therefore, under paragraph (e)(1) of this section, A is not a grantor of T with respect to the interest payments.

Example (7). A, B's brother, creates a trust, T, for B's benefit and contributes $50,000 to T. The trustee invests the $50,000 in stock of Company X. C, B's uncle, sells property with a fair market value of $1,000,000 to T in exchange for the stock when it has appreciated to a fair market value of $100,000. Under paragraph (e)(2)(ii) of this section, the $900,000 excess value is a gratuitous transfer by C. Therefore, under paragraph (e)(l) of this section, A is a grantor with respect to the portion of the trust valued at $100,000, and C is a grantor of T with respect to the portion of the trust valued at $900,000. In addition, A or C or both will be treated as the owners of the respective portions of the trust of which each person is a grantor if A or C or both retain powers over or interests in such portions under sections 673 through 677.

Example (8). G creates and funds a trust, T1, for the benefit of G's children and grandchildren. After G's death, under authority granted to the trustees in the trust instrument, the trustees of T1 transfer a portion of the assets of T1 to another trust, T2, and retain a power to revoke T2 and revest the assets of T2 in T1. Under paragraphs (e)(1) and (5) of this section, G is the grantor of T1 and T2. In addition, because the trustees of T1 have retained a power to revest the assets of T2 in T1, T1 is treated as the owner of T2 under section 678(a).

Example (9). G creates and funds a trust, T1, for the benefit of B. G retains a power to revest the assets of T1 in G within the meaning of section 676. Under the trust agreement, B is given a general power of appointment over the assets of T1. B exercises the general power of appointment with respect to one-half of the corpus of T1 in favor of a trust, T2, that is for the benefit of C, B's child. Under paragraph (e)(1) of this section, G is the grantor of T1, and under paragraphs (e)(1) and (5) of this section, B is the grantor of T2.

(7) The rules of this section are applicable to any transfer to a trust, or transfer of an interest in a trust, on or after August 10, 1999.

§ 1.671–3 Attribution or inclusion of income, deductions, and credits against tax.

(a) When a grantor or another person is treated under subpart E (section 671 and following) as the owner of any portion of a trust, there are included in computing his tax liability those items of income, deduction, and credit against tax attributable to or included in that portion. For example:

(1) If a grantor or another person is treated as the owner of an entire trust (corpus as well as ordinary income), he takes into account in computing his income tax liability all items of income, deduction, and credit (including capital gains and losses) to which he would have been entitled had the trust not been in existence during the period he is treated as owner.

(2) If the portion treated as owned consists of specific trust property and its income, all items directly related to that property are attributable to the portion. Items directly related to trust property not included in the portion treated as owned by the grantor or other person are governed by the provisions of subparts A through D (section 641 and following), part I, subchapter J, chapter 1 of the Code. Items that relate both to the portion treated as owned by the grantor and to the balance of the trust must be apportioned in a manner that is reasonable in the light of all the circumstances of each case, including the terms of the governing instrument, local law, and the practice of the trustee if it is reasonable and consistent.

(3) If the portion of a trust treated as owned by a grantor or another person consists of an undivided fractional interest in the trust, or of an interest represented by a dollar amount, a pro rata share of each item of income, deduction, and credit is normally allocated to the portion. Thus, where the portion owned consists of an interest in or a right to an amount of corpus only, a fraction of each item (including items allocated to corpus, such as capital gains) is attributed to the portion. The numerator of this fraction is the amount which is subject to the control of the grantor or other person and the denominator is normally the fair market value of the trust corpus at the beginning of the taxable year in question. The share not treated as owned by the grantor or other person is governed by the provisions of subparts A through D. See the last three sentences of paragraph (c) of this section for the principles applicable if the portion treated as owned consists of an interest in part of the ordinary income in contrast to an interest in corpus alone.

(b) If a grantor or another person is treated as the owner of a portion of a trust, that portion may or may not include both ordinary income and other income allocable to corpus. For example—

(1) Only ordinary income is included by reason of an interest in or a power over ordinary income alone. Thus, if a grantor is treated under section 673 as an owner by reason of a reversionary interest in ordinary income only, items of income allocable to corpus will not be included in the portion he is treated as owning. Similarly, if a grantor or another person is treated under sections 674–678 as an owner of a portion by reason of a power over ordinary income only, items of income allocable to corpus are not included in that portion. (See paragraph (c) of this section to determine the treatment of deductions and credits when only ordinary income is included in the portion.)

(2) Only income allocable to corpus is included by reason of an interest in or a power over corpus alone, if satisfaction of the interest or an exercise of the power will not result in an interest in or the exercise of a power over ordinary income which would itself cause that income to be included. For example, if a grantor has a reversionary interest in a trust which is not such as to require that he be treated as an owner under section 673, he may nevertheless be treated as an owner under section 677(a)(2) since any income allocable to corpus is accumulated for future distribution to him, but items of income included in determining ordinary income are not included in the portion he is treated as owning. Similarly, he may have a power over corpus which is such that he is treated as an owner under section 674 or 676(a), but ordinary income will not be included in the portion he owns, if his power can only affect income received after a period of time such that he would not be treated as an owner of the income if the power were a reversionary interest. (See paragraph (c) of this section to determine the treatment of deductions and credits when only income allocated to corpus is included in the portion.)

(3) Both ordinary income and other income allocable to corpus are included by reason of an interest in or a power over both ordinary income and corpus, or an interest in or a power over corpus alone which does not come within the provisions of subparagraph (2) of this paragraph. For example, if a grantor is treated under section 673 as the owner of a portion of a trust by reason of a reversionary interest in corpus, both ordinary income and other income allocable to corpus are included in the portion. Further, a grantor includes both ordinary income and other income allocable to corpus in the portion he is treated as owning if he is treated under section 674 or 676 as an owner because of a power over corpus which can affect income received within a period such that he would be treated as an owner under section 673 if the power were a reversionary interest. Similarly, a grantor or another person includes both ordinary income and other income allocable to corpus in the portion he is treated as owning if he is treated as an owner under section 675 or 678 because of a power over corpus.

(c) If only income allocable to corpus is included in computing a grantor's tax liability, he will take into account in that computation only those items of income, deductions, and credit which would not be included under subparts A through D in the computation of the tax liability of the current income beneficiaries if all distributable net income had actually been distributed to those beneficiaries. On the other hand, if the grantor or another person is treated as an owner solely because of his interest in or power over ordinary income alone, he will take into account in computing his tax liability those items which would be included in computing the tax liability of a current income beneficiary, including expenses allocable to corpus which enter into the computation of distributable net income. If the grantor or other person is treated as an owner because of his power over or right to a dollar amount of ordinary income, he will first take into account a portion of those items of income and expense entering into the computation of ordinary income under the trust instrument or local law sufficient to produce income of the dollar amount required. There will then be attributable to him a pro rata portion of other items entering into the computation of distributable net income under subparts A through D, such as expenses allocable to corpus, and a pro rata portion of credits of the trust. For examples of computations under this paragraph, see paragraph (g) of § 1.677(a)–1.

§ 1.671–4 Method of reporting.

(a) Portion of trust treated as owned by the grantor or another person. Except as provided in paragraphs (b) of this section and § 1.671–5, items of income, deduction, and credit attributable to any portion of a trust that, under the provisions of subpart E (section 671 and following), part I, subchapter J, chapter 1 of the Internal Revenue Code, is treated as owned by the grantor or another person, are not reported by the trust on Form 1041, "U.S. Income Tax Return for Estates and Trusts," but are shown on a separate statement to be attached to that form. Section 1.671–5 provides special reporting rules for widely held fixed investment trusts. Section 301.7701–4(e)(2) of this chapter provides guidance on how these reporting rules apply to an environmental remediation trust.

(b) Trust income taxed entirely to grantor. **(1)** In the case of a trust when

(i) The same individual is both grantor and trustee (or co-trustee), and

(ii) That individual is treated as owner for the taxable year of all of the assets of the trust by the application of section 676,

A Form 1041 should not be filed. Instead, all items of income, deduction, and credit from the trust should be reported on the individual's Form 1040 in accordance with its instructions. For provisions dealing with taxpayer identifying numbers, see § 301.6109–1 (Regulations on Procedure and Administration).

(2) In the case of a trust when

(i) A husband and wife are the sole grantors, and

(ii) One spouse is trustee or co-trustee with a third party or both spouses are trustees or co-trustees with a third party, and

(iii) One or both spouses are treated as owners of all of the assets of the trust for the taxable year by the application of section 676, and

(iv) The husband and wife for the taxable year make a single return jointly of income taxes under section 6013,

A Form 1041 should not be filed. Instead, all items of income, deduction, and credit from the trust should be reported on the spouses' Form 1040 in accordance with its instructions.

(3) The grantor of a trust described in § 1.671–(b) (1) or (2) who filed a Form 1041 on or before November 24, 1981 may continue to report income, deductions, and credits of the trust pursuant to § 1.671–4(a). Alternatively, the grantor of such a trust may file a final Form 1041 for the trust's current taxable year pursuant to § 1.671–4(a). In such a case, the grantor must write across the front of the Form 1041 a statement in substance saying "Pursuant to § 1.671–4(b), this is the final Form 1041 for this grantor trust." For the next taxable year, the grantor must furnish payers of income with his or her social security number, pursuant to § 301.6109–1(a)(2), and must follow the rule of § 1.671–4(b)(1) or (2), as the case may be.

(4) This paragraph (b) of this section shall not apply to a trust if the situs of the trust or any of the assets of the trust are not in the United States.

* * *

§ 1.672(a)–1 Definition of adverse party.

(a) Under section 672(a) an adverse party is defined as any person having a substantial beneficial interest in a trust which would be adversely affected by the exercise or nonexercise of a power which he possesses respecting the trust. A trustee is not an adverse party merely because of his interest as trustee. A person having a general power of appointment over the trust property is deemed to have a beneficial interest in the trust. An interest is a substantial interest if its value in relation to the total value of the property subject to the power is not insignificant.

(b) Ordinarily, a beneficiary will be an adverse party, but if his right to share in the income or corpus of a trust is limited to only a part, he may be an adverse party only as to that part. Thus, if A, B, C, and D are equal income beneficiaries of a trust and the grantor can revoke with A's consent, the grantor is treated as the owner of a portion which represents three-fourths of the trust; and items of income, deduction, and credit attributable to that portion are included in determining the tax of the grantor.

(c) The interest of an ordinary income beneficiary of a trust may or may not be adverse with respect to the exercise of a power over corpus. Thus, if the income of a trust is payable to A for life, with a power (which is not a general power of appointment) in A to appoint the corpus to the grantor either during his life or by will, A's interest is adverse to the return of the corpus to the grantor during A's life, but is not adverse to a return of the corpus after A's death. In other words, A's interest is adverse as to ordinary income but is not adverse as to income allocable to corpus. Therefore, assuming no other relevant facts exist, the grantor would not be taxable on the ordinary income of the trust under section 674, 676, or 677, but would be taxable under section 677 on income allocable to corpus (such as capital gains), since it may in the discretion of a nonadverse party be accumulated for future distribution to the grantor. Similarly, the interest of a contingent income beneficiary is adverse to a return of corpus to the grantor before the termination of his interest but not to a return of corpus after the termination of his interest.

(d) The interest of a remainderman is adverse to the exercise of any power over the corpus of a trust, but not to the exercise of a power over any income interest preceding his remainder. For example, if the grantor creates a trust which provides for income to be distributed to A for 10 years and then for the corpus to go to X if he is then living, a power exercisable by X to revest corpus in the grantor is a power exercisable by an adverse party; however, a power exercisable by X to distribute part or all of the ordinary income to the grantor may be a power exercisable by a nonadverse party (which would cause the ordinary income to be taxed to the grantor).

§ 1.672(b)–1 Nonadverse party.

A "nonadverse party" is any person who is not an adverse party.

§ 1.672(c)–1 Related or subordinate party.

Section 672(c) defines the term "related or subordinate party." The term, as used in sections 674(c) and 675(3), means any nonadverse party who is the grantor's spouse if living with the grantor; the grantor's father, mother, issue, brother or sister; an employee of the grantor; a corporation or any employee of a corporation in which the stock holdings of the grantor and the trust are significant from the viewpoint of voting control; or a subordinate employee of a corporation in which the grantor is an executive. For purposes of sections 674(c) and 675 (3), these persons are presumed to be subservient to the grantor in respect of the exercise or nonexercise of the powers conferred on them unless shown not to be subservient by a preponderance of the evidence.

§ 1.672(d)–1 Power subject to condition precedent.

Section 672(d) provides that a person is considered to have a power described in subpart E (section 671 and following), part I, subchapter J, chapter 1 of the Code, even though the exercise of the power is subject to a precedent giving of notice or takes effect only after the expiration of a certain period of time. However, although a person may be considered to have such a power, the grantor will nevertheless not be treated as an owner by reason of the power if its exercise can only affect beneficial enjoyment of income received after the expiration of a period of time such that, if the power were a reversionary interest, he would not be treated as an owner under section 673. See sections 674(b)(2), 676(b), and the last sentence of section 677(a). Thus, for example, if a grantor creates a trust for the benefit of his son and retains a power to revoke which takes effect only after the expiration of 2 years from the date of exercise, he is treated as an owner from the inception of the trust. However, if the grantor retains a power to revoke, exercisable at any time, which can only affect the beneficial enjoyment of the ordinary income of a trust received after the expiration of 10 years commencing with the date of the transfer in trust, or after the death of the income beneficiary, the power does not cause him to be treated as an owner with respect to ordinary income during the first 10 years of the trust or during the income beneficiary's life, as the case may be. See section 676(b).

* * *

§ 1.674(a)–1 Power to control beneficial enjoyment; scope of section 674.

(a) Under section 674, the grantor is treated as the owner of a portion of trust if the grantor or a nonadverse party has a power, beyond specified limits, to dispose of the beneficial enjoyment of the income or corpus, whether the power is a fiduciary power, a power of appointment, or any other power. Section 674(a) states in general terms that the grantor is treated as the owner in every case in which he or a nonadverse party can affect the beneficial enjoyment of a portion of a trust, the limitations being set forth as exceptions in subsections (b), (c), and (d) of section 674. These exceptions are discussed in detail in §§ 1.674(b)–1 through 1.674(d)–1. Certain limitations applicable to section 674(b), (c), and (d) are set forth in § 1.674(d)–2. Section 674(b) describes powers which are excepted regardless of who holds them. Section 674(c) describes additional powers of trustees which are excepted if at least half the trustees are independent, and if the grantor is not a trustee. Section 674(d) describes a further power which is excepted if it is held by trustees other than the grantor or his spouse (if living with the grantor).

(b) In general terms the grantor is treated as the owner of a portion of a trust if he or a nonadverse party or both has a power to dispose of the beneficial enjoyment of the corpus or income unless the power is one of the following:

(1) Miscellaneous powers over either ordinary income or corpus. (i) A power that can only affect the beneficial enjoyment of income (including capital gains) received after a period of time such that the grantor would not be treated as an owner under section 673 if the power were a reversionary interest (section 674(b)(2));

(ii) A testamentary power held by anyone (other than a testamentary power held by the grantor over accumulated income) (section 674(b)(3));

(iii) A power to choose between charitable beneficiaries or to affect the manner of their enjoyment of a beneficial interest (section 674(b)(4));

(iv) A power to allocate receipts and disbursements between income and corpus (section 674(b)(8)).

(2) Powers of distribution primarily affecting only one beneficiary. (i) A power to distribute corpus to or for a current income beneficiary, if the distribution must be charged against the share of corpus from which the beneficiary may receive income (section 674(b)(5)(B));

(ii) A power to distribute income to or for a current income beneficiary or to accumulate it either (a) if accumulated income must either be payable to the beneficiary from whom it was withheld or as described in paragraph (b)(6) of § 1.674(b)–1 (section 674(b)(6)); (b) if the power is to apply income to the support of a dependent of the grantor, and the income is not so applied (section 674(b)(1)); or (c) if the beneficiary is under 21 or under a legal disability and accumulated income is added to corpus (section 674(b)(7)).

(3) Powers of distribution affecting more than one beneficiary. A power to distribute corpus or income to or among one or more beneficiaries or to accumulate income, either (i) if the power is held by a trustee or trustees other than the grantor, at least half of whom are independent (section 674(c)), or (ii) if the power is limited by a reasonably definite standard in the trust instrument, and in the case of a power over income, if in addition the power is held by a trustee or trustees other than the grantor and the grantor's spouse living with the grantor (section 674(b)(5)(A) and (d)). (These powers include both powers to "sprinkle" income or corpus among current beneficiaries, and powers to shift income or corpus between current beneficiaries and remaindermen; however, certain of the powers described under subparagraph (2) of this paragraph can have the latter effect incidentally.)

(c) See section 671 and §§ 1.671–2 and 1.671–3 for rules for the treatment of income, deductions, and credits when a person is treated as the owner of all or only a portion of a trust.

§ 1.674(b)–1 Excepted powers exercisable by any person.

(a) Paragraph (b)(1) through (8) of this section sets forth a number of powers which may be exercisable by any person without causing the grantor to be treated as an owner of a trust under section 674(a). Further, with the exception of powers described in paragraph (b)(1) of this section, it is immaterial whether these powers are held in the capacity of trustee. It makes no difference under section 674(b) that the person holding the power is the grantor, or a related or subordinate party (with the qualifications noted in paragraph (b)(1) and (3) of this section).

(b) The exceptions referred to in paragraph (a) of this section are as follows (see, however, the limitations set forth in § 1.674(d)–2):

(1) Powers to apply income to support of a dependent. Section 674(b)(1) provides, in effect, that regardless of the general rule of section 674(a), the income of a trust will not be considered as taxable to the grantor merely because in the discretion of any person (other than a grantor who is not acting as a trustee or cotrustee) it may be used for the support of a beneficiary whom the grantor is legally obligated to support, except to the extent that it is in fact used for that purpose. See section 677(b) and the regulations thereunder.

(2) Powers affecting beneficial enjoyment only after a period.* Section 674(b)(2) provides an exception to section 674(a) if the exercise of a power can only affect the beneficial enjoyment of the income of a trust received after a period of time which is such that a grantor would not be treated as an owner under section 673 if the power were a reversionary interest. See §§ 1.673(a)–1 and 1.673 (b)–1. For example, if a trust created on January 1, 1955, provides for the payment of income to the grantor's son, and the grantor reserves the power to substitute other beneficiaries of income or corpus in lieu of his son on or after January 1, 1965, the grantor is not treated under section 674 as the owner of the trust with respect to ordinary income received before January 1, 1965. But the grantor will be treated as an owner on and after that date unless the power is relinquished. If the beginning of the period during which the grantor may substitute beneficiaries is postponed, the rules set forth in § 1.673(d)–1 are applicable in order to determine whether the grantor should be treated as an owner during the period following the postponement.

(3) Testamentary powers. Under paragraph (3) of section 674(b) a power in any person to control beneficial enjoyment exercisable only by will does not cause a grantor to be treated as an owner under section 674(a). However, this exception does not apply to income accumulated for testamentary disposition by the grantor or to income which may be accumulated for such distribution in the discretion of the grantor or a nonadverse party, or both, without the approval or consent of any adverse party. For example, if a trust instrument provides that the income is to be accumulated during the grantor's life and that the grantor may appoint the accumulated income by will, the grantor is treated as the owner of the trust. Moreover, if a trust instrument provides that the income is payable to another person for his life, but the grantor has a testamentary power of appointment over the remainder, and under the trust instrument and local law capital gains are added to corpus, the grantor is treated as the owner of a portion of the trust and capital gains and losses are included in that portion. (See § 1.671–3.)

(4) Powers to determine beneficial enjoyment of charitable beneficiaries. Under paragraph (4) of section 674(b) a power in any person to determine the beneficial enjoyment of corpus or income which is irrevocably payable (currently or in the future) for purposes specified in section 170(c) (relating to definition of charitable contributions) will not cause the grantor to be treated as an owner under section 674(a). For example, if a grantor creates a trust, the income of which is irrevocably payable solely to educational or other organizations that qualify under section 170(c), he is not treated as an owner under section 674 although he retains the power to allocate the income among such organizations.

(5) Powers to distribute corpus. Paragraph (5) of section 674(b) provides an exception to section 674(a) for powers to distribute corpus, subject to certain limitations, as follows:

(i) If the power is limited by a reasonably definite standard which is set forth in the trust instrument, it may extend to corpus distributions to any beneficiary or beneficiaries or class of beneficiaries (whether income beneficiaries or remaindermen) without causing the grantor to be treated as an owner under section 674. See section 674(b)(5)(A). It is not required that the standard consist of the needs and circumstances of the beneficiary. A clearly measurable standard under which the holder of a power is legally accountable is deemed a reasonably definite standard for this purpose. For instance, a power to distribute corpus for the education, support, maintenance, or health of the beneficiary; for his reasonable support and comfort; or to enable him to maintain his

*Editorial comment: The Regulations do not reflect changes made by the Tax Reform Act of 1986. See Sec. 674(b)(2).

accustomed standard of living; or to meet an emergency, would be limited by a reasonably definite standard. However, a power to distribute corpus for the pleasure, desire, or happiness of a beneficiary is not limited by a reasonably definite standard. The entire context of a provision of a trust instrument granting a power must be considered in determining whether the power is limited by a reasonably definite standard. For example, if a trust instrument provides that the determination of the trustee shall be conclusive with respect to the exercise or nonexercise of a power, the power is not limited by a reasonably definite standard. However, the fact that the governing instrument is phrased in discretionary terms is not in itself an indication that no reasonably definite standard exists.

(ii) If the power is not limited by a reasonably definite standard set forth in the trust instrument, the exception applies only if distributions of corpus may be made solely in favor of current income beneficiaries, and any corpus distribution to the current income beneficiary must be chargeable against the proportionate part of corpus held in trust for payment of income to that beneficiary as if it constituted a separate trust (whether or not physically segregated). See section 674(b)(5)(B).

(iii) This subparagraph may be illustrated by the following examples:

Example (1). A trust instrument provides for payment of the income to the grantor's two brothers for life, and for payment of the corpus to the grantor's nephews in equal shares. The grantor reserves the power to distribute corpus to pay medical expenses that may be incurred by his brothers or nephews. The grantor is not treated as an owner by reason of this power because section 674(b)(5)(A) excepts a power, exercisable by any person, to invade corpus for any beneficiary, including a remainderman, if the power is limited by a reasonably definite standard which is set forth in the trust instrument. However, if the power were also exercisable in favor of a person (for example, a sister) who was not otherwise a beneficiary of the trust, section 674(b)(5)(A) would not be applicable.

Example (2). The facts are the same as in example (1) except that the grantor reserves the power to distribute any part of the corpus to his brothers or to his nephews for their happiness. The grantor is treated as the owner of the trust. Paragraph (5)(A) of section 674(b) is inapplicable because the power is not limited by a reasonably definite standard. Paragraph (5)(B) is inapplicable because the power to distribute corpus permits a distribution of corpus to persons other than current income beneficiaries.

Example (3). A trust instrument provides for payment of the income to the grantor's two adult sons in equal shares for 10 years, after which the corpus is to be distributed to his grandchildren in equal shares. The grantor reserves the power to pay over to each son up to one-half of the corpus during the 10-year period, but any such payment shall proportionately reduce subsequent income and corpus payments made to the son receiving the corpus. Thus, if one-half of the corpus is paid to one son, all the income from the remaining half is thereafter payable to the other son. The grantor is not treated as an owner under section 674(a) by reason of this power because it qualifies under the exception of section 674(b)(5)(B).

(6) Powers to withhold income temporarily. (i) Section 674(b)(6) excepts a power which, in general, enables the holder merely to effect a postponement in the time when the ordinary income is enjoyed by a current income beneficiary. Specifically, there is excepted a power to distribute or apply ordinary income to or for a current income beneficiary or to accumulate the income, if the accumulated income must ultimately be payable either:

(a) To the beneficiary from whom it was withheld, his estate, or his appointees (or persons designated by name, as a class, or otherwise as alternate takers in default of appointment) under a power of appointment held by the beneficiary which does not exclude from the class of possible appointees any person other than the beneficiary, his estate, his creditors, or the creditors of his estate (section 674(b)(6)(A));

(b) To the beneficiary from whom it was withheld, or if he does not survive a date of distribution which could reasonably be expected to occur within his lifetime, to his appointees (or alternate takers in default of appointment) under any power of appointment, general or special, or if he has no power of appointment to one or more designated alternate takers (other than the grantor of the grantor's estate) whose shares have been irrevocably specified in the trust instrument (section 674(b)(6)(A) and the flush material following); or

(c) On termination of the trust, or in conjunction with a distribution of corpus which is augmented by the accumulated income, to the current income beneficiaries in shares which have been irrevocably specified in the trust instrument, or if any beneficiary does not survive a date of distribution which would reasonably be expected to occur within his lifetime, to his appointees (or alternate takers in default of appointment) under any power of appointment, general or special, or if he has no power of appointment to one or more designated alternate takers (other than the grantor or the grantor's estate) whose shares have been irrevocably specified in the trust instrument (section 674(b)(6)(B) and the flush material following).

(In the application of (a) of this subdivision, if the accumulated income of a trust is ultimately payable to the estate of the current income beneficiary or is ultimately payable to his appointees or takers in default of appointment, under a power of the type described in (a) of this subdivision, it need not be payable to the beneficiary from whom it was withheld under any circumstances. Furthermore, if a trust otherwise qualifies for the exception in (a) of this subdivision the trust income will not be considered to be taxable to the grantor under section 677 by reason of the existence of the power of appointment referred to in (a) of this subdivision.) In general, the exception in section 674(b)(6) is not applicable if the power is in substance one to shift ordinary income from one beneficiary to another. Thus, a power will not qualify for this exception if ordinary income may be distributed to beneficiary A, or may be added to corpus which is ultimately payable to beneficiary B, a remainderman who is not a current income beneficiary. However, section 674(b)(6)(B), and (c) of this subdivision, permit a limited power to shift ordinary income among current income beneficiaries, as illustrated in example (1) of this subparagraph.

(ii) The application of section 674(b)(6) may be illustrated by the following examples:

Example (1). A trust instrument provides that the income shall be paid in equal shares to the grantor's two adult daughters but the grantor reserves the power to withhold from either beneficiary any part of that beneficiary's share of income and to add it to the corpus of the trust until the younger daughter reaches the age of 30 years. When the younger daughter reaches the age of 30, the trust is to terminate and the corpus is to be divided equally between the two daughters or their estates. Although exercise of this power may permit the shifting of accumulated income from one beneficiary to the other (since the corpus with the accumulations is to be divided equally) the power is excepted under section 674(b)(6)(B) and subdivision (i)(c) of this subparagraph.

Example (2). The facts are the same as in example (1), except that the grantor of the trust reserves the power to distribute accumulated income to the beneficiaries in such shares as he chooses. The combined powers are not excepted by section 674(b)(6)(B) since income accumulated pursuant to the first power is neither required to be payable only in conjunction with a corpus distribution nor required to be payable in shares specified in the trust instrument. See, however, section 674(c) and § 1.674(c)–1 for the effect of such a power if it is exercisable only by independent trustees.

Example (3). A trust provides for payment of income to the grantor's adult son with the grantor retaining the power to accumulate the income until the grantor's death, when all accumulations are to be paid to the son. If the son predeceases the grantor, all accumulations are, at the death of the grantor, to be paid to his daughter, or if she is not living, to alternate takers (which do not include the grantor's estate) in specified shares. The power is excepted under section 674(b)(6)(A) since the date of distribution (the date of the grantor's death) may, in the usual case, reasonably be expected to occur during the beneficiary's (the son's) lifetime. It is not necessary that the accumulations be payable to the son's estate or his appointees if he should predecease the grantor for this exception to apply.

(7) Power to withhold income during disability. Section 674(b)(7) provides an exception for a power which, in general, will permit ordinary income to be withheld during the legal disability of an income beneficiary or while he is under 21. Specifically, there is excepted a power, exercisable only during the existence of a legal disability of any current income beneficiary or the period during which any income beneficiary is under the age of 21 years, to distribute or apply ordinary income to or for that beneficiary or to accumulate the income and add it to corpus. To qualify under this exception it is not necessary that the income ultimately be payable to the income beneficiary from whom it was withheld, his estate, or his appointees; that is, the accumulated income may be added to corpus and ultimately distributed to others. For example, the grantor is not treated as an owner under section 674 if the income of a trust is payable to his son for life, remainder to his grandchildren, although he reserves the power to accumulate income and add it to corpus while his son is under 21.

(8) Powers to allocate between corpus and income. Paragraph (8) of section 674(b) provides that a power to allocate receipts and disbursements between corpus and income, even though expressed in broad language, will not cause the grantor to be treated as an owner under the general rule of section 674(a).

§ 1.674(c)–1 Excepted powers exercisable only by independent trustees.

Section 674(c) provides an exception to the general rule of section 674(a) for certain powers that are exercisable by independent trustees. This exception is in addition to those provided for under section 674(b) which may be held by any person including an independent trustee. The powers to which section 674(c) apply are powers (a) to distribute, apportion, or accumulate income to or for a beneficiary or beneficiaries, or to, for, or within a class of beneficiaries, or (b) to pay out corpus to or for a beneficiary or beneficiaries or to or for a class of beneficiaries (whether or not income beneficiaries). In order for such a power to fall within the exception of section 674(c) it must be exercisable solely (without the approval or consent of any other person) by a trustee or trustees none of whom is the grantor and no more than half of whom are related or subordinate parties who are subservient to the wishes of the grantor. (See section 672(c) for definitions of these terms.) An example of the application of section 674(c) is a trust whose income is payable to the grantor's three adult sons with power in an independent trustee to allocate without restriction the amounts of income to be paid to each son each year. Such a power does not cause the grantor to be treated as the owner of the trust. See however, the limitations set forth in § 1.674(d)–2.

§ 1.674(d)–1 Excepted powers exercisable by any trustee other than grantor or spouse.

Section 674(d) provides an additional exception to the general rule of section 674(a) for a power to distribute, apportion, or accumulate income to or for a beneficiary or beneficiaries or to, for, or within a class of beneficiaries, whether or not the conditions of section 674(b)(6) or (7) are satisfied, if the power is solely exercisable (without the approval or consent of any other person) by a trustee or trustees none of whom is the grantor or spouse living with the grantor, and if the power is limited by a reasonably definite external standard set forth in the trust instrument (see paragraph (b)(5) of § 1.674(b)–1 with respect to what constitutes a reasonably definite standard). See, however, the limitations set forth in § 1.674(d)–2.

§ 1.674(d)–2 Limitations on exceptions in section 674(b), (c), and (d).

(a) Power to remove trustee. A power in the grantor to remove, substitute, or add trustees (other than a power exercisable only upon limited conditions which do not exist during the taxable year, such as the death or resignation of, or breach of fiduciary duty by, an existing trustee) may prevent a trust from qualifying under section 674(c) or (d). For example, if a grantor has an unrestricted power to remove an independent trustee and substitute any person including himself as trustee, the trust will not qualify under section 674(c) or (d). On the other hand if the grantor's power to remove, substitute, or add trustees is limited so that its exercise could not alter the trust in a manner that would disqualify it under section 674(c) or (d), as the case may be, the power itself does not disqualify the trust. Thus, for example, a power in the grantor to remove or discharge an independent trustee on the condition that he substitute another independent trustee will not prevent a trust from qualifying under section 674 (c).

(b) Power to add beneficiaries. The exceptions described in section 674(b)(5), (6), and (7), (c), and (d), are not applicable if any person has a power to add to the beneficiary or beneficiaries or to a class of beneficiaries designated to receive the income or corpus, except where the action is to provide for after-born or after-adopted children. This limitation does not apply to a power held by a beneficiary to substitute other beneficiaries to succeed to his interest in the trust (so that he would be an adverse party as to the exercise or nonexercise of that power). For example, the limitation does not apply to a power in a beneficiary of a nonspendthrift trust to assign his interest. Nor does the limitation apply to a power held by any person which would qualify as an exception under section 674(b)(3) (relating to testamentary powers).

§ 1.675–1 Administrative powers.

(a) General rule. Section 675 provides in effect that the grantor is treated as the owner of any portion of a trust if under the terms of the trust instrument or circumstances attendant on its operation administrative control is exercisable primarily for the benefit of the grantor rather than the beneficiaries of the trust. If a grantor retains a power to amend the administrative provisions of a trust instrument which is broad enough to permit an amendment causing the grantor to be treated as the owner of a portion of the trust under section 675, he will be treated as the owner of the portion from its inception. See section 671 and §§ 1.671–2 and 1.671–3 for rules for treatment of items of income, deduction, and credit when a person is treated as the owner of all or only a portion of a trust.

(b) Prohibited controls. The circumstances which cause administrative controls to be considered exercisable primarily for the benefit of the grantor are specifically described in paragraphs (1) through (4) of section 675 as follows:

(1) The existence of a power, exercisable by the grantor or a nonadverse party, or both, without the approval or consent of any adverse party, which enables the grantor or any other person to purchase, exchange, or otherwise deal with or dispose of the corpus or the income of the trust for less than adequate consideration in money or money's worth. Whether the existence of the power itself will constitute the holder an adverse party will depend on the particular circumstances.

(2) The existence of a power exercisable by the grantor or a nonadverse party, or both, which enables the grantor to borrow the corpus or income of the trust, directly or indirectly, without adequate interest or adequate security. However, this paragraph does not apply where a trustee (other than the grantor acting alone) is authorized under a general lending power to make loans to any person without regard to interest or security. A general lending power in the grantor, acting alone as trustee, under which he has power to determine interest rates and the adequacy of security is not in itself an indication that the grantor has power to borrow the corpus or income without adequate interest or security.

(3) The circumstance that the grantor has directly or indirectly borrowed the corpus or income of the trust and has not completely repaid the loan, including any interest, before the beginning of the taxable year. The preceding sentence does not apply to a loan which provides for adequate interest and adequate security, if it is made by a trustee other than the grantor or a related or subordinate trustee subservient to the grantor. See section 672(c) for definition of "a related or subordinate party."

(4) The existence of certain powers of administration exercisable in a nonfiduciary capacity by any nonadverse party without the approval or consent of any person in a fiduciary capacity. The term "powers of administration" means one or more of the following powers:

(i) A power to vote or direct the voting of stock or other securities of a corporation in which the holdings of the grantor and the trust are significant from the viewpoint of voting control;

(ii) A power to control the investment of the trust funds either by directing investments or reinvestments, or by vetoing proposed investments or reinvestments, to the extent that the trust funds consist of stocks or securities of corporations in which the holdings of the grantor and the trust are significant from the viewpoint of voting control; or

(iii) A power to reacquire the trust corpus by substituting other property of an equivalent value.

If a power is exercisable by a person as trustee, it is presumed that the power is exercisable in a fiduciary capacity primarily in the interests of the beneficiaries. This presumption may be rebutted only by clear and convincing proof that the power is not exercisable primarily in the interests of the beneficiaries. If a power is not exercisable by a person as trustee, the determination of whether the power is exercisable in a fiduciary or a nonfiduciary capacity depends on all the terms of the trust and the circumstances surrounding its creation and administration.

(c) Authority of trustee. The mere fact that a power exercisable by a trustee is described in broad language does not indicate that the trustee is authorized to purchase, exchange, or otherwise deal with or dispose of the trust property or income for less than an adequate and full consideration in money or money's worth, or is authorized to lend the trust property or income to the grantor without adequate interest. On the other hand, such authority may be indicated by the actual administration of the trust.

§ 1.676(a)–1 Power to revest title to portion of trust property in grantor; general rule.

If a power to revest in the grantor title to any portion of a trust is exercisable by the grantor or a nonadverse party, or both, without the approval or consent of an adverse party, the grantor is treated as the owner of that portion, except as provided in section 676(b) (relating to powers affecting beneficial enjoyment of income only after the expiration of certain periods of time). If the title to a portion of the trust will revest in the grantor upon the exercise of a power by the grantor or a nonadverse party, or both, the grantor is treated as the owner of that portion regardless of whether the power is a power to revoke, to terminate, to alter or amend, or to appoint. See section 671 and §§ 1.671–2 and 1.671–3 for rules for treatment of items of income, deduction, and credit when a person is treated as the owner of all or only a portion of a trust.

§ 1.676(b)–1 Powers exercisable only after a period of time.*

Section 676(b) provides an exception to the general rule of section 676(a) when the exercise of a power can only affect the beneficial enjoyment of the income of a trust received after the expiration of a period of time which is such that a grantor would not be treated as the owner of that portion, except as power were a reversionary interest. See §§ 1.673(a)–1 and 1.673(b)–1. Thus, for example, a grantor is excepted from the general rule of

*Editorial comment: The Regulations do not reflect changes made by the Tax Reform Act of 1986. See Sec. 676(b).

section 676(a) with respect to ordinary income if exercise of a power to revest corpus in him cannot affect the beneficial enjoyment of the income received within 10 years after the date of transfer of that portion of the trust. It is immaterial for this purpose that the power is vested at the time of the transfer. However, the grantor is subject to the general rule of section 676(a) after the expiration of the period unless the power is relinquished. Thus, in the above example, the grantor may be treated as the owner and be taxed on all income in the eleventh and succeeding years if exercise of the power can affect beneficial enjoyment of income received in those years. If the beginning of the period during which the grantor may revest is postponed, the rules set forth in § 1.673(d)–1 are applicable to determine whether the grantor should be treated as an owner during the period following the postponement.

§ 1.677(a)–1 Income for benefit of grantor; general rule.

(a) (1) Scope. Section 677 deals with the treatment of the grantor of a trust as the owner of a portion of the trust because he has retained an interest in the income from that portion. For convenience, "grantor" and "spouse" are generally referred to in the masculine and feminine genders, respectively, but if the grantor is a woman the reference to "grantor" is to her and the reference to "spouse" is to her husband. Section 677 also deals with the treatment of the grantor of a trust as the owner of a portion of the trust because the income from property transferred in trust after October 9, 1969, is, or may be, distributed to his spouse or applied to the payment of premiums on policies of insurance on the life of his spouse. However, section 677 does not apply when the income of a trust is taxable to a grantor's spouse under section 71 (relating to alimony and separate maintenance payments) or section 682 (relating to income of an estate or trust in case of divorce, etc.). See section 671–1 (b).

(2) Cross references. See section 671 and §§ 1.671–2 and 1.671–3 for rules for treatment of items of income, deduction, and credit when a person is treated as the owner of all or a portion of a trust.

(b) Income for benefit of grantor or his spouse; general rule—(1) Property transferred in trust prior to October 10, 1969. With respect to property transferred in trust prior to October 10, 1969, the grantor is treated, under section 677, in any taxable year as the owner (whether or not he is treated as an owner under section 674) of a portion of a trust of which the income for the taxable year or for a period not within the exception described in paragraph (e) of this section is, or in the discretion of the grantor or a nonadverse party, or both (without the approval or consent of any adverse party) may be:

(i) Distributed to the grantor;

(ii) Held or accumulated for future distribution to the grantor; or

(iii) Applied to the payment of premiums on policies of insurance on the life of the grantor, except policies of insurance irrevocably payable for a charitable purpose specified in section 170(c).

(2) Property transferred in trust after October 9, 1969. With respect to property transferred in trust after October 9, 1969, the grantor is treated, under section 677, in any taxable year as the owner (whether or not he is treated as an owner under section 674) of a portion of a trust of which the income for the taxable year or for a period not within the exception described in paragraph (e) of this section is, or in the discretion of the grantor, or his spouse, or a nonadverse party, or any combination thereof (without the approval or consent of any adverse party other than the grantor's spouse) may be:

(i) Distributed to the grantor or the grantor's spouse;

(ii) Held or accumulated for future distribution to the grantor or the grantor's spouse; or

(iii) Applied to the payment of premiums on policies of insurance on the life of the grantor or the grantor's spouse, except policies of insurance irrevocably payable for a charitable purpose specified in section 170(c).

With respect to the treatment of a grantor as the owner of a portion of a trust solely because its income is, or may be, distributed or held or accumulated for future distribution to a beneficiary who is his spouse or applied to the payment of premiums for insurance on the spouse's life, section 677(a) applies to the income of a trust solely during the period of the marriage of the grantor to a beneficiary. In the case of divorce or separation, see sections 71 and 682 and the regulations thereunder.

(c) Constructive distribution; cessation of interest. Under section 677 the grantor is treated as the owner of a portion of a trust if he has retained any interest which might, without the approval or consent of an adverse party, enable him to have the income from that portion distributed to him at some time either actually or constructively (subject to the exception described in paragraph (e) of this section). In the case of a transfer in trust after October 9, 1969, the grantor is also treated as the owner of a portion of a trust if he has granted or retained any interest which might, without the approval or consent of an adverse party (other than the grantor's spouse), enable his spouse to have the income from the portion at some time, whether or not within the grantor's lifetime, distributed to the spouse either actually or constructively. See paragraph (b)(2) of this section for additional rules relating to the income of a trust prior to the grantor's marriage to a beneficiary. Constructive distribution to the grantor or to his spouse includes payment on behalf of the grantor or his spouse to another in obedience to his or her direction and payment of premiums upon policies of insurance on the grantor's, or his spouse's, life (other than policies of insurance irrevocably payable for charitable purposes specified in section 170(c)). If the grantor (in the case of property transferred prior to Oct. 10, 1969) or the grantor and his spouse (in the case of property transferred after Oct. 9, 1969) are divested permanently and completely of every interest described in this paragraph, the grantor is not treated as an owner under section 677 after that divesting. The word "interest" as used in this paragraph does not include the possibility that the grantor or his spouse might receive back from a beneficiary an interest in a trust by inheritance. Further, with respect to transfers in trust prior to October 10, 1969, the word "interest" does not include the possibility that the grantor might receive back from a beneficiary an interest in a trust as a surviving spouse under a statutory right of election or a similar right.

(d) Discharge of legal obligation of grantor or his spouse. Under section 677 a grantor is, in general, treated as the owner of a portion of a trust whose income is, or in the discretion of the grantor or a non-adverse party, or both, may be applied in discharge of a legal obligation of the grantor (or his spouse in the case of property transferred in trust by the grantor after October 9, 1969). However, see § 1.677(b)–1 for special rules for trusts whose income may not be applied for the discharge of any legal obligation of the grantor or the grantor's spouse other than the support or maintenance of a beneficiary (other than the grantor's spouse) whom the grantor or grantor's spouse is legally obligated to support. See § 301.7701–4(e) of this chapter for rules on the classification of and application of section 677 to an environmental remediation trust.

(e) Exception for certain discretionary rights affecting income.* The last sentence of section 677 (a) provides that a grantor shall not be treated as the owner when a discretionary right can only affect the beneficial enjoyment of the income of a trust received after a period of time during which a grantor would not be treated as an owner under section 673 if the power were a reversionary interest. See §§ 1.673(a)–1 and 1.673(b)–1. For example, if the ordinary income of a trust is payable to B for 10 years and then in the grantor's discretion income or corpus may be paid to B or to the grantor (or his spouse in the case of property transferred in trust by the grantor after October 9, 1969), the grantor is not treated as an owner with respect to the ordinary income under section 677 during the first 10 years. He will be treated as an owner under section 677 after the expiration of the 10-year period unless the power is relinquished. If the beginning of the period during which the grantor may substitute beneficiaries is postponed, the rules set forth in § 1.673(d)–1 are applicable in determining whether the grantor should be treated as an owner during the period following the postponement.

(f) Accumulation of income. If income is accumulated in any taxable year for future distribution to the grantor (or his spouse in the case of property transferred in trust by the grantor after Oct. 9, 1969), section 677(a)(2) treats the grantor as an owner for that taxable year. The exception set forth in the last sentence of section 677(a) does not apply merely because the grantor (or his spouse in the case of property transferred in trust by the grantor after Oct. 9, 1969) must await the expiration of a period of time before he or she can receive or exercise discretion over previously accumulated income of the trust, even though the period is such that the grantor would not be treated as an owner under section 673 if a reversionary interest were involved. Thus, if income (including capital gains) of a trust is to be accumulated for 10 years* and then will be, or at the discretion of the grantor, or his spouse in the case of property transferred in trust after October 9, 1969, or a nonadverse party, may be, distributed to the grantor (or his spouse in the case of property transferred in trust after Oct. 9, 1969), the grantor is treated as the owner of the trust from its inception. If income attributable to transfers after October 9, 1969 is accumulated in any taxable year

*Editorial comment: The Regulations do not reflect changes made by the Tax Reform Act of 1986. See Sec. 677(a).

during the grantor's lifetime for future distribution to his spouse, section 677(a)(2) treats the grantor as an owner for that taxable year even though his spouse may not receive or exercise discretion over such income prior to the grantor's death.

(g) Examples. The application of section 677(a) may be illustrated by the following examples:

Example (1). G creates an irrevocable trust which provides that the ordinary income is to be payable to him for life and that on his death the corpus shall be distributed to B, an unrelated person. Except for the right to receive income, G retains no right or power which would cause him to be treated as an owner under sections 671 through 677. Under the applicable local law capital gains must be applied to corpus. During the taxable year 1970 the trust has the following items of gross income and deductions:

Dividends	$5,000
Capital gain	1,000
Expenses allocable to income	200
Expenses allocable to corpus	100

Since G has a right to receive income he is treated as an owner of a portion of the trust under section 677. Accordingly, he should include the $5,000 of dividends, $200 income expense, and $100 corpus expense in the computation of his taxable income for 1970. He should not include the $1,000 capital gain since that is not attributable to the portion of the trust that he owns. See § 1.671–3(b). The tax consequences of the capital gain are governed by the provisions of subparts A, B, C, and D (section 641 and following), part I, subchapter J, chapter 1 of the Code. Had the trust sustained a capital loss in any amount the loss would likewise not be included in the computation of G's taxable income, but would also be governed by the provisions of such subparts.

Example (2). G creates a trust which provides that the ordinary income is payable to his adult son. Ten years and one day* from the date of transfer or on the death of his son, whichever is earlier, corpus is to revert to G. In addition, G retains a discretionary right to receive $5,000 of ordinary income each year. (Absent the exercise of this right all the ordinary income is to be distributed to his son.) G retained no other right or power which would cause him to be treated as an owner under subpart E (section 671 and following). Under the terms of the trust instrument and applicable local law capital gains must be applied to corpus. During the taxable year 1970 the trust had the following items of income and deductions:

Dividends	$10,000
Capital gain	2,000
Expenses allocable to income	400
Expenses allocable to corpus	200

Since the capital gain is held or accumulated for future distributions to G, he is treated under section 677(a)(2) as an owner of a portion of the trust to which the gain is attributable. See § 1.671–3(b).

Therefore, he must include the capital gain in the computation of his taxable income. (Had the trust sustained a capital loss in any amount, G would likewise include that loss in the computation of his taxable income.) In addition, because of G's discretionary right (whether exercised or not) he is treated as the owner of a portion of the trust which will permit a distribution of income to him of $5,000. Accordingly, G includes dividends of $5,208.33 and income expenses of $208.33 in computing his taxable income, determined in the following manner:

Total dividends	$10,000.00
Less: Expenses allocable to income	400.00
Distributable income of the trust	9,600.00
Portion of dividends attributable to G (5,000/9,600 × $10,000)	5,208.33
Portion of income expenses attributable to G (5,000/9,600 × $400)	208.33
Amount of income subject to discretionary right	5,000.00

In accordance with § 1.671–3(c), G also takes into account $104.17 (5,000/9,600 × $200) of corpus expenses in computing his tax liability. The portion of the dividends and expenses of the trust not attributable to G are governed by the provisions of Subparts A through D.

§ 1.677(b)–1 Trusts for support.

(a) Section 677(b) provides that a grantor is not treated as the owner of a trust merely because its income may in the discretion of any person other than the grantor (except when he is acting as trustee or cotrustee) be applied or distributed for the support or maintenance of a beneficiary (other than the grantor's spouse in the case of income from property transferred in trust after October 9, 1969), such as the child of the grantor, whom the grantor or his spouse is legally obligated to support. If income of the current year of the trust is actually so applied or distributed the grantor may be treated as the owner of any portion of the trust under section 677 to that extent, even though it might have been applied or distributed for other purposes. In the case of property transferred to a trust before October 10, 1969, for the benefit of the grantor's spouse, the grantor may be treated as the owner to the extent income of the current year is actually applied for the support or maintenance of his spouse.

(b) If any amount applied or distributed for the support of a beneficiary, including the grantor's spouse in the case of property transferred in trust before October 10, 1969, whom the grantor is legally obligated to support is paid out of corpus or out of income other than income of the current year, the grantor is treated as a beneficiary of the trust, and the amount applied or distributed is considered to be an amount paid within the meaning of section 661(a)(2), taxable to the grantor under section 662. Thus, he is subject to the other relevant portions of subparts A through D (section 641 and following), part I, subchapter J, chapter 1 of the Code. Accordingly, the grantor may be taxed on an accumulation distribution or a capital gain distribution under subpart D (section 665 and following) of such part I. Those provisions are applied on the basis that the grantor is the beneficiary.

(c) For the purpose of determining the items of income, deduction, and credit of a trust to be included under this section in computing the grantor's tax liability, the income of the trust for the taxable year of distribution will be deemed to have been first distributed. For example, in the case of a trust reporting on the calendar year basis, a distribution made on January 1, 1956, will be deemed to have been made out of ordinary income of the trust for the calendar year 1956 to the extent of the income for that year even though the trust had received no income as of January 1, 1956. Thus, if a distribution of $10,000 is made on January 1, 1956, for the support of the grantor's dependent, the grantor will be treated as the owner of the trust for 1956 to that extent. If the trust received dividends of $5,000 and incurred expenses of $1,000 during that year but subsequent to January 1, he will take into account dividends of $5,000 and expenses of $1,000 in computing his tax liability for 1956. In addition, the grantor will be treated as a beneficiary of the trust with respect to the $6,000 ($10,000 less distributable income of $4,000 (dividends of $5,000 less expenses of $1,000)) paid out of corpus or out of other than income of the current year. See paragraph (b) of this section.

(d) The exception provided in section 677(b) relates solely to the satisfaction of the grantor's legal obligation to support or maintain a beneficiary. Consequently, the general rule of section 677(a) is applicable when in the discretion of the grantor or nonadverse parties income of a trust may be applied in discharge of a grantor's obligations other than his obligation of support or maintenance falling within section 677(b). Thus, if the grantor creates a trust the income of which may in the discretion of a nonadverse party be applied in the payment of the grantor's debts, such as the payment of his rent or other household expenses, he is treated as an owner of the trust regardless of whether the income is actually so applied.

(e) The general rule of section 677(a), and not section 677(b), is applicable if discretion to apply or distribute income of a trust rests solely in the grantor, or in the grantor in conjunction with other persons, unless in either case the grantor has such discretion as trustee or cotrustee.

(f) The general rule of section 677(a), and not section 677(b), is applicable to the extent that income is required, without any discretionary determination, to be applied to the support of a beneficiary whom the grantor is legally obligated to support.

§ 1.678(a)–1 Person other than grantor treated as substantial owner; general rule.

(a) Where a person other than the grantor of a trust has a power exercisable solely by himself to vest the corpus or the income of any portion of a testamentary or inter vivos trust in himself, he is treated under section 678(a) as the owner of that portion, except as provided in section 678(b) (involving taxation of the grantor) and section 678 (c) (involving an obligation of support). The holder of such a power also is treated as an owner of the trust even though he has partially released or otherwise modified the power so that he can no longer vest the corpus or income in himself, if he has retained such control of the trust as would, if retained by a grantor, subject the grantor to treatment as the owner under sections 671 to 677, inclusive. See section 671 and §§ 1.671–2 and 1.671–3 for rules for treatment of items of income, deduction, and credit where a person is treated as the owner of all or only a portion of a trust.

(b) Section 678(a) treats a person as an owner of a trust if he has a power exercisable solely by himself to apply the income or corpus for the satisfaction of his legal obligations, other than an obligation to support a dependent (see § 1.678(c)–1 subject to the limitation of section 678(b)). Section 678 does not apply if the power is not exercisable solely by himself. However, see § 1.662(a)–4 for principles applicable to income of a trust which, pursuant to the terms of the trust instrument, is used to satisfy the obligations of a person other than the grantor.

§ 1.678(b)–1 If grantor is treated as the owner.

Section 678(a) does not apply with respect to a power over income, as originally granted or thereafter modified, if the grantor of the trust is treated as the owner under sections 671 to 677, inclusive.

§ 1.678(c)–1 Trusts for support.

(a) Section 678(a) does not apply to a power which enables the holder, in the capacity of trustee or cotrustee, to apply the income of the trust to the support or maintenance of a person whom the holder is obligated to support, except to the extent the income is so applied. See paragraphs (a), (b), and (c) of § 1.677(b)–1 for applicable principles where any amount is applied for the support or maintenance of a person whom the holder is obligated to support.

(b) The general rule in section 678(a) (and not the exception in section 678(c)) is applicable in any case in which the holder of a power exercisable solely by himself is able, in any capacity other than that of trustee or cotrustee, to apply the income in discharge of his obligation of support or maintenance.

(c) Section 678(c) is concerned with the taxability of income subject to a power described in section 678(a). It has no application to the taxability of income which is either required to be applied pursuant to the terms of the trust instrument or is applied pursuant to a power which is not described in section 678(a), the taxability of such income being governed by other provisions of the Code. See § 1.662(a)–4.

§ 1.678(d)–1 Renunciation of power.

Section 678(a) does not apply to a power which has been renounced or disclaimed within a reasonable time after the holder of the power first became aware of its existence.

* * *

Income In Respect Of Decedents

§ 1.691(a)–1 Income in respect of a decedent.

(a) Scope of section 691. In general, the regulations under section 691 cover: (1) The provisions requiring that amounts which are not includible in gross income for the decedent's last taxable year or for a prior taxable year be included in the gross income of the estate or persons receiving such income to the extent that such amounts constitute "income in respect of a decedent"; (2) the taxable effect of a transfer of the right to such income; (3) the treatment of certain deductions and credit in respect of a decedent which are not allowable to the decedent for the taxable period ending with his death or for a prior taxable year; (4) the allowance to a recipient of income in respect of a decedent of a deduction for estate taxes attributable to the inclusion of the value of the right to such income in the decedent's estate; (5) special provisions with respect to installment obligations acquired from a decedent and with respect to the allowance of a deduction for estate taxes to a surviving annuitant under a joint and survivor annuity contract; and (6) special provisions relating to installment obligations transmitted at death when prior law applied to the transmission.

(b) General definition. In general, the term "income in respect of a decedent" refers to those amounts to which a decedent was entitled as gross income but which were not properly includible in computing his taxable income for the taxable year ending with the date of his death or for a previous taxable year under the method of accounting employed by the decedent. See the regulations under section 451. Thus, the term includes—

(1) All accrued income of a decedent who reported his income by use of the cash receipts and disbursements method;

(2) Income accrued solely by reason of the decedent's death in case of a decedent who reports his income by use of an accrual method of accounting; and

(3) Income to which the decedent had a contingent claim at the of his death.

See sections 736 and 753 and the regulations thereunder for "income in respect of a decedent" in the case of a deceased partner.

(c) Prior decedent. The term "income in respect of a decedent" also includes the amount of all items of gross income in respect of a prior decedent, if (1) the right to receive such amount was acquired by the decedent by reason of the death of the prior decedent or by bequest, devise, or inheritance from the prior decedent and if (2) the amount of gross income in respect of the prior decedent was not properly includible in computing the decedent's taxable income for the taxable year ending with the date of his death or for a previous taxable year. See example (2) of paragraph (b) of § 1.691(a)–2.

(d) Items excluded from gross income. Section 691 applies only to the amount of items of gross income in respect of a decedent, and items which are excluded from gross income under subtitle A of the Code are not within the provisions of section 691.

(e) Cross reference. For items deemed to be income in respect of a decedent for purposes of the deduction for estate taxes provided by section 691(c), see paragraph (c) of § 1.691(c)–1.

§ 1.691(a)–2 Inclusion in gross income by recipients.

(a) Under section 691(a)(1), income in respect of a decedent shall be included in the gross income, for the taxable year when received, of—

(1) The estate of the decedent, if the right to receive the amount is acquired by the decedent's estate from the decedent;

(2) The person who, by reason of the death of the decedent, acquires the right to receive the amount, if the right to receive the amount is not acquired by the decedent's estate from the decedent; or

(3) The person who acquires from the decedent the right to receive the amount by bequest, devise, or inheritance, if the amount is received after a distribution by the decedent's estate of such right.

These amounts are included in the income of the estate or of such persons when received by them whether or not they report income by use of the cash receipts and disbursements method.

(b) The application of paragraph (a) of this section may be illustrated by the following examples, in each of which it is assumed that the decedent kept his books by use of the cash receipts and disbursements method.

Example (1). The decedent was entitled at the date of his death to a large salary payment to be made in equal annual installments over five years. His estate, after collecting two installments, distributed the right to the remaining installment payments to the residuary legatee of the estate. The estate must include in its gross income the two installments received by it, and the legatee must include in his gross income each of the three installments received by him.

Example (2). A widow acquired, by bequest from her husband, the right to receive renewal commissions on life insurance sold by him in his lifetime, which commissions were payable over a period of years. The widow died before having received all of such commissions, and her son inherited the right to receive the rest of the commissions. The commissions received by the widow were includible in her gross income. The commissions received by the son were not includible in the widow's gross income but must be included in the gross income of the son.

Example (3). The decedent owned a Series E United States savings bond, with his wife as co-owner or beneficiary, but died before the payment of such bond. The entire amount of interest accruing on the bond and not includible in income by the decedent, not just the amount accruing after the death of the decedent, would be treated as income to his wife when the bond is paid.

Example (4). A, prior to his death, acquired 10,000 shares of the capital stock of the X Corporation at a cost of $100 per share. During his lifetime, A had entered into an agreement with X Corporation whereby X Corporation agreed to purchase and the decedent agreed that his executor would sell the 10,000 shares of X Corporation stock owned by him at the book value of the stock at the date of A's death. Upon A's death, the shares are sold by A's executor for $500 a share pursuant to the agreement. Since the sale of stock is consummated after A's death, there is no income in respect of a decedent with respect to the appreciation in value of A's stock to the date of his death. If, in this example, A had in fact sold the stock during his lifetime but payment had not been received before his death, any gain on the sale would constitute income in respect of a decedent when the proceeds were received.

Example (5). (1) A owned and operated an apple orchard. During his lifetime, A sold and delivered 1,000 bushels of apples to X, a canning factory, but did not receive payment before his death. A also entered into negotiations to sell 3,000 bushels of apples to Y, a canning factory, but did not complete the sale before his death. After A's death, the executor received payment from X. He also completed the sale to Y and transferred to Y 1,200 bushels of apples on hand at A's death and harvested and transferred an additional 1,800 bushels. The gain from the sale of apples by A to X constitutes income in respect of a decedent when received. On the other hand, the gain from the sale of apples by the executor to Y does not.

(2) Assume that, instead of the transaction entered into with Y, A had disposed of the 1,200 bushels of harvested apples by delivering them to Z, a cooperative association, for processing and sale. Each year the association commingles the fruit received from all of its members into a pool and assigns to each member a percentage interest in the pool based on the fruit delivered by him. After the fruit is processed and the products are sold, the association distributes the net proceeds from the pool to its members in proportion to their interests in the pool. After A's death, the association made distributions to the executor with respect to A's share of the proceeds from the pool in which A had an interest. Under such circumstances, the proceeds from the disposition of the 1,200 bushels of apples constitute income in respect of a decedent.

§ 1.691(a)–3 Character of gross income.

(a) The right to receive an amount of income in respect of a decedent shall be treated in the hands of the estate, or by the person entitled to receive such amount by bequest, devise, or inheritance from the decedent or by reason of his death, as if it had been acquired in the transaction by which the decedent (or a prior decedent) acquired such right, and shall be considered as having the same character it would have had if the decedent (or a prior decedent) had lived and received such amount. The provisions of section 1014(a), relating to the basis of property acquired from a decedent, do not apply to these amounts in the hands of the estate and such persons. See section 1014(c).

(b) The application of paragraph (a) of this section may be illustrated by the following:

(1) If the income would have been capital gain to the decedent, if he had lived and had received it, from the sale of property held for more than 1 year (6 months for taxable years beginning before 1977; 9 months for taxable years beginning in 1977), the income, when received, shall be treated in the hands of the estate or of such person as capital gain from the sale of the property, held for more than 1 year (6 months for taxable years beginning before 1977; 9 months for taxable years beginning in 1977), in the same manner as if such person had held the property for the period the decedent held it, and had made the sale.

* * *

§ 1.691(a)–4 Transfer of right to income in respect of a decedent.

(a) Section 691(a)(2) provides the rules governing the treatment of income in respect of a decedent (or a prior decedent) in the event a right to receive such income is transferred by the estate or person entitled thereto by bequest, devise, or inheritance, or by reason of the death of the decedent. In general, the transferor must include in his gross income for the taxable period in which the transfer occurs the amount of the consideration, if any, received for the right or the fair market value of the right at the time of the transfer, whichever is greater. Thus, upon a sale of such right by the estate or person entitled to receive it, the fair market value of the right or the amount received upon the sale, whichever is greater, is included in the gross income of the vendor. Similarly, if such right is disposed of by gift, the fair market value of the right at the time of the gift must be included in the gross income of the donor. In the case of a satisfaction of an installment obligation at other than face value, which is likewise considered a transfer under section 691(a)(2), see § 1.691(a)–5.

(b) If the estate of a decedent or any person transmits the right to income in respect of a decedent to another who would be required by section 691(a)(1) to include such income when received in his gross income, only the transferee will include such income when received in his gross income. In this situation, a transfer within the meaning of section 691(a)(2) has not occurred. This paragraph may be illustrated by the following:

(1) If a person entitled to income in respect of a decedent dies before receiving such income, only his estate or other person entitled to such income by bequest, devise, or inheritance from the latter decedent, or by reason of the death of the latter decedent, must include such amount in gross income when received.

(2) If a right to income in respect of a decedent is transferred by an estate to a specific or residuary legatee, only the specific or residuary legatee must include such income in gross income when received.

(3) If a trust to which is bequeathed a right of a decedent to certain payments of income terminates and transfers the right to a beneficiary, only the beneficiary must include such income in gross income when received.

If the transferee described in subparagraphs (1), (2), and (3) of this paragraph transfers his right to receive the amounts in the manner described in paragraph (a) of this section, the principles contained in paragraph (a) are applied to such transfer. On the other hand, if the transferee transmits his right in the manner described in this paragraph, the principles of this paragraph are again applied to such transfer.

§ 1.691(a)–5 Installment obligations acquired from decedent.

(a) Section 691(a)(4) has reference to an installment obligation which remains uncollected by a decedent (or a prior decedent) and which was originally acquired in a transaction the income from which was properly reportable by the decedent on the installment method under section 453. Under the provisions of section 691(a)(4), an amount equal to the excess of the face value of the obligation over its basis in the hands of the decedent (determined under section 453(d)(2) and the regulations thereunder) shall be considered an amount of income in respect of a decedent and shall be treated as such. The decedent's estate (or the person entitled to receive such income by bequest or inheritance from the decedent or by reason of the decedent's death) shall include in its gross income when received the same proportion of any payment in satisfaction of such obligations as would be returnable as income by the decedent if he had lived and received such payment. No gain on account of the transmission of such obligations by the decedent's death is required to be reported as income in the return of the decedent for the year of his death.* * *

(b) If an installment obligation described in paragraph (a) of this section is transferred within the meaning of section 691(a)(2) and paragraph (a) of § 1.691(a)–4, the entire installment obligation transferred shall be considered a right to income in respect of a decedent but the amount includible in the gross income of the transferor shall be reduced by an amount equal to the basis of the obligation in the hands of the decedent (determined under section 453(d)(2) and the regulations thereunder) adjusted, however, to take into account the receipt of any installment payments after the decedent's death and before such transfer. Thus, the amount includible in the gross income of the transferor shall be the fair market value of such obligation at the time of the transfer or the consideration received for the transfer of the installment obligation, whichever is greater, reduced by the basis of the obligation as described in the preceding sentence. For purposes of this paragraph, the term "transfer" in section 691(a)(2) and paragraph (a) of § 1.691(a)–4 includes the satisfaction of an installment obligation at other than face value.

(c) The application of this section may be illustrated by the following example:

Example. An heir of a decedent is entitled to collect an installment obligation with a face value of $100, a fair market value of $80, and a basis in the hands of the decedent of $60. If the heir collects the obligation at face value, the excess of the amount collected over the basis is considered income in respect of a decedent and includible in the gross income of the heir under section 691(a)(1). In this case, the amount includible would be $40 ($100 less $60). If the heir collects the obligation at $90, an amount other than face value, the entire obligation is considered a right to receive income in respect of a decedent but the amount ordinarily required to be included in the heir's gross income under section 691(a)(2) (namely, the consideration received in satisfaction of the installment obligation or its fair market value, whichever is greater) shall be reduced by the amount of the basis of the obligation in the hands of the decedent. In this case, the amount includible would be $30 ($90 less $60).

§ 1.691(b)–1 Allowance of deductions and credit in respect to decedents.

(a) Under section 691(b) the expenses, interest, and taxes described in sections 162, 163, 164, and 212 for which the decedent (or a prior decedent) was liable, which were not properly allowable as a deduction in his last taxable year or any prior taxable year, are allowed when paid—

(1) As a deduction by the estate; or

(2) If the estate was not liable to pay such obligation, as a deduction by the person who by bequest, devise, or inheritance from the decedent or by reason of the death of the decedent acquires, subject to such obligation, an interest in property of the decedent (or the prior decedent).

Similar treatment is given to the foreign tax credit provided by section 33.* For the purposes of subparagraph (2) of this paragraph, the right to receive an amount of gross income in respect of a decedent is considered property of the decedent; on the other hand, it is not necessary for a person, otherwise within the provisions of subparagraph (2) of this paragraph, to receive the right to any income in respect of a decedent. Thus, an heir who receives a right to income in respect of a decedent (by reason of the death of the decedent) subject to any income tax imposed by a foreign country during the decedent's life, which tax must be satisfied out of such income, is entitled to the credit provided by section 33* when he pays the tax. If a decedent who reported income by use of the cash receipts and disbursements method owned real property on which accrued taxes had become a lien, and if such property passed directly to the heir of the decedent in a jurisdiction in which real property does not become a part of a decedent's estate, the heir, upon paying such taxes, may take the same deduction under section 164 that would be allowed to the decedent if, while alive, he had made such payment.

(b) The deduction for percentage depletion is allowable only to the person (described in section 691(a)(1)) who receives the income in respect of the decedent to which the deduction relates, whether or not such person receives the property from which such income is derived. Thus, an heir who (by reason of the decedent's death) receives income derived from sales of units of mineral by the decedent (who reported income by use of the cash receipts and disbursements method) shall be allowed the deduction for percentage depletion, computed on the gross income from such number of units as if the heir had the same economic interest in the property as the decedent. Such heir need not also receive any interest in the mineral property other than such income. If the decedent did not compute his deduction for depletion on the basis of percentage depletion, any deduction for depletion to which the decedent was entitled at the date of his death would be allowable in

*Editorial comment: See Sec. 27 rather than Sec. 33.

computing his taxable income for his last taxable year, and there can be no deduction in respect of the decedent by any other person for such depletion.

§ 1.691(c)–1 Deduction for estate tax attributable to income in respect of a decedent.

(a) In general. A person who is required to include in gross income for any taxable year an amount of income in respect of a decedent may deduct for the same taxable year that portion of the estate tax imposed upon the decedent's estate which is attributable to the inclusion in the decedent's estate of the right to receive such amount. The deduction is determined as follows:

(1) Ascertain the net value in the decedent's estate of the items which are included under section 691 in computing gross income. This is the excess of the value included in the gross estate on account of the items of gross income in respect of the decedent (see § 1.691(a)–1 and paragraph (c) of this section) over the deductions from the gross estate for claims which represent the deductions and credit in respect of the decedent (see § 1.691(b)–1). But see section 691(d) and paragraph (b) of § 1.691(d)–1 for computation of the special value of a survivor's annuity to be used in computing the net value for estate tax purposes in cases involving joint and survivor annuities.

(2) Ascertain the portion of the estate tax attributable to the inclusion in the gross estate of such net value. This is the excess of the estate tax over the estate tax computed without including such net value in the gross estate. In computing the estate tax without including such net value in the gross estate, any estate tax deduction (such as the marital deduction) which may be based upon the gross estate shall be recomputed so as to take into account the exclusion of such net value from the gross estate. See example (2), paragraph (e) of § 1.691(d)–1.

For purposes of this section, the term "estate tax" means the tax imposed under section 2001 or 2101 * * *, reduced by the credits against such tax. Each person including in gross income an amount of income in respect of a decedent may deduct as his share of the portion of the estate tax (computed under subparagraph (2) of this paragraph) an amount which bears the same ratio to such portion as the value in the gross estate of the right to the income included by such person in gross income (or the amount included in gross income if lower) bears to the value in the gross estate of all the items of gross income in respect of the decedent.

(b) Prior decedent. If a person is required to include in gross income an amount of income in respect of a prior decedent, such person may deduct for the same taxable year that portion of the estate tax imposed upon the prior decedent's estate which is attributable to the inclusion in the prior decedent's estate of the value of the right to receive such amount. This deduction is computed in the same manner as provided in paragraph (a) of this section and is in addition to the deduction for estate tax imposed upon the decedent's estate which is attributable to the inclusion in the decedent's estate of the right to receive such amount.

* * *

PARTNERS AND PARTNERSHIPS

Determination Of Tax Liability

§ 1.701–1 Partners, not partnership, subject to tax.

Partners are liable for income tax only in their separate capacities. Partnerships as such are not subject to the income tax imposed by subtitle A but are required to make returns of income under the provisions of section 6031 and the regulations thereunder. For definition of the terms "partner" and "partnership", see sections 761 and 7701(a)(2), and the regulations thereunder. * * *

§ 1.701–2 Anti-abuse rule.

(a) Intent of subchapter K. Subchapter K is intended to permit taxpayers to conduct joint business (including investment) activities through a flexible economic arrangement without incurring an entity-level tax. Implicit in the intent of subchapter K are the following requirements—

(1) The partnership must be bona fide and each partnership transaction or series of related transactions (individually or collectively, the transaction) must be entered into for a substantial business purpose.

(2) The form of each partnership transaction must be respected under substance over form principles.

(3) Except as otherwise provided in this paragraph (a)(3), the tax consequences under subchapter K to each partner of partnership operations and of transactions between the partner and the partnership must accurately reflect the partners' economic agreement and clearly reflect the partner's income (collectively, *proper reflection of income*). However, certain provisions of subchapter K and the regulations thereunder were adopted to promote administrative convenience and other policy objectives, with the recognition that the application of those provisions to a transaction could, in some circumstances, produce tax results that do not properly reflect income. Thus, the proper reflection of income requirement of this paragraph (a)(3) is treated as satisfied with respect to a transaction that satisfies paragraphs (a)(1) and (2) of this section to the extent that the application of such a provision to the transaction and the ultimate tax results, taking into account all the relevant facts and circumstances, are clearly contemplated by that provision. See, for example, paragraph (d) *Example 6* of this section (relating to the value-equals-basis rule in § 1.704–1(b)(2)(iii)(c)), paragraph (d) *Example 9* of this section (relating to the election under section 754 to adjust basis in partnership property), and paragraph (d) *Examples 10 and 11* of this section (relating to the basis in property distributed by a partnership under section 732). See also, for example, §§ 1.704–3(e)(1) and 1.752–2(e)(4) (providing certain de minimis exceptions).

(b) Application of subchapter K rules. The provisions of subchapter K and the regulations thereunder must be applied in a manner that is consistent with the intent of subchapter K as set forth in paragraph (a) of this section (*intent of subchapter K*). Accordingly, if a partnership is formed or availed of in connection with a transaction a principal purpose of which is to reduce substantially the present value of the partners' aggregate federal tax liability in a manner that is inconsistent with the intent of subchapter K, the Commissioner can recast the transaction for federal tax purposes, as appropriate to achieve tax results that are consistent with the intent of subchapter K, in light of the applicable statutory and regulatory provisions and the pertinent facts and circumstances. Thus, even though the transaction may fall within the literal words of a particular statutory or regulatory provision, the Commissioner can determine, based on the particular facts and circumstances, that to achieve tax results that are consistent with the intent of subchapter K—

(1) The purported partnership should be disregarded in whole or in part, and the partnership's assets and activities should be considered, in whole or in part, to be owned and conducted, respectively, by one or more of its purported partners;

(2) One or more of the purported partners of the partnership should not be treated as a partner;

(3) The methods of accounting used by the partnership or a partner should be adjusted to reflect clearly the partnership's or the partner's income;

(4) The partnership's items of income, gain, loss, deduction, or credit should be reallocated; or

(5) The claimed tax treatment should otherwise be adjusted or modified.

(c) Facts and circumstances analysis: factors. Whether a partnership was formed or availed of with a principal purpose to reduce substantially the present value of the partners' aggregate federal tax liability in a manner inconsistent with the intent of subchapter K is determined based on all of the facts and circumstances, including a comparison of the purported business purpose for a transaction and the claimed tax benefits resulting from the transaction. The factors set forth below may be indicative, but do not necessarily establish, that a partnership was used in such a manner. These factors are illustrative only, and therefore may not be the only factors taken into account in making the determination under this section. Moreover, the weight given to any factor (whether specified in this paragraph or otherwise) depends on all the facts and circumstances. The presence or absence of any factor described in this paragraph does not create a presumption that a partnership was (or was not) used in such a manner. Factors include:

(1) The present value of the partners' aggregate federal tax liability is substantially less than had the partners owned the partnership's assets and conducted the partnership's activities directly;

(2) The present value of the partners' aggregate federal tax liability is substantially less than would be the case if purportedly separate transactions that are designed to achieve a particular end result are integrated and treated as steps in a single transaction. For example, this analysis may indicate that it was contemplated that a partner who was necessary to achieve the intended tax results and whose interest in the partnership was liquidated or disposed of (in whole or in part) would be a partner only temporarily in order to provide the claimed tax benefits to the remaining partners;

(3) One or more partners who are necessary to achieve the claimed tax results either have a nominal interest in the partnership, are substantially protected from any risk of loss from the partnership's activities (through distribution preferences, indemnity or loss guaranty agreements, or other arrangements), or have little or no participation in the profits from the partnership's activities other than a preferred return that is in the nature of a payment for the use of capital;

(4) Substantially all of the partners (measured by number or interests in the partnership) are related (directly or indirectly) to one another;

(5) Partnership items are allocated in compliance with the literal language of §§ 1.704–1 and 1.704–2 but with results that are inconsistent with the purpose of section 704(b) and those regulations. In this regard, particular scrutiny will be paid to partnerships in which income or gain is specially allocated to one or more partners that may be legally or effectively exempt from federal taxation (for example, a foreign person, an exempt organization, an insolvent taxpayer, or a taxpayer with unused federal tax attributes such as net operating losses, capital losses, or foreign tax credits);

(6) The benefits and burdens of ownership of property nominally contributed to the partnership are in substantial part retained (directly or indirectly) by the contributing partner (or a related party); or

(7) The benefits and burdens of ownership of partnership property are in substantial part shifted (directly or indirectly) to the distributee partner before or after the property is actually distributed to the distributee partner (or a related party).

(d) Examples. The following examples illustrate the principles of paragraphs (a), (b), and (c) of this section. The examples set forth below do not delineate the boundaries of either permissible or impermissible types of transactions. Further, the addition of any facts or circumstances that are not specifically set forth in an example (or the deletion of any facts or circumstances) may alter the outcome of the transaction described in the example. Unless otherwise indicated, parties to the transactions are not related to one another.

Example 1. Choice of entity; avoidance of entity-level tax; use of partnership consistent with the intent of subchapter K. **(i)** A and B form limited partnership PRS to conduct a bona fide business. A, the corporate general partner, has a 1% partnership interest. B, the individual limited partner, has a 99% interest. PRS is properly classified as a partnership under §§ 301.7701–2 and 301.7701–3. A and B chose limited partnership form as a means to provide B with limited liability without subjecting the income from the business operations to an entity-level tax.

(ii) Subchapter K is intended to permit taxpayers to conduct joint business activity through a flexible economic arrangement without incurring an entity-level tax. See paragraph (a) of this section. Although B has retained, indirectly, substantially all of the benefits and burdens of ownership of the money or property B contributed to PRS (see paragraph (c)(6) of this section), the decision to organize and conduct business through PRS under these circumstances is consistent with this intent. In addition, on these facts, the requirements of paragraphs (a)(1), (2), and (3) of this section have been satisfied. The Commissioner therefore cannot invoke paragraph (b) of this section to recast the transaction.

Example 2. Choice of entity; avoidance of subchapter S shareholder requirements; use of partnership consistent with

the intent of subchapter K. (i) A and B form partnership PRS to conduct a bona fide business. A is a corporation that has elected to be treated as an S corporation under subchapter S. B is a nonresident alien. PRS is properly classified as a partnership under §§ 301.7701–2 and 301.7701–3. Because section 1361(b) prohibits B from being a shareholder in A, A and B chose partnership form, rather than admit B as a shareholder in A, as a means to retain the benefits of subchapter S treatment for A and its shareholders.

(ii) Subchapter K is intended to permit taxpayers to conduct joint business activity through a flexible economic arrangement without incurring an entity-level tax. See paragraph (a) of this section. The decision to organize and conduct business through PRS is consistent with this intent. In addition, on these facts, the requirements of paragraphs (a)(1), (2), and (3) of this section have been satisfied. Although it may be argued that the form of the partnership transaction should not be respected because it does not reflect its substance (inasmuch as application of the substance over form doctrine arguably could result in B being treated as a shareholder of A, thereby invalidating A's subchapter S election), the facts indicate otherwise. The shareholders of A are subject to tax on their pro rata shares of A's income (see section 1361 et seq.), and B is subject to tax on B's distributive share of partnership income (see sections 871 and 875). Thus, the form in which this arrangement is cast accurately reflects its substance as a separate partnership and S corporation. The Commissioner therefore cannot invoke paragraph (b) of this section to recast the transaction.

Example 3. Choice of entity; avoidance of more restrictive foreign tax credit limitation, use of partnership consistent with the intent of subchapter K. (i) X, a domestic corporation, and Y, a foreign corporation, form partnership PRS under the laws of foreign Country A to conduct a bona fide joint business. X and Y each owns a 50% interest in PRS. PRS is properly classified as a partnership under §§ 301.7701–2 and 301.7701–3. PRS pays income taxes to Country A. X and Y chose partnership form to enable X to qualify for a direct foreign tax credit under section 901, with look-through treatment under § 1.904–5(h)(1). Conversely, if PRS were a foreign corporation for U.S. tax purposes, X would be entitled only to indirect foreign tax credits under section 902 with respect to dividend distributions from PRS. The look-through rules, however, would not apply, and pursuant to section 904(d)(1)(E) and § 1.904–4(g), the dividends and associated taxes would be subject to a separate foreign tax credit limitation for dividends from PRS, a noncontrolled section 902 corporation.

(ii) Subchapter K is intended to permit taxpayers to conduct joint business activity through a flexible economic arrangement without incurring an entity-level tax. See paragraph (a) of this section. The decision to organize and conduct business through PRS in order to take advantage of the look-through rules for foreign tax credit purposes, thereby maximizing X's use of its proper share of foreign taxes paid by PRS, is consistent with this intent. In addition, on these facts, the requirements of paragraphs (a)(1), (2), and (3) of this section have been satisfied. The Commissioner therefore cannot invoke paragraph (b) of this section to recast the transaction.

Example 4. Choice of entity; avoidance of gain recognition under sections 351(e) and 357(c); use of partnership consistent with the intent of subchapter K. (i) X, ABC, and DEF form limited partnership PRS to conduct a bona fide real estate management business. PRS is properly classified as a partnership under §§ 301.7701–2 and 301.7701–3. X, the general partner, is a newly formed corporation that elects to be treated as a real estate investment trust as defined in section 856. X offers its stock to the public and contributes substantially all of the proceeds from the public offering to PRS. ABC and DEF, the limited partners, are existing partnerships with substantial real estate holdings. ABC and DEF contribute all of their real property assets to PRS, subject to liabilities that exceed their respective aggregate bases in the real property contributed, and terminate under section 708(b)(1)(A). In addition, some of the former partners of ABC and DEF each have the right, beginning two years after the formation of PRS, to require the redemption of their limited partnership interests in PRS in exchange for cash or X stock (at X's option) equal to the fair market value of their respective interests in PRS at the time of the redemption. These partners are not compelled, as a legal or practical matter, to exercise their exchange rights at any time. X, ABC, and DEF chose to form a partnership rather than have ABC and DEF invest directly in X to allow ABC and DEF to avoid recognition of gain under sections 351(e) and 357(c). Because PRS would not be treated as an investment company within the meaning of section 351(e) if PRS were incorporated (so long as it did not elect under section 856), section 721(a) applies to the contribution of the real property to PRS. See section 721(b).

(ii) Subchapter K is intended to permit taxpayers to conduct joint business activity through a flexible economic arrangement without incurring an entity-level tax. See paragraph (a) of this section. The decision to organize and conduct business through PRS, thereby avoiding the tax consequences that would have resulted from contributing the existing partnerships' real estate assets to X (by applying the rules of sections 721, 731, and 752 in lieu of the rules of sections 351(e) and 357(c)), is consistent with this intent. In addition, on these facts, the requirements of paragraphs (a)(1), (2), and (3) of this section have been satisfied. Although it may be argued that the form of the transaction should not be respected because it does not reflect its substance (inasmuch as the present value of the partners' aggregate federal tax liability is substantially less than would be the case if the transaction were integrated and treated as a contribution of the encumbered assets by ABC and DEF directly to X, see paragraph (c)(2) of this section), the facts indicate otherwise. For example, the right of some of the former ABC and DEF partners after two years to exchange their PRS interests for cash or X stock (at X's option) equal to the fair market value of their PRS interest at that time would not require that right to be considered as exercised prior to its actual exercise. Moreover, X may make other real estate investments and other business decisions, including the decision to raise additional capital for those purposes. Thus, although it may be likely that some or all of the partners with the right to do so will, at some point, exercise their exchange rights, and thereby receive either cash or X stock, the form of the transaction as a separate partnership and real estate investment trust is respected under substance over form principles (see paragraph (a)(2) of this section). The Commissioner therefore cannot invoke paragraph (b) of this section to recast the transaction.

Example 5. Special allocations; dividends received deductions; use of partnership consistent with the intent of subchapter K. (i) Corporations X and Y contribute equal amounts to PRS, a bona fide partnership formed to make joint investments. PRS pays $100 for a share of common stock of Z, an unrelated corporation, which has historically paid an annual dividend of $6. PRS specially allocates the dividend income on the Z stock to X to the extent of the London Inter–Bank Offered Rate (LIBOR) on the record date, applied to X's contribution of $50, and allocates the remainder of the dividend income to Y. All other items of partnership income and loss are allocated equally between X and Y. The allocations under the partnership agreement have substantial economic effect within the meaning of § 1.704–1 (b)(2). In addition to avoiding an entity-level tax, a principal purpose for the formation of the partnership was to invest in the Z common stock and to allocate the dividend income from the stock to provide X with a floating-rate return based on LIBOR, while permitting X and Y to claim the dividends received deduction under section 243 on the dividends allocated to each of them.

(ii) Subchapter K is intended to permit taxpayers to conduct joint business activity through a flexible economic arrangement without incurring an entity-level tax. See paragraph (a) of this section. The decision to organize and conduct business through PRS is consistent with this intent. In addition, on these facts, the requirements of paragraphs (a)(1), (2), and (3) of this section have been satisfied. Section 704(b) and § 1.704–1 (b)(2) permit income realized by the partnership to be allocated validly to the partners separate from the partners' respective ownership of the capital to which the allocations relate, provided that the allocations satisfy both the literal requirements of the statute and regulations and the purpose of those provisions (see paragraph (c)(5) of this section). Section 704(e)(2) is not applicable to the facts of this example (otherwise, the allocations would be required to be proportionate to the partners' ownership of contributed capital). The Commissioner therefore cannot invoke paragraph (b) of this section to recast the transaction.

Example 6. Special allocations; nonrecourse financing; low-income housing credit; use of partnership consistent with the intent of subchapter K. (i) A and B, high-bracket taxpayers, and X, a corporation with net operating loss carryforwards, form general partnership PRS to own and operate a building that qualifies for the low-income housing credit provided by section 42. The project is financed with both cash contributions from the partners and nonrecourse indebtedness. The partnership agreement provides for special allocations of income and deductions, including the allocation of all depreciation deductions attributable to the building to A and B equally in a manner that is reasonably consistent with allocations that have substantial economic effect of some other significant partnership item attributable to the building. The section 42 credits are allocated to A and B in accordance with the allocation of depreciation deductions. PRS's allocations comply with all applicable regulations, including the requirements of §§ 1.704–1(b)(2)(ii) (pertaining to economic effect) and 1.704–2 (e) (requirements for allocations of nonrecourse deductions). The nonrecourse indebtedness is validly allocated to the partners under the rules of § 1.752–3, thereby increasing the basis of the partners' respective partnership interests. The basis increase created by the nonrecourse indebtedness enables A and B to deduct their distributive share of losses from the partnership (subject to all other applicable limitations under the Internal Revenue Code) against their nonpartnership income and to apply the credits against their tax liability.

(ii) At a time when the depreciation deductions attributable to the building are not treated as nonrecourse deductions under § 1.704–2(c) (because there is no net increase in partnership minimum gain during the year), the special allocation of depreciation deductions to A and B has substantial economic effect because of the value-equals-basis safe harbor contained in § 1.704–1(b)(2)(iii)(c) and the fact that A and B would bear the economic burden of any decline in the value of the building (to the extent of the partnership's investment in the building), notwithstanding that A and B believe it is unlikely that the building will decline in value (and, accordingly, they anticipate significant timing benefits through the special allocation). Moreover, in later years, when the depreciation deductions attributable to the building are treated as nonrecourse deductions under § 1.704.2(c), the special allocation of depreciation deductions to A and B is considered to be consistent with the partners' interests in the partnership under § 1.704–2(e).

(iii) Subchapter K is intended to permit taxpayers to conduct joint business activity through a flexible economic arrangement without incurring an entity-level tax. See paragraph (a) of this section. The decision to organize and conduct business through PRS is consistent with this intent. In addition, on these facts, the requirements of paragraphs (a)(1), (2), and (3) of this section have been satisfied. Section 704(b), § 1.704–1(b)(2), and § 1.704–2(e) allow partnership items of income, gain, loss, deduction, and credit to be allocated validly to the partners separate from the partners' respective ownership of the capital to which the allocations relate, provided that the allocations satisfy both the literal requirements of the statute and regulations and the purpose of those provisions (see paragraph (c)(5) of this section). Moreover, the application of the value-equals-basis safe harbor and the provisions of § 1.704–2(e) with respect to the allocations to A and B, and the tax results of the application of those provisions, taking into account all the facts and circumstances, are clearly contemplated. Accordingly, even if the allocations would not otherwise be considered to satisfy the proper reflection of income standard in paragraph (a)(3) of this section, that requirement will be treated as satisfied under these facts. Thus, even though the partners' aggregate federal tax liability may be substantially less than had the partners owned the partnership's assets directly (due to X's inability to use its allocable share of the partnership's losses and credits) (see paragraph (c)(1) of this section), the transaction is not inconsistent with the intent of subchapter K. The Commissioner therefore cannot invoke paragraph (b) of this section to recast the transaction.

Example 7. Partner with nominal interest; temporary partner; use of partnership not consistent with the intent of subchapter K. (i) Pursuant to a plan a principal purpose of which is to generate artificial losses and thereby shelter from federal taxation a substantial amount of income, X (a foreign corporation), Y (a domestic corporation), and Z (a promoter) form partnership PRS by contributing $9,000, $990, and $10, respectively, for proportionate interests (90.0%, 9.9%, and 0.1%, respectively) in the capital and profits of PRS. PRS purchases offshore equipment for $10,000 and validly leases the equipment offshore for a term representing most of its projected useful life. Shortly thereafter, PRS sells its rights to receive income under the lease to a third party for $9,000, and allocates the resulting $9,000 of income $8,100 to X, $891 to Y, and $9 to Z. PRS thereafter makes a distribution of $9,000 to X in complete liquidation of its interest. Under § 1.704–1(b)(2)(iv)(f), PRS restates the partners' capital accounts immediately before making the liquidating distribution to X to reflect its assets consisting of the offshore equipment worth $1,000 and $9,000 in cash. Thus, because the capital accounts immediately before the distribution reflect assets of $19,000 (that is, the initial capital contributions of $10,000 plus the $9,000 of income realized from the sale of the lease), PRS allocates a $9,000 book loss among the partners (for capital account purposes only), resulting in restated capital accounts for X, Y, and Z of $9,000, $990, and $10, respectively. Thereafter, PRS purchases real property by borrowing the $8,000 purchase price on a recourse basis, which increases Y's and Z's bases in their respective partnership interests from $1,881 and $19, to $9,801 and $99, respectively (reflecting Y's and Z's adjusted interests in the partnership of 99% and 1%, respectively). PRS subsequently sells the offshore equipment, subject to the lease, for $1,000 and allocates the $9,000 tax loss $8,910 to Y and $90 to Z. Y's and Z's bases in their partnership interests are therefore reduced to $891 and $9, respectively.

(ii) On these facts, any purported business purpose for the transaction is insignificant in comparison to the tax benefits that would result if the transaction were respected for federal tax purposes (see paragraph (c) of this section). Accordingly, the transaction lacks a substantial business purpose (see paragraph (a)(1) of this section). In addition, factors (1), (2), (3), and (5) of paragraph (c) of this section indicate that PRS was used with a principal purpose to reduce substantially the partners' tax liability in a manner inconsistent with the intent of subchapter K. On these facts, PRS is not bona fide (see paragraph (a)(1) of this section), and the transaction is not respected under applicable substance over form principles (see paragraph (a)(2) of this section) and does not properly reflect the income of Y (see paragraph (a)(3) of this section). Thus, PRS has been formed and availed of with a principal purpose of reducing substantially the present value of the partners' aggregate federal tax liability in a manner inconsistent with the intent of subchapter K. Therefore (in addition to possibly challenging the transaction under judicial principles or the validity of the allocations under § 1.704–1(b)(2) (see paragraph (h) of this section)), the Commissioner can recast the transaction as appropriate under paragraph (b) of this section.

Example 8. Plan to duplicate losses through absence of section 754 election; use of partnership not consistent with the intent of subchapter K. (i) A owns land with a basis of $100 and a fair market value of $60. A would like to sell the land to B. A and B devise a plan a principal purpose of which is to permit the duplication, for a substantial period of time, of the tax benefit of A's built-in loss in the land. To effect this plan, A, C (A's brother), and W (C's wife) form partner-ship PRS, to which A contributes the land, and C and W each contribute $30. All partnership items are shared in proportion to the partners' respective contributions to PRS. PRS invests the cash in an investment asset (that is not a marketable security within the meaning of section 731(c)). PRS also leases the land to B under a three-year lease pursuant to which B has the option to purchase the land from PRS upon the expiration of the lease for an amount equal to its fair market value at that time. All lease proceeds received are immediately distributed to the partners. In year 3, at a time when the values of the partnership's assets have not materially changed, PRS agrees with A to liquidate A's interest in exchange for the investment asset held by PRS. Under section 732(b), A's basis in the asset distributed equals $100, A's basis in A's partnership interest immediately before the distribution. Shortly thereafter, A sells the investment asset to X, an unrelated party, recognizing a $40 loss.

(ii) PRS does not make an election under section 754. Accordingly, PRS's basis in the land contributed by A remains $100. At the end of year 3, pursuant to the lease option, PRS sells the land to B for $60 (its fair market value). Thus, PRS recognizes a $40 loss on the sale, which is allocated equally between C and W. C's and W's bases in their partnership interests are reduced to $10 each pursuant to section 705. Their respective interests are worth $30 each. Thus, upon liquidation of PRS (or their interests therein), each of C and W will recognize $20 of gain. However, PRS's continued existence defers recognition of that gain indefinitely. Thus, if this arrangement is respected, C and W duplicate for their benefit A's built-in loss in the land prior to its contribution to PRS.

(iii) On these facts, any purported business purpose for the transaction is insignificant in comparison to the tax benefits that would result if the transaction were respected for federal tax purposes (see paragraph (c) of this section). Accordingly, the transaction lacks a substantial business purpose (see paragraph (a)(1) of this section). In addition, factors (1), (2), and (4) of paragraph (c) of this section indicate that PRS was used with a principal purpose to reduce substantially the partners' tax liability in a manner inconsistent with the intent of subchapter K. On these facts, PRS is not bona fide (see paragraph (a)(1) of this section), and the transaction is not respected under applicable substance over form principles (see paragraph (a)(2) of this section). Further, the tax consequences to the partners do not properly reflect the partners' income; and Congress did not contemplate application of section 754 to partnerships such as PRS, which was formed for a principal purpose of producing a double tax benefit from a single economic loss (see paragraph (a)(3) of this section). Thus, PRS has been formed and availed of with a principal purpose of reducing substantially the present value of the partners' aggregate federal tax liability in a manner inconsistent with the intent of subchapter K. Therefore (in addition to possibly challenging the transaction under judicial principles or other statutory authorities, such as the substance over form doctrine or the disguised sale rules under section 707 (see paragraph (h) of this section)), the Commissioner can recast the transaction as appropriate under paragraph (b) of this section.

Example 9. Absence of section 754 election; use of partnership consistent with the intent of subchapter K. (i) PRS is a bona fide partnership formed to engage in investment activities with contributions of cash from each partner. Several years after joining PRS, A, a partner with a capital account balance and basis in its partnership interest of $100, wishes to withdraw from PRS. The partnership agreement entitles A to receive the balance of A's capital account in cash or securities owned by PRS at the time of withdrawal, as mutually agreed to by A and the managing general partner, P. P and A agree to distribute to A $100 worth of nonmarketable securities (see section 731(c)) in which PRS has an aggregate basis of $20. Upon distribution, A's aggregate basis in the securities is $100 under section 732(b). PRS does not make an election to adjust the basis in its remaining assets under section 754. Thus, PRS's basis in its remaining assets is unaffected by the distribution. In contrast, if a section 754 election had been in effect for the year of the distribution, under these facts section 734(b) would have required PRS to adjust the basis in its remaining assets downward by the amount of the untaxed appreciation in the distributed property, thus reflecting that gain in PRS's retained assets. In selecting the assets to be distributed, A and P had a principal purpose to take advantage of the facts that (i) A's basis in the securities will be determined by reference to A's basis in its partnership interest under section 732(b), and (ii) because PRS will not make an election under section 754, the remaining partners of PRS will likely enjoy a federal tax timing advantage (i.e., from the $80 of additional basis in its assets that would have been eliminated if the section 754 election had been made) that is inconsistent with proper reflection of income under paragraph (a)(3) of this section.

(ii) Subchapter K is intended to permit taxpayers to con-duct joint business activity through a flexible economic arrangement without incurring an entity-level tax. See paragraph (a) of this section. The decision to organize and conduct business through PRS is consistent with this intent. In addition, on these facts, the requirements of paragraphs (a)(1) and (2) of this section have been satisfied. The validity of the tax treatment of this transaction is therefore dependent upon whether the transaction satisfies (or is treated as satisfying) the proper reflection of income standard under paragraph (a)(3) of this section. A's basis in the distributed securities is properly determined under section 732(b). The benefit to the remaining partners is a result of PRS not having made an election under section 754. Subchapter K is generally intended to produce tax consequences that achieve proper reflection of income. However, paragraph (a)(3) of this section provides that if the application of a provision of subchapter K produces tax results that do not properly reflect income, but application of that provision to the transaction and the ultimate tax results, taking into account all the relevant facts and circumstances, are clearly contemplated by that provision (and the transaction satisfies the requirements of paragraphs (a)(1) and (2) of this section), then the application of that provision to the transaction will be treated as satisfying the proper reflection of income standard.

(iii) In general, the adjustments that would be made if an election under section 754 were in effect are necessary to minimize distortions between the partners' bases in their partnership interests and the partnership's basis in its assets following, for example, a distribution to a partner. The electivity of section 754 is intended to provide administrative convenience for bona fide partnerships that are engaged in transactions for a substantial business purpose, by providing those partnerships the option of not adjusting their bases in their remaining assets following a distribution to a partner. Congress clearly recognized that if the section 754 election were not made, basis distortions may result. Taking into account all the facts and circumstances of the transaction, the electivity of section 754 in the context of the distribution from PRS to A, and the ultimate tax consequences that follow from the failure to make the election with respect to the transaction, are clearly contemplated by section 754. Thus, the tax consequences of this transaction will be treated as satisfying the proper reflection of income standard under paragraph (a)(3) of this section. The Commissioner therefore cannot invoke paragraph (b) of this section to recast the transaction.

Example 10. Basis adjustments under section 732; use of partnership consistent with the intent of subchapter K. (i) A, B, and C are partners in partnership PRS, which has for several years been engaged in substantial bona fide business activities. For valid business reasons, the partners agree that A's interest in PRS, which has a value and basis of $100, will be liquidated with the following assets of PRS: a nondepreciable asset with a value of $60 and a basis to PRS of $40, and related equipment with two years of cost recovery remaining and a value and basis to PRS of $40. Neither asset is described in section 751 and the transaction is not described in section 732(d). Under section 732(b) and (c), A's $100 basis in A's partnership interest will be allocated between the nondepreciable asset and the equipment received in the liquidating distribution in proportion to PRS's bases in those assets, or $50 to the nondepreciable asset and $50 to the equipment. Thus, A will have a $10 built-in gain in the nondepreciable asset ($60 value less $50 basis) and a $10 built-in loss in the equipment ($50 basis less $40 value), which it expects to recover rapidly through cost recovery deductions. In selecting the assets to be distributed to A, the partners had a principal purpose to take advantage of the fact that A's basis in the assets will be determined by reference to A's basis in A's partnership interest, thus, in effect, shifting a portion of A's basis from the nondepreciable asset to the equipment, which in turn would allow A to recover that portion of its basis more rapidly. This shift provides a federal tax timing advantage to A, with no offsetting detriment to B or C.

(ii) Subchapter K is intended to permit taxpayers to conduct joint business activity through a flexible economic arrangement without incurring an entity-level tax. See paragraph (a) of this section. The decision to organize and conduct business through PRS is consistent with this intent. In addition, on these facts, the requirements of paragraphs (a)(1) and (2) of this section have been satisfied. The validity of the tax treatment of this transaction is therefore dependent upon whether the transaction satisfies (or is treated as satisfying) the proper reflection of income standard under paragraph (a)(3) of this section. Subchapter K is generally intended to produce tax consequences that achieve proper reflection of income. However, paragraph (a)(3) of this section provides that if the application of a provision of subchapter K produces tax results that do not properly reflect income, but the application of that provision to the transaction and the ultimate tax results, taking into account all the relevant facts and circumstances, are clearly contemplated by that provision (and the transaction satisfies the requirements of paragraphs (a)(1) and (2) of this section), then the application of that provision to the transaction will be treated as satisfying the proper reflection of income standard.

(iii) A's basis in the assets distributed to it was determined under section 732(b) and (c). The transaction does not properly reflect A's income due to the basis distortions caused by the distribution and the shifting of basis from a nondepreciable to a depreciable asset. However, the basis rules under section 732, which in some situations can produce tax results that are inconsistent with the proper reflection of income standard (see paragraph (a)(3) of this section), are intended to provide simplifying administrative rules for bona fide partnerships that are engaged in transactions with a substantial business purpose. Taking into account all the facts and circumstances of the transaction, the application of the basis rules under section 732 to the distribution from PRS to A, and the ultimate tax consequences of the application of that provision of subchapter K, are clearly contemplated. Thus, the application of section 732 to this transaction will be treated as satisfying the proper reflection of income standard under paragraph (a)(3) of this section. The Commissioner therefore cannot invoke paragraph (b) of this section to recast the transaction.

Example 11. Basis adjustments under section 732; plan or arrangement to distort basis allocations artificially; use of partnership not consistent with the intent of subchapter K. **(i)** Partnership PRS has for several years been engaged in the development and management of commercial real estate projects. X, an unrelated party, desires to acquire undeveloped land owned by PRS, which has a value of $95 and a basis of $5. X expects to hold the land indefinitely after its acquisition. Pursuant to a plan a principal purpose of which is to permit X to acquire and hold the land but nevertheless to recover for tax purposes a substantial portion of the purchase price for the land, X contributes $100 to PRS for an interest therein. Subsequently (at a time when the value of the partnership's assets have not materially changed), PRS distributes to X in liquidation of its interest in PRS the land and another asset with a value and basis to PRS of $5. The second asset is an insignificant part of the economic transaction but is important to achieve the desired tax results. Under section 732(b) and (c), X's $100 basis in its partnership interest is allocated between the assets distributed to it in proportion to their bases to PRS, or $50 each. Thereafter, X plans to sell the second asset for its value of $5, recognizing a loss of $45. In this manner, X will, in effect, recover a substantial portion of the purchase price of the land almost immediately. In selecting the assets to be distributed to X, the partners had a principal purpose to take advantage of the fact that X's basis in the assets will be determined under section 732(b) and (c), thus, in effect, shifting a portion of X's basis economically allocable to the land that X intends to retain to an inconsequential asset that X intends to dispose of quickly. This shift provides a federal tax timing advantage to X, with no offsetting detriment to any of PRS's other partners.

(ii) Although section 732 recognizes that basis distortions can occur in certain situations, which may produce tax results that do not satisfy the proper reflection of income standard of paragraph (a)(3) of this section, the provision is intended only to provide ancillary, simplifying tax results for bona fide partnership transactions that are engaged in for substantial business purposes. Section 732 is not intended to serve as the basis for plans or arrangements in which inconsequential or immaterial assets are included in the distribution with a principal purpose of obtaining substantially favorable tax results by virtue of the statute's simplifying rules. The transaction does not properly reflect X's income due to the basis distortions caused by the distribution that result in shifting a significant portion of X's basis to this inconsequential asset. Moreover, the proper reflection of income standard contained in paragraph (a)(3) of this section is not treated as satisfied, because, taking into account all the facts and circumstances, the application of section 732 to this arrangement, and the ultimate tax consequences that would thereby result, were not clearly contemplated by that provision of subchapter K. In addition, by using a partnership (if respected), the partners' aggregate federal tax liability would be substantially less than had they owned the partnership's assets directly (see paragraph (c)(1) of this section). On these facts, PRS has been formed and availed of with a principal purpose to reduce the taxpayers' aggregate federal tax liability in a manner that is inconsistent with the intent of subchapter K. Therefore (in addition to possibly challenging the transaction under applicable judicial principles and statutory authorities, such as the disguised sale rules under section 707, see paragraph (h) of this section), the Commissioner can recast the transaction as appropriate under paragraph (b) of this section.

(e) Abuse of entity treatment—(1) General rule. The Commissioner can treat a partnership as an aggregate of its partners in whole or in part as appropriate to carry out the purpose of any provision of the Internal Revenue Code or the regulations promulgated thereunder.

(2) Clearly contemplated entity treatment. Paragraph (e)(1) of this section does not apply to the extent that—

(i) A provision of the Internal Revenue Code or the regulations promulgated thereunder prescribes the treatment of a partnership as an entity, in whole or in part, and

(ii) That treatment and the ultimate tax results, taking into account all the relevant facts and circumstances, are clearly contemplated by that provision.

(f) Examples. The following examples illustrate the principles of paragraph (e) of this section. The examples set forth below do not delineate the boundaries of either permissible or impermissible types of transactions. Further, the addition of any facts or circumstances that are not specifically set forth in an example (or the deletion of any facts or circumstances) may alter the outcome of the transaction described in the example. Unless otherwise indicated, parties to the transactions are not related to one another.

Example 1. Aggregate treatment of partnership appropriate to carry out purpose of section 163(e)(5). (i) Corporations X and Y are partners in partnership PRS, which for several years has engaged in substantial bona fide business activities. As part of these business activities, PRS issues certain high yield discount obligations to an unrelated third party. Section 163(e)(5) defers (and in certain circumstances disallows) the interest deductions on this type of obligation if issued by a corporation. PRS, X, and Y take the position that, because PRS is a partnership and not a corporation, section 163(e)(5) is not applicable.

(ii) Section 163(e)(5) does not prescribe the treatment of a partnership as an entity for purposes of that section. The purpose of section 163(e)(5) is to limit corporate-level interest deductions on certain obligations. The treatment of PRS as an entity could result in a partnership with corporate partners issuing those obligations and thereby circumventing the purpose of section 163(e)(5), because the corporate partner would deduct its distributive share of the interest on obligations that would have been deferred until paid or disallowed had the corporation issued its share of the obligation directly. Thus, under paragraph (e)(1) of this section, PRS is properly treated as an aggregate of its partners for purposes of applying section 163(e)(5) (regardless of whether any party has a tax avoidance purpose in having PRS issue the obligation). Each partner of PRS will therefore be treated as issuing its share of the obligations for purposes of determining the deductibility of its distributive share of any interest on the obligations. See also section 163(i)(5)(B).

Example 2. Aggregate treatment of partnership appropriate to carry out purpose of section 1059. (i) Corporations X and Y are partners in partnership PRS, which for several years has engaged in substantial bona fide business activities. As part of these business activities, PRS purchases 50 shares of Corporation Z common stock. Six months later, Corporation Z announces an extraordinary dividend (within the meaning of section 1059). Section 1059(a) generally provides that if any corporation receives an extraordinary dividend with respect to any share of stock and the corporation has not held the stock for more than two years before the dividend announcement date, the basis in the stock held by the corporation is reduced by the nontaxed portion of the dividend. PRS, X, and Y take the position that section 1059(a) is not applicable because PRS is a partnership and not a corporation.

(ii) Section 1059(a) does not prescribe the treatment of a partnership as an entity for purposes of that section. The purpose of section 1059(a) is to limit the benefits of the dividends received deduction with respect to extraordinary dividends. The treatment of PRS as an entity could result in corporate partners in the partnership receiving dividends through partnerships in circumvention of the intent of section 1059. Thus, under paragraph (e)(1) of this section, PRS is properly treated as an aggregate of its partners for purposes of applying section 1059 (regardless of whether any party had a tax avoidance purpose in acquiring the Z stock through PRS). Each partner of PRS will therefore be treated as owning its share of the stock. Accordingly, PRS must make appropriate adjustments to the basis of the Corporation Z stock, and the partners must also make adjustments to the basis in their respective interests in PRS under section 705(a)(2)(B). See also section 1059(g)(1).

Example 3. Prescribed entity treatment of partnership; determination of CFC status clearly contemplated. (i) X, a domestic corporation, and Y, a foreign corporation, intend to conduct a joint venture in foreign Country A. They form PRS, a bona fide domestic general partnership in which X owns a 40% interest and Y owns a 60% interest. PRS is properly classified as a partnership under §§ 301.7701–2 and 301.7701–3. PRS holds 100% of the voting stock of Z, a Country A entity that is classified as an association taxable as a corporation for federal tax purposes under § 301.7701–2. Z conducts its business operations in Country A. By investing in Z through a domestic partnership, X seeks to obtain the benefit of the look-through rules of section 904(d)(3) and, as a result, maximize its ability to claim credits for its proper share of Country A taxes expected to be incurred by Z.

(ii) Pursuant to sections 957(c) and 7701(a)(30), PRS is a United States person. Therefore, because it owns 10% or more of the voting stock of Z, PRS satisfies the definition of a U.S. shareholder under section 951(b). Under section 957(a), Z is a controlled foreign corporation (CFC) because more than 50% of the voting power or value of its stock is owned by PRS. Consequently, under section 904 (d)(3), X qualifies for look-through treatment in computing its credit for foreign taxes paid or accrued by Z. In contrast, if X and Y owned their interests in Z directly, Z would not be a CFC because only 40% of its stock would be owned by U.S. shareholders. X's credit for foreign taxes paid or accrued by Z in that case would be subject to a separate foreign tax credit limitation for dividends from Z, a noncontrolled section 902 corporation. See section 904(d)(1)(E) and § 1.904–4(g).

(iii) Sections 957(c) and 7701(a)(30) prescribe the treatment of a domestic partnership as an entity for purposes of defining a U.S. shareholder, and thus, for purposes of determining whether a foreign corporation is a CFC. The CFC rules prevent the deferral by U.S. shareholders of U.S. taxation of certain earnings of the CFC and reduce disparities that otherwise might occur between the amount of income subject to a particular foreign tax credit limitation when a taxpayer earns income abroad directly rather than indirectly through a CFC. The application of the look-through rules for foreign tax credit purposes is appropriately tied to CFC status. See sections 904(d)(2)(E) and 904(d)(3). This analysis confirms that Congress clearly contemplated that taxpayers could use a bona fide domestic partnership to subject themselves to the CFC regime, and the resulting application of the look-through rules of section 904(d)(3). Accordingly, under paragraph (e) of this section, the Commissioner cannot treat PRS as an aggregate of its partners for purposes of determining X's foreign tax credit limitation.

(g) Effective date. Paragraphs (a), (b), (c), and (d) of this section are effective for all transactions involving a partnership that occur on or after May 12, 1994. Paragraphs (e) and (f) of this section are effective for all transactions involving a partnership that occur on or after December 29, 1994.

(h) Scope and application. This section applies solely with respect to taxes under subtitle A of the Internal Revenue Code, and for purposes of this section, any reference to a federal tax is limited to any tax imposed under subtitle A of the Internal Revenue Code.

(i) Application of nonstatutory principles and other statutory authorities. The Commissioner can continue to assert and to rely upon applicable nonstatutory principles and other statutory and regulatory authorities to challenge transactions. This section does not limit the applicability of those principles and authorities.

§ 1.702–1 Income and credits of partner.

(a) General rule. Each partner is required to take into account separately in his return his distributive share, whether or not distributed, of each class or item of partnership income, gain, loss, deduction, or credit described in subparagraphs (1) through (9)* of this paragraph. (For the taxable year in which a partner includes his distributive share of partnership taxable income, see section 706(a) and § 1.706–1(a). Such distributive share shall be determined as provided in section 704 and § 1.704–1.) Accordingly, in determining his income tax:

(1) Each partner shall take into account, as part of his gains and losses from sales or exchanges of capital assets held for not more than 1 year (6 months for taxable years beginning before 1977; 9 months for taxable years beginning in 1977), his distributive share of the combined net amount of such gains and losses of the partnership.

(2) Each partner shall take into account, as part of his gains and losses from sales or exchanges of capital assets held for more than 1 year (6 months for taxable years beginning before 1977; 9 months for taxable years beginning in 1977), his distributive share of the combined net amount of such gains and losses of the partnership.

(3) Each partner shall take into account, as part of his gains and losses from sales or exchanges of property described in section 1231 (relating to property used in the trade or business and involuntary conversions), his distributive share of the combined net amount of such gains and losses of the partnership. The partnership shall not combine

*Editorial comment: Presently (a)(1) through (a)(8).

such items with items set forth in subparagraph (1) or (2) of this paragraph.

(4) Each partner shall take into account, as part of the charitable contributions paid by him, his distributive share of each class of charitable contributions paid by the partnership within the partnership's taxable year. Section 170 determines the extent to which such amount may be allowed as a deduction to the partner. For the definition of the term "charitable contribution", see section 170(c).

(5) Each partner shall take into account, as part of the dividends received by him from domestic corporations, his distributive share of dividends received by the partnership, with respect to which the partner is entitled to * * * an exclusion under section 116,* or a deduction under part VIII, subchapter B, chapter 1 of the Code.

* * *

(8) (i) Each partner shall take into account separately, as part of any class of income, gain, loss, deduction, or credit, his distributive share of the following items: Recoveries of bad debts, prior taxes, and delinquency amounts (section 111); gains and losses from wagering transactions (section 165(d)); soil and water conservation expenditures (section 175); non-business expenses as described in section 212; medical, dental, etc., expenses (section 213); * * * alimony, etc., payments (section 215); amounts representing taxes and interest paid to cooperative housing corporations (section 216); intangible drilling and developments costs (section 263(c)); * * * certain mining exploration expenditures (section 617); income, gain, or loss to the partnership under section 751(b); and any items of income, gain, loss, deduction, or credit subject to a special allocation under the partnership agreement which differs from the allocation of partnership taxable income or loss generally.

(ii) Each partner must also take into account separately the partner's distributive share of any partnership item which, if separately taken into account by any partner, would result in an income tax liability for that partner, or for any other person, different from that which would result if that partner did not take the item into account separately. Thus, if any partner is a controlled foreign corporation, as defined in section 957, items of income that would be gross subpart F income if separately taken into account by the controlled foreign corporation must be separately stated for all partners. Under section 911(a), if any partner is a bona fide resident of a foreign country who may exclude from gross income the part of the partner's distributive share which qualifies as earned income, as defined in section 911 (b), the earned income of the partnership for all partners must be separately stated. Similarly, all relevant items of income or deduction of the partnership must be separately stated for all partners in determining the applicability of section 183 (relating to activities not engaged in for profit) and the recomputation of tax thereunder for any partner. This paragraph (a)(8)(ii) applies to taxable years beginning on or after July 23, 2002.

(iii) Each partner shall aggregate the amount of his separate deductions or exclusions and his distributive share of partnership deductions or exclusions separately stated in determining the amount allowable to him of any deduction or exclusion under subtitle A of the Code as to which a limitation is imposed.* * *

(9) Each partner shall also take into account separately his distributive share of the taxable income or loss of the partnership, exclusive of items requiring separate computations under subparagraphs (1) through (8) of this paragraph. For limitation on allowance of a partner's distributive share of partnership losses, see section 704(d) and paragraph (d) of § 1.704–1.

(b) Character of items constituting distributive share. The character in the hands of a partner of any item of income, gain, loss, deduction, or credit described in section 702(a)(1) through (8) shall be determined as if such item were realized directly from the source from which realized by the partnership or incurred in the same manner as incurred by the partnership. For example, a partner's distributive share of gain from the sale of depreciable property used in the trade or business of the partnership shall be considered as gain from the sale of such depreciable property in the hands of the partner. Similarly, a partner's distributive share of partnership "hobby losses" (section 270)** or his distributive share of partnership charitable contributions to organizations qualifying under section 170(b)(1)(A) retains such character in the hands of the partner.

(c) Gross income of a partner. (1) Where it is necessary to determine the amount or character of the gross income of a partner, his gross income shall

*Editorial comment: The Regulations do not include the effect of the Tax Reform Act of 1986 which repealed the Sec. 116 exclusion.

**Editorial comment: See Sec. 183 rather than Sec. 270.

include the partner's distributive share of the gross income of the partnership, that is, the amount of gross income of the partnership from which was derived the partner's distributive share of partnership taxable income or loss (including items described in section 702(a)(1) through (8)). For example, a partner is required to include his distributive share of partnership gross income:

(i) In computing his gross income for the purpose of determining the necessity of filing a return (section 6012(a));

* * *

(iii) In computing the amount of gross income received from sources within possessions of the United States (section 931);

(iv) In determining a partner's "gross income from farming" (sections 175 and 6073), and

(v) In determining whether the de minimis or full inclusion rules of section 954(b)(3) apply.

(2) In determining the applicability of the 6-year period of limitation on assessment and collection provided in section 6501(e) (relating to omission of more than 25 percent of gross income), a partner's gross income includes his distributive share of partnership gross income (as described in section 6501(e)(1)(A)(i)). In this respect, the amount of partnership gross income from which was derived the partner's distributive share of any item of partnership income, gain, loss, deduction, or credit (as included or disclosed in the partner's return) is considered as an amount of gross income stated in the partner's return for the purposes of section 6501 (e). For example, A, who is entitled to one-fourth of the profits of the ABCD partnership, which has $10,000 gross income and $2,000 taxable income, reports only $300 as his distributive share of partnership profits. A should have shown $500 as his distributive share of profits, which amount was derived from $2,500 of partnership gross income. However, since A included only $300 on his return without explaining in the return the difference of $200, he is regarded as having stated in his return only $1,500 ($300/$500 of $2,500) as gross income from the partnership.

(d) Partners in community property States. If separate returns are made by a husband and wife domiciled in a community property State, and only one spouse is a member of the partnership, the part of his or her distributive share of any item or items listed in paragraph (a)(1) through (9)* of this section which is community property, or which is derived from community property, should be reported by the husband and wife in equal proportions.

(e) Special rules on requirement to separately state meal, travel, and entertainment expenses. Each partner shall take into account separately his or her distributive share of meal, travel, and entertainment expenses paid or incurred after December 31, 1986, by partnerships that have taxable years beginning before January 1, 1987, and ending with or within partner's taxable years beginning on or after January 1, 1987. In addition, with respect to skybox rentals under section 274(1)(2), each partner shall take into account separately his or her distributive share of rents paid or incurred after December 31, 1986, by partnerships that have taxable years beginning before January 1, 1989, and ending with or within partners' taxable years beginning on or after January 1, 1987.

(f) Cross reference. For special rules in accordance with the principles of section 702 applicable solely for the purpose of the tax imposed by section 56** (relating to the minimum tax for tax preferences) see § 1.58–2(a). In the case of a disposition of oil or gas property by the partnership, see the rules contained in section 613A(c)(7)(D) and regulation section 1.613A–3(e).

§ 1.702–2 Net operating loss deduction of partner.

For the purpose of determining a net operating loss deduction under section 172, a partner shall take into account his distributive share of items of income, gain, loss, deduction, or credit of the partnership. The character of any such item shall be determined as if such item were realized directly from the source from which realized by the partnership, or incurred in the same manner as incurred by the partnership. See section 702(b) and paragraph (b) of § 1.702–1. To the extent necessary to determine the allowance under section 172(d)(4) of the nonbusiness deductions of a partner (arising from both partnership and nonpartnership sources), the partner shall separately take into account his distributive share of the deductions of the partnership which are not attributable to a trade or business and combine such amount with his nonbusiness deductions from nonpartnership sources. Such partner shall also separately take into account his distributive share

*Editorial comment: Presently (a)(1) through (a)(8).

**Editorial comment: See Sec. 55 rather than Sec. 56.

of the gross income of the partnership not derived from a trade or business and combine such amount with his nonbusiness income from nonpartnership sources. See section 172 and the regulations thereunder.

§ 1.702–3T 4-year spread (temporary).

(a) Applicability. This section applies to a partner in a partnership if—

(1) The partnership is required by section 806 of the Tax Reform Act of 1986 (the 1986 Act). Pub.L. 99–514, 100 Stat. 2362, to change its taxable year for the first taxable year beginning after December 31, 1986 (partnership's year of change); and

(2) As a result of such change in taxable year, items from more than one taxable year of the partnership would, but for the provisions of this section, be included in the taxable year of the partner with or within which the partnership's year of change ends.

(b) Partner's treatment of items from the partnership's year of change—(1) In general. Except as provided in paragraph (c) of this section, if a partner's share of "income items" exceeds the partner's share of "expense items," the partner's share of each and every income and expense item shall be taken into account ratably (and retain its character) over the partner's first 4 taxable years beginning with the partner's taxable year with or within which the partnership's year of change ends.

(2) Definitions—(i) Income items. For purposes of this section, the term "income items" means the sum of—

(A) The partner's distributive share of taxable income (exclusive of separately stated items) from the partnership's year of change.

(B) The partner's distributive share of all separately stated income or gain items from the partnership's year of change, and

(C) Any amount includible in the partner's income under section 707(c) on account of payments during the partnership's year of change.

(ii) Expense items. For purposes of this section, the term "expense items" means the sum of—

(A) The partner's distributive share of taxable loss (exclusive of separately stated items) from the partnership's year of change, and

(B) The partner's distributive share of all separately stated items of loss or deduction from the partnership's year of change.

(c) Electing out of 4-year spread. A partner may elect out of the rules of paragraph (b) of this section by meeting the requirements of § 301.9100–7T of this chapter (temporary regulations relating to elections under the Tax Reform Act of 1986).

(d) Special rules for a partner that is a partnership or S corporation—(1) In general. Except as provided in paragraph (d)(2) of this section, a partner that is a partnership or S corporation may, if otherwise eligible, use the 4-year spread (with respect to partnership interests owned by the partner) described in this section.

(2) Certain partners prohibited from using 4-year spread—(i) In general. Except as provided in paragraph (d)(2)(ii) of this section, a partner that is a partnership or S corporation may not use the 4-year spread (with respect to partnership interests owned by the partner) if such partner is also changing its taxable year pursuant to section 806 of the 1986 Act.

(ii) Exception. If a partner's year of change does not include any income or expense items with respect to the partnership's year of change, such partner may, if otherwise eligible, use the 4-year spread (with respect to such partnership interest) described in this section even though the partner is a partnership or S corporation. See examples (13) and (14) in paragraph (h) of this section.

(e) Basis of partner's interest. The basis of a partner's interest in a partnership shall be determined as if the partner elected not to spread the partnership items over 4 years, regardless of whether such election was in fact made. Thus, for example, if a partner is eligible for the 4-year spread and does not elect out of the 4-year spread pursuant to paragraph (c) of this section, the partner's basis in the partnership interest will be increased in the first year of the 4-year spread period by an amount equal to the excess of the income items over the expense items. However, the partner's basis will not be increased again, with respect to the unamortized income and expense items, as they are amortized over the 4-year spread period.

(f) Effect on other provisions of the Code. Except as provided in paragraph (e) of this section, determinations with respect to a partner, for purposes of other provisions of the Code, must be made with regard to the manner in which partnership items are taken into account under the rules of this section. Thus, for example, a partner who does not elect out of the 4-year spread must take into account, for

purposes of determining net earnings from self-employment under section 1402(a) for a taxable year, only the ratable portion of partnership items for that taxable year.

(g) Treatment of dispositions—(1) In general. If a partnership interest is disposed of before the last taxable year in the 4-year spread period, unamortized income and expense items that are attributable to the interest disposed of and that would be taken into account by the partner for subsequent taxable years in the 4-year spread period shall be taken into account by the partner as determined under paragraph (g)(2) of this section. For purposes of this section, the term "disposed of" means any transfer, including (but not limited to) transfers by sale, exchange, gift, and by reason of death.

(2) Year unamortized items taken into account—(i) In general. If, at the end of a partner's taxable year, the fraction determined under paragraph (g)(2)(ii) of this section is—

(A) Greater than 2/3, the partner must continue to take the unamortized income and expense items into account ratably over the 4-year spread period;

(B) Greater than 1/3 but less than or equal to 2/3, the partner must, in addition to its ratable amortization, take into account in such year 50 percent of the income and expense items that would otherwise be unamortized at the end of such year (however, this paragraph (g)(2)(i)(B) is only applied once with respect to a partner's interest in a particular partnership); or

(C) Less than or equal to 1/3 the partner must take into account the entire balance of unamortized income and expense items in such year.

(ii) Determination of fraction. For purposes of paragraph (g)(2)(i) of this section, the numerator of the fraction is the partner's proportionate interest in the partnership at the end of the partner's taxable year and the denominator is the partner's proportionate interest in the partnership as of the last day of the partnership's year of change.

(h) Examples. The provisions of this section may be illustrated by the following examples.

Example (1). Assume that P1, a partnership with a taxable year ending September 30, is required by the 1986 Act to change its taxable year to a calendar year. All of the partners of P1 are individual taxpayers reporting on a calendar year. P1 is required to change to a calendar year for its taxable year beginning October 1, 1987, and to file a return for the short taxable year ending December 31, 1987. Based on the above facts, the partners of P1 are required to include the items from more than one taxable year of P1 in income for their 1987 taxable year. Thus, under paragraph (b) of this section, if a partner's share of income items exceeds the partner's share of expense items, the partner's share of each and every income and expense item shall be taken into account ratably by such partner in each of the partner's first four taxable years beginning with the partner's 1987 taxable year, unless such partner elects under paragraph (c) of this section to include all such amounts in his 1987 taxable year.

Example (2). Assume the same facts as in example (1), except P1 is a personal service corporation with all of its employee-owners reporting on a calendar year. Although P1 is required to change to a calendar year for its taxable year beginning October 1, 1987, neither P1 nor its employee-owners obtain the benefits of a 4-year spread. Pursuant to section 806(e)(2)(C) of the 1986 Act, the 4-year spread provision is only applicable to short taxable years of partnerships and S corporations required to change their taxable year under the 1986 Act.

Example (3). Assume the same facts as example (1) and that I is one of the individual partners of Pl. Further assume that I's distributive share of Pl's taxable income for the short taxable year ended December 31, 1987 (*i.e.*, Pl's year of change), is $10,000. In addition, I has $8,000 of separately stated expense from Pl's year of change. Since I's income items (*i.e.*, $10,000 of taxable income) exceed I's expense items (*i.e.*, $8,000 of separately stated expense) attributable to Pl's year of change, I is eligible for the 4-year spread provided by this section. If I does not elect out of the 4-year spread, I will recognize $2,500 of taxable income and $2,000 of separately stated expense in his 1987 calendar year return. Assuming I does not dispose of his partnership interest in Pl by December 31, 1989, the remaining $7,500 of taxable income and $6,000 of separately stated expense will be amortized (and retain its character) over I's next three taxable years (*i.e.*, 1988, 1989 and 1990).

Example (4). Assume the same facts as example (3), except that I disposes of his entire interest in P1 during 1988. Pursuant to paragraph (g) of this section, I would recognize $7,500 of taxable income and $6,000 of separately stated expense in his 1988 calendar year return.

Example (5). Assume the same facts as in example (3), except that I disposes of 50 percent of his interest in P1 during 1989. Pursuant to paragraph (g) of this section, I would recognize $3,750 of taxable income in his 1989 calendar year return ($2,500 ratable portion for 1989 plus 50 percent of the $2,500 of income items that would otherwise be unamortized at the end of 1989). I would also recognize $3,000 of separately stated expense items in 1989 ($2,000 ratable portion for 1989 plus 50 percent of the $2,000 of separately stated expense items that would otherwise be unamortized at the end of 1989).

Example (6). Assume the same facts as in example (1), except that X, a personal service service corporation as defined in section 441(i), is a partner of P1. X is a calendar year taxpayer, and thus is not required to change its taxable year under the 1986 Act. The same result occurs as in example (1) (*i.e.*, unless X elects to the contrary, X is required to include one fourth of its share of income and expense items from P1's year of change in the first four taxable years of X beginning with the 1987 taxable year).

Example (7). Assume the same facts as in example (6), except that X is a fiscal year personal service corporation with a taxable year ending September 30. X is required under the 1986 Act to change to a calendar year for its taxable year beginning October 1, 1987, and to file a return for its short year ending December 31, 1987. Based on the above facts, X is not required to include the items from more than one taxable year of P1 in any one taxable year of X. Thus, the provisions of this section do not apply to X, and X is required to include the full amount of income and expense items from P1's year of change in X's taxable income for X's short year ending December 31. Under section 443 of the Code, X is required to annualize the taxable income for its short year ending December 31, 1987.

Example (8). Assume that P2 is a partnership with a taxable year ending September 30. Under the 1986 Act, P2 would have been required to change its taxable year to a calendar year, effective for the taxable year beginning October 1, 1987. However, P2 properly changed its taxable year to a calendar year for the year beginning October 1, 1986, and filed a return for the short period ending December 31, 1986. The provisions of the 1986 Act do not apply to P2 because the short year ending December 31, 1986, was not required by the amendments made by section 806 of the 1986 Act. Thus, the partners of P2 are required to take all items of income and expense for the short taxable year ending December 31, 1986, into account for the taxable year with or within which such short year ends.

Example (9). Assume that P3 is a partnership with a taxable year ending March 31 and I, a calendar year individual, is a partner in P3. Under the 1986 Act, P3 would have been required to change its taxable year to a calendar year. However, under Rev.Proc. 87–32, P3 establishes and changes to a natural business year beginning with the taxable year ending June 30, 1987. Thus, P3 is required to change its taxable year under section 806 of the 1986 Act, and I is required to include items from more than one taxable year of P3 in one of her taxable years. Furthermore, I's share of P3's income items exceeds her share of P3's expense items for the short period April 1, 1987 through June 30, 1987. Accordingly, under this section, unless I elects to the contrary, I is required to take one fourth of her share of items of income and expense from P3's short taxable year ending June 30, 1987 into account for her taxable year ending December 31, 1987.

Example (10). Assume that P4 is a partnership with a taxable year ending March 31. Y, a C corporation, owns a 51 percent interest in the profits and capital of P4. Y reports its income on the basis of a taxable year ending March 31. P4 establishes and changes to a natural business year beginning with the taxable year ending June 30, 1987, under Rev.Proc. 87–32. Under the above facts, P4 is not required to change its taxable year because its March 31 taxable year was the taxable year of Y, the partner owning a majority of the partnership's profits and capital. Therefore, the remaining partners of P4 owning 49 percent of the profits and capital are not permitted the 4-year spread of the items of income and expense with respect to the short year, even though they may be required to include their distributive share of P4's items from more than one taxable year in one of their years.

Example (11). Assume that X and Y are C corporations with taxable years ending June 30. Each owns a 50-percent interest in the profits and capital of partnership P5. P5 has a taxable year ending March 31. Assume that P5 cannot establish a business purpose in order to retain a taxable year ending March 31, and thus P5 must change to a June 30 taxable year, the taxable year of its partners. Furthermore, assume that X's share of P5's income items exceeds its share of P5's expense items for P5's short taxable year ending June 30, 1987. Unless X elects out of the 4-year spread, the taxable year ending June 30, 1987, is the first of the four taxable years in which X must take into account its share of the items of income and expense resulting from P5's short taxable year ending June 30, 1987.

Example (12). Assume that I, an individual who reports income on the basis of the calendar year, is a partner in two partnerships, P6 and P7. Both partnerships have a taxable year ending September 30. Neither partnership can establish a business purpose for retaining its taxable year. Consequently, each partnership will change its taxable year to December 31, for the taxable year beginning October 1, 1987. The election to avoid a 4-year spread is made at the partner level; in addition, a partner may make such elections on a partnership-by-partnership basis. Thus, assuming I is eligible to obtain the 4-year spread with respect to income and expense items from partnerships P6 and P7, I may use the 4-year spread with respect to items from P6, while not using the 4-year spread with respect to items from P7.

Example (13). I, an individual taxpayer using a calendar year, owns an interest in P8, a partnership using a taxable year ending June 30. Furthermore, P8 owns an interest in P9, a partnership with a taxable year ending March 31. Under section 806 of the 1986 Act, P8 will be required to change to a taxable year ending December 31, while P9 will be required to change to a taxable year ending June 30. As a result, P8's year of change will be July 1 through December 31, 1987, while P9's year of change will be from April 1 through June 30, 1987. Since P9's year of change does not end with or within P8's year of change, paragraph (d)(2) of this section does not prevent P8 from obtaining a 4-year spread with respect to its interest in P9.

Example (14). The facts are the same as in example (13), except that P9 has a taxable year ending September 30, and under the 1986 Act P9 is required to change to a taxable year ending December 31. Therefore, P9's year of change will be from October 1, 1987 through December 31, 1987. Although P8's year of change from July 1, 1987 through December 31, 1987 includes two taxable years of P9 (*i.e.,* October 1, 1986 through September 30, 1987 and October 1, 1987 through December 31, 1987), paragraph (d)(2) of this section prohibits P8 from using the 4-year spread with respect to its interest in P9, because P9's year of change ends with or within P8's year of change.

§ 1.703–1 Partnership computations.

(a) Income and deductions. (1) The taxable income of a partnership shall be computed in the same manner as the taxable income of an individual, except as otherwise provided in this section. A partnership is required to state separately in its return the items described in section 702(a)(1) through (7)* and, in addition, to attach to its return a statement setting forth separately those items described in section 702(a)(8)** which the partner is required to take into account separately in determining his income tax. See paragraph (a)(8) of § 1.702.1. The partnership is further required to compute and to state separately in its return:

*Editorial comment: See Sec. 702(a)(1) through (6) instead.

**Editorial comment: See Sec. 702(a)(7) instead.

(i) As taxable income under section 702(a)(9),*** the total of all other items of gross income (not separately stated) over the total of all other allowable deductions (not separately stated), or

(ii) As loss under section 702(a)(9),*** the total of all other allowable deductions (not separately stated) over the total of all other items of gross income (not separately stated).

The taxable income or loss so computed shall be accounted for by the partners in accordance with their partnership agreement.

(2) The partnership is not allowed the following deductions:

(i) The standard deduction provided in section 141.*

(ii) The deduction for personal exemptions provided in section 151.

(iii) The deduction provided in section 164(a) for taxes, described in section 901, paid or accrued to foreign countries or possessions of the United States. Each partner's distributive share of such taxes shall be accounted for separately by him as provided in section 702(a)(6).

(iv) The deduction for charitable contributions provided in section 170. Each partner is considered as having paid within his taxable year his distributive share of any contribution or gift, payment of which was actually made by the partnership within its taxable year ending within or with the partner's taxable year. This item shall be accounted for separately by the partners as provided in section 702(a)(4). See also paragraph (b) of § 1.702–1.

(v) The net operating loss deduction provided in section 172. See § 1.702–2.

(vi) The additional itemized deductions for individuals provided in part VII, subchapter B, chapter 1 of the Code, as follows: Expenses for production of income (section 212); medical, dental, etc., expenses (section 213); expenses for care of certain dependents (section 214); alimony, etc., payments (section 215); and amounts representing taxes and interest paid to cooperative housing corporation (section 216). However, see paragraph (a)(8) of § 1.702–1.

(vii) The deduction for depletion under section 611 with respect to domestic oil or gas which is produced after December 31, 1974, and to which gross income from the property is attributable after such year.

***Editorial comment: See Sec. 702(a)(8) instead.

(b) Elections of the partnership—(1) General rule. Any elections (other than those described in subparagraph (2) of this paragraph) affecting the computation of income derived from a partnership shall be made by the partnership. For example, elections of methods of accounting, of computing depreciation, of treating soil and water conservation expenditures, and the option to deduct as expenses intangible drilling and development costs, shall be made by the partnership and not by the partners separately. All partnership elections are applicable to all partners equally, but any election made by a partnership shall not apply to any partner's non-partnership interests.

(2) Exceptions. (i) Each partner shall add his distributive share of taxes described in section 901 paid or accrued by the partnership to foreign countries or possessions of the United States (according to its method of treating such taxes) to any such taxes paid or accrued by him (according to his method of treating such taxes), and may elect to use the total amount either as a credit against tax or as a deduction from income.

(ii) Each partner shall add his distributive share of expenses described in section 615 or section 617 paid or accrued by the partnership to any such expenses paid or accrued by him and shall treat the total amount according to his method of treating such expenses, notwithstanding the treatment of the expenses by the partnership.

* * *

§ 1.704–1 Partner's distributive share.

(a) Effect of partnership agreement. A partner's distributive share of any item or class of items of income, gain, loss, deduction, or credit of the partnership shall be determined by the partnership agreement, unless otherwise provided by section 704 and paragraphs (b) through (e) of this section. For definition of partnership agreement see section 761(c).

(b) Determination of partner's distributive share—(o) Cross-references.

Heading	Section
Cross-references	1.704–1(b)(0)
In general	1.704–1(b)(1)
Basic principles	1.704–1(b)(1)(i)
Effective dates	1.704–1(b)(1)(ii)
Effect of other sections	1.704–1 (b)(1)(iii)

*Editorial comment: See Sec. 63 rather than Sec. 141.

(1) In general—(i) Basic principles. Under section 704(b) if a partnership agreement does not provide for the allocation of income, gain, loss, deduction, or credit (or item thereof) to a partner, or if the partnership agreement provides for the allocation of income, gain, loss, deduction, or credit (or item thereof) to a partner but such allocation does not have substantial economic effect, then the partner's distributive share of such income, gain, loss, deduction, or credit (or item thereof) shall be determined in accordance with such partner's interest in the partnership (taking into account all facts and circumstances). If the partnership agreement provides for the allocation of income, gain, loss, deduction, or credit (or item thereof) to a partner, there are three ways in which such allocation will be respected under section 704(b) and this paragraph. First, the allocation can have substantial economic effect in accordance with paragraph (b)(2) of this section. Second, taking into account all facts and circumstances, the allocation can be in accordance with the partner's interest in the partnership. See paragraph (b)(3) of this section. Third, the allocation can be deemed to be in accordance with the partner's interest in the partnership pursuant to one of the special rules contained in paragraph (b)(4) of this section and § 1.704–2. To the extent an allocation under the partnership agreement of income, gain, loss, deduction, or credit (or item thereof) to a partner does not have substantial economic effect, is not in accordance with the partner's interest in the partnership, and is not deemed to be in accordance with the partner's interest in the partnership, such income, gain, loss, deduction, or credit (or item thereof) will be reallocated in accordance with the partner's interest in the partnership (determined under paragraph (b)(3) of this section).

(ii) Effective dates. The provisions of this paragraph are effective for partnership taxable years beginning after December 31, 1975. However, for partnership taxable years beginning after December 31, 1975, but before May 1, 1986 (January 1, 1987, in the case of allocations of nonrecourse deductions as defined in paragraph (b)(4)(iv)(a) of this section), an allocation of income, gain, loss, deduction, or credit (or item thereof) to a partner that is not respected under this paragraph nevertheless will be respected under section 704(b) if such allocation has substantial economic effect or is in accordance with the partners' interests in the partnership as those terms have been interpreted under the relevant case law, the legislative history of section 210(d) of the Tax Reform Act of 1976, and the provisions of this paragraph in effect for partnership taxable years beginning before May 1, 1986.

(iii) Effect of other sections. The determination of a partner's distributive share of income, gain, loss, deduction, or credit (or item thereof) under section 704(b) and this paragraph is not conclusive as to the tax treatment of a partner with respect to such distributive share. For example, an allocation of loss or deduction to a partner that is respected under section 704(b) and this paragraph may not be deductible by such partner if the partner lacks the requisite motive for economic gain (see, *e.g., Goldstein v. Commissioner*, 364 F.2d 734 (2d Cir.1966)), or may be disallowed for that taxable year (and held in suspense) if the limitations of section 465 or section 704(d) are applicable. Similarly, an allocation that is respected under section 704(b) and this paragraph nevertheless may be reallocated under other provisions, such as section 482, section 704(e)(2), section 706(d) (and related assignment of income principles), and paragraph (b)(2)(ii) of § 1.751–1. If a partnership has a section 754 election in effect, a partner's distributive share of partnership income, gain, loss, or deduction may be affected as provided in § 1.743–1 (see paragraph (b)(2)(iv)(m)(2) of this section). A deduction that appears to be a nonrecourse deduction deemed to be in accordance with the partners' interests in the partnership may not be such because purported nonrecourse liabilities of the partnership in fact constitute equity rather than debt. The examples in paragraph (b)(5) of this section concern the validity of allocations under section 704(b) and this paragraph and, except as noted, do not address the effect of other sections or limitations on such allocations.

(iv) Other possible tax consequences. Allocations that are respected under section 704(b) and this paragraph may give rise to other tax consequences, such as those resulting from the application of section 61, section 83, section 751, section 2501, paragraph (f) of § 1.46–3, § 1.47–6, paragraph (b)(1) of § 1.721–1 (and related principles), and paragraph (e) of § 1.752–1. The examples in paragraph (b)(5) of this section concern the validity of allocations under section 704(b) and this paragraph and, except as noted, do not address other tax consequences that may result from such allocations.

(v) Purported allocations. Section 704(b) and this paragraph do not apply to a purported allocation if it is made to a person who is not a partner of the partnership (see section 7701 (a)(2) and paragraph (d) of § 301.7701–3) or to a person who is not receiving the purported allocation in his capacity as a partner (see section 707(a) and paragraph (a) of § 1.707–1).

(vi) Section 704(c) determinations. Section 704(c) and § 1.704–3 generally require that if property is contributed by a partner to a partnership, the partners' distributive shares of income, gain, loss, and deduction, as computed for tax purposes, with respect to the property are determined so as to take account of the variation between the adjusted tax basis and fair market value of the property. Although section 704(b) does not directly determine the partners' distributive shares of tax items governed by section 704(c), the partners' distributive shares of tax items may be determined under section 704(c) and § 1.704–3 (depending on the allocation method chosen by the partnership under § 1.704–3) with reference to the partners' distributive shares of the corresponding book items, as determined under section 704(b) and this paragraph. (See paragraphs (b)(2)(iv)(d) and (b)(4)(i) of this section.) See § 1.704–3 for methods of making allocations under section 704(c), and § 1.704–3T(d)(2) for a special rule in determining the amount of book items if the remedial allocation method is chosen by the partnership. See also paragraph (b)(5) Example (13)(i) of this section.

(vii) Bottom line allocations. Section 704(b) and this paragraph are applicable to allocations of income, gain, loss, deduction, and credit, allocations of specific items of income, gain, loss, deduction, and credit, and allocations of partnership net or "bottom line" taxable income and loss. An allocation to a partner of a share of partnership net or "bottom line" taxable income or loss shall be treated as an allocation to such partner of the same share of each item of income, gain, loss, and deduction that is taken into account in computing such net or "bottom line" taxable income or loss. See example (15)(i) of paragraph (b)(5) of this section.

(2) Substantial economic effect—(i) Two-part analysis. The determination of whether an allocation of income, gain, loss, or deduction (or item thereof) to a partner has substantial economic effect involves a two-part analysis that is made as of the end of the partnership taxable year to which the allocation relates. First, the allocation must have economic effect (within the meaning of paragraph (b)(2)(ii) of this section). Second, the economic effect of the allocation must be substantial (within the meaning of paragraph (b)(2)(iii) of this section).

(ii) Economic effect—(a) Fundamental principles. In order for an allocation to have economic effect, it must be consistent with the underlying economic arrangement of the partners. This means that in the event there is an economic benefit or economic burden that corresponds to an allocation, the partner to whom the allocation is made must receive such economic benefit or bear such economic burden.

(b) Three requirements. Based on the principles contained in paragraph (b)(2)(ii)(a) of this section, and except as otherwise provided in this paragraph, an allocation of income, gain, loss, or deduction (or item thereof) to a partner will have economic effect if, and only if, throughout the full term of the partnership, the partnership agreement provides—

(1) For the determination and maintenance of the partners' capital accounts in accordance with the rules of paragraph (b)(2)(iv) of this section.

(2) Upon liquidation of the partnership (or any partner's interest in the partnership), liquidating distributions are required in all cases to be made in accordance with the positive capital account balances of the partners, as determined after taking into account all capital account adjustments for the partnership taxable year during which such liquidation occurs (other than those made pursuant to this requirement (2) and requirement (3) of this paragraph (b)(2)(ii)(b)), by the end of such taxable year (or, if later, within 90 days after the date of such liquidation), and

(3) If such partner has a deficit balance in his capital account following the liquidation of his interest in the partnership, as determined after taking into account all capital account adjustments for the partnership taxable year during which such liquidation occurs (other than those made pursuant to this requirement (3)), he is unconditionally obligated to restore the amount of such deficit balance to the partnership by the end of such taxable year (or, if later, within 90 days after the date of such liquidation), which amount shall, upon liquidation of the partnership, be paid to creditors of the partnership or distributed to other partners in accordance with their positive capital account balances (in accordance with requirement (2) of this paragraph (b)(2)(ii)(b)).

For purposes of the preceding sentence, a partnership taxable year shall be determined without regard to section 706(c)(2)(A). Requirements (2) and (3) of this paragraph (b)(2)(ii)(b) are not violated if all or part of the partnership interest of one or more partners is purchased (other than in connection with the liquidation of the partnership) by the partnership or by one or more partners (or one or more persons related, within the meaning of section 267(b) (without modification by section 267(e)(1)) or section 707(b)(1), to a partner) pursuant to an agreement negotiated at arm's length by persons who at the time such agreement is entered into have materially adverse interests and if a principal purpose of such purchase and sale is not to avoid the principles of the second sentence of paragraph (b)(2)(ii)(a) of this section. In addition, requirement (2) of this paragraph (b)(2)(ii)(b) is not violated if, upon the liquidation of the partnership, the capital accounts of the partners are increased or decreased pursuant to paragraph (b)(2)(iv)(f) of this section as of the date of such liquidation and the partnership makes liquidating distributions within the time set out in that requirement (2) in the ratios of the partners' positive capital accounts, except that it does not distribute reserves reasonably required to provide for liabilities (contingent or otherwise) of the partnership and installment obligations owed to the partnership, so long as such withheld amounts are distributed as soon as practicable and in the ratios of the partners' positive capital account balances. See examples (1)(i) and (ii), (4)(i), (8)(i), and (16)(i) of paragraph (b)(5) of this section.

(c) Obligation to restore deficit. If a partner is not expressly obligated to restore the deficit balance in his capital account, such partner nevertheless will be treated as obligated to restore the deficit balance in his capital account (in accordance with requirement (3) of paragraph (b)(2)(ii)(b) of this section) to the extent of—

(1) The outstanding principal balance of any promissory note (of which such partner is the maker) contributed to the partnership by such partner (other than a promissory note that is readily tradable on an established securities market), and

(2) The amount of any unconditional obligation of such partner (whether imposed by the partnership agreement or by State or local law) to make subsequent contributions to the partnership (other than pursuant to a promissory note of which such partner is the maker),

provided that such note or obligation is required to be satisfied at a time no later than the end of the partnership taxable year in which such partner's interest is liquidated (or, if later, within 90 days after the date of such liquidation). If a promissory note referred to in the previous sentence is negotiable, a partner will be considered required to satisfy such note within the time period specified in such sentence if the partnership agreement provides that, in lieu of actual satisfaction, the partnership will retain such note and such partner will contribute to the partnership the excess, if any, of the outstanding principal balance of such note over its fair market value at the time of liquidation. See paragraph (b)(2)(iv)(d)(2) of this section. See examples (1)(ix) and (x) of paragraph (b)(5) of this section. A partner in no event will be considered obligated to restore the deficit balance in his capital account to the partnership (in accordance with requirement (3) of paragraph (b)(2)(ii)(b) of this section) to the extent such partner's obligation is not legally enforceable, or the facts and circumstances otherwise indicate a plan to avoid or circumvent such obligation. See paragraphs (b)(2)(ii)(f), (b)(2)(ii)(h), and (b)(4)(vi) of this section for other rules regarding such obligation.

For purposes of this paragraph (b)(2), if a partner contributes a promissory note to the partnership during a partnership taxable year beginning after December 29, 1988 and the maker of such note is a person related to such partner (within the meaning of § 1.752–1T(h), but without regard to subdivision (4) of that section), then such promissory note shall be treated as a promissory note of which such partner is the maker.

(d) Alternate test for economic effect. If—

(1) Requirements (1) and (2) of paragraph (b)(2)(ii)(b) of this section are satisfied, and

(2) The partner to whom an allocation is made is not obligated to restore the deficit balance in his capital account to the partnership (in accordance with requirement (3) of paragraph (b)(2)(ii)(b) of this section), or is obligated to restore only a limited dollar amount of such deficit balance, and

(3) The partnership agreement contains a "qualified income offset," such allocation will be considered to have economic effect under this paragraph (b)(2)(ii)(d) to the extent such allocation does not cause or increase a deficit balance in such partner's capital account (in excess of any limited dollar amount of such deficit balance that such partner is obligated to restore) as of the end of the partnership taxable year to which such allocation relates. In determining the extent to which the previous sentence is satisfied, such partner's capital account also shall be reduced for—

(4) Adjustments that, as of the end of such year, reasonably are expected to be made to such partner's capital account under paragraph (b)(2)(iv)(k) of this section for depletion allowances with respect to oil and gas properties of the partnership, and

(5) Allocations of loss and deduction that, as of the end of such year, reasonably are expected to be made to such partner pursuant to section 704(e)(2), section 706(d), and paragraph (b)(2)(ii) of § 751–1, and

(6) Distributions that, as of the end of such year, reasonably are expected to be made to such partner to the extent they exceed offsetting increases to such partner's capital account that reasonably are expected to occur during (or prior to) the partnership taxable years in which such distributions reasonably are expected to be made (other than increases pursuant to a minimum gain chargeback under paragraph (b)(4) (iv)(e) of this section or under § 1.704–2(f); however, increases to a partner's capital account pursuant to a minimum gain chargeback requirement are taken into account as an offset to distributions of nonrecourse liability proceeds that are reasonably expected to be made and that are allocable to an increase in partnership minimum gain) under § 1.704–2(f).

For purposes of determining the amount of expected distributions and expected capital account increases described in (6) above, the rule set out in paragraph (b)(2)(iii)(c) of this section concerning the presumed value of partnership property shall apply. The partnership agreement contains a "qualified income offset" if, and only if, it provides that a partner who unexpectedly receives an adjustment, allocation, or distribution described in (4), (5), or (6) above, will be allocated items of income and gain (consisting of a pro rata portion of each item of partnership income, including gross income, and gain for such year) in an amount and manner sufficient to eliminate such deficit balance as quickly as possible. Allocations of items of income and gain made pursuant to the immediately preceding sentence shall be deemed to be made in accordance with the partners' interests in the partnership if requirements (1) and (2) of paragraph (b)(2)(ii)(b) of this section are satisfied. See examples (1)(iii), (iv), (v), (vi), (viii), (ix), and (x), (15), and (16)(ii) of paragraph (b)(5) of this section.

(e) Partial economic effect. If only a portion of an allocation made to a partner with respect to a partnership taxable year has economic effect, both the portion that has economic effect and the portion that is reallocated shall consist of a proportionate share of all items that made up the allocation to such partner for such year. See examples (15)(ii) and (iii) of paragraph (b)(5) of this section.

(f) Reduction of obligation to restore. If requirements (1) and (2) of paragraph (b)(2)(ii)(b) of this section are satisfied, a partner's obligation to restore the deficit balance in his capital account (or any limited dollar amount thereof) to the partnership may be eliminated or reduced as of the end of a partnership taxable year without affecting the validity of prior allocations (see paragraph (b)(4)(vi) of this section) to the extent the deficit balance (if any) in such partner's capital account, after reduction for the items described in (4), (5), and (6) of paragraph (b)(2)(ii)(d) of this section, will not exceed the partner's remaining obligation (if any) to restore the deficit balance in his capital account. See example (1)(viii) of paragraph (b)(5) of this section.

(g) Liquidation defined. For purposes of this paragraph, a liquidation of a partner's interest in the partnership occurs upon the earlier of (1) the date upon which there is a liquidation of the partnership, or (2) the date upon which there is a liquidation of the partner's interest in the partnership under paragraph (d) of § 1.761–1. For purposes of this paragraph, the liquidation of a partnership occurs upon the earlier of (3) the date upon which the partnership is terminated under section 708(b)(1), or (4) the date upon which the partnership ceases to be a going concern (even though it may continue in existence for the purpose of winding up its affairs, paying its debts, and distributing any remaining balance to its partners). Requirements (2) and (3) of paragraph (b)(2)(ii)(b) of this section will be considered unsatisfied if the liquidation of a partner's interest in the partnership is delayed after its primary business activities have been terminated (for example, by continuing to engage in a relatively minor amount of business activity, if such actions themselves do not cause the partnership to terminate pursuant to section 708(b) (1)) for a principal purpose of deferring any distribution pursuant to requirement (2) of paragraph (b)(2) (ii)(b) of this section or deferring any partner's obligations under requirement (3) of paragraph (b)(2) (ii)(b) of this section.

(h) Partnership agreement defined. For purposes of this paragraph, the partnership agreement includes all agreements among the partners, or between one or more partners and the partnership, concerning affairs of the partnership and responsibilities of partners, whether oral or written, and whether or not embodied in a document referred to by the partners as the partnership agreement. Thus, in determining whether distributions are required in all cases to be made in accordance with the partners' positive capital account balances (requirement (2) of paragraph (b)(2)(ii)(b) of this section), and in determining the extent to which a partner is obligated to restore a deficit balance in his capital account (requirement (3) of paragraph (b)(2)(ii)(b) of this section), all arrangements among partners, or between one or more partners and the partnership relating to the partnership, direct and indirect, including puts, options, and other buy-sell agreements, and any other "stop-loss" arrangement, are considered to be part of the partnership agreement. (Thus, for example, if one partner who assumes a liability of the partnership is indemnified by another partner for a portion of such liability, the indemnifying partner (depending upon the particular facts) may be viewed as in effect having a partial deficit makeup obligation as a result of such indemnity agreement.) In addition, the partnership agreement includes provisions of Federal, State, or local law that govern the affairs of the partnership or are considered under such law to be a part of the partnership agreement (see the last sentence of paragraph (c) of § 1.761–1). For purposes of this paragraph (b)(2)(ii)(h), an agreement with a partner or a partnership shall include an agreement with a person related, within the meaning of section 267(b) (without modification by section 267(e)(1)) or section 707(b)(1), to such partner or partnership. For purposes of the preceding sentence, sections 267(b) and 707(b)(1) shall be applied for partnership taxable years beginning after December 29, 1988 by (1) substituting "80 percent or more" for "more than 50 percent" each place it appears in such sections, (2) excluding brothers and sisters from the members of a person's family, and (3) disregarding section 267(f)(1)(A).

(i) Economic effect equivalence. Allocations made to a partner that do not otherwise have economic effect under this paragraph (b)(2)(ii) shall nevertheless be deemed to have economic effect, provided that as of the end of each partnership taxable year a liquidation of the partnership at the end of such year or at the end of any future year would produce the same economic results to the partners as would occur if requirements (1), (2), and (3) of paragraph (b)(2)(ii)(b) of this section had been satisfied, regardless of the economic performance of the partnership. See examples (4)(ii) and (iii) of paragraph (b)(5) of this section.

(iii) Substantiality—**(a)** General rules. Except as otherwise provided in this paragraph (b)(2)(iii), the economic effect of an allocation (or allocations) is substantial if there is a reasonable possibility that the allocation (or allocations) will affect substantially the dollar amounts to be received by the partners from the partnership, independent of tax consequences. Notwithstanding the preceding sentence, the economic effect of an allocation (or allocations) is not substantial if, at the time the allocation becomes part of the partnership agreement, (1) the after-tax economic consequences of at least one partner may, in present value terms, be enhanced compared to such consequences if the allocation (or allocations) were not contained in the partnership agreement, and (2) there is a strong likelihood that the after-tax economic consequences of no partner will, in present value terms, be substantially diminished compared to such consequences if the allocation (or allocations) were not contained in the partnership agreement. In determining the after-tax economic benefit or detriment to a partner, tax consequences that result from the interaction of the allocation with such partner's tax attributes that are unrelated to the partnership will be taken into account. See examples (5) and (9) of paragraph (b)(5) of this section. The economic effect of an allocation is not substantial in the two situations described in paragraphs (b)(2)(iii)(b) and (c) of this section. However, even if an allocation is not described therein, its economic effect may be insubstantial under the general rules stated in this paragraph (b)(2)(iii)(a). References in this paragraph (b)(2)(iii) to allocations include capital account adjustments made pursuant to paragraph (b)(2)(iv)(k) of this section.

(b) Shifting tax consequences. The economic effect of an allocation (or allocations) in a partnership taxable year is not substantial if, at the time the allocation (or allocations) becomes part of the partnership agreement, there is a strong likelihood that—

(1) The net increases and decreases that will be recorded in the partners' respective capital accounts for such taxable year will not differ substantially from the net increases and decreases that would be recorded in such partners' respective capital accounts for such year if the allocations were not contained in the partnership agreement, and

(2) The total tax liability of the partners (for their respective taxable years in which the allocations will be taken into account) will be less than if the allocations were not contained in the partnership agreement (taking into account tax consequences that result from the interaction of the allocation (or allocations) with partner tax attributes that are unrelated to the partnership).

If, at the end of a partnership taxable year to which an allocation (or allocations) relates, the net increases and decreases that are recorded in the partners' respective capital accounts do not differ substantially from the net increases and decreases that would have been recorded in such partners' respective capital accounts had the allocation (or allocations) not been contained in the partnership agreement, and the total tax liability of the partners is (as described in (2) above) less than it would have been had the allocation (or allocations) not been contained in the partnership agreement, it will be presumed that, at the time the allocation (or allocations) became part of such partnership agreement, there was a strong likelihood that these results would occur. This presumption may be overcome by a showing of facts and circumstances that prove otherwise. See examples (6), (7)(ii) and (iii), and (10)(ii) of paragraph (b)(5) of this section.

(c) Transitory allocations. If a partnership agreement provides for the possibility that one or more allocations (the "original allocation(s)") will be largely offset by one or more other allocations (the "offsetting allocation(s)"), and, at the time the allocations become part of the partnership agreement, there is a strong likelihood that—

(1) The net increases and decreases that will be recorded in the partners' respective capital accounts for the taxable years to which the allocations relate will not differ substantially from the net increases and decreases that would be recorded in such partners' respective capital accounts for such years if the original allocation(s) and offsetting allocation(s) were not contained in the partnership agreement, and

(2) The total tax liability of the partners (for their respective taxable years in which the allocations will be taken into account) will be less than if the allocations were not contained in the partnership agreement (taking into account tax consequences that result from the interaction of the allocation (or allocations) with partner tax attributes that are unrelated to the partnership) the economic effect of the original allocation(s) and offsetting allocation(s) will not be substantial. If, at the end of a partnership taxable year to which an offsetting allocation(s) relates, the net increases and decreases recorded in the partners' respective capital accounts do not differ substantially from the net increases and decreases that would have been recorded in such partners' respective capital accounts had the original allocation(s) and the offsetting allocation(s) not been contained in the partnership agreement, and the total tax liability of the partners is (as described in (2) above) less than it would have been had such allocations not been contained in the partnership agreement, it will be presumed that, at the time the allocations became part of the partnership agreement, there was a strong likelihood that these results would occur. This presumption may be overcome by a showing of facts and circumstances that prove otherwise. See examples (1)(xi), (2), (3), (7), (8)(ii), and (17) of paragraph (b)(5) of this section. Notwithstanding the foregoing, the original allocation(s) and the offsetting allocation(s) will not be insubstantial (under this paragraph (b)(2)(iii)(c)) and, for purposes of paragraph (b)(2)(iii)(a), it will be presumed that there is a reasonable possibility that the allocations will affect substantially the dollar amounts to be received by the partners from the partnership if, at the time the allocations become part of the partnership agreement, there is a strong likelihood that the offsetting allocation(s) will not, in large part, be made within five years after the original allocation(s) is made (determined on a first-in, first-out basis). See example (2) of paragraph (b)(5) of this section. For purposes of applying the provisions of this paragraph (b)(2)(iii) (and paragraphs (b)(2)(ii)(d)(6) and (b)(3)(iii) of this section), the adjusted tax basis of partnership property (or, if partnership property is properly reflected on the books of the partnership at a book value that differs from its adjusted tax basis, the book value of such property) will be presumed to be the fair market value of such property, and adjustments to the adjusted tax basis (or book value) of such property will be presumed to be matched by corresponding changes in such property's fair market value. Thus, there cannot be a strong likelihood that the economic effect of an allocation (or allocations) will be largely offset by an allocation (or allocations) of gain or loss from the disposition of partnership property. See examples (1)(vi) and (xi) of paragraph (b)(5) of this section.

(iv) Maintenance of capital accounts—(a) In general. The economic effect test described in paragraph (b)(2)(ii) of this section requires an examination of the capital accounts of the partners of a partnership, as maintained under the partnership agreement. Except as otherwise provided in paragraph (b)(2)(ii)(i) of this section, an allocation of income, gain, loss, or deduction will not have economic effect under paragraph (b)(2)(ii) of this section, and will not be deemed to be in accordance with a partner's interest in the partnership under paragraph (b)(4) of this section, unless the capital accounts of the partners are determined and maintained throughout the full term of the partnership in accordance with the capital accounting rules of this paragraph (b)(2)(iv).

(b) Basic rules. Except as otherwise provided in this paragraph (b)(2)(iv), the partners' capital accounts will be considered to be determined and maintained in accordance with the rules of this paragraph (b)(2)(iv) if, and only if, each partner's capital account is increased by (1) the amount of money contributed by him to the partnership, (2) the fair market value of property contributed by him to the partnership (net of liabilities secured by such contributed property that the partnership is considered to assume or take subject to under section 752), and (3) allocations to him of partnership income and gain (or items thereof), including income and gain exempt from tax and income and gain described in paragraph (b)(2)(iv)(g) of this section, but excluding income and gain described in paragraph (b)(4)(i) of this section; and is decreased by (4) the amount of money distributed to him by the partnership, (5) the fair market value of property distributed to him by the partnership (net of liabilities secured by such distributed property that such partner is considered to assume or take subject to under section 752), (6) allocations to him of expenditures of the partnership described in section 705(a)(2)(B), and (7) allocations of partnership loss and deduction (or item thereof), including loss and deduction described in paragraph (b)(2)(iv)(g) of this section, but excluding items described in (6) above and loss or deduction described in paragraphs (b)(4)(i) or (b)(4)(iii) of this section; and is otherwise adjusted in accordance with the additional rules set forth in this paragraph (b)(2)(iv). For purposes of this paragraph, a partner who has more than one interest in a partnership shall have a single capital account that reflects all such interests, regardless of the class of interests owned by such partner (e.g., general or limited) and regardless of the time or manner in which such interests were acquired. For liabilities assumed before June 24, 2003, references to liabilities in this paragraph (b)(2)(iv)(b) shall include only liabilities secured by the contributed or distributed property that are taken into account under § 752(a) and (b).

(c) Treatment of liabilities. For purposes of this paragraph (b)(2)(iv), (1) money contributed by a partner to a partnership includes the amount of any partnership liabilities that are assumed by such partner (other than liabilities described in paragraph (b)(2)(iv)(b)(5) of this section that are assumed by a distributee partner) but does not include increases in such partner's share of partnership liabilities (see section 752(a)), and (2) money distributed to a partner by a partnership includes the amount of such partner's individual liabilities that are assumed by the partnership (other than liabilities described in paragraph (b)(2)(iv)(b)(2) of this section that are assumed by the partnership) but does not include decreases in such partner's share of partnership liabilities (see section 752(b)). For purposes of this paragraph (b)(2)(iv)(c), liabilities are considered assumed only to the extent the assuming party is thereby subjected to personal liability with respect to such obligation, the obligee is aware of the assumption and can directly enforce the assuming party's obligation, and, as between the assuming party and the party from whom the liability is assumed, the assuming party is ultimately liable.

(d) Contributed property—**(1)** In general. The basic capital accounting rules contained in paragraph (b)(2)(iv)(b) of this section require that a partner's capital account be increased by the fair market value of property contributed to the partnership by such partner on the date of contribution. See example (13)(i) of paragraph (b)(5) of this section. Consistent with section 752(c), section 7701(g) does not apply in determining such fair market value.

(2) Contribution of promissory notes. Notwithstanding the general rule of paragraph (b)(2)(iv)(b)(2) of this section, except as provided in this paragraph (b)(2)(iv)(d)(2), if a promissory note is contributed to a partnership by a partner who is the maker of such note, such partner's capital account will be increased with respect to such note only when there is a taxable disposition of such note by the partnership or when the partner makes principal payments on such note. See example (1)(ix) of paragraph (b)(5) of this section. The first sentence of this paragraph (b)(2)(iv)(d)(2) shall not apply if the note referred to therein is readily tradable on an established securities market. See also paragraph (b)(2)(ii)(c) of this section. Furthermore, a partner whose interest is liquidated will be considered as satisfying his obligation to restore the deficit balance in his capital account to the extent of (i) the fair market value, at the time of contribution, of any negotiable promissory note (of which such partner is the maker) that such partner contributes to the partnership on or after the date his interest is liquidated and within the time specified in paragraph (b)(2)(ii)(b)(3) of this section, and (ii) the fair market value, at the time of liquidation, of the unsatisfied portion of any negotiable promissory note (of which such partner is the maker) that such partner previously contributed to the partnership. For purposes of the preceding sentence, the fair market valuc of a note will be no less than the outstanding principal balance of such note, provided that such note bears interest at a rate no less than the applicable federal rate at the time of valuation.

(3) Section 704(c) considerations. Section 704(c) and § 1.704–3 govern the determination of the partners' distributive shares of income, gain, loss, and deduction, as computed for tax purposes, with respect to property contributed to a partnership (see paragraph (b)(1)(vi) of this section). In cases where section 704(c) and § 1.704–3 apply to partnership property, the capital accounts of the partners will not be considered to be determined and maintained in accordance with the rules of this paragraph (b)(2)(iv) unless the partnership agreement requires that the partners' capital accounts be adjusted in accordance with paragraph (b)(2)(iv)(g) of this section for allocations to them of income, gain, loss, and deduction (including depreciation, depletion, amortization, or other cost recovery) as computed for book purposes, with respect to the property. See, however, § 1.704–3T(d)(2) for a special rule in determining the amount of book items if the partnership chooses the remedial allocation method. See also Example (13)(i) of paragraph (b)(5) of this section. Capital accounts are not adjusted to reflect allocations under section 704(c) and § 1.704–3 (e.g., tax allocations of precontribution gain or loss).

(e) Distributed property—**(1)** In general. The basic capital accounting rules contained in paragraph (b)(2)(iv)(b) of this section require that a partner's capital account be decreased by the fair market value of property distributed by the partnership (without regard to section 7701(g)) to such partner (whether in connection with a liquidation or otherwise). To satisfy this requirement, the capital accounts of the partners first must be adjusted to reflect the manner in which the unrealized income, gain, loss, and deduction inherent in such property (that has not been reflected in the capital accounts previously) would be allocated among the partners if there were a taxable disposition of such property for the fair market value of such property (taking section 7701(g) into account) on the date of distribution. See example (14)(v) of paragraph (b)(5) of this section.

(2) Distribution of promissory notes. Notwithstanding the general rule of paragraph (b)(2)(iv) (b) (5), except as provided in this paragraph (b)(2) (iv) (e)(2), if a promissory note is distributed to a partner by a partnership that is the maker of such note, such partner's capital account will be decreased with respect to such note only when there is a taxable disposition of such note by the partner or when the partnership makes principal payments on the note. The previous sentence shall not apply if a note distributed to a partner by a partnership who is the maker of such note is readily tradable on an established securities market. Furthermore, the capital account of a partner whose interest in a partnership is liquidated will be reduced to the extent of (i) the fair market value, at the time of distribution, of any negotiable promissory note (of which such partnership is the maker) that such partnership distributes to the partner on or after the date such partner's interest is liquidated and within the time specified in paragraph (b)(2)(ii)(b)(2) of this section, and (ii) the fair market value, at the time of liquidation, of the unsatisfied portion of any negotiable promissory note (of which such partnership is the maker) that such partnership previously distributed to the partner. For purposes of the preceding sentence, the fair market value of a note will be no less than the outstanding principal balance of such note, provided that such note bears interest at a rate no less than the applicable federal rate at time of valuation.

(f) Revaluations of property. A partnership agreement may, upon the occurrence of certain events, increase or decrease the capital accounts of the partners to reflect a revaluation of partnership property (including intangible assets such as goodwill) on the partnership's books. Capital accounts so adjusted will not be considered to be determined and maintained in accordance with the rules of this paragraph (b)(2)(iv) unless—

(1) The adjustments are based on the fair market value of partnership property (taking section 7701(g) into account) on the date of adjustment, and

(2) The adjustments reflect the manner in which the unrealized income, gain, loss, or deduction inherent in such property (that has not been reflected in the capital accounts previously) would be allocated among the partners if there were a taxable disposition of such property for such fair market value on that date, and

(3) The partnership agreement requires that the partners' capital accounts be adjusted in accordance with paragraph (b)(2)(iv)(g) of this section for allocations to them of depreciation, depletion, amortization, and gain or loss, as computed for book purposes, with respect to such property, and

(4) The partnership agreement requires that the partners' distributive shares of depreciation, depletion, amortization, and gain or loss, as computed for tax purposes, with respect to such property be determined so as to take account of the variation between the adjusted tax basis and book value of such property in the same manner as under section 704(c) (see paragraph (b)(4)(i) of this section), and

(5) The adjustments are made principally for a substantial non-tax business purpose—

(i) In connection with a contribution of money or other property (other than a de minimis amount) to the partnership by a new or existing partner as consideration for an interest in the partnership, or

(ii) In connection with the liquidation of the partnership or a distribution of money or other property (other than a de minimis amount) by the partnership to a retiring or continuing partner as consideration for an interest in the partnership, or

(iii) Under generally accepted industry accounting practices, provided substantially all of the partnership's property (excluding money) consists of stock, securities, commodities, options, warrants, futures, or similar instruments that are readily tradable on an established securities market.

See examples (14) and (18) of paragraph (b)(5) of this section. If the capital accounts of the partners are not adjusted to reflect the fair market value of partnership property when an interest in the partnership is acquired from or relinquished to the partnership, paragraphs (b)(1)(iii) and (b)(1)(iv) of this section should be consulted regarding the potential tax consequences that may arise if the principles of section 704(c) are not applied to determine the partners' distributive shares of depreciation, depletion, amortization, and gain or loss as computed for tax purposes, with respect to such property.

(g) Adjustments to reflect book value—**(1)** In general. Under paragraphs (b)(2)(iv)(d) and (b)(2) (iv)(f) of this section, property may be properly reflected on the books of the partnership at a book value that differs from the adjusted tax basis of such property. In these circumstances, paragraphs (b)(2)(iv)(d)(3) and (b)(2)(iv)(f)(3) of this section provide that the capital accounts of the partners will not be considered to be determined and maintained in accordance with the rules of this paragraph (b)(2)(iv) unless the partnership agreement requires the partners' capital accounts to be adjusted in accordance with this paragraph (b)(2)(iv)(g) for allocations to them of depreciation, depletion, amortization, and gain or loss, as computed for book purposes, with respect to such property. In determining whether the economic effect of an allocation of book items is substantial, consideration will be given to the effect of such allocation on the determination of the partners' distributive shares of corresponding tax items under section 704(c) and paragraph (b)(4)(i) of this section. See example (17) of paragraph (b)(5) of this section. If an allocation of book items under the partnership agreement does not have substantial economic effect (as determined under paragraphs (b)(2)(ii) and (b)(2)(iii) of this section), or is not otherwise respected under this paragraph, such items will be reallocated in accordance with the partners' interests in the partnership, and such reallocation will be the basis upon which the partners' distributive shares of the corresponding tax items are determined under section 704(c) and paragraph (b)(4)(i) of this section. See examples (13), (14), and (18) of paragraph (b)(5) of this section.

(2) Payables and receivables. References in this paragraph (b)(2)(iv) and paragraph (b)(4)(i) of this section to book and tax depreciation, depletion, amortization, and gain or loss with respect to property that has an adjusted tax basis that differs from book value include, under analogous rules and principles, the unrealized income or deduction with respect to accounts receivable, accounts payable, and other accrued but unpaid items.

(3) Determining amount of book items. The partners' capital accounts will not be considered adjusted in accordance with this paragraph (b)(2)(iv)(g) unless the amount of book depreciation, depletion, or amortization for a period with respect to an item of partnership property is the amount that bears the same relationship to the book value of such property as the depreciation (or cost recovery deduction), depletion, or amortization computed for tax purposes with respect to such property for such period bears to the adjusted tax basis of such property. If such property has a zero adjusted tax basis, the book depreciation, depletion, or amortization may be determined under any reasonable method selected by the partnership.

(h) Determinations of fair market value. For purposes of this paragraph (b)(2)(iv), the fair market value assigned to property contributed to a partnership, property distributed by a partnership, or property otherwise revalued by a partnership, will be regarded as correct, provided that (1) such value is reasonably agreed to among the partners in arm's-length negotiations, and (2) the partners have sufficiently adverse interests. If, however, these conditions are not satisfied and the value assigned to such property is overstated or understated (by more than an insignificant amount), the capital accounts of the partners will not be considered to be determined and maintained in accordance with the rules of this paragraph (b)(2)(iv). Valuation of property contributed to the partnership, distributed by the partnership, or otherwise revalued by the partnership shall be on a property-by-property basis, except to the extent the regulations under section 704(c) permit otherwise.

(i) Section 705(a)(2)(B) expenditures—**(1)** In general. The basic capital accounting rules contained in paragraph (b)(2)(iv)(b) of this section require that a partner's capital account be decreased by allocations made to such partner of expenditures described in section 705(a)(2)(B). See example (11) of paragraph (b)(5) of this section. If an allocation of these expenditures under the partnership agreement does not have substantial economic effect (as determined under paragraphs (b)(2)(ii) and (b)(2)(iii) of this section), or is not otherwise respected under this paragraph, such expenditures will be reallocated in accordance with the partners' interest in the partnership.

(2) Expenses described in section 709. Except for amounts with respect to which an election is properly made under section 709(b), amounts paid or incurred to organize a partnership or to promote the sale of (or to sell) an interest in such a partnership shall, solely for purposes of this paragraph, be treated as section 705(a)(2)(B) expenditures, and upon liquidation of the partnership no further capital account adjustments will be made in respect thereof.

(3) Disallowed losses. If a deduction for a loss incurred in connection with the sale or exchange of partnership property is disallowed to the partnership under section 267(a)(1) or section 707(b), that deduction shall, solely for purposes of this paragraph, be treated as a section 705(a)(2)(B) expenditure.

(j) Basis adjustments to section 38 property. The capital accounts of the partners will not be considered to be determined and maintained in accordance with the rules of this paragraph (b)(2)(iv) unless such capital accounts are adjusted by the partners' shares of any upward or downward basis adjustments allocated to them under this paragraph (b)(2)(iv)(j). When there is a reduction in the adjusted tax basis of partnership section 38 property under section 48(q)(1) or section 48(q)(3), section 48(q)(6) provides for an equivalent downward adjustment to the aggregate basis of partnership interests (and no additional adjustment is made under section 705(a)(2)(B)). These downward basis adjustments shall be shared among the partners in the same proportion as the adjusted tax basis or cost of (or the qualified investment in) such section 38 property is allocated among the partners under paragraph (f) of § 1.46–3 (or paragraph (a)(4)(iv) of § 1.48–8). Conversely, when there is an increase in the adjusted tax basis of partnership section 38 property under section 48(q)(2), section 48(q)(6) provides for an equivalent upward adjustment to the aggregate basis of partnership interests. These upward adjustments shall be allocated among the partners in the same proportion as the investment tax credit from such property is recaptured by the partners under § 1.47–6.

* * *

(l) Transfers of partnership interests. The capital accounts of the partners will not be considered to be determined and maintained in accordance with the rules of this paragraph (b)(2)(iv) unless, upon the transfer of all or a part of an interest in the partnership, the capital account of the transferor that is attributable to the transferred interest carries over to the transferee partner. (See paragraph (b)(2)(iv)(m) of this section for rules concerning the effect of a section 754 election on the capital accounts of the partners.) If the transfer of an interest in a partnership causes a termination of the partnership under section 708(b(1)(B), the capital account of the transferee partner and the capital accounts of the other partners of the terminated partnership carry over to the new partnership that is formed as a result of the termination of the partnership under § 1.708–1 (b)(1)(iv). Moreover, the deemed contribution of assets and liabilities by the terminated partnership to a new partnership and the deemed liquidation that occur under § 1.708–1(b)(1)(iv) are disregarded for purposes of this paragraph (b)(2)(iv). See Example 13 of paragraph (b)(5) of this section and the example in § 1.708–1(b)(1)(iv). The previous three sentences apply to terminations of partnerships under section 708(b)(1)(B) occurring on or after May 9, 1997; however, the sentences may be applied to terminations occurring on or after May 9, 1996, provided that the partnership and its partners apply the sentences to the termination in a consistent manner.

(m) Section 754 elections—**(1)** In general. The capital accounts of the partners will not be considered to be determined and maintained in accordance with the rules of this paragraph (b)(2)(iv) unless, upon adjustment to the adjusted tax basis of partnership property under section 732, 734, or 743, the capital accounts of the partners are adjusted as provided in this paragraph (b)(2)(iv)(m).

(2) Section 743 adjustments. In the case of a transfer of all or a part of an interest in a partnership that has a section 754 election in effect for the partnership taxable year in which such transfer occurs, adjustments to the adjusted tax basis of partnership property under section 743 shall not be reflected in the capital account of the transferee partner or on the books of the partnership, and subsequent capital account adjustments for distributions (see paragraph (b)(2)(iv)(e)(1) of this section) and for depreciation, depletion, amortization, and gain or loss with respect to such property will disregard the effect of such basis adjustment. The preceding sentence shall not apply to the extent such basis adjustment is allocated to the common basis of partnership property under paragraph (b)(1) of § 1.734–2; in these cases, such basis adjustment shall, except as provided in paragraph (b)(2)(iv)(m)(5) of this section, give rise to adjustments to the capital accounts of the partners in accordance with their interests in the partnership under paragraph (b)(3) of this section. See examples (13)(iii) and (iv) of paragraph (b)(5) of this section.

(3) Section 732 adjustments. In the case of a transfer of all or a part of an interest in a partnership that does not have a section 754 election in effect for the partnership taxable year in which such transfer occurs, adjustments to the adjusted tax basis of partnership property under section 732(d) will be treated in the capital accounts of the partners in the same manner as section 743 basis adjustments are treated under paragraph (b)(2)(iv)(m)(2) of this section.

(4) Section 734 adjustments. Except as provided in paragraph (b)(2)(iv)(m)(5) of this section, in the case of a distribution of property in liquidation of a partner's interest in the partnership by a partnership that has a section 754 election in effect for the partnership taxable year in which the distribution occurs, the partner who receives the distribution that gives rise to the adjustment to the adjusted tax basis of partnership property under section 734 shall have a corresponding adjustment made to his capital account. If such distribution is made other than in liquidation of a partner's interest in the partnership, however, except as provided in paragraph (b)(2) (iv)(m)(5) of this section, the capital accounts of the partners shall be adjusted by the amount of the adjustment to the adjusted tax basis of partnership property under section 734, and such capital account adjustment shall be shared among the partners in the manner in which the unrealized income and gain that is displaced by such adjustment would have been shared if the property whose basis is adjusted were sold immediately prior to such adjustment for its recomputed adjusted tax basis.

(5) Limitations on adjustments. Adjustments may be made to the capital account of a partner (or his successor in interest) in respect of basis adjustments to partnership property under sections 732, 734, and 743 only to the extent that such basis adjustments (i) are permitted to be made to one or more items of partnership property under section 755, and (ii) result in an increase or a decrease in the amount at which such property is carried on the partnership's balance sheet, as computed for book purposes. For example, if the book value of partnership property exceeds the adjusted tax basis of such property, a basis adjustment to such property may be reflected in a partner's capital account only to the extent such adjustment exceeds the difference between the book value of such property and the adjusted tax basis of such property prior to such adjustment.

(n) Partnership level characterization. Except as otherwise provided in paragraph (b)(2)(iv)(k) of this section, the capital accounts of the partners will not be considered to be determined and maintained in accordance with the rules of this paragraph (b)(2)(iv) unless adjustments to such capital accounts in respect of partnership income, gain, loss, deduction, and section 705(a)(2)(B) expenditures (or item thereof) are made with reference to the Federal tax treatment of such items (and in the case of book items, with reference to the Federal tax treatment of the corresponding tax items) at the partnership level, without regard to any requisite or elective tax treatment of such items at the partner level (for example, under section 58(i)). However, a partnership that incurs mining exploration expenditures will determine the Federal tax treatment of income, gain, loss, and deduction with respect to the property to which such expenditures relate at the partnership level only after first taking into account the elections made by its partners under section 617 and section 703(b)(4).

(o) Guaranteed payments. Guaranteed payments to a partner under section 707(c) cause the capital account of the recipient partner to be adjusted only to the extent of such partner's distributive share of any partnership deduction, loss, or other downward capital account adjustment resulting from such payment.

(p) Minor discrepancies. Discrepancies between the balances in the respective capital accounts of the partners and the balances that would be in such respective capital accounts if they had been determined and maintained in accordance with this paragraph (b)(2)(iv) will not adversely affect the validity of an allocation, provided that such discrepancies are minor and are attributable to good faith error by the partnership.

(q) Adjustments where guidance is lacking. If the rules of this paragraph (b)(2)(iv) fail to provide guidance on how adjustments to the capital accounts of the partners should be made to reflect particular adjustments to partnership capital on the books of the partnership, such capital accounts will not be considered to be determined and maintained in accordance with those rules unless such capital account adjustments are made in a manner that (1) maintains equality between the aggregate governing capital accounts of the partners and the amount of partnership capital reflected on the partnership's balance sheet, as computed for book purposes, (2) is consistent with the underlying economic arrangement of the partners, and (3) is based, wherever practicable, on Federal tax accounting principles.

(r) Restatement of capital accounts. With respect to partnerships that began operating in a taxable year beginning before May 1, 1986, the capital accounts of the partners of which have not been determined and maintained in accordance with the rules of this paragraph (b)(2)(iv) since inception, such capital accounts shall not be considered to be determined and maintained in accordance with the rules of this paragraph (b)(2)(iv) for taxable years beginning after April 30, 1986, unless either—

(1) such capital accounts are adjusted, effective for the first partnership taxable year beginning after April 30, 1986, to reflect the fair market value of partnership property as of the first day of such taxable year, and in connection with such adjustment, the rules contained in paragraph (b)(2)(iv)(f)(2), (3), and (4) of this section are satisfied, or

(2) the differences between the balance in each partner's capital account and the balance that would be in such partner's capital account if capital accounts had been determined and maintained in accordance with this paragraph (b)(2)(iv) throughout the full term of the partnership are not significant (for example, such differences are solely attributable to a failure to provide for treatment of section 709 expenses in accordance with the rules of paragraph (b)(2)(iv)(i)(2) of this section or to a failure to follow the rules in paragraph (b)(2)(iv)(m) of this section), and capital accounts are adjusted to bring them into conformity with the rules of this paragraph (b)(2)(iv) no later than the end of the first partnership taxable year beginning after April 30, 1986.

With respect to a partnership that began operating in a taxable year beginning before May 1, 1986, modifications to the partnership agreement adopted on or before November 1, 1988, to make the capital account adjustments required to comply with this paragraph, and otherwise to satisfy the requirements of this paragraph, will be treated as if such modifications were included in the partnership agreement before the end of the first partnership taxable year beginning after April 30, 1986. However, compliance with the previous sentences will have no bearing on the validity of allocations that relate to partnership taxable years beginning before May 1, 1986.

(3) Partner's interest in the partnership—(i) In general. References in section 704(b) and this paragraph to a partner's interest in the partnership, or to the partner's interests in the partnership, signify the manner in which the partners have agreed to share the economic benefit or burden (if any) corresponding to the income, gain, loss, deduction, or credit (or item thereof) that is allocated. Except with respect to partnership items that cannot have economic effect (such as nonrecourse deductions of the partnership), this sharing arrangement may or may not correspond to the overall economic arrangement of the partners. Thus, a partner who has a 50 percent overall interest in the partnership may have a 90 percent interest in a particular item of income or deduction. (For example, in the case of an unexpected downward adjustment to the capital account of a partner who does not have a deficit make-up obligation that causes such partner to have a negative capital account, it may be necessary to allocate a disproportionate amount of gross income of the partnership to such partner for such year so as to bring that partner's capital account back up to zero.) The determination of a partner's interest in a partnership shall be made by taking into account all facts and circumstances relating to the economic arrangement of the partners. All partners' interests in the partnership are presumed to be equal (determined on a per capita basis). However, this presumption may be rebutted by the taxpayer or the Internal Revenue Service by establishing facts and circumstances that show that the partners' interests in the partnership are otherwise.

(ii) Factors considered. In determining a partner's interest in the partnership, the following factors are among those that will be considered:

(a) The partners' relative contributions to the partnership,

(b) The interests of the partners in economic profits and losses (if different than that in taxable income or loss),

(c) The interests of the partners in cash flow and other non-liquidating distributions, and

(d) The rights of the partners to distributions of capital upon liquidation.

The provisions of this subparagraph (b)(3) are illustrated by examples (1)(i) and (ii), (4)(i), (5)(i) and (ii), (6), (7), (8), (10)(ii), (16)(i), and (19)(iii) of paragraph (b)(5) of this section. See paragraph (b)(4)(i) of this section concerning rules for determining the partners' interests in the partnership with respect to certain tax items.

(iii) Certain determinations. If—

(a) Requirements (1) and (2) of paragraph (b)(2)(ii)(b) of this section are satisfied, and

(b) All or a portion of an allocation of income, gain, loss, or deduction made to a partner for a partnership taxable year does not have economic effect under paragraph (b)(2)(ii) of this section,

the partners' interests in the partnership with respect to the portion of the allocation that lacks economic effect will be determined by comparing the manner in which distributions (and contributions) would be made if all partnership property were sold at book value and the partnership were liquidated immediately following the end of the taxable year to which the allocation relates with the manner in which distributions (and contributions) would be made if all partnership property were sold at book value and the partnership were liquidated immediately following the end of the prior taxable year, and adjusting the result for the items described in (4), (5), and (6) of paragraph (b)(2)(ii)(d) of this section. A determination made under this paragraph (b)(3)(iii) will have no force if the economic effect of valid allocations made in the same manner is insubstantial under paragraph (b)(2)(iii) of this section. See examples

(1)(iv), (v), and (vi), and (15)(ii) and (iii) of paragraph (b)(5) of this section.

(4) Special rules—(i) Allocations to reflect revaluations. If partnership property is, under paragraphs (b)(2)(iv)(d) or (b)(2)(iv)(f) of this section, properly reflected in the capital accounts of the partners and on the books of the partnership at a book value that differs from the adjusted tax basis of such property, then depreciation, depletion, amortization, and gain or loss, as computed for book purposes, with respect to such property will be greater or less than the depreciation, depletion, amortization, and gain or loss, as computed for tax purposes, with respect to such property. In these cases the capital accounts of the partners are required to be adjusted solely for allocations of the book items to such partners (see paragraph (b)(2)(iv)(g) of this section), and the partners' shares of the corresponding tax items are not independently reflected by further adjustments to the partners' capital accounts. Thus, separate allocations of these tax items cannot have economic effect under paragraph (b)(2)(ii)(b)(1) of this section, and the partners' distributive shares of such tax items must (unless governed by section 704(c)) be determined in accordance with the partners' interests in the partnership. These tax items must be shared among the partners in a manner that takes account of the variation between the adjusted tax basis of such property and its book value in the same manner as variations between the adjusted tax basis and fair market value of property contributed to the partnership are taken into account in determining the partners' shares of tax items under section 704(c). See examples (14) and (18) of paragraph (b)(5) of this section.

(ii) Credits. Allocations of tax credits and tax credit recapture are not reflected by adjustments to the partners' capital accounts (except to the extent that adjustments to the adjusted tax basis of partnership section 38 property in respect of tax credits and tax credit recapture give rise to capital account adjustments under paragraph (b)(2)(iv)(j) of this section). Thus, such allocations cannot have economic effect under paragraph (b)(2)(ii)(b)(1) of this section, and the tax credits and tax credit recapture must be allocated in accordance with the partners' interests in the partnership as of the time the tax credit or credit recapture arises. With respect to the investment tax credit provided by section 38, allocations of cost or qualified investment made in accordance with paragraph (f) of § 1.46–3 and paragraph (a)(4)(iv) of § 1.48–8 shall be deemed to be made in accordance with the partners' interests in the partnership. With respect to other tax credits, if a partnership expenditure (whether or not deductible) that gives rise to a tax credit in a partnership taxable year also gives rise to valid allocations of partnership loss or deduction (or other downward capital account adjustments) for such year, then the partners' interests in the partnership with respect to such credit (or the cost giving rise thereto) shall be in the same proportion as such partners' respective distributive shares of such loss or deduction (and adjustments). See example (11) of paragraph (b)(5) of this section. Identical principles shall apply in determining the partners' interests in the partnership with respect to tax credits that arise from receipts of the partnership (whether or not taxable).

(iii) Excess percentage depletion. To the extent the percentage depletion in respect of an item of depletable property of the partnership exceeds the adjusted tax basis of such property, allocations of such excess percentage depletion are not reflected by adjustments to the partners' capital accounts. Thus, such allocations cannot have economic effect under paragraph (b)(2)(ii)(b)(1) of this section, and such excess percentage depletion must be allocated in accordance with the partners' interests in the partnership. The partners' interests in the partnership for a partnership taxable year with respect to such excess percentage depletion shall be in the same proportion as such partners' respective distributive shares of gross income from the depletable property (as determined under section 613(c)) for such year. See example (12) of paragraph (b)(5) of this section. See paragraphs (b)(2)(iv)(k) and (b)(4)(v) of this section for special rules concerning oil and gas properties of the partnership.

(iv) Allocations attributable to nonrecourse liabilities. The rules for allocations attributable to nonrecourse liabilities are contained in regulation section 1.704–2.

* * *

(vi) Amendments to partnership agreement. If an allocation has substantial economic effect under paragraph (b)(2) of this section or is deemed to be made in accordance with the partners' interests in the partnership under paragraph (b)(4) of this section under the partnership agreement that is effective for the taxable year to which such allocation relates, and such partnership agreement thereafter is modified, both the tax consequences of the modification and the facts and circumstances surrounding the modification will be closely scrutinized to determine whether the purported modification was part of the original agreement. If it is determined that the purported modification was part of the original agreement, prior allocations may be reallocated in a manner consistent with the modified terms of the agreement, and subsequent allocations may be reallocated to take account of such modified terms. For example, if a partner is obligated by the partnership agreement to restore the deficit balance in his capital account (or any limited dollar amount thereof) in accordance with requirement (3) of paragraph (b)(2)(ii)(b) of this section and, thereafter, such obligation is eliminated or reduced (other than as provided in paragraph (b) (2) (ii)(f) of this section), or is not complied with in a timely manner, such elimination, reduction, or non-compliance may be treated as if it always were part of the partnership agreement for purposes of making any reallocations and determining the appropriate limitations period.

(vii) Recapture. For special rules applicable to the allocation of recapture income or credit, see paragraph (e) of § 1.1245–1, paragraph (f) of § 1.1250–1, paragraph (c) of § 1.1254–1, and paragraph (a) of § 1.47–6.

(5) Examples. The operation of the rules in this paragraph is illustrated by the following examples:

Example (1). **(i)** A and B form a general partnership with cash contributions of $40,000 each, which cash is used to purchase depreciable personal property at a cost of $80,000. The partnership elects under section 48(q)(4) to reduce the amount of investment tax credit in lieu of adjusting the tax basis of such property. The partnership agreement provides that A and B will have equal shares of taxable income and loss (computed without regard to cost recovery deductions) and cash flow and that all cost recovery deductions on the property will be allocated to A. The agreement further provides that the partners' capital accounts will be determined and maintained in accordance with paragraph (b)(2)(iv) of the section, but that upon liquidation of the partnership, distributions will be made equally between the partners (regardless of capital account balances) and no partner will be required to restore the deficit balance in his capital account for distribution to partners with positive capital accounts balances. In the partnership's first taxable year, it recognizes operating income equal to its operating expenses and has an additional $20,000 cost recovery deduction, which is allocated entirely to A. That A and B will be entitled to equal distributions on liquidation, even though A is allocated the entire $20,000 cost recovery deduction, indicates A will not bear the full risk of the economic loss corresponding to such deduction if such loss occurs. Under paragraph (b)(2)(ii) of this section, the allocation lacks economic effect and will be disregarded. The partners made equal contributions to the partnership, share equally in other taxable income and loss and in cash flow, and will share equally in liquidation proceeds, indicating that their actual economic arrangement is to bear the risk imposed by the potential decrease in the value of the property equally. Thus, under paragraph (b)(3) of this section the partners' interests in the partnership are equal, and the cost recovery deduction will be reallocated equally between A and B.

(ii) Assume the same facts as in (i) except that the partnership agreement provides that liquidation proceeds will be distributed in accordance with capital account balances if the partnership is liquidated during the first five years of its existence but that liquidation proceeds will be distributed equally if the partnership is liquidated thereafter. Since the partnership agreement does not provide for the requirement contained in paragraph (b)(2)(ii)(b)(2) of this section to be satisfied throughout the term of the partnership, the partnership allocations do not have economic effect. Even if the partnership agreement provided for the requirement contained in paragraph (b)(2)(ii)(b)(2) to be satisfied throughout the term of the partnership, such allocations would not have economic effect unless the requirement contained in paragraph (b)(2)(ii)(b)(3) of this section or the alternate economic effect test contained in paragraph (b)(2)(ii)(d) of this section were satisfied.

(iii) Assume the same facts as in (i) except that distributions in liquidation of the partnership (or any partner's interest) are to be made in accordance with the partners' positive capital account balances throughout the term of the partnership (as set forth in paragraph (b)(2)(ii)(b)(2) of this section). Assume further that the partnership agreement contains a qualified income offset (as defined in paragraph (b)(2)(ii)(d) of this section) and that, as of the end of each partnership taxable year, the items described in paragraphs (b)(2)(ii)(d)(4), (5), and (6) of this section are not reasonably expected to cause or increase a deficit balance in A's capital account.

	A	B
Capital account upon formation.........	$40,000	$40,000
Less: year 1 cost recovery deduction..	(20,000)	0
Capital account at end of year 1	$20,000	$40,000

Under the alternate economic effect test contained in paragraph (b)(2)(ii)(d) of this section, the allocation of the $20,000 cost recovery deduction to A has economic effect.

(iv) Assume the same facts as in (iii) and that in the partnership's second taxable year it recognizes operating income equal to its operating expenses and has a $25,000 cost recovery deduction which, under the partnership agreement, is allocated entirely to A.

	A	B
Capital account at beginning of year 2..	$20,000	$40,000
Less: year 2 cost recovery deduction..	(25,000)	0
Capital account at end of year 2	($5,000)	$40,000

The allocation of the $25,000 cost recovery deduction to A satisfies that alternate economic effect test contained in paragraph (b)(2)(ii)(d) of this section only to the extent of $20,000. Therefore, only $20,000 of such allocation has economic effect, and the remaining $5,000 must be reallocated in accordance with the partners' interests in the partnership. Under the partnership agreement, if the property were sold immediately following the end of the partnership's second taxable year for $35,000 (its adjusted tax basis), the $35,000 would be distributed to B. Thus, B, and not A, bears the economic burden corresponding to $5,000 of the $25,000 cost recovery deduction allocated to A. Under paragraph (b)(3)(iii) of this section, $5,000 of such cost recovery deduction will be reallocated to B.

(v) Assume the same facts as in (iv) except that the cost recovery deduction for the partnership's second taxable year is $20,000 instead of $25,000. The allocation of such cost recovery deduction to A has economic effect under the alternate economic effect test contained in paragraph (b)(2)(ii)(d) of this section. Assume further that the property is sold for $35,000 immediately following the end of the partnership's second taxable year, resulting in a $5,000 taxable loss ($40,000 adjusted tax basis less $35,000 sales price), and the partnership is liquidated.

	A	B
Capital account at beginning of year 2	$20,000	$40,000
Less: year 2 cost recovery deduction	(20,000)	0
Capital account at end of year 2	0	$40,000
Less: loss on sale	(2,500)	(2,500)
Capital account before liquidation	($2,500)	$37,500

Under the partnership agreement the $35,000 sales proceeds are distributed to B. Since B bears the entire economic burden corresponding to the $5,000 taxable loss from the sale of the property, the allocation of $2,500 of such loss to A does not have economic effect and must be reallocated in accordance with the partners' interests in the partnership. Under paragraph (b)(3)(iii) of this section, such $2,500 loss will be reallocated to B.

(vi) Assume the same facts as in (iv) except that the cost recovery deduction for the partnership's second taxable year is $20,000 instead of $25,000, and that as of the end of the partnership's second taxable year it is reasonably expected that during its third taxable year the partnership will (1) have operating income equal to its operating expenses (but will have no cost recovery deductions), (2) borrow $10,000 (recourse) and distribute such amount $5,000 to A and $5,000 to B, and (3) thereafter sell the partnership property, repay the $10,000 liability, and liquidate. In determining the extent to which the alternate economic effect test contained in paragraph (b)(2)(ii)(d) of this section is satisfied as of the end of the partnership's second taxable year, the fair market value of partnership property is presumed to be equal to its adjusted tax basis (in accordance with paragraph (b)(2)(iii)(c) of this section). Thus, it is presumed that the selling price of such property during the partnership's third taxable year will be its $40,000 adjusted tax basis. Accordingly, there can be no reasonable expectation that there will be increases to A's capital account in the partnership's third taxable year that will offset the expected $5,000 distribution to A. Therefore, the distribution of the loan proceeds must be taken into account in determining to what extent the alternate economic effect test contained in paragraph (b)(2)(ii)(d) is satisfied.

	A	B
Capital account at beginning of year 2	$20,000	$40,000
Less: expected future distribution.	(5,000)	(5,000)
Less: year 2 cost recovery deduction	(20,000)	(0)
Hypothetical capital account at end of year 2	($5,000)	$35,000

Upon sale of the partnership property, the $40,000 presumed sales proceeds would be used to repay the $10,000 liability, and the remaining $30,000 would be distributed to B. Under these circumstances the allocation of the $20,000 cost recovery deduction to A in the partnership's second taxable year satisfies the alternate economic effect test contained in paragraph (b)(2)(ii)(d) of this section only to the extent of $15,000. Under paragraph (b)(3)(iii) of this section, the remaining $5,000 of such deduction will be reallocated to B. The results in this example would be the same even if the partnership agreement also provided that any gain (whether ordinary income or capital gain) upon the sale of the property would be allocated to A to the extent of the prior allocations of cost recovery deductions to him, and, at end of the partnership's second taxable year, the partners were confident that the gain on the sale of the property in the partnership's third taxable year would be sufficient to offset the expected $5,000 distribution to A.

(vii) Assume the same facts as in (iv) except that the partnership agreement also provides that any partner with a deficit balance in his capital account following the liquidation of his interest must restore that deficit to the partnership (as set forth in paragraph (b)(2)(ii)(b)(3) of this section). Thus, if the property were sold for $35,000 immediately after the end of the partnership's second taxable year, the $35,000 would be distributed to B, A would contribute $5,000 (the deficit balance in his capital account) to the partnership, and that $5,000 would be distributed to B. The allocation of the entire $25,000 cost recovery deduction to A in the partnership's second taxable year has economic effect.

(viii) Assume the same facts as in (vii) except that A's obligation to restore the deficit balance in his capital account is limited to a maximum of $5,000. The allocation of the $25,000 cost recovery deduction to A in the partnership's second taxable year has economic effect under the alternate economic effect test contained in paragraph (b)(2)(ii)(d) of this section. At the end of such year, A makes an additional $5,000 contribution to the partnership (thereby eliminating the $5,000 deficit balance in his capital account). Under paragraph (b)(2)(ii)(f) of this section, A's obligation to restore up to $5,000 of the deficit balance in his capital account may be eliminated after he contributes the additional $5,000 without affecting the validity of prior allocations.

(ix) Assume the same facts as in (iv) except that upon formation of the partnership A also contributes to the partnership his negotiable promissory note with a $5,000 principal balance. The note unconditionally obligates A to pay an additional $5,000 to the partnership at the earlier of (a) the beginning of the partnership's fourth taxable year, or (b) the end of the partnership taxable year in which A's interest is liquidated. Under paragraph (b)(2)(ii)(c) of this section, A is considered obligated to restore up to $5,000 of the deficit balance in his capital account to the partnership. Accordingly, under the alternate economic effect test contained in paragraph (b)(2)(ii)(d) of this section, the allocation of the $25,000 cost recovery deduction to A in the partnership's second taxable year has economic effect. The results in this example would be the same if (1) the note A contributed to the partnership were payable only at the end of the partnership's fourth taxable year (so that A would not be required to satisfy the note upon liquidation of his interest in the partnership), and (2) the partnership agreement provided that upon liquidation of A's interest, the partnership would retain A's note, and A would contribute to the partnership the excess of the outstanding principal balance of the note over its then fair market value.

(x) Assume the same facts as in (ix) except that A's obligation to contribute an additional $5,000 to the partnership is not evidenced by a promissory note. Instead, the partnership agreement imposes upon A the obligation to make an additional $5,000 contribution to the partnership at the earlier of (a) the beginning of the partnership's fourth taxable year, or (b) the end of the partnership taxable year in which A's interest is liquidated. Under paragraph (b)(2)(ii)(c) of this section, as a result of A's deferred contribution requirement, A is considered obligated to restore up to $5,000 of the deficit balance in his capital account to the partnership. Accordingly, under the alternate economic effect test contained in paragraph (b)(2)(ii)(d) of this section, the allocation of the $25,000 cost recovery deduction to A in the partnership's second taxable year has economic effect.

(xi) Assume the same facts as in (vii) except that the partnership agreement also provides that any gain (whether ordinary income or capital gain) upon the sale of the property will be allocated to A to the extent of the prior allocations to A of cost recovery deductions from such property, and additional gain will be allocated equally between A and B. At the time the allocations of cost recovery deductions were made to A, the partners believed there would be gain on the sale of the property in an amount sufficient to offset the allocations of cost recovery deductions to A. Nevertheless, the existence of the gain chargeback provision will not cause the economic effect of the allocations to be insubstantial under paragraph (b)(2)(iii)(c) of this sec-tion, since in testing whether the economic effect of such allocations is substantial, the recovery property is presumed to decrease in value by the amount of such deductions.

Example (2). C and D form a general partnership solely to acquire and lease machinery that is 5-year recovery property under section 168. Each contributes $100,000, and the partnership obtains an $800,000 recourse loan to purchase the machinery. The partnership elects under section 48(q)(4) to reduce the amount of investment tax credit in lieu of adjusting the tax basis of such machinery. The partnership, C, and D have calendar taxable years. The partnership agreement provides that the partners' capital accounts will be determined and maintained in accordance with paragraph (b)(2)(iv) of this section, distributions in liquidation of the partnership (or any partner's interest) will be made in accordance with the partners' positive capital account balances, and any partner with a deficit balance in his capital account following the liquidation of his interest must restore that deficit to the partnership (as set forth in paragraphs (b)(2)(ii)(b)(2) and (3) of this section). The partnership agreement further provides that (a) partnership net taxable loss will be allocated 90 percent to C and 10 percent to D until such time as there is partnership net taxable income, and therefore C will be allocated 90 percent of such taxable income until he has been allocated partnership net taxable income equal to the partnership net taxable loss previously allocated to him, (b) all further partnership net taxable income or loss will be allocated equally between C and D, and (c) distributions of operating cash flow will be made equally between C and D. The partnership enters into a 12-year lease with a financially secure corporation under which the partnership expects to have a net taxable loss in each of its first 5 partnership taxable years due to cost recovery deductions with respect to the machinery and net taxable income in each of its following 7 partnership taxable years, in part due to the absence of such cost recovery deductions. There is a strong likelihood that the partnership's net taxable loss in partnership taxable years 1 through 5 will be $100,000, $90,000, $80,000, $70,000, and $60,000, respectively, and the partnership's net taxable income in partnership taxable years 6 through 12 will be $40,000, $50,000, $60,000, $70,000, $80,000, $90,000, and $100,000, respectively. Even though there is a strong likelihood that the allocations of net taxable loss in years 1 through 5 will be largely offset by other allocations in partnership taxable years 6 through 12, and even if it is assumed that the total tax liability of the partners in years 1 through 12 will be less than if the allocations had not been provided in the partnership agreement, the economic effect of the allocations will not be insubstantial under paragraph (b)(2)(iii)(c) of this section. This is because at the time such allocations became part of the partnership agreement, there was a strong likelihood that the allocations of net taxable loss in years 1 through 5 would not be largely offset by allocations of income within 5 years (determined on a first-in, first-out basis). The year 1 allocation will not be offset until years 6, 7, and 8, the year 2 allocation will not be offset until years 8 and 9, the year 3 allocation will not be offset until years 9 and 10, the year 4 allocation will not be offset until years 10 and 11, and the year 5 allocation will not be offset until years 11 and 12.

Example (3). E and F enter into a partnership agreement to develop and market experimental electronic devices. E contributes $2,500 cash and agrees to devote his full-time services to the partnership. F contributes $100,000 cash and agrees to obtain a loan for the partnership for any additional capital needs. The partnership agreement provides that all deductions for research and experimental expenditures and interest on partnership loans are to be allocated to F. In addition, F will be allocated 90 percent, and E 10 percent, of partnership taxable income or loss, computed net of the deductions for such research and experimental expenditures and interest, until F has received allocations of such taxable income equal to the sum of such research and experimental expenditures, such interest expense, and his share of such taxable loss. Thereafter, E and F will share all taxable income and loss equally. Operating cash flow will be distributed equally between E and F. The partnership agreement also provides that E's and F's capital accounts will be determined and maintained in accordance with paragraph (b)(2)(iv) of this section, distributions in liquidation of the partnership (or any partner's interest) will be made in accordance with the partners' positive capital account balances, and any partner with a deficit balance in his capital account following the liquidation of his interest must restore that deficit to the partnership (as set forth in paragraphs (b)(2)(ii)(b)(2) and (3) of this section). These allocations have economic effect. In addition, in view of the nature of the partnership's activities, there is not a strong likelihood at the time the allocations become part of the partnership agreement that the economic effect of the allocations to F of deductions for research and experimental expenditures and interest on partnership loans will be largely offset by allocations to F of partnership net taxable income. The economic effect of the allocations is substantial.

Example (4). (i) G and H contribute $75,000 and $25,000, respectively, in forming a general partnership. The partnership agreement provides that all income, gain, loss, and deduction will be allocated equally between the partners, that the partners' capital accounts will be determined and maintained in accordance with paragraph (b)(2)(iv) of this section, but that all partnership distributions will, regardless of capital account balances, be made 75 percent to G and 25 percent to H. Following the liquidation of the partnership, neither partner is required to restore the deficit balance in his capital account to the partnership for distribution to partners with positive capital account balances. The allocations in the partnership agreement do not have economic effect. Since contributions were made in a 75/25 ratio and the partnership agreement indicates that all economic profits and losses of the partnership are to be shared in a 75/25 ratio, under paragraph (b)(3) of this section, partnership income, gain, loss, and deduction will be reallocated 75 percent to G and 25 percent to H.

(ii) Assume the same facts as in (i) except that the partnership maintains no capital accounts and the partnership agreement provides that all income, gain, loss, deduction, and credit will be allocated 75 percent to G and 25 percent to H. G and H are ultimately liable (under a State law right of contribution) for 75 percent and 25 percent, respectively, of any debts of the partnership. Although the allocations do not satisfy the requirements of paragraph (b)(2)(ii)(b) of this section, the allocations have economic effect under the economic effect equivalence test of paragraph (b)(2)(ii)(i) of this section.

(iii) Assume the same facts as in (i) except that the partnership agreement provides that any partner with a deficit balance in his capital account must restore that deficit to the partnership (as set forth in paragraph (b)(2)(ii)(b)(2) of this section). Although the allocations do not satisfy the requirements of paragraph (b)(2)(ii)(b) of this section, the allocations have economic effect under the economic effect equivalence test of paragraph (b)(2)(ii)(i) of this section.

Example (5). (i) Individuals I and J are the only partners of an investment partnership. The partnership owns corporate stocks, corporate debt instruments, and tax-exempt debt instruments. Over the next several years, I expects to be in the 50 percent marginal tax bracket, and J expects to be in the 15 percent marginal tax bracket. There is a strong likelihood that in each of the next several years the partnership will realize between $450 and $550 of tax-exempt interest and between $450 and $550 of a combination of taxable interest and dividends from its investments. I and J made equal capital contributions to the partnership, and they have agreed to share equally in gains and losses from the sale of the partnership's investment securities. I and J agree, however, that rather than share interest and dividends of the partnership equally, they will allocate the partnership's tax-exempt interest 80 percent to I and 20 percent to J and will distribute cash derived from interest received on the tax-exempt bonds in the same percentages. In addition, they agree to allocate 100 percent of the partnership's taxable interest and dividends to J and to distribute cash derived from interest and dividends received on the corporate stocks and debt instruments 100 percent to J. The partnership agreement further provides that the partners' capital accounts will be determined and maintained in accordance with paragraph (b)(2)(iv) of this section, distributions in liquidation of the partnership (or any partner's interest) will be made in accordance with the partner's positive capital account balances, and any partner with a deficit balance in his capital account following the liquidation of his interest must restore that deficit to the partnership (as set forth in paragraphs (b)(2)(ii)(b)(2) and (3) of this section). The allocation of taxable interest and dividends and tax-exempt interest has economic effect, but that economic effect is not substantial under the general rules set forth in paragraph (b)(2)(iii) of this section. Without the allocation I would be allocated between $225 and $275 of tax-exempt interest and between $225 and $275 of a combination of taxable interest and dividends, which (net of Federal income taxes he would owe on such income) would give I between $337.50 and $412.50 after tax. With the allocation, however, I will be allocated between $360 and $440 of tax-exempt interest and no taxable interest and dividends, which (net of Federal income taxes) will give I between $360 and $440 after tax. Thus, at the time the allocations became part of the partnership agreement, I is expected to enhance his after-tax economic consequences as a result of the allocations. On the other hand, there is a strong likelihood that neither I nor J will substantially diminish his after-tax economic consequences as a result of the allocations. Under the combination of likely investment outcomes least favorable for J, the partnership would realize $550 of tax-exempt interest and $450 of taxable interest and dividends, giving J $492.50 after tax (which is more than the $466.25 after tax J would have received if each of such amounts had been allocated equally between the partners). Under the combination of likely investment outcomes least favorable for I, the partnership would realize $450 of tax-exempt interest and $550 of taxable interest and dividends, giving I $360 after tax (which is not substantially less than the $362.50 he would have received if each of such amounts had been allocated equally between the partners). Accordingly, the allocations in the partnership agreement must be reallocated in accordance with the partners' interests in the partnership under paragraph (b)(3) of this section.

(ii) Assume the same facts as in (i). In addition, assume that in the first partnership taxable year in which the allocation arrangement described in (i) applies, the partnership realizes $450 of tax-exempt interest and $550 of taxable interest and dividends, so that, pursuant to the partnership agreement, I's capital account is credited with $360 (80 percent of the tax-exempt interest), and J's capital account is credited with $640 (20 percent of the tax-exempt interest and 100 percent of the taxable interest and dividends). The allocations of tax-exempt interest and taxable interest and dividends (which do not have substantial economic effect for the reasons stated in (i) will be disregarded and will be reallocated. Since under the partnership agreement I will receive 36 percent (360/1,000) and J will receive 64 percent (640/1,000) of the partnership's total investment income in such year, under paragraph (b)(3) of this section the partnership's tax-exempt interest and taxable interest and dividends each will be reallocated 36 percent to I and 64 percent to J.

Example (6). K and L are equal partners in a general partnership formed to acquire and operate property described in section 1231(b). The partnership, K, and L have calendar taxable years. The partnership agreement provides that the partners' capital accounts will be determined and maintained in accordance with paragraph (b)(2)(iv) of this section, that distributions in liquidation of the partnership (or any partner's interest) will be made in accordance with the partners' positive capital account balances, and that any partner with a deficit balance in his capital account following the liquidation of his interest must restore that deficit to the partnership (as set forth in paragraphs (b)(2)(ii)(b)(2) and (3) of this section). For a taxable year in which the partnership expects to incur a loss on the sale of a portion of such property, the partnership agreement is amended (at the beginning of the taxable year) to allocate such loss to K, who expects to have no gains from the sale of depreciable property described in section 1231(b) in that taxable year, and to allocate an equivalent amount of partnership loss and deduction for that year of a different character to L, who expects to have such gains. Any partnership loss and deduction in excess of these allocations will be allocated equally between K and L. The amendment is effective only for that taxable year. At the time the partnership agreement is amended, there is a strong likelihood that the partnership will incur deduction or loss in the taxable year other than loss from the sale of property described in section 1231(b) in an amount that will substantially equal or exceed the expected amount of the section 1231(b) loss. The allocations in such taxable year have economic effect. However, the economic effect of the allocations is insubstantial under the test described in paragraph (b)(2)(iii)(b) of this section because there is a strong likelihood, at the time the allocations become part of the partnership agreement, that the net increases and decreases to K's and L's capital accounts will be the same at the end of the taxable year to which they apply with such allocations in effect as they would have been in the absence of such allocations, and that the total taxes of K and L for such year will be reduced as a result of such allocations. If in fact the partnership incurs deduction or loss, other than loss from the sale of property described in section 1231 (b), in an amount at least equal to the section 1231(b) loss, the loss and deduction in such taxable year will be reallocated equally between K and L under paragraph (b)(3) of this section. If not, the loss from the sale of property described in section 1231(b) and the items of deduction and other loss realized in such year will be reallocated between K and L in proportion to the net decreases in their capital accounts due to the allocation of such items under the partnership agreement.

Example (7). (i) M and N are partners in the MN general partnership, which is engaged in an active business. Income, gain, loss, and deduction from MN's business is allocated equally between M and N. The partnership, M, and N have calendar taxable years. Under the partnership agreement the partners' capital accounts will be determined and maintained in accordance with paragraph (b)(2)(iv) of this section, distributions in liquidation of the partnership (or any partner's interest) will be made in accordance with the partner's positive capital account balances, and any partner with a deficit balance in his capital account following the liquidation of his interest must restore that deficit to the partnership (as set forth in paragraphs (b)(2)(ii)(b)(2) and (3) of this section). In order to enhance the credit standing of the partnership, the partners contribute surplus funds to the partnership, which the partners agree to invest in equal dollar amounts of tax-exempt bonds and corporate stock for the partnership's first 3 taxable years. M is expected to be in a higher marginal tax bracket than N during those 3 years. At the time the decision to make these investments is made, it is agreed that, during the 3-year period of the investment, M will be allocated 90 percent and N 10 percent of the interest income from the tax-exempt bonds as well as any gain or loss from the sale thereof, and that M will be allocated 10 percent and N 90 percent of the dividend income from the corporate stock as well as any gain or loss from the sale thereof. At the time the allocations concerning the investments become part of the partnership agreement, there is not a strong likelihood that the gain or loss from the sale of the stock will be substantially equal to the gain or loss from the sale of the tax-exempt bonds, but there is a strong likelihood that the tax-exempt interest and the taxable dividends realized from these investments during the 3-year period will not differ substantially. These allocations have economic effect, and the economic effect of the allocations of the gain or loss on the sale of the tax-exempt bonds and corporate stock is substantial. The economic effect of the allocations of the tax-exempt interest and the taxable dividends, however, is not substantial under the test described in paragraph (b)(2)(iii)(c) of this section because there is a strong likelihood, at the time the allocations become part of the partnership agreement, that at the end of the 3-year period to which such allocations relate, the net increases and decreases to M's and N's capital accounts will be the same with such allocations as they would have been in the absence of such allocations, and that the total taxes of M and N for the taxable years to which such allocations relate will be reduced as a result of such allocations. If in fact the amounts of the tax-exempt interest and taxable dividends earned by the partnership during the 3-year period are equal, the tax-exempt interest and taxable dividends will be reallocated to the partners in equal shares under paragraph (b)(3) of this section. If not, the tax-exempt interest and taxable dividends will be reallocated between M and N in proportion to the net increases in their capital accounts during such 3-year period due to the allocation of such items under the partnership agreement.

(ii) Assume the same facts as in (i) except that gain or loss from the sale of the tax-exempt bonds and corporate stock will be allocated equally between M and N and the partnership agreement provides that the 90/10 allocation arrangement with respect to the investment income applies only to the first $10,000 of interest income from the tax-exempt bonds and the first $10,000 of dividend income from the corporate stock, and only to the first taxable year of the partnership. There is a strong likelihood at the time the 90/10 allocation of the investment income became part of the partnership agreement that in the first taxable year of the partnership, the partnership will earn more than $10,000 of tax-exempt interest and more than $10,000 of taxable dividends. The allocations of tax-exempt interest and taxable dividends provided in the partnership agreement have economic effect, but under the test contained in paragraph (b)(2)(iii)(b) of this section, such economic effect is not substantial for the same reasons stated in (i) (but applied to the 1 taxable year, rather than to a 3-year period). If in fact the partnership realizes at least $10,000 of tax-exempt interest and at least $10,000 of taxable dividends in such year, the allocations of such interest income and dividend income will be reallocated equally between M and N under paragraph (b)(3) of this section. If not, the tax-exempt interest and taxable dividends will be reallocated between M and N in proportion to the net increases in their capital accounts due to the allocations of such items under the partnership agreement.

(iii) Assume the same facts as in (ii) except that at the time the 90/10 allocation of investment income becomes part of the partnership agreement, there is not a strong likelihood that (1) the partnership will earn $10,000 or more of tax-exempt interest and $10,000 or more of taxable dividends in the partnership's first taxable year, and (2) the amount of tax-exempt interest and taxable dividends earned during such year will be substantially the same. Under these facts the economic effect of the allocations generally will be substantial. (Additional facts may exist in certain cases, however, so that the allocation is insubstantial under the second sentence of paragraph (b)(2)(iii). See example (5) above.)

Example (8). (i) O and P are equal partners in the OP general partnership. The partnership, O, and P have calendar taxable years. Partner O has a net operating loss carryover from another venture that is due to expire at the end of the partnership's second taxable year. Otherwise, both partners expect to be in the 50 percent marginal tax bracket in the next several taxable years. The partnership agreement provides that the partners' capital accounts will be determined and maintained in accordance with paragraph (b)(2)(iv) of this section, distributions in liquidation of the partnership (or any partner's interest) will be made in accordance with the partners' positive capital account balances, and any partner with a deficit balance in his capital account following the liquidation of his interest must restore that deficit to the partnership (as set forth in paragraphs (b)(2)(ii)(b)(2) and (3) of this section).

The partnership agreement is amended (at the beginning of the partnership's second taxable year) to allocate all the partnership net taxable income for that year to O. Future partnership net taxable loss is to be allocated to O, and future partnership net taxable income to P, until the allocation of income to O in the partnership's second taxable year is offset. It is further agreed orally that in the event the partnership is liquidated prior to completion of such offset, O's capital account will be adjusted downward to the extent of one-half of the allocations of income to O in the partnership's second taxable year that have not been offset by other allocations, P's capital account will be adjusted upward by a like amount, and liquidation proceeds will be distributed in accordance with the partners' adjusted capital account balances. As a result of this oral amendment, all allocations of partnership net taxable income and net taxable loss made pursuant to the amendment executed at the beginning of the partnership's second taxable year lack economic effect and will be disregarded. Under the partnership agreement other allocations are made equally to O and P, and O and P will share equally in liquidation proceeds, indicating that the partners' interests in the partnership are equal. Thus, the disregarded allocations will be reallocated equally between the partners under paragraph (b)(3) of this section.

(ii) Assume the same facts as in (i) except that there is no agreement that O's and P's capital accounts will be adjusted downward and upward, respectively, to the extent of one-half of the partnership net taxable income allocated to O in the partnership's second taxable year that is not offset subsequently by other allocations. The income of the partnership is generated primarily by fixed interest payments received with respect to highly rated corporate bonds, which are expected to produce sufficient net taxable income prior to the end of the partnership's seventh taxable year to offset in large part the net taxable income to be allocated to O in the partnership's second taxable year. Thus, at the time the allocations are made part of the partnership agreement, there is a strong likelihood that the allocation of net taxable income to be made to O in the second taxable year will be offset in large part within 5 taxable years thereafter. These allocations have economic effect. However, the economic effect of the allocation of partnership net taxable income to O in the partnership's second taxable year, as well as the offsetting allocations to P, is not substantial under the test contained in paragraph (b)(2)(iii)(c) of this section because there is a strong likelihood that the net increases or decreases in O's and P's capital accounts will be the same at the end of the partnership's seventh taxable year with such allocations as they would have been in the absence of such allocations, and the total taxes of O and P for the taxable years to which such allocations relate will be reduced as a result of such allocations. If in fact the partnership, in its taxable years 3 through 7, realizes sufficient net taxable income to offset the amount allocated to O in the second taxable year, the allocations provided in the partnership agreement will be reallocated equally between the partners under paragraph (b)(3) of this section.

Example (9). Q and R form a limited partnership with contributions of $20,000 and $180,000, respectively. Q, the limited partner, is a corporation that has $2,000,000 of net operating loss carryforwards that will not expire for 8 years. Q does not expect to have sufficient income (apart from the income of the partnership) to absorb any of such net operating loss carryforwards. R, the general partner, is a corporation that expects to be in the 46 percent marginal tax bracket for several years. The partnership agreement provides that the partners' capital accounts will be determined and maintained in accordance with paragraph (b)(2)(iv) of this section, distributions in liquidation of the partnership (or any partner's interest) will be made in accordance with the partners' positive capital account balances, and any partner with a deficit balance in his capital account following the liquidation of his interest must restore that deficit to the partnership (as set forth in paragraphs (b)(2)(ii)(b)(2) and (3) of this section). The partnership's cash, together with the proceeds of an $800,000 loan, are invested in assets that are expected to produce taxable income and cash flow (before debt service) of approximately $150,000 a year for the first 8 years of the partnership's operations. In addition, it is expected that the partnership's total taxable income in its first 8 taxable years will not exceed $2,000,000. The partnership's $150,000 of cash flow in each of its first 8 years will be used to retire the $800,000 loan. The partnership agreement provides that partnership net taxable income will be allocated 90 percent to Q and 10 percent to R in the first through eighth partnership taxable years, and 90 percent to R and 10 percent to Q in all subsequent partnership taxable years. Net taxable loss will be allocated 90 percent to R and 10 percent to Q in all partnership taxable years. All distributions of cash from the partnership to partners (other than the priority distributions to Q described below) will be made 90 percent to R and 10 percent to Q. At the end of the partnership's eighth taxable year, the amount of Q's capital account in excess of one-ninth of R's capital account on such date will be designated as Q's "excess capital account." Beginning in the ninth taxable year of the partnership, the undistributed portion of Q's excess capital account will begin to bear interest which will be paid and deducted under section 707(c) at a rate of interest below the rate that the partnership can borrow from commercial lenders, and over the next several years (following the eight year) the partnership will make priority cash distributions to Q in prearranged percentages of Q's excess capital account designed to amortize Q's excess capital account and the interest thereon over a prearranged period. In addition, the partnership's agreement prevents Q from causing his interest in the partnership from being liquidated (and thereby receiving the balance in his capital account) without R's consent until Q's excess capital account has been eliminated. The below market rate of interest and the period over which the amortization will take place are prescribed such that, as of the end of the partnership's eighth taxable year, the present value of Q's right to receive such priority distributions is approximately 46 percent of the amount of Q's excess capital account as of such date. However, because the partnership's income for its first 8 taxable years will be realized approximately ratably over that period, the present value of Q's right to receive the priority distributions with respect to its excess capital account is, as of the date the partnership agreement is entered into, less than the present value of the additional Federal income taxes for which R would be liable if, during the partnership's first 8 taxable years, all partnership income were to be allocated 90 percent to R and 10 to Q. The allocations of partnership taxable income to Q and R in the first through eighth partnership taxable years have economic effect. However, such economic effect is not substantial under the general rules set forth in paragraph (b)(2)(iii) of this section. This is true because R may enhance his after-tax economic consequences, on a present value basis, as a result of the allocations to Q of 90 percent of partnership's income during taxable years 1 through 8, and there is a strong likelihood that neither R nor Q will substantially diminish its after-tax economic consequences, on a present value basis, as a result of such allocation. Accordingly, partnership taxable income for partnership taxable years 1 through 8 will be reallocated in accordance with the partners' interests in the partnership under paragraph (b)(3) of this section.

Example (10). (i) S and T form a general partnership to operate a travel agency. The partnership agreement provides that the partners' capital accounts will be determined and maintained in accordance with paragraph (b)(2)(iv) of this section, distributions in liquidation of the partnership (or any partner's interest) will be made in accordance with the partners' positive capital account balances, and any partner with a deficit balance in his capital account following the liquidation of his interest must restore that deficit to the partnership (as set forth in paragraphs (b)(2)(ii)(b)(2) and (3) of this section). The partnership agreement provides that T, a resident of a foreign country, will be allocated 90 percent, and S 10 percent, of the income, gain, loss, and deduction derived from operations conducted by T within his country, and all remaining income, gain, loss, and deduction will be allocated equally. The amount of such income, gain, loss, or deduction cannot be predicted with any reasonable certainty. The allocations provided by the partnership agreement have substantial economic effect.

(ii) Assume the same facts as in (i) except that the partnership agreement provides that all income, gain, loss, and deduction of the partnership will be shared equally, but that T will be allocated all income, gain, loss, and deduction derived from operations conducted by him within his country as a part of his equal share of partnership income, gain, loss, and deduction, upon to the amount of such share. Assume the total tax liability of S and T for each year to which these allocations relate will be reduced as a result of such allocation. These allocations have economic effect. However, such economic effect is not substantial under the test stated in paragraph (b)(2)(iii)(b) of this section because, at the time the allocations became part of the partnership agreement, there is a strong likelihood that the net increases and decreases to S's and T's capital accounts will be the same at the end of each partnership taxable year with such allocations as they would have been in the absence of such allocations, and that the total tax liability of S and T for each year to which such allocations relate will be reduced as a result of such allocations. Thus, all items of partnership income, gain, loss, and income, gain, loss, and deduction will be reallocated equally between S and T under paragraph (b)(3) of this section.

Example (11). (i) U and V share equally all income, gain, loss, and deduction of the UV general partnership, as well as all non-liquidating distributions made by the partnership. The partnership agreement provides that the partners' capital accounts will be determined and maintained in accordance with paragraph (b)(2)(iv) of this section, distributions in liquidation of the partnership (or any partner's interest) will be made in accordance with the partners' positive capital account balances, and any partner with a deficit balance in his capital account following the liquidation of his interest must restore such deficit to the partnership (as set forth in paragraphs (b)(2)(ii)(b)(2) and (3) of this section). The agreement further provides that the partners will be allocated equal shares of any section 705(a)(2)(B) expenditures of the partnership. In the partnership's first taxable year, it pays qualified first-year wages of $6,000 and is entitled to a $3,000 targeted jobs tax credit under sections 44B and 51 of the Code. Under section 280C the partnership must reduce its deduction for wages paid by the $3,000 credit claimed (which amount constitutes a section 705(a)(2)(B) expenditure). The partnership agreement allocates the credit to U. Although the allocations of wage deductions and section 705(a)(2)(B) expenditures have substantial economic effect, the allocation of tax credit cannot have economic effect since it cannot properly be reflected in the partners' capital accounts. Furthermore, the allocation is not in accordance with the special partners' interests in the partnership rule contained in paragraph (b)(4)(ii) of this section. Under that rule, since the expenses that gave rise to the credit are shared equally by the partners, the credit will be shared equally between U and V.

(ii) Assume the same facts as in (i) and that at the beginning of the partnership's second taxable year, the partnership agreement is amended to allocate to U all wage expenses incurred in that year (including wage expenses that constitute section 705(a)(2)(B) expenditures) whether or not such wages qualify for the credit. The partnership agreement contains no offsetting allocations. That taxable year the partnership pays $8,000 in total wages to its employees. Assume that the partnership has operating income equal to its operating expenses (exclusive of expenses for wages). Assume further that $6,000 of the $8,000 wage expense constitutes qualified first-year wages. U is allocated the $3,000 deduction and the $3,000 section 705(a)(2)(B) expenditure attributable to the $6,000 of qualified first-year wages, as well as the deduction for the other $2,000 in wage expenses. The allocations of wage deductions and section 705(a)(2)(B) expenditures have substantial economic effect. Furthermore, since the wage credit is allocated in the same proportion as the expenses that gave rise to the credit, and the allocation of those expenses has substantial economic effect, the allocation of such credit to U is in accordance with the special partners' interests in the partnership rule contained in paragraph (b)(4)(ii) of this section and is recognized thereunder.

* * *

Example (13). (i) Y and Z form a brokerage general partnership for the purpose of investing and trading in marketable securities. Y contributes cash of $10,000, and Z contributes securities of P corporation, which have an adjusted basis of $3,000 and a fair market value of $10,000. The partnership would not be an investment company under section 351(e) if it were incorporated. The partnership agreement provides that the partners' capital accounts will be determined and maintained in accordance with paragraph (b)(2)(iv) of this section, distributions in liquidation of the partnership (or any partner's interest) will be made in accordance with the partners' positive capital account balances, and any partner with a deficit balance in his capital account following the liquidation of his interest must restore that deficit to the partnership (as set forth in paragraphs (b)(2)(ii)(b)(2) and (3) of this section). The partnership uses the interim closing of the books method for purposes of section 706. The initial capital accounts of Y and Z are fixed at $10,000 each. The agreement further provides that all partnership distributions, income, gain, loss, deduction, and credit will be shared equally between Y and Z, except that the taxable gain attributable to the precontribution appreciation in the value of the securities of P corporation will be allocated to Z in accordance with section 704(c). During the partnership's first taxable year, it sells the securities of P corporation for $12,000, resulting in a $2,000 book gain ($12,000 less $10,000 book value) and a $9,000 taxable gain ($12,000 less $3,000 adjusted tax basis). The partnership has no other income, gain, loss, or deductions for the taxable year. The gain from the sale of the securities is allocated as follows:

	Y		Z	
	Tax	Book	Tax	Book
Capital account upon formation	$10,000	$10,000	$3,000	$10,000
Plus: gain	1,000	1,000	8,000	1,000
Capital account at end of year 1	$11,000	$11,000	$11,000	$11,000

The allocation of the $2,000 book gain, $1,000 each to Y and Z, has substantial economic effect. Furthermore, under section 704(c) the partners' distributive shares of the $9,000 taxable gain are $1,000 to Y and $8,000 to Z.

(ii) Assume the same facts as in (i) and that at the beginning of the partnership's second taxable year, it invests its $22,000 of cash in securities of G Corp. The G Corp. securities increase in value to $40,000, at which time Y sells 50 percent of his partnership interest (*i.e.*, a 25 percent interest in the partnership) to LK for $10,000. The partnership does not have a section 754 election in effect for the partnership taxable year during which such sale occurs. In accordance with paragraph (b)(2)(iv)(l) of this section, the partnership agreement provides that LK inherits 50 percent of Y's $11,000 capital account balance. Thus, following the sale, LK and Y each have a capital account of $5,500, and Z's capital account remains at $11,000. Prior to the end of the partnership's second taxable year, the securities are sold for their $40,000 fair market value, resulting in an $18,000 taxable gain ($40,000 less $22,000 adjusted tax basis). The partnership has no other income, gain, loss, or deduction in such taxable year. Under the partnership agreement the $18,000 taxable gain is allocated as follows:

	Y	Z	LK
Capital account before sale of securities	$5,500	$11,000	$5,500
Plus: gain	4,500	9,000	4,500
Capital account at end of year 2	$10,000	$20,000	$10,000

The allocation of the $18,000 taxable gain has substantial economic effect.

(iii) Assume the same facts as in (ii) except that the partnership has a section 754 election in effect for the partnership taxable year during which Y sells 50 percent of his interest to LK. Accordingly, under § 1.743–1 there is a $4,500 basis increase to the G Corp. securities with respect to LK. Notwithstanding this basis adjustment, as a result of the sale of the G Corp. securities, LK's capital account is, as in (ii), increased by $4,500. The fact that LK recognizes no taxable gain from such sale (due to his $4,500 section 743 basis adjustment) is irrelevant for capital accounting purposes since, in accordance with paragraph (b)(2)(iv)(m)(2) of this section, that basis adjustment is disregarded in the maintenance and computation of the partners' capital accounts.

(iv) Assume the same facts as in (iii) except that immediately following Y's sale of 50 percent of this interest to LK, the G Corp. securities decrease in value to $32,000 and are sold. The $10,000 taxable gain ($32,000 less $22,000 adjusted tax basis) is allocated as follows:

	Y	Z	LK
Capital account before sale of securities	$5,500	$11,000	$5,500
Plus: gain	2,500	5,000	2,500
Capital account at end of year 2	$8,000	$16,000	$8,000

The fact that LK recognizes a $2,000 taxable loss from the sale of the G Corp. securities (due to his $4,500 section 743 basis adjustment) is irrelevant for capital accounting purposes since, in accordance with paragraph (b)(2)(iv)(m)(2) of this section, that basis adjustment is disregarded in the maintenance and computation of the partners' capital accounts.

(v) Assume the same facts as in (ii) except that Y sells 100 percent of his partnership interest (i.e., a 50 percent interest in the partnership) to LK for $20,000. Under section 708(b)(1)(B) the partnership terminates. Under paragraph (b)(1)(iv) of § 1.708–1, there is a constructive liquidation of the partnership. Immediately preceding the constructive liquidation, the capital accounts of Z and LK equal $11,000 each (LK having inherited Y's $11,000 capital account) and the book value of the G Corp. securities is $22,000 (original purchase price of securities). Under paragraph (b)(2)(iv)(*l*) of this section, the deemed contribution of assets and liabilities by the terminated partnership to the new partnership and the deemed liquidation of the terminated partnership that occur under § 1.708–1(b)(1)(iv) in connection with the constructive liquidation of the terminated partnership are disregarded in the maintenance and computation of the partners' capital accounts. As a result, the capital accounts of Z and LK in the new partnership equal $11,000 each (their capital accounts in the terminated partnership immediately prior to the termination), and the book value of the G Corp. securities remains $22,000 (its book value immediately prior to the termination). This *Example 13*(v) applies to terminations of partnerships under section 708(b)(1)(B) occurring on or after May 9, 1997; however, this *Example 13*(v) may be applied to terminations occurring on or after May 9, 1996, provided that the partnership and its partners apply this *Example 13*(v) to the termination in a consistent manner.

Example (14). (i) MC and RW form a general partnership to which each contributes $10,000. The $20,000 is invested in securities of Ventureco (which are not readily tradable on an established securities market). In each of the partnership's taxable years, it recognizes operating income equal to its operating deductions (excluding gain or loss from the sale of securities). The partnership agreement provides that the partners' capital accounts will be determined and maintained in accordance with paragraph (b)(2)(iv) of this section, distributions in liquidation of the partnership (or any partner's interest) will be made in accordance with the partners' positive capital account balances, and any partner with a deficit balance in his capital account following the liquidation of his interest must restore that deficit to the partnership (as set forth in paragraphs (b)(2)(ii)(b)(2) and (3) of this section). The partnership uses the interim closing of the books method for purposes of section 706. Assume that the Ventureco securities subsequently appreciate in value to $50,000. At that time SK makes a $25,000 cash contribution to the partnership (thereby acquiring a one-third interest in the partnership), and the $25,000 is placed in a bank account. Upon SK's admission to the partnership, the capital accounts of MC and RW (which were $10,000 each prior to SK's admission) are, in accordance with paragraph (b)(2)(iv)(f) of this section, adjusted upward (to $25,000 each) to reflect their shares of the unrealized appreciation in the Ventureco securities that occurred before SK was admitted to the partnership. Immediately after SK's admission to the partnership, the securities are sold for their $50,000 fair market value, resulting in taxable gain of $30,000 ($50,000 less $20,000 adjusted tax basis) and no book gain or loss. An allocation of the $30,000 taxable gain cannot have economic effect since it cannot properly be reflected in the partners' book capital accounts. Under paragraph (b)(2)(iv)(f) of this section and the special partners' interests in the partnership rule contained in paragraph (b)(4)(i) of this section, unless the partnership agreement provides that the $30,000 taxable gain will, in accordance with section 704(c) principles, be shared $15,000 to MC and $15,000 to RW, the partners' capital accounts will not be considered maintained in accordance with paragraph (b)(2)(iv) of this section.

	MC		RW		SK	
	Tax	Book	Tax	Book	Tax	Book
Capital account following SK's admission.....	$10,000	$25,000	$10,000	$25,000	$25,000	$25,000
Plus: gain	15,000	0	15,000	0	0	0
Capital account following sale.......................	$25,000	$25,000	$25,000	$25,000	$25,000	$25,000

(ii) Assume the same facts as (i), except that after SK's admission to the partnership, the Ventureco securities appreciate in value to $74,000 and are sold, resulting in taxable gain of $54,000 ($74,000 less $20,000 adjusted tax basis) and book gain of $24,000 ($74,000 less $50,000 book value). Under the partnership agreement the $24,000 book gain (the appreciation in value occurring after SK became a partner) is allocated equally among MC, RW, and SK, and such allocations have substantial economic effect. An allocation of the $54,000 taxable gain cannot have economic effect since it cannot properly be reflected in the partners' book capital accounts. Under paragraph (b)(2)(iv)(f) of this section and the special partners' interests in the partnership rule contained in paragraph (b)(4)(i) of this section, unless the partnership agreement provides that the taxable gain will, in accordance with section 704(c) principles, be shared, $23,000 to MC, $23,000 to RW, and $8,000 to SK, the partners' capital accounts will not be considered maintained in accordance with paragraph (b)(2)(iv) of this section.

	MC		RW		SK	
	Tax	Book	Tax	Book	Tax	Book
Capital account following SK's admission.....	$10,000	$25,000	$10,000	$25,000	$25,000	$25,000
Plus: gain	23,000	8,000	23,000	8,000	8,000	8,000
Capital account following sale.......................	$33,000	$33,000	$33,000	$33,000	$33,000	$33,000

(iii) Assume the same facts as (i) except that after SK's admission to the partnership, the Ventureco securities depreciate in value to $44,000 and are sold, resulting in taxable gain of $24,000 ($44,000 less $20,000 adjusted tax basis) and a book loss of $6,000 ($50,000 book value less $44,000). Under the partnership agreement the $6,000 book loss is allocated equally among MC, RW, and SK, and such allocations have substantial economic effect. An allocation of the $24,000 taxable gain cannot have economic effect since it cannot properly be reflected in the partners' book capital accounts. Under paragraph (b)(2)(iv)(f) of this section and the special partners' interests in the partnership rule contained in paragraph (b)(4)(i) of this section, unless the partnership agreement provides that the $24,000 taxable gain will, in accordance with section 704(c) principles, be shared equally between MC and RW, the partners' capital accounts will not be considered maintained in accordance with paragraph (b)(2)(iv) of this section.

	MC		RW		SK	
	Tax	Book	Tax	Book	Tax	Book
Capital account follwoing SK's admission	$10,000	$25,000	$10,000	$25,000	$25,000	$25,000
Capital account following sale.......................	$22,000	$23,000	$22,000	$23,000	$25,000	$25,000

That SK bears an economic loss of $2,000 without a corresponding taxable loss is attributable entirely to the "ceiling rule." See paragraph (c)(2) of § 1.704–1.

(iv) Assume the same facts as in (ii) except that upon the admission of SK the capital accounts of MC and RW are not each adjusted upward from $10,000 to $25,000 to reflect the appreciation in the partnership's securities that occurred before SK was admitted to the partnership. Rather, upon SK's admission to the partnership, the partnership agreement is amended to provide that the first $30,000 of taxable gain upon the sale of such securities will be allocated equally between MC and RW, and that all other income, gain, loss, and deduction will be allocated equally between MC, RW, and SK. When the securities are sold for $74,000, the $54,000 of taxable gain is so allocated. These allocations of taxable gain have substantial economic effect. (If the agreement instead provides for all taxable gain (including the $30,000 taxable gain attributable to the appreciation in the securities prior to SK's admission to the partnership) to be allocated equally between MC, RW, and SK, the partners should consider whether, and to what extent, the provisions of paragraphs (b)(1)(iii) and (iv) of this section are applicable.)

(v) Assume the same facts as in (iv) except that instead of selling the securities, the partnership makes a distribution of the securities (which have a fair market value of $74,000). Assume the distribution does not give rise to a transaction described in section 707(a)(2)(B). In accordance with paragraph (b)(2)(iv)(e) of this section, the partners' capital accounts are adjusted immediately prior to the distribution to reflect how taxable gain ($54,000) would have been allocated had the securities been sold for their $74,000 fair market value, and capital account adjustments in respect of the distribution of the securities are made with reference to the $74,000 "booked-up" fair market value.

	MC	RW	SK
Capital account before adjustment	$10,000	$10,000	$25,000
Deemed sale adjustment	23,000	23,000	8,000
Less: distribution	(24,667)	(24,667)	(24,667)
Capital account after distribution	$8,333	$8,333	$8,333

(vi) Assume the same facts as in (i) except that the partnership does not sell the Ventureco securities. During the next 3 years the fair market value of the Ventureco securities remains at $50,000, and the partnership engages in no other investment activities. Thus, at the end of that period the balance sheet of the partnership and the partners' capital accounts are the same as they were at the beginning of such period. At the end of the 3 years, MC's interest in the partnership is liquidated for the $25,000 cash held by the partnership. Assume the distribution does not give rise to a transaction described in section 707(a)(2)(B). Assume further that the partnership has a section 754 election in effect for the taxable year during which such liquidation occurs. Under sections 734(b) and 755 the partnership increases the basis of the Ventureco securities by the $15,000 basis adjustment (the excess of $25,000 over the $10,000 adjusted tax basis of MC's partnership interest).

	MC		RW		SK	
	Tax	Book	Tax	Book	Tax	Book
Capital account before distribution	$10,000	$25,000	$10,000	$25,000	$25,000	$25,000
Plus: basis adjustment	15,000	0	0	0	0	0
Less: distribution	(25,000)	(25,000)	0	0	0	0
Capital account after liquidation	0	0	$10,000	$25,000	$25,000	$25,000

(vii) Assume the same facts as in (vi) except that the partnership has no section 754 election in effect for the taxable year during which such liquidation occurs.

	MC		RW		SK	
	Tax	Book	Tax	Book	Tax	Book
Capital account before distribution	$10,000	$25,000	$10,000	$25,000	$25,000	$25,000
Less: distribution	(25,000)	(25,000)	0	0	0	0
Capital account after liquidation	($15,000)	0	$10,000	$25,000	$25,000	$25,000

Following the liquidation of MC's interest in the partnership, the Ventureco securities are sold for their $50,000 fair market value, resulting in no book gain or loss but a $30,000 taxable gain. An allocation of this $30,000 taxable gain cannot have economic effect since it cannot properly be reflected in the partners' book capital accounts. Under paragraph (b)(2)(iv)(f) of this section and the special partners' interests in the partnership rule contained in paragraph (b)(4)(i) of this section, unless the partnership agreement provides that $15,000 of such taxable gain will, in accordance with section 704(c) principles, be included in RW's distributive share, the partners' capital accounts will not be considered maintained in accordance with paragraph (b)(2)(iv) of this section. The remaining $15,000 of such gain will, under paragraph (b)(3) of this section, be shared equally between RW and SK.

Example (15). (i) JB and DK form a limited partnership for the purpose of purchasing residential real estate to lease. JB, the limited partner, contributes $13,500, and DK, the general partner, contributes $1,500. The partnership, which uses the cash receipts and disbursements method of accounting, purchases a building for $100,000 (on leased land), incurring a recourse mortgage of $85,000 that requires the payment of interest only for a period of 3 years. The partnership agreement provides that partnership net taxable income and loss will be allocated 90 percent to JB and 10 percent to DK, the partners' capital accounts will be determined and maintained in accordance with paragraph (b)(2)(iv) of this section, distributions in liquidation of the partnership (or any partner's interest) will be made in accordance with the partners' positive capital account balances (as set forth in paragraph (b)(2)(ii)(b)(2) of this section), and JB is not required to restore any deficit balance in his capital account, but DK is so required. The partnership agreement contains a qualified income offset (as defined in paragraph (b)(2)(ii)(d) of this section). As of the end of each of the partnership's first 3 taxable years, the items described in paragraphs (b)(2)(ii)(d)(4), (5), and (6) of this section are not reasonably expected to cause or increase a deficit balance in JB's capital account. In the partnership's first taxable year, it has rental income of $10,000, operating expenses of $2,000, interest expense of $8,000, and cost recovery deductions of $12,000. Under the partnership agreement JB and DK are allocated $10,800 and $1,200, respectively, of the $12,000 net taxable loss incurred in the partnership's first taxable year.

	JB	DK
Capital account upon formation	$13,500	$1,500
Less: year 1 net loss	(10,800)	(1,200)
Capital account at end of year 1	$2,700	$300

The alternate economic effect test contained in paragraph (b)(2)(ii)(d) of this section is satisfied as of the end of the partnership's first taxable year. Thus, the allocation made in the partnership's first taxable year has economic effect.

(ii) Assume the same facts as in (i) and that in the partnership's second taxable year it again has rental income of $10,000, operating expenses of $2,000, interest expense of $8,000, and cost recovery deductions of $12,000. Under the partnership agreement JB and DK are allocated $10,800 and $1,200, respectively, of the $12,000 net taxable loss incurred in the partnership's second taxable year.

	JB	DK
Capital account at beginning of year 1	$2,700	$300
Less: year 2 net loss	(10,800)	(1,200)
Capital account at end of year 2	($8,100)	($900)

Only $2,700 of the $10,800 net taxable loss allocated to JB satisfies the alternate economic effect test contained in paragraph (b)(2)(ii)(d) of this section as of the end of the partnership's second taxable year. The allocation of such $2,700 net taxable loss to JB (consisting of $2,250 of rental income, $450 of operating expenses, $1,800 of interest expense, and $2,700 of cost recovery deductions) has economic effect. The remaining $8,100 of net taxable loss allocated by the partnership agreement to JB must be reallocated in accordance with the partners' interests in the partnership. Under paragraph (b)(3)(iii) of this section, the determination of the partners' interests in the remaining $8,100 net taxable loss is made by comparing how distributions (and contributions) would be made if the partnership sold its property at its adjusted tax basis and liquidated immediately following the end of the partnership's first taxable year with the results of such a sale and liquidation immediately following the end of the partnership's second taxable year. If the partnership's real property were sold for its $88,000 adjusted tax basis and the partnership were liquidated immediately following the end of the partnership's first taxable year, the $88,000 sales proceeds would be used to repay the $85,000 note, and there would be $3,000 remaining in the partnership, which would be used to make liquidating distributions to DK and JB of $300 and $2,700, respectively. If such property were sold for its $76,000 adjusted tax basis and the partnership were liquidated immediately following the end of the partnership's second taxable year, DK would be required to contribute $9,000 to the partnership in order for the partnership to repay the $85,000 note, and there would be no assets remaining in the partnership to distribute. A comparison of these outcomes indicates that JB bore $2,700 and DK $9,300 of the economic burden that corresponds to the $12,000 net taxable loss. Thus, in addition to the $1,200 net taxable loss allocated to DK under the partnership agreement, $8,100 of net taxable loss will be reallocated to DK under paragraph (b)(3)(iii) of this section. Similarly, for subsequent taxable years, absent an increase in JB's capital account, all net taxable loss allocated to JB under the partnership agreement will be reallocated to DK.

(iii) Assume the same facts as in (ii) and that in the partnership's third taxable year there is rental income of $35,000, operating expenses of $2,000, interest expenses of $8,000, and cost recovery deductions of $10,000. The capital accounts of the partners maintained on the books of the partnership do not take into account the reallocation to DK of the $8,100 net taxable loss in the partnership's second taxable year. Thus, an allocation of the $15,000 net taxable income, $13,500 to JB and $1,500 to DK (as dictated by the partnership agreement and as reflected in the capital accounts of the partners) does not have economic effect. The partners' interests in the partnership with respect to such $15,000 taxable gain again is made in the manner described in paragraph (b)(3)(iii) of this section. If the partnership's real property were sold for its $76,000 adjusted tax basis and the partnership were liquidated immediately following the end of the partnership's second taxable year, DK would be required to contribute $9,000 to the partnership in order for the partnership to repay the $85,000 note, and there would be no assets remaining to distribute. If such property were sold for its $66,000 adjusted tax basis and the partnership were liquidated immediately following the end of the partnership's third taxable year, the $91,000 ($66,000 sales proceeds plus $25,000 cash on hand) would be used to repay the $85,000 note and there would be $6,000 remaining in the partnership, which would be used to make liquidating distributions to DK and JB of $600 and $5,400, respectively. Accordingly, under paragraph (b)(3)(iii) of this section the $15,000 net taxable income in the partnership's third taxable year will be reallocated $9,600 to DK (minus $9,000 at end of the second taxable year to positive $600 at end of the third taxable year) and $5,400 to JB (zero at end of the second taxable year to positive $5,400 at end of the third taxable year).

Example (16). (i) KG and WN form a limited partnership for the purpose of investing in improved real estate. KG, the general partner, contributes $10,000 to the partnership, and WN, the limited partner, contributes $990,000 to the partnership. The $1,000,000 is used to purchase an apartment building on leased land. The partnership agreement provides that (1) the partners' capital accounts will be determined and maintained in accordance with paragraph (b)(2)(iv) of this section; (2) cash will be distributed first to WN until such time as he has received the amount of his original capital contribution ($990,000), next to KG until such time as he has received the amount of his original capital contribution ($10,000), and thereafter equally between WN and KG; (3) partnership net taxable income will be allocated 99 percent to WN and 1 percent to KG until the cumulative net taxable income allocated for all taxable years is equal to the cumulative net taxable loss previously allocated to the partners, and thereafter equally between WN and KG; (4) partnership net taxable loss will be allocated 99 percent to WN and 1 percent to KG, unless net taxable income has previously been allocated equally between WN and KG, in which case such net taxable loss first will be allocated equally until the cumulative net taxable loss allocated for all taxable years is equal to the cumulative net taxable income previously allocated to the partners; and (5) upon liquidation, WN is not required to restore any deficit balance in his capital account, but KG is so required. Since distributions in liquidation are not required to be made in accordance with the partners' positive capital account balances, and since WN is not required, upon the liquidation of his interest, to restore the deficit balance in his capital account to the partnership, the allocations provided by the partnership agreement do not have economic effect and will be reallocated in accordance with the partners' interests in the partnership under paragraph (b)(3) of this section.

(ii) Assume the same facts as in (i) except that the partnership agreement further provides that distributions in liquidation of the partnership (or any partner's interest) are to be made in accordance with the partners' positive capital account balances (as set forth in paragraph (b)(2)(ii)(b)(2) of this section). Assume further that the partnership agreement contains a qualified income offset (as defined in paragraph (b)(2)(ii)(d) of this section) and that, as of the end of each partnership taxable year, the items described in paragraphs (b)(2)(iii)(d)(4), (5), and (6) of this section are not reasonably expected to cause or increase a deficit balance in WN's capital account. The allocations provided by the partnership agreement have economic effect.

Example (17). FG and RP form a partnership with FG contributing cash of $100 and RP contributing property, with

2 years of cost recovery deductions remaining, that has an adjusted tax basis of $80 and a fair market value of $100. The partnership, FG, and RP have calendar taxable years. The partnership agreement provides that the partners' capital accounts will be determined and maintained in accordance with paragraph (b)(2)(iv) of this section, liquidation proceeds will be made in accordance with capital account balances, and each partner is liable to restore the deficit balance in his capital account to the partnership upon liquidation of his interest (as set forth in paragraphs (b)(2)(ii)(b)(2) and (3) of this section). FG expects to be in a substantially higher tax bracket than RP in the partnership's first taxable year. In the partnership's second taxable year, and in subsequent taxable years, it is expected that both will be in approximately equivalent tax brackets. The partnership agreement allocates all items equally except that all $50 of book depreciation is allocated to FG in the partnership's first taxable year and all $50 of book depreciation is allocated to RP in the partnership's second taxable year. If the allocation to FG of all book depreciation in the partnership's first taxable year is respected, FG would be entitled under section 704(c) to the entire cost recovery deduction ($40) for such year. Likewise, if the allocation to RP of all the book depreciation in the partnership's second taxable year is respected, RP would be entitled under section 704(c) to the entire cost recovery deduction ($40) for such year. The allocation of book depreciation to FG and RP in the partnership's first 2 taxable years has economic effect within the meaning of paragraph (b)(2)(ii) of this section. However, the economic effect of these allocations is not substantial under the test described in paragraph (b)(2)(iii)(c) of this section since there is a strong likelihood at the time such allocations became part of the partnership agreement that at the end of the 2-year period to which such allocations relate, the net increases and decreases to FG's and RP's capital accounts will be the same with such allocations as they would have been in the absence of such allocation, and the total tax liability of FG and RP for the taxable years to which the section 704(c) determinations relate would be reduced as a result of the allocations of book depreciation. As a result the allocations of book depreciation in the partnership agreement will be disregarded. FG and RP will be allocated such book depreciation in accordance with the partners' interests in the partnership under paragraph (b)(3) of this section. Under these facts the book depreciation deductions will be reallocated equally between the partners, and section 704(c) will be applied with reference to such reallocation of book depreciation.

Example (18). (i) WM and JL form a general partnership by each contributing $300,000 thereto. The partnership uses the $600,000 to purchase an item of tangible personal property, which it leases out. The partnership elects under section 48(q)(4) to reduce the amount of investment tax credit in lieu of adjusting the tax basis of such property. The partnership agreement provides that (1) the partners' capital account will be determined and maintained in accordance with paragraph (b)(2)(iv) of this section, (2) distributions in liquidation of the partnership (or any partner's interest) will be made in accordance with the partners' positive capital account balances (as set forth in paragraph (b)(2)(ii)(b)(2) of this section), (3) any partner with a deficit balance in his capital account following the liquidation of his interest must restore that deficit to the partnership (as set forth in paragraph (b)(2)(ii)(b)(3) of this section), (4) all income, gain, loss, and deduction of the partnership will be allocated equally between the partners, and (5) all nonliquidating distributions of the partnership will be made equally between the partners. Assume that in each of the partnership's taxable years, it recognizes operating income equal to its operating deductions (excluding cost recovery and depreciation deductions and gain or loss on the sale of its property). During its first 2 taxable years, the partnership has an additional $200,000 cost recovery deduction in each year. Pursuant to the partnership agreement these items are allocated equally between WM and JL.

	WM	JL
Capital account upon formation.........	$300,000	$300,000
Less: net loss for years 1 and 2.........	(200,000)	(200,000)
Capital account at end of year 2	$100,000	$100,000

The allocations made in the partnership's first 2 taxable years have substantial economic effect.

(ii) Assume the same facts as in (i) and that MK is admitted to the partnership at the beginning of the partnership's third taxable year. At the time of his admission, the fair market value of the partnership property is $600,000. MK contributes $300,000 to the partnership in exchange for an equal one-third interest in the partnership, and, as permitted under paragraph (b)(2)(iv)(g), the capital accounts of WM and JL are adjusted upward to $300,000 each to reflect the fair market value of partnership property. In addition, the partnership agreement is modified to provide that depreciation and gain or loss, as computed for tax purposes, with respect to the partnership property that appreciated prior to MK's admission will be shared among the partners in a manner that takes account of the variation between such property's $200,000 adjusted tax basis and its $600,000 book value in accordance with paragraph (b)(2)(iv)(f) and the special rule contained in paragraph (b)(4)(i) of this section. Depreciation and gain or loss, as computed for book purposes, with respect to such property will be allocated equally among the partners and, in accordance with paragraph (b)(2)(iv)(g) of this section, will be reflected in the partner's capital accounts, as will all other partnership income, gain, loss, and deduction. Since the requirements of (b)(2)(iv)(g) of this section are satisfied, the capital accounts of the partners (as adjusted) continue to be maintained in accordance with paragraph (b)(2)(iv) of this section.

(iii) Assume the same facts as in (ii) and that immediately after MK's admission to the partnership, the partnership property is sold for $600,000, resulting in a taxable gain of $400,000 ($600,000 less $200,000 adjusted tax basis) and no book gain or loss, and the partnership is liquidated. An allocation of the $400,000 taxable gain cannot have economic effect because such gain cannot properly be reflected in the partners' book capital accounts. Consistent with the special partners' interests in the partnership rule contained in paragraph (b)(4)(i) of this section, the partnership agreement provides that the $400,000 taxable gain will, in accordance with section 704(c) principles, be shared equally between WM and JL.

	WM		JL		MK	
	Tax	Book	Tax	Book	Tax	Book
Capital account at beginning of year 3	$100,000	$300,000	$100,000	$300,000	$300,000	$300,000
Plus: gain	200,000	0	200,000	0	0	0
Capital account before liquidation..................	$300,000	$300,000	$300,000	$300,000	$300,000	$300,000

The $900,000 of partnership cash ($600,000 sales proceeds plus $300,000 contributed by MK) is distributed equally among WM, JL, and MK in accordance with their adjusted positive capital account balances, each of which is $300,000.

(iv) Assume the same facts as in (iii) except that prior to liquidation the property appreciates and is sold for $900,000, resulting in a taxable gain of $700,000 ($900,000 less $200,000 adjusted tax basis) and a book gain of $300,000 ($900,000 less $600,000 book value). Under the partnership agreement the $300,000 of book gain is allocated equally among the partners, and such allocation has substantial economic effect.

	WM		JL		MK	
	Tax	Book	Tax	Book	Tax	Book
Capital account at beginning of year 3	$100,000	$300,000	$100,000	$300,000	$300,000	$300,000
Plus: gain	300,000	100,000	300,000	100,000	100,000	100,000
Capital account before liquidation	$400,000	$400,000	$400,000	$400,000	$400,000	$400,000

Consistent with the special partners' interests in the partnership rule contained in paragraph (b)(4)(i) of this section, the partnership agreement provides that the $700,000 taxable gain is, in accordance with section 704(c) principles, shared $300,000 to JL, $300,000 to WM, and $100,000 to MK. This ensures that (1) WM and JL share equally the $400,000 taxable gain that is attributable to appreciation in the property that occurred prior to MK's admission to the partnership in the same manner as it was reflected in their capital accounts upon MK's admission, and (2) WM, JL, and MK share equally the additional $300,000 taxable gain in the same manner as they shared the $300,000 book gain.

(v) Assume the same facts as in (ii) except that shortly after MK's admission the property depreciates and is sold for $450,000, resulting in a taxable gain of $250,000 ($450,000 less $200,000 adjusted tax basis) and a book loss of $150,000 ($450,000 less $600,000 book value). Under the partnership agreement these items are allocated as follows:

	WM		JL		MK	
	Tax	Book	Tax	Book	Tax	Book
Capital account at beginning of year 3	$100,000	$300,000	$100,000	$300,000	$300,000	$300,000
Plus: gain	125,000	0	125,000	0	0	0
Less: loss	0	(50,000)	0	(50,000)	0	(50,000)
Capital account before liquidation	$225,000	$250,000	$225,000	$250,000	$300,000	$250,000

The $150,000 book loss is allocated equally among the partners, and such allocation has substantial economic effect. Consistent with the special partners' interests in the partner-ship rule contained in paragraph (b)(4)(i) of this section, the partnership agreement provides that the $250,000 taxable gain is, in accordance with section 704(c) principles, shared equally between WM and JL. The fact that MK bears an economic loss of $50,000 without a corresponding taxable loss is attributable entirely to the "ceiling rule." See paragraph (c)(2) of § 1.704–1.

(vi) Assume the same facts as in (ii) except that the property depreciates and is sold for $170,000, resulting in a $30,000 taxable loss ($200,000 adjusted tax basis less $170,000) and a book loss of $430,000 ($600,000 book value less $170,000). The book loss of $430,000 is allocated equally among the partners ($143,333 each) and has substantial economic effect. Consistent with the special partners' interests in the partnership rule contained in paragraph (b)(4)(i) of this section, the partnership agreement provides that the entire $30,000 taxable loss is, in accordance with section 704(c) principles, included in MK's distributive share.

	WM		JL		MK	
	Tax	Book	Tax	Book	Tax	Book
Capital account at beginning of year 3	$100,000	$300,000	$100,000	$300,000	$300,000	$300,000
Less: loss	0	(143,333)	0	(143,333)	(30,000)	(143,333)
Capital account before liquidation	$100,000	$156,667	$100,000	$156,667	$270,000	$156,667

(vii) Assume the same facts as in (ii) and that during the partnership's third taxable year, the partnership has an additional $100,000 cost recovery deduction and $300,000 book depreciation deduction attributable to the property purchased by the partnership in its first taxable year. The $300,000 book depreciation deduction is allocated equally among the partners, and that allocation has substantial economic effect. Consistent with the special partners' interests in the partnership rule contained in paragraph (b)(4)(i) of this section, the partnership agreement provides that the $100,000 cost recovery deduction for the partnership's third taxable year is, in accordance with section 704 (c) principles, included in MK's distributive share. This is because under these facts those principles require MK to include the cost recovery deduction for such property in his distributive share up to the amount of the book depreciation deduction for such property properly allocated to him.

	WM		JL		MK	
	Tax	Book	Tax	Book	Tax	Book
Capital account at beginning of year 3	$100,000	$300,000	$100,000	$300,000	$300,000	$300,000
Less: recovery/depreciation deduction for year 3	0	(100,000)	0	(100,000)	(100,000)	(100,000)
Capital account at end of year 3	$100,000	$200,000	$100,000	$200,000	$200,000	$200,000

(viii) Assume the same facts as in (vii) except that upon MK's admission the partnership property has an adjusted tax basis of $220,000 (instead of $200,000), and thus the cost recovery deduction for the partnership's third taxable year is $110,000. Assume further that upon MK's admission WM and JL have adjusted capital account balances of $110,000 and $100,000, respectively. Consistent with the special partners' interests in the partnership rule contained in paragraph (b)(4)(i) of this section, the partnership agreement provides that the excess $10,000 cost recovery deduction ($110,000 less $100,000 included in MK's distributive share) is, in accordance with section 704(c) principles, shared equally between WM and JL and is so included in their respective distributive shares for the partnership's third taxable year.

(ix) Assume the same facts as in (vii) except that upon MK's admission the partnership agreement is amended to allocate the first $400,000 of book depreciation and loss on partnership property equally between WM and JL and the last $200,000 of such book depreciation and loss to MK. Assume such allocations have substantial economic effect. Pursuant to this amendment the $300,000 book depreciation deduction in the partnership's third taxable year is allocated equally between WM and JL. Consistent with the special partners' interests in the partnership rule contained in paragraph (b)(4)(i) of this section, the partnership agreement provides that the $100,000 cost recovery deduction is, in accordance with section 704(c) principles, shared equally between WM and JL. In the partnership's fourth taxable year, it has a $60,000 cost recovery deduction and a $180,000 book depreciation deduction. Under the amendment described above, the $180,000 book depreciation deduction is allocated $50,000 to WM, $50,000 to JL, and $80,000 to MK. Consistent with the special partners' interests in the partnership rule contained in paragraph (b)(4)(i) of this section, the partnership agreement provides that the $60,000 cost recovery deduction is, in accordance with section 704(c) principles, included entirely in MK's distributive share.

	WM		JL		MK	
	Tax	Book	Tax	Book	Tax	Book
Capital account at beginning of year 3	$100,000	$300,000	$100,000	$300,000	$300,000	$300,000
Less:						
(a) recovery/depreciation deduction for year 3	(50,000)	(150,000)	(50,000)	(150,000)	0	0
(b) recovery/depreciation deduction for year 4	0	(50,000)	0	(50,000)	(60,000)	(80,000)
Capital account at end of year 4	$50,000	$100,000	$50,000	$100,000	$240,000	$220,000

(x) Assume the same facts as in (vii) and that at the beginning of the partnership's third taxable year, the partnership purchases a second item of tangible personal property for $300,000 and elects under section 48(q)(4) to reduce the amount of investment tax credit in lieu of adjusting the tax basis of such property. The partnership agreement is amended to allocate the first $150,000 of cost recovery deductions and loss from such property to WM and the next $150,000 of cost recovery deductions and loss from such property equally between JL and MK. Thus, in the partnership's third taxable year it has, in addition to the items specified in (vii), a cost recovery and book depreciation deduction of $100,000 attributable to the newly acquired property, which is allocated entirely to WM.

As in (vii), the allocation of the $300,000 book depreciation attributable to the property purchased in the partnership's first taxable year equally among the partners has substantial economic effect, and consistent with the special partners' interests in the partnership rule contained in paragraph (b)(4)(i) of this section, the partnership agreement properly provides for the entire $100,000 cost recovery deduction attributable to such property to be included in MK's distributive share. Furthermore, the allocation to WM of the $100,000 cost recovery deduction attributable to the property purchased in the partnership's third taxable year has substantial economic effect.

	WM		JL		MK	
	Tax	Book	Tax	Book	Tax	Book
Capital account at beginning of year 3	$100,000	$300,000	$100,000	$300,000	$300,000	$300,000
Less:						
(a) recovery/depreciation deduction for property bought in year 1	0	(100,000)	0	(100,000)	(100,000)	(100,000)
(b) recovery/depreciation deduction for property bought in year 3	(100,000)	(100,000)	0	0	0	0
Capital account at end of year 3	0	$100,000	$100,000	$200,000	$200,000	$200,000

(xi) Assume the same facts as in (x) and that at the beginning of the partnership's fourth taxable year, the properties purchased in the partnership's first and third taxable years are disposed of for $90,000 and $180,000, respectively, and the partnership is liquidated. With respect to the property purchased in the first taxable year, there is a book loss of $210,000 ($300,000 book value less $90,000) and a taxable loss of $10,000 ($100,000 adjusted tax basis less $90,000). The book loss is allocated equally among the partners, and such allocation has substantial economic effect. Consistent with the special partners' interests in the partnership rule contained in paragraph (b)(4)(i) of this section, the partnership agreement provides that the taxable loss of $10,000 will, in accordance with section 704(c) principles, be included entirely in MK's distributive share. With respect to the property purchased in the partnership's third taxable year, there is a book and taxable loss of $20,000. Pursuant to the partnership agreement this loss is allocated entirely to WM, and such allocation has substantial economic effect.

	WM		JL		MK	
	Tax	Book	Tax	Book	Tax	Book
Capital account at beginning of year 4	0	$100,000	$100,000	$200,000	$200,000	$200,000
Less:						
(a) loss on property bought in year 1	0	(70,000)	0	(70,000)	(10,000)	(70,000)
(b) loss on property bought in year 3	(20,000)	(20,000)	0	0	0	0
Capital account before liquidation	($20,000)	$10,000	$100,000	$130,000	$190,000	$130,000

Partnership liquidation proceeds ($270,000) are properly distributed in accordance with the partners' adjusted positive book capital account balances ($10,000 to WM, $130,000 to JL and $130,000 to MK).

(xii) Assume the same facts as in (x) and that in the partnership's fourth taxable year it has a cost recovery deduction of $60,000 and book depreciation deduction of $180,000 attributable to the property purchased in the partnership's first taxable year, and a cost recovery and book depreciation deduction of $100,000 attributable to the property purchased in the partnership's third taxable year. The $180,000 book depreciation deduction attributable to the property purchased in the partnership's first taxable year is allocated equally among the partners, and such allocation has substantial economic effect. Consistent with the special partners' interests in the partnership rule contained in paragraph (b)(4)(i) of this section, the partnership agreement provides that the $60,000 cost recovery deduction attributable to the property purchased in the first taxable year is, in accordance with section 704(c) principles, included entirely in MK's distributive share. Furthermore, the $100,000 cost recovery deduction attributable to the property purchased in the third taxable year is allocated $50,000 to WM, $25,000 to JL, and $25,000 to MK, and such allocation has substantial economic effect.

	WM		JL		MK	
	Tax	Book	Tax	Book	Tax	Book
Capital account at beginning of year 4	0	$100,000	$100,000	$200,000	$200,000	$200,000
Less:						
(a) recovery/depreciation deduction for property bought in year 1	0	(60,000)	0	(60,000)	(60,000)	(60,000)
(b) recovery/depreciation deduction for property bought in year 3	(50,000)	(50,000)	(25,000)	(25,000)	(25,000)	(25,000)
Capital account at end of year 4	($50,000)	($10,000)	$75,000	$115,000	$115,000	$115,000

At the end of the partnership's fourth taxable year the adjusted tax bases of the partnership properties acquired in its first and third taxable years are $40,000 and $100,000, respectively. If the properties are disposed of at the beginning of the partnership's fifth taxable year for their adjusted tax bases, there would be no taxable gain or loss, a book loss of $80,000 on the property purchased in the partnership's first taxable year ($120,000 book value less $40,000), and cash available for distribution of $140,000.

	WM		JL		MK	
	Tax	Book	Tax	Book	Tax	Book
Capital account at beginning of year 5	($50,000)	($10,000)	$75,000	$115,000	$115,000	$115,000
Less: loss	0	(26,667)	0	(26,667)	0	(26,667)
Capital account before liquidation	($50,000)	($36,667)	$75,000	$88,333	$115,000	$88,333

If the partnership is then liquidated, the $140,000 of cash on hand plus the $36,667 balance that WM would be required to contribute to the partnership (the deficit balance in his book capital account) would be distributed equally between JL and MK in accordance with their adjusted positive book capital account balances.

(xiii) Assume the same facts as in (i). Any tax preferences under section 57(a)(12) attributable to the partnership's cost recovery deductions in the first 2 taxable years will be taken into account equally by WM and JL. If the partnership agreement instead provides that the partnership's cost recovery deductions in its first 2 taxable years are allocated 25 percent to WM and 75 percent to JL (and such allocations have substantial economic effect), the tax preferences attributable to such cost recovery deductions would be taken into account 25 percent by WM and 75 percent by JL. The conclusion in the previous sentence is unchanged even if the partnership's operating expenses (exclusive of cost recovery and depreciation deductions) exceed its operating income in each of the partnership's first 2 taxable years, the resulting net loss is allocated entirely to WM, and the cost recovery deductions are allocated 25 percent to WM and 75 percent to JL (provided such allocations have substantial economic effect). If the partnership agreement instead provides that all income, gain, loss, and deduction (including cost recovery and depreciations) are allocated equally between JL and WM, the tax preferences attributable to the cost recovery deductions would be taken into account equally by JL and WM. In this case, if the partnership has a $100,000 cost recovery deduction in its first taxable year and an additional net loss of $100,000 in its first taxable year (i.e., its operating expenses exceed its operating income by $100,000) and purports to categorize JL's $100,000 distributive share of partnership loss as being attributable to the cost recovery deduction and WM's $100,000 distributive share of partnership loss as being attributable to the net loss, the economic effect of such allocations is not substantial, and each partner will be allocated one-half of all partnership income, gain, loss, and deduction and will take into account one-half of the tax preferences attributable to the cost recovery deductions.

Example (19). **(i)** DG and JC form a general partnership for the purpose of drilling oil wells. DG contributes an oil lease, which has a fair market value and adjusted tax basis of $100,000. JC contributes $100,000 in cash, which is used to finance the drilling operations. The partnership agreement provides that DG is credited with a capital account of $100,000, and JC is credited with a capital account of $100,000. The agreement further provides that the partners' capital accounts will be determined and maintained in accordance with paragraph (b)(2)(iv) of this section, distributions in liquidation of the partnership (or any partner's interest) will be made in accordance with the partners' positive capital account balances, and any partner with a deficit balance in his capital account following the liquidation of his interest must restore such deficit to the partnership (as set forth in paragraphs (b)(2)(ii)(b)(2) and (3) of this section). The partnership chooses to adjust capital accounts on a simulated cost depletion basis and elects under section 48(q)(4) to reduce the amount of investment tax credit in lieu of adjusting the basis of its section 38 property. The agreement further provides that (1) all additional cash requirements of the partnership will be borne equally by DG and JC, (2) the deductions attributable to the property (including money) contributed by each partner will be allocated to such partner, (3) all other income, gain, loss, and deductions (and item thereof) will be allocated equally between DG and JC, and (4) all cash from operations will be distributed equally between DG and JC. In the partnership's first taxable year $80,000 of partnership intangible drilling cost deductions and $20,000 of cost recovery deductions on partnership equipment are allocated to JC, and the $100,000 basis of the lease is, for purposes of the depletion allowance under sections 611 and 613A(c)(7)(D), allocated to DG. The allocations of income, gain, loss, and deduction provided in the partnership agreement have substantial economic effect. Furthermore, since the allocation of the entire basis of the lease to DG will not result in capital account adjustments (under paragraph (b)(2)(iv)(k) of this section) the economic effect of which is insubstantial, and since all other partnership allocations are recognized under this paragraph, the allocation of the $100,000 adjusted basis of the lease to DG is, under paragraph (b)(4)(v) of this section, recognized as being in accordance with the partners' interests in partnership capital for purposes of section 613A(c)(7)(D).

(ii) Assume the same facts as in (i) except that the partnership agreement provides that (1) all additional cash requirements of the partnership for additional expenses will be funded by additional contributions from JC, (2) all cash from operations will first be distributed to JC until the excess of such cash distributions over the amount of such additional expense equals his initial $100,000 contributions, (3) all deductions attributable to such additional operating expenses will be allocated to JC, and (4) all income will be allocated to JC until the aggregate amount of income allocated to him equals the amount of partnership operating expenses funded by his initial $100,000 contribution plus the amount of additional operating expenses paid from contributions made solely by him. The allocations of income, gain, loss, and deduction provided in partnership agreement have economic effect. In addition, the economic effect of the allocations provided in the agreement is substantial. Because the partnership's drilling activities are sufficiently speculative, there is not a strong likelihood at the time the disproportionate allocations of loss and deduction to JC are provided for by the partnership agreement that the economic effect of such allocations will be largely offset by allocations of income. In addition, since the allocation of the entire basis of the lease to DG will not result in capital account adjustments (under paragraph (b)(2)(iv)(k) of this section) the economic effect of which is insubstantial, and since all other partnership allocations are recognized under this paragraph, the allocation of the adjusted basis of the lease to DG is, under paragraph (b)(4)(v) of this section, recognized as being in accordance with the partners' interests in partnership capital under section 613A(c)(7)(D).

(iii) Assume the same facts as in (i) except that all distributions, including those made upon liquidation of the partnership, will be made equally between DG and JC, and no partner is obligated to restore the deficit balance in his capital account to the partnership following the liquidation of his interest for distribution to partners with positive capital account balances. Since liquidation proceeds will be distributed equally between DG and JC irrespective of their capital account balances, and since no partner is required to restore the deficit balance in his capital account to the partnership upon liquidation (in accordance with paragraph (b)(2)(ii)(b)(3) of this section), the allocations of income, gain, loss, and deduction provided in the partnership agreement do not have economic effect and must be reallocated in accordance with the partners' interests in the partnership under paragraph (b)(3) of this section. Under these facts all partnership income, gain, loss, and deduction (and item thereof) will be reallocated equally between JC and DG. Furthermore, the allocation of the $100,000 adjusted tax basis of the lease of DG is not, under paragraph (b)(4)(v) of this section, deemed to be in accordance with the partners' interests in partnership capital under section 613A(c)(7)(D), and such basis must be reallocated in accordance with the partners' interests in partnership capital or income as determined under section 613A(c)(7)(D). The results in this example would be the same if JC's initial cash contribution were $1,000,000 (instead of $100,000), but in such case the partners should consider whether, and to what extent, the provisions of paragraph (b)(1) of § 1.721–1, and principles related thereto, may be applicable.

(iv) Assume the same facts as in (i) and that for the partnership's first taxable year the simulated depletion deduction with respect to the lease is $10,000. Since DG properly was allocated the entire depletable basis of the lease (such allocation having been recognized as being in accordance with DG's interest in partnership capital with respect to such lease), under paragraph (b)(2)(iv)(k)(1) of this section the partnership's $10,000 simulated depletion deduction is allocated to DG and will reduce his capital account accordingly. If (prior to any additional simulated depletion deductions) the lease is sold for $100,000, paragraph (b)(4)(v) of this section requires that the first $90,000 (i.e., the partnership's simulated adjusted basis in the lease) out of the $100,000 amount realized on such sale be allocated to DG (but does not directly affect his capital account). The partnership agreement allocates the remaining $10,000 amount realized equally between JC and DG (but such allocation does not directly affect their capital accounts). This allocation of the $10,000 portion of amount realized that exceeds the partnership's simulated adjusted basis in the lease will be treated as being in accordance with the partners' allocable shares of such amount realized under section 613A(c)(7)(D) because such allocation will not result in capital account adjustments (under paragraph (b)(2)(iv)(k) of this section) the economic effect of which is insubstantial, and all other partnership allocations are recognized under this paragraph. Under paragraph (b)(2)(iv)(k) of this section, the partners' capital accounts are adjusted upward by the partnership's simulated gain of $10,000 ($100,000 sales price less $90,000 simulated adjusted basis) in proportion to such partners' allocable shares of the $10,000 portion of the total amount realized that exceeds the partnership's $90,000 simulated adjusted basis ($5,000 to JC and $5,000 to DG). If the lease is sold for $50,000, under paragraph (b)(4)(v) of this section the entire $50,000 amount realized on the sale of the lease will be allocated to DG (but will not directly affect his capital account). Under paragraph (b)(2)(iv)(k) of this section the partners' capital accounts will be adjusted downward by the partnership's $40,000 simulated loss ($50,000 sales price less $90,000 simulated adjusted basis) in proportion to the partners' allocable shares of the total amount realized from the property that represents recovery of the partnership's simulated adjusted basis therein. Accordingly, DG's capital account will be reduced by such $40,000.

(c) Contributed property; cross-reference. See §§ 1.704–3 and 1.704–3T for methods of making allocations that take into account precontribution appreciation or diminution in value of property contributed by a partner to a partnership.

(d) Limitation on allowance of losses. (1) A partner's distributive share of partnership loss will be allowed only to the extent of the adjusted basis (before reduction by current year's losses) of such partner's interest in the partnership at the end of the partnership taxable year in which such loss occurred. A partner's share of loss in excess of his adjusted basis at the end of the partnership taxable year will not be allowed for that year. However, any loss so disallowed shall be allowed as a deduction at the end of the first succeeding partnership taxable year, and subsequent partnership taxable years, to the extent that the partner's adjusted basis for his partnership interest at the end of any such year exceeds zero (before reduction by such loss for such year).

(2) In computing the adjusted basis of a partner's interest for the purpose of ascertaining the extent to which a partner's distributive share of partnership loss shall be allowed as a deduction for the taxable year, the basis shall first be increased under section 705(a)(1) and decreased under section 705(a)(2), except for losses of the taxable year and losses previously disallowed. If the partner's distributive share of the aggregate of items of loss specified in section 702(a)(1), (2), (3), (8), and (9) exceeds the basis of the partner's interest computed under the preceding sentence, the limitation on losses under section 704(d) must be allocated to his distributive share of each such loss. This allocation shall be determined by taking the proportion that each loss bears to the total of all such losses. For purposes of the preceding sentence, the total losses for the taxable year shall be the sum of his distributive share of losses for the current year and his losses disallowed and carried forward from prior years.

(3) For the treatment of certain liabilities of the partner or partnership, see section 752 and § 1.752–1.

(4) The provisions of this paragraph may be illustrated by the following examples:

Example (1). At the end of the partnership taxable year 1955, partnership AB has a loss of $20,000. Partner A's distributive share of this loss is $10,000. At the end of such year, A's adjusted basis for his interest in the partnership (not taking into account his distributive share of the loss) is $6,000. Under section 704(d), A's distributive share of partnership loss is allowed to him (in his taxable year within or with which the partnership taxable year ends) only to the extent of his adjusted basis of $6,000. The $6,000 loss allowed for 1955 decreases the adjusted basis of A's interest to zero. Assume that, at the end of partnership taxable year 1956, A's share of partnership income has increased the adjusted basis of A's interest in the partnership to $3,000 (not taking into account the $4,000 loss disallowed in 1955). Of the $4,000 loss disallowed for the partnership taxable year 1955, $3,000 is allowed A for the partnership taxable year 1956, thus again decreasing the adjusted basis of his interest to zero. If, at the end of partnership taxable year 1957, A has an adjusted basis of his interest of at least $1,000 (not taking into account the disallowed loss of $1,000), he will be allowed the $1,000 loss previously disallowed.

Example (2). At the end of partnership taxable year 1955, partnership CD has a loss of $20,000. Partner C's distributive share of this loss is $10,000. The adjusted basis of his interest in the partnership (not taking into account his distributive share of such loss) is $6,000. Therefore, $4,000 of the loss is disallowed. At the end of partnership taxable year 1956, the partnership has no taxable income or loss, but owes $8,000 to a bank for money borrowed. Since C's share of this liability is $4,000, the basis of his partnership interest is increased from zero to $4,000. (See sections 752 and 722, and §§ 1.752–1 and 1.722–1.) C is allowed the $4,000 loss, disallowed for the preceding year under section 704(d), for his taxable year within or with which partnership taxable year 1956 ends.

Example (3). At the end of partnership taxable year 1955, partner C has the following distributive share of partnership items described in section 702(a): Long-term capital loss, $4,000;

short-term capital loss, $2,000; income as described in section 702 (a)(9), $4,000. Partner C's adjusted basis for his partnership interest at the end of 1955, before adjustment for any of the above items, is $1,000. As adjusted under section 705(a)(1)(A), C's basis is increased from $1,000 to $5,000 at the end of the year. C's total distributive share of partnership loss is $6,000. Since without regard to losses, C has a basis of only $5,000, C is allowed only $5,000/$6,000 of each loss, that is, $3,333 of his long-term capital loss, and $1,667 of his short-term capital loss. C must carry forward to succeeding taxable years $667 as a long-term capital loss and $333 as a short-term capital loss.

(e) Family partnerships—(1) In general—(i) Introduction. The production of income by a partnership is attributable to the capital or services, or both, contributed by the partners. The provisions of subchapter K, chapter 1 of the Code, are to be read in the light of their relationship to section 61, which requires, *inter alia*, that income be taxed to the person who earns it through his own labor and skill and the utilization of his own capital.

(ii) Recognition of donee as partner. With respect to partnerships in which capital is a material income-producing factor, section 704(e)(1) provides that a person shall be recognized as a partner for income tax purposes if he owns a capital interest in such a partnership whether or not such interest is derived by purchase or gift from any other person. If a capital interest in a partnership in which capital is a material income-producing factor is created by gift, section 704(e)(2) provides that the distributive share of the donee under the partnership agreement shall be includible in his gross income, except to the extent that such distributive share is determined without allowance of reasonable compensation for services rendered to the partnership by the donor, and except to the extent that the portion of such distributive share attributable to donated capital is proportionately greater than the share of the donor attributable to the donor's capital. For rules of allocation in such cases, see subparagraph (3) of this paragraph.

(iii) Requirement of complete transfer to donee. A donee or purchaser of a capital interest in a partnership is not recognized as a partner under the principles of section 704(e)(l) unless such interest is acquired in a *bona fide* transaction, not a mere sham for tax avoidance or evasion purposes, and the donee or purchaser is the real owner of such interest. To be recognized, a transfer must vest dominion and control of the partnership interest in the transferee. The existence of such dominion and control in the donee is to be determined from all the facts and circumstances. A transfer is not recognized if the transferor retains such incidents of ownership that the transferee has not acquired full and complete ownership of the partnership interest. Transactions between members of a family will be closely scrutinized, and the circumstances, not only at the time of the purported transfer but also during the periods preceding and following it, will be taken into consideration in determining the *bona fides* or lack of *bona fides* of the purported gift or sale. A partnership may be recognized for income tax purposes as to some partners but not as to others.

(iv) Capital as a material income-producing factor. For purposes of section 704(e)(1), the determination as to whether capital is a material income-producing factor must be made by reference to all the facts of each case. Capital is a material income-producing factor if a substantial portion of the gross income of the business is attributable to the employment of capital in the business conducted by the partnership. In general, capital is not a material income-producing factor where the income of the business consists principally of fees, commissions, or other compensation for personal services performed by members or employees of the partnership. On the other hand, capital is ordinarily a material income-producing factor if the operation of the business requires substantial inventories or a substantial investment in plant, machinery, or other equipment.

(v) Capital interest in a partnership. For purposes of section 704(e), a capital interest in a partnership means an interest in the assets of the partnership, which is distributable to the owner of the capital interest upon his withdrawal from the partnership or upon liquidation of the partnership. The mere right to participate in the earnings and profits of a partnership is not a capital interest in the partnership.

(2) Basic tests as to ownership—(i) In general. Whether an alleged partner who is a donee of a capital interest in a partnership is the real owner of such capital interest, and whether the donee has dominion and control over such interest, must be ascertained from all the facts and circumstances of the particular case. Isolated facts are not determinative; the reality of the donee's ownership is to be determined in the light of the transaction as a whole. The execution of legally sufficient and irrevocable deeds or other instruments of gift under State law is a factor to be taken into account but is not determinative of ownership by the donee for the purposes of section 704(e). The reality of the transfer and of the donee's ownership of the property attributed to him are to be ascertained from the conduct of the parties with respect to the alleged gift and not by any mechanical or formal test. Some of the more important factors to be considered in determining whether the donee has acquired ownership of the capital interest in a partnership are indicated in subdivisions (ii) to (x), inclusive, of this subparagraph.

(ii) Retained controls. The donor may have retained such controls of the interest which he has purported to transfer to the donee that the donor should be treated as remaining the substantial owner of the interest. Controls of particular significance include, for example, the following:

(a) Retention of control of the distribution of amounts of income or restrictions on the distributions of amounts of income (other than amounts retained in the partnership annually with the consent of the partners, including the donee partner, for the reasonable needs of the business). If there is a partnership agreement providing for a managing partner or partners, then amounts of income may be retained in the partnership without the acquiescence of all the partners if such amounts are retained for the reasonable needs of the business.

(b) Limitation of the right of the donee to liquidate or sell his interest in the partnership at his discretion without financial detriment.

(c) Retention of control of assets essential to the business (for example, through retention of assets leased to the alleged partnership).

(d) Retention of management powers inconsistent with normal relationships among partners. Retention by the donor of control of business management or of voting control, such as is common in ordinary business relationships, is not by itself to be considered as inconsistent with normal relationships among partners, provided the donee is free to liquidate his interest at his discretion without financial detriment. The donee shall not be considered free to liquidate his interest unless, considering all the facts, it is evident that the donee is independent of the donor and has such maturity and understanding of his rights as to be capable of deciding to exercise, and capable of exercising, his right to withdraw his capital interest from the partnership.

The existence of some of the indicated controls, though amounting to less than substantial ownership retained by the donor, may be considered along with other facts and circumstances as tending to show the lack of reality of the partnership interest of the donee.

(iii) Indirect controls. Controls inconsistent with ownership by the donee may be exercised indirectly as well as directly, for example, through a separate business organization, estate, trust, individual, or other partnership. Where such indirect controls exist, the reality of the donee's interest will be determined as if such controls were exercisable directly.

(iv) Participation in management. Substantial participation by the donee in the control and management of the business (including participation in the major policy decisions affecting the business) is strong evidence of a donee partner's exercise of dominion and control over his interest. Such participation presupposes sufficient maturity and experience on the part of the donee to deal with the business problems of the partnership.

(v) Income distributions. The actual distribution to a donee partner of the entire amount or a major portion of his distributive share of the business income for the sole benefit and use of the donee is substantial evidence of the reality of the donee's interest, provided the donor has not retained controls inconsistent with real ownership by the donee. Amounts distributed are not considered to be used for the donee's sole benefit if, for example, they are deposited, loaned, or invested in such manner that the donor controls or can control the use or enjoyment of such funds.

(vi) Conduct of partnership business. In determining the reality of the donee's ownership of a capital interest in a partnership, consideration shall be given to whether the donee is actually treated as a partner in the operation of the business. Whether or not the donee has been held out publicly as a partner in the conduct of the business, in relations with customers, or with creditors or other sources of financing, is of primary significance. Other factors of significance in this connection include:

(a) Compliance with local partnership, fictitious names, and business registration statutes.

(b) Control of business bank accounts.

(c) Recognition of the donee's rights in distributions of partnership property and profits.

(d) Recognition of the donee's interest in insurance policies, leases, and other business contracts and in litigation affecting business.

(e) The existence of written agreements, records, or memoranda, contemporaneous with the taxable year or years concerned, establishing the nature of the partnership agreement and the rights and liabilities of the respective partners.

(f) Filing of partnership tax returns as required by law.

However, despite formal compliance with the above factors, other circumstances may indicate that the donor has retained substantial ownership of the interest purportedly transferred to the donee.

(vii) Trustees as partners. A trustee may be recognized as a partner for income tax purposes under the principles relating to family partnerships generally as applied to the particular facts of the trust-partnership arrangement. A trustee who is unrelated to and independent of the grantor, and who participates as a partner and receives distribution of the income distributable to the trust, will ordinarily be recognized as the legal owner of the partnership interest which he holds in trust unless the grantor has retained controls inconsistent with such ownership. However, if the grantor is the trustee, or if the trustee is amenable to the will of the grantor, the provisions of the trust instrument (particularly as to whether the trustee is subject to the responsibilities of a fiduciary), the provisions of the partnership agreement, and the conduct of the parties must all be taken into account in determining whether the trustee in a fiduciary capacity has become the real owner of the partnership interest. Where the grantor (or person amenable to his will) is the trustee, the trust may be recognized as a partner only if the grantor (or such other person) in his participation in the affairs of the partnership actively represents and protects the interests of the beneficiaries in accordance with the obligations of a fiduciary and does not subordinate such interests to the interests of the grantor. Furthermore, if the grantor (or person amenable to his will) is the trustee, the following factors will be given particular consideration:

(a) Whether the trust is recognized as a partner in business dealings with customers and creditors, and

(b) Whether, if any amount of the partnership income is not properly retained for the reasonable needs of the business, the trust's share of such amount is distributed to the trust annually and paid to the beneficiaries or reinvested with regard solely to the interests of the beneficiaries.

(viii) Interests (not held in trust) of minor children. Except where a minor child is shown to be competent to manage his own property and participate in the partnership activities in accordance with his interest in the property, a minor child generally will not be recognized as a member of a partnership unless control of the property is exercised by another person as fiduciary for the sole benefit of the child, and unless there is such judicial supervision of the conduct of the fiduciary as is required by law. The use of the child's property or income for support for which a parent is legally responsible will be considered a use for the parent's benefit. "Judicial supervision of the conduct of the fiduciary" includes filing of such accountings and reports as are required by law of the fiduciary who participates in the affairs of the partnership on behalf of the minor. A minor child will be considered as competent to manage his own property if he actually has sufficient maturity and experience to be treated by disinterested persons as competent to enter business dealings and otherwise to conduct his affairs on a basis of equality with adult persons, notwithstanding legal disabilities of the minor under State law.

(ix) Donees as limited partners. The recognition of a donee's interest in a limited partnership will depend, as in the case of other donated interests, on whether the transfer of property is real and on whether the donee has acquired dominion and control over the interest purportedly transferred to him. To be recognized for Federal income tax purposes, a limited partnership must be organized and conducted in accordance with the requirements of the applicable State limited-partnership law. The absence of services and participation in management by a donee in a limited partnership is immaterial if the limited partnership meets all the other requirements prescribed in this paragraph. If the limited partner's right to transfer or liquidate his interest is subject to substantial restrictions (for example, where the interest of the limited partner is not assignable in a real sense or where such interest may be required to be left in the business for a long term of years), or if the general partner retains any other control which substantially limits any of the rights which would ordinarily be exercisable by unrelated limited partners in normal business relationships, such restrictions on the right to transfer or liquidate, or retention of other control, will be considered strong evidence as to the lack of reality of ownership by the donee.

(x) Motive. If the reality of the transfer of interest is satisfactorily established, the motives for the transaction are generally immaterial. However, the presence or absence of a tax-avoidance motive is one of many factors to be considered in determining the reality of the ownership of a capital interest acquired by gift.

(3) Allocation of family partnership income—(i) In general. (a) Where a capital interest in a partnership in which capital is a material income-producing factor is created by gift, the donee's distributive share shall be includible in his gross income, except to the extent that such share is determined without allowance of reasonable compensation for services rendered to the partnership by the donor, and except to the extent that the portion of such distributive share attributable to donated capital is proportionately greater than the distributive share attributable to the donor's capital. For the purpose of section 704, a capital interest in a partnership purchased by one member of a family from another shall be considered to be created by gift from the seller, and the fair market value of the purchased interest shall be considered to be donated capital. The "family" of any individual, for the purpose of the preceding sentence, shall include only his spouse, ancestors, and lineal descendants, and any trust for the primary benefit of such persons.

(b) To the extent that the partnership agreement does not allocate the partnership income in accordance with (a) of this subdivision, the distributive shares of the partnership income of the donor and donee shall be reallocated by making a reasonable allowance for the services of the donor and by attributing the balance of such income (other than a reasonable allowance for the services, if any, rendered by the donee) to the partnership capital of the donor and donee. The portion of income, if any, thus attributable to partnership capital for the taxable year shall be allocated between the donor and donee in accordance with their respective interests in partnership capital.

(c) In determining a reasonable allowance for services rendered by the partners, consideration shall be given to all the facts and circumstances of the business, including the fact that some of the partners may have greater managerial responsibility than others. There shall also be considered the amount that would ordinarily be paid in order to obtain comparable services from a person not having an interest in the partnership.

(d) The distributive share of partnership income, as determined under (b) of this subdivision, of a partner who rendered services to the partnership before entering the Armed Forces of the United States shall not be diminished because of absence due to military service. Such distributive share shall be adjusted to reflect increases or decreases in the capital interest of the absent partner. However, the partners may by agreement allocate a smaller share to the absent partner due to his absence.

(ii) Special rules. (a) The provisions of subdivision (i) of this subparagraph, relating to allocation of family partnership income, are applicable where the interest in the partnership is created by gift, indirectly or directly. Where the partnership interest is created indirectly, the term "donor" may include persons other than the nominal transferor. This rule may be illustrated by the following examples:

Example (1). A father gives property to his son who shortly thereafter conveys the property to a partnership consisting of the father and the son. The partnership interest of the son may be considered created by gift and the father may be considered the donor of the son's partnership interest.

Example (2). A father, the owner of a business conducted as a sole proprietorship, transfers the business to a partnership consisting of his wife and himself. The wife subsequently conveys her interest to their son. In such case, the father, as well as the mother, may be considered the donor of the son's partnership interest.

Example (3). A father makes a gift to his son of stock in the family corporation. The corporation is subsequently liquidated. The son later contributes the property received in the liquidation of the corporation to a partnership consisting of his father and himself. In such case, for purposes of section 704, the son's partnership interest may be considered created by gift and the father may be considered the donor of his son's partnership interest.

(b) The allocation rules set forth in section 704(e) and subdivision (i) of this subparagraph apply in any case in which the transfer or creation of the partnership interest has any of the substantial characteristics of a gift. Thus, allocation may be required where transfer of a partnership interest is made between members of a family (including collaterals) under a purported purchase agreement, if the characteristics of a gift are ascertained from the terms of the purchase agreement, the terms of any loan or credit arrangements made to finance the purchase, or from other relevant data.

(c) In the case of a limited partnership, for the purpose of the allocation provisions of subdivision (i) of this subparagraph, consideration shall be given to the fact that a general partner, unlike a limited partner, risks his credit in the partnership business.

(4) Purchased interest—(i) In general. If a purported purchase of a capital interest in a partnership does not meet the requirements of subdivision (ii) of this subparagraph, the ownership by the transferee of such capital interest will be recognized only if it qualifies under the requirements applicable to a transfer of a partnership interest by gifts. In a case not qualifying under subdivision (ii) of this subparagraph, if payment of any part of the purchase price is made out of partnership earnings, the transaction may be regarded in the same light as a purported gift subject to deferred enjoyment of income. Such a transaction may be lacking in reality either as a gift or as a *bona fide* purchase.

(ii) Tests as to reality of purchased interests. A purchase of a capital interest in a partnership, either directly or by means of a loan or credit extended by a member of the family, will be recognized as *bona fide* if:

(a) It can be shown that the purchase has the usual characteristics of an arm's-length transaction, considering all relevant factors, including the terms of the purchase agreement (as to price, due date of payment, rate of interest, and security, if any) and the terms of any loan or credit arrangement collateral to the purchase agreement; the credit standing of the purchaser (apart from relationship to the seller) and the capacity of the purchaser to incur a legally binding obligation; or

(b) It can be shown, in the absence of characteristics of an arm's-length transaction, that the purchase was genuinely intended to promote the success of the business by securing participation of the purchaser in the business or by adding his credit to that of the other participants.

However, if the alleged purchase price or loan has not been paid or the obligation otherwise discharged, the factors indicated in (a) and (b) of this subdivision shall be taken into account only as an aid in determining whether a *bona fide* purchase or loan obligation existed.

* * *

§ 1.704–2 Allocations attributable to nonrecourse liabilities.

(a) Table of contents. This paragraph contains a listing of the major headings of this § 1.704–2.

(2) Definition of and determination of partner nonrecourse deductions.

(3) Determination of partner nonrecourse debt minimum gain.

(4) Chargeback of partner nonrecourse debt minimum gain.

(5) Partner's share of partner nonrecourse debt minimum gain.

(6) Distribution of partner nonrecourse debt proceeds allocable to an increase in partner nonrecourse debt minimum gain.

(j) Ordering rules.

(1) Treatment of partnership losses and deductions.

(i) Partner nonrecourse deductions.

(ii) Partnership nonrecourse deductions.

(iii) Carryover to succeeding taxable year.

(2) Treatment of partnership income and gains.

(i) Minimum gain chargeback.

(ii) Chargeback attributable to decrease in partner nonrecourse debt minimum gain.

(iii) Carryover to succeeding taxable year.

(k) Tiered partnerships.

(1) Increase in upper-tier partnership's minimum gain.

(2) Decrease in upper-tier partnership's minimum gain.

(3) Nonrecourse debt proceeds distributed from the lower-tier partnership to the upper-tier partnership.

(4) Nonrecourse deductions of lower-tier partnership treated as depreciation by upper-tier partnership.

(5) Coordination with partner nonrecourse debt rules.

(l) Effective dates.

(1) In general.

(i) Prospective application.

(ii) Partnerships subject to temporary regulations.

(iii) Partnerships subject to former regulations.

(2) Special rule applicable to pre-January 30, 1989, related party nonrecourse debt.

(3) Transition rule for pre-March 1, 1984, partner nonrecourse debt.

(4) Election.

(m) Examples.

(b) **General principles and definitions—(1) Definition of and allocations of nonrecourse deductions.** Allocations of losses, deductions, or section 705(a)(2)(B) expenditures attributable to partnership nonrecourse liabilities ("nonrecourse deductions") cannot have economic effect because the creditor alone bears any economic burden that corresponds to those allocations. Thus, nonrecourse deductions must be allocated in accordance with the partners' interests in the partnership. Paragraph (e) of this section provides a test that deems allocations of nonrecourse deductions to be in accordance with the partners' interests in the partnership. If that test is not satisfied, the partners' distributive shares of nonrecourse deductions are determined under § 1.704–1(b)(3), according to the partners' overall economic interests in the partnership. See also paragraph (i) of this section for special rules regarding the allocation of deductions attributable to nonrecourse liabilities for which a partner bears the economic risk of loss (as described in paragraph (b)(4) of this section).

(2) **Definition of and allocations pursuant to a minimum gain chargeback.** To the extent a nonrecourse liability exceeds the adjusted tax basis of the partnership property it encumbers, a disposition of that property will generate gain that at least equals that excess ("partnership minimum gain"). An increase in partnership minimum gain is created by a decrease in the adjusted tax basis of property encumbered by a nonrecourse liability below the amount of that liability and by a partnership nonrecourse borrowing that exceeds the adjusted tax basis of the property encumbered by the borrowing. Partnership minimum gain decreases as reductions occur in the amount by which the nonrecourse liability exceeds the adjusted tax basis of the property encumbered by the liability. Allocations of gain attributable to a decrease in partnership minimum gain (a "minimum gain chargeback," as required under paragraph (f) of this section) cannot have economic effect because the gain merely offsets nonrecourse deductions previously claimed by the

partnership. Thus, to avoid impairing the economic effect of other allocations, allocations pursuant to a minimum gain chargeback must be made to the partners that either were allocated nonrecourse deductions or received distributions of proceeds attributable to a nonrecourse borrowing. Paragraph (e) of this section provides a test that, if met, deems allocations of partnership income pursuant to a minimum gain chargeback to be in accordance with the partners' interests in the partnership. If property encumbered by a nonrecourse liability is reflected on the partnership's books at a value that differs from its adjusted tax basis, paragraph (d)(3) of this section provides that minimum gain is determined with reference to the property's book basis. See also paragraph (i)(4) of this section for special rules regarding the minimum gain chargeback requirement for partner nonrecourse debt.

(3) Definition of nonrecourse liability. "Nonrecourse liability" means a nonrecourse liability as defined in § 1.752–1(a)(2) or a § 1.752–7 liability [as defined in § 1.752–7(b)(3)(i)] assumed by the partnership from a partner on or after June 24, 2003.

(4) Definition of partner nonrecourse debt. "Partner nonrecourse debt" or "partner nonrecourse liability" means any partnership liability to the extent the liability is nonrecourse for purposes of § 1.1001–2, and a partner or related person (within the meaning of § 1.752–4(b)) bears the economic risk of loss under § 1.752–2 because, for example, the partner or related person is the creditor or a guarantor.

(c) Amount of nonrecourse deductions. The amount of nonrecourse deductions for a partnership taxable year equals the net increase in partnership minimum gain during the year (determined under paragraph (d) of this section), reduced (but not below zero) by the aggregate distributions made during the year of proceeds of a nonrecourse liability that are allocable to an increase in partnership minimum gain (determined under paragraph (h) of this section). See paragraph (m), Examples (1)(i) and (vi), (2), and (3) of this section. However, increases in partnership minimum gain resulting from conversions, refinancings, or other changes to a debt instrument (as described in paragraph (g)(3)) do not generate nonrecourse deductions. Generally, nonrecourse deductions consist first of certain depreciation or cost recovery deductions and then, if necessary, a pro rata portion of other partnership losses, deductions, and section 705(a)(2)(B) expenditures for that year; excess nonrecourse deductions are carried over. See paragraphs (j)(1)(ii) and (iii) of this section for more specific ordering rules. See also paragraph (m), Example (1)(iv) of this section.

(d) Partnership minimum gain—(1) Amount of partnership minimum gain. The amount of partnership minimum gain is determined by first computing for each partnership nonrecourse liability any gain the partnership would realize if it disposed of the property subject to that liability for no consideration other than full satisfaction of the liability, and then aggregating the separately computed gains. The amount of partnership minimum gain includes minimum gain arising from a conversion, refinancing, or other change to a debt instrument, as described in paragraph (g)(3) of this section, only to the extent a partner is allocated a share of that minimum gain. For any partnership taxable year, the net increase or decrease in partnership minimum gain is determined by comparing the partnership minimum gain on the last day of the immediately preceding taxable year with the partnership minimum gain on the last day of the current taxable year. See paragraph (m). Examples (1)(i) and (iv), (2), and (3) of this section.

(2) Property subject to more than one liability. (i) In general. If property is subject to more than one liability, only the portion of the property's adjusted tax basis that is allocated to a nonrecourse liability under paragraph (d)(2)(ii) of this section is used to compute minimum gain with respect to that liability.

(ii) Allocating liabilities. If property is subject to two or more liabilities of equal priority, the property's adjusted tax basis is allocated among the liabilities in proportion to their outstanding balances. If property is subject to two or more liabilities of unequal priority, the adjusted tax basis is allocated first to the liability of the highest priority to the extent of its outstanding balance and then to each liability in descending order of priority to the extent of its outstanding balance, until fully allocated. See paragraph (m), Example (1)(v) and (vii) of this section.

(3) Partnership minimum gain if there is a book/tax disparity. If partnership property subject to one or more nonrecourse liabilities is, under § 1.704–1(b)(2)(iv)(d), (f), or (r), reflected on the partnership's books at a value that differs from its adjusted tax basis, the determinations under this section are made with reference to the property's book value. See section 704(c) and § 1.704–1(b)(4)(i) for principles that govern the treatment of a partner's share of minimum gain that is eliminated by the revaluation. See also paragraph (m), Example (3) of this section.

(4) Special rule for year of revaluation. If the partners' capital accounts are increased pursuant to § 1.704–1 (b)(2)(iv)(d), (f), or (r) to reflect a revaluation of partnership property subject to a nonrecourse liability, the net increase or decrease in partnership minimum gain for the partnership taxable year of the revaluation is determined by:

(i) First calculating the net decrease or increase in partnership minimum gain using the current year's book values and the prior year's partnership minimum gain amount; and

(ii) Then adding back any decrease in minimum gain arising solely from the revaluation. See paragraph (m), Example (3)(iii) of this section. If the partners' capital accounts are decreased to reflect a revaluation, the net increases or decreases in partnership minimum gain are determined in the same manner as in the year before the revaluation, but by using book values rather than adjusted tax bases. See section 7701(g) and § 1.704–1(b)(2)(iv)(f)(1) (property being revalued cannot be booked down below the amount of any nonrecourse liability to which the property is subject).

(e) Requirements to be satisfied. Allocations of nonrecourse deductions are deemed to be in accordance with the partners' interests in the partnership only if—

(1) Throughout the full term of the partnership requirements (1) and (2) of § 1.704–1(b)(2)(ii)(b) are satisfied (i.e., capital accounts are maintained in accordance with § 1.704–1(b)(2)(iv) and liquidating distributions are required to be made in accordance with positive capital account balances), and requirement (3) of either § 1.704–1(b)(2)(ii)(b) or § 1.704–1 (b)(2)(ii)(d) is satisfied (i.e., partners with deficit capital accounts have an unconditional deficit restoration obligation or agree to a qualified income offset);

(2) Beginning in the first taxable year of the partnership in which there are nonrecourse deductions and thereafter throughout the full term of the partnership, the partnership agreement provides for allocations of nonrecourse deductions in a manner that is reasonably consistent with allocations that have substantial economic effect of some other significant partnership item attributable to the property securing the nonrecourse liabilities;

(3) Beginning in the first taxable year of the partnership that it has nonrecourse deductions or makes a distribution of proceeds of a nonrecourse liability that are allocable to an increase in partnership minimum gain, and thereafter throughout the full term of the partnership, the partnership agreement contains a provision that complies with the minimum gain chargeback requirement of paragraph (f) of this section; and

(4) All other material allocations and capital account adjustments under the partnership agreement are recognized under § 1.704–1(b) (without regard to whether allocations of adjusted tax basis and amount realized under section 613A(c)(7)(D) are recognized under § 1.704–1(b)(4)(v)).

(f) Minimum gain chargeback requirement—(1) In general. If there is a net decrease in partnership minimum gain for a partnership taxable year, the minimum gain chargeback requirement applies and each partner must be allocated items of partnership income and gain for that year equal to that partner's share of the net decrease in partnership minimum gain (within the meaning of paragraph (g)(2)).

(2) Exception for certain conversions and refinancings. A partner is not subject to the minimum gain chargeback requirement to the extent the partner's share of the net decrease in partnership minimum gain is caused by a recharacterization of nonrecourse partnership debt as partially or wholly recourse debt or partner nonrecourse debt, and the partner bears the economic risk of loss (within the meaning of § 1.752–2) for the liability.

(3) Exception for certain capital contributions. A partner is not subject to the minimum gain chargeback requirement to the extent the partner contributes capital to the partnership that is used to repay the nonrecourse liability or is used to increase the basis of the property subject to the nonrecourse liability, and the partner's share of the net decrease in partnership minimum gain results from the repayment or the increase to the property's basis. See paragraph (m), Example (1)(iv) of this section.

(4) Waiver for certain income allocations that fail to meet minimum gain chargeback requirement if minimum gain chargeback distorts economic arrangement. In any taxable year that a partnership has a net decrease in partnership minimum gain, if the minimum gain chargeback requirement would cause a distortion in the economic arrangement among the partners and it is not expected that the partnership will have sufficient other income to correct that distortion, the Commissioner has the discretion, if requested by the partnership, to waive the minimum gain chargeback requirement. The following facts must be demonstrated in order for a request for a waiver to be considered:

(i) The partners have made capital contributions or received net income allocations that have restored the previous nonrecourse deductions and the distributions attributable to proceeds of a nonrecourse liability; and

(ii) The minimum gain chargeback requirement would distort the partners' economic arrangement as reflected in the partnership agreement and as evidenced over the term of the partnership by the partnership's allocations and distributions and the partners' contributions.

(5) Additional exceptions. The Commissioner may, by revenue ruling, provide additional exceptions to the minimum gain chargeback requirement.

(6) Partnership items subject to the minimum gain chargeback requirement. Any minimum gain chargeback required for a partnership taxable year consists first of certain gains recognized from the disposition of partnership property subject to one or more partnership nonrecourse liabilities and then if necessary consists of a pro rata portion of the partnership's other items of income and gain for that year. If the amount of the minimum gain chargeback requirement exceeds the partnership's income and gains for the taxable year, the excess carries over. See paragraphs (j)(2)(i) and (iii) of this section for more specific ordering rules.

(7) Examples. The following examples illustrate the provisions in § 1.704–2(f).

Example (1). Partnership AB consists of two partners, limited partner A and general partner B. Partner A contributes $90 and Partner B contributes $10 to the partnership. The partnership agreement has a minimum gain chargeback provision and provides that, except as otherwise required by section 704(c), all losses will be allocated 90 percent to A and 10 percent to B; and that all income will be allocated first to restore previous losses and thereafter 50 percent to A and 50 percent to B. Distributions are made first to return initial capital to the partners and then 50 percent to A and 50 percent to B. Final distributions are made in accordance with capital account balances. The partnership borrows $200 on a nonrecourse basis from an unrelated third party and purchases an asset for $300. The partnership's only tax item for each of the first three years is $100 of depreciation on the asset. A's and B's shares of minimum gain (under paragraph (g) of this section) and deficit capital account balances are $180 and $20 respectively at the end of the third year. In the fourth year, the partnership earns $400 of net operating income and allocates the first $300 to restore the previous losses (i.e., $270 to A and $30 to B); the last $100 is allocated $50 each. The partnership distributes $200 of the available cash that same year; the first $100 is distributed $90 to A and $10 to B to return their capital contributions; the last $100 is distributed $50 each to reflect their ratio for sharing profits.

	A	B
Capital account on formation	$90	$10
Less: net loss in years 1–3	($270)	($30)
Capital account at end of year 3	($180)	($20)
Allocation of operating income to restore nonrecourse deductions	$180	$20
Allocation of operating income to restore capital contributions	$90	$10
Allocation of operating income to reflect profits	$50	$50
Capital accounts after allocation of operating income	$140	$60
Distribution reflecting capital contribution	($90)	($10)
Distribution in profit-sharing ratio	($50)	($50)
Capital accounts following distribution	($0)	($0)

In the fifth year, the partnership sells the property for $300 and realizes $300 of gain. $200 of the proceeds are used to pay the nonrecourse lender. The partnership has $300 to distribute, and the partners expect to share that equally. Absent a waiver under paragraph (f)(4) of this section, the minimum gain chargeback would require the partnership to allocate the first $200 of the gain $180 to A and $20 to B, which would distort their economic arrangement. This allocation, together with the allocation of the $100 profit $50 to each partner, would result in A having a positive capital account balance of $230 and B having a positive capital account balance of $70. The allocation of income in year 4 in effect anticipated the minimum gain chargeback that did not occur until year 5. Assuming the partnership would not have sufficient other income to correct the distortion that would otherwise result, the partnership may request that the Commissioner exercise his or her discretion to waive the minimum gain chargeback requirement and recognize allocations that would allow A and B to share equally the gain on the sale of the property. These allocations would bring the partners' capital accounts to $150 each, allowing them to share the last $300 equally. The Commissioner may, in his or her discretion, permit this allocation pursuant to paragraph (f)(4) of this section because the minimum gain chargeback would distort the partners' economic arrangement over the term of the partnership as reflected in the partnership agreement and as evidenced by the partners' contributions and the partnership's allocations and distributions.

Example (2). A and B form a partnership, contribute $25 each to the partnership's capital, and agree to share all losses and profits 50 percent each. Neither partner has an unconditional deficit restoration obligation and all the requirements in paragraph (e) of this section are met. The partnership obtains a nonrecourse loan from an unrelated third party of $100 and purchases two assets, stock for $50 and depreciable property for $100. The nonrecourse loan is secured by the partnership's depreciable property. The partnership generates $20 of depreciation in each of the first five years as its only tax item. These deductions are properly treated as nonrecourse deductions and the allocation of these deductions 50 percent to A and 50 percent to B is deemed to be in accordance with the partners' interests in the partnership. At the end of year five, A and B each have a $25 deficit capital account and a $50 share of partnership minimum gain. In the beginning of year six, (at the lender's request), A guarantees the entire nonrecourse liability. Pursuant to paragraph (d)(1) of this section, the partnership has a net decrease in minimum gain of $100 and under paragraph (g)(2) of this section. A's and B's shares of that net decrease are $50 each. Under paragraph (f)(1) of this section (the minimum gain chargeback requirement), B is subject to a $50 minimum gain chargeback. Because the partnership has no gross income in year six, the entire $50 carries over as a minimum gain chargeback requirement to succeeding taxable years until there is enough income to cover the minimum gain chargeback requirement. Under the exception to the minimum gain chargeback in paragraph (f)(2) of this section, A is not subject to a minimum gain chargeback for A's $50 share of the net decrease because A bears the economic risk of loss for the liability. Instead, A's share of partner nonrecourse debt minimum gain is $50 pursuant to paragraph (i)(3) of this section. In year seven, the partnership earns $100 of net operating income and uses the money to repay the entire $100 nonrecourse debt (that A has guaranteed). Under paragraph (i)(3) of this section, the partnership has a net decrease in partner nonrecourse debt minimum gain of $50. B must be allocated $50 of the operating income pursuant to the carried over minimum gain chargeback requirement; pursuant to paragraph (i)(4) of this section, the other $50 of operating income must be allocated to A as a partner nonrecourse debt minimum gain chargeback.

(g) Shares of partnership minimum gain—(1) Partner's share of partnership minimum gain. Except as increased in paragraph (g)(3) of this section, a partner's share of partnership minimum gain at the end of any partnership taxable year equals:

(i) The sum of nonrecourse deductions allocated to that partner (and to that partner's predecessors in interest) up to that time and the distributions made to that partner (and to that partner's predecessors in interest) up to that time of proceeds of a nonrecourse liability allocable to an increase in partnership minimum gain (see paragraph (h)(l) of this section); minus

(ii) The sum of that partner's (and that partner's predecessors' in interest) aggregate share of the net decreases in partnership minimum gain plus their aggregate share of decreases resulting from revaluations of partnership property subject to one or more partnership nonrecourse liabilities.

For purposes of § 1.704–1(b)(2)(ii)(d), a partner's share of partnership minimum gain is added to the limited dollar amount, if any, of the deficit balance in the partner's capital account that the partner is obligated to restore. See paragraph (m), Examples (1)(i) and (3)(i) of this section.

(2) Partner's share of the net decrease in partnership minimum gain. A partner's share of the net decrease in partnership minimum gain is the amount of the total net decrease multiplied by the partner's percentage share of the partnership's minimum gain at the end of the immediately preceding taxable year. A partner's share of any decrease in partnership minimum gain resulting from a revaluation of partnership property equals the increase in the partner's capital account attributable to the revaluation to the extent the reduction in minimum gain is caused by the revaluation. See paragraph (m), Example (3)(ii) of this section.

(3) Conversions of recourse or partner nonrecourse debt into nonrecourse debt. A partner's share of partnership minimum gain is increased to the extent provided in this paragraph (g)(3) if a recourse or partner nonrecourse liability becomes partially or wholly nonrecourse. If a recourse liability becomes a nonrecourse liability, a partner has a share of the partnership's minimum gain that results from the conversion equal to the partner's deficit capital account (determined under § 1.704–1(b)(2)(iv)) to the extent the partner no longer bears the economic burden for the entire deficit capital account as a result of the conversion. For purposes of the preceding sentence, the determination of the extent to which a partner bears the economic burden for a deficit capital account is made by determining the consequences to the partner in the case of a complete liquidation of the partnership immediately after the conversion applying the rules described in § 1.704–1(b)(2)(iii)(c) that deem the value of partnership property to equal its basis, taking into account section 7701(g) in the case of property that secures nonrecourse indebtedness. If a partner nonrecourse debt becomes a nonrecourse liability, the partner's share of partnership minimum gain is increased to the extent the partner is not subject to the minimum gain chargeback requirement under paragraph (i)(4) of this section.

(h) Distribution of nonrecourse liability proceeds allocable to an increase in partnership minimum gain—(1) In general. If during its taxable year a partnership makes a distribution to the partners allocable to the proceeds of a nonrecourse liability, the distribution is allocable to an increase in partnership minimum gain to the extent the increase results from encumbering partnership property with aggregate nonrecourse liabilities that exceed the property's adjusted tax basis. See paragraph (m), Example (1)(vi) of this section. If the net increase in partnership minimum gain for a partnership taxable year is allocable to more than one nonrecourse liability, the net increase is allocated among the liabilities in proportion to the amount each liability contributed to the increase in minimum gain.

(2) Distribution allocable to nonrecourse liability proceeds. A partnership may use any reasonable method to determine whether a distribution by the partnership to one or more partners is allocable to proceeds of a nonrecourse liability. The rules prescribed under § 1.163–8T for allocating debt proceeds among expenditures (applying those rules to the partnership as if it were an individual) constitute a reasonable method for determining whether the nonrecourse liability proceeds are distributed to the partners and the partners to whom the proceeds are distributed.

(3) Option when there is an obligation to restore. A partnership may treat any distribution to a partner of the proceeds of a nonrecourse liability (that would otherwise be allocable to an increase in partnership minimum gain) as a distribution that is not allocable to an increase in partnership minimum gain to the extent the distribution does not cause or increase a deficit balance in the partner's capital account that exceeds the amount the partner is otherwise obligated to restore (within the meaning of § 1.704–1(b)(2)(ii)(c)) as of the end of the partnership taxable year in which the distribution occurs.

(4) Carryover to immediately succeeding taxable year. The carryover rule of this paragraph applies if the net increase in partnership minimum gain for a partnership taxable year that is allocable to a nonrecourse liability under paragraph (h)(2) of this section exceeds the distributions allocable to the proceeds of the liability ("excess allocable amount"), and all or part of the net increase in partnership minimum gain for the year is carried over as an increase in partnership minimum gain for the immediately succeeding taxable year (pursuant to paragraph (j)(1)(iii) of this section). If the carryover rule of this paragraph applies, the excess allocable amount (or the amount carried over under paragraph (j)(l)(iii) of this section, if less) is treated in the succeeding taxable year as an increase in partnership minimum gain that arose in that year as a result of incurring the nonrecourse liability to which the excess allocable amount is attributable. See paragraph (m), Example (1)(vi) of this section. If for a partnership taxable year there is an excess allocable amount with respect to more than one partnership nonrecourse liability, the excess allocable amount is allocated to each liability in proportion to the amount each liability contributed to the increase in minimum gain.

(i) Partnership nonrecourse liabilities where a partner bears the economic risk of loss—(1) In general. Partnership losses, deductions, or section 705(a)(2)(B) expenditures that are attributable to a particular partner nonrecourse liability ("partner nonrecourse deductions," as defined in paragraph (i)(2) of this section) must be allocated to the partner that bears the economic risk of loss for the liability. If more than one partner bears the economic risk of loss for a partner nonrecourse liability, any partner nonrecourse deductions attributable to that liability must be allocated among the partners according to the ratio in which they bear the economic risk of loss. If partners bear the economic risk of loss for different portions of a liability, each portion is treated as a separate partner nonrecourse liability.

(2) Definition of and determination of partner nonrecourse deductions. For any partnership taxable year, the amount of partner nonrecourse deductions with respect to a partner nonrecourse debt equals the net increase during the year in minimum gain attributable to the partner nonrecourse debt ("partner nonrecourse debt minimum gain"), reduced (but not below zero) by proceeds of the liability distributed during the year to the partner bearing the economic risk of loss for the liability that are both attributable to the liability and allocable to an increase in the partner nonrecourse debt minimum gain. See paragraph (m), Example (1)(viii) and (ix) of this section. The determination of which partnership items constitute the partner nonrecourse deductions with respect to a partner nonrecourse debt must be made in a manner consistent with the provisions of paragraphs (c) and (j)(1)(i) and (iii) of this section.

(3) Determination of partner nonrecourse debt minimum gain. For any partnership taxable year, the determination of partner nonrecourse debt minimum gain and the net increase or decrease in partner nonrecourse debt minimum gain must be made in a manner consistent with the provisions of paragraphs (d) and (g)(3) of this section.

(4) Chargeback of partner nonrecourse debt minimum gain. If during a partnership taxable year there is a net decrease in partner nonrecourse debt minimum gain, any partner with a share of that partner nonrecourse debt minimum gain (determined under paragraph (i)(5) of this section) as of the beginning of the year must be allocated items of income and gain for the year (and, if necessary, for succeeding years) equal to that partner's share of the net decrease in the partner nonrecourse debt minimum gain. A partner's share of the net decrease in partner nonrecourse debt minimum gain is determined in a manner consistent with the provisions of paragraph (g)(2) of this section. A partner is not subject to this minimum gain chargeback, however, to the extent the net decrease in partner nonrecourse debt minimum gain arises because a partner nonrecourse liabliltiy become partially or wholly a nonrecourse liability. The amount that would otherwise be subject to the partner nonrecourse debt minimum gain chargeback is added to the partner's share of partnership minimum gain under paragraph (g)(3) of this section. In addition, rules consistent with the provisions of paragraphs (f)(2), (3), (4), and (5) of this section apply with respect to partner nonrecourse debt in appropriate circumstances. The determination of which items of partnership income and gain must be allocated pursuant to this paragraph (i)(4) is made in a manner that is consistent with the provisions of paragraph (f)(6) of this section. See paragraph (j)(2)(ii) and (iii) of this section for more specific rules.

(5) Partner's share of partner nonrecourse debt minimum gain. A partner's share of partner nonrecourse debt minimum gain at the end of any partnership taxable year is determined in a manner consistent with the provisions of paragraphs (g)(1) and (g)(3) of this section with respect to each particular partner nonrecourse debt for which the partner bears the economic risk of loss. For purposes of § 1.704–1(b)(2)(ii)(d), a partner's share of partner nonrecourse debt minimum gain is added to the limited dollar amount, if any, of the deficit balance in the partner's capital account that the partner is obligated to restore, and the partner is not otherwise considered to have a deficit restoration obligation as a result of bearing the economic risk of loss for any partner nonrecourse debt. See paragraph (m), Example (1)(viii) of this section.

(6) Distribution of partner nonrecourse debt proceeds allocable to an increase in partner nonrecourse debt minimum gain. Rules consistent with the provisions of paragraph (h) of this section apply to distributions of the proceeds of partner nonrecourse debt.

(j) Ordering rules. For purposes of this section, the following ordering rules apply to partnership items.

Notwithstanding any other provision in this section and § 1.704–1, allocations of partner nonrecourse deductions, nonrecourse deductions, and minimum gain chargebacks are made before any other allocations.

(1) Treatment of partnership losses and deductions. (i) Partner nonrecourse deductions. Partnership losses, deductions, and section 705(a)(2)(B) expenditures are treated as partner nonrecourse deductions in the amount determined under paragraph (i)(2) of this section (determining partner nonrecourse deductions) in the following order:

(A) First, depreciation or cost recovery deductions with respect to property that is subject to partner nonrecourse debt;

(B) Then, if necessary, a pro rata portion of the partnership's other deductions, losses, and section 705(a)(2)(B) items.

Depreciation or cost recovery deductions with respect to property that is subject to a partnership nonrecourse liability is first treated as a partnership nonrecourse deduction and any excess is treated as a partner nonrecourse deduction under this paragraph (j)(1)(i).

(ii) Partnership nonrecourse deductions. Partnership losses, deductions, and section 705(a)(2)(B) expenditures are treated as partnership nonrecourse deductions in the amount determined under paragraph (c) of this section (determining nonrecourse deductions) in the following order:

(A) First, depreciation or cost recovery deductions with respect to property that is subject to partnership nonrecourse liabilities;

(B) Then, if necessary, a pro rata portion of the partnership's other deductions, losses, and section 705(a)(2)(B) items.

Depreciation or cost recovery deductions with respect to property that is subject to partner nonrecourse debt is first treated as a partner nonrecourse deduction and any excess is treated as a partnership nonrecourse deduction under this paragraph (j)(1)(ii). Any other item that is treated as a partner nonrecourse deduction will in no event be treated as a partnership nonrecourse deduction.

(iii) Carryover to succeeding taxable year. If the amount of partner nonrecourse deductions or nonrecourse deductions exceed the partnership's losses, deductions, and section 705(a)(2)(B) expenditures for the taxable year (determined under paragraphs (j)(1)(i) and (ii) of this section), the excess is treated as an increase in partner nonrecourse debt minimum gain or partnership minimum gain in the immediately succeeding partnership taxable year. See paragraph (m), Example (1)(vi) of this section.

(2) Treatment of partnership income and gains. (i) Minimum gain chargeback. Items of partnership income and gain equal to the minimum gain chargeback requirement (determined under paragraph

(f) of this section) are allocated as a minimum gain chargeback in the following order:

(A) First, gain from the disposition of property subject to partnership nonrecourse liabilities;

(B) Then, if necessary, a pro rata portion of the partnership's other items of income and gain for that year. Gain from the disposition of property subject to partner nonrecourse debt is allocated to satisfy a minimum gain chargeback requirement for partnership nonrecourse debt only to the extent not allocated under paragraph (j)(2)(ii) of this section.

(ii) Chargeback attributable to decrease in partner nonrecourse debt minimum gain. Items of partnership income and gain equal to the partner nonrecourse debt minimum gain chargeback (determined under paragraph (i)(4) of this section) are allocated to satisfy a partner nonrecourse debt minimum gain chargeback in the following order:

(A) First, gain from the disposition of property subject to partner nonrecourse debt;

(B) Then, if necessary, a pro rata portion of the partnership's other items of income and gain for that year. Gain from the disposition of property subject to a partnership nonrecourse liability is allocated to satisfy a partner nonrecourse debt minimum gain chargeback only to the extent not allocated under paragraph (j)(2)(i) of this section. An item of partnership income and gain that is allocated to satisfy a minimum gain chargeback under paragraph (f) of this section is not allocated to satisfy a minimum gain chargeback under paragraph (i)(4).

(iii) Carryover to succeeding taxable year. If a minimum gain chargeback requirement (determined under paragraphs (f) and (i)(4) of this section) exceeds the partnership's income and gains for the taxable year, the excess is treated as a minimum gain chargeback requirement in the immediately succeeding partnership taxable years until fully charged back.

(k) Tiered partnerships. For purposes of this section, the following rules determine the effect on partnership minimum gain when a partnership ("upper-tier partnership") is a partner in another partnership ("lower-tier partnership").

(1) Increase in upper-tier partnership's minimum gain. The sum of the nonrecourse deductions that the lower-tier partnership allocates to the upper-tier partnership for any taxable year of the upper-tier partnership, and the distributions made during that taxable year from the lower-tier partnership to the upper-tier partnership of proceeds of nonrecourse debt that are allocable to an increase in the lower-tier partnership's minimum gain, is treated as an increase in the upper-tier partnership's minimum gain.

(2) Decrease in upper-tier partnership's minimum gain. The upper-tier partnership's share for its taxable year of the lower-tier partnership's net decrease in its minimum gain is treated as a decrease in the upper-tier partnership's minimum gain for that taxable year.

(3) Nonrecourse debt proceeds distributed from the lower-tier partnership to the upper-tier partnership. All distributions from the lower-tier partnership to the upper-tier partnership during the upper-tier partnership's taxable year of proceeds of a nonrecourse liability allocable to an increase in the lower-tier partnership's minimum gain are treated as proceeds of a nonrecourse liability of the upper-tier partnership. The increase in the upper-tier partnership's minimum gain (under paragraph (k)(1) of this section) attributable to the receipt of those distributions is, for purposes of paragraph (h) of this section, treated as an increase in the upper-tier partnership's minimum gain arising from encumbering property of the upper-tier partnership with a nonrecourse liability of the upper-tier partnership.

(4) Nonrecourse deductions of lower-tier partnership treated as depreciation by upper-tier partnership. For purposes of paragraph (c) of this section, all nonrecourse deductions allocated by the lower-tier partnership to the upper-tier partnership for the upper-tier partnership's taxable year are treated as depreciation or cost recovery deductions with respect to property owned by the upper-tier partnership and subject to a nonrecourse liability of the upper-tier partnership with respect to which minimum gain increased during the year by the amount of the nonrecourse deductions.

(5) Coordination with partner nonrecourse debt rules. The lower-tier partnership's liabilities that are treated as the upper-tier partnership's liabilities under § 1.752–4(a) are treated as the upper-tier partnership's liabilities for purposes of applying paragraph (i) of this section. Rules consistent with the provisions of paragraphs (k)(1) through (k)(4) of this section apply to determine the allocations that the upper-tier partnership must make with respect to any liability that constitutes a nonrecourse debt for which one or more partners of the upper-tier partnership bear the economic risk of loss.

(l) Effective dates—(1) In general—(i) Prospective application. Except as otherwise provided in this paragraph (l), this section applies for partnership taxable years beginning on or after December 28, 1991. For the rules applicable to taxable years beginning after December 29, 1988, and before December 28, 1991, see former § 1.704–1T(b)(4)(iv). For the rules applicable to taxable years beginning on or before December 29, 1988, see former § 1.704–1 (b)(4)(iv).

(ii) Partnerships subject to temporary regulations. If a partnership agreement entered into after December 29, 1988, and before December 28, 1991, or a partnership agreement entered into on or before December 29, 1988, that elected to apply former § 1.704–1T(b)(4)(iv) (as contained in the CFR edition revised as of April 1, 1991), complied with the provisions of former § 1.704–1T(b)(4)(iv) before December 28, 1991—

(A) The provisions of former § 1.704–1T(b)(4)(iv) continue to apply to the partnership for any taxable year beginning on or after December 28, 1991 (unless the partnership makes an election under paragraph (l)(4) of this section) and ending before any subsequent material modification to the partnership agreement; and

(B) The provisions of this section do not apply to the partnership for any of those taxable years.

(iii) Partnerships subject to former regulations. If a partnership agreement entered into on or before December 29, 1988, complied with the provisions of former § 1.704–1(b)(4)(iv)(d) on or before that date—

(A) The provisions of former § 1.704–1(b)(4)(iv)(a) through (f) continue to apply to the partnership for any taxable year beginning after that date (unless the partnership made an election under § 1.704–1T(b)(4)(iv)(m)(4) in a partnership taxable year ending before December 28, 1991, or makes an election under paragraph (l)(4) of this section) and ending before any subsequent material modification to the partnership agreement; and

(B) The provisions of this section do not apply to the partnership for any of those taxable years.

(2) Special rule applicable to pre-January 30, 1989, related party nonrecourse debt. For purposes of this section and former § 1.704–1T(b)(4)(iv), if—

(i) A partnership liability would, but for this paragraph (l)(2) of this section, constitute a partner nonrecourse debt; and

(ii) Sections 1.752–1 through –3 or former §§ 1.752–1T through –3T (whichever is applicable) do not apply to the liability;

the liability is, notwithstanding paragraphs (i) and (b)(4) of this section, treated as a nonrecourse liability of the partnership, and not as a partner nonrecourse debt, to the extent the liability would be so treated under this section (or § 1.704–1T(b)(4)(iv)) if the determination of the extent to which one or more partners bears the economic risk of loss for the liability under § 1.752–1 or former § 1.752–1T were made without regard to the economic risk of loss that any partner would otherwise be considered to bear for the liability by reason of any obligation undertaken or interest as a creditor acquired prior to January 30, 1989, by a person related to the partner (within the meaning of § 1.752–4(b) or former § 1.752–1T(h)). For purposes of the preceding sentence, if a related person undertakes an obligation or acquires an interest as a creditor on or after January 30, 1989, pursuant to a written binding contract in effect prior to January 30, 1989, and at all times thereafter, the obligation or interest as a creditor is treated as if it were undertaken or acquired prior to January 30, 1989. However, for partnership taxable years beginning on or after December 29, 1988, a pre-January 30, 1989, liability, other than a liability subject to paragraph (l)(3) of this section or former § 1.704–1T(b)(4)(iv)(m)(3) (whichever is applicable), that is treated as grandfathered under former §§ 1.752–1T through –3T (whichever is applicable) will be treated as a nonrecourse liability for purposes of this section provided that all partners in the partnership consistently treat the liability as nonrecourse for partnership taxable years beginning on or after December 29, 1988.

(3) Transition rule for pre-March 1, 1984, partner nonrecourse debt. If a partnership liability would, but for this paragraph (l)(3) or former § 1.704–1T(b)(4)(iv), constitute a partner nonrecourse debt and the liability constitutes grandfathered partner nonrecourse debt that is appropriately treated as a nonrecourse liability of the partnership under § 1.752–1 (as in effect prior to December 29, 1988)—

(i) The liability is, notwithstanding paragraphs (i) and (b)(4) of this section, former § 1.704–1T(b)(4)(iv), and former § 1.704–1(b)(4)(iv), treated as a nonrecourse liability of the partnership for purposes of this section and for purposes of former § 1.704–1T(b)(4)(iv) and former § 1.704–1(b)(4)(iv) to the extent of the amount, if any, by which the smallest outstanding balance of the liability during the period beginning at the end of the first partnership taxable year ending on or after December 31, 1986, and ending at the time of any determination under this paragraph (l)(3)(i) or former § 1.704–1T (b)(4)(iv)(m)(3)(i) exceeds the aggregate amount of the adjusted basis (or book value) of partnership property allocable to the liability (determined in accordance with former § 1.704–1(b)(4)(iv)(c)(1) and (2) at the end of the first partnership taxable year ending on or after December 31, 1986); and

(ii) In applying this section to the liability, former § 1.704–1(b)(4)(iv)(c)(1) and (2) is applied as if all of the adjusted basis of partnership property allocable to the liability is allocable to the portion of the liability that is treated as a partner nonrecourse debt and as if none of the adjusted basis of partnership property that is allocable to the liability is allocable to the portion of the liability that is treated as a nonrecourse liability under this paragraph (l)(3) and former § 1.704–1T(b)(4)(iv)(m)(3)(i).

For purposes of the preceding sentence, a grandfathered partner debt is any partnership liability that was not subject to former §§ 1.752–1T and –3T but that would have been subject to those sections under § 1.752–4T(b) if the liability had arisen (other than pursuant to a written binding contract) on or after March 1, 1984. A partnership liability is not considered to have been subject to §§ 1.752–2T and –3T solely because a portion of the liability was treated as a liability to which those sections apply under § 1.752–4(e).

(4) Election. A partnership may elect to apply the provisions of this section to the first taxable year of the partnership ending on or after December 28, 1991. An election under this paragraph (l)(4) is made by attaching a written statement to the partnership return for the first taxable year of the partnership ending on or after December 28, 1991. The written statement must include the name, address, and taxpayer identification number of the partnership making the statement and must declare that an election is made under this paragraph (l)(4).

(m) Examples. The principles of this section are illustrated by the following examples:

Example 1. Nonrecourse deductions and partnership minimum gain. For Example 1, unless otherwise provided, the following facts are assumed. LP, the limited partner, and GP, the general partner, form a limited partnership to acquire and operate a commercial office building. LP contributes $180,000, and GP contributes $20,000. The partnership obtains an $800,000 nonrecourse loan and purchases the building (on leased land) for $1,000,000. The nonrecourse loan is secured only by the building, and no principal payments are due for 5 years. The partnership agreement provides that GP will be required to restore any deficit balance in GP's capital account following the liquidation of GP's interest (as set forth in § 1.704–1(b)(2)(ii)(b)(3)), and LP will not be required to restore any deficit balance in LP's capital account following the liquidation of LP's interest. The partnership agreement contains the following provisions required by paragraph (e) of this section; a qualified income offset (as defined in § 1.704–1(b)(2)(ii)(d)); a minimum gain chargeback (in accordance with paragraph (f) of this section); a provision that the partners' capital accounts will be determined and maintained in accordance with § 1.704–1(b)(2)(ii)(b)(1); and a provision that distributions will be made in accordance with partners' positive capital account balances (as set forth in § 1.704–1 (b)(2)(ii)(b)(2)). In addition, as of the end of each partnership taxable year discussed herein, the items described in § 1.704–1 (b)(2)(ii)(d)(4), (5), and (6) are not reasonably expected to cause or increase a deficit balance in LP's capital account. The partnership agreement provides that, except as otherwise required by its qualified income offset and minimum gain chargeback provisions, all partnership items will be allocated 90 percent to LP and 10 percent to GP until the first time when the partnership has recognized items of income and gain that exceed the items of loss and deduction it has recognized over its life, and all further partnership items will be allocated equally between LP and GP. Finally, the partnership agreement provides that all distributions, other than distributions in liquidation of the partnership or of a partner's interest in the partnership, will be made 90 percent to LP and 10 percent to GP until a total of $200,000 has been distributed, and thereafter all the distributions will be made equally to LP and GP. In each of the partnership's first 2 taxable years, it generates rental income of $95,000, operating expenses (including land lease payments) of $10,000, interest expense of $80,000, and a depreciation deduction of $90,000, resulting in a net taxable loss of $85,000 in each of those years. The allocations of these losses 90 per percent to LP and 10 percent to GP have substantial economic effect.

	LP	GP
Capital account on formation.................	$180,000	$20,000
Less: net loss in years 1 and 2..........	(153,000)	(17,000)
Capital account at end of year 2	27,000	3,000

In the partnership's third taxable year, it again generates rental income of $95,000, operating expenses of $10,000, interest expense of $80,000, and a depreciation deduction of $90,000, resulting in net taxable loss of $85,000. The partnership makes no distributions.

(i) Calculation of nonrecourse deductions and partnership minimum gain. If the partnership were to dispose of the building in full satisfaction of the nonrecourse liability at the end of the third year, it would realize $70,000 of gain ($800,000 amount realized less $730,000 adjusted tax basis). Because the amount of partnership minimum gain at the end of the third year (and the net increase in partnership minimum gain during the year) is $70,000, there are partnership nonrecourse deductions for that year of $70,000, consisting of depreciation deductions allowable with respect to the building of $70,000. Pursuant to the partnership agreement, all partnership items comprising the net taxable loss of $85,000, including the $70,000 nonrecourse deduction, are allocated 90 percent to LP and 10 percent to GP. The allocation of these items, other than the nonrecourse deductions, has substantial economic effect.

	LP	GP
Capital account at end of year 2	$27,000	$3,000
Less: net loss in year 3 (without nonrecourse deductions)	(13,500)	(1,500)
Less: nonrecourse deductions in year 3	(63,000)	(7,000)
Capital account at end of year 3	(49,500)	(5,500)

The allocation of the $70,000 nonrecourse deduction satisfies requirement (2) of paragraph (e) of this section because it is consistent with allocations having substantial economic effect of other significant partnership items attributable to the building. Because the remaining requirements of paragraph (e) of this section are satisfied, the allocation of nonrecourse deductions is deemed to be in accordance with the partners' interests in the partnership. At the end of the partnership's third taxable year, LP's and GP's shares of partnership minimum gain are $63,000 and $7,000, respectively. Therefore, pursuant to paragraph (g)(1) of this section, LP is treated as obligated to restore a deficit capital account balance of $63,000, so that in the succeeding year LP could be allocated up to an additional $13,500 of partnership deductions, losses, and section 705(a)(2)(B) items that are not nonrecourse deductions. Even though this allocation would increase a deficit capital account balance, it would be considered to have economic effect under the alternate economic effect test contained in § 1.704–1(b)(2)(ii)(d). If the partnership were to dispose of the building in full satisfaction of the nonrecourse liability at the beginning of the partnership's fourth taxable year (and had no other economic activity in that year), the partnership minimum gain would be decreased from $70,000 to zero, and the minimum gain chargeback would require that LP and GP be allocated $63,000 and $7,000, respectively, of the gain from that disposition.

(ii) Illustration of reasonable consistency requirement. Assume instead that the partnership agreement provides that all nonrecourse deductions of the partnership will be allocated equally between LP and GP. Furthermore, at the time the partnership agreement is entered into, there is a reasonable likelihood that over the partnership's life it will realize amounts of income and gain significantly in excess of amounts of loss and deduction (other than nonrecourse deductions). The equal allocation of excess income and gain has substantial economic effect.

	LP	GP
Capital account on formation................	$180,000	$20,000
Less: net loss in years 1 and 2	(153,000)	(17,000)
Less: net loss in year (without nonrecourse deductions)	(13,500)	(1,500)
Less: nonrecourse deductions in year 3	(35,000)	(35,000)
Capital account at end of year 3	(21,500)	(33,500)

The allocation of the $70,000 nonrecourse deduction equally between LP and GP satisfies requirement (2) of paragraph (e) of this section because the allocation is consistent with allocations, which will have substantial economic effect, of other significant partnership items attributable to the building. Because the remaining requirements of paragraph (e) of this section are satisfied, the allocation of nonrecourse deductions is deemed to be in accordance with the partners' interests in the partnership. The allocation to the nonrecourse deductions 75 percent to LP and 25 percent to GP (or in any other ratio between 90 percent to LP/10 percent to GP and 50 percent to LP/50 percent to GP) also would satisfy requirement (2) of paragraph (e) of this section.

(iii) Allocation of nonrecourse deductions that fails reasonable consistency requirement. Assume instead that the partnership agreement provides that LP will be allocated 99 percent, and GP 1 percent, of all nonrecourse deductions of the partnership. Allocating nonrecourse deductions this way does not satisfy requirement (2) of paragraph (e) of this section because the allocations are not reasonably consistent with allocations, having substantial economic effect, of any other significant partnership item attributable to the building. Therefore, the allocation of nonrecourse deductions will be disregarded, and the nonrecourse deductions of the partnership will be reallocated according to the partners' overall economic interests in the partnership, determined under § 1.704–1(b)(3)(ii).

(iv) Capital contribution to pay down nonrecourse debt. At the beginning of the partnership's fourth taxable year, LP contributes $144,000 and GP contributes $16,000 of additional capital to the partnership, which the partnership immediately uses to reduce the amount of its nonrecourse liability from $800,000 to $640,000. In addition, in the partnership's fourth taxable year, it generates rental income of $95,000, operating expenses of $10,000, interest expense of $64,000 (consistent with the debt reduction), and a depreciation deduction of $90,000, resulting in a net taxable loss of $69,000. If the partnership were to dispose of the building in full satisfaction of the nonrecourse liability at the end of that year, it would realize no gain ($640,000 amount realized less $640,000 adjusted tax basis). Therefore, the amount of partnership minimum gain at the end of the year is zero, which represents a net decrease in partnership minimum gain of $70,000 during the year. LP's and GP's shares of this net decrease are $63,000 and $7,000 respectively, so that at the end of the partnership's fourth taxable year, LP's and GP's shares of partnership minimum gain are zero. Although there has been a net decrease in partnership minimum gain, pursuant to paragraph (f)(3) of this section LP and GP are not subject to a minimum gain chargeback.

	LP	GP
Capital account at end of year 3	($49,500)	($5,500)
Plus: contribution................................	144,000	16,000
Less: net loss in year 4	(62,100)	(6,900)
Capital account at end of year 4	32,400	3,600
Minimum gain chargeback carryforward......................................	0	0

(v) Loans of unequal priority. Assume instead that the building acquired by the partnership is secured by a $700,000 nonrecourse loan and a $100,000 recourse loan, subordinate in priority to the nonrecourse loan. Under paragraph (d)(2) of this section, $700,000 of the adjusted basis of the building at the end of the partnership's third taxable year is allocated to the nonrecourse liability (with the remaining $30,000 allocated to the recourse liability) so that if the partnership disposed of the building in full satisfaction of the nonrecourse liability at the end of the year, it would realize no gain ($700,000 amount realized less $700,000 adjusted tax basis). Therefore, there is no minimum gain (or increase in minimum gain) at the end of the partnership's third taxable year. If, however, the $700,000 nonrecourse loan were subordinate in priority to the $100,000 recourse loan, under paragraph (d)(2) of this section, the first $100,000 of adjusted tax basis in the building would be allocated to the recourse liability, leaving only $630,000 of the adjusted basis of the building to be allocated to the $700,000 nonrecourse loan. In that case, the balance of the $700,000 nonrecourse liability would exceed the adjusted tax basis of the building by $70,000, so that there would be $70,000 of minimum gain (and a $70,000 increase in partnership minimum gain) in the partnership's third taxable year.

(vi) Nonrecourse borrowing; distribution of proceeds in subsequent year. The partnership obtains an additional nonrecourse loan of $200,000 at the end of its fourth taxable year, secured by a second mortgage on the building, and distributes $180,000 of this cash to its partners at the beginning of its fifth taxable year. In addition, in its fourth and fifth taxable years, the partnership again generates rental income of $95,000, operating expenses of $10,000, interest expense of $80,000 ($100,000 in the fifth taxable year reflecting the interest paid on both liabilities), and a depreciation deduction of $90,000, resulting in a net taxable loss of $85,000 ($105,000 in the fifth taxable year reflecting the interest paid on both liabilities). The partnership has distributed its $5,000 of operating cash flow in each year ($95,000 of rental income less $10,000 of operating expense and $80,000 of interest expenses) to LP and GP at the end of each year. If the partnership were to dispose of the building in full satisfaction of both nonrecourse liabilities at the end of its fourth taxable year, the partnership would realize $360,000 of gain ($1,000,000 amount realized less $640,000 adjusted tax basis). Thus, the net increase in partnership minimum gain during the partnership's fourth taxable year is $290,000 ($360,000 of minimum gain at the end of the fourth year less $70,000 of minimum gain at the end of the third year). Because the partnership did not distribute any of the proceeds of the loan it obtained in its fourth year during that year, the potential amount of partnership nonrecourse deductions for that year is $290,000. Under paragraph (c) of this section, if the partnership had distributed the proceeds of that loan to its partners at the end of its fourth year, the partnership's nonrecourse deductions for that year would have been reduced by the amount of that distribution because the proceeds of that loan are allocable to an increase in partnership minimum gain under paragraph (h)(1) of this section. Because the nonrecourse deductions of $290,000 for the partnership's fourth taxable year exceed its total deductions for that year, all $180,000 of the partnership's deductions for that year are treated as nonrecourse deductions, and the $110,000 excess nonrecourse deductions are treated as an increase in partnership minimum gain in the partnership's fifth taxable year under paragraph (c) of this section.

	LP	GP
Capital account at end of year 3 (including cash flow distributions)	($63,000)	($7,000)
Plus: rental income in year 4................	85,500	9,500
Less: nonrecourse deductions in year 4	(162,000)	(18,000)
Less: cash flow distributions in year 4..	(4,500)	(500)
Capital account at end of year 4	(144,000)	(16,000)

At the end of the partnership's fourth taxable year, LP's and GP's shares of partnership minimum gain are $225,000 and $25,000, respectively (because the $110,000 excess of nonrecourse deductions is carried forward to the next year). If the partnership were to dispose of the building in full satisfaction of the nonrecourse liabilities at the end of its fifth taxable year, the partnership would realize $450,000 of gain ($1,000,000 amount realized less 550,000 adjusted tax basis). Therefore, the net increase in partnership minimum gain during the partnership's fifth taxable year is $200,000 ($110,000 deemed increase plus the $90,000 by which minimum gain at the end of the fifth year exceeds minimum gain at the end of the fourth year ($450,000 less $360,000)). At the beginning of its fifth year, the partnership distributes $180,000 of the loan proceeds (retaining $20,000 to pay the additional interest expense). Under paragraph (h) of this section, the first $110,000 of this distribution (an amount equal to the deemed increase in partnership minimum gain for the year) is considered allocable to an increase in partnership minimum gain for the year. As a result, the amount of nonrecourse deductions for the partnership's fifth taxable year is $90,000 ($200,000 net increase in minimum gain less $110,000 distribution of nonrecourse liability proceeds allocable to an increase in partnership minimum gain), and the nonrecourse deductions consist solely of the $90,000 depreciation deduction allowable with respect to the building. As a result of the distributions during the partnership's fifth taxable year, the total distributions to the partners over the partnership's life equal $205,000. Therefore, the last $5,000 distributed to the partners during the fifth year will be divided equally between them under the partnership agreement. Thus, out of the $185,000 total distribution during the partnership's fifth taxable year, the first $180,000 is distributed 90 percent to LP and 10 percent to GP, and the last $5,000 is divided equally between them.

	LP	GP
Capital account at end of year 4	($144,000)	($16,000)
Less: net loss in year 5 (without nonrecourse deductions)................	(13,500)	(1,500)
Less: nonrecourse deductions in year 5	(81,000)	(9,000)
Less: distribution of loan proceeds	(162,000)	(18,000)
Less: cash flow distribution in year 5	(2,500)	(2,500)
Capital account at end of year 5	(403,000)	(47,000)

At the end of the partnership's fifth taxable year, LP's share of partnership minimum gain is $405,000 ($225,000 share of minimum gain at the end of the fourth year plus $81,000 of nonrecourse deductions for the fifth year and a $99,000 distribution of nonrecourse liability proceeds that are allocable to an increase in minimum gain) and GP's share of partnership minimum gain is $45,000 ($25,000 share of minimum gain at the end of the fourth year plus $9,000 of nonrecourse deductions for the fifth year and an $11,000 distribution of nonrecourse liability proceeds that are allocable to an increase in minimum gain).

(vii) Partner guarantee of nonrecourse debt. LP and GP personally guarantee the "first" $100,000 of the $800,000 nonrecourse loan (i.e., only if the building is worth less than $100,000 will they be called upon to make up any deficiency). Under paragraph (d)(2) of this section, only $630,000 of the adjusted tax basis of the building is allocated to the $700,000 nonrecourse portion of the loan because the collateral will be applied first to satisfy the $100,000 guaranteed portion, making it superior in priority to the remainder of the loan. On the other hand, if LP and GP were to guarantee the "last" $100,000 (i.e., if the building is worth less than $800,000, they will be called upon to make up the deficiency up to $100,000), $700,000 of the adjusted tax basis of the building would be allocated to the $700,000 nonrecourse portion of the loan because the guaranteed portion would be inferior in priority to it.

(viii) Partner nonrecourse debt. Assume instead that the $800,000 loan is made by LP, the limited partner. Under paragraph (b)(4) of this section, the $800,000 obligation does not constitute a nonrecourse liability of the partnership for purposes of this section because LP, a partner, bears the economic risk of loss for that loan within the meaning of § 1.752–2. Instead, the $800,000 loan constitutes a partner nonrecourse debt under paragraph (b)(4) of this section. In the partnership's third taxable year, partnership minimum gain would have increased by $70,000 if the debt were a nonrecourse liability of the partnership. Thus, under paragraph (i)(3) of this section, there is a net increase of $70,000 in the minimum gain attributable to the $800,000 partner nonrecourse debt for the partnership's third taxable year, and $70,000 of the $90,000 depreciation deduction from the building for the partnership's third taxable year constitutes a partner nonrecourse deduction with respect to the debt. See paragraph (i)(4) of this section. Under paragraph (i)(2) of this section, this partner nonrecourse deduction must be allocated to LP, the partner that bears the economic risk of loss for that liability.

(ix) Nonrecourse debt and partner nonrecourse debt of differing priorities. As in Example 1(viii) of this paragraph (m), the $800,000 loan is made to the partnership by LP, the limited partner, but the loan is a purchase money loan that "wraps around" a $700,000 underlying nonrecourse note (also secured by the building) issued by LP to an unrelated person in connection with LP's acquisition of the building. Under these circumstances, LP bears the economic risk of loss with respect to only $100,000 of the liability within the meaning of § 1.752–2. See § 1.752–2(f) (Example 6). Therefore, for purposes of paragraph (d) of this section, the $800,000 liability is treated as a $700,000 nonrecourse liability of the partnership and a $100,000 partner nonrecourse debt (inferior in priority to the $700,000 liability) of the partnership for which LP bears the economic risk of loss. Under paragraph (i)(2) of this section, $70,000 of the $90,000 depreciation deduction realized in the partnership's third taxable year constitutes a partner nonrecourse deduction that must be allocated to LP.

Example (2). Netting of increases and decreases in partnership minimum gain. For Example 2 unless otherwise provided, the following facts are assumed. X and Y form a general partnership to acquire and operate residential real properties. Each partner contributes $150,000 to the partnership. The partnership obtains a $1,500,000 nonrecourse loan and purchases 3 apartment buildings (on leased land) for $720,000 ("Property A"), $540,000 ("Property B"), and $540,000 ("Property C"). The nonrecourse loan is secured only by the 3 buildings, and no principal payments are due for 5 years. In each of the partnership's first 3 taxable years, it generates rental income of $225,000, operating expenses (including land lease payments) of $50,000, interest expense of $175,000, and depreciation deductions on the 3 properties of $150,000 ($60,000 on Property A and $45,000 on each of Property B and Property C), resulting in a net taxable loss of $150,000 in each of those years. The partnership makes no distributions to X or Y.

(i) Calculation of net increases and decreases in partnership minimum gain. If the partnership were to dispose of the 3 apartment buildings in full satisfaction of its nonrecourse liability at the end of its third taxable year, it would realize $150,000 of gain ($1,500,000 amount realized less $1,350,000 adjusted tax basis). Because the amount of partnership minimum gain at the end of that year (and the net increase in partnership minimum gain during that year) is $150,000, the amount of partnership nonrecourse deductions for that year is $150,000, consisting of depreciation deductions allowable with respect to the 3 apartment buildings of $150,000. The result would be the same if the partnership obtained 3 separate nonrecourse loans that were "cross-collateralized" (i.e., if each separate loan were secured by all 3 of the apartment buildings).

(ii) Netting of increases and decreases in partnership minimum gain when there is a disposition. At the beginning of the partnership's fourth taxable year, the partnership (with the permission of the nonrecourse lender) disposes of Property A for $835,000 and uses a portion of the proceeds to repay $600,000 of the nonrecourse liability (the principal amount attributable to Property A), reducing the balance to $900,000. As a result of the disposition, the partnership realizes gain of $295,000 ($835,000 amount realized less $540,000 adjusted tax basis). If the disposition is viewed in isolation, the partnership has generated minimum gain of $60,000 on the sale of Property A ($600,000 of debt reduction less $540,000 adjusted tax basis). However, during the partnership's fourth taxable year it also generates rental income of $135,000, operating expenses of $30,000, interest expense of $105,000, and depreciation deductions of $90,000 ($45,000 on each remaining building). If the partnership were to dispose of the remaining two buildings in full satisfaction of its nonrecourse liability at the end of the partnership's fourth taxable year, it would realize gain of $180,000 ($900,000 amount realized less $720,000 aggregate adjusted tax basis), which is the amount of partnership minimum gain at the end of the year. Because the partnership minimum gain increased from $150,000 to $180,000 during the partnership's fourth taxable year, the amount of partnership nonrecourse deductions for that year is $30,000, consisting of a ratable portion of depreciation deductions allowable with respect to the two remaining apartment buildings. No minimum gain chargeback is required for the taxable year, even though the partnership disposed of one of the properties subject to the nonrecourse liability during the year, because there is no net decrease in partnership minimum gain for the year. See paragraph (f)(1) of this section.

Example (3). Nonrecourse deductions and partnership minimum gain before third partner is admitted. For purposes of Example 3, unless otherwise provided, the following facts are assumed. Additional facts are given in each of Examples 3(ii), (iii), and (iv). A and B form a limited partnership to acquire and lease machinery that is 5-year recovery property. A, the limited partner, and B, the general partner, contribute $100,000 each to the partnership, which obtains an $800,000 nonrecourse loan and purchases the machinery for $1,000,000. The nonrecourse loan is secured only by the machinery. The principal amount of the loan is to be repaid $50,000 per year during each of the partnership's first 5 taxable years, with the remaining $550,000 of unpaid principal due on the first day of the partnership's sixth taxable year. The partnership agreement contains all of the provisions required by paragraph (e) of this section, and, as of the end of each partnership taxable year discussed herein, the items described in § 1.704–1(b)(2)(ii)(d)(4), (5), and (6) are not reasonably expected to cause or increase a deficit balance in A's or B's capital account. The partnership agreement provides that, except as otherwise required by its qualified income offset and minimum gain chargeback provisions, all partnership items will be allocated equally between A and B.

Finally, the partnership agreement provides that all distributions, other than distributions in liquidation of the partnership or of a partner's interest in the partnership, will be made equally between A and B. In the partnership's first taxable year it generates rental income of $130,000, interest expense of $80,000, and a depreciation deduction of $150,000, resulting in a net taxable loss of $100,000. In addition, the partnership repays $50,000 of the nonrecourse liability, reducing that liability to $750,000. Allocations of these losses equally between A and B have substantial economic effect.

	A	B
Capital account on formation	$100,000	$100,000
Less: net loss in year 1	(50,000)	(50,000)
Capital account at end of year 1	50,000	50,000

In the partnership's second taxable year, it generates rental income of $130,000, interest expense of $75,000, and a depreciation deduction of $220,000, resulting in a net taxable loss of $165,000. In addition, the partnership repays $50,000 of the nonrecourse liability, reducing that liability to $700,000, and distributes $2,500 of cash to each partner. If the partnership were to dispose of the machinery in full satisfaction of the nonrecourse liability at the end of that year, it would realize $70,000 of gain ($700,000 amount realized less $630,000 adjusted tax basis). Therefore, the amount of partnership minimum gain at the end of that year (and the net increase in partnership minimum gain during the year) is $70,000, and the amount of partnership nonrecourse deductions for the year is $70,000. The partnership nonrecourse deductions for its second taxable year consist of $70,000 of the depreciation deductions allowable with respect to the machinery. Pursuant to the partnership agreement, all partnership items comprising the net taxable loss of $165,000, including the $70,000 nonrecourse deduction, are allocated equally between A and B. The allocation of these items, other than the nonrecourse deductions, has substantial economic effect.

	A	B
Capital account at end of year 1	$50,000	$50,000
Less: net loss in year 2 (without nonrecourse deductions)	(47,500)	(47,500)
Less: nonrecourse deductions in year 2	(35,000)	(35,000)
Less: distribution	(2,500)	(2,500)
Capital account at end of year 2	(35,000)	(35,000)

(i) Calculation of nonrecourse deductions and partnership minimum gain. Because all of the requirements of paragraph (e) of this section are satisfied, the allocation of nonrecourse deductions is deemed to be made in accordance with the partners' interests in the partnership. At the end of the partnership's second taxable year, A's and B's shares of partnership minimum gain are $35,000 each. Therefore, pursuant to paragraph (g)(1) of this section, A and B are treated as obligated to restore deficit balances in their capital accounts of $35,000 each. If the partnership were to dispose of the machinery in full satisfaction of the nonrecourse liability at the beginning of the partnership's third taxable year (and had no other economic activity in that year), the partnership minimum gain would be decreased from $70,000 to zero. A's and B's shares of that net decrease would be $35,000 each. Upon that disposition, the minimum gain chargeback would require that A and B each be allocated $35,000 of that gain before any other allocation is made under section 704(b) with respect to partnership items for the partnership's third taxable year.

(ii) Nonrecourse deductions and restatement of capital accounts. (a) Additional facts. C is admitted to the partnership at the beginning of the partnership's third taxable year. At the time of C's admission, the fair market value of the machinery is $900,000. C contributes $100,000 to the partnership (the partnership invests $95,000 of this in undeveloped land and holds the other $5,000 in cash) in exchange for an interest in the partnership. In connection with C's admission to the partnership, the partnership's machinery is revalued on the partnership's books to reflect its fair market value of $900,000. Pursuant to § 1.704–1(b)(2)(iv)(f), the capital accounts of A and B are adjusted upwards to $100,000 each to reflect the revaluation of the partnership's machinery. This adjustment reflects the manner in which the partnership gain of $270,000 ($900,000 fair market value minus $630,000 adjusted tax basis) would be shared if the machinery were sold for its fair market value immediately prior to C's admission to the partnership.

	A	B
Capital account before C's admission	($35,000)	($35,000)
Deemed sale adjustment	135,000	135,000
Capital account adjusted for C's admission	100,000	100,000

The partnership agreement is modified to provide that, except as otherwise required by its qualified income offset and minimum gain chargeback provisions, partnership income, gain, loss, and deduction, as computed for book purposes, are allocated equally among the partners, and those allocations are reflected in the partners' capital accounts. The partnership agreement also is modified to provide that depreciation and gain or loss, as computed for tax purposes, with respect to the machinery will be shared among the partners in a manner that takes account of the variation between the property's $630,000 adjusted tax basis and its $900,000 book value, in accordance with § 1.704–1(b)(2)(iv)(f) and the special rule contained in § 1.704–1(b)(4)(i).

(b) Effect of revaluation. Because the requirements of § 1.704–1(b)(2)(iv)(g) are satisfied, the capital accounts of the partners (as adjusted) continue to be maintained in accordance with § 1.704–1(b)(2)(iv). If the partnership were to dispose of the machinery in full satisfaction of the nonrecourse liability immediately following the revaluation of the machinery, it would realize no book gain ($700,000 amount realized less $900,000 book value). As a result of the revaluation of the machinery upward by $270,000, under part (i) of paragraph (d)(4) of this section, the partnership minimum gain is reduced from $70,000 immediately prior to the revaluation to zero; but under part (ii) of paragraph (d)(4) of this section, the partnership minimum gain is increased by the $70,000 decrease arising solely from the revaluation. Accordingly, there is no net increase or decrease solely on account of the revaluation, and so no minimum gain chargeback is triggered. All future nonrecourse deductions that occur will be the nonrecourse deductions as calculated for book purposes, and will be charged to all 3 partners in accordance with the partnership agreement. For purposes of determining the partners' shares of minimum gain under paragraph (g) of this section, A's and B's shares of the decrease resulting from the revaluation are $35,000 each. However, as illustrated below, under section 704(c) principles, the tax capital accounts of A and B will eventually be charged $35,000 each, reflecting their 50 percent shares of the decrease in partnership minimum gain that resulted from the revaluation.

(iii) Allocation of nonrecourse deductions following restatement of capital accounts. (a) Additional facts. During the partnership's third taxable year, the partnership generates rental income of $130,000, interest expense of $70,000, a tax depreciation deduction of $210,000, and a book depreciation deduction (attributable to the machinery) of $300,000. As a result, the partnership has a net taxable loss of $150,000 and a net book loss of $240,000. In addition, the partnership repays $50,000 of the nonrecourse liability (after the data of C's admission), reducing the liability to $650,000 and distributes $5,000 of cash to each partner.

(b) Allocations. If the partnership were to dispose of the machinery in full satisfaction of the nonrecourse liability at the end of the year, $50,000 of book gain would result ($650,000 amount realized less $600,000 book basis). Therefore, the amount of partnership minimum gain at the end of the year is $50,000, which represents a net decrease in partnership minimum gain of $20,000 during the year. (This is so even though there would be an increase in partnership minimum gain in the partnership's third taxable year if minimum gain were computed with reference to the adjusted tax basis of the machinery.) Nevertheless, pursuant to paragraph (d)(4) of this section, the amount of nonrecourse deductions of the partnership for its third taxable year is $50,000 (the net increase in partnership minimum gain during the year determined by adding back the $70,000 decrease in partnership minimum gain attributable to the revaluation of the machinery to the $20,000 net decrease in partnership minimum gain during the year). The $50,000 of partnership nonrecourse deductions for the year consist of book depreciation deductions allowable with respect to the machinery of $50,000. Pursuant to the partnership agreement all partnership items comprising the net book loss of $240,000, including the $50,000 nonrecourse deduction, are allocated equally among the partners. The allocation of these items, other than the nonrecourse deductions, has substantial economic effect. Consistent with the special partners' interests in the partnership rule contained in § 1.704–1(b)(4)(i), the partnership agreement provides that the depreciation deduction for tax purposes of $210,000 for the partnership's third taxable year is, in accordance with section 704(c) principles, shared $55,000 to A, $55,000 to B, and $100,000 to C.

	A		B		C	
	Tax	Book	Tax	Book	Tax	Book
Capital account at beginning of year 3	(35,000)	$100,000	(35,000)	$100,000	$100,000	$100,000
Less: nonrecourse deductions	(9,166)	(16,666)	(9,166)	(16,666)	(16,666)	(16,666)

	A		B		C	
	Tax	Book	Tax	Book	Tax	Book
Less: items other than nonrecourse deductions in year 3	(25,834)	(63,334)	(25,834)	(63,334)	(63,334)	(63,334)
Less: distribution	(5,000)	(5,000)	(5,000)	(5,000)	(5,000)	(5,000)
Capital account at end of year 3	($75,000)	$15,000	($75,000)	$15,000	$15,000	$15,000

Because the requirements of paragraph (e) of this section are satisfied, the allocation of the nonrecourse deduction is deemed to be made in accordance with the partners' interests in the partnership. At the end of the partnership's third taxable year, A's, B's, and C's shares of partnership minimum gain are $16,666 each.

(iv) Subsequent allocation of nonrecourse deductions following restatement of capital accounts. (a) Additional facts. The partners' capital accounts at the end of the second and third taxable years of the partnership are as stated in Example 3(iii) of this paragraph (m). In addition, during the partnership's fourth taxable year the partnership generates rental income of $130,000, interest expense of $65,000, a tax depreciation deduction of $210,000, and a book depreciation deduction (attributable to the machinery) of $300,000. As a result, the partnership has a net taxable loss of $145,000 and a net book loss of $235,000. In addition, the partnership repays $50,000 of the nonrecourse liability, reducing that liability to $600,000, and distributes $5,000 of cash to each partner.

(b) Allocations. If the partnership were to dispose of the machinery in full satisfaction of the nonrecourse liability at the end of the fourth year, $300,000 of book gain would result ($600,000 amount realized less $300,000 book value). Therefore, the amount of partnership minimum gain as of the end of the year is $300,000, which represents a net increase in partnership minimum gain during the year of $250,000. Thus, the amount of partnership nonrecourse deductions for that year equals $250,000, consisting of book depreciation deductions of $250,000. Pursuant to the partnership agreement, all partnership items comprising the net book loss of $235,000, including the $250,000 nonrecourse deduction, are allocated equally among the partners. That allocation of all items, other than the nonrecourse deductions, has substantial economic effect. Consistent with the special partners' interests in the partnership rule contained in § 1.704–1(b)(4)(i), the partnership agreement provides that the depreciation deduction for tax purposes of $210,000 in the partnership's fourth taxable year is, in accordance with section 704(c) principles, allocated $55,000 to A, $55,000 to B, and $100,000 to C.

	A		B		C	
	Tax	Book	Tax	Book	Tax	Book
Capital account at end year 3	(75,000)	$15,000	(75,000)	$15,000	$15,000	$15,000
Less: nonrecourse deductions	(45,833)	(83,333)	(45,833)	(83,333)	(83,333)	(83,333)
Plus: items other than nonrecourse deduction in year 4	12,499	5,000	12,499	5,000	5,000	5,000
Less: distribution	(5,000)	(5,000)	(5,000)	(5,000)	(5,000)	(5,000)
Capital account at end of year 4	($113,334)	($68,333)	($113,333)	($68,333)	($68,333)	($68,333)

The allocation of the $250,000 nonrecourse deduction equally among A, B, and C satisfies requirement (2) of paragraph (e) of this section. Because all of the requirements of paragraph (e) of this section are satisfied, the allocation is deemed to be in accordance with the partners' interests in the partnership. At the end of the partnership's fourth taxable year A's, B's, and C's shares of partnership minimum gain are $100,000 each.

(v) Disposition of partnership property following restatement of capital accounts. (a) Additional facts. The partners' capital accounts at the end of the fourth taxable year of the partnership are as stated above in (iv). In addition, at the beginning of the partnership's fifth taxable year it sells the machinery for $650,000 (using $600,000 of the proceeds to repay the nonrecourse liability), resulting in a taxable gain of $440,000 ($650,000 amount realized less $210,000 adjusted tax basis) and a book gain of $350,000 ($650,000 amount realized less $300,000 book basis). The partnership has no other items of income, gain, loss, or deduction for the year.

(b) Effect of disposition. As a result of the sale, partnership minimum gain is reduced from $300,000 to zero, reducing A's, B's, and C's shares of partnership minimum gain to zero from $100,000 each. The minimum gain chargeback requires that A, B, and C each be allocated $100,000 of that gain (an amount equal to each partner's share of the net decrease in partnership minimum gain resulting from the sale) before any allocation is made to them under section 704(b) with respect to partnership items for the partnership's fifth taxable year. Thus, the allocation of the first $300,000 of book gain $100,000 to each of the partners is deemed to be in accordance with the partners' interests in the partnership under paragraph (e) of this section. The allocation of the remaining $50,000 of book gain equally among the partners has substantial economic effect. Consistent with the special partners' interests in the partnership rule contained in § 1.704–1(b)(4)(i), the partnership agreement provides that the $440,000 taxable gain is, in accordance with section 704(c) principles, allocated $161,667 to A, $161,667 to B, and $116,666 to C.

	A		B		C	
	Tax	Book	Tax	Book	Tax	Book
Capital account at end of year 4	($113,334)	($68,333)	($113,334)	($68,333)	($68,333)	($68,333)
Plus: minimum gain chargeback	138,573	100,000	138,573	100,000	100,000	100,000
Plus: additional gain	23,094	16,666	23,094	16,666	16,666	16,666
Capital account before liquidation	$48,333	$48,333	$48,333	$48,333	$48,333	$48,333

Example (4). Allocations of increase in partnership minimum gain among partnership properties. For Example 4, unless otherwise provided, the following facts are assumed. A partnership owns 4 properties, each of which is subject to a nonrecourse liability of the partnership. During a taxable year of the partnership, the following events take place. First, the partnership generates a depreciation deduction (for both book and tax purposes) with respect to Property W of $10,000 and repays $5,000 of the nonrecourse liability secured only by that property, resulting in an increase in minimum gain with respect to that liability of $5,000. Second, the partnership generates a depreciation deduction (for both book and tax purposes) with respect to Property X of $10,000 and repays none of the nonrecourse liability secured by that property, resulting in an increase in minimum gain with respect to that liability of $10,000. Third, the partnership generates a depreciation deduction (for both book and tax purposes) of $2,000 with respect to Property Y and repays $11,000 of the nonrecourse liability secured only by that property, resulting in a decrease in minimum gain with respect to that liability of $9,000 (although at the end of that year, there remains minimum gain with respect to that liability). Finally, the partnership borrows $5,000 on a nonrecourse basis, giving as the only security for that liability Property Z, a parcel of undeveloped land with an adjusted tax basis (and book value) of $2,000, resulting in a net increase in minimum gain with respect to that liability of $3,000.

(i) Allocation of increase in partnership minimum gain. The net increase in partnership minimum gain during that partnership taxable year is $9,000, so that the amount of nonrecourse deductions of the partnership for that taxable year is $9,000. Those nonrecourse deductions consist of $3,000 of depreciation deductions with respect to Property W and $6,000 of depreciation deductions with respect to Property X. See paragraph (c) of this section. The amount of nonrecourse deductions consisting of depreciation deductions is determined as follows. With respect to the nonrecourse liability secured by Property Z, for which there is no depreciation deduction, the amount of depreciation deductions that constitutes nonrecourse deductions is zero. Similarly, with respect to the nonrecourse liability secured by Property Y, for which there is no increase in minimum gain, the amount of depreciation deductions that constitutes nonrecourse deductions is zero. With respect to each of the nonrecourse liabilities secured by Properties W and X, which are secured by property for which there are depreciation deductions and for which there is an increase in minimum gain, the amount of depreciation deductions that constitutes nonrecourse deductions is determined by the following formula:

net increase in partnership minimum gain for that taxable year × total depreciation deductions for that taxable year on the specific property securing the nonrecourse liability to the extent minimum gain increased on that liability ÷ total depreciation deductions for that taxable year on all properties securing nonrecourse liabilities to the extent of the aggregate increase in minimum gain on all those liabilities.

Thus, for the liability secured by Property W, the amount is $9,000 times $5,000/$15,000, or $3,000. For the liability secured by Property X, the amount is $9,000 times $10,000/$15,000, or $6,000. (If one depreciable property secured two partnership nonrecourse liabilities, the amount of depreciation or book depreciation with respect to that property would be allocated among those liabilities in accordance with the method by which adjusted basis is allocated under paragraph (d)(2) of this section).

(ii) Alternative allocation of increase in partnership minimum gain among partnership properties. Assume instead that the loan secured by Property Z is $15,000 (rather than $5,000), resulting in a net increase in minimum gain with respect to that liability of $13,000. Thus, the net increase in partnership minimum gain is $19,000, and the amount of nonrecourse deductions of the partnership for that taxable year is $19,000. Those nonrecourse deductions consist of $5,000 of depreciation deductions with respect to Property W, $10,000 of depreciation deductions with respect to Property X, and a pro rata portion of the partnership's other items of deduction, loss, and section 705(a)(2)(B) expenditure for that year. The method for computing the amounts of depreciation deductions that constitute nonrecourse deductions is the same as in (i) of this Example 4 for the liabilities secured by Properties Y and Z. With respect to each of the nonrecourse liabilities secured by Properties W and X, the amount of depreciation deductions that constitutes nonrecourse deductions equals the total depreciation deductions with respect to the partnership property securing that particular liability to the extent of the increase in minimum gain with respect to that liability.

§ 1.704–3 Contributed property.

(a) In general—(1) General principles. The purpose of section 704(c) is to prevent the shifting of tax consequences among partners with respect to precontribution gain or loss. Under section 704(c), a partnership must allocate income, gain, loss, and deduction with respect to property contributed by a partner to the partnership so as to take into account any variation between the adjusted tax basis of the property and its fair market value at the time of contribution. Notwithstanding any other provision of this section, the allocations must be made using a reasonable method that is consistent with the purpose of section 704(c). For this purpose, an allocation method includes the application of all of the rules of this section (e.g., aggregation rules). An allocation method is not necessarily unreasonable merely because another allocation method would result in a higher aggregate tax liability. Paragraphs (b), (c), and (d) of this section describe allocation methods that are generally reasonable. Other methods may be reasonable in appropriate circumstances. Nevertheless, in the absence of specific published guidance, it is not reasonable to use an allocation method in which the basis of property contributed to the partnership is increased (or decreased) to reflect built-in gain (or loss), or a method under which the partnership creates tax allocations of income, gain, loss, or deduction independent of allocations affecting book capital accounts. See § 1.704–3T(d). Paragraph (e) of this section contains special rules and exceptions.

(2) Operating rules. Except as provided in paragraphs (e)(2) and (e)(3) of this section, section 704(c) and this section apply on a property-by-property basis. Therefore, in determining whether there is a disparity between adjusted tax basis and fair market value, the built-in gains and built-in losses on items of contributed property cannot be aggregated. A partnership may use different methods with respect to different items of contributed property, provided that the partnership and the partners consistently apply a single reasonable method for each item of contributed property and that the overall method or combination of methods are reasonable based on the facts and circumstances and consistent with the purpose of section 704(c). It may be unreasonable to use one method for appreciated property and another method for depreciated property. Similarly, it may be unreasonable to use the traditional method for built-in gain property contributed by a partner with a high marginal tax rate while using curative allocations for built-in gain property contributed by a partner with a low marginal tax rate. A new partnership formed as the result of the termination of a partnership under section 708(b)(1)(B) is not required to use the same method as the terminated partnership with respect to section 704(c) property deemed contributed to the new partnership by the terminated partnership under § 1.708–1(b)(1)(iv). The previous sentence applies to terminations of partnerships under section 708(b)(1)(B) occurring on or after May 9, 1997; however, the sentence may be applied to terminations occurring on or after May 9, 1996, provided that the partnership and its partners apply the sentence to the termination in a consistent manner.

(3) Definitions—(i) Section 704(c) property. Property contributed to a partnership is section 704(c) property if at the time of contribution its book value differs from the contributing partner's adjusted tax basis. For purposes of this section, book value is determined as contemplated by § 1.704–1(b). Therefore, book value is equal to fair market value at the time of contribution and is subsequently adjusted for cost recovery and other events that affect the basis of the property. For a partnership that maintains capital accounts in accordance with § 1.704–1(b)(2)(iv), the book value of property is initially the value used in determining the contributing partner's capital account under § 1.704–1(b)(2)(iv)(d), and is appropriately adjusted thereafter (e.g., for book cost recovery under §§ 1.704–1(b)(2)(iv)(g)(3) and 1.704–3T(d)(2) and other events that affect the basis of the property). A partnership that does not maintain capital accounts under § 1.704–1(b)(2)(iv) must comply with this section using a book capital account based on the same principles (i.e., a book capital account that reflects the fair market value of property at the time of contribution and that is subsequently adjusted for cost recovery and other events that affect the basis of the property). Property deemed contributed to a new partnership as the result of the termination of a partnership under section 708 (b)(1)(B) is treated as section 704(c) property in the hands of the new partnership only to the extent that the property was section 704(c) property in the hands of the terminated partnership immediately prior to the termination. See § 1.708–1(b)(1)(iv) for an example of the application of this rule. The previous two sentences apply to terminations of partnerships under section 708(b)(1)(B) occurring on or after May 9, 1997; however, the sentences may be applied to terminations occurring on or after May 9, 1996, provided that the partnership and its partners apply the sentences to the termination in a consistent manner.

(ii) Built-in gain and built-in loss. The built-in gain on section 704(c) property is the excess of the property's book value over the contributing partner's adjusted tax basis upon contribution. The built-in gain is thereafter reduced by decreases in the difference between the property's book value and adjusted tax basis. The built-in loss on section 704(c) property is the excess of the contributing partner's adjusted tax basis over the property's book value upon contribution. The built-in loss is thereafter reduced by decreases in the difference between the property's adjusted tax basis and book value. See § 1.460–4(k)(3)(v)(A) for a rule relating to the amount of built-in income or built-in loss attributable to a contract accounted for under a long-term contract method of accounting.

(4) Accounts payable and other accrued but unpaid items. Accounts payable and other accrued but unpaid items contributed by a partner using the cash receipts and disbursements method of accounting are treated as section 704(c) property for purposes of applying the rules of this section.

(5) Other provisions of the Internal Revenue Code. Section 704(c) and this section apply to a contribution of property to the partnership only if the contribution is governed by section 721, taking into account other provisions of the Internal Revenue Code. For example, to the extent that a transfer of property to a partnership is a sale under section 707, the transfer is not a contribution of property to which section 704(c) applies.

(6) Other applications of section 704(c) principles—(i) Revaluations under section 704(b). The principles of this section apply to allocations with respect to property for which differences between book value and adjusted tax basis are created when a partnership revalues partnership property pursuant to § 1.704–1(b)(2)(iv)(f) (reverse section 704(c) allocations). Partnerships are not required to use the same allocation method for reverse section 704 (c) allocations as for contributed property, even if at the time of revaluation the property is already subject to section 704(c) and paragraph (a) of this section. In addition, partnerships are not required to use the same allocation method for reverse section 704(c) allocations each time the partnership revalues its property. A partnership that makes allocations with respect to revalued property must use a reasonable method that is consistent with the purposes of section 704(b) and (c).

(ii) Basis adjustments. A partnership making adjustments under § 1.743–1(b) or 1.751–1(a)(2) must account for built-in gain or loss under section 704(c) in accordance with the principles of this section.

(7) Transfers of a partnership interest. If a contributing partner transfers a partnership interest, built-in gain or loss must be allocated to the transferee partner as it would have been allocated to the transferor partner. If the contributing partner transfers a portion of the partnership interest, the share of built-in gain or loss proportionate to the interest transferred must be allocated to the transferee partner. This rule does not apply to any person who acquired a partnership interest from a § 1.752–7 liability partner in a transaction to which paragraph (e)(1) of § 1.752–7 applies. See § 1.752–7(c)(1).

(8) Special rules.

(i) Disposition in a nonrecognition transaction. If a partnership disposes of section 704(c) property in a nonrecognition transaction the substituted basis property (within the meaning of section 7701(a)(42)) is treated as section 704(c) property with the same amount of built-in gain or loss as the section 704(c) property disposed of by the partnership. If gain or loss is recognized in such a transaction, appropriate adjustments must be made. The allocation method for the substituted basis property must be consistent with the allocation method chosen for the original property. If a partnership transfers an item of section 704 (c) property together with other property to a corporation under section 351, in order to preserve that item's built-in gain or loss, the basis in the stock received in exchange for the section 704(c) property is determined as if each item of section 704(c) property had been the only property transferred to the corporation by the partnership.

(ii) Disposition in an installment sale. If a partnership disposes of section 704(c) property in an installment sale as defined in section 453(b), the installment obligation received by the partnership is treated as the section 704(c) property with the same amount of built-in gain as the section 704(c) property disposed of by the partnership (with appropriate adjustments for any gain recognized on the installment sale). The allocation method for the installment obligation must be consistent with the allocation method chosen for the original property.

(iii) Contributed contracts. If a partner contributes to a partnership a contract that is section 704(c) property, and the partnership subsequently acquires property pursuant to the contract in a transaction in which less than all of the gain or loss is recognized, then the acquired property is treated as the section 704(c) property with the same amount of built-in gain or loss as the contract (with appropriate adjustments for any gain or loss recognized on the acquisition). For this purpose, the term contract includes, but is not limited to, options, forward contracts, and futures contracts. The allocation method for the acquired property must be consistent with the allocation method chosen for the contributed contract.

(iv) Capitalized amounts. To the extent that a partnership properly capitalizes all or a portion of an item as described in paragraph (a)(12) of this section, then the item or items to which such cost is properly capitalized is treated as section 704(c) property with the same amount of built-in loss as corresponds to the amount capitalized.

(9) Tiered partnerships. If a partnership contributes section 704(c) property to a second partnership (the lower-tier partnership), or if a partner that has contributed section 704(c) property to a partnership contributes that partnership interest to a second partnership (the upper-tier partnership), the upper-tier partnership must allocate its distributive share of lower-tier partnership items with respect to that section 704(c) property in a manner that takes into account the contributing partner's remaining built-in gain or loss. Allocations made under this paragraph will be considered to be made in a manner that meets the requirements of § 1.704–1(b)(2)(iv)(q) (relating to capital account adjustments where guidance is lacking).

(10) Anti-abuse rule. An allocation method (or combination of methods) is not reasonable if the contribution of property (or event that results in reverse section 704(c) allocations) and the corresponding allocation of tax items with respect to the property are made with a view to shifting the tax consequences of built-in gain or loss among the partners in a manner that substantially reduces the present value of the partners' aggregate tax liability.

(11) Contributing and noncontributing partners' recapture shares. For special rules applicable to the allocation of depreciation recapture with respect to property contributed by a partner to a partnership, see §§ 1.1245–1(e)(2) and 1.1250–1(f).

(12) § 1.752–7 liabilities. Except as otherwise provided in § 1.752–7, § 1.752–7 liabilities (within the meaning of § 1.752–7(b)(2)) are section 704(c) property (built-in loss property that at the time of contribution has a book value that differs from the contributing partner's adjusted tax basis) for purposes of applying the rules of this section. See § 1.752–7(c). To the extent that the built-in loss associated with the § 1.752–7 liability exceeds the cost of satisfying the § 1.752–7 liability (as defined in § 1.752–7(b)(3)), the excess creates a "ceiling rule" limitation, within the meaning of § 1.704–3(b)(1), subject to the methods of allocation set forth in § 1.704–3(b), (c) and (d).

(b) Traditional method—(1) In general. This paragraph (b) describes the traditional method of making section 704(c) allocations. In general, the traditional method requires that when the partnership has income, gain, loss, or deduction attributable to section 704(c) property, it must make appropriate allocations to the partners to avoid shifting the tax consequences of the built-in gain or loss. Under this rule, if the partnership sells section 704(c) property and recognizes gain or loss, built-in gain or loss on the property is allocated to the contributing partner. If the partnership sells a portion of, or an interest in, section 704(c) property, a proportionate part of the built-in gain or loss is allocated to the contributing partner. For section 704(c) property subject to amortization, depletion, depreciation, or other cost recovery, the allocation of deductions attributable to these items takes into account built-in gain or loss on the property. For example, tax allocations to the noncontributing partners of cost recovery deductions with respect to section 704(c) property generally must, to the extent possible, equal book allocations to those partners. However, the total income, gain, loss, or deduction allocated to the partners for a taxable year with respect to a property cannot exceed the total partnership income, gain, loss, or deduction with respect to that property for the taxable year (the ceiling rule). If a partnership has no property the allocations from which are limited by the ceiling rule, the traditional method is reasonable when used for all contributed property.

(2) Examples. The following examples illustrate the principles of the traditional method.

Example (1). Operation of the traditional method—(i) Calculation of built-in gain on contribution. A and B form partnership AB and agree that each will be allocated a 50 percent share of all partnership items and that AB will make allocations under section 704(c) using the traditional method under paragraph (b) of this section. A contributes depreciable property with an adjusted tax basis of $4,000 and a book value of $10,000, and B contributes $10,000 cash. Under paragraph (a)(3) of this section, A has built-in gain of $6,000, the excess of the partnership's book value for the property ($10,000) over A's adjusted tax basis in the property at the time of contribution ($4,000).

(ii) Allocation of tax depreciation. The property is depreciated using the straight-line method over a 10–year recovery period. Because the property depreciates at an annual rate of 10 percent, B would have been entitled to a depreciation deduction of $500 per year for both book and tax purposes if the adjusted tax basis of the property equalled its fair market value at the time of contribution. Although each partner is allocated $500 of book depreciation per year, the partnership is allowed a tax depreciation deduction of only $400 per year (10 percent of $4,000). The partnership can allocate only $400 of tax depreciation under the ceiling rule of paragraph (b)(1) of this section, and it must be allocated entirely to B. In AB's first year, the proceeds generated by the equipment exactly equal AB's operating expenses. At the end of that year, the book value of the property is $9,000 ($10,000 less the $1,000 book depreciation deduction), and the adjusted tax basis is $3,600 ($4,000 less the $400 tax depreciation deduction). A's built-in gain with respect to the property decreases to $5,400 ($9,000 book value less $3,600 adjusted tax basis). Also, at the end of AB's first year, A has a $9,500 book capital account and a $4,000 tax basis in A's partnership interest. B has a $9,500 book capital account and a $9,600 adjusted tax basis in B's partnership interest.

(iii) Sale of the property. If AB sells the property at the beginning of AB's second year for $9,000, AB realizes tax gain of $5,400 ($9,000, the amount realized, less the adjusted tax basis of $3,600). Under paragraph (b)(1) of this section, the entire $5,400 gain must be allocated to A because the property A contributed has that much built-in gain remaining. If AB sells the property at the beginning of AB's second year for $10,000, AB realizes tax gain of $6,400 ($10,000, the amount realized, less the adjusted tax basis of $3,600). Under paragraph (b)(1) of this section, only $5,400 of gain must be allocated to A to account for A's built-in gain. The remaining $1,000 of gain is allocated equally between A and B in accordance with the partnership agreement. If AB sells the property for less than the $9,000 book value, AB realizes tax gain of less than $5,400, and the entire gain must be allocated to A.

(iv) Termination and liquidation of partnership. If AB sells the property at the beginning of AB's second year for $9,000, and AB engages in no other transactions that year, A will recognize a gain of $5,400, and B will recognize no income or loss. A's adjusted tax basis for A's interest in AB will then be $9,400 ($4,000, A's original tax basis, increased by the gain of $5,400). B's adjusted tax basis for B's interest in AB will be $9,600 ($10,000, B's original tax basis, less the $400 depreciation deduction in the first partnership year). If the partnership then terminates and distributes its assets ($19,000 in cash) to A and B in proportion to their capital account balances, A will recognize a capital gain of $100 ($9,500, the amount distributed to A, less $9,400, the adjusted tax basis of A's interest). B will recognize a capital loss of $100 (the excess of B's adjusted tax basis, $9,600, over the amount received, $9,500).

Example (2). Unreasonable use of the traditional method—(i) Facts. C and D form partnership CD and agree that each will be allocated a 50 percent share of all partnership items and that CD will make allocations under section 704(c) using the traditional method under paragraph (b) of this section. C contributes equipment with an adjusted tax basis of $1,000 and a book value of $10,000, with a view to taking advantage of the fact that the equipment has only one year remaining on its cost recovery schedule although its remaining economic life is significantly longer. At the time of contribution, C has a built-in gain of $9,000 and the equipment is section 704(c) property. D contributes $10,000 of cash, which CD uses to buy securities. D has substantial net operating loss carryforwards that D anticipates will otherwise expire unused. Under § 1.704–1 (b)(2)(iv)(g)(3), the partnership must allocate the $10,000 of book depreciation to the partners in the first year of the partnership. Thus, there is $10,000 of book depreciation and $1,000 of tax depreciation in the partnership's first year. CD sells the equipment during the second year for $10,000 and recognizes a $10,000 gain ($10,000, the amount realized, less the adjusted tax basis of $0).

(ii) Unreasonable use of method—(A) At the beginning of the second year, both the book value and adjusted tax basis of the equipment are $0. Therefore, there is no remaining built-in gain. The $10,000 gain on the sale of the equipment in the second year is allocated $5,000 each to C and D. The interaction of the partnership's one-year write-off of the entire book value of the equipment and the use of the traditional method results in a shift of $4,000 of the precontribution gain in the equipment from C to D (D's $5,000 share of CD's $10,000 gain, less the $1,000 tax depreciation deduction previously allocated to D).

(B) The traditional method is not reasonable under paragraph (a)(10) of this section because the contribution of property is made, and the traditional method is used, with a view to shifting a significant amount of taxable income to a partner with a low marginal tax rate and away from a partner with a high marginal tax rate.

(C) Under these facts, if the partnership agreement in effect for the year of contribution had provided that tax gain from the sale of the property (if any) would always be allocated first to C to offset the effect of the ceiling rule limitation, the allocation method would not violate the anti-abuse rule of paragraph (a)(10) of this section. See paragraph (c)(3) of this section. Under other facts, (for example, if the partnership holds multiple section 704 (c) properties and either uses multiple allocation methods or uses a single allocation method where one or more of the properties are subject to the ceiling rule) the allocation to C may not be reasonable.

(c) Traditional method with curative allocations—(1) In general. To correct distortions created by the ceiling rule, a partnership using the traditional method under paragraph (b) of this section may make reasonable curative allocations to reduce or eliminate disparities between book and tax items of noncontributing partners. A curative allocation is an allocation of income, gain, loss, or deduction for tax purposes that differs from the partnership's allocation of the corresponding book item. For example, if a noncontributing partner is allocated less tax depreciation than book depreciation with respect to an item of section 704(c) property, the partnership may make a curative allocation to that partner of tax depreciation from another item of partnership property to make up the difference, notwithstanding that the corresponding book depreciation is allocated to the contributing partner. A partnership may limit its curative allocations to allocations of one or more particular tax items (e.g., only depreciation from a specific property or properties) even if the allocation of those available items does not offset fully the effect of the ceiling rule.

(2) Consistency. A partnership must be consistent in its application of curative allocations with respect to each item of section 704(c) property from year to year.

(3) Reasonable curative allocations—(i) Amount. A curative allocation is not reasonable to the extent it exceeds the amount necessary to offset the effect of the ceiling rule for the current taxable year or, in the case of a curative allocation upon disposition of the property, for prior taxable years.

(ii) Timing. The period of time over which the curative allocations are made is a factor in determining whether the allocations are reasonable. Notwithstanding paragraph (c)(3)(i) of this section, a partnership may make curative allocations in a taxable year to offset the effect of the ceiling rule for a prior taxable year if those allocations are made over a reasonable period of time, such as over the property's economic life, and are provided for under the partnership agreement in effect for the year of contribution. See paragraph (c)(4) Example 3(ii)(C) of this section.

(iii) Type—(A) In general. To be reasonable, a curative allocation of income, gain, loss, or deduction must be expected to have substantially the same effect on each partner's tax liability as the tax item limited by the ceiling rule. The expectation must exist at the time the section 704(c) property is obligated to be (or is) contributed to the partnership and the allocation with respect to that property becomes part of the partnership agreement. However, the expectation is tested at the time the allocation with respect to that property is actually made if the partnership agreement is not sufficiently specific as to the precise manner in which allocations are to be made with respect to that property. Under this paragraph (c), if the item limited by the ceiling rule is loss from the sale of property, a curative allocation of gain must be expected to have substantially the same effect as would an allocation to that partner of gain with respect to the sale of the property. If the item limited by the ceiling rule is depreciation or other cost recovery, a curative allocation of income to the contributing partner must be expected to have substantially the same effect as would an allocation to that partner of partnership income with respect to the contributed property. For example, if depreciation deductions with respect to leased equipment contributed by a tax-exempt partner are limited by the ceiling rule, a curative allocation of dividend or interest income to that partner generally is not reasonable, although a curative allocation of depreciation deductions from other leased equipment to the noncontributing partner is reasonable. Similarly, under this rule, if depreciation deductions apportioned to foreign source income in a particular statutory grouping under section 904(d) are limited by the ceiling rule, a curative allocation of income from another statutory grouping to the contributing partner generally is not reasonable, although a curative allocation of income from the same statutory grouping and of the same character is reasonable.

(B) Exception for allocation from disposition of contributed property. If cost recovery has been limited by the ceiling rule, the general limitation on character does not apply to income from the disposition of contributed property subject to the ceiling rule, but only if properly provided for in the partnership agreement in effect for the year of contribution or revaluation. For example, if allocations of depreciation deductions to a noncontributing partner have been limited by the ceiling rule, a curative allocation to the contributing partner of gain from the sale of that property, if properly provided for in the partnership agreement, is reasonable for purposes of paragraph (c)(3)(iii)(A) of this section even if not of the same character.

(4) Examples. The following examples illustrate the principles of this paragraph (c).

Example 1. Reasonable and unreasonable curative allocations (i) Facts. E and F form partnership EF and agree that each will be allocated a 50 percent share of all partnership items and that EF will make allocations under section 704(c) using the traditional method with curative allocations under paragraph (c) of this section. E contributes equipment with an adjusted tax basis of $4,000 and a book value of $10,000. The equipment has 10 years remaining on its cost recovery schedule and is depreciable using the straight-line method. At the time of contribution, E has a built-in gain of $6,000, and therefore, the equipment is section 704(c) property. F contributes $10,000 of cash, which EF uses to buy inventory for resale. In EF's first year, the revenue generated by the equipment equals EF's operating expenses. The equipment generates $1,000 of book depreciation and $400 of tax depreciation for each of 10 years. At the end of the first year EF sells all the inventory for $10,700, recognizing $700 of income. The partners anticipate that the inventory income will have substantially the same effect on their tax liabilities as income from E's contributed equipment. Under the traditional method of paragraph (b) of this section, E and F would each be allocated $350 of income from the sale of inventory for book and tax purposes and $500 of depreciation for book purposes. The $400 of tax depreciation would all be allocated to F. Thus, at the end of the first year, E and F's book and tax capital accounts would be as follows:

E		F		
Book	Tax	Book	Tax	
$10,000	$4,000	$10,000	$10,000	Initial contribution.
<500>	<0>	<500>	<400>	Depreciation.
350	350	350	350	Sales income.
9,850	4,350	9,850	9,950	

(ii) Reasonable curative allocation. Because the ceiling rule would cause a disparity of $100 between F's book and tax capital accounts, EF may properly allocate to E under paragraph (c) of this section an additional $100 of income from the sale of inventory for tax purposes. This allocation results in capital accounts at the end of EF's first year as follows:

E		F		
Book	Tax	Book	Tax	
$10,000	$4,000	$10,000	$10,000	Initial contribution.
<500>	<0>	<500>	<400>	Depreciation.
350	450	350	250	Sales income.
9,850	4,450	9,850	9,850	

(iii) Unreasonable curative allocation. (A) The facts are the same as in paragraphs (i) and (ii) of this Example 1, except that E and F choose to allocate all the income from the sale of the inventory to E for tax purposes, although they share it equally for book purposes. This allocation results in capital accounts at the end of EF's first year as follows:

E		F		
Book	Tax	Book	Tax	
$10,000	$4,000	$10,000	$10,000	Initial contribution.
<500>	<0>	<500>	<400>	Depreciation.
350	700	350	0	Sales income.
9,850	4,700	9,850	9,600	

(B) This curative allocation is not reasonable under paragraph (c)(3)(i) of this section because the allocation exceeds the amount necessary to offset the disparity caused by the ceiling rule.

Example 2. Curative allocations limited to depreciation (i) Facts. G and H form partnership GH and agree that each will be allocated a 50 percent share of all partnership items and that GH will make allocations under section 704(c) using the traditional method with curative allocations under paragraph (c) of this section, but only to the extent that the partnership has sufficient tax depreciation deductions. G contributes property G1, with an adjusted tax basis of $3,000 and a fair market value of $10,000, and H contributes property H1, with an adjusted tax basis of $6,000 and a fair market value of $10,000. Both properties have 5 years remaining on their cost recovery schedules and are depreciable using the straight-line method. At the time of contribution, G1 has a built-in gain of $7,000 and H1 has a built-in gain of $4,000, and therefore, both properties are section 704(c) property. G1 generates $600 of tax depreciation and $2,000 of book depreciation for each of five years. H1 generates $1,200 of tax depreciation and $2,000 of book depreciation for each of 5 years. In addition, the properties each generate $500 of operating income annually. G and H are each allocated $1,000 of book depreciation for each property. Under the traditional method of paragraph (b) of this section, G would be allocated $0 of tax depreciation for G1 and $1,000 for H1, and H would be allocated $600 of tax depreciation for G1 and $200 for H1. Thus, at the end of the first year, G and H's book and tax capital accounts would be as follows:

G		H		
Book	Tax	Book	Tax	
$10,000	$3,000	$10,000	$6,000	Initial contribution.
<1,000>	<0>	<1,000>	<600>	G1 depreciation.
<1,000>	<1,000>	<1,000>	<200>	H1 depreciation.
500	500	500	500	Operating income.
8,500	2,500	8,500	5,700	

(ii) Curative allocations. Under the traditional method, G is allocated more depreciation deductions than H, even though H contributed property with a smaller disparity reflected on GH's book and tax capital accounts. GH makes curative allocations to H of an additional $400 of tax depreciation each year, which reduces the disparities between G and H's book and tax capital accounts ratably each year. These allocations are reasonable provided the allocations meet the other requirements of this section. As a result of their agreement, at the end of the first year, G and H's capital accounts are as follows:

G		H		
Book	Tax	Book	Tax	
$10,000	$3,000	$10,000	$6,000	Initial contribution.
<1,000>	<0>	<1,000>	<600>	G1 depreciation.
<1,000>	<600>	<1,000>	<600>	H1 depreciation.
500	500	500	500	Operating income
8,500	2,900	8,500	5,300	

Example 3. Unreasonable use of curative allocations (i) Facts. J and K form partnership JK and agree that each will receive a 50 percent share of all partnership items and that JK will make allocations under section 704(c) using the traditional method with curative allocations under paragraph (c) of this section. J contributes equipment with an adjusted tax basis of $1,000 and a book value of $10,000, with a view to taking advantage of the fact that the equipment has only one year remaining on its cost recovery schedule although it has an estimated remaining economic life of 10 years. J has substantial net operating loss carryforwards that J anticipates will otherwise expire unused. At the time of contribution, J has a built-in gain of $9,000, and therefore, the equipment is section 704(c) property. K contributes $10,000 of cash, which JK uses to buy inventory for resale. In JK's first year, the revenues generated by the equipment exactly equal JK's operating

expenses. Under § 1.704–1(b)(2)(iv)(g)(3), the partnership must allocate the $10,000 of book depreciation to the partners in the first year of the partnership. Thus, there is $10,000 of book depreciation and $1,000 of tax depreciation in the partnership's first year. In addition, at the end of the first year JK sells all of the inventory for $18,000, recognizing $8,000 of income. The partners anticipate that the inventory income will have substantially the same effect on their tax liabilities as income from J's contributed equipment. Under the traditional method of paragraph (b) of this section, J and K's book and tax capital accounts at the end of the first year would be as follows:

J		K		
Book	Tax	Book	Tax	
$10,000	$1,000	$10,000	$10,000	Initial contribution.
<5,000>	<0>	<5,000>	<1,000>	Depreciation.
4,000	4,000	4,000	4,000	Sales income.
9,000	5,000	9,000	13,000	

(ii) Unreasonable use of method. (A) The use of curative allocations under these facts to offset immediately the full effect of the ceiling rule would result in the following book and tax capital accounts at the end of K's first year:

J		K		
Book	Tax	Book	Tax	
$10,000	$1,000	$10,000	$10,000	Initial contribution.
<5,000>	<0>	<5,000>	<1,000>	Depreciation.
4,000	8,000	4,000	0	Sales income.
9,000	9,000	9,000	9,000	

(B) This curative allocation is not reasonable under paragraph (a)(10) of this section because the contribution of property is made and the curative allocation method is used with a view to shifting a significant amount of partnership taxable income to a partner with a low marginal tax rate and away from a partner with a high marginal tax rate, within a period of time significantly shorter than the economic life of the property.

(C) The property has only one year remaining on its cost recovery schedule even though its economic life is considerably longer. Under these facts, if the partnership agreement had provided for curative allocations over a reasonable period of time, such as over the property's economic life, rather than over its remaining cost recovery period, the allocations would have been reasonable. See paragraph (c)(3)(ii) of this section. Thus, in this example, JK would make a curative allocation of $400 of sales income to J in the partnership's first year (10 percent of $4,000). J and K's book and tax capital accounts at the end of the first year would be as follows:

J		K		
Book	Tax	Book	Tax	
$10,000	$1,000	$10,000	$10,000	Initial contribution.
<5,000>	<0>	<5,000>	<1,000>	Depreciation.
4,000	4,400	4,000	3,600	Sales income.
9,000	5,400	9,000	12,600	

(d) Remedial allocation method. (1) In general. A partnership may adopt the remedial allocation method described in this paragraph to eliminate distortions caused by the ceiling rule. A partnership adopting the remedial allocation method eliminates those distortions by creating remedial items and allocating those items to its partners. Under the remedial allocation method, the partnership first determines the amount of book items under paragraph (d)(2) of this section and the partners' distributive shares of these items under section 704 (b). The partnership then allocates the corresponding tax items recognized by the partnership, if any, using the traditional method described in paragraph (b)(1) of this section. If the ceiling rule (as defined in paragraph (b)(1) of this section) causes the book allocation of an item to a noncontributing partner to differ from the tax allocation of the same item to the noncontributing partner, the partnership creates a remedial item of income, gain, loss, or deduction equal to the full amount of the difference and allocates it to the noncontributing partner. The partnership simultaneously creates an offsetting remedial item in an identical amount and allocates it to the contributing partner.

(2) Determining the amount of book items. Under the remedial allocation method, a partnership determines the amount of book items attributable to contributed property in the following manner rather than under the rules of § 1.704–1(b)(2)(iv)(g)(3). The portion of the partnership's book basis in the property equal to the adjusted tax basis in the property at the time of contribution is recovered in the same manner as the adjusted tax basis in the property is recovered (generally, over the property's remaining recovery period under section 168(i)(7) or other applicable Internal Revenue Code section). The remainder of the partnership's book basis in the property (the amount by which book basis exceeds adjusted tax basis) is recovered using any recovery period and depreciation (or other cost recovery) method (including first-year conventions) available to the partnership for newly purchased property (of the same type as the contributed property) that is placed in service at the time of contribution.

(3) Type. Remedial allocations of income, gain, loss, or deduction to the noncontributing partner have the same tax attributes as the tax item limited by the ceiling rule. The tax attributes of offsetting remedial allocations of income, gain, loss, or deduction to the contributing partner are determined by reference to the item limited by the ceiling rule. Thus, for example, if the ceiling rule limited item is loss from the sale of contributed property, the offsetting remedial allocation to the contributing partner must be gain from the sale of that property. Conversely, if the ceiling rule limited item is gain from the sale of contributed property, the offsetting remedial allocation to the contributing partner must be loss from the sale of that property. If the ceiling rule limited item is depreciation or other cost recovery from the contributed property, the offsetting remedial allocation to the contributing partner must be income of the type produced (directly or indirectly) by that property. Any partner level tax attributes are determined at the partner level. For example, if the ceiling rule limited item is depreciation from property used in a rental activity, the remedial allocation to the noncontributing partner is depreciation from property used in a rental activity and the offsetting remedial allocation to the contributing partner is ordinary income from that rental activity. Each partner then applies section 469 to the allocations as appropriate.

(4) Effect of remedial items. (i) Effect on partnership. Remedial items do not affect the partnership's computation of its taxable income under section 703 and do not affect the partnership's adjusted tax basis in partnership property.

(ii) Effect on partners. Remedial items are notional tax items created by the partnership solely for tax purposes and do not affect the partners' book capital accounts. Remedial items have the same effect as actual tax items on a partner's tax liability and on the partner's adjusted tax basis in the partnership interest.

(5) Limitations on use of methods involving remedial allocations. (i) Limitation on taxpayers. In the absence of published guidance, the remedial allocation method described in this paragraph (d) is the only reasonable section 704(c) method permitting the creation of notional tax items.

(ii) Limitation on Internal Revenue Service. In exercising its authority under paragraph (a)(10) of this section to make adjustments if a partnership's allocation method is not reasonable, the Internal Revenue Service will not require a partnership to use the remedial allocation method described in this paragraph (d) or any other method involving the creation of notional tax items.

(6) Adjustments to application of method. The Commissioner may, by published guidance, prescribe adjustments to the remedial allocation method under this paragraph (d) as necessary or appropriate. This guidance may, for example, prescribe adjustments to the remedial allocation method to prevent the duplication or omission of items of income or deduction or to reflect more clearly the partners' income or the income of a transferee of a partner.

(7) Examples. The following examples illustrate the principles of this paragraph (d).

Example 1. Remedial allocation method (i) Facts. On January 1, L and M form partnership LM and agree that each will be allocated a 50 percent share of all partnership items. The partnership agreement provides that LM will make allocations under section 704(c) using the remedial allocation method under this paragraph (d) and that the straight-line method will be used to recover excess book basis. L contributes depreciable property with an adjusted tax basis of $4,000 and a fair market value of $10,000. The property is depreciated using the straight-line method with a 10-year recovery period and has 4 years remaining on its recovery period. M contributes $10,000, which the partnership uses to purchase land. Except for the depreciation deductions, LM's expenses equal its income in each year of the 10 years commencing with the year the partnership is formed.

(ii) Years 1 through 4. Under the remedial allocation method of this paragraph (d), LM has book depreciation for each of its first 4 years of $1,600 [$1,000 ($4,000 adjusted tax basis divided by the 4-year remaining recovery period) plus $600 ($6,000 excess of book value over tax basis, divided by the NEW 10-year recovery period)]. (For the purpose of simplifying the example, the partnership's book depreciation is determined without regard to any first-year depreciation conventions.) Under the partnership agreement, L and M are each allocated 50 percent ($800) of the book depreciation. M is allocated $800 of tax depreciation and L is allocated the remaining $200 of tax depreciation ($1,000 – $800). See paragraph (d)(1) of this section. No remedial allocations are made because the ceiling rule does not result in a book allocation of depreciation to M different from the tax allocation. The allocations result in capital accounts at the end of LM's first 4 years as follows:

L		M		
Book	Tax	Book	Tax	
$10,000	$4,000	$10,000	$10,000	Initial contribution.
<3,200>	<800>	<3,200>	<3,200>	Depreciation.
$6,800	$ 3,200	$ 6,800	$ 6,800	

(iii) Subsequent years. (A) For each of years 5 through 10, LM has $600 of book depreciation ($6,000 excess of initial book value over adjusted tax basis divided by the 10-year recovery period that commenced in year 1), but no tax depreciation. Under the partnership agreement, the $600 of book depreciation is allocated equally to L and M. Because of the application of the ceiling rule in year 5, M would be allocated $300 of book depreciation, but no tax depreciation. Thus, at the end of LM's fifth year L's and M's book and tax capital accounts would be as follows:

L		M		
Book	Tax	Book	Tax	
$6,800	$ 3,200	$6,800	$6,800	End of year 4.
<300>		<300>		Depreciation.
$6,500	$ 3,200	$6,500	$6,800	

(B) Because the ceiling rule would cause an annual disparity of $300 between M's allocations of book and tax depreciation, LM must make remedial allocations of $300 of tax depreciation deductions to M under the remedial allocation method for each of years 5 through 10. LM must also make an offsetting remedial allocation to L of $300 of taxable income, which must be of the same type as income produced by the property. At the end of year 5, LM's capital accounts are as follows:

L		M		
Book	Tax	Book	Tax	
$6,800	$3,200	$6,800	$6,800	End of year 4.
<300>		<300>		Depreciation.
	300		<300>	Remedial allocations.
$6,500	$3,500	$6,500	$6,500	

(C) At the end of year 10, LM's capital accounts are as follows:

L		M		
Book	Tax	Book	Tax	
$6,500	$3,500	$6,500	$6,500	End of year 5.
<1,500>		<1,500>		Depreciation.
	1,500		<1,500>	Remedial allocations.
$5,000	$5,000	$5,000	$5,000	

Example 2. Remedial allocations on sale **(i) Facts.** N and P form partnership NP and agree that each will be allocated a 50 percent share of all partnership items. The partnership agreement provides that NP will make allocations under section 704(c) using the remedial allocation method under this paragraph (d). N contributes Blackacre (land) with an adjusted tax basis of $4,000 and a fair market value of $10,000. Because N has a built-in gain of $6,000, Blackacre is section 704(c) property. P contributes Whiteacre (land) with an adjusted tax basis and fair market value of $10,000. At the end of NP's first year, NP sells Blackacre to Q for $9,000 and recognizes a capital gain of $5,000 ($9,000 amount realized less $4,000 adjusted tax basis) and a book loss of $1,000 ($9,000 amount realized less $10,000 book basis). NP has no other items of income, gain, loss, or deduction. If the ceiling rule were applied, N would be allocated the entire $5,000 of tax gain and N and P would each be allocated $500 of book loss. Thus, at the end of NP's first year N's and P's book and tax capital accounts would be as follows:

N		P		
Book	Tax	Book	Tax	
$10,000	$4,000	$10,000	$10,000	Initial contribution.
<500>	5,000	<500>		Sale of Blackacre.
$9,500	$9,000	$9,500	$10,000	

(ii) Remedial allocation. Because the ceiling rule would cause a disparity of $500 between P's allocation of book and tax loss, NP must make a remedial allocation of $500 of capital loss to P and an offsetting remedial allocation to N of an additional $500 of capital gain. These allocations result in capital accounts at the end of NP's first year as follows:

N		P		
Book	Tax	Book	Tax	
$10,000	$4,000	$10,000	$10,000	Initial contribution.
<500>	5,000	<500>		Sale of Blackacre.
	500		<500>	Remedial allocations.
$9,500	$9,500	$9,500	$9,500	

Example 3. Remedial allocation where built-in gain property sold for book and tax loss **(i) Facts.** The facts are the same as in Example 2, except that at the end of NP's first year, NP sells Blackacre to Q for $3,000 and recognizes a capital loss of $1,000 ($3,000 amount realized less $4,000 adjusted tax basis) and a book loss of $7,000 ($3,000 amount realized less $10,000 book basis). If the ceiling rule were applied, P would be allocated the entire $1,000 of tax loss and N and P would each be allocated $3,500 of book loss. Thus, at the end of NP's first year, N's and P's book and tax capital accounts would be as follows:

N		P		
Book	Tax	Book	Tax	
$10,000	$4,000	$10,000	$10,000	Initial contribution.
<3,500>	0	<3,500>	<1,000>	Sale of Blackacre.
$6,500	$4,000	$4,500	$10,000	

(ii) Remedial allocation. Because the ceiling rule would cause a disparity of $2,500 between P's allocation of book and tax loss on the sale of Blackacre, NP must make a remedial allocation of $2,500 of capital loss to P and an offsetting remedial allocation to N of $2,500 of capital gain. These allocations result in capital accounts at the end of NP's first year as follows:

N		P		
Book	Tax	Book	Tax	
$10,000	$4,000	$10,000	$10,000	Initial contribution.
<3,500>	0	<3,500>	<1,000>	Sale of Blackacre.
	2,500		<2,500>	Remedial allocations.
$6,500	$6,500	$6,500	$6,500	

(e) Exceptions and special rules—(1) Small disparities—(i) General rule. If a partner contributes one or more items of property to a partnership within a single taxable year of the partnership, and the disparity between the book value of the property and the contributing partner's adjusted tax basis in the property is a small disparity, the partnership may—

(A) Use a reasonable section 704(c) method;

(B) Disregard the application of section 704(c) to the property; or

(C) Defer the application of section 704(c) to the property until the disposition of the property.

(ii) Definition of small disparity. A disparity between book value and adjusted tax basis is a small disparity if the book value of all properties contributed by one partner during the partnership taxable year does not differ from the adjusted tax basis by more than 15 percent of the adjusted tax basis, and the total gross disparity does not exceed $20,000.

(2) Aggregation. Each of the following types of property may be aggregated for purposes of making allocations under section 704(c) and this section if contributed by one partner during the partnership taxable year.

(i) Depreciable property. All property, other than real property, that is included in the same general asset account of the contributing partner and the partnership under section 168.

(ii) Zero-basis property. All property with a basis equal to zero, other than real property.

(iii) Inventory. For partnerships that do not use a specific identification method of accounting, each item of inventory, other than securities or similar investment interests (as defined in § 1.704–3T(e)(3)).

(3) Securities partnerships. [Reserved]

(f) Effective dates.—With the exception of paragraphs (a)(8)(ii), (a)(8)(iii) and (a)(11) of this section, this section applies to properties contributed to a partnership and to restatements pursuant to §1.704–1(b)(2)(iv)(f) on or after December 21, 1993. Paragraph (a)(11) of this section applies to properties contributed by a partner to a partnership on or after August 20, 1997. However, partnerships may rely on paragraph (a)(11) of this section for properties contributed before August 20, 1997, and disposed of on or after August 20, 1997. Paragraph (a)(8)(ii) applies to installment obligations received by a partnership in exchange for section 704(c) property on or after November 24, 2003. Paragraph (a)(8)(iii) applies to property acquired on or after November 24, 2003, by a partnership pursuant to a contract that is section 704(c) property. Except as otherwise provided in §1.752–7(k), paragraphs (a)(8)(iv) and (a)(12) apply to §1.752–7 liability transfers, as defined in §1.752–7(b)(4), occurring on or after June 24, 2003. See §1.752–7(k).

§ 1.704–3T Contributed property (temporary).

(a) through (c) [Reserved]

(d) Remedial allocation method—(1) In general. For contributions of property to a partnership and restatements pursuant to §1.704–1(b)(2)(iv)(f) on or after December 21, 1993, a partnership may adopt the remedial allocation method described in this paragraph by making reasonable remedial allocations to eliminate ceiling rule disparities between tax items of noncontributing partners and corresponding book items (as computed under paragraph (d)(2) of this section). Remedial allocations are tax allocations of income or gain that are offset by tax allocations of loss or deduction. These tax allocations are created by the partnership and have no effect on the partnership's book capital accounts. Under this method the partnership determines the amount of book items under paragraph (d)(2) of this section and determines the distributive share of these items under section 704(b). The partnership then makes tax allocations using the methodology set forth in § 1.704–3(b)(1) to avoid shifting the tax consequences of built-in gain or loss. If the ceiling rule (as defined in §1.704–3(b)(1)) results in a book allocation to a noncontributing partner different from the corresponding tax allocation, the partnership makes a remedial allocation of income, gain, loss, or deduction to the noncontributing partner equal to the full amount of the limitation caused by the ceiling rule, and a simultaneous, offsetting remedial allocation of deduction, loss, gain, or income to the contributing partner. In the absence of specific published guidance, the method described in this paragraph is the only reasonable section 704(c) method using remedial allocations.

(2) Determining the amount of book items. Under the remedial allocation method, for purposes of subchapter K the partnership determines the amount of book items in the following manner rather than under the rules of § 1.704–1(b)(2)(iv) (g)(3). The portion of the partnership's book basis in the property equal to the adjusted tax basis in the property at the time of contribution is recovered in the same manner as the adjusted tax basis in the property is recovered (generally, over the property's remaining recovery period under section 168(i)(7) or other applicable Internal Revenue Code section). The remainder of the partnership's book basis in the property (the amount by which book basis exceeds adjusted tax basis) is recovered using any applicable recovery period and depreciation (or other cost recovery) method available to the partnership for newly-purchased property placed in service at the time of contribution.

(3) Type. Remedial allocations of income, gain, loss, or deduction must have the same effect on each partner's tax liability as the tax item limited by the ceiling rule. This means that, when relevant, such attributes as the source, character, or (e.g., under section 469) nature of the item limited by the ceiling rule must be taken into account. Thus, if the item limited by the ceiling rule is loss from the sale of contributed property, the offsetting remedial allocation to the contributing partner must be gain from the sale of the property. If the item limited by the ceiling rule is depreciation or other cost recovery, the offsetting remedial allocation of income to the contributing partner must be of the same type of income that the contributed property produces.

(4) Limitation on adjustments by the Internal Revenue Service. In exercising its authority under § 1.704–3 to make adjustments if a partnership's allocation method is not reasonable, the Internal Revenue Service will not require a partnership to use the remedial allocation method described in this paragraph (d).

(5) Examples. The following examples illustrate the principles of this paragraph (d).

Example 1. Remedial allocation method— (i) Facts. L and M form partnership LM and agree that each will be allocated a 50 percent share of all partnership items. The partnership agreement provides that LM will make allocations under section 704(c) using the remedial allocation method under paragraph (d) of this section and that the straight-line method will be used to recover excess book basis. L contributes depreciable property with an adjusted tax basis of $4,000 and a fair market value of $10,000. The property is depreciable using the straight-line method with a 10-year recovery period and has 4 years remaining on its recovery period. M contributes $10,000, which the partnership uses to purchase land. Except for the depreciation deductions, LM's expenses equal its income in each year of the 10 years commencing with the year the partnership is formed.

(ii) Years 1 through 4. Under the remedial allocation method of paragraph (d) of this section; LM has book depreciation for each of its first 4 years of $1,600 [$1,000 ($4,000 tax basis divided by the 4-year remaining recovery period) plus $600 ($6,000 excess of book value over tax basis, divided by the new 10-year recovery period)]. Under the partnership agreement, L and M are each allocated 50 percent ($800) of the book depreciation. M is allocated $800 of tax depreciation and L is allocated the remaining $200 of tax depreciation ($1,000 – $800). See paragraph (d)(1) of this section. No remedial allocations are made because the ceiling rule does not result in a book allocation of depreciation to M different from the tax allocation. The allocations result in capital accounts at the end of LM's first 4 years as follows:

L		M		
Book	Tax	Book	Tax	
$10,000	$4,000	$10,000	$10,000	Initial contribution.
<3,200>	<800>	<3,200>	<3,200>	Depreciation.
6,800	3,200	6,800	6,800	

(iii) Subsequent Years. (A) For each of years 5 through 10, LM has $600 of book depreciation ($6,000 excess of initial book value over adjusted tax basis divided by the 10-year recovery period that commenced in year 1), but no tax depreciation. Under the partnership agreement, the $600 of book depreciation is allocated equally to L and M. Because of the application of the ceiling rule in year 5, M would be allocated $300 of book depreciation, but no tax depreciation. Thus, at the end of LM's fifth year L and M's book and tax capital accounts would be as follows:

L		M		
Book	Tax	Book	Tax	
$6,800	$3,200	$6,800	$6,800	End of year 4.
<300>	.....	<300>	.....	Depreciation.
6,500	3,200	6,500	6,800	

(B) Because the ceiling rule would cause an annual disparity of $300 between M's book and tax capital accounts, LM must make remedial allocations of $300 of tax depreciation deductions to M under the remedial allocation method, for each of years 5 through 10. LM must also make offsetting remedial tax allocations to L of $300 of income, which must be of the same type as income from the property. At the end of year 5, LM's capital accounts are as follows:

L		M		
Book	Tax	Book	Tax	
$6,800	$3,200	$6,800	$6,800	End of year 4.
<300>	.....	<300>	.....	Depreciation.
	300	.....	<300>	Remedial allocations.
6,500	3,500	6,500	6,500	

(C) At the end of year 10, LM's capital accounts are as follows:

L		M		
Book	Tax	Book	Tax	
$6,500	$3,500	$6,500	$6,500	End of year 5.
<1,500>	.....	<1,500>	.....	Depreciation.
	1,500	.....	<1,500>	Remedial allocations.
5,000	5,000	5,000	5,000	

Example 2. Remedial allocations on sale. (i) Facts. N and P form partnership NP and agree that each will be allocated a 50 percent share of all partnership items and that NP will make allocations under section 704(c) using the remedial allocation method under paragraph (d) of this section. N contributes Blackacre (land) with an adjusted tax basis of $4,000 and a book value of $10,000. Because N has a built-in gain of $6,000, Blackacre is section 704(c) property. P contributes Whiteacre (land) with an adjusted tax basis and book value of $10,000. At the end of NP's first year, NP sells Blackacre to Q for $9,000 and recognizes a capital gain of $5,000 ($9,000 amount realized, less $4,000 tax basis) and a book loss of $1,000 ($9,000 amount realized less $10,000 book basis). NP has no other items of income, gain, loss, or deduction. If the ceiling rule were applied, N would be allocated the entire $5,000 of tax gain and N and P would each be allocated $500 of book loss. Thus, at the end of NP's first year N and P's book and tax capital accounts would be as follows:

N		P		
Book	Tax	Book	Tax	
$10,000	$4,000	$10,000	$10,000	Initial contribution.
<500>	5,000	<500>	.....	Sale of Blackacre.
9,500	9,000	9,500	10,000	

(ii) **Remedial allocation.** Because the ceiling rule would cause a disparity of $500 between P's book and tax capital accounts, NP must make a remedial allocation of $500 of capital loss to P under the remedial allocation method, and an offsetting remedial allocation to N of an additional $500 of capital gain. These allocations result in capital accounts at the beginning of NP's second year as follows:

N		P		
Book	Tax	Book	Tax	
$10,000	$4,000	$10,000	$10,000	Initial contribution.
<500>	5,000	<500>	.....	Sale of Blackacre.
	500	.....	<500>	Remedial allocations.
9,500	9,500	9,500	9,500	

(e)(1) and **(2)** [Reserved]

(3) Special aggregation rule for securities partnerships—(i) General rule. The frequency of capital account restatements under § 1.704–1(b)(4)(i) and the number of partnership assets may make it impractical for securities partnerships to make reverse section 704(c) allocations on an asset-by-asset basis. Therefore, when making reverse section 704(c) allocations with respect to restatements made on or after December 21, 1993, it is generally reasonable for a securities partnership consistently to aggregate all gains and all losses from securities and similar investments (as defined in § 1.704–1(b)(2)(iv)(f)(5)(iii)). Gains must be aggregated separately from losses.

(ii) Securities partnership. For purposes of paragraph (e)(3)(i) of this section, a securities partnership is one that—

(A) If it were a domestic corporation would satisfy the requirements of section 851(b)(4);

(B) On each revaluation date, holds assets described in § 1.704–1(b)(2)(iv)(f)(5)(iii) that constitute at least 90 percent of the fair market value of its noncash assets;

(C) Either is registered with the Securities and Exchange Commission under the Investment Company Act of 1940, as amended (15 U.S.C. 80a–1 to 80b–2), as a Management Company, or does not have 50 percent or more of its capital interests held at any time during the current partnership taxable year by five or fewer persons, determined in accordance with section 707(b)(3), and

(D) Makes all of its book allocations in proportion to the partners' relative book capital accounts (except that the partnership may make reasonable special allocations to a partner that provides management services to the partnership).

(iii) Letter rulings. The Commissioner may, by letter ruling, permit partnerships not meeting the requirements of this paragraph (e)(3) to aggregate assets when making reverse section 704(c) allocations.

§ 1.704–4 Distribution of contributed property.

(a) Determination of gain and loss—(1) In general. A partner that contributes section 704(c) property to a partnership must recognize gain or loss under section 704(c)(1)(B) and this section on the distribution of such property to another partner within five years of its contribution to the partnership in an amount equal to the gain or loss that would have been allocated to such partner under section 704(c)(1)(A) and § 1.704–3 if the distributed property had been sold by the partnership to the distributee partner for its fair market value at the time of the distribution. See § 1.704–3(a)(3)(i) for a definition of section 704(c) property.

(2) Transactions to which section 704(c)(1)(B) applies. Section 704(c)(1)(B) and this section apply only to the extent that a distribution by a partnership is a distribution to a partner acting in the capacity of a partner within the meaning of section 731.

(3) Fair market value of property. The fair market value of the distributed section 704(c) property is the price at which the property would change hands between a willing buyer and a willing seller at the time of the distribution, neither being under any compulsion to buy or sell and both having reasonable knowledge of the relevant facts. The fair market value that a partnership assigns to distributed section 704(c) property will be regarded as correct, provided that the value is reasonably agreed to among the partners in an arm's-length negotiation and the partners have sufficiently adverse interests.

(4) Determination of five-year period—(i) General rule. The five-year period specified in paragraph (a)(1) of this section begins on and includes the date of contribution.

(ii) Section 708(b)(1)(B) terminations. A termination of the partnership under section 708(b)(1)(B) does not begin a new five-year period for each partner with respect to the built-in gain and built-in loss property that the terminated partnership is deemed to contribute to the new partnership under § 1.708–1(b)(1)(iv). See § 1.704–3(a)(3)(ii) for the definitions of built-in gain and built-in loss on section 704(c) property. This paragraph (a)(4)(ii) applies to terminations of partnerships under section 708(b)(1(B) occurring on or after May 9, 1997; however, this paragraph (a)(4)(ii) may be applied to terminations occurring on or after May 9, 1996, provided that the partnership and its partners apply this paragraph (a)(4)(ii) to the termination in a consistent manner.

(5) Examples. The following examples illustrate the rules of this paragraph (a). Unless otherwise specified, partnership income equals partnership expenses (other than depreciation deductions for contributed property) for each year of the partnership, the fair market value of partnership property does not change, all distributions by the partnership are subject to section 704(c)(1)(B), and all partners are unrelated.

Example 1. Recognition of gain. **(i)** On January 1, 1995, A, B, and C form partnership ABC as equal partners. A contributes $10,000 cash and Property A, nondepreciable real property with a fair market value of $10,000 and an adjusted tax basis of $4,000. Thus, there is a built-in gain of $6,000 on Property A at the time of contribution. B contributes $10,000 cash and Property B, nondepreciable real property with a fair market value and adjusted tax basis of $10,000. C contributes $20,000 cash.

(ii) On December 31, 1998, Property A and Property B are distributed to C in complete liquidation of C's interest in the partnership.

(iii) A would have recognized $6,000 of gain under section 704 (c)(1)(A) and § 1.704–3 on the sale of Property A at the time of the distribution ($10,000 fair market value less $4,000 adjusted tax basis). As a result, A must recognize $6,000 of gain on the distribution of Property A to C. B would not have recognized any gain or loss under section 704(c)(1)(A) and § 1.704–3 on the sale of Property B at the time of distribution because Property B was not section 704(c) property. As a result, B does not recognize any gain or loss on the distribution of Property B.

Example 2. Effect of post-contribution depreciation deductions **(i)** On January 1, 1995, A, B, and C form partnership ABC as equal partners. A contributes Property A, depreciable property with a fair market value of $30,000 and an adjusted tax basis of $20,000. Therefore, there is a built-in gain of $10,000 on Property A. B and C each contribute $30,000 cash. ABC uses the traditional method of making section 704(c) allocations described in § 1.704–3(b) with respect to Property A.

(ii) Property A is depreciated using the straight-line method over its remaining 10-year recovery period. The partnership has book depreciation of $3,000 per year (10 percent of the $30,000 book basis), and each partner is allocated $1,000 of book depreciation per year (one-third of the total annual book depreciation of $3,000). The partnership has a tax depreciation deduction of $2,000 per year (10 percent of the $20,000 tax basis in Property A). This $2,000 tax depreciation deduction is allocated equally between B and C, the noncontributing partners with respect to Property A.

(iii) At the end of the third year, the book value of Property A is $21,000 ($30,000 initial book value less $9,000 aggregate book depreciation) and the adjusted tax basis is $14,000 ($20,000 initial tax basis less $6,000 aggregate tax depreciation). A's remaining section 704(c)(1)(A) built-in gain with respect to Property A is $7,000 ($21,000 book value less $14,000 adjusted tax basis).

(iv) On December 31, 1997, Property A is distributed to B in complete liquidation of B's interest in the partnership. If Property A had been sold for its fair market value at the time of the distribution, A would have recognized $7,000 of gain under section 704(c)(1)(A) and § 1.704–3(b). Therefore, A recognizes $7,000 of gain on the distribution of Property A to B.

Example 3. Effect of remedial method. **(i)** On January 1, 1995, A, B, and C form partnership ABC as equal partners. A contributes Property A1, nondepreciable real property with a fair market value of $10,000 and an adjusted tax basis of $5,000, and Property A2, nondepreciable real property with a fair market value and adjusted tax basis of $10,000. B and C each contribute $20,000 cash. ABC uses the remedial method of making section 704(c) allocations described in §1.704–3(d) with respect to Property A1.

(ii) On December 31, 1998, when the fair market value of Property A1 has decreased to $7,000, Property A1 is distributed to C in a current distribution. If Property A1 had been sold by the partnership at the time of the distribution, ABC would have recognized the $2,000 of remaining built-in gain under section 704 (c)(1)(A) on the sale (fair market value of $7,000 less $5,000 adjusted tax basis). All of this gain would have been allocated to A. ABC would also have recognized a book loss of $3,000 ($10,000 original book value less $7,000 current fair market value of the property). Book loss in the amount of $2,000 would have been allocated equally between B and C. Under the remedial method, $2,000 of tax loss would also have been allocated equally to B and C to match their share of the book loss. As a result, $2,000 of gain would also have been allocated to A as an offsetting remedial allocation. A would have recognized $4,000 of total gain under section 704(c)(1)(A) on the sale of Property A1 ($2,000 of section 704(c) recognized gain plus $2,000 remedial gain). Therefore, A recognizes $4,000 of gain on the distribution of Property A1 to C under this section.

(b) Character of gain or loss—(1) General rule. Gain or loss recognized by the contributing partner under section 704(c)(1)(B) and this section has the same character as the gain or loss that would have resulted if the distributed property had been sold by the partnership to the distributee partner at the time of the distribution.

(2) Example. The following example illustrates the rule of this paragraph (b). Unless otherwise specified, partnership income equals partnership expenses (other than depreciation deductions for contributed property) for each year of the partnership, the fair market value of partnership property does not change, all distributions by the partnership are subject to section 704(c)(1)(B), and all partners are unrelated.

Example. Character of gain. **(i)** On January 1, 1995, A and B form partnership AB. A contributes $10,000 and Property A, nondepreciable real property with a fair market value of $10,000 and an adjusted tax basis of $4,000, in exchange for a 25 percent interest in partnership capital and profits. B contributes $60,000 cash for a 75 percent interest in partnership capital and profits.

(ii) On December 31, 1998, Property A is distributed to B in a current distribution. Property A is used in a trade or business of B.

(iii) A would have recognized $6,000 of gain under section 704 (c)(1)(A) on a sale of Property A at the time of the distribution (the difference between the fair market value ($10,000) and the adjusted tax basis ($4,000) of the property at that time). Because Property A is not a capital asset in the hands of Partner B and B holds more than 50 percent of partnership capital and profits, the character of the gain on a sale of Property A to B would have been ordinary income under section 707(b)(2). Therefore, the character of the gain to A on the distribution of Property A to B is ordinary income.

(c) Exceptions—(1) Property contributed on or before October 3, 1989. Section 704(c)(1)(B) and this section do not apply to property contributed to the partnership on or before October 3, 1989.

(2) Certain liquidations. Section 704(c)(1)(B) and this section do not apply to a distribution of an interest in section 704(c) property to a partner other than the contributing partner in a liquidation of the partnership if—

(i) The contributing partner receives an interest in the section 704(c) property contributed by that partner (and no other property); and

(ii) The built-in gain or loss in the interest distributed to the contributing partner, determined immediately after the distribution, is equal to or greater than the built-in gain or loss on the property that would have been allocated to the contributing partner under section 704(c)(1)(A) and § 1.704–3 on a sale of the contributed property to an unrelated party immediately before the distribution.

(3) Section 708(b)(1)(B) termination. Section 704(c)(1)(B) and this section do not apply to the deemed distribution of interests in a new partnership caused by the termination of a partnership under section 708(b)(l)(B). A subsequent distribution of section 704(c) property by the new partnership to a partner of the new partnership is subject to section 704(c)(1)(B) to the same extent that a distribution by the terminated partnership would have been subject to section 704(c)(1)(B). See also § 1.737–2(a) for a similar rule in the context of section 737. This paragraph (c)(3) applies to terminations of partnerships under section 708(b)(1)(B) occurring on or after May 9, 1997; however, this paragraph (c)(3) may be applied to terminations occurring on or after May 9, 1996, provided that the partnership and its partners apply this paragraph (c)(3) to the termination in a consistent manner.

(4) Complete transfer to another partnership. Section 704(c)(1)(B) and this section do not apply to a transfer by a partnership (transferor partnership) of all of its assets and liabilities to a second partnership (transferee partnership) in an exchange described in section 721, followed by a distribution of the interest in the transferee partnership in liquidation of the transferor partnership as part of the same plan or arrangement. A subsequent distribution of section 704(c) property by the transferee partnership to a partner of the transferee partnership is subject to section 704(c)(1)(B) to the same extent that a distribution by the transferor partnership would have been subject to section 704(c)(1)(B). See § 1.737–2(b) for a similar rule in the context of section 737.

(5) Incorporation of a partnership. Section 704 (c)(1)(B) and this section do not apply to an incorporation of a partnership by any method of incorporation (other than a method involving an actual distribution of partnership property to the partners followed by a contribution of that property to a corporation), provided that the partnership is liquidated as part of the incorporation transaction. See § 1.737–2(c) for a similar rule in the context of section 737.

(6) Undivided interests. Section 704(c)(1)(B) and this section do not apply to a distribution of an undivided interest in property to the extent that the undivided interest does not exceed the undivided interest, if any, contributed by the distributee partner in the same property. See § 1.737–2(d)(4) for the application of section 737 in a similar context. The portion of the undivided interest in property retained by the partnership after the distribution, if any, that is treated as contributed by the distributee partner, is reduced to the extent of the undivided interest distributed to the distributee partner.

(7) Example. The following example illustrates the rule of paragraph (c)(2) of this section. Unless otherwise specified, partnership income equals partnership expenses (other than depreciation deductions for contributed property) for each year of the partnership, the fair market value of partnership property does not change, all distributions by the partnership are subject to section 704(c)(1)(B), and all partners are unrelated.

Example. **(i)** On January 1, 1995, A and B form partnership AB, as equal partners. A contributes Property A, nondepreciable real property with a fair market value and adjusted tax basis of $20,000. B contributes Property B, nondepreciable real property with a fair market value of $20,000 and an adjusted tax basis of $10,000. Property B therefore has a built-in gain of $10,000 at the time of contribution.

(ii) On December 31, 1998, the partnership liquidates when the fair market value of Property A has not changed, but the fair market value of Property B has increased to $40,000.

(iii) In the liquidation, A receives Property A and a 25 percent interest in Property B. This interest in Property B has a fair market value of $10,000 to A, reflecting the fact that A was entitled to 50 percent of the $20,000 post-contribution appreciation in Property B. The partnership distributes to B a 75 percent interest in Property B with a fair market value of $30,000. B's basis in this portion of Property B is $10,000 under section 732(b). As a result, B has a built-in gain of $20,000 in this portion of Property B immediately after the distribution ($30,000 fair market value less $10,000 adjusted tax basis). This built-in gain is greater than the $10,000 of built-in gain in Property B at the time of contribution to the partnership. B therefore does not recognize any gain on the distribution of a portion of Property B to A under this section.

(d) Special rules—(1) Nonrecognition transactions, installment obligations, contributed contracts, and capitalized costs. (i) Property received by the partnership in exchange for section 704(c) property in a nonrecognition transaction is treated as the section 704(c) property for purposes of section 704(c)(1)(B) and this section to the extent that the property received is treated as section 704(c) property under § 1.704–3(a)(8). See § 1.737–2(d)(3) for a similar rule in the context of section 737.

* * *

(2) Transfers of a partnership interest. The transferee of all or a portion of the partnership interest of a contributing partner is treated as the contributing partner for purposes of section 704(c)(1)(B) and this section to the extent of the share of built-in gain or loss allocated to the transferee partner. See § 1.704–3(a)(7).

(3) Distributions of like-kind property. If section 704(c) property is distributed to a partner other than the contributing partner and like-kind property (within the meaning of section 1031) is distributed to the contributing partner no later than the earlier of (i) 180 days following the date of the distribution to the non-contributing partner, or (ii) the due date (determined with regard to extensions) of the contributing partner's income tax return for the taxable year of the distribution to the noncontributing partner, the amount of gain or loss, if any, that the contributing partner would otherwise have recognized under section 704(c)(1)(B) and this section is reduced by the amount of built-in gain or loss in the distributed likekind property in the hands of the contributing partner immediately after the distribution. The contributing partner's basis in the distributed like-kind property is determined as if the like-kind property were distributed in an unrelated distribution prior to the distribution of any other property distributed as part of the same distribution and is determined without regard to the increase in the contributing partner's adjusted tax basis in the partnership interest under section 704(c)(1)(B) and this section. See § 1.707–3 for provisions treating the distribution of the like-kind property to the contributing partner as a disguised sale in certain situations.

(4) Example. The following example illustrates the rules of this paragraph (d). Unless otherwise specified, partnership income equals partnership expenses (other than depreciation deductions for contributed property) for each year of the partnership, the fair market value of partnership property does not change, all distributions by the partnership are subject to section 704(c)(1)(B), and all partners are unrelated.

Example. Distribution of like-kind property. (i) On January 1, 1995, A, B, and C form partnership ABC as equal partners. A contributes Property A, nondepreciable real property with a fair market value of $20,000 and an adjusted tax basis of $10,000. B and C each contribute $20,000 cash. The partnership subsequently buys Property X, nondepreciable real property of a like-kind to Property A with a fair market value and adjusted tax basis of $8,000. The fair market value of Property X subsequently increases to $10,000.

(ii) On December 31, 1998, Property A is distributed to B in a current distribution. At the same time, Property X is distributed to A in a current distribution. The distribution of Property X does not result in the contribution of Property A being properly characterized as a disguised sale to the partnership under § 1.707–3. A's basis in Property X is $8,000 under section 732(a)(1). A therefore has $2,000 of built-in gain in Property X ($10,000 fair market value less $8,000 adjusted tax basis).

(iii) A would generally recognize $10,000 of gain under section 704(c)(1)(B) on the distribution of Property A, the difference between the fair market value ($20,000) of the property and its adjusted tax basis ($10,000). This gain is reduced, however, by the amount of the built-in gain of Property X in the hands of A. As a result, A recognizes only $8,000 of gain on the distribution of Property A to B under section 704(c)(1)(B) and this section.

(e) Basis adjustments—(1) Contributing partner's basis in the partnership interest. The basis of the contributing partner's interest in the partnership is increased by the amount of the gain, or decreased by the amount of the loss, recognized by the partner under section 704(c)(1)(B) and this section. This increase or decrease is taken into account in determining (i) the contributing partner's adjusted tax basis under section 732 for any property distributed to the partner in a distribution that is part of the same distribution as the distribution of the contributed property, other than like-kind property described in paragraph (d)(3) of this section (pertaining to the special rule for distributions of like-kind property), and (ii) the amount of the gain recognized by the contributing partner under section 731 or section 737, if any, on a distribution of money or property to the contributing partner that is part of the same distribution as the distribution of the contributed property. For a determination of basis in a distribution subject to section 737, see § 1.737–3(a).

(2) Partnership's basis in partnership property. The partnership's adjusted tax basis in the distributed section 704(c) property is increased or decreased immediately before the distribution by the amount of gain or loss recognized by the contributing partner under section 704(c)(1)(B) and this section. Any increase or decrease in basis is therefore taken into account in determining the distributee partner's adjusted tax basis in the distributed property under section 732. For a determination of basis in a distribution subject to section 737, see § 1.737–3(b).

(3) Section 754 adjustments. The basis adjustments to partnership property made pursuant to paragraph (e)(2) of this section are not elective and must be made regardless of whether the partnership has an election in effect under section 754. Any adjustments to the bases of partnership property (including the distributed section 704(c) property) under section 734(b) pursuant to a section 754 election must be made after (and must take into account) the adjustments to basis made under paragraph (e)(2) of this section. See § 1.737–3(c)(4) for a similar rule in the context of section 737.

(4) Example. The following example illustrates the rules of this paragraph (e). Unless otherwise specified, partnership income equals partnership expenses (other than depreciation deductions for contributed property) for each year of the partnership, the fair market value of partnership property does not change, all distributions by the partnership are subject to section 704(c)(1)(B), and all partners are unrelated.

Example. Basis adjustment. **(i)** On January 1, 1995, A, B, and C form partnership ABC as equal partners. A contributes $10,000 cash and Property A, nondepreciable real property with a fair market value of $10,000 and an adjusted tax basis of $4,000. B and C each contribute $20,000 cash.

(ii) On December 31, 1998, Property A is distributed to B in a current distribution.

(iii) Under paragraph (a) of this section, A recognizes $6,000 of gain on the distribution of Property A because that is the amount of gain that would have been allocated to A under section 704(c)(1)(A) and § 1.704–3 on a sale of Property A for its fair market value at the time of the distribution (fair market value of Property A ($10,000) less its adjusted tax basis at the time of distribution ($4,000)). The adjusted tax basis of A's partnership interest is increased from $14,000 to $20,000 to reflect this gain. The partnership's adjusted tax basis in Property A is increased from $4,000 to $10,000 immediately prior to its distribution to B. B's adjusted tax basis in Property A is therefore $10,000 under section 732(a)(1).

(f) Anti-abuse rule—(1) In general. The rules of section 704(c)(1)(B) and this section must be applied in a manner consistent with the purpose of section 704(c)(1)(B). Accordingly, if a principal purpose of a transaction is to achieve a tax result that is inconsistent with the purpose of section 704(c)(1)(B), the Commissioner can recast the transaction for federal tax purposes as appropriate to achieve tax results that are consistent with the purpose of section 704(c)(1)(B) and this section. Whether a tax result is inconsistent with the purpose of section 704(c)(1)(B) and this section must be determined based on all the facts and circumstances. See § 1.737–4 for an antiabuse rule and examples in the context of section 737.

(2) Examples. The following examples illustrate the anti-abuse rule of this paragraph (f). The examples set forth below do not delineate the boundaries of either permissible or impermissible types of transactions. Further, the addition of any facts or circumstances that are not specifically set forth in an example (or the deletion of any facts or circumstances) may alter the outcome of the transaction described in the example. Unless otherwise specified, partnership income equals partnership expenses (other than depreciation deductions for contributed property) for each year of the partnership, the fair market value of partnership property does not change, all distributions by the partnership are subject to section 704(c)(1)(B), and all partners are unrelated.

Example 1. Distribution in substance made within five-year period; results inconsistent with the purpose of section 704(c)(1)(B). **(i)** On January 1, 1995, A, B, and C form partnership ABC as equal partners. A contributes Property A, nondepreciable real property with a fair market value of $10,000 and an adjusted tax basis of $1,000. B and C each contributes $10,000 cash.

(ii) On December 31, 1998, the partners desire to distribute Property A to B in complete liquidation of B's interest in the partnership. If Property A were distributed at that time, however, A would recognize $9,000 of gain under section 704(c)(1)(B), the difference between the $10,000 fair market value and the $1,000 adjusted tax basis of Property A, because Property A was contributed to the partnership less than five years before December 31, 1998. On becoming aware of this potential gain recognition, and with a principal purpose of avoiding such gain, the partners amend the partnership agreement on December 31, 1998, and take any other steps necessary to provide that substantially all of the economic risks and benefits of Property A are borne by B as of December 31, 1998, and that substantially all of the economic risks and benefits of all other partnership property are borne by A and C. The partnership holds Property A until January 5, 2000, at which time it is distributed to B in complete liquidation of B's interest in the partnership.

(iii) The actual distribution of Property A occurred more than five years after the contribution of the property to the partnership. The steps taken by the partnership on December 31, 1998, however, are the functional equivalent of an actual distribution of Property A to B in complete liquidation of B's interest in the partnership as of that date. Section 704(c)(1)(B) requires recognition of gain when contributed section 704(c) property is in substance distributed to another partner within five years of its contribution to the partnership. Allowing a contributing partner to avoid section 704 (c)(1)(B) through arrangements such as those in this Example 1 that have the effect of a distribution of property within five years of the date of its contribution to the partnership would effectively undermine the purpose of section 704(c)(l)(B) and this section. As a result, the steps taken by the partnership on December 31, 1998, are treated as causing a distribution of Property A to B for purposes of section 704(c)(1)(B) on that date, and A recognizes gain of $9,000 under section 704(c)(1)(B) and this section at that time.

(iv) Alternatively, if on becoming aware of the potential gain recognition to A on a distribution of Property A on December 31, 1998, the partners had instead agreed that B would continue as a partner with no changes to the partnership agreement or to B's economic interest in partnership operations, the distribution of Property A to B on January 5, 2000, would not have been inconsistent with the purpose of section 704(c)(1)(B) and this section. In that situation, Property A would not have been distributed until after the expiration of the five-year period specified in section 704(c)(1)(B) and this section. Deferring the distribution of Property A until the end of the five-year period for a principal purpose of avoiding the recognition of gain under section 704(c)(1)(B) and this section is not inconsistent with the purpose of section 704(c)(1)(B). Therefore, A would not have recognized gain on the distribution of Property A in that case.

Example 2. Suspension of five-year period in manner consistent with the purpose of section 704(c)(1)(B). **(i)** A, B, and C form partnership ABC on January 1, 1995, to conduct bona fide business activities. A contributes Property A, nondepreciable real property with a fair market value of $10,000 and an adjusted tax basis of $1,000, in exchange for a 49.5 percent interest in partnership capital and profits. B contributes $10,000 in cash for a 49.5 percent interest in partnership capital and profits. C contributes cash for a 1 percent interest in partnership capital and profits. A and B are wholly owned subsidiaries of the same affiliated group and continue to control the management of Property A by virtue of their controlling interests in the partnership. The partnership is formed pursuant to a plan a principal purpose of which is to minimize the period of time that A would have to remain a partner with a potential acquiror of Property A.

(ii) On December 31, 1997, D is admitted as a partner to the partnership in exchange for $10,000 cash.

(iii) On January 5, 2000, Property A is distributed to D in complete liquidation of D's interest in the partnership.

(iv) The distribution of Property A to D occurred more than five years after the contribution of the property to the partnership. On these facts, however, a principal purpose of the transaction was to minimize the period of time that A would have to remain partners with a potential acquiror of Property A, and treating the five-year period of section 704(c)(l)(B) as running during a time when Property A was still effectively owned through the partnership by members of the contributing affiliated group of which A is a member is inconsistent with the purpose of section 704(c)(l)(B). Prior to the admission of D as a partner, the pooling of assets between A and B, on the one hand, and C, on the other hand, although sufficient to constitute ABC as a valid partnership for federal income tax purposes, is not a sufficient pooling of assets for purposes of running the five-year period with respect to the distribution of Property A to D. Allowing a contributing partner to avoid section 704(c)(1)(B) through arrangements such as those in this Example 2 would have the effect of substantially nullifying the five-year requirement of section 704(c)(1)(B) and this section and elevating the form of the transaction over its substance. As a result, with respect to the distribution of Property A to D, the five-year period of section 704(c)(1)(B) is tolled until the admission of D as a partner on December 31, 1997. Therefore, the distribution of Property A occurred before the end of the five-year period of section 704(c)(1)(B), and A recognizes gain of $9,000 under section 704(c)(1)(B) on the distribution.

(g) Effective date. This section applies to distributions by a partnership to a partner on or after January 9, 1995, except that paragraph (d)(1)(iv) applies to distributions by a partnership on or after June 24, 2003.

§ 1.705–1 Determination of basis of partner's interest.

(a) General rule. (1) Section 705 and this section provide rules for determining the adjusted basis of a partner's interest in a partnership. A partner is required to determine the adjusted basis of his interest in a partnership only when necessary for the determination of his tax liability or that of any other person. The determination of the adjusted basis of a partnership interest is ordinarily made as of the end of a partnership taxable year. Thus, for example, such year-end determination is necessary in ascertaining the extent to which a partner's distributive share of partnership losses may be allowed. See section 704 (d). However, where there has been a sale or exchange of all or a part of a partnership interest or a liquidation of a partner's entire interest in a partnership, the adjusted basis of the partner's interest should be determined as of the date of sale or exchange or liquidation. The adjusted basis of a partner's interest in a partnership is determined without regard to any amount shown in the partnership books as the partner's "capital," "equity," or similar account. For example, A contributes property with an adjusted basis to him of $400 (and a value of $1,000) to a partnership. B contributes $1,000 cash. While under their agreement each may have a "capital account" in the partnership of $1,000, the adjusted basis of A's interest is only $400 and B's interest $1,000.

(2) The original basis of a partner's interest in a partnership shall be determined under section 722 (relating to contributions to a partnership) or section 742 (relating to transfers of partnership interests). Such basis shall be increased under section 722 by any further contributions to the partnership and by the sum of the partner's distributive share for the taxable year and prior taxable years of—

(i) Taxable income of the partnership as determined under section 703(a),

(ii) Tax-exempt receipts of the partnership, and

(iii) The excess of the deductions for depletion over the basis of the depletable property, unless the property is an oil or gas property the basis of which has been allocated to partners under section 613A(c)(7)(D).

(3) The basis shall be decreased (but not below zero) by distributions from the partnership as provided in section 733 and by the sum of the partner's distributive share for the taxable year and prior taxable years of—

(i) Partnership losses (including capital losses), and

(ii) Partnership expenditures which are not deductible in computing partnership taxable income or loss and which are not capital expenditures.

(4) The basis shall be decreased (but not below zero) by the amount of the partner's deduction for depletion allowable under section 611 for any partnership oil and gas property to the extent the deduction does not exceed the proportionate share of the adjusted basis of the property allocated to the partner under section 613A(c)(7)(D).

(5) The basis shall be adjusted (but not below zero) to reflect any gain or loss to the partner resulting from a disposition by the partnership of a domestic oil or gas property after December 31, 1974.

(6) For the effect of liabilities in determining the amount of contributions made by a partner to a partnership or the amount of distributions made by a partnership to a partner, see section 752 and §1.752–1, relating to the treatment of certain liabilities. In determining the basis of a partnership interest on the effective date of subchapter K, chapter 1 of the Code, or any of the sections thereof, the partner's share of partnership liabilities on that date shall be included.

(7) For basis adjustments necessary to coordinate sections 705 and 1032 in certain situations in which a partnership disposes of stock or any position in stock to which section 1032 applies of a corporation that holds a direct or indirect interest in the partnership, see § 1.705–2.

(8) For basis adjustments necessary to coordinate sections 705 and 358(h), see § 1.358–7(b). For certain basis adjustments with respect to a § 1.752–7 liability assumed by a partnership from a partner, see § 1.752–7.

(b) Alternative rule. In certain cases, the adjusted basis of a partner's interest in a partnership may be determined by reference to the partner's share of the adjusted basis of partnership property which would be distributable upon termination of the partnership. The alternative rule may be used to determine the adjusted basis of a partner's interest where circumstances are such that the partner cannot practicably apply the general rule set forth in section 705(a) and paragraph (a) of this section, or where, from a consideration of all the facts, it is, in the opinion of the Commissioner, reasonable to conclude that the result produced will not vary substantially from the result obtainable under the general rule. Where the alternative rule is used, adjustments may be necessary in determining the adjusted basis of a partner's interest in a partnership. Adjustments would be required, for example, in order to reflect in a partner's share of the adjusted basis of partnership property any significant discrepancies arising as a result of contributed property, transfers of partnership interests, or distributions of property to the partners. The operation of the alternative rules may be illustrated by the following examples:

Example (1). The ABC partnership, in which A, B, and C are equal partners, owns various properties with a total adjusted basis of $1,500 and has earned and retained an additional $1,500. The total adjusted basis of partnership property is thus $3,000. Each partner's share in the adjusted basis of partnership property is one-third of this amount, or $1,000. Under the alternative rule, this amount represents each partner's adjusted basis for his partnership interest.

Example (2). Assume that partner A in example (1) of this paragraph sells his partnership interest to D for $1,250 at a time when the partnership property with an adjusted basis of $1,500 had appreciated in value to $3,000, and when the partnership also had $750 in cash. The total adjusted basis of all partnership property is $2,250 and the value of such property is $3,750. D's basis for his partnership interest is his cost, $1,250. However, his one-third share of the adjusted basis of partnership property is only $750. Therefore, for the purposes of the alternative rule, D has an adjustment of $500 in determining the basis of his interest. This amount represents the difference between the cost of his partnership interest and his share of partnership basis at the time of his purchase. If the partnership subsequently earns and retains an additional $1,500, its property will have an adjusted basis of $3,750. D's adjusted basis for his interest under the alternative rule is $1,750, determined by adding $500, his basis adjustment to $1,250 (his one-third share of the $3,750 adjusted basis of partnership property). If the partnership distributes $250 to each partner in a current distribution, D's adjusted basis for his interest will be $1,500 ($1,000, his one-third share of the remaining basis of partnership property, $3,000, plus his basis adjustment of $500).

Example (3). Assume that BCD partnership in example (2) of this paragraph continues to operate. In 1960, D proposes to sell his partnership interest and wishes to evaluate the tax consequences of such sale. It is necessary, therefore, to determine the adjusted basis of his interest in the partnership. Assume further that D cannot determine the adjusted basis of his interest under the general rule. The balance sheet of the BCD partnership is as follows:

Assets	Adjusted basis per books	Market Value
Cash	$3,000	$3,000
Receivables	4,000	4,000
Depreciable property	5,000	5,000
Land held for investment	18,000	30,000
Total	30,000	42,000

Liabilities and capital	Per books
Liabilities	$6,000
Capital accounts:	
B	4,500
C	4,500
D	15,000
Total	30,000

The $15,000 representing the amount of D's capital account does not reflect the $500 basis adjustment arising from D's purchase of his interest. See example (2) of this paragraph. The adjusted basis of D's partnership interest determined under the alternative rule is as follows:

D's share of the adjusted basis of partnership property (reduced by the amount of liabilities) at time of proposed sale	$15,000
D's share of partnership liabilities (under the partnership agreement liabilities are shared equally)	2,000
D's basis adjustment from example (2)	500
Adjusted basis of D's interest at the time of proposed sale, as determined under alternative rule	17,500

* * *

§ 1.706–1 Taxable years of partner and partnership.

(a) Year in which partnership income is includible. (1) In computing taxable income for a taxable year, a partner is required to include the partner's distributive share of partnership items set forth in section 702 and the regulations thereunder for any partnership taxable year ending within or with the partner's taxable year. A partner must also include in taxable income for a taxable year guaranteed payments under section 707(c) that are deductible by the partnership under its method of accounting in the partnership taxable year ending within or with the partner's taxable year.

(2) The rules of this paragraph (a)(1) may be illustrated by the following example:

Example. Partner A reports income using a calendar year, while the partnership of which A is a member reports its income using a fiscal year ending May 31. The partnership reports its income and deductions under the cash method of accounting. During the partnership taxable year ending May 31, 2002, the partnership makes guaranteed payments of $120,000 to A for services and for the use of capital. Of this amount, $70,000 was paid to A between June 1 and December 31, 2001, and the remaining $50,000 was paid to A between January 1 and May 31, 2002. The entire $120,000 paid to A is includible in A's taxable income for the calendar year 2002 (together with A's distributive share of partnership items set forth in section 702 for the partnership taxable year ending May 31, 2002).

(3) If a partner receives distributions under section 731 or sells or exchanges all or part of a partnership interest, any gain or loss arising therefrom does not constitute partnership income.

(b) Taxable year—(1) Partnership treated as a taxpayer. The taxable year of a partnership must be determined as though the partnership were a taxpayer.

(2) Partnership's taxable year—(i) Required taxable year. Except as provided in paragraph (b)(2)(ii) of this section, the taxable year of a partnership must be—

(A) The majority interest taxable year, as defined in section 706(b)(4);

(B) If there is no majority interest taxable year, the taxable year of all the principal partners of the partnership, as defined in 706(b)(3) (the principal partners' taxable year); or

(C) If there is no majority interest taxable year or principal partners' taxable year, the taxable year that produces the least aggregate deferral of income as determined under paragraph (b)(3) of this section.

(ii) Exceptions. A partnership may have a taxable year other than its required taxable year if it makes an election under section 444, elects to use a 52–53-week taxable year that ends with reference to its required taxable year or a taxable year elected under section 444, or establishes a business purpose for such taxable year and obtains approval of the Commissioner under section 442.

(3) Last aggregate deferral—(i) Taxable year that results in the least aggregate deferral of income. The taxable year that results in the least aggregate deferral of income will be the taxable year of one or more of the partners in the partnership which will result in the least aggregate deferral of income to the partners. The aggregate deferral for a particular year is equal to the sum of the products determined by multiplying the month(s) of deferral for each partner that would be generated by that year and each partner's interest in partnership profits for that year. The partner's taxable year that produces the lowest sum when compared to the other partner's taxable years is the taxable year that results in the least aggregate deferral of income to the partners. If the calculation results in more than one taxable year qualifying as the taxable year with the least aggregate deferral, the partnership may select any one of those taxable years as its taxable year. However, if one of the qualifying taxable years is also the partnership's existing taxable year, the partnership must maintain its existing taxable year. The determination of the taxable year that results in the least aggregate deferral of income generally must be made as of the beginning of the partnership's current taxable year. The director, however, may determine that the first day of the current taxable year is not the appropriate testing day and require the use of some other day or period that will more accurately reflect the ownership of the partnership and thereby the actual aggregate deferral to the partners where the partners engage in a transaction that has as its principal purpose the avoidance of the principles of this section. Thus, for example the preceding sentence would apply where there is a transfer of an interest in the partnership that results in a temporary transfer of that interest principally for purposes of qualifying for a specific taxable year under the principles of this section. For purposes of this section, deferral to each partner is measured in terms of months from the end of the partnership's taxable year forward to the end of the partner's taxable year.

(ii) Determination of the taxable year of a partner or partnership that uses a 52–53-week taxable year. For purposes of the calculation described in paragraph (b)(3)(i) of this section, the taxable year of a partner or partnership that uses a 52–53-week taxable year must be the same year determined under the rules of section 441(f) and the regulations thereunder with respect to the inclusion of income by the partner or partnership.

(iii) Special de minimis rule. If the taxable year that results in the least aggregate deferral produces an aggregate deferral that is less than .5 when compared to the aggregate deferral of the current taxable year, the partnership's current taxable year will be treated as the taxable year with the least aggregate deferral. Thus, the partnership will not be permitted to change its taxable year.

* * *

(iv) Examples. The principles of this section may be illustrated by the following examples:

Example (1). Partnership P is on a fiscal year ending June 30. Partner A reports income on the fiscal year ending June 30 and Partner B reports income on the fiscal year ending July 31. A and B each have a 50 percent interest in partnership profits. For its taxable year beginning July 1, 1987, the partnership will be required to retain its taxable year since the fiscal year ending June 30 results in the least aggregate deferral of income to the partners. This determination is made as follows:

Test 6/30	Year End	Interest in Partnership Profits	Months of Deferral for 6/30 Year End	Interest × Deferral
Partner A.....	6/30	.5	0	0
Partner B.....	7/31	.5	1	.5
Aggregate deferral				.5

Test 7/31	Year End	Interest in Partnership Profits	Months of Deferral for 7/31 Year End	Interest × Deferral
Partner A.....	6/30	.5	11	5.5
Partner B.....	7/31	.5	0	0
Aggregate deferral				5.5

Example (2). The facts are the same as in *Example (1)* except that A reports income on the calendar year and B reports on the fiscal year ending November 30. For the partnership's taxable year beginning July 1, 1987, the partnership is required to change its taxable year to a fiscal year ending November 30 because such year results in the least aggregate deferral of income to the partners. This determination is madę as follows:

Test 12/31	Year End	Interest in Partnership Profits	Months of Deferral for 12/31 Year End	Interest × Deferral
Partner A.....	12/31	.5	0	0
Partner B.....	11/30	.5	11	5.5
Aggregate deferral				5.5

Test 11/30	Year End	Interest in Partnership Profits	Months of Deferral for 11/30 Year End	Interest × Deferral
Partner A.....	12/31	.5	1	.5
Partner B.....	11/30	.5	0	0
Aggregate deferral				.5

Example (3). The facts are the same as in *Example (2)* except that B reports income on the fiscal year ending June 30. For the partnership's taxable year beginning July 1, 1987, each partner's taxable year will result in identical aggregate deferral of income. If the partnership's current taxable year was neither a fiscal year ending June 30 nor the calendar year, the partnership would select either the fiscal year ending June 30 or the calendar year as its taxable year. However, since the partnership's current taxable year ends June 30, it must retain its current taxable year. The determination is made as follows:

Test 12/31	Year End	Interest in Partnership Profits	Months of Deferral for 12/31 Year End	Interest × Deferral
Partner A.....	12/31	.5	0	0
Partner B.....	6/30	.5	6	3.0
Aggregate deferral				3.0

Test 6/30	Year End	Interest in Partnership Profits	Months of Deferral for 6/30 Year End	Interest × Deferral
Partner A.....	12/31	.5	6	3.0
Partner B.....	6/30	.5	0	0
Aggregate deferral				3.0

Example (4). The facts are the same as in *Example (1)* except that on December 31, 1987, Partner A sells a 4 percent interest in the partnership to Partner C, who reports income on the fiscal year ending June 30, and a 40 percent interest in the partnership to Partner D, who also reports income on the fiscal year ending June 30. The taxable year beginning July 1, 1987, is unaffected by the sale. However, for the taxable year beginning July 31, 1988, the partnership must determine the taxable year resulting in the least aggregate deferral as of July 1, 1988. In this case, the partnership will be required to retain its taxable year since the fiscal year ending June 30 continues to be the taxable year that results in the least aggregate deferral of income to the partners.

Example (5). The facts are the same as in *Example (4)* except that Partner D reports income on the fiscal year ending April 30. As in Example (4), the taxable year during which the sale took place is unaffected by the shifts in interests. However, for its taxable year beginning July 1, 1988, the partnership will be required to change its taxable year to the fiscal year ending April 30. This determination is made as follows:

Test 7/31	Year End	Interest in Partnership Profits	Months of Deferral for 7/31 Year End	Interest × Deferral
Partner A.....	6/30	.06	11	.66
Partner B.....	7/31	.5	0	0
Partner C.....	6/30	.04	11	.44
Partner D.....	4/30	.4	9	3.60
Aggregate deferral				4.70

Test 6/30	Year End	Interest in Partnership Profits	Months of Deferral for 6/30 Year End	Interest × Deferral
Partner A.....	6/30	.06	0	0
Partner B.....	7/31	.5	1	.5
Partner C.....	6/30	.04	0	0
Partner D.....	4/30	.4	10	4.0
Aggregate deferral				4.5

Test 4/30	Year End	Interest in Partnership Profits	Months of Deferral for 4/30 Year End	Interest × Deferral
Partner A.....	6/30	.06	2	.12
Partner B.....	7/31	.5	3	1.50
Partner C.....	6/30	.04	2	.08
Partner D.....	4/30	.4	0	0
Aggregate deferral				1.70

§ 1.706–1(b)(3) Test:	
Current taxable year (June 30)	4.5
Less: Taxable year producing the least aggregate deferral (April 30)	1.7
Additional aggregate deferral (greater than .5)	2.8

Example (6). (i) Partnership P has two partners, A who reports income on the fiscal year ending March 31, and B who reports income on the fiscal year ending July 31. A and B share profits equally. P has determined its taxable year under paragraph (b)(3) of this section to be the fiscal year ending March 31 as follows:

Test 3/31	Year End	Interest in Partnership Profits	Months of Deferral for 3/31 Year End	Interest × Deferral
Partner A.....	3/31	.5	0	0
Partner B.....	7/31	.5	4	2
Aggregate deferral				2

Test 7/31	Year End	Interest in Partnership Profits	Months of Deferral for 7/31 Year End	Interest × Deferral
Partner A.....	3/31	.5	8	4
Partner B.....	7/31	.5	0	0
Aggregate deferral				4

(ii) In May 1988, Partner A sells a 45 percent interest in the partnership to C, who reports income on the fiscal year ending April 30. For the taxable period beginning April 1, 1989, the fiscal year ending April 30 is the taxable year that produces the least aggregate deferral of income to the partners. However, under paragraph (b)(3)(iii) of this section the partnership is required to retain its fiscal year ending March 31. This determination is made as follows:

Test 3/31	Year End	Interest in Partnership Profits	Months of Deferral for 3/31 Year End	Interest × Deferral
Partner A.....	3/31	.05	0	0
Partner B.....	7/31	.5	4	2.00
Partner C.....	4/30	.45	1	.45
Aggregate deferral				2.45

Test 7/31	Year End	Interest in Partnership Profits	Months of Deferral for 7/31 Year End	Interest × Deferral
Partner A.....	3/31	.05	8	.40
Partner B.....	7/31	.5	0	0
Partner C.....	4/30	.45	9	4.05
Aggregate deferral				4.45

Test 4/30	Year End	Interest in Partnership Profits	Months of Deferral for 4/30 Year End	Interest × Deferral
Partner A.....	3/31	.05	11	.55
Partner B.....	7/31	.5	3	1.50
Partner C.....	4/30	.45	0	0
Aggregate deferral				2.05

§ 1.706–1(b)(3) Test:	
Current taxable year (3/31)	2.45
Less: Taxable year producing the least aggregate deferral (4/30)	2.05
Additional aggregate deferral (less than .5)	.40

(4) Measurement of partner's profits and capital interest—

(i) In general. The rules of this paragraph (b)(4) apply in determining the majority interest taxable year, the principal partners' taxable year, and the least aggregate deferral taxable year.

(ii) Profits interest—(A) In general. For purposes of section 706(b), a partner's interest in partnership profits is generally the partner's percentage share of partnership profits for the current partnership taxable year. If the partnership does not expect to have net income for the current partnership taxable year, then a partner's interest in partnership profits instead must be the partner's percentage share of partnership net income for the first taxable year in which the partnership expects to have a net income.

(B) Percentage share of partnership net income. The partner's percentage share of partnership net income for a partnership taxable year is the ratio of: the partner's distributive share of partnership net income for the taxable year, to the partnership's net income for the year. If a partner's percentage share of partnership net income for the taxable year depends on the amount or nature of partnership income for that year (due to, for example, preferred returns or special allocations of specific partnership items), then the partnership must make a reasonable estimate of the amount and nature of its income for the taxable year. This estimate must be based on all facts and circumstances known to the partnership as of the first day of the current partnership taxable year. The partnership must then use this estimate in determining the partners' interests in partnership profits for the taxable year.

(C) Distributive share. For purposes of this paragraph (b)(4)(ii), a partner's distributive share of partnership net income is determined by taking into account all rules and regulations affecting that determination, including, without limitation, sections 704(b), (c), and (e), 736, and 743.

(iii) Capital interest. Generally, a partner's interest in partnership capital is determined by reference to the assets of the partnership that the partner would be entitled to upon withdrawal from the partnership or upon liquidation of the partnership. If the partnership maintains capital accounts in accordance with § 1.704–1(b)(2)(iv), then for purposes of section 706(b), the partnership may assume that a partner's interest in partnership capital is the ratio of the partner's capital account to all partners' capital accounts as of the first day of the partnership taxable year.

(5) Taxable year of a partnership with taxexempt partners.—(i) Certain tax-exempt partners disregarded. In determining the taxable year (the current year) of a partnership under section 706(b) and the regulations thereunder, a partner that is taxexempt under section 501(a) shall be disregarded if such partner was not subject to tax, under chapter 1 of the Internal Revenue Code, on any income attributable to its investment in the partnership during the partnership's taxable year immediately preceding the current year. However, if a partner that is tax-exempt under section 501(a) was not a partner during the partnership's immediately preceding taxable year, such partner will be disregarded for the current year if the partnership reasonably believes that the partner will not be subject to tax, under chapter 1 of the Internal Revenue Code, on any income attributable to such partner's investment in the partnership during the current year.

(ii) Example. The provisions of paragraph (b)(5)(i) of this section may be illustrated by the following example:

Example. Assume that partnership A has historically used the calendar year as its taxable year. In addition, assume that A is owned by 5 partners, 4 calendar year individuals (each owning 10 percent of A's profits and capital) and a tax-exempt organization (owning 60 percent of A's profits and capital). The tax-exempt organization has never had unrelated business taxable income with respect to A and has historically used a June 30 fiscal year. Finally, assume that A desires to retain the calendar year for its taxable year beginning January 1, 2003. Under these facts and but for the special rule in paragraph (b)(5)(i) of this section, A would be required under section 706(b)(1)(B)(i) to change to a year ending June 30, for its taxable year beginning January 1, 2003. However, under the special rule provided in paragraph (b)(5)(i) of this section the partner that is tax-exempt is disregarded, and A must retain the calendar year, under section 706(b)(1)(B)(i), for its taxable year beginning January 1.

(iii) Effective date. The provisions of this paragraph (b)(5) are applicable for taxable years beginning on or after July 23, 2002. For taxable years beginning before July 23, 2002, see § 1.706–3T as contained in 26 CFR part 1 revised April 1, 2002.

* * *

(7) Adoption of taxable year. A newly-formed partnership may adopt, in accordance with §1.441–1(c), its required taxable year elected under section 444, or a 52–53-week taxable year ending with reference to its required taxable year or a taxable year elected under section 444 without securing the approval of the Commissioner. If a newly-formed partnership wants to adopt any other taxable year, it must establish a business purpose and secure the approval of the Commissioner under section 442.

(8) Change in taxable year—(i) Partnerships—(A) Approval required. An existing partnership may change its taxable year only by securing the approval of the Commissioner under section 442 or making an election under section 444. However, a partnership may obtain automatic approval for certain changes, including a change to its required taxable year, pursuant to administrative procedures published by the Commissioner.

(B) Short period tax return. A partnership that changes its taxable year must make its return for a short period in accordance with section 443, but must not annualize the partnership taxable income.

(C) Change in required taxable year. If a partnership is required to change to its majority interest taxable year, then no further change in the partnership's required taxable year is required for either of the two years following the year of the change. This limitation against a second change within a three-year period applies only if the first change was to the majority interest taxable year and does not apply following a change in the partnership's taxable year to the principal partners' taxable year or the least aggregate deferral taxable year.

(ii) Partners. Except as otherwise provided in the Internal Revenue Code or the regulations thereunder (e.g., section 859 regarding real estate investment trusts or § 1.442–2(c) regarding a subsidiary changing to its consolidated parent's taxable year), a partner may not change its taxable year without securing the approval of the Commissioner under section 442. However, certain partners may be eligible to obtain automatic approval to change their taxable years pursuant to the regulations or administrative procedures published by the Commissioner. A partner that changes its taxable year must make its return for a short period in accordance with section 443.

(9) Retention of taxable year. In certain cases, a partnership will be required to change its taxable year unless it obtains the approval of the Commissioner under section 442, or makes an election under section 444, to retain its current taxable year. For example, a partnership using a taxable year that corresponds to its required taxable year must obtain the approval of the Commissioner to retain such taxable year if its required taxable year changes as a result of a change in ownership, unless the partnership previously obtained approval for its current taxable year or, if appropriate, makes an election under section 444.

(10) Procedures for obtaining approval or making a section 444 election. See § 1.442–1(b) for procedures to obtain the approval of the Commissioner (automatically or otherwise) to adopt, change, or retain a taxable year. See §§ 1.444–1T and 1.444–2T for qualifications, and § 1.444–3T for procedures, for making an election under section 444.

* * *

(c) Closing of partnership year—(1) General rule. Section 706(c) and this paragraph provide rules governing the closing of partnership years. The closing of a partnership taxable year or a termination of a partnership for Federal income tax purposes is not necessarily governed by the "dissolution", "liquidation", etc., of a partnership under State or local law. The taxable year of a partnership shall not close as the result of the death of a partner, the entry of a new partner, the liquidation of a partner's entire interest in the partnership (as defined in section 761 (d)), or the sale or exchange of a partner's interest in the partnership, except in the case of a termination of a partnership and except as provided in subparagraph (2) of this paragraph. In the case of termination, the partnership taxable year closes for all partners as of the date of termination. See section 708(b) and paragraph (b) of § 1.708–1.

(2) Partner who retires or sells interest in partnership—(i) Disposition of entire interest. A partnership taxable year shall close with respect to a partner who sells or exchanges his entire interest in a partnership, and with respect to a partner whose entire interest is liquidated. However, a partnership taxable year with respect to a partner who dies shall not close prior to the end of such partnership taxable year, or the time when such partner's interest (held by his estate or other successor) is liquidated or sold or exchanged, whichever is earlier. See subparagraph (3) of this paragraph.

(ii) Inclusions in taxable income. In the case of a sale, exchange, or liquidation of a partner's entire interest in a partnership, the partner shall include in his taxable income for his taxable year within or with which his membership in the partnership ends, his distributive share of items described in section 702(a), and any guaranteed payments under section 707(c), for his partnership taxable year ending with the date of such sale, exchange, or liquidation. In order to avoid an interim closing of the partnership books, such partner's distributive share of items described in section 702(a) may, by agreement among the partners, be estimated by taking his *pro rata* part of the amount of such items he would have included in his taxable income had he remained a partner until the end of the partnership taxable year. The proration may be based on the portion of the taxable year that has elapsed prior to the sale, exchange, or liquidation, or may be determined under any other method that is reasonable. Any partner who is the transferee of such partner's interest shall include in his taxable income, as his distributive share of items described in section 702(a) with respect to the acquired interest, the *pro rata* part (determined by the method used by the transferor partner) of the amount of such items he would have included had he been a partner from the beginning of the taxable year of the partnership. The application of this subdivision may be illustrated by the following example:

Example. Assume that a partner selling his partnership interest on June 30, 1955, has an adjusted basis for his interest of $5,000 on that date; that his *pro rata* share of partnership income up to June 30 is $15,000; and that he sells his interest for $20,000. Under the provisions of section 706(c)(2), the partnership year with respect to him closes at the time of the sale. The $15,000 is includible in his income as his distributive share and, under section 705, it increases the basis of his partnership interest to $20,000, which is also the selling price of his interest. Therefore, no gain is realized on the sale of his partnership interest. The purchaser of this partnership interest shall include in his income as his distributive share his *pro rata* part of partnership income for the remainder of the partnership taxable year.

(3) Partner who dies. (i) When a partner dies, the partnership taxable year shall not close with respect to such partner prior to the end of the partnership taxable year. The partnership taxable year shall continue both for the remaining partners and the decedent partner. Where the death of a partner results in the termination of the partnership, the partnership taxable year shall close for all partners on the date of such termination under section 708(b)(1)(A). See also paragraph (b)(1)(i)(b) of § 1.708–1 for the continuation of a 2-member partnership under certain circumstances after the death of a partner. However, if the decedent partner's estate or other successor sells or exchanges its entire interest in the partnership, or if its entire interest is liquidated, the partnership taxable year with respect to the estate or other successor in interest shall close on the date of such sale or exchange, or the date of completion of the liquidation.

(ii) The last return of a decedent partner shall include only his share of partnership taxable income for any partnership taxable year or years ending within or with the last taxable year for such decedent partner (*i.e.*, the year ending with the date of his death). The distributive share of partnership taxable income for a partnership taxable year ending after the decedent's last taxable year is includible in the return of his estate or other successor in interest. If the estate or other successor in interest of a partner continues to share in the profits or losses of the partnership business, the distributives share thereof is includible in the taxable year of the estate or other successor in interest within or with which the taxable year of the partnership ends. See also paragraph (a)(1)(ii) of § 1.736–1. Where the estate or other successor in interest receives distributions, any gain or loss on such distributions is includible in its gross income for its taxable year in which the distribution is made.

(iii) If a partner (or a retiring partner), in accordance with the terms of the partnership agreement, designates a person to succeed to his interest in the partnership after his death, such designated person shall be regarded as a successor in interest of the deceased for purposes of this chapter. Thus, where a partner designates his widow as the successor in interest, her distributive share of income for the taxable year of the partnership ending within or with her taxable year may be included in a joint return in accordance with the provisions of sections 2 and 6013(a)(2) and (3).

(iv) If, under the terms of an agreement existing at the date of death of a partner, a sale or exchange of the decedent partner's interest in the partnership occurs upon that date, then the taxable year of the partnership with respect to such decedent partner shall close upon the date of death. See section 706(c)(2)(A)(i). The sale or exchange of a partnership interest does not, for the purpose of this rule, include any transfer of a partnership interest which occurs at death as a result of inheritance or any testamentary disposition.

(v) To the extent that any part of a distributive share of partnership income of the estate or other successor in interest of a deceased partner is attributable to the decedent for the period ending with the date of his death, such part of the distributive share is income in respect of the decedent under section 691. See section 691 and the regulations thereunder.

(vi) The provisions of this subparagraph may be illustrated by the following examples:

Example (1). B has a taxable year ending December 31 and is a member of partnership ABC, the taxable year of which ends on June 30. B dies on October 31, 1955. His estate (which as a new taxpayer may, under section 441 and the regulations thereunder, adopt any taxable year) adopts a taxable year ending October 31. The return of the decedent for the period January 1 to October 31, 1955, will include only his distributive share of taxable income of the partnership for its taxable year ending June 30, 1955. The distributive share of taxable income of the partnership for its taxable year ending June 30, 1956, arising from the interest of the decedent, will be includible in the return of the estate for its taxable year ending October 31, 1956. That part of the distributive share attributable to the decedent for the period ending with the date of his death (July 1 through October 31, 1955) is income in respect of a decedent under section 691.

Example (2). Assume the same facts as in example (1) of this subdivision, except that, prior to B's death, B and D had agreed that, upon B's death, D would purchase B's interest for $10,000. When B dies on October 31, 1955, the partnership taxable year beginning July 1, 1955, closes with respect to him. Therefore, the return for B's last taxable year (January 1 to October 31, 1955) will include his distributive share of taxable income of the partnership for its taxable year ending June 30, 1955, plus his distributive share of partnership taxable income for the period July 1 to October 31, 1955. See subdivision (iv) of this subparagraph.

Example (3). H is a member of a partnership having a taxable year ending December 31. Both H and his wife W are on a calendar year and file joint returns. H dies on March 31, 1955. Administration of the estate is completed and the estate, including the partnership interest, is distributed to W as legatee on November 30, 1955. Such distribution by the estate is not a sale or exchange of H's partnership interest. No part of the taxable income of the partnership for the taxable year ending December 31, 1955, which is allocable to H, will be included in H's taxable income for his last taxable year (January 1 through March 31, 1955) or in the taxable income of H's estate for the taxable year April 1 through November 30, 1955. The distributive share of partnership taxable income for the full calendar year that is allocable to H will be includible in the taxable income of W for her taxable year ending December 31, 1955, and she may file a joint return under sections 2 and 6013(a)(3). That part of the distributive share attributable to the decedent for the period ending with the date of his death (January 1 through March 31, 1955) is income in respect of a decedent under section 691.

Example (4). M is a member of partnership JKM which operates on a calendar year. M and his wife S file joint returns for calendar years. In accordance with the partnership agreement, M designated S to succeed to his interest in the partnership upon his death. M, who had withdrawn $10,000 from the partnership before his death, dies on October 20, 1955. S's distributive share of income for the taxable year 1955 is $15,000 ($10,000 of which represents the amount withdrawn by M). S shall include $15,000 in her income, even though M received $10,000 of this amount before his death. S may file a joint return with M for the year 1955 under sections 2 and 6013(a). That part of the $15,000 distributive share attributable to the decedent for the period ending with the date of his death (January 1 through October 20, 1955) is income in respect of a decedent under section 691.

(4) Disposition of less than entire interest. If a partner sells or exchanges a part of his interest in a partnership, or if the interest of a partner is reduced, the partnership taxable year shall continue to its normal end. In such case, the partner's distributive share of items which he is required to include in his taxable income under the provisions of section 702 (a) shall be determined by taking into account his varying interests in the partnership during the partnership taxable year in which such sale, exchange, or reduction of interest occurred.

(5) Transfer of interest by gift. The transfer of a partnership interest by gift does not close the partnership taxable year with respect to the donor. However, the income up to the date of gift attributable to the donor's interest shall be allocated to him under section 704(e)(2).

* * *

§ 1.707–0 Table of contents.

This section lists the captions that appear in §§ 1.707–1 through 1.707–9.

Section 1.707–1 Transactions between partner and partnership.

Section 1.707–2 Disguised payments for services [Reserved].

Section 1.707–3 Disguised sales of property to partnership; general rules

Section 1.707–4 Disguised sales of property to partnership; special rules applicable to guaranteed payments, preferred returns, operating cash flow distributions, and reimbursements of preformation expenditures.

Section 1.707–5 Disguised sales of property to partnership; special rules relating to liabilities.

(6) Qualified liability of a partner defined.

(7) Liability incurred within two years of transfer presumed to be in anticipation of the transfer.

(i) In general.

(ii) Disclosure of transfers of property subject to liabilities incurred within two years of the transfer.

(b) Treatment of debt-financed transfers of consideration by partnerships.

(1) In general.

(2) Partner's allocable share of liability.

(i) In general.

(ii) Debt-financed transfers made pursuant to a plan.

(A) In general.

(B) Special rule.

(iii) Reduction of partner's share of liability.

(c) Refinancings.

(d) Share of liability where assumption accompanied by transfer of money.

(e) Tiered partnerships and other related persons.

(f) Examples.

Section 1.707–6 Disguised sales of property by partnership to partner: general rules.

(a) In general.

(b) Special rules relating to liabilities.

(1) In general.

(2) Qualified liabilities.

(c) Disclosure rules.

(d) Examples.

Section 1.707–7 Disguised sales of partnership interests [Reserved].

Section 1.707–8 Disclosure of certain information.

(a) In general.

(b) Method of providing disclosure.

(c) Disclosure by certain partnerships.

Section 1.707–9 Effective dates and transitional rules.

(a) Sections 1.707–3 through 1.707–6.

(1) In general.

(2) Transfers occurring on or before April 24, 1991.

(3) Effective date of section 73 of the Tax Reform Act of 1984.

(b) Section 1.707–8 disclosure of certain information.

§ 1.707–1 Transactions between partner and partnership.

(a) **Partner not acting in capacity as partner.** A partner who engages in a transaction with a partnership other than in his capacity as a partner shall be treated as if he were not a member of the partnership with respect to such transaction. Such transactions include, for example, loans of money or property by the partnership to the partner or by the partner to the partnership, the sale of property by the partner to the partnership, the purchase of property by the partner from the partnership, and the rendering of services by the partnership to the partner or by the partner to the partnership. Where a partner retains the ownership of property but allows the partnership to use such separately owned property for partnership purposes (for example, to obtain credit or to secure firm creditors by guaranty, pledge, or other agreement) the transaction is treated as one between a partnership and a partner not acting in his capacity as a partner. However, transfers of money or property by a partner to a partnership as contributions, or transfers of money or property by a partnership to a partner as distributions, are not transactions included within the provisions of this section. In all cases, the substance of the transaction will govern rather than its form. See paragraph (c)(3) of § 1.731–1.

(b) **Certain sales or exchanges of property with respect to controlled partnerships—(1) Losses disallowed.** (i) No deduction shall be allowed for a loss on a sale or exchange of property (other than an interest in the partnership, directly or indirectly, between a partnership and a partner who owns, directly or indirectly, more than 50 percent of the capital interest or profits interest in such partnership. A loss on a sale or exchange of property, directly or indirectly, between two partnerships in which the same persons own, directly or indirectly, more than

50 percent of the capital interest or profits interest in each partnership shall not be allowed.

(ii) If a gain is realized upon the subsequent sale or exchange by a transferee of property with respect to which a loss was disallowed under the provisions of subdivision (i) of this subparagraph, section 267 (d) (relating to amount of gain where loss previously disallowed) shall apply as though the loss were disallowed under section 267(a)(1).

(2) Gains treated as ordinary income. Any gain recognized upon the sale or exchange, directly or indirectly, of property which, in the hands of the transferee immediately after the transfer, is property other than a capital asset, as defined in section 1221, shall be ordinary income if the transaction is between a partnership and a partner who owns, directly or indirectly, more than 80 percent* of the capital interest or profits interest in the partnership. This rule also applies where such a transaction is between partnerships in which the same persons own, directly or indirectly, more than 80 percent* of the capital interest or profits interest in each partnership. The term "property other than a capital asset" includes (but is not limited to) trade accounts receivable, inventory, stock in trade, and depreciable or real property used in the trade or business.

(3) Ownership of a capital or profits interest. In determining the extent of the ownership by a partner, as defined in section 761(b), of his capital interest or profits interest in a partnership, the rules for constructive ownership of stock provided in section 267(c)(1), (2), (4), and (5) shall be applied for the purpose of section 707(b) and this paragraph. Under these rules, ownership of a capital or profits interest in a partnership may be attributed to a person who is not a partner as defined in section 761(b) in order that another partner may be considered the constructive owner of such interest under section 267 (c). However, section 707(b)(1)(A) does not apply to a constructive owner of a partnership interest since he is not a partner as defined in section 761(b). For example, where trust T is a partner in the partnership ABT, and AW, A's wife, is the sole beneficiary of the trust, the ownership of a capital and profits interest in the partnership by T will be attributed to AW only for the purpose of further attributing the ownership of such interest to A. See section 267(c)(1) and (5). If A, B, and T are equal partners, then A will be considered as owning more than 50 percent of the capital and profits interest in the partnership, and losses on transactions between him and the partnership will be disallowed by section 707(b)(1)(A). However, a loss sustained by AW on a sale or exchange of property with the partnership would not be disallowed by section 707, but will be disallowed to the extent provided in paragraph (b) of § 1.267(b)–1. See section 267(a) and (b), and the regulations thereunder.

(c) Guaranteed payments. Payments made by a partnership to a partner for services or for the use of capital are considered as made to a person who is not a partner, to the extent such payments are determined without regard to the income of the partnership. However, a partner must include such payments as ordinary income for his taxable year within or with which ends the partnership taxable year in which the partnership deducted such payments as paid or accrued under its method of accounting. See section 706(a) and paragraph (a) of § 1.706–1. Guaranteed payments are considered as made to one who is not a member of the partnership only for the purposes of section 61(a) (relating to gross income) and section 162(a) (relating to trade or business expenses). For a guaranteed payment to be a partnership deduction, it must meet the same tests under section 162(a) as it would if the payment had been made to a person who is not a member of the partnership, and the rules of section 263 (relating to capital expenditures) must be taken into account. This rule does not affect the deductibility to the partnership of a payment described in section 736(a)(2) to a retiring partner or to a deceased partner's successor in interest. Guaranteed payments do not constitute an interest in partnership profits for purposes of sections 706(b)(3), 707(b), and 708(b). For the purposes of other provisions of the internal revenue laws, guaranteed payments are regarded as a partner's distributive share of ordinary income.* * * Similarly, a partner who receives guaranteed payments is not regarded as an employee of the partnership for the purposes of withholding of tax at source, deferred compensation plans, etc. The provisions of this paragraph may be illustrated by the following examples:

Example (1). Under the ABC partnership agreement, partner A is entitled to a fixed annual payment of $10,000 for services, without regard to the income of the partnership. His distributive share is 10 percent. After deducting the guaranteed payment, the partnership has $50,000 ordinary income. A must include $15,000

*Editorial comment: The Regulations do not reflect the effect of the Tax Reform Act of 1986 which substituted 50 percent for 80 percent. See Sec. 707(b).

as ordinary income for his taxable year within or with which the partnership taxable year ends ($10,000 guaranteed payment plus $5,000 distributive share).

Example (2). Partner C in the CD partnership is to receive 30 percent of partnership income as determined before taking into account any guaranteed payments, but not less than $10,000. The income of the partnership is $60,000, and C is entitled to $18,000 (30 percent of $60,000) as his distributive share. No part of this amount is a guaranteed payment. However, if the partnership had income of $20,000 instead of $60,000, $6,000 (30 percent of $20,000) would be partner C's distributive share, and the remaining $4,000 payable to C would be a guaranteed payment.

Example (3). Partner X in the XY partnership is to receive a payment of $10,000 for services, plus 30 percent of the taxable income or loss of the partnership. After deducting the payment of $10,000 to partner X, the XY partnership has a loss of $9,000. Of this amount, $2,700 (30 percent of the loss) is X's distributive share of partnership loss and, subject to section 704(d), is to be taken into account by him in his return. In addition, he must report as ordinary income the guaranteed payment of $10,000 made to him by the partnership.

Example (4). Assume the same facts as in example (3) of this paragraph, except that, instead of a $9,000 loss, the partnership has $30,000 in capital gains and no other items of income or deduction except the $10,000 paid X as a guaranteed payment. Since the items of partnership income or loss must be segregated under section 702(a), the partnership has a $10,000 ordinary loss and $30,000 in capital gains. X's 30 percent distributive shares of these amounts are $3,000 ordinary loss and $9,000 capital gain. In addition, X has received a $10,000 guaranteed payment which is ordinary income to him.

§ 1.707–2 Disguised payments for services. [Reserved]

§ 1.707–3 Disguised sales of property to partnership; general rules.

(a) Treatment of transfers as a sale—(1) In general. Except as otherwise provided in this section, if a transfer of property by a partner to a partnership and one or more transfers of money or other consideration by the partnership to that partner are described in paragraph (b)(1) of this section, the transfers are treated as a sale of property, in whole or in part, to the partnership.

(2) Definition and timing of sale. For purposes of §§ 1.707–3 through 1.707–5, the use of the term sale (or any variation of that word) to refer to a transfer of property by a partner to a partnership and a transfer of consideration by a partnership to a partner means a sale or exchange of that property, in whole or in part, to the partnership by the partner acting in a capacity other than as a member of the partnership, rather than a contribution and distribution to which sections 721 and 731, respectively, apply. A transfer that is treated as a sale under paragraph (a)(1) this section is treated as a sale for all purposes of the Internal Revenue Code (e.g., sections 453, 483, 1001, 1012, 1031 and 1274). The sale is considered to take place on the date that, under general principles of Federal tax law, the partnership is considered the owner of the property. If the transfer of money or other consideration from the partnership to the partner occurs after the transfer of property to the partnership; the partner and the partnership are treated as if, on the date of the sale, the partnership transferred to the partner an obligation to transfer to the partner money or other consideration.

(3) Application of disguised sale rules. If a person purports to transfer property to a partnership in a capacity as a partner, the rules of this section apply for purposes of determining whether the property was transferred in a disguised sale, even if it is determined after the application of the rules of this section that such person is not a partner. If after the application of the rules of this section to a purported transfer of property to a partnership, it is determined that no partnership exists because the property was actually sold, or it is otherwise determined that the contributed property is not owned by the partnership for tax purposes, the transferor of the property is treated as having sold the property to the person (or persons) that acquired ownership of the property for tax purposes.

(4) Deemed terminations under section 708. In applying the rules of this section, transfers resulting from a termination of a partnership under section 708 (b)(1)(B) are disregarded.

(b) Transfers treated as a sale—(1) In general. A transfer of property (excluding money or an obligation to contribute money) by a partner to a partnership and a transfer of money or other consideration (including the assumption of or the taking subject to a liability) by the partnership to the partner constitute a sale of property, in whole or in part, by the partner to the partnership only if based on all the facts and circumstances—

(i) The transfer of money or other consideration would not have been made but for the transfer of property; and

(ii) In cases in which the transfers are not made simultaneously, the subsequent transfer is not dependent on the entrepreneurial risks of partnership operations.

(2) Facts and circumstances. The determination of whether a transfer of property by a partner to the partnership and a transfer of money or other consideration by the partnership to the partner constitute a sale, in whole or in part, under paragraph (b)(1) of this section is made based on all the facts and circumstances in each case. The weight to be given each of the facts and circumstances will depend on the particular case. Generally, the facts and circumstances existing on the date of the earliest of such transfers are the ones considered in determining whether a sale exists under paragraph (b)(1) of this section. Among the facts and circumstances that may tend to prove the existence of a sale under paragraph (b)(1) of this section are the following:

(i) That the timing and amount of a subsequent transfer are determinable with reasonable certainty at the time of an earlier transfer;

(ii) That the transferor has a legally enforceable right to the subsequent transfer;

(iii) That the partner's right to receive the transfer of money or other consideration is secured in any manner, taking into account the period during which it is secured;

(iv) That any person has made or is legally obligated to make contributions to the partnership in order to permit the partnership to make the transfer of money or other consideration;

(v) That any person has loaned or has agreed to loan the partnership the money or other consideration required to enable the partnership to make the transfer, taking into account whether any such lending obligation is subject to contingencies related to the results of partnership operations;

(vi) That a partnership has incurred or is obligated to incur debt to acquire the money or other consideration necessary to permit it to make the transfer, taking into account the likelihood that the partnership will be able to incur that debt (considering such factors as whether any person has agreed to guarantee or otherwise assume personal liability for that debt);

(vii) That the partnership holds money or other liquid assets, beyond the reasonable needs of the business, that are expected to be available to make the transfer (taking into account the income that will be earned from those assets);

(viii) That partnership distributions, allocation or control of partnership operations is designed to effect an exchange of the burdens and benefits of ownership of property;

(ix) That the transfer of money or other consideration by the partnership to the partner is disproportionately large in relationship to the partner's general and continuing interest in partnership profits; and

(x) That the partner has no obligation to return or repay the money or other consideration to the partnership, or has such an obligation but it is likely to become due at such a distant point in the future that the present value of that obligation is small in relation to the amount of money or other consideration transferred by the partnership to the partner.

(c) Transfers made within two years presumed to be a sale—(1) In general. For purposes of this section, if within a two-year period a partner transfers property to a partnership and the partnership transfers money or other consideration to the partner (without regard to the order of the transfers), the transfers are presumed to be a sale of the property to the partnership unless the facts and circumstances clearly establish that the transfers do not constitute a sale.

(2) Disclosure of transfers made within two years. Disclosure to the Internal Revenue Service in accordance with § 1.707–8 is required if—

(i) A partner transfers property to a partnership and the partnership transfers money or other consideration to the partner with a two-year period (without regard to the order of the transfers);

(ii) The partner treats the transfers other than as a sale for tax purposes; and

(iii) The transfer of money or other consideration to the partner is not presumed to be a guaranteed payment for capital under § 1.707–4(a)(1)(ii), is not a reasonable preferred return within the meaning of § 1.707–4(a)(3), and is not an operating cash flow distribution within the meaning of § 1.707–4(b)(2).

(d) Transfers made more than two years apart presumed not to be a sale. For purposes of this section, if a transfer of money or other consideration to a partner by a partnership and the transfer of property to the partnership by that partner are more than two years apart, the transfers are presumed not to be a sale of the property to the partnership unless the facts and circumstances clearly establish that the transfers constitute a sale.

(e) Scope. This section and §§ 1.707–4 through 1.707–9 apply to contributions and distributions of property described in section 707(a)(2)(A) and transfers described in section 707(a)(2)(B) of the Internal Revenue Code.

(f) Examples. The following examples illustrate the application of this section.

Example 1. Treatment of simultaneous transfers as a sale. A transfers property X to partnership AB on April 9, 1992, in exchange for an interest in the partnership. At the time of the transfer, property X has a fair market value of $4,000,000 and an adjusted tax basis of $1,200,000. Immediately after the transfer, the partnership transfers $3,000,000 in cash to A. Assume that, under this section, the partnership's transfer of cash to A is treated as part of a sale of property X to the partnership. Because the amount of cash A receives on April 9, 1992, does not equal the fair market value of the property, A is considered to have sold a portion of property X with a value of $3,000,000 to the partnership in exchange for the cash. Accordingly, A must recognize $2,100,000 of gain ($3,000,000 amount realized less $900,000 adjusted tax basis ($1,200,000 multiplied by $3,000,000/$4,000,000)). Assuming A receives no other transfers that are treated as consideration for the sale of the property under this section, A is considered to have contributed to the partnership, in A's capacity as a partner, $1,000,000 of the fair market value of the property with an adjusted tax basis of $300,000.

Example 2. Treatment of transfers at different times as a sale. **(i)** The facts are the same as in Example 1, except that the $3,000,000 is transferred to A one year after A's transfer of property X to the partnership. Assume that under this section the partnership's transfer of cash to A is treated as part of a sale of property X to the partnership. Assume also that the applicable Federal short-term rate for April, 1992, is 10 percent, compounded semiannually.

(ii) Under paragraph (a)(2) of this section, A and the partnership are treated as if, on April 9, 1992, A sold a portion of property X to the partnership in exchange for an obligation to transfer $3,000,000 to A one year later. Section 1274 applies to this obligation because it does not bear interest and is payable more than six months after the date of the sale. As a result, A's amount realized from the receipt of the partnership's obligation will be the imputed principal amount of the partnership's obligation to transfer $3,000,000 to A, which equals $2,721,088 (the present value on April 9, 1992, of a $3,000,000 payment due one year later, determined using a discount rate of 10 percent, compounded semiannually). Therefore, A's amount realized from the receipt of the partnership's obligation is $2,721,088 (without regard to whether the sale is reported under the installment method). A is therefore considered to have sold only $2,721,088 of the fair market value of property X. The remainder of the $3,000,000 payment ($278,912) is characterized in accordance with the provisions of section 1272. Accordingly, A must recognize $1,904,761 of gain ($2,721,088 amount realized less $816,327 adjusted tax basis ($1,200,000 multiplied by $2,721,088/$4,000,000)) on the sale of property X to the partnership. The gain is reportable under the installment method of section 453 if the sale is otherwise eligible. Assuming A receives no other transfers that are treated as consideration for the sale of property under this section, A is considered to have contributed to the partnership, in A's capacity as a partner, $1,278,912 of the fair market value of property X with an adjusted tax basis of $383,673.

Example 3. Operation of presumption for transfers within two years. **(i)** C transfers undeveloped land to the CD partnership in exchange for an interest in the partnership. The partnership intends to construct a building on the land. At the time the land is transferred to the partnership, it is unencumbered and has an adjusted tax basis of $500,000 and a fair market value of $1,000,000. The partnership agreement provides that upon completing construction of the building the partnership will distribute $900,000 to C.

(ii) If, within two years of C's transfer of land to the partnership, a transfer is made to C pursuant to the provision requiring a distribution upon completion of the building, the transfer is presumed to be, under paragraph (c) of this section, part of a sale of the land to the partnership. C may rebut the presumption that the transfer is part of a sale if the facts and circumstances clearly establish that—

(A) The transfer to C would have been made without regard to C's transfer of land to the partnership; or

(B) The partnership's obligation or ability to make this transfer to C depends, at the time of the transfer to the partnership, on the entrepreneurial risks of partnership operations.

(iii) For example, if the partnership will be able to fund the transfer of cash to C only to the extent that permanent loan proceeds exceed the cost of constructing the building, the fact that excess permanent loan proceeds will be available only if the cost to complete the building is significantly less than the amount projected by a reasonable budget would be evidence that the transfer to C is not part of a sale. Similarly, a condition that limits the amount of the permanent loan to the cost of constructing the building (and thereby limits the partnership's ability to make a transfer to C) unless all or a substantial portion of the building is leased would be evidence that the transfer to C is not part of a sale, if a significant risk exists that the partnership may not be able to lease the building to that extent. Another factor that may prove that the transfer of cash to C is not part of a sale would be that, at the time the land is transferred to the partnership, no lender has committed to make a permanent loan to fund the transfer of cash to C.

(iv) Facts indicating that the transfer of cash to C is not part of a sale, however, may be offset by other factors. An offsetting factor to restrictions on the permanent loan proceeds may be that the permanent loan is to be a recourse loan and certain conditions to the loan are likely to be waived by the lender because of the creditworthiness of the partners or the value of the partnership's other assets. Similarly, the factor that no lender has committed to fund the transfer of cash to C may be offset by facts establishing that the partnership is obligated to attempt to obtain such a loan and that its ability to obtain such a loan is not significantly dependent on the value that will be added by successful completion of the building, or that the partnership reasonably anticipates that it will have (and will utilize) an alternative source to fund the transfer of cash to C if the permanent loan proceeds are inadequate.

Example 4. Operation of presumption for transfers within two years. E is a partner in the equal EF partnership. The partnership owns two parcels of unimproved real property (parcels 1 and 2). Parcels 1 and 2 are unencumbered. Parcel 1 has a fair market value of $500,000, and parcel 2 has a fair market value of $1,500,000. E transfers additional unencumbered, unimproved real property (parcel 3) with a fair market value of $1,000,000 to the partnership in exchange for an increased interest in partnership profits of 66⅔ percent. Immediately after this transfer, the partnership sells parcel 1 for $500,000 in a transaction not in the ordinary course of business. The partnership transfers the proceeds of the sale $333,333 to E and $166,667 to F in accordance with their respective partnership interests. The transfer of $333,333 to E is presumed to be, in accordance with paragraph (c) of this section, a sale, in part, of parcel 3 to the partnership. However, the facts of this example clearly establish that $250,000 of the transfer to E is not part of a sale of parcel 3 to the partnership because E would have been distributed $250,000 from the sale of parcel 1 whether or not E had transferred parcel 3 to the partnership. The transfer to E exceeds by $83,333 ($333,333 minus $250,000) the amount of the distribution that would have been made to E if E had not transferred parcel 3 to the partnership. Therefore, $83,333 of the transfer is presumed to be part of a sale of a portion of parcel 3 to the partnership by E.

Example 5. Operation of presumption for transfers more than two years apart. **(i)** G transfers undeveloped land to the GH partnership in exchange for an interest in the partnership. At the time the land is transferred to the partnership, it is unencumbered and has an adjusted tax basis of $500,000 and a fair market value of $1,000,000. H contributes $1,000,000 in cash in exchange for an interest in the partnership. Under the partnership agreement, the partnership is obligated to construct a building on the land. The projected construction cost is $5,000,000, which the partnership plans to fund with its $1,000,000 in cash and the proceeds of a construction loan secured by the land and improvements.

(ii) Shortly before G's transfer of the land to the partnership, the partnership secures commitments from lending institutions for construction and permanent financing. To obtain the construction loan, H guarantees completion of the building for a cost of $5,000,000. The partnership is not obligated to reimburse or indemnify H if H must make payment on the completion guarantee. The permanent loan will be funded upon completion of the building, which is expected to occur two years after G's transfer of the land. The amount of the permanent loan is to equal the lesser of $5,000,000 or 80 percent of the appraised value of the improved property at the time the permanent loan is closed. Under the partnership agreement, the partnership is obligated to apply the proceeds of the permanent loan to retire the construction loan and to hold any excess proceeds for transfer to G 25 months after G's transfer of the land to the partnership. The appraised value of the improved property at the time the permanent loan is closed is expected to exceed $5,000,000 only if the partnership is able to lease a substantial portion of the improvements by that time, and there is a significant risk that the partnership will not be able to achieve a satisfactory occupancy level. The partnership completes construction of the building for the projected cost of $5,000,000 approximately two years after G's transfer of the land. Shortly thereafter, the permanent loan is funded in the amount of $5,000,000. At the time of funding the land and building have an appraised value of $7,000,000. The partnership transfers the $1,000,000 excess permanent loan proceeds to G 25 months after G's transfer of the land to the partnership.

(iii) G's transfer of the land to the partnership and the partnership's transfer of $1,000,000 to G occurred more than two years apart. In accordance with paragraph (d) of this section, those transfers are presumed not to be a sale unless the facts and circumstances clearly establish that the transfers constitute a sale of the property, in whole or part, to the partnership. The transfer of $1,000,000 to G would not have been made but for G's transfer of the land to the partnership. In addition, at the time G transferred the land to the partnership, G had a legally enforceable right to receive a transfer from the partnership at a specified time an amount that equals the excess of the permanent loan proceeds over $4,000,000. In this case, however, there was a significant risk that the appraised value of the property would be insufficient to support a permanent loan in excess of $4,000,000 because of the risk that the partnership would not be able to achieve a sufficient occupancy level. Therefore, the facts of this example indicate that at the time G transferred the land to the partnership the subsequent transfer of $1,000,000 to G depended on the entrepreneurial risks of partnership operations. Accordingly, G's transfer of the land to the partnership is not treated as part of a sale.

Example 6. Rebuttal of presumption for transfers more than two years apart. The facts are the same as in Example 5, except that the partnership is able to secure a commitment for a permanent loan in the amount of $5,000,000 without regard to the appraised value of the improved property at the time the permanent loan is funded. Under these facts, at the time that G transferred the land to the partnership the subsequent transfer of $1,000,000 to G was not dependent on the entrepreneurial risks of partnership operations, because during the period before the permanent loan is funded, the permanent lender's obligation to make a loan in the amount necessary to fund the transfer is not subject to the contingencies related to the risks of partnership operations, and after the permanent loan is funded, the partnership holds liquid assets sufficient to make the transfer. Therefore, the facts and circumstances clearly establish that G's transfer of the land to the partnership is part of a sale.

Example 7. Operation of presumption for transfers more than two years apart. The facts are the same as in Example 6, except that H does not guarantee either that the improvements will be completed or that the cost to the partnership of completing the improvements will not exceed $5,000,000. Under these facts, if there is a significant risk that the improvements will not be completed, G's transfer of the land to the partnership will not be treated as part of a sale because the lender is required to make the permanent loan if the improvements are not completed. Similarly, the transfers will not be treated as a sale to the extent that there is a significant risk that the cost of constructing the improvements will exceed $5,000,000, because, in the absence of a guarantee of the cost of the improvements by H, the $5,000,000 proceeds of the permanent loan might not be sufficient to retire the construction loan and fund the transfer to G. In either case, the transfer of cash to G would be dependent on the entrepreneurial risks of partnership operations.

Example 8. Rebuttal of presumption for transfers more than two years apart. **(i)** On February 1, 1992, I, J, and K form partnership IJK. On formation of the partnership, I transfers an unencumbered office building with a fair market value of $50,000,000 and an adjusted tax basis of $20,000,000 to the partnership, and J and K each transfer United States government securities with a fair market value and an adjusted tax basis of $25,000,000 to the partnership. Substantially all of the rentable space in the office building is leased on a long-term basis. The partnership agreement provides that all items of income, gain, loss, and deduction from the office building are to be allocated 45 percent to J, 45 percent to K, and 10 percent to I. The partnership agreement also provides that all items of income, gain, loss, and deduction from the government securities are to be allocated 90 percent to I, 5 percent to J, and 5 percent to K. The partnership agreement requires that cash flow from the office building and government securities be allocated between partners in the same manner as the items of income, gain, loss, and deduction from those properties are allocated between them. The partnership agreement complies with the requirements of § 1.704–1 (b)(2)(ii)(b). It is not expected that the partnership will need to resort to the government securities or the cash flow therefrom to operate the office building. At the time the partnership is formed, I, J, and K contemplated that I's interest in the partnership would be liquidated sometime after January 31, 1994, in exchange for a transfer of the government securities and cash (if necessary). On March 1, 1995, the partnership transfers cash and the government securities to I in liquidation of I's interest in the partnership. The cash transferred to I represents the excess of I's share of the appreciation in the office building since the formation of the partnership over J's and K's share of the appreciation in the government securities since they are acquired by the partnership.

(ii) I's transfer of the office building to the partnership and the partnership's transfer of the government securities and cash to I occurred more than two years apart. Therefore, those transfers are presumed not to be a sale unless the facts and circumstances clearly establish that the transfers constitute a sale. Absent I's transfer of the office building to the partnership, I would not have received the government securities from the partnership. The facts (including the amount and nature of partnership assets) indicate that, at the time that I transferred the office building to the partnership, the timing of the transfer of the government securities to I was anticipated and was not dependent on the entrepreneurial risks of partnership operations. Moreover, the facts indicate that the partnership allocations were designed to effect an exchange of the burdens and benefits of ownership of the government securities in anticipation of the transfer of those securities to I and those burdens and benefits were effectively shifted to I on formation of the partnership. Accordingly, the facts and circumstances clearly establish that I sold the office building to the partnership on February 1, 1992, in exchange for the partnership's obligation to transfer the government securities to I and to make certain other cash transfers to I.

§ 1.707–4 Disguised sales of property to partnership; special rules applicable to guaranteed payments, preferred returns, operating cash flow distributions, and reimbursements of preformation expenditures.

(a) Guaranteed payments and preferred returns—(1) Guaranteed payment not treated as part of a sale—(i) In general. A guaranteed payment for capital made to a partner is not treated as part of a sale of property under § 1.707–3(a) (relating to treatment of transfers as a sale). A party's characterization of a payment as a guaranteed payment for capital will not control in determining whether a payment is, in fact, a guaranteed payment for capital. The term *guaranteed payment for capital* means any payment to a partner by a partnership that is determined without regard to partnership income and is for the use of that partner's capital. See section 707(c). For this purpose, one or more payments are not made for the use of a partner's capital if the payments are designed to liquidate all or part of the partner's interest in property contributed to the partnership rather than to provide the partner with a return on an investment in the partnership.

(ii) Reasonable guaranteed payments. Notwithstanding the presumption set forth in § 1.707–3(c) (relating to transfers made within two years of each other), for purposes of section 707(a)(2) and the regulations thereunder a transfer of money to a partner that is characterized by the parties as a guaranteed payment for capital, is determined without regard to the income of the partnership and is reasonable (within the meaning of paragraph (a)(3) of this section) is presumed to be a guaranteed payment for capital unless the facts and circumstances clearly establish that the transfer is not a guaranteed payment for capital and is part of a sale.

(iii) Unreasonable guaranteed payments. A transfer of money to a partner that is characterized by the parties as a guaranteed payment for capital but that is not reasonable (within the meaning of paragraph (a)(3) of this section) is presumed not to be a guaranteed payment for capital unless the facts and circumstances clearly establish that the transfer is a guaranteed payment for capital. A transfer that is not a guaranteed payment for capital is subject to the rules of § 1.707–3.

(2) Presumption regarding reasonable preferred returns. Notwithstanding the presumption set forth in § 1.707–3(c) (relating to transfers made within two years of each other), a transfer of money to a partner that is characterized by the parties as a preferred return and that is reasonable (within the meaning of paragraph (a)(3) of this section) is presumed not to be part of a sale of property to the partnership unless the facts and circumstances (including the likelihood and expected timing of the subsequent allocation of income or gain to support the preferred return) clearly establish that the transfer is part of a sale. The term *preferred return* means a preferential distribution of partnership cash flow to a partner with respect to capital contributed to the partnership by the partner that will be matched, to the extent available, by an allocation of income or gain.

(3) Definition of reasonable preferred returns and guaranteed payments—(i) In general. A transfer of money to a partner that is characterized as a preferred return or guaranteed payment for capital is reasonable only to the extent that the transfer is made to the partner pursuant to a written provision of a partnership agreement that provides for payment for the use of capital in a reasonable amount, and only to the extent that the payment is made for the use of capital after the date on which that provision is added to the partnership agreement.

(ii) Reasonable amount. A transfer of money that is made to a partner during any partnership taxable year and is characterized as a preferred return or guaranteed payment for capital is reasonable in amount if the sum of any preferred return and any guaranteed payment for capital that is payable for that year does not exceed the amount determined by multiplying either the partner's unreturned capital at the beginning of the year or, at the partner's option, the partner's weighted average capital balance for the year (with either amount appropriately adjusted, taking into account the relevant compounding periods, to reflect any unpaid preferred return or guaranteed payment for capital that is payable to the partner) by the safe harbor interest rate for that year. The safe harbor interest rate for a partnership's taxable year equals 150 percent of the highest applicable federal rate, at the appropriate compounding period or periods, in effect at any time from the time that the right to the preferred return or guaranteed payment for capital is first established pursuant to a binding, written agreement among the partners through the end of the taxable year. A partner's unreturned capital equals the excess of the aggregate amount of money and the fair market value of other consideration (net of liabilities) contributed by the partner to the partnership over the aggregate amount of money and the fair market value of other consideration (net of liabilities) distributed by the partnership to the partner other than transfers of money that are presumed to be guaranteed payments for capital under paragraph (a)(1)(ii) of this section, transfers of money that are reasonable preferred returns within the meaning of this paragraph (a)(3), and operating cash flow distributions within the meaning of paragraph (b)(2) of this section.

(4) Examples. The following examples illustrate the application of paragraph (a) of this section:

Example 1. Transfer presumed to be a guaranteed payment. **(i)** A transfers property with a fair market value of $100,000 to partnership AB. At the time of A's transfer, the partnership agreement is amended to provide that A is to receive a guaranteed payment for the use of A's capital of 10 percent (compounded annually) of the fair market value of the transferred property in each of the three years following the transfer. The partnership agreement provides that partnership net taxable income and loss will be allocated equally between partners A and B, and that partnership cash flow will be distributed in accordance with the allocation of partnership net taxable income and loss. The partnership would be allowed a deduction in the year paid if the transfers made to A are treated as guaranteed payments under section 707(c). Under the partnership agreement, that deduction would be allocated in the same manner as any other item of partnership deduction. The partnership agreement complies with the requirements of § 1.704–1(b)(2)(ii)(b). The partnership agreement does not provide for the payment of a preferred return and, other than the guaranteed payment to be paid to A, no transfer is expected to be made during the three year period following A's transfer that is not an operating cash flow distribution (within the meaning of paragraph (b)(2) of this section). Assume that the highest applicable federal rate in effect at the time of A's transfer is eight percent compounded annually.

(ii) The transfer of money to be made to A under the partnership agreement is characterized by the parties as a guaranteed payment for capital and is determined without regard to the income of the partnership. The transfer is also reasonable within the meaning of § 1.707–4(a)(3). The transfer, therefore, is presumed to be a guaranteed payment for capital. The presumption set forth in § 1.707–3(c) (relating to transfers made within two years of each other) thus does not apply to this transfer. The transfer will not be treated as part of a sale of property to the partnership unless the facts and circumstances clearly establish that the transfer is not a guaranteed payment for capital but is part of a sale.

(iii) The presumption that the transfer is a guaranteed payment for capital is not rebutted, because there are no facts indicating that the transfer is not a guaranteed payment for the use of capital.

Example 2. Transfers characterized as guaranteed payments treated as part of a sale. **(i)** C and D form partnership CD. C transfers property with a fair market value of $100,000 and an adjusted tax basis of $20,000 in exchange for a partnership interest. D is responsible for managing the day-to-day operations of the partnership and makes no capital contribution to the partnership upon its formation. The partnership agreement provides that C is to receive payments characterized as guaranteed payments and determined without regard to partnership income of $8,333 per year for the first four years of partnership operations for the use of C's capital. In addition, the partnership agreement provides that—

(A) Partnership net taxable income and loss will be allocated 75 percent to C and 25 percent to D; and

(B) All partnership cash flow (determined prior to consideration of the guaranteed payment) will be distributed 75 percent to C and 25 percent to D except that guaranteed payments that the partnership is obligated to make to C are payable solely out of D's share of the partnership's cash flow.

(ii) If D's share of the partnership's cash flow is not sufficient to make the guaranteed payment to C, then D is obligated to contribute any shortfall to the partnership, even in the event the partnership is liquidated. Thus, the effect of the guaranteed payment arrangement is that the guaranteed payment to C is funded entirely by D. The partnership agreement complies with the requirements of § 1.704–1(b)(2)(ii)(b). Assume that, at the time the partnership is formed, the partnership or D could borrow $25,000 pursuant to a loan requiring equal payments of principal and interest over a four-year term at the current market interest rate of approximately 12 percent (compounded annually). Assume that the highest applicable federal rate in effect at the time the partnership is formed is 10 percent compounded annually.

(iii) The transfer of money to be made to C under the partnership agreement is characterized by the parties as a guaranteed payment for capital and is determined without regard to the income of the partnership. The transfer is also reasonable within the meaning of § 1.707–4(a)(3). The transfer, therefore, is presumed to be a guaranteed payment for capital. The presumption set forth in § 1.707–3(c) (relating to transfers made within two years of each other) thus does not apply to this transfer. The transfer will not be treated as part of a sale of property to the partnership unless the facts and circumstances clearly establish that the transfer is not a guaranteed payment for capital and is part of a sale.

(iv) For the first four years of partnership operations, the total guaranteed payments made to C under the partnership agreement will equal $33,332. If the characterization of those payments as guaranteed payments for capital within the meaning of section 707 (c) were respected, C would be allocated $24,999 of the deductions that would be claimed by the partnership for those payments, thereby leaving the balance in C's capital account approximately $25,000 less than it would have been if the guaranteed payments had not been made. The guaranteed payments thus have the effect of offsetting approximately $25,000 of the credit made to C's capital account for the property transferred to the partnership by C. C's resulting capital account is approximately equivalent to the capital account C would have had if C had only contributed 75 percent of the property to the partnership. Furthermore, the effect of D's funding the guaranteed payment to C (either through reduced distributions of cash flow to D or additional contributions) is that D's capital account is approximately equivalent to the capital account D would have had if D had contributed 25 percent of the property (or contributed cash so that the partnership could purchase the 25 percent). Moreover, a $25,000 loan requiring equal payments of principal and interest over a four-year term at the current market interest rate of 12 percent (compounded annually), would have resulted in annual payments of principal and interest of $8,230.86. Consequently, the guaranteed payments effectively place the partners in the same economic position that they would have been in had D purchased a one-quarter interest in the property from C financed at the current market rate of interest, and then C and D each contributed their share of the property to the partnership. In view of the burden the guaranteed payments place on D's right to transfers of partnership cash flow and D's legal obligation to make contributions to the partnership to the extent necessary to fund the guaranteed payments, D has effectively purchased through the partnership a one-quarter interest in the property from C.

(v) Under these facts, the presumption that the transfers to C are guaranteed payments for capital is rebutted, because the facts and circumstances clearly establish that the transfers are part of a sale and not guaranteed payments for capital. Under § 1.707–3(a), C and the partnership are treated as if C sold a one-quarter interest in the property to the partnership in exchange for a promissory note evidencing the partnership's obligation to make the guaranteed payments.

(b) Presumption regarding operating cash flow distributions—(1) In general. Notwithstanding the presumption set forth in § 1.707–3(c) (relating to transfers made within two years of each other), an operating cash flow distribution is presumed not to be part of a sale of property to the partnership unless the facts and circumstances clearly establish that the transfer is part of a sale.

(2) Operating cash flow distributions—(i) In general. One or more transfers of money by the partnership to a partner during a taxable year of the partnership are operating cash flow distributions for purposes of paragraph (b)(1) of this section to the extent that those transfers are not presumed to be guaranteed payments for capital under paragraph (a)(1)(ii) of this section, are not reasonable preferred returns within the meaning of paragraph (a)(3) of this section, are not characterized by the parties as distributions to the partner acting in a capacity other than as a partner, and to the extent they do not exceed the product of the net cash flow of the partnership from operations for the year multiplied by the lesser of the partner's percentage interest in overall partnership profits for that year or the partner's percentage interest in overall partnership profits for the life of the partnership. For purposes of the preceding sentence, the net cash flow of the partnership from operations for a taxable year is an amount equal to the taxable income or loss of the partnership arising in the ordinary course of the partnership's business and investment activities, increased by tax exempt interest, depreciation, amortization, cost recovery allowances and other noncash charges deducted in determining such taxable income and decreased by—

(A) Principal payments made on any partnership indebtedness;

(B) Property replacement or contingency reserves actually established by the partnership;

(C) Capital expenditures when made other than from reserves or from borrowings the proceeds of which are not included in operating cash flow; and

(D) Any other cash expenditures (including preferred returns) not deducted in determining such taxable income or loss.

(ii) Operating cash flow safe harbor. For any taxable year, in determining a partner's operating cash flow distributions for the year, the partner may use the partner's smallest percentage interest under the terms of the partnership agreement in any material item of partnership income or gain that may be realized by the partnership in the three-year period beginning with such taxable year. This provision is merely intended to provide taxpayers with a safe harbor and is not intended to preclude a taxpayer from using a different percentage under the rules of paragraph (b)(2)(i) of this section.

(iii) Tiered partnerships. In the case of tiered partnerships, the upper-tier partnership must take into account its share of the net cash flow from operations of the lower-tier partnership applying principles similar to those described in paragraph (b)(2)(i) of this section, so that the amount of the upper-tier partnership's operating cash flow distributions is neither overstated nor understated.

(c) Accumulation of guaranteed payments, preferred returns, and operating cash flow distributions. Guaranteed payments for capital, preferred returns, and operating cash flow distributions presumed not to be part of a sale under the rules of paragraphs (a) and (b) of this section do not lose the benefit of the presumption by reason of being retained for distribution in a later year.

(d) Exception for reimbursements of preformation expenditures. A transfer of money or other consideration by the partnership to a partner is not treated as part of a sale of property by the partner to the partnership under § 1.707–3(a) (relating to treatment of transfers as a sale) to the extent that the transfer to the partner by the partnership is made to reimburse the partner for, and does not exceed the amount of, capital expenditures that—

(1) Are incurred during the two-year period preceding the transfer by the partner to the partnership; and

(2) Are incurred by the partner with respect to—

(i) Partnership organization and syndication costs described in section 709; or

(ii) Property contributed to the partnership by the partner, but only to the extent the reimbursed capital expenditures do not exceed 20 percent of the fair market value of such property at the time of the contribution. However, the 20 percent of fair market value limitation of this paragraph (d)(2)(ii) does not apply if the fair market value of the contributed property does not exceed 120 percent of the partner's adjusted basis in the contributed property at the time of contribution.

(e) Other exceptions. The Commissioner may provide by guidance published in the Internal Revenue Bulletin that other payments or transfers to a partner are not treated as part of a sale for purposes of section 707(a)(2) and the regulations thereunder.

§ 1.707–5 Disguised sales of property to partnership; special rules relating to liabilities.

(a) Liability assumed or taken subject to by partnership—(1) In general. For purposes of this section and §§ 1.707–3 and 1.707–4, if a partnership assumes or takes property subject to a qualified liability (as defined in paragraph (a)(6) of this section) of a partner, the partnership is treated as transferring consideration to the partner only to the extent provided in paragraph (a)(5) of this section. By contrast, if the partnership assumes or takes property subject to a liability of the partner other than a qualified liability, the partnership is treated as transferring consideration to the partner to the extent that the amount of the liability exceeds the partner's share of that liability immediately after the partnership assumes or takes subject to the liability as provided in paragraphs (a)(2), (3) and (4) of this section.

(2) Partner's share of liability. A partner's share of any liability of the partnership is determined under the following rules:

(i) Recourse liability. A partner's share of a recourse liability of the partnership equals the partner's share of the liability under the rules of section 752 and the regulations thereunder. A partnership liability is a recourse liability to the extent that the obligation is a recourse liability under § 1.752–1(a)(1) or would be treated as a recourse liability under that section if it were treated as a partnership liability for purposes of that section.

(ii) Nonrecourse liability. A partner's share of a nonrecourse liability of the partnership is determined by applying the same percentage used to determine the partner's share of the excess nonrecourse liability under § 1.752–3(a)(3). A partnership liability is a nonrecourse liability of the partnership to the extent that the obligation is a nonrecourse liability under § 1.752–1(a)(2) or would be a nonrecourse liability of the partnership under § 1.752–1(a)(2) if it were treated as a partnership liability for purposes of that section.

(3) Reduction of partner's share of liability. For purposes of this section, a partner's share of a liability, immediately after a partnership assumes or takes subject to the liability, is determined by taking into account a subsequent reduction in the partner's share if—

(i) At the time that the partnership assumes or takes subject to a liability, it is anticipated that the transferring partner's share of the liability will be subsequently reduced; and

(ii) The reduction of the partner's share of the liability is part of a plan that has as one of its principal purposes minimizing the extent to which the assumption of or taking subject to the liability is treated as part of a sale under § 1.707–3.

(4) Special rule applicable to transfers of encumbered property to a partnership by more than one partner pursuant to a plan. For purposes of paragraph (a)(1) of this section, if the partnership assumes or takes property or properties subject to the liabilities of more than one partner pursuant to a plan, a partner's share of the liabilities assumed or taken subject to by the partnership pursuant to that plan immediately after the transfers equals the sum of that partner's shares of the liabilities (other than that partner's qualified liabilities, as defined in paragraph (a)(6) of this section) assumed or taken subject to by the partnership pursuant to the plan. This paragraph (a)(4) does not apply to any liability assumed or taken subject to by the partnership with a principal purpose of reducing the extent to which any other liability assumed or taken subject to by the partnership is treated as a transfer of consideration under paragraph (a)(1) of this section.

(5) Special rule applicable to qualified liabilities. **(i)** If a transfer of property by a partner to a partnership is not otherwise treated as part of a sale, the partnership's assumption of or taking subject to a qualified liability in connection with a transfer of property is not treated as part of a sale. If a transfer of property by a partner to the partnership is treated as part of a sale without regard to the partnership's assumption of or taking subject to a qualified liability (as defined in paragraph (a)(6) of this section) in connection with the transfer of property, the partnership's assumption of or taking subject to that liability is treated as a transfer of consideration made pursuant to a sale of such property to the partnership only to the extent of the lesser of—

(A) The amount of consideration that the partnership would be treated as transferring to the partner under paragraph (a)(1) of this section if the liability were not a qualified liability; or

(B) The amount obtained by multiplying the amount of the qualified liability by the partner's net equity percentage with respect to that property.

(ii) A partner's net equity percentage with respect to an item of property equals the percentage determined by dividing—

(A) The aggregate transfers of money or other consideration to the partner by the partnership (other than any transfer described in this paragraph (a)(5)) that are treated as proceeds realized from the sale of the transferred property; by

(B) The excess of the fair market value of the property at the time it is transferred to the partnership over any qualified liability encumbering the property or, in the case of any qualified liability described in paragraph (a)(6)(i)(C) or (D) of this section, that is properly allocable to the property.

(6) Qualified liability of a partner defined. A liability assumed or taken subject to by a partnership in connection with a transfer of property to the partnership by a partner is qualified liability of the partner only to the extent—

(i) The liability is—

(A) A liability that was incurred by the partner more than two years prior to the earlier of the date the partner agrees in writing to transfer the property or the date the partner transfers the property to the partnership and that has encumbered the transferred property throughout that two-year period;

(B) A liability that was not incurred in anticipation of the transfer of the property to a partnership, but that was incurred by the partner within the two-year period prior to the earlier of the date the partner agrees in writing to transfer the property or the date the partner transfers the property to the partnership and that has encumbered the transferred property since it was incurred (see paragraph (a)(7) of this section for further rules regarding a liability incurred within two years of a property transfer or of a written agreement to transfer);

(C) A liability that is allocable under the rules of § 1.163–8T to capital expenditures with respect to the property; or

(D) A liability that was incurred in the ordinary course of the trade or business in which property transferred to the partnership was used or held but only if all the assets related to that trade or business are transferred other than assets that are not material to a continuation of the trade or business; and

(ii) If the liability is a recourse liability, the amount of the liability does not exceed the fair market value of the transferred property (less the amount of any other liabilities that are senior in priority and that either encumber such property or are liabilities described in paragraph (a)(6)(i)(C) or (D) of this section) at the time of the transfer.

(7) Liability incurred within two years of transfer presumed to be in anticipation of the transfer—(i) In general. For purposes of this section, if within a two-year period a partner incurs a liability (other than a liability described in paragraph (a)(6)(i)(C) or (D) of this section) and transfers property to a partnership or agrees in writing to transfer the property, and in connection with the transfer the partnership assumes or takes the property subject to the liability, the liability is presumed to be incurred in anticipation of the transfer unless the facts and circumstances clearly establish that the liability was not incurred in anticipation of the transfer.

(ii) Disclosure of transfers of property subject to liabilities incurred within two years of the transfer. If a partner treats a liability assumed or taken subject to by a partnership as a qualified liability under paragraph (a)(6)(i)(B) of this section, such treatment is to be disclosed to the Internal Revenue Service in accordance with § 1.707–8.

(b) Treatment of debt-financed transfers of consideration by partnerships—(1) In general. For purposes of § 1.707–3, if a partner transfers property to a partnership, and the partnership incurs a liability and all or a portion of the proceeds of that liability are allocable under § 1.163–8T to a transfer of money or other consideration to the partner made within 90 days of incurring the liability, the transfer of money or other consideration to the partner is taken into account only to the extent that the amount of money or the fair market value of the other consideration transferred exceeds that partner's allocable share of the partnership liability.

(2) Partner's allocable share of liability—(i) In general. A partner's allocable share of a partnership liability for purposes of paragraph (b)(1) of this section equals the amount obtained by multiplying the partner's share of the liability as described in paragraph (a)(2) of this section by the fraction determined by dividing—

(A) The portion of the liability that is allocable under § 1.163–8T to the money or other property transferred to the partner; by

(B) The total amount of the liability.

(ii) Debt-financed transfers made pursuant to a plan.—(A) In general. Except as provided in paragraph (b)(2)(iii) of this section, if a partnership transfers to more than one partner pursuant to a plan all or a portion of the proceeds of one or more partnership liabilities, paragraph (b)(1) of this section is applied by treating all of the liabilities incurred pursuant to the plan as one liability, and each partner's allocable share of those liabilities equals the amount obtained by multiplying the sum of the partner's shares of each of the respective liabilities (as defined in paragraph (a)(2) of this section) by the fraction obtained by dividing—

(1) The portion of those liabilities that is allocable under § 1.163–8T to the money or other consideration transferred to the partners pursuant to the plan; by

(2) The total amount of those liabilities.

(B) Special rule. Paragraph (b)(2)(ii)(A) of this section does not apply to any transfer of money or other property to a partner that is made with a principal purpose of reducing the extent to which any transfer is taken into account under paragraph (b)(1) of this section.

(iii) Reduction of partner's share of liability. For purposes of paragraph (b)(2) of this section, a partner's share of a liability, immediately after the partnership assumes or takes subject to the liability, is determined by taking into account a subsequent reduction in the partner's share if—

(A) It is anticipated that the partner's share of the liability that is allocable to a transfer of money or other consideration to the partner will be reduced subsequent to the transfer; and

(B) The reduction of the partner's share of the liability is part of a plan that has as one of its principal purposes minimizing the extent to which the partnership's distribution of the proceeds of the borrowing is treated as part of a sale.

(c) Refinancings. To the extent that the proceeds of a partner or partnership liability (the refinancing debt) are allocable under the rules of § 1.163–8T to payments discharging all or part of any other liability of that partner or of the partnership, as the case may be, the refinancing debt is treated as the other liability for purposes of applying the rules of this section.

(d) Share of liability where assumption accompanied by transfer of money. For purposes of §§ 1.707–3 through 1.707–5, if pursuant to a plan a partner pays or contributes money to the partnership and the partnership assumes or takes subject to one or more liabilities (other than qualified liabilities) of the partner, the amount of those liabilities that the partnership is treated as assuming or taking subject to is reduced (but not below zero) by the money transferred.

(e) Tiered partnerships and other related persons. If a lower-tier partnership succeeds to a liability of an upper-tier partnership, the liability in the lower-tier partnership retains the characterization as qualified or nonqualified that it had under these rules in the upper-tier partnership. A similar rule applies to other related party transactions involving liabilities to the extent provided by guidance published in the Internal Revenue Bulletin.

(f) Examples. The following examples illustrate the application of this section.

Example 1. Partnership's assumption of nonrecourse liability encumbering transferred property. **(i)** A and B form partnership AB, which will engage in renting office space. A transfers $500,000 in cash to the partnership, and B transfers an office building to the partnership. At the time it is transferred to the partnership, the office building has a fair market value of $1,000,000, an adjusted basis of $400,000, and is encumbered by a $500,000 liability, which B incurred 12 months earlier to finance the acquisition of other property. No facts rebut the presumption that the liability was incurred in anticipation of the transfer of the property to the partnership. Assume that this liability is a nonrecourse liability of the partnership within the meaning of section 752 and the regulations thereunder. The partnership agreement provides that partnership items will be allocated equally between A and B, including excess nonrecourse deductions under § 1.752–3(a)(3). The partnership agreement complies with the requirements of § 1.704–1(b)(2)(ii)(b).

(ii) The nonrecourse liability secured by the office building is not a qualified liability within the meaning of paragraph (a)(6) of this section. B would be allocated 50 percent of the excess nonrecourse liability under the partnership agreement. Accordingly, immediately after the partnership's assumption of that liability, B's share of the liability equals $250,000, which is equal to B's 50 percent share of the excess nonrecourse liability of the partnership as determined in accordance with B's share of partnership profits under § 1.752–3(a)(3).

(iii) The partnership's taking subject to the liability encumbering the office building is treated as a transfer of $250,000 of consideration to B (the amount by which the liability ($500,000) exceeds B's share of that liability immediately after taking subject to $250,000). B is treated as having sold $250,000 of the fair market value of the office building to the partnership in exchange for the partnership's taking subject to a $250,000 liability. This results in a gain of $150,000 ($250,000 minus ($250,000/ $ 1,000,000 multiplied by $400,000)).

Example 2. Partnership's assumption of recourse liability encumbering transferred property. **(i)** C transfers property Y to a partnership. At the time of its transfer to the partnership, property Y has a fair market value of $10,000,000 and is subject to an $8,000,000 liability that C incurred, immediately before transferring property Y to the partnership, in order to finance other expenditures. Upon the transfer of property Y to the partnership, the partnership assumed the liability encumbering that property. The partnership assumed this liability solely to acquire property Y. Under section 752 and the regulations thereunder, immediately after the partnership's assumption of the liability encumbering property Y, the liability is a recourse liability of the partnership and C's share of that liability is $7,000,000.

(ii) Under the facts of this example, the liability encumbering property Y is not a qualified liability.

Accordingly, the partnership's assumption of the liability results in a transfer of consideration to C in connection with C's transfer of property Y to the partnership in the amount of $1,000,000 (the excess of the liability assumed by the partnership ($8,000,000) over C's share of the liability immediately after the assumption ($7,000,000)). See paragraphs (a)(1) and (2) of this section.

Example 3. Subsequent reduction of transferring partner's share of liability. **(i)** The facts are the same as in Example 2. In addition, property Y is a fully leased office building, the rental income from property Y is sufficient to meet debt service, and the remaining term of the liability is ten years. It is anticipated that, three years after the partnership's assumption of the liability, C's share of the liability under section 752 will be reduced to zero because of a shift in the allocation of partnership losses pursuant to the terms of the partnership agreement. Under the partnership agreement, this shift in the allocation of partnership losses is dependent solely on the passage of time.

(ii) Under paragraph (a)(3) of this section, if the reduction in C's share of the liability was anticipated at the time of C's transfer, and the reduction was part of a plan that has as one of its principal purposes minimizing the extent of sale treatment under § 1.707–3 (i.e., a principal purpose of allocating a large percentage of losses to C in the first three years when losses were not likely to be realized was to minimize the extent to which C's transfer would be treated as part of a sale), C's share of the liability immediately after the assumption is treated as equal to C's reduced share.

Example 4. Trade payables as qualified liabilities. **(i)** D and E form partnership DE which will engage in a consulting business that requires no overhead and minimal cash on hand for daily operating expenses. Previously, D and E, as individual sole proprietors, operated separate consulting businesses. D and E each transfer to the partnership sufficient cash to cover daily operating expenses together with the goodwill and trade payables related to each sole proprietorship. Due to uncertainty over the collection rate on the trade receivables related to their sole proprietorships, D and E agree that none of the trade receivables will be transferred to the partnership.

(ii) Under the facts of this example, all the assets related to the consulting business (other than the trade receivables) together with the trade payables were transferred to partnership DE. The trade receivables retained by D and E are not material to a continuation of the trade or business by the partnership because D and E contributed sufficient cash to cover daily operating expenses. Accordingly, the trade payables transferred to the partnership constitute qualified liability under paragraph (a)(6) of this section.

Example 5. Partnership's assumption of a qualified liability as sole consideration. **(i)** F transfers property Z to a partnership. At the time of its transfer to the partnership, property Z has a fair market value of $165,000 and an adjusted tax basis of $75,000. Also, at the time of the transfer, property Z is subject to a $75,000 liability that F incurred more than two years before transferring property Z to the partnership. The liability has been secured by property Z since it was incurred by F. Upon the transfer of property Z to the partnership, the partnership assumed the liability encumbering that property. The partnership made no other transfers to F in consideration for the transfer of property Z to the partnership. Assume that, under section 752 and the regulations thereunder, immediately after the partnership's assumption of the liability encumbering property Z, the liability is a recourse liability of the partnership and F's share of that liability is $25,000.

(ii) The $75,000 liability secured by property Z is a qualified liability of F because F incurred the liability more than two years prior to the assumption of the liability by the partnership and the liability has encumbered property Z for more than two years prior to that assumption. See paragraph (a)(6) of this section. Therefore, since no other transfer to F was made as consideration for the transfer of property Z, under paragraph (a)(5) of this section, the partnership's assumption of the qualified liability of F encumbering property Z is not treated as part of a sale.

Example 6. Partnership's assumption of a qualified liability in addition to other consideration. **(i)** The facts are the same as in Example 5, except that the partnership makes a transfer to D of $30,000 in money that is consideration for F's transfer of property Z to the partnership under § 1.707–3.

(ii) As in Example 5, the $75,000 liability secured by property Z is a qualified liability of F. Since the partnership transferred $30,000 to F in addition to assuming the qualified liability under paragraph (a)(5) of this section, the partnership's assumption of this qualified liability is treated as a transfer of additional consideration to F to the extent of the lesser of—

(A) The amount that the partnership would be treated as transferring to F if the liability were not a qualified liability ($50,000 (i.e., the excess of the $75,000 qualified liability over F's $25,000 share of that liability)); or

(B) The amount obtained by multiplying the qualified liability ($75,000) by F's net equity percentage with respect to property Z (one-third).

(iii) F's net equity percentage with respect to property Z equals the fraction determined by dividing—

(A) The aggregate amount of money or other consideration (other than the qualified liability) transferred to F and treated as part of a sale of property Z under § 1.707–3(a) ($30,000 transfer of money); by

(B) F's net equity in property Z ($90,000 (i.e., the excess of the $165,000 fair market value over the $75,000 qualified liability)).

(iv) Accordingly, the partnership's assumption of the qualified liability of F encumbering property Z is treated as a transfer of $25,000 (one-third of $75,000) of consideration to F pursuant to a sale. Therefore, F is treated as having sold $55,000 of the fair market value of property Z to the partnership in exchange for $30,000 in money and the partnership's assumption of $25,000 of the qualified liability. Accordingly, F must recognize $30,000 of gain on the sale (the excess of the $55,000 amount realized over $25,000 of F's adjusted basis for property Z (i.e., one-third of F's adjusted basis for the property, because F is treated as having sold one-third of the property to the partnership)).

Example 7. Partnership's assumptions of liabilities encumbering properties transferred pursuant to a plan. **(i)** Pursuant to a plan, G and H transfer property 1 and property 2, respectively, to an existing partnership in exchange for interests in the partnership. At the time the properties are transferred to the partnership, property 1 has a fair market value of $10,000 and an adjusted tax basis of $6,000, and property 2 has a fair market value of $10,000 and an adjusted tax basis of $4,000. At the time properties 1 and 2 are transferred to the partnership, a $6,000 nonrecourse liability (liability 1) is secured by property 1 and a $7,000 recourse liability of F (liability 2) is secured by property 2. Properties 1 and 2 are transferred to the partnership, and the partnership takes subject to liability 1 and assumes liability 2. G and H incurred liabilities 1 and 2 immediately prior to transferring properties 1 and 2 to the partnership and used the proceeds for personal expenditures. The liabilities are not qualified liabilities. Assume that G and H are each allocated $2,000 of liability 1 in accordance with § 1.707–5(a)(2)(ii) (which determines a partner's share of a nonrecourse liability). Assume further that G's share of liability 2 is $3,500 and H's share is $0 in accordance with § 1.707–5(a)(2)(i) (which determines a partner's share of a recourse liability).

(ii) G and H transferred properties 1 and 2 to the partnership pursuant to a plan. Accordingly, the partnership's taking subject to liability 1 is treated as a transfer of only $500 of consideration to G, (the amount by which liability 1 ($6,000) exceeds G's share of liabilities 1 and 2 ($5,500)), and the partnership's assumption of liability 2 is treated as a transfer of only $5,000 of consideration to H (the amount by which liability 2 ($7,000) exceeds H's share of liabilities 1 and 2 ($2,000)). G is treated under the rule in § 1.707–3 as having sold $500 of the fair market value of property 1 in exchange for the partnership's taking subject to liability 1 and H is treated as having sold $5,000 of the fair market value of property 2 in exchange for the assumption of liability 2.

Example 8. Partnership's assumption of liability pursuant to a plan to avoid sale treatment of partnership assumption of another liability. **(i)** The facts are the same as in Example 7, except that—

(A) H transferred the proceeds of liability 2 to the partnership; and

(B) H incurred liability 2 in an attempt to reduce the extent to which the partnership's taking subject to liability 1 would be treated as a transfer of consideration to G (and thereby reduce the portion of G's transfer of property 1 to the partnership that would be treated as part of a sale).

(ii) Because the partnership assumed liability 2 with a principal purpose of reducing the extent to which the partnership's taking subject to liability 1 would be treated as a transfer of consideration to G, liability 2 is ignored in applying paragraph (a)(3) of this section. Accordingly, the partnership's taking subject to liability 1 is treated as a transfer of $4,000 of consideration to G (the amount by which liability 1 ($6,000) exceeds G's share of liability 1 ($2,000)). On the other hand, the partnership's assumption of liability 2 is not treated as a transfer of any consideration to H because H's share of that liability equals $7,000 as a result of H's transfer of $7,000 in money to the partnership.

Example 9. Partnership's assumptions of qualified liabilities encumbering properties transferred pursuant to a plan in addition to other consideration. **(i)** Pursuant to a plan, I transfers property 1 and J transfers property 2 plus $10,000 in cash to partnership IJ in exchange for equal interests in the partnership. At the time the properties are transferred to the partnership, property 1 has a fair market value of $100,000, an adjusted tax basis of $5,000, and is encumbered by a qualified liability of $50,000 (liability 1). Property 2 has a fair market value of $100,000, an adjusted tax basis of $5,000, and is encumbered by a qualified liability of $70,000 (liability 2). Pursuant to the plan, the partnership transferred to I $10,000 in cash. That amount is consideration for I's transfer of property 1 to the partnership under § 1.707–3. In accordance with § 1.707–5(a)(2), I and J are each allocated $25,000 of liability 1 and $35,000 of liability 2.

(ii) Because the partnership transferred $10,000 to I as consideration for the transfer of property, under § 1.707–5(a)(5), the partnership's assumption of liability 1 is treated as a transfer of additional consideration to I, even though liability 1 is a qualified liability, to the extent of the lesser of—

(A) The amount that the partnership would be treated as transferring to I if the liability were not a qualified liability; or

(B) The amount obtained by multiplying the qualified liability by I's net equity percentage with respect to property 1.

(iii) Because I and J transferred properties 1 and 2 to the partnership pursuant to a plan, treating I's qualified liability as a nonqualified liability under § 1.707–5(a)(5)(i)(A) enables I to apply the special rule applicable to transfers of encumbered property to a partnership by more than one partner pursuant to a plan under § 1.707–5(a)(4). Under this alternative test, the partnership's assumption of liability 1 encumbering property 1 is treated as a transfer of zero ($0) additional consideration to I pursuant to a sale. This is because the amount of liability 1 ($50,000) does not exceed the sum of I's share of liability 1 treated as a nonqualified liability ($25,000) and I's share of liability 2 ($35,000).

(iv) The alternative under § 1.707–5(a)(5)(i)(B) is the amount obtained by multiplying the qualified liability ($50,000) by I's net equity percentage with respect to property 1. I's net equity percentage with respect to property 1 equals one-fifth, the fraction determined by dividing—

(A) The aggregate amount of money or other consideration (other than the qualified liability) transferred to I and treated as part of a sale of property 1 under § 1.707–3(a) (the $10,000 transfer of money); by

(B) I's net equity in property 1 ($50,000 i.e., the excess of the $100,000 fair market value over the $50,000 qualified liability).

(v) Under this alternative test, the partnership's assumption of the qualified liability encumbering property 1 is treated as a transfer of $10,000 (one-fifth of the $50,000 qualified liability) of additional consideration to I pursuant to a sale.

(vi) Applying § 1.707–5(a)(5) to these facts, the partnership's assumption of liability 1 is treated as a transfer of additional consideration to I to the extent of the lesser of—

(A) zero; or

(B) $10,000.

(vii) Therefore, the partnership's assumption of I's qualified liability encumbering property 1 is not treated as a transfer of any additional consideration to I pursuant to a sale, and I is treated as having only received $10,000 of the fair market value of property 1 to the partnership in exchange for $10,000 in cash. Accordingly, I must recognize $9,500 of gain on the sale, that is, the excess of the $10,000 amount realized over $500 of I's adjusted tax basis for property 1 (one-tenth of I's adjusted tax basis for the property, because I is treated as having sold one-tenth of the property to the partnership). Since no other transfer to J was made as consideration for the transfer of property 2, the partnership's assumption of the qualified liability of J encumbering property 2 is not treated as part of a sale.

Example 10. Treatment of debt-financed transfers of consideration by partnership. **(i)** K transfers property Z to partnership KL in exchange for an interest therein on April 9, 1992. On September 13, 1992, the partnership incurs a liability of $20,000. On November 17, 1992, the partnership transfers $20,000 to K, and $10,000 of this transfer is allocable under the rules of § 1.163–8T to proceeds of the partnership liability incurred on September 13, 1992. The remaining $10,000 is paid from other partnership funds. Assume that, under section 752 and the corresponding regulations, the $20,000 liability incurred on September 13, 1992, is a recourse liability of the partnership and K's share of that liability is $10,000 on November 17, 1992.

(ii) Because a portion of the transfer made to K on November 17, 1992, is allocable under § 1.163–8T to proceeds of a partnership liability that was incurred by the partnership within 90 days of that transfer, K is required to take the transfer into account in applying the rules of this section and § 1.707–3 only to the extent that the amount of the transfer exceeds K's allocable share of the liability used to fund the transfer. K's allocable share of the $20,000 liability used to fund $10,000 of the transfer to K is $5,000 (K's share of the liability ($10,000) multiplied by the fraction obtained by dividing—

(A) The amount of the liability that is allocable to the distribution to K ($10,000); by

(B) The total amount of such liability ($20,000).

(iii) Therefore, K is required to take into account only $15,000 of the $20,000 partnership transfer to K for purposes of this section and § 1.707–3. Under these facts, assuming the within-two-year presumption is not rebutted, this $15,000 transfer will be treated under the rule in § 1.707–3 as part of a sale by K of property Z to the partnership.

Example 11. Borrowing against pool of receivables. **(i)** M generates receivables which have an adjusted basis of zero in the ordinary course of its business. For M to use receivables as security for a loan, a commercial lender requires M to transfer the receivables to a partnership in which M has a 90 percent interest. In January, 1992, M transfers to the partnership receivables with a face value of $100,000. N (who is not related to M) transfers $10,000 cash to the partnership in exchange for a 10 percent interest. The partnership borrows $80,000, secured by the receivables, and makes a distribution of $72,000 of the proceeds to M and $8,000 of the proceeds to N within 90 days of incurring the liability. M's share of the liability under § 1.707–5(a)(2) is $72,000 (90 percent × $80,000).

(ii) Because the transfer of the loan proceeds to M is allocable under § 1.163–8T to proceeds of a partnership loan that was incurred by the partnership within 90 days of that transfer, M is required to take the transfer into account in applying the rules of this section and § 1.707–3 only to the extent that the amount of the transfer ($72,000) exceeds M's allocable share of the liability used to fund the transfer. Because the distribution was a debt-financed transfer pursuant to a plan, M's allocable share of the liability is $72,000 ($72,000 × $80,000/80,000) under § 1.707–5(b)(2)(ii). Therefore, M is not required to take into account any of the loan proceeds for purposes of this section and § 1.707–3.

(iii) When the receivables are collected, M must be allocated the gain on the contributed receivables under section 704(c). However, the lender permits the partnership to distribute cash to the partners only to the extent of the value of new receivables contributed to the partnership. In 1993, M contributes additional receivables and receives a distribution of cash. The taxable income recognized by the partnership on the receivables is taxable income of the partnership arising in the ordinary course of the partnership's activities. To the extent the distribution does not exceed 90 percent

(M's percentage interest in overall partnership profits) of the partnership's operating cash flow under § 1.707–4(b), the distribution to M is presumed not to be a part of a sale of receivables by M to the partnership, and the presumption is not rebutted under these facts.

§ 1.707–6 Disguised sales of property by partnership to partner; general rules.

(a) In general. Rules similar to those provided in § 1.707–3 apply in determining whether a transfer of property by a partnership to a partner and one or more transfers of money or other consideration by that partner to the partnership are treated as a sale of property, in whole or in part, to the partner.

(b) Special rules relating to liabilities—(1) In general. Rules similar to those provided in § 1.707–5 apply to determine the extent to which an assumption of or taking subject to a liability by a partner, in connection with a transfer of property by a partnership, is considered part of a sale. Accordingly, if a partner assumes or takes property subject to a qualified liability (as defined in paragraph (b)(2) of this section) of a partnership, the partner is treated as transferring consideration to the partnership only to the extent provided in paragraph (b). If the partner assumes or takes subject to a liability that is not a qualified liability, the amount treated as consideration transferred to the partnership is the amount that the liability assumed or taken subject to by the partner exceeds the partner's share of that liability (determined under the rules of § 1.707–5(a)(2)) immediately before the transfer. Similar to the rules provided in § 1.707–5(a)(4), if more than one partner assumes or takes subject to a liability pursuant to a plan, the amount that is treated as a transfer of consideration by each partner is the amount by which all of the liabilities (other than qualified liabilities) assumed or taken subject to by the partner pursuant to the plan exceed the partner's share of all of those liabilities immediately before the assumption or taking subject to. This paragraph (b)(1) does not apply to any liability assumed or taken subject to by a partner with a principal purpose of reducing the extent to which any other liability assumed or taken subject to by a partner is treated as a transfer of consideration under this paragraph (b).

(2) Qualified liabilities. (i) If a transfer of property by a partnership to a partner is not otherwise treated as part of a sale, the partner's assumption of or taking subject to a qualified liability is not treated as part of a sale. If a transfer of property by a partnership to the partner is treated as part of a sale without regard to the partner's assumption of or taking subject to a qualified liability, the partner's assumption of or taking subject to that liability is treated as a transfer of consideration made pursuant to a sale of such property to the partner only to the extent of the lesser of—

(A) The amount of consideration that the partner would be treated as transferring to the partnership under paragraph (b) of this section if the liability were not a qualified liability; or

(B) The amount obtained by multiplying the amount of the liability at the time of its assumption or taking subject to by the partnership's net equity percentage with respect to that property.

(ii) A partnership's net equity percentage with respect to an item of property encumbered by a qualified liability equals the percentage determined by dividing—

(A) The aggregate transfers to the partnership from the partner (other than any transfer described in this paragraph (b)(2)) that are treated as the proceeds realized from the sale of the transferred property to the partner; by

(B) The excess of the fair market value of the property at the time it is transferred to the partner over any qualified liabilities of the partnership that are assumed or taken subject to by the partner at that time.

(iii) For purposes of this section, the definition of a qualified liability is that provided in § 1.707–5(a)(6) with the following exceptions—

(A) In applying the definition, the qualified liability is one that is originally an obligation of the partnership and is assumed or taken subject to by the partner in connection with a transfer of property to the partner; and

(B) If the liability was incurred by the partnership more than two years prior to the earlier of the date the partnership agrees in writing to transfer the property or the date the partnership transfers the property to the partner, that liability is a qualified liability whether or not it has encumbered the transferred property throughout the two-year period.

(c) Disclosure rules. Similar to the rules provided in §§ 1.707–3(c)(2) and 1.707–5(a)(7)(ii), a partnership is to disclose to the Internal Revenue Service, in accordance with § 1.707–8, the facts in the following circumstances:

(1) When a partnership transfers property to a partner and the partner transfers money or other consideration to the partnership within a two-year period (without regard to the order of the transfers) and the partnership treats the transfers as other than a sale for tax purposes; and

(2) When a partner assumes or takes subject to a liability of a partnership in connection with a transfer of property by the partnership to the partner, and the partnership incurred the liability within the two-year period prior to the earlier of the date the partnership agrees in writing to the transfer of property or the date the partnership transfers the property, and the partnership treats the liability as a qualified liability under rules similar to § 1.707–5(a)(6)(i)(B).

(d) Examples. The following examples illustrate the rules of this section.

Example 1. Sale of property by partnership to partner. **(i)** A is a member of a partnership. The partnership transfers property X to A. At the time of the transfer, property X has a fair market value of $1,000,000. One year after the transfer, A transfers $1,100,000 to the partnership. Assume that under the rules of section 1274 the imputed principal amount of an obligation to transfer $1,100,000 one year after the transfer of property X is $1,000,000 on the date of the transfer.

(ii) Since the transfer of $1,100,000 to the partnership by A is made within two years of the transfer of property X to A, under rules similar to those provided in § 1.707–3(c), the transfers are presumed to be a sale unless the facts and circumstances clearly establish otherwise. If no facts exist that would rebut this presumption, on the date that the partnership transfers property X to A, the partnership is treated as having sold property X to A in exchange for A's obligation to transfer $1,100,000 to the partnership one year later.

Example 2. Assumption of liability by partner **(i)** B is a member of an existing partnership. The partnership transfers property Y to B. On the date of the transfer, property Y has a fair market value of $1,000,000 and is encumbered by a nonrecourse liability of $600,000. B takes the property subject to the liability. The partnership incurred the nonrecourse liability six months prior to the transfer of property Y to B and used the proceeds to purchase an unrelated asset. Assume that, under rule of § 1.707–5(a)(2)(ii) (which determines a partner's share of a nonrecourse liability), B's share of the nonrecourse liability immediately before the transfer of property Y was $100,000.

(ii) The liability is not allocable under the rules of § 1.163–8T to capital expenditures with respect to the property transferred to B and was not incurred in the ordinary course of the trade or business in which the property transferred to the partner was used or held. Since the partnership incurred the nonrecourse liability within two years of the transfer to B, under rules similar to those provided in § 1.707–5(a)(5), the liability is presumed to be incurred in anticipation of the transfer unless the facts and circumstances clearly establish the contrary. Assuming no facts exist to rebut this presumption, the liability taken subject to by B is not a qualified liability. The partnership is treated as having received, on the date of the transfer of property Y to B, $500,000 ($600,000 liability assumed by B less B's share of the $100,000 liability immediately prior to the transfer) as consideration for the sale of one-half ($500,000/$1,000,000) of property Y to B. The partnership is also treated as having distributed to B, in B's capacity as a partner, the other one-half of property Y.

§ 1.707–7 Disguised sales of partnership interests. [Reserved]

§ 1.707–8 Disclosure of certain information.

(a) In general. The disclosure referred to in § 1.707–3(c)(2) (regarding certain transfers made within two years of each other), § 1.707–5(a)(7)(ii) (regarding a liability incurred within two years prior to a transfer of property), and § 1.707–6(c) (relating to transfers of property from a partnership to a partner in situations analogous to those listed above) is to be made in accordance with paragraph (b) of this section.

(b) Method of providing disclosure. Disclosure is to be made on a completed Form 8275 or on a statement attached to the return of the transferor of property for the taxable year of the transfer that includes the following:

(1) A caption identifying the statement as disclosure under section 707;

(2) An identification of the item (or group of items) with respect to which disclosure is made;

(3) The amount of each item; and

(4) The facts affecting the potential tax treatment of the item (or items) under section 707.

(c) Disclosure by certain partnerships. If more than one partner transfers property to a partnership pursuant to a plan, the disclosure required by this section may be made by the partnership on behalf of all the transferors rather than by each transferor separately.

§ 1.707–9 Effective dates and transitional rules.

(a) Sections 1.707–3 through 1.707–6—(1) In general. Except as provided in paragraph (a)(3) of this section, §§ 1.707–3 through 1.707–6 apply to any transaction with respect to which all transfers that are part of a sale of an item of property occur after April 24, 1991.

(2) Transfers occurring on or before April 24, 1991. Except as otherwise provided in paragraph (a)(3) of this section, in the case of any transaction with respect to which one or more of the transfers occurs on or before April 24, 1991, the determination of whether the transaction is a disguised sale of property (including a partnership interest) under section 707(a)(2) is to be made on the basis of the statute and the guidance provided regarding that provision in the legislative history of section 73 of the Tax Reform Act of 1984 (Pub.L. 98–369, 98 Stat. 494). See H.R.Rep. No. 861, 98th Cong., 2d Sess. 859–62 (1984); S.Prt. No. 169 (Vol. I), 98th Cong., 2d Sess. 223–32 (1984); H.R.Rep. No. 432 (Pt. 2), 98th Cong., 2d Sess. 1216–21 (1984).

(3) Effective date of section 73 of the Tax Reform Act of 1984. Sections 1.707–3 through 1.707–6 do not apply to any transfer of money or other consideration to which section 73(a) of the Tax Reform Act of 1984 (Pub.L. 98–369, 98 Stat. 494) does not apply pursuant to section 73(b) of that Act.

(b) Section 1.707–8 disclosure of certain information. The disclosure provisions described in § 1.707–8 apply to transactions with respect to which all transfers that are part of a sale of property occur after September 30, 1992.

§ 1.708–1 Continuation of partnership.

(a) General rule. For purposes of subchapter K, chapter 1 of the Code, an existing partnership shall be considered as continuing if it is not terminated.

(b) Termination—(1) General rule. (i) A partnership shall terminate when the operations of the partnership are discontinued and no part of any business, financial operation, or venture of the partnership continues to be carried on by any of its partners in a partnership. For example, on November 20, 1956, A and B, each of whom is a 20-percent partner in partnership ABC, sell their interests to C, who is a 60-percent partner. Since the business is no longer carried on by any of its partners in a partnership, the ABC partnership is terminated as of November 20, 1956. However, where partners DEF agree on April 30, 1957, to dissolve their partnership, but carry on the business through a winding up period ending September 30, 1957, when all remaining assets, consisting only of cash, are distributed to the partners, the partnership does not terminate because of cessation of business until September 30, 1957.

(a) Upon the death of one partner in a 2-member partnership, the partnership shall not be considered as terminated if the estate or other successor in interest of the deceased partner continues to share in the profits or losses of the partnership business.

(b) For the continuation of a partnership where payments are being made under section 736 (relating to payments to a retiring partner or a deceased partner's successor in interest), see paragraph (a)(6) of § 1.736–1.

(ii) A partnership shall terminate when 50-percent or more of the total interest in partnership capital and profits is sold or exchanged within a period of 12 consecutive months. Such sale or exchange includes a sale or exchange to another member of the partnership. However, a disposition of a partnership interest by gift (including assignment to a successor in interest), bequest, or inheritance, or the liquidation of a partnership interest, is not a sale or exchange for purposes of this subparagraph. Moreover, if the sale or exchange of an interest in a partnership (upper-tier partnership) that holds an interest in another partnership (lower-tier partnership) results in a termination of the upper-tier partnership, the upper-tier partnership is treated as exchanging its entire interest in the capital and profits of the lower-tier partnership. If the sale or exchange of an interest in an upper-tier partnership does not terminate the upper-tier partnership, the sale or exchange of an interest in the upper-tier partnership is not treated as a sale or exchange of a proportionate share of the upper-tier partnership's interest in the capital and profits of the lower-tier partnership. The previous two sentences apply to terminations of partnerships under section 708(b)(1)(B) occurring on or after May 9, 1997; however, the sentences may be applied to terminations occurring on or after May 9, 1996, provided that the partnership and its partners apply the sentences to the termination in a consistent manner. Furthermore, the contribution of property to a partnership does not constitute such a sale or exchange. See, however, paragraph (c)(3) of § 1.731–1. Fifty percent or more of the total interest in partnership capital and profits means 50 percent or more of the total interest in partnership capital plus 50 percent or more of the total interest in partnership profits. Thus, the sale of a 30-percent interest in partnership capital and a 60-percent interest in partnership profits is not the sale or exchange of 50 percent or more of the total interest in partnership capital and profits. If one or more partners sell or exchange interests aggregating 50-percent or more of the total interest in partnership capital and 50 percent or more of the total interest in partnership profits within a period of 12 consecutive months, such sale or exchange is considered as being within the provisions of this subparagraph. When interests are sold or exchanged on different dates, the percentages to be added are determined as of the date of each sale. For example, with respect to the ABC partnership, the sale by A on May 12, 1956, of a 30-percent interest in capital and profits to D, and the sale by B on March 27, 1957, of a 30-percent interest in capital and profits to E, is a sale of a 50 percent or more interest. Accordingly, the partnership is terminated as of March 27, 1957. However, if, on March 27, 1957, D instead of B, sold his 30-percent interest in capital and profits to E, there would be no termination since only one 30-percent interest would have been sold or exchanged within a 12-month period.

(iii) For purposes of subchapter K, chapter 1 of the Code, a partnership taxable year closes with respect to all partners on the date on which the partnership terminates. See section 706(c)(1) and paragraph (c)(1) of § 1.706–1. The date of termination is:

(a) For purposes of section 708(b)(1)(A), the date on which the winding up of the partnership affairs is completed.

(b) For purposes of section 708(b)(1)(B), the date of the sale or exchange of a partnership interest which, of itself or together with sales or exchanges in the preceding 12 months, transfers an interest of 50-percent or more in both partnership capital and profits.

(iv) If a partnership is terminated by a sale or exchange of an interest, the following is deemed to occur: The partnership contributes all of its assets and liabilities to a new partnership in exchange for an interest in the new partnership; and, immediately thereafter, the terminated partnership distributes interests in the new partnership to the purchasing partner and the other remaining partners in proportion to their respective interests in the terminated partnership in liquidation of the terminated partnership, either for the continuation of the business by the new partnership or for its dissolution and winding up. In the latter case, the new partnership terminates in accordance with (b)(1)(i) of this section. This paragraph (b)(1)(iv) applies to terminations of partnerships under section 708(b)(1)(B) occurring on or after May 9, 1997; however, this paragraph (b)(1)(iv) may be applied to terminations occurring on or after May 9, 1996, provided that the partnership and its partners apply this paragraph (b)(1)(iv) to the termination in a consistent manner. The provisions of this paragraph (b)(1)(iv) are illustrated by the following example:

Example. (i) A and B each contribute $10,000 cash to form AB, a general partnership, as equal partners. AB purchases depreciable Property X for $20,000. Property X increases in value to $30,000, at which time A sells its entire 50 percent interest to C for $15,000 in a transfer that terminates the partnership under section 708(b)(1)(B). At the time of the sale, Property X had an adjusted tax basis of $16,000 and a book value of $16,000 (original $20,000 tax basis and book value reduced by $4,000 of depreciation). In addition, A and B each had a capital account balance of $8,000 (original $10,000 capital account reduced by $2,000 of depreciation allocations with respect to Property X).

(ii) Following the deemed contribution of assets and liabilities by the terminated AB partnership to a new partnership (new AB) and the liquidation of the terminated AB partnership, the adjusted tax basis of Property X in the hands of new AB is $16,000. See Section 723. The book value of Property X in the hands of new partnership AB is also $16,000 (the book value of Property X immediately before the termination) and B and C each have a capital account of $8,000 in new AB (the balance of their capital accounts in AB prior to the termination). See § 1.704–1(b)(2)(iv)(l) (providing that the deemed contribution and liquidation with regard to the terminated partnership are disregarded in determining the capital accounts of the partners and the books of the new partnership). Additionally, under § 301.6109–1(d)(2)(iii) of this chapter, new AB retains the taxpayer identification number of the terminated AB partnership.

(iii) Property X was not section 704(c) property in the hands of terminated AB and is therefore not treated as section 704(c) property in the hands of new AB, even though Property X is deemed contributed to new AB at a time when the fair market value of Property X ($30,000) was different from its adjusted tax basis ($16,000). See § 1.704–3(a)(3)(i) (providing that property contributed to a new partnership under § 1.708–1(b)(l)(iv) is treated as section 704(c) property only to the extent that the property was section 704(c) property in the hands of the terminated partnership immediately prior to the termination).

(v) If a partnership is terminated by a sale or exchange of an interest in the partnership, a section 754 election (including a section 754 election made by the terminated partnership on its final return) that is in effect for the taxable year of the terminated partnership in which the sale occurs, applies with respect to the incoming partner. Therefore, the bases of partnership assets are adjusted pursuant to sections 743 and 755 prior to their deemed contribution to the new partnership. This paragraph (b)(1)(v) applies to terminations of partnerships under section 708(b)(1)(B) occurring on or after May 9, 1997; however, this paragraph (b)(1)(v) may be applied to terminations occurring on or after May 9, 1996, provided that the partnership and its partners apply this paragraph (b)(1)(v) to the termination in a consistent manner.

(2) Special rules—(i) Merger or consolidation. If two or more partnerships merge or consolidate into one partnership, the resulting partnership shall be considered a continuation of the merging or consolidating partnership the members of which own an interest of more than 50 percent in the capital and profits of the resulting partnership. If the resulting partnership can, under the preceding sentence, be considered a continuation of more than one of the merging or consolidating partnerships, it shall, unless the Commissioner permits otherwise, be considered the continuation of that partnership which is credited with the contribution of the greatest dollar value of assets to the resulting partnership. Any other merging or consolidating partnerships shall be considered as terminated. If the members of none of the merging or consolidating partnerships have an interest of more than 50 percent in the capital and profits of the resulting partnership, all of the merged or consolidated partnerships are terminated, and a new partnership results. The taxable years of such merging or consolidating partnerships which are considered terminated shall be closed in accordance with the provisions of section 706(c), and such partnerships shall file their returns for a taxable year ending upon the date of termination, *i.e.*, the date of merger or consolidation. The resulting partnership shall file a return for the taxable year of the merging or consolidating partnership that is considered as continuing. The return shall state that the resulting partnership is a continuation of such merging or consolidating partnership and shall include the names and addresses of the merged or consolidated partnerships. The respective distributive shares of the partners for the periods prior to and subsequent to the date of merger or consolidation shall be shown as a part of the return. The provisions of this subdivision may be illustrated by the following example:

Example. Partnership AB, in whose capital and profits A and B each own a 50-percent interest, and partnership CD, in whose capital and profits C and D each own a 50-percent interest, merge on September 30, 1955, and form partnership ABCD. Partners A, B, C, and D are on a calendar year; partnership AB is also on a calendar year; and partnership CD is on a fiscal year ending June 30th. After the merger, the partners have capital and profits interests as follows: A, 30 percent; B, 30 percent; C, 20 percent; and D, 20 percent. Since A and B together own an interest of more than 50 percent in the capital and profits of partnership ABCD, such partnership shall be considered a continuation of partnership AB and shall continue to file returns on a calendar year basis. Since C and D own an interest of less than 50 percent in the capital and profits of partnership ABCD, the taxable year of partnership CD closes as of September 30, 1955, the date of the merger, and CD partnership is terminated as of that date. Partnership ABCD is required to file a return for the taxable year January 1 to December 31, 1955, indicating thereon that, until September 30, 1955, it was partnership AB. Partnership CD is required to file a return for its final taxable year, July 1 through September 30, 1955.

(ii) Division of a partnership. Upon the division of a partnership into two or more partnerships, any resulting partnership or partnerships shall be considered a continuation of the prior partnership if its members had an interest of more than 50 percent in the capital and profits of the prior partnership. Any other resulting partnership will not be considered a continuation of the prior partnership but will be considered a new partnership. If the members of none of the resulting partnerships owned an interest of more than 50 percent in the capital and profits of the divided partnership, the divided partnership is terminated. Where members of a partnership which has been divided into two or more partnerships do not become members of a resulting partnership which is considered a continuation of the prior partnership, such partner's interests shall be considered liquidated as of the date of the division. The resulting partnership that is regarded as continuing shall file a return for the taxable year of the partnership that has been divided. The return shall state that the partnership is a continuation of the divided partnership and shall set forth separately the respective distributive shares of the partners for the periods prior to and subsequent to the date of division. The provisions of this subdivision may be illustrated by the following example:

Example. Partnership ABCD is in the real estate and insurance business. A owns a 40-percent interest, and B, C, and D each owns a 20-percent interest, in the capital and profits of the partnership. The partnership and the partners report their income on a calendar year. They agree to separate the real estate and insurance business as of November 1, 1955, and to form two partnerships; partnership AB to take over the real estate business, and partnership CD to take over the insurance business. Since members of resulting partnership AB owned more than a 50-percent interest in the capital and profits of partnership ABCD (A, 40 percent, and B, 20 percent), partnership AB shall be considered a continuation of partnership ABCD. Partnership AB is required to file a return for the taxable year January 1 to December 31, 1955, indicating thereon that until November 1, 1955, it was partnership ABCD. In forming partnership CD, partners C and D may contribute the property distributed to them in liquidation of their entire interests in divided partnership ABCD. Partnership CD will be required to file a return for the taxable year it adopts pursuant to section 706(b) and paragraph (b) of § 1.706–1.

§ 1.709–1 Treatment of organization and syndication costs.

(a) General rule. Except as provided in paragraph (b) of this section, no deduction shall be allowed under Chapter 1 of the Code to a partnership or to any partner for any amounts paid or incurred, directly or indirectly, in partnership taxable years beginning after December 31, 1975, to organize a partnership, or to promote the sale of, or to sell, an interest in the partnership.

(b) Amortization of organization expenses.* **(1)** Under section 709(b) of the Code, a partnership may elect to treat its organizational expenses (as defined in section 709(b)(2) and in § 1.709–2(a))

*Editorial comment: The Regulations do not reflect the effect of the American Jobs Creation Act of 2004 on organizational expenditures which provides the opportunity to elect limited expensing (i.e., maximum of $5,000 subject to a phaseout provision) with the balance being subject to amortization over an 180-month period. See § 709(b).

paid or incurred in partnership taxable years beginning after December 31, 1976, as deferred expenses. If a partnership elects to amortize organizational expenses, it must select a period of not less than 60 months, over which the partnership will amortize all such expenses on a straight line basis. This period must begin with the month in which the partnership begins business (as determined under § 1.709–2(c)). However, in the case of a partnership on the cash receipts and disbursements method of accounting, no deduction shall be allowed for a taxable year with respect to any such expenses that have not been paid by the end of that taxable year. Portions of such expenses which would have been deductible under section 709(b) in a prior taxable year if the expenses had been paid are deductible in the year of payment. The election is irrevocable and the period selected by the partnership in making its election may not be subsequently changed.

(2) If there is a winding up and complete liquidation of the partnership prior to the end of the amortization period, the unamortized amount of organizational expenses is a partnership deduction in its final taxable year to the extent provided under section 165 (relating to losses). However, there is no partnership deduction with respect to its capitalized syndication expenses.

(c) Time and manner of making election. The election to amortize organizational expenses provided by section 709(b) shall be made by attaching a statement to the partnership's return of income for the taxable year in which the partnership begins business. The statement shall set forth a description of each organizational expense incurred (whether or not paid) with the amount of the expense, the date each expense was incurred, the month in which the partnership began business, and the number of months (not less than 60) over which the expenses are to be amortized. A taxpayer on the cash receipts and disbursements method of accounting shall also indicate the amount paid before the end of the taxable year with respect to each such expense. Expenses less than $10 need not be separately listed, provided the total amount of these expenses is listed with the dates on which the first and last of such expenses were incurred, and, in the case of a taxpayer on the cash receipts and disbursements method of accounting, the aggregate amount of such expenses that was paid by the end of the taxable year is stated. In the case of a partnership which begins business in a taxable year that ends after March 31, 1983, the original return and statement must be filed (and the election made) not later than the date prescribed by law for filing the return (including any extensions of time) for that taxable year. Once an election has been made, an amended return (or returns) and statement (or statements) may be filed to include any organizational expenses not included in the partnership's original return and statement.

§ 1.709–2 Definitions.

(a) Organizational expenses. Section 709(b)(2) of the Internal Revenue Code defines organizational expenses as expenses which:

(1) Are incident to the creation of the partnership;

(2) Are chargeable to capital account; and

(3) Are of a character which, if expended incident to the creation of a partnership having an ascertainable life, would (but for section 709(a)) be amortized over such life.

An expenditure which fails to meet one or more of these three tests does not qualify as an organizational expense for purposes of section 709(b) and this section. To satisfy the statutory requirement described in paragraph (a)(1) of this section, the expense must be incurred during the period beginning at a point which is a reasonable time before the partnership begins business and ending with the date prescribed by law for filing the partnership return (determined without regard to any extensions of time) for the taxable year the partnership begins business. In addition, the expenses must be for creation of the partnership and not for operation or starting operation of the partnership trade or business. To satisfy the statutory requirement described in paragraph (a)(3) of this section, the expense must be for an item of a nature normally expected to benefit the partnership throughout the entire life of the partnership. The following are examples of organizational expenses within the meaning of section 709 and this section: Legal fees for services incident to the organization of the partnership, such as negotiation and preparation of a partnership agreement; accounting fees for services incident to the organization of the partnership; and filing fees. The following are examples of expenses that are not organizational expenses within the meaning of section 709 and this section (regardless of how the partnership characterizes them): Expenses connected with acquiring assets for the partnership or transferring assets to the partnership; expenses connected with the admission or removal of partners other than at the time the partnership is first organized; expenses connected with a contract relating to the operation of the partnership trade or business (even where the contract is between the partnership and one of its members); and syndication expenses.

(b) Syndication expenses. Syndication expenses are expenses connected with the issuing and marketing of interests in the partnership. Examples of syndication expenses are brokerage fees; registration fees; legal fees of the underwriter or placement agent and the issuer (the general partner or the partnership) for securities advice and for advice pertaining to the adequacy of tax disclosures in the prospectus or placement memorandum for securities law purposes; accounting fees for preparation of representations to be included in the offering materials; and printing costs of the prospectus, placement memorandum, and other selling and promotional material. These expenses are not subject to the election under section 709(b) and must be capitalized.

(c) Beginning business. The determination of the date a partnership begins business for purposes of section 709 presents a question of fact that must be determined in each case in light of all the circumstances of the particular case. Ordinarily, a partnership begins business when it starts the business operations for which it was organized. The mere signing of a partnership agreement is not alone sufficient to show the beginning of business.

If the activities of the partnership have advanced to the extent necessary to establish the nature of its business operations, it will be deemed to have begun business. Accordingly, the acquisition of operating assets which are necessary to the type of business contemplated may constitute beginning business for these purposes. The term "operating assets," as used herein, means assets that are in a state of readiness to be placed in service within a reasonable period following their acquisition.

Contributions, Distributions, and Transfers

Contributions to a Partnership

§ 1.721–1 Nonrecognition of gain or loss on contribution.

(a) No gain or loss shall be recognized either to the partnership or to any of its partners upon a contribution of property, including installment obligations, to the partnership in exchange for a partnership interest. This rule applies whether the contribution is made to a partnership in the process of formation or to a partnership which is already formed and operating. Section 721 shall not apply to a transaction between a partnership and a partner not acting in his capacity as a partner since such a transaction is governed by section 707. Rather than contributing property to a partnership, a partner may sell property to the partnership or may retain the ownership of property and allow the partnership to use it. In all cases, the substance of the transaction will govern, rather than its form. See paragraph (c)(3) of § 1.731–1. Thus, if the transfer of property by the partner to the partnership results in the receipt by the partner of money or other consideration, including a promissory obligation fixed in amount and time for payment, the transaction will be treated as a sale or exchange under section 707 rather than as a contribution under section 721. For the rules governing the treatment of liabilities to which contributed property is subject, see section 752 and § 1.752–1.

(b) **(1)** Normally, under local law, each partner is entitled to be repaid his contributions of money or other property to the partnership (at the value placed upon such property by the partnership at the time of the contribution) whether made at the formation of the partnership or subsequent thereto. To the extent that any of the partners gives up any part of his right to be repaid his contributions (as distinguished from a share in partnership profits) in favor of another partner as compensation for services (or in satisfaction of an obligation), section 721 does not apply. The value of an interest in such partnership capital so transferred to a partner as compensation for services constitutes income to the partner under section 61. The amount of such income is the fair market value of the interest in capital so transferred, either at the time the transfer is made for past services, or at the time the services have been rendered where the transfer is conditioned on the completion of the transferee's future services. The time when such income is realized depends on all the facts and circumstances, including any substantial restrictions or conditions on the compensated partner's right to withdraw or otherwise dispose of such interest. To the extent that an interest in capital representing compensation for services rendered by the decedent prior to his death is transferred after his death to the decedent's successor in interest, the fair market value of such interest is income in respect of a decedent under section 691.

(2) To the extent that the value of such interest is: (i) Compensation for services rendered to the partnership, it is a guaranteed payment for services under section 707(c); (ii) compensation for services rendered to a partner, it is not deductible by the partnership, but is deductible only by such partner to the extent allowable under this chapter.

(c) Underwritings of partnership interests—(1) In general. For the purpose of section 721, if a person acquires a partnership interest from an underwriter in exchange for cash in a qualified underwriting transaction, the person who acquires the partnership interest is treated as transferring cash directly to the partnership in exchange for the partnership interest and the underwriter is disregarded. A qualified underwriting transaction is a transaction in which a partnership issues partnership interests for cash in an underwriting in which either the underwriter is an agent of the partnership or the underwriter's ownership of the partnership interests is transitory.

(2) Effective date. This paragraph (c) is effective for qualified underwriting transactions occurring on or after May 1, 1996.

§ 1.722–1 Basis of contributing partner's interest.

The basis to a partner of a partnership interest acquired by a contribution of property, including money, to the partnership shall be the amount of money contributed plus the adjusted basis at the time of contribution of any property contributed. If the acquisition of an interest in partnership capital results in taxable income to a partner, such income shall constitute an addition to the basis of the partner's interest. See paragraph (b) of § 1.721–1. If the contributed property is subject to indebtedness or if liabilities of the partner are assumed by the partnership, the basis of the contributing partner's interest shall be reduced by the portion of the indebtedness assumed by the other partners, since the partnership's assumption of his indebtedness is treated as a distribution of money to the partner. Conversely, the assumption by the other partners of a portion of the contributor's indebtedness is treated as a contribution of money by them. See section 752 and § 1.752–1. The provisions of this section may be illustrated by the following examples:

Example (1). A acquired a 20-percent interest in a partnership by contributing property. At the time of A's contribution, the property had a fair market value of $10,000, an adjusted basis to A of $4,000, and was subject to a mortgage of $2,000. Payment of the mortgage was assumed by the partnership. The basis of A's interest in the partnership is $2,400, computed as follows:

Adjusted basis to A of property contributed	$4,000
Less portion of mortgage assumed by other partners which must be treated as a distribution (80 percent of $2,000)	1,600
Basis of A's interest	2,400

Example (2). If, in example (1) of this section, the property contributed by A was subject to a mortgage of $6,000, the basis of A's interest would be zero, computed as follows:

Adjusted basis to A of property contributed	$4,000
Less portion of mortgage assumed by other partners which must be treated as a distribution (80 percent of $6,000)	4,800
	(800)

See § 1.460-4(k)(3)(iv)(A) for a rules relating to basis adjustments required where a contract accounted for under a long-term contract method of accounting is transferred in a contribution to which section 721(a) applies. Since A's basis cannot be less than zero, the $800 in excess of basis, which is considered as a distribution of money under section 752(b), is treated as capital gain from the sale or exchange of a partnership interest. See section 731(a).

§ 1.723–1 Basis of property contributed to partnership.

The basis to the partnership of property contributed to it by a partner is the adjusted basis of such property to the contributing partner at the time of the contribution. Since such property has the same basis in the hands of the partnership as it had in the hands of the contributing partner, the holding period of such property for the partnership includes the period during which it was held by the partner. See section 1223(2). For elective adjustments to the basis of partnership property arising from distributions or transfers of partnership interests, see sections 732(d), 734(b), and 743(b).

Distributions by a Partnership

§ 1.731–1 Extent of recognition of gain or loss on distribution.

(a) Recognition of gain or loss to partner—(1) Recognition of gain. (i) Where money is distributed by a partnership to a partner, no gain shall be recognized to the partner except to the extent that the amount of money distributed exceeds the adjusted basis of the partner's interest in the partnership immediately before the distribution. This rule is applicable both to current distributions (i.e., distributions other than in liquidation of an entire interest) and to distributions in liquidation of a partner's entire interest in a partnership. Thus, if a partner with a basis for his interest of $10,000 receives a distribution of cash of $8,000 and property with a fair market value of $3,000, no gain is recognized to him. If $11,000 cash were distributed, gain would be recognized to the extent of $1,000. No gain shall be recognized to a distributee partner with respect to a distribution of property (other than money) until he sells or otherwise disposes of such property, except to the extent otherwise provided by section 736 (relating to payments to a retiring partner or a deceased partner's successor in interest) and section 751 (relating to unrealized receivables and inventory items). See section 731(c) and paragraph (c) of this section.

(ii) For the purposes of sections 731 and 705, advances or drawings of money or property against a partner's distributive share of income shall be treated as current distributions made on the last day of the partnership taxable year with respect to such partner.

(2) Recognition of loss. Loss is recognized to a partner only upon liquidation of his entire interest in the partnership, and only if the property distributed to him consists solely of money, unrealized receivables (as defined in section 751(c)), and inventory items (as defined in section 751(d)(2)). The term "liquidation of a partner's interest," as defined in section 761(d), is the termination of the partner's entire interest in the partnership by means of a distribution or a series of distributions. Loss is recognized to the distributee partner in such cases to the extent of the excess of the adjusted basis of such partner's interest in the partnership at the time of the distribution over the sum of—

(i) Any money distributed to him, and

(ii) The basis to the distributee, as determined under section 732, of any unrealized receivables and inventory items that are distributed to him.

If the partner whose interest is liquidated receives any property other than money, unrealized receivables, or inventory items, then no loss will be recognized. Application of the provisions of this subparagraph may be illustrated by the following examples:

Example (1). Partner A has a partnership interest in partnership ABC with an adjusted basis to him of $10,000. He retires from the partnership and receives, as a distribution in liquidation of his entire interest, his share of partnership property. This share is $5,000 cash and inventory with a basis to him (under section 732) of $3,000. Partner A realizes a capital loss of $2,000, which is recognized under section 731(a)(2).

Example (2). Partner B has a partnership interest in partnership BCD with an adjusted basis to him of $10,000. He retires from the partnership and receives, as a distribution in liquidation of his entire interest, his share of partnership property. This share is $4,000 cash, real property (used in the trade or business) with an adjusted basis to the partnership of $2,000, and unrealized receivables having a basis to him (under section 732) of $3,000. No loss will be recognized to B on the transaction because he received property other than money, unrealized receivables, and inventory items. As determined under section 732, the basis to B for the real property received is $3,000.

(3) Character of gain or loss. Gain or loss recognized under section 731(a) on a distribution is considered gain or loss from the sale or exchange of the partnership interest of the distributee partner, that is, capital gain or loss.

(b) Gain or loss recognized by partnership. A distribution of property (including money) by a partnership to a partner does not result in recognized gain or loss to the partnership under section 731. However, recognized gain or loss may result to the partnership from certain distributions which, under section 751(b), must be treated as a sale or exchange of property between the distributee partner and the partnership.

(c) Exceptions. (1) Section 731 does not apply to the extent otherwise provided by—

(i) Section 736 (relating to payments to a retiring partner or to a deceased partner's successor in interest) and

(ii) Section 751 (relating to unrealized receivables and inventory items).

For example, payments under section 736(a), which are considered as a distributive share or guaranteed payment, are taxable as such under that section.

(2) The receipt by a partner from the partnership of money or property under an obligation to repay the amount of such money or to return such property does not constitute a distribution subject to section 731 but is a loan governed by section 707(a). To the extent that such an obligation is canceled, the obligor partner will be considered to have received a distribution of money or property at the time of cancellation.

(3) If there is a contribution of property to a partnership and within a short period:

(i) Before or after such contribution other property is distributed to the contributing partner and the contributed property is retained by the partnership, or

(ii) After such contribution the contributed property is distributed to another partner,

such distribution may not fall within the scope of section 731. Section 731 does not apply to a distribution of property, if, in fact, the distribution was made in order to effect an exchange of property between two or more of the partners or between the partnership and a partner. Such a transaction shall be treated as an exchange of property.

* * *

§ 1.732–1 Basis of distributed property other than money.

(a) Distributions other than in liquidation of a partner's interest. The basis of property (other than money) received by a partner in a distribution from a partnership, other than in liquidation of his entire interest, shall be its adjusted basis to the partnership immediately before such distribution. However, the basis of the property to the partner shall not exceed the adjusted basis of the partner's interest in the partnership, reduced by the amount of any money distributed to him in the same transaction. The provisions of this paragraph may be illustrated by the following examples:

Example (1). Partner A, with an adjusted basis of $15,000 for his partnership interest, receives in a current distribution property having an adjusted basis of $10,000 to the partnership immediately before distribution, and $2,000 cash. The basis of the property in A's hands will be $10,000. Under sections 733 and 705, the basis of A's partnership interest will be reduced by the distribution to $3,000 ($15,000 less $2,000 cash, less $10,000, the basis of the distributed property to A).

Example (2). Partner R has an adjusted basis of $10,000 for his partnership interest. He receives a current distribution of $4,000 cash and property with an adjusted basis to the partnership of $8,000. The basis of the distributed property to partner R is limited to $6,000 ($10,000, the adjusted basis of his interest, reduced by $4,000, the cash distributed).

(b) Distribution in liquidation. Where a partnership distributes property (other than money) in liquidation of a partner's entire interest in the partnership, the basis of such property to the partner shall be an amount equal to the adjusted basis of his interest in the partnership reduced by the amount of any money distributed to him in the same transaction. Application of this rule may be illustrated by the following example:

Example. Partner B, with a partnership interest having an adjusted basis to him of $12,000, retires from the partnership and receives cash of $2,000, and real property with an adjusted basis to the partnership of $6,000 and a fair market value of $14,000. The basis of the real property to B is $10,000 (B's basis for his partnership interest, $12,000, reduced by $2,000, the cash distributed).

(c) Allocation of basis among properties distributed to a partner.

(1) General rule.—(i) Unrealized receivables and inventory items. The basis to be allocated to properties distributed to a partner under section 732 (a)(2) or (b) is allocated first to any unrealized receivables (as defined in section 751(c)) and inventory items (as defined in section 751(d)(2)) in an amount equal to the adjusted basis of each such property to the partnership immediately before the distribution. If the basis to be allocated is less than the sum of the adjusted bases to the partnership of the distributed unrealized receivables and inventory items, the adjusted basis of the distributed property must be decreased in the manner provided in paragraph (c)(2)(i) of this section. See § 1.460-4(k)(2)(iv)(D) for a rule determining the partnership's basis in a long-term contract accounted for under a long-term contract method of accounting.

(ii) Other distributed property. Any basis not allocated to unrealized receivables or inventory items under paragraph (c)(1)(i) of this section is allocated to any other property distributed to the partner in the same transaction by assigning to each distributed property an amount equal to the adjusted basis of the property to the partnership immediately before the distribution. However, if the sum of the adjusted bases to the partnership of such other distributed property does not equal the basis to be allocated among the distributed property, any increase or decrease required to make the amounts equal is allocated among the distributed property as provided in paragraph (c)(2) of this section.

(2) Adjustment to basis allocation.—(i) Decrease in basis. Any decrease to the basis of distributed property required under paragraph (c)(1) of this section is allocated first to distributed property with unrealized depreciation in proportion to each property's respective amount of unrealized depreciation before any decrease (but only to the extent of each property's unrealized depreciation). If the required decrease exceeds the amount of unrealized depreciation in the distributed property, the excess is allocated to the distributed property in proportion to the adjusted bases of the distributed property, as adjusted pursuant to the immediately preceding sentence.

(ii) Increase in basis. Any increase to the basis of distributed property required under paragraph (c)(1)(ii) of this section is allocated first to distributed property (other than unrealized receivables and inventory items) with unrealized appreciation in proportion to each property's respective amount of unrealized appreciation before any increase (but only to the extent of each property's unrealized appreciation). If the required increase exceeds the amount of unrealized appreciation in the distributed property, the excess is allocated to the distributed property (other than unrealized receivables or inventory items) in proportion to the fair market value of the distributed property.

(3) Unrealized receivables and inventory items. If the basis to be allocated upon a distribution in liquidation of the partner's entire interest in the partnership is greater than the adjusted basis to the partnership of the unrealized receivables and inventory items distributed to the partner, and if there is no other property distributed to which the excess can be allocated, the distributee partner sustains a capital loss under section 731(a)(2) to the extent of the unallocated basis of the partnership interest.

(4) Examples. The provisions of this paragraph (c) are illustrated by the following examples:

Example (1). A is a one-fourth partner in partnership PRS and has an adjusted basis in its partnership interest of $650. PRS distributes inventory items and Assets X and Y to A in liquidation of A's entire partnership interest. The distributed inventory items have a basis to the partnership of $100 and a fair market value of $200. Asset X has an adjusted basis to the partnership of $50 and a fair market value of $400. Asset Y has an adjusted basis to the partnership and a fair market value of $100. Neither Asset X nor Asset Y consists of inventory items or unrealized receivables. Under this paragraph (c), A's basis in its partnership interest is allocated first to the inventory items in an amount equal to their adjusted basis to the partnership. A, therefore, has an adjusted basis in the inventory items of $100. The remaining basis, $550, is allocated to the distributed property first in an amount equal to the property's adjusted basis to the partnership. Thus, Asset X is allocated $50 and Asset Y is allocated $100. Asset X is then allocated $350, the amount of unrealized appreciation in Asset X. Finally, the remaining basis, $50, is allocated to Assets X and Y in proportion to their fair market values: $40 to Asset X (400/500 × $50), and $10 to Asset Y (100/500 × $50). Therefore, after the distribution, A has an adjusted basis of $440 in Asset X and $110 in Asset Y.

Example (2). B is a one-fourth partner is partnership PRS and has an adjusted basis in its partnership interest of $200. PRS distributes Asset X and Asset Y to B in liquidation of its entire partnership interest. Asset X has an adjusted basis to the partnership and fair market value of $150. Asset Y has an adjusted basis to the partnership of $150 and a fair market value of $50. Neither of the assets consists of inventory items or unrealized receivables. Under this paragraph (c), B's basis is first assigned to the distributed property to the extent of the partnership's basis in each distributed property. Thus, Asset X and Asset Y are each assigned $150. Because the aggregate adjusted basis of the distributed property, $300, exceeds the basis to be allocated, $200, a decrease of $100 in the basis of the distributed property is required. Assets X and Y have unrealized depreciation of zero and $100, respectively. Thus, the entire decrease is allocated to Asset Y. After the distribution, B has an adjusted basis of $150 in Asset X and $50 in Asset Y.

Example (3). C, a partner in partnership PRS, receives a distribution in liquidation of its entire partnership interest of $6,000 cash, inventory items having an adjusted basis to the partnership of $6,000, and real property having an adjusted basis to the partnership of $4,000. C's basis in its partnership interest is $9,000. The cash distribution reduces C's basis to $3,000, which is allocated entirely to the inventory items. The real property has a zero basis in C's hands. The partnership bases not carried over to C for the distributed properties are lost unless an election under section 754 is in effect requiring the partnership to adjust the bases of remaining partnership properties under section 734(b).

Example (4). Assume the same facts as in Example 3 of this paragraph except C receives a distribution in liquidation of its entire partnership interest of $1,000 cash and inventory items having a basis to the partnership of $6,000. The cash distribution reduces C's basis to $8,000, which can be allocated only to the extent of $6,000 to the inventory items. The remaining $2,000 basis, not allocable to the distributed property, constitutes a capital loss to partner C under section 731(a)(2). If the election under section 754 is in effect, see section 734(b) for adjustment of the basis of undistributed partnership property.

(5) Effective date. This paragraph (c) applies to distributions of property from a partnership that occur on or after December 15, 1999.

(d) Special partnership basis to transferee under section 732(d). (1) (i) A transfer of a partnership interest occurs upon a sale or exchange of an interest or upon the death of a partner. Section 732(d) provides a special rule for the determination of the basis of property distributed to a transferee partner who acquired any part of his partnership interest in a transfer with respect to which the election under section 754 (relating to the optional adjustment to basis of partnership property) was not in effect.

(ii) Where an election under section 754 is in effect, see section 743(b) and § 1.743–1 and § 1.732–2.

(iii) If a transferee partner receives a distribution of property (other than money) from the partnership within 2 years after he acquired his interest or part thereof in the partnership by a transfer with respect to which the election under section 754 was not in effect, he may elect to treat as the adjusted partnership basis of such property the adjusted basis such property would have if the adjustment provided in section 743(b) were in effect.

(iv) If an election under section 732(d) is made upon a distribution of property to a transferee partner, the amount of the adjustment with respect to the transferee partner is not diminished by any depletion or depreciation of that portion of the basis of partnership property which arises from the special basis adjustment under section 732(d), since depletion or depreciation on such portion for the period prior to distribution is allowed or allowable only if the optional adjustment under section 743(b) is in effect.

(v) If property is distributed to a transferee partner who elects under section 732(d), and if such property is not the same property which would have had a special basis adjustment, then such special basis adjustment shall apply to any like property received in the distribution, provided that the transferee, in exchange for the property distributed, has relinquished his interest in the property with respect to which he would have had a special basis adjustment. This rule applies whether the property in which the transferee has relinquished his interest is retained or disposed of by the partnership. (For shift of transferee's special basis adjustment under section 743(b) to like property, see paragraph (b)(2)(ii) of § 1.743–1(g).)

(vi) The provisions of this paragraph (d)(1) may be illustrated by the following example:

Example (i) Transferee partner, T, purchased a one-fourth interest in partnership PRS for $17,000. At the time T purchased the partnership interest, the election under section 754 was not in effect and the partnership inventory had a basis to the partnership of $14,000 and a fair market value of $16,000. T's purchase price reflected $500 of this difference. Thus, $4,000 of the $17,000 paid by T for the partnership interest was attributable to T's share of partnership inventory with a basis of $3,500. Within 2 years after T acquired the partnership interest, T retired from the partnership and received in liquidation of its entire partnership interest the following property:

ASSETS		
	Adjusted basis to PRS	Fair market value
Cash	$1,500	$1,500
Inventory	3,500	4,000
Asset X	2,000	4,000
Asset Y	4,000	5,000

(ii) The fair market value of the inventory received by T was one-fourth of the fair market value of all partnership inventory and was T's share of such property. It is immaterial whether the inventory T received was on hand when T acquired the interest. In accordance with T's election under section 732(d), the amount of T's share of partnership basis that is attributable to partnership inventory is increased by $500 (one-fourth of the $2,000 difference between the fair market value of the property, $16,000, and its $14,000 basis to the partnership at the time T purchased its interest). This adjustment under section 732(d) applies only for purposes of distributions to T, and not for purposes of partnership depreciation, depletion, or gain or loss on disposition. Thus, the amount to be allocated among the properties received by T in the liquidating distribution is $15,500 ($17,000, T's basis for the partnership interest, reduced by the amount of cash received, $1,500). This amount is allocated as follows: The basis of the inventory items received is $4,000, consisting of the $3,500 common partnership basis, plus the basis adjustment of $500 which T would have had under section 743(b). The remaining basis of $11,500 ($15,500 minus $4,000) is allocated among the remaining property distributed to T by assigning to each property the adjusted basis to the partnership of such property and adjusting that basis by any required increase or decrease. Thus, the adjusted basis to T of Asset X is $5,111 ($2,000, the adjusted basis of Asset X to the partnership, plus $2,000, the amount of unrealized appreciation in Asset X, plus $1,111 ($4,000/$9,000 multiplied by $2,500). Similarly, the adjusted basis of Asset Y to T is $6,389 ($4,000, the adjusted basis of Asset Y to the partnership, plus $1,000, the amount of unrealized appreciation in Asset Y, plus, $1,389 ($5,000/$9,000 multiplied by $2,500)).

(2) A transferee partner who wishes to elect under section 732(d) shall make the election with his tax return—

(i) For the year of the distribution, if the distribution includes any property subject to the allowance for depreciation, depletion, or amortization, or

(ii) For any taxable year no later than the first taxable year in which the basis of any of the distributed property is pertinent in determining his income tax, if the distribution does not include any such property subject to the allowance for depreciation, depletion or amortization.

(3) A taxpayer making an election under section 732(d) shall submit with the return in which the election is made a schedule setting forth the following:

(i) That under section 732(d) he elects to adjust the basis of property received in a distribution; and

(ii) The computation of the special basis adjustment for the property distributed and the properties to which the adjustment has been allocated. For rules of allocation, see section 755.

(4) A partner who acquired any part of his partnership interest in a transfer to which the election provided in section 754 was not in effect, is required to apply the special basis rule contained in section 732(d) to a distribution to him, whether or not made within 2 years after the transfer, if at the time of his acquisition of the transferred interest—

(i) The fair market value of all partnership property (other than money) exceeded 110 percent of its adjusted basis to the partnership.

(ii) An allocation of basis under section 732(c) upon a liquidation of his interest immediately after the transfer of the interest would have resulted in a shift of basis from property not subject to an allowance for depreciation, depletion, or amortization, to property subject to such an allowance, and

(iii) A basis adjustment under section 743(b) would change the basis to the transferee partner of the property actually distributed.

(5) Required statements. If a transferee partner notifies a partnership that it plans to make the election under section 732(d) under paragraph (d)(3) of this section, or if a partnership makes a distribution to which paragraph (d)(4) of this section applies, the partnership must provide the transferee with such information as is necessary for the transferee properly to compute the transferee's basis adjustments under section 732(d).

(e) Exception. When a partnership distributes unrealized receivables (as defined in section 751(c)) or substantially appreciated inventory items (as defined in section 751(d)) in exchange for any part of a partner's interest in other partnership property (including money), or, conversely, partnership property (including money) other than unrealized receivables or substantially appreciated inventory items in exchange for any part of a partner's interest in the partnership's unrealized receivables or substantially appreciated inventory items, the distribution will be treated as a sale or exchange of property under the provisions of section 751(b). In such case, section 732 (including subsection(d) thereof) applies in determining the partner's basis of the property which he is treated as having sold to or exchanged with the partnership (as constituted after the distribution). The partner is considered as having received such property in a current distribution and, immediately thereafter, as having sold or exchanged it. See section 751(b) and paragraph (b) of § 1.751–1. However, section 732 does not apply in determining the basis of that part of property actually distributed to a partner which is treated as received by him in a sale or exchange under section 751(b). Consequently, the basis of such property shall be its cost to the partner.

§ 1.732–2 Special partnership basis of distributed property.

(a) Adjustments under section 734(b). In the case of a distribution of property to a partner, the partnership bases of the distributed properties shall reflect any increases or decreases to the basis of partnership property which have been made previously under section 734(b) (relating to the optional adjustment to basis of undistributed partnership property) in connection with previous distributions.

(b) Adjustments under section 743(b). In the case of a distribution of property to a partner who acquired any part of his interest in a transfer as to which an election under section 754 was in effect, then, for the purposes of section 732 (other than subsection (d) thereof), the adjusted partnership bases of the distributed property shall take into account, in addition to any adjustments under section 734(b), the transferee's special basis adjustment for the distributed property under section 743(b). The application of this paragraph may be illustrated by the following example:

Example. Partner D acquired his interest in partnership ABD from a previous partner. Since the partnership had made an election under section 754, a special basis adjustment with respect to D is applicable to the basis of partnership property in accordance with section 743(b). One of the assets of the partnership at the time D acquired his interest was property X, which is later distributed to D in a current distribution. Property X has an adjusted basis to the partnership of $1,000 and with respect to D it has a special basis adjustment of $500. Therefore, for purposes of section 732(a)(1), the adjusted basis of such property to the partnership with respect to D immediately before its distribution is $1,500. However, if property X is distributed to partner A, a nontransferee partner, its adjusted basis to the partnership for purposes of section 732(a)(1) is only $1,000. In such case, D's $500 special basis adjustment may shift over to other property. See § 1.743–1(g).

(c) Adjustments to basis of distributed inventory and unrealized receivables. Under section 732, the basis to be allocated to distributed properties shall be allocated first to any unrealized receivables and inventory items. If the distributee partner is a transferee of a partnership interest and has a special basis adjustment for unrealized receivables or inventory items under either section 743(b) or section 732 (d), then the partnership adjusted basis immediately prior to distribution of any unrealized receivables or inventory items distributed to such partner shall be determined as follows: If the distributee partner receives his entire share of the fair market value of the inventory items or unrealized receivables of the partnership, the adjusted basis of such distributed property to the partnership, for the purposes of section 732, shall take into account the entire amount of any special basis adjustment which the distributee partner may have for such assets. If the distributee partner receives less than his entire share of the fair market value of partnership inventory items or unrealized receivables, then, for purposes of section 732, the adjusted basis of such distributed property to the partnership shall take into account the same proportion of the distributee's special basis adjustment for unrealized receivables or inventory items as the value of such items distributed to him bears to his entire share of the total value of all such items of the partnership. The provisions of this paragraph may be illustrated by the following example:

Example. Partner C acquired his 40-percent interest in partnership AC from a previous partner. Since the partnership had made an election under section 754, C has a special basis adjustment to partnership property under section 743(b). C retires from the partnership when the adjusted basis of his partnership interest is $3,000. He receives from the partnership in liquidation of his entire interest, $1,000 cash, certain capital assets, depreciable property, and certain inventory items and unrealized receivables. C has a special basis adjustment of $800 with respect to partnership inventory items and of $200 with respect to unrealized receivables. The common partnership basis for the inventory items distributed to him is $500 and for the unrealized receivables is zero. If the value of inventory items and the unrealized receivables distributed to C in his 40 percent share of the total value of all partnership inventory items and unrealized receivables, then, for purposes of section 732, the adjusted basis of such property in C's hands will be $1,300 for the inventory items ($500 plus $800) and $200 for the unrealized receivables (zero plus $200). The remaining basis of $500, which constitutes the basis of the capital assets and depreciable property distributed to C, is determined as follows: $3,000 (total basis) less $1,000 cash, or $2,000 (the amount to be allocated to the basis of all distributed property), less $1,500 ($800 and $200 special basis adjustments, plus $500 common partnership basis, the amount allocated to inventory items and unrealized receivables). However, if the value of the inventory items and unrealized receivables distributed to C consisted of only 20 percent of the total fair market value of such property (*i.e.*, only one-half of C's 40-percent share), then only one-half of C's special basis adjustment of $800 for partnership inventory items and $200 for unrealized receivables would be taken into account. In that case, the basis of the inventory items in C's hands would be $650 ($250, the common partnership basis for inventory items distributed to him, plus $400, one-half of C's special basis adjustment for inventory items). The basis of the unrealized receivables in C's hands would be $100 (zero plus $100, one-half of C's special basis adjustment for unrealized receivables).

§ 1.732–3 Corresponding adjustment to basis of assets of a distributed corporation controlled by a corporate partner.

The determination of whether a corporate partner has control of a distributed corporation for purposes of section 732(f) shall be made by applying the special aggregate stock ownership rules of §1.1502-34.

§ 1.733–1 Basis of distributee partner's interest.

In the case of a distribution by a partnership to a partner other than in liquidation of a partner's entire interest, the adjusted basis to such partner of his interest in the partnership shall be reduced (but not below zero) by the amount of any money distributed to such partner and by the amount of the basis to him of distributed property other than money as determined under section 732 and §§ 1.732–1 and 1.732–2.

§ 1.734–1 Optional adjustment to basis of undistributed partnership property.

(a) General rule. A partnership shall not adjust the basis of partnership property as the result of a distribution of property to a partner, unless the election provided in section 754 (relating to optional adjustment to basis of partnership property) is in effect.*

(b) Method of adjustment—(1) Increase in basis. Where an election under section 754 is in effect and a distribution of partnership property is made, whether or not in liquidation of the partner's entire interest in the partnership, the adjusted basis of the remaining partnership assets shall be increased by—

(i) The amount of any gain recognized under section 731(a)(1) to the distributee partner, or

(ii) The excess of the adjusted basis to the partnership immediately before the distribution of any property distributed (including adjustments under section 743(b) or section 732(d) when applied) over the basis under section 732 (including such special basis adjustments) of such property to the distributee partner.

See § 1.460–4(k)(2)(iv)(D) for a rule determining the partnership's basis in a long-term contract accounted for under a long-term contract method of accounting. The provisions of this paragraph (b)(1) are illustrated by the following examples:

Example (1). Partner A has a basis of $10,000 for his one-third interest in partnership ABC. The partnership has no liabilities and has assets consisting of cash of $11,000 and property with a partnership basis of $19,000 and a value of $22,000. A receives $11,000 in cash in liquidation of his entire interest in the partnership. He has a gain of $1,000 under section 731(a)(1). If the election under section 754 is in effect, the partnership basis for the property becomes $20,000 ($19,000 plus $1,000).

*Editorial comment: The Regulations do not reflect the effect of the American Jobs Creation Act of 2004 which provides for a mandatory negative basis adjustment in certain circumstances (i.e., there is a "substantial basis reduction"). See §§ 734(a), (b), and (d).

Example (2). Partner D has a basis of $10,000 for his one-third interest in partnership DEF. The partnership balance sheet before the distribution shows the following:

ASSETS

	Adjusted basis	Value
Cash	$4,000	$4,000
Property X	11,000	11,000
Property Y	15,000	18,000
Total	30,000	33,000

LIABILITIES AND CAPITAL

	Adjusted basis	Value
Liabilities	$0	$0
Capital:		
D	10,000	11,000
E	10,000	11,000
F	10,000	11,000
Total	30,000	33,000

In liquidation of his entire interest in the partnership, D received property X with a partnership basis of $11,000. D's basis for property X is $10,000 under section 732(b). Where the election under section 754 is in effect, the excess of $1,000 (the partnership basis before the distribution less D's basis for property X after distribution) is added to the basis of property Y. The basis of property Y becomes $16,000 ($15,000 plus $1,000). If the distribution is made to a transferee partner who elects under section 732(d), see § 1.734–2.

(2) **Decrease in basis.*** Where the election provided in section 754 is in effect and a distribution is made in liquidation of a partner's entire interest, the partnership shall decrease the adjusted basis of the remaining partnership property by—

(i) The amount of loss, if any, recognized under section 731(a)(2) to the distributee partner, or

(ii) The excess of the basis of the distributed property to the distributee, as determined under section 732 (including adjustments under section 743 (b) or section 732(d) when applied) over the adjusted basis of such property to the partnership (including such special basis adjustments) immediately before such distribution.

The provisions of this subparagraph may be illustrated by the following examples:

Example (1). Partner G has a basis of $11,000 for his one-third interest in partnership GHI. Partnership assets consist of cash of $10,000 and property with a basis of $23,000 and a value of $20,000. There are no partnership liabilities. In liquidation of his entire interest in the partnership, G receives $10,000 in cash. He has a loss of $1,000 under section 731(a)(2). If the election under section 754 is in effect, the partnership basis for the property becomes $22,000 ($23,000 less $1,000).

Example (2). Partner J has a basis of $11,000 for his one-third interest in partnership JKL. The partnership balance sheet before the distribution shows the following:

ASSETS

	Adjusted basis	Value
Cash	$5,000	$5,000
Property X	10,000	10,000
Property Y	18,000	15,000
Total	33,000	30,000

LIABILITIES AND CAPITAL

	Adjusted basis	Value
Liabilities	$0	$0
Capital:		
J	11,000	10,000
K	11,000	10,000
L	11,000	10,000
Total	33,000	30,000

In liquidation of his entire interest in the partnership, J receives property X with a partnership basis of $10,000. J's basis for property X under section 732(b) is $11,000. Where the election under section 754 is in effect, the excess of $1,000 ($11,000 basis of property X to J, the distributee, less its $10,000 adjusted basis to the partnership immediately before the distribution) decreases the basis of property Y in the partnership. Thus, the basis of property Y becomes $17,000 ($18,000 less $1,000). If the distribution is made to a transferee partner who elects under section 732(d), see § 1.734–2.

(c) **Allocation of basis.** For allocation among the partnership properties of basis adjustments under section 734(b) and paragraph (b) of this section, see section 755 and § 1.755–1.

(d) **Returns.** A partnership which must adjust the bases of partnership properties under section 734 shall attach a statement to the partnership return for the year of the distribution setting forth the computation of the adjustment and the partnership properties to which the adjustment has been allocated.

*Editorial comment: The Regulations do not reflect the effect of the American Jobs Creation Act of 2004 which provides for a mandatory negative basis adjustment in certain circumstances (i.e., there is a "substantial basis reduction"). See §§ 734(a), (b), and (d).

(e) **Recovery of adjustments to basis of partnership property.**—(1) **Increases in basis.** For purposes of section 168, if the basis of a partnership's recovery property is increased as a result of the distribution of property to a partner, then the increased portion of the basis must be taken into account as if it were newly-purchased recovery property placed in service when the distribution occurs. Consequently, any applicable recovery period and method may be used to determine the recovery allowance with respect to the increased portion of the basis. However, no change is made for purposes of determining the recovery allowance under section 168 for the portion of the basis for which there is no increase.

(2) **Decreases in basis.** For purposes of section 168, if the basis of a partnership's recovery property is decreased as a result of the distribution of property to a partner, then the decrease in basis must be accounted for over the remaining recovery period of the property beginning with the recovery period in which the basis is decreased.

(3) **Effective date.** This paragraph (e) applies to distributions of property from a partnership that occur on or after December 15, 1999.

§ 1.734–2 Adjustment after distribution to transferee partner.

(a) In the case of a distribution of property by the partnership to a partner who has obtained all or part of his partnership interest by transfer, the adjustments to basis provided in section 743(b) and section 732(d) shall be taken into account in applying the rules under section 734(b). For determining the adjusted basis of distributed property to the partnership immediately before the distribution where there has been a prior transfer of a partnership interest with respect to which the election provided in section 754 or section 732(d) is in effect, see §§ 1.732–1 and 1.732–2.

(b) (1) If a transferee partner, in liquidation of his entire partnership interest, receives a distribution of property (including money) with respect to which he has no special basis adjustment, in exchange for his interest in property with respect to which he has a special basis adjustment, and does not utilize his entire special basis adjustment in determining the basis of the distributed property to him under section 732, the unused special basis adjustment of the distributee shall be applied as an adjustment to the partnership basis of the property retained by the partnership and as to which the distributee did not use his special basis adjustment. The provisions of this subparagraph may be illustrated by the following example:

Example. Upon the death of his father, partner S acquires by inheritance a half-interest in partnership ACS. Partners A and C each have a one-quarter interest. The assets of the partnership consist of $10,000 cash and land used in farming worth $10,000 with a basis of $1,000 to the partnership. Since the partnership had made the election under section 754 at the time of transfer, partner S had a special basis adjustment of $4,500 under section 743(b) with respect to his undivided half-interest in the real estate. The basis of S's partnership interest, in accordance with section 742, is $10,000. S retires from the partnership and receives $10,000 in cash in exchange for his entire interest. Since S has received no part of the real estate, his special basis adjustment of $4,500 will be allocated to the real estate, the remaining partnership property, and will increase its basis to the partnership to $5,500.

(2) The provisions of this paragraph do not apply to the extent that certain distributions are treated as sales or exchanges under section 751(b) (relating to unrealized receivables and substantially appreciated inventory items). See section 751(b) and paragraph (b) of § 1.751–1.

§ 1.735–1 Character of gain or loss on disposition of distributed property.

(a) **Sale or exchange of distributed property**—(1) **Unrealized receivables.** Any gain realized or loss sustained by a partner on a sale or exchange or other disposition of unrealized receivables (as defined in paragraph (c)(1) of § 1.751–1) received by him in a distribution from a partnership shall be considered gain or loss from the sale or exchange of property other than a capital asset.

(2) **Inventory items.** Any gain realized or loss sustained by a partner on a sale or exchange of inventory items (as defined in section 751(d)(2)) received in a distribution from a partnership shall be considered gain or loss from the sale or exchange of property other than a capital asset if such inventory items are sold or exchanged within 5 years from the date of the distribution by the partnership. The character of any gain or loss from a sale or exchange by the distributee partner of such inventory items after 5 years from the date of distribution shall be determined as of the date of such sale or exchange by reference to the character of the assets in his hands at that date (inventory items, capital assets, property used in a trade or business, etc.).

(b) **Holding period for distributed property.** A partner's holding period for property distributed to him by a partnership shall include the period such property was held by the partnership. The provisions of this paragraph do not apply for the purpose of determining the 5-year period described in section 735 (a)(2) and paragraph (a)(2) of this section. If the property has been contributed to the partnership by a partner, then the period that the property was held by such partner shall also be included. See section 1223 (2). For a partnership's holding period for contributed property, see § 1.723–1.

* * *

§ 1.736–1 Payments to a retiring partner or a deceased partner's successor in interest.*

(a) Payments considered as distributive share or guaranteed payment. (1) (i) Section 736 and this section apply only to payments made to a retiring partner or to a deceased partner's successor in interest in liquidation of such partner's entire interest in the partnership. See section 761(d). Section 736 and this section do not apply if the estate or other successor in interest of a deceased partner continues as a partner in its own right under local law. Section 736 and this section apply only to payments made by the partnership and not to transactions between the partners. Thus, a sale by partner A to partner B of his entire one-fourth interest in partnership ABCD would not come within the scope of section 736.

(ii) A partner retires when he ceases to be a partner under local law. However, for the purposes of subchapter K, chapter 1 of the Code, a retired partner or a deceased partner's successor will be treated as a partner until his interest in the partnership has been completely liquidated.

(2) When payments (including assumption of liabilities treated as a distribution of money under section 752) are made to a withdrawing partner, that is, a retiring partner or the estate or other successor in interest of a deceased partner, the amounts paid may represent several items. In part, they may represent the fair market value at the time of his death or retirement of the withdrawing partner's interest in all the assets of the partnership (including inventory) unreduced by partnership liabilities. Also, part of such payments may be attributable to his interest in unrealized receivables and part to an arrangement among the partners in the nature of mutual insurance. When a partnership makes such payments, whether or not related to partnership income, to retire the withdrawing partner's entire interest in the partnership, the payments must be allocated between (i) payments for the value of his interest in assets, except unrealized receivables and, under some circumstances, good will (section 736 (b)), and (ii) other payments (section 736(a)). The amounts paid for his interest in assets are treated in the same manner as a distribution in complete liquidation under sections 731, 732, and, where applicable, 751. See paragraph (b)(4)(ii) of § 1.751–1. The remaining partners are allowed no deduction for these payments since they represent either a distribution or a purchase of the withdrawing partner's capital interest by the partnership (composed of the remaining partners).

(3) Under section 736(a), the portion of the payments made to a withdrawing partner for his share of unrealized receivables, good will (in the absence of an agreement to the contrary), or otherwise not in exchange for his interest in assets under the rules contained in paragraph (b) of this section will be considered either—

(i) A distributive share of partnership income, if the amount of payment is determined with regard to income of the partnership; or

(ii) A guaranteed payment under section 707(c), if the amount of the payment is determined without regard to income of the partnership.

(4) Payments, to the extent considered as a distributive share of partnership income under section 736(a)(1), are taken into account under section 702 in the income of the withdrawing partner and thus reduce the amount of the distributive shares of the remaining partners. Payments, to the extent considered as guaranteed payments under section 736(a)(2), are deductible by the partnership under section 162(a) and are taxable as ordinary income to the recipient under section 61(a). See section 707(c).

(5) The amount of any payments under section 736(a) shall be included in the income of the recipient for his taxable year with or within which ends the partnership taxable year for which the payment is a distributive share, or in which the partnership is entitled to deduct such amount as a guaranteed payment. On the other hand, payments under section 736(b) shall be taken into account by the recipient for his taxable year in which such

*Editorial comment: The Regulations do not include the effect of the Revenue Reconciliation Act of 1993. See § 736(b)(3).

payments are made. See paragraph (b)(4) of this section.

(6) A retiring partner or a deceased partner's successor in interest receiving payments under section 736 is regarded as a partner until the entire interest of the retiring or deceased partner is liquidated. Therefore, if one of the members of a 2-man partnership retires under a plan whereby he is to receive payments under section 736, the partnership will not be considered terminated, nor will the partnership year close with respect to either partner, until the retiring partner's entire interest is liquidated, since the retiring partner continues to hold a partnership interest in the partnership until that time. Similarly, if a partner in a 2-man partnership dies, and his estate or other successor in interest receives payments under section 736, the partnership shall not be considered to have terminated upon the death of the partner but shall terminate as to both partners only when the entire interest of the decedent is liquidated. See section 708(b).

(b) Payments for interest in partnership. (1) Payments made in liquidation of the entire interest of a retiring partner or deceased partner shall, to the extent made in exchange for such partner's interest in partnership property (except for unrealized receivables and good will as provided in subparagraphs (2) and (3) of this paragraph), be considered as a distribution by the partnership (and not as a distributive share or guaranteed payment under section 736 (a)). Generally, the valuation placed by the partners upon a partner's interest in partnership property in an arm's length agreement will be regarded as correct. If such valuation reflects only the partner's net interest in the property (*i.e.*, total assets less liabilities), it must be adjusted so that both the value of the partner's interest in property and the basis for his interest take into account the partner's share of partnership liabilities. Gain or loss with respect to distributions under section 736(b) and this paragraph will be recognized to the distributee to the extent provided in section 731 and, where applicable, section 751.

(2) Payments made to a retiring partner or to the successor in interest of a deceased partner for his interest in unrealized receivables of the partnership in excess of their partnership basis, including any special basis adjustment for them to which such partner is entitled, shall not be considered as made in exchange for such partner's interest in partnership property. Such payments shall be treated as payments under section 736(a) and paragraph (a) of this section. For definition of unrealized receivables, see section 751(c).

(3) For the purposes of section 736(b) and this paragraph, payments made to a retiring partner or to a successor in interest of a deceased partner in exchange for the interest of such partner in partnership property shall not include any amount paid for the partner's share of good will of the partnership in excess of its partnership basis, including any special basis adjustments for it to which such partner is entitled, except to the extent that the partnership agreement provides for a reasonable payment with respect to such good will. Such payments shall be considered as payments under section 736(a). To the extent that the partnership agreement provides for a reasonable payment with respect to good will, such payments shall be treated under section 736(b) and this paragraph. Generally, the valuation placed upon good will by an arm's length agreement of the partners, whether specific in amount or determined by a formula, shall be regarded as correct.

(4) Payments made to a retiring partner or to a successor in interest of a deceased partner for his interest in inventory shall be considered as made in exchange for such partner's interest in partnership property for the purposes of section 736(b) and this paragraph. However, payments for an interest in substantially appreciated inventory items, as defined in section 751(d), are subject to the rules provided in section 751(b) and paragraph (b) of § 1.751–1. The partnership basis in inventory items as to a deceased partner's successor in interest does not change because of the death of the partner unless the partnership has elected the optional basis adjustment under section 754. But see paragraph (b)(3)(iii) of § 1.751–1.

(5) Where payments made under section 736 are received during the taxable year, the recipient must segregate that portion of each such payment which is determined to be in exchange for the partner's interest in partnership property and treated as a distribution under section 736(b) from that portion treated as a distributive share or guaranteed payment under section 736(a). Such allocation shall be made as follows—

(i) If a fixed amount (whether or not supplemented by any additional amounts) is to be received over a fixed number of years, the portion of each payment to be treated as a distribution under section 736(b) for the taxable year shall bear the same ratio to the total fixed agreed payments for such year (as distinguished from the amount actually received) as the total fixed agreed payments under section 736(b) bear to the total fixed agreed payments under section 736 (a) and (b). The balance, if any, of such amount received in the same taxable year shall be treated as a distributive share or a guaranteed payment under section 736(a)(1) or (2). However, if the total amount received in any one year is less than the amount considered as a distribution under section 736(b) for that year, then any unapplied portion shall be added to the portion of the payments for the following year or years which are to be treated as a distribution under section 736(b). For example, retiring partner W who is entitled to an annual payment of $6,000 for 10 years for his interest in partnership property, receives only $3,500 in 1955. In 1956, he receives $10,000. Of this amount, $8,500 ($6,000 plus $2,500 from 1955) is treated as a distribution under section 736(b) for 1956; $1,500, as a payment under section 736(a).

(ii) If the retiring partner or deceased partner's successor in interest receives payments which are not fixed in amount, such payments shall first be treated as payments in exchange for his interest in partnership property under section 736(b) to the extent of the value of that interest and, thereafter, as payments under section 736(a).

(iii) In lieu of the rules provided in subdivisions (i) and (ii) of this subparagraph, the allocation of each annual payment between section 736(a) and (b) may be made in any manner to which all the remaining partners and the withdrawing partner or his successor in interest agree, provided that the total amount allocated to property under section 736(b) does not exceed the fair market value of such property at the date of death or retirement.

(6) Except to the extent section 751(b) applies, the amount of any gain or loss with respect to payments under section 736(b) for a retiring or deceased partner's interest in property for each year of payment shall be determined under section 731. However, where the total of section 736(b) payments is a fixed sum, a retiring partner or a deceased partner's successor in interest may elect (in his tax return for the first taxable year for which he receives such payments), to report and to measure the amount of any gain or loss by the difference between—

(i) The amount treated as a distribution under section 736(b) in that year, and

(ii) The portion of the adjusted basis of the partner for his partnership interest attributable to such distribution (*i.e.*, the amount which bears the same proportion to the partner's total adjusted basis for his partnership interest as the amount distributed under section 736(b) in that year bears to the total amount to be distributed under section 736(b)).

A recipient who elects under this subparagraph shall attach a statement to his tax return for the first taxable year for which he receives such payments, indicating his election and showing the computation of the gain included in gross income.

(7) The provisions of this paragraph may be illustrated by the following examples:

Example (1). Partnership ABC is a personal service partnership and its balance sheet is as follows:

ASSETS

	Adjusted basis per books	Market value
Cash	$13,000	$13,000
Unrealized receivables	0	30,000
Capital and section 1231 assets	20,000	23,000
Total	33,000	66,000

LIABILITIES AND CAPITAL

	Adjusted basis per books	Market value
Liabilities	$3,000	$3,000
Capital:		
A	10,000	21,000
B	10,000	21,000
C	10,000	21,000
Total	33,000	66,000

Partner A retires from the partnership in accordance with an agreement whereby his share of liabilities ($1,000) is assumed. In addition he is to receive $9,000 in the year of retirement plus $10,000 in each of the two succeeding years. Thus, the total that A receives for his partnership interest is $30,000 ($29,000 in cash and $1,000 in liabilities assumed). Under the agreement terminating A's interest, the value of A's interest in section 736(b) partnership property is $12,000 (one-third of $36,000, the sum of $13,000 cash and $23,000, the fair market value of capital and section 1231 assets). A's share in unrealized receivables is not included in his interest in partnership property described in section 736(b). Since the basis of A's interest is $11,000 ($10,000 plus $1,000, his share of partnership liabilities), he will realize a capital gain of $1,000 ($12,000 minus $11,000) from the disposition of his interest in partnership property. The remaining $18,000 ($30,000 minus $12,000) will constitute payments under section 736(a)(2) which are taxable to A as guaranteed payments under section 707(c). The payment for the first year is $10,000, consisting of $9,000 in cash, plus $1,000 in liability assumed (section 752(b)). Thus, unless the partners agree otherwise under subparagraph (5)(iii) of this paragraph, each annual payment of $10,000 will be allocated as follows: $6,000 (18,000/30,000 of $10,000) is a section 736(a)(2) payment and $4,000 (12,000/30,000 of $10,000) is a payment for an interest in section 736(b) partnership property. (The partnership may deduct the $6,000 guaranteed payment made to A in each of the 3 years.) The gain on the payments for partnership property will be determined under section 731, as provided in subparagraph (6) of this paragraph. A will treat only $4,000 of each payment as a distribution in a series in liquidation of his entire interest and, under section 731, will have a capital gain of $1,000 when the last payment is made. However, if A so elects, as provided in subparagraph (6) of this paragraph, he may treat such gain as follows: Of each $4,000 payment attributable to A's interest in partnership property, $333 is capital gain (one-third of the total capital gain of $1,000), and $3,667 is a return of capital.

Example (2). Assume the same facts as in example (1) of this subparagraph except that the agreement between the partners provides for payments to A for 3 years of a percentage of annual income instead of a fixed amount. Unless the partners agree otherwise under subparagraph (5)(iii) of this paragraph, all payments received by A up to $12,000 shall be treated under section 736(b) as payments for A's interest in partnership property. His gain of $1,000 will be taxed only after he has received his full basis under section 731. Since the payments are not fixed in amount, the election provided in subparagraph (6) of this paragraph is not available. Any payments in excess of $12,000 shall be treated as a distributive share of partnership income to A under section 736(a)(1).

Example (3). Assume the same facts as in example (1) of this subparagraph except that the partnership agreement provides that the payment for A's interest in partnership property shall include payment for his interest in the good will of the partnership. At the time of A's retirement, the partners determine the value of partnership good will to be $9,000. The value of A's interest in partnership property described in section 736(b) is thus $15,000 (one-third of $45,000, the sum of $13,000 cash, plus $23,000, the value of capital and section 1231 assets, plus $9,000 good will). From the disposition of his interest in partnership property, A will realize a capital gain of $4,000 ($15,000 minus $11,000) the basis of his interest. The remaining $15,000 ($30,000 minus $15,000) will constitute payments under section 736(a)(2) which are taxable to A as guaranteed payments under section 707(c).

Example (4). Assume the same facts as in example (1) of this subparagraph except that the capital and section 1231 assets consist of an item of section 1245 property (as defined in section 1245(a)(3)). Assume further that under paragraph (c)(4) of § 1.751–1 the section 1245 property is an unrealized receivable to the extent of $2,000. Therefore, the value of A's interest in section 736(b) partnership property is only $11,333 (one-third of $34,000, the sum of $13,000 cash and $21,000, the fair market value of section 1245 property to the extent not an unrealized receivable). From the disposition of his interest in partnership property, A will realize a capital gain of $333 ($11,333 minus $11,000, the basis of his interest). The remaining $18,667 ($30,000 minus $11,333) will constitute payments under section 736(a)(2) which are taxable to A as guaranteed payments under section 707(c).

(c) Cross reference. See section 753 for treatment of payments under section 736(a) as income in respect of a decedent under section 691.

§ 1.737–1 Recognition of precontribution Gain.

(a) Determination of gain—(1) In general. A partner that receives a distribution of property (other than money) must recognize gain under section 737 and this section in an amount equal to the lesser of the excess distribution (as defined in paragraph (b) of this section) or the partner's net precontribution gain (as defined in paragraph (c) of this section). Gain recognized under section 737 and this section is in addition to any gain recognized under section 731.

(2) Transactions to which section 737 applies. Section 737 and this section apply only to the extent that a distribution by a partnership is a distribution to a partner acting in the capacity of a partner within the meaning of section 731, except that section 737 and this section do not apply to the extent that section 751(b) applies to the distribution.

(b) Excess distribution—(1) Definition. The excess distribution is the amount (if any) by which the fair market value of the distributed property (other than money) exceeds the distributee partner's adjusted tax basis in the partner's partnership interest.

(2) Fair market value of property. The fair market value of the distributed property is the price at which the property would change hands between a willing buyer and a willing seller at the time of the distribution, neither being under any compulsion to buy or sell and both having reasonable knowledge of the relevant facts. The fair market value that a partnership assigns to distributed property will be regarded as correct, provided that the value is reasonably agreed to among the partners in an arm's-length negotiation and the partners have sufficiently adverse interests.

(3) Distributee partner's adjusted tax basis—(i) General rule. In determining the amount of the excess distribution, the distributee partner's adjusted tax basis in the partnership interest includes any basis adjustment resulting from the distribution that is subject to section 737 (for example, adjustments required under section 752) and from any other distribution or transaction that is part of the same distribution, except for—

(A) The increase required under section 737(c)(1) for the gain recognized by the partner under section 737; and

(B) The decrease required under section 733(2) for any property distributed to the partner other than property previously contributed to the partnership by the distributee partner. See § 1.704–4(e)(1) for a rule in the context of section 704(c)(1)(B). See also § 1.737–3(b)(2) for a special rule for determining a partner's adjusted tax basis in distributed property previously contributed by the partner to the partnership.

(ii) Advances or drawings. The distributee partner's adjusted tax basis in the partnership interest is determined as of the last day of the partnership's taxable year if the distribution to which section 737 applies is properly characterized as an advance or drawing against the partner's distributive share of income. See § 1.731–1(a)(1)(ii).

(c) Net precontribution gain—(1) General rule. The distributee partner's net precontribution gain is the net gain (if any) that would have been recognized by the distributee partner under section 704(c)(1)(B) and § 1.704–4 if all property that had been contributed to the partnership by the distributee partner within five years of the distribution and is held by the partnership immediately before the distribution had been distributed by the partnership to another partner other than a partner who owns, directly or indirectly, more than 50 percent of the capital or profits interest in the partnership. See § 1.704–4 for provisions determining a contributing partner's gain or loss under section 704(c)(1)(B) on an actual distribution of contributed section 704(c) property to another partner.

(2) Special rules—(i) Property contributed on or before October 3, 1989. Property contributed to the partnership on or before October 3, 1989, is not taken into account in determining a partner's net precontribution gain. See § 1.704–4(c)(1) for a similar rule in the context of section 704(c)(1)(B).

(ii) Section 734(b)(1)(A) adjustments. For distributions to a distributee partner of money by a partnership with a section 754 election in effect that are part of the same distribution as the distribution of property subject to section 737, for purposes of paragraph (a) and (c)(1) of this section the distributee partner's net precontribution gain is reduced by the basis adjustments (if any) made to section 704(c) property contributed by the distributee partner under section 734(b)(1)(A). See § 1.737–3(c)(4) for rules regarding basis adjustments for partnerships with a section 754 election in effect.

(iii) Transfers of a partnership interest. The transferee of all or a portion of a contributing partner's partnership interest succeeds to the transferor's net precontribution gain, if any, in an amount proportionate to the interest transferred. **See § 1.704–3(a)(7) and § 1.704–4(d)(2) for similar provisions in the context of section 704(c)(1)(A) and section 704(c)(1)(B).**

(iv) Section 704(c)(1)(B) gain recognized in related distribution. A distributee partner's net precontribution gain is determined after taking into account any gain or loss recognized by the partner under section 704(c)(1)(B) and § 1.704–4 (or that would have been recognized by the partner except for the like-kind exception in section 704(c)(2) and § 1.704–4(d)(3)) on an actual distribution to another partner of section 704(c) property contributed by the distributee partner that is part of the same distribution as the distribution to the distributee partner.

(v) Section 704(c)(2) disregarded. A distributee partner's net precontribution gain is determined without regard to the provisions of section 704(c)(2) and § 1.704–4(d)(3) in situations in which the property contributed by the distributee partner is not actually distributed to another partner in a distribution related to the section 737 distribution.

(d) Character of gain. The character of the gain recognized by the distributee partner under section 737 and this section is determined by, and is proportionate to, the character of the partner's net precontribution gain. For this purpose, all gains and losses on section 704(c) property taken into account in determining the partner's net precontribution gain are netted according to their character. Character is determined at the partnership level for this purpose, and any character with a net negative amount is disregarded. The character of the partner's gain under section 737 is the same as, and in proportion to, any character with a net positive amount. Character for this purpose is determined as if the section 704(c) property had been sold by the partnership to an unrelated third party at the time of the distribution and includes any item that would have been taken into account separately by the contributing partner under section 702(a) and § 1.702–1(a).

(e) Examples. The following examples illustrate the provisions of this section. Unless otherwise specified, partnership income equals partnership expenses (other than depreciation deductions for contributed property) for each year of the partnership, the fair market value of partnership property does not change, all distributions by the partnership are subject to section 737, and all partners are unrelated.

Example (1). Calculation of excess distribution and net precontribution gain. (i) On January 1, 1995, A, B, and C form partnership ABC as equal partners. A contributes Property A, depreciable real property with a fair market value of $30,000 and an adjusted tax basis of $20,000. B contributes Property B, nondepreciable real property with a fair market value and adjusted tax basis of $30,000. C contributes $30,000 cash.

(ii) Property A has 10 years remaining on its cost recovery schedule and is depreciated using the straight-line method. The partnership uses the traditional method for allocating items under section 704(c) described in § 1.704–3(b)(1) for Property A. The partnership has book depreciation of $3,000 per year (10 percent of the $30,000 book basis in Property A) and each partner is allocated $1,000 of book depreciation per year (one-third of the total annual book depreciation of $3,000). The partnership also has tax depreciation of $2,000 per year (10 percent of the $20,000 adjusted tax basis in Property A). This $2,000 tax depreciation is allocated equally between B and C, the noncontributing partners with respect to Property A.

(iii) At the end of 1997, the book value of Property A is $21,000 ($30,000 initial book value less $9,000 aggregate book depreciation) and its adjusted tax basis is $14,000 ($20,000 initial tax basis less $6,000 aggregate tax depreciation).

(iv) On December 31, 1997, Property B is distributed to A in complete liquidation of A's partnership interest. The adjusted tax basis of A's partnership interest at that time is $20,000. The amount of the excess distribution is $10,000, the difference between the fair market value of the distributed Property B ($30,000) and A's adjusted tax basis in A's partnership interest ($20,000). A's net precontribution gain is $7,000, the difference between the book value of Property A ($21,000) and its adjusted tax basis at the time of the distribution ($14,000). A recognizes gain of $7,000 on the distribution, the lesser of the excess distribution and the net precontribution gain.

Example (2). Determination of distributee partner's basis. **(i)** On January 1, 1995, A, B, and C form general partnership ABC as equal partners. A contributes Property A, nondepreciable real property with a fair market value of $10,000 and an adjusted tax basis of $4,000. B and C each contributes $10,000 cash.

(ii) The partnership purchases Property B, nondepreciable real property with a fair market value of $9,000, subject to a $9,000 nonrecourse liability. This nonrecourse liability is allocated equally among the partners under section 752, increasing A's adjusted tax basis in A's partnership interest from $4,000 to $7,000.

(iii) On December 31, 1998, A receives $2,000 cash and Property B, subject to the $9,000 liability, in a current distribution.

(iv) In determining the amount of the excess distribution, the adjusted tax basis of A's partnership interest is adjusted to take into account the distribution of money and the shift in liabilities. A's adjusted tax basis is therefore increased to $11,000 for this purpose ($7,000 initial adjusted tax basis, less $2,000 distribution of money, less $3,000 (decrease in A's share of the $9,000 partnership liability), plus $9,000 (increase in A's individual liabilities)). As a result of this basis adjustment, the adjusted tax basis of A's partnership interest ($11,000) is greater than the fair market value of the distributed property ($9,000) and therefore, there is no excess distribution. A recognizes no gain under section 737.

Example (3). Net precontribution gain reduced for gain recognized under section 704(c)(1)(B). **(i)** On January 1, 1995, A, B, and C form partnership ABC as equal partners. A contributes Properties Al and A2, nondepreciable real properties located in the United States each with a fair market value of $10,000 and an adjusted tax basis of $6,000. B contributes Property B, nondepreciable real property located outside the United States, with a fair market value and adjusted tax basis of $20,000. C contributes $20,000 cash.

(ii) On December 31, 1998, Property B is distributed to A in complete liquidation of A's interest and, as part of the same distribution, Property A1 is distributed to B in a current distribution.

(iii) A's net precontribution gain before the distribution is $8,000 ($20,000 fair market value of Properties A1 and A2 less $12,000 adjusted tax basis of such properties). A recognizes $4,000 of gain under section 704(c)(1)(B) and § 1.704–4 on the distribution of Property A1 to B ($10,000 fair market value of Property A1 less $6,000 adjusted tax basis of Property A1). This gain is taken into account in determining A's excess distribution and net precontribution gain. As a result, A's net precontribution gain is reduced from $8,000 to $4,000, and the adjusted tax basis in A's partnership interest is increased by $4,000 to $16,000.

(iv) A recognizes gain of $4,000 on the receipt of Property B under section 737, an amount equal to the lesser of the excess distribution of $4,000 ($20,000 fair market value of Property B less $16,000 adjusted tax basis of A's interest in the partnership) and A's remaining net precontribution gain of $4,000.

Example (4). Character of gain. **(i)** On January 1, 1995, A, B, and C form partnership ABC as equal partners. A contributes the following nondepreciable property to the partnership:

	Fair market value	Adjusted tax basis
Property A1	$30,000	$20,000
Property A2	30,000	38,000
Property A3	10,000	9,000

(ii) The character of gain or loss on Property A1 and Property A2 is long-term, U.S.-source capital gain or loss. The character of gain on Property A3 is long-term, foreign-source capital gain. B contributes Property B, nondepreciable real property with a fair market value and adjusted tax basis of $70,000. C contributes $70,000 cash.

(iii) On December 31, 1998, Property B is distributed to A in complete liquidation of A's interest in the partnership. A recognizes $3,000 of gain under section 737, an amount equal to the excess distribution of $3,000 ($70,000 fair market value of Property B less $67,000 adjusted tax basis in A's partnership interest) and A's net precontribution gain of $3,000 ($70,000 aggregate fair market value of properties contributed by A less $67,000 aggregate adjusted tax basis of such properties).

(iv) In determining the character of A's gain, all gains and losses on property taken into account in determining A's net precontribution gain are netted according to their character and allocated to A's recognized gain under section 737 based on the relative proportions of the net positive amounts. U.S.-source and foreign-source gains must be netted separately because A would have been required to take such gains into account separately under section 702. As a result, A's net precontribution gain of $3,000 consists of $2,000 of net long-term, U.S.-source capital gain

($10,000 gain on Property A1 and $8,000 loss on Property A2) and $1,000 of net long-term, foreign-source capital gain ($1,000 gain on Property A3).

(v) The character of A's gain under paragraph (d) of this section is therefore $2,000 long-term, U.S.-source capital gain ($3,000 gain recognized under section 737 × $2,000 net long-term, U.S.-source capital gain/$3,000 total net precontribution gain) and $1,000 long-term, foreign-source capital gain ($3,000 gain recognized under section 737 × $1,000 net long-term, foreign-source capital gain/$3,000 total net precontribution gain).

§ 1.737–2 Exceptions and special rules.

(a) Section 708(b)(1)(B) terminations. Section 737 and this section do not apply to the deemed distribution of interests in a new partnership caused by the termination of a partnership under section 708 (b)(1)(B). A subsequent distribution of property by the new partnership to a partner of the new partnership that was formerly a partner of the terminated partnership is subject to section 737 to the same extent that a distribution from the terminated partnership would have been subject to section 737. See also § 1.704–4(c)(3) for a similar rule in the context of section 704(c)(1)(B). This paragraph (a) applies to terminations of partnerships under section 708(b)(1)(B) occurring on or after May 9, 1997; however, this paragraph (a) may be applied to terminations occurring on or after May 9, 1996, provided that the partnership and its partners apply this paragraph (a) to the termination in a consistent manner.

(b) Transfers to another partnership—(1) Complete transfer. Section 737 and this section do not apply to a transfer by a partnership (transferor partnership) of all of its assets and liabilities to a second partnership (transferee partnership) in an exchange described in section 721, followed by a distribution of the interest in the transferee partnership in liquidation of the transferor partnership as part of the same plan or arrangement. See § 1.704–4 (c)(4) for a similar rule in the context of section 704 (c)(1)(B).

(2) Certain divisive transactions. Section 737 and this section do not apply to a transfer by a partnership (transferor partnership) of all of the section 704(c) property contributed by a partner to a second partnership (transferee partnership) in an exchange described in section 721, followed by a distribution as part of the same plan or arrangement of an interest in the transferee partnership (and no other property) in complete liquidation of the interest of the partner that originally contributed the section 704(c) property to the transferor partnership.

(3) Subsequent distributions. A subsequent distribution of property by the transferee partnership to a partner of the transferee partnership that was formerly a partner of the transferor partnership is subject to section 737 to the same extent that a distribution from the transferor partnership would have been subject to section 737.

(c) Incorporation of a partnership. Section 737 and this section do not apply to an incorporation of a partnership by any method of incorporation (other than a method involving an actual distribution of partnership property to the partners followed by a contribution of that property to a corporation), provided that the partnership is liquidated as part of the incorporation transaction. See § 1.704–4(c)(5) for a similar rule in the context of section 704(c)(1)(B).

(d) Distribution of previously contributed property—(1) General rule. Any portion of the distributed property that consists of property previously contributed by the distributee partner (previously contributed property) is not taken into account in determining the amount of the excess distribution or the partner's net precontribution gain. The previous sentence applies on or after May 9, 1997. See § 1.737–3(b)(2) for a special rule for determining the basis of previously contributed property in the hands of a distributee partner who contributed the property to the partnership.

(2) Limitation for distribution of previously contributed interest in an entity. An interest in an entity previously contributed to the partnership is not treated as previously contributed property to the extent that the value of the interest is attributable to property contributed to the entity after the interest was contributed to the partnership. The preceding sentence does not apply to the extent that the property contributed to the entity was contributed to the partnership by the partner that also contributed the interest in the entity to the partnership.

(3) Nonrecognition transactions, installment sales, contributed contracts, and capitalized costs. (i) Property received by the partnership in exchange for contributed section 704(c) property in a nonrecognition transaction is treated as the contributed property with regard to the contributing partner for purposes of section 737 to the extent that the property received is treated as section 704(c) property under § 1.704–3 (a)(8). See § 1.704–4(d) (1) for a similar rule in the context of section 704(c) (1)(B).* * *

(4) Undivided interests. The distribution of an undivided interest in property is treated as the distribution of previously contributed property to the extent that the undivided interest does not exceed the undivided interest, if any, contributed by the distributee partner in the same property. See § 1.704–4(c)(6) for the application of section 704(c)(1)(B) in a similar context. The portion of the undivided interest in property retained by the partnership after the distribution, if any, that is treated as contributed by the distributee partner, is reduced to the extent of the undivided interest distributed to the distributee partner.

(e) Examples. The following examples illustrate the rules of this section. Unless otherwise specified, partnership income equals partnership expenses (other than depreciation deductions for contributed property) for each year of the partnership, the fair market value of partnership property does not change, all distributions by the partnership are subject to section 737, and all partners are unrelated.

Example (1). Distribution of previously contributed property. (i) On January 1, 1995, A, B, and C form partnership ABC as equal partners. A contributes the following nondepreciable real property to the partnership:

	Fair market value	Adjusted tax basis
Property Al	$20,000	$10,000
Property A2	10,000	6,000

(ii) A's total net precontribution gain on the contributed property is $14,000 ($10,000 on Property Al plus $4,000 on Property A2). B contributes $10,000 cash and Property B, nondepreciable real property with a fair market value and adjusted tax basis of $20,000. C contributes $30,000 cash.

(iii) On December 31, 1998, Property A2 and Property B are distributed to A in complete liquidation of A's interest in the partnership. Property A2 was previously contributed by A and is therefore not taken into account in determining the amount of the excess distribution or A's net precontribution gain. The adjusted tax basis of Property A2 in the hands of A is also determined under section 732 as if that property were the only property distributed to A.

(iv) As a result of excluding Property A2 from these determinations, the amount of the excess distribution is $10,000 ($20,000 fair market value of distributed Property B less $10,000 adjusted tax basis in A's partnership interest). A's net precontribution gain is also $10,000 ($14,000 total net precontribution gain less $4,000 gain with respect to previously contributed Property A2). A therefore recognizes $10,000 of gain on the distribution, the lesser of the excess distribution and the net precontribution gain.

Example (2). Distribution of a previously contributed interest in an entity. (i) On January 1, 1995, A, B, and C form partnership ABC as equal partners. A contributes Property A, nondepreciable real property with a fair market value of $10,000 and an adjusted tax basis of $5,000, and all of the stock of Corporation X with a fair market value and adjusted tax basis of $500. B contributes $500 cash and Property B, nondepreciable real property with a fair market value and adjusted tax basis of $10,000. Partner C contributes $10,500 cash. On December 31, 1996, ABC contributes Property B to Corporation X in a nonrecognition transaction under section 351.

(ii) On December 31, 1998, all of the stock of Corporation X is distributed to A in complete liquidation of A's interest in the partnership. The stock is treated as previously contributed property with respect to A only to the extent of the $500 fair market value of the Corporation X stock contributed by A. The fair market value of the distributed stock for purposes of determining the amount of the excess distribution is therefore $10,000 ($10,500 total fair market value of Corporation X stock less $500 portion treated as previously contributed property). The $500 fair market value and adjusted tax basis of the Corporation X stock is also not taken into account in determining the amount of the excess distribution and the net precontribution gain.

(iii) A recognizes $5,000 of gain under section 737, the amount of the excess distribution ($10,000 fair market value of distributed property less $5,000 adjusted tax basis in A's partnership interest) and A's net precontribution gain ($10,000 fair market value of Property A less $5,000 adjusted tax basis in Property A).

Example (3). Distribution of undivided interest in property. (i) On January 1, 1995, A and B form partnership AB as equal partners. A contributes $500 cash and an undivided one-half interest in Property X. B contributes $500 cash and an undivided one-half interest in Property X.

(ii) On December 31, 1998, an undivided one-half interest in Property X is distributed to A in a current distribution. The distribution of the undivided one-half interest in Property X is treated as a distribution of previously contributed property because A contributed an undivided one-half interest in Property X. As a result, A does not recognize any gain under section 737 on the distribution.

§ 1.737–3 Basis adjustments; Recovery rules.

(a) Distributee partner's adjusted tax basis in the partnership interest. The distributee partner's adjusted tax basis in the partnership interest is increased by the amount of gain recognized by the distributee partner under section 737 and this section. This increase is not taken into account in determining the amount of gain recognized by the partner under section 737(a)(1) and this section or in determining the amount of gain recognized by the partner under section 731(a) on the distribution of money in the same distribution or any related distribution. See § 1.704–4(e)(1) for a determination of the distributee partner's adjusted tax basis in a distribution subject to section 704(c)(1)(B).

(b) Distributee partner's adjusted tax basis in distributed property—(1) In general. The distributee partner's adjusted tax basis in the distributed property is determined under section 732(a) or (b) as applicable. The increase in the distributee partner's adjusted tax basis in the partnership interest under paragraph (a) of this section is taken into account in determining the distributee partner's adjusted tax basis in the distributed property other than property previously contributed by the partner. See § 1.704–4(e)(2) for a determination of basis in a distribution subject to section 704(c)(1)(B).

(2) Previously contributed property. The distributee partner's adjusted tax basis in distributed property that the partner previously contributed to the partnership is determined as if it were distributed in a separate and independent distribution prior to the distribution that is subject to section 737 and § 1.737–1.

(c) Partnership's adjusted tax basis in partnership property—(1) Increase in basis. The partnership's adjusted tax basis in eligible property is increased by the amount of gain recognized by the distributee partner under section 737.

(2) Eligible property. Eligible property is property that—

(i) Entered into the calculation of the distributee partner's net precontribution gain;

(ii) Has an adjusted tax basis to the partnership less than the property's fair market value at the time of the distribution;

(iii) Would have the same character of gain on a sale by the partnership to an unrelated party as the character of any of the gain recognized by the distributee partner under section 737; and

(iv) Was not distributed to another partner in a distribution subject to section 704(c)(1)(B) and § 1.704–4 that was part of the same distribution as the distribution subject to section 737.

(3) Method of adjustment. For the purpose of allocating the basis increase under paragraph (c)(2) of this section among the eligible property, all eligible property of the same character is treated as a single group. Character for this purpose is determined in the same manner as the character of the recognized gain is determined under § 1.737–1(d). The basis increase is allocated among the separate groups of eligible property in proportion to the character of the gain recognized under section 737. The basis increase is then allocated among property within each group in the order in which the property was contributed to the partnership by the partner, starting with the property contributed first, in an amount equal to the difference between the property's fair market value and its adjusted tax basis to the partnership at the time of the distribution. For property that has the same character and was contributed in the same (or a related) transaction, the basis increase is allocated based on the respective amounts of unrealized appreciation in such properties at the time of the distribution.

(4) Section 754 adjustments. The basis adjustments to partnership property made pursuant to paragraph (c)(1) of this section are not elective and must be made regardless of whether the partnership has an election in effect under section 754. Any adjustments to the bases of partnership property (including eligible property as defined in paragraph (c)(2) of this section) under section 734(b) pursuant to a section 754 election (other than basis adjustments under section 734(b)(1)(A) described in the following sentence) must be made after (and must take into account) the adjustments to basis made under paragraph (a) and paragraph (c)(1) of this section. Basis adjustments under section 734(b)(1)(A) that are attributable to distributions of money to the distributee partner that are part of the same distribution as the distribution of property subject to section 737 are made before the adjustments to basis under paragraph (a) and paragraph (c)(1) of this section. See § 1.737–1(c)(2)(ii) for the effect, if any, of basis adjustments under section 734(b)(1)(A) on a partner's net precontribution gain. See also § 1.704–4(e)(3) for a similar rule regarding basis adjustments pursuant to a section 754 election in the context of section 704(c)(1)(B).

(d) Recovery of increase to adjusted tax basis. Any increase to the adjusted tax basis of partnership property under paragraph (c)(1) of this section is recovered using any applicable recovery period and depreciation (or other cost recovery) method (including first-year conventions) available to the partnership for newly purchased property (of the type adjusted) placed in service at the time of the distribution.

(e) Examples. The following examples illustrate the rules of this section. Unless otherwise specified, partnership income equals partnership expenses (other than depreciation deductions for contributed property) for each year of the partnership, the fair market value of partnership property does not change, all distributions by the partnership are subject to section 737, and all partners are unrelated.

Example 1. Partner's basis in distributed property. **(i)** On January 1, 1995, A, B, and C form partnership ABC as equal partners. A contributes Property A, nondepreciable real property with a fair market value of $10,000 and an adjusted tax basis of $5,000. B contributes Property B, nondepreciable real property with a fair market value and adjusted tax basis of $10,000. C contributes $10,000 cash.

(ii) On December 31, 1998, Property B is distributed to A in complete liquidation of A's interest in the partnership. A recognizes $5,000 of gain under section 737, an amount equal to the excess distribution of $5,000 ($10,000 fair market value of Property B less $5,000 adjusted tax basis in A's partnership interest) and A's net precontribution gain of $5,000 ($10,000 fair market value of Property A less $5,000 adjusted tax basis of such property).

(iii) A's adjusted tax basis in A's partnership interest is increased by the $5,000 of gain recognized under section 737. This increase is taken into account in determining A's basis in the distributed property. Therefore, A's adjusted tax basis in distributed Property B is $10,000 under section 732(b).

Example 2. Partner's basis in distributed property in connection with gain recognized under section 704(c)(1)(B). **(i)** On January 1, 1995, A, B, and C form partnership ABC as equal partners. A contributes the following nondepreciable real property located in the United States to the partnership:

	Fair market value	Adjusted tax basis
Property Al	$10,000	5,000
Property A2	10,000	2,000

(ii) B contributes $10,000 cash and Property B, nondepreciable real property located outside the United States, with a fair market value and adjusted tax basis of $10,000. C contributes $20,000 cash.

(iii) On December 31, 1998, Property B is distributed to A in a current distribution and Property A1 is distributed to B in a current distribution. A recognizes $5,000 of gain under section 704(c)(1)(B) and § 1.704–4 on the distribution of Property Al to B, the difference between the fair market value of such property ($10,000) and the adjusted tax basis in distributed Property A1 ($5,000). The adjusted tax basis of A's partnership interest is increased by this $5,000 of gain under section 704(c)(1)(B) and § 1.704–4(e)(1).

(iv) The increase in the adjusted tax basis of A's partnership interest is taken into account in determining the amount of the excess distribution. As a result, there is no excess distribution because the fair market value of Property B ($10,000) is less than the adjusted tax basis of A's interest in the partnership at the time of distribution ($12,000). A therefore recognizes no gain under section 737 on the receipt of Property B. A's adjusted tax basis in Property B is $10,000 under section 732(a)(1). The adjusted tax basis of A's partnership interest is reduced from $12,000 to $2,000 under section 733. See Example 3 of § 1.737–1(e).

Example 3. Partnership's basis in partnership property after a distribution with section 737 gain. **(i)** On January 31, 1995, A, B, and C form partnership ABC as equal partners. A contributes the following nondepreciable property to the partnership:

	Fair market value	Adjusted tax basis
Property A1	$1,000	$ 500
Property A2	4,000	1,500
Property A3	4,000	6,000
Property A4	6,000	4,000

(ii) The character of gain or loss on Properties A1, A2, and A3 is long-term, U.S.-source capital gain or loss. The character of gain on Property A4 is long-term, foreign-source capital gain. B contributes Property B, nondepreciable real property with a fair market value and adjusted tax basis of $15,000. C contributes $15,000 cash.

(iii) On December 31, 1998, Property B is distributed to A in complete liquidation of A's interest in the partnership. A recognizes gain of $3,000 under section 737, an amount equal to the excess distribution of $3,000 ($15,000 fair market value of Property B less $12,000 adjusted tax basis in A's partnership interest) and A's net precontribution gain of $3,000 ($15,000 aggregate fair market value of the property contributed by A less $12,000 aggregate adjusted tax basis of such property).

(iv) $2,000 of A's gain is long-term, foreign-source capital gain ($3,000 total gain under section 737 × $2,000 net long-term, foreign-source capital gain/$3,000 total net precontribution gain). $1,000 of A's gain is long-term, U.S.-source capital gain ($3,000 total gain under section 737 × $1,000 net long-term, U.S.-source capital gain/$3,000 total net precontribution gain).

(v) The partnership must increase the adjusted tax basis of the property contributed by A by $3,000. All property contributed by A is eligible property. Properties Al, A2, and A3 have the same character and are grouped into a single group for purposes of allocating this basis increase. Property A4 is in a separate character group.

(vi) $2,000 of the basis increase must be allocated to long-term, foreign-source capital assets because $2,000 of the gain recognized by A was long-term, foreign-source capital gain. The adjusted tax basis of Property A4 is therefore increased from $4,000 to $6,000. $1,000 of the increase must be allocated to Properties A1 and A2 because $1,000 of the gain recognized by A is long-term, U.S.-source capital gain. No basis increase is allocated to Property A3 because its fair market value is less than its adjusted tax basis. The $1,000 basis increase is allocated between Properties A1 and A2 based on the unrealized appreciation in each asset before such basis adjustment. As a result, the adjusted tax basis of Property Al is increased by $167 ($1,000 × $500/$3,000) and the adjusted tax basis of Property A2 is increased by $833 ($1,000 × $2,500/3,000).

§ 1.737–4 Anti-abuse rule.

(a) In general. The rules of section 737 and §§ 1.737–1, 1.737–2, and 1.737–3 must be applied in a manner consistent with the purpose of section 737. Accordingly, if a principal purpose of a transaction is to achieve a tax result that is inconsistent with the purpose of section 737, the Commissioner can recast the transaction for federal tax purposes as appropriate to achieve tax results that are consistent with the purpose of section 737. Whether a tax result is inconsistent with the purpose of section 737 must be determined based on all the facts and circumstances. See § 1.704–4(f) for an anti-abuse rule and examples in the context of section 704(c)(1)(B). The anti-abuse rule and examples under section 704(c)(l)(B) and § 1.704–4(f) are relevant to section 737 and §§ 1.737–1, 1.737–2, and 1.737–3 to the extent that the net precontribution gain for purposes of section 737 is determined by reference to section 704(c)(1)(B).

(b) Examples. The following examples illustrate the rules of this section. The examples set forth below do not delineate the boundaries of either permissible or impermissible types of transactions. Further, the addition of any facts or circumstances that are not specifically set forth in an example (or the deletion of any facts or circumstances) may alter the outcome of the transaction described in the example. Unless otherwise specified, partnership income equals partnership expenses (other than depreciation deductions for contributed property) for each year of the partnership, the fair market value of partnership property does not change, all distributions by the partnership are subject to section 737, and all partners are unrelated.

Example 1. Increase in distributee partner's basis by temporary contribution; results inconsistent with the purpose of section 737. **(i)** On January 1, 1995, A, B, and C form partnership ABC as equal partners. A contributes Property A1, nondepreciable real property with a fair market value of $10,000 and an adjusted tax basis of $1,000. B contributes Property B, nondepreciable real property with a fair market value of $10,000 and an adjusted tax basis of $10,000. C contributes $10,000 cash.

(ii) On January 1, 1999, pursuant to a plan a principal purpose of which is to avoid gain under section 737, A transfers to the partnership Property A2, nondepreciable real property with a fair market value and adjusted tax basis of $9,000. A treats the transfer as a contribution to the partnership pursuant to section 721 and increases the adjusted tax basis of A's partnership interest from $1,000 to $10,000. On January 1, 1999, the partnership agreement is amended and all other necessary steps are taken so that substantially all of the economic risks and benefits of Property A2 are retained by A. On February 1, 1999, Property B is distributed to A in a current distribution. If the contribution of Property A2 is treated as a contribution to the partnership for purposes of section 737, there is no excess distribution because the fair market value of distributed Property B ($10,000) does not exceed the adjusted tax basis of A's interest in the partnership ($10,000), and therefore section 737 does not apply. A's adjusted tax basis in distributed Property B is $10,000 under section 732(a)(1) and the adjusted tax basis of A's partnership interest is reduced to zero under section 733.

(iii) On March 1, 2000, A receives Property A2 from the partnership in complete liquidation of A's interest in the partnership. A recognizes no gain on the distribution of Property A2 because the property was previously contributed property. See § 1.737–2(d).

(iv) Although A has treated the transfer of Property A2 as a contribution to the partnership that increased the adjusted tax basis of A's interest in the partnership, it would be inconsistent with the purpose of section 737 to recognize the transfer as a contribution to the partnership. Section 737 requires recognition of gain when the value of distributed property exceeds the distributee partner's adjusted tax basis in the partnership interest. Section 737 assumes that any contribution or other transaction that affects a partner's adjusted tax basis in the partnership interest is a contribution or transaction in substance and is not engaged in with a principal purpose of avoiding recognition of gain under section 737. Because the transfer of Property A2 to the partnership was not a contribution in substance and was made with a principal purpose of avoiding recognition of gain under section 737, the Commissioner can disregard the contribution of Property A2 for this purpose. As a result, A recognizes gain of $9,000 under section 737 on the receipt of Property B, an amount equal to the lesser of the excess distribution of $9,000 ($10,000 fair market value of distributed Property B less the $1,000 adjusted tax basis of A's partnership interest, determined without regard to the transitory contribution of Property A2) or A's net precontribution gain of $9,000 on Property Al.

Example 2. Increase in distributee partner's basis; section 752 liability shift; results consistent with the purpose of section 737. **(i)** On January 1, 1995, A and B form general partnership AB as equal partners. A contributes Property A, nondepreciable real property with a fair market value of $10,000 and an adjusted tax basis of $1,000. B contributes Property B, nondepreciable real property with a fair market value and adjusted tax basis of $10,000. The partnership also borrows $10,000 on a recourse basis and purchases Property C. The $10,000 liability is allocated equally between A and B under section 752, thereby increasing the adjusted tax basis in A's partnership interest to $6,000.

(ii) On December 31, 1998, the partners agree that A is to receive Property B in a current distribution. If A were to receive Property B at that time, A would recognize $4,000 of gain under section 737, an amount equal to the lesser of the excess distribution of $4,000 ($10,000 fair market value of Property B less $6,000 adjusted tax basis in A's partnership interest) or A's net precontribution gain of $9,000 ($10,000 fair market value of Property A less $1,000 adjusted tax basis of Property A).

(iii) With a principal purpose of avoiding such gain, A and B agree that A will be solely liable for the repayment of the $10,000 partnership liability and take the steps necessary so that the entire amount of the liability is allocated to A under section 752. The adjusted tax basis in A's partnership interest is thereby increased from $6,000 to $11,000 to reflect A's share of the $5,000 of liability previously allocated to B. As a result of this increase in A's adjusted tax basis, there is no excess distribution because the fair market value of distributed Property B ($10,000) is less than the adjusted tax basis of A's partnership interest. Recognizing A's increased adjusted tax basis as a result of the shift in liabilities is consistent with the purpose of section 737 and this section. Section 737 requires recognition of gain only when the value of the distributed property exceeds the distributee partner's adjusted tax basis in the partnership interest. The $10,000 recourse liability is a bona fide liability of the partnership that was undertaken for a substantial business purpose and A's and B's agreement that A will assume responsibility for repayment of that debt has substance. Therefore, the increase in A's adjusted tax basis in A's interest in the partnership due to the shift in partnership liabilities under section 752 is respected, and A recognizes no gain under section 737.

§ 1.737–5 Effective dates.

Sections 1.737–1, 1.737–2, 1.737–3, and 1.737–4 apply to distributions by a partnership to a partner on or after January 9, 1995, except that §1.737–2(d)(3)(iv) applies to distributions by a partnership to a partner on or after June 24, 2003.

Transfers of Interests In A Partnership

§ 1.741–1 Recognition and character of gain or loss on sale or exchange.

(a) The sale or exchange of an interest in a partnership shall, except to the extent section 751(a) applies, be treated as the sale or exchange of a capital asset, resulting in capital gain or loss measured by the difference between the amount realized and the adjusted basis of the partnership interest, as determined under section 705. For treatment of selling partner's distributive share up to date of sale, see section 706(c)(2). Where the provisions of section 751 require the recognition of ordinary income or loss with respect to a portion of the amount realized from such sale or exchange, the amount realized shall be reduced by the amount attributable under section 751 to unrealized receivables and substantially appreciated inventory items, and the adjusted basis of the transferor partner's interest in the partnership shall be reduced by the portion of such basis attributable to such unrealized receivables and substantially appreciated inventory items. See section 751 and § 1.751–1.

(b) Section 741 shall apply whether the partnership interest is sold to one or more members of the partnership or to one or more persons who are not members of the partnership. Section 741 shall also apply even though the sale of the partnership interest results in a termination of the partnership under section 708(b). Thus, the provisions of section 741 shall be applicable (1) to the transferor partner in a 2-man partnership when he sells his interest to the other partner, and (2) to all the members of a partnership when they sell their interests to one or more persons outside the partnership.

(c) See section 351 for nonrecognition of gain or loss upon transfer of a partnership interest to a corporation controlled by the transferor.

(d) For rules relating to the treatment of liabilities on the sale or exchange of interests in a partnership see §§ 1.752–1 and 1.1001–2.

(e) For rules relating to the capital gain or loss recognized when a partner sells or exchanges an interest in a partnership that holds appreciated collectibles or section 1250 property with section 1250 capital gain, see §1.1(h)–1. This paragraph (e) applies to transfers of interests in partnerships that occur on or after September 21, 2000.

(f) For rules relating to dividing the holding period of an interest in a partnership, see §1.1223–3. This paragraph (f) applies to transfers of partnership interests and distributions of property from a partnership that occur on or after September 21, 2000.

§ 1.742–1 Basis of transferee partner's interest.

The basis to a transferee partner of an interest in a partnership shall be determined under the general basis rules for property provided by part II (section 1011 and following), subchapter O, chapter 1 of the Code. Thus, the basis of a purchased interest will be its cost. The basis of a partnership interest acquired from a decedent is the fair market value of the interest at the date of his death or at the alternate valuation date, increased by his estate's or other successor's share of partnership liabilities, if any, on that date, and reduced to the extent that such value is attributable to items constituting income in respect of a decedent (see section 753 and paragraph (c)(3)(v) of § 1.706–1 and paragraph (b) of § 1.753–1) under section 691. See section 1014(c). For basis of contributing partner's interest, see section 722. The basis so determined is then subject to the adjustments provided in section 705.

§ 1.743–1 Optional adjustment to basis of partnership property.

(a) Generally. The basis of partnership property is adjusted as a result of the transfer of an interest in a partnership by sale or exchange or on the death of a partner only if the election provided by section 754 (relating to optional adjustments to the basis of partnership property) is in effect with respect to the partnership.* Whether or not the election provided in section 754 is in effect, the basis of partnership property is not adjusted as the result of a contribution of property, including money, to the partnership.

(b) Determination of adjustment. In the case of the transfer of an interest in a partnership, either by sale or exchange or as a result of the death of a partner, a partnership that has an election under section 754 in effect:

(1) Increases the adjusted basis of partnership property by the excess of the transferee's basis for the transferred partnership interest over the transferee's share of the adjusted basis to the partnership of the partnership's property; or

(2) Decreases the adjusted basis of partnership property by the excess of the transferee's share of the adjusted basis to the partnership of the partnership's property over the transferee's basis for the transferred partnership interest.

(c) Determination of transferee's basis in the transferred partnership interest. In the case of the transfer of a partnership interest by sale or exchange or as a result of the death of a partner, the transferee's basis in the transferred partnership interest is determined under section 742 and §1.742–1. See also section 752 and §§1.752–1 through 1.752–5.

(d) Determination of transferee's share of the adjusted basis to the partnership of the partnership's property. (1) Generally. A transferee's share of the adjusted basis to the partnership of partnership property is equal to the sum of the transferee's interest as a partner in the partnership's previously taxed capital, plus the transferee's share of partnership liabilities. Generally, a transferee's interest as a partner in the partnership's previously taxed capital is equal to:

(i) The amount of cash that the transferee would receive on a liquidation of the partnership following the hypothetical transaction, as defined in paragraph (d)(2) of this section (to the extent attributable to the acquired partnership interest); increased by

(ii) The amount of tax loss (including any remedial allocations under §1.704–3(d)), that would be allocated to the transferee from the hypothetical transaction (to the extent attributable to the acquired partnership interest); and decreased by

(iii) The amount of tax gain (including any remedial allocations under §1.704–3(d)), that would be allocated to the transferee from the hypothetical transaction (to the extent attributable to the acquired partnership interest).

(2) Hypothetical transaction defined. For purposes of paragraph (d)(1) of this section, the hypothetical transaction means the disposition by the partnership of all of the partnership's assets, immediately after the transfer of the partnership interest, in a fully taxable transaction for cash equal to the fair market value of the assets. See § 1.460–4 (k)(3)(v)(B) for a rule relating to the computation of income or loss that would be allocated to the transferee from a contract accounted for under a long-term contract method of accounting as a result of the hypothetical transaction.

(3) Examples. The provisions of this paragraph (d) are illustrated by the following examples:

Example (1). (i) A is a member of partnership PRS in which the partners have equal interests in capital and profits. The partnership has made an election under section 754, relating to the optional adjustment to the basis of partnership property. A sells its interest to T for $22,000. The balance sheet of the partnership at the date of sale shows the following:

ASSETS		
	Adjusted basis	Fair market value
Cash	$ 5,000	$ 5,000
Accounts receivable	10,000	10,000
Inventory	20,000	21,000
Depreciable assets	20,000	40,000
Total	55,000	76,000

LIABILITIES AND CAPITAL		
	Adjusted basis	Fair market value
Liabilities	$10,000	$10,000
Capital		
A	15,000	22,000
B	15,000	22,000
C	15,000	22,000
Total	55,000	76,000

(ii) The amount of the basis adjustment under section 743(b) is the difference between the basis of T's interest in the partnership and T's share of the adjusted basis to the partnership of the partnership's

*Editorial comment: The Regulations do not reflect the effect of the American Jobs Creation Act of 2004 which provides for a mandatory negative basis adjustment in certain circumstances (i.e., there is a "substantial built-in loss"). See §§ 743(a), (b), and (d).

property. Under section 742, the basis of T's interest is $25,333 (the cash paid for A's interest, $22,000, plus $3,333, T's share of partnership liabilities). T's interest in the partnership's previously taxed capital is $15,000 ($22,000, the amount of cash T would receive if PRS liquidated immediately after the hypothetical transaction, decreased by $7,000, the amount of tax gain allocated to T from the hypothetical transaction). T's share of the adjusted basis to the partnership of the partnership's property is $18,333 ($15,000 share of previously taxed capital, plus $3,333 share of the partnership's liabilities). The amount of the basis adjustment under section 743(b) to partnership property therefore, is $7,000, the difference between $25,333 and $18,333.

Example (2). A, B, and C form partnership PRS, to which A contributes land (Asset 1) with a fair market value of $1,000 and an adjusted basis to A of $400, and B and C each contribute $1,000 cash. Each partner has $1,000 credited to it on the books of the partnership as its capital contribution. The partners share in profits equally. During the partnership's first taxable year, Asset 1 appreciates in value to $1,300. A sells its one-third interest in the partnership to T for $1,100, when an election under section 754 is in effect. The amount of tax gain that would be allocated to T from the hypothetical transaction is $700 ($600 section 704(c) built-in gain, plus one-third of the additional gain). Thus, T's interest in the partnership's previously taxed capital is $400 ($1,100, the amount of cash T would receive if PRS liquidated immediately after the hypothetical transaction, decreased by $700, T's share of the gain from the hypothetical transaction). The amount of T's basis adjustment under section 743(b) to partnership property is $700 (the excess of $1,100, T's cost basis for its interest, over $400, T's share of the adjusted basis to the partnership of partnership property).

(e) Allocation of basis adjustment. For the allocation of the basis adjustment under this section among the individual items of partnership property, see section 755 and the regulations thereunder.

(f) Subsequent transfers. Where there has been more than one transfer of a partnership interest, a transferee's basis adjustment is determined without regard to any prior transferee's basis adjustment. In the case of a gift of an interest in a partnership, the donor is treated as transferring, and the donee as receiving, that portion of the basis adjustment attributable to the gifted partnership interest. The provisions of this paragraph (f) are illustrated by the following example:

Example (i) A, B, and C form partnership PRS. A and B each contribute $1,000 cash, and C contributes land with a basis and fair market value of $1,000. When the land has appreciated in value to $1,300, A sells its interest to T1 for $1,100 (one-third of $3,300, the fair market value of the partnership property). An election under section 754 is in effect; therefore T1 has a basis adjustment under section 743(b) of $100.

(ii) After the land has further appreciated in value to $1,600, T1 sells its interest to T2 for $1,200 (one-third of $3,600, the fair market value of the partnership property). T2 has a basis adjustment under section 743(b) of $200. This amount is determined without regard to any basis adjustment under section 743(b) that T1 may have had in the partnership assets.

(iii) During the following year, T2 makes a gift to T3 of fifty percent of T2's interest in PRS. At the time of the transfer, T2 has a $200 basis adjustment under section 743(b). T2 is treated as transferring $100 of the basis adjustment to T3 with the gift of the partnership interest.

(g) Distributions.—(1) Distribution of adjusted property to the transferee.

(i) Coordination with section 732. If a partnership distributes property to a transferee and the transferee has a basis adjustment for the property, the basis adjustment is taken into account under section 732. See §1.732–2(b).

(ii) Coordination with section 734. For certain adjustments to the common basis of remaining partnership property after the distribution of adjusted property to a transferee, see §1.734–2(b).

(2) Distribution of adjusted property to another partner.

(i) Coordination with section 732. If a partner receives a distribution of property with respect to which another partner has a basis adjustment, the distributee does not take the basis adjustment into account under section 732.

(ii) Reallocation of basis. A transferee with a basis adjustment in property that is distributed to another partner reallocates basis adjustment among the remaining items of partnership property under §1.755–1(c).

(3) Distributions in complete liquidation of a partner's interest. If a transferee receives a distribution of property (whether or not the transferee has a basis adjustment in such property) in liquidation of its interest in the partnership, the adjusted basis to the partnership of the distributed property immediately before the distribution includes the transferee's basis adjustment for the property in which the transferee relinquished an interest (either because it remained in the partnership or was distributed to another partner). Any basis adjustment for property in which the transferee is deemed to relinquish its interest is reallocated among the properties distributed to the transferee under §1.755–1(c).

(4) Coordination with other provisions. The rules of sections 704(c)(1)(B), 731, 737, and 751 apply before the rules of this paragraph (g).

(5) Example. The provisions of this paragraph (g) are illustrated by the following example:

Example (i) A, B, and C are equal partners in partnership PRS. Each partner originally contributed $10,000 in cash, and PRS used the contributions to purchase five nondepreciable capital assets. PRS has no liabilities. After five years, PRS's balance sheet appears as follows:

ASSETS		
	Adjusted basis	Fair market value
Asset 1	$10,000	$10,000
Asset 2	4,000	6,000
Asset 3	6,000	6,000
Asset 4	7,000	4,000
Asset 5	3,000	13,000
Total	30,000	39,000

CAPITAL		
	Adjusted basis	Fair market value
Partner A	$10,000	$13,000
Partner B	10,000	13,000
Partner C	10,000	13,000
Total	30,000	39,000

(ii) A sells its interest to T for $13,000 when PRS has an election in effect under section 754. T receives a basis adjustment under section 743(b) in the partnership property that is equal to $3,000 (the excess of T's basis in the partnership interest, $13,000, over T's share of the adjusted basis to the partnership of partnership property, $10,000). The basis adjustment is allocated under section 755, and the partnership's balance sheet appears as follows:

ASSETS			
	Adjusted basis	Fair market value	Basis adjustment
Asset 1	$10,000	$10,000	$0.00
Asset 2	4,000	6,000	666.67
Asset 3	6,000	6,000	0.00
Asset 4	7,000	4,000	(1,000.00)
Asset 5	3,000	13,000	3,333.33
Total	30,000	39,000	3,000.00

CAPITAL			
	Adjusted per books	Fair market value	Special basis
Partner T	$10,000	$13,000	$3,000
Partner B	10,000	13,000	0
Partner C	10,000	13,000	0
Total	30,000	39,000	3,000

(iii) Assume that PRS distributes Asset 2 to T in partial liquidation of T's interest in the partnership. T has a basis adjustment under section 743(b) of $666.67 in Asset 2. Under paragraph (g)(l)(i) of this section, T takes the basis adjustment into account under section 732. Therefore, T will have a basis in Asset 2 of $4,666.67 following the distribution.

(iv) Assume instead that PRS distributes Asset 5 to C in complete liquidation of C's interest in PRS. T has a basis adjustment under section 743(b) of $3,333.33 in Asset 5. Under paragraph (g)(2)(i) of this section, C does not take T's basis adjustment into account under section 732. Therefore, the partnership's basis for purposes of sections 732 and 734 is $3,000. Under paragraph (g)(2)(ii) of this section, T's $3,333.33 basis adjustment is reallocated among the remaining partnership assets under § 1.755–1(c).

(v) Assume instead that PRS distributes Asset 5 to T in complete liquidation of its interest in PRS. Under paragraph (g)(3) of this section, immediately prior to the distribution of Asset 5 to T, PRS must adjust the basis of Asset 5. Therefore, immediately prior to the distribution, PRS's basis in Asset 5 is equal to $6,000, which is the sum of (A) $3,000, PRS's common basis in Asset 5, plus (B) $3,333.33, T's basis adjustment to Asset 5, plus (C) ($333.33), the sum of T's basis adjustments in Assets 2 and 4. For purposes of sections 732 and 734, therefore, PRS will be treated as having a basis in Asset 5 equal to $6,000.

(h) Contributions of adjusted property.—(1) Section 721(a) transactions. If, in a transaction described in section 721(a), a partnership (the upper tier) contributes to another partnership (the lower tier) property with respect to which a basis adjustment has been made, the basis adjustment is treated as contributed to the lower-tier partnership, regardless of whether the lower-tier partnership makes a section 754 election. The lower tier's basis in the contributed assets and the upper tier's basis in the partnership interest received in the transaction are determined with reference to the basis adjustment. However, that portion of the basis of the upper tier's interest in the lower tier attributable to the basis adjustment must be segregated and allocated solely to the transferee partner for whom the basis adjustment was made. Similarly, that portion of the lower tier's basis in its assets attributable to the basis adjustment must be segregated and allocated solely to the upper tier and the transferee. A partner with a basis adjustment in property held by a partnership that terminates under section 708(b)(1) (B) will continue to have the same basis adjustment with respect to property deemed contributed by the terminated partnership to the new partnership under §1.708–1(b)(1)(iv), regardless of whether the new partnership makes a section 754 election.

(2) Section 351 transactions.—(i) Basis in transferred property. A corporation's adjusted tax basis in property transferred to the corporation by a partnership in a transaction described in section 351 is determined with reference to any basis adjustments to the property under section 743(b) (other than any basis adjustment that reduces a partner's gain under paragraph (h)(2)(ii) of this section).

(ii) Partnership gain. The amount of gain, if any, recognized by the partnership on a transfer of property by the partnership to a corporation in a transfer described in section 351 is determined without reference to any basis adjustment to the transferred property under section 743(b). The amount of gain, if any, recognized by the partnership on the transfer that is allocated to a partner with a basis adjustment in the transferred property is adjusted to reflect the partner's basis adjustment in the transferred property.

(iii) Basis in stock. The partnership's adjusted tax basis in stock received from a corporation in a transfer described in section 351 is determined without reference to the basis adjustment in property transferred to the corporation in the section 351 exchange. A partner with a basis adjustment in property transferred to the corporation, however, has a basis adjustment in the stock received by the partnership in the section 351 exchange in an amount equal to the partner's basis adjustment in the transferred property, reduced by any basis adjustment that reduced the partner's gain under paragraph (h)(2)(ii) of this section.

(iv) Example. The following example illustrates the principles of this paragraph (h)(2):

Example (i) A, B, and C are equal partners in partnership PRS. The partnership's only asset, Asset 1, has an adjusted tax basis of $60 and a fair market value of $120. Asset 1 is a nondepreciable capital asset and is not section 704(c) property. A has a basis in its partnership interest of $40, and a positive section 743(b) adjustment of $20 in Asset 1. In a transaction to which section 351 applies, PRS contributes Asset 1 to X, a corporation, in exchange for $15 in cash and X stock with a fair market value of $105.

(ii) Under paragraph (h)(2)(ii) of this section, PRS realizes $60 of gain on the transfer of Asset 1 to X ($120, its amount realized, minus $60, its adjusted basis), but recognizes only $15 of that gain under section 351(b)(1). Of this amount, $5 is allocated to each partner. A must use $5 of its basis adjustment in Asset 1 to offset A's share of PRS's gain. Under paragraph (h)(2)(iii) of this section, PRS's basis in the stock received from X is $60. However, A has a basis adjustment in the stock received by PRS equal to $15 (its basis adjustment in Asset 1, $20, reduced by the portion of the adjustment which reduced A's gain, $5). Under paragraph (h)(2)(i) of this section, X's basis in Asset 1 equals $90 (PRS's common basis in the asset, $60, plus the gain recognized by PRS under section 351(b)(1), $15, plus A's basis adjustment under section 743 (b), $20, less the portion of the adjustment which reduced A's gain, $5).

(i) [Reserved].

(j) Effect of basis adjustment.—(1) In general. The basis adjustment constitutes an adjustment to the basis of partnership property with respect to the transferee only. No adjustment is made to the common basis of partnership property. Thus, for purposes of calculating income, deduction, gain, and loss, the transferee will have a special basis for those partnership properties the bases of which are adjusted under section 743(b) and this section. The adjustment to the basis of partnership property under section 743(b) has no effect on the partnership's computation of any item under section 703.

(2) Computation of partner's distributive share of partnership items. The partnership first computes its items of income, deduction, gain, or loss at the partnership level under section 703. The partnership then allocates the partnership items among the partners, including the transferee, in accordance with section 704, and adjusts the partners' capital accounts accordingly. The partnership then adjusts the transferee's distributive share of the items of partnership income, deduction, gain, or loss, in accordance with paragraphs (j)(3) and (4) of this section, to reflect the effects of the transferee's basis adjustment under section 743(b). These adjustments to the transferee's distributive shares must be reflected on Schedules K and K-1 of the partnership's return (Form 1065). These adjustments to the transferee's distributive shares do not affect the transferee's capital account. See § 1.460–4(k)(3)(v)(B) for rules relating to the effect of a basis adjustment under section 743(b) that is allocated to a contract accounted for under a long-term contract method of accounting in determining the transferee's distributive share of income or loss from the contract.

(3) Effect of basis adjustment in determining items of income, gain, or loss.—(i) In general. The amount of a transferee's income, gain, or loss from the sale or exchange of a partnership asset in which the transferee has a basis adjustment is equal to the transferee's share of the partnership's gain or loss from the sale of the asset (including any remedial allocations under §1.704–3(d)), minus the amount of the transferee's positive basis adjustment for the partnership asset (determined by taking into account the recovery of the basis adjustment under paragraph (j)(4)(i)(B) of this section) or plus the amount of the transferee's negative basis adjustment for the partnership asset (determined by taking into account the recovery of the basis adjustment under paragraph (j)(4)(ii)(B) of this section).

(ii) Examples. The following examples illustrate the principles of this paragraph (j)(3):

Example (1). A and B form equal partnership PRS. A contributes nondepreciable property with a fair market value of $50 and an adjusted tax basis of $100. PRS will use the traditional allocation method under §1.704–3(b). B contributes $50 cash. A sells its interest to T for $50. PRS has an election in effect to adjust the basis of partnership property under section 754. T receives a negative $50 basis adjustment under section 743(b) that, under section 755, is allocated to the nondepreciable property. PRS then sells the property for $60. PRS recognizes a book gain of $10 (allocated equally between T and B) and a tax loss of $40. T will receive an allocation of $40 of tax loss under the principles of section 704(c). However, because T has a negative $50 basis adjustment in the nondepreciable property, T recognizes a $10 gain from the partnership's sale of the property.

Example (2). A and B form equal partnership PRS. A contributes nondepreciable property with a fair market value of $100 and an adjusted tax basis of $50. B contributes $100 cash. PRS will use the traditional allocation method under §1.704–3(b). A sells its interest to T for $100. PRS has an election in effect to adjust the basis of partnership property under section 754. Therefore, T receives a $50 basis adjustment under section 743 (b) that, under section 755, is allocated to the nondepreciable property. PRS then sells the nondepreciable property for $90. PRS recognizes a book loss of $10 (allocated equally between T and B) and a tax gain of $40. T will receive an allocation of the entire $40 of tax gain under the principles of section 704(c). However, because T has a $50 basis adjustment in the property, T recognizes a $10 loss from the partnership's sale of the property.

Example (3). A and B form equal partnership PRS. PRS will make allocations under section 704(c) using the remedial allocation method described in §1.704–3(d). A contributes nondepreciable property with a fair market value of $100 and an adjusted tax basis of $150. B contributes $100 cash. A sells its partnership interest to T for $100. PRS has an election in effect to adjust the basis of partnership property under section 754. T receives a negative $50 basis adjustment under section 743(b) that, under section 755, is allocated to the property. The partnership then sells the property for $120. The partnership recognizes a $20 book gain and a $30 tax loss. The book gain will be allocated equally between the partners. The entire $30 tax loss will be allocated to T under the principles of section 704(c). To match its $10 share of book gain, B will be allocated $10 of remedial gain, and T will be allocated an offsetting $10 of remedial loss. T was allocated a total of $40 of tax loss with respect to the property. However, because T has a negative $50 basis adjustment to the property, T recognizes a $10 gain from the partnership's sale of the property.

(4) Effect of basis adjustment in determining items of deduction.—(i) Increases.

(A) Additional deduction. The amount of any positive basis adjustment that is recovered by the transferee in any year is added to the transferee's distributive share of the partnership's depreciation or amortization deductions for the year. The basis adjustment is adjusted under section 1016(a)(2) to reflect the recovery of the basis adjustment.

(B) Recovery period.

(1) In general. Except as provided in paragraph (j)(4)(i)(B)(2) of this section, for purposes of section 168, if the basis of a partnership's recovery property is increased as a result of the transfer of a partnership interest, then the increased portion of the basis is taken into account as if it were newly-purchased recovery property placed in service when the transfer occurs. Consequently, any applicable recovery period and method may be used to determine the recovery allowance with respect to the increased portion of the basis. However, no change is made for purposes of determining the recovery allowance under section 168 for the portion of the basis for which there is no increase.

(2) Remedial allocation method. If a partnership elects to use the remedial allocation method described in §1.704–3(d) with respect to an item of the partnership's recovery property, then the portion of any increase in the basis of the item of the partnership's recovery property under section 743(b) that is attributable to section 704(c) built-in gain is recovered over the remaining recovery period for the partnership's excess book basis in the property as determined in the final sentence of §1.704–3(d)(2). Any remaining portion of the basis increase is recovered under paragraph (j)(4)(i)(B)(1) of this section.

(C) Examples. The provisions of this paragraph (j)(4)(i) are illustrated by the following examples:

Example (1). **(i)** A, B, and C are equal partners in partnership PRS, which owns Asset 1, an item of depreciable property that has a fair market value in excess of its adjusted tax basis. C sells its interest in PRS to T while PRS has an election in effect under section 754. PRS, therefore, increases the basis of Asset 1 with respect to T.

(ii) Assume that in the year following the transfer of the partnership interest to T, T's distributive share of the partnership's common basis depreciation deductions from Asset 1 is $1,000. Also assume that, under paragraph (j)(4)(i)(B) of this section, the amount of the basis adjustment under section 743(b) that T recovers during the year is $500. The total amount of depreciation deductions from Asset 1 reported by T is equal to $1,500.

Example (2). **(i)** A and B form equal partnership PRS. A contributes property with an adjusted basis of $100,000 and a fair market value of $500,000. B contributes $500,000 cash. When PRS is formed, the property has five years remaining in its recovery period. The partnership's adjusted basis of $100,000 will, therefore, be recovered over the five years remaining in the property' recovery period. PRS elects to use the remedial allocation method under §1.704–3(d) with respect to the property. If PRS had purchased the property at the time of the partnership's formation, the basis of the property would have been recovered over a 10-year period. The $400,000 of section 704(c) built-in gain will, therefore, be amortized under § 1.704–3(d) over a 10-year period beginning at the time of the partnership's formation.

(ii) **(A)** Except for the depreciation deductions, PRS's expenses equal its income in each year of the first two years commencing with the year the partnership is formed. After two years, A's share of the adjusted basis of partnership property is $120,000, while B's is $440,000:

Capital Accounts				
	A		B	
	Book	Tax	Book	Tax
Initial Contribution	$500,000	$100,000	$500,000	$500,000
Depreciation				
Year 1	(30,000)	—	(30,000)	(20,000)
Remedial	—	10,000	—	(10,000)
	470,000	110,000	470,000	470,000
Depreciation				
Year 2	(30,000)	—	(30,000)	(20,000)
Remedial	—	10,000	—	(10,000)
	440,000	120,000	440,000	440,000

(B) A sells its interest in PRS to T for its fair market value of $440,000. A valid election under section 754 is in effect with respect to the sale of the partnership interest. Accordingly, PRS makes an adjustment, pursuant to section 743(b), to increase the basis of partnership property. Under section 743(b), the amount of the basis adjustment is equal to $320,000. Under section 755, the entire basis adjustment is allocated to the property.

(iii) At the time of the transfer, $320,000 of section 704(c) built-in gain from the property was still reflected on the partnership's books, and all of the basis adjustment is attributable to section 704(c) built-in gain. Therefore, the basis adjustment will be recovered over the remaining recovery period for the section 704(c) built-in gain under §1.704–3(d).

(ii) Decreases.

(A) Reduced deduction. The amount of any negative basis adjustment allocated to an item of depreciable or amortizable property that is recovered in any year first decreases the transferee's distributive share of the partnership's depreciation or amortization deductions from that item of property for the year. If the amount of the basis adjustment recovered in any year exceeds the transferee's distributive share of the partnership's depreciation or amortization deductions from the item of property, then the transferee's distributive share of the partnership's depreciation or amortization deductions from other items of partnership property is decreased. The transfree then recognizes ordinary income to the extent of the excess, if any, of the amount of the basis adjustment recovered in any year over the transferee's distributive share of the partnership's depreciation or amortization deductions from all items of property.

(B) Recovery period. For purposes of section 168, if the basis of an item of a partnership's recovery property is decreased as the result of the transfer of an interest in the partnership, then the decrease is recovered over the remaining useful life of the item of the partnership's recovery property. The portion of the decrease that is recovered in any year during the recovery period is equal to the product of—

(1) The amount of the decrease to the item's adjusted basis (determined as of the date of the transfer); multiplied by

(2) A fraction, the numerator of which is the portion of the adjusted basis of the item recovered by the partnership in that year, and the denominator of which is the adjusted basis of the item on the date of the transfer (determined prior to any basis adjustments).

(C) Examples. The provisions of this paragraph (j)(4)(ii) are illustrated by the following examples:

Example (1). A, B, and C are equal partners in partnership PRS, which owns Asset 2, an item of depreciable property that has a fair market value that is less than its adjusted tax basis. C sells its interest in PRS to T while PRS has an election in effect under section 754. PRS, therefore, decreases the basis of Asset 2 with respect to T.

(ii) Assume that in the year following the transfer of the partnership interest to T, T's distributive share of the partnership's common basis depreciation deductions from Asset 2 is $1,000. Also assume that, under paragraph (j)(4)(ii)(B) of this section, the amount of the basis adjustment under section 743(b) that T recovers during the year is $500. The total amount of depreciation deductions from Asset 2 reported by T is equal to $500.

Example (2). (i) A and B form equal partnership PRS. A contributes property with an adjusted basis of $100,000 and a fair market value of $50,000. B contributes $50,000 cash. When PRS is formed, the property has five years remaining in its recovery period. The partnership's adjusted basis of $100,000 will, therefore, be recovered over the five years remaining in the property's recovery period. PRS uses the traditional allocation method under §1.704–3(b) with respect to the property. As a result, B will receive $5,000 of depreciation deductions from the property in each of years 1–5, and A, as the contributing partner, will receive $15,000 of depreciation deductions in each of these years.

(ii) Except for the depreciation deductions, PRS's expenses equal its income in each of the first two years commencing with the year the partnership is formed. After two years, A's share of the adjusted basis of partnership property is $70,000, while B's is $40,000. A sells its interest in PRS to T for its fair market value of $40,000. A valid election under section 754 is in effect with respect to the sale of the partnership interest. Accordingly, PRS makes an adjustment, pursuant to section 743(b), to decrease the basis of partnership property. Under section 743(b), the amount of the adjustment is equal to ($30,000). Under section 755, the entire adjustment is allocated to the property.

(iii) The basis of the property at the time of the transfer of the partnership interest was $60,000. In each of years 3 through 5, the partnership will realize depreciation deductions of $20,000 from the property. Thus, one third of the negative basis adjustment ($10,000) will be recovered in each of years 3 through 5. Consequently, T will be allocated, for tax purposes, depreciation of $15,000 each year from the partnership and will recover $10,000 of its negative basis adjustment. Thus, T's net depreciation deduction from the partnership in each year is $5,000.

Example (3). **(i)** A, B, and C are equal partners in partnership PRS, which owns Asset 2, an item of depreciable property that has a fair market value that is less than its adjusted tax basis. C sells its interest in PRS to T while PRS has an election in effect under section 754. PRS, therefore, decreases the basis of Asset 2 with respect to T.

(ii) Assume that in the year following the transfer of the partnership interest to T, T's distributive share of the partnership's common basis depreciation deductions from Asset 2 is $500. PRS allocates no other depreciation to T. Also assume that, under paragraph (j)(4)(ii)(B) of this section, the amount of the negative basis adjustment that T recovers during the year is $1,000. T will report $500 of ordinary income because the amount of the negative basis adjustment recovered during the year exceeds T's distributive share of the partnership's common basis depreciation deductions from Asset 2.

(5) Depletion. Where an adjustment is made under section 743(b) to the basis of partnership property subject to depletion, any depletion allowance is determined separately for each partner, including the transferee partner, based on the partner's interest in such property. See §1.702–1 (a)(8). For partnerships that hold oil and gas properties that are depleted at the partner level under section 613A(c)(7)(D), the transferee partner (and not the partnership) must make the basis adjustments, if any, required under section 743(b) with respect to such properties. See §1.613A–3(e)(6)(iv).

(6) Example. The provisions of paragraph (j)(5) of this section are illustrated by the following example:

Example. A, B, and C each contributes $5,000 cash to form partnership PRS, which purchases a coal property for $15,000. A, B, and C have equal interests in capital and profits. C subsequently sells its partnership interest to T for $100,000 when the election under section 754 is in effect. T has a basis adjustment under section 743(b) for the coal property of $95,000 (the difference between T's basis, $100,000, and its share of the basis of partnership property, $5,000). Assume that the depletion allowance computed under the percentage method would be $21,000 for the taxable year so that each partner would be entitled to $7,000 as its share of the deduction for depletion. However, under the cost depletion method, at an assumed rate of 10 percent, the allowance with respect to T's one-third interest which has a basis to him of $100,000 ($5,000 plus its basis adjustment of $95,000) is $10,000, although the cost depletion allowance with respect to the one-third interest of A and B in the coal property, each of which has a basis of $5,000, is only $500. For partners A and B, the percentage depletion is greater than cost depletion and each will deduct $7,000 based on the percentage depletion method. However, as to T, the transferee partner, the cost depletion method results in a greater allowance and T will, therefore, deduct $10,000 based on cost depletion. See section 613(a).

(k) Returns.—(1) Statement of adjustments.

(i) In general. A partnership that must adjust the bases of partnership properties under section 743(b) must attach a statement to the partnership return for the year of the transfer setting forth the name and taxpayer identification number of the transferee as well as the computation of the adjustment and the partnership properties to which the adjustment has been allocated.

(ii) Special rule. Where an interest is transferred in a partnership which holds oil and gas properties that are depleted at the partner level under section 613A(c)(7)(D), the transferee must attach a statement to the transferee's return for the year of the transfer, setting forth the computation of the basis adjustment under section 743(b) which is allocable to such properties and the specific properties to which the adjustment has been allocated.

(iii) Example. The provisions of paragraph (k)(1)(ii) of this section are illustrated by the following example:

Example (i) Partnership XYZ owns a single section 613A(c)(7)(D) domestic oil and gas property (Property) and other non-depletable assets. A, a partner in XYZ with an adjusted tax basis in Property of $100 (excluding any prior adjustments under section 743(b)), sells its partnership interest to B for $800 cash. Under §1.613A–3(e)(6)(iv), A's adjusted basis of $100 in Property carries over to B.

(ii) Under section 755, XYZ determines that Property accounts for 50% of the fair market value of all partnership assets. The remaining 50% of B's purchase price ($400) is attributable to non-depletable property. XYZ must provide a statement to B containing the portion of B's adjusted basis attributable to non-depletable property ($400). Under this paragraph (k)(1), XYZ must report basis adjustments under section 743(b) to non-depletable property. B must report basis adjustments under section 743(b) to Property.

(2) Requirement that transferee notify partnership.

(i) Sale or exchange. A transferee that acquires, by sale or exchange, an interest in a partnership with an election under section 754 in effect for the taxable year of the transfer, must notify the partnership, in writing, within 30 days of the sale or exchange. The written notice to the partnership must be signed under penalties of perjury and must include the names and addresses of the transferee and (if ascertainable) of the transferor, the taxpayer identification numbers of the transferee and (if ascertainable) of the transferor,the relationship (if any) between the transferee and the transferor, the date of the transfer, the amount of any liabilities assumed or taken subject to by the transferee, and the amount of any money, the fair market value of any other property delivered or to be delivered for the transferred interest in the partnership, and any other information necessary for the partnership to compute the transferee's basis.

(ii) Transfer on death. A transferee that acquires, on the death of a partner, an interest in a partnership with an election under section 754 in effect for the taxable year of the transfer, must notify the partnership, in writing, within one year of the death of the deceased partner. The written notice to the partnership must be signed under penalties of perjury and must include the names and addresses of the deceased partner and the transferee, the taxpayer identification numbers of the deceased partner and the transferee, the relationship (if any) between the transferee and the transferor, the deceased partner's date of death, the date on which the transferee became the owner of the partnership interest, the fair market value of the partnership interest on the applicable date of valuation set forth in section 1014, and the manner in which the fair market value of the partnership interest was determined.

(iii) Nominee reporting. If a partnership interest is transferred to a nominee which is required to furnish the statement under section 6031(c)(1) to the partnership, the nominee may satisfy the notice requirement contained in this paragraph (k)(2) by providing the statement required under §1.6031(c)–1T, provided that the statement satisfies all requirements of §1.6031(c)–1T and this paragraph (k)(2).

(3) Reliance. In making the adjustments under section 743(b) and any statement or return relating to such adjustments under this section, a partnership may rely on the written notice provided by a transferee pursuant to paragraph (k)(2) of this section to determine the transferee's basis in a partnership interest. The previous sentence shall not apply if any partner who has responsibility for federal income tax reporting by the partnership has knowledge of facts indicating that the statement is clearly erroneous.

(4) Partnership not required to make or report adjustments under section 743(b) until it has notice of the transfer. A partnership is not required to make the adjustments under section 743(b) (or any statement or return relating to those adjustments) with respect to any transfer until it has been notified of the transfer. For purposes of this section, a partnership is notified of a transfer when either—

(i) The partnership receives the written notice from the transferee required under paragraph (k)(2) of this section; or

(ii) Any partner who has responsibility for federal income tax reporting by the partnership has knowledge that there has been a transfer of a partnership interest.

(5) Effect on partnership of the failure of the transferee to comply. If the transferee fails to provide the partnership with the written notice required by paragraph (k)(2) of this section, the partnership must attach a statement to its return in the year that the partnership is otherwise notified of the transfer. This statement must set forth the name and taxpayer identification number (if ascertainable) of the transferee. In addition, the following statement must be prominently displayed in capital letters on the first page of the partnership's return for such year, and on the first page of any schedule or information statement relating to such transferee's share of income, credits, deductions, etc.: "RETURN FILED PURSUANT TO §1.743–1(k)(5)." The partnership will then be entitled to report the transferee's share of partnership items without adjustment to reflect the transferee's basis adjustment in partnership property. If, following the filing of a return pursuant to this paragraph (k)(5), the transferee provides the applicable written notice to the partnership, the partnership must make such adjustments as are necessary to adjust the basis of partnership property (as of the date of the transfer) in any amended return otherwise to be filed by the partnership or in the next annual partnership return of income to be regularly filed by the partnership. At such time, the partnership must also provide the transferee with such information as is necessary for the transferee to amend its prior returns to properly reflect the adjustment under section 743(b).

(l) Effective date. This section applies to transfers of partnership interests that occur on or after December 15, 1999.

Provisions Common To Part II, Subchapter K, Chapter 1 of The Code

§ 1.751–1 Unrealized receivables and inventory items.

(a) Sale or exchange of interest in a partnership—(1) Character of amount realized. To the extent that money or property received by a partner in exchange for all or part of his partnership interest is attributable to his share of the value of partnership unrealized receivables or substantially appreciated inventory items, the money or fair market value of the property received shall be considered as an amount realized from the sale or exchange of property other than a capital asset. The remainder of the total amount realized on the sale or exchange of the partnership interest is realized from the sale or exchange of a capital asset under section 741. For definition of "unrealized receivables" and "inventory items which have appreciated substantially in value," see section 751(c) and (d). Unrealized receivables and substantially appreciated inventory items are hereafter in this section referred to as "section 751 property." See paragraph (e) of this section.

(2) Determination of gain or loss. The income or loss realized by a partner upon the sale or exchange of its interest in section 751 property is the amount of income or loss from section 751 property (including any remedial allocations under §1.704–3(d)) that would have been allocated to the partner (to the extent attributable to the partnership interest sold or exchanged) if the partnership had sold all of its property in a fully taxable transaction for cash in an amount equal to the fair market value of such property (taking into account section 7701(g)) immediately prior to the partner's transfer of the interest in the partnership. Any gain or loss recognized that is attributable to section 751 property will be ordinary gain or loss. The difference between the amount of capital gain or loss that the partner would realize in the absence of section 751 and the amount of ordinary income or loss determined under this paragraph (a)(2) is the transferor's capital gain or loss on the sale of its partnership interest. See § 1.460–4(k)(2)(iv)(E) for rules relating to the amount of ordinary income or loss attributable to a contract accounted for under a long-term contract method of accounting.

(3) Statement required. A partner selling or exchanging any part of its interest in a partnership that has any section 751 property at the time of sale or exchange must submit with its income tax return for the taxable year in which the sale or exchange occurs a statement setting forth separately the following information:

(i) The date of the sale or exchange;

(ii) The amount of any gain or loss attributable to the section 751 property; and

(iii) The amount of any gain or loss attributable to capital gain or loss on the sale of the partnership interest.

(b) Certain distributions treated as sales or exchanges— (1) In general. (i) Certain distributions to which section 751(b) applies are treated in part as sales or exchanges of property between the partnership and the distributee partner, and not as distributions to which sections 731 through 736 apply. A distribution treated as a sale or exchange under section 751(b) is not subject to the provisions of section 707(b). Section 751(b) applies whether or not the distribution is in liquidation of the distributee partner's entire interest in the partnership. However, section 751(b) applies only to the extent that a partner either receives section 751 property in exchange for his relinquishing any part of his interest in other property, or receives other property in exchange for his relinquishing any part of his interest in section 751 property.

(ii) Section 751(b) does not apply to a distribution to a partner which is not in exchange for his interest in other partnership property. Thus, section 751(b) does not apply to the extent that a distribution consists of the distributee partner's share of section 751 property or his share of other property. Similarly, section 751(b) does not apply to current drawings or to advances against the partner's distributive share, or to a distribution which is, in fact, a gift or payment for services or for the use of capital. In determining whether a partner has received only his share of either section 751 property or of other property, his interest in such property remaining in the partnership immediately after a distribution must be taken into account. For example, the section 751 property in partnership ABC has a fair market value of $100,000 in which partner A has an interest of 30 percent, or $30,000. If A receives $20,000 of section 751 property in a distribution, and continues to have a 30-percent interest in the $80,000 of section 751 property remaining in the partnership after the distribution, only $6,000 ($30,000 minus $24,000 (30 percent of $80,000)) of the section 751 property received by him will be considered to be his share of such property. The remaining $14,000 ($20,000 minus $6,000) received is in excess of his share.

(iii) If a distribution is, in part, a distribution of the distributee partner's share of section 751 property, or of other property (including money) and, in part, a distribution in exchange of such properties, the distribution shall be divided for the purpose of applying section 751(b). The rules of section 751(b) shall first apply to the part of the distribution treated as a sale or exchange of such properties, and then the rules of sections 731 through 736 shall apply to the part of the distribution not treated as a sale or exchange. See paragraph (b)(4)(ii) of this section for treatment of payments under section 736(a).

(2) Distribution of section 751 property (unrealized receivables or substantially appreciated inventory items). (i) To the extent that a partner receives section 751 property in a distribution in exchange for any part of his interest in partnership property (including money) other than section 751 property, the transaction shall be treated as a sale or exchange of such properties between the distributee partner and the partnership (as constituted after the distribution).

(ii) At the time of the distribution, the partnership (as constituted after the distribution) realizes ordinary income or loss on the sale or exchange of the section 751 property. The amount of the income or loss to the partnership will be measured by the difference between the adjusted basis to the partnership of the section 751 property considered as sold to or exchanged with the partner, and the fair market value of the distributee partner's interest in other partnership property which he relinquished in the exchange. In computing the partners' distributive shares of such ordinary income or loss, the income or loss shall be allocated only to partners other than the distributee and separately taken into account under section 702(a)(8).

(iii) At the time of the distribution, the distributee partner realizes gain or loss measured by the difference between his adjusted basis for the property relinquished in the exchange (including any special basis adjustment which he may have) and the fair market value of the section 751 property received by him in exchange for his interest in other property which he has relinquished. The distributee's adjusted basis for the property relinquished is the basis such property would have had under section 732 (including subsection (d) thereof) if the distributee partner had received such property in a current distribution immediately before the actual distribution which is treated wholly or partly as a sale or exchange under section 751(b). The character of the gain or loss to the distributee partner shall be determined by the character of the property in which he relinquished his interest.

(3) Distribution of partnership property other than section 751 property. (i) To the extent that a partner receives a distribution of partnership property (including money) other than section 751 property in exchange for any part of his interest in section 751 property of the partnership, the distribution shall be treated as a sale or exchange of such properties between the distributee partner and the partnership (as constituted after the distribution).

(ii) At the time of the distribution, the partnership (as constituted after the distribution) realizes gain or loss on the sale or exchange of the property other than section 751 property. The amount of the gain to the partnership will be measured by the difference between the adjusted basis to the partnership of the distributed property considered as sold to or exchanged with the partner, and the fair market value of the distributee partner's interest in section 751 property which he relinquished in the exchange. The character of the gain or loss to the partnership is determined by the character of the distributed property treated as sold or exchanged by the partnership. In computing the partners' distributive shares of such gain or loss, the gain or loss shall be allocated only to partners other than the distributee and separately taken into account under section 702(a)(8).

(iii) At the time of the distribution, the distributee partner realizes ordinary income or loss on the sale or exchange of the section 751 property. The amount of the distributee partner's income or loss shall be measured by the difference between his adjusted basis for the section 751 property relinquished in the exchange (including any special basis adjustment which he may have), and the fair market value of other property (including money) received by him in exchange for his interest in the section 751 property which he has relinquished. The distributee partner's adjusted basis for the section 751 property relinquished is the basis such property would have had under section 732 (including subsection (d) thereof) if the distributee partner had received such property in a current distribution immediately before the actual distribution which is treated wholly or partly as a sale or exchange under section 751(b).

(4) Exceptions. (i) Section 751(b) does not apply to the distribution to a partner of property which the distributee partner contributed to the partnership. The distribution of such property is governed by the rules set forth in sections 731 through 736, relating to distributions by a partnership.

(ii) Section 751(b) does not apply to payments made to a retiring partner or to a deceased partner's successor in interest to the extent that, under section 736(a), such payments constitute a distributive share of partnership income or guaranteed payments. Payments to a retiring partner or to a deceased partner's successor in interest for his interest in unrealized receivables of the partnership in excess of their partnership basis, including any special basis adjustment for them to which such partner is entitled, constitute payments under section 736(a) and, therefore, are not subject to section 751(b). However, payments under section 736(b) which are considered as made in exchange for an interest in partnership property are subject to section 751(b) to the extent that they involve an exchange of substantially appreciated inventory items for other property. Thus, payments to a retiring partner or to a deceased partner's successor in interest under section 736 must first be divided between payments under section 736 (a) and section 736(b). The section 736(b) payments must then be divided, if there is an exchange of substantially appreciated inventory items for other property, between the payments treated as a sale or exchange under section 751(b) and payments treated as a distribution under sections 731 through 736. See subparagraph (1)(iii) of this paragraph, and section 736 and § 1.736–1.

(5) Statement required. A partnership which distributes section 751 property to a partner in exchange for his interest in other partnership property, or which distributes other property in exchange for any part of the partner's interest in section 751 property, shall submit with its return for the year of the distribution a statement showing the computation of any income, gain, or loss to the partnership under the provisions of section 751(b) and this paragraph. The distributee partner shall submit with his return a statement showing the computation of any income, gain, or loss to him. Such statement shall contain information similar to that required under paragraph (a)(3) of this section.

(c) Unrealized receivables.* **(1)** The term "unrealized receivables," as used in subchapter K, chapter 1 of the Code, means any rights (contractual or otherwise) to payment for—

(i) Goods delivered or to be delivered (to the extent that such payment would be treated as received for property other than a capital asset), or

(ii) Services rendered or to be rendered,

to the extent that income arising from such rights to payment was not previously includible in income under the method of accounting employed by the partnership. Such rights must have arisen under contracts or agreements in existence at the time of sale or distribution, although the partnership may not be able to enforce payment until a later time. For example, the term includes trade accounts receivable of a cash method taxpayer, and rights to payment for work or goods begun but incomplete at the time of the sale or distribution.

(2) The basis for such unrealized receivables shall include all costs or expenses attributable thereto paid or accrued but not previously taken into account under the partnership method of accounting.

(3) In determining the amount of the sale price attributable to such unrealized receivables, or their value in a distribution treated as a sale or exchange, full account shall be taken not only of the estimated cost of completing performance of the contract or agreement, but also of the time between the sale or distribution and the time of payment.

(4)(i) With respect to any taxable year of a partnership ending after September 12, 1966 (but only in respect of expenditures paid or incurred after that date), the term *unrealized receivables*, for purposes of this section and sections 731, 736, 741, and 751, also includes potential gain from mining property defined in section 617(f)(2). With respect to each item of partnership mining property so defined, the potential gain is the amount that would be treated as gain to which section 617(d)(1) would apply if (at the time of the transaction described in section 731, 736, 741, or 751, as the case may be) the item were sold by the partnership at its fair market value.

(ii) With respect to sales, exchanges, or other dispositions after December 31, 1975, in any taxable year of a partnership ending after that date, the term *unrealized receivables,* for purposes of this section and sections 731, 736, 741, and 751, also includes potential gain from stock in a DISC as described in section 992(a). With respect to stock in such a DISC, the potential gain is the amount that would be treated as gain to which section 995(c) would apply if (at the time of the transaction described in section 731, 736, 741, or 751, as the case may be) the stock were sold by the partnership at its fair market value.

(iii) With respect to any taxable year of a partnership beginning after December 31, 1962, the term *unrealized receivables,* for purposes of this section and sections 731, 736, 741, and 751, also includes potential gain from section 1245 property. With respect to each item of partnership section 1245 property (as defined in section 1245(a)(3)), potential gain from section 1245 property is the amount that would be treated as gain to which section 1245(a)(1) would apply if (at the time of the transaction described in section 731, 736, 741, or 751, as the case may be) the item of section 1245 property were sold by the partnership at its fair market value. See § 1.1245–1(e)(1). For example, if a partnership would recognize under section 1245(a)(1) gain of $600 upon a sale of one item of section 1245

*Editorial comment: The Regulations do not include the effect of the Revenue Reconciliation Act of 1993. See § 751(c).

property and gain of $300 upon a sale of its only other item of such property, the potential section 1245 income of the partnership would be $900.

(iv) With respect to transfers after October 9, 1975, and to sales, exchanges, and distributions taking place after that date, the term *unrealized receivables,* for purposes of this section and sections 731, 736, 741, and 751, also includes potential gain from stock in certain foreign corporations as described in section 1248. With respect to stock in such a foreign corporation, the potential gain is the amount that would be treated as gain to which section 1248(a) would apply if (at the time of the transaction described in section 731, 736, 741, or 751, as the case may be) the stock were sold by the partnership at its fair market value.

(v) With respect to any taxable year of a partnership ending after December 31, 1963, the term *unrealized receivables,* for purposes of this section and sections 731, 736, 741, and 751, also includes potential gain from section 1250 property. With respect to each item of partnership section 1250 property (as defined in section 1250(c)), potential gain from section 1250 property is the amount that would be treated as gain to which section 1250(a) would apply if (at the time of the transaction described in section 731, 736, 741, or 751, as the case may be) the item of section 1250 property were sold by the partnership at its fair market value. See § 1.1250–1(f)(1).

(vi) With respect to any taxable year of a partnership beginning after December 31, 1969, the term *unrealized receivables,* for purposes of this section and sections 731, 736, 741, and 751, also includes potential gain from farm recapture property as defined in section 1251(e)(1) (as in effect before enactment of the Tax Reform Act of 1984). With respect to each item of partnership farm recapture property so defined, the potential gain is the amount which would be treated as gain to which section 1251(c) (as in effect before enactment of the Tax Reform Act of 1984) would apply if (at the time of the transaction described in section 731, 736, 741, or 751, as the case may be) the item were sold by the partnership at its fair market value.

(vii) With respect to any taxable year of a partnership beginning after December 31, 1969, the term *unrealized receivables,* for purposes of this section and sections 731, 736, 741, and 751, also includes potential gain from farm land as defined in section 1252(a)(2). With respect to each item of partnership farm land so defined, the potential gain is the amount that would be treated as gain to which section 1252(a)(l) would apply if (at the time of the transaction described in section 731, 736, 741, or 751, as the case may be) the item were sold by the partnership at its fair market value.

(viii) With respect to transactions which occur after December 31, 1976; in any taxable year of a partnership ending after that date, the term *unrealized receivables,* for purposes of this section and sections 731, 736, 741, and 751, also includes potential gain from franchises, trademarks, or trade names referred to in section 1253(a). With respect to each such item so referred to in section 1253(a), the potential gain is the amount that would be treated as gain to which section 1253(a) would apply if (at the time of the transaction described in section 731, 736, 741, or 751, as the case may be) the items were sold by the partnership at its fair market value.

(ix) With respect to any taxable year of a partnership ending after December 31, 1975, the term *unrealized receivables,* for purposes of this section and sections 731, 736, 741, and 751, also includes potential gain under section 1254(a) from natural resource recapture property as defined in § 1.1254–1(b)(2). With respect to each separate partnership natural resource recapture property so described, the potential gain is the amount that would be treated as gain to which section 1254(a) would apply if (at the time of the transaction described in section 731, 736, 741, or 751, as the case may be) the property were sold by the partnership at its fair market value.

(5) For purposes of subtitle A of the Internal Revenue Code, the basis of any potential gain described in paragraph (c)(4) of this section is zero.

(6) (i) If (at the time of any transaction referred to in paragraph (c)(4) of this section) a partnership holds property described in paragraph (c)(4) of this section and if—

(A) A partner had a special basis adjustment under section 743(b) in respect of the property;

(B) The basis under section 732 of the property if distributed to the partner would reflect a special basis adjustment under section 732(d); or

(C) On the date a partner acquired a partnership interest by way of a sale or exchange (or upon the death of another partner) the partnership owned the property and an election under section 754 was in effect with respect to the partnership, the partner's share of any potential gain described in paragraph (c)(4) of this section is determined under paragraph (c)(6)(ii) of this section.

(ii) The partner's share of the potential gain described in paragraph (c)(4) of this section in respect of the property to which this paragraph (c)(6)(ii) applies is that amount of gain that the partner would recognize under section 617(d)(1), 995(c), 1245(a), 1248(a), 1250(a), 1251(c) (as in effect before the Tax Reform Act of 1984), 1252(a), 1253(a), or 1254(a) (as the case may be) upon a sale of the property by the partnership, except that, for purposes of this paragraph (c)(6) the partner's share of such gain is determined in a manner that is consistent with the manner in which the partner's share of partnership property is determined; and the amount of a potential special basis adjustment under section 732(d) is treated as if it were the amount of a special basis adjustment under section 743(b). For example, in determining, for purposes of this paragraph (c)(6), the amount of gain that a partner would recognize under section 1245 upon a sale of partnership property, the items allocated under § 1.1245–1(e)(3)(ii) are allocated to the partner in the same manner as the partner's share of partnership property is determined. See § 1.1250–1(f) for rules similar to those contained in § 1.1245–1(e)(3)(ii).

(d) Inventory items which have substantially appreciated in value—(1) Substantial appreciation.* Partnership inventory items shall be considered to have appreciated substantially in value if, at the time of the sale or distribution, the total fair market value of all the inventory items of the partnership exceeds 120 percent of the aggregate adjusted basis for such property in the hands of the partnership (without regard to any special basis adjustment of any partner) and, in addition, exceeds 10 percent of the fair market value of all partnership property other than money. The terms "inventory items which have appreciated substantially in value" or "substantially appreciated inventory items" refer to the aggregate of all partnership inventory items. These terms do not refer to specific partnership inventory items or to specific groups of such items. For example, any distribution of inventory items by a partnership the inventory items of which as a whole are substantially appreciated in value shall be a distribution of substantially appreciated inventory items for the purposes of section 751(b), even though the specific inventory items distributed may not be appreciated in value. Similarly, if the aggregate of partnership inventory items are not substantially appreciated in value, a distribution of specific inventory items, the value of which is more than 120 percent of their adjusted basis, will not constitute a distribution of substantially appreciated inventory items. For the purpose of this paragraph, the "fair market value" of inventory items has the same meaning as "market" value in the regulations under section 471, relating to general rule for inventories.

(2) Inventory items. The term "inventory items" as used in subchapter K, chapter 1 of the Code, includes the following types of property:

(i) Stock in trade of the partnership, or other property of a kind which would properly be included in the inventory of the partnership if on hand at the close of the taxable year, or property held by the partnership primarily for sale to customers in the ordinary course of its trade or business. See section 1221(1).

(ii) Any other property of the partnership which, on sale or exchange by the partnership, would be considered property other than a capital asset and other than property described in section 1231. Thus, accounts receivable acquired in the ordinary course of business for services or from the sale of stock in trade constitute inventory items (see section 1221(4)), as do any unrealized receivables.

(iii) Any other property retained by the partnership which, if held by the partner selling his partnership interest or receiving a distribution described in section 751(b), would be considered property described in subdivision (i) or (ii) of this subparagraph. Property actually distributed to the partner does not come within the provisions of section 751(d)(2)(C) and this subdivision.

(e) Section 751 property and other property. For the purposes of this section, "section 751 property" means unrealized receivables or substantially appreciated inventory items, and "other property" means all property (including money) except section 751 property.

* * *

(g) Examples. Application of the provisions of section 751 may be illustrated by the following examples:

Example (1). (i) (A) A and B are equal partners in personal service partnership PRS. B transfers its interest in PRS to T for $15,000 when PRS's balance sheet (reflecting a cash receipts and disbursements method of accounting) is as follows:

*Editorial comment: The Regulations do not include the effect of the Revenue Reconciliation Act of 1993. See § 751(d).

ASSETS

	Adjusted basis per books	Market value
Cash	$3,000	$3,000
Loans receivable	10,000	10,000
Capital assets	7,000	5,000
Unrealized receivables	0	14,000
Total	20,000	32,000

LIABILITIES AND CAPITAL

	Per books	Value
Liabilities	$2,000	$2,000
Capital:		
A	9,000	15,000
B	9,000	15,000
Total	20,000	32,000

(B) None of the assets owned by PRS is section 704(c) property, and the capital assets are nondepreciable. The total amount realized by B is $16,000, consisting of the cash received, $15,000, plus $1,000, B's share of the partnership liabilities assumed by T. See section 752. B's undivided half-interest in the partnership property includes a half-interest in the partnership's unrealized receivables items. B's basis for its partnership interest is $10,000 ($9,000, plus $1,000, B's share of partnership liabilities). If section 751(a) did not apply to the sale, B would recognize $6,000 of capital gain from the sale of the interest in PRS. However, section 751(a) does apply to the sale.

(ii) If PRS sold all of its section 751 property in a fully taxable transaction immediately prior to the transfer of B's partnership interest to T, B would have been allocated $7,000 of ordinary income from the sale of PRS's unrealized receivables. Therefore, B will recognize $7,000 of ordinary income with respect to the unrealized receivables. The difference between the amount of capital gain or loss that the partner would realize in the absence of section 751 ($6,000) and the amount of ordinary income or loss determined under paragraph (a)(2) of this section ($7,000) is the transferor's capital gain or loss on the sale of its partnership interest. In this case, B will recognize a $1,000 capital loss.

Example (2). (a) Facts. Partnership ABC makes a distribution to partner C in liquidation of his entire one-third interest in the partnership. At the time of the distribution, the balance sheet of the partnership, which uses the accrual method of accounting, is as follows:

ASSETS

	Adjusted basis per books	Market value
Cash	$15,000	$15,000
Accounts receivable	9,000	9,000
Inventory	21,000	30,000
Depreciable property	42,000	48,000
Land	9,000	9,000
Total	96,000	111,000

LIABILITIES AND CAPITAL

	Per books	Value
Current liabilities	$15,000	$15,000
Mortgage payable	21,000	21,000
Capital:		
A	20,000	25,000
B	20,000	25,000
C	20,000	25,000
Total	96,000	111,000

The distribution received by C consists of $10,000 cash and depreciable property with a fair market value of $15,000 and an adjusted basis to the partnership of $15,000.

(b) Presence of section 751 property. The partnership has no unrealized receivables, but the dual test provided in section 751(d)(1) must be applied to determine whether the inventory items of the partnership, in the aggregate, have appreciated substantially in value. The fair market value of all partnership inventory items, $39,000 (inventory $30,000, and accounts receivable $9,000), exceeds 120 percent of the $30,000 adjusted basis of such items to the partnership. The fair market value of the inventory items, $39,000, also exceeds 10 percent of the fair market value of all partnership property other than money (10 percent of $96,000 or $9,600). Therefore, the partnership inventory items have substantially appreciated in value.

(c) The properties exchanged. Since C's entire partnership interest is to be liquidated, the provisions of section 736 are applicable. No part of the payment, however, is considered as a distributive share or as a guaranteed payment under section 736(a) because the entire payment is made for C's interest in partnership property. Therefore, the entire payment is for an interest in partnership property under section 736(b), and, to the extent applicable, subject to the rules of section 751. In the distribution, C received his share of cash ($5,000) and $15,000 in depreciable property ($1,000 less than his $16,000 share). In addition, he received other partnership property ($5,000 cash and $12,000 liabilities assumed, treated as money distributed under section 752(b)) in exchange for his interest in accounts receivable ($3,000), inventory ($10,000), land ($3,000), and the balance of his interest in depreciable property ($1,000). Section 751(b) applies only to the extent of the exchange of other property for section 751 property (*i.e.,* inventory items, which include trade accounts receivable). The section 751 property exchanged has a fair market value of $13,000 ($3,000 in accounts receivable and $10,000 in inventory). Thus, $13,000 of the total amount C received is considered as received for the sale of section 751 property.

(d) Distributee partner's tax consequences. C's tax consequences on the distribution are as follows:

(1) The section 751(b) sale or exchange. C's share of the inventory items is treated as if he received them in a current distribution, and his basis for such items is $10,000 ($7,000 for inventory and $3,000 for accounts receivable) as determined under paragraph (b)(3)(iii) of this section. Then C is considered as having sold his share of inventory items to the partnership for $13,000. Thus, on the sale of his share of inventory items, C realizes $3,000 of ordinary income.

(2) The part of the distribution not under section 751(b). Section 751(b) does not apply to the balance of the distribution.

Before the distribution, C's basis for his partnership interest was $32,000 ($20,000 plus $12,000, his share of partnership liabilities). See section 752(a). This basis is reduced by $10,000, the basis attributed to the section 751 property treated as distributed to C and sold by him to the partnership. Thus, C has a basis of $22,000 for the remainder of his partnership interest. The total distribution to C was $37,000 ($22,000 in cash and liabilities assumed, and $15,000 in depreciable property). Since C received no more than his share of the depreciable property, none of the depreciable property constitutes proceeds of the sale under section 751(b). C did receive more than his share of money. Therefore, the sale proceeds, treated separately in subparagraph (1) of this paragraph of this example, must consist of money and therefore must be deducted from the money distribution. Consequently, in liquidation of the balance of C's interest, he receives depreciable property and $9,000 in money ($22,000 less $13,000). Therefore, no gain or loss is recognized to C on the distribution. Under section 732(b), C's basis for the depreciable property is $13,000 (the remaining basis of his partnership interest, $22,000, reduced by $9,000, the money received in the distribution).

(e) Partnership's tax consequences. The tax consequences to the partnership on the distribution are as follows:

(1) The section 751(b) sale or exchange. The partnership consisting of the remaining members has no ordinary income on the distribution since it did not give up any section 751 property in the exchange. Of the $22,000 money distributed (in cash and the assumption of C's share of liabilities), $13,000 was paid to acquire C's interest in inventory ($10,000 fair market value) and in accounts receivable ($3,000). Since under section 751(b) the partnership is treated as buying these properties, it has a new cost basis for the inventory and accounts receivable acquired from C. Its basis for C's share of inventory and accounts receivable is $13,000, the amount which the partnership is considered as having paid C in the exchange. Since the partnership is treated as having distributed C's share of inventory and accounts receivable to him, the partnership must decrease its basis for inventory and accounts receivable ($30,000) by $10,000, the basis of C's share treated as distributed to him, and then increase the basis for inventory and accounts receivable by $13,000 to reflect the purchase prices of the items acquired. Thus, the basis of the partnership inventory is increased from $21,000 to $24,000 in the transaction. (Note that the basis of property acquired in a section 751 (b) exchange is determined under section 1012 without regard to any elections of the partnership. See paragraph (e) of § 1.732–1.) Further, the partnership realizes no capital gain or loss on the portion of the distribution treated as a sale under section 751(b) since, to acquire C's interest in the inventory and accounts receivable, it gave up money and assumed C's share of liabilities.

(2) The part of the distribution not under section 751(b). In the remainder of the distribution to C which was not in exchange for C's interest in section 751 property, C received only other property as follows: $15,000 in depreciable property (with a basis to the partnership of $15,000) and $9,000 in money ($22,000 less $13,000 treated under subparagraph (1) of this paragraph of this example). Since this part of the distribution is not an exchange of section 751 property for other property, section 751(b) does not apply. Instead, the provisions which apply are sections 731 through 736, relating to distributions by a partnership. No gain or loss is recognized to the partnership on the distribution. (See section 731(b).) Further, the partnership makes no adjustment to the basis of remaining depreciable property unless an election under section 754 is in effect. (See section 734(a).) Thus, the basis of the depreciable property before the distribution, $42,000, is reduced by the basis of the depreciable property distributed, $15,000, leaving a basis for the depreciable property in the partnership of $27,000. However, if an election under section 754 is in effect, the partnership must make the adjustment required under section 734(b) as follows: Since the adjusted basis of the distributed property to the partnership had been $15,000, and is only $13,000 in C's hands (see paragraph (d)(2) of this example), the partnership will increase the basis of the depreciable property remaining in the partnership by $2,000 (the excess of the adjusted basis to the partnership of the distributed depreciable property immediately before the distribution over its basis to the distributee). Whether or not an election under section 754 is in effect, the basis for each of the remaining partner's partnership interests will be $38,000 ($20,000 original contribution, plus $12,000, each partner's original share of the liabilities, plus $6,000, the share of C's liabilities each assumed).

(f) Partnership trial balance. A trial balance of the AB partnership after the distribution in liquidation of C's entire interest would reflect the results set forth in the schedule below. Column I shows the amounts to be reflected in the records if an election is in effect under section 754 with respect to an optional adjustment under section 734(b) to the basis of undistributed partnership property. Column II shows the amounts to be reflected in the records where an election under section 754 is not in effect. Note that in column II, the total bases for the partnership assets do not equal the total of the bases for the partnership interests.

Example (3). (a) Facts. Assume that the distribution to partner C in example (2) of this paragraph in liquidation of his entire interest in partnership ABC consists of $5,000 in cash and $20,000 worth of partnership inventory with a basis of $14,000.

	I		II	
	Sec. 754, Election in effect		Sec. 754, Election not in effect	
	Basis	Fair market value	Basis	Fair market value
Cash	$5,000	$5,000	$5,000	$5,000
Accounts receivable	9,000	9,000	9,000	9,000

	I		II	
	Sec. 754, Election in effect		Sec. 754, Election not in effect	
	Basis	Fair market value	Basis	Fair market value
Inventory	24,000	30,000	24,000	30,000
Depreciable property	29,000	33,000	27,000	33,000
Land	9,000	9,000	9,000	9,000
	76,000	86,000	74,000	86,000
Current liabilities	15,000	15,000	15,000	15,000
Mortgage	21,000	21,000	21,000	21,000
Capital:				
	20,000	25,000	20,000	25,000
	20,000	25,000	20,000	25,000
	76,000	86,000	76,000	86,000

(b) Presence of section 751 property. For the same reason as stated in paragraph (b) of example (2), the partnership inventory items have substantially appreciated in value.

(c) The properties exchanged. In the distribution, C received his share of cash ($5,000) and his share of appreciated inventory items ($13,000). In addition, he received appreciated inventory with a fair market value of $7,000 (and with an adjusted basis to the partnership of $4,900) and $12,000 in money (liabilities assumed). C has relinquished his interest in $16,000 of depreciable property and $3,000 of land. Although C relinquished his interest in $3,000 of accounts receivable, such accounts receivable are inventory items and, therefore, that exchange was not an exchange of section 751 property for other property. Section 751(b) applies only to the extent of the exchange of other property for section 751 property (*i.e.*, depreciable property or land for inventory items). Assume that the partners agree that the $7,000 of inventory in excess of C's share was received by him in exchange for $7,000 of depreciable property.

(d) Distributee partner's tax consequences. C's tax consequence on the distributions are as follows:

(1) The section 751(b) sale or exchange. C is treated as if he had received his 7/16ths share of the depreciable property in a current distribution. His basis for that share is $6,125 (42,000/48,000 of $7,000), as determined under paragraph (b)(2)(iii) of this section. Then C is considered as having sold his 7/16ths share of depreciable property to the partnership for $7,000, realizing a gain of $875.

(2) The part of the distribution not under section 751(b). Section 751(b) does not apply to the balance of the distribution. Before the distribution, C's basis for his partnership interest was $32,000 ($20,000, plus $12,000, his share of partnership liabilities). See section 752(a). This basis is reduced by $6,125, the basis of property treated as distributed to C and sold by him to the partnership. Thus, C will have a basis of $25,875 for the remainder of his partnership interest. Of the $37,000 total distribution to C, $30,000 ($17,000 in money, including liabilities assumed, and $13,000 in inventory) is not within section 751(b). Under section 732(b), C's basis for the inventory with a fair market value of $13,000 (which had an adjusted basis to the partnership of $9,100) is limited to $8,875, the amount of the remaining basis for his partnership interest, $25,875, reduced by $17,000, the money received. Thus, C's total aggregate basis for the inventory received is $15,875 ($7,000 plus $8,875), and not its $14,000 basis in the hands of the partnership.

(e) Partnership's tax consequences. The tax consequences to the partnership on the distribution are as follows:

(1) The section 751(b) sale or exchange. The partnership consisting of the remaining members has $2,100 of ordinary income on the sale of the $7,000 of inventory which had a basis to the partnership of $4,900 (21,000/30,000 of $7,000). This $7,000 of inventory was paid to acquire 7/16ths of C's interest in the depreciable property. Since, under section 751(b), the partnership is treated as buying this property from C, it has a new cost basis for such property. Its basis for the depreciable property is $42,875 ($42,000 less $6,125, the basis of the 7/16ths share considered as distributed to C, plus $7,000, the partnership purchase price for this share).

(2) The part of the distribution not under section 751(b). In the remainder of the distribution to C which was not a sale or exchange of section 751 property for other property, the partnership realizes no gain or loss. See section 731(b). Further, under section 734(a), the partnership makes no adjustment to the basis of the accounts receivable or the 9/16ths interest in depreciable property which C relinquished. However, if an election under section 754 is in effect, the partnership must make the adjustment required under section 734(b) since the adjusted basis to the partnership of the inventory distributed had been $9,100, and C's basis for such inventory after distribution is only $8,875. The basis of the inventory remaining in the partnership must be increased by $225. Whether or not an election under section 754 is in effect, the basis for each of the remaining partnership interests will be $39,050 ($20,000 original contribution, plus $12,000, each partner's original share of the liabilities, plus $6,000, the share of C's liabilities now assumed, plus $1,050, each partner's share of ordinary income realized by the partnership upon that part of the distribution treated as a sale or exchange).

Example (4). (a) Facts. Assume the same facts as in example (3) of this paragraph, except that the partners did not identify the property which C relinquished in exchange for the $7,000 of inventory which he received in excess of his share.

(b) Presence of section 751 property. For the same reasons stated in paragraph (b) of example (2) of this paragraph, the partnership inventory items have substantially appreciated in value.

(c) The properties exchanged. The analysis stated in paragraph (c) of example (3) of this paragraph is the same in this example, except that, in the absence of a specific agreement among the partners as to the properties exchanged, C will be presumed to have sold to the partnership a proportionate amount of each property in which he relinquished an interest. Thus, in the absence of an agreement, C has received $7,000 of inventory in exchange for his release of 7/19ths of the depreciable property and 7/19ths of the land. ($7,000, fair market value of property released, over $19,000, the sum of the fair market values of C's interest in the land and C's interest in the depreciable property.)

(d) Distributee partner's tax consequences. C's tax consequences on the distribution are as follows:

(1) The section 751(b) sale or exchange. C is treated as if he had received his 7/19ths shares of the depreciable property and land in a current distribution. His basis for those shares is $6,263 (51,000/57,000 of $7,000, their fair market value), as determined under paragraph (b)(2)(iii) of this section. Then C is considered as having sold his 7/19ths shares of depreciable property and land to the partnership for $7,000, realizing a gain of $737.

(2) The part of the distribution not under section 751(b). Section 751(b) does not apply to the balance of the distribution. Before the distribution C's basis for his partnership interest was $32,000 ($20,000 plus $12,000, his share of partnership liabilities). See section 752(a). This basis is reduced by $6,263, the bases of C's shares of depreciable property and land treated as distributed to him and sold by him to the partnership. Thus, C will have a basis of $25,737 for the remainder of his partnership interest. Of the total $37,000 distributed to C, $30,000 ($17,000 in money, including liabilities assumed, and $13,000 in inventory) is not within section 751(b). Under section 732(b), C's basis for the inventory (with a fair market value of $13,000 and an adjusted basis to the partnership of $9,100) is limited to $8,737, the amount of the remaining basis for his partnership interest ($25,737 less $17,000), money received. Thus, C's total aggregate basis for the inventory he received is $15,737 ($7,000 plus $8,737), and not the $14,000 basis it had in the hands of the partnership.

(e) Partnership's tax consequences. The tax consequences to the partnership on the distribution are as follows:

(1) The section 751(b) sale or exchange. The partnership consisting of the remaining members has $2,100 of ordinary income on the sale of $7,000 of inventory which had a basis to the partnership of $4,900 (21,000/30,000 of $7,000). This $7,000 of inventory was paid to acquire 7/19ths of C's interest in the depreciable property and land. Since, under section 751(b), the partnership is treated as buying this property from C, it has a new cost basis for such property. The bases of the depreciable property and land would be $42,737 and $9,000, respectively. The basis for the depreciable property is computed as follows: The common partnership basis of $42,000 is reduced by the $5,158 basis (42,000/48,000 of $5,895) for C's 7/19ths interest constructively distributed and increased by $5,895 (16,000/19,000 of $7,000), the part of the purchase price allocated to the depreciable property. The basis of the land would be computed in the same way. The $9,000 original partnership basis is reduced by $1,105 basis (9,000/9,000 of $1,105) of land constructively distributed to C, and increased by $1,105 (3,000/19,000 of $7,000), the portion of the purchase price allocated to the land.

(2) The part of the distribution not under section 751(b). In the remainder of the distribution to C which was not a sale or exchange of section 751 property for other property, the partnership realizes no gain or loss. See section 731(b). Further, under section 734(a), the partnership makes no adjustment to the basis of the accounts receivable or the 12/16ths interests in depreciable property and land which C relinquished. However, if an election under section 754 is in effect, the partnership must make the adjustment required under section 734(b) since the adjusted basis to the partnership of the inventory distributed had been $9,100 and C's basis for such inventory after the distribution is only $8,737. The basis of the inventory remaining in the partnership must be increased by the difference of $363. Whether or not an election under section 754 is in effect, the basis for each of the remaining partnership interests will be $39,050 ($20,000 original contribution plus $12,000, each partner's original share of the liabilities, plus $6,000, the share of C's liabilities assumed, plus $1,050, each partner's share of ordinary income realized by the partnership upon the part of the distribution treated as a sale or exchange).

Example (5). (a) Facts. Assume that partner C in example (2) of this paragraph agrees to reduce his interest in capital and profits from one-third to one-fifth for a current distribution consisting of $5,000 in cash, and $7,500 of accounts receivable with a basis to the partnership of $7,500. At the same time, the total liabilities of the partnership are not reduced. Therefore, after the distribution, C's share of the partnership liabilities has been reduced by $4,800 from $12,000 (1/3 of $36,000) to $7,200 (1/5 of $36,000).

(b) Presence of section 751 property. For the same reasons as stated in paragraph (b) of example (2) of this paragraph, the partnership inventory items have substantially appreciated in value.

(c) The properties exchanged. C's interest in the fair market value of the partnership properties before and after the distribution can be illustrated by the following table:

	C's interest Fair Market Value		C received		C relinquished
Item	One-third before	One-fifth after	Distribution of share	In excess of share	
Cash	$5,000	$2,000	$3,000	$2,000	.....
Liabilities assumed	(12,000)	(7,200)	.....	4,800	.....
Inventory items:					
Accounts receivable	3,000	300	2,700	4,800	.....
Inventory	10,000	6,000	.....	.....	$4,000
Depreciable property	16,000	9,600	.....	.....	6,400
Land	3,000	1,800	.....	.....	1,200
Total	25,000	12,500	5,700	11,600	11,600

Although C relinquished his interest in $4,000 of inventory and received $4,800 of accounts receivable, both items constitute section 751 property and C has received only $800 of accounts receivable for $800 worth of depreciable property or for an $800 undivided interest in land. In the absence of an agreement identifying the properties exchanged, it is presumed C received $800 for proportionate shares of his interests in both depreciable property and land. To the extent that inventory was exchanged for accounts receivable, or to the extent cash was distributed for the release of C's interest in the balance of the depreciable property and land, the transaction does not fall within section 751(b) and is a current distribution under section 732(a). Thus, the remaining $6,700 of accounts receivable are received in a current distribution.

(d) Distributee partner's tax consequences. C's tax consequences on the distribution are as follows:

(1) The section 751(b) sale or exchange. Assuming that the partners paid $800 worth of accounts receivable for $800 worth of depreciable property, C is treated as if he received the depreciable property in a current distribution, and his basis for the $800 worth of depreciable property is $700 (42,000/48,000 of $800, its fair market value), as determined under paragraph (b)(2)(iii) of this section. Then C is considered as having sold his $800 share of depreciable property to the partnership for $800. On the sale of the depreciable property, C realizes a gain of $100. If, on the other hand, the partners had agreed that C exchanged an $800 interest in the land for $800 worth of accounts receivable, C would realize no gain or loss, because under paragraph (b)(2)(iii) of this section his basis for the land sold would be $800. In the absence of an agreement, the basis for the depreciable property and land (which C is considered as having received in a current distribution and then sold back to the partnership) would be $716 (51,000/57,000 of $800). In that case, on the sale of the balance of the $800 share of depreciable property and land, C would realize $84 of gain ($800 less $716).

(2) The part of the distribution not under section 751(b). Section 751(b) does not apply to the balance of the distribution. Under section 731, C does not realize either gain or loss on the balance of the distribution. The adjustments to the basis of C's interest are illustrated in the following table:

	If accounts receivable received for depreciable property	If accounts receivable received for land	If there is no agreement
Original basis for C's interest	$32,000	$32,000	$32,000
Less basis of property distributed prior to sec. 751(b) sale or exchange	–700	–800	–716
	31,300	31,200	31,284
Less money received in distribution	–9,800	–9,800	–9,800
	21,500	21,400	21,484
Less basis of property received in a current distribution under sec. 732	–6,700	–6,700	–6,700
Resulting basis for C's interest	14,800	14,700	14,784

C's basis for the $1,500 worth of accounts receivable which he received in the distribution will be $7,500, composed of $800 for the portion purchased in the section 751(b) exchange, plus $6,700, the basis carried over under section 732(a) for the portion received in the current distribution.

(e) Partnership's tax consequences. The tax consequences to the partnership on the distribution are as follows:

(1) The section 751(b) sale or exchange. The partnership realizes no gain or loss in the section 751 sale or exchange because it had a basis of $800 for the accounts receivable for which it received $800 worth of other property. If the partnership agreed to purchase $800 worth of depreciable property, the partnership basis of depreciable property becomes $42,100 ($42,000 less $700 basis of property constructively distributed to C, plus $800, price of property purchased). If the partnership purchased land with the accounts receivable, there would be no change in the basis of the land to the partnership because the basis of land distributed was equal to its purchase price. If there were no agreement, the basis of the depreciable property and land would be $51,084 (depreciable property, $42,084 and land $9,000). The basis for the depreciable property is computed as follows: The common partnership basis of $42,000 is reduced by the $590 basis (42,000/48,000 of $674) for C's $674 interest constructively distributed, and increased by $674 (6,400/7,600 of $800), the part of the purchase price allocated to the depreciable property. The basis of the land would be computed in the same way. The $9,000 original partnership basis is reduced by $126 basis (9,000/9,000 of $126) of the land constructively distributed to C, and increased by $126 (1,200/7,600 of $800), the portion of the purchase price allocated to the land.

(2) The part of the distribution not under section 751(b). The partnership will realize no gain or loss in the balance of the distribution under section 731. Since the property in C's hands after the distribution will have the same basis it had in the partnership, the basis of partnership property remaining in the partnership after the distribution will not be adjusted (whether or not an election under 754 is in effect).

Example (6). (a) Facts. Partnership ABC distributes to partner C, in liquidation of his entire one-third interest in the partnership, a machine which is section 1245 property with a recomputed basis (as defined in section 1245(a)(2)) of $18,000. At the time of the distribution, the balance sheet of the partnership is as follows:

ASSETS

	Adjusted basis per books	Market value
Cash	$3,000	$3,000
Machine (section 1245 property)	9,000	15,000
Land	18,000	27,000
Total	30,000	45,000

LIABILITIES AND CAPITAL

	Per books	Value
Liabilities	$0	$0
Capital:		
A	10,000	15,000
B	10,000	15,000
C	10,000	15,000
Total	30,000	45,000

(b) Presence of section 751 property. The section 1245 property is an unrealized receivable of the partnership to the extent of the potential section 1245 income in respect of the property. Since the fair market value of the property ($15,000) is lower than its recomputed basis ($18,000), the excess of the fair market value over its adjusted basis ($9,000), or $6,000, is the potential section 1245 income of the partnership in respect of the property. The partnership has no other section 751 property.

(c) The properties exchanged. In the distribution C received his share of section 751 property (potential section 1245 income of $2,000, *i.e.*, 1/3 of $6,000) and his share of section 1245 property (other than potential section 1245 income) with a fair market value of $3,000, *i.e.*, 1/3 of ($15,000 minus $6,000), and an adjusted basis of $3,000, *i.e.*, 1/3 of $9,000. In addition he received $4,000 of section 751 property (consisting of $4,000 ($6,000 minus $2,000) of potential section 1245 income) and section 1245 property (other than potential section 1245 income) with a fair market value of $6,000 ($9,000 minus $3,000) and an adjusted basis of $6,000 ($9,000 minus $3,000). C relinquished his interest in $1,000 of cash and $9,000 of land. Assume that the partners agree that the $4,000 of section 751 property in excess of C's share was received by him in exchange for $4,000 of land.

(d) Distributee partner's tax consequences. C's tax consequences on the distributions are as follows:

(1) The section 751(b) sale or exchange. C is treated as if he received in a current distribution 4/9ths of his share of the land with a basis of $2,667 (18,000/27,000 × $4,000). Then C is considered as having sold his 4/9ths share of the land to the partnership for $4,000, realizing a gain of $1,333. C's basis for the remainder of his partnership interest after the current distribution is $7,333, *i.e.*, the basis of his partnership interest before the current distribution ($10,000) minus the basis of the land treated as distributed to him ($2,667).

(2) The part of the distribution not under section 751(b). Of the $15,000 total distribution to C, $11,000 ($2,000 of potential section 1245 income and $9,000 section 1245 property other than potential section 1245 income) is not within section 751(b). Under section 732(b) and (c), C's basis for his share of potential section 1245 income is zero (see paragraph (c)(5) of this section) and his basis for $9,000 of section 1245 property (other than potential section 1245 income) is $7,333, *i.e.*, the amount of the remaining basis for his partnership interest ($7,333) reduced by the basis for his share of potential section 1245 income (zero). Thus C's total aggregate basis for the section 1245 property (fair market value of $15,000) distributed to him is $11,333 ($4,000 plus $7,333). For an illustration of the computation of his recomputed basis for the section 1245 property immediately after the distribution, see example (2) of paragraph (f)(3) of § 1.1245–4.

(e) Partnership's tax consequences. The tax consequences to the partnership on the distribution are as follows:

(1) The section 751(b) sale or exchange. Upon the sale of $4,000 potential section 1245 income, with a basis of zero, for 4/9ths of C's interest in the land, the partnership consisting of the remaining members has $4,000 ordinary income under sections 751 (b) and 1245(a)(1). See section 1245(b)(3) and (6)(A). The partnership's new basis for the land is $19,333, *i.e.*,, $18,000, less the basis of the 4/9ths share considered as distributed to C ($2,667), plus the partnership purchase price for this share ($4,000).

(2) The part of the distribution not under section 751(b). The analysis under this subparagraph should be made in accordance with the principles illustrated in paragraph (e)(2) of examples (3), (4), and (5) of this paragraph.

§ 1.752–0 Table of contents.

This section lists the major paragraphs that appear in §§ 1.752–1 through 1.752–7.

§ 1.752–1 Treatment of partnership liabilities.

§ 1.752–2 Partner's share of recourse liabilities.

(f) Examples.

(g) Time-value-of-money considerations.

(1) In general.

(2) Valuation of an obligation.

(3) Satisfaction of obligation with partner's promissory note.

(4) Example.

(h) Partner providing property as security for partnership liability.

(1) Direct pledge.

(2) Indirect pledge.

(3) Valuation.

(4) Partner's promissory note.

(i) Treatment of recourse liabilities in tiered partnerships.

(j) Anti-abuse rules.

(1) In general.

(2) Arrangements tantamount to a guarantee.

(3) Plan to circumvent or avoid the regulations.

(4) Example.

§ 1.752–3 Partner's share of nonrecourse liabilities.

(a) In general.

(b) Examples.

§ 1.752–4 Special rules.

(a) Tiered partnerships.

(b) Related person definition.

(1) In general.

(2) Person related to more than one partner.

(i) In general.

(ii) Natural persons.

(iii) Related partner exception.

(iv) Special rule where entity structured to avoid related person status.

(A) In general.

(B) Ownership interest.

(C) Example.

(c) Limitation.

(d) Time of determination.

§ 1.752–5 Effective dates and transition rules.

(a) In general.

(b) Election.

(1) In general.

(2) Time and manner of election.

(c) Effect of section 708(b)(1)(B) termination on determining date liabilities are incurred or assumed.

§ 1.752–6 Partnership assumption of partner's section 358(h)(3) liability after October 18, 1999, and before June 24, 2003.

(a) In general.

(b) Exceptions.

(1) In general.

(2) Transactions described in Notice 2000-44.

(c) Example.

(d) Effective date.

(1) In general.

(2) Election to apply § 1.752–7.

§ 1.752–7 Partnership assumption of partner's § 1.752–7 liability on or after June 24, 2003.

(a) Purpose and structure.

(b) Definitions.

(1) Assumption.

(2) Adjusted value.

(3) § 1.752–7 liability.

(i) In general.

(ii) Amount and share of § 1.752–7 liability.

(iii) Example.

(**4**) § 1.752–7 liability transfer.

(**i**) In general.

(**ii**) Terminations under section 708(b)(1)(B).

(**5**) § 1.752–7 liability partner.

(**i**) In general.

(**ii**) Tiered partnerships.

(**A**) Assumption by a lower-tier partnership.

(**B**) Distribution of partnership interest.

(**6**) Remaining built-in loss associated with a § 1.752–7 liability.

(**i**) In general.

(**ii**) Partial dispositions and assumptions.

(**7**) § 1.752–7 liability reduction.

(**i**) In general.

(**ii**) Partial dispositions and assumptions.

(**8**) Satisfaction of § 1.752–7 liability.

(**9**) Testing date.

(**10**) Trade or business.

(**i**) In general.

(**ii**) Examples.

(**c**) Application of section 704(b) and (c) to assumed § 1.752–7 liabilities.

(**1**) In general.

(**i**) Section 704(c).

(**ii**) Section 704(b).

(**2**) Example.

(**d**) Special rules for transfers of partnership interests, distributions of partnership assets, and assumptions of the § 1.752–7 liability after a § 1.752–7 liability transfer.

(**1**) In general.

(**2**) Exceptions.

(**i**) In general.

(**ii**) Examples.

(**e**) Transfer of § 1.752–7 liability partner's partnership interest.

(**1**) In general.

(**2**) Examples.

(**3**) Exception for nonrecognition transactions.

(**i**) In general.

(**ii**) Examples.

(**f**) Distribution in liquidation of § 1.752–7 liability partner's partnership interest.

(**1**) In general.

(**2**) Example.

(**g**) Assumption of § 1.752–7 liability by a partner other than § 1.752–7 liability partner.

(**1**) In general.

(**2**) Consequences to § 1.752–7 liability partner.

(**3**) Consequences to partnership.

(**4**) Consequences to assuming partner.

(**5**) Example.

(**h**) Notification by the partnership (or successor) of the satisfaction of the § 1.752–7 liability.

(**i**) Special rule for amounts that are capitalized prior to the occurrence of an event described in paragraphs (e), (f), or (g)

(**1**) In general.

(**2**) Example.

(**j**) Tiered partnerships.

(**1**) Look-through treatment.

(**2**) Trade or business exception.

(**3**) Partnership as a § 1.752–7 liability partner.

(**4**) Transfer of § 1.752–7 liability by partnership to another partnership or corporation after a transaction described in paragraphs (e), (f), or (g).

(**i**) In general.

(**ii**) Subsequent transfers.

(**5**) Example.

(**k**) Effective dates.

(**1**) In general.

(**2**) Election to apply this section to assumptions of liabilities occurring after October 18, 1999 and before June 24, 2003.

(**i**) In general.

(**ii**) Manner of making election.

(**iii**) Filing of amended returns.

(**iv**) Time for making election.

§ 1.752–1 Treatment of partnership liabilities.

(a) Definitions. For purposes of section 752, the following definitions apply:

(1) Recourse liability defined. A partnership liability is a recourse liability to the extent that any partner or related person bears the economic risk of loss for that liability under § 1.752–2.

(2) Nonrecourse liability defined. A partnership liability is a nonrecourse liability to the extent that no partner or related person bears the economic risk of loss for that liability under § 1.752–2.

(3) Related person. Related person means a person having a relationship to a partner that is described in § 1.752–4(b).

(4) Liability defined—

(i) In general. An obligation is a liability for purposes of section 752 and the regulations thereunder (§ 1.752–1 liability), only if, when, and to the extent that incurring the obligation—

(A) Creates or increases the basis of any of the obligor's assets (including cash);

(B) Gives rise to an immediate deduction to the obligor; or

(C) Gives rise to an expense that is not deductible in computing the obligor's taxable income and is not properly chargeable to capital.

(ii) Obligation. For purposes of this paragraph and § 1.752–7, an obligation is any fixed or contingent obligation to make payment without regard to whether the obligation is otherwise taken into account for purposes of the Internal Revenue Code. Obligations include, but are not limited to, debt obligations, environmental obligations, tort obligations, contract obligations, pension obligations, obligations under a short sale, and obligations under derivative financial instruments such as options, forward contracts, futures contracts, and swaps.

(iii) Other liabilities. For obligations that are not § 1.752–1 liabilities, see §§ 1.752–6 and 1.752–7.

(iv) Effective date. Except as otherwise provided in § 1.752–7(k), this paragraph (a)(4) applies to liabilities that are incurred or assumed by a partnership on or after June 24, 2003.

(b) Increase in partner's share of liabilities. Any increase in a partner's share of partnership liabilities, or any increase in a partner's individual liabilities by reason of the partner's assumption of partnership liabilities, is treated as a contribution of money by that partner to the partnership.

(c) Decrease in partner's share of liabilities. Any decrease in a partner's share of partnership liabilities, or any decrease in a partner's individual liabilities by reason of the partnership's assumption of the individual liabilities of the partner, is treated as a distribution of money by the partnership to that partner.

(d) Assumption of liability. Except as otherwise provided in paragraph (e) of this section, a person is considered to assume a liability only to the extent that:

(1) The assuming person is personally obligated to pay the liability; and

(2) If a partner or related person assumes a partnership liability, the person to whom the liability is owed knows of the assumption and can directly enforce the partner's or related person's obligation for the liability, and no other partner or person that is a related person to another partner would bear the economic risk of loss for the liability immediately after the assumption.

(e) Property subject to a liability. If property is contributed by a partner to the partnership or distributed by the partnership to a partner and the property is subject to a liability of the transferor, the transferee is treated as having assumed the liability, to the extent that the amount of the liability does not exceed the fair market value of the property at the time of the contribution or distribution.

(f) Netting of increases and decreases in liabilities resulting from same transaction. If, as a result of a single transaction, a partner incurs both an increase in the partner's share of the partnership liabilities (or the partner's individual liabilities) and a decrease in the partner's share of the partnership liabilities (or the partner's individual liabilities), only the net decrease is treated as a distribution from the partnership and only the net increase is treated as a contribution of money to the partnership. Generally, the contribution to or distribution from a partnership of property subject to a liability or the termination of the partnership under section 708(b) will require that increases and decreases in liabilities associated with the transaction be netted to determine if a partner will be deemed to have made a contribution or received a distribution as a result of the transaction. When two or more partnerships merge or consolidate under section 708(b)(2)(A), as described in §1.708–1 (c)(3)(i), increases and decreases in partnership liabilities associated with the merger or consolidation are netted by the partners in the terminating partnership and the resulting partnership to determine the effect of the merger under section 752.

(g) Example. The following example illustrates the principles of paragraphs (b), (c), (e), and (f) of this section.

Example (1). Property contributed subject to a liability, netting of increase and decrease in partner's share of liability. B contributes property with an adjusted basis of $1,000 to a general partnership in exchange for a one-third interest in the partnership. At the time of the contribution, the partnership does not have any liabilities outstanding and the property is subject to a recourse debt of $150 and has a fair market value in excess of $150. After the contribution, B remains personally liable to the creditor and none of the other partners bears any of the economic risk of loss for the liability under state law or otherwise. Under paragraph (e) of this section, the partnership is treated as having assumed the $150 liability. As a result, B's individual liabilities decrease by $150. At the same time, however, B's share of liabilities of the partnership increases by $150. Only the net increase or decrease in B's share of the liabilities of the partnership and B's individual liabilities is taken into account in applying section 752. Because there is no net change, B is not treated as having contributed money to the partnership or as having received a distribution of money from the partnership under paragraph (b) or (c) of this section. Therefore B's basis for B's partnership interest is $1,000 (B's basis for the contributed property).

* * *

(h) Sale or exchange of a partnership interest. If a partnership interest is sold or exchanged, the reduction in the transferor partner's share of partnership liabilities is treated as an amount realized under section 1001 and the regulations thereunder. For example, if a partner sells an interest in a partnership for $750 cash and transfers to the purchaser the partner's share of partnership liabilities in the amount of $250, the seller realizes $1,000 on the transaction.

(i) Bifurcation of partnership liabilities. If one or more partners bears the economic risk of loss as to part, but not all, of a partnership liability represented by a single contractual obligation, that liability is treated as two or more separate liabilities for purposes of section 752. The portion of the liability as to which one or more partners bear the economic risk of loss is a recourse liability and the remainder of the liability, if any, is a nonrecourse liability.

§ 1.752–2 Partner's share of recourse liabilities.

(a) In general. A partner's share of a recourse partnership liability equals the portion of that liability, if any, for which the partner or related person bears the economic risk of loss. The determination of the extent to which a partner bears the economic risk of loss for a partnership liability is made under the rules in paragraphs (b) through (j) of this section.

(b) Obligation to make a payment. (1) In general. Except as otherwise provided in this section, a partner bears the economic risk of loss for a partnership liability to the extent that, if the partnership constructively liquidated, the partner or related person would be obligated to make a payment to any person (or a contribution to the partnership) because that liability becomes due and payable and the partner or related person would not be entitled to reimbursement from another partner or person that is a related person to another partner. Upon a constructive liquidation, all of the following events are deemed to occur simultaneously:

(i) All of the partnership's liabilities become payable in full;

(ii) With the exception of property contributed to secure a partnership liability (see § 1.752–2(h)(2)), all of the partnership's assets, including cash, have a value of zero;

(iii) The partnership disposes of all of its property in a fully taxable transaction for no consideration (except relief from liabilities for which the creditor's right to repayment is limited solely to one or more assets of the partnership);

(iv) All items of income, gain, loss, or deduction are allocated among the partners; and

(v) The partnership liquidates.

(2) Treatment upon deemed disposition. For purposes of paragraph (b)(1) of this section, gain or loss on the deemed disposition of the partnership's assets is computed in accordance with the following:

(i) If the creditor's right to repayment of a partnership liability is limited solely to one or more assets of the partnership, gain or loss is recognized in an amount equal to the difference between the amount of the liability that is extinguished by the deemed disposition and the tax basis (or book value to the extent section 704(c) or § 1.704–1 (b)(4)(i) applies) in those assets.

(ii) A loss is recognized equal to the remaining tax basis (or book value to the extent section 704(c) or § 1.704–1 (b)(4)(i) applies) of all the partnership's assets not taken into account in paragraph (b)(2)(i) of this section.

(3) Obligations recognized. The determination of the extent to which a partner or related person has an obligation to make a payment under paragraph (b)(1) of this section is based on the facts and circumstances at the time of the determination. All statutory and contractual obligations relating to the partnership liability are taken into account for purposes of applying this section, including:

(i) Contractual obligations outside the partnership agreement such as guarantees, indemnifications, reimbursement agreements, and other obligations running directly to creditors or to other partners, or to the partnership;

(ii) Obligations to the partnership that are imposed by the partnership agreement, including the obligation to make a capital contribution and to restore a deficit capital account upon liquidation of the partnership; and

(iii) Payment obligations (whether in the form of direct remittances to another partner or a contribution to the partnership) imposed by state law including the governing state partnership statute.

To the extent that the obligation of a partner to make a payment with respect to a partnership liability is not recognized under this paragraph (b)(3), paragraph (b) of this section is applied as if the obligation did not exist.

(4) Contingent obligations. A payment obligation is disregarded if, taking into account all the facts and circumstances, the obligation is subject to contingencies that make it unlikely that the obligation will ever be discharged. If a payment obligation would arise at a future time after the occurrence of an event that is not determinable with reasonable certainty, the obligation is ignored until the event occurs.

(5) Reimbursement rights. A partner's or related person's obligation to make a payment with respect to a partnership liability is reduced to the extent that the partner or related person is entitled to reimbursement from another partner or a person who is a related person to another partner.

(6) Deemed satisfaction of obligation. For purposes of determining the extent to which a partner or related person has a payment obligation and the economic risk of loss, it is assumed that all partners and related persons who have obligations to make payments actually perform those obligations, irrespective of their actual net worth, unless the facts and circumstances indicate a plan to circumvent or avoid the obligation. See paragraphs (j) and (k) of this section.

(c) Partner or related person as lender—(1) In general. A partner bears the economic risk of loss for a partnership liability to the extent that the partner or a related person makes (or acquires an interest in) a nonrecourse loan to the partnership and the economic risk of loss for the liability is not borne by another partner.

(2) Wrapped debt. If a partnership liability is owed to a partner or related person and that liability includes (i.e., is "wrapped" around) a nonrecourse obligation encumbering partnership property that is owed to another person, the partnership liability will be treated as two separate liabilities. The portion of the partnership liability corresponding to the wrapped debt is treated as a liability owed to another person.

(d) De minimis exceptions—(1) Partner as lender. The general rule contained in paragraph (c)(1) of this section does not apply if a partner or related person whose interest (directly or indirectly through one or more partnerships including the interest of any related person) in each item of partnership income, gain, loss, deduction, or credit for every taxable year that the partner is a partner in the partnership is 10 percent or less, makes a loan to the partnership which constitutes qualified nonrecourse financing within the meaning of section 465(b)(6) (determined without regard to the type of activity financed).

(2) Partner as guarantor. The general rule contained in paragraph (b)(1) of this section does not apply if a partner or related person whose interest (directly or indirectly through one or more partnerships including the interest of any related person) in each item of partnership income, gain, loss, deduction, or credit for every taxable year that the partner is a partner in the partnership is 10 percent or less, guarantees a loan that would otherwise be a nonrecourse loan of the partnership and which would constitute qualified nonrecourse financing within the meaning of section 465(b)(6) (without regard to the type of activity financed) if the guarantor had made the loan to the partnership.

(e) Special rule for nonrecourse liability with interest guaranteed by a partner—(1) In general. For purposes of this section, if one or more partners or related persons have guaranteed the payment of more than 25 percent of the total interest that will accrue on a partnership nonrecourse liability over its remaining term, and it is reasonable to expect that the guarantor will be required to pay substantially all of the guaranteed future interest if the partnership fails to do so, then the liability is treated as two separate partnership liabilities. If this rule applies, the partner or related person that has guaranteed the payment of interest is treated as bearing the economic risk of loss for the partnership liability to the extent of the present value of the guaranteed future interest payments. The remainder of the stated principal amount of the partnership liability constitutes a nonrecourse liability. Generally, in applying this rule, it is reasonable to expect that the guarantor will be required to pay substantially all of the guaranteed future interest if, upon a default in payment by the partnership, the lender can enforce the interest guaranty without foreclosing on the property and thereby extinguishing the underlying debt. The guarantee of interest rule continues to apply even after the point at which the amount of guaranteed interest that will accrue is less than 25 percent of the total interest that will accrue on the liability.

(2) Computation of present value. The present value of the guaranteed future interest payments is computed using a discount rate equal to either the interest rate stated in the loan documents, or if interest is imputed under either section 483 or section 1274, the applicable federal rate, compounded semiannually. The computation takes into account any payment of interest that the partner or related person may be required to make only to the extent that the interest will accrue economically (determined in accordance with section 446 and the regulations thereunder) after the date of the interest guarantee. If the loan document contains a variable rate of interest that is an interest rate based on current values of an objective interest index, the present value is computed on the assumption that the interest determined under the objective interest index on the date of the computation will remain constant over the term of the loan. The term "objective interest index" has the meaning given to it in section 1275 and the regulations thereunder (relating to variable rate debt instruments). Examples of an objective interest index include the prime rate of a designated financial institution, LIBOR (London Interbank Offered Rate), and the applicable federal rate under section 1274(d).

(3) Safe harbor. The general rule contained in paragraph (e)(1) of this section does not apply to a partnership nonrecourse liability if the guarantee of interest by the partner or related person is for a period not in excess of the lesser of five years or one-third of the term of the liability.

(4) De minimis exception. The general rule contained in paragraph (e)(1) of this section does not apply if a partner or related person whose interest (directly or indirectly through one or more partnerships including the interest of any related person) in each item of partnership income, gain, loss, deduction, or credit for every taxable year that the partner is a partner in the partnership is 10 percent or less, guarantees the interest on a loan to that partnership which constitutes qualified nonrecourse financing within the meaning of section 465(b)(6) (determined without regard to the type of activity financed). An allocation of interest to the extent paid by the guarantor is not treated as a partnership item of deduction or loss subject to the 10 percent or less rule.

(f) Examples. The following examples illustrate the principles of paragraphs (a) through (e) of this section.

Example 1. Determining when a partner bears the economic risk of loss. A and B form a general partnership with each contributing $100 in cash. The partnership purchases an office building on leased land for $1,000 from an unrelated seller, paying $200 in cash and executing a note to the seller for the balance of $800. The note is a general obligation of the partnership, i.e., no partner has been relieved from personal liability. The partnership agreement provides that all items are allocated equally except that tax losses are specially allocated 90% to A and 10% to B and that capital accounts will be maintained in accordance with the regulations under section 704(b), including a deficit capital account restoration obligation on liquidation. In a constructive liquidation, the $800 liability becomes due and payable. All of the partnership's assets, including the building, are deemed to be worthless. The building is deemed sold for a value of zero. Capital accounts are adjusted to reflect the loss on the hypothetical disposition, as follows:

	A	B
Initial contribution	$100	$100
Loss on hypothetical sale	(900)	(100)
	($800)	$0

Other than the partners' obligation to fund negative capital accounts on liquidation, there are no other contractual or statutory payment obligations existing between the partners, the partnership and the lender. Therefore, $800 of the partnership liability is classified as a recourse liability because one or more partners bears the economic risk of loss for non-payment. B has no share of the $800 liability since the constructive liquidation produces no payment obligation for B. A's share of the partnership liability is $800 because A would have an obligation in that amount to make a contribution to the partnership.

Example 2. Recourse liability; deficit restoration obligation. C and D each contribute $500 in cash to the capital of a new general partnership, CD. CD purchases property from an unrelated seller for $1,000 in cash and a $9,000 mortgage note. The note is a general obligation of the partnership, i.e., no partner has been relieved from personal liability. The partnership agreement provides that profits and losses are to be divided 40% to C and 60% to D. C and D are required to make up any deficit in their capital accounts. In a constructive liquidation, all partnership assets are deemed to become worthless and all partnership liabilities become due and payable in full. The partnership is deemed to dispose of all its assets in a fully taxable transaction for no consideration. Capital accounts are adjusted to reflect the loss on the hypothetical disposition, as follows:

	C	D
Initial contribution	$500	$500
Loss on hypothetical sale	(4,000)	(6,000)
	($3,500)	($5,500)

C's capital account reflects a deficit that C would have to make up to $3,500 and D's Capital account reflects a deficit that D would have to make up of $5,500. Therefore, the $9,000 mortgage note is a recourse liability because one or more partners bear the economic risk of loss for the liability. C's share of the recourse liability is $3,500 and D's share is $5,500.

Example 3. Guarantee by limited partner; partner deemed to satisfy obligation. E and F form a limited partnership. E, the general partner, contributes $2,000 and F, the limited partner, contributes $8,000 in cash to the partnership. The partnership agreement allocates losses 20% to E and 80% to F until F's capital account is reduced to zero, after which all losses are allocated to E. The partnership purchases depreciable property for $25,000 using its $10,000 cash and a $15,000 recourse loan from a bank. F guarantees payment of the $15,000 loan to the extent the loan remains unpaid after the bank has exhausted its remedies against the partnership. In a constructive liquidation, the $15,000 liability becomes due and payable. All of the partnership's assets, including the depreciable property, are deemed to be worthless. The depreciable property is deemed sold for a value of zero. Capital accounts are adjusted to reflect the loss on the hypothetical disposition, as follows:

	E	F
Initial contribution	$2,000	$8,000
Loss on hypothetical sale	(17,000)	(8,000)
	($15,000)	$0

E, as a general partner, would be obligated by operation of law to make a net contribution to the partnership of $15,000. Because E is assumed to satisfy that obligation, it is also assumed that F would not have to satisfy F's guarantee. The $15,000 mortgage is treated as a recourse liability because one or more partners bear the economic risk of loss. E's share of the liability is $15,000, and F's share is zero. This would be so even if E's net worth at the time of the determination is less than $15,000, unless the facts and circumstances indicate a plan to circumvent or avoid E's obligation to contribute to the partnership.

Example 4. Partner guarantee with right of subrogation. G, a limited partner in the GH partnership, guarantees a portion of a partnership liability. The liability is a general obligation of the partnership, i.e., no partner has been relieved from personal liability. If under state law G is subrogated to the rights of the lender, G would have the right to recover the amount G paid to the recourse lender from the general partner. Therefore, G does not bear the economic risk of loss for the partnership liability.

Example 5. Bifurcation of partnership liability; guarantee of part of nonrecourse liability. A partnership borrows $10,000, secured by a mortgage on real property. The mortgage note contains an exoneration clause which provides that in the event of default, the holder's only remedy is to foreclose on the property. The holder may not look to any other partnership asset or to any partner to pay the liability. However, to induce the lender to make the loan, a partner guarantees payment of $200 of the loan principal. The exoneration clause does not apply to the partner's guarantee. If the partner paid pursuant to the guarantee, the partner would be subrogated to the rights of the lender with respect to $200 of the mortgage debt, but the partner is not otherwise entitled to reimbursement from the partnership or any partner. For purposes of section 752, $200 of the $10,000 mortgage liability is treated as a recourse liability of the partnership and $9,800 is treated as a nonrecourse liability of the partnership. The partner's share of the recourse liability of the partnership is $200.

Example 6. Wrapped debt. I, an individual, purchases real estate from an unrelated seller for $10,000, paying $1,000 in cash and giving a $9,000 purchase mortgage note on which I has no personal liability and as to which the seller can look only to the property for satisfaction. At a time when the property is worth $15,000, I sells the property to a partnership in which I is a general partner. The partnership pays for the property with a partnership purchase money mortgage note of $15,000 on which neither the partnership nor any partner (or person related to a partner) has personal liability. The $15,000 mortgage note is a wrapped debt that includes the $9,000 obligation to the original seller. The liability is a recourse liability to the extent of $6,000 because I is the creditor with respect to the loan and I bears the economic risk of loss for $6,000. I's share of the recourse liability is $6,000. The remaining $9,000 is treated as a partnership nonrecourse liability that is owed to the unrelated seller.

Example 7. Guarantee of interest by partner treated as part recourse and part nonrecourse. On January 1, 1992, a partnership obtains a $4,000,000 loan secured by a shopping center owned by the partnership. Neither the partnership nor any partner has any personal liability under the loan documents for repayment of the stated principal amount. Interest accrues at a 15 percent annual rate and is payable on December 31 of each year. The principal is payable in a lump sum on December 31, 2006. A partner guarantees payment of 50 percent of each interest payment required by the loan. The guarantee can be enforced without first foreclosing on the property. When the partnership obtains the loan, the present value (discounted at 15 percent, compounded annually) of the future interest payments is $3,508,422, and of the future principal payment is $491,578. If tested on that date, the loan would be treated as a partner-ship liability of $1,754,211 ($3,508,422 × .5) for which the guaranteeing partner bears the economic risk of loss and a partnership nonrecourse liability of $2,245,789 ($1,754,211 + $491,578).

Example 8. Contingent obligation not recognized. J and K form a general partnership with cash contributions of $2,500 each. J and K share partnership profits and losses equally. The partnership purchases an apartment building for its $5,000 of cash and a $20,000 nonrecourse loan from a commercial bank. The nonrecourse loan is secured by a mortgage on the building. The loan documents provide that the partnership will be liable for the outstanding balance of the loan on a recourse basis to the extent of any decrease in the value of the apartment building resulting from the partnership's failure properly to maintain the property. There are no facts that establish with reasonable certainty the existence of any liability on the part of the partnership (and its partners) for damages resulting from the partnership's failure properly to maintain the building. Therefore, no partner bears the economic risk of loss, and the liability constitutes a nonrecourse liability.

Under § 1.752–3, J and K share this nonrecourse liability equally because they share all profits and losses equally.

(g) Time-value-of-money considerations—(1) In general. The extent to which a partner or related person bears the economic risk of loss is determined by taking into account any delay in the time when a payment or contribution obligation with respect to a partnership liability is to be satisfied. If a payment obligation with respect to a partnership liability is not required to be satisfied within a reasonable time after the liability becomes due and payable, or if the obligation to make a contribution to the partnership is not required to be satisfied before the later of—

(i) The end of the year in which the partner's interest is liquidated, or

(ii) 90 days after the liquidation, the obligation is recognized only to the extent of the value of the obligation.

(2) Valuation of an obligation. The value of a payment or contribution obligation that is not required to be satisfied within the time period specified in paragraph (g)(1) of this section equals the entire principal balance of the obligation only if the obligation bears interest equal to or greater than the applicable federal rate under section 1274(d) at the time of valuation, commencing on—

(i) In the case of a payment obligation, the date that the partnership liability to a creditor or other person to whom the obligation relates becomes due and payable, or

(ii) In the case of a contribution obligation, the date of the liquidation of the partner's interest in the partnership. If the obligation does not bear interest at a rate at least equal to the applicable federal rate at the time of valuation, the value of the obligation is discounted to the present value of all payments due from the partner or related person (i.e., the imputed principal amount computed under section 1274(b)). For purposes of making this present value determination, the partnership is deemed to have constructively liquidated as of the date on which the payment obligation is valued and the payment obligation is assumed to be a debt instrument subject to the rules of section 1274 (i.e., the debt instrument is treated as if it were issued for property at the time of the valuation).

(3) Satisfaction of obligation with partner's promissory note. An obligation is not satisfied by the transfer to the obligee of a promissory note by a partner or related person unless the note is readily tradeable on an established securities market.

(4) Example. The following example illustrates the principle of paragraph (g) of this section.

Example. Value of obligation not required to be satisfied within specified time period. A, the general partner, and B, the limited partner, each contributes $10,000 to partnership AB. AB purchases property from an unrelated seller for $20,000 in cash and a $70,000 recourse purchase money note. The partnership agreement provides that profits and losses are to be divided equally. A and B are required to make up any deficit in their capital accounts. While A is required to restore any deficit balance in A's capital account within 90 days after the date of liquidation of the partnership, B is not required to restore any deficit for two years following the date of liquidation. The deficit in B's capital account will not bear interest during that two-year period. In a constructive liquidation, all partnership assets are deemed to become worthless and all partnership liabilities become due and payable in full. The partnership is deemed to dispose of all its assets in a fully taxable transaction for no consideration. Capital accounts are adjusted to reflect the loss on the hypothetical disposition, as follows:

	A	B
Initial contribution	$10,000	$10,000
Loss on hypothetical sale	(45,000)	(45,000)
	(35,000)	(35,000)

A's and B's capital accounts each reflect deficits of $35,000. B's obligation to make a contribution pursuant to B's deficit restoration obligation is recognized only to the extent of the fair market value of that obligation at the time of the constructive liquidation because B is not required to satisfy that obligation by the later of the end of the partnership taxable year in which B's interest is liquidated or within 90 days after the date of the liquidation. Because B's obligation does not bear interest, the fair market value is deemed to equal the imputed principal amount under section 1274(b). Under section 1274(b), the imputed principal amount of a debt instrument equals the present value of all payments due under the debt instrument. Assume the applicable federal rate with respect to B's obligation is 10 percent compounded semiannually. Using this discount rate, the present value of the $35,000 payment that B would be required to make two years after the constructive liquidation to restore the deficit balance in B's capital account equals $28,795. To the extent that B's deficit restoration obligation is not recognized, it is assumed that B's obligation does not exist. Therefore, A, as the sole general partner, would be obligated by operation of law to contribute an additional $6,205 of capital to the partnership. Accordingly, under paragraph (g) of this section, B bears the economic risk of loss for $28,795 and A bears the economic risk of loss for $41,205 ($35,000 + $6,205).

(h) Partner providing property as security for partnership liability—(1) Direct pledge. A partner is considered to bear the economic risk of loss for a partnership liability to the extent of the value of any of the partner's or related person's separate property (other than a direct or indirect interest in the partnership) that is pledged as security for the partnership liability.

(2) Indirect pledge. A partner is considered to bear the economic risk of loss for a partnership liability to the extent of the value of any property that the partner contributes to the partnership solely for the purpose of securing a partnership liability. Contributed property is not treated as contributed solely for the purpose of securing a partnership liability unless substantially all of the items of income, gain, loss, and deduction attributable to the contributed property are allocated to the contributing partner, and this allocation is generally greater than the partner's share of other significant items of partnership income, gain, loss, or deduction.

(3) Valuation. The extent to which a partner bears the economic risk of loss as a result of a direct pledge described in paragraph (h)(1) of this section or an indirect pledge described in paragraph (h)(2) of this section is limited to the net fair market value of the property (pledged property) at the time of the pledge or contribution. If a partner provides additional pledged property, the addition is treated as a new pledge and the net fair market value of the pledged property (including but not limited to the additional property) must be determined at that time. For purposes of this paragraph (h), if pledged property is subject to one or more other obligations, those obligations must be taken into account in determining the net fair market value of pledged property at the time of the pledge or contribution.

(4) Partner's promissory note. For purposes of paragraph (h)(2) of this section, a promissory note of the partner or related person that is contributed to the partnership shall not be taken into account unless the note is readily tradeable on an established securities market.

(i) Treatment of recourse liabilities in tiered partnerships. If a partnership (the "upper-tier partnership") owns (directly or indirectly through one or more partnerships) an interest in another partnership (the "lower-tier partnership"), the liabilities of the lower-tier partnership are allocated to the upper-tier partnership in an amount equal to the sum of the following—

(1) The amount of the economic risk of loss that the upper-tier partnership bears with respect to the liabilities; and

(2) Any other amount of the liabilities with respect to which partners of the upper-tier partnership bear the economic risk of loss.

(j) Anti-abuse rules—(1) In general. An obligation of a partner or related person to make a payment may be disregarded or treated as an obligation of another person for purposes of this section if facts and circumstances indicate that a principal purpose of the arrangement between the parties is to eliminate the partner's economic risk of loss with respect to that obligation or create the appearance of the partner or related person bearing the economic risk of loss when, in fact, the substance of the arrangement is otherwise. Circumstances with respect to which a payment obligation may be disregarded include, but are not limited to, the situations described in paragraphs (j)(2) and (j)(3) of this section.

(2) Arrangements tantamount to a guarantee. Irrespective of the form of a contractual obligation, a partner is considered to bear the economic risk of loss with respect to a partnership liability, or a portion thereof, to the extent that:

(i) The partner or related person undertakes one or more contractual obligations so that the partnership may obtain a loan;

(ii) The contractual obligations of the partner or related person eliminate substantially all the risk to the lender that the partnership will not satisfy its obligations under the loan; and

(iii) One of the principal purposes of using the contractual obligations is to attempt to permit partners (other than those who are directly or indirectly liable for the obligation) to include a portion of the loan in the basis of their partnership interests.

The partners are considered to bear the economic risk of loss for the liability in accordance with their relative economic burdens for the liability pursuant to the contractual obligations. For example, a lease between a partner and a partnership which is not on commercially reasonable terms may be tantamount to a guarantee by the partner of a partnership liability.

(3) Plan to circumvent or avoid the obligation. An obligation of a partner to make a payment is not recognized if the facts and circumstances evidence a plan to circumvent or avoid the obligation.

(4) Example. The following example illustrates the principle of paragraph (j)(3) of this section.

Example. Plan to circumvent or avoid obligation. A and B form a general partnership. A, a corporation, contributes $20,000 and B contributes $80,000 to the partnership. A is obligated to restore any deficit in its partnership capital account. The partnership agreement allocates losses 20% to A and 80% to B until B's capital account is reduced to zero, after which all losses are allocated to A. The partnership purchases depreciable property for $250,000 using its $100,000 cash and a $150,000 recourse loan from a bank. B guarantees payment of the $150,000 loan to the extent the loan remains unpaid after the bank has exhausted its remedies against the partnership. A is a subsidiary, formed by a parent of a consolidated group, with capital limited to $20,000 to allow the consolidated group to enjoy the tax losses generated by the property while at the same time limiting its monetary exposure for such losses. These facts, when considered together with B's guarantee, indicate a plan to circumvent or avoid A's obligation to contribute to the partnership. The rules of section 752 must be applied as if A's obligation to contribute did not exist. Accordingly, the $150,000 liability is a recourse liability that is allocated entirely to B.

* * *

§ 1.752–3 Partner's share of nonrecourse liabilities.

(a) In general. A partner's share of the nonrecourse liabilities of a partnership equals the sum of paragraphs (a)(1) through (a)(3) of this section as follows—

(1) The partner's share of partnership minimum gain determined in accordance with the rules of section 704(b) and the regulations thereunder;

(2) The amount of any taxable gain that would be allocated to the partner under section 704(c) (or in the same manner as section 704(c) in connection with a revaluation of partnership property) if the partnership disposed of (in a taxable transaction) all partnership property subject to one or more nonrecourse liabilities of the partnership in full satisfaction of the liabilities and for no other consideration; and

(3) The partner's share of the excess nonrecourse liabilities (those not allocated under paragraphs (a)(1) and (a)(2) of this section) of the partnership as determined in accordance with the partner's share of partnership profits. The partner's interest in partnership profits is determined by taking into account all facts and circumstances relating to the economic arrangement of the partners. The partnership agreement may specify the partners' interests in partnership profits for purposes of allocating excess nonrecourse liabilities provided the interests so specified are reasonably consistent with allocations (that have substantial economic effect under the section 704(b) regulations) of some other significant item of partnership income or gain. Alternatively, excess nonrecourse liabilities may be allocated among the partners in accordance with the manner in which it is reasonably expected that the deductions attributable to those nonrecourse liabilities will be allocated. Additionally, the partnership may first allocate an excess nonrecourse liability to a partner up to the amount of built-in gain that is allocable to the partner on section 704(c) property (as defined under §1.704–3(a)(3)(ii)) or property for which reverse section 704(c) allocations are applicable (as described in §1.704–3(a)(6)(i)) where such property is subject to the non-recourse liability to the extent that such built-in gain exceeds the gain described in paragraph (a)(2) of this section with respect to such property. This additional method does not apply for purposes of §1.707–5(a)(2)(ii). To the extent that a partnership uses this additional method and the entire amount of the excess nonrecourse liability is not allocated to the contributing partner, the partnership must allocate the remaining amount of the excess nonrecourse liability under one of the other methods in this paragraph (a)(3). Excess nonrecourse liabilities are not required to be allocated under the same method each year.

(b) Allocation of a single nonrecourse liability among multiple properties— (1) In general. For purposes of determining the amount of taxable gain under paragraph (a)(2) of this section, if a partnership holds multiple properties subject to a single nonrecourse liability, the partnership may allocate the liability among the multiple properties under any reasonable method. A method is not reasonable if it allocates to any item of property an amount of the liability that, when combined with any other liabilities allocated to the property, is in excess of the fair market value of the property at the time the liability is incurred. The portion of the nonrecourse liability allocated to each item of partnership property is then treated as a separate loan under paragraph (a)(2) of this section. In general, a partnership may not change the method of allocating a single nonrecourse liability under this paragraph (b) while any portion of the liability is outstanding. However, if one or more of the multiple properties subject to the liability is no longer subject to the liability, the portion of the liability allocated to that property must be reallocated among the properties still subject to the liability so that the amount of the liability allocated to any property does not exceed the fair market value of such property at the time of reallocation.

(2) Reductions in principal. For purposes of this paragraph (b), when the outstanding principal of a partnership liability is reduced, the reduction of outstanding principal is allocated among the multiple properties in the same proportion that the partnership liability originally was allocated to the properties under paragraph (b)(1) of this section.

(c) Examples. The following examples illustrate the principles of paragraph (a) of this section.

Example (1). Partner's share of nonrecourse liabilities. The AB partnership purchases depreciable property for a $1,000 purchase money note that is nonrecourse liability under the rules of this section. Assume that this is the only nonrecourse liability of the partnership, and that no principal payments are due on the purchase money note for a year. The partnership agreement provides that all items of income, gain, loss, and deduction are allocated equally. Immediately after purchasing the depreciable property, the partners share the nonrecourse liability equally because they have equal interests in partnership profits. A and B are each treated as if they contributed $500 to the partnership to reflect each partner's increase in his or her share of partnership liabilities (from $0 to $500). The minimum gain with respect to an item of partnership property subject to a nonrecourse liability equals the amount of gain that would be recognized if the partnership disposed of the property in full satisfaction of the nonrecourse liability and for no other consideration. Therefore, if the partnership claims a depreciation deduction of $200 for the depreciable property for the year it acquires that property partnership minimum gain for the year will increase by $200 (the excess of the $1,000 nonrecourse liability over the $800 adjusted tax basis of the property). See section 704(b) and the regulations thereunder. A and B each have a $100 share of partnership minimum gain at the end of that year because the depreciation deduction is treated as a nonrecourse deduction. See section 704(b) and the regulation thereunder. Accordingly, at the end of that year, A and B are allocated $100 each of the nonrecourse liability to match their shares of partnership minimum gain. The remaining $800 of the nonrecourse liability will be allocated equally between A and B ($400 each).

Example (2). Excess nonrecourse liabilities allocated consistently with reasonably expected deductions. The facts are the same as in Example 1 except that the partnership agreement provides that depreciation deductions will be allocated to A. The partners agree to allocate excess nonrecourse liabilities in accordance with the manner in which it is reasonably expected that the deductions attributable to those nonrecourse liabilities will be allocated. Assuming that the allocation of all of the depreciation deductions to A is valid under section 704(b), immediately after purchasing the depreciable property, A's share of the nonrecourse liability is $1,000. Accordingly, A is treated as if A contributed $1,000 to the partnership.

Example (3). Allocation of liability among multiple properties. **(i)** A and B are equal partners in a partnership (PRS). A contributes $70 of cash in exchange for a 50-percent interest in PRS. B contributes two items of property, X and Y, in exchange for a 50-percent interest in PRS. Property X has a fair market value (and book value) of $70 and an adjusted basis of $40, and is subject to a nonrecourse liability of $50. Property Y has a fair market value (and book value) of $120, an adjusted basis of $40, and is subject to a nonrecourse liability of $70. Immediately after the initial contributions, PRS refinances the two separate liabilities with a single $120 nonrecourse liability. All of the built-in gain attributable to Property X ($30) and Property Y ($80) is section 704(c) gain allocable to B.

(ii) The amount of the nonrecourse liability ($120) is less than the total book value of all of the properties that are subject to such liability ($70 + $120 = $190), so there is no partnership minimum gain. §1.704–2(d). Accordingly, no portion of the liability is allocated pursuant to paragraph (a)(1) of this section.

(iii) Pursuant to paragraph (b)(1) of this section, PRS decides to allocate the nonrecourse liability evenly between the Properties X and Y. Accordingly, each of Properties X and Y are treated as being subject to a separate $60 nonrecourse liability for purposes of applying paragraph (a)(2) of this section. Under paragraph (a)(2) of this section, B will be allocated $20 of the liability for each of Properties X and Y (in each case, $60 liability minus $40 adjusted basis.) As a result, a portion of the liability is allocated pursuant to paragraph (a)(2) of this section as follows:

Partner	Property	Tier 1	Tier 2
A	X	$0	$ 0
	Y	0	0
B	X	0	20
	Y	0	20

(iv) PRS has $80 of excess nonrecourse liability that it may allocate in any manner consistent with paragraph (a)(3) of this section. PRS determines to allocate the $80 of excess nonrecourse liabilities to the partners up to their share of the remaining section 704(c) gain on the properties, with any remaining amount of liabilities being allocated equally to A and B consistent with their equal interests in partnership profits. B has $70 of remaining section 704(c) gain ($10 on Property X and $60 on Property Y), and thus will be allocated $70 of the liability in accordance with this gain.

The remaining $10 is divided equally between A and B. Accordingly, the overall allocation of the $120 nonrecourse liability is as follows:

Partner	Tier1	Tier 2	Tier 3	Total
A	$0	$ 0	$ 5	$ 5
B	0	40	75	115

§ 1.752–4 Special rules.

(a) Tiered partnerships. An upper-tier partnership's share of the liabilities of a lower-tier partnership (other than any liability of the lower-tier partnership that is owed to the upper-tier partnership) is treated as a liability of the upper-tier partnership for purposes of applying section 752 and the regulations thereunder to the partners of the upper-tier partnership.

(b) Related person definition.— **(1) In general.** A person is related to a partner if the person and the partner bear a relationship to each other that is specified in section 267(b) or 707(b)(1), subject to the following modifications:

(i) Substitute "80 percent or more" for "more than 50 percent" each place it appears in those sections;

(ii) A person's family is determined by excluding brothers and sisters; and

(iii) Disregard sections 267(e)(1) and 267(f)(1) (A).

(2) Person related to more than one partner— (i) In general. If, in applying the related person rules in paragraph (b)(1) of this section, a person is related to more than one partner, paragraph (b)(1) of this section is applied by treating the person as related only to the partner with whom there is the highest percentage of related ownership. If two or more partners have the same percentage of related ownership and no other partner has a greater percentage, the liability is allocated equally among the partners having the equal percentages of related ownership.

(ii) Natural persons. For purposes of determining the percentage of related ownership between a person and a partner, natural persons who are related by virtue of being members of the same family are treated as having a percentage relationship of 100 percent with respect to each other.

(iii) Related partner exception. Notwithstanding paragraph (b)(1) of this section (which defines related person), persons owning interests directly or indirectly in the same partnership are not treated as related persons for purposes of determining the economic risk of loss borne by each of them for the liabilities of the partnership. This paragraph (iii) does not apply when determining a partner's interest under the de minimis rules in §§ 1.752–2(d) and (e).

(iv) Special rule where entity structured to avoid related person status— (A) In general. If—

(1) A partnership liability is owed to or guaranteed by another entity that is a partnership, an S corporation, a C corporation, or a trust;

(2) A partner or related person owns (directly or indirectly) a 20 percent or more ownership interest in the other entity; and

(3) A principal purpose of having the other entity act as a lender or guarantor of the liability was to avoid the determination that the partner that owns the interest bears the economic risk of loss for federal income tax purposes for all or part of the liability;

then the partner is treated as holding the other entity's interest as a creditor or guarantor to the extent of the partner's or related person's ownership interest in the entity.

(B) Ownership interest. For purposes of paragraph (b)(2)(iv)(A) of this section, a person's ownership interest in:

(1) A partnership equals the partner's highest percentage interest in any item of partnership loss or deduction for any taxable year;

(2) An S corporation equals the percentage of the outstanding stock in the S corporation owned by the shareholder;

(3) A C corporation equals the percentage of the fair market value of the issued and outstanding stock owned by the shareholder; and

(4) A trust equals the percentage of the actuarial interests owned by the beneficial owner of the trust.

(C) **Example. Entity structured to avoid related person status.** A, B, and C form a general partnership, ABC. A, B, and C are equal partners, each contributing $1,000 to the partnership. A and B want to loan money to ABC and have the loan treated as nonrecourse for purposes of section 752. A and B form partnership AB to which each contributes $50,000. A and B share losses equally in partnership AB. Partnership AB loans partnership ABC $100,000 on a nonrecourse basis secured by the property ABC buys with the loan. Under these facts and circumstances, A and B bear the economic risk of loss with respect to the partnership liability equally based on their percentage interest in losses of partnership AB.

(c) Limitation. The amount of an indebtedness is taken into account only once, even though a partner (in addition to the partner's liability for the indebtedness as a partner) may be separately liable therefor in a capacity other than as a partner.

(d) Time of determination. A partner's share of partnership liabilities must be determined whenever the determination is necessary in order to determine the tax liability of the partner or any other person. See § 1.705–1(a) for rules regarding when the adjusted basis of a partner's interest in the partnership must be determined.

* * *

§ 1.752–6 Partnership assumption of partner's section 358(h)(3) liability after October 18, 1999, and before June 24, 2003.

(a) In general. If, in a transaction described in section 721(a), a partnership assumes a liability (defined in section 358(h)(3)) of a partner (other than a liability to which section 752(a) and (b) apply), then, after application of section 752(a) and (b), the partner's basis in the partnership is reduced (but not below the adjusted value of such interest) by the amount (determined as of the date of the exchange) of the liability. For purposes of this section, the adjusted value of a partner's interest in a partnership is the fair market value of that interest increased by the partner's share of partnership liabilities under §§ 1.752–1 through 1.752–5.

(b) Exceptions.— (1) In general. Except as provided in paragraph (b)(2) of this section, the exceptions contained in section 358(h)(2)(A) and (B) apply to this section.

(2) Transactions described in Notice 2000–44. The exception contained in section 358(h)(2)(B) does not apply to an assumption of a liability (defined in section 358(h)(3)) by a partnership as part of a transaction described in, or a transaction that is substantially similar to the transactions described in, Notice 2000–44 (2000–2 C.B. 255). See § 601.601(d)(2) of this chapter.

(c) Example. The following example illustrates the principles of paragraph (a) of this section:

Example. In 1999, A and B form partnership PRS. A contributes property with a value and basis of $200, subject to a nonrecourse debt obligation of $50 and a fixed or contingent obligation of $100 that is not a liability to which section 752(a) and (b) applies, in exchange for a 50% interest in PRS. Assume that, after the contribution, A's share of partnership liabilities under §§ 1.752–1 through 1.752–5 is $25. Also assume that the $100 liability is not associated with a trade or business contributed by A to PRS or with assets contributed by A to PRS. After the contribution, A's basis in PRS is $175 (A's basis in the contributed land ($200) reduced by the nonrecourse debt assumed by PRS ($50), increased by A's share of partnership liabilities under §§ 1.752–1 through 1.752–5 ($25)). Because A's basis in the PRS interest is greater than the adjusted value of A's interest, $75 (the fair market value of A's interest ($50) increased by A's share of partnership liabilities ($25)), paragraph (a) of this section operates to reduce A's basis in the PRS interest (but not below the adjusted value of that interest) by the amount of liabilities described in section 358(h)(3) (other than liabilities to which section 752(a) and (b) apply) assumed by PRS. Therefore, A's basis in PRS is reduced to $75.

(d) Effective date— (1) In general. This section applies to assumptions of liabilities occurring after October 18, 1999, and before June 24, 2003.

(2) Election to apply § 1.752–7. The partnership may elect, under § 1.752–7(k)(2), to apply the provisions referenced in § 1.752–7 (k)(2) (ii) to all assumptions of liabilities by the partnership occurring after October 18, 1999, and before June 24, 2003. Section 1.752–7(k)(2) describes the manner in which the election is made.

§ 1.752–7 Partnership assumption of partner's § 1.752–7 liability on or after June 24, 2003.

(a) Purpose and structure. The purpose of this section is to prevent the acceleration or duplication of loss through the assumption of obligations not described in § 1.752–1 (a)(4)(i) in transactions involving partnerships. Under paragraph (c) of this section, any such obligation that is assumed by a partnership from a partner in a transaction governed by section 721(a) is treated as section 704(c) property. Paragraphs (e), (f), and (g) of this section provide rules for situations where a partnership assumes such an obligation from a partner and, subsequently, that partner transfers all or part of the partnership interest, that partner receives a distribution in liquidation of the partnership interest, or another partner assumes part or all of that obligation from the partnership. These rules prevent the duplication of loss by prohibiting the partnership and any person other than the partner from whom the obligation was assumed from claiming a deduction, loss, or capital expense to the extent of the built-in loss associated with the obligation. These rules also prevent the acceleration of loss by deferring the partner's deduction or loss attributable to the obligation (if any) until the satisfaction of the § 1.752–7 liability (within the meaning of paragraph (b)(8) of this section). Paragraph (d) of this section provides a number of exceptions to paragraphs (e), (f), and (g) of this section, including a de minimis exception. Paragraph (i) provides a special rule for situations in which an amount paid to satisfy a § 1.752–7 liability is capitalized into other partnership property. Paragraph (j) of this section provides special rules for tiered partnership transactions.

(b) Definitions. For purposes of this section, the following definitions apply:

(1) Assumption. The principles of § 1.752–1(d) and (e) apply in determining if a § 1.752–7 liability has been assumed.

(2) Adjusted value. The adjusted value of a partner's interest in a partnership is the fair market value of that interest increased by the partner's share of partnership liabilities under §§ 1.752–1 through 1.752–5.

(3) § 1.752–7 liability—

(i) In general. A § 1.752–7 liability is an obligation described in § 1.752—1 (a)(4)(ii) to the extent that either—

(A) The obligation is not described in § 1.752–1 (a)(4)(i); or

(B) The amount of the obligation (under paragraph (b)(3)(ii) of this section) exceeds the amount taken into account under § 1.752–1 (a)(4)(i).

(ii) Amount and share of § 1.752–7 liability. The amount of a § 1.752–7 liability (or, for purposes of paragraph (b)(3)(i) of this section, the amount of an obligation) is the amount of cash that a willing assignor would pay to a willing assignee to assume the § 1.752–7 liability in an arm's-length transaction. If the obligation arose under a contract in exchange for rights granted to the obligor under that contract, and those contractual rights are contributed to the partnership in connection with the partnership's assumption of the contractual obligation, then the amount of the § 1.752–7 liability or obligation is the amount of cash, if any, that a willing assignor would pay to a willing assignee to assume the entire contract. A partner's share of a partnership's § 1.752–7 liability is the amount of deduction that would be allocated to the partner with respect to the § 1.752–7 liability if the partnership disposed of all of its assets, satisfied all of its liabilities (other than § 1.752–7 liabilities), and paid an unrelated person to assume all of its § 1.752–7 liabilities in a fully taxable arm's-length transaction (assuming such payment would give rise to an immediate deduction to the partnership).

(iii) Example. In 2005, A, B, and C form partnership PRS. A contributes $10,000,000 in exchange for a 25% interest in PRS and PRS's assumption of a debt obligation. The debt obligation was issued for cash and the issue price was equal to the stated redemption price at maturity ($5,000,000). The debt obligation bears interest, payable quarterly, at a fixed rate of interest, which was a market rate of interest when the debt obligation was issued. At the time of the assumption, all accrued interest has been paid. Prior to the partnership assuming the obligation, interest rates decrease, resulting in the debt obligation bearing an above-market interest rate. Assume that, as a result of the decline in interest rates, A would have had to pay a willing assignee $6,000,000 to assume the debt obligation. The assumption of the debt obligation by PRS from A is treated as an assumption of a § 1.752–1 (a)(4)(i) liability in the amount of $5,000,000 (the portion of the total amount of the debt obligation that has created basis in A's assets, that is, the $5,000,000 that was issued in exchange for the debt obligation) and an assumption of a § 1.752–7 liability in the amount of $1,000,000 (the difference between the total obligation, $6,000,000, and the § 1.752–1 (a)(4)(i) liability, $5,000,000).

(4) § 1.752–7 liability transfer—

(i) In general. Except as provided in paragraph (b)(4)(ii) of this section, a § 1.752–7 liability transfer is any assumption of a § 1.752–7 liability by a partnership from a partner in a transaction governed by section 721(a).

(ii) Terminations under section 708(b)(1)(B). In determining if a deemed contribution of assets and assumption of liability as a result of a technical termination is treated as a § 1.752–7 liability transfer, only § 1.752–7 liabilities that were assumed by the terminating partnership as part of an earlier § 1.752–7 liability transfer are taken into account and, then, only to the extent of the remaining built-in loss associated with that § 1.752–7 liability.

(5) § 1.752–7 liability partner—

(i) In general. A § 1.752–7 liability partner is a partner from whom a partnership assumes a § 1.752–7 liability as part of a § 1.752–7 liability transfer or any person who acquires a partnership interest from the § 1.752–7 liability partner in a transaction to which paragraph (e)(3) of this section applies.

(ii) Tiered partnerships— (A) Assumption by a lower-tier partnership. If, in a § 1.752–7 liability transfer, a partnership (lower-tier partnership) assumes a §1.752–7 liability from another partnership (upper-tier partnership), then both the upper-tier partnership and the partners of the upper-tier partnership are § 1.752–7 liability partners. Therefore, paragraphs (e) and (f) of this section apply on a sale or liquidation of any partner's interest in the upper-tier partnership and on a sale or liquidation of the upper-tier partnership's interest in the lower-tier partnership. See paragraph (j) (3) of this section. If, in a § 1.752–7 liability transfer, the upper-tier partnership assumes a § 1.752–7 liability from a partner, and, subsequently, in another § 1.752–7 liability transfer, a lower-tier partnership assumes that § 1.752–7 liability from the upper-tier partnership, then the partner from whom the upper-tier partnership assumed the § 1.752–7 liability continues to be the § 1.752–7 liability partner of the lower-tier partnership with respect to the remaining built-in loss associated with that § 1.752–7 liability. Any new built-in loss associated with the § 1.752–7 liability that is created on the assumption of the § 1.752–7 liability from the upper-tier partnership by the lower-tier partnership is shared by all the partners of the upper-tier partnership in accordance with their interests in the upper-tier partnership, and each partner of the upper-tier partnership is treated as a § 1.752–7 liability partner with respect to that new built-in loss. See paragraph (e)(3)(ii), *Example 3* of this section.

(B) Distribution of partnership interest. If, in a transaction described in § 1.752–7(e)(3), an interest in a partnership (lower-tier partnership) that has assumed a § 1.752–7 liability is distributed by a partnership (upper-tier partnership) that is the § 1.752–7 liability partner with respect to that liability, then the persons receiving interests in the lower-tier partnership are § 1.752–7 liability partners with respect to the lower-tier partnership to the same extent that they were prior to the distribution.

* * *

§ 1.753–1 Partner receiving income in respect of decedent.

(a) Income in respect of a decedent under section 736(a). All payments coming within the provisions of section 736(a) made by a partnership to the estate or other successor in interest of a deceased partner are considered income in respect of the decedent under section 691. The estate or other successor in interest of a deceased partner shall be considered to have received income in respect of a decedent to the extent that amounts are paid by a third person in exchange for rights to future payments from the partnership under section 736 (a). When a partner who is receiving payments under section 736(a) dies, section 753 applies to any remaining payments under section 736(a) made to his estate or other successor in interest.

(b) Other income in respect of a decedent. When a partner dies, the entire portion of the distributive share which is attributable to the period ending with the date of his death and which is taxable to his estate or other successor constitutes income in respect of a decedent under section 691. This rule applies even though that part of the distributive share for the period before death which the decedent withdrew is not included in the value of the decedent's partnership interest for estate tax purposes. See paragraph (c)(3) of § 1.706–1.

(c) Example. The provisions of this section may be illustrated by the following example:

Example. A and the decedent B were equal partners in a business having assets (other than money) worth $40,000 with an adjusted basis of $10,000. Certain partnership business was well advanced towards completion before B's death and, after B's death but before the end of the partnership year, payment of $10,000 was made to the partnership for such work. The partnership agreement provided that, upon the death of one of the partners, all partnership property, including unfinished work, would pass to the surviving partner, and that the surviving partner would pay the estate of the decedent the undrawn balance of his share of partnership earnings to the date of death, plus $10,000 in each of the three years after death. B's share of earnings to the date of his death was $4,000, of which he had withdrawn $3,000. B's distributive share of partnership income of $4,000 to the date of his death is income in respect of a decedent (although only the $1,000 undrawn at B's death will be reflected in the value of B's partnership interest on B's estate tax return). Assume that the value of B's interest in partnership property at the date of his death was $22,000, composed of the following items: B's one-half share of the assets of $40,000, plus $2,000, B's interest in partnership cash. It should be noted that B's $1,000 undrawn share of earnings to the date of his death is not a separate item but will be paid from partnership assets. Under the partnership agreement, A is to pay B's estate a total of $31,000. The difference of $9,000 between the amount to be paid by A ($31,000) and the value of B's interest in partnership property ($22,000) comes within section 736(a) and, thus, also constitutes income in respect of a decedent. (However, the $17,000 difference between the $5,000 basis for B's share of the partnership property and its $22,000 value at the date of his death does not constitute income in respect of a decedent.) If, before the close of the partnership taxable year, A pays B's estate $11,000, of which they agree to allocate $3,000 as the payment under section 736(a), B's estate will include $7,000 in its gross income (B's $4,000 distributive share plus $3,000 payment under section 736(a)). In computing the deduction under section 691 (c), this $7,000 will be considered as the value for estate tax purposes of such income in respect of a decedent, even though only $4,000 ($1,000 of distributive share not withdrawn, plus $3,000, payment under section 736(a)) of this amount can be identified on the estate tax return as part of the partnership interest.

* * *

§ 1.754–1 Time and manner of making election to adjust basis of partnership property.

(a) In general. A partnership may adjust the basis of partnership property under sections 734(b) and 743(b) if it files an election in accordance with the rules set forth in paragraph (b) of this section. An election may not be filed to make the adjustments provided in either section 734(b) or section 743(b) alone, but such an election must apply to both sections. An election made under the provisions of this section shall apply to all property distributions and transfers of partnership interests taking place in the partnership taxable year for which the election is made and in all subsequent partnership taxable years unless the election is revoked pursuant to paragraph (c) of this section.

(b) Time and method of making election. (1) An election under section 754 and this section to adjust the basis of partnership property under sections 734(b) and 743(b), with respect to a distribution of property to a partner or a transfer of an interest in a partnership, shall be made in a written statement filed with the partnership return for the taxable year during which the distribution or transfer occurs. For the election to be valid, the return must be filed not later than the time prescribed by paragraph (e) of § 1.6031–1 (including extensions thereof) for filing the return for such taxable year (or before August 23, 1956, whichever is later). Notwithstanding the preceding two sentences, if a valid election has been made under section 754 and this section for a preceding taxable year and not revoked pursuant to paragraph (c) of this section, a new election is not required to be made. The statement required by this subparagraph shall (i) set forth the name and address of the partnership making the election, (ii) be signed by any one of the partners, and (iii) contain a declaration that the partnership elects under section 754 to apply the provisions of section 734(b) and section 743(b). For rules regarding extensions of time for filing elections, see § 1.9100–1.

(2) The principles of this paragraph may be illustrated by the following example:

Example. A, a U.S. citizen, is a member of partnership ABC, which has not previously made an election under section 754 to adjust the basis of partnership property. The partnership and the partners use the calendar year as the taxable year. A sells his interest in the partnership to D on January 1, 1971. The partnership may elect under section 754 and this section to adjust the basis of partnership property under sections 734(b) and 743(b). Unless an extension of time to make the election is obtained under the provisions of § 1.9100–1, the election must be made in a written statement filed with the partnership return for 1971 and must contain the information specified in subparagraph (1) of this paragraph. Such return must be filed by April 17, 1972 (unless an extension of time for filing the return is obtained). The election will apply to all distributions of property to a partner and transfers of an interest in the partnership occurring in 1971 and subsequent years, unless revoked pursuant to paragraph (c) of this section.

(c) Revocation of election.—(1) In general. A partnership having an election in effect under this section may revoke such election with the approval of the district director for the internal revenue district in which the partnership return is required to be filed. A partnership which wishes to revoke such an election shall file with the district director for the internal revenue district in which the partnership return is required to be filed an application setting forth the grounds on which the revocation is desired. The application shall be filed not later than 30 days after the close of the partnership taxable year with respect to which revocation is intended to take effect and shall be signed by any one of the partners. Examples of situations which may be considered sufficient reason for approving an application for revocation include a change in the nature of the partnership business, a substantial increase in the assets of the partnership, a change in the character of partnership assets, or an increased frequency of retirements or shifts of partnership interests, so that an increased administrative burden would result to the partnership from the election. However, no application for revocation of an election shall be approved when the purpose of the revocation is primarily to avoid stepping down the basis of partnership assets upon a transfer or distribution.

(2) Revocations effective on December 15, 1999. Notwithstanding paragraph (c)(1) of this section, any partnership having an election in effect under this section for its taxable year that includes December 15, 1999, may revoke such election effective for transfers or distributions occurring on or after December 15, 1999, by attaching a statement to the partnership's return for such year. For the revocation to be valid, the statement must be filed not later than the time prescribed by § 1.6031(a)–1 (e) (including extensions thereof) for filing the return for such taxable year, and must set forth the name and address of the partnership revoking the election, be signed by any one of the partners who is authorized to sign the partnership's federal income tax return, and contain a declaration that the partnership revokes its election under section 754 to apply the provisions of section 734(b) and 743(b). In addition, the following statement must be prominently displayed in capital letters on the first page of the partnership's return for such year: "RETURN FILED PURSUANT TO 1.754–1(c)(2).

§ 1.755–1 Rules for allocation of basis.

(a) In general— (1) Scope. This section provides rules for allocating basis adjustments under sections 743(b) and 734(b) among partnership property. If there is a basis adjustment to which this section applies, the basis adjustment is allocated among the partnership's assets as follows. First, the partnership must determine the value of each of its assets under paragraphs (a)(2) through (5) of this section. Second, the basis adjustment is allocated between the two classes of property described in section 755(b). These classes of property consist of capital assets and section 1231(b) property (capital gain property), and any other property of the partnership (ordinary income property). For purposes of this section, properties and potential gain treated as unrealized receivables under section 751(c) and the regulations thereunder shall be treated as separate assets that are ordinary income property. Third, the portion of the basis adjustment allocated to each class is allocated among the items within the class. Basis adjustments under section 743(b) are allocated among partnership assets under paragraph (b) of this section. Basis adjustments under section 734(b) are allocated among partnership assets under paragraph (c) of this section.

(2) Coordination of sections 755 and 1060. If there is a basis adjustment to which this section applies, and the assets of the partnership constitute a trade or business (as described in § 1.1060–1 (b)(2)), then the partnership is required to use the residual method to assign values to the partnership's section 197 intangibles. To do so, the partnership must, first, determine the value of partnership assets other than section 197 intangibles under paragraph (a)(3) of this section. The partnership then must determine partnership gross value under paragraph (a)(4) of this section. Last, the partnership must assign values to the partnership's section 197 intangibles under paragraph (a)(5) of this section. For purposes of this section, the term section 197 intangibles includes all section 197 intangibles (as defined in section 197), as well as any goodwill or going concern value that would not qualify as a section 197 intangible under section 197.

(3) Values of properties other than section 197 intangibles. For purposes of this section, the fair market value of each item of partnership property other than section 197 intangibles shall be determined on the basis of all the facts and circumstances, taking into account section 7701(g).

(4) Partnership gross value— (i) Basis adjustments under section 743(b)— (A) In general. Except as provided in paragraph (a)(4)(ii) of this section, in the case of a basis adjustment under section 743(b), partnership gross value generally is equal to the amount that, if assigned to all partnership property, would result in a liquidating distribution to the partner equal to the transferee's basis in the transferred partnership interest immediately following the relevant transfer (reduced by the amount, if any, of such basis that is attributable to partnership liabilities).

(B) Special situations. In certain circumstances, such as where income or loss with respect to particular section 197 intangibles are allocated differently among partners, partnership gross value may vary depending on the values of particular section 197 intangibles held by the partnership. In these special situations, the partnership must assign value, first, among section 197 intangibles (other than goodwill and going concern value) in a reasonable manner that is consistent with the ordering rule in paragraph (a)(5) of this section and would cause the appropriate liquidating distribution under paragraph (a)(4)(i)(A) of this section. If the actual fair market values, determined on the basis of all the facts and circumstances, of all section 197 intangibles (other than goodwill and going concern value) is not sufficient to cause the appropriate liquidating distribution, then the fair market value of goodwill and going concern value shall be presumed to equal an amount that if assigned to goodwill and going concern value would cause the appropriate liquidating distribution.

(C) Income in respect of a decedent. Solely for the purpose of determining partnership gross value under this paragraph (a)(4)(i), where a partnership interest is transferred as a result of the death of a partner, the transferee's basis in its partnership interest is determined without regard to section 1014(c), and is deemed to be adjusted for that portion of the interest, if any, that is attributable to items representing income in respect of a decedent under section 691.

(ii) Basis adjustments under section 743(b) resulting from substituted basis transactions. This paragraph (a)(4)(ii) applies to basis adjustments under section 743(b) that result from exchanges in which the transferee's basis in the partnership interest is determined in whole or in part by reference to the transferor's basis in the interest or to the basis of other property held at any time by the transferee (substituted basis transactions). In the case of a substituted basis transaction, partnership gross value equals the value of the entire partnership as a going concern, increased by the amount of partnership liabilities at the time of the exchange giving rise to the basis adjustment.

(iii) Basis adjustments under section 734(b). In the case of a basis adjustment under section 734(b), partnership gross value equals the value of the entire partnership as a going concern immediately following the distribution causing the adjustment, increased by the amount of partnership liabilities immediately following the distribution.

(5) Determining the values of section 197 intangibles— (i) Two classes. If the aggregate value of partnership property other than section 197 intangibles (as determined in paragraph (a)(3) of this section) is equal to or greater than partnership gross value (as determined in paragraph (a)(4) of this section), then all section 197 intangibles are deemed to have a value of zero for purposes of this section. In all other cases, the aggregate value of the partnership's section 197 intangibles (the residual section 197 intangibles value) is deemed to equal the excess of partnership gross value over the aggregate value of partnership property other than section 197 intangibles. The residual section 197 intangibles value must be allocated between two asset classes in the following order—

(A) Among section 197 intangibles other than goodwill and going concern value; and

(B) To goodwill and going concern value.

(ii) Values assigned to section 197 intangibles other than goodwill and going concern value. The fair market value assigned to a section 197 intangible (other than goodwill and going concern value) shall not exceed the actual fair market value (determined on the basis of all the facts and circumstances) of that asset on the date of the relevant transfer. If the residual section 197 intangibles value is less than the sum of the actual fair market values (determined on the basis of all the facts and circumstances) of all section 197 intangibles (other than goodwill and going concern value) held by the partnership, then the residual section 197 intangibles value must be allocated among the individual section 197 intangibles (other than goodwill and going concern value) as follows. The residual section 197 intangibles value is assigned first to any section 197 intangibles (other than goodwill and going concern value) having potential gain that would be treated as unrealized receivables under the flush language of section 751(c) (flush language receivables) to the extent of the basis of those section 197 intangibles and the amount of income arising from the flush language receivables that the partnership would recognize if the section 197 intangibles were sold for their actual fair market values (determined based on all the facts and circumstances) (collectively, the flush language receivables value). If the value assigned to section 197 intangibles (other than goodwill and going concern value) is less than the flush language receivables value, then the assigned value is allocated among the properties giving rise to the flush language receivables in proportion to the flush language receivables value in those properties. Any remaining residual section 197 intangibles value is allocated among the remaining portions of the section 197 intangibles (other than goodwill and going concern value) in proportion to the actual fair market values of such portions (determined based on all the facts and circumstances).

(iii) Value assigned to goodwill and going concern value. The fair market value of goodwill and going concern value is the amount, if any, by which the residual section 197 intangibles value exceeds the aggregate value of the partnership's section 197 intangibles (other than goodwill and going concern value).

(6) Examples. The provisions of paragraphs (a)(2) through (5) are illustrated by the following examples, which assume that the partnerships have an election in effect under section 754 at the time of the transfer and that the assets of each partnership constitute a trade or business (as described in § 1.1060–1(b)(2)). Except as provided, no partnership asset (other than inventory) is property described in section 751(a), and partnership liabilities are secured by all partnership assets. The examples are as follows:

Example 1. **(i)** A is the sole general partner in PRS, a limited partnership having three equal partners. PRS has goodwill and going concern value, two section 197 intangibles other than goodwill and going concern value (Intangible 1 and Intangible 2), and two other assets with fair market values (determined using all the facts and circumstances) as follows: inventory worth $1,000,000 and a building (a capital asset) worth $2,000,000. The fair market value of each of Intangible 1 and Intangible 2 is $50,000. PRS has one liability of $1,000,000, for which A bears the entire risk of loss under section 752 and the regulations thereunder. D purchases A's partnership interest for $650,000, resulting in a basis adjustment under section 743(b). After the purchase, D bears the entire risk of loss for PRS's liability under section 752 and the regulations thereunder. Therefore, D's basis in its interest in PRS is $1,650,000.

(ii) D's basis in the transferred partnership interest (reduced by the amount of such basis that is attributable to partnership liabilities) is $650,000 ($1,650,000–$1,000,000). Under paragraph (a)(4)(i) of this section, partnership gross value is $2,950,000 (the amount that, if assigned to all partnership property, would result in a liquidating distribution to D equal to $650,000).

(iii) Under paragraph (a)(3) of this section, the inventory has a fair market value of $1,000,000, and the building has a fair market value of $2,000,000. Thus, the aggregate value of partnership property other than section 197 intangibles, $3,000,000, is equal to or greater than partnership gross value, $2,950,000. Accordingly, under paragraphs (a)(3) and (5) of this section, the value assigned to each of the partnership's assets is as follows: inventory, $1,000,000; building, $2,000,000; Intangibles 1 and 2, $0; and goodwill and going concern value, $0. D's section 743(b) adjustment must be allocated under paragraph (b) of this section using these assigned fair market values.

Example 2. **(i)** Assume the same facts as in Example 1, except that the fair market values of Intangible 1 and Intangible 2 are each $300,000, and that D purchases A's interest in PRS for $1,000,000. After the purchase, D's basis in its interest in PRS is $2,000,000.

(ii) D's basis in the transferred partnership interest (reduced by the amount of such basis that is attributable to partnership liabilities) is $1,000,000 ($2,000,000–$1,000,000). Under paragraph (a)(4)(i) of this section, partnership gross value is $4,000,000 (the amount that, if assigned to all partnership property, would result in a liquidating distribution to D equal to $1,000,000).

(iii) Under paragraph (a)(5) of this section, the residual section 197 intangibles value is $1,000,000 (the excess of partnership gross value, $4,000,000, over the aggregate value of assets other than section 197 intangibles, $3,000,000 (the sum of the value of the inventory, $1,000,000, and the value of the building, $2,000,000)). The partnership must determine the values of section 197 assets by allocating the residual section 197 intangibles value among the partnership's assets. The residual section 197 intangibles value is assigned first to section 197 intangibles other than goodwill and going concern value, and then to goodwill and going concern value. Thus, $300,000 is assigned to each of Intangible 1 and Intangible 2, and $400,000 is assigned to goodwill and going concern value (the amount by which the residual section 197 intangibles value $1,000,000, exceeds the fair market value of section 197 intangibles other than goodwill and going concern value, $600,000). D's section 743(b) adjustment must be allocated under paragraph (b) of this section using these assigned fair market values.

Example 3. **(i)** Assume the same facts as in Example 1, except that the fair market values of Intangible 1 and Intangible 2 are each $300,000, and that D purchases A's interest in PRS for $750,000. After the purchase, D's basis in its interest in PRS is $1,750,000. Also assume that Intangible 1 was originally purchased for $300,000, and that its adjusted basis has been decreased to $50,000 as a result of amortization. Assume that, if PRS were to sell Intangible 1 for $300,000, it would recognize $250,000 of gain that would be treated as an unrealized receivable under the flush language in section 751(c).

(ii) D's basis in the transferred partnership interest (reduced by the amount of such basis that is attributable to partnership liabilities) is $750,000 ($1,750,000–$1,000,000). Under paragraph (a)(4)(i) of this section, partnership gross value is $3,250,000 (the amount that, if assigned to all partnership property, would result in a liquidating distribution to D equal to $750,000).

(iii) Under paragraph (a)(5) of this section, the residual section 197 intangibles value is $250,000 (the amount by which partnership gross value, $3,250,000, exceeds the aggregate value of partnership property other than section 197 intangibles, $3,000,000). Intangible 1 has potential gain that would be treated as unrealized receivables under the flush language of section 751 (c). The flush language receivables value in Intangible 1 is $300,000 (the sum of PRS's basis in Intangible 1, $50,000, and the amount of ordinary income, $250,000, that the partnership would recognize if Intangible 1 were sold for its actual fair market value). Because the residual 197 intangibles value, $250,000, is less than the flush language receivables value of Intangible 1, Intangible 1 is assigned a value of $250,000, and Intangible 2 and goodwill and going concern value are assigned a value of zero. D's section 743 (b) adjustment must be allocated under paragraph (b) of this section using these assigned fair market values.

Example 4. Assume the same facts as in Example 1, except that the fair market values of Intangible 1 and Intangible 2 are each $300,000, and that A does not sell its interest in PRS. Instead, A contributes its interest in PRS to E, a newly formed corporation wholly-owned by A, in a transaction described in section 351. Assume that the contribution results in a basis adjustment under section 743(b) (other than zero). PRS determines that its value as a going concern immediately following the contribution is $3,000,000. Under paragraph (a)(4)(ii) of this section, partnership gross value is $4,000,000 (the value of PRS as a going concern, $3,000,000, increased by the partnership's liability, $1,000,000., immediately after the contribution). Under paragraph (a)(5) of this section, the residual section 197 intangibles value is $1,000,000 (the amount by which partnership gross value, $4,000,000, exceeds the aggregate value of partnership property other than section 197 intangibles, $3,000,000). Of the residual section 197 intangibles value, $300,000 is assigned to each of Intangible 1 and Intangible 2, and $400,000 is assigned to goodwill and going concern value (the amount by which the residual section 197 intangibles value, $1,000,000, exceeds the fair market value of section 197 intangibles other than goodwill and going concern value, $600,000). E's section 743(b) adjustment must be allocated under paragraph (b)(5) of this section using these assigned fair market values.

Example 5. G is the sole general partner in PRS, a limited partnership having three equal partners (G, H, and I). PRS has goodwill and going concern value, two section 197 intangibles other than goodwill and going concern value (Intangible 1 and Intangible 2), and two capital assets with fair market values (determined using all the facts and circumstances) as follows: Vacant land worth $1,000,000, and a building worth $2,000,000. The fair market value of each of Intangible 1 and Intangible 2 is $300,000. PRS has one liability of $1,000,000, for which G bears the entire risk of loss under section 752 and the regulations thereunder. PRS distributes the land to H in liquidation of H's interest in PRS. Immediately prior to the distribution, PRS's basis in the land is $800,000, and H's basis in its interest in PRS is $750,000. The distribution causes the partnership to increase the basis of its remaining property by $50,000 under section 734(b)(1) (B). PRS determines that its value as a going concern immediately following the distribution is $2,000,000. Under paragraph (a)(4) (iii) of this section, partnership gross value is $3,000,000 (the value of PRS as a going concern, $2,000,000, increased by the partnership's liability, $1,000,000, immediately after the distribution). Under paragraph (a)(5) of this section, the residual section 197 intangibles value of PRS's section 197 intangibles is $1,000,000 (the amount by which partnership gross value, $3,000,000, exceeds the aggregate value of partnership property other than section 197 intangibles, $2,000,000). Of the residual section 197 intangibles value, $300,000 is assigned to each of Intangible 1 and Intangible 2, and $400,000 is assigned to goodwill and going concern value (the amount by which the residual section 197 intangibles value, $1,000,000, exceeds the fair market value of section 197 intangibles other than goodwill and going concern value, $600,000). PRS's section 734(b) adjustment must be allocated under paragraph (c) of this section using these assigned fair market values.

(b) Adjustments under section 743(b).— (1) Generally.— (i) Application. For basis adjustments under section 743(b) resulting from substituted basis transactions, paragraph (b)(5) of this section shall apply. For basis adjustments under section 743(b) resulting from all other transfers, paragraphs (b)(2) through (4) of this section shall apply. Except as provided in paragraph (b)(5) of this section, the portion of the basis adjustment allocated to one class of property may be an increase while the portion allocated to the other class is a decrease. This would be the case even though the total amount of the basis adjustment is zero. Except as provided in paragraph (b)(5) of this section, the portion of the basis adjustment allocated to one item of property within a class may be an increase while the portion allocated to another is a decrease. This would be the case even though the basis adjustment allocated to the class is zero.

(ii) Hypothetical transaction. For purposes of paragraphs (b)(2) through (b)(4) of this section, the allocation of the basis adjustment under section 743 (b) between the classes of property and among the items of property within each class are made based on the allocations of income, gain, or loss (including remedial allocations under §1.704–3(d)) that the transferee partner would receive (to the extent attributable to the acquired partnership interest) if, immediately after the transfer of the partnership interest, all of the partnership's property were disposed of in a fully taxable transaction for cash in an amount equal to the fair market value of such property (the hypothetical transaction). See § 1.460–4(k)(3)(v)(B) for a rule relating to the computation of income or loss that would be allocated to the transferee from a contract accounted for under a long-term contract method of accounting as a result of the hypothetical transaction.

(2) Allocations between classes of property. (i) **In general.** The amount of the basis adjustment allocated to the class of ordinary income property is equal to the total amount of income, gain, or loss (including any remedial allocations under §1.704–3(d)) that would be allocated to the transferee (to the extent attributable to the acquired partnership interest) from the sale of all ordinary income property in the hypothetical transaction. The amount of the basis adjustment to capital gain property is equal to—

(A) The total amount of the basis adjustment under section 743(b); less

(B) The amount of the basis adjustment allocated to ordinary income property under the preceding sentence; provided, however, that in no event may the amount of any decrease in basis allocated to capital gain property exceed the partnership's basis (or in the case of property subject to the remedial allocation method, the transferee's share of any remedial loss under §1.704–3(d) from the hypothetical transaction) in capital gain property. In the event that a decrease in basis allocated to capital gain property would otherwise exceed the partnership's basis in capital gain property, the excess must be applied to reduce the basis of ordinary income property.

(ii) Examples. The provisions of this paragraph (b)(2) are illustrated by the following examples:

Example (1). A and B form equal partnership PRS. A contributes $50,000 and Asset 1, a nondepreciable capital asset with a fair market value of $50,000 and an adjusted tax basis of $25,000. B contributes $100,000. PRS uses the cash to purchase Assets 2, 3, and 4. After a year, A sells its interest in PRS to T for $120,000. At the time of the transfer, A's share of the partnership's basis in partnership assets is $75,000. Therefore, T receives a $45,000 basis adjustment.

(ii) Immediately after the transfer of the partnership interest to T, the adjusted basis and fair market value of PRS's assets are as follows:

ASSETS

	Adjusted basis	Fair market value
Capital Gain Property:		
Asset 1	$25,000	$75,000
Asset 2	100,000	117,500
Ordinary Income Property:		
Asset 3	40,000	45,000
Asset 4	10,000	2,500
Total	175,000	240,000

(iii) If PRS sold all of its assets in a fully taxable transaction at fair market value immediately after the transfer of the partnership interest to T, the total amount of capital gain that would be allocated to T is equal to $46,250 ($25,000 section 704(c) built-in gain from Asset 1, plus fifty percent of the $42,500 appreciation in capital gain property). T would also be allocated a $1,250 ordinary loss from the sale of the ordinary income property.

(iv) The amount of the basis adjustment that is allocated to ordinary income property is equal to ($1,250) (the amount of the loss allocated to T from the hypothetical sale of the ordinary income property).

(v) The amount of the basis adjustment that is allocated to capital gain property is equal to $46,250 (the amount of the basis adjustment, $45,000, less ($1,250), the amount of loss allocated to T from the hypothetical sale of the ordinary income property).

Example (2). **(i)** A and B form equal partnership PRS. A and B each contribute $1,000 cash which the partnership uses to purchase Assets 1, 2, 3, and 4. After a year, A sells its partnership interest to T for $1,000. T's basis adjustment under section 743(b) is zero.

(ii) Immediately after the transfer of the partnership interest to T, the adjusted basis and fair market value of PRS's assets are as follows:

ASSETS

	Adjusted basis	Fair market value
Capital Gain Property:		
Asset 1	$500	$750
Asset 2	500	500
Ordinary Income Property:		
Asset 3	500	250
Asset 4	500	500
Total	2,000	2,000

(iii) If, immediately after the transfer of the partnership interest to T, PRS sold all of its assets in a fully taxable transaction at fair market value, T would be allocated a loss of $125 from the sale of the ordinary income property. Thus, the amount of the basis adjustment to ordinary income property is ($125). The amount of the basis adjustment to capital gain property is $125 (zero, the amount of the basis adjustment under section 743(b), less ($125), the amount of the basis adjustment allocated to ordinary income property).

(3) Allocation within the class. (i) Ordinary income property. The amount of the basis adjustment to each item of property within the class of ordinary income property is equal to—

(A) The amount of income, gain, or loss (including any remedial allocations under §1.704–3(d)) that would be allocated to the transferee (to the extent attributable to the acquired partnership interest) from the hypothetical sale of the item; reduced by

(B) The product of—

(1) Any decrease to the amount of the basis adjustment to ordinary income property required pursuant to the last sentence of paragraph (b)(2)(i) of this section; multiplied by

(2) A fraction, the numerator of which is the fair market value of the item of property to the partnership and the denominator of which is the total fair market value of all of the partnership's items of ordinary income property.

(ii) Capital gain property. The amount of the basis adjustment to each item of property within the class of capital gain property is equal to—

(A) The amount of income, gain, or loss (including any remedial allocations under §1.704–3(d)) that would be allocated to the transferee (to the extent attributable to the acquired partnership interest) from the hypothetical sale of the item; minus

(B) The product of—

(1) The total amount of gain or loss (including any remedial allocations under §1.704–3(d)) that would be allocated to the transferee (to the extent attributable to the acquired partnership interest) from the hypothetical sale of all items of capital gain property, minus the amount of the positive basis adjustment to all items of capital gain property or plus the amount of the negative basis adjustment to capital gain property; multiplied by

(2) A fraction, the numerator of which is the fair market value of the item of property to the partnership, and the denominator of which is the fair market value of all of the partnership's items of capital gain property.

(iii) Special rules—(A) Assets in which partner has no interest. An asset with respect to which the transferee partner has no interest in income, gain, losses, or deductions shall not be taken into account in applying paragraph (b)(3)(ii)(B) of this section.

(B) Limitation in decrease of basis. In no event may the amount of any decrease in basis allocated to an item of capital gain property under paragraph (b)(3)(ii)(B) of this section exceed the partnership's adjusted basis in that item (or in the case of property subject to the remedial allocation method, the transferee's share of any remedial loss under § 1.704–3(d) from the hypothetical transaction). In the event that a decrease in basis allocated under paragraph (b)(3)(ii)(B) of this section to an item of capital gain property would otherwise exceed the partnership's adjusted basis in that item, the excess must be applied to reduce the remaining basis, if any, of other capital gain assets pro rata in proportion to the bases of such assets (as adjusted under this paragraph (b)(3)).

(iv) Examples. The provisions of this paragraph (b)(3) are illustrated by the following examples:

Example (1). (i) Assume the same facts as Example 1 in paragraph (b)(2)(ii) of this section. Of the $45,000 basis adjustment, $46,250 was allocated to capital gain property. The amount allocated to ordinary income property was ($1,250).

(ii) Asset 1 is a capital gain asset, and T would be allocated $37,500 from the sale of Asset 1 in the hypothetical transaction. Therefore, the amount of the adjustment to Asset 1 is $37,500.

(iii) Asset 2 is a capital gain asset, and T would be allocated $8,750 from the sale of Asset 2 in the hypothetical transaction. Therefore, the amount of the adjustment to Asset 2 is $8,750.

(iv) Asset 3 is ordinary income property, and T would be allocated $2,500 from the sale of Asset 3 in the hypothetical transaction. Therefore, the amount of the adjustment to Asset 3 is $2,500.

(v) Asset 4 is ordinary income property, and T would be allocated ($3,750) from the sale of Asset 4 in the hypothetical transaction. Therefore, the amount of the adjustment to Asset 4 is ($3,750).

Example (2). (i) Assume the same facts as Example 1 in paragraph (b)(2)(ii) of this section, except that A sold its interest in PRS to T for $110,000 rather than $120,000. T, therefore, receives a basis adjustment under section 743(b) of $35,000. Of the $35,000 basis adjustment, ($1,250) is allocated to ordinary income property, and $36,250 is allocated to capital gain property.

(ii) Asset 3 is ordinary income property, and T would be allocated $2,500 from the sale of Asset 3 in the hypothetical transaction. Therefore, the amount of the adjustment to Asset 3 is $2,500.

(iii) Asset 4 is ordinary income property, and T would be allocated ($3,750) from the sale of Asset 4 in the hypothetical transaction. Therefore, the amount of the adjustment to Asset 4 is ($3,750).

(iv) Asset 1 is a capital gain asset, and T would be allocated $37,500 from the sale of Asset 1 in the hypothetical transaction. Asset 2 is a capital gain asset, and T would be allocated $8,750 from the sale of Asset 2 in the hypothetical transaction. The total amount of gain that would be allocated to T from the sale of the capital gain assets in the hypothetical transaction is $46,250, which exceeds the amount of the basis adjustment allocated to capital gain property by $10,000. The amount of the adjustment to Asset 1 is $33,604 ($37,500 minus $3,896 ($10,000 × $75,000/192,500)). The amount of the basis adjustment to Asset 2 is $2,646 ($8,750 minus $6,104 ($10,000 × $117,500/192,500)).

(4) Income in respect of a decedent. (i) In general. Where a partnership interest is transferred as a result of the death of a partner, under section 1014(c) the transferee's basis in its partnership interest is not adjusted for that portion of the interest, if any, which is attributable to items representing income in respect of a decedent under section 691. See §1.742–1. Accordingly, if a partnership interest is transferred as a result of the death of a partner, and the partnership holds assets representing income in respect of a decedent, no part of the basis adjustment under section 743(b) is allocated to these assets. See §1.743–1(b).

(ii) The provisions of this paragraph (b)(4) are illustrated by the following example:

Example. (i) A and B are equal partners in personal service partnership PRS. In 2004, as a result of B's death, B's partnership interest is transferred to T when PRS's balance sheet (reflecting a cash receipts and disbursements method of accounting) is as follows (based on all the facts and circumstances):

ASSETS

	Adjusted basis	Fair market value
Section 197 Intangible	$2,000	$5,000
Unrealized Receivables	0	15,000
Total	2,000	20,000

LIABILITIES AND CAPITAL

	Adjusted per books	Fair market value
Capital:		
A	1,000	10,000
B	1,000	10,000
Total	2,000	20,000

(ii) None of the assets owned by PRS is section 704(c) property, and the section 197 intangible is not amortizable. The fair market value of T's partnership interest on the applicable date of valuation set forth in section 1014 is $10,000. Of this amount, $2,500 is attributable to T's share of the partnership's section 197 intangible, and $7,500 is attributable to T's 50% share of the partnership's unrealized receivables. The partnership's unrealized receivables represent income in respect of a decedent. Accordingly, under section 1014(c), T's basis in its partnership interest is not adjusted for that portion of the interest which is attributable to the unrealized receivables. Therefore, T's basis in its partnership interest is $2,500.

(iii) Under paragraph (a)(4)(i)(C) of this section, solely for purposes of determining partnership gross value, T's basis in its partnership interest is deemed to be $10,000. Under paragraph (a)(4)(i) of this section, partnership gross value is $20,000 (the amount that, if assigned to all partnership property, would result in a liquidating distribution to T equal to $10,000).

(iv) Under paragraph (a)(5) of this section, the residual section 197 intangibles value is $5,000 (the excess of partnership gross value, $20,000, over the aggregate value of assets other than section 197 intangibles, $15,000). The residual section 197 intangibles value is assigned first to section 197 intangibles other than goodwill and going concern value, and then to goodwill and going concern value. Thus, $5,000 is assigned to the section 197 intangible, and $0 is assigned to goodwill and going concern value. T's section 743(b) adjustment must be allocated using these assigned fair market values.

(v) At the time of the transfer, B's share of the partnership's basis in partnership assets is $1,000. Accordingly, T receives a $1,500 basis adjustment under section 743(b). Under this paragraph (b)(4), the entire basis adjustment is allocated to the partnership's section 197 intangible.

(5) Substituted basis exchanges. (i) In general. This paragraph (b)(5) applies to basis adjustments under section 743(b) that result from exchanges in which the transferee's basis in the partnership interest is determined in whole or in part by reference to the transferor's basis in the interest. For exchanges on or after June 9, 2003, this paragraph (b)(5) also applies to basis adjustments under section 743(b) that result from exchanges in which the transferee's basis in the partnership interest is determined by reference to other property held at any time by the transferee. For example, this paragraph applies if a partnership interest is contributed to a corporation in a transaction to which section 351 applies or to a partnership in a transaction to which section 721(a) applies.

(ii) Allocations between classes of property. If the total amount of the basis adjustment under section 743(b) is zero, then no adjustment to the basis of partnership property will be made under this paragraph (b)(5). If there is an increase in basis to be allocated to partnership assets, such increase must be allocated to capital gain property or ordinary income property, respectively, only if the total amount of gain or loss (including any remedial allocations under §1.704–3(d)) that would be allocated to the transferee (to the extent attributable to the acquired partnership interest) from the hypothetical sale of all such property would result in a net gain or net income, as the case may be, to the transferee. Where, under the preceding sentence, an increase in basis may be allocated to both capital gain assets and ordinary income assets, the increase shall be allocated to each class in proportion to the net gain or net income, respectively, which would be allocated to the transferee from the sale of all assets in each class. If there is a decrease in basis to be allocated to partnership assets, such decrease must be allocated to capital gain property or ordinary income property, respectively, only if the total amount of gain or loss (including any remedial allocations under §1.704–3(d)) that would be allocated to the transferee (to the extent attributable to the acquired partnership interest) from the hypothetical sale of all such property would result in a net loss to the transferee. Where, under the preceding sentence, a decrease in basis may be allocated to both capital gain assets and ordinary income assets, the decrease shall be allocated to each class in proportion to the net loss which would be allocated to the transferee from the sale of all assets in each class.

(iii) Allocations within the classes.—(A) Increases. If there is an increase in basis to be allocated within a class, the increase must be allocated first to properties with unrealized appreciation in proportion to the transferee's share of the respective amounts of unrealized appreciation before such increase (but only to the extent of the transferee's share of each property's unrealized appreciation). Any remaining increase must be allocated among the properties within the class in proportion to the transferee's share of the amount that would be realized by the partnership upon the hypothetical sale of each asset in the class.

(B) Decreases. If there is a decrease in basis to be allocated within a class, the decrease must be allocated first to properties with unrealized depreciation in proportion to the transferee's shares of the respective amounts of unrealized depreciation before such decrease (but only to the extent of the transferee's share of each property's unrealized depreciation). Any remaining decrease must be allocated among the properties within the class in proportion to the transferee's shares of their adjusted bases (as adjusted under the preceding sentence).

(C) Limitation in decrease of basis. Where, as the result of a transaction to which this paragraph (b)(5) applies, a decrease in basis must be allocated to capital gain assets, ordinary income assets, or both, and the amount of the decrease otherwise allocable to a particular class exceeds the transferee's share of the adjusted basis to the partnership of all depreciated assets in that class, the transferee's negative basis adjustment is limited to the transferee's share of the partnership's adjusted basis in all depreciated assets in that class.

(D) Carryover adjustment. Where a transferee's negative basis adjustment under section 743(b) cannot be allocated to any asset, because the adjustment exceeds the transferee's share of the adjusted basis to the partnership of all depreciated assets in a particular class, the adjustment is made when the partnership subsequently acquires property of a like character to which an adjustment can be made.

(iv) Examples. The provisions of this paragraph (b)(5) are illustrated by the following examples:

Example (1). A is a member of partnership LTP, which has made an election under section 754. The three partners in LTP have equal interests in capital and profits. Solely in exchange for a partnership interest in UTP, A contributes its interest in LTP to UTP in a transaction described in section 721. At the time of the transfer, A's basis in its partnership interest ($5,000) equals its share of inside basis (also $5,000). Under section 723, UTP's basis in its interest in LTP is $5,000. LTP's only two assets on the date of contribution are inventory with a basis of $5,000 and a fair market value of $7,500, and a nondepreciable capital asset with a basis of $10,000 and a fair market value of $7,500. The amount of the basis adjustment under section 743(b) to partnership property is $0 ($5,000, UTP's basis in its interest in LTP, minus $5,000, UTP's share of LTP's basis in partnership assets). Because UTP acquired its interest in LTP in a substituted basis transaction, and the total amount of the basis adjustment under section 743(b) is zero, UTP receives no special basis adjustments under section 743(b) with respect to the partnership property of LTP.

Example (2). (i) A purchases a partnership interest in LTP at a time when an election under section 754 is not in effect. The three partners in LTP have equal interests in capital and profits. During a later year for which LTP has an election under section 754 in effect, and in a transaction that is unrelated to A's purchase of the LTP interest, A contributes its interest in LTP to UTP in a transaction described in section 721 (solely in exchange for a partnership interest in UTP). At the time of the transfer, A's adjusted basis in its interest in LTP is $20,433. Under section 721, A recognizes no gain or loss as a result of the contribution of its partnership interest to UTP. Under section 723, UTP's basis in its partnership interest in LTP is $20,433. The balance sheet of LTP on the date of the contribution shows the following:

ASSETS

	Adjusted basis	Fair market value
Cash	$5,000	$5,000
Accounts receivable	10,000	10,000
Inventory	20,000	21,000
Nondepreciable capital asset	20,000	40,000
Total	55,000	76,000

LIABILITIES AND CAPITAL

	Adjusted per books	Fair market value
Liabilities	$10,000	$10,000
Capital:		
A	15,000	22,000
B	15,000	22,000
C	15,000	22,000
Total	55,000	76,000

(ii) The amount of the basis adjustment under section 743(b) is the difference between the basis of UTP's interest in LTP and UTP's share of the adjusted basis to LTP of partnership property. UTP's interest in the previously taxed capital of LTP is $15,000 ($22,000, the amount of cash UTP would receive if LTP liquidated immediately after the hypothetical transaction, decreased by $7,000, the amount of tax gain allocated to UTP from the hypothetical transaction). UTP's share of the adjusted basis to LTP of partnership property is $18,333 ($15,000 share of previously taxed capital, plus $3,333 share of LTP's liabilities). The amount of the basis adjustment under section 743(b) to partnership property therefore, is $2,100 ($20,433 minus $18,333).

(iii) The total amount of gain that would be allocated to UTP from the hypothetical sale of capital gain property is $6,666.67 (one-third of the excess of the fair market value of LTP's nondepreciable capital asset, $40,000, over its basis, $20,000). The total amount of gain that would be allocated to UTP from the hypothetical sale of ordinary income property is $333.33 (one-third of the excess of the fair market value of LTP's inventory, $21,000, over its basis ($20,000). Under paragraph (b)(5), LTP must allocate $2,000 ($6,666.67 divided by $7,000 times $2,100) of UTP's basis adjustment to the nondepreciable capital asset. LTP must allocate $100 ($333.33 divided by $7,000 times $2,100) of UTP's basis adjustment to the inventory.

(c) Adjustments under section 734(b).*— **(1) Allocations between classes of property. (i) General rule.** Where there is a distribution of partnership property resulting in an adjustment to the basis of undistributed partnership property under section 734(b)(l)(B) or (b)(2)(B), the adjustment must be allocated to remaining partnership property of a character similar to that of the distributed property with respect to which the adjustment arose. Thus, when the partnership's adjusted basis of distributed capital gain property immediately prior to distribution exceeds the basis of the property to the distributee partner (as determined under section 732), the basis of the undistributed capital gain property remaining in the partnership is increased by an amount equal to the excess. Conversely, when the basis to the distributee partner (as determined under section 732) of distributed capital gain property exceeds the partnership's adjusted basis of such property immediately prior to the distribution, the basis of the undistributed capital gain property remaining in the partnership is decreased by an amount equal to such excess. Similarly, where there is a distribution of ordinary income property, and the basis of the property to the distributee partner (as determined under section 732) is not the same as the partnership's adjusted basis of the property immediately prior to distribution, the adjustment is made only to undistributed property of the same class remaining in the partnership.

(ii) Special rule. Where there is a distribution resulting in an adjustment under section 734(b)(1)(A) or (b)(2)(A) to the basis of undistributed partnership property, the adjustment is allocated only to capital gain property.

*Editorial comment: The Regulations do not reflect the effect of the American Jobs Creation Act of 2004 regarding no allocation of a basis decrease to stock of a corporate partner. See § 755(c).

(2) Allocations within the classes.— (i) Increases. If there is an increase in basis to be allocated within a class, the increase must be allocated first to properties with unrealized appreciation in proportion to their respective amounts of unrealized appreciation before such increase (but only to the extent of each property's unrealized appreciation). Any remaining increase must be allocated among the properties within the class in proportion to their fair market values.

(ii) Decreases. If there is a decrease in basis to be allocated within a class, the decrease must be allocated first to properties with unrealized depreciation in proportion to their respective amounts of unrealized depreciation before such decrease (but only to the extent of each property's unrealized depreciation). Any remaining decrease must be allocated among the properties within the class in proportion to their adjusted bases (as adjusted under the preceding sentence).

(3) Limitation in decrease of basis. Where a decrease in the basis of partnership assets is required under section 734(b)(2) and the amount of the decrease exceeds the adjusted basis to the partnership of property of the required character, the basis of such property is reduced to zero (but not below zero).

(4) Carryover adjustment. Where, in the case of a distribution, an increase or decrease in the basis of undistributed property cannot be made because the partnership owns no property of the character required to be adjusted, or because the basis of all the property of a like character has been reduced to zero, the adjustment is made when the partnership subsequently acquires property of a like character to which an adjustment can be made.

(5) Cross reference. See § 1.460–4(k)(3)(v)(B) for a rule relating to the computation of unrealized appreciation or depreciation in a contract accounted for under a long-term contract method of accounting.

(6) Example. The following example illustrates this paragraph (c):

Example (i) A, B, and C form equal partnership PRS. A contributes $50,000 and Asset 1, nondepreciable capital gain property with a fair market value of $50,000 and an adjusted tax basis of $25,000. B and C each contribute $100,000. PRS uses the cash to purchase Assets 2, 3, 4, 5, and 6. Assets 2 and 3 are nondepreciable capital assets, and Assets 4, 5, and 6 are inventory that has not appreciated substantially in value within the meaning of section 751(b)(3). Assets 4, 5, and 6 are the only assets held by the partnership which are subject to section 751. The partnership has an election in effect under section 754. After seven years, the adjusted basis and fair market value of PRS's assets are as follows:

ASSETS		
	Adjusted basis	Fair market value
Capital Gain Property:		
Asset 1	$ 25,000	$ 75,000
Asset 2	100,000	117,500
Asset 3	50,000	60,000
Ordinary Income Property:		
Asset 4	$ 40,000	$ 45,000
Asset 5	50,000	60,000
Asset 6	10,000	2,500
Total	275,000	360,000

(ii) **Allocation between classes.** Assume that PRS distributes Assets 3 and 5 to A in complete liquidation of A's interest in the partnership. A's basis in the partnership interest was $75,000. The partnership's basis in Assets 3 and 5 was $50,000 each. A's $75,000 basis in its partnership interest is allocated between Assets 3 and 5 under sections 732(b) and (c). A will, therefore, have a basis of $25,000 in Asset 3 (capital gain property), and a basis of $50,000 in Asset 5 (section 751 property). The distribution results in a $25,000 increase in the basis of capital gain property. There is no change in the basis of ordinary income property.

(iii) **Allocation within class.** The amount of the basis increase to capital gain property is $25,000 and must be allocated among the remaining capital gain assets in proportion to the difference between the fair market value and basis of each. The fair market value of Asset 1 exceeds its basis by $50,000. The fair market value of Asset 2 exceeds its basis by $17,500. Therefore, the basis of Asset 1 will be increased by $18,519 ($25,000, multiplied by $50,000, divided by $67,500), and the basis of Asset 2 will be increased by $6,481 ($25,000 multiplied by $17,500, divided by $67,500).

* * *

Definitions

§ 1.761–1 Terms defined.

(a) Partnership. The term partnership means a partnership as determined under §§ 301.7701–1, 301.7701–2, and 301.7701–3 of this chapter.

(b) Partner. The term "partner" means a member of a partnership.

(c) Partnership agreement. For the purposes of subchapter K, a partnership agreement includes the original agreement and any modifications thereof agreed to by all the partners or adopted in any other manner provided by the partnership agreement. Such agreement or modifications can be oral or written. A partnership agreement may be modified with respect to a particular taxable year subsequent to the close of such taxable year, but not later than the date (not including any extension of time) prescribed by law for the filing of the partnership return. As to any matter on which the partnership agreement, or any modification thereof, is silent, the provisions of local law shall be considered to constitute a part of the agreement.

(d) Liquidation of partner's interest. The term "liquidation of a partner's interest" means the termination of a partner's entire interest in a partnership by means of a distribution, or a series of distributions, to the partner by the partnership. A series of distributions will come within the meaning of this term whether they are made in one year or in more than one year. Where a partner's interest is to be liquidated by a series of distributions, the interest will not be considered as liquidated until the final distribution has been made. For the basis of property distributed in one liquidating distribution, or in a series of distributions in liquidation, see section 732(b). A distribution which is not in liquidation of a partner's entire interest, as defined in this paragraph, is a current distribution. Current distributions, therefore, include distributions in partial liquidation of a partner's interest, and distributions of the partner's distributive share. See paragraph (a)(1)(ii) of § 1.731–1.

(e) Distribution of partnership interest. For purposes of section 708(b)(1)(B) and § 1.708–1(b)(1)(iv), the deemed distribution of an interest in a new partnership by a partnership that terminates under section 708(b)(1)(B) is not a sale or exchange of an interest in the new partnership. However, the deemed distribution of an interest in a new partnership by a partnership that terminates under section 708(b)(1)(B) is treated as an exchange of the interest in the new partnership for purposes of section 743. This paragraph (e) applies to terminations of partnerships under section 708(b)(1)(B) occurring on or after May 9, 1997; however, this paragraph (e) may be applied to terminations occurring on or after May 9, 1997; however, this paragraph (e) may be applied to terminations occurring on or after May 9, 1996, provided that the partnership and its partners apply this paragraph (e) to the termination in a consistent manner.

§ 1.761–2 Exclusion of certain unincorporated organizations from the application of all or part of Subchapter K of Chapter 1 of the Code.

(a) Exclusion of eligible unincorporated organizations—(1) In general. Under conditions set forth in this section, an unincorporated organization described in subparagraph (2) or (3) of this paragraph may be excluded from the application of all or a part of the provisions of subchapter K of chapter 1 of the Code. Such organization must be availed of (i) for investment purposes only and not for the active conduct of a business, or (ii) for the joint production, extraction, or use of property, but not for the purpose of selling services or property produced or extracted. The members of such organization must be able to compute their income without the necessity of computing partnership taxable income. Any syndicate, group, pool, or joint venture which is classifiable as an association, or any group operating under an agreement which creates an organization classifiable as an association, does not fall within these provisions.

(2) Investing partnership. Where the participants in the joint purchase, retention, sale, or exchange of investment property—

(i) Own the property as coowners,

(ii) Reserve the right separately to take or dispose of their shares of any property acquired or retained, and

(iii) Do not actively conduct business or irrevocably authorize some person or persons acting in a representative capacity to purchase, sell, or exchange such investment property, although each separate participant may delegate authority to purchase, sell, or exchange his share of any such investment property for the time being for his account, but not for a period of more than a year, then

such group may be excluded from the application of the provisions of subchapter K under the rules set forth in paragraph (b) of this section.

(3) Operating agreements. Where the participants in the joint production, extraction, or use of property—

(i) Own the property as coowners, either in fee or under lease or other form of contract granting exclusive operating rights, and

(ii) Reserve the right separately to take in kind or dispose of their shares of any property produced, extracted, or used, and

(iii) Do not jointly sell services or the property produced or extracted, although each separate participant may delegate authority to sell his share of the property produced or extracted for the time being for his account, but not for a period of time in excess of the minimum needs of the industry, and in no event for more than 1 year, then

such group may be excluded from the application of the provisions of subchapter K under the rules set forth in paragraph (b) of this section. However, the preceding sentence does not apply to any unincorporated organization one of whose principal purposes is cycling, manufacturing, or processing for persons who are not members of the organization.

(b) Complete exclusion from subchapter K—(1) Time for making election for exclusion. Any unincorporated organization described in subparagraph (1) and either (2) or (3) of paragraph (a) of this section which wishes to be excluded from all of subchapter K must make the election provided in section 761(a) not later than the time prescribed by paragraph (e) of § 1.6031–1 (including extensions thereof) for filing the partnership return for the first taxable year for which exclusion from subchapter K is desired. Notwithstanding the prior sentence such organization may be deemed to have made the election in the manner prescribed in subparagraph (2)(ii) of this paragraph.

(2) Method of making election. (i) Except as provided in subdivision (ii) of this subparagraph, any unincorporated organization described in subparagraphs (1) and either (2) or (3) of paragraph (a) of this section which wishes to be excluded from all of subchapter K must make the election provided in section 761(a) in a statement attached to, or incorporated in, a properly executed partnership return, Form 1065, which shall contain the information required in this subdivision. Such return shall be filed with the internal revenue officer with whom a partnership return, Form 1065, would be required to be filed if no election were made. Where, for the purpose of determining such officer, it is necessary to determine the internal revenue district (or service center serving such district) in which the electing organization has its principal office or place of business, the principal office or place of business of the person filing the return shall be considered the principal office or place of business of the organization. The partnership return must be filed not later than the time prescribed by paragraph (e) of § 1.6031–1 (including extensions thereof) for filing the partnership return with respect to the first taxable year for which exclusion from subchapter K is desired. Such partnership return shall contain, in lieu of the information required by Form 1065 and by the instructions relating thereto, only the name or other identification and the address of the organization together with information on the return, or in the statement attached to the return, showing the names, addresses, and identification numbers of all the members of the organization; a statement that the organization qualifies under subparagraphs (1) and either (2) or (3) of paragraph (a) of this section; a statement that all of the members of the organization elect that it be excluded from all of subchapter K; and a statement indicating where a copy of the agreement under which the organization operates is available (or if the agreement is oral, from whom the provisions of the agreement may be obtained).

(ii) If an unincorporated organization described in subparagraphs (1) and either (2) or (3) of paragraph (a) of this section does not make the election provided in section 761(a) in the manner prescribed by subdivision (i) of this subparagraph, it shall nevertheless be deemed to have made the election if it can be shown from all the surrounding facts and circumstances that it was the intention of the members of such organization at the time of its formation to secure exclusion from all of subchapter K beginning with the first taxable year of the organization. Although the following facts are not exclusive, either one of such facts may indicate the requisite intent:

(a) At the time of the formation of the organization there is an agreement among the members that the organization be excluded from subchapter K beginning with the first taxable year of the organization, or

(b) The members of the organization owning substantially all of the capital interests report their respective shares of the items of income, deductions, and credits of the organization on their respective returns (making such elections as to individual items as may be appropriate) in a manner consistent with the exclusion of the organization from subchapter K beginning with the first taxable year of the organization.

(3) Effect of election—(i) In general. An election under this section to be excluded will be effective unless within 90 days after the formation of the organization (or by October 15, 1956, whichever is later) any member of the organization notifies the Commissioner that the member desires subchapter K to apply to such organization, and also advises the Commissioner that he has so notified all other members of the organization by registered or certified mail. Such election is irrevocable as long as the organization remains qualified under subparagraphs (1) and either (2) or (3) of paragraph (a) of this section, or unless approval of revocation of the election is secured from the Commissioner. Application for permission to revoke the election must be submitted to the Commissioner of Internal Revenue, Attention: T:I, Washington, D.C. 20224, no later than 30 days after the beginning of the first taxable year to which the revocation is to apply.

(ii) Special rule. Notwithstanding subdivision (i) of this subparagraph, an election deemed made pursuant to subparagraph (2)(ii) of this paragraph will not be effective in the case of an organization which had a taxable year ending on or before November 30, 1972, if any member of the organization notifies the Commissioner that the member desires subchapter K to apply to such organization, and also advises the Commissioner that he has so notified all other members of the organization by registered or certified mail. Such notification to the Commissioner must be made on or before January 2, 1973 and must include the names and addresses of all of the members of the organization.

(c) Partial exclusion from subchapter K. An unincorporated organization which wishes to be excluded from only certain sections of subchapter K must submit to the Commissioner, no later than 90 days after the beginning of the first taxable year for which partial exclusion is desired, a request for permission to be excluded from certain provisions of subchapter K. The request shall set forth the sections of subchapter K from which exclusion is sought and shall state that such organization qualifies under subparagraphs (1) and either (2) or (3) of paragraph (a) of this section, and that the members of the organization elect to be excluded to the extent indicated. Such exclusion shall be effective only upon approval of the election by the Commissioner and subject to the conditions he may impose.

(d) Cross reference. For requirements with respect to the filing of a return on Form 1065 by a partnership, see § 1.6031–1.

* * *

GAIN OR LOSS ON DISPOSITION OF PROPERTY

Determination Of Amount Of And Recognition Of Gain Or Loss

§ 1.1001–1 Computation of gain or loss.

(a) General rule. Except as otherwise provided in subtitle A of the Code, the gain or loss realized from the conversion of property into cash, or from the exchange of property for other property differing materially either in kind or in extent, is treated as income or as loss sustained. The amount realized from a sale or other disposition of property is the sum of any money received plus the fair market value of any property (other than money) received. The fair market value of property is a question of fact, but only in rare and extraordinary cases will property be considered to have no fair market value. The general method of computing such gain or loss is prescribed by section 1001(a) through (d) which contemplates that from the amount realized upon the sale or exchange there shall be withdrawn a sum sufficient to restore the adjusted basis prescribed by section 1011 and the regulations thereunder (*i.e.*, the cost or other basis adjusted for receipts, expenditures, losses, allowances, and other items chargeable against and applicable to such cost or other basis). The amount which remains after the adjusted basis has been restored to the taxpayer constitutes the realized gain. If the amount realized upon the sale or exchange is insuficient to restore to the taxpayer the adjusted basis of the property, a loss is sustained to the extent of the difference between such adjusted basis and the amount realized. The basis may be different depending upon whether gain or loss is being computed. For example, see section 1015(a) and the regulations thereunder. Section 1001(e) and paragraph (f) of this section prescribe the method of computing gain or loss upon the sale or other disposition of a term interest in property the adjusted basis (or a portion) of which is determined pursuant, or by reference, to section 1014 (relating to the basis of property acquired from a decedent) or section 1015 (relating to the basis of property acquired by gift or by a transfer in trust).

(b) Real estate taxes as amounts received. (1) Section 1001(b) and section 1012 state rules applicable in making an adjustment upon a sale of real property with respect to the real property taxes apportioned between seller and purchaser under section 164(d). Thus, if the seller pays (or agrees to pay) real property taxes attributable to the real property tax year in which the sale occurs, he shall not take into account, in determining the amount realized from the sale under section 1001(b), any amount received as reimbursement for taxes which are treated under section 164(d) as imposed upon the purchaser. Similarly, in computing the cost of the property under section 1012, the purchaser shall not take into account any amount paid to the seller as reimbursement for real property taxes which are treated under section 164(d) as imposed upon the purchaser. These rules apply whether or not the contract of sale calls for the purchaser to reimburse the seller for such real property taxes paid or to be paid by the seller.

(2) On the other hand, if the purchaser pays (or is to pay) an amount representing real property taxes which are treated under section 164(d) as imposed upon the seller, that amount shall be taken into account both in determining the amount realized from the sale under section 1001(b) and in computing the cost of the property under section 1012. It is immaterial whether or not the contract of sale specifies that the sale price has been reduced by, or is in any way intended to reflect, the taxes allocable to the seller. See also paragraph (b) of § 1.1012–1.

(3) Subparagraph (1) of this paragraph shall not apply to a seller who, in a taxable year prior to the taxable year of sale, pays an amount representing real property taxes which are treated under section 164(d) as imposed on the purchaser, if such seller has elected to capitalize such amount in accordance with section 266 and the regulations thereunder (relating to election to capitalize certain carrying charges and taxes).

(4) The application of this paragraph may be illustrated by the following examples:

Example (1). Assume that the contract price on the sale of a parcel of real estate is $50,000 and that real property taxes thereon in the amount of $1,000 for the real property tax year in which occurred the date of sale were previously paid by the seller. Assume further that $750 of the taxes are treated under section 164 (d) as imposed upon the purchaser and that he reimburses the seller in that amount in addition to the contract price. The amount realized by the seller is $50,000. Similarly, $50,000 is the purchaser's cost. If, in this example, the purchaser made no payment other than the contract price of $50,000, the amount realized by the seller would be $49,250, since the sales price would be deemed to include $750 paid to the seller in reimbursement for real property taxes imposed upon the purchaser. Similarly, $49,250 would be the purchaser's cost.

Example (2). Assume that the purchaser in example (1), above, paid all of the real property taxes. Assume further that $250 of the taxes are treated under section 164(d) as imposed upon the seller. The amount realized by the seller is $50,250. Similarly, $50,250 is the purchaser's cost, regardless of the taxable year in which the purchaser makes actual payment of the taxes.

Example (3). Assume that the seller described in the first part of example (1), above, paid the real property taxes of $1,000 in the taxable year prior to the taxable year of sale and elected under section 266 to capitalize the $1,000 of taxes. In such a case, the amount realized is $50,750. Moreover, regardless of whether the seller elected to capitalize the real property taxes, the purchaser in that case could elect under section 266 to capitalize the $750 of taxes treated under section 164(d) as imposed upon him, in which case his adjusted basis would be $50,750 (cost of $50,000 plus capitalized taxes of $570).

(c) Other rules. (1) Even though property is not sold or otherwise disposed of, gain is realized if the sum of all the amounts received which are required by section 1016 and other applicable provisions of subtitle A of the Code to be applied against the basis of the property exceeds such basis. Except as otherwise provided in section 301(c)(3)(B) with respect to distributions out of increase in value of property accrued prior to March 1, 1913, such gain is includible in gross income under section 61 as "income from whatever source derived". On the other hand, a loss is not ordinarily sustained prior to the sale or other disposition of the property, for the reason that until such sale or other disposition occurs there remains the possibility that the taxpayer may recover or recoup the adjusted basis of the property. Until some identifiable event fixes the actual sustaining of a loss and the amount thereof, it is not taken into account.

(2) The provisions of subparagraph (1) of this paragraph may be illustrated by the following example:

Example. A, an individual on a calendar year basis, purchased certain shares of stock subsequent to February 28, 1913, for $10,000. On January 1, 1954, A's adjusted basis for the stock had been reduced to $1,000 by reason of receipts and distributions described in sections 1016(a)(1) and 1016(a)(4). He received in 1954 a further distribution of $5,000, being a distribution covered by section 1016(a)(4), other than a distribution out of increase of value of property accrued prior to March 1, 1913. This distribution applied against the adjusted basis as required by section 1016(a)(4) exceeds that basis by $4,000. The $4,000 excess is a gain realized by A in 1954 and is includible in gross income in his return for that calendar year. In computing gain from the stock, as in adjusting basis, no distinction is made between items of receipts or distributions described in section 1016. If A sells the stock in 1955 for $5,000, he realizes in 1955 a gain of $5,000, since the adjusted basis of the stock for the purpose of computing gain or loss from the sale is zero.

(d) Installment sales. In the case of property sold on the installment plan, special rules for the taxation of the gain are prescribed in section 453.

(e) Transfers in part a sale and in part a gift. (1) Where a transfer of property is in part a sale and in part a gift, the transferor has a gain to the extent that the amount realized by him exceeds his adjusted basis in the property. However, no loss is sustained on such a transfer if the amount realized is less than the adjusted basis. For the determination of basis of property in the hands of the transferee, see § 1.1015–4. For the allocation of the adjusted basis of property in the case of a bargain sale to a charitable organization, see § 1.1011–2.

(2) Examples. The provisions of subparagraph (1) may be illustrated by the following examples:

Example (1). A transfers property to his son for $60,000. Such property in the hands of A has an adjusted basis of $30,000 (and a fair market value of $90,000). A's gain is $30,000, the excess of $60,000, the amount realized, over the adjusted basis, $30,000. He has made a gift of $30,000, the excess of $90,000, the fair market value, over the amount realized, $60,000.

Example (2). A transfers property to his son for $30,000. Such property in the hands of A has an adjusted basis of $60,000 (and a fair market value of $90,000). A has no gain or loss, and has made a gift of $60,000, the excess of $90,000, the fair market value, over the amount realized, $30,000.

Example (3). A transfers property to his son for $30,000. Such property in A's hands has an adjusted basis of $30,000 (and a fair market value of $60,000). A has no gain and has made a gift of $30,000, the excess of $60,000, the fair market value, over the amount realized, $30,000.

Example (4). A transfers property to his son for $30,000. Such property in A's hands has an adjusted basis of $90,000 (and a fair market value of $60,000). A has sustained no loss, and has made a gift of $30,000, the excess of $60,000, the fair market value, over the amount realized, $30,000.

* * *

§ 1.1001–2 Discharge of liabilities.

(a) Inclusion in amount realized—(1) In general. Except as provided in paragraph (a)(2) and (3) of this section, the amount realized from a sale or other disposition of property includes the amount of liabilities from which the transferor is discharged as a result of the sale or disposition.

(2) Discharge of indebtedness. The amount realized on a sale or other disposition of property that secures a recourse liability does not include amounts that are (or would be if realized and recognized) income from the discharge of indebtedness under section 61(a)(12). For situations where amounts arising from the discharge of indebtedness are not realized and recognized, see section 108 and § 1.61–12(b)(1).

(3) Liability incurred on acquisition. In the case of a liability incurred by reason of the acquisition of the property, this section does not apply to the extent that such liability was not taken into account in determining the transferor's basis for such property.

(4) Special rules. For purposes of this section—

(i) The sale or other disposition of property that secures a nonrecourse liability discharges the transferor from the liability;

(ii) The sale or other disposition of property that secures a recourse liability discharges the transferor from the liability if another person agrees to pay the liability (whether or not the transferor is in fact released from liability);

(iii) A disposition of property includes a gift of the property or a transfer of the property in satisfaction of liabilities to which it is subject;

(iv) Contributions and distributions of property between a partner and a partnership are not sales or other dispositions of property; and

(v) The liabilities from which a transferor is discharged as a result of the sale or disposition of a partnership interest include the transferor's share of the liabilities of the partnership.

(b) Effect of fair market value of security. The fair market value of the security at the time of sale or disposition is not relevant for purposes of determining under paragraph (a) of this section the amount of liabilities from which the taxpayer is discharged or treated as discharged. Thus, the fact that the fair market value of the property is less than the amount of the liabilities it secures does not prevent the full amount of those liabilities from being treated as money received from the sale or other disposition of the property. However, see paragraph (a)(2) of this section for a rule relating to certain income from discharge of indebtedness.

(c) Examples. The provisions of this section may be illustrated by the following examples. In each example assume the taxpayer uses the cash receipts and disbursements method of accounting, makes a return on the basis of the calendar year, and sells or disposes of all property which is security for a given liability.

Example (1). In 1976 A purchases an asset for $10,000. A pays the seller $1,000 in cash and signs a note payable to the seller for $9,000. A is personally liable for repayment with the seller having full recourse in the event of default. In addition, the asset which was purchased is pledged as security. During the years 1976 and 1977 A takes depreciation deductions on the asset in the amount of $3,100. During this same time period A reduces the outstanding principal on the note to $7,600. At the beginning of 1978 A sells the asset. The buyer pays A $1,600 in cash and assumes personal liability for the $7,600 outstanding liability. A becomes secondarily liable for repayment of the liability. A's amount realized is $9,200 ($1,600 + $7,600). Since A's adjusted basis in the asset is $6,900 ($10,000 – $3,100) A realizes a gain of $2,300 ($9,200 – $6,900).

Example (2). Assume the same facts as in example (1) except that A is not personally liable on the $9,000 note given to the seller and in the event of default the seller's only recourse is to the asset. In addition, on the sale of the asset by A, the purchaser takes the asset subject to the liability. Nevertheless, A's amount realized is $9,200 and A's gain realized is $2,300 on the sale.

Example (3). In 1975 L becomes a limited partner in partnership GL. L contributes $10,000 in cash to GL and L's distributive share of partnership income and loss is 10 percent. L is not entitled to receive any guaranteed payments. In 1978 M purchases L's entire interest in partnership GL. At the time of the sale L's adjusted basis in the partnership interest is $20,000. At that time L's proportionate share of liabilities, of which no partner has assumed personal liability, is $15,000. M pays $10,000 in cash for L's interest in the partnership. Under section 752(d) and this section, L's share of partnership liabilities, $15,000, is treated as money received. Accordingly, L's amount realized on the sale of the partnership interest is $25,000 ($10,000 + $15,000). L's gain realized on the sale is $5,000 ($25,000 – $20,000).

Example (4). In 1976 B becomes a limited partner in partnership BG. In 1978 B contributes B's entire interest in BG to a charitable organization described in section 170(c). At the time of the contribution all of the partnership liabilities are liabilities for which neither B nor G has assumed any personal liability and B's proportionate share of which is $9,000. The charitable organization does not pay any cash or other property to B, but takes the partnership interest subject to the $9,000 of liabilities. Assume that the contribution is treated as a bargain sale to a charitable organization and that under section 1011(b) $3,000 is determined to be the portion of B's basis in the partnership interest allocable to the sale. Under section 752(d) and this section, the $9,000 of liabilities is treated by B as money received, thereby making B's amount realized $9,000. B's gain realized is $6,000 ($9,000 – $3,000).

Example (5). In 1975 C, an individual, creates T, an irrevocable trust. Due to certain powers expressly retained by C, T is a "grantor trust" for purposes of subpart E of part 1 of subchapter J of the Code and therefore C is treated as the owner of the entire trust. T purchases an interest in P, a partnership. C, as owner of T, deducts the distributive share of partnership losses attributable to the partnership interest held by T. In 1978, when the adjusted basis of the partnership interest held by T is $1,200, C renounces the powers previously and expressly retained that initially resulted in T being classified as a grantor trust. Consequently, T ceases to be a grantor trust and C is no longer considered to be the owner of the trust. At the time of the renunciation all of P's liabilities are liabilities on which none of the partners have assumed any personal liability and the proportionate share of which of the interest held by T is $11,000. Since prior to the renunciation C was the owner of the entire trust, C was considered the owner of all the trust property for Federal income tax purposes, including the partnership interest. Since C was considered to be the owner of the partnership interest, C not T, was considered to be the partner in P during the time T was a "grantor trust". However, at the time C renounced the powers that gave rise to T's classification as a grantor trust, T no longer qualified as a grantor trust with the result that C was no longer considered to be the owner of the trust and trust property for Federal income tax purposes. Consequently, at that time, C is considered to have transferred ownership of the interest in P to T, now a separate taxable entity, independent of its grantor C. On the transfer, C's share of partnership liabilities ($11,000) is treated as money received. Accordingly, C's amount realized is $11,000 and C's gain realized is $9,800 ($11,000–$1,200).

Example (6). In 1977 D purchases an asset for $7,500. D pays the seller $1,500 in cash and signs a note payable to the seller for $6,000. D is not personally liable for repayment but pledges as security the newly purchased asset. In the event of default, the seller's only recourse is to the asset. During the years 1977 and 1978 D takes depreciation deductions on the asset totaling $4,200 thereby reducing D's basis in the asset to $3,300 ($7,500–$4,200). In 1979 D transfers the asset to a trust which is not a "grantor trust" for purposes of subpart E of part 1 of subchapter J of the Code. Therefore D is not treated as the owner of the trust. The trust takes the asset subject to the liability and in addition pays D $750 in cash. Prior to the transfer D had reduced the amount outstanding on the liability to $4,700. D's amount realized on the transfer is $5,450 ($4,700 + $750). Since D's adjusted basis is $3,300, D's gain realized is $2,150 ($5,450 – $3,300).

Example (7). In 1974 E purchases a herd of cattle for breeding purposes. The purchase price is $20,000 consisting of $1,000 cash and a $19,000 note. E is not personally liable for repayment of the liability and the seller's only recourse in the event of default is to the herd of cattle. In 1977 E transfers the herd back to the original seller thereby satisfying the indebtedness pursuant to a provision in the original sales agreement. At the time of the transfer the fair market value of the herd is $15,000 and the remaining principal balance on the note is $19,000. At that time E's adjusted basis in the herd is $16,500 due to a deductible loss incurred when a portion of the herd died as a result of disease. As a result of the indebtedness being satisfied, E's amount realized is $19,000 notwithstanding the fact that the fair market value of the herd was less than $19,000. E's realized gain is 2,500 ($19,000 – $16,500).

Example (8). In 1980, F transfers to a creditor an asset with a fair market value of $6,000 and the creditor discharges $7,500 of indebtedness for which F is personally liable. The amount realized on the disposition of the asset is its fair market value ($6,000). In addition, F has income from the discharge of indebtedness of $1,500 ($7,500 – $6,000).

* * *

Basis Rules Of General Application

§ 1.1011–1 Adjusted basis.

The adjusted basis for determining the gain or loss from the sale or other disposition of property is the cost or other basis prescribed in section 1012 or other applicable provisions of subtitle A of the Code, adjusted to the extent provided in sections 1016, 1017, and 1018 or as otherwise specifically provided for under applicable provisions of internal revenue laws.

* * *

§ 1.1012–1 Basis of property.

(a) General rule. In general, the basis of property is the cost thereof. The cost is the amount paid for such property in cash or other property. This general rule is subject to exceptions stated in subchapter O (relating to gain or loss on the disposition of property), subchapter C (relating to corporate distributions and adjustments), subchapter K (relating to partners and partnerships), and subchapter P (relating to capital gains and losses), chapter 1 of the Code.

(b) Real estate taxes as part of cost. In computing the cost of real property, the purchaser shall not take into account any amount paid to the seller as reimbursement for real property taxes which are treated under section 164(d) as imposed upon the purchaser. This rule applies whether or not the contract of sale calls for the purchaser to reimburse the seller for such real estate taxes paid or to be paid by the seller. On the other hand, where the purchaser pays (or assumes liability for) real estate taxes which are treated under section 164(d) as imposed upon the seller, such taxes shall be considered part of the cost of the property. It is immaterial whether or not the contract of sale specifies that the sale price has been reduced by, or is in any way intended to reflect, real estate taxes allocable to the seller under section 164 (d). For illustrations of the application of this paragraph, see paragraph (b) of § 1.1001–1.

(c) Sale of stock—(1) In general. If shares of stock in a corporation are sold or transferred by a taxpayer who purchased or acquired lots of stock on different dates or at different prices, and the lot from which the stock was sold or transferred cannot be adequately identified, the stock sold or transferred shall be charged against the earliest of such lots purchased or acquired in order to determine the cost or other basis of such stock and in order to determine the holding period of such stock for purposes of subchapter P, chapter 1 of the Code. If, on the other hand, the lot from which the stock is sold or transferred can be adequately identified, the rule stated in the preceding sentence is not applicable. As to what constitutes "adequate identification", see subparagraphs (2), (3), and (4) of this paragraph.

(2) Identification of stock. An adequate identification is made if it is shown that certificates representing shares of stock from a lot which was purchased or acquired on a certain date or for a certain price were delivered to the taxpayer's transferee. Except as otherwise provided in subparagraph (3) or (4) of this paragraph, such stock certificates delivered to the transferee constitute the stock sold or transferred by the taxpayer. Thus, unless the requirements of subparagraph (3) or (4) of this paragraph are met, the stock sold or transferred is charged to the lot to which the certificates delivered to the transferee belong, whether or not the taxpayer intends, or instructs his broker or other agent, to sell or transfer stock from a lot purchased or acquired on a different date or for a different price.

* * *

§ 1.1012–2 Transfers in part a sale and in part a gift.

For rules relating to basis of property acquired in a transfer which is in part a gift and in part a sale, see § 1.170A–4(c), § 1.1011–2(b), and § 1.105–4.

§ 1.1013–1 Property included in inventory.

The basis of property required to be included in inventory is the last inventory value of such property in the hands of the taxpayer. The requirements with respect to the valuation of an inventory are stated in subpart D (section 471 and following), part II, subchapter E, chapter 1 of the Code, and the regulations thereunder.

§ 1.1014–1 Basis of property acquired from a decedent.

(a) General rule. The purpose of section 1014 is, in general, to provide a basis for property acquired from a decedent which is equal to the value placed upon such property for purposes of the Federal estate tax. Accordingly, the general rule is that the basis of property acquired from a decedent is the fair market value of such property at the date of the decedent's death, or, if the decedent's executor so elects, at the alternate valuation date prescribed in section 2032 * * *. Property acquired from a decedent includes, principally, property acquired by bequest, devise, or inheritance, and, in the case of decedents dying after December 31, 1953, property required to be included in determining the value of the decedent's gross estate under any provision of the Internal Revenue Code of 1954 or the Internal Revenue Code of 1939. The general rule governing basis of property acquired from a decedent, as well as other rules prescribed elsewhere in this section, shall have no application if the property is sold, exchanged, or otherwise disposed of before the decedent's death by the person who acquired the property from the decedent. For general rules on the applicable valuation date where the executor of a decedent's estate elects under section 2032* * *, to value the decedent's gross estate at the alternate valuation date prescribed in such sections, see paragraph (e) of § 1.1014–3.

* * *

(c) Property to which section 1014 does not apply. Section 1014 shall have no application to the following classes of property:

(1) Property which constitutes a right to receive an item of income in respect of a decedent under section 691; and

* * *

§ 1.1014–2 Property acquired from a decedent.

(a) In general. The following property, except where otherwise indicated, is considered to have been acquired from a decedent and the basis thereof is determined in accordance with the general rule in § 1.1014–1:

(1) Without regard to the date of the decedent's death, property acquired by bequest, devise, or inheritance, or by the decedent's estate from the decedent, whether the property was acquired under the decedent's will or under the law governing the descent and distribution of the property of decedents.* * *

(2) Without regard to the date of the decedent's death, property transferred by the decedent during his lifetime in trust to pay the income for life to or on the order or direction of the decedent, with the right reserved to the decedent at all times before his death to revoke the trust.

(3) In the case of decedents dying after December 31, 1951, property transferred by the decedent during his lifetime in trust to pay the income for life to or on the order or direction of the decedent with the right reserved to the decedent at all times before his death to make any change in the enjoyment thereof through the exercise of a power to alter, amend, or terminate the trust.

(4) Without regard to the date of the decedent's death, property passing without full and adequate consideration under a general power of appointment exercised by the decedent by will. (See section 2041 (b) for definition of general power of appointment.)

(5) In the case of decedents dying after December 31, 1947, property which represents the surviving spouse's one-half share of community property held by the decedent and the surviving spouse under the community property laws of any State, Territory, or possession of the United States or any foreign country, if at least one-half of the whole of the community interest in that property was includible in determining the value of the decedent's gross estate under part III, chapter 11 of the Internal Revenue Code of 1954 (relating to the estate tax) * * *. It is not necessary for the application of this subparagraph that an estate tax return be required to be filed for the estate of the decedent or that an estate tax be payable.

* * *

(b) Property acquired from a decedent dying after December 31, 1953—(1) In general. In addition to the property described in paragraph (a) of this section, and except as otherwise provided in subparagraph (3) of this paragraph, in the case of a decedent dying after December 31, 1953, property shall also be considered to have been acquired from the decedent to the extent that both of the following conditions are met: (i) The property was acquired from the decedent by reason of death, form of ownership, or other conditions (including property acquired through the exercise or non-exercise of a power of appointment), and (ii) the property is includible in the decedent's gross estate under the provisions of the Internal Revenue Code of 1954, or the Internal Revenue Code of 1939, because of such acquisition. The basis of such property in the hands of the person who acquired it from the decedent shall be determined in accordance with the general rule in § 1.1014–1. See, however, § 1.1014–6 for special adjustments if such property is acquired before the death of the decedent. See also subparagraph (3) of this paragraph for a description of property not within the scope of this paragraph.

(2) Rules for the application of subparagraph (1) of this paragraph. Except as provided in subparagraph (3) of this paragraph, this paragraph generally includes all property acquired from a decedent, which is includible in the gross estate of the decedent if the decedent died after December 31, 1953. It is not necessary for the application of this paragraph that an estate tax return be required to be filed for the estate of the decedent or that an estate tax be payable. Property acquired prior to the death of a decedent which is includible in the decedent's gross estate, such as property transferred by a decedent in contemplation of death, and property held by a taxpayer and the decedent as joint tenants or as tenants by the entireties is within the scope of this paragraph. Also, this paragraph includes property acquired through the exercise or nonexercise of a power of appointment where such property is includible in the decedent's gross estate. It does not include property not includible in the decedent's gross estate such as property not situated in the United States acquired from a nonresident who is not a citizen of the United States.

(3) Exceptions to application of this paragraph. The rules in this paragraph are not applicable to the following property:

(i) Annuities described in section 72;

* * *

(iii) Property described in any paragraph other than paragraph (9) of section 1014(b). See paragraphs (a) and (c) of this section.

In illustration of subdivision (ii), assume that A acquired by gift stock of a character described in paragraph (c)(1) of this section from a donor and upon the death of the donor the stock was includible in the donor's estate as being a gift in contemplation of death. A's basis in the stock would not be determined by reference to its fair market value at the donor's death under the general rule in section 1014(a). Furthermore, the special basis rules prescribed in paragraph (c)(1) of this section are not applicable to such property acquired by gift in contemplation of death. It will be necessary to refer to the rules in section 1015(a) to determine the basis.

* * *

§ 1.1014–3 Other basis rules.

(a) Fair market value. For purposes of this section and § 1.1014–1, the value of property as of the date of the decedent's death as appraised for the purpose of the Federal estate tax or the alternate value as appraised for such purpose, whichever is applicable, shall be deemed to be its fair market value. If no estate tax return is required to be filed under section 6018 * * *, the value of the property appraised as of the date of the decedent's death for the purpose of State inheritance or transmission taxes shall be deemed to be its fair market value and no alternate valuation date shall be applicable.

(b) Property acquired from a decedent dying before March 1, 1913. If the decedent died before March 1, 1913, the fair market value on that date is taken in lieu of the fair market value on the date of death, but only to the same extent and for the same purposes as the fair market value on March 1, 1913, is taken under section 1053.

(c) Reinvestments by a fiduciary. The basis of property acquired after the death of the decedent by a fiduciary as an investment is the cost or other basis of such property to the fiduciary, and not the fair market value of such property at the death of the decedent. For example, the executor of an estate purchases stock of X company at a price of $100 per share with the proceeds of the sale of property acquired from a decedent. At the date of the decedent's death the fair market value of such stock was $98 per share. The basis of such stock to the executor or to a legatee, assuming the stock is distributed, is $100 per share.

(d) Reinvestments of property transferred during life. Where property is transferred by a decedent during life and the property is sold, exchanged, or otherwise disposed of before the decedent's death by the person who acquired the property from the decedent, the general rule stated in paragraph (a) of § 1.1014–1 shall not apply to such property. However, in such a case, the basis of any property acquired by such donee in exchange for the original property, or of any property acquired by the donee through reinvesting the proceeds of the sale of the original property, shall be the fair market value of the property thus acquired at the date of the decedent's death (or applicable alternate valuation date) if the property thus acquired is properly included in the decedent's gross estate for Federal estate tax purposes. These rules also apply to property acquired by the donee in any further exchanges or in further reinvestments. For example, on January 1, 1956, the decedent made a gift of real property to a trust for the benefit of his children, reserving to himself the power to revoke the trust at will. Prior to the decedent's death, the trustee sold the real property and invested the proceeds in stock of the Y Company at $50 per share. At the time of the decedent's death, the value of such stock was $75 per share. The corpus of the trust was required to be included in the decedent's gross estate owing to his reservation of the power of revocation. The basis of the Y company stock following the decedent's death is $75 per share. Moreover, if the trustee sold the Y Company stock before the decedent's death for $65 a share and reinvested the proceeds in Z company stock which increased in value to $85 per share at the time of the decedent's death, the basis of the Z company stock following the decedent's death would be $85 per share.

(e) Alternate valuation dates. Section 1014(a) provides a special rule applicable in determining the basis of property described in § 1.1014–2 where—

(1) The property is includible in the gross estate of a decedent who died after October 21, 1942, and

(2) The executor elects for estate tax purposes under section 2032, * * * to value the decedent's gross estate at the alternate valuation date prescribed in such sections.

In those cases, the value applicable in determining the basis of the property is not the value at the date of the decedent's death but (with certain limitations) the value at the date one year* after his death if not distributed, sold, exchanged, or otherwise disposed of in the meantime. If such property was distributed, sold, exchanged, or otherwise disposed of within one year* after the date of the decedent's death by the person who acquired it from the decedent, the value applicable in determining the basis is its value as of the date of such distribution, sale, exchange, or other disposition. For illustrations of the operation of this paragraph, see the estate tax regulations under section 2032.

* * *

§ 1.1015–1 Basis of property acquired by gift after December 31, 1920.

(a) General rule. (1) In the case of property acquired by gift after December 31, 1920 (whether by a transfer in trust or otherwise), the basis of the property for the purpose of determining gain is the same as it would be in the hands of the donor or the last preceding owner by whom it was not acquired by gift. The same rule applies in determining loss unless the basis (adjusted for the period prior to the date of gift in accordance with sections 1016 and 1017) is greater than the fair market value of the property at the time of the gift. In such case, the basis for determining loss is the fair market value at the time of the gift.

(2) The provisions of subparagraph (1) of this paragraph may be illustrated by the following example.

*Editorial comment: Presently 6 months rather than 1 year.

Example. A acquires by gift income-producing property which has an adjusted basis of $100,000 at the date of gift. The fair market value of the property at the date of gift is $90,000. A later sells the property for $95,000. In such case there is neither gain nor loss. The basis for determining loss is $90,000; therefore, there is no loss. Furthermore, there is no gain, since the basis for determining gain is $100,000.

(3) If the facts necessary to determine the basis of property in the hands of the donor or the last preceding owner by whom it was not acquired by gift are unknown to the donee, the district director shall, if possible, obtain such facts from such donor or last preceding owner, or any other person cognizant thereof. If the district director finds it impossible to obtain such facts, the basis in the hands of such donor or last preceding owner shall be the fair market value of such property as found by the district director as of the date or approximate date at which, according to the best information the district director is able to obtain, such property was acquired by such donor or last preceding owner. See paragraph (e) of this section for rules relating to fair market value.

* * *

(c) Time of acquisition. The date that the donee acquires an interest in property by gift is when the donor relinquishes dominion over the property and not necessarily when title to the property is acquired by the donee. Thus, the date that the donee acquires an interest in property by gift where he is a successor in interest, such as in the case of a remainderman of a life estate or a beneficiary of the distribution of the corpus of a trust, is the date such interests are created by the donor and not the date the property is actually acquired.

* * *

(e) Fair market value. For the purposes of this section, the value of property as appraised for the purpose of the Federal gift tax, or, if the gift is not subject to such tax, its value as appraised for the purpose of a State gift tax, shall be deemed to be the fair market value of the property at the time of the gift.

* * *

§ 1.1015–4 Transfers in part a gift and in part a sale.

(a) General rule. Where a transfer of property is in part a sale and in part a gift, the unadjusted basis of the property in the hands of the transferee is the sum of—

(1) Whichever of the following is the greater:

(i) The amount paid by the transferee for the property, or

(ii) The transferor's adjusted basis for the property at the time of the transfer, and

(2) The amount of increase, if any, in basis authorized by section 1015(d) for gift tax paid (see § 1.1015–5).

For determining loss, the unadjusted basis of the property in the hands of the transferee shall not be greater than the fair market value of the property at the time of such transfer. For determination of gain or loss of the transferor, see § 1.1001–1(e) and § 1.1011–2. For special rule where there has been a charitable contribution of less than a taxpayer's entire interest in property, see section 170(e)(2) and § 1.170A–4(c).

(b) Examples. The rule of paragraph (a) of this section is illustrated by the following examples:

Example (1). If A transfers property to his son for $30,000, and such property at the time of the transfer has an adjusted basis of $30,000 in A's hands (and a fair market value of $60,000), the unadjusted basis of the property in the hands of the son is $30,000.

Example (2). If A transfers property to his son for $60,000, and such property at the time of transfer has an adjusted basis of $30,000 in A's hands (and a fair market value of $90,000), the unadjusted basis of such property in the hands of the son is $60,000.

Example (3). If A transfers property to his son for $30,000, and such property at the time of transfer has an adjusted basis in A's hands of $60,000 (and a fair market value of $90,000), the unadjusted basis of such property in the hands of the son is $60,000.

Example (4). If A transfers property to his son for $30,000 and such property at the time of transfer has an adjusted basis of $90,000 in A's hands (and a fair market value of $60,000), the unadjusted basis of the property in the hands of the son is $90,000. However, since the adjusted basis of the property in A's hands at the time of the transfer was greater than the fair market value at that time, for the purpose of determining any loss on a later sale or other disposition of the property by the son its unadjusted basis in his hands is $60,000.

§ 1.1015–5 Increased basis for gift tax paid.

(a) General rule in the case of gifts made on or before December 31, 1976. (1) (i) Subject to the conditions and limitations provided in section 1015 (d), as added by the Technical Amendments Act of 1958, the basis (as determined under section 1015(a) and paragraph (a) of § 1.1015–1) of property acquired by gift is increased by the amount of gift tax paid with respect to the gift of such property. Under section 1015(d)(1)(A), such increase in basis applies to property acquired by gift on or after September 2, 1958 (the date of enactment of the Technical Amendments Act of 1958). Under section 1015(d)(1)(B), such increase in basis applies to property acquired by gift before September 2, 1958, and not sold, exchanged, or otherwise disposed of before such date. If section 1015(d)(1)(A) applies, the basis of the property is increased as of the date of the gift regardless of the date of payment of the gift tax. For example, if the property was acquired by gift on September 8, 1958, and sold by the donee on October 15, 1958, the basis of the property would be increased (subject to the limitation of section 1015 (d)) as of September 8, 1958 (the date of the gift), by the amount of gift tax applicable to such gift even though such tax was not paid until March 1, 1959. If section 1015(d)(1)(B) applies, any increase in the basis of the property due to gift tax paid (regardless of date of payment) with respect to the gift is made as of September 2, 1958. Any increase in basis under section 1015(d) can be no greater than the amount by which the fair market value of the property at the time of the gift exceeds the basis of such property in the hands of the donor at the time of the gift. See paragraph (b) of this section for rules for determining the amount of gift tax paid in respect of property transferred by gift.

* * *

(c) Special rule for increased basis for gift tax paid in the case of gifts made after December 31, 1976—(1) In general. With respect to gifts made after December 31, 1976 (other than gifts between spouses described in section 1015(e)), the increase in basis for gift tax paid is determined under section 1015(d)(6). Under section 1015(d)(6)(A), the increase in basis with respect to gift tax paid is limited to the amount (not in excess of the amount of gift tax paid) that bears the same ratio to the amount of gift tax paid as the net appreciation in value of the gift bears to the amount of the gift.

* * *

§ 1.1016–1 Adjustments to basis; scope of section.

Section 1016 and §§ 1.1016–2 to 1.1016–10, inclusive, contain the rules relating to the adjustments to be made to the basis of property to determine the adjusted basis as defined in section 1011. However, if the property was acquired from a decedent before his death, see § 1.1014–6 for adjustments on account of certain deductions allowed the taxpayer for the period between the date of acquisition of the property and the date of death of the decedent. * * *

§ 1.1016–2 Items properly chargeable to capital account.

(a) The cost or other basis shall be properly adjusted for any expenditure, receipt, loss, or other item, properly chargeable to capital account, including the cost of improvements and betterments made to the property. No adjustment shall be made in respect of any item which, under any applicable provision of law or regulation, is treated as an item not properly chargeable to capital account but is allowable as a deduction in computing net or taxable income for the taxable year. For example, in the case of oil and gas wells no adjustment may be made in respect of any intangible drilling and development expense allowable as a deduction in computing net or taxable income. See the regulations under section 263(c).

(b) The application of the foregoing provisions may be illustrated by the following example:

Example. A, who makes his returns on the calendar year basis, purchased property in 1941 for $10,000. He subsequently expended $6,000 for improvements. Disregarding, for the purpose of this example, the adjustments required for depreciation, the adjusted basis of the property is $16,000. If A sells the property in 1954 for $20,000, the amount of his gain will be $4,000.

(c) Adjustments to basis shall be made for carrying charges such as taxes and interest, with respect to property (whether real or personal, improved or unimproved, and whether productive or unproductive), which the taxpayer elects to treat as chargeable to capital account under section 266, rather than as an allowable deduction. The term "taxes" for this purpose includes duties and excise taxes but does not include income taxes.

* * *

§ 1.1016–3 Exhaustion, wear and tear, obsolescence, amortization, and depletion for periods since February 28, 1913.

(a) In general—(1) Adjustment where deduction is claimed. (i) For taxable periods beginning on or after January 1, 1952, the cost or other basis of property shall be decreased for exhaustion, wear and tear, obsolescence, amortization, and depletion by the greater of the following two amounts: (a) the amount allowed as deductions in computing taxable income, to the extent resulting in a reduction of the taxpayer's income taxes, or (b) the amount allowable for the years involved. See paragraph (b) of this section. Where the taxpayer makes an appropriate election the above rule is applicable for periods since February 28, 1913, and before January 1, 1952. See paragraph (d) of this section. For rule for such periods where no election is made, see paragraph (c) of this section.

(ii) The determination of the amount properly allowable for exhaustion, wear and tear, obsolescence, amortization, and depletion shall be made on the basis of facts reasonably known to exist at the end of the taxable year. A taxpayer is not permitted to take advantage in a later year of his prior failure to take any such allowance or his taking an allowance plainly inadequate under the known facts in prior years. In the case of depreciation, if in prior years the taxpayer has consistently taken proper deductions under one method, the amount allowable for such prior years shall not be increased even though a greater amount would have been allowable under another proper method. For rules governing losses on retirement of depreciable property, including rules for determining basis, see § 1.167(a)–8. * * *

(2) Adjustment for amount allowable where no depreciation deduction claimed. (i) If the taxpayer has not taken a depreciation deduction either in the taxable year or for any prior taxable year, adjustments to basis of the property for depreciation allowable shall be determined by using the straight-line method of depreciation. (See § 1.1016–4 for adjustments in the case of persons exempt from income taxation.)

(ii) For taxable years beginning after December 31, 1953, and ending after August 16, 1954, if the taxpayer with respect to any property has taken a deduction for depreciation properly under one of the methods provided in section 167(b) for one or more years but has omitted the deduction in other years, the adjustment to basis for the depreciation allowable in such a case will be the deduction under the method which was used by the taxpayer with respect to that property. Thus, if A acquired property in 1954 on which he properly computed his depreciation deduction under the method described in section 167(b)(2) (the declining-balance method) for the first year of its useful life but did not take a deduction in the second and third year of the asset's life, the adjustment to basis for depreciation allowable for the second and third year will be likewise computed under the declining-balance method.

* * *

(b) Adjustment for periods beginning on or after January 1, 1952. The decrease required by paragraph (a) of this section for deductions in respect of any period beginning on or after January 1, 1952, shall be whichever is the greater of the following amounts:

(1) The amount allowed as deductions in computing taxable income under subtitle A of the Code or prior income tax laws and resulting (by reason of the deductions so allowed) in a reduction for any taxable year of the taxpayer's taxes under subtitle A of the Code (other than chapter 2, relating to tax on self-employment income) or prior income, war-profits, or excess-profits tax laws; or

(2) The amount properly allowable as deductions in computing taxable income under subtitle A of the Code or prior income tax laws (whether or not the amount properly allowable would have caused a reduction for any taxable year of the taxpayer's taxes).

* * *

(e) Determination of amount allowed which reduced taxpayer's taxes. (1) As indicated in paragraphs (b) and (d) of this section, there are situations in which it is necessary to determine (for the purpose of ascertaining the basis adjustment required by paragraph (a) of this section) the extent to which the amount allowed as deductions resulted in a reduction for any taxable year of the taxpayer's taxes under subtitle A (other than chapter 2 relating to tax on self-employment income) of the Code, or prior income, war-profits, or excess-profits tax laws. This amount (amount allowed which resulted in a reduction of the taxpayer's taxes) is hereinafter referred to as the "tax-benefit amount allowed." For the purpose of determining whether the tax-benefit amount allowed exceeded the amount allowable, a determination must be made of that portion of the excess of the amount allowed over the amount allowable which, if disallowed, would not have resulted in an increase in any such tax previously determined. If the entire excess of the amount allowed over the amount allowable could be disallowed without any such increase in tax, the tax-benefit amount allowed shall not be considered to have exceeded the amount allowable. In such a case (if paragraph (b) or (d) of this section is applicable) the reduction in basis required by paragraph (a) of this section would be the amount properly allowable as a deduction. If only part of such excess could be disallowed without any such increase in tax, the tax-benefit amount allowed shall be considered to exceed the amount allowable to the extent of the remainder of such excess. In such a case (if paragraph (b) or (d) of this section is applicable), the reduction in basis required by paragraph (a) of this section would be the amount of the tax-benefit amount allowed.

(2) For the purpose of determining the tax-benefit amount allowed the tax previously determined shall be determined under the principles of section 1314. The only adjustments made in determining whether there would be an increase in tax shall be those resulting from the disallowance of the amount allowed. The taxable years for which the determination is made shall be the taxable year for which the deduction was allowed and any other taxable year which would be affected by the disallowance of such deduction. Examples of such other taxable years are taxable years to which there was a carryover or carryback of a net operating loss from the taxable year for which the deduction was allowed, and taxable years for which a computation under section 111 * * * was made by reference to the taxable year for which the deduction was allowed. In determining whether the disallowance of any part of the deduction would not have resulted in an increase in any tax previously determined, proper adjustment must be made for previous determinations under section 1311* * *.

(3) If a determination under section 1016(a)(2)(B) must be made with respect to several properties for each of which the amount allowed for the taxable year exceeded the amount allowable, the tax-benefit amount allowed with respect to each of such properties shall be an allocated portion of the tax-benefit amount allowed determined by reference to the sum of the amounts allowed and the sum of the amounts allowable with respect to such several properties.

(4) In the case of property held by a partnership or trust, the computation of the tax-benefit amount allowed shall take into account the tax benefit of the partners or beneficiaries, as the case may be, from the deduction by the partnership or trust of the amount allowed to the partnership or the trust. For this purpose, the determination of the amount allowed which resulted in a tax benefit to the partners or beneficiaries shall be made in the same manner as that provided above with respect to the taxes of the person holding the property.

(5) A taxpayer seeking to limit the adjustment to basis to the tax-benefit amount allowed for any period, in lieu of the amount allowed, must establish the tax-benefit amount allowed. A failure of adequate proof as to the tax-benefit amount allowed with respect to one period does not preclude the taxpayer from limiting the adjustment to basis to the tax-benefit amount allowed with respect to another period for which adequate proof is available. For example, a corporate transferee may have available adequate records with respect to the tax effect of the deduction of erroneous depreciation for certain taxable years, but may not have available adequate records with respect to the deduction of excessive depreciation for other taxable years during which the property was held by its transferor. In such case the corporate transferee shall not be denied the right to apply this section with respect to the erroneous depreciation for the period for which adequate proof is available.

(f) Determination of amount allowable in prior taxable years. (1) One of the factors in determining the adjustment to basis as of any date is the amount of depreciation, depletion, etc., allowable for periods prior to such date. The amount allowable for such prior periods is determined under the law applicable to such prior periods; all adjustments required by the law applicable to such periods are made in determining the adjusted basis of the property for the purpose of determining the amount allowable. Provisions corresponding to the rules in section 1016 (a)(2)(B) described in paragraphs (d) and (e) of this section, which limit adjustments to the "tax-benefit amount allowed" where an election is properly exercised, were first enacted by the Act of July 14, 1952 (66 Stat. 629). That law provided that corresponding rules are deemed to be includible in all revenue laws applicable to taxable years ending after December 31, 1931. Accordingly, those rules shall be taken into account in determining the amount of depreciation, etc., allowable for any taxable year ending after December 31, 1931. For example, if the adjusted basis of property held by the taxpayer since January 1, 1930, is determined as of January 1, 1955, and if an election was properly made under section 1020, or section 113(d) of the Internal Revenue Code of 1939, then the amount allowable which is taken into account in computing the adjusted basis as of January 1, 1955, shall be determined by taking those rules into account for all taxable years ending after December 31, 1931. The Act of July 14, 1952, made no change in the law applicable in determining the amount allowable for taxable years ending before January 1, 1932. If there was a final decision of a court prior to the enactment of the Act of July 14, 1952, determining the amount allowable for a particular taxable year, such determination shall be adjusted. In such case the adjustment shall be made only for the purpose of taking the provision of that law into account and only to the extent made necessary by such provisions.

* * *

§ 1.1016–5 Miscellaneous adjustments to basis.

(a) Certain stock distributions. (1) In the case of stock, the cost or other basis must be diminished by the amount of distributions previously made which, under the law applicable to the year in which the distribution was made, either were tax free or were applicable in reduction of basis (not including distributions made by a corporation which was classified as a personal service corporation under the provisions of the Revenue Act of 1918 (40 Stat. 1057) or the Revenue Act of 1921 (42 Stat. 227), out of its earnings or profits which were taxable in accordance with the provisions of section 218 of the Revenue Act of 1918 or the Revenue Act of 1921). For adjustments to basis in the case of certain corporate distributions, see section 301 and the regulations thereunder.

(2) The application of subparagraph (1) of this paragraph may be illustrated by the following example:

Example. A, who makes his returns upon the calendar year basis, purchased stock in 1923 for $5,000. He received in 1924 a distribution of $2,000 paid out of earnings and profits of the corporation accumulated before March 1, 1913. The adjusted basis for determining the gain or loss from the sale or other disposition of the stock in 1954 is $5,000 less $2,000, or $3,000, and the amount of the gain or loss from the sale or other disposition of the stock is the difference between $3,000 and the amount realized from the sale or other disposition.

(b) Amortizable bond premium. In the case of a tax-exempt bond, basis shall be reduced by the amount of the amortizable bond premium disallowable as a deduction under section 171(a)(2), or under section 125(a)(2) of the Internal Revenue Code of 1939 and, in the case of any other bond (as defined in section 171(d)), basis shall be reduced by the amount of the deductions allowable under section 171(a)(1), or under section 125(a)(1) of the Internal Revenue Code of 1939.

(c) Municipal bonds. In the case of a municipal bond (as defined in section 75(b)), basis shall be adjusted to the extent provided in section 75 * * * and the regulations thereunder.

(d) Sale or exchange of residence. Where the acquisition of a new residence results in the nonrecognition of any part of the gain on the sale, or exchange, or involuntary conversion of the old residence, the basis of the new residence shall be reduced by the amount of the gain not so recognized pursuant to section 1034(a), * * * and the regulations thereunder. See section 1034(e) and the regulations thereunder.

* * *

(h) Consent dividends.* * *

(2) In the case of amounts specified in a shareholder's consent to be treated as a consent dividend to which section 565 applies, the basis of the consent stock shall be increased by the amount which, under section 565(c)(2), is treated as contributed to the capital of the corporation.

* * *

§ 1.1016–10 Substituted basis.

(a) Whenever it appears that the basis of property in the hands of the taxpayer is a substituted basis, as defined in section 1016(b), the adjustments indicated in §§ 1.1016–1 to 1.1016–6, inclusive, shall be made after first making in respect of such substituted basis proper adjustments of a similar nature in respect of the period during which the property was held by the transferor, donor, or grantor, or during which the other property was held by the person for whom the basis is to be determined. In addition, whenever it appears that the basis of property in the hands of the taxpayer is a substituted basis, as defined in section 1016(b)(1), the adjustments indicated in §§ 1.1016–7 to 1.1016–9, inclusive, and in section 1017 shall also be made, whenever necessary, after first making in respect of such substituted basis a proper adjustment of a similar nature in respect of the period during which the property was held by the transferor, donor, or grantor. Similar rules shall also be applied in the case of a series of substituted bases.

(b) The application of this section may be illustrated by the following example:

Example. A, who makes his returns upon the calendar year basis, in 1935 purchased the X Building and subsequently gave it to his son B. B exchanged the X Building for the Y Building in a tax-free exchange, and then gave the Y Building to his wife C. C, in determining the gain from the sale or disposition of the Y Building in 1954, is required to reduce the basis of the building by deductions for depreciation which were successively allowed (but not less than the amount allowable) to A and B upon the X Building and to B upon the Y Building, in addition to the deductions for depreciation allowed (but not less than the amount allowable) to herself during her ownership of the Y Building.

§ 1.1017–1 Basis reduction following a discharge of indebtedness—

(a) General rule for section 108(b)(2)(E). This paragraph (a) applies to basis reductions under section 108(b)(2)(E) that are required by section 108(a) (1)(A) or (B) because the taxpayer excluded discharge of indebtedness (COD income) from gross income. A taxpayer must reduce in the following order, to the extent of the excluded COD income (but not below zero), the adjusted bases of property held on the first day of the taxable year following the taxable year that the taxpayer excluded COD income from gross income (in proportion to adjusted basis)—

(1) Real property used in a trade or business or held for investment, other than real property described in section 1221(1), that secured the discharged indebtedness immediately before the discharge;

(2) Personal property used in a trade or business or held for investment, other than inventory, accounts receivable, and notes receivable, that secured the discharged indebtedness immediately before the discharge;

(3) Remaining property used in a trade or business or held for investment, other than inventory, accounts receivable, notes receivable, and real property described in section 1221(1);

(4) Inventory, accounts receivable, notes receivable, and real property described in section 1221(1); and

(5) Property not used in a trade or business nor held for investment.

(b) Operating rules—(1) Prior tax-attribute reduction. The amount of excluded COD income applied to reduce basis does not include any COD income applied to reduce tax attributes under sections 108(b)(2)(A) through (D) and, if applicable, section 108(b)(5). For example, if a taxpayer excludes $100 of COD income from gross income under section 108(a) and reduces tax attributes by $40 under sections 108(b)(2)(A) through (D), the taxpayer is required to reduce the adjusted bases of property by $60 ($100 – $40) under section 108(b)(2)(E).

(2) Multiple discharged indebtednesses. If a taxpayer has COD income attributable to more than one discharged indebtedness resulting in the reduction of tax attributes under sections 108(b)(2)(A) through (D) and, if applicable, section 108(b)(5), paragraph (b)(1) of this section must be applied by allocating the tax-attribute reductions among the indebtednesses in proportion to the amount of COD income attributable to each discharged indebtedness. For example, if a taxpayer excludes $20 of COD income attributable to secured indebtedness A and excludes $80 of COD income attributable to unsecured indebtedness B (a total exclusion of $100), and if the taxpayer reduces tax indebtedness B (a total exclusion of $100), and if the taxpayer reduces tax attributes by $40 under sections 108(b)(2)(A) through (D), the taxpayer must reduce the amount of COD income attributable to secured indebtedness A to $12 ($20 – ($20/$100 × $40) and must reduce the amount of COD income attributable to unsecured indebtedness B to $48 ($80 – ($80/$100 × $40)).

(3) Limitation on basis reductions under section 108(b)(2)(E) in bankruptcy or insolvency. If COD income arises from a discharge of indebtedness in a title 11 case or while the taxpayer is insolvent, the amount of any basis reduction under section 108(b)(2)(E) shall not exceed the excess of—

(i) the aggregate of the adjusted bases of property and the amount of money held by the taxpayer immediately after the discharge; over

(ii) The aggregate of the liabilities of the taxpayer immediately after the discharge.

(4) Transactions to which section 381 applies. If a taxpayer realizes COD income that is excluded from gross income under section 108(a) either during or after a taxable year in which the taxpayer is the distributor or transferor of assets in a transaction described in section 381(a), the basis of property acquired by the acquiring corporation in the transaction must reflect the reductions required by section 1017 and this section. For this purpose, the basis of property of the distributor or transferor corporation immediately prior to the transaction described in section 381(a), but after the determination of tax for the year of the distribution or transfer of assets, will be available for reduction under section 108(b)(2). However, the basis of stock or securities of the acquiring corporation, if any, received by the taxpayer in exchange for the transferred assets shall not be available for reduction under section 108(b)(2). See § 1.108–7. This paragraph (b)(4) applies to discharges of indebtedness occurring on or after May 10, 2004.

(c) Modification of ordering rules for basis reductions under sections 108(b)(5) and 108(c)—(1) In general. The ordering rules prescribed in paragraph (a) of this section apply, with appropriate modifications, to basis reductions under sections 108(b) (5) and (c). Thus, a taxpayer that elects to reduce basis under section 108(b)(5) may, to the extent that the election applies, reduce only the adjusted basis of property described in paragraphs (a)(1), (2), and (3) of this section and, if an election is made under paragraph (f) of this section, paragraph (a)(4) of this section. Within paragraphs (a)(1), (2), (3), and (4) of this section, such a taxpayer may reduce only the adjusted bases of depreciable property. A taxpayer that elects to apply section 108 (c) may reduce only the adjusted basis of property described in paragraphs (a)(1) and (3) of this section and, within paragraphs (a)(1) and (3) of this section, may reduce only the adjusted bases of depreciable property. Furthermore, for basis reductions under section 108(c), a taxpayer must reduce the adjusted basis of the qualifying real property to the extent of the discharged qualified real property business indebtedness before reducing the adjusted bases of other depreciable real property. The term qualifying real property means real property with respect to which the indebtedness is qualified real property business indebtedness within the meaning of section 108(c)(3). See paragraphs (f) and (g) of this section for elections relating to section 1221(1) property and partnership interests.

(2) Partial basis reductions under section 108 (b)(5). If the amount of basis reductions under section 108(b)(5) is less than the amount of the COD income excluded from gross income under section 108(a), the taxpayer must reduce the balance of its tax attributes, including any remaining adjusted bases of depreciable and other property, by following the order rules under section 108(b)(2). For example, if a taxpayer excludes $100 of COD income from gross income under section 108(a) and elects to reduce the adjusted bases of depreciable property by $10 under section 108(b)(5), the taxpayer must reduce its remaining tax attributes by $90, starting with new operating losses under section 108(b)(2).

(3) Modification of fresh start rule for prior basis reductions under section 108(b)(5). After reducing the adjusted bases of depreciable property under section 108(b)(5), a taxpayer must compute the limitation on basis reductions under section 1017 (b)(2) using the aggregate of the remaining adjusted bases of property. For example, if, immediately after the discharge of indebtedness in a title 11 case, a taxpayer's adjusted bases of property is $100 and its undischarged indebtedness is $70, and if the taxpayer elects to reduce the adjusted bases of depreciable property by $10 under section 108(b)(5), section 1017(b)(2) limits any further basis reductions under section 108(b)(2)(E) to $20 (($100 – $10) – $70).

(d) Changes in security. If any property is added or eliminated as security for an indebtedness during the one-year period preceding the discharge of that indebtedness, such addition or elimination shall be disregarded where a principal purpose of the change is to affect the taxpayer's basis reductions under section 1017.

(e) Depreciable property. For purposes of this section, the term depreciable property means any property of a character subject to the allowance for depreciation or amortization, but only if the basis reduction would reduce the amount of depreciation or amortization which otherwise would be allowable for the period immediately following such reduction. Thus, for example, a lessor cannot reduce the basis of leased property where the lessee's obligation in respect of the property will restore to the lessor the loss due to depreciation during the term of the lease, since the lessor cannot take depreciation in respect of such property.

(f) Election to treat section 1221(1) real property as depreciable—(1) In general. For basis reductions under section 108(b)(5) and basis reductions relating to qualified farm indebtedness, a taxpayer may elect under sections 1017(b)(3)(E) and (4)(C), respectively, to treat real property described in section 1221(1) as depreciable property. This election is not available, however, for basis reductions under section 108(c).

(2) Time and manner. To make an election under section 1017(b)(3)(E) or (4)(C), a taxpayer must enter the appropriate information on Form 982, Reduction of Tax Attributes Due to Discharge of Indebtedness (and Section 1082 Basis Adjustment), and attach the form to a timely filed (including extensions) Federal income tax return for the taxable year in which the taxpayer has COD income that is excluded from gross income under section 108(a). An election under this paragraph (f) may be revoked only with the consent of the Commissioner.

(g) Partnerships—(1) Partnership COD income. For purposes of paragraph (a) of this section, a taxpayer must treat a distributive share of a partnership's COD income as attributable to a discharged indebtedness secured by the taxpayer's interest in that partnership.

(2) Partnership interest treated as depreciable property.

(i) In general. For purposes of making basis reductions, if a taxpayer makes an election under section 108(b)(5) (or 108(c)), the taxpayer must treat a partnership interest as depreciable property (or depreciable real property) to the extent of the partner's proportionate share of the partnership's basis in depreciable property (or depreciable real property), provided that the partnership consents to a corresponding reduction in the partnership's basis (inside basis) in depreciable property (or depreciable real property) with respect to such partner.

(ii) Request by partner and consent of partnership. (A) In general. Except as otherwise provided in this paragraph (g)(2)(ii), a taxpayer may choose whether or not to request that a partnership reduce the inside basis of its depreciable property (or depreciable real property) with respect to the taxpayer, and the partnership may grant or withhold such consent, in its sole discretion. A request by the taxpayer must be made before the due date (including extensions) for filing the taxpayer's Federal income tax return for the taxable year in which the taxpayer has COD income that is excluded from gross income under section 108(a).

(B) Request for consent required. A taxpayer must request a partnership's consent to reduce inside basis if, at the time of the discharge, the taxpayer owns (directly or indirectly) a greater than 50 percent interest in the capital and profits of the partnership, or if reductions to the basis of the taxpayer's depreciable property (or depreciable real property) are being made with respect to the taxpayer's distributive share of COD income of the partnership.

(C) Granting of request required. A partnership must consent to reduce its partners' shares of inside basis with respect to a discharged indebtedness if consent is requested with respect to that indebtedness by partners owning (directly or indirectly) an aggregate of more than 80 percent of the capital and profits interests of the partnership or five or fewer partners owning (directly or indirectly) an aggregate of more than 50 percent of the capital and profits interests of the partnership. For example, if there is a cancellation of partnership indebtedness that is secured by real property used in a partnership's trade or business, and if partners owning (in the aggregate) 90 percent of the capital and profits interests of the partnership elect to exclude the COD income under section 108(c), the partnership must make the appropriate reductions in those partners' shares of inside basis.

(iii) Partnership consent statement. (A) Partnership requirement. A consenting partnership must include with the Form 1065, U.S. Partnership Return of Income, for the taxable year following the year that ends with or within the taxable year the taxpayer excludes COD income from gross income under section 108(a), and must provide to the taxpayer on or before the due date of the taxpayer's return (including extensions) for the taxable year in which the taxpayer excludes COD income from gross income, a statement that—

(1) Contains the name, address, and taxpayer identification number of the partnership; and

(2) States the amount of the reduction of the partner's proportionate interest in the adjusted bases of the partnership's depreciable property or depreciable real property, whichever is applicable.

(B) Taxpayer's requirement. Statements described in paragraph (g)(2)(iii)(A) of this section must be attached to a taxpayer's timely filed (including extensions) Federal income tax return for the taxable year in which the taxpayer has COD income that is excluded from gross income under section 108(a).

(iv) Partner's share of partnership basis.—(A) In general. For purposes of this paragraph (g), a partner's proportionate share of the partnership's basis in depreciable property (or depreciable real property) is equal to the sum of—

(1) The partner's section 743(b) basis adjustments to items of partnership depreciable property (or depreciable real property); and

(2) The common basis depreciation deductions (but not including remedial allocations of depreciation deductions under §1.704–3(d)) that, under the terms of the partnership agreement effective for the taxable year in which the discharge of indebtedness occurs, are reasonably expected to be allocated to the partner over the property's remaining useful life. The assumptions made by a partnership in determining the reasonably expected allocation of depreciation deductions must be consistent for each partner. For example, a partnership may not treat the same depreciation deductions as being reasonably expected by more than one partner.

(B) Effective date. This paragraph (g)(2)(iv) applies to elections made under sections 108(b)(5) and 108(c) on or after December 15, 1999.

(v) Treatment of basis reduction.—(A) Basis adjustment. The amount of the reduction to the basis of depreciable partnership property constitutes an adjustment to the basis of partnership property with respect to the partner only. No adjustment is made to the common basis of partnership property. Thus, for purposes of income, deduction, gain, loss, and distribution, the partner will have a special basis for those partnership properties the bases of which are adjusted under section 1017 and this section.

(B) Recovery of adjustments to basis of partnership property. Adjustments to the basis of partnership property under this section are recovered in the manner described in §1.743–1.

(C) Effect of basis reduction. Adjustments to the basis of partnership property under this section are treated in the same manner and have the same effect as an adjustment to the basis of partnership property under section 743(b). The following example illustrate's this paragraph (g)(2)(v):

Example. **(i)** A, B, and C are equal partners in partnership PRS, which owns (among other things) Asset 1, an item of depreciable property with a basis of $30,000. A's basis in its partnership interest is $20,000. Under the terms of the partnership agreement, A's share of the depreciation deductions from Asset 1 over its remaining useful life will be $10,000. Under section 1017, A requests, and PRS agrees, to decrease the basis of Asset 1 with respect to A by $10,000.

(ii) In the year following the reduction of basis under section 1017, PRS amends its partnership agreement to provide that items of depreciation and loss from Asset 1 will be allocated equally between B and C. In that year, A's distributive share of the partnership's common basis depreciation deductions from Asset 1 is now $0. under §1.743–1(j)(4)(ii)(B), the amount of the section 1017 basis adjustment that A recovers during the year is $1,000. A will report $1,000 of ordinary income because A's distributive share of the partnership's common basis depreciation deductions from Asset 1 ($0) is insufficient to offset the amount of the section 1017 basis adjustment recovered by A during the year ($1,000).

(iii) In the following year, PRS sells Asset 1 for $15,000 and recognizes a $12,000 loss. This loss is allocated equally between B and C, and A's share of the loss is $0. Upon the sale of Asset 1, A recovers its entire remaining section 1017 basis adjustment ($9,000). A will report $9,000 of ordinary income.

(D) Effective date. This paragraph (g)(2)(v) applies to elections made under sections 108(b)(5) and 108(c) on or after December 15, 1999.

(3) Partnership basis reduction. The rules of this section (including this paragraph (g)) apply in determining the properties to which the partnership's basis reductions must be made.

(h) Special allocation rule for cases to which section 1398 applies. If a bankruptcy estate and a taxpayer to whom section 1398 applies (concerning only individuals under Chapter 7 or 11 of title 11 of the United States Code) hold property subject to basis reduction under section 108(b)(2)(E) or (5) on the first day of the taxable year following the taxable year of discharge, the bankruptcy estate must reduce all of the adjusted bases of its property before the taxpayer is required to reduce any adjusted bases of property.

(i) Effective date. This section applies to discharges of indebtedness occurring on or after October 22, 1998.

* * *

§ 1.1019–1 Property on which lessee has made improvements.

In any case in which a lessee of real property has erected buildings or made other improvements upon the leased property and the lease is terminated by forfeiture or otherwise resulting in the realization by such lessor of income which, were it not for the provisions of section 109, would be includible in gross income of the lessor, the amount so excluded from gross income shall not be taken into account in determining the basis or the adjusted basis of such property or any portion thereof in the hands of the lessor. If, however, in any taxable year beginning before January 1, 1942, there has been included in the gross income of the lessor an amount representing any part of the value of such property attributable to such buildings or improvements, the basis of each portion of such property shall be properly adjusted for the amount so included in gross income. For example, A leased in 1930 to B for a period of 25 years unimproved real property and in accordance with the terms of the lease B erected a building on the property. It was estimated that upon expiration of the lease the building would have a depreciated value of $50,000, which value the lessor elected to report (beginning in 1931) as income over the term of the lease. This method of reporting was used until 1942. In 1952 B forfeits the lease. The amount of $22,000 reported as income by A during the years 1931 to 1941, inclusive, shall be added to the basis of the property represented by the improvements in the hands of A. If in such case A did not report during the period of the lease any income attributable to the value of the building erected by the lessee and the lease was forfeited in 1940 when the building was worth $75,000, such amount, having been included in gross income under the law applicable to that year, is added to the basis of the property represented by the improvements in the hands of A. As to treatment of such property for the purposes of capital gains and losses, see subchapter P (section 1201 and following), chapter 1 of the Code.

* * *

Common Nontaxable Exchanges

§ 1.1031–0 Table of Contents.

This section lists the captions that appear in the regulations under section 1031.

§ 1.1031(a)–1 Property held for productive use in trade or business or for investment.

(a) In general—(1) Exchanges of property solely for property of a like kind. Section 1031(a)(1) provides an exception from the general rule requiring the recognition of gain or loss upon the sale or exchange of property. Under section 1031(a)(1), no gain or loss is recognized if property held for productive use in a trade or business or for investment is exchanged solely for property of a like kind to be held either for productive use in a trade or business or for investment. Under section 1031(a)(1), property held for productive use in a trade or business may be exchanged for property held for investment. Similarly, under section 1031(a)(1), property held for investment may be exchanged for property held for productive use in a trade or business. However, section 1031(a)(2) provides that section 1031(a)(1) does not apply to any exchange of—

(i) Stock in trade or other property held primarily for sale;

(ii) Stocks, bonds, or notes;

(iii) Other securities or evidences of indebtedness or interest;

(iv) Interests in a partnership;

(v) Certificates of trust or beneficial interests; or

(vi) Choses in action.

Section 1031(a)(1) does not apply to any exchange of interests in a partnership regardless of whether the interests exchanged are general or limited partnership interests or are interests in the same partnership or in different partnerships. An interest in a partnership that has in effect a valid election under section 761(a) to be excluded from the application of all of subchapter K is treated as an interest in each of the assets of the partnership and not as an interest in a partnership for purposes of section 1031(a)(2)(D) and paragraph (a)(1)(iv) of this section. An exchange of an interest in such a partnership does not qualify for nonrecognition of gain or loss under section 1031 with respect to any asset of the partnership that is described in section 1031(a)(2) or to the extent the exchange of assets of the partnership does not otherwise satisfy the requirements of section 1031(a).

(2) Exchanges of property not solely for property of a like kind. A transfer is not within the provisions of section 1031(a) if, as part of the consideration, the taxpayer receives money or property which does not meet the requirements of section 1031(a), but the transfer, if otherwise qualified, will be within the provisions of either section 1031(b) or (c). Similarly, a transfer is not within the provisions of section 1031(a) if, as part of the consideration, the other party to the exchange assumes a liability of the taxpayer (or acquires property from the taxpayer that is subject to a liability), but the transfer, if otherwise qualified, will be with-in the provisions of either section 1031(b) or (c). A transfer of property meeting the requirements of section 1031(a) may be within the provisions of section 1031(a) even though the taxpayer transfers in addition property not meeting the requirements of section 1031(a) or money. However, the nonrecognition treatment provided by section 1031(a) does not apply to the property transferred which does not meet the requirements of section 1031(a).

(b) Definition of "like kind." As used in section 1031(a), the words "like kind" have reference to the nature or character of the property and not to its grade or quality. One kind or class of property may not, under that section, be exchanged for property of a different kind or class. The fact that any real estate involved is improved or unimproved is not material, for that fact relates only to the grade or quality of the property and not to its kind or class. Unproductive real estate held by one other than a dealer for future use or future realization of the increment in value is held for investment and not primarily for sale. For additional rules for exchanges of personal property, see § 1.1031(a)–2.

(c) Examples of exchanges of property of a "like kind." No gain or loss is recognized if (1) a taxpayer exchanges property held for productive use in his trade or business, together with cash, for other property of like kind for the same use, such as a truck for a new truck or a passenger automobile for a new passenger automobile to be used for a like purpose; or (2) a taxpayer who is not a dealer in real estate exchanges city real estate for a ranch or farm, or exchanges a leasehold of a fee with 30 years or more to run for real estate, or exchanges improved real estate for unimproved real estate; or (3) a taxpayer exchanges investment property and cash for investment property of a like kind.

* * *

§ 1.1031(a)–2 Additional rules for exchanges of personal property.

(a) Introduction. Section 1.1031(a)–1(b) provides that the nonrecognition rules of section 1031 do not apply to an exchange of one kind or class of property for property of a different kind or class. This section contains additional rules for determining whether personal property has been exchanged for property of a like kind or like class. Personal properties of a like class are considered to be of a "like kind" for purposes of section 1031. In addition, an exchange of properties of a like kind may qualify under section 1031 regardless of whether the properties are also of a like class. In determining whether exchanged properties are of a like kind, no inference is to be drawn from the fact that the properties are not of a like class. Under paragraph (b) of this section, depreciable tangible personal properties are of a like class if they are either within the same General Asset Class (as defined in paragraph (b)(2) of this section) or within the same Product Class (as defined in paragraph (b)(3) of this section). Paragraph (c) of this section provides rules for exchanges of intangible personal property and nondepreciable personal property.

(b) Depreciable tangible personal property—(1) General rule. Depreciable tangible personal property is exchanged for property of a "like kind" under section 1031 if the property is exchanged for property of a like kind or like class. Depreciable tangible personal property is of a like class to other depreciable tangible personal property if the exchanged properties are either within the same General Asset Class or within the same Product Class. A single property may not be classified within more than one General Asset Class or within more than one Product Class. In addition, property classified within any General Asset Class may not be classified within a Product Class. A property's General Asset Class or Product Class is determined as of the date of the exchange.

(2) General Asset Classes. Except as provided in paragraphs (b)(4) and (b)(5) of this section, property within a General Asset Class consists of depreciable tangible personal property described in one of asset classes 00.11 through 00.28 and 00.4 of Rev.Proc. 87–56, 1987–2 C.B. 674. These General Asset Classes describe types of depreciable tangible personal property that frequently are used in many businesses. The General Asset Classes are as follows:

(i) Office furniture, fixtures, and equipment (asset class 00.11),

(ii) Information systems (computers and peripheral equipment) (asset class 00.12),

(iii) Data handling equipment, except computers (asset class 00.13),

(iv) Airplanes (airframes and engines), except those used in commercial or contract carrying of passengers or freight, and all helicopters (airframes and engines) (asset class 00.21),

(v) Automobiles, taxis (asset class 00.22),

(vi) Buses (asset class 00.23),

(vii) Light general purpose trucks (asset class 00.241),

(viii) Heavy general purpose trucks (asset class 00.242),

(ix) Railroad cars and locomotives, except those owned by railroad transportation companies (asset class 00.25),

(x) Tractor units for use over-the-road (asset class 00.26),

(xi) Trailers and trailer-mounted containers (asset class 00.27),

(xii) Vessels, barges, tugs, and similar water-transportation equipment, except those used in marine construction (asset class 00.28), and

(xiii) Industrial steam and electric generation and/or distribution systems (asset class 00.4).

(3) Product classes. Except as provided in paragraphs (b)(4) and (5) of this section, or as provided by the Commissioner in published guidance of general applicability, property within a product class consists of depreciable tangible personal property that is described in a 6-digit product class within Sectors 31, 32, and 33 (pertaining to manufacturing industries) of the *North American Industry Classification System* (NAICS), set forth in Executive Office of the President, Office of Management and Budget, North American Industry Classification System, United States, 2002 (NAICS Manual), as periodically updated. Copies of the NAICS Manual may be obtained from the National Technical Information Service, an agency of the U.S. Department of Commerce, and may be accessed on the internet. Sectors 31 through 33 of the NAICS Manual contain listings of specialized industries for the manufacture of described products and equipment. For this purpose, any 6-digit NAICS product class with a last digit of 9 (a miscellaneous category) is not a product class for purposes of this section. If a property is listed in more than one product class, the property is treated as listed in any one of those product classes. A property's 6-digit product class is referred to as the property's NAICS code.

(4) Modifications of NAICS product classes. The product classes of the NAICS Manual may be updated or otherwise modified from time to time as the manual is updated, effective on or after the date of the modification. The NAICS Manual generally is modified every five years, in years ending in a 2 or 7 (such as 2002, 2007, and 2012). The applicability date of the modified NAICS Manual is announced in the **Federal Register** and generally is January 1 of the year the NAICS Manual is modified. Taxpayers may rely on these modifications as they become effective in structuring exchanges under this section. Taxpayers may rely on the previous NAICS Manual for transfers of property made by a taxpayer during the one-year period following the effective date of the modification. For transfers of property made by a taxpayer on or after January 1, 1997, and on or before January 1, 2003, the NAICS Manual of 1997 may be used for determining product classes of the exchanged property.

(5) Administrative procedures for revising general asset classes and product classes. The Commissioner may, through published guidance of general applicability, supplement, modify, clarify, or update the guidance relating to the classification of properties provided in this paragraph. (b). (See § 601.601(d)(2) of this chapter.) For example, the Commissioner may determine not to follow (in whole or in part) a general asset class for purposes of identifying property of like class, may determine not to follow (in whole or in part) any modification of product classes published in the NAICS Manual, or may determine that other properties not listed within the same or in any product class or general asset class nevertheless are of a like class. The Commissioner also may determine that two items of property that are listed in separate product classes or in product classes with a last digit of 9 are of a like class, or that an item of property that has a NAICS code is of a like class to an item of property that does not have a NAICS code.

(6) No inference outside of section 1031. The rules provided in this section concerning the use of general asset classes or product classes are limited to exchanges under section 1031. No inference is intended with respect to the classification of property for other purposes, such as depreciation.

(7) Examples. The application of this paragraph (b) may be illustrated by the following examples:

Example 1. Taxpayer A transfers a personal computer (asset class 00.12) to B in exchange for a printer (asset class 00.12). With respect to A, the properties exchanged are within the same General Asset Class and therefore are of a like class.

Example 2. Taxpayer C transfers an airplane (asset class 00.21) to D in exchange for a heavy general purpose truck (asset class 00.242). The properties exchanged are not of a like class because they are within different General Asset Classes. Because each of the properties is within a General Asset Class, the properties may not be classified within a Product Class. The airplane and heavy general purpose truck are also not of a like kind. Therefore, the exchange does not qualify for nonrecognition of gain or loss under section 1031.

Example 3. Taxpayer E transfers a grader to F in exchange for a scraper. Neither property is within any of the general asset classes. However, both properties are within the same product class (NAICS code 333120). The grader and scraper are of a like class and deemed to be of a like kind for purposes of section 1031.

Example 4. Taxpayer G transfers a personal computer (asset class 00.12), an airplane (asset class 00.21) and a sanding machine (NAICS code 333210), to H in exchange for a printer (asset class 00.12), a heavy general purpose truck (asset class 00.242) and a lathe (NAICS code 333210). The personal computer and the printer are of a like class because they are within the same general asset class. The sanding machine and the lathe are of a like class because they are within the same product class (although neither property is within any of the general asset classes). The airplane and the heavy general purpose truck are neither within the same general asset class nor within the same product class, and are not of a like kind.

(8) Transition rule. Properties within the same product classes based on the 4-digit codes contained in Division D of the Executive Office of the President, Office of Management and Budget, Standard Industrial Classification Manual (1987), will be treated as property of a like class for transfers of property made by taxpayers on or before May 19, 2005.

(c) Intangible personal property and nondepreciable personal property—(1) General rule. An exchange of intangible personal property of nondepreciable personal property qualifies for nonrecognition of gain or loss under section 1031 only if the exchanged properties are of a like kind. No like classes are provided for these properties. Whether intangible personal property is of a like kind to other intangible personal property generally depends on the nature or character of the rights involved (e.g., a patent or a copyright) and also on the nature or character of the underlying property to which the intangible personal property relates.

(2) Goodwill and going concern value. The goodwill or going concern value of a business is not of a like kind to the goodwill or going concern value of another business.

(3) Examples. The application of this paragraph (c) may be illustrated by the following examples:

Example (1). Taxpayer K exchanges a copyright on a novel for a copyright on a different novel. The properties exchanged are of a like kind.

Example (2). Taxpayer J exchanges a copyright on a novel for a copyright on a song. The properties exchanged are not of a like kind.

* * *

§ 1.1031(a)–2T. Additional rules for exchanges of personal property (temporary).

(a) through (b)(2) [Reserved]. For further guidance, see § 1.1031(a)–2(a) through (b)(2).

(b) (3) Product classes. Except as provided in paragraphs (b)(4) and (b)(5) of this section, or as provided by the Commissioner in published guidance of general applicability, property within a product class consists of depreciable tangible personal property that is described in a 6-digit product class within Sectors 31, 32, and 33 (pertaining to manufacturing industries) of the North American Industry Classification System (NAICS), set forth in Executive Office of the President, Office of Management and Budget, North American Industry Classification System, United States, 2002 (NAICS Manual), as periodically updated. Copies of the NAICS Manual may be obtained from the National Technical Information Service, an agency of the U.S. Department of

Commerce, and may be accessed on the internet. Sectors 31 through 33 of the NAICS Manual contain listings of specialized industries for the manufacture of described products and equipment. For this purpose, any 6-digit NAICS product class with a last digit of 9 (a miscellaneous category) is not a product class for purposes of this section. If a property is listed in more than one product class, the property is treated as listed in any one of those product classes. A property's 6-digit product class is referred to as the property's NAICS code.

(4) Modifications of NAICS product classes. The product classes of the NAICS Manual may be updated or otherwise modified from time to time as the manual is updated, effective on or after the date of the modification. The NAICS Manual generally is modified every five years, in years ending in a 2 or 7 (such as 2002, 2007, and 2012). The applicability date of the modified NAICS Manual is announced in the Federal Register and generally is January 1 of the year the NAICS Manual is modified. Taxpayers may rely on these modifications as they become effective in structuring exchanges under this section. Taxpayers may rely on the previous NAICS Manual for transfers of property made by a taxpayer during the one-year period following the effective date of the modification. For transfers of property made by a taxpayer on or after January 1, 1997, and on or before January 1, 2003, the NAICS Manual of 1997 may be used for determining product classes of the exchanged property.

(5) Administrative procedures for revising general asset classes and product classes. The Commissioner may, through published guidance of general applicability, supplement, modify, clarify, or update the guidance relating to the classification of properties provided in this paragraph (b). (See § 601.601(d)(2) of this chapter.) For example, the Commissioner may determine not to follow (in whole or in part) a general asset class for purposes of identifying property of like class, may determine not to follow (in whole or in part) any modification of product classes published in the NAICS Manual, or may determine that other properties not listed within the same or in any product class or general asset class nevertheless are of a like class. The Commissioner also may determine that two items of property that are listed in separate product classes or in product classes with a last digit of 9 are of a like class, or that an item of property that has a NAICS code is of a like class to an item of property that does not have a NAICS code.

(6) No inference outside of section 1031. The rules provided in this section concerning the use of general asset classes or product classes are limited to exchanges under section 1031. No inference is intended with respect to the classification of property for other purposes, such as depreciation.

(7) Examples. The provisions of this paragraph (b) are illustrated by the following examples:

Example (1) and Example 2 [Reserved]. For further guidance, see § 1.1031(a)–2(b)(7), Example 1 and Example 2.

Example (3). Taxpayer E transfers a grader to F in exchange for a scraper. Neither property is within any of the general asset classes. However, both properties are within the same product class (NAICS code 333120). The grader and scraper are of a like class and deemed to be of a like kind for purposes of section 1031.

Example (4). Taxpayer G transfers a personal computer (asset class 00.12), an airplane (asset class 00.21) and a sanding machine (NAICS code 333210), to H in exchange for a printer (asset class 00.12), a heavy general purpose truck (asset class 00.242) and a lathe (NAICS code 333210). The personal computer and the printer are of a like class because they are within the same general asset class; the sanding machine and the lathe are of a like class because they are within the same product class (although neither property is within any of the general asset classes). The airplane and the heavy general purpose truck are neither within the same general asset class nor within the same product class, and are not of a like kind.

(8) Transition rule. Properties within the same product classes based on the 4-digit codes contained in Division D of the Executive Office of the President, Office of Management and Budget, Standard Industrial Classification Manual (1987), will be treated as property of a like class for transfers of property made by taxpayers on or before [the date these regulations are published as final regulations in the Federal Register].

(c) [Reserved]. For further guidance, see § 1.1031(a)–2(c).

(d) Effective dates. This section applies to transfers of property made by taxpayers on or after August 12, 2004. However, taxpayers may apply this section to transfers of property made by taxpayers on or after January 1, 1997, in taxable years for which the period of limitation for filing a claim for refund or credit under section 6511 has not expired. For all other exchanges occurring prior to August 12, 2004, see § 1.1031(a)–2(d).

§ 1.1031(b)–1 Receipt of other property or money in tax-free exchange.

(a) If the taxpayer receives other property (in addition to property permitted to be received without recognition of gain) or money—

(1) In an exchange described in section 1031(a) of property held for investment or productive use in trade or business for property of like kind to be held either for productive use or for investment,

(2) In an exchange described in section 1035(a) of insurance policies or annuity contracts,

(3) In an exchange described in section 1036(a) of common stock for common stock, or preferred stock for preferred stock, in the same corporation and not in connection with a corporate reorganization, or

(4) In an exchange described in section 1037(a) of obligations of the United States, issued under the Second Liberty Bond Act (31 U.S.C. 774 (2)), solely for other obligations issued under such Act, the gain, if any, to the taxpayer will be recognized under section 1031(b) in an amount not in excess of the sum of the money and the fair market value of the other property, but the loss, if any, to the taxpayer from such an exchange will not be recognized under section 1031(c) to any extent.

(b) The application of this section may be illustrated by the following examples:

Example (1). A, who is not a dealer in real estate, in 1954 exchanges real estate held for investment, which he purchased in 1940 for $5,000, for other real estate (to be held for productive use in trade or business) which has a fair market value of $6,000, and $2,000 in cash. The gain from the transaction is $3,000, but is recognized only to the extent of the cash received of $2,000.

* * *

(c) Consideration received in the form of an assumption of liabilities (or a transfer subject to a liability) is to be treated as "other property or money" for the purposes of section 1031(b). Where, on an exchange described in section 1031(b), each party to the exchange either assumes a liability of the other party or acquires property subject to a liability, then, in determining the amount of "other property or money" for purposes of section 1031(b), consideration given in the form of an assumption of liabilities (or a receipt of property subject to a liability) shall be offset against consideration received in the form of an assumption of liabilities (or a transfer subject to a liability). See § 1.1031(d)–2, examples (1) and (2).

§ 1.1031(b)–2 Safe harbor for qualified intermediaries.

(a) In the case of simultaneous transfers of like-kind properties involving a qualified intermediary (as defined in § 1.1031(k)–1(g)(4)(iii)), the qualified intermediary is not considered the agent of the taxpayer for purposes of section 1031(a). In such a case, the transfer and receipt of property by the taxpayer is treated as an exchange.

* * *

§ 1.1031(c)–1 Nonrecognition of loss.

Section 1031(c) provides that a loss shall not be recognized from an exchange of property described in section 1031(a), 1035(a), 1036(a), or 1037(a) where there is received in the exchange other property or money in addition to property permitted to be received without recognition of gain or loss. See example (4) of paragraph (a)(3) of § 1.1037–1 for an illustration of the application of this section in the case of an exchange of U.S. obligations described in section 1037(a).

§ 1.1031(d)–1 Property acquired upon a tax-free exchange.

(a) If, in an exchange of property solely of the type described in section 1031, section 1035(a), section 1036(a), or section 1037(a), no part of the gain or loss was recognized under the law applicable to the year in which the exchange was made, the basis of the property acquired is the same as the basis of the property transferred by the taxpayer with proper adjustments to the date of the exchange. If additional consideration is given by the taxpayer in the exchange, the basis of the property acquired shall be the same as the property transferred increased by the amount of additional consideration given (see section 1016 and the regulations thereunder).

(b) If, in an exchange of properties of the type indicated in section 1031, section 1035(a), section 1036(a), or section 1037(a), gain to the taxpayer was recognized under the provisions of section 1031(b) or a similar provision of a prior revenue law, on account of the receipt of money in the transaction, the basis of the property acquired is the basis of the property transferred (adjusted to the date of the exchange), decreased by the amount of money received and increased by the amount of gain recognized on the exchange. The application of this paragraph may be illustrated by the following example:

Example. A, an individual in the moving and storage business, in 1954 transfers one of his moving trucks with an adjusted basis in his hands of $2,500 to B in exchange for a truck (to be used in A's business) with a fair market value of $2,400 and $200 in cash. A realizes a gain of $100 upon the exchange, all of which is recognized under section 1031(b). The basis of the truck acquired by A is determined as follows:

Adjusted basis of A's former truck	$2,500
Less: Amount of money received	200
Difference	2,300
Plus: Amount of gain recognized	100
Basis of truck acquired by A	2,400

(c) If, upon an exchange of properties of the type described in section 1031, section 1035(a), section 1036(a), or section 1037(a), the taxpayer received other property (not permitted to be received without the recognition of gain) and gain from the transaction was recognized as required under section 1031(b), or a similar provision of a prior revenue law, the basis (adjusted to the date of the exchange) of the property transferred by the taxpayer, decreased by the amount of any money received and increased by the amount of gain recognized, must be allocated to and is the basis of the properties (other than money) received on the exchange. For the purpose of the allocation of the basis of the properties received, there must be assigned to such other property an amount equivalent to its fair market value at the date of the exchange. The application of this paragraph may be illustrated by the following example:

Example. A, who is not a dealer in real estate, in 1954 transfers real estate held for investment which he purchased in 1940 for $10,000 in exchange for other real estate (to be held for investment) which has a fair market value of $9,000, an automobile which has a fair market value of $2,000, and $1,500 in cash. A realizes a gain of $2,500, all of which is recognized under section 1031(b). The basis of the property received in exchange is the basis of the real estate A transfers ($10,000) decreased by the amount of money received ($1,500) and increased in the amount of gain that was recognized ($2,500), which results in a basis for the property received of $11,000. This basis of $11,000 is allocated between the automobile and the real estate received by A, the basis of the automobile being its fair market value at the date of the exchange, $2,000, and the basis of the real estate received being the remainder, $9,000.

(d) Section 1031(c) and, with respect to section 1031 and section 1036(a), similar provisions of prior revenue laws provide that no loss may be recognized on an exchange of properties of a type described in section 1031, section 1035(a), section 1036(a), or section 1037(a), although the taxpayer receives other property or money from the transaction. However, the basis of the property or properties (other than money) received by the taxpayer is the basis (adjusted to the date of the exchange) of the property transferred, decreased by the amount of money received. This basis must be allocated to the properties received, and for this purpose there must be allocated to such other property an amount of such basis equivalent to its fair market value at the date of the exchange.

(e) If, upon an exchange of properties of the type described in section 1031, section 1035(a), section 1036(a), or section 1037(a), the taxpayer also exchanged other property (not permitted to be transferred without the recognition of gain or loss) and gain or loss from the transaction is recognized under section 1002 or a similar provision of a prior revenue law, the basis of the property acquired is the total basis of the properties transferred (adjusted to the date of the exchange) increased by the amount of gain and decreased by the amount of loss recognized on the other property. For purposes of this rule, the taxpayer is deemed to have received in exchange for such other property an amount equal to its fair market value on the date of the exchange. The application of this paragraph may be illustrated by the following example:

Example. A exchanges real estate held for investment plus stock for real estate to be held for investment. The real estate transferred has an adjusted basis of $10,000 and a fair market value of $11,000. The stock transferred has an adjusted basis of $4,000 and a fair market value of $2,000. The real estate acquired has a fair market value of $13,000. A is deemed to have received a $2,000 portion of the acquired real estate in exchange for the stock, since $2,000 is the fair market value of the stock at the time of the exchange. A $2,000 loss is recognized under section 1002 on the exchange of the stock for real estate. No gain or loss is recognized on the exchange of the real estate since the property received is of the type permitted to be received without recognition of gain or loss. The basis of the real estate acquired by A is determined as follows:

Adjusted basis of real estate transferred	$10,000
Adjusted basis of stock transferred	4,000
	14,000
Less: Loss recognized on transfer of stock	2,000
Basis of real estate acquired upon the exchange	12,000

§ 1.1031(d)–1T Coordination of section 1060 with section 1031 (temporary).

If the properties exchanged under section 1031 are part of a group of assets which constitute a trade or business under section 1060, the like-kind property and other property or money which are treated as transferred in exchange for the like-kind property shall be excluded from the allocation rules of section 1060. However, section 1060 shall apply to property which is not like-kind property or other property or money which is treated as transferred in exchange for the like-kind property. For application of the section 1060 allocation rules to property which is not part of the like-kind exchange, see § 1.1060–1T(b), (d), and (g) Example (3).

§ 1.1031(d)–2 Treatment of assumption of liabilities.

For the purposes of section 1031(d), the amount of any liabilities of the taxpayer assumed by the other party to the exchange (or of any liabilities to which the property exchanged by the taxpayer is subject) is to be treated as money received by the taxpayer upon the exchange, whether or not the assumption resulted in a recognition of gain or loss to the taxpayer under the law applicable to the year in which the exchange was made. The application of this section may be illustrated by the following examples:

Example (1). B, an individual, owns an apartment house which has an adjusted basis in his hands of $500,000, but which is subject to a mortgage of $150,000. On September 1, 1954, he transfers the apartment house to C, receiving in exchange therefor $50,000 in cash and another apartment house with a fair market value on that date of $600,000. The transfer to C is made subject to the $150,000 mortgage. B realizes a gain of $300,000 on the exchange, computed as follows:

Value of property received		$600,000
Cash		50,000
Liabilities subject to which old property was transferred		150,000
Total consideration received		800,000
Less: Adjusted basis of property transferred		500,000
Gain realized		300,000

Under section 1031(b), $200,000 of the $300,000 gain is recognized. The basis of the apartment house acquired by B upon the exchange is $500,000 computed as follows:

Adjusted basis of property transferred		500,000
Less: Amount of money received:		
Cash	$50,000	
Amount of liabilities subject to which property was transferred	150,000	
		200,000
Difference		300,000
Plus: Amount of gain recognized upon the exchange		200,000
Basis of property acquired upon the exchange		500,000

Example (2). (a) D, an individual, owns an apartment house. On December 1, 1955, the apartment house owned by D has an adjusted basis in his hands of $100,000, a fair market value of $220,000, but is subject to a mortgage of $80,000. E, an individual, also owns an apartment house. On December 1, 1955, the apartment house owned by E has an adjusted basis of $175,000, a fair market value of $250,000, but is subject to a mortgage of $150,000. On December 1, 1955, D transfers his apartment house to E, receiving in exchange therefore $40,000 in cash and the apartment house owned by E. Each apartment house is transferred subject to the mortgage on it.

(b) D realizes a gain of $120,000 on the exchange, computed as follows:

Value of property received		$250,000
Cash		40,000
Liabilities subject to which old property was transferred		80,000
Total consideration received		370,000
Less:		
Adjusted basis of property transferred	$100,000	
Liabilities to which new property is subject	$150,000	
		250,000
Gain realized		120,000

For purposes of section 1031(b), the amount of "other property or money" received by D is $40,000. (Consideration received by D in the form of a transfer subject to a liability of $80,000 is offset by consideration given in the form of a receipt of property subject to a $150,000 liability. Thus, only the consideration received in the form of cash, $40,000, is treated as "other property or money" for purposes of section 1031(b).) Accordingly, under section 1031(b), $40,000 of the $120,000 gain is recognized. The basis of the apartment house acquired by D is $170,000, computed as follows:

Adjusted basis of property transferred		$100,000
Liabilities to which new property is subject		150,000
Total		250,000
Less: Amount of money received:		
Cash	$40,000	
Amount of liabilities subject to which property was transferred	80,000	
		120,000
Difference		130,000
Plus: Amount ot gain recognized upon the exchange		40,000
Basis of property acquired upon the exchange		170,000

(c) E realizes a gain of $75,000 on the exchange, computed as follows:

Value of property received		$220,000
Liabilities subject to which old property was transferred		150,000
Total consideration received		370,000
Less:		
Adjusted basis of property transferred	$175,000	
Cash	40,000	
Liabilities to which new properly is subject	80,000	
		295,000
Gain realized		75,000

For purposes of section 1031(b), the amount of "other property or money" received by E is $30,000. (Consideration received by E in the form of a transfer subject to a liability of $150,000 is offset by consideration given in the form of a receipt of property subject to an $80,000 liability and by the $40,000 cash paid by E. Although consideration received in the form of cash or other property is not offset by consideration given in the form of an assumption of liabilities or a receipt of property subject to a liability, consideration given in the form of cash or other property is offset against consideration received in the form of an assumption of liabilities or a transfer of property subject to a liability.) Accordingly, under section 1031(b), $30,000 of the $75,000 gain is recognized. The basis of the apartment house acquired by E is $175,000, computed as follows:

Adjusted basis of property transferred		$175,000
Cash		40,000
Liabilities to which new property is subject		80,000
Total		295,000
Less: Amount of money received:		
Amount of liabilities subject to which property was transferred	$150,000	
		150,000
Difference		145,000
Plus: Amount of gain recognized upon the exchange		30,000
Basis of property acquired upon the exchange		175,000

§ 1.1031(e)–1 Exchanges of livestock of different sexes.

Section 1031(e) provides that livestock of different sexes are not property of like kind. Section 1031(e) and this section are applicable to taxable years to which the Internal Revenue Code of 1954 applies.

§ 1.1031(j)–1 Exchanges of multiple properties.

(a) Introduction—(1) Overview. As a general rule, the application of section 1031 requires a property-by-property comparison for computing the gain recognized and basis of property received in a like-kind exchange. This section provides an exception to this general rule in the case of an exchange of multiple properties. An exchange is an exchange of multiple properties if, under paragraph (b)(2) of this section, more than one exchange group is created. In addition, an exchange is an exchange of multiple properties if only one exchange group is created but there is more than one property being transferred or received within that exchange group. Paragraph (b) of this section provides rules for computing the amount of gain recognized in an exchange of multiple properties qualifying for nonrecognition of gain or loss under section 1031. Paragraph (c) of this section provides rules for computing the basis of properties received in an exchange of multiple properties qualifying for nonrecognition of gain or loss under section 1031.

(2) General approach. (i) In general, the amount of gain recognized in an exchange of multiple properties is computed by first separating the properties transferred and the properties received by the taxpayer in the exchange into exchange groups in the manner described in paragraph (b)(2) of this section. The separation of the properties transferred and the properties received in the exchange into exchange groups involves matching up properties of a like kind of like class to the extent possible. Next, all liabilities assumed by the taxpayer as part of the transaction are offset by all liabilities of which the taxpayer is relieved as part of the transaction, with the excess liabilities assumed or relieved allocated in accordance with paragraph (b)(2)(ii) of this section. Then, the rules of section 1031 and the regulations thereunder are applied separately to each exchange group to determine the amount of gain recognized in the exchange. See §§ 1.1031(b)–1 and 1.1031(c)–1. Finally, the rules of section 1031 and the regulations thereunder are applied separately to each exchange group to determine the basis of the properties received in the exchange. See §§ 1.1031(d)–1 and 1.1031(d)–2.

(ii) For purposes of this section, the exchanges are assumed to be made at arms' length, so that the aggregate fair market value of the property received in the exchange equals the aggregate fair market value of the property transferred. Thus, the amount realized with respect to the properties transferred in each exchange group is assumed to equal their aggregate fair market value.

(b) Computation of gain recognized—(1) In general. In computing the amount of gain recognized in an exchange of multiple properties, the fair market value must be determined for each property transferred and for each property received by the taxpayer in the exchange. In addition, the adjusted basis must be determined for each property transferred by the taxpayer in the exchange.

(2) Exchange groups and residual group. The properties transferred and the properties received by the taxpayer in the exchange are separated into exchange groups and a residual group to the extent provided in this paragraph (b)(2).

(i) Exchange groups. Each exchange group consists of the properties transferred and received in the exchange, all of which are of a like kind or like class. If a property could be included in more than one exchange group, the taxpayer may include the property in any of those exchange groups. Property eligible for inclusion within an exchange group does not include money or property described in section

1031(a)(2) (i.e., stock in trade or other property held primarily for sale, stocks, bonds, notes, other securities or evidences of indebtedness or interest, interests in a partnership, certificates of trust or beneficial interests, or choses in action). For example, an exchange group may consist of all exchanged properties that are within the same General Asset Class or within the same Product Class (as defined in § 1.1031(a)–2(b)). Each exchange group must consist of at least one property transferred and at least one property received in the exchange.

(ii) Treatment of liabilities. **(A)** All liabilities assumed by the taxpayer as part of the exchange are offset against all liabilities of which the taxpayer is relieved as part of the exchange, regardless of whether the liabilities are recourse or non-recourse and regardless of whether the liabilities are secured by or otherwise relate to specific property transferred or received as part of the exchange. See §§ 1.1031 (b)–1(c) and 1.1031(d)–2. For purposes of this section, liabilities assumed by the taxpayer as part of the exchange consist of liabilities of the other party to the exchange assumed by the taxpayer and liabilities subject to which the other party's property is transferred in the exchange. Similarly, liabilities of which the taxpayer is relieved as part of the exchange consist of liabilities of the taxpayer assumed by the other party to the exchange and liabilities subject to which the taxpayer's property is transferred.

(B) If there are excess liabilities assumed by the taxpayer as part of the exchange (i.e., the amount of liabilities assumed by the taxpayer exceeds the amount of liabilities of which the taxpayer is relieved), the excess is allocated among the exchange groups (but not to the residual group) in proportion to the aggregate fair market value of the properties received by the taxpayer in the exchange groups. The amount of excess liabilities assumed by the taxpayer that are allocated to each exchange group may not exceed the aggregate fair market value of the properties received in the exchange group.

(C) If there are excess liabilities of which the taxpayer is relieved as part of the exchange (i.e., the amount of liabilities of which the taxpayer is relieved exceeds the amount of liabilities assumed by the taxpayer), the excess is treated as a Class I asset for purposes of making allocations to the residual group under paragraph (b)(2)(iii) of this section.

(D) Paragraphs (b)(2)(ii)(A), (B), and (C) of this section are applied in the same manner even if section 1031 and this section apply to only a portion of a larger transaction (such as a transaction described in section 1060(c) and § 1.1060–1T(b)). In that event, the amount of excess liabilities assumed by the taxpayer or the amount of excess liabilities of which the taxpayer is relieved is determined based on all liabilities assumed by the taxpayer and all liabilities of which the taxpayer is relieved as part of the larger transaction.

(iii) Residual group. If the aggregate fair market value of the properties transferred in all of the exchange groups differs from the aggregate fair market value of the properties received in all of the exchange groups (taking liabilities into account in the manner described in paragraph (b)(2)(ii) of this section), a residual group is created. The residual group consists of an amount of money or other property having an aggregate fair market value equal to that difference. The residual group consists of either money or other property transferred in the exchange or money or other property received in the exchange, but not both. For this purpose, other property includes property described in section 1031 (a)(2) (i.e., stock in trade or other property held primarily for sale, stocks, bonds, notes, other securities or evidences of indebtedness or interest, interests in a partnership, certificates of trust or beneficial interests, or choses in action), property transferred that is not of a like kind or like class with any property received, and property received that is not of a like kind or like class with any property transferred. The money and properties that are allocated to the residual group are considered to come from the following assets in the following order: first from Class I assets, then from Class II assets, then from Class III assets, and then from Class IV assets. The terms Class I assets, Class II assets, Class III assets, and Class IV assets have the same meanings as in § 1.1060–1T(d). Within each Class, taxpayers may choose which properties are allocated to the residual group.

(iv) Exchange group surplus and deficiency. For each of the exchange groups described in this section, an "exchange group surplus" or "exchange group deficiency," if any, must be determined. An exchange group surplus is the excess of the aggregate fair market value of the properties received (less the amount of any excess liabilities assumed by the taxpayer that are allocated to that exchange group), in an exchange group over the aggregate fair market value of the properties transferred in that exchange group. An exchange group deficiency is the excess of the aggregate fair market value of the properties transferred in an exchange group over the aggregate fair market value of the properties received (less the amount of any excess liabilities assumed by the taxpayer that are allocated to that exchange group) in that exchange group.

(3) Amount of gain recognized—**(i)** For purposes of this section, the amount of gain or loss realized with respect to each exchange group and the residual group is the difference between the aggregate fair market value of the properties transferred in that exchange group or residual group and the properties' aggregate adjusted basis. The gain realized with respect to each exchange group is recognized to the extent of the lesser of the gain realized and the amount of the exchange group deficiency, if any. Losses realized with respect to an exchange group are not recognized. See section 1031 (a) and (c). The total amount of gain recognized under section 1031 in the exchange is the sum of the amount of gain recognized with respect to each exchange group. With respect to the residual group, the gain or loss realized (as determined under this section) is recognized as provided in section 1001 or other applicable provisions of the Code.

(ii) The amount of gain or loss realized and recognized with respect to properties transferred by the taxpayer that are not within any exchange group or the residual group is determined under section 1001 and other applicable provisions of the Code, with proper adjustments made for all liabilities not allocated to the exchange groups or the residual group.

(c) Computation of basis of properties received. In an exchange of multiple properties qualifying for nonrecognition of gain or loss under section 1031 and this section, the aggregate basis of properties received in each of the exchange groups is the aggregate adjusted basis of the properties transferred by the taxpayer within that exchange group, increased by the amount of gain recognized by the taxpayer with respect to that exchange group, increased by the amount of the exchange group surplus or decreased by the amount of the exchange group deficiency, and increased by the amount, if any, of excess liabilities assumed by the taxpayer that are allocated to that exchange group. The resulting aggregate basis of each exchange group is allocated proportionately to each property received in the exchange group in accordance with its fair market value. The basis of each property received within the residual group (other than money) is equal to its fair market value.

(d) Examples. The application of this section may be illustrated by the following examples:

Example (1). (i) K exchanges computer A (asset class 00.12) and automobile A (asset class 00.22), both of which were held by K for productive use in its business, with W for printer B (asset class 00.12) and automobile B (asset class 00.22), both of which will be held by K for productive use in its business. K's adjusted basis and the fair market value of the exchanged properties are as follows:

	Adjusted basis	Fair market value
Computer A	$375	$1,000
Automobile A	1,500	4,000
Printer B	....	2,050
Automobile B	....	2,950

(ii) Under paragraph (b)(2) of this section, the properties exchanged are separated into exchange groups as follows:

(A) The first exchange group consists of computer A and printer B (both are within the same General Asset Class) and, as to K, has an exchange group surplus of $1050 because the fair market value of printer B ($2050) exceeds the fair market value of computer A ($1000) by that amount.

(B) The second exchange group consists of automobile A and automobile B (both are within the same General Asset Class) and, as to K, has an exchange group deficiency of $1050 because the fair market value of automobile A ($4000) exceeds the fair market value of automobile B ($2950) by that amount.

(iii) K recognizes gain on the exchange as follows:

(A) With respect to the first exchange group, the amount of gain realized is the excess of the fair market value of computer A ($1000) over its adjusted basis ($375), or $625. The amount of gain recognized is the lesser of the gain realized ($625) and the exchange group deficiency ($0), or $0.

(B) With respect to the second exchange group, the amount of gain realized is the excess of the fair market value of automobile A ($4000) over its adjusted basis ($1500), or $2500. The amount of gain recognized is the lesser of the gain realized ($2500) and the exchange group deficiency ($1050), or $1050.

(iv) The total amount of gain recognized by K in the exchange is the sum of the gains recognized with respect to both exchange groups ($0 + $1050), or $1050.

(v) The bases of the property received by K in the exchange, printer B and automobile B, are determined in the following manner:

(A) The basis of the property received in the first exchange group is the adjusted basis of the property transferred within the exchange group ($375), increased by the amount of gain recognized with respect to that exchange group ($0), increased by the amount of the exchange group surplus ($1050), and increased by the amount of excess liabilities assumed allocated to that exchange group ($0), or $1425. Because printer B was the only property received within the first exchange group, the entire basis of $1425 is allocated to printer B.

(B) The basis of the property received in the second exchange group is the adjusted basis of the property transferred within that exchange group ($1500), increased by the amount of gain recognized with respect to that exchange group ($1050), decreased by the amount of the exchange group deficiency ($1050), and increased by the amount of excess liabilities assumed allocated to that exchange group ($0), or $1500. Because automobile B was the only property received within the second exchange group, the entire basis of $1500 is allocated to automobile B.

Example (2). **(i)** F exchanges computer A (asset class 00.12) and automobile A (asset class 00.22), both of which were held by F for productive use in its business, with G for printer B (asset class 00.12) and automobile B (asset class 00.22), both of which will be held by F for productive use in its business, and corporate stock and $500 cash. The adjusted basis and fair market value of the properties are as follows:

	Adjusted basis	Fair market value
Computer A	$375	$1,000
Automobile A	3,500	4,000
Printer B	....	800
Automobile B	....	2,950
Corporate stock	....	750
Cash	....	500

(ii) Under paragraph (b)(2) of this section, the properties exchanged are separated into exchange groups as follows:

(A) The first exchange group consists of computer A and printer B (both are within the same General Asset Class) and, as to F, has an exchange group deficiency of $200 because the fair market value of computer A ($1000) exceeds the fair market value of printer B ($800) by that amount.

(B) The second exchange group consists of automobile A and automobile B (both are within the same General Asset Class) and, as to F, has an exchange group deficiency of $1050 because the fair market value of automobile A ($4000) exceeds the fair market value of automobile B ($2950) by that amount.

(C) Because the aggregate fair market value of the properties transferred by F in the exchange groups ($5,000) exceeds the aggregate fair market value of the properties received by F in the exchange groups ($3750) by $1250, there is a residual group in that amount consisting of the $500 cash and the $750 worth of corporate stock.

(iii) F recognizes gain on the exchange as follows:

(A) With respect to the first exchange group, the amount of gain realized is the excess of the fair market value of computer A ($1000) over its adjusted basis ($375), or $625. The amount of gain recognized is the lesser of the gain realized ($625) and the exchange group deficiency ($200), or $200.

(B) With respect to the second exchange group, the amount of gain realized is the excess of the fair market value of automobile A ($4000) over its adjusted basis ($3500), or $500. The amount of gain recognized is the lesser of the gain realized ($500) and the exchange group deficiency ($1050), or $500.

(C) No property transferred by F was allocated to the residual group. Therefore, F does not recognize gain or loss with respect to the residual group.

(iv) The total amount of gain recognized by F in the exchange is the sum of the gains recognized with respect to both exchange groups ($200 + $500), or $700.

(v) The bases of the properties received by F in the exchange (printer B, automobile B, and the corporate stock) are determined in the following manner:

(A) The basis of the property received in the first exchange group is the adjusted basis of the property transferred within that exchange group ($375), increased by the amount of gain recognized with respect to that exchange group ($200), decreased by the amount of the exchange group deficiency ($200), and increased by the amount of excess liabilities assumed allocated to that exchange group ($0), or $375. Because printer B was the only property received within the first exchange group, the entire basis of $375 is allocated to printer B.

(B) The basis of the property received in the second exchange group is the adjusted basis of the property transferred within that exchange group ($3500), increased by the amount of gain recognized with respect to that exchange group ($500), decreased by the amount of the exchange group deficiency ($1050), and increased by the amount of excess liabilities assumed allocated to that exchange group ($0), or $2950. Because automobile B was the only property received within the second exchange group, the entire basis of $2950 is allocated to automobile B.

(C) The basis of the property received within the residual group (the corporate stock) is equal to its fair market value or $750. Cash of $500 is also received within the residual group.

Example (3). **(i)** J and H enter into an exchange of the following properties. All of the property (except for the inventory) transferred by J was held for productive use in J's business. All of the property received by J will be held by J for productive use in its business.

J Transfers:			H Transfers:	
Property	Adjusted basis	Fair market value	Property	Fair market value
Computer A	$1,500	$ 5,000	Computer Z	$ 4,500
Computer B	500	3,000	Printer Y	2,500
Printer C	2,000	1,500	Real Estate X	1,000
Real Estate D	1,200	2,000	Real Estate W	4,000
Real Estate E	0	1,800	Grader V	2,000
Scraper F	3,300	2,500	Truck T	1,700
Inventory	1,000	1,700	Cash	1,800
Total	9,500	17,500	Total	17,500

(ii) Under paragraph (b)(2) of this section, the properties exchanged are separated into exchange groups as follows:

(A) The first exchange group consists of computer A, computer B, printer C, computer Z, and printer Y (all are within the same General Asset Class) and, as to J, has an exchange group deficiency of $2500 (($5000 + $3000 + $1500) – ($4500 + $2500)).

(B) The second exchange group consists of real estate D, E, X and W (all are of a like kind) and, as to J, has an exchange group surplus of $1200 (($1000 + $4000) – (2000 + $1800)).

(C) The third exchange group consists of scraper F and grader V (both are within the same Product Class (NAICS code 333120)) and, as to J, has an exchange group deficiency of $500 ($2500 – $2000).

(D) Because the aggregate fair market value of the properties transferred by J in the exchange groups ($15,800) exceeds the aggregate fair market value of the properties received by J in the exchange groups ($14,000) by $1800, there is a residual group in that amount consisting of the $1800 cash (a Class I asset).

(E) The transaction also includes a taxable exchange of inventory (which is property described in section 1031(a)(2)) for truck T (which is not of a like kind or like class to any property transferred in the exchange).

(iii) J recognizes gain on the transaction as follows:

(A) With respect to the first exchange group, the amount of gain realized is the excess of the aggregate fair market value of the properties transferred in the exchange group ($9500) over the aggregate adjusted basis ($4000), or $5500. The amount of gain recognized is the lesser of the gain realized ($5500) and the exchange group deficiency ($2500), or $2500.

(B) With respect to the second exchange group, the amount of gain realized is the excess of the aggregate fair market value of the properties transferred in the exchange group ($3800) over the aggregate adjusted basis ($1200), or $2600. The amount of gain recognized is the lesser of the gain realized ($2600) and the exchange group deficiency ($0), or $0.

(C) With respect to the third exchange group, a loss is realized in the amount of $800 because the fair market value of the property transferred in the exchange group ($2500) is less than its adjusted basis ($3300). Although a loss of $800 was realized, under section 1031(a) and (c) losses are not recognized.

(D) No property transferred by J was allocated to the residual group. Therefore, J does not recognize gain or loss with respect to the residual group.

(E) With respect to the taxable exchange of inventory for truck T, gain of $700 is realized and recognized by J (amount realized of $1700 (the fair market value of truck T) less the adjusted basis of the inventory ($1000)).

(iv) The total amount of gain recognized by J in the transaction is the sum of the gains recognized under section 1031 with respect to each exchange group ($2500 + $0 + $0) and any gain recognized outside of section 1031 ($700), or $3200.

(v) The bases of the property received by J in the exchange are determined in the following manner:

(A) The aggregate basis of the properties received in the first exchange group is the adjusted basis of the properties transferred within that exchange group ($4000), increased by the amount of gain recognized with respect to that exchange group ($2500), decreased by the amount of the exchange group deficiency ($2500), and increased by the amount of excess liabilities assumed allocated to that exchange group ($0), or $4000. This $4000 of basis is allocated proportionately among the assets received within the first exchange group in accordance with their fair market values: Computer Z's basis is $2571 ($4000 × $4500/$7000); printer Y's basis is $1429 ($4000 × $2500/$7000).

(B) The aggregate basis of the properties received in the second exchange group is the adjusted basis of the properties transferred within that exchange group ($1200), increased by the amount of gain recognized with respect to that exchange group ($0), increased by the amount of the exchange group surplus ($1200), and increased by the amount of excess liabilities assumed allocated to that exchange group ($0), or $2400. This $2400 of basis is allocated proportionately among the assets received within the second exchange group in accordance with their fair market values: Real estate X's basis is $480 ($2400 × $1000/$5000); real estate W's basis is $1920 ($2400 × $4000/$5000).

(C) The basis of the property received in the third exchange group is the adjusted basis of the property transferred within that exchange group ($3300), increased by the amount of gain recognized with respect to that exchange group ($0), decreased by the amount of the exchange group deficiency ($500), and increased by the amount of excess liabilities assumed allocated to that exchange group ($0), or $2800. Because grader V was the only property received within the third exchange group, the entire basis of $2800 is allocated to grader V.

(D) Cash of $1800 is received within the residual group.

(E) The basis of the property received in the taxable exchange (truck T) is equal to its cost of $1700.

Example (4). **(i)** B exchanges computer A (asset class 00.12), automobile A (asset class 00.22) and truck A (asset class 00.241), with C for computer R (asset class 00.12), automobile R (asset class 00.22), truck R (asset class 00.241) and $400 cash. All properties transferred by either B or C were held for productive use in the respective transferor's business. Similarly, all properties to be received by either B or C will be held for productive use in the respective recipient's business. Automobile A, automobile R and truck R are each secured by a nonrecourse liability and are transferred subject to such liability. The adjusted basis, fair market value, and liability secured by each property, if any, are as follows:

	Adjusted basis	Fair market value	Liability
B transfers:			
Computer A	$ 800	$1,500	$ 0
Automobile A	900	2,500	500
Truck A	700	2,000	0
C transfers:			
Computer R	1,100	1,600	0
Automobile R	2,100	3,100	750
Truck R	600	1,400	250
Cash	.....	400	.....

(ii) The tax treatment to B is as follows:

(A) **(1)** The first exchange group consists of computers A and R (both are within the same General Asset Class).

(2) The second exchange group consists of automobiles A and R (both are within the same General Asset Class).

(3) The third exchange group consists of trucks A and R (both are in the same General Asset Class).

(B) Under paragraph (b)(2)(ii) of this section, all liabilities assumed by B ($1000) are offset by all liabilities of which B is relieved ($500), resulting in excess liabilities assumed of $500. The excess liabilities assumed of $500 is allocated among the exchange groups in proportion to the fair market value of the properties received by B in the exchange groups as follows:

(1) $131 of excess liabilities assumed ($500 × $1600/$6100) is allocated to the first exchange group. The first exchange group has an exchange group deficiency of $31 because the fair market value of computer A ($1500) exceeds the fair market value of computer R less the excess liabilities assumed allocated to the exchange group ($1600 – $131) by that amount.

(2) $254 of excess liabilities assumed ($500 × $3100/$6100) is allocated to the second exchange group. The second exchange group has an exchange group surplus of $346 because the fair market value of automobile R less the excess liabilities assumed allocated to the exchange group ($3100 – $254) exceeds the fair market value of automobile A ($2500) by that amount.

(3) $115 of excess liabilities assumed ($500 × $1400/$6100) is allocated to the third exchange group. The third exchange group has an exchange group deficiency of $715 because the fair market value of truck A ($2000) exceeds the fair market value of truck R less the excess liabilities assumed allocated to the exchange group ($1400 – $115) by that amount.

(4) The difference between the aggregate fair market value of the properties transferred in all of the exchange groups, $6000, and the aggregate fair market value of the properties received in all of the exchange groups (taking excess liabilities assumed into account), $5600, is $400. Therefore there is a residual group in that amount consisting of $400 cash received.

(C) B recognizes gain on the exchange as follows:

(1) With respect to the first exchange group, the amount of gain realized is the excess of the fair market value of computer A ($1500) over its adjusted basis ($800), or $700. The amount of gain recognized is the lesser of the gain realized ($700) and the exchange group deficiency ($31), or $31.

(2) With respect to the second exchange group, the amount of gain realized is the excess of the fair market value of automobile A ($2500) over its adjusted basis ($900), or $1600.

The amount of gain recognized is the lesser of the gain realized ($1600) and the exchange group deficiency ($0), or $0.

(3) With respect to the third exchange group, the amount of gain realized is the excess of the fair market value of truck A ($2000) over its adjusted basis ($700), or $1300. The amount of gain recognized is the lesser of gain realized ($1300) and the exchange group deficiency ($715), or $715.

(4) No property transferred by B was allocated to the residual group. Therefore, B does not recognize gain or loss with respect to the residual group.

(D) The total amount of gain recognized by B in the exchange is the sum of the gains recognized under section 1031 with respect to each exchange group ($31 + $0 + $715), or $746.

(E) The bases of the property received by B in the exchange (computer R, automobile R, and truck R) are determined in the following manner:

(1) The basis of the property received in the first exchange group is the adjusted basis of the property transferred within that exchange group ($800), increased by the amount of gain recognized with respect to that exchange group ($31), decreased by the amount of the exchange group deficiency ($31), and increased by the amount of excess liabilities assumed allocated to that exchange group ($131), or $931. Because computer R was the only property received within the first exchange group, the entire basis of $931 is allocated to computer R.

(2) The basis of the property received in the second exchange group is the adjusted basis of the property transferred within that exchange group ($900), increased by the amount of gain recognized with respect to that exchange group ($0), increased by the amount of the exchange group surplus ($346), and increased by the amount of excess liabilities assumed allocated to that exchange group ($254), or $1500. Because automobile R was the only property received within the second exchange group, the entire basis of $1500 is allocated to automobile R.

(3) The basis of the property received in the third exchange group is the adjusted basis of the property transferred within that exchange group ($700), increased by the amount of gain recognized with respect to that exchange group ($715), decreased by the amount of the exchange group deficiency ($715), and increased by the amount of excess liabilities assumed allocated to that exchange group ($115), or $815. Because truck R was the only property received within the third exchange group, the entire basis of $815 is allocated to truck R.

(F) Cash of $400 is also received by B.

(iii) The tax treatment to C is as follows:

(A) **(1)** The first exchange group consists of computers R and A (both are within the same General Asset Class).

(2) The second exchange group consists of automobiles R and A (both are within the same General Asset Class).

(3) The third exchange group consists of trucks R and A (both are in the same General Asset Class).

(B) Under paragraph (b)(2)(ii) of this section, all liabilities of which C is relieved ($1000) are offset by all liabilities assumed by C ($500), resulting in excess liabilities relieved of $500. This excess liabilities relieved is treated as cash received by C.

(1) The first exchange group has an exchange group deficiency of $100 because the fair market value of computer R ($1600) exceeds the fair market value of computer A ($1500) by that amount.

(2) The second exchange group has an exchange group deficiency of $600 because the fair market value of automobile R ($3100) exceeds the fair market value of automobile A ($2500) by that amount.

(3) The third exchange group has an exchange group surplus of $600 because the fair market value of truck A ($2000) exceeds the fair market value of truck R ($1400) by that amount.

(4) The difference between the aggregate fair market value of the properties transferred by C in all of the exchange groups, $6100, and the aggregate fair market value of the properties received by C in all of the exchange groups, $6000, is $100. Therefore, there is a residual group in that amount, consisting of excess liabilities relieved of $100, which is treated as cash received by C.

(5) The $400 cash paid by C and $400 of the excess liabilities relieved which is treated as cash received by C are not within the exchange groups of the residual group.

(C) C recognizes gain on the exchange as follows:

(1) With respect to the first exchange group, the amount of gain realized is the excess of the fair market value of computer R

($1600) over its adjusted basis ($1100), or $500. The amount of gain recognized is the lesser of the gain realized ($500) and the exchange group deficiency ($100), or $100.

(2) With respect to the second exchange group, the amount of gain realized is the excess of the fair market value of automobile R ($3100) over its adjusted basis ($2100), or $1000. The amount of gain recognized is the lesser of the gain realized ($1000) and the exchange group deficiency ($600), or $600.

(3) With respect to the third exchange group, the amount of gain realized is the excess of the fair market value of truck R ($1400) over its adjusted basis ($600), or $800. The amount of gain recognized is the lesser of gain realized ($800) and the exchange group deficiency ($0), or $0.

(4) No property transferred by C was allocated to the residual group. Therefore, C does not recognize any gain with respect to the residual group.

(D) The total amount of gain recognized by C in the exchange is the sum of the gains recognized under section 1031 with respect to each exchange group ($100 + $600 + $0), or $700.

(E) The bases of the properties received by C in the exchange (computer A, automobile A, and truck A) are determined in the following manner:

(1) The basis of the property received in the first exchange group is the adjusted basis of the property transferred within that exchange group ($1100), increased by the amount of gain recognized with respect to that exchange group ($100), decreased by the amount of the exchange group deficiency ($100), and increased by the amount of excess liabilities assumed allocated to that exchange group ($0), or $1100. Because computer A was the only property received within the first exchange group, the entire basis of $1100 is allocated to computer A.

(2) The basis of the property received in the second exchange group is the adjusted basis of the property transferred within that exchange group ($2100), increased by the amount of gain recognized with respect to that exchange group deficiency ($600), decreased by the amount of the exchange group deficiency ($600), and increased by the amount of excess liabilities assumed allocated to that exchange group ($0), or $2100. Because automobile A was the only property received within the second exchange group, the entire basis of $2100 is allocated to automobile A.

(3) The basis of the property received in the third exchange group is the adjusted basis of the property transferred within that exchange group ($600), increased by the amount of gain recognized with respect to that exchange group ($0), increased by the amount of the exchange group surplus ($600), and increased by the amount of excess liabilities assumed allocated to that exchange group ($0), or $1200. Because truck A was the only property received within the third exchange group, the entire basis of $1200 is allocated to truck A.

Example (5). (i) U exchanges real estate A, real estate B, and grader A (NAICS code 333120) with V for real estate R and railroad car R (General Asset Class 00.25). All properties transferred by either U or V were held for productive use in the respective transferor's business. Similarly, all properties to be received by either U or V will be held for productive use in the respective recipient's business. Real estate R is secured by a recourse liability and is transferred subject to that liability. The adjusted basis, fair market value, and liability secured by each property, if any, are as follows:

	Adjusted basis	Fair market value	Liability
U Transfers:			
Real Estate A	$ 2000	$ 5000	....
Real Estate B	8000	13,500	....
Grader A	500	2000	....
V Transfers:			
Real Estate R	$20,000	$26,500	$7000
Railroad car R	1200	1000	....

(ii) The tax treatment to U is as follows:

(A) The exchange group consists of real estate A, real estate B, and real estate R.

(B) Under paragraph (b)(2)(ii) of this section, all liabilities assumed by U ($7000) are excess liabilities assumed. The excess liabilities assumed of $7000 is allocated to the exchange group.

(1) The exchange group has an exchange group surplus of $1000 because the fair market value of real estate R less the excess liabilities assumed allocated to the exchange group ($26,500–$7000) exceeds the aggregate fair market value of real estate A and B ($18,500) by that amount.

(2) The difference between the aggregate fair market value of the properties received in the exchange group (taking excess liabilities assumed into account), $19,500, and the aggregate fair market value of the properties transferred in the exchange group, $18,500, is $1000. Therefore, there is a residual group in that amount consisting of $1000 (or 50 percent of the fair market value) of grader A.

(3) The transaction also includes a taxable exchange of the 50 percent portion of grader A not allocated to the residual group (which is not of a like kind or like class to any property received by U in the exchange) for railroad car R (which is not of a like kind or like class to any property transferred by U in the exchange).

(C) U recognizes gain on the exchange as follows:

(1) With respect to the exchange group, the amount of the gain realized is the excess of the aggregate fair market value of real estate A and B ($18,500) over the aggregate adjusted basis ($10,000), or $8500. The amount of the gain recognized is the lesser of the gain realized ($8500) and the exchange group deficiency ($0), or $0.

(2) With respect to the residual group, the amount of gain realized and recognized is the excess of the fair market value of the 50 percent portion of grader A that is allocated to the residual group ($1000) over its adjusted basis ($250), or $750.

(3) With respect to the taxable exchange of the 50 percent portion of grader A not allocated to the residual group for railroad car R, gain of $750 is realized and recognized by U (amount realized of $1000 (the fair market value of railroad car R) less the adjusted basis of the 50 percent portion of grader A not allocated to the residual group ($250)).

(D) The total amount of gain recognized by U in the transaction is the sum of the gain recognized under section 1031 with respect to the exchange group ($0), any gain recognized with respect to the residual group ($750), and any gain recognized with respect to property transferred that is not in the exchange group or the residual group ($750), or $1500.

(E) The bases of the property received by U in the exchange (real estate R and railroad car R) are determined in the following manner:

(1) The basis of the property received in the exchange group is the aggregate adjusted basis of the property transferred within that exchange group ($10,000), increased by the amount of gain recognized with respect to that exchange group ($0), increased by the amount of the exchange group surplus ($1000), and increased by the amount of excess liabilities assumed allocated to that exchange group ($7000), or $18,000. Because real estate R is the only property received within the exchange group, the entire basis of $18,000 is allocated to real estate R.

(2) The basis of railroad car R is equal to its cost of $1000.

(iii) The tax treatment to V is as follows:

(A) The exchange group consists of real estate R, real estate A, and real estate B.

(B) Under paragraph (b)(2)(ii) of this section, the liabilities of which V is relieved ($7000) results in excess liabilities relieved of $7000 and is treated as cash received by V.

(1) The exchange group has an exchange group deficiency of $8000 because the fair market value of real estate R ($26,500) exceeds the aggregate fair market value of real estate A and B ($18,500) by that amount.

(2) The difference between the aggregate fair market value of the properties transferred by V in the exchange group, $26,500, and the aggregate fair market value of the properties received by V in the exchange group, $18,500, is $8000. Therefore, there is a residual group in that amount, consisting of the excess liabilities relieved of $7000, which is treated as cash received by V, and $1000 (or 50 percent of the fair market value) of grader A.

(3) The transaction also includes a taxable exchange of railroad car R (which is not of a like kind or like class to any property received by V in the exchange) for the 50 percent portion of grader A (which is not of a like kind or like class to any property transferred by V in the exchange) not allocated to the residual group.

(C) V recognizes gain on the exchange as follows:

(1) With respect to the exchange group, the amount of the gain realized is the excess of the fair market value of real estate R ($26,500) over its adjusted basis ($20,000), or $6500. The amount of the gain recognized is the lesser of the gain realized ($6500) and the exchange group deficiency ($8000), or $6500.

(2) No property transferred by V was allocated to the residual group. Therefore, V does not recognize gain or loss with respect to the residual group.

(3) With respect to the taxable exchange of railroad car R for the 50 percent portion of grader A not allocated to the exchange group or the residual group, a loss is realized and recognized in the amount of $200 (the excess of the $1200 adjusted basis of railroad car R over the amount realized of $1000 (fair market value of the 50 percent portion of grader A)).

(D) The basis of the property received by V in the exchange (real estate A, real estate B, and grader A) are determined in the following manner:

(1) The basis of the property received in the exchange group is the adjusted basis of the property transferred within that exchange group ($20,000), increased by the amount of gain recognized with respect to that exchange group ($6500), and decreased by the amount of the exchange group deficiency ($8000), or $18,500. This $18,500 of basis is allocated proportionately among the assets received within the exchange group in accordance with their fair market values: real estate A's basis is $5000 ($18,500 × $5000/$18,500); real estate B's basis is $13,500 ($18,500 × $13,500/$18,500).

(2) The basis of grader A is $2000.

(e) Effective date. Section 1.1031(j)–1 is effective for exchanges occurring on or after April 11, 1991.

§ 1.1031(k)–1 Treatment of deferred exchanges.

(a) Overview. This section provides rules for the application of section 1031 and the regulations thereunder in the case of a "deferred exchange." For purposes of section 1031 and this section, a deferred exchange is defined as an exchange in which, pursuant to an agreement, the taxpayer transfers property held for productive use in a trade or business or for investment (the "relinquished property") and subsequently receives property to be held either for productive use in a trade or business or for investment (the "replacement property"). In the case of a deferred exchange, if the requirements set forth in paragraphs (b), (c), and (d) of this section (relating to identification and receipt of replacement property) are not satisfied, the replacement property received by the taxpayer will be treated as property which is not of a like kind to the relinquished property. In order to constitute a deferred exchange, the transaction must be an exchange (i.e., a transfer of property for property, as distinguished from a transfer of property for money). For example, a sale of property followed by a purchase of property of a like kind does not qualify for nonrecognition of gain or loss under section 1031 regardless of whether the identification and receipt requirements of section 1031(a)(3) and paragraphs (b), (c), and (d) of this section are satisfied. The transfer of relinquished property in a deferred exchange is not within the provisions of section 1031(a) if, as part of the consideration, the taxpayer receives money or property which does not meet the requirements of section 1031(a), but the transfer, if otherwise qualified, will be within the provisions of either section 1031(b) or (c). See § 1.1031(a)–1(a)(2). In addition, in the case of a transfer of relinquished property in a deferred exchange, gain or loss may be recognized if the taxpayer actually or constructively receives money or property which does not meet the requirements of section 1031(a) before the taxpayer actually receives like-kind replacement property. If the taxpayer actually or constructively receives money or property which does not meet the requirements of section

1031(a) in the full amount of the consideration for the relinquished property, the transaction will constitute a sale, and not a deferred exchange, even though the taxpayer may ultimately receive like-kind replacement property. For purposes of this section, property which does not meet the requirements of section 1031(a) (whether by being described in section 1031(a)(2) or otherwise) is referred to as "other property." For rules regarding actual and constructive receipt, and safe harbors therefrom, see paragraphs (f) and (g), respectively, of this section. For rules regarding the determination of gain or loss recognized and the basis of property received in a deferred exchange, see paragraph (j) of this section.

(b) Identification and receipt requirements— (1) In general. In the case of a deferred exchange, any replacement property received by the taxpayer will be treated as property which is not of a like kind to the relinquished property if—

(i) The replacement property is not "identified" before the end of the "identification period," or

(ii) The identified replacement property is not received before the end of the "exchange period."

(2) Identification period and exchange period. **(i)** The identification period begins on the date the taxpayer transfers the relinquished property and ends at midnight on the 45th day thereafter.

(ii) The exchange period begins on the date the taxpayer transfers the relinquished property and ends at midnight on the earlier of the 180th day thereafter or the due date (including extensions) for the taxpayer's return of the tax imposed by chapter 1 of subtitle A of the Code for the taxable year in which the transfer of the relinquished property occurs.

(iii) If, as part of the same deferred exchange, the taxpayer transfers more than one relinquished property and the relinquished properties are transferred on different dates, the identification period and the exchange period are determined by reference to the earliest date on which any of the properties are transferred.

(iv) For purposes of this paragraph (b)(2), property is transferred when the property is disposed of within the meaning of section 1001(a).

(3) Example. This paragraph (b) may be illustrated by the following example.

Example. **(i)** M is a corporation that files its Federal income tax return on a calendar year basis. M and C enter into an agreement for an exchange of property that requires M to transfer property X to C. Under the agreement, M is to identify like-kind replacement property which C is required to purchase and to transfer to M. M transfers property X to C on November 16, 1992.

(ii) The identification period ends at midnight on December 31, 1992, the day which is 45 days after the date of transfer of property X. The exchange period ends at midnight on March 15, 1993, the due date for M's Federal income tax return for the taxable year in which M transferred property X. However, if M is allowed the automatic six-month extension for filing its tax return, the exchange period ends at midnight on May 15, 1993, the day which is 180 days after the date of transfer of property X.

(c) Identification of replacement property before the end of the identification period— (1) In general. For purposes of paragraph (b)(1)(i) of this section (relating to the identification requirement), replacement property is identified before the end of the identification period only if the requirements of this paragraph (c) are satisfied with respect to the replacement property. However, any replacement property that is received by the taxpayer before the end of the identification period will in all events be treated as identified before the end of the identification period.

(2) Manner of identifying replacement property. Replacement property is identified only if it is designated as replacement property in a written document signed by the taxpayer and hand delivered, mailed, telecopied, or otherwise sent before the end of the identification period to either—

(i) The person obliged to transfer the replacement property to the taxpayer (regardless of whether that person is a disqualified person as defined in paragraph (k) of this section); or

(ii) Any other person involved in the exchange other than the taxpayer or a disqualified person (as defined in paragraph (k) of this section).

Examples of persons involved in the exchange include any of the parties to the exchange, an intermediary, an escrow agent, and a title company. An identification of replacement property made in a written agreement for the exchange of properties signed by all parties thereto before the end of the identification period will be treated as satisfying the requirements of this paragraph (c)(2).

(3) Description of replacement property. Replacement property is identified only if it is unambiguously described in the written document or agreement. Real property generally is unambiguously described if it is described by a legal description, street address, or distinguishable name (e.g., the Mayfair Apartment Building). Personal property generally is unambiguously described if it is described by a specific description of the particular type of property. For example, a truck generally is unambiguously described if it is described by a specific make, model, and year.

(4) Alternative and multiple properties. **(i)** The taxpayer may identify more than one replacement property. Regardless of the number of relinquished properties transferred by the taxpayer as part of the same deferred exchange, the maximum number of replacement properties that the taxpayer may identify is—

(A) Three properties without regard to the fair market values of the properties (the "3-property rule"), or

(B) Any number of properties as long as their aggregate fair market value as of the end of the identification period does not exceed 200 percent of the aggregate fair market value of all the relinquished properties as of the date the relinquished properties were transferred by the taxpayer (the "200-percent rule").

(ii) If, as of the end of the identification period, the taxpayer has identified more properties as replacement properties than permitted by paragraph (c)(4)(i) of this section, the taxpayer is treated as if no replacement property had been identified. The preceding sentence will not apply, however, and an identification satisfying the requirements of paragraph (c)(4)(i) of this section will be considered made, with respect to—

(A) Any replacement property received by the taxpayer before the end of the identification period, and

(B) Any replacement property identified before the end of the identification period and received before the end of the exchange period, but only if the taxpayer receives before the end of the exchange period identified replacement property the fair market value of which is at least 95 percent of the aggregate fair market value of all identified replacement properties (the "95-percent rule").

For this purpose, the fair market value of each identified replacement property is determined as of the earlier of the date the property is received by the taxpayer or the last day of the exchange period.

(iii) For purposes of applying the 3-property rule, the 200-percent rule, and the 95-percent rule, all identifications of replacement property, other than identifications of replacement property that have been revoked in the manner provided in paragraph (c)(6) of this section, are taken into account. For example, if, in a deferred exchange, B transfers property X with a fair market value of $100,000 to C and B receives like-kind property Y with a fair market value of $50,000 before the end of the identification period, under paragraph (c)(l) of this section, property Y is treated as identified by reason of being received before the end of the identification period. Thus, under paragraph (c)(4)(i) of this section, B may identify either two additional replacement properties of any fair market value or any number of additional replacement properties as long as the aggregate fair market value of the additional replacement properties does not exceed $150,000.

(5) Incidental property disregarded. **(i)** Solely for purposes of applying this paragraph (c), property that is incidental to a larger item of property is not treated as property that is separate from the larger item of property. Property is incidental to a larger item of property if—

(A) In standard commercial transactions, the property is typically transferred together with the larger item of property, and

(B) The aggregate fair market value of all of the incidental property does not exceed 15 percent of the aggregate fair market value of the larger item of property.

(ii) This paragraph (c)(5) may be illustrated by the following examples.

Example 1. For purposes of paragraph (c) of this section, a spare tire and tool kit will not be treated as separate property from a truck with a fair market value of $10,000, if the aggregate fair market value of the spare tire and tool kit does not exceed $1,500. For purposes of the 3-property rule, the truck, spare tire, and tool kit are treated as 1 property. Moreover, for purposes of paragraph (c)(3) of this section (relating to the description of replacement property), the truck, spare tire, and tool kit are all considered to be unambiguously described if the make, model, and year of the truck are specified, even if no reference is made to the spare tire and tool kit.

Example 2. For purposes of paragraph (c) of this section, furniture, laundry machines, and other miscellaneous items of personal property will not be treated as separate property from an apartment building with a fair market value of $1,000,000, if the aggregate fair market value of the furniture, laundry machines, and other personal property does not exceed $150,000. For purposes of the 3-property rule, the apartment building, furniture, laundry machines, and other personal property are treated as 1 property. Moreover, for purposes of paragraph (c)(3) of this section (relating to the description of replacement property), the apartment building, furniture, laundry machines, and other personal property are all considered to be unambiguously described if the legal description, street address, or distinguishable name of the apartment building is specified, even if no reference is made to the furniture, laundry machines, and other personal property.

(6) Revocation of identification. An identification of replacement property may be revoked at any time before the end of the identification period. An identification of replacement property is revoked only if the revocation is made in a written document signed by the taxpayer and hand delivered, mailed, telecopied, or otherwise sent before the end of the identification period to the person to whom the identification of the replacement property was sent. An identification of replacement property that is made in a written agreement for the exchange of properties is treated as revoked only if the revocation is made in a written amendment to the agreement or in a written document signed by the taxpayer and hand delivered, mailed, telecopied, or otherwise sent before the end of the identification period to all of the parties to the agreement.

(7) Examples. This paragraph (c) may be illustrated by the following examples. Unless otherwise provided in an example, the following facts are assumed: B, a calendar year taxpayer, and C agree to enter into a deferred exchange. Pursuant to their agreement, B transfers real property X to C on May 17, 1991. Real property X, which has been held by B for investment, is unencumbered and has a fair market value on May 17, 1991, of $100,000. On or before July 1, 1991 (the end of the identification period), B is to identify replacement property that is of a like kind to real property X. On or before November 13, 1991 (the end of the exchange period), C is required to purchase the property identified by B and to transfer that property to B. To the extent the fair market value of the replacement property transferred to B is greater or less than the fair market value of real property X, either B or C, as applicable, will make up the difference by paying cash to the other party after the date the replacement property is received by B. No replacement property is identified in the agreement. When subsequently identified, the replacement property is described by legal description and is of a like kind to real property X (determined without regard to section 1031(a)(3) and this section). B intends to hold the replacement property received for investment.

Example 1. (i) On July 2, 1991, B identifies real property E as replacement property by designating real property E as replacement property in a written document signed by B and personally delivered to C.

(ii) Because the identification was made after the end of the identification period, pursuant to paragraph (b)(1)(i) of this section (relating to the identification requirement), real property E is treated as property which is not of a like kind to real property X.

Example 2. (i) C is a corporation of which 20 percent of the outstanding stock is owned by B. On July 1, 1991, B identifies real property F as replacement property by designating real property F as replacement property in a written document signed by B and mailed to C.

(ii) Because C is the person obligated to transfer the replacement property to B, real property F is identified before the end of the identification period. The fact that C is a "disqualified person" as defined in paragraph (k) of this section does not change this result.

(iii) Real property F would also have been treated as identified before the end of the identification period if, instead of sending the identification to C, B had designated real property F as replacement property in a written agreement for the exchange of properties signed by all parties thereto on or before July 1, 1991.

Example 3. (i) On June 3, 1991, B identifies the replacement property as "unimproved land located in Hood County with a fair market value not to exceed $100,000." The designation is made in a written document signed by B and personally delivered to C. On July 8, 1991, B and C agree that real property G is the property described in the June 3, 1991 document.

(ii) Because real property G was not unambiguously described before the end of the identification period, no replacement property is identified before the end of the identification period.

Example 4. (i) On June 28, 1991, B identifies real properties H, J, and K as replacement properties by designating these properties as replacement properties in a written document signed by B and personally delivered to C. The written document provides that by August 1, 1991, B will orally inform C which of the identified properties C is to transfer to B. As of July 1, 1991, the fair market values of real properties H, J, and K are $75,000, $100,000, and $125,000, respectively.

(ii) Because B did not identify more than three properties as replacement properties, the requirements of the 3-property rule are satisfied, and real properties H, J, and K are all identified before the end of the identification period.

Example 5. (i) On May 17, 1991, B identifies real properties L, M, N, and P as replacement properties by designating these properties as replacement properties in a written document signed by B and personally delivered to C. The written document provides that by July 2, 1991, B will orally inform C which of the identified properties C is to transfer to B. As of July 1, 1991, the fair market values of real properties L, M, N, and P are $30,000, $40,000, $50,000, and $60,000, respectively.

(ii) Although B identified more than three properties as replacement properties, the aggregate fair market value of the identified properties as of the end of the identification period ($180,000) did not exceed 200 percent of the aggregate fair market value of real property X (200% × $100,000 = $200,000). Therefore, the requirements of the 200-percent rule are satisfied, and real properties L, M, N, and P are all identified before the end of the identification period.

Example 6. (i) On June 21, 1991, B identifies real properties Q, R, and S as replacement properties by designating these properties as replacement properties in a written document signed by B and mailed to C. On June 24, 1991, B identifies real properties T and U as replacement properties in a written document signed by B and mailed to C. On June 28, 1991, B revokes the identification of real properties Q and R in a written document signed by B and personally delivered to C.

(ii) B has revoked the identification of real properties Q and R in the manner provided by paragraph (c)(6) of this section. Identifications of replacement property that have been revoked in the manner provided by paragraph (c)(6) of this section are not taken into account for purposes of applying the 3-property rule.

Thus, as of June 28, 1991, B has identified only replacement properties S, T, and U for purposes of the 3-property rule. Because B did not identify more than three properties as replacement properties for purposes of the 3-property rule, the requirements of that rule are satisfied, and real properties S, T, and U are all identified before the end of the identification period.

Example 7. (i) On May 20, 1991, B identifies real properties V and W as replacement properties by designating these properties as replacement properties in a written document signed by B and personally delivered to C. On June 4, 1991, B identifies real properties Y and Z as replacement properties in the same manner. On June 5, 1991, B telephones C and orally revokes the identification of real properties V and W. As of July 1, 1991, the fair market values of real properties V, W, Y, and Z are $50,000, $70,000, $90,000, and $100,000, respectively. On July 31, 1991, C purchases real properties Y and Z and transfers them to B.

(ii) Pursuant to paragraph (c)(6) of this section (relating to revocation of identification), the oral revocation of the identification of real properties V and W is invalid. Thus, the identification of real properties V and W is taken into account for purposes of determining whether the requirements of paragraph (c)(4) of this section (relating to the identification of alternative and multiple properties) are satisfied. Because B identified more than three properties and the aggregate fair market value of the identified properties as of the end of the identification period ($310,000) exceeds 200 percent of the fair market value of real property X (200% × $100,000 = $200,000), the requirements of paragraph (c)(4) of this section are not satisfied, and B is treated as if B did not identify any replacement property.

(d) Receipt of identified replacement property—(1) In general. For purposes of paragraph (b)(1)(ii) of this section (relating to the receipt requirement), the identified replacement property is received before the end of the exchange period only if the requirements of this paragraph (d) are satisfied with respect to the replacement property. In the case of a deferred exchange, the identified replacement property is received before the end of the exchange period if—

(i) The taxpayer receives the replacement property before the end of the exchange period, and

(ii) The replacement property received is substantially the same property as identified.

If the taxpayer has identified more than one replacement property, section 1031(a)(3)(B) and this paragraph (d) are applied separately to each replacement property.

(2) Examples. This paragraph (d) may be illustrated by the following examples. The following facts are assumed: B, a calendar year taxpayer, and C agree to enter into a deferred exchange. Pursuant to their agreement, B transfers real property X to C on May 17, 1991. Real property X, which has been held by B for investment, is unencumbered and has a fair market value on May 17, 1991, of $100,000. On or before July 1, 1991 (the end of the identification period), B is to identify replacement property that is of a like kind to real property X. On or before November 13, 1991 (the end of the exchange period), C is required to purchase the property identified by B and to transfer that property to B. To the extent the fair market value of the replacement property transferred to B is greater or less than the fair market value of real property X, either B or C, as applicable, will make up the difference by paying cash to the other party after the date the replacement property is received by B. The replacement property is identified in a manner that satisfies paragraph (c) of this section (relating to identification of replacement property) and is of a like kind to real property X (determined without regard to section 1031(a)(3) and this section). B intends to hold any replacement property received for investment.

Example 1. (i) In the agreement, B identifies real properties J, K, and L as replacement properties. The agreement provides that by July 26, 1991, B will orally inform C which of the properties C is to transfer to B.

(ii) As of July 1, 1991, the fair market values of real properties J, K, and L are $75,000, $100,000, and $125,000, respectively. On July 26, 1991, B instructs C to acquire real property K. On October 31, 1991, C purchases real property K for $100,000 and transfers the property to B.

(iii) Because real property K was identified before the end of the identification period and was received before the end of the exchange period, the identification and receipt requirements of section 1031(a)(3) and this section are satisfied with respect to real property K.

Example 2. (i) In the agreement, B identifies real property P as replacement property. Real property P consists of two acres of unimproved land. On October 15, 1991, the owner of real property P erects a fence on the property. On November 1, 1991, C purchases real property P and transfers it to B.

(ii) The erection of the fence on real property P subsequent to its identification did not alter the basic nature or character of real property P as unimproved land. B is considered to have received substantially the same property as identified.

Example 3. (i) In the agreement, B identifies real property Q as replacement property. Real property Q consists of a barn on two acres of land and has a fair market value of $250,000 ($187,500 for the barn and underlying land and $87,500 for the remaining land). As of July 26, 1991, real property Q remains unchanged and has a fair market value of $250,000. On that date, at B's direction, C purchases the barn and underlying land for $187,500 and transfers it to B, and B pays $87,500 to C.

(ii) The barn and underlying land differ in basic nature or character from real property Q as a whole, B is not considered to have received substantially the same property as identified.

Example 4. (i) In the agreement, B identifies real property R as replacement property. Real property R consists of two acres of unimproved land and has a fair market value of $250,000. As of October 3, 1991, real property R remains unimproved and has a fair market value of $250,000. On that date, at B's direction, C purchases 1½ acres of real property R for $187,500 and transfers it to B, and B pays $87,500 to C.

(ii) The portion of real property R that B received does not differ from the basic nature or character of real property R as a whole. Moreover, the fair market value of the portion of real property R that B received ($187,500) is 75 percent of the fair market value of real property R as of the date of receipt. Accordingly, B is considered to have received substantially the same property as identified.

(1) Special rules for identification and receipt of replacement property to be produced—(1) In general. A transfer of relinquished property in a deferred exchange will not fail to qualify for nonrecognition of gain or loss under section 1031 merely because the replacement property is not in existence or is being produced at the time the property is identified as replacement property. For purposes of this paragraph (e), the terms "produced" and "production" have the same meanings as provided in section 263A(g)(1) and the regulations thereunder.

(2) Identification of replacement property to be produced. (i) In the case of replacement property that is to be produced, the replacement property must be identified as provided in paragraph (c) of this section (relating to identification of replacement property). For example, if the identified replacement property consists of improved real property where the improvements are to be constructed, the description of the replacement property satisfies the requirements of paragraph (c)(3) of this section (relating to description of replacement property) if a legal description is provided for the underlying land and as much detail is provided regarding construction of the improvements as is practicable at the time the identification is made.

(ii) For purposes of paragraphs (c)(4)(i)(B) and (c)(5) of this section (relating to the 200-percent rule and incidental property), the fair market value of replacement property that is to be produced is its estimated fair market value as of the date it is expected to be received by the taxpayer.

(3) Receipt of replacement property to be produced. (i) For purposes of paragraph (d)(1)(ii) of this section (relating to receipt of the identified replacement property), in determining whether the replacement property received by the taxpayer is substantially the same property as identified where the identified replacement property is property to be produced, variations due to usual or typical production changes are not taken into account. However, if substantial changes are made in the property to be produced, the replacement property received will not be considered to be substantially the same property as identified.

(ii) If the identified replacement property is personal property to be produced, the replacement property received will not be considered to be substantially the same property as identified unless production of the replacement property received is completed on or before the date the property is received by the taxpayer.

(iii) If the identified replacement property is real property to be produced and the production of the property is not completed on or before the date the taxpayer receives the property, the property received will be considered to be substantially the same property as identified only if, had production been completed on or before the date the taxpayer receives the replacement property, the property received would have been considered to be substantially the same property as identified. Even so, the property received is considered to be substantially the same property as identified only to the extent the property received constitutes real property under local law.

(4) Additional rules. The transfer of relinquished property is not within the provisions of section 1031 (a) if the relinquished property is transferred in exchange for services (including production services). Thus, any additional production occurring with respect to the replacement property after the property is received by the taxpayer will not be treated as the receipt of property of a like kind.

(5) Example. This paragraph (e) may be illustrated by the following example.

Example. (i) B, a calendar year taxpayer, and C agree to enter into a deferred exchange. Pursuant to their agreement, B transfers improved real property X and personal property Y to C on May 17, 1991. On or before November 13, 1991 (the end of the exchange period), C is required to transfer to B real property M, on which C is constructing improvements, and personal property N, which C is producing. C is obligated to complete the improvements and production regardless of when properties M and N are transferred to B. Properties M and N are identified in a manner that satisfies paragraphs (c) (relating to identification of replacement property) and (e)(2) of this section. In addition, properties M and N are of a like kind, respectively, to real property X and personal property Y (determined without regard to section 1031(a)(3) and this section). On November 13, 1991, when construction of the improvements to property M is 20 percent completed and the production of property N is 90 percent completed, C transfers to B property M and property N. If construction of the improvements had been completed, property M would have been considered to be substantially the same property as identified. Under local law, property M constitutes real property to the extent of the underlying land and the 20 percent of the construction that is completed.

(ii) Because property N is personal property to be produced and production of property N is not completed before the date the property is received by B, property N is not considered to be substantially the same property as identified and is treated as property which is not of a like kind to property Y.

(iii) Property M is considered to be substantially the same property as identified to the extent of the underlying land and the 20 percent of the construction that is completed when property M is received by B. However, any additional construction performed by C with respect to property M after November 13, 1991, is not treated as the receipt of property of a like kind.

(f) Receipt of money or other property—(1) In general. A transfer of relinquished property in a deferred exchange is not within the provisions of section 1031(a) if, as part of the consideration, the taxpayer receives money or other property. However, such a transfer, if otherwise qualified, will be within the provisions of either section 1031(b) or (c). See § 1031(a)–1(a)(2). In addition, in the case of a transfer of relinquished property in a deferred exchange, gain or loss may be recognized if the taxpayer actually or constructively receives money or other property before the taxpayer actually receives like-kind replacement property. If the taxpayer actually or constructively receives money or other property in the full amount of the consideration for the relinquished property before the taxpayer actually receives like-kind replacement property, the transaction will constitute a sale and not a deferred exchange, even though the taxpayer may ultimately receive like-kind replacement property.

(2) Actual and constructive receipt. Except as provided in paragraph (g) of this section (relating to safe harbors), for purposes of section 1031 and this section, the determination of whether (or the extent to which) the taxpayer is in actual or constructive receipt of money or other property before the taxpayer actually receives like-kind replacement property is made under the general rules concerning actual and constructive receipt and without regard to the taxpayer's method of accounting. The taxpayer is in actual receipt of money or property at the time the taxpayer actually receives the money or property or receives the economic benefit of the money or property. The taxpayer is in constructive receipt of money or property at the time the money or property is credited to the taxpayer's account, set apart for the taxpayer, or otherwise made available so that the taxpayer may draw upon it at any time or so that the taxpayer can draw upon it if notice of intention to draw is given. Although the taxpayer is not in constructive receipt of money or property if the taxpayer's control of its receipt is subject to substantial limitations or restrictions, the taxpayer is in constructive receipt of the money or property at the time the limitations or restrictions lapse, expire, or are waived. In addition, actual or constructive receipt of money or property by an agent of the taxpayer (determined without regard to paragraph (k) of this section) is actual or constructive receipt by the taxpayer.

(3) Example. This paragraph (f) may be illustrated by the following example.

Example. (i) B, a calendar year taxpayer, and C agree to enter into a deferred exchange. Pursuant to the agreement, on May 17, 1991, B transfers real property X to C. Real property X, which has been held by B for investment, is unencumbered and has a fair market value on May 17, 1991, of $100,000. On or before July 1, 1991 (the end of the identification period), B is to identify replacement property that is of a like kind to real property X. On or before November 13, 1991 (the end of the exchange period), C is required to purchase the property identified by B and to transfer that property to B. At any time after May 17, 1991, and before C has purchased the replacement property, B has the right, upon notice, to demand that C pay $100,000 in lieu of acquiring and transferring the replacement property. Pursuant to the agreement, B identifies replacement property, and C purchases the replacement property and transfers it to B.

(ii) Under the agreement, B has the unrestricted right to demand the payment of $100,000 as of May 17, 1991. B is therefore in constructive receipt of $100,000 on that date. Because B is in constructive receipt of money in the full amount of the consideration for the relinquished property before B actually receives the like-kind replacement property, the transaction constitutes a sale, and the transfer of real property X does not qualify for nonrecognition of gain or loss under section 1031. B is treated as if B received the $100,000 in consideration for the sale of real property X and then purchased the like-kind replacement property.

(iii) If B's right to demand payment of the $100,000 were subject to a substantial limitation or restriction (e.g., the agreement provided that B had no right to demand payment before November 14, 1991 (the end of the exchange period)), then, for purposes of this section, B would not be in actual or constructive receipt of the money unless (or until) the limitation or restriction lapsed, expired, or was waived.

(g) Safe harbors—(1) In general. Paragraphs (g)(2) through (g)(5) of this section set forth four safe harbors the use of which will result in a determination that the taxpayer is not in actual or constructive receipt of money or other property for purposes of section 1031 and this section. More than one safe harbor can be used in the same deferred exchange, but the terms and conditions of each must be separately satisfied. For purposes of the safe harbor rules, the term "taxpayer" does not include a person or entity utilized in a safe harbor (e.g., a qualified intermediary). See paragraph (g)(8), Example 3(v), of this section.

(2) Security or guarantee arrangements. (i) In the case of a deferred exchange, the determination of whether the taxpayer is in actual or constructive receipt of money or other property before the taxpayer actually receives like-kind replacement property will be made without regard to the fact that the obligation of the taxpayer's transferee to transfer the replacement property to the taxpayer is or may be secured or guaranteed by one or more of the following—

(A) A mortgage, deed of trust, or other security interest in property (other than cash or a cash equivalent),

(B) A standby letter of credit which satisfies all of the requirements of § 15A.453–1(b)(3)(iii) and which may not be drawn upon in the absence of a default of the transferee's obligation to transfer like-kind replacement property to the taxpayer, or

(C) A guarantee of a third party.

(ii) Paragraph (g)(2)(i) of this section ceases to apply at the time the taxpayer has an immediate ability or unrestricted right to receive money or other property pursuant to the security or guarantee arrangement.

(3) Qualified escrow accounts and qualified trusts. (i) In the case of a deferred exchange, the determination of whether the taxpayer is in actual or constructive receipt of money or other property before the taxpayer actually receives like-kind replacement property will be made without regard to the fact that the obligation of the taxpayer's transferee to transfer the replacement property to the taxpayer is or may be secured by cash or a cash equivalent if the cash or cash equivalent is held in a qualified escrow account or in a qualified trust.

(ii) A qualified escrow account is an escrow account wherein—

(A) The escrow holder is not the taxpayer or a disqualified person (as defined in paragraph (k) of this section), and

(B) The escrow agreement expressly limits the taxpayer's rights to receive, pledge, borrow, or otherwise obtain the benefits of the cash or cash equivalent held in the escrow account as provided in paragraph (g)(6) of this section.

(iii) A qualified trust is a trust wherein—

(A) The trustee is not the taxpayer or a disqualified person (as defined in paragraph (k) of this section, except that for this purpose the relationship between the taxpayer and the trustee created by the qualified trust will not be considered a relationship under section 267(b)), and

(B) The trust agreement expressly limits the taxpayer's rights to receive, pledge, borrow, or otherwise obtain the benefits of the cash or cash equivalent held by the trustee as provided in paragraph (g)(6) of this section.

(iv) Paragraph (g)(3)(i) of this section ceases to apply at the time the taxpayer has an immediate ability or unrestricted right to receive, pledge, borrow, or otherwise obtain the benefits of the cash or cash equivalent held in the qualified escrow account or qualified trust. Rights conferred upon the taxpayer under state law to terminate or dismiss the escrow holder of a qualified escrow account or the trustee of a qualified trust are disregarded for this purpose.

(v) A taxpayer may receive money or other property directly from a party to the exchange, but not from a qualified escrow account or a qualified trust, without affecting the application of paragraph (g)(3)(i) of this section.

(4) Qualified intermediaries. (i) In the case of a taxpayer's transfer of relinquished property involving a qualified intermediary, the qualified intermediary is not considered the agent of the taxpayer for purposes of section 1031(a). In such a case, the taxpayer's transfer of relinquished property and subsequent receipt of like-kind replacement property is treated as an exchange, and the determination of whether the taxpayer is in actual or constructive receipt of money or other property before the taxpayer actually receives like-kind replacement property is made as if the qualified intermediary is not the agent of the taxpayer.

(ii) Paragraph (g)(4)(i) of this section applies only if the agreement between the taxpayer and the qualified intermediary expressly limits the taxpayer's rights to receive, pledge, borrow, or otherwise obtain the benefits of money or other property held by the qualified intermediary as provided in paragraph (g)(6) of this section.

(iii) A qualified intermediary is a person who—

(A) Is not the taxpayer or a disqualified person (as defined in paragraph (k) of this section), and

(B) Enters into a written agreement with the taxpayer (the "exchange agreement") and, as required by the exchange agreement, acquires the relinquished property from the taxpayer, transfers the relinquished property, acquires the replacement property, and transfers the replacement property to the taxpayer.

(iv) Regardless of whether an intermediary acquires and transfers property under general tax principles, solely for purposes of paragraph (g)(4)(iii)(B) of this section—

(A) An intermediary is treated as acquiring and transferring property if the intermediary acquires and transfers legal title to that property,

(B) An intermediary is treated as acquiring and transferring the relinquished property if the intermediary (either on its own behalf or as the agent of any party to the transaction) enters into an agreement with a person other than the taxpayer for the transfer of the relinquished property to that person and, pursuant to that agreement, the relinquished property is transferred to that person, and

(C) An intermediary is treated as acquiring and transferring replacement property if the intermediary (either on its own behalf or as the agent of any party to the transaction) enters into an agreement with the owner of the replacement property for the transfer of that property and, pursuant to that agreement, the replacement property is transferred to the taxpayer.

(v) Solely for purposes of paragraphs (g)(4)(iii) and (g)(4)(iv) of this section, an intermediary is treated as entering into an agreement if the rights of a party to the agreement are assigned to the intermediary and all parties to that agreement are notified in writing of the assignment on or before the date of the relevant transfer of property. For example, if a taxpayer enters into an agreement for the transfer of relinquished property and thereafter assigns its rights in that agreement to an intermediary and all parties to that agreement are notified in writing of the assignment on or before the date of the transfer of the relinquished property, the intermediary is treated as entering into that agreement. If the relinquished property is transferred pursuant to that agreement, the intermediary is treated as having acquired and transferred the relinquished property.

(vi) Paragraph (g)(4)(i) of this section ceases to apply at the time the taxpayer has an immediate ability or unrestricted right to receive, pledge, borrow, or otherwise obtain the benefits of money or other property held by the qualified intermediary. Rights conferred upon the taxpayer under state law to terminate or dismiss the qualified intermediary are disregarded for this purpose.

(vii) A taxpayer may receive money or other property directly from a party to the transaction other than the qualified intermediary without affecting the application of paragraph (g)(4)(i) of this section.

(5) Interest and growth factors. In the case of a deferred exchange, the determination of whether the taxpayer is in actual or constructive receipt of money or other property before the taxpayer actually receives the like-kind replacement property will be made without regard to the fact that the taxpayer is or may be entitled to receive any interest or growth factor with respect to the deferred exchange. The preceding sentence applies only if the agreement pursuant to which the taxpayer is or may be entitled to the interest or growth factor expressly limits the taxpayer's rights to receive the interest or growth factor as provided in paragraph (g)(6) of this section. For additional rules concerning interest or growth factors, see paragraph (h) of this section.

(6) Additional restrictions on safe harbors under paragraphs (g)(3) through (g)(5). (i) An agreement limits a taxpayer's rights as provided in this paragraph (g)(6) only if the agreement provides that the taxpayer has no rights, except as provided in paragraph (g)(6)(ii) and (g)(6)(iii) of this section, to receive, pledge, borrow, or otherwise obtain the benefits of money or other property before the end of the exchange period.

(ii) The agreement may provide that if the taxpayer has not identified replacement property by the end of the identification period, the taxpayer may have rights to receive, pledge, borrow, or otherwise obtain the benefits of money or other property at any time after the end of the identification period.

(iii) The agreement may provide that if the taxpayer has identified replacement property, the taxpayer may have rights to receive, pledge, borrow, or otherwise obtain the benefits of money or other property upon or after—

(A) The receipt by the taxpayer of all of the replacement property to which the taxpayer is entitled under the exchange agreement, or

(B) The occurrence after the end of the identification period of a material and substantial contingency that—

(1) Relates to the deferred exchange,

(2) Is provided for in writing, and

(3) Is beyond the control of the taxpayer and of any disqualified person (as defined in paragraph (k) of this section), other than the person obligated to transfer the replacement property to the taxpayer.

(7) Items disregarded in applying safe harbors under paragraphs (g)(3) through (g)(5). In determining whether a safe harbor under paragraphs (g)(3) through (g)(5) of this section ceases to apply and whether the taxpayer's rights to receive, pledge, borrow, or otherwise obtain the benefits of money or other property are expressly limited as provided in paragraph (g)(6) of this section, the taxpayer's receipt of or right to receive any of the following items will be disregarded—

(i) Items that a seller may receive as a consequence of the disposition of property and that are not included in the amount realized from the disposition of property (e.g., prorated rents), and

(ii) Transactional items that relate to the disposition of the relinquished property or to the acquisition of the replacement property and appear under local standards in the typical closing statements as the responsibility of a buyer or seller (e.g., commissions, prorated taxes, recording or transfer taxes, and title company fees).

(8) Examples. This paragraph (g) may be illustrated by the following examples. Unless otherwise provided in an example, the following facts are assumed: B, a calendar year taxpayer, and C agree to enter into a deferred exchange. Pursuant to their agreement, B is to transfer real property X to C on May 17, 1991. Real property X, which has been held by B for investment, is unencumbered and has a fair market value on May 17, 1991, of $100,000. On or before July 1, 1991 (the end of the identification period), B is to identify replacement property that is of a like kind to real property X. On or before November 13, 1991 (the end of the exchange period), C is required to purchase the property identified by B and to transfer that property to B. To the extent the fair market value of the replacement property transferred to B is greater or less than the fair market value property X, either B or C, as applicable, will make up the difference by paying cash to the other party after the date the replacement property is received by B. The replacement property is identified as provided in paragraph (c) of this section (relating to identification of replacement property) and is of a like kind to real property X (determined without regard to section 1031(a)(3) and this section). B intends to hold any replacement property received for investment.

Example 1. **(i)** On May 17, 1991, B transfers real property X to C. On the same day, C pays $10,000 to B and deposits $90,000 in escrow as security for C's obligation to perform under the agreement. The escrow agreement provides that B has no rights to receive, pledge, borrow, or otherwise obtain the benefits of the money in escrow before November 14, 1991, except that:

(A) if B fails to identify replacement property on or before July 1, 1991, B may demand the funds in escrow at any time after July 1, 1991; and

(B) if B identifies and receives replacement property, then B may demand the balance of the remaining funds in escrow at any time after B has received the replacement property.

The funds in escrow may be used to purchase the replacement property. The escrow holder is not a disqualified person as defined in paragraph (k) of this section. Pursuant to the terms of the agreement, B identifies replacement property, and C purchases the replacement property using the funds in escrow and transfers the replacement property to B.

(ii) C's obligation to transfer the replacement property to B was secured by cash held in a qualified escrow account because the escrow holder was not a disqualified person and the escrow agreement expressly limited B's rights to receive, pledge, borrow, or otherwise obtain the benefits of the money in escrow as provided in paragraph (g)(6) of this section. In addition, B did not have the immediate ability or unrestricted right to receive money or other property in escrow before B actually received the like-kind replacement property. Therefore, for purposes of section 1031 and this section, B is determined not to be in actual or constructive receipt of the $90,000 held in escrow before B received the like-kind replacement property. The transfer of real property X by B and B's acquisition of the replacement property qualify as an exchange under section 1031. See paragraph (j) of this section for determining the amount of gain or loss recognized.

Example 2. **(i)** On May 17, 1991, B transfers real property X to C, and C deposits $100,000 in escrow as security for C's obligation to perform under the agreement. Also on May 17, B identifies real property J as replacement property. The escrow agreement provides that no funds may be paid out without prior written approval of both B and C. The escrow agreement also provides that B has no rights to receive, pledge, borrow, or otherwise obtain the benefits of the money in escrow before November 14, 1991, except that:

(A) B may demand the funds in escrow at any time after the later of July 1, 1991, and the occurrence of any of the following events—

(1) real property J is destroyed, seized, requisitioned, or condemned, or

(2) a determination is made that the regulatory approval necessary for the transfer of real property J cannot be obtained in time for real property J to be transferred to B before the end of the exchange period;

(B) B may demand the funds in escrow at any time after August 14, 1991, if real property J has not been rezoned from residential to commercial use by that date; and

(C) B may demand the funds in escrow at the time B receives real property J or any time thereafter.

Otherwise, B is entitled to all funds in escrow after November 13, 1991. The funds in escrow may be used to purchase the replacement property. The escrow holder is not a disqualified person as described in paragraph (k) of this section. Real property J is not rezoned from residential to commercial use on or before August 14, 1991.

(ii) C's obligation to transfer the replacement property to B was secured by cash held in a qualified escrow account because the escrow holder was not a disqualified person and the escrow agreement expressly limited B's rights to receive, pledge, borrow, or otherwise obtain the benefits of the money in escrow as provided in paragraph (g)(6) of this section. From May 17, 1991, until August 15, 1991, B did not have the immediate ability or unrestricted right to receive money or other property before B actually received the like-kind replacement property. Therefore, for purposes of section 1031 and this section, B is determined not to be in actual or constructive receipt of the $100,000 in escrow from May 17, 1991, until August 15, 1991. However, on August 15, 1991, B had the unrestricted right, upon notice, to draw upon the $100,000 held in escrow. Thus, the safe harbor ceased to apply and B was in constructive receipt of the funds held in escrow. Because B constructively received the full amount of the consideration

($100,000) before B actually received the like-kind replacement property, the transaction is treated as a sale and not as a deferred exchange. The result does not change even if B chose not to demand the funds in escrow and continued to attempt to have real property J rezoned and to receive the property on or before November 13, 1991.

(iii) If real property J had been rezoned on or before August 14, 1991, and C had purchased real property J and transferred it to B on or before November 13, 1991, the transaction would have qualified for nonrecognition of gain or loss under section 1031(a).

Example 3. (i) On May 1, 1991, D offers to purchase real property X for $100,000. However, D is unwilling to participate in a like-kind exchange. B thus enters into an exchange agreement with C whereby B retains C to facilitate an exchange with respect to real property X. C is not a disqualified person as described in paragraph (k) of this section. The exchange agreement between B and C provides that B is to execute and deliver a deed conveying real property X to C who, in turn, is to execute and deliver a deed conveying real property X to D. The exchange agreement expressly limits B's rights to receive, pledge, borrow, or otherwise obtain the benefits of money or other property held by C as provided in paragraph (g)(6) of this section. On May 3, 1991, C enters into an agreement with D to transfer real property X to D for $100,000. On May 17, 1991, B executes and delivers to C a deed conveying real property X to C. On the same date, C executes and delivers to D a deed conveying real property X to D, and D deposits $100,000 in escrow. The escrow holder is not a disqualified person as defined in paragraph (k) of this section and the escrow agreement expressly limits B's rights to receive, pledge, borrow, or otherwise obtain the benefits of money or other property in escrow as provided in paragraph (g)(6) of this section. However, the escrow agreement provides that the money in escrow may be used to purchase replacement property. On June 3, 1991, B identifies real property K as replacement property. On August 9, 1991, E executes and delivers to C a deed conveying real property K to C and $80,000 is released from the escrow and paid to E. On the same date, C executes and delivers to B a deed conveying real property K to B, and the escrow holder pays B $20,000, the balance of the $100,000 sale price of real property X remaining after the purchase of real property K for $80,000.

(ii) B and C entered into an exchange agreement that satisfied the requirements of paragraph (g)(4)(iii)(B) of this section. Regardless of whether C may have acquired and transferred real property X under general tax principles, C is treated as having acquired and transferred real property X because C acquired and transferred legal title to real property X. Similarly, C is treated as having acquired and transferred real property K because C acquired and transferred legal title to real property K. Thus, C was a qualified intermediary. This result is reached for purposes of this section regardless of whether C was B's agent under state law.

(iii) Because the escrow holder was not a disqualified person and the escrow agreement expressly limited B's rights to receive, pledge, borrow, or otherwise obtain the benefits of money or other property in escrow as provided in paragraph (g)(6) of this section, the escrow account was a qualified escrow account. For purposes of section 1031 and this section, therefore, B is determined not to be in actual or constructive receipt of the funds in escrow before B received real property K.

(iv) The exchange agreement between B and C expressly limited B's rights to receive, pledge, borrow, or otherwise obtain the benefits of any money held by C as provided in paragraph (g)(6) of this section. Because C was a qualified intermediary, for purposes of section 1031 and this section B is determined not to be in actual or constructive receipt of any funds held by C before B received real property K. In addition, B's transfer of real property X and acquisition of real property K qualify as an exchange under section 1031. See paragraph (j) of this section for determining the amount of gain or loss recognized.

(v) If the escrow agreement had expressly limited C's rights to receive, pledge, borrow, or otherwise obtain the benefits of money or other property in escrow as provided in paragraph (g)(6) of this section, but had not expressly limited B's rights to receive, pledge, borrow, or otherwise obtain the benefits of that money or other property, the escrow account would not have been a qualified escrow account. Consequently, paragraph (g)(3)(i) of this section would not have been applicable in determining whether B was in actual or constructive receipt of that money or other property before B received real property K.

Example 4. (i) On May 1, 1991, B enters into an agreement to sell real property X to D for $100,000 on May 17, 1991. However, D is unwilling to participate in a like-kind exchange. B thus enters into an exchange agreement with C whereby B retains C to facilitate an exchange with respect to real property X. C is not a disqualified person as described in paragraph (k) of this section. In the exchange agreement between B and C, B assigns to C all of B's rights in the agreement with D. The exchange agreement expressly limits B's rights to receive, pledge, borrow, or otherwise obtain the benefits of money or other property held by C as provided in paragraph (g)(6) of this section. On May 17, 1991, B notifies D in writing of the assignment. On the same date, B executes and delivers to D a deed conveying real property X to D. D pays $10,000 to B and $90,000 to C. On June 1, 1991, B identifies real property L as replacement property. On July 5, 1991, B enters into an agreement to purchase real property L from E for $90,000, assigns its rights in that agreement to C, and notifies E in writing of the assignment. On August 9, 1991, C pays $90,000 to E, and E executes and delivers to B a deed conveying real property L to B.

(ii) The exchange agreement entered into by B and C satisfied the requirements of paragraph (g)(4)(iii)(B) of this section. Because B's rights in its agreements with D and E were assigned to C, and D and E were notified in writing of the assignment on or before the transfer of real properties X and L, respectively, C is treated as entering into those agreements. Because C is treated as entering into an agreement with D for the transfer of real property X and, pursuant to that agreement, real property X was transferred to D, C is treated as acquiring and transferring real property X. Similarly, because C is treated as entering into an agreement with E for the transfer of real property K and, pursuant to that agreement, real property K was transferred to B, C is treated as acquiring and transferring real property K. This result is reached for purposes of this section regardless of whether C was B's agent under state law and regardless of whether C is considered, under general tax principles, to have acquired title or beneficial ownership of the properties. Thus, C was a qualified intermediary.

(iii) The exchange agreement between B and C expressly limited B's rights to receive, pledge, borrow, or otherwise obtain the benefits of the money held by C as provided in paragraph (g)(6) of this section. Thus, B did not have the immediate ability or unrestricted right to receive money or other property held by C before B received real property L. For purposes of section 1031 and this section, therefore, B is determined not to be in actual or constructive receipt of the $90,000 held by C before B received real property L. In addition, the transfer of real property X by B and B's acquisition of real property L qualify as an exchange under section 1031. See paragraph (j) of this section for determining the amount of gain or loss recognized.

Example 5. **(i)** On May 1, 1991, B enters into an agreement to sell real property X to D for $100,000. However, D is unwilling to participate in a like-kind exchange. B thus enters into an agreement with C whereby B retains C to facilitate an exchange with respect to real property X. C is not a disqualified person as described in paragraph (k) of this section. The agreement between B and C expressly limits B's rights to receive, pledge, borrow, or otherwise obtain the benefits of money or other property held by C as provided in paragraph (g)(6) of this section. C neither enters into an agreement with D to transfer real property X to D nor is assigned B's rights in B's agreement to sell real property X to D. On May 17, 1991, B transfers real property X to D and instructs D to transfer the $100,000 to C. On June 1, 1991, B identifies real property M as replacement property. On August 9, 1991, C purchases real property L from E for $100,000, and E executes and delivers to C a deed conveying real property M to C. On the same date, C executes and delivers to B a deed conveying real property M to B.

(ii) Because B transferred real property X directly to D under B's agreement with D, C did not acquire real property X from B and transfer real property X to D. Moreover, because C did not acquire legal title to real property X, did not enter into an agreement with D to transfer real property X to D, and was not assigned B's rights in B's agreement to sell real property X to D, C is not treated as acquiring and transferring real property X. Thus, C was not a qualified intermediary and paragraph (g)(4)(i) of this section does not apply.

(iii) B did not exchange real property X for real property M. Rather, B sold real property X to D and purchased, through C, real property M. Therefore, the transfer of real property X does not qualify for nonrecognition of gain or loss under section 1031.

(h) Interest and growth factors—(1) In general. For purposes of this section, the taxpayer is treated as being entitled to receive interest or a growth factor with respect to a deferred exchange if the amount of money or property the taxpayer is entitled to receive depends upon the length of time elapsed between transfer of the relinquished property and receipt of the replacement property.

(2) Treatment as interest. If, as part of a deferred exchange, the taxpayer receives interest or a growth factor, the interest or growth factor will be treated as interest, regardless of whether it is paid to the taxpayer in cash or in property (including property of a like kind). The taxpayer must include the interest or growth factor in income according to the taxpayer's method of accounting.

(i) [Reserved]

(j) Determination of gain or loss recognized and the basis of property received in a deferred exchange—(1) In general. Except as otherwise provided, the amount of gain or loss recognized and the basis of property received in a deferred exchange is determined by applying the rules of section 1031 and the regulations thereunder. See §§ 1.1031(b)–1, 1.1031(c)–1, 1.1031(d)–1, 1.1031 (d)–1T, 1.1031(d)–2, and 1.1031(j)–1.

(2) Coordination with section 453—(i) Qualified escrow accounts and qualified trusts. Subject to the limitations of paragraphs (j)(2)(iv) and (v) of this section, in the case of a taxpayer's transfer of relinquished property in which the obligation of the taxpayer's transferee to transfer replacement property to the taxpayer is or may be secured by cash or a cash equivalent, the determination of whether the taxpayer has received a payment for purposes of section 453 and § 15a.453–1(b)(3)(i) of this chapter will be made without regard to the fact that the obligation is or may be so secured if the cash or cash equivalent is held in a qualified escrow account or a qualified trust. This paragraph (j)(2)(i) ceases to apply at the earlier of—

(A) The time described in paragraph (g)(3)(iv) of this section; or

(B) The end of the exchange period.

(ii) Qualified intermediaries. Subject to the limitations of paragraphs (j)(2)(iv) and (v) of this section, in the case of a taxpayer's transfer of relinquished property involving a qualified intermediary, the determination of whether the taxpayer has received a payment for purposes of section 453 and § 15a.453–1(b)(3)(i) of this chapter is made as if the qualified intermediary is not the agent of the taxpayer. For purposes of this paragraph (j)(2)(ii), a person who otherwise satisfies the definition of a qualified intermediary is treated as a qualified intermediary even though that person ultimately fails to acquire identified replacement property and transfer it to the taxpayer. This paragraph (j)(2)(ii) ceases to apply at the earlier of—

(A) The time described in paragraph (g)(4)(vi) of this section; or

(B) The end of the exchange period.

(iii) Transferee indebtedness. In the case of a transaction described in paragraph (j)(2)(ii) of this section, the receipt by the taxpayer of an evidence of indebtedness of the transferee of the qualified intermediary is treated as the receipt of an evidence of indebtedness of the person acquiring property from the taxpayer for purposes of section 453 and § 15a.453–1(b)(3)(i) of this chapter.

(iv) Bona fide intent requirement. The provisions of paragraphs (j)(2)(i) and (ii) of this section do not apply unless the taxpayer has a bona fide intent to enter into a deferred exchange at the beginning of the exchange period. A taxpayer will be treated as having a bona fide intent only if it is reasonable to believe, based on all the facts and circumstances as of the beginning of the exchange period, that like-kind replacement property will be acquired before the end of the exchange period.

(v) Disqualified property. The provisions of paragraphs (j)(2)(i) and (ii) of this section do not apply if the relinquished property is disqualified property. For purposes of this paragraph (j)(2), disqualified property means property that is not held for productive use in a trade or business or for investment or is property described in section 1031 (a)(2).

(vi) Examples. This paragraph (j)(2) may be illustrated by the following examples. Unless otherwise provided in an example, the following facts are assumed: B is a calendar year taxpayer who agrees to enter into a deferred exchange. Pursuant to the agreement, B is to transfer real property X. Real property X, which has been held by B for investment, is unencumbered and has a fair market value of $100,000 at the time of transfer. B's adjusted basis in real property X at that time is $60,000. B identifies a single like-kind replacement property before the end of the identification period, and B receives the replacement property before the end of the exchange period. The transaction qualifies as a like-kind exchange under section 1031.

Example 1. (i) On September 22, 1994, B transfers real property X to C and C agrees to acquire like-kind property and deliver it to B. On that date B has a bona fide intent to enter into a deferred exchange, C's obligation, which is not payable on demand or readily tradable, is secured by $100,000 in cash. The $100,000 is deposited by C in an escrow account that is a qualified escrow account under paragraph (g)(3) of this section. The escrow agreement provides that B has no rights to receive, pledge, borrow, or otherwise obtain the benefits of the cash deposited in the escrow account until the earlier of the date the replacement property is delivered to B or the end of the exchange period. On March 11, 1995, C acquires replacement property having a fair market value of $80,000 and delivers the replacement property to B. The $20,000 in cash remaining in the qualified escrow account is distributed to B at that time.

(ii) Under section 1031(b), B recognizes gain to the extent of the $20,000 in cash that B receives in the exchange. Under paragraph (j)(2)(i) of this section, the qualified escrow account is disregarded for purposes of section 453 and § 15a.453–1(b)(3)(i) of this chapter in determining whether B is in receipt of payment. Accordingly, B's receipt of C's obligation on September 22, 1994, does not constitute a payment. Instead, B is treated as receiving payment on March 11, 1995, on receipt of the $20,000 in cash from the qualified escrow account. Subject to the other requirements of sections 453 and 453A, B may report the $20,000 gain in 1995 under the installment method. See section 453(f)(6) for special rules for determining total contract price and gross profit in the case of an exchange described in section 1031(b).

Example 2. (i) D offers to purchase real property X but is unwilling to participate in a like-kind exchange. B thus enters into an exchange agreement with C whereby B retains C to facilitate an exchange with respect to real property X. On September 22, 1994, pursuant to the agreement, B transfers real property X to C who transfers it to D for $100,000 in cash. On that date B has a bona fide intent to enter into a deferred exchange. C is a qualified intermediary under paragraph (g)(4) of this section. The exchange agreement provides that B has no rights to receive, pledge, borrow, or otherwise obtain the benefits of the money held by C until the earlier of the date the replacement property is delivered to B or the end of the exchange period. On March 11, 1995, C acquires replacement property having a fair market value of $80,000 and delivers it, along with the remaining $20,000 from the transfer of real property X to B.

(ii) Under section 1031(b), B recognizes gain to the extent of the $20,000 cash B receives in the exchange. Under paragraph (j)(2)(ii) of this section, any agency relationship between B and C is disregarded for purposes of section 453 and § 15a.453–1(b)(3)(i) of this chapter in determining whether B is in receipt of payment. Accordingly, B is not treated as having received payment on September 22, 1994, on C's receipt of payment from D for the relinquished property. Instead, B is treated as receiving payment on March 11, 1995, on receipt of the $20,000 in cash from C. Subject to the other requirements of sections 453 and 453A, B may report the $20,000 gain in 1995 under the installment method.

Example 3. (i) D offers to purchase real property X but is unwilling to participate in a like-kind exchange. B enters into an exchange agreement with C whereby B retains C as a qualified intermediary to facilitate an exchange with respect to real property X. On December 1, 1994, pursuant to the agreement, B transfers real property X to C who transfers it to D for $100,000 in cash. On that date B has a bona fide intent to enter into a deferred exchange. The exchange agreement provides that B has no rights to receive, pledge, borrow, or otherwise obtain the benefits of the cash held by C until the earliest of the end of the identification period if B has not identified replacement property, the date the replacement property is delivered to B, or the end of the exchange period. Although B has a bona fide intent to enter into a deferred exchange at the beginning of the exchange period, B does not identify or acquire any replacement property. In 1995, at the end of the identification period, C delivers the entire $100,000 from the sale of real property X to B.

(ii) Under section 1001, B realizes gain to the extent of the amount realized ($100,000) over the adjusted basis in real property X ($60,000), or $40,000. Because B has a bona fide intent at the beginning of the exchange period to enter into a deferred exchange, paragraph (j)(2)(iv) of this section does not make paragraph (j)(2)(ii) of this section inapplicable even though B fails to acquire replacement property. Further, under paragraph (j)(2)(ii) of this section, C is a qualified intermediary even though C does not acquire and transfer replacement property to B. Thus, any agency relationship between B and C is disregarded for purposes of section 453 and § 15a.453–1(b)(3)(i) of this chapter in determining whether B is in receipt of payment. Accordingly, B is not treated as having received payment on December 1, 1994, on C's receipt of payment from D for the relinquished property. Instead, B is treated as receiving payment at the end of the identification period in 1995 on receipt of the $100,000 in cash from C. Subject to the other requirements of sections 453 and 453A, B may report the $40,000 gain in 1995 under the installment method.

Example 4. (i) D offers to purchase real property X but is unwilling to participate in a like-kind exchange. B thus enters into an exchange agreement with C whereby B retains C to facilitate an exchange with respect to real property X. C is qualified intermediary under paragraph (g)(4) of this section. On September 22, 1994, pursuant to the agreement, B transfers real property X to C who then transfers it to D for $80,000 in cash and D's 10-year installment obligation for $20,000. On that date B has a bona fide intent to enter into a deferred exchange. The exchange agreement provides that B has no rights to receive, pledge, borrow, or otherwise obtain the benefits of the money or other property held by C until the earlier of the date the replacement property is delivered to B or the end of the exchange period. D's obligation bears adequate stated interest and is not payable on demand or readily tradable. On March 11, 1995, C acquires replacement property having a fair market value of $80,000 and delivers it, along with the $20,000 installment obligation, to B.

(ii) Under section 1031(b), $20,000 of B's gain (i.e., the amount of the installment obligation B receives in the exchange) does not qualify for nonrecognition under section 1031(a). Under paragraphs (j)(2)(ii) and (iii) of this section, B's receipt of D's obligation is treated as the receipt of an obligation of the person acquiring the property for purposes of section 453 and § 15a.453–1 (b)(3)(i) of this chapter in determining whether B is in receipt of payment. Accordingly, B's receipt of the obligation is not treated as a payment. Subject to the other requirements of sections 453 and 453A, B may report the $20,000 gain under the installment method on receiving payments from D on the obligation.

Example 5. (i) B is a corporation that has held real property X to expand its manufacturing operations. However, at a meeting in November 1994, B's directors decide that real property X is not suitable for the planned expansion, and authorize a like-kind exchange of this property for property that would be suitable for the planned expansion. B enters into an exchange agreement with C whereby B retains C as a qualified intermediary to facilitate an exchange with respect to real property X. On November 28, 1994, pursuant to the agreement, B transfers real property X to C, who then transfers it to D for $100,000 in cash. The exchange agreement does not include any limitations or conditions that make it unreasonable to believe that like-kind replacement property will be acquired before the end of the exchange period. The exchange agreement provides that B has no rights to receive, pledge, borrow, or otherwise obtain the benefits of the cash held by C until the earliest of the end of the identification period, if B has not identified replacement property, the date the replacement property is delivered to B, or the end of the exchange period. In early January 1995, B's directors meet and decide that it is not feasible to proceed with the planned expansion due to a business downturn reflected in B's preliminary financial reports for the last quarter of 1994. Thus, B's directors instruct C to stop seeking replacement property. C delivers the $100,000 cash to B on January 12, 1995, at the end of the identification period. Both the decision to exchange real property X for other property and the decision to cease seeking replacement property because of B's business downturn are recorded in the minutes of the directors' meetings. There are no other facts or circumstances that would indicate whether, on November 28, 1994, B had a bona fide intent to enter into a deferred like-kind exchange.

(ii) Under section 1001, B realizes gain to the extent of the amount realized ($100,000) over the adjusted basis of real property X ($60,000), or $40,000. The directors' authorization of a like-kind exchange, the terms of the exchange agreement with C, and the absence of other relevant facts, indicate that B had a bona fide intent at the beginning of the exchange period to enter into a deferred like-kind exchange. Thus, paragraph (j)(2)(iv) of this section does not make paragraph (j)(2)(ii) of this section inapplicable, even though B fails to acquire replacement property. Further, under paragraph (j)(2)(ii) of this section, C is a qualified intermediary, even though C does not transfer replacement property to B. Thus, any agency relationship between B and C is disregarded for purposes of section 453 and § 15a.453–1(b)(3)(i) of this chapter in determining whether B is in receipt of payment. Accordingly, B is not treated as having received payment until January 12, 1995, on receipt of the $100,000 cash from C. Subject to the other requirements of sections 453 and 453A, B may report the $40,000 gain in 1995 under the installment method.

Example 6. (i) B has held real property X, for use in its trade or business, but decides to transfer that property because it is no longer suitable for B's planned expansion of its commercial enterprise. B and D agree to enter into a deferred exchange. Pursuant to their agreement, B transfers real property X to D on September 22, 1994, and D deposits $100,000 cash in a qualified escrow account as security for D's obligation under the agreement to transfer replacement property to B before the end of the exchange period. D's obligation is not payable on demand or readily tradable. The agreement provides that B is not required to accept any property that is not zoned for commercial use. Before the end of the identification period, B identifies real properties J, K, and L, all zoned for residential use, as replacement properties. Any one of these properties, rezoned for commercial use, would be suitable for B's planned expansion. In recent years, the zoning board with jurisdiction over properties J, K, and L has rezoned similar properties for commercial use. The escrow agreement provides that B has no rights to receive, pledge, borrow, or otherwise obtain the benefits of the money in the escrow account until the earlier of the time that the zoning board determines, after the end of the identification period, that it will not rezone the properties for commercial use or the end of the exchange period. On January 5, 1995, the zoning board decides that none of the properties will be rezoned for commercial use. Pursuant to the exchange agreement, B receives the $100,000 cash from the escrow on January 5, 1995. There are no other facts or circumstances that would indicate whether, on September 22, 1994, B had a bona fide intent to enter into a deferred like-kind exchange.

(ii) Under section 1001, B realizes gain to the extent of the amount realized ($100,000) over the adjusted basis of real property X ($60,000), or $40,000. The terms of the exchange agreement with D, the identification of properties J, K, and L, the efforts to have those properties rezoned for commercial purposes, and the absence of other relevant facts, indicate that B had a bona fide intent at the beginning of the exchange period to enter into a deferred exchange. Moreover, the limitations imposed in the exchange agreement on acceptable replacement property do not make it unreasonable to believe that like-kind replacement property would be acquired before the end of the exchange period. Therefore, paragraph (j)(2)(iv) of this section does not make paragraph (j)(2)(i) of this section inapplicable even though B fails to acquire replacement property. Thus, for purposes of section 453 and § 15a.453–1(b)(3)(i) of this chapter, the qualified escrow account is disregarded in determining whether B is in receipt of payment. Accordingly, B is not treated as having received payment on September 22, 1994, on D's deposit of the $100,000 cash into the qualified escrow account. Instead, B is treated as receiving payment on January 5, 1995. Subject to the other requirements of sections 453 and 453A, B may report the $40,000 gain in 1995 under the installment method.

(vii) Effective date. This paragraph (j)(2) is effective for transfers of property occurring on or after April 20, 1994. Taxpayers may apply this paragraph (j)(2) to transfers of property occurring before April 20, 1994, but on or after June 10, 1991, if those transfers otherwise meet the requirements of § 1.1031(k)–1. In addition, taxpayers may apply this paragraph (j)(2) to transfers of property occurring before June 10, 1991, but on or after May 16, 1990, if those transfers otherwise meet the requirements of § 1.1031(k)–1 or follow the guidance of 1A–237–84 published in 1990–1, C.B. See § 601.601(d)(2)(ii)(b) of this chapter.

(3) Examples. This paragraph (j) may be illustrated by the following examples. Unless otherwise provided in an example, the following facts are assumed: B, a calendar year taxpayer, and C agree to enter into a deferred exchange. Pursuant to their agreement, B is to transfer real property X to C on May 17, 1991. Real property X, which has been held by B for investment, is unencumbered and has a fair market value on May 17, 1991, of $100,000. B's adjusted basis in real property X is $40,000. On or before July 1, 1991 (the end of the identification period), B is to identify replacement property that is of a like kind to real property X. On or before November 13, 1991 (the end of the exchange period), C is required to purchase the property identified by B and to transfer that property to B. To the extent the fair market value of the replacement property transferred to B is greater or less than the fair market value of real property X, either B or C, as applicable, will make up the difference by paying cash to the other party after the date the replacement property is received. The replacement property is identified as provided in paragraph (c) of this section and is of a like kind to real property X (determined without regard to section 1031(a)(3) and this section). B intends to hold any replacement property received for investment.

Example 1. (i) On May 17, 1991, B transfers real property X to C and identifies real property R as replacement property. On June 3, 1991, C transfers $10,000 to B. On September 4, 1991, C purchases real property R for $90,000 and transfers real property R to B.

(ii) The $10,000 received by B is "money or other property" for purposes of section 1031 and the regulations thereunder. Under section 1031(b), B recognizes gain in the amount of $10,000. Under section 1031(d), B's basis in real property R is $40,000 (i.e., B's basis in real property X ($40,000), decreased in the amount of money received ($10,000), and increased in the amount of gain recognized ($10,000) in the deferred exchange).

Example 2. (i) On May 17, 1991, B transfers real property X to C and identifies real property S as replacement property, and C transfers $10,000 to B. On September 4, 1991, C purchases real property S for $100,000 and transfers real property S to B. On the same day, B transfers $10,000 to C.

(ii) The $10,000 received by B is "money or other property" for purposes of section 1031 and the regulations thereunder. Under section 1031(b), B recognizes gain in the amount of $10,000. Under section 1031(d), B's basis in real property S is $50,000 (i.e., B's basis in real property X ($40,000), decreased in the amount of money received ($10,000), increased in the amount of gain recognized ($10,000), and increased in the amount of the additional consideration paid by B ($10,000) in the deferred exchange).

Example 3. (i) Under the exchange agreement, B has the right at all times to demand $100,000 in cash in lieu of replacement property. On May 17, 1991, B transfers real property X to C and identifies real property T as replacement property. On September 4, 1991, C purchases real property T for $100,000 and transfers real property T to B.

(ii) Because B has the right on May 17, 1991, to demand $100,000 in cash in lieu of replacement property, B is in constructive receipt of the $100,000 on that date. Thus, the transaction is a sale and not an exchange, and the $60,000 gain realized by B in the transaction (i.e., $100,000 amount realized less $40,000 adjusted basis) is recognized. Under section 1031(d), B's basis in real property T is $100,000.

Example 4. (i) Under the exchange agreement, B has the right at all times to demand up to $30,000 in cash and the balance in replacement property instead of receiving replacement property in the amount of $100,000. On May 17, 1991, B transfers real property X to C and identifies real property U as replacement property. On September 4, 1991, C purchases real property U for $100,000 and transfers real property U to B.

(ii) The transaction qualifies as a deferred exchange under section 1031 and this section. However, because B had the right on May 17, 1991, to demand up to $30,000 in cash, B is in constructive receipt of $30,000 on that date. Under section 1031 (b), B recognizes gain in the amount of $30,000. Under section 1031(d), B's basis in real property U is $70,000 (i.e., B's basis in real property X ($40,000), decreased in the amount of money that B received ($30,000), increased in the amount of gain recognized ($30,000), and increased in the amount of additional consideration paid by B ($30,000) in the deferred exchange).

Example 5. (i) Assume real property X is encumbered by a mortgage of $30,000. On May 17, 1991, B transfers real property X to C and identifies real property V as replacement property, and C assumes the $30,000 mortgage on real property X. Real property V is encumbered by a $20,000 mortgage. On July 5, 1991, C purchases real property V for $90,000 by paying $70,000 and assuming the mortgage and transfers real property V to B with B assuming the mortgage.

(ii) The consideration received by B in the form of the liability assumed by C ($30,000) is offset by the consideration given by B in the form of the liability assumed by B ($20,000). The excess of the liability assumed by C over the liability assumed by B,

$10,000, is treated as "money or other property." See § 1.1031(b)–1(c). Thus, B recognizes gain under section 1031(b) in the amount of $10,000. Under section 1031(d), B's basis in real property V is $40,000 (i.e., B's basis in real property X ($40,000), decreased in the amount of money that B is treated as receiving in the form of the liability assumed by C ($30,000), increased in the amount of money that B is treated as paying in the form of the liability assumed by B ($20,000), and increased in the amount of the gain recognized ($10,000) in the deferred exchange).

(k) Definition of disqualified person. **(1)** For purposes of this section, a disqualified person is a person described in paragraph (k)(2), (k)(3), or (k)(4) of this section.

(2) The person is the agent of the taxpayer at the time of the transaction. For this purpose, a person who has acted as the taxpayer's employee, attorney, accountant, investment banker or broker, or real estate agent or broker within the 2-year period ending on the date of the transfer of the first of the relinquished properties is treated as an agent of the taxpayer at the time of the transaction. Solely for purposes of this paragraph (k)(2), performance of the following services will not be taken into account—

(i) Services for the taxpayer with respect to exchanges of property intended to qualify for nonrecognition of gain or loss under section 1031; and

(ii) Routine financial, title insurance, escrow, or trust services for the taxpayer by a financial institution, title insurance company, or escrow company.

(3) The person and the taxpayer bear a relationship described in either section 267(b) or section 707(b) (determined by substituting in each section "10 percent" for "50 percent" each place it appears).

(4) **(i)** The person and a person described in paragraph (k)(2) of this section bear a relationship described in either section 267(b) or section 707(b) (determined by substituting in each section "10 percent" for "50 percent" each place it appears).

* * *

(5) This paragraph (k) may be illustrated by the following examples. Unless otherwise provided, the following facts are assumed: On May 1, 1991, B enters into an exchange agreement (as defined in paragraph (g)(4)(iii)(B) of this section) with C whereby B retains C to facilitate an exchange with respect to real property X. On May 17, 1991, pursuant to the agreement, B executes and delivers to C a deed conveying real property X to C. C has no relationship to B described in paragraphs (k)(2), (k)(3), or (k)(4) of this section.

Example 1. **(i)** C is B's accountant and has rendered accounting services to B within the 2-year period ending on May 17, 1991, other than with respect to exchanges of property intended to qualify for nonrecognition of gain or loss under section 1031.

(ii) C is a disqualified person because C has acted as B's accountant within the 2-year period ending on May 17, 1991.

(iii) If C had not acted as B's accountant within the 2-year period ending on May 17, 1991, or if C had acted as B's accountant within that period only with respect to exchanges intended to qualify for nonrecognition of gain or loss under section 1031, C would not have been a disqualified person.

Example 2. **(i)** C, which is engaged in the trade or business of acting as an intermediary to facilitate deferred exchanges, is a wholly owned subsidiary of an escrow company that has performed routine escrow services for B in the past. C has previously been retained by B to act as an intermediary in prior section 1031 exchanges.

(ii) C is not a disqualified person notwithstanding the intermediary services previously provided by C to B (see paragraph (k)(2)(i) of this section) and notwithstanding the combination of C's relationship to the escrow company and the escrow services previously provided by the escrow company to B (see paragraph (k)(2)(ii) of this section).

Example 3. **(i)** C is a corporation that is only engaged in the trade or business of acting as an intermediary to facilitate deferred exchanges. Each of 10 law firms owns 10 percent of the outstanding stock of C. One of the 10 law firms that owns 10 percent of C is M. J is the managing partner of M and is the president of C. J, in his capacity as a partner in M, has also rendered legal advice to B within the 2-year period ending on May 17, 1991, on matters other than exchanges intended to qualify for nonrecognition of gain or loss under section 1031.

(ii) J and M are disqualified persons. C, however, is not a disqualified person because neither J nor M own, directly or indirectly, more than 10 percent of the stock of C. Similarly, J's participation in the management of C does not make C a disqualified person.

(l) [Reserved]

(m) Definition of fair market value. For purposes of this section, the fair market value of property means the fair market value of the property without regard to any liabilities secured by the property.

(n) No inference with respect to actual or constructive receipt rules outside of section 1031. The rules provided in this section relating to actual or constructive receipt are intended to be rules for determining whether there is actual or constructive receipt in the case of a deferred exchange. No inference is intended regarding the application of these rules for purposes of determining whether actual or constructive receipt exists for any other purpose.

(o) Effective date. This section applies to transfers of property made by a taxpayer on or after

June 10, 1991. However, a transfer of property made by a taxpayer on or after May 16, 1990, but before June 10, 1991, will be treated as complying with section 1031(a)(3) and this section if the deferred exchange satisfies either the provision of this section or the provisions of the notice of proposed rulemaking published in the Federal Register on May 16, 1990 (55 FR 20278).

§ 1.1032–1 Disposition by a corporation of its own capital stock.

(a) The disposition by a corporation of shares of its own stock (including treasury stock) for money or other property does not give rise to taxable gain or deductible loss to the corporation regardless of the nature of the transaction or the facts and circumstances involved. For example, the receipt by a corporation of the subscription price of shares of its stock upon their original issuance gives rise to neither taxable gain nor deductible loss, whether the subscription or issue price be equal to, in excess of, or less than, the par or stated value of such stock. Also, the exchange or sale by a corporation of its own shares for money or other property does not result in taxable gain or deductible loss, even though the corporation deals in such shares as it might in the shares of another corporation. A transfer by a corporation of shares of its own stock (including treasury stock) as compensation for services is considered, for purposes of section 1032(a), as a disposition by the corporation of such shares for money or other property.

(b) Section 1032(a) does not apply to the acquisition by a corporation of shares of its own stock except where the corporation acquires such shares in exchange for shares of its own stock (including treasury stock). See paragraph (e) of § 1.311–1, relating to treatment of acquisitions of a corporation's own stock. Section 1032(a) also does not relate to the tax treatment of the recipient of a corporation's stock.

(c) Where a corporation acquires shares of its own stock in exchange for shares of its own stock (including treasury stock) the transaction may qualify not only under section 1032(a), but also under section 368(a)(1)(E) (recapitalization) or section 305 (a) (distribution of stock and stock rights).

(d) For basis of property acquired by a corporation in connection with a transaction to which section 351 applies or in connection with a reorganization, see section 362. For basis of property acquired by a corporation in a transaction to which section 1032 applies but which does not qualify under any other non-recognition provision, see section 1012.

* * *

§ 1.1033(a)–1 Involuntary conversions; nonrecognition of gain.

(a) In general. Section 1033 applies to cases where property is compulsorily or involuntarily converted. An "involuntary conversion" may be the result of the destruction of property in whole or in part, the theft of property, the seizure of property, the requisition or condemnation of property, or the threat or imminence of requisition or condemnation of property. An "involuntary conversion" may be a conversion into similar property or into money or into dissimilar property. Section 1033 provides that, under certain specified circumstances, any gain which is realized from an involuntary conversion shall not be recognized. In cases where property is converted into other property similar or related in service or use to the converted property, no gain shall be recognized regardless of when the disposition of the converted property occurred and regardless of whether or not the taxpayer elects to have the gain not recognized. In other types of involuntary conversion cases, however, the proceeds arising from the disposition of the converted property must (within the time limits specified) be reinvested in similar property in order to avoid recognition of any gain realized. Section 1033 applies only with respect to gains; losses from involuntary conversions are recognized or not recognized without regard to this section.

* * *

§ 1.1033(a)–2 Involuntary conversion into similar property, into money or into dissimilar property.

(a) In general. The term "disposition of the converted property" means the destruction, theft, seizure, requisition, or condemnation of the converted property, or the sale or exchange of such property under threat or imminence of requisition or condemnation.

(b) Conversion into similar property. If property (as a result of its destruction in whole or in part, theft, seizure, or requisition or condemnation or threat or imminence thereof) is compulsorily or involuntarily converted only into property similar or related in service or use to the property so converted, no gain shall be recognized. Such nonrecognition of gain is mandatory.

(c) Conversion into money or into dissimilar property. **(1)** If property (as a result of its destruction in whole or in part, theft, seizure, or requisition or condemnation or threat or imminence thereof) is compulsorily or involuntarily converted into money or into property not similar or related in service or use to the converted property, the gain, if any, shall be recognized, at the election of the taxpayer, only to the extent that the amount realized upon such conversion exceeds the cost of other property purchased by the taxpayer which is similar or related in service or use to the property so converted, or the cost of stock of a corporation owning such other property which is purchased by the taxpayer in the acquisition of control of such corporation, if the taxpayer purchased such other property, or such stock, for the purpose of replacing the property so converted and during the period specified in subparagraph (3) of this paragraph. For the purposes of section 1033, the term "control" means the ownership of stock possessing at least 80 percent of the total combined voting power of all classes of stock entitled to vote and at least 80 percent of the total number of shares of all other classes of stock of the corporation.

(2) All of the details in connection with an involuntary conversion of property at a gain (including those relating to the replacement of the converted property, or a decision not to replace, or the expiration of the period for replacement) shall be reported in the return for the taxable year or years in which any of such gain is realized. An election to have such gain recognized only to the extent provided in subparagraph (1) of this paragraph shall be made by including such gain in gross income for such year or years only to such extent. If, at the time of filing such a return, the period within which the converted property must be replaced has expired, or if such an election is not desired, the gain should be included in gross income for such year or years in the regular manner. A failure to so include such gain in gross income in the regular manner shall be deemed to be an election by the taxpayer to have such gain recognized only to the extent provided in subparagraph (1) of this paragraph even though the details in connection with the conversion are not reported in such return. If, after having made an election under section 1033(a)(2), the converted property is not replaced within the required period of time, or replacement is made at a cost lower than was anticipated at the time of the election, or a decision is made not to replace, the tax liability for the year or years for which the election was made shall be recomputed. Such recomputation should be in the form of an "amended return". If a decision is made to make an election under section 1033(a)(2) after the filing of the return and the payment of the tax for the year or years in which any of the gain on an involuntary conversion is realized and before the expiration of the period within which the converted property must be replaced, a claim for credit or refund for such year or years should be filed. If the replacement of the converted property occurs in a year or years in which none of the gain on the conversion is realized, all of the details in connection with such replacement shall be reported in the return for such year or years.

(3) The period* referred to in subparagraphs (1) and (2) of this paragraph is the period of time commencing with the date of the disposition of the converted property, or the date of the beginning of the threat or imminence of requisition or condemnation of the converted property, whichever is earlier, and ending 2 years (or, in the case of a disposition occurring before Dec. 31, 1969, 1 year) after the close of the first taxable year in which any part of the gain upon the conversion is realized, or at the close of such later date as may be designated pursuant to an application of the taxpayer. Such application shall be made prior to the expiration of 2 years (or, in the case of a disposition occurring before Dec. 31, 1969, 1 year) after the close of the first taxable year in which any part of the gain from the conversion is realized, unless the taxpayer can show to the satisfaction of the district director—

(i) Reasonable cause for not having filed the application within the required period of time, and

(ii) The filing of such application was made within a reasonable time after the expiration of the required period of time. The application shall contain all of the details in connection with the involuntary conversion. Such application shall be made to the district director for the internal revenue district in which the return is filed for the first taxable year in which any of the gain from the involuntary conversion is realized. No extension of time shall be granted pursuant to such application unless the taxpayer can show reasonable cause for not being able to replace the converted property within the required period of time.

*Editorial comment: The Regulations do not reflect the effect of the American Jobs Creation Act of 2004 which provides for an extended replacement period for livestock sold on account of drought, flood, or other weather-related conditions. See § 1033(e).

See section 1033(g)(4) and § 1.1033(g)–1 for the circumstances under which, in the case of the conversion of real property held either for productive use in trade or business or for investment, the 2-year period referred to in this paragraph (c)(3) shall be extended to 3 years.

(4) Property or stock purchased before the disposition of the converted property shall be considered to have been purchased for the purpose of replacing the converted property only if such property or stock is held by the taxpayer on the date of the disposition of the converted property. Property or stock shall be considered to have been purchased only if, but for the provisions of section 1033(b), the unadjusted basis of such property or stock would be its cost to the taxpayer within the meaning of section 1012. If the taxpayer's unadjusted basis of the replacement property would be determined, in the absence of section 1033(b), under any of the exceptions referred to in section 1012, the unadjusted basis of the property would not be its cost within the meaning of section 1012. For example, if property similar or related in service or use to the converted property is acquired by gift and its basis is determined under section 1015, such property will not qualify as a replacement for the converted property.

(5) If a taxpayer makes an election under section 1033(a)(2), any deficiency, for any taxable year in which any part of the gain upon the conversion is realized, which is attributable to such gain may be assessed at any time before the expiration of three years from the date the district director with whom the return for such year has been filed is notified by the taxpayer of the replacement of the converted property or of an intention not to replace, or of a failure to replace, within the required period, notwithstanding the provisions of section 6212(c) or the provisions of any other law or rule of law which would otherwise prevent such assessment. If replacement has been made, such notification shall contain all of the details in connection with such replacement. Such notification should be made in the return for the taxable year or years in which the replacement occurs, or the intention not to replace is formed, or the period for replacement expires, if this return is filed with such district director. If this return is not filed with such district director, then such notification shall be made to such district director at the time of filing this return. If the taxpayer so desires, he may, in either event, also notify such district director before the filing of such return.

(6) If a taxpayer makes an election under section 1033(a)(2) and the replacement property or stock was purchased before the beginning of the last taxable year in which any part of the gain upon the conversion is realized, any deficiency, for any taxable year ending before such last taxable year, which is attributable to such election may be assessed at any time before the expiration of the period within which a deficiency for such last taxable year may be assessed, notwithstanding the provisions of section 6212(c) or 6501 or the provisions of any law or rule of law which would otherwise prevent such assessment.

(7) If the taxpayer makes an election under section 1033(a)(2), the gain upon the conversion shall be recognized to the extent that the amount realized upon such conversion exceeds the cost of the replacement property or stock, regardless of whether such amount is realized in one or more taxable years.

(8) The proceeds of a use and occupancy insurance contract, which by its terms insured against actual loss sustained of net profits in the business, are not proceeds of an involuntary conversion but are income in the same manner that the profits for which they are substituted would have been.

(9) There is no investment in property similar in character and devoted to a similar use if—

(i) The proceeds of unimproved real estate, taken upon condemnation proceedings, are invested in improved real estate.

(ii) The proceeds of conversion of real property are applied in reduction of indebtedness previously incurred in the purchase or a leasehold.

(iii) The owner of a requisitioned tug uses the proceeds to buy barges.

(10) If, in a condemnation proceeding, the Government retains out of the award sufficient funds to satisfy special assessments levied against the remaining portion of the plot or parcel of real estate affected for benefits accruing in connection with the condemnation, the amount so retained shall be deducted from the gross award in determining the amount of the net award.

(11) If, in a condemnation proceeding, the Government retains out of the award sufficient funds to satisfy liens (other than liens due to special assessments levied against the remaining portion of the plot or parcel of real estate affected for benefits accruing in connection with the condemnation) and mortgages against the property, and itself pays the same, the amount so retained shall not be deducted from the gross award in determining the amount of the net award. If, in a condemnation proceeding, the Government makes an award to a mortgagee to satisfy a mortgage on the condemned property, the amount of such award shall be considered as a part of the "amount realized" upon the conversion regardless of whether or not the taxpayer was personally liable for the mortgage debt. Thus, if a taxpayer has acquired property worth $100,000 subject to a $50,000 mortgage (regardless of whether or not he was personally liable for the mortgage debt) and, in a condemnation proceeding, the Government awards the taxpayer $60,000 and awards the mortgagee $50,000 in satisfaction of the mortgage, the entire $110,000 is considered to be the "amount realized" by the taxpayer.

(12) An amount expended for replacement of an asset, in excess of the recovery for loss, represents a capital expenditure and is not a deductible loss for income tax purposes.

§ 1.1033(a)–3 Involuntary conversion of principal residence.

Section 1033 shall apply in the case of property used by the taxpayer as his principal residence if the destruction, theft, seizure, requisition, or condemnation of such residence, or the sale or exchange of such residence under threat or imminence thereof, occurs before January 1, 1951, or after December 31, 1953. However, section 1033 shall not apply to the seizure, requisition, or condemnation (but not destruction), or the sale or exchange under threat or imminence thereof, of such residence property if the seizure, requisition, condemnation, sale, or exchange occurs after December 31, 1957, and if the taxpayer properly elects under section 1034(i) to treat the transaction as a sale (see paragraph (h)(2)(ii) of § 1.1034–1). See section 121 and paragraphs (d) and (g) of § 1.121–5 for special rules relating to the involuntary conversion of a principal residence of individuals who have attained age 65.*

§ 1.1033(b)–1 Basis of property acquired as a result of an involuntary conversion.

(a) The provisions of the first sentence of section 1033(b) may be illustrated by the following example:

Example. A's vessel which has an adjusted basis of $100,000 is destroyed in 1950 and A receives in 1951 insurance in the amount of $200,000. If A invests $150,000 in a new vessel, taxable gain to the extent of $50,000 would be recognized. The basis of the new vessel is $100,000; that is, the adjusted basis of the old vessel ($100,000) minus the money received by the taxpayer which was not expended in the acquisition of the new vessel ($50,000) plus the amount of gain recognized upon the conversion ($50,000). If any amount in excess of the proceeds of the conversion is expended in the acquisition of the new property, such amount may be added to the basis otherwise determined.

(b) The provisions of the last sentence of section 1033(b) may be illustrated by the following example:

Example. A taxpayer realizes $22,000 from the involuntary conversion of his barn in 1955; the adjusted basis of the barn to him was $10,000, and he spent in the same year $20,000 for a new barn which resulted in the nonrecognition of $10,000 of the $12,000 gain on the conversion. The basis of the new barn to the taxpayer would be $10,000—the cost of the new barn ($20,000) less the amount of the gain not recognized on the conversion ($10,000). The basis of the new barn would not be a substituted basis in the hands of the taxpayer within the meaning of section 1016(b)(2). If the replacement of the converted barn had been made by the purchase of two smaller barns which, together, were similar or related in service or use to the converted barn and which cost $8,000 and $12,000, respectively, then the basis of the two barns would be $4,000 and $6,000, respectively, the total basis of the purchased property ($10,000) allocated in proportion to their respective costs (8,000/20,000 of $10,000 or $4,000; and 12,000/20,000 of $10,000, or $6,000).

* * *

§ 1.1033(g)–1 Condemnation of real property held for productive use in trade or business or for investment.

(a) Special rule in general. This section provides special rules for applying section 1033 with respect to certain dispositions, occurring after December 31, 1957, of real property held either for productive use in trade or business or for investment (not including stock in trade or other property held primarily for sale). For this purpose, disposition means the seizure, requisition, or condemnation (but not destruction) of the converted property, or the sale or exchange of such property under threat or imminence of seizure, requisition, or condemnation. In such cases, for purposes of applying section 1033, the replacement of such property with property of like kind to be held either for productive use in trade or business or for investment shall be treated as property similar or related in service or use to the property so converted. For principles in determining whether the replacement property is property of like kind, see paragraph (b) of § 1.1031(a)–1.

* * *

*Editorial comment: This provision does not reflect the repeal of Secs. 121 and 1034 and the creation of a new Sec. 121 by the Taxpayer Relief Act of 1997.

§ 1.1035–1 Certain exchanges of insurance policies.

Under the provisions of section 1035 no gain or loss is recognized on the exchange of:

(a) A contract of life insurance for another contract of life insurance or for an endowment or annuity contract (section 1035(a)(l));

(b) A contract of endowment insurance for another contract of endowment insurance providing for regular payments beginning at a date not later than the date payments would have begun under the contract exchanged, or an annuity contract (section 1035(a)(2)); or

(c) An annuity contract for another annuity contract (section 1035(a)(3)), but section 1035 does not apply to such exchanges if the policies exchanged to not relate to the same insured. The exchange, without recognition of gain or loss, of an annuity contract for another annuity contract under section 1035(a)(3) is limited to cases where the same person or persons are the obligee or obligees under the contract received in exchange as under the original contract. This section and section 1035 do not apply to transactions involving the exchange of an endowment contract or annuity contract for a life insurance contract, nor an annuity contract for an endowment contract. In the case of such exchanges, any gain or loss shall be recognized. In the case of exchanges which would be governed by section 1035 except for the fact that the property received in exchange consists not only of property which could otherwise be received without the recognition of gain or loss, but also of other property or money, see section 1031 (b) and (c) and the regulations thereunder. Such an exchange does not come within the provisions of section 1035. Determination of the basis of property acquired in an exchange under section 1035(a) shall be governed by section 1031(d) and the regulations thereunder.

§ 1.1036–1 Stock for stock of the same corporation.

(a) Section 1036 permits the exchange, without the recognition of gain or loss, of common stock for common stock, or of preferred stock for preferred stock, in the same corporation. Section 1036 applies even though voting stock is exchanged for nonvoting stock or nonvoting stock is exchanged for voting stock. It is not limited to an exchange between two individual stockholders; it includes a transaction between a stockholder and the corporation. However, a transaction between a stockholder and the corporation may qualify not only under section 1036(a), but also under section 368(a)(1)(E) (recapitalization) or section 305(a) (distribution of stock and stock rights). The provisions of section 1036(a) do not apply if stock is exchanged for bonds, or preferred stock is exchanged for common stock, or common stock is exchanged for preferred stock, or common stock in one corporation is exchanged for common stock in another corporation. See paragraph (1) of § 1301–1 for certain transactions treated as distributions under section 301. See paragraph (e)(5) of § 1.368–2 for certain transactions which result in deemed distributions under section 305(c) to which sections 305(b)(4) and 301 apply.

(b) For rules relating to recognition of gain or loss where an exchange is not wholly in kind, see subsections (b) and (c) of section 1031. For rules relating to the basis of property acquired in an exchange described in paragraph (a) of this section, see subsection (d) of section 1031.

(c) A transfer is not within the provisions of section 1036(a) if as part of the consideration the other party to the exchange assumes a liability of the taxpayer (or if the property transferred is subject to a liability), but the transfer, if otherwise qualified, will be within the provisions of section 1031(b).

* * *

Transfers Between Spouses; Temporary Regulations

§ 1.1041–1T Treatment of transfer of property between spouses or incident to divorce (temporary).

Q–1 How is the transfer of property between spouses treated under section 1041?

A–1 Generally, no gain or loss is recognized on a transfer of property from an individual to (or in trust for the benefit of) a spouse or, if the transfer is incident to a divorce, a former spouse. The following questions and answers describe more fully the scope, tax consequences and other rules which apply to transfers of property under section 1041.

(a) Scope of section 1041 in general.

Q–2 Does section 1041 apply only to transfers of property incident to divorce?

A–2 No. Section 1041 is not limited to transfers of property incident to divorce. Section 1041 applies to any transfer of property between spouses regardless of whether the transfer is a gift or is a sale or exchange between spouses acting at arm's length (including a transfer in exchange for the relinquishment of property or marital rights or an exchange otherwise governed by another nonrecognition provision of the Code). A divorce or legal separation need not be contemplated between the spouses at the time of the transfer nor must a divorce or legal separation ever occur.

Example (1). A and B are married and file a joint return. A is the sole owner of a condominium unit. A sale or gift of the condominium from A to B is a transfer which is subject to the rules of section 1041.

Example (2). A and B are married and file separate returns. A is the owner of an independent sole proprietorship, X Company. In the ordinary course of business, X Company makes a sale of property to B. This sale is a transfer of property between spouses and is subject to the rules of section 1041.

Example (3). Assume the same facts as in example (2), except that X Company is a corporation wholly owned by A. This sale is not a sale between spouses subject to the rules of section 1041. However, in appropriate circumstances, general tax principles, including the step-transaction doctrine, may be applicable in recharacterizing the transaction.

Q–3 Do the rules of section 1041 apply to a transfer between spouses if the transferee spouse is a nonresident alien?

A–3 No. Gain or loss (if any) is recognized (assuming no other nonrecognition provision applies) at the time of a transfer of property if the property is transferred to a spouse who is a nonresident alien.

Q–4 What kinds of transfers are governed by section 1041?

A–4 Only transfers of property (whether real or personal, tangible or intangible) are governed by section 1041. Transfers of services are not subject to the rules of section 1041.

Q–5 Must the property transferred to a former spouse have been owned by the transferor spouse during the marriage?

A–5 No. A transfer of property acquired after the marriage ceases may be governed by section 1041.

(b) Transfer incident to the divorce.

Q–6 When is a transfer of property "incident to the divorce"?

A–6 A transfer of property is "incident to the divorce" in either of the following 2 circumstances—

(1) The transfer occurs not more than one year after the date on which the marriage ceases, or

(2) The transfer is related to the cessation of the marriage.

Thus, a transfer of property occurring not more than one year after the date on which the marriage ceases need not be related to the cessation of the marriage to qualify for section 1041 treatment. (See A–7 for transfers occurring more than one year after the cessation of the marriage.)

Q–7 When is a transfer of property "related to the cessation of the marriage"?

A–7 A transfer of property is treated as related to the cessation of the marriage if the transfer is pursuant to a divorce or separation instrument, as defined in section 71(b)(2), and the transfer occurs not more than 6 years after the date on which the marriage ceases. A divorce or separation instrument includes a modification or amendment to such decree or instrument. Any transfer not pursuant to a divorce or separation instrument and any transfer occurring more than 6 years after the cessation of the marriage is presumed to be not related to the cessation of the marriage. This presumption may be rebutted only by showing that the transfer was made to effect the division of property owned by the former spouses at the time of the cessation of the marriage. For example, the presumption may be rebutted by showing that (a) the transfer was not made within the one- and six-year periods described above because of factors which hampered an earlier transfer of the property, such as legal or business impediments to transfer or disputes concerning the value of the property owned at the time of the cessation of the marriage, and (b) the transfer is effected promptly after the impediment to transfer is removed.

Q–8 Do annulments and the cessations of marriages that are void *ab initio* due to violations of state law constitute divorces for purposes of section 1041?

A–8 Yes.

(c) Transfers on behalf of a spouse.

Q–9 May transfers of property to third parties on behalf of a spouse (or former spouse) qualify under section 1041?

A–9 Yes. There are three situations in which a transfer of property to a third party on behalf of a spouse (or former spouse) will qualify under section 1041, provided all other requirements of the section are satisfied. The first situation is where the transfer to the third party is required by a divorce or separation instrument. The second situation is where the transfer to the third party is pursuant to the written request of the other spouse (or former spouse). The third situation is where the transferor receives from the other spouse (or former spouse) a written consent or ratification of the transfer to the third party. Such consent or ratification must state that the parties intend the transfer to be treated as a transfer to the nontransferring spouse (or former spouse) subject to the rules of section 1041 and must be received by the transferor prior to the date of filing of the transferor's first return of tax for the taxable year in which the transfer was made. In the three situations described above, the transfer of property will be treated as made directly to the nontransferring spouse (or former spouse) and the nontransferring spouse will be treated as immediately transferring the property to the third party. The deemed transfer from the non-transferring spouse (or former spouse) to the third party is not a transaction that qualifies for nonrecognition of gain under section 1041. This A-9 shall not apply to transfers to which § 1.041–2 applies.

(d) Tax consequences of transfers subject to section 1041.

Q–10 How is the transferor of property under section 1041 treated for income tax purposes?

A–10 The transferor of property under section 1041 recognizes no gain or loss on the transfer even if the transfer was in exchange for the release of marital rights or other consideration. This rule applies regardless of whether the transfer is of property separately owned by the transferor or is a division (equal or unequal) of community property. Thus, the result under section 1041 differs from the result in *United States* v. Davis, 370 U.S. 65 (1962).

Q–11 How is the transferee of property under section 1041 treated for income tax purposes?

A–11 The transferee of property under section 1041 recognizes no gain or loss upon receipt of the transferred property. In all cases, the basis of the transferred property in the hands of the transferee is the adjusted basis of such property in the hands of the transferor immediately before the transfer. Even if the transfer is a bona fide sale, the transferee does not acquire a basis in the transferred property equal to the transferee's costs (the fair market value). This carryover basis rule applies whether the adjusted basis of the transferred property is less than, equal to, or greater than its fair market value at the time of transfer (or the value of any consideration provided by the transferee) and applies for purposes of determining loss as well as gain upon the subsequent disposition of the property by the transferee. Thus, this rule is different from the rule applied in section 1015(a) for determining the basis of property acquired by gift.

Q–12 Do the rules described in A–10 and A–11 apply even if the transferred property is subject to liabilities which exceed the adjusted basis of the property?

A–12 Yes. For example, assume A owns property having a fair market value of $10,000 and an adjusted basis of $1,000. In contemplation of making a transfer of this property incident to a divorce from B, A borrows $5,000 from a bank, using the property as security for the borrowing. A then transfers the property to B and B assumes, or takes the property subject to, the liability to pay the $5,000 debt. Under section 1041, A recognizes no gain or loss upon the transfer of the property, and the adjusted basis of the property in the hands of B is $1,000.

Q–13 Will a transfer under section 1041 result in a recapture of investment tax credits with respect to the property transferred?

A–13 In general, no. Property transferred under section 1041 will not be treated as being disposed of by, or ceasing to be section 38 property with respect to, the transferor. However, the transferee will be subject to investment tax credit recapture if, upon or after the transfer, the property is disposed of by, or ceases to be section 38 property with respect to, the transferee. For example, as part of a divorce property settlement, B receives a car from A that has been used in A's business for two years and for which an investment tax credit was taken by A. No part of A's business is transferred to B and B's use of the car is solely personal. B is subject to recapture of the investment tax credit previously taken by A.

(e) Notice and recordkeeping requirement with respect to transactions under section 1041.

Q–14 Does the transferor of property in a transaction described in section 1041 have to supply, at the time of the transfer, the transferee with records sufficient to determine the adjusted basis and holding period of the property at the time of the transfer and (if applicable) with notice that the property transferred under section 1041 is potentially subject to recapture of the investment tax credit?

A–14 Yes. A transferor of property under section 1041 must, at the time of the transfer, supply the transferee with records sufficient to determine the adjusted basis and holding period of the property as of the date of the transfer. In addition, in the case of a transfer of property which carries with it a potential liability for investment tax credit recapture, the transferor must, at the time of the transfer, supply the transferee with records sufficient to determine the amount and period of such potential liability. Such records must be preserved and kept accessible by the transferee.

(f) Property settlements—effective dates, transitional periods and elections.

Q–15 When does section 1041 become effective?

A–15 Generally, section 1041 applies to all transfers after July 18, 1984. However, it does not apply to transfers after July 18, 1984 pursuant to instruments in effect on or before July 18, 1984. (See A–16 with respect to exceptions to the general rule.)

Q–16 Are there any exceptions to the general rule stated in A–15 above?

A–16 Yes. Two transitional rules provide exceptions to the general rule stated in A–15. First, section 1041 will apply to transfers after July 18, 1984 under instruments that were in effect on or before July 18, 1984 if both spouses (or former spouses) elect to have section 1041 apply to such transfers. Second, section 1041 will apply to all transfers after December 31, 1983 (including transfers under instruments in effect on or before July 18, 1984) if both spouses (or former spouses) elect to have section 1041 apply. (See A–18 relating to the time and manner of making the elections under the first or second transitional rule.)

Q–17 Can an election be made to have section 1041 apply to some, but not all, transfers made after December 31, 1983, or some but not all, transfers made after July 18, 1984 under instruments in effect on or before July 18, 1984?

A–17 No. Partial elections are not allowed. An election under either of the two elective transitional rules applies to all transfers governed by that election whether before or after the election is made, and is irrevocable.

(g) Property settlements—time and manner of making the elections under section 1041.

Q–18 How do spouses (or former spouses) elect to have section 1041 apply to transfers after December 31, 1983, or to transfers after July 18, 1984 under instruments in effect on or before July 18, 1984?

A–18 In order to make an election under section 1041 for property transfers after December 31, 1983, or property transfers under instruments that were in effect on or before July 18, 1984, both spouses (or former spouses) must elect the application of the rules of section 1041 by attaching to the transferor's first filed income tax return for the taxable year in which the first transfer occurs, a statement signed by both spouses (or former spouses) which includes each spouse's social security number and is in substantially the form set forth at the end of this answer.

In addition, the transferor must attach a copy of such statement to his or her return for each subsequent taxable year in which a transfer is made that is governed by the transitional election. A copy of the signed statement must be kept by both parties.

The election statements shall be in substantially the following form:

In the case of an election regarding transfers after 1983:

Section 1041 Election

The undersigned hereby elect to have the provisions of section 1041 of the Internal Revenue Code apply to all qualifying transfers of property after December 31, 1983. The undersigned understand that section 1041 applies to all property transferred between spouses, or former spouses incident to divorce. The parties further understand that the effects for Federal income tax purposes of having section 1041 apply are that (1) no gain or loss is recognized by the transferor spouse or former spouse as a result of this transfer; and (2) the basis of the transferred property in the hands of the transferee is the adjusted basis of the property in the hands of the transferor immediately before the transfer, whether or not the adjusted basis of the transferred property is less than, equal to, or greater than its fair market value at the time of the transfer. The undersigned understand that if the transferee spouse or former spouse disposes of the property in a transaction in which gain is recognized, the amount of gain which is taxable may be larger than it would have been if this election had not been made.

In the case of an election regarding preexisting decrees:

Section 1041 Election

The undersigned hereby elect to have the provisions of section 1041 of the Internal Revenue Code apply to all qualifying transfers of property after July 18, 1984 under any instrument in effect on or before July 18, 1984. The undersigned understand that section 1041 applies to all property transferred between spouses, or former spouses incident to the divorce. The parties further understand that the effects for Federal income tax purposes of having section 1041 apply are that (1) no gain or loss is recognized by the transferor spouse or former spouse as a result of this transfer; and (2) the basis of the transferred property in the hands of the transferee is the adjusted basis of the property in the hands of the transferor immediately before the transfer, whether or not the adjusted basis of the transferred property is less than, equal to, or greater than its fair market value at the time of the transfer. The undersigned understand that if the transferee spouse or former spouse disposes of the property in a transaction in which gain is recognized, the amount of gain which is taxable may be larger than it would have been if this election had not been made.

§ 1.1041–2 Redemptions of stock.

(a) In general—(1) Redemptions of stock not resulting in constructive distributions. Notwithstanding Q&A–9 of § 1.1041–1T(c), if a corporation redeems stock owned by a spouse or former spouse (transferor spouse), and the transferor spouse's receipt of property in respect of such redeemed stock is not treated, under applicable tax law, as resulting in a constructive distribution to the other spouse or former spouse (nontransferor spouse), then the form of the stock redemption shall be respected for Federal income tax purposes. Therefore, the transferor spouse will be treated as having received a distribution from the corporation in redemption of stock.

(2) Redemptions of stock resulting in constructive distributions. Notwithstanding Q&A–9 of § 1.104–1T(c), if a corporation redeems stock owned by a transferor spouse, and the transferor spouse's receipt of property in respect of such redeemed stock is treated, under applicable tax law, as resulting in a constructive distribution to the non transferor spouse, then the redeemed stock shall be deemed first to be transferred by the transferor spouse to the nontransferor spouse and then to be transferred by the nontransferor spouse to the redeeming corporation. Any property actually received by the transferor spouse from the redeeming corporation in respect of the redeemed stock shall be deemed first to be transferred by the corporation to the nontransferor spouse in redemption of such spouse's stock and then to be transferred by the nontransferor spouse to the transferor spouse.

(b) Tax consequences—(1) Transfers described in paragraph (a)(1) of this section. Section 1041 will not apply to any of the transfers described in paragraph (a) (1) of this section. See section 302 for rules relating to the tax consequences of certain redemptions; redemptions characterized as distributions under section 302(d) will be subject to section 301 if received from a Subchapter C corporation or section 1368 if received from a Subchapter S corporation.

(2) Transfers described in paragraph (a)(2) of this section. The tax consequences of each deemed transfer described in paragraph (a)(2) of this section are determined under applicable provisions of the Internal Revenue Code as if the spouses had actually made such transfers. Accordingly, section 1041 applies to any deemed transfer of the stock and redemption proceeds between the transferor spouse and the nontransferor spouse, provided the requirements of section 1041 are otherwise satisfied with respect to such deemed transfer. Section 1041, however, will not apply to any deemed transfer of stock by the nontransferor spouse to the redeeming corporation in exchange for the redemption proceeds. See section 302 for rules relating to the tax consequences of certain redemptions; redemptions characterized as distributions under section 302(d) will be subject to section 301 if received from a Subchapter C corporation or section 1368 if received from a Subchapter S corporation.

(c) Special rules in case of agreements between spouses or former spouses—(1) Transferor spouse taxable. Notwithstanding applicable tax law, a transferor spouse's receipt of property in respect of the redeemed stock shall be treated as a distribution to the transferor spouse in redemption of such stock for purposes of paragraph (a)(1) of this section, and shall not be treated as resulting in a constructive distribution to the nontransferor spouse for purposes of paragraph (a)(2) of this section, if a divorce or separation instrument, or a valid written agreement between the transferor spouse and the nontransferor spouse, expressly provides that—

(i) Both spouses or former spouses intend for the redemption to be treated, for Federal income tax purposes, as a redemption distribution to the transferor spouse; and

(ii) Such instrument or agreement supersedes any other instrument or agreement concerning the purchase, sale, redemption, or other disposition of the stock that is the subject of the redemption.

(2) Nontransferor spouse taxable. Notwithstanding applicable tax law, a transferor spouse's receipt of property in respect of the redeemed stock shall be treated as resulting in a constructive distribution to the nontransferor spouse for purposes of paragraph (a)(2) of this section, and shall not be treated as a distribution to the transferor spouse in redemption of such stock for purposes of paragraph (a)(1) of this section, if a divorce or separation instrument, or a valid written agreement between the transferor spouse and the nontransferor spouse, expressly provides that—

(i) Both spouses or former spouses intend for the redemption to be treated, for Federal income tax purposes, as resulting in a constructive distribution to the nontransferor spouse; and

(ii) Such instrument or agreement supersedes any other instrument or agreement concerning the purchase, sale, redemption, or other disposition of the stock that is the subject of the redemption.

(3) Execution of agreements. For purposes of this paragraph (c), a divorce or separation instrument must be effective, or a valid written agreement must be executed by both spouses or former spouses, prior to the date on which the transferor spouse (in the case of paragraph (c)(1) of this section) or the nontransferor spouse (in the cases of paragraph (c)(2) of this section) files such spouse's first timely filed Federal income tax return for the year that includes the date of the stock redemption, but no later than the date such return is due (including extensions).

(d) Examples. The provisions of this section may be illustrated by the following examples:

Example 1. Corporation X has 100 shares outstanding. A and B each own 50 shares. A and B divorce. The divorce instrument requires B to purchase A's shares, and A to sell A's shares to B, in exchange for $100x. Corporation X redeems A's shares for $100x. Assume that, under applicable tax law, B has a primary and unconditional obligation to purchase A's stock, and therefore the stock redemption results in a constructive distribution to B. Also assume that the special rule of paragraph (c)(1) of this section does not apply. Accordingly, under paragraphs (a)(2) and (b)(2) of this section, A shall be treated as transferring A's stock of Corporation X to B in a transfer to which section 1041 applies (assuming the requirements of section 1041 are otherwise satisfied), B shall be treated as transferring the Corporation X stock B is deemed to have received from A to Corporation X in exchange for $100x in an exchange to which section 1041 does not apply and sections 302(d) and 301 apply, and B shall be treated as transferring the $100x to A in a transfer to which section 1041 applies.

Example 2. Assume the same facts as Example 1, except that the divorce instrument provides as follows: "A and B agree that the redemption will be treated for Federal income tax purposes as a redemption distribution to A." The divorce instrument further provides that it "supersedes all other instruments or agreements concerning the purchase, sale, redemption, or other disposition of the stock that is the subject of the redemption." By virtue of the special rule of paragraph (c)(1) of this section and under paragraphs (a)(1) and (b)(1) of this section, the tax consequences of the redemption shall be determined in accordance with its form as a redemption of A's shares by Corporation X and shall not be treated as resulting in a constructive distribution to B. See section 302.

Example 3. Assume the same facts as Example 1, except that the divorce instrument requires A to sell A's shares to Corporation X in exchange for a note. B guarantees Corporation X's payment of the note. Assume that, under applicable tax law, B does not have a primary and unconditional obligation to purchase A's stock, and therefore the stock redemption does not result in a constructive distribution to B. Also assume that the special rule of paragraph (c)(2) of this section does not apply. Accordingly, under paragraphs (a)(l) and (b)(1) of this section, the tax consequences of the redemption shall be determined in accordance with its form as a redemption of A's shares by Corporation X. See section 302.

* * *

§ 1.1042–1T Questions and answers relating to the sales of stock to employee stock ownership plans or certain cooperatives (temporary).

Q–1: What does section 1042 provide?

A–1: **(a)** Section 1042 provides rules under which a taxpayer may elect not to recognize gain in certain cases where "qualified securities" are sold to a qualifying employee stock ownership plan or worker-owned cooperative in taxable years of the seller beginning after July 18, 1984, and "qualified replacement property" is purchased by the taxpayer within the "replacement period." If the requirements of Q&A-2 of this section are met, and if the taxpayer makes an election under section 1042(a) in accordance with Q&A-3 of this section, the gain realized by the taxpayer on the sale of the qualified securities is recognized only to the extent that the amount realized on such sale exceeds the cost to the taxpayer of the qualified replacement property.

(b) Under section 1042, the term "qualified securities" means employer securities (as defined in section 409(1)) with respect to which each of the following requirements is satisfied: (1) The employer securities were issued by a domestic corporation; (2) for at least one year before and immediately after the sale, the domestic corporation that issued the employer securities (and each corporation that is a member of a "controlled group of corporations" with such corporation for purposes of section 409(1)) has no stock outstanding that is readily tradeable on an established market; (3) as of the time of the sale, the employer securities have been held by the taxpayer for more than 1 year; and (4) the employer securities were not received by the taxpayer in a distribution from a plan described in section 401(a) or in a transfer pursuant to an option or other right to acquire stock to which section 83, 422, 422A, 423, or 424* applies.

*Editorial comment: The reference is now Sec. 83, 422, or 423. The Regulations do not reflect the effect of the Revenue Reconciliation Act of 1990 which repealed Secs. 422 and 424 and which redesignated Sec. 422A as Sec. 422 and Sec. 425 as Sec. 424.

(c) The term "replacement period" means the period which begins 3 months before the date on which the sale of qualified securities occurs and which ends 12 months after the date of such sale. A replacement period may include any period which occurs prior to July 19, 1984.

(d) The term "qualified replacement property" means any securities (as defined in section 165(g)(2)) issued by a domestic corporation which does not, for the taxable year of such corporation in which the securities are purchased by the taxpayer, have passive investment income (as defined in section 1362(d)(3)(D)) that exceeds 25 percent of the gross receipts of such corporation for the taxable year preceding the taxable year of purchase. In addition, securities of the domestic corporation that issued the employer securities qualifying under section 1042 (and of any corporation that is a member of a "controlled group of corporations" with such corporation for purposes of section 409(1)) will not qualify as "qualified replacement property."

(e) For purposes of section 1042(a), there is a "purchase" of qualified replacement property only if the basis of such property is determined by reference to its cost to the taxpayer. If the basis of the qualified replacement property is determined by reference to its basis in the hands of the transferor thereof or another person, or by reference to the basis of property (other than cash or its equivalent) exchanged for such property, then the basis of such property is not determined solely by reference to its cost to the taxpayer.

Q–2: What is a sale of qualified securities for purposes of section 1042(b)?

A–2: **(a)** Under section 1042(b), a sale of qualified securities is one under which all of the following requirements are met:

(1) The qualified securities are sold to an employee stock ownership plan (as defined in section 4975(e)(7)) maintained by the corporation that issued the qualified securities (or by a member of the "controlled group of corporations" with such corporation for purposes of section 409(1)) or to an eligible worker-owned cooperative (as defined in section 1042(c)(2));

(2) The employee stock ownership plan or eligible worker-owned cooperative owns, immediately after the sale, 30 percent or more of the total value of the employer securities (within the meaning of section 409(1) outstanding as of such time;

(3) No portion of the assets of the employee stock ownership plan or eligible worker-owned cooperative attributable to qualified securities that are sold to the plan or cooperative by the taxpayer or by any other person in a sale with respect to which an election under section 1042(a) is made accrue under the plan or are allocated by the cooperative, either directly or indirectly and either concurrently with or at any time thereafter, for the benefit of (i) the taxpayer; (ii) any person who is a member of the family of the taxpayer (within the meaning of section 267(c)(4)); or (iii) any person who owns (after the application of section 318(a)), at any time after July 18, 1984, and until immediately after the sale, more than 25 percent of in value of the outstanding portion of any class of stock of the corporation that issued the qualified securities (or of any member of the "controlled group of corporations" with such corporation for purposes of section 409(1)). For purposes of this calculation, stock that is owned, directly or indirectly, by or for a qualified plan shall not be treated as outstanding.

(4) The taxpayer files with the Secretary (as part of the required election described in Q&A-3 of this section) a verified written statement of the domestic corporation (or corporations) whose employees are covered by the plan acquiring the qualified securities or of any authorized officer of the eligible worker-owned cooperative, consenting to the application of section 4978(a) with respect to such corporation or cooperative.

(b) For purposes of determining whether paragraph (a)(2) of this section is satisfied, sales of qualified securities by two or more taxpayers may be treated as a single sale if such sales are made as part of a single, integrated transaction under a prearranged agreement between the taxpayers.

(c) For purposes of determining whether paragraph (a)(3) of this section is satisfied with respect to the prohibition against an accrual or allocation of qualified securities, the accrual or allocation of any benefits or contributions or other assets that are not attributable to qualified securities sold to the employee stock ownership plan or eligible worker-owned cooperative in a sale with respect to which an election under section 1042(a) is made (including any accrual or allocation under any other plan or arrangement maintained by the corporation or any member of "the controlled group of corporations" with such corporation for purposes of section 409(1)) must be made without regard to the allocation of such qualified securities. Paragraph (a)(3) of this section above may be illustrated in part by the following example: Individuals A, B, and C own 50, 25, and 25, respectively, of the 100 outstanding shares of common stock of Corporation X. Such shares constitute qualified securities as defined in Q&A-1 of this section. A and B, but not C, are employees of Corporation X. For the benefit of all its employees, Corporation X establishes an employee stock ownership plan that obtains a loan meeting the exemption requirements of section 4975(d)(3). The loan proceeds are used by the plan to purchase the 100 shares of qualified securities from A, B, and C, all of whom elect nonrecognition treatment under section 1042(a) with respect to the gain realized on their sale of such securities. Under the requirements of paragraph (a)(3) of this section, no part of the assets of the plan attributable to the 100 shares of qualified securities may accrue under the plan (or under any other plan or arrangement maintained by Corporation X) for the benefit of A or B or any person who is a member of the family of A or B (as determined under section 267(c)(4)). Furthermore, no other assets of the plan or assets of the employer may accrue for the benefit of such individuals in lieu of the receipt of assets attributable to such qualified securities.

(d) A sale under section 1042(a) shall not include any sale of securities by a dealer or underwriter in the ordinary course of its trade or business as a dealer or underwriter, whether or not guaranteed.

Q–3: What is the time and manner for making the election under section 1042(a)?

A–3: **(a)** The election not to recognize the gain realized upon the sale of qualified securities to the extent provided under section 1042(a) shall be made in a "statement of election" attached to the taxpayer's income tax return filed on or before the due date (including extensions of time) for the taxable year in which the sale occurs. If a taxpayer does not make a timely election under this section to obtain section 1042(a) nonrecognition treatment with respect to the sale of qualified securities, it may not subsequently make an election on an amended return or otherwise. Also, an election once made is irrevocable.

(b) The statement of election shall provide that the taxpayer elects to treat the sale of securities as a sale of qualified securities under section 1042(a), and shall contain the following information:

(1) A description of the qualified securities sold, including the type and number of shares;

(2) The date of the sale of the qualified securities;

(3) The adjusted basis of the qualified securities;

(4) The amount realized upon the sale of the qualified securities;

(5) The identity of the employee stock ownership plan or eligible worker-owned cooperative to which the qualified securities were sold; and

(6) If the sale was part of a single, interrelated transaction under a prearranged agreement between taxpayers involving other sales of qualified securities, the names and taxpayer identification numbers of the other taxpayers under the agreement and the number of shares sold by the other taxpayers. See Q&A–2 of this section.

If the taxpayer has purchased qualified replacement property at the time of the election, the taxpayer must attach as part of the statement of election a "statement of purchase" describing the qualified replacement property, the date of the purchase, and the cost of the property, and declaring such property to be the qualified replacement property with respect to the sale of qualified securities. Such statement of purchase must be notarized by the later of thirty days after the purchase or March 6, 1986. In addition, the statement of election must be accompanied by the verified written statement of consent required under Q&A–2 of this section with respect to the qualified securities sold.

(c) If the taxpayer has not purchased qualified replacement property at the time of the filing of the statement of election, a timely election under this Q&A shall not be considered to have been made unless the taxpayer attaches the notarized statement of purchase described above to the taxpayer's income tax return filed for the taxable year following the year for which the election under section 1042(a) was made. Such notarized statement of purchase shall be filed with the district director or the director of the regional service center with whom such election was originally filed, if the return is not filed with such director.

Q–4: What is the basis of qualified replacement property?

A–4: If a taxpayer makes an election under section 1042(a), the basis of the qualified replacement property purchased by the taxpayer during the replacement period shall be reduced by an amount equal to the amount of gain which was not recognized. If more than one item of qualified replacement property is purchased, the basis of each of such items shall be reduced by an amount determined by multiplying the total gain not recognized by reason of the application of section 1042(a) by a fraction, the numerator of which is the cost of such item of property and the denominator of which is the total cost of all such items of property.

For the rule regarding the holding period of qualified replacement property, see section 1223(13).

Q–5: What is the statute of limitations for the assessment of a deficiency relating to the gain on the sale of qualified security?

A–5: **(a)** If any gain is realized by the taxpayer on the sale of any qualified securities and such gain has not been recognized under section 1042(a) in accordance with the requirements of this section, the statutory period provided in section 6501(a) for the assessment of any deficiency with respect to such gain shall not expire prior to the expiration of 3 years from the date of receipt, by the district director or director of regional service center with whom the statement of election under 1042(a) was originally filed, of:

(1) A notarized statement of purchase as described in Q&A-3;

(2) A written statement of the taxpayer's intention not to purchase qualified replacement property within the replacement period; or

(3) A written statement of the taxpayer's failure to purchase qualified replacement property within the replacement period.

In those situations when a taxpayer is providing a written statement of an intention not to purchase or of a failure to purchase qualified replacement property, the statement shall be accompanied, where appropriate, by an amended return for the taxable year in which the gain from the sale of the qualified securities was realized, in order to reflect the inclusion in gross income for that year of gain required to be recognized in connection with such sale.

(b) Any gain from the sale of qualified securities which is required to be recognized due to a failure to meet the requirements under section 1042 shall be included in the gross income for the taxable year in which the gain was realized. If any gain from the sale of qualified securities is not recognized under section 1042(a) in accordance with the requirements of this section, any deficiency attributable to any portion of such gain may be assessed at any time before the expiration of the 3-year period described in this Q&A, notwithstanding the provision of any law or rule of law which would otherwise prevent such assessment.

Q–6: When does section 1042 become effective?

A–6: Section 1042 applies to sales of qualified securities in taxable years of sellers beginning after July 18, 1984.

* * *

Special Rules

* * *

§ 1.1060–1 Special allocation rules for certain asset acquisitions.

(a) Scope—(1) In general. This section prescribes rules relating to the requirements of section 1060, which, in the case of an applicable asset acquisition, requires the transferor (the seller) and the transferee (the purchaser) each to allocate the consideration paid or received in the transaction among the assets transferred in the same manner as amounts are allocated under section 338(b)(5) (relating to the allocation of adjusted grossed-up basis among the assets of the target corporation when a section 338 election is made). In the case of an applicable asset acquisition described in paragraph (b)(1) of this section, sellers and purchasers must allocate the consideration under the residual method as described in §§1.338–6 and 1.338–7 in order to determine, respectively, the amount realized from, and the basis in, each of the transferred assets. For rules relating to distributions of partnership property or transfers of partnership interests which are subject to section 1060(d), see §1.755–2T.

* * *

(3) Outline of topics. In order to facilitate the use of this section, this paragraph (a)(3) lists the major paragraphs in this section as follows:

(a) Scope.
(1) In general.

(2) Effective date.

(3) Outline of topics.

(b) Applicable asset acquisition.
(1) In general.

(2) Assets constituting a trade or business.

(i) In general.

(ii) Goodwill or going concern value.

(iii) Factors indicating goodwill or going concern value.

(3) Examples.

(4) Asymmetrical transfers of assets.

(5) Related transactions.

(6) More than a single trade or business.

(7) Covenant entered into by the seller.

(8) Partial non-recognition exchanges.

(c) Allocation of consideration among assets under the residual method.

(1) Consideration.

(2) Allocation of consideration among assets.

(3) Certain costs.

(4) Effect of agreement between parties.

(d) Examples.

(e) Reporting requirements.

(1) Applicable asset acquisitions.

(i) In general.

(ii) Time and manner of reporting.

(A) In general.

(B) Additional reporting requirement.

(2) Transfers of interests in partnerships.

* * *

(b) Applicable asset acquisition—(1) In general. An applicable asset acquisition is any transfer, whether direct or indirect, of a group of assets if the assets transferred constitute a trade or business in the hands of either the seller or the purchaser and, except as provided in paragraph (b)(8) of this section, the purchaser's basis in the transferred assets is determined wholly by reference to the purchaser's consideration.

(2) Assets constituting a trade or business—(i) In general. For purposes of this section, a group of assets constitutes a trade or business if—

(A) the use of such assets would constitute an active trade or business under section 355; or

(B) Its character is such that goodwill or going concern value could under any circumstance attach to such group.

(ii) Goodwill or going concern value. Goodwill is the value of a trade or business attributable to the expectancy of continued customer patronage. This expectancy may be due to the name or reputation of a trade or business or any other factor. Going concern value is the additional value that attaches to property because of its existence as an integral part of an ongoing business activity. Going concern value includes the value attributable to the ability of a trade or business (or a part of a trade or business) to continue functioning or generating income without interruption notwithstanding a change in ownership. It also includes the value that is attributable to the immediate use or availability of an acquired trade or business, such as, for example, the use of the revenues or net earnings that otherwise would not be received during any period if the acquired trade or business were not available or operational.

(iii) Factors indicating goodwill or going concern value. In making the determination in this paragraph (b)(2), all the facts and circumstances surrounding the transaction are taken into account. Whether sufficient consideration is available to allocate to goodwill or going concern value after the residual method is applied is not relevant in determining whether goodwill or going concern value could attach to a group of assets. Factors to be considered include—

(A) The presence of any intangible assets (whether or not those assets are section 197 intangibles), provided, however, that the transfer of such an asset in the absence of other assets will not be a trade or business for purposes of section 1060;

(B) The existence of an excess of the total consideration over the aggregate book value of the tangible and intangible assets purchased (other than goodwill and going concern value) as shown in the financial accounting books and records of the purchaser; and

(C) Related transactions, including lease agreements, licenses, or other similar agreements between the purchaser and seller (or managers, directors, owners, or employees of the seller) in connection with the transfer.

(3) Examples. The following examples illustrate paragraphs (b)(1) and (2) of this section.

Example 1. S is a high grade machine shop that manufactures microwave connectors in limited quantities. It is a successful company with a reputation within the industry and among its customers for manufacturing unique, high quality products. Its tangible assets consist primarily of ordinary machinery for working metal and plating. It has no secret formulas or patented drawings of value. P is a company that designs, manufactures, and markets electronic components. It wants to establish an immediate presence in the microwave industry, an area in which it previously has not been engaged. P is acquiring assets of a number of smaller companies and hopes that these assets will collectively allow it to offer a broad product mix. P acquires the assets of S in order to augment its product mix and to promote its presence in the microwave industry. P will not use the assets acquired from S to manufacture microwave connectors. The assets transferred are assets that constitute a trade or business in the hands of the seller. Thus, P's purchase of S's assets is an applicable asset acquisition. The fact that P will not use the assets acquired from S to continue the business of S does not affect this conclusion.

Example 2. S, a sole proprietor who operates a car wash, both leases the building housing the car wash and sells all of the car wash equipment to P. S's use of the building and the car wash equipment constitute a trade or business. P begins operating a car wash in the building it leases from S. Because the assets transferred together with the asset leased are assets which constitute a trade or business, P's purchase of S's assets is an applicable asset acquisition.

Example 3. S, a corporation, owns a retail store business in State X and conducts activities in connection with that business enterprise that meet the active trade or business requirement of section 355. P is a minority shareholder of S. S distributes to P all the assets of S used in S's retail business in State X in complete redemption of P's stock in S held by P. The distribution of S's assets in redemption of P's stock is treated as a sale or exchange under sections 302(a) and 302(b)(3), and P's basis in the assets distributed to it is determined wholly by reference to the consideration paid, the S stock. Thus, S's distribution of assets constituting a trade or business to P is an applicable asset acquisition.

Example 4. S is a manufacturing company with an internal financial bookkeeping department. P is in the business of providing a financial bookkeeping service on a contract basis. As part of an agreement for P to begin providing financial bookkeeping services to S, P agrees to buy all of the assets associated with S's internal bookkeeping operations and provide employment to any of S's bookkeeping department employees who choose to accept a position with P. In addition to selling P the assets associated with its bookkeeping operation, S will enter into a long term contract with P for bookkeeping services. Because assets transferred from S to P, along with the related contract for bookkeeping services, are a trade or business in the hands of P, the sale of the bookkeeping assets from S to P is an applicable asset acquisition.

(4) Asymmetrical transfers of assets. If, under general principles of tax law, a seller is not treated as transferring the same assets as the purchaser is treated as acquiring, the assets acquired by the purchaser constitute a trade or business, and, except as provided in paragraph (b)(8) of this section, the purchaser's basis in the transferred assets is determined wholly by reference to the purchaser's consideration, then the purchaser is subject to section 1060.

(5) Related transactions. Whether the assets transferred constitute a trade or business is determined by aggregating all transfers from the seller to the purchaser in a series of related transactions. Except as provided in paragraph (b)(8) of this section, all assets transferred from the seller to the purchaser in a series of related transactions are included in the group of assets among which the consideration paid or received in such series is allocated under the residual method.

The principles of §1.338–1(c) are also applied in determining which assets are included in the group of assets among which the consideration paid or received is allocated under the residual method.

(6) More than a single trade or business. If the assets transferred from a seller to a purchaser include more than one trade or business, then, in applying this section, all of the assets transferred (whether or not transferred in one transaction or a series of related transactions and whether or not part of a trade or business) are treated as a single trade or business.

(7) Covenant entered into by the seller. If, in connection with an applicable asset acquisition, the seller enters into a covenant (e.g., a covenant not to compete) with the purchaser, that covenant is treated as an asset transferred as part of a trade or business.

(8) Partial non-recognition exchanges. A transfer may constitute an applicable asset acquisition notwithstanding the fact that no gain or loss is recognized with respect to a portion of the group of assets transferred. All of the assets transferred, including the non-recognition assets, are taken into account in determining whether the group of assets constitutes a trade or business. The allocation of consideration under paragraph (c) of this section is done without taking to account either the non-recognition assets or the amount of money or other property that is treated as transferred in exchange for the non-recognition assets (together, the non-recognition exchange property). The basis in and gain or loss recognized with respect to the non-recognition exchange property are determined under such rules as would otherwise apply to an exchange of such property. The amount of the money and other property treated as exchanged for non-recognition assets is the amount by which the fair market value of the non-recognition assets transferred by one party exceeds the fair market value of the non-recognition assets transferred by the other (to the extent of the money and the fair market value of property transferred in the exchange). The money and other property that are treated as transferred in exchange for the non-recognition assets (and which are not included among the assets to which section 1060 applies) are considered to come from the following assets in the following order: First from Class I assets, then from Class II assets, then from Class III assets, then from Class IV assets, then from Class V assets, then from Class VI assets, and then from Class VII assets. For this purpose, liabilities assumed (or to which a non-recognition exchange property is subject) are treated as Class I assets. See Example 1 in paragraph (d) of this section for an example of the application of section 1060 to a single transaction which is, in part, a non-recognition exchange.

(c) Allocation of consideration among assets under the residual method—(1) Consideration. The seller's consideration is the amount, in the aggregate, realized from selling the assets in the applicable asset acquisition under section 1001(b). The purchaser's consideration is the amount, in the aggregate, of its cost of purchasing the assets in the applicable asset acquisition that is properly taken into account in basis.

(2) Allocation of consideration among assets. For purposes of determining the seller's amount realized for each of the assets sold in an applicable asset acquisition, the seller allocates consideration to all the assets sold by using the residual method under §§1.338–6 and 1.338–7, substituting consideration for ADSP. For purposes of determining the purchaser's basis in each of the assets purchased in an applicable asset acquisition, the purchaser allocates consideration to all the assets purchased by using the residual method under §§1.338–6 and 1.338–7, substituting consideration for AGUB. In allocating consideration, the rules set forth in paragraphs (c)(3) and (4) of this section apply in addition to the rules in §§1.338–6 and 1.338–7.

(3) Certain costs. The seller and purchaser each adjusts the amount allocated to an individual asset to take into account the specific identifiable costs incurred in transferring that asset in connection with the applicable asset acquisition (e.g., real estate transfer costs or security interest perfection costs). Cost so allocated increase, or decrease, as appropriate, the total consideration that is allocated under the residual method. No adjustment is made to the amount allocated to an individual asset for general costs associated with the applicable asset acquisition as a whole or with groups of assets included therein (e.g., non-specific appraisal fees or accounting fees). These latter amounts are taken into account only indirectly through their effect on the total consideration to be allocated.

* * *

(4) Effect of agreement between parties. If, in connection with an applicable asset acquisition, the seller and purchaser agree in writing as to the allocation of any amount of consideration to, or as to the fair market value of, any of the assets, such agreement is binding on them to the extent provided in this paragraph (c)(4). Nothing in this paragraph (c)(4) restricts the Commissioner's authority to challenge the allocations or values arrived at in an allocation agreement. This paragraph (c)(4) does not apply if the parties are able to refute the allocation or valuation under the standards set forth in *Commissioner v. Danielson*, 378 F.2d 771 (3d Cir.), cert. denied, 389 U.S. 858 (1967) (a party wishing to challenge the tax consequences of an agreement as construed by the Commissioner must offer proof that, in an action between the parties to the agreement, would be admissible to alter that construction or show its unenforceability because of mistake, undue influence, fraud, duress, etc.).

(d) Examples. The following examples illustrate this section:

Example 1. (i) On January 1, 2001, A transfers assets X, Y, and Z to B in exchange for assets D, E, and F plus $1,000 cash.

(ii) Assume the exchange of assets constitutes an exchange of like-kind property to which section 1031 applies. Assume also that goodwill or going concern value could under any circumstances attach to each of the DEF and XYZ groups of assets and, therefore, each group constitutes a trade or business under section 1060.

(iii) Assume the fair market values of the assets and the amount of money transferred are as follows:

By A		By B	
Asset	Fair market value	Asset	Fair market value
X	$ 400	D	$ 40
Y	400	E	30
Z	200	F	30
		Cash (amount)	1,000
Total	$1,000	Total	$1,100

(iv) Under paragraph (b)(8) of this section, for purposes of allocating consideration under paragraph (c) of this section, the like-kind assets exchanged and any money or other property that are treated as transferred in exchange for the like-kind property are excluded from the application of section 1060.

(v) Since assets X, Y, and Z are like-kind property, they are excluded from the application of the section 1060 allocation rules.

(vi) Since assets D, E, and F are like-kind property, they are excluded from the application of the section 1060 allocation rules. Thus, the allocation rules of section 1060 do not apply in determining B's gain or loss with respect to the disposition of assets D, E, and F, and the allocation rules of section 1060 and paragraph (c) of this section are not applied to determine A's bases of assets D, E, and F. In addition, $900 of the $1,000 cash B gave to A for A's like-kind assets is treated as transferred in exchange for the like-kind property in order to equalize the fair market values of the like-kind assets. Therefore, $900 of the cash is excluded from the application of the section 1060 allocation rules.

(vii) $100 of the cash is allocated under section 1060 and paragraph (c) of this section.

(viii) A received $100 that must be allocated under section 1060 and paragraph (c) of this section. Since A transferred no Class I, II, III, IV, V, or VI assets to which section 1060 applies, in determining its amount realized for the part of the exchange to which section

1031 does not apply, the $100 is allocated to Class VII assets (goodwill and going concern value).

(ix) B gave A $100 that must be allocated under section 1060 and paragraph (c) of this section. Since B received from A no Class I, II, III, IV, V, or VI assets to which section 1060 applies, the $100 consideration is allocated by B to Class VII assets (goodwill and going concern value).

Example 2. (i) On January 1, 2001, S, a sole proprietor, sells to P, a corporation, a group of assets that constitutes a trade or business under paragraph (b)(2) of this section. S, who plans to retire immediately, also executes in P's favor a covenant not to compete. P pays S $3,000 in cash and assumes $1,000 in liabilities. Thus, the total consideration is $4,000.

(ii) On the purchase date, P and S also execute a separate agreement that states that the fair market values of the Class II, Class III, Class V, and Class VI assets S sold to P are as follows:

Asset class	Asset	Fair market value
II	Actively traded securities	$500
	Total Class II	500
III	Accounts receivable	200
	Total Class III	200
V	Furniture and fixtures	800
	Building	800
	Land	200
	Equipment	400
	Total Class V	2,200
VI	Covenant not to compete	900
	Total Class VI	900

(iii) P and S each allocate the consideration in the transaction among the assets transferred under paragraph (c) of this section in accordance with the agreed upon fair market values of the assets, so that $500 is allocated to Class II assets, $200 is allocated to the Class III asset, $2,200 is allocated to Class V assets, $900 is allocated to Class VI assets, and $200 ($4,000 total consideration less $3,800 allocated to assets in Classes II, III, V, and VI) is allocated to the Class VII assets (goodwill and going concern value).

(iv) In connection with the examination of P's return, the Commissioner, in determining the fair market values of the assets transferred, may disregard the parties' agreement. Assume that the Commissioner correctly determines that the fair market value of the covenant not to compete was $500. Since the allocation of consideration among Class II, III, V, and VI assets results in allocation up to the fair market value limitation, the $600 of unallocated consideration resulting from the Commissioner's redetermination of the value of the covenant not to compete is allocated to Class VII assets (goodwill and going concern value).

* * *

Wash Sales Of Stock Or Securities

§ 1.1091–1 Losses from wash sales of stock or securities.

(a) A taxpayer cannot deduct any loss claimed to have been sustained from the sale or other disposition of stock or securities if, within a period beginning 30 days before the date of such sale or disposition and ending 30 days after such date (referred to in this section as the 61-day period), he has acquired (by purchase or by an exchange upon which the entire amount of gain or loss was recognized by law), or has entered into a contract or option so to acquire, substantially identical stock or securities. However, this prohibition does not apply (1) in the case of a taxpayer, not a corporation, if the sale or other disposition of stock or securities is made in connection with the taxpayer's trade or business, or (2) in the case of a corporation, a dealer in stock or securities, if the sale or other disposition of stock or securities is made in the ordinary course of its business as such dealer.

(b) Where more than one loss is claimed to have been sustained within the taxable year from the sale or other disposition of stock or securities, the provisions of this section shall be applied to the losses in the order in which the stock or securities the disposition of which resulted in the respective losses were disposed of (beginning with the earliest disposition). If the order of disposition of stock or securities disposed of at a loss on the same day cannot be determined, the stock or securities will be considered to have been disposed of in the order in which they were originally acquired (beginning with the earliest acquisition).

(c) Where the amount of stock or securities acquired within the 61-day period is less than the amount of stock or securities sold or otherwise disposed of, then the particular shares of stock or securities the loss from the sale or other disposition of which is not deductible shall be those with which the stock or securities acquired are matched in accordance with the following rule: The stock or securities acquired will be matched in accordance with the order of their acquisition (beginning with the earliest acquisition) with an equal number of the shares of stock or securities sold or otherwise disposed of.

(d) Where the amount of stock or securities acquired within the 61-day period is not less than the amount of stock or securities sold or otherwise disposed of, then the particular shares of stock or securities the acquisition of which resulted in the nondeductibility of the loss shall be those with which the stock or securities disposed of are matched in accordance with the following rule: The stock or securities sold or otherwise disposed of will be matched with an equal number of the shares of stock or securities acquired in accordance with the order of acquisition (beginning with the earliest acquisition) of the stock or securities acquired.

(e) The acquisition of any share of stock or any security which results in the nondeductibility of a loss under the provisions of this section shall be disregarded in determining the deductibility of any other loss.

(f) The word "acquired" as used in this section means acquired by purchase or by an exchange upon which the entire amount of gain or loss was recognized by law, and comprehends cases where the taxpayer has entered into a contract or option within the 61-day period to acquire by purchase or by such an exchange.

(g) For purposes of determining under this section the 61-day period applicable to a short sale of stock or securities, the principles of paragraph (a) of § 1.1233–1 for determining the consummation of a short sale shall generally apply except that the date of entering into the short sale shall be deemed to be the date of sale if, on the date of entering into the short sale, the taxpayer owns (or on or before such date has entered into a contract or option to acquire) stock or securities identical to those sold short and subsequently delivers such stock or securities to close the short sale.

(h) The following examples illustrate the application of this section:

Example (1). A, whose taxable year is the calendar year, on December 1, 1954, purchased 100 shares of common stock in the M Company for $10,000 and on December 15, 1954, purchased 100 additional shares for $9,000. On January 3, 1955, he sold the 100 shares purchased on December 1, 1954, for $9,000. Because of the provisions of section 1091, no loss from the sale is allowable as a deduction.

Example (2). A, whose taxable year is the calendar year, on September 21, 1954, purchased 100 shares of the common stock of the M Company for $5,000. On December 21, 1954, he purchased 50 shares of substantially identical stock for $2,750, and on December 27, 1954, he purchased 25 additional shares of such stock for $1,125. On January 3, 1955, he sold for $4,000 the 100 shares purchased on September 21, 1954. There is an indicated loss of $1,000 on the sale of the 100 shares. Since, within the 61-day period, A purchased 75 shares of substantially identical stock, the loss on the sale of 75 of the shares ($3,750 – $3,000, or $750) is not allowable as a deduction because of the provisions of section 1091. The loss on the sale of the remaining 25 shares ($1,250 – $1,000, or $250) is deductible subject to the limitations provided in sections 267 and 1211. The basis of the 50 shares purchased December 21, 1954, the acquisition of which resulted in the nondeductibility of the loss ($500) sustained on 50 of the 100 shares sold on January 3, 1955, is $2,500 (the cost of 50 of the shares sold on January 3, 1955) + $750 (the difference between the purchase price ($2,750) of the 50 shares acquired on December 21, 1954, and the selling price ($2,000) of 50 of the shares sold on January 3, 1955), or $3,250. Similarly, the basis of the 25 shares purchased on December 27, 1954, the acquisition of which resulted in the nondeductibility of the loss ($250) sustained on 25 of the shares sold on January 3, 1955, is $1,250 + $125, or $1,375. See § 1.1091–2.

Example (3). A, whose taxable year is the calendar year, on September 15, 1954, purchased 100 shares of the stock of the M Company for $5,000. He sold these shares on February 1, 1956, for $4,000. On each of the four days from February 15, 1956, to February 18, 1956, inclusive, he purchased 50 shares of substantially identical stock for $2,000. There is an indicated loss of $1,000 from the sale of the 100 shares on February 1, 1956, but, since within the 61-day period A purchased not less than 100 shares of substantially identical stock, the loss is not deductible. The particular shares of stock the purchase of which resulted in the nondeductibility of the loss are the first 100 shares purchased within such period, that is, the 50 shares purchased on February 15, 1956, and the 50 shares purchased on February 16, 1956. In determining the period for which the 50 shares purchased on February 15, 1956, and the 50 shares purchased on February 16, 1956, were held, there is to be included the period for which the 100 shares purchased on September 15, 1954, and sold on February 1, 1956, were held.

§ 1.1091–2 Basis of stock or securities acquired in "wash sales."

(a) In general. The application of section 1091(d) may be illustrated by the following examples:

Example (1). A purchased a share of common stock of the X Corporation for $100 in 1935, which he sold January 15, 1955, for $80. On February 1, 1955, he purchased a share of common stock of the same corporation for $90. No loss from the sale is recognized under section 1091. The basis of the new share is $110; that is, the basis of the old share ($100) increased by $10, the excess of the price at which the new share was acquired ($90) over the price at which the old share was sold ($80).

Example (2). A purchased a share of common stock of the Y Corporation for $100 in 1935, which he sold January 15, 1955, for $80. On February 1, 1955, he purchased a share of common stock of the same corporation for $70. No loss from the sale is recognized under section 1091. The basis of the new share is $90; that is, the basis of the old share ($100) decreased by $10, the excess of the price at which the old share was sold ($80) over the price at which the new share was acquired ($70).

* * *

CAPITAL GAINS AND LOSSES

Treatment of Capital Gains*

* * *

Treatment of Capital Losses

§ 1.1211–1 Limitation on capital losses.

(a) Corporations— (1) General rule. In the case of a corporation, there shall be allowed as a deduction an amount equal to the sum of:

(i) Losses sustained during the taxable year from sales or exchanges of capital assets, plus

(ii) The aggregate of all losses sustained in other taxable years which are treated as a short-term capital loss in such taxable year pursuant to section 1212(a)(1),

but only to the extent of gains from such sales or exchanges of capital assets in such taxable year.

* * *

(b) Taxpayers other than corporations— (1) General rule. In the case of a taxpayer other than a corporation, there shall be allowed as a deduction an amount equal to the sum of:

(i) Losses sustained during the taxable year from sales or exchanges of capital assets, plus

(ii) The aggregate of all losses sustained in other taxable years which are treated either as a short-term capital loss or as a long-term capital loss in such taxable year pursuant to section 1212(b), but only to the extent of gains from sales or exchanges of capital assets in such taxable year, plus (if such losses exceed such gains) the additional allowance or transitional additional allowance deductible under section 1211(b) from ordinary income for such taxable year. The additional allowance deductible under section 1211 (b) shall be determined by application of subparagraph (2) of this paragraph, and the transitional additional allowance by application of subparagraph (3) of this paragraph.

(2) Additional allowance. Except as otherwise provided by subparagraph (3) of this paragraph, the additional allowance deductible under section 1211 (b) for taxable years beginning after December 31, 1969, shall be the least of:

(i) The taxable income for the taxable year reduced, but not below zero, by the zero bracket amount (in the case of taxable years beginning before January 1, 1977, the taxable income for the taxable year);**

(ii) $3,000 ($2,000 for taxable years beginning in 1977; $1,000 for taxable years beginning before January 1, 1977); or

(iii) The sum of the excess of the net short-term capital loss over the net long-term capital gain, plus one-half*** of the excess of the net long-term capital loss over the net short-term capital gain.

* * *

(7) Married taxpayers filing separate returns— (i) In general. In the case of a husband or a wife who files a separate return for a taxable year beginning after December 31, 1969, the $3,000, $2,000, and $1,000 amounts specified in subparagraphs (2)(ii) and (3)(i)(b) of this paragraph shall instead be $1,500, $1,000, and $500, respectively.

* * *

§ 1.1212–1 Capital loss carryovers and carrybacks.

* * *

(b) Taxpayers other than corporations for taxable years beginning after December 31, 1963— (1) In general.*** If a taxpayer other than a corporation sustains a net capital loss for any taxable year beginning after December 31, 1963, the portion thereof which is a short-term capital loss carryover shall be carried over to the succeeding taxable year and treated as a short-term capital loss sustained in such succeeding taxable year, and the portion thereof

*Omitted

**Editorial comment: The Regulations do not reflect the effect of the Tax Reform Act of 1986. See Sec. 1211(b).

***Editorial comment: The Regulations do not reflect the effect of the Technical and Miscellaneous Revenue Act of 1988. See Sec. 1212(b)(2).

which constitutes a long-term capital loss carryover shall be carried over to the succeeding taxable year and treated as a long-term capital loss sustained in such succeeding taxable year. The carryovers are included in the succeeding taxable year in the determination of the amount of the short-term capital loss, the net short-term capital gain or loss, the long-term capital loss, and the net long-term capital gain or loss in such year, the net capital loss in such year, and the capital loss carryovers from such year. For purposes of this subparagraph:

(i) A short-term capital loss carryover is the excess of the net short-term capital loss for the taxable year over the net long-term capital gain for such year, and

(ii) A long-term capital loss carryover is the excess of the net long-term capital loss for the taxable year over the net short-term capital gain for such year.

(2) Special rules for determining a net short-term capital gain or loss for purposes of carryover—* * *

(ii) Taxable years beginning after December 31, 1969. In determining a net short-term capital gain or loss of a taxable year beginning after December 31, 1969—

(a) For purposes of computing a short-term capital loss carryover to the succeeding taxable year, an amount equal to the additional allowance for the taxable year (determined as provided in section 1211(b) and § 1.121–1(b)(2)) is treated as a short-term capital gain occurring in such year, and

(b) For purposes of computing a long-term capital loss carryover to the succeeding taxable year, an amount equal to the sum of the additional allowance for the taxable year (determined as provided in section 1211(b) and § 1.1211–1(b)(2)), plus the excess of such additional allowance over the net short-term capital loss (determined without regard to section 1212(b)(2) for such year) is treated as a short-term capital gain in such year.

The rules provided in this subdivision are for the purpose of taking into account the additional allowance deductible for the current taxable year under section 1211(b) and § 1.1211–1 (b)(2) in determining the amount and character of capital loss carryovers from the current taxable year to the succeeding taxable year. Their practical application to a determination of the amount and character of capital loss carryovers from the current taxable year to the succeeding taxable year involves identification of the net long-term and net short-term capital loss components of the additional allowance deductible in the current taxable year as provided by § 1.1211–1 (b)(2)(iii). To the extent that the additional allowance is composed of net short-term capital losses, such losses are treated as a short-term capital gain in the current taxable year in determining the capital loss carryovers to the succeeding year. To the extent that the additional allowance is composed of net long-term capital losses applied pursuant to the provisions of § 1.1211–1(b)(2)(iii), an amount equal to twice the amount of such component of the additional allowance is treated as a short-term capital gain in the current taxable year. See paragraph (4) of this section for transitional rules if any part of the additional allowance is composed of net long-term capital losses carried to the current taxable year from a taxable year beginning before January 1, 1970.

* * *

(c) Husband and wife. (1) The following rules shall be applied in computing capital loss carryovers by husband and wife:

(i) If a husband and wife making a joint return for any taxable year made separate returns for the preceding year, any capital loss carryovers of each spouse from such preceding taxable year may be carried forward to the taxable year in accordance with paragraph (a) or (b) of this section.

(ii) If a joint return was made for the preceding taxable year, any capital loss carryover from such preceding taxable year may be carried forward to the taxable year in accordance with paragraph (a) or (b) of this section.

* * *

(v) If separate returns are made both for the taxable year and the preceding taxable year, any capital loss carryover of each spouse may be carried forward by such spouse in accordance with paragraph (a) or (b) of this section.

* * *

§ 1.1221–1 Meaning of terms.

(a) The term "capital assets" includes all classes of property not specifically excluded by section 1221. In determining whether property is a "capital asset", the period for which held is immaterial.

(b) Property used in the trade or business of a taxpayer of a character which is subject to the allowance for depreciation provided in section 167 and real property used in the trade or business of a taxpayer is excluded from the term "capital assets". Gains and losses from the sale or exchange of such property are not treated as gains and losses from the sale or exchange of capital assets, except to the extent provided in section 1231. See § 1.1231–1. Property held for the production of income, but not used in a trade or business of the taxpayer, is not excluded from the term "capital assets" even though depreciation may have been allowed with respect to such property under section 23(1) of the Internal Revenue Code of 1939 before its amendment by section 121(c) of the Revenue Act of 1942 (56 Stat. 819). However, gain or loss upon the sale or exchange of land held by a taxpayer primarily for sale to customers in the ordinary course of his business, as in the case of a dealer in real estate, is not subject to the provisions of subchapter P (section 1201 and following), chapter 1 of the Code.

(c) (1) A copyright, a literary, musical,* or artistic composition, and similar property are excluded from the term "capital assets" if held by a taxpayer whose personal efforts created such property, or if held by a taxpayer in whose hands the basis of such property is determined, for purposes of determining gain from a sale or exchange, in whole or in part by reference to the basis of such property in the hands of a taxpayer whose personal efforts created such property. For purposes of this subparagraph, the phrase "similar property" includes for example, such property as a theatrical production, a radio program, a newspaper cartoon strip, or any other property eligible for copyright protection (whether under statute or common law), but does not include a patent or an invention, or a design which may be protected only under the patent law and not under the copyright law.

(2) In the case of sales and other dispositions occurring after July 25, 1969, a letter, a memorandum, or similar property is excluded from the term "capital asset" if held by (i) a taxpayer whose personal efforts created such property, (ii) a taxpayer for whom such property was prepared or produced, or (iii) a taxpayer in whose hands the basis of such property is determined, for purposes of determining gain from a sale or exchange, in whole or in part by reference to the basis of such property in the hands of a taxpayer described in subdivision (i) or (ii) of this subparagraph. In the case of a collection of letters, memorandums, or similar property held by a person who is a taxpayer described in subdivision (i), (ii), or (iii) of this subparagraph as to some of such letters, memorandums, or similar property but not as to others, this subparagraph shall apply only to those letters, memorandums, or similar property as to which such person is a taxpayer described in such subdivision. For purposes of this subparagraph, the phrase "similar property" includes, for example, such property as a draft of a speech, a manuscript, a research paper, an oral recording of any type, a transcript of an oral recording, a transcript of an oral interview or of dictation, a personal or business diary, a log or journal, a corporate archive, including a corporate charter, office correspondence, a financial record, a drawing, a photograph, or a dispatch. A letter, memorandum, or property similar to a letter or memorandum, addressed to a taxpayer shall be considered as prepared or produced for him. This subparagraph does not apply to property, such as a corporate archive, office correspondence, or a financial record, sold or disposed of as part of a going business if such property has no significant value separate and apart from its relation to and use in such business; it also does not apply to any property to which subparagraph (1) of this paragraph applies (i. e., property to which section 1221(3) applied before its amendment by section 514(a) of the Tax Reform Act of 1969 (83 Stat. 643)).

(3) For purposes of this paragraph, in general, property is created in whole or in part by the personal efforts of a taxpayer if such taxpayer performs literary, theatrical, musical, artistic, or other creative or productive work which affirmatively contributes to the creation of the property, or if such taxpayer directs and guides others in the performance of such work. A taxpayer, such as corporate executive, who merely has administrative control of writers, actors, artists, or personnel and who does not substantially engage in the direction and guidance of such persons in the performance of their work, does not create property by his personal efforts. However, for purposes of subparagraph (2) of this paragraph, a letter or memorandum, or property similar to a letter or memorandum, which is prepared by personnel who are under the administrative control of a taxpayer, such as a corporate executive, shall be deemed to have been prepared or produced for him whether or not such letter, memorandum, or similar property is reviewed by him.

(4) For the application of section 1231 to the sale or exchange of property to which this paragraph

*Editorial comment: The Regulations do not reflect the effect of the Tax Increase Prevention and Reconciliation Act of 2005 which provided that the taxpayer can elect to treat the sale or exchange of self-created musical works as capital assets. See Sec. 1221(b)(3).

applies, see § 1.1231–1. For the application of section 170 to the charitable contribution of property to which this paragraph applies, see section 170(e) and the regulations thereunder.

(d) Section 1221(4) excludes from the definition of "capital asset" accounts or notes receivable acquired in the ordinary course of trade or business for services rendered or from the sale of stock in trade or inventory or property held for sale to customers in the ordinary course of trade or business. Thus, if a taxpayer acquires a note receivable for services rendered, reports the fair market value of the note as income, and later sells the note for less than the amount previously reported, the loss is an ordinary loss. On the other hand, if the taxpayer later sells the note for more than the amount originally reported, the excess is treated as ordinary income.

* * *

§ 1.1222–1 Other terms relating to capital gains and losses.

(a) The phrase "short-term" applies to the category of gains and losses arising from the sale or exchange of capital assets held for 1 year (6 months for taxable years beginning before 1977; 9 months for taxable years beginning in 1977) or less; the phrase "long-term" to the category of gains and losses arising from the sale or exchange of capital assets held for more than 1 year (6 months for taxable years beginning before 1977; 9 months for taxable years beginning in 1977). The fact that some part of a loss from the sale or exchange of a capital asset may be finally disallowed because of the operation of section 1211 does not mean that such loss is not "taken into account in computing taxable income" within the meaning of that phrase as used in sections 1222(2) and 1222(4).

(b) (1) In the definition of "net short-term capital gain", as provided in section 1222(5), the amounts brought forward to the taxable year under section 1212 (other than section 1212(b)(1)(B)) are short-term capital losses for such taxable year.

(2) In the definition of "net long-term capital gain," as provided in section 1222(7), the amounts brought forward to the taxable year under section 1212(b)(1)(B) are long-term capital losses for such taxable year.

(c) Gains and losses from the sale or exchange of capital assets held for not more than 1 year (6 months for taxable years beginning before 1977; 9 months for taxable years beginning in 1977) (described as short-term capital gains and short-term capital losses) shall be segregated from gains and losses arising from the sale or exchange of such assets held for more than 1 year (6 months for taxable years beginning before 1977; 9 months for taxable years beginning in 1977) (described as long-term capital gains and long-term capital losses).

(d) (1) The term capital gain net income (net capital gain for taxable years beginning before January 1, 1977) means the excess of the gains from sales or exchanges of capital assets over the losses from sales or exchanges of capital assets, which losses include any amounts carried to the taxable year pursuant to section 1212(a) or section 1212(b).

* * *

(e) The term "net capital loss" means the excess of the losses from sales or exchanges of capital assets over the sum allowed under section 1211. However, in the case of a corporation, amounts which are short-term capital losses under § 1.1212–1(a) are excluded in determining such "net capital loss".

* * *

§ 1.1223–1 Determination of period for which capital assets are held.

(a) The holding period of property received in an exchange by a taxpayer includes the period for which the property which he exchanged was held by him, if the property received has the same basis in whole or in part for determining gain or loss in the hands of the taxpayer as the property exchanged. However, this rule shall apply, in the case of exchanges after March 1, 1954, only if the property exchanged was at the time of the exchange a capital asset in the hands of the taxpayer or property used in his trade or business as defined in section 1231(b). For the purposes of this paragraph, the term "exchange" includes the following transactions: (1) An involuntary conversion described in section 1033, and (2) a distribution to which section 355 (or so much of section 356 as relates to section 355) applies. Thus, if property acquired as the result of a compulsory or involuntary conversion of other property of the taxpayer has under section 1033(c) the same basis in whole or in part in the hands of the taxpayer as the property so converted, its acquisition is treated as an exchange and the holding period of the newly acquired property shall include the period during which the converted property was held by the taxpayer. Thus, also, where stock of a controlled corporation is received by a taxpayer pursuant to a distribution to which section 355 (or so much of section 356 as relates to section 355) applies, the distribution is treated as an exchange and the period for which the taxpayer has held the stock of the controlled corporation shall include the period for which he held the stock of the distributing corporation with respect to which such distribution was made.

(b) The holding period of property in the hands of a taxpayer shall include the period during which the property was held by any other person, if such property has the same basis in whole or in part in the hands of the taxpayer for determining gain or loss from a sale or exchange as it would have in the hands of such other person. For example, the period for which property acquired by gift after December 31, 1920, was held by the donor must be included in determining the period for which the property was held by the taxpayer if, under the provisions of section 1015, such property has, for the purpose of determining gain or loss from the sale or exchange, the same basis in the hands of the taxpayer as it would have in the hands of the donor.

* * *

(d) If the acquisition of stock or securities resulted in the nondeductibility (under section 1091, relating to wash sales) of the loss from the sale or other disposition of substantially identical stock or securities, the holding period of the newly acquired securities shall include the period for which the taxpayer held the securities with respect to which the loss was not allowable.

(e) The period for which the taxpayer has held stock, or stock subscription rights, received on a distribution shall be determined as though the stock dividend, or stock right, as the case may be, were the stock in respect of which the dividend was issued if the basis for determining gain or loss upon the sale or other disposition of such stock dividend or stock right is determined under section 307. * * *

(f) The period for which the taxpayer has held stock or securities issued to him by a corporation pursuant to the exercise by him of rights to acquire such stock or securities from the corporation will, in every case and whether or not the receipt of taxable gain was recognized in connection with the distribution of the rights, begin with and include the day upon which the rights to acquire such stock or securities were exercised. A taxpayer will be deemed to have exercised rights received from a corporation to acquire stock or securities therein where there is an expression of assent to the terms of such rights made by the taxpayer in the manner requested or authorized by the corporation.

(g) The period for which the taxpayer has held a residence, the acquisition of which resulted under the provisions of section 1034 in the nonrecognition of any part of the gain realized on the sale or exchange of another residence, shall include the period for which such other residence had been held as of the date of such sale or exchange. See § 1.1034–1. * * *

(h) If a taxpayer accepts delivery of a commodity in satisfaction of a commodity futures contract, the holding period of the commodity shall include the period for which the taxpayer held the commodity futures contract, if such futures contract was a capital asset in his hands.

(i) If shares of stock in a corporation are sold from lots purchased at different dates or at different prices and the identity of the lots cannot be determined, the rules prescribed by the regulations under section 1012 for determining the cost or other basis of such stocks so sold or transferred shall also apply for the purpose of determining the holding period of such stock.

(j) In the case of a person acquiring property, or to whom property passed, from a decedent (within the meaning of section 1014(b)) dying after December 31, 1970, such person shall be considered to have held the property for more than 1 year (6 months for taxable years beginning before 1977; 9 months for taxable years beginning in 1977) if the property:

(1) Has a basis in the hands of such person which is determined in whole or in part under section 1014, and

(2) Is sold or otherwise disposed of by such person within 6 months after the decedent's death.

The provisions of this paragraph apply to sales of such property included in the decedent's gross estate for the purposes of the estate tax by the executor or administrator of the estate and to sales of such property by other persons who have acquired property from the decedent. The provisions of this paragraph may also be applicable to cases involving joint tenancies, community property, and properties transferred in contemplation of death. Thus, if a surviving joint tenant, who acquired property by right of survivorship, sells or otherwise disposes of such property within 6 months after the date of the decedent's death, and the basis of the property in his hands is determined in whole or in part under section 1014, the property shall be considered to have been held by the surviving joint tenant for more than 6 months. Similarly, a surviving spouse's share of community property shall be considered to have been held by her for more than 6 months if it is sold or otherwise disposed of within 6 months after the date of the decedent's death, regardless of when the property was actually acquired by the marital community. For the purposes of this paragraph, it is immaterial that the sale or other disposition produces gain or loss. If property is considered to have been held for more than 6 months by reason of this paragraph, it also is considered to have been held for that period for purposes of section 1231 (if that section is otherwise applicable).

* * *

Special Rules For Determining Capital Gains And Losses

§ 1.1231–1 Gains and losses from the sale or exchange of certain property used in the trade or business.

(a) In general. Section 1231 provides that, subject to the provisions of paragraph (e) of the section, a taxpayer's gains and losses from the disposition (including involuntary conversion) of assets described in that section as "property used in the trade or business" and from the involuntary conversion of capital assets held for more than 6 months shall be treated as long-term capital gains and losses if the total gains exceed the total losses. If the total gains do not exceed the total losses, all such gains and losses are treated as ordinary gains and losses. Therefore, if the taxpayer has no gains subject to section 1231, a recognized loss from the condemnation (or from a sale or exchange under threat of condemnation) of even a capital asset held for more than 1 year (6 months for taxable years beginning before 1977; 9 months for taxable years beginning in 1977) is an ordinary loss. Capital assets subject to section 1231 treatment include only capital assets involuntarily converted. The noncapital assets subject to section 1231 treatment are (1) depreciable business property and business real property held for more than 1 year (6 months for taxable years beginning before 1977; 9 months for taxable years beginning in 1977) other than stock in trade and certain copyrights and artistic property and, in the case of sales and other dispositions occurring after July 25, 1969, other than a letter, memorandum, or property similar to a letter or memorandum; (2) timber, coal, and iron ore, which do not otherwise meet the requirements of section 1231 but with respect to which section 631 applies; and (3) certain livestock and unharvested crops. See paragraph (c) of this section.

(b) Treatment of gains and losses. For the purpose of applying section 1231, a taxpayer must aggregate his recognized gains and losses from:

(1) The sale, exchange, or involuntary conversion of property used in the trade or business (as defined in section 1231(b)), and

(2) The involuntary conversion (but not sale or exchange) of capital assets held for more than 1 year (6 months for taxable years beginning before 1977; 9 months for taxable years beginning in 1977).

If the gains to which section 1231 applies exceed the losses to which the section applies, the gains and losses are treated as long-term capital gains and losses and are subject to the provisions of parts I and II (section 1201 and following), subchapter P, chapter 1 of the Code, relating to capital gains and losses. If the gains to which section 1231 applies do not exceed the losses to which the section applies, the gains and losses are treated as ordinary gains and losses. Therefore, in the latter case, a loss from the involuntary conversion of a capital asset held for more than 1 year (6 months for taxable years beginning before 1977; 9 months for taxable years beginning in 1977) is treated as an ordinary loss and is not subject to the limitation on capital losses in section 1211. The phrase "involuntary conversion" is defined in paragraph (e) of this section.

(c) Transactions to which section applies. Section 1231 applies to recognized gains and losses from the following:

(1) The sale, exchange, or involuntary conversion of property held for more than 1 year (6 months for taxable years beginning before 1977; 9 months for taxable years beginning in 1977) and used in the taxpayer's trade or business, which is either real property or is of a character subject to the allowance for depreciation under section 167 (even though fully depreciated), and which is not:

(i) Property of a kind which would properly be includible in the inventory of the taxpayer if on hand at the close of the taxable year, or property held by the taxpayer primarily for sale to customers in the ordinary course of business;

(ii) A copyright, a literary, musical, or artistic composition, or similar property, or (in the case of sales and other dispositions occurring after July 25, 1969) a letter, memorandum, or property similar to a letter or memorandum, held by a taxpayer described in section 1221(3); or

(iii) Livestock held for draft, breeding, dairy, or sporting purposes, except to the extent included under paragraph (4) of this paragraph, or poultry.

(2) The involuntary conversion of capital assets held for more than 1 year (6 months for taxable years beginning before 1977; 9 months for taxable years beginning in 1977).

(3) The cutting or disposal of timber, or the disposal of coal or iron ore, to the extent considered arising from a sale or exchange by reason of the provisions of section 631 and the regulations thereunder.

(4) The sale, exchange, or involuntary conversion of livestock if the requirements of § 1.1231–2 are met.

(5) The sale, exchange, or involuntary conversion of unharvested crops on land which is (i) used in the taxpayer's trade or business and held for more than 1 year (6 months for taxable years beginning before 1977; 9 months for taxable years beginning in 1977), and (ii) sold or exchanged at the same time and to the same person. See paragraph (f) of this section.

For purposes of section 1231, the phrase "property used in the trade or business" means property described in this paragraph (other than property described in subparagraph (2) of this paragraph). Notwithstanding any of the provisions of this paragraph, section 1231(a) does not apply to gains and losses under the circumstances described in paragraph (e)(2) or (3) of this section.

(d) Extent to which gains and losses are taken into account. All gains and losses to which section 1231 applies must be taken into account in determining whether and to what extent the gains exceed the losses. For the purpose of this computation, the provisions of section 1211 limiting the deduction of capital losses do not apply, and no losses are excluded by that section. With that exception, gains are included in the computations under section 1231 only to the extent that they are taken into account in computing gross income, and losses are included only to the extent that they are taken into account in computing taxable income. The following are examples of gains and losses not included in the computations under section 1231:

(1) Losses of a personal nature which are not deductible by reason of section 165(c) or (d), such as losses from the sale of property held for personal use;

(2) Losses which are not deductible under section 267 (relating to losses with respect to transactions between related taxpayers) or section 1091 (relating to losses from wash sales);

(3) Gain on the sale of property (to which section 1231 applies) reported for any taxable year on the installment method under section 453, except to the extent the gain is to be reported under section 453 for the taxable year; and

(4) Gains and losses which are not recognized under section 1002, such as those to which sections 1031 through 1036, relating to common nontaxable exchanges, apply.

(e) Involuntary conversion— (1) General rule. For purposes of section 1231, the terms "compulsory or involuntary conversion" and "involuntary conversion" of property mean the conversion of property into money or other property as a result of complete or partial destruction, theft or seizure, or an exercise of the power of requisition or condemnation, or the threat or imminence thereof. Losses upon the complete or partial destruction, theft, seizure, requisition, or condemnation of property are treated as losses upon an involuntary conversion whether or not there is a conversion of the property into other property or money and whether or not the property is uninsured, partially insured, or totally insured. For example, if a capital asset held for more than 1 year (6 months for taxable years beginning before 1977; 9 months for taxable years beginning in 1977), with an adjusted basis of $400, but not held for the production of income, is stolen, and the loss which is sustained in the taxable year 1956 is not compensated for by insurance or otherwise, section 1231 applies to the $400 loss. For certain exceptions to this subparagraph, see subparagraphs (2) and (3) of this paragraph.

* * *

(3) Exclusion of gains and losses from certain involuntary conversions. Notwithstanding the provisions of subparagraph (1) of this paragraph, if for any taxable year beginning after December 31, 1969, the recognized losses from the involuntary conversion as a result of fire, storm, shipwreck, or other casualty, or from theft, of any property used in the trade or business or of any capital asset held for more than 1 year (6 months for taxable years beginning before 1977; 9 months for taxable years beginning in 1977) exceed the recognized gains from the involuntary conversion of any such property as a result of fire, storm, shipwreck, or other casualty, or from theft, such gains and losses are not gains and losses to which section 1231 applies and shall not be taken into account in applying the provisions of this section. The net loss, in effect, will be treated as an ordinary loss. This subparagraph shall apply whether such property is uninsured, partially insured, or totally insured and, in the case of a capital asset held for more than 1 year (6 months for taxable years beginning before 1977; 9 months for taxable years beginning in 1977), whether the property is property used in the trade or business, property held for the production of income, or a personal asset.

* * *

§ 1.1233–1 Gains and losses from short sales.

(a) General. **(1)** For income tax purposes, a short sale is not deemed to be consummated until delivery of property to close the short sale. Whether the recognized gain or loss from a short sale is capital gain or loss or ordinary gain or loss depends upon whether the property so delivered constitutes a capital asset in the hands of the taxpayer.

(2) Thus, if a dealer in securities makes a short sale of X Corporation stock, ordinary gain or loss results on closing of the short sale if the stock used to close the short sale was stock which he held primarily for sale to customers in the ordinary course of his trade or business. If the stock used to close the short sale was a capital asset in his hands, or if the taxpayer in this example was not a dealer, a capital gain or loss would result.

(3) Generally, the period for which a taxpayer holds property delivered to close a short sale determines whether long-term or short-term capital gain or loss results.

(4) Thus, if a taxpayer makes a short sale of shares of stock and covers the short sale by purchasing and delivering shares which he held for not more than 1 year (6 months for taxable years beginning before 1977; 9 months for taxable years beginning in 1977), the recognized gain or loss would be considered short-term capital gain or loss. If the short sale is made through a broker and the broker borrows property to make a delivery, the short sale is not deemed to be consummated until the obligation of the seller created by the short sale is finally discharged by delivery of property to the broker to replace the property borrowed by the broker.

(5) For rules for determining the date of sale for purposes of applying under section 1091 the 61-day period applicable to a short sale of stock or securities at a loss, see paragraph (g) of § 1.1091–1.

(b) Hedging transactions. Under section 1233 (g), the provisions of section 1233 and this section shall not apply to any bona fide hedging transaction in commodity futures entered into by flour millers, producers of cloth, operators of grain elevators, etc., for the purpose of their business. Gain or loss from a short sale of commodity futures which does not qualify as a hedging transaction shall be considered gain or loss from the sale or exchange of a capital asset if the commodity future used to close the short sale constitutes a capital asset in the hands of the taxpayer as explained in paragraph (a) of this section.

(c) Special short sales—(1) General. Section 1233 provides rules as to the tax consequences of a short sale of property if gain or loss from the short sale is considered as gain or loss from the sale or exchange of a capital asset under section 1233(a) and paragraph (a) of this section and if, at the time of the short sale or on or before the date of the closing of the short sale, the taxpayer holds property substantially identical to that sold short. The term "property" is defined for purposes of such rules to include only stocks and securities (including stocks and securities dealt with on a "when issued" basis) and commodity futures, which are capital assets in the hands of the taxpayer. Certain restrictions on the application of the section to commodity futures are provided in section 1233(e) and paragraph (d)(2) of this section. Section 1233(f) contains special provisions governing the operation of rule (2) in subparagraph (2) of this paragraph in the case of a purchase and short sale of stock (as defined in subparagraph (3) qualifying as an arbitrage operation. See paragraph (f) of this section for detailed rules relating to arbitrage operations in stocks and securities.

(2) Treatment of special short sales. The first two rules, which are set forth in section 1233(b), are applicable whenever property substantially identical to that sold short has been held by the taxpayer on the date of the short sale for not more than 1 year (6 months for taxable years beginning before 1977; 9 months for taxable years beginning in 1977) (determined without regard to rule (2), contained in this subparagraph, relating to the holding period) or is acquired by him after the short sale and on or before the date of the closing thereof. These rules are:

Rule (1). Any gain upon the closing of such short sale shall be considered as a gain upon the sale or exchange of a capital asset held for not more than 1 year (6 months for taxable years beginning before 1977; 9 months for taxable years beginning in 1977) (notwithstanding the period of time any property used to close such short sale has been held); and

Rule (2). The holding period of such substantially identical property shall be considered to begin (notwithstanding the provisions of section 1223) on the date of the closing of such short sale or on the date of a sale, gift, or other disposition of such property, whichever date occurs first.

(3) Options to sell. For the purpose of rule (1) and rule (2) in subparagraph (2) of this paragraph, the acquisition of an option to sell property at a fixed price shall be considered a short sale, and the exercise or failure to exercise such option shall be considered as a closing of such short sale, except that any option to sell property at a fixed price acquired on or after August 17, 1954 (the day after enactment of the Internal Revenue Code of 1954), shall not be considered a short sale and the exercise or failure to exercise such option shall not be considered as the closing of a short sale provided that the option and property identified as intended to be used in its exercise are acquired on the same date. This exception shall not apply, if the option is exercised, unless it is exercised by the sale of the property so identified. In the case of any option not exercised which falls within this exception, the cost of such option shall be added to the basis of the property with which such option is identified. If the option itself does not specifically identify the property intended to be used in exercising the option, then the identification of such property shall be made by appropriate entries in the taxpayer's records within 15 days after the date such property is acquired or before November 17, 1956, whichever expiration date later occurs.

(4) Treatment of losses. The third rule, which is set forth in section 1233(d), is applicable whenever property substantially identical to that sold short has been held by the taxpayer on the date of the short sale for more than 1 year (6 months for taxable years beginning before 1977; 9 months for taxable years beginning in 1977). This rule is:

Rule (3). Any loss upon the closing of such short sale shall be considered as a loss upon the sale or exchange of a capital asset held for more than 1 year (6 months for taxable years beginning before 1977; 9 months for taxable years beginning in 1977), not withstanding the period of time any property used to close such short sale has been held. For the purpose of this rule, the acquisition of an option to sell property at a fixed price is not considered a short sale, and the exercise or failure to exercise such option is not considered as a closing of a short sale.

(5) Application of rules. Rules (1) and (3) contained in subparagraphs (2) and (4) of this paragraph do not apply to the gain or loss attributable to so much of the property sold short as exceeds in quantity the substantially identical property referred to in section 1233 (b) and (d), respectively. Except as otherwise provided in section 1233(f), rule (2) in subparagraph (2) of this paragraph applies to the substantially identical property referred to in section 1233(b) in the order of the dates of the acquisition of such property, but only to so much of such property as does not exceed the quantity sold short. If property substantially identical to that sold short has been held by the taxpayer on the date of the short sale for not more than 1 year (6 months for taxable years beginning before 1977; 9 months for taxable years beginning in 1977), or is acquired by him after the short sale and on or before the date of the closing thereof, and if property substantially identical to that sold short has been held by the taxpayer on the date of the short sale for more than 1 year (6 months for taxable years beginning before 1977; 9 months for taxable years beginning in 1977), all three rules are applicable.

(6) Examples. The following examples illustrate the application of these rules to short sales of stock in the case of a taxpayer who makes his return on the basis of the calendar year:

Example (1). A buys 100 shares of X stock at $10 per share on February 1, 1955, sells short 100 shares of X stock at $16 per share on July 1, 1955, and closes the short sale on August 2, 1955, by delivering the 100 shares of X stock purchased on February 1, 1955, to the lender of the stock used to effect the short sale. Since 100 shares of X stock had been held by A on the date of the short sale for not more than 6 months, the gain of $600 realized upon the closing of the short sale is, by application of rule (1) in subparagraph (2) of this paragraph, a short-term capital gain.

Example (2). A buys 100 shares of X stock at $10 per share on February 1, 1955, sells short 100 shares of X stock at $16 per share on July 1, 1955, closes the short sale on August 1, 1955, with 100 shares of X stock purchased on that date at $18 per share, and on August 2, 1955, sells at $18 per share the 100 shares of X stock purchased on February 1, 1955. The $200 loss sustained upon the closing of the short sale is a short-term capital loss to which section 1233(d) has no application. By application of rule (2) in subparagraph (2) of this paragraph, however, the holding period of the 100 shares of X stock purchased on February 1, 1955, and sold on August 2, 1955 is considered to begin on August 1, 1955, the date of the closing of the short sale. The $800 gain realized upon the sale of such stock is, therefore, a short-term capital gain.

* * *

§ 1.1234–1 Options to buy or sell.

(a) Sale or exchange— (1) Capital assets. Gain or loss from the sale or exchange of an option (or privilege) to buy or sell property which is (or if acquired would be) a capital asset in the hands of the taxpayer holding the option is considered as gain or loss from the sale or exchange of a capital asset (unless, under the provisions of subparagraph (2) of this paragraph, the gain or loss is subject to the provisions of section 1231). The period for which the taxpayer has held the option determines whether the capital gain or loss is short-term or long-term.

(2) Section 1231 transactions. Gain or loss from the sale or exchange of an option to buy or sell property is considered a gain or loss subject to the provisions of section 1231 if, had the sale or exchange been of the property subject to the option, held by the taxpayer for the length of time he held the option, the sale or exchange would have been subject to the provisions of section 1231.

(3) Other property. Gain or loss from the sale or exchange of an option to buy or sell property which is not (or if acquired would not be) a capital asset in the hands of the taxpayer holding the option is considered ordinary income or loss (unless under the provisions of subparagraph (2) of this paragraph, the gain or loss is subject to the provisions of section 1231).

(b) Failure to exercise option. If the holder of an option to buy or sell property incurs a loss on failure to exercise the option, the option is deemed to have been sold or exchanged on the date that it expired. Any such loss to the holder of an option is treated under the general rule provided in paragraph (a) of this section. In general, any gain to the grantor of an option arising from the failure of the holder to exercise it, and any gain or loss realized by the grantor of an option as a result of a closing transaction, such as repurchasing the option from the holder, is considered ordinary income or loss. However, for the treatment of gain or loss from a closing transaction with respect to or gain on the lapse of an option granted in stock, securities, commodities or commodity futures, see section 1234(b) and § 1.1234–3. For special rules for grantors of straddles applicable to certain options granted on or before September 1, 1976, see § 1.1234–2.

(c) Certain options to sell property at a fixed price. Section 1234 does not apply to a loss on the failure to exercise an option to sell property at a fixed price which is acquired on the same day on which the property identified as intended to be used in exercising the option is acquired. Such a loss is not recognized, but the cost of the option is added to the basis of the property with which it is identified. See section 1233(c) and the regulations thereunder.

(d) Dealers in options to buy or sell. Any gain or loss realized by a dealer in options from the sale or exchange or an option to buy or sell property is considered ordinary income or loss under paragraph (a)(3) of this section. A dealer in options to buy or sell property is considered a dealer in the property subject to the option.

(e) Other exceptions. Section 1234 does not apply to gain resulting from the sale or exchange of an option:

(1) To the extent that the gain is in the nature of compensation (see sections 61 and 421, and the regulations thereunder, relating to employee stock options);

(2) If the option is treated as section 306 stock (see section 306 and the regulations thereunder, relating to dispositions of certain stock);

(3) To the extent that the gain is a distribution of earnings or profits taxable as a dividend (see section 301 and the regulations thereunder, relating to distributions of property); or

(4) Acquired by the taxpayer before March 1, 1954, if in the hands of the taxpayer such option is a capital asset (whether or not the property to which the option relates is, or would be if acquired by the taxpayer, a capital asset in the hands of the taxpayer).

(f) Limitations on effect of section. Losses to which section 1234 applies are subject to the limitations on losses under sections 165(c) and 1211 when applicable. Section 1234 does not permit the deduction of any loss which is disallowed under any other provision of law. In addition, section 1234 does not apply to an option to lease property, but does apply to an option to buy or sell a lease. Thus, an option to obtain all the right, title, and interest of a lessee in leased property is subject to the provisions of section 1234, but an option to obtain a sublease from the lessee is not. Furthermore, if section 1234 applies to an option to buy or sell a lease, it is the character the lease itself, if acquired, would have in the hands of the taxpayer, and not the character of the property leased, which determines the treatment of gain or loss experienced by the taxpayer with respect to such an option.

(g) Examples. The rules set forth in this section may be illustrated by the following examples:

Example (1). A taxpayer is considering buying a new house for his residence and acquires an option to buy a certain house at a fixed price. Although the property goes up in value, the taxpayer decides he does not want the house for his residence and sells the option for more than he paid for it. The gain which taxpayer realized is a capital gain since the property, if acquired, would have been a capital asset in his hands.

Example (2). Assume the same facts as in example (1), except that the property goes down in value, and the taxpayer decides not to purchase the house. He sells the option at a loss. While this is a capital loss under section 1234, it is not a deductible loss because of the provisions of section 165(c).

Example (3). A dealer in industrial property acquires an option to buy an industrial site and fails to exercise the option. The loss is an ordinary loss since he would have held the property for sale to customers in the ordinary course of his trade or business if he had acquired it.

* * *

§ 1.1235–1 Sale or exchange of patents.

(a) General rule. Section 1235 provides that a transfer (other than by gift, inheritance, or devise) of all substantial rights to a patent, or of an undivided interest in all such rights to a patent, by a holder to a person other than a related person constitutes the sale or exchange of a capital asset held for more than 1 year (6 months for taxable years beginning before 1977; 9 months for taxable years beginning in 1977), whether or not payments therefor are:

(1) Payable periodically over a period generally coterminous with the transferee's use of the patent, or

(2) Contingent on the productivity, use, or disposition of the property transferred.

(b) Scope of section 1235. If a transfer is not one described in paragraph (a) of this section, section 1235 shall be disregarded in determining whether or not such transfer is the sale or exchange of a capital asset. For example, a transfer by a person other than a holder or a transfer by a holder to a related person is not governed by section 1235. The tax consequences of such transfers shall be determined under other provisions of the internal revenue laws.

(c) Special rules—(1) Payments for infringement. If section 1235 applies to the transfer of all substantial rights to a patent (or an undivided interest therein), amounts received in settlement of, or as the award of damages in, a suit for compensatory damages for infringement of the patent shall be considered payments attributable to a transfer to which section 1235 applies to the extent that such amounts relate to the interest transferred. For taxable years beginning before January 1, 1964, see section 1304, as in effect before such date, and § 1.1304A–1 for treatment of compensatory damages for patent infringement.

(2) Payments to an employee. Payments received by an employee as compensation for services rendered as an employee under an employment contract requiring the employee to transfer to the employer the rights to any invention by such employee are not attributable to a transfer to which section 1235 applies. However, whether payments received by an employee from his employer (under an employment contract or otherwise) are attributable to the transfer by the employee of all substantial rights to a patent (or an undivided interest therein) or are compensation for services rendered the employer by the employee is a question of fact. In determining which is the case, consideration shall be given not only to all the facts and circumstances of the employment relationship but also to whether the amount of such payments depends upon the production, sale, or use by, or the value to, the employer of the patent rights transferred by the employee. If it is determined that payments are attributable to the transfer of patent rights, and all other requirements under section 1235 are met, such payments shall be treated as proceeds derived from the sale of a patent.

(3) Successive transfers. The applicability of section 1235 to transfers of undivided interest in patents, or to successive transfers of such rights, shall be determined separately with respect to each transfer. For example, X, who is a holder, and Y, who is not a holder, transfer their respective two-thirds and one-third undivided interests in a patent to Z. Assume the transfer by X qualifies under section 1235 and that X in a later transfer acquires all the rights with respect to Y's interest, including the rights to payments from Z. One-third of all the payments thereafter received by X from Z are not attributable to a transfer to which section 1235 applies.

(d) Payor's treatment of payments in a transfer under section 1235. Payments made by the transferee of patent rights pursuant to a transfer satisfying the requirements of section 1235 are payments of the purchase price for the patent rights and are not the payment of royalties.

* * *

§ 1.1235–2 Definition of terms.

For the purposes of section 1235 and § 1.1235–1:

(a) Patent. The term "patent" means a patent granted under the provisions of title 35 of the United States Code, or any foreign patent granting rights generally similar to those under a United States patent. It is not necessary that the patent or patent application for the invention be in existence if the requirements of section 1235 are otherwise met.

(b) All substantial rights to a patent. (1) The term "all substantial rights to a patent" means all rights (whether or not then held by the grantor) which are of value at the time the rights to the patent (or an undivided interest therein) are transferred. The term "all substantial rights to a patent" does not include a grant of rights to a patent:

(i) Which is limited geographically within the country of issuance;

(ii) Which is limited in duration by the terms of the agreement to a period less than the remaining life of the patent;

(iii) Which grants rights to the grantee, in fields of use within trades or industries, which are less than all the rights covered by the patent, which exist and have value at the time of the grant; or

(iv) Which grants to the grantee less than all the claims or inventions covered by the patent which exist and have value at the time of the grant.

The circumstances of the whole transaction, rather than the particular terminology used in the instrument of transfer, shall be considered in determining whether or not all substantial rights to a patent are transferred in a transaction.

(2) Rights which are not considered substantial for purposes of section 1235 may be retained by the holder. Examples of such rights are:

(i) The retention by the transferor of legal title for the purpose of securing performance or payment by the transferee in a transaction involving transfer of an exclusive license to manufacture, use, and sell for the life of the patent;

(ii) The retention by the transferor of rights in the property which are not inconsistent with the passage of ownership, such as the retention of a security interest (such as a vendor's lien), or a reservation in the nature of a condition subsequent (such as a provision for forfeiture on account of nonperformance).

(3) Examples of rights which may or may not be substantial, depending upon the circumstances of the whole transaction in which rights to a patent are transferred, are:

(i) The retention by the transferor of an absolute right to prohibit sublicensing or subassignment by the transferee;

(ii) The failure to convey to the transferee the right to use or to sell the patent property.

(4) The retention of a right to terminate the transfer at will is the retention of a substantial right for the purposes of section 1235.

(c) Undivided interest. A person owns an "undivided interest" in all substantial rights to a patent when he owns the same fractional share of each and every substantial right to the patent. It does not include, for example, a right to the income from a patent, or a license limited geographically, or a license which covers some, but not all, of the valuable claims or uses covered by the patent. A transfer limited in duration by the terms of the instrument to a period less than the remaining life of the patent is not a transfer of an undivided interest in all substantial rights to a patent.

(d) Holder. **(1)** The term "holder" means any individual:

(i) Whose efforts created the patent property and who would qualify as the "original and first" inventor, or joint inventor, within the meaning of title 35 of the United States Code, or

(ii) Who has acquired his interest in the patent property in exchange for a consideration paid to the inventor in money or money's worth prior to the actual reduction of the invention to practice (see paragraph (e) of this section), provided that such individual was neither the employer of the inventor nor related to him (see paragraph (f) of this section). The requirement that such individual is neither the employer of the inventor nor related to him must be satisfied at the time when the substantive rights as to the interest to be acquired are determined, and at the time when the consideration in money or money's worth to be paid is definitely fixed. For example, if prior to the actual reduction to practice of an invention an individual who is neither the employer of the inventor nor related to him agrees to pay the inventor a sum of money definitely fixed as to amount in return for an undivided one-half interest in rights to a patent and at a later date, when such individual has become the employer of the inventor, he pays the definitely fixed sum of money pursuant to the earlier agreement, such individual will not be denied the status of a holder because of such employment relationship.

(2) Although a partnership cannot be a holder, each member of a partnership who is an individual may qualify as a holder as to his share of a patent owned by the partnership. For example, if an inventor who is a member of a partnership composed solely of individuals uses partnership property in the development of his invention with the understanding that the patent when issued will become partnership property, each of the inventor's partners during this period would qualify as a holder. If, in this example, the partnership were not composed solely of individuals, nevertheless, each of the individual partners' distributive shares of income attributable to the transfer of all substantial rights to the patent or an undivided interest therein, would be considered proceeds from the sale or exchange of a capital asset held for more than 1 year (6 months for taxable years beginning before 1977; 9 months for taxable years beginning in 1977).

(3) An individual may qualify as a holder whether or not he is in the business of making inventions or in the business of buying and selling patents.

(e) Actual reduction to practice. For the purposes of determining whether an individual is a holder under paragraph (d) of this section, the term "actual reduction to practice" has the same meaning as it does under section 102(g) of title 35 of the United States Code. Generally, an invention is reduced to actual practice when it has been tested and operated successfully under operating conditions. This may occur either before or after application for a patent but cannot occur later than the earliest time that commercial exploitation of the invention occurs.

(f) Related person. **(1)** The term "related person" means one whose relationship to another person at the time of the transfer is described in section 267 (b), except that the term does not include a brother or sister, whether of the whole or the half blood. Thus, if a holder transfers all his substantial rights to a patent to his brother or sister, or both, such transfer is not to a related person.

* * *

§ 1.1236–1 Dealers in securities.

(a) Capital gains. Section 1236(a) provides that gain realized by a dealer in securities from the sale or exchange of a security (as defined in paragraph (c) of this section) shall not be considered as gain from the sale or exchange of a capital asset unless:

(1) The security is, before the expiration of the thirtieth day after the date of its acquisition, clearly identified in the dealer's records as a security held for investment or,*

(2) The security is not held by the dealer primarily for sale to customers in the ordinary course of his trade or business at any time after the identification referred to in subparagraph (1) of this paragraph has been made.

Unless both of these requirements are met, the gain is considered as gain from the sale of assets held by the dealer primarily for sale to customers in the course of his business.

(b) Ordinary losses. Section 1236(b) provides that a loss sustained by a dealer in securities from the sale or exchange of a security shall not be considered a loss from the sale or exchange of property which is not a capital asset if at any time after November 19, 1951, the security has been clearly identified in the dealer's records as a security held for investment. Once a security has been identified after November 19, 1951, as being held by the dealer for investment, it shall retain that character for purposes of determining loss on its ultimate disposition, even though at the time of its disposition the dealer holds it primarily for sale to his customers in the ordinary course of his business. * * *

(c) Definitions— (1) Security. For the purposes of this section, the term "security" means any share of stock in any corporation, any certificate of stock or interest in any corporation, any note, bond, debenture, or other evidence of indebtedness, or any evidence of any interest in, or right to subscribe to or purchase, any of the foregoing.

(2) Dealer in securities. For definition of a "dealer in securities," see the regulations under section 471.

(d) Identification of security in dealer's records. **(1)** A security is clearly identified in the dealer's records as a security held for investment when there is an accounting separation of the security from other securities, as by making appropriate entries in the dealer's books of account to distinguish the security from inventories and to designate it as an investment and by (i) indicating with such entries, to the extent feasible, the individual serial number of, or other characteristic symbol imprinted upon, the individual security, or (ii) adopting any other method of identification satisfactory to the Commissioner.

* * *

§ 1.1237–1 Real property subdivided for sale.

(a) General rule— (1) Introductory. This section provides a special rule for determining whether the taxpayer holds real property primarily for sale to customers in the ordinary course of his business

*Editorial comment: The Regulations do not reflect the effect of the Deficit Reduction Act of 1984. See Sec. 1236(a)(1).

under section 1221(1). This rule is to permit taxpayers qualifying under it to sell real estate from a single tract held for investment without the income being treated as ordinary income merely because of subdividing the tract or of active efforts to sell it. The rule is not applicable to dealers in real estate or to corporations, except a corporation making such sales in a taxable year beginning after December 31, 1954, if such corporation qualifies under the provisions of paragraph (c)(5)(iv) of this section.

(2) When subdividing and selling activities are to be disregarded. When its conditions are met, section 1237 provides that if there is no other substantial evidence that a taxpayer holds real estate primarily for sale to customers in the ordinary course of his business, he shall not be considered a real estate dealer holding it primarily for sale merely because he has (i) subdivided the tract into lots (or parcels) and (ii) engaged in advertising, promotion, selling activities or the use of sales agents in connection with the sale of lots in such subdivision. Such subdividing and selling activities shall be disregarded in determining the purpose for which the taxpayer held real property sold from a subdivision whenever it is the only substantial evidence indicating that the taxpayer has ever held the real property sold primarily for sale to customers in the ordinary course of his business.

(3) When subdividing and selling activities are to be taken into account. When other substantial evidence tends to show that the taxpayer held real property for sale to customers in the ordinary course of his business, his activities in connection with the subdivision and sale of the property sold shall be taken into account in determining the purpose for which the taxpayer held both the subdivided property and any other real property. For example, such other evidence may consist of the taxpayer's selling activities in connection with other property in prior years during which he was engaged in subdividing or selling activities with respect to the subdivided tract, his intention in prior years (or at the time of acquiring the property subdivided) to hold the tract primarily for sale in his business, his subdivision of other tracts in the same year, his holding other real property for sale to customers in the same year, or his construction of a permanent real estate office which he could use in selling other real property. On the other hand, if the only evidence of the taxpayer's purpose in holding real property consisted of not more than one of the following, in the year in question, such fact would not be considered substantial other evidence:

(i) Holding a real estate dealer's license;

(ii) Selling other real property which was clearly investment property;

(iii) Acting as a salesman for a real estate dealer, but without any financial interest in the business; or

(iv) Mere ownership of other vacant real property without engaging in any selling activity whatsoever with respect to it.

If more than one of the above exists, the circumstances may or may not constitute substantial evidence that the taxpayer held real property for sale in his business, depending upon the particular facts in each case.

(4) Section 1237 not exclusive. (i) The rule in section 1237 is not exclusive in its application. Section 1237 has no application in determining whether or not real property is held by a taxpayer primarily for sale in his business if any requirement under the section is not met. Also, even though the conditions of section 1237 are met, the rules of section 1237 are not applicable if without regard to section 1237 the real property sold would not have been considered real property held primarily for sale to customers in the ordinary course of his business. Thus, the district director may at all times conclude from convincing evidence that the taxpayer held the real property solely as an investment. Furthermore, whether or not the conditions of section 1237 are met, the section has no application to losses realized upon the sale of realty from subdivided property.

(ii) If, owing solely to the application of section 1237, the real property sold is deemed not to have been held primarily for sale in the ordinary course of business, any gain realized upon such sale shall be treated as ordinary income to the extent provided in section 1237(b)(1) and (2) and paragraph (e) of this section. Any additional gain realized upon the sale shall be treated as gain arising from the sale of a capital asset or, if the circumstances so indicate, as gain arising from the sale of real property used in the trade or business as defined in section 1231(b)(1). For the relationship between sections 1237 and 1231, see paragraph (f) of this section.

(5) Principal conditions of qualification. Before section 1237 applies, the taxpayer must meet three basic conditions, more fully explained later: He cannot have held any part of the tract at any time previously for sale in the ordinary course of his business, nor in the year of sale held any other real estate for sale to customers; he cannot make substantial improvements on the tract which increase the value of the lot sold substantially; and he must have owned the property 5 years, unless he inherited it. However, the taxpayer may make certain improvements if they are necessary to make the property marketable if he elects neither to add their cost to the basis of the property, or of any other property, nor to deduct the cost as an expense, and he has held the property at least 10 years. If the requirements of section 1237 are met, gain (but not more than 5 percent of the selling price of each lot) shall be treated as ordinary income in and after the year in which the sixth lot or parcel is sold.

(b) Disqualification arising from holding real property primarily for sale—(1) General rule. Section 1237 does not apply to any transaction if the taxpayer either:

(i) Held the lot sold (or the tract of which it was a part) primarily for sale in the ordinary course of his business in a prior year, or

(ii) Holds other real property primarily for sale in the ordinary course of his business in the same year in which such lot is sold.

Where either of these elements is present, section 1237 shall be disregarded in determining the proper treatment of any gain arising from such sale.

(2) Method of applying general rule. For purposes of this paragraph, in determining whether the lot sold was held primarily for sale in the ordinary course of business in a prior year, the principles of section 1237 shall be applied, whether or not section 1237 was effective for such prior year, if the sale of the lot occurs after December 31, 1953, or, in the case of a corporation meeting the requirements of paragraph (c)(5)(iv) of this section, if the sale of the lot occurs in a taxable year beginning after December 31, 1954. Whether, on the other hand, the taxpayer holds other real property for sale in the ordinary course of his business in the same year such lot was sold shall be determined without regard to the application of section 1237 to such other real property.

(3) Attribution rules with respect to the holding of property. The taxpayer is considered as holding property which he owns individually, jointly, or as a member of a partnership. He is not generally considered as holding property owned by members of his family, an estate or trust, or a corporation. See, however, paragraph (c)(5)(iv)(c) of this section for an exception to this rule. The purpose for which a prior owner held the lot or tract, or his activities, are immaterial except to the extent they indicate the purpose for which the taxpayer has held the lot or tract. See paragraph (d) of this section for rules relating to the determination of the period for which the property is held. The principles of this subparagraph may be illustrated by the following example:

Example. A dealer in real property held a tract of land for sale to customers in the ordinary course of his business for 5 years. He then made a gift of it to his son. As a result of the operation of section 1223(2) the son will have held the property for the period of time required by section 1237. However, he will not qualify for the benefits of section 1237 because, there being no evidence to the contrary, the circumstances involved establish that the son holds the property for sale to customers, as did his father.

(c) Disqualification arising from substantial improvements—(1) General rule. Section 1237 will not apply if the taxpayer or certain others make improvements on the tract which are substantial and which substantially increase the value of the lot sold. Certain improvements are not substantial within the meaning of section 1237(a)(2) if they are necessary to make the lot marketable at the prevailing local price and meet the other conditions of section 1237(b)(3). See subparagraph (5) of this paragraph.

(2) Improvements made or deemed to be made by the taxpayer. Certain improvements made by the taxpayer or made under a contract of sale between the taxpayer and the buyer make section 1237 inapplicable.

(i) For the purposes of section 1237(a)(2) the taxpayer is deemed to have made any improvements on the tract while he held it which are made by:

(a) The taxpayer's whole or half brothers and sisters, spouse, ancestors and lineal descendants.

(b) A corporation controlled by the taxpayer. A corporation is controlled by the taxpayer if he controls, as the result of direct ownership, constructive ownership, or otherwise, more than 50 percent of the corporation's voting stock.

(c) A partnership of which the taxpayer was a member at the time the improvements were made.

(d) A lessee if the improvement takes the place of a payment of rental income. See section 109 and the regulations thereunder.

(e) A Federal, State, or local government, or political subdivision thereof, if the improvement results in an increase in the taxpayer's basis for the property, as it would, for example, from a special tax assessment for paving streets.

(ii) The principles of subdivision (i) of this subparagraph may be illustrated by the following example:

Example. A held a tract of land for 3 years during which he made substantial improvements thereon which substantially enhanced the value of every lot on the tract. A then made a gift of the tract to his son. The son made no further improvements on the tract but held it for 3 years and then sold several lots therefrom. The son is not entitled to the benefits of section 1237 since under section 1237(a)(2) he is deemed to have made the substantial improvements made by his father, and under section 1223(2) he is treated as having held the property for the period during which his father held it. Thus, the disqualifying improvements are deemed to have been made by the son while the tract was held by him. See paragraph (d) of this section for rules relating to the determination of the period for which the property is held.

(iii) The taxpayer is also charged with making any improvements made pursuant to a contract of sale entered into between the taxpayer and the buyer. Therefore, the buyer, as well as the taxpayer, may make improvements which prevent the application of section 1237.

(a) If a contract of sale obligates either the taxpayer or the buyer to make a substantial improvement which would substantially increase the value of the lot, the taxpayer may not claim the application of section 1237 unless the obligation to improve the lot ceases (for any reason other than that the improvement has been made) before or within the period, prescribed by section 6511, within which the taxpayer may file a claim for credit or refund of an overpayment of his tax on the gain from the sale of the lot. The following example illustrates this rule:

Example. In 1956, A sells several lots from a tract he has subdivided for sale. Section 1237 would apply to the sales of these lots except that in the contract of sale, A agreed to install sewers, hard surface roads, and other utilities which would increase the value of the lots substantially. If in 1957, instead of requiring the improvements, the buyer releases A from this obligation, A may then claim the application of section 1237 to the sale of lots in 1956 in computing his income tax for 1956, since the period of limitations in which A may file a claim for credit or refund of an overpayment of his 1956 income tax has not expired.

(b) An improvement is made pursuant to a contract if the contract imposes an obligation on either party to make the improvement, but not if the contract merely places restrictions on the improvements, if any, either party may make. The following example illustrates this rule:

Example. B sells several lots from a tract which he has subdivided. Each contract of sale prohibits the purchaser from building any structure on his lot except a personal residence costing $15,000 or more. Even if the purchasers build such residences, that does not preclude B from applying section 1237 to the sales of such lots, since the contracts did not obligate the purchasers to make any improvements.

(iv) Improvements made by a bona fide lessee (other than as rent) or by others not described in section 1237(a)(2) do not preclude the use of section 1237.

(3) When improvements substantially enhance the value of the lot sold. Before a substantial improvement will preclude the use of section 1237, it must substantially enhance the value of the lot sold.

(i) The increase in value to be considered is only the increase attributable to the improvement or improvements. Other changes in the market price of the lot, not arising from improvements made by the taxpayer, shall be disregarded. The difference between the value of the lot, including improvements, when the improvement has been completed and an appraisal of its value if unimproved at that time, will disclose the value added by the improvements.

(ii) Whether improvements have substantially increased the value of a lot depends upon the circumstances in each case. If improvements increase the value of a lot by 10 percent or less, such increase will not be considered as substantial, but if the value of the lot is increased by more than 10 percent, then all relevant factors must be considered to determine whether, under such circumstances, the increase is substantial.

(iii) Improvement may increase the value of some lots in a tract without equally affecting other lots in the same tract. Only the lots whose value was substantially increased are ineligible for application of the rule established by section 1237.

(4) When an improvement is substantial. To prevent the application of section 1237, the improvement itself must be substantial in character. Among the improvements considered substantial are shopping centers, other commercial or residential buildings, and the installation of hard surface roads or utilities such as sewers, water, gas, or electric lines. On the other hand a temporary structure used as a field office, surveying, filling, draining, leveling and clearing operations, and the construction of minimum all-weather access roads, including gravel roads where required by the climate, are not substantial improvements.

(5) Special rules relating to substantial improvements. Under certain conditions a taxpayer, including a corporation to which subdivision (iv) of this subparagraph applies, may obtain the benefits of section 1237 whether or not substantial improvements have been made. In addition, an individual taxpayer may, under certain circumstances elect to have substantial improvements treated as necessary and not substantial.

(i) When an improvement is not considered substantial. An improvement will not be considered substantial if all of the following conditions are met:

(a) The taxpayer has held the property for 10 years. The full 10-year period must elapse, whether or not the taxpayer inherited the property. Although the taxpayer must hold the property 10 years, he need not hold it for 10 years after subdividing it. See paragraph (d) of this section for rules relating to the determination of the period for which the property is held.

(b) The improvement consists of the building or installation of water, sewer, or drainage facilities (either surface, sub-surface, or both) or roads, including hard surface roads, curbs, and gutters.

(c) The district director with whom the tax-payer must file his return is satisfied that, without such improvement, the lot sold would not have brought the prevailing local price for similar building sites.

(d) The taxpayer elects, as provided in subdivision (iii) of this subparagraph, not to adjust the basis of the lot sold or any other property held by him for any part of the cost of such improvement attributable to such lot and not to deduct any part of such cost as an expense.

(ii) Meaning of "similar building site". A "similar building site" is any real property in the immediate vicinity whose size, terrain, and other characteristics are comparable to the taxpayer's property. For the purpose of determining whether a tract is marketable at the prevailing local price for similar building sites, the taxpayer shall furnish the district director with sufficient evidence to enable him to compare (a) the value of the taxpayer's property in an unimproved state with (b) the amount for which similar building sites, improved by the installation of water, sewer, or drainage facilities or roads, have recently been sold, reduced by the present cost of such improvements. Such comparison may be made and expressed in terms of dollars per square foot, dollars per acre, or dollars per front foot, or in any other suitable terms depending upon the practice generally followed by real estate dealers in the taxpayer's locality. The taxpayer shall also furnish evidence, where possible, of the best bona fide offer received for the tract or a lot thereof just before making the improvement, to assist the district director in determining the value of the tract or lot if it had been sold in its unimproved state. * * *

(d) Holding period required—(1) General rules. To apply section 1237, the taxpayer must either have inherited the lot sold or have held it for 5 years. Generally, the provisions of section 1223 are applicable in determining the period for which the taxpayer has held the property. The provisions of this subparagraph may be illustrated by the following examples:

Example (1). A held a tract of land for 3 years under circumstances otherwise qualifying for section 1237 treatment. He made a gift of the tract to B at a time when the fair market value of the tract exceeded A's basis for the tract. B held the tract for 2 more years under similar circumstances. B then sold 4 lots from the tract. B is entitled to the benefits of section 1237 since under section 1223(2) he held the lots for 5 years and all the other requirements of section 1237 are met.

Example (2). C purchased all the stock in a corporation in 1955. The corporation purchased an unimproved tract of land in 1957. In 1961 the corporation was liquidated under section 333 and C acquired the tract of land. For purposes of section 1237, C's holding period commenced on the date the corporation actually acquired the land in 1957 and not on the date C purchased the stock.

(2) Rules relating to property acquired upon death. If the taxpayer inherited the property there is no 5-year holding period required under section 1237. However, any holding period required by any other provision of the Code, such as section 1222, is nevertheless applicable. For purposes of section 1237, neither the survivor's one-half of community property, nor property acquired by survivorship in a joint tenancy, is property acquired by devise or inheritance. The holding period for the surviving joint tenant begins on the date the property was originally acquired.

(e) Tax consequences if section 1237 applies—(1) Introductory. Where there is no substantial evidence other than subdivision and related selling activities that real property is held for sale in the ordinary course of taxpayer's business and section 1237 applies, section 1237(b)(1) provides a special rule for computing taxable gain. For the relationship between sections 1237 and 1231, see paragraph (f) of this section.

(2) Characterization of gain and its relation to selling expenses. (i) When the taxpayer has sold less than 6 lots or parcels from the same tract up to the end of his taxable year, the entire gain will be capital gain. (Where the land is used in a trade or business, see paragraph (f) of this section.) In computing the number of lots or parcels sold, two or more contiguous lots sold to a single buyer in a single sale will be counted as only one parcel. The following example illustrates this rule:

Example. A meets all the conditions of section 1237 in subdividing and selling a single tract. In 1956 he sells 4 lots to B, C, D, and E. In the same year F buys 3 adjacent lots. Since A has sold only 5 lots or parcels from the tract, any gain A realizes on the sales will be capital gain.

(ii) If the taxpayer has sold the sixth lot or parcel from the same tract within the taxable year, then the amount, if any, by which 5 percent of the selling price of each lot exceeds the expenses incurred in connection with its sale or exchange, shall, to the extent it represents gain, be ordinary income. Any part of the gain not treated as ordinary income will be treated as capital gain. (Where the land is used in a trade or business, see paragraph (f) of this section.) Five percent of the selling price of each lot sold from the tract in the taxable year the sixth lot is sold and thereafter is, to the extent it represents gain, considered ordinary income. However, all expenses of sale of the lot are to be deducted first from the 5 percent of the gain which would otherwise be considered ordinary income, and any remainder of such expenses shall reduce the gain upon the sale or exchange which would otherwise be considered capital gain. Such expenses cannot be deducted as ordinary business expenses from other income. The 5-percent rule applies to all lots sold from the tract in the year the sixth lot or parcel is sold. Thus, if the taxpayer sells the first 6 lots of a single tract in one year, 5 percent of the selling price of each lot sold shall be treated as ordinary income and reduced by the selling expenses. On the other hand, if the taxpayer sells the first 3 lots of a single tract in 1955, and the next 3 lots in 1956, only the gain realized from the sales made in 1956 shall be so treated. For the effect of a 5-year interval between sales, see paragraph (g)(2) of this section. The operation of this subdivision may be illustrated by the following examples:

Example (1). Assume the selling price of the sixth lot of a tract is $10,000, the basis of the lot in the hands of the taxpayer is $5,000, and the expenses of sale are $750. The amount of gain realized by the taxpayer is $4,250, of which the amount of ordinary income attributable to the sale is zero, computed as follows:

Selling price		$10,000
Basis		5,000
Excess over basis		5,000
5 percent of selling price	$500	
Expenses of sale	750	
Amount of gain realized treated as ordinary income		0
Excess over basis		5,000
5 percent of selling price	500	
Excess of expenses over 5 percent of selling price	250	
		750
Amount of gain realized from sale of property not held for sale in ordinary course of business		4,250

Example (2). Assume the same facts as in Example (1), except that the expenses of sale of such sixth lot are $300. The amount of gain realized by the taxpayer is $4,700, of which the amount of ordinary income attributable to the sale is $200, computed as follows:

Selling price		$10,000
Basis		5,000
Excess over basis		5,000
5 percent of selling price	$500	
Expenses of sale	300	
Amount of gain realized treated as ordinary income		200
Excess over basis		5,000
5 percent of selling price	500	
Excess of expenses over 5 percent of selling price	0	
		500
Amount of gain realized from sale of property not held for sale in ordinary course of business		4,500

(iii) In the case of an exchange, the term "selling price" shall mean the fair market value of property received plus any sum of money received in exchange for the lot. See section 1031 for those exchanges in which no gain is recognized. For the purpose of subsections (b) and (c) of section 1237 and paragraphs (e) and (g) of this section, an exchange shall be treated as a sale or exchange whether or not gain or loss is recognized with respect to such exchange.

(f) Relationship of section 1237 and section 1231. Application of section 1237 to a sale of real property may, in some cases, result in the property being treated as real property used in the trade or business, as described in section 1231(b)(1). Thus, assuming section 1237 is otherwise applicable, if the lot sold would be considered property described in section 1231(b)(1) except for the fact that the taxpayer subdivided the tract of which it was a part, then evidence of such subdivision and connected sales activities shall be disregarded and the lot sold shall be considered real property used in the trade or business. Under such circumstances, any gain or loss realized from the sale shall be treated as gain or loss arising from the sale of real property used in the trade or business.

(g) Definition of "tract"—(1) Aggregation of properties. For the purposes of section 1237, the term "tract" means either (i) a single piece of real property or (ii) two or more pieces of real property if they were contiguous at any time while held by the taxpayer, or would have been contiguous but for the interposition of a road, street, railroad, stream, or similar property. Properties are contiguous if their boundaries meet at one or more points. The single piece of contiguous properties need not have been conveyed by a single deed. The taxpayer may have assembled them over a period of time and may hold them separately, jointly, or as a partner, or in any combination of such forms of ownership.

(2) When a subdivision will be considered a new tract. If the taxpayer sells or exchanges no lots from the tract for a period of 5 years after the sale or exchange of at least 1 lot in the tract, then the remainder of the tract shall be deemed a new tract for the purpose of counting the number of lots sold from the same tract under section 1237(b)(1). The pieces in the new tract need not be contiguous. The 5-year period is measured between the dates of the sales or exchanges.

* * *

§ 1.1239–1 Gain from sale or exchange of depreciable property between certain related taxpayers after October 4, 1976.

(a) In general. In the case of a sale or exchange of property, directly or indirectly, between related persons after October 4, 1976 (other than a sale or exchange made under a binding contract entered into on or before that date), any gain recognized by the transferor shall be treated as ordinary income if such property is, in the hands of the transferee, subject to the allowance for depreciation provided in section 167. This rule also applies to property which would be subject to the allowance for depreciation provided in section 167 except that the purchaser has elected a different form of deduction, such as those allowed under sections 169, 188, and 191.

(b) Related persons.* For purposes of paragraph (a) of this section, the term "related persons" means:

(1) A husband and wife,

(2) An individual and a corporation 80 percent or more in value of the outstanding stock of which is owned, directly or indirectly, by or for such individual, or

(3) Two or more corporations 80 percent or more in value of the outstanding stock of each of which is owned, directly or indirectly, by or for the same individual.

(c) Rules of construction—(1) Husband and wife. * * *

(2) Sales between commonly controlled corporations. In general, in the case of a sale or exchange of depreciable property between related corporations (within the meaning of paragraph (b)(3) of this section), gain which is treated as ordinary income by reason of this section shall be taxable to the transferor corporation rather than to a controlling shareholder. However, such gain shall be treated as ordinary income taxable to a controlling shareholder rather than the transferor corporation if the transferor corporation is used by a controlling shareholder as a mere conduit to make a sale to another controlled corporation, or the entity of the corporate transferor is otherwise properly disregarded for tax purposes. Sales between two or more corporations that are related within the meaning of paragraph (b)(3) of this section may also be subject to the rules of section 482 (relating to allocation of income between or among organizations, trades, or businesses which are commonly owned or controlled), and to rules requiring constructive dividend treatment to the controlling shareholder in appropriate circumstances.

(3) Relationship determination for transfers made after January 6, 1983—taxpayer and an 80-percent owned entity. For purposes of paragraph (b)(2) of this section with respect to transfers made after January 6, 1983—

(i) If the transferor is an entity, the transferee and such entity are related if the entity is an 80-percent owned entity with respect to such transferee either immediately before or immediately after the sale or exchange of depreciable property, and

(ii) If the transferor is not an entity, the transferee and such transferor are related if the transferee is an 80-percent owned entity with respect to such transferor immediately after the sale or exchange of depreciable property.

(4) Relationship determination for transfers made after January 6, 1983—two 80-percent owned entities. For purposes of paragraph (b)(3) of this section, with respect to transfers made after January 6, 1983, two entities are related if the same shareholder both owns 80 percent or more in value of the stock of the transferor before the sale or exchange of depreciable property and owns 80 percent or more in value of the stock of the transferee immediately after the sale or exchange of depreciable property.

*Editorial comment: The Regulations do not reflect the effect of the Tax Reform Act of 1986. See Sec. 1239(b) and (c).

(5) Ownership of stock. For purposes of determining the ownership of stock under this section, the constructive ownership rules of section 318 shall be applied, except that section 318(a)(2)(C) (relating to attribution of stock ownership from a corporation) and section 318(a)(3)(C) (relating to attribution of stock ownership to a corporation) shall be applied without regard to the 50-percent limitation contained therein. The application of the constructive ownership rules of section 318 to section 1239 is illustrated by the following examples:

Example (1). A, an individual, owns 79 percent of the stock (by value) of Corporation X, and a trust for A's children owns the remaining 21 percent of the stock. A's children are deemed to own the stock owned for their benefit by the trust in proportion to their actuarial interests in the trust (section 318(a)(2)(B)). A, in turn, constructively owns the stock so deemed to be owned by his children (section 318(a)(1)(A)(ii)). Thus, A is treated as owning all the stock of Corporation X, and any gain A recognizes from the sale of depreciable property to Corporation X is treated under section 1239 as ordinary income.

Example (2). Y Corporation owns 100 percent in value of the stock of Z Corporation. Y Corporation sells depreciable property at a gain to Z Corporation. P and his daughter, D, own 80 percent in value of the Y Corporation stock. Under the constructive ownership rules of section 318, as applied to section 1239, P and D are each considered to own the stock in Z Corporation owned by Y Corporation. Also, P and D are each considered to own the stock in Y Corporation owned by the other. As a result, both P and D constructively own 80 percent or more in value of the stock of both Y and Z Corporations. Thus, the sale between Y and Z is governed by section 1239 and produces ordinary income to Y.

§ 1.1241–1 Cancellation of lease or distributor's agreement.

(a) In general. Section 1241 provides that proceeds received by lessees or distributors from the cancellation of leases or of certain distributorship agreements are considered as amounts received in exchange therefor. Section 1241 applies to leases of both real and personal property. Distributorship agreements to which section 1241 applies are described in paragraph (c) of this section. Section 1241 has no application in determining whether or not a cancellation not qualifying under that section is a sale or exchange. Further, section 1241 has no application in determining whether or not a lease or a distributorship agreement is a capital asset, even though its cancellation qualifies as an exchange under section 1241.

(b) Definition of "cancellation". The term "cancellation" of a lease or a distributor's agreement, as used in section 1241, means a termination of all the contractual rights of a lessee or distributor with respect to particular premises or a particular distributorship, other than by the expiration of the lease or agreement in accordance with its terms. A payment made in good faith for a partial cancellation of a lease or a distributorship agreement is recognized as an amount received for cancellation under section 1241 if the cancellation relates to a severable economic unit, such as a portion of the premises covered by a lease, a reduction in the unexpired term of a lease or distributorship agreement, or a distributorship in one of several areas or of one of several products. Payments made for other modifications of leases or distributorship agreements, however, are not recognized as amounts received for cancellation under section 1241.

* * *

§ 1.1244(a)–1 Loss on small business stock treated as ordinary loss.

(a) In general. Subject to certain conditions and limitations, section 1244 provides that a loss on the sale or exchange (including a transaction treated as a sale or exchange, such as worthlessness) of "section 1244 stock" which would otherwise be treated as a loss from the sale or exchange of a capital asset shall be treated as a loss from the sale or exchange of an asset which is not a capital asset (referred to in this section and §§ 1.1244(b)–1 to 1.1244(e)–1, inclusive, as an "ordinary loss"). Such a loss shall be allowed as a deduction from gross income in arriving at adjusted gross income. The requirements that must be satisfied in order that stock may be considered section 1244 stock are described in §§ 1.1244(c)–1 and 1.1244(c)–2. These requirements relate to the stock itself and the corporation issuing such stock. In addition, the taxpayer who claims an ordinary loss deduction pursuant to section 1244 must satisfy the requirements of paragraph (b) of this section.

(b) Taxpayers entitled to ordinary loss. The allowance of an ordinary loss deduction for a loss of section 1244 stock is permitted only to the following two classes of taxpayers:

(1) An individual sustaining the loss to whom the stock was issued by a small business corporation, or

(2) An individual who is a partner in a partnership at the time the partnership acquired the stock in an issuance from a small business corporation and whose distributive share of partnership items reflects the loss sustained by the partnership. The ordinary loss deduction is limited to the lesser of the partner's distributive share at the time of the issuance of the stock or the partner's distributive share at the time

the loss is sustained. In order to claim a deduction under section 1244 the individual, or the partnership, sustaining the loss must have continuously held the stock from the date of issuance. A corporation, trust, or estate is not entitled to ordinary loss treatment under section 1244 regardless of how the stock was acquired. An individual who acquires stock from a shareholder by purchase, gift, devise, or in any other manner is not entitled to an ordinary loss under section 1244 with respect to this stock.

Thus, ordinary loss treatment is not available to a partner to whom the stock is distributed by the partnership. Stock acquired through an investment banking firm, or other person, participating in the sale of an issue may qualify for ordinary loss treatment only if the stock is not first issued to the firm or person. Thus, for example, if the firm acts as a selling agent for the issuing corporation the stock may qualify. On the other hand, stock purchased by an investment firm and subsequently resold does not qualify as section 1244 stock in the hands of the person acquiring the stock from the firm.

(c) Examples. The provisions of paragraph (b) of this section may be illustrated by the following examples:

Example (1). A and B, both individuals, and C, a trust, are equal partners in a partnership to which a small business corporation issues section 1244 stock. The partnership sells the stock at a loss. A's and B's distributive share of the loss may be treated as an ordinary loss pursuant to section 1244, but C's distributive share of the loss may not be so treated.

Example (2). The facts are the same as in example (1) except that the section 1244 stock is distributed by the partnership to partner A and he subsequently sells the stock at a loss. Section 1244 is not applicable to the loss since A did not acquire the stock by issuance from the small business corporation.

§ 1.1244(b)–1 Annual limitation.

(a) In general. Subsection (b) of section 1244 imposes a limitation on the aggregate amount of loss that for any taxable year may be treated as an ordinary loss by a taxpayer by reason of that section. In the case of a partnership, the limitation is determined separately as to each partner. Any amount of loss in excess of the applicable limitation is treated as loss from the sale or exchange of a capital asset.

(b) Amount of loss— (1) Taxable years beginning after December 31, 1978. For any taxable year beginning after December 31, 1978, the maximum amount that may be treated as an ordinary loss under section 1244 is:

(i) $50,000, or

(ii) $100,000, if a husband and wife file a joint return under section 6013. These limitations on the maximum amount of ordinary loss apply whether the loss or losses are sustained on pre-November 1978 stock (as defined in § 1.1244(c)–1(a)(1)), post-November 1978 stock (as defined in § 1.1244(c)–1 (a)(2)), or on any combination of pre-November 1978 stock and post-November 1978 stock. The limitation referred to in (ii) applies to a joint return whether the loss or losses are sustained by one or both spouses.

* * *

(4) Examples. The provisions of this section may be illustrated by the following examples:

* * *

Example (2). For the taxable year ending December 31, 1979, B, a married taxpayer who files a joint return, sustains a $90,000 loss on post-November 1978 stock in Corporation X. In the same taxable year, C, B's spouse, sustains a $25,000 loss on post-November 1978 stock in Corporation Y. Both losses qualify under section 1244. B and C's ordinary loss is limited to $100,000 under paragraph (b)(1)(ii). The remaining $15,000 of loss is treated as loss from the sale or exchange of a capital asset.

* * *

§ 1.1244(c)–1 Section 1244 stock defined.

(a) In general. For purposes of §§ 1.1244(a)–1 to 1.244(e)–1, inclusive:

(1) The term "pre-November 1978 stock" means stock issued after June 30, 1958, and on or before November 6, 1978.

(2) The term "post-November 1978 stock" means stock issued after November 6, 1978.

In order that stock may qualify as section 1244 stock, the requirements described in paragraphs (b) through (e) of this section must be satisfied. In addition, the requirements of paragraph (f) of this section must be satisfied in the case of pre-November 1978 stock. Whether these requirements have been met is determined at the time the stock is issued, except for the requirement in paragraph (e) of this section. Whether the requirement in paragraph (e) of this section, relating to gross receipts of the corporation, has been satisfied is determined at the time a loss is sustained. Therefore, at the time of issuance it cannot be said with certainty that stock will qualify for the benefits of section 1244.

(b) Common stock.* Only common stock, either voting or nonvoting, in a domestic corporation may qualify as section 1244 stock. * * *

(c) Small business corporation. At the time the stock is issued (or, in the case of pre-November 1978 stock, at the time of adoption of the plan described in paragraph (f)(1) of this section) the corporation must be a "small business corporation". See § 1.1244(c)–2 for the definition of a small business corporation.

(d) Issued for money or other property. (1) The stock must be issued to the taxpayer for money or other property transferred by the taxpayer to the corporation. However, stock issued in exchange for stock or securities, including stock or securities, of the issuing corporation, cannot qualify as section 1244 stock, except as provided in § 1.1244(d)–3, relating to certain cases where stock is issued in exchange for section 1244 stock. Stock issued for services rendered or to be rendered to, or for the benefit of, the issuing corporation does not qualify as section 1244 stock. Stock issued in consideration for cancellation of indebtedness of the corporation shall be considered issued in exchange for money or other property unless such indebtedness is evidenced by a security, or arises out of the performance of personal services.

(2) The following examples illustrate situations where stock fails to qualify as section 1244 stock as a result of the rules in subparagraph (1) of this paragraph:

Example (1). A taxpayer owns stock of Corporation X issued to him prior to July 1, 1958. Under a plan adopted in 1977, he exchanges his stock for a new issuance of stock of Corporation X. The stock received by the taxpayer in the exchange may not qualify as section 1244 stock even if the corporation has adopted a valid plan and is a small business corporation.

Example (2). A taxpayer owns stock in Corporation X. Corporation X merges into Corporation Y. In exchange for his stock, Corporation Y issues shares of its stock to the taxpayer. The stock in Corporation Y does not qualify as section 1244 stock even if the stock exchanged by the taxpayer did qualify.

Example (3). Corporation X transfers part of its business assets to Corporation Y, a new corporation, and all of the stock of Corporation Y is issued directly to the shareholders of Corporation X. Since the Corporation Y stock was not issued to the shareholders for a transfer by them of money or other property, none of the Corporation Y stock in the hands of the shareholders can qualify.

(e) Gross receipts. (1) (i) (a) Except as provided in subparagraph (2) of this paragraph, stock will not qualify under section 1244, if 50 percent or more of the gross receipts of the corporation, for the period consisting of the five most recent taxable years of the corporation ending before the date the loss on such stock is sustained by the shareholders, is derived from royalties, rents, dividends, interest, annuities, and sales or exchanges of stock or securities. If the corporation has not been in existence for five taxable years ending before such date, the percentage test referred to in the preceding sentence applies to the period of the taxable years ending before such date during which the corporation has been in existence; and if the loss is sustained during the first taxable year of the corporation such test applies to the period beginning with the first day of such taxable year and ending on the day before the loss is sustained. The test under this paragraph shall be made on the basis of total gross receipts, except that gross receipts from the sales or exchanges of stock or securities shall be taken into account only to the extent of gains therefrom. The term "gross receipts" as used in section 1244(c)(1)(C) is not synonymous with "gross income". Gross receipts means the total amount received or accrued under the method of accounting used by the corporation in computing its taxable income. Thus, the total amount of receipts is not reduced by returns and allowances, cost, or deductions. For example, gross receipts will include the total amount received or accrued during the corporation's taxable year from the sale or exchange (including a sale or exchange to which section 337 applies) of any kind of property, from investments, and for services rendered by the corporation. However, gross receipts does not include amounts received in nontaxable sales or exchanges (other than those to which section 337 applies), except to the extent that gain is recognized by the corporation, nor does that term include amounts received as a loan, as a repayment of a loan, as a contribution to capital, or on the issuance by the corporation of its own stock.

(b) The meaning of the term "gross receipts" as used in section 1244(c)(1)(C) may be further illustrated by the following examples:

Example (1). A corporation on the accrual method sells property (other than stock or securities) and receives payment partly in money and partly in the form of a note payable at a future

*Editorial comment: The Regulations do not reflect the effect of the Deficit Reduction Act of 1984 which repealed the common stock requirement. See Sec. 1244(c)(1).

time. The amount of the money and the face amount of the note would be considered gross receipts in the taxable year of the sale and would not be reduced by the adjusted basis of the property, the costs of sale, or any other amount.

Example (2). A corporation has a long-term contract as defined in paragraph (a) of § 1.451–3 with respect to which it reports income according to the percentage-of-completion method as described in paragraph (b)(1) of § 1.451–3. The portion of the gross contract price which corresponds to the percentage of the entire contract which has been completed during the taxable year shall be included in gross receipts for such year.

Example (3). A corporation which regularly sells personal property on the installment plan elects to report its taxable income from the sale of property (other than stock or securities) on the installment method in accordance with section 453. The installment payments actually received in a given taxable year of the corporation shall be included in gross receipts for such year.

(ii) The term "royalties" as used in subdivision (i) of this subparagraph means all royalties, including mineral, oil, and gas royalties (whether or not the aggregate amount of such royalties constitutes 50 percent or more of the gross income of the corporation for the taxable year), and amounts received for the privilege of using patents, copyrights, secret processes and formulas, good will, trademarks, trade brands, franchises, and other like property. The term "royalties" does not include amounts received upon the disposal of timber, coal, or domestic iron ore with a retained economic interest to which the special rules of section 631(b) and (c) apply or amounts received from the transfer of patent rights to which section 1235 applies. For the definition of "mineral, oil, or gas royalties", see paragraph (b)(11)(ii) and (iii) of § 1.543–1. For purposes of this subdivision, the gross amount of royalties shall not be reduced by any part of the cost of the rights under which they are received or by any amount allowable as a deduction in computing taxable income.

(iii) The term "rents" as used in subdivision (i) of this subparagraph means amounts received for the use of, or right to use, property (whether real or personal) of the corporation, whether or not such amounts constitute 50 percent or more of the gross income of the corporation for the taxable year. The term "rents" does not include payments for the use or occupancy of rooms or other space where significant services are also rendered to the occupant, such as for the use or occupancy of rooms or other quarters in hotels, boarding houses, or apartment houses furnishing hotel services, or in tourist homes, motor courts, or motels. Generally, services are considered rendered to the occupant if they are primarily for his convenience and are other than those usually or customarily rendered in connection with the rental of rooms or other space for occupancy only. The supplying of maid service, for example, constitutes such services; whereas the furnishing of heat and light, the cleaning of public entrances, exits, stairways, and lobbies, the collection of trash, etc., are not considered as services rendered to the occupant. Payments for the use or occupancy of entire private residences or living quarters in duplex or multiple housing units, of offices in an office building, etc., are generally "rents" under section 1244(c)(1)(C). Payments for the parking of automobiles ordinarily do not constitute rents. Payments for the warehousing of goods or for the use of personal property do not constitute rents if significant services are rendered in connection with such payments.

(iv) The term "dividends" as used in subdivision (i) of this subparagraph includes dividends as defined in section 316, amounts required to be included in gross income under section 551 (relating to foreign personal holding company income taxed to United States shareholders), and consent dividends determined as provided in section 565.

(v) The term "interest" as used in subdivision (i) of this subparagraph means any amounts received for the use of money (including tax-exempt interest).

(vi) The term "annuities" as used in subdivision (i) of this subparagraph means the entire amount received as an annuity under an annuity, endowment, or life insurance contract, regardless of whether only part of such amount would be includible in gross income under section 72.

(vii) For purposes of subdivision (i) of this subparagraph, gross receipts from the sales or exchanges of stock or securities are taken into account only to the extent of gains therefrom. Thus, the gross receipts from the sale of a particular share of stock will be the excess of the amount realized over the adjusted basis of such share. If the adjusted basis should equal or exceed the amount realized on the sale or exchange of a certain share of stock, bond, etc., there would be no gross receipts resulting from the sale of such security. Losses on sales or exchanges of stock or securities do not offset gains on the sales or exchanges of other stock or securities for purposes of computing gross receipts from such sales or exchanges. Gross receipts from the sale or exchange of stocks and securities include gains received from such sales or exchanges by a corporation even though such corporation is a regular dealer in stocks and securities. For the meaning of the term "stocks or securities", see paragraph (b)(5)(i) of § 1.543–1.

(2) The requirement of subparagraph (1) of this paragraph need not be satisfied if for the applicable period the aggregate amount of deductions allowed to the corporation exceeds the aggregate amount of its gross income. But for this purpose the deductions allowed by section 172, relating to the net operating loss deduction, and by sections 242, 243, 244, and 245, relating to certain special deductions for corporations, shall not be taken into account. Notwithstanding the provisions of this subparagraph and of subparagraph (1) of this paragraph, pursuant to the specific delegation of authority granted in section 1244(e) to prescribe such regulations as may be necessary to carry out the purposes of section 1244, ordinary loss treatment will not be available with respect to stock of a corporation which is not largely an operating company within the five most recent taxable years (or such lesser period as the corporation is in existence) ending before the date of the loss. Thus, for example, assume that a person who is not a dealer in real estate forms a corporation which issues stock to him which meets all the formal requirements of section 1244 stock. The corporation then acquires a piece of unimproved real estate which it holds as an investment. The property declines in value and the stockholder sells his stock at a loss. The loss does not qualify for ordinary loss treatment under section 1244 but must be treated as a capital loss.

(3) In applying subparagraphs (1) and (2) of this paragraph to a successor corporation in a reorganization described in section 368(a)(1)(F), such corporation shall be treated as the same corporation as its predecessor. See paragraph (d)(2) of § 1.1244(d)–3.

* * *

§ 1.1244(c)–2 Small business corporation defined.

(a) In general. A corporation is treated as a small business corporation if it is a domestic corporation that satisfies the requirements described in paragraph (b) or (c) of this section. The requirements of paragraph (b) of this section apply if a loss is sustained on post-November 1978 stock. The requirements of paragraph (c) of this section apply if a loss is sustained on pre-November 1978 stock. If losses are sustained on both pre-November 1978 stock and post-November 1978 stock in the same taxable year, the requirements of paragraph (b) of this section are applied to the corporation at the time of the issuance of the stock (as required by paragraph (b) in the case of a loss on post-November 1978 stock) in order to determine whether the loss on post-November 1978 stock qualifies as a section 1244 loss, and the requirements of paragraph (c) of this section are applied to the corporation at the time of the adoption of the plan (as required by paragraph (c) in the case of a loss on pre-November 1978 stock) in order to determine whether the loss on pre-November 1978 stock qualifies as a section 1244 loss. For definition of domestic corporation, see section 7701 (a)(4) and the regulations under that section.

(b) Post-November 1978 stock—(1) Amount received by corporation for stock. Capital receipts of a small business corporation may not exceed $1,000,000. For purposes of this paragraph the term "capital receipts" means the aggregate dollar amount received by the corporation for its stock, as a contribution to capital, and as paid-in surplus. If the $1,000,000 limitation is exceeded, the rules of subparagraph (2) of this paragraph (b) apply. In making these determinations, (i) property is taken into account at its adjusted basis to the corporation (for determining gain) as of the date received by the corporation, and (ii) this aggregate amount is reduced by the amount of any liability to which the property was subject and by the amount of any liability assumed by the corporation at the time the property was received. Capital receipts are not reduced by distributions to shareholders, even though the distributions may be capital distributions.

(2) Requirement of designation in event $1,000,000 limitation exceeded. (i) If capital receipts exceed $1,000,000, the corporation shall designate as section 1244 stock certain shares of post-November 1978 common stock issued for money or other property in the transitional year. For purposes of this paragraph, the term "transitional year" means the first taxable year in which capital receipts exceed $1,000,000 and in which the corporation issues stock. This designation shall be made in accordance with the rules of subdivision (iii) of this paragraph (b)(2). The amount received for designated stock shall not exceed $1,000,000 less amounts received—

(A) In exchange for stock in years prior to the transitional year;

(B) As contributions to capital in years prior to the transitional year; and

(C) As paid-in surplus in years prior to the transitional year.

(ii) Post-November 1978 common stock issued for money or other property before the transitional year qualifies as section 1244 stock without affirmative designation by the corporation. Post-November 1978 common stock issued after the transitional year does not qualify as section 1244 stock.

(iii) The corporation shall make the designation required by subdivision (i), of this paragraph (b)(2) not later than the 15th day of the third month following the close of the transitional year. However, in the case of post-November 1978 common stock issued on or before June 2, 1981 the corporation shall make the required designation by August 3, 1981 or by the 15th day of the 3rd month following the close of the transitional year, whichever is later. The designation shall be made by entering the numbers of the qualifying share certificates on the corporation's records. If the shares do not bear serial numbers or other identifying numbers or letters, or are not represented by share certificates, the corporation shall make an alternative designation in writing at the time of issuance, or, in the case of post-November 1978 common stock issued on or before June 2, 1981 by August 3, 1981. This alternative designation may be made in any manner sufficient to identify the shares qualifying for section 1244 treatment. If the corporation fails to make a designation by share certificate number or an alternative written designation as described, the rules of subparagraph (3) of this paragraph (b) apply.

* * *

§ 1.1244(d)–1 Contributions of property having basis in excess of value.

(a) In general. **(1)** Section 1244(d)(1)(A) provides a special rule which limits the amount of loss on section 1244 stock that may be treated as an ordinary loss. This rule applies only when section 1244 stock is issued by a corporation in exchange for property that, immediately before the exchange, has an adjusted basis (for determining loss) in excess of its fair market value. If section 1244 stock is issued in exchange for such property and the basis of such stock in the hands of the taxpayer is determined by reference to the basis of such property, then for purposes of section 1244, the basis of such stock shall be reduced by an amount equal to the excess, at the time of the exchange, of the adjusted basis of the property over its fair market value.

(2) The provisions of section 1244(d)(1)(A) do not affect the basis of stock for purposes other than section 1244. Such provisions are to be used only in determining the portion of the total loss sustained that may be treated as an ordinary loss pursuant to section 1244.

(b) Transfer of more than one item. If a taxpayer exchanges several items of property for stock in a single transaction so that the basis of the property transferred is allocated evenly among the shares of stock received, the computation under this section should be made by reference to the aggregate fair market value and the aggregate basis of the property transferred.

(c) Examples. The provisions of this section may be illustrated by the following examples:

Example (1). B transfers property with an adjusted basis of $1,000 and a fair market value of $250 to a corporation for 10 shares of section 1244 stock in an exchange that qualifies under section 351. The basis of B's stock is $1,000 ($100 per share), but, solely for purposes of section 1244, the total basis of the stock must be reduced by $750, the excess of the adjusted basis of the property exchanged over its fair market value. Thus, the basis of such stock for purposes of section 1244 is $250 and the basis of each share for such purposes is $25. If B sells his 10 shares for $250, he will recognize a loss of $750, all of which must be treated as a capital loss. If he sells the 10 shares for $200, then $50 of his total loss of $800 will be treated as an ordinary loss under section 1244, assuming the various requirements of such section are satisfied, and the remaining $750 will be a capital loss.

* * *

§ 1.1244(d)–2 Increases in basis of section 1244 stock.

(a) In general. If subsequent to the time of its issuance there is for any reason, including the operation of section 1376(a), an increase in the basis of section 1244 stock, such increase shall be treated as allocable to stock which is not section 1244 stock. Therefore, a loss on stock, the basis of which has been increased subsequent to its issuance, must be apportioned between the part that qualifies as section 1244 stock and the part that does not so qualify. Only the loss apportioned to the part that so qualifies may be treated as an ordinary loss pursuant to section 1244. The amount of loss apportioned to the part that qualifies is the amount which bears the same ratio to the total loss as the basis of the stock which is treated as allocated to section 1244 stock bears to the total basis of the stock.

(b) Example. The provisions of paragraph (a) of this section may be illustrated by the following example:

Example. For $10,000 a corporation issues 100 shares of section 1244 stock to X. X later contributes $2,000 to the capital of the corporation and this increases the total basis of his 100 shares to $12,000. Subsequently, he sells the 100 shares for $9,000. Of the $3,000 loss, $2,500 is allocated to the portion of the stock that qualifies as section 1244 stock ($10,000/$12,000 of $3,000), and the remaining $500 is allocated to the portion of the stock that does not so qualify. Therefore, to the extent of $2,500, the loss may be treated as an ordinary loss assuming the various requirements of section 1244 stock are satisfied. However, the remaining $500 loss must be treated as a capital loss.

§ 1.1244(d)–3 Stock dividends, recapitalizations, changes in name, etc.

(a) In general. Section 1244(c)(1) provides that stock may not qualify for the benefits of section 1244 unless it is issued to the taxpayer for money or other property not including stock or securities. However, section 1244(d)(2) authorizes exceptions to this rule. The exceptions may apply in three situations: (1) The receipt of a stock dividend; (2) the exchange of stock for stock pursuant to a reorganization described in section 368(a)(1)(E); and (3) the exchange of stock for stock pursuant to a reorganization described in section 368(a)(1)(F).

* * *

§ 1.1244(d)–4 Net operating loss deduction.

(a) General rule. For purpose of section 172, relating to the net operating loss deduction, any amount of loss that is treated as an ordinary loss under section 1244 (taking into account the annual dollar limitation of that section) shall be treated as attributable to the trade or business of the taxpayer. Therefore, this loss is allowable in determining the taxpayer's net operating loss for a taxable year and is not subject to the application of section 172(d)(4), relating to nonbusiness deductions. A taxpayer may deduct the maximum of ordinary loss permitted under section 1244(b) even though all or a portion of the taxpayer's net operating loss carryback or carryover for the taxable year was, when incurred, a loss on section 1244 stock.

(b) Example. The provisions of this section may be illustrated by the following example:

Example. A, a single individual, computes a net operating loss of $15,000 for 1980 in accordance with the rules of § 1.172–3, relating to net operating loss in case of a taxpayer other than a corporation. Included within A's computation of this net operating loss is a deduction arising under section 1244 for a loss on small business stock. A had no taxable income in 1977, 1978, or 1979. Assume that A can carry over the entire $15,000 loss under the rules of section 172. In 1981 A has gross income of $75,000 and again sustains a loss on section 1244 stock. The amount of A's 1981 loss on section 1244 stock is $50,000. A may deduct the full $50,000 as an ordinary loss under section 1244 and the full $15,000 as a net operating loss carryover in 1981.

* * *

§ 1.1245–1 General rule for treatment of gain from dispositions of certain depreciable property.

(a) General. (1) In general, section 1245(a)(1) provides that, upon a disposition of an item of section 1245 property, the amount by which the lower of (i) the "recomputed basis" of the property, or (ii) the amount realized on a sale, exchange, or involuntary conversion (or the fair market value of the property on any other disposition), exceeds the adjusted basis of the property shall be treated as gain from the sale or exchange of property which is neither a capital asset nor property described in section 1231 (that is, shall be recognized as ordinary income). The amount of such gain shall be determined separately for each item of section 1245 property. In general, the term "recomputed basis" means the adjusted basis of property plus all adjustments reflected in such adjusted basis on account of depreciation allowed or allowable for all periods after December 31, 1961. See section 1245(a) (2) and § 1.1245–2. Generally, the ordinary income treatment applies even though in the absence of section 1245 no gain would be recognized under the Code. For example, if a corporation distributes section 1245 property as a dividend, gain may be recognized as ordinary income to the corporation even though, in the absence of section 1245, section 311(a) would preclude any recognition of gain to the corporation. For the definition of "section 1245 property", see section 1245(a)(3) and § 1.1245–3. For exceptions and limitations to the application of section 1245(a)(1), see section 1245(b) and § 1.1245–4.

(2) Section 1245(a)(1) applies to dispositions of section 1245 property in taxable years beginning after December 31, 1962, except that:

(i) In respect of section 1245 property which is an elevator or escalator, section 1245(a)(1) applies to dispositions after December 31, 1963, and

(ii) In respect of section 1245 property which is livestock (described in subparagraph (4) of § 1.1245–3(a)), section 1245(a)(1) applies to dispositions made in taxable years beginning after December 31, 1969, and (iii) [reserved].

(3) For purposes of this section and §§ 1.1245–2 through 1.1245–6, the term "disposition" includes a sale in a sale-and-leaseback transaction and a transfer upon the foreclosure of a security interest, but such term does not include a mere transfer of title to a creditor upon creation of a security interest or to a debtor upon termination of a security interest. Thus, for example, a disposition occurs upon a sale of property pursuant to a conditional sales contract even though the seller retains legal title to the property for purposes of security but a disposition does not occur when the seller ultimately gives up his security interest following payment by the purchaser.

(4) For purposes of applying section 1245, the facts and circumstances of each disposition shall be considered in determining what is the appropriate item of section 1245 property. A taxpayer may treat any number of units of section 1245 property in any particular depreciation account (as defined in § 1.167 (a)–7) as one item of section 1245 property as long as it is reasonably clear, from the best estimates obtainable on the basis of all the facts and circumstances, that the amount of gain to which section 1245(a)(1) applies is not less than the total of the gain under section 1245(a)(1) which would be computed separately for each unit. Thus, for example, if 50 units of section 1245 property X, 25 units of section 1245 property Y, and other property are accounted for in one depreciation account, and if each such unit is sold at a gain in one transaction in which the total gain realized on the sale exceeds the sum of the adjustments reflected in the adjusted basis (as defined in paragraph (a)(2) of § 1.1245–2) of each such unit on account of depreciation allowed or allowable for periods after December 31, 1961, all 75 units may be treated as one item of section 1245 property. If, however, 5 such units of section 1245 property Y were sold at a loss, then only 70 of such units (50 of X plus the 20 of Y sold at a gain) may be treated as one item of section 1245 property.

(5) In case of a sale, exchange, or involuntary conversion of section 1245 and non-section 1245 property in one transaction, the total amount realized upon the disposition shall be allocated between the section 1245 property and the non-section 1245 property in proportion to their respective fair market values. In general, if a buyer and seller have adverse interests as to the allocation of the amount realized between the section 1245 property and the non-section 1245 property, any arm's length agreement between the buyer and the seller will establish the allocation. In the absence of such an agreement, the allocation shall be made by taking into account the appropriate facts and circumstances. Some of the facts and circumstances which shall be taken into account to the extent appropriate include, but are not limited to, a comparison between the section 1245 property and all the property disposed of in such transaction of (i) the original cost and reproduction cost of construction, erection, or production, (ii) the remaining economic useful life, (iii) state of obsolescence, and (iv) anticipated expenditures to maintain, renovate, or to modernize.

(b) Sale, exchange, or involuntary conversion.

(1) In the case of a sale, exchange, or involuntary conversion of section 1245 property, the gain to which section 1245(a)(1) applies is the amount by which (i) the lower of the amount realized upon the disposition of the property or the recomputed basis of the property, exceeds (ii) the adjusted basis of the property.

(2) The provisions of this paragraph may be illustrated by the following examples:

Example (1). On January 1, 1964, Brown purchases section 1245 property for use in his manufacturing business. The property has a basis for depreciation of $3,300. After taking depreciation deductions of $1,300 (the amount allowable), Brown realizes after selling expenses the amount of $2,900 upon sale of the property on January 1, 1969. Brown's gain is $900 ($2,900 amount realized minus $2,000 adjusted basis). Since the amount realized upon disposition of the property ($2,900) is lower than its recomputed basis ($3,300, i.e., $2,000 adjusted basis plus $1,300 in depreciation deductions), the entire gain is treated as ordinary income under section 1245(a)(1) and not as gain from the sale or exchange of property described in section 1231.

Example (2). Assume the same facts as in example (1) except that Brown exchanges the section 1245 property for land which has a fair market value of $3,700, thereby realizing a gain of $1,700 ($3,700 amount realized minus $2,000 adjusted basis). Since the recomputed basis of the property ($3,300) is lower than the amount realized upon its disposition ($3,700), the excess of recomputed basis over adjusted basis, or $1,300, is treated as ordinary income under section 1245(a)(l). The remaining $400 of the gain may be treated as gain from the sale or exchange of property described in section 1231.

(c) Other dispositions. (1) In the case of a disposition of section 1245 property other than by way of a sale, exchange, or involuntary conversion, the gain to which section 1245(a)(1) applies is the amount by which (i) the lower of the fair market value of the property on the date of disposition or the recomputed basis of the property, exceeds (ii) the adjusted basis of the property. If property is transferred by a corporation to a shareholder for an amount less than its fair market value in a sale or exchange, for purposes of applying section 1245 such transfer shall be treated as a disposition other than by way of a sale, exchange, or involuntary conversion.

(2) The provisions of this paragraph may be illustrated by the following examples:

Example (1). X Corporation distributes section 1245 property to its shareholders as a dividend. The property has an adjusted basis of $2,000 to the corporation, a recomputed basis of $3,300, and a fair market value of $3,100. Since the fair market value of the property ($3,100) is lower than its recomputed basis ($3,300), the excess of fair market value over adjusted basis, or $1,100, is treated under section 1245(a)(1) as ordinary income to the corporation even though, in the absence of section 1245, section 311(a) would preclude recognition of gain to the corporation.

Example (2). Assume the same facts as in example (1) except that X Corporation distributes the section 1245 property to its shareholders in complete liquidation of the corporation. Assume further that section 1245(b)(3) does not apply and that the fair market value of the property is $3,800 at the time of the distribution. Since the recomputed basis of the property ($3,300) is lower than its fair market value ($3,800), the excess of recomputed basis over adjusted basis, or $1,300, is treated under section 1245 (a)(1) as ordinary income to the corporation even though, in the absence of section 1245, section 336* would preclude recognition of gain to the corporation.

(d) Losses. Section 1245(a)(1) does not apply to losses. Thus, section 1245(a)(1) does not apply if a loss is realized upon a sale, exchange, or involuntary conversion of property, all of which is considered section 1245 property, nor does the section apply to a disposition of such property other than by way of sale, exchange, or involuntary conversion if at the time of the disposition the fair market value of such property is not greater than its adjusted basis.

(e) Treatment of partnership and partners. (1) The manner of determining the amount of gain recognized under section 1245(a)(1) to a partnership may be illustrated by the following example:

Example. A partnership sells for $63 section 1245 property which has an adjusted basis to the partnership of $30 and a recomputed basis to the partnership of $60. The partnership recognizes under section 1245(a)(1) gain of $30, i.e., the lower of the amount realized ($63) or recomputed basis ($60), minus adjusted basis ($30). This result would not be changed if one or more partners had, in respect of the property, a special basis adjustment described in section 743(b) or had taken depreciation deductions in respect of such special basis adjustment.

(2) (i) Unless subparagraph (e)(3) of this section applies, a partner's distributive share of gain recognized under section 1245(a)(1) by the partnership is equal to the lesser of the partner's share of total gain from the disposition of the property (gain limitation) or the partner's share of depreciation or amortization with respect to the property (as determined under paragraph (e)(2)(ii) of this section). Any gain recognized under section 1245(a)(1) by the partnership that is not allocated under the first sentence of this paragraph (e)(2)(i) (excess depreciation recapture) is allocated among the partners whose shares of total gain from the disposition of the property exceed their shares of depreciation or amortization with respect to the property. Excess depreciation recapture is allocated among those partners in proportion to their relative shares of the total gain (including gain recognized under section 1245(a)(l)) from the disposition of the property that is allocated to the partners who are not subject to the gain limitation. See Example 2 of paragraph (e)(2)(iii) of this section.

(ii) (A) Subject to the adjustments described in paragraphs (e)(2)(ii)(B) and (e)(2)(ii)(C) of this section, a partner's share of depreciation or amortization with respect to property equals the total amount of allowed or allowable depreciation or amortization previously allocated to that partner with respect to the property.

(B) If a partner transfers a partnership interest, a share of depreciation or amortization must be allocated to the transferee partner as it would have been allocated to the transferor partner. If the partner transfers a portion of the partnership interest, a share of depreciation or amortization proportionate to the interest transferred must be allocated to the transferee partner.

(C) (1) A partner's share of depreciation or amortization with respect to property contributed by the partner includes the amount of depreciation or amortization allowed or allowable to the partner for the period before the property is contributed.

* * *

§ 1.1245–2 Definition of recomputed basis.

(a) General rule— (1) Recomputed basis defined. The term "recomputed basis" means, with respect to any property, an amount equal to the sum of:

(i) The adjusted basis of the property, as defined in section 1011, plus

(ii) The amount of the adjustments reflected in the adjusted basis.

(2) Definition of adjustments reflected in adjusted basis. The term "adjustments reflected in the adjusted basis" means:

(i) With respect to any property other than property described in subdivision (ii), (iii), or (iv) of this subparagraph, the amount of the adjustments attributable to periods after December 31, 1961,

*Editorial comment: The Regulations do not include the change made to Sec. 336 by the Tax Reform Act of 1986.

(ii) With respect to an elevator or escalator, the amount of the adjustments attributable to periods after June 30, 1963,

(iii) With respect to livestock (described in subparagraph (4) of § 1.1245–3(a)), the amount of the adjustments attributable to periods after December 31, 1969, or

(iv) [Reserved]

which are reflected in the adjusted basis of such property on account of deductions allowed or allowable for depreciation or amortization (within the meaning of subparagraph (3) of this paragraph). For cases where the taxpayer can establish that the amount allowed for any period was less than the amount allowable, see subparagraph (7) of this paragraph. For determination of adjusted basis of property in a multiple asset account, see paragraph (c)(3) of § 1.167(a)–8.

(3) Meaning of "depreciation or amortization". (i) For purposes of subparagraph (2) of this paragraph, the term "depreciation or amortization" includes allowances (and amounts treated as allowances) for depreciation (or amortization in lieu thereof), * * *

(4) Adjustments of other taxpayers or in respect of other property. (i) For purposes of subparagraph (2) of this paragraph, the adjustments reflected in adjusted basis on account of depreciation or amortization which must be taken into account in determining recomputed basis are not limited to those adjustments on account of depreciation or amortization with respect to the property disposed of, nor are such adjustments limited to those on account of depreciation or amortization allowed or allowable to the taxpayer disposing of such property. Except as provided in subparagraph (7) of this paragraph, all such adjustments are taken into account, whether the deductions were allowed or allowable in respect of the same or other property and whether to the taxpayer or to any other person. For manner of determining the amount of adjustments reflected in the adjusted basis of property immediately after certain dispositions, see paragraph (c) of this section.

(ii) The provisions of this subparagraph may be illustrated by the following example:

Example. On January 1, 1966, Jones purchases machine X for use in his trade or business. The machine, which is section 1245 property, has a basis for depreciation of $10,000. After taking depreciation deductions of $2,000 (the amount allowable), Jones transfers the machine to his son as a gift on January 1, 1968. Since the exception for gifts in section 1245(b)(1) applies, Jones does not recognize gain under section 1245(a)(1). The son's adjusted basis for the machine is $8,000. On January 1, 1969, after taking a depreciation deduction of $1,000 (the amount allowable), the son exchanges machine X for machine Y in a like kind exchange described in section 1031. Since the exception for like kind exchanges in section 1245(b)(4) applies, the son does not recognize gain under section 1245(a)(1). The son's adjusted basis for machine Y is $7,000. In 1969, the son takes a depreciation deduction of $1,000 (the amount allowable) in respect of machine Y. The son sells machine Y on June 30, 1970. No depreciation was allowed or allowable for 1970, the year of the sale. The recomputed basis of machine Y on June 30, 1970, is determined in the following manner:

Adjusted basis		$6,000
Adjustments reflected in the adjusted basis:		
Depreciation deducted by Jones for 1966 and 1967 on machine X	2,000	
Depreciation deducted by son for 1968 on machine X	1,000	
Depreciation deducted by son for 1969 on machine Y	1,000	
Total adjustments reflected in the adjusted basis		$4,000
Recomputed basis		10,000

* * *

(7) Depreciation or amortization allowed or allowable. For purposes of determining recomputed basis, generally all adjustments (for periods after Dec. 31, 1961, or, in the case of property described in subparagraph (2)(ii), (iii), or (iv) of this paragraph, for periods after the applicable date) attributable to allowed or allowable depreciation or amortization must be taken into account. See section 1016(a)(2) and the regulations thereunder for the meaning of "allowed" and "allowable". However, if a taxpayer can establish by adequate records or other sufficient evidence that the amount allowed for depreciation or amortization for any period was less than the amount allowable for such period, the amount to be taken into account for such period shall be the amount allowed. No adjustment is to be made on account of the tax imposed by section 56 (relating to the minimum tax for tax preferences). See paragraph (b) of this section (relating to records to be kept and information to be filed). For example, assume that in the year 1967 it becomes necessary to determine the recomputed basis of property, the $500 adjusted basis of which reflects adjustments of $1,000 with respect to depreciation deductions allowable for periods after December 31, 1961. If the taxpayer can establish by adequate records or other sufficient evidence that he had been allowed deductions amounting to only $800 for the period, then in determining recomputed basis the amount added to adjusted basis with respect to the $1,000 adjustments to basis for the period will be only $800.

* * *

§ 1.1245–3 Definition of section 1245 property.

(a) In general. (1) The term "section 1245 property" means any property (other than livestock excluded by the effective date limitation in subparagraph (4) of this paragraph) which is or has been property of a character subject to the allowance for depreciation provided in section 167 and which is either:

(i) Personal property (within the meaning of paragraph (b) of this section),

(ii) Property described in section 1245(a)(3)(B) (see paragraph (c) of this section), or

(iii) An elevator or an escalator within the meaning of subparagraph (C) of section 48(a)(1) (relating to the definition of "section 38 property" for purposes of the investment credit), but without regard to the limitations in such subparagraph (C).

* * *

§ 1.1245–4 Exceptions and limitations.

(a) Exception for gifts—(1) General rule. Section 1245(b)(1) provides that no gain shall be recognized under section 1245(a)(1) upon a disposition by gift. For purposes of this paragraph, the term "gift" means, except to the extent that subparagraph (3) of this paragraph applies, a transfer of property which, in the hands of the transferee, has a basis determined under the provisions of section 1015(a) or (d) (relating to basis of property acquired by gifts). For reduction in amount of charitable contribution in case of a gift of section 1245 property, see section 170(e) and the regulations thereunder.

* * *

(b) Exception for transfers at death—(1) General rule. Section 1245(b)(2) provides that, except as provided in section 691 (relating to income in respect of a decedent), no gain shall be recognized under section 1245(a)(1) upon a transfer at death. For purposes of this paragraph, the term "transfer at death" means a transfer of property which, in the hands of the transferee, has a basis determined under the provisions of section 1014(a) (relating to basis of property acquired from a decedent) because of the death of the transferor. For recomputed basis of property acquired in a transfer at death, see paragraph (c)(1)(iv) of § 1.1245–2.

(2) Examples. The provisions of this paragraph may be illustrated by the following examples:

Example (1). Smith owns section 1245 property which, upon Smith's death, is inherited by his son. Since the property is described in section 1014(b)(1), its basis in the hands of the son is determined under the provisions of section 1014(a). Therefore, section 1245(a)(1) does not apply to the transfer at Smith's death.

* * *

(c) Limitation for certain tax-free transactions—(1) Limitation on amount of gain. Section 1245(b)(3) provides that upon a transfer of property described in subparagraph (2) of this paragraph, the amount of gain taken into account by the transferor under section 1245(a)(1) shall not exceed the amount of gain recognized to the transferor on the transfer (determined without regard to section 1245). For purposes of this subparagraph, in case of a transfer of both section 1245 property and non-section 1245 property in one transaction, the amount realized from the disposition of the section 1245 property (as determined under paragraph (a)(5) of § 1.1245–1) shall be deemed to consist of that portion of the fair market value of each property acquired which bears the same ratio to the fair market value of such acquired property as the amount realized from the disposition of the section 1245 property bears to the total amount realized. The preceding sentence shall be applied solely for purposes of computing the portion of the total gain (determined without regard to section 1245) which shall be recognized as ordinary income under section 1245(a)(1). For determination of the recomputed basis of the section 1245 property in the hands of the transferee, see paragraph (c)(2) of § 1.1245–2. Section 1245(b)(3) does not apply to a disposition of property to an organization (other than a cooperative described in section 521) which is exempt from the tax imposed by chapter 1 of the Code.

(2) Transfers covered. The transfers referred to in subparagraph (1) of this paragraph are transfers of property in which the basis of the property in the hands of the transferee is determined by reference to its basis in the hands of the transferor by reason of the application of any of the following provisions:

(i) Section 332 (relating to distributions in complete liquidation of an 80-percent-or-more controlled subsidiary corporation). See subparagraph (3) of this paragraph.

(ii) Section 351 (relating to transfer to a corporation controlled by transferor).

(iii) Section 361 (relating to exchanges pursuant to certain corporate reorganizations).

(iv) Section 371(a) (relating to exchanges pursuant to certain receivership and bankruptcy proceedings).*

(v) Section 374(a) (relating to exchanges pursuant to certain railroad reorganizations).*

(vi) Section 721 (relating to transfers to a partnership in exchange for a partnership interest).

(vii) Section 731 (relating to distributions by a partnership to a partner). For special carryover basis rule, see section 1245(b)(6)(A) and paragraph (f)(1) of this section.

(3) Complete liquidation of subsidiary. In the case of a distribution in complete liquidation of an 80-percent-or-more controlled subsidiary to which section 332 applies, the limitation provided in section 1245(b)(3) is confined to instances in which the basis of the property in the hands of the transferee is determined, under section 334(b)(1), by reference to its basis in the hands of the transferor. Thus, for example, the limitation of section 1245(b)(3) may apply in respect of a liquidating distribution of section 1245 property by an 80-percent-or-more controlled corporation to the parent corporation, but does not apply in respect of a liquidating distribution of section 1245 property to a minority shareholder. Section 1245(b)(3) does not apply to a liquidating distribution of property by an 80-percent-or-more controlled subsidiary to is parent if the parent's basis for the property is determined, under section 334(b)(2), by reference to its basis for the stock of the subsidiary.

(4) Examples. The provisions of this paragraph may be illustrated by the following examples:

Example (1). Section 1245 property, which is owned by Smith, has a fair market value of $10,000, a recomputed basis of $8,000, and an adjusted basis of $4,000. Smith transfers the property to a corporation in exchange for stock in the corporation worth $9,000 plus $1,000 in cash in a transaction qualifying under section 351. Without regard to section 1245, Smith would recognize $1,000 gain under section 351(b), and the corporation's basis for the property would be determined under section 362(a) by reference to its basis in the hands of Smith. Since the recomputed basis of the property disposed of ($8,000) is lower than the amount realized ($10,000), the excess of recomputed basis over adjusted basis ($4,000), or $4,000, would be treated as ordinary income under section 1245(a)(1) if the provisions of section 1245(b)(3) did not apply. However, section 1245(b)(3) limits the gain taken into account by Smith under section 1245(a)(1) to $1,000. If, instead, Smith transferred the property to the corporation solely in exchange for stock of the corporation worth $10,000, then, because of the application of section 1245(b)(3), Smith would not take any gain into account under section 1245(a)(1). If, however, Smith transferred the property to the corporation for stock worth $5,000 and $5,000 cash, only $4,000 of the $5,000 gain under section 351(b) would be treated as ordinary income under section 1245(a)(1).

Example (2). Assume the same facts as in example (1) except that Smith contributes the property to a new partnership in which he has a one-half interest. Since, without regard to section 1245, no gain would be recognized to Smith under section 721, and by reason of the application of section 721 the partnership's basis for the property would be determined under section 723 by reference to its basis in the hands of Smith, the application of section 1245(b)(3) results in no gain being taken into account by Smith under section 1245(a)(1).

Example (3). Assume the same facts as in example (2) except that the property is subject to a $9,000 mortgage. Since under section 752(b) (relating to decrease in partner's liabilities) Smith is treated as receiving a distribution in money of $4,500 (one-half of liability assumed by partnership), and since the basis of Smith's partnership interest is $4,000 (the adjusted basis of the contributed property), the $4,500 distribution results in his realizing $500 gain under section 731(a) (relating to distributions by a partnership), determined without regard to section 1245. Accordingly, the application of section 1245(b)(3) limits the gain taken into account by Smith under section 1245(a)(1) to $500.

(d) Limitation for like kind exchanges and involuntary conversions—(1) General rule. Section 1245(b)(4) provides that if property is disposed of and gain (determined without regard to section 1245) is not recognized in whole or in part under section 1031 (relating to like kind exchanges) or section 1033 (relating to involuntary conversions), then the amount of gain taken into account by the transferor under section 1245(a)(1) shall not exceed the sum of:

(i) The amount of gain recognized on such disposition (determined without regard to section 1245), plus

(ii) The fair market value of property acquired which is not section 1245 property and which is not taken into account under subdivision (i) of this subparagraph (that is, the fair market value of non-section 1245 property acquired which is qualifying

*Editorial comment: The Regulations do not reflect the repeal of Secs. 371 and 374 by the Revenue Reconciliation Act of 1990.

property under section 1031 or 1033, as the case may be).

(2) Examples. The provisions of subparagraph (1) of this paragraph may be illustrated by the following examples:

Example (1). Smith exchanges machine A for machine B in a like kind exchange as to which no gain is recognized under section 1031(a). Both machines are section 1245 property. No gain is recognized under section 1245(a)(1) because of the limitation contained in section 1245(b)(4). The result would be the same if machine A were involuntarily converted into machine B in a transaction as to which no gain is recognized under section 1033(a)(1).

* * *

§ 1.1245–5 Adjustments to basis.

In order to reflect gain recognized under section 1245(a)(1), the following adjustments to the basis of property shall be made:

(a) Property acquired in like kind exchange or involuntary conversion. (1) If property is acquired in a transaction to which section 1245(b)(4) applies, its basis shall be determined under the rules of section 1031(d) or 1033(c).

(2) The provisions of this paragraph may be illustrated by the following example:

Example. Jones exchanges property A, which is section 1245 property with an adjusted basis of $10,000, for property B, which has a fair market value of $9,000, and property C, which has a fair market value of $3,500, in a like kind exchange as to which no gain would be recognized under section 1031(a). Upon the exchange $2,500 gain is recognized under section 1245(a)(1), since property C is not section 1245 property. See section 1245(b)(4). Under the rules of section 1031(d), the basis of the properties received in the exchange is $12,500 (i.e., the basis of property transferred, $10,000, plus the amount of gain recognized, $2,500), of which the amount allocated to property C is $3,500 (the fair market value thereof), and the residue, $9,000, is allocated to property B.

* * *

§ 1.1245–6 Relation of section 1245 to other sections.

(a) General. The provisions of section 1245 apply notwithstanding any other provision of subtitle A of the Code. Thus, unless an exception or limitation under section 1245(b) applies, gain under section 1245(a)(1) is recognized notwithstanding any contrary nonrecognition provision or income characterizing provision. For example, since section 1245 overrides section 1231 (relating to property used in the trade or business), the gain recognized under section 1245(a)(1) upon a disposition will be treated as ordinary income and only the remaining gain, if any, from the disposition may be considered as gain from the sale or exchange of a capital asset if section 1231 is applicable. See example (2) of paragraph (b)(2) of § 1.1245–1. For effect of section 1245 on basis provisions of the Code, see § 1.1245–5.

(b) Nonrecognition sections overridden. The nonrecognition provisions of subtitle A of the Code which section 1245 overrides include, but are not limited to, sections 267(d), 311(a), 336,* 337, 501(a), 512(b)(5), and 1039. See section 1245(b) for the extent to which section 1245(a)(1) overrides sections 332, 351, 361, 371(a)**, 374(a)**, 721, 731, 1031, 1033, 1071, and 1081(b)(1) and (d)(1)(A). For limitation on amount of adjustments reflected in adjusted basis of property disposed of by an organization exempt from income taxes (within the meaning of section 501(a)), see paragraph (a)(8) of § 1.1245–2.

* * *

§ 1.1250–1 Gain from dispositions of certain depreciable realty.

(a) Dispositions after December 31, 1969—(1) Ordinary income. (i) In general, section 1250(a)(1) provides that, upon a disposition of an item of section 1250 property after December 31, 1969, the applicable percentage of the lower of:

(a) The additional depreciation (as defined in § 1.1250–2) attributable to periods after December 31, 1969 in respect of the property, or

(b) The excess of the amount realized on a sale, exchange, or involuntary conversion (or the fair market value of the property on any other disposition) over the adjusted basis of the property,

shall be treated as gain from the sale or exchange of property which is neither a capital asset nor property described in section 1231 (that is, shall be recognized as ordinary income). The amount of such gain shall be determined separately for each item

*Editorial comment: The Regulations do not include the change made to Sec. 336 by the Tax Reform Act of 1986.

**Editorial comment: The Regulations do not reflect the repeal of Secs. 371 and 374 by the Revenue Reconciliation Act of 1990.

(see subparagraph (2)(ii) of this paragraph) of section 1250 property. If the amount determined under (b) of this subdivision exceeds the amount determined under (a) of this subdivision, then such excess shall be treated as provided in subdivision (ii) of this subparagraph. For relation of section 1250 to other provisions, see paragraph (c) of this section.

(ii) If the amount determined under subdivision (i)(b) of this subparagraph exceeds the amount determined under subdivision (i)(a) of this subparagraph, then the applicable percentage of the lower of:

(a) The additional depreciation attributable to periods before January 1, 1970, or

(b) Such excess,

Shall also be recognized as ordinary income.

(iii) If gain would be recognized upon a disposition of an item of section 1250 property under subdivisions (i) and (ii) of this subparagraph, and if section 1250(d) applies, then the gain recognized shall be considered as recognized first under subdivision (i) of this subparagraph. (See example (3)(i) of paragraph (c)(4) of § 1.1250–3.)

(2) Meaning of terms. (i) For purposes of section 1250, the term "disposition" shall have the same meaning as in paragraph (a)(3) of § 1.1245–1. "Section 1250 property" is, in general, depreciable real property other than section 1245 property. See paragraph (e) of this section. See paragraph (d)(1) of this section for meaning of the term "applicable percentage." If, however, the property is considered to have two or more elements with separate periods (for example, because units thereof are placed in service on different dates, improvements are made to the property, or because of the application of paragraph (h) of § 1.1250–3), see the special rules of § 1.1250–5.

(ii) For purposes of applying section 1250, the facts and circumstances of each disposition shall be considered in determining what is the appropriate item of section 1250 property. In general, a building is an item of section 1250 property, but in an appropriate case more than one building may be treated as a single item. For example, if two or more buildings or structures on a single tract or parcel (or contiguous tracts or parcels) of land are operated as an integrated unit (as evidenced by their actual operation, management, financing, and accounting), they may be treated as a single item of section 1250 property. For the manner of determining whether an expenditure shall be treated as an addition to capital account of an item of section 1250 property or as a separate item of section 1250 property, see paragraph (d)(2)(iii) of § 1.1250–5.

(3) Sale, exchange, or involuntary conversion after December 31, 1969. (i) In the case of a disposition of section 1250 property by a sale, exchange, or involuntary conversion after December 31, 1969, the gain to which section 1250(a)(1) applies is the applicable percentage for the property (determined under paragraph (d)(1) of this section) multiplied by the lower of (a) the additional depreciation in respect of the property attributable to periods after December 31, 1969, or (b) the excess (referred to as "gain realized") of the amount realized over the adjusted basis of the property.

(ii) In addition to gain recognized under section 1250(a)(1) and subdivision (i) of this subparagraph, gain may also be recognized under section 1250(a)(2) and this subdivision if the gain realized exceeds the additional depreciation attributable to periods after December 31, 1969. In such a case, the amount of gain recognized under section 1250(a)(2) and this subdivision is the applicable percentage for the property (determined under paragraph (d)(2) of this section) multiplied by the lower of (a) the additional depreciation attributable to periods before January 1, 1970, or (b) the excess (referred to as "remaining gain") of the gain realized over the additional depreciation attributable to periods after December 31, 1969.

(iii) The provisions of this subparagraph may be illustrated by the following examples:

Example (1). Section 1250 property which has an adjusted basis of $500,000 is sold for $650,000 after December 31, 1969, and thus the gain realized is $150,000. At the time of the sale the additional depreciation in respect of the property attributable to periods after December 31, 1969, is $190,000 and the applicable percentage is 100 percent (paragraph (d)(1)(i)(e) of this section). Since the gain realized ($150,000), is lower than the additional depreciation ($190,000), the amount of gain recognized as ordinary income under section 1250(a)(1) is $150,000 (that is, 100 percent of $150,000). No gain is recognized under section 1250(a)(2).

Example (2). Section 1250 property which has an adjusted basis of $440,000 is sold for $500,000 on December 31, 1974, and thus the gain realized is $60,000. The property was acquired on March 31, 1966. At the time of the sale, the additional depreciation attributable to periods after December 31, 1969, is $20,000, and the additional depreciation attributable to periods before January 1, 1970, is $60,000. The property qualified as residential rental property for each taxable year ending after December 31, 1969, and the applicable percentage is 95 percent (paragraph (d)(1)(i)(c) of this section). The applicable percentage under paragraph (d)(2) of this section is 15 percent. Since the additional depreciation attributable to periods after December 31, 1969 ($20,000), is lower than the gain realized ($60,000), the amount of gain recognized as ordinary income under section 1250(a)(1) is $19,000 (that is, 95 percent of $20,000). In addition, gain is recognized under section 1250(a)(2) since there is remaining gain of $40,000 (that is, the gain realized ($60,000) minus the additional depreciation attributable to periods after December 31, 1969 ($20,000)). Since the remaining gain of $40,000 is lower than the additional depreciation attributable to periods before January 1, 1970 ($60,000), the amount of gain recognized as ordinary income under section 1250(a)(2) is $6,000 (that is, 15 percent of $40,000). The remaining $35,000 (that is, gain realized $60,000, minus gain recognized under section 1250(a), $25,000) of the gain may be treated as gain from the sale or exchange of property described in section 1231.

(4) Other dispositions after December 31, 1969. **(i)** In the case of a disposition of section 1250 property after December 31, 1969, other than by way of a sale, exchange, or involuntary conversion, the gain to which section 1250(a)(1) applies is the applicable percentage for the property (determined under paragraph (d)(1) of this section) multiplied by the lower of (a) the additional depreciation in respect of the property attributable to periods after December 31, 1969, or (b) the excess (referred to as "potential gain") of the fair market value of the property over its adjusted basis. In addition, if the potential gain exceeds the additional depreciation attributable to periods after December 31, 1969, then the gain to which section 1250(a)(2) applies is the applicable percentage for the property (determined under paragraph (d)(2) of this section) multiplied by the lower of (c) the additional depreciation attributable to periods before January 1, 1970, or (d) the excess (referred to as "remaining potential gain") of the potential gain over the additional depreciation attributable to periods after December 31, 1969. If property is transferred by a corporation to a shareholder for an amount less than its fair market value in a sale or exchange, for purposes of applying section 1250 such transfer shall be treated as a disposition other than by way of a sale, exchange, or involuntary conversion.

(ii) The provisions of this subparagraph may be illustrated by the following examples:

Example (1). Section 1250 property having an adjusted basis of $500,000 and a fair market value of $550,000 is distributed by a corporation to a stockholder in complete liquidation of the corporation after December 31, 1969, and thus the potential gain is $50,000. At the time of the liquidation, the additional depreciation for the property attributable to periods after December 31, 1969, is $80,000 and the applicable percentage is 100 percent (paragraph (d)(1)(i)(e) of this section). Since the potential gain of $50,000 is lower than the additional depreciation attributable to periods after December 31, 1969 ($80,000), the amount of gain recognized as ordinary income under section 1250(a)(1) is $50,000 (that is, 100 percent of $50,000) even though in the absence of section 1250, section 336 would preclude recognition of gain to the corporation.

Example (2). The facts are the same as in example (1) except that the fair market value of the property is $650,000, and thus the potential gain is $150,000. Since the additional depreciation attributable to periods after December 31, 1969 ($80,000), is lower than the potential gain of $150,000, the amount of gain recognized as ordinary income under section 1250(a)(l) is $80,000 (that is, 100 percent of $80,000). In addition, section 1250(a)(2) applies since there is remaining potential gain of $70,000, that is, potential gain ($150,000) minus additional depreciation attributable to periods after December 31, 1969 ($80,000). The additional depreciation attributable to periods before January 1, 1970, is $90,000 and the applicable percentage under paragraph (d)(2) of this section is 50 percent. Since the remaining potential gain of $70,000 is lower than the additional depreciation attributable to periods before January 1, 1970 ($90,000), the amount of gain recognized as ordinary income under section 1250(a)(2) is $35,000 (that is, 50 percent of $70,000). Thus under section 1250(a), $115,000 (that is, $80,000 under section 1250(a)(1), plus $35,000 under section 1250(a)(2)) is recognized as ordinary income, even though in the absence of section 1250, section 336* would preclude recognition of gain to the corporation.

(5) Instances of nonapplication. **(i)** Section 1250(a)(1) does not apply to losses. Thus, section 1250(a)(1) does not apply if a loss is realized upon a sale, exchange, or involuntary conversion of property, all of which is considered section 1250 property, nor does the section apply to a disposition of such property other than by way of sale, exchange, or involuntary conversion if at the time of the disposition the fair market value of such property is not greater than its adjusted basis.

(ii) In general, in the case of section 1250 property with a holding period under section 1223 of more than 1 year, section 1250(a)(1) does not apply if for periods after December 31, 1969, there are no "depreciation adjustments in excess of straight line" (as computed under section 1250(b) and paragraph (b) of § 1.1250–2).

(6) Allocation rules. **(i)** In the case of a sale, exchange, or involuntary conversion of section 1250 property and nonsection 1250 property in one transaction after December 31, 1969, the total amount realized upon the disposition shall be allocated between the section 1250 property and the other property in proportion to their respective fair market values. Such allocation shall be made in accordance with the principles set forth in paragraph (a)(5) of § 1.1245–1 (relating to allocation between section 1245 property and nonsection 1245 property).

(ii) If an item of section 1250 property has two (or more) applicable percentages because one subdivision of paragraph (d)(1)(i) of this section applies to one portion of the taxpayer's holding period (determined under § 1.1250–4) and another subdivision of such paragraph applies with respect to another such portion, then the gain realized on a sale, exchange, or involuntary conversion, or the potential gain in the case of any other disposition, shall be allocated to each such portion of the taxpayer's holding period after December 31, 1969, in the same proportion as the additional depreciation with respect to such item for such portion bears to the additional depreciation with respect to such item for the entire holding period after December 31, 1969.

* * *

(c) Relation of section 1250 to other provisions—(1) General. The provisions of section 1250 apply notwithstanding any other provision of subtitle A of the Code. See section 1250(i). Thus, unless an exception or limitation under section 1250(d) and § 1.1250–3 applies, gain under section 1250(a) is recognized notwithstanding any contrary nonrecognition provision or income characterizing provision. For example, since section 1250 overrides section 1231 (relating to property used in the trade or business), the gain recognized under section 1250 (a) upon a disposition will be treated as ordinary income and only the remaining gain, if any, from the disposition may be considered as gain from the sale or exchange of a capital asset if section 1231 is applicable. See the example in paragraph (b)(3)(ii) of this section.

(2) Nonrecognition sections overridden. The nonrecognition provisions of subtitle A of the Code which section 1250 overrides include, but are not limited to, sections 267(d), 311(a), 336,* 337, 501 (a), and 512(b)(5). See section 1250(d) for the extent to which section 1250(a) overrides sections 332, 351, 361, 371(a), ** 374(a), ** 721, 731, 1031, 1033, 1039, 1071, and 1081 (b)(1) and (d)(1)(A). For amount of additional depreciation in respect of property disposed of by an organization exempt from income taxes (within the meaning of section 501(a)), see paragraph (d)(6) of § 1.1250–2.

* * *

(4) Treatment of gain not recognized under section 1250. Section 1250 does not prevent gain which is not recognized under section 1250 from being considered as gain under another provision of the Code, such as, for example, section 1239 (relating to gain from sale of depreciable property between certain related persons). Thus, for example, if section 1250 property which has an adjusted basis of $10,000 is sold for $17,500 in a transaction to which section 1239 applies, and if $5,000 of the gain would be recognized under section 1250(a) then the remaining $2,500 of the gain would be treated as ordinary income under section 1239.

* * *

(d) Applicable percentage—(1) Definition for purposes of section 1250(a)(1). (i) For purposes of section 1250(a)(1), the term "applicable percentage" means—

(a) In the case of property disposed of pursuant to a written contract which was, on July 24, 1969, and at all times thereafter binding on the owner of the property, 100 percent minus 1 percentage point for each full month the property was held after the date on which the property was held 20 full months;

(b) In the case of property constructed, reconstructed, or acquired by the taxpayer before January 1, 1975, with respect to which a mortgage is insured under section 221(d)(3) or 236 of the National Housing Act, or housing is financed or assisted by direct loan or tax abatement under similar provisions of State or local laws, and with respect to which the owner is subject to the restrictions described in section 1039(b)(1)(B) (relating to approved dispositions of certain Government-assisted housing projects), 100 percent minus 1 percentage point for each full month of the taxpayer's holding period for the property (determined under § 1.1250–4) during which the property qualified under this sentence, beginning after the date on which the property so qualified for 20 full months.

(c) In the case of residential rental property (as defined in section 167(j)(2)(B)) other than that covered by (a) and (b) of this subdivision, 100 percent minus 1 percentage point for each full month of the taxpayer's holding period for the property (determined under § 1.1250–4) included within a taxable year for which the property qualified as residential rental property, beginning after the date on which the property so qualified for 100 full months.

*Editorial comment: The Regulations do not include the change made to Sec. 336 by the Tax Reform Act of 1986.

**Editorial comment: The Regulations do not reflect the repeal of Secs. 371 and 374 by the Revenue Reconciliation Act of 1990.

(d) In the case of property with respect to which a deduction was allowed under section 167(k) (relating to the depreciation of expenditures to rehabilitate low-income rental housing), 100 percent minus 1 percentage point for each full month of the taxpayer's holding period (determined under § 1.1250–4) beginning 100 full months after the date on which the property was placed in service.

(e) In the case of all other property, 100 percent.

The provisions of (a), (b), and (c) of this subdivision shall not apply with respect to additional depreciation described in section 1250(b)(4). If the taxpayer's holding period under § 1.1250–4 includes a period before January 1, 1970, such period shall be taken into account in applying each provision of this subdivision.

* * *

(3) Holding period. For purposes of this paragraph, the holding period of property shall be determined under the rules of § 1.1250–4, and not under the rules of section 1223, notwithstanding that the property was acquired on or before December 31, 1963. In the case of a disposition of section 1250 property which consists of 2 or more elements (within the meaning of paragraph (c) of § 1.1250–5), the holding period for each element shall be determined under the rules of paragraph (a)(2)(ii) of § 1.1250–5.

(4) Full month. For purposes of this paragraph, the term "full month" (or "full months") means the period beginning on a date in 1 month and terminating on the date before the corresponding date in the next succeeding month (or in another succeeding month), or, if a particular succeeding month does not have such a corresponding date, terminating on the last day of such particular succeeding month.

* * *

(e) Section 1250 property—(1) Definition. The term "section 1250 property" means any real property (other than section 1245 property, as defined in section 1245(a)(3) and § 1.1245–3) which is or has been property of a character subject to the allowance for depreciation provided in section 167. See section 1250(c).

(2) Character of property. For purposes of subparagraph (1) of this paragraph, the term "is or has been property of a character subject to the allowance for depreciation provided in section 167" shall have the same meaning as when used in paragraph (a)(1) and (3) of § 1.1245–3. Thus, if a father uses a house in his trade or business during a period after December 31, 1963, and then gives the house to his son as a gift for the son's personal use, the house is section 1250 property in the hands of the son. For exception to the application of section 1250 (a) upon disposition of a principal residence, see section 1250(d)(7).

(3) Real property. (i) For purposes of subparagraph (1) of this paragraph, the term "real property" means any property which is not personal property within the meaning of paragraph (b) of § 1.1245—3. The term section 1250 property includes three types of depreciable real property. The first type is intangible real property. For purposes of this paragraph, a leasehold of land or of section 1250 property is intangible real property, and accordingly such a leasehold is section 1250 property. However, a fee simple interest in land is not depreciable, and therefore is not section 1250 property. The second type is a building or its structural components within the meaning of paragraph (c) of § 1.1245–3. The third type is all other tangible real property except (a) "property described in section 1245(a)(3)(B)" as defined in paragraph (c)(1) of § 1.1245–3 (relating to property used as an integral part of a specified activity or as a specified facility), and (b) property described in section 1245(a)(3)(D). An elevator or escalator (within the meaning of section 1245(a)(3) (C)) is not section 1250 property.

* * *

§ 1.1250–3 Exceptions and limitations.

(a) Exception for gifts—(1) General rule. Section 1250(d)(l) provides that no gain shall be recognized under section 1250(a) upon a disposition by gift. For purposes of this paragraph, the term "gift" shall have the same meaning as in paragraph (a) of § 1.1245–4. For reduction in amount of charitable contribution in case of a gift of section 1250 property, see section 170(e) and paragraph (c) (3) of § 1.170–1.

(2) Disposition in part a sale or exchange and in part a gift. Where a disposition of property is in part a sale or exchange and in part a gift, the disposition shall be subject to the provisions of § 1.1250–1 and the gain to which section 1250(a) applies, shall be computed under that section.

(3) Treatment of property in hands of transferee. If property is disposed of in a transaction which is a gift:

(i) The additional depreciation for the property in the hands of the transferee immediately after the disposition shall be an amount equal to (a) the amount of the additional depreciation for the property in the hands of the transferor immediately before the disposition, minus (b) the amount of any gain (in case the disposition is in part a sale or exchange and in part a gift) which would have been taken into account under section 1250(a) by the transferor upon the disposition if the applicable percentage had been 100 percent.

(ii) For purposes of computing the applicable percentage, the holding period under section 1250(e)(2) of property received as a gift in the hands of the transferee includes the transferor's holding period,

(iii) In case of a disposition which is in part a sale or exchange and in part a gift, if the adjusted basis of the property in the hands of the transferee exceeds its adjusted basis immediately before the transfer, the excess is an addition to capital account under paragraph (d)(2)(ii) of § 1.1250–5 (relating to property with 2 or more elements), and

* * *

(b) Exception for transfers at death—(1) General rule. Section 1250(d)(2) provides that, except as provided in section 691 (relating to income in respect of a decedent), no gain shall be recognized under section 1250(a) upon a transfer at death. For purposes of this paragraph, the term "transfer at death" shall have the same meaning as in paragraph (b)of § 1.1245–4.

(2) Treatment of transferee. (i) If as of the date a person acquires property from a decedent such person's basis is determined, by reason of the application of section 1014(a), solely by reference to the fair market value of the property on the date of the decedent's death or on the applicable date provided in section 2032 (relating to alternate valuation date), then (a) on the date of death the additional depreciation for the property is zero, and (b) for purposes of computing applicable percentage the holding period of the property under section 1250 (e)(1)(A) is deemed to begin on the day after the date of death.

(ii) If property is acquired in a transfer at death to which section 1250(d)(2) applies, the amount of the additional depreciation for the property in the hands of the transferee immediately after the transfer shall be the amount (if any) of the additional depreciation in respect of the property allowed the transferee before the decedent's death, but only to the extent that the basis of the property (determined under section 1014(a)) is required to be reduced under the second sentence of section 1014(b)(9) (relating to adjustments to basis where property is acquired from a decedent prior to his death) by depreciation adjustments referred to in paragraph (d)(1) of § 1.1250–2 which give rise to such additional depreciation. For treatment of such property as having a special element with additional depreciation so computed, see paragraph (c)(5)(i) of § 1.1250–5 (relating to property with two or more elements). For purposes of determining applicable percentage, such special element shall have a holding period which includes the transferee's holding period for such property for the period before the decedent's death.

* * *

(c) Limitation for certain tax-free transactions—(1) General. Section 1250(d)(3) provides that upon a transfer of property described in subparagraph (2) of this paragraph, the amount of gain taken into account by the transferor under section 1250(a) shall not exceed the amount of gain recognized to the transferor on the transfer (determined without regard to section 1250). For purposes of this subparagraph, in case of a transfer of both section 1250 property and nonsection 1250 property in one transaction, the amount realized from the disposition of the section 1250 property shall be deemed to consist of that portion of the fair market value of each property acquired which bears the same ratio to the fair market value of such acquired property as the amount realized from the disposition of the section 1250 property bears to the total amount realized. The preceding sentence shall be applied solely for purposes of computing the portion of the total gain (determined without regard to section 1250) which shall be recognized as ordinary income under section 1250(a). Section 1250(d)(3) does not apply to a disposition of property to an organization (other than a cooperative described in section 521) which is exempt from the tax imposed by chapter 1 of the Code.

(2) Transfers covered. The transfers described in this subparagraph are transfers of property in which the basis of the property in the hands of the transferee is determined by reference to its basis in the hands of the transferor by reason of the application of any of the following provisions:

(i) Section 332 (relating to distributions in complete liquidation of an 80 percent or more controlled subsidiary corporation). For application of section 1250(d)(3) to such a complete liquidation, the principles of paragraph (c)(3) of § 1.1245–4 shall apply.

(ii) Section 351 (relating to transfer to a corporation controlled by transferor).

(iii) Section 361 (relating to exchanges pursuant to certain corporate reorganizations).

* * *

(vi) Section 721 (relating to transfers to a partnership in exchange for a partnership interest).

(vii) Section 731 (relating to distributions by a partnership to a partner). For special carryover basis rule, see section 1250(d)(6)(A) and paragraph (f)(1) of this section.

(3) Treatment of property in hands of transferee. In the case of a transfer described in subparagraph (2) (other than subdivision (vii) thereof) of this paragraph—

(i) The additional depreciation for the property in the hands of the transferee immediately after the disposition shall be an amount equal to (a) the amount of the additional depreciation for the property in the hands of the transferor immediately before the disposition, minus (b) the amount of additional depreciation necessary to produce an amount equal to the gain taken into account under section 1250(a) by the transferor upon the disposition (taking into account the applicable percentage for the property),

(ii) For purposes of computing applicable percentage, the holding period under section 1250(e)(2) of the property in the hands of the transferee includes the transferor's holding period,

(iii) If the adjusted basis of the property in the hands of the transferee exceeds its adjusted basis immediately before the transferee, the excess is an addition to capital account under paragraph (d)(2)(ii) of § 1.1250–5 (relating to property with 2 or more elements), and

(iv) If the property disposed of consists of 2 or more elements within the meaning of paragraph (c) of § 1.1250–5, see paragraph (e)(1) of § 1.1250–5 for the amount of additional depreciation and the holding period for each element in the hands of the transferee.

* * *

(d) Limitation for like kind exchanges and involuntary conversions—(1) Limitation on gain.

(i) Under section 1250(d)(4)(A), if property is disposed of and gain (determined without regard to section 1250) is not recognized in whole or in part under section 1031 (relating to like kind exchanges) or section 1033 (relating to involuntary conversions), then the amount of gain taken into account by the transferor under section 1250(a) shall not exceed the greater of the two limitations set forth in subdivisions (ii) and (iii) of this subparagraph. Immediately after the transfer the basis of the acquired property shall be determined under subparagraph (2), (3), or (4) (whichever is applicable) of this paragraph, and its additional depreciation shall be computed under subparagraph (5) of this paragraph. The holding period of the acquired property for purposes of computing applicable percentage, which is determined under section 1250(e)(1), does not include the holding period of the property disposed of. In the case of a disposition of section 1250 property and other property in one transaction, see subparagraph (6) of this paragraph. In case of a disposition described in section 1250(d)(4)(A) of a portion of this item of property, see subparagraph (7) of this paragraph.

(ii) For purposes of this subparagraph, the first limitation is the sum of:

(a) The amount of gain recognized on the disposition under section 1031 or 1033 (determined without regard to section 1250), plus

(b) An amount equal to the cost of any stock purchased in a corporation which (without regard to section 1250) would result in nonrecognition of gain under section 1033(a)(3)(A).

(iii) For purposes of this subparagraph, the second limitation is the excess (if any) of:

(a) The amount of gain which would (without regard to section 1250(d)(4)) be taken into account under section 1250(a), over

(b) The fair market value (or cost in the case of a transaction described in section 1033(a)(3)) of the section 1250 property acquired in the transaction.

* * *

(2) Basis of property purchased upon involuntary conversion into money.

(i) If section 1250 property is purchased in a compulsory or involuntary conversion to which section 1033(a)(3) applies, and if by reason of the application of section 1250(d) (4)(A) all or part of the gain computed under section 1250(a) is not taken into account, then the basis of the section 1250 property and other purchased property shall be determined under the rules prescribed in this subparagraph. See section 1250(d) (4)(D).

(ii) The total basis of all purchased property, the acquisition of which results in the nonrecognition of any part of the gain realized upon the transaction, shall be (a) its cost, reduced by (b) the portion of the total gain realized which was not recognized. To the extent that section 1250(d)(4)(A)(i) prevents the purchase of stock from resulting in nonrecognition of gain, the basis of purchased stock is its cost.

(iii) If purchased property consists of both section 1250 property and other property, the total basis computed under subdivision (ii) of this subparagraph shall be allocated between the section 1250 property (treated as a class) and the other property (treated as a class) in proportion to their respective costs, except that for purposes of this subdivision (but not subdivision (iv) of this subparagraph) the cost of the section 1250 property shall be deemed to be the excess of (a) its actual cost, over (b) the gain not taken into account under section 1250(a) by reason of the application of section 1250(d)(4)(A).

* * *

(3) Basis of property acquired upon involuntary conversion into similar property. If property is involuntarily converted into property similar or related in service or use in a transaction to which section 1033(a)(1) applies, and if by reason of the application of section 1250(d)(4)(A) all or part of the gain computed under section 1250(a) is not taken into account, then:

(i) The total basis of the acquired property shall be determined under the first sentence of section 1033(c), and

* * *

(4) Basis of property acquired in like kind exchange. If section 1250 property is transferred in an exchange described in section 1031(a) or (b), and if by reason of the application of section 1250(d)(4)(A) all or part of the gain computed under section 1250(a) is not taken into account, then:

(i) The total basis of the property (including non-section 1250 property) acquired of the type permitted to be received under section 1031 without recognition of gain or loss shall be determined under section 1031(d), and

* * *

(5) Additional depreciation for property acquired in like kind exchange or involuntary conversion. (i) If property is disposed of in a transaction described in section 1031 or 1033, and if by reason of the application of section 1250(d)(4)(A) all or part of the gain computed under section 1250(a) is not taken into account, then the additional depreciation for the acquired property immediately after the transaction (as computed under section 1250(d)(4)(E)) shall be an amount equal to the amount of gain computed under section 1250(a) which was not taken into account by reason of the application of section 1250(d)(4)(A).

* * *

§ 1.1250–4 Holding period.

(a) General. In general, for purposes only of determining the applicable percentage (as defined in sec. 1250(1)(C) and (2)(B)) of section 1250 property, the holding period of the property shall be determined under the rules of section 1250(e) and this section and not under the rules of section 1223. If the property is treated as consisting of two or more elements (within the meaning of paragraph (c)(1) of § 1.1250–5), see paragraph (a)(2)(ii) of § 1.1250–5 for application of this section to determination of holding period of each element. Section 1250(e) does not affect the determination of the amount of additional depreciation in respect of section 1250 property.

(b) Beginning of holding period. (1) For the purpose of determining the applicable percentage, in the case of property acquired by the taxpayer (other than by means of a transaction referred to in paragraph (c) or (d) of this section), the holding period of the property shall begin on the day after the date of its acquisition. See section 1250(e)(1)(A). Thus, for example, if a taxpayer purchases section 1250 property on January 1, 1965, the holding period of the property begins on January 2, 1965. If he sells the property on October 1, 1966, the holding period on the day of the sale is 21 full months, and, accordingly, the applicable percentage is 99 percent. This result would not be changed even if the property initially had been used solely as the taxpayer's residence for a portion of the 21-month period. If, however, the property were sold on September 30, 1966, the holding period would be only 20 full months.

(2) For the purpose of determining the applicable percentage in the case of property constructed, reconstructed, or erected by the taxpayer, the holding period of the property shall begin on the first day of the month during which the property is placed in service. See section 1250(e)(1)(B). Thus, for example, if a taxpayer constructs section 1250 property and places it in service on January 15, 1965, its holding period begins on January 1, 1965. If the taxpayer sells the property on December 31, 1966, its holding period on the day of sale is 24 full months, and, accordingly, the applicable percentage is 96 percent. For purposes of this subparagraph, property is placed in service on the date on which it is first used, whether in a trade or business, in the production of income, or in a personal activity. Thus, for example, a residence constructed by a taxpayer for his personal use is placed in service on the date it is occupied as a residence. For purposes of determining the date property is placed in service, it is immaterial when the period begins for depreciation with respect to the property under any depreciation practice under which depreciation begins in any month other than the month in which the property is placed in service. If one or more units of a single property are placed in service on different dates before the completion of the property, see paragraph (c)(3) of § 1.1250–5 (relating to treatment of each such unit as an element).

(c) Property with transferred basis. Under section 1250(e)(2), if the basis of property acquired in a transaction described in this subparagraph is determined by reference to its basis in the hands of the transferor, then the holding period of the property in the hands of the transferee shall include the holding period of the property in the hands of the transferor. The transactions described in this subparagraph are:

(1) A gift described in section 1250(d)(1).

(2) Certain transfers at death to the extent provided in paragraph (b)(2)(ii) of § 1.1250–3.

(3) Certain tax-free transactions to which section 1250(d)(3) applies. For application of section 1250 (d)(3) and (e)(2) to a distribution by a partnership to a partner, see paragraph (f)(1) of § 1.1250–3.

(4) A transfer described in paragraph (e)(4) of § 1.1250–3 (relating to transaction under section 1081 (d)(1)(A)).

* * *

READJUSTMENT OF TAX BETWEEN YEARS AND SPECIAL LIMITATIONS

Claim of Right

§ 1.1341–1 Restoration of amounts received or accrued under claim of right.

(a) In general. **(1)** If, during the taxable year, the taxpayer is entitled under other provisions of chapter 1 of the Internal Revenue Code of 1954 to a deduction of more than $3,000 because of the restoration to another of an item which was included in the taxpayer's gross income for a prior taxable year (or years) under a claim of right, the tax imposed by chapter 1 of the Internal Revenue Code of 1954 for the taxable year shall be the tax provided in paragraph (b) of this section.

(2) For the purpose of this section "income included under a claim of right" means an item included in gross income because it appeared from all the facts available in the year of inclusion that the taxpayer had an unrestricted right to such item, and "restoration to another" means a restoration resulting because it was established after the close of such prior taxable year (or years) that the taxpayer did not have an unrestricted right to such item (or portion thereof).

(3) For purposes of determining whether the amount of a deduction described in section 1341(a) (2) exceeds $3,000 for the taxable year, there shall be taken into account the aggregate of all such deductions with respect to each item of income (described in section 1341(a)(1)) of the same class.

(b) Determination of tax. **(1)** Under the circumstances described in paragraph (a) of this section, the tax imposed by chapter 1 of the Internal Revenue Code of 1954 for the taxable year shall be the lesser of:

(i) The tax for the taxable year computed under section 1341(a)(4), that is, with the deduction taken into account, or

(ii) The tax for the taxable year computed under section 1341(a)(5), that is, without taking such deduction into account, minus the decrease in tax (net of any increase in tax imposed by section 56, relating to the minimum tax for tax preferences) (under chapter 1 of the Internal Revenue Code of 1954, under chapter 1 (other than subchapter E) and subchapter E of chapter 2 of the Internal Revenue Code of 1939, or under the corresponding provisions of prior revenue laws) for the prior taxable year (or years) which would result solely from the exclusion from gross income of all or that portion of the income included under a claim of right to which the deduction is attributable. For the purpose of this subdivision, the amount of the decrease in tax is not limited to the amount of the tax for the taxable year. See paragraph (i) of this section where the decrease in tax for the prior taxable year (or years) exceeds the tax for the taxable year.

(iii) For purposes of computing, under section 1341(a)(4) and subdivision (i) of this subparagraph, the tax for a taxable year beginning after December 31, 1961, if the deduction of the amount of the restoration results in a net operating loss for the taxable year of restoration, such net operating loss shall, pursuant to section 1341(b)(4)(A), be carried back to the same extent and in the same manner as is provided under section 172 (relating to the net operating loss deduction) and the regulations thereunder. If the aggregate decrease in tax for the taxable year (or years) to which such net operating loss is carried back is greater than the excess of:

(a) The amount of decrease in tax for a prior taxable year (or years) computed under section 1341 (a)(5)(B), over

(b) The tax for the taxable year computed under section 1341(a)(5)(A),

the tax imposed for the taxable year under chapter 1 shall be the tax determined under section 1341(a)(4) and subdivision (i) of this subparagraph. If the tax imposed for the taxable year is determined under section 1341(a)(4) and subdivision (i) of this subparagraph, the decrease in tax for the taxable year (or years) to which the net operating loss is carried back shall be an overpayment of tax for the taxable year (or years) to which the net operating loss is carried back and shall be refunded or credited as an overpayment for such taxable year (or years). See section 6511(d)(2), relating to special period of limitation with respect to net operating loss carrybacks.

(2) Except as otherwise provided in section 1341(b)(4)(B) and paragraph (d)(1)(ii) and (4)(ii) of this section, if the taxpayer computes his tax for the taxable year under the provisions of section 1341(a)(5) and subparagraph (1)(ii) of this paragraph, the amount of the restoration shall not be taken into account in computing taxable income or loss for the taxable year, including the computation of any net operating loss carryback or carryover or any capital loss carryover. However, the amount of such restoration shall be taken into account in adjusting earnings and profits for the current taxable year.

(3) If the tax determined under subparagraph (1) (i) of this paragraph is the same as the tax determined under subparagraph (1)(ii) of this paragraph, the tax imposed for the taxable year under chapter 1 shall be the tax determined under subparagraph (1)(i) of this paragraph, and section 1341 and this section shall not otherwise apply.

(4) After it has been determined whether the tax imposed for a taxable year of restoration beginning after December 31, 1961, shall be computed under the provisions of section 1341(a)(4) or under the provisions of section 1341(a)(5), the net operating loss, if any, which remains after the application of section 1341(b)(4)(A) or the net operating loss or capital loss, if any, which remains after the application of section 1341(b)(4)(B) shall be taken into account in accordance with the following rules:

(i) If it is determined that section 1341(a)(4) and subparagraph (1)(i) of this paragraph apply, then that portion, if any, of the net operating loss for the taxable year which remains after the application of section 1341(b)(4)(A) and subparagraph (1)(iii) of this paragraph shall be taken into account under section 172 for taxable years subsequent to the taxable year of restoration to the same extent and in the same manner as a net operating loss sustained in such taxable year of restoration. Thus, if the net operating loss for the taxable year of restoration (computed with the deduction referred to in section 1341(a)(4)) exceeds the taxable income (computed with the modifications prescribed in section 172) for the taxable year (or years) to which it is carried back, such excess shall be available as a carryover to taxable years subsequent to the taxable year of restoration.

(ii) If it is determined that section 1341(a)(5) and subparagraph (1)(ii) of this paragraph apply, then that portion, if any, of a net operating loss or capital loss which remains after the application of section 1341(b)(4)(B) and paragraph (d)(4) of this section shall be taken into account under section 172 or section 1212, as the case may be, for taxable years subsequent to the taxable year of restoration to the same extent and in the same manner as a net operating loss or capital loss sustained in the prior taxable year (or years). For example, if the net operating loss for the prior taxable year (computed with the exclusion referred to in section 1341(a)(5)(B)) exceeds the taxable income (computed with the modifications prescribed in section 172) for prior taxable years to which such net operating loss is carried back or carried over (including for this purpose the taxable year of restoration), such excess shall be available as a carryover to taxable years subsequent to the taxable year of restoration in accordance with the rules prescribed in section 172 which are applicable to such prior taxable year (or years).

(c) Application to deductions which are capital in nature. Section 1341 and this section shall also apply to a deduction which is capital in nature otherwise allowable in the taxable year. If the deduction otherwise allowable is capital in nature, the determination of whether the taxpayer is entitled to the benefits of section 1341 and this section shall be made without regard to the net capital loss limitation imposed by section 1211. For example, if a taxpayer restores $4,000 in the taxable year and such amount is a long-term capital loss, the taxpayer will, nevertheless, be considered to have met the $3,000 deduction requirement for purposes of applying this section, although the full amount of the loss might not be allowable as a deduction for the taxable year. However, if the tax for the taxable year is computed with the deduction taken into account, the deduction allowable will be subject to the limitation on capital losses provided in section 1211, and the capital loss carryover provided in section 1212.

(d) Determination of decrease in tax for prior taxable years—(1) Prior taxable years. (i) Except as otherwise provided in subdivision (ii) of this subparagraph, the prior taxable year (or years) referred to in paragraph (b) of this section is the year (or years) in which the item to which the deduction is attributable was included in gross income under a claim of right and, in addition, any other prior taxable year (or years) the tax for which will be affected by the exclusion from gross income in such prior taxable year (or years) of such income.

(ii) For purposes of applying section 1341(b)(4)(B) in computing the amount of the decrease referred to in paragraph (b)(1)(ii) of this section for any taxable year beginning after December 31, 1961, the term "prior taxable year (or years)" includes the taxable year of restoration. Under section 1341(b)(4)(B), for taxable years of restoration beginning after December 31, 1961, in any case where the exclusion referred to in section 1341(a)(5)(B) and paragraph (b)(1)(ii) of this section results in a net operating loss or capital loss for the prior taxable year (or years), such loss shall, for purposes of computing the decrease in tax for the prior taxable year (or years) under such section 1341(a) (5)(B) and such paragraph (b)(1)(ii) of this section, be carried back and carried over to the same extent and in the same manner as is provided under section 172 (relating to the net operating loss deduction) or section 1212 (relating to capital loss carryover), except that no carryover beyond the taxable year shall be taken into account. See subparagraph (4) of this paragraph for rules relating to the computation of the amount of decrease in tax.

(2) Amount of exclusion from gross income in prior taxable years. (i) The amount to be excluded from gross income for the prior taxable year (or years) in determining the decrease in tax under section 1341(a)(5)(B) and paragraph (b)(1)(ii) of this section shall be the amount restored in the taxable year, but shall not exceed the amount included in gross income in the prior taxable year (or years) under the claim of right to which the deduction for the restoration is attributable, and shall be adjusted as provided in subdivision (ii) of this subparagraph.

(ii) If the amount included in gross income for the prior taxable year (or years) under the claim of right in question was reduced in such year (or years) by a deduction allowed under section 1202 (or section 117(b) of the Internal Revenue Code of 1939 or corresponding provisions of prior revenue laws), then the amount determined under subdivision (i) of this subparagraph to be excluded from gross income for such year (or years) shall be reduced in the same proportion that the amount included in gross income under a claim of right was reduced.

(iii) The determination of the amount of the exclusion from gross income of the prior taxable year shall be made without regard to the capital loss limitation contained in section 1211 applicable in computing taxable income for the current taxable year. The amount of the exclusion from gross income in a prior taxable year (or years) shall not exceed the amount which would, but for the application of section 1211, be allowable as a deduction in the taxable year of restoration.

* * *

(3) **Determination of amount of deduction attributable to prior taxable years.** (i) If the deduction otherwise allowable for the taxable year relates to income included in gross income under a claim of right in more than one prior taxable year and the amount attributable to each such prior taxable year cannot be readily identified, then the portion attributable to each such prior taxable year shall be that proportion of the deduction otherwise allowable for the taxable year which the amount of the income included under the claim of right in question for the prior taxable year bears to the total of all such income included under the claim of right for all such prior taxable years.

(ii) The rule provided in subdivision (i) of this subparagraph may be illustrated as follows:

Example. Under a claim of right, A included in his gross income over a period of three taxable years an aggregate of $9,000 for services to a certain employer, in amounts as follows: $2,000 for taxable year 1952, $4,000 for taxable year 1953, and $3,000 for taxable year 1954. In 1955 it is established that A must restore $6,750 of these amounts to his employer, and that A is entitled to a deduction of this amount in the taxable year 1955. The amount of the deduction attributable to each of the prior taxable years cannot be identified. Accordingly, the amount of the deduction attributable to each prior taxable year is:

1952—$6,750 × $2,000 ÷ $9,000 = $1,500

1953—$6,750 × $4,000 ÷ $9,000 = $3,000

1954—$6,750 × $3,000 ÷ $9,000 = $2,250

(4) **Computation of amount of decrease in tax.** (i) In computing the amount of decrease in tax for a prior taxable year (or years) resulting from the exclusion from gross income of the income included under a claim of right, there must first be ascertained the amount of tax previously determined for the taxpayer for such prior taxable year (or years). The tax previously determined shall be the sum of the amounts shown by the taxpayer on his return or returns, plus any amounts which have been previously assessed (or collected without assessment) as deficiencies or which appropriately should be assessed or collected, reduced by the amount of any refunds or credits which have previously been made or which appropriately should be made. For taxable years beginning after December 31, 1961, if the provisions of section 1341(b)(4)(B) are applicable, the tax previously determined shall include the tax for the taxable year of restoration computed without taking the deduction for the amount of the restoration into account. After the tax previously determined has been ascertained, a recomputation must then be made to determine the decrease in tax, if any, resulting from the exclusion from gross income of all or that portion of the income included under a claim of right to which the deduction otherwise allowable in the taxable year is attributable.

(ii) No item other than the exclusion of the income previously included under a claim of right shall be considered in computing the amount of decrease in tax if reconsideration of such other item is prevented by the operation of any provision of the internal revenue laws or any other rule of law. However, if the amounts of other items in the return are dependent upon the amount of adjusted gross income, taxable income, or net income (such as charitable contributions, foreign tax credit, deductions for depletion, and net operating loss), appropriate adjustment shall be made as part of the computation of the decrease in tax. For the purpose of determining the decrease in tax for the prior taxable year (or years) which would result from the exclusion from gross income of the item included under a claim of right, the exclusion of such item shall be given effect not only in the prior taxable year in which it was included in gross income but in all other prior taxable years (including the taxable year of restoration if such year begins after December 31, 1961, and section 1341(b)(4)(B) applies, see subparagraph (1)(ii) of this paragraph) affected by the inclusion of the item (for example, prior taxable years affected by a net operating loss carryback or carryover or capital loss carryover).

* * *

(e) **Method of accounting.** The provisions of section 1341 and this section shall be applicable in the case of a taxpayer on the cash receipts and disbursements method of accounting only to the taxable year in which the item of income included in a prior year (or years) under a claim of right is actually repaid. However, in the case of a taxpayer on the cash receipts and disbursements method of accounting who constructively received an item of income under a claim of right and included such item of income in gross income in a prior year (or years), the provisions of section 1341 and this section shall be applicable to the taxable year in which the taxpayer is required to relinquish his right to receive such item of income. Such provisions shall be applicable in the case of other taxpayers only to the taxable year which is the proper taxable year (under the method of accounting used by the taxpayer in computing taxable income) for taking into account the deduction resulting from the restoration of the item of income included in a prior year (or years) under a claim of right. For example, if the taxpayer is on an accrual method of accounting, the provisions of this section shall apply to the year in which the obligation properly accrues for the repayment of the item included under a claim of right.

(f) Inventory items, stock in trade, and property held primarily for sale in the ordinary course of trade or business. **(1)** Except for amounts specified in subparagraphs (2) and (3) of this paragraph, the provisions of section 1341 and this section do not apply to deductions attributable to items which were included in gross income by reason of the sale or other disposition of stock in trade of the taxpayer (or other property of a kind which would properly have been included in the inventory of the taxpayer if on hand at the close of the prior taxable year) or property held by the taxpayer primarily for sale to customers in the ordinary course of the taxpayer's trade or business. This section is, therefore, not applicable to sales returns and allowances and similar items.

* * *

(g) Bad debts. The provisions of section 1341 and this section do not apply to deductions attributable to bad debts.

(h) Legal fees and other expenses. Section 1341 and this section do not apply to legal fees or other expenses incurred by a taxpayer in contesting the restoration of an item previously included in income. This rule may be illustrated by the following example:

Example. A sold his personal residence to B in a prior taxable year and realized a capital gain on the sale. C claimed that under an agreement with A he was entitled to a 5-percent share of the purchase price since he brought the parties together and was instrumental in closing the sale. A rejected C's demand and included the entire amount of the capital gain in gross income for the year of sale. C instituted action and in the taxable year judgment is rendered against A who pays C the amount involved. In addition, A pays legal fees in the taxable year which were incurred in the defense of the action. Section 1341 applies to the payment of the 5-percent share of the purchase price to C. However, the payment of the legal fees, whether or not otherwise deductible, does not constitute an item restored for purposes of section 1341(a) and paragraph (a) of this section.

(i) Refunds. If the decrease in tax for the prior taxable year (or years) determined under section 1341(a)(5)(B) and paragraph (b)(1)(ii) of this section exceeds the tax imposed by chapter 1 of the Code for the taxable year computed without the deduction, and for taxable years beginning after December 31, 1961, if such excess is greater than the decrease in tax for the taxable year (or years) to which the net operating loss described in section 1341(b)(4)(A) and paragraph (b)(1)(iii) of this section is carried back, such excess shall be considered to be a payment of tax for the taxable year of restoration. Such payment is deemed to have been made on the last day prescribed by law for the payment of tax for the taxable year and shall be refunded or credited in the same manner as if it were an overpayment of tax for such taxable year. However, no interest shall be allowed or paid if such an excess results from the application of section 1341(a)(5)(B) in the case of a deduction described in paragraph (f)(3) of this section (relating to payments or repayments pursuant to price redetermination). If the tax for the taxable year of restoration is computed under section 1341 (a)(4) and results in a decrease in tax for the taxable year (or years) to which a net operating loss described in section 1341(b)(4)(A) is carried back, see paragraph (b)(1)(iii) of this section.

* * *

ELECTION OF CERTAIN SMALL BUSINESS CORPORATIONS AS TO TAXABLE STATUS

* * *

§ 1.1375–1 Tax imposed when passive investment income of corporation having Subchapter C earnings and profits exceed 25 percent of gross receipts.

(a) General rule. For taxable years beginning after 1981, section 1375(a) imposes a tax on the income of certain S corporations that have passive investment income. In the case of a taxable year beginning during 1982, an electing small business corporation may elect to have the rules under this section not apply. See the regulations under section 1362 for rules on the election. For purposes of this section, the term "S corporation" shall include an electing small business corporation under prior law. This tax shall apply to an S corporation for a taxable year if the S corporation has—

(1) Subchapter C earnings and profits at the close of such taxable year, and

(2) Gross receipts more than 25 percent of which are passive investment income.

If the S corporation has no Subchapter C earnings and profits at the close of the taxable year (because, for example, such earnings and profits were distributed in accordance with section 1368), the tax shall not be imposed even though the S corporation has passive investment income for the taxable year. If the tax is imposed, the tax shall be computed by multiplying the excess net passive income (as defined in paragraph (b) of this section) by the highest rate of tax specified in section 11(b).

(b) Definitions—(1) Excess net passive income—(i) In general. The term "excess net passive income" is defined in section 1375(b)(1), and can be expressed by the following formula:

$$ENPI = NPI \times \frac{PII - (.25 \times GR)}{PII}$$

Where:
ENPI = excess net passive income
NPI = net passive income
PII = passive investment income
GR = total gross receipts

(ii) Limitation. The amount of the excess net passive income for any taxable year shall not exceed the corporation's taxable income for the taxable year (determined in accordance with section 1374(d) and § 1.1374–1(d)).

(2) Net passive income. The term "net passive income" means—

(i) Passive investment income, reduced by

(ii) The deductions allowable under Chapter 1 of the Internal Revenue Code of 1954* which are directly connected (within the meaning of paragraph (b)(3) of this section) with the production of such income (other than deductions allowable under section 172 and Part VIII of Subchapter B).

(3) Directly connected—(i) In general. For purposes of paragraph (b)(2)(ii) of this section, to be directly connected with the production of income, an item of deduction must have proximate and primary relationship to the income. Expenses, depreciation, and similar items attributable solely to such income qualify for deduction.

(ii) Allocation of deduction. If an item of deduction is attributable (within the meaning of paragraph (b)(3)(i) of this section) in part to passive investment income and in part to income other than passive investment income, the deduction shall be allocated between the two types of items on a reasonable basis. The portion of any deduction so allocated to passive investment income shall be treated as proximately and primarily related to such income.

(4) Other definitions. The terms "Subchapter C earnings and profits," "passive investment income," and "gross receipts" shall have the same meaning given these terms in section 1362(d)(3) and the regulations thereunder.

(c) Special rules—

(1) Disallowance of credits. No credit is allowed under Part IV of Subchapter A of Chapter 1 of the Code (other than section 34) against the tax imposed by section 1375(a) and this section.

(2) Coordination with section 1374. If any gain—

(i) Is taken into account in determining passive income for purposes of this section, and

(ii) Is taken into account under section 1374,

the amount of such gain taken into account under section 1374(b) and § 1.1374–1 (b)(1) and (2) in determining the amount of tax shall be reduced by the portion of the excess net passive income for the taxable year which is attributable (on a pro rata basis) to such gain. For purposes of the preceding sentence, the portion of excess net passive income for the taxable year which is attributable to such capital gain is equal to the amount determined by multiplying the excess net passive income by the following fraction:

$$\frac{NCG - E}{NPI}$$

Where:
NCG = net capital gain
NPI = net passive income
E = expense attributable to net capital gain

(d) Waiver of tax in certain cases—

(1) In general. If an S corporation establishes to the satisfaction of the Commissioner that—

(i) It determined in good faith that it had no Subchapter C earnings and profits at the close of the taxable year, and

*Editorial comment: The Regulations do not reflect the effect of the Tax Reform Act of 1986 which changed the title to the Internal Revenue Code of 1986.

(ii) During a reasonable period of time after it was determined that it did have Subchapter C earnings and profits at the close of such taxable year such earnings and profits were distributed,

the Commissioner may waive the tax imposed by section 1375 for such taxable year. The S corporation has the burden of establishing that under the relevant facts and circumstances the Commissioner should waive the tax.

For example, if an S corporation establishes that in good faith and using due diligence it determined that it had no Subchapter C earnings and profits at the close of a taxable year, but it was later determined on audit that it did have Subchapter C earnings and profits at the close of such taxable year, and if the corporation establishes that it distributed such earnings and profits within a reasonable time after the audit, it may be appropriate for the Commissioner to waive the tax on passive income for such taxable year.

(2) Corporation's request for a waiver. A request for waiver of the tax imposed by section 1375 shall be made in writing to the district director and shall contain all relevant facts to establish that the requirements of paragraph (d)(1) of this section are met. Such request shall contain a description of how and on what date the S corporation in good faith and using due diligence determined that it had no Subchapter C earnings and profits at the close of the taxable year, a description of how and on what date it was determined that the S corporation had Subchapter C earnings and profits at the close of the year and a description (including dates) of any steps taken to distribute such earnings and profits. If the earnings and profits have not yet been distributed, the request shall contain a timetable for distribution and an explanation of why such timetable is reasonable. On the date the waiver is to become effective, all Subchapter C earnings and profits must have been distributed.

(e) Reduction in pass-thru for tax imposed on excess net passive income. See section 1366(f)(3) for a special rule reducing each item of the corporation's passive investment income for purposes of section 1366(a) if a tax is imposed on the corporation under section 1375.

(f) Examples. The following examples illustrates the principles of this section:

Example (1). Assume Corporation M, an S corporation, has for its taxable year total gross receipts of $200,000, passive investment income of $100,000, $60,000 of which is interest income, and expenses directly connected with the production of such interest income in the amount of $10,000. Assume also that at the end of the taxable year Corporation M has Subchapter C earnings and profits. Since more than 25 percent of the Corporation M's total gross receipts are passive investment income, and since Corporation M has Subchapter C earnings and profits at the end of the taxable year, Corporation M will be subject to the tax imposed by section 1375. The amount of excess net passive investment income is $45,000 ($90,000 × (50,^{000}/$_{100}$,000)). Assume that the other $40,000 of passive investment income is attributable to net capital gain and that there are no expenses directly connected with such gain. Under these facts, $20,000 of the excess net passive income is attributable to the net capital gain ($45,000 × ($40,000/$90,000)). Accordingly, the amount of gain taken into account under section 1374(b)(1) and the taxable income of Corporation M under section 1374(b)(2) shall be reduced by $20,000.

Example (2). Assume an S corporation with Subchapter C earnings and profits has tax-exempt income of $400, its only passive income, gross receipts of $1,000 and taxable income of $250 and there are no expenses associated with the tax-exempt income. The corporation's excess net income for the taxable year would total $150 (400 × (400–^{250}/$_{400}$)). This amount is subject to the tax imposed by section 1375, not withstanding that such amount is otherwise tax-exempt income.

* * *

§ 1.1378–1 Taxable year of S corporation.

(a) In general. The taxable year of an S corporation must be a permitted year. A permitted year is the required taxable year (i.e., a taxable year ending on December 31), a taxable year elected under section 444, a 52–53-week taxable year ending with reference to the required taxable year or a taxable year elected under section 444, or any other taxable year for which the corporation establishes a business purpose to the satisfaction of the Commissioner under section 442.

(b) Adoption of taxable year. An electing S corporation may adopt, in accordance with § 1.441–1 (c), its required taxable year, a taxable year elected under section 444, or a 52–53-week taxable year ending with reference to its required taxable year or a taxable year elected under section 444 without the approval of the Commissioner. See § 1.441–1. An electing S corporation that wants to adopt any other taxable year, must establish a business purpose and obtain the approval of the Commissioner under section 442.

(c) Change in taxable year—

(1) Approval required. An S corporation or electing S corporation that wants to change its taxable year must obtain the approval of the Commissioner under section 442 or make an election under section 444. However, an S corporation or electing S corporation may obtain automatic approval for certain changes, including a change to its required taxable year, pursuant to administrative procedures published by the Commissioner.

(2) **Short period tax return.** An S corporation or electing S corporation that changes its taxable year must make its return for a short period in accordance with section 443, but must not annualize the corporation's taxable income.

(d) **Retention of taxable year.** In certain cases, an S corporation or electing S corporation will be required to change its taxable year unless it obtains the approval of the Commissioner under section 442, or makes an election under section 444, to retain its current taxable year. For example, a corporation using a June 30 fiscal year that elects to be an S corporation and, as a result, is required to use the calendar year must obtain the approval of the Commissioner to retain its current fiscal year.

(e) **Procedures for obtaining approval or making a section 444 election.**

(1) **In general.** See § 1.442–1(b) for procedures to obtain the approval of the Commissioner (automatically or otherwise) to adopt, change, or retain a taxable year. See §§ 1.444–1T and 1.444–2T for qualification's, and 1.444–3T for procedures, for making an election under section 444.

(2) **Special rules for election S corporations.** An electing S corporation that wants to adopt, change to, or retain a taxable year other than its required taxable year must request approval of the Commissioner on Form 2553, "Election by a Small Business Corporation," when the election to be an S corporation is filed pursuant to section 1362(b) and § 1.1362–6. See § 1.1362–6(a)(2)(i) for the manner of making an election to be an S corporation. If such corporation receives permission to adopt, change to, or retain a taxable year other than its required taxable year, the election to be an S corporation will be effective. Denial of the request renders the election ineffective unless the corporation agrees that, in the event the request to adopt, change to, or retain a taxable year other than its required taxable year is denied, it will adopt, change to, or retain its required taxable year or, if applicable, make an election under section 444.

(f) **Effective date.** The rules of this section are applicable for taxable years ending on or after May 17, 2002.

CONSOLIDATED RETURNS

RETURNS AND PAYMENT OF TAX
CONSOLIDATED RETURN REGULATIONS

* * *

§ 1.1502–1 Definitions.

(a) Group. The term "group" means an affiliated group of corporations as defined in section 1504. See § 1.1502–75(d) as to when a group remains in existence. Except as thc context otherwise requires, references to a group are references to a consolidated group (as defined in paragraph (b) of this section).

(b) Member. The term "member" means a corporation (including the common parent) which is included within such group.

(c) Subsidiary. The term "subsidiary" means a corporation other than the common parent which is a member of such group.

(d) Consolidated return year. The term "consolidated return year" means a taxable year for which a consolidated return is filed or required to be filed by such group.

(e) Separate return year. The term "separate return year" means a taxable year of a corporation for which it files a separate return or for which it joins in the filing of a consolidated return by another group.

(f) Separate return limitation year—(1) In general. Except as provided in subparagraphs (2) and (3) of this paragraph, the term "separate return limitation year" means any separate return year of a member or of a predecessor of such member. The term "predecessor" means a transferor or distributor of assets to a member in a transaction to which section 381(a) applies.

(2) Exceptions. The term "separate return limitation year" shall not include:

(i) A separate return year of the corporation which is the common parent for the consolidated return year to which the tax attribute is to be carried (except as provided in § 1.1502–75(d)(2)(ii) and subparagraph (3) of this paragraph),

(ii) A separate return year of any corporation which was a member of the group for each day of such year, or

(iii) A separate return year of a predecessor of any member if such predecessor was a member of the group for each day of such year,

provided that an election under section 1562(a) (relating to the privilege to elect multiple surtax exemptions) was never effective (or is no longer effective as a result of a termination of such election) for such year. An election under section 1562(a) which is effective for a taxable year beginning in 1963 and ending in 1964 shall be disregarded.

* * *

RELATED RULES

§ 1.1551–1 Disallowance of surtax exemption and accumulated earnings credit.

(a) In general. If:

(1) Any corporation transfers, on or after January 1, 1951, and before June 13, 1963, all or part of its property (other than money) to a transferee corporation,

(2) Any corporation transfers, directly or indirectly, after June 12, 1963, all or part of its property (other than money) to a transferee corporation, or

(3) Five or fewer individuals are in control of a corporation and one or more of them transfer, directly or indirectly, after June 12, 1963, property (other than money) to a transferee corporation, and the transferee was created for the purpose of acquiring such property or was not actively engaged in business at the time of such acquisition, and if after such transfer the transferor or transferors are in control of the transferee during any part of the taxable year of the transferee, then for such taxable year of the transferee the Secretary or his delegate may disallow the surtax exemption defined in section 11(d)* or the accumulated earnings credit of $150,000** * * * provided in paragraph (2) or (3) of section 535(c), unless the transferee establishes by the clear preponderance of the evidence that the securing

*Editorial comment: The beneficial rates presently appear in Sec. 11(b) rather than Sec. 11(d).

**Editorial comment: The $150,000 amount has been replaced with $250,000 in most cases. See Sec. 535(c)(2).

of such exemption or credit was not a major purpose of the transfer.

(b) Purpose of section 1551. The purpose of section 1551 is to prevent avoidance or evasion of the surtax imposed by section 11(c)* or of the accumulated earnings tax imposed by section 531. It is not intended, however, that section 1551 be interpreted as delimiting or abrogating any principle of law established by judicial decision, or any existing provisions of the Code, such as sections 269 and 482, which have the effect of preventing the avoidance or evasion of income taxes. Such principles of law and such provisions of the Code, including section 1551, are not mutually exclusive, and in appropriate cases they may operate together or they may operate separately.

(c) Application of section 269(b) to cases covered by section 1551. The provisions of section 269(b) and the authority of the district director thereunder, to the extent not inconsistent with the provisions of section 1551, are applicable to cases covered by section 1551. Pursuant to the authority provided in section 269(b) the district director may allow to the transferee any part of a surtax exemption or accumulated earnings credit for a taxable year for which such exemption or credit would otherwise be disallowed under section 1551(a); or he may apportion such exemption or credit among the corporations involved. * * *

(d) Actively engaged in business. For purposes of this section, a corporation maintaining an office for the purpose of preserving its corporate existence is not considered to be "actively engaged in business" even though such corporation may be deemed to be "doing business" for other purposes. Similarly, for purposes of this section, a corporation engaged in winding up its affairs, prior to an acquisition to which section 1551 is applicable, is not considered to be "actively engaged in business."

(e) Meaning and application of the term "control"—(1) In general. For purposes of this section, the term "control" means:

(i) With respect to a transferee corporation described in paragraph (a)(1) or (2) of this section, the ownership by the transferor corporation, its shareholders, or both, of stock possessing either (a) at least 80 percent of the total combined voting power of all classes of stock entitled to vote, or (b) at least 80 percent of the total value of shares of all classes of stock.

(ii) With respect to each corporation described in paragraph (a)(3) of this section, the ownership by five or fewer individuals of stock possessing (a) at least 80 percent of the total combined voting power of all classes of stock entitled to vote or at least 80 percent of the total value of shares of all classes of the stock of each corporation, and (b) more than 50 percent of the total combined voting power of all classes of stock entitled to vote or more than 50 percent of the total value of shares of all classes of stock of each corporation, taking into account the stock ownership of each such individual only to the extent such stock ownership is identical with respect to each such corporation.

(2) Special rules. In determining for purposes of this section whether stock possessing at least 80 percent (or more than 50 percent in the case of subparagraph (1)(ii)(b) of this paragraph) of the total combined voting power of all classes of stock entitled to vote is owned, all classes of such stock shall be considered together; it is not necessary that at least 80 percent (or more than 50 percent) of each class of voting stock be owned. Likewise, in determining for purposes of this section whether stock possessing at least 80 percent (or more than 50 percent) of the total value of shares of all classes of stock is owned, all classes of stock of the corporation shall be considered together; it is not necessary that at least 80 percent (or more than 50 percent) of the value of shares of each class be owned. The fair market value of a share shall be considered as the value to be used for purposes of this computation. With respect to transfers described in paragraph (a)(2) or (3) of this section, the ownership of stock shall be determined in accordance with the provisions of section 1563(e) and the regulations thereunder. With respect to transfers described in paragraph (a)(1) of this section, the ownership of stock shall be determined in accordance with the provisions of section 544 and the regulations thereunder, except that constructive ownership under section 544(a)(2) shall be determined only with respect to the individual's spouse and minor children. * * *

(3) Example. This paragraph may be illustrated by the following example:

*Editorial comment: See the corporate tax rates in Sec. 11(b) rather than Sec. 11(c).

Example. On January 1, 1964, individual A, who owns 50 percent of the voting stock of corporation X, and individual B, who owns 30 percent of such voting stock, transfer property (other than money) to corporation Y (newly created for the purpose of acquiring such property) in exchange for all of Y's voting stock. After the transfer, A and B own the voting stock of corporations X and Y in the following proportions:

Individual	Corp. X	Corp. Y	Identical ownership
A	50	30	30
B	30	50	30
Total	80	80	60

The transfer of property by A and B to corporation Y is a transfer described in paragraph (a)(3) of this section since (i) A and B own at least 80 percent of the voting stock of corporations X and Y, and (ii) taking into account each such individual's stock ownership only to the extent such ownership is identical with respect to each such corporation, A and B own more than 50 percent of the voting stock of corporations X and Y.

(f) Taxable year of allowance or disallowance—(1) In general. The district director's authority with respect to cases covered by section 1551 is not limited to the taxable year of the transferee corporation in which the transfer of property occurs. Such authority extends to the taxable year in which the transfer occurs or any subsequent taxable year of the transferee corporation if, during any part of such year, the transferor or transferors are in control of the transferee.

* * *

(g) Nature of transfer—* * *

(2) Corporate transfers after June 12, 1963. A direct or indirect transfer made after June 12, 1963, by any corporation of all or part of its assets to a transferee corporation, whether or not such transfer qualifies as a reorganization under section 368, is within the scope of section 1551(a)(2) except that section 1551(a)(2) does not apply to a transfer of money only. For example, if a transferor corporation transfers property to its shareholders or to a subsidiary, the transfer of that property by the shareholders or the subsidiary to a transferee corporation as part of the same transaction is a transfer of property by the transferor corporation to which section 1551(a)(2) applies. A transfer of property pursuant to a purchase by a transferee corporation from a transferor corporation controlling the transferee is within the scope of section 1551(a)(2), whether or not the purchase follows a transfer of cash from the controlling corporation.

(3) Other transfers after June 12, 1963. A direct or indirect transfer made after June 12, 1963, by five or fewer individuals to a transferee corporation, whether or not such transfer qualifies under one or more other provisions of the Code (for example, section 351), is within the scope of section 1551(a) (3) except that section 1551(a)(3) does not apply to a transfer of money only. Thus, if one of five or fewer individuals who are in control of a corporation transfers property (other than money) to a controlled transferee corporation, the transfer is within the scope of section 1551(a)(3) notwithstanding that the other individuals transfer nothing or transfer only money.

(4) Examples. This paragraph may be illustrated by the following examples:

Example (1). Individuals A and B each owns 50 percent of the voting stock of corporation X. On January 15, 1964, A and B each acquires property (other than money) from X and, as part of the same transaction, each transfers such property to his wholly owned corporation (newly created for the purpose of acquiring such property). A and B retain substantial continuing interests in corporation X. The transfers to the two newly created corporations are within the scope of section 1551(a)(2).

Example (2). Corporation W organizes corporation X, a wholly owned subsidiary, for the purpose of acquiring the properties of corporation Y. Pursuant to a reorganization qualifying under section 368(a)(1)(C), substantially all of the properties of corporation Y are transferred on June 15, 1963, to corporation X solely in exchange for voting stock of corporation W. There is a transfer of property from W to X within the meaning of section 1551(a)(2).

Example (3). Individuals A and B, each owning 50 percent of the voting stock of corporation X, organize corporation Y to which each transfers money only in exchange for 50 percent of the stock of Y. Subsequently, Y uses such money to acquire other property from A and B after June 12, 1963. Such acquisition is within the scope of section 1551(a)(3).

Example (4). Individual A owns 55 percent of the stock of corporation X. Another 25 percent of corporation X's stock is owned in the aggregate by individuals B, C, D, and E. On June 15, 1963, individual A transfers property to corporation Y (newly created for the purpose of acquiring such property) in exchange for 60 percent of the stock of Y, and B, C, and D acquire all of the remaining stock of Y. The transfer is within the scope of section 1551(a)(3).

(h) Purpose of transfer. In determining, for purposes of this section, whether the securing of the surtax exemption* or accumulated earnings credit constituted "a major purpose" of the transfer, all circumstances relevant to the transfer shall be considered. "A major purpose" will not be inferred from the mere purchase of inventory by a subsidiary from a centralized warehouse maintained by its parent corporation or by another subsidiary of the parent corporation. For disallowance of the surtax exemption and accumulated earnings credit under section 1551, it is not necessary that the obtaining of either such credit or exemption, or both, have been

*Editorial comment: See the beneficial tax rates in Sec. 11(b).

the sole or principal purpose of the transfer of the property. It is sufficient if it appears, in the light of all the facts and circumstances, that the obtaining of such exemption or credit, or both, was one of the major considerations that prompted the transfer. Thus, the securing of the surtax exemption or the accumulated earnings credit may constitute "a major purpose" of the transfer, notwithstanding that such transfer was effected for a valid business purpose and qualified as a reorganization within the meaning of section 368. The taxpayer's burden of establishing by the clear preponderance of the evidence that the securing of either such exemption or credit or both was not "a major purpose" of the transfer may be met, for example, by showing that the obtaining of such exemption, or credit, or both, was not a major factor in relationship to the other consideration or considerations which prompted the transfer.

* * *

CERTAIN CONTROLLED CORPORATIONS

* * *

§ 1.1561–1 Limitations on certain multiple tax benefits in the case of certain controlled corporations.

(a) In general. Part II (section 1561 and following), subchapter B, chapter 6 of the Code, provides rules relating to certain controlled corporations. In general, section 1561 provides that the component members of a controlled group of corporations on a December 31, for their taxable years which include such December 31, shall be limited for purposes of subtitle A to

(1) One surtax exemption under section 11(d),*

(2) One $150,000** amount for purposes of computing the accumulated earnings credit under section 535(c)(2) and (3), and* * *

* * *

For certain definitions (including the definition of a "controlled group of corporations" and a "component member") and special rules for purposes of part II of subchapter B, see section 1563 and the regulations thereunder.

(b) Tax avoidance. The provisions of part II, subchapter B, chapter 6 do not delimit or abrogate any principle of law established by judicial decision, or any existing provisions of the code, such as sections 269, 482, and 1551, which have the effect of preventing the avoidance or evasion of income taxes.

(c) Special rules. (1) For purposes of sections 1561 and 1563 and the regulations thereunder, the term "corporation" includes an electing small business corporation (as defined in section 1371(b)).† However, for the treatment of an electing small business corporation as an excluded member of a controlled group of corporations, see paragraph (b)(2)(ii) of § 1.1563–1.

* * *

§ 1.1561–2 Determination of amount of tax benefits.

(a) Surtax exemption. (1) If a corporation is a component member of a controlled group of corporations on December 31, the surtax exemption under section 11(d)* of such corporation for the taxable year which includes such December 31 shall be an amount equal to:

(i) $50,000†† divided by the number of corporations which are component members of such group on such December 31, or

(ii) If an apportionment plan is adopted under § 1.1561–3 which is effective with respect to such taxable year such portion of $50,000†† as is apportioned to such member in accordance with such plan.

(2) In the case of a controlled group of corporations which includes component members which join in the filing of a consolidated return and other component members which do not join in the filing of such a return, and where there is no apportionment plan effective under § 1.1561–3 apportioning the $50,000†† amount among the component members

*Editorial comment: The beneficial tax rates (or surtax exemption) appear in Sec. 11(b) rather than Sec. 11(d).

**Editorial comment: The $150,000 amount has been replaced with $250,000 in most cases. See Sec. 535(c)(2).

***Editorial comment: The Regulations do not include the effect of the Tax Reform Act of 1986 with respect to the Sec. 59A environmental tax and the Sec. 55 alternative minimum tax.

†Editorial comment: See Sec. 1361 rather than Sec. 1371.

††Editorial comment: Presently $75,000 rather than $50,000.

filing the consolidated return and the other component members of the controlled group, each component member of the controlled group, (including each component member which joins in filing the consolidated return) shall be treated as a separate corporation for purposes of equally apportioning the $50,000†† amount under subparagraph (1)(i) of this paragraph. In such case, the surtax exemption of the corporations filing the consolidated return shall be the sum of the amounts apportioned to each component member which joins in filing the consolidated return.

* * *

(c) Accumulated earnings credit. (1) Except as provided in subparagraph (2) of this paragraph, if a corporation is a component member of a controlled group on a December 31, the amount for purposes of computing the accumulated earnings credit under section 535(c)(2) and (3) of such corporation shall be an amount equal to $150,000* divided by the number of corporations which are component members of such group on such December 31. In the case of a controlled group of corporations which includes component members which join in the filing of a consolidated return and other component members which do not join in the filing of such a return, each component member of the controlled group (including each component member which joins in filing the consolidated return) shall be treated as a separate corporation for purposes of equally apportioning the $150,000* amount under this subparagraph. In such case, the amount for purposes of computing the accumulated earnings credit for the component members filing the consolidated return shall be the sum of the amounts apportioned to each component member which joins in filing the consolidated return.

(2) If, with respect to any component member of the controlled group, the amount determined under subparagraph (1) of this paragraph exceeds the sum of (i) such member's accumulated earnings and profits as of the close of the preceding taxable year, plus (ii) such member's earnings and profits for the taxable year which are retained (within the meaning of section 535(c)(1)), then any such excess shall be subtracted from the amount determined under subparagraph (1) of this paragraph with respect to such member and shall be divided equally among those remaining component members of the controlled group that do not have such an excess (until no such excess remains to be divided among those remaining members that have not had such an excess). The excess so divided among such remaining members shall be added to the amount determined under subparagraph (1) with respect to such members. If a controlled group of corporations includes component members which join in the filing of a consolidated return and other component members which do not join in filing such return, the component members filing the consolidated return shall be treated as a single corporation for purposes of this subparagraph.

(3) A controlled group may not adopt an apportionment plan, as provided in § 1.1561–3, with respect to the amounts computed under the provisions of this paragraph.

(4) The provisions of this paragraph may be illustrated by the following example:

Example. A controlled group is composed of four component member corporations, W, X, Y, and Z. Each corporation files a separate income tax return on the basis of a calendar year. The sum of the earnings and profits for the taxable year ending December 31, 1975, which are retained plus the sum of the accumulated earnings and profits (as of the close of the preceding taxable year) is $15,000, $75,000, $37,500, and $300,000 for W, X, Y, and Z, respectively. The amounts determined under this paragraph for W, X, Y, and Z for 1975 are $15,000, $48,750, $37,500, and $48,750, respectively, computed as follows:

	Component members			
	W	X	Y	Z
Earnings and profits	$15,000	$75,000	$37,500	$300,000
Amount computed under subparagraph (1)	37,500	37,500	37,500	37,500
Excess	22,500	0	0	0
Allocation of excess	.....	7,500	7,500	7,500
New excess	.....	.....	7,500	.....
Reallocation of new excess	.....	3,750	.....	3,750
Amount to be used for purposes of section 535(c)(2) and (3)	15,000	48,750	37,500	48,750

*Editorial comment: The $150,000 amount has been replaced with $250,000 in most cases. See Sec. 535(c)(2).

††Editorial comment: Presently $75,000 rather than $50,000.

* * *

§ 1.1561–3 Apportionment of surtax exemption.

(a) In general. **(1)** In the case of corporations which are component members of a controlled group of corporations on a December 31, the single $50,000* surtax exemption under section 11(d)** may be apportioned among such members (for the taxable year of each such member which includes such December 31) if all such members consent, in the manner provided in paragraph (b) of this section, to an apportionment plan with respect to such December 31. Such plan shall provide for the apportionment of a fixed dollar amount to one or more of such members, but in no event shall the sum of the amounts so apportioned exceed $50,000.* An apportionment plan shall not be considered as adopted with respect to a particular December 31 until each component member which is required to consent to the plan under paragraph (b)(1) of this section filed the original of a statement described in such paragraph (or, the original of a statement incorporating its consent is filed on its behalf). In the case of a return filed before a plan is adopted, the surtax exemption** for purposes of such return shall be equally apportioned in accordance with the rules provided in §1.1561–2(a)(1)(i). (If a valid apportionment plan is adopted after the return is filed and within the time prescribed by subparagraph (2) of this paragraph, such return should be amended (or a claim for refund should be made) to reflect the change from equal apportionment.)

(2) A controlled group may adopt an apportionment plan with respect to a particular December 31 only if, at the time such plan is sought to be adopted, there is at least one year remaining in the statutory period (including any extensions thereof) for the assessment of a deficiency against any corporation the tax liability of which would be increased by the adoption of such plan. If there is less than one year remaining with respect to any such corporation, the director of the service center with which such corporation files its income tax return will ordinarily, upon request, enter into an agreement to extend such statutory period for the limited purpose of assessing any deficiency against such corporation attributable to the adoption of such apportionment plan.

(3)(i) The amount apportioned to a component member of a controlled group of corporations in an apportionment plan adopted with respect to a particular December 31 shall constitute such member's surtax exemption** for its taxable year including the particular December 31, and for all taxable years of such members including succeeding December 31's, unless the apportionment plan is amended in accordance with paragraph (c) of this section or is terminated under subdivision (ii) of this subparagraph. Thus, the apportionment plan (including any amendments thereof) has a continuing effect and need not be renewed annually.

(ii) If an apportionment plan is adopted with respect to a particular December 31, such plan shall terminate with respect to a succeeding December 31, if:

(a) The controlled group ceases to remain in existence during the calendar year ending on such succeeding December 31,

(b) Any corporation which was a component member of such group on the particular December 31 is not a component member of such group on such succeeding December 31, or

(c) Any corporation which was not a component member of such group on the particular December 31 is a component member of such group on such succeeding December 31.

An apportionment plan, once terminated with respect to a December 31, is no longer effective. Accordingly, unless a new apportionment plan is adopted, the surtax exemption** of the component members of the controlled group for their taxable years which include such December 31 and all December 31's thereafter will be determined in accordance with the rules provided in paragraph (a)(1)(i) of § 1.1561–2.

* * *

§ 1.1563–1 Definition of controlled group of corporations and component members.

(a) Controlled group of corporations—(1) In general. For purposes of sections 1561 through 1563 and the regulations thereunder, the term "controlled group of corporations" means any group of corporations which is either a "parent-subsidiary controlled group" (as defined in subparagraph (2) of this

*Editorial comment: Presently $75,000 rather than $50,000.

**Editorial comment: The beneficial tax rates and the related amounts appear in Sec. 11(b) rather than Sec. 11(d).

paragraph), a "brother-sister controlled group" (as defined in subparagraph (3) of this paragraph), a "combined group" (as defined in subparagraph (4) of this paragraph), or an "insurance group" (as defined in subparagraph (5) of this paragraph). For the exclusion of certain stock for purposes of applying the definitions contained in this paragraph, see section 1563(c) and § 1.1563–2.

(2) Parent-subsidiary controlled group. (i) The term "parent-subsidiary controlled group" means one or more chains of corporations connected through stock ownership with a common parent corporation if:

(a) Stock possessing at least 80 percent of the total combined voting power of all classes of stock entitled to vote or at least 80 percent of the total value of shares of all classes of stock of each of the corporations, except the common parent corporation, is owned (directly and with the application of paragraph (b)(1) of § 1.1563–3, relating to options) by one or more of the other corporations; and

(b) The common parent corporation owns (directly and with the application of paragraph (b)(1) of § 1.1563–3, relating to options) stock possessing at least 80 percent of the total combined voting power of all classes of stock entitled to vote or at least 80 percent of the total value of shares of all classes of stock of at least one of the other corporations, excluding, in computing such voting power or value, stock owned directly by such other corporations.

(ii) The definition of a parent-subsidiary controlled group of corporations may be illustrated by the following examples:

Example (1). P Corporation owns stock possessing 80 percent of the total combined voting power of all classes of stock entitled to vote of S Corporation. P is the common parent of a parent-subsidiary controlled group consisting of member corporations P and S.

Example (2). Assume the same facts as in example (1). Assume further that S owns stock possessing 80 percent of the total value of shares of all classes of stock of T Corporation. P is the common parent of a parent-subsidiary controlled group consisting of member corporations P, S, and T. The result would be the same if P, rather than S, owned the T stock.

Example (3). L Corporation owns 80 percent of the only class of stock of M Corporation and M, in turn, owns 40 percent of the only class of stock of O Corporation. L also owns 80 percent of the only class of stock of N Corporation and N, in turn, owns 40 percent of the only class of stock of O. L is the common parent of a parent-subsidiary controlled group consisting of member corporations L, M, N, and O.

Example (4). X Corporation owns 75 percent of the only class of stock of Y and Z Corporations; Y owns all the remaining stock of Z; and Z owns all the remaining stock of Y. Since intercompany stockholdings are excluded (that is, are not treated as outstanding) for purposes of determining whether X owns stock possessing at least 80 percent of the voting power or value of at least one of the other corporations, X is treated as the owner of stock possessing 100 percent of the voting power and value of Y and of Z for purposes of subdivision (i)(b) of this subparagraph. Also, stock possessing 100 percent of the voting power and value of Y and Z is owned by the other corporations in the group within the meaning of subdivision (i)(a) of this subparagraph. (X and Y together own stock possessing 100 percent of the voting power and value of Z, and X and Z together own stock possessing 100 percent of the voting power and value of Y.) Therefore, X is the common parent of a parent-subsidiary controlled group of corporations consisting of member corporations X, Y, and Z.

(3) Brother-sister controlled group.** **(i)** The term "brother-sister controlled group" means two or more corporations if the same five or fewer persons who are individuals, estates, or trusts own (directly and with the application of the rules contained in paragraph (b) of § 1.1563–3), stock possessing:

(a) At least 80 percent of the total combined voting power of all classes of stock entitled to vote or at least 80 percent of the total value of shares of all classes of the stock of each corporation; and

(b) More than 50 percent of the total combined voting power of all classes of stock entitled to vote or more than 50 percent of the total value of shares of all classes of stock of each corporation, taking into account the stock ownership of each such person only to the extent such stock ownership is identical with respect to each such corporation.

The five or fewer persons whose stock ownership is considered for purposes of the 80 percent requirement must be the same persons whose stock ownership is considered for purposes of the more-than-50 percent requirement.

(ii) The principles of this subparagraph may be illustrated by the following examples:* and **

*Editorial comment: The Regulations now reflect the effect of the Supreme Court decision in *U.S. v. Vogel Fertilizer Co.* [102 S.Ct. 821 (1982)].

**Editorial comment: The Regulations do not reflect the effect of the American Jobs Creation Act of 2004 which deleted the 80% requirement in defining a brother-sister controlled group under § 1563. See § 1563(a)(2).

Example (1). The outstanding stock of corporations P, Q, R, S, and T, which have only one class of stock outstanding is owned by the following unrelated individuals.

Individuals	P	Q	R	S	T	Identical ownership
	Corporations					
A	55%	51%	55%	55%	55%	51%.
B	45%	49%	.....	.....	.....	(45% in P & Q).
C	.....	.....	45%	.....	.....	
D	.....	.....	.....	45%	.....	
E	.....	.....	.....	.....	45%	
Total	100%	100%	100%	100%	100%	

Corporations P and Q are members of a brother-sister controlled group of corporations. Although the more-than-50 percent identical ownership requirement is met for all 5 corporations, corporations R, S, and T are not members because at least 80 percent of the stock of each of those corporations is not owned by the same 5 or fewer persons whose stock ownership is considered for purposes of the more-than-50 percent identical ownership requirement.

Example (2). The outstanding stock of corporations U and V, which have only one class of stock outstanding, is owned by the following unrelated individuals:

Individuals	U (percent)	V (percent)
	Corporations	
A	12	12
B	12	12
C	12	12
D	12	12
E	13	13
F	13	13
G	13	13
H	13	13
Total	100	100

Any group of five of the shareholders will own more than 50 percent of the stock in each corporation, in identical holdings. However, U and V are not members of brother-sister controlled group because at least 80 percent of the stock of each corporation is not owned by the same five or fewer persons.

Example (3). Corporation X and Y each have two classes of stock outstanding, voting common and non-voting common. (None of this stock is excluded from the definition of stock under section 1563(c).) Unrelated individuals A and B own the following percentages of the class of stock entitled to vote (voting) and of the total value of shares of all classes of stock (value) in each of corporations X and Y:

Individuals	X	Y
	Corporations	
A	100% voting, 60% value.	75% voting, 60% value.
B	0% voting, 10% value.	25% voting, 10% value.

No other shareholder of X owns (or is considered to own) any stock in Y. X and Y are a brother-sister controlled group of corporations. The group meets the more-than-50 percent ownership requirements because A and B own more than 50 percent of the total value of shares of all classes of stock of X and Y in identical holdings. (The group also meets the more-than-50 percent ownership requirement because of A's voting stock ownership.) The group meets the 80 percent requirement because A and B own at least 80 percent of the total combined voting power of all classes of stock entitled to vote.

Example (4). Assume the same facts as in example (3) except that the value of the stock owned by A and B is not more than 50 percent of the total value of shares of all classes of stock of each corporation in identical holdings. X and Y are not a brother-sister controlled group of corporations. The group meets the more-than-50 percent ownership requirement because A owns more than 50 percent of the total combined voting power of the voting stock of each corporation. For purposes of the 80 percent requirement, B's voting stock in Y cannot be combined with A's voting stock in Y since B, who does not own any voting stock in X, is not a person whose ownership is considered for purposes of the more-than-50 percent requirement. Because no other shareholder owns stock in both X and Y, these other shareholders' stock ownership is not counted towards meeting either the more-than-50 percent ownership requirement or the 80-percent ownership requirement.

* * *

(4) Combined group. **(i)** The term "combined group" means any group of three or more corporations, if:

(a) Each such corporation is a member of either a parent-subsidiary controlled group of corporations or a brother-sister controlled group of corporations, and

(b) At least one of such corporations is the common parent of a parent-subsidiary controlled group and also is a member of a brother-sister controlled group.

(ii) The definition of a combined group of corporations may be illustrated by the following examples:

Example (1). Smith, an individual, owns stock possessing 80 percent of the total combined voting power of all classes of the stock of corporations X and Y. Y, in turn, owns stock possessing 80 percent of the total combined voting power of all classes of the stock of corporation Z. Since:

(a) X, Y, and Z are each members of either a parent-subsidiary or brother-sister controlled group of corporations, and

(b) Y is the common parent of a parent-subsidiary controlled group of corporations consisting of Y and Z, and also is a member of a brother-sister controlled group of corporations consisting of X and Y,

X, Y, and Z are members of the same combined group.

Example (2). Assume the same facts as in example (1), and further assume that corporation X owns 80 percent of the total value of shares of all classes of stock of corporation T, X, Y, Z, and T are members of the same combined group.

* * *

(6) Voting power of stock. For purposes of § 1.1562–5, this section, and §§ 1.1563–2 and 1.1563–3, in determining whether the stock owned by a person (or persons) possesses a certain percentage of the total combined voting power of all classes of stock entitled to vote of a corporation, consideration will be given to all the facts and circumstances of each case. A share of stock will generally be considered as possessing the voting power accorded to such share by the corporate charter, bylaws, or share certificate. On the other hand, if there is any agreement, whether express or implied, that a shareholder will not vote his stock in a corporation, the formal voting rights possessed by his stock may be disregarded in determining the percentage of the total combined voting power possessed by the stock owned by other shareholders in the corporation, if the result is that the corporation becomes a component member of a controlled group of corporations. Moreover, if a shareholder agrees to vote his stock in a corporation in the manner specified by another shareholder in the corporation, the voting rights possessed by the stock owned by the first shareholder may be considered to be possessed by the stock owned by such other shareholder if the result is that the corporation becomes a component member of a controlled group of corporations.

(b) Component members—(1) In general. For purposes of sections 1561 through 1563 and the regulations thereunder, a corporation is a component member of a controlled group of corporations on a December 31 (and with respect to the taxable year which includes such December 31) if such corporation:

(i) Is a member of such controlled group on such December 31 and is not treated as an excluded member under subparagraph (2) of this paragraph, or

(ii) Is not a member of such controlled group on such December 31 but is treated as an additional member under subparagraph (3) of this paragraph.

*Editorial comment: Presently Sec. 1361 and Sec. 1374 rather than Sec. 1371 and Sec. 1378.

(2) Excluded members. (i) A corporation, which is a member of a controlled group of corporations on the December 31 included within its taxable year, but was a member of such group for less than one-half of the number of days in such taxable year which precede such December 31, shall be treated as an excluded member of such group on such December 31.

(ii) A corporation which is a member of a controlled group of corporations on any December 31 shall be treated as an excluded member of such group on such date if, for its taxable year including such date, such corporation is:

(a) Exempt from taxation under section 501(a) (except a corporation which has unrelated business taxable income for such taxable year which is subject to tax under section 511) or 521,

(b) A foreign corporation not subject to taxation under section 882(a) for the taxable year,

(c) An electing small business corporation (as defined in section 1371(b))* not subject to the tax imposed by section 1378,*

* * *

§ 1.1563–3 Rules for determining stock ownership.

(a) In general. In determining stock ownership for purposes of §§ 1.1562–5, 1.1563–1, 1.1563–2, and this section, the constructive ownership rules of paragraph (b) of this section apply to the extent such rules are referred to in such sections. The application of such rules shall be subject to the operating rules and special rules contained in paragraphs (c) and (d) of this section.

(b) Constructive ownership—(1) Options. If a person has an option to acquire any outstanding stock of a corporation, such stock shall be considered as owned by such person. For purposes of this subparagraph, an option to acquire such an option, and each one of a series of such options, shall be considered as an option to acquire such stock. For example, assume Smith owns an option to purchase 100 shares of the outstanding stock of M Corporation. Under this subparagraph, Smith is considered to own such 100 shares. The result would be the same if Smith owned an option to acquire the option (or one of a series of options) to purchase 100 shares of M stock.

(2) Attribution from partnerships. **(i)** Stock owned, directly or indirectly, by or for a partnership shall be considered as owned by any partner having an interest of 5 percent or more in either the capital or profits of the partnership in proportion to his interest in capital or profits, whichever such proportion is the greater.

(ii) The provisions of this subparagraph may be illustrated by the following example:

Example. Green, Jones, and White, unrelated individuals, are partners in the GJW partnership. The partners' interests in the capital and profits of the partnership are as follows:

Partner	Capital	Profits
	Percent	Percent
Green	36	25
Jones	60	71
White	4	4

The GJW partnership owns the entire outstanding stock (100 shares) of X Corporation. Under this subparagraph, Green is considered to own the X stock owned by the partnership in proportion to his interest in capital (36 percent) or profits (25 percent), whichever such proportion is the greater. Therefore, Green is considered to own 36 shares of the X stock. However, since Jones has a greater interest in the profits of the partnership, he is considered to own the X stock in proportion to his interest in such profits. Therefore, Jones is considered to own 71 shares of the X stock. Since White does not have an interest of 5 percent or more in either the capital or profits of the partnership, he is not considered to own any shares of the X stock.

(3) Attribution from estates or trusts. **(i)** Stock owned, directly or indirectly, by or for an estate or trust shall be considered as owned by any beneficiary who has an actuarial interest of 5 percent or more in such stock, to the extent of such actuarial interest. For purposes of this subparagraph, the actuarial interest of each beneficiary shall be determined by assuming the maximum exercise of discretion by the fiduciary in favor of such beneficiary and the maximum use of such stock to satisfy his rights as a beneficiary. A beneficiary of an estate or trust who cannot under any circumstances receive any interest in stock held by the estate or trust, including the proceeds from the disposition thereof, or the income therefrom, does not have an actuarial interest in such stock. Thus, where stock owned by a decedent's estate has been specifically bequeathed to certain beneficiaries and the remainder of the estate is bequeathed to other beneficiaries, the stock is attributable only to the beneficiaries to whom it is specifically bequeathed. Similarly, a remainderman of a trust who cannot under any circumstances receive any interest in the stock of a corporation which is a part of the corpus of the trust (including any accumulated income therefrom or the proceeds from a disposition thereof) does not have an actuarial interest in such stock. However, an income beneficiary of a trust does have an actuarial interest in stock if he has any right to the income from such stock even though under the terms of the trust instrument such stock can never be distributed to him. The factors and methods prescribed in § 20.2031–7 of this chapter (Estate Tax Regulations) for use in ascertaining the value of an interest in property for estate tax purposes shall be used for purposes of this subdivision in determining a beneficiary's actuarial interest in stock owned directly or indirectly by or for a trust.

(ii) For the purposes of this subparagraph, property of a decedent shall be considered as owned by his estate if such property is subject to administration by the executor or administrator for the purposes of paying claims against the estate and expenses of administration notwithstanding that, under local law, legal title to such property vests in the decedent's heirs, legatees or devisees immediately upon death. With respect to an estate, the term "beneficiary" includes any person entitled to receive property of the decedent pursuant to a will or pursuant to laws of descent and distribution. A person shall no longer be considered a beneficiary of an estate when all the property to which he is entitled has been received by him, when he no longer has a claim against the estate arising out of having been a beneficiary, and when there is only a remote possibility that it will be necessary for the estate to seek the return of property or to seek payment from him by contribution or otherwise to satisfy claims against the estate or expenses of administration. When pursuant to the preceding sentence, a person ceases to be a beneficiary, stock owned by the estate shall not thereafter be considered owned by him.

(iii) Stock owned, directly or indirectly, by or for any portion of a trust of which a person is considered the owner under subpart E, part I, subchapter J of the Code (relating to grantors and others treated as substantial owners) is considered as owned by such person.

(iv) This subparagraph does not apply to stock owned by any employees' trust described in section 401(a) which is exempt from tax under section 501(a).

(4) Attribution from corporations. **(i)** Stock owned, directly or indirectly, by or for a corporation shall be considered as owned by any person who owns (within the meaning of section 1563(d)) 5 percent or more in value or its stock in that proportion which the value of the stock which such person so owns bears to the value of all the stock in such corporation.

(ii) The provisions of this subparagraph may be illustrated by the following example:

Example. Brown, an individual, owns 60 shares of the 100 shares of the only class of outstanding stock of corporation P. Smith, an individual, owns 4 shares of the P stock, and corporation X owns 36 shares of the P stock. Corporation P owns, directly and indirectly, 50 shares of the stock of corporation S. Under this subparagraph, Brown is considered to own 30 shares of the S stock ($^{60}/_{100} \times 50$), and X is considered to own 18 shares of the S stock ($^{36}/_{100} \times 50$). Since Smith does not own 5 percent or more in value of the P stock, he is not considered as owning any of the S stock owned by P. If, in this example, Smith's wife had owned directly 1 share of the P stock, Smith (and his wife) would each own 5 shares of the P stock, and therefore Smith (and his wife) would be considered as owning 2.5 shares of the S stock ($^{5}/_{100} \times 50$).

(5) Spouse. (i) Except as provided in subdivision (ii) of this subparagraph, an individual shall be considered to own the stock owned, directly or indirectly, by or for his spouse, other than a spouse who is legally separated from the individual under a decree of divorce, whether interlocutory or final, or a decree of separate maintenance.

(ii) An individual shall not be considered to own stock in a corporation owned, directly or indirectly, by or for his spouse on any day of a taxable year of such corporation, provided that each of the following conditions are satisfied with respect to such taxable year:

(a) Such individual does not, at any time during such taxable year, own directly any stock in such corporation.

(b) Such individual is not a member of the board of directors or an employee of such corporation and does not participate in the management of such corporation at any time during such taxable year.

(c) Not more than 50 percent of such corporation's gross income for such taxable year was derived from royalties, rents, dividends, interest, and annuities.

(d) Such stock in such corporation is not, at any time during such taxable year, subject to conditions which substantially restrict or limit the spouse's right to dispose of such stock and which run in favor of the individual or his children who have not attained the age of 21 years. The principles of paragraph (b)(2)(iii) of § 1.1563–2 shall apply in determining whether a condition is a condition described in the preceding sentence.

(iii) For purposes of subdivision (ii)(c) of this subparagraph, the gross income of a corporation for a taxable year shall be determined under section 61 and the regulations thereunder. The terms "royalties", "rents", "dividends", "interest", and "annuities" shall have the same meanings such terms are given for purposes of section 1244(c). See paragraph (e)(1)(ii), (iii), (iv), (v), and (vi) of § 1.1244(c)–1.

(6) Children, grandchildren, parents, and grandparents. (i) An individual shall be considered to own the stock owned, directly or indirectly, by or for his children who have not attained the age of 21 years, and, if the individual has not attained the age of 21 years, the stock owned, directly or indirectly, by or for his parents.

(ii) If an individual owns (directly, and with the application of the rules of this paragraph but without regard to this subdivision) stock possessing more than 50 percent of the total combined voting power of all classes of stock entitled to vote or more than 50 percent of the total value of shares of all classes of stock in a corporation, then such individual shall be considered to own the stock in such corporation owned, directly or indirectly, by or for his parents, grandparents, grandchildren, and children who have attained the age of 21 years. In determining whether the stock owned by an individual possesses the requisite percentage of the total combined voting power of all classes of stock entitled to vote of a corporation, see paragraph (a)(6) of § 1.1563–1.

(iii) For purposes of section 1563, and §§ 1.1563–1 through 1.1563–4, a legally adopted child of an individual shall be treated as a child of such individual by blood.

* * *

PROCEDURE AND ADMINISTRATION

INFORMATION AND RETURNS

Returns and Records

Records, Statements, and Special Returns

§ 1.6001–1 Records.

(a) In general. Except as provided in paragraph (b) of this section, any person subject to tax under subtitle A of the Code (including a qualified State individual income tax which is treated pursuant to section 6361(a) as if it were imposed by chapter 1 of subtitle A), or any person required to file a return of information with respect to income, shall keep such permanent books of account or records, including inventories, as are sufficient to establish the amount of gross income, deductions, credits, or other matters required to be shown by such person in any return of such tax or information.

(b) Farmers and wage-earners. Individuals deriving gross income from the business of farming, and individuals whose gross income includes salaries, wages, or similar compensation for personal services rendered, are required with respect to such income to keep such records as will enable the district director to determine the correct amount of income subject to the tax. It is not necessary, however, that with respect to such income individuals keep the books of account or records required by paragraph (a) of this section. For rules with respect to the records to be kept in substantiation of traveling and other business expenses of employees, see § 1.162–17.

* * *

(d) Notice by district director requiring returns statements, or the keeping of records. The district director may require any person, by notice served upon him, to make such returns, render such statements, or keep such specific records as will enable the district director to determine whether or not such person is liable for tax under subtitle A of the Code, including qualified State individual income taxes, which are treated pursuant to section 6361(a) as if they were imposed by chapter 1 of subtitle A.

(e) Retention of records. The books or records required by this section shall be kept at all times available for inspection by authorized internal revenue officers or employees, and shall be retained so long as the contents thereof may become material in the administration of any internal revenue law.

* * *

Tax Returns Or Statements

§ 1.6011–1 General requirement of return, statement, or list.

(a) General rule. Every person subject to any tax, or required to collect any tax, under subtitle A of the Code, shall make such returns or statements as are required by the regulations in this chapter. The return or statement shall include therein the information required by the applicable regulations or forms.

(b) Use of prescribed forms. Copies of the prescribed return forms will so far as possible be furnished taxpayers by district directors. A taxpayer will not be excused from making a return, however, by the fact that no return form has been furnished to him. Taxpayers not supplied with the proper forms should make application therefor to the district director in ample time to have their returns prepared, verified, and filed on or before the due date with the internal revenue office where such returns are required to be filed. Each taxpayer should carefully prepare his return and set forth fully and clearly the information required to be included therein. Returns which have not been so prepared will not be accepted as meeting the requirements of the Code. In the absence of a prescribed form, a statement made by a taxpayer disclosing his gross income and the deductions therefrom may be accepted as a tentative return, and, if filed within the prescribed time, the statement so made will relieve the taxpayer from liability for the addition to tax imposed for the delinquent filing of the return, provided that without unnecessary delay such a tentative return is supplemented by a return made on the proper form.

* * *

Subchapter B—Estate and Gift Taxes

PART 20—ESTATE TAX; ESTATES OF DECEDENTS DYING AFTER AUGUST 16, 1954

INTRODUCTION

* * *

§ 20.0–2 General description of tax.

(a) Nature of tax. The Federal estate tax is neither a property tax nor an inheritance tax. It is a tax imposed upon the transfer of the entire taxable estate and not upon any particular legacy, devise, or distributive share. Escheat of a decedent's property to the State for lack of heirs is a transfer which causes the property to be included in the decedent's gross estate.

(b) Method of determining tax; estate of citizen or resident—(1) In general. Subparagraphs (2) to (5) of this paragraph contain a general description of the method to be used in determining the Federal estate tax imposed upon the transfer of the estate of a decedent who was a citizen or resident of the United States at the time of his death.

(2) Gross estate. The first step in determining the tax is to ascertain the total value of the decedent's gross estate. The value of the gross estate includes the value of all property to the extent of the interest therein of the decedent at the time of his death. (For certain exceptions in the case of real property situated outside the United States, see paragraphs (a) and (c) of § 20.2031–1.) In addition, the gross estate may include property in which the decedent did not have an interest at the time of his death. A decedent's gross estate for Federal estate tax purposes may therefore be very different from the same decedent's estate for local probate purposes. Examples of items which may be included in a decedent's gross estate and not in his probate estate are the following: certain property transferred by the decedent during his lifetime without adequate consideration; property held jointly by the decedent and others; property over which the decedent had a general power of appointment; proceeds of certain policies of insurance on the decedent's life; annuities; and dower or curtesy of a surviving spouse or a statutory estate in lieu thereof. For a detailed explanation of the method of ascertaining the value of the gross estate, see sections 2031 through 2044, and the regulations thereunder.

(3) Taxable estate. The second step in determining the tax is to ascertain the value of the decedent's taxable estate. The value of the taxable estate is determined by subtracting from the value of the gross estate the authorized exemption and deductions. Under various conditions and limitations, deductions are allowable for expenses, indebtedness, taxes, losses, charitable transfers, and transfers to a surviving spouse. For a detailed explanation of the method of ascertaining the value of the taxable estate, see sections 2051 through 2056, and the regulations thereunder.

(4) Gross estate tax. The third step is the determination of the gross estate tax. This is accomplished by the application of certain rates to the value of the decedent's taxable estate. In this connection, see section 2001 and the regulations thereunder.

(5) Net estate tax payable. The final step is the determination of the net estate tax payable. This is done by subtracting from the gross estate tax the authorized credits against tax. Under certain conditions and limitations, credits are allowable for the following (computed in the order stated below):

(i) State death taxes paid in connection with the decedent's estate (section 2011);

(ii) Gift taxes paid on inter-vivos transfers by the decedent of property included in his gross estate (section 2012);

(iii) Foreign death taxes paid in connection with the decedent's estate (section 2014); and

(iv) Federal estate taxes paid on transfers of property to the decedent (section 2013).

Sections 2015 and 2016 contain certain further rules for the application of the credits for State and foreign death taxes. For a detailed explanation of the credits against tax, see sections 2011 through 2016, and the regulations thereunder.

* * *

ESTATES OF CITIZENS OR RESIDENTS

* * *

Credits Against Tax

§ 20.2011–1 Credit for State death taxes.*

(a) In general. A credit is allowed under section 2011 against the Federal estate tax for estate, inheritance, legacy or succession taxes actually paid to any State, Territory, or the District of Columbia,* * * (hereinafter referred to as "State death taxes"). The credit, however, is allowed only for State death taxes paid (1) with respect to property included in the decedent's gross estate, and (2) with respect to the decedent's estate. The amount of the credit is subject to the limitation described in paragraph (b) of this section. It is subject to further limitations described in § 20.2011–2 if a deduction is allowed under section 2053(d) for State death taxes paid with respect to a charitable gift. * * *

(b) Amount of credit. (1) If the decedent's taxable estate does not exceed $40,000, the credit for State death taxes is zero. If the decedent's taxable estate does exceed $40,000, the credit for State death taxes is limited to an amount computed in accordance with the following table:

TABLE FOR COMPUTATION OF MAXIMUM CREDIT FOR STATE DEATH TAXES

(A)—Taxable estate equal to or more than—	(B)—Taxable estate less than—	(C)—Credit on amount in column (A)	(D)—Rates of credit on excess over amount in column (A) (percent)
$40,000	$90,000	.....	0.8
90,000	140,000	$400	1.6
140,000	240,000	1,200	2.4
240,000	440,000	3,600	3.2
440,000	640,000	10,000	4.0
640,000	840,000	18,000	4.8
840,000	1,040,000	27,600	5.6
1,040,000	1,540,000	38,800	6.4
1,540,000	2,040,000	70,800	7.2
2,040,000	2,540,000	106,800	8.0
2,540,000	3,040,000	146,800	8.8
3,040,000	3,540,000	190,800	9.6
3,540,000	4,040,000	238,800	10.4
4,040,000	5,040,000	290,800	11.2
5,040,000	6,040,000	402,800	12.0
6,040,000	7,040,000	522,800	12.8
7,040,000	8,040,000	650,800	13.6
8,040,000	9,040,000	786,800	14.4
9,040,000	10,040,000	930,800	15.2
10,040,000	.....	1,082,800	16.0

(2) Subparagraph (1) of this paragraph may be illustrated by the following example:

Example. (i) The decedent died January 1, 1955, leaving a taxable estate of $150,000. On January 1, 1956, inheritance taxes totaling $2,500 were actually paid to a State with respect to property included in the decedent's gross estate. Reference to the table discloses that the specified amount in column (A) nearest to but less than the value of the decedent's taxable estate is $140,000. The maximum credit in respect of this amount, as indicated in column (C), is $1,200. The amount by which the taxable estate exceeds the same specified amount is $10,000. The maximum credit in respect of this amount, computed at the rate of 2.4 percent indicated in column (D), is $240. Thus, the maximum credit in respect of the decedent's taxable estate of $150,000 is $1,440, even though $2,500 in inheritance taxes was actually paid to the State.

(ii) If, in subdivision (i) of this example, the amount actually paid to the State was $950, the credit for State death taxes would be limited to $950. If, in subdivision (i) of this example, the decedent's taxable estate was $35,000, no credit for State death taxes would be allowed.

* * *

§ 20.2011–2 Limitation on credit if a deduction for State death taxes is allowed under section 2053(d).

If a deduction is allowed under section 2053(d) for State death taxes paid with respect to a charitable gift, the credit for State death taxes is subject to special limitations. Under these limitations, the credit cannot exceed the least of the following:

(a) The amount of State death taxes paid other than those for which a deduction is allowed under section 2053(d);

(b) The amount indicated in section 2011(b) to be the maximum credit allowable with respect to the decedent's taxable estate; or

(c) An amount, A, which bears the same ratio to B (the amount which would be the maximum credit allowable under section 2011(b) if the deduction under section 2053(d) for State death taxes were not allowed in computing the decedent's taxable estate) as C (the amount of State death taxes paid other than those for which a deduction is allowed under section 2053(d)) bears to D (the total amount of State death taxes paid). For the purpose of this computation, in determining what the decedent's taxable estate would be if the deduction for State death taxes under section 2053(d) were not allowed, adjustment

*Editorial comment: The Regulations do not reflect the effect of the Tax Relief Reconciliation Act of 2001 which repealed the state death tax credit. The repeal used a phaseout approach which commenced in 2002 and was completed in 2005.

must be made for the decrease in the deduction for charitable gifts under section 2055 or 2106(a)(2)(for estates of nonresidents not citizens) by reason of any increase in Federal estate tax which would be charged against the charitable gifts.

The application of this section may be illustrated by the following example:

Example. The decedent died January 1, 1955, leaving a gross estate of $925,000. Expenses, indebtedness, etc., amounted to $25,000. The decedent bequeathed $400,000 to his son with the direction that the son bear the State death taxes on the bequest. The residuary estate was left to a charitable organization. Except as noted above, all Federal and State death taxes were payable out of the residuary estate. The State imposed death taxes of $60,000 on the son's bequest and death taxes of $75,000 on the bequest to charity. No death taxes were imposed by a foreign country with respect to any property in the gross estate. The decedent's taxable estate (determined without regard to the limitation imposed by section 2011(e)(2)(B) is computed as follows:

* * *

Gross estate				$925,000.00
Expenses, indebtedness, etc			$25,000.00	
Exemption			60,000.00	
Deduction under section 2053(d)			75,000.00	
Charitable deduction:				
Gross estate		$925,000.00		
Expenses, etc	$25,000.00			
Bequest to son	400,000.00			
State death tax paid from residue	75,000.00			
Federal estate tax paid from residue	122,916.67	622,916.67	302,083.33	462,083.33
Taxable estate				462,916.67

If the deduction under section 2053(d) were not allowed, the decedent's taxable estate would be computed as follows:

Gross estate				$925,000.00
Expenses, indebtedness, etc			$25,000.00	
Exemption			60,000.00	
Charitable deduction:				
Gross estate		$925,000.00		
Expenses, etc	$25,000.00			
Bequest to son	400,000.00			
State death tax paid from residue	75,000.00			
Federal estate tax paid from residue	155,000.00	655,000.00	270,000.00	355,000.00
Taxable estate				570,000.00

On a taxable estate of $570,000, the maximum credit allowable under section 2011(b) would be $15,200. Under these facts, the credit for State death taxes is determined as follows:

(1) Amount of State death taxes paid other than those for which a deduction is allowed under section 2053(d) ($135,000–$75,000)	$60,000.00
(2) Amount indicated in section 2011(b) to be the maximum credit allowable with respect to the decedent's taxable estate of $462,916.67	10,916.67
(3) Amount determined by use of the ratio described in paragraph (c) above [($60,000 ÷ $135,000) × $15,200]	6,755.56
(4) Credit for State death taxes (least of subparagraphs (1) through (3) above)	6,755.56

§ 20.2013–1 Credit for tax on prior transfers.

(a) In general. A credit is allowed under section 2013 against the Federal estate tax imposed on the present decedent's estate for Federal estate tax paid on the transfer of property to the present decedent from a transferor who died within ten years before, or within two years after, the present decedent's death. See § 20.2013–5 for definition of the terms "property" and "transfer". There is no requirement that the transferred property be identified in the estate of the present decedent or that the property be in existence at the time of the decedent's death. It is sufficient that the transfer of the property was subjected to Federal estate tax in the estate of the transferor and that the transferor died within the prescribed period of time. The executor must submit such proof as may be requested by the district director in order to establish the right of the estate to the credit.

(b) Limitations on credit. The credit for tax on prior transfers is limited to the smaller of the following amounts:

(1) The amount of the Federal estate tax attributable to the transferred property in the transferor's estate, computed as set forth in § 20.2013–2; or

(2) The amount of the Federal estate tax attributable to the transferred property in the decedent's estate, computed as set forth in § 20.2013–3.

Rules for valuing property for purposes of the credit are contained in § 20.2013–4.

(c) **Percentage reduction.** If the transferor died within the two years before, or within the two years after, the present decedent's death, the credit is the smaller of the two limitations described in paragraph (b) of this section. If the transferor predeceased the present decedent by more than two years, the credit is a certain percentage of the smaller of the two limitations described in paragraph (b) of this section, determined as follows:

(1) 80 percent, if the transferor died within the third or fourth years preceding the present decedent's death;

(2) 40 percent, if the transferor died within the fifth or sixth years preceding the present decedent's death;

(3) 40 percent, if the transferor died within the seventh or eighth years preceding the present decedent's death; and

(4) 20 percent, if the transferor died within the ninth or tenth years preceding the present decedent's death.

The word "within" as used in this paragraph means "during". Therefore, if a death occurs on the second anniversary of another death, the first death is considered to have occurred within the two years before the second death. If the credit for tax on prior transfers relates to property received from two or more transferors, the provisions of this paragraph are to be applied separately with respect to the property received from each transferor. * * *

§ 20.2015–1 Credit for death taxes on remainders.

(a) If the executor of an estate elects under section 6163(a) to postpone the time for payment of any portion of the Federal estate tax attributable to a reversionary or remainder interest in property, credit is allowed under sections 2011 and 2014 against that portion of the Federal estate tax for State death taxes and foreign death taxes attributable to the reversionary or remainder interest if the State death taxes or foreign death taxes are paid and if credit therefor is claimed either—

(1) Within the time provided for in sections 2011 and 2014, or

(2) Within the time for payment of the tax imposed by section 2001 or 2101 as postponed under section 6163(a) and as extended under section 6163(b)(on account of undue hardship) or, if the precedent interest terminated before July 5, 1958, within 60 days after the termination of the preceding interest or interests in the property.

The allowance of credit, however, is subject to the other limitations contained in sections 2011 and 2014 and, in the case of the estate of a decedent who was a nonresident not a citizen of the United States, in section 2102(b).

(b) In applying the rule stated in paragraph (a) of this section, credit for State death taxes or foreign death taxes paid within the time provided in sections 2011 and 2014 is applied first to the portion of the Federal estate tax payment of which is not postponed, and any excess is applied to the balance of the Federal estate tax. However, credit for State death taxes or foreign death taxes not paid within the time provided in section 2011 and 2014 is allowable only against the portion of the Federal estate tax attributable to the reversionary or remainder interest, and only for State or foreign death taxes attributable to that interest. If a State death tax or a foreign death tax is imposed upon both a reversionary or remainder interest and upon other property, without a definite apportionment of the tax, the amount of the tax deemed attributable to the reversionary or remainder interest is an amount which bears the same ratio to the total tax as the value of the reversionary or remainder interest bears to the value of the entire property with respect to which the tax was imposed. In applying this ratio, adjustments consistent with those required under paragraph (c) of § 20.6163–1 must be made.

(c) The application of this section may be illustrated by the following examples:

Example (1). One-third of the Federal estate tax was attributable to a remainder interest in real property located in State Y, and two-thirds of the Federal estate tax was attributable to other property located in State X. The payment of the tax attributable to the remainder interest was postponed under the provisions of section 6163(a). The maximum credit allowable for State death taxes under the provisions of section 2011 is $12,000. Therefore, of the maximum credit allowable, $4,000 is attributable to the remainder interest and $8,000 is attributable to the other property. Within the 4-year period provided for in section 2011, inheritance tax in the amount of $9,000 was paid to State X in connection with the other property. With respect to this $9,000, $8,000 (the maximum amount allowable) is allowed as a credit against the Federal estate tax attributable to the other property, and $1,000 is allowed as a credit against the postponed tax. The life estate or other precedent interest expired after July 4, 1958. After the expiration of the 4-year period but before the expiration of the period of postponement elected under section 6163(a) and of the period of extension granted under section 6163(b) for payment of the tax, inheritance tax in the amount of $5,000 was paid to State Y in connection with the remainder interest. As the maximum credit allowable with respect to the remainder interest is $4,000 and $1,000 has already been allowed as a credit, an additional $3,000 will be credited against the Federal estate tax attributable to the remainder interest. It should be noted that if the life estate or other precedent interest had expired after the expiration of the 4-year period but before July 5, 1958, the same result would be reached only if the inheritance tax had been paid to State Y before the expiration of 60 days after the termination of the life estate or other precedent interest.

Example (2). The facts are the same as in example (1), except that within the 4-year period inheritance tax in the amount of $2,500 was paid to State Y with respect to the remainder interest and inheritance tax in the amount of $7,500 was paid to State X with respect to the other property. The amount of $8,000 is allowed as a credit against the Federal estate tax attributable to the other property and the amount of $2,000 is allowed as a credit against the postponed tax. The life estate or other precedent interest expired after July 4, 1958. After the expiration of the 4-year period but before the expiration of the period of postponement elected under section 6163(a) and of the period of extension granted under section 6163(b) for payment of the tax, inheritance tax in the amount of $5,000 was paid to State Y in connection with the remainder interest. As the maximum credit allowable with respect to the remainder interest is $4,000 and $2,000 already has been allowed as a credit, an additional $2,000 will be credited against the Federal estate tax attributable to the remainder interest. It should be noted that if the life estate or other precedent interest had expired after the expiration of the 4-year period but before July 5, 1958, the same result would be reached only if the inheritance tax had been paid to State Y before the expiration of 60 days after the termination of the life estate or other precedent interest.

Example (3). The facts are the same as in example (2), except that no payment was made to State Y within the 4-year period. The amount of $7,500 is allowed as a credit against the Federal estate tax attributable to the other property. After termination of the life interest additional credit will be allowed in the amount of $4,000 against the Federal estate tax attributable to the remainder interest. Since the payment of $5,000 was made to State Y following the expiration of the 4-year period, no part of the payment may be allowed as a credit against the Federal estate tax attributable to the other property.

* * *

Gross Estate

§ 20.2031–0 Table of contents.

This section lists the section headings and undesignated center headings that appear in the regulations under section 2031.

§ 20.2031–1 Definition of gross estate; valuation of property.

(a) Definition of gross estate. Except as otherwise provided in this paragraph the value of the gross estate of a decedent who was a citizen or resident of the United States at the time of his death is the total value of the interests described in sections 2033 through 2044.* * * In the case of a decedent dying after October 16, 1962, real property situated outside the United States which comes within the scope of sections 2033 through 2044 is included in the gross estate to the same extent as any other property coming within the scope of those sections. In arriving at the value of the gross estate the interests described in sections 2033 through 2044 are valued as described in this section, §§ 20.2031–2 through 20.2031–9 and § 20.2032–1. The contents of sections 2033 through 2044 are, in general, as follows:

(1) Sections 2033 and 2034 are concerned mainly with interests in property passing through the decedent's probate estate. Section 2033 includes in the decedent's gross estate any interest that the decedent had in property at the time of his death. Section 2034 provides that any interest of the decedent's surviving spouse in the decedent's property, such as dower or curtesy, does not prevent the inclusion of such property in the decedent's gross estate.

(2) Sections 2035 through 2038 deal with interests in property transferred by the decedent during his life under such circumstances as to bring the interests within the decedent's gross estate. Section 2035 includes in the decedent's gross estate property transferred in contemplation of death, even though the decedent had not interest in, or control over, the property at the time of his death. Section 2036 provides for the inclusion of transferred property with respect to which the decedent retained the income or the power to designate who shall enjoy the income. Section 2037 includes in the decedent's gross estate certain transfers under which the beneficial enjoyment of the property could be obtained only by surviving the decedent. Section 2038 provides for the inclusion of transferred property if the decedent had at the time of his death the power to change the beneficial enjoyment of the property. It should be noted that there is considerable overlap in the application of sections 2036 through 2038 with respect to reserved powers, so that transferred property may be includible in the decedent's gross estate in varying degrees under more than one of those sections.

(3) Sections 2039 through 2042 deal with special kinds of property and powers. Sections 2039 and 2040 concern annuities and jointly held property respectively. Section 2041 deals with powers held by the decedent over the beneficial enjoyment of property not originating with the decedent. Section 2042 concerns insurance under policies on the life of the decedent.

(4) Section 2043 concerns the sufficiency of consideration for transfers made by the decedent during his life. This has a bearing on the amount to be included in the decedent's gross estate under sections 2035 through 2038, and 2041. Section 2044 deals with retroactivity.

(b) Valuation of property in general. The value of every item of property includible in a decedent's gross estate under sections 2031 through 2044 is its fair market value at the time of the decedent's death, except that if the executor elects the alternate valuation method under section 2032, it is the fair market value thereof at the date, and with the adjustments, prescribed in that section. The fair market value is the price at which the property would change hands between a willing buyer and a willing seller, neither being under any compulsion to buy or to sell and both having reasonable knowledge of relevant facts. The fair market value of a particular item of property includible in the decedent's gross estate is not to be determined by a forced sale price. Nor is the fair market value of an item of property to be determined by the sale price of the item in a market other than that in which such item is most commonly sold to the public, taking into account the location of the item wherever appropriate. Thus, in the case of an item of property includible in the decedent's gross estate, which is generally obtained by the public in the retail market, the fair market value of such an item of property is the price at which the item or a comparable item would be sold at retail. For example, the fair market value of an automobile (an article generally obtained by the public in the retail market) includible in the decedent's gross estate is the price for which an automobile of the same or approximately the same description, make, model, age, condition, etc., could be purchased by a member of the general public and not the price for which the particular automobile of the decedent would be purchased by a dealer in used automobiles. Examples of items of property which are generally sold to the public at retail may be found in §§ 20.2031–6 and 20.2031–8. The value is generally to be determined by ascertaining as a basis the fair market value as of the applicable valuation date of each unit of property. For example, in the case of shares of stock or bonds, such unit of property is generally a share of stock or a bond. Livestock, farm machinery, harvested and growing crops must generally be itemized and the value of each item separately returned. Property shall not be returned at the value at which it is assessed for local tax purposes unless that value represents the fair market value as of the applicable valuation date. All relevant facts and elements of value as of the applicable valuation date shall be considered in every case. The value of items of property which were held by the decedent for sale in the course of a business generally should be reflected in the value of the business. For valuation of interests in businesses, see § 20.2031–3. See § 20.2031–2 and §§ 20.2031–4 through 20.2031–8 for further information concerning the valuation of other particular kinds of property. For certain circumstances under which the sale of an item of property at a price below its fair market value may result in a deduction for the estate, see paragraph (d)(2) of § 20.2053–3.

* * *

§ 20.2031–2 Valuation of stocks and bonds.

(a) In general. The value of stocks and bonds is the fair market value per share or bond on the applicable valuation date.

(b) Based on selling prices. (1) In general, if there is a market for stocks or bonds, on a stock exchange, in an over-the-counter market, or otherwise, the mean between the highest and lowest quoted selling prices on the valuation date is the fair market value per share or bond. If there were no sales on the valuation date but there were sales on dates within a reasonable period both before and after the valuation date, the fair market value is determined by taking a weighted average of the means between the highest and lowest sales on the nearest date before and the nearest date after the valuation date. The average is to be weighted inversely by the respective numbers of trading days between the selling dates and the valuation date. If the stocks or bonds are listed on more than one exchange, the records of the exchange where the stocks or bonds are principally dealt in should be employed if such records are available in a generally available listing or publication of general circulation. In the event that such records are not so available and such stocks or bonds are listed on a composite listing of combined exchanges available in a generally available listing or publication of general circulation, the records of such combined exchanges should be employed. In valuing listed securities, the executor should be careful to consult accurate records to obtain values as of the applicable valuation date. If quotations of unlisted securities are obtained from brokers, or evidence as to their sale is obtained from officers of the issuing companies, copies of the letters furnishing such quotations or evidence of sale should be attached to the return.

(2) If it is established with respect to bonds for which there is a market on a stock exchange, that the highest and lowest selling prices are not available for the valuation date in a generally available listing or publication of general circulation but that closing selling prices are so available, the fair market value per bond is the mean between the quoted closing selling price on the valuation date and the quoted closing selling price on the trading day before the valuation date. If there were no sales on the trading day before the valuation date but there were sales on a date within a reasonable period before the valuation date, the fair market value is determined by taking a weighted average of the quoted closing selling price on the valuation date and the quoted closing selling price on the nearest date before the valuation date. The closing selling price for the valuation date is to be weighted by the number of trading days between the previous selling date and the valuation date. If there were no sales within a reasonable period before the valuation date but there were sales on the valuation date, the fair market value is the closing selling price on such valuation date. If there were no sales on the valuation date but there were sales on dates within a reasonable period both before and after the valuation date, the fair market value is determined by taking a weighted average of the quoted closing selling prices on the nearest date before and the nearest date after the valuation date. The average is to be weighted inversely by the respective numbers of trading days between the selling dates and the valuation date. If the bonds are listed on more than one exchange, the records of the exchange where the bonds are principally dealt in should be employed. In valuing listed securities, the executor should be careful to consult accurate records to obtain values as of the applicable valuation date.

* * *

(c) Based on bid and asked prices. If the provisions of paragraph (b) of this section are inapplicable because actual sales are not available during a reasonable period beginning before and ending after the valuation date, the fair market value may be determined by taking the mean between the bona fide bid and asked prices on the valuation date, or if none, by taking a weighted average of the means between the bona fide bid and asked prices on the nearest trading date before and the nearest trading date after the valuation date, if both such nearest dates are within a reasonable period. The average is to be determined in the manner described in paragraph (b) of this section.

(d) Based on incomplete selling prices or bid and asked prices. If the provisions of paragraphs (b) and (c) of this section are inapplicable because no actual sale prices or bona fide bid and asked prices are available on a date within a reasonable period before the valuation date, but such prices are available on a date within a reasonable period after the valuation date, or vice versa, then the mean between the highest and lowest available sale prices or bid and asked prices may be taken as the value.

(e) Where selling prices or bid and asked prices do not reflect fair market value. If it is established that the value of any bond or share of stock determined on the basis of selling or bid and asked prices as provided under paragraphs (b), (c), and (d) of this section does not reflect the fair market value thereof, then some reasonable modification of that basis or other relevant facts and elements of value are considered in determining the fair market value. Where sales at or near the date of death are few or of a sporadic nature, such sales alone may not indicate fair market value. In certain exceptional cases, the size of the block of stock to be valued in relation to the number of shares changing hands in sales may be relevant in determining whether selling prices reflect the fair market value of the block of stock to be valued. If the executor can show that the block of stock to be valued is so large in relation to the actual sales on the existing market that it could not be liquidated in a reasonable time without depressing the market, the price at which the block could be sold as such outside the usual market, as through an underwriter, may be a more accurate indication of value than market quotations. Complete data in support of any allowance claimed due to the size of the block of stock being valued shall be submitted with the return. On the other hand, if the block of stock to be valued represents a controlling interest, either actual or effective, in a going business, the price at which other lots change hands may have little relation to its true value.

(f) Where selling prices or bid and asked prices are unavailable. If the provisions of paragraphs (b), (c), and (d) of this section are inapplicable because actual sale prices and bona fide bid and asked prices are lacking, then the fair market value is to be determined by taking the following factors into consideration:

(1) In the case of corporate or other bonds, the soundness of the security, the interest yield, the date of maturity, and other relevant factors; and

(2) In the case of shares of stock, the company's net worth, prospective earning power and dividend-paying capacity, and other relevant factors.

Some of the "other relevant factors" referred to in subparagraphs (1) and (2) of this paragraph are: The good will of the business; the economic outlook in the particular industry; the company's position in the industry and its management; the degree of control of the business represented by the block of stock to be valued; and the values of securities of corporations engaged in the same or similar lines of business which are listed on a stock exchange. However, the weight to be accorded such comparisons or any other evidentiary factors considered in the determination of a value depends upon the facts of each case. In addition to the relevant factors described above, consideration shall also be given to nonoperating assets, including proceeds of life insurance policies payable to or for the benefit of the company, to the extent such nonoperating assets have not been taken into account in the determination of net worth, prospective earning power and dividend-earning capacity. Complete financial and other data upon which the valuation is based should be submitted with the return, including copies of reports of any examinations of the company made by accountants, engineers, or any technical experts as of or near the applicable valuation date.

* * *

§ 20.2031–3 Valuation of interests in businesses.

The fair market value of any interest of a decedent in a business, whether a partnership or a proprietorship, is the net amount which a willing purchaser whether an individual or a corporation, would pay for the interest to a willing seller, neither being under any compulsion to buy or to sell and both having reasonable knowledge of relevant facts. The net value is determined on the basis of all relevant factors including—

(a) A fair appraisal as of the applicable valuation date of all the assets of the business, tangible and intangible, including good will;

(b) The demonstrated earning capacity of the business; and

(c) The other factors set forth in paragraphs (f) and (h) of § 20.2031–2 relating to the valuation of corporate stock, to the extent applicable.

Special attention should be given to determining an adequate value of the good will of the business in all cases in which the decedent has not agreed, for an adequate and full consideration in money or money's worth, that his interest passes at his death to, for example, his surviving partner or partners. Complete financial and other data upon which the valuation is based should be submitted with the return, including copies of reports of examinations of the business made by accountants, engineers, or any technical experts as of or near the applicable valuation date.

* * *

§ 20.2031–4 Valuation of notes.

The fair market value of notes, secured or unsecured, is presumed to be the amount of unpaid principal, plus interest accrued to the date of death, unless the executor establishes that the value is lower or that the notes are worthless. However, items of interest shall be separately stated on the estate tax return. If not returned at face value, plus accrued interest, satisfactory evidence must be submitted that the note is worth less than the unpaid amount (because of the interest rate, date of maturity, or other cause), or that the note is uncollectible, either in whole or in part (by reason of the insolvency of the party or parties liable, or for other cause), and that any property pledged or mortgaged as security is insufficient to satisfy the obligation.

§ 20.2031–5 Valuation of cash on hand or on deposit.

The amount of cash belonging to the decedent at the date of his death, whether in his possession or in the possession of another, or deposited with a bank, is included in the decedent's gross estate. If bank checks outstanding at the time of the decedent's death and given in discharge of bona fide legal obligations of the decedent incurred for an adequate and full consideration in money or money's worth are subsequently honored by the bank and charged to the decedent's account, the balance remaining in the account may be returned, but only if the obligations are not claimed as deductions from the gross estate.

§ 20.2031–6 Valuation of household and personal effects.

(a) General rule. The fair market value of the decedent's household and personal effects is the price which a willing buyer would pay to a willing seller, neither being under any compulsion to buy or to sell and both having reasonable knowledge of relevant facts. A room by room itemization of household and personal effects is desirable. All the articles should be named specifically, except that a number of articles contained in the same room, none of which has a value in excess of $100, may be grouped. A separate value should be given for each article named. In lieu of an itemized list, the executor may furnish a written statement, containing a declaration that it is made under penalties of perjury, setting forth the aggregate value as appraised by a competent appraiser or appraisers of recognized standing and ability, or by a dealer or dealers in the class of personalty involved.

(b) Special rule in cases involving a substantial amount of valuable articles. Notwithstanding the provisions of paragraph (a) of this section, if there are included among the household and personal effects articles having marked artistic or intrinsic value of a total value in excess of $3,000 (*e.g.*, jewelry, furs, silverware, paintings, etchings, engravings, antiques, books, statuary, vases, oriental rugs, coin or stamp collections), the appraisal of an expert or experts, under oath, shall be filed with the return. The appraisal shall be accompanied by a written statement of the executor containing a declaration that it is made under the penalties of perjury as to the completeness of the itemized list of such property and as to the disinterested character and the qualifications of the appraiser or appraisers.

(c) Disposition of household effects prior to investigation. If it is desired to effect distribution or sale of any portion of the household or personal effects of the decedent in advance of an investigation by an officer of the Internal Revenue Service, information to that effect shall be given to the district director. The statement to the district director shall be accompanied by an appraisal of such property, under oath, and by a written statement of the executor, containing a declaration that it is made under the penalties of perjury, regarding the completeness of the list of such property and the qualifications of the appraiser, as heretofore described. If a personal inspection by an officer of the Internal Revenue Service is not deemed necessary, the executor will be so advised. This procedure is designed to facilitate disposition of such property and to obviate future expense and inconvenience to the estate by affording the district director an opportunity to make an investigation should one be deemed necessary prior to sale or distribution.

(d) Additional rules if an appraisal involved. If, pursuant to paragraphs (a), (b), and (c) of this section, expert appraisers are employed, care should be taken to see that they are reputable and of recognized competency to appraise the particular class of property involved. In the appraisal, books in sets by standard authors should be listed in separate groups. In listing paintings having artistic value, the size, subject, and artist's name should be stated. In the case of oriental rugs, the size, make, and general condition should be given. Sets of silverware should be listed in separate groups. Groups or individual pieces of silverware should be weighed and the weights given in troy ounces. In arriving at the value of silverware, the appraisers should take into consideration its antiquity, utility, desirability, condition, and obsolescence.

§ 20.2031–7 Valuation of annuities, interests for life or term of years, and remainder or reversionary interests.

(a) In general. Except as otherwise provided in paragraph (b) of this section and § 20.7520–3(b) (pertaining to certain limitations on the use of prescribed tables), the fair market value of annuities, life estates, terms of years, remainders, and reversionary interests for estates of decedents is the present value of such interests, determined under paragraph (d) of this section. The regulations in this and in related sections provide tables with standard actuarial factors and examples that illustrate how to use the tables to compute the present value of ordinary annuity, life, and remainder interests in property. These sections also refer to standard and special actuarial factors that may be necessary to compute the present value of similar interests in more unusual fact situations.

(b) Commercial annuities and insurance contracts. The value of annuities issued by companies regularly engaged in their sale, and of insurance policies on the lives of persons other than the decedent, is determined under § 20.2031–8. See § 20.2042–1 with respect to insurance policies on the decedent's life.

* * *

§ 20.2032–1 Alternate valuation.*

(a) In general. In general, section 2032 provides for the valuation of a decedent's gross estate at a date other than the date of the decedent's death. More specifically, if an executor elects the alternate valuation method under section 2032, the property included in the decedent's gross estate on the date of his death is valued as of whichever of the following dates is applicable:

(1) Any property distributed, sold, exchanged, or otherwise disposed of within 6 months (1 year, if the decedent died on or before December 31, 1970) after the decedent's death is valued as of the date on which it is first distributed, sold, exchanged, or otherwise disposed of;

(2) Any property not distributed, sold, exchanged, or otherwise disposed of within 6 months (1 year, if the decedent died on or before December 31, 1970) after the decedent's death is valued as of the date 6 months (1 year, if the decedent died on or before December 31, 1970) after the date of the decedent's death;

(3) Any property, interest, or estate which is affected by mere lapse of time is valued as of the date of the decedent's death, but adjusted for any difference in its value not due to mere lapse of time as of the date 6 months (1 year, if the decedent died on or before December 31, 1970) after the decedent's death, or as of the date of its distribution, sale, exchange, or other disposition, whichever date first occurs.

(b) Method and effect of election—(1) In general. The election to use the alternate valuation method is made on the return of tax imposed by section 2001. For purposes of this paragraph (b), the term *return of tax imposed by section 2001* means the last estate tax return filed by the executor on or before the due date of the return (including extensions of time to file actually granted) or, if a timely return is not filed, the first estate tax return filed by the executor after the due date, provided the return is filed no later than 1 year after the due date (including extensions of time to file actually granted). Once the election is made, it is irrevocable, provided that an election may be revoked on a subsequent return filed on or before the due date of the return (including extensions of time to file actually granted). The election may be made only if it will decrease both the value of the gross estate and the sum (reduced by allowable credits) of the estate tax and the generation-skipping transfer tax payable by reason of the decedent's death with respect to the property includible in the decedent's gross estate. If the election is made, the alternate valuation method applies to all property included in the gross estate and cannot be applied to only a portion of the property.

(2) Protective election. If, based on the return of tax as filed, use of the alternate valuation method would not result in a decrease in both the value of the gross estate and the sum (reduced by allowable credits) of the estate tax and the generation-skipping transfer tax liability payable by reason of the decedent's death with respect to the property

*Editorial comment: The filing requirement under Sec. 6018 was increased by the Economic Recovery Tax Act of 1981. For 1986 and thereafter, the amount is $600,000 through 1997. The Taxpayer Relief Act of 1997 increases the amount using a transitional approach as follows: $625,000 in 1998, $650,000 in 1999, $675,000 in 2000 and 2001, $700,000 in 2002 and 2003, $850,000 in 2004, $950,000 in 2005, and $1,000,000 in 2006 and thereafter. The Tax Relief Reconciliation Act of 2001 modifies the filing requirement using a transition approach as follows: $1,000,000 in 2002 and 2003, $1,500,000 in 2004 and 2005, $2,000,000 in 2006, 2007, and 2008, and $3,500,000 in 2009 and 2010.

includible in the decedent's gross estate, a protective election may be made to use the alternate valuation method if it is subsequently determined that such a decrease would occur. A protective election is made on the return of tax imposed by section 2001. The protective election is irrevocable as of the due date of the return (including extensions of time actually granted). The protective election becomes effective on the date on which it is determined that use of the alternate valuation method would result in a decrease in both the value of the gross estate and in the sum (reduced by allowable credits) of the estate tax and generation-skipping transfer tax liability payable by reason of the decedent's death, with respect to the property includible in the decedent's gross estate.

(3) Requests for extension of time to make the election. A request for an extension of time to make the election or protective election pursuant to §§ 301.9100–1 and 301.9100–3 of this chapter will not be granted unless the return of tax imposed by 2001 is filed no later than 1 year after the due date of the return (including extensions of time actually granted).

(c) Meaning of "distributed, sold, exchanged, or otherwise disposed of". (1) The phrase "distributed, sold, exchanged, or otherwise disposed of" comprehends all possible ways by which property ceases to form a part of the gross estate. For example, money on hand at the date of the decedent's death which is thereafter used in the payment of funeral expenses, or which is thereafter invested, falls within the term "otherwise disposed of." The term also includes the surrender of a stock certificate for corporate assets in complete or partial liquidation of a corporation pursuant to section 331. The term does not, however, extend to transactions which are mere changes in form. Thus, it does not include a transfer of assets to a corporation in exchange for its stock in a transaction with respect to which no gain or loss would be recognizable for income tax purposes under section 351. Nor does it include an exchange of stock or securities in a corporation for stock or securities in the same corporation or another corporation in a transaction, such as a merger, recapitalization, reorganization or other transaction described in section 368(a) or 355, with respect to which no gain or loss is recognizable for income tax purposes under section 354 or 355.

(2) Property may be "distributed" either by the executor, or by a trustee of property included in the gross estate under section 2035 through 2038, or section 2041. Property is considered as "distributed" upon the first to occur of the following:

(i) The entry of an order or decree of distribution, if the order or decree subsequently becomes final;

(ii) The segregation or separation of the property from the estate or trust so that it becomes unqualifiedly subject to the demand or disposition of the distributee; or

(iii) The actual paying over or delivery of the property to the distributee.

(3) Property may be "sold, exchanged, or otherwise disposed of" by: (i) The executor; (ii) a trustee or other donee to whom the decedent during his lifetime transferred property included in his gross estate under sections 2035 through 2038, or section 2041; (iii) an heir or devisee to whom title to property passes directly under local law; (iv) a surviving joint tenant or tenant by the entirety; or (v) any other person. If a binding contract for the sale, exchange, or other disposition of property is entered into, the property is considered as sold, exchanged, or otherwise disposed of on the effective date of the contract, unless the contract is not subsequently carried out substantially in accordance with its terms. The effective date of a contract is normally the date it is entered into (and not the date it is consummated, or the date legal title to the property passes) unless the contract specifies a different effective date.

(d) "Included property" and "excluded property". If the executor elects the alternate valuation method under section 2032, all property interests existing at the date of decedent's death which form a part of his gross estate as determined under sections 2033 through 2044 are valued in accordance with the provisions of this section. Such property interests are referred to in this section as "included property". Furthermore, such property interests remain "included property" for the purpose of valuing the gross estate under the alternate valuation method even though they change in form during the alternate valuation period by being actually received, or disposed of, in whole or in part, by the estate. On the other hand, property earned or accrued (whether received or not) after the date of the decedent's death and during the alternate valuation period with respect to any property interest existing at the date of the decedent's death, which does not represent a form of "included property" itself or the receipt of "included property" is excluded in valuing the gross estate under the alternate valuation method. Such property is referred to in this section as "excluded property". Illustrations of "included property" and "excluded property" are contained in the subparagraphs (1) to (4) of this paragraph:

(1) Interest-bearing obligations. Interest-bearing obligations, such as bonds or notes, may comprise two elements of "included property" at the date of the decedent's death, namely, (i) the principal of the obligation itself, and (ii) interest accrued to the date of death. Each of these elements is to be separately valued as of the applicable valuation date. Interest accrued after the date of death and before the subsequent valuation date constitutes "excluded property". However, any part payment or principal made between the date of death and the subsequent valuation date, or any advance payment of interest for a period after the subsequent valuation date made during the alternate valuation period which has the effect of reducing the value of the principal obligation as of the subsequent valuation date, will be included in the gross estate, and valued as of the date of such payment.

(2) Leased property. The principles set forth in subparagraph (1) of this paragraph with respect to interest-bearing obligations also apply to leased realty or personalty which is included in the gross estate and with respect to which an obligation to pay rent has been reserved. Both the realty or personalty itself and the rents accrued to the date of death constitute "included property", and each is to be separately valued as of the applicable valuation date. Any rent accrued after the date of death and before the subsequent valuation date is "excluded property". Similarly, the principle applicable with respect to interest paid in advance is equally applicable with respect to advance payments of rent.

(3) Noninterest-bearing obligations. In the case of noninterest-bearing obligations sold at a discount, such as savings bonds, the principal obligation and the discount amortized to the date of death are property interests existing at the date of death and constitute "included property". The obligation itself is to be valued at the subsequent valuation date without regard to any further increase in value due to amortized discount. The additional discount amortized after death and during the alternate valuation period is the equivalent of interest accruing during that period and is, therefore, not to be included in the gross estate under the alternate valuation method.

(4) Stock of a corporation. Shares of stock in a corporation and dividends declared to stockholders of record on or before the date of the decedent's death and not collected at the date of death constitute "included property" of the estate. On the other hand, ordinary dividends out of earnings and profits (whether in cash, shares of the corporation, or other property) declared to stockholders of record after the date of the decedent's death are "excluded property" and are not to be valued under the alternate valuation method. If, however, dividends are declared to stockholders of record after the date of the decedent's death with the effect that the shares of stock at the subsequent valuation date do not reasonably represent the same "included property" of the gross estate as existed at the date of the decedent's death, the dividends are "included property", except to the extent that they are out of earnings of the corporation after the date of the decedent's death. For example, if a corporation makes a distribution in partial liquidation to stockholders of record during the alternate valuation period which is not accompanied by a surrender of a stock certificate for cancellation, the amount of the distribution received on stock included in the gross estate is itself "included property", except to the extent that the distribution was out of earnings and profits since the date of the decedent's death. Similarly, if a corporation, in which the decedent owned a substantial interest and which possessed at the date of the decedent's death accumulated earnings and profits equal to its paid-in capital, distributed all of its accumulated earnings and profits as a cash dividend to shareholders of record during the alternate valuation period, the amount of the dividends received on stock includible in the gross estate will be included in the gross estate under the alternate valuation method. Likewise, a stock dividend distributed under such circumstances is "included property."

* * *

(f) Mere lapse of time. In order to eliminate changes in value due only to mere lapse of time, section 2032(a)(3) provides that any interest or estate "affected by mere lapse of time" is included in a decedent's gross estate under the alternate valuation method at its value as of the date of the decedent's death, but with adjustment for any difference in its value as of the subsequent valuation date not due to mere lapse of time. Properties, interests, or estates which are "affected by mere lapse of time" include patents, estates for the life of a person other than the decedent, remainders, reversions, and other like properties, interests, or estates. The phrase "affected by mere lapse of time" has no reference to obligations for the payment of money, whether or not interest-bearing, the value of which changes with the passing of time. However, such an obligation, like any other property, may become affected by lapse of time when made the subject of a bequest or transfer which itself is creative of an interest or estate so affected. The application of this paragraph is illustrated in subparagraphs (1) and (2) of this paragraph:

(1) Life estates, remainders, and similar interests. The values of life estates, remainders, and similar interests are to be obtained by applying the methods prescribed in § 20.2031–7, using (i) the age of each person, the duration of whose life may affect the value of the interest, as of the date of the decedent's death, and (ii) the value of the property as of the alternate date. For example, assume that the decedent or his estate was entitled to receive property upon the death of his elder brother who was entitled to receive the income therefrom for life. At the date of the decedent's death, the property was worth $50,000 and the elder brother was 31 years old. The value of the decedent's remainder interest at the date of the decedent's death would, as explained in paragraph (d) of § 20.2031–7, be $2,373 ($50,000 × .04746). If, because of economic conditions, the property declined in value and was worth only $40,000 6 months after the date of the decedent's death, the value of the remainder interest would be $1,898.40 ($40,000 × .04746), even though the elder brother may be 32 years old on the alternate date.

(2) Patents. To illustrate the alternate valuation of a patent, assume that the decedent owned a patent which, on the date of the decedent's death, had an unexpired term of ten years and a value of $78,000. Six months after the date of the decedent's death, the patent was sold, because of lapse of time and other causes, for $60,000. The alternate value thereof would be obtained by dividing $60,000 by 0.95 (ratio of the remaining life of the patent at the alternate date to the remaining life of the patent at the date of the decedent's death), and would, therefore, be $63,157.89.

(g) Effect of election on deductions. If the executor elects the alternate valuation method under section 2032, any deduction for administration expenses under section 2053(b) (pertaining to property not subject to claims) or losses under section 2054 * * * is allowed only to the extent that it is not otherwise in effect allowed in determining the value of the gross estate. Furthermore, the amount of any charitable deduction under section 2055 * * * or the amount of any marital deduction under section 2056 is determined by the value of the property with respect to which the deduction is allowed as of the date of the decedent's death, adjusted, however, for any difference in its value as of the date 6 months (1 year, if the decedent died on or before December 31, 1970) after death, or as of the date of its distribution, sale, exchange, or other disposition, whichever first occurs. However, no such adjustment may take into account any difference in value due to lapse of time or to the occurrence or nonoccurrence of a contingency.

(h) Effective date. Paragraph (b) of this section is applicable to decedents dying on or after January 4, 2005. However, pursuant to section 7805(b)(7), taxpayers may elect to apply paragraph (b) of this section retroactively if the period of limitations for filing a claim for a credit or refund of Federal estate or generation-skipping transfer tax under section 6511 has not expired.

§ 20.2032A–3 Material participation requirements for valuation of certain farm and closely-held business real property.

(a) In general. Under section 2032A, an executor may, for estate tax purposes, make a special election concerning valuation of qualified real property (as defined in section 2032A(b)) used as a farm for farming purposes or in another trade or business. If this election is made, the property will be valued on the basis of its value for its qualified use in farming or the other trade or business, rather than its fair market value determined on the basis of highest and best use (irrespective of whether its highest and best use is the use in farming or other business). For the special valuation rules of section 2032A to apply, the deceased owner and/or a member of the owner's family (as defined in section 2032A(e)(2)) must materially participate in the operation of the farm or other business. Whether the required material participation occurs is a factual determination, and the types of activities and financial risks which will support such a finding will vary with the mode of ownership of both the property itself and of any business in which it is used. Passively collecting rents, salaries, draws, dividends, or other income from the farm or other business is not sufficient for material participation, nor is merely advancing capital and reviewing a crop plan or other business proposal and financial reports each season or business year.

(b) Types of qualified property—(1) In general. Real property valued under section 2032A must pass from the decedent to a qualified heir or be acquired from the decedent by a qualified heir. The real property may be owned directly or may be owned indirectly through ownership of an interest in a corporation, a partnership, or a trust. Where the ownership is indirect, however, the decedent's interest in the business must, in addition to meeting the tests for qualification under section 2032A, qualify under the tests of section 6166(b)(1) as an interest in a closely-held business on the date of the decedent's death and for sufficient other time (combined with periods of direct ownership) to equal at least 5 years of the 8 year period preceding the death. All specially valued property must be used in a trade or business. Directly owned real property that is leased by a decedent to a separate closely held business is considered to be qualified real property, but only if the separate business qualifies as a closely held business under section 6166(b)(1) with respect to the decedent on the date of his or her death and for sufficient other time (combined with periods during which the property was operated as a proprietorship) to equal at least 5 years of the 8 year period preceding the death. For example, real property owned by the decedent and leased to a farming corporation or partnership owned and operated entirely by the decedent and fewer than 15 members of the decedent's family is eligible for special use valuation. Under section 2032A, the term trade or business applies only to an active business such as a manufacturing, mercantile, or service enterprise, or to the raising of agricultural or horticultural commodities, as distinguished from passive investment activities. The mere passive rental of property "to a party other than a member of the decedent's family" will not qualify. The decedent "or a member of the decedent's family" must own an equity interest in the farm operation. A trade or business is not necessarily present even though an office and regular hours are maintained for management of income producing assets, as the term "business" is not as broad under section 2032A as under section 162. Additionally, no trade or business is present in the case of activities not engaged in for profit. See section 183.

(2) Structures and other real property improvements. Qualified real property includes residential buildings and other structures and real property improvements occupied or used on a regular basis by the owner or lessee of real property (or by employees of the owner or lessee) for the purpose of operating the farm or other closely held business. A farm residence occupied by the decedent owner of the specially valued property is considered to be occupied for the purpose of operating the farm even though a family member (not the decedent) was the person materially participating in the operation of the farm as required under section 2032A(b)(l)(C).

(c) **Period material participation must last.** The required participation must last—

(1) For periods totalling 5 years or more during the 8 years immediately preceding the date of the decedent's death; and

(2) For periods totalling 5 years or more during any 8 year period ending after the date of the decedent's death (up to a maximum of 15 years after decedent's death, when the additional estate tax provisions of section 2032A(c) cease to apply).

In determining whether the material participation requirement is satisfied, no exception is made for periods during which real property is held by the decedent's estate. Additionally, contemporaneous material participation by 2 or more family members during a period totalling a year will not result in that year being counted as 2 or more years for purposes of satisfying the requirements of this paragraph (c). Death of a qualified heir (as defined in section 2032A(e)(l)) before the requisite time has passed ends any material participation requirement for that heir's portion of the property as to the original decedent's estate if the heir received a separate, joint or other undivided property interest from the decedent. If qualified heirs receive successive interests in specially valued property (*e.g.* life estate and remainder interests) from the decedent, the material participation requirement does not end with respect to any part of the property until the death of the last qualified heir (or, if earlier, the expiration of 15 years from the date of the decedent's death). The requirements of section 2032A will fully apply to an heir's estate if an election under this section is made for the same property by the heir's executor. In general, to determine whether the required participation has occurred, brief periods (*e.g.*, periods of 30 days or less) during which there was no material participation may be disregarded. This is so only if these periods were both preceded and followed by substantial periods (*e.g.* periods of more than 120 days) in which there was uninterrupted material participation. See paragraph (e)(1) of this section which provides a special rule for periods when little or no activity is necessary to manage fully a farm.

(d) Period property must be owned by decedent and family members. Only real property which is actually owned by any combination of the decedent, members of the decedent's family, and qualified closely held businesses for periods totalling at least 5 of the 8 years preceding the date of decedent's death may be valued under section 2032A. For example, replacement property acquired in like-kind exchange under section 1031 is considered to be owned only from the date on which the replacement property is actually acquired. On the other hand, replacement property acquired as a result of an involuntary conversion in a transfer that would meet the requirements of section 2032A(h) if it occurred after the date of the decedent's death is considered to have been owned from the date in which the involuntarily converted property was acquired. Property transferred from a proprietorship to a corporation or a partnership during the 8-year period ending on the date of the decedent's death is considered to be continuously owned to the extent of the decedent's equity interest in the corporation or partnership if, (1) the transfer meets the requirements of section 351 or 721, respectively, and (2) the decedent's interest in the corporation or partnership meets the requirements for indirectly held property contained in paragraph (b)(1) of this section. Likewise, property transferred to a trust is considered to be continuously owned if the beneficial ownership of the trust property is such that the requirements of section 6166(b)(1)(C) would be so satisfied if the property were owned by a corporation and all beneficiaries having vested interests in the trust were shareholders in the corporation. Any periods following the transfer during which the interest in the corporation, partnership, or trust does not meet the requirements of section 6166(b)(1) may not be counted for purposes of satisfying the ownership requirements of this paragraph (d).

(e) Required activities—(1) In general. Actual employment of the decedent (or of a member of the decedent's family) on a substantially full-time basis (35 hours a week or more) or to any lesser extent necessary personally to manage fully the farm or business in which the real property to be valued under section 2032A is used constitutes material participation. For example, many farming operations require only seasonal activity. Material participation is present as long as all necessary functions are performed even though little or no actual activity occurs during nonproducing seasons. In the absence of this direct involvement in the farm or other business, the activities of either the decedent or family members must meet the standards prescribed in this paragraph and those prescribed in the regulations issued under section 1402(a)(1). Therefore, if the participant (or participants) is self-employed with respect to the farm or other trade or business, his or her income from the farm or other business must be earned income for purposes of the tax on self-employment income before the participant is considered to be materially participating under section 2032A. Payment of the self-employment tax is not conclusive as to the presence of material participation. If no self-employment taxes have been paid, however, material participation is presumed not to have occurred unless the executor demonstrates to the satisfaction of the Internal Revenue Service that material participation did in fact occur and informs the Service of the reason no such tax was paid. In addition, all such taxes (including interest and penalties) determined to be due must be paid. In determining whether the material participation requirement is satisfied, the activities of each participant are viewed separately from the activities of all other participants, and at any given time, the activities of at least one participant must be material. If the involvement is less than full-time, it must be pursuant to an arrangement providing for actual participation in the production or management of production where the land is used by any nonfamily member, or any trust or business entity, in farming or another business. The arrangement may be oral or written, but must be formalized in some manner capable of proof. Activities not contemplated by the arrangement will not support a finding of material participation under section 2032A, and activities of any agent or employee other than a family member may not be considered in determining the presence of material participation. Activities of family members are considered only if the family relationship existed at the time the activities occurred.

(2) Factors considered. No single factor is determinative of the presence of material participation, but physical work and participation in management decisions are the principal factors to be considered. As a minimum, the decedent and/or a family member must regularly advise or consult with the other managing party on the operation of the business. While they need not make all final management decisions alone, the decedent and/or family members must participate in making a substantial number of these decisions. Additionally, production activities on the land should be inspected regularly by the family participant, and funds should be advanced and financial responsibility assumed for a substantial portion of the expense involved in the operation of the farm or other business in which the real property is used. In the case of a farm, the furnishing by the owner or other family members of a substantial portion of the machinery, implements, and livestock used in the production activities is an important factor to consider in finding material participation. With farms, hotels, or apartment buildings, the operation of which qualifies as a trade or business, the participating decedent or heir's maintaining his or her principal place of residence on the premises is a factor to consider in determining whether the overall participation is material. Retention of a professional farm manager will not by itself prevent satisfaction of the material participation requirement by the decedent and family members. However, the decedent and/or a family member must personally materially participate under the terms of arrangement with the professional farm manager to satisfy this requirement.

(f) Special rules for corporations, partnerships, and trusts—(1) Required arrangement. With indirectly owned property as with property that is directly owned, there must be an arrangement calling for material participation in the business by the decedent owner or a family member. Where the real property is indirectly owned, however, even full-time involvement must be pursuant to an arrangement between the entity and the decedent or family member specifying the services to be performed. Holding an office in which certain material functions are inherent may constitute the necessary arrangement for material participation. Where property is owned by a trust, the arrangement will generally be found in one or more of four situations. First, the arrangement may result from appointment as a trustee. Second, the arrangement may result from an employer-employee relationship in which the participant is employed by a qualified closely held business owned by the trust in a position requiring his or her material participation in its activities. Third, the participants may enter into a contract with the trustees to manage, or take part in managing, the real property for the trust. Fourth, where the trust agreement expressly grants the management rights to the beneficial owner, that grant is sufficient to constitute the arrangement required under this section.

(2) Required activities. The same participation standards apply under section 2032A where property is owned by a qualified closely held business as where the property is directly owned. In the case of a corporation, a partnership, or a trust where the participating decedent and/or family members are employees and thereby not subject to self-employment income taxes, they are to be viewed as if they were self-employed, and their activities must be activities that would subject them to self-employment income taxes were they so. Where property is owned by a corporation, a partnership or a trust, participation in the management and operation of the real property itself as a component of the closely held business is the determinative factor. Nominally holding positions as a corporate officer or director and receiving a salary therefrom or merely being listed as a partner and sharing in profits and losses will not alone support a finding of material participation. This is so even though, as partners, the participants pay self-employment income taxes on their distributive shares of partnership earnings under § 1.1402(a)–2. Further, it is especially true for corporate directors in states where the board of directors need not be an actively functioning entity or need only act informally. Corporate offices held by an owner are, however, factors to be considered with all other relevant facts in judging the degree of participation. When real property is directly owned and is leased to a corporation or partnership in which the decedent owns an interest which qualified as an interest in a trade or business within the meaning of section 6166(b)(1), the presence of material participation is determined by looking at the activities of the participant with regard to the property in whatever capacity rendered. During any periods when qualified real property is held by an estate, material participation is to be determined in the same manner as if the property were owned by a trust.

(g) Examples. The rules for determining material participation may be illustrated by the following examples. Additional illustrations may be found in examples (1) through (6) in § 1.1402(a)–4.

Example (1). A, the decedent, actively operated his 100-acre farm on a full-time basis for 20 years. He then leased it to B for the 10 years immediately preceding his death. By the terms of the lease, A was to consult with B on where crops were to be planted, to supervise marketing of the crop, and to share equally with B in expenses and earnings. A was present on the farm each spring for consultation; however, once planting was completed, he left for his retirement cottage where he remained until late summer, at which time he returned to the farm to supervise the marketing operation. A at all times maintained the farm home in which he had lived for the time he had owned the farm and lived there when at the farm. In light of his activities, assumption of risks, and valuable knowledge of proper techniques for the particular land gained over 20 years of full-time farming on the land involved, A is deemed to have materially participated in the farming business.

Example (2). D is the 70-year old widow of farmer C. She lives on a farm for which special valuation has been elected and has lived there for 20 years. D leases the land to E under an arrangement calling for her participation in the operation of the farm. D annually raises a vegetable garden, chickens, and hogs. She also inspects the tobacco fields (which produce approximately 50 percent of farm income) weekly and informs E if she finds any work that needs to be done. D and E share expenses and income equally. Other decisions such as what fields to plant and when to plant and harvest crops are left to E, but D does occasionally make suggestions. During the harvest season, D prepares and serves meals for all temporary farm help. D is deemed to participate materially in the farm operations based on her farm residence and her involvement with the main money crop.

Example (3). Assume that D in example (2) moved to a nursing home 1 year after her husband's death. E completely operated the farm for her for 6 years following her move. If E is not a member of D's family, material participation ceases when D moves; however, if E is a member of D's family, E's material participation will prevent disqualification even if D owns the property. Further, upon D's death, the section 2032A valuation could be elected for her estate if E were a member of her family and the other requirements of section 2032A were satisfied.

Example (4). F, a qualified heir, owned a specially valued farm. He contracted with G to manage the farm for him as F, a lawyer, lived and worked 15 miles away in a nearby town. F supplied all machinery and equipment and assumed financial responsibility for the expenses of the farm operation. The contract specified that G was to submit a crop plan and a list of expenses and earnings for F's approval. It also called for F to inspect the farm regularly and to approve all expenditures over $100. In practice, F visited the farm weekly during the growing season to inspect and discuss operations. He actively participated in making important management decisions such as what fields to plant or pasture and how to utilize the subsidy program. F is deemed to have materially participated in the farm operation as his personal involvement amounted to more than managing an investment. Had F not regularly inspected the farm and participated in management decisions, however, he would not be considered to be materially participating. This would be true even though F did assume financial responsibility for the operation and did review annual crop plans.

Example (5). Decedent I owned 90 percent of all outstanding stock of X Corporation, a qualified closely-held business which owns real property to be specially valued. I held no formal position in the corporation and there was no arrangement for him to participate in daily business operations. I regularly spent several hours each day at the corporate offices and made decisions on many routine matters. I is not deemed to have materially participated in the X Corporation despite his activity because there was no arrangement requiring him to act in the manner in which he did.

Example (6). Decedent J was a senior partner in the law firm of X, Y, and Z, which is a qualified closely held business owning the building in which its offices are located. J ceased to practice law actively 5 years before his death in 1977; however, he remained a full partner and annually received a share of firm profits. J is not deemed to have materially participated under section 2032A even though he still may have reported his distributive share of partnership income for self-employment income tax purposes if the payments were not made pursuant to any retirement agreement. This is so because J does not meet the requirement of actual personal material participation.

Example (7). K, the decedent, owned a tree farm. He contracted with L, a professional forester, to manage the property for him as K, a doctor, lived and worked in a town 50 miles away. The activities of L are not considered in determining whether K materially participated in the tree farm operation. During the 5 years preceding K's death, there was no need for frequent inspections of the property or consultation concerning it, in as much as most of the land had been reforested and the trees were in the beginning stages of their growing cycle. However, once every year, L submitted for K's approval a proposed plan for the management of the property over the next year. K actively participated in making important management decisions, such as where and whether a pre-commercial thinning should be conducted, whether the timber was adequately protected from fire and disease, whether fire lines needed to be plowed around the new trees, and whether boundary lines were properly maintained around the property. K inspected the property at least twice every year and assumed financial responsibility for the expenses of the tree farm. K also reported his income from the tree farm as earned income for purposes of the tax on self-employment income. Over a period of several years, K had harvested and marketed timber from certain tracts of the tree farm and had supervised replanting of the areas where trees were removed. K's history of harvesting, marketing, and replanting of trees showed him to be in the business of tree farming rather than merely passively investing in timber land. If the history of K's tree farm did not show such an active business operation, however, the tree farm would not qualify for special use valuation. In light of all these facts, K is deemed to have materially participated in the farm as his personal involvement amounted to more than managing an investment.

Example (8). Decedent M died on January 1, 1978, owning a farm for which special use valuation under section 2032A has been elected. M owned the farm real property for 15 years before his death. During the 4 years preceding M's death (January 1, 1974 through December 31, 1977), the farm was rented to N, a non-family member, and neither M nor any member of his family materially participated in the farming operation. From January 1, 1970, until December 31, 1973, both M and his daughter, O, materially participated in the farming operation. The material participation requirement of section 2032A(b)(1)(C)(ii) is not satisfied because material participation did not occur for periods aggregating at least 5 different years of the 8 years preceding M's death.

§ 20.2032A–4 Method of valuing farm real property.

(a) In general. Unless the executor of the decedent's estate elects otherwise under section 2032A(e)(7)(B)(ii) or fails to document comparable rented farm property meeting the requirements of this section, the value of the property which is used for farming purposes and which is subject to an election under section 2032A is determined by—

(1) Subtracting the average annual state and local real estate taxes on actual tracts of comparable real property in the same locality from the average annual gross cash rental for that same comparable property, and

(2) Dividing the result so obtained by the average annual effective interest rate charged on new Federal land bank loans.

The computation of each average annual amount is to be based on the 5 most recent calendar years ending before the date of the decedent's death.

(b) Gross cash rental—(1) Generally. Gross cash rental is the total amount of cash received for the use of actual tracts of comparable farm real property in the same locality as the property being specially valued during the period of one calendar year. This amount is not diminished by the amount of any expenses or liabilities associated with the farm operation or the lease. See, paragraph (d) of this section for a definition of comparable property and rules for property on which buildings or other improvements are located and farms including multiple property types. Only rentals from tracts of comparable farm property which are rented solely for an amount of cash which is not contingent upon production are acceptable for use in valuing real property under section 2032A(e)(7). The rentals considered must result from an arm's-length transaction as defined in this section. Additionally, rentals received under leases which provide for payment solely in cash are not acceptable as accurate measures of cash rental value if involvement by the lessor (or a member of the lessor's family who is other than a lessee) in the management or operation of the farm to an extent which amounts to material participation under the rules of section 2032A is contemplated or actually occurs. In general, therefore, rentals for any property which qualifies for special use valuation cannot be used to compute gross cash rentals under this section because the total amount received by the lessor does not reflect the true cash rental value of the real property.

(2) Special rules—(i) Documentation required of executor. The executor must identify to the Internal Revenue Service actual comparable property for all specially valued property and cash rentals from that property if the decedent's real property is valued under section 2032A(e)(7). If the executor does not identify such property and cash rentals, all specially valued real property must be valued under the rules of section 2032A(e)(8) if special use valuation has been elected. See, however, § 20.2032A–8 (d) for a special rule for estates electing section 2032A treatment on or before August 30, 1980.

(ii) Arm's-length transaction required. Only those cash rentals which result from a lease entered into in an arm's-length transaction are acceptable under section 2032A(e)(7). For these purposes, lands leased from the Federal government, or any state or local government, which are leased for less than the amount that would be demanded by a private individual leasing for profit are not leased in an arm's-length transaction. Additionally, leases between family members (as defined in section 2032A(e)(2)) which do not provide a return on the property commensurate with that received under leases between unrelated parties in the locality are not acceptable under this section.

(iii) In-kind rents, statements of appraised rental value, and area averages. Rents which are paid wholly or partly in kind (*e.g.*, crop shares) may not be used to determine the value of real property under section 2032A(e)(7). Likewise, appraisals or other statements regarding rental value as well as area-wide averages of rentals (*i.e.*, those compiled by the United States Department of Agriculture) may not be used under section 2032A(e)(7) because they are not true measures of the actual cash rental value of comparable property in the same locality as the specially valued property.

(iv) Period for which comparable real property must have been rented solely for cash. Comparable real property rented solely for cash must be identified for each of the five calendar years preceding the year of the decedent's death if section 2032A(e)(7) is used to value the decedent's real property. Rentals from the same tract of comparable property need not be used for each of these 5 years, however, provided an actual tract of property meeting the requirements of this section is identified for each year.

(v) Leases under which rental of personal property is included. No adjustment to the rents actually received by the lessor is made for the use of any farm equipment or other personal property the use of which is included under a lease for comparable real property unless the lease specifies the amount of the total rental attributable to the personal property and that amount is reasonable under the circumstances.

(c) State and local real estate taxes. For purposes of the farm valuation formula under section 2032A(e)(7) state and local taxes are taxes which are assessed by a state or local government and which are allowable deductions under section 164. However, only those taxes on the comparable real property from which cash rentals are determined may be used in the formula valuation.

(d) Comparable real property defined. Comparable real property must be situated in the same locality as the specially valued property. This requirement is not to be viewed in terms of mileage or political divisions alone, but rather is to be judged according to generally accepted real property valuation rules. The determination of properties which are comparable is a factual one and must be based on numerous factors, no one of which is determinative. It will, therefore, frequently be necessary to value farm property in segments where there are different uses or land characteristics included in the specially valued farm. For example, if section 2032A(e)(7) is used, rented property on which comparable buildings or improvements are located must be identified for specially valued property on which buildings or other real property improvements are located. In cases involving multiple areas or land characteristics, actual comparable property for each segment must be used, and the rentals and taxes from all such properties combined (using generally accepted real property valuation rules) for use in the valuation formula given in this section. However, any premium or discount resulting from the presence of multiple uses or other characteristics in one farm is also to be reflected. All factors generally considered in real estate valuation are to be considered in determining comparability under section 2032A. While not intended as an exclusive list, the following factors are among those to be considered in determining comparability—

(1) Similarity of soil as determined by any objective means, including an official soil survey reflected in a soil productivity index;

(2) Whether the crops grown are such as would deplete the soil in a similar manner;

(3) The types of soil conservation techniques that have been practiced on the two properties;

(4) Whether the two properties are subject to flooding;

(5) The slope of the land;

(6) In the case of livestock operations, the carrying capacity of the land;

(7) Where the land is timbered, whether the timber is comparable to that on the subject property;

(8) Whether the property as a whole is unified or whether it is segmented, and where segmented, the availability of the means necessary for movement among the different segments;

(9) The number, types, and conditions of all buildings and other fixed improvements located on the properties and their location as it effects efficient management and use of property and value per se; and

(10) Availability of, and type of, transportation facilities in terms of costs and of proximity of the properties to local markets.

(e) Effective interest rate defined—(1) Generally. The annual effective interest rate on new Federal land bank loans is the average billing rate charged on new agricultural loans to farmers and ranchers in the farm credit district in which the real property to be valued under section 2032A is located, adjusted as provided in paragraph (e)(2) of this section. This rate is to be a single rate for each district covering the period of one calendar year and is to be computed to the nearest one-hundredth of one percent. In the event that the district billing rates of interest on such new agricultural loans change during a year, the rate for that year is to be weighed to reflect the portion of the year during which each such rate was charged. If a district's billing rate on such new agricultural loans varies according to the amount of the loan, the rate applicable to a loan in an amount resulting from dividing the total dollar amount of such loans closed during the year by the total number of the loans closed is to be used under section 2032A. Applicable rates may be obtained from the district director of internal revenue.

(2) Adjustment to billing rate of interest. The billing rate of interest determined under this paragraph is to be adjusted to reflect the increased cost of borrowing resulting from the required purchase of land bank association stock. For section 2032A purposes, the rate of required stock investment is the average of the percentages of the face amount of new agricultural loans to farmers and ranchers required to be invested in such stock by the applicable district bank during the year. If this percentage changes during a year, the average is to be adjusted to reflect the period when each percentage requirement was effective. The percentage is viewed as a reduction in the loan proceeds actually received from the amount upon which interest is charged.

(3) Example. The determination of the effective interest rate for any year may be illustrated as follows:

Example. District X of the Federal land bank system charged an 8 percent billed interest rate on new agricultural loans for 8 months of the year, 1976, and an 8.75 percent rate for 4 months of the year. The average billing rate, was therefore, 8.25 percent [(1.08 × $^{8}/_{12}$) + (1.0875 × $^{4}/_{12}$) = 1.0825]. The district required stock equal to 5 percent of the face amount of the loan to be purchased as a precondition to receiving a loan. Thus, the borrower only received 95 percent of the funds upon which he paid interest. The applicable annual interest rate for 1976 of 8.68 percent is computed as follows:

8.25 percent × 1.00 (total loan amount) = 8.25 percent (billed interest rate) divided by 0.95 (percent of loan proceeds received by borrower) = 8.68 percent (effective interest rate for 1976).

* * *

§ 20.2033–1 Property in which the decedent had an interest.

(a) In general. The gross estate of a decedent who was a citizen or resident of the United States at the time of his death includes under section 2033 the value of all property, whether real or personal, tangible or intangible, and wherever situated, beneficially owned by the decedent at the time of his death. * * * Real property is included whether it came into the possession and control of the executor or administrator or passed directly to heirs or devisees. Various statutory provisions which exempt bonds, notes, bills, and certificates of indebtedness of the Federal Government or its agencies and the interest thereon from taxation are generally not applicable to the estate tax, since such tax is an excise tax on the transfer of property at death and is not a tax on the property transferred.

(b) Miscellaneous examples. A cemetery lot owned by the decedent is part of his gross estate, but its value is limited to the salable value of that part of the lot which is not designed for the interment of the decedent and the members of his family. Property subject to homestead or other exemptions under local law is included in the gross estate. Notes or other claims held by the decedent are likewise included even though they are cancelled by the decedent's will. Interest and rents accrued at the date of the decedent's death constitute a part of the gross estate. Similarly, dividends which are payable to the decedent or his estate by reason of the fact that on or before the date of the decedent's death he was a stockholder of record (but which have not been collected at death) constitute a part of the gross estate.

§ 20.2034–1 Dower or curtesy interests.

A decedent's gross estate includes under section 2034 any interest in property of the decedent's surviving spouse existing at the time of the decedent's death as dower or curtesy, or any interest created by statute in lieu thereof (although such other interest may differ in character from dower or curtesy). Thus, the full value of property is included in the decedent's gross estate, without deduction of such an interest of the surviving husband or wife, and without regard to when the right to such an interest arose.

* * *

§ 20.2036–1 Transfers with retained life estate.

(a) In general. A decedent's gross estate includes under section 2036 the value of any interest in property transferred by the decedent after March 3, 1931, whether in trust or otherwise, except to the extent that the transfer was for an adequate and full consideration in money or money's worth (see § 20.2043–1), if the decedent retained or reserved (1) for his life, or (2) for any period not ascertainable without reference to his death (if the transfer was made after June 6, 1932), or (3) for any period which does not in fact end before his death:

(i) The use, possession, right to the income, or other enjoyment of the transferred property, or

(ii) The right, either alone or in conjunction with any other person or persons, to designate the person or persons who shall possess or enjoy the transferred property or its income (except that, if the transfer was made before June 7, 1932, the right to designate must be retained by or reserved to the decedent alone).

If the decedent retained or reserved an interest or right with respect to all of the property transferred by him, the amount to be included in his gross estate under section 2036 is the value of the entire property, less only the value of any outstanding income interest which is not subject to the decedent's interest or right and which is actually being enjoyed by another person at the time of the decedent's death.

If the decedent retained or reserved an interest or right with respect to a part only of the property transferred by him, the amount to be included in his gross estate under section 2036 is only a corresponding proportion of the amount described in the preceding sentence. An interest or right is treated as having been retained or reserved if at the time of the transfer there was an understanding, express, or implied, that the interest or right would later be conferred.

(b) Meaning of terms.(1) A reservation by the decedent "for any period not ascertainable without reference to his death" may be illustrated by the following examples:

(i) A decedent reserved the right to receive the income from transferred property in quarterly payments, with the proviso that no part of the income between the last quarterly payment and the date of the decedent's death was to be received by the decedent or his estate; and

(ii) A decedent reserved the right to receive the income from transferred property after the death of another person who was in fact enjoying the income at the time of the decedent's death. In such a case, the amount to be included in the decedent's gross estate under this section does not include the value of the outstanding income interest of the other person. It may be noted that if the other person predeceased the decedent, the reservation by the decedent may be considered to be either for his life, or for a period which does not in fact end before his death.

(2) The "use, possession, right to the income, or other enjoyment of the transferred property" is considered as having been retained by or reserved to the decedent to the extent that the use, possession, right to the income, or other enjoyment is to be applied toward the discharge of a legal obligation of the decedent, or otherwise for his pecuniary benefit. The term "legal obligation" includes a legal obligation to support a dependent during the decedent's lifetime.

(3) The phrase "right * * * to designate the person or persons who shall possess or enjoy the transferred property or the income therefrom" includes a reserved power to designate the person or persons to receive the income from the transferred property, or to possess or enjoy nonincome-producing property, during the decedent's life or during any other period described in paragraph (a) of this section. With respect to such a power, it is immaterial (i) whether the power was exercisable alone or only in conjunction with another person or persons, whether or not having an adverse interest; (ii) in what capacity the power was exercisable by the decedent or by another person or persons in conjunction with the decedent; and (iii) whether the exercise of the power was subject to a contingency beyond the decedent's control which did not occur before his death (*e.g.*, the death of another person during the decedent's lifetime). The phrase, however, does not include a power over the transferred property itself which does not affect the enjoyment of the income received or earned during the decedent's life. (See, however, section 2038 for the inclusion of property in the gross estate on account of such a power.) Nor does the phrase apply to a power held solely by a person other than the decedent. But, for example, if the decedent reserved the unrestricted power to remove or discharge a trustee at any time and appoint himself as trustee, the decedent is considered as having the powers of the trustee.

§ 20.2037–1 Transfers taking effect at death.

(a) In general. A decedent's gross estate includes under section 2037 the value of any interest in property transferred by the decedent after September 7, 1916, whether in trust or otherwise, except to the extent that the transfer was for an adequate and full consideration in money or money's worth (see § 20.2043–1), if—

(1) Possession or enjoyment of the property could, through ownership of the interest, have been obtained only by surviving the decedent,

(2) The decedent had retained a possibility (referred to in this section as a "reversionary interest") that the property, other than the income alone, would return to the decedent or his estate or would be subject to a power of disposition by him, and

(3) The value of the reversionary interest immediately before the decedent's death exceeded 5 percent of the value of the entire property.

* * *

(b) Condition of survivorship. As indicated in paragraph (a) of this section, the value of an interest in transferred property is not included in a decedent's gross estate under section 2037 unless possession or enjoyment of the property could, through ownership of such interest, have been obtained only by surviving the decedent. Thus, property is not included in the decedent's gross estate if, immediately before the decedent's death, possession or enjoyment of the property could have been obtained by any beneficiary either by surviving the decedent or through the occurrence of some other event such as the expiration of a term of years. However, if a consideration of the terms and circumstances of the transfer as a whole indicates that the "other event" is unreal and if the death of the decedent does, in fact, occur before the "other event", the beneficiary will be considered able to possess or enjoy the property only by surviving the decedent. Notwithstanding the foregoing, an interest in transferred property is not includible in a decedent's gross estate under section 2037 if possession or enjoyment of the property could have been obtained by any beneficiary during the decedent's life through the exercise of a general power of appointment (as defined in section 2041) which in fact was exercisable immediately before the decedent's death. See examples (5) and (6) in paragraph (e) of this section.

(c) Retention of reversionary interest.(1) As indicated in paragraph (a) of this section, the value of an interest in transferred property is not included in a decedent's gross estate under section 2037 unless the decedent had retained a reversionary interest in the property, and the value of the reversionary interest immediately before the death of the decedent exceeded 5 percent of the value of the property.

(2) For purposes of section 2037, the term "reversionary interest" includes a possibility that property transferred by the decedent may return to him or his estate and a possibility that property transferred by the decedent may become subject to a power of disposition by him. The term is not used in a technical sense, but has reference to any reserved right under which the transferred property shall or may be returned to the grantor. Thus, it encompasses an interest arising either by the express terms of the instrument of transfer or by operation of law. (See, however, paragraph (f) of this section with respect to transfers made before October 8, 1949.) The term "reversionary interest" does not include rights to income only, such as the right to receive the income from a trust after the death of another person. (However, see section 2036 for the inclusion of property in the gross estate on account of such rights.) Nor does the term "reversionary interest" include the possibility that the decedent during his lifetime might have received back an interest in transferred property by inheritance through the estate of another person. Similarly, a statutory right of a spouse to receive a portion of whatever estate a decedent may leave at the time of his death is not a "reversionary interest".

(3) For purposes of this section, the value of the decedent's reversionary interest is computed as of the moment immediately before his death, without regard to whether or not the executor elects the alternate valuation method under section 2032 and without regard to the fact of the decedent's death. The value is ascertained in accordance with recognized valuation principles for determining the value for estate tax purposes of future or conditional interests in property. (See §§ 20.2031–1, 20.2031–7, and 20.2031–9). For example, if the decedent's reversionary interest was subject to an outstanding life estate in his wife, his interest is valued according to the actuarial rules set forth in § 20.2031–7. On the other hand, if the decedent's reversionary interest was contingent on the death of his wife without issue surviving and if it cannot be shown that his wife is incapable of having issue (so that his interest is not subject to valuation according to the actuarial rules in § 20.2031–7), his interest is valued according to the general rules set forth in § 20.2031–1. A possibility that the decedent may be able to dispose of property under certain conditions is considered to have the same value as a right of the decedent to the return of the property under those same conditions.

(4) In order to determine whether or not the decedent retained a reversionary interest in transferred property of a value in excess of 5 percent, the value of the reversionary interest is compared with the value of the transferred property, including interests therein which are not dependent upon survivorship of the decedent. For example, assume that the decedent, A, transferred property in trust with the income payable to B for life and with the remainder payable to C if A predeceases B, but with the property to revert to A if B predeceases A. Assume further that A does, in fact, predecease B. The value of A's reversionary interest immediately before his death is compared with the value of the trust corpus, without deduction of the value of B's outstanding life estate. If, in the above example, A had retained a reversionary interest in one-half only of the trust corpus, the value of his reversionary interest would be compared with the value of one-half of the trust corpus, again without deduction of any part of the value of B's outstanding life estate.

(d) Transfers partly taking effect at death. If separate interests in property are transferred to one or more beneficiaries, paragraphs (a) to (c) of this section are to be separately applied with respect to each interest. For example, assume that the decedent transferred an interest in Blackacre to A which could be possessed or enjoyed only by surviving the decedent, and that the decedent transferred an interest in Blackacre to B which could be possessed or enjoyed only on the occurrence of some event unrelated to the decedent's death. Assume further that the decedent retained a reversionary interest in Blackacre of a value in excess of 5 percent. Only the value of the interest transferred to A is includible in the decedent's gross estate. Similar results would obtain if possession or enjoyment of the entire property could have been obtained only by surviving the decedent, but the decedent had retained a reversionary interest in a part only of such property.

(e) **Examples.** The provisions of paragraphs (a) to (d) of this section may be further illustrated by the following examples.* * *

Example (1). The decedent transferred property in trust with the income payable to his wife for life and, at her death, remainder to the decedent's then surviving children, or if none, to the decedent or his estate. Since each beneficiary can possess or enjoy the property without surviving the decedent, no part of the property is includible in the decedent's gross estate under section 2037, regardless of the value of the decedent's reversionary interest. (However, see section 2033 for inclusion of the value of the reversionary interest in the decedent's gross estate.)

Example (2). The decedent transferred property in trust with the income to be accumulated for the decedent's life, and at his death, principal and accumulated income to be paid to the decedent's then surviving issue, or, if none, to A or A's estate. Since the decedent retained no reversionary interest in the property, no part of the property is includible in the decedent's gross estate, even though possession or enjoyment of the property could be obtained by the issue only by surviving the decedent.

Example (3). The decedent transferred property in trust with the income payable to his wife for life and with the remainder payable to the decedent or, if he is not living at his wife's death, to his daughter or her estate. The daughter cannot obtain possession or enjoyment of the property without surviving the decedent. Therefore, if the decedent's reversionary interest immediately before his death exceeded 5 percent of the value of the property, the value of the property, less the value of the wife's outstanding life estate, is includible in the decedent's gross estate.

Example (4). The decedent transferred property in trust with the income payable to his wife for life and with the remainder payable to his son or, if the son is not living at the wife's death, to the decedent or, if the decedent is not then living, to X or X's estate. Assume that the decedent was survived by his wife, his son, and X. Only X cannot obtain possession or enjoyment of the property without surviving the decedent. Therefore, if the decedent's reversionary interest immediately before his death exceeded 5 percent of the value of the property, the value of X's remainder interest (with reference to the time immediately after the decedent's death) is includible in the decedent's gross estate.

Example (5). The decedent transferred property in trust with the income to be accumulated for a period of 20 years or until the decedent's prior death, at which time the principal and accumulated income was to be paid to the decedent's son if then surviving. Assume that the decedent does, in fact, die before the expiration of the 20-year period. If, at the time of the transfer, the decedent was 30 years of age, in good health, etc., the son will be considered able to possess or enjoy the property without surviving the decedent. If, on the other hand, the decedent was 70 years of age at the time of the transfer, the son will not be considered able to possess or enjoy the property without surviving the decedent. In this latter case, if the value of the decedent's reversionary interest (arising by operation of law) immediately before his death exceeded 5 percent of the value of the property, the value of the property is includible in the decedent's gross estate.

Example (6). The decedent transferred property in trust with the income to be accumulated for his life and, at his death, the principal and accumulated income to be paid to the decedent's then surviving children. The decedent's wife was given the unrestricted power to alter, amend, or revoke the trust. Assume that the wife survived the decedent but did not, in fact, exercise her power during the decedent's lifetime. Since possession or enjoyment of the property could have been obtained by the wife during the decedent's lifetime under the exercise of a general power of appointment, which was, in fact, exercisable immediately before the decedent's death, no part of the property is includible in the decedent's gross estate.

* * *

§ 20.2038–1 Revocable transfers.

(a) **In general.** A decedent's gross estate includes under section 2038 the value of any interest in property transferred by the decedent, whether in trust or otherwise, if the enjoyment of the interest was subject at the date of the decedent's death to any change through the exercise of a power by the decedent to alter, amend, revoke, or terminate, or if the decedent relinquished such a power in contemplation of death. However, section 2038 does not apply—

(1) To the extent that the transfer was for an adequate and full consideration in money or money's worth (see § 20.2043–1);

(2) If the decedent's power could be exercised only with the consent of all parties having an interest (vested or contingent) in the transferred property, and if the power adds nothing to the rights of the parties under local law; or

(3) To a power held solely by a person other than the decedent. But, for example, if the decedent had the unrestricted power to remove or discharge a trustee at any time and appoint himself trustee, the

decedent is considered as having the powers of the trustee. However, this result would not follow if he only had the power to appoint himself trustee under limited conditions which did not exist at the time of his death. (See last two sentences of paragraph (b) of this section.)

Except as provided in this paragraph, it is immaterial in what capacity the power was exercisable by the decedent or by another person or persons in conjunction with the decedent; whether the power was exercisable alone or only in conjunction with another person or persons, whether or not having an adverse interest* * *; and at what time or from what source the decedent acquired his power* * *. Section 2038 is applicable to any power affecting the time or manner of enjoyment of property or its income, even though the identity of the beneficiary is not affected. For example, section 2038 is applicable to a power reserved by the grantor of a trust to accumulate income or distribute it to A, and to distribute corpus to A, even though the remainder is vested in A or his estate, and no other person has any beneficial interest in the trust. However, only the value of an interest in property subject to a power to which section 2038 applies is included in the decedent's gross estate under section 2038.

(b) Date of existence of power. A power to alter, amend, revoke, or terminate will be considered to have existed at the date of the decedent's death even though the exercise of the power was subject to a precedent giving of notice or even though the alteration, amendment, revocation, or termination would have taken effect only on the expiration of a stated period after the exercise of the power, whether or not on or before the date of the decedent's death notice had been given or the power had been exercised. In determining the value of the gross estate in such cases, the full value of the property transferred subject to the power is discounted for the period required to elapse between the date of the decedent's death and the date upon which the alteration, amendment, revocation, or termination could take effect. In this connection, see especially § 20.2031–7. However, section 2038 is not applicable to a power the exercise of which was subject to a contingency beyond the decedent's control which did not occur before his death (*e.g.*, the death of another person during the decedent's life). See, however, section 2036(a)(2) for the inclusion of property in the decedent's gross estate on account of such a power.

* * *

§ 20.2039–1 Annuities.

(a) In general. A decedent's gross estate includes under section 2039(a) and (b) the value of an annuity or other payment receivable by any beneficiary by reason of surviving the decedent under certain agreements or plans to the extent that the value of the annuity or other payment is attributable to contributions made by the decedent or his employer. Section 2039(a) and (b), however, has no application to an amount which constitutes the proceeds of insurance under a policy on the decedent's life. Paragraph (b) of this section describes the agreements or plans to which section 2039(a) and (b) applies; paragraph (c)* of this section provides rules for determining the amount includible in the decedent's gross estate; and paragraph (d)* of this section distinguishes proceeds of life insurance. The fact that an annuity or other payment is not includible in a decedent's gross estate under section 2039(a) and (b) does not mean that it is not includible under some other section of part III of subchapter A of chapter 11. * * *

(b) Agreements or plans to which section 2039(a) and (b) applies.(1) Section 2039(a) and (b) applies to the value of an annuity or other payment receivable by any beneficiary under any form of contract or agreement entered into after March 3, 1931, under which—

(i) An annuity or other payment was payable to the decedent, either alone or in conjunction with another person or persons, for his life or for any period not ascertainable without reference to his death or for any period which does not in fact end before his death, or

(ii) The decedent possessed, for his life or for any period not ascertainable without reference to his death or for any period which does not in fact end before his death, the right to receive such an annuity or other payment, either alone or in conjunction with another person or persons.

*Editorial comment: The Regulations do not reflect the repeal of this provision.

The term "annuity or other payment" as used with respect to both the decedent and the beneficiary has reference to one or more payments extending over any period of time. The payments may be equal or unequal, conditional or unconditional, periodic or sporadic. The term "contract or agreement" includes any arrangement, understanding or plan, or any combination of arrangements, understandings or plans arising by reason of the decedent's employment. An annuity or other payment "was payable" to the decedent if, at the time of his death, the decedent was in fact receiving an annuity or other payment, whether or not he had an enforceable right to have payments continued. The decedent "possessed the right to receive" an annuity or other payment if, immediately before his death, the decedent had an enforceable right to receive payments at some time in the future, whether or not, at the time of his death, he had a present right to receive payments. In connection with the preceding sentence, the decedent will be regarded as having had "an enforceable right to receive payments at some time in the future" so long as he had complied with his obligations under the contract or agreement up to the time of his death. For the meaning of the phrase "for his life or for any period not ascertainable without reference to his death or for any period which does not in fact end before his death", see section 2036 and § 20.2036–1.

(2) The application of this paragraph is illustrated and more fully explained in the following examples. In each example: (i) It is assumed that all transactions occurred after March 3, 1931, and (ii) the amount stated to be includible in the decedent's gross estate is determined in accordance with the provisions of paragraph (c) of this section.

Example (1). The decedent purchased an annuity contract under the terms of which the issuing company agreed to pay an annuity to the decedent for his life and, upon his death, to pay a specified lump sum to his designated beneficiary. The decedent was drawing his annuity at the time of his death. The amount of the lump sum payment to the beneficiary is includible in the decedent's gross estate under section 2039(a) and (b).

Example (2). Pursuant to a retirement plan, the employer made contributions to a fund which was to provide the employee, upon his retirement at age 60, with an annuity for life, and which was to provide the employee's wife, upon his death after retirement, with a similar annuity for life. The benefits under the plan were completely forfeitable during the employee's life, but upon his death after retirement, the benefits to the wife were forfeitable only upon her remarriage. The employee had no right to originally designate or to ever change the employer's designation of the surviving beneficiary. The retirement plan at no time met the requirements of section 401(a) (relating to qualified plans). Assume that the employee died at age 61 after the employer started payment of his annuity as described above. The value of the wife's annuity is includible in the decedent's gross estate under section 2039(a) and (b). Includibility in this case is based on the fact that the annuity to the decedent "was payable" at the time of his death. The fact that the decedent's annuity was forfeitable is of no consequence since, at the time of his death, he was in fact receiving payments under the plan. Nor is it important that the decedent had no right to choose the surviving beneficiary. The element of forfeitability in the wife's annuity may be taken into account only with respect to the valuation of the annuity in the decedent's gross estate.

Example (3). Pursuant to a retirement plan, the employer made contributions to a fund which was to provide the employee, upon his retirement at age 60, with an annuity of $100 per month for life, and which was to provide his designated beneficiary, upon the employee's death after retirement, with a similar annuity for life. The plan also provided that (a) upon the employee's separation from service before retirement, he would have a nonforfeitable right to receive a reduced annuity starting at age 60, and (b) upon the employee's death before retirement, a lump sum payment representing the amount of the employer's contributions credited to the employee's account would be paid to the designated beneficiary. The plan at no time met the requirements of section 401(a) (relating to qualified plans). Assume that the employee died at age 49 and that the designated beneficiary was paid the specified lump sum payment. Such amount is includible in the decedent's gross estate under section 2039(a) and (b). Since immediately before his death, the employee had an enforceable right to receive an annuity commencing at age 60, he is considered to have "possessed the right to receive" an annuity as that term is used in section 2039(a). If, in this example, the employee would not be entitled to any benefits in the event of his separation from service before retirement for any reason other than death, the result would be the same so long as the decedent had complied with his obligations under the contract up to the time of his death. In such case, he is considered to have had, immediately before his death, an enforceable right to receive an annuity commencing at age 60.

Example (4). Pursuant to a retirement plan, the employee made contributions to a fund which was to provide the employee, upon his retirement at age 60, with an annuity for life, and which was to provide his designated beneficiary, upon the employee's death after retirement, with a similar annuity for life. The plan provided, however, that no benefits were payable in the event of the employee's death before retirement. The retirement plan at no time met the requirements of section 401(a) (relating to qualified plans). Assume that the employee died at age 59 but that the employer nevertheless started payment of an annuity in a slightly reduced amount to the designated beneficiary. The value of the annuity is not includible in the decedent's gross estate under section 2039(a) and (b). Since the employee died before reaching the retirement age, the employer was under no obligation to pay the annuity to the employee's designated beneficiary. Therefore, the annuity was not paid under a "contract or agreement" as that term is used in section 2039(a). If, however, it can be established that the employer has consistently paid an annuity under such circumstances, the annuity will be considered as having been paid under a "contract or agreement".

Example (5). The employer made contributions to a retirement fund which were credited to the employee's individual account. Under the plan, the employee was to receive one-half the amount credited to his account upon his retirement at age 60, and his designated beneficiary was to receive the other one-half upon the employee's death after retirement. If the employee should die before reaching the retirement age, the entire amount credited to his account at such time was to be paid to the designated beneficiary. The retirement plan at no time met the requirements of section 401(a) (relating to qualified plans). Assume that the employee received one-half the amount credited to his account upon reaching the retirement age and that he died shortly thereafter. Since the employee received all that he was entitled to receive under the plan before his death, no amount was payable to him for his life or for any period not ascertainable without reference to his death, or for any period which did not in fact end before his death. Thus, the amount of the payment to the designated beneficiary is not includible in the decedent's gross estate under section 2039(a) and (b). If, in this example, the employee died before reaching the retirement age, the amount of the payment to the designated beneficiary would be includible in the decedent's gross estate under section 2039(a) and (b). In this latter case, the decedent possessed the right to receive lump sum payment for a period which did not in fact end before his death.

Example (6). The employer made contributions to two different funds set up under two different plans. One plan was to provide the employee upon his retirement at age 60, with an annuity for life, and the other plan was to provide the employee's designated beneficiary, upon the employee's death, with a similar annuity for life. Each plan was established at a different time and each plan was administered separately in every respect. Neither plan at any time met the requirements of section 401(a) (relating to qualified plans). The value of the designated beneficiary's annuity is includible in the employee's gross estate. All rights and benefits accruing to an employee and to others by reason of the employment (except rights and benefits accruing under certain plans meeting the requirements of section 401(a) (see § 20.2039–2)) are considered together in determining whether or not section 2039(a) and (b) applies. The scope of section 2039(a) and (b) cannot be limited by indirection.

(c) Amount includible in the gross estate. The amount to be included in a decedent's gross estate under section 2039(a) and (b) is an amount which bears the same ratio to the value at the decedent's death of the annuity or other payment receivable by the beneficiary as the contribution made by the decedent, or made by his employer (or former employer) for any reason connected with his employment, to the cost of the contract or agreement bears to its total cost. In applying this ratio, the value at the decedent's death of the annuity or other payment is determined in accordance with the rules set forth in §§ 20.2031–1, 20.2031–7, 20.2031–8, and 20.2031–9. The application of this paragraph may be illustrated by the following examples:

Example (1). On January 1, 1945, the decedent and his wife each contributed $15,000 to the purchase price of an annuity contract under the terms of which the issuing company agreed to pay an annuity to the decedent and his wife for their joint lives and to continue the annuity to the survivor for his life. Assume that the value of the survivor's annuity at the decedent's death (computed under § 20.2031–8) is $20,000. Since the decedent contributed one-half of the cost of the contract, the amount to be included in his gross estate under section 2039(a) and (b) is $10,000.

Example (2). Under the terms of an employment contract entered into on January 1, 1945, the employer and the employee made contributions to a fund which was to provide the employee, upon his retirement at age 60, with an annuity for life, and which was to provide his designated beneficiary, upon the employee's death after retirement, with a similar annuity for life. The retirement fund at no time formed part of a plan meeting the requirements of section 401(a) (relating to qualified plans). Assume that the employer and the employee each contributed $5,000 to the retirement fund. Assume further, that the employee died after retirement at which time the value of the survivor's annuity was $8,000. Since the employer's contributions were made by reason of the decedent's employment, the amount to be included in his gross estate under section 2039(a) and (b) is the entire $8,000. If, in the above example, only the employer made contributions to the fund, the amount to be included in the gross estate would still be $8,000.

* * *

§ 20.2040–1 Joint interests.*

(a) In general. A decedent's gross estate includes under section 2040 the value of property held jointly at the time of the decedent's death by the decedent and another person or persons with right of survivorship, as follows:

(1) To the extent that the property was acquired by the decedent and the other joint owner or owners by gift, devise, bequest, or inheritance, the decedent's fractional share of the property is included.

(2) In all other cases, the entire value of the property is included except such part of the entire value as is attributable to the amount of the consideration in money or money's worth furnished by the other joint owner or owners. See § 20.2043–1 with respect to adequacy of consideration. Such part of the entire value is that portion of the entire value of the property at the decedent's death (or at the alternate valuation date described in section 2032 which the consideration in money or money's worth furnished by the other joint owner or owners bears to the total cost of acquisition and capital additions. In determining the consideration furnished by the other joint owner or owners, there is taken into account only that portion of such consideration which is shown not to be attributable to money or other property acquired by the other joint owner or owners from the decedent for less than a full and adequate consideration in money or money's worth.

*Editorial comment: The Regulations do not include the effect of the Tax Reform Act of 1976 and subsequent legislation.

The entire value of jointly held property is included in a decedent's gross estate unless the executor submits facts sufficient to show that property was not acquired entirely with consideration furnished by the decedent, or was acquired by the decedent and the other joint owner or owners by gift, bequest, devise, or inheritance.

(b) Meaning of "property held jointly". Section 2040 specifically covers property held jointly by the decedent and any other person (or persons), property held by the decedent and spouse as tenants by the entirety, and a deposit of money, or a bond or other instrument, in the name of the decedent and any other person and payable to either or the survivor. The section applies to all classes of property, whether real or personal, and regardless of when the joint interests were created. Furthermore, it makes no difference that the survivor takes the entire interest in the property by right of survivorship and that no interest therein forms a part of the decedent's estate for purposes of administration. The section has no application to property held by the decedent and any other person (or persons) as tenants in common.

(c) Examples. The application of this section may be explained in the following examples in each of which it is assumed that the other joint owner or owners survived the decedent:

(1) If the decedent furnished the entire purchase price of the jointly held property, the value of the entire property is included in his gross estate;

(2) If the decedent furnished a part only of the purchase price, only a corresponding portion of the value of the property is so included;

(3) If the decedent furnished no part of the purchase price, no part of the value of the property is so included;

(4) If the decedent, before the acquisition of the property by himself and the other joint owner, gave the latter a sum of money or other property which thereafter became the other joint owner's entire contribution to the purchase price, then the value of the entire property is so included, notwithstanding the fact that the other property may have appreciated in value due to market conditions between the time of the gift and the time of the acquisition of the jointly held property;

(5) If the decedent, before the acquisition of the property by himself and the other joint owner, transferred to the latter for less than an adequate and full consideration in money or money's worth other income-producing property, the income from which belonged to and became the other joint owner's entire contribution to the purchase price, then the value of the jointly held property less that portion attributable to the income which the other joint owner did furnish is included in the decedent's gross estate;

(6) If the property originally belonged to the other joint owner and the decedent purchased his interest from the other joint owner, only that portion of the value of the property attributable to the consideration paid by the decedent is included;

(7) If the decedent and his spouse acquired the property by will or gift as tenants by the entirety, one-half of the value of the property is included in the decedent's gross estate; and

(8) If the decedent and his two brothers acquired the property by will or gift as joint tenants, one-third of the value of the property is so included.

§ 20.2041–1 Powers of appointment; in general.

(a) Introduction. A decedent's gross estate includes under section 2041 the value of property in respect of which the decedent possessed, exercised, or released certain powers of appointment. This section contains rules of general application; § 20.2041–2 contains rules specifically applicable to general powers of appointment created on or before October 21, 1942; and § 20.2041–3 sets forth specific rules applicable to powers of appointment created after October 21, 1942.

(b) Definition of "power of appointment"—(1) In general. The term "power of appointment" includes all powers which are in substance and effect powers of appointment regardless of the nomenclature used in creating the power and regardless of local property law connotations. For example, if a trust instrument provides that the beneficiary may appropriate or consume the principal of the trust, the power to consume or appropriate is a power of appointment. Similarly, a power given to a decedent to affect the beneficial enjoyment of trust property or its income by altering, amending, or revoking the trust instrument or terminating the trust is a power of appointment. If the community property laws of a State confer upon the wife a power of testamentary disposition over property in which she does not have a vested interest she is considered as having a power of appointment. A power in a donee to remove or discharge a trustee and appoint himself may be a power of appointment. For example, if under the terms of a trust instrument, the trustee or his successor has the power to appoint the principal of the trust for the benefit of individuals including himself, and the decedent has the unrestricted power to remove or discharge the trustee at any time and appoint any other person including himself, the decedent is considered as having a power of appointment. However, the decedent is not considered to have a power of appointment if he only had the power to appoint a successor, including himself, under limited conditions which did not exist at the time of his death, without an accompanying unrestricted power of removal. Similarly, a power to amend only the administrative provisions of a trust instrument, which cannot substantially affect the beneficial enjoyment of the trust property or income, is not a power of appointment. The mere power of management, investment, custody of assets, or the power to allocate receipts and disbursements as between income and principal, exercisable in a fiduciary capacity, whereby the holder has no power to enlarge or shift any of the beneficial interests therein except as an incidental consequence of the discharge of such fiduciary duties is not a power of appointment. Further, the right in a beneficiary of a trust to assent to a periodic accounting, thereby relieving the trustee from further accountability, is not a power of appointment if the right of assent does not consist of any power or right to enlarge or shift the beneficial interest of any beneficiary therein.

(2) Relation to other sections. For purposes of §§ 20.2041–1 to 20.2041–3, the term "power of appointment" does not include powers reserved by the decedent to himself within the concept of sections 2036 through 2038. (See §§ 20.2036–1 to 20.2038–1.) No provision of section 2041 or of §§ 20.2041–1 to 20.2041–3 is to be construed as in any way limiting the application of any other section of the Internal Revenue Code or of these regulations. The power of the owner of a property interest already possessed by him to dispose of his interest, and nothing more, is not a power of appointment, and the interest is includible in his gross estate to the extent it would be includible under section 2033 or some other provision of part III of subchapter A of chapter 11. For example, if a trust created by S provides for payment of the income to A for life with power in A to appoint the remainder by will and, in default of such appointment for payment of the income to A's widow, W, for her life and for payment of the remainder to A's estate, the value of A's interest in the remainder is includible in his gross estate under section 2033 regardless of its includibility under section 2041.

(3) Powers over a portion of property. If a power of appointment exists as to part of an entire group of assets or only over a limited interest in property, section 2041 applies only to such part or interest. For example, if a trust created by S provides for the payment of income to A for life, then to W for life, with power in A to appoint the remainder by will and in default of appointment for payment of the remainder to B or his estate, and if A dies before W, section 2041 applies only to the value of the remainder interest excluding W's life estate. If A dies after W, section 2041 would apply to the value of the entire property. If the power were only over one-half the remainder interest, section 2041 would apply only to one-half the value of the amounts described above.

(c) Definition of "general power of appointment"—(1) In general. The term "general power of appointment" as defined in section 2041(b)(1) means any power of appointment exercisable in favor of the decedent, his estate, his creditors, or the creditors of his estate, except (i) joint powers, to the extent provided in §§ 20.2041–2 and 20.2041–3, and (ii) certain powers limited by an ascertainable standard, to the extent provided in subparagraph (2) of this paragraph. A power of appointment exercisable to meet the estate tax, or any other taxes, debts, or charges which are enforceable against the estate, is included within the meaning of a power of appointment exercisable in favor of the decedent's estate, his creditors, or the creditors of his estate. A power of appointment exercisable for the purpose of discharging a legal obligation of the decedent or for his pecuniary benefit is considered a power of appointment exercisable in favor of the decedent or his creditors. However, for purposes of §§ 20.2041–1 to 20.2041–3, a power of appointment not otherwise considered to be a general power of appointment is not treated as a general power of appointment merely by reason of the fact that an appointee may, in fact, be a creditor of the decedent or his estate. A power of appointment is not a general power if by its terms it is either—

(a) Exercisable only in favor of one or more designated persons or classes other than the decedent or his creditors, or the decedent's estate or the creditors of his estate, or

(b) Expressly not exercisable in favor of the decedent or his creditors, or the decedent's estate or the creditors of his estate.

A decedent may have two powers under the same instrument, one of which is a general power of appointment and the other of which is not. For example, a beneficiary may have a power to withdraw trust corpus during his life, and a testamentary power to appoint the corpus among his descendants. The testamentary power is not a general power of appointment.

(2) Powers limited by an ascertainable standard. A power to consume, invade, or appropriate income or corpus, or both, for the benefit of the decedent which is limited by an ascertainable standard relating to the health, education, support, or maintenance of the decedent is, by reason of section 2041(b)(1)(A), not a general power of appointment. A power is limited by such a standard if the extent of the holder's duty to exercise and not to exercise the power is reasonably measurable in terms of his needs for health, education, or support (or any combination of them). As used in this subparagraph, the words "support" and "maintenance" are synonymous and their meaning is not limited to the bare necessities of life. A power to use property for the comfort, welfare, or happiness of the holder of the power is not limited by the requisite standard. Examples of powers which are limited by the requisite standard are powers exercisable for the holder's "support," "support in reasonable comfort," "maintenance in health and reasonable comfort," "support in his accustomed manner of living," "education, including college and professional education," "health," and "medical, dental, hospital and nursing expenses and expenses of invalidism." In determining whether a power is limited by an ascertainable standard, it is immaterial whether the beneficiary is required to exhaust his other income before the power can be exercised.

* * *

(d) Definition of "exercise." Whether a power of appointment is in fact exercised may depend upon local law. For example, the residuary clause of a will may be considered under local law as an exercise of a testamentary power of appointment in the absence of evidence of a contrary intention drawn from the whole of the testator's will. However, regardless of local law, a power of appointment is considered as exercised for purposes of section 2041 even though the exercise is in favor of the taker in default of appointment, and irrespective of whether the appointed interest and the interest in default of appointment are identical or whether the appointee renounces any right to take under the appointment. A power of appointment is also considered as exercised even though the disposition cannot take effect until the occurrence of an event after the exercise takes place, if the exercise is irrevocable and, as of the time of the exercise, the condition was not impossible of occurrence. For example, if property is left in trust to A for life, with a power in B to appoint the remainder by will, and B dies before A, exercising his power by appointing the remainder to C if C survives A, B is considered to have exercised his power if C is living at B's death. On the other hand, a testamentary power of appointment is not considered as exercised if it is exercised subject to the occurrence during the decedent's life of an express or implied condition which did not in fact occur. Thus, if in the preceding example, C dies before B, B's power of appointment would not be considered to have been exercised. Similarly, if a trust provides for income to A for life, remainder as A appoints by will, and A appoints a life estate in the property to B and does not otherwise exercise his power, but B dies before A, A's power is not considered to have been exercised.

(e) Time of creation of power. A power of appointment created by will is, in general, considered as created on the date of the testator's death. However, section 2041(b)(3) provides that a power of appointment created by a will executed on or before October 21, 1942, is considered a power created on or before that date if the testator dies before July 1, 1949, without having republished the will, by codicil or otherwise, after October 21, 1942. A power of appointment created by an inter vivos instrument is considered as created on the date the instrument takes effect. Such a power is not considered as created at some future date merely because it is not exercisable on the date the instrument takes effect, or because it is revocable, or because the identity of its holders is not ascertainable until after the date the instrument takes effect. However, if the holder of a power exercises it by creating a second power, the second power is considered as created at the time of the exercise of the first. The application of this paragraph may be illustrated by the following examples:

Example (1). A created a revocable trust before October 22, 1942, providing for payment of income to B for life with remainder as B shall appoint by will. Even though A dies after October 21, 1942, without having exercised his power of revocation, B's power of appointment is considered a power created before October 22, 1942.

Example (2). C created an irrevocable inter vivos trust before October 22, 1942, naming T as trustee and providing for payment of income to D for life with remainder to E. T was given the power to pay corpus to D and the power to appoint a successor trustee. If T resigns after October 21, 1942, and appoints D as successor trustee, D is considered to have a power of appointment created before October 22, 1942.

Example (3). F created an irrevocable inter vivos trust before October 22, 1942, providing for payment of income to G for life with remainder as G shall appoint by will, but in default of appointment income to H for life with remainder as H shall appoint by will. If G died after October 21, 1942, without having exercised his power of appointment, H's power of appointment is considered a power created before October 22, 1942, even though it was only a contingent interest until G's death.

Example (4). If in example (3) above G had exercised his power of appointment by creating a similar power in J, J's power of appointment would be considered a power created after October 21, 1942.

* * *

§ 20.2041–3 Powers of appointment created after October 21, 1942.

(a) In general.(1) Property subject to a power of appointment created after October 21, 1942, is includible in the gross estate of the holder of the power under varying conditions depending on whether the power is (i) general in nature, (ii) possessed at death, or (iii) exercised or released. See paragraphs (b), (c), and (d) of § 20.2041–1 for the definition of various terms used in this section. See paragraph (c) of this section for the rules applicable to determine the extent to which joint powers created after October 21, 1942, are to be treated as general powers of appointment.

(2) If the power is a general power of appointment, the value of an interest in property subject to such a power is includible in a decedent's gross estate under section 2041(a)(2) if either—

(i) The decedent has the power at the time of his death (and the interest exists at the time of his death), or

(ii) The decedent exercised or released the power, or the power lapsed, under the circumstances and to the extent described in paragraph (d) of this section.

(3) If the power is not a general power of appointment, the value of property subject to the power is includible in the holder's gross estate under section 2041(a)(3) only if it is exercised to create a further power under certain circumstances (see paragraph (e) of this section).

(b) Existence of power at death. For purposes of section 2041(a)(2), a power of appointment is considered to exist on the date of a decedent's death even though the exercise of the power is subject to the precedent giving of notice, or even though the exercise of the power takes effect only on the expiration of a stated period after its exercise, whether or not on or before the decedent's death notice has been given or the power has been exercised. However, a power which by its terms is exercisable only upon the occurrence during the decedent's lifetime of an event or a contingency which did not in fact take place or occur during such time is not a power in existence on the date of the decedent's death. For example, if a decedent was given a general power of appointment exercisable only after he reached a certain age, only if he survived another person, or only if he died without descendants, the power would not be in existence on the date of the decedent's death if the condition precedent to its exercise had not occurred.

(c) Joint powers created after October 21, 1942. The treatment of a power of appointment created after October 21, 1942, which is exercisable only in conjunction with another person is governed by section 2041(b)(1)(C), which provides as follows:

(1) Such a power is not considered a general power of appointment if it is not exercisable by the decedent except with the consent or joinder of the creator of the power.

(2) Such power is not considered a general power of appointment if it is not exercisable by the decedent except with the consent or joinder of a person having a substantial interest in the property subject to the power which is adverse to the exercise of the power in favor of the decedent, his estate, his creditors, or the creditors of his estate. An interest adverse to the exercise of a power is considered as substantial if its value in relation to the total value of the property subject to the power is not insignificant. For this purpose, the interest is to be valued in accordance with the actuarial principles set forth in § 20.2031–7 or, if it is not susceptible to valuation under those provisions, in accordance with the general principles set forth in § 20.2031–1. A taker in default of appointment under a power has an interest which is adverse to an exercise of the power. A coholder of the power has no adverse interest merely because of his joint possession of the power nor merely because he is a permissible appointee under a power. However, a coholder of a power is considered as having an adverse interest where he may possess the power after the decedent's death and may exercise it at that time in favor of himself, his estate, his creditors, or the creditors of his estate. Thus, for example, if X, Y, and Z held a power jointly to appoint among a group of persons which includes themselves and if on the death of X the power will pass to Y and Z jointly, then Y and Z are considered to have interests adverse to the exercise of the power in favor of X. Similarly, if on Y's death the power will pass to Z, Z is considered to have an interest adverse to the exercise of the power in favor of Y. The application of this subparagraph may be further illustrated by the following additional examples in each of which it is assumed that the value of the interest in question is substantial:

Example (1). The decedent and R were trustees of a trust under the terms of which the income was to be paid to the decedent for life and then to M for life, and the remainder was to be paid to R. The trustees had power to distribute corpus to the decedent. Since R's interest was substantially adverse to an exercise of the power in favor of the decedent the latter did not have a general power of appointment. If M and the decedent were the trustees, M's interest would likewise have been adverse.

Example (2). The decedent and L were trustees of a trust under the terms of which the income was to be paid to L for life and then to M for life, and the remainder was to be paid to the decedent. The trustees had power to distribute corpus to the decedent during L's life. Since L's interest was adverse to an exercise of the power in favor of the decedent, the decedent did not have a general power of appointment. If the decedent and M were the trustees, M's interest would likewise have been adverse.

Example (3). The decedent and L were trustees of a trust under the terms of which the income was to be paid to L for life. The trustees could designate whether corpus was to be distributed to the decedent or to A after L's death. L's interest was not adverse to an exercise of the power in favor of the decedent, and the decedent therefore had a general power of appointment.

(3) A power which is exercisable only in conjunction with another person, and which after application of the rules set forth in subparagraphs (1) and (2) of this paragraph constitutes a general power of appointment, will be treated as though the holders of the power who are permissible appointees of the property were joint owners of property subject to the power. The decedent, under this rule, will be treated as possessed of a general power of appointment over an aliquot share of the property to be determined with reference to the number of joint holders, including the decedent, who (or whose estates or creditors) are permissible appointees. Thus, for example, if X, Y, and Z hold an unlimited power jointly to appoint among a group of persons, including themselves, but on the death of X the power does not pass to Y and Z jointly, then Y and Z are not considered to have interests adverse to the exercise of the power in favor of X. In this case X is considered to possess a general power of appointment as to one-third of the property subject to the power.

(d) Releases, lapses, and disclaimers of general powers of appointment.(1) Property subject to a general power of appointment created after October 21, 1942, is includible in the gross estate of a decedent under section 2041(a)(2) even though he does not have the power at the date of his death, if during his life he exercised or released the power under circumstances such that, if the property subject to the power had been owned and transferred by the decedent, the property would be includible in the decedent's gross estate under section 2035, 2036, 2037, or 2038. Further, section 2041(b)(2) provides that the lapse of a power of appointment is considered to be a release of the power to the extent set forth in subparagraph (3) of this paragraph. A release of a power of appointment need not be formal or express in character. The principles set forth in § 20.2041–2 for determining the application of the pertinent provisions of sections 2035 through 2038 to a particular exercise of a power of appointment are applicable for purposes of determining whether or not an exercise or release of a power of appointment created after October 21, 1942, causes the property to be included in a decedent's gross estate under section 2041(a)(2). If a general power of appointment created after October 21, 1942, is partially released, a subsequent exercise or release of the power under circumstances described in the first sentence of this subparagraph, or its possession at death will nevertheless cause the property subject to the power to be included in the gross estate of the holder of the power.

(2) Section 2041(a)(2) is not applicable to the complete release of a general power of appointment created after October 21, 1942, whether exercisable during life or by will, if the release was not made in contemplation of death within the meaning of section 2035, and if after the release the holder of the power retained no interest in or control over the property subject to the power which would cause the property to be included in his gross estate under sections 2036 through 2038 if the property had been transferred by the holder.

(3) The failure to exercise a power of appointment created after October 21, 1942, within a specified time, so that the power lapses, constitutes a release of the power. However, section 2041(b)(2) provides that such a lapse of a power of appointment during any calendar year during the decedent's life is treated as a release for purposes of inclusion of property in the gross estate under section 2041(a)(2) only to the extent that the property which could have been appointed by exercise of the lapsed power exceeds the greater of (i) $5,000 or (ii) 5 percent of the aggregate value, at the time of the lapse, of the assets out of which, or the proceeds of which, the exercise of the lapsed power could have been satisfied. For example, assume that A transferred $200,000 worth of securities in trust providing for payment of income to B for life with remainder to B's issue. Assume further that B was given a noncumulative right to withdraw $10,000 a year from the principal of the trust fund (which neither increased nor decreased in value prior to B's death). In such case, the failure of B to exercise his right of withdrawal will not result in estate tax with respect to the power to withdraw $10,000 which lapses each year before the year of B's death. At B's death there will be included in his gross estate the $10,000 which he was entitled to withdraw for the year in which his death occurs less any amount which he may have taken during that year. However, if in the above example B had possessed the right to withdraw $15,000 of the principal annually, the failure to exercise such power in any year will be considered a release of the power to the extent of the excess of the amount subject to withdrawal over 5 percent of the trust fund (in this example, $5,000, assuming that the trust fund is worth $200,000 at the time of the lapse). Since each lapse is treated as though B had exercised dominion over the trust property by making a transfer of principal reserving the income therefrom for his life, the value of the trust property (but only to the extent of the excess of the amount subject to withdrawal over 5 percent of the trust fund) is includible in B's gross estate (unless before B's death he has disposed of his right to the income under circumstances to which sections 2035 through 2038 would not be applicable). The extent to which the value of the trust property is included in the decedent's gross estate is determined as provided in subparagraph (4) of this paragraph.

(4) The purpose of section 2041(b)(2) is to provide a determination, as of the date of the lapse of the power, of the proportion of the property over which the power lapsed which is an exempt disposition for estate tax purposes and the proportion which, if the other requirements of sections 2035 through 2038 are satisfied, will be considered as a taxable disposition. Once the taxable proportion of any disposition at the date of lapse has been determined, the valuation of that proportion as of the date of the decedent's death (or, if the executor has elected the alternate valuation method under section 2032, the value as of the date therein provided), is to be ascertained in accordance with the principles which are applicable to the valuation of transfers of property by the decedent under the corresponding provisions of sections 2035 through 2038. For example, if the life beneficiary of a trust had a right exercisable only during one calendar year to draw down $50,000 from the corpus of a trust, which he did not exercise, and if at the end of the year the corpus was worth $800,000, the taxable portion over which the power lapsed is $10,000 (the excess of $50,000 over 5 percent of the corpus), or 1/80 of the total value. On the decedent's death, if the total value of the corpus of the trust (excluding income accumulated after the lapse of the power) on the applicable valuation date was $1,200,000, $15,000 (1/80 of $1,200,000) would be includible in the decedent's gross estate. However, if the total value was then $600,000, only $7,500 (1/80 of $600,000) would be includible.

(5) If the failure to exercise a power, such as a right of withdrawal, occurs in more than a single year, the proportion of the property over which the power lapsed which is treated as a taxable disposition will be determined separately for each such year. The aggregate of the taxable proportions for all such years, valued in accordance with the above principles, will be includible in the gross estate by reason of the lapse. The includible amount, however, shall not exceed the aggregate value of the assets out of which, or the proceeds of which, the exercise of the power could have been satisfied, valued as of the date of the decedent's death (or, if the executor has elected the alternate valuation method under section 2032, the value as of the date therein provided).

(6) **(i)** A disclaimer or renunciation of a general power of appointment created in a taxable transfer after December 31, 1976, in the person disclaiming is not considered a release of the power if the disclaimer or renunciation is a qualified disclaimer as described in section 2518 and the corresponding regulations. If the disclaimer or renunciation is not a qualified disclaimer, it is considered a release of the power by the disclaimant.

(ii) The disclaimer or renunciation of a general power of appointment created in a taxable transfer before January 1, 1977, in the person disclaiming is not considered to be a release of the power. The disclaimer or renunciation must be unequivocal and effective under local law. A disclaimer is a complete and unqualified refusal to accept the rights to which one is entitled. There can be no disclaimer or renunciation of a power after its acceptance. In the absence of facts to the contrary, the failure to renounce or disclaim within a reasonable time after learning of its existence will be presumed to constitute an acceptance of the power. In any case where a power is purported to be disclaimed or renounced as to only a portion of the property subject to the power, the determination as to whether or not there has been a complete and unqualified refusal to accept the rights to which one is entitled will depend on all the facts and circumstances of the particular case, taking into account the recognition and effectiveness of such a disclaimer under local law. Such rights refer to the incidents of the power and not to other interests of the decedent in the property. If effective under local law, the power may be disclaimed or renounced without disclaiming or renouncing such other interests.

(e) Successive powers.(1) Property subject to a power of appointment created after October 21, 1942, which is not a general power, is includible in the gross estate of the holder of the power under section 2041(a)(3) if the power is exercised, and if both of the following conditions are met:

(i) If the exercise is (a) by will, or (b) by a disposition which is of such nature that if it were a transfer of property owned by the decedent, the property would be includible in the decedent's gross estate under sections 2035 through 2037; and

(ii) If the power is exercised by creating another power of appointment which, under the terms of the instruments creating and exercising the first power and under applicable local law, can be validly exercised so as to (a) postpone the vesting of any estate or interest in the property for a period ascertainable without regard to the date of the creation of the first power, or (b) (if the applicable rule against perpetuities is stated in terms of suspension of ownership or of the power of alienation, rather than of vesting) suspend the absolute ownership or the power of alienation of the property for a period ascertainable without regard to the date of the creation of the first power.

(2) For purposes of the application of section 2041(a)(3), the value of the property subject to the second power of appointment is considered to be its value unreduced by any precedent or subsequent interest which is not subject to the second power. Thus, if a decedent has a power to appoint by will $100,000 to a group of persons consisting of his children and grandchildren and exercises the power by making an outright appointment of $75,000 and by giving one appointee a power to appoint $25,000, no more than $25,000 will be includible in the decedent's gross estate under section 2041(a)(3). If, however, the decedent appoints the income from the entire fund to a beneficiary for life with power in the beneficiary to appoint the remainder by will, the entire $100,000 will be includible in the decedent's gross estate under section 2041(a)(3) if the exercise of the second power can validly postpone the vesting of any estate or interest in the property or can suspend the absolute ownership or power of alienation of the property for a period ascertainable without regard to the date of the creation of the first power.

(f) Examples. The application of this section may be further illustrated by the following examples, in each of which it is assumed, unless otherwise stated, that S has transferred property in trust after October 21, 1942, with the remainder payable to R at L's death, and that neither L nor R has any interest in or power over the enjoyment of the trust property except as is indicated separately in each example:

Example (1). Income is directed to be paid to L during his lifetime at the end of each year, if living. L has an unrestricted power during his lifetime to cause the income to be distributed to any other person, but no power to cause it to be accumulated. At L's death, no part of the trust property is includible in L's gross estate since L had a power to dispose of only his income interest, a right otherwise possessed by him.

Example (2). Income is directed to be accumulated during L's life but L has a noncumulative power to distribute $10,000 of each year's income to himself. Unless L's power is limited to himself. Unless L's power is limited by an ascertainable standard (relating to his health, etc.), as defined in paragraph (c)(2) of § 20.2041–1, he has a general power of appointment over $10,000 of each year's income, the lapse of which may cause a portion of any income not distributed to be included in his gross estate under section 2041.

See subparagraphs (3), (4), and (5) of paragraph (d) of this section. Thus, if the trust income during the year amounts to $20,000, L's failure to distribute any of the income to himself constitutes a lapse as to $5,000 (*i.e.*, the amount by which $10,000 exceeds $5,000). If L's power were cumulative (*i.e.*, if the power did not lapse at the end of each year but lapsed only by reason of L's death), the total accumulations which L chose not to distribute to himself immediately before his death would be includible in his gross estate under section 2041.

Example (3). L is entitled to all the income during his lifetime and has an unrestricted power to cause corpus to be distributed to himself. L had a general power of appointment over the corpus of the trust, and the entire corpus as of the time of his death is includible in his gross estate under section 2041.

Example (4). Income was payable to L during his lifetime. R has an unrestricted power to cause corpus to be distributed to L. R dies before L. In such case, R has only a power to dispose of his remainder interest, the value of which is includible in his gross estate under section 2033, and nothing in addition would be includible under section 2041. If in this example R's remainder were contingent on his surviving L, nothing would be includible in his gross estate under either section 2033 or 2041. While R would have a power of appointment, it would not be a general power.

Example (5). Income was payable to L during his lifetime. R has an unrestricted power to cause corpus to be distributed to himself. R dies before L. While the value of R's remainder interest is includible in his gross estate under section 2033, R also has a general power of appointment over the entire trust corpus. Under such circumstances, the entire value of the trust corpus is includible in R's gross estate under section 2041.

§ 20.2042–1 Proceeds of life insurance.

(a) In general.(1) Section 2042 provides for the inclusion in a decedent's gross estate of the proceeds of insurance on the decedent's life (i) receivable by or for the benefit of the estate (see paragraph (b) of this section) and (ii) receivable by other beneficiaries (see paragraph (c) of this section). The term "insurance" refers to life insurance of every description, including death benefits paid by fraternal beneficial societies operating under the lodge system.

(2) Proceeds of life insurance which are not includible in the gross estate under section 2042 may, depending upon the facts of the particular case, be includible under some other section of part III of subchapter A of chapter 11. For example, if the decedent possessed incidents of ownership in an insurance policy on his life but gratuitously transferred all rights in the policy in contemplation of death, the proceeds would be includible under section 2035. Section 2042 has no application to the inclusion in the gross estate of the value of rights in an insurance policy on the life of a person other than the decedent, or the value of rights in a combination annuity contract and life insurance policy on the decedent's life (*i.e.*, a "retirement income" policy with death benefit or an "endowment" policy) under which there was no insurance element at the time of the decedent's death (see paragraph (d) of § 20.2039–1).

(3) Except as provided in paragraph (c)(6), the amount to be included in the gross estate under section 2042 is the full amount receivable under the policy. If the proceeds of the policy are made payable to a beneficiary in the form of an annuity for life or for a term of years, the amount to be included in the gross estate is the one sum payable at death under an option which could have been exercised either by the insured or by the beneficiary, or if no option was granted, the sum used by the insurance company in determining the amount of the annuity.

(b) Receivable by or for the benefit of the estate. (1) Section 2042 requires the inclusion in the gross estate of the proceeds of insurance on the decedent's life receivable by the executor or administrator, or payable to the decedent's estate. It makes no difference whether or not the estate is specifically named as the beneficiary under the terms of the policy. Thus, if under the terms of an insurance policy the proceeds are receivable by another beneficiary but are subject to an obligation, legally binding upon the other beneficiary, to pay taxes, debts, or other charges enforceable against the estate, then the amount of such proceeds required for the payment in full (to the extent of the beneficiary's obligation) of such taxes, debts, or other charges is includible in the gross estate. Similarly, if the decedent purchased an insurance policy in favor of another person or a corporation as collateral security for a loan or other accommodation, its proceeds are considered to be receivable for the benefit of the estate. The amount of the loan outstanding at the date of the decedent's death, with interest accrued to that date, will be deductible in determining the taxable estate. See § 20.2053–4.

(2) If the proceeds of an insurance policy made payable to the decedent's estate are community assets under the local community property law and, as a result, one-half of the proceeds belongs to the decedent's spouse, then only one-half of the proceeds is considered to be receivable by or for the benefit of the decedent's estate.

(c) Receivable by other beneficiaries. (1) Section 2042 requires the inclusion in the gross estate of the proceeds of insurance on the decedent's life not receivable by or for the benefit of the estate if the decedent possessed at the date of his death any of the incidents of ownership in the policy, exercisable either alone or in conjunction with any other person. However, if the decedent did not possess any of such incidents of ownership at the time of his death nor transfer them in contemplation of death, no part of the proceeds would be includible in his gross estate under section 2042. Thus, if the decedent owned a policy of insurance on his life and, 4 years before his death, irrevocably assigned his entire interest in the policy to his wife retaining no reversionary interest therein (see subparagraph (3) of this paragraph), the proceeds of the policy would not be includible in his gross estate under section 2042.

(2) For purposes of this paragraph, the term "incidents of ownership" is not limited in its meaning to ownership of the policy in the technical legal sense. Generally speaking, the term has reference to the right of the insured or his estate to the economic benefits of the policy. Thus, it includes the power to change the beneficiary, to surrender or cancel the policy, to assign the policy, to revoke an assignment, to pledge the policy for a loan, or to obtain from the insurer a loan against the surrender value of the policy, etc. See subparagraph (6) of this paragraph for rules relating to the circumstances under which incidents of ownership held by a corporation are attributable to a decedent through his stock ownership.

(3) The term "incidents of ownership" also includes a reversionary interest in the policy or its proceeds, whether arising by the express terms of the policy or other instrument or by operation of law, but only if the value of the reversionary interest immediately before the death of the decedent exceeded 5 percent of the value of the policy.

As used in this subparagraph, the term "reversionary interest" includes a possibility that the policy or its proceeds may return to the decedent or his estate and a possibility that the policy or its proceeds may become subject to a power of disposition by him. In order to determine whether or not the value of a reversionary interest immediately before the death of the decedent exceeded 5 percent of the value of the policy, the principles contained in paragraph (c)(3) and (4) of § 20.2037–1, insofar as applicable, shall be followed under this subparagraph. In that connection, there must be specifically taken into consideration any incidents of ownership held by others immediately before the decedent's death which would affect the value of the reversionary interest. For example, the decedent would not be considered to have a reversionary interest in the policy of a value in excess of 5 percent if the power to obtain the cash surrender value existed in some other person immediately before the decedent's death and was exercisable by such other person alone and in all events. The terms "reversionary interest" and "incidents of ownership" do not include the possibility that the decedent might receive a policy or its proceeds by inheritance through the estate of another person, or as a surviving spouse under a statutory right of election or a similar right.

(4) A decedent is considered to have an "incident of ownership" in an insurance policy on his life held in trust if, under the terms of the policy, the decedent (either alone or in conjunction with another person or persons) has the power (as trustee or otherwise) to change the beneficial ownership in the policy or its proceeds, or the time or manner of enjoyment thereof, even though the decedent has no beneficial interest in the trust. Moreover, assuming the decedent created the trust, such a power may result in the inclusion in the decedent's gross estate under section 2036 or 2038 of other property transferred by the decedent to the trust if, for example, the decedent has the power to surrender the insurance policy and if the income otherwise used to pay premiums on the policy would become currently payable to a beneficiary of the trust in the event that the policy were surrendered.

(5) As an additional step in determining whether or not a decedent possessed any incidents of ownership in a policy or any part of a policy, regard must be given to the effect of the State or other applicable law upon the terms of the policy. For example, assume that the decedent purchased a policy of insurance on his life with funds held by him and his surviving wife as community property, designating their son as beneficiary but retaining the right to surrender the policy. Under the local law, the proceeds upon surrender would have inured to the marital community. Assuming that the policy is not surrendered and that the son receives the proceeds on the decedent's death, the wife's transfer of her one-half interest in the policy was not considered absolute before the decedent's death. Upon the wife's prior death, one-half of the value of the policy would have been included in her gross estate. Under these circumstances, the power of surrender possessed by the decedent as agent for his wife with respect to one-half of the policy is not, for purposes of this section, an "incident of ownership", and the decedent is, therefore, deemed to possess an incident of ownership in only one-half of the policy.

(6) In the case of economic benefits of a life insurance policy on the decedent's life that are reserved to a corporation of which the decedent is the sole or controlling stockholders, the corporations' incidents of ownership will not be attributed to the decedent through his stock ownership to the extent the proceeds of the policy are payable to the corporation. Any proceeds payable to a third party for a valid business purpose, such as in satisfaction of a business debt of the corporation, so that the net worth of the corporation is increased by the amount of such proceeds, shall be deemed to be payable to the corporation for purposes of the preceding sentence. See § 20.203–2(f) for a rule providing that the proceeds of certain life insurance policies shall be considered in determining the value of the decedent's stock. Except as hereinafter provided with respect to a group-term life insurance policy, if any part of the proceeds of the policy are not payable to or for the benefit of the corporation, and thus are not taken into account in valuing the decedent's stock holdings in the corporation for purposes of section 2031, any incidents of ownership held by the corporation as to that part of the proceeds will be attributed to the decedent through his stock ownership where the decedent is the sole or controlling stockholder. Thus, for example, if the decedent is the controlling stockholder in a corporation, and the corporation owns a life insurance policy on his life, the proceeds of which are payable to the decedent's spouse, the incidents of ownership held by the corporation will be attributed to the decedent through his stock ownership and the proceeds will be included in his gross estate under section 2042. If in this example the policy proceeds had been payable 40 percent to decedent's spouse and 60 percent to the corporation, only 40 percent of the proceeds would be included in decedent's gross estate under section 2042. For purposes of this subparagraph, the decedent will not be deemed to be the controlling stockholder of a corporation unless, at the time of his death, he owned stock possessing more than 50 percent of the total combined voting power of the corporation. Solely for purposes of the preceding sentence, a decedent shall be considered to be the owner of only the stock with respect to which legal title was held, at the time of his death, by (i) the decedent (or his agent or nominee); (ii) the decedent and another person jointly (but only the proportionate number of shares which corresponds to the portion of the total consideration which is considered to be furnished by the decedent for purposes of section 2040 and the regulations thereunder); and (iii) by a trustee of a voting trust (to the extent of the decedent's beneficial interest therein) or any other trust with respect to which the decedent was treated as an owner under subpart E, part I, subchapter J, chapter 1 of the Code immediately prior to his death. In the case of group-term life insurance, as defined in the regulations under section 79, the power to surrender or cancel a policy held by a corporation shall not be attributed to any decedent through his stock ownership.

§ 20.2043–1 Transfers for insufficient consideration.

(a) In general. The transfers, trusts, interests, rights or powers enumerated and described in sections 2035 through 2038 and section 2041 are not subject to the Federal estate tax if made, created, exercised, or relinquished in a transaction which constituted a bona fide sale for an adequate and full consideration in money or money's worth. To constitute a bona fide sale for an adequate and full consideration in money or money's worth, the transfer must have been made in good faith, and the price must have been an adequate and full equivalent reducible to a money value. If the price was less than such a consideration, only the excess of the fair market value of the property (as of the applicable valuation date) over the price received by the decedent is included in ascertaining the value of his gross estate.

(b) Marital rights and support obligations. For purposes of chapter 11, a relinquishment or promised relinquishment or dower, curtesy, or of a statutory estate created in lieu of dower or curtesy, or of other marital rights in the decedent's property or estate, is not to any extent a consideration in "money or money's worth."

* * *

§ 20.2046–1 Disclaimed property.

This section shall apply to the disclaimer or renunciation of a taxable transfer creating an interest in the person disclaiming made after December 31, 1976. If a qualified disclaimer is made with respect to such a transfer, the Federal estate tax provisions are to apply with respect to the property interest disclaimed as if the interest had never been transferred to the person making the disclaimer. See section 2518 and the corresponding regulations for rules relating to a qualified disclaimer.

* * *

Taxable Estate

§ 20.2053–1 Deductions for expenses, indebtedness, and taxes; in general.*

(a) General rule. In determining the taxable estate of a decedent who was a citizen or resident of the United States at the time of his death, there are allowed as deductions under section 2053(a) and (b) amounts falling within the following two categories (subject to the limitations contained in this section and in §§ 20.2053–2 through 20.2053–9):

(1) First category. Amounts which are payable out of property subject to claims and which are allowable by the law of the jurisdiction, whether within or without the United States, under which the estate is being administered for—

(i) Funeral expenses;

(ii) Administration expenses;

(iii) Claims against the estate (including taxes to the extent set forth in § 20.2053–6 and charitable pledges to the extent set forth in § 20.2053–5); and

(iv) Unpaid mortgages on, or any indebtedness in respect of, property, the value of the decedent's interest in which is included in the value of the gross estate undiminished by the mortgage or indebtedness.

As used in this subparagraph, the phrase "allowable by the law of the jurisdiction" means allowable by the law governing the administration of decedents' estates. The phrase has no reference to amounts allowable as deductions under a law which imposes a State death tax. See further §§ 20.2053–2 through 20.2053–7.

(2) Second category. Amounts representing expenses incurred in administering property which is inluded in the gross estate but which is not subject to claims and which—

(i) Would be allowed as deductions in the first category if the property being administered were subject to claims; and

(ii) Were paid before the expiration of the period of limitation for assessment provided in section 6501.

See further § 20.2053–8.

(b) Provisions applicable to both categories—(1) In general. If the item is not one of those described in paragraph (a) of this section, it is not deductible merely because payment is allowed by the local law. If the amount which may be expended for the particular purpose is limited by the local law no deduction in excess of that limitation is permissible.

(2) Effect of court decree. The decision of a local court as to the amount and allowability under local law of a claim or administration expense will ordinarily be accepted if the court passes upon the facts upon which deductibility depends. If the court does not pass upon those facts, its decree will, of course, not be followed. For example, if the question before the court is whether a claim should be allowed, the decree allowing it will ordinarily be accepted as establishing the validity and amount of the claim. However, the decree will not necessarily be accepted even though it purports to decide the facts upon which deductibility depends. It must appear that the court actually passed upon the merits of the claim. This will be presumed in all cases of an active and genuine contest. If the result reached appears to be unreasonable, this is some evidence that there was not such a contest, but it may be rebutted by proof to the contrary. If the decree was rendered by consent, it will be accepted, provided the consent was a bona fide recognition of the validity of the claim (and not a mere cloak for a gift) and was accepted by the court as satisfactory evidence upon the merits. It will be presumed that the consent was of this character, and was so accepted, if given by all parties having an interest adverse to the claimant. The decree will not be accepted if it is at variance with the law of the State; as, for example, an allowance made to an executor in excess of that prescribed by statute. On the other hand, a deduction for the amount of a bona fide indebtedness of the decedent, or of a reasonable expense of administration, will not be denied because no court decree has been entered if the amount would be allowable under local law.

(3) Estimated amounts. An item may be entered on the return for deduction though its exact amount is not then known, provided it is ascertainable with reasonable certainty, and will be paid. No deduction may be taken upon the basis of a vague or uncertain estimate. If the amount of a liability was not

*Editorial comment: The Regulations do not reflect the effect of the Tax Relief Reconciliation Act of 2001 which provides for a state death tax deduction. The deduction became effective in 2005 after the repeal of the state death tax credit was complete. See §2058(a).

ascertainable at the time of final audit of the return by the district director and, as a consequence, it was not allowed as a deduction in the audit, and subsequently the amount of the liability is ascertained, relief may be sought by a petition to the Tax Court or a claim for refund as provided by sections 6213(a) and 6511, respectively.

(c) Provision applicable to first category only. Deductions of the first category (described in paragraph (a)(1) of this section) are limited under section 2053(a) to amounts which would be property allowable out of property subject to claims by the law of the jurisdiction under which the decedent's estate is being administered. Further, the total allowable amount of deductions of the first category is limited by section 2053(c)(2) to the sum of—

(1) The value of property included in the decedent's gross estate and subject to claims, plus

(2) Amounts paid, out of property not subject to claims against the decedent's estate, within 9 months (15 months in the case of the estate of a decedent dying before January 1, 1971) after the decedent's death (the period within which the estate tax return must be filed under section 6075), or within any extension of time for filing the return granted under section 6081.

The term "property subject to claims" is defined in section 2053(c)(2) as meaning the property includible in the gross estate which, or the avails of which, under the applicable law, would bear the burden of the payment of these deductions in the final adjustment and settlement of the decedent's estate. However, for the purposes of this definition, the value of property subject to claims is first reduced by the amount of any deduction allowed under section 2054 for any losses from casualty or theft incurred during the settlement of the estate attributable to such property. The application of this paragraph may be illustrated by the following examples:

Example (1). The only item in the gross estate is real property valued at $250,000 which the decedent and his surviving spouse held as tenants by the entirety. Under the local law this real property is not subject to claims. Funeral expenses of $1,200 and debts of the decedent in the amount of $1,500 are allowable under local law. Before the prescribed date for filing the estate tax return, the surviving spouse paid the funeral expenses and $1,000 of the debts. The remaining $500 of the debts was paid by her after the prescribed date for filing the return. The total amount allowable as deductions under section 2053 is limited to $2,200, the amount paid prior to the prescribed date for filing the return.

Example (2). The only two items in the gross estate were a bank deposit of $20,000 and insurance in the amount of $150,000. The insurance was payable to the decedent's surviving spouse and under local law was not subject to claims. Funeral expenses of $1,000 and debts in the amount of $29,000 were allowable under local law. A son was executor of the estate and before the prescribed date for filing the estate tax return he paid the funeral expenses of $9,000 of the debts, using therefor $5,000 of the bank deposit and $5,000 supplied by the surviving spouse. After the prescribed date for filing the return, the executor paid the remaining $20,000 of the debts, using for that purpose the $15,000 left in the bank account plus an additional $5,000 supplied by the surviving spouse. The total amount allowable as deductions under section 2053 is limited to $25,000 ($20,000 of property subject to claims plus the $5,000 additional amount which, before the prescribed date for filing the return, was paid out of property not subject to claims).

(d) Disallowance of double deductions. See section 642(g) and § 1.642(g)–1 with respect to the disallowance for income tax purposes of certain deductions unless the right to take such deductions for estate tax purposes is waived.

§ 20.2053–2 Deduction for funeral expenses.

Such amounts for funeral expenses are allowed as deductions from a decedent's gross estate as (a) are actually expended, (b) would be properly allowable out of property subject to claims under the laws of the local jurisdiction, and (c) satisfy the requirements of paragraph (c) of § 20.2053–1. A reasonable expenditure for a tombstone, monument, or mausoleum, or for a burial lot, either for the decedent or his family, including a reasonable expenditure for its future care, may be deducted under this heading, provided such an expenditure is allowable by the local law. Included in funeral expenses is the cost of transportation of the person bringing the body to the place of burial.

§ 20.2053–3 Deduction for expenses of administering estate.

(a) In general. The amounts deductible from a decedent's gross estate as "administration expenses" of the first category (see paragraphs (a) and (c) of § 20.2053–1) are limited to such expenses as are actually and necessarily, incurred in the administration of the decedent's estate; that is, in the collection of assets, payment of debts, and distribution of property to the persons entitled to it. The expenses contemplated in the law are such only as attend the settlement of an estate and the transfer of the property of the estate to individual beneficiaries or to a trustee, whether the trustee is the executor or some other person. Expenditures not essential to the proper settlement of the estate, but incurred for the individual benefit of the heirs, legatees, or devisees, may not be taken as deductions. Administration expenses include (1) executor's commissions; (2) attorney's fees; and (3) miscellaneous expenses. Each of these classes is considered separately in paragraphs (b) through (d) of this section.

(b) Executor's commissions.(1) The executor or administrator, in filing the estate tax return, may deduct his commissions in such an amount as has actually been paid or in an amount which at the time of filing the estate tax return may reasonably be expected to be paid, but no deduction may be taken if no commissions are to be collected. If the amount of the commissions has not been fixed by decree of the proper court, the deduction will be allowed on the final audit of the return, to the extent that all three of the following conditions are satisfied:

(i) The district director is reasonably satisfied that the commissions claimed will be paid;

(ii) The amount claimed as a deduction is within the amount allowable by the laws of the jurisdiction in which the estate is being administered; and

(iii) It is in accordance with the usually accepted practice in the jurisdiction to allow such an amount in estates of similar size and character.

If the deduction is disallowed in whole or in part on final audit, the disallowance will be subject to modification as the facts may later require. If the deduction is allowed in advance of payment and payment is thereafter waived, it shall be the duty of the executor to notify the district director and to pay the resulting tax, together with interest.

(2) A bequest or devise to the executor in lieu of commissions is not deductible. If, however, the decedent fixed by his will the compensation payable to the executor for services to be rendered in the administration of the estate, deduction may be taken to the extent that the amount so fixed does not exceed the compensation allowable by the local law or practice.

(3) Except to the extent that a trustee is in fact performing services with respect to property subject to claims which would normally be performed by an executor, amounts paid as trustees' commissions do not constitute expenses of administration under the first category, and are only deductible as expenses of the second category to the extent provided in § 20.2053–8.

(c) Attorney's fees.(1) The executor or administrator, in filing the estate tax return, may deduct such an amount of attorney's fees as has actually been paid, or an amount which at the time of filing may reasonably be expected to be paid. If on the final audit of a return the fees claimed have not been awarded by the proper court and paid, the deduction will, nevertheless, be allowed, if the district director is reasonably satisfied that the amount claimed will be paid and that it does not exceed a reasonable remuneration for the services rendered, taking into account the size and character of the estate and the local law and practice. If the deduction is disallowed in whole or in part on final audit, the disallowance will be subject to modification as the facts may later require.

(2) A deduction for attorneys' fees incurred in contesting an asserted deficiency or in prosecuting a claim for refund should be claimed at the time the deficiency is contested or the refund claim is prosecuted. A deduction for reasonable attorneys' fees actually paid in contesting an asserted deficiency or in prosecuting a claim for refund will be allowed even though the deduction, as such, was not claimed in the estate tax return or in the claim for refund. A deduction for these fees shall not be denied, and the sufficiency of a claim for refund shall not be questioned, solely by reason of the fact that the amount of the fees to be paid was not established at the time that the right to the deduction was claimed.

(3) Attorneys' fees incurred by beneficiaries incident to litigation as to their respective interests are not deductible if the litigation is not essential to the proper settlement of the estate within the meaning of paragraph (a) of this section. An attorney's fee not meeting this test is not deductible as an administration expense under section 2053 and this section, even if it is approved by a probate court as an expense payable or reimbursable by the estate.

(d) Miscellaneous administration expenses. (1) Miscellaneous administration expenses include such expenses as court costs, surrogates' fees, accountants' fees, appraisers' fees, clerk hire, etc. Expenses necessarily incurred in preserving and distributing the estate are deductible, including the cost of storing or maintaining property of the estate, if it is impossible to effect immediate distribution to the beneficiaries. Expenses for preserving and caring for the property may not include outlays for additions or improvements; nor will such expenses be allowed for a longer period than the executor is reasonably required to retain the property.

(2) Expenses for selling property of the estate are deductible if the sale is necessary in order to pay the decedent's debts, expenses of administration, or taxes, to preserve the estate, or to effect distribution. The phrase "expenses for selling property" includes brokerage fees and other expenses attending the sale, such as the fees of an auctioneer if it is reasonably necessary to employ one. Where an item included in the gross estate is disposed of in a bona fide sale (including a redemption) to a dealer in such items at a price below its fair market value, for purposes of this paragraph there shall be treated as an expense for selling the item whichever of the following amounts is the lesser: (i) The amount by which the fair market value of the property on the applicable valuation date exceeds the proceeds of the sale, or (ii) the amount by which the fair market value of the property on the date of the sale exceeds the proceeds of the sale. The principles used in determining the value at which an item of property is included in the gross estate shall be followed in arriving at the fair market value of the property for purposes of this paragraph. See §§ 20.2031–1 through 20.2031–9.

§ 20.2053–4 Deduction for claims against the estate; in general.

The amounts that may be deducted as claims against a decedent's estate are such only as represent personal obligations of the decedent existing at the time of his death, whether or not then matured, and interest thereon which had accrued at the time of death. Only interest accrued at the date of the decedent's death is allowable even though the executor elects the alternate valuation method under section 2032. Only claims enforceable against the decedent's estate may be deducted. Except as otherwise provided in § 20.2053–5 with respect to pledges or subscriptions, section 2053(c)(1)(A) provides that the allowance of a deduction for a claim founded upon a promise or agreement is limited to the extent that the liability was contracted bona fide and for an adequate and full consideration in money or money's worth. See § 20.2043–1. Liabilities imposed by law or arising out of torts are deductible.

§ 20.2053–5 Deductions for charitable, etc., pledges or subscriptions.

A pledge or a subscription, evidenced by a promissory note or otherwise, even though enforceable against the estate, is deductible only to the extent that—

(a) Liability therefor was contracted bona fide and for an adequate and full consideration in cash or its equivalent, or

(b) It would have constituted an allowable deduction under section 2055 (relating to charitable, etc., deductions) if it had been a bequest.

§ 20.2053–6 Deduction for taxes.

(a) In general. Taxes are deductible in computing a decedent's gross estate only as claims against the estate (except to the extent that excise taxes may be allowable as administration expenses), and only to the extent not disallowed by section 2053(c)(1)(B) (see the remaining paragraphs of this section). However, see § 20.2053–9 with respect to the deduction allowed for certain State death taxes on charitable, etc., transfers.

(b) Property taxes. Property taxes are not deductible unless they accrued before the decedent's death. However, they are not deductible merely because they have accrued in an accounting sense. Property taxes in order to be deductible must be an enforceable obligation of the decedent at the time of his death.

(c) Death taxes. No estate, succession, legacy or inheritance tax payable by reason of the decedent's death is deductible, except as provided in § 20.2053–9 with respect to certain State death taxes on charitable, etc., transfers. However, see sections 2011 and 2014 and the regulations thereunder with respect to credits for death taxes.

(d) Gift taxes. Unpaid gift taxes on gifts made by a decedent before his death are deductible. If a gift is considered as made one-half by the decedent and one-half by his spouse under section 2513, the entire amount of the gift tax, unpaid at the decedent's death, attributable to a gift in fact made by the decedent is deductible. No portion of the tax attributable to a gift in fact made by the decedent's spouse is deductible except to the extent that the obligation is enforced against the decedent's estate and his estate has no effective right of contribution against his spouse. (See section 2012 and § 20.2012–1 with respect to credit for gift taxes paid upon gifts of property included in a decedent's gross estate.)

(e) Excise taxes. Excise taxes incurred in selling property of a decedent's estate are deductible as an expense of administration if the sale is necessary in order to (1) pay the decedent's debts, expenses of administration, or taxes, (2) preserve the estate, or (3) effect distribution. Excise taxes incurred in distributing property of the estate in kind are also deductible.

(f) Income taxes. Unpaid income taxes are deductible if they are on income property includible in an income tax return of the decedent for a period before his death. Taxes on income received after the decedent's death are not deductible. If income received by a decedent during his lifetime is included in a joint income tax return filed by the decedent and his spouse, or by the decedent's estate and his surviving spouse, the portion of the joint liability for the period covered by the return for which a deduction will be allowed is the amount for which the decedent's estate would be liable under local law, as between the decedent and his spouse, after enforcement of any effective right of reimbursement or contribution. In the absence of evidence to the contrary, the deductible amount is presumed to be an amount bearing the same ratio to the total joint tax liability for the period covered by the return that the amount of income tax for which the decedent would have been liable if he had filed a separate return for that period bears to the total of the amounts for which the decedent and his spouse would have been liable if they had both filed separate returns for that period. Thus, in the absence of evidence to the contrary, the deductible amount equals:

Decedent's separate tax ÷ Both separate taxes × Joint tax.

However, the deduction cannot in any event exceed the lesser of—

(1) The decedent's liability for the period (as determined in this paragraph) reduced by the amounts already contributed by the decedent toward payment of the joint liability, or

(2) If there is an enforceable agreement between the decedent and his spouse or between the executor and the spouse relative to the payment of the joint liability, the amount which pursuant to the agreement is to be contributed by the estate toward payment of the joint liability.

If the decedent's estate and his surviving spouse are entitled to a refund on account of an overpayment of a joint income tax liability, the overpayment is an asset includible in the decedent's gross estate under section 2033 in the amount to which the estate would be entitled under local law, as between the estate and the surviving spouse. In the absence of evidence to the contrary, the includible amount is presumed to be the amount by which the decedent's contributions toward payment of the joint tax exceeds his liability determined in accordance with the principles set forth in this paragraph (other than subparagraph (1) of this paragraph).

§ 20.2053–7 Deduction for unpaid mortgages.

A deduction is allowed from a decedent's gross estate of the full unpaid amount of a mortgage upon, or of any other indebtedness in respect of, any property of the gross estate, including interest which had accrued thereon to the date of death, provided the value of the property, undiminished by the amount of the mortgage or indebtedness, is included in the value of the gross estate. If the decedent's estate is liable for the amount of the mortgage or indebtedness, the full value of the property subject to the mortgage or indebtedness must be included as part of the value of the gross estate; the amount of the mortgage or indebtedness being in such case allowed as a deduction. But if the decedent's estate is not so liable, only the value of the equity of redemption (or the value of the property, less the mortgage or indebtedness) need be returned as part of the value of the gross estate. In no case may the deduction on account of the mortgage or indebtedness exceed the liability therefor contracted bona fide and for an adequate and full consideration in money or money's worth. See § 20.2043–1. Only interest accrued to the date of the decedent's death is allowable even though the alternate valuation method under section 2032 is selected. In any case where real property situated outside the United States no deduction may be taken of any mortgage thereon or any other indebtedness does not form a part of the gross estate, in respect thereof.

§ 20.2053–8 Deduction for expenses in administering property not subject to claims.

(a) Expenses incurred in administering property included in a decedent's gross estate but not subject to claims fall within the second category of deductions set forth in § 20.2053–1, and may be allowed as deductions if they—

(1) Would be allowed as deductions in the first category if the property being administered were subject to claims; and

(2) Were paid before the expiration of the period of limitation for assessment provided in section 6501.

Usually, these expenses are incurred in connection with the administration of a trust established by a decedent during his lifetime. They may also be incurred in connection with the collection of other assets or the transfer or clearance of title to other property included in a decedent's gross estate for estate tax purposes but not included in his probate estate.

(b) These expenses may be allowed as deductions only to the extent that they would be allowed as deductions under the first category if the property were subject to claims. See § 20.2053–3. The only expenses in administering property not subject to claims which are allowed as deductions are those occasioned by the decedent's death and incurred in settling the decedent's interest in the property or vesting good title to the property in the beneficiaries. Expenses not coming within the description in the preceding sentence but incurred on behalf of the transferees are not deductible.

(c) The principles set forth in paragraphs (b), (c), and (d) of § 20.2053–3 (relating to the allowance of executor's commissions, attorney's fees, and miscellaneous administration expenses of the first category) are applied in determining the extent to which trustee's commissions, attorney's and accountant's fees, and miscellaneous administration expenses are allowed in connection with the administration of property not subject to claims.

(d) The application of this section may be illustrated by the following examples:

Example (1). In 1940, the decedent made an irrevocable transfer of property to the X Trust Company, as trustee. The instrument of transfer provided that the trustee should pay the income from the property to the decedent for the duration of his life and upon his death, distribute the corpus of the trust among designated beneficiaries. The property was included in the decedent's gross estate under the provisions of section 2036. Three months after the date of death, the trustee distributed the trust corpus among the beneficiaries, except for $6,000 which it withheld. The amount withheld represented $5,000 which it retained as trustee's commissions in connection with the termination of the trust and $1,000 which it had paid to an attorney for representing it in connection with the termination. Both the trustee's commissions and the attorney's fees were allowable under the law of the jurisdiction in which the trust was being administered, were reasonable in amount, and were in accord with local custom. Under these circumstances, the estate is allowed a deduction of $6,000.

Example (2). In 1945, the decedent made an irrevocable transfer of property to Y Trust Company, as trustee. The instrument of transfer provided that the trustee should pay the income from the property to the decedent during his life. If the decedent's wife survived him, the trust was to continue for the duration of her life, with Y Trust Company and the decedent's son as co-trustees, and with income payable to the decedent's wife for the duration of her life. Upon the death of both the decedent and his wife, the corpus is to be distributed among designated remaindermen. The decedent was survived by his wife. The property was included in the decedent's gross estate under the provisions of section 2036. In accordance with local custom, the trustee made an accounting to the court as of the date of the decedent's death. Following the death of the decedent, a controversy arose among the remaindermen as to their respective rights under the instrument of transfer, and a suit was brought in court to which the trustee was made a party. As part of the accounting, the court approved the following expenses which the trustee had paid within 3 years following the date of death: $10,000, trustee's commissions; $5,000, accountant's fees; $25,000, attorney's fees; and $2,500, representing fees paid to the guardian of a remainderman who was a minor. The trustee's commissions and accountant's fees were for services in connection with the usual issues involved in a trust accounting as also were one-half of the attorney's and guardian's fees. The remainder of the attorney's and guardian's fees were for services performed in connection with the suit brought by the remaindermen. The amount allowed as a deduction is the $28,750 ($10,000, trustee's commissions; $5,000, accountant's fees; $12,500, attorney's fees; and $1,250, guardian's fees) incurred as expenses in connection with the usual issues involved in a trust accounting. The remaining expenses are not allowed as deductions since they were incurred on behalf of the transferees.

Example (3). Decedent in 1950 made an irrevocable transfer of property to the Z Trust Company, as trustee. The instrument of transfer provided that the trustee should pay the income from the property to the decedent's wife for the duration of her life. If the decedent survived his wife the trust corpus was to be returned to him but if he did not survive her, then upon the death of the wife, the trust corpus was to be distributed among their children. The decedent predeceased his wife and the transferred property, less the value of the wife's outstanding life estate, was included in his gross estate under the provisions of section 2037 since his reversionary interest therein immediately before his death was in excess of 5 percent of the value of the property. At the wife's request, the court ordered the trustee to render an accounting of the trust property as of the date of the decedent's death. No deduction will be allowed the decedent's estate for any of the expenses incurred in connection with the trust accounting, since the expenses were incurred on behalf of the wife.

Example (4). If, in the preceding example, the decedent died without other property and no executor or administrator of his estate was appointed, so that it was necessary for the trustee to prepare an estate tax return and participate in its audit, or if the trustee required accounting proceedings for its own protection in accordance with local custom, trustees', attorneys', and guardians' fees in connection with the estate tax or accounting proceedings would be deductible to the same extent that they would be deductible if the property were subject to claims. Deductions incurred under similar circumstances by a surviving joint tenant or the recipient of life insurance proceeds would also be deductible.

§ 20.2053–9 Deduction for certain State death taxes.

(a) General rule. A deduction is allowed a decedent's estate under section 2053(d) for the amount of any estate, succession, legacy, or inheritance tax imposed by a State, Territory, or the District of Columbia, * * * but only if (1) the conditions stated in paragraph (b) of this section are met, and (2) an election is made in accordance with the provisions of paragraph (c) of this section. See section 2011(e) and § 20.2011–2 for the effect which the allowance of this deduction has upon the credit for State death taxes.

(b) Condition for allowance of deduction. **(1)** The deduction is not allowed unless either—

(i) The entire decrease in the Federal estate tax resulting from the allowance of the deduction inures solely to the benefit of a charitable, etc., transferee described in section 2055 or 2106(a)(2), or

(ii) The Federal estate tax is equitably apportioned among all the transferees (including the decedent's surviving spouse and the charitable, etc., transferees) of property included in the decedent's gross estate.

For allowance of the credit, it is sufficient if either of these conditions is satisfied. Thus, in a case where the entire decrease in Federal estate tax inures to the benefit of a charitable transferee, the deduction is allowable even though the Federal estate tax is not equitably apportioned among all the transferees of property included in the decedent's gross estate. Similarly, if the Federal estate tax is equitably apportioned among all the transferees of property included in the decedent's gross estate, the deduction is allowable even though a noncharitable transferee receives some benefit from the allowance of the deduction.

(2) For purposes of this paragraph, the Federal estate tax is considered to be equitably apportioned among all the transferees (including the decedent's surviving spouse and the charitable, etc., transferees) of property included in the decedent's gross estate only if each transferee's share of the tax is based upon the net amount of his transfer subjected to the tax (taking into account any exemptions, credits, or deductions allowed by chapter 11). See examples (2) through (5) of paragraph (e) of this section.

(c) Exercise of election. The election to take a deduction for a State death tax imposed upon a transfer for charitable, etc., uses shall be exercised by the executor by the filing of a written notification to that effect with the district director of internal revenue in whose district the estate tax return for the decedent's estate was filed. The notification shall be filed before the expiration of the period of limitation for assessment provided in section 6501 (usually 3 years from the last day for filing the return). The election may be revoked by the executor by the filing of a written notification to that effect with the district director at any time before the expiration of such period.

(d) Amount of State death tax imposed upon a transfer. If a State death tax is imposed upon the transfer of the decedent's entire estate and not upon the transfer of a particular share thereof, the State death tax imposed upon a transfer for charitable, etc., uses is deemed to be an amount, E, which bears the same ratio to F (the amount of the State death tax imposed with respect to the transfer of the entire estate) as G (the value of the charitable, etc., transfer, reduced as provided in the next sentence) bears to H (the total value of the properties, interests, and benefits subjected to the State death tax received by all persons interested in the estate, reduced as provided in the last sentence of this paragraph). In arriving at amount G of the ratio, the value of the charitable, etc., transfer is reduced by the amount of any deduction or exclusion allowed with respect to such property in determining the amount of the State death tax. In arriving at amount H of the ratio, the total value of the properties, interests, and benefits subjected to State death tax received by all persons interested in the estate is reduced by the amount of all deductions and exclusions allowed in determining the amount of the State death tax on account of the nature of a beneficiary or a beneficiary's relationship to the decedent.

(e) Examples. The application of this section may be illustrated by the following examples:

Example (1). The decedent's gross estate was valued at $200,000. He bequeathed $90,000 to a nephew, $10,000 to Charity A, and the remainder of his estate to Charity B. State inheritance tax in the amount of $13,500 was imposed upon the bequest to the nephew, $1,500 upon the bequest to Charity A, and $15,000 upon the bequest to Charity B. Under the will and local law, each legatee is required to pay the State inheritance tax on his bequest, and the Federal estate tax is to be paid out of the residuary estate. Since the entire burden of paying the Federal estate tax falls on Charity B, it follows that the decrease in the Federal estate tax resulting from the allowance of deductions for State death taxes in the amounts of $1,500 and $15,000 would inure solely for the benefit of Charity B. Therefore, deductions of $1,500 and $15,000 are allowable under section 2053(d). If, in this example, the State death taxes as well as the Federal estate tax were to be paid out of the residuary estate, the result would be the same.

* * *

§ 20.2054–1 Deduction for losses from casualties or theft.

A deduction is allowed for losses incurred during the settlement of the estate arising from fires, storms, shipwrecks, or other casualties, or from theft, if the losses are not compensated for by insurance or otherwise. If the loss is partly compensated for, the excess of the loss over the compensation may be deducted. Losses which are not of the nature described are not deductible. In order to be deductible a loss must occur during the settlement of the estate. If a loss with respect to an asset occurs after its distribution to the distributee it may not be deducted. Notwithstanding the foregoing, no deduction is allowed under this section if the estate has waived its right to take such a deduction pursuant to the provisions of section 642(g) in order to permit its allowance for income tax purposes. See further § 1.642(g)–1.

§ 20.2055–1 Deduction for transfers for public, charitable, and religious uses; in general.

(a) General rule. A deduction is allowed under section 2055(a) from the gross estate of a decedent who was a citizen or resident of the United States at the time of his death for the value of property included in the decedent's gross estate and transferred by the decedent during his lifetime or by will—

(1) To or for the use of the United States, any State, Territory, any political subdivision thereof, or the District of Columbia, for exclusively public purposes;

(2) To or for the use of any corporation or association organized and operated exclusively for religious, charitable, scientific, literary, or educational purposes (including the encouragement of art and the prevention of cruelty to children or animals), if no part of the net earnings of the corporation or association inures to the benefit of any private stockholder or individual (other than as a legitimate object of such purposes), if the organization is not disqualified for tax exemption under section 501(c)(3) by reason of attempting to influence legislation, and if, in the case of transfers made after December 31, 1969, it does not participate in, or intervene in (including the publishing or distributing of statements), any political campaign on behalf of or in opposition to any candidate for public office;

(3) To a trustee or trustees, or a fraternal society, order, or association operating under the lodge system, if the transferred property is to be used exclusively for religious, charitable, scientific, literary, or educational purposes (or for the prevention of cruelty to children or animals), if no substantial part of the activities of such transferee is carrying on propaganda, or otherwise attempting, to influence legislation, and if, in the case of transfers made after December 31, 1969, such transferee does not participate in, or intervene in (including the publishing or distributing of statements), any political campaign on behalf of any candidate for public office; or

(4) To or for the use of any veterans' organization incorporated by act of Congress, or of any of its departments, local chapters, or posts, no part of the net earnings of which inures to the benefit of any private shareholder or individual.

The deduction is not limited, in the case of estates of citizens or residents of the United States, to transfers to domestic corporations or associations, or to trustees for use within the United States. Nor is the deduction subject to percentage limitations such as are applicable to the charitable deduction under the income tax. An organization will not be considered to meet the requirements of subparagraph (2) or (3) of this paragraph if such organization engages in any activity which would cause it to be classified as an "action" organization under paragraph (c)(3) of § 1.501(c)(3)–1 of this chapter (Income Tax Regulations). See §§ 20.2055–4 and 20.2055–5 for rules relating to the disallowance of deductions to trusts and organizations which engage in certain prohibited transactions or whose governing instruments do not contain certain specified requirements.

(b) Powers of appointment—(1) General rule. A deduction is allowable under section 2055(b) for the value of property passing to or for the use of a transferee described in paragraph (a) of this section by the exercise, failure to exercise, release or lapse of a power of appointment by reason of which the property is includible in the decedent's gross estate under section 2041.

(2) Certain bequests subject to power of appointment. For the allowance of a deduction in the case of a bequest in trust where the decedent's surviving spouse (i) was over 80 years of age at the date of decedent's death, (ii) was entitled for life to all of the net income from the trust, and (iii) had a power of appointment over the corpus of the trust exercisable by will in favor of, among others, a charitable organization, see section 2055(b)(2). See also section 6503(e) for suspension of the period of limitations for assessment or collection of any deficiency attributable to the allowance of the deduction.

* * *

§ 20.2055–2 Transfers not exclusively for charitable purposes.

* * *

(b) Transfers subject to a condition or a power. **(1)** If, as of the date of a decedent's death, a transfer for charitable purposes is dependent upon the performance of some act or the happening of a precedent event in order that it might become effective, no deduction is allowable unless the possibility that the charitable transfer will not become effective is so remote as to be negligible. If an estate or interest has passed to, or is vested in, charity at the time of a decedent's death and the estate or interest would be defeated by the subsequent performance of some act or the happening of some event, the possibility of occurrence of which appeared at the time of the decedent's death to be so remote as to be negligible, the deduction is allowable. If the legatee, devisee, donee, or trustee is empowered to divert the property or fund, in whole or in part, to a use or purpose which would have rendered it, to the extent that it is subject to such power, not deductible had it been directly so bequeathed, devised, or given by the decedent, the deduction will be limited to that portion, if any, of the property or fund which is exempt from an exercise of the power.

(2) The application of this paragraph may be illustrated by the following examples:

Example (1). In 1965, A dies leaving certain property in trust in which charity is to receive the income for the life of his widow. The assets placed in trust by the decedent consist of stock in a corporation the fiscal policies of which are controlled by the decedent and his family. The trustees of the trust and the remaindermen are members of the decedent's family, and the governing instrument contains no adequate guarantee of the request income to the charitable organization. Under such circumstances, no deduction will be allowed. Similarly, if the trustees are not members of the decedent's family but have no power to sell or otherwise dispose of the closely held stock, or otherwise insure the requisite enjoyment of income to the charitable organization, no deduction will be allowed.

Example (2). C dies leaving a tract of land to a city government for as long as the land is used by the city for a public park. If the city accepts the tract and if, on the date of C's death, the possibility that the city will not use the land for a public park is so remote as to be negligible, a deduction will be allowed.

(c) Disclaimers—(1) Decedents dying after December 31, 1976. In the case of a bequest, devise, or transfer made by a decedent dying after December 31, 1976, the amount of a bequest, devise or transfer for which a deduction is allowable under section 2055 includes an interest which falls into the bequest, devise or transfer as the result of either—

(i) A qualified disclaimer (see section 2518 and the corresponding regulations for rules relating to a qualified disclaimer), or

(ii) The complete termination of a power to consume, invade, or appropriate property for the benefit of an individual by reason of the death of such individual or for any other reason, if the termination occurs within the period of time (including extensions) for filing the decedent's Federal estate tax return and before such power has been exercised.

* * *

(d) Payments in compromise. If a charitable organization assigns or surrenders a part of a transfer to it pursuant to a compromise agreement in settlement of a controversy, the amount so assigned or surrendered is not deductible as a transfer to that charitable organization.

(e) Limitation applicable to decedents dying after December 31, 1969—(1) Disallowance of deduction—(i) In general. In the case of decedents dying after December 31, 1969, where an interest in property passes or has passed from the decedent for charitable purposes and an interest (other than an interest which is extinguished upon the decedent's death) in the same property passes or has passed from the decedent for private purposes (for less than an adequate and full consideration in money or money's worth) after October 9, 1969, no deduction is allowed under section 2055 for the value of the interest which passes or has passed for charitable purposes unless the interest in property is a deductible interest described in subparagraph (2) of this paragraph. The principles of section 2056 and the regulations thereunder shall apply for purposes of determining under this paragraph (e)(1)(i) whether an interest in property passes or has passed from the decedent. If however, as of the date of a decedent's death, a transfer for a private purpose is dependent upon the performance of some act on the happening of a precedent event in order that it might become effective, an interest in property will be considered to pass for a private purpose unless the possibility of occurrence of such act or event is so remote as to be negligible. The application of this paragraph (e)(1)(i) may be illustrated by the following examples, in each of which it is assumed that the interest in property which passes for private purposes does not pass for an adequate and full consideration in money or money's worth:

Example (1). In 1973, H creates a trust which is to pay the income of the trust to W for her life, the reversionary interest in the trust being retained by H. H predeceases W in 1975. H's will provide that the residue of his estate (including the reversionary interest in the trust) is to be transferred to charity. For purposes of this paragraph (e)(1)(i), interests in the same property have passed from H for charitable purposes and for private purposes.

Example (2). In 1973, H creates a trust which is to pay the income of the trust to W for her life and upon termination of the life estate to transfer the remainder to S. S predeceases W in 1975. S's will provides that the residue of his estate (including the remainder interest in the trust) is to be transferred to charity. For purposes of this paragraph (e)(l)(i), interests in the same property have not passed from H or S for charitable purposes and for private purposes.

Example (3). H transfers Blackacre to A by gift, reserving the right to the rentals of Blackacre for a term of 20 years. H dies within the 20-year term, bequeathing the right to the remaining rentals to charity. For purposes of this subparagraph the term "property" refers to Blackacre, and the right to rentals from Blackacre consist of an interest in Blackacre. An interest in Blackacre has passed from H for charitable purposes and for private purposes.

Example (4). H bequeaths the residue of his estate in trust for the benefit of A and a charity. An annuity of $5,000 a year is to be paid to charity for 20 years. Upon termination of the 20-year term the corpus is to be distributed to A if living. However, if A should die during the 20-year term, the corpus is to be distributed to charity upon termination of the term. An interest in the residue of the estate has passed from H for charitable purposes. In addition, an interest in the residue of the estate has passed from H for private purposes, unless the possibility that A will survive the 20-year term is so remote as to be negligible.

Example (5). H bequeaths the residue of his estate in trust. Under the terms of the trust an annuity of $5,000 a year is to be paid to charity for 20 years. Upon termination of the term, the corpus is to pass to such of A's children and their issue as A may appoint. However, if A should die during the 20-year term without exercising the power of appointment, the corpus is to be distributed to charity upon termination of the term. Since the possible appointees include private persons, an interest in the residue of the estate is considered to have passed from H for private purposes.

Example (6). H devises Blackacre to X Charity. Under applicable local law, W, H's widow, is entitled to elect a dower interest in Blackacre. W elects to take her dower interest in Blackacre. For purposes of this paragraph (e)(1)(i), interests in the same property have passed from H for charitable purposes and for private purposes. If, however, W does not elect to take her dower interest in Blackacre, then, for purposes of this paragraph (e)(l)(i), interests in the same property have not passed from H for charitable purposes and for private purposes.

(ii) Works of art and copyrights treated as separate properties—(a) In general. For purposes of paragraphs (e)(1)(i) and (e)(2) of this section, in the case of decedents dying after December 31, 1981, if a decedent makes a qualified contribution of a work of art, the work of art and the copyright on such work of art shall be treated as separate properties. Thus, a deduction is allowable under section 2055 for a qualified contribution of a work of art, whether or not the related copyright is simultaneously transferred to a charitable organization.

* * *

(2) Deductible interests. A deductible interest for purposes of subparagraph (1) of this paragraph is a charitable interest in property where—

(i) Undivided portion of decedent's entire interest. The charitable interest is an undivided portion, not in trust, of the decedent's entire interest in property. An undivided portion of a decedent's entire interest in property must consist of a fraction or percentage of each and every substantial interest or right owned by the decedent in such property and must extend over the entire term of the decedent's interest in such property and in other property into which such property is converted. For example, if the decedent transferred a life estate in an office building to his wife for her life and retained a reversionary interest in the office building, the devise by the decedent of one-half of that reversionary interest to charity while his wife is still alive will not be considered the transfer of a deductible interest; because an interest in the same property has already passed from the decedent for private purposes, the reversionary interest will not be considered the decedent's entire interest in the property. If, on the other hand, the decedent had been given a life estate in Blackacre for the life of his wife and the decedent had no other interest in Blackacre at any time during his life, the devise by the decedent of one-half of that life estate to charity would be considered the transfer of a deductible interest; because the life estate would be considered the decedent's entire interest in the property, the devise would be of an undivided portion of such entire interest. An undivided portion of a decedent's entire interest in the property includes an interest in property whereby the charity is given the right, as a tenant in common with the decedent's devisee or legatee, to possession, dominion, and control of the property for a portion of each year appropriate to its interest in such property. However, except as provided in paragraphs (e)(2)(ii), (iii), and (iv) of this section, for purposes of this subdivision a charitable contribution of an interest in property not in trust where the decedent transfers some specific rights to one party and transfers other substantial rights to another party will not be considered a contribution of an undivided portion of the decedent's entire interest in property. A bequest to charity made on or before December 17, 1980, of an open space easement in gross in perpetuity shall be considered the transfer to charity of an undivided portion of the decedent's entire interest in the property. For the definition of an open space easement in gross in perpetuity, see § 1.170A–7(b)(1)(ii) of this chapter (Income Tax Regulations).

(ii) Remainder interest in personal residence. The charitable interest is a remainder interest, not in trust, in a personal residence. Thus, for example, if the decedent devises to charity a remainder interest in a personal residence and bequeaths to his surviving spouse a life estate in such property, the value of the remainder interest is deductible under section 2055. For purposes of this subdivision, the term "personal residence" means any property which was used by the decedent as his personal residence even though it was not used as his principal residence. For example, a decedent's vacation home may be a personal residence for purposes of this subdivision. The term "personal residence" also includes stock owned by the decedent as a tenant-stockholder in a cooperative housing corporation (as those terms are defined in section 216(b)(1) and (2)) if the dwelling which the decedent was entitled to occupy as such stockholder was used by him as his personal residence.

(iii) Remainder interest in a farm. The charitable interest is a remainder interest, not in trust, in a farm. Thus, for example, if the decedent devises to charity a remainder interest in a farm and bequeaths to his daughter a life estate in such property, the value of the remainder interest is deductible under section 2055. For purposes of this subdivision, the term "farm" means any land used by the decedent or his tenant for the production of crops, fruits, or other agricultural products or for the sustenance of livestock. The term "livestock" includes cattle, hogs, horses, mules, donkeys, sheep, goats, captive fur-bearing animals, chickens, turkeys, pigeons, and other poultry. A farm includes the improvements thereon.

(iv) Qualified conservation contribution. The charitable interest is a qualified conservation contribution. For the definition of a qualified conservation contribution, see § 1.170A–14.

(v) Charitable remainder trusts and pooled income funds. The charitable interest is a remainder interest in a trust which is a charitable remainder annuity trust, as defined in section 664(d)(1) and § 1.664–2 of this chapter; a charitable remainder unitrust, as defined in section 664(d)(2) and (3) and § 1.664–3 of this chapter; or a pooled income fund, as defined in section 642(c)(5) and § 1.642(c)–5 of this chapter. The charitable organization to or for the use of which the remainder interest passes must meet the requirements of both section 2055(a) and section 642(c) (5)(A), section 664(d)(1)(C), or section 664(d)(2)(C), whichever applies. For example, the charitable organization to which the remainder interest in a charitable remainder annuity trust passes may not be a foreign corporation.

(vi) Guaranteed annuity interest.(a) The charitable interest is a guaranteed annuity interest, whether or not such interest is in trust. For purposes of this subdivision (vi), the term "guaranteed annuity interest" means the right pursuant to the instrument of transfer to receive a guaranteed annuity. A guaranteed annuity is an arrangement under which a determinable amount is paid periodically, but not less often than annually, for a specified term or for the life or lives of an individual or individuals, each of whom must be living at the date of death of the decedent and can be ascertained at such date. For example, the annuity may be paid for the life of A plus a term of years. An amount is determinable if the exact amount which must be paid under the conditions specified in the instrument of transfer can be ascertained as of the appropriate valuation date. For example, the amount to be paid may be a stated sum for a term, or for the life of an individual, at the expiration of which it may be changed by a specified amount, but it may not be redetermined by reference to a fluctuating index such as the cost of living index. In further illustration, the amount to be paid may be expressed in terms of a fraction or a percentage of the net fair market value, as finally determined for Federal estate tax purposes, of the residue of the estate on the appropriate valuation date, or it may be expressed in terms of a fraction or percentage of the cost of living index on the appropriate valuation date.

(b) A charitable interest is a guaranteed annuity interest only if it is a guaranteed annuity interest in every respect. For example, if the charitable interest is the right to receive from a trust each year a payment equal to the lesser of a sum certain or a fixed percentage of the net fair market value of the trust assets, determined annually, such interest is not a guaranteed annuity interest.

(c) Where a charitable interest in the form of a guaranteed annuity interest is not in trust, the interest will be considered a guaranteed annuity interest only if it is to be paid by an insurance company or by an organization regularly engaged in issuing annuity contracts.

(d) Where a charitable interest in the form of a guaranteed annuity interest is in trust, the governing instrument of the trust may provide that income of the trust which is in excess of the amount required to pay the guaranteed annuity interest shall be paid to or for the use of a charity. Nevertheless, the amount of the deduction under section 2055 shall be limited to the fair market value of the guaranteed annuity interest as determined under paragraph (f)(2)(iv) of this section.

(e) Where a charitable interest in the form of a guaranteed annuity interest is in trust and the present value, on the appropriate valuation date, of all the income interests for a charitable purpose exceeds 60 percent of the aggregate fair market value of all amounts in such trust (after the payment of estate taxes and all other liabilities), the charitable interest will not be considered a guaranteed annuity interest unless the governing instrument of the trust prohibits both the acquisition and the retention of assets which would give rise to a tax under section 4944 if the trustee had acquired such assets.

(f) Where a charitable interest in the form of a guaranteed annuity interest is in trust, the charitable interest generally is not a guaranteed annuity interest if any amount may be paid by the trust for a private purpose before the expiration of all the charitable annuity interests. There are two exceptions to this general rule. First, the charitable interest is a guaranteed annuity interest if the amount payable for a private purpose is in the form of a guaranteed annuity interest and the trust's governing instrument does not provide for any preference or priority in the payment of the private annuity as opposed to the charitable annuity. Second, the charitable interest is a guaranteed annuity interest if under the trust's governing instrument the amount that may be paid for a private purpose is payable only from a group of assets that are devoted exclusively to private purposes and to which section 4947(a)(2) is inapplicable by reason of section 4947(a)(2)(B). For purposes of this paragraph (e)(2)(vi)(f), an amount is not paid for a private purpose if it is paid for an adequate and full consideration in money or money's worth. See § 53.4947–1(c) of this chapter for rules relating to the inapplicability of section 4947(a)(2) to segregated amounts in a split-interest trust.

* * *

(vii) Unitrust interest.(a) The charitable interest is a unitrust interest, whether or not such interest is in trust. For purposes of this subdivision (vii), the term "unitrust interest" means the right pursuant to the instrument of transfer to receive payment, not less often than annually, of a fixed percentage of the net fair market value, determined annually, of the property which funds the unitrust interest. In computing the net fair market value of the property which funds the unitrust interest, all assets and liabilities shall be taken into account without regard to whether particular items are taken into account in determining the income from the property. The net fair market value of the property which funds the unitrust interest may be determined on any one date during the year or by taking the average of valuations made on more than one date during the year, provided that the same valuation date or dates and valuation methods are used each year. Where the charitable interest is a unitrust interest to be paid by a trust and the governing instrument of the trust does not specify the valuation date or dates, the trustee shall select such date or dates and shall indicate his selection on the first return on Form 1041 which the trust is required to file. Payments under a unitrust interest may be paid for a specified term or for the life or lives of an individual or individuals, each of whom must be living at the date of death of the decedent and can be ascertained at such date. For example, the unitrust interest may be paid for the life of A plus a term of years.

(b) A charitable interest is a unitrust interest only if it is a unitrust interest in every respect. For example, if the charitable interest is the right to receive from a trust each year a payment equal to the lesser of a sum certain or a fixed percentage of the net fair market value of the trust assets, determined annually, such interest is not a unitrust interest.

(c) Where a charitable interest in the form of a unitrust interest is not in trust, the interest will be considered a unitrust interest only if it is to be paid by an insurance company or by an organization regularly engaged in issuing interests otherwise meeting the requirements of a unitrust interest.

(d) Where a charitable interest in the form of a unitrust interest is in trust, the governing instrument of the trust may provide that income of the trust which is in excess of the amount required to pay the unitrust interest shall be paid to or for the use of a charity. Nevertheless, the amount of the deduction under section 2055 shall be limited to the fair market value of the unitrust interest as determined under paragraph (f)(2)(v) of this section.

(e) Where a charitable interest in the form of a unitrust interest is in trust, the charitable interest generally is not a unitrust interest if any amount may be paid by the trust for a private purpose before the expiration of all the charitable unitrust interests. There are two exceptions to this general rule. First, the charitable interest is a unitrust interest if the amount payable for a private purpose is in the form of a unitrust interest and the trust's governing instrument does not provide for any preference or priority in the payment of the private unitrust interest as opposed to the charitable unitrust interest. Second, the charitable interest is a unitrust interest if under the trust's governing instrument the amount that may be paid for a private purpose is payable only from a group of assets that are devoted exclusively to private purposes and to which section 4947(a)(2) is inapplicable by reason of section 4947(a)(2)(B). For purposes of this paragraph (e)(2)(vii)(e), an amount is not paid for a private purpose if it is paid for an adequate and full consideration in money or money's worth. See § 53.4947–1(c) of this chapter for rules relating to the inapplicability of section 4947(a)(2) to segregated amounts in a split-interest trust.

(f) For rules relating to certain governing instrument requirements and to the imposition of certain excise taxes where the unitrust interest is in trust and for rules governing payment of private income interests by a split-interest trust, see section 4947(a)(2) and (b)(3)(A), and the regulations thereunder.

* * *

§ 20.2056(a)–1 Marital deduction; in general.

(a) In general. A deduction is allowed under section 2056 from the gross estate of a decedent for the value of any property interest which passes from the decedent to the decedent's surviving spouse if the interest is a *deductible interest* as defined in § 20.2056(a)–2. With respect to decedents dying in certain years, a deduction is allowed under section 2056 only to the extent that the total of the deductible interests does not exceed the applicable limitations set forth in paragraph (c) of this section. The deduction allowed under section 2056 is referred to as the *marital deduction.* See also sections 2056(d) and 2056A for special rules applicable in the case of decedents dying after November 10, 1988, if the decedent's surviving spouse is not a citizen of the United States at the time of the decedent's death. In such cases, the marital deduction may not be allowed unless the property passes to a qualified domestic trust as described in section 2056A(a).

(b) Requirements for marital deduction—(1) In general. To obtain the marital deduction with respect to any property interest, the executor must establish the following facts—

(i) The decedent was survived by a spouse (see § 20.2056(c)–2(e));

(ii) The property interest passed from the decedent to the spouse (see §§ 20.2056(b)–5 through 20.2056(b)–8 and 20.2056(c)–1 through 20.2056(c)–3);

(iii) The property interest is a *deductible interest* (see § 20.2056(a)–2); and

(iv) The value of the property interest (see § 20.2056(b)–4).

(2) Burden of establishing requisite facts. The executor must provide the facts relating to any applicable limitation on the amount of the allowable marital deduction under § 20.2056(a)–1(c), and must submit proof necessary to establish any fact required under paragraph (b)(1), including any evidence requested by the district director.

(c) Marital deduction; limitation on aggregate deductions—(1) Estates of decedents dying before 1977. In the case of estates of decedents dying before January 1, 1977, the marital deduction is limited to one-half of the value of the *adjusted gross estate*, as that term was defined under section 2056(c)(2) prior to repeal by the Economic Recovery Tax Act of 1981.

(2) Estates of decedents dying after December 31, 1976, and before January 1, 1982—Except as provided in § 2002(d)(1) of the Tax Reform Act of 1976 (Pub.L. 94–455), in the case of decedents dying after December 31, 1976, and before January 1, 1982, the marital deduction is limited to the greater of—

(i) $250,000; or

(ii) One-half of the value of the decedent's adjusted gross estate, adjusted for inter vivos gifts to the spouse as prescribed by section 2056(c)(1)(B) prior to repeal by the Economic Recovery Tax Act of 1981 (Pub.L. 97–34).

(3) Estates of decedents dying after December 31, 1981. In the case of estates of decedents dying after December 31, 1981, the marital deduction is limited as prescribed in paragraph (c)(2) of this section if the provisions of § 403(e)(3) of Pub.L. 97–34 are satisfied.

§ 20.2056(a)–2 Marital deduction; "deductible interests" and "nondeductible interests."

(a) In general. Property interests which passed from a decedent to his surviving spouse fall within two general categories: (1) Those with respect to which the marital deduction is authorized, and (2) those with respect to which the marital deduction is not authorized. These categories are referred to in this section and other sections of the regulations under section 2056 as "deductible interests" and "nondeductible interests," respectively (see paragraph (b) of this section). Subject to any applicable limitations set forth in §§ 20.2056(a)–1(c), the amount of the marital deduction is the aggregate value of the "deductible interests."

(b) Deductible interests. An interest passing to a decedent's surviving spouse is a "deductible interest" if it does not fall within one of the following categories of "nondeductible interests;"

(1) Any property interest which passed from the decedent to his surviving spouse is a "nondeductible interest" to the extent it is not included in the decedent's gross estate.

(2) If a deduction is allowed under section 2053 (relating to deductions for expenses and indebtedness) by reason of the passing of a property interest from the decedent to his surviving spouse, such interest is, to the extent of the deduction under section 2053, a "nondeductible interest." Thus, a property interest which passed from the decedent to his surviving spouse in satisfaction of a deductible claim of the spouse against the estate is, to the extent of the claim, a "nondeductible interest" (see § 20.2056(b)–4). Similarly, amounts deducted under section 2053(a)(2) for commissioners allowed to the surviving spouse as executor are "nondeductible interests." As to the valuation, for the purpose of the marital deduction, of any property interest which passed from the decedent to his surviving spouse subject to a mortgage or other encumbrance, see § 20.2056(b)–4.

(3) If during settlement of the estate a loss deductible under section 2054 occurs with respect to a property interest, then that interest is, to the extent of the deductible loss, a "nondeductible interest" for the purpose of the marital deduction.

(4) A property interest passing to a decedent's surviving spouse which is a "terminable interest," as defined in § 20.2056(b)–1, is a "nondeductible interest" to the extent specified in that section.

§ 20.2056(b)–1 Marital deduction; limitation in case of life estate or other "terminable interest."

(a) In general. Section 2056(b) provides that no marital deduction is allowed with respect to certain property interests, referred to generally as "terminable interests," passing from a decedent to his surviving spouse. The phrase "terminable interest" is defined in paragraph (b) of this section. However, the fact that an interest in property passing to a decedent's surviving spouse is a "terminable interest" makes it nondeductible only (1) under the circumstances described in paragraph (c) of this section, and (2) if it does not come within one of the exceptions referred to in paragraph (d) of this section.

(b) "Terminable interests." A "terminable interest" in property is an interest which will terminate or fail on the lapse of time or on the occurrence or the failure to occur of some contingency. Life estates, terms for years, annuities, patents, and copyrights are therefore terminable interests. However, a bond, note, or similar contractual obligation, the discharge of which would not have the effect of an annuity or a term for years, is not a terminable interest.

(c) Nondeductible terminable interests.(1) A property interest which constitutes a terminable interest, as defined in paragraph (b) of this section, is nondeductible if—

(i) Another interest in the same property passed from the decedent to some other person for less than an adequate and full consideration in money or money's worth, and

(ii) By reason of its passing, the other person or his heirs or assigns may possess or enjoy any part of the property after the termination or failure of the spouse's interest.

(2) Even though a property interest which constitutes a terminable interest is not nondeductible by reason of the rules stated in subparagraph (1) of this paragraph, such an interest is nondeductible if—

(i) The decedent has directed his executor or a trustee to acquire such an interest for the decedent's surviving spouse (see further paragraph (f) of this section), or

(ii) Such an interest passing to the decedent's surviving spouse may be satisfied out of a group of assets which includes a nondeductible interest (see further § 20.2056(b)–2). In this case, however, full nondeductibility may not result.

(d) Exceptions. A property interest passing to a decedent's surviving spouse is deductible (if it is not otherwise disqualified under § 20.2056(a)–2) even though it is a terminable interest, and even though an interest therein passed from the decedent to another person, if it is a terminable interest only because—

(1) It is conditioned on the spouse's surviving for a limited period, in the manner described in § 20.2056(b)–3;

(2) It is a right to income for life with a general power of appointment, meeting the requirements set forth in § 20.2056(b)–5;

(3) It consists of life insurance or annuity payments held by the insurer with a general power of appointment in the spouse, meeting the requirements set forth in § 20.2056(b)–6;

(4) It is qualified terminable interest property, meeting the requirements set forth in § 20.2056(b)–7; or

(5) It is an interest in a qualified charitable remainder trust in which the spouse is the only noncharitable beneficiary, meeting the requirements set forth in § 20.2056(b)–8.

(e) Miscellaneous principles.(1) In determining whether an interest passed from the decedent to some other person, it is immaterial whether interests in the same property passed to the decedent's spouse and another person at the same time, or under the same instrument.

(2) In determining whether an interest in the same property passed from the decedent both to his surviving spouse and to some other person, a distinction is to be drawn between "property," as such term is used in section 2056, and an "interest in property." The term "property" refers to the underlying property in which various interests exist; each such interest is not for this purpose to be considered as "property."

(3) Whether or not an interest is nondeductible because it is a terminable interest is to be determined by reference to the property interests which actually passed from the decedent. Subsequent conversions of the property are immaterial for this purpose. Thus, where a decedent bequeathed his estate to his wife for life with remainder to his children, the interest which passed to his wife is a nondeductible interest, even though the wife agrees with the children to take a fractional share of the estate in fee in lieu of the life interest in the whole, or sells the life estate for cash, or acquires the remainder interest of the children either by purchase or gift.

(4) The terms "passed from the decedent," "passed from the decedent to his surviving spouse," and "passed from the decedent to a person other than his surviving spouse" are defined in §§ 20.2056(c)–1 through 20.2056(c)–3.

(f) Direction to acquire a terminable interest. No marital deduction is allowed with respect to a property interest which a decedent directs his executor or a trustee to covert after his death into a terminable interest for his surviving spouse. The marital deduction is not allowed even though no interest in the property subject to the terminable interest passes to another person and even though the interest would otherwise come within the exceptions described in §§ 20.2056(b)–5 and 20.2056(b)–6 (relating to life estates and life insurance and annuity payments with powers of appointment). However, a general investment power, authorizing investments in both terminable interests and other property, is not a direction to invest in a terminable interest.

(g) Examples. The application of this section may be illustrated by the following examples. In each example, it is assumed that the executor made no election under section 2056(b)(7) (even if under the specific facts the election would have been available), that any property interest passing from the decedent to a person other than the surviving spouse passed for less than full and adequate consideration in money or money's worth, and that section 2056(b)(8) is inapplicable.

Example (1). H (the decedent) devised real property to W (his surviving wife) for life, with remainder to A and his heirs. The interest which passed from H to W is a nondeductible interest since it will terminate upon her death and A (or his heirs or assigns) will thereafter possess or enjoy the property.

Example (2). H bequeathed the residue of his estate in trust for the benefit of W and A. The trust income is to be paid to W for life, and upon her death the corpus is to be distributed to A or his issue. However, if A should die without issue, leaving W surviving, the corpus is then to be distributed to W. The interest which passed from H to W is a nondeductible interest since it will terminate in the event of her death if A or his issue survive, and A or his issue will thereafter possess or enjoy the property.

Example (3). H during his lifetime purchased an annuity contract providing for payments to himself for life and then to W for life if she should survive him. Upon the death of the survivor of H and W, the excess, if any, of the cost of the contract over the annuity payments theretofore made was to be refunded to A. The interest which passed from H to W is a nondeductible interest since A may possess or enjoy a part of the property following the termination of the interest of W. If, however, the contract provided for no refund upon the death of the survivor of H and W, or provided that any refund was to go to the estate of the survivor, then the interest which passed from H to W is (to the extent it is included in H's gross estate) a deductible interest.

Example (4). H, in contemplation of death, transferred a residence to A for life with remainder to W provided W survives A, but if W predeceases A, the property is to pass to B and his heirs. If it is assumed that H died during A's lifetime, and the value of the residence was included in determining the value of his gross estate, the interest which passed from H to W is a nondeductible interest since it will terminate if W predeceases A and the property will thereafter be possessed or enjoyed by B (or his heirs or assigns). This result is not affected by B's assignment of his interest during H's lifetime, whether made in favor of W or another person, since the term "assigns" (as used in section 2056(b)(1)(B)) includes such an assignee. However, if it is assumed that A predeceased H, the interest of B in the property was extinguished, and, viewed as of the time of the subsequent death of H, the interest which passed from him to W is the entire interest in the property and, therefore, a deductible interest.

Example (5). H transferred real property to A by gift (reserving the right to the rentals) of the property for a term of 20 years. H died within the 20-year term, bequeathing the right to the remaining rentals to a trust for the benefit of W. The terms of the trust satisfy the five conditions stated in § 20.2056(b)–5, so that the property interest which passed in trust is considered to have passed from H to W. However, the interest is a nondeductible interest since it will terminate upon the expiration of the term and A will thereafter possess or enjoy the property.

Example (6). H bequeathed a patent to W and A as tenants in common. In this case, the interest of W will terminate upon the expiration of the term of the patent, but possession or enjoyment of the property by A must necessarily cease at the same time. Therefore, since A's possession or enjoyment cannot outlast the termination of W's interest, the latter is a deductible interest.

Example (7). A decedent bequeathed $100,000 to his wife, subject to a direction to his executor to use the bequest for the purchase of an annuity for the wife. The bequest is a nondeductible interest.

Example (8). Assume that pursuant to local law an allowance for support is payable to the decedent's surviving spouse during the period of the administration of the decedent's estate, but that upon her death or remarriage during such period her right to any further allowance will terminate. Assume further that the surviving spouse is sole beneficiary of the decedent's estate. Under such circumstances, the allowance constitutes a deductible interest since any part of the allowance not receivable by the surviving spouse during her lifetime will pass to her estate under the terms of the decedent's will. If, in this example, the decedent bequeathed only one-third of his residuary estate to his surviving spouse, then two-thirds of the allowance for support would constitute a nondeductible terminable interest.

§ 20.2056(b)–2 Marital deduction; interest in unidentified assets.

(a) In general. Section 2056(b)(2) provides that if an interest passing to a decedent's surviving spouse may be satisfied out of assets (or their proceeds) which include a particular asset that would be a nondeductible interest if it passed from the decedent to his spouse, the value of the interest passing to the spouse is reduced, for the purpose of the marital deduction, by the value of the particular asset.

(b) Application of section 2056(b)(2). In order for section 2056(b)(2) to apply, two circumstances must coexist, as follows:

(1) The property interest which passed from the decedent to his surviving spouse must be payable out of a group of assets included in the gross estate. Examples of property interests payable out of a group of assets are a general legacy, a bequest of the residue of the decedent's estate or of a proportion of the residue, and a right to a share of the corpus of a trust upon its termination.

(2) The group of assets out of which the property interest is payable must include one or more particular assets which, if passing specifically to the surviving spouse, would be nondeductible interests. Therefore, section 2056(b)(2) is not applicable merely because the group of assets includes a terminable interest, but would only be applicable if the terminable interest were nondeductible under the provisions of § 20.2056(b)–1.

(c) Interest nondeductible if circumstances present. If both of the circumstances set forth in paragraph (b) of this section are present, the property interest payable out of the group of assets is (except as to any excess of its value over the aggregate value of the particular asset or assets which would not be deductible if passing specifically to the surviving spouse) a nondeductible interest.

(d) Example. The application of this section may be illustrated by the following example:

Example. A decedent bequeathed one-third of the residue of his estate to his wife. The property passing under the decedent's will included a right to the rentals of an office building for a term of years, reserved by the decedent under a deed of the building by way of gift to his son. The decedent did not make a specific bequest of the right to such rentals. Such right, if passing specifically to the wife, would be a nondeductible interest (see example (5) of paragraph (g) of § 20.2056(b)–1). It is assumed that the value of the bequest of one-third of the residue of the estate to the wife was $85,000, and that the right to the rentals was included in the gross estate at a value of $60,000. If the decedent's executor had the right under the decedent's will or local law to assign the entire lease in satisfaction of the bequest, the bequest is a nondeductible interest to the extent of $60,000. If the executor could only assign a one-third interest in the lease in satisfaction of the bequest, the bequest is a nondeductible interest to the extent of $20,000. If the decedent's will provided that his wife's bequest could not be satisfied with a nondeductible interest, the entire bequest is a deductible interest. If, in this example, the asset in question had been foreign real estate not included in the decedent's gross estate, the results would be the same.

§ 20.2056(b)–3 Marital deduction; interest of spouse conditioned on survival for limited Period.

(a) In general. Generally, no marital deduction is allowable if the interest passing to the surviving spouse is a terminable interest as defined in paragraph (b) of § 20.2056(b)(1). However, section 2056(b)(3) provides an exception to this rule so as to allow a deduction if (1) the only condition under which it will terminate is the death of the surviving spouse within 6 months after the decedent's death, or her death as a result of a common disaster which also resulted in the decedent's death, and (2) the condition does not in fact occur.

(b) Six months' survival. If the only condition which will cause the interest taken by the surviving spouse to terminate is the death of the surviving spouse and the condition is of such nature that it can occur only within 6 months following the decedent's death, the exception provided by section 2056(b)(3) will apply, provided the condition does not in fact occur. However, if the condition (unless it relates to death as a result of a common disaster) is one which may occur either within the 6-month period or thereafter, the exception provided by section 2056(b)(3) will not apply.

(c) Common disaster. If a property interest passed from the decedent to his surviving spouse subject to the condition that she does not die as a result of a common disaster which also resulted in the decedent's death, the exception provided by section 2056(b)(3) will not be applied in the final audit of the return if there is still a possibility that the surviving spouse may be deprived of the property interest by operation of the common disaster provision as given effect by the local law.

(d) Examples. The application of this section may be illustrated by the following examples:

Example (1). A decedent bequeathed his entire estate to his spouse on condition that she survive him by 6 months. In the event his spouse failed to survive him by 6 months, his estate was to go to his niece and her heirs. The decedent was survived by his spouse. It will be observed that, as of the time of the decedent's death, it was possible that the niece would, by reason of the interest which passed to her from the decedent possess or enjoy the estate after the termination of the interest which passed to the spouse. Hence, under the general rule set forth in § 20.2056(b)–1, the interest which passed to the spouse would be regarded as a nondeductible interest. If the surviving spouse in fact died within 6 months after the decedent's death, that general rule is to be applied, and the interest which passed to the spouse is a nondeductible interest. However, if the spouse in fact survived the decedent by 6 months, thus extinguishing the interest of the niece, the case comes within the exception provided by section 2056(b)(3), and the interest which passed to the spouse is a deductible interest. (It is assumed for the purpose of this example that no other factor which would cause the interest to be nondeductible is present.)

Example (2). The facts are the same as in example (1) except that the will provided that the estate was to go to the niece either in case the decedent and his spouse should both die as a result of a common disaster, or in case the spouse should fail to survive the decedent by 3 months. It is assumed that the decedent was survived by his spouse. In this example, the interest which passed from the decedent to his surviving spouse is to be regarded as a nondeductible interest if the surviving spouse in fact died either within 3 months after the decedent's death or as a result of a common disaster which also resulted in the decedent's death. However, if the spouse in fact survived the decedent by 3 months, and did not thereafter die as a result of a common disaster which also resulted in the decedent's death, the exception provided under section 2056(b)(3) will apply and the interest will be deductible.

Example (3). The facts are the same as in example (1) except that the will provided that the estate was to go to the niece if the decedent and his spouse should both die as a result of a common disaster and if the spouse failed to survive the decedent by 3 months. If the spouse in fact survived the decedent by 3 months, the interest of the niece is extinguished, and the interest passing to the spouse is a deductible interest.

Example (4). A decedent devised and bequeathed his residuary estate to his wife if she was living on the date of distribution of his estate. The devise and bequest is a nondeductible interest even though distribution took place within 6 months after the decedent's death and the surviving spouse in fact survived the date of distribution.

§ 20.2056(b)–4 Marital deduction; valuation of interest passing to surviving spouse.

(a) In general. The value, for the purpose of the marital deduction, of any deductible interest which passed from the decedent to his surviving spouse is to be determined as of the date of the decedent's death, except that if the executor elects the alternate valuation method under section 2032 the valuation is to be determined as of the date of the decedent's death but with the adjustment described in paragraph (a)(3) of § 20.2032–1. The marital deduction may be taken only with respect to the net value of any deductible interest which passed from the decedent to his surviving spouse, the same principles being applicable as if the amount of a gift to the spouse were being determined.

(b) Property interest subject to an encumbrance or obligation. If a property interest passed from the decedent to his surviving spouse subject to a mortgage or other encumbrance, or if an obligation is imposed upon the surviving spouse by the decedent in connection with the passing of a property interest, the value of the property interest is to be reduced by the amount of the mortage, other encumbrance, or obligation. However, if under the terms of the decedent's will or under local law the executor is required to discharge, out of other assets of the decedent's estate, a mortgage or other encumbrance on property passing from the decedent to his surviving spouse, or is required to reimburse the surviving spouse for the amount of the mortgage or other encumbrance, the payment or reimbursement constitutes an additional interest passing to the surviving spouse. The passing of a property interest subject to the imposition of an obligation by the decedent does not include a bequest, devise, or transfer in lieu of dower, curtesy, or of a statutory estate created in lieu of dower or curtesy, or of other marital rights in the decedent's property or estate. The passing of a property interest subject to the imposition of an obligation by the decedent does, however, include a bequest, etc., in lieu of the interest of his surviving spouse under community property laws unless such interest was, immediately prior to the deceden's death, a mere expectancy. The following examples are illustrative of property interests which passed from the decedent to his surviving spouse subject to the imposition of an obligation by the decedent:

Example (1). A decedent devised a residence valued at $25,000 to his wife, with a direction that she pay $5,000 to his sister. For the purpose of the marital deduction, the value of the property interest passing to the wife is only $20,000.

Example (2). A decedent devised real property to his wife in satisfaction of a debt owing to her. The debt is a deductible claim under section 2053. Since the wife is obligated to relinquish the claim as a condition to acceptance of the devise, the value of the devise is, for the purpose of the marital deduction, to be reduced by the amount of the claim.

Example (3). A decedent bequeathed certain securities to his wife in lieu of her interest in property held by them as community property under the law of the State of their residence. The wife elected to relinquish her community property interest and to take the bequest. For the purpose of the marital deduction, the value of the bequest is to be reduced by the value of the community property interest relinquished by the wife.

(c) Effect of death taxes.(1) In the determination of the value of any property interest which passed from the decedent to his surviving spouse, there must be taken into account the effect which the Federal estate tax, or any estate, succession, legacy, or inheritance tax, has upon the net value to the surviving spouse of the property interest.

(2) For example, assume that the only bequest to the surviving spouse is $100,000 and the spouse is required to pay a State inheritance tax in the amount of $1,500. If no other death taxes affect the net value of the bequest, the value, for the purpose of the marital deduction, is $98,500.

(3) As another example, assume that a decedent devised real property to his wife having a value for Federal estate tax purposes of $100,000 and also bequeathed to her a nondeductible interest for life under a trust. The State of residence valued the real property at $90,000 and the life interest at $30,000, and imposed an inheritance tax (at graduated rates) of $4,800 with respect to the two interests. If it is assumed that the inheritance tax on the devise is required to be paid by the wife, the amount of tax to be ascribed to the devise is:

$$(90,000 \div 120,000) \times \$4,800 = \$3,600.$$

Accordingly, if no other death taxes affect the net value of the bequest, the value, for the purpose of the marital deduction, is $100,000 less $3,600, or $96,400.

(4) If the decedent bequeaths his residuary estate, or a portion of it, to his surviving spouse, and his will contains a direction that all death taxes shall be payable out of the residuary estate, the value of the bequest, for the purpose of the marital deduction, is based upon the amount of the residue as reduced pursuant to such direction, if the residuary estate, or a portion of it, is bequeathed to the surviving spouse, and by the local law the Federal estate tax is payable out of the residuary estate, the value of the bequest, for the purpose of the marital deduction, may not exceed its value as reduced by the Federal estate tax. Methods of computing the deduction, under such circumstances, are set forth in supplemental instructions to the estate tax return.

(d) Effect of administration expenses.—(1) Definitions.(i) Management expenses. Estate management expenses are expenses that are incurred in connection with the investment of estate assets or with their preservation or maintenance during a reasonable period of administration. Examples of these expenses could include investment advisory fees, stock brokerage commissions, custodial fees, and interest.

(ii) Transmission expenses. Estate transmission expenses are expenses that would not have been incurred but for the decedent's death and the consequent necessity of collecting the decedent's assets, paying the decedent's debts and death taxes, and distributing the decedent's property to those who are entitled to receive it. Estate transmission expenses include any administration expense that is not a management expense. Examples of these expenses could include executor commissions and attorney fees (except to the extent of commissions or fees specifically related to investment, preservation, or maintenance of the assets), probate fees, expenses incurred in construction proceedings and defending against will contests, and appraisal fees.

(iii) Marital share. The marital share is the property or interest in property that passed from the decedent for which a deduction is allowable under section 2056(a). The marital share includes the income produced by the property or interest in property during the period of administration if the income, under the terms of the governing instrument or applicable local law, is payable to the surviving spouse or is to be added to the principal of the property interest passing to, or for the benefit of, the surviving spouse.

(2) Effect of transmission expenses. For purposes of determining the marital deduction, the value of the marital share shall be reduced by the amount of the estate transmission expenses paid from the marital share.

(3) Effect of management expenses attributable to the marital share. For purposes of determining the marital deduction, the value of the marital share shall not be reduced by the amount of the estate management expenses attributable to and paid from the marital share. Pursuant to section 2056(b)(9), however, the amount of the allowable marital deduction shall be reduced by the amount of any such management expenses that are deducted under section 2053 on the decedent's Federal estate tax return.

(4) Effect of management expenses not attributable to the marital share. For purposes of determining the marital deduction, the value of the marital share shall be reduced by the amount of the estate management expenses paid from the marital share but attributable to a property interest not included in the marital share.

(5) Examples. The following examples illustrate the application of this paragraph (d):

Example (1). The decedent dies after 2006 having made no lifetime gifts. The decedent makes a bequest of shares of ABC Corporation stock to the decedent's child. The bequest provides that the child is to receive the income from the shares from the date of the decedent's death. The value of the bequeathed shares on the decedent's date of death is $3,000,000. The residue of the estate is bequeathed to a trust for which the executor properly makes an election under section 2056(b)(7) to treat as qualified terminable interest property. The value of the residue on the decedent's date of death, before the payment of administration expenses and Federal and State estate taxes, is $6,000,000. Under applicable local law, the executor has the discretion to pay administration expenses from the income or principal of the residuary estate. All estate taxes are to be paid from the residue. The State estate tax equals the State death tax credit available under section 2011.

During the period of administration, the estate incurs estate transmission expenses of $400,000, which the executor charges to the residue. For purposes of determining the marital deduction, the value of the residue is reduced by the Federal and State estate taxes and by the estate transmission expenses. If the transmission expenses are deducted on the Federal estate tax return, the marital deduction is $3,500,000 ($6,000,000 minus $400,000 transmission expenses and minus $2,100,000 Federal and State estate taxes). If the transmission expenses are deducted on the estate's Federal income tax return rather than on the estate tax return, the marital deduction is $3,011,111 ($6,000,000 minus $400,000 transmission expenses and minus $2,588,889 Federal and State estate taxes).

Example (2). The facts are the same as in Example 1, except that, instead of incurring estate transmission expenses, the estate incurs estate management expenses of $400,000 in connection with the residue property passing for the benefit of the spouse. The executor charges these management expenses to the residue. In determining the value of the residue passing to the spouse for marital deduction purposes, a reduction is made for Federal and State estate taxes payable from the residue but no reduction is made for the estate management expenses. If the management expenses are deducted on the estate's income tax return, the net value of the property passing to the spouse is $3,900,000 ($6,000,000 minus $2,100,000 Federal and State estate taxes). A marital deduction is claimed for that amount, and the taxable estate is $5,100,000.

Example (3). The facts are the same as in Example 1, except that the estate management expenses of $400,000 are incurred in connection with the bequest of ABC Corporation stock to the decedent's child. The executor charges these management expenses to the residue. For purposes of determining the marital deduction, the value of the residue is reduced by the Federal and State estate taxes and by the management expenses. The management expenses reduce the value of the residue because they are charged to the property passing to the spouse even though they were incurred with respect to stock passing to the child. If the management expenses are deducted on the estate's Federal income tax return, the marital deduction is $3,011,111 ($6,000,000 minus $400,000 management expenses and minus $2,588,889 Federal and State estate taxes). If the management expenses are deducted on the estate's Federal estate tax return, rather than on the estate's Federal income tax return, the marital deduction is $3,500,000 ($6,000,000 minus $400,000 management expenses and minus $2,100,000 in Federal and State estate taxes).

Example (4). The decedent, who dies in 2000, has a gross estate of $3,000,000. Included in the gross estate are proceeds of $150,000 from a policy insuring the decedent's life and payable to the decedent's child as beneficiary. The applicable credit amount against the tax was fully consumed by the decedent's lifetime gifts. Applicable State law requires the child to pay any estate taxes attributable to the life insurance policy. Pursuant to the decedent's will, the rest of the decedent's estate passes outright to the surviving spouse. During the period of administration, the estate incurs estate management expenses of $150,000 in connection with the property passing to the spouse. The value of the property passing to the spouse is $2,850,000 ($3,000,000 less the insurance proceeds of $150,000 passing to the child). For purposes of determining the marital deduction, if the management expenses are deducted on the estate's income tax return, the marital deduction is $2,850,000 ($3,000,000 less $150,000) and there is a resulting taxable estate of $150,000 ($3,000,000 less a marital deduction of $2,850,000). Suppose, instead, the management expenses of $150,000 are deducted on the estate's estate tax return under section 2053 as expenses of administration. In such a situation, claiming a marital deduction of $2,850,000 would be taking a deduction for the same $150,000 in property under both sections 2053 and 2056 and would shield from estate taxes the $150,000 in insurance proceeds passing to the decedent's child. Therefore, in accordance with section 2056(b)(9), the marital deduction is limited to $2,700,000, and the resulting taxable estate is $150,000.

Example (5). The decedent dies after 2006 having made no lifetime gifts. The value of the decedent's residuary estate on the decedent's date of death is $3,000,000, before the payment of administration expenses and Federal and State estate taxes. The decedent's will provides a formula for dividing the decedent's residuary estate between two trusts to reduce the estate's Federal estate taxes to zero. Under the formula, one trust, for the benefit of the decedent's child, is to be funded with that amount of property equal in value to so much of the applicable exclusion amount under section 2010 that would reduce the estate's Federal estate tax to zero. The other trust, for the benefit of the surviving spouse, satisfies the requirements of section 2056(b)(7) and is to be funded with the remaining property in the estate. The State estate tax equals the State death tax credit available under section 2011. During the period of administration, the estate incurs transmission expenses of $200,000. The transmission expenses of $200,000 reduce the value of the residue to $2,800,000. If the transmission expenses are deducted on the Federal estate tax return, then the formula divides the residue so that the value of the property passing to the child's trust is $1,000,000 and the value of the property passing to the marital trust is $1,800,000. The allowable marital deduction is $1,800,000. The applicable exclusion amount shields from Federal estate tax the entire $1,000,000 passing to the child's trust so that the amount of Federal and State estate taxes is zero. Alternatively, if the transmission expenses are deducted on the estate's Federal income tax return, the formula divides the residue so that the value of the property passing to the child's trust is $800,000 and the value of the property passing to the marital trust is $2,000,000. The allowable marital deduction is $2,000,000. The applicable exclusion amount shields from Federal estate tax the entire $800,000 passing to the child's trust so that the amount of Federal and State estate taxes remains zero.

Example (6). The facts are the same as in Example 5, except that the decedent's will provides that the child's trust is to be funded with that amount of property equal in value to the applicable exclusion amount under section 2010 allowable to the decedent's estate. The residue of the estate, after the payment of any debts, expenses, and Federal and State estate taxes, is to pass to the marital trust. The applicable exclusion amount in this case is $1,000,000, so the value of the property passing to the child's trust is $1,000,000. After deducting the $200,000 of transmission expenses, the residue of the estate is $1,800,000 less any estate taxes. If the transmission expenses are deducted on the Federal estate tax return, the allowable marital deduction is $1,800,000, the taxable estate is zero, and the Federal and State estate taxes are zero. Alternatively, if the transmission expenses are deducted on the estate's Federal income tax return, the net value of the property passing to the spouse is $1,657,874 ($1,800,000 minus $142,106 estate taxes). A marital deduction is claimed for that amount, the taxable estate is $1,342,106, and the Federal and State estate taxes total $142,106.

Example (7). The decedent, who dies in 2000, makes an outright pecuniary bequest of $3,000,000 to the decedent's surviving spouse, and the residue of the estate, after the payment of all debts, expenses, and Federal and State estate taxes, passes to the decedent's child. Under the terms of the governing instrument and applicable local law, a beneficiary of a pecuniary bequest is not entitled to any income on the bequest. During the period of administration, the estate pays estate transmission expenses from the income earned by the property that will be distributed to the surviving spouse in satisfaction of the pecuniary bequest. The income earned on this property is not part of the marital share. Therefore, the allowable marital deduction is $3,000,000, unreduced by the amount of the estate transmission expenses.

(6) Effective date. The provisions of this paragraph (d) apply to estates of decedents dying on or after December 3, 1999.

(e) Remainder interests. If the income from property is made payable to another individual for life, or for a term of years, with remainder absolutely to the surviving spouse or to her estate, the marital deduction is based upon the present value of the remainder. The present value of the remainder is to be determined in accordance with the rules stated in § 20.2031–7.* * *

§ 20.2056(b)–5 Marital deduction; life estate with power of appointment in surviving spouse.

(a) In general. Section 2056(b)(5) provides that if an interest in property passes from the decedent to his surviving spouse (whether or not in trust) and the spouse is entitled for life to all the income from the entire interest or all the income from a specific portion of the entire interest, with a power in her to appoint the entire interest or the specific portion, the interest which passes to her is a deductible interest, to the extent that it satisfies all five of the conditions set forth below (see paragraph (b) of this section if one or more of the conditions is satisfied as to only a portion of the interest):

(1) The surviving spouse must be entitled for life to all of the income from the entire interest or a specific portion of the entire interest, or to a specific portion of all the income from the entire interest.

(2) The income payable to the surviving spouse must be payable annually or at more frequent intervals.

(3) The surviving spouse must have the power to appoint the entire interest or the specific portion to either herself or her estate.

(4) The power in the surviving spouse must be exercisable by her alone and (whether exercisable by will or during life) must be exercisable in all events.

(5) The entire interest or the specific portion must not be subject to a power in any other person to appoint any part to any person other than the surviving spouse.

(b) Specific portion; deductible amount. If either the right to income or the power of appointment passing to the surviving spouse pertains only to a specific portion of a property interest passing from the decedent, the marital deduction is allowed only to the extent that the rights in the surviving spouse meet all of the five conditions described in paragraph (a) of this section. While the rights over the income and the power must coexist as to the same interest in property, it is not necessary that the rights over the income or the power as to such interest be in the same proportion. However, if the rights over income meeting the required conditions set forth in paragraph (a)(1) and (2) of the section extend over a smaller share of the property interest than the share with respect to which the power of appointment requirements set forth in paragraph (a)(3) through (5) of this section are satisfied, the deductible interest is limited to the smaller share. Correspondingly, if a power of appointment meeting all the requirements extends to a smaller portion of the property interest than the portion over which the income rights pertain, the deductible interest cannot exceed the value of the portion to which such power of appointment applies. Thus, if the decedent leaves to his surviving spouse the right to receive annually all of the income from a particular property interest and a power of appointment meeting the specifications prescribed in paragraph (a)(3) through (5) of this section as to only one-half of the property interest, then only one-half of the property interest is treated as a deductible interest. Correspondingly, if the income interest of the spouse satisfying the requirements extends to only one-fourth of the property interest and a testamentary power of appointment satisfying the requirements extends to all of the property interest, then only one-fourth of the interest in the spouse qualifies as a deductible interest. Further, if the surviving spouse has no right to income from a specific portion of a property interest but a testamentary power of appointment which meets the necessary conditions over the entire interest, then none of the interest qualifies for the deduction. In addition, if, from the time of the decedent's death, the surviving spouse has a power of appointment meeting all of the required conditions over three-fourths of the entire property interest and the prescribed income rights over the entire interest, but with a power in another person to appoint one-half of the entire interest, the value of the interest in the surviving spouse over only one-half of the property interest will qualify as a deductible interest.

(c) Meaning of specific portion—(1) In general. Except as provided in paragraphs (c)(2) and (c)(3) of this section, a partial interest in property is not treated as a specific portion of the entire interest. In addition, any specific portion of an entire interest in property is nondeductible to the extent the specific portion is subject to invasion for the benefit of any person other than the surviving spouse, except in the case of a deduction allowable under section 2056(b)(5), relating to the exercise of a general power of appointment by the surviving spouse.

(2) Fraction or percentage share. Under section 2056(b)(10), a partial interest in property is treated as a specific portion of the entire interest if the rights of the surviving spouse in income, and the required rights as to the power described in § 20.2056(b)–5(a), constitute a fractional or percentage share of the entire property interest, so that the surviving spouse's interest reflects its proportionate share of the increase or decrease in the value of the entire property interest to which the income rights and the power relate. Thus, if the spouse's right to income and the spouse's power extend to a specified fraction or percentage of the property, or the equivalent, the interest is in a specific portion of the property. In accordance with paragraph (b) of this section, if the spouse has the right to receive the income from a specific portion of the trust property (after applying paragraph (c)(3) of this section) but has a power of appointment over a different specific portion of the property (after applying paragraph (c)(3) of this section), the marital deduction is limited to the lesser specific portion.

(3) Special rule in the case of estates of decedents dying on or before October 24, 1992, and certain decedents dying after October 24, 1992, with wills or revocable trusts executed on or prior to that date.

(i) In the case of estates of decedents within the purview of the effective date and transitional rules contained in paragraphs (c)(3)(ii) and (iii) of this section:

(A) A specific sum payable annually, or at more frequent intervals, out of the property and its income that is not limited by the income of the property is treated as the right to receive the income from a specific portion of the property. The specific portion, for purposes of paragraph (c)(2) of this section, is the portion of the property that, assuming the interest rate generally applicable for the valuation of annuities at the time of the decedent's death, would produce income equal to such payments. However, a pecuniary amount payable annually to a surviving spouse is not treated as a right to the income from a specific portion of the trust property for purposes of this paragraph (c)(3)(i)(A) if any person other than the surviving spouse may receive, during the surviving spouse's lifetime, any distribution of the property. To determine the applicable interest rate for valuing annuities, see sections 2031 and 7520 and the regulations under those sections.

(B) The right to appoint a pecuniary amount out of a larger fund (or trust corpus) is considered the right to appoint a specific portion of such fund or trust for purposes of paragraph (c)(2) in an amount equal to such pecuniary amount.

(ii) The rules contained in paragraphs (c)(3)(i)(A) and (B) of this section apply with respect to estates of decedents dying on or before October 24, 1992.

(iii) The rules contained in paragraphs (c)(3)(i)(A) and (B) of this section apply in the case of decedents dying after October 24, 1992, if property passes to the spouse pursuant to a will or revocable trust agreement executed on or before October 24, 1992, and either—

(A) On that date, the decedent was under a mental disability to change the disposition of the property and did not regain competence to dispose of such property before the date of death; or

(B) The decedent dies prior to October 24, 1995.

(iv) Notwithstanding paragraph (c)(3)(iii) of this section, paragraphs (c)(3)(i)(A) and (B) of this section do not apply if the will or revocable trust is amended after October 24, 1992, in any respect that increases the amount of the transfer qualifying for the marital deduction or alters the terms by which the interest so passes to the surviving spouse of the decedent.

(4) Local law. A partial interest in property is treated as a specific portion of the entire interest if it is shown that the surviving spouse has rights under local law that are identical to those the surviving spouse would have acquired had the partial interest been expressed in terms satisfying the requirements of paragraph (c)(2) (or paragraph (c)(3) if applicable) of this section.

(5) Examples. The following examples illustrate the application of paragraphs (a) through (c)(4) of this section:

Example 1. Spouse entitled to the lesser of an annuity or a fraction of trust income. The decedent, D, died prior to October 24, 1992. D bequeathed in trust 500 identical shares of X company stock, valued for estate tax purposes at $500,000. The trust provides that during the lifetime of D's spouse, S, the trustee is to pay annually to S the lesser of one-half of the trust income or $20,000. Any trust income not paid to S is to be accumulated in the trust and may not be distributed during S's lifetime. S has a testamentary general power of appointment over the entire trust principal. The applicable interest rate for valuing annuities as of D's date of death under section 7520 is 10 percent. For purposes of paragraphs (a) through (c) of this section, S is treated as receiving all of the income from the lesser of—

(i) One half of the stock ($250,000); or

(ii) $200,000, the specific portion of the stock which, as determined in accordance with § 20.2056(b)–5(c)(3)(i)(A), would produce annual income of $20,000 (20,000/.10). Accordingly, the marital deduction is limited to $200,000 (200,000/500,000 or 2/5 of the value of the trust).

Example 2. Spouse possesses power and income interest over different specific portions of trust. The facts are the same as in Example 1 except that S's testamentary general power of appointment is exercisable over only ¼ of the trust principal. Consequently, under section 2056(b)(5), the marital deduction is allowable only for the value of ¼ of the trust ($125,000); i.e., the lesser of the value of the portion with respect to which S is deemed to be entitled to all of the income (2/5 of the trust or $200,000), or the value of the portion with respect to which S possesses the requisite power of appointment (¼ of the trust or $125,000).

Example 3. Power of appointment over pecuniary amount. The decedent, D, died prior to October 24, 1992. D bequeathed property valued at $400,000 for estate tax purposes in trust. The trustee is to pay annually to D's spouse, S, one-fourth of the trust income. Any trust income not paid to S is to be accumulated in the trust and may not be distributed during S's lifetime. The will gives S a testamentary general power of appointment over the sum of $160,000. Because D died prior to October 24, 1992, S's power of appointment over $160,000 is treated as a power of appointment over a specific portion of the entire trust interest. The marital deduction allowable under section 2056(b)(5) is limited to $100,000; that is, the lesser of—

(1) The value of the trust corpus ($400,000);

(2) The value of the trust corpus over which S has a power of appointment ($160,000); or

(3) That specific portion of the trust with respect to which S is entitled to all the income ($100,000).

Example 4. Power of appointment over shares of stock constitutes a power over a specific portion. Under D's will, 250 shares of Y company stock were bequeathed in trust pursuant to which all trust income was payable annually to S, D's spouse, for life. S was given a testamentary general power of appointment over 100 shares of stock. The trust provides that if the trustee sells the Y company stock, S's general power of appointment is exercisable with respect to the sale proceeds or the property in which the proceeds are reinvested. Because the amount of property represented by a single share of stock would be altered if the corporation split its stock, issued stock dividends, made a distribution of capital, etc., a power to appoint 100 shares at the time of S's death is not necessarily a power to appoint the entire interest that the 100 shares represented on the date of D's death. If it is shown that, under local law, S has a general power to appoint not only the 100 shares designated by D but also 100/250 of any distributions by the corporation that are included in trust principal, the requirements of paragraph (c)(2) of this section are satisfied and S is treated as having a general power to appoint 100/250 of the entire interest in the 250 shares. In that case, the marital deduction is limited to 40 percent of the trust principal. If local law does not give S that power, the 100 shares would not constitute a specific portion under § 20.2056(b)–5(c) (including § 20.2056(b)–5(c)(3)(i)(B)). The nature of the asset is such that a change in the capitalization of the corporation could cause an alteration in the original value represented by the shares at the time of D's death and, thus, it does not represent a specific portion of the trust.

(d) Meaning of entire interest. Because a marital deduction is allowed for each separate qualifying interest in property passing from the decedent to the decedent's surviving spouse (subject to any applicable limitations in § 20.2056(a)–l(c)), for purposes of paragraphs (a) and (b) of this section, each property interest with respect to which the surviving spouse received any rights is considered separately in determining whether the surviving spouse's rights extend to the entire interest or to a specific portion of the entire interest. A property interest which consists of several identical units of property (such as a block of 250 shares of stock, whether the ownership is evidenced by one or several certificates) is considered one property interest, unless certain of the units are to be segregated and accorded different treatment, in which case each segregated group of items is considered a separate property interest. The bequest of a specified sum of money constitutes the bequest of a separate property interest if immediately following distribution by the executor and thenceforth it, and the investments made with it, must be so segregated or accounted for as to permit its identification as a separate item of property. The application of this paragraph may be illustrated by the following examples:

Example (1). The decedent transferred to a trustee three adjoining farms, Blackacre, Whiteacre, and Greenacre. His will provided that during the lifetime of the surviving spouse the trustee should pay her all of the income from the trust. Upon her death, all of Blackacre, a one-half interest in Whiteacre, and a one-third interest in Greenacre were to be distributed to the person or persons appointed by her in her will. The surviving spouse is considered as being entitled to all of the income from the entire interest in Blackacre, all of the income from the entire interest in Whiteacre, and all of the income from the entire interest in Greenacre. She also is considered as having a power of appointment over the entire interest in Blackacre, over one-half of the entire interest in Whiteacre, and over one-third of the entire interest in Greenacre.

Example (2). The decedent bequeathed $250,000 to C, as trustee. C is to invest the money and pay all of the income from the investments to W, the decedent's surviving spouse, annually. W was given a general power, exercisable by will, to appoint one-half of the corpus of the trust. Here, immediately following distribution by the executor, the $250,000 will be sufficiently segregated to permit its identification as a separate item, and the $250,000 will constitute an entire property interest. Therefore, W has a right to income and a power of appointment such that one-half of the entire interest is a deductible interest.

Example (3). The decedent bequeathed 100 shares of Z corporation stock to D, as trustee. W, the decedent's surviving spouse, is to receive all of the income of the trust annually and is given a general power, exercisable by will, to appoint out of the trust corpus the sum of $25,000. In this case the $25,000 is not, immediately following distribution, sufficiently segregated to permit its identification as a separate item of property in which the surviving spouse has the entire interest. Therefore, the $25,000 does not constitute the entire interest in a property for the purpose of paragraphs (a) and (b) of this section.

(e) Application of local law. In determining whether or not the conditions set forth in paragraph (a)(1) through (5) of this section are satisfied by the instrument of transfer, regard is to be had to the applicable provisions of the law of the jurisdiction under which the interest passes and, if the transfer is in trust, the applicable provisions of the law governing the administration of the trust. For example, silence of a trust instrument as to the frequency of payment will not be regarded as a failure to satisfy the condition set forth in paragraph (a)(2) of this section that income must be payable to the surviving spouse annually or more frequently unless the applicable law permits payment to be made less frequently than annually. The principles outlined in this paragraph and paragraphs (f) and (g) of this section which are applied in determining whether transfers in trust meet such conditions are equally applicable in ascertaining whether, in the case of interests not in trust, the surviving spouse has the equivalent in rights over income and over the property.

(f) Right to income.(1) If an interest is transferred in trust, the surviving spouse is "entitled for life to all of the income from the entire interest or a specific portion of the entire interest", for the purpose of the condition set forth in paragraph (a)(1) of this section, if the effect of the trust is to give her substantially that degree of beneficial enjoyment of the trust property during her life which the principles of the law of trusts accord to a person who is unqualifiedly designated as the life beneficiary of a trust. Such degree of enjoyment is given only if it was the decedent's intention, as manifested by the terms of the trust instrument and the surrounding circumstances, that the trust should produce for the surviving spouse during her life such an income, or that the spouse should have such use of the trust property as is consistent with the value of the trust corpus and with its preservation. The designation of the spouse as sole income beneficiary for life of the entire interest or a specific portion of the entire interest will be sufficient to qualify the trust unless the terms of the trust and the surrounding circumstances considered as a whole evidence an intention to deprive the spouse of the requisite degree of enjoyment. In determining whether a trust evidences that intention, the treatment required or permitted with respect to individual items must be considered in relation to the entire system provided for the administration of the trust. In addition, the surviving spouse's interest shall meet the condition set forth in paragraph (a)(1) of this section if the spouse is entitled to income as determined by applicable local law that provides for a reasonable apportionment between the income and remainder beneficiaries of the total return of the trust and that meets the requirements of § 1.643(b)–1 of this chapter.

(2) If the over-all effect of a trust is to give to the surviving spouse such enforceable rights as will preserve to her the requisite degree of enjoyment, it is immaterial whether that result is effected by rules specifically stated in the trust instrument, or, in their absence, by the rules for the management of the trust property and the allocation of receipts and expenditures supplied by the State law. For example, a provision in the trust instrument for amortization of bond premium by appropriate periodic charges to interest will not disqualify the interest passing in trust even though there is no State law specifically authorizing amortization, or there is a State law denying amortization which is applicable only in the absence of such a provision in the trust instrument.

(3) In the case of a trust, the rules to be applied by the trustee in allocation of receipts and expenses between income and corpus must be considered in relation to the nature and expected productivity of the assets passing in trust, the nature and frequency of occurrence of the expected receipts, and any provisions as to change in the form of investments. If it is evident from the nature of the trust assets and the rules provided for management of the trust that the allocation to income of such receipts as rents, ordinary cash dividends, and interest will give to the spouse the substantial enjoyment during life required by the statute, provisions that such receipts as stock dividends and proceeds from the conversion of trust assets shall be treated as corpus will not disqualify the interest passing in trust. Similarly, provision for a depletion charge against income in the case of trust assets which are subject to depletion will not disqualify the interest passing in trust, unless the effect is to deprive the spouse of the requisite beneficial enjoyment. The same principle is applicable in the case of depreciation, trustees' commissions, and other charges.

(4) Provisions granting administrative powers to the trustee will not have the effect of disqualifying an interest passing in trust unless the grant of powers evidences the intention to deprive the surviving spouse of the beneficial enjoyment required by the statute. Such an intention will not be considered to exist if the entire terms of the instrument are such that the local courts will impose reasonable limitations upon the exercise of the powers. Among the powers which if subject to reasonable limitations will not disqualify the interest passing in trust are the power to determine the allocation or apportionment of receipts and disbursements between income and corpus, the power to apply the income or corpus for the benefit of the spouse, and the power to retain the assets passing to the trust. For example, a power to retain trust assets which consist substantially of unproductive property will not disqualify the interest if the applicable rules for the administration of the trust require, or permit the spouse to require, that the trustee either make the property productive or convert it within a reasonable time. Nor will such a power disqualify the interest if the applicable rules for administration of the trust require the trustee to use the degree of judgment and care in the exercise of the power which a prudent man would use if he were owner of the trust assets. Further, a power to retain a residence or other property for the personal use of the spouse will not disqualify the interest passing in trust.

(5) An interest passing in trust will not satisfy the condition set forth in paragraph (a)(1) of this section that the surviving spouse be entitled to all the income if the primary purpose of the trust is to safeguard property without providing the spouse with the required beneficial enjoyment. Such trusts include not only trusts which expressly provide for the accumulation of the income but also trusts which indirectly accomplish a similar purpose. For example, assume that the corpus of a trust consists substantially of property which is not likely to be income producing during the life of the surviving spouse and that the spouse cannot compel the trustee to convert or otherwise deal with the property as described in subparagraph (4) of this paragraph. An interest passing to such a trust will not qualify unless the applicable rules for the administration require, or permit the spouse to require, that the trustee provide the required beneficial enjoyment such as by payments to the spouse out of other assets of the trust.

(6) If a trust is created during the decedent's life, it is immaterial whether or not the interest passing in trust satisfied the conditions set forth in paragraph (a)(1) through (5) of this section prior to the decedent's death. If a trust may be terminated during the life of the surviving spouse, under her exercise of a power of appointment or by distribution of the corpus to her, the interest passing in trust satisfies the condition set forth in paragraph (a)(1) of this section (that the spouse be entitled to all the income) if she (i) is entitled to the income until the trust terminates, or (ii) has the right, exercisable in all events, to have the corpus distributed to her at any time during her life.

(7) An interest passing in trust fails to satisfy the condition set forth in paragraph (a)(1) of this section, that the spouse be entitled to all the income, to the extent that the income is required to be accumulated in whole or in part or may be accumulated in the discretion of any person other than the surviving spouse; to the extent that the consent of any person other than the surviving spouse is required as a condition precedent to distribution of the income; or to the extent that any person other than the surviving spouse has the power to alter the terms of the trust so as to deprive her of her right to the income. An interest passing in trust will not fail to satisfy the condition that the spouse be entitled to all the income merely because its terms provide that the right of the surviving spouse to the income shall not be subject to assignment, alienation, pledge, attachment or claims of creditors.

(8) In the case of an interest passing in trust, the terms "entitled for life" and "payable annually or at more frequent intervals," as used in the conditions set forth in paragraph (a)(1) and (2) of this section, require that under the terms of the trust the income referred to must be currently (at least annually; see paragraph (e) of this section) distributable to the spouse or that she must have such command over the income that it is virtually hers. Thus, the conditions in paragraph (a)(1) and (2) of this section are satisfied in this respect if, under the terms of the trust instrument, the spouse has the right exercisable annually (or more frequently) to require distribution to herself of the trust income, and otherwise the trust income is to be accumulated and added to corpus. Similarly, as respects the income for the period between the last distribution date and the date of the spouse's death, it is sufficient if that income is subject to the spouse's power to appoint. Thus, if the trust instrument provides that income accrued or undistributed on the date of the spouse's death is to be disposed of as if it had been received after her death, and if the spouse has a power of appointment over the trust corpus, the power necessarily extends to the undistributed income.

(9) An interest is not to be regarded as failing to satisfy the conditions set forth in paragraph (a)(1) and (2) of this section (that the spouse be entitled to all the income and that it be payable annually or more frequently) merely because the spouse is not entitled to the income from estate assets for the period before distribution of those assets by the executor, unless the executor is, by the decedent's will, authorized or directed to delay distribution beyond the period reasonably required for administration of the decedent's estate. As to the valuation of the property interest passing to the spouse in trust where the right to income is expressly postponed, see § 20.2056(b)–4.

(g) Power of appointment in surviving spouse. **(1)** The conditions set forth in paragraph (a)(3) and (4) of this section, that is, that the surviving spouse must have a power of appointment exercisable in favor of herself or her estate and exercisable alone and in all events are not met unless the power of the surviving spouse to appoint the entire interest or a specific portion of it falls within one of the following categories:

(i) A power so to appoint fully exercisable in her own favor at any time following the decedent's death (as, for example, an unlimited power to invade); or

(ii) A power so to appoint exercisable in favor of her estate. Such a power, if exercisable during life, must be fully exercisable at any time during life, or, if exercisable by will, must be fully exercisable irrespective of the time of her death (subject in either case to the provisions of § 20.2053(b)–3, relating to interests conditioned on survival for a limited period); or

(iii) A combination of the powers described under subdivisions (i) and (ii) of this subparagraph. For example, the surviving spouse may, until she attains the age of 50 years, have a power to appoint to herself and thereafter have a power to appoint to her estate. However, the condition that the spouse's power must be exercisable in all events is not satisfied unless irrespective of when the surviving spouse may die the entire interest or a specific portion of it will at the time of her death be subject to one power or the other (subject to the exception in § 20.2053(b)–3, relating to interests contingent on survival for a limited period).

(2) The power of the surviving spouse must be a power to appoint the entire interest or a specific portion of it as unqualified owner (and free of the trust if a trust is involved, or free of the joint tenancy if a joint tenancy is involved) or to appoint the entire interest or a specific portion of it as a part of her estate (and free of the trust if a trust is involved), that is, in effect, to dispose of it to whomsoever she pleases. Thus, if the decedent devised property to a son and the surviving spouse as joint tenants with right of survivorship and under local law the surviving spouse has a power of severance exercisable without consent of the other joint tenant, and by exercising this power could acquire a one-half interest in the property as a tenant in common, her power of severance will satisfy the conditions set forth in paragraph (a)(3) of this section that she have a power of appointment in favor of herself or her estate. However, if the surviving spouse entered into a binding agreement with the decedent to exercise the power only in favor of their issue, that condition is not met. An interest passing in trust will not be regarded as failing to satisfy the condition merely because takers in default of the surviving spouse's exercise of the power are designated by the decedent. The decedent may provide that, in default of exercise of the power, the trust shall continue for an additional period.

(3) A power is not considered to be a power exercisable by a surviving spouse alone and in all events as required by paragraph (a)(4) of this section if the exercise of the power in the surviving spouse to appoint the entire interest or a specific portion of it to herself or to her estate requires the joinder or consent of any other person. The power is not "exercisable in all events", if it can be terminated during the life of the surviving spouse by any event other than her complete exercise or release of it. Further, a power is not "exercisable in all events" if it may be exercised for a limited purpose only. For example, a power which is not exercisable in the event of the spouse's remarriage is not exercisable in all events. Likewise, if there are any restrictions, either by the terms of the instrument or under applicable local law, on the exercise of a power to consume property (whether or not held in trust) for the benefit of the spouse, the power is not exercisable in all events. Thus, if a power of invasion is exercisable only for the spouse's support, or only for her limited use, the power is not exercisable in all events. In order for a power of invasion to be exercisable in all events, the surviving spouse must have the unrestricted power exercisable at any time during her life to use all or any part of the property subject to the power, and to dispose of it in any manner, including the power to dispose of it by gift (whether or not she has power to dispose of it by will).

(4) The power in the surviving spouse is exercisable in all events only if it exists immediately following the decedent's death. For example, if the power given to the surviving spouse is exercisable during life, but cannot be effectively exercised before distribution of the assets by the executor, the power is not exercisable in all events. Similarly, if the power is exercisable by will, but cannot be effectively exercised in the event the surviving spouse dies before distribution of the assets by the executor, the power is not exercisable in all events. However, an interest will not be disqualified by the mere fact that, in the event the power is exercised during administration of the estate, distribution of the property to the appointee will be delayed for the period of administration. If the power is in existence at all times following the decedent's death, limitations of a formal nature will not disqualify an interest. Examples of formal limitations on a power exercisable during life are requirements that an exercise must be in a particular form, that it must be filed with a trustee during the spouse's life, that reasonable notice must be given, or that reasonable intervals must elapse between successive partial exercises. Examples of formal limitations on a power exercisable by will are that it must be exercised by a will executed by the surviving spouse after the decedent's death or that exercise must be by specific reference to the power.

(5) If the surviving spouse has the requisite power to appoint to herself or her estate, it is immaterial that she also has one or more lesser powers. Thus, if she has a testamentary power to appoint to her estate, she may also have a limited power of withdrawal or of appointment during her life. Similarly, if she has an unlimited power of withdrawal, she may have a limited testamentary power.

(h) Requirement of survival for a limited period. A power of appointment in the surviving spouse will not be treated as failing to meet the requirements of paragraph (a)(3) of this section even though the power may terminate, if the only conditions which would cause the termination are those described in paragraph (a) of § 20.2056(b)–3, and if those conditions do not in fact occur. Thus, the entire interest or a specific portion of it will not be disqualified by reason of the fact that the exercise of the power in the spouse is subject to a condition of survivorship described in § 20.2056(b)–3 if the terms of the condition, that is, the survivorship of the surviving spouse, or the failure to die in a common disaster, are fulfilled.

(i) [Reserved]

(j) Existence of a power in another. Paragraph (a)(5) of this section provides that a transfer described in paragraph (a) is nondeductible to the extent that the decedent created a power in the trustee or in any other person to appoint a part of the interest to any person other than the surviving spouse. However, only powers in other persons which are in opposition to that of the surviving spouse will cause a portion of the interest to fail to satisfy the condition set forth in paragraph (a)(5) of this section. Thus, a power in a trustee to distribute corpus to or for the benefit of a surviving spouse will not disqualify the trust. Similarly, a power to distribute corpus to the spouse for the support of minor children will not disqualify the trust if she is legally obligated to support such children. The application of this paragraph may be illustrated by the following examples:

Example (1). Assume that a decedent created a trust, designating his surviving spouse as income beneficiary for life with an unrestricted power in the spouse to appoint the corpus during her life. The decedent further provided that in the event the surviving spouse should die without having exercised the power, the trust should continue for the life of his son with a power in the son to appoint the corpus. Since the power in the son could become exercisable only after the death of the surviving spouse, the interest is not regarded as failing to satisfy the condition set forth in paragraph (a)(5) of this section.

Example (2). Assume that the decedent created a trust, designating his surviving spouse as income beneficiary for life and as donee of a power to appoint by will the entire corpus. The decedent further provided that the trustee could distribute 30 percent of the corpus to the decedent's son when he reached the age of 35 years. Since the trustee has a power to appoint 30 percent of the entire interest for the benefit of a person other than the surviving spouse, only 70 percent of the interest placed in trust satisfied the condition set forth in paragraph (a)(5) of this section. If, in this case, the surviving spouse had a power, exercisable by her will, to appoint only one-half of the corpus as it was constituted at the time of her death, it should be noted that only 35 percent of the interest placed in the trust would satisfy the condition set forth in paragraph (a)(3) of this section.

§ 20.2056(b)–6 Marital deduction; life insurance or annuity payments with power of appointment in surviving spouse.

(a) In general. Section 2056(b)(6) provides that an interest in property passing from a decedent to his surviving spouse, which consists of proceeds held by an insurer under the terms of a life insurance, endowment, or annuity contract, is a "deductible interest" to the extent that is satisfied all five of the following conditions (see paragraph (b) of this section if one or more of the conditions is satisfied as to only a portion of the proceeds):

(1) The proceeds, or a specific portion of the proceeds, must be held by the insurer subject to an agreement either to pay the entire proceeds or a specific portion thereof in installments, or to pay interest thereon, and all or a specific portion of the installments or interest payable during the life of the surviving spouse must be payable only to her.

(2) The installments or interest payable to the surviving spouse must be payable annually, or more frequently, commencing not later than 13 months after the decedent's death.

(3) The surviving spouse must have the power to appoint all or a specific portion of the amounts so held by the insurer to either herself or her estate.

(4) The power in the surviving spouse must be exercisable by her alone and (whether exercisable by will or during life) must be exercisable in all events.

(5) The amounts or the specific portion of the amounts payable under such contract must not be subject to a power in any other person to appoint any part thereof to any person other than the surviving spouse.

(b) Specific portion; deductible interest. If the right to receive interest or installment payments or the power of appointment passing to the surviving spouse pertains only to a specific portion of the proceeds held by the insurer, the marital deduction is allowed only to the extent that the rights of the surviving spouse in the specific portion meet the five conditions described in paragraph (a) of this section. While the rights to interest, or to receive payment in installments, and the power must coexist as to the proceeds of the same contract, it is not necessary that the rights to each be in the same proportion. If the rights to interest meeting the required conditions set forth in paragraph (a)(1) and (2) of this section extend over a smaller share of the proceeds than the share with respect to which the power of appointment requirements set forth in paragraph (a)(3) through (5) of this section are satisfied, the deductible interest is limited to the smaller share. Similarly, if the portion of the proceeds payable in installments is a smaller portion of the proceeds than the portion to which the power of appointment meeting such requirements relates, the deduction is limited to the smaller portion. In addition, if a power of appointment meeting all the requirements extends to a smaller portion of the proceeds than the portion over which the interest or installment rights pertain, the deductible interest cannot exceed the value of the portion to which such power of appointment applies. Thus, if the contract provides that the insurer is to retain the entire proceeds and pay all of the interest thereon annually to the surviving spouse and if the surviving spouse has a power of appointment meeting the specifications prescribed in paragraph (a)(3) through (5) of this section, as to only one-half of the proceeds held, then only one-half of the proceeds may be treated as a deductible interest. Correspondingly, if the rights of the spouse to receive installment payments or interest satisfying the requirements extend to only one-fourth of the proceeds and a testamentary power of appointment satisfying the requirements of paragraph (a)(3) through (5) of this section extends to all of the proceeds, then only one-fourth of the proceeds qualifies as a deductible interest. Further, if the surviving spouse has no right to installment payments (or interest) over any portion of the proceeds but a testamentary power of appointment which meets the necessary conditions over the entire remaining proceeds, then none of the proceeds qualifies for the deduction. In addition, if, from the time of the decedent's death, the surviving spouse has a power of appointment meeting all of the required conditions over three-fourths of the proceeds and the right to receive interest from the entire proceeds, but with a power in another person to appoint one-half of the entire proceeds, the value of the interest in the surviving spouse over only one-half of the proceeds will qualify as a deductible interest.

(c) Applicable principles.(1) The principles set forth in paragraph (c) of § 20.2056(b)–5 for determining what constitutes a "specific portion of the entire interest" for the purpose of section 2056(b)(5) are applicable in determining what constitutes a "specific portion of all such amounts" for the purpose of section 2056(b)(6). However, the interest in the proceeds passing to the surviving spouse will not be disqualified by the fact that the installment payments or interest to which the spouse is entitled or the amount of the proceeds over which the power of appointment is exercisable may be expressed in terms of a specific sum rather than a fraction or a percentage of the proceeds provided it is shown that such sums are a definite or fixed percentage or fraction of the total proceeds.

(2) The provisions of paragraph (a) of this section are applicable with respect to a property interest which passed from the decedent in the form of proceeds of a policy of insurance upon the decedent's life, a policy of insurance upon the life of a person who predeceased the decedent, a matured endowment policy, or an annuity contract, but only in case the proceeds are to be held by the insurer. With respect to proceeds under any such contract which are to be held by a trustee, with power of appointment in the surviving spouse, see § 20.2056(b)–5. As to the treatment of proceeds not meeting the requirements of § 20.2056(b)–5 or of this section, see § 20.2056(a)–2.

(3) In the case of a contract under which payments by the insurer commenced during the decedent's life, it is immaterial whether or not the conditions in subparagraphs (1) through (5) of paragraph (a) of this section were satisfied prior to the decedent's death.

(d) Payments of installments or interest. The conditions in subparagraphs (1) and (2) of paragraph (a) of this section relative to the payments of installments or interest to the surviving spouse are satisfied if, under the terms of the contract, the spouse has the right exercisable annually (or more frequently) to require distribution to herself of installments of the proceeds or a specific portion thereof, as the case may be, and otherwise such proceeds or interest are to be accumulated and held by the insurer pursuant to the terms of the contract. A contract which otherwise requires the insurer to make annual or more frequent payments to the surviving spouse following the decedent's death, will not be disqualified merely because the surviving spouse must comply with certain formalities in order to obtain the first payment. For example, the contract may satisfy the conditions in subparagraphs (1) and (2) of paragraph (a) of this section even though it requires the surviving spouse to furnish proof of death before the first payment is made. The condition in paragraph (a)(1) of this section is satisfied where interest on the proceeds or a specific portion thereof is payable, annually or more frequently, for a term, or until the occurrence of a specified event, following which the proceeds or a specific portion thereof are to be paid in annual or more frequent installments.

(e) Powers of appointment.(1) In determining whether the terms of the contract satisfy the conditions in subparagraph (3), (4), or (5) of paragraph (a) of this section relating to a power of appointment in the surviving spouse or any other person, the principles stated in § 20.2056(b)–5 are applicable. As stated in § 20.2056(b)–5, the surviving spouse's power to appoint is "exercisable in all events" only if it is in existence immediately following the decedent's death, subject, however, to the operation of § 20.2056(b)–3 relating to interests conditioned on survival for a limited period.

(2) For examples of formal limitations on the power which will not disqualify the contract, see paragraph (g)(4) of § 20.2056(b)–5. If the power is exercisable from the moment of the decedent's death, the contract is not disqualified merely because the insurer may require proof of the decedent's death as a condition to making payment to the appointee. If the submission of proof of the decedent's death is a condition to the exercise of the power, the power will not be considered "exercisable in all events" unless in the event the surviving spouse had died immediately following the decedent, her power to appoint would have been considered to exist at the time of her death, within the meaning of section 2041(a)(2). See paragraph (b) of § 20.2041–3.

(3) It is sufficient for the purposes of the condition in paragraph (a)(3) of this section that the surviving spouse have the power to appoint amounts held by the insurer to herself or her estate if the surviving spouse has the unqualified power, exercisable in favor of herself or her estate, to appoint amounts held by the insurer which are payable after her death. Such power to appoint need not extend to installments or interest which will be paid to the spouse during her life. Further, the power to appoint need not be a power to require payment in a single sum. For example, if the proceeds of a policy are payable in installments, and if the surviving spouse has the power to direct that all installments payable after her death be paid to her estate, she has the requisite power.

(4) It is not necessary that the phrase "power to appoint" be used in the contract. For example, the condition in paragraph (a)(3) of this section that the surviving spouse have the power to appoint amounts held by the insurer to herself or her estate is satisfied by terms of a contract which give the surviving spouse a right which is, in substance and effect, a power to appoint to herself or her estate, such as a right to withdraw the amount remaining in the fund held by the insurer, or a right to direct that any amount held by the insurer under the contract at her death shall be paid to her estate.

* * *

§ 20.2056(c)–1 Marital deduction; definition of passed from the decedent.

(a) In general. The following rules are applicable in determining the person to whom any property interest "passed from the decedent":

(1) Property interests devolving upon any person (or persons) as surviving coowner with the decedent under any form of joint ownership under which the right of survivorship existed are considered as having passed from the decedent to such person (or persons).

(2) Property interests at any time subject to the decedent's power to appoint (whether alone or in conjunction with any person) are considered as having passed from the decedent to the appointee under his exercise of the power, or, in case of the lapse, release or nonexercise of the power, as having passed from the decedent to the taker in default of exercise.

(3) The dower or curtesy interest (or statutory interest in lieu thereof) of the decedent's surviving spouse is considered as having passed from the decedent to his spouse.

(4) The proceeds of insurance upon the life of the decedent are considered as having passed from the decedent to the person who, at the time of the decedent's death, was entitled to receive the proceeds.

(5) Any property interest transferred during life, bequeathed or devised by the decedent, or inherited from the decedent, is considered as having passed to the person to whom he transferred, bequeathed, or devised the interest, or to the person who inherited the interest from him.

(6) The survivor's interest in an annuity or other payment described in section 2039 (see §§ 20.2039–1 and 20.2039–2) is considered as having passed from the decedent to the survivor only to the extent that the value of such interest is included in the decedent's gross estate under that section. If only a portion of the entire annuity or other payment is included in the decedent's gross estate and the annuity or other payment is payable to more than one beneficiary, then the value of the interest considered to have passed to each beneficiary is that portion of the amount payable to each beneficiary that the amount of the annuity or other payment included in the decedent's gross estate bears to the total value of the annuity or other payment payable to all beneficiaries.

(b) Expectant interest in property under community property laws. If before the decedent's death the decedent's surviving spouse had merely an expectant interest in property held by her and the decedent under community property laws, that interest is considered as having passed from the decedent to the spouse.

§ 20.2056(c)–2 Marital deduction; definition of "passed from the decedent to his surviving spouse."

(a) In general. In general, the definition stated in § 20.2056(c)–1 is applicable in determining the property interests which "passed from the decedent to his surviving spouse." Special rules are provided, however, for the following:

(1) In the case of certain interests with income for life to the surviving spouse with power of appointment in her (see § 20.2056(b)–5);

(2) In the case of certain interests with income for life to the surviving spouse that the executor elects to treat as qualified terminable interest property (see § 20.2056(b)–7);

(3) In the case of proceeds held by the insurer under a life insurance, endowment, or annuity contract with power of appointment in the surviving spouse (see § 20.2056(b)–6);

(4) In case of the disclaimer of an interest by the surviving spouse or by any other person (see § 20.2056(d)–1);

(5) In case of an election by the surviving spouse (see paragraph (c) of this section); and

(6) In case of a controversy involving the decedent's will, see paragraph (d) of this section.

A property interest is considered as passing to the surviving spouse only if it passes to the spouse as beneficial owner, except to the extent otherwise provided in §§ 20.2056(b)–5 through 20.2056(b)–7. For this purpose, where a property interest passed from the decedent in trust, such interest is considered to have passed from him to his surviving spouse to the extent of her beneficial interest therein. The deduction may not be taken with respect to a property interest which passed to such spouse merely as trustee, or subject to a binding agreement by the spouse to dispose of the interest in favor of a third person. An allowance or award paid to a surviving spouse pursuant to local law for her support during the administration of the decedent's estate constitutes a property interest passing from the decedent to his surviving spouse. In determining whether or not such an interest is deductible, however, see generally the terminable interest rules of § 20.2056(b)–1 and especially example (8) of paragraph (g) of that section.

(b) Examples. The following illustrate the provisions of paragraph (a) of this section:

(1) A property interest bequeathed in trust by H (the decedent) is considered as having passed from him to W (his surviving spouse)—

(i) If the trust income is payable to W for life and upon her death the corpus is distributable to her executors or administrators;

(ii) If W is entitled to the trust income for a term of years following which the corpus is to be paid to W or her estate;

(iii) If the trust income is to be accumulated for a term of years or for W's life and the augmented fund paid to W or her estate; or

(iv) If the terms of the transfer satisfy the requirements of § 20.2056(b)–5 or 20.2056(b)–7.

(2) If H devised property—

(i) To A for life with remainder absolutely to W or her estate, the remainder interest is considered to have passed from H to W;

(ii) To W for life with remainder to her estate, the entire property is considered as having passed from H to W; or

(iii) Under conditions which satisfy the provisions of § 20.2056(b)–5, the entire property is considered as having passed from H to W.

(3) Proceeds of insurance upon the life of H are considered as having passed from H to W if the terms of the contract—

(i) Meet the requirements of § 20.2056(b)–6;

(ii) Provide that the proceeds are payable to W in a lump sum;

(iii) Provide that the proceeds are payable in installments to W for life and after her death any remaining installments are payable to her estate;

(iv) Provide that interest on the proceeds is payable to W for life and upon her death the principal amount is payable to her estate; or

(v) Provide that the proceeds are payable to a trustee under an arrangement whereby the requirements of § 20.2056(b)–5 or 20.2056(b)–7 are satisfied.

(c) Effect of election by surviving spouse. This paragraph contains rules applicable if the surviving spouse may elect between a property interest offered to her under the decedent's will or other instrument and a property interest to which she is otherwise entitled (such as dower, a right in the decedent's estate, or her interest under community property laws) of which adverse disposition was attempted by the decedent under the will or other instrument. If the surviving spouse elects to take against the will or other instrument, then the property interests offered thereunder are not considered as having "passed from the decedent to his surviving spouse" and the dower or other property interest retained by her is considered as having so passed (if it otherwise so qualifies under this section). If the surviving spouse elects to take under the will or other instrument, then the dower or other property interest relinquished by her is not considered as having "passed from the decedent to his surviving spouse" (irrespective of whether it otherwise comes within the definition stated in paragraph (a) of this section) and the interest taken under the will or other instrument is considered as having so passed (if it otherwise so qualifies). As to the valuation of the property interest taken under the will or other instrument, see paragraph (b) of § 20.2056(b)–4.

(d) Will contests. (1) If as a result of a controversy involving the decedent's will, or involving any bequest or devise thereunder, his surviving spouse assigns or surrenders a property interest in settlement of the controversy, the interest so assigned or surrendered is not considered as having "passed from the decedent to his surviving spouse."

(2) If as a result of the controversy involving the decedent's will, or involving any bequest or devise thereunder, a property interest is assigned or surrendered to the surviving spouse, the interest so acquired will be regarded as having "passed from the decedent to his surviving spouse" only if the assignment or surrender as a bona fide recognition of enforceable rights of the surviving spouse in the decedent's estate. Such a bona fide recognition will be presumed where the assignment or surrender was pursuant to a decision of a local court upon the merits in an adversary proceeding following a genuine and active contest. However, such a decree will be accepted only to the extent that the court passed upon the facts upon which deductibility of the property interest depends. If the assignment or surrender was pursuant to a decree rendered by consent, or pursuant to an agreement not to contest the will or not to probate the will, it will not necessarily be accepted as a bona fide evaluation of the rights of the spouse.

(e) Survivorship. If the order of deaths of the decedent and his spouse cannot be established by proof, a presumption (whether supplied by local law, the decedent's will, or otherwise) that the decedent was survived by his spouse will be recognized as satisfying paragraph (b)(1) of § 20.2056(a)–1, but only to the extent that it has the effect of giving to the spouse an interest in property includible in her gross estate under part III of subchapter A of chapter 11. Under these circumstances, if an estate tax return is required to be filed for the estate of the decedent's spouse, the marital deduction will not be allowed in the final audit of the estate tax return of the decedent's estate with respect to any property interest which has not been finally determined to be includible in the gross estate of his spouse.

§ 20.2056(c)–3 Marital deduction; definition of passed from the decedent to a person other than his surviving spouse.

The expression "passed from the decedent to a person other than his surviving spouse" refers to any property interest which, under the definition stated in § 20.2056(c)–1 is considered as having "passed from the decedent" and which under the rules referred to in § 20.2056(c)–2 is not considered as having "passed from the decedent to his surviving spouse." Interests which passed to a person other than the surviving spouse include interests so passing under the decedent's exercise, release, or nonexercise of a nontaxable power to appoint. It is immaterial whether the property interest which passed from the decedent to a person other than his surviving spouse is included in the decedent's gross estate. The term "person other than his surviving spouse" includes the possible unascertained takers of a property interest, as, for example, the members of a class to be ascertained in the future. As another example, assume that the decedent created a power of appointment over a property interest, which does not come within the purview of § 20.2056(b)–5 or § 20.2056(b)–6. In such a case, the term "person other than his surviving spouse" refers to the possible appointees and possible takers in default (other than the spouse) of such property interest. Whether or not there is a possibility that the "person other than his surviving spouse" (or the heirs or assigns of such person) may possess or enjoy the property following termination or failure of the interest therein which passed from the decedent to his surviving spouse is to be determined as of the time of the decedent's death.

* * *

§ 20.2056(d)–1 Marital deduction; special rules for marital deduction if surviving spouse is not a United States citizen.

Rules pertaining to the application of section 2056(d), including certain transition rules, are contained in §§ 20.2056A–1 through 20.2056A–13.

§ 20.2056(d)–2 Marital deduction; effect of disclaimers of post-December 31, 1976 transfers.

(a) Disclaimer by a surviving spouse. If a surviving spouse disclaims an interest in property passing to such spouse from the decedent in a taxable transfer made after December 31, 1976, the efficacy of the disclaimer will be determined by section 2518 and the corresponding regulations. If a qualified disclaimer is determined to have been made by the surviving spouse, the property interest disclaimed is treated as if such interest had never been transferred to the surviving spouse.

(b) Disclaimer by a person other than a surviving spouse. If an interest in property passes to one other than the surviving spouse from a decedent in a taxable transfer made after December 31, 1976, and—

(1) The person other than the surviving spouse makes a qualified disclaimer with respect to such interest in property, and

(2) The surviving spouse is entitled to such interest in property as a result of such disclaimer, the disclaimed interest is treated as passing directly from the decedent to the surviving spouse. If the disclaimer is not a qualified disclaimer, the interest in property is considered as passing from the decedent to the person who made the disclaimer as if the disclaimer had not been made. See section 2518 and the corresponding regulations for rules relating to a qualified disclaimer.

* * *

PART 25—GIFT TAX; GIFTS MADE AFTER DECEMBER 31, 1954

GIFT TAX*

* * *

DETERMINATION OF TAX LIABILITY

§ 25.2501–1 Imposition of tax.

(a) In general. (1) The tax applies to all transfers by gift of property, wherever situated, by an individual who is a citizen or resident of the United States, to the extent the value of the transfers exceeds the amount of the exclusions authorized by section 2503 and the deductions authorized by sections 2521 (as in effect prior to its repeal by the Tax Reform Act of 1976), 2522, and 2523. For each "calendar period" (as defined in § 25.2502–1(c)(1)), the tax described in this paragraph (a) is imposed on the transfer of property by gift during such calendar period.

* * *

§ 25.2502–1 Rate of tax.

(a) Computation of tax. The rate of tax is determined by the total of all gifts made by the donor during the calendar period and all the preceding calendar periods since June 6, 1932. See § 25.2502–1(c)(1) for the definition of "calendar period" and § 25.2502–1(c)(2) for the definition of "preceding calendar periods." The following six steps are to be followed in computing the tax:

(1) First step. Ascertain the amount of the "taxable gifts" (as defined in § 25.2503–1) for the calendar period for which the return is being prepared.

(2) Second step. Ascertain "the aggregate sum of the taxable gifts for each of the preceding calendar periods" (as defined in § 25.2504–1), considering only those gifts made after June 6, 1932.

(3) Third step. Ascertain the total amount of the taxable gifts, which is the sum of the amounts determined in the first and second steps. See § 25.2702–6 for an adjustment to the total amount of an individual's taxable gifts where the individual's current taxable gifts include the transfer of certain interests in trust that were previously valued under the provisions of section 2702.

(4) Fourth step. Compute the tentative tax on the total amount of taxable gifts (as determined in the third step) using the rate schedule in effect at the time the gift (for which the return is being filed) is made.

(5) Fifth step. Compute the tentative tax on the aggregate sum of the taxable gifts for each of the preceding calendar periods (as determined in the second step), using the same rate schedule set forth in the fourth step of this paragraph (a).

(6) Sixth step. Subtract the amount determined in the fifth step from the amount determined in the fourth step. The amount remaining is the gift tax for the calendar period for which the return is being prepared.

(b) Rate of tax. The tax is computed in accordance with the rate schedule in effect at the time the gift was made as set forth in section 2001(c) or corresponding provisions of prior law.

(c) Definitions.(1) The term "calendar period" means:

(i) Each calendar year for the calendar years 1932 (but only that portion of such year after June 6, 1932) through 1970;

(ii) Each calendar quarter for the first calendar quarter of the calendar year 1971 through the last calendar quarter of calendar year 1981; or

(iii) Each calendar year for the calendar year 1982 and each succeeding calendar year.

(2) The term "preceding calendar periods" means all calendar periods ending prior to the calendar period for which the tax is being computed.

(d) Examples. The following examples illustrate the application of this section with respect to gifts made by citizens or residents of the United States:

* * *

Example (6). A makes gifts (other than gifts of future interests in property) during the calendar year 1982 of $160,000 to B and

*Omitted

$100,000 to C. Two exclusions of $10,000 each are allowable, in accordance with the provisions of section 2503(b), which results in taxable gifts for 1982 of $240,000. In the first calendar quarter of 1978, A made taxable gifts totaling $100,000 on which gift tax was paid. For the calendar year 1969, A made taxable gifts totaling $50,000. The full amount of A's specific exemption provided under section 2521, which was in effect at the time, was claimed and allowed in 1968. The computation of the gift tax for the calendar period 1982 (following the steps set forth in paragraph (a) of this section) is shown below.

(1) Amount of taxable gifts for the calendar year 1982, $240,000.

(2) Total amount of taxable gifts for preceding calendar periods ($100,000 + $50,000), $150,000.

(3) Total taxable gifts, $390,000.

(4) Tax computed on item 3 (in accordance with the rate schedule in effect for the year 1982), $118,400.

(5) Tax computed on item 2 (using same rate schedule), $38,800.

(6) Tax for year 1982 (Item 4 minus item 5), $79,600.

§ 25.2502–2 Donor primarily liable for tax.

Section 2502(d)* provides that the donor shall pay the tax. If the donor dies before the tax is paid the amount of the tax is a debt due the United States from the decedent's estate and his executor or administrator is responsible for its payment out of the estate. (See § 25.6151–1 for the time and place for paying the tax.) If there is no duly qualified executor or administrator, the heirs, legatees, devisees, and distributees are liable for and required to pay the tax to the extent of the value of their inheritances, bequests, devises, or distributive shares of the donor's estate. If a husband and wife effectively signify consent, under section 2513, to have gifts made to a third party during any "calendar period" (as defined in § 25.2502–1(c)(1)) considered as made one-half by each, the liability with respect to the gift tax of each spouse for that calendar period is joint and several (see § 25.2513–4). As to the personal liability of the donee, see paragraph (b) of § 301.6324–1 of this chapter (Regulations on Procedure and Administration). As to the personal liability of the executor or administrator, see section 3467 of the Revised Statutes (31 U.S.C. 192), which reads as follows:

*Editorial comment: See Sec. 2502(c) rather than Sec. 2502(d).

Every executor, administrator, or assignee, or other person, who pays, in whole or in part, any debt due by the person or estate for whom or for which he acts before he satisfies and pays the debts due to the United States from such person or estate, shall become answerable in his own person and estate to the extent of such payments for the debts so due to the United States, or for so much thereof as may remain due and unpaid.

As used in such section 3467, the word "debt" includes a beneficiary's distributive share of an estate. Thus if an executor pays a debt due by the estate which is being administered by him or distributes any portion of the estate before there is paid all of the gift tax which he has a duty to pay, the executor is personally liable, to the extent of the payment or distribution, for so much of the gift tax as remains due and unpaid.

§ 25.2503–1 General definition of "taxable gifts" and of "total amount of gifts."

The term "taxable gifts" means the "total amount of gifts" made by the donor during the "calendar period" (as defined in § 25.2502–1(c)(1)) less the deductions provided for in sections * * * 2522, and 2523 * * *, charitable, etc., gifts and the marital deduction, respectively. The term "total amount of gifts" means the sum of the values of the gifts made during the calendar period less the amounts excludable under section 2503(b). See § 25.2503–2. The entire value of any gift of a future interest in property must be included in the total amount of gifts for the calendar period in which the gift is made. See § 25.2503–3.

§ 25.2503–2 Exclusions from gifts.

(a) Gifts made after December 31, 1981. Except as provided in paragraph (f) of this section (involving gifts to a noncitizen spouse), the first $10,000** of gifts made to any one donee during calendar year 1982 or any calendar year thereafter, except gifts of future interests in property as defined in §§ 25.2503–3 and 25.2503–4, is excluded in determining the total amount of gifts for the calendar year. In the case of a gift in trust, the beneficiary of the trust is the donee.

* * *

§ 25.2503–3 Future interests in property.

(a) No part of the value of a gift of a future interest may be excluded in determining the total

**Editorial comment: The $10,000 amount is subject to indexing. For 2012, the indexed amount is $13,000 and for 2013, the indexed amount is $14,000.

amount of gifts made during the "calendar period" (as defined in § 25.2502–1(c)(1)). "Future interest" is a legal term, and includes reversions, remainders, and other interests or estates, whether vested or contingent, and whether or not supported by a particular interest or estate, which are limited to commence in use, possession, or enjoyment at some future date or time. The term has no reference to such contractual rights as exist in a bond, note (though bearing no interest until maturity), or in a policy of life insurance, the obligations of which are to be discharged by payments in the future. But a future interest or interests in such contractual obligations may be created by the limitations contained in a trust or other instrument of transfer used in effecting a gift.

(b) An unrestricted right to the immediate use, possession, or enjoyment of property or the income from property (such as a life estate or term certain) is a present interest in property. An exclusion is allowable with respect to a gift of such an interest (but not in excess of the value of the interest). If a donee has received a present interest in property, the possibility that such interest may be diminished by the transfer of a greater interest in the same property to the donee through the exercise of a power is disregarded in computing the value of the present interest, to the extent that no part of such interest will at any time pass to any other person (see example (4) of paragraph (c) of this section). For an exception to the rule disallowing an exclusion for gifts of future interests in the case of certain gifts to minors, see § 25.2503–4.

(c) The operation of this section may be illustrated by the following examples:

Example (1). Under the terms of a trust created by A the trustee is directed to pay the net income to B, so long as B shall live. The trustee is authorized in his discretion to withhold payments of income during any period he deems advisable and add such income to the trust corpus. Since B's right to receive the income payments is subject to the trustee's discretion, it is not a present interest and no exclusion is allowable with respect to the transfer in trust.

Example (2). C transfers certain insurance policies on his own life to a trust created for the benefit of D. Upon C's death the proceeds of the policies are to be invested and the net income therefrom paid to D during his lifetime. Since the income payments to D will not begin until after C's death the transfer in trust represents a gift of a future interest in property against which no exclusion is allowable.

Example (3). Under the terms of a trust created by E the net income is to be distributed to E's three children in such shares as the trustee, in his uncontrolled discretion deems advisable. While the terms of the trust provide that all of the net income is to be distributed, the amount of income any one of the three beneficiaries will receive rests entirely within the trustee's discretion and cannot be presently ascertained. Accordingly, no exclusions are allowable with respect to the transfers to the trust.

Example (4). Under the terms of a trust the net income is to be paid to F for life, with the remainder payable to G on F's death. The trustee has the uncontrolled power to pay over the corpus to F at any time. Although F's present right to receive the income may be terminated, no other person has the right to such income interest. Accordingly, the power in the trustee is disregarded in determining the value of F's present interest. The power would not be disregarded to the extent that the trustee during F's life could distribute corpus to persons other than F.

Example (5). The corpus of a trust created by J consists of certain real property, subject to a mortgage. The terms of the trust provide that the net income from the property is to be used to pay the mortgage. After the mortgage is paid in full the net income is to be paid to K during his lifetime. Since K's right to receive the income payments will not begin until after the mortgage is paid in full the transfer in trust represents a gift of a future interest in property against which no exclusion is allowable.

Example (6). L pays premiums on a policy of insurance on his life, all the incidents of ownership in the policy (including the right to surrender the policy) are vested in M. The payment of premiums by L constitutes a gift of a present interest in property.

§ 25.2503–4 Transfer for the benefit of a minor.

(a) Section 2503(c) provides that no part of a transfer for the benefit of a donee who has not attained the age of 21 years on the date of the gift will be considered a gift of a future interest in property if the terms of the transfer satisfy all of the following conditions:

(1) Both the property itself and its income may be expended by or for the benefit of the donee before he attains the age of 21 years;

(2) Any portion of the property and its income not disposed of under subparagraph (1) of this paragraph will pass to the donee when he attains the age of 21 years; and

(3) Any portion of the property and its income not disposed of under subparagraph (1) of this paragraph will be payable either to the estate of the donee or as he may appoint under a general power of appointment as defined in section 2514(c) if he dies before attaining the age of 21 years.

(b) Either a power of appointment exercisable by the donee by will or a power of appointment exercisable by the donee during his lifetime will satisfy the conditions set forth in paragraph (a)(3) of this section. However, if the transfer is to qualify for the exclusion under this section, there must be no restrictions of substance (as distinguished from formal restrictions of the type described in paragraph (g)(4) of § 25.2523(e)–1 by the terms of the instrument of transfer on the exercise of the power by the donee. However, if the minor is given a power of appointment exercisable during lifetime or is given a power of appointment exercisable by will, the fact that under the local law a minor is under a disability to exercise an *inter vivos* power or to execute a will does not cause the transfer to fail to satisfy the conditions of section 2503(c). Further, a transfer does not fail to satisfy the conditions of section 2503 (c) by reason of the mere fact that—

(1) There is left to the discretion of a trustee the determination of the amounts, if any, of the income or property to be expended for the benefit of the minor and the purpose for which the expenditure is to be made, provided there are no substantial restrictions under the terms of the trust instrument on the exercise of such discretion;

(2) The donee, upon reaching age 21, has the right to extend the term of the trust; or

(3) The governing instrument contains a disposition of the property or income not expended during the donee's minority to persons other than the donee's estate in the event of the default of appointment by the donee.

(c) A gift to a minor which does not satisfy the requirements of section 2503(c) may be either a present or a future interest under the general rules of § 25.2503–3. Thus, for example, a transfer of property in trust with income required to be paid annually to a minor beneficiary and corpus to be distributed to him upon his attaining the age of 21 is a gift of a present interest with respect to the right to income but is a gift of a future interest with respect to the right to corpus.

§ 25.2503–6 Exclusion for certain qualified transfer for tuition or medical expenses.

(a) In general. Section 2503(e) provides that any qualified transfer after December 31, 1981, shall not be treated as a transfer of property by gift for purposes of chapter 12 of subtitle B of the Code. Thus, a qualified transfer on behalf of any individual is excluded in determining the total amount of gifts in calendar year 1982 and subsequent years. This exclusion is available in addition to the $10,000 annual gift tax exclusion. Furthermore, an exclusion for a qualified transfer is permitted without regard to the relationship between the donor and the donee.

(b) Qualified transfers—(1) Definition. For purposes of this paragraph, the term "qualified transfer" means any amount paid on behalf of an individual—

(i) As tuition to a qualifying educational organization for the education or training of that individual, or

(ii) To any person who provides medical care with respect to that individual as payment for the qualifying medical expenses arising from such medical care.

(2) Tuition expenses. For purposes of paragraph (b)(1)(i) of this section, a qualifying educational organization is one which normally maintains a regular faculty and curriculum and normally has a regularly enrolled body of pupils or students in attendance at the place where its educational activities are regularly carried on. See section 170(b)(1)(A)(ii) and the regulations thereunder. The unlimited exclusion is permitted for tuition expenses of full-time or part-time students paid directly to the qualifying educational organization providing the education. No unlimited exclusion is permitted for amounts paid for books, supplies, dormitory fees, board, or other similar expenses which do not constitute direct tuition costs.

(3) Medical expenses. For purposes of paragraph (b)(1)(ii) of this section, qualifying medical expenses are limited to those expenses defined in section 213(d) * * * and include expenses incurred for the diagnosis, cure, mitigation, treatment or prevention of disease, or for the purpose of affecting any structure or function of the body or for transportation primarily for and essential to medical care. In addition, the unlimited exclusion from the gift tax includes amounts paid for medical insurance on behalf of any individual. The unlimited exclusion from the gift tax does not apply to amounts paid for medical care that are reimbursed by the donee's insurance. Thus, if payment for a medical expense is reimbursed by the donee's insurance company, the donor's payment for that expense, to the extent of the reimbursement amount, is not eligible for the unlimited exclusion from the gift tax and the gift is treated as having been made on the date the reimbursement is received by the donee.

(c) Examples. The provisions of paragraph (b) of this section may be illustrated by the following examples.

Example (1). In 1982, A made a tuition payment directly to a foreign university on behalf of B. A had no legal obligation to make this payment. The foreign university is described in section 170(b)(1)(A)(ii) of the Code. A's tuition payment is exempt from the gift tax under section 2503(e) of the Code.

Example (2). A transfers $100,000 to a trust the provisions of which state that the funds are to be used for tuition expenses incurred by A's grandchildren. A's transfer to the trust is a completed gift for Federal gift tax purposes and is not a direct transfer to an educational organization as provided in paragraph (b)(2) of this section and does not qualify for the unlimited exclusion from gift tax under section 2503(e).

Example (3). C was seriously injured in an automobile accident in 1982. D, who is unrelated to C, paid C's various medical expenses by checks made payable to the physician. D also paid the hospital for C's hospital bills. These medical and hospital expenses were types described in section 213 of the Code and were not reimbursed by insurance or otherwise. Because the medical and hospital bills paid in 1982 for C were medical expenses within the meaning of section 213 of the Code, and since they were paid directly by D to the person rendering the medical care, they are not treated as transfers subject to the gift tax.

Example (4). Assume the same facts as in example (2) except that instead of making the payments directly to the medical service provided, D reimbursed C for the medical expenses which C had previously paid. The payments made by D to C do not qualify for the exclusion under section 2503(e) of the Code and are subject to the gift tax on the date the reimbursement is received by C to the extent the reimbursement and all other gifts from D to C during the year of the reimbursement exceed the $10,000 annual exclusion provided in section 2503(b).

§ 25.2504–1 Taxable gifts for preceding calendar periods.

(a) In order to determine the correct gift tax liability for any calendar period it is necessary to ascertain the correct amount, if any, of the aggregate sum of the taxable gifts for each of the "preceding calendar periods" (as defined in § 25.2502–l(c)(2)). See paragraph (a) of § 25.2502–1. The term "aggregate sum of the taxable gifts for each of the preceding calendar periods" means the correct aggregate of such gifts, not necessarily that returned for those calendar periods and in respect of which tax was paid. All transfers that constituted gifts in prior calendar periods under the laws, including the provisions of law relating to exclusions from gifts, in effect at the time the transfers were made are included in determining the amount of taxable gifts for preceding calendar periods. The deductions other than for the specific exemption (see paragraph (b) of this section) allowed by the laws in effect at the time the transfers were made also are taken into account in determining the aggregate sum of the taxable gifts for preceding calendar periods. (The allowable exclusion from a gift is $5,000 for years before 1939, $4,000 for the calendar years 1939 through 1942, $3,000 for the calendar years 1943 through 1981, and $10,000 thereafter.)

(b) In determining the aggregate sum of the taxable gifts for the "preceding calendar periods" (as defined in § 25.2502–1(c)(2)), the total of the amounts allowed as deductions for the specific exemption, under section 2521 (as in effect prior to its repeal by the Tax Reform Act of 1976) and the corresponding provisions of prior laws, shall not exceed $30,000. Thus, if the only prior gifts by a donor were made in 1940 and 1941 (at which time the specific exemption allowable was $40,000), and if in the donor's returns for those years the donor claimed deductions totaling $40,000 for the specific exemption and reported taxable gifts totaling $110,000, then in determining the aggregate sum of the taxable gifts for the preceding calendar periods, the deductions for the specific exemption cannot exceed $30,000, and the donor's taxable gifts for such periods will be $120,000 (instead of the $110,000 reported on the donor's returns). (The allowable deduction for the specific exemption was $50,000 for calendar years before 1936, $40,000 for calendar years 1936 through 1942, and $30,000 for 1943 through 1976.)

(c) If the donor and the donor's spouse consented to have gifts made to third parties considered as made one-half by each spouse, pursuant to the provisions of section 2513 or section 1000(f) of the Internal Revenue Code of 1939 (which corresponds to Section 2513), these provisions shall be taken into account in determining the aggregate sum of the taxable gifts for the preceding calendar periods (under paragraph (a) of this section).

(d) If interpretations of the gift tax law in preceding calendar periods resulted in the erroneous inclusion of property for gift tax purposes that should have been excluded, or the erroneous exclusion of property that should have been included, adjustments must be made in order to arrive at the correct aggregate of taxable gifts for the preceding calendar periods (under paragraph (a) of this section). * * *

§ 25.2504–2 Determination of gifts for preceding calendar periods.

(a) Gifts made before August 6, 1997. If the time has expired within which a tax may be assessed under chapter 12 of the Internal Revenue Code (or under corresponding provisions of prior laws) on the transfer of property by gift made during a preceding calendar period, as defined in §25.2502–1 (c)(2), the gift was made prior to August 6, 1997, and a tax has been assessed or paid for such prior calendar period, the value of the gift, for purposes of arriving at the correct amount of the taxable gifts for the preceding calendar periods (as defined under §25.2504–1(a)), is the value used in computing the tax for the last preceding calendar period for which a tax was assessed or paid under chapter 12 of the Internal Revenue Code or the corresponding provisions of prior laws. However, this rule does not apply where no tax was paid or assessed for the prior calendar period. Furthermore, this rule does not apply to adjustments involving issues other than valuation. See §25.2504–1(d).

(b) Gifts made or section 2701(d) taxable events occurring after August 5, 1997. If the time has expired under section 6501 within which a gift tax may be assessed under chapter 12 of the Internal Revenue Code (or under corresponding provisions of prior laws) on the transfer of property by gift made during a preceding calendar period, as defined in §25.2502–1(c)(2), or with respect to an increase in taxable gifts required under section 2701(d) and §25.2701–4, and the gift was made, or the section 2701(d) taxable event occurred, after August 5, 1997, the amount of the taxable gift or the amount of the increase in taxable gifts, for purposes of determining the correct amount of taxable gifts for the preceding calendar periods (as defined in §25.2504–1(a)), is the amount that is finally determined for gift tax purposes (within the meaning of §20.2001–1(c) of this chapter) and such amount may not be thereafter adjusted. The rule of this paragraph (b) applies to adjustments involving all issues relating to the gift including valuation issues and legal issues involving the interpretation of the gift tax law. For purposes of determining if the time has expired within which a gift tax may be assessed, see §301.6501(c)–1(e) and (f) of this chapter.

(c) Examples. The following examples illustrate the rules of paragraphs (a) and (b) of this section:

Example (1).(i) Facts. In 1996, A transferred closely-held stock in trust for the benefit of B, A's child. A timely filed a Federal gift tax return reporting the 1996 transfer to B. No gift tax was assessed or paid as a result of the gift tax annual exclusion and the application of A's available unified credit. In 2001, A transferred additional closely-held stock to the trust. A's Federal gift tax return reporting the 2001 transfer was timely filed and the transfer was adequately disclosed under §301.6501(c)–1(f)(2) of this chapter. In computing the amount of taxable gifts, A claimed annual exclusions with respect to the transfers in 1996 and 2001. In 2003, A transfers additional property to B and timely files a Federal gift tax return reporting the gift.

(ii) Application of the rule limiting adjustments to prior gifts. Under section 2504(c), in determining A's 2003 gift tax liability, the amount of A's 1996 gift can be adjusted for purposes of computing prior taxable gifts, since that gift was made prior to August 6, 1997, and therefore, the provisions of the paragraph (a) of this section apply. Adjustments can be made with respect to the valuation of the gift and legal issues presented (for example, the availability of the annual exclusion with respect to the gift). However, A's 2001 transfer was adequately disclosed on a timely filed gift tax return and, thus, under paragraph (b) of this section, the amount of the 2001 taxable gift by A may not be adjusted (either with respect to the valuation of the gift or any legal issue) for purposes of computing prior taxable gifts in determining A's 2003 gift tax liability.

Example (2).(i) Facts. In 1996, A transferred closely-held stock to B, A's child. A timely filed a Federal gift tax return reporting the 1996 transfer to B and paid gift tax on the value of the gift reported on the return. On August 1, 1997, A transferred additional closely-held stock to B in exchange for a promissory note signed by B. Also, on September 10, 1997, A transferred closely-held stock to C, A's other child. On April 15, 1998, A timely filed a gift tax return for 1997 reporting the September 10, 1997, transfer to C and, under §301.6501(c)–1(f)(2) of this chapter, adequately disclosed that transfer and paid gift tax with respect to the transfer. However, A believed that the transfer to B on August 1, 1997, was for full and adequate consideration and A did not report the transfer to B on the 1997 Federal gift tax return. In 2002, A transfers additional property to B and timely files a Federal gift tax return reporting the gift.

(ii) Application of the rule limiting adjustments to prior gifts. Under section 2504(c), in determining A's 2002 gift tax liability, the value of A's 1996 gift cannot be adjusted for purposes of computing the value of prior taxable gifts, since that gift was made prior to August 6, 1997, and a timely filed Federal gift tax return was filed on which a gift tax was assessed and paid. However, A's prior taxable gifts can be adjusted to reflect the August 1, 1997, transfer because, although a gift tax return for 1997 was timely filed and gift tax was paid, under §301.6501(c)–1(f) of this chapter the period for assessing gift tax with respect to the August 1, 1997, transfer did not commence to run since the transfer was not adequately disclosed on the 1997 gift tax return. Accordingly, a gift tax may be assessed with respect to the August 1, 1997, transfer and the amount of the gift would be reflected in prior taxable gifts for purposes of computing A's gift tax liability for 2002. A's September 10, 1997, transfer to C was adequately disclosed on a timely filed gift tax return and, thus, under paragraph (b) of this section, the amount of the September 10, 1997, taxable gift by A may not be adjusted for purposes of computing prior taxable gifts in determining A's 2002 gift tax liability.

Example (3).(i) Facts. In 1994, A transferred closely-held stock to B and C, A's children. A timely filed a Federal gift tax return reporting the 1994 transfers to B and C and paid gift tax on the value of the gifts reported on the return. Also in 1994, A transferred closely-held stock to B in exchange for a bona fide promissory note signed by B. A believed that the transfer to B in exchange for the promissory note was for full and adequate consideration and A did not report that transfer to B on the 1994 Federal gift tax return. In 2002, A transfers additional property to B and timely files a Federal gift tax return reporting the gift.

(ii) Application of the rule limiting adjustments to prior gifts. Under section 2504(c), in determining A's 2002 gift tax liability, the value of A's 1994 gifts cannot be adjusted for purposes of computing prior taxable gifts because those gifts were made prior to August 6, 1997, and a timely filed Federal gift tax return was filed with respect to which a gift tax was assessed and paid, and the period of limitations on assessment has expired. The provisions of paragraph (a) of this section apply to the 1994 transfers. However, for purposes of determining A's adjusted taxable gifts in computing A's estate tax liability, the gifts may be adjusted. See §20.2001–1(a) of this chapter.

(d) Effective dates. Paragraph (a) of this section applies to transfers of property by gift made prior to August 6, 1997. Paragraphs (b) and (c) of this section apply to transfers of property by gift made after August 5, 1997, if the gift tax return for the calendar period in which the transfer is reported is filed after December 3, 1999.

TRANSFERS

§ 25.2511–1 Transfers in general.

(a) The gift tax applies to a transfer by way of gift whether the transfer is in trust or otherwise, whether the gift is direct or indirect, and whether the property is real or personal, tangible or intangible. For example, a taxable transfer may be effected by the creation of a trust, the forgiving of a debt, the assignment of a judgment, the assignment of the benefits of an insurance policy, or the transfer of cash, certificates of deposit, or Federal, State or municipal bonds. Statutory provisions which exempt bonds, notes, bills and certificates of indebtedness of the Federal Government or its agencies and the interest thereon from taxation are not applicable to the gift tax, since the gift tax is an excise tax on the transfer, and is not a tax on the subject of the gift.

* * *

(c) (1) The gift tax also applies to gifts indirectly made. Thus, any transaction in which an interest in property is gratuitously passed or conferred upon another, regardless of the means or device employed, constitutes a gift subject to tax. See further § 25.2512–8 relating to transfers for insufficient consideration. However, in the case of a taxable transfer creating an interest in the person disclaiming made after December 31, 1976, this paragraph (c)(1) shall not apply to the donee if, as a result of a qualified disclaimer by the donee, the property passes to a different donee. Nor shall it apply to a donor if, as a result of a qualified disclaimer by the donee, a completed transfer of an interest in property is not effected. See section 2518 and the corresponding regulations for rules relating to a qualified disclaimer.

(2) In the case of taxable transfers creating an interest in the person disclaiming made before January 1, 1977, where the law governing the administration of the decedent's estate gives a beneficiary, heir, or next-of-kin a right completely and unqualifiedly to refuse to accept ownership of property transferred from a decedent (whether the transfer is effected by the decedent's will or by the law of descent and distribution), a refusal to accept ownership does not constitute the making of a gift if the refusal is made within a reasonable time after knowledge of the existence of the transfer. The refusal must be unequivocal and effective under the local law. There can be no refusal of ownership of property after its acceptance. In the absence of the facts to the contrary, if a person fails to refuse to accept a transfer to him of ownership of a decedent's property within a reasonable time after learning of the existence of the transfer, he will be presumed to have accepted the property. Where the local law does not permit such a refusal, any disposition by the beneficiary, heir, or next-of-kin whereby ownership is transferred gratuitously to another constitutes the making of a gift by the beneficiary, heir, or next-of-kin. In any case where a refusal is purported to relate to only a part of the property, the determination of whether or not there has been a complete and unqualified refusal to accept ownership will depend on all of the facts and circumstances in each particular case, taking into account the recognition and effectiveness of such a purported refusal under the local law. In illustration, if Blackacre was devised to A under the decedent's will (which also provided that all lapsed legacies and devises shall go to B, the residuary beneficiary), and under the local law A could refuse to accept ownership in which case title would be considered as never having passed to A, A's refusal to accept Blackacre within a reasonable time of learning of the devise will not constitute the making of a gift by A to B. However, if a decedent who owned Greenacre died intestate with C and D as his only heirs, and under local law the heir of a decedent cannot, by refusal to accept, prevent himself from becoming an owner of intestate property, any gratuitous disposition by C (by whatever term it is known) whereby he gives up his ownership of a portion of Greenacre and D acquires the whole thereof constitutes the making of a gift by C to D.

(d) If a joint income tax return is filed by a husband and wife for a taxable year, the payment by one spouse of all or part of the income tax liability for such year is not treated as resulting in a transfer that is subject to gift tax. The same rule is applicable to the payment of gift tax for a "calendar period" (as defined in § 25.2502–1(c)(1)) in the case of a husband and wife who have consented to have the gifts made considered as made half by each of them in accordance with the provisions of section 2513.

(e) If a donor transfers by gift less than his entire interest in property, the gift tax is applicable to the interest transferred. The tax is applicable, for example, to the transfer of an undivided half interest in property, or to the transfer of a life estate when the grantor retains the remainder interest, or vice versa.

However, if the donor's retained interest is not susceptible of measurement on the basis of generally accepted valuation principles, the gift tax is applicable to the entire value of the property subject to the gift. Thus if a donor, aged 65 years, transfers a life estate in property to A, aged 25 years, with remainder to A's issue, or in default of issue, with reversion to the donor, the gift tax will normally be applicable to the entire value of the property.

(f) If a donor is the owner of only a limited interest in property, and transfers his entire interest, the interest is in every case to be valued by the rules set forth in §§ 25.2512–1 through 25.2512–7. If the interest is a remainder or reversion or other future interest, it is to be valued on the basis of actuarial principles set forth in § 25.2512–5, or if it is not susceptible of valuation in that manner, in accordance with the principles set forth in § 25.2512–1.

(g) (1) Donative intent on the part of the transferor is not an essential element in the application of the gift tax to the transfer. The application of the tax is based on the objective facts of the transfer and the circumstances under which it is made, rather than on the subjective motives of the donor. However, there are certain types of transfers to which the tax is not applicable. It is applicable only to a transfer of a beneficial interest in property. It is not applicable to a transfer of bare legal title to a trustee. A transfer by a trustee of trust property in which he has no beneficial interest does not constitute a gift by the trustee (but such a transfer may constitute a gift by the creator of the trust, if until the transfer he had the power to change the beneficiaries by amending or revoking the trust). The gift tax is not applicable to a transfer for a full and adequate consideration in money or money's worth, or to ordinary business transactions, described in § 25.2512–8.

(2) If a trustee has a beneficial interest in trust property, a transfer of the property by the trustee is not a taxable transfer if it is made pursuant to a fiduciary power the exercise or nonexercise of which is limited by a reasonably fixed or ascertainable standard which is set forth in the trust instrument. A clearly measurable standard under which the holder of a power is legally accountable is such a standard for this purpose. For instance, a power to distribute corpus for the education, support, maintenance, or health of the beneficiary; for his reasonable support and comfort; to enable him to maintain his accustomed standard of living; or to meet an emergency, would be such a standard. However, a power to distribute corpus for the pleasure, desire, or happiness of a beneficiary is not such a standard. The entire context of a provision of a trust instrument granting a power must be considered in determining whether the power is limited by a reasonably definite standard. For example, if a trust instrument provides that the determination of the trustee shall be conclusive with respect to the exercise or nonexercise of a power, the power is not limited by a reasonably definite standard. However, the fact that the governing instrument is phrased in discretionary terms is not in itself an indication that no such standard exists.

(h) The following are examples of transactions resulting in taxable gifts and in each case it is assumed that the transfers were not made for an adequate and full consideration in money or money's worth:

(1) A transfer of property by a corporation to B is a gift to B from the stockholders of the corporation. If B himself is a stockholder, the transfer is a gift to him from the other stockholders but only to the extent it exceeds B's own interest in such amount as a shareholder. A transfer of property by B to a corporation generally represents gifts by B to the other individual shareholders of the corporation to the extent of their proportionate interests in the corporation. However, there may be an exception to this rule, such as a transfer made by an individual to a charitable, public, political or similar organization which may constitute a gift to the organization as a single entity, depending upon the facts and circumstances in the particular case.

(2) The transfer of property to B if there is imposed upon B the obligation of paying a commensurate annuity to C is a gift to C.

(3) The payment of money or the transfer of property to B in consideration of B's promise to render a service to C is a gift to C, or to both B and C, depending on whether the service to be rendered to C is or is not an adequate and full consideration in money or money's worth for that which is received by B. See section 2512(b) and the regulations thereunder.

(4) If A creates a joint bank account for himself and B (or a similar type of ownership by which A can regain the entire fund without B's consent), there is a gift to B when B draws upon the account for his own benefit, to the extent of the amount drawn without any obligation to account for a part of the proceeds to A. Similarly, if A purchases a United States savings bond registered as payable to "A or B," there is a gift to B when B surrenders the bond for cash without any obligation to account for a part of the proceeds to A.

(5) If A with his own funds purchases property and has the title conveyed to himself and B as joint owners, with rights of survivorship (other than a joint ownership described in example (4)) but which rights may be defeated by either party severing his interest, there is a gift to B in the amount of half the value of the property. However, see § 25.2515–1 relative to the creation of a joint tenancy (or tenancy by the entirety) between husband and wife in real property with rights of survivorship which, unless the donor elects otherwise is not considered as a transfer includible for Federal gift tax purposes at the time of the creation of the joint tenancy. See § 25.2515–2 with respect to determining the extent to which the creation of a tenancy by the entirety constitutes a taxable gift if the donor elects to have the creation of the tenancy so treated. See also § 25.2523(d)–1 with respect to the marital deduction allowed in the case of the creation of a joint tenancy or a tenancy by the entirety.

(6) If A is possessed of a vested remainder interest in property, subject to being divested only in the event he should fail to survive one or more individuals or the happening of some other event, an irrevocable assignment of all or any part of his interest would result in a transfer includible for Federal gift tax purposes. See especially paragraph (e) of § 25.2512–5 or paragraph (e) of § 25.2512–9, whichever is applicable, for the valuation of an interest of this type.

(7) If A, without retaining a power to revoke the trust or to change the beneficial interests therein, transfers property in trust whereby B is to receive the income for life and at his death the trust is to terminate and the corpus is to be returned to A, provided A survives, but if A predeceases B the corpus is to pass to C, A has made a gift equal to the total value of the property less the value of his retained interest. See paragraph (e) of § 25.2512–5 or paragraph (e) of § 25.2512–9, whichever is applicable, for the valuation of the donor's retained interest.

(8) If the insured purchases a life insurance policy, or pays a premium on a previously issued policy, the proceeds of which are payable to a beneficiary or beneficiaries other than his estate, and with respect to which the insured retains no reversionary interest in himself or his estate and no power to revest the economic benefits in himself or his estate or to change the beneficiaries or their proportionate benefits (or if the insured relinquishes by assignment, by designation of a new beneficiary or otherwise, every such power that was retained in a previously issued policy), the insured has made a gift of the value of the policy, or to the extent of the premium paid, even though the right of the assignee or beneficiary to receive the benefits is conditioned upon his surviving the insured. For the valuation of life insurance policies see § 25.2512–6.

(9) Where property held by a husband and wife as community property is used to purchase insurance upon the husband's life and a third person is revocably designated as beneficiary and under the State law the husband's death is considered to make absolute the transfer by the wife, there is a gift by the wife at the time of the husband's death of half the amount of the proceeds of such insurance.

(10) If under a pension plan (pursuant to which he has an unqualified right to an annuity) an employee has an option to take either a retirement annuity for himself alone or a smaller annuity for himself with a survivorship annuity payable to his wife, an irrevocable election by the employee to take the reduced annuity in order that an annuity may be paid, after the employee's death, to his wife results in the making of a gift. However, see section 2517 and the regulations thereunder for the exemption from gift tax of amounts attributable to employers' contributions under qualified plans and certain other contracts.

§ 25.2511–2 Cessation of donor's dominion and control.

(a) The gift tax is not imposed upon the receipt of the property by the donee, nor is it necessarily determined by the measure of enrichment resulting to the donee from the transfer, nor is it conditioned upon ability to identify the donee at the time of the transfer. On the contrary, the tax is a primary and personal liability of the donor, is an excise upon his act of making the transfer, is measured by the value of the property passing from the donor, and attaches regardless of the fact that the identity of the donee may not then be known or ascertainable.

(b) As to any property, or part thereof or interest therein, of which the donor has so parted with dominion and control as to leave in him no power to change its disposition, whether for his own benefit or for the benefit of another, the gift is complete. But if upon a transfer of property (whether in trust or otherwise) the donor reserves any power over its disposition, the gift may be wholly incomplete, or may be partially complete and partially incomplete, depending upon all the facts in the particular case. Accordingly, in every case of a transfer of property subject to a reserved power, the terms of the power must be examined and its scope determined. For example, if a donor transfers property to another in trust to pay the income to the donor or accumulate it in the discretion of the trustee, and the donor retains a testamentary power to appoint the remainder among his descendants, no portion of the transfer is a completed gift. On the other hand, if the donor had not retained the testamentary power of appointment, but instead provided that the remainder should go to X or his heirs, the entire transfer would be a completed gift. However, if the exercise of the trustee's power in favor of the grantor is limited by a fixed or ascertainable standard (see paragraph (g)(2) of § 25.2511–1), enforceable by or on behalf of the grantor, then the gift is incomplete to the extent of the ascertainable value of any rights thus retained by the grantor.

(c) A gift is incomplete in every instance in which a donor reserves the power to revest the beneficial title to the property in himself. A gift is also incomplete if and to the extent that a reserved power gives the donor the power to name new beneficiaries or to change the interests of the beneficiaries as between themselves unless the power is a fiduciary power limited by a fixed or ascertainable standard. Thus, if an estate for life is transferred but, by an exercise of a power, the estate may be terminated or cut down by the donor to one of less value, and without restriction upon the extent to which the estate may be so cut down, the transfer constitutes an incomplete gift. If in this example the power was confined to the right to cut down the estate for life to one for a term of five years, the certainty of an estate for not less than that term results in a gift to that extent complete.

(d) A gift is not considered incomplete, however, merely because the donor reserves the power to change the manner or time of enjoyment. Thus, the creation of a trust the income of which is to be paid annually to the donee for a period of years, the corpus being distributable to him at the end of the period, and the power reserved by the donor being limited to a right to require that, instead of the income being so payable, it should be accumulated and distributed with the corpus to the donee at the termination of the period, constitutes a completed gift.

(e) A donor is considered as himself having a power if it is exercisable by him in conjunction with any person not having a substantial adverse interest in the disposition of the transferred property or the income therefrom. A trustee, as such, is not a person having an adverse interest in the disposition of the trust property or its income.

(f) The relinquishment or termination of a power to change the beneficiaries of transferred property, occurring otherwise than by the death of the donor (the statute being confined to transfers by living donors), is regarded as the event that completes the gift and causes the tax to apply. For example, if A transfers property in trust for the benefit of B and C but reserves the power as trustee to change the proportionate interests of B and C, and if A thereafter has another person appointed trustee in place of himself, such later relinquishment of the power by A to the new trustee completes the gift of the transferred property, whether or not the new trustee has a substantial adverse interest. The receipt of income or of other enjoyment of the transferred property by the transferee or by the beneficiary (other than by the donor himself) during the interim between the making of the initial transfer and the relinquishment or termination of the power operates to free such income or other enjoyment from the power, and constitutes a gift of such income or of such other enjoyment taxable as of the "calendar period" (as defined in § 25.2502–1(c)(1)) of its receipt. If property is transferred in trust to pay the income to A for life with remainder to B, powers to distribute corpus to A, and to withhold income from A for future distribution to B, are powers to change the beneficiaries of the transferred property.

(g) If a donor transfers property to himself as trustee (or to himself and some other person, not possessing a substantial adverse interest, as trustees), and retains no beneficial interest in the trust property and no power over it except fiduciary powers, the exercise or nonexercise of which is limited by a fixed or ascertainable standard, to change the beneficiaries of the transferred property, the donor has made a completed gift and the entire value of the transferred property is subject to the gift tax.

(h) If a donor delivers a properly indorsed stock certificate to the donee or the donee's agent, the gift is completed for gift tax purposes on the date of delivery. If the donor delivers the certificate to his bank or broker as his agent, or to the issuing corporation or its transfer agent, for transfer into the name of the donee, the gift is completed on the date the stock is transferred on the books of the corporation.

(i) [Reserved]

(j) If the donor contends that a power is of such nature as to render the gift incomplete, and hence not subject to the tax as of the "calendar period" (as defined in § 25.2502–(l)(c)(l)) of the initial transfer, see §301.6501(c)(l)(f)(5).

* * *

§ 25.2512–0 Table of contents.

This section lists the section headings that appear in the regulations under section 2512.

Actuarial Tables Applicable Before May 1, 1989

§ 25.2512–1 Valuation of property; in general.

Section 2512 provides that if a gift is made in property, its value at the date of the gift shall be considered the amount of the gift. The value of the property is the price at which such property would change hands between a willing buyer and a willing seller, neither being under any compulsion to buy or to sell, and both having reasonable knowledge of relevant facts. The value of a particular item of property is not the price that a forced sale of the property would produce. Nor is the fair market value of an item of property the sale price in a market other than that in which such item is most commonly sold to the public, taking into account the location of the item wherever appropriate. Thus, in the case of an item of property made the subject of a gift, which is generally obtained by the public in the retail market, the fair market value of such an item of property is the price at which the item or a comparable item would be sold at retail. For example, the value of an automobile (an article generally obtained by the public in the retail market) which is the subject of a gift, is the price for which an automobile of the same or approximately the same description, make, model, age, condition, etc., could be purchased by a member of the general public and not the price for which the particular automobile of the donor would be purchased by a dealer in used automobiles. Examples of items of property which are generally sold to the public at retail may be found in § 25.2512–6. The value is generally to be determined by ascertaining as a basis the fair market value at the time of the gift of each unit of the property. For example, in the case of shares of stocks or bonds, such unit of property is generally a share or a bond. Property shall not be returned at the value at which it is assessed for local tax purposes unless that value represents the fair market value thereof on the date of the gift. All relevant facts and elements of value as of the time of the gift shall be considered. Where the subject of a gift is an interest in a business, the value of items of property in the inventory of the business generally should be reflected in the value of the business. For valuation of interests in businesses, see § 25.2512–3. See § 25.2512–2 and §§ 25.2512–4 through 25.2512–6 for further information concerning the valuation of other particular kinds of property. See section 2701 and the regulations at § 25.2701 for special rules for valuing transfers of an interest in a corporation or a partnership and for the treatment of unpaid qualified payments at the subsequent transfer of an applicable retained interest by the transferor or by an applicable family member. See section 2704(b) and the regulations at § 25.2704–2 for special valuation rules where an interest in property is subject to an applicable restriction.

§ 25.2512–2 Stocks and bonds.

(a) In general. The value of stocks and bonds is the fair market value per share or bond on the date of the gift.

(b) Based on selling prices. (1) In general, if there is a market for stocks or bonds, on a stock exchange, in an over-the-counter market or otherwise, the mean between the highest and lowest quoted selling prices on the date of the gift is the fair market value per share or bond. If there were no sales on the date of the gift but there were sales on dates within a reasonable period both before and after the date of the gift, the fair market value is determined by taking a weighted average of the means between the highest and lowest sales on the nearest date before and the nearest date after the date of the gift. The average is to be weighted inversely by the respective numbers of trading days between the selling dates and the date of the gift. If the stocks or bonds are listed on more than one exchange, the records of the exchange where the stocks or bonds are principally dealt in should be employed if such records are available in a generally available listing or publication of general circulation. In the event that such records are not so available and such stocks or bonds are listed on a composite listing of combined exchanges available in a generally available listing or publication of general circulation, the records of such combined exchanges should be employed. In valuing listed securities, the donor should be careful to consult accurate records to obtain values as of the date of the gift. If quotations of unlisted securities are obtained from brokers, or evidence as to their sale is obtained from the officers of the issuing companies, copies of letters furnishing such quotations or evidence of sale should be attached to the return.

(2) If it is established with respect to bonds for which there is a market on a stock exchange, that the highest and lowest selling prices are not available for the date of the gift in a generally available listing or publication of general circulation but that closing prices are so available, the fair market value per bond is the mean between the quoted closing selling price on the date of the gift and the quoted closing selling price on the trading day before the date of the gift. If there were no sales on the trading day before the date of the gift but there were sales on dates within a reasonable period before the date of the gift, the fair market value is determined by taking a weighted average of the quoted closing selling prices on the date of the gift and the nearest date before the date of the gift. The closing selling price for the date of the gift is to be weighted by the respective number of trading days between the previous selling date and the date of the gift. If there were no sales within a reasonable period before the date of the gift but there were sales on the date of the gift, the fair market value is the closing selling price on the date of the gift. If there were no sales on the date of the gift but there were sales within a reasonable period both before and after the date of the gift, the fair market value is determined by taking a weighted average of the quoted closing selling prices on the nearest date before and the nearest date after the date of the gift. The average is to be weighed inversely by the respective numbers of trading days between the selling dates and the date of the gift. If the bonds are listed on more than one exchange, the records of the exchange where the bonds are principally dealt in should be employed. In valuing listed securities, the donor should be careful to consult accurate records to obtain values as of the date of the gift.

* * *

(c) Based on bid and asked prices. If the provisions of paragraph (b) of this section are inapplicable because actual sales are not available during reasonable period beginning before and ending after the date of the gift, the fair market value may be determined by taking the mean between the bona fide bid and asked prices on the date of the gift, or if none, by taking a weighted average of the means between the bona fide bid and asked prices on the nearest trading date before and the nearest trading date after the date of the gift, if both such nearest dates are within a reasonable period. The average is to be determined in the manner described in paragraph (b) of this section.

(d) Where selling prices and bid and asked prices are not available for dates both before and after the date of gift. If the provisions of paragraphs (b) and (c) of this section are inapplicable because no actual sale prices or quoted bona fide bid and asked prices are available on a date within a reasonable period before the date of the gift, but such prices are available on a date within a reasonable period after the date of the gift, or vice versa, then the mean between the highest and lowest available sale prices or bid and asked prices may be taken as the value.

(e) Where selling prices or bid and asked prices do not represent fair market value. In cases in which it is established that the value per bond or share of any security determined on the basis of the selling or bid and asked prices as provided under paragraphs (b), (c), and (d) of this section does not represent the fair market value thereof, then some reasonable modification of the value determined on that basis or other relevant facts and elements of value shall be considered in determining fair market value. Where sales at or near the date of the gift are few or of a sporadic nature, such sales alone may not indicate fair market value. In certain exceptional cases, the size of the block of securities made the subject of each separate gift in relation to the number of shares changing hands in sales may be relevant in determining whether selling prices reflect the fair market value of the block of stock to be valued. If the donor can show that the block of stock to be valued, with reference to each separate gift, is so large in relation to the actual sales on the existing market that it could not be liquidated in a reasonable time without depressing the market, the price at which the block could be sold as such outside the usual market, as through an underwriter, may be a more accurate indication of value than market quotations. Complete data in support of any allowance claimed due to the size of the block of stock being valued should be submitted with the return. On the other hand, if the block of stock to be valued represents a controlling interest, either actual or effective, in a going business, the price at which other lots change hands may have little relation to its true value.

(f) Where selling prices or bid and asked prices are unavailable. If the provisions of paragraphs (b), (c), and (d) of this section are inapplicable because actual sale prices and bona fide bid and asked prices are lacking, then the fair market value is to be determined by taking the following factors into consideration:

(1) In the case of corporate or other bonds, the soundness of the security, the interest yield, the date of maturity, and other relevant factors; and

(2) In the case of shares of stock, the company's net worth, prospective earning power and dividend-paying capacity, and other relevant factors.

Some of the "other relevant factors" referred to in subparagraphs (1) and (2) of this paragraph are: The goodwill of the business; the economic outlook in the particular industry; the company's position in the industry and its management; the degree of control of the business represented by the block of stock to be valued; and the values of securities of corporations engaged in the same or similar lines of business which are listed on a stock exchange. However, the weight to be accorded such comparisons or any other evidentiary factors considered in the determination of a value depends upon the facts of each case. Complete financial and other data upon which the valuation is based should be submitted with the return, including copies of reports of any examinations of the company made by accountants, engineers, or any technical experts as of or near the date of the gift.

§ 25.2512–3 Valuation of interest in businesses.

(a) Care should be taken to arrive at an accurate valuation of any interest in a business which the donor transfers without an adequate and full consideration in money or money's worth. The fair market value of any interest in a business, whether a partnership or a proprietorship, is the net amount which a willing purchaser, whether an individual or a corporation, would pay for the interest to a willing seller, neither being under any compulsion to buy or to sell and both having reasonable knowledge of the relevant facts. The net value is determined on the basis of all relevant factors including—

(1) A fair appraisal as of the date of the gift of all the assets of the business, tangible and intangible, including good will;

(2) The demonstrated earning capacity of the business; and

(3) The other factors set forth in paragraph (f) of § 25.2512–2 relating to the valuation of corporate stock, to the extent applicable.

Special attention should be given to determining an adequate value of the good will of the business. Complete financial and other data upon which the valuation is based should be submitted with the return, including copies of reports of examinations of the business made by accountants, engineers, or any technical experts as of or near the date of the gift.

§ 25.2512–4 Valuation of notes.

The fair market value of notes, secured or unsecured, is presumed to be the amount of unpaid principal, plus accrued interest to the date of the gift, unless the donor establishes a lower value. Unless returned at face value, plus accrued interest, it must be shown by satisfactory evidence that the note is worth less than the unpaid amount (because of the interest rate, or date of maturity, or other cause), or that the note is uncollectible in part (by reason of the insolvency of the party or parties liable, or for other cause), and that the property, if any, pledged or mortgaged as security is insufficient to satisfy it.

§ 25.2512–5 Valuation of annuities, unitrust interests, interests for life or term of years, and remainder or reversionary interests.

(a) In general. Except as otherwise provided in paragraph (b) of this section and § 25.7520–3(b), the fair market value of annuities, unitrust interests, life estates, terms of years, remainders, and reversions transferred by gift is the present value of the interests determined under paragraph (d) of this section. Section 20.2031–7 of this chapter (Estate Tax Regulations) and related sections provide tables with standard actuarial factors and examples that illustrate how to use the tables to compute the present value of ordinary annuity, life and remainder interests in property. These sections also refer to standard and special actuarial factors that may be necessary to compute the present value of similar interests in more unusual fact situations. These factors and examples are also generally applicable for gift tax purposes in computing the values of taxable gifts.

(b) Commercial annuities and insurance contracts. The value of life insurance contracts and contracts for the payment of annuities issued by companies regularly engaged in their sale is determined under § 25.2512–6.

* * *

(e) Effective date. This section applies after April 30, 1999.

* * *

§ 25.2512–7 Effect of excise tax.

If jewelry, furs or other property, the purchase of which is subject to an excise tax, is purchased at retail by a taxpayer and made the subject of gifts within a reasonable time after purchase, the purchase price, including the excise tax, is considered to be the fair market value of the property on the date of the gift, in the absence of evidence that the market price of similar articles has increased or decreased in the meantime. Under other circumstances, the excise tax is taken into account in determining the fair market value of property to the extent, and only to the extent, that it affects the price at which the property would change hands between a willing buyer and a willing seller, as provided in § 25.2512–1.

§ 25.2512–8 Transfers for insufficient consideration.

Transfers reached by the gift tax are not confined to those only which, being without a valuable consideration, accord with the common law concept of gifts, but embrace as well sales, exchanges, and other dispositions of property for a consideration to the extent that the value of the property transferred by the donor exceeds the value in money or money's worth of the consideration given therefor. However, a sale, exchange, or other transfer of property made in the ordinary course of business (a transaction which is bona fide, at arm's length, and free from any donative intent), will be considered as made for an adequate and full consideration in money or money's worth. A consideration not reducible to a value in money or money's worth, as love and affection, promise of marriage, etc., is to be wholly disregarded, and the entire value of the property transferred constitutes the amount of the gift. Similarly, a relinquishment or promised relinquishment of dower or curtesy, or of a statutory estate created in lieu of dower or curtesy, or of other marital rights in the spouse's property or estate, shall not be considered to any extent a consideration "in money or money's worth." See, however, section 2516 and the regulations thereunder with respect to certain transfers incident to a divorce. See also sections 2701, 2702, 2703 and 2704 and the regulations at §§ 25.2701–0 through 25.2704–3 for special rules for valuing transfers of business interests, transfers in trust, and transfers pursuant to options and purchase agreements.

* * *

§ 25.2513–1 Gifts by husband or wife to third party considered as made one-half by each.

(a) A gift made by one spouse to a person other than his (or her) spouse may, for the purpose of the gift tax, be considered as made one-half by his spouse, but only if at the time of the gift each spouse was a citizen or resident of the United States. For purposes of this section, an individual is to be considered as the spouse of another individual only if he was married to such individual at the time of the gift and does not remarry during the remainder of the "calendar period" (as defined in § 25.2502–l(c)(l)).

(b) The provisions of this section will apply to gifts made during a particular "calendar period" (as defined in § 25.2502–1(c)(1)) only if both spouses signify their consent to treat all gifts made to third parties during that calendar period by both spouses while married to each other as having been made one-half by each spouse. As to the manner and time for signifying consent, see § 25.2513–2. Such consent, if signified with respect to any calendar period, is effective with respect to all gifts made to third parties during such calendar period except as follows:

(1) If the consenting spouses were not married to each other during a portion of the calendar period, the consent is not effective with respect to any gifts made during such portion of the calendar period. Where the consent is signified by an executor or administrator of a deceased spouse, the consent is not effective with respect to gifts made by the surviving spouse during the portion of the calendar period that his spouse was deceased.

(2) If either spouse was a nonresident not a citizen of the United States during any portion of the calendar period, the consent is not effective with respect to any gift made during that portion of the calendar period.

(3) The consent is not effective with respect to a gift by one spouse of a property interest over which he created in his spouse a general power of appointment (as defined in section 2514(c)).

(4) If one spouse transferred property in part to his spouse and in part to third parties, the consent is effective with respect to the interest transferred to third parties only insofar as such interest is ascertainable at the time of the gift and hence severable from the interest transferred to his spouse. See § 25.2512–5 for the principles to be applied in the valuation of annuities, life estates, terms for years, remainders and reversions.

(5) The consent applies alike to gifts made by one spouse alone and to gifts made partly by each spouse, provided such gifts were to third parties and do not fall within any of the exceptions set forth in subparagraphs (1) through (4) of this paragraph. The consent may not be applied only to a portion of the property interest constituting such gifts. For example, a wife may not treat gifts made by her spouse from his separate property to third parties as having been made one-half by her if her spouse does not consent to treat gifts made by her to third parties during the same calendar period as having been made one-half by him. If the consent is effectively signified on either the husband's return or the wife's return, all gifts made by the spouses to third parties (except as described in subparagraphs (1) through (4) of this paragraph), during the calendar period will be treated as having been made one-half by each spouse.

(c) If a husband and wife consent to have the gifts made to third party donees considered as made one-half by each spouse, and only one spouse makes gifts during the "calendar period" (as defined in § 25.2502–1(c)(1)), the other spouse is not required to file a gift tax return provided: (1) The total value of the gifts made to each third party donee since the beginning of the calendar year is not in excess of $20,000 ($6,000 for calendar years prior to 1982), and (2) no portion of the property transferred constitutes a gift of a future interest. If a transfer made by either spouse during the calendar period to a third-party represents a gift of a future interest in property and the spouses consent to have the gifts considered as made one-half by each, a gift tax return for such calendar period must be filed by each spouse regardless of the value of the transfer. (See § 25.2503–3 for the definition of a future interest.)

(d) The following examples illustrate the application of this section relating to the requirements for the filing of a return, assuming that a consent was effectively signified:

(1) A husband made gifts valued at $7,000 during the second quarter of 1971 to a third party and his wife made no gifts during this time. Each spouse is required to file a return for the second calendar quarter of 1971.

(2) A husband made gifts valued at $5,000 to each of two third parties during the year 1970 and his wife made no gifts. Only the husband is required to file a return. (See § 25.6019–2.)

(3) During the third quarter of 1971, a husband made gifts valued at $5,000 to a third party, and his wife made gifts valued at $2,000 to the same third party. Each spouse is required to file a return for the third calendar quarter of 1971.

(4) A husband made gifts valued at $5,000 to a third party and his wife made gifts valued at $3,000 to another third party during the year 1970. Only the husband is required to file a return for the calendar year 1970. (See § 25.6019–2.)

(5) A husband made gifts valued at $2,000 during the first quarter of 1971 to third parties which represented gifts of future interests in property (see § 25.2503–3), and his wife made no gifts during such calendar quarter. Each spouse is required to file a return for the first calendar quarter of 1971.

§ 25.2513–2 Manner and time of signifying consent.

(a) **(1)** Consent to the application of the provisions of section 2513 with respect to a "calendar period" (as defined in § 25.2502–1(c)(1)) shall, in order to be effective, be signified by both spouses. If both spouses file gift tax returns within the time for signifying consent, it is sufficient if—

(i) The consent of the husband is signified on the wife's return, and the consent of the wife is signified on the husband's return;

(ii) The consent of each spouse is signified on his own return; or

(iii) The consent of both spouses is signified on one of the returns.

If only one spouse files a gift tax return within the time provided for signifying consent, the consent of both spouses shall be signified on that return. However, wherever possible, the notice of the consent is to be shown on both returns and it is preferred that the notice be executed in the manner described in subdivision (i) of this subparagraph. The consent may be revoked only as provided in § 25.2513–3. If one spouse files more than one gift tax return for a calendar period on or before the due date of the return, the last return so filed shall, for the purpose of determining whether a consent has been signified, be considered as the return. (See §§ 25.6075–1 and 25.6075–2 for the due date of a gift tax return.)

* * *

(b) **(1)** With respect to gifts made after December 31, 1981, or before January 1, 1971, the consent may be signified at any time following the close of the calendar year, subject to the following limitations:

(i) The consent may not be signified after the 15th day of April following the close of the calendar year, unless before such 15th day no return has been filed for the year by either spouse, in which case the consent may not be signified after a return for the year is filed by either spouse; and

(ii) The consent may not be signified for a calendar year after a notice of deficiency in gift tax for that year has been sent to either spouse in accordance with the provisions of section 6212(a).

* * *

§ 25.2513–3 Revocation of consent.

(a) **(1)** With respect to gifts made after December 31, 1981, or before January 1, 1971, if the consent to the application of the provisions of section 2513 for a calendar year was effectively signified on or before the 15th day of April following the close of the calendar year, either spouse may revoke the consent by filing in duplicate a signed statement of revocation, but only if the statement is filed on or before such 15th day of April. Therefore, a consent that was not effectively signified until after the 15th day of April following the close of the calendar year to which it applies may not be revoked.

* * *

(b) Except as provided in paragraph (b) of § 301.6091–1 of this chapter (relating to hand-carried documents), the statement referred to in paragraph (a) of this section shall be filed with the internal revenue officer with whom the gift tax return is required to be filed, or with whom the gift tax return would be required to be filed if a return were required.

§ 25.2513–4 Joint and several liability for tax.

If consent to the application of the provisions of section 2513 is signified as provided in § 25.2513–2, and not revoked as provided in § 25.2513–3, the liability with respect to the entire gift tax of each spouse for such "calendar period" (as defined in § 25.2502–1(c)(l)) is joint and several. See paragraph (d) of § 25.2511–1.

§ 25.2514–1 Transfers under power of appointment.

(a) **Introductory.** **(1)** Section 2514 treats the exercise of a general power of appointment created on or before October 21, 1942, as a transfer of property for purposes of the gift tax. The section also treats as a transfer of property the exercise or complete release of a general power of appointment created after October 21, 1942, and under certain circumstances the exercise of a power of appointment (not a general power of appointment) created after October 21, 1942, by the creation of another power of appointment. See paragraph (d) of § 25.2514–3. Under certain circumstances, also, the failure to exercise a power of appointment created after October 21, 1942, within a specified time, so that the power lapses, constitutes a transfer of property. Paragraphs (b) through (e) of this section contain definitions of certain terms used in §§ 25.2514–2 and 25.2514–3. See § 25.2514–2 for specific rules applicable to certain powers created on or before October 21, 1942. See § 25.2514–3 for specific rules applicable to powers created after October 21, 1942.

(b) Definition of "power of appointment"—(1) In general. The term "power of appointment" includes all powers which are in substance and effect powers of appointment received by the donee of the power from another person, regardless of the nomenclature used in creating the power and regardless of local property law connotations. For example, if a trust instrument provides that the beneficiary may appropriate or consume the principal of the trust, the power to consume or appropriate is a power of appointment. Similarly, a power given to a donee to affect the beneficial enjoyment of a trust property or its income by altering, amending or revoking the trust instrument or terminating the trust is a power of appointment. A power in a donee to remove or discharge a trustee and appoint himself may be a power of appointment. For example, if under the terms of a trust instrument, the trustee or his successor has the power to appoint the principal of the trust for the benefit of individuals including himself, and A, another person, has the unrestricted power to remove or discharge the trustee at any time and appoint any other person, including himself, A is considered as having a power of appointment. However, he would not be considered to have a power of appointment if he only had the power to appoint a successor, including himself, under limited conditions which did not exist at the time of exercise, release or lapse of the trustee's power, without an accompanying unrestricted power of removal. Similarly, a power to amend only the administrative provisions of a trust instrument, which cannot substantially affect the beneficial enjoyment of the trust property or income, is not a power of appointment. The mere power of management, investment, custody of assets, or the power to allocate receipts and disbursements as between income and principal, exercisable in a fiduciary capacity, whereby the holder has no power to enlarge or shift any of the beneficial interests therein except as an incidental consequence of the discharge of such fiduciary duties is not a power of appointment. Further, the right in a beneficiary of a trust to assent to a periodic accounting, thereby relieving the trustee from further accountability, is not a power of appointment if the right of assent does not consist of any power or right to enlarge or shift the beneficial interest of any beneficiary therein.

(2) Relation to other sections. For purposes of §§ 25.2514–1 through 25.2514–3, the term "power of appointment" does not include powers reserved by a donor to himself. No provision of section 2514 or of §§ 25.2514–1 through 25.2514–3 is to be construed as in any way limiting the application of any other section of the Internal Revenue Code or of these regulations. The power of the owner of a property interest already possessed by him to dispose of his interest, and nothing more, is not a power of appointment, and the interest is includible in the amount of his gifts to the extent it would be includible under section 2511 or other provisions of the Internal Revenue Code. For example, if a trust created by S provides for payment of the income to A for life with power in A to appoint the entire trust property by deed during her lifetime to a class consisting of her children, and a further power to dispose of the entire corpus by will to anyone, including her estate, and A exercises the inter vivos power in favor of her children, she has necessarily made a transfer of her income interest which constitutes a taxable gift under section 2511(a), without regard to section 2514. This transfer also results in a relinquishment of her general power to appoint by will which constitutes a transfer under section 2514 if the power was created after October 21, 1942.

(3) Powers over a portion of property. If a power of appointment exists as to part of an entire group of assets or only over a limited interest in property, section 2514 applies only to such part or interest.

(c) Definition of "general power of appointment"—(1) In general. The term "general power of appointment" as defined in section 2514(c) means any power of appointment exercisable in favor of the person possessing the power (referred to as the "possessor"), his estate, his creditors, or the creditors of his estate, except (i) joint powers, to the extent provided in §§ 25.2514–2 and 25.2514–3 and (ii) certain powers limited by an ascertainable standard, to the extent provided in subparagraph (2) of this paragraph. A power of appointment exercisable to meet the estate tax, or any other taxes, debts, or charges which are enforceable against the possessor or his estate, is included within the meaning of a power of appointment exercisable in favor of the possessor, his estate, his creditors, or the creditors of his estate. A power of appointment exercisable for the purpose of discharging a legal obligation of the possessor or for his pecuniary benefit is considered a power of appointment exercisable in favor of the possessor or his creditors. However, for purposes of

§§ 25.2514–1 through 25.2514–3, a power of appointment not otherwise considered to be a general power of appointment is not treated as a general power of appointment merely by reason of the fact that an appointee may, in fact, be a creditor of the possessor or his estate. A power of appointment is not a general power if by its terms it is either—

(a) Exercisable only in favor of one or more designated persons or classes other than the possessor or his creditors, or the possessor's estate, or the creditors of his estate, or

(b) Expressly not exercisable in favor of the possessor or his creditors, the possessor's estate, or the creditors of his estate.

A beneficiary may have two powers under the same instrument, one of which is a general power of appointment and the other of which is not. For example, a beneficiary may have a general power to withdraw a limited portion of trust corpus during his life, and a further power exercisable during his lifetime to appoint the corpus among his children. The latter power is not a general power of appointment (but its exercise may result in the exercise of the former power; see paragraph (d) of this section).

(2) Powers limited by an ascertainable standard. A power to consume, invade, or appropriate income or corpus, or both, for the benefit of the possessor which is limited by an ascertainable standard relating to the health, education, support, or maintenance of the possessor is, by reason of section 2514(c)(l), not a general power of appointment. A power is limited by such a standard if the extent of the possessor's duty to exercise and not to exercise the power is reasonably measurable in terms of his needs for health, education, or support (or any combination of them). As used in this subparagraph, the words "support" and "maintenance" are synonymous and their meaning is not limited to the bare necessities of life. A power to use property for the comfort, welfare, or happiness of the holder of the power is not limited by the requisite standard. Examples of powers which are limited by the requisite standard are powers exercisable for the holder's "support," "support in reasonable comfort," "maintenance in health and reasonable comfort," "support in his accustomed manner of living," "education, including college and professional education," "health," and "medical, dental, hospital and nursing expenses and expenses of invalidism." In determining whether a power is limited by an ascertainable standard, it is immaterial whether the beneficiary is required to exhaust his other income before the power can be exercised.

* * *

(d) Definition of "exercise." Whether a power of appointment is in fact exercised may depend upon local law. However, regardless of local law, a power of appointment is considered as exercised for purposes of section 2514 even though the exercise is in favor of the taker in default of appointment, and irrespective of whether the appointed interest and the interest in default of appointment are identical or whether the appointee renounces any right to take under the appointment. A power of appointment is also considered as exercised even though the disposition cannot take effect until the occurrence of an event after the exercise takes place, if the exercise is irrevocable and, as of the time of the exercise, the condition was not impossible of occurrence. For example, if property is left in trust to A for life, with a power in A to appoint the remainder by an instrument filed with the trustee during his life, and A exercises his power by appointing the remainder to B in the event that B survives A, A is considered to have exercised his power if the exercise was irrevocable. Furthermore, if a person holds both a presently exercisable general power of appointment and a presently exercisable nongeneral power of appointment over the same property, the exercise of the nongeneral power is considered the exercise of the general power only to the extent that immediately after the exercise of the nongeneral power the amount of money or property subject to being transferred by the exercise of the general power is decreased. For example, assume A has a noncumulative annual power to withdraw the greater of $5,000 or 5 percent of the value of a trust having a value of $300,000 and a lifetime nongeneral power to appoint all or a portion of the trust corpus to A's child or grandchildren. If A exercises the nongeneral power by appointing $150,000 to A's child, the exercise of the nongeneral power is treated as the exercise of the general power to the extent of $7,500 (maximum exercise of general power before the exercise of the nongeneral power, 5% of $300,000 or $15,000, less maximum exercise of the general power after the exercise of the nongeneral power, 5% of $150,000 or $7,500).

(e) Time of creation of power. A power of appointment created by will is, in general, considered as created on the date of the testator's death. However, section 2514(f) provides that a power of appointment created by a will executed on or before October 21, 1942, is considered a power created on or before that date if the testator dies before July 1, 1949, without having republished the will, by codicil or otherwise, after October 21, 1942. A power of appointment created by an inter vivos instrument is considered as created on the date the instrument takes effect. Such a power is not considered as created at some future date merely because it is not exercisable on the date the instrument takes effect, or because it is revocable, or because the identity of its holders is not ascertainable until after the date the instrument takes effect. However, if the holder of a power exercises it by creating a second power, the second power is considered as created at the time of the exercise of the first. The application of this paragraph may be illustrated by the following examples:

Example (1). A created a revocable trust before October 22, 1942, providing for payment of income to B for life with remainder as B shall appoint by deed or will. Even though A dies after October 21, 1942, without having exercised his power of revocation, B's power of appointment is considered a power created before October 22, 1942.

Example (2). C created an irrevocable inter vivos trust before October 22, 1942, naming T as trustee and providing for payment of income to D for life with remainder to E. T was given the power to pay corpus to D and the power to appoint a successor trustee. If T resigns after October 21, 1942, and appoints D as successor trustee, D is considered to have a power of appointment created before October 22, 1942.

Example (3). F created an irrevocable inter vivos trust before October 22, 1942, providing for payment of income to G for life with remainder as G shall appoint by deed or will, but in default of appointment income to H for life with remainder as H shall appoint by deed or will. If G died after October 21, 1942, without having exercised his power of appointment, H's power of appointments is considered a power created before October 22, 1942, even though it was only a contingent interest until G's death.

Example (4). If in example (3) above G had exercised by will his power of appointment, by creating a similar power in J, J's power of appointment would be considered a power created after October 21, 1942.

* * *

§ 25.2514–3 Powers of appointment created after October 21, 1942.

(a) In general. The exercise, release, or lapse (except as provided in paragraph (c) of this section) of a general power of appointment created after October 21, 1942, is deemed to be a transfer of property by the individual possessing the power. The exercise of a power of appointment that is not a general power is considered to be a transfer if it is exercised to create a further power under certain circumstances (see paragraph (d) of this section). See paragraph (c) of § 25.2514–1 for the definition of various terms used in this section. See paragraph (b) of this section for the rules applicable to determine the extent to which joint powers created after October 21, 1942, are to be treated as general powers of appointment.

(b) Joint powers created after October 21, 1942. The treatment of a power of appointment created after October 21, 1942, which is exercisable only in conjunction with another person is governed by section 2514(c)(3), which provides as follows:

(1) Such a power is not considered as a general power of appointment if it is not exercisable by the possessor except with the consent or joinder of the creator of the power.

(2) Such power is not considered as a general power of appointment if it is not exercisable by the possessor except with the consent or joinder of a person having a substantial interest in the property subject to the power which is adverse to the exercise of the power in favor of the possessor, his estate, his creditors, or the creditors of his estate. An interest adverse to the exercise of a power is considered as substantial if its value in relation to the total value of the property subject to the power is not insignificant. For this purpose, the interest is to be valued in accordance with the actuarial principles set forth in § 25.2512–5 or, if it is not susceptible to valuation under those provisions, in accordance with the general principles set forth in § 25.2512–1. A taker in default of appointment under a power has an interest which is adverse to an exercise of the power. A coholder of the power has no adverse interest merely because of his joint possession of the power nor merely because he is a permissible appointee under a power. However, a coholder of a power is considered as having an adverse interest where he may possess the power after the possessor's death and may exercise it at that time in favor of himself, his estate, his creditors, or the creditors of his estate. Thus, for example, if X, Y, and Z held a power jointly to appoint among a group of persons which includes themselves and if on the death of X the power will pass to Y and Z jointly, then Y and Z are considered to have interests adverse to the exercise of the power in favor of X. Similarly, if on Y's death the power will pass to Z, Z is considered to have an interest adverse to the exercise of the power in favor of Y. The application of this subparagraph may be further illustrated by the following examples in each of which it is assumed that the value of the interest in question is substantial:

Example (1). The taxpayer and R are trustees of a trust under which the income is to be paid to the taxpayer for life and then to M for life, and R is remainderman. The trustees have power to distribute corpus to the taxpayer. Since R's interest is substantially adverse to an exercise of the power in favor of the taxpayer, the latter does not have a general power of appointment. If M and the taxpayer were trustees, M's interest would likewise be adverse.

Example (2). The taxpayer and L are trustees of a trust under which the income is to be paid to L for life and then to M for life, and the taxpayer is remainderman. The trustees have power to distribute corpus to the taxpayer during L's life. Since L's interest is adverse to an exercise of the power in favor of the taxpayer, the taxpayer does not have a general power of appointment. If the taxpayer and M were trustees, M's interest would likewise be adverse.

Example (3). The taxpayer and L are trustees of a trust under which the income is to be paid to L for life. The trustees can designate whether corpus is to be distributed to the taxpayer or to A after L's death. L's interest is not adverse to an exercise of the power in favor of the taxpayer, and the taxpayer therefore has a general power of appointment.

(3) A power which is exercisable only in conjunction with another person, and which after application of the rules set forth in subparagraphs (1) and (2) of this paragraph, constitutes a general power of appointment, will be treated as though the holders of the power who are permissible appointees of the property were joint owners of property subject to the power. The possessor, under this rule, will be treated as possessed of a general power of appointment over an aliquot share of the property to be determined with reference to the number of joint holders, including the possessor, who (or whose estates or creditors) are permissible appointees. Thus, for example, if X, Y, and Z hold an unlimited power jointly to appoint among a group of persons, including themselves, but on the death of X the power does not pass to Y and Z jointly, then Y and Z are not considered to have interests adverse to the exercise of the power in favor of X. In this case, X is considered to possess a general power of appointment as to one-third of the property subject to the power.

(c) Partial releases, lapses, and disclaimers of general powers of appointment created after October 21, 1942—(1) Partial release of power. The general principles set forth in § 25.2511–2 for determining whether a donor of property (or of a property right or interest) has divested himself of all or any portion of his interest therein to the extent necessary to effect a completed gift are applicable in determining whether a partial release of a power of appointment constitutes a taxable gift. Thus, if a general power of appointment is partially released so that thereafter the donor may still appoint among a limited class of persons not including himself the partial release does not effect a complete gift, since the possessor of the power has retained the right to designate the ultimate beneficiaries of the property over which he holds the power and since it is only the termination of such control which completes a gift.

(2) Powers partially released before June 1, 1951. If a general power of appointment created after October 21, 1942, was partially released prior to June 1, 1951, so that it no longer represented a general power of appointment, as defined in paragraph (c) of § 25.2514–1, the subsequent exercise, release, or lapse of the partially released power at any time thereafter will not constitute the exercise or release of a general power of appointment. For example, assume that A created a trust in 1943 under which B possessed a general power of appointment. By an instrument executed in 1948 such general power of appointment was reduced in scope by B to an excepted power. The inter vivos exercise in 1955, or in any "calendar period" (as defined in § 25.2502–1(c)(1)) thereafter, of such excepted power is not considered an exercise or release of a general power of appointment for purposes of the gift tax.

(3) Power partially released after May 31, 1951. If a general power of appointment created after October 21, 1942, was partially released after May 31, 1951, the subsequent exercise, release or a lapse of the power at any time thereafter, will constitute the exercise or release of a general power of appointment for gift tax purposes.

(4) Release or lapse of power. A release of a power of appointment need not be formal or express in character. For example, the failure to exercise a general power of appointment created after October 21, 1942, within a specified time so that the power lapses, constitutes a release of the power. In any case where the possessor of a general power of appointment is incapable of validly exercising or releasing a power, by reason of minority, or otherwise, and the power may not be validly exercised or released on his behalf, the failure to exercise or release the power is not a lapse of the power. If a trustee has in his capacity as trustee a power which is considered as a general power of appointment, his resignation or removal as trustee will cause a lapse of his power. However, section 2514(e) provides that a lapse during any calendar year is considered as a release so as to be subject to the gift tax only to the extent that the property which could have been appointed by exercise of the lapsed power of appointment exceeds the greater of (i) $5,000, or (ii) 5 percent of the aggregate value, at the time of the lapse, of the assets out of which, or the proceeds of which, the exercise of the lapsed power could be satisfied. For example, if an individual has a noncumulative right to withdraw $10,000 a year from the principal of a trust fund, the failure to exercise this right of withdrawal in a particular year will not constitute a gift if the fund at the end of the year equals or exceeds $200,000. If, however, at the end of the particular year the fund should be worth only $100,000, the failure to exercise the power will be considered a gift to the extent of $5,000, the excess of $10,000 over 5 percent of a fund of $100,000. Where the failure to exercise a power, such as a right of withdrawal, occurs in more than a single year, the value of the taxable transfer will be determined separately for each year.

(5) Disclaimer of power created after December 31, 1976. A disclaimer or renunciation of a general power of appointment created in a taxable transfer after December 31, 1976, in the person disclaiming is not considered a release of the power for gift tax purposes if the disclaimer or renunciation is a qualified disclaimer as described in section 2518 and the corresponding regulations. If the disclaimer or renunciation is not a qualified disclaimer, it is considered a release of the power.

(6) Disclaimer of power created before January 1, 1977. A disclaimer or renunciation of a general power of appointment created in a taxable transfer before January 1, 1977, in the person disclaiming is not considered a release of the power. The disclaimer or renunciation must be unequivocal and effective under local law. A disclaimer is a complete and unqualified refusal to accept the rights to which one is entitled. There can be no disclaimer or renunciation of a power after its acceptance. In the absence of facts to the contrary, the failure to renounce or disclaim within a reasonable time after learning of the existence of a power shall be presumed to constitute an acceptance of the power. In any case where a power is purported to be disclaimed or renounced as to only a portion of the property subject to the power, the determination as to whether there has been a complete and unqualified refusal to accept the rights to which one is entitled will depend on all the facts and circumstances of the particular case, taking into account the recognition and effectiveness of such a disclaimer under local law. Such rights refer to the incidents of the power and not to other interests of the possessor of the power in the property. If effective under local law, the power may be disclaimed or renounced without disclaiming or renouncing such other interests.

(d) Creation of another power in certain cases. Paragraph (d) of section 2514 provides that there is a transfer for purposes of the gift tax of the value of property (or of property rights or interests) with respect to which a power of appointment, which is not a general power of appointment, created after October 21, 1942, is exercised by creating another power of appointment which, under the terms of the instruments creating and exercising the first power and under applicable local law, can be validly exercised so as to (1) postpone the vesting of any estate or interest in the property for a period ascertainable without regard to the date of the creation of the first power, or (2) (if the applicable rule against perpetuities is stated in terms of suspensions of ownership or of the power of alienation, rather than of vesting) suspend the absolute ownership or the power of alienation of the property for a period ascertainable without regard to the date of the creation of the first power. For the purpose of section 2514(d), the value of the property subject to the second power of appointment is considered to be its value unreduced by any precedent or subsequent interest which is not subject to the second power. Thus, if a donor has a power to appoint $100,000 among a group consisting of his children or grandchildren and during his lifetime exercises the power by making an outright appointment of $75,000 and by giving one appointee a power to appoint $25,000, no more than $25,000 will be considered a gift under section 2514(d). If, however, the donor appoints the income from the entire fund to a beneficiary for life with power in the beneficiary to appoint the remainder, the entire $100,000 will be considered a gift under section 2514(d), if the exercise of the second power can validly postpone the vesting of any estate or interest in the property or can suspend the absolute ownership or power of alienation of the property for a period ascertainable without regard to the date of the creation of the first power.

(e) Examples. The application of this section may be further illustrated by the following examples in each of which it is assumed, unless otherwise stated, that S has transferred property in trust after October 21, 1942, with the remainder payable to R at L's death, and that neither L nor R has any interest in or power over the enjoyment of the trust property except as is indicated separately in each example:

Example (1). The income is payable to L for life. L has the power to cause the income to be paid to R. The exercise of the right constitutes the making of a transfer of property under section 2511. L's power does not constitute a power of appointment since it is only a power to dispose of his income interest, a right otherwise possessed by him.

Example (2). The income is to be accumulated during L's life. L has the power to have the income distributed to himself. If L's power is limited by an ascertainable standard (relating to health, etc.) as defined in paragraph (c)(2) of § 25.2514–1, the lapse of such power will not constitute a transfer of property for gift tax purposes. If L's power is not so limited, its lapse or release during L's lifetime may constitute a transfer of property for gift tax purposes. See especially paragraph (c)(4) of § 25.2514–3.

Example (3). The income is to be paid to L for life. L has a power, exercisable at any time, to cause the corpus to be distributed to himself. L has a general power of appointment over the remainder interest, the release of which constitutes a transfer for gift tax purposes of the remainder interest. If in this example L had a power to cause the corpus to be distributed only to X, L would have a power of appointment which is not a general power of appointment, the exercise or release of which would not constitute a transfer of property for purposes of the gift tax. Although the exercise or release of the nongeneral power is not taxable under this section, see § 25.2514–1(b)(2) for the gift tax consequences of the transfer of the life income interest.

Example (4). The income is payable to L for life. R has the right to cause the corpus to be distributed to L at any time. R's power is not a power of appointment, but merely a right to dispose of his remainder interest, a right already possessed by him. In such a case, the exercise of the right constitutes the making of a transfer of property under section 2511 of the value, if any, of his remainder interest. See paragraph (e) of § 25.251–1.

Example (5). The income is to be paid to L. R has the right to appoint the corpus to himself at any time. R's general power of appointment over the corpus includes a general power to dispose of L's income interest therein. The lapse or release of R's general power over the income interest during his life may constitute the making of a transfer of property. See especially paragraph (c)(4) of § 25.2514-3.

* * *

§ 25.2516–1 Certain property settlements.

(a) Section 2516 provides that transfers of property or interests in property made under the terms of a written agreement between spouses in settlement of their marital or property rights are deemed to be for an adequate and full consideration in money or money's worth and, therefore, exempt from the gift tax (whether or not such agreement is approved by a divorce decree), if the spouses obtain a final decree of divorce from each other within two years after entering into the agreement.

* * *

§ 25.2516–2 Transfers in settlement of support obligations.

Transfers to provide a reasonable allowance for the support of children (including legally adopted children) of a marriage during minority are not subject to the gift tax if made pursuant to an agreement which satisfies the requirements of section 2516.

* * *

§ 25.2518–1 Qualified disclaimers of property; In general.

(a) Applicability—(1) In general. The rules described in §§ 25.2518–1 through 25.2518–3 apply to the qualified disclaimer of an interest in property which is created in the person disclaiming by a taxable transfer made after December 31, 1976. In general, a qualified disclaimer is an irrevocable and unqualified refusal to accept the ownership of an interest in property. For rules relating to the determination of when a transfer occurs, see § 25.2518–2 (c)(3) and (4).

(2) Example. The provisions of paragraph (a)(1) of this section may be illustrated by the following example:

Example. W creates an irrevocable trust on December 10, 1968, and retains the right to receive the income for life. Upon the death of W, which occurs after December 31, 1976, the trust property is distributable to W's surviving issue, per stirpes. The creation of the remainder interest in the trust was a taxable transfer. Therefore, section 2518 does not apply to the disclaimer of the remainder interest because the taxable transfer was made prior to January 1, 1977. If, however, W had also retained the power to designate the person or persons to receive the trust principal at her death, and as a result no taxable gift was made of the remainder interest at the time of the creation of the trust, section 2518 would apply to any disclaimer made after W's death with respect to an interest in the trust property.

(b) Effect of a qualified disclaimer. If a person makes a qualified disclaimer as described in section 2518(b) and § 25.2518–2, for purposes of the Federal estate, gift, and generation-skipping transfer tax provisions, the disclaimed interest in property is treated as if it had never been transferred to the person making the qualified disclaimer. Instead, it is considered as passing directly from the transferor of the property to the person entitled to receive the property as a result of the disclaimer. Accordingly, a person making a qualified disclaimer is not treated as making a gift. Similarly, the value of a decedent's gross estate for purposes of the Federal estate tax does not include the value of property with respect to which the decedent, or the decedent's executor or administrator on behalf of the decedent, has made a qualified disclaimer. If the disclaimer is not a qualified disclaimer, for the purposes of the Federal estate, gift, and generation-skipping transfer tax provisions, the disclaimer is disregarded and the disclaimant is treated as having received the interest.

(c) Effect of local law—(1) In general—(i) Interests created before 1982. A disclaimer of an interest created in a taxable transfer before 1982 which otherwise meets the requirements of a qualified disclaimer under section 2518 and the corresponding regulations but which, by itself, is not effective under applicable local law to divest ownership of the disclaimed property from the disclaimant and vest it in another, is nevertheless treated as a qualified disclaimer under section 2518 if, under applicable local law, the disclaimed interest in property is transferred, as a result of attempting the disclaimer, to another person without any direction on the part of the disclaimant. An interest in property will not be considered to be transferred without any direction on the part of the disclaimant if, under applicable local law, the disclaimant has any discretion (whether or not such discretion is exercised) to determine who will receive such interest. Actions by the disclaimant which are required under local law merely to divest owner-ship of the property from the disclaimant and vest ownership in another person will not disqualify the disclaimer for purposes of section 2518(a). See § 25.2518–2(d)(1) for rules relating to the immediate vesting of title in the disclaimant.

(ii) Interests created after 1981. [Reserved].

(2) Creditor's claims. The fact that a disclaimer is voidable by the disclaimant's creditors has no effect on the determination of whether such disclaimer constitutes a qualified disclaimer. However, a disclaimer that is wholly void or that is voided by the disclaimant's creditors cannot be a qualified disclaimer.

(3) Examples. The provisions of paragraphs (c)(1) and (2) of this section may be illustrated by the following examples:

Example (1). F dies testate in State Y on June 17, 1978. G and H are beneficiaries under the will. The will provides that any disclaimed property is to pass to the residuary estate. H has no interest in the residuary estate. Under the applicable laws of State Y, a disclaimer must be made within 6 months of the death of the testator. Seven months after F's death, H disclaimed the real property H received under the will. The disclaimer statute of State Y has a provision stating that an untimely disclaimer will be treated as an assignment of the interest disclaimed to those persons who would have taken had the disclaimer been valid. Pursuant to this provision, the disclaimed property became part of the residuary estate. Assuming the remaining requirements of section 2518 are met, H has made a qualified disclaimer for purposes of section 2518(a).

Example (2). Assume the same facts as in example (1) except that the law of State Y does not treat an ineffective disclaimer as a transfer to alternative takers. H assigns the disclaimed interest by deed to those who would have taken had the disclaimer been valid. Under these circumstances, H has not made a qualified disclaimer for purposes of section 2518(a) because the disclaimant directed who would receive the property.

Example (3). Assume the same facts as in example (1) except that the law of State Y requires H to pay a transfer tax in order to effectuate the transfer under the ineffective disclaimer provision. H pays the transfer tax. H has make a qualified disclaimer for purposes of section 2518(a).

(d) Cross-reference. For rules relating to the effect of qualified disclaimers on the estate tax charitable and marital deductions, see §§ 20.2055–2(c) and 20.2056(d)–1 respectively. For rules relating to the effect of a qualified disclaimer of a general power of appointment, see § 20.2041–3(d).

§ 25.2518–2 Requirements for a qualified disclaimer.

(a) In general. For the purposes of section 2518(a), a disclaimer shall be a qualified disclaimer only if it satisfies the requirements of this section. In general, to be a qualified disclaimer—

(1) The disclaimer must be irrevocable and unqualified:

(2) The disclaimer must be in writing;

(3) The writing must be delivered to the person specified in paragraph (b)(2) of this section within the time limitations specified in paragraph (c)(1) of this section;

(4) The disclaimant must not have accepted the interest disclaimed or any of its benefits; and

(5) The interest disclaimed must pass either to the spouse of the decedent or to a person other than the disclaimant without any direction on the part of the person making the disclaimer.

(b) Writing—(1) Requirements. A disclaimer is a qualified disclaimer only if it is in writing. The writing must identify the interest in property disclaimed and be signed either by the disclaimant or by the disclaimant's legal representative.

(2) Delivery. The writing described in paragraph (b)(1) of this section must be delivered to the transferor of the interest, the transferor's legal representative, the holder of the legal title to the property to which the interest relates, or the person in possession of such property.

(c) Time limit—(1) In general. A disclaimer is a qualified disclaimer only if the writing described in paragraph (b)(1) of this section is delivered to the persons described in paragraph (b)(2) of this section no later than the date which is 9 months after the later of—

(i) The date on which the transfer creating the interest in the disclaimant is made, or

(ii) The day on which the disclaimant attains age 21.

(2) A timely mailing of a disclaimer treated as a timely delivery. Although section 7502 and the regulations under that section apply only to documents to be filed with the Service, a timely mailing of a disclaimer to the person described in paragraph (b)(2) of this section is treated as a timely delivery if the mailing requirements under paragraphs (c)(l), (c)(2) and (d) of § 301.7502–1 are met. Further, if the last day of the period specified in paragraph (c)(1) of this section falls on Saturday, Sunday or a legal holiday (as defined in paragraph (b) of § 301.7503–1), then the delivery of the writing described in paragraph (b)(1) of this section shall be considered timely if delivery is made on the first succeeding day which is not Saturday, Sunday or a legal holiday. See paragraph (d)(3) of this section for rules applicable to the exception for individuals under 21 years of age.

(3) Transfer. For purposes of the time limitation described in paragraph (c)(1)(i) of this section, the 9-month period for making a disclaimer generally is to be determined with reference to the taxable transfer creating the interest in the disclaimant. With respect to inter vivos transfers, a taxable transfer occurs when there is a completed gift for Federal gift tax purposes regardless of whether a gift tax is imposed on the completed gift. Thus, gifts qualifying for the gift tax annual exclusion under section 2503(b) are regarded as taxable transfers for this purpose. With respect to transfers made by a decedent at death or transfers which become irrevocable at death, a taxable transfer occurs upon the date of the decedent's death. However, where there is a taxable transfer of an interest for Federal gift tax purposes and such interest is later included in the transferor's gross estate for Federal estate tax purposes, the 9-month period for making a qualified disclaimer is determined with reference to the earlier taxable transfer. In the case of a general power of appointment, the holder of the power has a 9-month period after the creation of the power in which to disclaim. A person to whom any interest in property passes by reason of the exercise or lapse of a general power may disclaim such interest within a 9-month period after the exercise or lapse. In the case of a nongeneral power of appointment, the holder of the power, permissible appointees, or takers in default of appointment must disclaim within a 9-month period after the original taxable transfer that created or authorized the creation of the power. If the transfer is for the life of an income beneficiary with succeeding interests to other persons, both the life tenant and the other remaindermen, whether their interests are vested or contingent, must disclaim no later than 9 months after the original taxable transfer. In the case of a remainder interest in property which an executor elects to treat as qualified terminable interest property under section 2056(b)(7), the remainderman must disclaim within 9 months of the transfer creating the interest, rather than 9 months from the date such interest is subject to tax under section 2044 or 2519. A person who receives an interest in property as the result of a qualified disclaimer of the interest must disclaim the previously disclaimed interest no later than 9 months after the date of the taxable transfer creating the interest in the preceding disclaimant. Thus, if A were to make a qualified disclaimer of a specific bequest and as a result of the qualified disclaimer the property passed as part of the residue, the beneficiary of the residue could make a qualified disclaimer no later than 9 months after the date of the testator's death. See paragraph (d)(3) of this section for the time limitation rule with reference to recipients who are under 21 years of age.

(4) Joint property—(i) In general. Except as otherwise provided in paragraph (c)(4)(ii) of this section, a qualified disclaimer under section 2518(a) of an interest or any portion of an interest in a joint tenancy or a tenancy by the entirety must be made no later than 9 months after the transfer creating the tenancy. Thus, a surviving joint tenant cannot disclaim any part of the interest, including the survivorship interest, if more than 9 months have passed since the transfer creating the joint tenancy. In addition, a joint tenant cannot make a qualified disclaimer of any portion of the joint interest attributable to consideration furnished by that tenant.

(ii) Tenancies in real property between spouses created before 1982. In the case of joint tenancies between spouses or a tenancy by the entirety in real property created after 1976 and before 1982 where no election was made under section 2515, the surviving spouse must make a qualified disclaimer no later than 9 months after the date of death of the first spouse to die. Such a qualified disclaimer will be effective for—

(A) The entire joint interest (except any portion attributable to consideration furnished by the surviving spouse) if the date of death of the deceased spouse is before 1982; or

(B) One-half the value of the joint interest if the date of death of the deceased spouse is after 1981. See examples (7) and (8) under paragraph (c)(5) of this section.

(5) Examples. The provisions of paragraphs (c)(1) through (c)(4) of this section may be illustrated by the following examples. For purposes of the following examples, assume that all beneficiaries are over 21 years of age.

Example (1). On May 13, 1978, in a transfer which constitutes a completed gift for Federal gift tax purposes, A creates a trust in which B is given a lifetime interest in the income from the trust. B is also given a nongeneral testamentary power of appointment over the corpus of the trust. The power of appointment may be exercised in favor of any of the issue of A and B. If there are no surviving issue at B's death or if the power is not exercised, the corpus is to pass to E. On May 13, 1978, A and B have two surviving children, C and D. If A, B, C or D wishes to make a qualified disclaimer, the disclaimer must be made no later than 9 months after May 13, 1978.

Example (2). Assume the same facts as in example (1) except that B is given a general power of appointment over the corpus of the trust. B exercises the general power of appointment in favor of C upon B's death on June 17, 1989. C may make a qualified disclaimer no later than 9 months after June 17, 1989. If B had died without exercising the general power of appointment, E could have made a qualified disclaimer no later than 9 months after June 17, 1989.

Example (3). F creates a trust on April 1, 1978, in which F's child G is to receive the income from the trust for life. Upon G's death, the corpus of the trust is to pass to G's child H. If either G or H wishes to make a qualified disclaimer, it must be made no later than 9 months after April 1, 1978.

Example (4). A creates a trust on February 15, 1978, in which B is named the income beneficiary for life. The trust further provides that upon B's death the proceeds of the trust are to pass to C, if then living. If C predeceases D, the proceeds shall pass to D or D's estate. To have timely disclaimers for purposes of section 2518, B, C, and D must disclaim their respective interests no later than 9 months after February 15, 1978.

Example (5). A, a resident of State Q, dies on January 10, 1979, devising certain real property to B. The disclaimer laws of State Q require that a disclaimer be made within a reasonable time after a transfer. B disclaims the entire interest in real property on November 10, 1979. Although B's disclaimer may be effective under State Q law, it is not a qualified disclaimer under section 2518 because the disclaimer was made later than 9 months after the taxable transfer to B.

Example (6). A creates a revocable trust on June 1, 1980, in which B and C are given the income interest for life. Upon the death of the last income beneficiary, the remainder interest is to pass to D. The creation of the trust is not a completed gift for Federal gift tax purposes, but each distribution of trust income to B and C is a completed gift at the date of distribution. B and C disclaim each income distribution no later than 9 months after the date of the particular distribution. In order to disclaim an income distribution in the form of a check, the recipient must return the check to the trustee uncashed along with a written disclaimer. A dies on September 1, 1982, causing the trust to become irrevocable, and the trust corpus is includible in A's gross estate for Federal estate tax purposes under section 2038. If B or C wishes to make a qualified disclaimer of his income interest, he must do so no later than 9 months after September 1, 1982. If D wishes to make a qualified disclaimer of his remainder interest, he must do so no later than 9 months after September 1, 1982.

Example (7). On March 1, 1977, H and W purchase a tract of vacant land which is conveyed to them as tenants by the entirety. The entire consideration is paid by H. H does not elect, under section 2515, to have the transaction treated as a transfer for purposes of Chapter 12. H dies on June 1, 1981. On October 1, 1981, W disclaims the property. Assuming the other requirements of section 2518(b) are satisfied, W has made a qualified disclaimer because the transfer which created W's interest is treated as not occurring until H's death since no election was made under section 2515. Had an election been made under section 2515, then W's disclaimer of any of W's interest in the property would not be a qualified disclaimer.

Example (8). Assume the same facts as in example (7) except that H dies on September 3, 1984. W has until 9 months after September 3, 1984 to make a qualified disclaimer, but she can only make a qualified disclaimer of one-half of the joint interest.

Example (9). On July 1, 1980, B transfers $10,000 to a bank account which is held jointly by B and C. Assume the transfer is not a completed gift for Federal gift tax purposes. The funds in the bank account may be withdrawn in full by either B or C at any time. C never receives funds from the bank account. B dies on August 15, 1989, and C disclaims the amount in the bank account on October 15, 1989. Assuming the remaining requirements of section 2518 (b) are satisfied, C made a qualified disclaimer under section 2518 (a) because it was made no later than 9 months after the taxable transfer that created an interest in C.

Example (10). H and W reside in State X, a community property state. On April 1, 1978, H and W purchase real property with community funds. The property is not held by H and W as jointly owned property with rights of survivorship. H and W hold the property until January 3, 1985, when H dies. H devises his portion of the property to W. On March 15, 1985, W disclaims the portion of the property devised to her by H. Assuming all the other requirements of section 2518 (b) have been met, W has made a qualified disclaimer of the interest devised to her by H. However, W could not disclaim the interest in the property that she acquired on April 1, 1978.

(d) No acceptance of benefits—(1) Acceptance. A qualified disclaimer cannot be made with respect to an interest in property if the disclaimant has accepted the interest or any of its benefits, expressly or impliedly, prior to making the disclaimer. Acceptance is manifested by an affirmative act which is consistent with ownership of the interest in property. Acts indicative of acceptance include using the property or the interest in property; accepting dividends, interest, or rents from the property; and directing others to act with respect to the property or interest in property. However, merely taking delivery of an instrument of title, without more, does not constitute acceptance. Moreover, a disclaimant is not considered to have accepted property merely because under applicable local law title to the property vests immediately in the disclaimant upon the death of a decedent. The acceptance of one interest in property will not, by itself, constitute an acceptance of any other separate interests created by the transferor and held by the disclaimant in the same property. In the case of residential property, held in joint tenancy by some or all of the residents, a joint tenant will not be considered to have accepted the joint interest merely because the tenant resided on the property prior to disclaiming his interest in the property. The exercise of a power of appointment to any extent by the donee of the power is an acceptance of its benefits. In addition, the acceptance of any consideration in return for making the disclaimer is an acceptance of the benefits of the entire interest disclaimed.

(2) Fiduciaries. If a beneficiary who disclaims an interest in property is also a fiduciary, actions taken by such person in the exercise of fiduciary powers to preserve or maintain the disclaimed property shall not be treated as an acceptance of such property or any of its benefits. Under this rule, for example, an executor who is also a beneficiary may direct the harvesting of a crop or the general maintenance of a home. A fiduciary, however, cannot retain a wholly discretionary power to direct the enjoyment of the disclaimed interest. For example, a fiduciary's disclaimer of a beneficial interest does not meet the requirements of a qualified disclaimer if the fiduciary exercised or retains a discretionary power to allocate enjoyment of that interest among members of a designated class. See paragraph (e) of this section for rules relating to the effect of directing the redistribution of disclaimed property.

(3) Under 21 years of age. A beneficiary who is under 21 years of age has until 9 months after his twenty-first birthday in which to make a qualified disclaimer of his interest in property. Any actions taken with regard to an interest in property by a beneficiary or a custodian prior to the beneficiary's twenty-first birthday will not be an acceptance by the beneficiary of the interest.

(4) Examples. The provisions of paragraphs (d)(1), (2) and (3) of this section may be illustrated by the following examples:

Example (1). On April 9, 1977, A established a trust for the benefit of B, then age 22. Under the terms of the trust, the current income of the trust is to be paid quarterly to B. Additionally, one half the principal is to be distributed to B when B attains the age of 30 years. The balance of the principal is to be distributed to B when B attains the age of 40 years. Pursuant to the terms of the trust, B received a distribution of income on June 30, 1977. On August 1, 1977, B disclaimed B's right to receive both the income from the trust and the principal of the trust, B's disclaimer of the income interest is not a qualified disclaimer for purposes of section 2518(a) because B accepted income prior to making the disclaimer. B's disclaimer of the principal, however, does satisfy section 2518(b)(3). See also § 25.2518–3 for rules relating to the disclaimer of less than an entire interest in property.

Example (2). B is the recipient of certain property devised to B under the will of A. The will stated that any disclaimed property was to pass to C. B and C entered into negotiations in which it was decided that B would disclaim all interest in the real property that was devised to B. In exchange, C promised to let B live in the family home for life. B's disclaimer is not a qualified disclaimer for purposes of section 2518(a) because B accepted consideration for making the disclaimer.

Example (3). A received a gift of Blackacre on December 25, 1978. A never resided on Blackacre but when property taxes on Blackacre became due on July 1, 1979, A paid them out personal funds. On August 15, 1979, A disclaimed the gift of Blackacre. Assuming all the requirements of section 2518 (b) have been met, A has made a qualified disclaimer of Blackacre. Merely paying the property taxes does not constitute an acceptance of Blackacre even though A's personal funds were used to pay the taxes.

Example (4). A died on February 15, 1978. Pursuant to A's will, B received a farm in State Z. B requested the executor to sell the farm and to give the proceeds to B. The executor then sold the farm pursuant to B's request. B then disclaimed $50,000 of the proceeds from the sale of the farm. B's disclaimer is not a qualified disclaimer. By requesting the executor to sell the farm B accepted the farm even though the executor may not have been legally obligated to comply with B's request. See also § 25.2518–3 for rules relating to the disclaimer of less than an entire interest in property.

Example (5). Assume the same facts as in example (4) except that instead of requesting the executor to sell the farm, B pledged the farm as security for a short-term loan which was paid off prior to distribution of the estate. B then disclaimed his interest in the farm. B's disclaimer is not a qualified disclaimer. By pledging the farm as security for the loan, B accepted the farm.

Example (6). A delivered 1,000 shares of stock in Corporation X to B as a gift on February 1, 1980. A had the shares registered in B's name on that date. On April 1, 1980, B disclaimed the interest in the 1,000 shares. Prior to making the disclaimer, B did not pledge the shares, accept any dividends or otherwise commit any acts indicative of acceptance. Assuming the remaining requirements of section 2518 are satisfied, B's disclaimer is a qualified disclaimer.

Example (7). On January 1, 1980, A created an irrevocable trust in which B was given a testamentary general power of appointment over the trust's corpus. B executed a will on June 1, 1980, in which B provided for the exercise of the power of appointment. On September 1, 1980, B disclaimed the testamentary power of appointment. Assuming the remaining requirements of section 2518 (b) are satisfied, B's disclaimer of the testamentary power of appointment is a qualified disclaimer.

Example (8). H and W reside in X, a community property state. On January 1, 1981, H and W purchase a residence with community funds. They continue to reside in the house until H dies testate on February 1, 1990. Although H could devise his portion of the residence to any person, H devised his portion of the residence to W. On September 1, 1990, W disclaims the portion of the residence devised to her pursuant to H's will but continues to live in the residence. Assuming the remaining requirements of section 2518(b) are satisfied, W's disclaimer is a qualified disclaimer under section 2518 (a). W's continued occupancy of the house prior to making the disclaimer will not by itself be treated as an acceptance of the benefits of the portion of the residence devised to her by H.

Example (9). In 1979, D established a trust for the benefit of D's minor children E and F. Under the terms of the trust, the trustee is given the power to make discretionary distributions of current income and corpus to both children. The corpus of the trust is to be distributed equally between E and F when E becomes 35 years of age. Prior to attaining the age of 21 years on April 8, 1982, E receives several distributions of income from the trust. E receives no distributions of income between April 8, 1982 and August 15, 1982, which is the date on which E disclaims all interest in the income from the trust. As a result of the disclaimer the income will be distributed to F. If the remaining requirements of section 2518 are met, E's disclaimer is a qualified disclaimer under section 2518(a). To have a qualified disclaimer of the interest in corpus, E must disclaim the interest no later than 9 months after April 8, 1982, E's 21st birthday.

Example (10). Assume the same facts as in example (9) except that E accepted a distribution of income on May 13, 1982. E's disclaimer is not a qualified disclaimer under section 2518 because by accepting an income distribution after attaining the age of 21, E accepted benefits from the income interest.

Example (11). F made a gift of 10 shares of stock to G as custodian for H under the State X Uniform Gifts to Minors Act. At the time of the gift, H was 15 years old. At age 18, the local age of majority, the 10 shares were delivered to and registered in the name of H. Between the receipt of the shares and H's 21st birthday, H received dividends from the shares. Within 9 months of attaining age 21, H disclaimed the 10 shares. Assuming H did not accept any dividends from the shares after attaining age 21, the disclaimer by H is a qualified disclaimer under section 2518.

(e) Passage without direction by the disclaimant of beneficial enjoyment of disclaimed interest— (1) In general. A disclaimer is not a qualified disclaimer unless the disclaimed interest passes without any direction on the part of the disclaimant to a person other than the disclaimant (except as provided in paragraph (e)(2) of this section). If there is an express or implied agreement that the disclaimed interest in property is to be given or bequeathed to a person specified by the disclaimant, the disclaimant shall be treated as directing the transfer of the property interest. The requirements of a qualified disclaimer under section 2518 are not satisfied if—

(i) The disclaimant, either alone or in conjunction with another, directs the redistribution or transfer of the property or interest in property to another person (or has the power to direct the redistribution or transfer of the property or interest in property to another person unless such power is limited by an ascertainable standard); or

(ii) The disclaimed property or interest in property passes to or for the benefit of the disclaimant as a result of the disclaimer (except as provided in paragraph (e)(2) of this section).

If a power of appointment is disclaimed, the requirements of this paragraph (e)(1) are satisfied so long as there is no direction on the part of the disclaimant with respect to the transfer of the interest subject to the power or with respect to the transfer of the power to another person. A person may make a qualified disclaimer of a beneficial interest in property even if after such disclaimer the disclaimant has a fiduciary power to distribute to designated beneficiaries, but only if the power is subject to an ascertainable standard. See examples (11) and (12) of paragraph (e)(5) of this section.

(2) Disclaimer by surviving spouse. In the case of a disclaimer made by a decedent's surviving spouse with respect to property transferred by the decedent, the disclaimer satisfies the requirements of this paragraph (e) if the interest passes as a result of the disclaimer without direction on the part of the surviving spouse either to the surviving spouse or to another person. If the surviving spouse, however, retains the right to direct the beneficial enjoyment of the disclaimed property in a transfer that is not subject to Federal estate and gift tax (whether as trustee or otherwise), such spouse will be treated as directing the beneficial enjoyment of the disclaimed property, unless such power is limited by an ascertainable standard. See examples (4), (5), and (6) in paragraph (e)(5) of this section.

(3) Partial failure of disclaimer. If a disclaimer made by a person other than the surviving spouse is not effective to pass completely an interest in property to a person other than the disclaimant because—

(i) The disclaimant also has a right to receive such property as an heir at law, residuary beneficiary, or by any other means; and

(ii) The disclaimant does not effectively disclaim these rights, the disclaimer is not a qualified disclaimer with respect to the portion of the disclaimed property which the disclaimant has a right to receive. If the portion of the disclaimed interest in property which the disclaimant has a right to receive is not severable property or an undivided portion of the property, then the disclaimer is not a qualified disclaimer with respect to any portion of the property. Thus, for example, if a disclaimant who is not a surviving spouse receives a specific bequest of a fee simple interest in property and as a result of the disclaimer of the entire interest, the property passes to a trust in which the disclaimant has a remainder interest, then the disclaimer will not be a qualified disclaimer unless the remainder interest in the property is also disclaimed. See § 25.2518–3 (a)(l)(ii) for the definition of severable property.

(4) Effect of precatory language. Precatory language in a disclaimer naming takers of disclaimed property will not be considered as directing the redistribution or transfer of the property or interest in property to such persons if the applicable State law gives the language no legal effect.

(5) Examples. The provisions of this paragraph (e) may be illustrated by the following examples:

Example (1). A, a resident of State X, died on July 30, 1978. Pursuant to A's will, B, A's son and heir at law, received the family home. In addition, B and C each received 50 percent of A's residuary estate. B disclaimed the home. A's will made no provision for the distribution of property in the case of a beneficiary's disclaimer. Therefore, pursuant to the disclaimer laws of State X, the disclaimed property became part of the residuary estate. Because B's 50 percent share of the residuary estate will be increased by 50 percent of the value of the family home, the disclaimed property will not pass solely to another person. Consequently, B's disclaimer of the family home is a qualified disclaimer only with respect to the 50 percent portion that passes solely to C. Had B also disclaimed B's 50 percent interest in the residuary estate, the disclaimer would have been a qualified disclaimer under section 2518 of the entire interest in the home (assuming the remaining requirements of a qualified disclaimer were satisfied). Similarly, if under the laws of State X, the disclaimer has the effect of divesting B of all interest in the home, both as devisee and as a beneficiary of the residuary estate, including any property resulting from its sale, the disclaimer would be a qualified disclaimer of B's entire interest in the home.

Example (2). D, a resident of State Y, died testate on June 30, 1978. E, an heir at law of D, received specific bequests of certain severable personal property from D. E disclaimed the property transferred by D under the will. The will made no provision for the distribution of property in the case of a beneficiary's disclaimer. The disclaimer laws of State Y provide that such property shall pass to the decedent's heirs at law in the same manner as if the disclaiming beneficiary had died immediately before the testator's death. Because State Y's law treats E as predeceasing D, the property disclaimed by E does not pass to E as an heir at law or otherwise. Consequently, if the remaining requirements of section 2518(b) are satisfied, E's disclaimer is a qualified disclaimer under section 2518(a).

Example (3). Assume the same facts as in example (2) except that State Y has no provision treating the disclaimant as predeceasing the testator. E's disclaimer satisfies section 2518 (b)(4) only to the extent that E does not have a right to receive the property as an heir at law. Had E disclaimed both the share E received under D's will and E's intestate share, the requirement of section 2518 (b)(4) would have been satisfied.

Example (4). B died testate on February 13, 1980. B's will established both a marital trust and a nonmarital trust. The decedent's surviving spouse, A, is an income beneficiary of the marital trust and has a testamentary general power of appointment over its assets. A is also an income beneficiary of the nonmarital trust, but has no power to appoint or invade the corpus. The provisions of the will specify that any portion of the marital trust disclaimed is to be added to the nonmarital trust. A disclaimed 30 percent of the marital trust. (See § 25.2518–3(b) for rules relating to the disclaimer of an undivided portion of an interest in property.) Pursuant to the will, this portion of the marital trust property was transferred to the nonmarital trust without any direction on the part of A. This disclaimer by A satisfies section 2518(b)(4).

Example (5). Assume the same facts as in example (4) except that A, the surviving spouse, has both an income interest in the nonmarital trust and a testamentary nongeneral power to appoint among designated beneficiaries. This power is not limited by an ascertainable standard. The requirements of section 2518(b)(4) are not satisfied unless A also disclaims the nongeneral power to appoint the portion of the trust corpus that is attributable to the property that passed to the nonmarital trust as a result of A's disclaimer. Assuming that the fair market value of the disclaimed property on the date of the disclaimer is $250,000 and that the fair market value of the nonmarital trust (including the disclaimed property) immediately after the disclaimer is $750,000, A must disclaim the power to appoint one-third of the nonmarital trust's corpus. The result is the same regardless of whether the nongeneral power is testamentary or inter vivos.

Example (6). Assume the same facts as in example (4) except that A has both an income interest in the nonmarital trust and a power to invade corpus if needed for A's health or maintenance. In addition, an independent trustee has power to distribute to A any portion of the corpus which the trustee determines to be desirable for A's happiness. Assuming the other requirements of section 2518 are satisfied. A may make a qualified disclaimer of interests in the marital trust without disclaiming any of A's interests in the nonmarital trust.

Example (7). B died testate on June 1, 1980. B's will created both a marital trust and a nonmarital trust. The decedent's surviving spouse, C, is an income beneficiary of the marital trust and has a testamentary general power of appointment over its assets. C is an income beneficiary of the nonmarital trust, and additionally has the noncumulative right to withdraw yearly the greater of $5,000 or 5 percent of the aggregate value of the principal. The provisions of the will specify that any portion of the marital trust disclaimed is to be added to the nonmarital trust. C disclaims 50 percent of the marital trust corpus. Pursuant to the will, this amount is transferred to the nonmarital trust. Assuming the remaining requirements of section 2518(b) are satisfied, C's disclaimer is a qualified disclaimer.

Example (8). A, a resident of State X, died on July 19, 1979. A was survived by a spouse B, and three children, C, D, and E. Pursuant to A's will, B received one-half of A's estate and the children received equal shares of the remaining one-half of the estate. B disclaimed the entire interest B had received. The will made no provisions for the distribution of property in the case of a beneficiary's disclaimer. The disclaimer laws of State X provide that under these circumstances disclaimed property passes to the decedent's heirs at law in the same manner as if the disclaiming beneficiary had died immediately before the testator's death. As a result, C, D, and E are A's only remaining heirs at law, and will divide the disclaimed property equally among themselves. B's disclaimer includes language stating that "it is my intention that C, D, and E will share equally in the division of this property as a result of my disclaimer." State X considers these to be precatory words and gives them no legal effect. B's disclaimer meets all other requirements imposed by State X on disclaimers, and is considered an effective disclaimer under which the property will vest solely in C, D, and E in equal shares without any further action required by B. Therefore, B is not treated as directing the redistribution or transfer of the property. If the remaining requirements of section 2518 are met, B's disclaimer is a qualified disclaimer.

Example (9). C died testate on January 1, 1979. According to C's will, D was to receive 1/3 of the residuary estate with any disclaimed property going to E. D was also to receive a second 1/3 of the residuary estate with any disclaimed property going to F. Finally, D was to receive a final 1/3 of the residuary estate with any disclaimed property going to G. D specifically states that he is disclaiming the interest in which the disclaimed property is designated to pass to E. D has effectively directed that the disclaimed property will pass to E and therefore D's disclaimer is not a qualified disclaimer under section 2518(a).

Example (10). Assume the same facts as in example (9) except that C's will also states that D was to receive Blackacre and Whiteacre. C's will further provides that if D disclaimed Blackacre then such property was to pass to E and that if D disclaimed Whiteacre then Whiteacre was to pass to F. D specifically disclaims Blackacre with the intention that it pass to E. Assuming the other requirements of section 2518 are met, D has made a qualified disclaimer of Blackacre. Alternatively, D could disclaim an undivided portion of both Blackacre and Whiteacre. Assuming the other requirements of section 2518 are met, this would also be a qualified disclaimer.

Example (11). G creates an irrevocable trust on February 16, 1983, naming H, I and J as the income beneficiaries for life and F as the remainderman. F is also named the trustee and as trustee has the discretionary power to invade the corpus and make discretionary distributions to H, I or J during their lives. F disclaims the remainder interest on August 8, 1983, but retains his discretionary power to invade the corpus. F has not made a qualified disclaimer because F retains the power to direct enjoyment of the corpus and the retained fiduciary power is not limited by an ascertainable standard.

Example (12). Assume the same facts as in example (11) except that F may only invade the corpus to make distributions for the health, maintenance or support of H, I or J during their lives. If the other requirements of section 2518(b) are met, F has made a qualified disclaimer of the remainder interest because the retained fiduciary power is limited by an ascertainable standard.

§ 25.2518–3 Disclaimer of less than an entire interest.

(a) Disclaimer of a partial interest—(1) In general—(i) Interest. If the requirements of this section are met, the disclaimer of all or an undivided portion of any separate interest in property may be a qualified disclaimer even if the disclaimant has another interest in the same property. In general, each interest in property that is separately created by the transferor is treated as a separate interest. For example, if an income interest in securities is bequeathed to A for life, then to B for life, with the remainder interest in such securities bequeathed to A's estate, and if the remaining requirements of section 2518(b) are met, A could make a qualified disclaimer of either the income interest or the remainder, or an undivided portion of either interest. A could not, however, make a qualified disclaimer of the income interest for a certain number of years. Further, where local law merges interests separately created by the transferor, a qualified disclaimer will be allowed only if there is a disclaimer of the entire merged interest or an undivided portion of such merged interest. See example (12) in paragraph (d) of this section. See § 25.2518–3(b) for rules relating to the disclaimer of an undivided portion. Where the merger of separate interests would occur but for the creation by the transferor of a nominal interest (as defined in paragraph (a)(1)(iv) of this section), a qualified disclaimer will be allowed only if there is a disclaimer of all the separate interests, or an undivided portion of all such interests, which would have merged but for the nominal interest.

(ii) Severable property. A disclaimant shall be treated as making a qualified disclaimer of a separate interest in property if the disclaimer relates to severable property and the disclaimant makes a disclaimer which would be a qualified disclaimer if such property were the only property in which the disclaimant had an interest. If applicable local law does not recognize a purported disclaimer of severable property, the disclaimant must comply with the requirements of paragraph (c)(1) of § 25.2518–1 in order to make a qualified disclaimer of the severable property. Severable property is property which can be divided into separate parts each of which, after severance, maintains a complete and independent existence. For example, a legatee of shares of corporate stock may accept some shares of the stock and make a qualified disclaimer of the remaining shares.

(iii) Powers of appointment. A power of appointment with respect to property is treated as a separate interest in such property and such power of appointment with respect to all or an undivided portion of such property may be disclaimed independently from any other interests separately created by the transferor in the property if the requirements of section 2518(b) are met. See example (21) of paragraph (d) of this section. Further, a disclaimer of a power of appointment with respect to property is a qualified disclaimer only if any right to direct the beneficial enjoyment of the property which is retained by the disclaimant is limited by an ascertainable standard. See example (9) of paragraph (d) of this section.

(iv) Nominal interest. A nominal interest is an interest in property created by the transferor that—

(A) Has an actuarial value (as determined under § 20.2031–10) of less than 5 percent of the total value of the property at the time of the taxable transfer creating the interest,

(B) Prevents the merger under local law or two or more other interests created by the transferor, and

(C) Can be clearly shown from all the facts and circumstances to have been created primarily for the purpose of preventing the merger of such other interests.

Factors to be considered in determining whether an interest is created primarily for the purpose of preventing merger include (but are not limited to) the following: the relationship between the transferor and the interest holder; the age difference between the interest holder and the beneficiary whose interests would have merged; the interest holder's state of health at the time of the taxable transfer; and, in the case of a contingent remainder, any other factors which indicate that the possibility of the interest vesting as a fee simple is so remote as to be negligible.

(2) In trust. A disclaimer is not a qualified disclaimer under section 2518 if the beneficiary disclaims income derived from specific property transferred in trust while continuing to accept income derived from the remaining properties in the same trust unless the disclaimer results in such property being removed from the trust and passing, without any direction on the part of the disclaimant, to persons other than the disclaimant or to the spouse of the decedent. Moreover, a disclaimer of both an income interest and a remainder interest in specific trust assets is not a qualified disclaimer if the beneficiary retains interests in other trust property unless, as a result of the disclaimer, such assets are removed from the trust and pass, without any direction on the part of the disclaimant, to persons other than the disclaimant or to the spouse of the decedent. The disclaimer of an undivided portion of an interest in a trust may be a qualified disclaimer. See also paragraph (b) of this section for rules relating to the disclaimer of an undivided portion of an interest in property.

(b) Disclaimer of undivided portion. A disclaimer of an undivided portion of a separate interest in property which meets the other requirements of a qualified disclaimer under section 2518(b) and the corresponding regulations is a qualified disclaimer. An undivided portion of a disclaimant's separate interest in property must consist of a fraction or percentage of each and every substantial interest or right owned by the disclaimant in such property and must extend over the entire term of the disclaimant's interest in such property and in other property into which such property is converted. A disclaimer of some specific rights while retaining other rights with respect to an interest in the property is not a qualified disclaimer of an undivided portion of the disclaimant's interest in property. Thus, for example, a disclaimer made by the devisee of a fee simple interest in Blackacre is not a qualified disclaimer if the disclaimant disclaims a remainder interest in Blackacre but retains a life estate.

(c) Disclaimer of a pecuniary amount. A disclaimer of a specific pecuniary amount out of a pecuniary or nonpecuniary bequest or gift which satisfies the other requirements of a qualified disclaimer under section 2518(b) and the corresponding regulations is a qualified disclaimer provided that no income or other benefit of the disclaimed amount inures to the benefit of the disclaimant either prior to or subsequent to the disclaimer. Thus, following the disclaimer of a specific pecuniary amount from a bequest or gift, the amount disclaimed and any income attributable to such amount must be segregated from the portion of the gift or bequest that was not disclaimed. Such a segregation of assets making up the disclaimer of a pecuniary amount must be made on the basis of the fair market value of the assets on the date of the disclaimer or on a basis that is fairly representative of value changes that may have occurred between the date of transfer and the date of the disclaimer. A pecuniary amount distributed to the disclaimant from the bequest or gift prior to the disclaimer shall be treated as a distribution of corpus from the bequest or gift. However, the acceptance of a distribution from the gift or bequest shall also be considered to be an acceptance of a proportionate amount of income earned by the bequest or gift. The proportionate share of income considered to be accepted by the disclaimant shall be determined at the time of the disclaimer according to the following formula:

$$\frac{\text{Total amount of distributions received by the disclaimant out of the gift or bequest}}{\text{Total value of the gift or bequest on the date of transfer}} \times \text{Total amount of income earned by the gift or bequest between date of transfer and date of disclaimer}$$

See examples (17), (18), and (19) in § 25.2518-3(d) for illustrations of the rules set forth in this paragraph (c).

* * *

DEDUCTIONS

* * *

§ 25.2522(a)–1 Charitable and similar gifts; citizens or residents.

(a) In determining the amount of taxable gifts for the "calendar period" (as defined in § 25.2502–1(c)(1)) there may be deducted, in the case of a donor who was a citizen or resident of the United States at the time the gifts were made, all gifts included in the "total amount of gifts" made by the donor during the calendar period (see section 2503 and the regulations thereunder) and made to or for the use of:

(1) The United States, any State, Territory, or any political subdivision thereof, or the District of Columbia, for exclusively public purposes.

(2) Any corporation, trust, community chest, fund, or foundation organized and operated exclusively for religious, charitable, scientific, literary, or educational purposes, including the encouragement of art and the prevention of cruelty to children or animals, if no part of the net earnings of the organization inures to the benefit of any private shareholder or individual, if the organization is not disqualified for taxexemption under section 501 (c)(3) by reason of attempting to influence legislation, and if, in the case of gifts made after December 31, 1969, it does not participate in, or intervene in (including the publishing or distributing of statements), any political campaign on behalf of or in opposition to any candidate for public office.

(3) A fraternal society, order, or association, operating under the lodge system, provided the gifts are to be used by the society, order or association exclusively for one or more of the purposes set forth in subparagraph (2) of this paragraph.

(4) Any post or organization of war veterans or auxiliary unit or society thereof, if organized in the United States or any of its possessions, and if no part of its net earnings inures to the benefit of any private shareholder or individual.

The deduction is not limited to gifts for use within the United States, or to gifts to or for the use of domestic corporations, trusts, community chests, funds, or foundations, or fraternal societies, orders, or associations operating under the lodge system. An organization will not be considered to meet the requirements of subparagraph (2) of this paragraph, or of paragraph (b)(2) or (3) of this section, if such organization engages in any activity which would cause it to be classified as an "action" organization under paragraph (c)(3) of § 1.501(c)(3)–1 of this chapter (Income Tax Regulations). For the deductions for charitable and similar gifts made by a nonresident who was not a citizen of the United States at the time the gifts were made, see § 25.2522(b)–1. See §§ 25.2522(c)–1 and 25.2522(c)–2 for rules relating to the disallowance of deductions to trusts and organizations which engage in certain prohibited transactions or whose governing instruments do not contain certain specified requirements.

(b) The deduction under section 2522 is not allowed for a transfer to a corporation, trust, community chest, fund, or foundation unless the organization or trust meets the following four tests:

(1) It must be organized and operated exclusively for one or more of the specified purposes.

(2) It must not, by a substantial part of its activities, attempt to influence legislation by propaganda or otherwise.

(3) In the case of gifts made after December 31, 1969, it must not participate in, or intervene in (including the publishing or distributing of statements), any political campaign on behalf of any candidate for public office.

(4) Its net earnings must not inure in whole or in part to the benefit of private shareholders or individuals other than as legitimate objects of the exempt purposes.

For further limitations see § 25.2522(c)–1, relating to gifts to trusts and organizations which have engaged in a prohibited transaction described in section 681(b)(2) or section 503(c).

(c) In order to prove the right to the charitable, etc., deduction provided by section 2522 the donor must submit such data as may be requested by the Internal Revenue Service. As to the extent the deductions provided by this section are allowable, see section 2524.

* * *

§ 25.2522(c)–2 Disallowance of charitable, etc., deductions in the case of gifts made after December 31, 1969.

(a) Organizations subject to section 507(c) tax. Section 508(d)(1) provides that, in the case of gifts made after December 31, 1969, a deduction which would otherwise be allowable under section 2522 for a gift to or for the use of an organization upon which the tax provided by section 507(c) has been imposed shall not be allowed if the gift is made by the donor after notification is made under section 507(a) or if the donor is a substantial contributor (as defined in section 507(d)(2)) who makes such gift in his taxable year (as defined in section 441) which includes the first day on which action is taken by such organization that culminates in the imposition of the tax under section 507(c) and any subsequent taxable year. This paragraph does not apply if the entire amount of the unpaid portion of the tax imposed by section 507(c) is abated under section 507(g) by the Commissioner or his delegate.

(b) Taxable private foundations, section 4947 trusts, etc. Section 508(d)(2) provides that, in the case of gifts made after December 31, 1969, a deduction which would otherwise be allowable under section 2522 shall not be allowed if the gift is made to or for the use of—

(1) A private foundation or a trust described in section 4947(a)(2) in a taxable year of such organization for which such organization fails to meet the governing instrument requirements of section 508(e) (determined without regard to section 508(e)(2)(B) and (C)), or

(2) Any organization in a period for which it is not treated as an organization described in section 501(c)(3) by reason of its failure to give notification under section 508(a) of its status to the Commissioner.

For additional rules, see § 1.508–2(b)(1) of this chapter (Income Tax Regulations).

(c) Foreign organizations with substantial support from foreign sources. Section 4948(c)(4) provides that, in the case of gifts made after December 31, 1969, a deduction which would otherwise be allowable under section 2522 for a gift to or for the use of a foreign organization which has received substantially all of its support (other than gross investment income) from sources without the United States shall not be allowed if the gift is made (1) after the date on which the Commissioner has published notice that he has notified such organization that it has engaged in a prohibited transaction, or (2) in a taxable year of such organization for which it is not exempt from taxation under section 501(a) because it has engaged in a prohibited transaction after December 31, 1969.

§ 25.2522(c)–3 Transfers not exclusively for charitable, etc., purposes in the case of gifts made after July 31, 1969.

(a) Remainders and similar interests. If a trust is created or property is transferred for both a charitable and a private purpose, deduction may be taken of the value of the charitable beneficial interest only insofar as that interest is presently ascertainable, and hence severable from the noncharitable interest.

(b) Transfers subject to a condition or a power.

(1) If, as of the date of the gift, a transfer for charitable purposes is dependent upon the performance of some act or of the happening of a precedent event in order that it might become effective, no deduction is allowable unless the possibility that the charitable transfer will not become effective is so remote as to be negligible. If an estate or interest has passed to, or is vested in, charity on the date of the gift and the estate or interest would be defeated by the performance of some act or the happening of some event, the possibility of occurrence of which appeared on such date to be so remote as to be negligible, the deduction is allowable. If the donee or trustee is empowered to divert the property or fund, in whole or in part, to a use or purpose which would have rendered it, to the extent that it is subject to such power, not deductible had it been directly so given by the donor, the deduction will be limited to that portion, if any, of the property or fund which is exempt from an exercise of the power.

(2) The application of this paragraph may be illustrated by the following examples:

Example (1). In 1965, A transfers certain property in trust in which charity is to receive the income for his life. The assets placed in trust by the donor consist of stock in a corporation the fiscal policies of which are controlled by the donor and his family. The trustees of the trust and the remainderman are members of the donor's family and the governing instrument contains no adequate guarantee of the requisite income to the charitable organization. Under such circumstances, no deduction will be allowed. Similarly, if the trustees are not members of the donor's family but have no power to sell or otherwise dispose of the closely held stock, or otherwise insure the requisite enjoyment of income to the charitable organization, no deduction will be allowed.

Example (2). C transfers a tract of land to a city government for as long as the land is used by the city for a public park. If on the date of gift the city does plan to use the land for a public park and the possibility that the city will not use the land for a public park is so remote as to be negligible, a deduction will be allowed.

(c) Transfers of partial interest in property—(1) Disallowance of deduction—(i) In general. If a donor transfers an interest in property after July 31, 1969, for charitable purposes and an interest in the same property is retained by the donor, or is transferred or has been transferred for private purposes after such date (for less than an adequate and full consideration in money or money's worth), no deduction is allowed under section 2522 for the value of the interest which is transferred or has been transferred for charitable purposes unless the interest in property is a deductible interest described in subparagraph (2) of this paragraph. The principles that are used in applying section 2523 and the regulations thereunder shall apply for purposes of determining under this paragraph (c)(1)(i) whether an interest in property is retained by the donor, or is transferred or has been transferred by the donor. If, however, as of the date of the gift, a retention of any interest by a donor, or a transfer for a private purpose, is dependent upon the performance of some act or the happening of a precedent event in order that it may become effective, an interest in property will be considered retained by the donor, or transferred for a private purpose, unless the possibility of occurrence of such act or event is so remote as to be negligible. The application of this paragraph (c)(1)(i) may be illustrated by the following examples, in each of which it is assumed that the property interest which is transferred for private purposes is not transferred for an adequate and full consideration in money or money's worth:

Example (1). In 1973, H creates a trust which is to pay the income of the trust to W for her life, the reversionary interest in the trust being retained by H. In 1975, H gives the reversionary interest to charity, while W is still living. For purposes of this paragraph (c)(l)(i), interests in the same property have been transferred by H for charitable purposes and for private purposes.

Example (2). In 1973, H creates a trust which is to pay the income of the trust to W for her life and upon termination of the life estate to transfer the remainder to S. In 1975, S gives his remainder interest to charity, while W is still living. For purposes of this paragraph (c)(1)(i), interests in the same property have not been transferred by H or S for charitable purposes and for private purposes.

Example (3). H transfers Blackacre to A by gift, reserving the right to the rentals of Blackacre for a term of 20 years. After 4 years H transfers the right to the remaining rentals to charity. For purposes of this paragraph (c)(1)(i) the term "property" refers to Blackacre, and the right to rentals from Blackacre consist of an interest in Blackacre. An interest in Blackacre has been transferred by H for charitable purposes and for private purposes.

Example (4). H transfers property in trust for the benefit of A and a charity. An annuity of $5,000 a year is to be paid to charity for 20 years. Upon termination of the 20-year term the corpus is to be distributed to A if living. However, if A should die during the 20-year term, the corpus is to be distributed to charity upon termination of the term. An interest in property has been transferred by H for charitable purposes. In addition, an interest in the same property has been transferred by H for private purposes unless the possibility that A will survive the 20-year term is so remote as to be negligible.

Example (5). H transfers property in trust, under the terms of which an annuity of $5,000 a year is to be paid to charity for 20 years. Upon termination of the term, the corpus is to pass to such of A's children and their issue as A may appoint. However, if A should die during the 20-year term without exercising the power of appointment, the corpus is to be distributed to charity upon termination of the term. Since the possible appointees include private persons, an interest in the corpus of the trust is considered to have been transferred by H for private purposes.

(ii) Works of art and copyright treated as separate properties. For purposes of paragraphs (c)(1)(i) and (c)(2) of this section, rules similar to the rules in § 20.2055–2(e)(1)(ii) shall apply in the case of transfers made after December 31, 1981.

(2) Deductible interests. A deductible interest for purposes of subparagraph (1) of this paragraph is a charitable interest in property where—

(i) Undivided portion of donor's entire interest. The charitable interest is an undivided portion, not in trust, of the donor's entire interest in property. An undivided portion of a donor's entire interest in property must consist of a fraction or percentage of each and every substantial interest or right owned by the donor in such property and must extend over the entire term of the donor's interest in such property and in other property into which such property is converted. For example, if the donor have a life estate in an office building to his wife for her life and retained a reversionary interest in the office building, the gift by the donor of one-half of that reversionary interest to charity while his wife is still alive will not be considered the transfer of a deductible interest; because an interest in the same property has already passed from the donor for private purposes, the reversionary interest will not be considered the donor's entire interest in the property. If, on the other hand, the donor had been given a life estate in Blackacre for the life of his wife and the donor had no other interest in Blackacre on or before the time of gift, the gift by the donor of one-half of that life estate to charity would be considered the transfer of a deductible interest; because the life estate would be considered the donor's entire interest in the property, the gift would be of an undivided portion of such entire interest. An undivided portion of a donor's entire interest in property includes an interest in property whereby the charity is given the right, as a tenant in common with the donor, to possession, dominion, and control of the property for a portion of each year appropriate to its interest in such property. However, except as provided in paragraphs (e)(2)(ii), (iii), and (iv) of this section, for purposes of this subdivision a charitable contribution of an interest in property not in trust where the decedent transfers some specific rights to one party and transfers other substantial rights to another party will not be considered a contribution of an undivided portion of the decedent's entire interest in property. Thus, for example, a deduction is not allowable for the value of an immediate and perpetual gift not in trust of an interest in original historic motion picture films to a charitable organization where the donor retains the exclusive right to make reproductions of such films and to exploit such reproductions commercially. A gift to charity made on or before December 17, 1980, of an open space easement in gross in perpetuity shall be considered the transfer to charity of an undivided portion of the donor's entire interest in property.

(ii) Remainder interest in a personal residence. The charitable interest is an irrevocable remainder interest, not in trust, in a personal residence. Thus, for example, if the donor gives to charity a remainder interest in a personal residence and retains an estate in such property for life or a term of years the value of such remainder interest is deductible under section 2522. For purposes of this subdivision, the term "personal residence" means any property which is used by the donor as his personal residence even though it is not used as his principal residence. For example, a donor's vacation home may be a personal residence for purposes of this subdivision. The term "personal residence" also includes stock owned by the donor on the date of gift as a tenant-stockholder in a cooperative housing corporation (as those terms are defined in section 216(b)(1) and (2)) if the dwelling which the donor is entitled to occupy as such stockholder is used by him as his personal residence.

(iii) Remainder interest in a farm. The charitable interest is an irrevocable remainder interest, not in trust, in a farm. Thus, for example, if the donor gives to charity a remainder interest in a farm and retains an estate in such property for life or a term of years, the value of such remainder interest is deductible under section 2522. For purposes of this subdivision, the term "farm" means any land used by the donor or his tenant for the production of crops, fruits, or other agricultural products or for the sustenance of livestock. The term "livestock" includes cattle, hogs, horses, mules, donkeys, sheep, goats, captive fur-bearing animals, chickens, turkeys, pigeons, and other poultry. A farm includes the improvements thereon.

(iv) Qualified conservation contribution. The charitable interest is a qualified conservation contribution. For the definition of a qualified conservation contribution, see § 1.170A–14.

(v) Charitable remainder trust and pooled income funds. The charitable interest is a remainder interest in a trust which is a charitable remainder annuity trust, as defined in section 664(d)(1) and § 1.664–2 of this chapter; a charitable remainder unitrust, as defined in section 664(d)(2) and (3) and § 1.664–3 of this chapter; or a pooled income fund, as defined in section 642(c)(5) and § 1.642(c)–5 of this chapter. The charitable organization to or for the use of which the remainder interest is transferred must meet the requirements of both section 2522(a) or (b) and section 642(c)(5)(A), section 664(d)(1)(C), or section 664(d)(2)(C), whichever applies. For example, the charitable organization to which the remainder interest in a charitable remainder annuity trust is transferred may not be a foreign corporation.

(vi) Guaranteed annuity interest.(a) The charitable interest is a guaranteed annuity interest, whether or not such interest is in trust. For purposes of this subdivision (v), the term "guaranteed annuity interest" means an irrevocable right pursuant to the instrument of transfer to receive a guaranteed annuity. A guaranteed annuity is an arrangement under which a determinable amount is paid periodically, but not less often than annually, for a specified term or for the life or lives of a named individual or individuals, each of whom must be living at the date of the gift and can be ascertained at such date. For example, the annuity may be paid for the life of A plus a term of years. An amount is determinable if the exact amount which must be paid under the conditions specified in the instrument of transfer can be ascertained as of the date of gift. For example, the amount to be paid may be a stated sum for a term, or for the life of an individual, at the expiration of which it may be changed by a specified amount, but it may not be redetermined by reference to a fluctuating index such as the cost of living index. In further illustration, the amount to be paid may be expressed as a fraction or percentage of the cost of living index on the date of gift.

(b) A charitable interest is a guaranteed annuity interest only if it is a guaranteed annuity interest in every respect. For example, if the charitable interest is the right to receive from a trust each year a payment equal to the lesser of a sum certain or a fixed percentage of the net fair market value of the trust assets, determined annually, such interest is not a guaranteed annuity interest.

(c) Where a charitable interest in the form of a guaranteed annuity interest is not in trust, the interest will be considered a guaranteed annuity interest only if it is to be paid by an insurance company or by an organization regularly engaged in issuing annuity contracts.

(d) Where a charitable interest in the form of a guaranteed annuity interest is in trust, the governing instrument of the trust may provide that income of the trust which is in excess of the amount required to pay the guaranteed annuity interest shall be paid to or for the use of a charity. Nevertheless, the amount of the deduction under section 2522 shall be limited to the fair market value of the guaranteed annuity interest as determined under paragraph (d)(2)(iv) of this section.

(e) Where a charitable interest in the form of a guaranteed annuity interest is in trust and the present value on the date of gift of all income interests for a charitable purpose exceeds 60 percent of the aggregate fair market value of all amounts in such trust (after the payment of liabilities), the charitable interest will not be considered a guaranteed annuity interest unless the governing instrument of the trust prohibits both the acquisition and the retention of assets which would give rise to a tax under section 4944 if the trustee had acquired such assets. The requirement in this (e) for a prohibition in the governing instrument against the retention of assets which would give rise to a tax under section 4944 if the trustee had acquired the assets shall not apply to a gift made on or before May 21, 1972.

(f) Where a charitable interest in the form of a guaranteed annuity interest is in trust, and the gift of such interest is made after May 21, 1972, the charitable interest generally is not a guaranteed annuity interest if any amount may be paid by the trust for a private purpose before the expiration of all the charitable annuity interests. There are two exceptions to this general rule. First, the charitable interest is a guaranteed annuity interest if the amount payable for a private purpose is in the form of a guaranteed annuity interest and the trust's governing instrument does not provide for any preference or priority in the payment of the private annuity as opposed to the charitable annuity. Second, the charitable interest is a guaranteed annuity interest if under the trust's governing instrument the amount that may be paid for a private purpose is payable only from a group of assets that are devoted exclusively to private purposes and to which section 4947(a)(2) is inapplicable by reason of section 4947(a)(2)(B). For purposes of this paragraph (c)(2)(vi)(f), an amount is not paid for a private purpose if it is paid for an adequate and full consideration in money or money's worth. See § 53.4947–1(c) of this chapter for rules relating to the inapplicability of section 4947(a)(2) to segregated amounts in a split-interest trust.

(g) For rules relating to certain governing instrument requirements and to the imposition of certain excise taxes where the guaranteed annuity interest is in trust and for rules governing payment of private income interests by a split-interest trust, see section 4947(a)(2) and (b)(3)(A), and the regulations thereunder.

(vii) Unitrust interest.(a) The charitable interest is a unitrust interest, whether or not such interest is in trust. For purposes of this subdivision (vi), the term "unitrust interest" means an irrevocable right pursuant to the instrument of transfer to receive payment, not less often than annually, of a fixed percentage of the net fair market value, determined annually, of the property which funds the unitrust interest. In computing the net fair market value of the property which funds the unitrust interest, all assets and liabilities shall be taken into account without regard to whether particular items are taken into account in determining the income from the property. The net fair market value of the property which funds the unitrust interest may be determined on any one date during the year or by taking the average of valuations made on more than one date during the year, provided that the same valuation date or dates and valuation methods are used each year. Where the charitable interest is a unitrust interest to be paid by a trust and the governing instrument of the trust does not specify the valuation date or dates, the trustee shall select such date or dates and shall indicate his selection on the first return on Form 1041 which the trust is required to file. Payments under a unitrust interest may be paid for a specified term or for the life or lives of an individual or individuals, each of whom must be living at the date of the gift and can be ascertained at such date. For example, the unitrust interest may be paid for the life of A plus a term of years.

(b) A charitable interest is a unitrust interest only if it is a unitrust interest in every respect. For example, if the charitable interest is the right to receive from a trust each year a payment equal to the lesser of a sum certain or a fixed percentage of the net fair market value of the trust assets, determined annually, such interest is not a unitrust interest.

(c) Where a charitable interest in the form of a unitrust interest is not in trust, the interest will be considered a unitrust interest only if it is to be paid by an insurance company or by an organization regularly engaged in issuing interests otherwise meeting the requirements of a unitrust interest.

(d) Where a charitable interest in the form of a unitrust interest is in trust, the governing instrument of the trust may provide that income of the trust which is in excess of the amount required to pay the unitrust interest shall be paid to or for the use of a charity. Nevertheless, the amount of the deduction under section 2522 shall be limited to the fair market value of the unitrust interest as determined under paragraph (d)(2)(v) of this section.

(e) Where a charitable interest in the form of a unitrust interest is in trust, the charitable interest generally is not a unitrust interest if any amount may be paid by the trust for a private purpose before the expiration of all the charitable unitrust interests. There are two exceptions to this general rule. First, the charitable interest is a unitrust interest if the amount payable for a private purpose is in the form of a unitrust interest and the trust's governing instrument does not provide for any preference or priority in the payment of the private unitrust interest as opposed to the charitable unitrust interest. Second, the charitable interest is a unitrust interest if under the trust's governing instrument the amount that may be paid for a private purpose is payable only from a group of assets that are devoted exclusively to private purposes and to which section 4947(a)(2) is inapplicable by reason of section 4947(a)(2)(B). For purposes of this paragraph (c)(2)(vii)(e), an amount is not paid for a private purpose if it is paid for an adequate and full consideration in money or money's worth. See § 53.4947–1(c) of this chapter for rules relating to the inapplicability of section 4947(a)(2) to segregated amounts in a split-interest trust.

(f) For rules relating to certain governing instrument requirements and to the imposition of certain excise taxes where the unitrust interest is in trust and for rules governing payment of private income interests by a split-interest trust, see sections 4947(a)(2) and (b)(3)(A), and the regulations thereunder.

(d) Valuation of charitable interest—(1) In general. The amount of the deduction in the case of a contribution of a partial interest in property to which this section applies is the fair market value of the partial interest on the date of gift. The fair market value of an annuity, life estate, term for years, remainder, reversion or unitrust interest is its present value.

(2) Certain transfers after July 31, 1969. In the case of a transfer after July 31, 1969, of an interest described in subdivision (iv), (v), or (vi) of paragraph (c)(2) of this section, the present value of such interest is to be determined under the following rules:

(i) The present value of a remainder interest in a charitable remainder annuity trust is to be determined under § 1.664–2(c) of this chapter (Income Tax Regulations).

(ii) The present value of a remainder interest in a charitable remainder unitrust is to be determined under § 1.664–4 of this chapter.

(iii) The present value of a remainder interest in a pooled income fund is to be determined under § 1.642(c)–6 of this chapter.

(iv) The present value of a guaranteed annuity interest described in paragraph (c)(2)(v) of this section is to be determined under § 25.2512–5 or 25.2512–9, whichever is appropriate, except that, if the annuity is issued by a company regularly engaged in the sale of annuities, the present value is to be determined under § 25.2512–6. If by reason of all the conditions and circumstances surrounding a transfer of an income interest in property in trust it appears that the charity may not receive the beneficial enjoyment of the interest, a deduction will be allowed under section 2522 only for the minimum amount it is evident the charity will receive.

Example (1). In 1975, B transfers $20,000 in trust with the requirement that a designated charity be paid a guaranteed annuity interest (as defined in paragraph (c)(2)(v) of this section) of $4,100 a year, payable annually at the end of each year for a period of 6 years and that the remainder be paid to his children. The fair market value of an annuity of $4,100 a year for a period of 6 years is $20,160.93 ($4,100 × 4.9173), as determined under Table B in § 25.2512–9(f). The deduction with respect to the guaranteed annuity interest will be limited to $20,000, which is the minimum amount it is evident the charity will receive.

Example (2). In 1975, C transfers $40,000 in trust with the requirement that D, an individual, and X Charity be paid simultaneously guaranteed annuity interests (as defined in paragraph (c)(2)(v) of this section) of $5,000 a year each, payable annually at the end of each year, for a period of 5 years and that the remainder be paid to C's children. The fair market value of two annuities of $5,000 each a year for a period of 5 years is $42,124 ([$5,000 × 4.2124] × 2), as determined under Table B in § 25.2512–9(f). The trust instrument provides that in the event the trust fund is insufficient to pay both annuities in a given year, the trust fund will be evenly divided between the charitable and private annuitants. The deduction with respect to the charitable annuity will be limited to $20,000, which is the minimum amount it is evident the charity will receive.

Example (3). In 1975, D transfers $65,000 in trust with the requirement that a guaranteed annuity interest (as defined in paragraph (c)(2)(v) of this section) of $5,000 a year, payable annually at the end of each year, be paid to Y Charity for a period of 10 years and that a guaranteed annuity interest (as defined in paragraph (c)(2)(v) of this section) of $5,000 a year, payable annually at the end of each year, be paid to W, his wife, aged 62, for 10 years or until her prior death. The annuities are to be paid simultaneously, and the remainder is to be paid to D's children. The fair market value of the private annuity is $33,877 ($5,000 × 6.7754), as determined pursuant to § 25.2512–9(e) and by the use of factors involving one life and a term of years as published in Publication 723A (12–70). The fair market value of the charitable annuity is $36,800.50 ($5,000 × 7.3601), as determined under Table B in § 25.2512–9(f). It is not evident from the governing instrument of the trust or from local law that the trustee would be required to apportion the trust fund between the wife and charity in the event the fund were insufficient to pay both annuities in a given year. Accordingly, the deduction with respect to the charitable annuity will be limited to $31,123 ($65,000 less $33,877 [the value of the private annuity]), which is the minimum amount it is evident the charity will receive.

(v) The present value of a unitrust interest described in paragraph (c)(2)(vi) of this section is to be determined by subtracting the present value of all interests in the transferred property other than the unitrust interest from the fair market value of the transferred property.

(3) Other transfers. The present value of an interest not described in paragraph (d)(2) of this section is to be determined under § 25.2512–5.

(4) Special computations. If the interest transferred is such that its present value is to be determined by a special computation, a request for a special factor, accompanied by a statement of the date of birth and sex of each individual the duration of whose life may affect the value of the interest, and by copies of the relevant instruments, may be submitted by the donor to the Commissioner who may, if conditions permit, supply the factor requested. If the Commissioner furnishes the factor, a copy of the letter supplying the factor must be attached to the tax return in which the deduction is claimed. If the Commissioner does not furnish the factor, the claim for deduction must be supported by a full statement of the computation of the present value made in accordance with the principles set forth in this paragraph.

* * *

§ 25.2523(a)–1 Gift to spouse; In general.

(a) In general. In determining the amount of taxable gifts for the calendar quarter (with respect to gifts made after December 31, 1970, and before January 1, 1982), or calendar year (with respect to gifts made before January 1, 1971, or after December 31, 1981), a donor may deduct the value of any property interest transferred by gift to a donee who at the time of the gift is the donor's spouse, except as limited by paragraphs (b) and (c) of this section. See § 25.2502–1(c)(1) for the definition of calendar quarter. This deduction is referred to as the *marital deduction.* In the case of gifts made prior to July 14, 1988, no marital deduction is allowed with respect to a gift if, at the time of the gift, the donor is a nonresident not a citizen of the United States. Further, in the case of gifts made on or after July 14, 1988, no marital deduction is allowed (regardless of the donor's citizenship or residence) for transfers to a spouse who is not a citizen of the United States at the time of the transfer. However, for certain special rules applicable in the case of estate and gift tax treaties, see section 7815(d)(14) of Public Law 101–239. The donor must submit any evidence necessary to establish the donor's right to the marital deduction.

(b) "Deductible interests" and "nondeductible interests"—(1) In general. The property interests transferred by a donor to his spouse consist of either transfers with respect to which the marital deduction is authorized (as described in subparagraph (2) of this paragraph) or transfers with respect to which the marital deduction is not authorized (as described in subparagraph (3) of this paragraph). These transfers are referred to in this section and in §§ 25.2523(b)–1 through 25.2523(f)–1 as "deductible interests" and "nondeductible interests", respectively.

(2) "Deductible interest". A property interest transferred by a donor to his spouse is a "deductible interest" if it does not fall within either class of "nondeductible interests" described in subparagraph (3) of this paragraph.

(3) "Nondeductible interests".(i) A property interest transferred by a donor to his spouse which is a "terminable interest", as defined in § 25.2523(b)–1, is a "nondeductible interest" to the extent specified in that section.

(ii) Any property interest transferred by a donor to the donor's spouse is a *nondeductible interest* to the extent it is not required to be included in a gift tax return for a calendar quarter (for gifts made after December 31, 1970, and before January 1, 1982) or calendar year (for gifts made before January 1, 1971, or after December 31, 1981). See §§ 25.2515–1 (relating to tenancies by the entirety) and 25.2516–1 (relating to property settlements followed by divorce) for some, but not necessarily all, of the situations in which property is transferred by a donor to his spouse and not included in the total amount of gifts made during the calendar quarter or calendar year.

* * *

§ 25.2523(b)–1 Life estate or other terminable interest.

(a) In general.(1) The provisions of section 2523(b) generally disallow a marital deduction with respect to certain property interests (referred to generally as terminable interests and defined in paragraph (a)(3) of this section) transferred to the donee spouse under the circumstances described in paragraph (a)(2) of this section, unless the transfer comes within the purview of one of the exceptions set forth in § 25.2523(d)–1 (relating to certain joint interests); § 25.2523(e)–1 (relating to certain life estates with powers of appointment); § 25.2523(f)–1 (relating to certain qualified terminable interest property); or § 25.2523(g)–1 (relating to certain qualified charitable remainder trusts).

(2) If a donor transfers a terminable interest in property to the donee spouse, the marital deduction is disallowed with respect to the transfer if the donor spouse also—

(i) Transferred an interest in the same property to another donee (see paragraph (b) of this section), or

(ii) Retained an interest in the same property in himself (see paragraph (c) of this section), or

(iii) Retained a power to appoint an interest in the same property (see paragraph (d) of this section).

Notwithstanding the preceding sentence, the marital deduction is disallowed under these circumstances only if the other donee, the donor, or the possible appointee, may, by reason of the transfer or retention, possess or enjoy any part of the property after the termination or failure of the interest therein transferred to the donee spouse.

(3) For purposes of this section, a distinction is to be drawn between "property," as such term is used in section 2523, and an "interest in property." The "property" referred to is the underlying property in which various interests exist; each such interest is not, for this purpose, to be considered as "property." A "terminable interest" in property is an interest which will terminate or fail on the lapse of time or on the occurrence or failure to occur of some contingency. Life estates, terms for years, annuities, patents, and copyrights are therefore terminable interests. However, a bond, note, or similar contractual obligation, the discharge of which would not have the effect of an annuity or term for years, is not a terminable interest.

(b) Interest in property which another donee may possess or enjoy.(1) Section 2523(b) provides that no marital deduction shall be allowed with respect to the transfer to the donee spouse of a "terminable interest" in property, in case—

(i) The donor transferred (for less than an adequate and full consideration in money or money's worth) an interest in the same property to any person other than the donee spouse (or the estate of such spouse), and

(ii) By reason of such transfer, such person (or his heirs or assigns) may possess or enjoy any part of such property after the termination or failure of the interest therein transferred to the donee spouse.

(2) In determining whether the donor transferred an interest in property to any person other than the donee spouse, it is immaterial whether the transfer to the person other than the donee spouse was made at the same time as the transfer to such spouse, or at any earlier time.

(3) Except as provided in § 25.2523(e)–1 or 25.2523(f)–1, if at the time of the transfer it is impossible to ascertain the particular person or persons who may receive a property interest transferred by the donor, such interest is considered as transferred to a person other than the donee spouse for the purpose of section 2523(b). This rule is particularly applicable in the case of the transfer of a property interest by the donor subject to a reserved power. See § 25.2511–2. Under this rule, any property interest over which the donor reserved a power to revest the beneficial title in himself, or over which the donor reserved the power to name new beneficiaries or to change the interests of the beneficiaries as between themselves, is for the purpose of section 2523(b), considered as transferred to a "person other than the donee spouse." The following examples, in which it is assumed that the donor did not make an election under sections 2523(f)(2)(C) and (f)(4), illustrate the application of the provisions of this paragraph (b)(3):

Example (1). If a donor transferred property in trust naming his wife as the irrevocable income beneficiary for 10 years, and providing that, upon the expiration of that term, the corpus should be distributed among his wife and children in such proportions as the trustee should determine, the right to the corpus, for the purpose of the marital deduction, is considered as transferred to a "person other than the donee spouse."

Example (2). If, in the above example, the donor had provided that, upon the expiration of the 10-year term, the corpus was to be paid to his wife, but also reserved the power to revest such corpus in himself, the right to corpus, for the purpose of the marital deduction, is considered as transferred to a "person other than the donee spouse."

(4) The term "person other than the donee spouse" includes the possible unascertained takers of a property interest, as, for example, the members of a class to be ascertained in the future. As another example, assume that the donor created a power of appointment over a property interest, which does not come within the purview of § 25.2523(e)–1. In such a case, the term "person other than the donee spouse" refers to the possible appointees and takers in default (other than the spouse) of such property interest.

(5) An exercise or release at any time by the donor (either alone or in conjunction with any person) of a power to appoint an interest in property, even though not otherwise a transfer by him is considered as a transfer by him in determining, for the purpose of section 2523(b), whether he transferred an interest in such property to a person other than the donee spouse.

(6) The following examples illustrate the application of this paragraph. In each example, it is assumed that the donor made no election under sections 2523(f)(2)(C) and (f)(4) and that the property interest that the donor transferred to a person other than the donee spouse is not transferred for adequate and full consideration in money or money's worth:

Example 1. H (the donor) transferred real property to W (his wife) for life, with remainder to A and his heirs. No marital deduction may be taken with respect to the interest transferred to W, since it will terminate upon her death and A (or his heirs or assigns) will thereafter possess or enjoy the property.

Example 2. H transferred property for the benefit of W and A. The income was payable to W for life and upon her death the principal was to be distributed to A or his issue. However, if A should die without issue, leaving W surviving, the principal was then to be distributed to W. No marital deduction may be taken with respect to the interest transferred to W, since it will terminate in the event of his issue will thereafter possess or enjoy the property.

Example 3. H purchased for $100,000 a life annuity for W. If the annuity payments made during the life of W should be less than $100,000, further payments were to be made to A. No marital deduction may be taken with respect to the interest transferred to W; since A may possess or enjoy a part of the property following the termination of W's interest. If, however, the contract provided for no continuation of payments, and provided for no refund upon the death of W, or provided that any refund was to go to the estate of W, then a marital deduction may be taken with respect to the gift.

Example 4. H transferred property to A for life with remainder to W provided W survives A, but if W predeceases A, the property is to pass to B and his heirs. No marital deduction may be taken with respect to the interest transferred to W.

Example 5. H transferred real property to A, reserving the right to the rentals of the property for a term of 20 years. H later transferred the right to the remaining rentals to W. No marital deduction may be taken with respect to the interest since it will terminate upon the expiration of the balance of the 20-year term and A will thereafter possess or enjoy the property.

Example 6. H transferred a patent to W and A as tenants in common. In this case, the interest of W will terminate upon the expiration of the term of the patent, but possession and enjoyment of the property by A must necessarily cease at the same time. Therefore, since A's possession or enjoyment cannot outlast the termination of W's interest, the provisions of section 2523(b) do not disallow the marital deduction with respect to the interest.

(c) Interest in property which the donor may possess or enjoy. **(1)** Section 2523(b) provides that no marital deduction is allowed with respect to the transfer to the donee spouse of a "terminable interest" in property, if—

(i) The donor retained in himself an interest in the same property, and

(ii) By reason of such retention, the donor (or his heirs or assigns) may possess or enjoy any part of the property after the termination or failure of the interest transferred to the donee spouse.* * *

(2) In general, the principles illustrated by the examples under paragraph (b) of this section are applicable in determining whether the marital deduction may be taken with respect to a property interest transferred to the donee spouse subject to the retention by the donor of an interest in the same property. The application of this paragraph may be further illustrated by the following example, in which it is assumed that the donor made no election under sections 2523(f)(2)(C) and (f)(4).

Example. The donor purchased three annuity contracts for the benefit of his wife and himself. The first contract provided for payments to the wife for life, with refund to the donor in case the aggregate payments made to the wife were less than the cost of the contract. The second contract provided for payments to the donor for life, and then to the wife for life if she survived the donor. The third contract provided for payments to the donor and his wife for their joint lives and then to the survivor of them for life. No marital deduction may be taken with respect to the gifts resulting from the purchases of the contracts since, in the case of each contract, the donor may possess or enjoy a part of the property after the termination or failure of the interest transferred to the wife.

(d) Interest in property over which the donor retained a power to appoint.(1) Section 2523(b) provides that no marital deduction is allowed with respect to the transfer to the donee spouse of a terminable interest" in property if—

(i) The donor had, immediately after the transfer, a power to appoint an interest in the same property, and

(ii) The donor's power was exercisable (either alone or in conjunction with any person) in such manner that the appointee may possess or enjoy any part of the property after the termination or failure of the interest transferred to the donee spouse.

(2) For the purposes of section 2523(b), the donor is to be considered as having, immediately after the transfer to the donee spouse, such a power to appoint even though the power cannot be exercised until after the lapse of time, upon the occurrence of an event or contingency, or upon the failure of an event or contingency to occur. It is immaterial whether the power retained by the donor was a taxable power of appointment under section 2514.

(3) The principles illustrated by the examples under paragraph (b) of this section are generally applicable in determining whether the marital deduction may be taken with respect to a property interest transferred to the donee spouse subject to retention by the donor of a power to appoint an interest in the same property. The application of this paragraph may be further illustrated by the following example:

Example. The donor, having a power of appointment over certain property, appointed a life estate to his spouse. No marital deduction may be taken with respect to such transfer, since, if the retained power to appoint the remainder interest is exercised, the appointee thereunder may possess or enjoy the property after the termination or failure of the interest taken by the donee spouse.

§ 25.2523(c)–1 Interest in unidentified assets.

(a) Section 2523(c) provides that if an interest passing to a donee spouse may be satisfied out of a group of assets (or their proceeds) which include a particular asset that would be a nondeductible interest if it passed from the donor to his spouse, the value of the interest passing to the spouse is reduced, for the purpose of the marital deduction, by the value of the particular asset.

(b) In order for this section to apply, two circumstances must coexist, as follows:

(1) The property interest transferred to the donee spouse must be payable out of a group of assets. An example of a property interest payable out of a group of assets is a right to a share of the corpus of a trust upon its termination.

(2) The group of assets out of which the property interest is payable must include one or more particular assets which, if transferred by the donor to the donee spouse, would not qualify for the marital deduction. Therefore, section 2523(c) is not applicable merely because a group of assets includes a terminable interest, but would only be applicable if the terminable interest were nondeductible under the provisions of § 25.2523(b)–1.

(c) If both of the circumstances set forth in paragraph (b) of this section exist, only a portion of the property interest passing to the spouse is a deductible interest. The portion qualifying as a deductible interest is an amount equal to the excess, if any, of the value of the property interest passing to the spouse over the aggregate value of the asset (or assets) that if transferred to the spouse would not qualify for the marital deduction. See paragraph (c) of § 25.2523(a)–1 to determine the percentage of the deductible interest allowable as a marital deduction. The application of this section may be illustrated by the following example:

Example. H was absolute owner of a rental property and on July 1, 1950, transferred it to A by gift, reserving the income for a period of 20 years. On July 1, 1955, he created a trust to last for a period of 10 years. H was to receive the income from the trust and at the termination of the trust the trustee is to turn over to H's wife, W, property having a value of $100,000. The trustee has absolute discretion in deciding which properties in the corpus he shall turn over to W in satisfaction of the gift to her. The trustee received two items of property from H. Item (1) consisted of shares of corporate stock. Item (2) consisted of the right to receive the income from the rental property during the unexpired portion of the 20-year term. Assume that at the termination of the trust on July 1, 1965, the value of the right to the rental income for the then unexpired term of 5 years (item (2)) will be $30,000. Since item (2) is a nondeductible interest and the trustee can turn it over to W in partial satisfaction of her gift, only $70,000 of the $100,000 receivable by her on July 1, 1965, will be considered as property with respect to which a marital deduction is allowable. The present value on July 1, 1955, of the right to receive $70,000 at the end of 10 years is $49,624.33 ($70,000 × 0.708919, as found in Table II of § 25.2512–5). The value of the property qualifying for the marital deduction, therefore, is $49,624.33 and a marital deduction is allowed for one-half of that amount, or $24,812.17.

§ 25.2523(d)–1 Joint interests.

Section 2523(d) provides that if a property interest is transferred to the donee spouse as sole joint tenant with the donor or as a tenant by the entirety, the interest of the donor in the property which exists solely by reason of the possibility that the donor may survive the donee spouse, or that there may occur a severance of the tenancy, is not for the purposes of section 2523(b), to be considered as an interest retained by the donor in himself. Under this provision, the fact that the donor may, as surviving tenant, possess or enjoy the property after the termination of the interest transferred to the donee spouse does not preclude the allowance of the marital deduction with respect to the latter interest. Thus, if the donor purchased real property in the name of the donor and the donor's spouse as tenants by the entirety or as joint tenants with rights of survivorship, a marital deduction is allowable with respect to the value of the interest of the donee spouse in the property (subject to the limitations set forth in § 25.2523(a)–1). See paragraph (c) of § 25.2523(b)–1, and section 2524.

§ 25.2523(e)–1 Marital deduction; life estate with power of appointment in donee spouse.

(a) In general. Section 2523(e) provides that if an interest in property is transferred by a donor to his spouse (whether or not in trust) and the spouse is entitled for life to all the income from a specific portion of the entire interest, with a power in her to appoint the entire interest of all the income from interest or the specific portion, the interest transferred to her is a deductible interest, to the extent that it satisfies all five of the conditions set forth below (see paragraph (b) of this section if one or more of the conditions is satisfied as to only a portion of the interest):

(1) The donee spouse must be entitled for life to all of the income from the entire interest or a specific portion of the entire interest, or to a specific portion of all the income from the entire interest.

(2) The income payable to the donee spouse must be payable annually or at more frequent intervals.

(3) The donee spouse must have the power to appoint the entire interest of the specific portion to either herself or her estate.

(4) The power in the donee spouse must be exercisable by her alone and (whether exercisable by will or during life) must be exercisable in all events.

(5) The entire interest or the specific portion must not be subject to a power in any other person to appoint any part to any person other than the donee spouse.

(b) Specific portion; deductible amount. If either the right to income or the power of appointment given to the donee spouse pertains only to a specific portion of a property interest, the portion of the interest which qualifies as a deductible interest is limited to the extent that the rights in the donee spouse meet all of the five conditions described in paragraph (a) of this section. While the rights over the income and the power must coexist as to the same interest in property, it is not necessary that the rights over the income or the power as to such interest be in the same proportion. However, if the rights over income meeting the required conditions set forth in paragraph (a)(1) and (2) of this section extend over a smaller share of the property interest than the share with respect to which the power of appointment requirements set forth in paragraph (a)(3) through (5) of this section are satisfied, the deductible interest is limited to the smaller share. Conversely, if a power of appointment meeting all the requirements extends to a smaller portion of the property interest than the portion over which the income rights pertain, the deductible interest cannot exceed the value of the portion to which such power of appointment applies. Thus, if the donor gives to the donee spouse the right to receive annually all of the income from a particular property interest and a power of appointment meeting the specifications prescribed in paragraph (a)(3) through (5) of this section as to only one-half of the property interest, then only one-half of the property interest is treated as a deductible interest. Correspondingly, if the income interest of the spouse satisfying the requirements extends to only one-fourth of the property interest and a testamentary power of appointment satisfying the requirements extends to all of the property interest, then only one-fourth of the interest in the spouse qualifies as a deductible interest. Further, if the donee spouse has no right to income from a specific portion of a property interest but a testamentary power of appointment which meets the necessary conditions over the entire interest, then none of the interest qualifies for the deduction. In addition, if, from the time of the transfer, the donee spouse has a power of appointment meeting all of the required conditions over three-fourths of the entire property interest and the prescribed income rights over the entire interest, but with a power in another person to appoint one-half of the entire interest, the value of the interest in the donee spouse over only one-half of the property interest will qualify as a deductible interest.

(c) Meaning of specific portion—(1) In general. Except as provided in paragraphs (c)(2) and (c)(3) of this section, a partial interest in property is not treated as a *specific portion* of the entire interest. In addition, any specific portion of an entire interest in property is nondeductible to the extent the specific portion is subject to invasion for the benefit of any person other than the donee spouse, except in the case of a deduction allowable under section 2523(e), relating to the exercise of a general power of appointment by the donee spouse.

(2) Fraction or percentage share. Under section 2523(e), a partial interest in property is treated as a specific portion of the entire interest if the rights of the donee spouse in income, and the required rights as to the power described in § 25.2523(e)–1(a), constitute a fractional or percentage share of the entire property interest, so that the donee spouse's interest reflects its proportionate share of the increase or decrease in the value of the entire property interest to which the income rights and the power relate. Thus, if the spouse's right to income and the spouse's power extend to a specified fraction or percentage of the property, or its equivalent, the interest is in a specific portion of the property. In accordance with paragraph (b) of this section, if the spouse has the right to receive the income from a specific portion of the trust property (after applying paragraph (c)(3) of this section) but has a power of appointment over a different specific portion of the property (after applying paragraph (c)(3) of this section), the marital deduction is limited to the lesser specific portion.

(3) Special rule in the case of gifts made on or before October 24, 1992. In the case of gifts within the purview of the effective date rule contained in paragraph (c)(3)(iii) of this section:

(i) A specific sum payable annually, or at more frequent intervals, out of the property and its income that is not limited by the income of the property is treated as the right to receive the income from a specific portion of the property. The specific portion, for purposes of paragraph (c)(2) of this section, is the portion of the property that, assuming the interest rate generally applicable for the valuation of annuities at the time of the donor's gift, would produce income equal to such payments. However, a pecuniary amount payable annually to a donee spouse is not treated as a right to the income from a specific portion of trust property for purposes of this paragraph (c)(3)(i) if any person other than the donee spouse may receive, during the donee spouse's lifetime, any distribution of the property. To determine the applicable interest rate for valuing annuities, see sections 2512 and 7520 and the regulations under those sections.

(ii) The right to appoint a pecuniary amount out of a larger fund (or trust corpus) is considered the right to appoint a specific portion of such fund or trust in an amount equal to such pecuniary amount.

(iii) The rules contained in paragraphs (c)(3)(i) and (ii) of this section apply with respect to gifts made on or before October 24, 1992.

(4) Local law. A partial interest in property is treated as a specific portion of the entire interest if it is shown that the donee spouse has rights under local law that are identical to those the donee spouse would have acquired had the partial interest been expressed in terms satisfying the requirements of paragraph (c)(2) of this section (or paragraph (c)(3) of this section if applicable).

(5) Examples. The following examples illustrate the application of paragraphs (b) and (c) of this section, where D, the donor, transfers property to D's spouse, S:

Example 1. Spouse entitled to the lesser of an annuity or a fraction of trust income. Prior to October 24, 1992, D transferred in trust 500 identical shares of X Company stock, valued for gift tax purposes at $500,000. The trust provided that during the lifetime of D's spouse, S, the trustee is to pay annually to S the lesser of one-half of the trust income or $20,000. Any trust income not paid to S is to be accumulated in the trust and may not be distributed during S's lifetime. S has a testamentary general power of appointment over the entire trust principal. The applicable interest rate for valuing annuities as of the date of D's gift under section 7520 is 10 percent. For purposes of paragraphs (a) through (c) of this section, S is treated as receiving all of the income from the lesser of one-half of the stock ($250,000), or $200,000, the specific portion of the stock which, as determined in accordance with § 25.2523(e)–1(c)(3)(i) of this chapter, would produce annual income of $20,000 (20,000/.10). Accordingly, the marital deduction is limited to $200,000 (200,000/500,000 or 2/5 of the value of the trust.)

Example 2. Spouse possesses power and income interest over different specific portions of trust. The facts are the same as in Example 1 except that S's testamentary general power of appointment is exercisable over only ¼ of the trust principal. Consequently, under section 2523(e), the marital deduction is allowable only for the value of ¼ of the trust ($125,000); i.e., the lesser of the value of the portion with respect to which S is deemed to be entitled to all of the income (2/5 of the trust or $200,000), or the value of the portion with respect to which S possesses the requisite power of appointment (¼ of the trust or $125,000).

Example 3. Power of appointment over shares of stock constitutes a power over a specific portion. D transferred 250 identical shares of Y company stock to a trust under the terms of which trust income is to be paid annually to S, during S's lifetime. S was given a testamentary general power of appointment over 100 shares of stock. The trust provides that if the trustee sells the Y company stock, S's general power of appointment is exercisable with respect to the sale proceeds or the property in which the proceeds are reinvested. Because the amount of property represented by a single share of stock would be altered if the corporation split its stock, issued stock dividends, made a distribution of capital, etc., a power to appoint 100 shares at the time of S's death is not necessarily a power to appoint the entire interest that the 100 shares represented on the date of D's gift. If it is shown that, under local law, S has a general power to appoint not only the 100 shares designated by D but also 100/250 of any distributions by the corporation that are included in trust principal, the requirements of paragraph (c)(2) of this section are satisfied and S is treated as having a general power to appoint 100/250 of the entire interest in the 250 shares. In that case, the marital deduction is limited to 40 percent of the trust principal. If local law does not give S that power, the 100 shares would not constitute a specific portion under § 25.2523(e)–1(c) (including § 25.2523(e)–1(c)(3)(ii)). The nature of the asset is such that a change in the capitalization of the corporation could cause an alteration in the original value represented by the shares at the time of the transfer and is thus not a specific portion of the trust.

(d) Definition of "entire interest". Since a marital deduction is allowed for each qualifying separate interest in property transferred by the donor to the donee spouse, for purposes of paragraphs (a) and (b) of this section, each property interest with respect to which the donee spouse received some rights is considered separately in determining whether her rights extend to the entire interest or to a specific portion of the entire interest. A property interest which consists of several identical units of property (such as a block of 250 shares of stock, whether the ownership is evidenced by one or several certificates) is considered one property interest, unless certain of the units are to be segregated and accorded different treatment, in which case each segregated group of items is considered a separate property interest. The bequest of a specified sum of money constitutes the bequest of a separate property interest if immediately following the transfer and thenceforth it, and the investments made with it, must be so segregated or accounted for as to permit its identification as a separate item of property. The application of this paragraph may be illustrated by the following examples:

Example (1). The donor transferred to a trustee three adjoining farms, Blackacre, Whiteacre, and Greenacre. The trust instrument provided that during the lifetime of the donee spouse the trustee should pay her all of the income from the trust. Upon her death, all of Blackacre, a one-half interest in Whiteacre, and a one-third interest in Greenacre were to be distributed to the person or persons appointed by her in her will. The donee spouse is considered as being entitled to all of the income from the entire interest in Blackacre, all of the income from the entire interest in Whiteacre, and all of the income from the entire interest in Greenacre. She also is considered as having a power of appointment over the entire interest in Blackacre, over one-half of the entire interest in Whiteacre, and over one-third of the entire interest in Greenacre.

Example (2). The donor transferred $250,000 to C, as trustee. C is to invest the money and pay all of the income from the investments to W, the donor's spouse, annually. W was given a general power, exercisable by will, to appoint one-half of the corpus of the trust. Here, immediately following establishment of the trust, the $250,000 will be sufficiently segregated to permit its identification as a separate item, and the $250,000 will constitute an entire property interest. Therefore, W has a right to income and a power of appointment such that one-half of the entire interest is a deductible interest.

Example (3). The donor transferred 100 shares of Z Corporation stock to D, as trustee. W, the donor's spouse, is to receive all of the income of the trust annually and is given a general power, exercisable by will, to appoint out of the trust corpus the sum of $25,000. In this case the $25,000 is not, immediately following establishment of the trust, sufficiently segregated to permit its identification as a separate item of property in which the donee spouse has the entire interest. Therefore, the $25,000 does not constitute the entire interest in a property for the purpose of paragraphs (a) and (b) of this section.

(e) Application of local law. In determining whether or not the conditions set forth in paragraph (a)(1) through (5) of this section are satisfied by the instrument of transfer, regard is to be had to the applicable provisions of the law of the jurisdiction under which the interest passes and, if the transfer is in trust, the applicable provisions of the law governing the administration of the trust. For example, silence of a trust instrument as to the frequency of payment will not be regarded as a failure to satisfy the condition set forth in paragraph (a)(2) of this section that income must be payable to the donee spouse annually or more frequently unless the applicable law permits payment to be made less frequently than annually. The principles outlined in this paragraph and paragraphs (f) and (g) of this section which are applied in determining whether transfers in trust meet such conditions are equally applicable in ascertaining whether, in the case of interests not in trust, the donee spouse has the equivalent in rights over income and over the property.

(f) Right to income.(1) If an interest is transferred in trust, the donee spouse is "entitled for life to all of the income from the entire interest or a specific portion of the entire interest," for the purpose of the condition set forth in paragraph (a)(l) of this section, if the effect of the trust is to give her substantially that degree of beneficial enjoyment of the trust property during her life which the principles of the law of trust accord to a person who is unqualifiedly designated as the life beneficiary of a trust. Such degree of enjoyment is given only if it was the donor's intention, as manifested by the terms of the trust instrument and the surrounding circumstances, that the trust should produce for the donee spouse during her life such an income, or that the spouse should have such use of the trust property as is consistent with the value of the trust corpus and with its preservation. The designation of the spouse as sole income beneficiary for life of the entire interest or a specific portion of the entire interest will be sufficient to qualify the trust unless the terms of the trust and the surrounding circumstances considered as a whole evidence an intention to deprive the spouse of the requisite degree of enjoyment. In determining whether a trust evidences that intention, the treatment required or permitted with respect to individual items must be considered in relation to the entire system provided for the administration of the trust. In addition, the spouse's interest shall meet the condition set forth in paragraph (a)(1) of this section if the spouse is entitled to income as determined by applicable local law that provides for a reasonable apportionment between the income and remainder beneficiaries of the total return of the trust and that meets the requirements of 1.643(b)–1 of this chapter.

(2) If the over-all effect of a trust is to give to the donee spouse such enforceable rights as will preserve to her the requisite degree of enjoyment, it is immaterial whether that result is effected by rules specifically stated in the trust instrument, or, in their absence, by the rules for the management of the trust property and the allocation of receipts and expenditures supplied by the State law. For example, a provision in the trust instrument for amortization of bond premium by appropriate periodic charges to interest will not disqualify the interest transferred in trust even though there is no State law specifically authorizing amortization or there is a State law denying amortization which is applicable only in the absence of such a provision in the trust instrument.

(3) In the case of a trust, the rules to be applied by the trustee in allocation of receipts and expenses between income and corpus must be considered in relation to the nature and expected productivity of the assets transferred in trust, the nature and frequency of occurrence of the expected receipts, and any provisions as to change in the form of investments. If it is evident from the nature of the trust assets and the rules provided for management of the trust that the allocation to income of such receipts as rents, ordinary cash dividends and interest will give to the spouse the substantial enjoyment during life required by the statute, provisions that such receipts as stock dividends and proceeds from the conversion of trust assets shall be treated as corpus will not disqualify the interest transferred in trust. Similarly, provision for a depletion charge against income in the case of trust assets which are subject to depletion will not disqualify the interest transferred in trust, unless the effect is to deprive the spouse of the requisite beneficial enjoyment. The same principle is applicable in the case of depreciation, trustees' commissions, and other charges.

(4) Provisions granting administrative powers to the trustees will not have the effect of disqualifying an interest transferred in trust unless the grant of powers evidences the intention to deprive the donee spouse of the beneficial enjoyment required by the statute. Such an intention will not be considered to exist if the entire terms of the instrument are such that the local courts will impose reasonable limitations upon the exercise of the powers. Among the powers which if subject to reasonable limitations will not disqualify the interest transferred in trust are the power to determine the allocation or apportionment of receipts and disbursements between income and corpus, the power to apply the income or corpus for the benefit of the spouse, and the power to retain the assets transferred to the trust. For example, a power to retain trust assets which consist substantially of unproductive property will not disqualify the interest if the applicable rules for the administration of the trust require, or permit the spouse to require, that the trustee either make the property productive or convert it within a reasonable time. Nor will such a power disqualify the interest if the applicable rules for administration of the trust require the trustee to use the degree of judgment and care in the exercise of the power which a prudent man would use if he were owner of the trust assets. Further, a power to retain a residence for the spouse or other property for the personal use of the spouse will not disqualify the interest transferred in trust.

(5) An interest transferred in trust will not satisfy the condition set forth in paragraph (a)(1) of this section that the donee spouse be entitled to all the income if the primary purpose of the trust is to safeguard property without providing the spouse with the required beneficial enjoyment. Such trusts include not only trusts which expressly provide for the accumulation of the income but also trusts which indirectly accomplish a similar purpose. For example, assume that the corpus of a trust consists substantially of property which is not likely to be income producing during the life of the donee spouse and that the spouse cannot compel the trustee to convert or otherwise deal with the property as described in subparagraph (4) of this paragraph. An interest transferred to such a trust will not qualify unless the applicable rules for the administration require, or permit the spouse to require, that the trustee provide the required beneficial enjoyment, such as by payments to the spouse out of other assets of the trust.

(6) If a trust may be terminated during the life of the donee spouse, under her exercise of a power of appointment or by distribution of the corpus to her, the interest transferred in trust satisfies the condition set forth in paragraph (a)(1) of this section (that the spouse be entitled to all the income) if she (i) is entitled to the income until the trust terminates, or (ii) has the right, exercisable in all events, to have the corpus distributed to her at any time during her life.

(7) An interest transferred in trust fails to satisfy the condition set forth in paragraph (a)(1) of this section, that the spouse be entitled to all the income, to the extent that the income is required to be accumulated in whole or in part or may be accumulated in the discretion of any person other than the donee spouse; to the extent that the consent of any person other than the donee spouse is required as a condition precedent to distribution of the income; or to the extent that any person other than the donee spouse has the power to alter the terms of the trust so as to deprive her of her right to the income. An interest transferred in trust will not fail to satisfy the condition that the spouse be entitled to all the income merely because its terms provide that the right of the donee spouse to the income shall not be subject to assignment, alienation, pledge, attachment or claims of creditors.

(8) In the case of an interest transferred in trust, the terms "entitled for life" and "payable annually or at more frequent intervals", as used in the conditions set forth in paragraph (a)(l) and (2) of this section, require that under the terms of the trust the income referred to must be currently (at least annually; see paragraph (e) of this section) distributable to the spouse or that she must have such command over the income that it is virtually hers. Thus, the conditions in paragraph (a)(1) and (2) of this section are satisfied in this respect if, under the terms of the trust instrument, the donee spouse has the right exercisable annually (or more frequently) to require distribution to herself of the trust income, and otherwise the trust income is to be accumulated and added to corpus. Similarly, as respects the income for the period between the last distribution date and the date of the spouse's death, it is sufficient if that income is subject to the spouse's power to appoint. Thus, if the trust instrument provides that income accrued or undistributed on the date of the spouse's death is to be disposed of as if it had been received after her death, and if the spouse has a power of appointment over the trust corpus, the power necessarily extends to the undistributed income.

(g) Power of appointment in donee spouse.(1) The conditions set forth in paragraph (a)(3) and (4) of this section, that is, that the donee spouse must have a power of appointment exercisable in favor of herself or her estate and exercisable alone and in all events, are not met unless the power of the donee spouse to appoint the entire interest or a specific portion of it falls within one of the following categories:

(i) A power so to appoint fully exercisable in her own favor at any time during her life (as, for example, an unlimited power to invade); or

(ii) A power so to appoint exercisable in favor of her estate. Such a power, if exercisable during life, must be fully exercisable at any time during life, or if exercisable by will, must be fully exercisable irrespective of the time of her death; or

(iii) A combination of the powers described under subdivisions (i) and (ii) of this subparagraph. For example, the donee spouse may, until she attains the age of 50 years, have a power to appoint to herself and thereafter have a power to appoint to her estate. However, the condition that the spouse's power must be exercisable in all events is not satisfied unless irrespective of when the donee spouse may die the entire interest or a specific portion of it will at the time of her death be subject to one power or the other.

(2) The power of the donee spouse must be a power to appoint the entire interest or a specific portion of it as unqualified owner (and free of the trust if a trust is involved, or free of the joint tenancy if a joint tenancy is involved) or to appoint the entire interest or a specific portion of it as a part of her estate (and free of the trust if a trust is involved), that is, in effect, to dispose of it to whomsoever she pleases. Thus, if the donor transferred property to a son and the donee spouse as joint tenants with right of survivorship and under local law the donee spouse has a power of severance exercisable without consent of the other joint tenant, and by exercising this power could acquire a one-half interest in the property as a tenant in common, her power of severance will satisfy the condition set forth in paragraph (a)(3) of this section that she have a power of appointment in favor of herself or her estate. However, if the donee spouse entered into a binding agreement with the donor to exercise the power only in favor of their issue, that condition is not met. An interest transferred in trust will not be regarded as failing to satisfy the condition merely because takers in default of the donee spouse's exercise of the power are designated by the donor. The donor may provide that, in default of exercise of the power, the trust shall continue for an additional period.

(3) A power is not considered to be a power exercisable by a donee spouse alone and in all events as required by paragraph (a)(4) of this section if the exercise of the power in the donee spouse to appoint the entire interest or a specific portion of it to herself or to her estate requires the joinder or consent of any other person. The power is not "exercisable in all events", if it can be terminated during the life of the donee spouse by any event other than her complete exercise or release of it. Further, a power is not "exercisable in all events" if it may be exercised for a limited purpose only. For example, a power which is not exercisable in the event of the spouse's remarriage is not exercisable in all events. Likewise, if there are any restrictions, either by the terms of the instrument or under applicable local law, on the exercise of a power to consume property (whether or not held in trust) for the benefit of the spouse, the power is not exercisable in all events. Thus, if a power of invasion is exercisable only for the spouse's support, or only for her limited use, the power is not exercisable in all events. In order for a power of invasion to be exercisable in all events, the donee spouse must have the unrestricted power exercisable at any time during her life to use all or any part of the property subject to the power, and to dispose of it in any manner, including the power to dispose of it by gift (whether or not she has power to dispose of it by will).

(4) If the power is in existence at all times following the transfer of the interest, limitations of a formal nature will not disqualify the interest. Examples of formal limitations on a power exercisable during life are requirements that an exercise must be in a particular form, that it must be filed with a trustee during the spouse's life, that reasonable notice must be given, or that reasonable intervals must elapse between successive partial exercises. Examples of formal limitations on a power exercisable by will are that it must be exercised by a will executed by the donee spouse after the making of the gift or that exercise must be by specific reference to the power.

(5) If the donee spouse has the requisite power to appoint to herself or her estate, it is immaterial that she also has one or more lesser powers. Thus, if she has a testamentary power to appoint to her estate, she may also have a limited power of withdrawal or of appointment during her life. Similarly, if she has an unlimited power of withdrawal, she may have a limited testamentary power.

(h) Existence of a power in another. Paragraph (a)(5) of this section provides that a transfer described in paragraph (a) is nondeductible to the extent that the donor created a power in the trustee or in any other person to appoint a part of the interest to any person other than the donee spouse. However, only powers in other persons which are in opposition to that of the donee spouse will cause a portion of the interest to fail to satisfy the condition set forth in paragraph (a)(5) of this section. Thus, a power in a trustee to distribute corpus to or for the benefit of the donee spouse will not disqualify the trust. Similarly, a power to distribute corpus to the spouse for the support of minor children will not disqualify the trust if she is legally obligated to support such children. The application of this paragraph may be illustrated by the following examples:

Example (1). Assume that a donor created a trust, designating his spouse as income beneficiary for life with an unrestricted power in the spouse to appoint the corpus during her life. The donor further provided that in the event the donee spouse should die without having exercised the power, the trust should continue for the life of his son with a power in the son to appoint the corpus. Since the power in the son could become exercisable only after the death of the donee spouse, the interest is not regarded as failing to satisfy the condition set forth in paragraph (a)(5) of this section.

Example (2). Assume that the donor created a trust, designating his spouse as income beneficiary for life and as donee of a power to appoint by will the entire corpus. The donor further provided that the trustee could distribute 30 percent of the corpus to the donor's son when he reached the age of 35 years. Since the trustee has a power to appoint 30 percent of the entire interest for the benefit of a person other than the donee spouse, only 70 percent of the interest placed in trust satisfied the condition set forth in paragraph (a)(5) of this section. If, in this case, the donee spouse had a power, exercisable by her will, to appoint only one-half of the corpus as it was constituted at the time of her death, it should be noted that only 35 percent of the interest placed in the trust would satisfy the condition set forth in paragraph (a)(3) of this section.

* * *

§ 25.2524–1 Extent of deductions.

Under the provisions of section 2524, the charitable deduction provided for in section 2522 and the marital deduction provided for in section 2523 are allowable only to the extent that the gifts, with respect to which those deductions are authorized, are included in the "total amount of gifts" made during the "calendar period" (as defined in § 25.2502–1(c)(1)), computed as provided in section 2503 and § 25.2503–1 (*i.e.*, the total gifts less exclusions). * * *

* * *

Subchapter F—Procedure and Administration

PART 301—PROCEDURE AND ADMINISTRATION

DEFINITIONS

§ 301.7701–1 Classification of organizations for federal tax purposes.

(a) Organizations for federal tax purposes.— (1) In general. The Internal Revenue Code prescribes the classification of various organizations for federal tax purposes. Whether an organization is an entity separate from its owners for federal tax purposes is a matter of federal tax law and does not depend on whether the organization is recognized as an entity under local law.

(2) Certain joint undertakings give rise to entities for federal tax purposes. A joint venture or other contractual arrangement may create a separate entity for federal tax purposes if the participants carry on a trade, business, financial operation, or venture and divide the profits therefrom. For example, a separate entity exists for federal tax purposes if co-owners of an apartment building lease space and in addition provide services to the occupants either directly or through an agent. Nevertheless, a joint undertaking merely to share expenses does not create a separate entity for federal tax purposes. For example, if two or more persons jointly construct a ditch merely to drain surface water from their properties, they have not created a separate entity for federal tax purposes. Similarly, mere co-ownership of property that is maintained, kept in repair, and rented or leased does not constitute a separately entity for federal tax purposes. For example, if an individual owner, or tenants in common, of farm property lease it to a farmer for a cash rental or a share of the crops, they do not necessarily create a separate entity for federal tax purposes.

(3) Certain local law entities not recognized. An entity formed under local law is not always recognized as a separate entity for federal tax purposes. For example, an organization wholly owned by a State is not recognized as a separate entity for federal tax purposes if it is an integral part of the State. Similarly, tribes incorporated under section 17 of the Indian Reorganization Act of 1934, as amended, 25 U.S.C. 477, or under section 3 of the Oklahoma Indian Welfare Act, as amended, 25 U.S.C. 503, are not recognized as separate entities for federal tax purposes.

(4) Single owner organizations. Under §§ 301.7701–2 and 301.7701–3, certain organizations that have a single owner can choose to be recognized or disregarded as entities separate from their owners.

(b) Classification of organizations. The classification of organizations that are recognized as separate entities is determined under §§ 301.7701–2, 301.7701–3, and 301.7701–4 unless a provision of the Internal Revenue Code (such as section 860A addressing Real Estate Mortgage Investment Conduits (REMICs)) provides for special treatment of that organization. For the classification of organizations as trusts, see § 301.7701–4. That section provides that trusts generally do not have associates or an objective to carry on business for profit. Sections 301.7701–2 and 301.7701–3 provide rules for classifying organizations that are not classified as trusts.

(c) Qualified cost sharing arrangements. A qualified cost sharing arrangement that is described in § 1.482–7 of this chapter and any arrangement that is treated by the Commissioner as a qualified cost sharing arrangement under § 1.482–7 of this chapter is not recognized as a separate entity for purposes of the Internal Revenue Code. See § 1.482–7 of this chapter for the proper treatment of qualified cost sharing arrangements.

(d) Domestic and foreign entities. For purposes of this section and §§ 301.7701–2 and 301.7701–3, an entity is a domestic entity if it is created or organized in the United States or under the law of the United States or of any State; an entity is foreign if it is not domestic. See sections 7701(a)(4) and (a)(5).

(e) State. For purposes of this section and § 301.7701–2, the term State includes the District of Columbia.

(f) Effective date. The rules of this section are effective as of January 1, 1997.

* * *

§ 301.7701–4 Trusts.

(a) Ordinary trusts. In general, the term “trust” as used in the Internal Revenue Code refers to an arrangement created either by a will or by an inter vivos declaration whereby trustees take title to property for the purpose of protecting or conserving it for the beneficiaries under the ordinary rules applied in chancery or probate courts. Usually the beneficiaries of such a trust do no more than accept the benefits thereof and are not the voluntary planners or creators of the trust arrangement. However, the beneficiaries of such a trust may be the persons who create it and it will be recognized as a trust under the Internal Revenue Code if it was created for the purpose of protecting or conserving the trust property for beneficiaries who stand in the same relation to the trust as they would if the trust had been created by others for them. Generally speaking, an arrangement will be treated as a trust under the Internal Revenue Code if it can be shown that the purpose of the arrangement is to vest in trustees responsibility for the protection and conservation of property for beneficiaries who cannot share in the discharge of this responsibility and, therefore, are not associates in a joint enterprise for the conduct of business for profit.

(b) Business trusts. There are other arrangements which are known as trusts because the legal title to property is conveyed to trustees for the benefit of beneficiaries, but which are not classified as trusts for purposes of the Internal Revenue Code because they are not simply arrangements to protect or conserve the property for the beneficiaries. These trusts, which are often known as business or commercial trusts, generally are created by the beneficiaries simply as a device to carry on a profit-making business which normally would have been carried on through business organizations that are classified as corporations or partnerships under the Internal Revenue Code. However, the fact that the corpus of the trust is not supplied by the beneficiaries is not sufficient reason in itself for classifying the arrangement as an ordinary trust rather than as an association or partnership. The fact that any organization is technically cast in the trust form, by conveying title to property to trustees for the benefit of persons designated as beneficiaries, will not change the real character of the organization if, applying the principles set forth in §§ 301.7701–2 and 301.7701–3, the organization more nearly resembles an association or a partnership than a trust.

(c) Certain investment trusts—(1) An "investment" trust will not be classified as a trust if there is a power under the trust agreement to vary the investment of the certificate holders. See Commissioner v. North American Bond Trust, 122 F. 2d 545 (2d Cir. 1941), cert. denied, 314 U.S. 701 (1942). An investment trust with a single class of ownership interests, representing undivided beneficial interests in the assets of the trust, will be classified as a trust if there is no power under the trust agreement to vary the investment of the certificate holders. An investment trust with multiple classes of ownership interests will ordinarily be classified as an association or a partnership under § 301.7701–2; however, an investment trust with multiple classes of ownership interests, in which there is no power under the trust agreement to vary the investment of the certificate holders, will be classified as a trust if the trust is formed to facilitate direct investment in the assets of the trust and the existence of multiple classes of ownership interests is incidental to that purpose.

(2) The provisions of paragraph (c)(1) of this section may be illustrated by the following examples:

Example (1). A corporation purchases a portfolio of residential mortgages and transfers the mortgages to a bank under a trust agreement. At the same time, the bank as trustee delivers to the corporation certificates evidencing rights to payments from the pooled mortgages; the corporation sells the certificates to the public. The trustee holds legal title to the mortgages in the pool for the benefit of the certificate holders but has no power to reinvest proceeds attributable to the mortgages in the pool or to vary investments in the pool in any other manner. There are two classes of certificates. Holders of class A certificates are entitled to all payments of mortgage principal, both scheduled and prepaid, until their certificates are retired; holders of class B certificates receive payments of principal only after all class A certificates have been retired. The different rights of the class A and class B certificates serve to shift to the holders of the class A certificates, in addition to the earlier scheduled payments of principal, the risk that mortgages in the pool will be prepaid so that the holders of the class B certificates will have "call protection" (freedom from premature termination of their interests on account of prepayments). The trust thus serves to create investment interests with respect to the mortgages held by the trust that differ significantly from direct investment in the mortgages. As a consequence, the existence of multiple classes of trust ownership is not incidental to any purpose of the trust to facilitate direct investment, and accordingly, the trust is classified as an association or a partnership under § 301.7701–2.

* * *

(3) Liquidating trusts. Certain organizations which are commonly known as liquidating trusts are treated as trusts for purposes of the Internal Revenue Code. An organization will be considered a liquidating trust if it is organized for the primary purpose of liquidating and distributing the assets transferred to it, and if its activities are all reasonably necessary to, and consistent with, the accomplishment of that purpose. A liquidating trust is treated as a trust for purposes of the Internal Revenue Code because it is formed with the objective of liquidating particular assets and not as an organization having as its purpose the carrying on of a profit-making business which normally would be conducted through business organizations classified as corporations or partnerships. However, if the liquidation is unreasonably prolonged or if the liquidation purpose becomes so obscured by business activities that the declared purpose of liquidation can be said to be lost or abandoned, the status of the organization will no longer be that of a liquidating trust. Bondholders' protective committees, voting trusts, and other agencies formed to protect the interests of security holders during insolvency, bankruptcy, or corporate reorganization proceedings are analogous to liquidating trusts but if subsequently utilized to further the control or profitable operation of a going business on a permanent continuing basis, they will lose their classification as trusts for purposes of the Internal Revenue Code.

* * *

§ 301.7701–16 Other terms.

For a definition of the term "withholding agent" see § 1.144–7(a). Any other terms that are defined in section 7701 and that are not defined in §§ 301.7701–1 to 301.7701–15, inclusive, shall, when used in this chapter, have the meanings assigned to them in section 7701.

* * *

GLOSSARY OF TAX TERMS

The key terms in this glossary have been defined to reflect their conventional use in the field of taxation. The definitions may therefore be incomplete for other purposes.

A

Abandoned spouse. The abandoned spouse provision enables a married taxpayer with a dependent child whose spouse did not live in the taxpayer's home during the last six months of the tax year to file as a head of household rather than as married filing separately.

Accelerated cost recovery system (ACRS). A method in which the cost of tangible property is recovered over a prescribed period of time. Enacted by the Economic Recovery Tax Act (ERTA) of 1981 and substantially modified by the Tax Reform Act (TRA) of 1986 (the modified system is referred to as MACRS), the approach disregards salvage value, imposes a period of cost recovery that depends upon the classification of the asset into one of various recovery periods, and prescribes the applicable percentage of cost that can be deducted each year. §168.

Accelerated death benefits. The amount received from a life insurance policy by the insured who is terminally ill or chronically ill. Any realized gain may be excluded from the gross income of the insured if the policy is surrendered to the insurer or is sold to a licensed viatical settlement provider. §101(g).

Accident and health benefits. Employee fringe benefits provided by employers through the payment of health and accident insurance premiums or the establishment of employer-funded medical reimbursement plans. Employers generally are entitled to a deduction for such payments, whereas employees generally exclude such fringe benefits from gross income. §§105 and 106.

Accountable plan. An accountable plan is a type of expense reimbursement plan that requires an employee to render an adequate accounting to the employer and return any excess reimbursement or allowance. If the expense qualifies, it will be treated as a deduction *for* AGI.

Accounting income. The accountant's concept of income is generally based upon the realization principle. Financial accounting income may differ from taxable income (e.g., accelerated depreciation might be used for Federal income tax and straight-line depreciation for financial accounting purposes). Differences are included in a reconciliation of taxable and accounting income on either Schedule M–1 or M–3 of Form 1120 for corporations.

Accounting method. The method under which income and expenses are determined for tax purposes. Important accounting methods include the cash basis and the accrual basis. Special methods are available for the reporting of gain on installment sales, recognition of income on construction projects (the completed contract and percentage of completion methods), and the valuation of inventories (last-in, first-out and first-in, first-out). §§446–474.

Accounting period. The period of time, usually a year, used by a taxpayer for the determination of tax liability. Unless a fiscal year is chosen, taxpayers must determine and pay their income tax liability by using the calendar year (January 1 through December 31) as the period of measurement. An example of a fiscal year is July 1 through June 30. A change in accounting period (e.g., from a calendar year to a fiscal year) generally requires the consent of the IRS. Some new taxpayers, such as a newly formed corporation, are free to select either an initial calendar or a fiscal year without the consent of the IRS. §§441–444.

Accrual method. A method of accounting that reflects expenses incurred and income earned for any one tax year. In contrast to the cash basis of accounting, expenses need not be paid to be deductible, nor need income be received to be taxable. Unearned income (e.g., prepaid interest and rent) generally is taxed in the year of receipt regardless of the method of accounting used by the taxpayer. §446(c)(2).

Accumulated adjustments account (AAA). An account that aggregates an S corporation's post-1982 income, loss, and deductions for the tax year (including nontaxable income and nondeductible losses and expenses). After the year-end income and expense adjustments are made, the account is reduced by distributions made during the tax year. §1368(e).

Accumulated earnings and profits. Net undistributed taxbasis earnings of a corporation aggregated from March 1, 1913, to the end of the prior tax year. Used to determine the amount of dividend income associated with a distribution to shareholders. §316 and Reg. §1.316–2.

Accuracy-related penalty. Major civil taxpayer penalties relating to the accuracy of tax return data, including misstatements stemming from taxpayer negligence and improper valuation of income and deductions, are coordinated under this umbrella term. The penalty usually equals 20 percent of the understated tax liability. §6662.

ACE adjustment. An adjustment in computing corporate alternative minimum taxable income (AMTI), computed at 75 percent of the excess of adjusted current earnings (ACE) over unadjusted AMTI. ACE computations reflect longer and slower cost recovery deductions and other restrictions on the timing of certain recognition events. Exempt interest, life insurance proceeds, and other receipts that are included in earnings and profits but not in taxable income also increase the ACE adjustment. If unadjusted AMTI exceeds ACE, the ACE adjustment is negative. The negative adjustment is limited to the aggregate of the positive adjustments under ACE for prior years, reduced by any previously claimed negative adjustments. §56(c).

Acquiescence. Agreement by the IRS on the results reached in certain judicial decisions; sometimes abbreviated *Acq.* or *A.*

Acquisition indebtedness. Debt incurred in acquiring, constructing, or substantially improving a qualified residence of the taxpayer. The interest on such loans is deductible as qualified residence interest. However, interest on such debt is deductible only on the portion of the indebtedness that does not exceed $1,000,000 ($500,000 for married persons filing separate returns). §163(h)(3).

Active income. Active income includes wages, salary, commissions, bonuses, profits from a trade or business in which the taxpayer is a material participant, gain on the sale or other disposition of assets used in an active trade or business, and income from intangible property if the taxpayer's personal efforts significantly contributed to the creation of the property. The passive activity loss rules require classification of income and losses into three categories with active income being one of them. §469.

Ad valorem tax. A tax imposed on the value of property. The most common ad valorem tax is that imposed by states, counties, and cities on real estate. Ad valorem taxes can be imposed on personal property as well.

Additional depreciation. The excess of the amount of depreciation actually deducted over the amount that would have been deducted had the straight-line method been used. §1250(b). See also *Section 1250 recapture.*

Additional first-year depreciation. See *fifty percent additional first-year depreciation* and *one hundred percent additional first-year depreciation.*

Adjusted basis. The cost or other basis of property reduced by depreciation allowed or allowable and increased by capital improvements. Other special adjustments are provided in §1016 and the related Regulations. §§1012, 1014, and 1015.

Adoption expenses credit. A provision intended to assist taxpayers who incur nonrecurring costs directly associated with the adoption process such as legal costs, social service review costs, and transportation costs. Up to $12,970 ($12,970 for a child with special needs regardless of the actual adoption expenses) of costs incurred to adopt an eligible child qualify for the credit. A taxpayer may claim the credit in the year qualifying expenses are paid or incurred if the expenses are paid during or after the year in which the adoption is finalized. For qualifying expenses paid or incurred in a tax year prior to the year the adoption is finalized, the credit must be claimed in the tax year following the tax year during which the expenses are paid or incurred. §23, §36C.

Aggregate concept. The theory of partnership taxation under which, in certain cases, a partnership is treated as a mere extension of each partner. This is also referred to as the conduit concept.

Alimony and separate maintenance payments. Alimony deductions result from the payment of a legal obligation arising from the termination of a marital relationship. Payments designated as alimony generally are included in the gross income of the recipient and are deductible *for* AGI by the payer. §§71 and 215.

Alimony recapture. The amount of alimony that previously has been included in the gross income of the recipient and deducted by the payor that now is deducted by the recipient and included in the gross income of the payor as the result of front-loading. §71(f).

All events test. For accrual method taxpayers, income is earned when (1) all the events have occurred that fix the right to receive the income and (2) the amount can be determined with reasonable accuracy. Accrual of income cannot be postponed simply because a portion of the income may have to be returned in a subsequent period. The all events test also is utilized to determine when expenses can be deducted by an accrual basis taxpayer. The application of the test could cause a variation between the treatment of an item for accounting and for tax purposes. For example, a reserve for warranty expense may be properly accruable under generally accepted accounting principles but not be deductible under the Federal income tax law. Because of the application of the all events test, the deduction becomes available in the year the warranty obligation becomes fixed and the amount is determinable with reasonable certainty. Reg §§1.446–1 (c)(1)(ii) and 1.461–1(a)(2).

Allocate. The assignment of income for various tax purposes. A multistate corporation's nonbusiness income usually is allocated to the state where the nonbusiness assets are located; it is not apportioned with the rest of the entity's income. The income and expense items of an estate or trust are allocated between income and corpus components. Specific items of income, expense, gain, loss, and credit can be allocated to specific partners, if a substantial economic nontax purpose for the allocation is established.

Alternate valuation date. Property passing from a decedent by death may be valued for estate tax purposes as of the date of death or the alternate valuation date. The alternate valuation date is six months after the date of death or the date the property is disposed of by the estate, whichever comes first. To use the alternate valuation date, the executor or administrator of the estate must make an affirmative election. Election of the alternate valuation date is not available unless it decreases the amount of the gross estate *and* reduces the estate tax liability. §2032.

Alternative depreciation system (ADS). A cost recovery system that produces a smaller deduction than would be calculated under ACRS or MACRS. The alternative system must be used in certain instances and can be elected in other instances. §168(g). See also *cost recovery.*

Alternative minimum tax (AMT). The AMT is a fixed percentage of the alternative minimum tax base (AMTB). AMTB generally starts with the taxpayer's adjusted gross income (for individuals) or taxable income (for other taxpayers). To this amount, the taxpayer (1) adds designated preference items (e.g., tax-exempt interest income on private activity bonds), (2) makes other specified adjustments (e.g., to reflect a longer, straight-line cost recovery deduction), (3) subtracts certain AMT itemized deductions for individuals (e.g., interest incurred on housing but not taxes paid), and (4) subtracts an exemption amount (e.g., $40,000 on a corporate return). The taxpayer must pay the greater of the resulting AMT (reduced by only certain tax credits) or the regular income tax (reduced by all allowable tax credits). The AMT does not apply to certain small C corporations. AMT preferences and adjustments are assigned to partners and S corporation shareholders. §55.

Alternative minimum tax credit. The AMT can result from timing differences that give rise to positive adjustments in calculating the AMT base. To provide equity for the taxpayer when these timing differences reverse, the regular income tax liability may be reduced by a tax credit for a prior year's minimum tax liability attributable to timing differences. §53.

Alternative tax. An option that is allowed in computing the tax on net capital gain. For the corporate taxpayer, the rate is 35 percent (the same as the highest regular corporate tax rate). Thus, for corporate taxpayers, the alternative tax does not produce a beneficial result. For noncorporate taxpayers, the rate is usually 15 percent (but is 25 percent for unrecaptured §1250 gain and 28 percent for collectibles and §1202 gain). However, if the noncorporate taxpayer is in the 10 or 15 percent tax bracket, the alternative tax rate is 0 percent in 2008, 2009, 2010, 2011, 2012, and 2013 and 5 percent in 2007 and prior years (rather than 15 percent). Certain high income taxpayers (i.e., in the 39.6 percent tax bracket) have an alternative tax rate of 20 percent. Alternative tax treatment also is available for certain dividends. §§1(h) and 1201. See also *unrecaptured §1250 gain (25 percent gain).*

Alternative tax NOL deduction (ATNOLD). In calculating the AMT, the taxpayer is allowed to deduct NOL carryovers and carrybacks. However, for this purpose, a special calculation is required that is referred to as the ATNOLD. The regular income tax is modified for AMT adjustments and preferences to produce the ATNOLD. §56(d).

American opportunity credit. This credit replaces the Hope credit for 2009, 2010, 2011, 2012, and 2013 and applies for qualifying expenses for the first four years of postsecondary education. Qualified expenses include tuition and related expenses and books and other course materials. Room and board are ineligible for the credit. The maximum credit available per student is $2,500 (100 percent of the first $2,000 of qualified expenses and 25 percent of the next $2,000 of qualified expenses). Eligible students include the taxpayer, taxpayer's spouse, and taxpayer's dependents. To qualify for the credit, a student must take at least one-half the full-time course load for a least one academic term at a qualifying educational institution. The credit is phased out for higher income taxpayers. §25A. See also *HOPE scholarship credit* and *lifetime learning credit.*

Amortization. The tax deduction for the cost or other basis of an intangible asset over the asset's estimated useful life. Examples of amortizable intangibles include patents, copyrights, and leasehold interests. The intangible goodwill can be amortized for income tax purposes over a 15-year period. §197.

Amount realized. The amount received by a taxpayer upon the sale or exchange of property. Amount realized is the sum of the cash and the fair market value of any property or services received by the taxpayer, plus any related debt assumed by the buyer. Determining the amount realized is the starting point for arriving at realized gain or loss. §1001(b).

AMT adjustments. In calculating AMTI, certain adjustments are added to or deducted from taxable income. These adjustments generally reflect timing differences. §56.

AMT exclusions. A credit that can be used to reduce the regular income tax liability in future tax years is available in connection with the AMT (AMT credit). The credit is applicable only with respect to the AMT that results from timing differences. It is not available in connection with AMT exclusions, which include the standard deduction, personal exemptions, medical expenses deductible in calculating the regular income tax that are not deductible in computing the AMT, other itemized deductions that are not allowable for AMT purposes, excess percentage depletion, and tax-exempt interest on specified private activity bonds. §53.

Annual exclusion. In computing the taxable gifts for the year, each donor excludes the first $13,000 (in 2012) and $14,000 (in 2013) of a gift to each donee. Usually, the annual exclusion is not available for gifts of future interests. §2503(b).

Annuity. A fixed sum of money payable to a person at specified times for a specified period of time or for life. If the party making the payment (i.e., the obligor) is regularly engaged in this type of business (e.g., an insurance company), the arrangement is classified as a commercial annuity. A so-called private annuity involves an obligor that is not regularly engaged in selling annuities (e.g., a charity or family member). §72.

Apportion. The assignment of the business income of a multistate corporation to specific states for income taxation. Usually, the apportionment procedure accounts for the property, payroll, and sales activity levels of the various states, and a proportionate assignment of the entity's total income is made, using a three-factor apportionment formula. These activities indicate the commercial domicile of the corporation, relative to that income. Some states exclude nonbusiness income from the apportionment procedure; they allocate nonbusiness income to the states where the nonbusiness assets are located.

Archer medical savings account. See *medical savings account (MSA)* and *health savings account (HSA).*

Assignment of income. A procedure whereby a taxpayer attempts to avoid the recognition of income by assigning to another the property that generates the income. Such a procedure will not avoid the recognition of income by the taxpayer making the assignment if it can be said that the income was earned at the point of the transfer. In this case, usually referred to as an anticipatory assignment of income, the income will be taxed to the person who earns it.

Assumption of liabilities. In a corporate formation, corporate takeover, or asset purchase, the new owner often takes assets and agrees to assume preexisting debt. Such actions do not create boot received on the transaction for the new shareholder, unless there is no *bona fide* business purpose for the exchange, or the principal purpose of the debt assumption is the avoidance of tax liabilities. Gain is recognized to the extent that liabilities assumed exceed the aggregated bases of the transferred assets of a shareholder. §357.

At-risk limitation. Generally, a taxpayer can deduct losses related to a trade or business, S corporation, partnership, or investment asset only to the extent of the at-risk amount. §465.

Attribution. Under certain circumstances, the tax law applies attribution (constructive ownership) rules to assign to one taxpayer the ownership interest of another taxpayer. If, for example, the stock of Gold Corporation is held 60 percent by Marsha and 40 percent by Sidney, Marsha may be deemed to own 100 percent of Gold Corporation if Marsha and Sidney are mother and son. In that case, the stock owned by Sidney is attributed to Marsha. Stated differently, Marsha has a 60 percent direct and a 40 percent indirect interest in Gold Corporation. It can also be said that Marsha is the constructive owner of Sidney's interest. §§267, 318, and 707(b).

Automatic mileage method. Automobile expenses are generally deductible only to the extent the automobile is used in business or for the production of income. Personal commuting expenses are not deductible. The taxpayer may deduct actual expenses (including depreciation and insurance), or the standard (automatic) mileage rate may be used (56.5 cents for 2013 and 55.5 cents for 2012). Automobile expenses incurred for medical purposes or in connection with job-related moving expenses are deductible to the extent of actual out-of-pocket expenses or at the rate of 24 cents per mile for 2013, and 23 cents per mile for 2012. For charitable activities, the rate is 14 cents per mile.

B

Bad debts. A deduction is permitted if a business account receivable subsequently becomes partially or completely worthless, providing the income arising from the debt previously was included in income. Available methods are the specific charge-off method and the reserve method. However, except for certain financial institutions, TRA of 1986 repealed the use of the reserve method for 1987 and thereafter. If the reserve method is used, partially or totally worthless accounts are charged to the reserve. A nonbusiness bad debt deduction is allowed as a short-term capital loss if the loan did not arise in connection with the creditor's trade or business activities. Loans between related parties (family members) generally are classified as nonbusiness. §166.

Basis in partnership interest. The acquisition cost of the partner's ownership interest in the partnership. Includes purchase price and associated debt acquired from other partners and in the course of the entity's trade or business. §§705 and 721.

Boot. Cash or property of a type not included in the definition of a nontaxable exchange. The receipt of boot causes an otherwise nontaxable transfer to become taxable to the extent of the lesser of the fair market value of the boot or the realized gain on the transfer. For example, see transfers to controlled corporations under §351(b) and like-kind exchanges under §1031(b).

Branch profits tax. A tax on the effectively connected earnings and profits of the U.S. branch of a foreign corporation. The tax is levied in addition to the usual §11 tax, in an amount equal to 30 percent of the dividend equivalent amount. Treaties can override the tax or reduce the withholding percentage. Earnings reinvested in the U.S. operations of the entity are not subject to the tax until repatriation.

Brother-sister controlled group. More than one corporation owned by the same shareholders. If, for example, Chris and Pat each own one-half of the stock in Wren Corporation and Redbird Corporation, Wren and Redbird form a brother-sister controlled group. §1563.

Built-in gains tax. A penalty tax designed to discourage a shift of the incidence of taxation on unrealized gains from a C corporation to its shareholders, via an S election. Under this provision, any recognized gain during the first 10 years of S status generates a corporate-level tax on a base not to exceed the aggregate untaxed built-in gains brought into the S corporation upon its election from C corporation taxable years. §1374.

Business bad debt. A tax deduction allowed for obligations obtained in connection with a trade or business that have become either partially or completely worthless. In contrast to nonbusiness bad debts, business bad debts are deductible as business expenses. §166.

Business energy credit. A 10 percent tax credit is available to businesses that invest in certain energy property. The purpose of the credit is to create incentives for conservation and to penalize the increased use of oil and gas. The business energy tax credit applies to equipment with an estimated useful life of at least three years that uses fuel or feedstock other than oil or natural gas (e.g., solar, geothermal). §§46(2) and 48(a).

C

C corporation. A separate taxable entity, subject to the rules of Subchapter C of the Code. This business form may create a double taxation effect relative to its shareholders. The entity is subject to the regular corporate tax and a number of penalty taxes at the Federal level.

Cafeteria plan. An employee benefit plan under which an employee is allowed to select from among a variety of employer-provided fringe benefits. Some of the benefits may be taxable, and some may be statutory nontaxable benefits (e.g., health and accident insurance and group term life insurance). The employee is taxed only on the taxable benefits selected. A cafeteria benefit plan is also referred to as a flexible benefit plan. §125.

Capital account. The financial accounting analog of a partner's tax basis in the entity.

Capital asset. Broadly speaking, all assets are capital except those specifically excluded by the Code. Major categories of noncapital assets include property held for resale in the normal course of business (inventory), trade accounts and notes receivable, and depreciable property and real estate used in a trade or business (§1231 assets). §1221.

Capital contribution. Various means by which a shareholder makes additional funds available to the corporation (placed at the risk of the business), sometimes without the receipt of additional stock. If no stock is received, the contributions are added to the basis of the shareholder's existing stock investment and do not generate gross income to the corporation. §118.

Capital gain. The gain from the sale or exchange of a capital asset.

Capital gain property. Property contributed to a charitable organization that, if sold rather than contributed, would have resulted in long-term capital gain to the donor.

Capital interest. Usually, the percentage of the entity's net assets that a partner would receive on liquidation. Typically determined by the partner's capital sharing ratio.

Capital loss. The loss from the sale or exchange of a capital asset.

Capital sharing ratio. A partner's percentage ownership of the entity's capital.

Cash method. See *cash receipts method.*

Cash receipts method. A method of accounting under which the taxpayer generally reports income when cash is collected and reports expenses when cash payments are made. However, for fixed assets, the cash basis taxpayer claims deductions through depreciation or amortization in the same manner as an accrual basis taxpayer. Prepaid expenses must be capitalized and amortized if the life of the asset extends "substantially beyond" the end of the tax year (i.e., the one-year rule). §446(c)(1). See also *constructive receipt.*

Casualty loss. A casualty is defined as "the complete or partial destruction of property resulting from an identifiable event of a sudden, unexpected or unusual nature" (e.g., floods, storms, fires, auto accidents). Individuals may deduct a casualty loss only if the loss is incurred in a trade or business or in a transaction entered into for profit or arises from fire, storm, shipwreck, or other casualty or from theft. Individuals usually deduct personal casualty losses as itemized deductions subject to a $100 ($500 for 2009) nondeductible amount and to an annual floor equal to 10 percent of adjusted gross income that applies after the $100 ($500 for 2009) per casualty floor has been applied. Special rules are provided for the netting of certain casualty gains and losses. §165.

Charitable contributions. Contributions are deductible (subject to various restrictions and ceiling limitations) if made to qualified nonprofit charitable organizations. A cash basis taxpayer is entitled to a deduction solely in the year of payment. Accrual basis corporations may accrue contributions at year-end if payment is properly authorized before the end of the year and payment is made within two and one-half months after the end of the year. §170.

Check-the-box regulations. A business entity can elect to be taxed as a sole proprietorship, partnership, S corporation, or C corporation by indicating its preference on the tax return. Legal structure and operations are irrelevant in this regard. Thus, by using the check-the-box rules prudently, an entity can select the most attractive tax results offered by the Code, without being bound by legal forms. Not available if the entity is incorporated under state law.

Child tax credit. A tax credit based solely on the number of qualifying children under age 17. The maximum credit available is $1,000 per child. A qualifying child must be claimed as a dependent on a parent's tax return in order to qualify for the credit. Taxpayers who qualify for the child tax credit may also qualify for a supplemental credit. The supplemental credit is treated as a component of the earned income credit and is therefore refundable. The credit is phased out for higher-income taxpayers. §24.

Circuit Court of Appeals. Any of 13 Federal courts that consider tax matters appealed from the U.S. Tax Court, a U.S. District Court, or the U.S. Court of Federal Claims. Appeal from a U.S. Court of Appeals is to the U.S. Supreme Court by *Certiorari.*

Circulation expenditures. Expenditures of establishing or increasing the circulation of a periodical that may be either expensed or capitalized. If such expenses are expensed, an adjustment will occur for AMT purposes, since the expenses are deducted over a three-year period for AMT purposes. Over the three-year period, both positive and negative AMT adjustments will be produced. §§56 and 173.

Claim of right doctrine. A judicially imposed doctrine applicable to both cash and accrual basis taxpayers that holds that an amount is includible in income upon actual or constructive receipt if the taxpayer has an unrestricted claim to the payment. For the tax treatment of amounts repaid when previously included in income under the claim of right doctrine, see §1341.

Closely held corporation. A corporation where stock ownership is not widely dispersed. Rather, a few shareholders are in control of corporate policy and are in a position to benefit personally from that policy.

Closing agreement. In a tax dispute, the parties sign a closing agreement to spell out the terms under which the matters are settled. The agreement is binding on both the IRS and the taxpayer, for the disputed year and for all future years.

Collectibles. A special type of capital asset, the gain from which is taxed at a maximum rate of 28 percent if the holding period is more than one year. Examples include art, rugs, antiques, gems, metals, stamps, some coins and bullion, and alcoholic beverages held for investment. §§1(h)(5) and 408(m)(2).

Community property. Louisiana, Texas, New Mexico, Arizona, California, Washington, Idaho, Nevada, and Wisconsin have community property systems. Alaska residents can elect community property status for assets. The rest of the states are common law property jurisdictions. The difference between common law and community property systems centers around the property rights possessed by married persons. In a common law system, each spouse owns whatever he or she earns. Under a community property system, one-half of the earnings of each spouse is considered owned by the other spouse. Assume, for example, Jeff and Alice are husband and wife and their only income is the $50,000 annual salary Jeff receives. If they live in New York (a common law state), the $50,000 salary belongs to Jeff. If, however, they live in Texas (a community property state), the $50,000 salary is owned one-half each by Jeff and Alice.

Compensatory damages. Damages received or paid by the taxpayer can be classified as compensatory damages or as punitive damages. Compensatory damages are those paid to compensate one for harm caused by another. Compensatory damages are excludable from the recipient's gross income. §104.

Complete termination redemption. Sale or exchange treatment is available relative to this type of redemption. The shareholder must retire all of his or her outstanding shares in the corporation (ignoring family attribution rules), and cannot hold an interest, other than that of a creditor, for the 10 years following the redemption. §302(b)(3).

Completed contract method. A method of reporting gain or loss on certain long-term contracts. Under this method of accounting, gross income and expenses are recognized in the tax year in which the contract is completed. §460.

Complex trust. Not a simple trust. Such trusts may have charitable beneficiaries, accumulate income, and distribute corpus. §§661–663.

Constructive dividend. A taxable benefit derived by a shareholder from his or her corporation that is not actually called a dividend. Examples include unreasonable compensation, excessive rent payments, bargain purchases of corporate property, and shareholder use of corporate property. Constructive dividends generally are found in closely held corporations.

Constructive liquidation scenario. The means by which recourse debt is shared among partners in basis determination.

Constructive receipt. If income is unqualifiedly available although not physically in the taxpayer's possession, it is subject to the income tax. An example is accrued interest on a savings account. Under the constructive receipt of income concept, the interest is taxed to a depositor in the year available, rather than the year actually withdrawn. The fact that the depositor uses the cash basis of accounting for tax purposes is irrelevant. See Reg. §1.451–2.

Control. Holding a specified level of stock ownership in a corporation. For §351, the new shareholder(s) must hold at least 80 percent of the total combined voting power of all voting classes of stock and at least 80 percent of the shares of all nonvoting classes. Other tax provisions require different levels of control to bring about desired effects, such as 50 or 100 percent.

Controlled foreign corporation (CFC). A non-U.S. corporation in which more than 50 percent of the total combined voting power of all classes of stock entitled to vote or the total value of the stock of the corporation is owned by "U.S. shareholders" on any day during the taxable year of the foreign corporation. For purposes of this definition, a U.S. shareholder is any U.S. person who owns, or is considered to own, 10 percent or more of the total combined voting power of all classes of voting stock of the foreign corporation. Stock owned directly, indirectly, and constructively is used in this measure.

Controlled group. A controlled group of corporations is required to share the lower-level corporate tax rates and various other tax benefits among the members of the group. A controlled group may be either a brother-sister or a parent-subsidiary group. §§1561 and 1563.

Corporate liquidation. Occurs when a corporation distributes its net assets to its shareholders and ceases to be a going concern. Generally, a shareholder recognizes capital gain or loss upon the liquidation of the entity, regardless of the corporation's balance in its earnings and profits account. However, the distributing corporation recognizes gain and loss on assets that it distributes to shareholders in kind. §§331–338.

Corpus. The body or principal of a trust. Suppose, for example, Grant transfers an apartment building into a trust, income payable to Ruth for life, remainder to Shawn upon Ruth's death. Corpus of the trust is the apartment building.

Correspondence audit. An audit conducted by the IRS by mail. Typically, the IRS writes to the taxpayer requesting the verification of a particular deduction or exemption. The completion of a special form or the remittance of copies of records or other support is all that is requested of the taxpayer.

Cost depletion. Depletion that is calculated based on the adjusted basis of the asset. The adjusted basis is divided by the expected recoverable units to determine the depletion per unit. The depletion per unit is multiplied by the units sold during the tax year to calculate cost depletion. §§611 and 612.

Cost recovery. The portion of the cost of an asset written off under ACRS (or MACRS), which replaced the depreciation system as a method for writing off the cost of an asset for most assets placed in service after 1980 (after 1986 for MACRS). §168. See also *alternative depreciation system, fifty percent additional first-year depreciation,* and *one hundred percent additional first-year depreciation.*

Court of original jurisdiction. The Federal courts are divided into courts of original jurisdiction and appellate courts. A dispute between a taxpayer and the IRS is first considered by a court of original jurisdiction (i.e., a trial court). The four Federal courts of original jurisdiction are the U.S. Tax Court, U.S. District Court, the Court of Federal Claims, and the Small Cases Division of the U.S. Tax Court.

Coverdell Education Savings Account (CESA). A savings account established to pay for qualified education expenses (i.e., tuition, fees, books, supplies, related equipment, room and board if the student's course load is at least one-half of the full-time course load). The maximum annual contribution to the savings account of a beneficiary is $2,000. The maximum annual contribution is subject to phaseout beginning at $95,000 for single taxpayers and $190,000 for married couples who file a joint return. Contributions are not deductible and cannot be made to a savings account once the beneficiary attains age 18. Distributions used to pay for qualified education expenses for a designated beneficiary are tax-free. §530.

Credit for certain retirement plan contributions. A nonrefundable credit is available based on eligible contributions of up to $2,000 to certain qualified retirement plans, such as traditional and Roth IRAs and §401(k) plans. The benefit provided by this credit is in addition to any deduction or exclusion that otherwise is available resulting from the qualifying contribution. The amount of the credit depends on the taxpayer's AGI and filing status. §25B.

Credit for child and dependent care expenses. A tax credit ranging from 20 percent to 35 percent of employment-related expenses (child and dependent care expenses) for amounts of up to $6,000 is available to individuals who are employed (or deemed to be employed) and maintain a household for a dependent child under age 13, disabled spouse, or disabled dependent. §21.

Credit for employer-provided child care. A nonrefundable credit is available to employers who provide child care facilities to their employees during normal working hours. The credit, limited to $150,000, is comprised of two components. The portion of the credit for qualified child care expenses is equal to 25 percent of these expenses while the portion of the credit for qualified child care resource and referral services is equal to 10 percent of these expenses. Any qualifying expenses otherwise deductible by the taxpayer must be reduced by the amount of the credit. In addition, the taxpayer's basis for any property used for qualifying purposes is reduced by the amount of the credit. §45F.

Credit for small employer pension plan startup costs. A nonrefundable credit available to small businesses based on administrative costs associated with establishing and maintaining certain qualified plans. While such qualifying costs generally are deductible as ordinary and necessary business expenses, the availability of the credit is intended to lower the costs of starting a qualified retirement program, and therefore encourage qualifying businesses to establish retirement plans for their employees. The credit is available for eligible employers at the rate of 50 percent of qualified startup costs. The maximum credit is $500 (based on a maximum $1,000 of qualifying expenses). §45E.

Current earnings and profits. Net tax-basis earnings of a corporation aggregated during the current tax year. A corporate distribution is deemed to be first from the entity's current earnings and profits and then from accumulated earnings and profits. Shareholders recognize dividend income to the extent of the earnings and profits of the corporation. A dividend results to the extent of current earnings and profits, even if there is a larger negative balance in accumulated earnings and profits. §312.

D

***De minimis* fringe.** Benefits provided to employees that are too insignificant to warrant the time and effort required to account for the benefits received by each employee and the value of those benefits. Such amounts are excludable from the employee's gross income. §132.

Death benefit. A payment made by an employer to the beneficiary or beneficiaries of a deceased employee on account of the death of the employee. §101.

Death tax. A tax imposed on property transferred by the death of the owner. §2001.

Debt-financed income. Included in computations of the unrelated business income of an exempt organization, the gross income generated from debt-financed property. §514.

Deduction for qualified tuition and related expenses. Taxpayers are allowed a deduction of up to $4,000 for higher education expenses. Certain taxpayers are not eligible for the deduction: those whose AGI exceeds a specified amount and those who can be claimed as a dependent by another taxpayer. These expenses are classified as a deduction *for* AGI and they need not be employment related. §222.

Deductions for adjusted gross income. The Federal income tax is not imposed upon gross income. Rather, it is imposed upon taxable income. Congressionally identified deductions for individual taxpayers are subtracted either from gross income to arrive at adjusted gross income or from adjusted gross income to arrive at the tax base, taxable income. §§62 and 63.

Deductions from adjusted gross income. See *deductions for adjusted gross income.*

Dependency exemption. The tax law provides an exemption for each individual taxpayer and an additional exemption for the taxpayer's spouse if a joint return is filed. An individual may also claim a dependency exemption for each dependent, provided certain tests are met. The amount of the personal and dependency exemptions is $3,900 in 2013 ($3,800 in 2012). The exemption was subject to phaseout once adjusted gross income exceeds certain statutory threshold amounts. Beginning in 2006, this reduction is subject to phaseout over a 4-year period. For 2009, two-thirds of the reduction in the exemption amount is phased out and for 2010 all of the reduction is phased out. Under the sunset provision, the phaseout of personal and dependency exemptions was scheduled to be reinstated in 2011. The Tax Relief Act (TRA) of 2010 put off the reinstatement for two years (i.e., 2011 and 2012). For 2013, the American Taxpayer Relief Act of 2012 reinstated the phaseout of personal and dependency exemptions. §§151 and 152. See also *qualifying child* and *qualifying relative.*

Depletion. The process by which the cost or other basis of a natural resource (e.g., an oil or gas interest) is recovered upon extraction and sale of the resource. The two ways to determine the depletion allowance are the cost and percentage (or statutory) methods. Under cost depletion, each unit of production sold is assigned a portion of the cost or other basis of the interest. This is determined by dividing the cost or other basis by the total units expected to be recovered. Under percentage (or statutory) depletion, the tax law provides a special percentage factor for different types of minerals and other natural resources. This percentage is multiplied by the gross income from the interest to arrive at the depletion allowance. §§611–613A.

Depreciation. The deduction for the cost or other basis of a tangible asset over the asset's estimated useful life. §167.

Determination letter. Upon the request of a taxpayer, the IRS will comment on the tax status of a completed transaction. Determination letters frequently are used to clarify employee status, determine whether a retirement or profit sharing plan qualifies under the Code, and determine the tax-exempt status of certain nonprofit organizations.

Disabled access credit. A tax credit designed to encourage small businesses to make their facilities more accessible to disabled individuals. The credit is equal to 50 percent of the eligible expenditures that exceed $250 but do not exceed $10,250. Thus, the maximum amount for the credit is $5,000. The adjusted basis for depreciation is reduced by the amount of the credit. To qualify, the facility must have been placed in service before November 6, 1990. §44.

Disaster area loss. A casualty sustained in an area designated as a disaster area by the President of the United States. In such an event, the disaster loss may be treated as having occurred in the taxable year immediately preceding the year in which the disaster actually occurred. Thus, immediate tax benefits are provided to victims of a disaster. §165(i).

Disclaimers. Rejections, refusals, or renunciations of claims, powers, or property. Section 2518 sets forth the conditions required to avoid gift tax consequences as the result of a disclaimer.

Disguised sale. When a partner contributes property to the entity and soon thereafter receives a distribution from the partnership, the transactions are collapsed, and the distribution is seen as a purchase of the asset by the partnership. §707(a)(2)(B).

Disproportionate distribution. A distribution from a partnership to one or more of its partners in which at least one partner's interest in partnership hot assets is increased or decreased. For example, a distribution of cash to one partner and hot assets to another changes both partners' interest in hot assets and is disproportionate. The intent of rules for taxation of disproportionate distributions is to ensure each partner eventually recognizes his or her proportionate share of partnership ordinary income. §§731 and 751.

Disproportionate redemption. Sale or exchange treatment is available relative to this type of stock redemption. After the exchange, the shareholder owns less than 80 percent of his or her pre-redemption interest in the corporation, and owns only a minority interest in the entity. §302(b)(2).

Distributable net income (DNI). The measure that determines the nature and amount of the distributions from estates and trusts that the beneficiaries must include in income. DNI also limits the amount that estates and trusts can claim as a deduction for such distributions. §643(a).

Dividend equivalent amount (DEA). The amount subject to the branch profits tax, it is equal to the effectively connected E&P of the U.S. branch of a foreign corporation, reduced/(increased) by an increase/(reduction) in U.S. net equity.

Dividends received deduction. A deduction allowed a shareholder that is a corporation for dividends received from a domestic corporation. The deduction usually is 70 percent of the dividends received, but it could be 80 or 100 percent depending upon the ownership percentage held by the recipient corporation. §§243–246.

Domestic production activities deduction (DPAD). See also *production activities deduction (PAD).*

Domestic production gross receipts (DPGR). A key component in computing the domestic production activities deduction (DPAD). Includes receipts from the sale and other disposition of qualified production property produced in significant part within the U.S. DPGR is defined in §199(c)(4). See also *production activities deduction (PAD).*

E

Earned income credit. A tax credit designed to provide assistance to certain low-income individuals who generally have a qualifying child. This is a refundable credit. To receive the most beneficial treatment, the taxpayer must have qualifying children. However, it is possible to qualify for the credit without having a child. To calculate the credit for a taxpayer with one or more children for 2013, a statutory rate of 34 percent for one child (40 percent for two children and 45 percent for three or more children) is multiplied by the earned income (subject to a statutory maximum of $9,560 with one qualifying child, $13,430 with two qualifying children, and $13,430 for three or more qualifying children). Once the earned income exceeds certain thresholds, the credit is phased out using a 15.98 percent rate for one qualifying child and a 21.06 percent rate for two or more qualifying children. For the qualifying taxpayer without children, the credit is calculated on a maximum earned income of $6,370 applying a 7.65 percent rate with the phaseout beginning later applying the same rate.

Earnings and profits (E&P). Measures the economic capacity of a corporation to make a distribution to shareholders that is not a return of capital. Such a distribution results in dividend income to the shareholders to the extent of the corporation's current and accumulated earnings and profits. §§312 and 316.

Economic effect test. Requirements that must be met before a special allocation may be used by a partnership. The premise behind the test is that each partner who receives an allocation of income or loss from a partnership bears the economic benefit or burden of the allocation. Reg. §1.704–1(b).

Economic income. The change in the taxpayer's net worth, as measured in terms of market values, plus the value of the assets the taxpayer consumed during the year. Because of the impracticality of this income model, it is not used for tax purposes.

Economic performance test. One of the requirements that must be satisfied in order for an accrual basis taxpayer to deduct an expense. The accrual basis taxpayer first must satisfy the all events test. That test is not deemed satisfied until economic performance occurs. This occurs when property or services are provided to the taxpayer, or in the case in which the taxpayer is required to provide property or services, whenever the property or services are actually provided by the taxpayer.

Education expenses. Employees may deduct education expenses that are incurred either (1) to maintain or improve existing job-related skills or (2) to meet the express requirements of the employer or the requirements imposed by law to retain employment status. The expenses are not deductible if the education is required to meet the minimum educational standards for the taxpayer's job or if the education qualifies the individual for a new trade or business. See a limited exception to the preceding sentence in §222. Reg. §1.162–5. See also *HOPE scholarship credit, American opportunity credit, and lifetime learning credit.*

Educational savings bonds. U.S. Series EE bonds whose proceeds are used for qualified higher educational expenses for the taxpayer, the taxpayer's spouse, or a dependent. The interest may be excluded from gross income, provided the taxpayer's adjusted gross income does not exceed certain amounts. §135.

Effectively connected. Income of a nonresident alien or foreign corporation that is attributable to the operation of a U.S. trade or business under either the asset-use or business-activities test.

e-file. The electronic filing of a tax return. The filing is either direct or indirect. As to direct, the taxpayer goes online using a computer and tax return preparation software. Indirect filing occurs when a taxpayer utilizes an authorized IRS e-file provider. The provider often is the tax return preparer.

Electing large partnership. A partnership with 100 or more partners may elect to be subject to simplified tax reporting and audit procedures. The election allows the partnership to combine certain income and expense amounts and report net amounts to the partners. The result is fewer "pass-through" items to the partners, which makes the partners' tax returns easier to prepare. As an example, an electing large partnership with a long-term capital gain and a short-term capital loss would offset the two amounts and allocate the net amount among the partners. §§771–777.

Employment taxes. Employment taxes are those taxes that an employer must pay on account of its employees. Employment taxes include FICA (Federal Insurance Contributions Act) and FUTA (Federal Unemployment Tax Act) taxes. Employment taxes are paid to the IRS in addition to income tax withholdings at specified intervals. Such taxes can be levied on the employees, the employer, or both.

Enrolled agent (EA). A tax practitioner who has gained admission to practice before the IRS by passing an IRS examination.

Entertainment expenses. These expenses are deductible only if they are directly related to or associated with a trade or business. Various restrictions and documentation requirements have been imposed upon the deductibility of entertainment expenses to prevent abuses by taxpayers. See, for example, the provision contained in §274(n) that disallows 50 percent of entertainment expenses. §274.

Entity concept. The theory of partnership taxation under which a partnership is treated as a separate and distinct entity from the partners and has its own tax attributes.

Estate tax. A tax imposed on the right to transfer property by death. Thus, an estate tax is levied on the decedent's estate and not on the heir receiving the property. §2001.

Excess lobbying expenditure. An excise tax is applied on otherwise tax-exempt organizations with respect to the excess of total lobbying expenditures over grass roots lobbying expenditures for the year. §501(h).

Excise tax. A tax on the manufacture, sale, or use of goods; on the carrying on of an occupation or activity; or on the transfer of property. Thus, the Federal estate and gift taxes are, theoretically, excise taxes.

Exclusion amount. The value of assets that is equal to the credit allowed for gifts or transfers by death. Thus, if the unified transfer tax credit is $2,045,800 (in 2013), the exclusion amount is $5,250,000 (in 2013). Often called the *exemption equivalent amount.* Any exclusion amount unused by a deceased spouse may be used by the surviving spouse. §§2010 and 2505. See also *unified tax credit.*

Exemption equivalent amount. The taxable amount (currently $5,250,000 for *gift tax* and *estate tax*) that is the equivalent of the *unified transfer tax credit* allowed. See *exclusion amount.*

Exempt organization. An organization that is either partially or completely exempt from Federal income taxation. §501.

Expenses in respect of a decedent. Deductions accrued at the moment of death but not recognizable on the final income tax return of a decedent because of the method of accounting used. Such items are allowed as deductions on the estate tax return and on the income tax return of the estate (Form 1041) or the heir (Form 1040). An example of a deduction in respect of a decedent is interest expense accrued to the date of death by a cash basis debtor. §691.

Extraordinary personal services. These are services provided by individuals where the customers' use of the property is incidental to their receipt of the services. For example, a patient's use of a hospital bed is incidental to his or her receipt of medical services. This is one of the six exceptions to determine whether an activity is a passive rental activity. §469.

Extraterritorial income. A device by which the United States encourages outbound (export) sales, services, and leases. An exclusion from gross income is computed under §114 for certain transactions of U.S. taxpayers.

F

Fair market value. The amount at which property would change hands between a willing buyer and a willing seller, neither being under any compulsion to buy or to sell, and both having reasonable knowledge of the relevant facts. Reg. §§1.1001–1(a) and 20.2031–1(b).

Federal District Court. A Federal District Court is a trial court for purposes of litigating Federal tax matters. It is the only trial court in which a jury trial can be obtained.

Feeder organization. An entity that carries on a trade or business for the benefit of an exempt organization. However, such a relationship does not result in the feeder organization itself being tax-exempt. §502.

FICA tax. An abbreviation that stands for Federal Insurance Contributions Act, commonly referred to as the Social Security tax. The FICA tax is comprised of the Social Security tax (old age, survivors, and disability insurance) and the Medicare tax (hospital insurance) and is imposed on both employers and employees. The employer is responsible for withholding from the employee's wages the Social Security tax at a rate of 4.2 percent (6.2 percent for other than 2011 or 2012) on a maximum wage base of $106,800 in 2011 and $110,100 in 2012, and the Medicare tax at a rate of 1.45 percent (no maximum wage base). The employer is required to match the employee's contribution. The employer's contribution is still at the 6.2% rate for 2011 and 2012. The maximum wage base for 2013 is $113,700. The 6.2 percent employee rate applies in 2013. §3101.

Field audit. An audit conducted by the IRS on the business premises of the taxpayer or in the office of the tax practitioner representing the taxpayer.

Fifty percent additional first-year depreciation. This provision, which was effective for property acquired after December 31, 2007 and before January 1, 2009, provided for an additional cost recovery deduction of 50 percent in the tax year that qualified property was placed in service. Qualified property included most types of new property other than buildings. The property had to be placed in service before January 1, 2009 and the taxpayer had to be the original user. The taxpayer can elect to forgo the bonus depreciation. The American Recovery and Reinvestment Tax Act of 2009 extended the additional first-year depreciation provision for an additional year. The Small Business Jobs Act of 2010 extended the additional first-year depreciation for an additional year. For 2011, the percentage is increased to 100 percent. For 2012, the percentage reverts to 50 percent. The American Taxpayer Relief Act of 2012 reinstated bonus depreciation for 2013 using a 50 percent rate. §168(k). See also *cost recovery allowance* and *one hundred percent additional first-year depreciation.*

Finalized Regulation. The U.S. Treasury Department Regulations (abbreviated Reg.) represent the position of the IRS as to how the Internal Revenue Code is to be interpreted. Their purpose is to provide taxpayers and IRS personnel with rules of general and specific application to the various provisions of the tax law. Regulations are published in the *Federal Register* and in all tax services.

FIRPTA. Under the Foreign Investment in Real Property Tax Act, gains or losses realized by nonresident aliens and non-U.S. corporations on the disposition of U.S. real estate create U.S.-source income and are subject to U.S. income tax.

Fiscal year. A fiscal year is a 12-month period ending on the last day of a month other than December. In certain circumstances, a taxpayer is permitted to elect a fiscal year instead of being required to use a calendar year. §441.

Flat tax. In its pure form, a flat tax would eliminate all exclusions, deductions, and credits and impose a one-rate tax on gross income.

Flexible spending plan. An employee benefit plan that allows the employee to take a reduction in salary in exchange for the employer paying benefits that can be provided by the employer without the employee being required to recognize income (e.g., medical and child care benefits). §125.

Foreign earned income exclusion. The Code allows exclusions for earned income generated outside the United States to alleviate any tax base and rate disparities among countries. In addition, the exclusion is allowed for housing expenditures incurred by the taxpayer's employer with respect to the non-U.S. assignment, and self-employed individuals can deduct foreign housing expenses incurred in a trade or business. The exclusion is limited to $97,600 for 2013 ($95,100 in 2012). §911.

Foreign tax credit. A U.S. citizen or resident who incurs or pays income taxes to a foreign country on income subject to U.S. tax may be able to claim some of these taxes as a credit against the U.S. income tax. §§27 and 901–905.

Franchise. An agreement that gives the transferee the right to distribute, sell, or provide goods, services, or facilities within a specified area. The cost of obtaining a franchise may be amortized over a statutory period of 15 years. In general, the franchisor's gain on the sale of franchise rights is an ordinary gain because the franchisor retains a significant power, right, or continuing interest in the subject of the franchise. §§197 and 1253.

Franchise tax. A tax levied on the right to do business in a state as a corporation. Although income considerations may come into play, the tax usually is based on the capitalization of the corporation.

Fraud. Tax fraud falls into two categories: civil and criminal. Under civil fraud, the IRS may impose as a penalty an amount equal to as much as 75 percent of the underpayment [§6651(f)]. Fines and/or imprisonment are prescribed for conviction of various types of criminal tax fraud (§§7201–7207). Both civil and criminal fraud involve a specific intent on the part of the taxpayer to evade the tax; mere negligence is not enough. Criminal fraud requires the additional element of willfulness (i.e., done deliberately and with evil purpose). In practice, it becomes difficult to distinguish between the degree of intent necessary to support criminal, rather than civil, fraud. In either situation, the IRS has the burden of proving fraud.

Fruit and tree metaphor. The courts have held that an individual who earns income from property or services cannot assign that income to another. For example, a father cannot assign his earnings from commissions to his child and escape income tax on those amounts.

Functional currency. The currency of the economic environment in which the taxpayer carries on most of its activities, and in which the taxpayer transacts most of its business.

FUTA tax. An employment tax levied on employers. Jointly administered by the Federal and state governments, the tax provides funding for unemployment benefits. FUTA applies at a rate of 6.2 percent on the first $7,000 of covered wages paid during the year for each employee. The Federal government allows a credit for FUTA paid (or allowed under a merit rating system) to the state. The credit cannot exceed 5.4 percent of the covered wages. §3301.

Future interest. An interest that will come into being at some future time. It is distinguished from a present interest, which already exists. Assume that Dan transfers securities to a newly created trust. Under the terms of the trust instrument, income from the securities is to be paid each year to Wilma for her life, with the securities passing to Sam upon Wilma's death. Wilma has a present interest in the trust since she is currently entitled to receive the income from the securities. Sam has a future interest since he must wait for Wilma's death to benefit from the trust. The annual exclusion of $13,000 is not allowed for a gift of a future interest. §2503(b).

G

General business credit. The summation of various nonrefundable business credits, including the tax credit for rehabilitation expenditures, business energy credit, work opportunity credit, research activities credit, low-income housing credit, disabled access credit, small employer pension plan startup costs credit, and employer-provided child care credit. The amount of general business credit that can be used to reduce the tax liability is limited to the taxpayer's net income tax reduced by the greater of (1) the tentative minimum tax or (2) 25 percent of the net regular tax liability that exceeds $25,000. Unused general business credits can be carried back 1 year and forward 20 years. §38.

General partnership. A partnership that is owned by one or more general partners. Creditors of a general partnership can collect amounts owed them from both the partnership assets and the assets of the partners individually.

Gift. A transfer of property for less than adequate consideration. Gifts usually occur in a personal setting (such as between members of the same family). They are excluded from the income tax base but may be subject to a transfer tax. §§102 and 2501.

Gift tax. A tax imposed on the transfer of property by gift. The tax is imposed upon the donor of a gift and is based on the fair market value of the property on the date of the gift. §2501.

Goodwill. The reputation and built-up business of a company. For accounting purposes, goodwill has no basis unless it is purchased. In the purchase of a business, goodwill generally is the difference between the purchase price and the fair market value of the assets acquired. The intangible asset goodwill can be amortized for tax purposes over a 15-year period. Reg. §1.167(a)–3 and §197.

Grantor. A transferor of property. The creator of a trust is usually referred to as the grantor of the trust.

Grantor trust. A trust under which the grantor retains control over the income or corpus (or both) to such an extent that he or she is treated as the owner of the property and its income for income tax purposes. Income from a grantor trust is taxable to the grantor and not to the beneficiary who receives it. §§671–679.

Grass roots expenditures. Exempt organizations are prohibited from engaging in political activities, but spending incurred to influence the opinions of the general public relative to specific legislation is permitted by the law. §501(h).

Gross estate. The property owned or previously transferred by a decedent that is subject to the Federal estate tax. The gross estate can be distinguished from the probate estate, which is property actually subject to administration by the administrator or executor of an estate. §§2031–2046.

Gross income. Income subject to the Federal income tax. Gross income does not include all economic income. That is, certain exclusions are allowed (e.g., interest on municipal bonds). For a manufacturing or merchandising business, gross income usually means gross profit (gross sales or gross receipts less cost of goods sold). §61 and Reg. §1.61–3(a).

Group term life insurance. Life insurance coverage provided by an employer for a group of employees. Such insurance is renewable on a year-to-year basis, and typically no cash surrender value is built up. The premiums paid by the employer on the insurance are not taxed to the employees on coverage of up to $50,000 per person. §79 and Reg. §1.79–1(b).

Guaranteed payments. Payments made by a partnership to a partner for services rendered or for the use of capital to the extent that the payments are determined without regard to the income of the partnership. The payments are treated as though they were made to a nonpartner and thus are usually deductible by the entity. §707(c).

H

Half-year convention. The half-year convention is a cost recovery convention that assumes all property is placed in service at mid-year and thus provides for a half-year's cost recovery for that year. §168.

Head of household. An unmarried individual who maintains a household for another and satisfies certain conditions set forth in §2(b). This status enables the taxpayer to use a set of income tax rates that are lower than those applicable to other unmarried individuals but higher than those applicable to surviving spouses and married persons filing a joint return.

Health savings account (HSA). A medical savings account created in legislation enacted in December 2003 that is designed to replace and expand Archer Medical Savings Accounts. See also *medical savings account (MSA)*.

Hobby losses. Losses from an activity not engaged in for profit. The Code restricts the amount of losses that an individual can deduct for hobby activities so that these transactions cannot be used to offset income from other sources. §183.

Holding period. The period of time during which property has been held for income tax purposes. The holding period is significant in determining whether gain or loss from the sale or exchange of a capital asset is long term or short term. §1223.

Home equity loans. Loans that utilize the personal residence of the taxpayer as security. The interest on such loans is deductible as qualified residence interest. However, interest is deductible only on the portion of the loan that does not exceed the lesser of (1) the fair market value of the residence, reduced by the acquisition indebtedness, or (2) $100,000 ($50,000 for married persons filing separate returns). A major benefit of a home equity loan is that there are no tracing rules regarding the use of the loan proceeds. §163(h)(3).

HOPE scholarship credit. A tax credit for qualifying expenses paid for the first two years of postsecondary education. Room, board, and book costs are ineligible for the credit. The maximum credit available for 2008 is $1,800 per year per student, computed as 100 percent of the first $1,200 of qualifying expenses, plus 50 percent of the second $1,200 of qualifying expenses. Eligible students include the taxpayer, taxpayer's spouse, and taxpayer's dependents. To qualify for the credit, a student must take at least one-half the full-time course load for at least one academic term at a qualifying educational institution. The credit is phased out for higher-income taxpayers. For 2009, 2010, 2011, 2012, and 2013, the Hope scholarship credit is replaced with the American Opportunity credit. §25A. See *American opportunity credit* and *lifetime learning credit.*

Hot assets. Unrealized receivables and substantially appreciated inventory under §751. When hot assets are present, the sale of a partnership interest or the disproportionate distribution of the assets can cause ordinary income to be recognized.

Hybrid method. A combination of the accrual and cash methods of accounting. That is, the taxpayer may account for some items of income on the accrual method (e.g., sales and cost of goods sold) and other items (e.g., interest income) on the cash method. §446.

I

Imputed interest. For certain long-term sales of property, the IRS can convert some of the gain from the sale into interest income if the contract does not provide for a minimum rate of interest to be paid by the purchaser. The application of this procedure has the effect of forcing the seller to recognize less long-term capital gain and more ordinary income (interest income). §483 and the related Regulations and §7872.

Inbound taxation. U.S. tax effects when a non-U.S. person begins an investment or business activity in the United States.

Incentive stock option (ISO). A type of stock option that receives favorable tax treatment. If various qualification requirements can be satisfied, there are no recognition tax consequences when the stock option is granted. However, the spread (the excess of the fair market value at the date of exercise over the option price) is a tax preference item for purposes of the alternative minimum tax. The gain on disposition of the stock resulting from the exercise of the stock option will be classified as long-term capital gain if certain holding period requirements are met (the employee must not dispose of the stock within two years after the option is granted or within one year after acquiring the stock). §422.

Income. For tax purposes, an increase in wealth that has been realized.

Income in respect of a decedent (IRD). Income earned by a decedent at the time of death but not reportable on the final income tax return because of the method of accounting that appropriately is utilized. Such income is included in the gross estate and is taxed to the eventual recipient (either the estate or heirs). The recipient is, however, allowed an income tax deduction for the estate tax attributable to the income. §691.

Independent contractor. A self-employed person as distinguished from one who is employed as an employee.

Individual retirement account (IRA). A type of retirement plan to which an individual with earned income can contribute a statutory maximum. The maximum amount is $5,000 in 2009, 2010, 2011, and 2012 and increases to $5,500 in 2013. IRAs can be classified as traditional IRAs or Roth IRAs. With a traditional IRA, an individual can contribute and deduct a maximum of $5,500 in 2013. The deduction is a deduction *for* AGI. However, if the individual is an active participant in another qualified retirement plan, the deduction is phased out proportionally between certain AGI ranges (note that the phaseout limits the amount of the deduction and not the amount of the contribution). With a Roth IRA, an individual can contribute a maximum of $5,000 in 2009, 2010, 2011, and 2012. The amount increases to $5,500 in 2013. No deduction is permitted. However, if a five-year holding period requirement is satisfied and if the distribution is a qualified distribution, the taxpayer can make tax-free withdrawals from a Roth IRA. The maximum annual contribution is phased out proportionally between certain AGI ranges. §§219, 408, and 408A.

Inheritance tax. A tax imposed on the right to receive property from a decedent. Thus, theoretically, an inheritance tax is imposed on the heir. The Federal estate tax is imposed on the estate.

Inside basis. A partnership's basis in the assets it owns.

Installment method. A method of accounting enabling certain taxpayers to spread the recognition of gain on the sale of property over the collection period. Under this procedure, the seller arrives at the gain to be recognized by computing the gross profit percentage from the sale (the gain divided by the contract price) and applying it to each payment received. §453.

Intangible drilling and development costs (IDC). Taxpayers may elect to expense or capitalize (subject to amortization) intangible drilling and development costs. However, ordinary income recapture provisions apply to oil and gas properties on a sale or other disposition if the expense method is elected. §§263(c) and 1254(a).

Intermediate sanctions. The IRS can assess excise taxes on disqualified persons and organization managers associated with so-called public charities engaging in excess benefit transactions. An excess benefit transaction is one in which a disqualified person engages in a non-fair market value transaction with the exempt organization or receives unreasonable compensation. Prior to the idea of intermediate sanctions, the only option available to the IRS was to revoke the organization's exempt status. §4958.

Interpretive Regulation. A Regulation issued by the Treasury Department that purports to explain the meaning of a particular Code Section. An interpretive Regulation is given less deference than a legislative Regulation.

Investment income. Consisting of virtually the same elements as portfolio income, a measure by which to justify a deduction for interest on investment indebtedness. §§163 and 469.

Investment interest. Payment for the use of funds used to acquire assets that produce investment income. The deduction for investment interest is limited to net investment income for the tax year. §163(d).

Investor losses. Losses on stock and securities. If stocks and bonds are capital assets in the hands of the holder, a capital loss materializes as of the last day of the taxable year in which the stocks or bonds become worthless. Under certain circumstances involving stocks and bonds of affiliated corporations, an ordinary loss is permitted upon worthlessness.

Involuntary conversion. The loss or destruction of property through theft, casualty, or condemnation. Any gain realized on an involuntary conversion can, at the taxpayer's election, be deferred for Federal income tax purposes if the owner reinvests the proceeds within a prescribed period of time in property that is similar or related in service or use. §1033.

IRAs (traditional). See *Individual retirement account (IRA).*

Itemized deductions. Personal and employee expenditures allowed by the Code as deductions from adjusted gross income. Examples include certain medical expenses, interest on home mortgages, state income taxes, and charitable contributions. Itemized deductions are reported on Schedule A of Form 1040. Certain miscellaneous itemized deductions are reduced by 2 percent of the taxpayer's adjusted gross income. In addition, a taxpayer whose adjusted gross income exceeds a certain level (indexed annually) must reduce the itemized deductions by 3 percent of the excess of adjusted gross income over that level. Medical, casualty and theft, and investment interest deductions are not subject to the 3 percent reduction. The 3 percent reduction may not reduce itemized deductions that are subject to the reduction to below 20 percent of their initial amount. Beginning in 2006, this reduction was subject to phaseout over a 4-year period. For 2009, two-thirds of the reduction in itemized deductions is phased out and for 2010 all of the reduction is phased out. Under the sunset provision, the phaseout of itemized deductions was scheduled to be reinstated beginning in 2011. The Tax Relief Act (TRA) of 2010 put off the reinstatement for two years (i.e., 2011 and 2012). For 2013, the American Taxpayer Relief Act of 2012 reinstated the phaseout for itemized deductions. §§67, 68, 163, 164, 170, and 213.

J

Joint tenants. Two or more persons having undivided ownership of property with the right of survivorship. Right of survivorship gives the surviving owner full ownership of the property. Suppose Bob and Tami are joint tenants of a tract of land. Upon Bob's death, Tami becomes the sole owner of the property. For the estate tax consequences upon the death of a joint tenant, see §2040.

K

Keogh plan. A retirement plan that is available to self-employed taxpayers; also referred to as an H.R. 10 plan. Under such plans in 2011, a taxpayer may deduct each year up to either 100 percent of net earnings from self-employment or $49,000, whichever is less. For 2012, the amount is increased to $50,000. For 2013, the amount is increased to $51,000. If the plan is a profit-sharing plan, the percentage is 25 percent.

Kiddie tax. Passive income, such as interest and dividends, that is recognized by a child under age 19 (under age 24 if a full-time student) is taxed to him or her at the rates that would have applied had the income been incurred by the child's parents, generally to the extent that the income exceeds $2,000. The additional tax is assessed regardless of the source of the income or the income's underlying property. If the child's parents are divorced, the custodial parent's rates are used. The parents' rates reflect any applicable alternative minimum tax and the phaseouts of lower tax brackets and other deductions. §1(g).

L

Least aggregate deferral method. An algorithm set forth in the Regulations to determine the tax year for a partnership or §corporation with owners whose tax years differ. The tax year selected is the one that produces the least aggregate deferral of income for the owners. Reg. §1.706–1T.

Legislative Regulation. Some Code Sections give the Secretary of the Treasury or his delegate the authority to prescribe Regulations to carry out the details of administration or to otherwise complete the operating rules. Regulations issued pursuant to this type of authority truly possess the force and effect of law. In effect, Congress is almost delegating its legislative powers to the Treasury Department.

Lessee. One who rents property from another. In the case of real estate, the lessee is also known as the tenant.

Lessor. One who rents property to another. In the case of real estate, the lessor is also known as the landlord.

Letter ruling. The written response of the IRS to a taxpayer's request for interpretation of the revenue laws, with respect to a proposed transaction (e.g., concerning the tax-free status of a reorganization). Not to be relied on as precedent by other than the party who requested the ruling.

Liabilities in excess of basis. On the contribution of capital to a corporation, an investor recognizes gain on the exchange to the extent that contributed assets carry liabilities with a face amount in excess of the tax basis of the contributed assets. This rule keeps the investor from holding the investment asset received with a negative basis. §357(c).

Life insurance proceeds. A specified sum (the face value or maturity value of the policy) paid to the designated beneficiary of the policy by the life insurance company upon the death of the insured.

Lifetime learning credit. A tax credit for qualifying expenses for taxpayers pursuing education beyond the first two years of postsecondary education. Individuals who are completing their last two years of undergraduate studies, pursuing graduate or professional degrees, or otherwise seeking new job skills or maintaining existing job skills are all eligible for the credit. Eligible individuals include the taxpayer, taxpayer's spouse, and taxpayer's dependents. The maximum credit is 20 percent of the first $10,000 of qualifying expenses and is computed per taxpayer. The credit is phased out for higher-income taxpayers. §25A. See *HOPE scholarship credit* and *American opportunity credit.*

Like-kind exchange. An exchange of property held for productive use in a trade or business or for investment (except inventory and stocks and bonds) for other investment or trade or business property. Unless non-like-kind property (boot) is received, the exchange is fully nontaxable. §1031.

Limited expensing. See *Section 179 expensing.*

Limited liability company (LLC). A form of entity allowed by all of the states. The entity is taxed as a partnership in which all members or owners of the LLC are treated much like limited partners. There are no restrictions on ownership, all members may participate in management, and none has personal liability for the entity's debts.

Limited liability partnership (LLP). A form of entity allowed by many of the states, where a general partnership registers with the state as an LLP. Owners are general partners, but a partner is not liable for any malpractice committed by other partners. The personal assets of the partners are at risk for the entity's contractual liabilities, such as accounts payable. The personal assets of a specific partner are at risk for his or her own professional malpractice and tort liability, and for malpractice and torts committed by those whom he or she supervises.

Limited partnership. A partnership in which some of the partners are limited partners. At least one of the partners in a limited partnership must be a general partner.

Liquidating distribution. A distribution by a partnership or corporation that is in complete liquidation of the entity's trade or business activities. Typically, such distributions generate capital gain or loss to the investors without regard, for instance, to the earnings and profits of the corporation or to the partnership's basis in the distributed property. They can, however, lead to recognized gain or loss at the corporate level.

Listed property. The term listed property includes (1) any passenger automobile, (2) any other property used as a means of transportation, (3) any property of a type generally used for purposes of entertainment, recreation, or amusement, (4) any computer or peripheral equipment (with an exception for exclusive business use), (5) any cellular telephone (or other similar telecommunications equipment), and (6) any other property of a type specified in the Regulations. If listed property is predominantly used for business, the taxpayer is allowed to use the statutory percentage method of cost recovery. Otherwise, the straight-line cost recovery method must be used. §280F.

Lobbying expenditure. An expenditure made for the purpose of influencing legislation. Such payments can result in the loss of the exempt status of, and the imposition of Federal income tax on, an exempt organization. §501(h).

Long-term care insurance. Insurance that helps pay the cost of care when the insured is unable to care for himself or herself. Such insurance is generally thought of as insurance against the cost of an aged person entering a nursing home. The employer can provide the insurance, and the premiums may be excluded from the employee's gross income. §7702B.

Long-term contract. A building, installation, construction, or manufacturing contract that is entered into but not completed within the same tax year. A manufacturing contract is a long-term contract only if the contract is to manufacture (1) a unique item not normally carried in finished goods inventory or (2) items that normally require more than 12 calendar months to complete. The two available methods to account for long-term contracts are the percentage of completion method and the completed contract method. The completed contract method can be used only in limited circumstances. §460.

Long-term nonpersonal use capital assets. Includes investment property with a long-term holding period. Such property disposed of by casualty or theft may receive §1231 treatment.

Low-income housing credit. Beneficial treatment to owners of low-income housing is provided in the form of a tax credit. The calculated credit is claimed in the year the building is placed in service and in the following nine years. §42.

M

Majority interest partners. Partners who have more than a 50 percent interest in partnership profits and capital, counting only those partners who have the same taxable year, are referred to as majority interest partners. The term is of significance in determining the appropriate taxable year of a partnership. §706(b).

Marital deduction. A deduction allowed against the taxable estate or taxable gifts upon the transfer of property from one spouse to another. §§2056 and 2523.

Marriage penalty. The additional tax liability that results for a married couple when compared with what their tax liability would be if they were not married and filed separate returns.

Material participation. If an individual taxpayer materially participates in a nonrental trade or business activity, any loss from that activity is treated as an active loss that can be offset against active income. Material participation is achieved by meeting any one of seven tests provided in the Regulations. §469(h) and Reg. §1.469–5T.

Meaningful reduction test. A decrease in the shareholder's voting control. Used to determine whether a redemption qualifies for sale or exchange treatment. §302(b)(2).

Medical expenses. Medical expenses of an individual, spouse, and dependents are allowed as an itemized deduction to the extent that such amounts (less insurance reimbursements) exceed 10 percent (or 7.5 percent if at least age 65) of adjusted gross income. §213.

Medical savings account (MSA). A plan available to employees of small firms (50 or fewer employees) with high-deductible health insurance. The employee can place money in the fund and then deduct the contributions (within limits) from gross income. If the employer contributes to the fund, the employee can exclude the contribution from gross income. Income earned from the fund and withdrawals for medical care are not subject to tax. §§106(b) and 220. See also *health savings account (HSA)*.

Mid-month convention. A cost recovery convention that assumes property is placed in service in the middle of the month that it is actually placed in service. §168.

Mid-quarter convention. A cost recovery convention that assumes property placed in service during the year is placed in service at the middle of the quarter in which it is actually placed in service. The mid-quarter convention applies if more than 40 percent of the value of property (other than eligible real estate) is placed in service during the last quarter of the year. §168.

Miscellaneous itemized deductions. A special category of itemized deductions that includes such expenses as professional dues, tax return preparation fees, job-hunting costs, unreimbursed employee business expenses, and certain investment expenses. Such expenses are deductible only to the extent they exceed 2 percent of adjusted gross income. §67.

Modified accelerated cost recovery system (MACRS). A method in which the cost of tangible property is recovered over a prescribed period of time. Enacted by the Economic Recovery Tax Act (ERTA) of 1981 and substantially modified by the Tax Reform Act (TRA) of 1986 (the modified system is referred to as MACRS), the approach disregards salvage value, imposes a period of cost recovery that depends upon the classification of the asset into one of various recovery periods, and prescribes the applicable percentage of cost that can be deducted each year. §168.

Modified adjusted gross income. A key determinant in computing the domestic production activities deduction (DPAD). The deduction is limited to a percentage of the *lesser of* qualified production activities income (QPAI) or modified adjusted gross income. Aside from limited changes required by §199(d)(2)(A), modified adjusted gross income is AGI as usually determined but without any domestic production activities deduction (DPAD). See also *production activities deduction (PAD).*

Moving expenses. A deduction *for* AGI is permitted to employees and self-employed individuals provided certain tests are met. The taxpayer's new job must be at least 50 miles farther from the old residence than the old residence was from the former place of work. In addition, an employee must be employed on a full-time basis at the new location for 39 weeks in the 12-month period following the move. Deductible moving expenses include the cost of moving the household and personal effects, transportation, and lodging expenses during the move. The cost of meals during the move is not deductible. Qualified moving expenses that are paid (or reimbursed) by the employer can be excluded from the employee's gross income. In this case, the related deduction by the employee is not permitted. §§62(a)(15), 132(a)(6), and 217.

Multiple support agreement. To qualify for a dependency exemption, the support test must be satisfied. This requires that over 50 percent of the support of the potential dependent be provided by the taxpayer. Where no one person provides more than 50 percent of the support, a multiple support agreement enables a taxpayer to still qualify for the dependency exemption. Any otherwise eligible person who contributed more than 10 percent of the support is entitled to claim the exemption if each person in the group who contributed more than 10 percent files a written consent (Form 2120). Each person who is a party to the multiple support agreement must meet all the other requirements for claiming the dependency exemption. §152(d).

N

National sales tax. Intended as a replacement for the current Federal income tax. Unlike a value added tax (VAT), which is levied on the manufacturer, it would be imposed on the consumer upon the final sale of goods and services. To keep the tax from being regressive, low-income taxpayers would be granted some kind of credit or exemption.

Negligence. Failure to exercise the reasonable or ordinary degree of care of a prudent person in a situation that results in harm or damage to another. Code §6651 imposes a penalty on taxpayers who exhibit negligence or intentional disregard of rules and Regulations with respect to the underpayment of certain taxes.

Net capital gain. The excess of the net long-term capital gain for the tax year over the net short-term capital loss. The net capital gain of an individual taxpayer is eligible for the alternative tax. §1222(11).

Net capital loss. The excess of the losses from sales or exchanges of capital assets over the gains from sales or exchanges of such assets. Up to $3,000 per year of the net capital loss may be deductible by noncorporate taxpayers against ordinary income. The excess net capital loss carries over to future tax years. For corporate taxpayers, the net capital loss cannot be offset against ordinary income, but it can be carried back three years and forward five years to offset net capital gains. §§1211, 1212, and 1221(10).

Net investment income. The excess of investment income over investment expenses. Investment expenses are those deductible expenses directly connected with the production of investment income. Investment expenses do not include investment interest. The deduction for investment interest for the tax year is limited to net investment income. §163(d).

Net operating loss. To mitigate the effect of the annual accounting period concept, §172 allows taxpayers to use an excess loss of one year as a deduction for certain past or future years. In this regard, a carryback period of 2 years and a carryforward period of 20 years usually are allowed.

Nexus. A multistate corporation's taxable income can be apportioned to a specific state only if the entity has established a sufficient presence, or nexus, with that state. State law, which often follows the Uniform Division of Income for Tax Purposes Act (UDITPA), specifies various activities that lead to nexus in various states.

Ninety-day letter. Commonly referred to as the 90-day letter, this notice is sent to a taxpayer upon request, upon the expiration of the 30-day letter, or upon exhaustion by the taxpayer of his or her administrative remedies before the IRS. The notice gives the taxpayer 90 days in which to file a petition with the U.S. Tax Court. If a petition is not filed, the IRS will demand payment of the assessed deficiency. §§6211–6216.

No-additional-cost services. Services that the employer may provide the employee at no additional cost to the employer. Generally, the benefit is the ability to utilize the employer's excess capacity (e.g., vacant seats on an airliner). Such amounts are excludable from the recipient's gross income. §132(a)(1).

Nonaccountable plan. An expense reimbursement plan that does not have an accountability feature. The result is that employee expenses must be claimed as deductions *from* AGI. An exception is moving expenses that are deductions *for* AGI.

Nonacquiescence. Disagreement by the IRS on the result reached in certain judicial decisions. *Nonacq*. or *NA*.

Nonbusiness bad debt. A bad debt loss that is not incurred in connection with a creditor's trade or business. The loss is classified as a short-term capital loss and is allowed only in the year the debt becomes entirely worthless. In addition to family loans, many investor losses are nonbusiness bad debts. §166(d).

Nonliquidating distribution. A payment made by a partnership or corporation to the entity's owner is a nonliquidating distribution when the entity's legal existence does not cease thereafter. If the payor is a corporation, such a distribution can result in dividend income to the shareholders. If the payor is a partnership, the partner usually assigns a basis in the distributed property that is equal to the lesser of the partner's basis in the partnership interest or the basis of the distributed asset to the partnership. In this regard, the partner first assigns basis to any cash that he or she receives in the distribution. The partner's remaining basis, if any, is assigned to the noncash assets according to their relative bases to the partnership.

Nonrecourse debt. Debt secured by the property that it is used to purchase. The purchaser of the property is not personally liable for the debt upon default. Rather, the creditor's recourse is to repossess the related property. Nonrecourse debt generally does not increase the purchaser's at-risk amount.

Nonrefundable credit. A nonrefundable credit is a credit that is not paid if it exceeds the taxpayer's tax liability. Some nonrefundable credits qualify for carryback and carryover treatment.

Nonresident alien. An individual who is neither a citizen nor a resident of the United States. Citizenship is determined under the immigration and naturalization laws of the United States. Residency is determined under §7701(b) of the Internal Revenue Code.

Nontaxable exchange. A transaction in which realized gains or losses are not recognized. The recognition of gain or loss is postponed (deferred) until the property received in the non-taxable exchange is subsequently disposed of in a taxable transaction. Examples are §1031 like-kind exchanges and §1033 involuntary conversions.

Not essentially equivalent redemption. Sale or exchange treatment is given to this type of redemption. Although various safe-harbor tests are failed, the nature of the redemption is such that dividend treatment is avoided, because it represents a meaningful reduction in the shareholder's interest in the corporation. §302(b)(1).

O

Occupational tax. A tax imposed on various trades or businesses. A license fee that enables a taxpayer to engage in a particular occupation.

Offer in compromise. A settlement agreement offered by the IRS in a tax dispute, especially where there is doubt as to the collectibility of the full deficiency. Offers in compromise can include installment payment schedules, as well as reductions in the tax and penalties owed by the taxpayer.

Office audit. An audit conducted by the IRS in the agent's office.

Office-in-the-home expenses. Employment and business-related expenses attributable to the use of a residence (e.g., den or office) are allowed only if the portion of the residence is exclusively used on a regular basis as a principal place of business of the taxpayer or as a place of business that is used by patients, clients, or customers. If the expenses are incurred by an employee, the use must be for the convenience of the employer as opposed to being merely appropriate and helpful. §280A.

One hundred percent additional first-year depreciation. The Tax Relief Act of 2010 provides for a cost recovery deduction of 100 percent in the tax year qualified property is placed in service. Qualified property includes most types of new property other than buildings. This provision is effective for property acquired after December 31, 2010, and placed in service before January 1, 2012. For 2012, the percentage reverts to 50 percent and remains at 50 percent for 2013. See also *cost recovery allowance* and *fifty percent additional first-year depreciation.*

One-year rule for prepaid expenses. Taxpayers who use the cash method are required to use the accrual method for deducting certain prepaid expenses (i.e., must capitalize the item and can deduct only when used). If a prepayment will not be consumed or expire by the end of the tax year following the year of payment, the prepayment must be capitalized and prorated over the benefit period. Conversely, if the prepayment will be consumed by the end of the tax year following the year of payment, it can be expensed when paid. To obtain the current deduction under the one-year rule, the payment must be a required payment rather than a voluntary payment.

Options. The sale or exchange of an option to buy or sell property results in capital gain or loss if the property is a capital asset. Generally, the closing of an option transaction results in short-term capital gain or loss to the writer of the call and the purchaser of the call option. §1234.

Ordinary and necessary. An ordinary expense is one that is common and accepted in the general industry or type of activity in which the taxpayer is engaged. It comprises one of the tests for the deductibility of expenses incurred or paid in connection with a trade or business; for the production or collection of income; for the management, conservation, or maintenance of property held for the production of income; or in connection with the determination, collection, or refund of any tax. §§162(a) and 212. A necessary expense is one that is appropriate and helpful in furthering the taxpayer's business or income-producing activity. §§162(a) and 212.

Ordinary income property. Property contributed to a charitable organization that, if sold rather than contributed, would have resulted in other than long-term capital gain to the donor (i.e., ordinary income property and short-term capital gain property). Examples are inventory and capital assets held for less than the long-term holding period.

Organizational expenditures. Items incurred early in the life of a corporate entity, qualifying for a special treatment under Federal tax law. A corporation can elect to immediately expense the first $5,000 (subject to phaseout) of organizational expenditures and generally amortize the balance over a period of 180 months. Amortizable expenditures exclude those incurred to obtain capital (underwriting fees) or assets (subject to cost recovery). Typically, amortizable expenditures include legal and accounting fees and state incorporation payments. Such items must be incurred by the end of the entity's first tax year. §§248 and 709.

Original issue discount. The difference between the issue price of a debt obligation (e.g., a corporate bond) and the maturity value of the obligation when the issue price is *less than* the maturity value. OID represents interest and must be amortized over the life of the debt obligation using the effective interest method. The difference is not considered to be original issue discount for tax purposes when it is less than one-fourth of 1 percent of the redemption price at maturity multiplied by the number of years to maturity. §§1272 and 1273(a)(3).

Outbound taxation. U.S. tax effects when a U.S. person begins an investment or business activity outside the United States.

Outside basis. A partner's basis in his or her partnership interest.

P

Parent-subsidiary controlled group. A controlled or affiliated group of corporations, where at least one corporation is at least 80 percent owned by one or more of the others. The affiliated group definition under §1504 is more difficult to meet. §1563.

Partnership. For income tax purposes, a partnership includes a syndicate, group, pool, or joint venture, as well as ordinary partnerships. In an ordinary partnership, two or more parties combine capital and/or services to carry on a business for profit as co-owners. §7701(a)(2).

Passive investment income (PII). Gross receipts from royalties, certain rents, dividends, interest, annuities, and gains from the sale or exchange of stock and securities. With certain exceptions, if the passive investment income of an S corporation exceeds 25 percent of the corporation's gross receipts for three consecutive years, S status is lost.

Passive loss. Any loss from (1) activities in which the taxpayer does not materially participate or (2) rental activities (subject to certain exceptions). Net passive losses cannot be used to offset income from nonpassive sources. Rather, they are suspended until the taxpayer either generates net passive income (and a deduction of such losses is allowed) or disposes of the underlying property (at which time the loss deductions are allowed in full). One relief provision allows landlords who actively participate in the rental activities to deduct up to $25,000 of passive losses annually. However, a phaseout of the $25,000 amount commences when the landlord's AGI exceeds $100,000. Another relief provision applies for material participation in a real estate trade or business. §469.

Patent. A patent is an intangible asset that may be amortized over a statutory 15-year period as a §197 intangible. The sale of a patent usually results in favorable long-term capital gain treatment. §§197 and 1235.

Payroll factor. The proportion of a multistate corporation's total payroll that is traceable to a specific state. Used in determining the taxable income that is to be apportioned to that state.

Percentage depletion. Percentage depletion is depletion based on a statutory percentage applied to the gross income from the property. The taxpayer deducts the greater of cost depletion or percentage depletion. §613.

Percentage of completion method. A method of reporting gain or loss on certain long-term contracts. Under this method of accounting, the gross contract price is included in income as the contract is completed. §460.

Personal casualty gain. The recognized gain from any involuntary conversion of personal use property arising from fire, storm, shipwreck, or other casualty, or from theft. §165.

Personal casualty loss. The recognized loss from any involuntary conversion of personal use property arising from fire, storm, shipwreck, or other casualty, or from theft. §165.

Personal exemption. The tax law provides an exemption for each individual taxpayer and an additional exemption for the taxpayer's spouse if a joint return is filed. An individual may also claim a dependency exemption for each dependent, provided certain tests are met. The amount of the personal and dependency exemptions is $3,900 in 2013 ($3,800 in 2012). The exemption is subject to phaseout once adjusted gross income exceeds certain statutory threshold amounts. Beginning in 2006, this reduction is subject to phaseout over a 4-year period. For 2009, two-thirds of the reduction in the exemption amount is phased out and for 2010 all of the reduction is phased out. Under the sunset provision, the phaseout of personal and dependency exemptions was scheduled to be reinstated in 2011. The Tax Relief Act (TRA) of 2010 put off the reinstatement for two years (i.e., 2011 and 2012). For 2013, the American Taxpayer Relief Act of 2012 reinstated the phaseout of personal and dependency exemptions. §§151 and 152. See also *qualifying child* and *qualifying relative.*

Personal residence. If a residence has been owned and used by the taxpayer as the principal residence for at least two years during the five-year period ending on the date of sale, up to $250,000 of realized gain is excluded from gross income. For a married couple filing a joint return, the $250,000 is increased to $500,000 if either spouse satisfies the ownership requirement and both spouses satisfy the use requirement. §121.

Personal service corporation (PSC). A corporation whose principal activity is the performance of personal services (e.g., health, law, engineering, architecture, accounting, actuarial science, performing arts, or consulting) and where such services are substantially performed by the employee-owners. The 35 percent statutory income tax rate applies to PSCs. §§11, 269A, 280H, and 444.

Personalty. All property that is not attached to real estate (realty) and is movable. Examples of personalty are machinery, automobiles, clothing, household furnishings, inventory, and personal effects.

Points. Loan origination fees that may be deductible as interest by a buyer of property. A seller of property who pays points reduces the selling price by the amount of the points paid for the buyer. While the seller is not permitted to deduct this amount as interest, the buyer may do so. §461(g).

Portfolio income. Income from interest, dividends, rentals, royalties, capital gains, or other investment sources. Net passive losses cannot be used to offset net portfolio income. §469.

Precedent. A previously decided court decision that is recognized as authority for the disposition of future decisions.

Precontribution gain or loss. Partnerships allow for a variety of special allocations of gain or loss among the partners, but gain or loss that is—*built in*—on an asset contributed to the partnership is assigned specifically to the contributing partner. §704(c)(1)(A).

Prepaid income. See *unearned (prepaid) income.*

Previously taxed income (PTI). Under prior law, the undistributed taxable income of an S corporation was taxed to the shareholders as of the last day of the corporation's tax year and usually could be withdrawn by the shareholders without tax consequences at some later point in time. The role of PTI has been taken over by the accumulated adjustments account. See also *accumulated adjustments account.*

Principal partner. A partner with a 5 percent or greater interest in partnership capital or profits. §706(b)(3).

Private activity bond. Interest on state and local bonds is excludable from gross income. §103. Certain such bonds are labeled private activity bonds. Although the interest on such bonds is excludable for regular income tax purposes, it is treated as a tax preference in calculating the AMT. However, such bonds issued in 2009 or 2010 are not AMT tax preferences.

Private foundation. An exempt organization that is subject to additional statutory restrictions on its activities and on contributions made to it. Excise taxes may be levied on certain prohibited transactions, and the Code places more stringent restrictions on the deductibility of contributions to private foundations. §509.

Probate estate. The property of a decedent that is subject to administration by the executor or administrator of an estate.

Procedural Regulation. A Regulation issued by the Treasury Department that is a housekeeping-type instruction indicating information that taxpayers should provide the IRS as well as information about the internal management and conduct of the IRS itself.

Production activities deduction (PAD). A deduction origianlly based on 3% of the lesser of qualified production activities income (QPAI) or modified adjusted gross income but not to exceed 50% of the W-2 production wages paid. In the case of a corporate taxpayer, taxable income is substituted for modified AGI. The deduction rate increased to 6% for 2007 to 2009 and increased to 9% for 2010 and thereafter. §199. See also *qualified production activities income (QPAI).*

Profit and loss sharing ratios. Specified in the partnership agreement and used to determine each partner's allocation of ordinary taxable income and separately stated items. Profits and losses can be shared in different ratios. The ratios can be changed by amending the partnership agreement. §704(a).

Profits interest. A partner's percentage allocation of partnership operating results, determined by the profit and loss sharing ratios.

Property. Assets defined in the broadest legal sense. Property includes the unrealized receivables of a cash basis taxpayer, but not services rendered. §351.

Property dividend. Generally treated in the same manner as a cash distribution, measured by the fair market value of the property on the date of distribution. The portion of the distribution representing E & P is a dividend; any excess is treated as a return of capital. Distribution of appreciated property causes the distributing corporation to recognize gain. The distributing corporation does not recognize loss on property that has depreciated in value. §§301, 311, and 316.

Property factor. The proportion of a multistate corporation's total property that is traceable to a specific state. Used in determining the taxable income that is to be apportioned to that state.

Proportionate distribution. A distribution in which each partner in a partnership receives a pro rata share of hot assets being distributed. For example, a distribution of $10,000 of hot assets equally to two 50 percent partners is a proportionate distribution. §751.

Proposed Regulation. A Regulation issued by the Treasury Department in proposed, rather than final, form. The interval between the proposal of a Regulation and its finalization permits taxpayers and other interested parties to comment on the propriety of the proposal.

Public Law 86–272. A congressional limit on the ability of the state to force a multistate corporation to assign income to that state. Under P.L. 86–272, where orders for tangible personal property are both filled and delivered outside the state, the entity must establish more than the mere solicitation of such orders before any income can be apportioned to the state.

Punitive damages. Damages received or paid by the taxpayer can be classified as compensatory damages or as punitive damages. Punitive damages are those awarded to punish the defendant for gross negligence or the intentional infliction of harm. Such damages are includible in gross income. §104.

Q

Qualified business unit (QBU). A subsidiary, branch, or other business entity that conducts business using a currency other than the U.S. dollar.

Qualified dividend income. Dividends that are eligible for the beneficial 0 percent (5% prior to 2008) or 15 percent tax rate. The American Taxpayer Relief Act of 2012 increased the tax rate from 15 percent to 20 percent for certain high-income taxpayers (i.e., tax bracket is 39.6 percent). Excluded are certain dividends from foreign corporations, dividends from tax-exempt entities, and dividends that do not satisfy the holding period requirement. A dividend from a foreign corporation is eligible for qualified dividend status only if one of the following requirements are met: (1) the foreign corporation's stock is traded on an established U.S. securities market, or (2) the foreign corporation is eligible for the benefits of a comprehensive income tax treaty between its country of incorporation and the United States. To satisfy the holding period requirement, the stock on which the dividend is paid must have been held for more than 60 days during the 120-day period beginning 60 days before the ex-dividend date.

Qualified employee discounts. Discounts offered employees on merchandise or services that the employer ordinarily sells or provides to customers. The discounts must be generally available to all employees. In the case of property, the discount cannot exceed the employer's gross profit (the sales price cannot be less than the employer's cost). In the case of services, the discounts cannot exceed 20 percent of the normal sales price. §132(a)(2).

Qualified nonrecourse debt. Debt issued on realty by a bank, retirement plan, or governmental agency. Included in the at-risk amount by the investor. §465(b)(6).

Qualified production activities income (QPAI). A key determinant in computing the domestic production activities deduction (DPAD). It consists of domestic production gross receipts (DPGR) reduced by cost of goods sold and other assignable expenses. Thus, QPAI represents the profit derived from production activities. §199. See also *production activities deduction (PAD)* and *domestic production gross receipts (DPGR).*

Qualified real property business indebtedness. Indebtedness that was incurred or assumed by the taxpayer in connection with real property used in a trade or business and is secured by such real property. The taxpayer must not be a C corporation. For qualified real property business indebtedness, the taxpayer may elect to exclude some or all of the income realized from cancellation of debt on qualified real property. If the election is made, the basis of the property must be reduced by the amount excluded. The amount excluded cannot be greater than the excess of the principal amount of the outstanding debt over the fair market value (net of any other debt outstanding on the property) of the property securing the debt. §108(c).

Qualified residence interest. A term relevant in determining the amount of interest expense the individual taxpayer may deduct as an itemized deduction for what otherwise would be disallowed as a component of personal interest (consumer interest). Qualified residence interest consists of interest paid on qualified residences (principal residence and one other residence) of the taxpayer. Debt that qualifies as qualified residence interest is limited to $1 million of debt to acquire, construct, or substantially improve qualified residences (acquisition indebtedness) plus $100,000 of other debt secured by qualified residences (home equity indebtedness). The home equity indebtedness may not exceed the fair market value of a qualified residence reduced by the acquisition indebtedness for that residence. §163(h)(3).

Qualified small business corporation. A C corporation that has aggregate gross assets not exceeding $50 million and that is conducting an active trade or business. §1202.

Qualified small business stock. Stock in a qualified small business corporation, purchased as part of an original issue after August 10, 1993. The shareholder may exclude from gross income 50 percent of the realized gain on the sale of the stock, if he or she held the stock for more than five years. §1202.

Qualified terminable interest property (QTIP). Generally, the marital deduction (for gift and estate tax purposes) is not available if the interest transferred will terminate upon the death of the transferee spouse and pass to someone else. Thus, if Jim (the husband) places property in trust, life estate to Mary (the wife), and remainder to their children upon Mary's death, this is a terminable interest that will not provide Jim (or Jim's estate) with a marital deduction. If, however, the transfer in trust is treated as qualified terminable interest property (the QTIP election is made), the terminable interest restriction is waived and the marital deduction becomes available. In exchange for this deduction, the surviving spouse's gross estate must include the value of the QTIP election assets, even though he or she has no control over the ultimate disposition of the asset. Terminable interest property qualifies for this election if the donee (or heir) is the only beneficiary of the asset during his or her lifetime and receives income distributions relative to the property at least annually. For gifts, the donor spouse is the one who makes the QTIP election. For property transferred by death, the executor of the estate of the deceased spouse has the right to make the election. §§2056(b)(7) and 2523(f).

Qualified transportation fringes. Transportation benefits provided by the employer to the employee. Such benefits include (1) transportation in a commuter highway vehicle between the employee's residence and the place of employment, (2) a transit pass, and (3) qualified parking. Qualified transportation fringes are excludable from the employee's gross income to the extent categories (1) and (2) above do not exceed $245 per month in 2013 ($125 in 2012) and category (3) does not exceed $245 per month in 2013 ($240 in 2012). These amounts are indexed annually for inflation. §132(a)(5).

Qualified tuition program. A program that allows college tuition to be prepaid for a beneficiary. When the tuition is used, nothing must be included in gross income if used for qualified higher education expenses. §529.

Qualified tuition reduction plan. A type of fringe benefit plan that is available to employees of nonprofit educational institutions. Such employees (and the spouse and dependent children) are allowed to exclude from gross income a tuition waiver pursuant to a qualified tuition reduction plan. The exclusion applies to undergraduate tuition. In limited circumstances, the exclusion also applies to the graduate tuition of teaching and research assistants. §117(d).

Qualifying child. An individual who, as to the taxpayer, satisfies the relationship, abode, and age tests. To be claimed as a dependent, such individual must also meet the citizenship and joint return tests and not be self-supporting. §§152(a)(1) and (c). See also *dependency exemption* and *personal exemption.*

Qualifying relative. An individual who, as to the taxpayer, satisfies the relationship, gross income, support, citizenship, and joint return tests. Such an individual can be claimed as a dependent of the taxpayer. §§152(a)(2) and (d). See also *dependency exemption* and *personal exemption.*

R

Realized gain or loss. The difference between the amount realized upon the sale or other disposition of property and the adjusted basis of the property. §1001.

Realty. Real estate.

Reasonable cause. Relief from taxpayer and preparer penalties often is allowed where reasonable cause is found for the taxpayer's actions. For example, reasonable cause for the late filing of a tax return might be a flood that damaged the taxpayer's record-keeping systems and made a timely completion of the return difficult.

Reasonableness. The Code includes a reasonableness requirement with respect to the deduction of salaries and other compensation for services. What constitutes reasonableness is a question of fact. If an expense is unreasonable, the amount that is classified as unreasonable is not allowed as a deduction. The question of reasonableness generally arises with respect to closely held corporations where there is no separation of ownership and management. §162(a)(1).

Recognized gain or loss. The portion of realized gain or loss subject to income taxation. §1001.

Recourse debt. Debt for which the lender may both foreclose on the property and assess a guarantor for any payments due under the loan. A lender may also make a claim against the assets of any general partner in a partnership to which debt is issued, without regard to whether the partner has guaranteed the debt.

Recovery of capital doctrine. When a taxable sale or exchange occurs, the seller may be permitted to recover his or her investment (or other adjusted basis) in the property before gain or loss is recognized.

Redemption to pay death taxes. Sale or exchange treatment is available relative to this type of redemption, to the extent of the proceeds up to the total amount paid by the estate or heir for death taxes and administration expenses. The stock value must exceed 35 percent of the value of the decedent's adjusted gross estate. In meeting this test, one can combine shareholdings in corporations where the decedent held at least 20 percent of the outstanding shares. §303.

Refundable credit. A refundable credit is a credit that is paid to the taxpayer even if the amount of the credit (or credits) exceeds the taxpayer's tax liability.

Regular corporation. See *C corporation.*

Rehabilitation expenditures credit. A credit that is based on expenditures incurred to rehabilitate industrial and commercial buildings and certified historic structures. The credit is intended to discourage businesses from moving from older, economically distressed areas to newer locations and to encourage the preservation of historic structures. §47.

Rehabilitation expenditures credit recapture. When property that qualifies for the rehabilitation expenditures credit is disposed of or ceases to be used in the trade or business of the taxpayer, some or all of the tax credit claimed on the property may be recaptured as additional tax liability. The amount of the recapture is the difference between the amount of the credit claimed originally and what should have been claimed in light of the length of time the property was actually held or used for qualifying purposes. §50.

Related corporation. See *controlled group.*

Related parties. Various Code Sections define related parties and often include a variety of persons within this (usually detrimental) category. Generally, related parties are accorded different tax treatment from that applicable to other taxpayers who enter into similar transactions. For instance, realized losses that are generated between related parties are not recognized in the year of the loss. However, these deferred losses can be used to offset recognized gains that occur upon the subsequent sale of the asset to a nonrelated party. Other uses of a related-party definition include the conversion of gain upon the sale of a depreciable asset into all ordinary income (§1239) and the identification of constructive ownership of stock relative to corporate distributions, redemptions, liquidations, reorganizations, and compensation.

Rental activity. Any activity where payments are received principally for the use of tangible property is a rental activity. Temporary Regulations provide that in certain circumstances activities involving rentals of real and personal property are not to be *treated* as rental activities. The Temporary Regulations list six exceptions. Temp. Reg. §1.469–1T(e)(3)(ii).

Reorganization. Occurs, among other instances, when one corporation acquires another in a merger or acquisition, a single corporation divides into two or more entities, a corporation makes a substantial change in its capital structure, or a corporation undertakes a change in its legal name or domicile. The exchange of stock and other securities in a corporate reorganization can be effected favorably for tax purposes if certain statutory requirements are followed strictly. Tax consequences include the nonrecognition of any gain that is realized by the shareholders except to the extent of boot received. §368.

Research activities credit. A tax credit whose purpose is to encourage research and development. It consists of three components: the incremental research activities credit, the basic research credit and the energy credit. The incremental research activities credit is equal to 20 percent of the excess qualified research expenditures over the base amount. The basic research credit is equal to 20 percent of the excess of basic research payments over the base amount. §41.

Research and experimental expenditures. The Code provides three alternatives for the tax treatment of research and experimentation expenditures. They may be expensed in the year paid or incurred, deferred subject to amortization, or capitalized. If the taxpayer does not elect to expense such costs or to defer them subject to amortization (over 60 months), the expenditures must be capitalized. §174. Three types of research activities credits are available: the basic research credit, the incremental research activities credit, and the energy credit. The rate for each type is 20 percent. §41.

Reserve method. A method of accounting whereby an allowance is permitted for estimated uncollectible accounts. Actual write-offs are charged to the reserve, and recoveries of amounts previously written off are credited to the reserve. The Code permits only certain financial institutions to use the reserve method. §166.

Residential rental real estate. Buildings for which at least 80 percent of the gross rents are from dwelling units (e.g., an apartment building). This type of building is distinguished from nonresidential (commercial or industrial) buildings in applying the recapture of depreciation provisions. The term also is relevant in distinguishing between buildings that are eligible for a 27.5-year life versus a 39-year life for MACRS purposes. Generally, residential buildings receive preferential treatment. §168.

Revenue Agent's Report. A Revenue Agent's Report (RAR) reflects any adjustments made by the agent as a result of an audit of the taxpayer. The RAR is mailed to the taxpayer along with the 30-day letter, which outlines the appellate procedures available to the taxpayer.

Revenue neutrality. A description that characterizes tax legislation when it neither increases nor decreases the revenue result. Thus, any tax revenue losses are offset by tax revenue gains.

Revenue Procedure. A matter of procedural importance to both taxpayers and the IRS concerning the administration of the tax laws is issued as a Revenue Procedure (abbreviated Rev.Proc.). A Revenue Procedure is first published in an *Internal Revenue Bulletin* (I.R.B.) and later transferred to the appropriate *Cumulative Bulletin* (C.B.). Both the *Internal Revenue Bulletins* and the *Cumulative Bulletins* are published by the U.S. Government Printing Office.

Revenue Ruling. A Revenue Ruling (abbreviated Rev. Rul.) is issued by the National Office of the IRS to express an official interpretation of the tax law as applied to specific transactions. It is more limited in application than a Regulation. A Revenue Ruling is first published in an *Internal Revenue Bulletin* (I.R.B.) and later transferred to the appropriate *Cumulative Bulletin* (C.B.). Both the *Internal Revenue Bulletins* and the *Cumulative Bulletins* are published by the U.S. Government Printing Office.

Reversionary interest. The property that reverts to the grantor after the expiration of an intervening income interest. Assume Phil places real estate in trust with income to Junior for 11 years, and upon the expiration of this term, the property returns to Phil. Under these circumstances, Phil holds a reversionary interest in the property. A reversionary interest is the same as a remainder interest, except that, in the latter case, the property passes to someone other than the original owner (e.g., the grantor of a trust) upon the expiration of the intervening interest.

Roth IRAs. See *Individual retirement account (IRA).*

S

S corporation. The designation for a small business corporation. §§1361–1379. See also *Subchapter S.*

Sale or exchange. A requirement for the recognition of capital gain or loss. Generally, the seller of property must receive money or relief from debt in order to have sold the property. An exchange involves the transfer of property for other property. Thus, collection of a debt is neither a sale nor an exchange. The term *sale or exchange* is not defined by the Code.

Sales factor. The proportion of a multistate corporation's total sales that is traceable to a specific state. Used in determining the taxable income that is to be apportioned to that state.

Sales tax. A state- or local-level tax on the retail sale of specified property. Generally, the purchaser pays the tax, but the seller collects it, as an agent for the government. Various taxing jurisdictions allow exemptions for purchases of specific items, including certain food, services, and manufacturing equipment. If the purchaser and seller are in different states, a use tax usually applies.

Schedule M–1. On the Form 1120, a reconciliation of book net income with Federal taxable income. Accounts for timing and permanent differences in the two computations, such as depreciation differences, exempt income, and nondeductible items. On Forms 1120S and 1065, the Schedule M–1 reconciles book income with the owners' aggregate ordinary taxable income.

Schedule M-3. An *expanded* reconciliation of book net income with Federal taxable income (see *Schedule* M-1). Applies to corporations with total assets of $10 million or more.

Scholarships. Scholarships are generally excluded from the gross income of the recipient unless the payments are a disguised form of compensation for services rendered. However, the Code imposes restrictions on the exclusion. The recipient must be a degree candidate. The excluded amount is limited to amounts used for tuition, fees, books, supplies, and equipment required for courses of instruction. Amounts received for room and board are not eligible for the exclusion. §117.

Section 121 exclusion. If a residence has been owned and used by the taxpayer as the principal residence for at least two years during the five-year period ending on the date of sale, up to $250,000 of realized gain is excluded from gross income. For a married couple filing a joint return, the $250,000 is increased to $500,000 if either spouse satisfies the ownership requirement and both spouses satisfy the use requirement.

Section 179 expensing. The ability to deduct a capital expenditure in the year an asset is placed in service rather than over the asset's useful life or cost recovery period. The annual ceiling on the deduction is $500,000 in 2013 ($500,000 for 2012). However, the deduction is reduced dollar for dollar when §179 property placed in service during the taxable year exceeds $2 million in 2013 ($2 million in 2012). In addition, the amount expensed under §179 cannot exceed the aggregate amount of taxable income derived from the conduct of any trade or business by the taxpayer.

Section 338 election. When a corporation acquires at least 80 percent of a subsidiary in a 12-month period, it can elect to treat the acquisition of such stock as an asset purchase. The acquiring corporation's basis in the subsidiary's assets then is the cost of the stock. The subsidiary is deemed to have sold its assets for an amount equal to the grossed-up basis in its stock. §338.

Section 401(k) plan. A cash or deferred arrangement plan that allows participants to elect to receive up to $17,500 in 2013 ($17,000 in 2012) in cash (taxed currently) or to have a contribution made on their behalf to a profit sharing or stock bonus plan (excludible from gross income). The plan may also be in the form of a salary reduction agreement between the participant and the employer.

Section 1231 gains and losses. If the combined gains and losses from the taxable dispositions of §1231 assets plus the net gain from business involuntary conversions (of both §1231 assets and long-term capital assets) is a gain, the gains and losses are treated as long-term capital gains and losses. In arriving at §1231 gains, however, the depreciation recapture provisions (e.g., §§1245 and 1250) are first applied to produce ordinary income. If the net result of the combination is a loss, the gains and losses from §1231 assets are treated as ordinary gains and losses. §1231(a).

Section 1231 lookback. In order for gain to be classified as §1231 gain, the gain must survive the §1231 lookback. To the extent of nonrecaptured §1231 losses for the five prior tax years, the gain is classified as ordinary income. §1231(c).

Section 1231 property. Depreciable assets and real estate used in trade or business and held for the required long-term holding period. Under certain circumstances, the classification also includes timber, coal, domestic iron ore, livestock (held for draft, breeding, dairy, or sporting purposes), and unharvested crops. §1231(b).

Section 1244 stock. Stock issued under §1244 by qualifying small business corporations. If §1244 stock becomes worthless, the shareholders may claim an ordinary loss rather than the usual capital loss, within statutory limitations.

Section 1245 property. Property that is subject to the recapture of depreciation under §1245. For a definition of §1245 property, see §1245(a)(3).

Section 1245 recapture. Upon a taxable disposition of §1245 property, ali depreciation claimed on the property is recaptured as ordinary income (but not to exceed recognized gain from the disposition).

Section 1250 property. Real estate that is subject to the recapture of depreciation under §1250. For a definition of §1250 property, see §1250(c).

Section 1250 recapture. Upon a taxable disposition of §1250 property, some of the depreciation or cost recovery claimed on the property may be recaptured as ordinary income. See also *additional depreciation.*

Securities. Generally, stock, debt, and other financial assets. To the extent securities other than the stock of the transferee corporation are received in a §351 exchange, the new shareholder realizes a gain.

Self-employment retirement plan. A designation for retirement plans available to self-employed taxpayers. Also referred to as H.R. 10 and Keogh plans. Under such plan, a taxpayer may deduct each year up to either 100 percent of net earnings from self-employment or $51,000 in 2013 ($50,000 in 2012), whichever is less. If the plan is a profit sharing plan, the percentage is 25 percent.

Self-employment tax. In 2011 and 2012, a tax of 10.4 percent is levied on individuals with net earnings from self-employment (up to $106,800 in 2011 and $110,100 in 2012) to provide Social Security benefits (i.e., the old age, survivors, and disability insurance portion) for such individuals. For 2010 and 2013, the tax rate is 12.4 percent. In addition, in 2012 (and 2011), a tax of 2.9 percent is levied on individuals with net earnings from self-employment (with no statutory ceiling) to provide Medicare benefits (i.e., the hospital insurance portion) for such individuals. If a self-employed individual also receives wages from an employer that are subject for FICA, the self-employment tax will be reduced if total income subject to Social Security is more than $106,800 in 2011, $110,100 in 2012, or $113,700 in 2013. A partial deduction is allowed in calculating the self-employment tax. Individuals with net earnings of $400 or more from self-employment are subject to this tax. §§1401 and 1402.

Separately stated item. Any item of a partnership or S corporation that might be taxed differently to any two owners of the entity. These amounts are not included in ordinary income of the entity, but are instead reported separately to the owners; tax consequences are determined at the owner level. §§702 and 1363.

Severance tax. A tax imposed upon the extraction of natural resources.

Short sale. A short sale occurs when a taxpayer sells borrowed property (usually stock) and repays the lender with substantially identical property either held on the date of the short sale or purchased after the sale. No gain or loss is recognized until the short sale is closed, and such gain or loss is generally short term. §1233.

Short taxable year (short period). A tax year that is less than 12 months. A short taxable year may occur in the initial reporting period, in the final tax year, or when the taxpayer changes tax years. §443.

Significant participation activity. There are seven tests to determine whether an individual has achieved material participation in an activity, one of which is based on more than 500 hours of participation in significant participation activities. A significant participation activity is one in which the individual's participation exceeds 100 hours during the year. Reg. §1.469–5T.

Simple trust. Simple trusts are those that are not complex trusts. Such trusts may not have a charitable beneficiary, accumulate income, or distribute corpus. §§651 and 652.

Small business corporation. A corporation that satisfies the definition of §1361(b), §1244(c), or both. Satisfaction of §1361(b) permits an §election, and satisfaction of §1244 enables the shareholders of the corporation to claim an ordinary loss on the worthlessness of stock.

Small business stock. See *small business corporation.*

Small Cases Division of the U.S. Tax Court. Jurisdiction is limited to claims of $50,000 or less. There is no appeal from this court.

Special allocation. Any amount for which an agreement exists among the partners of a partnership outlining the method used for spreading the item among the partners.

Specific charge-off method. A method of accounting for bad debts in which a deduction is permitted only when an account becomes partially or completely worthless. §166.

Sprinkling trust. When a trustee has the discretion to either distribute or accumulate the entity accounting income of the trust and to distribute it among the trust's income beneficiaries in varying magnitudes, a sprinkling trust exists. The trustee can sprinkle the income of the trust.

Standard deduction. The individual taxpayer can either itemize deductions or take the standard deduction. The amount of the standard deduction depends on the taxpayer's filing status (single, head of household, married filing jointly, surviving spouse, or married filing separately). For 2013, the amount of the standard deduction ranges from $6,100 (married filing separately and for unmarried) to $12,200 (married filing jointly). For 2012, the amounts are $5,950 and $11,900, respectively. Additional standard deductions of either $1,200 (for married taxpayers) or $1,500 (for single taxpayers) are available for 2013, if the taxpayer is either blind or age 65 or over. For 2012, the amounts are $1,150 and $1,450, respectively. Limitations exist on the amount of the standard deduction of a taxpayer who is another taxpayer's dependent. The standard deduction amounts are adjusted for inflation each year. §63(c).

Startup expenditures. Expenditures paid or incurred associated with the creation of a business prior to the beginning of business. Examples of such expenditures include advertising, salaries and wages, travel and other expenses incurred in lining up prospective distributors, suppliers, or customers, and salaries and fees to executives, consultants, and professional service providers. A taxpayer may elect to immediately expense the first $5,000 ($10,000 in 2010) (subject to phaseout) of startup expenditures and generally amortize the balance over a period of 180 months.

Statute of limitations. Provisions of the law that specify the maximum period of time in which action may be taken on a past event. Code §§6501–6504 contain the limitation periods applicable to the IRS for additional assessments, and §§6511–6515 relate to refund claims by taxpayers.

Statutory employee. Statutory employees are considered selfemployed independent contractors for purposes of reporting income and expenses on their tax returns. Generally, a statutory employee must meet three tests:

- It is understood from a service contract that the services will be performed by the person.
- The person does not have a substantial investment in facilities (other than transportation used to perform the services).
- The services involve a continuing relationship with the person for whom they are performed.

For further information on statutory employees, see Circular E *Employer's Tax Guide* IRS Publication 15.

Stock dividend. Not taxable if pro rata distributions of stock or stock rights on common stock. Section 305 governs the taxability of stock dividends and sets out five exceptions to the general rule that stock dividends are nontaxable.

Stock redemption. A corporation buys back its own stock from a specified shareholder. Typically, the corporation recognizes any realized gain on the noncash assets that it uses to effect a redemption, and the shareholder obtains a capital gain or loss upon receipt of the purchase price. §302.

Stock rights. Assets that convey to the holder the power to purchase corporate stock at a specified price, often for a limited period of time. Stock rights received may be taxed as a distribution of earnings and profits. After the right is exercised, the basis of the acquired share includes the investor's purchase price or gross income, if any, to obtain the right. Disposition of the right also is a taxable event, with basis often assigned from the shares held prior to the issuance of the right. §§305 and 307.

Subchapter S. Sections 1361–1379 of the Internal Revenue Code. An elective provision permitting certain small business corporations (§1361) and their shareholders (§1362) to elect to be treated for income tax purposes in accordance with the operating rules of §§1363–1379. However, some S corporations usually avoid the corporate income tax, and corporate losses can be claimed by the shareholders.

Subpart F. That subpart of the Code that identifies the current tax treatment of income earned by a controlled foreign corporation. Certain types of income are included in U.S. gross income by U.S. shareholders of such an entity as they are generated, not when they are repatriated.

Substantial authority. Taxpayer understatement penalties are waived where substantial authority existed for the disputed position taken on the return.

Surviving spouse. When a husband or wife predeceases the other spouse, the survivor is known as a surviving spouse. Under certain conditions, a surviving spouse may be entitled to use the income tax rates in §1(a) (those applicable to married persons filing a joint return) for the two years after the year of death of his or her spouse. §2.

Syndication costs. Incurred in promoting and marketing partnership interests for sale to investors. Examples include legal and accounting fees, printing costs for prospectus and placement documents, and state registration fees. These items are capitalized by the partnership as incurred, with no amortization thereof allowed. §709.

T

Tax avoidance. The minimization of one's tax liability by taking advantage of legally available tax planning opportunities. Tax avoidance can be contrasted with tax evasion, which entails the reduction of tax liability by illegal means.

Tax benefit rule. A provision that limits the recognition of income from the recovery of an expense or loss properly deducted in a prior tax year to the amount of the deduction that generated a tax saving. Assume that last year Gary, age 66, had medical expenses of $3,000 and adjusted gross income of $30,000. Because of the 7.5 percent limitation, Gary could deduct only $750 of these expenses [$3,000 – (7.5% $30,000)]. If, this year, Gary is reimbursed by his insurance company for $900 of these expenses, the tax benefit rule limits the amount of income from the reimbursement to $750 (the amount previously deducted with a tax saving). §111.

Tax credit for the elderly or disabled. An elderly (age 65 and over) or disabled taxpayer may receive a tax credit amounting to 15 percent of $5,000 ($7,500 for qualified married individuals filing jointly). This amount is reduced by Social Security benefits, excluded pension benefits, and one-half of the taxpayer's adjusted gross income in excess of $7,500 ($10,000 for married taxpayers filing jointly). §22.

Tax credits. Tax credits are amounts that directly reduce a taxpayer's tax liability. The tax benefit received from a tax credit is not dependent on the taxpayer's marginal tax rate, whereas the benefit of a tax deduction or exclusion is dependent on the taxpayer's tax bracket.

Tax haven. A country in which either locally sourced income or residents of the country are subject to a low rate of taxation.

Tax preferences. Various items that may result in the imposition of the alternative minimum tax. §57.

Tax rate schedules. Rate schedules that are used by upperincome taxpayers and those not permitted to use the tax table. Separate rate schedules are provided for married individuals filing jointly, head of household, single taxpayers, estates and trusts, and married individuals filing separate returns. §1.

Tax research. The method used to determine the best available solution to a situation that possesses tax consequences. Both tax and nontax factors are considered.

Tax shelters. The typical tax shelter generated large losses in the early years of the activity. Investors would offset these losses against other types of income and, therefore, avoid paying income taxes on this income. These tax shelter investments could then be sold after a few years and produce capital gain income, which is taxed at a lower rate than ordinary income. The passive activity loss rules and the at-risk rules now limit tax shelter deductions.

Tax table. A tax table that is provided for taxpayers with less than $100,000 of taxable income. Separate columns are provided for single taxpayers, married taxpayers filing jointly, head of household, and married taxpayers filing separately. §3.

Tax treaty. An agreement between the U.S. Department of State and another country, designed to alleviate double taxation of income and asset transfers, and to share administrative information useful to tax agencies in both countries. The United States has income tax treaties with over 40 countries, and transfer tax treaties with about 20.

Taxable estate. The taxable estate is the gross estate of a decedent reduced by the deductions allowed by §§2053–2056 (e.g., administration expenses, marital and charitable deductions). The taxable estate is subject to the unified transfer tax at death. §2051.

Taxable gift. The amount of a gift that is subject to the unified transfer tax. Thus, a taxable gift has been adjusted by the annual exclusion and other appropriate deductions (e.g., marital and charitable). §2053.

Taxable year. The annual period over which income is measured for income tax purposes. Most individuals use a calendar year, but many businesses use a fiscal year based on the natural business year. §441.

Technical advice memoranda (TAMs). TAMs are issued by the National Office of the IRS in response to questions raised by IRS field personnel during audits. They deal with completed rather than proposed transactions and are often requested for questions related to exempt organizations and employee plans.

Temporary Regulation. A Regulation issued by the Treasury Department in temporary form. When speed is critical, the Treasury Department issues Temporary Regulations that take effect immediately. These Regulations have the same authoritative value as Final Regulations and may be cited as precedent for three years. Temporary Regulations are also issued as proposed Regulations.

Tenants by the entirety. Essentially, a joint tenancy between husband and wife.

Tenants in common. A form of ownership where each tenant (owner) holds an undivided interest in property. Unlike a joint tenancy or a tenancy by the entirety, the interest of a tenant in common does not terminate upon that individual's death (there is no right of survivorship). Assume Tim and Cindy acquire real estate as equal tenants in common, each having furnished one-half of the purchase price. Upon Tim's death, his one-half interest in the property passes to his estate or heirs, not to Cindy.

Terminable interest. An interest in property that terminates upon the death of the holder or upon the occurrence of some other specified event. The transfer of a terminable interest by one spouse to the other may not qualify for the marital deduction. §§2056(b) and 2523(b).

Theft loss. A loss from larceny, embezzlement, or robbery. It does not include misplacement of items. §165.

Thin capitalization. When debt owed by a corporation to the shareholders becomes too large in relation to the corporation's capital structure (i.e., stock and shareholder equity), the IRS may contend that the corporation is thinly capitalized. In effect, this means that some or all of the debt is reclassified as equity. The immediate result is to disallow any interest deduction to the corporation on the reclassified debt. To the extent of the corporation's earnings and profits, interest payments and loan repayments on the reclassified debt are treated as dividends to the shareholders. §385.

Thirty-day letter. A letter that accompanies an *RAR* (Revenue Agent's Report) issued as a result of an IRS audit of a taxpayer (or the rejection of a taxpayer's claim for refund). The letter outlines the taxpayer's appeal procedure before the IRS. If the taxpayer does not request any such procedures within the 30-day period, the IRS will issue a statutory notice of deficiency (the 90-day letter).

Throwback rule. If there is no income tax in the state to which a sale otherwise would be apportioned, the sale essentially is exempt from state income tax, even though the seller is domiciled in a state that levies an income tax. Nonetheless, if the seller's state has adopted a throwback rule, the sale is attributed to the *seller's* state, and the transaction is subjected to a state-level tax.

Transportation expenses. Transportation expenses for an employee include only the cost of transportation (taxi fares, automobile expenses, etc.) in the course of employment when the employee is not away from home in travel status. Commuting expenses are not deductible.

Travel expenses. Travel expenses include meals (generally subject to a 50 percent disallowance) and lodging and transportation expenses while away from home in the pursuit of a trade or business (including that of an employee).

Treaty shopping. An international investor attempts to use the favorable aspects of a tax treaty to his or her advantage, often elevating the form of the transaction over its substance (e.g., by establishing only a nominal presence in the country offering the favorable treaty terms).

U

UDITPA. The Uniform Division of Income for Tax Purposes Act has been adopted in some form by many of the states. The Act develops criteria by which the total taxable income of a multistate corporation can be assigned to specific states.

Unearned (prepaid) income. Income received but not yet earned. Normally, such income is taxed when received, even for accrual basis taxpayers. However, in certain cases involving advance payments for goods and services, income may be deferred. See Revenue Procedure 2004-34 (I.R.B. No. 22, 991) and Reg. §1.451-5. See also *accrual method.*

Unified transfer tax credit. A credit allowed against any unified transfer tax. §§2010 and 2505. See also *exclusion amount.*

Unified transfer tax. Rates applicable to transfers by gift and death made after 1976. §2001(c).

Unitary theory. Sales, property, and payroll of related corporations are combined for nexus and apportionment purposes, and the worldwide income of the unitary entity is apportioned to the state. Subsidiaries and other affiliated corporations found to be part of the corporation's unitary business (because they are subject to overlapping ownership, operation, or management) are included in the apportionment procedure. This approach can be limited if a water's edge election is in effect.

Unrealized receivables. Amounts earned by a cash basis taxpayer but not yet received. Because of the method of accounting used by the taxpayer, these amounts have no income tax basis. When unrealized receivables are distributed to a partner, they generally convert a transaction from nontaxable to taxable or convert otherwise capital gain to ordinary income. §751.

Unreasonable compensation. A deduction is allowed for "reasonable" salaries or other compensation for personal services actually rendered. To the extent compensation is "excessive" ("unreasonable"), no deduction is allowed. The problem of unreasonable compensation usually is limited to closely held corporations, where the motivation is to pay out profits in some form that is deductible to the corporation. Deductible compensation therefore becomes an attractive substitute for nondeductible dividends when the shareholders also are employed by the corporation. §162.

Unrecaptured §1250 gain (25 percent gain). Gain from the sale of depreciable real estate held more than one year. The gain is equal to or less than the depreciation taken on such property and is reduced by §1245 and §1250 gain. See also *alternative tax.*

Unrelated business income. Income recognized by an exempt organization that is generated from activities not related to the exempt purpose of the entity. For instance, the pharmacy located in a hospital often generates unrelated business income. §§511 and 512.

Unrelated business income tax. Levied on the unrelated business income of an exempt organization. §511.

U.S. Court of Federal Claims. A trial court (court of original jurisdiction) that decides litigation involving Federal tax matters. Appeal from this court is to the Court of Appeals for the Federal Circuit.

U.S. shareholder. For purposes of classification of an entity as a controlled foreign corporation, a U.S. person who owns, or is considered to own, 10 percent or more of the total combined voting power of all classes of voting stock of a foreign corporation. Stock owned directly, indirectly, and constructively is counted for this purpose.

U.S. Supreme Court. The highest appellate court or the court of last resort in the Federal court system and in most states. Only a small number of tax decisions of the U.S.

Courts of Appeal are reviewed by the U.S. Supreme Court under its certiorari procedure. The Supreme Court usually grants certiorari to resolve a conflict among the Courts of Appeal (e.g., two or more appellate courts have assumed opposing positions on a particular issue) or when the tax issue is extremely important (e.g., size of the revenue loss to the Federal government).

U.S. Tax Court. The U.S. Tax Court is one of four trial courts of original jurisdiction that decides litigation involving Federal income, death, or gift taxes. It is the only trial court where the taxpayer must not first pay the deficiency assessed by the IRS. The Tax Court will not have jurisdiction over a case unless a statutory notice of deficiency (90-day letter) has been issued by the IRS and the taxpayer files the petition for hearing within the time prescribed.

U.S. trade or business. A set of activities that is carried on in a regular, continuous, and substantial manner. A non-U.S. taxpayer is subject to U.S. tax on the taxable income that is effectively connected with a U.S. trade or business.

Use tax. A sales tax that is collectible by the seller where the purchaser is domiciled in a different state.

V

Vacation home. The Code places restrictions upon taxpayers who rent their residences or vacation homes for part of the tax year. The restrictions may result in a scaling down of expense deductions for the taxpayers. §280A.

Value added tax (VAT). A national sales tax that taxes the increment in value as goods move through the production process. A VAT is much used in other countries but has not yet been incorporated as part of the U.S. Federal tax structure.

Voluntary revocation. The owners of a majority of shares in an S corporation elect to terminate the S status of the entity, as of a specified date. The day on which the revocation is effective is the first day of the corporation's C tax year. §1362.

W

W–2 wages. The domestic production activities deduction (DPAD) cannot exceed 50% of the W–2 wages paid for any particular year that are properly allocable to domestic production gross receipts. Prop.Reg. §1.199–2(f)(2) provides several methods for calculating the W–2 wages, but the payments must involve common law employees. §199. See also *production activities deduction (PAD).*

Wash sale. A loss from the sale of stock or securities that is disallowed because the taxpayer, within 30 days before or after the sale, has acquired stock or securities substantially identical to those sold. §1091.

Water's edge election. A limitation on the worldwide scope of the unitary theory. If a corporate water's edge election is in effect, the state can consider only the activities that occur within the boundaries of the United States in the apportionment procedure.

Welfare-to-work credit. A tax credit available to employers hiring individuals who have been long-term recipients of family assistance welfare benefits. In general, long-term recipients are those individuals who are certified by a designated local agency as being members of a family receiving assistance under a public aid program for at least an 18-month period ending on the hiring date. The welfare-to-work credit is available for qualified wages paid in the first two years of employment. The maximum credit is equal to $9,000 per qualified employee, computed as 40 percent of the first $10,000 of qualified wages paid in the first year of employment, plus 50 percent of the first $10,000 of qualified wages paid in the second year of employment. Starting in 2007, the welfare-to-work credit became part of the work opportunity tax credit. §51.

Wherewithal to pay. This concept recognizes the inequity of taxing a transaction when the taxpayer lacks the means with which to pay the tax. Under it, there is a correlation between the imposition of the tax and the ability to pay the tax. It is particularly suited to situations in which the taxpayer's economic position has not changed significantly as a result of the transaction.

Working condition fringe. A type of fringe benefit received by the employee that is excludable from the employee's gross income. It consists of property or services provided (paid or reimbursed) by the employer for which the employee could take a tax deduction if the employee had paid for them. §132(a)(3).

Work opportunity tax credit. Employers are allowed a tax credit equal to 40 percent of the first $6,000 of wages (per eligible employee) for the first year of employment. Eligible employees include certain hard-to-employ individuals (e.g., qualified ex-felons, high-risk youth, food stamp recipients, and veterans). The employer's deduction for wages is reduced by the amount of the credit taken. For qualified summer youth employees, the 40 percent rate is applied to the first $3,000 of qualified wages. See the *welfare-to-work credit* for the calculation for long-term recipients of family assistance welfare benefits. §51.

Worthless securities. A loss (usually capital) is allowed for a security that becomes worthless during the year. The loss is deemed to have occurred on the last day of the year. Special rules apply to securities of affiliated companies and small business stock. §165.

Writ of Certiorari. Appeal from a U.S. Court of Appeals to the U.S. Supreme Court is by Writ of Certiorari. The Supreme Court need not accept the appeal, and it usually does not (*cert. den.*) unless a conflict exists among the lower courts that must be resolved or a constitutional issue is involved.

INDEX

ESTATE TAX

References are to Sections

GENERATION-SKIPPING TRANSFER TAX

References are to Sections

GIFT TAX

References are to Sections

INCOME TAX

References are to Sections